PETERSON'S®
GRADUATE PROGRAMS IN THE BIOLOGICAL/BIOMEDICAL SCIENCES & HEALTH-RELATED MEDICAL PROFESSIONS

2019

PETERSON'S®

PETERSON'S®

About Peterson's®

Peterson's® has been your trusted educational publisher for over 50 years. It's a milestone we're quite proud of, as we continue to offer the most accurate, dependable, high-quality educational content in the field, providing you with everything you need to succeed. No matter where you are on your academic or professional path, you can rely on Peterson's for its books, online information, expert test-prep tools, the most up-to-date education exploration data, and the highest quality career success resources—everything you need to achieve your education goals. For our complete line of products, visit **www.petersons.com**.

For more information about Peterson's range of educational products, contact Peterson's, 8740 Lucent Blvd., Suite 400 Highlands Ranch, CO 80129, or find us online at **www.petersons.com.**

ISSN 1093-8443
ISBN: 978-0-7689-4223-1

Printed in the United States of America

10 9 8 7 6 5 4 3 2 1   20 19 18

Fifty-third Edition

CONTENTS

A Note from the Peterson's Editors

The six volumes of Peterson's *Graduate and Professional Programs*, the only annually updated reference work of its kind, provide wide-ranging information on the graduate and professional programs offered by accredited colleges and universities in the United States, U.S. territories, and Canada and by those institutions outside the United States that are accredited by U.S. accrediting bodies. More than 44,000 individual academic and professional programs at nearly 2,300 institutions are listed. Peterson's *Graduate and Professional Programs* have been used for more than fifty years by prospective graduate and professional students, placement counselors, faculty advisers, and all others interested in postbaccalaureate education.

Graduate & Professional Programs: An Overview contains information on institutions as a whole, while the other books in the series are devoted to specific academic and professional fields:

- ***Graduate Programs in the Biological/Biomedical Sciences & Health-Related Medical Professions***
- ***Graduate Programs in Business, Education, Information Studies, Law & Social Work***
- ***Graduate Programs in Engineering & Applied Sciences***
- ***Graduate Programs in the Humanities, Arts & Social Sciences***
- ***Graduate Programs in the Physical Sciences, Mathematics, Agricultural Sciences, the Environment & Natural Resources***

The books may be used individually or as a set. For example, if you have chosen a field of study but do not know what institution you want to attend or if you have a college or university in mind but have not chosen an academic field of study, it is best to begin with the Overview guide.

Graduate & Professional Programs: An Overview presents several directories to help you identify programs of study that might interest you; you can then research those programs further in the other books in the series by using the Directory of Graduate and Professional Programs by Field, which lists 500 fields and gives the names of those institutions that offer graduate degree programs in each.

For geographical or financial reasons, you may be interested in attending a particular institution and will want to know what it has to offer. You should turn to the Directory of Institutions and Their Offerings, which lists the degree programs available at each institution. As in the Directory of Graduate and Professional Programs by Field, the level of degrees offered is also indicated.

All books in the series include advice on graduate education, including topics such as admissions tests, financial aid, and accreditation. **The Graduate Adviser** includes two essays and information about accreditation. The first essay, "The Admissions Process," discusses general admission requirements, admission tests, factors to consider when selecting a graduate school or program, when and how to apply, and how admission decisions are made. Special information for international students and tips for minority students are also included. The second essay, "Financial Support," is an overview of the broad range of support available at the graduate level. Fellowships, scholarships, and grants; assistantships and internships; federal and private loan programs, as well as Federal Work-Study; and the GI bill are detailed. This essay concludes with advice on applying for need-based financial aid. "Accreditation and Accrediting Agencies" gives information on accreditation and its purpose and lists institutional accrediting agencies first and then specialized accrediting agencies relevant to each volume's specific fields of study.

With information on more than 40,000 graduate programs in more than 500 disciplines, Peterson's *Graduate and Professional Programs* give you all the information you need about the programs that are of interest to you in three formats: **Profiles** (capsule summaries of basic information), **Displays** (information that an institution or program wants to emphasize), and **Close-Ups** (written by administrators, with more expansive information than the **Profiles**, emphasizing different aspects of the programs). By using these various formats of program information, coupled with **Appendixes** and **Indexes** covering directories and subject areas for all six books, you will find that these guides provide the most comprehensive, accurate, and up-to-date graduate study information available.

Peterson's publishes a full line of resources with information you need to guide you through the graduate admissions process. Peterson's publications can be found at college libraries and career centers and your local bookstore or library—or visit us on the Web at www.petersons.com.

Colleges and universities will be pleased to know that Peterson's helped you in your selection. Admissions staff members are more than happy to answer questions, address specific problems, and help in any way they can. The editors at Peterson's wish you great success in your graduate program search!

NOTICE: Certain portions of or information contained in this book have been submitted and paid for by the educational institution identified, and such institutions take full responsibility for the accuracy, timeliness, completeness and functionality of such contents. Such portions or information include (i) each display ad that comprises a half page of information covering a single educational institution or program and (ii) each two-page description or Close-Up of a graduate school or program that appear in the different sections of this guide. The "Close-Ups and Displays" are listed in various sections throughout the book.

THE GRADUATE ADVISER

The Admissions Process

Generalizations about graduate admissions practices are not always helpful because each institution has its own set of guidelines and procedures. Nevertheless, some broad statements can be made about the admissions process that may help you plan your strategy.

Factors Involved in Selecting a Graduate School or Program

Selecting a graduate school and a specific program of study is a complex matter. Quality of the faculty; program and course offerings; the nature, size, and location of the institution; admission requirements; cost; and the availability of financial assistance are among the many factors that affect one's choice of institution. Other considerations are job placement and achievements of the program's graduates and the institution's resources, such as libraries, laboratories, and computer facilities. If you are to make the best possible choice, you need to learn as much as you can about the schools and programs you are considering before you apply.

The following steps may help you narrow your choices.

- Talk to alumni of the programs or institutions you are considering to get their impressions of how well they were prepared for work in their fields of study.
- Remember that graduate school requirements change, so be sure to get the most up-to-date information possible.
- Talk to department faculty members and the graduate adviser at your undergraduate institution. They often have information about programs of study at other institutions.
- Visit the websites of the graduate schools in which you are interested to request a graduate catalog. Contact the department chair in your chosen field of study for additional information about the department and the field.
- Visit as many campuses as possible. Call ahead for an appointment with the graduate adviser in your field of interest and be sure to check out the facilities and talk to students.

General Requirements

Graduate schools and departments have requirements that applicants for admission must meet. Typically, these requirements include undergraduate transcripts (which provide information about undergraduate grade point average and course work applied toward a major), admission test scores, and letters of recommendation. Most graduate programs also ask for an essay or personal statement that describes your personal reasons for seeking graduate study. In some fields, such as art and music, portfolios or auditions may be required in addition to other evidence of talent. Some institutions require that the applicant have an undergraduate degree in the same subject as the intended graduate major.

Most institutions evaluate each applicant on the basis of the applicant's total record, and the weight accorded any given factor varies widely from institution to institution and from program to program.

The Application Process

You should begin the application process at least one year before you expect to begin your graduate study. Find out the application deadline for each institution (many are provided in the **Profile** section of this guide). Go to the institution's website and find out if you can apply online. If not, request a paper application form. Fill out this form thoroughly and neatly. Assume that the school needs all the information it is requesting and that the admissions officer will be sensitive to the neatness and overall quality of what you submit. Do not supply more information than the school requires.

The institution may ask at least one question that will require a three- or four-paragraph answer. Compose your response on the assumption that the admissions officer is interested in both what you think and how you express yourself. Keep your statement brief and to the point, but, at the same time, include all pertinent information about your past experiences and your educational goals. Individual statements vary greatly in style and content, which helps admissions officers differentiate among applicants. Many graduate departments give considerable weight to the statement in making their admissions decisions, so be sure to take the time to prepare a thoughtful and concise statement.

If recommendations are a part of the admissions requirements, carefully choose the individuals you ask to write them. It is generally best to ask current or former professors to write the recommendations, provided they are able to attest to your intellectual ability and motivation for doing the work required of a graduate student. It is advisable to provide stamped, preaddressed envelopes to people being asked to submit recommendations on your behalf.

Completed applications, including references, transcripts, and admission test scores, should be received at the institution by the specified date.

Be advised that institutions do not usually make admissions decisions until all materials have been received. Enclose a self-addressed postcard with your application, requesting confirmation of receipt. Allow at least ten days for the return of the postcard before making further inquiries.

If you plan to apply for financial support, it is imperative that you file your application early.

ADMISSION TESTS

The major testing program used in graduate admissions is the Graduate Record Examinations (GRE®) testing program, sponsored by the GRE Board and administered by Educational Testing Service, Princeton, New Jersey.

The Graduate Record Examinations testing program consists of a General Test and six Subject Tests. The General Test measures critical thinking, verbal reasoning, quantitative reasoning, and analytical writing skills. It is offered as an Internet-based test (iBT) in the United States, Canada, and many other countries.

The GRE® revised General Test's questions were designed to reflect the kind of thinking that students need to do in graduate or business school and demonstrate that students are indeed ready for graduate-level work.

- **Verbal Reasoning**—Measures ability to analyze and evaluate written material and synthesize information obtained from it, analyze relationships among component parts of sentences, and recognize relationships among words and concepts.
- **Quantitative Reasoning**—Measures problem-solving ability, focusing on basic concepts of arithmetic, algebra, geometry, and data analysis.
- **Analytical Writing**—Measures critical thinking and analytical writing skills, specifically the ability to articulate and support complex ideas clearly and effectively.

The computer-delivered GRE® revised General Test is offered year-round at Prometric™ test centers and on specific dates at testing locations outside of the Prometric test center network. Appointments are scheduled on a first-come, first-served basis. The GRE® revised General Test is also offered as a paper-based test three times a year in areas where computer-based testing is not available.

You can take the computer-delivered GRE® revised General Test once every twenty-one days, up to five times within any continuous rolling twelve-month period (365 days)—even if you canceled your scores on a previously taken test. You may take the paper-based GRE® revised General Test as often as it is offered.

Three scores are reported on the revised General Test:

1. A **Verbal Reasoning score** is reported on a 130–170 score scale, in 1-point increments.
2. A **Quantitative Reasoning score** is reported on a 130–170 score scale, in 1-point increments.
3. An **Analytical Writing score** is reported on a 0–6 score level, in half-point increments.

The GRE® Subject Tests measure achievement and assume undergraduate majors or extensive background in the following six disciplines:

- Biology
- Chemistry
- Literature in English
- Mathematics
- Physics
- Psychology

The Subject Tests are available three times per year as paper-based administrations around the world. Testing time is approximately 2 hours and 50 minutes. You can obtain more information about the GRE® by visiting the ETS website at **www.ets.org** or consulting the *GRE® Information Bulletin*. The *Bulletin* can be obtained at many undergraduate colleges. You can also download it from the ETS website or obtain it by contacting Graduate Record Examinations, Educational Testing Service, P.O. Box 6000, Princeton, NJ 08541-6000; phone: 609-771-7670 or 866-473-4373.

If you expect to apply for admission to a program that requires any of the GRE® tests, you should select a test date well in advance of the application deadline. Scores on the computer-based General Test are reported within ten to fifteen days; scores on the paper-based Subject Tests are reported within six weeks.

Another testing program, the Miller Analogies Test® (MAT®), is administered at more than 500 Controlled Testing Centers in the United States, Canada, and other countries. The MAT® computer-based test is now available. Testing time is 60 minutes. The test consists of 120 partial analogies. You can obtain the *Candidate Information Booklet,* which contains a list of test centers and instructions for taking the test, from **www.milleranalogies.com** or by calling 800-328-5999 (toll-free).

Check the specific requirements of the programs to which you are applying.

How Admission Decisions Are Made

The program you apply to is directly involved in the admissions process. Although the final decision is usually made by the graduate dean (or an associate) or the faculty admissions committee, recommendations from faculty members in your intended field are important. At some institutions, an interview is incorporated into the decision process.

A Special Note for International Students

In addition to the steps already described, there are some special considerations for international students who intend to apply for graduate study in the United States. All graduate schools require an indication of competence in English. The purpose of the Test of English as a Foreign Language (TOEFL®) is to evaluate the English proficiency of people who are nonnative speakers of English and want to study at colleges and universities where English is the language of instruction. The TOEFL® is administered by Educational Testing Service (ETS) under the general direction of a policy board established by the College Board and the Graduate Record Examinations Board.

The TOEFL iBT® assesses four basic language skills: listening, reading, writing, and speaking. The Internet-based test is administered at secure, official test centers. The testing time is approximately 4 hours.

The TOEFL® is also offered in a paper-based format in areas of the world where internet-based testing is not available. In 2017, ETS launched a revised TOEFL® paper-based Test, that more closely aligned to the TOEFL iBT® test. This revised paper-based test consists of three sections—listening, reading, and writing. The testing time is approximately 3 hours.

You can obtain more information for both versions of the TOEFL® by visiting the ETS website at **www.ets.org/toefl**. Information can also be obtained by contacting TOEFL® Services, Educational Testing Service, P.O. Box 6151, Princeton, NJ 08541-6151. Phone: 609-771-7100 or 877-863-3546 (toll free).

International students should apply especially early because of the number of steps required to complete the admissions process. Furthermore, many United States graduate schools have a limited number of spaces for international students, and many more students apply than the schools can accommodate.

International students may find financial assistance from institutions very limited. The U.S. government requires international applicants to submit a certification of support, which is a statement attesting to the applicant's financial resources. In addition, international students *must* have health insurance coverage.

Tips for Minority Students

Indicators of a university's values in terms of diversity are found both in its recruitment programs and its resources directed to student success. Important questions: Does the institution vigorously recruit minorities for its graduate programs? Is there funding available to help with the costs associated with visiting the school? Are minorities represented in the institution's brochures or website or on their faculty rolls? What campus-based resources or services (including assistance in locating housing or career counseling and placement) are available? Is funding available to members of underrepresented groups?

At the program level, it is particularly important for minority students to investigate the "climate" of a program under consideration. How many minority students are enrolled and how many have graduated? What opportunities are there to work with diverse faculty and mentors whose research interests match yours? How are conflicts resolved or concerns addressed? How interested are faculty in building strong and supportive relations with students? "Climate" concerns should be addressed by posing questions to various individuals, including faculty members, current students, and alumni.

Information is also available through various organizations, such as the Hispanic Association of Colleges & Universities (HACU), and publications such as *Diverse Issues in Higher Education* and *Hispanic Outlook* magazine. There are also books devoted to this topic, such as *The Multicultural Student's Guide to Colleges* by Robert Mitchell.

Financial Support

The range of financial support at the graduate level is very broad. The following descriptions will give you a general idea of what you might expect and what will be expected of you as a financial support recipient.

Fellowships, Scholarships, and Grants

These are usually outright awards of a few hundred to many thousands of dollars with no service to the institution required in return. Fellowships and scholarships are usually awarded on the basis of merit and are highly competitive. Grants are made on the basis of financial need or special talent in a field of study. Many fellowships, scholarships, and grants not only cover tuition, fees, and supplies but also include stipends for living expenses with allowances for dependents. However, the terms of each should be examined because some do not permit recipients to supplement their income with outside work. Fellowships, scholarships, and grants may vary in the number of years for which they are awarded.

In addition to the availability of these funds at the university or program level, many excellent fellowship programs are available at the national level and may be applied for before and during enrollment in a graduate program. A listing of many of these programs can be found at the Council of Graduate Schools' website, **https://cgsnet.org/**. There is a wealth of information in the "Programs" and "Awards" sections.

Assistantships and Internships

Many graduate students receive financial support through assistantships, particularly involving teaching or research duties. It is important to recognize that such appointments should not be viewed simply as employment relationships but rather should constitute an integral and important part of a student's graduate education. As such, the appointments should be accompanied by strong faculty mentoring and increasingly responsible apprenticeship experiences. The specific nature of these appointments in a given program should be considered in selecting that graduate program.

TEACHING ASSISTANTSHIPS

These usually provide a salary and full or partial tuition remission and may also provide health benefits. Unlike fellowships, scholarships, and grants, which require no service to the institution, teaching assistantships require recipients to provide the institution with a specific amount of undergraduate teaching, ideally related to the student's field of study. Some teaching assistants are limited to grading papers, compiling bibliographies, taking notes, or monitoring laboratories. At some graduate schools, teaching assistants must carry lighter course loads than regular full-time students.

RESEARCH ASSISTANTSHIPS

These are very similar to teaching assistantships in the manner in which financial assistance is provided. The difference is that recipients are given basic research assignments in their disciplines rather than teaching responsibilities. The work required is normally related to the student's field of study; in most instances, the assistantship supports the student's thesis or dissertation research.

ADMINISTRATIVE INTERNSHIPS

These are similar to assistantships in application of financial assistance funds, but the student is given an assignment on a part-time basis, usually as a special assistant with one of the university's administrative offices. The assignment may not necessarily be directly related to the recipient's discipline.

RESIDENCE HALL AND COUNSELING ASSISTANTSHIPS

These assistantships are frequently assigned to graduate students in psychology, counseling, and social work, but they may be offered to students in other disciplines, especially if the student has worked in this capacity during his or her undergraduate years. Duties can vary from being available in a dean's office for a specific number of hours for consultation with undergraduates to living in campus residences and being responsible for both counseling and administrative tasks or advising student activity groups. Residence hall assistantships often include a room and board allowance and, in some cases, tuition assistance and stipends. Contact the Housing and Student Life Office for more information.

Health Insurance

The availability and affordability of health insurance is an important issue and one that should be considered in an applicant's choice of institution and program. While often included with assistantships and fellowships, this is not always the case and, even if provided, the benefits may be limited. It is important to note that the U.S. government requires international students to have health insurance.

The GI Bill

This provides financial assistance for students who are veterans of the United States armed forces. If you are a veteran, contact your local Veterans Administration office to determine your eligibility and to get full details about benefits. There are a number of programs that offer educational benefits to current military enlistees. Some states have tuition assistance programs for members of the National Guard. Contact the VA office at the college for more information.

Federal Work-Study Program (FWS)

Employment is another way some students finance their graduate studies. The federally funded Federal Work-Study Program provides eligible students with employment opportunities, usually in public and private nonprofit organizations. Federal funds pay up to 75 percent of the wages, with the remainder paid by the employing agency. FWS is available to graduate students who demonstrate financial need. Not all schools have these funds, and some only award them to undergraduates. Each school sets its application deadline and workstudy earnings limits. Wages vary and are related to the type of work done. You must file the Free Application for Federal Student Aid (FAFSA) to be eligible for this program.

Loans

Many graduate students borrow to finance their graduate programs when other sources of assistance (which do not have to be repaid) prove insufficient. You should always read and understand the terms of any loan program before submitting your application.

FEDERAL DIRECT LOANS

Federal Direct Loans. The Federal Direct Loan Program offers a variable-fixed interest rate loan to graduate students with the Department of Education acting as the lender. Students receive a new rate with each new loan, but that rate is fixed for the life of the loan. Beginning with loans made on or after July 1, 2013, the interest rate for loans made each July 1st to June 30th period are determined based on the last 10-year Treasury note auction prior to June 1st of that year, plus an added percentage. The interest rate can be no higher than 9.5%.

Beginning July 1, 2012, the Federal Direct Loan for graduate students is an unsubsidized loan. Under the *unsubsidized* program, the grad borrower pays the interest on the loan from the day proceeds are issued and is responsible for paying interest during all periods. If the borrower chooses not to pay the interest while in school, or during the grace periods, deferment, or forbearance, the interest accrues and will be capitalized.

Graduate students may borrow up to $20,500 per year through the Direct Loan Program, up to a cumulative maximum of $138,500, including undergraduate borrowing. No more than $65,500 of the $138,500 can be from subsidized loans, including loans the grad borrower may have received for periods of enrollment that began before July 1, 2012, or for prior undergraduate borrowing. You may borrow up to the cost of attendance at the school in which you are enrolled or will attend, minus estimated financial assistance from other federal, state, and private sources, up to a maximum of $20,500. Grad borrowers who reach the aggregate loan limit over the course of their education cannot receive additional loans; however, if they repay some of their loans to bring the outstanding balance below the aggregate limit, they could be eligible to borrow again, up to that limit.

Under the *subsidized* Federal Direct Loan Program, repayment begins six months after your last date of enrollment on at least a half-time basis. Under the *unsubsidized* program, repayment of interest begins within thirty days from disbursement of the loan proceeds, and repayment of the principal begins six months after your last enrollment on at least a half-time basis. Some borrowers may choose to defer interest payments while they are in school. The accrued interest is added to the loan balance when the borrower begins repayment. There are several repayment options.

Federal Perkins Loans. The Federal Perkins Loan is available to students demonstrating financial need and is administered directly by the school. Not all schools have these funds, and some may award them to undergraduates only. Eligibility is determined from the information you provide on the FAFSA. The school will notify you of your eligibility.

Eligible graduate students may borrow up to $8,000 per year, up to a maximum of $60,000, including undergraduate borrowing (even if your previous Perkins Loans have been repaid). The interest rate for Federal Perkins Loans is 5 percent, and no interest accrues while you remain in school at least half-time. Students who are attending less than half-time need to check with their school to determine the length of their grace period. There are no guarantee, loan, or disbursement fees. Repayment begins nine months after your last date of enrollment on at least a half-time basis and may extend over a maximum of ten years with no prepayment penalty.

Federal Direct Graduate PLUS Loans. Effective July 1, 2006, graduate and professional students are eligible for Graduate PLUS loans. This program allows students to borrow up to the cost of attendance, less any other aid received. These loans have a fixed interest rate (7.6% for loans first disbursed on or after July 1, 2018, and before July 1, 2019) and interest begins to accrue at the time of disbursement. Beginning with loans made on or after July 1, 2013, the interest rate for loans made each July 1st to June 30th period are determined based on the last 10-year Treasury note auction prior to June 1st of that year. The interest rate can be no higher than 10.5%. The PLUS loans do involve a credit check; a PLUS borrower may obtain a loan with a cosigner if his or her credit is not good enough. Grad PLUS loans may be deferred while a student is in school and for the six months following a drop below half-time enrollment. For more information, you should contact a representative in your college's financial aid office.

Deferring Your Federal Loan Repayments. If you borrowed under the Federal Direct Loan Program, Federal Direct PLUS Loan Program, or the Federal Perkins Loan Program for previous undergraduate or graduate study, your payments may be deferred when you return to graduate school, depending on when you borrowed and under which program.

There are other deferment options available if you are temporarily unable to repay your loan. Information about these deferments is provided at your entrance and exit interviews. If you believe you are eligible for a deferment of your loan payments, you must contact your lender or loan servicer to request a deferment. The deferment must be filed prior to the time your payment is due, and it must be re-filed when it expires if you remain eligible for deferment at that time.

SUPPLEMENTAL (PRIVATE) LOANS

Many lending institutions offer supplemental loan programs and other financing plans, such as the ones described here, to students seeking additional assistance in meeting their education expenses. Some loan programs target all types of graduate students; others are designed specifically for business, law, or medical students. In addition, you can use private loans not specifically designed for education to help finance your graduate degree.

If you are considering borrowing through a supplemental or private loan program, you should carefully consider the terms and be sure to read the fine print. Check with the program sponsor for the most current terms that will be applicable to the amounts you intend to borrow for graduate study. Most supplemental loan programs for graduate study offer unsubsidized, credit-based loans. In general, a credit-ready borrower is one who has a satisfactory credit history or no credit history at all. A creditworthy borrower generally must pass a credit test to be eligible to borrow or act as a cosigner for the loan funds.

Many supplemental loan programs have minimum and maximum annual loan limits. Some offer amounts equal to the cost of attendance minus any other aid you will receive for graduate study. If you are planning to borrow for several years of graduate study, consider whether there is a cumulative or aggregate limit on the amount you may borrow. Often this cumulative or aggregate limit will include any amounts you borrowed and have not repaid for undergraduate or previous graduate study.

The combination of the annual interest rate, loan fees, and the repayment terms you choose will determine how much you will repay over time. Compare these features in combination before you decide which loan program to use. Some loans offer interest rates that are adjusted monthly, quarterly, or annually. Some offer interest rates that are lower during the in-school, grace, and deferment periods and then increase when you begin repayment. Some programs include a loan origination fee, which is usually deducted from the principal amount you receive when the loan is disbursed and must be repaid along with the interest and other principal when you graduate, withdraw from school, or drop below half-time study. Sometimes the loan fees are reduced if you borrow with a qualified cosigner. Some programs allow you to defer interest and/or principal payments while you are enrolled in graduate school. Many programs allow you to capitalize your interest payments; the interest due on your loan is added to the outstanding balance of your loan, so you don't have to repay immediately, but this increases the amount you owe. Other programs allow you to pay the interest as you go, which reduces the amount you later have to repay. The private loan market is very competitive, and your financial aid office can help you evaluate these programs.

Applying for Need-Based Financial Aid

Schools that award federal and institutional financial assistance based on need will require you to complete the FAFSA and, in some cases, an institutional financial aid application.

If you are applying for federal student assistance, you **must** complete the FAFSA. A service of the U.S. Department of Education, the FAFSA is free to all applicants. Most applicants apply online at **www.fafsa.ed.gov**. Paper applications are available at the financial aid office of your local college.

After your FAFSA information has been processed, you will receive a Student Aid Report (SAR). If you provided an e-mail address on the FAFSA, this will be sent to you electronically; otherwise, it will be mailed to your home address.

Follow the instructions on the SAR if you need to correct information reported on your original application. If your situation changes after you file your FAFSA, contact your financial aid officer to discuss amending your information. You can also appeal your financial aid award if you have extenuating circumstances.

If you would like more information on federal student financial aid, visit the FAFSA website or download the most recent version of *Do You Need Money for College* at www.studentaid.ed.gov/sa/sites/default/files/2018-19-do-you-need-money.pdf. This guide is also available in Spanish.

The U.S. Department of Education also has a toll-free number for questions concerning federal student aid programs. The number is 1-800-4-FED AID (1-800-433-3243). If you are hearing impaired, call toll-free, 1-800-730-8913.

Summary

Remember that these are generalized statements about financial assistance at the graduate level. Because each institution allots its aid differently, you should communicate directly with the school and the specific department of Interest to you. It is not unusual, for example, to find that an endowment vested within a specific department supports one or more fellowships. You may fit its requirements and specifications precisely.

Accreditation and Accrediting Agencies

Colleges and universities in the United States, and their individual academic and professional programs, are accredited by nongovernmental agencies concerned with monitoring the quality of education in this country. Agencies with both regional and national jurisdictions grant accreditation to institutions as a whole, while specialized bodies acting on a nationwide basis—often national professional associations—grant accreditation to departments and programs in specific fields.

Institutional and specialized accrediting agencies share the same basic concerns: the purpose an academic unit—whether university or program—has set for itself and how well it fulfills that purpose, the adequacy of its financial and other resources, the quality of its academic offerings, and the level of services it provides. Agencies that grant institutional accreditation take a broader view, of course, and examine university-wide or college-wide services with which a specialized agency may not concern itself.

Both types of agencies follow the same general procedures when considering an application for accreditation. The academic unit prepares a self-evaluation, focusing on the concerns mentioned above and usually including an assessment of both its strengths and weaknesses; a team of representatives of the accrediting body reviews this evaluation, visits the campus, and makes its own report; and finally, the accrediting body makes a decision on the application. Often, even when accreditation is granted, the agency makes a recommendation regarding how the institution or program can improve. All institutions and programs are also reviewed every few years to determine whether they continue to meet established standards; if they do not, they may lose their accreditation.

Accrediting agencies themselves are reviewed and evaluated periodically by the U.S. Department of Education and the Council for Higher Education Accreditation (CHEA). Recognized agencies adhere to certain standards and practices, and their authority in matters of accreditation is widely accepted in the educational community.

This does not mean, however, that accreditation is a simple matter, either for schools wishing to become accredited or for students deciding where to apply. Indeed, in certain fields the very meaning and methods of accreditation are the subject of a good deal of debate. For their part, those applying to graduate school should be aware of the safeguards provided by regional accreditation, especially in terms of degree acceptance and institutional longevity. Beyond this, applicants should understand the role that specialized accreditation plays in their field, as this varies considerably from one discipline to another. In certain professional fields, it is necessary to have graduated from a program that is accredited in order to be eligible for a license to practice, and in some fields the federal government also makes this a hiring requirement. In other disciplines, however, accreditation is not as essential, and there can be excellent programs that are not accredited. In fact, some programs choose not to seek accreditation, although most do.

Institutions and programs that present themselves for accreditation are sometimes granted the status of candidate for accreditation, or what is known as "preaccreditation." This may happen, for example, when an academic unit is too new to have met all the requirements for accreditation. Such status signifies initial recognition and indicates that the school or program in question is working to fulfill all requirements; it does not, however, guarantee that accreditation will be granted.

Institutional Accrediting Agencies—Regional

MIDDLE STATES COMMISSION ON HIGHER EDUCATION

Accredits institutions in Delaware, District of Columbia, Maryland, New Jersey, New York, Pennsylvania, Puerto Rico, and the Virgin Islands.

Dr. Elizabeth Sibolski, President
Middle States Commission on Higher Education
3624 Market Street, Second Floor West
Philadelphia, Pennsylvania 19104
Phone: 267-284-5000
Fax: 215-662-5501
E-mail: info@msche.org
Website: www.msche.org

NEW ENGLAND ASSOCIATION OF SCHOOLS AND COLLEGES

Accredits institutions in Connecticut, Maine, Massachusetts, New Hampshire, Rhode Island, and Vermont.

Dr. Barbara E. Brittingham, President/Director
Commission on Institutions of Higher Education
3 Burlington Woods Drive, Suite 100
Burlington, Massachusetts 01803-4531
Phone: 855-886-3272 or 781-425-7714
Fax: 781-425-1001
E-mail: cihe@neasc.org
Website: https://cihe.neasc.org

THE HIGHER LEARNING COMMISSION

Accredits institutions in Arizona, Arkansas, Colorado, Illinois, Indiana, Iowa, Kansas, Michigan, Minnesota, Missouri, Nebraska, New Mexico, North Dakota, Ohio, Oklahoma, South Dakota, West Virginia, Wisconsin, and Wyoming.

Dr. Barbara Gellman-Danley, President
The Higher Learning Commission
230 South LaSalle Street, Suite 7-500
Chicago, Illinois 60604-1413
Phone: 800-621-7440 or 312-263-0456
Fax: 312-263-7462
E-mail: info@hlcommission.org
Website: www.hlcommission.org

NORTHWEST COMMISSION ON COLLEGES AND UNIVERSITIES

Accredits institutions in Alaska, Idaho, Montana, Nevada, Oregon, Utah, and Washington.

Dr. Sandra E. Elman, President
8060 165th Avenue, NE, Suite 100
Redmond, Washington 98052
Phone: 425-558-4224
Fax: 425-376-0596
E-mail: selman@nwccu.org
Website: www.nwccu.org

SOUTHERN ASSOCIATION OF COLLEGES AND SCHOOLS

Accredits institutions in Alabama, Florida, Georgia, Kentucky, Louisiana, Mississippi, North Carolina, South Carolina, Tennessee, Texas, and Virginia.

Dr. Belle S. Wheelan, President
Commission on Colleges
1866 Southern Lane
Decatur, Georgia 30033-4097
Phone: 404-679-4500 Ext. 4504
Fax: 404-679-4558
E-mail: questions@sacscoc.org
Website: www.sacscoc.org

WESTERN ASSOCIATION OF SCHOOLS AND COLLEGES

Accredits institutions in California, Guam, and Hawaii.

Jamienne S. Studley, President
WASC Senior College and University Commission
985 Atlantic Avenue, Suite 100
Alameda, California 94501
Phone: 510-748-9001
Fax: 510-748-9797
E-mail: wasc@wscuc.org
Website: https://www.wscuc.org/

Institutional Accrediting Agencies—Other

ACCREDITING COUNCIL FOR INDEPENDENT COLLEGES AND SCHOOLS
Michelle Edwards, President
750 First Street NE, Suite 980
Washington, DC 20002-4223
Phone: 202-336-6780
Fax: 202-842-2593
E-mail: info@acics.org
Website: www.acics.org

DISTANCE EDUCATION ACCREDITING COMMISSION (DEAC)
Leah Matthews, Executive Director
1101 17th Street NW, Suite 808
Washington, DC 20036-4704
Phone: 202-234-5100
Fax: 202-332-1386
E-mail: info@deac.org
Website: www.deac.org

Specialized Accrediting Agencies

ACUPUNCTURE AND ORIENTAL MEDICINE
Mark S. McKenzie, LAc MsOM DiplOM, Executive Director
Accreditation Commission for Acupuncture and Oriental Medicine
8941 Aztec Drive, Suite 2
Eden Prairie, Minnesota 55347
Phone: 952-212-2434
Fax: 301-313-0912
E-mail: info@acaom.org
Website: www.acaom.org

ALLIED HEALTH
Kathleen Megivern, Executive Director
Commission on Accreditation of Allied Health Education Programs (CAAHEP)
25400 US Hwy 19 North, Suite 158
Clearwater, Florida 33763
Phone: 727-210-2350
Fax: 727-210-2354
E-mail: mail@caahep.org
Website: www.caahep.org

ART AND DESIGN
Karen P. Moynahan, Executive Director
National Association of Schools of Art and Design (NASAD)
Commission on Accreditation
11250 Roger Bacon Drive, Suite 21
Reston, Virginia 20190-5248
Phone: 703-437-0700
Fax: 703-437-6312
E-mail: info@arts-accredit.org
Website: http://nasad.arts-accredit.org

ATHLETIC TRAINING EDUCATION
Pamela Hansen, CAATE Director of Accreditation
Commission on Accreditation of Athletic Training Education (CAATE)
6850 Austin Center Blvd., Suite 100
Austin, Texas 78731-3184
Phone: 512-733-9700
E-mail: pamela@caate.net
Website: www.caate.net

AUDIOLOGY EDUCATION
Meggan Olek, Director
Accreditation Commission for Audiology Education (ACAE)
11480 Commerce Park Drive, Suite 220
Reston, Virginia 20191
Phone: 202-986-9500
Fax: 202-986-9550
E-mail: info@acaeaccred.org
Website: https://acaeaccred.org/

AVIATION
Dr. Gary J. Northam, President
Aviation Accreditation Board International (AABI)
3410 Skyway Drive
Auburn, Alabama 36830
Phone: 334-844-2431
Fax: 334-844-2432
E-mail: gary.northam@auburn.edu
Website: www.aabi.aero

BUSINESS
Stephanie Bryant, Executive Vice President and Chief Accreditation Officer
AACSB International—The Association to Advance Collegiate Schools of Business
777 South Harbour Island Boulevard, Suite 750
Tampa, Florida 33602
Phone: 813-769-6500
Fax: 813-769-6559
E-mail: stephanie.bryant@aacsb.edu
Website: www.aacsb.edu

BUSINESS EDUCATION
Dr. Phyllis Okrepkie, President
International Assembly for Collegiate Business Education (IACBE)
11374 Strang Line Road
Lenexa, Kansas 66215
Phone: 913-631-3009
Fax: 913-631-9154
E-mail: iacbe@iacbe.org
Website: www.iacbe.org

CHIROPRACTIC
Dr. Craig S. Little, President
Council on Chiropractic Education (CCE)
Commission on Accreditation
8049 North 85th Way
Scottsdale, Arizona 85258-4321
Phone: 480-443-8877 or 888-443-3506
Fax: 480-483-7333
E-mail: cce@cce-usa.org
Website: www.cce-usa.org

CLINICAL LABORATORY SCIENCES
Dianne M. Cearlock, Ph.D., Chief Executive Officer
National Accrediting Agency for Clinical Laboratory Sciences
5600 North River Road, Suite 720
Rosemont, Illinois 60018-5119
Phone: 773-714-8880 or 847-939-3597
Fax: 773-714-8886
E-mail: info@naacls.org
Website: www.naacls.org

CLINICAL PASTORAL EDUCATION
Trace Haythorn, Ph.D., Executive Director/CEO
Association for Clinical Pastoral Education, Inc.
One West Court Square, Suite 325
Decatur, Georgia 30030-2576
Phone: 678-363-6226
Fax: 404-320-0849
E-mail: acpe@acpe.edu
Website: www.acpe.edu

DANCE
Karen P. Moynahan, Executive Director
National Association of Schools of Dance (NASD)
Commission on Accreditation
11250 Roger Bacon Drive, Suite 21
Reston, Virginia 20190-5248
Phone: 703-437-0700
Fax: 703-437-6312
E-mail: info@arts-accredit.org
Website: http://nasd.arts-accredit.org

DENTISTRY
Dr. Kathleen T. O'Loughlin, Executive Director

Commission on Dental Accreditation
American Dental Association
211 East Chicago Avenue
Chicago, Illinois 60611
Phone: 312-440-2500
E-mail: accreditation@ada.org
Website: www.ada.org

DIETETICS AND NUTRITION
Mary B. Gregoire, Ph.D., Executive Director; RD, FADA, FAND
Academy of Nutrition and Dietetics
Accreditation Council for Education in Nutrition and Dietetics (ACEND)
120 South Riverside Plaza
Chicago, Illinois 60606-6995
Phone: 800-877-1600 or 312-899-0040
E-mail: acend@eatright.org
Website: www.eatright.org/cade

EDUCATION PREPARATION
Christopher Koch, President
Council for the Accreditation of Educator Preparation (CAEP)
1140 19th Street NW, Suite 400
Washington, DC 20036
Phone: 202-223-0077
Fax: 202-296-6620
E-mail: caep@caepnet.org
Website: www.caepnet.org

ENGINEERING
Michael Milligan, Ph.D., PE, Executive Director
Accreditation Board for Engineering and Technology, Inc. (ABET)
415 North Charles Street
Baltimore, Maryland 21201
Phone: 410-347-7700
E-mail: accreditation@abet.org
Website: www.abet.org

FORENSIC SCIENCES
Nancy J. Jackson, Director of Development and Accreditation
American Academy of Forensic Sciences (AAFS)
Forensic Science Education Program Accreditation Commission (FEPAC)
410 North 21st Street
Colorado Springs, Colorado 80904
Phone: 719-636-1100
Fax: 719-636-1993
E-mail: njackson@aafs.org
Website: www.fepac-edu.org

FORESTRY
Carol L. Redelsheimer
Director of Science and Education
Society of American Foresters
10100 Laureate Way
Bethesda, Maryland 20814-2198
Phone: 301-897-8720 or 866-897-8720
Fax: 301-897-3690
E-mail: membership@safnet.org
Website: www.eforester.com

HEALTHCARE MANAGEMENT
Commission on Accreditation of Healthcare Management Education (CAHME)
Anthony Stanowski, President and CEO
6110 Executive Boulevard, Suite 614
Rockville, Maryland 20852
Phone: 301-298-1820
E-mail: info@cahme.org
Website: www.cahme.org

HEALTH INFORMATICS AND HEALTH MANAGEMENT
Angela Kennedy, EdD, MBA, RHIA, Chief Executive Officer
Commission on Accreditation for Health Informatics and Information Management Education (CAHIIM)
233 North Michigan Avenue, 21st Floor
Chicago, Illinois 60601-5800
Phone: 312-233-1134
Fax: 312-233-1948
E-mail: info@cahiim.org
Website: www.cahiim.org

HUMAN SERVICE EDUCATION
Dr. Elaine Green, President
Council for Standards in Human Service Education (CSHSE)
3337 Duke Street
Alexandria, Virginia 22314
Phone: 571-257-3959
E-mail: info@cshse.org
Website: www.cshse.org

INTERIOR DESIGN
Holly Mattson, Executive Director
Council for Interior Design Accreditation
206 Grandview Avenue, Suite 350
Grand Rapids, Michigan 49503-4014
Phone: 616-458-0400
Fax: 616-458-0460
E-mail: info@accredit-id.org
Website: www.accredit-id.org

JOURNALISM AND MASS COMMUNICATIONS
Patricia Thompson, Executive Director
Accrediting Council on Education in Journalism and Mass Communications (ACEJMC)
201 Bishop Hall
P.O. Box 1848
University, MS 38677-1848
Phone: 662-915-5504
E-mail: pthomps1@olemiss.edu
Website: www.acejmc.org

LANDSCAPE ARCHITECTURE
Nancy Somerville, Executive Vice President, CEO
American Society of Landscape Architects (ASLA)
636 Eye Street, NW
Washington, DC 20001-3736
Phone: 202-898-2444
Fax: 202-898-1185
E-mail: info@asla.org
Website: www.asla.org

LAW
Barry Currier, Managing Director of Accreditation & Legal Education
American Bar Association
321 North Clark Street, 21st Floor
Chicago, Illinois 60654
Phone: 312-988-6738
Fax: 312-988-5681
E-mail: legaled@americanbar.org
Website: https://www.americanbar.org/groups/legal_education/accreditation.html

LIBRARY
Karen O'Brien, Director
Office for Accreditation
American Library Association
50 East Huron Street
Chicago, Illinois 60611-2795
Phone: 800-545-2433, ext. 2432 or 312-280-2432
Fax: 312-280-2433
E-mail: accred@ala.org
Website: http://www.ala.org/aboutala/offices/accreditation/

MARRIAGE AND FAMILY THERAPY
Tanya A. Tamarkin, Director of Educational Affairs
Commission on Accreditation for Marriage and Family Therapy Education (COAMFTE)
American Association for Marriage and Family Therapy
112 South Alfred Street
Alexandria, Virginia 22314-3061

Phone: 703-838-9808
Fax: 703-838-9805
E-mail: coa@aamft.org
Website: www.aamft.org

MEDICAL ILLUSTRATION
Kathleen Megivern, Executive Director
Commission on Accreditation of Allied Health Education Programs (CAAHEP)
25400 US Highway 19 North, Suite 158
Clearwater, Florida 33756
Phone: 727-210-2350
Fax: 727-210-2354
E-mail: mail@caahep.org
Website: www.caahep.org

MEDICINE
Liaison Committee on Medical Education (LCME)
Robert B. Hash, M.D., LCME Secretary
American Medical Association
Council on Medical Education
330 North Wabash Avenue, Suite 39300
Chicago, Illinois 60611-5885
Phone: 312-464-4933
E-mail: lcme@aamc.org
Website: www.ama-assn.org

Liaison Committee on Medical Education (LCME)
Heather Lent, M.A., Director
Accreditation Services
Association of American Medical Colleges
655 K Street, NW
Washington, DC 20001-2399
Phone: 202-828-0596
E-mail: lcme@aamc.org
Website: www.lcme.org

MUSIC
Karen P. Moynahan, Executive Director
National Association of Schools of Music (NASM)
Commission on Accreditation
11250 Roger Bacon Drive, Suite 21
Reston, Virginia 20190-5248
Phone: 703-437-0700
Fax: 703-437-6312
E-mail: info@arts-accredit.org
Website: http://nasm.arts-accredit.org/

NATUROPATHIC MEDICINE
Daniel Seitz, J.D., Ed.D., Executive Director
Council on Naturopathic Medical Education
P.O. Box 178
Great Barrington, Massachusetts 01230
Phone: 413-528-8877
E-mail: https://cnme.org/contact-us/
Website: www.cnme.org

NURSE ANESTHESIA
Francis R.Gerbasi, Ph.D., CRNA, COA Executive Director
Council on Accreditation of Nurse Anesthesia Educational Programs (CoA-NAEP)
American Association of Nurse Anesthetists
222 South Prospect Avenue
Park Ridge, Illinois 60068-4001
Phone: 847-655-1160
Fax: 847-692-7137
E-mail: accreditation@coa.us.com
Website: http://www.coacrna.org

NURSE EDUCATION
Jennifer L. Butlin, Executive Director
Commission on Collegiate Nursing Education (CCNE)
One Dupont Circle, NW, Suite 530
Washington, DC 20036-1120
Phone: 202-887-6791
Fax: 202-887-8476
E-mail: jbutlin@aacn.nche.edu
Website: www.aacn.nche.edu/accreditation

Marsal P. Stoll, Chief Executive Officer
Accreditation Commission for Education in Nursing (ACEN)
3343 Peachtree Road, NE, Suite 850
Atlanta, Georgia 30326
Phone: 404-975-5000
Fax: 404-975-5020
E-mail: mstoll@acenursing.org
Website: www.acenursing.org

NURSE MIDWIFERY
Heather L. Maurer, M.A., Executive Director
Accreditation Commission for Midwifery Education (ACME)
American College of Nurse-Midwives
8403 Colesville Road, Suite 1550
Silver Spring, Maryland 20910
Phone: 240-485-1800
Fax: 240-485-1818
E-mail: info@acnm.org
Website: www.midwife.org/Program-Accreditation

NURSE PRACTITIONER
Gay Johnson, CEO
National Association of Nurse Practitioners in Women's Health
Council on Accreditation
505 C Street, NE
Washington, DC 20002
Phone: 202-543-9693 Ext. 1
Fax: 202-543-9858
E-mail: info@npwh.org
Website: www.npwh.org

NURSING
Marsal P. Stoll, Chief Executive Director
Accreditation Commission for Education in Nursing (ACEN)
3343 Peachtree Road, NE, Suite 850
Atlanta, Georgia 30326
Phone: 404-975-5000
Fax: 404-975-5020
E-mail: info@acenursing.org
Website: www.acenursing.org

OCCUPATIONAL THERAPY
Heather Stagliano, DHSc, OTR/L, Executive Director
The American Occupational Therapy Association, Inc.
4720 Montgomery Lane, Suite 200
Bethesda, Maryland 20814-3449
Phone: 301-652-6611 Ext. 2682
TDD: 800-377-8555
Fax: 240-762-5150
E-mail: accred@aota.org
Website: www.aoteonline.org

OPTOMETRY
Joyce L. Urbeck, Administrative Director
Accreditation Council on Optometric Education (ACOE)
American Optometric Association
243 North Lindbergh Boulevard
St. Louis, Missouri 63141-7881
Phone: 314-991-4100, Ext. 4246
Fax: 314-991-4101
E-mail: accredit@aoa.org
Website: www.theacoe.org

OSTEOPATHIC MEDICINE
Director, Department of Accreditation
Commission on Osteopathic College Accreditation (COCA)
American Osteopathic Association
142 East Ontario Street
Chicago, Illinois 60611
Phone: 312-202-8048
Fax: 312-202-8202
E-mail: predoc@osteopathic.org
Website: www.aoacoca.org

PHARMACY
Peter H. Vlasses, PharmD, Executive Director
Accreditation Council for Pharmacy Education
135 South LaSalle Street, Suite 4100
Chicago, Illinois 60603-4810
Phone: 312-664-3575
Fax: 312-664-4652
E-mail: csinfo@acpe-accredit.org
Website: www.acpe-accredit.org

PHYSICAL THERAPY
Sandra Wise, Senior Director
Commission on Accreditation in Physical Therapy Education (CAPTE)
American Physical Therapy Association (APTA)
1111 North Fairfax Street
Alexandria, Virginia 22314-1488
Phone: 703-706-3245
Fax: 703-706-3387
E-mail: accreditation@apta.org
Website: www.capteonline.org

PHYSICIAN ASSISTANT STUDIES
Sharon L. Luke, Executive Director
Accredittion Review Commission on Education for the Physician Assistant, Inc. (ARC-PA)
12000 Findley Road, Suite 275
Johns Creek, Georgia 30097
Phone: 770-476-1224
Fax: 770-476-1738
E-mail: arc-pa@arc-pa.org
Website: www.arc-pa.org

PLANNING
Jesmarie Soto Johnson, Executive Director
American Institute of Certified Planners/Association of Collegiate Schools of Planning/American Planning Association
Planning Accreditation Board (PAB)
2334 West Lawrence Avenue, Suite 209
Chicago, Illinois 60625
Phone: 773-334-7200
E-mail: smerits@planningaccreditationboard.org
Website: www.planningaccreditationboard.org

PODIATRIC MEDICINE
Heather Stagliano, OTR/L, DHSc, Executive Director
Council on Podiatric Medical Education (CPME)
American Podiatric Medical Association (APMA)
9312 Old Georgetown Road
Bethesda, Maryland 20814-1621
Phone: 301-581-9200
Fax: 301-571-4903
Website: www.cpme.org

PSYCHOLOGY AND COUNSELING
Jacqueline Remondet, Associate Executive Director, CEO of the Accrediting Unit,
Office of Program Consultation and Accreditation
American Psychological Association
750 First Street, NE
Washington, DC 20002-4202
Phone: 202-336-5979 or 800-374-2721
TDD/TTY: 202-336-6123
Fax: 202-336-5978
E-mail: apaaccred@apa.org
Website: www.apa.org/ed/accreditation

Kelly Coker, Executive Director
Council for Accreditation of Counseling and Related Educational Programs (CACREP)
1001 North Fairfax Street, Suite 510
Alexandria, Virginia 22314
Phone: 703-535-5990
Fax: 703-739-6209
E-mail: cacrep@cacrep.org
Website: www.cacrep.org

Richard M. McFall, Executive Director
Psychological Clinical Science Accreditation System (PCSAS)
1101 East Tenth Street
IU Psychology Building
Bloomington, Indiana 47405-7007
Phone: 812-856-2570
Fax: 812-322-5545
E-mail: rmmcfall@pcsas.org
Website: www.pcsas.org

PUBLIC HEALTH
Laura Rasar King, M.P.H., MCHES, Executive Director
Council on Education for Public Health
1010 Wayne Avenue, Suite 220
Silver Spring, Maryland 20910
Phone: 202-789-1050
Fax: 202-789-1895
E-mail: Lking@ceph.org
Website: www.ceph.org

PUBLIC POLICY, AFFAIRS AND ADMINISTRATION
Crystal Calarusse, Chief Accreditation Officer
Commission on Peer Review and Accreditation
Network of Schools of Public Policy, Affairs, and Administration (NASPAA-COPRA)
1029 Vermont Avenue, NW, Suite 1100
Washington, DC 20005
Phone: 202-628-8965
Fax: 202-626-4978
E-mail: copra@naspaa.org
Website: accreditation.naspaa.org

RADIOLOGIC TECHNOLOGY
Leslie Winter, Chief Executive Officer Joint Review Committee on Education in Radiologic Technology (JRCERT)
20 North Wacker Drive, Suite 2850
Chicago, Illinois 60606-3182
Phone: 312-704-5300
Fax: 312-704-5304
E-mail: mail@jrcert.org
Website: www.jrcert.org

REHABILITATION EDUCATION
Frank Lane, Ph.D., Executive Director
Council for Accreditation of Counseling and Related Educational Programs (CACREP)
1001 North Fairfax Street, Suite 510
Alexandria, Virginia 22314
Phone: 703-535-5990
Fax: 703-739-6209
E-mail: cacrep@cacrep.org
Website: www.cacrep.org

RESPIRATORY CARE
Thomas Smalling, Executive Director
Commission on Accreditation for Respiratory Care (CoARC)
1248 Harwood Road
Bedford, Texas 76021-4244
Phone: 817-283-2835
Fax: 817-354-8519
E-mail: tom@coarc.com
Website: www.coarc.com

SOCIAL WORK
Dr. Stacey Borasky, Director of Accreditation
Office of Social Work Accreditation
Council on Social Work Education
1701 Duke Street, Suite 200
Alexandria, Virginia 22314
Phone: 703-683-8080
Fax: 703-519-2078
E-mail: info@cswe.org
Website: www.cswe.org

SPEECH-LANGUAGE PATHOLOGY AND AUDIOLOGY
Kimberlee Moore, Accreditation Executive Director
American Speech-Language-Hearing Association
Council on Academic Accreditation in Audiology and Speech-Language Pathology
2200 Research Boulevard #310
Rockville, Maryland 20850-3289
Phone: 301-296-5700
Fax: 301-296-8750
E-mail: accreditation@asha.org
Website: http://caa.asha.org

TEACHER EDUCATION
Christopher A. Koch, President
National Council for Accreditation of Teacher Education (NCATE)
Teacher Education Accreditation Council (TEAC)
1140 19th Street, Suite 400
Washington, DC 20036
Phone: 202-223-0077
Fax: 202-296-6620
E-mail: caep@caepnet.org
Website: www.ncate.org

TECHNOLOGY
Michale S. McComis, Ed.D., Executive Director
Accrediting Commission of Career Schools and Colleges
2101 Wilson Boulevard, Suite 302
Arlington, Virginia 22201
Phone: 703-247-4212
Fax: 703-247-4533
E-mail: mccomis@accsc.org
Website: www.accsc.org

TECHNOLOGY, MANAGEMENT, AND APPLIED ENGINEERING
Kelly Schild, Director of Accreditation
The Association of Technology, Management, and Applied Engineering (ATMAE)
275 N. York Street, Suite 401
Elmhurst, Illinois 60126
Phone: 630-433-4514
Fax: 630-563-9181
E-mail: Kelly@atmae.org
Website: www.atmae.org

THEATER
Karen P. Moynahan, Executive Director
National Association of Schools of Theatre Commission on Accreditation
11250 Roger Bacon Drive, Suite 21
Reston, Virginia 20190
Phone: 703-437-0700
Fax: 703-437-6312
E-mail: info@arts-accredit.org
Website: http://nast.arts-accredit.org/

THEOLOGY
Dr. Bernard Fryshman, Executive VP
Emeritus and Interim Executive Director
Association of Advanced Rabbinical and Talmudic Schools (AARTS)
Accreditation Commission
11 Broadway, Suite 405
New York, New York 10004
Phone: 212-363-1991
Fax: 212-533-5335
E-mail: k.sharfman.aarts@gmail.com

Frank Yamada, Executive Director
Association of Theological Schools in the United States and Canada (ATS)
Commission on Accrediting
10 Summit Park Drive
Pittsburgh, Pennsylvania 15275
Phone: 412-788-6505
Fax: 412-788-6510
E-mail: ats@ats.edu
Website: www.ats.edu

Dr. Timothy Eaton, President
Transnational Association of Christian Colleges and Schools (TRACS)
Accreditation Commission
15935 Forest Road
Forest, Virginia 24551
Phone: 434-525-9539
Fax: 434-525-9538
E-mail: info@tracs.org
Website: www.tracs.org

VETERINARY MEDICINE
Dr. Karen Brandt, Director of Education and Research
American Veterinary Medical Association (AVMA)
Council on Education
1931 North Meacham Road, Suite 100
Schaumburg, Illinois 60173-4360
Phone: 847-925-8070 Ext. 6674
Fax: 847-285-5732
E-mail: info@avma.org
Website: www.avma.org

How to Use These Guides

As you identify the particular programs and institutions that interest you, you can use both the ***Graduate & Professional Programs: An Overview*** volume and the specialized volumes in the series to obtain detailed information.

- ***Graduate Programs in the Biological/Biomedical Sciences & Health-Related Professions***
- ***Graduate Programs in Business, Education, Information Studies, Law & Social Work***
- ***Graduate Programs in Engineering & Applied Sciences***
- ***Graduate Programs the Humanities, Arts & Social Sciences***
- ***Graduate Programs in the Physical Sciences, Mathematics, Agricultural Sciences, the Environment & Natural Resources***

Each of the specialized volumes in the series is divided into sections that contain one or more directories devoted to programs in a particular field. If you do not find a directory devoted to your field of interest in a specific volume, consult "Directories and Subject Areas" (located at the end of each volume). After you have identified the correct volume, consult the "Directories and Subject Areas in This Book" index, which shows (as does the more general directory) what directories cover subjects not specifically named in a directory or section title.

Each of the specialized volumes in the series has a number of general directories. These directories have entries for the largest unit at an institution granting graduate degrees in that field. For example, the general Engineering and Applied Sciences directory in the ***Graduate Programs in Engineering & Applied Sciences*** volume consists of **Profiles** for colleges, schools, and departments of engineering and applied sciences.

General directories are followed by other directories, or sections, that give more detailed information about programs in particular areas of the general field that has been covered. The general Engineering and Applied Sciences directory, in the previous example, is followed by nineteen sections with directories in specific areas of engineering, such as Chemical Engineering, Industrial/Management Engineering, and Mechanical Engineering.

Because of the broad nature of many fields, any system of organization is bound to involve a certain amount of overlap. Environmental studies, for example, is a field whose various aspects are studied in several types of departments and schools. Readers interested in such studies will find information on relevant programs in the ***Graduate Programs in the Biological/Biomedical Sciences & Health-Related Professions*** volume under Ecology and Environmental Biology and Environmental and Occupational Health; in the ***Graduate Programs in the Physical Sciences, Mathematics, Agricultural Sciences, the Environment & Natural Resources*** volume under Environmental Management and Policy and Natural Resources; and in the ***Graduate Programs in Engineering & Applied Sciences*** volume under Energy Management and Policy and Environmental Engineering. To help you find all of the programs of interest to you, the introduction to each section within the specialized volumes includes, if applicable, a paragraph suggesting other sections and directories with information on related areas of study.

Directory of Institutions with Programs in the Physical Sciences, Mathematics, Agricultural Sciences, the Environment & Natural Resources

This directory lists institutions in alphabetical order and includes beneath each name the academic fields in which each institution offers graduate programs. The degree level in each field is also indicated, provided that the institution has supplied that information in response to Peterson's Annual Survey of Graduate and Professional Institutions.

An M indicates that a master's degree program is offered; a D indicates that a doctoral degree program is offered; an O signifies that other advanced degrees (e.g., certificates or specialist degrees) are offered; and an * (asterisk) indicates that a **Close-Up** and/or **Display** is located in this volume. See the index, "Close-Ups and Displays," for the specific page number.

Profiles of Academic and Professional Programs in the Specialized Volumes

Each section of **Profiles** has a table of contents that lists the Program Directories, **Displays**, and **Close-Ups.** Program Directories consist of the **Profiles** of programs in the relevant fields, with **Displays** following if programs have chosen to include them. **Close-Ups,** which are more individualized statements, are also listed for those graduate schools or programs that have chosen to submit them.

The **Profiles** found in the 500 directories in the specialized volumes provide basic data about the graduate units in capsule form for quick reference. To make these directories as useful as possible, **Profiles** are generally listed for an institution's smallest academic unit within a subject area. In other words, if an institution has a College of Liberal Arts that administers many related programs, the **Profile** for the individual program (e.g., Program in History), not the entire College, appears in the directory.

There are some programs that do not fit into any current directory and are not given individual **Profiles.** The directory structure is reviewed annually in order to keep this number to a minimum and to accommodate major trends in graduate education.

The following outline describes the **Profile** information found in the guides and explains how best to use that information. Any item that does not apply to or was not provided by a graduate unit is omitted from its listing. The format of the **Profiles** is constant, making it easy to compare one institution with another and one program with another.

A ★ graphic next to the school's name indicates the institution has additional detailed information in a "Premium Profile" on Petersons.com. After reading their information here, you can learn more about the school by visiting www.petersons.com and searching for that particular college or university's graduate program.

Identifying Information. The institution's name, in boldface type, is followed by a complete listing of the administrative structure for that field of study. (For example, University of Akron, Buchtel College of Arts and Sciences, Department of Theoretical and Applied Mathematics, Program in Mathematics.) The last unit listed is the one to which all information in the **Profile** pertains. The institution's city, state, and ZIP code follow.

Offerings. Each field of study offered by the unit is listed with all postbaccalaureate degrees awarded. Degrees that are not preceded by a specific concentration are awarded in the general field listed in the unit name. Frequently, fields of study are broken down into subspecializations, and those appear following the degrees awarded; for example, "Offerings in secondary education (M.Ed.), including English education, mathematics education, science education." Students enrolled in the M.Ed. program would be able to specialize in any of the three fields mentioned.

Professional Accreditation. Some **Profiles** indicate whether a program is professionally accredited. Because it is possible for a program to receive or lose professional accreditation at any time, students entering fields in which accreditation is important to a career should verify the status of programs by contacting either the chairperson or the appropriate accrediting association.

Jointly Offered Degrees. Explanatory statements concerning programs that are offered in cooperation with other institutions are included in the list of degrees offered. This occurs most commonly on a regional basis (for example, two state universities offering a cooperative Ph.D. in special education) or where the specialized nature of the institutions encourages joint efforts (a J.D./M.B.A. offered by a law school at an institution with no formal business programs and an institution with a business school but lacking a law school). Only programs that are truly cooperative are listed; those involving only limited course work at another institution are not. Interested students should contact the heads of such units for further information.

Program Availability. This may include the following: part-time, evening/weekend, online only, 100% online, blended/hybrid learning, and/or minimal on-campus study. When information regarding the availability of part-time or evening/weekend study appears in the **Profile**, it means that students are able to earn a degree exclusively through such study. Blended/hybrid learning describes those courses in which some traditional in-class time has been replaced by online learning activities. Hybrid courses take advantage of the best features of both face-to-face and online learning.

Faculty. Figures on the number of faculty members actively involved with graduate students through teaching or research are separated into full- and part-time as well as men and women whenever the information has been supplied.

Students. Figures for the number of students enrolled in graduate and professional programs pertain to the semester of highest enrollment from the 2017–18 academic year. These figures are broken down into full- and part-time and men and women whenever the data have been supplied. Information on the number of matriculated students enrolled in the unit who are members of a minority group or are international students appears here. The average age of the matriculated students is followed by the number of applicants, the percentage accepted, and the number enrolled for fall 2017.

Degrees Awarded. The number of degrees awarded in the calendar year is listed. Many doctoral programs offer a terminal master's degree if students leave the program after completing only part of the requirements for a doctoral degree; that is indicated here. All degrees are classified into one of four types: master's, doctoral, first professional, and other advanced degrees. A unit may award one or several degrees at a given level; however, the data are only collected by type and may therefore represent several different degree programs.

Degree Requirements. The information in this section is also broken down by type of degree, and all information for a degree level pertains to all degrees of that type unless otherwise specified. Degree requirements are collected in a simplified form to provide some very basic information on the nature of the program and on foreign language, thesis or dissertation, comprehensive exam, and registration requirements. Many units also provide a short list of additional requirements, such as fieldwork or an internship. For complete information on graduation requirements, contact the graduate school or program directly.

Entrance Requirements. Entrance requirements are broken down into the four degree levels of master's, doctoral, first professional, and other advanced degrees. Within each level, information may be provided in two basic categories: entrance exams and other requirements. The entrance exams are identified by the standard acronyms used by the testing agencies, unless they are not well known. Other entrance requirements are quite varied, but they often contain an undergraduate or graduate grade point average (GPA). Unless otherwise stated, the GPA is calculated on a 4.0 scale and is listed as a minimum required for admission. Additional exam requirements/recommendations for international students may be listed here. Application deadlines for domestic and international students, the application fee, and whether electronic applications are accepted may be listed here. Note that the deadline should be used for reference only; these dates are subject to change, and students interested in applying should always contact the graduate unit directly about application procedures and deadlines.

Expenses. The typical cost of study for the 2018–2019 academic year (2017–18 if 2018–19 figures were not available) is given in two basic categories: tuition and fees. Cost of study may be quite complex at a graduate institution. There are often sliding scales for part-time study, a different cost for first-year students, and other variables that make it impossible to completely cover the cost of study for each graduate program. To provide the most usable information, figures are given for full-time study for a full year where available and for part-time study in terms of a per-unit rate (per credit, per semester hour, etc.). Occasionally, variances may be noted in tuition and fees for reasons such as the type of program, whether courses are taken during the day or evening, whether courses are at the master's or doctoral level, or other institution-specific reasons. Respondents were also given the opportunity to provide more specific and detailed tuition and fees information at the unit level. When provided, this information will appear in place of any typical costs entered elsewhere on the university-level survey. Expenses are usually subject to change; for exact costs at any given time, contact your chosen schools and programs directly. Keep in mind that the tuition of Canadian institutions is usually given in Canadian dollars.

Financial Support. This section contains data on the number of awards administered by the institution and given to graduate students during the 2017–18 academic year. The first figure given represents the total number of students receiving financial support enrolled in that unit. If the unit has provided information on graduate appointments, these are broken down into three major categories: fellowships give money to graduate students to cover the cost of study and living expenses and are not based on a work obligation or research commitment, research assistantships provide stipends to graduate students for assistance in a formal research project with a faculty member, and teaching assistantships provide stipends to graduate students for teaching or for assisting faculty members in teaching undergraduate classes. Within each category, figures are given for the total number of awards, the average yearly amount per award, and whether full or partial tuition reimbursements are awarded. In addition to graduate appointments, the availability of several other financial aid sources is covered in this section. Tuition waivers are routinely part of a graduate appointment, but units sometimes waive part or all of a student's tuition even if a graduate appointment is not available. Federal Work Study is made available to students who demonstrate need and meet the federal guidelines; this form of aid normally includes 10 or more hours of work per week in an office of the institution. Institutionally sponsored loans are low-interest loans available to graduate students to cover both educational and living expenses. Career-related internships or fieldwork offer money to students who are participating in a formal off-campus research project or practicum. Grants, scholarships, traineeships, unspecified assistantships, and other awards may also be noted. The availability of financial support to part-time students is also indicated here.

Some programs list the financial aid application deadline and the forms that need to be completed for students to be eligible for financial awards. There are two forms: FAFSA, the Free Application for Federal Student Aid, which is required for federal aid, and the CSS PROFILE®.

Faculty Research. Each unit has the opportunity to list several keyword phrases describing the current research involving faculty members and graduate students. Space limitations prevent the unit from listing complete information on all research programs. The total expenditure for funded research from the previous academic year may also be included.

Unit Head and Application Contact. The head of the graduate program for each unit may be listed with academic title, phone and fax numbers, and e-mail address. In addition to the unit head's contact information, many graduate programs also list a separate contact for application and admission information, followed by the graduate school, program, or department's website. If no unit head or application contact is given, you should contact the overall institution for information on graduate admissions.

Displays and Close-Ups

The **Displays** and **Close-Ups** are supplementary insertions submitted by deans, chairs, and other administrators who wish to offer an additional, more individualized statement to readers. A number of graduate school and program administrators have attached a **Display** ad near the **Profile** listing. Here you will find information that an institution or program wants to emphasize. The **Close-Ups** are by their very nature more expansive and flexible than the **Profiles**, and the administrators who have written them may emphasize different aspects of their programs. All of the **Close-Ups** are organized in the same way (with the exception of a few that describe research and training opportunities instead of degree programs), and in each one you will find information on the same basic topics, such as programs of study, research facilities, tuition and fees, financial aid, and application procedures. If an institution or program has submitted a **Close-Up**, a boldface cross-reference appears below its **Profile**. As with the **Displays**, all of the **Close-Ups** in the guides have been submitted by choice; the absence of a **Display** or **Close-Up** does not reflect any type of editorial judgment on the part of Peterson's, and their presence in the guides should not be taken as an indication of status, quality, or approval. Statements regarding a university's objectives and accomplishments are a reflection of its own beliefs and are not the opinions of the Peterson's editors.

Appendixes

This section contains two appendixes. The first, "Institutional Changes Since the 2018 Edition," lists institutions that have closed, merged, or changed their name or status since the last edition of the guides. The second, "Abbreviations Used in the Guides," gives abbreviations of degree names, along with what those abbreviations stand for. These appendixes are identical in all six volumes of ***Peterson's Graduate and Professional Programs***.

Indexes

There are three indexes presented here. The first index, "Close-Ups and Displays," gives page references for all programs that have chosen to place **Close-Ups** and **Displays** in this volume. It is arranged alphabetically by institution; within institutions, the arrangement is alphabetical by subject area. It is not an index to all programs in the book's directories of **Profiles**; readers must refer to the directories themselves for **Profile** information on programs that have not submitted the additional, more individualized statements. The second index, "Directories and Subject Areas in Other Books in This Series", gives book references for the directories in the specialized volumes and also includes cross-references for subject area names not used in the directory structure, for example, "Computing Technology (see Computer Science)." The third index, "Directories and Subject Areas in This Book," gives page references for the directories in this volume and cross-references for subject area names not used in this volume's directory structure.

Data Collection Procedures

The information published in the directories and Profiles of all the books is collected through Peterson's Annual Survey of Graduate and Professional Institutions. The survey is sent each spring to nearly 2,300 institutions offering postbaccalaureate degree programs, including accredited institutions in the United States, U.S. territories, and Canada and those institutions outside the United States that are accredited by U.S. accrediting bodies. Deans and other administrators complete these surveys, providing information on programs in the 500 academic and professional fields covered in the guides as well as overall institutional information. While every effort has been made to ensure the accuracy and completeness of the data, information is sometimes unavailable or changes occur after publication deadlines. All usable information received in time for publication has been included. The omission of any particular item from a directory or Profile signifies either that the item is not applicable to the institution or program or that information was not available. Profiles of programs scheduled to begin during the 2018–19 academic year cannot, obviously, include statistics on enrollment or, in many cases, the number of faculty members. If no usable data were submitted by an institution, its name, address, and program name appear in order to indicate the availability of graduate work.

Criteria for Inclusion in This Guide

To be included in this guide, an institution must have full accreditation or be a candidate for accreditation (preaccreditation) status by an institutional or specialized accrediting body recognized by the U.S. Department of Education or the Council for Higher Education Accreditation (CHEA). Institutional accrediting bodies, which review each institution as a whole, include the six regional associations of schools and colleges (Middle States, New England, North Central, Northwest, Southern, and Western), each of which is responsible for a specified portion of the United States and its territories. Other institutional accrediting bodies are national in scope and accredit specific kinds of institutions (e.g., Bible colleges, independent colleges, and rabbinical and Talmudic schools). Program registration by the New York State Board of Regents is considered to be the equivalent of institutional accreditation, since the board requires that all programs offered by an institution meet its standards before recognition is granted. A Canadian institution must be chartered and authorized to grant degrees by the provincial government, affiliated with a chartered institution, or accredited by a recognized U.S. accrediting body. This guide also includes institutions outside the United States that are accredited by these U.S. accrediting bodies. There are recognized specialized or professional accrediting bodies in more than fifty different fields, each of which is authorized to accredit institutions or specific programs in its particular field. For specialized institutions that offer programs in one field only, we designate this to be the equivalent of institutional accreditation. A full explanation of the accrediting process and complete information on recognized institutional (regional and national) and specialized accrediting bodies can be found online at **www.chea.org** or at **www.ed.gov/admins/finaid/accred/index.html.**

NOTICE: Certain portions of or information contained in this book have been submitted and paid for by the educational institution identified, and such institutions take full responsibility for the accuracy, timeliness, completeness and functionality of such contents. Such portions or information include (i) each display ad that comprises a half page of information covering a single educational institution or program and (ii) each two-page description or Close-Up of a graduate school or program that appear in the different sections of this guide. The "Close-Ups and Displays" are listed in various sections throughout the book.

DIRECTORY OF INSTITUTIONS WITH PROGRAMS IN THE BIOLOGICAL/ BIOMEDICAL SCIENCES & HEALTH-RELATED MEDICAL PROFESSIONS

ABILENE CHRISTIAN UNIVERSITY
Communication Disorders M
Health Services Management and Hospital Administration M
Nursing and Healthcare Administration D
Nursing Education D
Nursing—General D
Nutrition M,O
Occupational Therapy M

ACADEMY FOR FIVE ELEMENT ACUPUNCTURE
Acupuncture and Oriental Medicine M

ACADEMY OF CHINESE CULTURE AND HEALTH SCIENCES
Acupuncture and Oriental Medicine M

ACADIA UNIVERSITY
Biological and Biomedical Sciences—General M

ACUPUNCTURE & INTEGRATIVE MEDICINE COLLEGE, BERKELEY
Acupuncture and Oriental Medicine M

ACUPUNCTURE AND MASSAGE COLLEGE
Acupuncture and Oriental Medicine M

ADELPHI UNIVERSITY
Adult Nursing M
Biological and Biomedical Sciences—General M
Communication Disorders M,D
Community Health M,O
Health Services Management and Hospital Administration M
Nursing and Healthcare Administration M,O
Nursing Education M,O
Nursing—General D
Nutrition M,D,O
Public Health—General M

ADLER UNIVERSITY
Community Health M

ADVENTIST UNIVERSITY OF HEALTH SCIENCES
Health Services Management and Hospital Administration M
Nurse Anesthesia M
Occupational Therapy M
Physical Therapy D
Physician Assistant Studies M

ALABAMA AGRICULTURAL AND MECHANICAL UNIVERSITY
Biological and Biomedical Sciences—General M,D
Communication Disorders M
Nutrition M

ALABAMA COLLEGE OF OSTEOPATHIC MEDICINE
Osteopathic Medicine D

ALABAMA STATE UNIVERSITY
Allied Health—General M,D
Biological and Biomedical Sciences—General M,D
Microbiology M,D
Occupational Therapy M
Physical Therapy D
Rehabilitation Sciences M

ALASKA PACIFIC UNIVERSITY
Health Services Management and Hospital Administration M

ALBANY COLLEGE OF PHARMACY AND HEALTH SCIENCES
Cell Biology M
Clinical Laboratory Sciences/Medical Technology M
Health Services Research M,D
Molecular Biology M
Pharmaceutical Sciences M,D
Pharmacology M,D
Pharmacy M,D

ALBANY MEDICAL COLLEGE
Allopathic Medicine D
Bioethics M,D,O
Cardiovascular Sciences M,D
Cell Biology M,D
Immunology M,D
Microbiology M,D
Molecular Biology M,D
Neuroscience M,D
Nurse Anesthesia M
Pharmacology M,D
Physician Assistant Studies M

ALBANY STATE UNIVERSITY
Family Nurse Practitioner Studies M
Health Services Management and Hospital Administration M
Nursing Education M
Nursing—General M

ALBERT EINSTEIN COLLEGE OF MEDICINE
Allopathic Medicine D
Anatomy D
Biochemistry D
Biological and Biomedical Sciences—General D
Biophysics D
Cell Biology D
Clinical Research D
Computational Biology D
Developmental Biology D
Genetics D
Genomic Sciences D
Immunology D
Microbiology D
Molecular Biology D
Molecular Genetics D
Molecular Pharmacology D
Neuroscience D
Pathology D
Physiology D
Structural Biology D
Systems Biology D

ALBERTUS MAGNUS COLLEGE
Health Services Management and Hospital Administration M

ALCORN STATE UNIVERSITY
Biological and Biomedical Sciences—General M
Nursing—General M

ALDERSON BROADDUS UNIVERSITY
Physician Assistant Studies M

ALLEN COLLEGE
Adult Nursing M,D
Community Health Nursing M,D
Family Nurse Practitioner Studies M,D
Gerontological Nursing M,D
Nursing and Healthcare Administration M,D
Nursing Education M,D
Nursing Informatics M,D
Nursing—General M,D
Occupational Therapy M,D
Psychiatric Nursing M,D
Public Health—General M,D

ALLIANT INTERNATIONAL UNIVERSITY–SAN DIEGO
Neuroscience M,D,O

ALLIANT INTERNATIONAL UNIVERSITY–SAN FRANCISCO
Pharmacology M

ALVERNIA UNIVERSITY
Family Nurse Practitioner Studies M,D,O
Gerontological Nursing M,D,O
Nursing and Healthcare Administration M,D,O
Nursing Education M,D,O
Nursing—General M,D,O
Occupational Therapy M

ALVERNO COLLEGE
Family Nurse Practitioner Studies M,D
Nursing—General M,D
Psychiatric Nursing M,D

AMERICAN ACADEMY OF ACUPUNCTURE AND ORIENTAL MEDICINE
Acupuncture and Oriental Medicine M,D

AMERICAN COLLEGE OF ACUPUNCTURE AND ORIENTAL MEDICINE
Acupuncture and Oriental Medicine M

AMERICAN COLLEGE OF HEALTHCARE SCIENCES
Allied Health—General M,O
Health Promotion M,O
Nutrition M,O
Physiology M,O

AMERICAN INTERCONTINENTAL UNIVERSITY ONLINE
Health Services Management and Hospital Administration M

AMERICAN INTERNATIONAL COLLEGE
Family Nurse Practitioner Studies M,D,O
Nursing and Healthcare Administration M,D,O
Nursing Education M,D,O
Occupational Therapy M,D,O
Physical Therapy M,D,O

AMERICAN MUSEUM OF NATURAL HISTORY–RICHARD GILDER GRADUATE SCHOOL
Biological and Biomedical Sciences—General D

AMERICAN PUBLIC UNIVERSITY SYSTEM
Nursing—General M,D

AMERICAN SENTINEL UNIVERSITY
Health Services Management and Hospital Administration M
Nursing—General M

AMERICAN UNIVERSITY
Biological and Biomedical Sciences—General M
Biopsychology M,D,O
Health Promotion M
Health Services Management and Hospital Administration M,O
Neuroscience M,D,O
Nutrition M,O

AMERICAN UNIVERSITY OF ARMENIA
Public Health—General M

AMERICAN UNIVERSITY OF BEIRUT
Allopathic Medicine M,D
Biochemistry M,D
Biological and Biomedical Sciences—General M,D
Cell Biology M,D
Clinical Research M,D
Community Health Nursing M
Community Health M,D
Environmental and Occupational Health M,D
Epidemiology M,D
Gerontological Nursing M
Health Promotion M,D
Health Services Management and Hospital Administration M,D
Health Services Research M,D
Immunology M,D
Microbiology M,D
Molecular Biology M,D
Neuroscience M,D
Nursing and Healthcare Administration M
Nursing—General M
Nutrition M,D
Oral and Dental Sciences M,D
Pharmacology M,D
Physiology M,D
Psychiatric Nursing M
Public Health—General M,D

AMERICAN UNIVERSITY OF HEALTH SCIENCES
Clinical Research M

ANDERSON UNIVERSITY (SC)
Family Nurse Practitioner Studies M,D
Health Services Management and Hospital Administration M
Nursing and Healthcare Administration M,D
Nursing Education M,D
Nursing—General M,D
Psychiatric Nursing M,D

ANDREWS UNIVERSITY
Allied Health—General M
Biological and Biomedical Sciences—General M
Communication Disorders M
Nursing—General M,D
Nutrition M,O
Physical Therapy D
Public Health—General M,O

ANGELO STATE UNIVERSITY
Biological and Biomedical Sciences—General M
Family Nurse Practitioner Studies M
Nursing Education M
Nursing—General M
Physical Therapy D

ANTIOCH UNIVERSITY MIDWEST
Health Services Management and Hospital Administration M

ANTIOCH UNIVERSITY NEW ENGLAND
Conservation Biology M

AOMA GRADUATE SCHOOL OF INTEGRATIVE MEDICINE
Acupuncture and Oriental Medicine M,D

APPALACHIAN COLLEGE OF PHARMACY
Pharmacy D

APPALACHIAN STATE UNIVERSITY
Biological and Biomedical Sciences—General M
Cell Biology M
Communication Disorders M
Molecular Biology M
Nutrition M

AQUINAS INSTITUTE OF THEOLOGY
Health Services Management and Hospital Administration M,D,O

ARCADIA UNIVERSITY
Physical Therapy D
Physician Assistant Studies M
Public Health—General M

ARGOSY UNIVERSITY, ATLANTA
Biopsychology M,D,O
Health Services Management and Hospital Administration M,D
Public Health—General M

ARGOSY UNIVERSITY, CHICAGO
Health Services Management and Hospital Administration M,D
Neuroscience D
Public Health—General M

ARGOSY UNIVERSITY, HAWAI'I
Health Services Management and Hospital Administration M,D,O
Pharmacology M,O
Public Health—General M

ARGOSY UNIVERSITY, LOS ANGELES
Health Services Management and Hospital Administration M,D
Public Health—General M

ARGOSY UNIVERSITY, NORTHERN VIRGINIA
Health Services Management and Hospital Administration M,D,O
Public Health—General M

ARGOSY UNIVERSITY, ORANGE COUNTY
Health Services Management and Hospital Administration M,D,O
Public Health—General M

ARGOSY UNIVERSITY, PHOENIX
Health Services Management and Hospital Administration M,D
Neuroscience M,D
Public Health—General M

ARGOSY UNIVERSITY, SEATTLE
Health Services Management and Hospital Administration M,D
Public Health—General M

ARGOSY UNIVERSITY, TAMPA
Health Services Management and Hospital Administration M,D
Neuroscience M,D
Public Health—General M

ARGOSY UNIVERSITY, TWIN CITIES
Biopsychology M,D,O
Health Services Management and Hospital Administration M,D
Public Health—General M

ARIZONA SCHOOL OF ACUPUNCTURE AND ORIENTAL MEDICINE
Acupuncture and Oriental Medicine M

ARIZONA STATE UNIVERSITY AT THE TEMPE CAMPUS
Animal Behavior M,D
Biochemistry M,D
Biological and Biomedical Sciences—General M,D
Cell Biology M,D
Communication Disorders M,D
Community Health M,D,O
Conservation Biology M,D
Evolutionary Biology M,D
Family Nurse Practitioner Studies M,D,O
Gerontological Nursing M,D,O
Health Promotion M,D
Health Services Management and Hospital Administration M,D
International Health M,D,O
Microbiology M,D
Molecular Biology M,D
Neuroscience M,D
Nursing and Healthcare Administration M,D,O
Nursing Education M,D,O
Nursing—General M,D,O
Nutrition M,D
Plant Biology M,D
Psychiatric Nursing M,D,O
Public Health—General M,D,O

ARKANSAS STATE UNIVERSITY
Biological and Biomedical Sciences—General M,O
Communication Disorders M,O
Health Services Management and Hospital Administration M,D,O
Molecular Biology M,D
Nurse Anesthesia M,D,O
Nursing—General M,D,O
Occupational Therapy D
Physical Therapy D

ARKANSAS TECH UNIVERSITY
Nursing—General M

ASHLAND UNIVERSITY
Family Nurse Practitioner Studies D
Health Services Management and Hospital Administration M
Nursing—General D

ASHWORTH COLLEGE
Health Services Management and Hospital Administration M

ASPEN UNIVERSITY
Forensic Nursing M
Nursing and Healthcare Administration M
Nursing Education M
Nursing Informatics M
Nursing—General M

ASSUMPTION COLLEGE
Health Services Management and Hospital Administration M,O

ATHABASCA UNIVERSITY
Allied Health—General M,O
Nursing and Healthcare Administration M,O
Nursing—General M,O

ATLANTIC INSTITUTE OF ORIENTAL MEDICINE
Acupuncture and Oriental Medicine M,D

ATLANTIS UNIVERSITY
Health Services Management and Hospital Administration M

A.T. STILL UNIVERSITY
Allied Health—General M,D,O
Biological and Biomedical Sciences—General M,D
Communication Disorders M,D,O
Dentistry M,D,O
Health Services Management and Hospital Administration M,D,O
International Health M,D,O
Occupational Therapy M,D,O
Oral and Dental Sciences M,D,O
Osteopathic Medicine M,D
Physical Therapy M,D,O
Physician Assistant Studies M,D,O
Public Health—General M,D,O

AUBURN UNIVERSITY
Biochemistry M,D
Biological and Biomedical Sciences—General M,D
Botany M,D
Cell Biology M,D
Communication Disorders M,D
Entomology M,D
Molecular Biology M,D
Nursing Education M
Nursing—General M
Nutrition M,D,O
Pharmaceutical Sciences M,D
Pharmacy D
Plant Pathology M,D
Veterinary Medicine D
Zoology M,D

AUBURN UNIVERSITY AT MONTGOMERY
Family Nurse Practitioner Studies M

Nursing Education	M
Nursing—General	M

AUGSBURG UNIVERSITY

Family Nurse Practitioner Studies	M,D
Nursing—General	M,D
Physician Assistant Studies	M
Transcultural Nursing	M,D

AUGUSTA UNIVERSITY

Acute Care/Critical Care Nursing	D
Allied Health—General	D
Allopathic Medicine	D
Anatomy	D
Biochemistry	D
Cancer Biology/Oncology	D
Cardiovascular Sciences	D
Cell Biology	D
Clinical Research	M
Dentistry	D
Environmental and Occupational Health	M
Family Nurse Practitioner Studies	D
Genomic Sciences	D
Gerontological Nursing	D
Molecular Medicine	D
Neuroscience	D
Nurse Anesthesia	D
Nursing and Healthcare Administration	M,D
Nursing—General	D
Occupational Therapy	M
Oral and Dental Sciences	M,D
Pediatric Nursing	D
Pharmacology	D
Physical Therapy	D
Physician Assistant Studies	M
Physiology	D
Psychiatric Nursing	D
Public Health—General	M
Rehabilitation Sciences	D

AUSTIN PEAY STATE UNIVERSITY

Biological and Biomedical Sciences—General	M
Clinical Laboratory Sciences/Medical Technology	M
Family Nurse Practitioner Studies	M
Nursing and Healthcare Administration	M
Nursing Education	M
Nursing Informatics	M
Nursing—General	M
Public Health—General	M

AVILA UNIVERSITY

Health Services Management and Hospital Administration	M

AZUSA PACIFIC UNIVERSITY

Adult Nursing	M,D
Family Nurse Practitioner Studies	M,D
Gerontological Nursing	M,D
Nursing and Healthcare Administration	M,D
Nursing Education	M,D
Nursing—General	M,D
Pediatric Nursing	M,D
Physical Therapy	D
Psychiatric Nursing	M,D
Public Health—General	M

BAKER COLLEGE CENTER FOR GRADUATE STUDIES–ONLINE

Health Services Management and Hospital Administration	M,D

BALDWIN WALLACE UNIVERSITY

Communication Disorders	M
Health Services Management and Hospital Administration	M
Physician Assistant Studies	M
Public Health—General	M

BALL STATE UNIVERSITY

Biological and Biomedical Sciences—General	M,D
Communication Disorders	M,D
Family Nurse Practitioner Studies	M,D,O
Gerontological Nursing	M,D,O
Health Promotion	M
Neuroscience	M,D,O
Nursing Education	M,D,O
Nursing—General	M,D,O
Nutrition	M
Physiology	M

BANK STREET COLLEGE OF EDUCATION

Maternal and Child Health	M

BARRY UNIVERSITY

Acute Care/Critical Care Nursing	M,O
Anatomy	M
Biological and Biomedical Sciences—General	M
Communication Disorders	M
Family Nurse Practitioner Studies	M,O
Health Services Management and Hospital Administration	M,O
Nurse Anesthesia	M
Nursing and Healthcare Administration	M,D,O
Nursing Education	M,O
Nursing—General	M,D,O
Occupational Therapy	M
Physician Assistant Studies	M
Podiatric Medicine	D
Public Health—General	M

BARUCH COLLEGE OF THE CITY UNIVERSITY OF NEW YORK

Health Services Management and Hospital Administration	M

BASTYR UNIVERSITY

Acupuncture and Oriental Medicine	M,D
Maternal and Child Health	M,O
Naturopathic Medicine	D,O
Nurse Midwifery	M,O
Nutrition	M,O

BAYLOR COLLEGE OF MEDICINE

Allopathic Medicine	D
Biochemistry	D
Biological and Biomedical Sciences—General	M,D
Biophysics	D
Cancer Biology/Oncology	D
Cardiovascular Sciences	D
Cell Biology	D
Clinical Laboratory Sciences/Medical Technology	M,D
Computational Biology	D
Developmental Biology	D
Genetics	D
Human Genetics	D
Immunology	D
Microbiology	D
Molecular Biology	D
Molecular Biophysics	D
Molecular Medicine	D
Molecular Physiology	D
Neuroscience	D
Nurse Anesthesia	D
Pharmacology	D
Physician Assistant Studies	M
Structural Biology	D
Translational Biology	D
Virology	D

BAYLOR UNIVERSITY

Allied Health—General	M,D
Biochemistry	M,D
Biological and Biomedical Sciences—General	M,D
Communication Disorders	M
Community Health	M,D
Ecology	D
Emergency Medical Services	D
Environmental Biology	M,D
Family Nurse Practitioner Studies	M,D
Health Services Management and Hospital Administration	M
Maternal and Child/Neonatal Nursing	M,D
Nurse Midwifery	M,D
Nursing—General	M,D
Nutrition	M,D
Physical Therapy	D
Physiology	M,D

BAY PATH UNIVERSITY

Occupational Therapy	M,D
Physician Assistant Studies	M

BELHAVEN UNIVERSITY (MS)

Health Services Management and Hospital Administration	M

BELLARMINE UNIVERSITY

Family Nurse Practitioner Studies	M,D
Nursing and Healthcare Administration	M,D
Nursing Education	M,D
Nursing—General	M,D
Physical Therapy	M,D

BELLEVUE UNIVERSITY

Health Services Management and Hospital Administration	M

BELLIN COLLEGE

Family Nurse Practitioner Studies	M
Nursing Education	M
Nursing—General	M

BELMONT UNIVERSITY

Allied Health—General	M,D
Health Services Management and Hospital Administration	M
Nursing—General	M,D
Occupational Therapy	M,D
Pharmaceutical Administration	D
Pharmacy	D
Physical Therapy	M,D
Public Health—General	D

BEMIDJI STATE UNIVERSITY

Biological and Biomedical Sciences—General	M

BENEDICTINE UNIVERSITY

Health Promotion	M
Health Services Management and Hospital Administration	M
Nursing—General	M
Nutrition	M
Public Health—General	M

BENNINGTON COLLEGE

Allied Health—General	O

BETHEL COLLEGE

Nursing—General	M

BETHEL UNIVERSITY (MN)

Nurse Midwifery	M,D,O
Nursing Education	M,D,O
Physician Assistant Studies	M,D,O

BETHEL UNIVERSITY (TN)

Physician Assistant Studies	M

BINGHAMTON UNIVERSITY, STATE UNIVERSITY OF NEW YORK

Biological and Biomedical Sciences—General	M,D
Biopsychology	D
Community Health Nursing	M,D,O
Family Nurse Practitioner Studies	M,D,O
Gerontological Nursing	M,D,O
Health Services Management and Hospital Administration	M,D
Nursing—General	M,D,O
Pharmacy	D
Psychiatric Nursing	M,D,O

BIOLA UNIVERSITY

Communication Disorders	M,O

BLACK HILLS STATE UNIVERSITY

Genomic Sciences	M

BLESSING-RIEMAN COLLEGE OF NURSING & HEALTH SCIENCES

Nursing and Healthcare Administration	M
Nursing Education	M
Nursing—General	M

BLOOMSBURG UNIVERSITY OF PENNSYLVANIA

Adult Nursing	M,D
Biological and Biomedical Sciences—General	M
Communication Disorders	M,D
Community Health	M,D
Family Nurse Practitioner Studies	M,D
Nurse Anesthesia	M,D
Nursing and Healthcare Administration	M,D
Nursing—General	M,D

BLUFFTON UNIVERSITY

Health Services Management and Hospital Administration	M

BOISE STATE UNIVERSITY

Biological and Biomedical Sciences—General	M,D
Environmental and Occupational Health	M,O
Gerontological Nursing	M,D,O
Health Promotion	M,O
Molecular Biology	M,D
Nursing—General	M,D,O
Public Health—General	M,D,O

BOSTON COLLEGE

Adult Nursing	M,D
Biochemistry	M,D
Biological and Biomedical Sciences—General	D
Gerontological Nursing	M,D
Maternal and Child/Neonatal Nursing	M,D
Nurse Anesthesia	M,D
Nursing—General	M,D
Pediatric Nursing	M,D
Psychiatric Nursing	M,D
Women's Health Nursing	M,D

BOSTON UNIVERSITY

Allied Health—General	M,D
Allopathic Medicine	D
Anatomy	M,D
Biochemistry	M,D
Biological and Biomedical Sciences—General	M,D
Biophysics	M,D
Biopsychology	M
Cell Biology	M,D
Clinical Research	M
Communication Disorders	M,D
Community Health	M,D
Dentistry	M,D,O
Environmental and Occupational Health	M,D
Epidemiology	M,D
Genetics	D
Genomic Sciences	D
Health Services Management and Hospital Administration	M,D
Health Services Research	M,D
Immunology	D
International Health	M,D
Medical Imaging	M
Microbiology	D
Molecular Biology	M,D
Molecular Medicine	D
Neurobiology	M,D
Neuroscience	D
Nutrition	M,D
Occupational Therapy	D
Oral and Dental Sciences	M,D
Pathology	M,D
Pharmaceutical Sciences	D
Pharmacology	M,D
Physical Therapy	M,D
Physician Assistant Studies	M
Physiology	M,D
Public Health—General	M,D
Rehabilitation Sciences	M,D
Translational Biology	D

BOWIE STATE UNIVERSITY

Family Nurse Practitioner Studies	M
Nursing and Healthcare Administration	M
Nursing Education	M
Nursing—General	M

BOWLING GREEN STATE UNIVERSITY

Biological and Biomedical Sciences—General	M,D
Communication Disorders	M,D
Public Health—General	M

BRADLEY UNIVERSITY

Biochemistry	M
Biological and Biomedical Sciences—General	M
Family Nurse Practitioner Studies	M,D,O
Health Services Management and Hospital Administration	M,D,O
Nursing and Healthcare Administration	M,D,O
Nursing Education	M,D,O
Nursing—General	M,D,O
Nutrition	M
Physical Therapy	D

BRANDEIS UNIVERSITY

Biochemistry	M,D
Biological and Biomedical Sciences—General	M,D,O
Biophysics	M,D
Cell Biology	M,D
Genetics	M,D
Health Services Management and Hospital Administration	M
International Health	M,D
Microbiology	M,D
Molecular Biology	M,D
Neurobiology	M,D
Neuroscience	M,D

BRANDMAN UNIVERSITY

Health Services Management and Hospital Administration	M
Nursing—General	D

BRENAU UNIVERSITY

Family Nurse Practitioner Studies	M
Health Services Management and Hospital Administration	M
Nursing and Healthcare Administration	M
Nursing Education	M
Occupational Therapy	M

BRIAR CLIFF UNIVERSITY

Nursing—General	M,D,O

BRIDGEWATER STATE UNIVERSITY

Communication Disorders	M
Health Promotion	M

BRIGHAM YOUNG UNIVERSITY

Biochemistry	M,D
Biological and Biomedical Sciences—General	M,D
Communication Disorders	M
Developmental Biology	M,D
Family Nurse Practitioner Studies	M
Health Promotion	M,D
Health Services Management and Hospital Administration	M
Microbiology	M,D
Molecular Biology	M,D
Neuroscience	M,D
Nursing—General	M
Nutrition	M
Physiology	M,D
Public Health—General	M

BROADVIEW UNIVERSITY–WEST JORDAN

Health Services Management and Hospital Administration	M

BROCK UNIVERSITY

Allied Health—General	M,D
Biological and Biomedical Sciences—General	M,D
Neuroscience	M,D

BROOKLINE COLLEGE

Nursing and Healthcare Administration	M
Nursing—General	M

BROOKLYN COLLEGE OF THE CITY UNIVERSITY OF NEW YORK

Biological and Biomedical Sciences—General	M
Communication Disorders	M,D
Community Health	M
Health Services Management and Hospital Administration	M
Nutrition	M
Public Health—General	M

BROWN UNIVERSITY

Allopathic Medicine	D
Biochemistry	M,D
Biological and Biomedical Sciences—General	M,D
Cell Biology	M,D
Community Health	M,D
Ecology	D
Epidemiology	M,D
Evolutionary Biology	D
Health Services Research	D
Molecular Biology	M,D
Molecular Pharmacology	M,D
Neuroscience	D
Pathobiology	M,D
Physiology	M,D
Public Health—General	M

BRYAN COLLEGE

Health Services Management and Hospital Administration	M

BRYAN COLLEGE OF HEALTH SCIENCES

Nurse Anesthesia	M

BRYANT UNIVERSITY

Physician Assistant Studies	M

BUCKNELL UNIVERSITY

Animal Behavior	M
Biological and Biomedical Sciences—General	M

*M—masters degree; D—doctorate; O—other advanced degree; *—Close-Up and/or Display*

BUFFALO STATE COLLEGE, STATE UNIVERSITY OF NEW YORK
- Biological and Biomedical Sciences—General M
- Communication Disorders M

BUTLER UNIVERSITY
- Pharmaceutical Sciences M,D
- Pharmacy M,D
- Physician Assistant Studies M,D

CABARRUS COLLEGE OF HEALTH SCIENCES
- Occupational Therapy M

CABRINI UNIVERSITY
- Biological and Biomedical Sciences—General M,D

CALIFORNIA BAPTIST UNIVERSITY
- Adult Nursing M
- Communication Disorders M
- Family Nurse Practitioner Studies M
- Health Promotion M
- Health Services Management and Hospital Administration M
- Nursing and Healthcare Administration M
- Nursing Education M
- Nursing—General M,D
- Physician Assistant Studies M
- Public Health—General M

CALIFORNIA COAST UNIVERSITY
- Health Services Management and Hospital Administration M

CALIFORNIA HEALTH SCIENCES UNIVERSITY
- Pharmacy D

CALIFORNIA INSTITUTE OF INTEGRAL STUDIES
- Acupuncture and Oriental Medicine M,D
- Ecology M,D,O

CALIFORNIA INSTITUTE OF TECHNOLOGY
- Biochemistry M,D
- Biological and Biomedical Sciences—General D
- Biophysics D
- Cell Biology D
- Developmental Biology D
- Genetics D
- Immunology D
- Molecular Biology D
- Molecular Biophysics M,D
- Neurobiology D
- Neuroscience M,D

CALIFORNIA INTERCONTINENTAL UNIVERSITY
- Health Services Management and Hospital Administration M,D

CALIFORNIA NORTHSTATE UNIVERSITY
- Allopathic Medicine D
- Pharmacy D

CALIFORNIA POLYTECHNIC STATE UNIVERSITY, SAN LUIS OBISPO
- Biochemistry M
- Biological and Biomedical Sciences—General M*
- Nutrition M*

CALIFORNIA STATE POLYTECHNIC UNIVERSITY, POMONA
- Biological and Biomedical Sciences—General M

CALIFORNIA STATE UNIVERSITY, BAKERSFIELD
- Biological and Biomedical Sciences—General M
- Family Nurse Practitioner Studies M
- Health Services Management and Hospital Administration M
- Nursing—General M

CALIFORNIA STATE UNIVERSITY, CHICO
- Biological and Biomedical Sciences—General M
- Communication Disorders M
- Health Services Management and Hospital Administration M
- Nursing—General M
- Nutrition M

CALIFORNIA STATE UNIVERSITY, DOMINGUEZ HILLS
- Biological and Biomedical Sciences—General M
- Nursing—General M
- Occupational Therapy M

CALIFORNIA STATE UNIVERSITY, EAST BAY
- Biochemistry M
- Biological and Biomedical Sciences—General M
- Communication Disorders M
- Health Services Management and Hospital Administration M

CALIFORNIA STATE UNIVERSITY, FRESNO
- Biological and Biomedical Sciences—General M
- Communication Disorders M
- Health Promotion M
- Health Services Management and Hospital Administration M
- Nursing—General M,D
- Physical Therapy D
- Public Health—General M

CALIFORNIA STATE UNIVERSITY, FULLERTON
- Biological and Biomedical Sciences—General M
- Communication Disorders M
- Environmental and Occupational Health M
- Health Promotion M
- Nurse Anesthesia M,D
- Nursing and Healthcare Administration M,D
- Nursing Education M,D
- Nursing—General M,D
- Public Health—General M
- School Nursing M,D
- Women's Health Nursing M,D

CALIFORNIA STATE UNIVERSITY, LONG BEACH
- Biochemistry M
- Biological and Biomedical Sciences—General M
- Communication Disorders M
- Health Services Management and Hospital Administration M
- Microbiology M
- Nursing—General M,D,O
- Nutrition M
- Physical Therapy D
- Public Health—General M

CALIFORNIA STATE UNIVERSITY, LOS ANGELES
- Biochemistry M
- Biological and Biomedical Sciences—General M
- Communication Disorders M
- Health Services Management and Hospital Administration M,O
- Nursing—General M,O
- Nutrition M,O

CALIFORNIA STATE UNIVERSITY, NORTHRIDGE
- Biochemistry M
- Biological and Biomedical Sciences—General M
- Communication Disorders M
- Environmental and Occupational Health M
- Epidemiology M
- Health Services Management and Hospital Administration M
- Industrial Hygiene M
- Physical Therapy M
- Public Health—General M

CALIFORNIA STATE UNIVERSITY, SACRAMENTO
- Biochemistry M
- Biological and Biomedical Sciences—General M
- Cell Biology M
- Communication Disorders M
- Conservation Biology M
- Developmental Biology M
- Molecular Biology M
- Nursing—General M
- Physical Therapy D

CALIFORNIA STATE UNIVERSITY, SAN BERNARDINO
- Biological and Biomedical Sciences—General M
- Health Services Management and Hospital Administration M
- Nursing—General M
- Public Health—General M

CALIFORNIA STATE UNIVERSITY, SAN MARCOS
- Biological and Biomedical Sciences—General M
- Communication Disorders M
- Family Nurse Practitioner Studies M
- Nursing and Healthcare Administration M
- Nursing Education M
- Nursing—General M
- Psychiatric Nursing M
- Public Health—General M

CALIFORNIA STATE UNIVERSITY, STANISLAUS
- Conservation Biology M
- Ecology M
- Gerontological Nursing M
- Nursing Education M
- Nursing—General M

CALIFORNIA UNIVERSITY OF PENNSYLVANIA
- Communication Disorders M
- Health Services Management and Hospital Administration M
- Nursing and Healthcare Administration M
- Nursing Education M
- Nursing—General M
- Nutrition M

CAMBRIDGE COLLEGE
- Health Services Management and Hospital Administration M
- School Nursing M,D,O

CAMPBELL UNIVERSITY
- Osteopathic Medicine D
- Pharmaceutical Sciences M,D
- Pharmacy M,D
- Physical Therapy M,D
- Physician Assistant Studies M,D

CANADIAN COLLEGE OF NATUROPATHIC MEDICINE
- Naturopathic Medicine O

CANADIAN MEMORIAL CHIROPRACTIC COLLEGE
- Acupuncture and Oriental Medicine O
- Chiropractic D,O

CANISIUS COLLEGE
- Allied Health—General M,O
- Communication Disorders M,O
- Community Health M,O
- Nutrition M,O
- Zoology M

CAPELLA UNIVERSITY
- Environmental and Occupational Health M,D
- Epidemiology D
- Gerontological Nursing M
- Health Services Management and Hospital Administration M,D
- Nursing and Healthcare Administration M
- Nursing Education M,D
- Nursing—General M,D

CAPITAL UNIVERSITY
- Nursing and Healthcare Administration M
- Nursing—General M

CARDINAL STRITCH UNIVERSITY
- Health Services Management and Hospital Administration M
- Nursing—General M

CARIBBEAN UNIVERSITY
- Gerontological Nursing M,D
- Pediatric Nursing M,D

CARLETON UNIVERSITY
- Biological and Biomedical Sciences—General M,D
- Neuroscience M,D

CARLOS ALBIZU UNIVERSITY
- Communication Disorders M,D

CARLOS ALBIZU UNIVERSITY, MIAMI CAMPUS
- Communication Disorders M,D

CARLOW UNIVERSITY
- Family Nurse Practitioner Studies M,O
- Health Services Management and Hospital Administration M
- Nursing and Healthcare Administration M
- Nursing Education M
- Nursing—General D
- Women's Health Nursing M,O

CARNEGIE MELLON UNIVERSITY
- Biochemistry M,D
- Biological and Biomedical Sciences—General M,D
- Biophysics M,D
- Biopsychology D
- Cell Biology M,D
- Computational Biology M,D
- Developmental Biology M,D
- Genetics M,D
- Health Services Management and Hospital Administration M
- Molecular Biology M,D
- Molecular Biophysics D
- Neurobiology M,D
- Neuroscience D
- Structural Biology M,D

CARROLL UNIVERSITY
- Occupational Therapy M
- Physical Therapy D
- Physician Assistant Studies M

CARSON-NEWMAN UNIVERSITY
- Family Nurse Practitioner Studies M
- Nursing Education M
- Nursing—General M

CASE WESTERN RESERVE UNIVERSITY
- Acute Care/Critical Care Nursing M
- Allopathic Medicine D
- Anatomy M
- Anesthesiologist Assistant Studies M
- Biochemistry M,D
- Bioethics M
- Biological and Biomedical Sciences—General M,D
- Biophysics M,D
- Cancer Biology/Oncology D
- Cell Biology D
- Clinical Research M,D
- Communication Disorders M,D
- Dentistry D
- Epidemiology D
- Family Nurse Practitioner Studies M
- Genomic Sciences M,D
- Gerontological Nursing M
- Health Services Management and Hospital Administration M
- Human Genetics M,D
- Immunology D
- Maternal and Child/Neonatal Nursing M
- Medical/Surgical Nursing M
- Microbiology D
- Molecular Biology D
- Molecular Medicine D
- Neuroscience D
- Nurse Anesthesia M
- Nurse Midwifery M
- Nursing Education M
- Nursing—General M,D
- Nutrition M,D
- Oral and Dental Sciences M,O
- Pathology M,D
- Pediatric Nursing M
- Pharmacology D
- Physician Assistant Studies M

- Physiology M,D
- Psychiatric Nursing M
- Public Health—General M
- Virology D
- Women's Health Nursing M

THE CATHOLIC UNIVERSITY OF AMERICA
- Biological and Biomedical Sciences—General M,D
- Cell Biology M,D
- Clinical Laboratory Sciences/Medical Technology M,D
- Health Services Management and Hospital Administration M
- Microbiology M,D
- Nursing—General M,D,O

CEDAR CREST COLLEGE
- Nursing and Healthcare Administration M
- Nursing Education M
- Nursing—General M
- Nutrition O

CEDARS-SINAI MEDICAL CENTER
- Biological and Biomedical Sciences—General M,D
- Medical Imaging M,D
- Translational Biology M,D

CEDARVILLE UNIVERSITY
- Family Nurse Practitioner Studies M,D
- Health Services Management and Hospital Administration M,D
- International Health M,D
- Nursing Education M,D
- Pharmacy M,D

CENTRAL CONNECTICUT STATE UNIVERSITY
- Biological and Biomedical Sciences—General M,D
- Hospice Nursing M
- Molecular Biology M,O
- Nursing—General M

CENTRAL METHODIST UNIVERSITY
- Nursing and Healthcare Administration M
- Nursing Education M
- Nursing—General M

CENTRAL MICHIGAN UNIVERSITY
- Biological and Biomedical Sciences—General M
- Communication Disorders M,D
- Conservation Biology M
- Health Services Management and Hospital Administration M,D,O
- International Health M,D,O
- Neuroscience M,D
- Nutrition M,D,O
- Physical Therapy M,D
- Physician Assistant Studies M,D
- Rehabilitation Sciences M,D

CENTRAL WASHINGTON UNIVERSITY
- Biological and Biomedical Sciences—General M
- Botany M
- Ecology M
- Microbiology M
- Nutrition M
- Physiology M

CHAMPLAIN COLLEGE
- Health Services Management and Hospital Administration M

CHAPMAN UNIVERSITY
- Communication Disorders M
- Nutrition M
- Pharmaceutical Sciences M,D
- Pharmacy M,D
- Physical Therapy D
- Physician Assistant Studies M

CHARLES R. DREW UNIVERSITY OF MEDICINE AND SCIENCE
- Allopathic Medicine D
- Public Health—General M

CHATHAM UNIVERSITY
- Biological and Biomedical Sciences—General M
- Environmental Biology M
- Nursing and Healthcare Administration M,D
- Nursing Education M,D
- Nursing—General M,D
- Occupational Therapy M,D
- Physical Therapy D
- Physician Assistant Studies M

THE CHICAGO SCHOOL OF PROFESSIONAL PSYCHOLOGY: ONLINE
- Health Services Management and Hospital Administration M
- Pharmacology M

CHICAGO STATE UNIVERSITY
- Biological and Biomedical Sciences—General M
- Nursing—General M
- Occupational Therapy M
- Pharmacy D
- Public Health—General M

CHRISTIAN BROTHERS UNIVERSITY
- Physician Assistant Studies M

THE CITADEL, THE MILITARY COLLEGE OF SOUTH CAROLINA
- Biological and Biomedical Sciences—General M,O
- Medical Microbiology M,O

CITY COLLEGE OF THE CITY UNIVERSITY OF NEW YORK

Biochemistry	M,D
Biological and Biomedical Sciences—General	M,D

CLAREMONT GRADUATE UNIVERSITY

Botany	M,D
Computational Biology	M,D
Health Promotion	M,D
Public Health—General	M,D

CLARION UNIVERSITY OF PENNSYLVANIA

Communication Disorders	M
Family Nurse Practitioner Studies	M
Health Services Management and Hospital Administration	M
Nursing—General	M,D
Rehabilitation Sciences	M

CLARK ATLANTA UNIVERSITY

Biological and Biomedical Sciences—General	M,D

CLARKE UNIVERSITY

Family Nurse Practitioner Studies	D
Nursing and Healthcare Administration	D
Nursing—General	D
Physical Therapy	D
Psychiatric Nursing	D

CLARKSON COLLEGE

Adult Nursing	M,O
Family Nurse Practitioner Studies	M,O
Nursing and Healthcare Administration	M,O
Nursing Education	M,O
Nursing—General	M,O

CLARKSON UNIVERSITY

Bioethics	M,O
Biological and Biomedical Sciences—General	M
Health Services Management and Hospital Administration	M,O
Health Services Research	M
Nursing and Healthcare Administration	M,O
Occupational Therapy	M
Physical Therapy	D
Physician Assistant Studies	M

CLARK UNIVERSITY

Biochemistry	D
Biological and Biomedical Sciences—General	M,D
Community Health	M
International Health	M

CLAYTON STATE UNIVERSITY

Biological and Biomedical Sciences—General	M
Family Nurse Practitioner Studies	M
Nursing—General	M

CLEARY UNIVERSITY

Health Services Management and Hospital Administration	M,O

CLEMSON UNIVERSITY

Biological and Biomedical Sciences—General	M,D
Clinical Research	M,D,O
Entomology	M,D
Environmental and Occupational Health	M,D
Family Nurse Practitioner Studies	M,D,O
Genetics	M,D,O
Gerontological Nursing	M,D,O
International Health	M,D,O
Microbiology	M,D
Molecular Biology	D
Nursing—General	M,D,O
Plant Biology	M,D
Public Health—General	M,D,O
Toxicology	M,D
Veterinary Sciences	M,D

CLEVELAND STATE UNIVERSITY

Allied Health—General	M
Bioethics	M,O
Biological and Biomedical Sciences—General	M,D
Communication Disorders	M
Health Services Management and Hospital Administration	M
Molecular Medicine	M,D
Nursing Education	D
Nursing—General	M,D
Occupational Therapy	M
Physical Therapy	D
Physician Assistant Studies	M
Public Health—General	M

CLEVELAND UNIVERSITY–KANSAS CITY

Chiropractic	D
Health Promotion	M

COLD SPRING HARBOR LABORATORY

Biological and Biomedical Sciences—General	D

THE COLLEGE AT BROCKPORT, STATE UNIVERSITY OF NEW YORK

Biological and Biomedical Sciences—General	M,O
Community Health	M
Health Services Management and Hospital Administration	M,O
Public Health—General	M

COLLEGE OF CHARLESTON

Marine Biology	M

COLLEGE OF MOUNT SAINT VINCENT

Family Nurse Practitioner Studies	M,O
Nursing and Healthcare Administration	M,O
Nursing Education	M,O
Nursing—General	M,O

THE COLLEGE OF NEW JERSEY

International Health	M
Nursing—General	M,O
Public Health—General	M

THE COLLEGE OF NEW ROCHELLE

Acute Care/Critical Care Nursing	M,O
Family Nurse Practitioner Studies	M,O
Nursing and Healthcare Administration	M,O
Nursing Education	M,O
Nursing—General	M,O

COLLEGE OF SAINT ELIZABETH

Health Services Management and Hospital Administration	M
Nursing—General	M
Nutrition	M,O
Public Health—General	M

COLLEGE OF SAINT MARY

Nursing—General	M
Occupational Therapy	M

THE COLLEGE OF SAINT ROSE

Communication Disorders	M

THE COLLEGE OF ST. SCHOLASTICA

Nursing—General	M,O
Occupational Therapy	M
Physical Therapy	D

COLLEGE OF STATEN ISLAND OF THE CITY UNIVERSITY OF NEW YORK

Adult Nursing	M,D,O
Biological and Biomedical Sciences—General	M
Gerontological Nursing	M,D,O
Health Services Management and Hospital Administration	M
Neuroscience	M
Nursing—General	D
Physical Therapy	D

THE COLLEGE OF WILLIAM AND MARY

Biological and Biomedical Sciences—General	M
Clinical Laboratory Sciences/Medical Technology	M,D
Computational Biology	M,D
Medical Physics	M,D
Neuroscience	M,D

COLORADO MESA UNIVERSITY

Family Nurse Practitioner Studies	M,D,O
Nursing Education	M,D,O
Nursing—General	M,D,O

COLORADO SCHOOL OF TRADITIONAL CHINESE MEDICINE

Acupuncture and Oriental Medicine	M

COLORADO STATE UNIVERSITY

Biochemistry	M,D
Biological and Biomedical Sciences—General	M,D
Botany	M,D
Conservation Biology	M,D
Entomology	M,D
Environmental and Occupational Health	M,D
Epidemiology	M,D
Immunology	M,D
Microbiology	M,D
Nutrition	M,D
Occupational Therapy	M,D
Pathology	M,D
Plant Pathology	M,D
Veterinary Medicine	D
Veterinary Sciences	M,D
Zoology	M,D

COLORADO STATE UNIVERSITY–GLOBAL CAMPUS

Health Services Management and Hospital Administration	M

COLORADO STATE UNIVERSITY–PUEBLO

Biochemistry	M
Biological and Biomedical Sciences—General	M
Nursing—General	M

COLUMBIA COLLEGE OF NURSING

Nursing—General	M

COLUMBIA SOUTHERN UNIVERSITY

Environmental and Occupational Health	M
Health Services Management and Hospital Administration	M

COLUMBIA UNIVERSITY

Acute Care/Critical Care Nursing	M,O
Adult Nursing	M,O
Allopathic Medicine	M,D
Anatomy	M,D
Biochemistry	M,D
Bioethics	M
Biological and Biomedical Sciences—General	M,D,O*
Biophysics	M,D
Cell Biology	M,D
Community Health	M,D
Conservation Biology	M,D
Dentistry	D
Developmental Biology	M,D
Ecology	M,D
Environmental and Occupational Health	M,D
Epidemiology	M,D
Evolutionary Biology	M,D
Family Nurse Practitioner Studies	M,O
Genetics	M,D
Gerontological Nursing	M,O
Health Services Management and Hospital Administration	M
Maternal and Child Health	M,D
Medical Physics	M,D
Microbiology	M,D
Molecular Biology	D
Neurobiology	D
Nurse Anesthesia	M,O
Nurse Midwifery	M
Nursing—General	M,D,O
Nutrition	M,D
Occupational Therapy	M,D
Oral and Dental Sciences	M,D,O
Pathobiology	M,D
Pathology	M,D
Pediatric Nursing	M,O
Pharmaceutical Administration	M
Pharmacology	M,D
Physical Therapy	D
Physiology	M,D
Psychiatric Nursing	M,O
Public Health—General	M,D
Structural Biology	D
Toxicology	M,D

COLUMBUS STATE UNIVERSITY

Biological and Biomedical Sciences—General	M
Family Nurse Practitioner Studies	M
Health Services Management and Hospital Administration	M
Nursing and Healthcare Administration	M
Nursing Education	M
Nursing Informatics	M
Nursing—General	M

CONCORDIA UNIVERSITY (CANADA)

Biological and Biomedical Sciences—General	M,D,O
Genomic Sciences	M,D,O

CONCORDIA UNIVERSITY IRVINE

Health Services Management and Hospital Administration	M
Nursing—General	M

CONCORDIA UNIVERSITY, ST. PAUL

Allied Health—General	M,D
Health Services Management and Hospital Administration	M
Physical Therapy	M,D

CONCORDIA UNIVERSITY WISCONSIN

Family Nurse Practitioner Studies	M,D
Health Services Management and Hospital Administration	M
Nursing—General	M,D
Occupational Therapy	M
Pharmacy	M,D
Physical Therapy	D
Rehabilitation Sciences	M

CONCORD UNIVERSITY

Health Promotion	M

COPENHAGEN BUSINESS SCHOOL

Health Services Management and Hospital Administration	M,D

COPPIN STATE UNIVERSITY

Family Nurse Practitioner Studies	M,O
Nursing—General	M,O

CORNELL UNIVERSITY

Animal Behavior	D
Biochemistry	M,D
Biological and Biomedical Sciences—General	D
Biophysics	D
Biopsychology	D
Cell Biology	D
Computational Biology	D
Conservation Biology	M,D
Developmental Biology	D
Ecology	M,D
Entomology	M,D
Evolutionary Biology	D
Genetics	D
Genomic Sciences	D
Health Services Management and Hospital Administration	M,D
Microbiology	D
Molecular Biology	M,D
Neurobiology	D
Nutrition	M,D
Physiology	M,D
Plant Biology	M,D
Plant Molecular Biology	M,D
Plant Pathology	M,D
Plant Physiology	M,D
Toxicology	M,D
Veterinary Medicine	D

COX COLLEGE

Family Nurse Practitioner Studies	M
Nursing and Healthcare Administration	M
Nursing Education	M
Nursing—General	M

CREIGHTON UNIVERSITY

Adult Nursing	M,D,O
Allied Health—General	M,D
Allopathic Medicine	D
Anatomy	M
Bioethics	M
Biological and Biomedical Sciences—General	M,D
Dentistry	D
Emergency Medical Services	M
Family Nurse Practitioner Studies	M,D,O
Gerontological Nursing	M,D,O
Health Promotion	M
Health Services Management and Hospital Administration	M
Immunology	M,D
Maternal and Child/Neonatal Nursing	M,D,O
Medical Microbiology	M,D
Medical Physics	M
Nursing and Healthcare Administration	M,D,O
Nursing—General	M,D,O
Occupational Therapy	D
Pediatric Nursing	M,D,O
Pharmaceutical Sciences	M,D
Pharmacology	M,D
Pharmacy	D
Physical Therapy	D
Psychiatric Nursing	M,D,O
Public Health—General	M

CURRY COLLEGE

Nursing—General	M

DAEMEN COLLEGE

Adult Nursing	M,D,O
Community Health	M
Epidemiology	M
Health Services Management and Hospital Administration	M
Medical/Surgical Nursing	M,D,O
Nursing and Healthcare Administration	M,D,O
Nursing Education	M,D,O
Nursing—General	M,D,O
Physical Therapy	D,O
Physician Assistant Studies	M
Public Health—General	M

DALHOUSIE UNIVERSITY

Allopathic Medicine	M,D
Anatomy	M,D
Biochemistry	M,D
Biological and Biomedical Sciences—General	M,D
Biophysics	M,D
Botany	M
Communication Disorders	M,D
Community Health	M
Ecology	M
Environmental Biology	M
Epidemiology	M
Health Services Management and Hospital Administration	M,D
Immunology	M,D
Microbiology	M,D
Neurobiology	M,D
Neuroscience	M,D
Nursing—General	M,D
Occupational Therapy	M
Oral and Dental Sciences	
Pathology	M,D
Pharmacology	M,D
Physical Therapy	M
Physiology	M,D
Plant Pathology	M
Plant Physiology	M

DALLAS BAPTIST UNIVERSITY

Health Services Management and Hospital Administration	M

DARTMOUTH COLLEGE

Allopathic Medicine	D
Biochemistry	M,D
Biological and Biomedical Sciences—General	D
Cell Biology	D
Ecology	D
Environmental Biology	D
Epidemiology	M,D
Evolutionary Biology	D
Genetics	D
Health Services Management and Hospital Administration	M,D
Health Services Research	M,D
Immunology	D
Microbiology	D
Molecular Biology	D
Molecular Medicine	
Molecular Pathogenesis	D
Neuroscience	D
Public Health—General	M

DAVENPORT UNIVERSITY

Health Services Management and Hospital Administration	M
Public Health—General	M

DELAWARE STATE UNIVERSITY

Biological and Biomedical Sciences—General	M
Neuroscience	M,D
Nursing—General	M

DELTA STATE UNIVERSITY

Biological and Biomedical Sciences—General	M
Family Nurse Practitioner Studies	M,D
Health Services Management and Hospital Administration	M,D
Nursing Education	M,D
Nursing—General	M,D

DEPAUL UNIVERSITY

Biological and Biomedical Sciences—General	M,D
Family Nurse Practitioner Studies	M,D
Nursing—General	M,D

*M—masters degree; D—doctorate; O—other advanced degree; *—Close-Up and/or Display*

- Public Health—General M

DESALES UNIVERSITY
- Family Nurse Practitioner Studies M,D,O
- Health Services Management and Hospital Administration M
- Nurse Anesthesia M,D,O
- Nurse Midwifery M,D,O
- Nursing and Healthcare Administration M,D,O
- Nursing Education M,D,O
- Nursing—General M,D,O

DES MOINES UNIVERSITY
- Anatomy M
- Biological and Biomedical Sciences—General M
- Health Services Management and Hospital Administration M
- Osteopathic Medicine D
- Physical Therapy D
- Physician Assistant Studies M
- Podiatric Medicine D
- Public Health—General M

DOMINICAN COLLEGE
- Allied Health—General M,D
- Family Nurse Practitioner Studies M,D
- Health Services Management and Hospital Administration M
- Occupational Therapy M
- Physical Therapy M,D

DOMINICAN UNIVERSITY OF CALIFORNIA
- Biological and Biomedical Sciences—General M
- Clinical Laboratory Sciences/Medical Technology M
- Occupational Therapy M

DONGGUK UNIVERSITY LOS ANGELES
- Acupuncture and Oriental Medicine M

DRAGON RISES COLLEGE OF ORIENTAL MEDICINE
- Acupuncture and Oriental Medicine M

DRAKE UNIVERSITY
- Occupational Therapy M,D
- Pharmacy M,D

DREW UNIVERSITY
- Biological and Biomedical Sciences—General M,D,O
- Health Services Management and Hospital Administration M,D,O

DREXEL UNIVERSITY
- Acute Care/Critical Care Nursing M
- Allied Health—General M,D,O
- Allopathic Medicine D
- Biochemistry M,D
- Biological and Biomedical Sciences—General M,D,O
- Biopsychology M,D
- Cell Biology M,D
- Emergency Medical Services M
- Epidemiology M,D,O
- Family Nurse Practitioner Studies M
- Genetics M,D
- Immunology M,D
- Microbiology M,D
- Molecular Biology M,D
- Molecular Medicine M
- Neuroscience M,D
- Nurse Anesthesia M
- Nursing and Healthcare Administration M
- Nursing Education M
- Nursing—General M,D
- Pathobiology M,D
- Pediatric Nursing M
- Pharmaceutical Sciences M
- Pharmacology M,D
- Physical Therapy M,D,O
- Physician Assistant Studies M
- Psychiatric Nursing M
- Public Health—General M,D,O
- Veterinary Sciences M
- Women's Health Nursing M

DUKE UNIVERSITY
- Acute Care/Critical Care Nursing M,D,O
- Adult Nursing M,D,O
- Allopathic Medicine D
- Anatomy D
- Biochemistry D
- Bioethics M
- Biological and Biomedical Sciences—General M,D
- Biopsychology D
- Cancer Biology/Oncology D
- Cell Biology D,O
- Clinical Laboratory Sciences/Medical Technology M
- Clinical Research M
- Computational Biology D,O
- Developmental Biology O
- Ecology D,O
- Environmental and Occupational Health O
- Family Nurse Practitioner Studies M,D,O
- Genetics D
- Genomic Sciences D
- Gerontological Nursing M,D,O
- Health Services Management and Hospital Administration M,O
- Immunology D
- International Health M
- Maternal and Child/Neonatal Nursing M,D,O
- Medical Physics M,D
- Microbiology D
- Molecular Biology D,O
- Molecular Biophysics O
- Molecular Genetics D
- Neurobiology D
- Neuroscience D,O
- Nurse Anesthesia M,D,O
- Nursing and Healthcare Administration M,D,O
- Nursing Education M,D,O
- Nursing Informatics M,D,O
- Nursing—General D
- Pathology M,D
- Pediatric Nursing M,D,O
- Pharmacology D
- Physical Therapy D
- Physician Assistant Studies M
- Structural Biology O
- Toxicology O
- Women's Health Nursing M,D,O

DUQUESNE UNIVERSITY
- Allied Health—General M,D,O
- Bioethics M,D,O
- Biological and Biomedical Sciences—General D
- Communication Disorders M,D
- Family Nurse Practitioner Studies M,O
- Forensic Nursing M,O
- Health Services Management and Hospital Administration M,D
- Medicinal and Pharmaceutical Chemistry M,D
- Nursing Education M,O
- Nursing—General M,D,O
- Occupational Therapy M,D
- Pharmaceutical Administration M
- Pharmaceutical Sciences M,D
- Pharmacology M,D
- Pharmacy D
- Physical Therapy M,D
- Physician Assistant Studies M,D
- Rehabilitation Sciences M,D

D'YOUVILLE COLLEGE
- Anatomy M
- Chiropractic D
- Family Nurse Practitioner Studies M,D,O
- Health Services Management and Hospital Administration M,D,O
- Nursing—General M,D,O
- Nutrition M
- Occupational Therapy M
- Pharmacy D
- Physical Therapy D,O
- Physician Assistant Studies M

EAST CAROLINA UNIVERSITY
- Allied Health—General M,D,O
- Allopathic Medicine D
- Biological and Biomedical Sciences—General M
- Biophysics M,D
- Communication Disorders M,D
- Dentistry D
- Environmental and Occupational Health M,D,O
- Health Physics/Radiological Health M,D
- Health Promotion M
- Health Services Management and Hospital Administration M,O
- Maternal and Child Health M,D,O
- Medical Physics M,D
- Molecular Biology M
- Nursing—General M,D
- Nutrition M
- Occupational Therapy M,D,O
- Pharmacology D
- Physical Therapy D
- Physician Assistant Studies M
- Public Health—General M,D,O
- Rehabilitation Sciences M,D,O

EASTERN ILLINOIS UNIVERSITY
- Biological and Biomedical Sciences—General M
- Communication Disorders M
- Nutrition M

EASTERN KENTUCKY UNIVERSITY
- Allied Health—General M
- Biological and Biomedical Sciences—General M
- Communication Disorders M
- Community Health M
- Ecology M
- Environmental and Occupational Health M
- Family Nurse Practitioner Studies M
- Health Promotion M
- Health Services Management and Hospital Administration M
- Industrial Hygiene M
- Nursing—General M
- Nutrition M
- Occupational Therapy M

EASTERN MENNONITE UNIVERSITY
- Biological and Biomedical Sciences—General M
- Health Services Management and Hospital Administration M
- Nursing and Healthcare Administration M,D
- Nursing—General M,D
- School Nursing M,D

EASTERN MICHIGAN UNIVERSITY
- Adult Nursing M,O
- Biological and Biomedical Sciences—General M
- Clinical Research M,O
- Communication Disorders M
- Health Promotion M,O
- Health Services Management and Hospital Administration M,O
- Nursing and Healthcare Administration M,O
- Nursing Education M,O
- Nutrition M
- Occupational Therapy M
- Physician Assistant Studies M
- Physiology M

EASTERN NEW MEXICO UNIVERSITY
- Biochemistry M
- Biological and Biomedical Sciences—General M
- Communication Disorders M
- Nursing—General M

EASTERN UNIVERSITY
- Health Services Management and Hospital Administration M
- School Nursing M,O

EASTERN VIRGINIA MEDICAL SCHOOL
- Allopathic Medicine D
- Biological and Biomedical Sciences—General M,D
- Medical/Surgical Nursing M
- Physician Assistant Studies M
- Public Health—General M
- Reproductive Biology M
- Vision Sciences O

EASTERN WASHINGTON UNIVERSITY
- Biological and Biomedical Sciences—General M
- Communication Disorders M
- Dental Hygiene M
- Occupational Therapy M
- Physical Therapy D
- Public Health—General M

EAST STROUDSBURG UNIVERSITY OF PENNSYLVANIA
- Biological and Biomedical Sciences—General M
- Communication Disorders M
- Public Health—General M
- Rehabilitation Sciences M

EAST TENNESSEE STATE UNIVERSITY
- Allied Health—General M
- Allopathic Medicine D
- Anatomy D
- Biochemistry D
- Biological and Biomedical Sciences—General M,D
- Communication Disorders M,D
- Community Health M,D,O
- Environmental and Occupational Health M,D,O
- Epidemiology M,D,O
- Family Nurse Practitioner Studies M,D,O
- Gerontological Nursing M,D,O
- Health Services Management and Hospital Administration M,D,O
- International Health M,D,O
- Microbiology M,D
- Nursing and Healthcare Administration M,D,O
- Nursing Education M,D,O
- Nursing—General M,D,O
- Nutrition M
- Pediatric Nursing M,D,O
- Pharmaceutical Sciences D
- Pharmacology D
- Pharmacy D
- Physical Therapy D
- Physiology D
- Psychiatric Nursing M,D,O
- Public Health—General M,D,O
- Women's Health Nursing M,D,O

EAST WEST COLLEGE OF NATURAL MEDICINE
- Acupuncture and Oriental Medicine M

EDGEWOOD COLLEGE
- Nursing—General M,D

EDINBORO UNIVERSITY OF PENNSYLVANIA
- Communication Disorders M
- Family Nurse Practitioner Studies M,D
- Nursing Education M,D
- Nursing—General M,D

EDP UNIVERSITY OF PUERTO RICO–SAN SEBASTIAN
- Nursing—General M

EDWARD VIA COLLEGE OF OSTEOPATHIC MEDICINE–CAROLINAS CAMPUS
- Osteopathic Medicine D

EDWARD VIA COLLEGE OF OSTEOPATHIC MEDICINE–VIRGINIA CAMPUS
- Osteopathic Medicine D

ELIZABETH CITY STATE UNIVERSITY
- Biological and Biomedical Sciences—General M

ELIZABETHTOWN COLLEGE
- Occupational Therapy M

ELMEZZI GRADUATE SCHOOL OF MOLECULAR MEDICINE
- Molecular Medicine D

ELMHURST COLLEGE
- Communication Disorders M
- Health Services Management and Hospital Administration M
- Nursing—General M
- Occupational Therapy M
- Public Health—General M

ELMS COLLEGE
- Acute Care/Critical Care Nursing M,D
- Biological and Biomedical Sciences—General M
- Family Nurse Practitioner Studies M,D
- Gerontological Nursing M,D
- Health Services Management and Hospital Administration M,O
- Nursing and Healthcare Administration M,D
- Nursing Education M,D
- Nursing—General M,D

ELON UNIVERSITY
- Physical Therapy D
- Physician Assistant Studies M

EMBRY-RIDDLE AERONAUTICAL UNIVERSITY–WORLDWIDE
- Environmental and Occupational Health M

EMERSON COLLEGE
- Communication Disorders M

EMMANUEL COLLEGE (UNITED STATES)
- Nursing and Healthcare Administration M,O
- Nursing Education M,O
- Nursing—General M,O

EMORY & HENRY COLLEGE
- Occupational Therapy M,D
- Physical Therapy M,D
- Physician Assistant Studies M,D

EMORY UNIVERSITY
- Adult Nursing M
- Allied Health—General M,D
- Allopathic Medicine D
- Anesthesiologist Assistant Studies M
- Animal Behavior D
- Biochemistry D
- Bioethics M
- Biological and Biomedical Sciences—General D
- Biophysics D
- Cancer Biology/Oncology D
- Cell Biology D
- Clinical Research M
- Developmental Biology D
- Ecology D
- Environmental and Occupational Health M,D
- Epidemiology M,D
- Evolutionary Biology D
- Family Nurse Practitioner Studies M
- Genetics D
- Health Promotion M
- Health Services Management and Hospital Administration M,D
- Health Services Research M,D
- Human Genetics M
- Immunology D
- International Health M
- Microbiology D
- Molecular Biology D
- Molecular Genetics D
- Molecular Pathogenesis D
- Neuroscience D
- Nurse Midwifery M
- Nursing and Healthcare Administration M
- Nursing—General M,D
- Nutrition M,D
- Pediatric Nursing M
- Pharmacology D
- Physical Therapy D
- Physician Assistant Studies M
- Public Health—General M,D
- Women's Health Nursing M

EMPEROR'S COLLEGE OF TRADITIONAL ORIENTAL MEDICINE
- Acupuncture and Oriental Medicine M,D

EMPORIA STATE UNIVERSITY
- Biological and Biomedical Sciences—General M
- Botany M
- Cell Biology M
- Environmental Biology M
- Microbiology M
- Zoology M

ENDICOTT COLLEGE
- Family Nurse Practitioner Studies M,O
- International Health M,O
- Nursing and Healthcare Administration M,O
- Nursing Education M,O
- Nursing—General M,O

EVERGLADES UNIVERSITY
- Public Health—General M

EXCELSIOR COLLEGE
- Health Services Management and Hospital Administration M,O
- Nursing and Healthcare Administration M
- Nursing Education M
- Nursing Informatics M
- Nursing—General M
- Public Health—General M

FAIRFIELD UNIVERSITY
- Family Nurse Practitioner Studies M,D
- Nurse Anesthesia M,D
- Nursing and Healthcare Administration M,D
- Nursing—General M,D
- Psychiatric Nursing M,D

FAIRLEIGH DICKINSON UNIVERSITY, FLORHAM CAMPUS
- Biological and Biomedical Sciences—General M
- Gerontological Nursing M
- Health Services Management and Hospital Administration M
- Nursing—General M
- Pharmacology M,O

- Pharmacy D
- Psychiatric Nursing M

FAIRLEIGH DICKINSON UNIVERSITY, METROPOLITAN CAMPUS
- Biological and Biomedical Sciences—General M
- Clinical Laboratory Sciences/Medical Technology M
- Health Services Management and Hospital Administration M
- Nursing—General M,D,O
- Pharmaceutical Administration M,O

FAIRMONT STATE UNIVERSITY
- Health Promotion M

FELICIAN UNIVERSITY
- Adult Nursing M,O
- Family Nurse Practitioner Studies M,O
- Gerontological Nursing M,O
- Health Services Management and Hospital Administration M
- Nursing and Healthcare Administration M,D,O
- Nursing Education M,O
- Nursing—General M,D,O

FERRIS STATE UNIVERSITY
- Allied Health—General M
- Health Services Management and Hospital Administration M
- Nursing and Healthcare Administration M
- Nursing Education M
- Nursing Informatics M
- Nursing—General M
- Optometry D
- Pharmacy D
- Public Health—General M

FIELDING GRADUATE UNIVERSITY
- Neuroscience O

FISK UNIVERSITY
- Biological and Biomedical Sciences—General M

FITCHBURG STATE UNIVERSITY
- Biological and Biomedical Sciences—General M
- Forensic Nursing M,O

FIVE BRANCHES UNIVERSITY
- Acupuncture and Oriental Medicine M,D

FLORIDA AGRICULTURAL AND MECHANICAL UNIVERSITY
- Allied Health—General M,D
- Health Services Research M,D
- Medicinal and Pharmaceutical Chemistry M,D
- Nursing and Healthcare Administration M,D
- Nursing—General M,D
- Occupational Therapy M
- Pharmaceutical Administration M,D
- Pharmaceutical Sciences M,D
- Pharmacology M,D
- Pharmacy D
- Physical Therapy D
- Public Health—General M,D
- Toxicology M,D

FLORIDA ATLANTIC UNIVERSITY
- Biological and Biomedical Sciences—General M,D
- Communication Disorders M
- Health Promotion M
- Health Services Management and Hospital Administration M
- Neuroscience D
- Nursing and Healthcare Administration M,D,O
- Nursing—General M,D,O

FLORIDA COLLEGE OF INTEGRATIVE MEDICINE
- Acupuncture and Oriental Medicine M

FLORIDA GULF COAST UNIVERSITY
- Allied Health—General M,D
- Nurse Anesthesia M
- Nursing Education M
- Occupational Therapy M
- Physical Therapy D
- Physician Assistant Studies M

FLORIDA INSTITUTE OF TECHNOLOGY
- Biochemistry M
- Biological and Biomedical Sciences—General M,D
- Cell Biology M,D
- Conservation Biology M
- Ecology M,D
- Health Services Management and Hospital Administration M
- Marine Biology M,D
- Molecular Biology M,D

FLORIDA INTERNATIONAL UNIVERSITY
- Adult Nursing M,D
- Allopathic Medicine M,D
- Biological and Biomedical Sciences—General M,D
- Communication Disorders M
- Environmental and Occupational Health M,D
- Epidemiology M,D
- Health Promotion M,D
- Health Services Management and Hospital Administration M,D
- Neuroscience M,D
- Nurse Anesthesia M,D
- Nursing—General M,D
- Nutrition M,D
- Occupational Therapy M
- Pediatric Nursing M,D
- Physical Therapy D
- Physician Assistant Studies M,D
- Psychiatric Nursing M,D
- Public Health—General M,D

FLORIDA NATIONAL UNIVERSITY
- Family Nurse Practitioner Studies M
- Health Services Management and Hospital Administration M
- Nursing and Healthcare Administration M
- Nursing Education M
- Nursing—General M

FLORIDA SOUTHERN COLLEGE
- Adult Nursing M
- Family Nurse Practitioner Studies M
- Gerontological Nursing M
- Nursing and Healthcare Administration M
- Nursing Education M
- Nursing—General M

FLORIDA STATE UNIVERSITY
- Allopathic Medicine D
- Biochemistry M,D
- Biological and Biomedical Sciences—General M,D
- Biopsychology M,D
- Cell Biology M,D
- Communication Disorders M,D
- Ecology M,D
- Evolutionary Biology M,D
- Family Nurse Practitioner Studies D,O
- Molecular Biology M,D
- Molecular Biophysics D
- Neuroscience M,D
- Nursing—General D,O
- Nutrition M,D
- Psychiatric Nursing D,O
- Public Health—General M
- Structural Biology D

FONTBONNE UNIVERSITY
- Communication Disorders M

FORDHAM UNIVERSITY
- Biological and Biomedical Sciences—General M,D,O
- Clinical Research M
- Conservation Biology M,D,O
- Health Services Management and Hospital Administration M,D

FORT HAYS STATE UNIVERSITY
- Biological and Biomedical Sciences—General M
- Communication Disorders M
- Nursing—General M

FORT VALLEY STATE UNIVERSITY
- Environmental and Occupational Health M
- Public Health—General M

FRAMINGHAM STATE UNIVERSITY
- Health Services Management and Hospital Administration M
- Nursing and Healthcare Administration M
- Nursing Education M
- Nursing—General M
- Nutrition M

FRANCISCAN MISSIONARIES OF OUR LADY UNIVERSITY
- Family Nurse Practitioner Studies M
- Health Services Management and Hospital Administration M,D
- Nurse Anesthesia D
- Nursing—General M,D
- Nutrition M,D
- Physical Therapy M,D
- Physician Assistant Studies M,D

FRANCISCAN UNIVERSITY OF STEUBENVILLE
- Nursing—General M

FRANCIS MARION UNIVERSITY
- Family Nurse Practitioner Studies M
- Health Services Management and Hospital Administration M
- Nursing Education M
- Nursing—General M
- Physician Assistant Studies M

FRANKLIN PIERCE UNIVERSITY
- Health Services Management and Hospital Administration M,D,O
- Nursing and Healthcare Administration M,D,O
- Nursing Education M,D,O
- Physical Therapy M,D,O
- Physician Assistant Studies M,D,O

FRESNO PACIFIC UNIVERSITY
- Family Nurse Practitioner Studies M
- Nursing—General M

FRIENDS UNIVERSITY
- Health Services Management and Hospital Administration M

FRONTIER NURSING UNIVERSITY
- Family Nurse Practitioner Studies M,D,O
- Nurse Midwifery M,D,O
- Nursing—General M,D,O*
- Psychiatric Nursing M,D,O
- Women's Health Nursing M,D,O

FROSTBURG STATE UNIVERSITY
- Biological and Biomedical Sciences—General M
- Conservation Biology M
- Ecology M
- Nursing and Healthcare Administration M
- Nursing Education M
- Nursing—General M

GALLAUDET UNIVERSITY
- Communication Disorders M,D,O
- Neuroscience M,D,O

GANNON UNIVERSITY
- Environmental and Occupational Health M
- Family Nurse Practitioner Studies M,O
- Nurse Anesthesia M,O
- Nursing and Healthcare Administration M
- Nursing—General D
- Occupational Therapy M,D
- Physical Therapy D
- Physician Assistant Studies M

GARDNER-WEBB UNIVERSITY
- Family Nurse Practitioner Studies M,D
- Nursing—General M,D
- Physician Assistant Studies M

GEISINGER COMMONWEALTH SCHOOL OF MEDICINE
- Allopathic Medicine D
- Biological and Biomedical Sciences—General M

GEORGE FOX UNIVERSITY
- Physical Therapy D

GEORGE MASON UNIVERSITY
- Adult Nursing M,D,O
- Biochemistry M,D
- Biological and Biomedical Sciences—General M,D,O
- Community Health M,O
- Computational Biology M,D,O
- Ecology M,D
- Epidemiology M,O
- Family Nurse Practitioner Studies M,D,O
- Gerontological Nursing M,D,O
- Health Promotion M,O
- Health Services Management and Hospital Administration M,D,O
- Health Services Research M,D,O
- International Health M,O
- Neuroscience M,D,O
- Nursing Education M,D,O
- Nursing—General M,D,O
- Nutrition M,O
- Psychiatric Nursing M,D,O
- Public Health—General M,O
- Rehabilitation Sciences D,O
- Systems Biology M,D,O

GEORGETOWN UNIVERSITY
- Acute Care/Critical Care Nursing M,D
- Allopathic Medicine D
- Biochemistry M,D
- Biological and Biomedical Sciences—General M,D
- Epidemiology M,O
- Family Nurse Practitioner Studies M,D
- Health Physics/Radiological Health M
- Health Promotion M,D
- Immunology M,D
- Infectious Diseases M,D
- International Health M,D
- Microbiology M,D
- Molecular Biology M,D
- Neuroscience D
- Nurse Anesthesia M,D
- Nurse Midwifery M,D
- Nursing Education M,D
- Nursing—General M,D
- Pharmacology M,D
- Physiology M,D
- Public Health—General M,D
- Radiation Biology M

THE GEORGE WASHINGTON UNIVERSITY
- Adult Nursing M,D,O
- Allopathic Medicine D
- Biochemistry D
- Biological and Biomedical Sciences—General M,D
- Communication Disorders M
- Community Health M,D
- Environmental and Occupational Health D
- Epidemiology M
- Family Nurse Practitioner Studies M,D,O
- Health Services Management and Hospital Administration M,D,O
- Health Services Research M,D,O
- Immunology D
- Infectious Diseases M,D,O
- International Health M,D
- Microbiology M,D,O
- Molecular Medicine D
- Nursing and Healthcare Administration M,D,O
- Nursing Education M,D,O
- Nursing—General M,D,O
- Physical Therapy D
- Physician Assistant Studies M
- Public Health—General M,D
- Systems Biology D
- Toxicology M,O

GEORGIA CAMPUS–PHILADELPHIA COLLEGE OF OSTEOPATHIC MEDICINE
- Osteopathic Medicine D
- Pharmacy D*
- Physical Therapy D*

GEORGIA COLLEGE & STATE UNIVERSITY
- Biological and Biomedical Sciences—General M
- Health Promotion M
- Nursing—General M,D,O

GEORGIA INSTITUTE OF TECHNOLOGY
- Biological and Biomedical Sciences—General M,D
- Health Physics/Radiological Health M,D
- Health Services Management and Hospital Administration M
- Physiology M,D

GEORGIA SOUTHERN UNIVERSITY
- Allied Health—General M,D,O
- Biological and Biomedical Sciences—General M
- Community Health M,D
- Environmental and Occupational Health M,D,O
- Epidemiology M,D
- Family Nurse Practitioner Studies M
- Health Services Management and Hospital Administration M,D
- Nursing Education O
- Nursing—General D
- Nutrition O
- Psychiatric Nursing M
- Public Health—General M,D

GEORGIA SOUTHERN UNIVERSITY–ARMSTRONG CAMPUS
- Adult Nursing M,O
- Communication Disorders M
- Family Nurse Practitioner Studies M,O
- Gerontological Nursing M,O
- Health Services Management and Hospital Administration M
- Nursing—General M,O
- Physical Therapy D
- Public Health—General M

GEORGIA SOUTHWESTERN STATE UNIVERSITY
- Family Nurse Practitioner Studies M,O
- Nursing and Healthcare Administration M,O
- Nursing Education M,O
- Nursing Informatics M,O
- Nursing—General M,O

GEORGIA STATE UNIVERSITY
- Adult Nursing M,D,O
- Allied Health—General M
- Biochemistry M,D
- Biological and Biomedical Sciences—General M,D
- Cell Biology M,D
- Communication Disorders M,D
- Environmental Biology M,D
- Family Nurse Practitioner Studies M,D,O
- Health Services Management and Hospital Administration M,D,O
- Microbiology M,D
- Molecular Biology M,D
- Molecular Genetics M,D
- Neurobiology M,D
- Neuroscience D
- Nursing and Healthcare Administration M,D,O
- Nursing Informatics M,D,O
- Nursing—General M,D,O
- Nutrition M
- Pediatric Nursing M,D,O
- Physical Therapy D
- Physiology M,D
- Psychiatric Nursing M,D,O
- Public Health—General M,D,O
- Women's Health Nursing M,D,O

GERSTNER SLOAN KETTERING GRADUATE SCHOOL OF BIOMEDICAL SCIENCES
- Biological and Biomedical Sciences—General D
- Cancer Biology/Oncology D*

GODDARD COLLEGE
- Health Promotion M

GOLDEY-BEACOM COLLEGE
- Health Services Management and Hospital Administration M

GOLDFARB SCHOOL OF NURSING AT BARNES-JEWISH COLLEGE
- Acute Care/Critical Care Nursing M
- Gerontological Nursing M
- Nurse Anesthesia M
- Nursing and Healthcare Administration M
- Nursing—General M

GONZAGA UNIVERSITY
- Nursing—General M,D
- Physiology M,D

GOSHEN COLLEGE
- Family Nurse Practitioner Studies M
- Nursing—General M

GOUCHER COLLEGE
- Biological and Biomedical Sciences—General O

GOVERNORS STATE UNIVERSITY
- Communication Disorders M
- Environmental Biology M
- Health Services Management and Hospital Administration M

*M—masters degree; D—doctorate; O—other advanced degree; *—Close-Up and/or Display*

Nursing—General M
Occupational Therapy M
Physical Therapy D

GRACELAND UNIVERSITY (IA)
Family Nurse Practitioner Studies M,D,O
Gerontological Nursing M,D,O
Nursing Education M,D,O
Nursing—General M,D,O

THE GRADUATE CENTER, CITY UNIVERSITY OF NEW YORK
Biochemistry D
Biological and Biomedical Sciences—General D
Biopsychology D
Communication Disorders D
Neuroscience D
Nursing—General D

GRAMBLING STATE UNIVERSITY
Family Nurse Practitioner Studies M,O
Health Services Management and Hospital Administration M
Nursing—General M,O

GRAND CANYON UNIVERSITY
Acute Care/Critical Care Nursing M,D,O
Family Nurse Practitioner Studies M,D,O
Health Services Management and Hospital Administration M,D,O
Nursing Education M,D,O
Nursing—General M,D,O
Public Health—General M,D,O

GRAND VALLEY STATE UNIVERSITY
Allied Health—General M,D
Biological and Biomedical Sciences—General M
Cancer Biology/Oncology M
Cell Biology M
Communication Disorders M
Health Services Management and Hospital Administration M
Molecular Biology M
Nursing and Healthcare Administration M,D
Nursing Education M,D
Nursing—General M,D
Nutrition M
Occupational Therapy M
Physical Therapy D
Physician Assistant Studies M
Public Health—General M

GRAND VIEW UNIVERSITY
Nursing and Healthcare Administration M,O
Nursing Education M,O

GRANTHAM UNIVERSITY
Health Services Management and Hospital Administration M
Nursing and Healthcare Administration M
Nursing Education M
Nursing Informatics M
Nursing—General M

GWYNEDD MERCY UNIVERSITY
Adult Nursing M,D
Family Nurse Practitioner Studies M,D
Gerontological Nursing M,D
Health Services Management and Hospital Administration M
Nursing Education M,D
Nursing—General M,D
Oncology Nursing M,D
Pediatric Nursing M,D

HAMPTON UNIVERSITY
Allied Health—General M
Biological and Biomedical Sciences—General M
Communication Disorders M
Community Health Nursing M,D
Environmental Biology M
Family Nurse Practitioner Studies M,D
Medical Physics M,D
Nursing and Healthcare Administration M,D
Nursing Education M,D
Nursing—General M,D
Physical Therapy D

HARDING UNIVERSITY
Allied Health—General M,D
Communication Disorders M
Pharmacy D
Physical Therapy D
Physician Assistant Studies M

HARDIN-SIMMONS UNIVERSITY
Family Nurse Practitioner Studies M
Maternal and Child/Neonatal Nursing M
Nursing Education M
Nursing—General M
Physical Therapy D
Physician Assistant Studies M,D

HARVARD UNIVERSITY
Allopathic Medicine D
Biochemistry D
Biological and Biomedical Sciences—General M,D,O
Biophysics D*
Biopsychology D
Cell Biology D
Computational Biology M
Dentistry M,D,O
Environmental and Occupational Health M,D
Epidemiology M,D
Evolutionary Biology D
Genetics M,D
Health Promotion M,D
Health Services Management and Hospital Administration M,D
International Health M,D
Medical Physics D
Microbiology D
Molecular Biology D
Molecular Genetics D
Molecular Pharmacology D
Neurobiology D
Neuroscience D
Nutrition D
Oral and Dental Sciences M,D,O
Pathology D
Public Health—General M,D*
Systems Biology D

HAWAI`I PACIFIC UNIVERSITY
Nursing—General M,D
Public Health—General M

HEC MONTREAL
Medical Microbiology D

HERZING UNIVERSITY ONLINE
Health Services Management and Hospital Administration M
Nursing and Healthcare Administration M
Nursing Education M
Nursing—General M

HIGH POINT UNIVERSITY
Pharmacy M,D
Physical Therapy M,D
Physician Assistant Studies M,D

HILBERT COLLEGE
Health Services Management and Hospital Administration M

HODGES UNIVERSITY
Health Services Management and Hospital Administration M

HOFSTRA UNIVERSITY
Allopathic Medicine D
Bioethics M,D,O
Biological and Biomedical Sciences—General M
Communication Disorders M,D,O
Family Nurse Practitioner Studies M
Gerontological Nursing M
Health Services Management and Hospital Administration M,O
Medical Physics M
Molecular Medicine D
Nursing and Healthcare Administration M,D,O
Nursing—General M
Occupational Therapy M,O
Physician Assistant Studies M
Psychiatric Nursing M
Public Health—General M,O

HOLY FAMILY UNIVERSITY
Health Services Management and Hospital Administration M
Nursing and Healthcare Administration M
Nursing Education M
Nursing—General M

HOLY NAMES UNIVERSITY
Family Nurse Practitioner Studies M,O
Nursing and Healthcare Administration M,O
Nursing Informatics M,O
Nursing—General M,O

HOOD COLLEGE
Biological and Biomedical Sciences—General M
Environmental Biology M,O
Immunology M
Microbiology M
Molecular Biology M

HOWARD UNIVERSITY
Allied Health—General M,D
Allopathic Medicine D
Anatomy M,D
Biochemistry M,D
Biological and Biomedical Sciences—General M,D
Biophysics D
Biopsychology M,D
Communication Disorders M,D
Dentistry D,O
Family Nurse Practitioner Studies M
Microbiology D
Molecular Biology M,D
Nursing Education M
Nursing—General M
Nutrition M,D
Occupational Therapy M,D
Oral and Dental Sciences D,O
Pharmacology M,D
Pharmacy D
Physical Therapy M,D
Physician Assistant Studies M,D
Physiology D
Public Health—General M

HUMBOLDT STATE UNIVERSITY
Biological and Biomedical Sciences—General M

HUNTER COLLEGE OF THE CITY UNIVERSITY OF NEW YORK
Adult Nursing M
Animal Behavior M,O
Biochemistry M,D
Biological and Biomedical Sciences—General M,D
Communication Disorders M
Community Health Nursing M
Family Nurse Practitioner Studies D
Gerontological Nursing M,D
Nursing—General M,D,O
Nutrition M
Physical Therapy D
Psychiatric Nursing M,D,O
Public Health—General M

HUNTINGTON UNIVERSITY
Occupational Therapy M,D

HUNTINGTON UNIVERSITY OF HEALTH SCIENCES
Nutrition M,D

HUSSON UNIVERSITY
Community Health Nursing M,O
Family Nurse Practitioner Studies M,O
Health Services Management and Hospital Administration M
Nursing—General M,O
Pharmacology M,D
Pharmacy M,D
Physical Therapy D
Psychiatric Nursing M,O

ICAHN SCHOOL OF MEDICINE AT MOUNT SINAI
Allopathic Medicine D
Bioethics M
Biological and Biomedical Sciences—General M,D
Clinical Research M,D
Community Health M,D
Neuroscience M,D
Public Health—General M,D

IDAHO STATE UNIVERSITY
Allied Health—General M,D,O
Biological and Biomedical Sciences—General M,D
Communication Disorders M,D
Community Health O
Dental Hygiene M
Dentistry O
Health Physics/Radiological Health M,D
Medical Microbiology M,D
Medicinal and Pharmaceutical Chemistry M,D
Microbiology M,D
Nursing—General M,D
Occupational Therapy M
Oral and Dental Sciences O
Pharmaceutical Administration M,D
Pharmaceutical Sciences M,D
Pharmacology M,D
Pharmacy M,D
Physical Therapy D
Physician Assistant Studies M
Public Health—General M

IGLOBAL UNIVERSITY
Health Services Management and Hospital Administration M

ILLINOIS COLLEGE OF OPTOMETRY
Optometry D

ILLINOIS INSTITUTE OF TECHNOLOGY
Biochemistry M,D
Biological and Biomedical Sciences—General M,D
Cell Biology M,D
Health Physics/Radiological Health M,D
Medical Imaging M,D
Microbiology M,D
Molecular Biology M,D
Molecular Biophysics M,D

ILLINOIS STATE UNIVERSITY
Animal Behavior M,D
Bacteriology M,D
Biochemistry M,D
Biological and Biomedical Sciences—General M,D
Biophysics M,D
Botany M,D
Cell Biology M,D
Communication Disorders M
Conservation Biology M,D
Developmental Biology M,D
Ecology M,D
Entomology M,D
Evolutionary Biology M,D
Family Nurse Practitioner Studies M,D,O
Genetics M,D
Immunology M,D
Microbiology M,D
Molecular Biology M,D
Molecular Genetics M,D
Neurobiology M,D
Neuroscience M,D
Nursing—General M,D,O
Parasitology M,D
Physiology M,D
Plant Biology M,D
Plant Molecular Biology M,D
Structural Biology M,D
Zoology M,D

IMMACULATA UNIVERSITY
Health Promotion M
Neuroscience M,D,O
Nursing and Healthcare Administration M
Nursing Education M
Nursing—General M
Nutrition M

INDEPENDENCE UNIVERSITY
Community Health Nursing M
Community Health M
Gerontological Nursing M
Health Promotion M
Health Services Management and Hospital Administration M
Nursing and Healthcare Administration M
Nursing—General M
Public Health—General M

INDIANA STATE UNIVERSITY
Biological and Biomedical Sciences—General M,D
Cell Biology M,D
Communication Disorders M,D,O
Ecology M,D
Environmental and Occupational Health M
Evolutionary Biology M,D
Family Nurse Practitioner Studies M,D
Molecular Biology M,D
Nursing and Healthcare Administration M,D
Nursing Education M,D
Nursing—General M,D
Occupational Therapy M,D
Physical Therapy M,D
Physician Assistant Studies M,D
Physiology M,D

INDIANA TECH
Health Services Management and Hospital Administration M

INDIANA UNIVERSITY BLOOMINGTON
Biochemistry M,D
Biological and Biomedical Sciences—General M,D
Cell Biology M,D
Communication Disorders M,D
Community Health M,D
Ecology M,D,O
Environmental and Occupational Health M,D
Epidemiology M,D
Evolutionary Biology M,D
Genetics M,D
Health Promotion M,D
Health Services Management and Hospital Administration M,D
Medical Physics M,D
Microbiology M,D
Molecular Biology M,D
Neuroscience D
Nutrition M,D
Optometry M,D
Plant Biology M,D
Public Health—General M,D
Toxicology M,D,O
Zoology M,D

INDIANA UNIVERSITY EAST
Nursing—General M

INDIANA UNIVERSITY KOKOMO
Family Nurse Practitioner Studies M
Health Services Management and Hospital Administration M,O
Nursing and Healthcare Administration M
Nursing Education M
Nursing—General M

INDIANA UNIVERSITY NORTHWEST
Health Services Management and Hospital Administration M,O

INDIANA UNIVERSITY OF PENNSYLVANIA
Biological and Biomedical Sciences—General M
Communication Disorders M
Environmental and Occupational Health M,D
Health Services Management and Hospital Administration M,D
Nursing and Healthcare Administration M
Nursing Education M
Nursing—General D
Nutrition M

INDIANA UNIVERSITY–PURDUE UNIVERSITY FORT WAYNE
Adult Nursing M,O
Biological and Biomedical Sciences—General M
Family Nurse Practitioner Studies M,O
Gerontological Nursing M,O
Nursing and Healthcare Administration M,O
Nursing Education M,O
Nursing—General M,O

INDIANA UNIVERSITY–PURDUE UNIVERSITY INDIANAPOLIS
Acute Care/Critical Care Nursing M
Allopathic Medicine M,D
Anatomy M,D
Biochemistry M,D
Bioethics M,D,O
Biological and Biomedical Sciences—General M,D
Cell Biology M,D
Community Health M,D,O
Dentistry M,D,O
Environmental and Occupational Health M,D,O
Epidemiology M,D,O
Family Nurse Practitioner Studies M
Gerontological Nursing M
Health Services Management and Hospital Administration M,D,O
Immunology M,D
International Health M,D,O
Microbiology M,D
Molecular Biology M,D
Molecular Genetics M,D
Neurobiology D
Nursing and Healthcare Administration M,D
Nursing Education M
Nursing—General M,D
Nutrition M,D
Occupational Therapy M,D
Pathology M,D

- Pediatric Nursing M
- Pharmacology M,D
- Physical Therapy M,D
- Public Health—General M,D,O
- Rehabilitation Sciences M,D
- Toxicology M,D

INDIANA UNIVERSITY SOUTH BEND
- Family Nurse Practitioner Studies M
- Health Services Management and Hospital Administration M,O
- Nursing—General M

INDIANA WESLEYAN UNIVERSITY
- Health Services Management and Hospital Administration M,O
- Nursing and Healthcare Administration M
- Nursing Education M
- Nursing—General M

INSTITUTE OF CLINICAL ACUPUNCTURE AND ORIENTAL MEDICINE
- Acupuncture and Oriental Medicine M

INSTITUTE OF PUBLIC ADMINISTRATION
- Health Services Management and Hospital Administration M,O

INSTITUTE OF TAOIST EDUCATION AND ACUPUNCTURE
- Acupuncture and Oriental Medicine M

INSTITUT FRANCO-EUROPÉEN DE CHIROPRAXIE
- Chiropractic D

INSTITUTO TECNOLOGICO DE SANTO DOMINGO
- Allopathic Medicine M,D
- Bioethics M,O
- Health Promotion M,O
- Maternal and Child Health M,O
- Nutrition M,O

INTER AMERICAN UNIVERSITY OF PUERTO RICO, ARECIBO CAMPUS
- Acute Care/Critical Care Nursing M
- Medical/Surgical Nursing M
- Nurse Anesthesia M
- Nursing—General M

INTER AMERICAN UNIVERSITY OF PUERTO RICO, BARRANQUITAS CAMPUS
- Acute Care/Critical Care Nursing M
- Biological and Biomedical Sciences—General M
- Medical/Surgical Nursing M
- Nursing—General M

INTER AMERICAN UNIVERSITY OF PUERTO RICO, BAYAMÓN CAMPUS
- Ecology M

INTER AMERICAN UNIVERSITY OF PUERTO RICO, METROPOLITAN CAMPUS
- Clinical Laboratory Sciences/Medical Technology M
- Microbiology M
- Molecular Biology M

INTER AMERICAN UNIVERSITY OF PUERTO RICO SCHOOL OF OPTOMETRY
- Optometry D

IONA COLLEGE
- Communication Disorders M
- Health Services Management and Hospital Administration M,O

IOWA STATE UNIVERSITY OF SCIENCE AND TECHNOLOGY
- Biological and Biomedical Sciences—General M,D
- Biophysics M,D
- Cell Biology M,D
- Computational Biology M,D
- Developmental Biology M,D
- Ecology M,D
- Entomology M,D
- Evolutionary Biology M,D
- Genetics M,D
- Immunology M,D
- Microbiology M,D
- Molecular Biology M,D
- Molecular Genetics M,D
- Neuroscience M,D
- Nutrition M,D
- Pathology M,D
- Plant Biology M,D
- Plant Pathology M,D
- Structural Biology M,D
- Toxicology M,D
- Veterinary Medicine M
- Veterinary Sciences M,D

IRELL & MANELLA GRADUATE SCHOOL OF BIOLOGICAL SCIENCES
- Biochemistry D
- Biological and Biomedical Sciences—General D*
- Cancer Biology/Oncology D
- Cell Biology D
- Developmental Biology D
- Genetics D
- Immunology D
- Molecular Biology D
- Neuroscience D
- Pharmaceutical Sciences D

ITHACA COLLEGE
- Allied Health—General M,D
- Communication Disorders M
- Occupational Therapy M
- Physical Therapy D

JACKSON STATE UNIVERSITY
- Biological and Biomedical Sciences—General M
- Communication Disorders M
- Public Health—General M,D
- Rehabilitation Sciences M

JACKSONVILLE STATE UNIVERSITY
- Biological and Biomedical Sciences—General M
- Nursing—General M

JACKSONVILLE UNIVERSITY
- Adult Nursing M,D,O
- Allied Health—General M,D
- Communication Disorders M
- Dentistry M,O
- Family Nurse Practitioner Studies M
- Gerontological Nursing M,D,O
- Nursing and Healthcare Administration M
- Nursing Education M
- Nursing Informatics M
- Nursing—General M,D
- Occupational Therapy D
- Oral and Dental Sciences M,O
- Psychiatric Nursing M

JAMES MADISON UNIVERSITY
- Biological and Biomedical Sciences—General M
- Communication Disorders M,D
- Family Nurse Practitioner Studies M,D
- Gerontological Nursing M,D
- Nurse Midwifery M,D
- Nursing and Healthcare Administration M,D
- Nursing—General M,D
- Nutrition M
- Occupational Therapy M
- Physician Assistant Studies M
- Physiology M
- Psychiatric Nursing M,D

JEFFERSON COLLEGE OF HEALTH SCIENCES
- Nursing and Healthcare Administration M
- Nursing Education M
- Nursing—General M
- Occupational Therapy M
- Physician Assistant Studies M

JOHN CARROLL UNIVERSITY
- Biological and Biomedical Sciences—General M

JOHNS HOPKINS UNIVERSITY
- Allopathic Medicine D
- Anatomy D
- Biochemistry M,D
- Bioethics M,D
- Biological and Biomedical Sciences—General M,D
- Biophysics D
- Cardiovascular Sciences M,D
- Cell Biology D
- Clinical Research M,D
- Community Health Nursing
- Community Health M,D
- Developmental Biology D
- Environmental and Occupational Health M,D
- Epidemiology M,D
- Evolutionary Biology D
- Family Nurse Practitioner Studies D
- Genetics M,D
- Gerontological Nursing D
- Health Services Management and Hospital Administration M,D
- Immunology M,D
- Infectious Diseases M,D
- International Health M,D
- Microbiology M,D
- Molecular Biology M,D
- Molecular Biophysics D
- Molecular Medicine D
- Neuroscience D
- Nursing and Healthcare Administration M,D
- Nursing Education O
- Nursing—General M,D,O*
- Nutrition M,D
- Pathobiology D
- Pathology D
- Pediatric Nursing D,O
- Pharmaceutical Sciences M
- Pharmacology D
- Physiology D
- Psychiatric Nursing O
- Public Health—General M,D

JOHNSON & WALES UNIVERSITY
- Occupational Therapy D
- Physician Assistant Studies M

KANSAS CITY UNIVERSITY OF MEDICINE AND BIOSCIENCES
- Bioethics M
- Biological and Biomedical Sciences—General M
- Osteopathic Medicine D

KANSAS STATE UNIVERSITY
- Biochemistry M,D
- Biological and Biomedical Sciences—General M,D
- Communication Disorders M,D,O
- Entomology M,D
- Genetics M,D
- Nutrition M,D
- Pathobiology M,D
- Physiology M,D
- Plant Pathology M,D
- Public Health—General M,D,O
- Veterinary Medicine D
- Veterinary Sciences M,O

KEAN UNIVERSITY
- Communication Disorders M,D
- Community Health Nursing M
- Health Services Management and Hospital Administration M
- Nursing and Healthcare Administration M,D
- Nursing—General M
- Occupational Therapy M
- Physical Therapy D

KECK GRADUATE INSTITUTE
- Biological and Biomedical Sciences—General M,D,O
- Pharmacy D

KEISER UNIVERSITY
- Family Nurse Practitioner Studies M
- Health Services Management and Hospital Administration M
- Nursing—General M
- Occupational Therapy M
- Physician Assistant Studies M

KENNESAW STATE UNIVERSITY
- Biochemistry M
- Biological and Biomedical Sciences—General M
- Health Services Management and Hospital Administration M
- Nursing and Healthcare Administration M
- Nursing Education M
- Nursing—General M,D

KENT STATE UNIVERSITY
- Adult Nursing M,D
- Biological and Biomedical Sciences—General M,D
- Botany M,D
- Cell Biology M,D
- Communication Disorders M,D,O
- Ecology M,D
- Environmental and Occupational Health M,D
- Epidemiology M,D
- Family Nurse Practitioner Studies M,D
- Genetics M,D
- Gerontological Nursing M,D
- Health Promotion M,D
- Health Services Management and Hospital Administration M,D
- Molecular Biology M,D
- Neuroscience M,D
- Nursing and Healthcare Administration M,D
- Nursing Education M,D
- Nursing—General M,D
- Nutrition M
- Pediatric Nursing M,D
- Pharmacology M,D
- Physiology M,D
- Podiatric Medicine D
- Psychiatric Nursing M,D
- Public Health—General M,D

KENTUCKY STATE UNIVERSITY
- Nursing—General M,D

KETTERING COLLEGE
- Physician Assistant Studies M

KEUKA COLLEGE
- Gerontological Nursing M
- Nursing Education M
- Nursing—General M
- Occupational Therapy M

KING'S COLLEGE
- Health Services Management and Hospital Administration M
- Physician Assistant Studies M

KING UNIVERSITY
- Family Nurse Practitioner Studies M,D
- Health Services Management and Hospital Administration M
- Nursing and Healthcare Administration M,D
- Nursing Education M,D
- Nursing—General M,D
- Pediatric Nursing M,D

KUTZTOWN UNIVERSITY OF PENNSYLVANIA
- Biological and Biomedical Sciences—General M,D

LAKE ERIE COLLEGE
- Health Services Management and Hospital Administration M

LAKE ERIE COLLEGE OF OSTEOPATHIC MEDICINE
- Biological and Biomedical Sciences—General M,D,O
- Osteopathic Medicine M,D,O
- Pharmacy M,D,O

LAKE FOREST GRADUATE SCHOOL OF MANAGEMENT
- Health Services Management and Hospital Administration M

LAKEHEAD UNIVERSITY
- Biological and Biomedical Sciences—General M
- Health Services Research M

LAKELAND UNIVERSITY
- Health Services Management and Hospital Administration M

LAMAR UNIVERSITY
- Biological and Biomedical Sciences—General M
- Communication Disorders M,D
- Health Services Management and Hospital Administration M
- Nursing and Healthcare Administration M
- Nursing Education M
- Nursing—General M
- Public Health—General M

LANDER UNIVERSITY
- Nursing—General M

LANGSTON UNIVERSITY
- Physical Therapy D

LA ROCHE COLLEGE
- Nurse Anesthesia M,D
- Nursing and Healthcare Administration M
- Nursing Education M
- Nursing—General M

LA SALLE UNIVERSITY
- Adult Nursing M,D,O
- Communication Disorders M
- Community Health Nursing M,D,O
- Family Nurse Practitioner Studies M,D,O
- Gerontological Nursing M,D,O
- Nurse Anesthesia M,D,O
- Nursing and Healthcare Administration M,D,O
- Nursing Education M,D,O
- Nursing—General M,D,O
- Public Health—General M
- School Nursing M,D,O

LASELL COLLEGE
- Health Services Management and Hospital Administration M,O
- Rehabilitation Sciences M

LAURENTIAN UNIVERSITY
- Biochemistry M
- Biological and Biomedical Sciences—General M,D
- Ecology M,D
- Nursing—General M
- Public Health—General D

LAWRENCE TECHNOLOGICAL UNIVERSITY
- Health Services Management and Hospital Administration M,D,O

LEBANESE AMERICAN UNIVERSITY
- Pharmacy D

LEBANON VALLEY COLLEGE
- Communication Disorders M
- Health Services Management and Hospital Administration M
- Physical Therapy D

LEE UNIVERSITY
- Biological and Biomedical Sciences—General M,O

LEHIGH UNIVERSITY
- Biochemistry M,D
- Biological and Biomedical Sciences—General M,D
- Cell Biology M,D
- Environmental and Occupational Health M,O
- Health Services Management and Hospital Administration M,O
- Molecular Biology M,D

LEHMAN COLLEGE OF THE CITY UNIVERSITY OF NEW YORK
- Adult Nursing M
- Biological and Biomedical Sciences—General M
- Communication Disorders M
- Gerontological Nursing M
- Health Promotion M
- Maternal and Child/Neonatal Nursing M
- Nursing—General M
- Nutrition M
- Pediatric Nursing M

LE MOYNE COLLEGE
- Family Nurse Practitioner Studies M,O
- Nursing and Healthcare Administration M,O
- Nursing Education M,O
- Nursing Informatics M,O
- Nursing—General M,O
- Occupational Therapy M
- Physician Assistant Studies M

LENOIR-RHYNE UNIVERSITY
- Health Services Management and Hospital Administration M
- Nursing and Healthcare Administration M
- Nursing Education M
- Nursing—General M
- Occupational Therapy M
- Physician Assistant Studies M
- Public Health—General M

LESLEY UNIVERSITY
- Ecology M,D,O

*M—masters degree; D—doctorate; O—other advanced degree; *—Close-Up and/or Display*

LETOURNEAU UNIVERSITY
Health Services Management and Hospital Administration M

LEWIS & CLARK COLLEGE
Communication Disorders M

LEWIS UNIVERSITY
Adult Nursing M,D
Computational Biology M
Environmental and Occupational Health M
Family Nurse Practitioner Studies M,D
Health Services Management and Hospital Administration M
Nursing and Healthcare Administration M,D
Nursing Education M,D
Nursing—General M,D
School Nursing M,D

LIBERTY UNIVERSITY
Anatomy M,D
Biological and Biomedical Sciences—General M,D
Biopsychology M,D
Cell Biology M,D
Epidemiology M,D
Family Nurse Practitioner Studies M,D
Health Promotion M,D,O
International Health M,D
Molecular Medicine M,D
Nursing and Healthcare Administration M,D
Nursing Education M,D
Nursing Informatics M,D
Nursing—General M,D
Nutrition M,D
Osteopathic Medicine D
Public Health—General M,D

LIFE CHIROPRACTIC COLLEGE WEST
Chiropractic D

LIFE UNIVERSITY
Chiropractic D
Nutrition M

LINCOLN MEMORIAL UNIVERSITY
Family Nurse Practitioner Studies M
Nurse Anesthesia M
Nursing—General M
Osteopathic Medicine D
Psychiatric Nursing M

LINDENWOOD UNIVERSITY
Communication Disorders M,D,O
Health Promotion M
Health Services Management and Hospital Administration M,O
Nursing—General M

LINDENWOOD UNIVERSITY–BELLEVILLE
Health Services Management and Hospital Administration M

LIPSCOMB UNIVERSITY
Clinical Laboratory Sciences/Medical Technology M
Health Services Management and Hospital Administration M,O
Molecular Biology M
Nutrition M
Pharmacy M,D

LOCK HAVEN UNIVERSITY OF PENNSYLVANIA
Health Promotion M
Health Services Management and Hospital Administration M
Physician Assistant Studies M

LOGAN UNIVERSITY
Chiropractic D
Nutrition M,D
Rehabilitation Sciences M,D

LOMA LINDA UNIVERSITY
Adult Nursing M
Allied Health—General M,D
Allopathic Medicine M,D
Anatomy D
Biochemistry M,D
Bioethics M,O
Communication Disorders M,D
Dentistry M,D,O
Environmental and Occupational Health M
Epidemiology M,D
Gerontological Nursing M
Health Services Management and Hospital Administration M
International Health M
Microbiology M,D
Nursing and Healthcare Administration M
Nursing Education M
Nursing—General D
Nutrition M,D
Occupational Therapy M,D
Oral and Dental Sciences M,O
Pathology D
Pediatric Nursing M
Pharmacology D
Pharmacy D
Physical Therapy M,D
Physician Assistant Studies M
Physiology D
Public Health—General M,D
Rehabilitation Sciences M,D

LONDON METROPOLITAN UNIVERSITY
Biological and Biomedical Sciences—General M,D
Health Services Management and Hospital Administration M,D
Immunology M,D
Nutrition M,D
Pharmacology M,D
Public Health—General M,D

LONG ISLAND UNIVERSITY–BRENTWOOD CAMPUS
Family Nurse Practitioner Studies M,O
Health Services Management and Hospital Administration M,O

LONG ISLAND UNIVERSITY–HUDSON
Health Services Management and Hospital Administration M,O
Pharmaceutical Sciences M,O
Pharmacy M,O

LONG ISLAND UNIVERSITY–LIU BROOKLYN
Adult Nursing M,O
Biological and Biomedical Sciences—General M,D,O
Communication Disorders M,D,O
Community Health M,D,O
Family Nurse Practitioner Studies M,O
Health Services Management and Hospital Administration M,O
Nursing Education M,O
Nursing—General M,O
Occupational Therapy M,D,O
Pharmaceutical Sciences M,D
Pharmacology M,D
Pharmacy M,D
Physical Therapy M,D,O
Physician Assistant Studies M,D,O
Public Health—General M,D,O
Toxicology M,D

LONG ISLAND UNIVERSITY–LIU POST
Allied Health—General M,O
Biological and Biomedical Sciences—General M,O
Communication Disorders M,D,O
Family Nurse Practitioner Studies M,O
Health Services Management and Hospital Administration M,O
Nursing Education M,O
Nutrition M,O

LONGWOOD UNIVERSITY
Communication Disorders M

LOUISIANA STATE UNIVERSITY AND AGRICULTURAL & MECHANICAL COLLEGE
Biochemistry M,D
Biological and Biomedical Sciences—General M,D
Biopsychology M,D
Communication Disorders M,D
Entomology M,D
Medical Physics M,D
Nutrition M,D
Plant Pathology M,D
Toxicology M,D
Veterinary Medicine D
Veterinary Sciences M,D

LOUISIANA STATE UNIVERSITY HEALTH SCIENCES CENTER
Allopathic Medicine M,D
Anatomy D
Biological and Biomedical Sciences—General D
Cell Biology D
Communication Disorders M,D
Community Health Nursing M,D,O
Community Health M,D
Dentistry D
Developmental Biology D
Environmental and Occupational Health M,D
Epidemiology M,D
Family Nurse Practitioner Studies M,D,O
Gerontological Nursing M,D,O
Health Services Management and Hospital Administration M,D
Human Genetics D
Immunology D
Maternal and Child/Neonatal Nursing M,D,O
Microbiology D
Neurobiology D
Neuroscience D
Nurse Anesthesia M,D,O
Nursing and Healthcare Administration M,D,O
Nursing Education M,D,O
Nursing—General M,D,O
Occupational Therapy M
Parasitology D
Pharmacology D
Physical Therapy D
Physician Assistant Studies M
Physiology D
Public Health—General M,D

LOUISIANA STATE UNIVERSITY HEALTH SCIENCES CENTER AT SHREVEPORT
Allopathic Medicine D
Anatomy M,D
Biochemistry M,D
Biological and Biomedical Sciences—General M
Cell Biology M,D
Immunology M,D
Microbiology M,D
Molecular Biology M,D
Pharmacology M,D
Physiology M,D

LOUISIANA STATE UNIVERSITY IN SHREVEPORT
Biological and Biomedical Sciences—General M
Health Services Management and Hospital Administration M
Public Health—General M

LOUISIANA TECH UNIVERSITY
Biological and Biomedical Sciences—General M,D,O
Communication Disorders M,D,O
Molecular Biology M,D,O
Nutrition M,D,O

LOURDES UNIVERSITY
Nurse Anesthesia M
Nursing and Healthcare Administration M
Nursing Education M

LOYOLA MARYMOUNT UNIVERSITY
Bioethics M

LOYOLA UNIVERSITY CHICAGO
Adult Nursing M,D,O
Biochemistry M,D
Bioethics M,D,O
Biological and Biomedical Sciences—General M,D
Cell Biology M,D
Clinical Research M
Family Nurse Practitioner Studies M,D,O
Health Services Management and Hospital Administration M
Immunology M,D
Infectious Diseases M,D,O
Microbiology M,D
Molecular Biology M,D
Molecular Pharmacology M,D
Molecular Physiology M,D
Neuroscience M,D
Nursing and Healthcare Administration M,D,O
Nursing—General M,D,O
Nutrition M,D,O
Physiology M,D
Public Health—General M,O
Women's Health Nursing M,D,O

LOYOLA UNIVERSITY MARYLAND
Communication Disorders M

LOYOLA UNIVERSITY NEW ORLEANS
Family Nurse Practitioner Studies M,D
Nursing—General M,D

MADONNA UNIVERSITY
Adult Nursing M
Health Services Management and Hospital Administration M
Hospice Nursing M
Nursing and Healthcare Administration M
Nursing—General M

MAHARISHI UNIVERSITY OF MANAGEMENT
Physiology D

MALONE UNIVERSITY
Family Nurse Practitioner Studies M
Nursing—General M

MANCHESTER UNIVERSITY
Genomic Sciences M
Pharmacy D

MANHATTANVILLE COLLEGE
Biological and Biomedical Sciences—General M,O
Health Promotion M,O

MANSFIELD UNIVERSITY OF PENNSYLVANIA
Nursing—General M

MARIAN UNIVERSITY (IN)
Family Nurse Practitioner Studies M,D
Nurse Anesthesia M,D
Nursing Education M,D
Nursing—General M,D
Osteopathic Medicine M,D

MARIAN UNIVERSITY (WI)
Adult Nursing M
Nursing Education M
Nursing—General M

MARIETTA COLLEGE
Physician Assistant Studies M

MARIST COLLEGE
Physical Therapy D

MARQUETTE UNIVERSITY
Acute Care/Critical Care Nursing M,D,O
Adult Nursing M,D,O
Biological and Biomedical Sciences—General M,D
Cardiovascular Sciences M
Cell Biology M,D
Communication Disorders M,O
Dentistry D
Developmental Biology M,D
Ecology M,D
Family Nurse Practitioner Studies M,D,O
Genetics M,D
Gerontological Nursing M,D,O
Microbiology M,D
Molecular Biology M,D
Neuroscience M,D
Nurse Midwifery M,D,O
Nursing and Healthcare Administration M,D,O
Nursing—General M,D,O
Oral and Dental Sciences M,O
Pediatric Nursing M,D,O
Physical Therapy D
Physician Assistant Studies M
Physiology M,D
Rehabilitation Sciences M,D

MARSHALL B. KETCHUM UNIVERSITY
Optometry M,D
Pharmacy M,D
Vision Sciences M,D

MARSHALL UNIVERSITY
Allopathic Medicine D
Biological and Biomedical Sciences—General M,D
Communication Disorders M
Health Services Management and Hospital Administration M
Nurse Anesthesia D
Nursing—General M,O
Nutrition M,O
Pharmacy D
Physical Therapy D
Public Health—General M

MARY BALDWIN UNIVERSITY
Occupational Therapy D

MARYLAND UNIVERSITY OF INTEGRATIVE HEALTH
Acupuncture and Oriental Medicine M,D,O
Health Promotion M,O
Naturopathic Medicine D
Nutrition M,D,O

MARYMOUNT UNIVERSITY
Allied Health—General M,D,O
Family Nurse Practitioner Studies M,D,O
Health Promotion M
Health Services Management and Hospital Administration M
Nursing—General M,D,O
Physical Therapy D

MARYVILLE UNIVERSITY OF SAINT LOUIS
Acute Care/Critical Care Nursing M,D
Adult Nursing M,D
Allied Health—General M,D,O
Communication Disorders M
Family Nurse Practitioner Studies M,D
Gerontological Nursing M,D
Health Services Management and Hospital Administration M,O
Nursing—General M,D
Occupational Therapy M
Pediatric Nursing M,D
Physical Therapy D

MARYWOOD UNIVERSITY
Communication Disorders M
Health Services Management and Hospital Administration M
Nutrition M,O
Physician Assistant Studies M

MASSACHUSETTS INSTITUTE OF TECHNOLOGY
Biochemistry D
Biological and Biomedical Sciences—General M,D
Cell Biology D
Communication Disorders M,D
Computational Biology D
Developmental Biology D
Environmental Biology M,D,O
Genetics D
Genomic Sciences M,D
Immunology D
Medical Physics M,D
Microbiology D
Molecular Biology M,D,O
Molecular Toxicology D
Neurobiology D
Neuroscience D
Structural Biology D
Systems Biology D
Toxicology M,D

MAYO CLINIC GRADUATE SCHOOL OF BIOMEDICAL SCIENCES
Biochemistry M,D
Clinical Laboratory Sciences/Medical Technology M,D
Genetics D
Immunology D
Molecular Biology M,D
Molecular Pharmacology M,D
Neuroscience M,D
Physiology M,D
Virology D

MAYO CLINIC SCHOOL OF HEALTH SCIENCES
Nurse Anesthesia D
Physical Therapy D

MAYO CLINIC SCHOOL OF MEDICINE
Allopathic Medicine D

MCGILL UNIVERSITY
Allopathic Medicine M,D
Anatomy M,D
Biochemistry M,D
Bioethics M,D,O
Biological and Biomedical Sciences—General M,D
Cell Biology M,D
Communication Disorders M,D
Community Health M,D,O
Dentistry M,D,O
Entomology M,D
Environmental and Occupational Health M,D,O
Epidemiology M,D,O
Family Nurse Practitioner Studies M,D,O
Health Services Management and Hospital Administration M,D,O
Human Genetics M,D
Immunology M,D
Medical Physics M,D
Microbiology M,D
Neuroscience M,D

- Nursing—General M,D,O
- Nutrition M,D,O
- Oral and Dental Sciences M,D,O
- Parasitology M,D,O
- Pathology M,D
- Pharmacology M,D
- Physiology M,D
- Rehabilitation Sciences M,D,O

MCKENDREE UNIVERSITY
- Nursing and Healthcare Administration M
- Nursing Education M
- Nursing—General M

MCMASTER UNIVERSITY
- Biochemistry M,D
- Biological and Biomedical Sciences—General M,D
- Cancer Biology/Oncology M,D
- Cardiovascular Sciences M,D
- Cell Biology M,D
- Genetics M,D
- Health Physics/Radiological Health M,D
- Health Services Research M,D
- Immunology M,D
- Medical Physics M,D
- Molecular Biology M,D
- Neuroscience M,D
- Nursing—General M,D
- Nutrition M,D
- Occupational Therapy M
- Pharmacology M,D
- Physical Therapy M
- Physiology M,D
- Rehabilitation Sciences M,D
- Virology M,D

MCMURRY UNIVERSITY
- Family Nurse Practitioner Studies M
- Nursing Education M
- Nursing—General M

MCNEESE STATE UNIVERSITY
- Family Nurse Practitioner Studies M
- Health Promotion M
- Nursing Education M
- Nursing—General M,O
- Nutrition M
- Psychiatric Nursing M,O

MCPHS UNIVERSITY
- Acupuncture and Oriental Medicine M
- Health Services Management and Hospital Administration M
- Nursing—General M
- Optometry D
- Pharmaceutical Sciences M,D
- Pharmacology M,D
- Pharmacy D
- Physical Therapy D
- Physician Assistant Studies M

MEDICAL COLLEGE OF WISCONSIN
- Allopathic Medicine D
- Biochemistry D
- Bioethics M,O
- Biological and Biomedical Sciences—General M,D,O
- Clinical Laboratory Sciences/Medical Technology M
- Clinical Research
- Community Health D
- Neuroscience D
- Pharmacology D
- Pharmacy D
- Physiology D
- Public Health—General M,D,O
- Toxicology D

MEDICAL UNIVERSITY OF SOUTH CAROLINA
- Adult Nursing M,D
- Allied Health—General M,D
- Allopathic Medicine D
- Biochemistry M,D
- Biological and Biomedical Sciences—General M,D
- Cancer Biology/Oncology D
- Cardiovascular Sciences D
- Cell Biology D
- Clinical Research M
- Dentistry D
- Developmental Biology D
- Epidemiology M,D
- Family Nurse Practitioner Studies M,D
- Genetics D
- Gerontological Nursing M,D
- Health Services Management and Hospital Administration M,D
- Immunology M,D
- International Health M
- Maternal and Child/Neonatal Nursing M,D
- Medical Imaging D
- Medicinal and Pharmaceutical Chemistry D
- Microbiology M,D
- Molecular Biology M,D
- Molecular Pharmacology M,D
- Neuroscience M,D
- Nurse Anesthesia M
- Nursing and Healthcare Administration M
- Nursing Education M
- Nursing—General D
- Occupational Therapy M
- Pathobiology D
- Pathology M,D
- Pharmacy D
- Physical Therapy D
- Physician Assistant Studies M
- Rehabilitation Sciences D

- Toxicology D

MEHARRY MEDICAL COLLEGE
- Allopathic Medicine D
- Biochemistry D
- Biological and Biomedical Sciences—General D
- Cancer Biology/Oncology D
- Dentistry D
- Environmental and Occupational Health M
- Health Services Management and Hospital Administration M
- Immunology D
- Microbiology D
- Neuroscience D
- Pharmacology D
- Public Health—General M

MEMORIAL UNIVERSITY OF NEWFOUNDLAND
- Biochemistry M,D
- Biological and Biomedical Sciences—General M,D,O
- Biopsychology M,D
- Cancer Biology/Oncology M,D
- Cardiovascular Sciences M,D
- Clinical Research M
- Community Health M,D,O
- Epidemiology M,D,O
- Human Genetics M,D
- Immunology M,D
- Neuroscience M,D
- Nursing—General M,D
- Pharmaceutical Sciences M,D

MERCER UNIVERSITY
- Allopathic Medicine M,D
- Environmental and Occupational Health M,D
- Family Nurse Practitioner Studies M,D,O
- Gerontological Nursing M,D,O
- Nursing and Healthcare Administration M,D
- Nursing—General M,D,O
- Pharmaceutical Sciences D
- Pharmacy D
- Physical Therapy M,D
- Physician Assistant Studies M,D
- Public Health—General M,D

MERCY COLLEGE
- Allied Health—General M,D
- Communication Disorders M
- Health Services Management and Hospital Administration M
- Nursing and Healthcare Administration M
- Nursing Education M
- Nursing—General M
- Occupational Therapy M
- Physical Therapy D
- Physician Assistant Studies M

MERCY COLLEGE OF OHIO
- Health Services Management and Hospital Administration M
- Nursing—General M

MERCYHURST UNIVERSITY
- Physician Assistant Studies M

MEREDITH COLLEGE
- Nutrition M,O

MERRIMACK COLLEGE
- Health Promotion M

MESSIAH COLLEGE
- Nursing Education M

METHODIST UNIVERSITY
- Physician Assistant Studies M

METROPOLITAN STATE UNIVERSITY
- Nursing and Healthcare Administration M,D
- Nursing Education M,D
- Nursing—General M,D
- Oral and Dental Sciences M,D

MGH INSTITUTE OF HEALTH PROFESSIONS
- Communication Disorders M,O
- Gerontological Nursing M,D,O
- Nursing Education M,D,O
- Nursing—General M,D,O
- Occupational Therapy D
- Pediatric Nursing M,D,O
- Physical Therapy M,D,O
- Physician Assistant Studies M
- Psychiatric Nursing M,D,O
- Women's Health Nursing M,D,O

MIAMI REGIONAL UNIVERSITY
- Nursing and Healthcare Administration M
- Nursing Education M
- Nursing—General M

MIAMI UNIVERSITY
- Biochemistry M,D
- Biological and Biomedical Sciences—General M,D
- Communication Disorders M
- Microbiology M,D

MICHIGAN STATE UNIVERSITY
- Allopathic Medicine D
- Biochemistry M,D
- Biological and Biomedical Sciences—General M,D
- Cell Biology M,D
- Clinical Laboratory Sciences/Medical Technology M
- Communication Disorders M,D
- Ecology D
- Entomology M,D
- Epidemiology M,D
- Evolutionary Biology D
- Genetics M,D
- Microbiology M,D
- Molecular Biology M,D
- Molecular Genetics M,D
- Neuroscience M,D
- Nursing—General M,D
- Nutrition M,D
- Osteopathic Medicine D
- Pathobiology M,D
- Pathology M,D
- Pharmacology M,D
- Physiology M,D
- Plant Biology M,D
- Plant Pathology M,D
- Public Health—General M
- Structural Biology D
- Systems Biology D
- Toxicology M,D
- Veterinary Medicine D
- Veterinary Sciences M,D
- Zoology M,D

MICHIGAN TECHNOLOGICAL UNIVERSITY
- Biochemistry M,D,O
- Biological and Biomedical Sciences—General M,D
- Ecology M,D
- Molecular Biology M,D,O

MIDAMERICA NAZARENE UNIVERSITY
- Nursing and Healthcare Administration M
- Nursing Education M
- Nursing—General M
- Public Health—General M

MIDDLE GEORGIA STATE UNIVERSITY
- Gerontological Nursing M

MIDDLE TENNESSEE SCHOOL OF ANESTHESIA
- Nurse Anesthesia M,D

MIDDLE TENNESSEE STATE UNIVERSITY
- Biological and Biomedical Sciences—General M
- Family Nurse Practitioner Studies M,O
- Molecular Biology D
- Nursing and Healthcare Administration M
- Nursing Education M
- Nursing—General M,O

MIDWEST COLLEGE OF ORIENTAL MEDICINE
- Acupuncture and Oriental Medicine M,O

MIDWESTERN STATE UNIVERSITY
- Biological and Biomedical Sciences—General M
- Community Health M,O
- Family Nurse Practitioner Studies M
- Health Physics/Radiological Health M
- Health Services Management and Hospital Administration M,O
- Nursing Education M
- Nursing—General M
- Psychiatric Nursing M

MIDWESTERN UNIVERSITY, DOWNERS GROVE CAMPUS
- Biological and Biomedical Sciences—General M
- Dentistry D
- Occupational Therapy M
- Optometry D
- Osteopathic Medicine D
- Pharmacy D
- Physical Therapy D
- Physician Assistant Studies M

MIDWESTERN UNIVERSITY, GLENDALE CAMPUS
- Allied Health—General M,D
- Biological and Biomedical Sciences—General M
- Cardiovascular Sciences M
- Communication Disorders M
- Dentistry D
- Nurse Anesthesia M
- Occupational Therapy M
- Optometry D
- Osteopathic Medicine D
- Pharmacy D
- Physical Therapy D
- Physician Assistant Studies M
- Podiatric Medicine D

MIDWIVES COLLEGE OF UTAH
- Nurse Midwifery M

MILLERSVILLE UNIVERSITY OF PENNSYLVANIA
- Family Nurse Practitioner Studies M,O
- Nursing Education M,O
- Nursing—General D

MILLIGAN COLLEGE
- Health Services Management and Hospital Administration M,O
- Occupational Therapy M
- Physician Assistant Studies M

MILLIKIN UNIVERSITY
- Family Nurse Practitioner Studies M,D
- Nurse Anesthesia M,D
- Nursing Education M,D
- Nursing—General M,D

MILLS COLLEGE
- Biological and Biomedical Sciences—General O

MILWAUKEE SCHOOL OF ENGINEERING
- Cardiovascular Sciences M
- Clinical Laboratory Sciences/Medical Technology M
- Health Services Management and Hospital Administration M
- Nursing and Healthcare Administration M
- Perfusion M

MINNESOTA STATE UNIVERSITY MANKATO
- Allied Health—General M,D,O
- Biological and Biomedical Sciences—General M
- Communication Disorders M
- Community Health M,O
- Family Nurse Practitioner Studies M,D
- Nursing Education M,D
- Nursing—General M,D

MINNESOTA STATE UNIVERSITY MOORHEAD
- Communication Disorders M,D,O
- Health Services Management and Hospital Administration M,O
- Nursing—General M,O

MINOT STATE UNIVERSITY
- Communication Disorders M

MISERICORDIA UNIVERSITY
- Allied Health—General M,D
- Communication Disorders M
- Health Services Management and Hospital Administration M
- Nursing—General M,D
- Occupational Therapy M,D
- Physical Therapy D

MISSISSIPPI COLLEGE
- Biochemistry M
- Biological and Biomedical Sciences—General M
- Health Services Management and Hospital Administration M

MISSISSIPPI STATE UNIVERSITY
- Biochemistry M,D
- Biological and Biomedical Sciences—General M,D
- Genetics M,D
- Molecular Biology M,D
- Nutrition M,D
- Veterinary Medicine D
- Veterinary Sciences M,D

MISSISSIPPI UNIVERSITY FOR WOMEN
- Communication Disorders M,D,O
- Nursing—General M,D,O
- Public Health—General M,D,O

MISSISSIPPI VALLEY STATE UNIVERSITY
- Environmental and Occupational Health M

MISSOURI SOUTHERN STATE UNIVERSITY
- Dental Hygiene M
- Nursing—General M

MISSOURI STATE UNIVERSITY
- Biological and Biomedical Sciences—General M
- Cell Biology M
- Communication Disorders M,D
- Family Nurse Practitioner Studies M,D
- Health Services Management and Hospital Administration M
- Molecular Biology M
- Nurse Anesthesia D
- Nursing Education M,D
- Nursing—General M,D
- Nutrition M,D,O
- Occupational Therapy M
- Physical Therapy D
- Physician Assistant Studies M
- Public Health—General M

MISSOURI UNIVERSITY OF SCIENCE AND TECHNOLOGY
- Biological and Biomedical Sciences—General M
- Environmental Biology M

MISSOURI WESTERN STATE UNIVERSITY
- Biological and Biomedical Sciences—General M
- Nursing and Healthcare Administration M,O
- Nursing Education M,O
- Nursing—General M,O

MOLLOY COLLEGE
- Communication Disorders M
- Family Nurse Practitioner Studies M,D,O
- Gerontological Nursing M,D,O
- Health Services Management and Hospital Administration M,D,O
- Nursing Education M,D,O
- Nursing—General M,D,O
- Pediatric Nursing M,D,O
- Psychiatric Nursing M,D,O

MONMOUTH UNIVERSITY
- Adult Nursing M,D,O
- Communication Disorders M,D,O
- Family Nurse Practitioner Studies M,D,O

*M—masters degree; D—doctorate; O—other advanced degree; *—Close-Up and/or Display*

Forensic Nursing	M,D,O
Gerontological Nursing	M,D,O
Nursing and Healthcare Administration	M,D,O
Nursing Education	M,D,O
Nursing—General	M,D,O
Physician Assistant Studies	M,D,O
Psychiatric Nursing	M,D,O
School Nursing	M,D,O

MONROE COLLEGE

Community Health	M
Epidemiology	M
Health Services Management and Hospital Administration	M
Public Health—General	M

MONTANA STATE UNIVERSITY

Biochemistry	M,D
Biological and Biomedical Sciences—General	M,D
Ecology	M,D
Family Nurse Practitioner Studies	M,D,O
Immunology	M,D
Infectious Diseases	M,D
Microbiology	M,D
Neuroscience	M,D
Nursing and Healthcare Administration	M,D,O
Nursing Education	M,D,O
Nursing—General	M,D,O
Plant Pathology	M,D
Psychiatric Nursing	M,D,O

MONTANA STATE UNIVERSITY BILLINGS

Health Services Management and Hospital Administration	M

MONTANA TECH OF THE UNIVERSITY OF MONTANA

Industrial Hygiene	M

MONTCLAIR STATE UNIVERSITY

Biochemistry	M
Biological and Biomedical Sciences—General	M
Communication Disorders	M,D
Ecology	M
Evolutionary Biology	M
Marine Biology	M
Molecular Biology	M,O
Nutrition	M,O
Pharmacology	M
Physiology	M
Public Health—General	M

MORAVIAN COLLEGE

Acute Care/Critical Care Nursing	M
Allied Health—General	M
Health Services Management and Hospital Administration	M
Nursing and Healthcare Administration	M
Nursing Education	M
Nursing—General	M

MOREHEAD STATE UNIVERSITY

Biological and Biomedical Sciences—General	M

MOREHOUSE SCHOOL OF MEDICINE

Allopathic Medicine	D
Biological and Biomedical Sciences—General	M,D
Clinical Research	M
Public Health—General	M

MORGAN STATE UNIVERSITY

Biological and Biomedical Sciences—General	M,D
Environmental Biology	D
Nursing—General	M,D
Public Health—General	M,D

MORNINGSIDE COLLEGE

Family Nurse Practitioner Studies	M
Gerontological Nursing	M
Nursing—General	M

MOUNT ALLISON UNIVERSITY

Biochemistry	M
Biological and Biomedical Sciences—General	M

MOUNT ALOYSIUS COLLEGE

Health Services Management and Hospital Administration	M

MOUNT CARMEL COLLEGE OF NURSING

Acute Care/Critical Care Nursing	M,D
Adult Nursing	M,D
Family Nurse Practitioner Studies	M,D
Gerontological Nursing	M,D
Nursing and Healthcare Administration	M,D
Nursing Education	M,D
Nursing—General	M,D

MOUNT MARTY COLLEGE

Nurse Anesthesia	M
Nursing—General	M

MOUNT MARY UNIVERSITY

Nursing and Healthcare Administration	M
Nutrition	M
Occupational Therapy	M,D

MOUNT MERCY UNIVERSITY

Nursing and Healthcare Administration	M
Nursing Education	M
Nursing—General	M

MOUNT ST. JOSEPH UNIVERSITY

Health Promotion	M,O
Health Services Management and Hospital Administration	D
Nursing and Healthcare Administration	M
Nursing Education	M
Nursing—General	M,D
Physical Therapy	D

MOUNT SAINT MARY COLLEGE

Adult Nursing	M,O
Family Nurse Practitioner Studies	M,O
Health Services Management and Hospital Administration	M
Nursing and Healthcare Administration	M,O
Nursing Education	M,O
Nursing—General	M,O

MOUNT SAINT MARY'S UNIVERSITY (CA)

Health Services Management and Hospital Administration	M,D,O
Nursing—General	M,D,O
Physical Therapy	M,D,O

MOUNT ST. MARY'S UNIVERSITY (MD)

Health Services Management and Hospital Administration	M

MOUNT SAINT VINCENT UNIVERSITY

Nutrition	M

MURRAY STATE UNIVERSITY

Biological and Biomedical Sciences—General	M
Communication Disorders	M,O
Environmental and Occupational Health	M
Family Nurse Practitioner Studies	D
Nurse Anesthesia	D
Nursing—General	D
Nutrition	M,O

NAROPA UNIVERSITY

Ecology	M

NATIONAL AMERICAN UNIVERSITY (TX)

Health Services Management and Hospital Administration	M,D
Nursing and Healthcare Administration	M,D
Nursing Education	M,D
Nursing Informatics	M,D

NATIONAL COLLEGE OF MIDWIFERY

Nurse Midwifery	M,D

NATIONAL UNIVERSITY

Biological and Biomedical Sciences—General	M,O
Family Nurse Practitioner Studies	M,O
Health Promotion	M,O
Health Services Management and Hospital Administration	M,O
Nurse Anesthesia	M,O
Nursing and Healthcare Administration	M,O
Nursing Informatics	M,O
Psychiatric Nursing	M,O
Public Health—General	M,O

NATIONAL UNIVERSITY OF HEALTH SCIENCES

Acupuncture and Oriental Medicine	M,D
Chiropractic	M,D
Medical Imaging	M,D

NATIONAL UNIVERSITY OF NATURAL MEDICINE

Acupuncture and Oriental Medicine	M,D
Clinical Research	M
International Health	M
Naturopathic Medicine	M,D
Nutrition	M

NAZARETH COLLEGE OF ROCHESTER

Communication Disorders	M
Physical Therapy	D

NEBRASKA METHODIST COLLEGE

Health Promotion	M
Health Services Management and Hospital Administration	M
Nursing and Healthcare Administration	M
Nursing Education	M
Nursing—General	M

NEBRASKA WESLEYAN UNIVERSITY

Nursing—General	M

NEUMANN UNIVERSITY

Adult Nursing	M,O
Gerontological Nursing	M,O
Nursing—General	M,O
Physical Therapy	D

NEW CHARTER UNIVERSITY

Health Services Management and Hospital Administration	M

NEW ENGLAND COLLEGE

Health Services Management and Hospital Administration	M

NEW ENGLAND COLLEGE OF OPTOMETRY

Optometry	M,D
Vision Sciences	M,D

NEW ENGLAND INSTITUTE OF TECHNOLOGY

Occupational Therapy	M
Public Health—General	M

NEW JERSEY CITY UNIVERSITY

Allied Health—General	M
Community Health	M
Health Services Management and Hospital Administration	M

NEW JERSEY INSTITUTE OF TECHNOLOGY

Biological and Biomedical Sciences—General	M,D,O
Health Services Management and Hospital Administration	M,D
Medicinal and Pharmaceutical Chemistry	M,D,O
Pharmaceutical Administration	M,D
Pharmacology	M,D

NEWMAN UNIVERSITY

Nurse Anesthesia	M

NEW MEXICO INSTITUTE OF MINING AND TECHNOLOGY

Biological and Biomedical Sciences—General	M,D

NEW MEXICO STATE UNIVERSITY

Biological and Biomedical Sciences—General	M,D
Communication Disorders	M,D,O
Entomology	M
Family Nurse Practitioner Studies	M,D,O
Molecular Biology	M,D
Nursing and Healthcare Administration	M,D,O
Nursing—General	M,D,O
Plant Pathology	M
Psychiatric Nursing	M,D,O
Public Health—General	M,O

NEW YORK ACADEMY OF ART

Anatomy	M

NEW YORK CHIROPRACTIC COLLEGE

Acupuncture and Oriental Medicine	M
Anatomy	M
Chiropractic	D*
Nutrition	M

NEW YORK COLLEGE OF HEALTH PROFESSIONS

Acupuncture and Oriental Medicine	M

NEW YORK COLLEGE OF PODIATRIC MEDICINE

Podiatric Medicine	D

NEW YORK COLLEGE OF TRADITIONAL CHINESE MEDICINE

Acupuncture and Oriental Medicine	M

NEW YORK INSTITUTE OF TECHNOLOGY

International Health	O
Nutrition	M
Occupational Therapy	M
Osteopathic Medicine	O
Physical Therapy	D
Physician Assistant Studies	M

NEW YORK MEDICAL COLLEGE

Allopathic Medicine	D
Biochemistry	M,D
Biological and Biomedical Sciences—General	M,D
Cell Biology	M,D
Communication Disorders	M,D,O
Environmental and Occupational Health	M,D,O
Epidemiology	M,D,O
Health Services Management and Hospital Administration	M,D,O
Immunology	M,D
Industrial Hygiene	M,D,O
International Health	M,D,O
Microbiology	M,D
Molecular Biology	M,D
Pathology	M,D
Pharmacology	M,D
Physical Therapy	M,D,O
Physiology	M,D
Public Health—General	M,D,O

NEW YORK UNIVERSITY

Acute Care/Critical Care Nursing	M,D,O
Adult Nursing	M,D,O
Allopathic Medicine	M,D
Bioethics	M
Biological and Biomedical Sciences—General	M,D,O
Cancer Biology/Oncology	M,D
Cell Biology	D
Clinical Research	M
Communication Disorders	M,D
Community Health	M,D
Computational Biology	D
Dentistry	D
Developmental Biology	M,D
Environmental and Occupational Health	M,D*
Epidemiology	M,D
Family Nurse Practitioner Studies	M,D,O
Genetics	M,D
Genomic Sciences	D
Gerontological Nursing	M,D,O
Health Promotion	M,D,O
Health Services Management and Hospital Administration	M,D,O
Immunology	M,D
International Health	M,D
Medical Imaging	D
Microbiology	M,D
Molecular Biology	M,D
Molecular Genetics	M,D
Molecular Pharmacology	D
Molecular Toxicology	M,D
Neurobiology	M,D
Neuroscience	D
Nurse Midwifery	M,D,O
Nursing and Healthcare Administration	M,O
Nursing Education	M,O
Nursing Informatics	M,O
Nursing—General	M,D,O
Nutrition	M,D
Occupational Therapy	M,D
Oral and Dental Sciences	M,D,O
Pediatric Nursing	M,D,O
Physical Therapy	M,D,O
Physiology	D
Plant Biology	M,D
Psychiatric Nursing	M,D,O
Public Health—General	M,D
Rehabilitation Sciences	M,D
Structural Biology	D
Toxicology	M,D

NIAGARA UNIVERSITY

Health Services Management and Hospital Administration	M

NICHOLLS STATE UNIVERSITY

Environmental Biology	M
Family Nurse Practitioner Studies	M
Marine Biology	M
Nursing and Healthcare Administration	M
Nursing Education	M
Nursing—General	M
Psychiatric Nursing	M

NORTH CAROLINA AGRICULTURAL AND TECHNICAL STATE UNIVERSITY

Biological and Biomedical Sciences—General	M
Environmental and Occupational Health	M
Nutrition	M

NORTH CAROLINA CENTRAL UNIVERSITY

Biological and Biomedical Sciences—General	M
Communication Disorders	M

NORTH CAROLINA STATE UNIVERSITY

Biochemistry	D
Biological and Biomedical Sciences—General	M,D,O
Botany	M,D
Cell Biology	M,D
Entomology	M,D
Epidemiology	M,D
Genetics	M,D
Genomic Sciences	M,D
Infectious Diseases	M,D
Microbiology	M,D
Molecular Toxicology	M,D
Nutrition	M,D
Pathology	M,D
Pharmacology	M,D
Physiology	M,D
Plant Biology	M,D
Plant Pathology	M,D
Toxicology	M,D
Veterinary Medicine	M,D
Veterinary Sciences	M,D
Zoology	M,D

NORTH DAKOTA STATE UNIVERSITY

Biochemistry	M,D
Biological and Biomedical Sciences—General	M,D
Botany	M,D
Cell Biology	D
Community Health	M
Conservation Biology	M,D
Entomology	M,D
Genomic Sciences	M,D
Infectious Diseases	M
Microbiology	M,D
Molecular Biology	D
Molecular Pathogenesis	M,D
Nursing—General	D
Nutrition	M,D
Pathology	M,D
Pharmacy	M,D
Plant Pathology	M,D
Public Health—General	M*
Zoology	M,D

NORTHEASTERN ILLINOIS UNIVERSITY

Biological and Biomedical Sciences—General	M
Cell Biology	M
Ecology	M
Molecular Biology	M

NORTHEASTERN STATE UNIVERSITY

Communication Disorders	M
Nursing and Healthcare Administration	M
Nursing Education	M
Occupational Therapy	M
Optometry	D

NORTHEASTERN UNIVERSITY

Acute Care/Critical Care Nursing	M,D,O
Allied Health—General	M,D,O
Biological and Biomedical Sciences—General	M,D
Communication Disorders	M,D,O
Family Nurse Practitioner Studies	M,D,O
Gerontological Nursing	M,D,O
Marine Biology	M,D
Maternal and Child/Neonatal Nursing	M,D,O
Nursing and Healthcare Administration	M,D,O
Nursing—General	M,D,O
Nutrition	M
Pediatric Nursing	M,D,O
Pharmaceutical Sciences	M,D,O
Pharmacology	M,D,O
Pharmacy	M,D,O
Psychiatric Nursing	M,D,O

NORTHEAST OHIO MEDICAL UNIVERSITY

Allopathic Medicine	D
Bioethics	M,D,O

- Health Services Management and Hospital Administration M,D,O
- Pharmaceutical Administration M,D,O
- Pharmaceutical Sciences M,D,O
- Pharmacy D
- Public Health—General M,D,O

NORTHERN ARIZONA UNIVERSITY
- Allied Health—General M,D,O
- Biological and Biomedical Sciences—General M,D
- Communication Disorders M
- Family Nurse Practitioner Studies M,D,O
- Nursing—General M,D,O
- Occupational Therapy D
- Physical Therapy D
- Physician Assistant Studies M

NORTHERN ILLINOIS UNIVERSITY
- Biochemistry M,D
- Biological and Biomedical Sciences—General M,D
- Communication Disorders M,D
- Nursing—General M,D
- Nutrition M
- Physical Therapy D
- Public Health—General M

NORTHERN KENTUCKY UNIVERSITY
- Allied Health—General M
- Nursing—General M,D,O

NORTHERN MICHIGAN UNIVERSITY
- Biological and Biomedical Sciences—General M
- Clinical Laboratory Sciences/Medical Technology M
- Molecular Genetics M
- Nursing—General D

NORTH PARK UNIVERSITY
- Adult Nursing M
- Nursing and Healthcare Administration M
- Nursing—General M

NORTHWESTERN HEALTH SCIENCES UNIVERSITY
- Acupuncture and Oriental Medicine M
- Chiropractic D
- Nutrition M

NORTHWESTERN STATE UNIVERSITY OF LOUISIANA
- Health Physics/Radiological Health M
- Nursing—General M

NORTHWESTERN UNIVERSITY
- Allopathic Medicine
- Biochemistry D
- Biological and Biomedical Sciences—General D
- Biophysics D
- Biopsychology D
- Cell Biology D
- Clinical Laboratory Sciences/Medical Technology M
- Clinical Research M,O
- Communication Disorders M,D
- Developmental Biology D
- Epidemiology D
- Health Services Management and Hospital Administration M,D
- Health Services Research D
- International Health M
- Molecular Biology D
- Neurobiology M,D
- Neuroscience D
- Physical Therapy D
- Physiology M
- Plant Biology M,D
- Public Health—General M
- Rehabilitation Sciences D
- Structural Biology D
- Systems Biology D

NORTHWEST MISSOURI STATE UNIVERSITY
- Biological and Biomedical Sciences—General M,O

NORTHWEST NAZARENE UNIVERSITY
- Nursing and Healthcare Administration M

NORWICH UNIVERSITY
- Nursing and Healthcare Administration M
- Nursing Education M
- Nursing—General M

NOTRE DAME OF MARYLAND UNIVERSITY
- Pharmacy D

NOVA SOUTHEASTERN UNIVERSITY
- Adult Nursing M,D
- Allied Health—General M,D
- Allopathic Medicine D
- Anesthesiologist Assistant Studies M,D
- Biological and Biomedical Sciences—General M,D
- Communication Disorders M,D
- Dentistry M,D
- Family Nurse Practitioner Studies M,D
- Gerontological Nursing M,D
- Marine Biology M,D
- Nursing Education M,D
- Nursing Informatics M,D
- Nursing—General M,D
- Nutrition M,D,O
- Occupational Therapy M,D
- Optometry M,D
- Osteopathic Medicine M,D,O
- Pharmacy M,D*
- Physical Therapy M,D
- Physician Assistant Studies M,D
- Psychiatric Nursing M,D
- Public Health—General M,D,O

OAKLAND UNIVERSITY
- Allied Health—General M,D,O
- Biological and Biomedical Sciences—General M,D,O
- Environmental and Occupational Health M
- Family Nurse Practitioner Studies M,O
- Gerontological Nursing M,O
- Maternal and Child Health D,O
- Medical Physics M,O
- Nurse Anesthesia M,O
- Nursing—General M,D,O
- Physical Therapy D,O

OCCIDENTAL COLLEGE
- Biological and Biomedical Sciences—General M

OHIO CHRISTIAN UNIVERSITY
- Health Services Management and Hospital Administration M

OHIO DOMINICAN UNIVERSITY
- Health Services Management and Hospital Administration M
- Physician Assistant Studies M

OHIO NORTHERN UNIVERSITY
- Pharmacy D

THE OHIO STATE UNIVERSITY
- Allied Health—General M
- Allopathic Medicine D
- Anatomy M,D
- Biochemistry M,D
- Biological and Biomedical Sciences—General M,D
- Biophysics M,D
- Cell Biology M,D
- Communication Disorders M,D
- Dental Hygiene M,D
- Dentistry M,D
- Developmental Biology M,D
- Ecology M,D
- Entomology M,D
- Evolutionary Biology M,D
- Genetics M,D
- Health Services Management and Hospital Administration M,D
- Microbiology M,D
- Molecular Biology M,D
- Molecular Genetics M,D
- Neuroscience D
- Nursing—General M,D
- Nutrition M,D
- Occupational Therapy M
- Optometry M,D
- Oral and Dental Sciences M,D
- Pharmaceutical Administration M,D
- Pharmacology M,D
- Pharmacy M,D
- Physical Therapy D
- Plant Pathology M,D
- Public Health—General M,D
- Rehabilitation Sciences D
- Veterinary Sciences M,D

OHIO UNIVERSITY
- Biochemistry M,D
- Biological and Biomedical Sciences—General M,D
- Cell Biology M,D
- Communication Disorders M,D
- Ecology M,D
- Environmental Biology M,D
- Evolutionary Biology M,D
- Family Nurse Practitioner Studies M,D
- Health Services Management and Hospital Administration M
- Microbiology M,D
- Molecular Biology D
- Neuroscience M,D
- Nursing and Healthcare Administration M,D
- Nursing Education M,D
- Nursing—General M,D
- Nutrition M
- Osteopathic Medicine D
- Physical Therapy D
- Physiology M,D
- Plant Biology M,D
- Public Health—General M

OKLAHOMA BAPTIST UNIVERSITY
- Nursing Education M
- Nursing—General M

OKLAHOMA CHRISTIAN UNIVERSITY
- Health Services Management and Hospital Administration M

OKLAHOMA CITY UNIVERSITY
- Nursing Education M,D
- Nursing—General M,D

OKLAHOMA STATE UNIVERSITY
- Biochemistry M,D
- Biological and Biomedical Sciences—General M,D
- Botany M,D
- Communication Disorders M
- Ecology M,D
- Entomology M,D
- Evolutionary Biology M,D
- Microbiology M,D
- Molecular Biology M,D
- Molecular Genetics M,D
- Nutrition M,D
- Plant Biology M,D
- Plant Pathology M,D
- Veterinary Medicine D
- Veterinary Sciences M,D

OKLAHOMA STATE UNIVERSITY CENTER FOR HEALTH SCIENCES
- Biological and Biomedical Sciences—General M,D
- Health Services Management and Hospital Administration M
- Osteopathic Medicine D
- Toxicology M

OKLAHOMA WESLEYAN UNIVERSITY
- Nursing and Healthcare Administration M
- Nursing Education M

OLD DOMINION UNIVERSITY
- Adult Nursing M,D
- Allied Health—General M,D
- Biochemistry M,D
- Biological and Biomedical Sciences—General M,D
- Communication Disorders M
- Community Health M
- Dental Hygiene M
- Ecology D
- Family Nurse Practitioner Studies M
- Gerontological Nursing M,D
- Health Promotion M
- Health Services Research D
- Immunology M
- Industrial Hygiene M
- Maternal and Child/Neonatal Nursing M,D
- Microbiology M
- Nurse Anesthesia D
- Nursing and Healthcare Administration M,D
- Nursing Education M,D
- Nursing—General D
- Pediatric Nursing M,D
- Physical Therapy D
- Public Health—General M
- Rehabilitation Sciences D

OLIVET NAZARENE UNIVERSITY
- Family Nurse Practitioner Studies M
- Nursing—General M

OREGON COLLEGE OF ORIENTAL MEDICINE
- Acupuncture and Oriental Medicine M,D

OREGON HEALTH & SCIENCE UNIVERSITY
- Allopathic Medicine D
- Biochemistry M,D
- Biological and Biomedical Sciences—General M,D,O
- Biopsychology D
- Cancer Biology/Oncology D
- Cell Biology D
- Clinical Research M,O
- Community Health Nursing M,O
- Computational Biology M,D,O
- Dentistry D,O
- Developmental Biology D
- Family Nurse Practitioner Studies M
- Genetics D
- Gerontological Nursing M
- Health Services Management and Hospital Administration M,O
- Immunology D
- Microbiology D
- Molecular Biology M,D
- Molecular Medicine M,D
- Neuroscience D
- Nurse Anesthesia M
- Nurse Midwifery M
- Nursing and Healthcare Administration M
- Nursing Education M,O
- Nursing—General M,D,O
- Nutrition M,O
- Oral and Dental Sciences M,D,O
- Pediatric Nursing M
- Pharmacology D
- Physician Assistant Studies M
- Physiology D
- Psychiatric Nursing M

OREGON STATE UNIVERSITY
- Allied Health—General M,D
- Biochemistry M,D
- Biological and Biomedical Sciences—General M,D
- Biophysics M,D
- Botany M,D
- Cell Biology M,D
- Computational Biology M,D
- Conservation Biology M,D
- Ecology M,D
- Environmental and Occupational Health M,D
- Environmental Biology M,D
- Epidemiology M,D
- Genetics M,D
- Genomic Sciences M,D
- Health Physics/Radiological Health M,D
- Health Promotion M,D
- Health Services Management and Hospital Administration M,D
- Immunology M,D
- International Health M,D
- Medical Imaging M,D
- Medical Physics M,D
- Microbiology M,D
- Molecular Biology M,D
- Molecular Toxicology M,D
- Nutrition M,D
- Parasitology M,D
- Pharmaceutical Sciences M,D
- Pharmacy D
- Physiology M,D
- Plant Molecular Biology D
- Plant Pathology M,D
- Plant Physiology M,D
- Public Health—General M,D
- Systems Biology M,D
- Toxicology M,D
- Veterinary Medicine D
- Virology M,D

OTTERBEIN UNIVERSITY
- Family Nurse Practitioner Studies M,D,O
- Nurse Anesthesia M,D,O
- Nursing and Healthcare Administration M,D,O
- Nursing Education M,D,O
- Nursing—General M,D,O

OUR LADY OF THE LAKE UNIVERSITY
- Communication Disorders M
- Health Services Management and Hospital Administration M

PACE UNIVERSITY
- Biochemistry M
- Biological and Biomedical Sciences—General M,O
- Family Nurse Practitioner Studies M,D,O
- Health Services Management and Hospital Administration M
- Molecular Biology M
- Nursing and Healthcare Administration M,D,O
- Nursing—General M,D,O
- Physician Assistant Studies M

PACIFIC COLLEGE OF ORIENTAL MEDICINE
- Acupuncture and Oriental Medicine M,D

PACIFIC COLLEGE OF ORIENTAL MEDICINE–CHICAGO
- Acupuncture and Oriental Medicine M

PACIFIC COLLEGE OF ORIENTAL MEDICINE–NEW YORK
- Acupuncture and Oriental Medicine M

PACIFIC LUTHERAN UNIVERSITY
- Family Nurse Practitioner Studies D
- Nursing—General M,D

PACIFIC NORTHWEST UNIVERSITY OF HEALTH SCIENCES
- Osteopathic Medicine D

PACIFIC UNIVERSITY
- Communication Disorders M,D
- Health Services Management and Hospital Administration M
- Occupational Therapy D
- Optometry M,D
- Pharmacy D
- Physical Therapy M,D
- Physician Assistant Studies M
- Vision Sciences M,D

PALM BEACH ATLANTIC UNIVERSITY
- Family Nurse Practitioner Studies M,D
- Nursing and Healthcare Administration M,D
- Nursing—General M,D
- Pharmacy D

PALMER COLLEGE OF CHIROPRACTIC
- Anatomy M
- Chiropractic D
- Clinical Research M

PALO ALTO UNIVERSITY
- Biopsychology D

PARKER UNIVERSITY
- Chiropractic D

PARK UNIVERSITY
- Health Services Management and Hospital Administration M,O
- International Health M,O

PENN STATE GREAT VALLEY
- Health Services Management and Hospital Administration M,O

PENN STATE HARRISBURG
- Health Services Management and Hospital Administration M,D,O

PENN STATE HERSHEY MEDICAL CENTER
- Allopathic Medicine M,D
- Anatomy M,D
- Biochemistry M,D
- Biological and Biomedical Sciences—General M,D
- Cell Biology D
- Developmental Biology D
- Genomic Sciences
- Health Services Research M
- Immunology M,D
- Molecular Genetics M,D
- Molecular Medicine D
- Molecular Toxicology D
- Neurobiology D
- Neuroscience M,D
- Public Health—General M,D
- Veterinary Sciences M
- Virology M,D

PENN STATE UNIVERSITY PARK
- Biochemistry M,D
- Biological and Biomedical Sciences—General M,D
- Biopsychology M,D
- Cell Biology M,D
- Communication Disorders M,D,O

*M—masters degree; D—doctorate; O—other advanced degree; *—Close-Up and/or Display*

Ecology M,D
Entomology M,D
Health Services Management and Hospital Administration M,D
Molecular Biology M,D
Nursing—General M,D
Nutrition M,D
Pathobiology M,D
Physiology M,D
Plant Biology M,D
Plant Pathology M,D

PENNSYLVANIA COLLEGE OF HEALTH SCIENCES
Health Services Management and Hospital Administration M
Nursing and Healthcare Administration M
Nursing Education M

PENSACOLA CHRISTIAN COLLEGE
Nursing—General M,D,O

PFEIFFER UNIVERSITY
Health Services Management and Hospital Administration M

PHILADELPHIA COLLEGE OF OSTEOPATHIC MEDICINE
Biological and Biomedical Sciences—General M
Biopsychology M,D,O
Health Services Management and Hospital Administration M,D,O
Osteopathic Medicine D
Physician Assistant Studies M
Public Health—General M,D,O

PHOENIX INSTITUTE OF HERBAL MEDICINE & ACUPUNCTURE
Acupuncture and Oriental Medicine M

PITTSBURG STATE UNIVERSITY
Biological and Biomedical Sciences—General M
Nursing Education M,D
Nursing—General M,D

PLYMOUTH STATE UNIVERSITY
Health Promotion M,O

POINT LOMA NAZARENE UNIVERSITY
Acute Care/Critical Care Nursing M
Biological and Biomedical Sciences—General M
Family Nurse Practitioner Studies M
Gerontological Nursing M
Health Services Management and Hospital Administration M
Nursing—General M,D,O
Pediatric Nursing M

POINT PARK UNIVERSITY
Health Services Management and Hospital Administration M

PONCE HEALTH SCIENCES UNIVERSITY
Allopathic Medicine D
Biological and Biomedical Sciences—General D
Epidemiology M,D
Public Health—General M,D

PONTIFICAL CATHOLIC UNIVERSITY OF PUERTO RICO
Biological and Biomedical Sciences—General M
Clinical Laboratory Sciences/Medical Technology O
Medical/Surgical Nursing M
Nursing—General M
Psychiatric Nursing M

PONTIFICIA UNIVERSIDAD CATOLICA MADRE Y MAESTRA
Allopathic Medicine D

PORTLAND STATE UNIVERSITY
Biological and Biomedical Sciences—General M,D
Communication Disorders M
Health Promotion M,D
Health Services Management and Hospital Administration M,D,O
Public Health—General M,D

POST UNIVERSITY
Health Services Management and Hospital Administration M

PRAIRIE VIEW A&M UNIVERSITY
Nursing—General M,D

PRESBYTERIAN COLLEGE
Pharmacy D

PRINCETON UNIVERSITY
Computational Biology D
Ecology D
Evolutionary Biology D
Marine Biology D
Molecular Biology D
Neuroscience D

PURDUE UNIVERSITY
Allied Health—General M,D
Anatomy M,D
Biochemistry M,D
Biological and Biomedical Sciences—General M,D
Biophysics M,D
Botany M,D
Cancer Biology/Oncology D
Cell Biology M,D
Communication Disorders M,D
Developmental Biology M,D
Ecology M,D
Entomology M,D
Environmental and Occupational Health M,D
Epidemiology M,D
Evolutionary Biology M,D
Family Nurse Practitioner Studies M,D,O
Genetics M,D
Genomic Sciences D
Gerontological Nursing M,D,O
Health Physics/Radiological Health M,D
Immunology M,D
Medical Physics M,D
Medicinal and Pharmaceutical Chemistry D
Microbiology M,D
Molecular Biology M,D
Molecular Pharmacology D
Neurobiology M,D
Neuroscience D
Nursing—General M,D,O
Nutrition M,D
Pathobiology M,D
Pathology M,D
Pediatric Nursing M,D,O
Pharmaceutical Administration M,D,O
Pharmaceutical Sciences M,D
Pharmacology M,D
Pharmacy D
Physiology M,D
Plant Pathology M,D
Plant Physiology M,D
Public Health—General M,D
Systems Biology D
Toxicology M,D
Veterinary Medicine D
Veterinary Sciences M,D
Virology M,D

PURDUE UNIVERSITY GLOBAL
Health Services Management and Hospital Administration M,O
Nursing and Healthcare Administration M
Nursing Education M
Nursing—General M

PURDUE UNIVERSITY NORTHWEST
Acute Care/Critical Care Nursing M
Adult Nursing M
Biological and Biomedical Sciences—General M
Family Nurse Practitioner Studies M
Nursing and Healthcare Administration M
Nursing—General M

QUEENS COLLEGE OF THE CITY UNIVERSITY OF NEW YORK
Biological and Biomedical Sciences—General M,O
Communication Disorders M,O
Neuroscience M
Nutrition M,O

QUEEN'S UNIVERSITY AT KINGSTON
Allopathic Medicine D
Anatomy M,D
Biochemistry M,D
Biological and Biomedical Sciences—General M,D
Cancer Biology/Oncology M,D
Cardiovascular Sciences M,D
Cell Biology M,D
Epidemiology M,D
Family Nurse Practitioner Studies M,D,O
Health Services Management and Hospital Administration M,D
Immunology M,D
Microbiology M,D
Molecular Biology M,D
Molecular Medicine M,D
Neurobiology M,D
Neuroscience M,D
Nursing—General M,D,O
Occupational Therapy M,D
Pathology M,D
Pediatric Nursing M,D,O
Pharmaceutical Sciences M,D
Pharmacology M,D
Physical Therapy M,D
Physiology M,D
Public Health—General M,D
Rehabilitation Sciences M,D
Reproductive Biology M,D
Toxicology M,D
Women's Health Nursing M,D,O

QUEENS UNIVERSITY OF CHARLOTTE
Nursing and Healthcare Administration M
Nursing Education M
Nursing—General M

QUINNIPIAC UNIVERSITY
Adult Nursing D
Allied Health—General M
Allopathic Medicine D
Anesthesiologist Assistant Studies M
Biological and Biomedical Sciences—General M
Cardiovascular Sciences M
Cell Biology M
Community Health D
Family Nurse Practitioner Studies D
Health Physics/Radiological Health M
Health Services Management and Hospital Administration M
Molecular Biology M
Nurse Anesthesia D
Nursing and Healthcare Administration D
Nursing—General D
Pathology M
Perfusion M
Physician Assistant Studies M

RADFORD UNIVERSITY
Communication Disorders M
Nursing—General D
Occupational Therapy M
Physical Therapy D

RAMAPO COLLEGE OF NEW JERSEY
Family Nurse Practitioner Studies M
Nursing and Healthcare Administration M
Nursing Education M
Nursing—General M

REGENT UNIVERSITY
Health Services Management and Hospital Administration M,D,O

REGIS COLLEGE (MA)
Family Nurse Practitioner Studies M,D,O
Health Services Management and Hospital Administration M,D,O
Nursing Education M,D,O
Nursing—General M,D,O
Occupational Therapy M,D,O

REGIS UNIVERSITY
Allied Health—General M,D,O
Biological and Biomedical Sciences—General M
Environmental Biology M
Health Services Management and Hospital Administration M,D,O
Maternal and Child/Neonatal Nursing M,D,O
Nursing and Healthcare Administration M,D,O
Nursing Education M,D,O
Occupational Therapy M,D,O
Pharmacy M,D,O
Physical Therapy M,D,O

RENSSELAER POLYTECHNIC INSTITUTE
Biochemistry M,D
Biological and Biomedical Sciences—General M,D
Biophysics M,D

RESEARCH COLLEGE OF NURSING
Adult Nursing M
Family Nurse Practitioner Studies M
Gerontological Nursing M
Nursing and Healthcare Administration M
Nursing—General M

RESURRECTION UNIVERSITY
Nursing—General M

RHODE ISLAND COLLEGE
Biological and Biomedical Sciences—General M,O
Health Services Management and Hospital Administration M
Nursing—General M,D

RICE UNIVERSITY
Biochemistry M,D
Cell Biology M,D
Ecology M,D
Evolutionary Biology M,D
Health Services Management and Hospital Administration M

RIVIER UNIVERSITY
Family Nurse Practitioner Studies M,D
Nursing and Healthcare Administration M,D
Nursing Education M,D
Nursing—General M,D
Psychiatric Nursing M,D
Public Health—General M,D

ROBERT MORRIS UNIVERSITY
Nursing—General M,D

ROBERT MORRIS UNIVERSITY ILLINOIS
Health Services Management and Hospital Administration M

ROBERTS WESLEYAN COLLEGE
Health Services Management and Hospital Administration M
Nursing and Healthcare Administration M
Nursing Education M
Nursing Informatics M
Nursing—General M

ROCHESTER INSTITUTE OF TECHNOLOGY
Biological and Biomedical Sciences—General M
Environmental and Occupational Health M
Health Services Management and Hospital Administration M,O
Occupational Therapy M

THE ROCKEFELLER UNIVERSITY
Biological and Biomedical Sciences—General M,D*

ROCKHURST UNIVERSITY
Communication Disorders M
Health Services Management and Hospital Administration M,O
Occupational Therapy M
Physical Therapy D

ROCKY MOUNTAIN COLLEGE
Physician Assistant Studies M

ROCKY MOUNTAIN UNIVERSITY OF HEALTH PROFESSIONS
Communication Disorders D
Family Nurse Practitioner Studies D
Occupational Therapy D
Physical Therapy D
Physician Assistant Studies M
Physiology D

ROCKY VISTA UNIVERSITY
Biological and Biomedical Sciences—General M
Osteopathic Medicine D
Physician Assistant Studies M

ROGER WILLIAMS UNIVERSITY
Health Services Management and Hospital Administration M

ROLLINS COLLEGE
Public Health—General M

ROOSEVELT UNIVERSITY
Pharmacy D

ROSALIND FRANKLIN UNIVERSITY OF MEDICINE AND SCIENCE
Allied Health—General M,D,O
Allopathic Medicine D
Anatomy D
Biochemistry D
Biological and Biomedical Sciences—General M,D
Biophysics M,D
Cell Biology D
Health Promotion M
Health Services Management and Hospital Administration M,O
Immunology D
Microbiology D
Molecular Biology D
Molecular Pharmacology M,D
Neuroscience D
Nurse Anesthesia D
Nutrition M
Pathology M
Pharmacy D
Physical Therapy M,D
Physician Assistant Studies M
Physiology M,D
Podiatric Medicine D

ROSEMAN UNIVERSITY OF HEALTH SCIENCES
Dentistry M,D,O
Pharmacy D

ROWAN UNIVERSITY
Allopathic Medicine D
Biological and Biomedical Sciences—General M
Health Promotion M
Nursing—General M
Osteopathic Medicine D
Pharmaceutical Sciences M
School Nursing M,D,O

RUSH UNIVERSITY
Adult Nursing D,O
Allopathic Medicine D
Anatomy M,D
Biochemistry M,D
Cell Biology M,D
Clinical Laboratory Sciences/Medical Technology M
Communication Disorders M,D
Community Health Nursing D
Family Nurse Practitioner Studies D
Gerontological Nursing D,O
Health Services Management and Hospital Administration M,D
Immunology M,D
Maternal and Child/Neonatal Nursing D,O
Medical Physics M,D
Microbiology M,D
Neuroscience M,D
Nurse Anesthesia D,O
Nursing and Healthcare Administration M
Nursing—General D
Nutrition D
Occupational Therapy M
Pediatric Nursing D,O
Perfusion M
Pharmaceutical Sciences M,D
Pharmacology M,D
Physical Therapy M
Physician Assistant Studies M
Physiology D
Psychiatric Nursing D
Virology M,D

RUTGERS UNIVERSITY–CAMDEN
Biological and Biomedical Sciences—General M
Computational Biology M,D
Family Nurse Practitioner Studies D
Gerontological Nursing D
Health Services Management and Hospital Administration M,O
Nursing—General D
Physical Therapy D
Public Health—General M,O

RUTGERS UNIVERSITY–NEWARK
Adult Nursing M,D,O
Allied Health—General M,D,O
Allopathic Medicine D
Biochemistry M,D
Biological and Biomedical Sciences—General M,D,O
Biopsychology D
Cancer Biology/Oncology D,O
Cell Biology D
Clinical Laboratory Sciences/Medical Technology M
Computational Biology M
Dentistry M,D,O
Developmental Biology D,O
Epidemiology M,O
Family Nurse Practitioner Studies M,D,O
Health Physics/Radiological Health M
Health Services Management and Hospital Administration M,D,O
Immunology D

Infectious Diseases	D,O
Medical Imaging	M
Microbiology	D
Molecular Biology	M,D
Molecular Genetics	D
Molecular Medicine	D
Molecular Pathology	D
Neuroscience	D
Nurse Anesthesia	M,D,O
Nursing Informatics	M
Nursing—General	M,D,O
Nutrition	M,D,O
Occupational Health Nursing	M,D,O
Oral and Dental Sciences	M,D,O
Pathology	D
Pharmaceutical Administration	M
Pharmacology	D
Physical Therapy	D
Physician Assistant Studies	M
Physiology	D
Public Health—General	M,O
Transcultural Nursing	M,D,O
Women's Health Nursing	M,D,O

RUTGERS UNIVERSITY–NEW BRUNSWICK

Allopathic Medicine	D
Biochemistry	M,D
Biological and Biomedical Sciences—General	M,D
Biopsychology	D
Cancer Biology/Oncology	M,D
Cell Biology	M,D
Clinical Laboratory Sciences/Medical Technology	M
Computational Biology	D
Developmental Biology	M,D
Ecology	M,D
Entomology	M,D
Environmental and Occupational Health	M,D,O
Environmental Biology	M,D
Epidemiology	M,D,O
Evolutionary Biology	M,D
Genetics	M,D
Health Services Management and Hospital Administration	M,D,O
Immunology	M,D
Marine Biology	M,D
Medical Microbiology	M,D
Medicinal and Pharmaceutical Chemistry	M,D
Microbiology	M,D
Molecular Biology	M,D
Molecular Biophysics	D
Molecular Genetics	M,D
Molecular Pharmacology	M,D
Molecular Physiology	M,D
Neuroscience	M,D
Nutrition	M,D
Pharmaceutical Sciences	M,D
Pharmacy	M,D
Physiology	M,D
Plant Biology	M,D
Plant Molecular Biology	M,D
Plant Pathology	M,D
Public Health—General	M,D
Reproductive Biology	M,D
Systems Biology	D
Toxicology	M,D
Translational Biology	M
Virology	M,D

SACRED HEART UNIVERSITY

Communication Disorders	M
Family Nurse Practitioner Studies	M,D,O
Molecular Biology	M
Nursing and Healthcare Administration	M,D,O
Nursing Education	M,D,O
Nursing—General	M,D,O
Nutrition	M
Occupational Therapy	M
Physical Therapy	D
Physician Assistant Studies	M
Public Health—General	M

SAGE GRADUATE SCHOOL

Family Nurse Practitioner Studies	M
Gerontological Nursing	M,O
Health Services Management and Hospital Administration	M
Nursing Education	D
Nursing—General	M,D,O
Nutrition	M,O
Occupational Therapy	M
Physical Therapy	D
Psychiatric Nursing	M,O

SAGINAW VALLEY STATE UNIVERSITY

Family Nurse Practitioner Studies	M,D
Health Services Management and Hospital Administration	M
Nursing—General	M
Occupational Therapy	M

ST. AMBROSE UNIVERSITY

Communication Disorders	M
Health Services Management and Hospital Administration	M,D
Occupational Therapy	D
Physical Therapy	D
Physician Assistant Studies	M
Public Health—General	M

SAINT ANTHONY COLLEGE OF NURSING

Nursing—General	M

ST. CATHERINE UNIVERSITY

Adult Nursing	M,D
Gerontological Nursing	M,D
Health Services Management and Hospital Administration	M
International Health	M
Nursing Education	M,D
Nursing—General	M,D
Occupational Therapy	M,D
Pediatric Nursing	M,D
Physical Therapy	D
Physician Assistant Studies	M
Public Health—General	M

ST. CLOUD STATE UNIVERSITY

Biological and Biomedical Sciences—General	M
Communication Disorders	M

SAINT FRANCIS MEDICAL CENTER COLLEGE OF NURSING

Family Nurse Practitioner Studies	M,D,O
Gerontological Nursing	M,D,O
Maternal and Child/Neonatal Nursing	M,D,O
Medical/Surgical Nursing	M,D,O
Nursing and Healthcare Administration	M,D,O
Nursing Education	M,D,O
Nursing—General	M,D,O
Psychiatric Nursing	M,D,O

SAINT FRANCIS UNIVERSITY

Biological and Biomedical Sciences—General	M
Cancer Biology/Oncology	M
Nursing and Healthcare Administration	M
Nursing Education	M
Nursing—General	M
Occupational Therapy	M
Physical Therapy	D
Physician Assistant Studies	M

ST. FRANCIS XAVIER UNIVERSITY

Biological and Biomedical Sciences—General	M

ST. JOHN FISHER COLLEGE

Biological and Biomedical Sciences—General	M
Nursing—General	M,D,O
Pharmacy	D

ST. JOHN'S UNIVERSITY (NY)

Biological and Biomedical Sciences—General	M,D
Communication Disorders	M,D
Pharmaceutical Administration	M
Pharmaceutical Sciences	M,D
Pharmacy	M,D
Public Health—General	M
Toxicology	M

ST. JOSEPH'S COLLEGE, LONG ISLAND CAMPUS

Adult Nursing	M
Gerontological Nursing	M
Health Services Management and Hospital Administration	M
Nursing Education	M
Nursing—General	M

ST. JOSEPH'S COLLEGE, NEW YORK

Adult Nursing	M
Gerontological Nursing	M
Health Services Management and Hospital Administration	M
Nursing Education	M
Nursing—General	M

SAINT JOSEPH'S COLLEGE OF MAINE

Family Nurse Practitioner Studies	M,O
Health Services Management and Hospital Administration	M
Nursing and Healthcare Administration	M,O
Nursing Education	M,O
Nursing—General	M,O

SAINT JOSEPH'S UNIVERSITY

Biological and Biomedical Sciences—General	M
Communication Disorders	M,D,O
Health Services Management and Hospital Administration	M,O

SAINT LEO UNIVERSITY

Health Services Management and Hospital Administration	M,D

ST. LOUIS COLLEGE OF PHARMACY

Pharmacy	D

SAINT LOUIS UNIVERSITY

Allied Health—General	M,D,O
Allopathic Medicine	D
Anatomy	M,D
Biochemistry	D
Bioethics	D,O
Biological and Biomedical Sciences—General	M,D*
Communication Disorders	M
Community Health	M
Computational Biology	M
Dentistry	M
Health Services Management and Hospital Administration	M,D
Immunology	D
Microbiology	D
Molecular Biology	D
Nursing—General	M,D,O
Nutrition	M
Occupational Therapy	M
Oral and Dental Sciences	M
Pathology	D
Pharmacology	D
Physical Therapy	M,D
Physician Assistant Studies	M
Physiology	D
Public Health—General	M,D

SAINT MARY-OF-THE-WOODS COLLEGE

Health Services Management and Hospital Administration	M
Nursing—General	M

SAINT MARY'S COLLEGE

Adult Nursing	D
Communication Disorders	M
Family Nurse Practitioner Studies	D
Gerontological Nursing	D
Nursing—General	D

SAINT MARY'S UNIVERSITY OF MINNESOTA

Health Services Management and Hospital Administration	M
Nurse Anesthesia	M

ST. NORBERT COLLEGE

Health Services Management and Hospital Administration	M

SAINT PETER'S UNIVERSITY

Adult Nursing	M,D,O
Health Services Management and Hospital Administration	M
Nursing and Healthcare Administration	M,D,O
Nursing—General	M,D,O

ST. THOMAS UNIVERSITY

Health Services Management and Hospital Administration	M,O

SAINT VINCENT COLLEGE

Nurse Anesthesia	M,D

SAINT XAVIER UNIVERSITY

Communication Disorders	M
Health Services Management and Hospital Administration	M,O
Nursing—General	M,O

SALEM STATE UNIVERSITY

Gerontological Nursing	M
Nursing and Healthcare Administration	M
Nursing Education	M
Nursing—General	M
Occupational Therapy	M

SALISBURY UNIVERSITY

Biological and Biomedical Sciences—General	M
Family Nurse Practitioner Studies	D
Nursing and Healthcare Administration	M,D
Nursing Education	M
Nursing—General	M,D
Physiology	M

SALUS UNIVERSITY

Communication Disorders	M,D,O
Occupational Therapy	M,O
Optometry	D
Physician Assistant Studies	M
Public Health—General	M
Rehabilitation Sciences	M,O
Vision Sciences	M,O

SALVE REGINA UNIVERSITY

Health Services Management and Hospital Administration	M,O
Nursing—General	D

SAMFORD UNIVERSITY

Communication Disorders	M,D
Family Nurse Practitioner Studies	M,D
Health Services Management and Hospital Administration	M
Nurse Anesthesia	M,D
Nursing and Healthcare Administration	M,D
Nursing Informatics	M,D
Nursing—General	M,D
Nutrition	M
Pharmacy	D
Physical Therapy	M,D
Public Health—General	M

SAM HOUSTON STATE UNIVERSITY

Allied Health—General	M
Biological and Biomedical Sciences—General	M
Nutrition	M

SAMUEL MERRITT UNIVERSITY

Family Nurse Practitioner Studies	M,D,O
Nurse Anesthesia	M,D,O
Nursing and Healthcare Administration	M,D,O
Nursing—General	M,D,O
Occupational Therapy	D
Physical Therapy	D
Physician Assistant Studies	M
Podiatric Medicine	D

SAN DIEGO STATE UNIVERSITY

Biochemistry	M,D
Biological and Biomedical Sciences—General	M,D
Cell Biology	M,D
Communication Disorders	M,D
Ecology	M,D
Emergency Medical Services	M,D
Environmental and Occupational Health	M,D
Epidemiology	M,D
Health Physics/Radiological Health	M
Health Promotion	M,D
Health Services Management and Hospital Administration	M,D
International Health	M,D
Microbiology	M
Molecular Biology	M,D
Nursing—General	M
Nutrition	M
Pharmaceutical Administration	M
Physical Therapy	D
Public Health—General	M,D
Toxicology	M,D

SANFORD BURNHAM PREBYS MEDICAL DISCOVERY INSTITUTE

Biological and Biomedical Sciences—General	D

SAN FRANCISCO STATE UNIVERSITY

Acute Care/Critical Care Nursing	M,O
Biochemistry	M
Biological and Biomedical Sciences—General	M
Cell Biology	M
Communication Disorders	M
Community Health Nursing	M,O
Community Health	M
Developmental Biology	M
Ecology	M
Family Nurse Practitioner Studies	M,O
Health Services Management and Hospital Administration	M
Marine Biology	M
Microbiology	M
Molecular Biology	M
Nursing and Healthcare Administration	M,O
Nursing—General	M,O
Pediatric Nursing	M,O
Physical Therapy	D
Physiology	M
Public Health—General	M
Women's Health Nursing	M,O

SAN JOSE STATE UNIVERSITY

Biological and Biomedical Sciences—General	M
Communication Disorders	M,D
Ecology	M
Family Nurse Practitioner Studies	M
Molecular Biology	M
Nursing—General	M
Nutrition	M
Occupational Therapy	M
Physiology	M
Public Health—General	M

SAN JUAN BAUTISTA SCHOOL OF MEDICINE

Allopathic Medicine	M,D
Public Health—General	M,D

SARAH LAWRENCE COLLEGE

Human Genetics	M
Public Health—General	M

SAYBROOK UNIVERSITY

Nutrition	M,D,O

THE SCRIPPS RESEARCH INSTITUTE

Biological and Biomedical Sciences—General	D

SEATTLE INSTITUTE OF ORIENTAL MEDICINE

Acupuncture and Oriental Medicine	M

SEATTLE PACIFIC UNIVERSITY

Adult Nursing	M,O
Family Nurse Practitioner Studies	M,O
Gerontological Nursing	M,O
Nursing and Healthcare Administration	M,O
Nursing Education	M,O
Nursing Informatics	M,O
Nursing—General	M,O

SEATTLE UNIVERSITY

Nursing—General	D

SETON HALL UNIVERSITY

Adult Nursing	M,D
Allied Health—General	D
Allopathic Medicine	D
Biochemistry	M,D
Biological and Biomedical Sciences—General	M,D
Communication Disorders	M
Gerontological Nursing	M,D
Health Services Management and Hospital Administration	M,D
International Health	M,O
Microbiology	M,D
Molecular Biology	M,D
Neuroscience	M,D
Nursing and Healthcare Administration	M,D
Nursing Education	M,D
Nursing—General	M,D
Occupational Therapy	M
Pediatric Nursing	M,D
Physical Therapy	D
Physician Assistant Studies	M
School Nursing	M,D

SETON HILL UNIVERSITY

Health Services Management and Hospital Administration	M
Oral and Dental Sciences	M,O
Physician Assistant Studies	M

SHAWNEE STATE UNIVERSITY

Occupational Therapy	M

SHENANDOAH UNIVERSITY

Adult Nursing	M,D,O

*M—masters degree; D—doctorate; O—other advanced degree; *—Close-Up and/or Display*

Allied Health—General M,D,O
Family Nurse Practitioner Studies M,D,O
Gerontological Nursing M,D,O
Health Services Management and Hospital Administration M,D,O
Nurse Midwifery M,D,O
Nursing and Healthcare Administration M,D,O
Nursing Education M,D,O
Nursing—General M,D,O
Pharmacy D
Physical Therapy M,D,O
Physician Assistant Studies M,D,O
Psychiatric Nursing M,D,O
Public Health—General M,D,O

SHERMAN COLLEGE OF CHIROPRACTIC
Chiropractic D

SHIPPENSBURG UNIVERSITY OF PENNSYLVANIA
Biological and Biomedical Sciences—General M
Health Services Management and Hospital Administration M,D,O

SIENA HEIGHTS UNIVERSITY
Health Services Management and Hospital Administration M,O

SIMMONS COLLEGE
Family Nurse Practitioner Studies M,D,O
Health Promotion M,D,O
Health Services Management and Hospital Administration M
Nursing—General M,D,O
Nutrition M,D,O
Physical Therapy M,D,O
Public Health—General M

SIMON FRASER UNIVERSITY
Biochemistry M,D,O
Biological and Biomedical Sciences—General M,D,O
Entomology M,D,O
International Health M,D,O
Molecular Biology M,D,O
Public Health—General M,D,O
Toxicology M,D,O

SLIPPERY ROCK UNIVERSITY OF PENNSYLVANIA
Physical Therapy D
Physician Assistant Studies M
Public Health—General M

SMITH COLLEGE
Biological and Biomedical Sciences—General M

SONOMA STATE UNIVERSITY
Biochemistry M
Biological and Biomedical Sciences—General M
Family Nurse Practitioner Studies M
Health Promotion M
Nursing—General M
Occupational Therapy M
Physical Therapy M

SOUTH BAYLO UNIVERSITY
Acupuncture and Oriental Medicine M

SOUTH CAROLINA STATE UNIVERSITY
Allied Health—General M
Biological and Biomedical Sciences—General M
Communication Disorders M
Health Services Management and Hospital Administration M
Nutrition M

SOUTH COLLEGE
Pharmacy D
Physician Assistant Studies M

SOUTH DAKOTA STATE UNIVERSITY
Biological and Biomedical Sciences—General M,D
Microbiology M,D
Nursing—General M,D
Nutrition M,D
Pharmaceutical Sciences M,D
Pharmacy D
Veterinary Sciences M,D

SOUTHEASTERN LOUISIANA UNIVERSITY
Biological and Biomedical Sciences—General M
Communication Disorders M
Nursing—General M,D

SOUTHEASTERN OKLAHOMA STATE UNIVERSITY
Environmental and Occupational Health M

SOUTHEASTERN UNIVERSITY (FL)
Health Services Management and Hospital Administration M,D

SOUTHEAST MISSOURI STATE UNIVERSITY
Biological and Biomedical Sciences—General M
Communication Disorders M
Nursing—General M

SOUTHERN ADVENTIST UNIVERSITY
Acute Care/Critical Care Nursing M,D
Adult Nursing M,D
Family Nurse Practitioner Studies M,D
Gerontological Nursing M,D
Health Services Management and Hospital Administration M
Nursing Education M,D
Nursing—General M,D
Psychiatric Nursing M,D

SOUTHERN ARKANSAS UNIVERSITY–MAGNOLIA
Psychiatric Nursing M

SOUTHERN CALIFORNIA UNIVERSITY OF HEALTH SCIENCES
Acupuncture and Oriental Medicine M,D
Chiropractic D

SOUTHERN COLLEGE OF OPTOMETRY
Optometry D

SOUTHERN CONNECTICUT STATE UNIVERSITY
Biological and Biomedical Sciences—General M
Communication Disorders M
Family Nurse Practitioner Studies M,D
Nursing Education M,D
Nursing—General M,D
Public Health—General M

SOUTHERN ILLINOIS UNIVERSITY CARBONDALE
Biochemistry M,D
Biological and Biomedical Sciences—General M,D
Communication Disorders M
Community Health M
Health Services Management and Hospital Administration M
Medical Physics M
Microbiology M,D
Molecular Biology M,D
Nutrition M
Pharmacology M,D
Physician Assistant Studies M
Physiology M,D
Plant Biology M,D
Zoology M,D

SOUTHERN ILLINOIS UNIVERSITY EDWARDSVILLE
Biological and Biomedical Sciences—General M
Communication Disorders M
Dentistry D
Family Nurse Practitioner Studies M,D,O
Nurse Anesthesia D
Nursing and Healthcare Administration M,O
Nursing Education M,O
Nursing—General M,D,O
Pharmacy D

SOUTHERN METHODIST UNIVERSITY
Biological and Biomedical Sciences—General M,D
Cell Biology M,D
Health Promotion M,D
Molecular Biology M,D
Physiology M,D

SOUTHERN NAZARENE UNIVERSITY
Health Services Management and Hospital Administration M
Nursing and Healthcare Administration M
Nursing Education M
Nursing—General M

SOUTHERN NEW HAMPSHIRE UNIVERSITY
Health Services Management and Hospital Administration M,D,O
Nursing and Healthcare Administration M,O
Nursing Education M,O
Nursing—General M,O

SOUTHERN UNIVERSITY AND AGRICULTURAL AND MECHANICAL COLLEGE
Biochemistry M
Biological and Biomedical Sciences—General M
Communication Disorders M
Family Nurse Practitioner Studies M,D,O
Gerontological Nursing M,D,O
Nursing and Healthcare Administration M,D,O
Nursing Education M,D,O
Nursing—General M,D,O

SOUTH UNIVERSITY (AL)
Health Services Management and Hospital Administration M
Nursing—General M

SOUTH UNIVERSITY
Family Nurse Practitioner Studies M
Health Services Management and Hospital Administration M
Nursing—General M
Occupational Therapy D

SOUTH UNIVERSITY
Adult Nursing M
Family Nurse Practitioner Studies M
Health Services Management and Hospital Administration M
Nursing Education M
Nursing—General M
Physician Assistant Studies M

SOUTH UNIVERSITY (GA)
Anesthesiologist Assistant Studies M
Health Services Management and Hospital Administration M
Nursing Education M
Nursing—General M
Pharmacy
Physician Assistant Studies M

SOUTH UNIVERSITY (SC)
Health Services Management and Hospital Administration M
Nursing—General M
Pharmacy D

SOUTH UNIVERSITY
Nursing—General M

SOUTH UNIVERSITY
Family Nurse Practitioner Studies M
Nursing—General M

SOUTHWEST ACUPUNCTURE COLLEGE
Acupuncture and Oriental Medicine M

SOUTHWEST BAPTIST UNIVERSITY
Health Services Management and Hospital Administration M
Physical Therapy D

SOUTHWEST COLLEGE OF NATUROPATHIC MEDICINE AND HEALTH SCIENCES
Naturopathic Medicine D

SOUTHWESTERN OKLAHOMA STATE UNIVERSITY
Allied Health—General M
Microbiology M
Pharmacy D

SPALDING UNIVERSITY
Adult Nursing M,D,O
Family Nurse Practitioner Studies M,D,O
Nursing and Healthcare Administration M,D,O
Nursing Education M,D,O
Nursing—General M,D,O
Occupational Therapy M
Pediatric Nursing M,D,O

SPRING ARBOR UNIVERSITY
Nursing—General M

SPRINGFIELD COLLEGE
Health Promotion M,D,O
Occupational Therapy M
Physical Therapy D
Physician Assistant Studies M

SPRING HILL COLLEGE
Nursing and Healthcare Administration M,O
Nursing—General M,O

STANBRIDGE UNIVERSITY
Nursing—General M
Occupational Therapy M

STANFORD UNIVERSITY
Allopathic Medicine D
Biochemistry D
Biological and Biomedical Sciences—General M,D
Biophysics D
Clinical Research M,D
Developmental Biology M,D
Ecology M,D
Epidemiology M,D
Genetics D
Health Services Research M,D
Immunology D
Microbiology D
Physiology D
Structural Biology D
Systems Biology D

STATE UNIVERSITY OF NEW YORK AT FREDONIA
Biological and Biomedical Sciences—General M,O
Communication Disorders M,O

STATE UNIVERSITY OF NEW YORK AT NEW PALTZ
Communication Disorders M

STATE UNIVERSITY OF NEW YORK AT PLATTSBURGH
Communication Disorders M

STATE UNIVERSITY OF NEW YORK COLLEGE AT CORTLAND
Communication Disorders M
Community Health M

STATE UNIVERSITY OF NEW YORK COLLEGE AT ONEONTA
Biological and Biomedical Sciences—General M
Nutrition M

STATE UNIVERSITY OF NEW YORK COLLEGE AT POTSDAM
Community Health M

STATE UNIVERSITY OF NEW YORK COLLEGE OF ENVIRONMENTAL SCIENCE AND FORESTRY
Biochemistry M,D
Conservation Biology M,D
Ecology M,D
Entomology M,D
Environmental Biology M,D
Plant Pathology M,D

STATE UNIVERSITY OF NEW YORK COLLEGE OF OPTOMETRY
Optometry D
Vision Sciences D

STATE UNIVERSITY OF NEW YORK COLLEGE OF TECHNOLOGY AT DELHI
Nursing and Healthcare Administration M
Nursing Education M
Nursing—General M

STATE UNIVERSITY OF NEW YORK DOWNSTATE MEDICAL CENTER
Allopathic Medicine M,D
Biological and Biomedical Sciences—General M,D
Cell Biology D
Community Health M
Family Nurse Practitioner Studies M,O
Medical/Surgical Nursing M,O
Molecular Biology D
Neuroscience D
Nurse Anesthesia M
Nurse Midwifery M,O
Nursing—General M,O
Occupational Therapy M
Public Health—General M

STATE UNIVERSITY OF NEW YORK EMPIRE STATE COLLEGE
Nursing Education M

STATE UNIVERSITY OF NEW YORK POLYTECHNIC INSTITUTE
Family Nurse Practitioner Studies M,O
Nursing Education M,O

STATE UNIVERSITY OF NEW YORK UPSTATE MEDICAL UNIVERSITY
Allopathic Medicine D
Anatomy M,D
Biochemistry M,D
Biological and Biomedical Sciences—General M,D
Cell Biology M,D
Clinical Laboratory Sciences/Medical Technology M
Family Nurse Practitioner Studies M,O
Immunology M,D
Microbiology M,D
Molecular Biology M,D
Neuroscience D
Nursing—General M,O
Pharmacology D
Physical Therapy D
Physiology M,D

STEPHEN F. AUSTIN STATE UNIVERSITY
Biological and Biomedical Sciences—General M
Communication Disorders M

STEPHENS COLLEGE
Physician Assistant Studies M,O

STEVENS INSTITUTE OF TECHNOLOGY
Biochemistry M,D,O
Pharmaceutical Sciences M,O

STEVENSON UNIVERSITY
Biological and Biomedical Sciences—General M
Health Services Management and Hospital Administration M
Nursing and Healthcare Administration M
Nursing Education M
Nursing—General M

STOCKTON UNIVERSITY
Communication Disorders M
Nursing—General M
Occupational Therapy M
Physical Therapy D

STONY BROOK UNIVERSITY, STATE UNIVERSITY OF NEW YORK
Adult Nursing M,D,O
Allopathic Medicine D
Anatomy D
Biochemistry M,D
Bioethics
Biological and Biomedical Sciences—General M,D,O
Biophysics D
Cell Biology M,D
Community Health M,D,O
Dentistry D,O
Developmental Biology M,D
Ecology M,D
Evolutionary Biology M,D
Family Nurse Practitioner Studies M,D,O
Genetics D
Gerontological Nursing M,D,O
Health Promotion M,O
Health Services Management and Hospital Administration M,D,O
Immunology M,D
Maternal and Child/Neonatal Nursing M,D,O
Medical Physics M,D
Microbiology D
Molecular Biology M,D
Molecular Genetics D
Molecular Physiology D
Neuroscience M,D
Nurse Midwifery M,D,O
Nursing and Healthcare Administration M,D,O
Nursing Education M,O
Nursing—General M,D,O
Nutrition M,O
Occupational Therapy M,D,O
Oral and Dental Sciences M,D,O
Pathology M,D
Pediatric Nursing M,D,O
Pharmacology M,D
Pharmacy D
Physical Therapy M,D,O
Physician Assistant Studies M,D,O
Physiology D
Psychiatric Nursing M,D,O
Public Health—General M,O
Rehabilitation Sciences M,D,O
Structural Biology D
Women's Health Nursing M,D,O

STRATFORD UNIVERSITY (VA)
Health Services Management and Hospital Administration M,D

STRAYER UNIVERSITY
Health Services Management and Hospital Administration M

SUFFOLK UNIVERSITY

Community Health	M
Health Services Management and Hospital Administration	M

SULLIVAN UNIVERSITY

Pharmacy	D

SUL ROSS STATE UNIVERSITY

Biological and Biomedical Sciences—General	M

SWEDISH INSTITUTE, COLLEGE OF HEALTH SCIENCES

Acupuncture and Oriental Medicine	M

SYRACUSE UNIVERSITY

Biological and Biomedical Sciences—General	M,D
Communication Disorders	M,D
Environmental and Occupational Health	O
Health Services Management and Hospital Administration	O
International Health	M
Neuroscience	M,D
Nutrition	M,D

TARLETON STATE UNIVERSITY

Biological and Biomedical Sciences—General	M
Clinical Laboratory Sciences/Medical Technology	M
Nursing and Healthcare Administration	M
Nursing Education	M
Nursing—General	M
Public Health—General	M

TEACHERS COLLEGE, COLUMBIA UNIVERSITY

Biological and Biomedical Sciences—General	M,D
Communication Disorders	M,D,O
Community Health	M,D,O
Neuroscience	M,D
Nursing and Healthcare Administration	M,D
Nursing Education	M,D,O
Nutrition	M,D,O
Physiology	M,D

TEMPLE UNIVERSITY

Adult Nursing	D
Allied Health—General	M,D
Allopathic Medicine	D
Biological and Biomedical Sciences—General	M,D
Communication Disorders	M,D
Dentistry	D
Environmental and Occupational Health	M,D
Epidemiology	M,D
Family Nurse Practitioner Studies	D
Health Services Management and Hospital Administration	M
Medicinal and Pharmaceutical Chemistry	M,D
Nursing—General	D
Occupational Therapy	M,D
Oral and Dental Sciences	M,O
Pharmaceutical Administration	M
Pharmaceutical Sciences	M,D
Pharmacy	M,D
Physical Therapy	D
Podiatric Medicine	D
Public Health—General	M,D
Rehabilitation Sciences	M,D

TENNESSEE STATE UNIVERSITY

Allied Health—General	M,D,O
Biological and Biomedical Sciences—General	D
Communication Disorders	M
Family Nurse Practitioner Studies	M,O
Nursing—General	M,O
Occupational Therapy	M
Physical Therapy	D
Public Health—General	M

TENNESSEE TECHNOLOGICAL UNIVERSITY

Acute Care/Critical Care Nursing	D
Biological and Biomedical Sciences—General	M,D
Family Nurse Practitioner Studies	M,D
Gerontological Nursing	D
Health Promotion	M
Nursing and Healthcare Administration	M,D
Nursing Education	M
Nursing—General	M,D
Psychiatric Nursing	D
Women's Health Nursing	D

TEXAS A&M INTERNATIONAL UNIVERSITY

Biological and Biomedical Sciences—General	M
Family Nurse Practitioner Studies	M
Nursing—General	M

TEXAS A&M UNIVERSITY

Allopathic Medicine	M,D
Biochemistry	M,D
Biological and Biomedical Sciences—General	M,D,O
Community Health	M,D
Dental Hygiene	M,D,O
Dentistry	M,D,O
Entomology	M,D
Environmental and Occupational Health	M,D
Epidemiology	M,D
Family Nurse Practitioner Studies	M
Forensic Nursing	M
Health Promotion	M,D
Health Services Management and Hospital Administration	M,D
Health Services Research	M,D
Marine Biology	M,D
Microbiology	M,D
Nursing and Healthcare Administration	M,D
Nursing Education	M
Nursing—General	M
Nutrition	M,D
Oral and Dental Sciences	M,D,O
Pharmacy	D
Plant Pathology	M,D
Public Health—General	M,D,O
Veterinary Medicine	M,D
Veterinary Sciences	M,D

TEXAS A&M UNIVERSITY–COMMERCE

Biological and Biomedical Sciences—General	M,O

TEXAS A&M UNIVERSITY–CORPUS CHRISTI

Biological and Biomedical Sciences—General	M,D
Family Nurse Practitioner Studies	M,D
Health Services Management and Hospital Administration	M,D
Marine Biology	M,D
Nursing and Healthcare Administration	M,D
Nursing Education	M,D
Nursing—General	M,D

TEXAS A&M UNIVERSITY–KINGSVILLE

Biological and Biomedical Sciences—General	M
Communication Disorders	M

TEXAS CHIROPRACTIC COLLEGE

Chiropractic	D

TEXAS CHRISTIAN UNIVERSITY

Adult Nursing	M,O
Allied Health—General	M,D,O
Biochemistry	M,D
Biological and Biomedical Sciences—General	M,D
Biophysics	M,D
Communication Disorders	M
Family Nurse Practitioner Studies	D
Gerontological Nursing	M,O
Health Services Management and Hospital Administration	M,O
Neuroscience	M,D
Nurse Anesthesia	D
Nursing and Healthcare Administration	M,D,O
Nursing Education	M,O
Nursing—General	M,D,O
Pediatric Nursing	M,D,O

TEXAS HEALTH AND SCIENCE UNIVERSITY

Acupuncture and Oriental Medicine	M,D
Health Services Management and Hospital Administration	M,D

TEXAS SOUTHERN UNIVERSITY

Biological and Biomedical Sciences—General	M
Health Services Management and Hospital Administration	M
Pharmaceutical Sciences	M,D
Pharmacy	D
Toxicology	M,D

TEXAS STATE UNIVERSITY

Allied Health—General	M,D
Biochemistry	M
Biological and Biomedical Sciences—General	M
Communication Disorders	M
Conservation Biology	M
Family Nurse Practitioner Studies	M
Health Services Management and Hospital Administration	M
Marine Biology	M,D
Nutrition	M
Physical Therapy	D

TEXAS TECH UNIVERSITY

Biological and Biomedical Sciences—General	M,D
Health Services Management and Hospital Administration	M,D
Microbiology	M,D
Nutrition	M,D
Toxicology	M,D
Zoology	M,D

TEXAS TECH UNIVERSITY HEALTH SCIENCES CENTER

Acute Care/Critical Care Nursing	M,D,O
Allopathic Medicine	D
Biological and Biomedical Sciences—General	M,D
Cell Biology	M,D
Communication Disorders	M,D
Family Nurse Practitioner Studies	M,D,O
Gerontological Nursing	M,D,O
Health Services Management and Hospital Administration	M
Molecular Pathology	M
Nursing and Healthcare Administration	M,D,O
Nursing Education	M,D,O
Nursing—General	M,D,O
Occupational Therapy	M
Pediatric Nursing	M,D,O
Pharmaceutical Sciences	M,D
Physical Therapy	D
Physician Assistant Studies	M
Rehabilitation Sciences	D

TEXAS TECH UNIVERSITY HEALTH SCIENCES CENTER EL PASO

Allopathic Medicine	D
Biological and Biomedical Sciences—General	M
Nursing General	M

TEXAS WESLEYAN UNIVERSITY

Nurse Anesthesia	M,D

TEXAS WOMAN'S UNIVERSITY

Acute Care/Critical Care Nursing	M,D
Adult Nursing	M,D
Allied Health—General	M,D
Biological and Biomedical Sciences—General	M,D
Communication Disorders	M
Dental Hygiene	M,D
Family Nurse Practitioner Studies	M,D
Gerontological Nursing	M,D
Health Services Management and Hospital Administration	M
Molecular Biology	M,D
Nursing and Healthcare Administration	M,D
Nursing Education	M,D
Nursing—General	M,D
Nutrition	M,D
Occupational Therapy	M,D
Pediatric Nursing	M,D
Physical Therapy	D
Women's Health Nursing	M,D

THOMAS EDISON STATE UNIVERSITY

Nursing and Healthcare Administration	M
Nursing Education	M
Nursing Informatics	M
Nursing—General	M,D
Public Health—General	M

THOMAS JEFFERSON UNIVERSITY

Allopathic Medicine	D
Biochemistry	D
Biological and Biomedical Sciences—General	M,D,O
Cancer Biology/Oncology	D
Cell Biology	M,D
Clinical Laboratory Sciences/Medical Technology	M
Clinical Research	M,O
Developmental Biology	M
Genetics	D
Genomic Sciences	D
Health Physics/Radiological Health	M
Health Services Management and Hospital Administration	M,D,O
Health Services Research	M,D,O
Human Genetics	M
Immunology	D
Infectious Diseases	O
Microbiology	M,D
Molecular Pharmacology	D
Neuroscience	D
Nurse Midwifery	M
Nursing—General	M,D
Occupational Therapy	M,D
Pharmacology	M
Pharmacy	D
Physical Therapy	D
Physician Assistant Studies	M
Public Health—General	M,O
Toxicology	M

THOMAS UNIVERSITY

Nursing—General	M

TIFFIN UNIVERSITY

Health Services Management and Hospital Administration	M

TOURO COLLEGE

Communication Disorders	M,D
Occupational Therapy	M,D
Physical Therapy	M,D
Physician Assistant Studies	M,D

TOURO UNIVERSITY CALIFORNIA

Osteopathic Medicine	M,D
Pharmacy	M,D
Public Health—General	M,D

TOWSON UNIVERSITY

Allied Health—General	M
Biological and Biomedical Sciences—General	M
Communication Disorders	M,D
Environmental and Occupational Health	D
Health Services Management and Hospital Administration	M,O
Nursing Education	O
Nursing—General	O
Occupational Therapy	M
Physician Assistant Studies	M

TRENT UNIVERSITY

Biological and Biomedical Sciences—General	M,D

TREVECCA NAZARENE UNIVERSITY

Health Services Management and Hospital Administration	M
Physician Assistant Studies	M

TRIDENT UNIVERSITY INTERNATIONAL

Clinical Research	M,D,O
Environmental and Occupational Health	M,D,O
Health Services Management and Hospital Administration	M,D,O
International Health	M,D,O
Public Health—General	M,D,O

TRINE UNIVERSITY

Physical Therapy	D
Physician Assistant Studies	M

TRINITY INTERNATIONAL UNIVERSITY

Bioethics	M,D

TRINITY UNIVERSITY

Health Services Management and Hospital Administration	M

TRINITY WASHINGTON UNIVERSITY

Public Health—General	M

TRINITY WESTERN UNIVERSITY

Health Services Management and Hospital Administration	M,O
Nursing—General	M

TRI-STATE COLLEGE OF ACUPUNCTURE

Acupuncture and Oriental Medicine	M,O

TROPICAL AGRICULTURE RESEARCH AND HIGHER EDUCATION CENTER

Conservation Biology	M,D

TROY UNIVERSITY

Adult Nursing	M,D
Biological and Biomedical Sciences—General	M,O
Family Nurse Practitioner Studies	M,D
Health Services Management and Hospital Administration	M
Maternal and Child Health	M,D
Nursing Informatics	M,D
Nursing—General	M,D

TRUETT MCCONNELL UNIVERSITY

Biological and Biomedical Sciences—General	M

TRUMAN STATE UNIVERSITY

Biological and Biomedical Sciences—General	M
Communication Disorders	M

TUFTS UNIVERSITY

Allopathic Medicine	D
Biochemistry	D
Biological and Biomedical Sciences—General	M,D,O
Cancer Biology/Oncology	D
Cell Biology	D
Clinical Laboratory Sciences/Medical Technology	M,D,O
Dentistry	D
Developmental Biology	D
Environmental and Occupational Health	M,D
Epidemiology	M,D,O
Genetics	D
Health Services Management and Hospital Administration	M,D,O
Immunology	D
Infectious Diseases	M,D
Microbiology	D
Molecular Biology	D
Molecular Medicine	D
Neuroscience	M,D
Nutrition	M,D,O
Occupational Therapy	M,D,O
Oral and Dental Sciences	M,O
Pathology	M,D
Physician Assistant Studies	M,D,O
Public Health—General	M,D,O
Reproductive Biology	M,D
Structural Biology	D
Veterinary Medicine	M,D

TULANE UNIVERSITY

Allopathic Medicine	D
Biochemistry	M
Biological and Biomedical Sciences—General	M,D
Cell Biology	M,D
Community Health	M,D
Ecology	M,D
Environmental and Occupational Health	M,D
Epidemiology	M,D
Evolutionary Biology	M,D
Health Promotion	M
Health Services Management and Hospital Administration	M,D
Human Genetics	M
Immunology	M
International Health	M,D
Microbiology	M
Molecular Biology	M,D
Neuroscience	M,D
Parasitology	M,D,O
Pharmacology	M
Physiology	M
Public Health—General	M,D
Structural Biology	M,D

TUSCULUM COLLEGE

Family Nurse Practitioner Studies	M
Nursing—General	M

TUSKEGEE UNIVERSITY

Biological and Biomedical Sciences—General	M,D
Nutrition	M
Occupational Therapy	M
Veterinary Medicine	M,D
Veterinary Sciences	M,D

UNIFORMED SERVICES UNIVERSITY OF THE HEALTH SCIENCES

Allopathic Medicine	M,D

*M—masters degree; D—doctorate; O—other advanced degree; *—Close-Up and/or Display*

Biological and Biomedical Sciences—General M,D
Cell Biology M,D
Environmental and Occupational Health M,D
Family Nurse Practitioner Studies M,D
Gerontological Nursing M,D
Health Services Management and Hospital Administration M,D
Immunology D
Infectious Diseases D*
International Health M,D
Molecular Biology M,D*
Neuroscience D*
Nurse Anesthesia M,D
Nursing—General M,D
Psychiatric Nursing M,D
Public Health—General M,D
Women's Health Nursing M,D
Zoology M,D

UNION COLLEGE (NE)
Physician Assistant Studies M

UNION INSTITUTE & UNIVERSITY
Health Promotion M
Health Services Management and Hospital Administration M

UNION UNIVERSITY
Family Nurse Practitioner Studies M,D,O
Nurse Anesthesia M,D,O
Nursing and Healthcare Administration M,D,O
Nursing Education M,D,O
Nursing—General M,D,O
Pharmacy D

UNITED STATES UNIVERSITY
Family Nurse Practitioner Studies M

UNIVERSIDAD ADVENTISTA DE LAS ANTILLAS
Medical/Surgical Nursing M

UNIVERSIDAD AUTONOMA DE GUADALAJARA
Allopathic Medicine D
Environmental and Occupational Health M,D

UNIVERSIDAD CENTRAL DEL CARIBE
Allopathic Medicine M,D
Anatomy M,D
Biochemistry M,D
Biological and Biomedical Sciences—General M,D
Cell Biology M,D
Immunology M,D
Microbiology M,D
Molecular Biology M,D
Pharmacology M,D
Physiology M,D

UNIVERSIDAD CENTRAL DEL ESTE
Allopathic Medicine D
Dentistry D

UNIVERSIDAD DE CIENCIAS MEDICAS
Allopathic Medicine M,D,O
Anatomy M,D,O
Biological and Biomedical Sciences—General M,D,O
Community Health M,D,O
Environmental and Occupational Health M,D,O
Health Services Management and Hospital Administration M,D,O
Pharmacy M,D,O

UNIVERSIDAD DE IBEROAMERICA
Acute Care/Critical Care Nursing M,D
Allopathic Medicine M,D
Health Services Management and Hospital Administration M,D
Neuroscience M,D

UNIVERSIDAD DE LAS AMÉRICAS PUEBLA
Clinical Laboratory Sciences/Medical Technology M

UNIVERSIDAD DEL TURABO
Adult Nursing M,O
Communication Disorders M
Environmental Biology M,D
Family Nurse Practitioner Studies M,O
Health Promotion M
Naturopathic Medicine D

UNIVERSIDAD IBEROAMERICANA
Allopathic Medicine D
Dentistry M,D

UNIVERSIDAD METROPOLITANA
Nursing and Healthcare Administration M,O
Nursing—General M,O
Oncology Nursing M,O

UNIVERSIDAD NACIONAL PEDRO HENRIQUEZ URENA
Allopathic Medicine D
Dentistry D
Ecology M

UNIVERSITÉ DE MONCTON
Biochemistry M
Biological and Biomedical Sciences—General M
Nutrition M

UNIVERSITÉ DE MONTRÉAL
Allopathic Medicine D
Biochemistry M,D,O
Bioethics M,D,O
Biological and Biomedical Sciences—General M,D
Cell Biology M,D
Communication Disorders M,O
Community Health M,D,O
Dental Hygiene O
Environmental and Occupational Health M
Genetics O
Health Services Management and Hospital Administration M,O
Immunology M,D
Microbiology M,D
Molecular Biology M,D
Neuroscience M,D
Nursing—General M,D,O
Nutrition M,D,O
Occupational Therapy O
Optometry D
Oral and Dental Sciences M,O
Pathology M,D
Pharmaceutical Sciences M,D,O
Pharmacology M,D
Physiology M,D
Public Health—General M,D,O
Rehabilitation Sciences O
Toxicology O
Veterinary Medicine D
Veterinary Sciences M,D
Virology D
Vision Sciences M,O

UNIVERSITÉ DE SHERBROOKE
Allopathic Medicine D
Biochemistry M,D
Biological and Biomedical Sciences—General M,D,O
Biophysics M,D
Cell Biology M,D
Clinical Laboratory Sciences/Medical Technology M,D
Immunology M,D
Microbiology M,D
Pharmacology M,D
Physiology M,D
Radiation Biology M,D

UNIVERSITÉ DU QUÉBEC À CHICOUTIMI
Genetics M

UNIVERSITÉ DU QUÉBEC À MONTRÉAL
Biological and Biomedical Sciences—General M,D
Environmental and Occupational Health O

UNIVERSITÉ DU QUÉBEC À RIMOUSKI
Nursing—General M,O

UNIVERSITÉ DU QUÉBEC À TROIS-RIVIÈRES
Biophysics M,D
Chiropractic D
Nursing—General M,O

UNIVERSITÉ DU QUÉBEC EN ABITIBI-TÉMISCAMINGUE
Biological and Biomedical Sciences—General M,D

UNIVERSITÉ DU QUÉBEC EN OUTAOUAIS
Nursing—General M,O

UNIVERSITÉ DU QUÉBEC, INSTITUT NATIONAL DE LA RECHERCHE SCIENTIFIQUE
Biological and Biomedical Sciences—General M,D
Immunology M,D
Medical Microbiology M,D
Microbiology M,D
Virology M,D

UNIVERSITÉ LAVAL
Allopathic Medicine D,O
Anatomy O
Anesthesiologist Assistant Studies O
Biochemistry M,D,O
Biological and Biomedical Sciences—General M,D,O
Cancer Biology/Oncology O
Cardiovascular Sciences O
Cell Biology M,D
Communication Disorders M
Community Health M,D,O
Dentistry D
Emergency Medical Services O
Environmental and Occupational Health O
Epidemiology M,D
Health Physics/Radiological Health O
Immunology M,D
Infectious Diseases O
Microbiology M,D
Molecular Biology M,D
Neurobiology M,D
Nursing—General M,D,O
Nutrition M,D
Oral and Dental Sciences M,O
Pathology O
Pharmaceutical Sciences M,D,O
Physiology M,D
Plant Biology M,D

UNIVERSITY AT ALBANY, STATE UNIVERSITY OF NEW YORK
Biological and Biomedical Sciences—General M,D
Environmental and Occupational Health M,D
Epidemiology M,D
Health Services Management and Hospital Administration M,D,O
Neuroscience M,D
Public Health—General M,D
Toxicology M,D

UNIVERSITY AT BUFFALO, THE STATE UNIVERSITY OF NEW YORK
Adult Nursing M,D,O
Allied Health—General M,D,O
Allopathic Medicine D
Anatomy M,D
Biochemistry M,D
Biological and Biomedical Sciences—General M,D
Biophysics M,D
Cancer Biology/Oncology M
Cell Biology M,D
Clinical Laboratory Sciences/Medical Technology M
Communication Disorders M,D
Community Health M,D,O
Dentistry D
Ecology M,D,O
Epidemiology M,D
Evolutionary Biology M,D,O
Family Nurse Practitioner Studies M,D,O
Genetics M,D
Genomic Sciences M,D
Gerontological Nursing M,D,O
Health Services Management and Hospital Administration M,D
Immunology M,D
Medical Physics M,D
Medicinal and Pharmaceutical Chemistry M,D
Microbiology M,D
Molecular Biology D
Molecular Biophysics M,D
Molecular Pharmacology D
Neuroscience M,D
Nurse Anesthesia M,D,O
Nursing and Healthcare Administration M,D,O
Nursing—General M,D,O
Nutrition M,D,O
Occupational Therapy M
Oral and Dental Sciences M,D,O
Pathology M,D
Pharmaceutical Sciences M,D
Pharmacology M,D
Pharmacy D
Physical Therapy D
Physiology M,D
Psychiatric Nursing M,D,O
Public Health—General M,D
Rehabilitation Sciences O
Structural Biology M,D
Toxicology M,D

THE UNIVERSITY OF AKRON
Biological and Biomedical Sciences—General M,D
Communication Disorders M,D
Health Services Management and Hospital Administration M
Nursing—General M,D
Public Health—General M,D

THE UNIVERSITY OF ALABAMA
Biological and Biomedical Sciences—General M,D
Communication Disorders M
Community Health M
Health Promotion M,D
Nursing—General M,D
Nutrition M

THE UNIVERSITY OF ALABAMA AT BIRMINGHAM
Adult Nursing M,D
Allied Health—General M,D,O
Allopathic Medicine D
Biochemistry D
Biological and Biomedical Sciences—General M,D
Cancer Biology/Oncology D
Cell Biology D
Clinical Laboratory Sciences/Medical Technology M,D
Community Health M
Dentistry D
Developmental Biology D
Environmental and Occupational Health M,D
Epidemiology M,D
Family Nurse Practitioner Studies M,D
Genetics D
Genomic Sciences D
Gerontological Nursing M,D
Health Promotion D
Health Services Management and Hospital Administration M,D
Health Services Research M,D
Immunology D
Industrial Hygiene M,D
Maternal and Child Health M,D
Microbiology D
Molecular Biology D
Molecular Medicine D
Neuroscience M,D
Nurse Anesthesia M,D
Nursing and Healthcare Administration M,D
Nursing Informatics M,D
Nursing—General M,D
Nutrition M,D
Occupational Therapy M,O
Optometry D
Oral and Dental Sciences M
Pathobiology D
Pediatric Nursing M,D
Physical Therapy D
Physician Assistant Studies M
Psychiatric Nursing M,D
Public Health—General M,D
Rehabilitation Sciences D
Structural Biology D
Toxicology M,D
Vision Sciences M,D
Women's Health Nursing M,D

THE UNIVERSITY OF ALABAMA IN HUNTSVILLE
Acute Care/Critical Care Nursing M,D,O
Biological and Biomedical Sciences—General M,D
Family Nurse Practitioner Studies M,D,O
Gerontological Nursing M,D,O
Health Services Management and Hospital Administration M,D,O
Nursing Education M,D,O
Nursing—General M,D,O

UNIVERSITY OF ALASKA ANCHORAGE
Biological and Biomedical Sciences—General M
Health Services Management and Hospital Administration M
Public Health—General M

UNIVERSITY OF ALASKA FAIRBANKS
Biochemistry M,D
Biological and Biomedical Sciences—General M,D,O
Marine Biology M,D
Neuroscience M,D

UNIVERSITY OF ALBERTA
Biochemistry M,D
Biological and Biomedical Sciences—General M,D
Cancer Biology/Oncology M,D
Cell Biology M,D
Clinical Laboratory Sciences/Medical Technology M,D
Communication Disorders M,D
Community Health M,D
Conservation Biology M,D
Dental Hygiene O
Dentistry D
Ecology M,D
Environmental and Occupational Health M,D
Environmental Biology M,D
Epidemiology M,D
Evolutionary Biology M,D
Genetics M,D
Health Physics/Radiological Health M,D
Health Promotion M,O
Health Services Management and Hospital Administration M,D
Health Services Research M,D
Immunology M,D
International Health M,D
Maternal and Child/Neonatal Nursing D
Medical Microbiology M,D
Medical Physics M,D
Microbiology M,D
Molecular Biology M,D
Neuroscience M,D
Nursing—General M,D
Occupational Therapy M,D
Oral and Dental Sciences M,D
Pathology M,D
Pharmaceutical Sciences M,D
Pharmacology M,D
Pharmacy M,D
Physical Therapy M,D
Physiology M,D
Plant Biology M,D
Public Health—General M,D
Rehabilitation Sciences D
Vision Sciences M,D

THE UNIVERSITY OF ARIZONA
Allopathic Medicine M,D
Biochemistry M,D
Biological and Biomedical Sciences—General M,D
Cancer Biology/Oncology D
Cell Biology D
Communication Disorders M,D,O
Ecology M,D
Entomology M,D
Epidemiology M,D
Evolutionary Biology M,D
Family Nurse Practitioner Studies M,D,O
Genetics M,D
Immunology D
Medical Physics M
Microbiology D
Molecular Biology D
Molecular Medicine M,D
Neuroscience D
Nursing—General M,D,O
Nutrition M,D
Perfusion M,D
Pharmaceutical Sciences M,D
Pharmacology M,D
Pharmacy D
Physiology M,D
Plant Pathology M,D
Public Health—General M,D

UNIVERSITY OF ARKANSAS
Biological and Biomedical Sciences—General M,D
Cell Biology M,D
Communication Disorders M
Community Health M,D
Entomology M,D
Health Promotion M,D
Molecular Biology M,D
Nursing—General M
Plant Pathology M

UNIVERSITY OF ARKANSAS AT LITTLE ROCK
Biological and Biomedical Sciences—General M

UNIVERSITY OF ARKANSAS FOR MEDICAL SCIENCES
Allopathic Medicine D
Biochemistry M,D,O

Biological and Biomedical Sciences—General	M,D,O
Communication Disorders	M,D
Environmental and Occupational Health	M,D,O
Epidemiology	M,D,O
Health Physics/Radiological Health	M,D
Health Promotion	M,D,O
Health Services Management and Hospital Administration	M,D,O
Health Services Research	M,D,O
Immunology	M,D,O
Microbiology	M,D,O
Molecular Biology	M,D,O
Molecular Biophysics	M,D,O
Neurobiology	M,D,O
Nursing—General	D
Nutrition	M,D,O
Pharmacology	M,D,O
Pharmacy	M,D
Physician Assistant Studies	M,D
Physiology	M,D,O
Public Health—General	M,D,O
Toxicology	M,D,O

UNIVERSITY OF ARKANSAS–FORT SMITH

Health Services Management and Hospital Administration	M

UNIVERSITY OF BALTIMORE

Health Services Management and Hospital Administration	M

UNIVERSITY OF BRIDGEPORT

Acupuncture and Oriental Medicine	M
Chiropractic	D
Dental Hygiene	M
Naturopathic Medicine	D
Nutrition	M
Physician Assistant Studies	M

THE UNIVERSITY OF BRITISH COLUMBIA

Allopathic Medicine	M,D
Biochemistry	M,D
Biopsychology	M,D
Botany	M,D
Cell Biology	M,D
Communication Disorders	M,D
Dentistry	D
Developmental Biology	M,D
Genetics	M,D
Health Services Management and Hospital Administration	M,D
Immunology	M,D
Infectious Diseases	M,D
Microbiology	M,D
Molecular Biology	M,D
Neuroscience	M,D
Nursing—General	M,D
Nutrition	M,D
Occupational Therapy	M
Oral and Dental Sciences	M,D
Pathology	M,D
Pharmaceutical Sciences	M,D
Pharmacology	M,D
Pharmacy	M,D
Physical Therapy	M
Public Health—General	M,D
Rehabilitation Sciences	M,D
Reproductive Biology	M,D
Zoology	M,D

UNIVERSITY OF CALGARY

Allopathic Medicine	D
Biochemistry	M,D
Biological and Biomedical Sciences—General	M,D
Cancer Biology/Oncology	M,D
Cardiovascular Sciences	M,D
Community Health	M,D
Genetics	M,D
Immunology	M,D
Infectious Diseases	M,D
Microbiology	M,D
Molecular Biology	M,D
Molecular Genetics	M,D
Neuroscience	M,D
Nursing—General	M,D,O
Pathology	M,D
Physiology	M,D

UNIVERSITY OF CALIFORNIA, BERKELEY

Allopathic Medicine	
Biochemistry	D
Biological and Biomedical Sciences—General	D
Biophysics	D
Cell Biology	D
Clinical Research	O
Environmental and Occupational Health	M,D
Epidemiology	M,D
Health Services Management and Hospital Administration	D
Immunology	D
Infectious Diseases	M,D
Microbiology	D
Molecular Biology	D
Molecular Toxicology	D
Neuroscience	D
Nutrition	M,D
Optometry	D,O
Physiology	M,D
Plant Biology	D
Public Health—General	M,D
Vision Sciences	M,D

UNIVERSITY OF CALIFORNIA, DAVIS

Allopathic Medicine	D
Animal Behavior	D
Biochemistry	M,D
Biophysics	M,D
Cell Biology	M,D
Clinical Research	M
Developmental Biology	M,D
Ecology	M,D
Entomology	M,D
Epidemiology	M,D
Evolutionary Biology	D
Genetics	M,D
Immunology	M,D
Maternal and Child Health	M
Microbiology	M,D
Molecular Biology	M,D
Neuroscience	D
Nutrition	M,D
Pathology	M,D
Pharmacology	M,D
Physiology	M,D
Plant Biology	M,D
Plant Pathology	M,D
Toxicology	M,D
Veterinary Medicine	D
Veterinary Sciences	M,O
Zoology	M

UNIVERSITY OF CALIFORNIA, IRVINE

Allopathic Medicine	D
Anatomy	M,D
Biochemistry	M,D
Biological and Biomedical Sciences—General	M,D
Biophysics	D
Cell Biology	M,D
Computational Biology	D
Developmental Biology	M,D
Ecology	M,D
Environmental and Occupational Health	M,D
Epidemiology	M,D
Evolutionary Biology	M,D
Genetics	D
Health Services Management and Hospital Administration	M
Medicinal and Pharmaceutical Chemistry	D
Microbiology	M,D
Molecular Biology	M,D
Molecular Genetics	M,D
Neurobiology	M,D
Neuroscience	D
Nursing—General	M
Pathology	D
Pharmaceutical Sciences	D
Physiology	D
Public Health—General	M,D
Systems Biology	D
Toxicology	M,D
Translational Biology	M

UNIVERSITY OF CALIFORNIA, LOS ANGELES

Allopathic Medicine	D
Anatomy	M,D
Biochemistry	M,D
Biological and Biomedical Sciences—General	M,D
Cell Biology	M,D
Clinical Research	M
Community Health	M,D
Dentistry	D,O
Developmental Biology	M,D
Ecology	M,D
Environmental and Occupational Health	M,D
Epidemiology	M,D
Evolutionary Biology	M,D
Health Services Management and Hospital Administration	M,D
Human Genetics	M,D
Immunology	M,D
Medical Physics	M,D
Microbiology	M,D
Molecular Biology	M,D
Molecular Genetics	M,D
Molecular Physiology	D
Molecular Toxicology	D
Neurobiology	M,D
Neuroscience	D
Nursing—General	M,D
Oral and Dental Sciences	M,D
Pathology	M,D
Pharmacology	M,D
Physiology	M,D
Public Health—General	M,D
Toxicology	D

UNIVERSITY OF CALIFORNIA, MERCED

Biochemistry	M,D
Biological and Biomedical Sciences—General	M,D
Systems Biology	M,D

UNIVERSITY OF CALIFORNIA, RIVERSIDE

Allopathic Medicine	D
Biochemistry	M,D
Biological and Biomedical Sciences—General	M,D
Botany	M,D
Cell Biology	M,D
Developmental Biology	M,D
Entomology	M,D
Evolutionary Biology	M,D
Genetics	D
Genomic Sciences	D
International Health	M,D
Microbiology	M,D
Molecular Biology	M,D
Neuroscience	D
Plant Biology	M,D
Plant Molecular Biology	M,D
Plant Pathology	M,D
Toxicology	M,D

UNIVERSITY OF CALIFORNIA, SAN DIEGO

Allopathic Medicine	D
Biochemistry	M,D
Biological and Biomedical Sciences—General	M,D*
Biophysics	M,D
Clinical Laboratory Sciences/Medical Technology	M,D
Clinical Research	M
Communication Disorders	D
Epidemiology	D
Health Services Management and Hospital Administration	M
International Health	D
Neuroscience	M,D
Pharmacy	D
Public Health—General	D
Systems Biology	D*

UNIVERSITY OF CALIFORNIA, SAN FRANCISCO

Allopathic Medicine	D
Biochemistry	D
Biological and Biomedical Sciences—General	D
Biophysics	D
Cell Biology	D
Dentistry	D
Developmental Biology	D
Genetics	D
Genomic Sciences	D
Medical Imaging	M
Medicinal and Pharmaceutical Chemistry	D
Molecular Biology	D
Neuroscience	D
Nursing—General	M,D
Oral and Dental Sciences	M,D
Pharmaceutical Sciences	D
Pharmacology	D
Pharmacy	D
Physical Therapy	D

UNIVERSITY OF CALIFORNIA, SANTA BARBARA

Biochemistry	D
Biophysics	D
Cell Biology	M,D
Developmental Biology	M,D
Ecology	M,D
Evolutionary Biology	M,D
Marine Biology	M,D
Molecular Biology	M,D
Neuroscience	D

UNIVERSITY OF CALIFORNIA, SANTA CRUZ

Biochemistry	M,D
Cell Biology	M,D
Developmental Biology	M,D
Ecology	M,D
Environmental Biology	M,D
Evolutionary Biology	M,D
Molecular Biology	M,D
Toxicology	M,D

UNIVERSITY OF CENTRAL ARKANSAS

Adult Nursing	M,O
Biological and Biomedical Sciences—General	M
Communication Disorders	M,D
Family Nurse Practitioner Studies	M,O
Nursing and Healthcare Administration	M,O
Nursing Education	M,O
Nursing—General	M,O
Nutrition	M
Occupational Therapy	M
Physical Therapy	D

UNIVERSITY OF CENTRAL FLORIDA

Acute Care/Critical Care Nursing	M,D,O
Allopathic Medicine	M,D
Biological and Biomedical Sciences—General	M,D
Communication Disorders	M,D,O
Conservation Biology	M,D
Family Nurse Practitioner Studies	M,D,O
Gerontological Nursing	M,D,O
Health Services Management and Hospital Administration	M,O
Nursing Education	M,D,O
Nursing—General	M,D,O
Physical Therapy	D
Physiology	M

UNIVERSITY OF CENTRAL MISSOURI

Biological and Biomedical Sciences—General	M,D,O
Communication Disorders	M,D,O
Environmental and Occupational Health	M,D,O
Industrial Hygiene	M,D,O
Nursing—General	M,D,O

UNIVERSITY OF CENTRAL OKLAHOMA

Biological and Biomedical Sciences—General	M
Communication Disorders	M
Health Promotion	M
Nursing—General	M
Nutrition	M

UNIVERSITY OF CHARLESTON

Pharmacy	D
Physician Assistant Studies	M

UNIVERSITY OF CHICAGO

Allopathic Medicine	D
Anatomy	D
Biological and Biomedical Sciences—General	D
Biophysics	D
Cancer Biology/Oncology	D
Cell Biology	D
Developmental Biology	D
Ecology	D
Evolutionary Biology	D
Genetics	D
Genomic Sciences	D
Health Promotion	M,D
Health Services Management and Hospital Administration	M,O
Human Genetics	D
Immunology	D
Medical Physics	D
Microbiology	D
Molecular Biology	D
Molecular Biophysics	D
Neurobiology	D
Neuroscience	D
Nutrition	D
Systems Biology	D
Zoology	D

UNIVERSITY OF CINCINNATI

Acute Care/Critical Care Nursing	M,D
Adult Nursing	M,D
Allopathic Medicine	D
Biochemistry	M,D
Biological and Biomedical Sciences—General	M,D,O
Biophysics	D
Cancer Biology/Oncology	D
Cell Biology	D
Communication Disorders	M,D
Developmental Biology	D
Environmental and Occupational Health	M,D
Epidemiology	M,D
Genomic Sciences	M,D
Gerontological Nursing	M,D
Health Physics/Radiological Health	M
Health Promotion	M,D
Health Services Research	M
Immunology	M,D
Industrial Hygiene	M,D
Maternal and Child/Neonatal Nursing	M,D
Medical Imaging	M,D
Medical Physics	M
Microbiology	M,D
Molecular Biology	M,D
Molecular Genetics	M,D
Molecular Medicine	D
Molecular Toxicology	M,D
Neuroscience	D
Nurse Anesthesia	M,D
Nurse Midwifery	M,D
Nursing and Healthcare Administration	M,D
Nursing—General	M,D
Nutrition	M
Occupational Health Nursing	M,D
Pathobiology	D
Pathology	D
Pediatric Nursing	M,D
Pharmaceutical Sciences	M,D
Pharmacology	D
Pharmacy	D
Physical Therapy	D
Public Health—General	M,D
Systems Biology	D
Women's Health Nursing	M,D

UNIVERSITY OF COLORADO BOULDER

Biochemistry	M,D
Cell Biology	M,D
Communication Disorders	M,D
Developmental Biology	M,D
Ecology	M,D
Evolutionary Biology	M,D
Molecular Biology	M,D
Physiology	M,D

UNIVERSITY OF COLORADO COLORADO SPRINGS

Adult Nursing	M,D
Gerontological Nursing	M,D
Nursing—General	M,D

UNIVERSITY OF COLORADO DENVER

Adult Nursing	M,D
Allopathic Medicine	D
Anatomy	M,D
Anesthesiologist Assistant Studies	M
Biochemistry	D
Biological and Biomedical Sciences—General	M,D
Biophysics	M
Cancer Biology/Oncology	D
Cell Biology	M,D
Clinical Laboratory Sciences/Medical Technology	M,D
Clinical Research	M,D
Community Health	M,D,O
Computational Biology	M,D
Dentistry	D,O
Developmental Biology	M,D
Ecology	M
Environmental and Occupational Health	M
Epidemiology	M,D
Family Nurse Practitioner Studies	M,D
Genetics	D
Genomic Sciences	D
Health Services Management and Hospital Administration	M
Health Services Research	M,D
Immunology	D
International Health	M
Microbiology	D

*M—masters degree; D—doctorate; O—other advanced degree; *—Close-Up and/or Display*

Molecular Biology	D
Molecular Genetics	D
Neuroscience	D
Nurse Midwifery	M,D
Nursing and Healthcare Administration	M,D
Nursing—General	M,D
Oral and Dental Sciences	D,O
Pediatric Nursing	M,D
Pharmaceutical Sciences	D
Pharmacology	D
Pharmacy	D
Physical Therapy	D
Physician Assistant Studies	M
Psychiatric Nursing	M,D
Public Health—General	M,D
Rehabilitation Sciences	D
Systems Biology	M,D
Toxicology	D
Women's Health Nursing	M,D

UNIVERSITY OF CONNECTICUT

Biophysics	M,D
Biopsychology	M,D
Botany	M,D
Cell Biology	M,D
Communication Disorders	M,D
Developmental Biology	M,D
Ecology	M,D
Environmental and Occupational Health	O
Genetics	M,D
Genomic Sciences	M,D
Gerontological Nursing	O
Health Services Management and Hospital Administration	M,D
Maternal and Child/Neonatal Nursing	O
Medicinal and Pharmaceutical Chemistry	M,D
Microbiology	M,D
Molecular Biology	M,D
Neurobiology	M,D
Neuroscience	M,D
Nursing—General	D,O*
Nutrition	M,D
Pathobiology	M,D
Pharmaceutical Sciences	M,D
Pharmacology	M,D
Pharmacy	D
Physical Therapy	D
Physiology	M,D
Structural Biology	M,D
Toxicology	M,D

UNIVERSITY OF CONNECTICUT HEALTH CENTER

Allopathic Medicine	D
Anatomy	D
Biochemistry	D
Biological and Biomedical Sciences—General	D
Cell Biology	D
Clinical Research	M
Dentistry	D,O
Developmental Biology	D
Genetics	D
Immunology	D
Molecular Biology	D
Neuroscience	D
Oral and Dental Sciences	M
Public Health—General	M

UNIVERSITY OF DALLAS

Health Services Management and Hospital Administration	M,D

UNIVERSITY OF DAYTON

Biochemistry	M
Biological and Biomedical Sciences—General	M,D
Physical Therapy	D
Physician Assistant Studies	M

UNIVERSITY OF DELAWARE

Adult Nursing	M,O
Biochemistry	M,D
Biological and Biomedical Sciences—General	M,D
Cancer Biology/Oncology	M,D
Cell Biology	M,D
Communication Disorders	M
Developmental Biology	M,D
Ecology	M,D
Entomology	M,D
Evolutionary Biology	M,D
Family Nurse Practitioner Studies	M,O
Genetics	M,D
Gerontological Nursing	M,O
Health Promotion	M
HIV/AIDS Nursing	M,O
Maternal and Child/Neonatal Nursing	M,O
Microbiology	M,D
Molecular Biology	M,D
Neuroscience	D
Nursing and Healthcare Administration	M,O
Nursing—General	M,O
Nutrition	M
Oncology Nursing	M,O
Pediatric Nursing	M,O
Physical Therapy	D
Physiology	M,D
Psychiatric Nursing	M,O
Women's Health Nursing	M,O

UNIVERSITY OF DENVER

Biological and Biomedical Sciences—General	M,D
Cell Biology	M,D
Ecology	M,D
Evolutionary Biology	M,D
Health Services Management and Hospital Administration	M,O
International Health	M,D,O
Molecular Biology	M,D

UNIVERSITY OF DETROIT MERCY

Allied Health—General	M,D,O
Dentistry	M,D,O
Family Nurse Practitioner Studies	M,D,O
Health Services Management and Hospital Administration	M,D,O
Nurse Anesthesia	M,D,O
Nursing Education	M,D,O
Nursing—General	M,D,O
Oral and Dental Sciences	M,D,O
Physician Assistant Studies	M,D,O

UNIVERSITY OF EAST-WEST MEDICINE

Acupuncture and Oriental Medicine	M,D

UNIVERSITY OF EVANSVILLE

Health Services Management and Hospital Administration	M
Physical Therapy	D

THE UNIVERSITY OF FINDLAY

Health Services Management and Hospital Administration	M,D
Occupational Therapy	M,D
Pharmacy	M,D
Physical Therapy	M,D
Physician Assistant Studies	M,D

UNIVERSITY OF FLORIDA

Allied Health—General	M,D,O
Allopathic Medicine	D
Biochemistry	D
Biological and Biomedical Sciences—General	M,D
Botany	M,D
Cell Biology	M,D
Clinical Laboratory Sciences/Medical Technology	M,D
Clinical Research	M,D,O
Communication Disorders	M,D
Dentistry	D,O
Ecology	M,D,O
Environmental and Occupational Health	M,D,O
Epidemiology	M,D,O
Genetics	D
Health Services Management and Hospital Administration	M,D
Health Services Research	M,D
Immunology	D
International Health	M,D
Medical Physics	M,D,O
Medicinal and Pharmaceutical Chemistry	M,D
Microbiology	M,D
Molecular Biology	M,D
Molecular Genetics	M,D
Neuroscience	D
Nursing—General	M,D
Nutrition	M,D
Occupational Therapy	M
Oral and Dental Sciences	M,D,O
Pharmaceutical Administration	M,D
Pharmaceutical Sciences	M,D
Pharmacology	M,D
Pharmacy	M,D
Physical Therapy	D
Physician Assistant Studies	M
Physiology	M,D
Plant Biology	M,D
Plant Molecular Biology	M,D
Plant Pathology	M,D
Public Health—General	M,D,O
Rehabilitation Sciences	D
Toxicology	M,D,O
Veterinary Medicine	D
Veterinary Sciences	M,D,O
Zoology	M,D

UNIVERSITY OF GEORGIA

Biochemistry	M,D
Biological and Biomedical Sciences—General	D
Cell Biology	M,D
Communication Disorders	M,D,O
Ecology	M,D
Entomology	M,D
Environmental and Occupational Health	M,D
Genetics	M,D
Genomic Sciences	M,D
Health Promotion	M,D
Infectious Diseases	D
Microbiology	M,D
Molecular Biology	M,D
Neuroscience	D
Nutrition	M,D
Pathology	M,D
Pharmaceutical Administration	D
Pharmaceutical Sciences	M,D
Pharmacology	M,D
Pharmacy	M,D,O
Physiology	M,D
Plant Biology	M,D
Plant Pathology	M,D
Public Health—General	D
Veterinary Medicine	M,D

UNIVERSITY OF GUAM

Biological and Biomedical Sciences—General	M
Marine Biology	M

UNIVERSITY OF GUELPH

Acute Care/Critical Care Nursing	M,D,O
Anatomy	M,D
Anesthesiologist Assistant Studies	M,D,O
Biochemistry	M,D
Biological and Biomedical Sciences—General	M,D
Biophysics	M,D
Botany	M,D
Cardiovascular Sciences	M,D,O
Cell Biology	M,D
Ecology	M,D
Emergency Medical Services	M,D,O
Entomology	M,D
Environmental Biology	M,D
Epidemiology	M,D
Evolutionary Biology	M,D
Immunology	M,D,O
Infectious Diseases	M,D,O
Medical Imaging	M,D,O
Microbiology	M,D
Molecular Biology	M,D
Molecular Genetics	M,D
Neuroscience	M,D,O
Nutrition	M,D
Pathology	M,D,O
Pharmacology	M,D
Physiology	M,D
Plant Pathology	M,D
Toxicology	M,D
Veterinary Medicine	M,D,O
Veterinary Sciences	M,D,O
Vision Sciences	M,D,O
Zoology	M,D

UNIVERSITY OF HARTFORD

Biological and Biomedical Sciences—General	M
Community Health Nursing	M
Neuroscience	M
Nursing Education	M
Nursing—General	M
Physical Therapy	M,D

UNIVERSITY OF HAWAII AT HILO

Conservation Biology	M
Marine Biology	M
Nursing—General	D
Pharmaceutical Sciences	D*
Pharmacology	M
Pharmacy	D

UNIVERSITY OF HAWAII AT MANOA

Adult Nursing	M,D,O
Allopathic Medicine	D
Biological and Biomedical Sciences—General	M,D
Botany	M,D
Communication Disorders	M
Community Health Nursing	M,D,O
Developmental Biology	M,D
Entomology	M,D
Epidemiology	D
Family Nurse Practitioner Studies	M,D,O
Genetics	M,D
Marine Biology	M,D
Medical Microbiology	M,D
Microbiology	M,D
Molecular Biology	M,D
Nursing and Healthcare Administration	M,D,O
Nursing—General	M,D,O
Nutrition	M,D
Physiology	M,D
Plant Pathology	M,D
Public Health—General	M,D,O
Reproductive Biology	M,D
Zoology	M,D

UNIVERSITY OF HOLY CROSS

Biological and Biomedical Sciences—General	M,D
Health Services Management and Hospital Administration	M,D

UNIVERSITY OF HOUSTON

Biochemistry	M,D
Biological and Biomedical Sciences—General	M,D
Communication Disorders	M
Family Nurse Practitioner Studies	M
Nursing and Healthcare Administration	M
Nursing Education	M
Nursing—General	M
Nutrition	M,D
Optometry	D
Pharmaceutical Administration	M,D
Pharmaceutical Sciences	M,D
Pharmacology	M,D
Pharmacy	M,D
Vision Sciences	M,D

UNIVERSITY OF HOUSTON–CLEAR LAKE

Biological and Biomedical Sciences—General	M
Health Services Management and Hospital Administration	M

UNIVERSITY OF HOUSTON–VICTORIA

Biological and Biomedical Sciences—General	M

UNIVERSITY OF IDAHO

Biochemistry	M,D
Biological and Biomedical Sciences—General	M,D
Computational Biology	M,D
Entomology	M,D
Microbiology	M,D
Plant Pathology	M,D
Veterinary Sciences	M,D

UNIVERSITY OF ILLINOIS AT CHICAGO

Acute Care/Critical Care Nursing	M,O
Adult Nursing	M,O
Allied Health—General	M,D,O
Allopathic Medicine	D
Anatomy	M
Biochemistry	D
Biological and Biomedical Sciences—General	M,D
Biophysics	M,D
Cell Biology	M,D
Community Health Nursing	M,O
Community Health	M,D
Dentistry	D
Environmental and Occupational Health	M,D
Epidemiology	M,D
Family Nurse Practitioner Studies	M,O
Genetics	D
Gerontological Nursing	M,O
Health Services Management and Hospital Administration	M,D
Health Services Research	M,D
Immunology	D
Maternal and Child/Neonatal Nursing	M,O
Medicinal and Pharmaceutical Chemistry	M,D
Microbiology	D
Molecular Biology	D
Molecular Genetics	D
Neuroscience	M,D
Nurse Midwifery	M,O
Nursing and Healthcare Administration	M,O
Nursing—General	M,D,O
Nutrition	M,D
Occupational Health Nursing	M,O
Occupational Therapy	M,D
Oral and Dental Sciences	M,D
Pediatric Nursing	M,O
Pharmaceutical Administration	M,D
Pharmaceutical Sciences	M,D
Pharmacology	D
Pharmacy	D
Physical Therapy	M,D
Physiology	M,D
Public Health—General	M,D
School Nursing	M,O
Toxicology	M,D
Women's Health Nursing	M,O

UNIVERSITY OF ILLINOIS AT SPRINGFIELD

Biological and Biomedical Sciences—General	M
Community Health	M,O
Environmental and Occupational Health	M,O
Epidemiology	M,O
Public Health—General	M,O

UNIVERSITY OF ILLINOIS AT URBANA–CHAMPAIGN

Biochemistry	M,D
Biological and Biomedical Sciences—General	M,D
Biophysics	M,D
Cell Biology	D
Communication Disorders	M,D
Community Health	M,D
Computational Biology	M,D
Conservation Biology	M,D
Developmental Biology	D
Ecology	M,D
Entomology	M,D
Evolutionary Biology	M,D
Health Services Management and Hospital Administration	M,D
Microbiology	M,D
Molecular Physiology	M,D
Neuroscience	D
Nutrition	M,D
Pathobiology	M,D
Physiology	M,D
Plant Biology	M,D
Public Health—General	M,D
Rehabilitation Sciences	M,D
Veterinary Medicine	D
Veterinary Sciences	M,D
Zoology	M,D

UNIVERSITY OF INDIANAPOLIS

Biological and Biomedical Sciences—General	M
Family Nurse Practitioner Studies	M,D
Maternal and Child/Neonatal Nursing	M,D
Nurse Midwifery	M,D
Nursing and Healthcare Administration	M,D
Nursing Education	M,D
Nursing—General	M,D
Occupational Therapy	M,D
Physical Therapy	M,D
Public Health—General	M
Women's Health Nursing	M,D

THE UNIVERSITY OF IOWA

Allopathic Medicine	D
Anatomy	D
Bacteriology	M,D
Biochemistry	M,D
Biological and Biomedical Sciences—General	M,D
Biophysics	M,D
Cell Biology	M,D
Clinical Research	M,D
Communication Disorders	M,D
Community Health	M,D
Computational Biology	M,D,O
Dentistry	M,D,O
Environmental and Occupational Health	M,D,O
Epidemiology	M,D
Evolutionary Biology	M,D
Genetics	M,D
Health Services Management and Hospital Administration	M,D
Immunology	M,D
Industrial Hygiene	M,D,O
Medicinal and Pharmaceutical Chemistry	M,D
Microbiology	M,D
Molecular Biology	D
Neurobiology	M,D
Neuroscience	D
Nursing—General	M,D
Oral and Dental Sciences	M,D,O

Pathology	M
Pharmaceutical Sciences	M,D
Pharmacology	M,D
Pharmacy	M,D
Physical Therapy	M,D
Physician Assistant Studies	M
Physiology	M,D
Public Health—General	M,D,O
Radiation Biology	M
Rehabilitation Sciences	M,D
Toxicology	M,D
Translational Biology	M,D
Virology	M,D

UNIVERSITY OF JAMESTOWN

Physical Therapy	D

THE UNIVERSITY OF KANSAS

Adult Nursing	M,D,O
Allied Health—General	M,D,O
Allopathic Medicine	D
Anatomy	M,D
Biochemistry	D
Biological and Biomedical Sciences—General	D
Biophysics	D
Cancer Biology/Oncology	M,D
Cell Biology	M,D
Clinical Research	M
Communication Disorders	M,D
Community Health Nursing	M,D,O
Community Health	M,D,O
Computational Biology	D
Developmental Biology	D
Ecology	M,D
Epidemiology	M
Evolutionary Biology	M,D
Gerontological Nursing	M,D,O
Health Promotion	M,D,O
Health Services Management and Hospital Administration	M,D
Medicinal and Pharmaceutical Chemistry	M,D
Microbiology	M,D
Molecular Biology	D
Neuroscience	M,D
Nurse Anesthesia	D
Nurse Midwifery	M,D,O
Nursing—General	M,D,O
Nutrition	M,D,O
Occupational Therapy	M,D
Pathology	M,D
Pharmacology	M,D
Pharmacy	M,D
Physical Therapy	D
Physiology	D
Psychiatric Nursing	M,D,O
Public Health—General	M
Rehabilitation Sciences	M,D
Toxicology	M,D

UNIVERSITY OF KENTUCKY

Allied Health—General	M,D
Allopathic Medicine	D
Anatomy	D
Biochemistry	D
Biological and Biomedical Sciences—General	M,D
Clinical Research	M
Communication Disorders	M
Dentistry	D
Entomology	M,D
Epidemiology	D
Health Physics/Radiological Health	M
Health Promotion	M,D
Health Services Management and Hospital Administration	M
Immunology	D
Medical Physics	M
Microbiology	D
Neurobiology	D
Nursing—General	D
Nutrition	M,D
Oral and Dental Sciences	M
Pharmaceutical Sciences	M,D
Pharmacology	D
Pharmacy	D
Physical Therapy	D
Physician Assistant Studies	M
Physiology	D
Plant Pathology	M,D
Public Health—General	M,D
Rehabilitation Sciences	D
Toxicology	M,D
Veterinary Sciences	M,D

UNIVERSITY OF LA VERNE

Health Services Management and Hospital Administration	M,D,O
Health Services Research	M
Public Health—General	M

UNIVERSITY OF LETHBRIDGE

Biochemistry	M,D
Biological and Biomedical Sciences—General	M,D
Molecular Biology	M,D
Neuroscience	M,D
Nursing—General	M,D

UNIVERSITY OF LOUISIANA AT LAFAYETTE

Biological and Biomedical Sciences—General	M,D
Communication Disorders	M,D
Environmental Biology	M,D
Evolutionary Biology	M,D
Family Nurse Practitioner Studies	M,D
Nursing and Healthcare Administration	M
Nursing Education	M,D
Nursing—General	M,D

UNIVERSITY OF LOUISIANA AT MONROE

Biological and Biomedical Sciences—General	M
Communication Disorders	M
Occupational Therapy	M
Pharmacy	D
Toxicology	D

UNIVERSITY OF LOUISVILLE

Allopathic Medicine	D
Anatomy	M,D
Biochemistry	M,D
Bioethics	M,D
Biological and Biomedical Sciences—General	M,D
Communication Disorders	M,D
Community Health	M
Dentistry	M,D
Environmental Biology	M,D
Epidemiology	M,D
Family Nurse Practitioner Studies	M,D
Gerontological Nursing	M,D
Health Services Management and Hospital Administration	M
Immunology	M,D
Maternal and Child/Neonatal Nursing	M,D
Microbiology	M,D
Molecular Genetics	M,D
Neurobiology	M,D
Nursing and Healthcare Administration	M,D
Nursing Education	M,D
Nursing—General	M,D
Oral and Dental Sciences	M,D
Pharmacology	M,D
Physiology	M,D
Psychiatric Nursing	M,D
Public Health—General	M,D
Toxicology	M,D
Women's Health Nursing	M,D

UNIVERSITY OF LYNCHBURG

Allopathic Medicine	D
Health Promotion	M
Physical Therapy	D
Physician Assistant Studies	M
Public Health—General	M

UNIVERSITY OF MAINE

Biological and Biomedical Sciences—General	M,D
Botany	M,D
Communication Disorders	M
Entomology	M,D
Family Nurse Practitioner Studies	M,O
Microbiology	M,D
Molecular Biology	M,D
Nursing Education	M,O
Nursing—General	M,O
Plant Pathology	M,D
Zoology	M,D

UNIVERSITY OF MANAGEMENT AND TECHNOLOGY

Health Services Management and Hospital Administration	M

THE UNIVERSITY OF MANCHESTER

Biochemistry	M,D
Biological and Biomedical Sciences—General	M,D
Biophysics	M,D
Cancer Biology/Oncology	M,D
Cell Biology	M,D
Communication Disorders	M,D
Dentistry	M,D
Developmental Biology	M,D
Ecology	M,D
Environmental Biology	M,D
Evolutionary Biology	M,D
Genetics	M,D
Immunology	M,D
Microbiology	M,D
Molecular Biology	M,D
Molecular Genetics	M,D
Neurobiology	M,D
Neuroscience	M,D
Nurse Midwifery	M,D
Nursing—General	M,D
Optometry	M,D
Oral and Dental Sciences	M,D
Pharmaceutical Sciences	M,D
Pharmacology	M,D
Pharmacy	M,D
Physiology	M,D
Public Health—General	M,D
Structural Biology	M,D
Toxicology	M,D
Vision Sciences	M,D

UNIVERSITY OF MANITOBA

Allopathic Medicine	M
Anatomy	M,D
Biochemistry	M,D
Biological and Biomedical Sciences—General	M,D,O
Botany	M,D
Cancer Biology/Oncology	M
Community Health	M,D,O
Dentistry	D
Ecology	M,D
Entomology	M,D
Human Genetics	M,D
Immunology	M,D
Infectious Diseases	M,D
Maternal and Child Health	M
Medical Microbiology	M,D
Microbiology	M,D
Nursing—General	M
Nutrition	M,D
Occupational Therapy	M,D
Oral and Dental Sciences	M,D
Pathology	M
Pharmaceutical Sciences	M,D
Pharmacology	M,D
Physical Therapy	M,D
Physiology	M,D
Plant Physiology	M,D
Rehabilitation Sciences	M,D
Zoology	M,D

UNIVERSITY OF MARY

Bioethics	M
Cardiovascular Sciences	M
Family Nurse Practitioner Studies	M,D
Health Services Management and Hospital Administration	M
Nursing and Healthcare Administration	M,D
Nursing Education	M,D
Nursing—General	M,D
Occupational Therapy	M
Physical Therapy	D

UNIVERSITY OF MARY HARDIN-BAYLOR

Family Nurse Practitioner Studies	M,D,O
Nursing Education	M,D,O
Nursing—General	M,D,O
Physical Therapy	D

UNIVERSITY OF MARYLAND, BALTIMORE

Allied Health—General	M
Allopathic Medicine	D
Biochemistry	M,D
Biological and Biomedical Sciences—General	M,D,O
Cancer Biology/Oncology	D
Cell Biology	M,D
Clinical Laboratory Sciences/Medical Technology	M
Clinical Research	M,D,O
Community Health Nursing	M,D,O
Dentistry	D,O
Epidemiology	M,D,O
Family Nurse Practitioner Studies	M,D,O
Genomic Sciences	M,D
Gerontological Nursing	M,D,O
Health Services Research	M,D
Human Genetics	M,D
Immunology	D
International Health	M,D,O
Maternal and Child/Neonatal Nursing	M,D,O
Microbiology	D
Molecular Biology	M,D
Molecular Medicine	D
Neurobiology	D
Neuroscience	D
Nurse Anesthesia	M,D,O
Nursing and Healthcare Administration	M,D,O
Nursing Education	M,D,O
Nursing Informatics	M,D,O
Nursing—General	M,D,O
Oral and Dental Sciences	M,D,O
Pathology	M
Pediatric Nursing	M,D,O
Pharmaceutical Administration	M,D
Pharmaceutical Sciences	D
Pharmacology	M,D
Pharmacy	M,D
Physical Therapy	D
Psychiatric Nursing	M,D,O
Rehabilitation Sciences	D
Toxicology	M,D

UNIVERSITY OF MARYLAND, BALTIMORE COUNTY

Biological and Biomedical Sciences—General	M,D
Cell Biology	D
Epidemiology	M,D,O
Health Services Management and Hospital Administration	M,D,O
Molecular Biology	M,D
Neuroscience	D

UNIVERSITY OF MARYLAND, COLLEGE PARK

Biochemistry	M,D
Biological and Biomedical Sciences—General	M,D
Biophysics	D
Cell Biology	M,D
Communication Disorders	M,D
Computational Biology	D
Conservation Biology	M
Ecology	M,D
Entomology	M,D
Environmental and Occupational Health	M
Epidemiology	M,D
Evolutionary Biology	M,D
Genomic Sciences	D
Health Services Management and Hospital Administration	M,D
Maternal and Child Health	M,D
Molecular Biology	D
Molecular Genetics	M,D
Neuroscience	M,D
Nutrition	M,D
Plant Biology	M,D
Public Health—General	M,D
Veterinary Medicine	D
Veterinary Sciences	M,D

UNIVERSITY OF MARYLAND EASTERN SHORE

Pharmaceutical Sciences	M,D
Physical Therapy	D
Rehabilitation Sciences	M
Toxicology	M,D

UNIVERSITY OF MARYLAND UNIVERSITY COLLEGE

Health Services Management and Hospital Administration	M

UNIVERSITY OF MASSACHUSETTS AMHERST

Adult Nursing	M,D
Animal Behavior	M,D
Biochemistry	M,D
Biological and Biomedical Sciences—General	M,D
Cell Biology	M,D
Communication Disorders	M,D
Community Health Nursing	M,D
Community Health	M,D
Developmental Biology	D
Environmental and Occupational Health	M,D
Environmental Biology	M,D
Epidemiology	M,D
Evolutionary Biology	M,D
Family Nurse Practitioner Studies	M,D
Genetics	M,D
Gerontological Nursing	M,D
Health Services Management and Hospital Administration	M,D
Microbiology	M,D*
Molecular Biophysics	D
Neuroscience	M,D
Nursing and Healthcare Administration	M,D
Nursing—General	M,D
Nutrition	M,D
Physiology	M,D
Plant Biology	M,D
Plant Molecular Biology	M,D
Plant Physiology	M,D
Public Health—General	M,D

UNIVERSITY OF MASSACHUSETTS BOSTON

Biological and Biomedical Sciences—General	M,D
Nursing—General	M,D
Vision Sciences	M

UNIVERSITY OF MASSACHUSETTS DARTMOUTH

Biochemistry	M,D
Biological and Biomedical Sciences—General	M,D
Community Health Nursing	M,D
Health Services Management and Hospital Administration	M
Marine Biology	M,D
Nursing—General	M,D

UNIVERSITY OF MASSACHUSETTS LOWELL

Allied Health—General	M,D
Biochemistry	M,D
Biological and Biomedical Sciences—General	M
Clinical Laboratory Sciences/Medical Technology	M
Family Nurse Practitioner Studies	M
Gerontological Nursing	M
Health Physics/Radiological Health	M
Health Promotion	D
Nursing—General	M,D
Physical Therapy	D

UNIVERSITY OF MASSACHUSETTS MEDICAL SCHOOL

Adult Nursing	M,D,O
Allopathic Medicine	D
Biochemistry	M,D
Biological and Biomedical Sciences—General	M,D
Cancer Biology/Oncology	M,D
Clinical Research	M,D
Computational Biology	M,D
Family Nurse Practitioner Studies	M,D,O
Gerontological Nursing	M,D,O
Health Services Research	M,D
Immunology	M,D
Microbiology	M,D
Molecular Pharmacology	M,D
Neuroscience	M,D
Nursing and Healthcare Administration	M,D,O
Nursing Education	M,D,O
Nursing—General	M,D,O
Translational Biology	M,D

UNIVERSITY OF MEMPHIS

Allied Health—General	M,O
Biological and Biomedical Sciences—General	M,D
Communication Disorders	M,D
Environmental and Occupational Health	M,D
Epidemiology	M,D
Family Nurse Practitioner Studies	M,O
Health Promotion	M,O
Health Services Management and Hospital Administration	M,D
Nursing and Healthcare Administration	M,O
Nursing Education	M,O
Nursing—General	M,O
Nutrition	M,O
Public Health—General	M,D

UNIVERSITY OF MIAMI

Acute Care/Critical Care Nursing	M,D
Adult Nursing	M,D
Allopathic Medicine	D
Biochemistry	D
Biological and Biomedical Sciences—General	M,D
Biophysics	D

*M—masters degree; D—doctorate; O—other advanced degree; *—Close-Up and/or Display*

Cancer Biology/Oncology	D
Cell Biology	D
Community Health	D
Developmental Biology	D
Environmental and Occupational Health	M
Epidemiology	M,D
Evolutionary Biology	M,D
Family Nurse Practitioner Studies	M,D
Genetics	M,D
Immunology	D
Marine Biology	M,D
Microbiology	D
Molocular Biology	D
Neuroscience	M,D
Nurse Anesthesia	M,D
Nurse Midwifery	M,D
Nursing—General	M,D
Nutrition	M
Pharmacology	D
Physical Therapy	D
Physiology	D
Public Health—General	M,D

UNIVERSITY OF MICHIGAN

Allopathic Medicine	D
Biochemistry	M,D
Biological and Biomedical Sciences—General	M,D
Biophysics	D
Biopsychology	D
Cancer Biology/Oncology	M,D
Cell Biology	M,D
Clinical Research	M
Dental Hygiene	M
Dentistry	D
Developmental Biology	M,D
Ecology	M,D
Environmental and Occupational Health	M,D
Epidemiology	M,D
Evolutionary Biology	M,D
Health Physics/Radiological Health	M,D,O
Health Promotion	M,D
Health Services Management and Hospital Administration	M,D
Human Genetics	M,D
Immunology	M,D
Industrial Hygiene	M,D
International Health	M,D
Medicinal and Pharmaceutical Chemistry	D
Microbiology	M,D
Molecular Biology	M,D
Molecular Pathology	D
Neuroscience	D
Nursing—General	M,D,O
Nutrition	M,D
Oral and Dental Sciences	M,D
Pathology	D
Pediatric Nursing	M,D,O
Pharmaceutical Administration	D
Pharmaceutical Sciences	D
Pharmacology	M,D
Pharmacy	D
Physiology	M,D
Public Health—General	M,D
Toxicology	M,D

UNIVERSITY OF MICHIGAN–FLINT

Biological and Biomedical Sciences—General	M
Family Nurse Practitioner Studies	M,D,O
Health Services Management and Hospital Administration	M,O
Neuroscience	D,O
Nurse Anesthesia	D
Nursing—General	M,D,O
Physical Therapy	D,O
Psychiatric Nursing	M,D,O
Public Health—General	M

UNIVERSITY OF MINNESOTA, DULUTH

Allopathic Medicine	D
Biochemistry	M,D
Biological and Biomedical Sciences—General	M,D
Biophysics	M,D
Communication Disorders	M
Immunology	M,D
Medical Microbiology	M,D
Molecular Biology	M,D
Pharmacology	M,D
Pharmacy	M,D
Physiology	M,D
Toxicology	M,D

UNIVERSITY OF MINNESOTA ROCHESTER

Computational Biology	M,D
Occupational Therapy	M,D

UNIVERSITY OF MINNESOTA, TWIN CITIES CAMPUS

Allopathic Medicine	M,D
Animal Behavior	M,D
Biochemistry	D
Biological and Biomedical Sciences—General	M
Biophysics	M,D
Biopsychology	D
Cancer Biology/Oncology	D
Cell Biology	M,D
Clinical Laboratory Sciences/Medical Technology	M
Clinical Research	M
Communication Disorders	M,D
Community Health	M
Conservation Biology	M,D
Dentistry	D
Developmental Biology	M,D
Ecology	M,D
Entomology	M,D
Environmental and Occupational Health	M,D,O
Epidemiology	M,D
Evolutionary Biology	M,D
Family Nurse Practitioner Studies	M,D
Genetics	M,D
Gerontological Nursing	M,D
Health Services Management and Hospital Administration	M,D
Health Services Research	M,D
Immunology	D
Industrial Hygiene	M,D
Infectious Diseases	M,D
International Health	M,D
Maternal and Child Health	M
Medical Physics	M,D
Medicinal and Pharmaceutical Chemistry	M,D
Microbiology	D
Molecular Biology	M,D
Neurobiology	M,D
Neuroscience	M,D
Nurse Anesthesia	M,D
Nurse Midwifery	M,D
Nursing and Healthcare Administration	M,D
Nursing Informatics	M,D
Nursing—General	M,D
Nutrition	M,D
Occupational Health Nursing	M,D
Oral and Dental Sciences	M,D,O
Pediatric Nursing	M,D
Pharmaceutical Administration	M,D
Pharmaceutical Sciences	M,D
Pharmacology	M,D
Pharmacy	D
Physical Therapy	M,D
Physiology	D
Plant Biology	M,D
Plant Pathology	M,D
Psychiatric Nursing	M,D
Public Health—General	M,D,O
Structural Biology	D
Toxicology	M,D
Veterinary Medicine	D
Veterinary Sciences	M,D
Virology	D
Women's Health Nursing	M,D

UNIVERSITY OF MISSISSIPPI

Biological and Biomedical Sciences—General	M,D
Communication Disorders	M,D
Health Promotion	M,D
Medicinal and Pharmaceutical Chemistry	M,D
Nutrition	M,D
Pharmaceutical Administration	M,D
Pharmaceutical Sciences	M,D
Pharmacology	M,D
Pharmacy	M,D
Toxicology	M,D

UNIVERSITY OF MISSISSIPPI MEDICAL CENTER

Allied Health—General	M
Allopathic Medicine	D
Anatomy	M,D
Biochemistry	D
Biological and Biomedical Sciences—General	M,D
Biophysics	D
Dentistry	M,D
Microbiology	D
Neuroscience	D
Nursing—General	M,D
Occupational Therapy	M
Oral and Dental Sciences	M,D
Pathology	D
Pharmacology	D
Physical Therapy	M
Physiology	D
Toxicology	D

UNIVERSITY OF MISSOURI

Adult Nursing	M,D,O
Allopathic Medicine	D
Anatomy	M,D
Biochemistry	M,D
Biological and Biomedical Sciences—General	M,D
Communication Disorders	M,D
Community Health	M,D
Ecology	M,D
Evolutionary Biology	M,D
Family Nurse Practitioner Studies	M,D,O
Gerontological Nursing	M,D,O
Health Physics/Radiological Health	M
Health Services Management and Hospital Administration	M,D
Immunology	D
Microbiology	D
Nursing and Healthcare Administration	M,D,O
Nursing—General	M,D,O
Nutrition	M,D
Occupational Therapy	M
Pathobiology	M,D
Pathology	M,D
Pediatric Nursing	M,D,O
Pharmacology	M,D
Physical Therapy	D
Physiology	M,D
Psychiatric Nursing	M,D,O
Veterinary Medicine	M,D
Veterinary Sciences	M

UNIVERSITY OF MISSOURI–KANSAS CITY

Adult Nursing	M,D
Allopathic Medicine	M,D
Biochemistry	D
Biological and Biomedical Sciences—General	M,D
Biophysics	D
Cell Biology	D
Dental Hygiene	M,D,O
Dentistry	M,D,O
Family Nurse Practitioner Studies	M,D
Gerontological Nursing	M,D
Maternal and Child/Neonatal Nursing	M,D
Molecular Biology	D
Nursing and Healthcare Administration	M,D
Nursing Education	M,D
Nursing—General	M,D
Oral and Dental Sciences	M,D,O
Pediatric Nursing	M,D
Pharmacy	D
Women's Health Nursing	M,D

UNIVERSITY OF MISSOURI–ST. LOUIS

Adult Nursing	D,O
Biochemistry	M,D
Biological and Biomedical Sciences—General	M,D,O
Family Nurse Practitioner Studies	D,O
Gerontological Nursing	D,O
Neuroscience	M,D,O
Nursing—General	D,O
Optometry	D
Pediatric Nursing	D,O
Psychiatric Nursing	D,O
Women's Health Nursing	D,O

UNIVERSITY OF MOBILE

Nursing and Healthcare Administration	M,D
Nursing Education	M,D
Nursing—General	M,D

UNIVERSITY OF MONTANA

Animal Behavior	M,D,O
Biochemistry	D
Biological and Biomedical Sciences—General	M,D
Cell Biology	D
Communication Disorders	M,O
Community Health	M
Developmental Biology	D
Ecology	M,D
Immunology	D
Medicinal and Pharmaceutical Chemistry	M,D
Microbiology	D
Molecular Biology	D
Neuroscience	M,D
Pharmaceutical Sciences	M,D
Pharmacy	M,D
Physical Therapy	D
Public Health—General	M,O
Toxicology	M,D
Zoology	M,D

UNIVERSITY OF MONTEVALLO

Communication Disorders	M

UNIVERSITY OF MOUNT OLIVE

Nursing—General	M

UNIVERSITY OF MOUNT UNION

Physical Therapy	D
Physician Assistant Studies	M

UNIVERSITY OF NEBRASKA AT KEARNEY

Biological and Biomedical Sciences—General	M
Communication Disorders	M

UNIVERSITY OF NEBRASKA AT OMAHA

Biological and Biomedical Sciences—General	M,O
Communication Disorders	M

UNIVERSITY OF NEBRASKA–LINCOLN

Biochemistry	M,D
Biological and Biomedical Sciences—General	M,D
Biopsychology	M,D
Communication Disorders	M,D
Entomology	M,D
Health Promotion	M,D
Nutrition	M,D
Toxicology	M,D
Veterinary Sciences	M,D

UNIVERSITY OF NEBRASKA MEDICAL CENTER

Allied Health—General	M,D,O
Allopathic Medicine	D,O
Anatomy	M,D
Biochemistry	M
Biological and Biomedical Sciences—General	M,D
Cancer Biology/Oncology	D
Cell Biology	M,D
Clinical Laboratory Sciences/Medical Technology	M,O
Dentistry	M,D,O
Environmental and Occupational Health	D
Epidemiology	D
Genetics	M,D
Health Promotion	D
Health Services Management and Hospital Administration	M,D
Health Services Research	M,D
Immunology	M,D
Infectious Diseases	M,D
Molecular Biology	M
Molecular Genetics	M,D
Molecular Medicine	D
Neuroscience	D
Nursing—General	D
Nutrition	O
Oral and Dental Sciences	M,D
Pathology	M,D
Perfusion	M
Pharmaceutical Sciences	M,D
Pharmacology	D
Pharmacy	D
Physical Therapy	D
Physician Assistant Studies	M
Physiology	D
Public Health—General	M
Toxicology	D

UNIVERSITY OF NEVADA, LAS VEGAS

Allied Health—General	M,D,O
Biochemistry	M,D
Biological and Biomedical Sciences—General	M,D
Community Health	M,D,O
Dentistry	M,D,O
Family Nurse Practitioner Studies	M,D,O
Health Physics/Radiological Health	M,D,O
Health Services Management and Hospital Administration	M
Nursing Education	M,D,O
Nursing—General	M,D,O
Nutrition	M,D
Oral and Dental Sciences	M,D,O
Physical Therapy	D
Public Health—General	M,D,O

UNIVERSITY OF NEVADA, RENO

Allopathic Medicine	D
Biochemistry	M,D
Biological and Biomedical Sciences—General	M
Cell Biology	M,D
Communication Disorders	M,D
Conservation Biology	D
Ecology	D
Environmental and Occupational Health	M,D
Evolutionary Biology	D
Molecular Biology	M,D
Molecular Pharmacology	D
Nursing—General	M,D
Nutrition	M
Physiology	D
Public Health—General	M,D

UNIVERSITY OF NEW BRUNSWICK FREDERICTON

Biological and Biomedical Sciences—General	M,D
Health Services Research	M
Nursing Education	M
Nursing—General	M

UNIVERSITY OF NEW BRUNSWICK SAINT JOHN

Biological and Biomedical Sciences—General	M,D

UNIVERSITY OF NEW ENGLAND

Biological and Biomedical Sciences—General	M
Dentistry	D
Health Services Management and Hospital Administration	M,D,O
Nurse Anesthesia	M,D
Nutrition	M,D,O
Occupational Therapy	M,D
Osteopathic Medicine	D
Pharmacy	D
Physical Therapy	M,D
Physician Assistant Studies	M,D
Public Health—General	M,D,O

UNIVERSITY OF NEW HAMPSHIRE

Biochemistry	M,D
Biological and Biomedical Sciences—General	M,D
Communication Disorders	M
Conservation Biology	M
Evolutionary Biology	D
Family Nurse Practitioner Studies	M,D,O
Genetics	M,D
Marine Biology	M,D
Microbiology	M,D
Nursing—General	M,D,O
Nutrition	M,D
Occupational Therapy	M,O
Psychiatric Nursing	M,D,O
Public Health—General	M,O

UNIVERSITY OF NEW HAVEN

Cell Biology	M
Ecology	M
Environmental and Occupational Health	M
Health Services Management and Hospital Administration	M,O
Molecular Biology	M
Nutrition	M,O

UNIVERSITY OF NEW MEXICO

Allied Health—General	M,D,O
Allopathic Medicine	D
Biochemistry	M,D
Biological and Biomedical Sciences—General	M,D
Cell Biology	M,D
Clinical Laboratory Sciences/Medical Technology	M,O
Communication Disorders	M
Community Health	M
Dental Hygiene	M
Epidemiology	M
Genetics	M,D
Health Services Management and Hospital Administration	M
Microbiology	M,D
Molecular Biology	M,D
Neuroscience	M,D
Nursing—General	M,D
Nutrition	M
Occupational Therapy	M
Pathology	M,D
Pharmaceutical Sciences	M,D
Pharmacy	D
Physical Therapy	D
Physician Assistant Studies	M
Physiology	M,D
Public Health—General	M
Toxicology	M,D

UNIVERSITY OF NEW ORLEANS
Biological and Biomedical Sciences—General M
Health Services Management and Hospital Administration M

UNIVERSITY OF NORTH ALABAMA
Health Promotion M
Health Services Management and Hospital Administration M
Nursing—General M

THE UNIVERSITY OF NORTH CAROLINA AT CHAPEL HILL
Adult Nursing M,D,O
Allied Health—General M,D
Allopathic Medicine D
Biochemistry M,D
Biological and Biomedical Sciences—General M,D
Biophysics M,D
Biopsychology D
Botany M,D
Cell Biology M,D
Clinical Research M,D
Communication Disorders M,D
Computational Biology D
Dental Hygiene M,D
Dentistry D
Developmental Biology M,D
Ecology M,D
Environmental and Occupational Health M,D
Epidemiology M,D
Evolutionary Biology M,D
Family Nurse Practitioner Studies M,D,O
Genetics M,D
Gerontological Nursing M,D,O
Health Promotion M
Health Services Management and Hospital Administration M,D
Immunology M,D
Maternal and Child Health M,D
Microbiology M,D
Molecular Biology M,D
Molecular Physiology D
Neurobiology D
Neuroscience D
Nursing and Healthcare Administration M,D,O
Nursing Education M,D,O
Nursing Informatics M,D,O
Nursing—General M,D,O
Nutrition M,D
Occupational Health Nursing M
Occupational Therapy M,D
Oral and Dental Sciences M,D
Pathology D
Pediatric Nursing M,D,O
Pharmaceutical Administration M,D
Pharmaceutical Sciences M,D
Pharmacology D
Pharmacy M,D
Physical Therapy D
Psychiatric Nursing M,D,O
Public Health—General M,D
Toxicology M,D

THE UNIVERSITY OF NORTH CAROLINA AT CHARLOTTE
Acute Care/Critical Care Nursing M,D,O
Biological and Biomedical Sciences—General M,D
Community Health M,D,O
Family Nurse Practitioner Studies M,D,O
Gerontological Nursing M,D,O
Health Services Management and Hospital Administration M,D,O
Health Services Research D
Nurse Anesthesia M,D,O
Nursing and Healthcare Administration M,D,O
Nursing Education M,D,O
Nursing—General M,D,O
Public Health—General M,D,O

THE UNIVERSITY OF NORTH CAROLINA AT GREENSBORO
Adult Nursing M,D,O
Biochemistry M
Biological and Biomedical Sciences—General M
Communication Disorders M,D
Community Health M,D
Gerontological Nursing M,D,O
Nurse Anesthesia M,D,O
Nursing and Healthcare Administration M,D,O
Nursing Education M,D,O
Nursing—General M,D,O
Nutrition M,D

THE UNIVERSITY OF NORTH CAROLINA AT PEMBROKE
Health Services Management and Hospital Administration M
Nursing and Healthcare Administration M
Nursing Education M
Nursing—General M

THE UNIVERSITY OF NORTH CAROLINA WILMINGTON
Biological and Biomedical Sciences—General M,D
Clinical Research M,D,O
Family Nurse Practitioner Studies M,D,O
Marine Biology M,D
Nursing Education M,D,O
Nursing—General M,D,O

UNIVERSITY OF NORTH DAKOTA
Biological and Biomedical Sciences—General M,D
Clinical Laboratory Sciences/Medical Technology M,D
Communication Disorders M
Community Health Nursing M,D,O
Family Nurse Practitioner Studies M,D,O
Genetics M,D
Gerontological Nursing M,D,O
Nurse Anesthesia M,D,O
Nursing Education M,D,O
Nursing—General M,D,O
Occupational Therapy M
Physical Therapy D
Physician Assistant Studies M
Psychiatric Nursing M,D,O
Public Health—General M
Zoology M,D

UNIVERSITY OF NORTHERN BRITISH COLUMBIA
Community Health M,D,O

UNIVERSITY OF NORTHERN COLORADO
Acute Care/Critical Care Nursing M,D
Biological and Biomedical Sciences—General M
Communication Disorders M,D
Community Health M
Family Nurse Practitioner Studies M,D
Health Services Management and Hospital Administration M
International Health M
Nursing Education M,D
Nursing—General M,D
Public Health—General M
Rehabilitation Sciences M,D

UNIVERSITY OF NORTHERN IOWA
Allied Health—General M,D
Biological and Biomedical Sciences—General M
Communication Disorders M
Community Health M
Health Promotion M

UNIVERSITY OF NORTH FLORIDA
Allied Health—General M,D,O
Biological and Biomedical Sciences—General M
Communication Disorders M
Community Health M,O
Family Nurse Practitioner Studies M,D,O
Nurse Anesthesia M,D,O
Nursing—General M,D,O
Nutrition M
Physical Therapy M,D
Public Health—General M,O

UNIVERSITY OF NORTH GEORGIA
Family Nurse Practitioner Studies M,O
Nursing Education M
Physical Therapy D

UNIVERSITY OF NORTH TEXAS
Biochemistry M,D,O
Biological and Biomedical Sciences—General M,D,O
Communication Disorders M,D,O
Health Services Management and Hospital Administration M,D,O
Molecular Biology M,D,O

UNIVERSITY OF NORTH TEXAS HEALTH SCIENCE CENTER AT FORT WORTH
Anatomy M,D
Biochemistry M,D
Biological and Biomedical Sciences—General M,D
Cancer Biology/Oncology M,D
Epidemiology M,D,O
Genetics M,D
Health Services Management and Hospital Administration M,D,O
Health Services Research M,D,O
Immunology M,D
International Health M,D,O
Microbiology M,D
Neuroscience M,D
Osteopathic Medicine D
Pharmaceutical Sciences M,D
Pharmacology M,D
Physical Therapy M,D
Physician Assistant Studies M,D
Physiology M,D
Public Health—General M,D,O
Rehabilitation Sciences M,D

UNIVERSITY OF NOTRE DAME
Biochemistry M,D
Biological and Biomedical Sciences—General M,D
Cell Biology M,D
Ecology M,D
Evolutionary Biology M,D
Genetics M,D
Molecular Biology M,D
Parasitology M,D
Physiology M,D

UNIVERSITY OF OKLAHOMA
Biochemistry M,D
Biological and Biomedical Sciences—General D
Ecology M,D
Evolutionary Biology M,D
Health Promotion M,D
Health Services Management and Hospital Administration M,O
Microbiology M,D
Neurobiology M,D
Plant Biology M,D

Structural Biology M,D

UNIVERSITY OF OKLAHOMA HEALTH SCIENCES CENTER
Allied Health—General M,D,O
Allopathic Medicine D
Biochemistry M,D
Biological and Biomedical Sciences—General M,D
Biopsychology M,D
Cell Biology M,D
Communication Disorders M,D,O
Dentistry D,O
Environmental and Occupational Health M,D
Epidemiology M,D
Health Physics/Radiological Health M,D
Health Promotion M,D
Health Services Management and Hospital Administration M,D
Immunology M,D
Medical Physics M,D
Microbiology M,D
Molecular Biology M,D
Neuroscience M,D
Nursing—General M
Nutrition M
Occupational Therapy M
Oral and Dental Sciences M
Pathology D
Pharmaceutical Sciences M,D
Pharmacy D
Physical Therapy M
Physician Assistant Studies M
Physiology M,D
Public Health—General M,D
Radiation Biology M,D
Rehabilitation Sciences M

UNIVERSITY OF OREGON
Biochemistry M,D
Biological and Biomedical Sciences—General M,D
Biopsychology M,D
Communication Disorders M,D
Ecology M,D
Evolutionary Biology M,D
Genetics M,D
Marine Biology M,D
Molecular Biology M,D
Neuroscience M,D
Physiology M,D

UNIVERSITY OF OTTAWA
Allopathic Medicine M,D
Biochemistry M,D
Biological and Biomedical Sciences—General M,D
Cell Biology M,D
Communication Disorders M
Community Health D,O
Epidemiology M
Health Services Management and Hospital Administration M
Health Services Research D,O
Immunology M,D
Microbiology M,D
Molecular Biology M,D
Nursing—General M,D,O
Public Health—General D
Rehabilitation Sciences M

UNIVERSITY OF PENNSYLVANIA
Acute Care/Critical Care Nursing M
Adult Nursing M
Allopathic Medicine D
Biochemistry D
Bioethics M
Biological and Biomedical Sciences—General M,D
Cancer Biology/Oncology D
Cell Biology D
Clinical Laboratory Sciences/Medical Technology M
Computational Biology D
Dentistry D
Developmental Biology D
Environmental and Occupational Health M
Epidemiology M
Family Nurse Practitioner Studies M,O
Genetics D
Genomic Sciences D
Gerontological Nursing M
Health Services Management and Hospital Administration M,D
Health Services Research M
Human Genetics M
Immunology D
International Health M
Maternal and Child/Neonatal Nursing M
Medical Physics M,D
Microbiology D
Molecular Biology D
Molecular Biophysics D
Neuroscience D
Nurse Anesthesia M
Nurse Midwifery M
Nursing and Healthcare Administration M,D
Nursing—General M,D,O
Pediatric Nursing M
Pharmacology D
Physiology D
Psychiatric Nursing M
Public Health—General M
Veterinary Medicine D
Virology D
Women's Health Nursing M

UNIVERSITY OF PHOENIX–BAY AREA CAMPUS
Gerontological Nursing M,D
Health Services Management and Hospital Administration M,D
Nursing and Healthcare Administration M,D
Nursing Education M,D
Nursing Informatics M,D
Nursing—General M,D

UNIVERSITY OF PHOENIX–CENTRAL VALLEY CAMPUS
Community Health M
Health Services Management and Hospital Administration M
Nursing—General M

UNIVERSITY OF PHOENIX–HAWAII CAMPUS
Community Health M
Family Nurse Practitioner Studies M
Health Services Management and Hospital Administration M
Nursing Education M
Nursing—General M

UNIVERSITY OF PHOENIX–HOUSTON CAMPUS
Health Services Management and Hospital Administration M
Nursing—General M

UNIVERSITY OF PHOENIX–LAS VEGAS CAMPUS
Allied Health—General M

UNIVERSITY OF PHOENIX–ONLINE CAMPUS
Family Nurse Practitioner Studies M,O
Health Services Management and Hospital Administration M,D,O
Nursing Education M,O
Nursing—General M,D,O

UNIVERSITY OF PHOENIX–PHOENIX CAMPUS
Family Nurse Practitioner Studies M,O
Gerontological Nursing M,O
Health Services Management and Hospital Administration M,O
Nursing Education M,O
Nursing Informatics M,O
Nursing—General M,O

UNIVERSITY OF PHOENIX–SACRAMENTO VALLEY CAMPUS
Family Nurse Practitioner Studies M
Health Services Management and Hospital Administration M
Nursing Education M
Nursing—General M

UNIVERSITY OF PHOENIX–SAN ANTONIO CAMPUS
Health Services Management and Hospital Administration M
Nursing—General M

UNIVERSITY OF PHOENIX–SAN DIEGO CAMPUS
Nursing Education M
Nursing—General M

UNIVERSITY OF PIKEVILLE
Health Services Management and Hospital Administration M
Optometry D
Osteopathic Medicine D

UNIVERSITY OF PITTSBURGH
Acute Care/Critical Care Nursing M,D
Allopathic Medicine D
Bioethics M
Biological and Biomedical Sciences—General M,D
Cell Biology D
Clinical Laboratory Sciences/Medical Technology D
Clinical Research M,O
Communication Disorders M,D
Community Health M,D,O
Computational Biology D
Dentistry M,D,O
Developmental Biology D
Ecology D
Environmental and Occupational Health M,D
Epidemiology M,D
Evolutionary Biology D
Family Nurse Practitioner Studies M,D
Gerontological Nursing M,D
Health Services Management and Hospital Administration M,D,O
Health Services Research M
Human Genetics M,D,O
Immunology D
Infectious Diseases M,D
International Health M,D,O
Maternal and Child/Neonatal Nursing M,D
Microbiology M,D
Molecular Biology D
Molecular Biophysics D
Molecular Genetics D
Molecular Pathology D
Molecular Pharmacology D
Molecular Physiology D
Neuroscience D
Nurse Anesthesia D
Nurse Midwifery D
Nursing and Healthcare Administration M,D
Nursing Informatics M,D

*M—masters degree; D—doctorate; O—other advanced degree; *—Close-Up and/or Display*

Nursing—General	D
Nutrition	M
Occupational Therapy	M,D
Oral and Dental Sciences	M,D,O
Pathology	D
Pediatric Nursing	M,D
Pharmaceutical Administration	M
Pharmaceutical Sciences	M,D
Pharmacy	D
Physical Therapy	M,D
Physician Assistant Studies	M,D
Psychiatric Nursing	M,D
Public Health—General	M,D,O
Rehabilitation Sciences	M,D
Structural Biology	D
Systems Biology	D
Vision Sciences	M,D

UNIVERSITY OF PORTLAND

Family Nurse Practitioner Studies	M,D
Health Services Management and Hospital Administration	M
Nursing Education	M,D
Nursing—General	M,D

UNIVERSITY OF PRINCE EDWARD ISLAND

Anatomy	M,D
Bacteriology	M,D
Biological and Biomedical Sciences—General	M,D
Epidemiology	M,D
Immunology	M,D
Parasitology	M,D
Pathology	M,D
Pharmacology	M,D
Physiology	M,D
Toxicology	M,D
Veterinary Medicine	D
Veterinary Sciences	M,D
Virology	M,D

UNIVERSITY OF PUERTO RICO–MAYAGÜEZ

Biological and Biomedical Sciences—General	M

UNIVERSITY OF PUERTO RICO–MEDICAL SCIENCES CAMPUS

Acute Care/Critical Care Nursing	M
Adult Nursing	M
Allied Health—General	M,D,O
Allopathic Medicine	D
Anatomy	M,D
Biochemistry	M,D
Biological and Biomedical Sciences—General	M,D
Clinical Laboratory Sciences/Medical Technology	M,O
Clinical Research	M,O
Communication Disorders	M,D
Community Health Nursing	M
Dentistry	D
Environmental and Occupational Health	M
Epidemiology	M
Family Nurse Practitioner Studies	M
Gerontological Nursing	M
Health Promotion	O
Health Services Management and Hospital Administration	M
Health Services Research	M
Industrial Hygiene	M
Maternal and Child Health	M
Maternal and Child/Neonatal Nursing	M
Microbiology	M,D
Nurse Midwifery	M,O
Nursing—General	M
Nutrition	M,D,O
Occupational Therapy	M
Oral and Dental Sciences	O
Pediatric Nursing	M
Pharmaceutical Sciences	M,D
Pharmacology	M,D
Pharmacy	M
Physical Therapy	M
Physiology	M,D
Psychiatric Nursing	M
Toxicology	M,D

UNIVERSITY OF PUERTO RICO–RÍO PIEDRAS

Biological and Biomedical Sciences—General	M,D
Cell Biology	M,D
Ecology	M,D
Evolutionary Biology	M,D
Genetics	M,D
Molecular Biology	M,D
Neuroscience	M,D
Nutrition	M

UNIVERSITY OF PUGET SOUND

Occupational Therapy	M,D
Physical Therapy	D

UNIVERSITY OF REDLANDS

Communication Disorders	M

UNIVERSITY OF REGINA

Biochemistry	M,D
Biological and Biomedical Sciences—General	M,D
Biophysics	M,D
Cancer Biology/Oncology	M,D
Health Services Management and Hospital Administration	M,D,O
Nursing—General	M,D

UNIVERSITY OF RHODE ISLAND

Acute Care/Critical Care Nursing	M,D,O
Adult Nursing	M,D,O
Biochemistry	M,D
Biological and Biomedical Sciences—General	M,D
Cell Biology	M,D
Clinical Laboratory Sciences/Medical Technology	M,D
Communication Disorders	M
Ecology	M,D
Evolutionary Biology	M,D
Family Nurse Practitioner Studies	M,D,O
Gerontological Nursing	M,D,O
Health Services Management and Hospital Administration	M,D,O
Marine Biology	M,D
Medical Physics	M,D
Medicinal and Pharmaceutical Chemistry	M,D
Microbiology	M,D
Molecular Biology	M,D
Molecular Genetics	M,D
Nursing Education	M,D,O
Nursing—General	M,D,O
Nutrition	M
Pharmaceutical Sciences	M,D
Pharmacology	M,D
Pharmacy	D
Physical Therapy	D
Toxicology	M,D

UNIVERSITY OF ROCHESTER

Acute Care/Critical Care Nursing	M,D
Adult Nursing	M,D
Allopathic Medicine	D
Anatomy	D
Biochemistry	D
Biological and Biomedical Sciences—General	M,D
Biophysics	D
Clinical Research	M
Computational Biology	D
Ecology	M,D
Epidemiology	D
Family Nurse Practitioner Studies	M,D
Genetics	M,D
Genomic Sciences	D
Gerontological Nursing	M,D
Health Services Management and Hospital Administration	M,D
Health Services Research	D
Immunology	M,D
Maternal and Child/Neonatal Nursing	M,D
Microbiology	M,D
Molecular Biology	M,D
Neurobiology	D
Neuroscience	D
Nursing and Healthcare Administration	M,D
Nursing Education	M,D
Nursing—General	M,D
Oral and Dental Sciences	M
Pathology	D
Pediatric Nursing	M,D
Pharmacology	M,D
Physiology	M,D
Psychiatric Nursing	M,D
Public Health—General	M
Structural Biology	D
Toxicology	D

UNIVERSITY OF ST. AUGUSTINE FOR HEALTH SCIENCES

Health Services Management and Hospital Administration	M
Nursing and Healthcare Administration	M
Nursing Education	M
Nursing Informatics	M
Nursing—General	M,D
Occupational Therapy	M,D
Physical Therapy	D

UNIVERSITY OF ST. FRANCIS (IL)

Family Nurse Practitioner Studies	M,D,O
Nursing and Healthcare Administration	M,D,O
Nursing Education	M,D,O
Nursing—General	M,D,O
Physician Assistant Studies	M,O
Psychiatric Nursing	M,D,O

UNIVERSITY OF SAINT FRANCIS (IN)

Environmental and Occupational Health	M
Family Nurse Practitioner Studies	M,D,O
Health Services Management and Hospital Administration	M
Nurse Anesthesia	M,D,O
Nursing—General	M,D,O
Physician Assistant Studies	M

UNIVERSITY OF SAINT JOSEPH

Biochemistry	M
Biological and Biomedical Sciences—General	M
Family Nurse Practitioner Studies	M,D
Nursing Education	M,D
Nursing—General	M,D
Nutrition	M
Pharmacy	D
Psychiatric Nursing	M,D
Public Health—General	M

UNIVERSITY OF SAINT MARY

Health Services Management and Hospital Administration	M
Nursing and Healthcare Administration	M
Nursing Education	M
Nursing—General	M
Physical Therapy	D

UNIVERSITY OF ST. THOMAS (MN)

Health Services Management and Hospital Administration	M

UNIVERSITY OF SAN DIEGO

Adult Nursing	M,D
Family Nurse Practitioner Studies	M,D
Gerontological Nursing	M,D
Nursing and Healthcare Administration	M,D
Nursing—General	M,D
Pediatric Nursing	M,D
Psychiatric Nursing	M,D

UNIVERSITY OF SAN FRANCISCO

Biological and Biomedical Sciences—General	M
Health Services Management and Hospital Administration	M
Nursing—General	D
Public Health—General	M

UNIVERSITY OF SASKATCHEWAN

Allopathic Medicine	D
Anatomy	M,D
Biochemistry	M,D
Biological and Biomedical Sciences—General	M,D
Cell Biology	M,D
Community Health	M,D
Dentistry	D
Epidemiology	M,D
Health Services Management and Hospital Administration	M
Immunology	M,D
Microbiology	M,D
Nursing—General	M
Pathology	M,D
Pharmaceutical Sciences	M,D
Pharmacology	M,D
Physiology	M,D
Reproductive Biology	M,D
Toxicology	M,D,O
Veterinary Medicine	M,D
Veterinary Sciences	M,D

THE UNIVERSITY OF SCRANTON

Biochemistry	M
Family Nurse Practitioner Studies	M,D,O
Health Services Management and Hospital Administration	M
Nurse Anesthesia	M,D,O
Nursing and Healthcare Administration	M,D,O
Nursing—General	M,D,O
Occupational Therapy	M
Physical Therapy	D

UNIVERSITY OF SIOUX FALLS

Health Services Management and Hospital Administration	M

UNIVERSITY OF SOUTH AFRICA

Acute Care/Critical Care Nursing	M,D
Health Services Management and Hospital Administration	M,D
Maternal and Child/Neonatal Nursing	M,D
Medical/Surgical Nursing	M,D
Nurse Midwifery	M,D
Public Health—General	M,D

UNIVERSITY OF SOUTH ALABAMA

Allied Health—General	M,D
Allopathic Medicine	D
Biological and Biomedical Sciences—General	M,D
Communication Disorders	M,D
Environmental and Occupational Health	M
Nursing and Healthcare Administration	M,D,O
Nursing Education	M,D,O
Nursing—General	M,D,O
Occupational Therapy	M
Physical Therapy	D
Physician Assistant Studies	M
Toxicology	M

UNIVERSITY OF SOUTH CAROLINA

Acute Care/Critical Care Nursing	M,O
Adult Nursing	M,O
Allopathic Medicine	D
Biochemistry	M,D
Biological and Biomedical Sciences—General	M,D,O
Cell Biology	M,D
Communication Disorders	M,D
Community Health Nursing	M
Developmental Biology	M,D
Ecology	M,D
Environmental and Occupational Health	M,D
Epidemiology	M,D
Evolutionary Biology	M,D
Family Nurse Practitioner Studies	M
Health Promotion	M,D,O
Health Services Management and Hospital Administration	M,D
Industrial Hygiene	M,D
Medical/Surgical Nursing	M
Molecular Biology	M,D
Nurse Anesthesia	M
Nursing and Healthcare Administration	M
Nursing—General	M,O
Pediatric Nursing	M
Pharmaceutical Sciences	M,D
Pharmacy	D
Psychiatric Nursing	M,O
Public Health—General	M
Rehabilitation Sciences	M,O
Women's Health Nursing	M

UNIVERSITY OF SOUTH DAKOTA

Allied Health—General	M,D,O
Allopathic Medicine	D,O
Bioethics	D,O
Biological and Biomedical Sciences—General	M,D
Cardiovascular Sciences	M,D
Cell Biology	M,D
Communication Disorders	M,D
Health Services Management and Hospital Administration	M,O
Immunology	M,D
Microbiology	M,D
Molecular Biology	M,D
Neuroscience	M,D
Occupational Therapy	M,D
Pharmacology	M,D
Physical Therapy	D
Physician Assistant Studies	M
Physiology	M,D
Public Health—General	M

UNIVERSITY OF SOUTHERN CALIFORNIA

Allopathic Medicine	D
Biochemistry	M
Biological and Biomedical Sciences—General	M,D,O
Biophysics	M,D
Cancer Biology/Oncology	D
Cell Biology	D
Clinical Research	M,D,O
Computational Biology	D
Dentistry	D
Developmental Biology	D
Environmental and Occupational Health	M
Environmental Biology	M,D
Epidemiology	M,D
Evolutionary Biology	D
Genomic Sciences	D
Health Promotion	M
Health Services Management and Hospital Administration	M,O
Health Services Research	D
Immunology	M
International Health	M,O
Marine Biology	M,D
Medical Imaging	M,D
Medical Microbiology	D
Microbiology	M
Molecular Biology	M,D
Molecular Pharmacology	M,D
Neurobiology	D
Neuroscience	M,D
Nurse Anesthesia	D
Occupational Therapy	M,D
Oral and Dental Sciences	M,D,O
Pathology	M,D
Pharmaceutical Administration	M
Pharmaceutical Sciences	M,D,O
Pharmacy	D
Physical Therapy	M,D
Physician Assistant Studies	M
Physiology	M
Public Health—General	M
Toxicology	M,D

UNIVERSITY OF SOUTHERN INDIANA

Family Nurse Practitioner Studies	M,D,O
Health Services Management and Hospital Administration	M
Nursing and Healthcare Administration	M,D,O
Nursing Education	M,D,O
Nursing—General	M,D,O
Occupational Therapy	M
Psychiatric Nursing	M,D,O

UNIVERSITY OF SOUTHERN MAINE

Adult Nursing	M,D,O
Biological and Biomedical Sciences—General	M
Family Nurse Practitioner Studies	M,D,O
Gerontological Nursing	M,D,O
Health Services Management and Hospital Administration	M
Immunology	M
Molecular Biology	M
Nursing and Healthcare Administration	M,D,O
Nursing Education	M,D,O
Nursing—General	M,D,O
Occupational Therapy	M
Psychiatric Nursing	M,D,O
Public Health—General	M,O

UNIVERSITY OF SOUTHERN MISSISSIPPI

Biochemistry	M,D
Biological and Biomedical Sciences—General	M,D
Clinical Laboratory Sciences/Medical Technology	M
Communication Disorders	M,D
Epidemiology	M
Health Services Management and Hospital Administration	M
Nursing—General	M,D,O
Nutrition	M
Public Health—General	M

UNIVERSITY OF SOUTH FLORIDA

Acute Care/Critical Care Nursing	M,D,O
Adult Nursing	M,D,O
Allopathic Medicine	M,D
Anatomy	M,D
Bioethics	O
Biological and Biomedical Sciences—General	M,D
Cancer Biology/Oncology	M,D
Cardiovascular Sciences	O
Cell Biology	M,D
Clinical Research	M,D,O
Communication Disorders	M,D,O
Community Health	M,D,O
Computational Biology	M,D
Ecology	M,D
Environmental and Occupational Health	M,D,O
Environmental Biology	M,D
Epidemiology	M,D,O
Evolutionary Biology	M,D
Family Nurse Practitioner Studies	M,D,O
Gerontological Nursing	M,D,O
Health Services Management and Hospital Administration	M,D,O

Immunology M,D
Infectious Diseases M,D
International Health M,D,O
Maternal and Child Health O
Medical Microbiology M,D
Medical Physics M,D
Microbiology M,D
Molecular Biology M,D
Molecular Medicine M,D
Molecular Pharmacology M,D
Neuroscience M,D,O
Nurse Anesthesia M,D,O
Nursing Education M,D,O
Nursing—General M,D,O
Nutrition M,D,O
Occupational Health Nursing M,D,O
Oncology Nursing M,D,O
Pathology M,D
Pediatric Nursing M,D,O
Pharmaceutical Sciences M,D
Pharmacy M,D,O
Physical Therapy D
Physiology M,D
Public Health—General M,D,O*
Rehabilitation Sciences D
Toxicology O

THE UNIVERSITY OF TAMPA
Adult Nursing M
Family Nurse Practitioner Studies M
Nursing—General M
Nutrition M

THE UNIVERSITY OF TENNESSEE
Anatomy M,D
Animal Behavior M,D
Biochemistry M,D
Bioethics M,D
Biological and Biomedical Sciences—General M,D
Communication Disorders M,D,O
Community Health M,D
Ecology M,D
Entomology M,D
Evolutionary Biology M,D
Genetics M,D
Genomic Sciences M,D
Health Promotion M
Health Services Management and Hospital Administration M
Microbiology M,D
Nursing—General M,D
Nutrition M
Physiology M,D
Plant Pathology M,D
Plant Physiology M,D
Public Health—General M
Veterinary Medicine D

THE UNIVERSITY OF TENNESSEE AT CHATTANOOGA
Family Nurse Practitioner Studies M,D,O
Gerontological Nursing M,D,O
Nurse Anesthesia M,D,O
Nursing Education M,D,O
Nursing—General M,D,O
Occupational Therapy D
Physical Therapy D

THE UNIVERSITY OF TENNESSEE AT MARTIN
Nutrition M

THE UNIVERSITY OF TENNESSEE HEALTH SCIENCE CENTER
Allied Health—General M,D
Allopathic Medicine D
Biological and Biomedical Sciences—General M,D
Clinical Laboratory Sciences/Medical Technology M,D
Communication Disorders M,D
Dentistry D
Epidemiology M,D
Family Nurse Practitioner Studies D,O
Gerontological Nursing D,O
Health Services Research M,D
Nursing—General M,D,O
Occupational Therapy M,D
Oral and Dental Sciences M,D
Pathology M,D
Pediatric Nursing D,O
Pharmaceutical Sciences M,D
Pharmacology M,D
Pharmacy M,D
Physical Therapy M,D
Physician Assistant Studies M,D
Psychiatric Nursing D,O

THE UNIVERSITY OF TENNESSEE–OAK RIDGE NATIONAL LABORATORY
Biological and Biomedical Sciences—General M,D
Genomic Sciences M,D

THE UNIVERSITY OF TEXAS AT ARLINGTON
Biological and Biomedical Sciences—General M,D
Family Nurse Practitioner Studies M,D
Health Services Management and Hospital Administration M
Nursing and Healthcare Administration M,D
Nursing Education M,D
Nursing—General M,D

THE UNIVERSITY OF TEXAS AT AUSTIN
Adult Nursing M,D
Allopathic Medicine D
Animal Behavior D
Biochemistry D
Biological and Biomedical Sciences—General M,D
Biopsychology D
Cell Biology D
Clinical Laboratory Sciences/Medical Technology M,D
Communication Disorders M,D
Community Health Nursing M,D
Ecology D
Evolutionary Biology D
Family Nurse Practitioner Studies M,D
Gerontological Nursing M,D
Maternal and Child/Neonatal Nursing M,D
Medicinal and Pharmaceutical Chemistry M,D
Microbiology D
Molecular Biology D
Neurobiology D
Neuroscience D
Nursing and Healthcare Administration M,D
Nursing Education M,D
Nursing—General M,D
Nutrition M,D
Pediatric Nursing M,D
Pharmaceutical Sciences M,D
Pharmacology M,D
Pharmacy D
Plant Biology M,D
Psychiatric Nursing M,D
Toxicology M,D

THE UNIVERSITY OF TEXAS AT DALLAS
Biochemistry M,D
Biological and Biomedical Sciences—General M,D
Cell Biology M,D
Communication Disorders M,D
Health Services Management and Hospital Administration M,D
Molecular Biology M,D
Neuroscience M,D

THE UNIVERSITY OF TEXAS AT EL PASO
Allied Health—General D
Biochemistry M,D
Biological and Biomedical Sciences—General M,D
Communication Disorders M
Family Nurse Practitioner Studies M,D,O
Health Services Management and Hospital Administration M,D,O
Nursing and Healthcare Administration M,D,O
Nursing Education M,D,O
Nursing—General M,D,O
Occupational Therapy M
Physical Therapy D
Public Health—General M,O

THE UNIVERSITY OF TEXAS AT SAN ANTONIO
Biological and Biomedical Sciences—General M,D
Cell Biology M,D
Ecology M
Molecular Biology M,D
Neurobiology M,D
Translational Biology D

THE UNIVERSITY OF TEXAS AT TYLER
Biological and Biomedical Sciences—General M
Environmental and Occupational Health M
Family Nurse Practitioner Studies M,D
Health Services Management and Hospital Administration M
Nursing and Healthcare Administration M,D
Nursing Education M,D
Nursing—General M,D
Pharmacy D

THE UNIVERSITY OF TEXAS HEALTH SCIENCE CENTER AT HOUSTON
Allopathic Medicine D
Biochemistry M,D
Biological and Biomedical Sciences—General M,D
Cancer Biology/Oncology M,D
Cell Biology M,D
Community Health M,D,O
Dentistry M,D
Environmental and Occupational Health M,D,O
Epidemiology M,D,O
Genetics M,D
Genomic Sciences M,D,O
Health Promotion M,D,O
Health Services Management and Hospital Administration M,D,O
Immunology M,D
Infectious Diseases M,D
Maternal and Child Health M,D,O
Medical Physics M,D
Microbiology M,D
Neuroscience M,D
Nursing—General M,D
Pharmacology M,D
Public Health—General M,D,O

THE UNIVERSITY OF TEXAS HEALTH SCIENCE CENTER AT SAN ANTONIO
Acute Care/Critical Care Nursing M,D,O
Allopathic Medicine M,D
Biochemistry M,D
Biological and Biomedical Sciences—General D
Cell Biology M,D
Clinical Laboratory Sciences/Medical Technology D
Clinical Research M
Communication Disorders M,D
Community Health Nursing M,D,O
Dentistry M,D,O
Family Nurse Practitioner Studies M,D,O
Gerontological Nursing M,D,O
Immunology M,D
Medical Physics D
Microbiology M,D
Molecular Medicine M,D
Neuroscience D
Nursing and Healthcare Administration M,D,O
Nursing Education M,D,O
Nursing—General M,D,O
Occupational Therapy M,D
Pediatric Nursing M,D,O
Pharmacology D
Physical Therapy M,D
Physician Assistant Studies M,D
Psychiatric Nursing M,D,O
Structural Biology M,D
Toxicology M

THE UNIVERSITY OF TEXAS MD ANDERSON CANCER CENTER
Genetics M

THE UNIVERSITY OF TEXAS MEDICAL BRANCH
Allied Health—General M,D
Allopathic Medicine D
Biochemistry D
Biological and Biomedical Sciences—General M,D
Biophysics D
Cell Biology M,D
Clinical Laboratory Sciences/Medical Technology M,D
Computational Biology D
Immunology M,D
Microbiology M,D
Molecular Biophysics D
Neuroscience D
Nursing—General M,D
Occupational Therapy M
Pathology D
Pharmacology M,D
Physical Therapy M,D
Physician Assistant Studies M
Physiology M,D
Public Health—General M
Rehabilitation Sciences D
Structural Biology D
Toxicology M,D
Translational Biology M,D

THE UNIVERSITY OF TEXAS OF THE PERMIAN BASIN
Biological and Biomedical Sciences—General M

THE UNIVERSITY OF TEXAS RIO GRANDE VALLEY
Adult Nursing M,O
Allopathic Medicine D
Biological and Biomedical Sciences—General M
Clinical Laboratory Sciences/Medical Technology M
Communication Disorders M
Family Nurse Practitioner Studies M,O
Health Services Management and Hospital Administration M
Nursing and Healthcare Administration M,O
Nursing Education M,O
Nursing—General M,O
Nutrition M
Occupational Therapy M
Physician Assistant Studies M
Psychiatric Nursing M,O

THE UNIVERSITY OF TEXAS SOUTHWESTERN MEDICAL CENTER
Allopathic Medicine D
Biochemistry D
Biological and Biomedical Sciences—General M,D
Cancer Biology/Oncology D
Cell Biology D
Developmental Biology D
Genetics D
Immunology D
Microbiology D
Molecular Biophysics D
Neuroscience D
Nutrition M
Physical Therapy D
Physician Assistant Studies M

UNIVERSITY OF THE CUMBERLANDS
Physician Assistant Studies M

UNIVERSITY OF THE DISTRICT OF COLUMBIA
Cancer Biology/Oncology M
Communication Disorders M
Nutrition M

UNIVERSITY OF THE INCARNATE WORD
Biological and Biomedical Sciences—General M
Health Services Management and Hospital Administration M,D
Nursing—General M,D
Nutrition M
Optometry D
Osteopathic Medicine M,D
Pharmacy D
Physical Therapy D

UNIVERSITY OF THE PACIFIC
Biological and Biomedical Sciences—General M
Communication Disorders M,D
Dentistry M,D,O
Pharmaceutical Sciences M,D
Pharmacy D
Physical Therapy M,D

UNIVERSITY OF THE SACRED HEART
Environmental and Occupational Health M
Occupational Health Nursing M

UNIVERSITY OF THE SCIENCES
Biochemistry M,D
Cell Biology M
Health Services Management and Hospital Administration M,D
Medicinal and Pharmaceutical Chemistry M,D
Occupational Therapy M,D
Pharmaceutical Administration M
Pharmaceutical Sciences M,D
Pharmacology M,D
Pharmacy D
Physical Therapy D
Public Health—General M
Toxicology M,D

THE UNIVERSITY OF TOLEDO
Biochemistry M,D
Biological and Biomedical Sciences—General M,D,O
Cancer Biology/Oncology M,D
Cardiovascular Sciences M,D
Communication Disorders M,D,O
Community Health Nursing M,O
Ecology M,D
Environmental and Occupational Health M,D,O
Epidemiology M,O
Family Nurse Practitioner Studies M,O
Genomic Sciences M,O
Health Promotion M,D,O
Health Services Management and Hospital Administration M,O
Immunology M,D
Industrial Hygiene M,D,O
International Health M,O
Medical Physics M,D
Medicinal and Pharmaceutical Chemistry M,D
Neuroscience M,D
Nursing and Healthcare Administration M,O
Nursing Education M,O
Nursing—General M,D,O
Nutrition M,O
Occupational Therapy M,D
Oral and Dental Sciences M
Pathology M,O
Pediatric Nursing M,O
Pharmaceutical Administration M
Pharmaceutical Sciences M
Pharmacology M,D
Pharmacy M,D
Physical Therapy M,D
Physician Assistant Studies M
Public Health—General M,D,O

UNIVERSITY OF TORONTO
Allopathic Medicine M,D
Biochemistry M,D
Bioethics M,D
Biophysics M,D
Cell Biology M,D
Communication Disorders M,D
Community Health M,D
Dentistry D
Ecology M,D
Environmental and Occupational Health M,D
Epidemiology M,D
Evolutionary Biology M,D
Health Physics/Radiological Health M,D
Health Promotion M,D
Health Services Management and Hospital Administration M
Immunology M,D
Molecular Genetics M,D
Nursing—General M,D
Nutrition M,D
Occupational Therapy M
Oral and Dental Sciences M,D
Pathobiology M,D
Pharmaceutical Sciences M,D
Pharmacology M,D
Physical Therapy M
Physiology M,D
Public Health—General M,D
Rehabilitation Sciences M,D
Systems Biology M,D

THE UNIVERSITY OF TULSA
Biochemistry M,D
Biological and Biomedical Sciences—General M,D
Communication Disorders M
Family Nurse Practitioner Studies D
Gerontological Nursing D
Nursing—General D
Rehabilitation Sciences M

UNIVERSITY OF UTAH
Allopathic Medicine D
Anatomy D
Biochemistry M,D
Biological and Biomedical Sciences—General M,D,O
Cancer Biology/Oncology M,D
Clinical Laboratory Sciences/Medical Technology M

*M—masters degree; D—doctorate; O—other advanced degree; *—Close-Up and/or Display*

Communication Disorders	M,D
Dentistry	D
Gerontological Nursing	M,O
Health Promotion	M,D
Health Services Management and Hospital Administration	M,D
Health Services Research	M,D
Human Genetics	M,D
Medical Physics	M,D
Medicinal and Pharmaceutical Chemistry	M,D
Molecular Biology	D
Neurobiology	D
Neuroscience	D
Nursing—General	M,D
Nutrition	M,D
Occupational Therapy	M,D
Pathology	M,D
Pharmaceutical Administration	M,D
Pharmaceutical Sciences	M,D
Pharmacology	D
Pharmacy	D
Physical Therapy	D
Physician Assistant Studies	M
Physiology	M,D
Public Health—General	M,D
Rehabilitation Sciences	D
Toxicology	D

UNIVERSITY OF VERMONT

Allied Health—General	M,D,O
Allopathic Medicine	M,D,O
Biochemistry	M,D
Biological and Biomedical Sciences—General	M,D
Cell Biology	D
Clinical Laboratory Sciences/Medical Technology	M,D,O
Communication Disorders	M
Community Health	M
Entomology	M,D,O
Environmental and Occupational Health	M,O
Epidemiology	M,O
Health Promotion	M
Health Services Management and Hospital Administration	M,O
International Health	M,O
Molecular Biology	D
Neuroscience	D
Nursing—General	M,D,O
Nutrition	M
Pathology	M
Pharmacology	M,D
Physical Therapy	D
Plant Biology	M,D
Plant Pathology	M,D,O
Public Health—General	M,O
Rehabilitation Sciences	D
Veterinary Sciences	M,D

UNIVERSITY OF VICTORIA

Biochemistry	M,D
Biological and Biomedical Sciences—General	M,D
Family Nurse Practitioner Studies	M,D
Medical Physics	M,D
Microbiology	M,D
Nursing and Healthcare Administration	M,D
Nursing Education	M,D
Nursing—General	M,D

UNIVERSITY OF VIRGINIA

Acute Care/Critical Care Nursing	M,D
Allopathic Medicine	M,D
Biochemistry	D
Biological and Biomedical Sciences—General	M,D
Biophysics	M,D
Cell Biology	D
Clinical Research	M
Communication Disorders	M,D
Community Health	M,D
Health Services Management and Hospital Administration	M
Health Services Research	M
Microbiology	D
Molecular Genetics	D
Molecular Physiology	M,D
Neuroscience	D
Nursing and Healthcare Administration	M,D
Nursing—General	M,D
Pathology	D
Pharmacology	D
Physiology	D
Psychiatric Nursing	M,D
Public Health—General	M,D

UNIVERSITY OF WASHINGTON

Allopathic Medicine	D
Animal Behavior	M,D
Biochemistry	D
Bioethics	M
Biological and Biomedical Sciences—General	M,D
Biophysics	D
Cell Biology	D
Clinical Laboratory Sciences/Medical Technology	M
Clinical Research	M,D
Communication Disorders	M,D
Community Health	M,D
Dentistry	M,D,O
Ecology	M,D
Environmental and Occupational Health	M,D
Epidemiology	M,D
Genetics	M,D,O
Genomic Sciences	D
Health Services Management and Hospital Administration	M
Health Services Research	M,D
Immunology	D
International Health	M,D
Maternal and Child Health	M,D
Medicinal and Pharmaceutical Chemistry	D
Microbiology	D
Molecular Biology	D
Neurobiology	D
Neuroscience	M,D
Nursing—General	M,D,O
Nutrition	M,D
Occupational Therapy	M,D
Oral and Dental Sciences	M,D,O
Pathobiology	D
Pathology	D
Pharmaceutical Sciences	M,D
Pharmacology	D
Pharmacy	M,D
Physical Therapy	M,D
Physiology	D
Public Health—General	M
Rehabilitation Sciences	M,D
Structural Biology	D
Toxicology	M,D
Veterinary Sciences	M

UNIVERSITY OF WASHINGTON, BOTHELL

Nursing—General	M

UNIVERSITY OF WASHINGTON, TACOMA

Community Health Nursing	M
Nursing and Healthcare Administration	M
Nursing Education	M
Nursing—General	M

UNIVERSITY OF WATERLOO

Biochemistry	M,D
Biological and Biomedical Sciences—General	M,D
Optometry	M,D
Public Health—General	M,D
Vision Sciences	M,D

THE UNIVERSITY OF WEST ALABAMA

Conservation Biology	M

THE UNIVERSITY OF WESTERN ONTARIO

Allopathic Medicine	M,D
Anatomy	M,D
Biochemistry	M,D
Biological and Biomedical Sciences—General	M,D
Biophysics	M,D
Cell Biology	M,D
Communication Disorders	M
Dentistry	D
Epidemiology	M,D
Health Services Management and Hospital Administration	M,D
Immunology	M,D
Microbiology	M,D
Neuroscience	M,D
Nursing—General	M,D
Occupational Therapy	M
Oral and Dental Sciences	M
Pathology	M,D
Physical Therapy	M,O
Physiology	M,D

UNIVERSITY OF WESTERN STATES

Chiropractic	D

UNIVERSITY OF WEST FLORIDA

Biological and Biomedical Sciences—General	M
Health Promotion	M
Health Services Management and Hospital Administration	M
Nursing—General	M
Public Health—General	M

UNIVERSITY OF WEST GEORGIA

Biological and Biomedical Sciences—General	M,O
Communication Disorders	M,D,O
Health Services Management and Hospital Administration	M,D,O
Nursing Education	M,D,O
Nursing—General	M,D,O

UNIVERSITY OF WINDSOR

Biochemistry	M,D
Biological and Biomedical Sciences—General	M,D
Biopsychology	M,D
Nursing—General	M

UNIVERSITY OF WISCONSIN–EAU CLAIRE

Adult Nursing	M,D
Communication Disorders	M
Family Nurse Practitioner Studies	M,D
Gerontological Nursing	M,D
Nursing and Healthcare Administration	M,D
Nursing Education	M,D
Nursing—General	M,D

UNIVERSITY OF WISCONSIN–GREEN BAY

Nursing and Healthcare Administration	M

UNIVERSITY OF WISCONSIN–LA CROSSE

Biological and Biomedical Sciences—General	M
Cancer Biology/Oncology	M
Cell Biology	M
Community Health	M
Medical Microbiology	M
Microbiology	M
Molecular Biology	M
Nurse Anesthesia	M
Occupational Therapy	M
Physical Therapy	D
Physician Assistant Studies	M
Physiology	M
Public Health—General	M
Rehabilitation Sciences	M

UNIVERSITY OF WISCONSIN–MADISON

Adult Nursing	D
Allopathic Medicine	D
Bacteriology	M
Biochemistry	M,D
Biological and Biomedical Sciences—General	
Biophysics	D
Biopsychology	D
Botany	M,D
Cancer Biology/Oncology	D
Cell Biology	D
Clinical Research	M,D
Communication Disorders	M,D
Conservation Biology	M
Ecology	M
Entomology	M,D
Environmental Biology	M,D
Epidemiology	M,D
Genetics	M,D
Gerontological Nursing	D
Medical Microbiology	D
Medical Physics	M,D
Microbiology	D
Molecular Biology	D
Molecular Pathology	D
Neuroscience	D
Nursing—General	D
Nutrition	M,D
Occupational Therapy	M,D
Pathology	D
Pediatric Nursing	D
Pharmaceutical Administration	M,D
Pharmaceutical Sciences	M,D
Pharmacology	D
Pharmacy	D
Physical Therapy	D
Physician Assistant Studies	M
Physiology	M,D
Plant Pathology	M,D
Psychiatric Nursing	D
Public Health—General	M
Toxicology	M,D
Veterinary Medicine	M,D
Veterinary Sciences	M,D
Zoology	M,D

UNIVERSITY OF WISCONSIN–MILWAUKEE

Allied Health—General	M,D,O
Biochemistry	M,D
Biological and Biomedical Sciences—General	M,D
Cell Biology	M,D
Communication Disorders	M
Community Health	D
Environmental and Occupational Health	M,D,O
Epidemiology	M,D,O
Family Nurse Practitioner Studies	M,D,O
Health Promotion	M,D,O
Health Services Management and Hospital Administration	M,D
Medical Imaging	D
Microbiology	M,D
Molecular Biology	M,D
Nursing—General	M,D,O*
Nutrition	M,D
Occupational Therapy	M
Physical Therapy	M,D
Public Health—General	M,D,O
Rehabilitation Sciences	D

UNIVERSITY OF WISCONSIN–OSHKOSH

Adult Nursing	M
Biological and Biomedical Sciences—General	M
Botany	M
Family Nurse Practitioner Studies	M
Health Services Management and Hospital Administration	M
Microbiology	M
Nursing—General	M
Zoology	M

UNIVERSITY OF WISCONSIN–PARKSIDE

Health Promotion	M
Molecular Biology	M

UNIVERSITY OF WISCONSIN–RIVER FALLS

Communication Disorders	M

UNIVERSITY OF WISCONSIN–STEVENS POINT

Communication Disorders	M,D
Health Promotion	M
Nutrition	M

UNIVERSITY OF WISCONSIN–STOUT

Conservation Biology	M
Industrial Hygiene	M
Nutrition	M

UNIVERSITY OF WISCONSIN–WHITEWATER

Communication Disorders	M
Environmental and Occupational Health	M

UNIVERSITY OF WYOMING

Botany	M,D
Cell Biology	D
Communication Disorders	M
Community Health	M,D
Computational Biology	D
Ecology	M,D
Entomology	M,D
Genetics	D
Health Promotion	M
Health Services Management and Hospital Administration	M,D
Microbiology	D
Molecular Biology	M,D
Nursing—General	M
Nutrition	M
Pathobiology	M
Pharmacy	M,D
Physiology	M,D
Reproductive Biology	M,D
Zoology	M,D

URBANA UNIVERSITY–A BRANCH CAMPUS OF FRANKLIN UNIVERSITY

Nursing—General	M

URSULINE COLLEGE

Adult Nursing	M,D
Family Nurse Practitioner Studies	M,D
Gerontological Nursing	M,D
Health Services Management and Hospital Administration	M
Medical/Surgical Nursing	M,D
Nursing Education	M,D
Nursing—General	M,D

UTAH STATE UNIVERSITY

Biochemistry	M,D
Biological and Biomedical Sciences—General	M,D
Communication Disorders	M,D,O
Ecology	M,D
Health Promotion	M,D
Nutrition	M,D
Public Health—General	M,D
Toxicology	M,D
Veterinary Sciences	M,D

UTAH VALLEY UNIVERSITY

Nursing—General	M

UTICA COLLEGE

Health Services Management and Hospital Administration	M
Occupational Therapy	M
Physical Therapy	D

VALDOSTA STATE UNIVERSITY

Communication Disorders	M,D,O
Family Nurse Practitioner Studies	M
Gerontological Nursing	M
Health Services Management and Hospital Administration	M
Nursing—General	M
Psychiatric Nursing	M

VALPARAISO UNIVERSITY

Health Services Management and Hospital Administration	M
Nursing Education	M,D,O
Nursing—General	M,D,O
Physician Assistant Studies	M,D,O
Public Health—General	M,D,O

VAN ANDEL INSTITUTE GRADUATE SCHOOL

Genetics	D
Molecular Genetics	D

VANDERBILT UNIVERSITY

Acute Care/Critical Care Nursing	M,D,O
Adult Nursing	M,D,O
Allopathic Medicine	M,D
Biochemistry	M,D
Biological and Biomedical Sciences—General	M,D
Biophysics	M,D
Cell Biology	M,D
Communication Disorders	M,D
Developmental Biology	M,D
Family Nurse Practitioner Studies	M,D,O
Gerontological Nursing	M,D,O
Health Physics/Radiological Health	M,D
Health Services Management and Hospital Administration	M
Human Genetics	D
Immunology	M,D
Maternal and Child/Neonatal Nursing	M,D,O
Microbiology	M,D
Molecular Biology	M,D
Molecular Physiology	M,D
Nurse Midwifery	M,D,O
Nursing and Healthcare Administration	M,D,O
Nursing Informatics	M,D,O
Nursing—General	M,D,O
Pathology	D
Pediatric Nursing	M,D,O
Pharmacology	D
Psychiatric Nursing	M,D,O
Public Health—General	M
Women's Health Nursing	M,D,O

VANGUARD UNIVERSITY OF SOUTHERN CALIFORNIA

Nursing—General	M

VILLANOVA UNIVERSITY

Adult Nursing	M,D,O
Biological and Biomedical Sciences—General	M
Family Nurse Practitioner Studies	M,D,O
Gerontological Nursing	M,D,O
Health Services Management and Hospital Administration	M
Nurse Anesthesia	M,D,O
Nursing Education	M,D,O
Nursing—General	M,D,O
Pediatric Nursing	M,D,O

VIRGINIA COMMONWEALTH UNIVERSITY

Adult Nursing	M,D,O
Allied Health—General	D
Allopathic Medicine	D
Anatomy	M
Biochemistry	M,D

Biological and Biomedical Sciences—General	M,D,O
Clinical Laboratory Sciences/Medical Technology	M,D
Dentistry	M,D
Family Nurse Practitioner Studies	M
Health Physics/Radiological Health	D
Health Services Management and Hospital Administration	M,D
Health Services Research	D
Human Genetics	M,D
Immunology	M,D
Medical Physics	M,D
Medicinal and Pharmaceutical Chemistry	M,D
Microbiology	M,D
Molecular Biology	M,D
Molecular Genetics	M,D
Neurobiology	M
Neuroscience	M,D,O
Nurse Anesthesia	M,D
Nursing and Healthcare Administration	M,D,O
Nursing Education	M,D,O
Nursing—General	M,D,O
Occupational Therapy	M,D
Pediatric Nursing	M,D,O
Pharmaceutical Administration	M,D
Pharmaceutical Sciences	M,D
Pharmacology	M,D,O
Pharmacy	D
Physical Therapy	M,D
Physiology	M,D
Psychiatric Nursing	M,D,O
Rehabilitation Sciences	D
Systems Biology	D
Toxicology	M,D,O
Women's Health Nursing	M,D,O

VIRGINIA INTERNATIONAL UNIVERSITY

Health Services Management and Hospital Administration	M,O

VIRGINIA POLYTECHNIC INSTITUTE AND STATE UNIVERSITY

Biochemistry	M,D
Biological and Biomedical Sciences—General	M,D
Entomology	M,D
Genetics	M,D
Nutrition	M,D
Plant Pathology	M,D
Plant Physiology	M,D
Public Health—General	M,D
Veterinary Medicine	M,D
Veterinary Sciences	M,D

VIRGINIA STATE UNIVERSITY

Biological and Biomedical Sciences—General	M
Community Health	M,D

VITERBO UNIVERSITY

Health Services Management and Hospital Administration	M
Nursing—General	D

WAGNER COLLEGE

Family Nurse Practitioner Studies	M,D,O
Microbiology	M
Nursing Education	M,D,O
Nursing—General	M,D,O

WAKE FOREST UNIVERSITY

Allopathic Medicine	D
Anatomy	D
Biochemistry	D
Biological and Biomedical Sciences—General	M,D
Cancer Biology/Oncology	D
Genomic Sciences	D
Health Services Research	M
Immunology	D
Microbiology	D
Molecular Genetics	D
Molecular Medicine	M,D
Neurobiology	D
Neuroscience	D
Nurse Anesthesia	M
Pathobiology	M,D
Pharmacology	D
Physiology	D

WALDEN UNIVERSITY

Adult Nursing	M,D,O
Clinical Research	M,D,O
Community Health	M,D,O
Epidemiology	M,D,O
Family Nurse Practitioner Studies	M,D,O
Gerontological Nursing	M,D,O
Health Promotion	M,D,O
Health Services Management and Hospital Administration	M,D,O
International Health	M,D,O
Nursing and Healthcare Administration	M,D,O
Nursing Education	M,D,O
Nursing Informatics	M,D,O
Nursing—General	M,D,O
Public Health—General	M,D,O

WALLA WALLA UNIVERSITY

Biological and Biomedical Sciences—General	M

WALSH UNIVERSITY

Adult Nursing	M,D
Health Services Management and Hospital Administration	M
Nursing and Healthcare Administration	M,D
Nursing Education	M,D
Nursing—General	M,D
Physical Therapy	D

WASHBURN UNIVERSITY

Nursing and Healthcare Administration	M,D,O
Nursing—General	M,D,O

WASHINGTON ADVENTIST UNIVERSITY

Health Services Management and Hospital Administration	M
Nursing and Healthcare Administration	M
Nursing Education	M
Nursing—General	M

WASHINGTON STATE UNIVERSITY

Allopathic Medicine	M,D
Biochemistry	M,D
Bioethics	M,D,O
Biological and Biomedical Sciences—General	M,D
Biophysics	M,D
Communication Disorders	M
Community Health	M,D,O
Entomology	M,D
Family Nurse Practitioner Studies	M,D,O
Genetics	M,D
Health Services Management and Hospital Administration	M
Immunology	M,D
Infectious Diseases	M,D
Neuroscience	M,D
Nursing—General	M,D,O
Nutrition	M
Pharmacy	M,D
Plant Pathology	M,D
Psychiatric Nursing	M,D,O
Veterinary Medicine	D
Veterinary Sciences	M,D

WASHINGTON UNIVERSITY IN ST. LOUIS

Allopathic Medicine	D
Biochemistry	D
Bioethics	M
Biological and Biomedical Sciences—General	D
Cell Biology	D
Clinical Research	M
Communication Disorders	M,D
Computational Biology	D
Developmental Biology	D
Ecology	D
Environmental Biology	D
Epidemiology	M,D
Evolutionary Biology	D
Genetics	M,D
Genomic Sciences	M
Health Services Research	M,O
Human Genetics	D
Immunology	D
International Health	M,D
Microbiology	D
Molecular Biology	D
Molecular Biophysics	D
Molecular Genetics	D
Molecular Pathogenesis	D
Neuroscience	D
Occupational Therapy	M,D
Physical Therapy	D
Plant Biology	D
Public Health—General	M,D
Rehabilitation Sciences	D
Systems Biology	D

WAYLAND BAPTIST UNIVERSITY

Health Services Management and Hospital Administration	M,D

WAYNESBURG UNIVERSITY

Health Services Management and Hospital Administration	M,D
Nursing and Healthcare Administration	M,D
Nursing Education	M,D
Nursing Informatics	M,D
Nursing—General	M,D

WAYNE STATE UNIVERSITY

Acute Care/Critical Care Nursing	M,D
Adult Nursing	M,D
Allopathic Medicine	D
Anatomy	M,D,O
Biochemistry	M,D,O
Biological and Biomedical Sciences—General	M,D
Biopsychology	M,D,O
Cancer Biology/Oncology	M,D,O
Cell Biology	M,D,O
Communication Disorders	M,D
Community Health Nursing	M,D
Computational Biology	M,D
Genomic Sciences	M,D,O
Gerontological Nursing	M,D
Health Services Management and Hospital Administration	M,D
Health Services Research	M,D
Immunology	M,D,O
Maternal and Child/Neonatal Nursing	M,D
Medical Imaging	M,D,O
Medical Physics	M,D,O
Medicinal and Pharmaceutical Chemistry	M,D
Microbiology	M,D,O
Molecular Biology	M,D,O
Molecular Genetics	M,D,O
Molecular Medicine	M,D,O
Neuroscience	M,D,O
Nurse Anesthesia	M,D,O
Nurse Midwifery	M,D
Nursing—General	M,D
Nutrition	M,D,O
Occupational Therapy	M
Pathology	M,D,O
Pediatric Nursing	M,D,O
Pharmaceutical Sciences	M,D
Pharmacology	M,D,O
Pharmacy	D
Physical Therapy	D
Physician Assistant Studies	M
Physiology	M,D,O
Psychiatric Nursing	M,D
Public Health—General	M,D,O
Toxicology	M,D
Women's Health Nursing	M,D

WEBER STATE UNIVERSITY

Health Physics/Radiological Health	M
Health Services Management and Hospital Administration	M
Nursing and Healthcare Administration	M
Nursing Education	M
Nursing—General	M

WEBSTER UNIVERSITY

Communication Disorders	M
Health Services Management and Hospital Administration	M,D,O
Nurse Anesthesia	D
Nursing Education	M
Nursing—General	M

WEILL CORNELL MEDICINE

Biochemistry	M,D
Biological and Biomedical Sciences—General	M,D
Biophysics	M,D
Cell Biology	M,D
Computational Biology	D
Epidemiology	M
Health Services Research	M
Immunology	M,D
Molecular Biology	M,D
Neuroscience	M,D
Pharmacology	M,D
Physician Assistant Studies	M
Physiology	M,D
Structural Biology	M,D
Systems Biology	M,D

WESLEYAN UNIVERSITY

Biochemistry	D
Biological and Biomedical Sciences—General	D
Cell Biology	D
Developmental Biology	D
Ecology	D
Evolutionary Biology	D
Genetics	D
Genomic Sciences	D
Molecular Biology	D
Molecular Biophysics	D
Neurobiology	D

WESLEY COLLEGE

Nursing—General	M

WEST CHESTER UNIVERSITY OF PENNSYLVANIA

Biological and Biomedical Sciences—General	M,O
Communication Disorders	M
Gerontological Nursing	M,D,O
Health Services Management and Hospital Administration	M,O
Nursing Education	M,D,O
Nursing—General	M,D,O
Nutrition	M
Public Health—General	M,O
School Nursing	M,D,O

WEST COAST UNIVERSITY

Family Nurse Practitioner Studies	M,D
Health Services Management and Hospital Administration	M,D
Nursing—General	M,D
Occupational Therapy	M,D
Pharmacy	M,D
Physical Therapy	M,D

WESTERN CAROLINA UNIVERSITY

Biological and Biomedical Sciences—General	M
Communication Disorders	M
Health Services Management and Hospital Administration	M
Nursing—General	M,D,O
Physical Therapy	D

WESTERN CONNECTICUT STATE UNIVERSITY

Adult Nursing	M,D
Gerontological Nursing	M,D
Health Services Management and Hospital Administration	M
Nursing Education	D
Nursing—General	M,D

WESTERN GOVERNORS UNIVERSITY

Health Services Management and Hospital Administration	M
Nursing and Healthcare Administration	M
Nursing Education	M
Nursing Informatics	M

WESTERN ILLINOIS UNIVERSITY

Biological and Biomedical Sciences—General	M,O
Communication Disorders	M
Ecology	D
Marine Biology	M,O
Public Health—General	M
Zoology	M,O

WESTERN KENTUCKY UNIVERSITY

Biological and Biomedical Sciences—General	M
Communication Disorders	M
Health Services Management and Hospital Administration	M
Nursing—General	M
Physical Therapy	D
Public Health—General	M

WESTERN MICHIGAN UNIVERSITY

Biological and Biomedical Sciences—General	M,D,O
Communication Disorders	M,D
Health Services Management and Hospital Administration	M,D,O
Nursing—General	M
Occupational Therapy	M
Physician Assistant Studies	M
Physiology	M
Rehabilitation Sciences	M

WESTERN NEW ENGLAND UNIVERSITY

Occupational Therapy	D
Pharmacy	D

WESTERN NEW MEXICO UNIVERSITY

Occupational Therapy	M

WESTERN UNIVERSITY OF HEALTH SCIENCES

Allied Health—General	M,D
Biological and Biomedical Sciences—General	M
Dentistry	D
Nursing and Healthcare Administration	M
Nursing—General	M,D
Optometry	D
Osteopathic Medicine	D
Pharmaceutical Sciences	M
Pharmacy	D
Physical Therapy	D
Physician Assistant Studies	M
Podiatric Medicine	D
Veterinary Medicine	D

WESTERN WASHINGTON UNIVERSITY

Biological and Biomedical Sciences—General	M
Communication Disorders	M

WESTFIELD STATE UNIVERSITY

Physician Assistant Studies	M

WEST LIBERTY UNIVERSITY

Biological and Biomedical Sciences—General	M
Physician Assistant Studies	M
Zoology	M

WESTMINSTER COLLEGE (UT)

Family Nurse Practitioner Studies	M
Nurse Anesthesia	M
Nursing—General	M
Public Health—General	M

WEST TEXAS A&M UNIVERSITY

Biological and Biomedical Sciences—General	M
Communication Disorders	M
Family Nurse Practitioner Studies	M
Nursing—General	M

WEST VIRGINIA SCHOOL OF OSTEOPATHIC MEDICINE

Osteopathic Medicine	D

WEST VIRGINIA UNIVERSITY

Allopathic Medicine	M,D
Biochemistry	M,D
Biological and Biomedical Sciences—General	M,D
Cancer Biology/Oncology	M,D
Communication Disorders	M,D
Dental Hygiene	M,D
Dentistry	M,D
Developmental Biology	M,D
Entomology	M,D
Environmental and Occupational Health	M,D
Epidemiology	M,D
Genetics	M,D
Immunology	M,D
Industrial Hygiene	M,D
Molecular Biology	M,D
Nursing—General	M,D,O
Nutrition	M,D
Occupational Therapy	M,D
Oral and Dental Sciences	M,D
Pathology	M,D
Pharmaceutical Sciences	D
Pharmacy	D
Physical Therapy	M,D
Plant Pathology	M,D
Public Health—General	M,D

WEST VIRGINIA WESLEYAN COLLEGE

Family Nurse Practitioner Studies	M,O
Nurse Midwifery	M,O
Nursing and Healthcare Administration	M,O
Nursing Education	M,O
Nursing—General	M,O
Psychiatric Nursing	M,O

WHEELING JESUIT UNIVERSITY

Nursing—General	M
Physical Therapy	D

WICHITA STATE UNIVERSITY

Allied Health—General	M,D
Biological and Biomedical Sciences—General	M
Communication Disorders	M,D
Nursing—General	M,D
Physical Therapy	D
Physician Assistant Studies	M

*M—masters degree; D—doctorate; O—other advanced degree; *—Close-Up and/or Display*

WIDENER UNIVERSITY
Health Services Management and Hospital Administration M
Nursing—General M,D,O
Physical Therapy M,D

WILFRID LAURIER UNIVERSITY
Biological and Biomedical Sciences—General M
Health Promotion M
Neuroscience M,D

WILKES UNIVERSITY
Health Services Management and Hospital Administration M
Nursing—General M,D
Pharmacy D

WILLIAM CAREY UNIVERSITY
Nursing—General M
Osteopathic Medicine D

WILLIAM JAMES COLLEGE
Community Health M,D,O
International Health M,D,O

WILLIAM PATERSON UNIVERSITY OF NEW JERSEY
Adult Nursing M,D,O
Biological and Biomedical Sciences—General M,D,O
Communication Disorders M,D,O
Gerontological Nursing M,D,O
Nursing Education M,D,O
Nursing—General M,D,O
School Nursing M,D,O

WILLIAM WOODS UNIVERSITY
Health Services Management and Hospital Administration M,D,O

WILMINGTON UNIVERSITY
Adult Nursing M,D
Family Nurse Practitioner Studies M,D
Gerontological Nursing M,D
Health Services Management and Hospital Administration M,D
Nursing and Healthcare Administration M,D
Nursing—General M,D

WILSON COLLEGE
Health Services Management and Hospital Administration M
Nursing and Healthcare Administration M
Nursing Education M
Nursing—General M

WINGATE UNIVERSITY
Health Services Management and Hospital Administration M
Pharmacy D
Physical Therapy D
Physician Assistant Studies M

WINONA STATE UNIVERSITY
Acute Care/Critical Care Nursing M,D,O
Adult Nursing M,D,O
Family Nurse Practitioner Studies M,D,O
Gerontological Nursing M,D,O
Nursing and Healthcare Administration M,D,O
Nursing Education M,D,O
Nursing—General M,D,O

WINSTON-SALEM STATE UNIVERSITY
Family Nurse Practitioner Studies M,D
Health Services Management and Hospital Administration M
Nursing Education M,D
Nursing—General M,D
Occupational Therapy M
Physical Therapy D

WINTHROP UNIVERSITY
Biological and Biomedical Sciences—General M
Nutrition M,O

WOLFORD COLLEGE
Nurse Anesthesia M,D

WON INSTITUTE OF GRADUATE STUDIES
Acupuncture and Oriental Medicine M,O

WOODS HOLE OCEANOGRAPHIC INSTITUTION
Marine Biology D

WORCESTER POLYTECHNIC INSTITUTE
Biochemistry M,D
Biological and Biomedical Sciences—General M,D
Computational Biology M,D

WORCESTER STATE UNIVERSITY
Communication Disorders M
Community Health Nursing M
Health Services Management and Hospital Administration M
Nursing Education M
Occupational Therapy M

WORLD MEDICINE INSTITUTE
Acupuncture and Oriental Medicine M

WRIGHT STATE UNIVERSITY
Acute Care/Critical Care Nursing M
Adult Nursing M
Allopathic Medicine D
Anatomy M
Biochemistry M
Biological and Biomedical Sciences—General M,D
Family Nurse Practitioner Studies M
Gerontological Nursing M
Health Promotion M
Immunology M
Maternal and Child/Neonatal Nursing M
Microbiology M
Molecular Biology M
Neuroscience M
Nursing and Healthcare Administration M
Nursing—General M
Pediatric Nursing M
Pharmacology M
Physiology M
Psychiatric Nursing M
Public Health—General M
School Nursing M
Toxicology M

XAVIER UNIVERSITY
Health Services Management and Hospital Administration M*
Nursing—General M,D,O
Occupational Therapy M

XAVIER UNIVERSITY OF LOUISIANA
Pharmacy D

YALE UNIVERSITY
Allopathic Medicine D
Biochemistry D
Biological and Biomedical Sciences—General D
Biophysics D
Cell Biology D
Computational Biology D
Developmental Biology D
Ecology D
Environmental and Occupational Health M,D
Epidemiology M,D
Evolutionary Biology D
Genetics D
Genomic Sciences D
Health Services Management and Hospital Administration M,D
Immunology D
Infectious Diseases D
International Health M,D
Microbiology D
Molecular Biology D
Molecular Biophysics D
Molecular Medicine D
Molecular Physiology D
Neurobiology D
Neuroscience D
Nursing—General M,D,O
Pathology M,D
Pharmacology D
Physician Assistant Studies M
Physiology D
Plant Biology D
Public Health—General M,D
Virology D

YESHIVA UNIVERSITY
Communication Disorders M

YORK COLLEGE OF PENNSYLVANIA
Gerontological Nursing M
Health Services Management and Hospital Administration M
Nurse Anesthesia M
Nursing—General M

YORK COLLEGE OF THE CITY UNIVERSITY OF NEW YORK
Pharmaceutical Sciences M
Physician Assistant Studies M

YORK UNIVERSITY
Biological and Biomedical Sciences—General M,D
Nursing—General M

YO SAN UNIVERSITY OF TRADITIONAL CHINESE MEDICINE
Acupuncture and Oriental Medicine M

YOUNGSTOWN STATE UNIVERSITY
Anatomy M
Biochemistry M
Biological and Biomedical Sciences—General M
Environmental Biology M
Health Services Management and Hospital Administration M
Microbiology M
Molecular Biology M
Nursing—General M
Physical Therapy D
Physiology M

ACADEMIC AND PROFESSIONAL PROGRAMS IN THE BIOLOGICAL AND BIOMEDICAL SCIENCES

Section 1
Biological and Biomedical Sciences

This section contains a directory of institutions offering graduate work in biological and biomedical sciences, followed by in-depth entries submitted by institutions that chose to prepare detailed program descriptions. Additional information about programs listed in the directory but not augmented by an in-depth entry may be obtained by writing directly to the dean of a graduate school or chair of a department at the address given in the directory.

Programs in fields related to the biological and biomedical sciences may be found throughout this book. In the other guides in this series:

Graduate Programs in the Humanities, Arts & Social Sciences

See *Psychology and Counseling* and *Sociology, Anthropology, and Archaeology*

Graduate Programs in the Physical Sciences, Mathematics, Agricultural Sciences, the Environment & Natural Resources

See *Chemistry, Marine Sciences and Oceanography,* and *Mathematical Sciences*

Graduate Programs in Engineering & Applied Sciences

See *Agricultural Engineering and Bioengineering, Biomedical Engineering and Biotechnology, Civil and Environmental Engineering, Management of Engineering and Technology,* and *Ocean Engineering*

CONTENTS

Program Directory

Featured Schools: Displays and Close-Ups

See also:

Biological and Biomedical Sciences—General

Acadia University, Faculty of Pure and Applied Science, Department of Biology, Wolfville, NS B4P 2R6, Canada. Offers M Sc. *Degree requirements:* For master's, comprehensive exam, thesis. *Entrance requirements:* For master's, minimum B-average in last 2 years of major. Additional exam requirements/recommendations for international students: Required—TOEFL (minimum score 580 paper-based; 93 iBT), IELTS (minimum score 6.5). *Application deadline:* For fall admission, 2/1 priority date for domestic and international students. Applications are processed on a rolling basis. Application fee: $50. *Financial support:* Application deadline: 2/1. *Faculty research:* Respiration physiology, estuaries and fisheries, limnology, plant biology, conservation biology. *Unit head:* Dr. Brian Williams, Head Advisor, 902-585-1424, E-mail: brian.williams@acadiau.ca. *Application contact:* Lisa Taul, Administrative Secretary, 902-585-1334, Fax: 902-585-1059, E-mail: lisa.taul@acadiau.ca.
Website: http://biology.acadiau.ca/

Adelphi University, College of Arts and Sciences, Department of Biology, Garden City, NY 11530-0701. Offers biology (MS); biotechnology (MS). *Program availability:* Part-time, evening/weekend. *Faculty:* 17 full-time (8 women), 28 part-time/adjunct (14 women). *Students:* 32 full-time (22 women), 11 part-time (7 women); includes 23 minority (5 Black or African American, non-Hispanic/Latino; 1 American Indian or Alaska Native, non-Hispanic/Latino; 11 Asian, non-Hispanic/Latino; 5 Hispanic/Latino; 1 Two or more races, non-Hispanic/Latino), 6 international. Average age 26. 105 applicants, 46% accepted, 14 enrolled. In 2017, 8 master's awarded. *Degree requirements:* For master's, thesis or alternative. *Entrance requirements:* For master's, bachelor's degree in biology or allied sciences, essay, 3 letters of recommendation, official transcripts. Additional exam requirements/recommendations for international students: Required—TOEFL (minimum score 550 paper-based; 80 iBT), IELTS (minimum score 6.5). *Application deadline:* For fall admission, 5/1 for international students; for spring admission, 12/1 for international students. Applications are processed on a rolling basis. Application fee: $50. Electronic applications accepted. *Expenses:* Contact institution. *Financial support:* Research assistantships with full and partial tuition reimbursements, teaching assistantships, career-related internships or fieldwork, institutionally sponsored loans, scholarships/grants, traineeships, and unspecified assistantships available. Support available to part-time students. Financial award application deadline: 2/15; financial award applicants required to submit FAFSA. *Faculty research:* Plant-animal interactions, physiology (plant, cornea), reproductive behavior, topics in evolution, fish biology. *Unit head:* Dr. Alan Schoenfeld, Chair, 516-877-4211, E-mail: schoenfeld@adelphi.edu. *Application contact:* E-mail: graduateadmissions@adelphi.edu.
Website: http://academics.adelphi.edu/artsci/bio/index.php

Alabama Agricultural and Mechanical University, School of Graduate Studies, College of Agricultural, Life and Natural Sciences, Department of Biological and Environmental Sciences, Huntsville, AL 35811. Offers biology (MS); plant and soil science (MS, PhD). *Program availability:* Evening/weekend. Terminal master's awarded for partial completion of doctoral program. *Degree requirements:* For master's, thesis optional; for doctorate, one foreign language, thesis/dissertation optional. *Entrance requirements:* For master's, GRE General Test, BS in agriculture; for doctorate, GRE General Test, master's degree. Additional exam requirements/recommendations for international students: Required—TOEFL (minimum score 500 paper-based; 61 iBT). Electronic applications accepted. *Faculty research:* Plant breeding, cytogenetics, crop production, soil chemistry and fertility, remote sensing.

Alabama State University, College of Science, Mathematics and Technology, Department of Biological Sciences, Montgomery, AL 36101-0271. Offers biology (MS); microbiology (PhD). *Faculty:* 13 full-time (4 women), 7 part-time/adjunct (4 women). *Students:* 12 full-time (9 women), 21 part-time (11 women); includes 25 minority (23 Black or African American, non-Hispanic/Latino; 1 Asian, non-Hispanic/Latino; 1 Two or more races, non-Hispanic/Latino), 2 international. Average age 22. 11 applicants, 91% accepted, 5 enrolled. In 2017, 2 doctorates awarded. *Degree requirements:* For master's, one foreign language, comprehensive exam, thesis; for doctorate, 3 foreign languages, thesis/dissertation. *Entrance requirements:* For master's, GRE General Test, GRE Subject Test, writing competency test. Additional exam requirements/recommendations for international students: Required—TOEFL (minimum score 500 paper-based). *Application deadline:* For fall admission, 4/15 for domestic and international students; for spring admission, 11/15 for domestic and international students; for summer admission, 3/15 for domestic and international students. Applications are processed on a rolling basis. Application fee: $25. Electronic applications accepted. *Expenses:* Tuition, state resident: part-time $412 per credit hour. Tuition, nonresident: part-time $824 per credit hour. *Required fees:* $685 per semester. *Financial support:* Research assistantships and scholarships/grants available. Financial award application deadline: 6/30; financial award applicants required to submit FAFSA. *Faculty research:* Salmonella pseudomonas, cancer cells. *Unit head:* Dr. Boakai K. Robertson, Chair, 334-229-4467, Fax: 334-229-1007, E-mail: bkrobertson@alasu.edu. *Application contact:* Dr. William Person, Dean of Graduate Studies, 334-229-4274, Fax: 334-229-4928, E-mail: wperson@alasu.edu.
Website: http://www.alasu.edu/academics/colleges—departments/science-mathematics-technology/biological-sciences-department/index.aspx

Albert Einstein College of Medicine, Graduate Programs in the Biomedical Sciences, Bronx, NY 10461. Offers PhD, MD/PhD. *Degree requirements:* For doctorate, thesis/dissertation. *Entrance requirements:* For doctorate, GRE General Test. Additional exam requirements/recommendations for international students: Required—TOEFL. *Application deadline:* For fall admission, 12/15 for domestic students. Applications are processed on a rolling basis. Application fee: $75. Electronic applications accepted. *Financial support:* Fellowships available. *Unit head:* Dr. Victoria H. Freedman, Associate Dean for Graduate Studies, 718-430-2872, Fax: 718-430-8655. *Application contact:* Salvatore Calabro, Director of Graduate Admissions, 718-430-2345, Fax: 718-430-8655, E-mail: phd@einstein.yu.edu.
Website: https://www.einstein.yu.edu/education/phd/

Albert Einstein College of Medicine, Medical Scientist Training Program, Bronx, NY 10461. Offers MD/PhD. *Application deadline:* For fall admission, 11/1 for domestic students. Application fee: $75. *Financial support:* Fellowships available. *Unit head:* Dr. Myles Akabas, MD, Director, 718-430-2128, Fax: 718-430-8655, E-mail: myles.akabas@einstein.yu.edu. *Application contact:* Sheila Cleeton, Executive Director and Registrar, Einstein Graduate Division, 718-430-2128, Fax: 718-430-8655, E-mail: sheila.cleeton@einstein.yu.edu.
Website: http://www.einstein.yu.edu/education/mstp/

Alcorn State University, School of Graduate Studies, School of Arts and Sciences, Department of Biology, Lorman, MS 39096-7500. Offers MS.

American Museum of Natural History–Richard Gilder Graduate School, Program in Comparative Biology, New York, NY 10024. Offers PhD. *Degree requirements:* For doctorate, thesis/dissertation, qualifying examination. *Entrance requirements:* For doctorate, GRE General Test (taken within the past five years); GRE Subject Test (recommended), BA, BS, or equivalent degree from accredited institution; official transcripts; essay;. Additional exam requirements/recommendations for international students: Required—TOEFL (minimum score 600 paper-based; 100 iBT), IELTS (minimum score 7).

American University, College of Arts and Sciences, Department of Biology, Washington, DC 20016-8007. Offers biology (MS); biotechnology (MA). *Program availability:* Part-time. *Faculty:* 19 full-time (10 women). *Students:* 13 full-time (7 women), 11 part-time (7 women); includes 5 minority (2 Black or African American, non-Hispanic/Latino; 1 Asian, non-Hispanic/Latino; 1 Hispanic/Latino; 1 Two or more races, non-Hispanic/Latino), 3 international. Average age 27. 31 applicants, 84% accepted, 7 enrolled. In 2017, 10 master's awarded. *Degree requirements:* For master's, comprehensive exam, thesis (for some programs). *Entrance requirements:* For master's, GRE General Test, GRE Subject Test, statement of purpose, transcripts, 2 letters of recommendation, resume. Additional exam requirements/recommendations for international students: Required—TOEFL (minimum score 600 paper-based; 100 iBT). *Application deadline:* For fall admission, 3/1 for domestic students; for spring admission, 11/1 for domestic students. Application fee: $55. Electronic applications accepted. *Expenses:* Contact institution. *Financial support:* Research assistantships, teaching assistantships, institutionally sponsored loans, and unspecified assistantships available. Financial award application deadline: 2/1; financial award applicants required to submit FAFSA. *Faculty research:* Neurobiology, cave biology, population genetics, vertebrate physiology. *Unit head:* Dr. Katie DeCicco-Skinner, Department Chair, 202-885-2193, E-mail: decicco@american.edu. *Application contact:* Jonathan Harper, Assistant Director, Graduate Recruitment, 202-855-3622, E-mail: jharper@american.edu.
Website: http://www.american.edu/cas/biology/

American University of Beirut, Graduate Programs, Faculty of Arts and Sciences, 1107 2020, Lebanon. Offers anthropology (MA); Arab and Middle Eastern history (PhD); Arabic language and literature (MA, PhD); archaeology (MA); art history and curating (MA); biology (MS); cell and molecular biology (PhD); chemistry (MS); clinical psychology (MA); computational sciences (MS); computer science (MS); economics (MA); education (MA), including administration and policy studies, elementary education, mathematics education, psychology school guidance, psychology test and measurements, science education, teaching English as a foreign language; English language (MA); English literature (MA); environmental policy planning (MS); financial economics (MAFE); general psychology (MA); geology (MS); history (MA); Islamic studies (MA); mathematics (MS); media studies (MA); Middle East studies (MA); philosophy (MA); physics (MS); political studies (MA); public administration (MA); public policy and international affairs (MA); sociology (MA); theoretical physics (PhD). *Program availability:* Part-time. *Faculty:* 108 full-time (36 women), 5 part-time/adjunct (4 women). *Students:* 251 full-time (180 women), 233 part-time (172 women). Average age 26. 425 applicants, 65% accepted, 121 enrolled. In 2017, 47 master's, 2 doctorates awarded. *Degree requirements:* For master's, one foreign language, comprehensive exam, thesis (for some programs), project; for doctorate, one foreign language, comprehensive exam, thesis/dissertation. *Entrance requirements:* For master's, GRE General Test (for some programs); for doctorate, GRE General Test (GRE Subject Test for theoretical physics). Additional exam requirements/recommendations for international students: Required—TOEFL (minimum score 583 paper-based; 97 iBT), IELTS (minimum score 7). *Application deadline:* For fall admission, 2/8 for domestic students; for spring admission, 11/3 for domestic students. Application fee: $50. Electronic applications accepted. *Expenses:* Contact institution. *Financial support:* In 2017–18, 29 fellowships, 40 research assistantships were awarded; teaching assistantships, scholarships/grants, tuition waivers (full and partial), and unspecified assistantships also available. Financial award application deadline: 4/4. *Unit head:* Dr. Nadia Maria El Cheikh, Dean, Faculty of Arts and Sciences, 961-1-374374 Ext. 3800, Fax: 961-1-744461, E-mail: nmcheikh@aub.edu.lb. *Application contact:* Rima Rassi, Graduate Studies Officer, 961-1-350000 Ext. 3833, Fax: 961-1-744461, E-mail: rr46@aub.edu.lb.
Website: http://www.aub.edu.lb/fas/pages/default.aspx

American University of Beirut, Graduate Programs, Faculty of Medicine, Beirut, Lebanon. Offers biochemistry (MS); biomedical engineering (MS); biomedical sciences (PhD); health research (MS); human morphology (MS); medicine (MD); microbiology and immunology (MS); neuroscience (MS); orthodontics (clinical) (MS); pharmacology and therapeutics (MS); physiology (MS). *Program availability:* Part-time. *Faculty:* 335 full-time (117 women), 54 part-time/adjunct (5 women). *Students:* 513 full-time (274 women). Average age 23. 527 applicants, 47% accepted, 169 enrolled. In 2017, 18 master's, 98 doctorates awarded. *Degree requirements:* For master's, one foreign language, comprehensive exam, thesis (for some programs); for doctorate, one foreign language, comprehensive exam, thesis/dissertation. *Entrance requirements:* For doctorate, MCAT (for MD); GRE (for PhD). Additional exam requirements/recommendations for international students: Required—TOEFL (minimum score 600 paper-based; 100 iBT), IELTS (minimum score 7.5). *Application deadline:* Applications are processed on a rolling basis. Application fee: $75. Electronic applications accepted. *Expenses:* Contact institution. *Financial support:* In 2017–18, 302 students received support. Fellowships, research assistantships, teaching assistantships, institutionally sponsored loans, scholarships/grants, tuition waivers, and unspecified assistantships available. *Unit head:* Dr. Mohamed Sayegh, Dean, 961-1-135000 Ext. 4700, Fax: 961-1-744489, E-mail: msayegh@aub.edu.lb. *Application contact:* Dr. Salim Kanaan, Director, Admission's Office, 961-1-350000 Ext. 2594, Fax: 961-1-750775, E-mail: sk00@aub.edu.lb.

Andrews University, School of Graduate Studies, College of Arts and Sciences, Department of Biology, Berrien Springs, MI 49104. Offers MAT, MS. *Faculty:* 7 full-time (3 women). *Students:* 7 full-time (3 women), 1 (woman) part-time; includes 1 minority (Hispanic/Latino), 2 international. Average age 27. 10 applicants, 60% accepted, 6 enrolled. In 2017, 2 master's awarded. *Degree requirements:* For master's, comprehensive exam, thesis. *Entrance requirements:* For master's, GRE Subject Test. Additional exam requirements/recommendations for international students: Required—TOEFL (minimum score 550 paper-based). *Application deadline:* Applications are processed on a rolling basis. Application fee: $40. *Financial support:* Fellowships, research assistantships, teaching assistantships, career-related internships or fieldwork, Federal Work-Study, and institutionally sponsored loans available. Financial award application deadline: 3/15. *Faculty research:* Manatee habitat characterization, seabird habitat dynamics. *Unit head:* Dr. Thomas Goodwin, Chairman, 269-471-3243. *Application contact:* Justina Clayburn, Supervisor of Graduate Admission, 800-253-2874, Fax: 269-471-6321, E-mail: graduate@andrews.edu.

Angelo State University, College of Graduate Studies and Research, College of Science and Engineering, Department of Biology, San Angelo, TX 76909. Offers MS.

Program availability: Part-time, evening/weekend. *Students:* 7 full-time (5 women), 9 part-time (5 women); includes 3 minority (1 Black or African American, non-Hispanic/Latino; 1 Asian, non-Hispanic/Latino; 1 Hispanic/Latino). Average age 26. *Degree requirements:* For master's, comprehensive exam, thesis optional. *Entrance requirements:* For master's, GRE General Test, essay. *Application deadline:* For fall admission, 7/15 priority date for domestic students, 6/10 for international students; for spring admission, 12/1 priority date for domestic students, 11/1 for international students. Applications are processed on a rolling basis. Application fee: $40 ($50 for international students). Electronic applications accepted. *Expenses:* Tuition, state resident: full-time $3856. Tuition, nonresident: full-time $11,324. *Required fees:* $2650. *Financial support:* Research assistantships, teaching assistantships, career-related internships or fieldwork, Federal Work-Study, scholarships/grants, and unspecified assistantships available. Support available to part-time students. Financial award application deadline: 3/1. *Faculty research:* Texas poppy-mallow project, Chisos hedgehog cactus, skunks, reptiles, amphibians, rodents, seed germination, mammals. *Unit head:* Dr. Russell Wilke, Chair, 325-486-6638, Fax: 325-942-2184, E-mail: russell.wilke@angelo.edu.
Website: http://www.angelo.edu/dept/biology/

Appalachian State University, Cratis D. Williams Graduate School, Department of Biology, Boone, NC 28608. Offers cell and molecular biology (MS). *Program availability:* Part-time. *Degree requirements:* For master's, comprehensive exam, thesis. *Entrance requirements:* For master's, GRE General Test, 3 letters of recommendation. Additional exam requirements/recommendations for international students: Required—TOEFL (minimum score 570 paper-based; 79 iBT), IELTS (minimum score 6.5). Electronic applications accepted. *Faculty research:* Aquatic and terrestrial ecology, animal and plant physiology, behavior and systematics, immunology and cell biology, molecular biology and microbiology.

Arizona State University at the Tempe campus, College of Liberal Arts and Sciences, School of Life Sciences, Tempe, AZ 85287-4601. Offers animal behavior (PhD); applied ethics (biomedical and health ethics) (MA); biology (MS, PhD), including biology, biology and society, complex adaptive systems science (PhD), plant biology and conservation (MS); environmental life sciences (PhD); evolutionary biology (PhD); history and philosophy of science (PhD); human and social dimensions of science and technology (PhD); microbiology (PhD); molecular and cellular biology (PhD); neuroscience (PhD). Terminal master's awarded for partial completion of doctoral program. *Degree requirements:* For master's, thesis (for some programs), interactive Program of Study (iPOS) submitted before completing 50 percent of required credit hours; for doctorate, variable foreign language requirement, comprehensive exam, thesis/dissertation, interactive Program of Study (iPOS) submitted before completing 50 percent of required credit hours. *Entrance requirements:* For master's and doctorate, GRE, minimum GPA of 3.0 or equivalent in last 2 years of work leading to bachelor's degree. Additional exam requirements/recommendations for international students: Required—TOEFL (minimum score 600 paper-based; 100 iBT). Electronic applications accepted.

Arkansas State University, Graduate School, College of Sciences and Mathematics, Department of Biological Sciences, State University, AR 72467. Offers biological sciences (MA); biology (MS); biology education (MSE, SCCT); biotechnology (PSM). *Program availability:* Part-time. *Degree requirements:* For master's, comprehensive exam, thesis (for some programs); for SCCT, comprehensive exam. *Entrance requirements:* For master's, GRE General Test, appropriate bachelor's degree, letters of reference, interview, official transcripts, immunization records, statement of educational objectives and career goals, teaching certificate (for MSE); for SCCT, GRE General Test or MAT, interview, master's degree, letters of reference, official transcript, personal statement, immunization records. Additional exam requirements/recommendations for international students: Required—TOEFL (minimum score 550 paper-based; 79 iBT), IELTS (minimum score 6), PTE (minimum score 56). Electronic applications accepted.

A.T. Still University, Kirksville College of Osteopathic Medicine, Kirksville, MO 63501. Offers biomedical sciences (MS); osteopathic medicine (DO). *Accreditation:* AOsA. *Faculty:* 37 full-time (6 women), 30 part-time/adjunct (6 women). *Students:* 716 full-time (309 women), 10 part-time (5 women); includes 133 minority (18 Black or African American, non-Hispanic/Latino; 1 American Indian or Alaska Native, non-Hispanic/Latino; 43 Asian, non-Hispanic/Latino; 36 Hispanic/Latino; 35 Two or more races, non-Hispanic/Latino), 1 international. Average age 27. 4,481 applicants, 9% accepted, 183 enrolled. In 2017, 13 master's, 172 doctorates awarded. *Degree requirements:* For master's, thesis; for doctorate, Level 1 and 2 COMLEX-PE and CE exams. *Entrance requirements:* For master's, GRE, MCAT, or DAT, minimum undergraduate GPA of 2.65 (cumulative and science); for doctorate, MCAT, bachelor's degree with minimum GPA of 2.8 (cumulative and science) or 90 semester hours with minimum GPA of 3.5 (cumulative and science) and MCAT (minimum score 500). Additional exam requirements/recommendations for international students: Required—TOEFL. *Application deadline:* For fall admission, 2/1 for domestic students; for summer admission, 2/1 for domestic students. Applications are processed on a rolling basis. Application fee: $70. Electronic applications accepted. Application fee is waived when completed online. *Financial support:* In 2017–18, 142 students received support, including 22 fellowships with full tuition reimbursements available (averaging $55,455 per year); Federal Work-Study and scholarships/grants also available. Financial award application deadline: 6/1; financial award applicants required to submit FAFSA. *Faculty research:* Practice-based research network, antibiotic resistance, staphylococcus aureus, bacterial virulence and environmental survival, excitability of the exercise pressor reflex, clinical trials. *Total annual research expenditures:* $127,751. *Unit head:* Dr. Margaret Wilson, Dean, 660-626-2354, Fax: 660-626-2080, E-mail: mwilson@atsu.edu. *Application contact:* Donna Sparks, Director, Admissions Processing, 660-626-2117, Fax: 660-626-2969, E-mail: admissions@atsu.edu.
Website: http://www.atsu.edu/kcom/

Auburn University, Graduate School, College of Sciences and Mathematics, Department of Biological Sciences, Auburn University, AL 36849. Offers botany (MS); zoology (MS). *Faculty:* 37 full-time (16 women), 1 (woman) part-time/adjunct. *Students:* 42 full-time (19 women), 65 part-time (43 women); includes 15 minority (8 Black or African American, non-Hispanic/Latino; 1 Asian, non-Hispanic/Latino; 2 Hispanic/Latino; 4 Two or more races, non-Hispanic/Latino), 15 international. Average age 27. 83 applicants, 41% accepted, 23 enrolled. In 2017, 22 master's, 7 doctorates awarded. *Entrance requirements:* For master's and doctorate, GRE General Test. Additional exam requirements/recommendations for international students: Required—TOEFL. Application fee: $50 ($60 for international students). Electronic applications accepted. *Expenses:* Tuition, state resident: full-time $10,974; part-time $519 per credit hour. Tuition, nonresident: full-time $29,658; part-time $1557 per credit hour. *Required fees:* $816 per semester. Tuition and fees vary according to degree level and program. *Financial support:* Research assistantships and teaching assistantships available. Financial award applicants required to submit FAFSA. *Unit head:* Dr. Jason E. Bond, Chair, 334-844-3906, Fax: 334-844-1645. *Application contact:* Dr. George Flowers, Dean of the Graduate School, 334-844-2125.

Austin Peay State University, College of Graduate Studies, College of Science, Technology, Engineering and Mathematics, Department of Biology, Clarksville, TN 37044. Offers clinical laboratory science (MS). *Program availability:* Part-time. *Faculty:* 12 full-time (5 women). *Students:* 1 full-time (0 women), 27 part-time (15 women); includes 3 minority (2 Hispanic/Latino; 1 Two or more races, non-Hispanic/Latino), 1 international. Average age 27. 24 applicants, 71% accepted, 13 enrolled. In 2017, 16 master's awarded. *Degree requirements:* For master's, comprehensive exam, thesis optional. *Entrance requirements:* For master's, GRE General Test, 3 letters of recommendation, minimum undergraduate GPA of 2.75. Additional exam requirements/recommendations for international students: Required—TOEFL (minimum score 500 paper-based). *Application deadline:* For fall admission, 8/8 priority date for domestic students. Applications are processed on a rolling basis. Application fee: $45 ($50 for international students). Electronic applications accepted. *Expenses:* Tuition, state resident: full-time $7686; part-time $427 per credit hour. Tuition, nonresident: full-time $20,268; part-time $1126 per credit hour. *Required fees:* $1529; $76.45 per credit hour. *Financial support:* Research assistantships with full tuition reimbursements, career-related internships or fieldwork, Federal Work-Study, institutionally sponsored loans, scholarships/grants, and unspecified assistantships available. Support available to part-time students. Financial award application deadline: 4/1; financial award applicants required to submit FAFSA. *Faculty research:* Molecular basis of microbial pathogenesis, avian ecology, aquatic toxicology, endocrinology, aquatic biology. *Unit head:* Dr. Don Dailey, Chair, 931-221-7781, Fax: 931-221-6323, E-mail: daileyd@apsu.edu. *Application contact:* Megan Mitchell, Coordinator of Graduate Admissions, 800 859-4723, Fax: 931-221-7641, E-mail: gradadmissions@apsu.edu.
Website: http://www.apsu.edu/biology/

Ball State University, Graduate School, College of Sciences and Humanities, Department of Biology, Program in Biology, Muncie, IN 47306. Offers MA, MS. *Program availability:* Part-time. *Students:* 14 full-time (4 women), 25 part-time (9 women); includes 4 minority (1 Black or African American, non-Hispanic/Latino; 3 Two or more races, non-Hispanic/Latino). Average age 24. 33 applicants, 91% accepted, 20 enrolled. In 2017, 17 master's awarded. *Entrance requirements:* For master's, minimum baccalaureate GPA of 2.75 or 3.0 in latter half of baccalaureate, transcripts of all prior coursework, three letters of recommendation. Additional exam requirements/recommendations for international students: Required—TOEFL (minimum score 550 paper-based; 79 iBT), IELTS (minimum score 6.5). *Application deadline:* Applications are processed on a rolling basis. Application fee: $60. Electronic applications accepted. *Financial support:* Research assistantships with partial tuition reimbursements, teaching assistantships with partial tuition reimbursements, and unspecified assistantships available. Financial award application deadline: 3/1; financial award applicants required to submit FAFSA. *Unit head:* Dr. Kemuel Badger, Chairman, 765-285-8820, Fax: 765-285-0001, E-mail: kbadger@bsu.edu. *Application contact:* Dr. David LeBlanc, Graduate Advisor, 765-285-8832, Fax: 765-285-8820, E-mail: dleblanc@bsu.edu.
Website: http://www.bsu.edu/biology

Ball State University, Graduate School, College of Sciences and Humanities, Interdepartmental Program in Environmental Sciences, Muncie, IN 47306. Offers environmental science (PhD), including biology, chemistry, geological sciences. *Program availability:* Part-time. *Students:* 2 full-time (0 women), 7 part-time (1 woman), 3 international. Average age 33. 4 applicants, 25% accepted. In 2017, 1 doctorate awarded. *Degree requirements:* For doctorate, thesis/dissertation. *Entrance requirements:* For doctorate, GRE General Test, minimum cumulative GPA of 3.0 (chemistry), 3.2 (biology and geological sciences); acknowledged arrangement for doctoral environmental sciences research with faculty mentor; three letters of recommendation. Additional exam requirements/recommendations for international students: Required—TOEFL (minimum score 550 paper-based; 79 iBT), IELTS (minimum score 6.5). *Application deadline:* Applications are processed on a rolling basis. Application fee: $60. Electronic applications accepted. *Financial support:* Research assistantships with partial tuition reimbursements and teaching assistantships with partial tuition reimbursements available. Financial award application deadline: 3/1; financial award applicants required to submit FAFSA. *Unit head:* Dr. Jeffry Grigsby, Director, 765-285-2486, Fax: 765-285-6505, E-mail: jgrigsby@bsu.edu.
Website: http://cms.bsu.edu/Academics/CollegesandDepartments/EnvironmentalScience.aspx

Barry University, College of Health Sciences, Programs in Biology and Biomedical Sciences, Miami Shores, FL 33161-6695. Offers biology (MS); biomedical sciences (MS). *Program availability:* Part-time, evening/weekend. *Degree requirements:* For master's, comprehensive exam, thesis (for some programs). *Entrance requirements:* For master's, GRE General Test or Florida Teacher's Certification Exam (biology); GRE General Test, MCAT, or DAT (biomedical sciences). Electronic applications accepted. *Faculty research:* Genetics, immunology, anthropology.

Baylor College of Medicine, Graduate School of Biomedical Sciences, Houston, TX 77030-3498. Offers MS, PhD, MD/PhD. Terminal master's awarded for partial completion of doctoral program. *Degree requirements:* For master's, thesis; for doctorate, thesis/dissertation, public defense. *Entrance requirements:* For doctorate, GRE General Test, GRE Subject Test (strongly recommended), minimum GPA of 3.0. Additional exam requirements/recommendations for international students: Required—TOEFL. Electronic applications accepted. *Faculty research:* Cell and molecular biology of cardiac muscle, structural biophysics, gene expression and regulation, human genomes, viruses.

Baylor University, Graduate School, College of Arts and Sciences, Department of Biology, Waco, TX 76798. Offers biology (MA, MS, PhD); environmental biology (MS); limnology (MS). *Program availability:* Part-time. *Faculty:* 13 full-time (3 women). *Students:* 47 full-time (24 women), 2 part-time (1 woman); includes 7 minority (2 Black or African American, non-Hispanic/Latino; 1 Asian, non-Hispanic/Latino; 1 Hispanic/Latino; 3 Two or more races, non-Hispanic/Latino), 6 international. In 2017, 6 master's awarded. *Degree requirements:* For master's, thesis (for some programs); for doctorate, thesis/dissertation. *Entrance requirements:* For master's and doctorate, GRE General Test. Additional exam requirements/recommendations for international students: Required—TOEFL. *Application deadline:* For fall admission, 2/15 priority date for domestic and international students. Applications are processed on a rolling basis. Application fee: $25. *Financial support:* Research assistantships with full and partial tuition reimbursements, teaching assistantships with full and partial tuition reimbursements, career-related internships or fieldwork, Federal Work-Study, institutionally sponsored loans, and tuition waivers (full and partial) available. Support available to part-time students. Financial award application deadline: 2/28. *Faculty research:* Terrestrial ecology, aquatic ecology, genetics. *Unit head:* Dr. Ryan King, Graduate Program Director, 254-710-2150, Fax: 254-710-2969, E-mail: ryan_s_king@baylor.edu. *Application contact:* Tamara Lehmann, Academic Support Associate, 254-710-2578, Fax: 254-710-2969, E-mail: tamara_lehmann@baylor.edu.
Website: http://www.baylor.edu/biology/

Baylor University, Graduate School, Institute of Biomedical Studies, Waco, TX 76798. Offers MS, PhD. *Faculty:* 19 part-time/adjunct (4 women). *Students:* 22 full-time (8 women); includes 4 minority (1 Black or African American, non-Hispanic/Latino; 1 Asian, non-Hispanic/Latino; 2 Hispanic/Latino), 11 international. Average age 24. 69 applicants, 10% accepted, 5 enrolled. In 2017, 2 master's, 5 doctorates awarded. *Entrance requirements:* For master's and doctorate, GRE General Test. Additional exam requirements/recommendations for international students: Required—TOEFL (minimum

score 550 paper-based). *Application deadline:* For spring admission, 2/15 for domestic and international students. Applications are processed on a rolling basis. Application fee: $25. Electronic applications accepted. *Financial support:* In 2017–18, 22 students received support. Research assistantships, teaching assistantships, and tuition waivers available. *Unit head:* Dr. Bob Kane, Acting Graduate Program Director, 254-710-4556, Fax: 254-710-2199, E-mail: bob_kane@baylor.edu. *Application contact:* Rhonda Bellert, Administrative Associate, 254-710-2514, Fax: 254-710-2199, E-mail: rhonda_bellert@baylor.edu.
Website: http://www.baylor.edu/biomedical/

Bemidji State University, School of Graduate Studies, Bemidji, MN 56601. Offers biology (MS); education (MS); English (MA, MS); environmental studies (MS); mathematics (MS); mathematics (elementary and middle level education) (MS); special education (M Sp Ed). *Program availability:* Part-time, online learning. *Degree requirements:* For master's, comprehensive exam, thesis (for some programs). *Entrance requirements:* For master's, GRE; GMAT, letters of recommendation, letters of interest. Additional exam requirements/recommendations for international students: Required—TOEFL (minimum score 550 paper-based; 80 iBT). Electronic applications accepted. *Expenses:* Contact institution. *Faculty research:* Human performance, sport, and health: physical education teacher education, continuum models, spiritual health, intellectual health, resiliency, health priorities; psychology: health psychology, college student drinking behavior, micro-aggressions, infant cognition, false memories, leadership assessment; biology: structure and dynamics of forest communities, aquatic and riverine ecology, interaction between animal populations and aquatic environments, cellular motility.

Binghamton University, State University of New York, Graduate School, Harpur College of Arts and Sciences, Department of Biological Sciences, Binghamton, NY 13902-6000. Offers MA, MS, PhD. *Program availability:* Part-time. *Faculty:* 26 full-time (11 women). *Students:* 32 full-time (17 women), 40 part-time (17 women); includes 12 minority (4 Asian, non-Hispanic/Latino; 5 Hispanic/Latino; 3 Two or more races, non-Hispanic/Latino), 12 international. Average age 27. 72 applicants, 39% accepted, 17 enrolled. In 2017, 18 master's, 6 doctorates awarded. Terminal master's awarded for partial completion of doctoral program. *Degree requirements:* For master's, thesis; for doctorate, comprehensive exam, thesis/dissertation. *Entrance requirements:* For master's and doctorate, GRE General Test. Additional exam requirements/recommendations for international students: Required—TOEFL (minimum score 550 paper-based; 100 iBT). *Application deadline:* For fall admission, 1/15 priority date for domestic and international students; for spring admission, 10/15 priority date for domestic and international students. Application fee: $75. Electronic applications accepted. *Financial support:* In 2017–18, 41 students received support, including 3 research assistantships with full tuition reimbursements available (averaging $19,000 per year), 37 teaching assistantships with full tuition reimbursements available (averaging $17,500 per year); career-related internships or fieldwork, Federal Work-Study, institutionally sponsored loans, scholarships/grants, health care benefits, tuition waivers (full and partial), and unspecified assistantships also available. Financial award applicants required to submit FAFSA. *Unit head:* Dr. Curt M. Pueschel, Chairperson, 607-777-2602, E-mail: curtp@binghamton.edu. *Application contact:* Ben Balkaya, Assistant Dean and Director, 607-777-2151, Fax: 607-777-2501, E-mail: balkaya@binghamton.edu.

Bloomsburg University of Pennsylvania, School of Graduate Studies, College of Science and Technology, Department of Biological and Allied Health Sciences, Program in Biology, Bloomsburg, PA 17815-1301. Offers MS. *Degree requirements:* For master's, thesis optional. *Entrance requirements:* For master's, minimum QPA of 3.0, 2 letters of recommendation, personal statement, undergraduate degree in biology. Additional exam requirements/recommendations for international students: Required—TOEFL (minimum score 550 paper-based), IELTS. Electronic applications accepted. *Expenses:* Tuition, state resident: full-time $10,000; part-time $500 per credit hour. Tuition, nonresident: full-time $15,000; part-time $750 per credit hour. *Required fees:* $2484; $110.75 per credit hour. $75 per term. Tuition and fees vary according to program.

Boise State University, College of Arts and Sciences, Department of Biological Sciences, Boise, ID 83725-0399. Offers biology (MA, MS); biomolecular sciences (PhD); raptor biology (MS). *Program availability:* Part-time. *Faculty:* 26. *Students:* 51 full-time (23 women), 10 part-time (5 women); includes 7 minority (1 Black or African American, non-Hispanic/Latino; 1 American Indian or Alaska Native, non-Hispanic/Latino; 1 Asian, non-Hispanic/Latino; 3 Hispanic/Latino; 1 Native Hawaiian or other Pacific Islander, non-Hispanic/Latino), 6 international. Average age 30. 45 applicants, 27% accepted, 10 enrolled. In 2017, 13 master's awarded. *Degree requirements:* For master's, thesis. *Entrance requirements:* For master's, GRE General Test, minimum GPA of 3.0. Additional exam requirements/recommendations for international students: Required—TOEFL (minimum score 550 paper-based; 80 iBT), IELTS (minimum score 6). *Application deadline:* For fall admission, 1/15 for domestic and international students; for spring admission, 10/1 for domestic and international students. Application fee: $65 ($95 for international students). Electronic applications accepted. *Expenses:* Tuition, state resident: full-time $6471; part-time $390 per credit. Tuition, nonresident: full-time $21,787; part-time $685 per credit. *Required fees:* $2283; $100 per term. Part-time tuition and fees vary according to course load and program. *Financial support:* Research assistantships, teaching assistantships, institutionally sponsored loans, and unspecified assistantships available. Financial award application deadline: 1/15; financial award applicants required to submit FAFSA. *Faculty research:* Soil and stream microbial ecology, avian ecology. *Unit head:* Dr. Kevin Feris, Chair, 208-426-4267, E-mail: kevinferis@boisestate.edu. *Application contact:* Dr. Ian Roberts, Graduate Coordinator, 208-426-3208, E-mail: iroberts@boisestate.edu.
Website: http://biology.boisestate.edu/graduate-programs/

Boston College, Graduate School of Arts and Sciences, Department of Biology, Chestnut Hill, MA 02467-3800. Offers PhD, MBA/MS. *Degree requirements:* For doctorate, thesis/dissertation. *Entrance requirements:* For doctorate, GRE General Test, GRE Subject Test. Additional exam requirements/recommendations for international students: Required—TOEFL (minimum score 600 paper-based; 100 iBT), IELTS (minimum score 8). Electronic applications accepted. *Faculty research:* Molecular cell biology and genetics, cell cycle, neurobiology, developmental biology, structural and cellular biochemistry, vector biology, infectious disease, bioinformatics.

Boston University, Graduate School of Arts and Sciences, Department of Biology, Boston, MA 02215. Offers MA, PhD. *Students:* 61 full-time (41 women), 4 part-time (2 women); includes 11 minority (1 Black or African American, non-Hispanic/Latino; 5 Asian, non-Hispanic/Latino; 4 Hispanic/Latino; 1 Two or more races, non-Hispanic/Latino), 13 international. Average age 26. 246 applicants, 17% accepted, 19 enrolled. In 2017, 10 master's, 11 doctorates awarded. Terminal master's awarded for partial completion of doctoral program. *Degree requirements:* For master's, thesis (for some programs); for doctorate, comprehensive exam, thesis/dissertation. *Entrance requirements:* For master's and doctorate, GRE General Test, GRE Subject Test (recommended), 3 letters of recommendation, transcripts, personal statement, curriculum vitae. Additional exam requirements/recommendations for international students: Required—TOEFL (minimum score 550 paper-based; 84 iBT). *Application deadline:* For fall admission, 12/7 for domestic and international students. Application fee: $95. Electronic applications accepted. *Financial support:* In 2017–18, 50 students received support, including 13 fellowships with full tuition reimbursements available (averaging $22,000 per year), 12 research assistantships with full tuition reimbursements available (averaging $22,000 per year), 49 teaching assistantships with full tuition reimbursements available (averaging $22,000 per year); Federal Work-Study, scholarships/grants, traineeships, and health care benefits also available. Financial award application deadline: 12/7. *Unit head:* Kim McCall, Chair, 617-353-5444, Fax: 617-358-0442, E-mail: kmccall@bu.edu. *Application contact:* Christina Honeycutt, Academic Administrator, 617-353-2432, Fax: 617-353-6340, E-mail: cjhoney@bu.edu.
Website: http://www.bu.edu/biology/

Boston University, School of Medicine, Division of Graduate Medical Sciences, Program in Biomedical Sciences, Boston, MA 02118. Offers PhD. *Entrance requirements:* For doctorate, GRE. *Financial support:* Fellowships, research assistantships, and teaching assistantships available. *Unit head:* Dr. Linda Hyman, Associate Provost, 617-638-5255, Fax: 617-638-5740. *Application contact:* GMS Office of Admissions, 617-638-5255, E-mail: askgms@bu.edu.
Website: http://www.bumc.bu.edu/gms/pibs/

Bowling Green State University, Graduate College, College of Arts and Sciences, Department of Biological Sciences, Bowling Green, OH 43403. Offers MS, PhD. *Program availability:* Part-time. *Degree requirements:* For master's, thesis or alternative; for doctorate, comprehensive exam, thesis/dissertation. *Entrance requirements:* For master's and doctorate, GRE General Test. Additional exam requirements/recommendations for international students: Required—TOEFL. Electronic applications accepted. *Faculty research:* Aquatic ecology, endocrinology and neurophysiology, nitrogen fixation, photosynthesis.

Bradley University, The Graduate School, College of Liberal Arts and Sciences, Department of Biology, Peoria, IL 61625-0002. Offers MS. *Program availability:* Part-time. *Degree requirements:* For master's, comprehensive exam, thesis. *Entrance requirements:* For master's, GRE. Additional exam requirements/recommendations for international students: Required—TOEFL (minimum score 550 paper-based; 79 iBT), IELTS (minimum score 6.5). Electronic applications accepted.

Brandeis University, Graduate School of Arts and Sciences, Department of Physics, Waltham, MA 02454-9110. Offers physics (MS, PhD); quantitative biology (PhD). *Program availability:* Part-time. *Faculty:* 15 full-time (3 women), 1 part-time/adjunct (0 women). *Students:* 51 full-time (18 women); includes 3 minority (1 Asian, non-Hispanic/Latino; 2 Hispanic/Latino), 24 international. Average age 26. 165 applicants, 15% accepted, 10 enrolled. In 2017, 5 master's, 7 doctorates awarded. Terminal master's awarded for partial completion of doctoral program. *Degree requirements:* For master's, thesis optional, qualifying exam, 1-year residency; for doctorate, comprehensive exam, thesis/dissertation, qualifying and advanced exams. *Entrance requirements:* For master's and doctorate, GRE General Test; GRE Subject Test (recommended), resume, letters of recommendation, statement of purpose, transcripts. Additional exam requirements/recommendations for international students: Required—PTE (minimum score 68), TOEFL (minimum score 600 paper-based, 100 iBT) or IELTS (7). *Application deadline:* For fall admission, 1/15 priority date for domestic students. Applications are processed on a rolling basis. Application fee: $75. Electronic applications accepted. *Expenses: Tuition:* Full-time $48,720. *Required fees:* $88. Tuition and fees vary according to course load, degree level, program and student level. *Financial support:* In 2017–18, 53 students received support, including 21 fellowships with full tuition reimbursements available (averaging $30,000 per year), 31 research assistantships with full tuition reimbursements available (averaging $30,000 per year), 3 teaching assistantships with partial tuition reimbursements available (averaging $2,500 per year); Federal Work-Study, scholarships/grants, health care benefits, and tuition waivers (partial) also available. Support available to part-time students. Financial award application deadline: 1/15; financial award applicants required to submit FAFSA. *Faculty research:* Astrophysics, condensed-matter and biophysics, high energy and gravitational theory, particle physics, microfluidics, radio astronomy, string theory. *Unit head:* Dr. Craig Blocker, Department Chair, 781-736-2352, E-mail: blocker@brandeis.edu. *Application contact:* Rachel Krebs, Department Administrator, 781-736-2352, E-mail: scigradoffice@brandeis.edu.
Website: http://www.brandeis.edu/gsas/programs/physics.html

Brandeis University, Graduate School of Arts and Sciences, Program in Biochemistry and Biophysics, Waltham, MA 02454-9110. Offers biochemistry and biophysics (MS, PhD); quantitative biology (PhD). *Faculty:* 11 full-time (5 women). *Students:* 35 full-time (14 women); includes 8 minority (4 Asian, non-Hispanic/Latino; 2 Hispanic/Latino; 2 Two or more races, non-Hispanic/Latino), 6 international. Average age 27. 77 applicants, 25% accepted, 16 enrolled. In 2017, 1 master's, 6 doctorates awarded. Terminal master's awarded for partial completion of doctoral program. *Degree requirements:* For master's, thesis; for doctorate, thesis/dissertation, qualifying exams. *Entrance requirements:* For master's, GRE General Test, resume, letters of recommendation, statement of purpose, transcripts; for doctorate, GRE General Test, resume, letters of recommendation, statement of purpose, transcripts, list of previous research experience. Additional exam requirements/recommendations for international students: Required—PTE (minimum score 68), TOEFL (minimum score 600 paper-based, 100 iBT) or IELTS (7). *Application deadline:* For fall admission, 12/1 priority date for domestic students. Applications are processed on a rolling basis. Application fee: $75. Electronic applications accepted. *Expenses: Tuition:* Full-time $48,720. *Required fees:* $88. Tuition and fees vary according to course load, degree level, program and student level. *Financial support:* In 2017–18, 39 students received support, including 17 fellowships with full tuition reimbursements available (averaging $33,000 per year), 21 research assistantships with full tuition reimbursements available (averaging $33,000 per year); Federal Work-Study, scholarships/grants, health care benefits, and tuition waivers (partial) also available. Financial award application deadline: 4/15; financial award applicants required to submit FAFSA. *Faculty research:* Macromolecular chemistry, structure and function, biochemistry, biophysics, biological macromolecules. *Unit head:* Dr. Dagmar Ringe, Director of Graduate Studies, 781-736-4902, E-mail: scigradoffice@brandeis.edu. *Application contact:* Rachel Krebs, Department Administrator, 781-736-2352, E-mail: scigradoffice@brandeis.edu.
Website: http://www.brandeis.edu/gsas/programs/bio.html

Brandeis University, Graduate School of Arts and Sciences, Program in Molecular and Cell Biology, Waltham, MA 02454-9110. Offers genetics (PhD); microbiology (PhD); molecular and cell biology (MS, PhD); molecular biology (PhD); neurobiology (PhD); quantitative biology (PhD). *Faculty:* 27 full-time (13 women), 3 part-time/adjunct (2 women). *Students:* 47 full-time (29 women), 2 part-time (1 woman); includes 10 minority (1 American Indian or Alaska Native, non-Hispanic/Latino; 2 Asian, non-Hispanic/Latino; 6 Hispanic/Latino; 1 Two or more races, non-Hispanic/Latino), 11 international. Average age 27. 138 applicants, 25% accepted, 18 enrolled. In 2017, 11 master's, 8 doctorates awarded. Terminal master's awarded for partial completion of doctoral program. *Degree requirements:* For master's, thesis optional, research project, research lab, or project lab; for doctorate, comprehensive exam, thesis/dissertation, journal clubs; research seminar; colloquia; qualifying exam. *Entrance requirements:* For master's, GRE General Test, transcripts, resume, letters of recommendation, statement of purpose; for

doctorate, GRE General Test, transcripts, resume, letters of recommendation, statement of purpose, list of previous research experience. Additional exam requirements/recommendations for international students: Required—PTE (minimum score 68), TOEFL (minimum score 600 paper-based, 100 iBT) or IELTS (7). *Application deadline:* For fall admission, 12/1 priority date for domestic students; for spring admission, 11/15 for domestic students, 10/15 for international students. Applications are processed on a rolling basis. Application fee: $75. Electronic applications accepted. *Expenses: Tuition:* Full-time $48,720. *Required fees:* $88. Tuition and fees vary according to course load, degree level, program and student level. *Financial support:* In 2017–18, 46 students received support, including 20 fellowships with full tuition reimbursements available (averaging $33,000 per year), 19 research assistantships with full tuition reimbursements available (averaging $33,000 per year); scholarships/grants and tuition waivers (partial) also available. Financial award application deadline: 4/15; financial award applicants required to submit FAFSA. *Faculty research:* Molecular biology, genetics and development; structural and cell biology; neurobiology. *Unit head:* Dr. James Haber, Co-Chair, 781-736-2462, E-mail: haber@brandeis.edu. *Application contact:* Jena Pitman-Leung, Department Administrator, 781-736-2352, E-mail: scigradoffice@brandeis.edu.
Website: http://www.brandeis.edu/gsas/programs/mcbio.html

Brandeis University, Graduate School of Arts and Sciences, Program in Neuroscience, Waltham, MA 02454-9110. Offers neuroscience (MS, PhD); quantitative biology (PhD). *Faculty:* 24 full-time (8 women). *Students:* 65 full-time (34 women); includes 16 minority (2 Black or African American, non-Hispanic/Latino; 1 American Indian or Alaska Native, non-Hispanic/Latino; 4 Asian, non-Hispanic/Latino; 8 Hispanic/Latino; 1 Two or more races, non-Hispanic/Latino), 14 international. Average age 27. 182 applicants, 18% accepted, 19 enrolled. In 2017, 3 master's, 5 doctorates awarded. Terminal master's awarded for partial completion of doctoral program. *Degree requirements:* For master's, thesis optional, research project; for doctorate, comprehensive exam, thesis/dissertation, qualifying exams, teaching experience, journal club, research seminars. *Entrance requirements:* For master's, GRE General Test, transcripts, statement of purpose, resume, letters of recommendation; for doctorate, GRE General Test, transcripts, statement of purpose, resume, letters of recommendation, listing of previous research experience. Additional exam requirements/recommendations for international students: Required—PTE (minimum score 68), TOEFL (minimum score 600 paper-based, 100 iBT) or IELTS (7). *Application deadline:* For fall admission, 12/1 priority date for domestic students. Applications are processed on a rolling basis. Application fee: $75. Electronic applications accepted. *Expenses: Tuition:* Full-time $48,720. *Required fees:* $88. Tuition and fees vary according to course load, degree level, program and student level. *Financial support:* In 2017–18, 62 students received support, including 23 fellowships with full tuition reimbursements available (averaging $33,000 per year), 30 research assistantships with full tuition reimbursements available (averaging $33,000 per year); Federal Work-Study, scholarships/grants, health care benefits, and tuition waivers (partial) also available. Financial award application deadline: 4/15; financial award applicants required to submit FAFSA. *Faculty research:* Behavioral/cognitive neuroscience, cellular and molecular neuroscience, computational neuroscience and systems neuroscience, and developmental neuroscience. *Unit head:* Dr. Avi Rodal, Director of Graduate Studies, 781-736-2459, E-mail: arodal@brandeis.edu. *Application contact:* Jena Pitman-Leung, Academic Administrator, 781-736-2352, E-mail: scigradoffice@brandeis.edu.
Website: http://www.brandeis.edu/gsas/programs/neuroscience.html

Brandeis University, Graduate School of Arts and Sciences, Program in Premedical Studies, Waltham, MA 02454-9110. Offers Postbaccalaureate Certificate. *Students:* 7 full-time (3 women), 2 part-time (both women). Average age 24. 50 applicants, 32% accepted, 3 enrolled. In 2017, 8 Postbaccalaureate Certificates awarded. *Entrance requirements:* For degree, GRE General Test, ACT, or SAT, resume, letters of recommendation, transcripts, statement of purpose, interview. *Application deadline:* For fall admission, 5/15 for domestic students; for summer admission, 4/15 for domestic students. Application fee: $75. Electronic applications accepted. *Expenses:* $8,650 per semester tuition; $88 fees. *Financial support:* In 2017–18, 1 student received support. Applicants required to submit FAFSA. *Faculty research:* Health profession preparation, pre-medical, pre-veterinary, pre-dental, pre-optometry, pre-osteopathic. *Unit head:* Kate Stutz, Director of Pre-Health Advising, 781-736-3470, E-mail: stutz@brandeis.edu. *Application contact:* Jean Deo, Department Administrator, 781-736-3716, E-mail: jdeo@brandeis.edu.
Website: http://www.brandeis.edu/gsas/programs/premed.html

Brigham Young University, Graduate Studies, College of Life Sciences, Department of Biology, Provo, UT 84602. Offers biological science education (MS); biology (MS, PhD). *Faculty:* 25 full-time (2 women). *Students:* 36 full-time (14 women); includes 5 minority (3 Hispanic/Latino; 2 Native Hawaiian or other Pacific Islander, non-Hispanic/Latino), 5 international. Average age 29. 22 applicants, 50% accepted, 9 enrolled. In 2017, 5 master's, 3 doctorates awarded. *Degree requirements:* For master's, comprehensive exam, thesis, prospectus, defense of research, defense of thesis; for doctorate, comprehensive exam, thesis/dissertation, prospectus, defense of research, defense of dissertation. *Entrance requirements:* For master's and doctorate, GRE General Test, minimum cumulative GPA of 3.0 for undergraduate degree. Additional exam requirements/recommendations for international students: Required—TOEFL (minimum score 580 paper-based; 85 iBT). *Application deadline:* For fall admission, 1/15 for domestic and international students. Application fee: $50. Electronic applications accepted. *Expenses:* $10,320 per academic year, $405 per credit hour for members of the Church of Jesus Christ of Latter-day Saints; $20,640 for the year, $810 per credit hour for those who are not members of the Church. *Financial support:* In 2017–18, 32 students received support, including 2 fellowships with full tuition reimbursements available (averaging $30,000 per year), 62 research assistantships with full and partial tuition reimbursements available (averaging $6,494 per year), 35 teaching assistantships with full and partial tuition reimbursements available (averaging $6,653 per year); career-related internships or fieldwork, institutionally sponsored loans, scholarships/grants, tuition waivers (full and partial), and unspecified assistantships also available. Financial award application deadline: 3/1; financial award applicants required to submit FAFSA. *Faculty research:* Systematics, bioinformatics, ecology, evolution. *Unit head:* Dr. Dennis K. Shiozawa, Chair, 801-422-4972, E-mail: dennis_shiozawa@byu.edu. *Application contact:* Gentri Glaittli, Graduate Program Manager, 801-422-7137, E-mail: biogradmanager@byu.edu.
Website: http://biology.byu.edu/

Brock University, Faculty of Graduate Studies, Faculty of Mathematics and Science, Program in Biological Sciences, St. Catharines, ON L2S 3A1, Canada. Offers M Sc, PhD. *Program availability:* Part-time. *Degree requirements:* For master's, thesis; for doctorate, thesis/dissertation. *Entrance requirements:* For master's, honors B Sc in biology, minimum undergraduate GPA of 3.0; for doctorate, M Sc. Additional exam requirements/recommendations for international students: Required—TOEFL (minimum score 550 paper-based; 80 iBT), IELTS (minimum score 6.5), TWE (minimum score 4). Electronic applications accepted. *Faculty research:* Viticulture, neurobiology, ecology, molecular biology, molecular genetics.

Brooklyn College of the City University of New York, School of Education, Program in Middle Childhood Science Education, Brooklyn, NY 11210-2889. Offers biology (MA); chemistry (MA); earth science (MA); general science (MA); physics (MA). *Program availability:* Part-time, evening/weekend. *Entrance requirements:* For master's, LAST, interview, previous course work in education and mathematics, resume, 2 letters of recommendation, essay. Additional exam requirements/recommendations for international students: Required—TOEFL (minimum score 500 paper-based; 61 iBT). Electronic applications accepted. *Faculty research:* Geometric thinking, mastery of basic facts, problem-solving strategies, history of mathematics.

Brooklyn College of the City University of New York, School of Natural and Behavioral Sciences, Department of Biology, Brooklyn, NY 11210-2889. Offers MA. *Degree requirements:* For master's, one foreign language, comprehensive exam, thesis. *Entrance requirements:* For master's, minimum GPA of 3.0, 2 letters of recommendation. Additional exam requirements/recommendations for international students: Required—TOEFL (minimum score 500 paper-based; 61 iBT). Electronic applications accepted. *Faculty research:* Evolutionary biology, molecular biology of development, cell biology, comparative endocrinology, ecology.

Brown University, Graduate School, Division of Biology and Medicine, Providence, RI 02912. Offers AM, M Sc, MA, MPH, Sc M, MD, PhD, MD/PhD. *Program availability:* Part-time. Terminal master's awarded for partial completion of doctoral program. *Degree requirements:* For doctorate, thesis/dissertation. *Entrance requirements:* For master's and doctorate, GRE General Test. Additional exam requirements/recommendations for international students: Required—TOEFL. Electronic applications accepted.

Bucknell University, Graduate Studies, College of Arts and Sciences, Department of Biology, Lewisburg, PA 17837. Offers MS. *Degree requirements:* For master's, thesis. *Entrance requirements:* For master's, GRE General Test, GRE Subject Test, minimum GPA of 3.0. Additional exam requirements/recommendations for international students: Required—TOEFL (minimum score 600 paper-based).

Buffalo State College, State University of New York, The Graduate School, Faculty of Natural and Social Sciences, Department of Biology, Buffalo, NY 14222-1095. Offers biology (MA); secondary education (MS Ed), including biology. *Program availability:* Evening/weekend. *Degree requirements:* For master's, thesis (for some programs), project. *Entrance requirements:* For master's, minimum GPA of 2.75. Additional exam requirements/recommendations for international students: Required—TOEFL (minimum score 550 paper-based).

Cabrini University, Academic Affairs, Radnor, PA 19087. Offers accounting (M Acc); autism spectrum disorder (M Ed); biological sciences (MS), including civic leadership; criminology and criminal justice (MA); curriculum, instruction, and assessment (M Ed); educational leadership (M Ed, Ed D), including curriculum and instructional leadership (Ed D), preK-12 leadership (Ed D); English as a second language (M Ed); organizational leadership (DBA, PhD); preK to 4 (M Ed); reading specialist (M Ed); secondary education (M Ed), including biology, chemistry, English, English/communication, mathematics, social studies; special education grades 7-12 (M Ed); special education preK-8 (M Ed); teaching and learning (M Ed). *Program availability:* Part-time, evening/weekend. *Faculty:* 23 full-time (17 women), 46 part-time/adjunct (38 women). *Students:* 60 full-time (35 women), 559 part-time (435 women); includes 93 minority (66 Black or African American, non-Hispanic/Latino; 1 American Indian or Alaska Native, non-Hispanic/Latino; 8 Asian, non-Hispanic/Latino; 15 Hispanic/Latino; 3 Two or more races, non-Hispanic/Latino), 4 international. Average age 33. 290 applicants, 82% accepted, 154 enrolled. In 2017, 283 master's awarded. *Degree requirements:* For master's, comprehensive exam (for some programs), thesis (for some programs); for doctorate, comprehensive exam (for some programs), thesis/dissertation. *Entrance requirements:* For master's, professional resume, personal statement, two recommendations, official transcripts; for doctorate, official transcripts, minimum master's GPA of 3.0, two recommendations, interview with admissions committee. Additional exam requirements/recommendations for international students: Required—TOEFL (minimum score 80 iBT). *Application deadline:* For fall admission, 8/26 for domestic students, 8/1 for international students; for winter admission, 1/13 for domestic students, 12/20 for international students; for spring admission, 1/13 for domestic students, 12/20 for international students; for summer admission, 5/20 for domestic students, 4/30 for international students. Applications are processed on a rolling basis. Application fee: $50. Electronic applications accepted. Application fee is waived when completed online. *Expenses:* Contact institution. *Financial support:* In 2017–18, 1,459 students received support. Tuition waivers and unspecified assistantships available. Financial award application deadline: 5/1; financial award applicants required to submit FAFSA. *Unit head:* Dr. Maliha Zaman, 610-902-8502, Fax: 610-902-8797, E-mail: msz37@cabrini.edu. *Application contact:* Diane Greenwood, Director of Graduate Admissions, 610-902-8291, E-mail: diane.l.greenwood@cabrini.edu.
Website: http://cabrini.edu/graduate

California Institute of Technology, Division of Biology, Pasadena, CA 91125-0001. Offers biochemistry and molecular biophysics (PhD); cell biology and biophysics (PhD); developmental biology (PhD); genetics (PhD); immunology (PhD); molecular biology (PhD); neurobiology (PhD). *Degree requirements:* For doctorate, thesis/dissertation, qualifying exam. *Entrance requirements:* For doctorate, GRE General Test. Additional exam requirements/recommendations for international students: Required—TOEFL. Electronic applications accepted. *Faculty research:* Molecular genetics of differentiation and development, structure of biological macromolecules, molecular and integrative neurobiology.

★ **California Polytechnic State University, San Luis Obispo,** College of Science and Mathematics, Department of Biological Sciences, San Luis Obispo, CA 93407. Offers MA, MS. *Program availability:* Part-time. *Faculty:* 8 full-time (3 women). *Students:* 29 full-time (18 women), 10 part-time (8 women); includes 9 minority (1 Asian, non-Hispanic/Latino; 7 Hispanic/Latino; 1 Two or more races, non-Hispanic/Latino), 1 international. Average age 26. 96 applicants, 28% accepted, 21 enrolled. In 2017, 21 master's awarded. *Degree requirements:* For master's, comprehensive exam (for some programs), thesis (for some programs). *Entrance requirements:* For master's, GRE. Additional exam requirements/recommendations for international students: Required—TOEFL (minimum score 80 iBT). *Application deadline:* For fall admission, 2/1 for domestic and international students. Applications are processed on a rolling basis. Application fee: $55. Electronic applications accepted. *Expenses:* Tuition, state resident: full-time $7176; part-time $4164 per year. *Required fees:* $3690; $3219 per year. $1073 per trimester. *Financial support:* Fellowships, research assistantships, teaching assistantships, career-related internships or fieldwork, and Federal Work-Study available. Support available to part-time students. Financial award application deadline: 3/2; financial award applicants required to submit FAFSA. *Faculty research:* Ancient fossil DNA, restoration ecology microbe biodiversity indices, biological inventories. *Unit head:* Dr. Emily Taylor, Graduate Coordinator, 805-756-2616, Fax: 805-756-1419, E-mail: etaylor@calpoly.edu.
Website: http://bio.calpoly.edu/

See Display on the next page and Close-Up on page 105.

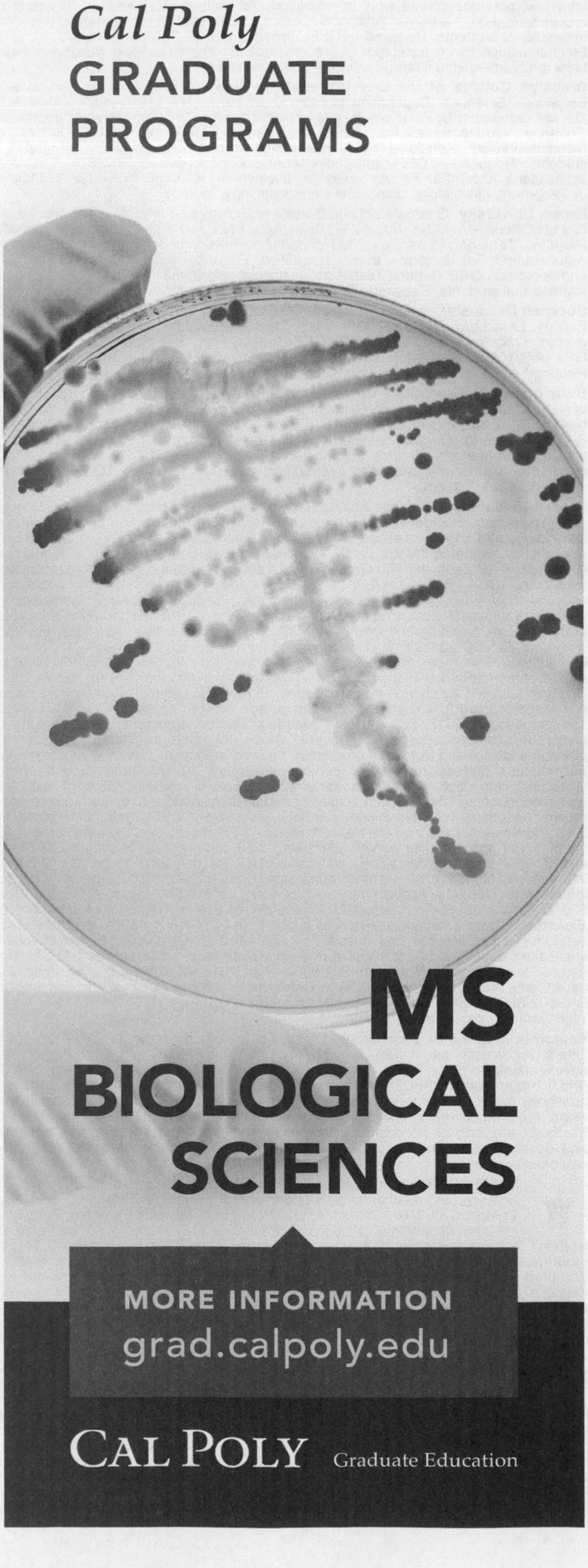

California State Polytechnic University, Pomona, Program in Biological Sciences, Pomona, CA 91768-2557. Offers MS. *Program availability:* Part-time, evening/weekend. *Students:* 37 full-time (21 women), 45 part-time (21 women); includes 51 minority (1 Black or African American, non-Hispanic/Latino; 16 Asian, non-Hispanic/Latino; 29 Hispanic/Latino; 5 Two or more races, non-Hispanic/Latino), 7 international. Average age 27. 47 applicants, 60% accepted, 20 enrolled. In 2017, 24 master's awarded. *Entrance requirements:* Additional exam requirements/recommendations for international students: Required—TOEFL (minimum score 550 paper-based). *Application deadline:* Applications are processed on a rolling basis. Application fee: $55. Electronic applications accepted. *Expenses:* Contact institution. *Financial support:* Application deadline: 3/2; applicants required to submit FAFSA. *Unit head:* Dr. Robert J. Talmadge, Professor/Graduate Coordinator, 909-869-3025, Fax: 909-869-4078, E-mail: rjtalmadge@cpp.edu. *Application contact:* Deborah L. Brandon, Executive Director of Admissions and Enrollment Planning, 909-869-3427, Fax: 909-869-5315, E-mail: dlbrandon@cpp.edu.
Website: http://www.cpp.edu/~sci/biological-sciences/graduate-studies/index.shtml

California State University, Bakersfield, Division of Graduate Studies, School of Natural Sciences, Mathematics, and Engineering, Program in Biology, Bakersfield, CA 93311. Offers MS. *Faculty:* 7 full-time (4 women). *Students:* 12 full-time (10 women), 5 part-time (3 women); includes 7 minority (2 Asian, non-Hispanic/Latino; 5 Hispanic/Latino). Average age 27. 5 applicants, 100% accepted, 3 enrolled. In 2017, 6 master's awarded. *Entrance requirements:* For master's, GRE, minimum undergraduate GPA of 3.0 in last 90 quarter units, 3 letters of recommendation. Additional exam requirements/recommendations for international students: Required—TOEFL. *Application deadline:* Applications are processed on a rolling basis. *Expenses:* Tuition, state resident: full-time $7176; part-time $4164 per year. *Financial support:* In 2017–18, fellowships (averaging $1,850 per year) were awarded; Federal Work-Study, scholarships/grants, and tuition waivers (full and partial) also available. Financial award application deadline: 3/2; financial award applicants required to submit FAFSA. *Unit head:* Dr. Anna L. Jacobsen, Graduate Coordinator, 661-654-2572, E-mail: ajacobsen@csub.edu. *Application contact:* Debbie Blowers, Assistant Director of Admissions and Evaluations, 661-654-3381, E-mail: dblowers@csub.edu.
Website: https://www.csub.edu/biology/index.html

California State University, Chico, Office of Graduate Studies, College of Natural Sciences, Department of Biological Sciences, Chico, CA 95929-0722. Offers MS. *Degree requirements:* For master's, thesis, independent research project resulting in a thesis. *Entrance requirements:* For master's, GRE, two letters of recommendation, statement of purpose, resume. Additional exam requirements/recommendations for international students: Required—TOEFL (minimum score 550 paper-based; 80 iBT), IELTS (minimum score 6.5), PTE (minimum score 59). Electronic applications accepted.

California State University, Dominguez Hills, College of Natural and Behavioral Sciences, Department of Biology, Carson, CA 90747-0001. Offers MS. *Program availability:* Part-time, evening/weekend. *Degree requirements:* For master's, thesis. *Entrance requirements:* For master's, minimum GPA of 2.75. Additional exam requirements/recommendations for international students: Required—TOEFL (minimum score 550 paper-based). Electronic applications accepted. *Faculty research:* Cancer biology, infectious diseases, ecology of native plants, remediation, community ecology.

California State University, East Bay, Office of Graduate Studies, College of Science, Department of Biological Sciences, Hayward, CA 94542-3000. Offers marine science (MA, MS), including biological science, marine science (MS). *Program availability:* Part-time. *Faculty:* 16 full-time (9 women), 4 part-time/adjunct (2 women). *Students:* 13 full-time (9 women), 21 part-time (16 women); includes 14 minority (3 Black or African American, non-Hispanic/Latino; 8 Asian, non-Hispanic/Latino; 3 Hispanic/Latino), 6 international. Average age 29. 39 applicants, 41% accepted, 13 enrolled. In 2017, 16 master's awarded. *Degree requirements:* For master's, thesis. *Entrance requirements:* For master's, GRE General and Subject Tests, minimum GPA of 3.0 in field, 2.75 overall; 3 letters of reference; statement of purpose. Additional exam requirements/recommendations for international students: Required—TOEFL (minimum score 550 paper-based). *Application deadline:* For fall admission, 4/15 for domestic and international students. Applications are processed on a rolling basis. Application fee: $55. Electronic applications accepted. *Financial support:* Fellowships, teaching assistantships, career-related internships or fieldwork, Federal Work-Study, institutionally sponsored loans, and scholarships/grants available. Support available to part-time students. Financial award application deadline: 3/2; financial award applicants required to submit FAFSA. *Unit head:* Dr. Donald Gailey, Chair, 510-885-3471, Fax: 510-885-4747, E-mail: donald.gailey@csueastbay.edu. *Application contact:* Prof. Maria Nieto, Interim Graduate Coordinator, 510-885-4757, Fax: 510-885-4747, E-mail: maria.nieto@csueastbay.edu.
Website: http://www20.csueastbay.edu/csci/departments/biology/

California State University, Fresno, Division of Research and Graduate Studies, College of Science and Mathematics, Department of Biology, Fresno, CA 93740-8027. Offers biology (MS); biotechnology (MBT). *Program availability:* Part-time, evening/weekend. *Degree requirements:* For master's, thesis. *Entrance requirements:* For master's, GRE General Test, GRE Subject Test, minimum GPA of 2.5 in last 60 units. Additional exam requirements/recommendations for international students: Required—TOEFL. Electronic applications accepted. *Faculty research:* Genome neuroscience, ecology conflict resolution, biomechanics, cell death, vibrio cholera.

California State University, Fullerton, Graduate Studies, College of Natural Science and Mathematics, Department of Biological Science, Fullerton, CA 92831-3599. Offers biology (MS); biotechnology (MBT). *Program availability:* Part-time. *Faculty:* 22 full-time (12 women). *Students:* 7 full-time (4 women), 46 part-time (28 women); includes 27 minority (2 Black or African American, non-Hispanic/Latino; 11 Asian, non-Hispanic/Latino; 13 Hispanic/Latino; 1 Two or more races, non-Hispanic/Latino), 5 international. Average age 26. 52 applicants, 29% accepted, 7 enrolled. *Entrance requirements:* For master's, GRE General and Subject Tests, MCAT, or DAT, minimum GPA of 3.0 in biology. Application fee: $55. *Financial support:* Research assistantships, teaching assistantships, career-related internships or fieldwork, Federal Work-Study, institutionally sponsored loans, and scholarships/grants available. Support available to part-time students. Financial award application deadline: 3/1; financial award applicants required to submit FAFSA. *Faculty research:* Glycosidase release and the block to polyspermy in ascidian eggs. *Unit head:* Karen Lau, Department Coordinator, 657-278-2461, E-mail: skarl@fullerton.edu. *Application contact:* Admissions/Applications, 657-278-2371.

California State University, Fullerton, Graduate Studies, College of Natural Science and Mathematics, Department of Chemistry and Biochemistry, Fullerton, CA 92831-3599. Offers biology (MS); chemistry (MA, MS). *Program availability:* Part-time. *Faculty:* 7 full-time (4 women). *Students:* 3 full-time (0 women), 16 part-time (6 women); includes 8 minority (3 Asian, non-Hispanic/Latino; 4 Hispanic/Latino; 1 Two or more races, non-Hispanic/Latino), 1 international. Average age 25. 34 applicants, 44% accepted, 7 enrolled. *Degree requirements:* For master's, thesis, departmental qualifying exam. *Entrance requirements:* For master's, minimum GPA of 2.5 in last 60 units of course work, major in chemistry or related field. Application fee: $55. *Financial support:* Research assistantships, teaching assistantships, career-related internships or fieldwork, Federal Work-Study, institutionally sponsored loans, and scholarships/grants available. Support available to part-time students. Financial award application deadline: 3/1; financial award applicants required to submit FAFSA. *Unit head:* Dr. Peter De Lijser, Chair, 657-278-3621, E-mail: pdelijser@fullerton.edu. *Application contact:* Admissions/Applications, 657-278-2371.

California State University, Long Beach, Graduate Studies, College of Natural Sciences and Mathematics, Department of Biological Sciences, Long Beach, CA 90840. Offers biology (MS); microbiology (MS). *Program availability:* Part-time. *Entrance requirements:* For master's, GRE Subject Test, minimum GPA of 3.0. Electronic applications accepted.

California State University, Los Angeles, Graduate Studies, College of Natural and Social Sciences, Department of Biological Sciences, Los Angeles, CA 90032-8530. Offers biology (MS). *Program availability:* Part-time, evening/weekend. *Degree requirements:* For master's, comprehensive exam or thesis. *Entrance requirements:* Additional exam requirements/recommendations for international students: Required—TOEFL (minimum score 500 paper-based). *Faculty research:* Ecology, environmental biology, cell and molecular biology, physiology, medical microbiology.

California State University, Northridge, Graduate Studies, College of Science and Mathematics, Department of Biology, Northridge, CA 91330. Offers MS. *Students:* 26 full-time (9 women), 40 part-time (27 women); includes 21 minority (5 Asian, non-Hispanic/Latino; 13 Hispanic/Latino; 3 Two or more races, non-Hispanic/Latino), 3 international. Average age 27. 58 applicants, 38% accepted, 16 enrolled. In 2017, 31 master's awarded. *Degree requirements:* For master's, thesis, seminar. *Entrance requirements:* For master's, GRE Subject Test, GRE General Test. Additional exam requirements/recommendations for international students: Required—TOEFL. *Application deadline:* For fall admission, 3/15 priority date for domestic students; for spring admission, 10/15 priority date for domestic students. Application fee: $55. *Financial support:* Research assistantships, teaching assistantships, Federal Work-Study, institutionally sponsored loans, tuition waivers (partial), and unspecified assistantships available. Support available to part-time students. Financial award applicants required to submit FAFSA. *Faculty research:* Cell adhesion, cancer research, fishery research. *Unit head:* Dr. Larry Allen, Chair, 818-677-3356.
Website: http://www.csun.edu/~hfbio002/

California State University, Sacramento, College of Natural Sciences and Mathematics, Department of Biological Sciences, Sacramento, CA 95819. Offers biological conservation (MS); molecular and cellular biology (MS); stem cell (MA). *Program availability:* Part-time. *Students:* 25 full-time (15 women), 20 part-time (14 women); includes 11 minority (2 Black or African American, non-Hispanic/Latino; 1 American Indian or Alaska Native, non-Hispanic/Latino; 8 Asian, non-Hispanic/Latino), 1 international. Average age 29. 82 applicants, 29% accepted, 18 enrolled. In 2017, 11 master's awarded. *Degree requirements:* For master's, thesis or project; writing proficiency exam. *Entrance requirements:* For master's, GRE, bachelor's degree in biology or equivalent; minimum GPA of 2.75 in all biology courses, 3.0 in all upper-division biology courses. Additional exam requirements/recommendations for international students: Required—TOEFL (minimum score 550 paper-based; 80 iBT); Recommended—IELTS, TSE. *Application deadline:* For fall admission, 2/1 for domestic and international students. Applications are processed on a rolling basis. Application fee: $55. Electronic applications accepted. *Expenses:* Contact institution. *Financial support:* Teaching assistantships, career-related internships or fieldwork, Federal Work-Study, and scholarships/grants available. Support available to part-time students. Financial award application deadline: 3/1; financial award applicants required to submit FAFSA. *Unit head:* Dr. Shannon Datwyler, Chair, 916-278-6535, Fax: 916-278-6993, E-mail: datwyler@csus.edu. *Application contact:* Jose Martinez, Graduate Admissions Supervisor, 916-278-7871, E-mail: martinj@skymail.csus.edu.
Website: http://www.csus.edu/bios

California State University, San Bernardino, Graduate Studies, College of Natural Sciences, Program in Biology, San Bernardino, CA 92407. Offers MS. *Program availability:* Part-time. *Faculty:* 10 full-time (3 women). *Students:* 4 full-time (1 woman), 13 part-time (5 women); includes 2 minority (both Asian, non-Hispanic/Latino). Average age 33. 10 applicants, 50% accepted, 3 enrolled. In 2017, 7 master's awarded. *Application deadline:* For fall admission, 5/1 for domestic students; for winter admission, 10/16 for domestic students; for spring admission, 1/22 for domestic students. Application fee: $55. *Faculty research:* Ecology, molecular biology, physiology, cell biology, neurobiology. *Unit head:* Dr. Michael Chao, Chair, 909-537-5388, E-mail: mchao@csusb.edu. *Application contact:* Dr. Dorota Huizinga, Dean of Graduate Studies, 909-537-3064, E-mail: dorota.huizinga@csusb.edu.

California State University, San Marcos, College of Science and Mathematics, Program in Biology, San Marcos, CA 92096-0001. Offers MS. *Program availability:* Part-time. *Entrance requirements:* For master's, GRE General Test, minimum GPA of 2.75 in mathematics and science or 3.0 in last 35 units of mathematics and science, bachelor's degree in the biological or related sciences. Additional exam requirements/recommendations for international students: Required—TOEFL, TWE. *Application deadline:* For fall admission, 2/15 for domestic students; for spring admission, 10/15 for domestic students. Application fee: $55. *Expenses:* Tuition, state resident: full-time $7176. Tuition, nonresident: full-time $9504. *Faculty research:* Gene regulation of life states, carbon cycling, genetic markers of viral infection, neurobiology. *Unit head:* Julie Jameson, Graduate Program Coordinator, 760-750-8274, E-mail: jjameson@csusm.edu. *Application contact:* Dr. Deborah Kristan, Graduate Advisor, 760-750-4638, E-mail: dkristan@csusm.edu.
Website: http://www.csusm.edu/biology/bioms/

Carleton University, Faculty of Graduate Studies, Faculty of Science, Department of Biology, Ottawa, ON K1S 5B6, Canada. Offers M Sc, PhD. Programs offered jointly with University of Ottawa. *Degree requirements:* For master's, thesis, seminar; for doctorate, comprehensive exam, thesis/dissertation, seminar. *Entrance requirements:* For master's, honors degree in science; for doctorate, M Sc. Additional exam requirements/recommendations for international students: Required—TOEFL. *Faculty research:* Biochemical, structural, and genetic regulation in cells; behavioral ecology; insect taxonomy; physiology of cells.

Carnegie Mellon University, Mellon College of Science, Department of Biological Sciences, Pittsburgh, PA 15213-3891. Offers biochemistry (PhD); biophysics (PhD); cell and developmental biology (PhD); computational biology (MS, PhD); genetics (PhD); molecular biology (PhD); neuroscience (PhD); structural biology (PhD). *Degree requirements:* For doctorate, comprehensive exam, thesis/dissertation. *Entrance requirements:* For doctorate, GRE General Test, GRE Subject Test, interview. Electronic applications accepted. *Faculty research:* Genetic structure, function, and regulation; protein structure and function; biological membranes; biological spectroscopy.

Case Western Reserve University, School of Graduate Studies, Department of Biology, Cleveland, OH 44106. Offers MS, PhD. *Program availability:* Part-time. *Faculty:* 25 full-time (13 women), 4 part-time/adjunct (all women). *Students:* 74 full-time (30 women), 5 part-time (4 women); includes 12 minority (3 Black or African American, non-Hispanic/Latino; 4 Asian, non-Hispanic/Latino; 4 Hispanic/Latino; 1 Two or more races, non-Hispanic/Latino), 26 international. Average age 28. 99 applicants, 46% accepted, 16 enrolled. In 2017, 9 master's, 2 doctorates awarded. Terminal master's awarded for partial completion of doctoral program. *Degree requirements:* For master's, thesis or alternative; for doctorate, thesis/dissertation. *Entrance requirements:* For master's and doctorate, GRE General Test, GRE Subject Test, statement of objectives; three letters of recommendation. Additional exam requirements/recommendations for international students: Required—TOEFL (minimum score 577 paper-based; 90 iBT); Recommended—IELTS (minimum score 7). *Application deadline:* For fall admission, 12/15 priority date for domestic students. Applications are processed on a rolling basis. Application fee: $50. Electronic applications accepted. *Expenses: Tuition:* Full-time $43,854; part-time $1827 per credit hour. *Required fees:* $50; $50 per credit hour. Tuition and fees vary according to course load and program. *Financial support:* Fellowships, research assistantships, teaching assistantships, career-related internships or fieldwork, Federal Work-Study, scholarships/grants, tuition waivers, unspecified assistantships, and stipends available. Financial award application deadline: 12/15; financial award applicants required to submit CSS PROFILE or FAFSA. *Faculty research:* Cellular, developmental, and molecular biology; genetics; genetic engineering; biotechnology; ecology. *Unit head:* Mark Willis, Professor and Chair, Department of Biology, 216-368-4358, Fax: 216-368-4762, E-mail: mark.willis@case.edu. *Application contact:* Julia Brown-Allen, Graduate Coordinator/Graduate Recruiter, 216-368-3556, Fax: 216-368-4672, E-mail: julia.brown@case.edu.
Website: http://biology.case.edu/

Case Western Reserve University, School of Medicine and School of Graduate Studies, Graduate Programs in Medicine, Medical Scientist Training Program, Cleveland, OH 44106. Offers MD/PhD. *Entrance requirements:* Additional exam requirements/recommendations for international students: Required—TOEFL. Electronic applications accepted. *Expenses: Tuition:* Full-time $43,854; part-time $1827 per credit hour. *Required fees:* $50; $50 per credit hour. Tuition and fees vary according to course load and program. *Faculty research:* Biochemistry, molecular biology, immunology, genetics, neurosciences.

The Catholic University of America, School of Arts and Sciences, Department of Biology, Washington, DC 20064. Offers biotechnology (MS); cell and microbial biology (MS, PhD), including cell biology; clinical laboratory science (MS, PhD); MSLS/MS. MSLS/MS offered jointly with Department of Library and Information Science. *Program availability:* Part-time. *Faculty:* 10 full-time (4 women), 7 part-time/adjunct (1 woman). *Students:* 24 full-time (18 women), 43 part-time (20 women); includes 7 minority (2 Black or African American, non-Hispanic/Latino; 3 Asian, non-Hispanic/Latino; 2 Two or more races, non-Hispanic/Latino), 48 international. Average age 31. 56 applicants, 61% accepted, 18 enrolled. In 2017, 7 master's, 1 doctorate awarded. Terminal master's awarded for partial completion of doctoral program. *Degree requirements:* For master's and doctorate, comprehensive exam. *Entrance requirements:* For master's and doctorate, GRE General Test, GRE Subject Test, statement of purpose, official copies of academic transcripts, three letters of recommendation. Additional exam requirements/recommendations for international students: Required—TOEFL (minimum score 550 paper-based; 80 iBT). *Application deadline:* For fall admission, 7/15 priority date for domestic students, 7/1 for international students; for spring admission, 11/15 priority date for domestic students, 11/1 for international students. Applications are processed on a rolling basis. Application fee: $55. Electronic applications accepted. *Expenses:* Contact institution. *Financial support:* Fellowships, research assistantships, teaching assistantships, Federal Work-Study, scholarships/grants, tuition waivers (full and partial), and unspecified assistantships available. Financial award application deadline: 2/1; financial award applicants required to submit FAFSA. *Faculty research:* Virus structure and assembly, hepatic and epithelial cell biology, drug resistance and genome stabilization in yeast, biophysics of ion-conductive nanostructures, eukaryotic gene regulation, cancer and vaccine research. *Total annual research expenditures:* $1.7 million. *Unit head:* Dr. Venigalla Rao, Chair, 202-319-5271, Fax: 202-319-5721, E-mail: rao@cua.edu. *Application contact:* Dr. Steven Brown, Director of Graduate Admissions, 202-319-5057, Fax: 202-319-6533, E-mail: cua-admissions@cua.edu.
Website: http://biology.cua.edu/

Cedars-Sinai Medical Center, Graduate Programs, Los Angeles, CA 90048. Offers biomedical and translational sciences (PhD); magnetic resonance in medicine (MS). *Faculty:* 60 full-time (15 women). *Students:* 40 full-time (26 women); includes 12 minority (2 Black or African American, non-Hispanic/Latino; 4 Asian, non-Hispanic/Latino; 4 Hispanic/Latino; 2 Native Hawaiian or other Pacific Islander, non-Hispanic/Latino). Average age 29. 55 applicants, 15% accepted, 8 enrolled. *Degree requirements:* For doctorate, comprehensive exam, thesis/dissertation. *Entrance requirements:* For doctorate, GRE, 3 letters of recommendation. Additional exam requirements/recommendations for international students: Required—TOEFL (minimum score 550 paper-based; 80 iBT), IELTS (minimum score 6.5). *Application deadline:* For fall admission, 1/31 for domestic students. Application fee: $35. Electronic applications accepted. *Financial support:* Health care benefits and annual stipends (averaging $36,000) available. *Faculty research:* Regenerative medicine, immunology and host-pathogen interactions, cancer biology, genomics, tissue fibrosis and repair, neurosciences, metabolism, heart biology. *Total annual research expenditures:* $36 million. *Application contact:* Emma Yates Casler, Program Coordinator, 310-423-8294, E-mail: yatese@cshs.org.
Website: https://www.cedars-sinai.edu/Education/Graduate-Research-Education/

Central Connecticut State University, School of Graduate Studies, School of Engineering, Science and Technology, Department of Biology, New Britain, CT 06050-4010. Offers biological sciences (MA), including ecology and environmental sciences, general biology; biology (DNP-A). *Program availability:* Part-time, evening/weekend. *Faculty:* 7 full-time (2 women), 2 part-time/adjunct (both women). *Students:* 101 full-time (57 women), 19 part-time (13 women); includes 32 minority (11 Black or African American, non-Hispanic/Latino; 11 Asian, non-Hispanic/Latino; 3 Hispanic/Latino; 7 Two or more races, non-Hispanic/Latino). Average age 30. 54 applicants, 91% accepted, 41 enrolled. In 2017, 53 master's awarded. *Degree requirements:* For master's, comprehensive exam, thesis or alternative. *Entrance requirements:* For master's, minimum undergraduate GPA of 2.7, essay, letters of recommendation. Additional exam requirements/recommendations for international students: Required—TOEFL (minimum score 550 paper-based; 79 iBT); Recommended—IELTS (minimum score 6.5). *Application deadline:* For fall admission, 8/1 for domestic students, 5/1 for international students; for spring admission, 11/1 for domestic and international students. Applications are processed on a rolling basis. Application fee: $50. Electronic applications accepted. *Expenses: Tuition, area resident:* Full-time $6757. Tuition, state resident: full-time $9750; part-time $374 per credit. Tuition, nonresident: full-time $18,102; part-time $374 per credit. *Required fees:* $4635; $255 per credit. *Financial support:* In 2017–18, 6 students received support. Career-related internships or fieldwork, Federal Work-Study, scholarships/grants, and unspecified assistantships available. Support available to part-time students. Financial award application deadline: 3/1; financial award applicants required to submit FAFSA. *Faculty research:* Environmental science, anesthesia, health sciences, zoology, animal behavior. *Unit head:* Dr. Douglas Carter, Chair, 860-832-2645, E-mail: carterd@ccsu.edu. *Application contact:* Patricia Gardner, Associate Director of Graduate Studies, 860-832-2350, Fax: 860-832-2362.
Website: http://www.ccsu.edu/biology/

Biological and Biomedical Sciences—General

Central Michigan University, College of Graduate Studies, College of Science and Technology, Department of Biology, Mount Pleasant, MI 48859. Offers biology (MS); conservation biology (MS). *Program availability:* Part-time. *Degree requirements:* For master's, thesis or alternative. *Entrance requirements:* For master's, GRE, bachelor's degree with a major in biological science, minimum GPA of 3.0. Electronic applications accepted. *Faculty research:* Conservation biology, morphology and taxonomy of aquatic plants, molecular biology and genetics, microbials and invertebrate ecology, vertebrates.

Central Washington University, School of Graduate Studies and Research, College of the Sciences, Department of Biological Sciences, Ellensburg, WA 98926. Offers botany (MS); microbiology and parasitology (MS); stream ecology and fisheries (MS); terrestrial ecology (MS). *Program availability:* Part-time. *Entrance requirements:* For master's, GRE General Test, minimum GPA of 3.0. Additional exam requirements/recommendations for international students: Required—TOEFL (minimum score 550 paper-based; 79 iBT). *Application deadline:* For fall admission, 2/1 priority date for domestic students; for winter admission, 10/1 for domestic students; for spring admission, 1/1 for domestic students. Applications are processed on a rolling basis. Application fee: $50. Electronic applications accepted. *Financial support:* Application deadline: 3/1; applicants required to submit FAFSA. *Unit head:* Dr. Kristina A. Ernest, Graduate Coordinator, 509-963-2805, E-mail: kristina.ernest@cwu.edu. *Application contact:* Justine Eason, Admissions Program Coordinator, 509-963-3103, Fax: 509-963-1799, E-mail: masters@cwu.edu.

Chatham University, Program in Biology, Pittsburgh, PA 15232-2826. Offers environmental biology (MS); human biology (MS). *Program availability:* Part-time. *Faculty:* 1 full-time (0 women), 2 part-time/adjunct (1 woman). *Students:* 51 full-time (39 women), 9 part-time (6 women); includes 23 minority (10 Black or African American, non-Hispanic/Latino; 1 American Indian or Alaska Native, non-Hispanic/Latino; 9 Asian, non-Hispanic/Latino; 3 Hispanic/Latino), 5 international. Average age 25. 180 applicants, 60% accepted, 39 enrolled. In 2017, 52 master's awarded. *Degree requirements:* For master's, thesis optional. *Entrance requirements:* For master's, 3 letters of recommendation. Additional exam requirements/recommendations for international students: Required—TOEFL (minimum score 600 paper-based; 100 iBT), IELTS (minimum score 7), TWE. *Application deadline:* For fall admission, 4/1 priority date for domestic and international students; for spring admission, 11/1 priority date for domestic students, 10/1 priority date for international students. Applications are processed on a rolling basis. Application fee: $45. Electronic applications accepted. Application fee is waived when completed online. *Expenses: Tuition:* Full-time $16,740; part-time $930 per credit. *Required fees:* $486; $27 per credit. $243 per semester. *Financial support:* Applicants required to submit FAFSA. *Faculty research:* Molecular evolution of iron homeostasis, characteristics of soil bacterial communities, gene flow through seed movement, role of gonadotropins in spermatogonial proliferation, phosphatide/inositol metabolism in epithelial cells. *Unit head:* Dr. Lisa Lambert, Director, 412-365-1217, E-mail: lambert@chatham.edu. *Application contact:* Ashlee Bartko, Senior Assistant Director of Graduate Admission, 412-365-1115, Fax: 412-365-1609, E-mail: gradadmissions@chatham.edu.
Website: http://www.chatham.edu/departments/sciences/graduate/biology

Chicago State University, School of Graduate and Professional Studies, College of Arts and Sciences, Department of Biological Sciences, Chicago, IL 60628. Offers MS. *Program availability:* Part-time, evening/weekend. *Entrance requirements:* For master's, minimum GPA of 3.0, 15 credit hours in biological sciences. *Application deadline:* For fall admission, 7/1 for domestic students; for spring admission, 11/10 for domestic students. Applications are processed on a rolling basis. Application fee: $25. *Faculty research:* Molecular genetics of gene complexes, mammalian immune cell function, genetics of agriculturally important microbes, environmental toxicology, neuromuscular physiology. *Unit head:* Dr. Mark Erhart, Graduate Advisor, 773-995-2432, E-mail: ma-erhart@csu.edu. *Application contact:* Graduate Studies Office, 773-995-2404.
Website: http://www.csu.edu/cas/bioandprehealth/index.htm

The Citadel, The Military College of South Carolina, Citadel Graduate College, School of Science and Mathematics, Department of Biology, Charleston, SC 29409. Offers biology (MA); environmental studies (Graduate Certificate). *Accreditation:* NCATE (one or more programs are accredited). *Program availability:* Part-time, evening/weekend. *Entrance requirements:* For master's, GRE (minimum combined score of 290 verbal and quantitative) or MAT (minimum raw score of 396), official transcript reflecting highest degree earned from regionally-accredited college or university; for Graduate Certificate, official transcript reflecting highest degree earned from regionally-accredited college or university. Additional exam requirements/recommendations for international students: Required—TOEFL (minimum score 550 paper-based; 79 iBT). Electronic applications accepted. *Expenses:* Tuition, state resident: part-time $587 per credit hour. Tuition, nonresident: part-time $988 per credit hour. *Required fees:* $90 per term.

The Citadel, The Military College of South Carolina, Citadel Graduate College, Zucker Family School of Education, Charleston, SC 29409. Offers elementary/secondary school administration and supervision (M Ed); elementary/secondary school counseling (M Ed); interdisciplinary STEM education (M Ed); literacy education (M Ed, Graduate Certificate); middle grades (MAT), including English, mathematics, science, social studies; physical education (grades K-12) (MAT); school superintendency (Ed S); secondary education (MAT), including biology, English, mathematics, social studies; student affairs (Graduate Certificate); student affairs and college counseling (M Ed). *Accreditation:* NCATE. *Program availability:* Part-time, evening/weekend, 100% online, blended/hybrid learning. *Degree requirements:* For master's, comprehensive exam (for some programs). *Entrance requirements:* For master's, GRE (minimum combined verbal and quantitative score of 290) or MAT (minimum score 396). Additional exam requirements/recommendations for international students: Required—TOEFL (minimum score 550 paper-based; 79 iBT). Electronic applications accepted. *Expenses:* Tuition, state resident: part-time $587 per credit hour. Tuition, nonresident: part-time $988 per credit hour. *Required fees:* $90 per term.

City College of the City University of New York, Graduate School, Division of Science, Department of Biology, New York, NY 10031-9198. Offers MS, PhD. PhD program offered jointly with Graduate School and University Center of the City University of New York. *Program availability:* Part-time. Terminal master's awarded for partial completion of doctoral program. *Degree requirements:* For master's, thesis or alternative; for doctorate, one foreign language, thesis/dissertation, teaching experience. *Entrance requirements:* For doctorate, GRE General Test. Additional exam requirements/recommendations for international students: Required—TOEFL (minimum score 500 paper-based; 61 iBT). Electronic applications accepted. *Faculty research:* Animal behavior, ecology, genetics, neurobiology, molecular biology.

Clark Atlanta University, School of Arts and Sciences, Department of Biology, Atlanta, GA 30314. Offers MS, PhD. *Program availability:* Part-time. *Faculty:* 15 full-time (7 women), 5 part-time/adjunct (all women). *Students:* 14 full-time (7 women), 5 part-time (4 women); includes 13 minority (12 Black or African American, non-Hispanic/Latino; 1 Asian, non-Hispanic/Latino), 6 international. Average age 31. 26 applicants, 62% accepted, 6 enrolled. In 2017, 2 master's, 9 doctorates awarded. Terminal master's awarded for partial completion of doctoral program. *Degree requirements:* For master's, one foreign language, thesis; for doctorate, 2 foreign languages, thesis/dissertation. *Entrance requirements:* For master's, GRE General Test, minimum GPA of 2.5; for doctorate, GRE General Test, minimum graduate GPA of 3.0. Additional exam requirements/recommendations for international students: Required—TOEFL (minimum score 500 paper-based; 61 iBT). *Application deadline:* For fall admission, 4/1 for domestic and international students; for spring admission, 11/1 for domestic and international students. Applications are processed on a rolling basis. Application fee: $40 ($55 for international students). Electronic applications accepted. *Financial support:* Research assistantships, career-related internships or fieldwork, Federal Work-Study, scholarships/grants, traineeships, and unspecified assistantships available. Support available to part-time students. Financial award application deadline: 4/30; financial award applicants required to submit FAFSA. *Faculty research:* Regulation of amino-DNA, cellular regulations. *Unit head:* Dr. Paul Musey, Interim Chairperson, 404-880-6829, E-mail: pmusey@cau.edu.

Clarkson University, School of Arts and Sciences, Program in Basic Science, Potsdam, NY 13699. Offers basic science (MS), including biology. *Students:* 3 full-time (1 woman), 1 (woman) part-time; includes 2 minority (both Asian, non-Hispanic/Latino), 1 international. 6 applicants, 67% accepted, 2 enrolled. In 2017, 2 master's awarded. *Entrance requirements:* For master's, GRE. Additional exam requirements/recommendations for international students: Required—TOEFL (minimum score 550 paper-based, 80 iBT) or IELTS (6.5). *Application deadline:* Applications are processed on a rolling basis. Application fee: $50. Electronic applications accepted. *Expenses: Tuition:* Full-time $24,210; part-time $1345 per credit hour. Tuition and fees vary according to campus/location and program. *Financial support:* Scholarships/grants and unspecified assistantships available. *Unit head:* Dr. Charles Thorpe, Interim Dean of Arts and Sciences, 315-268-6544. *Application contact:* Dan Capogna, Director of Graduate Admissions, 518-631-9910, E-mail: graduate@clarkson.edu.
Website: https://www.clarkson.edu/academics/graduate

Clark University, Graduate School, Department of Biology, Worcester, MA 01610-1477. Offers MA, PhD. *Faculty:* 11 full-time (3 women), 3 part-time/adjunct (1 woman). *Students:* 30 full-time (20 women); includes 3 minority (2 Asian, non-Hispanic/Latino; 1 Hispanic/Latino), 7 international. Average age 26. 34 applicants, 32% accepted, 10 enrolled. In 2017, 1 doctorate awarded. Terminal master's awarded for partial completion of doctoral program. *Degree requirements:* For doctorate, thesis/dissertation. *Entrance requirements:* For doctorate, GRE General Test. Additional exam requirements/recommendations for international students: Required—TOEFL (minimum score 575 paper-based; 90 iBT), IELTS (minimum score 6.5). *Application deadline:* For fall admission, 1/15 priority date for domestic students. Application fee: $75. Electronic applications accepted. *Financial support:* Fellowships, research assistantships, teaching assistantships, scholarships/grants, and tuition waivers (full and partial) available. *Faculty research:* Nitrogen assimilation in marine algae, polyporale taxonomies, fungal evolutionary history, drug discovery, taste sensitivities, biodiversity inventories. *Unit head:* Dr. Justin Thackeray, Chair, 508-793-7563, E-mail: jthackeray@clarku.edu. *Application contact:* Paula Kupstas, Department Secretary, 508-793-7173, Fax: 528-793-7174, E-mail: pkupstas@clarku.edu.
Website: http://www.clarku.edu/departments/biology/

Clayton State University, School of Graduate Studies, College of Arts and Sciences, Program in Education, Morrow, GA 30260-0285. Offers biology (MAT); English (MAT); history (MAT); mathematics (MAT). *Accreditation:* NCATE. *Entrance requirements:* For master's, GRE, GACE, 2 official copies of transcripts, 3 recommendation letters, statement of purpose. Additional exam requirements/recommendations for international students: Required—TOEFL (minimum score 550 paper-based). Electronic applications accepted.

Clemson University, Graduate School, College of Science, Department of Biological Sciences, Clemson, SC 29634. Offers biological sciences (MS, PhD); biological sciences for science educators (MBS); environmental toxicology (MS, PhD); microbiology (MS, PhD). *Program availability:* Part-time, 100% online. *Faculty:* 46 full-time (15 women), 9 part-time/adjunct (4 women). *Students:* 136 full-time (86 women), 546 part-time (386 women); includes 76 minority (26 Black or African American, non-Hispanic/Latino; 2 American Indian or Alaska Native, non-Hispanic/Latino; 10 Asian, non-Hispanic/Latino; 20 Hispanic/Latino; 18 Two or more races, non-Hispanic/Latino), 34 international. Average age 35. 245 applicants, 75% accepted, 143 enrolled. In 2017, 182 master's, 12 doctorates awarded. *Degree requirements:* For master's, comprehensive exam (for some programs), thesis (for some programs); for doctorate, comprehensive exam, thesis/dissertation. *Entrance requirements:* For master's and doctorate, GRE General Test, unofficial transcripts, letters of recommendation. Additional exam requirements/recommendations for international students: Required—TOEFL (minimum score 100 iBT), IELTS (minimum score 7.5), PTE (minimum score 72). *Application deadline:* For fall admission, 1/5 for domestic and international students. Application fee: $80 ($90 for international students). Electronic applications accepted. *Expenses:* $5,174 per semester full-time resident, $9,714 per semester full-time non-resident, $511 per credit hour part-time resident, $1,017 per credit hour part-time non-resident; $741 per credit hour online; other fees may apply per session. *Financial support:* In 2017–18, 47 students received support, including 2 fellowships with partial tuition reimbursements available (averaging $17,000 per year), 8 research assistantships with partial tuition reimbursements available (averaging $23,063 per year), 37 teaching assistantships with partial tuition reimbursements available (averaging $21,662 per year). Financial award application deadline: 1/5. *Faculty research:* Microbiology, cell and developmental biology, evolutionary biology, ecology, molecular biology. *Total annual research expenditures:* $1.5 million. *Unit head:* Dr. Robert Cohen, Department Chair, 864-656-1112, Fax: 864-656-0435, E-mail: rscohen@clemson.edu. *Application contact:* Jay Lyn Martin, Student Services Program Coordinator, 864-656-3587, Fax: 864-656-0435, E-mail: jaylyn@clemson.edu.
Website: http://www.clemson.edu/science/departments/biosci/

Cleveland State University, College of Graduate Studies, College of Sciences and Health Professions, Department of Biological, Geological, and Environmental Sciences, Cleveland, OH 44115. Offers MS, PhD. *Program availability:* Part-time. *Faculty:* 18 full-time (5 women), 54 part-time/adjunct (22 women). *Students:* 56 full-time (34 women), 13 part-time (7 women); includes 8 minority (3 Black or African American, non-Hispanic/Latino; 3 Asian, non-Hispanic/Latino; 1 Hispanic/Latino; 1 Two or more races, non-Hispanic/Latino), 27 international. Average age 29. 56 applicants, 54% accepted, 16 enrolled. In 2017, 8 master's, 8 doctorates awarded. Terminal master's awarded for partial completion of doctoral program. *Entrance requirements:* For master's, GRE General Test, 3 letters of recommendation; for doctorate, GRE General Test, 3 letters of recommendation; 1-2 page essay; statement of career goals and research interests. Additional exam requirements/recommendations for international students: Required—TOEFL (minimum score 550 paper-based; 78 iBT), IELTS. *Application deadline:* Applications are processed on a rolling basis. Application fee: $40. Electronic applications accepted. *Financial support:* In 2017–18, 33 students received support, including 1 fellowship with full tuition reimbursement available (averaging $21,000 per year), 14 research assistantships with full tuition reimbursements available (averaging $11,800 per year), 29 teaching assistantships with full tuition reimbursements available (averaging $9,500 per year); tuition waivers (full and partial) and unspecified assistantships also available. Financial award applicants required to submit FAFSA. *Faculty research:* Cardiopulmonary pathology, signaling pathways and RNA

interference, toxoplasmosis, plant ecology, biology and biochemistry of nitric oxide. *Unit head:* Dr. Crystal M. Weyman, Chairperson/Professor, 216-687-6971, Fax: 216-687-6972, E-mail: c.weyman@csuohio.edu. *Application contact:* Dr. Girish C. Shukla, Associate Professor and Graduate Program Director, 216-687-2395, Fax: 216-687-6972, E-mail: g.shukla@csuohio.edu.
Website: http://www.csuohio.edu/sciences/bges

Cold Spring Harbor Laboratory, Watson School of Biological Sciences, Cold Spring Harbor, NY 11724. Offers PhD. *Faculty:* 55 full-time (11 women). *Students:* 44 full-time (22 women); includes 7 minority (1 Black or African American, non-Hispanic/Latino; 2 Asian, non-Hispanic/Latino; 3 Hispanic/Latino; 1 Two or more races, non-Hispanic/Latino), 22 international. Average age 27. 202 applicants, 13% accepted, 8 enrolled. In 2017, 9 doctorates awarded. *Degree requirements:* For doctorate, comprehensive exam, thesis/dissertation, lab rotations, teaching experience, qualifying exam, postdoctoral proposals. *Entrance requirements:* For doctorate, GRE (recommended). *Application deadline:* For fall admission, 12/1 for domestic and international students. Application fee: $60. Electronic applications accepted. *Financial support:* In 2017–18, 44 students received support, including 44 fellowships with full tuition reimbursements available (averaging $34,000 per year); scholarships/grants, traineeships, health care benefits, and tuition waivers (full) also available. Financial award application deadline: 12/1. *Faculty research:* Genetics and genomics, neurobiology, cancer, plant biology, molecular biology, quantitative biology, bioinformatics. *Unit head:* Dr. Alexander Gann, Dean, 516-367-6890. *Application contact:* Admissions and Recruitment Manager, 516-367-6890, E-mail: gradschool@cshl.edu.
Website: https://www.cshl.edu/education/phd-program/

The College at Brockport, State University of New York, School of Arts and Sciences, Department of Biology, Brockport, NY 14420-2997. Offers MS, PSM. *Program availability:* Part-time. *Faculty:* 6 full-time (1 woman). *Students:* 8 full-time (6 women), 6 part-time (2 women); includes 2 minority (1 Black or African American, non-Hispanic/Latino; 1 Asian, non-Hispanic/Latino). 12 applicants, 83% accepted, 7 enrolled. In 2017, 2 master's awarded. *Degree requirements:* For master's, comprehensive exam, thesis or alternative. *Entrance requirements:* For master's, letters of recommendation, minimum GPA of 3.0, scientific writing sample, statement of objectives. Additional exam requirements/recommendations for international students: Required—TOEFL (minimum score 550 paper-based; 79 iBT), IELTS (minimum score 6.5). *Application deadline:* For fall admission, 7/15 priority date for domestic and international students; for spring admission, 11/15 priority date for domestic and international students; for summer admission, 6/15 priority date for domestic and international students. Application fee: $50. Electronic applications accepted. *Expenses:* Tuition, state resident: full-time $10,870; part-time $453 per credit hour. Tuition, nonresident: full-time $22,210. *Required fees:* $988; $246 per semester. *Financial support:* In 2017–18, 8 teaching assistantships with full tuition reimbursements (averaging $6,000 per year) were awarded; Federal Work-Study, scholarships/grants, and unspecified assistantships also available. Support available to part-time students. Financial award application deadline: 3/15; financial award applicants required to submit FAFSA. *Faculty research:* Microbiology, molecular genetics, cellular biology, developmental biology, animal physiology. *Unit head:* Dr. Rey Sia, Chairperson, 585-395-2783, Fax: 585-395-2741, E-mail: rsia@brockport.edu. *Application contact:* Dr. Adam Rich, Graduate Program Director, 585-395-5740, Fax: 585-395-2741, E-mail: arich@brockport.edu.
Website: http://www.brockport.edu/biology/graduate/

The College at Brockport, State University of New York, School of Education, Health, and Human Services, Department of Education and Human Development, Program in Inclusive Generalist Education, Brockport, NY 14420-2997. Offers biology (MS Ed, AGC), chemistry (MS Ed, AGC); English (MS Ed, Advanced Certificate); mathematics (MS Ed, Advanced Certificate); science (MS Ed, Advanced Certificate); social studies (MS Ed, Advanced Certificate). *Students:* 61 part-time (30 women); includes 2 minority (1 Black or African American, non-Hispanic/Latino; 1 Asian, non-Hispanic/Latino). 41 applicants, 78% accepted, 25 enrolled. In 2017, 12 master's, 3 AGCs awarded. *Degree requirements:* For master's, thesis or alternative. *Entrance requirements:* For master's, edTPA, GRE or MAT, minimum GPA of 3.0, letters of recommendation, statement of objectives, academic major (or equivalent) in program discipline, current resume. Additional exam requirements/recommendations for international students: Required—TOEFL (minimum score 550 paper-based; 79 iBT), IELTS (minimum score 6.5). *Application deadline:* For fall admission, 3/15 priority date for domestic and international students; for spring admission, 10/15 priority date for domestic and international students; for summer admission, 3/15 for domestic and international students. Application fee: $80. Electronic applications accepted. *Expenses:* Tuition, state resident: full-time $10,870; part-time $453 per credit hour. Tuition, nonresident: full-time $22,210. *Required fees:* $988; $246 per semester. *Financial support:* Federal Work-Study, scholarships/grants, and unspecified assistantships available. Support available to part-time students. Financial award application deadline: 3/15; financial award applicants required to submit FAFSA. *Unit head:* Dr. Sue Robb, Chairperson, 585-395-5935, Fax: 585-395-2171, E-mail: srobb@brockport.edu. *Application contact:* Anne Walton, Coordinator of Graduate Advisement, 585-395-2326, Fax: 585-395-2172, E-mail: awalton@brockport.edu.
Website: https://www.brockport.edu/academics/education_human_development/department.html

College of Staten Island of the City University of New York, Graduate Programs, Division of Science and Technology, Program in Biology, Staten Island, NY 10314-6600. Offers biology (MS), including biotechnology, general biology. *Program availability:* Part-time, evening/weekend. *Faculty:* 7 full-time, 1 part-time/adjunct. *Students:* 31. 44 applicants, 50% accepted, 16 enrolled. In 2017, 13 master's awarded. *Degree requirements:* For master's, 30 credits (for general biology and biotechnology tracks). *Entrance requirements:* For master's, GRE (recommended), BS in biology from accredited college; minimum overall GPA of 2.75, 3.0 in undergraduate science and mathematics courses; two letters of recommendation. Additional exam requirements/recommendations for international students: Required—TOEFL (minimum score 550 paper-based; 79 iBT), IELTS (minimum score 6.5). *Application deadline:* For fall admission, 7/1 for domestic and international students; for spring admission, 11/25 for domestic and international students. Applications are processed on a rolling basis. Application fee: $125. Electronic applications accepted. *Expenses:* Tuition, state resident: full-time $10,450; part-time $440 per credit. Tuition, nonresident: full-time $19,320; part-time $440 per credit. *Required fees:* $181.10 per semester. Tuition and fees vary according to program. *Faculty research:* Gene regulatory network, transcriptional regulation and epigenetics; developmental biology and evolution; biogeography, conservation, species responses and abundance; ecological process and computational biology; cancer biology. *Unit head:* Dr. Jianying Gu, 718-982-4123, E-mail: jianying.gu@csi.cuny.edu. *Application contact:* Sasha Spence, Associate Director for Graduate Admissions, 718-982-2019, Fax: 718-982-2500, E-mail: sasha.spence@csi.cuny.edu.
Website: https://www.csi.cuny.edu/sites/default/files/pdf/admissions/grad/pdf/Biology%20Fact%20Sheet.pdf

College of Staten Island of the City University of New York, Graduate Programs, School of Education, Program in Adolescence Education, Staten Island, NY 10314-6600. Offers adolescence education (MS Ed), including biology, English, mathematics, social studies. *Program availability:* Part-time, evening/weekend. *Faculty:* 23 full-time, 6 part-time/adjunct. *Students:* 87. 45 applicants, 67% accepted, 23 enrolled. In 2017, 21 master's awarded. *Degree requirements:* For master's, thesis, educational research project supervised by faculty. *Entrance requirements:* For master's, GRE General Test or an approved equivalent examination, relevant bachelor's degree, minimum overall GPA of 3.0, two letters of recommendation, one- or two-page personal statement. Additional exam requirements/recommendations for international students: Required—TOEFL (minimum score 550 paper-based; 79 iBT), IELTS (minimum score 6.5). *Application deadline:* For fall admission, 4/25 for domestic and international students; for spring admission, 11/25 for domestic and international students. Applications are processed on a rolling basis. Application fee: $125. Electronic applications accepted. *Expenses:* Tuition, state resident: full-time $10,450; part-time $440 per credit. Tuition, nonresident: full-time $19,320; part-time $440 per credit. *Required fees:* $181.10 per semester. Tuition and fees vary according to program. *Faculty research:* Development and assessment of TPACK (technological pedagogical content knowledge), technology and differentiation in stem classrooms, teacher effectiveness and student achievement, teacher knowledge, knowledge transfer from college to classroom. *Unit head:* Diane Brescia, 718-982-3877, E-mail: diane.brescia@csi.cuny.edu. *Application contact:* Sasha Spence, Associate Director for Graduate Admissions, 718-982-2019, Fax: 718-982-2500, E-mail: sasha.spence@csi.cuny.edu.
Website: http://www.csi.cuny.edu/catalog/graduate/graduate-programs-in-education.htm#o2608

The College of William and Mary, Faculty of Arts and Sciences, Department of Biology, Williamsburg, VA 23187-8795. Offers MS. *Faculty:* 28 full-time (12 women), 1 (woman) part-time/adjunct. *Students:* 16 full-time (9 women); includes 2 minority (1 Black or African American, non-Hispanic/Latino; 1 Two or more races, non-Hispanic/Latino), 1 international. Average age 23. 42 applicants, 24% accepted, 10 enrolled. In 2017, 9 master's awarded. *Degree requirements:* For master's, comprehensive exam, thesis (for some programs). *Entrance requirements:* For master's, GRE Subject Test (recommended for students who have not earned bachelor's degree in biology), GRE General Test, minimum GPA of 3.0. Additional exam requirements/recommendations for international students: Required—TOEFL. *Application deadline:* For fall admission, 2/1 priority date for domestic and international students. Application fee: $50. Electronic applications accepted. *Financial support:* In 2017–18, 15 teaching assistantships with full tuition reimbursements (averaging $18,240 per year) were awarded; Federal Work-Study, institutionally sponsored loans, and unspecified assistantships also available. Financial award application deadline: 2/1; financial award applicants required to submit FAFSA. *Faculty research:* Cellular and molecular biology, genetics, ecology, organismal biology, physiology. *Total annual research expenditures:* $2.2 million. *Unit head:* Dr. Eric L. Bradley, Chair, 757-221-2220, E-mail: elbrad@wm.edu. *Application contact:* Dr. Matthias Leu, Graduate Director, 757-221-7497, E-mail: mleu@wm.edu.
Website: http://www.wm.edu/biology/

Colorado State University, College of Natural Sciences, Department of Biology, Fort Collins, CO 80523-1878. Offers botany (MS, PhD). *Faculty:* 32 full-time (13 women), 8 part-time/adjunct (5 women). *Students:* 16 full-time (9 women), 20 part-time (8 women); includes 3 minority (1 Asian, non-Hispanic/Latino; 2 Hispanic/Latino), 4 international. Average age 30. 28 applicants, 36% accepted, 7 enrolled. In 2017, 6 master's, 3 doctorates awarded. Terminal master's awarded for partial completion of doctoral program. *Degree requirements:* For master's, thesis, defense; for doctorate, comprehensive exam, thesis/dissertation. *Entrance requirements:* For master's and doctorate, transcripts, minimum GPA of 3.0; recommendation letters. Additional exam requirements/recommendations for international students: Required—TOEFL (minimum score 550 paper-based; 80 iBT), IELTS (minimum score 6.5). *Application deadline:* For fall admission, 1/1 for domestic and international students; for spring admission, 10/1 for domestic and international students. Application fee: $60 ($70 for international students). Electronic applications accepted. *Expenses:* Tuition, state resident: full-time $9917. Tuition, nonresident: full-time $24,312. *Required fees:* $2284. Tuition and fees vary according to course load and program. *Financial support:* In 2017–18, 80 students received support, including 15 research assistantships with full and partial tuition reimbursements available (averaging $20,524 per year), 69 teaching assistantships with full and partial tuition reimbursements available (averaging $18,656 per year); fellowships with full and partial tuition reimbursements available, career-related internships or fieldwork, health care benefits, and unspecified assistantships also available. Financial award applicants required to submit FAFSA. *Faculty research:* Cell and molecular biology, organismal biology, ecology and evolutionary biology. *Total annual research expenditures:* $7 million. *Unit head:* Dr. Michael F. Antolin, Department Chair and Professor, 970-491-7011, Fax: 970-491-0649, E-mail: michael.antolin@colostate.edu. *Application contact:* Dorothy Ramirez, Graduate Coordinator, 970-491-1923, Fax: 970-491-0649, E-mail: dramirez@colostate.edu.
Website: http://www.biology.colostate.edu/

Colorado State University, College of Veterinary Medicine and Biomedical Sciences, Department of Biomedical Sciences, Fort Collins, CO 80523-1680. Offers biomedical sciences (PhD); reproductive technology (MS). *Faculty:* 39 full-time (14 women), 3 part-time/adjunct (2 women). *Students:* 97 full-time (74 women), 34 part-time (17 women); includes 25 minority (2 Black or African American, non-Hispanic/Latino; 1 American Indian or Alaska Native, non-Hispanic/Latino; 4 Asian, non-Hispanic/Latino; 13 Hispanic/Latino; 5 Two or more races, non-Hispanic/Latino), 10 international. Average age 26. 230 applicants, 54% accepted, 87 enrolled. In 2017, 74 master's, 1 doctorate awarded. Terminal master's awarded for partial completion of doctoral program. *Degree requirements:* For master's, comprehensive exam (for some programs), thesis (for some programs); for doctorate, comprehensive exam (for some programs), thesis/dissertation. *Entrance requirements:* For master's and doctorate, GRE, minimum GPA of 3.0; bachelor's degree; resume/curriculum vitae; statement of purpose; recommendations. Additional exam requirements/recommendations for international students: Required—TOEFL (minimum score 550 paper-based; 80 iBT), IELTS (minimum score 6.5). *Application deadline:* For fall admission, 4/1 for domestic and international students; for spring admission, 9/1 for domestic and international students; for summer admission, 1/1 for domestic and international students. Applications are processed on a rolling basis. Application fee: $60 ($70 for international students). Electronic applications accepted. *Expenses:* $120 per credit hour. *Financial support:* In 2017–18, 20 research assistantships (averaging $22,812 per year), 7 teaching assistantships (averaging $23,844 per year) were awarded; fellowships, scholarships/grants, traineeships, health care benefits, and unspecified assistantships also available. *Faculty research:* Ion channels in arterial smooth muscle and their impact on arterial function; characterizing the communication between the developing fetus and the utero-placental unit; viral diseases that affect domestic and wild animals and spillover into human populations; the proopiomelanocortin neurons in the arcuate nucleus of the hypothalamus; neurotransmitter release in Central Nervous System Disease. *Total annual research expenditures:* $5 million. *Unit head:* Dr. Colin Clay, Department Head, 970-491-3259, E-mail: colin.clay@colostate.edu. *Application contact:* Erin Bisenius, Graduate Education Coordinator, 970-491-6188, E-mail: erin.bisenius@colostate.edu.
Website: http://csu-cvmbs.colostate.edu/academics/bms/Pages/default.aspx

Biological and Biomedical Sciences—General

Colorado State University–Pueblo, College of Science and Mathematics, Pueblo, CO 81001-4901. Offers applied natural science (MS), including biochemistry, biology, chemistry. *Program availability:* Part-time, evening/weekend. *Degree requirements:* For master's, comprehensive exam (for some programs), thesis (for some programs), internship report (if non-thesis). *Entrance requirements:* For master's, GRE General Test (minimum score 1000), 2 letters of reference, minimum GPA of 3.0. Additional exam requirements/recommendations for international students: Required—TOEFL (minimum score 500 paper-based), IELTS (minimum score 5). *Faculty research:* Fungal cell walls, molecular biology, bioactive materials synthesis, atomic force microscopy-surface chemistry, nanoscience.

Columbia University, College of Physicians and Surgeons, New York, NY 10032. Offers M Phil, MA, MS, DN Sc, DPT, Ed D, MD, OTD, PhD, Adv C, MBA/MS, MD/DDS, MD/MPH, MD/MS, MD/PhD, MPH/MS. *Program availability:* Part-time. *Entrance requirements:* For master's, GRE General Test. Additional exam requirements/recommendations for international students: Required—TOEFL. *Expenses:* Contact institution.

Columbia University, Graduate School of Arts and Sciences, Department of Biological Sciences, New York, NY 10027. Offers PhD. *Degree requirements:* For doctorate, comprehensive exam, thesis/dissertation, teaching experience. *Entrance requirements:* For doctorate, GRE General Test, GRE Subject Test (recommended), letters of recommendation. Additional exam requirements/recommendations for international students: Required—TOEFL (minimum score 600 paper-based; 100 iBT). *Expenses: Tuition:* Full-time $44,864; part-time $1704 per credit. *Required fees:* $2370 per semester. One-time fee: $105.

See Display below and Close-Up on page 107.

Columbus State University, Graduate Studies, College of Letters and Sciences, Department of Earth and Space Sciences, Columbus, GA 31907-5645. Offers natural sciences (MS), including biology, chemistry, environmental science, geosciences. *Program availability:* Part-time, evening/weekend. *Faculty:* 5 full-time (2 women), 4 part-time/adjunct (0 women). *Students:* 15 full-time (9 women), 6 part-time (4 women); includes 4 minority (2 Black or African American, non-Hispanic/Latino; 1 Hispanic/Latino; 1 Two or more races, non-Hispanic/Latino). Average age 26. 25 applicants, 40% accepted, 5 enrolled. In 2017, 5 master's awarded. *Degree requirements:* For master's, thesis. *Entrance requirements:* For master's, GRE General Test, minimum GPA of 3.0. Additional exam requirements/recommendations for international students: Required—TOEFL (minimum score 550 paper-based; 79 iBT). *Application deadline:* For fall admission, 6/30 priority date for domestic students, 5/1 for international students; for spring admission, 11/1 for domestic and international students; for summer admission, 3/1 for domestic and international students. Applications are processed on a rolling basis. Application fee: $50. Electronic applications accepted. *Expenses:* Tuition, state resident: full-time $3708; part-time $2472 per year. Tuition, nonresident: full-time $14,418; part-time $9612 per year. *International tuition:* $19,218 full-time. *Required fees:* $1605. Tuition and fees vary according to program. *Financial support:* In 2017–18, 2 students received support, including 14 research assistantships with partial tuition reimbursements available (averaging $3,000 per year); career-related internships or fieldwork, Federal Work-Study, institutionally sponsored loans, scholarships/grants, and unspecified assistantships also available. Support available to part-time students. Financial award application deadline: 5/1; financial award applicants required to submit FAFSA. *Unit head:* Dr. Clint Barineau, Department Chair, 706-569-3026, E-mail: barineau_clinton@columbusstate.edu. *Application contact:* Catrina Smith-Edmond, Assistant Director for Graduate and Global Admission, 706-507-8824, Fax: 706-568-5091, E-mail: smithedmond_catrina@columbusstate.edu.
Website: http://ess.columbusstate.edu/

Concordia University, School of Graduate Studies, Faculty of Arts and Science, Department of Biology, Montréal, QC H3G 1M8, Canada. Offers biology (M Sc, PhD); biotechnology and genomics (Diploma). *Degree requirements:* For master's, thesis; for doctorate, thesis/dissertation, pedagogical training. *Entrance requirements:* For master's, honors degree in biology; for doctorate, M Sc in life science. *Faculty research:* Cell biology, animal physiology, ecology, microbiology/molecular biology, plant physiology/biochemistry and biotechnology.

Cornell University, Graduate School, Biomedical and Biological Sciences PhD Program, Ithaca, NY 14853. Offers PhD. *Degree requirements:* For doctorate, comprehensive exam, thesis/dissertation. *Entrance requirements:* For doctorate, GRE General Test. Additional exam requirements/recommendations for international students: Required—TOEFL (minimum score 550 paper-based; 77 iBT). Electronic applications accepted. *Expenses:* Contact institution.

Creighton University, School of Medicine and Graduate School, Graduate Programs in Medicine, Department of Biomedical Sciences, Omaha, NE 68178-0001. Offers MS, PhD, MD/PhD. Terminal master's awarded for partial completion of doctoral program. *Degree requirements:* For master's, thesis; for doctorate, thesis/dissertation. *Entrance requirements:* For master's, GRE General Test (minimum 50th percentile), three recommendations; for doctorate, GRE General Test (minimum score: 50th percentile), three recommendations. Additional exam requirements/recommendations for international students: Required—TOEFL. Electronic applications accepted. Part-time tuition and fees vary according to course load, degree level, campus/location and program. *Faculty research:* Molecular biology and gene transfection.

Dalhousie University, Faculty of Graduate Studies and Faculty of Medicine, Graduate Programs in Medicine, Halifax, NS B3H 4R2, Canada. Offers M Sc, PhD. *Degree requirements:* For master's, thesis; for doctorate, thesis/dissertation. *Entrance requirements:* Additional exam requirements/recommendations for international students: Required—1 of 5 approved tests: TOEFL, IELTS, CANTEST, CAEL, Michigan English Language Assessment Battery. Electronic applications accepted. *Expenses:* Contact institution.

Dalhousie University, Faculty of Science, Department of Biology, Halifax, NS B3H 4R2, Canada. Offers M Sc, PhD. Terminal master's awarded for partial completion of doctoral program. *Degree requirements:* For master's, thesis; for doctorate, thesis/dissertation. *Entrance requirements:* Additional exam requirements/recommendations for international students: Required—TOEFL, IELTS, CANTEST, CAEL, or Michigan English Language Assessment Battery. Electronic applications accepted. *Faculty research:* Marine biology, ecology, animal physiology, plant physiology, microbiology (cell, molecular, genetics, development).

Dartmouth College, Graduate Program in Molecular and Cellular Biology, Department of Biological Sciences, Hanover, NH 03755. Offers PhD, MBA/PhD, MD/PhD. *Faculty:* 22 full-time (6 women), 1 (woman) part-time/adjunct. *Entrance requirements:* For doctorate, GRE General Test, letters of recommendation. *Application deadline:* For fall admission, 12/8 for domestic students. Application fee: $75. Electronic applications accepted. *Financial support:* Fellowships and health care benefits available. *Unit head:* Dr. Thomas Jack, Chair and Professor, 603-646-3367, E-mail: biology@dartmouth.edu. *Application contact:* Janet Cheney, Program Coordinator, 603-650-1612, E-mail: mcb@dartmouth.edu.
Website: http://www.dartmouth.edu/~mcb/

Delaware State University, Graduate Programs, Department of Biological Sciences, Program in Biological Sciences, Dover, DE 19901-2277. Offers MS. *Entrance requirements:* For master's, GRE, prerequisite undergraduate courses. Additional exam requirements/recommendations for international students: Required—TOEFL.

Delta State University, Graduate Programs, College of Arts and Sciences, Division of Biological and Physical Sciences, Cleveland, MS 38733-0001. Offers natural sciences (MSNS). *Program availability:* Part-time. *Degree requirements:* For master's, research project or thesis. *Entrance requirements:* For master's, GRE General Test.

DePaul University, College of Science and Health, Chicago, IL 60604. Offers applied mathematics (MS); applied statistics (MS); biological sciences (MA, MS); chemistry (MS); environmental science (MS); mathematics education (MA); mathematics for teaching (MS); nursing (MS); nursing practice (DNP); physics (MS); polymer and coatings science (MS); psychology (MS); pure mathematics (MS); science education (MS); MA/PhD. *Accreditation:* AACN. *Application deadline:* Applications are processed on a rolling basis. Application fee: $40. Electronic applications accepted. *Financial support:* Applicants required to submit FAFSA. *Unit head:* Dr. Gerald P. Koocher, Dean, 773-325-8300. *Application contact:* Ann Spittle, Director of Graduate Admission, 773-325-7315, Fax: 312-476-3244, E-mail: graddepaul@depaul.edu.
Website: http://csh.depaul.edu/

Des Moines University, College of Osteopathic Medicine, Program in Biomedical Sciences, Des Moines, IA 50312-4104. Offers MS.

Dominican University of California, School of Health and Natural Sciences, Program in Biological Sciences, San Rafael, CA 94901-2298. Offers MS. *Faculty:* 5 full-time (3 women), 6 part-time/adjunct (3 women). *Students:* 17 full-time (10 women), 3 part-time (1 woman); includes 11 minority (5 Asian, non-Hispanic/Latino; 4 Hispanic/Latino; 2 Two or more races, non-Hispanic/Latino). Average age 26. 10 applicants, 100% accepted, 8 enrolled. In 2017, 9 master's awarded. *Degree requirements:* For master's, thesis. *Entrance requirements:* For master's, GRE, BS in biology, biological sciences or biomedical sciences; minimum GPA of 3.0 in last 60 units. Additional exam requirements/recommendations for international students: Required—TOEFL (minimum score 550 paper-based; 80 iBT), IELTS (minimum score 6.5). *Application deadline:* For fall admission, 3/15 priority date for domestic and international students. Applications are processed on a rolling basis. Application fee: $0. Electronic applications accepted. *Expenses:* $1,080 per unit. *Financial support:* In 2017–18, 11 students received support. Research assistantships, career-related internships or fieldwork, and scholarships/grants available. Financial award application deadline: 3/2; financial award applicants required to submit FAFSA. *Unit head:* Dr. Maggie Louie, Program Director, 415-485-3248, E-mail: maggie.louie@dominican.edu. *Application contact:* Michael Lavigna, Assistant Director of Graduate Admissions, 415-485-3253, Fax: 415-485-3214, E-mail: gradmissions@dominican.edu.
Website: https://www.dominican.edu/academics/hns/sciencemath/graduate/ms-in-biological-sciences

Drew University, Caspersen School of Graduate Studies, Madison, NJ 07940-1493. Offers conflict resolution and leadership (Certificate), including community leadership, moderation, peace building; education (M Ed); finance (MA); history and culture (MA, PhD), including American history, book history, British history, European history, Holocaust and genocide (M Litt, MA, D Litt, PhD), intellectual history, Irish history, print culture, public history; K-12 education (MAT), including art, biology, chemistry, elementary education, English, French, Italian, math, secondary education, special education, teacher of students with disabilities; liberal studies (M Litt, D Litt), including history, Holocaust and genocide (M Litt, MA, D Litt, PhD), Irish/Irish-American studies, literature (M Litt, MMH, D Litt, DMH, CMH), religion, spirituality, teaching in the two-year college, writing; medical humanities (MMH, DMH, CMH), including arts, health, healthcare, literature (M Litt, MMH, D Litt, DMH, CMH), scientific research; poetry (MFA). *Program availability:* Part-time, evening/weekend. *Faculty:* 4 full-time (2 women), 29 part-time/adjunct (15 women). *Students:* 77 full-time (42 women), 175 part-time (114 women); includes 39 minority (12 Black or African American, non-Hispanic/Latino; 6 Asian, non-Hispanic/Latino; 16 Hispanic/Latino; 5 Two or more races, non-Hispanic/Latino), 11 international. Average age 41. 126 applicants, 75% accepted, 52 enrolled. In 2017, 38 master's, 23 doctorates, 35 other advanced degrees awarded. Terminal master's awarded for partial completion of doctoral program. *Degree requirements:* For master's and other advanced degree, thesis (for some programs); for doctorate, one foreign language, comprehensive exam (for some programs), thesis/dissertation. *Entrance requirements:* For master's, PRAXIS Core and Subject Area tests (for MAT), GRE/GMAT (for M Fin), resume, transcripts, writing sample, personal statement, letters of recommendation; for doctorate, GRE (PhD in history and culture), resume, transcripts, writing sample, personal statement, letters of recommendation; for other advanced degree, resume, transcripts, personal statement. Additional exam requirements/recommendations for international students: Required—TOEFL (minimum score 587 paper-based; 80 iBT), IELTS (minimum score 6), TWE (minimum score 4). *Application deadline:* For fall admission, 8/1 for domestic students, 6/1 for international students; for spring admission, 12/1 for domestic students, 10/1 for international students. Applications are processed on a rolling basis. Application fee: $35. Electronic applications accepted. *Financial support:* Fellowships, research assistantships, teaching assistantships, career-related internships or fieldwork, Federal Work-Study, scholarships/grants, and unspecified assistantships available. Support available to part-time students. Financial award applicants required to submit FAFSA. *Faculty research:* Irish history and culture, conflict resolution and leadership. *Application contact:* Leanne Horinko, Director of Caspersen Admissions, 973-408-3280, E-mail: gradm@drew.edu.
Website: http://www.drew.edu/caspersen

Drexel University, College of Arts and Sciences, Department of Biology, Philadelphia, PA 19104-2875. Offers biological sciences (MS, PhD). *Program availability:* Part-time. *Degree requirements:* For doctorate, thesis/dissertation. *Entrance requirements:* For master's and doctorate, GRE General Test. Additional exam requirements/recommendations for international students: Required—TOEFL. Electronic applications accepted. *Faculty research:* Genetic engineering, physiological ecology.

Drexel University, College of Medicine, Biomedical Graduate Programs, Philadelphia, PA 19129. Offers MLAS, MMS, MS, PhD, Certificate, MD/PhD. *Program availability:* Part-time. Terminal master's awarded for partial completion of doctoral program. *Degree requirements:* For master's, comprehensive exam; for doctorate, thesis/dissertation, qualifying exam. *Entrance requirements:* For master's and doctorate, GRE General Test. Additional exam requirements/recommendations for international students: Required—TOEFL. Electronic applications accepted. *Expenses:* Contact institution.

Drexel University, College of Medicine, MD/PhD Program, Philadelphia, PA 19104-2875. Offers MD/PhD. Electronic applications accepted.

Drexel University, School of Biomedical Engineering, Science and Health Systems, Program in Biomedical Science, Philadelphia, PA 19104-2875. Offers MS, PhD. *Degree requirements:* For master's, thesis (for some programs); for doctorate, thesis/dissertation. Electronic applications accepted.

Duke University, Graduate School, Department of Biology, Durham, NC 27708. Offers PhD. *Degree requirements:* For doctorate, one foreign language, thesis/dissertation. *Entrance requirements:* For doctorate, GRE General Test, GRE Subject Test (recommended). Additional exam requirements/recommendations for international students: Required—TOEFL (minimum score 577 paper-based; 90 iBT) or IELTS (minimum score 7). Electronic applications accepted.

Duke University, School of Medicine, Program in Biomedical Sciences, Durham, NC 27710. Offers MS. *Faculty:* 18 part-time/adjunct (10 women). *Students:* 40 full-time (24 women); includes 21 minority (10 Black or African American, non-Hispanic/Latino; 7 Asian, non-Hispanic/Latino; 4 Hispanic/Latino). In 2017, 41 master's awarded. *Entrance requirements:* For master's, GRE, BS from accredited institution; minimum GPA of 3.2. *Application deadline:* For fall admission, 3/15 priority date for domestic students. Applications are processed on a rolling basis. Application fee: $75. Electronic applications accepted. *Financial support:* In 2017–18, 37 students received support. Scholarships/grants available. Financial award application deadline: 5/1; financial award applicants required to submit FAFSA. *Unit head:* Dr. Kathy Andolsek, Professor in Family Medicine, 919-668-3883, Fax: 919-681-0720, E-mail: kathryn.andolsek@duke.edu. *Application contact:* Christie T. McCray, Administrative Coordinator, 919-684-8653, Fax: 919-681-0720, E-mail: christie.mccray@duke.edu.
Website: https://medschool.duke.edu/education/degree-programs-and-admissions/master-biomedical-sciences

Duquesne University, Bayer School of Natural and Environmental Sciences, Department of Biological Sciences, Pittsburgh, PA 15282-0001. Offers PhD. *Faculty:* 14 full-time (4 women), 2 part-time/adjunct (0 women). *Students:* 34 full-time (18 women), 1 (woman) part-time; includes 3 minority (1 Black or African American, non-Hispanic/Latino; 1 Hispanic/Latino; 1 Two or more races, non-Hispanic/Latino), 8 international. Average age 28. 21 applicants, 43% accepted, 7 enrolled. In 2017, 3 doctorates awarded. *Degree requirements:* For doctorate, thesis/dissertation. *Entrance requirements:* For doctorate, GRE General Test; GRE Subject Test in biology, biochemistry, or cell and molecular biology (recommended), BS or MS in biological sciences or related field, 3 letters of recommendation, statement of purpose, official transcripts. Additional exam requirements/recommendations for international students: Required—TOEFL (minimum score 95 iBT) or IELTS. *Application deadline:* For fall admission, 1/15 for domestic and international students. Applications are processed on a rolling basis. Application fee: $0. Electronic applications accepted. *Expenses:* $1,312 per credit. *Financial support:* In 2017–18, 27 students received support, including 1 fellowship with full tuition reimbursement available (averaging $24,200 per year), 3 research assistantships with full tuition reimbursements available (averaging $24,200 per year), 21 teaching assistantships with full tuition reimbursements available (averaging $24,200 per year); scholarships/grants, tuition waivers (partial), and unspecified assistantships also available. Financial award application deadline: 5/31. *Faculty research:* Cell and developmental biology, molecular biology and genetics, evolution, ecology, physiology and microbiology. *Total annual research expenditures:* $813,716. *Unit head:* Dr. Joseph McCormick, Chair, 412-396-4775, Fax: 412-396-5907, E-mail: mccormick@duq.edu. *Application contact:* Heather Costello, Graduate Academic Advisor, 412-396-6339, E-mail: costelloh@duq.edu.
Website: http://www.duq.edu/academics/schools/natural-and-environmental-sciences/academic-programs/biological-sciences

East Carolina University, Graduate School, Thomas Harriot College of Arts and Sciences, Department of Biology, Greenville, NC 27858-4353. Offers biology (MS); molecular biology and biotechnology (MS). *Program availability:* Part-time. *Students:* 39 full-time (24 women), 16 part-time (8 women); includes 8 minority (5 Black or African American, non-Hispanic/Latino; 2 Asian, non-Hispanic/Latino; 1 Two or more races, non-Hispanic/Latino). Average age 26. 52 applicants, 54% accepted, 17 enrolled. In 2017, 8 master's awarded. *Degree requirements:* For master's, comprehensive exam, thesis. *Entrance requirements:* For master's, GRE General Test, GRE Subject Test. Additional exam requirements/recommendations for international students: Recommended—TOEFL, IELTS. *Application deadline:* For fall admission, 6/1 priority date for domestic students, 3/1 priority date for international students; for spring admission, 10/15 priority date for domestic students. Applications are processed on a rolling basis. Application fee: $75. Electronic applications accepted. *Expenses:* Tuition, state resident: full-time $4749; part-time $297 per credit hour. Tuition, nonresident: full-time $17,898; part-time $1119 per credit hour. *Required fees:* $2691; $224 per credit hour. Part-time tuition and fees vary according to course load and program. *Financial support:* Fellowships with partial tuition reimbursements, research assistantships with partial tuition reimbursements, teaching assistantships with partial tuition reimbursements, career-related internships or fieldwork, Federal Work-Study, scholarships/grants, and unspecified assistantships available. Support available to part-time students. Financial award application deadline: 3/1. *Faculty research:* Biotechnology, biochemistry, bioinformatics, microbiology, cell biology. *Unit head:* Dr. Jeff McKinnon, Chair, 252-328-6718, E-mail: mckinnonj@ecu.edu. *Application contact:* Dean of Graduate School, 252-328-6012, Fax: 252-328-6071, E-mail: gradschool@ecu.edu.
Website: http://www.ecu.edu/cs-cas/biology/

Eastern Illinois University, Graduate School, College of Liberal Arts and Sciences, Department of Biological Sciences, Charleston, IL 61920. Offers MS. *Program availability:* Part-time, evening/weekend. *Degree requirements:* For master's, comprehensive exam (for some programs), thesis (for some programs). *Entrance requirements:* For master's, GMAT or GRE. Additional exam requirements/recommendations for international students: Required—TOEFL (minimum score 500 paper-based; 61 iBT), IELTS (minimum score 6). *Application deadline:* For fall admission, 5/15 for domestic and international students; for spring admission, 10/15 for domestic and international students. Applications are processed on a rolling basis. Application fee: $30. Electronic applications accepted. *Financial support:* Research assistantships with full tuition reimbursements, teaching assistantships with full tuition reimbursements, career-related internships or fieldwork, Federal Work-Study, and unspecified assistantships available. Support available to part-time students. Financial award application deadline: 3/1; financial award applicants required to submit FAFSA. *Unit head:* Gary A. Bulla, Chair, 217-581-3499, Fax: 217-581-7141, E-mail: gabulla@eiu.edu. *Application contact:* Britto Nathan, Graduate Coordinator, 217-581-6891, Fax: 217-581-7141, E-mail: bpnathan@eiu.edu.
Website: http://www.eiu.edu/biologygrad/

Eastern Kentucky University, The Graduate School, College of Arts and Sciences, Department of Biological Sciences, Richmond, KY 40475-3102. Offers biological sciences (MS); ecology (MS). *Program availability:* Part-time. *Degree requirements:* For master's, thesis. *Entrance requirements:* For master's, GRE General Test, minimum GPA of 2.5. *Faculty research:* Systematics, ecology, and biodiversity; animal behavior; protein structure and molecular genetics; biomonitoring and aquatic toxicology; pathogenesis of microbes and parasites.

Eastern Mennonite University, Program in Biomedicine, Harrisonburg, VA 22802-2462. Offers MA. *Application deadline:* For fall admission, 7/31 for domestic students; for spring admission, 11/9 for domestic students. Applications are processed on a rolling basis. Application fee: $50. Electronic applications accepted. *Unit head:* Kim Gingerich Brenneman, Chair, 540-432-4429, E-mail: brennkg@emu.edu. *Application contact:* Don A. Yoder, Director of Seminary and Graduate Admissions, 540-432-4257, Fax: 540-432-4598, E-mail: yoderda@emu.edu.
Website: http://www.emu.edu/ma-biomed/

Eastern Michigan University, Graduate School, College of Arts and Sciences, Department of Biology, Ypsilanti, MI 48197. Offers community college biology teaching

(MS); general biology (MS). *Program availability:* Part-time, evening/weekend, online learning. *Faculty:* 24 full-time (7 women). *Students:* 7 full-time (3 women), 26 part-time (11 women); includes 7 minority (1 Black or African American, non-Hispanic/Latino; 3 Asian, non-Hispanic/Latino; 1 Hispanic/Latino; 2 Two or more races, non-Hispanic/Latino), 3 international. Average age 27. 57 applicants, 61% accepted, 18 enrolled. In 2017, 23 master's awarded. *Entrance requirements:* For master's, GRE General Test, GRE Subject Test. Additional exam requirements/recommendations for international students: Required—TOEFL. *Application deadline:* Applications are processed on a rolling basis. Application fee: $45. *Financial support:* Fellowships, research assistantships with full tuition reimbursements, teaching assistantships with full tuition reimbursements, career-related internships or fieldwork, Federal Work-Study, institutionally sponsored loans, scholarships/grants, tuition waivers (partial), and unspecified assistantships available. Support available to part-time students. Financial award applicants required to submit FAFSA. *Unit head:* Dr. Marianne Laporte, Department Head, 734-487-4242, Fax: 734-487-9235, E-mail: mlaporte@emich.edu. *Application contact:* Dr. David Kass, Graduate Coordinator, 734-487-4242, Fax: 734-487-9235, E-mail: dkass@emich.edu.
Website: http://www.emich.edu/biology

Eastern New Mexico University, Graduate School, College of Liberal Arts and Sciences, Department of Biology, Portales, NM 88130. Offers MS. *Program availability:* Part-time. *Degree requirements:* For master's, comprehensive exam, thesis optional. *Entrance requirements:* For master's, GRE, minimum GPA of 3.0, 2 letters of recommendation, statement of research interest, bachelor's degree related to field of study or proof of common knowledge. Additional exam requirements/recommendations for international students: Required—TOEFL (minimum score 550 paper-based; 79 iBT), IELTS (minimum score 6). *Application deadline:* For fall admission, 7/20 priority date for domestic students, 6/20 priority date for international students; for spring admission, 12/15 priority date for domestic students, 11/15 priority date for international students. Applications are processed on a rolling basis. Application fee: $10. Electronic applications accepted. *Financial support:* Applicants required to submit FAFSA. *Unit head:* Dr. Matthew Barlow, Graduate Coordinator, 575-562-2543, E-mail: matthew.barlow@enmu.edu. *Application contact:* Sharon Potter, Department Secretary, Biology and Physical Sciences, 575-562-2174, Fax: 575-562-2192, E-mail: sharon.potter@enmu.edu.
Website: https://www.enmu.edu/academics/colleges-departments/college-liberal-arts-sciences/home-department-of-biology

Eastern Virginia Medical School, Doctoral Program in Biomedical Sciences, Norfolk, VA 23501-1980. Offers PhD. *Degree requirements:* For doctorate, thesis/dissertation. *Entrance requirements:* For doctorate, GRE General Test. Additional exam requirements/recommendations for international students; Required—TOEFL. Electronic applications accepted. *Expenses:* Contact institution.

Eastern Virginia Medical School, Master's Program in Biomedical Sciences Research, Norfolk, VA 23501-1980. Offers MS. *Degree requirements:* For master's, comprehensive exam (for some programs), thesis optional. *Entrance requirements:* For master's, GRE. Additional exam requirements/recommendations for international students: Required—TOEFL. Electronic applications accepted. *Expenses:* Contact institution.

Eastern Virginia Medical School, Master's Program in Clinical Embryology and Andrology, Norfolk, VA 23501-1980. Offers MS. *Program availability:* Online learning. *Entrance requirements:* Additional exam requirements/recommendations for international students: Required—TOEFL (minimum score 550 paper-based; 80 iBT). Electronic applications accepted. *Expenses:* Contact institution.

Eastern Virginia Medical School, Medical Master's Program in Biomedical Sciences, Norfolk, VA 23501-1980. Offers MS. *Entrance requirements:* For master's, MCAT. Electronic applications accepted. *Expenses:* Contact institution.

Eastern Washington University, Graduate Studies, College of Science, Technology, Engineering and Mathematics, Department of Biology, Cheney, WA 99004-2431. Offers MS. *Faculty:* 14. *Students:* 20 full-time (11 women), 1 part-time (0 women); includes 1 minority (Hispanic/Latino), 1 international. Average age 29. 14 applicants, 64% accepted, 8 enrolled. In 2017, 7 master's awarded. *Degree requirements:* For master's, comprehensive exam, thesis. *Entrance requirements:* For master's, GRE General Test, minimum GPA of 3.0. Additional exam requirements/recommendations for international students: Required—TOEFL (minimum score 580 paper-based; 92 iBT), IELTS (minimum score 7), PTE (minimum score 63). *Application deadline:* For fall admission, 4/1 priority date for domestic students; for spring admission, 1/15 for domestic students. Applications are processed on a rolling basis. Application fee: $75. Electronic applications accepted. *Expenses:* Tuition, state resident: full-time $11,191; part-time $373.06 per credit. Tuition, nonresident: full-time $25,995; part-time $866.52 per credit. *Financial support:* In 2017–18, 14 students received support. Teaching assistantships with partial tuition reimbursements available, career-related internships or fieldwork, Federal Work-Study, institutionally sponsored loans, scholarships/grants, health care benefits, tuition waivers (partial), and unspecified assistantships available. Support available to part-time students. Financial award application deadline: 2/1; financial award applicants required to submit FAFSA. *Faculty research:* Ecology of Eastern Washington Channeled Scablands, Columbia River fisheries, biotechnology applied to vaccines, role of mycorrhiza in plant nutrition, exercise and estrous cycles. *Unit head:* Dr. Robin O'Quinn, 509-359-2339, E-mail: biologymasters@ewu.edu.
Website: http://www.ewu.edu/cshe/programs/biology.xml

East Stroudsburg University of Pennsylvania, Graduate and Extended Studies, College of Arts and Sciences, Department of Biological Sciences, East Stroudsburg, PA 18301-2999. Offers biology (MS). *Program availability:* Part-time, evening/weekend. *Faculty:* 10 full-time (2 women). *Students:* 9 full-time (5 women), 3 part-time (2 women); includes 1 minority (Hispanic/Latino), 1 international. Average age 27. 10 applicants, 80% accepted, 4 enrolled. In 2017, 4 master's awarded. *Degree requirements:* For master's, comprehensive exam, thesis or alternative. *Entrance requirements:* For master's, GRE, resume, undergraduate major in life science (or equivalent), completion of organic chemistry (minimum two semesters), 3 letters of recommendation, letter of intent. Additional exam requirements/recommendations for international students: Recommended—TOEFL (minimum score 560 paper-based; 83 iBT), IELTS. *Application deadline:* For fall admission, 7/31 for domestic students, 6/30 priority date for international students; for spring admission, 11/30 for domestic students, 10/31 for international students. Applications are processed on a rolling basis. Application fee: $50. Electronic applications accepted. *Expenses:* Tuition, state resident: full-time $4500; part-time $3000 per credit. Tuition, nonresident: full-time $6750; part-time $4500 per credit. *Required fees:* $2642; $1756 per credit. $878 per semester. Tuition and fees vary according to course load, campus/location and program. *Financial support:* Research assistantships with tuition reimbursements, Federal Work-Study, and unspecified assistantships available. Support available to part-time students. Financial award application deadline: 3/1; financial award applicants required to submit FAFSA. *Unit head:* Terry Masters, Chair, 570-422-3709, Fax: 570-422-3724, E-mail: tmasters@esu.edu. *Application contact:* Kevin Quintero, Associate Director, Graduate and Extended Studies, 570-422-3890, Fax: 570-422-3711, E-mail: kquintero@esu.edu.
Website: http://www4.esu.edu/academics/departments/biology/graduate_programs/index.cfm

East Tennessee State University, Quillen College of Medicine, Department of Biomedical Sciences, Johnson City, TN 37614. Offers anatomy (PhD); biochemistry (PhD); microbiology (PhD); pharmaceutical sciences (PhD); pharmacology (PhD); physiology (PhD); quantitative biosciences (PhD). In 2017, 5 doctorates awarded. *Degree requirements:* For doctorate, comprehensive exam, thesis/dissertation, comprehensive qualifying exam; one-year residency. *Entrance requirements:* For doctorate, GRE General Test, GRE Subject Test, 3 letters of recommendation, minimum of 60 credit hours beyond the baccalaureate degree. Additional exam requirements/recommendations for international students: Required—TOEFL (minimum score 550 paper-based; 79 iBT). *Application deadline:* For fall admission, 6/1 priority date for domestic students, 4/29 for international students; for spring admission, 11/1 for domestic students, 9/29 for international students; for summer admission, 3/15 for domestic students, 2/1 for international students. Applications are processed on a rolling basis. Application fee: $55 ($65 for international students). Electronic applications accepted. *Expenses:* Contact institution. *Financial support:* Research assistantships with full tuition reimbursements, career-related internships or fieldwork, institutionally sponsored loans, scholarships/grants, and unspecified assistantships available. Financial award application deadline: 7/1; financial award applicants required to submit FAFSA. *Faculty research:* Cardiovascular, infectious disease, neurosciences, cancer, immunology. *Unit head:* Theo Hagg, Chair, 423-439-6294, Fax: 423-439-2140, E-mail: haggt1@etsu.edu. *Application contact:* Theo Hagg, Chair, 423-439-6294, Fax: 423-439-2140, E-mail: haggt1@etsu.edu.
Website: http://www.etsu.edu/com/dbms/

East Tennessee State University, School of Graduate Studies, College of Arts and Sciences, Department of Biological Sciences, Johnson City, TN 37614. Offers biology (MS); biomedical sciences (MS); microbiology (MS). *Degree requirements:* For master's, comprehensive exam, thesis. *Entrance requirements:* For master's, GRE General Test or GRE Subject Test, minimum GPA of 3.0, undergraduate degree in life or physical sciences, two letters of recommendation; course in calculus and/or course in probability and statistics (recommended). Additional exam requirements/recommendations for international students: Required—TOEFL (minimum score 550 paper-based; 79 iBT). *Application deadline:* For fall admission, 6/1 for domestic students, 4/29 for international students; for spring admission, 11/1 for domestic students, 9/29 for international students; for summer admission, 3/15 for domestic students, 2/1 for international students. Application fee: $55 ($65 for international students). Electronic applications accepted. *Financial support:* Teaching assistantships with full tuition reimbursements, institutionally sponsored loans, scholarships/grants, and unspecified assistantships available. Financial award application deadline: 7/1; financial award applicants required to submit FAFSA. *Faculty research:* Neuroethology, chronobiology, molecular biology, behavioral ecology, systematics, paleo botany. *Unit head:* Dr. Joseph Bidwell, Chair, 423-439-4329, Fax: 423-439-5958, E-mail: bidwell@etsu.edu. *Application contact:* Dr. Joseph Bidwell, Chair, 423-439-4329, Fax: 423-439-5958, E-mail: bidwell@etsu.edu.
Website: http://www.etsu.edu/cas/biology/

Elizabeth City State University, Master of Science in Biology Program, Elizabeth City, NC 27909-7806. Offers biological sciences (MS); biology education (MS). *Program availability:* Part-time, evening/weekend. *Faculty:* 8 full-time (1 woman), 1 (woman) part-time/adjunct. *Students:* 3 full-time (1 woman), 17 part-time (11 women); includes 14 minority (12 Black or African American, non-Hispanic/Latino; 1 Asian, non-Hispanic/Latino; 1 Two or more races, non-Hispanic/Latino). Average age 30. 10 applicants, 70% accepted, 5 enrolled. In 2017, 10 master's awarded. *Degree requirements:* For master's, thesis. *Entrance requirements:* For master's, GRE, minimum GPA of 3.0, 3 letters of recommendation, 2 official transcripts from all undergraduate/graduate schools attended, typewritten one-page expository description of student educational preparation, research interests and career aspirations. Additional exam requirements/recommendations for international students: Required—TOEFL (minimum score 550 paper-based, 80 iBT) or IELTS (minimum score 6.5). *Application deadline:* For fall admission, 7/15 priority date for domestic and international students; for spring admission, 11/15 priority date for domestic and international students; for summer admission, 3/15 priority date for domestic and international students. Applications are processed on a rolling basis. Application fee: $30. Electronic applications accepted. Tuition and fees vary according to course load and program. *Financial support:* In 2017–18, 18 students received support. Scholarships/grants available. Financial award application deadline: 6/30; financial award applicants required to submit FAFSA. *Faculty research:* Apoptosis and cancer, plant bioengineering, development of biofuels, microbial degradation, developmental toxicology. *Unit head:* Dr. Gloria Payne, Chair, 252-335-3595, Fax: 252-335-3697, E-mail: gepayne@ecsu.edu.
Website: https://www.ecsu.edu/academics/department/natural-sciences/

Elms College, Division of Natural Sciences, Mathematics and Technology, Chicopee, MA 01013-2839. Offers biomedical sciences (MS). *Faculty:* 4 full-time (2 women), 1 (woman) part-time/adjunct. *Students:* 16 full-time (10 women); includes 9 minority (5 Black or African American, non-Hispanic/Latino; 4 Asian, non-Hispanic/Latino), 1 international. Average age 24. 21 applicants, 95% accepted, 16 enrolled. *Entrance requirements:* Additional exam requirements/recommendations for international students: Required—TOEFL. *Application deadline:* Applications are processed on a rolling basis. Application fee: $30. *Expenses: Tuition:* Full-time $13,860; part-time $770 per credit hour. *Required fees:* $200. Tuition and fees vary according to degree level and program. *Financial support:* Applicants required to submit FAFSA. *Unit head:* Dr. Goose Gosselin, Chair, Division of Natural Sciences and Mathematics, 413-265-2216, E-mail: gosseling@elms.edu. *Application contact:* School of Graduate and Professional Studies, 413-265-2445, E-mail: graduateeducation@elms.edu.

Emory University, Laney Graduate School, Division of Biological and Biomedical Sciences, Atlanta, GA 30322-1100. Offers PhD. *Degree requirements:* For doctorate, comprehensive exam, thesis/dissertation. *Entrance requirements:* For doctorate, GRE General Test, minimum GPA of 3.0 in science course work (recommended). Additional exam requirements/recommendations for international students: Required—TOEFL. Electronic applications accepted. *Expenses:* Contact institution. *Faculty research:* Biochemistry, cancer; genetics; immunology and microbiology; neuroscience and pharmacology; nutrition; population biology and ecology.

Emporia State University, Department of Biological Sciences, Emporia, KS 66801-5415. Offers botany (MS); environmental biology (MS); forensic science (MS); general biology (MS); microbial and cellular biology (MS); zoology (MS). *Program availability:* Part-time. *Faculty:* 13 full-time (3 women), 1 part-time/adjunct (0 women). *Students:* 20 full-time (11 women), 15 part-time (3 women); includes 3 minority (2 Hispanic/Latino; 1 Two or more races, non-Hispanic/Latino), 17 international. 17 applicants, 59% accepted, 8 enrolled. In 2017, 21 master's awarded. *Degree requirements:* For master's, comprehensive exam or thesis. *Entrance requirements:* For master's, GRE, appropriate undergraduate degree, interview, letters of reference. Additional exam requirements/recommendations for international students: Required—TOEFL (minimum score 520 paper-based; 68 iBT). *Application deadline:* For fall admission, 8/15 priority date for domestic students. Applications are processed on a rolling basis. Application fee: $30 ($75 for international students). Electronic applications accepted. *Expenses:* Tuition, state resident: full-time $6084; part-time $253.50 per credit hour. Tuition, nonresident: full-time $18,924; part-time $788.50 per credit hour. *Required fees:* $1943; $80.95 per

credit hour. Tuition and fees vary according to campus/location. *Financial support:* In 2017–18, 7 research assistantships with full tuition reimbursements (averaging $9,747 per year), 15 teaching assistantships with full tuition reimbursements (averaging $7,499 per year) were awarded; career-related internships or fieldwork, Federal Work-Study, institutionally sponsored loans, health care benefits, and unspecified assistantships also available. Financial award application deadline: 3/15; financial award applicants required to submit FAFSA. *Faculty research:* Fisheries, range, and wildlife management; aquatic, plant, grassland, vertebrate, and invertebrate ecology; mammalian and plant systematics, taxonomy, and evolution; immunology, virology, and molecular biology. *Unit head:* Dr. Tim Burnett, Interim Chair, 620-341-5910, Fax: 620-341-5608, E-mail: tburnett@emporia.edu.
Website: http://www.emporia.edu/info/degrees-courses/grad/biology

Fairleigh Dickinson University, Florham Campus, Maxwell Becton College of Arts and Sciences, Department of Biological and Allied Health Sciences, Program in Biology, Madison, NJ 07940-1099. Offers MS. *Expenses: Tuition:* Full-time $22,410; part-time $1245 per credit. *Required fees:* $888; $414 per unit. Tuition and fees vary according to course load, degree level and program.

Fairleigh Dickinson University, Metropolitan Campus, University College: Arts, Sciences, and Professional Studies, School of Natural Sciences, Program in Biology, Teaneck, NJ 07666-1914. Offers MS. *Expenses: Tuition:* Full-time $22,410; part-time $1245 per credit. *Required fees:* $888; $414 per unit. Tuition and fees vary according to course load, degree level and program.

Fisk University, Division of Graduate Studies, Department of Biology, Nashville, TN 37208-3051. Offers MA. *Program availability:* Part-time. *Degree requirements:* For master's, comprehensive exam, thesis. *Entrance requirements:* For master's, GRE. Electronic applications accepted. *Faculty research:* Cell biology, topographical imaging, serotonin receptors in rats, enzyme assays, developmental biology.

Fitchburg State University, Division of Graduate and Continuing Education, Programs in Biology and Teaching Biology (Secondary Level), Fitchburg, MA 01420-2697. Offers biology (MA). *Accreditation:* NCATE. *Program availability:* Part-time, evening/weekend. *Faculty:* 1 (woman) full-time. *Students:* 4 part-time (1 woman); includes 1 minority (Black or African American, non-Hispanic/Latino). Average age 34. 1 applicant, 100% accepted, 1 enrolled. In 2017, 5 master's awarded. *Entrance requirements:* Additional exam requirements/recommendations for international students: Required—TOEFL (minimum score 550 paper-based; 79 iBT). *Application deadline:* For fall admission, 7/15 for international students; for spring admission, 12/1 for international students. Applications are processed on a rolling basis. Application fee: $50. Electronic applications accepted. *Expenses:* Contact institution. *Financial support:* In 2017–18, research assistantships with partial tuition reimbursements (averaging $5,500 per year) were awarded; Federal Work-Study, scholarships/grants, and unspecified assistantships also available. Support available to part-time students. Financial award application deadline: 3/1; financial award applicants required to submit FAFSA. *Unit head:* Dr. Lisa Grimm, Chair, 978-665-3245, Fax: 978-665-3658, E-mail: gce@fitchburgstate.edu. *Application contact:* Jinawa McNeil, Director of Admissions, 978-665-3140, Fax: 978-665-4540, E-mail: admissions@fitchburgstate.edu.

Florida Atlantic University, Charles E. Schmidt College of Medicine, Boca Raton, FL 33431-0991. Offers biomedical science (MS); medicine (MD). *Program availability:* Part-time. *Students:* 277 full-time (127 women), 17 part-time (12 women); includes 109 minority (25 Black or African American, non-Hispanic/Latino; 43 Asian, non-Hispanic/Latino; 36 Hispanic/Latino; 5 Two or more races, non-Hispanic/Latino), 2 international. Average age 25. 3,714 applicants, 2% accepted, 84 enrolled. In 2017, 25 master's, 62 doctorates awarded. *Degree requirements:* For master's, thesis (for some programs); for doctorate, comprehensive exam. *Entrance requirements:* For master's, GRE, minimum GPA of 3.0; for doctorate, MCAT, AMCAS application, letters of recommendation, interview. *Application deadline:* For fall admission, 5/1 for domestic students, 3/15 for international students; for spring admission, 10/1 for domestic and international students. Application fee: $30. Electronic applications accepted. *Expenses:* Contact institution. *Financial support:* Fellowships and research assistantships available. Financial award applicants required to submit FAFSA. *Faculty research:* Osteoarthritis, aging, breast cancer, HIV/AIDS, cardio metabolic risk in psychiatry. *Unit head:* Deborah Roski, Senior Director of Administration, 561-297-2142, E-mail: dsalerno@health.fau.edu.
Website: http://med.fau.edu/

Florida Atlantic University, Charles E. Schmidt College of Science, Department of Biological Sciences, Boca Raton, FL 33431-0991. Offers biology (MS, MST). *Program availability:* Part-time. *Faculty:* 42 full-time (16 women), 1 part-time/adjunct (0 women). *Students:* 88 full-time (47 women), 65 part-time (38 women); includes 43 minority (6 Black or African American, non-Hispanic/Latino; 7 Asian, non-Hispanic/Latino; 20 Hispanic/Latino; 10 Two or more races, non-Hispanic/Latino), 13 international. Average age 28. 113 applicants, 30% accepted, 34 enrolled. In 2017, 43 master's awarded. *Degree requirements:* For master's, thesis (for some programs). *Entrance requirements:* For master's, GRE General Test, minimum GPA of 3.0. Additional exam requirements/recommendations for international students: Required—TOEFL (minimum score 500 paper-based; 61 iBT), IELTS (minimum score 6). *Application deadline:* For fall admission, 3/15 for domestic and international students; for spring admission, 10/1 for domestic and international students. Application fee: $30. *Expenses:* Tuition, state resident: full-time $7400; part-time $369.82 per credit. Tuition, nonresident: full-time $20,496; part-time $1042.81 per credit. *Financial support:* Fellowships, research assistantships, teaching assistantships, career-related internships or fieldwork, and Federal Work-Study available. *Faculty research:* Ecology of the Everglades, molecular biology and biotechnology, marine biology. *Unit head:* Rodney K. Murphey, Chair, E-mail: rmurphey@fau.edu.
Website: http://www.science.fau.edu/biology/

Florida Institute of Technology, College of Science, Program in Biological Sciences, Melbourne, FL 32901-6975. Offers biological science (PhD); biotechnology (MS); cell and molecular biology (MS); ecology (MS); marine biology (MS). *Program availability:* Part-time. *Students:* Average age 26. 230 applicants, 24% accepted, 21 enrolled. In 2017, 27 master's, 3 doctorates awarded. *Degree requirements:* For master's, thesis (for some programs), research, seminar, internship, or summer lab; for doctorate, comprehensive exam, thesis/dissertation, dissertations seminar, publications. *Entrance requirements:* For master's, GRE General Test, 3 letters of recommendation; statement of objectives; bachelor's degree in biology, chemistry, biochemistry or equivalent; for doctorate, GRE General Test, resume, 3 letters of recommendation, minimum GPA of 3.2, statement of objectives. Additional exam requirements/recommendations for international students: Required—TOEFL (minimum score 550 paper-based; 79 iBT). *Application deadline:* For fall admission, 3/1 for domestic students, 4/1 for international students; for spring admission, 9/1 for domestic and international students. Applications are processed on a rolling basis. Electronic applications accepted. *Expenses: Tuition:* Part-time $1241 per credit hour. Part-time tuition and fees vary according to campus/location. *Financial support:* Career-related internships or fieldwork, institutionally sponsored loans, tuition waivers (partial), unspecified assistantships, and tuition remissions available. Support available to part-time students. Financial award application deadline: 3/1; financial award applicants required to submit FAFSA. *Faculty research:* Initiation of protein synthesis in eukaryotic cells, fixation of radioactive carbon, changes in DNA molecule, endangered or threatened avian and mammalian species, hydro acoustics and feeding preference of the West Indian manatee. *Unit head:* Dr. Richard B. Aronson, Department Head, 321-674-8034, Fax: 321-674-7238, E-mail: raronson@fit.edu. *Application contact:* Cheryl A. Brown, Associate Director of Graduate Admissions, 321-674-7581, Fax: 321-723-9468, E-mail: cbrown@fit.edu.
Website: http://cos.fit.edu/biology/

Florida International University, College of Arts, Sciences, and Education, Department of Biological Sciences, Miami, FL 33199. Offers MS, PhD. *Program availability:* Part-time. *Faculty:* 49 full-time (18 women), 30 part-time/adjunct (18 women). *Students:* 82 full-time (44 women), 18 part-time (5 women); includes 34 minority (4 Black or African American, non-Hispanic/Latino; 1 Asian, non-Hispanic/Latino; 26 Hispanic/Latino; 3 Two or more races, non-Hispanic/Latino), 18 international. Average age 30. 69 applicants, 20% accepted, 13 enrolled. In 2017, 3 master's, 15 doctorates awarded. *Degree requirements:* For master's, thesis; for doctorate, comprehensive exam, thesis/dissertation. *Entrance requirements:* For master's, GRE General Test, 2 letters of recommendation, minimum GPA of 3.0, faculty sponsor; for doctorate, GRE General Test, 3 letters of recommendation, faculty sponsor with dissertation advisor status, minimum GPA of 3.0. Additional exam requirements/recommendations for international students: Required—TOEFL (minimum score 550 paper-based; 80 iBT). *Application deadline:* For fall admission, 2/1 priority date for domestic and international students; for spring admission, 8/1 priority date for domestic and international students. Applications are processed on a rolling basis. Application fee: $30. Electronic applications accepted. *Expenses:* Tuition, state resident: full-time $8912; part-time $446 per credit hour. Tuition, nonresident: full-time $21,393; part-time $992 per credit hour. *Required fees:* $390; $195 per semester. *Financial support:* Institutionally sponsored loans and scholarships/grants available. Financial award application deadline: 3/1; financial award applicants required to submit FAFSA. *Unit head:* Dr. Steven Oberbauer, Chair, 305-348-2580, E-mail: steven.oberbauer@fiu.edu. *Application contact:* Nanett Rojas, Assistant Director, Graduate Admissions, 305-348-7442, Fax: 305-348-7441, E-mail: gradadm@fiu.edu.
Website: http://casgroup.fiu.edu/biology/

Florida International University, Herbert Wertheim College of Medicine, Miami, FL 33199. Offers biomedical sciences (PhD); medicine (MD); physician assistant studies (MPAS). *Accreditation:* LCME/AMA. *Faculty:* 84 full-time (45 women), 83 part-time/adjunct (28 women). *Students:* 638 full-time (364 women); includes 418 minority (42 Black or African American, non-Hispanic/Latino; 124 Asian, non-Hispanic/Latino; 228 Hispanic/Latino; 24 Two or more races, non-Hispanic/Latino), 12 international. Average age 26. 5,410 applicants, 7% accepted, 170 enrolled. In 2017, 115 doctorates awarded. *Entrance requirements:* For doctorate, MCAT (minimum score of 25), minimum overall GPA of 3.0; 3 letters of recommendation, 2 from basic science faculty (biology, chemistry, physics, math) and 1 from any other faculty member. *Application deadline:* For fall admission, 12/15 for domestic students. Application fee: $160. Electronic applications accepted. *Expenses:* Contact institution. *Financial support:* Institutionally sponsored loans and scholarships/grants available. Financial award application deadline: 3/1; financial award applicants required to submit FAFSA. *Unit head:* Dr. John Rock, Dean, 305-348-0570, E-mail: med.admissions@fiu.edu. *Application contact:* Cristina M. Arabatzis, Assistant Director of Admissions, 305-348-0639, Fax: 305-348-0650, E-mail: carabatz@fiu.edu.
Website: http://medicine.fiu.edu/

Florida State University, The Graduate School, College of Arts and Sciences, Department of Biological Science, Tallahassee, FL 32306-4295. Offers cell and molecular biology (MS, PhD); ecology and evolutionary biology (MS, PhD); science teaching (MST). *Faculty:* 51 full-time (16 women). *Students:* 119 full-time (58 women); includes 10 minority (4 Black or African American, non-Hispanic/Latino; 1 Hispanic/Latino; 1 Native Hawaiian or other Pacific Islander, non-Hispanic/Latino; 4 Two or more races, non-Hispanic/Latino), 29 international. Average age 29. 163 applicants, 25% accepted, 25 enrolled. In 2017, 6 master's, 10 doctorates awarded. Terminal master's awarded for partial completion of doctoral program. *Degree requirements:* For master's, comprehensive exam, thesis, teaching experience, seminar presentations; for doctorate, comprehensive exam, thesis/dissertation, teaching experience; seminar presentations. *Entrance requirements:* For master's and doctorate, GRE General Test, minimum upper-division GPA of 3.0. Additional exam requirements/recommendations for international students: Required—TOEFL (minimum score 600 paper-based; 92 iBT). *Application deadline:* For fall admission, 12/1 for domestic and international students. Application fee: $30. Electronic applications accepted. *Financial support:* In 2017–18, 130 students received support, including 9 fellowships with full tuition reimbursements available (averaging $30,000 per year), 29 research assistantships with full tuition reimbursements available (averaging $23,000 per year), 85 teaching assistantships with full tuition reimbursements available (averaging $23,000 per year); scholarships/grants, traineeships, and unspecified assistantships also available. Financial award application deadline: 12/1; financial award applicants required to submit FAFSA. *Faculty research:* Cell and molecular biology and genetics, ecology and evolutionary biology, neuroscience, plant science, structural biology. *Unit head:* Dr. Thomas A. Houpt, Professor and Associate Chair, 850-644-4906, Fax: 850-644-4783, E-mail: houpt@bio.fsu.edu. *Application contact:* Jessica Webber, Graduate Coordinator, 850-644-3023, Fax: 850-644-9829, E-mail: gradinfo@bio.fsu.edu.
Website: http://www.bio.fsu.edu/

Florida State University, The Graduate School, College of Arts and Sciences, Department of Mathematics, Tallahassee, FL 32306-4510. Offers applied and computational mathematics (MS, PhD); biomathematics (MS, PhD); financial mathematics (MS, PhD), including actuarial science (MS); pure mathematics (MS, PhD). *Program availability:* Part-time. *Faculty:* 34 full-time (4 women). *Students:* 114 full-time (31 women); includes 8 minority (1 Black or African American, non-Hispanic/Latino; 1 Asian, non-Hispanic/Latino; 2 Hispanic/Latino; 4 Two or more races, non-Hispanic/Latino), 74 international. 160 applicants, 61% accepted, 43 enrolled. In 2017, 18 master's, 24 doctorates awarded. Terminal master's awarded for partial completion of doctoral program. *Degree requirements:* For master's, comprehensive exam (for some programs), thesis optional; for doctorate, comprehensive exam, thesis/dissertation, candidacy exam (including written qualifying examinations which differ by degree concentration). *Entrance requirements:* For master's and doctorate, GRE General Test, minimum upper-division GPA of 3.0, 4-year bachelor's degree. Additional exam requirements/recommendations for international students: Required—TOEFL (minimum score 550 paper-based; 80 iBT), IELTS (minimum score 6.5). *Application deadline:* For fall admission, 12/15 priority date for domestic and international students; for spring admission, 4/30 for domestic and international students. Application fee: $30. Electronic applications accepted. *Financial support:* In 2017–18, 104 students received support, including 2 fellowships with full tuition reimbursements available (averaging $24,053 per year), 10 research assistantships with full tuition reimbursements available (averaging $20,053 per year), 83 teaching assistantships with full tuition reimbursements available (averaging $20,053 per year); career-related internships or fieldwork, institutionally sponsored loans, scholarships/grants, health care benefits, tuition waivers (full and partial), and unspecified assistantships also available. Financial award application deadline: 12/15; financial award applicants required to submit FAFSA. *Faculty research:*

Biological and Biomedical Sciences—General

Low-dimensional and geometric topology, mathematical modeling in neuroscience, computational stochastics and Monte Carlo methods, mathematical physics, applied analysis. *Total annual research expenditures:* $1.3 million. *Unit head:* Dr. Philip L. Bowers, Chairperson, 850-644-2202, Fax: 850-644-4053, E-mail: bowers@math.fsu.edu. *Application contact:* Elizabeth Scott, Graduate Advisor and Admissions Coordinator, 850-644-2278, Fax: 850-644-4053, E-mail: emscott2@fsu.edu.
Website: http://www.math.fsu.edu/

Florida State University, The Graduate School, College of Arts and Sciences, Department of Scientific Computing, Tallahassee, FL 32306-4120. Offers computational science (MS, PhD), including atmospheric science (PhD), biochemistry (PhD), biological science (PhD), computational science (PhD), geological science (PhD), materials science (PhD), physics (PhD). *Program availability:* Part-time. *Faculty:* 12 full-time (2 women). *Students:* 37 full-time (6 women), 3 part-time (1 woman); includes 14 minority (9 Asian, non-Hispanic/Latino; 1 Hispanic/Latino; 4 Two or more races, non-Hispanic/Latino). Average age 27. 43 applicants, 23% accepted, 9 enrolled. In 2017, 5 master's, 5 doctorates awarded. Terminal master's awarded for partial completion of doctoral program. *Degree requirements:* For master's, thesis (for some programs); for doctorate, comprehensive exam, thesis/dissertation. *Entrance requirements:* For master's and doctorate, GRE General Test, knowledge of at least one object-oriented computing language, 3 letters of recommendation, resume, statement of purpose. Additional exam requirements/recommendations for international students: Required—TOEFL (minimum score 550 paper-based; 80 iBT). *Application deadline:* For fall admission, 1/15 for domestic and international students. Applications are processed on a rolling basis. Application fee: $30. Electronic applications accepted. *Financial support:* In 2017–18, 32 students received support, including 10 research assistantships with full tuition reimbursements available (averaging $26,670 per year), 23 teaching assistantships with full tuition reimbursements available (averaging $23,000 per year); scholarships/grants, health care benefits, tuition waivers (full), and unspecified assistantships also available. Financial award application deadline: 1/15. *Faculty research:* Morphometrics, mathematical and systems biology, mining proteomic and metabolic data, computational materials research, computational fluid dynamics, astrophysics, deep learning, computational neuroscience. *Total annual research expenditures:* $500,000. *Unit head:* Dr. Gordon Erlebacher, Chair, 850-644-7024, E-mail: gerlebacher@fsu.edu. *Application contact:* David Amwake, Administrative Specialist, 850-644-2273, Fax: 850-644-0098, E-mail: damwake@fsu.edu.
Website: http://www.sc.fsu.edu

Fordham University, Graduate School of Arts and Sciences, Department of Biological Sciences, New York, NY 10458. Offers biological sciences (MS, PhD); conservation biology (Graduate Certificate). *Program availability:* Part-time, evening/weekend. *Faculty:* 18 full-time (2 women). *Students:* 46 full-time (30 women); includes 4 minority (1 Asian, non-Hispanic/Latino; 3 Hispanic/Latino), 9 international. Average age 29. 64 applicants, 50% accepted, 15 enrolled. In 2017, 7 master's, 5 doctorates, 3 other advanced degrees awarded. Terminal master's awarded for partial completion of doctoral program. *Degree requirements:* For master's, one foreign language, comprehensive exam, thesis optional; for doctorate, one foreign language, comprehensive exam, thesis/dissertation. *Entrance requirements:* For master's and doctorate, GRE General Test, GRE Subject Test (recommended). Additional exam requirements/recommendations for international students: Required—TOEFL (minimum score 550 paper-based). *Application deadline:* For fall admission, 1/4 priority date for domestic students; for spring admission, 11/1 for domestic students. Application fee: $70. Electronic applications accepted. *Financial support:* In 2017–18, 28 students received support, including 4 fellowships with tuition reimbursements available (averaging $31,000 per year), 42 teaching assistantships with tuition reimbursements available (averaging $29,270 per year); Federal Work-Study, institutionally sponsored loans, scholarships/grants, tuition waivers (full and partial), and unspecified assistantships also available. Support available to part-time students. Financial award application deadline: 1/4; financial award applicants required to submit FAFSA. *Faculty research:* Avian ecology, behavioral ecology, and conservation biology; plant, community and ecosystem responses to invasive organisms; neurobiology and ion channel disorders; biochemical, physiological and morphological basis of pattern formation; behavioral, physiological and biochemical adaptations of mammals to extreme environments; evolutionary ecology, functional morphology and ichthyology; genotypic response to biogeographic and anthropogenic factors; community-based sustainable resource use. *Total annual research expenditures:* $1.5 million. *Unit head:* Dr. James Lewis, Chair, 718-817-3642, Fax: 718-817-3645, E-mail: jdlewis@fordham.edu. *Application contact:* Travis Stratton, Interim Director of Graduate Admissions, 718-817-4417, Fax: 718-817-3566, E-mail: tstrattion@fordham.edu.

Fort Hays State University, Graduate School, College of Science, Technology and Mathematics, Department of Biological Sciences, Program in Biology, Hays, KS 67601-4099. Offers MS. *Program availability:* Part-time. *Degree requirements:* For master's, comprehensive exam, thesis optional. *Entrance requirements:* Additional exam requirements/recommendations for international students: Required—TOEFL (minimum score 550 paper-based). Electronic applications accepted.

Frostburg State University, College of Liberal Arts and Sciences, Department of Biology, Frostburg, MD 21532. Offers applied ecology and conservation biology (MS); fisheries and wildlife management (MS). *Program availability:* Part-time, evening/weekend. *Faculty:* 10 full-time (3 women), 1 part-time/adjunct (0 women). *Students:* 12 full-time (9 women), 7 part-time (5 women). Average age 28. 21 applicants, 57% accepted, 4 enrolled. In 2017, 4 master's awarded. *Degree requirements:* For master's, thesis. *Entrance requirements:* For master's, GRE General Test, resume. Additional exam requirements/recommendations for international students: Required—TOEFL. *Application deadline:* For fall admission, 7/15 priority date for domestic students. Applications are processed on a rolling basis. Application fee: $45. Electronic applications accepted. *Expenses:* Tuition, state resident: part-time $433 per credit hour. Tuition, nonresident: part-time $557 per credit hour. *Required fees:* $121 per credit hour. $27 per term. *Financial support:* In 2017–18, 15 research assistantships with full tuition reimbursements (averaging $5,000 per year) were awarded; career-related internships or fieldwork and Federal Work-Study also available. Financial award application deadline: 4/1; financial award applicants required to submit FAFSA. *Faculty research:* Molecular and morphological evolution, ecology and behavior of birds, conservation genetics of amphibians and fishes, biology of endangered species. *Unit head:* Dr. David Puthoff, Department Chair, 301-687-4172, E-mail: dpputhoff@frostburg.edu. *Application contact:* Vickie Mazer, Director, Graduate Services, 301-687-7053, Fax: 301-687-4597, E-mail: vmmazer@frostburg.edu.

Geisinger Commonwealth School of Medicine, Graduate Programs in Medicine, Scranton, PA 18509. Offers biomedical sciences (MBS). *Program availability:* Part-time, evening/weekend. *Entrance requirements:* For master's, MCAT, DAT, GRE, bachelor's degree; coursework in biology with lab, organic chemistry with lab, inorganic chemistry with lab, physics with lab, and English; official transcripts; three letters of recommendation. Electronic applications accepted.

George Mason University, College of Science, School of Systems Biology, Manassas, VA 20110. Offers bioinformatics and computational biology (MS, PhD, Certificate); bioinformatics management (MS, PSM); biology (MS); biosciences (PhD); personalized medicine (Certificate). *Faculty:* 12 full-time (4 women), 2 part-time/adjunct (0 women). *Students:* 107 full-time (54 women), 89 part-time (44 women); includes 64 minority (6 Black or African American, non-Hispanic/Latino; 35 Asian, non-Hispanic/Latino; 14 Hispanic/Latino; 9 Two or more races, non-Hispanic/Latino), 37 international. Average age 31. 141 applicants, 79% accepted, 64 enrolled. In 2017, 27 master's, 8 doctorates, 4 other advanced degrees awarded. *Degree requirements:* For master's, comprehensive exam (for some programs), research project or thesis; for doctorate, comprehensive exam, thesis/dissertation. *Entrance requirements:* For master's, GRE, resume; 3 letters of recommendation; expanded goals statement; 2 copies of official transcripts; bachelor's degree in related field with minimum GPA of 3.0 in last 60 hours; for doctorate, GRE, self-assessment form; resume; 3 letters of recommendation; expanded goals statement; 2 copies of official transcripts; bachelor's degree in related field with minimum GPA of 3.0 in last 60 hours; for Certificate, resume; 2 copies of official transcripts. Additional exam requirements/recommendations for international students: Required—TOEFL (minimum score 575 paper-based; 88 iBT), IELTS (minimum score 6.5), PTE (minimum score 59). Application fee: $75 ($80 for international students). Electronic applications accepted. *Expenses:* Tuition, state resident: full-time $11,228; part-time $459.50 per credit. Tuition, nonresident: full-time $30,932; part-time $1280.50 per credit. *Required fees:* $3252; $135.50 per credit. Part-time tuition and fees vary according to course load and program. *Financial support:* In 2017–18, 51 students received support, including 15 fellowships (averaging $3,902 per year), 14 research assistantships with tuition reimbursements available (averaging $16,679 per year), 38 teaching assistantships with tuition reimbursements available (averaging $15,754 per year); career-related internships or fieldwork, Federal Work-Study, scholarships/grants, unspecified assistantships, and health care benefits (for full-time research or teaching assistantship recipients) also available. Support available to part-time students. Financial award application deadline: 3/1; financial award applicants required to submit FAFSA. *Faculty research:* Functional genomics of chronic human diseases, ecology of vector-borne infectious diseases, neurogenetics, molecular biology, computational modeling, proteomics, chronic metabolic diseases, nanotechnology. *Total annual research expenditures:* $766,416. *Unit head:* Dr. Iosif Vaisman, Director, 703-993-8431, Fax: 703-993-8976, E-mail: ivaisman@gmu.edu. *Application contact:* Diane St. Germain, Graduate Student Services Coordinator, 703-993-4263, Fax: 703-993-8976, E-mail: dstgerma@gmu.edu.
Website: http://ssb.gmu.edu/

George Mason University, Schar School of Policy and Government, Program in Biodefense, Arlington, VA 22201. Offers MS, PhD, Certificate. *Program availability:* Evening/weekend, 100% online. *Faculty:* 3 full-time (1 woman), 10 part-time/adjunct (4 women). *Students:* 21 full-time (14 women), 36 part-time (24 women); includes 12 minority (4 Asian, non-Hispanic/Latino; 6 Hispanic/Latino; 2 Two or more races, non-Hispanic/Latino), 1 international. Average age 30. 37 applicants, 59% accepted, 16 enrolled. In 2017, 15 master's, 3 doctorates, 4 other advanced degrees awarded. *Degree requirements:* For master's, thesis, project; for doctorate, comprehensive exam, thesis/dissertation. *Entrance requirements:* For master's, GRE (taken in the past five years), transcripts from all previous institutions attended in the U.S.; goals statement; two letters of recommendation; current resume; writing sample; for doctorate, GRE (taken in the past five years), official transcript from all colleges and universities attended; current resume; two letters of recommendation; statement of goals (not to exceed 500 words); writing sample (approximately 10-25 pages in length). Additional exam requirements/recommendations for international students: Required—TOEFL (minimum score 575 paper-based; 88 iBT), IELTS (minimum score 6.5), PTE (minimum score 59). *Application deadline:* For fall admission, 2/1 priority date for domestic and international students; for spring admission, 11/1 priority date for domestic and international students. Application fee: $75 ($80 for international students). Electronic applications accepted. *Expenses:* $795 per credit in-state tuition, $1,516 out-of-state. *Financial support:* In 2017–18, 6 students received support, including 1 fellowship, 5 research assistantships with tuition reimbursements available (averaging $15,009 per year); career-related internships or fieldwork, Federal Work-Study, scholarships/grants, unspecified assistantships, and health care benefits (for full-time research or teaching assistantship recipients) also available. Support available to part-time students. Financial award application deadline: 3/1; financial award applicants required to submit FAFSA. *Faculty research:* Weapons of mass destruction; global health security; homeland security; terrorism; genome editing and synthetic biology. *Unit head:* Gregory Koblentz, Director, 703-993-1266, Fax: 703-993-1399, E-mail: gkoblent@gmu.edu. *Application contact:* Stephanie Ellis, Graduate Admissions Coordinator, 703-993-4478, E-mail: sellis11@gmu.edu.

Georgetown University, Graduate School of Arts and Sciences, Department of Biology, Washington, DC 20057. Offers PhD. Terminal master's awarded for partial completion of doctoral program. *Degree requirements:* For doctorate, comprehensive exam, thesis/dissertation. *Entrance requirements:* For doctorate, GRE General Test, GRE Subject Test (biology). Additional exam requirements/recommendations for international students: Required—TOEFL (minimum score 550 paper-based). Electronic applications accepted. *Faculty research:* Parasitology, ecology, evaluation and behavior, neuroscience and development, cell and molecular biology, immunology.

Georgetown University, National Institutes of Health Sponsored Programs, GU-NIH Graduate Partnership Programs in Biomedical Sciences, Washington, DC 20057. Offers MS, PhD, MD/PhD, MS/PhD. *Entrance requirements:* For doctorate, GRE General Test. Additional exam requirements/recommendations for international students: Required—TOEFL.

The George Washington University, Columbian College of Arts and Sciences, Department of Biological Sciences, Washington, DC 20052. Offers MS, PhD. *Program availability:* Part-time, evening/weekend. *Faculty:* 5 full-time (1 woman), 25 part-time/adjunct (9 women). *Students:* 29 full-time (18 women), 14 part-time (6 women); includes 8 minority (1 Black or African American, non-Hispanic/Latino; 2 Asian, non-Hispanic/Latino; 4 Hispanic/Latino; 1 Two or more races, non-Hispanic/Latino), 8 international. Average age 28. 87 applicants, 22% accepted, 14 enrolled. In 2017, 3 master's, 9 doctorates awarded. Terminal master's awarded for partial completion of doctoral program. *Degree requirements:* For master's, comprehensive exam; for doctorate, thesis/dissertation, general exam. *Entrance requirements:* For master's and doctorate, GRE General Test, minimum GPA of 3.0. Additional exam requirements/recommendations for international students: Required—TOEFL (minimum score 550 paper-based; 80 iBT). *Application deadline:* For fall admission, 1/2 priority date for domestic and international students; for spring admission, 10/1 priority date for domestic and international students. Applications are processed on a rolling basis. Application fee: $75. Electronic applications accepted. *Expenses: Tuition:* Full-time $28,800; part-time $1655 per credit hour. *Required fees:* $45; $2.75 per credit hour. *Financial support:* In 2017–18, 25 students received support. Fellowships with full tuition reimbursements available, teaching assistantships with full tuition reimbursements available, Federal Work-Study, and tuition waivers available. Financial award application deadline: 1/2. *Faculty research:* Systematics, evolution, ecology, developmental biology, cell/molecular biology. *Total annual research expenditures:* $900,000. *Unit head:* Dr. Diana Lipscomb, Chair, 202-994-5828, Fax: 202-994-6100, E-mail: biodl@gwu.edu.

The George Washington University, Columbian College of Arts and Sciences, Institute for Biomedical Sciences, Washington, DC 20037. Offers biochemistry and systems biology (PhD); microbiology and immunology (PhD); molecular medicine (PhD), including molecular and cellular oncology, neurosciences, pharmacology and physiology. *Program availability:* Part-time, evening/weekend. *Students:* Average age 27. *Degree requirements:* For doctorate, thesis/dissertation. *Entrance requirements:* For doctorate, GRE General Test, minimum GPA of 3.0. Additional exam requirements/recommendations for international students: Required—TOEFL (minimum score 600 paper-based; 80 iBT). *Application deadline:* For fall admission, 12/15 priority date for domestic and international students. Applications are processed on a rolling basis. Application fee: $60. Electronic applications accepted. *Expenses: Tuition:* Full-time $28,800; part-time $1655 per credit hour. *Required fees:* $45; $2.75 per credit hour. *Financial support:* In 2017–18, 24 students received support. Fellowships with full tuition reimbursements available, Federal Work-Study, institutionally sponsored loans, and tuition waivers available. *Unit head:* Dr. Linda L. Werling, Director, 202-994-2918, Fax: 202-994-0967, E-mail: lwerling@gwu.edu. *Application contact:* 202-994-2179, Fax: 202-994-0967, E-mail: gwibs@gwu.edu.
Website: http://smhs.gwu.edu/ibs/

Georgia College & State University, Graduate School, College of Arts and Sciences, Department of Biology, Milledgeville, GA 31061. Offers MS. *Program availability:* Part-time. *Faculty:* 26 full-time (12 women). *Students:* 21 full-time (14 women), 4 part-time (2 women); includes 12 minority (4 Black or African American, non-Hispanic/Latino; 4 Asian, non-Hispanic/Latino; 1 Hispanic/Latino; 3 Two or more races, non-Hispanic/Latino), 1 international. Average age 25. 12 applicants, 92% accepted, 7 enrolled. In 2017, 15 master's awarded. *Degree requirements:* For master's, thesis or alternative, minimum GPA of 3.0. *Entrance requirements:* For master's, GRE (minimum score of 800 under the old system and 286 under the new scoring system), 30 hours of undergraduate course work in biological science, 2 transcripts, certificate of immunization. *Application deadline:* For fall admission, 7/1 priority date for domestic students, 4/1 for international students; for spring admission, 11/1 priority date for domestic students, 9/1 for international students; for summer admission, 4/1 priority date for domestic students. Applications are processed on a rolling basis. Application fee: $40. Electronic applications accepted. *Expenses:* $288 per credit hour full-time in-state, $2,592 per semester; $1,027 per credit hour full-time out-of-state, $9,243 per semester; $343 per semester fees. *Financial support:* In 2017–18, 17 students received support. Traineeships and unspecified assistantships available. Support available to part-time students. Financial award application deadline: 3/1; financial award applicants required to submit FAFSA. *Faculty research:* Molecular genetics, cell biology, environmental microbiology, microbial ecology. *Unit head:* Dr. Indiren Pillay, Chair, 478-445-0809, E-mail: indiren.pillayll@gcsu.edu. *Application contact:* Dr. Alfred Mead, Graduate Coordinator, 478-445-1091, E-mail: al.mead@gcsu.edu.

Georgia Institute of Technology, Graduate Studies, College of Sciences, School of Biological Sciences, Atlanta, GA 30332-0001. Offers applied physiology (PhD); biology (MS, PhD); prosthetics and orthotics (MS). *Program availability:* Part-time. Terminal master's awarded for partial completion of doctoral program. *Degree requirements:* For master's, thesis; for doctorate, thesis/dissertation, qualifying exam. *Entrance requirements:* For master's and doctorate, GRE General Test. Additional exam requirements/recommendations for international students: Required—TOEFL (minimum score 600 paper-based; 100 iBT). Electronic applications accepted. *Faculty research:* Microbiology, molecular and cell biology, ecology.

Georgia Southern University, Jack N. Averitt College of Graduate Studies, College of Science and Mathematics, Program in Biology, Statesboro, GA 30460. Offers MS. *Program availability:* Part-time. *Faculty:* 76 full-time (26 women). *Students:* 34 full-time (21 women), 12 part-time (5 women); includes 7 minority (2 Black or African American, non-Hispanic/Latino; 2 Asian, non-Hispanic/Latino; 3 Hispanic/Latino). Average age 26. 30 applicants, 50% accepted, 13 enrolled. In 2017, 11 master's awarded. *Degree requirements:* For master's, comprehensive exam, thesis optional, terminal exam. *Entrance requirements:* For master's, GRE General Test, GRE Subject Test (preferred), minimum GPA of 2.8, BS in biology, 2 letters of reference. Additional exam requirements/recommendations for international students: Required—TOEFL (minimum score 550 paper-based; 80 iBT), IELTS (minimum score 6). *Application deadline:* For fall admission, 4/1 priority date for domestic and international students; for spring admission, 10/1 priority date for domestic students, 10/1 for international students. Applications are processed on a rolling basis. Application fee: $50. Electronic applications accepted. *Expenses:* Tuition, state resident: full-time $4986; part-time $3324 per year. Tuition, nonresident: full-time $21,982; part-time $15,352 per year. *Required fees:* $2092; $1802 per credit hour. $901 per semester. Tuition and fees vary according to course load, campus/location and program. *Financial support:* In 2017–18, 21 students received support, including 13 research assistantships with full tuition reimbursements available (averaging $10,000 per year), 31 teaching assistantships with full tuition reimbursements available (averaging $10,000 per year); career-related internships or fieldwork, Federal Work-Study, scholarships/grants, tuition waivers (full), and unspecified assistantships also available. Support available to part-time students. Financial award application deadline: 4/15; financial award applicants required to submit FAFSA. *Faculty research:* Behavior, evolution and ecology, molecular biology, physiology, parasitology, vector-borne diseases, natural resources, coastal plain science. *Total annual research expenditures:* $420,563. *Unit head:* Dr. Checo Colon-Gaud, Program Coordinator, 912-478-0053, Fax: 912-478-0845, E-mail: jccolongaud@georgiasouthern.edu.
Website: http://www.bio.georgiasouthern.edu

Georgia State University, College of Arts and Sciences, Department of Biology, Atlanta, GA 30302-3083. Offers applied and environmental microbiology (MS, PhD), including applied and environmental microbiology, bioinformatics (MS); cellular and molecular biology and physiology (MS, PhD), including bioinformatics (MS), cellular and molecular biology and physiology; molecular genetics and biochemistry (MS, PhD), including bioinformatics (MS), molecular genetics and biochemistry; neurobiology and behavior (MS, PhD), including bioinformatics (MS), neurobiology and behavior. *Program availability:* Part-time. *Faculty:* 48 full-time (27 women). *Students:* 251 full-time (155 women), 22 part-time (12 women); includes 131 minority (76 Black or African American, non-Hispanic/Latino; 31 Asian, non-Hispanic/Latino; 16 Hispanic/Latino; 8 Two or more races, non-Hispanic/Latino), 63 international. Average age 27. 190 applicants, 54% accepted, 71 enrolled. In 2017, 75 master's, 21 doctorates awarded. Terminal master's awarded for partial completion of doctoral program. *Degree requirements:* For master's, comprehensive exam (for some programs), thesis optional; for doctorate, comprehensive exam, thesis/dissertation. *Entrance requirements:* For master's, GRE. *Application deadline:* For fall admission, 6/1 priority date for domestic and international students; for spring admission, 10/1 priority date for domestic and international students. Applications are processed on a rolling basis. Application fee: $50. Electronic applications accepted. *Expenses:* Tuition, state resident: full-time $7020. Tuition, nonresident: full-time $22,518. *Required fees:* $2128. Tuition and fees vary according to degree level and program. *Financial support:* In 2017–18, fellowships with full tuition reimbursements (averaging $2,200 per year), research assistantships with full tuition reimbursements (averaging $20,000 per year), teaching assistantships with full tuition reimbursements (averaging $5,400 per year) were awarded; unspecified assistantships also available. Financial award application deadline: 3/1; financial award applicants required to submit FAFSA. *Faculty research:* Applied and environmental microbiology, cell biology and immunology, molecular pathogenesis, protein modeling, neurobiology and behavior. *Unit head:* Dr. Charles Derby, Director of Graduate Studies, 404-413-5393, E-mail: cderby@gsu.edu.
Website: http://biology.gsu.edu/

Georgia State University, College of Arts and Sciences, MD/PhD Program, Atlanta, GA 30302-3083. Offers MD/PhD. *Expenses:* Tuition, state resident: full-time $7020. Tuition, nonresident: full-time $22,518. *Required fees:* $2128. Tuition and fees vary according to degree level and program. *Unit head:* Dr. William J. Long, Dean, 404-413-5114, Fax: 404-413-5117, E-mail: long@gsu.edu. *Application contact:* Amber Amari, Director, Graduate and Scheduling Services, 404-413-5037, E-mail: aamari@gsu.edu.

Georgia State University, College of Education and Human Development, Department of Middle and Secondary Education, Atlanta, GA 30302-3083. Offers curriculum and instruction (Ed D); English education (MAT); mathematics education (M Ed, MAT); middle level education (MAT); reading, language and literacy education (M Ed, MAT), including reading instruction (M Ed); science education (M Ed, MAT), including biology (MAT), broad field science (MAT), chemistry (MAT), earth science (MAT), physics (MAT); social studies education (M Ed, MAT), including economics (MAT), geography (MAT), history (MAT), political science (MAT); teaching and learning (PhD), including language and literacy, mathematics education, music education, science education, social studies education, teaching and teacher education. *Accreditation:* NCATE. *Program availability:* Part-time, evening/weekend, online learning. *Faculty:* 24 full-time (18 women). *Students:* 179 full-time (110 women), 192 part-time (133 women); includes 193 minority (130 Black or African American, non-Hispanic/Latino; 1 American Indian or Alaska Native, non-Hispanic/Latino; 23 Asian, non-Hispanic/Latino; 25 Hispanic/Latino; 14 Two or more races, non-Hispanic/Latino), 6 international. Average age 33. 175 applicants, 58% accepted, 83 enrolled. In 2017, 81 master's, 17 doctorates awarded. *Entrance requirements:* For master's, GRE; GACE I (for initial teacher preparation programs), baccalaureate degree or equivalent, resume, goals statement, two letters of recommendation, minimum undergraduate GPA of 2.5; proof of initial teacher certification in the content area (for M Ed); for doctorate, GRE, resume, goals statement, writing sample, two letters of recommendation, minimum graduate GPA of 3.3, interview. *Application deadline:* For fall admission, 1/15 priority date for domestic and international students; for spring admission, 10/1 for domestic and international students. Application fee: $50. Electronic applications accepted. *Expenses:* Tuition, state resident: full-time $7020. Tuition, nonresident: full-time $22,518. *Required fees:* $2128. Tuition and fees vary according to degree level and program. *Financial support:* In 2017–18, fellowships with full tuition reimbursements (averaging $19,667 per year), research assistantships with full tuition reimbursements (averaging $5,436 per year), teaching assistantships with full tuition reimbursements (averaging $2,779 per year) were awarded; career-related internships or fieldwork, Federal Work-Study, scholarships/grants, health care benefits, tuition waivers (full and partial), and unspecified assistantships also available. Financial award application deadline: 3/15. *Faculty research:* Teacher education in language and literacy, mathematics, science, and social studies in urban middle and secondary school settings; learning technologies in school, community, and corporate settings; multicultural education and education for social justice; urban education; international education. *Unit head:* Dr. Dana L. Fox, Chair, 404-413-8060, Fax: 404-413-8063, E-mail: dfox@gsu.edu. *Application contact:* Bobbie Turner, Administrative Coordinator, 404-413-8405, Fax: 404-413-8063, E-mail: bnturner@gsu.edu.
Website: http://mse.education.gsu.edu/

Gerstner Sloan Kettering Graduate School of Biomedical Sciences, Program in Cancer Biology, New York, NY 10021. Offers PhD. *Faculty:* 126 full-time (25 women). *Students:* 70 full-time (28 women); includes 11 minority (1 Black or African American, non-Hispanic/Latino; 5 Asian, non-Hispanic/Latino; 5 Hispanic/Latino), 29 international. 228 applicants, 17% accepted, 14 enrolled. In 2017, 7 doctorates awarded. *Degree requirements:* For doctorate, thesis/dissertation. *Entrance requirements:* For doctorate, GRE, transcripts, three letters of recommendation. Additional exam requirements/recommendations for international students: Required—TOEFL. *Application deadline:* For fall admission, 12/1 for domestic and international students. Electronic applications accepted. *Financial support:* In 2017–18, 70 students received support. Teaching assistantships and fellowship package including stipend ($38,655), full-tuition scholarship, first-year allowance, and comprehensive medical and dental insurance available. *Faculty research:* Structural biology, computational biology, genomics, immunology, chemical biology. *Unit head:* Linda Burnley, Associate Dean, 646-888-6639, E-mail: burnleyl@sloankettering.edu. *Application contact:* Main Office, 646-888-6639, Fax: 646-422-2351, E-mail: gradstudies@sloankettering.edu.

See Display on page 166 and Close-Up on page 207.

Goucher College, Post-Baccalaureate Premedical Program, Baltimore, MD 21204-2794. Offers Certificate. *Entrance requirements:* For degree, GRE, SAT or ACT. *Application deadline:* Applications are processed on a rolling basis. Application fee: $60. Electronic applications accepted. *Expenses:* Contact institution. *Financial support:* Fellowships, institutionally sponsored loans, and scholarships/grants available. Financial award application deadline: 3/1; financial award applicants required to submit FAFSA. *Unit head:* Betsy Merideth, Director, 800-414-3437, Fax: 410-337-6461, E-mail: bmerideth@goucher.edu. *Application contact:* Theresa Reifsnider, Program Assistant, 800-414-3437, Fax: 410-337-6461, E-mail: pbpm@goucher.edu.
Website: http://www.goucher.edu/postbac/

The Graduate Center, City University of New York, Graduate Studies, Program in Biology, New York, NY 10016-4039. Offers PhD. *Faculty:* 78 full-time (24 women). *Students:* 139 full-time (82 women); includes 43 minority (9 Black or African American, non-Hispanic/Latino; 21 Asian, non-Hispanic/Latino; 10 Hispanic/Latino; 3 Two or more races, non-Hispanic/Latino), 23 international. Average age 32. 151 applicants, 28% accepted, 18 enrolled. In 2017, 17 doctorates awarded. *Degree requirements:* For doctorate, thesis/dissertation, teaching experience. *Entrance requirements:* For doctorate, GRE General Test. Additional exam requirements/recommendations for international students: Required—TOEFL. *Application deadline:* For fall admission, 1/1 for domestic students. Application fee: $125. Electronic applications accepted. *Financial support:* In 2017–18, 100 students received support, including 157 fellowships, 1 research assistantship, 1 teaching assistantship; career-related internships or fieldwork, Federal Work-Study, institutionally sponsored loans, and tuition waivers (full and partial) also available. Financial award application deadline: 4/15; financial award applicants required to submit FAFSA. *Unit head:* Cathy Savage-Dunn, Executive Officer, 212-817-8101, Fax: 212-817-1504, E-mail: csavagedunn@gc.cuny.edu. *Application contact:* Executive Officer, 212-817-8100, Fax: 212-817-1504, E-mail: biology@gc.cuny.edu.

Grand Valley State University, College of Liberal Arts and Sciences, Biology Department, Allendale, MI 49401-9403. Offers MS. *Program availability:* Part-time. *Faculty:* 15 full-time (6 women). *Students:* 25 full-time (13 women), 15 part-time (5 women); includes 5 minority (1 Black or African American, non-Hispanic/Latino; 2 American Indian or Alaska Native, non-Hispanic/Latino; 1 Hispanic/Latino; 1 Two or more races, non-Hispanic/Latino). Average age 26. 15 applicants, 100% accepted, 13 enrolled. In 2017, 12 master's awarded. *Degree requirements:* For master's, comprehensive exam, thesis or alternative. *Entrance requirements:* For master's, GRE General Test, 3 letters of reference, 500-word essay, minimum GPA of 3.0. Additional exam requirements/recommendations for international students: Required—TOEFL (minimum iBT score of 80), IELTS (6.5), or Michigan English Language Assessment Battery (77). *Application deadline:* For winter admission, 1/15 priority date for domestic students. Applications are processed on a rolling basis. Application fee: $30. Electronic applications accepted. *Expenses:* $657 per credit hour. *Financial support:* In 2017–18, 29 students received support, including 5 fellowships, 26 research assistantships with full and partial tuition reimbursements available (averaging $8,000 per year); career-related internships or fieldwork, scholarships/grants, and unspecified assistantships also available. Financial award application deadline: 1/15. *Faculty research:* Natural resources conservation biology, aquatic sciences, terrestrial ecology, behavioral biology. *Unit head:* Dr. Neil MacDonald, Director, 616-331-2697, Fax: 616-331-3446, E-mail: macdonan@gvsu.edu. *Application contact:* Dr. Eric Snyder, Graduate Program Director, 616-331-2417, Fax: 616-331-3446, E-mail: snydeeri@gvsu.edu.

Grand Valley State University, College of Liberal Arts and Sciences, Department of Biomedical Sciences, Allendale, MI 49401-9403. Offers MHS. *Program availability:* Part-time. *Faculty:* 24 full-time (6 women), 1 part-time/adjunct (0 women). *Students:* 4 full-time (1 woman), 15 part-time (8 women); includes 2 minority (both Black or African American, non-Hispanic/Latino). Average age 25. 21 applicants, 57% accepted, 5 enrolled. In 2017, 7 master's awarded. *Degree requirements:* For master's, comprehensive exam, project or thesis. *Entrance requirements:* For master's, GRE General Test, MCAT, or DAT, minimum GPA of 3.0; 3 letters of reference; completion of undergraduate courses in anatomy, physiology, microbiology, and statistics; coursework in chemistry (recommended); personal statement. Additional exam requirements/recommendations for international students: Required—TOEFL (minimum iBT score of 80), IELTS (6.5), or Michigan English Language Assessment Battery (77). *Application deadline:* For fall admission, 2/1 priority date for domestic and international students. Applications are processed on a rolling basis. Application fee: $30. Electronic applications accepted. *Expenses:* $657 per credit hour. *Financial support:* In 2017–18, 1 student received support, including 1 research assistantship with full and partial tuition reimbursement available (averaging $8,000 per year); fellowships, scholarships/grants, and unspecified assistantships also available. Financial award application deadline: 2/1. *Faculty research:* Cell regulation, neurobiology, parasitology, virology, microbial pathogenicity. *Unit head:* Dr. Daniel Bergman, Chair, 616-331-8837, Fax: 616-331-2090, E-mail: bergmand@gvsu.edu. *Application contact:* Dr. Derek Thomas, Graduate Program Director/Recruiting Contact, 616-331-2812, Fax: 616-331-2090, E-mail: thomasde@gvsu.edu.

Hampton University, School of Science, Department of Biological Sciences, Hampton, VA 23668. Offers biology (MS); environmental science (MS). *Program availability:* Part-time. *Students:* 1 (woman) full-time, 1 (woman) part-time; both minorities (both Black or African American, non-Hispanic/Latino). Average age 24. 7 applicants. In 2017, 2 master's awarded. *Degree requirements:* For master's, comprehensive exam (for some programs), thesis optional. *Entrance requirements:* For master's, GRE General Test. *Application deadline:* For fall admission, 6/1 priority date for domestic students, 6/1 for international students; for spring admission, 11/1 priority date for domestic students, 11/1 for international students; for summer admission, 4/1 priority date for domestic students, 2/1 priority date for international students. Applications are processed on a rolling basis. Application fee: $35. Electronic applications accepted. *Expenses: Tuition:* Full-time $22,630; part-time $575 per semester hour. *Required fees:* $70. Tuition and fees vary according to program. *Financial support:* Fellowships, research assistantships, teaching assistantships, career-related internships or fieldwork, Federal Work-Study, institutionally sponsored loans, scholarships/grants, and stipends available. Support available to part-time students. Financial award application deadline: 6/30; financial award applicants required to submit FAFSA. *Faculty research:* Molecular mechanisms responsible for initiation, promotion, and progression of breast, colon, prostate, thyroid, and skin cancers; isolation and characterization of bacteria in natural and contaminated environments and study of probable uses in biocontrol, diabetes, and hypertension. *Unit head:* Dr. Jermel Watkins, Chair, 757-727-5267, E-mail: jermel.watkins@hamptonu.edu.

Harvard University, Extension School, Cambridge, MA 02138-3722. Offers applied sciences (CAS); biotechnology (ALM); educational technologies (ALM); educational technology (CET); English for graduate and professional studies (DGP); environmental management (ALM, CEM); information technology (ALM); journalism (ALM); liberal arts (ALM); management (ALM, CM); mathematics for teaching (ALM); museum studies (ALM); premedical studies (Diploma); publication and communication (CPC). *Program availability:* Part-time, evening/weekend. *Degree requirements:* For master's, thesis. *Entrance requirements:* For master's, 3 completed graduate courses with grade of B or higher. Additional exam requirements/recommendations for international students: Required—TOEFL (minimum score 600 paper-based), TWE (minimum score 5). *Expenses:* Contact institution.

Harvard University, Graduate School of Arts and Sciences, Department of Organismic and Evolutionary Biology, Cambridge, MA 02138. Offers biology (PhD). *Degree requirements:* For doctorate, 2 foreign languages, public presentation of thesis research, exam. *Entrance requirements:* For doctorate, GRE General Test, GRE Subject Test (recommended), 7 courses in biology, chemistry, physics, mathematics, computer science, or geology. Additional exam requirements/recommendations for international students: Required—TOEFL.

Harvard University, Graduate School of Arts and Sciences, Division of Medical Sciences, Boston, MA 02115. Offers biological chemistry and molecular pharmacology (PhD); cell biology (PhD); genetics (PhD); microbiology and molecular genetics (PhD); pathology (PhD), including experimental pathology. *Degree requirements:* For doctorate, thesis/dissertation. *Entrance requirements:* For doctorate, GRE General Test, GRE Subject Test. Additional exam requirements/recommendations for international students: Required—TOEFL.

Harvard University, Harvard T.H. Chan School of Public Health, PhD Program in Biological Sciences in Public Health, Boston, MA 02115. Offers PhD. *Students:* 53 full-time (33 women); includes 17 minority (5 Black or African American, non-Hispanic/Latino; 7 Asian, non-Hispanic/Latino; 4 Hispanic/Latino; 1 Two or more races, non-Hispanic/Latino), 6 international. Average age 29. 112 applicants, 11% accepted, 9 enrolled. In 2017, 8 doctorates awarded. *Degree requirements:* For doctorate, qualifying examination, dissertation/defense. *Entrance requirements:* For doctorate, GRE General Test. Additional exam requirements/recommendations for international students: Recommended—TOEFL (minimum score 600 paper-based; 100 iBT), IELTS (minimum score 7). Electronic applications accepted. *Financial support:* Fellowships, research assistantships, teaching assistantships, institutionally sponsored loans, health care benefits, and tuition waivers (full) available. Financial award application deadline: 1/1. *Faculty research:* Nutrition biochemistry, molecular and cellular toxicology, cardiovascular disease, cancer biology, immunology and infectious diseases, environmental health physiology. *Unit head:* Deirdre Duckett, Assistant Director, E-mail: bph@hsph.harvard.edu.
Website: http://www.hsph.harvard.edu/admissions/degree-programs/doctor-of-philosophy/phd-in-biological-sciences-and-public-health/

See Display on page 777 and Close-Up on page 841.

Hofstra University, College of Liberal Arts and Sciences, Programs in Biology, Hempstead, NY 11549. Offers biology (MA, MS); urban ecology (MA, MS). *Program availability:* Part-time, evening/weekend. *Students:* 17 full-time (10 women), 7 part-time (3 women); includes 18 minority (7 Black or African American, non-Hispanic/Latino; 1 American Indian or Alaska Native, non-Hispanic/Latino; 2 Asian, non-Hispanic/Latino; 6 Hispanic/Latino; 2 Two or more races, non-Hispanic/Latino). Average age 25. 18 applicants, 78% accepted, 8 enrolled. In 2017, 11 master's awarded. *Degree requirements:* For master's, thesis, minimum GPA of 3.0. *Entrance requirements:* For master's, GRE, bachelor's degree in biology or equivalent, 2 letters of recommendation, essay. Additional exam requirements/recommendations for international students: Required—TOEFL (minimum score 550 paper-based; 80 iBT). *Application deadline:* Applications are processed on a rolling basis. Application fee: $75. Electronic applications accepted. *Expenses: Tuition:* Full-time $1292. *Required fees:* $970. Tuition and fees vary according to program. *Financial support:* In 2017–18, 23 students received support, including 18 fellowships with full and partial tuition reimbursements available (averaging $4,355 per year); research assistantships with full and partial tuition reimbursements available, career-related internships or fieldwork, Federal Work-Study, institutionally sponsored loans, scholarships/grants, tuition waivers (full and partial), and unspecified assistantships also available. Support available to part-time students. Financial award applicants required to submit FAFSA. *Faculty research:* Cellular communication through extracellular vesicle release; endocytic trafficking of g protein-coupled receptors in human diseases like vascular inflammation and cancer; ecological factors that promote the evolution of parental care behaviors; neurobiological, genetic, and hormonal regulation of mate choice and maternal behaviors in female songbirds and amphibians; applied and environmental microbiology; the scholarship of teaching and learning; biology education; metacognition. *Unit head:* Dr. Peter Daniel, Chairperson, 516-463-6718, Fax: 516-463-5112, E-mail: peter.c.daniel@hofstra.edu. *Application contact:* Sunil Samuel, Assistant Vice President of Admissions, 516-463-4723, Fax: 516-463-4664, E-mail: graduateadmission@hofstra.edu.
Website: http://www.hofstra.edu/hclas

Hood College, Graduate School, Program in Biomedical Science, Frederick, MD 21701-8575. Offers biomedical science (MS), including biotechnology/molecular biology, microbiology/immunology/virology. *Program availability:* Part-time, evening/weekend. *Faculty:* 5 full-time (3 women), 1 (woman) part-time/adjunct. *Students:* 13 full-time (6 women), 73 part-time (39 women); includes 21 minority (12 Black or African American, non-Hispanic/Latino; 6 Asian, non-Hispanic/Latino; 2 Hispanic/Latino; 1 Two or more races, non-Hispanic/Latino), 6 international. Average age 30. 24 applicants, 92% accepted, 14 enrolled. In 2017, 13 master's awarded. *Degree requirements:* For master's, thesis or alternative. *Entrance requirements:* For master's, bachelor's degree in biology; minimum GPA of 3.0; undergraduate course work in cell biology, chemistry, organic chemistry, and genetics. Additional exam requirements/recommendations for international students: Required—TOEFL (minimum score 575 paper-based; 89 iBT), IELTS (minimum score 6). *Application deadline:* For fall admission, 8/15 priority date for domestic students, 8/5 for international students; for spring admission, 12/1 priority date for domestic students, 12/1 for international students; for summer admission, 5/1 priority date for domestic students, 4/15 for international students. Applications are processed on a rolling basis. Application fee: $35. Electronic applications accepted. *Expenses:* $500 per credit plus $110 comprehensive fee per semester, plus any applicable lab fees by course. *Financial support:* Research assistantships with full tuition reimbursements, tuition waivers (partial), and unspecified assistantships available. Financial award applicants required to submit FAFSA. *Faculty research:* Molecular signaling in cell tumor initiation, biomedical ethics, genetic and biochemical approaches to study regulation of gene expression. *Unit head:* Dr. April M. Boulton, Dean of the Graduate School, 301-696-3600, E-mail: gofurther@hood.edu. *Application contact:* Larbi Bricha, Assistant Director of Graduate Admissions, 301-696-3600, E-mail: gofurther@hood.edu.
Website: http://www.hood.edu/graduate

Howard University, Graduate School, Department of Biology, Washington, DC 20059-0002. Offers MS, PhD. *Program availability:* Part-time. *Degree requirements:* For master's, thesis, qualifying exams; for doctorate, thesis/dissertation, qualifying exams. *Entrance requirements:* For master's and doctorate, GRE General Test, minimum GPA of 3.0. Additional exam requirements/recommendations for international students: Required—TOEFL. Electronic applications accepted. *Faculty research:* Physiology, molecular biology, cell biology, microbiology, environmental biology.

Humboldt State University, Academic Programs, College of Natural Resources and Sciences, Department of Biological Sciences, Arcata, CA 95521-8299. Offers MS. *Degree requirements:* For master's, project or thesis. *Entrance requirements:* For master's, GRE General Test, appropriate bachelor's degree, minimum GPA of 2.5, 3 letters of recommendation. Additional exam requirements/recommendations for international students: Required—TOEFL (minimum score 500 paper-based). *Faculty research:* Plant ecology, DNA sequencing, invertebrates.

Hunter College of the City University of New York, Graduate School, School of Arts and Sciences, Department of Biological Sciences, New York, NY 10065-5085. Offers MA, PhD. PhD offered jointly with The Graduate Center, City University of New York. *Program availability:* Part-time. Terminal master's awarded for partial completion of doctoral program. *Degree requirements:* For master's, one foreign language, comprehensive exam or thesis. *Entrance requirements:* For master's, GRE, 1 year of course work in organic chemistry (including laboratory), college physics, and calculus; undergraduate major in biology, botany, physiology, zoology, chemistry or physics. Additional exam requirements/recommendations for international students: Required—TOEFL. *Faculty research:* Analysis of prokaryotic and eukaryotic DNA, protein structure, mammalian DNA replication, oncogene expression, neuroscience.

Icahn School of Medicine at Mount Sinai, Graduate School of Biomedical Sciences, New York, NY 10029-6504. Offers biomedical sciences (MS, PhD); clinical research education (MS, PhD); community medicine (MPH); genetic counseling (MS); neurosciences (PhD); MD/PhD. Terminal master's awarded for partial completion of doctoral program. *Degree requirements:* For master's, thesis; for doctorate, comprehensive exam, thesis/dissertation. *Entrance requirements:* For master's, GRE General Test; for doctorate, GRE General Test, GRE Subject Test, 3 years of college pre-med course work. Additional exam requirements/recommendations for international students: Required—TOEFL. Electronic applications accepted. *Faculty research:* Cancer, genetics and genomics, immunology, neuroscience, developmental and stem cell biology, translational research.

Idaho State University, Office of Graduate Studies, College of Science and Engineering, Department of Biological Sciences, Pocatello, ID 83209-8007. Offers biology (MNS, MS, DA, PhD); clinical laboratory science (MS); microbiology (MS). *Accreditation:* NAACLS. *Program availability:* Part-time. *Degree requirements:* For master's, comprehensive exam, thesis; for doctorate, comprehensive exam, thesis/dissertation, 9 credits of internship (for DA). *Entrance requirements:* For master's, GRE General Test, minimum GPA of 3.0 in all upper division classes; for doctorate, GRE General Test, GRE Subject Test (biology), diagnostic exam (DA), minimum GPA of 3.0 in all upper division classes. Additional exam requirements/recommendations for international students: Required—TOEFL (minimum score 550 paper-based; 80 iBT). Electronic applications accepted. *Faculty research:* Ecology, plant and animal physiology, plant and animal developmental biology, immunology, molecular biology, bioinfomatics.

Illinois Institute of Technology, Graduate College, College of Science, Department of Biology, Chicago, IL 60616. Offers applied life sciences (MS); biochemistry (MS); biology (MS, PhD); cell and molecular biology (MS); microbiology (MS); molecular biochemistry and biophysics (MS, PhD). *Program availability:* Part-time, evening/weekend, online learning. Terminal master's awarded for partial completion of doctoral program. *Degree requirements:* For master's, comprehensive exam, thesis (for some programs); for doctorate, comprehensive exam, thesis/dissertation. *Entrance requirements:* For master's, GRE General Test (minimum score 300 Quantitative and Verbal, 2.5 Analytical Writing), minimum undergraduate GPA of 3.0; for doctorate, GRE General Test (minimum score 310 Quantitative and Verbal, 3.0 Analytical Writing); GRE Subject Test (strongly recommended), minimum undergraduate GPA of 3.0. Additional exam requirements/recommendations for international students: Required—TOEFL (minimum score 550 paper-based; 80 iBT). Electronic applications accepted. *Faculty research:* Macromolecular crystallography, insect immunity and basic cell biology, improvement of bacterial strains for enhanced biodesulfurization of petroleum, programmed cell death in cancer cells.

Illinois State University, Graduate School, College of Arts and Sciences, School of Biological Sciences, Normal, IL 61790. Offers animal behavior (MS); bacteriology (MS); biochemistry (MS); biological sciences (MS); biology (PhD); biophysics (MS); biotechnology (MS); botany (MS, PhD); cell biology (MS); conservation biology (MS); developmental biology (MS); ecology (MS, PhD); entomology (MS); evolutionary biology (MS); genetics (MS, PhD); immunology (MS); microbiology (MS, PhD); molecular biology (MS); molecular genetics (MS); neurobiology (MS); neuroscience (MS); parasitology (MS); physiology (MS, PhD); plant biology (MS); plant molecular biology (MS); plant sciences (MS); structural biology (MS); zoology (MS, PhD). *Program availability:* Part-time. *Degree requirements:* For master's, thesis or alternative; for doctorate, variable foreign language requirement, thesis/dissertation, 2 terms of residency. *Entrance requirements:* For master's, GRE General Test, minimum GPA of 2.6 in last 60 hours of course work; for doctorate, GRE General Test. *Faculty research:* Redoc balance and drug development in schistosoma mansoni, control of the growth of listeria monocytogenes at low temperature, regulation of cell expansion and microtubule function by SPRI, CRUI: physiology and fitness consequences of different life history phenotypes.

Indiana State University, College of Graduate and Professional Studies, College of Arts and Sciences, Department of Biology, Terre Haute, IN 47809. Offers cellular and molecular biology (PhD); ecology, systematics and evolution (PhD); life sciences (MS); physiology (PhD); science education (MS). *Degree requirements:* For master's, thesis optional; for doctorate, comprehensive exam, thesis/dissertation. *Entrance requirements:* For master's and doctorate, GRE General Test. Electronic applications accepted.

Indiana University Bloomington, University Graduate School, College of Arts and Sciences, Department of Biology, Bloomington, IN 47405. Offers biology teaching (MAT); biotechnology (MA); evolution, ecology, and behavior (MA, PhD); genetics (PhD); microbiology (MA, PhD); molecular, cellular, and developmental biology (PhD); plant sciences (MA, PhD); zoology (MA, PhD). Terminal master's awarded for partial completion of doctoral program. *Degree requirements:* For master's, thesis, oral defense; for doctorate, thesis/dissertation, oral defense. *Entrance requirements:* For master's and doctorate, GRE General Test. Additional exam requirements/recommendations for international students: Required—TOEFL (minimum score 100 iBT). Electronic applications accepted. *Faculty research:* Evolution, ecology and behavior; microbiology; molecular biology and genetics; plant biology.

Indiana University of Pennsylvania, School of Graduate Studies and Research, College of Natural Sciences and Mathematics, Department of Biology, Program in Biology, Indiana, PA 15705. Offers MS. *Program availability:* Part-time. *Faculty:* 15 full-time (4 women). *Students:* 19 full-time (13 women), 16 part-time (11 women); includes 4 minority (2 Black or African American, non-Hispanic/Latino; 2 Hispanic/Latino), 12 international. Average age 26. 42 applicants, 67% accepted, 8 enrolled. In 2017, 15 master's awarded. *Degree requirements:* For master's, comprehensive exam, thesis optional. *Entrance requirements:* For master's, 2 letters of recommendation. Additional exam requirements/recommendations for international students: Required—TOEFL (minimum score 550 paper-based). *Application deadline:* Applications are processed on a rolling basis. Application fee: $50. Electronic applications accepted. *Expenses:* Tuition, state resident: full-time $12,000; part-time $500 per credit. Tuition, nonresident: full-time $18,000; part-time $750 per credit. *Required fees:* $4073; $165.55 per credit. $64 per term. *Financial support:* In 2017–18, 8 research assistantships with tuition reimbursements (averaging $5,385 per year) were awarded; fellowships with full tuition reimbursements, career-related internships or fieldwork, Federal Work-Study, scholarships/grants, and unspecified assistantships also available. Financial award application deadline: 4/15; financial award applicants required to submit FAFSA. *Unit head:* Dr. Josiah Townsend, Graduate Coordinator, 724-357-2587, E-mail: josiah.townsend@iup.edu.
Website: http://www.iup.edu/grad/biology/default.aspx

Indiana University–Purdue University Fort Wayne, College of Arts and Sciences, Department of Biology, Fort Wayne, IN 46805-1499. Offers MS. *Program availability:* Part-time, evening/weekend. *Degree requirements:* For master's, thesis optional. *Entrance requirements:* For master's, GRE General Test, minimum GPA of 3.0, major or minor in biology, three letters of recommendation. Additional exam requirements/recommendations for international students: Required—TOEFL (minimum score 550 paper-based; 79 iBT), TWE. Electronic applications accepted. *Faculty research:* Photosynthates, unicellular green algae, Chinook salmon.

Indiana University–Purdue University Indianapolis, School of Science, Department of Biology, Indianapolis, IN 46202. Offers MS, PhD. PhD offered jointly with Purdue University. *Program availability:* Part-time, evening/weekend. Terminal master's awarded for partial completion of doctoral program. *Degree requirements:* For master's, thesis (for some programs); for doctorate, thesis/dissertation. *Entrance requirements:* For master's and doctorate, GRE General Test. *Faculty research:* Cell and model membranes, cell and molecular biology, immunology, oncology, developmental biology.

Inter American University of Puerto Rico, Barranquitas Campus, Program in Education, Barranquitas, PR 00794. Offers curriculum and teaching (M Ed), including biology, English as a second language, history, Spanish; educational leadership and management (MA); elementary education (M Ed); information and library service technology (M Ed); special education (MA). *Accreditation:* TEAC. *Program availability:* Part-time, evening/weekend. *Faculty:* 1 full-time (0 women), 3 part-time/adjunct (2 women). *Students:* 17 full-time (16 women), 2 part-time (both women); all minorities (all Hispanic/Latino). Average age 34. 9 applicants, 89% accepted, 8 enrolled. In 2017, 5 master's awarded. *Degree requirements:* For master's, 2 foreign languages, comprehensive exam, thesis (for some programs). *Entrance requirements:* For master's, GRE or EXADEP, bachelor's degree or its equivalent from accredited institution, official academic transcript from institution that conferred bachelor's degree, minimum GPA of 2.5, two recommendation letters, interview (for some programs), essay (for some programs). *Application deadline:* Applications are processed on a rolling basis. Application fee: $31. Electronic applications accepted. *Expenses:* $3,392 full-time tuition plus $652 fees. *Financial support:* Applicants required to submit FAFSA. *Unit head:* Juan A. Negron-Berrios, PhD, Chancellor, 787-857-3600 Ext. 2002, Fax: 787-857-2125, E-mail: janegron@br.inter.edu. *Application contact:* Aramilda Cartagena-Santiago, Dean of Students, 787-857-3600 Ext. 2009, Fax: 787-857-2125, E-mail: aramildacartagena@br.inter.edu.

Iowa State University of Science and Technology, Department of Biomedical Sciences, Ames, IA 50011. Offers MS, PhD. *Entrance requirements:* For master's and doctorate, GRE General Test. Additional exam requirements/recommendations for international students: Required—TOEFL (minimum score 590 paper-based; 79 iBT), IELTS (minimum score 6.5). Electronic applications accepted. *Faculty research:* Cerebella research; endocrine physiology; memory, learning and associated diseases; ion-channels and dry resistance; glia-neuron signaling; neurobiology of pain.

Irell & Manella Graduate School of Biological Sciences, Graduate Program, Duarte, CA 91010. Offers brain metastatic cancer (PhD); cancer and stem cell metabolism (PhD); cancer biology (PhD); cancer biology and developmental therapeutics (PhD); cell biology (PhD); chemical biology (PhD); chromosomal break repair (PhD); diabetes and pancreatic progenitor cell biology (PhD); DNA repair and cancer biology (PhD); germline epigenetic remodeling and endocrine disruptors (PhD); hematology and hematopoietic cell transplantation (PhD); hematology and immunology (PhD); inflammation and cancer (PhD); micrornas and gene regulation in cardiovascular disease (PhD); mixed chimrism for reversal of autoimmunity (PhD); molecular and cellular biology (PhD); molecular biology and genetics (PhD); nanoparticle mediated twist1 silencing in metastatic cancer (PhD); neuro-oncology and stem cell biology (PhD); neuroscience (PhD); RNA directed therapies for HIV-1 (PhD); small RNA-induced transcriptional gene activation (PhD); stem cell regulation by the microenvironment (PhD); translational oncology and pharmaceutical sciences (PhD); tumor biology (PhD). *Degree requirements:* For doctorate, comprehensive exam, thesis/dissertation, qualifying exams, two advanced courses. *Entrance requirements:* For doctorate, GRE General Test; GRE Subject Test (recommended), 2 years of course work in chemistry (general and organic); 1 year of course work each in biochemistry, general biology, and general physics; 2 semesters of course work in mathematics; significant research laboratory experience. Additional exam requirements/recommendations for international students: Required—TOEFL. Electronic applications accepted. *Faculty research:* Cancer biology, diabetes, stem cell biology, neuroscience, immunology.

See Display on the next page and Close-Up on page 109.

Jackson State University, Graduate School, College of Science, Engineering and Technology, Department of Biology, Jackson, MS 39217. Offers biology (MS); environmental science (MS). *Program availability:* Part-time, evening/weekend. *Degree requirements:* For master's, comprehensive exam, thesis. *Entrance requirements:* For master's, GRE General Test. Additional exam requirements/recommendations for international students: Required—TOEFL (minimum score 520 paper-based; 67 iBT). *Faculty research:* Comparative studies on the carbohydrate composition of marine macroalgae, host-parasite relationship between the spruce budworm and entomepathogen fungus.

Jacksonville State University, College of Graduate Studies and Continuing Education, College of Arts and Sciences, Department of Biology, Jacksonville, AL 36265-1602. Offers MS. *Program availability:* Part-time, evening/weekend. *Degree requirements:* For master's, comprehensive exam, thesis (for some programs). *Entrance requirements:* For master's, GRE General Test or MAT. Additional exam requirements/recommendations for international students: Required—TOEFL (minimum score 500 paper-based; 61 iBT). Electronic applications accepted.

James Madison University, The Graduate School, College of Science and Mathematics, Program in Biology, Harrisonburg, VA 22801. Offers MS. *Program availability:* Part-time. *Students:* 20 full-time (11 women), 3 part-time (0 women); includes 4 minority (2 Black or African American, non-Hispanic/Latino; 2 Hispanic/Latino). Average age 30. In 2017, 11 master's awarded. Application fee: $55. Electronic applications accepted. *Expenses:* Tuition, state resident: full-time $10,512; part-time $438 per credit hour. Tuition, nonresident: full-time $28,358; part-time $1162 per credit hour. *Required fees:* $1128. *Financial support:* In 2017–18, 16 students received support. Fellowships, Federal Work-Study, and 16 assistantships (averaging $7911) available. Financial award application deadline: 3/1; financial award applicants required to submit FAFSA. *Faculty research:* Evolutionary ecology, gene regulation, microbial ecology, plant development, biomechanics. *Unit head:* Dr. Joanna B. Mott, Department Head, 540-568-6225, E-mail: mottjb@jmu.edu. *Application contact:* Lynette D. Michael, Director of Graduate Admissions and Student Records, 540-568-6131 Ext. 6395, E-mail: michaeld@jmu.edu.
Website: http://www.jmu.edu/biology/index.shtml

John Carroll University, Graduate Studies, Department of Biology, University Heights, OH 44118. Offers MA, MS. *Program availability:* Part-time. *Degree requirements:* For master's, essay or thesis, seminar. *Entrance requirements:* For master's, undergraduate major in biology, 1 semester of biochemistry, minimum GPA of 2.5. *Application deadline:* For fall admission, 8/15 priority date for domestic students; for spring admission, 1/3 for domestic students. Applications are processed on a rolling basis. Application fee: $25 ($35 for international students). Electronic applications accepted. *Expenses: Tuition:* Full-time $16,238; part-time $788 per credit hour. One-time fee: $200. Part-time tuition and fees vary according to course load and program. *Financial support:* In 2017–18, 13 students received support. Teaching assistantships with full tuition reimbursements available available. Financial award application deadline: 3/1; financial award applicants required to submit FAFSA. *Faculty research:* Algal ecology, systematics, molecular genetics, neurophysiology, behavioral ecology. *Unit head:* Dr. Rebecca E. Drenovsky, Chairperson, 216-397-4251, Fax: 216-397-4482, E-mail: drenovsky@jcu.edu. *Application contact:* Dr. Ralph A. Saporito, Graduate Program Director, 216-397-4492, Fax: 216-397-4492, E-mail: rsaporito@jcu.edu.

Johns Hopkins University, National Institutes of Health Sponsored Programs, Baltimore, MD 21218. Offers biology (PhD), including biochemistry, biophysics, cell biology, developmental biology, genetic biology, molecular biology; cell, molecular, and developmental biology and biophysics (PhD). *Degree requirements:* For doctorate, comprehensive exam, thesis/dissertation. *Entrance requirements:* For doctorate, GRE General Test. Additional exam requirements/recommendations for international students: Required—TOEFL (minimum score 600 paper-based), TWE. Electronic applications accepted. *Faculty research:* Protein and nucleic acid biochemistry and biophysical chemistry, molecular biology and development.

Johns Hopkins University, School of Education, Master's Programs in Education, Baltimore, MD 21218. Offers counseling (MS), including clinical mental health counseling, school counseling; education (MS), including educational studies, gifted education, reading, school administration and supervision, technology for educators; elementary education (MAT); health professions (M Ed); intelligence analysis (MS); organizational leadership (MS); secondary education (MAT), including biology, chemistry, earth/space science, English, physics, social studies; special education (MS), including early childhood special education, general special education studies, mild to moderate disabilities, severe disabilities. *Program availability:* Part-time, evening/weekend, 100% online, blended/hybrid learning. *Degree requirements:* For master's, comprehensive exam (for some programs), portfolio, capstone project and/or internship;

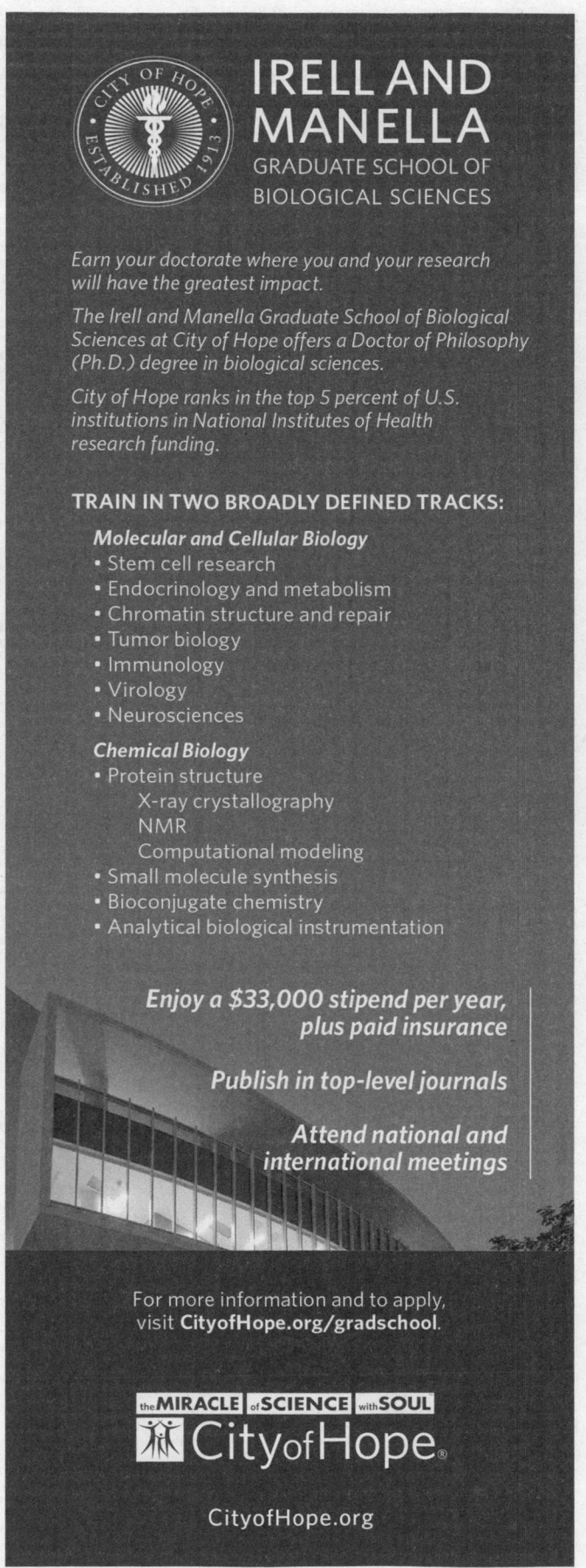

PRAXIS II (subject area assessments) for initial teacher preparation programs that lead to licensure. *Entrance requirements:* For master's, GRE (for full-time programs only); PRAXIS I/core or state-approved alternative (for initial teacher preparation programs that lead to licensure), minimum of bachelor's degree from regionally- or nationally-accredited institution; minimum GPA of 3.0 in all previous programs of study; official transcripts from all post-secondary institutions attended; essay; curriculum vitae/resume; letters of recommendation (3 for full-time programs, 2 for part-time programs); dispositions survey. Additional exam requirements/recommendations for international students: Required—TOEFL (minimum score 600 paper-based; 100 iBT), IELTS (minimum score 7). Electronic applications accepted. *Expenses:* Contact institution.

Johns Hopkins University, School of Medicine, Graduate Programs in Medicine, Baltimore, MD 21218. Offers MA, PhD. *Degree requirements:* For doctorate, thesis/dissertation. *Entrance requirements:* Additional exam requirements/recommendations for international students: Required—TOEFL. Electronic applications accepted. *Expenses:* Contact institution.

Johns Hopkins University, Zanvyl Krieger School of Arts and Sciences, Chemistry-Biology Interface Program, Baltimore, MD 21218. Offers chemical biology (MS, PhD). *Faculty:* 28 full-time (6 women). *Students:* 34 full-time (10 women); includes 10 minority (4 Asian, non-Hispanic/Latino; 3 Hispanic/Latino; 3 Two or more races, non-Hispanic/Latino). Average age 25. 86 applicants, 17% accepted, 5 enrolled. In 2017, 4 master's, 3 doctorates awarded. Terminal master's awarded for partial completion of doctoral program. *Degree requirements:* For master's, comprehensive exam, 8 one-semester courses, oral exam; for doctorate, comprehensive exam, thesis/dissertation, 8 one-semester courses, research proposal, oral exam. *Entrance requirements:* For doctorate, GRE General Test; GRE Subject Test in biochemistry, cell and molecular biology, biology or chemistry (strongly recommended), 3 letters of recommendation, transcripts, statement of purpose, resume/curriculum vitae, interview. Additional exam requirements/recommendations for international students: Required—TOEFL (minimum score 600 paper-based). *Application deadline:* For fall admission, 1/15 for domestic and international students. Applications are processed on a rolling basis. Application fee: $75. Electronic applications accepted. *Expenses:* $10,434 tuition. *Financial support:* Fellowships, teaching assistantships, Federal Work-Study, scholarships/grants, health care benefits, unspecified assistantships, and stipends (averaging $32,470) available. Financial award application deadline: 4/15; financial award applicants required to submit FAFSA. *Faculty research:* Enzyme mechanisms, inhibitors, and metabolic pathways; DNA replication, damaged, and repair; using small molecules to probe signal transduction, gene regulation, angiogenesis, and other biological processes; synthetic methods and medicinal chemistry; synthetic modeling of metalloenzymes. *Unit head:* Dr. Steve Rokita, Director, 410-516-5793, Fax: 410-516-8420, E-mail: rokita@jhu.edu. *Application contact:* Lauren McGhee, Academic Program Administrator, 410-516-7427, Fax: 410-516-8420, E-mail: lauren.mcghee@jhu.edu.
Website: http://www.cbi.jhu.edu

Johns Hopkins University, Zanvyl Krieger School of Arts and Sciences, Program in Cell, Molecular, Developmental Biology, and Biophysics, Baltimore, MD 21218. Offers PhD. Terminal master's awarded for partial completion of doctoral program. *Degree requirements:* For doctorate, comprehensive exam, thesis/dissertation. *Entrance requirements:* For doctorate, GRE General Test. Additional exam requirements/recommendations for international students: Required—TOEFL (minimum score 600 paper-based), IELTS, TWE. Electronic applications accepted. *Faculty research:* Cell biology, molecular biology and development, biochemistry, developmental biology, biophysics, genetics.

Kansas City University of Medicine and Biosciences, College of Biosciences, Kansas City, MO 64106-1453. Offers bioethics (MA); biomedical sciences (MS). *Program availability:* Part-time. *Degree requirements:* For master's, comprehensive exam, thesis (for some programs). *Entrance requirements:* For master's, MCAT, GRE.

Kansas State University, Graduate School, College of Arts and Sciences, Division of Biology, Manhattan, KS 66506. Offers biology (MS). Terminal master's awarded for partial completion of doctoral program. *Degree requirements:* For master's, thesis; for doctorate, thesis/dissertation. *Entrance requirements:* For master's, GRE General Test, minimum undergraduate GPA of 3.0; for doctorate, GRE General Test, minimum GPA of 3.0. Additional exam requirements/recommendations for international students: Required—TOEFL (minimum score 550 paper-based). Electronic applications accepted. *Faculty research:* Ecology, genetics, developmental biology, microbiology, cell biology.

Kansas State University, Graduate School, College of Veterinary Medicine, Department of Diagnostic Medicine/Pathobiology, Manhattan, KS 66506. Offers biomedical science (MS); diagnostic medicine/pathobiology (PhD). Terminal master's awarded for partial completion of doctoral program. *Degree requirements:* For doctorate, thesis/dissertation. *Entrance requirements:* For master's and doctorate, interviews. Additional exam requirements/recommendations for international students: Required—TOEFL (minimum score 550 paper-based). Electronic applications accepted. *Faculty research:* Infectious disease of animals, food safety and security, epidemiology and public health, toxicology, pathology.

Keck Graduate Institute, School of Applied Life Sciences, Claremont, CA 91711. Offers applied life sciences (PhD); bioscience (MBS); bioscience management (Certificate). *Degree requirements:* For master's, comprehensive exam, project. *Entrance requirements:* For master's, GRE General Test or MCAT. Additional exam requirements/recommendations for international students: Required—TOEFL. Electronic applications accepted. *Faculty research:* Computational biology, drug discovery and development, molecular and cellular biology, biomedical engineering, biomaterials and tissue engineering.

Kennesaw State University, College of Science and Mathematics, Program in Integrative Biology, Kennesaw, GA 30144. Offers MS. *Degree requirements:* For master's, thesis. *Entrance requirements:* For master's, GRE, two letters of recommendation, official transcript, statement of interest. Additional exam requirements/recommendations for international students: Required—TOEFL (minimum score 550 paper-based; 80 iBT), IELTS (minimum score 6.5). *Application deadline:* For fall admission, 2/1 for domestic and international students. Application fee: $60. Electronic applications accepted. *Financial support:* Research assistantships with full tuition reimbursements and unspecified assistantships available. Financial award application deadline: 4/1; financial award applicants required to submit FAFSA. *Unit head:* Dr. Joe Dirnberger, Coordinator, 470-578-6546, E-mail: jdirnber@kennesaw.edu. *Application contact:* Admissions Counselor, 470-578-4377, Fax: 470-578-9172, E-mail: ksugrad@kennesaw.edu.
Website: http://csm.kennesaw.edu/msib/

Kent State University, College of Arts and Sciences, Department of Biological Sciences, Kent, OH 44242-0001. Offers biological sciences (MA, MS, PhD), including botany (MS, PhD), cell biology (MS, PhD), ecology (MS, PhD), physiology (MS, PhD). *Program availability:* Part-time. *Faculty:* 28 full-time (10 women), 3 part-time/adjunct (2 women). *Students:* 55 full-time (37 women), 10 part-time (6 women); includes 6 minority (3 Black or African American, non-Hispanic/Latino; 1 Asian, non-Hispanic/Latino; 2 Two or more races, non-Hispanic/Latino), 12 international. Average age 28. 27 applicants, 56% accepted, 11 enrolled. In 2017, 4 master's, 6 doctorates awarded. Terminal

master's awarded for partial completion of doctoral program. *Degree requirements:* For master's, thesis (for some programs), departmental seminar presentation about research (for MS); for doctorate, thesis/dissertation, departmental seminar presentation about research, admitted to doctoral candidacy following written and oral candidacy. *Entrance requirements:* For master's, GRE, minimum GPA of 3.0, official transcripts, goal statement, three letters of recommendation, list of up to five potential faculty advisors, undergraduate coursework roughly equivalent to a biology minor; for doctorate, GRE, official transcripts, goal statement, three letters of recommendation, list of up to five potential faculty advisors, baccalaureate degree with strong background in biology and related subjects such as chemistry and mathematics. Additional exam requirements/recommendations for international students: Required—TOEFL (minimum score 587 paper-based, 94 iBT), Michigan English Language Assessment Battery (minimum score 82), IELTS (7.0), or PTE (65). *Application deadline:* For fall admission, 12/15 for domestic students, 12/5 for international students. Applications are processed on a rolling basis. Application fee: $45 ($70 for international students). Electronic applications accepted. *Expenses:* Tuition, state resident: full-time $11,310; part-time $515 per credit hour. Tuition, nonresident: full-time $20,396; part-time $928 per credit hour. *International tuition:* $18,544 full-time. *Financial support:* Research assistantships with full tuition reimbursements, teaching assistantships with full tuition reimbursements, Federal Work-Study, scholarships/grants, and unspecified assistantships available. Financial award application deadline: 12/15. *Unit head:* Dr. James L. Blank, Dean, 330-672-2650, E-mail: jblank@kent.edu. *Application contact:* Dr. Heather K. Caldwell, Associate Professor and Graduate Coordinator, 330-672-3636, E-mail: hcaldwel@kent.edu.
Website: http://www.kent.edu/biology

Kent State University, College of Arts and Sciences, School of Biomedical Sciences, Kent, OH 44242-0001. Offers biological anthropology (PhD); biomedical mathematics (MS, PhD); cellular and molecular biology (MS, PhD), including cellular biology and structures, molecular biology and genetics; neurosciences (MS, PhD); pharmacology (MS, PhD); physiology (MS, PhD). *Faculty:* 22 full-time (9 women), 3 part-time/adjunct (1 woman). *Students:* 75 full-time (46 women); includes 8 minority (1 Black or African American, non-Hispanic/Latino; 3 Asian, non-Hispanic/Latino; 2 Hispanic/Latino; 2 Two or more races, non-Hispanic/Latino), 25 international. Average age 28. 70 applicants, 23% accepted, 13 enrolled. In 2017, 23 master's, 5 doctorates awarded. Terminal master's awarded for partial completion of doctoral program. *Degree requirements:* For master's, thesis; for doctorate, comprehensive exam, thesis/dissertation. *Entrance requirements:* For master's, GRE, bachelor's degree, transcripts, minimum GPA of 3.0, goal statement, three letters of recommendation, academic preparation adequate to perform graduate work in the desired field; for doctorate, GRE, master's degree, minimum GPA of 3.0, transcripts, goal statement, three letters of recommendation. Additional exam requirements/recommendations for international students: Required—TOEFL (minimum score 600 paper-based, 100 iBT), Michigan English Language Assessment Battery (minimum score 85), IELTS (minimum score 7.0) or PTE (minimum score 68). *Application deadline:* For fall admission, 1/1 for domestic and international students. Applications are processed on a rolling basis. Application fee: $45 ($70 for international students). Electronic applications accepted. *Expenses:* Tuition, state resident: full-time $11,310; part-time $515 per credit hour. Tuition, nonresident: full-time $20,396; part-time $928 per credit hour. *International tuition:* $18,544 full-time. *Financial support:* Research assistantships with full tuition reimbursements, teaching assistantships, and unspecified assistantships available. Financial award application deadline: 1/1. *Unit head:* Dr. Ernest J. Freeman, Director, School of Biomedical Sciences, 330-672-2363, E-mail: efreema2@kent.edu.
Website: http://www.kent.edu/biomedical/

Kutztown University of Pennsylvania, College of Education, Program in Secondary Education, Kutztown, PA 19530-0730. Offers biology (M Ed); curriculum and instruction (M Ed); English (M Ed); mathematics (M Ed); middle level (M Ed); social studies (M Ed); teaching (M Ed); transformational teaching and learning (Ed D). *Accreditation:* NCATE. *Program availability:* Part-time, evening/weekend, 100% online, blended/hybrid learning. *Faculty:* 4 full-time (3 women), 1 part-time/adjunct (0 women). *Students:* 33 full-time (21 women), 76 part-time (49 women); includes 6 minority (3 Black or African American, non-Hispanic/Latino; 3 Hispanic/Latino). Average age 32. 76 applicants, 91% accepted, 43 enrolled. In 2017, 31 master's awarded. *Degree requirements:* For master's, comprehensive exam, thesis optional; for doctorate, thesis/dissertation. *Entrance requirements:* For master's, GRE General Test, minimum undergraduate major GPA of 3.0, 3 letters of recommendation, copy of PRAXIS II or valid instructional I or II teaching certificate; for doctorate, master's or specialist degree in education or related field from regionally-accredited institution of higher learning with minimum graduate GPA of 3.25, significant educational experience, employment in an education setting (preferred). Additional exam requirements/recommendations for international students: Required—TOEFL (minimum score 550 paper-based, 79 iBT), IELTS (minimum score 6.5), or PTE (minimum score 53). *Application deadline:* For fall admission, 8/1 for domestic and international students; for spring admission, 12/1 for domestic and international students. Application fee: $35. Electronic applications accepted. *Expenses:* Tuition, state resident: part-time $500 per credit. Tuition, nonresident: part-time $750 per credit. *Required fees:* $115 per credit. One-time fee: $50 part-time. Tuition and fees vary according to degree level. *Financial support:* Career-related internships or fieldwork, Federal Work-Study, scholarships/grants, and unspecified assistantships available. Financial award application deadline: 3/1; financial award applicants required to submit FAFSA. *Unit head:* Dr. Theresa Stahler, Department Chair, 610-683-4259, Fax: 610-683-1338, E-mail: stahler@kutztown.edu. *Application contact:* Dr. Patricia Walsh Coates, Graduate Coordinator, 610-638-4289, Fax: 610-683-1338, E-mail: coates@kutztown.edu.
Website: https://www.kutztown.edu/academcs/graduate-programs/secondary-education.htm

Lake Erie College of Osteopathic Medicine, Professional Programs, Erie, PA 16509-1025. Offers biomedical sciences (Postbaccalaureate Certificate); medical education (MS); osteopathic medicine (DO); pharmacy (Pharm D). *Accreditation:* ACPE; AOsA. *Degree requirements:* For doctorate, comprehensive exam, National Osteopathic Medical Licensing Exam, Levels 1 and 2; for Postbaccalaureate Certificate, comprehensive exam, North American Pharmacist Licensure Examination (NAPLEX). *Entrance requirements:* For doctorate, MCAT, minimum GPA of 3.2, letters of recommendation; for Postbaccalaureate Certificate, PCAT, letters of recommendation, minimum GPA of 3.5. Electronic applications accepted. *Faculty research:* Cardiac smooth and skeletal muscle mechanics, chemotherapeutics and vitamins, osteopathic manipulation.

Lakehead University, Graduate Studies, Faculty of Social Sciences and Humanities, Department of Biology, Thunder Bay, ON P7B 5E1, Canada. Offers M Sc. *Program availability:* Part-time, evening/weekend. *Degree requirements:* For master's, thesis, department seminary, oral examination. *Entrance requirements:* For master's, minimum B average. Additional exam requirements/recommendations for international students: Required—TOEFL. *Faculty research:* Systematics and biogeography, wildlife parasitology, plant physiology and biochemistry, plant ecology, fishery biology.

Lamar University, College of Graduate Studies, College of Arts and Sciences, Department of Biology, Beaumont, TX 77701. Offers MS. *Program availability:* Part-time, evening/weekend. *Faculty:* 14 full-time (4 women), 2 part-time/adjunct (both women). *Students:* 4 full-time (all women), 7 part-time (3 women); includes 4 minority (1 Black or African American, non-Hispanic/Latino; 2 Asian, non-Hispanic/Latino; 1 Two or more races, non-Hispanic/Latino), 3 international. Average age 27. 5 applicants, 100% accepted. *Degree requirements:* For master's, thesis. *Entrance requirements:* For master's, GRE General Test, minimum GPA of 2.5 in last 60 hours of undergraduate course work. Additional exam requirements/recommendations for international students: Required—TOEFL (minimum score 550 paper-based; 79 iBT), IELTS (minimum score 6.5). *Application deadline:* For fall admission, 8/10 for domestic students, 7/1 for international students; for spring admission, 1/5 for domestic students, 12/1 for international students. Applications are processed on a rolling basis. Application fee: $25 ($50 for international students). Electronic applications accepted. *Expenses:* Contact institution. *Financial support:* In 2017–18, 3 teaching assistantships (averaging $6,200 per year) were awarded. Financial award application deadline: 4/1. *Faculty research:* Microbiology, limnology, vertebrate ecology, invertebrate hemoglobin, ornithology. *Unit head:* Dr. Paul Nicoletto, Chair, 409-880-8262, Fax: 409-880-7147. *Application contact:* Deidre Mayer, Interim Director, Admissions and Academic Services, 409-880-8888, Fax: 409-880-7419, E-mail: gradmissions@lamar.edu.
Website: http://artssciences.lamar.edu/biology

Laurentian University, School of Graduate Studies and Research, Programme in Biology, Sudbury, ON P3E 2C6, Canada. Offers biology (M Sc); boreal ecology (PhD). *Program availability:* Part-time. *Degree requirements:* For master's, thesis. *Entrance requirements:* For master's, honors degree with second class or better. *Faculty research:* Recovery of acid-stressed lakes, effects of climate change, origin and maintenance of biocomplexity, radionuclide dynamics, cytogenetic studies of plants.

Lee University, Program in Education, Cleveland, TN 37320-3450. Offers art (MAT); curriculum and instruction (M Ed, Ed S); early childhood (MAT); educational leadership (M Ed, Ed S); elementary education (MAT); English and math (MAT); English and science (MAT); English and social studies (MAT); higher education administration (MS); history (MAT); history and economics (MAT); math and science (MAT); math and social studies (MAT); middle grades (MAT); science and social studies (MASW); secondary education (MAT); Spanish (MAT); special education (M Ed, MAT); TESOL (MAT). *Accreditation:* NCATE. *Program availability:* Part-time. *Faculty:* 15 full-time (7 women), 8 part-time/adjunct (3 women). *Students:* 28 full-time (21 women), 77 part-time (48 women); includes 12 minority (7 Black or African American, non-Hispanic/Latino; 2 Hispanic/Latino; 3 Two or more races, non-Hispanic/Latino), 1 international. Average age 31. 35 applicants, 83% accepted, 22 enrolled. In 2017, 54 master's, 4 other advanced degrees awarded. *Degree requirements:* For master's, variable foreign language requirement, thesis optional, internship. *Entrance requirements:* For master's, MAT or GRE General Test, minimum undergraduate GPA of 2.75, 3 letters of recommendation, interview, writing sample, official transcripts, background check; for Ed S, minimum undergraduate and master's GPA of 2.75, official transcripts for undergraduate and master's degrees. Additional exam requirements/recommendations for international students: Required—TOEFL (minimum score 61 iBT). *Application deadline:* For fall admission, 6/1 priority date for domestic and international students; for spring admission, 11/1 priority date for domestic and international students; for summer admission, 4/1 priority date for domestic and international students. Applications are processed on a rolling basis. Application fee: $25. Electronic applications accepted. *Expenses: Tuition:* Full-time $12,780; part-time $710 per credit hour. *Required fees:* $60; $60 per term. Tuition and fees vary according to program. *Financial support:* In 2017–18, 32 students received support. Career-related internships or fieldwork, Federal Work-Study, institutionally sponsored loans, scholarships/grants, and unspecified assistantships available. Financial award application deadline: 3/1; financial award applicants required to submit FAFSA. *Unit head:* Dr. William Kamm, Director, 423-614-8544, E-mail: wkamm@leeuniversity.edu. *Application contact:* Crystal Keeter, Graduate Education Secretary, 423-614-8544, E-mail: ckeeter@leeuniversity.edu.
Website: http://www.leeuniversity.edu/academics/graduate/education

Lehigh University, College of Arts and Sciences, Department of Biological Sciences, Bethlehem, PA 18015. Offers biochemistry (PhD); cell and molecular biology (PhD); integrative biology (PhD); molecular biology (MS). *Program availability:* 100% online. *Faculty:* 18 full-time (8 women). *Students:* 38 full-time (20 women), 21 part-time (15 women); includes 12 minority (2 Black or African American, non-Hispanic/Latino; 1 American Indian or Alaska Native, non-Hispanic/Latino; 1 Asian, non-Hispanic/Latino; 6 Hispanic/Latino; 2 Two or more races, non-Hispanic/Latino), 10 international. Average age 28. 33 applicants, 42% accepted, 4 enrolled. In 2017, 8 master's, 4 doctorates awarded. Terminal master's awarded for partial completion of doctoral program. *Degree requirements:* For master's, thesis optional; for doctorate, comprehensive exam, thesis/dissertation. *Entrance requirements:* For doctorate, GRE General Test. Additional exam requirements/recommendations for international students: Required—TOEFL (minimum score 85 iBT). *Application deadline:* For fall admission, 7/15 for domestic and international students; for spring admission, 12/1 for domestic and international students; for summer admission, 4/30 for domestic and international students. Application fee: $75. Electronic applications accepted. *Expenses:* $1,460 per credit. *Financial support:* In 2017–18, 39 students received support, including 8 fellowships with full tuition reimbursements available (averaging $27,600 per year), 17 research assistantships with full tuition reimbursements available (averaging $27,600 per year), 23 teaching assistantships with full tuition reimbursements available (averaging $27,600 per year); health care benefits and tuition waivers also available. Financial award application deadline: 12/1; financial award applicants required to submit CSS PROFILE or FAFSA. *Faculty research:* Gene expression, cytoskeleton and cell structure, cell cycle and growth regulation, neuroscience, animal behavior, microbiology. *Total annual research expenditures:* $1.8 million. *Unit head:* Dr. Linda Lowe-Krentz, Chairperson, 610-758-5084, Fax: 610-758-4004, E-mail: lij0@lehigh.edu. *Application contact:* Dr. Amber Rice, Graduate Coordinator, 610-758-5509, Fax: 610-758-4004, E-mail: amr511@lehigh.edu.
Website: http://www.lehigh.edu/~inbios/

Lehman College of the City University of New York, School of Natural and Social Sciences, Department of Biological Sciences, Program in Biology, Bronx, NY 10468-1589. Offers MA.

Liberty University, School of Health Sciences, Lynchburg, VA 24515. Offers anatomy and cell biology (PhD); biomedical sciences (MS); epidemiology (MPH); exercise science (MS), including clinical, community physical activity, human performance, nutrition; global health (MPH); health promotion (MPH); medical sciences (MA), including biopsychology, business management, health informatics, molecular medicine, public health; nutrition (MPH). *Program availability:* Part-time, online learning. *Students:* 542 full-time (394 women), 696 part-time (541 women); includes 402 minority (286 Black or African American, non-Hispanic/Latino; 10 American Indian or Alaska Native, non-Hispanic/Latino; 34 Asian, non-Hispanic/Latino; 46 Hispanic/Latino; 1 Native Hawaiian or other Pacific Islander, non-Hispanic/Latino; 25 Two or more races, non-Hispanic/Latino), 59 international. Average age 32. 1,592 applicants, 40% accepted, 297 enrolled. In 2017, 204 master's awarded. *Degree requirements:* For master's, thesis (for some programs); for doctorate, thesis/dissertation. *Entrance requirements:* For doctorate, MAT or GRE, minimum GPA of 3.25 in master's program, 2-3 recommendations, writing samples (for some programs), letter of intent, professional vitae. Additional exam requirements/recommendations for international students: Required—TOEFL (minimum score 600 paper-based; 100 iBT). Application fee: $50. *Financial support:* Applicants required to submit FAFSA. *Unit head:* Dr. Ralph Linstra, Dean. *Application contact:* Jay Bridge, Director of Admissions, 800-424-9595, Fax: 800-628-7977, E-mail: gradadmissions@liberty.edu.

London Metropolitan University, Graduate Programs, London, United Kingdom. Offers applied psychology (M Sc); architecture (MA); biomedical science (M Sc); blood science (M Sc); cancer pharmacology (M Sc); computer networking and cyber security (M Sc); computing and information systems (M Sc); conference interpreting (MA); counter-terrorism studies (M Sc); creative, digital and professional writing (MA); crime, violence and prevention (M Sc); criminology (M Sc); curating contemporary art (MA); data analytics (M Sc); digital media (MA); early childhood studies (MA); education (MA, Ed D); financial services law, regulation and compliance (LL M); food science (M Sc); forensic psychology (M Sc); health and social care management and policy (M Sc); human nutrition (M Sc); human resource management (MA); human rights and international conflict (MA); information technology (M Sc); intelligence and security studies (M Sc); international oil, gas and energy law (LL M); international relations (MA); interpreting (MA); learning and teaching in higher education (MA); legal practice (LL M); media and entertainment law (LL M); organizational and consumer psychology (M Sc); psychological therapy (M Sc); psychology of mental health (M Sc); public health (M Sc); public policy and management (MPA); security studies (M Sc); social work (M Sc); spatial planning and urban design (MA); sports therapy (M Sc); supporting older children and young people with dyslexia (MA); teaching languages (MA), including Arabic, English; translation (MA); woman and child abuse (MA).

Long Island University–LIU Brooklyn, Richard L. Conolly College of Liberal Arts and Sciences, Brooklyn, NY 11201-8423. Offers biology (MS); chemistry (MS); clinical psychology (PhD); creative writing (MFA); English (MA); media arts (MA, MFA); political science (MA); psychology (MA); social science (MS); United Nations (Advanced Certificate); urban studies (MA); writing and production for television (MFA). *Program availability:* Part-time. *Faculty:* 32 full-time (13 women), 17 part-time/adjunct (6 women). *Students:* 178 full-time (123 women), 143 part-time (96 women); includes 128 minority (65 Black or African American, non-Hispanic/Latino; 22 Asian, non-Hispanic/Latino; 31 Hispanic/Latino; 10 Two or more races, non-Hispanic/Latino), 54 international. Average age 30. 629 applicants, 38% accepted, 74 enrolled. In 2017, 147 master's, 9 doctorates, 8 other advanced degrees awarded. Terminal master's awarded for partial completion of doctoral program. *Degree requirements:* For master's, comprehensive exam (for some programs), thesis (for some programs); for doctorate, thesis/dissertation. *Entrance requirements:* For doctorate, GRE. Additional exam requirements/recommendations for international students: Required—TOEFL (minimum score 550 paper-based, 79 iBT) or IELTS. *Application deadline:* Applications are processed on a rolling basis. Application fee: $50. Electronic applications accepted. *Expenses: Tuition:* Full-time $21,618; part-time $1201 per credit. *Required fees:* $1840; $920 per term. Tuition and fees vary according to course load. *Financial support:* In 2017–18, 214 students received support, including 120 fellowships with full and partial tuition reimbursements available (averaging $915 per year), 5 research assistantships with full and partial tuition reimbursements available (averaging $2,300 per year), 136 teaching assistantships with full and partial tuition reimbursements available (averaging $2,300 per year); career-related internships or fieldwork, Federal Work-Study, institutionally sponsored loans, scholarships/grants, and unspecified assistantships also available. Support available to part-time students. Financial award application deadline: 2/15; financial award applicants required to submit FAFSA. *Faculty research:* Quantum gravity and astrophysics; string theory; pharmaceutical biotechnology with a focus on molecular details of drug susceptibility/resistance mechanisms; entomology, population and community ecology, agroecology, and biodiversity; psychotherapy process-outcome, particularly therapeutic alliance development, the role of common factors, and the study of treatment failures; personality pathology, borderline personality disorder and pathological narcissism. *Unit head:* Dr. Scott Krawczyk, Dean, 718-488-1003, E-mail: scott.krawczyk@liu.edu. *Application contact:* Bayu Sutrisno, Graduate Admissions Counselor, 718-488-1564, Fax: 718-780-6110, E-mail: bayu.sutrisno@liu.edu.

Long Island University–LIU Post, College of Liberal Arts and Sciences, Brookville, NY 11548-1300. Offers applied mathematics (MS); behavior analysis (MA); biology (MS); criminal justice (MS); earth science (MS); English (MA); environmental sustainability (MS); genetic counseling (MS); history (MA); interdisciplinary studies (MA, MS); political science (MA); psychology (MA). *Program availability:* Part-time, evening/weekend, blended/hybrid learning. *Faculty:* 41 full-time (21 women), 24 part-time/adjunct (13 women). *Students:* 173 full-time (124 women), 62 part-time (35 women); includes 54 minority (11 Black or African American, non-Hispanic/Latino; 13 Asian, non-Hispanic/Latino; 23 Hispanic/Latino; 7 Two or more races, non-Hispanic/Latino), 12 international. Average age 28. 368 applicants, 54% accepted, 74 enrolled. In 2017, 89 master's, 15 other advanced degrees awarded. Terminal master's awarded for partial completion of doctoral program. *Degree requirements:* For master's, comprehensive exam (for some programs), thesis (for some programs). *Entrance requirements:* Additional exam requirements/recommendations for international students: Required—TOEFL, IELTS, or PTE. *Application deadline:* Applications are processed on a rolling basis. Application fee: $50. Electronic applications accepted. *Expenses: Tuition:* Full-time $21,618; part-time $1201 per credit. *Required fees:* $1840; $920 per term. Tuition and fees vary according to course load. *Financial support:* In 2017–18, 165 students received support. Fellowships, research assistantships, teaching assistantships, career-related internships or fieldwork, Federal Work-Study, scholarships/grants, tuition waivers (partial), and unspecified assistantships available. Support available to part-time students. Financial award application deadline: 2/15; financial award applicants required to submit FAFSA. *Faculty research:* Biology, environmental sustainability, mathematics, psychology, genetic counseling. *Unit head:* Dr. Nathaniel Bowditch, Dean, 516-299-2234, Fax: 516-299-4140, E-mail: nathaniel.bowditch@liu.edu. *Application contact:* Rita Langdon, Graduate Admissions, 516-299-2900, Fax: 516-299-2137, E-mail: post-enroll@liu.edu.
Website: http://liu.edu/CWPost/Academics/Schools/CLAS

Long Island University–LIU Post, School of Health Professions and Nursing, Brookville, NY 11548-1300. Offers biomedical science (MS); cardiovascular perfusion (MS); clinical lab sciences (MS); clinical laboratory management (MS); dietetic internship (Advanced Certificate); family nurse practitioner (MS, Advanced Certificate); forensic social work (Advanced Certificate); gerontology (Advanced Certificate); health administration (MPA); non-profit management (Advanced Certificate); nursing education (MS); nutrition (MS); public administration (MPA); social work (MSW). *Program availability:* Part-time, blended/hybrid learning. *Faculty:* 23 full-time (17 women), 33 part-time/adjunct (19 women). *Students:* 228 full-time (174 women), 227 part-time (185 women); includes 172 minority (76 Black or African American, non-Hispanic/Latino; 1 American Indian or Alaska Native, non-Hispanic/Latino; 44 Asian, non-Hispanic/Latino; 48 Hispanic/Latino; 3 Two or more races, non-Hispanic/Latino), 60 international. Average age 31. 392 applicants, 67% accepted, 138 enrolled. In 2017, 180 master's, 26 other advanced degrees awarded. *Degree requirements:* For master's, comprehensive exam (for some programs), thesis (for some programs). *Entrance requirements:* Additional exam requirements/recommendations for international students: Required—TOEFL (minimum score 85 iBT) or IELTS (7.5). *Application deadline:* Applications are processed on a rolling basis. Application fee: $50. Electronic applications accepted. *Expenses: Tuition:* Full-time $21,618; part-time $1201 per credit. *Required fees:* $1840; $920 per term. Tuition and fees vary according to course load. *Financial support:* In 2017–18, 102 students received support. Research assistantships, teaching assistantships, career-related internships or fieldwork, Federal Work-Study, scholarships/grants, and unspecified assistantships available. Support available to part-time students. Financial award application deadline: 2/15; financial award applicants required to submit FAFSA. *Faculty research:* Antibiotic resistance, evidence-based practice, family care, interprofessional learning, simulation learning. *Unit head:* Dr. Stacy Gropack, Dean, 516-299-2485, Fax: 516-299-2527, E-mail: post-shpn@liu.edu. *Application contact:* Kathy Riley, Associate Director of Graduate Admissions, 516-299-2900, Fax: 516-299-2137, E-mail: post-enroll@liu.edu.
Website: http://liu.edu/post/health

Louisiana State University and Agricultural & Mechanical College, Graduate School, College of Science, Department of Biological Sciences, Baton Rouge, LA 70803. Offers biochemistry (MS, PhD); biological science (MS, PhD); science (MNS). *Faculty:* 57 full-time (12 women). *Students:* 123 full-time (54 women), 3 part-time (1 woman); includes 20 minority (7 Black or African American, non-Hispanic/Latino; 4 Asian, non-Hispanic/Latino; 7 Hispanic/Latino; 2 Two or more races, non-Hispanic/Latino), 46 international. Average age 29. 70 applicants, 24% accepted, 17 enrolled. In 2017, 1 master's, 18 doctorates awarded. *Financial support:* In 2017–18, 10 fellowships (averaging $37,093 per year), 15 research assistantships (averaging $24,248 per year), 94 teaching assistantships (averaging $22,610 per year) were awarded. *Total annual research expenditures:* $8.6 million.

Louisiana State University Health Sciences Center, School of Graduate Studies in New Orleans, New Orleans, LA 70112-2223. Offers PhD, MD/PhD. *Faculty:* 159 full-time (45 women). *Students:* 70 full-time (41 women); includes 18 minority (6 Black or African American, non-Hispanic/Latino; 10 Asian, non-Hispanic/Latino; 2 Hispanic/Latino), 6 international. Average age 26. 58 applicants, 34% accepted, 15 enrolled. In 2017, 15 doctorates awarded. Terminal master's awarded for partial completion of doctoral program. *Degree requirements:* For doctorate, comprehensive exam, thesis/dissertation. *Entrance requirements:* For doctorate, GRE General Test. Additional exam requirements/recommendations for international students: Recommended—TOEFL, IELTS. *Application deadline:* For fall admission, 4/1 for domestic and international students. Applications are processed on a rolling basis. Application fee: $30. *Expenses:* Contact institution. *Financial support:* In 2017–18, 61 students received support. Tuition waivers (full) and unspecified assistantships available. Financial award application deadline: 4/1. *Unit head:* Dr. Joseph M. Moerschbaecher, III, Head, 504-568-2211, Fax: 504-568-2361. *Application contact:* Leigh Smith-Vaniz, Coordinator of Student Affairs, 504-568-2211, Fax: 504-568-5588, E-mail: lsmi30@lsuhsc.edu.
Website: http://graduatestudies.lsuhsc.edu

Louisiana State University Health Sciences Center at Shreveport, Master of Science in Biomedical Sciences Program, Shreveport, LA 71130-3932. Offers MS. Terminal master's awarded for partial completion of doctoral program. *Degree requirements:* For master's, thesis, seminar and journal club presentations, research component. *Entrance requirements:* For master's, GRE. Additional exam requirements/recommendations for international students: Required—TOEFL, IELTS. *Faculty research:* Cardiovascular, cancer, neuroscience, genetics, virology, immunology.

Louisiana State University in Shreveport, College of Arts and Sciences, Program in Biological Sciences, Shreveport, LA 71115-2399. Offers MS. *Program availability:* Part-time, evening/weekend. *Students:* 25 full-time (13 women), 10 part-time (6 women); includes 12 minority (6 Black or African American, non-Hispanic/Latino; 3 Hispanic/Latino; 3 Two or more races, non-Hispanic/Latino), 2 international. Average age 28. 76 applicants, 89% accepted, 15 enrolled. In 2017, 22 master's awarded. *Degree requirements:* For master's, comprehensive exam (for some programs), thesis optional. *Entrance requirements:* For master's, GRE. Additional exam requirements/recommendations for international students: Required—TOEFL (minimum score 550 paper-based; 61 iBT). *Application deadline:* For fall admission, 6/30 for domestic and international students; for spring admission, 11/30 for domestic and international students; for summer admission, 4/30 for domestic and international students. Applications are processed on a rolling basis. Application fee: $20 ($30 for international students). Electronic applications accepted. *Expenses:* Tuition, state resident: full-time $3098; part-time $344 per credit hour. Tuition, nonresident: full-time $9923; part-time $1103 per credit hour. *Required fees:* $384 per semester. Tuition and fees vary according to program. *Financial support:* Applicants required to submit FAFSA. *Unit head:* Dr. Tara Williams-Hart, Director, 318-797-5220, E-mail: tara.williams-hart@lsus.edu. *Application contact:* Mary Catherine Harvison, Director of Admissions, 318-797-2400, Fax: 318-797-5286, E-mail: mary.harvison@lsus.edu.
Website: http://www.lsus.edu/academics/graduate-studies/graduate-programs/master-of-science-in-biological-sciences

Louisiana Tech University, Graduate School, College of Applied and Natural Sciences, Ruston, LA 71272. Offers biology (MS); dietetics (Graduate Certificate); health informatics (MHI); molecular science and nanotechnology (MS, PhD). *Program availability:* Part-time. *Faculty:* 56 full-time (31 women), 10 part-time/adjunct (4 women). *Students:* 75 full-time (49 women), 32 part-time (23 women); includes 32 minority (19 Black or African American, non-Hispanic/Latino; 4 Asian, non-Hispanic/Latino; 8 Hispanic/Latino; 1 Two or more races, non-Hispanic/Latino), 9 international. Average age 29. 46 applicants, 67% accepted, 10 enrolled. In 2017, 36 master's, 1 doctorate, 15 other advanced degrees awarded. *Degree requirements:* For master's, comprehensive exam (for some programs), thesis (for some programs); for doctorate, comprehensive exam, thesis/dissertation. *Entrance requirements:* For master's and doctorate, GRE General Test, transcript with bachelor's degree awarded; for Graduate Certificate, transcript with bachelor's degree awarded. Additional exam requirements/recommendations for international students: Required—TOEFL (minimum score 550 paper-based; 80 iBT), IELTS (minimum score 6.5). *Application deadline:* For fall admission, 8/1 priority date for domestic students, 6/1 for international students; for winter admission, 11/1 priority date for domestic students, 9/1 for international students; for spring admission, 2/1 priority date for domestic students, 12/1 for international students; for summer admission, 5/1 priority date for domestic students, 3/1 for international students. Applications are processed on a rolling basis. Application fee: $40. Electronic applications accepted. *Expenses:* Tuition, state resident: full-time $5146. Tuition, nonresident: full-time $10,147. *International tuition:* $10,267 full-time. *Required fees:* $2273. *Financial support:* In 2017–18, 19 students received support, including 19 research assistantships with partial tuition reimbursements available (averaging $8,817 per year); career-related internships or fieldwork, Federal Work-Study, scholarships/grants, and unspecified assistantships also available. Financial award application deadline: 2/1. *Faculty research:* Developmentally appropriate practices in early childhood education, maternal and child nutrition, nutrition and cardiovascular disease, and early intervention for infants and toddlers; research in cell and molecular biology; health promotion in emerging adults, insulin pump use, forensic

nursing, qualitative research, empathy in nursing students, civility in nursing education, and STI education; gene expression data analysis and data mining, knowledge discovery for health related data. *Unit head:* Dr. Gary A. Kennedy, Dean, 318-257-4287, Fax: 318-257-5060, E-mail: kennedy@latech.edu.
Website: http://ans.latech.edu/

Louisiana Tech University, Graduate School, College of Education, Ruston, LA 71272. Offers counseling and guidance (MA), including clinical mental health counseling, human services, orientation and mobility; counseling psychology (PhD); curriculum and instruction (M Ed); cyber education (Graduate Certificate); dynamics of domestic and family violence (Graduate Certificate); early childhood education - PreK-3 (MAT); educational leadership (M Ed, Ed D); elementary education and special education mild/moderate grades 1-5 (MAT); higher education administration (Graduate Certificate); industrial/organizational psychology (MA, PhD); kinesiology (MS); middle school education (MAT), including mathematics; orientation and mobility (Graduate Certificate); rehabilitation teaching for the blind (Graduate Certificate); secondary education (MAT), including agriculture, biology, business, chemistry, English; special education: visually impaired (MAT); teacher leader education (Graduate Certificate); visual impairments - blind education (Graduate Certificate). *Accreditation:* NCATE. *Program availability:* Part-time. *Faculty:* 28 full-time (16 women), 23 part-time/adjunct (22 women). *Students:* 269 full-time (192 women), 194 part-time (150 women); includes 127 minority (94 Black or African American, non-Hispanic/Latino; 2 American Indian or Alaska Native, non-Hispanic/Latino; 6 Asian, non-Hispanic/Latino; 16 Hispanic/Latino; 1 Native Hawaiian or other Pacific Islander, non-Hispanic/Latino; 8 Two or more races, non-Hispanic/Latino), 8 international. Average age 34. 226 applicants, 74% accepted, 60 enrolled. In 2017, 5 master's, 2 doctorates, 1 other advanced degree awarded. *Degree requirements:* For master's, thesis; for doctorate, thesis/dissertation. *Entrance requirements:* For master's and doctorate, GRE General Test. Additional exam requirements/recommendations for international students: Required—TOEFL (minimum score 550 paper-based; 80 iBT), IELTS (minimum score 6.5). *Application deadline:* For fall admission, 9/1 priority date for domestic students, 6/1 for international students; for winter admission, 11/1 priority date for domestic students, 9/1 for international students; for spring admission, 2/1 priority date for domestic students, 12/1 for international students; for summer admission, 5/1 priority date for domestic students, 3/1 for international students. Application fee: $40. Electronic applications accepted. *Expenses:* Tuition, state resident: full-time $5146. Tuition, nonresident: full-time $10,147. *International tuition:* $10,267 full-time. *Required fees:* $2273. *Financial support:* In 2017–18, 40 students received support, including 23 research assistantships (averaging $10,346 per year), 15 teaching assistantships (averaging $6,887 per year); fellowships and career-related internships or fieldwork also available. Financial award application deadline: 2/1. *Faculty research:* Blindness and the best methods for increasing independence for individuals who are blind or visually impaired; educating and investigating factors contributing to improvements in human performance across the lifespan and a reduction in injury rates during training. *Total annual research expenditures:* $2.1 million. *Unit head:* Dr. Don Schillinger, Dean, 318-257-3712, E-mail: dschill@latech.edu. *Application contact:* Dr. Dawn Basinger, Associate Dean of Academic Affairs, 318-257-2977, Fax: 318-257-2379, E-mail: dbasing@latech.edu.
Website: http://education.latech.edu/

Loyola University Chicago, Graduate School, Department of Biology, Chicago, IL 60660. Offers MA, MS. *Faculty:* 21 full-time (8 women). *Students:* 76 full-time (34 women); includes 30 minority (6 Black or African American, non-Hispanic/Latino; 15 Asian, non-Hispanic/Latino; 5 Hispanic/Latino; 4 Two or more races, non-Hispanic/Latino). Average age 25. 301 applicants, 42% accepted, 63 enrolled. In 2017, 66 master's awarded. *Degree requirements:* For master's, thesis. *Entrance requirements:* For master's, GRE General Test, GRE Subject Test, 3 letters of recommendation, BS in biology. Additional exam requirements/recommendations for international students: Required—TOEFL. *Application deadline:* For fall admission, 6/1 for domestic and international students. Applications are processed on a rolling basis. Application fee: $50. Electronic applications accepted. Tuition and fees vary according to course load, degree level and program. *Financial support:* In 2017–18, 7 students received support, including 7 fellowships with full tuition reimbursements available (averaging $16,000 per year); Federal Work-Study and institutionally sponsored loans also available. Financial award application deadline: 2/1; financial award applicants required to submit FAFSA. *Faculty research:* Evolution, systematics, development, organismal biology, aquatic biology, molecular biology and genetics, cell biology, neurobiology. *Total annual research expenditures:* $2.5 million. *Unit head:* Dr. Terry Grande, Graduate Program Director, 773-583-5649, Fax: 773-508-3646, E-mail: tgrande@luc.edu. *Application contact:* Jill Schur, Director of Graduate Enrollment Management, 312-915-8902, E-mail: gradinfo@luc.edu.
Website: http://www.luc.edu/biology/

Loyola University Chicago, Graduate School, Integrated Program in Biomedical Sciences, Maywood, IL 60141. Offers biochemistry and molecular biology (MS, PhD); cell and molecular physiology (MS, PhD); infectious disease and immunology (MS); integrative cell biology (MS, PhD); microbiology and immunology (MS, PhD); molecular pharmacology and therapeutics (MS, PhD); neuroscience (MS, PhD). *Faculty:* 84 full-time (32 women). *Students:* 126 full-time (65 women), 1 (woman) part-time; includes 36 minority (5 Black or African American, non-Hispanic/Latino; 14 Asian, non-Hispanic/Latino; 14 Hispanic/Latino; 3 Two or more races, non-Hispanic/Latino), 13 international. Average age 26. 748 applicants, 34% accepted, 124 enrolled. In 2017, 41 master's, 18 doctorates awarded. *Degree requirements:* For master's, thesis; for doctorate, comprehensive exam, thesis/dissertation. *Entrance requirements:* For doctorate, GRE. Additional exam requirements/recommendations for international students: Required—TOEFL (minimum score 94 iBT), IELTS (minimum score 7.5). *Application deadline:* For fall admission, 2/7 for domestic students. Applications are processed on a rolling basis. Electronic applications accepted. *Expenses:* Contact institution. *Financial support:* In 2017–18, 20 students received support. Schmitt Fellowships and yearly tuition scholarships (averaging $25,032) available. Financial award application deadline: 6/15; financial award applicants required to submit FAFSA. *Unit head:* Dr. Leanne L. Cribbs, Associate Dean, Graduate Education, 708-327-2817, Fax: 708-216-8216, E-mail: lcribbs@luc.edu. *Application contact:* Margarita Quesada, Graduate Program Secretary, 708-216-3532, Fax: 708-216-8216, E-mail: mquesad@luc.edu.
Website: http://ssom.luc.edu/graduate_school/degree-programs/ipbsphd/

Manhattanville College, School of Education, Program in Middle Childhood/Adolescence Education (Grades 5-12), Purchase, NY 10577-2132. Offers biology (MAT, Advanced Certificate); biology and special education (MPS); chemistry (MAT, Advanced Certificate); chemistry and special education (MPS); earth science (Advanced Certificate); education for sustainability (Advanced Certificate); English (MAT, Advanced Certificate); English and special education (MPS); literacy and special education (MPS); literacy specialist (MPS); math and special education (MPS); mathematics (MAT, Advanced Certificate); physics (MAT, Advanced Certificate); social studies (MAT); social studies and special education (MPS); special education generalist (MPS). *Program availability:* Part-time, evening/weekend. *Faculty:* 2 full-time (both women), 5 part-time/adjunct (1 woman). *Students:* 8 full-time (7 women), 28 part-time (16 women); includes 4 minority (1 Asian, non-Hispanic/Latino; 2 Hispanic/Latino; 1 Two or more races, non-Hispanic/Latino). Average age 31. 7 applicants, 86% accepted, 4 enrolled. In 2017, 13 master's, 1 other advanced degree awarded. *Degree requirements:* For master's, comprehensive exam (for some programs), thesis (for some programs), student teaching, research seminars, portfolios, internships, writing assessment; for Advanced Certificate, comprehensive exam (for some programs). *Entrance requirements:* For master's, GRE or MAT (for programs leading to certification), minimum GPA of 3.0, 2 letters of recommendation, interview, essay (2-3 page personal statement that describes reasons for choosing teaching or educational leadership as profession and philosophy of education), proof of immunization (for those born after 1957). Additional exam requirements/recommendations for international students: Required—TOEFL (minimum score 600 paper-based; 110 iBT); Recommended—IELTS (minimum score 8). *Application deadline:* Applications are processed on a rolling basis. Application fee: $75. Electronic applications accepted. *Expenses:* $915 per credit. *Financial support:* Teaching assistantships, career-related internships or fieldwork, Federal Work-Study, institutionally sponsored loans, scholarships/grants, and unspecified assistantships available. Financial award application deadline: 3/15; financial award applicants required to submit FAFSA. *Faculty research:* Education for sustainability. *Unit head:* Dr. Shelly Wepner, Dean, 914-323-3153, Fax: 914-323-5493, E-mail: shelly.wepner@mville.edu. *Application contact:* Alissa Wilson, Director, Graduate Admissions, 914-323-3150, Fax: 914-694-1732, E-mail: edschool@mville.edu.
Website: http://www.mville.edu/programs#/search/19

Marquette University, Graduate School, College of Arts and Sciences, Department of Biology, Milwaukee, WI 53201-1881. Offers cell biology (MS, PhD); developmental biology (MS, PhD); ecology (MS, PhD); epithelial physiology (MS, PhD); genetics (MS, PhD); microbiology (MS, PhD); molecular biology (MS, PhD); muscle and exercise physiology (MS, PhD); neuroscience (PhD). Terminal master's awarded for partial completion of doctoral program. *Degree requirements:* For master's, comprehensive exam, thesis, 1 year of teaching experience or equivalent; for doctorate, thesis/dissertation, 1 year of teaching experience or equivalent, qualifying exam. *Entrance requirements:* For master's and doctorate, GRE General Test, GRE Subject Test, official transcripts from all current and previous colleges/universities except Marquette, statement of professional goals and aspirations, three letters of recommendation. Additional exam requirements/recommendations for international students: Required—TOEFL (minimum score 530 paper-based). Electronic applications accepted. *Faculty research:* Neurobiology, neuroendocrinology, epithelial physiology, neuropeptide interactions, synaptic transmission.

Marshall University, Academic Affairs Division, College of Science, Department of Biological Science, Huntington, WV 25755. Offers MA, MS. *Students:* 28 full-time (13 women), 2 part-time (1 woman); includes 1 minority (Asian, non-Hispanic/Latino). Average age 27. In 2017, 12 master's awarded. *Degree requirements:* For master's, thesis (for some programs). *Entrance requirements:* For master's, GRE General Test. Application fee: $40. *Financial support:* Career-related internships or fieldwork available. *Unit head:* Dr. David Mallory, Chairperson, 304-696-2353, E-mail: mallory@marshall.edu. *Application contact:* Information Contact, 304-746-1900, Fax: 304-746-1902, E-mail: services@marshall.edu.

Marshall University, Joan C. Edwards School of Medicine and Academic Affairs Division, Program in Biomedical Sciences, Huntington, WV 25755. Offers MS, PhD. *Faculty:* 39 full-time (12 women), 3 part-time/adjunct (0 women). *Students:* 49 full-time (25 women), 2 part-time (1 woman); includes 3 minority (all Black or African American, non-Hispanic/Latino), 11 international. Average age 26. 64 applicants, 69% accepted, 23 enrolled. Terminal master's awarded for partial completion of doctoral program. *Degree requirements:* For master's, comprehensive exam, thesis optional; for doctorate, thesis/dissertation, written and oral qualifying exams. *Entrance requirements:* For master's, GRE General Test or MCAT (medical science), 1 year of course work in biology, physics, chemistry, and organic chemistry and associated labs; for doctorate, GRE General Test, 1 year of course work in biology, physics, chemistry, and organic chemistry and associated labs. Additional exam requirements/recommendations for international students: Required—TOEFL (minimum score 525 paper-based). *Application deadline:* Applications are processed on a rolling basis. Application fee: $30 ($40 for international students). *Expenses:* Contact institution. *Financial support:* Research assistantships with tuition reimbursements, career-related internships or fieldwork, Federal Work-Study, and institutionally sponsored loans available. Support available to part-time students. Financial award application deadline: 5/1; financial award applicants required to submit FAFSA. *Faculty research:* Neurosciences, cardiopulmonary science, molecular biology, toxicology, endocrinology. *Unit head:* Dr. Richard M. Niles, Associate Dean for Research and Graduate Education, 304-696-7272, Fax: 304-696-7171, E-mail: niles@marshall.edu. *Application contact:* Dr. Vernon E. Reichenbecher, Director of Graduate Studies, 304-696-7272, Fax: 304-696-7171, E-mail: reichenb@marshall.edu.
Website: http://www.marshall.edu/graduate/

Massachusetts Institute of Technology, School of Engineering, Harvard-MIT Health Sciences and Technology Program, Cambridge, MA 02139. Offers health sciences and technology (SM, PhD, Sc D), including bioastronautics (PhD, Sc D), bioinformatics and integrative genomics (PhD, Sc D), medical engineering and medical physics (PhD, Sc D), speech and hearing bioscience and technology (PhD, Sc D). Terminal master's awarded for partial completion of doctoral program. *Degree requirements:* For doctorate, comprehensive exam, thesis/dissertation. *Entrance requirements:* For doctorate, GRE General Test. Additional exam requirements/recommendations for international students: Required—TOEFL, IELTS. Electronic applications accepted. *Faculty research:* Biomedical imaging, drug delivery, medical devices, medical diagnostics, regenerative biomedical technologies.

Massachusetts Institute of Technology, School of Science, Department of Biology, Cambridge, MA 02139. Offers biochemistry (PhD); biological oceanography (PhD); biology (PhD); biophysical chemistry and molecular structure (PhD); cell biology (PhD); computational and systems biology (PhD); developmental biology (PhD); genetics (PhD); immunology (PhD); microbiology (PhD); molecular biology (PhD); neurobiology (PhD). *Degree requirements:* For doctorate, comprehensive exam, thesis/dissertation, teaching assistantship during two semesters. *Entrance requirements:* For doctorate, GRE General Test. Additional exam requirements/recommendations for international students: Required—TOEFL, IELTS. Electronic applications accepted. *Faculty research:* Cellular, developmental and molecular (plant and animal) biology; biochemistry, bioengineering, biophysics and structural biology; classical and molecular genetics, stem cell and epigenetics; immunology and microbiology; cancer biology, molecular medicine, neurobiology and human disease; computational and systems biology.

McGill University, Faculty of Graduate and Postdoctoral Studies, Faculty of Medicine, Department of Medicine, Montréal, QC H3A 2T5, Canada. Offers experimental medicine (M Sc, PhD), including bioethics (M Sc), experimental medicine.

McGill University, Faculty of Graduate and Postdoctoral Studies, Faculty of Science, Department of Biology, Montréal, QC H3A 2T5, Canada. Offers bioinformatics (M Sc, PhD); environment (M Sc, PhD); neo-tropical environment (M Sc, PhD).

McMaster University, Faculty of Health Sciences, Department of Biochemistry and Biomedical Sciences, Hamilton, ON L8S 4M2, Canada. Offers M Sc, PhD. Terminal master's awarded for partial completion of doctoral program. *Degree requirements:* For master's, thesis; for doctorate, comprehensive exam, thesis/dissertation. *Entrance requirements:* For master's and doctorate, minimum B+ average. Additional exam requirements/recommendations for international students: Required—TOEFL (minimum score 550 paper-based). *Faculty research:* Molecular and cell biology, biomolecular structure and function, molecular pharmacology and toxicology.

McMaster University, Faculty of Health Sciences and School of Graduate Studies, Program in Medical Sciences, Hamilton, ON L8S 4M2, Canada. Offers blood and vascular (M Sc, PhD); genetics and cancer (M Sc, PhD); immunity and infection (M Sc, PhD); metabolism and nutrition (M Sc, PhD); neurosciences and behavioral sciences (M Sc, PhD); physiology/pharmacology (M Sc, PhD); MD/PhD. *Degree requirements:* For master's, thesis; for doctorate, comprehensive exam, thesis/dissertation. *Entrance requirements:* For master's, honors B Sc, B+ average in related field; for doctorate, M Sc, minimum B+ average. Additional exam requirements/recommendations for international students: Required—TOEFL (minimum score 580 paper-based; 92 iBT).

McMaster University, School of Graduate Studies, Faculty of Science, Department of Biology, Hamilton, ON L8S 4M2, Canada. Offers M Sc, PhD. *Program availability:* Part-time. *Degree requirements:* For master's, thesis; for doctorate, comprehensive exam, thesis/dissertation. *Entrance requirements:* Additional exam requirements/recommendations for international students: Required—TOEFL (minimum score 550 paper-based).

Medical College of Wisconsin, Graduate School, Milwaukee, WI 53226-0509. Offers MA, MPH, MS, PhD, Graduate Certificate, MD/PhD. *Program availability:* Part-time, evening/weekend, online learning. *Degree requirements:* For master's, comprehensive exam (for some programs), thesis (for some programs); for doctorate, comprehensive exam, thesis/dissertation. *Entrance requirements:* For master's and doctorate, GRE General Test. Additional exam requirements/recommendations for international students: Required—TOEFL. *Application deadline:* For fall admission, 1/15 priority date for domestic students, 1/15 for international students; for spring admission, 12/1 priority date for domestic students, 12/1 for international students. Applications are processed on a rolling basis. Application fee: $50. Electronic applications accepted. *Financial support:* Research assistantships with full tuition reimbursements, career-related internships or fieldwork, Federal Work-Study, institutionally sponsored loans, scholarships/grants, traineeships, health care benefits, unspecified assistantships, and all full time PhD seekers receive a full tuition scholarship plus cost of living stipend available. Financial award application deadline: 2/15; financial award applicants required to submit FAFSA. *Faculty research:* Clinical and translational science, genomics and proteomics, cancer. *Unit head:* Dr. Ravindra P. Misra, Dean, 414-955-8218, Fax: 414-955-6555, E-mail: gradschool@mcw.edu. *Application contact:* Dr. Ravindra P. Misra, Dean, 414-955-8218, Fax: 414-955-6555, E-mail: gradschool@mcw.edu.
Website: http://www.mcw.edu/graduateschool.htm

Medical College of Wisconsin, Interdisciplinary Program in Biomedical Sciences, Milwaukee, WI 53226-0509. Offers PhD. *Application deadline:* For fall admission, 12/15 priority date for domestic students. Applications are processed on a rolling basis. *Unit head:* Dr. Joseph C. Besharse, Director, 414-955-8063, Fax: 414-955-6517, E-mail: biomed@mcw.edu. *Application contact:* Dr. Joseph C. Besharse, Director, 414-955-8063, Fax: 414-955-6517, E-mail: biomed@mcw.edu.
Website: http://www.mcw.edu/BiomedicalGraduateProgram.htm

Medical University of South Carolina, College of Graduate Studies, Charleston, SC 29425. Offers MS, PhD, DMD/PhD, MD/PhD, Pharm D/PhD. Terminal master's awarded for partial completion of doctoral program. *Degree requirements:* For master's, thesis; for doctorate, thesis/dissertation, oral and written exams. *Entrance requirements:* For doctorate, GRE General Test, interview. Additional exam requirements/recommendations for international students: Required—TOEFL (minimum score 600 paper-based; 100 iBT). Electronic applications accepted. *Expenses:* Contact institution. *Faculty research:* Cell signaling and cancer biology, drug discovery and toxicology, biochemistry and genetics, macromolecular structure, neurosciences, microbiology and immunology.

Meharry Medical College, School of Graduate Studies, Program in Biomedical Sciences, Nashville, TN 37208-9989. Offers biochemistry and cancer biology (PhD); microbiology and immunology (PhD); neuroscience (PhD); pharmacology (PhD); MD/PhD. *Degree requirements:* For doctorate, comprehensive exam, thesis/dissertation. *Entrance requirements:* For doctorate, GRE General Test, GRE Subject Test.

Memorial University of Newfoundland, Faculty of Medicine and School of Graduate Studies, Graduate Programs in Medicine, St. John's, NL A1C 5S7, Canada. Offers M Sc, PhD, Diploma, MD/PhD. *Program availability:* Part-time. *Degree requirements:* For master's, thesis; for doctorate, comprehensive exam, thesis/dissertation, oral defense of thesis. *Entrance requirements:* For master's, MD or B Sc; for doctorate, MD or M Sc; for Diploma, bachelor's degree in health-related field. Additional exam requirements/recommendations for international students: Required—TOEFL (minimum score 550 paper-based). Electronic applications accepted. *Faculty research:* Human genetics, community health, clinical epidemial, cancer, immunology, cardiovascular and immol sciences, applied health services research, neuroscience.

Memorial University of Newfoundland, School of Graduate Studies, Department of Biology, St. John's, NL A1C 5S7, Canada. Offers M Sc, PhD. *Program availability:* Part-time. *Degree requirements:* For master's, thesis; for doctorate, comprehensive exam, thesis/dissertation, oral defense of thesis. *Entrance requirements:* For master's, honors degree (minimum 2nd class standing) in related field; for doctorate, M Sc. Electronic applications accepted. *Faculty research:* Northern flora and fauna, especially cold ocean and boreal environments.

Miami University, College of Arts and Science, Department of Biology, Oxford, OH 45056. Offers MA, MAT, MS, PhD. *Program availability:* Online learning. *Students:* 85 full-time (41 women), 821 part-time (691 women); includes 139 minority (16 Black or African American, non-Hispanic/Latino; 3 American Indian or Alaska Native, non-Hispanic/Latino; 21 Asian, non-Hispanic/Latino; 59 Hispanic/Latino; 1 Native Hawaiian or other Pacific Islander, non-Hispanic/Latino; 39 Two or more races, non-Hispanic/Latino), 24 international. Average age 33. In 2017, 229 master's, 14 doctorates awarded. *Application deadline:* For fall admission, 1/1 for domestic and international students. Application fee: $50. Electronic applications accepted. *Expenses:* Tuition, state resident: full-time $13,812; part-time $575 per credit hour. Tuition, nonresident: full-time $30,860; part-time $1286 per credit hour. *Financial support:* Scholarships/grants available. *Unit head:* Dr. Thomas Crist, Chair, 513-529-3100, E-mail: biology@miamioh.edu.
Website: http://miamioh.edu/cas/academics/departments/biology/

Michigan State University, College of Human Medicine and The Graduate School, Graduate Programs in Human Medicine, East Lansing, MI 48824. Offers biochemistry and molecular biology (MS, PhD); epidemiology (MS, PhD); microbiology (MS); microbiology and molecular genetics (PhD); pharmacology and toxicology (MS, PhD); physiology (MS, PhD); public health (MPH). *Entrance requirements:* Additional exam requirements/recommendations for international students: Required—TOEFL.

Michigan State University, College of Osteopathic Medicine and The Graduate School, Graduate Studies in Osteopathic Medicine, East Lansing, MI 48824. Offers biochemistry and molecular biology (MS, PhD); microbiology (MS); microbiology and molecular genetics (PhD); pharmacology and toxicology (MS, PhD), including integrative pharmacology (MS), pharmacology and toxicology, pharmacology and toxicology-environmental toxicology (PhD); physiology (MS, PhD).

Michigan State University, College of Veterinary Medicine and The Graduate School, Graduate Programs in Veterinary Medicine, Program in Comparative Medicine and Integrative Biology, East Lansing, MI 48824. Offers comparative medicine and integrative biology (MS, PhD); comparative medicine and integrative biology–environmental toxicology (PhD). *Entrance requirements:* Additional exam requirements/recommendations for international students: Required—TOEFL. Electronic applications accepted.

Michigan Technological University, Graduate School, College of Sciences and Arts, Department of Biological Sciences, Houghton, MI 49931. Offers MS, PhD. *Program availability:* Part-time. *Faculty:* 28 full-time (9 women), 12 part-time/adjunct. *Students:* 34 full-time (17 women), 11 part-time (4 women); includes 4 minority (1 Black or African American, non-Hispanic/Latino; 1 Hispanic/Latino; 2 Two or more races, non-Hispanic/Latino), 19 international. Average age 28. 117 applicants, 16% accepted, 11 enrolled. In 2017, 7 master's, 5 doctorates awarded. Terminal master's awarded for partial completion of doctoral program. *Degree requirements:* For master's, comprehensive exam (for some programs), thesis (for some programs); for doctorate, comprehensive exam, thesis/dissertation. *Entrance requirements:* For master's and doctorate, GRE, statement of purpose, personal statement, official transcripts, 2 letters of recommendation, resume/curriculum vitae. Additional exam requirements/recommendations for international students: Required—TOEFL (minimum score 85 iBT) or IELTS (recommended minimum score of 6.5). *Application deadline:* For fall admission, 1/15 priority date for domestic and international students; for spring admission, 9/15 priority date for domestic and international students. Applications are processed on a rolling basis. Electronic applications accepted. *Expenses:* Tuition, state resident: full-time $17,100; part-time $950 per credit. Tuition, nonresident: full-time $17,100; part-time $950 per credit. *Required fees:* $248; $124 per term. Tuition and fees vary according to course load and program. *Financial support:* In 2017–18, 25 students received support, including 3 fellowships with tuition reimbursements available (averaging $15,790 per year), 8 research assistantships with tuition reimbursements available (averaging $15,790 per year), 9 teaching assistantships with tuition reimbursements available (averaging $15,790 per year); career-related internships or fieldwork, Federal Work-Study, scholarships/grants, health care benefits, unspecified assistantships, and cooperative program also available. Financial award applicants required to submit FAFSA. *Faculty research:* Aquatic ecology, phytotechnologies, microbiomes, micro-RNA and human diseases, Genomics. *Total annual research expenditures:* $1.8 million. *Unit head:* Dr. Chandrashekhar P. Joshi, Chair, 906-487-2738, Fax: 906-487-3167, E-mail: cpjoshi@mtu.edu. *Application contact:* Tori Connors, Departmental Coordinator, 906-487-1628, Fax: 906-487-3167, E-mail: tconnors@mtu.edu.
Website: http://www.mtu.edu/biological/

Middle Tennessee State University, College of Graduate Studies, College of Basic and Applied Sciences, Department of Biology, Murfreesboro, TN 37132. Offers MS. *Program availability:* Part-time, evening/weekend, online learning. *Degree requirements:* For master's, comprehensive exam, thesis. *Entrance requirements:* For master's, GRE. Additional exam requirements/recommendations for international students: Required—TOEFL (minimum score 525 paper-based; 71 iBT) or IELTS (minimum score 6). Electronic applications accepted. *Faculty research:* Molecular biosciences.

Midwestern State University, Billie Doris McAda Graduate School, College of Science and Mathematics, Department of Biology, Wichita Falls, TX 76308. Offers MS. *Program availability:* Part-time, evening/weekend. *Degree requirements:* For master's, comprehensive exam, thesis. *Entrance requirements:* For master's, GRE General Test, MAT or GMAT. Additional exam requirements/recommendations for international students: Required—TOEFL (minimum score 550 paper-based). Electronic applications accepted. *Faculty research:* Molecular analysis of flora and fauna, mineral toxicity in plants, embryonic patterning and cell signaling, animal physiology, mammalogy.

Midwestern University, Downers Grove Campus, College of Graduate Studies, Master of Arts Program in Biomedical Sciences, Downers Grove, IL 60515-1235. Offers MA. *Entrance requirements:* For master's, GRE General Test, MCAT, PCAT, DAT, OAT or other professional exam, bachelor's degree, minimum cumulative GPA of 2.75.
Website: http://www.midwestern.edu/Programs_and_Admission/IL_Master_of_Arts_in_Biomedical_Sciences.html

Midwestern University, Downers Grove Campus, College of Graduate Studies, Program in Biomedical Sciences, Downers Grove, IL 60515-1235. Offers MBS. *Program availability:* Part-time. *Entrance requirements:* For master's, GRE General Test, MCAT or PCAT, 2 letters of recommendation. *Application deadline:* Applications are processed on a rolling basis. Application fee: $50.
Website: http://www.midwestern.edu/Programs_and_Admission/IL_Master_of_Biomedical_Sciences.html

Midwestern University, Glendale Campus, College of Health Sciences, Arizona Campus, MA Program in Biomedical Sciences, Glendale, AZ 85308. Offers MA. *Entrance requirements:* For master's, GRE General Test, MCAT, or other professional exam, bachelor's degree, minimum cumulative GPA of 2.75.

Midwestern University, Glendale Campus, College of Health Sciences, Arizona Campus, MBS Program in Biomedical Sciences, Glendale, AZ 85308. Offers MBS. Application fee: $50. *Expenses:* Contact institution.

Mills College, Graduate Studies, Pre-Medical Studies Program, Oakland, CA 94613-1000. Offers Certificate. *Program availability:* Part-time. *Faculty:* 7 full-time (4 women), 6 part-time/adjunct (5 women). *Students:* 43 full-time (31 women), 25 part-time (14 women); includes 20 minority (2 Black or African American, non-Hispanic/Latino; 8 Asian, non-Hispanic/Latino; 5 Hispanic/Latino; 5 Two or more races, non-Hispanic/Latino), 3 international. Average age 27. 211 applicants, 50% accepted, 42 enrolled. In 2017, 32 Certificates awarded. *Entrance requirements:* For degree, SAT/ACT or GRE General Test, bachelor's degree in a non-science area. Additional exam requirements/recommendations for international students: Required—TOEFL (minimum score 550 paper-based; 80 iBT) or IELTS (minimum score 6). *Application deadline:* For fall admission, 2/1 priority date for domestic students, 12/15 for international students. Applications are processed on a rolling basis. Application fee: $50. Electronic applications accepted. *Expenses:* Contact institution. *Financial support:* In 2017–18, 38 students received support, including 38 fellowships with tuition reimbursements available (averaging $5,732 per year), 5 teaching assistantships with tuition reimbursements available; institutionally sponsored loans and scholarships/grants also available. Support available to part-time students. Financial award application deadline: 2/1; financial award applicants required to submit FAFSA. *Faculty research:* Antifungal compounds and their modes of action, organic chemistry-spectroscopy and organic chemistry reaction mechanisms, oceanography, physics and chemistry education, cell-cell and cell-extracellular matrix interactions. *Total annual research expenditures:* $1.7 million. *Unit head:* Dr. John Brabson, Chair of Pre-Medical Program, 510-430-2203, Fax: 510-430-2159, E-mail: johnb@mills.edu. *Application contact:* Robynne Lofton, Director of Admissions, 510-430-3295, Fax: 510-430-2159, E-mail: grad-admission@mills.edu.
Website: http://www.mills.edu/premed

Minnesota State University Mankato, College of Graduate Studies and Research, College of Science, Engineering and Technology, Department of Biological Sciences, Mankato, MN 56001. Offers biology (MS); biology education (MS); environmental sciences (MS). *Program availability:* Part-time. *Degree requirements:* For master's, one foreign language, comprehensive exam, thesis or alternative. *Entrance requirements:* For master's, minimum GPA of 3.0 during previous 2 years of course work. Additional exam requirements/recommendations for international students: Required—TOEFL. Electronic applications accepted.

Mississippi College, Graduate School, College of Arts and Sciences, School of Science and Mathematics, Department of Biological Sciences, Clinton, MS 39058. Offers biological science (M Ed); biology (MCS); biology-biological sciences (MS); biology-medical sciences (MS). *Program availability:* Part-time. *Degree requirements:* For master's, comprehensive exam, thesis optional. *Entrance requirements:* For master's, GRE General Test, minimum GPA of 2.5. Additional exam requirements/recommendations for international students: Recommended—TOEFL, IELTS. Electronic applications accepted.

Mississippi State University, College of Arts and Sciences, Department of Biological Sciences, Mississippi State, MS 39762. Offers biological sciences (MS, PhD); general biology (MS). MS in general biology offered online only. *Program availability:* Blended/hybrid learning. *Faculty:* 18 full-time (7 women), 1 part-time/adjunct (0 women). *Students:* 51 full-time (23 women), 40 part-time (30 women); includes 6 minority (2 Black or African American, non-Hispanic/Latino; 1 Asian, non-Hispanic/Latino; 1 Hispanic/Latino; 2 Two or more races, non-Hispanic/Latino), 19 international. Average age 31. 86 applicants, 49% accepted, 34 enrolled. In 2017, 17 master's, 2 doctorates awarded. Terminal master's awarded for partial completion of doctoral program. *Degree requirements:* For master's, one foreign language, thesis, comprehensive oral or written exam; for doctorate, one foreign language, thesis/dissertation, comprehensive oral or written exam. *Entrance requirements:* For master's, GRE General Test, minimum GPA of 2.75 on last 60 hours of undergraduate courses; for doctorate, GRE General Test. Additional exam requirements/recommendations for international students: Required—TOEFL (minimum score 550 paper-based; 79 iBT); Recommended—IELTS (minimum score 6.5). *Application deadline:* For fall admission, 7/1 for domestic students, 5/1 for international students; for spring admission, 11/1 for domestic students, 9/1 for international students. Applications are processed on a rolling basis. Application fee: $60 ($80 for international students). Electronic applications accepted. *Expenses:* Tuition, state resident: full-time $8318; part-time $462.12 per credit hour. Tuition, nonresident: full-time $22,358; part-time $1242.12 per credit hour. *Required fees:* $110; $12.24 per credit hour. $6.12 per semester. *Financial support:* In 2017–18, 8 research assistantships with partial tuition reimbursements (averaging $17,450 per year), 47 teaching assistantships with partial tuition reimbursements (averaging $16,370 per year) were awarded; Federal Work-Study, institutionally sponsored loans, scholarships/grants, and unspecified assistantships also available. Financial award application deadline: 4/1; financial award applicants required to submit FAFSA. *Faculty research:* Botany, zoology, microbiology, ecology. *Total annual research expenditures:* $6.6 million. *Unit head:* Dr. Angus Dawe, Professor and Head, 662-325-3120, Fax: 662-325-7939, E-mail: dawe@biology.msstate.edu. *Application contact:* Marina Hunt, Admissions and Enrollment Assistant, 662-325-5188, E-mail: mhunt@grad.msstate.edu.
Website: http://www.biology.msstate.edu

Missouri State University, Graduate College, College of Natural and Applied Sciences, Department of Biology, Springfield, MO 65897. Offers biology (MS); natural and applied science (MNAS), including biology (MNAS, MS Ed); secondary education (MS Ed), including biology (MNAS, MS Ed). *Faculty:* 18 full-time (3 women), 7 part-time/adjunct (2 women). *Students:* 21 full-time (12 women), 20 part-time (16 women); includes 5 minority (1 Asian, non-Hispanic/Latino; 3 Hispanic/Latino; 1 Two or more races, non-Hispanic/Latino), 5 international. Average age 26. 28 applicants, 46% accepted, 13 enrolled. In 2017, 20 master's awarded. *Degree requirements:* For master's, comprehensive exam, thesis or alternative. *Entrance requirements:* For master's, GRE (MS, MNAS), 24 hours of course work in biology (MS); minimum GPA of 3.0 (MS, MNAS); 9-12 teacher certification (MS Ed). Additional exam requirements/recommendations for international students: Required—TOEFL (minimum score 550 paper-based; 79 iBT), IELTS (minimum score 6). *Application deadline:* For fall admission, 7/20 priority date for domestic students, 5/1 for international students; for spring admission, 12/20 priority date for domestic students, 9/1 for international students; for summer admission, 5/20 priority date for domestic students. Applications are processed on a rolling basis. Application fee: $35 ($50 for international students). Electronic applications accepted. *Expenses:* Tuition, state resident: full-time $2915; part-time $2021 per credit hour. Tuition, nonresident: full-time $5354; part-time $3647 per credit hour. *International tuition:* $11,992 full-time. *Required fees:* $173; $173 per credit hour. Tuition and fees vary according to class time, course level, course load, degree level, campus/location and program. *Financial support:* In 2017–18, 2 research assistantships with full tuition reimbursements (averaging $10,672 per year), 26 teaching assistantships with full tuition reimbursements (averaging $9,746 per year) were awarded; Federal Work-Study, institutionally sponsored loans, scholarships/grants, and unspecified assistantships also available. Financial award application deadline: 3/31; financial award applicants required to submit FAFSA. *Faculty research:* Hibernation physiology of bats, behavioral ecology of salamanders, mussel conservation, plant evolution and systematics, cellular/molecular mechanisms involved in migraine pathology. *Unit head:* Dr. S. Alicia Mathis, Department Head, 417-836-5126, Fax: 417-836-6934, E-mail: biology@missouristate.edu. *Application contact:* Stephanie Praschan, Director, Graduate Enrollment Management, 417-836-5330, Fax: 417-836-6200, E-mail: stephaniepraschan@missouristate.edu.
Website: http://biology.missouristate.edu/

Missouri University of Science and Technology, Department of Biological Sciences, Rolla, MO 65409. Offers applied and environmental biology (MS). *Faculty:* 10 full-time (3 women). *Students:* 10 full-time (6 women), 6 part-time (5 women); includes 1 minority (Hispanic/Latino), 6 international. Average age 28. 19 applicants, 68% accepted, 7 enrolled. In 2017, 8 master's awarded. *Entrance requirements:* For master's, GRE (minimum score 600 quantitative, 4 writing). Additional exam requirements/recommendations for international students: Required—TOEFL (minimum score 570 paper-based). Application fee: $50. *Expenses:* Tuition, state resident: full-time $7391; part-time $3696 per year. Tuition, nonresident: full-time $21,712; part-time $10,857 per year. *Required fees:* $728; $564 per unit. Tuition and fees vary according to course load. *Financial support:* In 2017–18, 6 research assistantships (averaging $1,810 per year), 1 teaching assistantship (averaging $1,814 per year) were awarded; institutionally sponsored loans and unspecified assistantships also available. *Total annual research expenditures:* $306,173. *Unit head:* Dr. David Duvernell, Chair, 573-341-6988, Fax: 573-341-4821, E-mail: duvernelld@mst.edu. *Application contact:* Debbie Schwertz, Admissions Coordinator, 573-341-6013, Fax: 573-341-6271, E-mail: schwertz@mst.edu.
Website: http://biosci.mst.edu/

Missouri Western State University, Program in Applied Science, St. Joseph, MO 64507-2294. Offers chemistry (MAS); engineering technology management (MAS); industrial life science (MAS); sport and fitness management (MAS). *Accreditation:* AACSB. *Program availability:* Part-time. *Students:* 37 full-time (16 women), 20 part-time (9 women); includes 8 minority (6 Black or African American, non-Hispanic/Latino; 1 Asian, non-Hispanic/Latino; 1 Two or more races, non-Hispanic/Latino), 10 international. Average age 27. 28 applicants, 86% accepted, 16 enrolled. In 2017, 32 master's awarded. *Entrance requirements:* Additional exam requirements/recommendations for international students: Recommended—TOEFL (minimum score 79 iBT), IELTS (minimum score 6). *Application deadline:* For fall admission, 7/15 for domestic and international students; for spring admission, 10/1 for domestic and international students; for summer admission, 3/15 for domestic students. Applications are processed on a rolling basis. Application fee: $45 ($50 for international students). Electronic applications accepted. *Expenses:* Tuition, state resident: full-time $6391; part-time $336 per credit hour. Tuition, nonresident: full-time $11,483; part-time $604 per credit hour. *Required fees:* $542; $99 per credit hour. $176 per semester. One-time fee: $45. Tuition and fees vary according to course load and program. *Financial support:* Scholarships/grants and unspecified assistantships available. Support available to part-time students. *Unit head:* Dr. Benjamin D. Caldwell, Dean of the Graduate School, 816-271-4394, Fax: 816-271-4525, E-mail: graduate@missouriwestern.edu.

Montana State University, The Graduate School, College of Letters and Science, Department of Cell Biology and Neuroscience, Bozeman, MT 59717. Offers biological sciences (PhD); neuroscience (MS, PhD). *Program availability:* Part-time. *Degree requirements:* For master's, comprehensive exam; for doctorate, comprehensive exam, thesis/dissertation. *Entrance requirements:* For master's and doctorate, GRE General Test. Additional exam requirements/recommendations for international students: Required—TOEFL (minimum score 550 paper-based). Electronic applications accepted. *Faculty research:* Development of the nervous system, neuronal mechanisms of visual perception, ion channel biophysics, mechanisms of sensory coding, neuroinformatics.

Montclair State University, The Graduate School, College of Science and Mathematics, Program in Biology, Montclair, NJ 07043-1624. Offers biological science/education (MS); biology (MS); ecology and evolution (MS); physiology (MS).

Morehead State University, Graduate Programs, College of Science and Technology, Department of Biology and Chemistry, Morehead, KY 40351. Offers biology (MS); biology regional analysis (MS). *Program availability:* Part-time. *Degree requirements:* For master's, comprehensive exam, thesis optional, oral and written final exams. *Entrance requirements:* For master's, GRE General Test, minimum GPA of 3.0 in biology, 2.5 overall; undergraduate major/minor in biology, environmental science, or equivalent. Additional exam requirements/recommendations for international students: Required—TOEFL (minimum score 525 paper-based). Electronic applications accepted. *Faculty research:* Atherosclerosis, RNA evolution, cancer biology, water quality/ecology, immunoparasitology.

Morehouse School of Medicine, Graduate Programs in Biomedical Sciences, Atlanta, GA 30310-1495. Offers biomedical research (MS); biomedical sciences (PhD); biomedical technology (MS); medical sciences (MS). *Degree requirements:* For master's, thesis (for some programs); for doctorate, thesis/dissertation. *Entrance requirements:* For doctorate, GRE General Test. Additional exam requirements/recommendations for international students: Required—TOEFL (minimum score 550 paper-based). Electronic applications accepted. *Expenses:* Contact institution.

Morgan State University, School of Graduate Studies, School of Computer, Mathematical, and Natural Sciences, Department of Biology, Baltimore, MD 21251. Offers bioenvironmental science (PhD); biology (MS). *Degree requirements:* For master's, comprehensive exam, thesis. *Entrance requirements:* For master's, minimum GPA of 3.0. *Application deadline:* For fall admission, 2/1 priority date for domestic students; for spring admission, 10/1 priority date for domestic students. *Expenses:* Tuition, state resident: part-time $433 per credit. Tuition, nonresident: part-time $851 per credit. *Required fees:* $81.50 per credit. *Unit head:* Dr. James Wachira, Program Coordinator, 443-885-3632, E-mail: james.wachira@morgan.edu. *Application contact:* Dr. Dean Campbell, Graduate Recruitment Specialist, 443-885-3185, Fax: 443-885-8226, E-mail: dean.campbell@morgan.edu.
Website: https://www.morgan.edu/biology

Mount Allison University, Department of Biology, Sackville, NB E4L 1E4, Canada. Offers M Sc. *Degree requirements:* For master's, thesis. *Entrance requirements:* For master's, honors degree. Full-time tuition and fees vary according to campus/location and student level. *Financial support:* Fellowships available. *Faculty research:* Field ecology, animal physiology, molecular ecology, microbiology, developmental biology, genetics. *Unit head:* Suzie Currie, Head, 506-364-2260, E-mail: scurrie@mta.ca.
Website: http://www.mta.ca/Community/Academics/Faculty_of_Science/Biology/Biology/

Murray State University, Jesse D. Jones College of Science, Engineering and Technology, Department of Biology, Murray, KY 42071. Offers MS. *Program availability:* Part-time. *Faculty:* 15 full-time (3 women), 1 (woman) part-time/adjunct. *Students:* 7 full-time (4 women), 6 part-time (2 women), 1 international. Average age 30. 14 applicants, 29% accepted, 4 enrolled. In 2017, 5 master's awarded. *Entrance requirements:* For master's, GRE or GMAT, minimum university GPA of 2.75. Additional exam requirements/recommendations for international students: Required—TOEFL (minimum score 527 paper-based; 71 iBT). *Application deadline:* Applications are processed on a rolling basis. Application fee: $40 ($50 for international students). Electronic applications accepted. *Expenses:* Tuition, state resident: full-time $9504. Tuition, nonresident: full-time $26,811. *International tuition:* $14,400 full-time. Tuition and fees vary according to course load, degree level and reciprocity agreements. *Financial support:* In 2017–18, 13 research assistantships, 4 teaching assistantships were awarded; Federal Work-Study and unspecified assistantships also available. Financial award applicants required to submit FAFSA. *Unit head:* Dr. Claire Fuller, Chair, Department of Biology, 270-809-2786, Fax: 270-809-2788, E-mail: cfuller@murraystate.edu. *Application contact:* Kaitlyn Burzynski, Interim Assistant Director for Graduate Admission and Records, 270-809-5732, Fax: 270-809-3780, E-mail: msu.graduateadmissions@murraystate.edu.
Website: http://www.murraystate.edu/academics/CollegesDepartments/CollegeOfScienceEngineeringandTechnology/CollegeOfSciencePrograms/biologyDept/index.aspx

National University, College of Letters and Sciences, La Jolla, CA 92037-1011. Offers biology (MS); counseling psychology (MA), including licensed professional clinical counseling, marriage and family therapy; creative writing (MFA); English (MA); film studies (MA); forensic and crime scene investigations (Certificate); forensic sciences (MFS); human behavior (MA); mathematics for educators (MS); performance psychology (MA); strategic communications (MA). *Program availability:* Part-time, evening/weekend, 100% online, blended/hybrid learning. *Degree requirements:* For master's, thesis (for some programs). *Entrance requirements:* For master's, interview, minimum GPA of 2.5. Additional exam requirements/recommendations for international students: Required—TOEFL (minimum score 550 paper-based; 79 iBT), IELTS (minimum score 6). *Application deadline:* Applications are processed on a rolling basis. Application fee: $60 ($65 for international students). Electronic applications accepted. *Expenses: Tuition:* Part-time $430 per quarter hour. *Financial support:* Career-related internships or fieldwork, institutionally sponsored loans, scholarships/grants, and tuition waivers (partial) available. Support available to part-time students. Financial award

application deadline: 6/30; financial award applicants required to submit FAFSA. *Unit head:* Dr. Carol Richardson, Dean, 858-642-8450, E-mail: cols@nu.edu. *Application contact:* Brandon Jouganatos, Interim Vice President for Enrollment Services, 800-628-8648, E-mail: advisor@nu.edu.
Website: http://www.nu.edu/OurPrograms/CollegeOfLettersAndSciences.html

New Jersey Institute of Technology, College of Science and Liberal Arts, Newark, NJ 07102. Offers applied mathematics (MS); applied physics (MS, PhD); applied statistics (MS, Certificate); biology (MS, PhD); biostatistics (MS); chemistry (MS, PhD); environmental and sustainability policy (MS); environmental science (MS, PhD); history (MA, MAT); materials science and engineering (MS, PhD); mathematical and computational finance (MS); mathematical sciences (PhD); pharmaceutical chemistry (MS); professional and technical communications (MS); technical communication essentials (Certificate). *Program availability:* Part-time, evening/weekend. *Students:* Average age 28. 504 applicants, 64% accepted, 65 enrolled. In 2017, 81 master's, 18 doctorates, 1 other advanced degree awarded. Terminal master's awarded for partial completion of doctoral program. *Entrance requirements:* For master's, GRE General Test; for doctorate, GRE General Test, minimum graduate GPA of 3.5. Additional exam requirements/recommendations for international students: Required—TOEFL (minimum score 550 paper-based; 79 iBT). *Application deadline:* For fall admission, 6/1 priority date for domestic students, 5/1 priority date for international students; for spring admission, 11/15 priority date for domestic and international students. Applications are processed on a rolling basis. Application fee: $75. Electronic applications accepted. *Expenses:* Contact institution. *Financial support:* In 2017–18, 106 students received support, including 8 fellowships (averaging $3,436 per year), 51 research assistantships (averaging $23,452 per year), 91 teaching assistantships (averaging $25,553 per year); scholarships/grants, traineeships, and unspecified assistantships also available. Financial award application deadline: 1/15. *Faculty research:* Biophotonics and bioimaging, morphogenetic patterning, embryogenesis, biological fluid dynamics, applied research in the mathematical sciences. *Unit head:* Dr. Kevin Belfield, Dean, 973-596-3676, Fax: 973-565-0586, E-mail: kevin.d.belfield@njit.edu. *Application contact:* Stephen Eck, Director of Admissions, 973-596-3300, Fax: 973-596-3461, E-mail: admissions@njit.edu.
Website: http://csla.njit.edu/

New Mexico Institute of Mining and Technology, Center for Graduate Studies, Department of Biology, Socorro, NM 87801. Offers biology (MS); geobiology (PhD). *Program availability:* Part-time. *Degree requirements:* For master's, thesis. *Entrance requirements:* For master's, GRE General Test. Additional exam requirements/recommendations for international students: Required—TOEFL (minimum score 540 paper-based). *Application deadline:* For fall admission, 3/1 priority date for domestic students; for spring admission, 6/1 priority date for domestic students. Applications are processed on a rolling basis. Application fee: $16 ($30 for international students). Electronic applications accepted. *Expenses:* Tuition, state resident: full-time $6406; part-time $356 per credit. Tuition, nonresident: full-time $21,190; part-time $1177 per credit. *Required fees:* $1030. *Financial support:* Fellowships, research assistantships, teaching assistantships with full and partial tuition reimbursements, Federal Work-Study, institutionally sponsored loans, and unspecified assistantships available. Financial award application deadline: 3/1; financial award applicants required to submit CSS PROFILE or FAFSA. *Faculty research:* Molecular biology, evolution and evolutionary ecology, immunology, endocrinology. *Unit head:* Dr. Snezna Rogelj, Chair, 575-835-5608, Fax: 575-835-5668, E-mail: snezna@nmt.edu. *Application contact:* Dr. Lorie Liebrock, Dean of Graduate Studies, 575-835-5513, Fax: 575-835-5476, E-mail: graduate@nmt.edu.
Website: http://www.nmt.edu/academics/biology/index.php

New Mexico State University, College of Arts and Sciences, Department of Biology, Las Cruces, NM 88003. Offers biology (MS, PhD); biotechnology (MS). *Program availability:* Part-time. *Faculty:* 21 full-time (10 women). *Students:* 50 full-time (27 women), 7 part-time (4 women); includes 15 minority (1 American Indian or Alaska Native, non-Hispanic/Latino; 2 Asian, non-Hispanic/Latino; 9 Hispanic/Latino; 3 Two or more races, non-Hispanic/Latino), 15 international. Average age 31. 34 applicants, 53% accepted, 11 enrolled. In 2017, 11 master's, 6 doctorates awarded. *Entrance requirements:* For master's and doctorate, GRE. Additional exam requirements/recommendations for international students: Required—TOEFL (minimum score 550 paper-based; 79 iBT), IELTS (minimum score 6.5). *Application deadline:* For fall admission, 1/15 priority date for domestic students, 1/15 for international students; for spring admission, 10/4 priority date for domestic students, 10/4 for international students. Applications are processed on a rolling basis. Application fee: $40 ($50 for international students). Electronic applications accepted. *Expenses:* Tuition, state resident: full-time $4390. Tuition, nonresident: full-time $15,309. *Required fees:* $853. *Financial support:* In 2017–18, 48 students received support, including 2 fellowships (averaging $4,390 per year), 12 research assistantships (averaging $22,467 per year), 30 teaching assistantships (averaging $18,180 per year); career-related internships or fieldwork, Federal Work-Study, scholarships/grants, traineeships, health care benefits, and unspecified assistantships also available. Support available to part-time students. Financial award application deadline: 3/1. *Faculty research:* Microbiology, cell and organismal physiology, ecology and ethology, evolution, genetics, developmental biology. *Total annual research expenditures:* $2.4 million. *Unit head:* Dr. Michele K. Nishiguchi, Department Head, 575-646-3611, Fax: 575-646-5665, E-mail: nish@nmsu.edu. *Application contact:* Dr. Jennifer Curtiss, Associate Professor, 575-646-3611, Fax: 575-646-5665, E-mail: curtij01@nmsu.edu.
Website: http://bio.nmsu.edu

New York Medical College, Graduate School of Basic Medical Sciences, Valhalla, NY 10595. Offers biochemistry and molecular biology (MS, PhD); cell biology (MS, PhD); microbiology and immunology (MS, PhD); pathology (MS, PhD); pharmacology (MS, PhD); physiology (MS, PhD); MD/PhD. *Program availability:* Part-time, evening/weekend. *Faculty:* 70 full-time (17 women), 25 part-time/adjunct (9 women). *Students:* 116 full-time (63 women), 25 part-time (11 women); includes 65 minority (17 Black or African American, non-Hispanic/Latino; 1 American Indian or Alaska Native, non-Hispanic/Latino; 23 Asian, non-Hispanic/Latino; 21 Hispanic/Latino; 3 Two or more races, non-Hispanic/Latino), 27 international. Average age 27. 273 applicants, 56% accepted, 59 enrolled. In 2017, 32 master's, 3 doctorates awarded. *Degree requirements:* For master's, thesis; for doctorate, comprehensive exam, thesis/dissertation. *Entrance requirements:* For master's, GRE General Test, MCAT, or DAT; for doctorate, GRE General Test. Additional exam requirements/recommendations for international students: Required—TOEFL. *Application deadline:* For fall admission, 7/1 priority date for domestic students, 5/1 priority date for international students; for spring admission, 12/1 priority date for domestic students, 9/15 priority date for international students. Applications are processed on a rolling basis. Application fee: $75 ($100 for international students). Electronic applications accepted. *Expenses:* $1,125 per credit, $655 fees. *Financial support:* Fellowships, research assistantships, Federal Work-Study, institutionally sponsored loans, scholarships/grants, tuition waivers, and health benefits (for PhD candidates only) available. Support available to part-time students. Financial award application deadline: 4/30; financial award applicants required to submit FAFSA. *Faculty research:* Cardiovascular science, infectious diseases, neuroscience, cancer, cell signaling. *Unit head:* Dr. Francis L. Belloni, Dean, 914-594-4110, Fax: 914-594-4944, E-mail: francis_belloni@nymc.edu. *Application contact:* Valerie Romeo-Messana, Director of Admissions, 914-594-4110, Fax: 914-594-4944, E-mail: v_romeomessana@nymc.edu.
Website: https://www.nymc.edu/graduate-school-of-basic-medical-sciences-gsbms/gsbms-academics/

New York University, Graduate School of Arts and Science, Department of Biology, New York, NY 10012-1019. Offers biology (PhD); biomedical journalism (MS); cancer and molecular biology (PhD); computational biology (PhD); computers in biological research (MS); developmental genetics (PhD); general biology (MS); immunology and microbiology (PhD); molecular genetics (PhD); neurobiology (PhD); oral biology (MS); plant biology (PhD); recombinant DNA technology (MS); MS/MBA. *Program availability:* Part-time. *Students:* Average age 27. 394 applicants, 56% accepted, 77 enrolled. In 2017, 68 master's, 9 doctorates awarded. Terminal master's awarded for partial completion of doctoral program. *Degree requirements:* For master's, thesis or alternative, qualifying paper; for doctorate, comprehensive exam, thesis/dissertation. *Entrance requirements:* For master's and doctorate, GRE General Test. Additional exam requirements/recommendations for international students: Required—TOEFL. *Application deadline:* For fall admission, 12/1 priority date for domestic students, 12/1 for international students. Application fee: $100. *Expenses: Tuition:* Full-time $41,352; part-time $19,968 per year. *Required fees:* $2496; $1628 per unit. $814 per term. Tuition and fees vary according to course load and program. *Financial support:* Fellowships, research assistantships, teaching assistantships, career-related internships or fieldwork, Federal Work-Study, institutionally sponsored loans, scholarships/grants, health care benefits, and unspecified assistantships available. Financial award application deadline: 12/1; financial award applicants required to submit FAFSA. *Faculty research:* Genomics, molecular and cell biology, development and molecular genetics, molecular evolution of plants and animals. *Unit head:* Stephen Small, Chair, 212-998-8200, Fax: 212-995-4015, E-mail: biology.admissions@nyu.edu. *Application contact:* Ken Birnbaum, Director of Graduate Studies, PhD Programs, 212-998-8200, Fax: 212-995-4015, E-mail: biology.admissions@nyu.edu.
Website: http://biology.as.nyu.edu/

New York University, Graduate School of Arts and Science, Department of Environmental Medicine, New York, NY 10012-1019. Offers environmental health sciences (MS, PhD), including biostatistics (PhD), environmental hygiene (MS), epidemiology (PhD), ergonomics and biomechanics (PhD), exposure assessment and health effects (PhD), molecular toxicology/carcinogenesis (PhD), toxicology. *Program availability:* Part-time. *Students:* Average age 30. 79 applicants, 44% accepted, 20 enrolled. In 2017, 8 master's, 6 doctorates awarded. Terminal master's awarded for partial completion of doctoral program. *Degree requirements:* For master's, thesis or alternative; for doctorate, one foreign language, thesis/dissertation, oral and written exams. *Entrance requirements:* For master's and doctorate, GRE General Test, minimum GPA of 3.0; bachelor's degree in biological, physical, or engineering science. Additional exam requirements/recommendations for international students: Required—TOEFL. *Application deadline:* For fall admission, 12/18 for domestic and international students. Application fee: $100. *Expenses: Tuition:* Full-time $41,352; part-time $19,968 per year. *Required fees:* $2496; $1628 per unit. $814 per term. Tuition and fees vary according to course load and program. *Financial support:* Fellowships, teaching assistantships, career-related internships or fieldwork, Federal Work-Study, institutionally sponsored loans, and health care benefits available. Financial award application deadline: 12/18; financial award applicants required to submit FAFSA. *Unit head:* Dr. Max Costa, Chair, 845-731-3661, Fax: 845-351-4510, E-mail: ehs@env.med.nyu.edu. *Application contact:* Dr. Jerome J. Solomon, Director of Graduate Studies, 845-731-3661, Fax: 845-351-4510, E-mail: ehs@env.med.nyu.edu.
Website: http://environmental-medicine.med.nyu.edu/

See Close-Up on page 843.

New York University, School of Medicine and Graduate School of Arts and Science, Medical Scientist Training Program, New York, NY 10016. Offers MD/PhD. *Faculty:* 207 full-time (51 women). *Students:* 85 full-time (36 women); includes 31 minority (5 Black or African American, non-Hispanic/Latino; 17 Asian, non-Hispanic/Latino; 8 Hispanic/Latino; 1 Native Hawaiian or other Pacific Islander, non-Hispanic/Latino). 434 applicants, 14% accepted, 14 enrolled. *Application deadline:* For fall admission, 10/15 for domestic students. Applications are processed on a rolling basis. Application fee: $100. Electronic applications accepted. *Expenses:* All tuition and fees are waived. *Financial support:* In 2017–18, 25 fellowships with full tuition reimbursements were awarded; health care benefits, tuition waivers (full), and unspecified assistantships also available. *Faculty research:* Biomedical sciences. *Unit head:* Dr. Naoko Tanese, Associate Dean for Biomedical Sciences/Director, Sackler Institute of Graduate Biomedical Sciences, 212-263-8945, E-mail: naoko.tanese@nyumc.org. *Application contact:* Heather Petrucci, Program Manager, 212-263-5648, E-mail: sackler-info@nyumc.org.
Website: https://med.nyu.edu/research/sackler-institute-graduate-biomedical-sciences/md-phd-program

New York University, Steinhardt School of Culture, Education, and Human Development, Department of Teaching and Learning, New York, NY 10012. Offers clinically rich integrated science (MA), including clinically rich integrated science, teaching biology grades 7-12, teaching chemistry 7-12, teaching physics 7-12; early childhood and childhood education (MA), including childhood education, early childhood education, early childhood education/early childhood special education; English education (MA, PhD, Advanced Certificate), including clinically-based English education, grades 7-12 (MA), English education (PhD, Advanced Certificate), English education, grades 7-12 (MA); environmental conservation education (MA); literacy education (MA), including literacy 5-12, literacy B-6; mathematics education (MA), including teachers of mathematics 7-12; multilingual/multicultural studies (MA, PhD, Advanced Certificate), including bilingual education, foreign language education (MA), teaching English to speakers of other languages (MA, PhD), teaching foreign languages, 7-12 (MA), teaching French as a foreign language (MA), teaching Spanish as a foreign language (MA); social studies education (MA), including teaching art/social studies 7-12, teaching social studies 7-12; special education (MA), including childhood, early childhood; teaching and learning (Ed D, PhD). *Program availability:* Part-time. *Students:* Average age 25. 926 applicants, 68% accepted, 210 enrolled. In 2017, 290 master's, 10 doctorates, 2 other advanced degrees awarded. *Entrance requirements:* For doctorate, GRE General Test, interview; for Advanced Certificate, master's degree. Additional exam requirements/recommendations for international students: Required—TOEFL (minimum score 100 iBT). *Application deadline:* For fall admission, 12/1 priority date for domestic and international students; for spring admission, 10/1 for domestic and international students. Applications are processed on a rolling basis. Application fee: $75. Electronic applications accepted. *Expenses: Tuition:* Full-time $41,352; part-time $19,968 per year. *Required fees:* $2496; $1628 per unit. $814 per term. Tuition and fees vary according to course load and program. *Financial support:* Fellowships with full and partial tuition reimbursements, research assistantships with full and partial tuition reimbursements, teaching assistantships with full and partial tuition reimbursements, career-related internships or fieldwork, Federal Work-Study, institutionally sponsored loans, scholarships/grants, tuition waivers (partial), and unspecified assistantships

available. Support available to part-time students. Financial award application deadline: 2/1; financial award applicants required to submit FAFSA. *Faculty research:* Cultural contexts for literacy learning, school restructuring, parenting and education, teacher learning, language assessment. *Unit head:* Dr. Susan Neuman, Chairperson, 212-998-5460, Fax: 212-995-4049. *Application contact:* 212-998-5030, Fax: 212-995-4328, E-mail: steinhardt.gradadmissions@nyu.edu.
Website: http://steinhardt.nyu.edu/teachlearn/

North Carolina Agricultural and Technical State University, School of Graduate Studies, College of Arts and Sciences, Department of Biology, Greensboro, NC 27411. Offers biology (MS); biology education (MAT). *Program availability:* Part-time, evening/weekend. *Degree requirements:* For master's, comprehensive exam, thesis (for some programs), qualifying exam. *Entrance requirements:* For master's, GRE General Test, personal statement. *Faculty research:* Physical ecology, cytochemistry, botany, parasitology, microbiology.

North Carolina Central University, College of Arts and Sciences, Department of Biological and Biomedical Sciences, Durham, NC 27707-3129. Offers MS. *Degree requirements:* For master's, one foreign language, comprehensive exam, thesis. *Entrance requirements:* For master's, GRE, minimum GPA of 3.0 in major, 2.5 overall. Additional exam requirements/recommendations for international students: Required—TOEFL. *Application deadline:* For fall admission, 8/1 for domestic students. Application fee: $30. *Expenses:* Tuition, state resident: full-time $2770; part-time $692.50 per credit hour. Tuition, nonresident: full-time $9247; part-time $2311.75 per credit hour. *Financial support:* Application deadline: 5/1; applicants required to submit FAFSA. *Unit head:* Porche' L. Spence, Program Coordinator, 919-530-5474, Fax: 919-530-7773, E-mail: plspence@nccu.edu. *Application contact:* Porche' L. Spence, Program Coordinator, 919-530-5474, Fax: 919-530-7773, E-mail: plspence@nccu.edu.

North Carolina State University, College of Veterinary Medicine, Program in Comparative Biomedical Sciences, Raleigh, NC 27695. Offers cell biology (MS, PhD); infectious disease (MS, PhD); pathology (MS, PhD); pharmacology (MS, PhD); population medicine (MS, PhD). *Program availability:* Part-time. *Degree requirements:* For master's, thesis; for doctorate, thesis/dissertation. *Entrance requirements:* For master's and doctorate, GRE General Test. Additional exam requirements/recommendations for international students: Required—TOEFL (minimum score 550 paper-based). Electronic applications accepted. *Expenses:* Contact institution. *Faculty research:* Infectious diseases, cell biology, pharmacology and toxicology, genomics, pathology and population medicine.

North Carolina State University, Graduate School, College of Agriculture and Life Sciences, Raleigh, NC 27695. Offers M Tox, MAE, MB, MBAE, MFG, MFM, MFS, MG, MMB, MN, MP, MS, MZS, Ed D, PhD, Certificate. *Program availability:* Part-time. Electronic applications accepted.

North Dakota State University, College of Graduate and Interdisciplinary Studies, College of Science and Mathematics, Department of Biological Sciences, Fargo, ND 58102. Offers biology (MS); botany (MS, PhD); zoology (MS, PhD). *Entrance requirements:* For master's and doctorate, GRE General Test. Additional exam requirements/recommendations for international students: Required—TOEFL. *Application deadline:* For fall admission, 1/15 for domestic students. Applications are processed on a rolling basis. Application fee: $35. Electronic applications accepted. *Expenses:* Tuition, state resident: full-time $4323; part-time $360.21 per credit. Tuition, nonresident: full-time $6484; part-time $540.31 per credit. *Required fees:* $668; $55.70 per credit. Part-time tuition and fees vary according to degree level, program and reciprocity agreements. *Financial support:* Application deadline: 4/15; applicants required to submit FAFSA. *Faculty research:* Comparative endocrinology, physiology, behavioral ecology, plant cell biology, aquatic biology. *Unit head:* Dr. Katie Reindl, Graduate Coordinator, 701-231-7087, E-mail: katie.reindl@ndsu.edu. *Application contact:* Elizabeth Worth, Marketing, Recruitment, and Public Relations Coordinator, 701-231-8476, Fax: 701-231-6524, E-mail: elizabeth.worth@ndsu.edu.
Website: http://www.ndsu.edu/biology/

Northeastern Illinois University, College of Graduate Studies and Research, College of Arts and Sciences, Program in Biology, Chicago, IL 60625. Offers biology (MS), including cell biology, ecology, molecular biology, organismal biology. *Program availability:* Part-time, evening/weekend. *Degree requirements:* For master's, comprehensive exam, thesis optional. *Entrance requirements:* For master's, minimum GPA of 2.75. Additional exam requirements/recommendations for international students: Required—TOEFL (minimum score 550 paper-based; 79 iBT). *Application deadline:* For fall admission, 4/1 priority date for domestic students; for spring admission, 8/15 for domestic students. Applications are processed on a rolling basis. Application fee: $30. Electronic applications accepted. *Expenses:* Tuition, state resident: full-time $7274; part-time $404.11 per credit hour. Tuition, nonresident: full-time $14,548; part-time $808.23 per credit hour. *Required fees:* $1284. *Financial support:* Applicants required to submit FAFSA. *Faculty research:* Paleoecology and freshwater biology, protein biosynthesis and targeting, microbial growth and physiology, molecular biology of antibody production, reptilian neurobiology. *Unit head:* Dr. John Kasmer, Department Chair, 773-442-5717, E-mail: j-kasmer@neiu.edu. *Application contact:* Martha Narvaez, Graduate Admission Representative, 773-442-6006, E-mail: m-narvaez@neiu.edu.

Northeastern University, College of Science, Boston, MA 02115-5096. Offers applied mathematics (MS); bioinformatics (MS); biology (PhD); biotechnology (MS); chemistry and chemical biology (MS, PhD); environmental science and policy (MS); marine and environmental sciences (PhD); marine biology (MS); mathematics (MS, PhD); operations research (MSOR); physics (MS, PhD); psychology (PhD). *Program availability:* Part-time. Terminal master's awarded for partial completion of doctoral program. *Degree requirements:* For master's, comprehensive exam (for some programs), thesis; for doctorate, comprehensive exam (for some programs), thesis/dissertation. *Entrance requirements:* For master's, GRE General Test. *Application deadline:* Applications are processed on a rolling basis. Application fee: $75. Electronic applications accepted. *Expenses:* Contact institution. *Financial support:* Fellowships with tuition reimbursements, research assistantships with tuition reimbursements, teaching assistantships with tuition reimbursements, career-related internships or fieldwork, scholarships/grants, health care benefits, tuition waivers (full and partial), and unspecified assistantships available. Support available to part-time students. Financial award applicants required to submit FAFSA. *Unit head:* Dr. Kenneth Henderson, Dean, 617-373-5089, E-mail: k.henderson@northeastern.edu. *Application contact:* Graduate Student Services, 617-373-4275, E-mail: gradcos@northeastern.edu.
Website: https://cos.northeastern.edu/

Northern Arizona University, College of Engineering, Forestry, and Natural Sciences, Department of Biological Sciences, Flagstaff, AZ 86011. Offers biology (MS, PhD). *Faculty:* 65 full-time (24 women), 2 part-time/adjunct (both women). *Students:* 106 full-time (63 women), 12 part-time (7 women); includes 18 minority (1 Black or African American, non-Hispanic/Latino; 1 American Indian or Alaska Native, non-Hispanic/Latino; 3 Asian, non-Hispanic/Latino; 9 Hispanic/Latino; 4 Two or more races, non-Hispanic/Latino), 9 international. Average age 30. 67 applicants, 63% accepted, 40 enrolled. In 2017, 21 master's, 6 doctorates awarded. *Degree requirements:* For master's, variable foreign language requirement, comprehensive exam (for some programs), thesis, oral defense, individualized research; for doctorate, variable foreign language requirement, comprehensive exam, thesis/dissertation, oral defense, individualized research. *Entrance requirements:* For master's and doctorate, GRE General Test. Additional exam requirements/recommendations for international students: Required—TOEFL (minimum score 80 iBT), IELTS (minimum score 6.5). *Application deadline:* For fall admission, 1/15 for domestic and international students; for spring admission, 10/1 for domestic and international students. Application fee: $65. Electronic applications accepted. *Expenses:* Tuition, state resident: full-time $9240; part-time $458 per credit hour. Tuition, nonresident: full-time $21,588; part-time $1199 per credit hour. *Required fees:* $1021; $14 per credit hour. $646 per semester. Tuition and fees vary according to course load, campus/location and program. *Financial support:* In 2017–18, 121 students received support, including 5 fellowships with full and partial tuition reimbursements available (averaging $16,582 per year), 17 research assistantships with full and partial tuition reimbursements available (averaging $16,582 per year), 101 teaching assistantships with full and partial tuition reimbursements available (averaging $16,582 per year); institutionally sponsored loans, health care benefits, tuition waivers (full and partial), and unspecified assistantships also available. Financial award application deadline: 2/1; financial award applicants required to submit FAFSA. *Faculty research:* Genetic levels of trophic levels, plant hybrid zones, insect biodiversity, natural history and cognition of wild jays. *Unit head:* Jason Wilder, Chair, 928-523-5286, Fax: 928-523-7500, E-mail: jason.wilder@nau.edu. *Application contact:* Judi Irons, Administrative Assistant, 928-523-0896, Fax: 928-523-7500, E-mail: judith.irons@nau.edu.
Website: https://nau.edu/biological-sciences/

Northern Illinois University, Graduate School, College of Liberal Arts and Sciences, Department of Biological Sciences, De Kalb, IL 60115-2854. Offers MS, PhD. *Program availability:* Part-time. *Faculty:* 30 full-time (6 women), 7 part-time/adjunct (1 woman). *Students:* 40 full-time (26 women), 18 part-time (10 women); includes 3 minority (2 Asian, non-Hispanic/Latino; 1 Hispanic/Latino), 12 international. Average age 29. 46 applicants, 50% accepted, 12 enrolled. In 2017, 19 master's, 8 doctorates awarded. Terminal master's awarded for partial completion of doctoral program. *Degree requirements:* For master's, comprehensive exam, thesis optional; for doctorate, thesis/dissertation, candidacy exam, dissertation defense. *Entrance requirements:* For master's, GRE General Test, bachelor's degree in related field, minimum GPA of 2.75; for doctorate, GRE General Test, bachelor's or master's degree in related field; minimum undergraduate GPA of 2.75, graduate 3.2. Additional exam requirements/recommendations for international students: Required—TOEFL (minimum score 550 paper-based). *Application deadline:* For fall admission, 6/1 for domestic students, 5/1 for international students; for spring admission, 11/1 for domestic students, 10/1 for international students. Applications are processed on a rolling basis. Application fee: $40. Electronic applications accepted. *Financial support:* In 2017–18, 13 research assistantships with full tuition reimbursements, 33 teaching assistantships with full tuition reimbursements were awarded; fellowships with full tuition reimbursements, career-related internships or fieldwork, Federal Work-Study, scholarships/grants, tuition waivers (full), and unspecified assistantships also available. Support available to part-time students. Financial award applicants required to submit FAFSA. *Faculty research:* Plant molecular biology, neurosecretory control, ethnobotany, organellar genomes, carbon metabolism. *Unit head:* Dr. Barrie P. Bode, Chair, 815-753-1753, Fax: 815-753-0461, E-mail: bodebp@niu.edu. *Application contact:* Dr. Thomas Sims, Director of Graduate Studies, 815-753-7873.
Website: http://www.bios.niu.edu/

Northern Michigan University, Office of Graduate Education and Research, College of Arts and Sciences, Department of Biology, Marquette, MI 49855-5301. Offers biology (MS); integrated biosciences (MS). *Program availability:* Part-time. *Degree requirements:* For master's, thesis. *Entrance requirements:* For master's, GRE, minimum GPA of 3.0; references; coursework in biology and other sciences; faculty member as mentor. Additional exam requirements/recommendations for international students: Required—TOEFL (minimum score 550 paper-based; 79 iBT), IELTS (minimum score 6.5). *Application deadline:* For fall admission, 5/1 for domestic students; for winter admission, 12/1 for domestic students; for spring admission, 3/17 for domestic students. Applications are processed on a rolling basis. Application fee: $50. Electronic applications accepted. *Expenses:* Tuition, state resident: full-time $9417; part-time $542 per credit hour. Tuition, nonresident: full-time $12,873; part-time $758 per credit hour. Tuition and fees vary according to course load, degree level and program. *Financial support:* Career-related internships or fieldwork, Federal Work-Study, institutionally sponsored loans, tuition waivers, and unspecified assistantships available. Support available to part-time students. Financial award application deadline: 3/1; financial award applicants required to submit FAFSA. *Faculty research:* Evolutionary genetics, neurobiology, conservation biology, fisheries and wildlife, microbiology. *Unit head:* John Rebers, Head, 906-227-1585, E-mail: jrebers@nmu.edu. *Application contact:* John Rebers, Head, 906-227-1585, E-mail: jrebers@nmu.edu.
Website: http://www.nmu.edu/biology/

Northwestern University, Feinberg School of Medicine, Combined MD/PhD Medical Scientist Training Program, Evanston, IL 60208. Offers MD/PhD. Application must be made to both The Graduate School and the Medical School. *Accreditation:* LCME/AMA. Electronic applications accepted. *Faculty research:* Cardiovascular epidemiology, cancer epidemiology, nutritional interventions for the prevention of cardiovascular disease and cancer, women's health, outcomes research.

Northwestern University, Feinberg School of Medicine and Interdepartmental Programs, Driskill Graduate Program in Life Sciences, Chicago, IL 60611. Offers biostatistics (PhD); epidemiology (PhD); health and biomedical informatics (PhD); health services and outcomes research (PhD); healthcare quality and patient safety (PhD); translational outcomes in science (PhD). *Degree requirements:* For doctorate, comprehensive exam, thesis/dissertation, written and oral qualifying exams. *Entrance requirements:* For doctorate, GRE General Test. Additional exam requirements/recommendations for international students: Required—TOEFL (minimum score 600 paper-based). Electronic applications accepted.

Northwestern University, The Graduate School, Interdisciplinary Biological Sciences Program (IBiS), Evanston, IL 60208. Offers biochemistry (PhD); bioengineering and biotechnology (PhD); biotechnology (PhD), cell and molecular biology (PhD); developmental and systems biology (PhD); nanotechnology (PhD); neurobiology (PhD); structural biology and biophysics (PhD). *Degree requirements:* For doctorate, thesis/dissertation, qualifying exam. *Entrance requirements:* For doctorate, GRE General Test. Additional exam requirements/recommendations for international students: Required—TOEFL (minimum score 600 paper-based). Electronic applications accepted. *Faculty research:* Biophysics/structural biology, cell/molecular biology, synthetic biology, developmental systems biology, chemical biology/nanotechnology.

Northwest Missouri State University, Graduate School, College of Arts and Sciences, Maryville, MO 64468-6001. Offers biology (MS); elementary mathematics specialist (MS Ed); English (MA); English education (MS Ed); English pedagogy (MA); geographic information science (MS, Certificate); history (MS Ed); mathematics (MS); mathematics education (MS Ed); teaching: science (MS Ed). *Program availability:* Part-time. *Faculty:* 67 full-time (21 women). *Students:* 11 full-time (5 women), 70 part-time (39 women);

includes 9 minority (2 Black or African American, non-Hispanic/Latino; 1 American Indian or Alaska Native, non-Hispanic/Latino; 3 Hispanic/Latino; 3 Two or more races, non-Hispanic/Latino). Average age 34. 33 applicants, 42% accepted, 10 enrolled. In 2017, 19 master's, 7 other advanced degrees awarded. *Degree requirements:* For master's, comprehensive exam. *Entrance requirements:* For master's, GRE General Test, writing sample. Additional exam requirements/recommendations for international students: Required—TOEFL (minimum score 550 paper-based). *Application deadline:* For fall admission, 7/1 for domestic and international students; for spring admission, 11/15 for domestic and international students. Applications are processed on a rolling basis. Application fee: $0 ($50 for international students). Electronic applications accepted. *Expenses:* Tuition, state resident: full-time $4551; part-time $252.86 per credit hour. Tuition, nonresident: full-time $9103; part-time $505.72 per credit hour. *Required fees:* $2453; $136.25 per credit hour. Tuition and fees vary according to course load and program. *Financial support:* Research assistantships with full tuition reimbursements, teaching assistantships with full tuition reimbursements, and administrative assistantships, tutorial assistantships available. Financial award application deadline: 4/1; financial award applicants required to submit FAFSA. *Unit head:* Dr. Michael Steiner, Dean, 660-562-1107.
Website: https://www.nwmissouri.edu/academics/undergraduate/majors/liberal-arts-sciences.htm

Nova Southeastern University, College of Medical Sciences, Fort Lauderdale, FL 33314-7796. Offers biomedical sciences (MBS). *Faculty:* 30 full-time (12 women), 1 part-time/adjunct (0 women). *Students:* 53 full-time (29 women); includes 31 minority (4 Black or African American, non-Hispanic/Latino; 7 Asian, non-Hispanic/Latino; 19 Hispanic/Latino; 1 Two or more races, non-Hispanic/Latino), 3 international. Average age 25. 350 applicants, 11% accepted, 40 enrolled. In 2017, 10 master's awarded. *Entrance requirements:* For master's, MCAT, DAT, minimum GPA of 2.5. *Application deadline:* Applications are processed on a rolling basis. Application fee: $50. *Expenses:* Contact institution. *Financial support:* Application deadline: 4/15; applicants required to submit FAFSA. *Faculty research:* Neurophysiology, mucosal immunology, allergies involving the lungs, cardiovascular physiology, parasitology. *Total annual research expenditures:* $2,000. *Unit head:* Dr. Harold E. Laubach, Dean, 954-262-1303, Fax: 954-262-1802, E-mail: harold@nova.edu. *Application contact:* Dr. Lori B. Dribin, Assistant Dean for Student Affairs, 954-262-1341, Fax: 954-262-1802, E-mail: lorib@nova.edu.

Nova Southeastern University, Halmos College of Natural Sciences and Oceanography, Fort Lauderdale, FL 33314-7796. Offers biological sciences (MS), including health studies; marine biology and oceanography (PhD), including marine biology, oceanography. *Program availability:* Part-time, evening/weekend, blended/hybrid learning. *Faculty:* 17 full-time (3 women), 22 part-time/adjunct (11 women). *Students:* 29 full-time (18 women), 149 part-time (93 women); includes 29 minority (5 Black or African American, non-Hispanic/Latino; 6 Asian, non-Hispanic/Latino; 12 Hispanic/Latino; 6 Two or more races, non-Hispanic/Latino), 5 international. Average age 30. 78 applicants, 73% accepted, 34 enrolled. In 2017, 46 master's, 1 doctorate awarded. *Degree requirements:* For master's, thesis; for doctorate, comprehensive exam, thesis/dissertation, departmental qualifying exam. *Entrance requirements:* For master's, GRE General Test, 3 letters of recommendation; BS/BA in natural science (for marine biology program); BS/BA in biology (for biological sciences program); minor in the natural sciences or equivalent (for coastal zone management and marine environmental sciences); for doctorate, GRE General Test, master's degree. Additional exam requirements/recommendations for international students: Required—TOEFL (minimum score 550 paper-based); Recommended—IELTS. *Application deadline:* Applications are processed on a rolling basis. Application fee: $50. Electronic applications accepted. *Expenses:* Contact institution. *Financial support:* In 2017–18, 101 students received support, including 6 fellowships with full and partial tuition reimbursements available (averaging $25,000 per year), 40 research assistantships with full and partial tuition reimbursements available (averaging $20,000 per year), 8 teaching assistantships with tuition reimbursements available (averaging $15,000 per year); career-related internships or fieldwork, Federal Work-Study, scholarships/grants, health care benefits, tuition waivers (full and partial), and unspecified assistantships also available. Support available to part-time students. Financial award application deadline: 4/15; financial award applicants required to submit FAFSA. *Faculty research:* Physical and biological oceanography, molecular and microbiology, ecology and evolution, coral reefs, marine ecosystems. *Total annual research expenditures:* $5 million. *Unit head:* Dr. Richard Dodge, Dean, 954-262-3600, Fax: 954-262-4020, E-mail: dodge@nsu.nova.edu. *Application contact:* Dr. Bernhard Riegl, Chair, Department of Marine and Environmental Sciences, 954-262-3600, Fax: 954-262-4020, E-mail: rieglb@nova.edu.
Website: http://cnso.nova.edu

Oakland University, Graduate Study and Lifelong Learning, College of Arts and Sciences, Department of Biological Sciences, Rochester, MI 48309-4479. Offers biological and biomedical sciences (PhD); biology (MA, MS); biomedical sciences (Graduate Certificate). *Program availability:* Part-time. *Faculty:* 19 full-time (9 women). *Students:* 37 full-time (18 women), 8 part-time (6 women); includes 3 minority (1 Black or African American, non-Hispanic/Latino; 2 Asian, non-Hispanic/Latino), 6 international. Average age 26. 80 applicants, 33% accepted, 18 enrolled. In 2017, 6 master's, 3 doctorates, 2 other advanced degrees awarded. *Degree requirements:* For master's, thesis. *Entrance requirements:* For master's, GRE Subject Test, GRE General Test, minimum GPA of 3.0. Additional exam requirements/recommendations for international students: Required—TOEFL (minimum score 550 paper-based). *Application deadline:* Applications are processed on a rolling basis. Application fee: $0. Electronic applications accepted. *Expenses:* Contact institution. *Financial support:* Federal Work-Study, institutionally sponsored loans, and tuition waivers available. Financial award application deadline: 3/1; financial award applicants required to submit FAFSA. *Unit head:* Dr. Doug Wendell, Chair, 248-370-4457, Fax: 248-370-4225, E-mail: wendell@oakland.edu.
Website: http://www2.oakland.edu/biology

Occidental College, Department of Biology, Los Angeles, CA 90041-3314. Offers MA. *Program availability:* Part-time. *Degree requirements:* For master's, thesis, final exam. *Entrance requirements:* For master's, GRE General Test, GRE Subject Test, minimum GPA of 3.0. Additional exam requirements/recommendations for international students: Required—TOEFL (minimum score 625 paper-based). *Application deadline:* For fall admission, 3/1 for domestic students; for spring admission, 10/1 for domestic students. Applications are processed on a rolling basis. Application fee: $60. *Expenses:* Contact institution. *Financial support:* Fellowships, Federal Work-Study, institutionally sponsored loans, and scholarships/grants available. Support available to part-time students. Financial award application deadline: 3/1; financial award applicants required to submit FAFSA. *Unit head:* Department Chair, 323-259-2697, E-mail: biology@oxy.edu. *Application contact:* Susan Molik, Academic Services Assistant, Graduate Office, 323-259-2921, Fax: 323-341-4988, E-mail: molik@oxy.edu.

The Ohio State University, College of Medicine, Biomedical Sciences Graduate Program, Columbus, OH 43210. Offers PhD. *Students:* 117 full-time (50 women). Average age 27. In 2017, 21 doctorates awarded. *Degree requirements:* For doctorate, thesis/dissertation. *Entrance requirements:* For doctorate, GRE General Test. Additional exam requirements/recommendations for international students: Required—TOEFL (minimum score 600 paper-based; 100 iBT), Michigan English Language Assessment Battery (minimum score 86); Recommended—IELTS (minimum score 8). *Application deadline:* For fall admission, 12/1 for domestic students, 11/1 for international students; for summer admission, 12/1 priority date for domestic students, 11/1 priority date for international students. Applications are processed on a rolling basis. Application fee: $60 ($70 for international students). Electronic applications accepted. *Financial support:* Fellowships with full tuition reimbursements, research assistantships with full tuition reimbursements, scholarships/grants, and unspecified assistantships available. Financial award application deadline: 1/15. *Unit head:* Dr. Jeffrey Parvin, MD, Co-Director, 614-292-0523, Fax: 614-292-6226, E-mail: bsgp@osumc.edu. *Application contact:* Graduate and Professional Admissions, 614-292-9444, Fax: 614-292-3895, E-mail: gpadmissions@osu.edu.
Website: http://medicine.osu.edu/bsgp

The Ohio State University, Graduate School, College of Arts and Sciences, Division of Natural and Mathematical Sciences, Department of Mathematics, Columbus, OH 43210. Offers actuarial and quantitative risk management (MAQRM); computational sciences (MMS); mathematical biosciences (MMS); mathematics (PhD); mathematics for educators (MMS). *Faculty:* 64. *Students:* 142 full-time (22 women); includes 7 minority (all Asian, non-Hispanic/Latino), 75 international. Average age 25. In 2017, 33 master's, 11 doctorates awarded. *Degree requirements:* For master's, thesis optional; for doctorate, one foreign language, thesis/dissertation. *Entrance requirements:* For master's, GRE General Test; for doctorate, GRE General Test (recommended), GRE Subject Test (mathematics). Additional exam requirements/recommendations for international students: Required—TOEFL (minimum score 550 paper-based; 79 iBT), Michigan English Language Assessment Battery (minimum score 82); Recommended—IELTS (minimum score 7). *Application deadline:* For fall admission, 12/15 priority date for domestic and international students. Applications are processed on a rolling basis. Application fee: $60 ($70 for international students). Electronic applications accepted. *Financial support:* Fellowships, research assistantships, teaching assistantships, Federal Work-Study, institutionally sponsored loans, and unspecified assistantships available. Support available to part-time students. *Unit head:* Dr. Luis Casian, Chair and Professor, 614-292-7173, E-mail: casian.1@osu.edu. *Application contact:* Erin Anthony, Graduate Studies Coordinator, 614-292-6274, Fax: 614-292-1479, E-mail: grad-info@math.osu.edu.
Website: http://www.math.osu.edu/

Ohio University, Graduate College, College of Arts and Sciences, Department of Biological Sciences, Athens, OH 45701-2979. Offers biological sciences (MS, PhD); cell biology and physiology (MS, PhD); ecology and evolutionary biology (MS, PhD); exercise physiology and muscle biology (MS, PhD); microbiology (MS, PhD); neuroscience (MS, PhD). Terminal master's awarded for partial completion of doctoral program. *Degree requirements:* For master's, comprehensive exam, thesis, 1 quarter of teaching experience; for doctorate, comprehensive exam, thesis/dissertation, 2 quarters of teaching experience. *Entrance requirements:* For master's, GRE General Test, names of three faculty members whose research interests most closely match the applicant's interest; for doctorate, GRE General Test, essay concerning prior training, research interest and career goals, plus names of three faculty members whose research interests most closely match the applicant's interest. Additional exam requirements/recommendations for international students: Required—TOEFL (minimum score 620 paper-based; 105 iBT) or IELTS (minimum score 7.5). Electronic applications accepted. *Faculty research:* Ecology and evolutionary biology, exercise physiology and muscle biology, neurobiology, cell biology, physiology.

Oklahoma State University, College of Arts and Sciences, Department of Integrative Biology, Stillwater, OK 74078. Offers MS, PhD. *Faculty:* 27 full-time (11 women), 3 part-time/adjunct (all women). *Students:* 5 full-time (3 women), 56 part-time (29 women); includes 9 minority (1 Black or African American, non-Hispanic/Latino; 3 Hispanic/Latino; 5 Two or more races, non-Hispanic/Latino), 5 international. Average age 29. 24 applicants, 67% accepted, 13 enrolled. In 2017, 8 master's, 8 doctorates awarded. *Entrance requirements:* For master's and doctorate, GRE General Test. Additional exam requirements/recommendations for international students: Required—TOEFL (minimum score 550 paper-based; 79 iBT). *Application deadline:* For fall admission, 3/1 priority date for international students; for spring admission, 8/1 priority date for international students. Applications are processed on a rolling basis. Application fee: $40 ($75 for international students). Electronic applications accepted. *Expenses:* Tuition, state resident: full-time $4019; part-time $2679.60 per year. Tuition, nonresident: full-time $15,286; part-time $10,190.40 per year. *Required fees:* $2129; $1419 per unit. Tuition and fees vary according to program. *Financial support:* Research assistantships, teaching assistantships, career-related internships or fieldwork, Federal Work-Study, scholarships/grants, health care benefits, tuition waivers (partial), and unspecified assistantships available. Support available to part-time students. Financial award application deadline: 3/1; financial award applicants required to submit FAFSA. *Unit head:* Dr. Loren Smith, Department Head, 405-744-5555, Fax: 405-744-7824, E-mail: loren.smith@okstate.edu.
Website: http://integrativebiology.okstate.edu/

Oklahoma State University Center for Health Sciences, Program in Biomedical Sciences, Tulsa, OK 74107-1898. Offers MS, PhD, DO/PhD. *Degree requirements:* For master's, thesis; for doctorate, thesis/dissertation, comprehensive, oral and written exam. *Entrance requirements:* For master's, GRE General Test, minimum GPA of 3.0; for doctorate, GRE General Test, MCAT, minimum GPA of 3.0. Additional exam requirements/recommendations for international students: Required—TOEFL (minimum score 79 iBT). Electronic applications accepted. *Expenses:* Contact institution. *Faculty research:* Neuroscience, cell biology, cell signaling, infectious disease, virology, neurotoxicology.

Old Dominion University, College of Sciences, Master of Science in Biology Program, Norfolk, VA 23529. Offers biology (MS); microbiology and immunology (MS). *Program availability:* Part-time. *Faculty:* 22 full-time (4 women), 22 part-time/adjunct (2 women). *Students:* 18 full-time (11 women), 15 part-time (11 women); includes 4 minority (2 Black or African American, non-Hispanic/Latino; 2 Asian, non-Hispanic/Latino). Average age 28. 28 applicants, 25% accepted, 6 enrolled. In 2017, 10 master's awarded. *Degree requirements:* For master's, comprehensive exam, thesis optional, 31 credits. *Entrance requirements:* For master's, GRE General Test, MCAT, minimum GPA of 3.0. Additional exam requirements/recommendations for international students: Required—TOEFL (minimum score 550 paper-based; 79 iBT). *Application deadline:* For fall admission, 2/1 priority date for domestic and international students; for winter admission, 6/1 priority date for domestic and international students; for spring admission, 10/1 priority date for domestic and international students. Application fee: $50. Electronic applications accepted. *Expenses:* Tuition, state resident: full-time $8928; part-time $496 per credit. Tuition, nonresident: full-time $22,482; part-time $1249 per credit. *Required fees:* $66 per semester. *Financial support:* In 2017–18, 11 students received support, including 2 fellowships (averaging $6,575 per year), 10 research assistantships with partial tuition reimbursements available (averaging $15,000 per year), 9 teaching assistantships with partial tuition reimbursements available (averaging $15,000 per year); career-related internships or fieldwork and scholarships/grants also available. Support available to part-time students. Financial award application deadline: 2/1; financial award applicants required to submit FAFSA. *Faculty research:* Ecology and systematics of vertebrates, marine biology, molecular and cellular microbiology and

immunology, vector-borne diseases, human and ecological physiology. *Total annual research expenditures:* $2 million. *Unit head:* Dr. Robert Ratzlaff, Graduate Program Director, 757-683-4361, Fax: 757-683-5283, E-mail: biolgpd@odu.edu. *Application contact:* William Heffelfinger, Director of Graduate Admissions, 757-683-5554, Fax: 757-683-3255, E-mail: gradadmit@odu.edu.
Website: http://sci.odu.edu/biology/academics/bio-ms.shtml

Old Dominion University, College of Sciences, Program in Biomedical Sciences, Norfolk, VA 23529. Offers PhD. *Faculty:* 29 full-time (8 women). *Students:* 8 full-time (4 women), 8 part-time (6 women); includes 3 minority (2 Black or African American, non-Hispanic/Latino; 1 Hispanic/Latino), 7 international. Average age 33. 17 applicants, 12% accepted, 2 enrolled. In 2017, 2 doctorates awarded. *Degree requirements:* For doctorate, comprehensive exam, thesis/dissertation. *Entrance requirements:* For doctorate, GRE General Test, minimum GPA of 3.0. Additional exam requirements/recommendations for international students: Required—TOEFL (minimum score 84 iBT). *Application deadline:* For fall admission, 12/15 priority date for domestic and international students. Application fee: $50. Electronic applications accepted. *Expenses:* Tuition, state resident: full-time $8928; part-time $496 per credit. Tuition, nonresident: full-time $22,482; part-time $1249 per credit. *Required fees:* $66 per semester. *Financial support:* In 2017–18, 2 fellowships with full tuition reimbursements (averaging $18,000 per year), 2 research assistantships with full tuition reimbursements (averaging $18,000 per year), 4 teaching assistantships with full tuition reimbursements (averaging $15,000 per year) were awarded; career-related internships or fieldwork, scholarships/grants, tuition waivers (full), and unspecified assistantships also available. Support available to part-time students. Financial award application deadline: 12/15; financial award applicants required to submit FAFSA. *Faculty research:* Systems biology and biophysics, pure and applied biomedical sciences, biological chemistry, clinical chemistry, cell biology and molecular pathogenesis. *Unit head:* Dr. Lesley Greene, Graduate Program Director, 757-683-6596, E-mail: lgreene@odu.edu. *Application contact:* Kristi Rehrauer, Graduate Program Assistant, 757-683-6979, E-mail: krehraue@odu.edu.

Oregon Health & Science University, School of Medicine, Graduate Programs in Medicine, Portland, OR 97239-3098. Offers MBA, MBI, MCR, MPAS, MS, MSCNU, PhD, Certificate. *Program availability:* Part-time. *Faculty:* 470. *Students:* 355 full-time (206 women), 358 part-time (182 women); includes 179 minority (16 Black or African American, non-Hispanic/Latino; 5 American Indian or Alaska Native, non-Hispanic/Latino; 90 Asian, non-Hispanic/Latino; 38 Hispanic/Latino; 30 Two or more races, non-Hispanic/Latino), 54 international. Average age 33. In 2017, 153 master's, 34 doctorates, 78 other advanced degrees awarded. Terminal master's awarded for partial completion of doctoral program. *Entrance requirements:* For master's, GRE General Test (minimum scores: 153 Verbal/148 Quantitative/4.5 Analytical), MCAT or GMAT (for some programs); for doctorate, GRE General Test (minimum scores: 153 Verbal/148 Quantitative/4.5 Analytical). *Financial support:* Fellowships, research assistantships, teaching assistantships, scholarships/grants, health care benefits, and full-tuition and stipends (for PhD students) available. Financial award application deadline: 3/1; financial award applicants required to submit FAFSA. *Unit head:* Dr. Allison Fryer, Associate Dean for Graduate Studies, 503-494-6222, E-mail: somgrad@ohsu.edu. *Application contact:* Lorie Gookin, Admissions Coordinator, 503-494-6222, E-mail: somgrad@ohsu.edu.

Oregon State University, College of Science, Program in Integrative Biology, Corvallis, OR 97331. Offers behavioral ecology (MS, PhD). Terminal master's awarded for partial completion of doctoral program. *Entrance requirements:* For master's and doctorate, GRE. Additional exam requirements/recommendations for international students: Required—TOEFL (minimum score 80 iBT), IELTS (minimum score 6.5). *Application deadline:* For fall admission, 12/15 for domestic and international students. Application fee: $75 ($85 for international students). Electronic applications accepted. *Faculty research:* Ecology and evolutionary biology, physiology and behavior, development and cell biology. *Unit head:* Robert T. Mason, Head, 541-737-5335, E-mail: masonr@science.oregonstate.edu. *Application contact:* Graduate Admissions Coordinator, 541-737-5335, E-mail: ib@science.oregonstate.edu.
Website: http://ib.oregonstate.edu/

Oregon State University, Interdisciplinary/Institutional Programs, Program in Comparative Health Sciences, Corvallis, OR 97331. Offers biomedical sciences (MS, PhD). *Entrance requirements:* For master's and doctorate, GRE. Additional exam requirements/recommendations for international students: Required—TOEFL (minimum score 80 iBT), IELTS (minimum score 6.5). *Application deadline:* For fall admission, 12/10 for domestic and international students. Application fee: $75 ($85 for international students). *Unit head:* Lynette Hawthorne, Administrative Assistant, E-mail: lynette.hawthorne@oregonstate.edu. *Application contact:* Carolyn Cowan, Assistant to the Department Head, 541-737-6921, E-mail: carolyn.cowan@oregonstate.edu.

Pace University, School of Education, New York, NY 10038. Offers adolescent education (MST), including biology, chemistry, earth science, English, foreign languages, mathematics, physics, social studies; childhood education (MST); early childhood development, learning and intervention (MST); educational technology studies (MS); inclusive adolescent education (MST), including biology, chemistry, earth science, English, foreign languages, mathematics, physics, social studies; integrated instruction for educational technology (Certificate); integrated instruction for literacy and technology (Certificate); literacy (MS Ed); special education (MS Ed). *Accreditation:* NCATE. *Program availability:* Part-time, evening/weekend, 100% online, blended/hybrid learning. *Faculty:* 19 full-time (13 women), 86 part-time/adjunct (49 women). *Students:* 91 full-time (76 women), 548 part-time (401 women); includes 247 minority (112 Black or African American, non-Hispanic/Latino; 2 American Indian or Alaska Native, non-Hispanic/Latino; 31 Asian, non-Hispanic/Latino; 93 Hispanic/Latino; 1 Native Hawaiian or other Pacific Islander, non-Hispanic/Latino; 8 Two or more races, non-Hispanic/Latino), 6 international. Average age 30. 188 applicants, 86% accepted, 114 enrolled. In 2017, 213 master's, 8 other advanced degrees awarded. *Degree requirements:* For master's and Certificate, certification exams. *Entrance requirements:* For master's, GRE (for initial certification programs only), teaching certificate (for MS Ed in literacy and special education programs only). Additional exam requirements/recommendations for international students: Required—TOEFL (minimum score 88 iBT), IELTS or PTE. *Application deadline:* For fall admission, 8/1 priority date for domestic students, 6/1 for international students; for spring admission, 12/1 priority date for domestic students, 10/1 for international students. Applications are processed on a rolling basis. Application fee: $70. Electronic applications accepted. *Expenses:* Contact institution. *Financial support:* In 2017–18, 17 students received support, including 17 research assistantships with partial tuition reimbursements available (averaging $6,020 per year); career-related internships or fieldwork, Federal Work-Study, scholarships/grants, and unspecified assistantships also available. Financial award application deadline: 9/1; financial award applicants required to submit FAFSA. *Faculty research:* STEM education, TESOL, teacher education, special education, language and literary development. *Total annual research expenditures:* $29,706. *Unit head:* Dr. Xiao-Lei Wang, Dean, School of Education, 914-773-3876, E-mail: xwang@pace.edu. *Application contact:* Susan Ford-Goldschein, Director of Graduate Admissions, 212-346-1531, Fax: 212-346-1585, E-mail: graduateadmission@pace.edu.
Website: http://www.pace.edu/school-of-education

Penn State Hershey Medical Center, College of Medicine, Graduate School Programs in the Biomedical Sciences, Hershey, PA 17033. Offers MPH, MS, Dr PH, PhD, MD/PhD, PhD/MBA. Terminal master's awarded for partial completion of doctoral program. *Degree requirements:* For master's, thesis or alternative; for doctorate, comprehensive exam, thesis/dissertation, oral exam. *Entrance requirements:* For master's, GRE; for doctorate, GRE, minimum GPA of 3.0. Additional exam requirements/recommendations for international students: Required—TOEFL (minimum score 550 paper-based; 81 iBT). *Application deadline:* Applications are processed on a rolling basis. Application fee: $65. Electronic applications accepted. *Expenses:* Contact institution. *Financial support:* In 2017–18, research assistantships with full tuition reimbursements (averaging $27,802 per year) were awarded; fellowships with full tuition reimbursements, career-related internships or fieldwork, scholarships/grants, health care benefits, tuition waivers (full), and unspecified assistantships also available. *Unit head:* Dr. Charles Lang, Associate Dean of Graduate Studies, 717-531-8892, Fax: 717-531-0786, E-mail: grad-hmc@psu.edu. *Application contact:* Kristin E. Smith, Director of Graduate Admissions, 717-531-1045, Fax: 717-531-0786, E-mail: kec17@psu.edu.

Penn State University Park, Graduate School, Eberly College of Science, Department of Biology, University Park, PA 16802. Offers MS, PhD. *Unit head:* Dr. Douglas R. Cavener, Dean, 814-865-9591, Fax: 814-865-3634. *Application contact:* Lori Hawn, Director, Graduate Student Services, 814-865-1795, Fax: 814-863-4627, E-mail: l-gswww@lists.psu.edu.
Website: http://bio.psu.edu/

Penn State University Park, Graduate School, Intercollege Graduate Programs, Program in Molecular, Cellular, and Integrative Biosciences, University Park, PA 16802. Offers MS, PhD. *Unit head:* Dr. Regina Vasilatos-Younken, Dean, 814-865-2516, Fax: 814-863-4627. *Application contact:* Lori Hawn, Director, Graduate Student Services, 814-865-1795, Fax: 814-863-4627, E-mail: l-gswww@lists.psu.edu.
Website: http://www.huck.psu.edu/content/graduate-programs/molecular-cellular-and-integrative-biosciences

Philadelphia College of Osteopathic Medicine, Graduate and Professional Programs, Graduate Programs in Biomedical Sciences, Philadelphia, PA 19131-1694. Offers MS. *Program availability:* Evening/weekend. *Faculty:* 25 full-time (14 women). *Students:* 108 full-time (64 women); includes 30 minority (9 Black or African American, non-Hispanic/Latino; 4 Asian, non-Hispanic/Latino; 2 Hispanic/Latino; 15 Two or more races, non-Hispanic/Latino). Average age 26. 362 applicants, 57% accepted, 79 enrolled. In 2017, 43 master's awarded. *Degree requirements:* For master's, thesis optional. *Entrance requirements:* For master's, GRE, MCAT, DAT, OAT, PCAT, pre-medical prerequisite coursework; biochemistry (recommended). Additional exam requirements/recommendations for international students: Required—TOEFL (minimum score 79 iBT). *Application deadline:* Applications are processed on a rolling basis. Application fee: $75. Electronic applications accepted. *Expenses:* Contact institution. *Financial support:* In 2017–18, 59 students received support. Federal Work-Study, institutionally sponsored loans, and scholarships/grants available. Financial award application deadline: 3/15; financial award applicants required to submit FAFSA. *Faculty research:* Neuroscience and neurodegenerative disorders, inflammation and allergic response to food allergens, cardiovascular function and disease, bone and joint disorders, cancer biology. *Total annual research expenditures:* $533,489. *Unit head:* Dr. Marcus Bell, Chair, 215-871-6834, Fax: 215-871-6865, E-mail: marcusbe@pcom.edu. *Application contact:* Kevin A. Zajac, Assistant Director of Admissions, 215-871-6700, Fax: 215-871-6719, E-mail: kevinzaj@pcom.edu.
Website: http://www.pcom.edu

Pittsburg State University, Graduate School, College of Arts and Sciences, Department of Biology, Pittsburg, KS 66762. Offers MS. *Faculty:* 16. *Students:* 11 (7 women); includes 1 minority (Two or more races, non-Hispanic/Latino), 2 international. In 2017, 5 master's awarded. *Degree requirements:* For master's, thesis or alternative. *Entrance requirements:* For master's, letter of intent. Additional exam requirements/recommendations for international students: Required—TOEFL (minimum score 520 paper-based; 68 iBT), IELTS (minimum score 6), PTE (minimum score 47). *Application deadline:* For fall admission, 6/1 for international students; for spring admission, 10/15 for international students; for summer admission, 4/1 for international students. Applications are processed on a rolling basis. Application fee: $35 ($60 for international students). Electronic applications accepted. *Expenses:* Contact institution. *Financial support:* In 2017–18, 5 teaching assistantships with full tuition reimbursements (averaging $5,500 per year) were awarded; fellowships, research assistantships, career-related internships or fieldwork, Federal Work-Study, and unspecified assistantships also available. Financial award application deadline: 2/1; financial award applicants required to submit FAFSA. *Unit head:* Dr. Dixie Smith, Chairperson, 620-235-4741, E-mail: dsmith@pittstate.edu. *Application contact:* Lisa Allen, Assistant Director of Graduate and Continuing Studies, 620-235-4223, Fax: 620-235-4219, E-mail: lallen@pittstate.edu.

Point Loma Nazarene University, Department of Biology, San Diego, CA 92106-2899. Offers MS. *Program availability:* Part-time. *Faculty:* 5 full-time (3 women). *Students:* 3 full-time (1 woman), 15 part-time (11 women); includes 10 minority (5 Asian, non-Hispanic/Latino; 2 Hispanic/Latino; 3 Two or more races, non-Hispanic/Latino), 1 international. Average age 31. 7 applicants, 71% accepted, 5 enrolled. In 2017, 7 master's awarded. *Degree requirements:* For master's, comprehensive exam (for some programs), thesis (for some programs). *Entrance requirements:* For master's, major field test in biology or GRE Subject Test (biology), BA/BS in science field, letters of recommendation, essay, interview. Additional exam requirements/recommendations for international students: Required—TOEFL. *Application deadline:* For fall admission, 7/26 priority date for domestic students; for spring admission, 11/29 priority date for domestic students; for summer admission, 5/23 priority date for domestic students. Application fee: $50. Electronic applications accepted. *Expenses:* Contact institution. *Financial support:* Available to part-time students. Applicants required to submit FAFSA. *Faculty research:* Biology education, immunology, angiogenesis, population genetics. *Unit head:* Dr. Dianne Anderson, Director of Master's Program in Biology, 619-849-2705, E-mail: dianneanderson@pointloma.edu. *Application contact:* Maira Lopes, Enrollment Advisor, 619-948-2885, E-mail: mairalopes@pointloma.edu.
Website: https://www.pointloma.edu/graduate-studies/programs/general-biology-ms

Ponce Health Sciences University, Program in Biomedical Sciences, Ponce, PR 00732-7004. Offers PhD. *Degree requirements:* For doctorate, one foreign language, comprehensive exam, thesis/dissertation. *Entrance requirements:* For doctorate, GRE General Test, proficiency in Spanish and English, minimum overall GPA of 3.0, 3 letters of recommendation, minimum of 35 credits in science.

Pontifical Catholic University of Puerto Rico, College of Sciences, Department of Biology, Ponce, PR 00717-0777. Offers environmental sciences (MS). *Degree requirements:* For master's, thesis. *Entrance requirements:* For master's, GRE, 2 letters of recommendation, interview, minimum GPA of 2.75.

Portland State University, Graduate Studies, College of Liberal Arts and Sciences, Department of Biology, Portland, OR 97207-0751. Offers MA, MS, PhD. *Faculty:* 21 full-time (9 women), 4 part-time/adjunct (0 women). *Students:* 52 full-time (36 women), 18 part-time (11 women); includes 10 minority (4 Asian, non-Hispanic/Latino; 2 Hispanic/

Latino; 1 Native Hawaiian or other Pacific Islander, non-Hispanic/Latino; 3 Two or more races, non-Hispanic/Latino), 2 international. Average age 30. 69 applicants, 25% accepted, 14 enrolled. In 2017, 8 master's, 3 doctorates awarded. *Degree requirements:* For master's, one foreign language, thesis; for doctorate, thesis/dissertation. *Entrance requirements:* For master's, GRE General Test, GRE Subject Test, minimum GPA of 3.0 in upper-division course work or 2.75 overall, 2 letters of reference; for doctorate, GRE General Test, GRE Subject Test, minimum GPA of 3.5 in science. Additional exam requirements/recommendations for international students: Required—TOEFL (minimum score 550 paper-based; 80 iBT). *Application deadline:* For fall admission, 2/15 for domestic and international students; for winter admission, 9/1 for domestic students, 7/1 for international students; for spring admission, 11/1 for domestic and international students. Application fee: $65. *Expenses:* Tuition, state resident: full-time $14,436; part-time $401 per credit. Tuition, nonresident: full-time $21,780; part-time $605 per credit. *Required fees:* $1380; $22 per credit. $119 per quarter. One-time fee: $325. Tuition and fees vary according to program. *Financial support:* In 2017–18, 44 students received support, including 10 research assistantships with full and partial tuition reimbursements available (averaging $18,001 per year), 33 teaching assistantships (averaging $23,000 per year); Federal Work-Study, scholarships/grants, tuition waivers (full and partial), and unspecified assistantships also available. Support available to part-time students. Financial award application deadline: 3/1; financial award applicants required to submit FAFSA. *Faculty research:* Genetic diversity and natural population, vertebrate temperature regulation, water balance and sensory physiology, trace elements and aquatic ecology, molecular genetics. *Total annual research expenditures:* $2.4 million. *Unit head:* Dr. Michael Bartlett, Chair, 503-725-3858, E-mail: micb@pdx.edu.
Website: https://www.pdx.edu/biology/

Purdue University, Graduate School, Biomedical Sciences Interdisciplinary Graduate Program, West Lafayette, IN 47907. Offers PhD. Program offered jointly by School of Veterinary Medicine and Weldon School of Biomedical Engineering. *Students:* 9 full-time (7 women); includes 4 minority (2 Asian, non-Hispanic/Latino; 2 Two or more races, non-Hispanic/Latino), 4 international. Average age 26. 18 applicants, 22% accepted, 4 enrolled. *Degree requirements:* For doctorate, thesis/dissertation, seminars, teaching experience. *Entrance requirements:* For doctorate, GRE General Test (minimum scores: verbal 550, quantitative 700), minimum undergraduate GPA of 3.0. Additional exam requirements/recommendations for international students: Required—TOEFL (minimum score 550 paper-based; 77 iBT); Recommended—TWE. *Application deadline:* For fall admission, 12/15 priority date for domestic and international students. Applications are processed on a rolling basis. Application fee: $60 ($75 for international students). Electronic applications accepted. *Financial support:* Fellowships, research assistantships, and teaching assistantships available. Support available to part-time students. *Unit head:* Harm HogenEsch, Head of the Graduate Program, 765-496-3485, Fax: 765-496-1261, E-mail: hogenesch@purdue.edu. *Application contact:* Sandra M. May, Graduate Contact for Admissions, 765-494-7054, E-mail: smmay@purdue.edu.
Website: http://www.gradschool.purdue.edu/BSDT/

Purdue University, Graduate School, College of Science, Department of Biological Sciences, West Lafayette, IN 47907. Offers biochemistry (PhD); biophysics (PhD); cell and developmental biology (PhD); ecology, evolutionary and population biology (MS, PhD), including ecology, evolutionary biology, population biology; genetics (MS, PhD); microbiology (MS, PhD); molecular biology (PhD); neurobiology (MS, PhD); plant physiology (PhD). *Faculty:* 42 full-time (13 women), 3 part-time/adjunct (0 women). *Students:* 115 full-time (58 women), 6 part-time (4 women); includes 17 minority (1 Black or African American, non-Hispanic/Latino; 6 Asian, non-Hispanic/Latino; 9 Hispanic/Latino; 1 Two or more races, non-Hispanic/Latino), 60 international. Average age 27. 165 applicants, 12% accepted, 15 enrolled. In 2017, 5 master's, 16 doctorates awarded. Terminal master's awarded for partial completion of doctoral program. *Degree requirements:* For master's, thesis (for some programs); for doctorate, thesis/dissertation, seminars, teaching experience. *Entrance requirements:* For master's, GRE General Test (minimum analytical writing score of 3.5), minimum undergraduate GPA of 3.0; for doctorate, GRE General Test (minimum analytical writing score of 3.5), minimum undergraduate GPA of 3.5. Additional exam requirements/recommendations for international students: Required—TOEFL minimum score 600 paper-based; 107 iBT (for MS), 80 iBT (for PhD). *Application deadline:* For fall admission, 12/7 for domestic and international students. Applications are processed on a rolling basis. Application fee: $60 ($75 for international students). Electronic applications accepted. *Financial support:* Fellowships, research assistantships, and teaching assistantships available. Support available to part-time students. Financial award application deadline: 2/15; financial award applicants required to submit FAFSA. *Unit head:* Stephen Konieczny, Head, 765-494-4407, E-mail: sfk@purdue.edu. *Application contact:* Georgina E. Rupp, Graduate Coordinator, 765-494-8142, E-mail: ruppg@purdue.edu.
Website: http://www.bio.purdue.edu/

Purdue University, Graduate School, PULSe - Purdue University Life Sciences Program, West Lafayette, IN 47907. Offers biomolecular structure and biophysics (PhD); biotechnology (PhD); chemical biology (PhD); chromatin and regulation of gene expression (PhD); integrative neuroscience (PhD); integrative plant sciences (PhD); membrane biology (PhD); microbiology (PhD); molecular evolutionary and cancer biology (PhD); molecular evolutionary genetics (PhD); molecular virology (PhD). *Students:* 60 full-time (29 women); includes 6 minority (4 Hispanic/Latino; 2 Two or more races, non-Hispanic/Latino), 36 international. Average age 25. 127 applicants, 39% accepted, 25 enrolled. *Entrance requirements:* For doctorate, GRE, minimum undergraduate GPA of 3.0. Additional exam requirements/recommendations for international students: Required—TOEFL (minimum score 550 paper-based; 77 iBT). *Application deadline:* For fall admission, 1/15 priority date for domestic and international students. Applications are processed on a rolling basis. Application fee: $60 ($75 for international students). Electronic applications accepted. *Financial support:* In 2017–18, research assistantships with tuition reimbursements (averaging $22,500 per year), teaching assistantships with tuition reimbursements (averaging $22,500 per year) were awarded. *Unit head:* Dr. Jason R. Cannon, Head of the Graduate Program, 765-494-0794, E-mail: cannonjr@purdue.edu. *Application contact:* Lindsey Springer, Graduate Contact for Admissions, 765-496-9667, E-mail: lbcampbe@purdue.edu.
Website: http://www.gradschool.purdue.edu/pulse

Purdue University Northwest, Graduate Studies Office, School of Engineering, Mathematics, and Science, Department of Biological Sciences, Hammond, IN 46323-2094. Offers biology (MS); biology teaching (MS); biotechnology (MS). *Entrance requirements:* For master's, GRE. Additional exam requirements/recommendations for international students: Required—TOEFL. Electronic applications accepted. *Faculty research:* Cell biology, molecular biology, genetics, microbiology, neurophysiology.

Queens College of the City University of New York, Division of Education, Department of Secondary Education and Youth Services, Queens, NY 11367-1597. Offers adolescent biology (MAT); art (MS Ed); biology (MS Ed, AC); chemistry (MS Ed, AC); earth sciences (MS Ed, AC); English (MS Ed, AC); French (MS Ed); Italian (MS Ed, AC); literacy education (MS Ed); mathematics (MS Ed, AC); music (MS Ed, AC); physics (MS Ed, AC); social studies (MS Ed, AC); Spanish (MS Ed, AC). *Program availability:* Part-time, evening/weekend. *Students:* 28 full-time (16 women), 349 part-time (202 women); includes 165 minority (18 Black or African American, non-Hispanic/Latino; 56 Asian, non-Hispanic/Latino; 83 Hispanic/Latino; 8 Two or more races, non-Hispanic/Latino), 14 international. Average age 29. *Degree requirements:* For master's, research project. *Entrance requirements:* For master's, minimum GPA of 3.0. Additional exam requirements/recommendations for international students: Required—TOEFL, IELTS. *Application deadline:* For fall admission, 4/1 for domestic students; for spring admission, 11/1 for domestic students. Applications are processed on a rolling basis. Application fee: $125. Electronic applications accepted. *Financial support:* Career-related internships or fieldwork available. Financial award application deadline: 4/1; financial award applicants required to submit FAFSA. *Unit head:* Dr. Eleanor Armour-Thomas, Chairperson, 718-997-5150, E-mail: eleanor.armour-thomas@qc.cuny.edu. *Application contact:* Elizabeth D'Amico-Ramirez, Assistant Director of Graduate Admissions, 718-997-5203, E-mail: elizabeth.damicoramirez@qc.cuny.edu.

Queens College of the City University of New York, Mathematics and Natural Sciences Division, Department of Biology, Queens, NY 11367-1597. Offers MA. *Program availability:* Part-time. *Faculty:* 18 full-time (6 women), 31 part-time/adjunct (16 women). *Students:* 3 full-time (all women), 18 part-time (12 women); includes 10 minority (6 Asian, non-Hispanic/Latino; 3 Hispanic/Latino; 1 Native Hawaiian or other Pacific Islander, non-Hispanic/Latino), 2 international. Average age 29. 26 applicants, 69% accepted, 9 enrolled. In 2017, 4 master's awarded. *Degree requirements:* For master's, thesis, qualifying exam. *Entrance requirements:* For master's, minimum GPA of 3.0. Additional exam requirements/recommendations for international students: Required—TOEFL (minimum score 100 iBT), IELTS (minimum score 7). *Application deadline:* For fall admission, 4/1 for domestic students; for spring admission, 11/1 for domestic students. Applications are processed on a rolling basis. Application fee: $125. Electronic applications accepted. *Financial support:* Career-related internships or fieldwork, Federal Work-Study, institutionally sponsored loans, tuition waivers (partial), and unspecified assistantships available. Support available to part-time students. Financial award application deadline: 4/1; financial award applicants required to submit FAFSA. *Faculty research:* Developmental genetics, evolutionary ecology, urban ecology and conservation, cell signaling pathways, molecular biology. *Unit head:* Daniel Weinstein, Chair, 718-997-4552, E-mail: daniel.weinstein@qc.cuny.edu. *Application contact:* David C Lahti, Graduate Advisor, Department of Biology, 718-997-3422, E-mail: david.lahti@qc.cuny.edu.

Queen's University at Kingston, School of Graduate Studies, Faculty of Arts and Sciences, Department of Biology, Kingston, ON K7L 3N6, Canada. Offers M Sc, PhD. *Program availability:* Part-time. *Degree requirements:* For master's, thesis; for doctorate, comprehensive exam, thesis/dissertation. *Entrance requirements:* Additional exam requirements/recommendations for international students: Required—TOEFL. *Faculty research:* Limnology, plant morphogenesis, nitrogen fixation, cell cycle, genetics.

Quinnipiac University, School of Health Sciences, Program in Biomedical Sciences, Hamden, CT 06518-1940. Offers MHS. *Program availability:* Part-time, evening/weekend. *Faculty:* 10 full-time (4 women), 12 part-time/adjunct (4 women). *Students:* 74 full-time (46 women), 14 part-time (6 women); includes 31 minority (14 Black or African American, non-Hispanic/Latino; 10 Asian, non-Hispanic/Latino; 6 Hispanic/Latino; 1 Two or more races, non-Hispanic/Latino), 20 international. 117 applicants, 62% accepted, 35 enrolled. In 2017, 29 master's awarded. *Degree requirements:* For master's, comprehensive exam, thesis optional. *Entrance requirements:* For master's, minimum GPA of 2.75; bachelor's degree in biological, medical, or health sciences. Additional exam requirements/recommendations for international students: Required—TOEFL (minimum score 575 paper-based; 90 iBT), IELTS (minimum score 6.5). *Application deadline:* For fall admission, 7/30 priority date for domestic students, 4/30 priority date for international students; for spring admission, 12/15 priority date for domestic students, 9/30 priority date for international students. Applications are processed on a rolling basis. Application fee: $45. Electronic applications accepted. *Financial support:* Federal Work-Study, scholarships/grants, and unspecified assistantships available. Financial award application deadline: 6/1; financial award applicants required to submit FAFSA. *Faculty research:* ACL injury mechanism and running injuries and performance; transcriptional activators upstream stimulatory factor (USF); identification of novel antimicrobials; vaccines, formites and opportunistic pathogens; molecular biology of the Lyme Disease agent, Borrelia burgdorferi; molecular and microscopic techniques in host-pathogen interactions; non-invasive vascular biology, external pneumatic compression, sports performance. *Unit head:* Dwayne Boucaud, Program Director, 203-582-3768, E-mail: graduate@qu.edu. *Application contact:* Office of Graduate Admissions, 800-462-1944, Fax: 203-582-3443, E-mail: graduate@qu.edu.
Website: https://www.qu.edu/schools/health-sciences/programs/mhs-biomedical-sciences.html

Regis University, Regis College, Denver, CO 80221-1099. Offers biomedical sciences (MS); developmental practice (MDP); education (MA); environmental biology (MS). *Accreditation:* TEAC. *Program availability:* Part-time. *Degree requirements:* For master's, thesis (for some programs), capstone presentation. *Entrance requirements:* For master's, official transcript reflecting baccalaureate degree awarded from U.S.-based regionally-accredited college or university. Additional exam requirements/recommendations for international students: Required—TOEFL (minimum score 550 paper-based; 82 iBT). Electronic applications accepted. *Expenses:* Contact institution.

Rensselaer Polytechnic Institute, Graduate School, School of Science, Program in Biology, Troy, NY 12180-3590. Offers MS, PhD. *Faculty:* 21 full-time (8 women), 2 part-time/adjunct (1 woman). *Students:* 13 full-time (3 women), 1 part-time (0 women); includes 1 minority (Black or African American, non-Hispanic/Latino), 3 international. Average age 27. 91 applicants, 18% accepted, 5 enrolled. In 2017, 1 master's, 5 doctorates awarded. Terminal master's awarded for partial completion of doctoral program. *Degree requirements:* For master's, comprehensive exam, thesis optional; for doctorate, comprehensive exam, thesis/dissertation. *Entrance requirements:* For master's and doctorate, GRE. Additional exam requirements/recommendations for international students: Required—TOEFL (minimum score 570 paper-based; 88 iBT), IELTS (minimum score 6.5), PTE (minimum score 60). *Application deadline:* For fall admission, 1/1 priority date for domestic and international students. Applications are processed on a rolling basis. Application fee: $75. Electronic applications accepted. *Expenses: Tuition:* Full-time $52,550; part-time $2125 per credit hour. *Required fees:* $2890. *Financial support:* In 2017–18, research assistantships (averaging $23,000 per year), teaching assistantships (averaging $23,000 per year) were awarded; fellowships also available. Financial award application deadline: 1/1. *Faculty research:* Biochemistry; bioinformatics; biophysics; cancer biology; computational biology; ecology and environmental sciences; microbiology; molecular, cell, and developmental biology; neuroscience; stem cells; structural biology. *Total annual research expenditures:* $1.4 million. *Unit head:* Dr. George Makhatadze, Graduate Program Director, 518-276-4417, E-mail: makhag@rpi.edu.
Website: https://science.rpi.edu/biology/graduate

Rhode Island College, School of Graduate Studies, Faculty of Arts and Sciences, Department of Biology, Providence, RI 02908-1991. Offers biology (MA); modern biological sciences (CGS). *Program availability:* Part-time. *Faculty:* 6. *Students:* 1 full-time (0 women), 4 part-time (1 woman). Average age 31. In 2017, 1 other advanced degree awarded. *Degree requirements:* For master's, thesis. *Entrance requirements:* For master's, GRE General and Subject Tests. Additional exam requirements/

recommendations for international students: Recommended—TOEFL (minimum score 550 paper-based; 79 iBT). *Application deadline:* For fall admission, 3/1 for domestic students. Applications are processed on a rolling basis. Application fee: $50. Electronic applications accepted. *Expenses:* Tuition, state resident: full-time $9768; part-time $407 per credit. Tuition, nonresident: full-time $19,008; part-time $792 per credit. *Required fees:* $696; $29 per credit. One-time fee: $200 full-time; $100 part-time. Tuition and fees vary according to course load. *Financial support:* In 2017–18, 3 teaching assistantships with full tuition reimbursements (averaging $2,917 per year) were awarded; career-related internships or fieldwork, Federal Work-Study, scholarships/grants, health care benefits, and unspecified assistantships also available. Support available to part-time students. Financial award application deadline: 5/15; financial award applicants required to submit FAFSA. *Unit head:* Dr. Rebeka Merson, Chair, 401-456-8010, E-mail: biology@ric.edu.
Website: http://www.ric.edu/biology/index.php

Rochester Institute of Technology, Graduate Enrollment Services, College of Science, School of Life Sciences, Rochester, NY 14623. Offers MS. *Program availability:* Part-time. *Students:* 21 full-time (11 women), 12 part-time (4 women); includes 2 minority (1 Black or African American, non-Hispanic/Latino; 1 Two or more races, non-Hispanic/Latino), 6 international. Average age 27. 51 applicants, 33% accepted, 10 enrolled. In 2017, 8 master's awarded. *Entrance requirements:* For master's, GRE (for some programs), minimum GPA of 3.0 (recommended). *Application deadline:* For fall admission, 2/15 priority date for domestic and international students; for spring admission, 12/15 priority date for domestic and international students. Applications are processed on a rolling basis. Application fee: $65. Electronic applications accepted. *Expenses:* $1,815 per credit hour. *Financial support:* In 2017–18, 26 students received support. Research assistantships with partial tuition reimbursements available, teaching assistantships with partial tuition reimbursements available, career-related internships or fieldwork, scholarships/grants, and unspecified assistantships available. Support available to part-time students. Financial award applicants required to submit FAFSA. *Faculty research:* Gene expression analysis and genomic sequence analysis; computational biology and evolution; machine learning of big data in biology; metabolomics; aquatic ecology, global warming; microbial degradation of pharmaceuticals; GIS applications; nutrition of migratory birds. *Unit head:* Dr. André O. Hudson, School Head, 585-475-4259, E-mail: aohsbi@rit.edu. *Application contact:* Diane Ellison, Senior Associate Vice President, Graduate Enrollment Services, 585-475-2229, Fax: 585-475-7164, E-mail: gradinfo@rit.edu.
Website: http://www.rit.edu/science/gsols

The Rockefeller University, The David Rockefeller Graduate Program in Bioscience, New York, NY 10021-6399. Offers MS, PhD. *Faculty:* 79 full-time (11 women). *Students:* 232 full-time (92 women); includes 50 minority (6 Black or African American, non-Hispanic/Latino; 23 Asian, non-Hispanic/Latino; 20 Hispanic/Latino; 1 Native Hawaiian or other Pacific Islander, non-Hispanic/Latino), 72 international. Average age 25. 786 applicants, 10% accepted, 26 enrolled. In 2017, 9 master's, 23 doctorates awarded. Terminal master's awarded for partial completion of doctoral program. *Degree requirements:* For master's, thesis; for doctorate, thesis/dissertation. *Entrance requirements:* For doctorate, GRE General Test; GRE Subject Test (strongly recommended), three letters of recommendation, official college or university transcripts, personal essay. Additional exam requirements/recommendations for international students: Required—TOEFL. *Application deadline:* For fall and winter admission, 12/1 for domestic and international students. Application fee: $50. Electronic applications accepted. Application fee is waived when completed online. *Financial support:* In 2017–18, 232 students received support, including 232 fellowships with full tuition reimbursements available; institutionally sponsored loans, scholarships/grants, traineeships, and health care benefits also available. *Unit head:* Dr. Sidney Strickland, Dean of Graduate and Postgraduate Studies/Vice President, 212-327-8086, Fax: 212-327-8505, E-mail: phd@rockefeller.edu. *Application contact:* Kristen Cullen, Graduate Admissions Administrator/Registrar, 212-327-8086, Fax: 212-327-8505, E-mail: phd@rockefeller.edu.
Website: http://www.rockefeller.edu/graduate/

See Display below and Close-Up on page 111.

Rocky Vista University, Program in Biomedical Sciences, Parker, CO 80134. Offers MS. *Entrance requirements:* For master's, GRE, MCAT, PCAT, or DAT, U.S. citizenship or permanent residency, bachelor's degree, minimum science and overall GPA of 2.75, resume, two letters of recommendation. Application fee: $50. *Unit head:* Dr. Francina Deason Towne, Director, 720-875-2837, E-mail: ftowne@rvu.edu. *Application contact:* Dr. Francina Deason Towne, Director, 720-875-2837, E-mail: ftowne@rvu.edu.
Website: http://www.rvu.edu/rvu-co/msbs/

Rosalind Franklin University of Medicine and Science, College of Health Professions, Department of Interprofessional Healthcare Studies, Biomedical Sciences Program, North Chicago, IL 60064-3095. Offers MS. *Entrance requirements:* For master's, MCAT, DAT, OAT, PCAT or GRE, BS in chemistry, physics, biology. Additional exam requirements/recommendations for international students: Required—TOEFL.

Rosalind Franklin University of Medicine and Science, School of Graduate and Postdoctoral Studies - Interdisciplinary Graduate Program in Biomedical Sciences, North Chicago, IL 60064-3095. Offers MS, PhD, DPM/PhD, MD/PhD. Terminal master's awarded for partial completion of doctoral program. *Degree requirements:* For master's, comprehensive exam, thesis, publication; for doctorate, comprehensive exam, thesis/dissertation. *Entrance requirements:* For master's and doctorate, GRE General Test. Additional exam requirements/recommendations for international students: Required—TOEFL, TWE. Electronic applications accepted. *Expenses:* Contact institution. *Faculty research:* Extracellular matrix, nutrition and mood, neuropsychopharmacology, membrane transport, brain metabolism.

Rowan University, Graduate School, College of Science and Mathematics, Department of Biological Science, Glassboro, NJ 08028-1701. Offers MS. Electronic applications accepted. *Expenses:* Tuition, state resident: full-time $15,020; part-time $751 per semester hour. Tuition, nonresident: full-time $15,020; part-time $751 per semester hour. *Required fees:* $3158; $157.90 per semester hour. Tuition and fees vary according to course load, campus/location and program.

Rutgers University–Camden, Graduate School of Arts and Sciences, Program in Biology, Camden, NJ 08102. Offers MS. *Program availability:* Part-time, evening/weekend. *Degree requirements:* For master's, comprehensive exam, thesis (for some programs), 30 credits. *Entrance requirements:* For master's, GRE General Test, GRE Subject Test (recommended), 3 letters of recommendation; statement of personal, professional and academic goals; biology or related undergraduate degree (preferred). Additional exam requirements/recommendations for international students: Required—TOEFL, IELTS. Electronic applications accepted. *Faculty research:* Neurobiology, biochemistry, ecology, developmental biology, biological signaling mechanisms.

Rutgers University–Newark, Graduate School of Biomedical Sciences, Newark, NJ 07107. Offers biodefense (Certificate); biomedical engineering (PhD); biomedical sciences (multidisciplinary) (PhD); cellular biology, neuroscience and physiology (PhD), including neuroscience, physiology, biophysics, cardiovascular biology, molecular pharmacology, stem cell biology; infection, immunity and inflammation (PhD), including immunology, infectious disease, microbiology, oral biology; molecular biology, genetics and cancer (PhD), including biochemistry, molecular genetics, cancer biology, radiation biology, bioinformatics; neuroscience (Certificate); pharmacological sciences

(Certificate); stem cell (Certificate); DMD/PhD; MD/PhD. PhD in biomedical engineering offered jointly with New Jersey Institute of Technology. *Program availability:* Part-time, evening/weekend. Terminal master's awarded for partial completion of doctoral program. *Degree requirements:* For doctorate, thesis/dissertation, qualifying exam. *Entrance requirements:* For doctorate, GRE General Test. Additional exam requirements/recommendations for international students: Required—TOEFL. Electronic applications accepted.

Rutgers University–Newark, Graduate School, Program in Biology, Newark, NJ 07102. Offers MS, PhD. *Program availability:* Part-time, evening/weekend. Terminal master's awarded for partial completion of doctoral program. *Degree requirements:* For master's, comprehensive exam, thesis optional; for doctorate, thesis/dissertation, qualifying exam. *Entrance requirements:* For master's, GRE General Test, minimum undergraduate B average; for doctorate, GRE General Test, GRE Subject Test, minimum B average. Electronic applications accepted. *Faculty research:* Cell-cytoskeletal elements, development and regeneration in the nervous system, cellular trafficking, environmental stressors and their impact on development, opportunistic parasitic infections in AIDS.

Rutgers University–Newark, Graduate School, Program in Computational Biology, Newark, NJ 07102. Offers MS. Program offered jointly with New Jersey Institute of Technology. *Entrance requirements:* For master's, GRE, minimum undergraduate B average. Additional exam requirements/recommendations for international students: Required—TOEFL.

Rutgers University–New Brunswick, Graduate School-New Brunswick, BioMaPS Institute for Quantitative Biology, Piscataway, NJ 08854-8097. Offers computational biology and molecular biophysics (PhD). *Degree requirements:* For doctorate, comprehensive exam, thesis/dissertation. *Entrance requirements:* For doctorate, GRE. Additional exam requirements/recommendations for international students: Required—TOEFL. Electronic applications accepted. *Faculty research:* Structural biology, systems biology, bioinformatics, translational medicine, genomics.

Rutgers University–New Brunswick, Graduate School of Biomedical Sciences, Piscataway, NJ 08854-5635. Offers biochemistry and molecular biology (MS, PhD); biomedical engineering (MS, PhD); biomedical science (MS); cellular and molecular pharmacology (MS, PhD); clinical and translational science (MS); environmental sciences/exposure assessment (PhD); molecular genetics, microbiology and immunology (MS, PhD); neuroscience (MS, PhD); physiology and integrative biology (MS, PhD); toxicology (PhD); MD/PhD. Terminal master's awarded for partial completion of doctoral program. *Degree requirements:* For master's, thesis (for some programs), ethics training; for doctorate, comprehensive exam, thesis/dissertation, ethics training. *Entrance requirements:* For master's, GRE General Test, MCAT, DAT; for doctorate, GRE General Test. Additional exam requirements/recommendations for international students: Required—TOEFL. Electronic applications accepted.

St. Cloud State University, School of Graduate Studies, College of Science and Engineering, Department of Biology, St. Cloud, MN 56301-4498. Offers MA, MS. *Degree requirements:* For master's, comprehensive exam (for some programs), thesis or alternative. *Entrance requirements:* For master's, GRE General Test, minimum GPA of 2.75. Additional exam requirements/recommendations for international students: Recommended—TOEFL (minimum score 550 paper-based), IELTS (minimum score 6.5). *Application deadline:* For fall admission, 6/1 priority date for domestic students, 4/1 for international students; for spring admission, 10/1 priority date for domestic students, 8/1 for international students. Applications are processed on a rolling basis. Application fee: $35. Electronic applications accepted. *Expenses:* Tuition, state resident: full-time $8220; part-time $398.75 per credit. Tuition, nonresident: full-time $11,948; part-time $605.79 per credit. Tuition and fees vary according to degree level, campus/location, program and reciprocity agreements. *Financial support:* Federal Work-Study, scholarships/grants, and unspecified assistantships available. Financial award application deadline: 3/1.
Website: http://www.stcloudstate.edu/biology/

Saint Francis University, Medical Science Program, Loretto, PA 15940-0600. Offers MMS. *Program availability:* Part-time, evening/weekend, online learning. *Faculty:* 2 full-time (both women), 16 part-time/adjunct (10 women). *Students:* 42 full-time (29 women), 45 part-time (30 women); includes 41 minority (6 Black or African American, non-Hispanic/Latino; 5 Asian, non-Hispanic/Latino; 23 Hispanic/Latino; 1 Native Hawaiian or other Pacific Islander, non-Hispanic/Latino; 6 Two or more races, non-Hispanic/Latino). Average age 31. 59 applicants, 100% accepted, 57 enrolled. In 2017, 107 master's awarded. *Degree requirements:* For master's, thesis or alternative, successful completion of affiliate PA program, minimum GPA of 2.8 in program. *Entrance requirements:* For master's, enrollment in affiliate PA program, bachelor's degree with minimum GPA of 2.5, resume, transcript. Additional exam requirements/recommendations for international students: Recommended—TOEFL (minimum score 80 iBT). *Application deadline:* For fall admission, 6/15 for domestic students; for spring admission, 11/15 for domestic students; for summer admission, 3/15 for domestic students. Applications are processed on a rolling basis. Application fee: $0. Electronic applications accepted. *Expenses:* Contact institution. *Financial support:* Available to part-time students. Applicants required to submit FAFSA. *Faculty research:* Health care policy, physician assistant practice roles, health promotion/disease prevention, public health epidemiology. *Application contact:* Jean A. Kline, Administrative Assistant, 814-472-3357, Fax: 814-472-3066, E-mail: jkline@francis.edu.
Website: http://francis.edu/master-of-medical-science/

St. Francis Xavier University, Graduate Studies, Department of Biology, Antigonish, NS B2G 2W5, Canada. Offers M Sc. *Degree requirements:* For master's, thesis. *Entrance requirements:* For master's, 2 letters of recommendation. Additional exam requirements/recommendations for international students: Required—TOEFL (minimum score 580 paper-based). *Faculty research:* Cellular, whole organism, and population levels; marine photosynthesis; biophysical mechanisms; aquatic biology.

St. John Fisher College, Ralph C. Wilson Jr. School of Education, Program in Adolescence Education and Special Education, Rochester, NY 14618-3597. Offers adolescence education: biology with special education (MS Ed); adolescence education: chemistry with special education (MS Ed); adolescence education: English with special education (MS Ed); adolescence education: French with special education (MS Ed); adolescence education: math with special education (MS Ed); adolescence education: physics with special education (MS Ed); adolescence education: social studies with special education (MS Ed); adolescence education: Spanish with special education (MS Ed). *Program availability:* Part-time, evening/weekend. *Faculty:* 5 full-time (4 women), 7 part-time/adjunct (6 women). *Students:* 15 full-time (3 women), 4 part-time (all women); includes 4 minority (2 Black or African American, non-Hispanic/Latino; 1 Hispanic/Latino; 1 Two or more races, non-Hispanic/Latino). Average age 27. 34 applicants, 85% accepted, 12 enrolled. In 2017, 19 master's awarded. *Degree requirements:* For master's, field experiences, student teaching. *Entrance requirements:* For master's, LAST, 2 letters of recommendation, personal statement, current resume. Additional exam requirements/recommendations for international students: Required—TOEFL (minimum score 575 paper-based; 80 iBT). *Application deadline:* Applications are processed on a rolling basis. Application fee: $30. Electronic applications accepted. *Expenses:* Contact institution. *Financial support:* Scholarships/grants available. Financial award applicants required to submit FAFSA. *Faculty research:* Arts and humanities, urban schools, constructivist learning, at-risk students, mentoring. *Unit head:* Dr. Susan Hildenbrand, Program Director, 585-385-7297, E-mail: shildenbrand@sjfc.edu. *Application contact:* Michelle Gosier, Director of Transfer and Graduate Admissions, 585-385-8064, E-mail: mgosier@sjfc.edu.

St. John's University, St. John's College of Liberal Arts and Sciences, Department of Biological Sciences, Queens, NY 11439. Offers MS, PhD. *Program availability:* Part-time, evening/weekend. *Faculty:* 14 full-time (5 women), 17 part-time/adjunct (4 women). *Students:* 30 full-time (18 women), 4 part-time (3 women); includes 13 minority (8 Asian, non-Hispanic/Latino; 4 Hispanic/Latino; 1 Two or more races, non-Hispanic/Latino), 18 international. Average age 26. 71 applicants, 44% accepted, 12 enrolled. In 2017, 11 master's, 2 doctorates awarded. *Degree requirements:* For master's, variable foreign language requirement, comprehensive exam, thesis optional; for doctorate, variable foreign language requirement, comprehensive exam, thesis/dissertation. *Entrance requirements:* For master's, GRE, letters of recommendation, transcripts, resume, personal statement; for doctorate, GRE General Test, letters of recommendation, transcripts, resume, personal statement. Additional exam requirements/recommendations for international students: Required—TOEFL (minimum score 80 iBT), IELTS (minimum score 6.5). *Application deadline:* For fall admission, 5/1 for domestic students; for spring admission, 11/1 for domestic students. Applications are processed on a rolling basis. Application fee: $70. Electronic applications accepted. *Expenses: Tuition:* Full-time $44,280; part-time $1230 per credit. *Required fees:* $340; $340 per credit. Tuition and fees vary according to course load, degree level and program. *Financial support:* Fellowships, research assistantships, teaching assistantships, scholarships/grants, and unspecified assistantships available. Support available to part-time students. Financial award application deadline: 2/1; financial award applicants required to submit FAFSA. *Faculty research:* Regulation of gene transcription, immunology and inflammation, cancer research, infectious diseases, molecular control of developmental processes. *Total annual research expenditures:* $837,326. *Unit head:* Dr. Ales Vancura, Chair, 718-990-1679, E-mail: vancuraa@stjohns.edu. *Application contact:* Robert Medrano, Director of Graduate Admission, 718-990-1601, Fax: 718-990-5686, E-mail: gradhelp@stjohns.edu.
Website: https://www.stjohns.edu/academics/schools-and-colleges/st-johns-college-liberal-arts-and-sciences/biological-sciences

Saint Joseph's University, College of Arts and Sciences, Department of Biology, Philadelphia, PA 19131-1395. Offers MA, MS. *Program availability:* Part-time. *Faculty:* 14 full-time (6 women), 2 part-time/adjunct (0 women). *Students:* 5 full-time (1 woman), 12 part-time (5 women); includes 1 minority (Black or African American, non-Hispanic/Latino), 6 international. Average age 25. 33 applicants, 39% accepted, 7 enrolled. In 2017, 7 master's awarded. *Degree requirements:* For master's, comprehensive exam (for some programs), thesis (for some programs), minimum GPA of 3.0, completion of degree within 5 years. *Entrance requirements:* For master's, GRE, 2 letters of recommendation, transcript, personal statement, resume. Additional exam requirements/recommendations for international students: Required—TOEFL (minimum score 550 paper-based; 80 iBT), IELTS (minimum score 6.5). *Application deadline:* For fall admission, 3/15 priority date for domestic and international students; for spring admission, 11/1 for international students. Applications are processed on a rolling basis. Application fee: $35. Electronic applications accepted. *Expenses:* Contact institution. *Financial support:* Scholarships/grants and unspecified assistantships available. Financial award application deadline: 5/1; financial award applicants required to submit FAFSA. *Faculty research:* Molecular regulation of sleep in vertebrate and invertebrate models; microbial pathogenesis; global change biology; molecular evolution in microbial and plant systems. *Unit head:* Dr. Karen Snetselaar, Graduate Director, 610-660-3131, E-mail: gradcas@sju.edu. *Application contact:* Graduate Admissions, College of Arts and Sciences, 610-660-3131, E-mail: gradcas@sju.edu.
Website: http://sju.edu/majors-programs/graduate-arts-sciences/masters/biology-ma-and-ms

Saint Louis University, Graduate Programs, College of Arts and Sciences and Graduate Programs, Department of Biology, St. Louis, MO 63103. Offers MS, MS-R, PhD. *Degree requirements:* For master's, comprehensive exam, thesis (for some programs); for doctorate, thesis/dissertation, preliminary exams. *Entrance requirements:* For master's, GRE General Test, letters of recommendation, resume; for doctorate, GRE General Test, letters of recommendation, resumé, statement, transcripts. Additional exam requirements/recommendations for international students: Required—TOEFL (minimum score 550 paper-based). Electronic applications accepted. *Faculty research:* Systematics, speciation, evolution, community ecology, conservation biology, molecular signaling.

★ **Saint Louis University,** Graduate Programs, School of Medicine, Graduate Programs in Biomedical Sciences, St. Louis, MO 63103. Offers MS-R, PhD. *Faculty:* 122 full-time (43 women), 3 part-time/adjunct (0 women). *Students:* 89 full-time (53 women), 5 part-time (3 women); includes 6 minority (2 Black or African American, non-Hispanic/Latino; 1 Asian, non-Hispanic/Latino; 3 Hispanic/Latino), 18 international. Average age 27. 179 applicants, 22% accepted, 19 enrolled. *Degree requirements:* For doctorate, comprehensive exam, thesis/dissertation. *Entrance requirements:* For doctorate, GRE. Additional exam requirements/recommendations for international students: Required—TOEFL. *Application deadline:* For fall admission, 2/1 for domestic and international students. Applications are processed on a rolling basis. Application fee: $40. Electronic applications accepted. *Expenses:* Tuition is free; $100 per year student activity fee. *Financial support:* In 2017–18, 57 students received support, including 8 fellowships with full tuition reimbursements available (averaging $24,270 per year); Federal Work-Study, scholarships/grants, traineeships, tuition waivers, and unspecified assistantships also available. Support available to part-time students. Financial award application deadline: 6/1; financial award applicants required to submit FAFSA. *Faculty research:* Biochemistry and molecular biology, physiology and pharmacology, virology, pathology, immunology. *Unit head:* Dr. Willis K. Samson, Director, 314-977-8677, Fax: 314-977-8670, E-mail: samsonwk@slu.edu. *Application contact:* Gary U. Behrman, Associate Dean of Graduate School Admissions, 314-977-3827, Fax: 314-977-3943, E-mail: behrmang@slu.edu.
Website: http://medschool.slu.edu/gpbs

See Display on the next page and Close-Up on page 113.

Salisbury University, Program in Applied Biology, Salisbury, MD 21801-6837. Offers MS. *Program availability:* Part-time. *Faculty:* 9 full-time (4 women). *Students:* 8 full-time (4 women), 1 part-time (0 women); includes 1 minority (Native Hawaiian or other Pacific Islander, non-Hispanic/Latino). Average age 25. 5 applicants, 60% accepted, 3 enrolled. In 2017, 2 master's awarded. *Degree requirements:* For master's, comprehensive exam, thesis optional. *Entrance requirements:* For master's, GRE, three letters of recommendation; transcripts from all colleges and universities attended; personal statement; resume; minimum GPA of 3.0; contact with prospective graduate advisor. Additional exam requirements/recommendations for international students: Required—TOEFL (minimum score 550 paper-based; 79 iBT), IELTS (minimum score 6.5). *Application deadline:* For fall admission, 3/1 for domestic and international students; for

spring admission, 10/1 for domestic and international students. Application fee: $65. Electronic applications accepted. *Expenses:* $392 per credit hour resident; $703 per credit hour non-resident; $92 per credit hour fees. *Financial support:* In 2017–18, 5 students received support, including 9 teaching assistantships with full tuition reimbursements available (averaging $13,000 per year); career-related internships or fieldwork and scholarships/grants also available. Support available to part-time students. Financial award application deadline: 3/1; financial award applicants required to submit FAFSA. *Faculty research:* Animal behavior; microbiology; ecology and evolution; genetics and molecular biology; neuroscience. *Unit head:* Dr. Dana Price, Graduate Program Director, Applied Biology, 410-543-6498, E-mail: dlprice@salisbury.edu. *Application contact:* Sandy Ramses, Program Management Specialist, 410-543-6054, E-mail: shramses@salisbury.edu.
Website: http://www.salisbury.edu/gsr/gradstudies/MSBIOpage.html

Sam Houston State University, College of Sciences, Department of Biological Sciences, Huntsville, TX 77341. Offers MA, MS. *Program availability:* Part-time. *Degree requirements:* For master's, comprehensive exam, thesis (for some programs). *Entrance requirements:* For master's, GRE General Test, letters of recommendation, statement of purpose. Additional exam requirements/recommendations for international students: Required—TOEFL (minimum score 550 paper-based; 78 iBT), IELTS (minimum score 6.5). Electronic applications accepted.

San Diego State University, Graduate and Research Affairs, College of Sciences, Department of Biology, San Diego, CA 92182. Offers biology (MA, MS), including ecology (MS), molecular biology (MS), physiology (MS), systematics/evolution (MS); cell and molecular biology (PhD); ecology (MS, PhD); microbiology (MS). Terminal master's awarded for partial completion of doctoral program. *Degree requirements:* For master's, thesis; for doctorate, thesis/dissertation. *Entrance requirements:* For master's, GRE General Test, GRE Subject Test, resume or curriculum vitae, 2 letters of recommendation. Additional exam requirements/recommendations for international students: Required—TOEFL. Electronic applications accepted.

Sanford Burnham Prebys Medical Discovery Institute, Graduate School of Biomedical Sciences, La Jolla, CA 92037. Offers PhD. *Faculty:* 52. *Students:* 31 full-time (19 women). In 2017, 5 doctorates awarded. *Degree requirements:* For doctorate, thesis/dissertation. *Entrance requirements:* For doctorate, GRE General Test. Additional exam requirements/recommendations for international students: Recommended—TOEFL, IELTS. *Application deadline:* For fall admission, 12/1 for domestic students. Application fee: $60. *Financial support:* Scholarships/grants and health care benefits available. *Faculty research:* Cancer, immunity, neuroscience and aging, disorders of metabolism, childhood diseases. *Unit head:* Dr. Guy Salvesen, Dean, 858-646-3114. *Application contact:* Andrew Bankston, Program Manager, Graduate School, 858-646-3100, E-mail: gsbs@sbp.edu.

San Francisco State University, Division of Graduate Studies, College of Science and Engineering, Department of Biology, San Francisco, CA 94132-1722. Offers cell and molecular biology (MS); ecology, evolution, and conservation biology (MS); interdisciplinary marine and estuarine science (MS); marine biology (MS); microbiology (MS); physiology and behavioral biology (MS); science (PSM), including biotechnology, stem cell science. *Application deadline:* Applications are processed on a rolling basis. *Unit head:* Dr. Laura Burrus, Chair, 415-338-7680, Fax: 415-338-2295, E-mail: lburrus@sfsu.edu. *Application contact:* Dr. Diana Chu, Graduate Coordinator, 415-405-3487, Fax: 415-338-2295, E-mail: chud@sfsu.edu.
Website: http://biology.sfsu.edu/

San Jose State University, Graduate Studies and Research, College of Science, San Jose, CA 95192-0099. Offers bioinformatics (MS); biological sciences (MA, MS), including ecology and evolution (MS), molecular biology and microbiology (MS), physiology (MS); biotechnology (MBT); chemistry (MA, MS); computer science (MS); geology (MS); marine science (MS); mathematics (MA, MS), including mathematics education (MA); medical products development management (MS); meteorology (MS); physics (MS), including computational physics, modern optics, physics; statistics (MS). MS in marine science offered through Moss Landing Marine Labs. *Program availability:* Part-time. *Faculty:* 78 full-time (27 women), 25 part-time/adjunct (13 women). *Students:* 154 full-time (76 women), 212 part-time (102 women); includes 135 minority (4 Black or African American, non-Hispanic/Latino; 78 Asian, non-Hispanic/Latino; 27 Hispanic/Latino; 1 Native Hawaiian or other Pacific Islander, non-Hispanic/Latino; 25 Two or more races, non-Hispanic/Latino), 135 international. Average age 28. 1,156 applicants, 26% accepted, 179 enrolled. In 2017, 196 master's awarded. *Degree requirements:* For master's, comprehensive exam (for some programs), thesis (for some programs), directed reading, colloquium, project, writing project, statistical consulting. *Entrance requirements:* Additional exam requirements/recommendations for international students: Required—TOEFL (minimum score 550 paper-based; 80 iBT), IELTS (minimum score 6.5), TWE, PTE (minimum score 53). *Application deadline:* For fall admission, 2/1 for domestic and international students. Applications are processed on a rolling basis. Application fee: $55. Electronic applications accepted. *Expenses:* Tuition, state resident: full-time $7176. Tuition, nonresident: full-time $16,680. Tuition and fees vary according to course load and program. *Financial support:* Fellowships, research assistantships, career-related internships or fieldwork, Federal Work-Study, scholarships/grants, traineeships, tuition waivers (full and partial), and unspecified assistantships available. Support available to part-time students. Financial award application deadline: 4/28; financial award applicants required to submit FAFSA. *Unit head:* Dr. Michael Kaufman, Dean, 408-924-4800, Fax: 408-924-4815, E-mail: michael.kaufman@sjsu.edu.
Website: http://www.sjsu.edu/science/

The Scripps Research Institute, Kellogg School of Science and Technology, La Jolla, CA 92037. Offers chemical and biological sciences (PhD). *Degree requirements:* For doctorate, thesis/dissertation. *Entrance requirements:* For doctorate, GRE General Test, GRE Subject Test, 3 letters of recommendation, official transcripts. Additional exam requirements/recommendations for international students: Required—TOEFL. Electronic applications accepted. *Faculty research:* Molecular structure and function, plant biology, immunology, bioorganic chemistry and molecular design, synthetic organic chemistry and natural product synthesis.

Seton Hall University, College of Arts and Sciences, Department of Biological Sciences, South Orange, NJ 07079-2697. Offers biology (MS); biology/business administration (MS); microbiology (MS); molecular bioscience (PhD); molecular bioscience/neuroscience (PhD). *Program availability:* Part-time, evening/weekend. *Degree requirements:* For master's, thesis optional; for doctorate, comprehensive exam, thesis/dissertation. *Entrance requirements:* For master's, GRE or undergraduate degree (BS in biological sciences) with minimum GPA of 3.0 from accredited U.S. institution; for doctorate, GRE. Additional exam requirements/recommendations for international students: Required—TOEFL. Electronic applications accepted. *Faculty research:* Neurobiology, genetics, immunology, molecular biology, cellular physiology, toxicology, microbiology, bioinformatics.

Shippensburg University of Pennsylvania, School of Graduate Studies, College of Arts and Sciences, Department of Biology, Shippensburg, PA 17257-2299. Offers MS. *Program availability:* Part-time, evening/weekend. *Faculty:* 11 full-time (4 women). *Students:* 13 full-time (8 women), 7 part-time (4 women), 3 international. Average age 26. 20 applicants, 85% accepted, 7 enrolled. In 2017, 21 master's awarded. *Degree requirements:* For master's, thesis optional, oral thesis defense, seminar, minimum QPA of 3.0. *Entrance requirements:* For master's, minimum GPA of 2.75; essay; 500-word statement of purpose; 33 credits of course work in biology; minimum of 3 courses with

labs including both inorganic and organic chemistry or biochemistry; completion of math through calculus (including a statistics course) and two lab courses in physics. Additional exam requirements/recommendations for international students: Required—TOEFL (minimum iBT score 80) or IELTS (minimum score 6.5). *Application deadline:* For fall admission, 4/30 for international students; for spring admission, 9/30 for international students. Applications are processed on a rolling basis. Application fee: $45. Electronic applications accepted. *Expenses:* Tuition, state resident: part-time $500 per credit. Tuition, nonresident: part-time $750 per credit. *Required fees:* $145 per credit. *Financial support:* In 2017–18, 9 students received support. Career-related internships or fieldwork, scholarships/grants, unspecified assistantships, and resident hall director and student payroll positions available. Support available to part-time students. Financial award application deadline: 3/1; financial award applicants required to submit FAFSA. *Unit head:* Dr. Tim J. Maret, Professor and Program Coordinator, 717-477-1401, Fax: 717-477-4064, E-mail: tjmare@ship.edu. *Application contact:* Maya T. Mapp, Director of Admissions, 717-477-1231, Fax: 717-477-4016, E-mail: mtmapp@ship.edu.
Website: http://www.ship.edu/biology/

Simon Fraser University, Office of Graduate Studies and Postdoctoral Fellows, Faculty of Science, Department of Biological Sciences, Burnaby, BC V5A 1S6, Canada. Offers bioinformatics (Graduate Diploma); biological sciences (M Sc, PhD); environmental toxicology (MET); pest management (MPM). *Degree requirements:* For master's, thesis; for doctorate, thesis/dissertation, candidacy exam; for Graduate Diploma, practicum. *Entrance requirements:* For master's, minimum GPA of 3.0 (on scale of 4.33) or 3.33 based on last 60 credits of undergraduate courses; for doctorate, minimum GPA of 3.5 (on scale of 4.33); for Graduate Diploma, minimum GPA of 2.5 (on scale of 4.33) or 2.67 based on last 60 credits of undergraduate courses. Additional exam requirements/recommendations for international students: Recommended—TOEFL (minimum score 580 paper-based; 93 iBT), IELTS (minimum score 7), TWE (minimum score 5). Electronic applications accepted. *Faculty research:* Cell biology, wildlife ecology, environmental and evolutionary physiology, environmental toxicology, pest management.

Smith College, Graduate and Special Programs, Department of Biological Sciences, Northampton, MA 01063. Offers MAT, MS. *Program availability:* Part-time. *Students:* 1 (woman) full-time, 5 part-time (4 women); includes 2 minority (1 Black or African American, non-Hispanic/Latino; 1 Hispanic/Latino). Average age 26. 8 applicants, 75% accepted, 4 enrolled. In 2017, 4 master's awarded. *Degree requirements:* For master's, one foreign language, thesis (for some programs). *Entrance requirements:* For master's, GRE General Test (for MS). Additional exam requirements/recommendations for international students: Required—TOEFL (minimum score 595 paper-based; 97 iBT), IELTS. *Application deadline:* For fall admission, 1/15 for domestic and international students. Application fee: $60. *Expenses: Tuition:* Full-time $37,440; part-time $1560 per credit. Tuition and fees vary according to course load and program. *Financial support:* In 2017–18, 6 students received support, including 5 research assistantships with full tuition reimbursements available (averaging $13,850 per year); fellowships, scholarships/grants, and human resources employee benefit also available. Support available to part-time students. Financial award application deadline: 1/15; financial award applicants required to submit CSS PROFILE or FAFSA. *Unit head:* Jesse Bellemare, Graduate Student Advisor, 413-585-3812, E-mail: jbellema@smith.edu. *Application contact:* Ruth Morgan, Program Assistant, 413-585-3050, Fax: 413-585-3054, E-mail: rmorgan@smith.edu.
Website: http://www.smith.edu/biology/

Sonoma State University, School of Science and Technology, Department of Biology, Rohnert Park, CA 94928. Offers biochemistry (MA). *Program availability:* Part-time. *Degree requirements:* For master's, thesis or alternative, oral exam. *Entrance requirements:* For master's, GRE General Test, GRE Subject Test, minimum GPA of 3.0. Additional exam requirements/recommendations for international students: Required—TOEFL (minimum score 500 paper-based). *Application deadline:* For fall admission, 11/30 for domestic students. Applications are processed on a rolling basis. Application fee: $55. *Financial support:* Fellowships, research assistantships, teaching assistantships, career-related internships or fieldwork, Federal Work-Study, and tuition waivers (full) available. Financial award application deadline: 3/2; financial award applicants required to submit FAFSA. *Faculty research:* Plant physiology, comparative physiology, community ecology, restoration ecology, marine ecology, conservation genetics, primate behavior, behavioral ecology, developmental biology, plant and animal systematics. *Unit head:* Dr. Richard Whitkus, Department Chair, 707-664-2303, E-mail: whitkus@sonoma.edu. *Application contact:* Dr. Derek Girman, Graduate Adviser, 707-664-3055, E-mail: girman@sonoma.edu.
Website: http://www.sonoma.edu/biology/

South Carolina State University, College of Graduate and Professional Studies, Department of Education, Orangeburg, SC 29117-0001. Offers early childhood education (MAT); education (M Ed); elementary education (M Ed, MAT); English (MAT); general science/biology (MAT); mathematics (MAT); secondary education (M Ed), including biology education, business education, counselor education, English education, home economics education, industrial education, mathematics education, science education, social studies education; special education (M Ed), including emotionally handicapped, learning disabilities, mentally handicapped. *Accreditation:* NCATE. *Program availability:* Part-time, evening/weekend. *Faculty:* 11 full-time (6 women), 4 part-time/adjunct (2 women). *Students:* 26 full-time (18 women), 22 part-time (17 women); includes 41 minority (all Black or African American, non-Hispanic/Latino), 1 international. Average age 33. 25 applicants, 100% accepted, 19 enrolled. In 2017, 6 master's awarded. *Degree requirements:* For master's, thesis optional, departmental qualifying exam. *Entrance requirements:* For master's, GRE General Test, NTE, interview, teaching certificate. *Application deadline:* For fall admission, 6/15 priority date for domestic students, 6/15 for international students; for spring admission, 11/1 for domestic and international students. Application fee: $25. Electronic applications accepted. *Expenses:* Tuition, state resident: full-time $9388; part-time $607 per credit hour. Tuition, nonresident: full-time $19,968; part-time $1194 per credit hour. *Required fees:* $766; $766 per credit hour. *Financial support:* Fellowships, career-related internships or fieldwork, Federal Work-Study, and scholarships/grants available. Financial award application deadline: 6/1. *Unit head:* Dr. Charlie Spell, Interim Chair, Department of Education, 803-536-8963, Fax: 803-516-4568, E-mail: cspell@scsu.edu. *Application contact:* Curtis Foskey, Coordinator of Graduate Studies, 803-536-8419, Fax: 803-536-8812, E-mail: cfoskey@scsu.edu.

South Dakota State University, Graduate School, College of Agriculture and Biological Sciences, Department of Animal and Range Sciences, Brookings, SD 57007. Offers animal science (MS, PhD); biological sciences (PhD). *Program availability:* Part-time. *Degree requirements:* For master's, thesis, oral exam; for doctorate, comprehensive exam, thesis/dissertation, preliminary oral and written exams. *Entrance requirements:* Additional exam requirements/recommendations for international students: Required—TOEFL (minimum score 550 paper-based; 79 iBT). *Faculty research:* Ruminant and nonruminant nutrition, meat science, reproductive physiology, range utilization, ecology genetics, muscle biology, animal production.

South Dakota State University, Graduate School, College of Agriculture and Biological Sciences, Department of Biology and Microbiology, Brookings, SD 57007. Offers biological sciences (MS, PhD). *Program availability:* Part-time. *Degree requirements:* For master's, thesis (for some programs), oral exam; for doctorate, comprehensive exam, thesis/dissertation, oral exam. *Entrance requirements:* For master's and doctorate, GRE General Test. Additional exam requirements/recommendations for international students: Required—TOEFL (minimum score 600 paper-based; 100 iBT). *Faculty research:* Ecosystem ecology; plant, animal and microbial genomics; animal infectious disease, microbial bioproducts.

South Dakota State University, Graduate School, College of Agriculture and Biological Sciences, Department of Dairy Science, Brookings, SD 57007. Offers animal sciences (MS, PhD); biological sciences (MS, PhD). *Program availability:* Part-time. *Degree requirements:* For master's, thesis, oral exam; for doctorate, comprehensive exam, thesis/dissertation, preliminary oral and written exams. *Entrance requirements:* Additional exam requirements/recommendations for international students: Required—TOEFL (minimum score 550 paper-based). *Faculty research:* Dairy cattle nutrition, energy metabolism, food safety, dairy processing technology.

South Dakota State University, Graduate School, College of Agriculture and Biological Sciences, Department of Veterinary and Biomedical Sciences, Brookings, SD 57007. Offers biological sciences (MS, PhD). *Program availability:* Part-time, evening/weekend. *Degree requirements:* For master's, thesis (for some programs), oral exam; for doctorate, comprehensive exam, thesis/dissertation, preliminary oral and written exams. *Entrance requirements:* Additional exam requirements/recommendations for international students: Required—TOEFL (minimum score 525 paper-based; 71 iBT). *Faculty research:* Infectious disease, food animal, virology, immunology.

South Dakota State University, Graduate School, College of Engineering, Department of Agricultural and Biosystems Engineering, Brookings, SD 57007. Offers biological sciences (MS, PhD); engineering (MS). PhD offered jointly with Iowa State University of Science and Technology. *Program availability:* Part-time. *Degree requirements:* For master's, thesis (for some programs), oral exam; for doctorate, thesis/dissertation, preliminary oral and written exams. *Entrance requirements:* For master's and doctorate, engineering degree. Additional exam requirements/recommendations for international students: Required—TOEFL (minimum score 550 paper-based; 79 iBT). *Faculty research:* Water resources, food engineering, natural resources engineering, machine design, bioprocess engineering.

South Dakota State University, Graduate School, College of Pharmacy and Allied Health Professions, Department of Pharmaceutical Sciences, Brookings, SD 57007. Offers biological science (MS); pharmaceutical sciences (PhD). *Degree requirements:* For master's, thesis, oral exam; for doctorate, comprehensive exam, thesis/dissertation, oral exam. *Entrance requirements:* For master's and doctorate, GRE General Test. Additional exam requirements/recommendations for international students: Required—TOEFL (minimum score 550 paper-based). *Faculty research:* Drugs of abuse, anti-cancer drugs, sustained drug delivery, drug metabolism.

Southeastern Louisiana University, College of Science and Technology, Department of Biological Sciences, Hammond, LA 70402. Offers biology (MS). *Program availability:* Part-time. *Faculty:* 10 full-time (3 women). *Students:* 20 full-time (10 women), 3 part-time (1 woman); includes 5 minority (1 Asian, non-Hispanic/Latino; 3 Hispanic/Latino; 1 Two or more races, non-Hispanic/Latino), 2 international. Average age 25. 28 applicants, 50% accepted, 8 enrolled. In 2017, 13 master's awarded. *Degree requirements:* For master's, comprehensive exam, thesis (for some programs). *Entrance requirements:* For master's, GRE, two letters of recommendation, curriculum vita, letter of intent. Additional exam requirements/recommendations for international students: Required—TOEFL (minimum score 500 paper-based; 61 iBT). *Application deadline:* For fall admission, 7/15 priority date for domestic students, 6/1 priority date for international students; for spring admission, 12/1 priority date for domestic students, 10/1 priority date for international students. Applications are processed on a rolling basis. Application fee: $20 ($30 for international students). Electronic applications accepted. *Expenses:* Tuition, state resident: full-time $6684. Tuition, nonresident: full-time $19,162. *Required fees:* $2088. *Financial support:* In 2017–18, 11 students received support, including 5 fellowships (averaging $10,800 per year), 1 research assistantship (averaging $10,100 per year), 9 teaching assistantships (averaging $10,100 per year); career-related internships or fieldwork, Federal Work-Study, institutionally sponsored loans, scholarships/grants, traineeships, and unspecified assistantships also available. Support available to part-time students. Financial award application deadline: 5/1; financial award applicants required to submit FAFSA. *Faculty research:* Evolutionary biology, ecology, molecular biology, morphology and physiology, microbiology and immunology. *Unit head:* Dr. Christopher Beachy, Department Head, 985-549-3740, Fax: 985-549-3851, E-mail: christopher.beachy@southeastern.edu. *Application contact:* Amanda Harper, Graduate Admissions Analyst, 985-549-5620, Fax: 985-549-5632, E-mail: admissions@southeastern.edu.
Website: http://www.southeastern.edu/acad_research/depts/biol

Southeast Missouri State University, School of Graduate Studies, Department of Biology, Cape Girardeau, MO 63701-4799. Offers MNS. *Program availability:* Part-time. *Faculty:* 15 full-time (5 women). *Students:* 15 full-time (7 women), 22 part-time (9 women), 5 international. Average age 26. 18 applicants, 67% accepted, 12 enrolled. In 2017, 10 master's awarded. *Degree requirements:* For master's, comprehensive exam (for some programs), thesis (for some programs), thesis and oral defense, or research paper and comprehensive exam. *Entrance requirements:* For master's, minimum undergraduate GPA of 2.5, 2.75 in last 30 hours of undergraduate course work in science and mathematics; 2 letters of recommendation; faculty sponsor agreement. Additional exam requirements/recommendations for international students: Required—TOEFL (minimum score 550 paper-based; 79 iBT), IELTS (minimum score 6), PTE (minimum score 53). *Application deadline:* For fall admission, 4/1 for domestic and international students; for spring admission, 10/1 for domestic and international students; for summer admission, 4/1 for domestic students. Applications are processed on a rolling basis. Application fee: $30 ($40 for international students). Electronic applications accepted. *Expenses:* Tuition, state resident: part-time $270.34 per credit hour. Tuition, nonresident: part-time $504 per credit hour. *Required fees:* $33.40 per credit hour. *Financial support:* In 2017–18, 11 students received support, including 15 teaching assistantships with full tuition reimbursements available; career-related internships or fieldwork, Federal Work-Study, scholarships/grants, traineeships, tuition waivers (full), and unspecified assistantships also available. Financial award application deadline: 6/30; financial award applicants required to submit FAFSA. *Faculty research:* Wildlife toxicology, population and community ecology, drosophila genetics, herpetology (climate change, reproductive biology), floristics and plant evolutionary ecology, microbial physiology. *Unit head:* Dr. James E. Champine, Department of Biology Chair/Professor, 573-651-2171, Fax: 573-651-2382, E-mail: jchampine@semo.edu. *Application contact:* Dr. Rebecka Brasso, Assistant Professor, 573-651-2358, Fax: 573-651-2382, E-mail: dsiegel@semo.edu.
Website: http://www.semo.edu/biology/

Southern Connecticut State University, School of Graduate Studies, School of Arts and Sciences, Department of Biology, New Haven, CT 06515-1355. Offers MS. *Program availability:* Part-time, evening/weekend. *Degree requirements:* For master's, thesis optional. *Entrance requirements:* For master's, previous course work in biology, chemistry, and mathematics; interview. Electronic applications accepted.

Southern Illinois University Carbondale, Graduate School, College of Science, Biological Sciences Program, Carbondale, IL 62901-4701. Offers MS. *Degree requirements:* For master's, thesis or alternative. *Entrance requirements:* For master's, GRE General Test, minimum GPA of 2.7. Additional exam requirements/ recommendations for international students: Required—TOEFL. *Faculty research:* Molecular mechanisms of mutagenesis, reproductive endocrinology, avian energetics and nutrition, developmental plant physiology.

Southern Illinois University Carbondale, Graduate School, Graduate Programs in Medicine, Carbondale, IL 62901-4701. Offers molecular, cellular and systemic physiology (MS); molecular, cellular, and systemic physiology (PhD); pharmacology (MS, PhD); physician assistant studies (MSPA). Terminal master's awarded for partial completion of doctoral program. *Degree requirements:* For master's, thesis; for doctorate, thesis/dissertation. *Entrance requirements:* For master's, GRE, minimum GPA of 3.0; for doctorate, GRE, minimum GPA of 3.25. Additional exam requirements/ recommendations for international students: Required—TOEFL. *Faculty research:* Cardiovascular physiology, neurophysiology of hearing.

Southern Illinois University Edwardsville, Graduate School, College of Arts and Sciences, Department of Biological Sciences, Program in Biology, Edwardsville, IL 62026. Offers MA, MS. *Program availability:* Part-time, evening/weekend. *Degree requirements:* For master's, thesis (for some programs). *Entrance requirements:* For master's, GRE. Additional exam requirements/recommendations for international students: Required—TOEFL (minimum score 550 paper-based; 79 iBT), IELTS (minimum score 6.5). Electronic applications accepted.

Southern Methodist University, Dedman College of Humanities and Sciences, Department of Biological Sciences, Dallas, TX 75275. Offers molecular and cellular biology (MA, MS, PhD). Terminal master's awarded for partial completion of doctoral program. *Degree requirements:* For master's, thesis (for MS), oral exam; for doctorate, thesis/dissertation, qualifying exam. *Entrance requirements:* For master's, GRE General Test (minimum score 1200), minimum GPA of 3.0; for doctorate, GRE General Test (minimum score: 1200), minimum GPA of 3.0. Additional exam requirements/ recommendations for international students: Required—TOEFL (minimum score 550 paper-based). *Application deadline:* For fall admission, 2/1 priority date for domestic and international students; for spring admission, 11/30 priority date for domestic and international students. Applications are processed on a rolling basis. Application fee: $60. Electronic applications accepted. *Financial support:* Applicants required to submit FAFSA. *Faculty research:* Free radicals and aging, protein structure, chromatin structure, signal processes, retroviral pathogenesis. *Unit head:* Dr. Robert Harrod, Advisor for Graduate Studies, 214-768-3864, E-mail: rharrod@smu.edu. *Application contact:* Dr. Pia Vogel, Graduate Advisor, 214-768-1790, Fax: 214-768-3955, E-mail: pvogel@smu.edu. Website: http://smu.edu/biology/Graduate.asp

Southern University and Agricultural and Mechanical College, Graduate School, College of Sciences, Department of Biology, Baton Rouge, LA 70813. Offers MS. *Degree requirements:* For master's, comprehensive exam, thesis. *Entrance requirements:* For master's, GRE General Test. Additional exam requirements/ recommendations for international students: Required—TOEFL (minimum score 525 paper-based). *Faculty research:* Toxicology, neuroendocrinology, mycotoxin, virology.

Stanford University, School of Humanities and Sciences, Department of Biology, Stanford, CA 94305-2004. Offers MS, PhD. Terminal master's awarded for partial completion of doctoral program. *Degree requirements:* For doctorate, thesis/ dissertation, oral exam. *Entrance requirements:* For master's, GRE General Test; for doctorate, GRE General Test, GRE Subject Test. Additional exam requirements/ recommendations for international students: Required—TOEFL. Electronic applications accepted. *Expenses: Tuition:* Full-time $48,987; part-time $10,620 per quarter. One-time fee: $400. Tuition and fees vary according to program.

Stanford University, School of Medicine, Graduate Programs in Medicine, Stanford, CA 94305-2004. Offers MS, PhD. Terminal master's awarded for partial completion of doctoral program. *Degree requirements:* For master's, thesis; for doctorate, thesis/dissertation. *Entrance requirements:* For master's, GRE General Test or MCAT. Additional exam requirements/recommendations for international students: Required—TOEFL. Electronic applications accepted. *Expenses: Tuition:* Full-time $48,987; part-time $10,620 per quarter. One-time fee: $400. Tuition and fees vary according to program.

State University of New York at Fredonia, College of Liberal Arts and Sciences, Fredonia, NY 14063-1136. Offers biology (MS); English (MA); English education 7-12 (MA); interdisciplinary studies (MA, MS); math education (MS Ed); professional writing (CAS); speech pathology (MS); MA/MS. *Program availability:* Part-time, evening/ weekend. *Students:* 73 full-time (62 women), 9 part-time (6 women); includes 7 minority (1 Black or African American, non-Hispanic/Latino; 1 Asian, non-Hispanic/Latino; 2 Hispanic/Latino; 1 Native Hawaiian or other Pacific Islander, non-Hispanic/Latino; 2 Two or more races, non-Hispanic/Latino). Average age 24. 200 applicants, 25% accepted, 43 enrolled. In 2017, 41 master's, 1 other advanced degree awarded. *Degree requirements:* For master's, comprehensive exam (for some programs), thesis (for some programs). *Entrance requirements:* For master's, GRE. Additional exam requirements/ recommendations for international students: Required—TOEFL (minimum score 79 iBT), IELTS (minimum score 6.5). *Application deadline:* Applications are processed on a rolling basis. Application fee: $75. Electronic applications accepted. *Expenses:* Tuition, state resident: full-time $8154. Tuition, nonresident: full-time $16,650. *Required fees:* $1209. *Financial support:* In 2017–18, 5 students received support, including 14 teaching assistantships with full and partial tuition reimbursements available (averaging $5,957 per year); tuition waivers (full and partial) and unspecified assistantships also available. *Faculty research:* Immunology/microbiology, applied human physiology, ecology and evolution, invertebrate biology, molecular biology, biochemistry, physiology, animal behavior, science education, vertebrate physiology, cell biology, plant biology, developmental biology, aquatic ecology, bilingual language acquisition, bilingual language acquisition and disorders, augmentative and alternate communication with ALS, World War I, Zweig, environmental literature, editing, adolescent literature, pedagogy. *Unit head:* Dr. Andy Karafa, Dean, 716-673-3173, Fax: 716-673-3338, E-mail: andy.karafa@gmail.com. *Application contact:* Wendy S. Dunst, Interim Graduate Recruitment and Admissions Associate, 716-673-3808, Fax: 716-673-3712, E-mail: wendy.dunst@fredonia.edu. Website: http://www.fredonia.edu/clas/

State University of New York College at Oneonta, Graduate Programs, Department of Biology, Oneonta, NY 13820-4015. Offers biology (MS); lake management (MS). *Program availability:* Part-time, evening/weekend. *Degree requirements:* For master's, comprehensive exam. *Entrance requirements:* For master's, GRE General Test, GRE Subject Test.

State University of New York Downstate Medical Center, School of Graduate Studies, Brooklyn, NY 11203-2098. Offers MS, PhD, MD/PhD. *Degree requirements:* For doctorate, thesis/dissertation. *Entrance requirements:* For doctorate, GRE. Additional exam requirements/recommendations for international students: Required—TOEFL. *Faculty research:* Cellular and molecular neurobiology, role of oncogenes in early cardiogenesis, mechanism of gene regulation, cardiovascular physiology, yeast molecular genetics.

State University of New York Upstate Medical University, College of Graduate Studies, Syracuse, NY 13210. Offers MS, PhD, MD/PhD. Terminal master's awarded for partial completion of doctoral program. *Degree requirements:* For master's, thesis; for doctorate, comprehensive exam, thesis/dissertation. *Entrance requirements:* For master's, GRE General Test, interview; for doctorate, GRE General Test, telephone interview. Additional exam requirements/recommendations for international students: Required—TOEFL. Electronic applications accepted. *Faculty research:* Cancer, disorders of the nervous system, infectious diseases, diabetes/metabolic disorders/ cardiovascular diseases.

Stephen F. Austin State University, Graduate School, College of Sciences and Mathematics, Department of Biology, Nacogdoches, TX 75962. Offers MS. *Degree requirements:* For master's, comprehensive exam, thesis optional. *Entrance requirements:* For master's, GRE General Test, minimum GPA of 2.8 in last 60 hours, 2.5 overall. Additional exam requirements/recommendations for international students: Required—TOEFL.

Stevenson University, Program in Forensic Science, Owings Mills, MD 21153. Offers biology (MS); chemistry (MS); crime scene investigation (MS). Program offered in partnership with Maryland State Police Forensic Sciences Division. *Program availability:* Part-time. *Faculty:* 4 full-time (3 women), 4 part-time/adjunct (2 women). *Students:* 22 full-time (16 women), 21 part-time (18 women); includes 23 minority (19 Black or African American, non-Hispanic/Latino; 1 American Indian or Alaska Native, non-Hispanic/ Latino; 3 Two or more races, non-Hispanic/Latino). Average age 28. 18 applicants, 100% accepted, 18 enrolled. In 2017, 26 master's awarded. *Degree requirements:* For master's, capstone course. *Entrance requirements:* For master's, bachelor's degree in a natural science from regionally-accredited institution; official college transcripts from all previous academic work; minimum cumulative GPA of 3.0 in past academic work. *Application deadline:* Applications are processed on a rolling basis. Application fee: $0. Electronic applications accepted. *Expenses:* Contact institution. *Financial support:* Unspecified assistantships available. Financial award applicants required to submit FAFSA. *Unit head:* John Tobin, PhD, Coordinator, 443-352-4142, Fax: 443-394-0538, E-mail: jtobin@stevenson.edu. *Application contact:* William Wellein, Enrollment Counselor, 443-352-5843, Fax: 443-394-0538, E-mail: wwellein@stevenson.edu. Website: http://www.stevenson.edu

Stony Brook University, State University of New York, Stony Brook Medicine, School of Medicine and Graduate School, Graduate Programs in Medicine, Stony Brook, NY 11794. Offers MS, PhD, Advanced Certificate. *Students:* 123 full-time (55 women), 10 part-time (5 women); includes 47 minority (10 Black or African American, non-Hispanic/ Latino; 16 Asian, non-Hispanic/Latino; 20 Hispanic/Latino; 1 Two or more races, non-Hispanic/Latino), 14 international. 206 applicants, 41% accepted, 48 enrolled. In 2017, 49 master's, 11 doctorates awarded. *Degree requirements:* For doctorate, thesis/ dissertation, exam. *Entrance requirements:* For doctorate, GRE General Test. Additional exam requirements/recommendations for international students: Required—TOEFL. *Application deadline:* For fall admission, 1/15 for domestic students; for spring admission, 10/1 for domestic students. Application fee: $100. Electronic applications accepted. *Expenses:* Contact institution. *Financial support:* In 2017–18, 29 fellowships, 29 research assistantships were awarded; teaching assistantships, career-related internships or fieldwork, and Federal Work-Study also available. Financial award application deadline: 3/15. *Unit head:* Dr. Kenneth Kaushansky, Dean and Senior Vice President of Health Sciences, 631-444-2121, Fax: 631-632-6621. *Application contact:* Melissa Jordan, Assistant Dean, 631-632-9712, Fax: 631-632-7243, E-mail: melissa.jordan@stonybrook.edu.

Stony Brook University, State University of New York, Stony Brook Medicine, School of Medicine, Medical Scientist Training Program, Stony Brook, NY 11794. Offers MD/ PhD. *Entrance requirements:* Additional exam requirements/recommendations for international students: Required—TOEFL. *Application deadline:* For fall admission, 12/1 for domestic students. *Expenses:* Tuition, state resident: full-time $10,870; part-time $453 per credit. Tuition, nonresident: full-time $22,210; part-time $925 per credit. *Financial support:* Tuition waivers (full) available. *Unit head:* Dr. Michael A. Frohman, Director, 631-444-3050, Fax: 631-444-9749, E-mail: michael.frohman@stonybrook.edu. *Application contact:* Carron Allen, Program Administrator, 631-444-3219, Fax: 631-444-3492, E-mail: carron.allen@stonybrook.edu. Website: http://www.pharm.stonybrook.edu/mstp/

Sul Ross State University, College of Arts and Sciences, Department of Biology, Alpine, TX 79832. Offers MS. *Program availability:* Part-time. *Degree requirements:* For master's, thesis optional. *Entrance requirements:* For master's, GRE General Test, minimum GPA of 2.5 in last 60 hours of undergraduate work. *Faculty research:* Plant-animal interaction, Chihuahuan desert biology, insect biological control, plant and animal systematics, wildlife biology.

Syracuse University, College of Arts and Sciences, Department of Biology, Syracuse, NY 13244. Offers biology (MS, PhD); neuroscience (PhD). Terminal master's awarded for partial completion of doctoral program. *Degree requirements:* For master's, thesis; for doctorate, thesis/dissertation. *Entrance requirements:* For master's and doctorate, GRE General Test, GRE Subject Test (recommended), BS or BA, at least a minimal background in both physical and biological sciences, three letters of recommendation, personal statement, transcripts. Additional exam requirements/recommendations for international students: Required—TOEFL (minimum score 100 iBT). *Application deadline:* For fall admission, 12/15 priority date for domestic and international students. Application fee: $75. Electronic applications accepted. *Financial support:* Fellowships with full tuition reimbursements, research assistantships with tuition reimbursements, teaching assistantships with tuition reimbursements, and scholarships/grants available. Financial award application deadline: 12/15; financial award applicants required to submit FAFSA. *Faculty research:* Cell signaling, plant ecosystem ecology, aquatic ecology, genetics and molecular biology of color vision, ion transport by cell membranes. *Unit head:* Dr. Ramesh Raina, Professor, Biology/Department Chair, 315-443-4546, E-mail: raraina@syr.edu. *Application contact:* Lynn Fall, Graduate Program Administrator, 315-443-9154, E-mail: biology@syr.edu. Website: http://biology.syr.edu/

Syracuse University, School of Education, Programs in Science Education, Syracuse, NY 13244. Offers biology (MS); chemistry (MS, PhD). *Program availability:* Part-time. *Students:* Average age 38. In 2017, 4 doctorates awarded. *Degree requirements:* For doctorate, comprehensive exam, thesis/dissertation. *Entrance requirements:* For master's, GRE General Test or MAT, official transcripts from previous academic institutions, 3 letters of recommendation (preferably from faculty), personal statement that makes a clear and compelling argument for why applicant wants to teach secondary science; for doctorate, GRE General Test or MAT, master's degree, interview. Additional exam requirements/recommendations for international students: Required—TOEFL (minimum score 100 iBT). *Application deadline:* For fall admission, 1/15 priority date for domestic and international students; for spring admission, 10/15 priority date for domestic and international students. Applications are processed on a rolling basis. Application fee: $75. Electronic applications accepted. *Financial support:* Fellowships with full tuition reimbursements, research assistantships, teaching assistantships, and scholarships/grants available. Financial award application deadline: 1/15. *Faculty research:* Diverse field experiences and theoretical and practical knowledge in research-

based science teaching, biology, chemistry, earth science, and physics. *Unit head:* Dr. Sharon Dotger, Program Coordinator, 315-443-9138, E-mail: sdotger@syr.edu. *Application contact:* Speranza Migliore, Graduate Admissions Recruiter, 315-443-2505, E-mail: gradrcrt@syr.edu.
Website: http://soe.syr.edu/academic/teaching_and_leadership/graduate/masters/science_education/

Tarleton State University, College of Graduate Studies, College of Science and Technology, Department of Biological Sciences, Stephenville, TX 76402. Offers biology (MS). *Program availability:* Part-time, evening/weekend. *Faculty:* 11 full-time (3 women). *Students:* 13 full-time (8 women), 7 part-time (4 women); includes 3 minority (1 Black or African American, non-Hispanic/Latino; 2 Hispanic/Latino). Average age 26. 12 applicants, 100% accepted, 9 enrolled. In 2017, 9 master's awarded. *Degree requirements:* For master's, comprehensive exam, thesis (for some programs). *Entrance requirements:* For master's, GRE General Test, minimum GPA of 3.0. Additional exam requirements/recommendations for international students: Required—TOEFL (minimum score 550 paper-based; 80 iBT), IELTS (minimum score 6). *Application deadline:* For fall admission, 8/15 priority date for domestic students; for spring admission, 1/7 for domestic students. Applications are processed on a rolling basis. Application fee: $45 ($145 for international students). Electronic applications accepted. *Expenses:* Contact institution. *Financial support:* Research assistantships, teaching assistantships, career-related internships or fieldwork, and Federal Work-Study available. Support available to part-time students. Financial award application deadline: 5/1; financial award applicants required to submit FAFSA. *Unit head:* Dr. Allan Nelson, Department Head, 254-968-9158, E-mail: nelson@tarleton.edu. *Application contact:* Information Contact, 254-968-9104, Fax: 254-968-9670, E-mail: gradoffice@tarleton.edu.
Website: http://www.tarleton.edu/degrees/masters/ms-biology/

Teachers College, Columbia University, Department of Mathematics, Science and Technology, New York, NY 10027-6696. Offers biology 7-12 (MA); chemistry 7-12 (MA); communication and education (MA, Ed D); computing in education (MA); earth science 7-12 (MA); instructional technology and media (Ed M, MA, Ed D); mathematics education (Ed M, MA, Ed D, Ed DCT, PhD); physics 7-12 (MA); science and dental education (MA); science education (Ed M, MS, Ed DCT, PhD); supervisor/teacher of science education (MA); technology specialist (MA). *Program availability:* Part-time, evening/weekend, online learning. *Students:* 187 full-time (129 women), 228 part-time (153 women); includes 143 minority (42 Black or African American, non-Hispanic/Latino; 64 Asian, non-Hispanic/Latino; 25 Hispanic/Latino; 12 Two or more races, non-Hispanic/Latino), 125 international. Average age 32. 484 applicants, 59% accepted, 141 enrolled. Terminal master's awarded for partial completion of doctoral program. *Degree requirements:* For doctorate, thesis/dissertation. *Unit head:* Prof. Erica Walker, Chair, E-mail: ewalker@tc.columbia.edu. *Application contact:* David Estrella, Director of Admission, 212-678-3305, E-mail: estrella@tc.columbia.edu.
Website: http://www.tc.columbia.edu/mathematics-science-and-technology/

Temple University, College of Science and Technology, Department of Biology, Philadelphia, PA 19122. Offers biology (MS, PSM, PhD); biotechnology (MS). *Faculty:* 46 full-time (16 women), 2 part-time/adjunct (both women). *Students:* 80 full-time (42 women), 28 part-time (12 women); includes 26 minority (1 Black or African American, non-Hispanic/Latino; 14 Asian, non-Hispanic/Latino; 7 Hispanic/Latino; 4 Two or more races, non-Hispanic/Latino), 19 international. 103 applicants, 53% accepted, 36 enrolled. In 2017, 32 master's, 4 doctorates awarded. Terminal master's awarded for partial completion of doctoral program. *Entrance requirements:* For master's and doctorate, GRE General Test, minimum GPA of 3.0. Additional exam requirements/recommendations for international students: Required—TOEFL (minimum score 550 paper-based; 79 iBT). *Application deadline:* For fall admission, 1/15 for domestic students, 12/15 for international students; for spring admission, 10/15 for domestic students, 8/1 for international students. Applications are processed on a rolling basis. Application fee: $60. *Expenses:* Tuition, state resident: full-time $16,164; part-time $898 per credit hour. Tuition, nonresident: full-time $22,158; part-time $1231 per credit hour. *Required fees:* $890; $445 per semester. Full-time tuition and fees vary according to course load, degree level, campus/location and program. *Financial support:* Fellowships, research assistantships, teaching assistantships, Federal Work-Study, and tuition waivers (full) available. Financial award application deadline: 1/15; financial award applicants required to submit FAFSA. *Faculty research:* Membrane proteins, genetics, molecular biology, neuroscience, aquatic biology. *Unit head:* Dr. Allen Nicholson, Chair, 215-204-9048, Fax: 215-204-6646, E-mail: biology@temple.edu.
Website: https://bio.cst.temple.edu/

Temple University, Lewis Katz School of Medicine, Philadelphia, PA 19122-6096. Offers biomedical sciences (MS); MD/MA; MD/MBA; MD/MPH; MD/PhD. *Faculty:* 20 full-time (7 women). *Students:* 1,078 full-time (551 women), 25 part-time (21 women); includes 411 minority (74 Black or African American, non-Hispanic/Latino; 210 Asian, non-Hispanic/Latino; 95 Hispanic/Latino; 1 Native Hawaiian or other Pacific Islander, non-Hispanic/Latino; 31 Two or more races, non-Hispanic/Latino), 27 international. 159 applicants, 34% accepted, 36 enrolled. In 2017, 16 master's, 217 doctorates awarded. Terminal master's awarded for partial completion of doctoral program. *Degree requirements:* For master's, thesis optional; for doctorate, thesis/dissertation (for some programs), research seminars (for PhD). *Entrance requirements:* For master's, GRE General Test, minimum undergraduate GPA of 3.0; for doctorate, GRE General Test (for PhD); MCAT (for MD), minimum undergraduate GPA of 3.0. Additional exam requirements/recommendations for international students: Required—TOEFL. *Application deadline:* For fall admission, 2/15 for domestic and international students. Application fee: $60. Electronic applications accepted. *Expenses:* Contact institution. *Financial support:* Fellowships, research assistantships, scholarships/grants, and health care benefits available. Financial award application deadline: 2/15; financial award applicants required to submit FAFSA. *Faculty research:* Translational medicine, molecular biology and immunology of autoimmune disease and cancer, cardiovascular and pulmonary disease pathophysiology, biology of substance abuse, causes and consequences of obesity, molecular mechanisms of neurological dysfunction. *Unit head:* Larry R. Kaiser, Dean, 215-707-8773, Fax: 215-707-5072, E-mail: sks@temple.edu. *Application contact:* Jacob Ufberg, Associate Dean of Admissions, 215-707-5308, E-mail: tusmgrad@temple.edu.
Website: http://www.temple.edu/medicine/

Tennessee State University, The School of Graduate Studies and Research, College of Agriculture, Human and Natural Sciences, Department of Biological Sciences, Nashville, TN 37209-1561. Offers PhD. *Degree requirements:* For doctorate, thesis/dissertation. *Entrance requirements:* For doctorate, GRE General Test, GRE Subject Test. *Faculty research:* Cellular and molecular biology and agrobiology.

Tennessee Technological University, College of Graduate Studies, College of Arts and Sciences, Department of Biology, Cookeville, TN 38505. Offers fish, game, and wildlife management (MS). *Program availability:* Part-time. *Faculty:* 22 full-time (2 women). *Students:* 2 full-time (1 woman), 18 part-time (9 women); includes 3 minority (all Hispanic/Latino), 1 international. 20 applicants, 50% accepted, 6 enrolled. In 2017, 9 master's awarded. *Degree requirements:* For master's, thesis. *Entrance requirements:* For master's, GRE. Additional exam requirements/recommendations for international students: Required—TOEFL (minimum score 527 paper-based; 71 iBT), IELTS (minimum score 5.5), PTE (minimum score 48), or TOEIC (Test of English as an International Communication). *Application deadline:* For fall admission, 8/1 for domestic students, 5/1 for international students; for spring admission, 12/1 for domestic students, 10/1 for international students; for summer admission, 5/1 for domestic students, 2/1 for international students. Applications are processed on a rolling basis. Application fee: $35 ($40 for international students). Electronic applications accepted. *Expenses:* Tuition, state resident: full-time $9925; part-time $565 per credit hour. Tuition, nonresident: full-time $22,993; part-time $1291 per credit hour. *Financial support:* In 2017–18, 7 research assistantships, 14 teaching assistantships (averaging $7,500 per year) were awarded. Financial award application deadline: 4/1. *Faculty research:* Aquatics, environmental studies. *Unit head:* Dr. Robert Kissell, Chairperson, 931-372-3134, Fax: 931-372-6257, E-mail: rkissell@tntech.edu. *Application contact:* Shelia K. Kendrick, Coordinator of Graduate Studies, 931-372-3808, Fax: 931-372-3497, E-mail: skendrick@tntech.edu.

Tennessee Technological University, College of Graduate Studies, College of Interdisciplinary Studies, School of Environmental Studies, Department of Environmental Sciences, Cookeville, TN 38505. Offers agriculture (PhD); biology (PhD); chemistry (PhD); geosciences (PhD); integrated research (PhD). *Program availability:* Part-time. *Students:* 2 full-time (1 woman), 15 part-time (4 women); includes 1 minority (Asian, non-Hispanic/Latino), 4 international. 10 applicants, 30% accepted, 2 enrolled. In 2017, 2 doctorates awarded. *Degree requirements:* For doctorate, comprehensive exam, thesis/dissertation. *Entrance requirements:* For doctorate, GRE. Additional exam requirements/recommendations for international students: Required—TOEFL (minimum score 527 paper-based; 71 iBT), IELTS (minimum score 5.5), PTE (minimum score 48), or TOEIC (Test of English as an International Communication). *Application deadline:* For fall admission, 7/1 for domestic students, 5/1 for international students; for spring admission, 12/1 for domestic students, 10/2 for international students; for summer admission, 5/1 for domestic students, 2/1 for international students. Applications are processed on a rolling basis. Application fee: $35 ($40 for international students). Electronic applications accepted. *Expenses:* Tuition, state resident: full-time $9925; part-time $565 per credit hour. Tuition, nonresident: full-time $22,993; part-time $1291 per credit hour. *Financial support:* Fellowships, research assistantships, and teaching assistantships available. Financial award application deadline: 4/1. *Unit head:* Dr. Hayden Mattingly, Interim Director, 931-372-6246, E-mail: hmattingly@tntech.edu. *Application contact:* Shelia K. Kendrick, Coordinator of Graduate Studies, 931-372-3808, Fax: 931-372-3497, E-mail: skendrick@tntech.edu.

Texas A&M International University, Office of Graduate Studies and Research, College of Arts and Sciences, Department of Biology and Chemistry, Laredo, TX 78041. Offers biology (MS). *Degree requirements:* For master's, comprehensive exam, thesis (for some programs). *Entrance requirements:* Additional exam requirements/recommendations for international students: Required—TOEFL (minimum score 79 iBT).

Texas A&M University, College of Dentistry, Dallas, TX 75266-0677. Offers advanced education in general dentistry (Certificate); biomedical sciences (MS); dental hygiene (MS); dental public health (Certificate); endodontics (Certificate); maxillofacial surgery (Certificate); oral and maxillofacial pathology (Certificate); oral and maxillofacial radiology (Certificate); oral and maxillofacial surgery (Certificate); oral biology (MS, PhD); orthodontics (Certificate); pediatric dentistry (Certificate); periodontics (Certificate); prosthodontics (Certificate). *Accreditation:* ADA; SACS/CC. *Faculty:* 44. *Enrollment:* 499 full-time matriculated graduate/professional students (251 women), 37 part-time matriculated graduate/professional students (12 women). *Students:* 499 full-time (251 women), 37 part-time (12 women); includes 275 minority (54 Black or African American, non-Hispanic/Latino; 2 American Indian or Alaska Native, non-Hispanic/Latino; 100 Asian, non-Hispanic/Latino; 109 Hispanic/Latino; 10 Two or more races, non-Hispanic/Latino), 30 international. Average age 27. In 2017, 18 master's, 2 doctorates, 101 other advanced degrees awarded. *Entrance requirements:* Additional exam requirements/recommendations for international students: Required—TOEFL (minimum score 550 paper-based; 79 iBT). Application fee: $35. Electronic applications accepted. *Expenses:* Contact institution. *Financial support:* In 2017–18, 235 students received support, including 32 research assistantships with tuition reimbursements available (averaging $8,712 per year), 43 teaching assistantships with tuition reimbursements available (averaging $14,231 per year); career-related internships or fieldwork, institutionally sponsored loans, scholarships/grants, traineeships, health care benefits, tuition waivers (full and partial), and unspecified assistantships also available. Support available to part-time students. Financial award applicants required to submit FAFSA. *Unit head:* Dr. Lawrence E. Wolinsky, Dean, 214-828-8300, E-mail: wolinsky@tamhsc.edu. *Application contact:* Ernestine S. Lacy, Associate Dean for Student Affairs and Student Diversity, 214-828-8374, Fax: 214-874-4572, E-mail: eslacy@tamhsc.edu.
Website: http://www.dentistry.tamhsc.edu/

Texas A&M University, College of Science, Department of Biology, College Station, TX 77843. Offers biology (MS, PhD); microbiology (MS, PhD). *Faculty:* 39. *Students:* 89 full-time (48 women), 5 part-time (3 women); includes 10 minority (2 Black or African American, non-Hispanic/Latino; 3 Asian, non-Hispanic/Latino; 3 Hispanic/Latino; 2 Two or more races, non-Hispanic/Latino), 40 international. Average age 29. 109 applicants, 28% accepted, 19 enrolled. In 2017, 5 master's, 19 doctorates awarded. *Degree requirements:* For master's, thesis or alternative; for doctorate, comprehensive exam, thesis/dissertation. *Entrance requirements:* For master's and doctorate, GRE General Test. Additional exam requirements/recommendations for international students: Required—TOEFL. *Application deadline:* For fall admission, 12/1 for domestic students. Applications are processed on a rolling basis. Application fee: $50 ($90 for international students). Electronic applications accepted. *Expenses:* Contact institution. *Financial support:* In 2017–18, 87 students received support, including 4 fellowships with tuition reimbursements available (averaging $25,816 per year), 41 research assistantships with tuition reimbursements available (averaging $14,313 per year), 45 teaching assistantships with tuition reimbursements available (averaging $13,974 per year); career-related internships or fieldwork, institutionally sponsored loans, scholarships/grants, traineeships, health care benefits, tuition waivers (full and partial), and unspecified assistantships also available. Support available to part-time students. Financial award application deadline: 4/1; financial award applicants required to submit FAFSA. *Faculty research:* Biological clocks, cell, molecular and developmental biology, ecology and evolutionary biology, genetics and genomics, microbiology. *Unit head:* Dr. Tom McKnight, Department Head, 979-845-3896, Fax: 979-845-2891, E-mail: mcknight@bio.tamu.edu. *Application contact:* Dr. Arne Lekven, Graduate Advisor, 979-458-3461, Fax: 979-845-2891, E-mail: alekven@bio.tamu.edu.
Website: http://www.bio.tamu.edu/index.html

Texas A&M University–Commerce, College of Science and Engineering, Commerce, TX 75429. Offers biological sciences (MS); broadfield science biology (MS); broadfield science chemistry (MS); broadfield science physics (MS); chemistry (MS); computational linguistics (Graduate Certificate); computational science (MS); computer science (MS); environmental science (Graduate Certificate); mathematics (MS); physics (MS); technology management (MS). *Program availability:* Part-time, 100% online, blended/hybrid learning. *Faculty:* 46 full-time (5 women), 14 part-time/adjunct (1 woman). *Students:* 257 full-time (103 women), 251 part-time (99 women); includes 77

minority (23 Black or African American, non-Hispanic/Latino; 1 American Indian or Alaska Native, non-Hispanic/Latino; 12 Asian, non-Hispanic/Latino; 31 Hispanic/Latino; 10 Two or more races, non-Hispanic/Latino), 289 international. Average age 29. 481 applicants, 52% accepted, 105 enrolled. In 2017, 341 master's awarded. *Degree requirements:* For master's, comprehensive exam, thesis optional. *Entrance requirements:* For master's, GRE, official transcripts, letters of recommendation, resume, statement of goals. Additional exam requirements/recommendations for international students: Required—TOEFL (minimum score 550 paper-based, 79 iBT), IELTS (minimum score 6). *Application deadline:* For fall admission, 6/1 priority date for international students; for spring admission, 10/15 priority date for international students; for summer admission, 3/15 priority date for international students. Applications are processed on a rolling basis. Application fee: $50 ($75 for international students). Electronic applications accepted. *Expenses:* Contact institution. *Financial support:* In 2017–18, 66 students received support, including 11 research assistantships with partial tuition reimbursements available (averaging $8,000 per year), 41 teaching assistantships with partial tuition reimbursements available (averaging $8,000 per year); scholarships/grants, health care benefits, and unspecified assistantships also available. Financial award application deadline: 5/1; financial award applicants required to submit FAFSA. *Faculty research:* Regenerative medicine, catalytic materials and processes, nuclear theory/astrophysics, image processing/recognition. *Total annual research expenditures:* $1.7 million. *Unit head:* Dr. Brent L. Donham, Dean, 903-886-5390, Fax: 903-886-5199, E-mail: brent.donham@tamuc.edu. *Application contact:* Dayla Burgin, Graduate Student Services Coordinator, 903-886-5134, E-mail: dayla.burgin@tamuc.edu.
Website: http://www.tamuc.edu/academics/graduateSchool/programs/sciences/default.aspx

Texas A&M University–Corpus Christi, College of Graduate Studies, College of Science and Engineering, Program in Biology, Corpus Christi, TX 78412. Offers MS, PhD. *Program availability:* Part-time, evening/weekend. *Students:* 8 full-time (all women), 5 part-time (3 women); includes 3 minority (all Hispanic/Latino). Average age 32. 6 applicants, 50% accepted, 3 enrolled. In 2017, 6 master's awarded. *Degree requirements:* For master's, comprehensive exam, thesis. *Entrance requirements:* For master's, GRE (taken within 5 years), essay (up to 1,000 words), 3 letters of recommendation. Additional exam requirements/recommendations for international students: Required—TOEFL (minimum score 550 paper-based; 79 iBT), IELTS (minimum score 6.5). *Application deadline:* For fall admission, 5/15 for domestic students, 4/15 for international students; for spring admission, 10/15 for domestic students, 9/15 for international students; for summer admission, 3/1 for domestic students, 2/1 for international students. Applications are processed on a rolling basis. Application fee: $50 ($70 for international students). Electronic applications accepted. *Expenses:* Tuition, state resident: full-time $3568; part-time $198.24 per credit hour. Tuition, nonresident: full-time $11,038; part-time $613.24 per credit hour. *Required fees:* $2129; $1422.58 per semester. Tuition and fees vary according to program. *Financial support:* Research assistantships, teaching assistantships, institutionally sponsored loans, scholarships/grants, health care benefits, and unspecified assistantships available. Support available to part-time students. Financial award application deadline: 3/15. *Unit head:* Dr. Kim Withers, Coordinator, 361-825-5907, Fax: 361-825-2742, E-mail: kim.withers@tamucc.edu. *Application contact:* Graduate Admissions Coordinator, 361-825-2177, Fax: 361-825-2755, E-mail: gradweb@tamucc.edu.
Website: http://www.biol.tamucc.edu/ms/

Texas A&M University–Kingsville, College of Graduate Studies, College of Arts and Sciences, Department of Biological and Health Sciences, Kingsville, TX 78363. Offers biology (MS). *Entrance requirements:* Additional exam requirements/recommendations for international students: Required—TOEFL (minimum score 550 paper-based; 79 iBT); Recommended—IELTS (minimum score 6). Electronic applications accepted.

Texas Christian University, College of Science and Engineering, Department of Biology, Fort Worth, TX 76129. Offers MA, MS, PhD. *Program availability:* Part-time. *Faculty:* 12 full-time (4 women). *Students:* 17 full-time (6 women), 1 (woman) part-time; includes 2 minority (both Black or African American, non-Hispanic/Latino). Average age 26. 28 applicants, 50% accepted, 10 enrolled. In 2017, 8 master's awarded. *Degree requirements:* For master's, thesis (for some programs); for doctorate, thesis/dissertation. *Entrance requirements:* For master's, GRE General Test. Additional exam requirements/recommendations for international students: Required—TOEFL (minimum score 560 paper-based). *Application deadline:* For fall admission, 2/1 priority date for domestic students, 1/15 for international students; for spring admission, 9/1 priority date for domestic students, 8/15 for international students. Applications are processed on a rolling basis. Application fee: $60. Electronic applications accepted. *Financial support:* In 2017–18, 13 students received support, including 13 teaching assistantships with full tuition reimbursements available (averaging $16,000 per year). Financial award application deadline: 2/1. *Faculty research:* Invasive species, anthrax, mercury contamination in food webs, ecological impacts of wind turbines, Alzheimer's disease. *Total annual research expenditures:* $729,849. *Unit head:* Dr. Michael Chumley, Chairperson, 817-257-8777, E-mail: m.chumley@tcu.edu. *Application contact:* Dr. Amanda Hale, Associate Professor, 817-257-6182, E-mail: a.hale@tcu.edu.
Website: http://www.bio.tcu.edu/

Texas Southern University, School of Science and Technology, Department of Biology, Houston, TX 77004-4584. Offers MS. *Program availability:* Part-time, evening/weekend. *Degree requirements:* For master's, one foreign language, comprehensive exam, thesis. *Entrance requirements:* For master's, GRE General Test, minimum GPA of 2.5. Additional exam requirements/recommendations for international students: Required—TOEFL. Electronic applications accepted. *Faculty research:* Microbiology, cell and molecular biology, biochemistry, biochemical virology, biophysics.

Texas State University, The Graduate College, College of Science and Engineering, Program in Biology, San Marcos, TX 78666. Offers MA, MS. *Program availability:* Part-time. *Faculty:* 17 full-time (10 women), 3 part-time/adjunct (0 women). *Students:* 32 full-time (15 women), 13 part-time (8 women); includes 20 minority (3 Black or African American, non-Hispanic/Latino; 16 Hispanic/Latino; 1 Two or more races, non-Hispanic/Latino), 6 international. Average age 28. 43 applicants, 53% accepted, 16 enrolled. In 2017, 12 master's awarded. *Degree requirements:* For master's, comprehensive exam, thesis (for some programs). *Entrance requirements:* For master's, GRE General Test (recommended minimum score in at least the 50th percentile on both the verbal and quantitative portions), baccalaureate degree in biology or related discipline from regionally-accredited university with minimum GPA of 3.0 on last 60 undergraduate semester hours, current curriculum vitae, statement of purpose with aspirations and academic goals, 3 letters of recommendation, letter of intent to mentor from faculty member of Biology Department. Additional exam requirements/recommendations for international students: Required—TOEFL (minimum score 550 paper-based; 78 iBT), IELTS (minimum score 6.5). *Application deadline:* For fall admission, 2/1 priority date for domestic and international students; for spring admission, 10/15 for domestic students, 10/1 for international students; for summer admission, 4/15 for domestic students, 3/15 for international students. Applications are processed on a rolling basis. Application fee: $40 ($90 for international students). Electronic applications accepted. *Expenses:* Tuition, state resident: full-time $7868; part-time $3934 per semester. Tuition, nonresident: full-time $17,828; part-time $8914 per semester. *Required fees:* $2092; $1435 per semester. Tuition and fees vary according to course load. *Financial support:* In 2017–18, 28 students received support, including 2 research assistantships (averaging $13,866 per year), 31 teaching assistantships (averaging $12,759 per year); Federal Work-Study, institutionally sponsored loans, scholarships/grants, health care benefits, and unspecified assistantships also available. Support available to part-time students. Financial award application deadline: 3/1; financial award applicants required to submit FAFSA. *Unit head:* Dr. David Lemke, Graduate Advisor, 512-245-2178, E-mail: dl10@txstate.edu. *Application contact:* Dr. Andrea Golato, Dean of the Graduate School, 512-245-2581, Fax: 512-245-8365, E-mail: jw02@swt.edu.
Website: http://www.bio.txstate.edu/Graduate-Programs/M-S—Biology.html

Texas Tech University, Graduate School, College of Arts and Sciences, Department of Biological Sciences, Lubbock, TX 79409-3131. Offers biology (MS, PhD); environmental sustainability and natural resource management (PSM); microbiology (MS); zoology (MS, PhD). *Program availability:* Part-time, blended/hybrid learning. *Faculty:* 44 full-time (16 women). *Students:* 103 full-time (56 women), 13 part-time (5 women); includes 12 minority (2 Black or African American, non-Hispanic/Latino; 2 Asian, non-Hispanic/Latino; 6 Hispanic/Latino; 2 Two or more races, non-Hispanic/Latino), 51 international. Average age 29. 77 applicants, 36% accepted, 17 enrolled. In 2017, 13 master's, 10 doctorates awarded. *Degree requirements:* For master's, comprehensive exam, thesis or alternative; for doctorate, comprehensive exam, thesis/dissertation. *Entrance requirements:* For master's and doctorate, GRE General Test. Additional exam requirements/recommendations for international students: Required—TOEFL (minimum score 550 paper-based; 79 iBT). *Application deadline:* For fall admission, 6/1 priority date for domestic students, 1/15 priority date for international students; for spring admission, 9/1 priority date for domestic students, 6/15 priority date for international students. Applications are processed on a rolling basis. Application fee: $60. Electronic applications accepted. *Expenses:* Contact institution. *Financial support:* In 2017–18, 110 students received support, including 85 fellowships (averaging $1,960 per year), 28 research assistantships (averaging $8,365 per year), 93 teaching assistantships (averaging $15,744 per year); Federal Work-Study and health care benefits also available. Financial award application deadline: 2/15; financial award applicants required to submit FAFSA. *Faculty research:* Biodiversity, genomics and evolution; climate change in arid ecosystems, plant biology and biotechnology; animal communication and behavior; microbiomes, zoonosis and emerging diseases. *Total annual research expenditures:* $1.7 million. *Unit head:* Dr. Ron Chesser, Chair, 806-834-0121, Fax: 806-742-2963, E-mail: ron.chesser@ttu.edu. *Application contact:* Dr. Lou Densmore, Graduate Adviser, 806-834-6479, Fax: 806-742-2963, E-mail: lou.densmore@ttu.edu.
Website: http://www.depts.ttu.edu/biology/

Texas Tech University Health Sciences Center, Graduate School of Biomedical Sciences, Lubbock, TX 79430-0002. Offers MS, PhD, MD/PhD, MS/PhD. Terminal master's awarded for partial completion of doctoral program. *Degree requirements:* For master's, thesis; for doctorate, thesis/dissertation. *Entrance requirements:* For master's and doctorate, GRE General Test, minimum GPA of 3.0. Additional exam requirements/recommendations for international students: Required—TOEFL (minimum score 550 paper-based). Electronic applications accepted. *Faculty research:* Genetics of neurological disorders, hemodynamics to prevent DVT, toxin A synthesis, DA neurons, peroxidases.

Texas Tech University Health Sciences Center El Paso, Graduate School of Biomedical Sciences, El Paso, TX 79905. Offers MS.

Texas Woman's University, Graduate School, College of Arts and Sciences, Department of Biology, Denton, TX 76204. Offers biology (MS); molecular biology (PhD). PhD in molecular biology offered through cooperative program of the Federation of North Texas Area Universities (The University of North Texas, Texas Woman's University, and Texas A&M Commerce). *Program availability:* Part-time. *Faculty:* 15 full-time (10 women), 1 part-time/adjunct (0 women). *Students:* 1 full-time (0 women), 40 part-time (29 women); includes 5 minority (1 Black or African American, non-Hispanic/Latino; 2 Asian, non-Hispanic/Latino; 1 Hispanic/Latino; 1 Two or more races, non-Hispanic/Latino), 22 international. Average age 33. 19 applicants, 53% accepted, 2 enrolled. In 2017, 3 doctorates awarded. Terminal master's awarded for partial completion of doctoral program. *Degree requirements:* For master's, comprehensive exam, thesis (for some programs), professional paper or thesis; for doctorate, comprehensive exam, thesis/dissertation, 1-year residency. *Entrance requirements:* For master's, GRE General Test (preferred minimum score 148 [425 old version] verbal, 140 [425 old version] quantitative), 3 letters of reference; letter of interest; for doctorate, GRE General Test (preferred minimum score 153 [500 old version] verbal, 144 [500 old version] quantitative), 3 letters of reference, letter of interest. Additional exam requirements/recommendations for international students: Required—TOEFL (minimum score 550 paper-based; 79 iBT); Recommended—IELTS (minimum score 6.5), TSE (minimum score 53). *Application deadline:* For fall admission, 3/1 priority date for domestic and international students; for spring admission, 11/1 priority date for domestic students, 7/1 priority date for international students; for summer admission, 5/1 priority date for domestic students, 2/1 priority date for international students. Applications are processed on a rolling basis. Application fee: $50 ($75 for international students). Electronic applications accepted. *Expenses:* $7,520 per year full-time in-state; $16,820 per year full-time out-of-state. *Financial support:* In 2017–18, 15 students received support, including 1 research assistantship (averaging $31,488 per year), 15 teaching assistantships (averaging $29,092 per year); career-related internships or fieldwork, institutionally sponsored loans, scholarships/grants, traineeships, health care benefits, and unspecified assistantships also available. Support available to part-time students. Financial award application deadline: 3/1; financial award applicants required to submit FAFSA. *Faculty research:* Electron microscopy, protein degradation, sensory neuroscience, transcription regulation, virus: host interactions. *Unit head:* Dr. Ron Hovis, Interim Chair, 940-898-2351, Fax: 940-898-2382, E-mail: biology@twu.edu. *Application contact:* Korie Hawkins, Associate Director of Admissions, Graduate Recruitment, 940-898-3188, Fax: 940-898-3081, E-mail: admissions@twu.edu.
Website: http://www.twu.edu/biology

Thomas Jefferson University, Jefferson College of Biomedical Sciences, Philadelphia, PA 19107. Offers MS, PhD, Certificate, MD/PhD. *Program availability:* Part-time, evening/weekend. *Faculty:* 169 full-time (52 women), 39 part-time/adjunct (18 women). *Students:* 125 full-time (67 women), 144 part-time (88 women); includes 44 minority (16 Black or African American, non-Hispanic/Latino; 1 American Indian or Alaska Native, non-Hispanic/Latino; 15 Asian, non-Hispanic/Latino; 10 Hispanic/Latino; 2 Two or more races, non-Hispanic/Latino), 35 international. 356 applicants, 43% accepted, 78 enrolled. In 2017, 26 master's, 26 doctorates awarded. Terminal master's awarded for partial completion of doctoral program. *Degree requirements:* For master's, thesis; for doctorate, comprehensive exam, thesis/dissertation. *Entrance requirements:* For master's, GRE or MCAT; for doctorate, GRE or MCAT, minimum GPA of 3.2. Additional exam requirements/recommendations for international students: Required—TOEFL (minimum score 100 iBT), IELTS (minimum score 7). *Application deadline:* Applications are processed on a rolling basis. Application fee: $50. Electronic applications accepted. *Financial support:* Fellowships, Federal Work-Study, institutionally sponsored loans, scholarships/grants, and traineeships available. Support available to part-time students.

Financial award application deadline: 5/1; financial award applicants required to submit FAFSA. *Unit head:* Dr. Gerald B. Grunwald, Dean, 215-503-4191, Fax: 215-503-6690, E-mail: gerald.grunwald@jefferson.edu. *Application contact:* Marc E. Stearns, Senior Associate Director of Admissions, 215-503-0155, Fax: 215-503-3433, E-mail: jgsbs-info@jefferson.edu.
Website: http://www.jefferson.edu/university/biomedical-sciences.html

Towson University, Jess and Mildred Fisher College of Science and Mathematics, Program in Biology, Towson, MD 21252-0001. Offers MS. *Program availability:* Part-time, evening/weekend. *Students:* 12 full-time (9 women), 31 part-time (18 women); includes 12 minority (6 Black or African American, non-Hispanic/Latino; 4 Asian, non-Hispanic/Latino; 1 Hispanic/Latino; 1 Two or more races, non-Hispanic/Latino), 1 international. *Degree requirements:* For master's, thesis optional. *Entrance requirements:* For master's, GRE General Test (for thesis students), minimum GPA of 3.0; 24 credits in related course work; 3 letters of recommendation; minimum 24 units in biology; coursework in chemistry, organic chemistry, and physics; personal statement; official transcripts. *Application deadline:* For fall admission, 1/17 for domestic students, 5/15 for international students; for spring admission, 10/15 for domestic students, 12/1 for international students. Applications are processed on a rolling basis. Application fee: $45. Electronic applications accepted. *Expenses:* Tuition, state resident: full-time $7960; part-time $398 per unit. Tuition, nonresident: full-time $16,480; part-time $824 per unit. *Required fees:* $2600; $130 per year. $390 per term. *Financial support:* Application deadline: 4/1. *Unit head:* Dr. Peko Tsuji, Graduate Program Co-Director, 410-704-4117, E-mail: ptsuji@towson.edu. *Application contact:* Coverley Beidleman, Assistant Director of Graduate Admissions, 410-704-5630, Fax: 410-704-3030, E-mail: cbeidleman@towson.edu.
Website: http://www.towson.edu/fcsm/departments/biology/gradbiology/

Trent University, Graduate Studies, Program in Applications of Modeling in the Natural and Social Sciences, Peterborough, ON K9J 7B8, Canada. Offers applications of modeling in the natural and social sciences (MA); biology (M Sc, PhD); chemistry (M Sc); computer studies (M Sc); geography (M Sc, PhD); physics (M Sc). *Program availability:* Part-time. *Degree requirements:* For master's, thesis. *Entrance requirements:* For master's, honours degree. *Faculty research:* Computation of heat transfer, atmospheric physics, statistical mechanics, stress and coping, evolutionary ecology.

Trent University, Graduate Studies, Program in Environmental and Life Sciences and Program in Applications of Modeling in the Natural and Social Sciences, Department of Biology, Peterborough, ON K9J 7B8, Canada. Offers M Sc, PhD. *Program availability:* Part-time. *Degree requirements:* For master's, thesis; for doctorate, thesis/dissertation. *Entrance requirements:* For master's, honours degree; for doctorate, master's degree. *Faculty research:* Aquatic and behavioral ecology, hydrology and limnology, human impact on ecosystems, behavioral ecology of birds, ecology of fish.

Troy University, Graduate School, College of Arts and Sciences, Program in Biomedical Sciences, Troy, AL 36082. Offers MS, Certificate. *Program availability:* Part-time, evening/weekend. *Faculty:* 8 full-time (1 woman), 1 (woman) part-time/adjunct. *Students:* 10 full-time (6 women), 9 part-time (5 women); includes 5 minority (3 Black or African American, non-Hispanic/Latino; 2 Asian, non-Hispanic/Latino). Average age 27. 21 applicants, 76% accepted, 8 enrolled. In 2017, 7 master's awarded. *Degree requirements:* For master's, comprehensive exam. *Entrance requirements:* For master's, GRE (minimum score of 850 on old exam or 290 on new exam), MAT (minimum score of 385), or GMAT (minimum score of 380), baccalaureate degree, official transcripts, two letters of recommendation, 500-word personal statement. Additional exam requirements/recommendations for international students: Required—TOEFL (minimum score 523 paper-based; 70 iBT), IELTS (minimum score 6). *Application deadline:* For fall admission, 6/1 for international students; for spring admission, 10/15 for international students. Applications are processed on a rolling basis. Application fee: $50. Electronic applications accepted. *Expenses:* Tuition, state resident: part-time $417 per credit hour. Tuition, nonresident: part-time $834 per credit hour. *Required fees:* $42 per credit hour. $50 per semester. Tuition and fees vary according to campus/location. *Financial support:* Fellowships, career-related internships or fieldwork, and scholarships/grants available. Support available to part-time students. Financial award applicants required to submit FAFSA. *Unit head:* Dr. Glenn Cohen, Chairman, Department of Biology, 334-670-3660, Fax: 334-670-3626, E-mail: gcohen@troy.edu. *Application contact:* Jessica A. Kimbro, Director of Graduate Admissions, 334-670-3178, E-mail: jacord@troy.edu.

Truett McConnell University, Pilgram Marpeck School of Science, Technology, Engineering and Mathematics, Cleveland, GA 30528. Offers biology (MS). *Program availability:* Part-time. *Faculty:* 2 full-time (0 women). *Students:* 1 (woman) full-time. *Degree requirements:* For master's, thesis. *Entrance requirements:* For master's, GRE, minimum STEM GPA of 3.0, personal statement, letters of recommendation. *Application deadline:* For fall admission, 8/1 for domestic students; for spring admission, 12/1 for domestic students; for summer admission, 5/1 for domestic students. Applications are processed on a rolling basis. Electronic applications accepted. *Expenses: Tuition:* Part-time $325 per credit hour. *Required fees:* $910 per year. $455 per semester. *Financial support:* Teaching assistantships available. Financial award applicants required to submit FAFSA. *Unit head:* Dr. Robert Bowen, Dean, 706-865-2134 Ext. 6400, E-mail: rbowen@truett.edu. *Application contact:* Jim Dunnington, Coordinator of Online and Graduate Admissions, 706-865-2134 Ext. 2131, E-mail: jdunnington@truett.edu.
Website: https://truett.edu/degrees/master-science-biology/

Truman State University, Graduate School, School of Arts and Letters, Program in Biology, Kirksville, MO 63501-4221. Offers MS. *Degree requirements:* For master's, comprehensive exam, thesis. *Entrance requirements:* For master's, GRE General Test, minimum GPA of 3.0. Additional exam requirements/recommendations for international students: Required—TOEFL (minimum score 550 paper-based). Electronic applications accepted.

Tufts University, Cummings School of Veterinary Medicine, North Grafton, MA 01536. Offers animals and public policy (MS); biomedical sciences (PhD), including digestive diseases, infectious diseases, neuroscience and reproductive biology, pathology; conservation medicine (MS); veterinary medicine (DVM); DVM/MPH; DVM/MS. *Accreditation:* AVMA (one or more programs are accredited). *Degree requirements:* For master's, thesis (for some programs); for doctorate, comprehensive exam, thesis/dissertation (for some programs). *Entrance requirements:* For master's and doctorate, GRE General Test. Additional exam requirements/recommendations for international students: Required—TOEFL or IELTS. Electronic applications accepted. *Expenses:* Contact institution. *Faculty research:* Oncology, veterinary ethics, international veterinary medicine, veterinary genomics, pathogenesis of Clostridium difficile, wildlife fertility control.

Tufts University, Graduate School of Arts and Sciences, Department of Biology, Medford, MA 02155. Offers biology (MS, PhD); soft materials robotics (PhD). *Program availability:* Part-time. *Students:* 60 full-time (39 women), 4 part-time (1 woman); includes 13 minority (5 Asian, non-Hispanic/Latino; 7 Hispanic/Latino; 1 Two or more races, non-Hispanic/Latino), 13 international. Average age 26. 168 applicants, 18% accepted, 15 enrolled. In 2017, 8 master's, 8 doctorates awarded. Terminal master's awarded for partial completion of doctoral program. *Degree requirements:* For master's, thesis (for some programs); for doctorate, comprehensive exam, thesis/dissertation. *Entrance requirements:* For master's and doctorate, GRE General Test. Additional exam requirements/recommendations for international students: Required—TOEFL (minimum score 550 paper-based; 80 iBT), IELTS (minimum score 6.5). *Application deadline:* For fall admission, 12/15 for domestic and international students; for spring admission, 10/15 for domestic and international students. Applications are processed on a rolling basis. Application fee: $85. Electronic applications accepted. *Expenses:* Contact institution. *Financial support:* Fellowships, research assistantships, teaching assistantships, Federal Work-Study, scholarships/grants, tuition waivers (full and partial), and unspecified assistantships available. Financial award application deadline: 1/15. *Unit head:* Dr. Catherine Freudenreich, Graduate Program Director, 617-627-4037. *Application contact:* Office of Graduate Admissions, 617-627-3395, E-mail: gradadmissions@tufts.edu.
Website: http://www.ase.tufts.edu/biology

Tufts University, Sackler School of Graduate Biomedical Sciences, Boston, MA 02111. Offers MS, PhD, Certificate, DVM/PhD, MD/PhD. Terminal master's awarded for partial completion of doctoral program. *Degree requirements:* For master's, comprehensive exam (for some programs), thesis; for doctorate, thesis/dissertation. *Entrance requirements:* For master's and doctorate, GRE General Test (for some programs), letters of reference, resume, personal statement; for Certificate, letters of reference, resume, personal statement. Additional exam requirements/recommendations for international students: Required—TOEFL or IELTS. Electronic applications accepted. *Expenses:* Contact institution.

Tulane University, School of Medicine and School of Liberal Arts, Graduate Programs in Biomedical Sciences, New Orleans, LA 70118-5669. Offers MS, PhD, MD/PhD. *Degree requirements:* For doctorate, thesis/dissertation. *Entrance requirements:* For master's, GRE General Test, minimum B average in undergraduate course work; for doctorate, GRE General Test. Additional exam requirements/recommendations for international students: Required—TOEFL. *Expenses:* Contact institution.

Tuskegee University, Graduate Programs, College of Arts and Sciences, Department of Biology, Tuskegee, AL 36088. Offers MS. *Degree requirements:* For master's, thesis. *Entrance requirements:* For master's, GRE General Test, GRE Subject Test. Additional exam requirements/recommendations for international students: Required—TOEFL (minimum score 500 paper-based).

Tuskegee University, Graduate Programs, Program in Integrative Biosciences, Tuskegee, AL 36088. Offers PhD. *Degree requirements:* For doctorate, thesis/dissertation. *Entrance requirements:* For doctorate, GRE General Test, GRE Subject Test, minimum cumulative GPA of 3.0, 3.4 in upper-division courses; 3 letters of recommendation; resume or curriculum vitae. Additional exam requirements/recommendations for international students: Required—TOEFL (minimum score 500 paper-based). Electronic applications accepted.

Uniformed Services University of the Health Sciences, F. Edward Hebert School of Medicine, Graduate Programs in the Biomedical Sciences and Public Health, Bethesda, MD 20814. Offers emerging infectious diseases (PhD); medical and clinical psychology (PhD), including clinical psychology, medical psychology; medicine (MS, PhD), including health professions education; molecular and cell biology (MS, PhD); neuroscience (PhD); preventive medicine and biometrics (MPH, MS, MSPH, MTMH, PhD), including environmental health sciences (PhD), healthcare administration and policy (MS), medical zoology (PhD), public health (MPH, MSPH), tropical medicine and hygiene (MTMH). *Students:* Average age 25. 598 applicants, 17% accepted, 77 enrolled. In 2017, 19 master's, 50 doctorates awarded. Terminal master's awarded for partial completion of doctoral program. *Degree requirements:* For master's, comprehensive exam, thesis or alternative; for doctorate, comprehensive exam, thesis/dissertation, qualifying exam. *Entrance requirements:* For master's, GRE General Test; for doctorate, GRE General Test, minimum GPA of 3.0. *Application deadline:* For fall admission, 12/1 priority date for domestic students. Application fee: $0. Electronic applications accepted. *Expenses:* There are no tuition charges or fees for graduate students at USU. *Financial support:* In 2017–18, 50 fellowships (averaging $43,000 per year) were awarded; research assistantships, career-related internships or fieldwork, scholarships/grants, and health care benefits also available. *Unit head:* Dr. Gregory Mueller, Associate Dean, 301-295-3507, E-mail: gregory.mueller@usuhs.edu. *Application contact:* Tina Finley, Administrative Officer, 301-295-3642, Fax: 301-295-6772, E-mail: netina.finley@usuhs.edu.
Website: http://www.usuhs.mil/graded

Universidad Central del Caribe, School of Medicine, Program in Biomedical Sciences, Bayamón, PR 00960-6032. Offers anatomy and cell biology (MA, MS); biochemistry (MS); biomedical sciences (MA); cellular and molecular biology (PhD); microbiology and immunology (MA, MS); pharmacology (MS); physiology (MS).

Universidad de Ciencias Medicas, Graduate Programs, San Jose, Costa Rica. Offers dermatology (SP); family health (MS); health service center administration (MHA); human anatomy (MS); medical and surgery (MD); occupational medicine (MS); pharmacy (Pharm D). *Program availability:* Part-time. *Degree requirements:* For master's, thesis; for doctorate and SP, comprehensive exam. *Entrance requirements:* For master's, MD or bachelor's degree; for doctorate, admissions test; for SP, admissions test, MD.

Université de Moncton, Faculty of Sciences, Department of Biology, Moncton, NB E1A 3E9, Canada. Offers M Sc. *Degree requirements:* For master's, one foreign language, thesis. *Entrance requirements:* For master's, minimum GPA of 3.0. Electronic applications accepted. *Faculty research:* Terrestrial ecology, aquatic ecology, marine biology, aquaculture, ethology, biotechnology.

Université de Montréal, Faculty of Arts and Sciences, Department of Biological Sciences, Montréal, QC H3C 3J7, Canada. Offers M Sc, PhD. *Program availability:* Part-time. *Degree requirements:* For master's, thesis; for doctorate, thesis/dissertation, general exam. *Entrance requirements:* For doctorate, MS in biology or related field. Electronic applications accepted. *Faculty research:* Fresh water ecology, plant biotechnology, neurobiology, genetics, cell physiology.

Université de Montréal, Faculty of Medicine, Programs in Biomedical Sciences, Montréal, QC H3C 3J7, Canada. Offers M Sc, PhD. *Degree requirements:* For master's, thesis; for doctorate, thesis/dissertation, general exam. *Entrance requirements:* For master's and doctorate, proficiency in French, knowledge of English. Electronic applications accepted.

Université de Sherbrooke, Faculty of Medicine and Health Sciences, Graduate Programs in Medicine, Sherbrooke, QC J1H 5N4, Canada. Offers M Sc, PhD. *Program availability:* Part-time. Terminal master's awarded for partial completion of doctoral program. *Degree requirements:* For master's, thesis; for doctorate, thesis/dissertation. Electronic applications accepted. *Expenses:* Contact institution.

Université de Sherbrooke, Faculty of Sciences, Department of Biology, Sherbrooke, QC J1K 2R1, Canada. Offers M Sc, PhD, Diploma. *Degree requirements:* For master's, thesis; for doctorate, comprehensive exam, thesis/dissertation. *Entrance requirements:* For doctorate, master's degree. Electronic applications accepted. *Faculty research:* Microbiology, ecology, molecular biology, cell biology, biotechnology.

Université du Québec à Montréal, Graduate Programs, Program in Biology, Montréal, QC H3C 3P8, Canada. Offers M Sc, PhD. *Program availability:* Part-time. *Degree requirements:* For master's, thesis; for doctorate, thesis/dissertation. *Entrance requirements:* For master's, appropriate bachelor's degree or equivalent, proficiency in French; for doctorate, appropriate master's degree or equivalent, proficiency in French.

Université du Québec en Abitibi-Témiscamingue, Graduate Programs, Program in Environmental Sciences, Rouyn-Noranda, QC J9X 5E4, Canada. Offers biology (MS); environmental sciences (PhD); sustainable forest ecosystem management (MS).

Université du Québec, Institut National de la Recherche Scientifique, Graduate Programs, INRS - Institut Armand-Frappier, Laval, QC G1K 9A9, Canada. Offers applied microbiology (M Sc); biology (PhD); experimental health sciences (M Sc); virology and immunology (M Sc, PhD). *Program availability:* Part-time. *Faculty:* 48 full-time. *Students:* 149 full-time (89 women), 18 part-time (11 women), 86 international. Average age 30. 29 applicants, 93% accepted, 25 enrolled. In 2017, 16 master's, 13 doctorates awarded. *Degree requirements:* For master's, thesis; for doctorate, thesis/dissertation. *Entrance requirements:* For master's, appropriate bachelor's degree, proficiency in French; for doctorate, appropriate master's degree, proficiency in French. *Application deadline:* For fall admission, 3/30 for domestic and international students; for winter admission, 11/1 for domestic and international students; for spring admission, 3/1 for domestic and international students. Application fee: $45 Canadian dollars. Electronic applications accepted. *Financial support:* In 2017–18, fellowships (averaging $16,500 per year) were awarded; research assistantships also available. *Faculty research:* Immunity, infection and cancer; toxicology and environmental biotechnology; molecular pharmacochemistry. *Unit head:* Pierre Talbot, Director, 450-687-5010 Ext. 4300, Fax: 450-686-5501, E-mail: pierre.talbot@iaf.inrs.ca. *Application contact:* Sylvie Richard, Registrar, 418-654-2518, Fax: 418-654-3858, E-mail: sylvie.richard@adm.inrs.ca.
Website: http://www.iaf.inrs.ca

Université Laval, Faculty of Medicine, Graduate Programs in Medicine, Québec, QC G1K 7P4, Canada. Offers M Sc, PhD, Diploma. *Degree requirements:* For doctorate, comprehensive exam, thesis/dissertation. *Entrance requirements:* For doctorate, knowledge of French, comprehension of written English; for Diploma, knowledge of French. Electronic applications accepted.

Université Laval, Faculty of Sciences and Engineering, Department of Biology, Programs in Biology, Québec, QC G1K 7P4, Canada. Offers M Sc, PhD. Terminal master's awarded for partial completion of doctoral program. *Degree requirements:* For master's, thesis; for doctorate, comprehensive exam, thesis/dissertation. *Entrance requirements:* For master's and doctorate, knowledge of French and English. Electronic applications accepted.

University at Albany, State University of New York, College of Arts and Sciences, Department of Biological Sciences, Albany, NY 12222-0001. Offers forensic biology (MS). *Faculty:* 22 full-time (8 women). *Students:* 28 full-time (18 women), 36 part-time (20 women); includes 8 minority (2 Black or African American, non-Hispanic/Latino; 4 Asian, non-Hispanic/Latino; 1 Hispanic/Latino; 1 Two or more races, non-Hispanic/Latino), 10 international. 88 applicants, 31% accepted, 18 enrolled. In 2017, 4 master's awarded. *Degree requirements:* For master's, one foreign language. *Entrance requirements:* For master's, GRE General Test. Additional exam requirements/recommendations for international students: Required—TOEFL (minimum score 550 paper-based). *Application deadline:* For fall admission, 2/15 priority date for domestic students, 5/1 for international students; for spring admission, 11/1 for domestic and international students. Applications are processed on a rolling basis. Application fee: $75. Electronic applications accepted. *Expenses:* Tuition, state resident: full-time $10,870; part-time $453 per credit hour. Tuition, nonresident: full-time $22,210; part-time $925 per credit hour. *Required fees:* $84.68 per credit hour. $508.06 per semester. Part-time tuition and fees vary according to course load and program. *Financial support:* Fellowships, research assistantships, teaching assistantships, and minority assistantships available. Financial award application deadline: 5/1. *Faculty research:* Interferon, neural development, RNA self-splicing, behavioral ecology, DNA repair enzymes. *Unit head:* Glyne Griffith, Chair, 518-442-4300, Fax: 518-442-4354, E-mail: ggriffith@albany.edu. *Application contact:* Michael DeRensis, Director, Graduate Admissions, 518-442-3980, Fax: 518-442-3922, E-mail: graduate@albany.edu.
Website: http://www.albany.edu/biology/

University at Albany, State University of New York, School of Public Health, Department of Biomedical Sciences, Albany, NY 12222-0001. Offers MS, PhD. *Faculty:* 24 full-time (9 women), 8 part-time/adjunct (3 women). *Students:* 18 full-time (10 women), 21 part-time (14 women); includes 8 minority (1 Black or African American, non-Hispanic/Latino; 1 Asian, non-Hispanic/Latino; 3 Hispanic/Latino; 3 Two or more races, non-Hispanic/Latino), 5 international. 33 applicants, 42% accepted, 12 enrolled. In 2017, 4 doctorates awarded. *Degree requirements:* For master's, thesis; for doctorate, comprehensive exam, thesis/dissertation. *Entrance requirements:* For master's and doctorate, GRE General Test, 3 letters of reference. Additional exam requirements/recommendations for international students: Required—TOEFL (minimum score 600 paper-based). *Application deadline:* For fall admission, 1/1 for domestic and international students; for winter admission, 4/1 for domestic and international students; for spring admission, 10/30 for domestic students, 11/1 for international students. Applications are processed on a rolling basis. Application fee: $75. Electronic applications accepted. *Expenses:* Tuition, state resident: full-time $10,870; part-time $453 per credit hour. Tuition, nonresident: full-time $22,210; part-time $925 per credit hour. *Required fees:* $84.68 per credit hour. $508.06 per semester. Part-time tuition and fees vary according to course load and program. *Financial support:* Fellowships with full tuition reimbursements, research assistantships with full tuition reimbursements, teaching assistantships with tuition reimbursements, scholarships/grants, traineeships, health care benefits, tuition waivers (partial), and unspecified assistantships available. Financial award application deadline: 1/1. *Faculty research:* Gene expression; RNA processing; membrane transport; immune response regulation; etiology of AIDS, Lyme disease, epilepsy. *Unit head:* Dr. Janice Pata, Chair, 518-402-2750, E-mail: ipata@albany.edu.
Website: http://www.wadsworth.org/sph/bms/

University at Buffalo, the State University of New York, Graduate School, College of Arts and Sciences, Department of Biological Sciences, Buffalo, NY 14260. Offers MA, MS, PhD. *Faculty:* 28 full-time (9 women). *Students:* 79 full-time (36 women); includes 19 minority (4 Black or African American, non-Hispanic/Latino; 11 Asian, non-Hispanic/Latino; 2 Hispanic/Latino; 2 Two or more races, non-Hispanic/Latino), 25 international. Average age 26. 132 applicants, 49% accepted, 31 enrolled. In 2017, 19 master's, 8 doctorates awarded. Terminal master's awarded for partial completion of doctoral program. *Degree requirements:* For master's, independent research project, written report, oral presentation; for doctorate, comprehensive exam, thesis/dissertation, thesis research, oral defense. *Entrance requirements:* For master's, GRE (for MS); GRE, MCAT, DAT, or equivalent test (for MA), solid foundation in biology, math through calculus, chemistry through organic, general physics; for doctorate, GRE, solid foundation in biology, math through calculus, chemistry through organic, general physics; previous research experience. Additional exam requirements/recommendations for international students: Required—TOEFL (minimum score 95 iBT) or IELTS (minimum score 6.5). *Application deadline:* For fall admission, 1/2 priority date for domestic and international students; for spring admission, 12/15 for domestic and international students. Applications are processed on a rolling basis. Application fee: $75. Electronic applications accepted. *Financial support:* In 2017–18, 48 students received support, including 12 fellowships (averaging $4,500 per year), 11 research assistantships with full tuition reimbursements available (averaging $25,000 per year), 36 teaching assistantships with full tuition reimbursements available (averaging $22,800 per year); health care benefits also available. Financial award application deadline: 1/2. *Faculty research:* Regulation of gene expression, signaling and sensory transduction, evolutionary phylogenomics, neuroscience, fungal biology. *Total annual research expenditures:* $1.9 million. *Unit head:* Dr. Stephen J. Free, Chair, 716-645-4904, Fax: 716-645-2975, E-mail: free@buffalo.edu. *Application contact:* Dr. Laura Rusche, Director of Graduate Studies, 716-645-5198, Fax: 716-645-2975, E-mail: lrusche@buffalo.edu.
Website: http://arts-sciences.buffalo.edu/biological-sciences.html

University at Buffalo, the State University of New York, Graduate School, Jacobs School of Medicine and Biomedical Sciences, Graduate Programs in Medicine and Biomedical Sciences, PhD Program in Biomedical Sciences, Buffalo, NY 14260. Offers PhD. *Students:* 13 full-time (6 women); includes 2 minority (1 Black or African American, non-Hispanic/Latino; 1 Hispanic/Latino), 1 international. 239 applicants, 18% accepted, 13 enrolled. *Degree requirements:* For doctorate, comprehensive exam, thesis/dissertation. *Entrance requirements:* For doctorate, GRE General Test, 3 letters of recommendation. Additional exam requirements/recommendations for international students: Required—TOEFL (minimum score 600 paper-based; 100 iBT), IELTS (minimum score 7.5). *Application deadline:* For fall admission, 1/10 priority date for domestic and international students. Applications are processed on a rolling basis. Application fee: $85. Electronic applications accepted. *Financial support:* In 2017–18, 13 students received support, including 6 fellowships (averaging $5,000 per year), 13 research assistantships with full tuition reimbursements available (averaging $27,000 per year); scholarships/grants and health care benefits also available. Financial award application deadline: 1/10. *Faculty research:* Molecular, cell and structural biology; pharmacology and toxicology; neurosciences; microbiology; pathogenesis and disease; bioinformatics; bioengineering. *Unit head:* Dr. Mark Sutton, Director, 716-829-3398, Fax: 716-829-2437, E-mail: smbs-gradprog@buffalo.edu. *Application contact:* Elizabeth A. White, Administrative Director, 716-829-3399, Fax: 716-829-2437, E-mail: bethw@buffalo.edu.
Website: http://medicine.buffalo.edu/phdprogram

The University of Akron, Graduate School, Buchtel College of Arts and Sciences, Department of Biology, Akron, OH 44325. Offers biology (MS); integrated bioscience (PhD). *Program availability:* Part-time. *Faculty:* 18 full-time (3 women). *Students:* 14 full-time (8 women). Average age 25. 15 applicants, 67% accepted, 5 enrolled. In 2017, 10 master's awarded. *Degree requirements:* For master's, thesis optional, oral defense of thesis, oral exam, seminars; for doctorate, thesis/dissertation, oral defense of dissertation, seminars. *Entrance requirements:* For master's, GRE General Test, GRE Subject Test (biology), or MCAT, baccalaureate degree in biology or equivalent training; minimum GPA of 3.0 overall and in biology (minimum 32 semester credit hours or equivalent); competence in chemistry and mathematics; letter of interest indicating proposed area of specialization and possible advisers; for doctorate, GRE General Test, minimum GPA of 3.0; three letters of recommendation; career goals and research interest statement. Additional exam requirements/recommendations for international students: Required—TOEFL (minimum score 79 iBT), IELTS (minimum score 6.5). *Application deadline:* For fall admission, 1/1 for domestic and international students. Applications are processed on a rolling basis. Application fee: $45 ($70 for international students). Electronic applications accepted. *Financial support:* In 2017–18, 6 research assistantships with full tuition reimbursements, 18 teaching assistantships with full tuition reimbursements were awarded. Financial award application deadline: 1/10. *Faculty research:* Behavior/neuroscience, ecology-evolution, genetics, molecular biology, physiology. *Total annual research expenditures:* $1.3 million. *Unit head:* Dr. Stephen Weeks, Chair, 330-972-7156, E-mail: scweeks@uakron.edu. *Application contact:* Dr. Todd Blackledge, Graduate Director, 330-972-4264, E-mail: blackledge@uakron.edu.
Website: http://www.uakron.edu/biology/

The University of Alabama, Graduate School, College of Arts and Sciences, Department of Biological Sciences, Tuscaloosa, AL 35487. Offers MS, PhD. *Faculty:* 40 full-time (19 women), 1 (woman) part-time/adjunct. *Students:* 59 full-time (25 women), 3 part-time (1 woman); includes 8 minority (1 Black or African American, non-Hispanic/Latino; 1 Asian, non-Hispanic/Latino; 2 Hispanic/Latino; 4 Two or more races, non-Hispanic/Latino), 18 international. Average age 27. 66 applicants, 38% accepted, 15 enrolled. In 2017, 16 master's, 7 doctorates awarded. Terminal master's awarded for partial completion of doctoral program. *Degree requirements:* For master's, comprehensive exam, thesis optional; for doctorate, comprehensive exam, thesis/dissertation, written and oral candidacy exams. *Entrance requirements:* For master's and doctorate, GRE General Test, minimum GPA of 3.0. Additional exam requirements/recommendations for international students: Required—TOEFL (minimum score 550 paper-based; 80 iBT). *Application deadline:* For fall admission, 12/5 priority date for domestic and international students; for spring admission, 12/5 priority date for domestic students, 9/5 priority date for international students. Applications are processed on a rolling basis. Application fee: $50 ($60 for international students). Electronic applications accepted. *Financial support:* In 2017–18, 23 fellowships with full tuition reimbursements (averaging $18,000 per year), 21 research assistantships with full tuition reimbursements (averaging $21,000 per year), 52 teaching assistantships with full tuition reimbursements (averaging $17,000 per year) were awarded; scholarships/grants, health care benefits, and unspecified assistantships also available. Financial award application deadline: 7/1; financial award applicants required to submit FAFSA. *Faculty research:* Molecular and cellular biology, developmental genetics, ecology, evolutionary biology, systematics. *Total annual research expenditures:* $1.5 million. *Unit head:* Dr. Janis O'Donnell, Chair, 205-348-9810, E-mail: jodonnel@bama.ua.edu. *Application contact:* Dr. Stevan Marcus, Graduate Program Director, 205-348-8094, Fax: 205-348-1786, E-mail: smarcus@as.ua.edu.
Website: http://bsc.ua.edu

The University of Alabama at Birmingham, College of Arts and Sciences, Program in Biology, Birmingham, AL 35294. Offers MS, PhD. Terminal master's awarded for partial completion of doctoral program. *Degree requirements:* For master's, comprehensive exam (for some programs), thesis (for some programs); for doctorate, thesis/dissertation. *Entrance requirements:* For master's and doctorate, GRE General Test, previous course work in biology, calculus, organic chemistry, and physics; letters of recommendation. Additional exam requirements/recommendations for international students: Required—TOEFL, TWE. Electronic applications accepted.

The University of Alabama at Birmingham, Joint Health Sciences, Program in Basic Medical Sciences, Birmingham, AL 35294. Offers MSBMS. *Entrance requirements:* For master's, GRE. Electronic applications accepted.

The University of Alabama in Huntsville, School of Graduate Studies, College of Science, Department of Biological Sciences, Huntsville, AL 35899. Offers biology (MS); biotechnology science and engineering (PhD); education (MS). *Program availability:*

Part-time, evening/weekend. *Degree requirements:* For master's, comprehensive exam, thesis or alternative, oral and written exams. *Entrance requirements:* For master's, GRE General Test, previous course work in biochemistry and organic chemistry, minimum GPA of 3.0. Additional exam requirements/recommendations for international students: Required—TOEFL (minimum score 550 paper-based; 80 iBT), IELTS (minimum score 6.5). Electronic applications accepted. *Faculty research:* Physiology, microbiology, genomics and protemics, ecology and evolution, drug discovery.

University of Alaska Anchorage, College of Arts and Sciences, Department of Biological Sciences, Anchorage, AK 99508. Offers MS. *Program availability:* Part-time. *Degree requirements:* For master's, comprehensive exam, thesis. *Entrance requirements:* For master's, GRE General Test, GRE Subject Test, bachelor's degree in biology, chemistry or equivalent science. Additional exam requirements/ recommendations for international students: Required—TOEFL (minimum score 550 paper-based). *Application deadline:* For fall admission, 7/1 priority date for domestic and international students; for spring admission, 11/1 priority date for domestic and international students. Applications are processed on a rolling basis. Application fee: $45. *Expenses:* Tuition, state resident: part-time $489 per credit hour. Tuition, nonresident: part-time $1028 per credit hour. *Financial support:* Research assistantships, teaching assistantships, Federal Work-Study, scholarships/grants, traineeships, health care benefits, and unspecified assistantships available. Support available to part-time students. Financial award application deadline: 4/1; financial award applicants required to submit FAFSA. *Faculty research:* Taxonomy and vegetative analysis in Alaskan ecosystems, fish environment and seafood, biochemistry, arctic ecology, vertebrate ecology.
Website: http://www.uaa.alaska.edu/biological-sciences/

University of Alaska Fairbanks, College of Natural Sciences and Mathematics, Department of Biology and Wildlife, Fairbanks, AK 99775-6100. Offers biological sciences (MS, PhD); wildlife biology and conservation (MS). *Program availability:* Part-time. *Degree requirements:* For master's, comprehensive exam, thesis, oral defense of thesis; for doctorate, comprehensive exam, thesis/dissertation, oral defense of dissertation. *Entrance requirements:* For master's and doctorate, GRE General Test, GRE Subject Test (biology), bachelor's degree from accredited institution with minimum cumulative undergraduate and major GPA of 3.0. Additional exam requirements/ recommendations for international students: Required—TOEFL (minimum score 550 paper-based; 79 iBT), TWE. Electronic applications accepted. *Faculty research:* Plant-herbivore interactions, plant metabolic defenses, insect manufacture of glycerol, ice nucleators, structure and functions of arctic and subarctic freshwater ecosystems.

University of Alberta, Faculty of Graduate Studies and Research, Department of Biological Sciences, Edmonton, AB T6G 2E1, Canada. Offers environmental biology and ecology (M Sc, PhD); microbiology and biotechnology (M Sc, PhD); molecular biology and genetics (M Sc, PhD); physiology and cell biology (M Sc, PhD); plant biology (M Sc, PhD); systematics and evolution (M Sc, PhD). Terminal master's awarded for partial completion of doctoral program. *Degree requirements:* For master's, thesis; for doctorate, thesis/dissertation. *Entrance requirements:* Additional exam requirements/recommendations for international students: Required—TOEFL.

University of Alberta, Faculty of Medicine and Dentistry and Faculty of Graduate Studies and Research, Graduate Programs in Medicine, Edmonton, AB T6G 2E1, Canada. Offers M Sc, MD, PhD. *Program availability:* Part-time. *Degree requirements:* For doctorate, thesis/dissertation (for some programs). *Faculty research:* Basic, clinical, and applied biomedicine.

The University of Arizona, College of Agriculture and Life Sciences, School of Animal and Comparative Biomedical Sciences, Tucson, AZ 85721. Offers MS, PhD. *Degree requirements:* For master's, thesis; for doctorate, comprehensive exam, thesis/ dissertation. *Entrance requirements:* For master's and doctorate, GRE, minimum GPA of 3.0, 3 letters of recommendation, letter of intent. Additional exam requirements/ recommendations for international students: Required—TOEFL (minimum score 550 paper-based; 79 iBT). Electronic applications accepted.

The University of Arizona, College of Science and Eller College of Management, Program in Applied Biosciences, Tucson, AZ 85721. Offers PSM. *Program availability:* Part-time. *Degree requirements:* For master's, thesis or alternative, internship, colloquium, business courses. *Entrance requirements:* For master's, 3 letters of recommendation. Additional exam requirements/recommendations for international students: Required—TOEFL (minimum score 600 paper-based; 90 iBT). Electronic applications accepted. *Faculty research:* Biotechnology, bioinformatics, pharmaceuticals, agriculture, oncology.

University of Arkansas, Graduate School, J. William Fulbright College of Arts and Sciences, Department of Biological Sciences, Fayetteville, AR 72701. Offers MA, MS, PhD. In 2017, 6 master's, 5 doctorates awarded. *Degree requirements:* For doctorate, one foreign language, thesis/dissertation. *Entrance requirements:* For master's and doctorate, GRE Subject Test. *Application deadline:* For fall admission, 8/1 for domestic students, 4/1 for international students; for spring admission, 12/1 for domestic students, 10/1 for international students; for summer admission, 4/15 for domestic students, 3/1 for international students. Applications are processed on a rolling basis. Application fee: $60. Electronic applications accepted. *Expenses:* Tuition, state resident: full-time $3782. Tuition, nonresident: full-time $10,238. *Financial support:* In 2017–18, 27 research assistantships, 8 teaching assistantships were awarded; fellowships with tuition reimbursements, career-related internships or fieldwork, and Federal Work-Study also available. Support available to part-time students. Financial award application deadline: 4/1; financial award applicants required to submit FAFSA. *Unit head:* Dr. David McNabb, Chair, 479-575-3251, Fax: 479-575-4010, E-mail: dmcnabb@uark.edu.
Website: https://fulbright.uark.edu/departments/biology/

University of Arkansas at Little Rock, Graduate School, College of Arts, Letters, and Sciences, Department of Biology, Little Rock, AR 72204-1099. Offers MS.

University of Arkansas for Medical Sciences, Graduate School, Little Rock, AR 72205. Offers biochemistry and molecular biology (MS, PhD); bioinformatics (MS, PhD); cellular physiology and molecular biophysics (MS, PhD); clinical nutrition (MS); interdisciplinary biomedical sciences (MS, PhD, Certificate); interdisciplinary toxicology (MS); microbiology and immunology (PhD); neurobiology and developmental sciences (PhD); pharmacology (PhD); MD/PhD. Bioinformatics programs hosted jointly with the University of Arkansas at Little Rock. *Program availability:* Part-time. Terminal master's awarded for partial completion of doctoral program. *Degree requirements:* For master's, comprehensive exam (for some programs), thesis (for some programs); for doctorate, thesis/dissertation. *Entrance requirements:* For master's and doctorate, GRE. Additional exam requirements/recommendations for international students: Required—TOEFL. Electronic applications accepted. *Expenses:* Contact institution.

University of Calgary, Cumming School of Medicine and Faculty of Graduate Studies, Medical Science Graduate Program, Calgary, AB T2N 1N4, Canada. Offers cancer biology (M Sc, PhD); critical care medicine (M Sc, PhD); joint injury and arthritis (M Sc, PhD); molecular and medical genetics (M Sc, PhD); mountain medicine and high altitude physiology (M Sc, PhD); pathologists' assistant (M Sc, PhD). *Degree requirements:* For master's, thesis; for doctorate, thesis/dissertation, candidacy exam. *Entrance requirements:* For master's, minimum undergraduate GPA of 3.2; for doctorate, minimum graduate GPA of 3.2. Additional exam requirements/recommendations for international students: Required—TOEFL (minimum score 600 paper-based). Electronic applications accepted. *Faculty research:* Cancer biology, immunology, joint injury and arthritis, medical education, population genomics.

University of Calgary, Faculty of Graduate Studies, Faculty of Science, Department of Biological Sciences, Calgary, AB T2N 1N4, Canada. Offers M Sc, PhD. *Program availability:* Part-time. *Degree requirements:* For master's, thesis; for doctorate, thesis/ dissertation, candidacy exam. *Entrance requirements:* Additional exam requirements/ recommendations for international students: Required—TOEFL. Electronic applications accepted. *Faculty research:* Biochemistry; cellular, molecular, and microbial biology; botany; ecology; zoology.

University of California, Berkeley, Graduate Division, College of Letters and Science, Department of Integrative Biology, Berkeley, CA 94720-1500. Offers PhD. *Degree requirements:* For doctorate, thesis/dissertation, oral qualifying exam. *Entrance requirements:* For doctorate, GRE General Test, GRE Subject Test, 3 letters of recommendation. Additional exam requirements/recommendations for international students: Required—TOEFL. Electronic applications accepted. *Faculty research:* Morphology, physiology, development of plants and animals, behavior, ecology.

University of California, Irvine, Francisco J. Ayala School of Biological Sciences, Irvine, CA 92697. Offers MS, PhD, MD/PhD. *Students:* 302 full-time (160 women), 3 part-time (1 woman); includes 125 minority (4 Black or African American, non-Hispanic/ Latino; 1 American Indian or Alaska Native, non-Hispanic/Latino; 53 Asian, non-Hispanic/Latino; 54 Hispanic/Latino; 13 Two or more races, non-Hispanic/Latino), 45 international. Average age 26. 913 applicants, 23% accepted, 102 enrolled. In 2017, 54 master's, 44 doctorates awarded. *Entrance requirements:* For master's and doctorate, GRE General Test, GRE Subject Test, minimum GPA of 3.0. Additional exam requirements/recommendations for international students: Required—TOEFL (minimum score 550 paper-based). *Application deadline:* For fall admission, 12/15 for domestic and international students. Applications are processed on a rolling basis. Application fee: $105 ($125 for international students). Electronic applications accepted. *Financial support:* Fellowships with full tuition reimbursements, research assistantships with full tuition reimbursements, teaching assistantships with full tuition reimbursements, career-related internships or fieldwork, institutionally sponsored loans, scholarships/grants, traineeships, health care benefits, and unspecified assistantships available. Financial award application deadline: 3/1; financial award applicants required to submit FAFSA. *Faculty research:* Molecular biology and biochemistry, developmental and cell biology, physiology and biophysics, neurosciences, ecology and evolutionary biology. *Unit head:* Prof. Frank Laferla, Dean, 949-824-5315, Fax: 949-824-3035, E-mail: laferla@uci.edu. *Application contact:* Prof. R. Michael Mulligan, Associate Dean, 949-824-8433, Fax: 949-824-4709, E-mail: rmmullig@uci.edu.
Website: http://www.bio.uci.edu/

University of California, Los Angeles, David Geffen School of Medicine and Graduate Division, Graduate Programs in Medicine, Los Angeles, CA 90095. Offers MS, PhD, MD/PhD. Terminal master's awarded for partial completion of doctoral program. *Degree requirements:* For doctorate, thesis/dissertation, written and oral qualifying exams. Electronic applications accepted. *Expenses:* Contact institution.

University of California, Los Angeles, Graduate Division, College of Letters and Science, Department of Ecology and Evolutionary Biology, Los Angeles, CA 90095. Offers MA, PhD. Terminal master's awarded for partial completion of doctoral program. *Degree requirements:* For master's, comprehensive exam or thesis; for doctorate, thesis/dissertation, oral and written qualifying exams; 3 quarters of teaching experience. *Entrance requirements:* For master's and doctorate, GRE General Test, GRE Subject Test (biology), bachelor's degree; minimum undergraduate GPA of 3.0 (or its equivalent if letter grade system not used). Additional exam requirements/recommendations for international students: Required—TOEFL. Electronic applications accepted.

University of California, Merced, Graduate Division, School of Natural Sciences, Merced, CA 95343. Offers applied mathematics (MS, PhD); chemistry and chemical biology (MS, PhD); physics (MS, PhD); quantitative and systems biology (MS, PhD). *Faculty:* 71 full-time (27 women). *Students:* 208 full-time (75 women); includes 71 minority (5 Black or African American, non-Hispanic/Latino; 24 Asian, non-Hispanic/ Latino; 33 Hispanic/Latino; 1 Native Hawaiian or other Pacific Islander, non-Hispanic/ Latino; 8 Two or more races, non-Hispanic/Latino), 52 international. Average age 28. 293 applicants, 45% accepted, 51 enrolled. In 2017, 9 master's, 18 doctorates awarded. Terminal master's awarded for partial completion of doctoral program. *Degree requirements:* For master's, variable foreign language requirement, comprehensive exam, thesis or alternative; for doctorate, variable foreign language requirement, comprehensive exam, thesis/dissertation. *Entrance requirements:* For master's and doctorate, GRE. Additional exam requirements/recommendations for international students: Required—TOEFL (minimum score 550 paper-based; 80 iBT); Recommended—IELTS (minimum score 7). *Application deadline:* For fall admission, 1/ 15 for domestic and international students. Application fee: $90 ($110 for international students). Electronic applications accepted. *Expenses:* Tuition, state resident: full-time $11,502; part-time $5751 per semester. Tuition, nonresident: full-time $26,604; part-time $13,302 per semester. *Required fees:* $564 per semester. *Financial support:* In 2017–18, 170 students received support, including 19 fellowships with full tuition reimbursements available (averaging $23,832 per year), 32 research assistantships with full tuition reimbursements available (averaging $16,429 per year), 148 teaching assistantships with full tuition reimbursements available (averaging $16,038 per year); scholarships/grants, traineeships, and health care benefits also available. Financial award application deadline: 1/15. *Faculty research:* Computational science, soft matter physics, applied math, environmental and biological systems, biological and materials chemistry. *Total annual research expenditures:* $4.2 million. *Unit head:* Dr. Elizabeth Dumont, Dean, 209-228-4487, Fax: 209-228-4060, E-mail: edumont@ucmerced.edu. *Application contact:* Tsu Ya, Director of Graduate Admissions and Academic Services, 209-228-4521, Fax: 209-228-6906, E-mail: tya@ucmerced.edu.

University of California, Riverside, Graduate Division, Department of Evolution, Ecology, and Organismal Biology, Riverside, CA 92521-0102. Offers evolution, ecology and organismal biology (MS, PhD). *Faculty:* 40 full-time (14 women). Terminal master's awarded for partial completion of doctoral program. *Degree requirements:* For master's, thesis, oral defense of thesis; for doctorate, comprehensive exam, thesis/dissertation, 3 quarters of teaching experience, qualifying exams. *Entrance requirements:* For master's and doctorate, GRE General Test, minimum GPA of 3.2. Additional exam requirements/ recommendations for international students: Required—TOEFL (minimum score 550 paper-based, 80 iBT) or IELTS; Recommended—TWE. *Application deadline:* For fall admission, 1/5 priority date for domestic and international students; for winter admission, 11/15 for domestic students, 9/1 for international students; for spring admission, 3/1 for domestic students, 12/1 for international students. Application fee: $80 ($100 for international students). Electronic applications accepted. *Expenses:* Tuition, state resident: full-time $5746. Tuition, nonresident: full-time $10,780. Tuition and fees vary according to campus/location and program. *Financial support:* Fellowships, research assistantships, teaching assistantships, career-related internships or fieldwork, Federal Work-Study, institutionally sponsored loans, scholarships/grants, tuition waivers (full and partial), and unspecified assistantships available. Financial award application deadline:

1/5; financial award applicants required to submit FAFSA. *Faculty research:* Ecology, evolutionary biology, physiology, quantitative genetics, conservation biology, systems biology. *Unit head:* Dr. Helen Regan, Department Chair, E-mail: helen.regan@ucr.edu. *Application contact:* Dawn Loyola, Director of Graduate Student Advising, 800-735-0717, E-mail: eeobgrad@ucr.edu.
Website: http://www.biology.ucr.edu/

University of California, Riverside, Graduate Division, Program in Biomedical Sciences, Riverside, CA 92521-0102. Offers PhD. *Degree requirements:* For doctorate, thesis/dissertation, qualifying exams. *Entrance requirements:* For doctorate, GRE General Test, minimum GPA of 3.2. Additional exam requirements/recommendations for international students: Required—TOEFL (minimum score 550 paper-based; 80 iBT). Electronic applications accepted. *Expenses:* Contact institution. *Faculty research:* Cancer cell biology; chronic inflammatory and autoimmune disease; cytokine, chemokine and endocrine biology in health and disease; microbiology, parasitology and vector borne diseases; neurodegeneration.

University of California, San Diego, Graduate Division, Department of Physics, La Jolla, CA 92093. Offers biophysics (PhD); computational neuroscience (PhD); computational science (PhD); multi-scale biology (PhD); physics (MS, PhD); quantitative biology (PhD). *Students:* 149 full-time (28 women). 514 applicants, 20% accepted, 28 enrolled. In 2017, 8 master's, 20 doctorates awarded. *Degree requirements:* For doctorate, comprehensive exam, thesis/dissertation, 1-quarter teaching assistantship. *Entrance requirements:* For doctorate, GRE General Test, GRE Subject Test, statement of purpose, three letters of reference. Additional exam requirements/recommendations for international students: Required—TOEFL (minimum score 550 paper-based; 80 iBT), IELTS (minimum score 7). *Application deadline:* For fall admission, 12/20 for domestic students. Application fee: $105 ($125 for international students). Electronic applications accepted. *Financial support:* Fellowships, research assistantships, teaching assistantships, scholarships/grants, and unspecified assistantships available. Financial award applicants required to submit FAFSA. *Faculty research:* Astrophysics/astronomy, biological physics, condensed matter/material science, elementary particles, plasma physics. *Unit head:* Benjamin Grinstein, Chair, 858-534-6857, E-mail: chair@physics.ucsd.edu. *Application contact:* Saixious Dominguez-Kilday, Graduate Admissions Coordinator, 858-534-3293, E-mail: skilday@physics.ucsd.edu.
Website: http://physics.ucsd.edu/

★ **University of California, San Diego,** Graduate Division, Division of Biological Sciences, La Jolla, CA 92093-0348. Offers anthropogeny (PhD); bioinformatics (PhD), biology (PhD), interdisciplinary environmental research (PhD); multi-scale biology (PhD); quantitative biology (PhD). PhD in biology offered jointly with San Diego State University. *Students:* 335 full-time (191 women), 6 part-time (1 woman). 728 applicants, 28% accepted, 139 enrolled. In 2017, 35 doctorates awarded. *Degree requirements:* For doctorate, comprehensive exam, thesis/dissertation, 3 quarters of teaching assistantship. *Entrance requirements:* For doctorate, GRE General Test; GRE Subject Test in biology, biochemistry, cell and molecular biology, or chemistry (recommended). Additional exam requirements/recommendations for international students: Required—TOEFL (minimum score 550 paper-based; 80 iBT), IELTS (minimum score 7). *Application deadline:* For fall admission, 11/28 for domestic students. Application fee: $105 ($125 for international students). Electronic applications accepted. *Financial support:* Fellowships, research assistantships, teaching assistantships, scholarships/grants, traineeships, and unspecified assistantships available. Financial award applicants required to submit FAFSA. *Faculty research:* Molecular, cellular and developmental biology, genetics, behavior and evolution; microbiology; bioinformatics; signal transduction; quantitative biology, neurobiology. *Unit head:* Jens Lykke-Andersen, Chair, 858-822-3659. *Application contact:* Brandon Keith, Program Coordinator, 858-534-8983, E-mail: biogradprog@ucsd.edu.
Website: http://biology.ucsd.edu/

See Close-Up on page 115.

University of California, San Diego, School of Medicine and Graduate Division, Graduate Studies in Biomedical Sciences, La Jolla, CA 92093-0685. Offers anthropogeny (PhD); bioinformatics (PhD); biomedical science (PhD); multi-scale biology (PhD). *Students:* 171 full-time (90 women). 459 applicants, 20% accepted, 30 enrolled. In 2017, 31 doctorates awarded. *Degree requirements:* For doctorate, comprehensive exam, thesis/dissertation, 1-quarter teaching assistantship. *Entrance requirements:* For doctorate, GRE General Test; GRE Subject Test in either biology, biochemistry, cell and molecular biology or chemistry (recommended). Additional exam requirements/recommendations for international students: Required—TOEFL (minimum score 550 paper-based; 80 iBT), IELTS (minimum score 7). *Application deadline:* For fall admission, 12/1 for domestic students. Application fee: $105 ($125 for international students). Electronic applications accepted. *Financial support:* Fellowships, research assistantships, teaching assistantships, scholarships/grants, traineeships, unspecified assistantships, and stipends available. Financial award applicants required to submit FAFSA. *Faculty research:* Genetics, microbiology and immunology, molecular cell biology, molecular pharmacology, molecular pathology. *Unit head:* Arshad Desai, Chair, 858-534-9698, E-mail: abdesai@ucsd.edu. *Application contact:* Leanne Nordeman, Graduate Coordinator, 858-534-3982, E-mail: biomedsci@ucsd.edu.
Website: http://biomedsci.ucsd.edu

University of California, San Diego, School of Medicine, Medical Scientist Training Program, La Jolla, CA 92093. Offers MD/PhD. *Financial support:* Fellowships, research assistantships, scholarships/grants, and traineeships available. Financial award applicants required to submit FAFSA. *Unit head:* Paul A. Insel, Director, 858-534-2295. *Application contact:* Mary Alice Kiisel, Assistant, 858-534-0689, E-mail: mstp@ucsd.edu.

University of California, San Francisco, Graduate Division, Biomedical Sciences Graduate Program, San Francisco, CA 94143. Offers PhD. *Degree requirements:* For doctorate, thesis/dissertation. *Entrance requirements:* For doctorate, GRE General Test, three letters of recommendation, official transcripts. Additional exam requirements/recommendations for international students: Required—TOEFL, IELTS. *Faculty research:* Cancer biology and cell signaling, developmental and stem cell biology, human genetics, immunology, neurobiology, tissue/organ biology and endocrinology, vascular and cardiac biology, virology and microbial pathogenesis.

University of California, San Francisco, School of Medicine, San Francisco, CA 94143-0410. Offers MD, PhD, MD/MPH, MD/MS, MD/PhD. *Accreditation:* LCME/AMA (one or more programs are accredited). *Entrance requirements:* For doctorate, MCAT (for MD), interview (for MD). Electronic applications accepted. *Expenses:* Contact institution. *Faculty research:* Neurosciences, human genetics, developmental biology, social/behavioral/policy sciences, immunology.

University of Central Arkansas, Graduate School, College of Natural Sciences and Math, Department of Biological Science, Conway, AR 72035-0001. Offers MS. *Program availability:* Part-time. *Degree requirements:* For master's, comprehensive exam, thesis optional. *Entrance requirements:* For master's, GRE General Test, minimum GPA of 2.7. Additional exam requirements/recommendations for international students: Required—TOEFL (minimum score 550 paper-based; 80 iBT). *Application deadline:* For fall admission, 3/1 priority date for domestic students; for spring admission, 10/1 priority date for domestic students. Applications are processed on a rolling basis. Application fee: $25 ($50 for international students). Electronic applications accepted. *Financial support:* Research assistantships with partial tuition reimbursements, teaching assistantships with partial tuition reimbursements, and unspecified assistantships available. Financial award application deadline: 2/15; financial award applicants required to submit FAFSA.
Website: http://uca.edu/biology/

University of Central Florida, College of Community Innovation and Education, School of Teacher Education, Program in Teacher Education, Orlando, FL 32816. Offers art education (MAT); English language (MAT); mathematics education (MAT); middle school mathematics (MAT); middle school science (MAT); science education (MAT), including biology, chemistry, physics; social science education (MAT). *Accreditation:* NCATE. *Program availability:* Part-time, evening/weekend. *Students:* 11 full-time (9 women), 28 part-time (23 women); includes 15 minority (5 Black or African American, non-Hispanic/Latino; 2 Asian, non-Hispanic/Latino; 6 Hispanic/Latino; 2 Two or more races, non-Hispanic/Latino), 2 international. Average age 29. In 2017, 6 master's awarded. *Degree requirements:* For master's, thesis or alternative. *Entrance requirements:* For master's, Florida Teacher Certification Examination/General Knowledge Test or GRE General Test. Additional exam requirements/recommendations for international students: Required—TOEFL. *Application deadline:* For spring admission, 12/1 for domestic students; for summer admission, 4/15 for domestic students. Application fee: $30. Electronic applications accepted. *Expenses:* Tuition, state resident: part-time $288.16 per credit hour. Tuition, nonresident: part-time $1073.31 per credit hour. Tuition and fees vary according to program. *Financial support:* Fellowships, research assistantships, teaching assistantships, career-related internships or fieldwork, Federal Work-Study, institutionally sponsored loans, tuition waivers (partial), and unspecified assistantships available. Financial award application deadline: 3/1; financial award applicants required to submit FAFSA. *Unit head:* Dr. Michael Hynes, Director, 407-823-2005, E-mail: mychael.hynes@ucf.edu. *Application contact:* Associate Director, Graduate Admissions, 407-823-2766, Fax: 407-823-6442, E-mail: gradadmissions@ucf.edu.
Website: http://www.graduatecatalog.ucf.edu/programs/program.aspx?id=9727&program=Teacher%20Education%20MAT

University of Central Florida, College of Medicine, Burnett School of Biomedical Sciences, Orlando, FL 32816. Offers biomedical sciences (MS, PhD); biotechnology (MS). *Faculty:* 69 full-time (30 women), 5 part-time/adjunct (2 women). *Students:* 91 full-time (56 women), 11 part-time (5 women); includes 37 minority (10 Black or African American, non-Hispanic/Latino; 6 Asian, non-Hispanic/Latino; 19 Hispanic/Latino; 3 Two or more races, non-Hispanic/Latino), 26 international. Average age 27. 196 applicants, 36% accepted, 44 enrolled. In 2017, 20 master's, 8 doctorates awarded. *Degree requirements:* For master's, comprehensive exam, thesis or alternative. *Entrance requirements:* For master's, GRE, letters of recommendation, resume, professional/goal statement. Additional exam requirements/recommendations for international students: Required—TOEFL. *Application deadline:* For fall admission, 1/15 for domestic students. Application fee: $30. Electronic applications accepted. *Expenses:* Tuition, state resident: part-time $288.16 per credit hour. Tuition, nonresident: part-time $1073.31 per credit hour. Tuition and fees vary according to program. *Financial support:* In 2017–18, 53 students received support, including 20 fellowships with partial tuition reimbursements available (averaging $13,780 per year), 52 research assistantships with partial tuition reimbursements available (averaging $10,670 per year), 12 teaching assistantships with partial tuition reimbursements available (averaging $12,067 per year); scholarships/grants and health care benefits also available. Financial award application deadline: 3/1; financial award applicants required to submit FAFSA. *Unit head:* Dr. Griffith Parks, Director, 407-226-7001, E-mail: griffith.parks@ucf.edu. *Application contact:* Associate Director, Graduate Admissions, 407-823-2766, Fax: 407-823-6442, E-mail: gradadmissions@ucf.edu.
Website: https://med.ucf.edu/biomed/

University of Central Missouri, The Graduate School, Warrensburg, MO 64093. Offers accountancy (MA); accounting (MBA); applied mathematics (MS); aviation safety (MA); biology (MS); business administration (MBA); career and technical education leadership (MS); college student personnel administration (MS); communication (MA); computer science (MS); counseling (MS); criminal justice (MS); educational leadership (Ed D); educational technology (MS); elementary and early childhood education (MSE); English (MA); environmental studies (MA); finance (MBA); history (MA); human services/educational technology (Ed S); human services/learning resources (Ed S); human services/professional counseling (Ed S); industrial hygiene (MS); industrial management (MS); information systems (MBA); information technology (MS); kinesiology (MS); library science and information services (MS); literacy education (MSE); marketing (MBA); mathematics (MS); music (MA); occupational safety management (MS); psychology (MS); rural family nursing (MS); school administration (MSE); social gerontology (MS); sociology (MA); special education (MSE); speech language pathology (MS); superintendency (Ed S); teaching (MAT); teaching English as a second language (MA); technology (MS); technology management (PhD); theatre (MA). *Program availability:* Part-time, 100% online, blended/hybrid learning. *Faculty:* 337 full-time (145 women), 41 part-time/adjunct (28 women). *Students:* 785 full-time (398 women), 1,633 part-time (1,063 women); includes 231 minority (102 Black or African American, non-Hispanic/Latino; 4 American Indian or Alaska Native, non-Hispanic/Latino; 16 Asian, non-Hispanic/Latino; 52 Hispanic/Latino; 57 Two or more races, non-Hispanic/Latino), 692 international. Average age 30. In 2017, 2,605 master's, 122 other advanced degrees awarded. *Degree requirements:* For master's and Ed S, comprehensive exam (for some programs), thesis (for some programs). *Entrance requirements:* Additional exam requirements/recommendations for international students: Required—TOEFL (minimum score 550 paper-based; 79 iBT). *Application deadline:* For fall admission, 6/1 priority date for domestic and international students; for spring admission, 10/1 priority date for domestic and international students; for summer admission, 4/1 priority date for domestic and international students. Applications are processed on a rolling basis. Application fee: $30 ($75 for international students). Electronic applications accepted. *Expenses:* Tuition, state resident: full-time $8771; part-time $292.35 per credit hour. Tuition, nonresident: full-time $17,541; part-time $584.70 per credit hour. *Required fees:* $372; $24.78 per credit hour. *Financial support:* In 2017–18, 99 students received support. Research assistantships, teaching assistantships, career-related internships or fieldwork, Federal Work-Study, scholarships/grants, and administrative and laboratory assistantships available. Support available to part-time students. Financial award application deadline: 3/1; financial award applicants required to submit FAFSA. *Unit head:* Shellie Hewitt, Director of Graduate and International Student Services, 660-543-4621, Fax: 660-543-4778, E-mail: hewitt@ucmo.edu. *Application contact:* 660-543-4621, E-mail: admit_intl@ucmo.edu.
Website: http://www.ucmo.edu/graduate/

University of Central Oklahoma, The Jackson College of Graduate Studies, College of Mathematics and Science, Department of Biology, Edmond, OK 73034-5209. Offers MS. *Program availability:* Part-time. *Faculty:* 15 full-time (4 women), 1 (woman) part-time/adjunct. *Students:* 6 full-time (3 women), 22 part-time (15 women); includes 4 minority (1 Asian, non-Hispanic/Latino; 2 Hispanic/Latino; 1 Two or more races, non-Hispanic/Latino), 3 international. Average age 29. 13 applicants, 92% accepted, 10

enrolled. In 2017, 1 master's awarded. *Degree requirements:* For master's, thesis. *Entrance requirements:* For master's, GRE General Test, GRE Subject Test (biology), faculty commitment to mentor. Additional exam requirements/recommendations for international students: Required—TOEFL (minimum score 550 paper-based; 79 iBT), IELTS (minimum score 6.5). *Application deadline:* For fall admission, 7/15 for international students; for spring admission, 11/15 for international students. Applications are processed on a rolling basis. Application fee: $60. Electronic applications accepted. *Expenses:* Tuition, state resident: full-time $5375; part-time $268.75 per credit hour. Tuition, nonresident: full-time $13,295; part-time $664.75 per credit hour. *Required fees:* $626; $31.30 per credit hour. One-time fee: $50. Tuition and fees vary according to program. *Financial support:* In 2017–18, 14 students received support, including 10 research assistantships with partial tuition reimbursements available (averaging $3,605 per year), 12 teaching assistantships with partial tuition reimbursements available (averaging $4,949 per year); Federal Work-Study, scholarships/grants, tuition waivers (partial), and unspecified assistantships also available. Financial award application deadline: 3/31; financial award applicants required to submit FAFSA. *Unit head:* Dr. Bob Brennan, Chair, 405-974-2461, Fax: 405-974-3824. *Application contact:* Dr. Michelle Haynie, Graduate Advisor, 405-974-5774, Fax: 405-974-3824, E-mail: gradcoll@uco.edu.
Website: http://www.biology.uco.edu/

University of Chicago, Division of the Biological Sciences, Biochemistry and Molecular Biology Department, Chicago, IL 60637. Offers PhD, MD/PhD. *Students:* 24 full-time (13 women). 65 applicants, 35% accepted, 5 enrolled. In 2017, 8 doctorates awarded. *Degree requirements:* For doctorate, thesis/dissertation, ethics class, 2 teaching assistantships. *Entrance requirements:* For doctorate, GRE General Test, transcripts, statement of purpose, 3 letters of recommendation. Additional exam requirements/recommendations for international students: Required—TOEFL (minimum score 600 paper-based; 104 iBT), IELTS (minimum score 7). *Application deadline:* For fall admission, 12/1 for domestic and international students. Application fee: $90. Electronic applications accepted. *Financial support:* In 2017–18, 26 students received support, including fellowships with full tuition reimbursements available (averaging $31,000 per year), research assistantships with full tuition reimbursements available (averaging $31,000 per year); institutionally sponsored loans, scholarships/grants, traineeships, and health care benefits also available. Financial award application deadline: 12/1. *Faculty research:* Molecular biology, gene expression, and DNA-protein interactions; membrane biochemistry, molecular endocrinology, and transmembrane signaling; enzyme mechanisms, physical biochemistry, and structural biology. *Total annual research expenditures:* $5 million. *Unit head:* Dr. Tobin Sosnick, Chair, E-mail: trsosnic@uchicago.edu. *Application contact:* Lisa Anderson, Graduate Student Administrator, 773-834-3586, Fax: 773-702-0439, E-mail: landerso@bsd.uchicago.edu.
Website: http://bmb.uchospitals.edu/

University of Cincinnati, Graduate School, College of Medicine, Biomedical Sciences Flex Option Program, Cincinnati, OH 45221. Offers PhD. *Degree requirements:* For doctorate, thesis/dissertation, qualifying exam. *Entrance requirements:* For doctorate, GRE, 2 letters of recommendation. Additional exam requirements/recommendations for international students: Required—TOEFL. Electronic applications accepted. *Expenses: Tuition, area resident:* Full-time $14,468. Tuition, state resident: full-time $14,968; part-time $754 per credit hour. Tuition, nonresident: full-time $24,210; part-time $1311 per credit hour. *International tuition:* $26,460 full-time. *Required fees:* $3958; $84 per credit hour. One-time fee: $85 full-time. Tuition and fees vary according to course load, degree level and program. *Faculty research:* Environmental health, developmental biology, cell and molecular biology, immunobiology, molecular genetics.

University of Cincinnati, Graduate School, College of Medicine, Graduate Programs in Biomedical Sciences, Cincinnati, OH 45221. Offers MS, PhD, Graduate Certificate. Terminal master's awarded for partial completion of doctoral program. *Degree requirements:* For master's, thesis; for doctorate, thesis/dissertation, qualifying exam. *Entrance requirements:* For master's and doctorate, GRE General Test. Additional exam requirements/recommendations for international students: Required—TOEFL (minimum score 600 paper-based; 100 iBT). Electronic applications accepted. *Expenses:* Contact institution. *Faculty research:* Cancer, cardiovascular, metabolic disorders, neuroscience, computational medicine.

University of Cincinnati, Graduate School, College of Medicine, Physician Scientist Training Program, Cincinnati, OH 45221. Offers MD/PhD. *Entrance requirements:* Additional exam requirements/recommendations for international students: Required—TOEFL. Electronic applications accepted. *Expenses: Tuition, area resident:* Full-time $14,468. Tuition, state resident: full-time $14,968; part-time $754 per credit hour. Tuition, nonresident: full-time $24,210; part-time $1311 per credit hour. *International tuition:* $26,460 full-time. *Required fees:* $3958; $84 per credit hour. One-time fee: $85 full-time. Tuition and fees vary according to course load, degree level and program.

University of Cincinnati, Graduate School, McMicken College of Arts and Sciences, Department of Biological Sciences, Cincinnati, OH 45221-0006. Offers MS, PhD. *Program availability:* Part-time. Terminal master's awarded for partial completion of doctoral program. *Degree requirements:* For master's, thesis; for doctorate, comprehensive exam, thesis/dissertation. *Entrance requirements:* For master's and doctorate, GRE General Test, BS in biology, chemistry, or equivalent. Additional exam requirements/recommendations for international students: Required—TOEFL (minimum score 600 paper-based; 100 iBT). Electronic applications accepted. *Expenses: Tuition, area resident:* Full-time $14,468. Tuition, state resident: full-time $14,968; part-time $754 per credit hour. Tuition, nonresident: full-time $24,210; part-time $1311 per credit hour. *International tuition:* $26,460 full-time. *Required fees:* $3958; $84 per credit hour. One-time fee: $85 full-time. Tuition and fees vary according to course load, degree level and program. *Faculty research:* Physiology and development, cell and molecular, ecology and evolutionary.

University of Colorado Denver, College of Liberal Arts and Sciences, Department of Integrative Biology, Denver, CO 80217. Offers biology (MS); integrative and systems biology (PhD). *Program availability:* Part-time. *Faculty:* 21 full-time (7 women), 2 part-time/adjunct (both women). *Students:* 29 full-time (17 women), 13 part-time (5 women); includes 8 minority (2 Asian, non-Hispanic/Latino; 3 Hispanic/Latino; 1 Native Hawaiian or other Pacific Islander, non-Hispanic/Latino; 2 Two or more races, non-Hispanic/Latino), 1 international. Average age 29. 38 applicants, 34% accepted, 13 enrolled. In 2017, 9 master's awarded. *Degree requirements:* For master's, comprehensive exam, thesis, 30-32 credit hours; for doctorate, comprehensive exam, thesis/dissertation. *Entrance requirements:* For master's, GRE General Test (minimum score in 50th percentile in each section), BA/BS from accredited institution awarded within the last 10 years; minimum undergraduate GPA of 3.0; prerequisite courses: 1 year each of general biology and general chemistry; 1 semester each of general genetics, general ecology, and cell biology; and a structure/function course; for doctorate, GRE, minimum undergraduate GPA of 3.2, three letters of recommendation, official transcripts from all universities and colleges attended. Additional exam requirements/recommendations for international students: Required—TOEFL (minimum score 537 paper-based; 75 iBT); Recommended—IELTS (minimum score 6.5). *Application deadline:* For fall admission, 1/15 for domestic and international students. Application fee: $50 ($75 for international students). Electronic applications accepted. *Financial support:* In 2017–18, 27 students received support. Fellowships, research assistantships, teaching assistantships, Federal Work-Study, institutionally sponsored loans, scholarships/grants, and traineeships available. Financial award application deadline: 4/1; financial award applicants required to submit FAFSA. *Faculty research:* Molecular developmental biology; quantitative ecology, biogeography, and population dynamics; environmental signaling and endocrine disruption; speciation, the evolution of reproductive isolation, and hybrid zones; evolutionary, behavioral, and conservation ecology. *Unit head:* Dr. John Swallow, Chair, 303-556-6154, E-mail: john.swallow@ucdenver.edu. *Application contact:* Dr. Michael Wunder, Graduate Advisor, 303-556-8870, E-mail: michael.wunder@ucdenver.edu.
Website: http://www.ucdenver.edu/academics/colleges/CLAS/Departments/biology/Programs/MasterofScience/Pages/BiologyMasterOfScience.aspx

University of Colorado Denver, School of Medicine, Biomedical Sciences Program, Aurora, CO 80045. Offers MS, PhD. *Students:* 27 full-time (11 women), 9 part-time (5 women); includes 12 minority (1 Black or African American, non-Hispanic/Latino; 5 Asian, non-Hispanic/Latino; 5 Hispanic/Latino; 1 Two or more races, non-Hispanic/Latino), 3 international. Average age 27. 57 applicants, 35% accepted, 15 enrolled. In 2017, 11 master's awarded. Terminal master's awarded for partial completion of doctoral program. *Degree requirements:* For master's and doctorate, comprehensive exam. *Entrance requirements:* For master's, GRE, three letters of recommendation; for doctorate, GRE, minimum undergraduate GPA of 3.0; prerequisite coursework in organic chemistry, biology, biochemistry, physics, and calculus; letters of recommendation; interview. Additional exam requirements/recommendations for international students: Required—TOEFL (minimum score 550 paper-based; 80 iBT). *Application deadline:* For fall admission, 12/1 for domestic students, 11/1 for international students. Application fee: $50 ($75 for international students). Electronic applications accepted. *Unit head:* Heide Ford, Director, 303-724-3509, E-mail: heide.ford@ucdenver.edu. *Application contact:* Elizabeth Bowen, Program Administrator, 303-724-3565, E-mail: elizabeth.bowen@ucdenver.edu.
Website: http://www.ucdenver.edu/academics/colleges/Graduate-School/academic-programs/Biomedical/Pages/home.aspx

University of Connecticut Health Center, Graduate School and School of Medicine, Combined Degree Program in Biomedical Sciences, Farmington, CT 06030. Offers MD/PhD. *Entrance requirements:* Additional exam requirements/recommendations for international students: Required—TOEFL (minimum score 600 paper-based). *Expenses:* Contact institution.

University of Connecticut Health Center, Graduate School, Programs in Biomedical Sciences, Farmington, CT 06030. Offers PhD, DMD/PhD, MD/PhD. *Degree requirements:* For doctorate, comprehensive exam, thesis/dissertation. *Entrance requirements:* For doctorate, GRE General Test. Additional exam requirements/recommendations for international students: Required—TOEFL (minimum score 600 paper-based). Electronic applications accepted.

University of Connecticut Health Center, Graduate School, Programs in Biomedical Sciences - Integrated, Farmington, CT 06030. Offers PhD, DMD/PhD, MD/PhD. *Degree requirements:* For doctorate, comprehensive exam, thesis/dissertation. *Entrance requirements:* For doctorate, GRE General Test. Additional exam requirements/recommendations for international students: Required—TOEFL (minimum score 600 paper-based). Electronic applications accepted.

University of Dayton, Department of Biology, Dayton, OH 45469. Offers MS, PhD. *Faculty:* 18 full-time (7 women). *Students:* 21 full-time (14 women); includes 3 minority (1 Black or African American, non-Hispanic/Latino; 2 Asian, non-Hispanic/Latino), 7 international. Average age 27. 30 applicants, 7% accepted. In 2017, 1 master's, 1 doctorate awarded. Terminal master's awarded for partial completion of doctoral program. *Degree requirements:* For master's, comprehensive exam, thesis; for doctorate, comprehensive exam, thesis/dissertation, candidacy exam, one first-author paper accepted/published. *Entrance requirements:* For master's and doctorate, GRE, minimum undergraduate GPA of 3.0. Additional exam requirements/recommendations for international students: Required—TOEFL (minimum score 550 paper-based; 80 iBT); Recommended—IELTS. *Application deadline:* For fall admission, 1/31 for domestic and international students. Applications are processed on a rolling basis. Application fee: $50 for international students. Electronic applications accepted. *Expenses:* Contact institution. *Financial support:* In 2017–18, 2 research assistantships with full tuition reimbursements (averaging $20,200 per year), 18 teaching assistantships with full tuition reimbursements (averaging $20,200 per year) were awarded; career-related internships or fieldwork, institutionally sponsored loans, and unspecified assistantships also available. Financial award application deadline: 3/1; financial award applicants required to submit FAFSA. *Faculty research:* Cancer genetics, organ development and disease, cryobiology, evolution and development, landscape ecology, microbial interaction, biofilms. *Application contact:* Dr. Amit Singh, Director, Biology Graduate Programs, 937-229-2894, Fax: 937-229-2021, E-mail: asingh1@udayton.edu.
Website: https://www.udayton.edu/artssciences/academics/biology/grad/index.php

University of Delaware, College of Arts and Sciences, Department of Biological Sciences, Newark, DE 19716. Offers biotechnology (MS); cancer biology (MS, PhD); cell and extracellular matrix biology (MS, PhD); cell and systems physiology (MS, PhD); developmental biology (MS, PhD); ecology and evolution (MS, PhD); microbiology (MS, PhD); molecular biology and genetics (MS, PhD). Terminal master's awarded for partial completion of doctoral program. *Degree requirements:* For master's, thesis, preliminary exam; for doctorate, comprehensive exam, thesis/dissertation, preliminary exam. *Entrance requirements:* For master's and doctorate, GRE General Test. Additional exam requirements/recommendations for international students: Required—TOEFL (minimum score 600 paper-based); Recommended—TWE. Electronic applications accepted. *Faculty research:* Microorganisms, bone, cancer metastasis, developmental biology, cell biology, DNA.

University of Denver, Division of Natural Sciences and Mathematics, Department of Biological Sciences, Denver, CO 80208. Offers biology, ecology and evolution (MS, PhD); biomedical sciences (PSM); cell and molecular biology (MS, PhD). *Program availability:* Part-time. *Students:* Average age 25. 71 applicants, 44% accepted, 18 enrolled. In 2017, 7 master's, 3 doctorates awarded. Terminal master's awarded for partial completion of doctoral program. *Degree requirements:* For master's, comprehensive exam (for some programs), thesis; for doctorate, one foreign language, comprehensive exam (for some programs), thesis/dissertation. *Entrance requirements:* For master's and doctorate, GRE General Test, bachelor's degree in biology or related field, transcripts, personal statement, three letters of recommendation. Additional exam requirements/recommendations for international students: Required—TOEFL (minimum score 550 paper-based; 80 iBT). *Application deadline:* For fall admission, 1/1 priority date for domestic and international students. Applications are processed on a rolling basis. Application fee: $65. Electronic applications accepted. *Expenses:* Contact institution. *Financial support:* In 2017–18, 35 students received support, including 5 research assistantships with tuition reimbursements available (averaging $18,667 per year), 14 teaching assistantships with tuition reimbursements available (averaging $18,095 per year); Federal Work-Study, institutionally sponsored loans, scholarships/grants, and unspecified assistantships also available. Support available to part-time students. Financial award application deadline: 2/15; financial award applicants required to submit FAFSA. *Faculty research:* Molecular

biology, cell biology, neurobiology, ecology, molecular evolution. *Unit head:* Dr. Joseph Angleson, Associate Professor and Chair, 303-871-3463, Fax: 303-871-3471, E-mail: jangleso@du.edu. *Application contact:* Randi Flageolle, Assistant to the Chair, 303-871-3457, Fax: 303-871-3471, E-mail: rflageol@du.edu.
Website: http://www.du.edu/nsm/departments/biologicalsciences

University of Florida, College of Medicine and Graduate School, Interdisciplinary Program in Biomedical Sciences, Gainesville, FL 32610-0229. Offers MS, PhD, MD/PhD. *Degree requirements:* For doctorate, comprehensive exam, thesis/dissertation. *Entrance requirements:* For doctorate, GRE General Test, minimum GPA of 3.0, biochemistry before enrollment. Additional exam requirements/recommendations for international students: Required—TOEFL, IELTS. Electronic applications accepted. *Expenses:* Contact institution.

University of Georgia, Biomedical and Health Sciences Institute, Athens, GA 30602. Offers neuroscience (PhD). *Entrance requirements:* For doctorate, GRE, official transcripts, 3 letters of recommendation, statement of interest. Additional exam requirements/recommendations for international students: Required—TOEFL.

University of Guam, Office of Graduate Studies, College of Natural and Applied Sciences, Program in Biology, Mangilao, GU 96923. Offers tropical marine biology (MS). *Degree requirements:* For master's, comprehensive exam, thesis. *Entrance requirements:* For master's, GRE General Test, GRE Subject Test. Additional exam requirements/recommendations for international students: Required—TOEFL. *Faculty research:* Maintenance and ecology of coral reefs.

University of Guelph, Graduate Studies, College of Biological Science, Guelph, ON N1G 2W1, Canada. Offers M Sc, PhD. *Program availability:* Part-time. *Degree requirements:* For master's, thesis (for some programs); for doctorate, comprehensive exam (for some programs), thesis/dissertation. *Entrance requirements:* Additional exam requirements/recommendations for international students: Required—TOEFL (minimum score 550 paper-based). Electronic applications accepted.

University of Hartford, College of Arts and Sciences, Department of Biology, West Hartford, CT 06117-1599. Offers biology (MS); neuroscience (MS). *Program availability:* Part-time, evening/weekend. *Degree requirements:* For master's, comprehensive exam, thesis optional, oral exams. *Entrance requirements:* For master's, GRE or MCAT. Additional exam requirements/recommendations for international students: Required—TOEFL (minimum score 550 paper-based). Electronic applications accepted. *Faculty research:* Neurobiology of aging, central actions of neural steroids, neuroendocrine control of reproduction, retinopathies in sharks, plasticity in the central nervous system.

University of Hawaii at Manoa, John A. Burns School of Medicine and Office of Graduate Education, Graduate Programs in Biomedical Sciences, Honolulu, HI 96822. Offers MS, PhD. *Program availability:* Part-time. Terminal master's awarded for partial completion of doctoral program. *Degree requirements:* For master's, thesis optional; for doctorate, comprehensive exam, thesis/dissertation. *Entrance requirements:* For master's and doctorate, GRE General Test. Additional exam requirements/recommendations for international students: Required—TOEFL (minimum score 500 paper-based; 61 iBT), IELTS (minimum score 5). *Expenses:* Contact institution.

University of Holy Cross, Graduate Programs, New Orleans, LA 70131-7399. Offers biomedical sciences (MS); Catholic theology (MA); counseling (MA, PhD), including community counseling (MA), marriage and family counseling (MA), school counseling (MA); educational leadership (M Ed); executive leadership (Ed D); management (MS), including healthcare management, operations management; teaching and learning (M Ed). *Accreditation:* ACA; NCATE. *Program availability:* Part-time, evening/weekend, online learning. *Faculty:* 7 full-time (4 women), 8 part-time/adjunct (3 women). *Students:* 67 full-time (55 women), 69 part-time (55 women); includes 51 minority (46 Black or African American, non-Hispanic/Latino; 2 American Indian or Alaska Native, non-Hispanic/Latino; 1 Asian, non-Hispanic/Latino; 2 Hispanic/Latino). Average age 30. 20 applicants, 50% accepted. In 2017, 28 degrees awarded. *Degree requirements:* For master's, thesis. *Entrance requirements:* For master's, GRE General Test, minimum GPA of 2.7. *Application deadline:* For fall admission, 9/1 for domestic students. Application fee: $15. *Expenses: Tuition:* Full-time $10,890; part-time $605 per credit hour. *Required fees:* $1624; $812 per semester. One-time fee: $50. *Financial support:* Federal Work-Study and tuition waivers (partial) available. Support available to part-time students. Financial award application deadline: 6/1. *Unit head:* Dr. Myles Seghers, Dean of Humanities, Education, and Counseling, 504-394-7744 Ext. 214, Fax: 504-391-2421, E-mail: mseghers@olhcc.edu. *Application contact:* Anne-Katherine Lene, Director of Student Enrollment, 504-394-7744 Ext. 110, Fax: 504-391-2421, E-mail: aklene@olhcc.edu.

University of Houston, College of Natural Sciences and Mathematics, Department of Biology and Biochemistry, Houston, TX 77204. Offers biochemistry (MA, PhD); biology (MA). Terminal master's awarded for partial completion of doctoral program. *Degree requirements:* For master's, comprehensive exam (for some programs), thesis optional; for doctorate, comprehensive exam (for some programs), thesis/dissertation. *Entrance requirements:* For master's and doctorate, GRE. Additional exam requirements/recommendations for international students: Required—TOEFL (minimum score 550 paper-based; 79 iBT), IELTS (minimum score 6.5). Electronic applications accepted. *Faculty research:* Cell and molecular biology, ecology and evolution, biochemical and biophysical sciences, chemical biology.

University of Houston–Clear Lake, School of Science and Computer Engineering, Program in Biological Sciences, Houston, TX 77058-1002. Offers MS. *Program availability:* Part-time, evening/weekend. *Entrance requirements:* For master's, GRE General Test. Additional exam requirements/recommendations for international students: Required—TOEFL (minimum score 550 paper-based).

University of Houston–Victoria, School of Arts and Sciences, Program in Biomedical Sciences, Victoria, TX 77901-4450. Offers biological sciences (MS); biomedical sciences (MS); forensic science (MS).

University of Idaho, College of Graduate Studies, College of Science, Department of Biological Sciences, Moscow, ID 83844. Offers biology (MS, PhD); microbiology, molecular biology and biochemistry (PhD). *Faculty:* 19 full-time (6 women). *Students:* 22. Average age 28. In 2017, 2 master's, 6 doctorates awarded. *Degree requirements:* For doctorate, thesis/dissertation. *Entrance requirements:* For master's and doctorate, GRE, minimum GPA of 3.0. Additional exam requirements/recommendations for international students: Required—TOEFL (minimum score 79 iBT). *Application deadline:* For fall admission, 8/1 for domestic students; for spring admission, 12/15 for domestic students. Applications are processed on a rolling basis. Application fee: $60. Electronic applications accepted. *Expenses:* Tuition, state resident: full-time $6722; part-time $430 per credit hour. Tuition, nonresident: full-time $23,046; part-time $1337 per credit hour. *Required fees:* $2142; $63 per credit hour. *Financial support:* Research assistantships and teaching assistantships available. Financial award applicants required to submit FAFSA. *Faculty research:* Animal behavior development, germ cell development, intraflagellar transport, molecular mechanisms, molecular chaperones. *Unit head:* Dr. James J. Nagler, Chair, 208-885-6280, E-mail: biosci@uidaho.edu. *Application contact:* Sean Scoggin, Graduate Recruitment Coordinator, 208-885-4723, Fax: 208-885-4406, E-mail: graduateadmissions@uidaho.edu.
Website: https://www.uidaho.edu/sci/biology

University of Illinois at Chicago, College of Liberal Arts and Sciences, Department of Biological Sciences, Chicago, IL 60607-7128. Offers MS, PhD. *Degree requirements:* For master's, thesis; for doctorate, thesis/dissertation, preliminary exam. *Entrance requirements:* For master's and doctorate, GRE General Test, GRE Subject Test, previous course work in physics, calculus, and organic chemistry; minimum GPA of 2.75. Additional exam requirements/recommendations for international students: Required—TOEFL. Electronic applications accepted. *Expenses:* Contact institution. *Faculty research:* Classical and molecular genetic analysis, modulation of synaptic transmission, molecular ecology, landscape genetics, conservation biology, ecophysiology, plant nutrition and global climate change, predator-prey interactions and urban wildlife, genetic studies of Drosophila, glutamate signaling in Drosophila, molecular mechanisms of exocytosis and endocytosis, global change biology, plant and ecosystem physiology, isotope ecology, respiration, community.

University of Illinois at Chicago, College of Medicine and Graduate College, Graduate Programs in Medicine, Chicago, IL 60607-7128. Offers MHPE, MS, PhD, MD/MS, MD/PhD. *Program availability:* Part-time. Terminal master's awarded for partial completion of doctoral program. *Degree requirements:* For master's, thesis; for doctorate, thesis/dissertation. *Entrance requirements:* For master's and doctorate, GRE General Test. *Expenses:* Contact institution.

University of Illinois at Springfield, Graduate Programs, College of Liberal Arts and Sciences, Program in Biology, Springfield, IL 62703-5407. Offers MS. *Program availability:* Part-time, evening/weekend. *Faculty:* 8 full-time (2 women). *Students:* 2 part-time (both women); includes 1 minority (Hispanic/Latino). Average age 35. *Degree requirements:* For master's, oral presentation of the written thesis or comprehensive examination. *Entrance requirements:* For master's, GRE General Test, GRE Subject Test (biology), minimum undergraduate GPA of 3.0; letter that discusses academic and career goals including how goals fit with departmental specialties; 2 letters of reference. Additional exam requirements/recommendations for international students: Required—TOEFL (minimum score 500 paper-based; 61 iBT). *Application deadline:* Applications are processed on a rolling basis. Application fee: $60 ($75 for international students). Electronic applications accepted. *Expenses:* Tuition, state resident: full-time $7896; part-time $329 per credit hour. Tuition, nonresident: full-time $16,200; part-time $675 per credit hour. Tuition and fees vary according to program. *Financial support:* In 2017–18, research assistantships with full tuition reimbursements (averaging $10,249 per year), teaching assistantships with full tuition reimbursements (averaging $10,303 per year) were awarded; fellowships, career-related internships or fieldwork, Federal Work-Study, scholarships/grants, health care benefits, and unspecified assistantships also available. Support available to part-time students. Financial award application deadline: 11/15; financial award applicants required to submit FAFSA. *Unit head:* Dr. James Bonacum, Program Administrator, 217-206-6035, Fax: 217-206-7205, E-mail: jbona1@uis.edu.
Website: http://www.uis.edu/biology

University of Illinois at Urbana–Champaign, Graduate College, College of Liberal Arts and Sciences, School of Chemical Sciences, Champaign, IL 61820. Offers MA, MS, PhD, MS/JD, MS/MBA. *Expenses:* Contact institution.

University of Illinois at Urbana–Champaign, Graduate College, College of Liberal Arts and Sciences, School of Integrative Biology, Champaign, IL 61820. Offers MS, MST, PSM, PhD. *Program availability:* Part-time, online learning.

University of Indianapolis, Graduate Programs, College of Arts and Sciences, Department of Biology, Indianapolis, IN 46227-3697. Offers human biology (MS). *Program availability:* Part-time, evening/weekend. *Degree requirements:* For master's, thesis. *Entrance requirements:* For master's, GRE General Test, 3 letters of recommendation; minimum GPA of 3.0; BA/BS in anthropology, biology, human biology or closely-related field; resume. Additional exam requirements/recommendations for international students: Required—TOEFL (minimum score 550 paper-based).

The University of Iowa, Graduate College, College of Liberal Arts and Sciences, Department of Biology, Iowa City, IA 52242-1324. Offers biology (MS, PhD); cell and developmental biology (MS, PhD); evolution (MS, PhD); genetics (MS, PhD); neurobiology (MS, PhD). Terminal master's awarded for partial completion of doctoral program. *Degree requirements:* For master's, thesis optional, exam; for doctorate, comprehensive exam, thesis/dissertation. *Entrance requirements:* For master's and doctorate, GRE General Test, minimum GPA of 3.0. Additional exam requirements/recommendations for international students: Required—TOEFL (minimum score 600 paper-based; 100 iBT). Electronic applications accepted. *Faculty research:* Neurobiology, evolutionary biology, genetics, cell and developmental biology.

The University of Iowa, Roy J. and Lucille A. Carver College of Medicine and Graduate College, Graduate Programs in Medicine, Iowa City, IA 52242-1316. Offers MA, MPAS, MS, DPT, PhD, JD/MHA, MBA/MHA, MD/JD, MD/PhD, MHA/MA, MHA/MS, MPH/MHA, MS/MA, MS/MS. *Program availability:* Part-time. *Degree requirements:* For doctorate, thesis/dissertation. Electronic applications accepted. *Expenses:* Contact institution.

The University of Iowa, Roy J. and Lucille A. Carver College of Medicine and Graduate College, Medical Scientist Training Program, Iowa City, IA 52242-1316. Offers MD/PhD. Electronic applications accepted. Application fee is waived when completed online. *Faculty research:* Structure and function of ion channels, molecular genetics of human disease, neurobiology of pain, viral immunology and immunopathology, epidemiology of aging and cancer, human learning and memory, structural enzymology.

The University of Kansas, University of Kansas Medical Center, School of Medicine, Interdisciplinary Graduate Program in Biomedical Sciences (IGPBS), Kansas City, KS 66160. Offers PhD, MD/PhD. *Students:* 15 full-time (11 women); includes 2 minority (both Asian, non-Hispanic/Latino), 5 international. Average age 27. 120 applicants, 14% accepted, 15 enrolled. Terminal master's awarded for partial completion of doctoral program. *Degree requirements:* For doctorate, comprehensive exam, thesis/dissertation. *Entrance requirements:* For doctorate, GRE. Additional exam requirements/recommendations for international students: Required—TOEFL. *Application deadline:* For fall admission, 12/1 priority date for domestic and international students. Applications are processed on a rolling basis. Application fee: $60. Electronic applications accepted. *Financial support:* In 2017–18, 1 student received support, including 3 research assistantships with full tuition reimbursements available (averaging $24,000 per year), 18 teaching assistantships with full tuition reimbursements available (averaging $24,000 per year); scholarships/grants and unspecified assistantships also available. Financial award application deadline: 3/1; financial award applicants required to submit FAFSA. *Faculty research:* Cardiovascular biology, neurosciences, signal transduction and cancer biology, molecular biology and genetics, developmental biology. *Unit head:* Dr. Michael J. Werle, Director, 913-588-7491, Fax: 913-588-2710, E-mail: mwerle@kumc.edu. *Application contact:* Martin J. Graham, Coordinator, 913-588-2719, Fax: 913-588-5242, E-mail: mgraham4@kumc.edu.
Website: http://www.kumc.edu/igpbs.html

University of Kentucky, Graduate School, College of Arts and Sciences, Program in Biology, Lexington, KY 40506-0032. Offers MS, PhD. *Degree requirements:* For master's, comprehensive exam, thesis optional; for doctorate, comprehensive exam, thesis/dissertation. *Entrance requirements:* For master's, GRE General Test, minimum undergraduate GPA of 2.75; for doctorate, GRE General Test, minimum graduate GPA of 3.0. Additional exam requirements/recommendations for international students: Required—TOEFL (minimum score 550 paper-based). Electronic applications accepted. *Faculty research:* General biology, microbiology, &ITDrosophila&RO molecular genetics, molecular virology, multiple loci inheritance.

University of Kentucky, Graduate School, Graduate School Programs from the College of Medicine, Lexington, KY 40506-0032. Offers MS, PhD, MD/PhD. *Degree requirements:* For master's, comprehensive exam, thesis (for some programs); for doctorate, comprehensive exam, thesis/dissertation. *Entrance requirements:* For master's, GRE General Test, minimum undergraduate GPA of 2.75; for doctorate, GRE General Test, minimum undergraduate GPA of 3.0. Additional exam requirements/recommendations for international students: Required—TOEFL (minimum score 550 paper-based). Electronic applications accepted.

University of Lethbridge, School of Graduate Studies, Lethbridge, AB T1K 3M4, Canada. Offers addictions counseling (M Sc); agricultural biotechnology (M Sc); agricultural studies (M Sc, MA); anthropology (MA); archaeology (M Sc, MA); art (MA, MFA); biochemistry (M Sc); biological sciences (M Sc); biomolecular science (PhD); biosystems and biodiversity (PhD); Canadian studies (MA); chemistry (M Sc); computer science (M Sc); computer science and geographical information science (M Sc); counseling (MC); counseling psychology (M Ed); dramatic arts (MA); earth, space, and physical science (PhD); economics (MA); education (MA, PhD); educational leadership (M Ed); English (MA); environmental science (M Sc); evolution and behavior (PhD); exercise science (M Sc); French (MA); French/German (MA); French/Spanish (MA); general education (M Ed); geography (M Sc, MA); German (MA); health sciences (M Sc); individualized multidisciplinary (M Sc, MA); kinesiology (M Sc, MA); management (M Sc), including accounting, finance, human resource management and labor relations, information systems, international management, marketing, policy and strategy; mathematics (M Sc); music (M Mus, MA); Native American studies (MA); neuroscience (M Sc, PhD); new media (MA, MFA); nursing (M Sc, MN); philosophy (MA); physics (M Sc); political science (MA); psychology (M Sc, MA); religious studies (MA); sociology (MA); theatre and dramatic arts (MFA); theoretical and computational science (PhD); urban and regional studies (MA); women and gender studies (MA). *Program availability:* Part-time, evening/weekend. *Degree requirements:* For master's, thesis (for some programs); for doctorate, comprehensive exam, thesis/dissertation. *Entrance requirements:* For master's, GMAT (for M Sc in management), bachelor's degree in related field, minimum GPA of 3.0 during previous 20 graded semester courses, 2 years' teaching or related experience (M Ed); for doctorate, master's degree, minimum graduate GPA of 3.5. Additional exam requirements/recommendations for international students: Required—TOEFL (minimum score 580 paper-based; 93 iBT). Electronic applications accepted. *Faculty research:* Movement and brain plasticity, gibberellin physiology, photosynthesis, carbon cycling, molecular properties of main-group ring components.

University of Louisiana at Lafayette, College of Sciences, Department of Biology, Lafayette, LA 70504. Offers biology (MS); environmental and evolutionary biology (PhD). Terminal master's awarded for partial completion of doctoral program. *Degree requirements:* For master's, thesis; for doctorate, 2 foreign languages, comprehensive exam, thesis/dissertation. *Entrance requirements:* For master's, GRE General Test, minimum GPA of 2.75; for doctorate, GRE General Test, GRE Subject Test, minimum GPA of 3.0. Additional exam requirements/recommendations for international students: Required—TOEFL (minimum score 550 paper-based). *Application deadline:* For fall admission, 5/15 for domestic and international students; for spring admission, 10/1 for domestic and international students. Applications are processed on a rolling basis. Application fee: $25 ($30 for international students). Electronic applications accepted. *Financial support:* Application deadline: 5/1. *Faculty research:* Structure and ultrastructure, system biology, ecology, processes, environmental physiology. *Unit head:* Dr. Scott France, Graduate Admissions Chair, 337-482-6320, E-mail: france@louisiana.edu. *Application contact:* Dr. Paul Leberg, Graduate Coordinator, 337-482-6750, Fax: 337-482-5834, E-mail: leberg@louisiana.edu.

University of Louisiana at Monroe, Graduate School, College of Arts, Education, and Sciences, Department of Biology, Monroe, LA 71209-0001. Offers MS. *Faculty:* 6 full-time (2 women). *Students:* 25 full-time (11 women), 3 part-time (1 woman); includes 9 minority (5 Black or African American, non-Hispanic/Latino; 2 Hispanic/Latino; 2 Two or more races, non-Hispanic/Latino), 4 international. Average age 25. 18 applicants, 28% accepted, 4 enrolled. *Degree requirements:* For master's, thesis optional. *Entrance requirements:* For master's, GRE General Test, minimum GPA of 2.5. Additional exam requirements/recommendations for international students: Required—TOEFL (minimum score 500 paper-based; 61 iBT); Recommended—IELTS (minimum score 5.5). *Application deadline:* For fall admission, 8/24 priority date for domestic students, 3/1 for international students; for winter admission, 12/14 priority date for domestic students, 4/1 for international students; for spring admission, 1/19 for domestic students, 8/1 for international students. Applications are processed on a rolling basis. Application fee: $20 ($30 for international students). Electronic applications accepted. *Expenses:* Tuition, state resident: full-time $6489; part-time $479 per hour. Tuition, nonresident: full-time $12,100; part-time $479 per hour. *Required fees:* $8860; $802 per hour. $3273 per semester. *Financial support:* In 2017–18, 22 students received support. Teaching assistantships, career-related internships or fieldwork, Federal Work-Study, and unspecified assistantships available. Financial award application deadline: 4/1; financial award applicants required to submit FAFSA. *Faculty research:* Fish systematics and zoogeography, taxonomy and distribution of Louisiana plants, aquatic biology, secondary succession, microbial ecology. *Unit head:* Dr. Sushma Krishnamurthy, Head, 318-342-1813, Fax: 318-342-1790, E-mail: krishnamurthy@ulm.edu. *Application contact:* Dr. Kim Marie Tolson, Graduate Coordinator, 318-342-1805, Fax: 318-342-1790, E-mail: tolson@ulm.edu.
Website: http://www.ulm.edu/biology/

University of Louisville, Graduate School, College of Arts and Sciences, Department of Biology, Louisville, KY 40292-0001. Offers biology (MS); environmental biology (PhD). *Program availability:* Part-time. *Faculty:* 25 full-time (9 women), 6 part-time/adjunct (3 women). *Students:* 38 full-time (17 women), 7 part-time (4 women); includes 9 minority (1 Asian, non-Hispanic/Latino; 4 Hispanic/Latino; 4 Two or more races, non-Hispanic/Latino), 11 international. Average age 29. 32 applicants, 50% accepted, 13 enrolled. In 2017, 6 master's, 1 doctorate awarded. Terminal master's awarded for partial completion of doctoral program. *Degree requirements:* For master's, comprehensive exam, thesis (for some programs); for doctorate, comprehensive exam, thesis/dissertation. *Entrance requirements:* For master's, GRE, MCAT, or DAT; for doctorate, GRE. Additional exam requirements/recommendations for international students: Required—TOEFL (minimum score 550 paper-based; 83 iBT), IELTS (minimum score 6.5). *Application deadline:* For fall admission, 1/15 priority date for domestic and international students; for spring admission, 12/1 for domestic and international students; for summer admission, 4/15 for domestic and international students. Applications are processed on a rolling basis. Application fee: $65. Electronic applications accepted. *Expenses:* Tuition, state resident: full-time $12,246; part-time $681 per credit hour. Tuition, nonresident: full-time $25,486; part-time $1417 per credit hour. *Required fees:* $196. Tuition and fees vary according to course load, program and reciprocity agreements. *Financial support:* In 2017–18, 2 fellowships with full tuition reimbursements (averaging $22,000 per year), 2 research assistantships with full tuition reimbursements (averaging $22,000 per year), 24 teaching assistantships with full tuition reimbursements (averaging $22,000 per year) were awarded; unspecified assistantships also available. Financial award application deadline: 1/15. *Faculty research:* Molecular, microbiology, ecology, animal behavior, evolution. *Total annual research expenditures:* $744,439. *Unit head:* Dr. Ronald Fell, Chair, 502-852-6771, Fax: 502-852-0725, E-mail: rdfell@louisville.edu. *Application contact:* Latonia Craig, Director of Graduate Recruitment and Diversity Retention, 502-852-5207, E-mail: gradadm@louisville.edu.
Website: http://louisville.edu/biology

University of Maine, Graduate School, College of Natural Sciences, Forestry, and Agriculture, Department of Molecular and Biomedical Sciences, Orono, ME 04469. Offers microbiology (PhD). *Faculty:* 11 full-time (5 women), 7 part-time/adjunct (3 women). *Students:* 18 full-time (10 women), 5 part-time (4 women); includes 2 minority (both Asian, non-Hispanic/Latino), 5 international. Average age 29. 25 applicants, 28% accepted, 6 enrolled. In 2017, 3 master's, 2 doctorates awarded. *Degree requirements:* For master's, thesis (for some programs); for doctorate, comprehensive exam, thesis/dissertation. *Entrance requirements:* For master's and doctorate, GRE General Test. Additional exam requirements/recommendations for international students: Required—TOEFL (minimum score 580 paper-based; 92 iBT), IELTS (minimum score 7). *Application deadline:* For fall admission, 1/15 for domestic and international students; for spring admission, 9/15 for domestic and international students. Applications are processed on a rolling basis. Application fee: $65. Electronic applications accepted. *Expenses:* Tuition, state resident: full-time $7722; part-time $429 per credit hour. Tuition, nonresident: full-time $25,146; part-time $1397 per credit hour. *Required fees:* $1162; $581 per credit hour. *Financial support:* In 2017–18, 19 students received support, including 1 fellowship with full tuition reimbursement available (averaging $23,100 per year), 7 research assistantships with full tuition reimbursements available (averaging $23,300 per year), 11 teaching assistantships with full tuition reimbursements available (averaging $21,700 per year); tuition waivers (full and partial) also available. Financial award application deadline: 3/1. *Faculty research:* Immunology and microbiology, bioinformatics, molecular and cellular toxicology, zebrafish, signal transduction, protein biochemistry. *Total annual research expenditures:* $1.6 million. *Unit head:* Dr. Robert Gundersen, Chair, 207-581-2802, Fax: 207-581-2801. *Application contact:* Scott G. Delcourt, Assistant Vice President for Graduate Studies and Senior Associate Dean, 207-581-3291, Fax: 207-581-3232, E-mail: graduate@maine.edu.
Website: http://umaine.edu/biomed/

University of Maine, Graduate School, College of Natural Sciences, Forestry, and Agriculture, School of Biology and Ecology, Orono, ME 04469. Offers biological sciences (PhD); botany and plant pathology (MS); entomology (MS); zoology (MS, PhD). *Program availability:* Part-time. *Faculty:* 30 full-time (16 women), 2 part-time/adjunct (1 woman). *Students:* 61 full-time (40 women), 22 part-time (11 women); includes 7 minority (1 American Indian or Alaska Native, non-Hispanic/Latino; 3 Asian, non-Hispanic/Latino; 3 Hispanic/Latino), 14 international. Average age 30. 69 applicants, 87% accepted, 28 enrolled. In 2017, 7 master's, 9 doctorates awarded. Terminal master's awarded for partial completion of doctoral program. *Degree requirements:* For master's, thesis (for some programs); for doctorate, comprehensive exam, thesis/dissertation. *Entrance requirements:* For master's and doctorate, GRE General Test. Additional exam requirements/recommendations for international students: Required—TOEFL (minimum score 80 iBT), IELTS (minimum score 6.5). *Application deadline:* For fall admission, 2/1 priority date for domestic students. Applications are processed on a rolling basis. Application fee: $65. Electronic applications accepted. *Expenses:* Tuition, state resident: full-time $7722; part-time $429 per credit hour. Tuition, nonresident: full-time $25,146; part-time $1397 per credit hour. *Required fees:* $1162; $581 per credit hour. *Financial support:* In 2017–18, 92 students received support, including 2 fellowships with full tuition reimbursements available (averaging $25,000 per year), 47 research assistantships with full tuition reimbursements available (averaging $19,800 per year), 32 teaching assistantships with full tuition reimbursements available (averaging $15,200 per year); career-related internships or fieldwork, Federal Work-Study, institutionally sponsored loans, tuition waivers (full and partial), and unspecified assistantships also available. Financial award application deadline: 3/1. *Faculty research:* Ecology and evolution (aquatic, terrestrial, paleo); development and genetics; biomedical research; ecophysiology and stress; invasion ecology and pest management. *Total annual research expenditures:* $3.1 million. *Unit head:* Dr. Andrei Aloykhin, Director, 207-581-2977, Fax: 207-581-2537. *Application contact:* Scott G. Delcourt, Assistant Vice President for Graduate Studies and Senior Associate Dean, 207-581-3291, Fax: 207-581-3232, E-mail: graduate@maine.edu.
Website: http://sbe.umaine.edu/

University of Maine, Graduate School, Graduate School of Biomedical Science and Engineering, Orono, ME 04469. Offers bioinformatics (PSM); biomedical engineering (PhD); biomedical science (PhD). *Faculty:* 160 full-time (48 women). *Students:* 34 full-time (17 women), 16 part-time (9 women); includes 1 minority (Two or more races, non-Hispanic/Latino), 13 international. Average age 29. 39 applicants, 41% accepted, 15 enrolled. In 2017, 3 doctorates awarded. *Degree requirements:* For doctorate, comprehensive exam, thesis/dissertation. *Entrance requirements:* For doctorate, GRE General Test, master's degree. Additional exam requirements/recommendations for international students: Required—TOEFL (minimum score 90 iBT), IELTS (minimum score 7). *Application deadline:* For fall admission, 1/1 priority date for domestic and international students. Application fee: $65. *Expenses:* Tuition, state resident: full-time $7722; part-time $429 per credit hour. Tuition, nonresident: full-time $25,146; part-time $1397 per credit hour. *Required fees:* $1162; $581 per credit hour. *Financial support:* In 2017–18, 47 students received support, including 3 fellowships with full tuition reimbursements available (averaging $28,300 per year), 28 research assistantships with full tuition reimbursements available (averaging $25,000 per year), 5 teaching assistantships with full tuition reimbursements available (averaging $15,200 per year); scholarships/grants and unspecified assistantships also available. Financial award application deadline: 3/1. *Faculty research:* Molecular and cellular biology, neuroscience, biomedical engineering, toxicology, bioinformatics and computational biology. *Total annual research expenditures:* $1.4 million. *Unit head:* Dr. David Neivandt, Director, 207-581-2803. *Application contact:* Scott G. Delcourt, Assistant Vice President for Graduate Studies and Senior Associate Dean, 207-581-3291, Fax: 207-581-3232, E-mail: graduate@maine.edu.
Website: http://gsbse.umaine.edu/

The University of Manchester, School of Biological Sciences, Manchester, United Kingdom. Offers adaptive organismal biology (M Phil, PhD); animal biology (M Phil, PhD); biochemistry (M Phil, PhD); bioinformatics (M Phil, PhD); biomolecular sciences (M Phil, PhD); biotechnology (M Phil, PhD); cell biology (M Phil, PhD); cell matrix research (M Phil, PhD); channels and transporters (M Phil, PhD); developmental biology (M Phil, PhD); environmental biology (M Phil, PhD); evolutionary biology (M Phil, PhD); gene expression (M Phil, PhD); genetics (M Phil, PhD); history of science, technology and medicine (M Phil, PhD); immunology (M Phil, PhD); integrative neurobiology and behavior (M Phil, PhD); membrane trafficking (M Phil, PhD); microbiology (M Phil, PhD); molecular and cellular neuroscience (M Phil, PhD); molecular biology (M Phil, PhD);

molecular cancer studies (M Phil, PhD); neuroscience (M Phil, PhD); ophthalmology (M Phil, PhD); optometry (M Phil, PhD); organelle function (M Phil, PhD); pharmacology (M Phil, PhD); physiology (M Phil, PhD); plant sciences (M Phil, PhD); stem cell research (M Phil, PhD); structural biology (M Phil, PhD); systems neuroscience (M Phil, PhD); toxicology (M Phil, PhD).

The University of Manchester, School of Chemical Engineering and Analytical Science, Manchester, United Kingdom. Offers biocatalysis (M Phil, PhD); chemical engineering (M Phil, PhD); chemical engineering and analytical science (M Phil, D Eng, PhD); colloids, crystals, interfaces and materials (M Phil, PhD); environment and sustainable technology (M Phil, PhD); instrumentation (M Phil, PhD); multi-scale modeling (M Phil, PhD); process integration (M Phil, PhD); systems biology (M Phil, PhD).

The University of Manchester, School of Materials, Manchester, United Kingdom. Offers advanced aerospace materials engineering (M Sc); advanced metallic systems (PhD); biomedical materials (M Phil, M Sc, PhD); ceramics and glass (M Phil, M Sc, PhD); composite materials (M Sc, PhD); corrosion and protection (M Phil, M Sc, PhD); materials (M Phil, PhD); metallic materials (M Phil, M Sc, PhD); nanostructural materials (M Phil, M Sc, PhD); paper science (M Phil, M Sc, PhD); polymer science and engineering (M Phil, M Sc, PhD); technical textiles (M Sc); textile design, fashion and management (M Phil, M Sc, PhD); textile science and technology (M Phil, M Sc, PhD); textiles (M Phil, PhD); textiles and fashion (M Ent).

The University of Manchester, School of Medicine, Manchester, United Kingdom. Offers M Phil, PhD.

University of Manitoba, Faculty of Graduate Studies, Faculty of Science, Department of Biological Sciences, Winnipeg, MB R3T 2N2, Canada. Offers botany (M Sc, PhD); ecology (M Sc, PhD); zoology (M Sc, PhD).

University of Manitoba, Max Rady College of Medicine and Faculty of Graduate Studies, Graduate Programs in Medicine, Winnipeg, MB R3T 2N2, Canada. Offers M Sc, MPH, PhD, G Dip, MD/PhD. *Accreditation:* LCME/AMA. *Program availability:* Part-time. *Expenses:* Contact institution.

University of Maryland, Baltimore, Graduate School, Graduate Program in Life Sciences, Baltimore, MD 21201. Offers biochemistry and molecular biology (MS, PhD), including biochemistry; cellular and molecular biomedical science (MS); clinical research (Postbaccalaureate Certificate); epidemiology (PhD); gerontology (PhD); molecular medicine (PhD), including cancer biology, cell and molecular physiology, human genetics and genomic medicine, molecular toxicology and pharmacology; molecular microbiology and immunology (PhD); neuroscience (PhD); physical rehabilitation science (PhD); toxicology (MS, PhD); MD/MS; MD/PhD. *Students:* 251 full-time (153 women), 53 part-time (37 women); includes 88 minority (29 Black or African American, non-Hispanic/Latino; 34 Asian, non-Hispanic/Latino; 16 Hispanic/Latino; 9 Two or more races, non-Hispanic/Latino), 47 international. Average age 29. 579 applicants, 23% accepted, 46 enrolled. In 2017, 22 master's, 52 doctorates awarded. *Degree requirements:* For master's, comprehensive exam (for some programs), thesis (for some programs); for doctorate, comprehensive exam, thesis/dissertation. *Entrance requirements:* For master's and doctorate, GRE. Additional exam requirements/recommendations for international students: Required—TOEFL (minimum score 80 iBT); Recommended—IELTS (minimum score 7). *Application deadline:* For fall admission, 12/15 for domestic students, 1/15 for international students. Application fee: $75. Electronic applications accepted. *Expenses:* Tuition, state resident: full-time $13,990; part-time $661 per credit. Tuition, nonresident: full-time $30,484; part-time $1310 per credit. *Required fees:* $1894; $94 per credit. $415 per semester. Part-time tuition and fees vary according to course load, degree level and program. *Financial support:* In 2017–18, research assistantships with partial tuition reimbursements (averaging $26,000 per year) were awarded; fellowships, scholarships/grants, health care benefits, and unspecified assistantships also available. Financial award application deadline: 3/1; financial award applicants required to submit FAFSA. *Faculty research:* Cancer, reproduction, cardiovascular, immunology. *Unit head:* Dr. Dudley Strickland, Assistant Dean for Graduate Studies, 410-706-8010. *Application contact:* Keith T. Brooks, Assistant Dean, 410-706-7131, Fax: 410-706-3473, E-mail: kbrooks@umaryland.edu.
Website: http://lifesciences.umaryland.edu

University of Maryland, Baltimore County, The Graduate School, College of Natural and Mathematical Sciences, Department of Biological Sciences, Program in Biological Sciences, Baltimore, MD 21250. Offers MS, PhD. *Faculty:* 26 full-time (11 women). *Students:* 40 full-time (22 women), 1 (woman) part-time; includes 10 minority (2 Black or African American, non-Hispanic/Latino; 5 Asian, non-Hispanic/Latino; 3 Hispanic/Latino), 14 international. Average age 30. 155 applicants, 30% accepted, 6 enrolled. In 2017, 4 master's, 5 doctorates awarded. Terminal master's awarded for partial completion of doctoral program. *Degree requirements:* For master's, thesis; for doctorate, thesis/dissertation. *Entrance requirements:* For master's, GRE General Test, minimum GPA of 3.0; for doctorate, GRE General Test, GRE Subject Test, minimum GPA of 3.0. Additional exam requirements/recommendations for international students: Required—TOEFL (minimum score 80 iBT), IELTS (minimum score 6.5). *Application deadline:* For fall admission, 4/15 priority date for domestic and international students. Application fee: $50. Electronic applications accepted. *Expenses: Required fees:* $132. *Financial support:* In 2017–18, 41 students received support, including 4 fellowships with full tuition reimbursements available (averaging $24,000 per year), 10 research assistantships with full tuition reimbursements available (averaging $24,000 per year), 27 teaching assistantships with full tuition reimbursements available (averaging $24,000 per year); health care benefits also available. *Faculty research:* Bioinformatics, synthetic biology, biofuels, age related changes in traits, vision science, evolutionary biology of organisms, cell migration. *Unit head:* Dr. Michelle Starz-Gaiano, Director, 410-455-2217, Fax: 410-455-3875, E-mail: biograd@umbc.edu. *Application contact:* Brandy Darcey, Graduate Program Coordinator, 410-455-3669, E-mail: bdarcey@umbc.edu.

University of Maryland, College Park, Academic Affairs, College of Computer, Mathematical and Natural Sciences, Department of Biology, PhD Program in Biological Sciences, College Park, MD 20742. Offers behavior, ecology, evolution, and systematics (PhD); computational biology, bioinformatics, and genomics (PhD); molecular and cellular biology (PhD); physiological systems (PhD). *Degree requirements:* For doctorate, comprehensive exam, thesis/dissertation, thesis work presentation in seminar. *Entrance requirements:* For doctorate, GRE General Test; GRE Subject Test in biology (recommended), academic transcripts, statement of purpose/research interests, 3 letters of recommendation. Additional exam requirements/recommendations for international students: Required—TOEFL. Electronic applications accepted.

University of Maryland, College Park, Academic Affairs, College of Computer, Mathematical and Natural Sciences, Department of Biology, Program in Biology, College Park, MD 20742. Offers MS, PhD. *Program availability:* Part-time, evening/weekend. Terminal master's awarded for partial completion of doctoral program. *Degree requirements:* For master's, comprehensive exam, thesis optional; for doctorate, thesis/dissertation, oral exam.

University of Maryland, College Park, Academic Affairs, College of Computer, Mathematical and Natural Sciences, Program in Life Sciences, College Park, MD 20742. Offers MLS. *Degree requirements:* For master's, scholarly paper. *Entrance requirements:* For master's, 1 year of teaching experience, letters of recommendation. Electronic applications accepted. *Faculty research:* Genetic engineering, gene therapy, ecology, biocomplexity.

University of Massachusetts Amherst, Graduate School, College of Natural Sciences, Department of Animal Biotechnology and Biomedical Sciences, Amherst, MA 01003. Offers MS, PhD. *Program availability:* Part-time. Terminal master's awarded for partial completion of doctoral program. *Degree requirements:* For master's, thesis or alternative; for doctorate, comprehensive exam, thesis/dissertation. *Entrance requirements:* For doctorate, GRE General Test. Additional exam requirements/recommendations for international students: Required—TOEFL (minimum score 550 paper-based; 80 iBT), IELTS (minimum score 6.5). Electronic applications accepted.

University of Massachusetts Boston, College of Science and Mathematics, Program in Biology, Boston, MA 02125-3393. Offers MS, PhD. *Program availability:* Part-time, evening/weekend. *Faculty:* 38 full-time (15 women), 19 part-time/adjunct (11 women). *Students:* 31 full-time (22 women), 32 part-time (18 women); includes 8 minority (3 Black or African American, non-Hispanic/Latino; 1 Asian, non-Hispanic/Latino; 3 Hispanic/Latino; 1 Two or more races, non-Hispanic/Latino), 12 international. Average age 31. 74 applicants, 23% accepted, 12 enrolled. In 2017, 3 master's, 5 doctorates awarded. *Entrance requirements:* For master's, GRE General Test, GRE Subject Test, minimum GPA of 2.75. *Application deadline:* For fall admission, 3/1 for domestic students; for spring admission, 11/1 for domestic students. *Expenses:* Tuition, state resident: full-time $17,375. Tuition, nonresident: full-time $33,915. *Required fees:* $355. *Financial support:* Research assistantships, teaching assistantships, career-related internships or fieldwork, Federal Work-Study, and unspecified assistantships available. Support available to part-time students. Financial award application deadline: 3/1; financial award applicants required to submit FAFSA. *Faculty research:* Microbial ecology, population and conservation genetics energetics of insect locomotion, science education, evolution and ecology of marine invertebrates. *Unit head:* Dr. Greg Beck, Director, 617-287-6600. *Application contact:* Graduate Admissions Coordinator, 617-287-6400, Fax: 617-287-6236, E-mail: bos.gadm@dpc.umassp.edu.

University of Massachusetts Boston, College of Science and Mathematics, Program in Biotechnology and Biomedical Sciences, Boston, MA 02125-3393. Offers MS. *Program availability:* Part-time, evening/weekend. *Students:* 3 full-time (all women), 2 part-time (1 woman); includes 1 minority (Asian, non-Hispanic/Latino), 1 international. Average age 28. 33 applicants, 9% accepted, 3 enrolled. In 2017, 2 master's awarded. *Entrance requirements:* For master's, GRE General Test, GRE Subject Test, minimum GPA of 2.75, 3.0 in science and math. *Application deadline:* For fall admission, 3/1 for domestic students; for spring admission, 11/1 for domestic students. *Expenses:* Tuition, state resident: full-time $17,375. Tuition, nonresident: full-time $33,915. *Required fees:* $355. *Financial support:* Research assistantships, teaching assistantships, career-related internships or fieldwork, Federal Work-Study, and unspecified assistantships available. Support available to part-time students. Financial award application deadline: 3/1; financial award applicants required to submit FAFSA. *Faculty research:* Evolutionary and molecular immunology, molecular genetics, tissue culture, computerized laboratory technology. *Unit head:* Dr. Greg Beck, Director, 617-287-6600. *Application contact:* Graduate Admissions Coordinator, 617-287-6400, Fax: 617-287-6236, E-mail: bos.gadm@dpc.umassp.edu.

University of Massachusetts Boston, College of Science and Mathematics, Program in Integrative Biosciences, Boston, MA 02125-3393. Offers PhD. *Students:* 2 full-time (1 woman), 2 part-time (0 women); includes 2 minority (1 Asian, non-Hispanic/Latino; 1 Hispanic/Latino), 1 international. Average age 28. 9 applicants, 22% accepted, 1 enrolled. *Expenses:* Tuition, state resident: full-time $17,375. Tuition, nonresident: full-time $33,915. *Required fees:* $355. *Unit head:* Dr. William Hagar, Interim Dean, 617-287-5777. *Application contact:* Graduate Admissions Coordinator, 617-287-6400, Fax: 617-287-6236, E-mail: bos.gadm@dpc.umassp.edu.
Website: https://www.umb.edu/academics/csm/interdisciplinary_programs/integrative_biosciences_phd

University of Massachusetts Dartmouth, Graduate School, College of Arts and Sciences, Department of Biology, North Dartmouth, MA 02747-2300. Offers biology (MS); integrative biology (PhD); marine biology (MS). *Program availability:* Part-time. *Faculty:* 19 full-time (9 women), 1 (woman) part-time/adjunct. *Students:* 15 full-time (11 women), 6 part-time (3 women); includes 4 minority (2 Asian, non-Hispanic/Latino; 1 Hispanic/Latino; 1 Two or more races, non-Hispanic/Latino), 1 international. Average age 26. 25 applicants, 52% accepted, 7 enrolled. In 2017, 6 master's awarded. *Degree requirements:* For master's, thesis; for doctorate, comprehensive exam, thesis/dissertation. *Entrance requirements:* For master's and doctorate, GRE, statement of purpose (minimum of 300 words), resume, official transcripts, 3 letters of recommendation. Additional exam requirements/recommendations for international students: Required—TOEFL (minimum score 550 paper-based; 79 iBT), IELTS (minimum score 6.5). *Application deadline:* For fall admission, 1/15 priority date for domestic students, 12/15 priority date for international students. Application fee: $60. Electronic applications accepted. *Expenses:* Tuition, state resident: full-time $15,449; part-time $643.71 per credit. Tuition, nonresident: full-time $27,880; part-time $1161.67 per credit. *Required fees:* $405; $25.88 per credit. Tuition and fees vary according to course load and reciprocity agreements. *Financial support:* In 2017–18, 7 research assistantships (averaging $16,027 per year), 10 teaching assistantships (averaging $18,375 per year) were awarded; tuition waivers (full), unspecified assistantships, and instructional assistantships also available. Support available to part-time students. Financial award application deadline: 3/1; financial award applicants required to submit FAFSA. *Faculty research:* Quality of the antibody for pathogen recognition, evolution of social systems, mechanism of cell polarization, transmission of apicomplexan infection in Atlantic sea scallops, antibody mediated protection. *Total annual research expenditures:* $2.1 million. *Unit head:* Whitney Hable, Graduate Program Director, Biology/Marine Biology, 508-999-8206, E-mail: whable@umassd.edu. *Application contact:* Steven Briggs, Director of Marketing and Recruitment for Graduate Studies, 508-999-8604, Fax: 508-999-8183, E-mail: graduate@umassd.edu.
Website: http://www.umassd.edu/cas/biology

University of Massachusetts Lowell, College of Sciences, Department of Biological Sciences, Lowell, MA 01854. Offers MS. *Program availability:* Part-time. *Degree requirements:* For master's, thesis. *Entrance requirements:* For master's, GRE General Test. Electronic applications accepted.

University of Massachusetts Medical School, Graduate School of Biomedical Sciences, Worcester, MA 01655-0115. Offers biomedical sciences (PhD), including biochemistry and molecular pharmacology, bioinformatics and computational biology, cancer biology, immunology and microbiology, interdisciplinary, neuroscience, translational science; biomedical sciences (millennium program) (PhD); clinical and population health research (PhD); clinical investigation (MS). *Faculty:* 1,316 full-time (526 women), 357 part-time/adjunct (229 women). *Students:* 347 full-time (180 women); includes 61 minority (10 Black or African American, non-Hispanic/Latino; 1 American Indian or Alaska Native, non-Hispanic/Latino; 35 Asian, non-Hispanic/Latino; 15

Hispanic/Latino), 130 international. Average age 29. 608 applicants, 28% accepted, 54 enrolled. In 2017, 6 master's, 51 doctorates awarded. Terminal master's awarded for partial completion of doctoral program. *Degree requirements:* For master's, comprehensive exam, thesis; for doctorate, comprehensive exam, thesis/dissertation. *Entrance requirements:* For master's, MD, PhD, DVM, or PharmD; for doctorate, GRE General Test, bachelor's degree. Additional exam requirements/recommendations for international students: Required—TOEFL (minimum score 90 iBT) or IELTS (minimum score 7.0). *Application deadline:* For fall admission, 12/15 for domestic and international students. Applications are processed on a rolling basis. Application fee: $80. Electronic applications accepted. Application fee is waived when completed online. *Expenses:* $14,883 in-state tuition and mandatory fees; $31,486 out-of-state. *Financial support:* In 2017–18, 15 fellowships with partial tuition reimbursements (averaging $29,000 per year), 296 research assistantships with full tuition reimbursements (averaging $31,212 per year) were awarded; institutionally sponsored loans and scholarships/grants also available. Financial award application deadline: 5/15. *Faculty research:* RNA biology, molecular/cell/developmental/metabolic biology, bioinformatics and computational biology, clinical/translational research, infectious disease and immunology. *Total annual research expenditures:* $279 million. *Unit head:* Dr. Mary Ellen Lane, Dean, 508-856-4018, E-mail: maryellen.lane@umassmed.edu. *Application contact:* Dr. Kendall Knight, Assistant Vice Provost for Admissions, 508-856-5628, Fax: 508-856-3659, E-mail: kendall.knight@umassmed.edu.
Website: http://www.umassmed.edu/gsbs/

University of Memphis, Graduate School, College of Arts and Sciences, Department of Biology, Memphis, TN 38152. Offers MS, PhD. *Faculty:* 16 full-time (3 women), 1 (woman) part-time/adjunct. *Students:* 33 full-time (18 women), 20 part-time (12 women); includes 10 minority (5 Black or African American, non-Hispanic/Latino; 2 Asian, non-Hispanic/Latino; 2 Hispanic/Latino; 1 Two or more races, non-Hispanic/Latino), 9 international. Average age 29. 27 applicants, 33% accepted, 6 enrolled. In 2017, 6 doctorates awarded. Terminal master's awarded for partial completion of doctoral program. *Degree requirements:* For master's, comprehensive exam, thesis (for some programs); for doctorate, one foreign language, comprehensive exam, thesis/dissertation. *Entrance requirements:* For master's, GRE General Test; for doctorate, GRE General Test, master's degree. Additional exam requirements/recommendations for international students: Required—TOEFL (minimum score 550 paper-based; 79 iBT). *Application deadline:* For fall admission, 2/1 for domestic and international students; for spring admission, 9/15 for domestic and international students. Applications are processed on a rolling basis. Application fee: $35 ($60 for international students). Electronic applications accepted. *Expenses:* Contact institution. *Financial support:* In 2017–18, 16 students received support, including 8 research assistantships with full tuition reimbursements available (averaging $20,006 per year), 29 teaching assistantships with full tuition reimbursements available (averaging $20,380 per year); Federal Work-Study, scholarships/grants, and unspecified assistantships also available. Financial award application deadline: 2/1; financial award applicants required to submit FAFSA. *Faculty research:* Protein trafficking and signal transduction; animal behavior and communication, neurobiology, and circadian clock function; phylogenetics, evolution, and ecology; causation and prevention of cancer; reproductive biology. *Unit head:* Dr. Randall Bayer, Chairman, 901-678-2581, Fax: 901-678-4746, E-mail: rbayer@memphis.edu. *Application contact:* Dr. Charles Lessman, Professor and Graduate Coordinator, 901-678-2963, Fax: 901-678-4457, E-mail: grad_studies_coordinator@memphis.edu.
Website: http://www.memphis.edu/biology/

University of Miami, Graduate School, College of Arts and Sciences, Department of Biology, Coral Gables, FL 33124. Offers biology (MS, PhD); genetics and evolution (MS, PhD). Terminal master's awarded for partial completion of doctoral program. *Degree requirements:* For master's, comprehensive exam (for some programs), thesis (for some programs); for doctorate, thesis/dissertation, oral and written qualifying exam. *Entrance requirements:* For master's, GRE General Test, 3 letters of recommendation, research papers; for doctorate, GRE General Test, 3 letters of recommendation, research papers, sponsor letter. Additional exam requirements/recommendations for international students: Required—TOEFL (minimum score 550 paper-based; 59 iBT). Electronic applications accepted. *Faculty research:* Neuroscience to ethology; plants, vertebrates and mycorrhizae; phylogenies, life histories and species interactions; molecular biology, gene expression and populations; cells, auditory neurons and vertebrate locomotion.

University of Michigan, Medical School and Rackham Graduate School, Medical Scientist Training Program, Ann Arbor, MI 48109. Offers MD/PhD. *Accreditation:* LCME/AMA. *Students:* 97 full-time (43 women); includes 46 minority (2 Black or African American, non-Hispanic/Latino; 1 American Indian or Alaska Native, non-Hispanic/Latino; 33 Asian, non-Hispanic/Latino; 9 Hispanic/Latino; 1 Native Hawaiian or other Pacific Islander, non-Hispanic/Latino). Average age 28. 433 applicants, 8% accepted, 10 enrolled. *Application deadline:* For fall admission, 10/15 for domestic students. Applications are processed on a rolling basis. Application fee: $160. Electronic applications accepted. *Expenses:* Tuition, state resident: full-time $22,368; part-time $1201 per credit hour. Tuition, nonresident: full-time $45,156; part-time $2467 per credit hour. *Required fees:* $376 per term. Tuition and fees vary according to course load, degree level and program. *Financial support:* In 2017–18, 97 students received support, including 84 fellowships with full tuition reimbursements available (averaging $30,600 per year), 8 research assistantships with full tuition reimbursements available (averaging $30,600 per year), 5 teaching assistantships with full tuition reimbursements available (averaging $30,600 per year); scholarships/grants, traineeships, and health care benefits also available. *Unit head:* Dr. Ronald J. Koenig, Director, 734-764-6176, Fax: 734-764-8180, E-mail: rkoenig@umich.edu. *Application contact:* Laurie Koivupalo, Administrative Associate, 734-764-6176, Fax: 734-764-8180, E-mail: lkoivupl@umich.edu.
Website: https://medicine.umich.edu/medschool/education/md-phd-program/about-mstp

University of Michigan, Rackham Graduate School, Program in Biomedical Sciences (PIBS), Ann Arbor, MI 48109-5619. Offers MS, PhD. *Faculty:* 548 full-time. *Students:* 72 full-time (42 women); includes 28 minority (6 Black or African American, non-Hispanic/Latino; 7 Asian, non-Hispanic/Latino; 15 Hispanic/Latino), 6 international. Average age 24. 869 applicants, 22% accepted, 72 enrolled. *Degree requirements:* For doctorate, thesis/dissertation, oral defense of dissertation, preliminary exam. *Entrance requirements:* For doctorate, GRE General Test, 3 letters of recommendation, personal statement, academic statement of purpose (aka research statement), transcripts that resulted in a degree. Additional exam requirements/recommendations for international students: Required—TOEFL (minimum score 84 iBT). *Application deadline:* For fall admission, 12/1 for domestic and international students. Application fee: $75 ($90 for international students). Electronic applications accepted. *Expenses:* $11,207 pre-candidate, Michigan resident; $22,624 pre-candidate, non-Michigan resident. *Financial support:* In 2017–18, 73 students received support, including 73 fellowships with full tuition reimbursements available (averaging $30,600 per year); scholarships/grants, health care benefits, and unspecified assistantships also available. Financial award application deadline: 12/1. *Faculty research:* Genetics, cellular and molecular biology, microbial pathogenesis, cancer biology, neuroscience, microbiology, biophysics, bioinformatics, cell and developmental biology, molecular and integrative physiology. *Unit head:* Dr. Scott Barolo, Associate Professor, Cell and Developmental Biology/Director of the Program in Biomedical Sciences, 734-615-7005, Fax: 734-647-7022, E-mail: sbarolo@umich.edu. *Application contact:* Michelle DiMondo, Academic Affairs and Student Success Coordinator, 734-647-5773, Fax: 734-647-7022, E-mail: mdimondo@umich.edu.
Website: http://medicine.umich.edu/phd

University of Michigan–Flint, College of Arts and Sciences, Program in Biology, Flint, MI 48502-1950. Offers MS. *Program availability:* Part-time. *Faculty:* 24 full-time (13 women), 1 (woman) part-time/adjunct. *Students:* 8 full-time (6 women), 15 part-time (9 women); includes 1 minority (Hispanic/Latino), 1 international. Average age 29. 15 applicants, 80% accepted, 8 enrolled. In 2017, 4 master's awarded. *Degree requirements:* For master's, thesis optional. *Entrance requirements:* For master's, GRE, bachelor's degree in biology or related life science from accredited institution; minimum overall undergraduate and prerequisite GPA of 3.0; completion of following prerequisites at an accredited university: cell biology, ecology, general physics, and genetics. Additional exam requirements/recommendations for international students: Required—TOEFL (minimum score 84 iBT), IELTS (minimum score 6.5). *Application deadline:* For fall admission, 8/1 for domestic students, 5/1 for international students; for winter admission, 11/15 for domestic students, 9/1 for international students; for spring admission, 3/15 for domestic students, 1/1 for international students; for summer admission, 5/15 for domestic students. Applications are processed on a rolling basis. Application fee: $55. Electronic applications accepted. *Expenses:* Contact institution. *Financial support:* Federal Work-Study, scholarships/grants, and unspecified assistantships available. Support available to part-time students. Financial award application deadline: 3/1; financial award applicants required to submit FAFSA. *Faculty research:* Research and assisting with the capture of invasive feral swine in Michigan. *Unit head:* Dr. Joseph Sucic, Director, 810-762-3360, Fax: 810-762-3310, E-mail: jsucic@umflint.edu. *Application contact:* Bradley T. Maki, Director of Graduate Admissions, 810-762-3171, Fax: 810-766-6789, E-mail: bmaki@umflint.edu.
Website: https://www.umflint.edu/graduateprograms/biology

University of Minnesota, Duluth, Graduate School, Swenson College of Science and Engineering, Department of Biology, Integrated Biosciences Program, Duluth, MN 55812-2496. Offers MS, PhD. Terminal master's awarded for partial completion of doctoral program. *Degree requirements:* For master's, thesis, seminar; for doctorate, comprehensive exam, thesis/dissertation, written and oral exam, seminar, written thesis. *Entrance requirements:* For master's, GRE, 1 year of biology, physics, and chemistry; 1 semester of calculus; for doctorate, GRE, 1 year each of chemistry, biology, physics, calculus, and advanced chemistry. Additional exam requirements/recommendations for international students: Required—TOEFL (minimum score 550 paper-based; 79 iBT). Electronic applications accepted. *Faculty research:* Ecology, organizational and population biology; cell, molecular and physiological biology.

University of Minnesota, Twin Cities Campus, Graduate School, College of Biological Sciences, Biological Science Program, Minneapolis, MN 55455-0213. Offers MBS. *Program availability:* Part-time, evening/weekend. *Entrance requirements:* For master's, 2 years of work experience. Electronic applications accepted. *Expenses:* Contact institution.

University of Mississippi, Graduate School, College of Liberal Arts, University, MS 38677. Offers anthropology (MA); biology (MS, PhD); chemistry (MS, DA, PhD); creative writing (MFA); documentary expression (MFA); economics (MA, PhD); English (MA, PhD); experimental psychology (PhD); history (MA, PhD); mathematics (MS, PhD); modern languages (MA); music (MM); philosophy (MA); physics (MA, MS, PhD); political science (MA, PhD); Southern studies (MA); studio art (MFA). *Program availability:* Part-time. *Faculty:* 465 full-time (207 women), 82 part-time/adjunct (46 women). *Students:* 466 full-time (229 women), 72 part-time (34 women); includes 87 minority (38 Black or African American, non-Hispanic/Latino; 18 Asian, non-Hispanic/Latino; 24 Hispanic/Latino; 7 Two or more races, non-Hispanic/Latino), 121 international. Average age 29. *Degree requirements:* For doctorate, thesis/dissertation. *Entrance requirements:* For master's, GRE General Test, minimum GPA of 3.0; for doctorate, GRE General Test. Additional exam requirements/recommendations for international students: Required—TOEFL. *Application deadline:* For fall admission, 2/1 priority date for domestic students; for spring admission, 10/1 for domestic students. Applications are processed on a rolling basis. Application fee: $50. Electronic applications accepted. *Financial support:* Fellowships, research assistantships, teaching assistantships, career-related internships or fieldwork, Federal Work-Study, institutionally sponsored loans, scholarships/grants, and unspecified assistantships available. Financial award application deadline: 3/1; financial award applicants required to submit FAFSA. *Unit head:* Dr. Lee Michael Cohen, Dean, 662-915-7177, Fax: 662-915-5792, E-mail: libarts@olemiss.edu. *Application contact:* Dr. Christy M. Wyandt, Associate Dean of Graduate School, 662-915-7474, Fax: 662-915-7577, E-mail: cwyandt@olemiss.edu.

University of Mississippi Medical Center, School of Graduate Studies in the Health Sciences, Jackson, MS 39216-4505. Offers MS, PhD, MD/PhD. *Program availability:* Part-time. Terminal master's awarded for partial completion of doctoral program. *Degree requirements:* For master's, thesis (for some programs); for doctorate, comprehensive exam, thesis/dissertation, first authored publication. *Entrance requirements:* For master's and doctorate, GRE. Additional exam requirements/recommendations for international students: Required—TOEFL (minimum score 550 paper-based; 79 iBT), IELTS (minimum score 6.5), PTE (minimum score 53). *Faculty research:* Immunology; protein chemistry and biosynthesis; cardiovascular, renal, and endocrine physiology; rehabilitation therapy on immune system/hypothalamic/adrenal axis interaction.

University of Missouri, College of Veterinary Medicine and Office of Research and Graduate Studies, Graduate Programs in Veterinary Medicine, Department of Biomedical Sciences, Columbia, MO 65211. Offers biomedical sciences (MS, PhD); comparative medicine (MS); veterinary medicine and surgery (MS); DVM/PhD. *Entrance requirements:* For master's and doctorate, GRE General Test, minimum GPA of 3.0; 10 hours each of biology and chemistry; 3 hours each of physics, biochemistry, and calculus. *Expenses:* Tuition, state resident: full-time $6480. Tuition, nonresident: full-time $17,744. *Required fees:* $1108. Tuition and fees vary according to course load, campus/location and program. *Faculty research:* Anatomy (gross or microscopic); physiology/pharmacology (molecular, cellular and integrative); biochemistry/molecular biology; endocrinology; toxicology; exercise biology including cardiac, vascular and muscle biology; cardiovascular biology including neuroendocrine regulation; membrane transport biology including cystic fibrosis and cardiac disease; reproductive biology.
Website: http://biomed.missouri.edu/

University of Missouri, Office of Research and Graduate Studies, College of Arts and Science, Division of Biological Sciences, Columbia, MO 65211. Offers evolutionary biology and ecology (MA, PhD). Terminal master's awarded for partial completion of doctoral program. *Entrance requirements:* For master's and doctorate, GRE General Test (minimum score 1200 verbal and quantitative), minimum GPA of 3.0. Additional exam requirements/recommendations for international students: Required—TOEFL. *Expenses:* Tuition, state resident: full-time $6480. Tuition, nonresident: full-time $17,744. *Required fees:* $1108. Tuition and fees vary according to course load, campus/location and program. *Financial support:* Fellowships, research assistantships, teaching assistantships, institutionally sponsored loans, traineeships, health care benefits, and unspecified assistantships available.
Website: http://biology.missouri.edu/graduate-studies/

University of Missouri, School of Medicine and Office of Research and Graduate Studies, Graduate Programs in Medicine, Columbia, MO 65211. Offers family and community medicine (MS); health administration (MS); medical pharmacology and physiology (MS, PhD); molecular microbiology and immunology (MS, PhD); pathology and anatomical sciences (MS, PhD). *Program availability:* Part-time. *Degree requirements:* For doctorate, thesis/dissertation. *Entrance requirements:* For master's and doctorate, GRE General Test, minimum GPA of 3.0. Additional exam requirements/recommendations for international students: Required—TOEFL. *Application deadline:* Applications are processed on a rolling basis. *Expenses:* Contact institution. *Financial support:* Fellowships, research assistantships, teaching assistantships, career-related internships or fieldwork, and institutionally sponsored loans available.
Website: http://som.missouri.edu/departments.shtml

University of Missouri–Kansas City, School of Biological Sciences, Kansas City, MO 64110-2499. Offers biology (MA); cell biology and biophysics (PhD); cellular and molecular biology (MS); molecular biology and biochemistry (PhD). PhD (interdisciplinary) offered through the School of Graduate Studies. *Program availability:* Part-time, evening/weekend. *Degree requirements:* For doctorate, comprehensive exam, thesis/dissertation. *Entrance requirements:* For master's, GRE, minimum GPA of 3.0; for doctorate, GRE General Test. Additional exam requirements/recommendations for international students: Required—TOEFL (minimum score 550 paper-based; 80 iBT). *Faculty research:* Structural biology, molecular genetics.

University of Missouri–St. Louis, College of Arts and Sciences, Department of Biology, St. Louis, MO 63121. Offers MS, PhD, Certificate. *Program availability:* Part-time. *Faculty:* 19 full-time (8 women), 7 part-time/adjunct (1 woman). *Students:* 32 full-time (21 women), 21 part-time (13 women); includes 4 minority (3 Asian, non-Hispanic/Latino; 1 Two or more races, non-Hispanic/Latino), 25 international. 43 applicants, 58% accepted, 14 enrolled. *Degree requirements:* For master's, thesis or alternative; for doctorate, thesis/dissertation, 1 semester of teaching experience. *Entrance requirements:* For master's, 3 letters of recommendation; for doctorate, GRE General Test, 3 letters of recommendation. Additional exam requirements/recommendations for international students: Required—TOEFL (minimum score 79 iBT), IELTS (minimum score 6.5). *Application deadline:* For fall admission, 12/15 priority date for domestic and international students; for spring admission, 12/1 for domestic and international students. Application fee: $50 ($40 for international students). Electronic applications accepted. *Expenses:* Tuition, state resident: part-time $476.50 per credit hour. Tuition, nonresident: part-time $1169.70 per credit hour. *Financial support:* Fellowships with full tuition reimbursements, research assistantships with tuition reimbursements, teaching assistantships with tuition reimbursements, career-related internships or fieldwork, and Federal Work-Study available. Support available to part-time students. Financial award application deadline: 2/1. *Faculty research:* Molecular biology, microbial genetics, animal behavior, tropical ecology, plant systematics. *Unit head:* Dr. Wendy Olivas, Chair, 314-516-4241, Fax: 314-516-6233, E-mail: olivasw@umsl.edu. *Application contact:* 314-516-5458, Fax: 314-516-7015, E-mail: gradadm@umsl.edu.
Website: http://www.umsl.edu/~biology/

University of Montana, Graduate School, College of Health Professions and Biomedical Sciences, Skaggs School of Pharmacy, Department of Biomedical and Pharmaceutical Sciences, Missoula, MT 59812. Offers biomedical sciences (PhD); medicinal chemistry (MS, PhD); molecular and cellular toxicology (MS, PhD); neuroscience (PhD); pharmaceutical sciences (MS). *Accreditation:* ACPE. *Degree requirements:* For master's, oral defense of thesis; for doctorate, research dissertation defense. *Entrance requirements:* For master's and doctorate, GRE General Test. Additional exam requirements/recommendations for international students: Required—TOEFL (minimum score 540 paper-based). Electronic applications accepted. *Faculty research:* Cardiovascular pharmacology, medicinal chemistry, neurosciences, environmental toxicology, pharmacogenetics, cancer.

University of Montana, Graduate School, College of Humanities and Sciences, Division of Biological Sciences, Missoula, MT 59812. Offers cellular, molecular and microbial biology (PhD), including cellular and developmental biology, microbial evolution and ecology, microbiology and immunology, molecular biology and biochemistry; organismal biology and ecology (MS, PhD); systems ecology (MS, PhD). Terminal master's awarded for partial completion of doctoral program. *Degree requirements:* For master's, thesis; for doctorate, thesis/dissertation. *Entrance requirements:* For master's and doctorate, GRE General Test. Additional exam requirements/recommendations for international students: Required—TOEFL. *Faculty research:* Biochemistry/microbiology, organismal biology, ecology.

University of Nebraska at Kearney, College of Natural and Social Sciences, Department of Biology, Kearney, NE 68849. Offers biology (MS); science/math education (MA Ed). *Program availability:* Part-time, evening/weekend, 100% online. *Degree requirements:* For master's, comprehensive exam, thesis optional. *Entrance requirements:* For master's, GRE (for thesis option and for online program applicants if undergraduate GPA is below 2.75), letter of interest. Additional exam requirements/recommendations for international students: Recommended—TOEFL (minimum score 550 paper-based; 79 iBT), IELTS (minimum score 6.5). Electronic applications accepted. *Expenses:* Contact institution. *Faculty research:* Pollution injury, molecular biology-viral gene expression, prairie range condition modeling, evolution of symbiotic nitrogen fixation, geographic information systems (GIS), molecular genetics of aging.

University of Nebraska at Omaha, Graduate Studies, College of Arts and Sciences, Department of Biology, Omaha, NE 68182. Offers biology (MS); business for bioscientists (Certificate). *Program availability:* Part-time. *Degree requirements:* For master's, comprehensive exam (for some programs), thesis (for some programs). *Entrance requirements:* For master's, GRE General Test, minimum GPA of 3.0, transcripts, 24 undergraduate biology hours, 3 letters of recommendation, statement of purpose. Additional exam requirements/recommendations for international students: Required—TOEFL, IELTS, PTE. Electronic applications accepted.

University of Nebraska–Lincoln, Graduate College, College of Agricultural Sciences and Natural Resources, School of Veterinary Medicine and Biomedical Sciences, Lincoln, NE 68588. Offers veterinary science (MS). MS, PhD offered jointly with University of Nebraska Medical Center. *Program availability:* Online learning. *Degree requirements:* For master's, thesis optional; for doctorate, comprehensive exam, thesis/dissertation. *Entrance requirements:* For master's, GRE General Test; for doctorate, GRE General Test, MCAT, or VCAT. Additional exam requirements/recommendations for international students: Required—TOEFL (minimum score 550 paper-based). Electronic applications accepted. *Faculty research:* Virology, immunobiology, molecular biology, mycotoxins, ocular degeneration.

University of Nebraska–Lincoln, Graduate College, College of Arts and Sciences, School of Biological Sciences, Lincoln, NE 68588. Offers MA, MS, PhD. *Degree requirements:* For master's, thesis optional; for doctorate, comprehensive exam, thesis/dissertation. *Entrance requirements:* For master's and doctorate, GRE General Test. Additional exam requirements/recommendations for international students: Required—TOEFL (minimum score 550 paper-based). Electronic applications accepted. *Faculty research:* Behavior, botany, and zoology; ecology and evolutionary biology; genetics; cellular and molecular biology; microbiology.

University of Nebraska Medical Center, Interdisciplinary Graduate Program in Biomedical Sciences, Omaha, NE 68198-5840. Offers MS, PhD. *Faculty:* 222 full-time (60 women). *Students:* 20 full-time (8 women); includes 3 minority (1 Black or African American, non-Hispanic/Latino; 2 Asian, non-Hispanic/Latino), 6 international. Average age 24. 89 applicants, 31% accepted, 20 enrolled. *Degree requirements:* For doctorate, comprehensive exam, thesis/dissertation. *Entrance requirements:* Additional exam requirements/recommendations for international students: Required—TOEFL (minimum score 95 iBT); Recommended—IELTS (minimum score 7). *Application deadline:* For fall admission, 5/15 for domestic students, 3/15 for international students; for summer admission, 2/15 for domestic students, 12/15 for international students. Applications are processed on a rolling basis. Electronic applications accepted. *Expenses:* Contact institution. *Financial support:* In 2017–18, 20 students received support. Health care benefits, tuition waivers (full), and unspecified assistantships available. Financial award application deadline: 5/15. *Unit head:* Kimberly Rothgeb, IGPBS Program Coordinator, 402-559-3362, Fax: 402-559-5368, E-mail: krothgeb@unmc.edu.
Website: http://www.unmc.edu/igpbs/

University of Nebraska Medical Center, Medical Sciences Interdepartmental Area, Omaha, NE 68198-4000. Offers applied behavior analysis (PhD); clinical translational research (MS, PhD); health practice and medical education research (MS); oral biology (MS, PhD). *Program availability:* Part-time. *Faculty:* 170 full-time, 20 part-time/adjunct. *Students:* 48 full-time (31 women), 59 part-time (37 women); includes 34 minority (1 Black or African American, non-Hispanic/Latino; 30 Asian, non-Hispanic/Latino; 3 Hispanic/Latino). Average age 32. 68 applicants, 34% accepted, 23 enrolled. In 2017, 26 master's, 915 doctorates awarded. Terminal master's awarded for partial completion of doctoral program. *Degree requirements:* For master's, comprehensive exam, thesis; for doctorate, comprehensive exam, thesis/dissertation. *Entrance requirements:* For master's, GRE General Test; for doctorate, GRE General Test, MCAT, DAT, LSAT. Additional exam requirements/recommendations for international students: Required—TOEFL (minimum score 550 paper-based; 80 iBT). *Application deadline:* For fall admission, 6/1 for domestic students, 4/1 for international students; for spring admission, 10/1 for domestic students, 9/1 for international students. Applications are processed on a rolling basis. Application fee: $60. Electronic applications accepted. *Expenses:* Contact institution. *Financial support:* In 2017–18, 72 students received support, including 1 fellowship with full tuition reimbursement available (averaging $23,400 per year), 37 research assistantships with full tuition reimbursements available (averaging $23,400 per year), 2 teaching assistantships with full tuition reimbursements available (averaging $23,400 per year); scholarships/grants and health care benefits also available. Financial award application deadline: 3/15; financial award applicants required to submit FAFSA. *Faculty research:* Molecular genetics, oral biology, veterinary pathology, newborn medicine, immunology, clinical research. *Unit head:* Dr. Laura Bilek, Graduate Committee Chair, 402-559-6923, E-mail: lbilek@unmc.edu. *Application contact:* Rhonda Sheibal-Carver, Interdisciplinary Programs Coordinator, 402-559-5141, E-mail: rhonda.sheibalcarver@unmc.edu.
Website: https://www.unmc.edu/msia/index.html

University of Nevada, Las Vegas, Graduate College, College of Sciences, School of Life Sciences, Las Vegas, NV 89154-4004. Offers biological sciences (MS, PhD). *Program availability:* Part-time. *Faculty:* 20 full-time (4 women), 2 part-time/adjunct (1 woman). *Students:* 41 full-time (18 women), 9 part-time (5 women); includes 16 minority (1 Asian, non-Hispanic/Latino; 8 Hispanic/Latino; 7 Two or more races, non-Hispanic/Latino), 8 international. Average age 30. 34 applicants, 41% accepted, 11 enrolled. In 2017, 7 master's, 1 doctorate awarded. *Degree requirements:* For master's, thesis; for doctorate, comprehensive exam, thesis/dissertation. *Entrance requirements:* For master's and doctorate, GRE General Test, bachelor's degree. Additional exam requirements/recommendations for international students: Required—TOEFL (minimum score 550 paper-based; 80 iBT), IELTS (minimum score 7). *Application deadline:* For fall admission, 1/15 for domestic students. Application fee: $60 ($95 for international students). Electronic applications accepted. *Expenses:* $275 per credit, $850 per course, $7,969 per year resident, $22,157 per year non-resident, $7,094 non-resident fee (7 credits or more), $1,307 annual health insurance fee. *Financial support:* In 2017–18, 48 students received support, including 1 fellowship with partial tuition reimbursement available (averaging $15,000 per year), 20 research assistantships with full and partial tuition reimbursements available (averaging $18,757 per year), 28 teaching assistantships with full and partial tuition reimbursements available (averaging $20,415 per year); institutionally sponsored loans, scholarships/grants, health care benefits, and unspecified assistantships also available. Financial award application deadline: 3/15; financial award applicants required to submit FAFSA. *Faculty research:* Biodiversity, evolution, and ecology; bioinformatics and quantitative biology; cell, developmental and molecular biology; environmental and medical microbiology. *Total annual research expenditures:* $2.5 million. *Unit head:* Dr. Donald Price, Director/Professor, 702-895-2053, Fax: 702-895-3956, E-mail: donald.price@unlv.edu. *Application contact:* Dr. Andrew Andres, Graduate Coordinator, 702-895-1778, Fax: 702-895-3956, E-mail: andrew.andres@unlv.edu.
Website: http://sols.unlv.edu/

University of Nevada, Reno, Graduate School, College of Science, Department of Biology, Reno, NV 89557. Offers MS. *Degree requirements:* For master's, thesis optional. *Entrance requirements:* For master's, GRE General Test, minimum GPA of 2.75. Additional exam requirements/recommendations for international students: Required—TOEFL (minimum score 500 paper-based; 61 iBT), IELTS (minimum score 6). Electronic applications accepted. *Faculty research:* Gene expression, stress protein genes, secretory proteins, conservation biology, behavioral ecology.

University of New Brunswick Fredericton, School of Graduate Studies, Faculty of Science, Department of Biology, Fredericton, NB E3B 5A3, Canada. Offers M Sc, PhD. *Program availability:* Part-time. *Degree requirements:* For master's, thesis; for doctorate, thesis/dissertation. *Entrance requirements:* For master's, minimum GPA of 3.0; undergraduate degree (B Sc or equivalent preferred); for doctorate, minimum GPA of 3.0; undergraduate and/or master's degree in related discipline. Additional exam requirements/recommendations for international students: Required—TWE (minimum score 4), TOEFL (minimum score 600 paper-based) or IELTS (minimum score 7). Electronic applications accepted. *Faculty research:* Evolutionary biology, aquatic ecology, wildlife and conservation biology, marine biology, algae and plant biology.

University of New Brunswick Saint John, Department of Biology, Saint John, NB E2L 4L5, Canada. Offers M Sc, PhD. *Program availability:* Part-time. *Degree requirements:* For master's, thesis; for doctorate, comprehensive exam, thesis/dissertation. *Entrance requirements:* For master's, B Sc, minimum GPA of 3.0; for doctorate, M Sc, minimum GPA of 3.0. Additional exam requirements/recommendations for international students: Required—TOEFL (minimum score 600 paper-based), TWE (minimum score 4). Electronic applications accepted. *Faculty research:* Marine and environmental biology (including assessing impacts of anthropogenic stressors on aquatic and terrestrial systems using molecular through ecological endpoints), evolution, natural products chemistry.

University of New England, College of Arts and Sciences, Biddeford, ME 04005-9526. Offers biological sciences (MS); marine sciences (MS). *Program availability:* Part-time. *Faculty:* 30 full-time (17 women), 2 part-time/adjunct (1 woman). *Students:* 14 full-time

(11 women), 6 part-time (3 women); includes 1 minority (Asian, non-Hispanic/Latino). Average age 25. 29 applicants, 34% accepted, 8 enrolled. In 2017, 4 master's awarded. *Application deadline:* Applications are processed on a rolling basis. Electronic applications accepted. Tuition and fees vary according to degree level, program and student level. *Financial support:* Fellowships, research assistantships, teaching assistantships, career-related internships or fieldwork, scholarships/grants, traineeships, and unspecified assistantships available. Financial award application deadline: 5/1; financial award applicants required to submit FAFSA. *Unit head:* Dr. Jeanne A.K. Hey, Dean, College of Arts and Sciences, 207-602-2371, Fax: 207-602-5973, E-mail: jhey@une.edu. *Application contact:* Scott Steinberg, Dean of University Admissions, 207-221-4225, Fax: 207-523-1925, E-mail: ssteinberg@une.edu.
Website: http://www.une.edu/cas/programs/graduate

University of New Hampshire, Graduate School, College of Life Sciences and Agriculture, Department of Biological Sciences, Durham, NH 03824. Offers integrative and organismal biology (MS, PhD); marine biology (MS, PhD). *Program availability:* Part-time. *Students:* 11 full-time (7 women), 25 part-time (19 women); includes 2 minority (both Two or more races, non-Hispanic/Latino), 2 international. Average age 26. 42 applicants, 21% accepted, 6 enrolled. In 2017, 2 master's awarded. *Entrance requirements:* For master's and doctorate, GRE General Test. Additional exam requirements/recommendations for international students: Required—TOEFL (minimum score 550 paper-based; 80 iBT). *Application deadline:* For fall admission, 3/15 for domestic and international students; for spring admission, 12/1 for domestic students. Application fee: $65. Electronic applications accepted. *Financial support:* In 2017–18, 32 students received support, including 11 research assistantships, 21 teaching assistantships; fellowships also available. Financial award application deadline: 2/15. *Unit head:* Don Chandler, Chair, 603-862-1735. *Application contact:* Diane Lavalliere, Senior Academic and Student Support Assistant, 603-862-2100, E-mail: diane.lavalliere@unh.edu.
Website: http://www.colsa.unh.edu/dbs

University of New Mexico, Graduate Studies, College of Arts and Sciences, Program in Biology, Albuquerque, NM 87131. Offers MS, PhD. *Faculty:* 34 full-time (11 women). *Students:* 54 full-time (32 women), 39 part-time (21 women); includes 27 minority (2 American Indian or Alaska Native, non-Hispanic/Latino; 2 Asian, non-Hispanic/Latino; 21 Hispanic/Latino; 2 Two or more races, non-Hispanic/Latino), 4 international. Average age 31. 80 applicants, 31% accepted, 25 enrolled. In 2017, 9 master's, 6 doctorates awarded. *Degree requirements:* For master's, comprehensive exam, thesis optional; for doctorate, comprehensive exam, thesis/dissertation. *Entrance requirements:* For master's and doctorate, GRE General Test, minimum GPA of 3.2, letters of recommendation. Additional exam requirements/recommendations for international students: Required—TOEFL (minimum score 550 paper-based; 79 iBT). *Application deadline:* For fall admission, 1/3 priority date for domestic and international students. Applications are processed on a rolling basis. Application fee: $50. Electronic applications accepted. *Financial support:* Fellowships with full tuition reimbursements, research assistantships with full tuition reimbursements, teaching assistantships with full tuition reimbursements, Federal Work-Study, scholarships/grants, health care benefits, and unspecified assistantships available. Financial award application deadline: 1/3; financial award applicants required to submit FAFSA. *Faculty research:* Aquatic ecology, behavioral ecology, botany, cell biology, comparative biology, conservation biology, developmental biology, ecology, evolutionary biology, genetics, genomics, global change biology, immunology, invertebrate biology, mathematical biology, microbiology, molecular evolution, paleo biology, parasitology, physiological ecology, plant biology, systematics, vertebrate biology. *Total annual research expenditures:* $10.8 million. *Unit head:* Dr. Robert D. Miller, Chair, 505-277-2496, Fax: 505-277-0304, E-mail: rdmiller@unm.edu. *Application contact:* Cheryl Martin, Graduate Program Coordinator, 505-277-1712, Fax: 505-277-0304, E-mail: cherylm@unm.edu.
Website: http://biology.unm.edu/

University of New Mexico, Graduate Studies, Health Sciences Center, Program in Biomedical Sciences, Albuquerque, NM 87131-5196. Offers biochemistry and molecular biology (MS, PhD); cell biology and physiology (MS, PhD); molecular genetics and microbiology (MS, PhD); neuroscience (MS, PhD); pathology (MS, PhD); toxicology (MS, PhD). *Program availability:* Part-time. *Students:* Average age 29. 61 applicants, 16% accepted, 10 enrolled. In 2017, 11 master's, 14 doctorates awarded. Terminal master's awarded for partial completion of doctoral program. *Degree requirements:* For master's, thesis; for doctorate, comprehensive exam, thesis/dissertation, qualifying exam at the end of year 1/core curriculum. *Entrance requirements:* For master's and doctorate, GRE General Test, minimum undergraduate GPA of 3.0. Additional exam requirements/recommendations for international students: Required—TOEFL. *Application deadline:* For fall admission, 3/1 priority date for domestic and international students. Applications are processed on a rolling basis. Application fee: $50. Electronic applications accepted. *Financial support:* Fellowships, research assistantships with full tuition reimbursements, teaching assistantships, career-related internships or fieldwork, Federal Work-Study, institutionally sponsored loans, scholarships/grants, traineeships, health care benefits, and unspecified assistantships available. Financial award application deadline: 1/1; financial award applicants required to submit FAFSA. *Faculty research:* Infectious disease/immunity, cancer biology, cardiovascular and metabolic diseases, brain and behavioral illness, environmental health. *Unit head:* Dr. Helen J. Hathaway, Program Director, 505-272-1887, Fax: 505-272-2412, E-mail: hhathaway@salud.unm.edu. *Application contact:* Mary Fenton, Admissions Coordinator, 505-272-1887, Fax: 505-272-2412, E-mail: mfenton@salud.unm.edu.

University of New Orleans, Graduate School, College of Sciences, Department of Biological Sciences, New Orleans, LA 70148. Offers MS. *Degree requirements:* For master's, one foreign language, thesis. *Entrance requirements:* For master's, GRE General Test. Additional exam requirements/recommendations for international students: Required—TOEFL (minimum score 550 paper-based; 79 iBT), IELTS (minimum score 6.5). *Application deadline:* For fall admission, 7/1 priority date for domestic students, 6/1 for international students; for spring admission, 11/1 priority date for domestic students, 10/1 for international students. Applications are processed on a rolling basis. Application fee: $20. Electronic applications accepted. *Financial support:* Application deadline: 5/15; applicants required to submit FAFSA. *Faculty research:* Biochemistry, genetics, vertebrate and invertebrate systematics and ecology, cell and mammalian physiology, morphology. *Unit head:* Dr. Steven G. Johnson, Chairperson, 504-280-6741, Fax: 504-280-6121, E-mail: sgjohnso@uno.edu. *Application contact:* Dr. Bernard Rees, Graduate Coordinator, 504-280-6309, Fax: 504-280-6121, E-mail: brees@uno.edu.
Website: http://biology.uno.edu

The University of North Carolina at Chapel Hill, Graduate School, College of Arts and Sciences, Department of Biology, Chapel Hill, NC 27599. Offers botany (MA, MS, PhD); cell biology, development, and physiology (MA, MS, PhD); cell motility and cytoskeleton (PhD); ecology and behavior (MA, MS, PhD); genetics and molecular biology (MA, MS, PhD); morphology, systematics, and evolution (MA, MS, PhD). Terminal master's awarded for partial completion of doctoral program. *Degree requirements:* For master's, comprehensive exam, thesis (for some programs); for doctorate, comprehensive exam, thesis/dissertation. *Entrance requirements:* For master's, GRE General Test, GRE Subject Test, 2 semesters of calculus or statistics; 2 semesters of physics, organic chemistry; 3 semesters of biology; for doctorate, GRE General Test, GRE Subject Test, 2 semesters calculus or statistics, 2 semesters physics, organic chemistry, 3 semesters of biology. Additional exam requirements/recommendations for international students: Required—TOEFL (minimum score 550 paper-based). Electronic applications accepted. *Faculty research:* Gene expression, biomechanics, yeast genetics, plant ecology, plant molecular biology.

The University of North Carolina at Chapel Hill, School of Medicine and Graduate School, Graduate Programs in Medicine, Chapel Hill, NC 27599. Offers MS, Au D, DPT, PhD, MD/PhD. *Program availability:* Online learning. Terminal master's awarded for partial completion of doctoral program. *Degree requirements:* For master's, comprehensive exam; for doctorate, thesis/dissertation. Electronic applications accepted. *Expenses:* Contact institution.

The University of North Carolina at Charlotte, College of Liberal Arts and Sciences, Department of Biological Sciences, Charlotte, NC 28223-0001. Offers MS, PhD. *Program availability:* Part-time. *Faculty:* 25 full-time (8 women). *Students:* 42 full-time (27 women), 11 part-time (6 women); includes 7 minority (1 Black or African American, non-Hispanic/Latino; 4 Asian, non-Hispanic/Latino; 2 Two or more races, non-Hispanic/Latino), 13 international. Average age 27. 49 applicants, 31% accepted, 11 enrolled. In 2017, 5 master's, 2 doctorates awarded. Terminal master's awarded for partial completion of doctoral program. *Degree requirements:* For master's, comprehensive exam, thesis or project; for doctorate, thesis/dissertation. *Entrance requirements:* For master's, GRE General Test, BS or BA from accredited university; minimum overall GPA of 3.0; personal statement; for doctorate, GRE General Test, BS or BA from accredited university; minimum overall GPA of 3.0. Additional exam requirements/recommendations for international students: Required—TOEFL (minimum score 523 paper-based, 70 iBT) or IELTS (6.5). *Application deadline:* For fall admission, 1/15 for domestic and international students; for spring admission, 10/1 for domestic and international students. Applications are processed on a rolling basis. Application fee: $75. Electronic applications accepted. *Expenses:* Tuition, state resident: full-time $4337. Tuition, nonresident: full-time $17,771. *Required fees:* $3211. Tuition and fees vary according to course load and program. *Financial support:* In 2017–18, 41 students received support, including 6 fellowships (averaging $42,959 per year), 8 research assistantships (averaging $8,476 per year), 27 teaching assistantships (averaging $9,583 per year); career-related internships or fieldwork, institutionally sponsored loans, scholarships/grants, and unspecified assistantships also available. Support available to part-time students. Financial award application deadline: 3/1; financial award applicants required to submit FAFSA. *Total annual research expenditures:* $1.9 million. *Unit head:* Dr. Pinku Mukherjee, Chair, 704-687-5465, E-mail: pmukherj@uncc.edu. *Application contact:* Kathy B. Giddings, Director of Graduate Admissions, 704-687-5503, Fax: 704-687-1668, E-mail: gradadm@uncc.edu.
Website: http://biology.uncc.edu/

The University of North Carolina at Greensboro, Graduate School, College of Arts and Sciences, Department of Biology, Greensboro, NC 27412-5001. Offers MS. *Degree requirements:* For master's, thesis. *Entrance requirements:* For master's, GRE General Test, GRE Subject Test. Additional exam requirements/recommendations for international students: Required—TOEFL. Electronic applications accepted. *Faculty research:* Environmental biology, biochemistry, animal ecology, vertebrate reproduction.

The University of North Carolina Wilmington, College of Arts and Sciences, Department of Biology and Marine Biology, Wilmington, NC 28403-3297. Offers biology (MS); marine biology (MS, PhD). *Program availability:* Part-time. *Faculty:* 39 full-time (12 women), 2 part-time/adjunct (0 women). *Students:* 4 full-time (3 women), 71 part-time (44 women); includes 7 minority (1 Black or African American, non-Hispanic/Latino; 3 Asian, non-Hispanic/Latino; 2 Hispanic/Latino; 1 Two or more races, non-Hispanic/Latino), 2 international. Average age 29. 72 applicants, 31% accepted, 22 enrolled. In 2017, 16 master's, 2 doctorates awarded. *Degree requirements:* For master's, comprehensive exam, thesis; for doctorate, comprehensive exam, thesis/dissertation. *Entrance requirements:* For master's, GRE General Test, 3 recommendations, research interests form and statement, resume or curriculum vitae, baccalaureate degree from biology-related field; for doctorate, GRE General Test, 3 recommendations, resume or curriculum vitae, summary of MS thesis research, statement of PhD research interests, copies of publications, master's degree or BS and 1 year of completed work in the MS in biology program. Additional exam requirements/recommendations for international students: Required—TOEFL (minimum score 550 paper-based; 79 iBT), IELTS (minimum score 6.5). *Application deadline:* For fall admission, 6/15 for domestic students; for spring admission, 11/30 for domestic students. Applications are processed on a rolling basis. Application fee: $75. Electronic applications accepted. *Expenses:* Tuition, state resident: full-time $4626; part-time $226.76 per credit hour. Tuition, nonresident: full-time $17,834; part-time $874.22 per credit hour. *Required fees:* $2124. Tuition and fees vary according to program. *Financial support:* Research assistantships with tuition reimbursements, teaching assistantships with tuition reimbursements, and scholarships/grants available. Support available to part-time students. Financial award application deadline: 1/1; financial award applicants required to submit FAFSA. *Faculty research:* Ecology, physiology, cell and molecular biology, systematics, biomechanics. *Unit head:* Dr. Heather Koopman, Chair, 910-962-7199, E-mail: koopmanh@uncw.edu. *Application contact:* Dr. Stephen Kinsey, Graduate Coordinator, 910-962-7398, Fax: 910-962-4066, E-mail: kinseys@uncw.edu.
Website: http://www.uncw.edu/bio/graduate.html

University of North Dakota, Graduate School, College of Arts and Sciences, Department of Biology, Grand Forks, ND 58202. Offers biology (MS); fisheries/wildlife (PhD); genetics (PhD); zoology (PhD). Terminal master's awarded for partial completion of doctoral program. *Degree requirements:* For master's, thesis, final exam; for doctorate, comprehensive exam, thesis/dissertation, final exam. *Entrance requirements:* For master's, GRE General Test, GRE Subject Test, minimum GPA of 3.0; for doctorate, GRE General Test, GRE Subject Test, minimum GPA of 3.5. Additional exam requirements/recommendations for international students: Required—TOEFL (minimum score 550 paper-based; 79 iBT), IELTS (minimum score 6.5). Electronic applications accepted. *Faculty research:* Population biology, wildlife ecology, RNA processing, hormonal control of behavior.

University of Northern Colorado, Graduate School, College of Natural and Health Sciences, School of Biology, Program in Biological Sciences, Greeley, CO 80639. Offers MS. *Program availability:* Part-time. *Degree requirements:* For master's, comprehensive exam. *Entrance requirements:* For master's, GRE General Test, 3 letters of recommendation. Electronic applications accepted.

University of Northern Iowa, Graduate College, College of Humanities, Arts and Sciences, Department of Biology, Cedar Falls, IA 50614. Offers MS. *Program availability:* Part-time. *Degree requirements:* For master's, comprehensive exam (for some programs), thesis or alternative. *Entrance requirements:* For master's, minimum GPA of 3.0; 3 letters of recommendation. Additional exam requirements/recommendations for international students: Required—TOEFL (minimum score 500 paper-based; 61 iBT). Electronic applications accepted.

University of North Florida, College of Arts and Sciences, Department of Biology, Jacksonville, FL 32224. Offers MA, MS. *Program availability:* Part-time. *Degree requirements:* For master's, thesis (for some programs). *Entrance requirements:* For master's, GRE General Test, minimum GPA of 3.0 in last 60 hours, letters of recommendation. Additional exam requirements/recommendations for international students: Required—TOEFL (minimum score 570 paper-based). Electronic applications accepted.

University of North Texas, Robert B. Toulouse School of Graduate Studies, Denton, TX 76203-5459. Offers accounting (MS); applied anthropology (MA, MS); applied behavior analysis (Certificate); applied geography (MA); applied technology and performance improvement (M Ed, MS); art education (MA); art history (MA); art museum education (Certificate); arts leadership (Certificate); audiology (Au D); behavior analysis (MS); behavioral science (PhD); biochemistry and molecular biology (MS); biology (MA, MS); biomedical engineering (MS); business analysis (MS); chemistry (MS); clinical health psychology (PhD); communication studies (MA, MS); computer engineering (MS); computer science (MS); counseling (M Ed, MS), including clinical mental health counseling (MS), college and university counseling, elementary school counseling, secondary school counseling; creative writing (MA); criminal justice (MS); curriculum and instruction (M Ed); decision sciences (MBA); design (MA, MFA), including fashion design (MFA), innovation studies, interior design (MFA); early childhood studies (MS); economics (MS); educational leadership (M Ed, Ed D); educational psychology (MS, PhD), including family studies (MS), gifted and talented (MS), human development (MS), learning and cognition (MS), research, measurement and evaluation (MS); electrical engineering (MS); emergency management (MPA); engineering technology (MS); English (MA); English as a second language (MA); environmental science (MS); finance (MBA, MS); financial management (MPA); French (MA); health services management (MBA); higher education (M Ed, Ed D); history (MA, MS); hospitality management (MS); human resources management (MPA); information science (MS); information systems (PhD); information technologies (MBA); interdisciplinary studies (MA, MS); international studies (MA); international sustainable tourism (MS); jazz studies (MM); journalism (MA, MJ, Graduate Certificate), including interactive and virtual digital communication (Graduate Certificate), narrative journalism (Graduate Certificate), public relations (Graduate Certificate); kinesiology (MS); linguistics (MA); local government management (MPA); logistics (PhD); logistics and supply chain management (MBA); long-term care, senior housing, and aging services (MA); management (PhD); marketing (MBA); mathematics (MA, MS); mechanical and energy engineering (MS, PhD); music (MA), including ethnomusicology, music theory, musicology, performance; music composition (PhD); music education (MM Ed, PhD); nonprofit management (MPA); operations and supply chain management (MBA); performance (MM, DMA); philosophy (MA); political science (MA); professional and technical communication (MA); radio, television and film (MA, MFA); rehabilitation counseling (Certificate); sociology (MA); Spanish (MA); special education (M Ed); speech-language pathology (MA); strategic management (MBA); studio art (MFA); teaching (M Ed); MBA/MS. *Program availability:* Part-time, evening/weekend, online learning. Terminal master's awarded for partial completion of doctoral program. *Degree requirements:* For master's, variable foreign language requirement, comprehensive exam (for some programs), thesis (for some programs); for doctorate, variable foreign language requirement, comprehensive exam (for some programs), thesis/dissertation; for other advanced degree, variable foreign language requirement, comprehensive exam (for some programs). *Entrance requirements:* For master's and doctorate, GRE, GMAT. Additional exam requirements/recommendations for international students: Required—TOEFL (minimum score 550 paper-based; 79 iBT). Electronic applications accepted.

University of North Texas Health Science Center at Fort Worth, Graduate School of Biomedical Sciences, Fort Worth, TX 76107-2699. Offers biochemistry and cancer biology (MS, PhD); biotechnology (MS); cell biology, immunology and microbiology (MS, PhD); clinical research management (MS); forensic genetics (MS); genetics (MS, PhD); integrative physiology (MS, PhD); medical sciences (MS); pharmaceutical sciences and pharmacotherapy (MS, PhD); pharmacology and neuroscience (MS, PhD); structural anatomy and rehabilitation sciences (MS, PhD); DO/MS; DO/PhD. Terminal master's awarded for partial completion of doctoral program. *Degree requirements:* For master's, thesis; for doctorate, thesis/dissertation. *Entrance requirements:* For master's and doctorate, GRE General Test. Additional exam requirements/recommendations for international students: Required—TOEFL. *Expenses:* Contact institution. *Faculty research:* Alzheimer's disease, aging, eye diseases, cancer, cardiovascular disease.

University of Notre Dame, Graduate School, College of Science, Department of Biological Sciences, Notre Dame, IN 46556. Offers aquatic ecology, evolution and environmental biology (MS, PhD); cellular and molecular biology (MS, PhD); genetics (MS, PhD); physiology (MS, PhD); vector biology and parasitology (MS, PhD). Terminal master's awarded for partial completion of doctoral program. *Degree requirements:* For master's, comprehensive exam, thesis; for doctorate, comprehensive exam, thesis/dissertation, candidacy exam. *Entrance requirements:* For master's and doctorate, GRE General Test. Additional exam requirements/recommendations for international students: Required—TOEFL (minimum score 600 paper-based; 80 iBT). Electronic applications accepted. *Faculty research:* Tropical disease, molecular genetics, neurobiology, evolutionary biology, aquatic biology.

University of Oklahoma, College of Arts and Sciences and School of Aerospace and Mechanical Engineering and Department of Chemistry and Biochemistry, Program in Cellular and Behavioral Neurobiology, Norman, OK 73019. Offers cellular and behavioral neurobiology (PhD), including biology, chemistry and biochemistry, psychology. *Students:* 5 full-time (2 women), 1 (woman) part-time, 1 international. Average age 27. 8 applicants, 13% accepted, 1 enrolled. In 2017, 1 doctorate awarded. *Degree requirements:* For doctorate, comprehensive exam, thesis/dissertation, 2-3 lab rotations plus requirements of particular home department to which student applies. *Entrance requirements:* For doctorate, GRE General Test; GRE Subject Test in chemistry (recommended for applicants to chemistry and biochemistry), transcripts, 3 letters of recommendation, personal statement; publications (for psychology). Additional exam requirements/recommendations for international students: Required—TOEFL (minimum score 79 iBT) or IELTS (minimum score 6.5). Application fee: $50 ($100 for international students). Electronic applications accepted. *Expenses:* Tuition, state resident: full-time $5119; part-time $213.30 per credit hour. Tuition, nonresident: full-time $19,778; part-time $824.10 per credit hour. *Required fees:* $3458; $133.55 per credit hour. $126.50 per semester. *Financial support:* In 2017–18, 5 students received support. Fellowships with full tuition reimbursements available, research assistantships with full tuition reimbursements available, teaching assistantships with full tuition reimbursements available, scholarships/grants, health care benefits, and unspecified assistantships available. Financial award application deadline: 6/1; financial award applicants required to submit FAFSA. *Faculty research:* Behavioral neurobiology, cellular neurobiology, molecular neurobiology, developmental neurobiology, cell signaling. *Unit head:* Dr. Ari Berkowitz, Director, Graduate Program, 405-325-3492, Fax: 405-325-6202, E-mail: ari@ou.edu.
Website: http://www.ou.edu/cbn

University of Oklahoma Health Sciences Center, College of Medicine and Graduate College, Graduate Programs in Medicine, Oklahoma City, OK 73190. Offers biochemistry and molecular biology (MS, PhD), including biochemistry, molecular biology; cell biology (MS, PhD); medical sciences (MS); microbiology and immunology (MS, PhD), including immunology, microbiology; neuroscience (MS, PhD); pathology (PhD); physiology (MS, PhD); psychiatry and behavioral sciences (MS, PhD), including biological psychology; radiological sciences (MS, PhD), including medical radiation physics; MD/PhD. *Program availability:* Part-time. Terminal master's awarded for partial completion of doctoral program. *Degree requirements:* For doctorate, thesis/dissertation. *Entrance requirements:* For doctorate, GRE General Test, 3 letters of recommendation. Additional exam requirements/recommendations for international students: Required—TOEFL. *Expenses:* Contact institution. *Faculty research:* Behavior and drugs, structure and function of endothelium, genetics and behavior, gene structure and function, action of antibiotics.

University of Oregon, Graduate School, College of Arts and Sciences, Department of Biology, Eugene, OR 97403. Offers ecology and evolution (MA, MS, PhD); marine biology (MA, MS, PhD); molecular, cellular and genetic biology (PhD); neuroscience and development (PhD). Terminal master's awarded for partial completion of doctoral program. *Degree requirements:* For master's, thesis (for some programs); for doctorate, thesis/dissertation. *Entrance requirements:* For master's and doctorate, GRE General Test, minimum GPA of 3.2. Additional exam requirements/recommendations for international students: Required—TOEFL. *Faculty research:* Developmental neurobiology; evolution, population biology, and quantitative genetics; regulation of gene expression; biochemistry of marine organisms.

University of Ottawa, Faculty of Graduate and Postdoctoral Studies, Faculty of Science, Ottawa-Carleton Institute of Biology, Ottawa, ON K1N 6N5, Canada. Offers M Sc, PhD. M Sc, PhD offered jointly with Carleton University. *Program availability:* Part-time. *Degree requirements:* For master's, thesis, seminar; for doctorate, comprehensive exam, thesis/dissertation, seminar. *Entrance requirements:* For master's, honors B Sc degree or equivalent, minimum B average; for doctorate, honors B Sc with minimum B+ average or M Sc with minimum B+ average. Electronic applications accepted. *Faculty research:* Physiology/biochemistry, cellular and molecular biology, ecology, behavior and systematics.

University of Pennsylvania, Perelman School of Medicine, Biomedical Graduate Studies, Philadelphia, PA 19104. Offers MS, PhD, MD/PhD, VMD/PhD. *Faculty:* 1,121. *Students:* 883 full-time (496 women), 23 part-time (18 women); includes 323 minority (33 Black or African American, non-Hispanic/Latino; 146 Asian, non-Hispanic/Latino; 102 Hispanic/Latino; 42 Two or more races, non-Hispanic/Latino), 94 international. 1,591 applicants, 22% accepted, 181 enrolled. In 2017, 79 master's, 135 doctorates awarded. Application fee: $80. *Financial support:* In 2017–18, 651 students received support. *Unit head:* Dr. Michael Nusbaum, Director, 215-898-1585, E-mail: nusbaum@mail.med.upenn.edu. *Application contact:* Aislinn Wallace, Admissions Coordinator, 215-746-6349, E-mail: aislinnw@mail.med.upenn.edu.
Website: http://www.med.upenn.edu/bgs/

University of Pennsylvania, School of Arts and Sciences, Graduate Group in Biology, Philadelphia, PA 19104. Offers PhD. *Faculty:* 50 full-time (13 women), 2 part-time/adjunct (1 woman). *Students:* 50 full-time (24 women); includes 8 minority (4 Asian, non-Hispanic/Latino; 2 Hispanic/Latino; 2 Two or more races, non-Hispanic/Latino), 20 international. Average age 28. 126 applicants, 18% accepted, 11 enrolled. In 2017, 9 doctorates awarded.
Website: http://www.bio.upenn.edu

University of Pittsburgh, Kenneth P. Dietrich School of Arts and Sciences, Department of Biological Sciences, Pittsburgh, PA 15260. Offers ecology and evolution (PhD); molecular, cellular, and developmental biology (PhD). *Program availability:* Online learning. *Faculty:* 29 full-time (8 women). *Students:* 51 full-time (32 women); includes 3 minority (1 Black or African American, non-Hispanic/Latino; 1 Asian, non-Hispanic/Latino; 1 Hispanic/Latino), 9 international. Average age 23. 151 applicants, 19% accepted, 9 enrolled. In 2017, 6 doctorates awarded. *Degree requirements:* For doctorate, comprehensive exam, thesis/dissertation, completion of research integrity module. *Entrance requirements:* For doctorate, GRE General Test, GRE Subject Test. Additional exam requirements/recommendations for international students: Required—TOEFL (minimum score 90 iBT). *Application deadline:* For fall admission, 1/2 priority date for domestic students, 12/9 priority date for international students. Applications are processed on a rolling basis. Application fee: $0 ($50 for international students). Electronic applications accepted. *Financial support:* In 2017–18, 34 fellowships with full tuition reimbursements (averaging $34,776 per year), 72 research assistantships with full tuition reimbursements (averaging $28,800 per year), 34 teaching assistantships with full tuition reimbursements (averaging $28,367 per year) were awarded; Federal Work-Study, traineeships, health care benefits, and tuition waivers also available. *Faculty research:* Molecular biology; ecology and evolution; microbiology; biochemistry; structural biology. *Total annual research expenditures:* $8.2 million. *Unit head:* Dr. Jeffrey G. Lawrence, Professor/Chair, 412-624-4350, Fax: 412-624-4349, E-mail: jlawrenc@pitt.edu. *Application contact:* Cathleen M. Barr, Graduate Administrator, 412-624-4268, Fax: 412-624-4349, E-mail: cbarr@pitt.edu.
Website: http://www.biology.pitt.edu

University of Pittsburgh, School of Computing and Information, Program in Computational Modeling and Simulation, Pittsburgh, PA 15260. Offers biological science (PhD). *Program availability:* Part-time. *Faculty:* 21 full-time (3 women). *Students:* 5 full-time (2 women), 3 international. Average age 23. Terminal master's awarded for partial completion of doctoral program. *Degree requirements:* For master's, comprehensive exam, thesis; for doctorate, comprehensive exam, thesis/dissertation, preliminary exam. *Entrance requirements:* For doctorate, GRE General Test, GRE Subject Test, statement of purpose, transcripts for all college-level institutions attended, three letters of reference. Additional exam requirements/recommendations for international students: Required—TOEFL (minimum score 600 paper-based; 90 iBT), IELTS (minimum score 7). *Application deadline:* For fall admission, 1/15 for domestic and international students. Application fee: $0 ($50 for international students). Electronic applications accepted. *Expenses:* $21,748 full-time resident per year, $877 part-time per credit; $35,904 full-time non-resident per year, $1,468 part-time per credit; $830 full-time academic fees per year, $265 part-time per term. *Financial support:* In 2017–18, 4 fellowships with full tuition reimbursements (averaging $34,344 per year), 1 research assistantship with full tuition reimbursement (averaging $27,930 per year) were awarded; teaching assistantships and tuition waivers (full) also available. *Faculty research:* Modeling of geological systems, electronic structure, chemical reaction mechanisms, computation economics, machine learning methods. *Unit head:* Kenneth D. Jordan, Professor, 412-624-8690, E-mail: jordan@pitt.edu. *Application contact:* Christie D. Hay, Graduate Administrator, 412-624-5501, Fax: 412-624-8611, E-mail: cmspadm@pitt.edu.
Website: http://www.cmsp.pitt.edu/

University of Pittsburgh, School of Medicine, Graduate Programs in Medicine, Biomedical Sciences Master's Program, Pittsburgh, PA 15260. Offers MS. *Faculty:* 10 full-time (3 women). *Students:* 44 full-time (24 women); includes 22 minority (7 Black or African American, non-Hispanic/Latino; 6 Asian, non-Hispanic/Latino; 4 Hispanic/Latino; 5 Two or more races, non-Hispanic/Latino), 3 international. Average age 25. 115 applicants, 38% accepted, 44 enrolled. *Degree requirements:* For master's, comprehensive exam, capstone project. *Entrance requirements:* Additional exam

requirements/recommendations for international students: Required—TOEFL (minimum score 100 iBT), IELTS (minimum score 7). *Application deadline:* For fall admission, 6/1 priority date for domestic and international students. Applications are processed on a rolling basis. Application fee: $50. Electronic applications accepted. *Expenses:* $26,782 in-state, $42,006 out-of-state. *Faculty research:* The vascular system, peptide hormones, signal transduction. *Unit head:* Dr. Alessandro Bisello, Director, 412-383-3265, E-mail: bmppitt@pitt.edu. *Application contact:* Larissa Kocelko, Administrative Specialist, 412-383-8716, E-mail: lrk31@pitt.edu.
Website: http://bmp.pitt.edu

University of Pittsburgh, School of Medicine, Graduate Programs in Medicine, Interdisciplinary Biomedical Graduate Program, Pittsburgh, PA 15260. Offers PhD. *Faculty:* 221 full-time (52 women). *Students:* 16 full-time (9 women); includes 3 minority (1 Asian, non-Hispanic/Latino; 2 Hispanic/Latino), 4 international. Average age 24. 350 applicants, 21% accepted, 16 enrolled. *Degree requirements:* For doctorate, comprehensive exam, thesis/dissertation. *Entrance requirements:* For doctorate, GRE General Test, minimum GPA of 3.2, 3 letters of recommendation, official transcripts, baccalaureate degree. Additional exam requirements/recommendations for international students: Required—TOEFL (minimum score 600 paper-based; 100 iBT), IELTS (minimum score 7). *Application deadline:* For fall admission, 12/1 priority date for domestic and international students. Application fee: $50. Electronic applications accepted. *Expenses:* $26,782 in-state, $42,006 out-of-state. *Financial support:* In 2017–18, 16 students received support. Traineeships available. *Faculty research:* Cell biology and molecular physiology, cellular and molecular pathology, molecular genetics and developmental biology, molecular pharmacology. *Unit head:* Dr. John Horn, Director, 412-648-8957, Fax: 412-648-1077, E-mail: gradstudies@medschool.pitt.edu. *Application contact:* Carol Williams, Admissions and Recruiting Manager, 412-648-8957, Fax: 412-648-1077, E-mail: gradstudies@medschool.pitt.edu.
Website: http://www.gradbiomed.pitt.edu/

University of Prince Edward Island, Faculty of Science, Charlottetown, PE C1A 4P3, Canada. Offers environmental sciences (M Sc, PhD); human biology (M Sc); molecular and macromolecular sciences (M Sc, PhD); sustainable design engineering (M Sc). *Degree requirements:* For master's, thesis. *Entrance requirements:* Additional exam requirements/recommendations for international students: Required—TOEFL (minimum score 550 paper-based; 80 iBT), Canadian Academic English Language Assessment, Michigan English Language Assessment Battery, Canadian Test of English for Scholars and Trainees. *Faculty research:* Ecology and wildlife biology, molecular, genetics and biotechnology, organometallic, bio-organic, supramolecular and synthetic organic chemistry, neurobiology and stoke materials science.

University of Puerto Rico–Mayagüez, Graduate Studies, College of Arts and Sciences, Department of Biology, Mayagüez, PR 00681-9000. Offers MS. *Program availability:* Part-time. *Degree requirements:* For master's, one foreign language, comprehensive exam, thesis. *Entrance requirements:* For master's, BS in biology or its equivalent; minimum GPA of 3.0 in biology courses. Electronic applications accepted. *Faculty research:* Genetics, molecular biology, microbiology, immunology, botany.

University of Puerto Rico–Medical Sciences Campus, School of Medicine, Biomedical Sciences Graduate Program, San Juan, PR 00936-5067. Offers MS, PhD. Terminal master's awarded for partial completion of doctoral program. *Degree requirements:* For master's, one foreign language, thesis; for doctorate, one foreign language, comprehensive exam, thesis/dissertation. *Entrance requirements:* For master's and doctorate, GRE General Test, GRE Subject Test, interview, 3 letters of recommendation, minimum GPA of 3.0. Electronic applications accepted. *Expenses:* Contact institution.

University of Puerto Rico–Río Piedras, College of Natural Sciences, Department of Biology, San Juan, PR 00931-3300. Offers ecology/systematics (MS, PhD); evolution/genetics (MS, PhD); molecular/cellular biology (MS, PhD); neuroscience (MS, PhD). *Program availability:* Part-time. *Degree requirements:* For master's, one foreign language, comprehensive exam, thesis; for doctorate, one foreign language, comprehensive exam, thesis/dissertation. *Entrance requirements:* For master's, GRE Subject Test, interview, minimum GPA of 3.0, letter of recommendation; for doctorate, GRE Subject Test, interview, master's degree, minimum GPA of 3.0, letter of recommendation. *Faculty research:* Environmental, poblational and systematic biology.

University of Regina, Faculty of Graduate Studies and Research, Faculty of Science, Department of Biology, Regina, SK S4S 0A2, Canada. Offers M Sc, PhD. *Program availability:* Part-time. *Faculty:* 15 full-time (4 women), 17 part-time/adjunct (1 woman). *Students:* 39 full-time (26 women), 6 part-time (3 women). 21 applicants, 38% accepted. In 2017, 7 master's, 3 doctorates awarded. *Degree requirements:* For master's, thesis; for doctorate, comprehensive exam, thesis/dissertation. *Entrance requirements:* Additional exam requirements/recommendations for international students: Required—TOEFL (minimum score 580 paper-based; 80 iBT), IELTS (minimum score 6.5), PTE (minimum score 59). *Application deadline:* Applications are processed on a rolling basis. Application fee: $100. Electronic applications accepted. *Expenses:* CAD$10,681 per year (for M Sc); CAD$9,930 per year (for PhD). *Financial support:* In 2017–18, fellowships (averaging $6,375 per year), teaching assistantships (averaging $2,562 per year) were awarded; research assistantships and scholarships/grants also available. Financial award application deadline: 6/15. *Faculty research:* Aquatic and terrestrial ecology, molecular and population genetics, developmental biology, microbiology, plant physiology and morphology. *Unit head:* Dr. Harold Weger, Department Head, 306-585-4479, Fax: 306-337-2410.
Website: http://www.uregina.ca/science/biology/

University of Rhode Island, Graduate School, College of the Environment and Life Sciences, Department of Biological Sciences, Kingston, RI 02881. Offers cell and molecular biology (MS, PhD); earth and environmental sciences (MS, PhD); ecology and ecosystem sciences (MS, PhD); evolutionary and marine biology (MS, PhD); sustainable agriculture and food systems (MS, PhD). *Program availability:* Part-time. *Faculty:* 18 full-time (10 women). *Students:* 99 full-time (56 women), 16 part-time (12 women); includes 10 minority (4 Black or African American, non-Hispanic/Latino; 3 Asian, non-Hispanic/Latino; 2 Hispanic/Latino; 1 Two or more races, non-Hispanic/Latino), 21 international. 151 applicants, 22% accepted, 26 enrolled. In 2017, 18 master's, 9 doctorates awarded. *Entrance requirements:* Additional exam requirements/recommendations for international students: Required—TOEFL. *Application deadline:* For fall admission, 1/15 for domestic and international students. Application fee: $65. Electronic applications accepted. *Expenses:* Tuition, state resident: full-time $12,706; part-time $786 per credit. Tuition, nonresident: full-time $25,216; part-time $1401 per credit. *Required fees:* $1598; $45 per credit. One-time fee: $30 part-time. *Financial support:* In 2017–18, 4 research assistantships with tuition reimbursements (averaging $12,698 per year) were awarded. Financial award application deadline: 1/15; financial award applicants required to submit FAFSA. *Faculty research:* Physiological constraints on predators in the Antarctic, effects of CO2 absorption in salt water particularly as it impacts pteropods. *Unit head:* Dr. Evan Preisser, Chair, 401-874-2120, E-mail: preisser@uri.edu.
Website: http://web.uri.edu/bio/

University of Rochester, School of Arts and Sciences, Department of Biology, Rochester, NY 14627. Offers biology (MS); ecology, genetics, and genomics (PhD); molecular, cellular, and developmental biology evolution (PhD). *Faculty:* 21 full-time (6 women). *Students:* 42 full-time (17 women), 4 part-time (all women); includes 6 minority (1 Asian, non-Hispanic/Latino; 3 Hispanic/Latino; 2 Two or more races, non-Hispanic/Latino), 22 international. Average age 27. 119 applicants, 22% accepted, 11 enrolled. In 2017, 6 master's, 5 doctorates awarded. Terminal master's awarded for partial completion of doctoral program. *Degree requirements:* For master's, comprehensive exam (for some programs), thesis (for some programs); for doctorate, thesis/dissertation, qualifying exam. *Entrance requirements:* For master's and doctorate, GRE General Test, GRE Subject Test (highly recommended), personal statement, transcripts, three letters of recommendation. Additional exam requirements/recommendations for international students: Required—TOEFL. *Application deadline:* For fall admission, 1/2 for domestic and international students. Application fee: $60. Electronic applications accepted. *Expenses:* $1,596 per credit hour. *Financial support:* In 2017–18, 36 students received support, including 1 fellowship (averaging $23,000 per year), 20 research assistantships (averaging $28,000 per year), 15 teaching assistantships (averaging $28,000 per year); health care benefits and tuition waivers (full) also available. Financial award application deadline: 1/1. *Faculty research:* Evolution, ecology, genetics, cellular biology, molecular biology. *Total annual research expenditures:* $6.7 million. *Unit head:* Michael Welte, Professor and Chair, 585-276-3897, E-mail: michael.welte@rochester.edu. *Application contact:* Cynthia Landry, Administrative Assistant, 585-275-7991, E-mail: cynthia.landry@rochester.edu.
Website: https://www.sas.rochester.edu/bio/graduate/index.html

University of Rochester, School of Medicine and Dentistry, Graduate Programs in Medicine and Dentistry, Interdepartmental Program in Translational Biomedical Science, Rochester, NY 14627. Offers PhD.

University of Saint Joseph, Department of Biology, West Hartford, CT 06117-2700. Offers MS. *Program availability:* Part-time, online learning. *Degree requirements:* For master's, comprehensive exam, thesis or alternative. *Entrance requirements:* For master's, 2 letters of recommendation. *Application deadline:* Applications are processed on a rolling basis. Application fee: $50. Electronic applications accepted. Application fee is waived when completed online. *Financial support:* Unspecified assistantships available. Support available to part-time students. Financial award applicants required to submit FAFSA.
Website: https://www.usj.edu/academics/schools/sasbe/biology/

University of San Francisco, College of Arts and Sciences, Program in Biology, San Francisco, CA 94117-1080. Offers MS. *Degree requirements:* For master's, thesis. *Entrance requirements:* For master's, GRE General Test, GRE Subject Test (recommended), BS in biology or the equivalent. Additional exam requirements/recommendations for international students: Required—TOEFL, IELTS, PTE.

University of Saskatchewan, College of Graduate Studies and Research, College of Arts and Science, Department of Biology, Saskatoon, SK S7N 5A2, Canada. Offers M Sc, PhD. *Degree requirements:* For master's, thesis (for some programs); for doctorate, comprehensive exam (for some programs), thesis/dissertation. *Entrance requirements:* Additional exam requirements/recommendations for international students: Required—TOEFL (minimum score 80 iBT); Recommended—IELTS (minimum score 6.5). Electronic applications accepted.

University of Saskatchewan, Western College of Veterinary Medicine and College of Graduate Studies and Research, Graduate Programs in Veterinary Medicine, Department of Veterinary Biomedical Sciences, Saskatoon, SK S7N 5A2, Canada. Offers veterinary anatomy (M Sc); veterinary biomedical sciences (M Vet Sc); veterinary physiological sciences (M Sc, PhD). *Degree requirements:* For master's, thesis; for doctorate, comprehensive exam (for some programs), thesis/dissertation. *Entrance requirements:* Additional exam requirements/recommendations for international students: Required—TOEFL (minimum score 80 iBT); Recommended—IELTS (minimum score 6.5). Electronic applications accepted. *Faculty research:* Toxicology, animal reproduction, pharmacology, chloride channels, pulmonary pathobiology.

University of South Alabama, College of Arts and Sciences, Department of Biological Sciences, Mobile, AL 36688. Offers MS. *Program availability:* Part-time. *Faculty:* 8 full-time (4 women). *Students:* 9 full-time (4 women). Average age 26. 10 applicants, 20% accepted, 2 enrolled. In 2017, 2 master's awarded. *Degree requirements:* For master's, comprehensive exam, thesis. *Entrance requirements:* For master's, GRE minimum score of 300 (or MCAT with minimum score of 24 for applicants planning to enter a cellular/molecular area), minimum undergraduate GPA of 2.8 in all biological courses taken; undergraduate major in biology, botany, or zoology. Additional exam requirements/recommendations for international students: Required—TOEFL (minimum score 600 paper-based; 100 iBT). *Application deadline:* For fall admission, 7/1 priority date for domestic students, 6/1 priority date for international students; for spring admission, 12/1 priority date for domestic students, 11/1 priority date for international students; for summer admission, 5/1 priority date for domestic students, 4/1 for international students. Applications are processed on a rolling basis. Application fee: $35. Electronic applications accepted. *Expenses:* Tuition, state resident: full-time $10,104; part-time $421 per semester hour. Tuition, nonresident: full-time $20,208; part-time $842 per semester hour. *Financial support:* Fellowships, research assistantships, teaching assistantships, career-related internships or fieldwork, Federal Work-Study, institutionally sponsored loans, scholarships/grants, and unspecified assistantships available. Support available to part-time students. Financial award application deadline: 3/31; financial award applicants required to submit FAFSA. *Faculty research:* Marine biology, molecular biochemistry, plant taxonomy, fungal biology. *Unit head:* Dr. Tim Sherman, Chair, Biology, 251-460-6331, E-mail: tsherman@southalabama.edu.
Website: http://www.southalabama.edu/colleges/artsandsci/biology/

University of South Alabama, College of Medicine and Graduate School, Interdisciplinary Graduate Program in Basic Medical Sciences, Mobile, AL 36688-0002. Offers PhD. *Faculty:* 16 full-time (3 women). *Students:* 41 full-time (28 women), 3 part-time (0 women); includes 6 minority (5 Black or African American, non-Hispanic/Latino; 1 Hispanic/Latino), 8 international. Average age 29. 26 applicants, 38% accepted, 8 enrolled. In 2017, 7 doctorates awarded. *Degree requirements:* For doctorate, comprehensive exam, thesis/dissertation. *Entrance requirements:* For doctorate, GRE, two semesters or three quarters of undergraduate work in physics, general chemistry, organic chemistry, biology, English composition, and mathematics (including statistics and calculus) with minimum GPA of 3.0. Additional exam requirements/recommendations for international students: Required—TOEFL (minimum score 600 paper-based; 100 iBT). *Application deadline:* For fall admission, 3/31 for domestic and international students. Application fee: $75. Electronic applications accepted. *Expenses:* Contact institution. *Financial support:* In 2017–18, research assistantships with full tuition reimbursements (averaging $23,000 per year) were awarded; fellowships, teaching assistantships, career-related internships or fieldwork, institutionally sponsored loans, scholarships/grants, and unspecified assistantships also available. Support available to part-time students. Financial award application deadline: 3/31; financial award applicants required to submit FAFSA. *Faculty research:* Microcirculation, molecular biology, cell biology, growth control. *Unit head:* Dr. Mark Taylor, Director of

College of Medicine Graduate Studies, 251-460-6153, Fax: 251-460-6071, E-mail: mtaylor@southalabama.edu. *Application contact:* Lanette Flagge, Academic Advisor, 251-460-6153, Fax: 251-461-6071, E-mail: lflagge@southalabama.edu.
Website: http://www.usahealthsystem.com/PHDinBasicMedicalSciences

University of South Alabama, Graduate School, Program in Environmental Toxicology, Mobile, AL 36688. Offers basic medical sciences (MS); biology (MS); chemistry (MS); environmental toxicology (MS); exposure route and chemical transport (MS). *Faculty:* 3 full-time (0 women), 1 (woman) part-time/adjunct. *Students:* 9 full-time (2 women), 2 part-time (both women); includes 1 minority (Black or African American, non-Hispanic/Latino). Average age 26. 7 applicants, 29% accepted, 2 enrolled. In 2017, 3 master's awarded. *Degree requirements:* For master's, comprehensive exam, research project or thesis. *Entrance requirements:* For master's, GRE, BA/BS in related discipline, minimum undergraduate GPA of 3.0. Additional exam requirements/recommendations for international students: Required—TOEFL (minimum score 525 paper-based; 71 iBT). *Application deadline:* For fall admission, 7/15 for domestic students, 6/15 for international students; for spring admission, 12/1 for domestic students, 11/1 for international students. Application fee: $35. Electronic applications accepted. *Expenses:* Tuition, state resident: full-time $10,104; part-time $421 per semester hour. Tuition, nonresident: full-time $20,208; part-time $842 per semester hour. *Financial support:* Fellowships, research assistantships, teaching assistantships, career-related internships or fieldwork, Federal Work-Study, institutionally sponsored loans, scholarships/grants, and unspecified assistantships available. Support available to part-time students. Financial award application deadline: 3/31; financial award applicants required to submit FAFSA. *Unit head:* Dr. Harold Pardue, Dean of the Graduate School, 251-460-6310, E-mail: hpardue@southalabama.edu. *Application contact:* Dr. David Forbes, Chair, Chemistry, 251-460-6181, E-mail: dforbes@southalabama.edu.
Website: http://www.southalabama.edu/graduatemajors/etox/index.html

University of South Carolina, The Graduate School, College of Arts and Sciences, Department of Biological Sciences, Columbia, SC 29208. Offers biology (MS, PhD); biology education (IMA, MAT); ecology, evolution and organismal biology (MS, PhD); molecular, cellular, and developmental biology (MS, PhD). IMA and MAT offered in cooperation with the College of Education. Terminal master's awarded for partial completion of doctoral program. *Degree requirements:* For master's, one foreign language, thesis (for some programs); for doctorate, one foreign language, thesis/dissertation. *Entrance requirements:* For master's and doctorate, GRE General Test, minimum GPA of 3.0 in [illegible]. Electronic applications accepted. *Faculty research:* Marine ecology, population and evolutionary biology, molecular biology and genetics, development.

University of South Carolina, School of Medicine and The Graduate School, Graduate Programs in Medicine, Columbia, SC 29208. Offers biomedical science (MBS, PhD); genetic counseling (MS); nurse anesthesia (MNA); rehabilitation counseling (MRC, Certificate), including psychiatric rehabilitation (Certificate), rehabilitation counseling (MRC). Terminal master's awarded for partial completion of doctoral program. *Degree requirements:* For master's, comprehensive exam, thesis (for some programs), practicum; for doctorate, comprehensive exam, thesis/dissertation. *Entrance requirements:* For master's, doctorate, and Certificate, GRE General Test. Electronic applications accepted. *Expenses:* Contact institution. *Faculty research:* Cardiovascular diseases, oncology, neuroscience, psychiatric rehabilitation, genetics.

University of South Carolina, School of Medicine and The Graduate School, Graduate Programs in Medicine, Graduate Program in Biomedical Science, Doctoral Program in Biomedical Science, Columbia, SC 29208. Offers PhD. *Degree requirements:* For doctorate, comprehensive exam, thesis/dissertation. *Entrance requirements:* For doctorate, GRE General Test. Electronic applications accepted. *Faculty research:* Cancer, neuroscience, cardiovascular, reproductive, immunology.

University of South Carolina, School of Medicine and The Graduate School, Graduate Programs in Medicine, Graduate Program in Biomedical Science, Master's Program in Biomedical Science, Columbia, SC 29208. Offers MBS. *Degree requirements:* For master's, comprehensive exam, thesis. *Entrance requirements:* For master's, GRE General Test. Electronic applications accepted. *Faculty research:* Cardiovascular diseases, oncology, reproductive biology, neuroscience, microbiology.

University of South Dakota, Graduate School, College of Arts and Sciences, Department of Biology, Vermillion, SD 57069. Offers MS, PhD. *Degree requirements:* For master's, comprehensive exam (for some programs), thesis (for some programs); for doctorate, comprehensive exam, thesis/dissertation. *Entrance requirements:* For master's, GRE Subject Test, GRE General Test, minimum GPA of 2.7; for doctorate, GRE General Test, GRE Subject Test, minimum GPA of 2.7. Additional exam requirements/recommendations for international students: Required—TOEFL (minimum score 550 paper-based; 70 iBT). *Application deadline:* Applications are processed on a rolling basis. Application fee: $35. Electronic applications accepted. *Financial support:* Fellowships with partial tuition reimbursements, research assistantships with partial tuition reimbursements, teaching assistantships with partial tuition reimbursements, Federal Work-Study, and unspecified assistantships available. Support available to part-time students. Financial award applicants required to submit FAFSA. *Faculty research:* Evolutionary and ecological informatics, neuroscience, stress physiology. *Application contact:* Graduate School, 605-658-6140, Fax: 605-677-6118, E-mail: grad@usd.edu.
Website: http://www.usd.edu/biology

University of South Dakota, Graduate School, Sanford School of Medicine and Graduate School, Biomedical Sciences Graduate Program, Vermillion, SD 57069. Offers cardiovascular research (MS, PhD); cellular and molecular biology (MS, PhD); molecular microbiology and immunology (MS, PhD); neuroscience (MS, PhD); physiology and pharmacology (MS, PhD). Terminal master's awarded for partial completion of doctoral program. *Degree requirements:* For master's, thesis; for doctorate, comprehensive exam, thesis/dissertation. *Entrance requirements:* For master's and doctorate, GRE General Test, minimum GPA of 3.0. Additional exam requirements/recommendations for international students: Required—TOEFL (minimum score 550 paper-based; 80 iBT), IELTS (minimum score 6). *Application deadline:* For fall admission, 1/15 priority date for domestic students, 3/15 for international students. Applications are processed on a rolling basis. Application fee: $35. Electronic applications accepted. *Expenses:* Contact institution. *Financial support:* In 2017–18, 44 students received support. Fellowships with partial tuition reimbursements available, research assistantships with tuition reimbursements available, teaching assistantships, and unspecified assistantships available. Financial award application deadline: 4/15; financial award applicants required to submit FAFSA. *Faculty research:* Molecular biology, microbiology, neuroscience, cellular biology, physiology. *Total annual research expenditures:* $7.4 million. *Unit head:* 605-658-6322, Fax: 605-677-6381, E-mail: biomed@usd.edu.
Website: http://www.usd.edu/medicine/basic-biomedical-sciences/graduate

University of Southern California, Graduate School, Dana and David Dornsife College of Letters, Arts and Sciences, Department of Biological Sciences, Los Angeles, CA 90089. Offers biology (MS); computational molecular biology (MS); integrative and evolutionary biology (PhD); marine biology and biological oceanography (MS, PhD), including marine and environmental biology (MS), marine biology and biological oceanography (PhD); molecular and computational biology (PhD), including biology, computational biology and bioinformatics, molecular biology; neurobiology (PhD). Terminal master's awarded for partial completion of doctoral program. *Degree requirements:* For master's, comprehensive exam (for some programs), research paper; for doctorate, thesis/dissertation, qualifying examination, dissertation defense. *Entrance requirements:* For master's, GRE, 3 letters of recommendation, personal statement, resume, minimum GPA of 3.0; for doctorate, GRE, 3 letters of recommendation, resume, minimum GPA of 3.0. Additional exam requirements/recommendations for international students: Required—TOEFL (minimum score 600 paper-based; 100 iBT). Electronic applications accepted. *Faculty research:* Microarray data analysis, microbial ecology and genetics, integrative organismal and behavioral biology and ecology, stem cell pluipotency, cancer cell biology.

University of Southern California, Keck School of Medicine and Graduate School, Graduate Programs in Medicine, Los Angeles, CA 90033. Offers MPAP, MPH, MS, PhD, Certificate. *Faculty:* 320 full-time (114 women), 54 part-time/adjunct (28 women). *Students:* 943 full-time (652 women), 82 part-time (62 women); includes 486 minority (51 Black or African American, non-Hispanic/Latino; 2 American Indian or Alaska Native, non-Hispanic/Latino; 245 Asian, non-Hispanic/Latino; 159 Hispanic/Latino; 6 Native Hawaiian or other Pacific Islander, non-Hispanic/Latino; 23 Two or more races, non-Hispanic/Latino), 177 international. Average age 26. 2,191 applicants, 32% accepted, 402 enrolled. In 2017, 328 master's, 19 doctorates awarded. Terminal master's awarded for partial completion of doctoral program. *Entrance requirements:* For master's, GRE General Test, minimum GPA of 3.0; for doctorate, GRE General Test (minimum combined Verbal and Quantitative score of 1000), minimum GPA of 3.0. Additional exam requirements/recommendations for international students: Required—TOEFL (minimum score 600 paper-based; 100 iBT). *Application deadline:* Applications are processed on a rolling basis. Application fee: $90. Electronic applications accepted. *Expenses:* Contact institution. *Financial support:* Fellowships, research assistantships, teaching assistantships, career-related internships or fieldwork, Federal Work-Study, institutionally sponsored loans, scholarships/grants, traineeships, and health care benefits available. Support available to part-time students. Financial award applicants required to submit CSS PROFILE or FAFSA. *Unit head:* Dr. Ite Offringa, Associate Dean for Graduate Affairs, 323-442-1607, Fax: 323-442-1199, E-mail: ilaird@usc.edu. *Application contact:* Marisela Zuniga, Administrative Coordinator, 323-442-1607, Fax: 323-442-1199, E-mail: mzuniga@usc.edu.
Website: http://keck.usc.edu/

University of Southern Maine, College of Science, Technology, and Health, Program in Biology, Portland, ME 04103. Offers MS. *Faculty research:* Salt marsh plant ecology, marine microbial ecology, brain development, ecophysiology of marine cyanobacteria, evolution of mammalian social behavior.

University of Southern Mississippi, College of Science and Technology, Department of Biological Sciences, Hattiesburg, MS 39406-0001. Offers MS, PhD. *Students:* 14 full-time (9 women). 39 applicants, 41% accepted, 14 enrolled. Terminal master's awarded for partial completion of doctoral program. *Degree requirements:* For master's, comprehensive exam, thesis; for doctorate, comprehensive exam, thesis/dissertation. *Entrance requirements:* For master's, GRE General Test, minimum GPA of 3.0 on last 60 hours; for doctorate, GRE General Test, minimum GPA of 3.5. Additional exam requirements/recommendations for international students: Required—TOEFL, IELTS. *Application deadline:* For fall admission, 3/1 priority date for domestic students, 3/1 for international students; for spring admission, 1/10 priority date for domestic and international students. Applications are processed on a rolling basis. Application fee: $60. *Expenses:* Tuition, state resident: full-time $3830. *Financial support:* Research assistantships with full tuition reimbursements, teaching assistantships with full tuition reimbursements, Federal Work-Study, scholarships/grants, health care benefits, and unspecified assistantships available. Financial award application deadline: 3/15; financial award applicants required to submit FAFSA. *Unit head:* Dr. Janet Donaldson, Chair, 601-266-4748, Fax: 601-266-5797. *Application contact:* Dr. Jake Schaefer, Graduate Program Coordinator, 601-266-4928, Fax: 601-266-5797.
Website: https://www.usm.edu/biological-sciences

University of South Florida, College of Arts and Sciences, Department of Cell Biology, Microbiology, and Molecular Biology, Tampa, FL 33620-9951. Offers biology (MS), including cell biology, microbiology and molecular biology; cancer biology (PhD); cancer chemical biology (PhD); cancer immunology and immunotherapy (PhD); cell and molecular biology (PhD); microbiology (MS). *Faculty:* 19 full-time (6 women). *Students:* 81 full-time (55 women), 4 part-time (2 women); includes 12 minority (1 Black or African American, non-Hispanic/Latino; 2 Asian, non-Hispanic/Latino; 5 Hispanic/Latino; 4 Two or more races, non-Hispanic/Latino), 29 international. Average age 27. 159 applicants, 18% accepted, 23 enrolled. In 2017, 21 master's, 10 doctorates awarded. *Degree requirements:* For master's, thesis or alternative; for doctorate, comprehensive exam, thesis/dissertation. *Entrance requirements:* For master's and doctorate, GRE General Test, minimum GPA of 3.0, extensive background in biology or chemistry. Additional exam requirements/recommendations for international students: Required—TOEFL (minimum score 570 paper-based; 79 iBT) or IELTS (minimum score 6.5). *Application deadline:* For fall admission, 11/30 priority date for domestic and international students; for spring admission, 7/1 priority date for domestic students, 7/1 for international students. Application fee: $30. *Financial support:* In 2017–18, 10 students received support. Career-related internships or fieldwork, health care benefits, and unspecified assistantships available. Financial award application deadline: 4/1. *Faculty research:* Cell biology, microbiology and molecular biology: basic and applied science in bacterial pathogenesis, genome integrity and mechanisms of aging, structural and computational biology; cancer biology: immunology, cancer control, signal transduction, drug discovery, genomics. *Total annual research expenditures:* $1.8 million. *Unit head:* Dr. James Garey, Professor/Chair, 813-974-7103, Fax: 813-974-1614, E-mail: garey@usf.edu. *Application contact:* Dr. Kenneth Wright, Associate Professor of Cancer Biology, H. Lee Moffitt Cancer Center and Research Institute, 813-745-3918, Fax: 813-974-1614, E-mail: ken.wright@moffitt.org.
Website: http://biology.usf.edu/cmmb/

University of South Florida, College of Arts and Sciences, Department of Integrative Biology, Tampa, FL 33620-9951. Offers biology (MS), including ecology and evolution (MS, PhD), environmental and ecological microbiology (MS, PhD), physiology and morphology (MS, PhD); integrative biology (PhD), including ecology and evolution (MS, PhD), environmental and ecological microbiology (MS, PhD), physiology and morphology (MS, PhD). *Program availability:* Part-time. *Faculty:* 14 full-time (5 women). *Students:* 21 full-time (11 women), 1 (woman) part-time; includes 1 minority (Asian, non-Hispanic/Latino), 2 international. Average age 30. 35 applicants, 17% accepted, 5 enrolled. In 2017, 7 master's, 5 doctorates awarded. *Degree requirements:* For master's, comprehensive exam, thesis (for some programs); for doctorate, comprehensive exam, thesis/dissertation. *Entrance requirements:* For master's and doctorate, GRE General Test, minimum GPA of 3.0 in last 60 hours of BS. *Application deadline:* For fall admission, 11/30 priority date for domestic and international students; for spring admission, 7/1 priority date for domestic and international students. Application fee: $30. Electronic applications accepted. *Financial support:* In 2017–18, 7 students received

support. Research assistantships, teaching assistantships, and unspecified assistantships available. Financial award application deadline: 6/30; financial award applicants required to submit FAFSA. *Faculty research:* Marine ecology, ecosystem responses to urbanization, biomechanical and physiological mechanisms of animal movement, population biology and conservation, microbial ecology and public health microbiology, natural diversity of parasites and herbivores; ecosystems, vertebrates, disturbance ecology, functional and ecological morphology of feeding in fishes, rare amphibians and reptiles, genomics in ecological experiments, ecotoxicology, global carbon cycle, plant-animal interactions. *Total annual research expenditures:* $1.9 million. *Unit head:* Dr. Valerie Harwood, Professor and Chair, 813-974-1524, Fax: 813-974-3263, E-mail: vharwood@usf.edu. *Application contact:* Dr. Stephen Deban, Associate Professor and Graduate Program Director, 813-974-2242, E-mail: sdeban@usf.edu.
Website: http://biology.usf.edu/ib/grad/

University of South Florida, Morsani College of Medicine and College of Graduate Studies, Graduate Programs in Medical Sciences, Tampa, FL 33620-9951. Offers advanced athletic training (MS); athletic training (MS); bioinformatics and computational biology (MSBCB); biotechnology (MSB); health informatics (MSHI); medical sciences (MSMS, PhD), including aging and neuroscience (MSMS), allergy, immunology and infectious disease (PhD), anatomy, biochemistry and molecular biology, clinical and translational research, health science (MSMS), interdisciplinary medical sciences (MSMS), medical microbiology and immunology (MSMS), metabolic and nutritional medicine (MSMS), microbiology and immunology (PhD), molecular medicine, molecular pharmacology and physiology (PhD), neuroscience (PhD), pathology and cell biology (PhD), women's health (MSMS). *Students:* 372 full-time (212 women), 216 part-time (142 women); includes 257 minority (78 Black or African American, non-Hispanic/Latino; 1 American Indian or Alaska Native, non-Hispanic/Latino; 79 Asian, non-Hispanic/Latino; 84 Hispanic/Latino; 15 Two or more races, non-Hispanic/Latino), 62 international. Average age 28. 1,048 applicants, 46% accepted, 309 enrolled. In 2017, 351 master's, 56 doctorates awarded. Terminal master's awarded for partial completion of doctoral program. *Degree requirements:* For master's, comprehensive exam, thesis; for doctorate, comprehensive exam, thesis/dissertation. *Entrance requirements:* For master's, GRE General Test or GMAT, bachelor's degree or equivalent from regionally-accredited university with minimum GPA of 3.0 in upper-division sciences coursework; prerequisites in general biology, general chemistry, general physics, organic chemistry, quantitative analysis, and integral and differential calculus; for doctorate, GRE General Test, bachelor's degree from regionally-accredited university with minimum GPA of 3.0 in upper-division sciences coursework; 3 letters of recommendation; personal interview; 1-2 page personal statement; prerequisites in biology, chemistry, physics, organic chemistry, quantitative analysis, and integral/differential calculus. Additional exam requirements/recommendations for international students: Required—TOEFL (minimum score 550 paper-based; 79 iBT) or IELTS (minimum score 6.5). *Application deadline:* For fall admission, 2/1 priority date for domestic students, 2/1 for international students. Application fee: $30. Electronic applications accepted. *Expenses:* Contact institution. *Financial support:* In 2017–18, 109 students received support. *Faculty research:* Anatomy, biochemistry, cancer biology, cardiovascular disease, cell biology, immunology, microbiology, molecular biology, neuroscience, pharmacology, physiology. *Total annual research expenditures:* $45.3 million. *Unit head:* Dr. Michael Barber, Professor/Associate Dean for Graduate and Postdoctoral Affairs, 813-974-9908, Fax: 813-974-4317, E-mail: mbarber@health.usf.edu. *Application contact:* Dr. Eric Bennett, Graduate Director, PhD Program in Medical Sciences, 813-974-1545, Fax: 813-974-4317, E-mail: esbennet@health.usf.edu.
Website: http://health.usf.edu/nocms/medicine/graduatestudies/

The University of Tennessee, Graduate School, College of Arts and Sciences, Program in Life Sciences, Knoxville, TN 37996. Offers genome science and technology (MS, PhD); plant physiology and genetics (MS, PhD). *Degree requirements:* For doctorate, one foreign language, thesis/dissertation. *Entrance requirements:* For master's and doctorate, GRE General Test, minimum GPA of 2.7. Additional exam requirements/recommendations for international students: Required—TOEFL. Electronic applications accepted.

The University of Tennessee, Graduate School, Intercollegiate Programs, Program in Comparative and Experimental Medicine, Knoxville, TN 37996. Offers MS, PhD. *Degree requirements:* For master's, thesis; for doctorate, thesis/dissertation. *Entrance requirements:* For master's and doctorate, GRE General Test, minimum GPA of 2.7. Additional exam requirements/recommendations for international students: Required—TOEFL. Electronic applications accepted.

The University of Tennessee Health Science Center, College of Graduate Health Sciences, Memphis, TN 38163. Offers biomedical engineering (MS, PhD); biomedical sciences (PhD); dental sciences (MDS); epidemiology (MS); health outcomes and policy research (PhD); laboratory research and management (MS); nursing science (PhD); pharmaceutical sciences (PhD); pharmacology (MS); speech and hearing science (PhD); DDS/PhD; DNP/PhD; MD/PhD; Pharm D/PhD. MS and PhD programs in biomedical engineering offered jointly with University of Memphis. *Faculty:* 528 full-time (176 women). *Students:* 258 full-time (130 women); includes 87 minority (14 Black or African American, non-Hispanic/Latino; 68 Asian, non-Hispanic/Latino; 5 Hispanic/Latino). Average age 28. 673 applicants, 17% accepted, 102 enrolled. In 2017, 23 master's, 30 doctorates awarded. Terminal master's awarded for partial completion of doctoral program. *Degree requirements:* For master's, comprehensive exam, thesis; for doctorate, thesis/dissertation, oral and written preliminary and comprehensive exams. *Entrance requirements:* For master's and doctorate, GRE General Test, minimum GPA of 3.0. Additional exam requirements/recommendations for international students: Recommended—TOEFL (minimum score 79 iBT), IELTS (minimum score 6.5). *Application deadline:* For winter admission, 1/1 for domestic and international students; for spring admission, 3/1 for domestic and international students. Applications are processed on a rolling basis. Application fee: $0. Electronic applications accepted. *Expenses:* Contact institution. *Financial support:* In 2017–18, 150 students received support, including 150 research assistantships (averaging $25,000 per year); fellowships, institutionally sponsored loans, scholarships/grants, health care benefits, and tuition waivers (full and partial) also available. Support available to part-time students. *Faculty research:* Cell biology, epidemiology, biomedical engineering, speech and hearing science, health policy, pharmaceutical sciences, dental sciences, nursing science, pharmacology. *Unit head:* Dr. Donald B. Thomason, Dean, 901-448-5538, E-mail: dthomaso@uthsc.edu. *Application contact:* Dr. Isaac O. Donkor, Associate Dean for Student Affairs, 901-448-5538, E-mail: idonkor@uthsc.edu.
Website: http://grad.uthsc.edu/

The University of Tennessee–Oak Ridge National Laboratory, Graduate Program in Genome Science and Technology, Knoxville, TN 37966. Offers life sciences (MS, PhD). *Degree requirements:* For master's, thesis; for doctorate, comprehensive exam, thesis/dissertation. *Entrance requirements:* For master's and doctorate, GRE General Test. Additional exam requirements/recommendations for international students: Required—TOEFL. Electronic applications accepted. *Faculty research:* Genetics/genomics, structural biology/proteomics, computational biology/bioinformatics, bioanalytical technologies.

The University of Texas at Arlington, Graduate School, College of Science, Department of Biology, Arlington, TX 76019. Offers biology (MS); quantitative biology (PhD). *Program availability:* Part-time, evening/weekend. *Degree requirements:* For master's, thesis, oral defense of thesis; for doctorate, comprehensive exam, thesis/dissertation, oral defense of dissertation. *Entrance requirements:* For master's and doctorate, GRE General Test. Additional exam requirements/recommendations for international students: Required—TOEFL (minimum score 550 paper-based; 79 iBT). Electronic applications accepted. *Faculty research:* Cellular and microbiology, comparative genomics, evolution and ecology.

The University of Texas at Austin, Graduate School, College of Natural Sciences, School of Biological Sciences, Austin, TX 78712-1111. Offers ecology, evolution and behavior (PhD); microbiology (PhD); plant biology (MA, PhD). *Entrance requirements:* For master's and doctorate, GRE General Test. Electronic applications accepted.

The University of Texas at Dallas, School of Natural Sciences and Mathematics, Department of Biological Sciences, Richardson, TX 75080. Offers bioinformatics and computational biology (MS); biotechnology (MS); molecular and cell biology (MS, PhD). *Program availability:* Part-time, evening/weekend. *Faculty:* 22 full-time (4 women), 3 part-time/adjunct (2 women). *Students:* 107 full-time (64 women), 26 part-time (11 women); includes 24 minority (3 Black or African American, non-Hispanic/Latino; 12 Asian, non-Hispanic/Latino; 5 Hispanic/Latino; 4 Two or more races, non-Hispanic/Latino), 76 international. Average age 27. 307 applicants, 23% accepted, 45 enrolled. In 2017, 37 master's, 9 doctorates awarded. *Degree requirements:* For master's, thesis optional; for doctorate, thesis/dissertation, publishable paper. *Entrance requirements:* For master's and doctorate, GRE (minimum combined score of 1000 on verbal and quantitative). Additional exam requirements/recommendations for international students: Required—TOEFL (minimum score 550 paper-based; 80 iBT). *Application deadline:* For fall admission, 7/15 for domestic students, 5/1 priority date for international students; for spring admission, 11/15 for domestic students, 9/1 priority date for international students. Applications are processed on a rolling basis. Application fee: $50 ($100 for international students). Electronic applications accepted. *Expenses:* Tuition, state resident: full-time $12,916; part-time $718 per credit hour. Tuition, nonresident: full-time $25,252; part-time $1403 per credit hour. *Financial support:* In 2017–18, 78 students received support, including 14 research assistantships with partial tuition reimbursements available (averaging $25,380 per year), 59 teaching assistantships with partial tuition reimbursements available (averaging $17,265 per year); fellowships with partial tuition reimbursements available, career-related internships or fieldwork, Federal Work-Study, institutionally sponsored loans, scholarships/grants, and unspecified assistantships also available. Support available to part-time students. Financial award application deadline: 4/30; financial award applicants required to submit FAFSA. *Faculty research:* Role of mitochondria in neurodegenerative diseases, protein-DNA interactions in site-specific recombination, eukaryotic gene expression, bio-nanotechnology, sickle cell research. *Unit head:* Dr. Stephen Spiro, Department Head, 972-883-6032, Fax: 972-883-4551, E-mail: stephen.spiro@utdallas.edu. *Application contact:* Dr. Lawrence Reitzer, Graduate Advisor, 972-883-2502, Fax: 972-883-4551, E-mail: reitzer@utdallas.edu.
Website: http://www.utdallas.edu/biology/

The University of Texas at El Paso, Graduate School, College of Science, Department of Biological Sciences, El Paso, TX 79968-0001. Offers bioinformatics (MS); biological sciences (MS, PhD). *Program availability:* Part-time, evening/weekend. *Degree requirements:* For master's, thesis; for doctorate, thesis/dissertation. *Entrance requirements:* For master's, GRE, minimum GPA of 3.0, letters of recommendation; for doctorate, GRE, statement of purpose, letters of recommendation. Additional exam requirements/recommendations for international students: Required—TOEFL; Recommended—IELTS. *Application deadline:* For fall admission, 8/1 priority date for domestic students, 3/1 for international students; for spring admission, 11/1 priority date for domestic students, 9/1 for international students. Applications are processed on a rolling basis. Application fee: $45 ($80 for international students). Electronic applications accepted. *Financial support:* Fellowships with partial tuition reimbursements, research assistantships with partial tuition reimbursements, teaching assistantships with partial tuition reimbursements, institutionally sponsored loans, scholarships/grants, health care benefits, tuition waivers (partial), and unspecified assistantships available. Support available to part-time students. Financial award application deadline: 3/15; financial award applicants required to submit FAFSA.

The University of Texas at San Antonio, College of Sciences, Department of Biology, San Antonio, TX 78249-0617. Offers biology (MS); biotechnology (MS); cell and molecular biology (PhD); neurobiology (PhD). *Faculty:* 37 full-time (10 women), 1 part-time/adjunct (0 women). *Students:* 111 full-time (64 women), 50 part-time (25 women); includes 76 minority (5 Black or African American, non-Hispanic/Latino; 1 American Indian or Alaska Native, non-Hispanic/Latino; 11 Asian, non-Hispanic/Latino; 55 Hispanic/Latino; 1 Native Hawaiian or other Pacific Islander, non-Hispanic/Latino; 3 Two or more races, non-Hispanic/Latino), 30 international. Average age 27. 153 applicants, 55% accepted, 57 enrolled. In 2017, 17 master's, 3 doctorates awarded. Terminal master's awarded for partial completion of doctoral program. *Degree requirements:* For master's, comprehensive exam, thesis or alternative; for doctorate, comprehensive exam, thesis/dissertation. *Entrance requirements:* For master's, GRE General Test, bachelor's degree with 18 credit hours in field of study or in another appropriate field of study; for doctorate, GRE General Test, 3 letters of recommendation, statement of purpose, resume. Additional exam requirements/recommendations for international students: Required—TOEFL (minimum score 500 paper-based; 100 iBT), IELTS (minimum score 5). *Application deadline:* For fall admission, 6/15 for domestic students, 3/1 for international students; for spring admission, 10/15 for domestic students, 9/15 for international students. Application fee: $50 ($90 for international students). Electronic applications accepted. *Expenses:* Tuition, state resident: full-time $5495. Tuition, nonresident: full-time $21,938. *Required fees:* $1915. Tuition and fees vary according to program. *Faculty research:* Development of human and veterinary vaccines against a fungal disease, mammalian germ cells and stem cells, dopamine neuron physiology and addiction, plant biochemistry, dendritic computation and synaptic plasticity. *Total annual research expenditures:* $9.1 million. *Unit head:* Dr. Garry Sunter, Chair, 210-458-5479, E-mail: garry.sunter@utsa.edu.
Website: http://bio.utsa.edu/

The University of Texas at Tyler, College of Arts and Sciences, Department of Biology, Tyler, TX 75799-0001. Offers biology (MS); interdisciplinary studies (MSIS). *Degree requirements:* For master's, comprehensive exam, thesis, oral qualifying exam, thesis defense. *Entrance requirements:* For master's, GRE General Test, GRE Subject Test, bachelor's degree in biology or equivalent. Additional exam requirements/recommendations for international students: Required—TOEFL. Electronic applications accepted. *Faculty research:* Phenotypic plasticity and heritability of life history traits, invertebrate ecology and genetics, systematics and phylogenetics of reptiles, hibernation physiology in turtles, landscape ecology, host-microbe interaction, outer membrane proteins in bacteria.

The University of Texas Health Science Center at Houston, MD Anderson UTHealth Graduate School, Houston, TX 77225-0036. Offers biochemistry and cell biology (PhD); biomedical sciences (MS); cancer biology (PhD); genetic counseling (MS); genetics and epigenetics (PhD); immunology (PhD); medical physics (MS, PhD); microbiology and infectious diseases (PhD); neuroscience (PhD); quantitative sciences (PhD); therapeutics and pharmacology (PhD); MD/PhD. Terminal master's awarded for partial completion of doctoral program. *Degree requirements:* For master's, thesis; for doctorate, thesis/dissertation. *Entrance requirements:* For master's and doctorate, GRE General Test. Additional exam requirements/recommendations for international students: Required—TOEFL. Electronic applications accepted. *Faculty research:* Biomedical sciences.

The University of Texas Health Science Center at San Antonio, Graduate School of Biomedical Sciences, Integrated Biomedical Sciences Program, San Antonio, TX 78229-3900. Offers PhD. *Degree requirements:* For doctorate, comprehensive exam, thesis/dissertation.

The University of Texas Medical Branch, Graduate School of Biomedical Sciences, Galveston, TX 77555. Offers MA, MMS, MPH, MS, PhD, MD/PhD. Terminal master's awarded for partial completion of doctoral program. *Degree requirements:* For master's, comprehensive exam (for some programs), thesis or alternative; for doctorate, comprehensive exam, thesis/dissertation. *Entrance requirements:* For master's and doctorate, GRE General Test, 3 letters of recommendation. Additional exam requirements/recommendations for international students: Required—TOEFL (minimum score 550 paper-based; 80 iBT), IELTS (minimum score 6.5). Electronic applications accepted. *Expenses:* Contact institution.

The University of Texas of the Permian Basin, Office of Graduate Studies, College of Arts and Sciences, Department of Biology, Odessa, TX 79762-0001. Offers MS. *Program availability:* Part-time, evening/weekend. *Degree requirements:* For master's, comprehensive exam, thesis or alternative. *Entrance requirements:* For master's, GRE General Test. Additional exam requirements/recommendations for international students: Required—TOEFL (minimum score 550 paper-based).

The University of Texas Rio Grande Valley, College of Sciences, Department of Biology, Edinburg, TX 78539. Offers MS. *Program availability:* Part-time, evening/weekend. *Faculty:* 18 full-time (6 women), 1 part-time/adjunct (0 women). *Students:* 31 full-time (20 women), 27 part-time (15 women); includes 43 minority (42 Hispanic/Latino; 1 Two or more races, non-Hispanic/Latino). Average age 26. 17 applicants, 71% accepted, 10 enrolled. In 2017, 21 master's awarded. *Degree requirements:* For master's, comprehensive exam, thesis optional, minimum GPA of 3.0 overall and in all higher biology courses. *Entrance requirements:* For master's, GRE General Test, 24 hours of undergraduate courses in biological sciences or closely-related disciplines with minimum GPA of 3.0. Additional exam requirements/recommendations for international students: Required—TOEFL or IELTS. *Application deadline:* For fall admission, 6/1 for domestic and international students; for spring admission, 11/1 for domestic students, 10/1 for international students; for summer admission, 5/1 for domestic students, 3/1 for international students. Applications are processed on a rolling basis. Application fee: $50 ($100 for international students). Electronic applications accepted. *Expenses:* Tuition, state resident: full-time $5550; part-time $417 per credit hour. Tuition, nonresident: full-time $13,020; part-time $832 per credit hour. *Required fees:* $1169. *Financial support:* Application deadline: 6/1. *Faculty research:* Flora and fauna of South Padre Island, plant taxonomy of Rio Grande Valley. *Unit head:* Kristine Lowe, Interim Chair, E-mail: kristine.lowe@utrgv.edu.
Website: http://portal.utpa.edu/utpa_main/daa_home/cose_home/biology_home/biology_graduate

The University of Texas Southwestern Medical Center, Southwestern Graduate School of Biomedical Sciences, Clinical Science Program, Dallas, TX 75390. Offers MCS, MSCS. *Program availability:* Part-time. *Degree requirements:* For master's, 1-year clinical research project. *Entrance requirements:* For master's, graduate degree in biomedical science. Electronic applications accepted.

The University of Texas Southwestern Medical Center, Southwestern Graduate School of Biomedical Sciences, Division of Basic Science, Dallas, TX 75390. Offers biological chemistry (PhD); biomedical engineering (MS, PhD); cancer biology (PhD); cell regulation (PhD); genetics and development (PhD); immunology (PhD); integrative biology (PhD); molecular biophysics (PhD); molecular microbiology (PhD); neuroscience (PhD); MD/PhD. *Degree requirements:* For doctorate, thesis/dissertation, qualifying exam. *Entrance requirements:* For doctorate, GRE General Test, research experience. Additional exam requirements/recommendations for international students: Required—TOEFL. Electronic applications accepted.

The University of Texas Southwestern Medical Center, Southwestern Graduate School of Biomedical Sciences, Medical Scientist Training Program, Dallas, TX 75390. Offers PhD, MD/PhD. Electronic applications accepted.

University of the Incarnate Word, School of Mathematics, Science, and Engineering, San Antonio, TX 78209-6397. Offers applied statistics (MS); biology (MA, MS); mathematics (MA), including teaching; multidisciplinary sciences (MA); nutrition (MS). *Program availability:* Part-time, evening/weekend. *Faculty:* 9 full-time (4 women), 3 part-time/adjunct (1 woman). *Students:* 42 full-time (33 women), 6 part-time (5 women); includes 27 minority (2 Black or African American, non-Hispanic/Latino; 1 American Indian or Alaska Native, non-Hispanic/Latino; 1 Asian, non-Hispanic/Latino; 23 Hispanic/Latino), 6 international. In 2017, 13 master's awarded. *Degree requirements:* For master's, comprehensive exam (for some programs), thesis optional, capstone. *Entrance requirements:* For master's, GRE, recommendation letter. Additional exam requirements/recommendations for international students: Required—TOEFL (minimum score 560 paper-based; 83 iBT). *Application deadline:* Applications are processed on a rolling basis. Application fee: $20. Electronic applications accepted. *Expenses: Tuition:* Full-time $16,470; part-time $915 per credit hour. Tuition and fees vary according to degree level, program and student level. *Financial support:* In 2017–18, 1 research assistantship (averaging $5,000 per year) was awarded; Federal Work-Study, scholarships/grants, tuition waivers (partial), and unspecified assistantships also available. Financial award applicants required to submit FAFSA. *Faculty research:* Neural morphallaxis in lumbriculus variegatus, igneous and metamorphic petrology, applied cloud and precipitation physics, DNA-protein interactions, evolution of adenoviruses and picornaviruses. *Unit head:* Dr. Carlos A. Garcia, Dean, 210-829-2717, Fax: 210-829-3153, E-mail: cagarci9@uiwtx.edu. *Application contact:* Johnny Garcia, Graduate Admissions Counselor, 210-805-3554, Fax: 210-829-3921, E-mail: admis@uiwtx.edu.
Website: http://www.uiw.edu/smse/index.htm

University of the Pacific, College of the Pacific, Department of Biological Sciences, Stockton, CA 95211-0197. Offers MS. *Faculty:* 16 full-time (5 women), 2 part-time/adjunct (1 woman). *Students:* 1 (woman) full-time, 26 part-time (13 women); includes 13 minority (7 Asian, non-Hispanic/Latino; 4 Hispanic/Latino; 2 Two or more races, non-Hispanic/Latino), 2 international. Average age 25. 22 applicants, 55% accepted, 10 enrolled. In 2017, 8 master's awarded. *Degree requirements:* For master's, thesis. *Entrance requirements:* For master's, GRE General Test, GRE Subject Test. Additional exam requirements/recommendations for international students: Required—TOEFL. *Application deadline:* For fall admission, 3/1 priority date for domestic students; for spring admission, 10/1 priority date for domestic students. Applications are processed on a rolling basis. Application fee: $75. *Financial support:* Teaching assistantships and institutionally sponsored loans available. Support available to part-time students. Financial award application deadline: 3/1; financial award applicants required to submit FAFSA. *Unit head:* Dr. Craig Vierra, Co-Chairman, 209-946-2181, E-mail: cvierra@pacific.edu. *Application contact:* Information Contact, 209-946-2181.
Website: http://www.pacific.edu/Academics/Schools-and-Colleges/College-of-the-Pacific/Academics/Departments-and-Programs/Biological-Sciences/Academics/Graduate

The University of Toledo, College of Graduate Studies, College of Medicine and Life Sciences, Interdepartmental Programs, Toledo, OH 43606-3390. Offers bioinformatics and proteomics/genomics (MSBS); biomarkers and bioinformatics (Certificate); biomarkers and diagnostics (PSM); human donation sciences (MSBS); medical sciences (MSBS); MD/MSBS. *Degree requirements:* For master's, thesis or alternative. *Entrance requirements:* For master's, GRE, minimum undergraduate GPA of 3.0, three letters of recommendation, statement of purpose, transcripts from all prior institutions attended, resume; for Certificate, minimum undergraduate GPA of 3.0, three letters of recommendation, statement of purpose, transcripts from all prior institutions attended, resume. Additional exam requirements/recommendations for international students: Required—TOEFL (minimum score 550 paper-based; 80 iBT). Electronic applications accepted.

The University of Toledo, College of Graduate Studies, College of Natural Sciences and Mathematics, Department of Biological Sciences, Toledo, OH 43606-3390. Offers biology (MS, PhD). *Program availability:* Part-time. *Degree requirements:* For master's, thesis or alternative; for doctorate, thesis/dissertation. *Entrance requirements:* For master's and doctorate, GRE General Test, GRE Subject Test, minimum cumulative point-hour ratio of 2.7 for all previous academic work, three letters of recommendation, statement of purpose, transcripts from all prior institutions attended. Additional exam requirements/recommendations for international students: Required—TOEFL (minimum score 550 paper-based; 80 iBT). Electronic applications accepted. *Faculty research:* Biochemical parasitology, physiological ecology, animal physiology.

The University of Toledo, College of Graduate Studies, College of Natural Sciences and Mathematics, Department of Environmental Sciences, Toledo, OH 43606-3390. Offers biology (MS, PhD), including ecology; geology (MS), including earth surface processes. *Program availability:* Part-time. *Degree requirements:* For master's, thesis or alternative. *Entrance requirements:* For master's, GRE General Test, minimum cumulative point-hour ratio of 2.7 for all previous academic work, three letters of recommendation, statement of purpose, transcripts from all prior institutions attended. Additional exam requirements/recommendations for international students: Required—TOEFL (minimum score 550 paper-based; 80 iBT). Electronic applications accepted. *Faculty research:* Environmental geochemistry, geophysics, petrology and mineralogy, paleontology, geohydrology.

The University of Tulsa, Graduate School, College of Engineering and Natural Sciences, Department of Biological Science, Tulsa, OK 74104-3189. Offers MS, MTA, PhD, JD/MS. *Program availability:* Part-time. *Faculty:* 11 full-time (2 women). *Students:* 16 full-time (6 women), 7 part-time (2 women); includes 7 minority (4 American Indian or Alaska Native, non-Hispanic/Latino; 3 Hispanic/Latino), 6 international. Average age 31. 25 applicants, 28% accepted, 6 enrolled. In 2017, 2 master's, 4 doctorates awarded. Terminal master's awarded for partial completion of doctoral program. *Degree requirements:* For master's, thesis, oral exams; for doctorate, comprehensive exam, thesis/dissertation. *Entrance requirements:* For master's and doctorate, GRE General Test. Additional exam requirements/recommendations for international students: Required—TOEFL (minimum score 550 paper-based; 80 iBT), IELTS (minimum score 6). *Application deadline:* Applications are processed on a rolling basis. Application fee: $55. Electronic applications accepted. *Expenses: Tuition:* Full-time $22,230. *Required fees:* $2000. Tuition and fees vary according to course load and program. *Financial support:* In 2017–18, 27 students received support, including 20 fellowships with full tuition reimbursements available (averaging $5,341 per year), 4 research assistantships with full tuition reimbursements available (averaging $14,080 per year), 10 teaching assistantships with full tuition reimbursements available (averaging $13,500 per year); career-related internships or fieldwork, Federal Work-Study, scholarships/grants, health care benefits, tuition waivers (full and partial), and unspecified assistantships also available. Support available to part-time students. Financial award application deadline: 2/1; financial award applicants required to submit FAFSA. *Faculty research:* Aerobiology, animal behavior and behavioral ecology, cell and molecular biology, ecology, developmental biology, genetics, herpetology, glycobiology, immunology, microbiology, morphology, mycology, ornithology, molecular systematic and virology. *Total annual research expenditures:* $232,593. *Unit head:* Dr. Estelle Levetin, Chairperson, 918-631-2764, Fax: 918-631-2762, E-mail: estelle-levetin@utulsa.edu. *Application contact:* Dr. Harrington Wells, Advisor, 918-631-3071, Fax: 918-631-2762, E-mail: harrington-wells@utulsa.edu.
Website: http://engineering.utulsa.edu/academics/biological-science/

University of Utah, Graduate School, College of Science, Department of Biology, Salt Lake City, UT 84112. Offers MS, PhD. *Program availability:* Part-time. *Faculty:* 44 full-time (9 women), 25 part-time/adjunct (12 women). *Students:* 55 full-time (24 women), 20 part-time (7 women); includes 12 minority (1 Black or African American, non-Hispanic/Latino; 5 Asian, non-Hispanic/Latino; 4 Hispanic/Latino; 2 Two or more races, non-Hispanic/Latino), 15 international. Average age 24. 142 applicants, 14% accepted, 14 enrolled. In 2017, 2 master's, 7 doctorates awarded. Terminal master's awarded for partial completion of doctoral program. *Entrance requirements:* For master's and doctorate, GRE General Test, minimum GPA of 3.0. Additional exam requirements/recommendations for international students: Required—TOEFL (minimum score 500 paper-based; 80 iBT). Application fee: $55 ($65 for international students). Electronic applications accepted. Application fee is waived when completed online. *Financial support:* In 2017–18, 82 students received support. Fellowships, research assistantships, teaching assistantships, career-related internships or fieldwork, scholarships/grants, traineeships, and health care benefits available. Financial award application deadline: 3/15; financial award applicants required to submit FAFSA. *Faculty research:* Ecology, evolutionary biology, cell and developmental biology, physiology and organismal biology, molecular biology, biochemistry, microbiology, plant biology, neurobiology, genetics. *Total annual research expenditures:* $10.4 million. *Unit head:* Dr. M. Denise Dearing, Department Chair, 801-585-1298, E-mail: denise.dearing@utah.edu. *Application contact:* Shannon Nielsen, Administrative Program Coordinator, 801-581-5636, Fax: 801-581-4668, E-mail: shannon.nielsen@bioscience.utah.edu.
Website: http://www.biology.utah.edu

University of Utah, School of Medicine and Graduate School, Graduate Programs in Medicine, Salt Lake City, UT 84112-1107. Offers M Phil, M Stat, MPAS, MPH, MS, MSPH, PhD, Certificate. *Program availability:* Part-time. *Degree requirements:* For doctorate, thesis/dissertation. *Entrance requirements:* For doctorate, MCAT. Electronic applications accepted. *Faculty research:* Molecular biology, biochemistry, cell biology, immunology, bioengineering.

University of Vermont, Graduate College, College of Arts and Sciences, Department of Biology, Burlington, VT 05405. Offers biology (MS, PhD); biology education (MST). *Students:* 31 (21 women); includes 2 minority (both Hispanic/Latino), 6 international. 26 applicants, 35% accepted, 2 enrolled. In 2017, 1 master's, 3 doctorates awarded.

Degree requirements: For master's, thesis; for doctorate, thesis/dissertation. *Entrance requirements:* For master's and doctorate, GRE General Test. Additional exam requirements/recommendations for international students: Required—TOEFL (minimum score 550 paper-based, 90 iBT) or IELTS (6.5). *Application deadline:* For fall admission, 12/15 for domestic and international students. Application fee: $65. Electronic applications accepted. *Expenses:* Tuition, state resident: full-time $11,628; part-time $646 per credit. Tuition, nonresident: full-time $29,340; part-time $1630 per credit. *Required fees:* $1994; $10 per credit. Tuition and fees vary according to course load and program. *Financial support:* In 2017–18, 30 students received support, including 5 research assistantships with full tuition reimbursements available (averaging $22,000 per year), 25 teaching assistantships with full tuition reimbursements available (averaging $20,000 per year); fellowships and health care benefits also available. Financial award application deadline: 3/1. *Application contact:* Dr. Nicholas Gotelli, Coordinator, 802-656-2922, E-mail: nicholas.gotelli@uvm.edu.
Website: https://www.uvm.edu/cas/biology/graduate-programs-overview

University of Vermont, Graduate College, Cross-College Interdisciplinary Program, Cellular, Molecular and Biomedical Sciences Program, Burlington, VT 05405. Offers PhD. *Students:* 48 (26 women). Average age 29. 74 applicants, 35% accepted, 9 enrolled. In 2017, 6 doctorates awarded. *Degree requirements:* For doctorate, thesis/dissertation. *Entrance requirements:* For doctorate, GRE General Test. Additional exam requirements/recommendations for international students: Required—TOEFL (minimum score 550 paper-based; 100 iBT), IELTS (minimum score 7). *Application deadline:* For fall admission, 12/1 for domestic and international students. Application fee: $65. Electronic applications accepted. *Expenses:* Tuition, state resident: full-time $11,628; part-time $646 per credit. Tuition, nonresident: full-time $29,340; part-time $1630 per credit. *Required fees:* $1994; $10 per credit. Tuition and fees vary according to course load and program. *Financial support:* In 2017–18, 16 research assistantships with full tuition reimbursements (averaging $28,000 per year), 33 teaching assistantships with full tuition reimbursements (averaging $28,000 per year) were awarded; fellowships and career-related internships or fieldwork also available. Financial award application deadline: 3/1. *Faculty research:* Cancer biology and genome stability, genomics and computational biology, immunology and microbial pathogenesis, stem cell and developmental biology, lung and cardiovascular biology. *Unit head:* Dr. Matthew Poynter, Director, 802-656-8045, E-mail: cmb@uvm.edu. *Application contact:* Jessica Lalime, Administrator, 802-656-9673, E-mail: cmb@uvm.edu.
Website: https://www.uvm.edu/cmb

University of Vermont, The Robert Larner, MD College of Medicine and Graduate College, Graduate Programs in Medicine, Program in Medical Science, Burlington, VT 05405. Offers MS. *Students:* 33 part-time (12 women). 167 applicants, 55% accepted, 33 enrolled. In 2017, 17 master's awarded. *Entrance requirements:* For master's, MCAT or GRE. Additional exam requirements/recommendations for international students: Required—TOEFL (minimum iBT score of 90) or IELTS (6.5). *Application deadline:* For fall admission, 6/15 for domestic and international students; for summer admission, 2/15 for domestic and international students. Application fee: $65. Electronic applications accepted. *Expenses:* Tuition, state resident: full-time $11,628; part-time $646 per credit. Tuition, nonresident: full-time $29,340; part-time $1630 per credit. *Required fees:* $1994; $10 per credit. Tuition and fees vary according to course load and program. *Unit head:* Dr. Karen Lounsbury, Director, 802-656-9925, E-mail: karen.lounsbury@med.uvm.edu.
Website: https://learn.uvm.edu/program/uvm-master-of-medical-science-degree/

University of Victoria, Faculty of Graduate Studies, Faculty of Science, Department of Biology, Victoria, BC V8W 2Y2, Canada. Offers M Sc, PhD. *Degree requirements:* For master's, thesis, seminar; for doctorate, thesis/dissertation, seminar, candidacy exam. *Entrance requirements:* For master's and doctorate, GRE General Test, minimum B+ average in previous 2 years of biology course work. Additional exam requirements/recommendations for international students: Required—TOEFL (minimum score 575 paper-based), IELTS (minimum score 7). Electronic applications accepted. *Faculty research:* Neurobiology of vertebrates and invertebrates, physiology, reproduction and tissue culture of forest trees, evolution and ecology, cell and molecular biology, molecular biology of environmental health.

University of Virginia, College and Graduate School of Arts and Sciences, Department of Biology, Charlottesville, VA 22903. Offers MA, MS, PhD. *Faculty:* 37 full-time (9 women), 2 part-time/adjunct (1 woman). *Students:* 57 full-time (31 women); includes 3 minority (1 Black or African American, non-Hispanic/Latino; 1 Hispanic/Latino; 1 Two or more races, non-Hispanic/Latino), 25 international. Average age 26. 86 applicants, 21% accepted, 9 enrolled. In 2017, 2 master's, 4 doctorates awarded. *Degree requirements:* For master's, thesis; for doctorate, thesis/dissertation. *Entrance requirements:* For master's and doctorate, GRE General Test, GRE Subject Test (recommended), 2 letters of recommendation. Additional exam requirements/recommendations for international students: Required—TOEFL (minimum score 600 paper-based; 90 iBT), IELTS (minimum score 7). *Application deadline:* For fall admission, 12/21 for domestic and international students. Applications are processed on a rolling basis. Application fee: $60. Electronic applications accepted. *Financial support:* Fellowships, research assistantships, and teaching assistantships available. Financial award applicants required to submit FAFSA. *Faculty research:* Ecology and evolution, neurobiology and behavior, molecular genetics, cell development. *Unit head:* George Bloom, Chair, 434-243-3543 Ext. 434, Fax: 434-982-5626, E-mail: gsb4g@virginia.edu. *Application contact:* Robert Cox, Director of Graduate Studies in Biology, 434-982-1987 Ext. 434, Fax: 434-982-5626, E-mail: rmc3u@virginia.edu.
Website: http://bio.as.virginia.edu/

University of Virginia, School of Medicine, Department of Molecular Physiology and Biological Physics, Program in Biological and Physical Sciences, Charlottesville, VA 22903. Offers MS. In 2017, 17 master's awarded. *Entrance requirements:* For master's, GRE General Test. Additional exam requirements/recommendations for international students: Required—TOEFL. *Application deadline:* Applications are processed on a rolling basis. Application fee: $60. Electronic applications accepted. *Financial support:* Applicants required to submit FAFSA. *Unit head:* Dr. Mark Yeager, Chair, 434-924-5108, Fax: 434-982-1616, E-mail: my3r@virginia.edu. *Application contact:* Director of Graduate Studies, E-mail: physiograd@virginia.edu.
Website: http://www.healthsystem.virginia.edu/internet/physio/

University of Washington, Graduate School, College of Arts and Sciences, Department of Biology, Seattle, WA 98195. Offers PhD.

University of Washington, Graduate School, School of Medicine, Graduate Programs in Medicine, Seattle, WA 98195. Offers MA, MOT, MPO, MS, DPT, PhD. *Program availability:* Part-time. *Degree requirements:* For doctorate, thesis/dissertation. *Entrance requirements:* For doctorate, GRE. Electronic applications accepted. *Expenses:* Contact institution.

University of Waterloo, Graduate Studies, Faculty of Science, Department of Biology, Waterloo, ON N2L 3G1, Canada. Offers M Sc, PhD. *Program availability:* Part-time. *Degree requirements:* For master's, thesis, seminar; for doctorate, comprehensive exam, thesis/dissertation, seminar. *Entrance requirements:* For master's, honor's degree; for doctorate, master's degree. Additional exam requirements/recommendations for international students: Required—TOEFL, IELTS, PTE. Electronic applications accepted. *Faculty research:* Biosystematics, ecology and limnology, molecular and cellular biology, biochemistry, physiology.

The University of Western Ontario, Faculty of Graduate Studies, Biosciences Division, Department of Biology, London, ON N6A 5B8, Canada. Offers M Sc, PhD. *Degree requirements:* For master's, thesis; for doctorate, thesis/dissertation. *Entrance requirements:* For doctorate, M Sc or equivalent. Additional exam requirements/recommendations for international students: Required—TOEFL. *Faculty research:* Ecology systematics, plant biochemistry and physiology, yeast genetics, molecular biology.

University of West Florida, Hal Marcus College of Science and Engineering, Department of Biology, Pensacola, FL 32514-5750. Offers MS. *Degree requirements:* For master's, thesis. *Entrance requirements:* For master's, GRE (minimum score: verbal 450, quantitative 550), official transcripts; BS in biology or related field; letter of interest; three letters of recommendation from individuals who can evaluate applicant's academic ability. Additional exam requirements/recommendations for international students: Required—TOEFL (minimum score 550 paper-based).

University of West Georgia, College of Science and Mathematics, Carrollton, GA 30118. Offers biology (MS); computer science (MS); geographic information systems (Postbaccalaureate Certificate); mathematics (MS). *Program availability:* Part-time, evening/weekend, 100% online, blended/hybrid learning. *Faculty:* 47 full-time (16 women). *Students:* 19 full-time (9 women), 68 part-time (23 women); includes 24 minority (15 Black or African American, non-Hispanic/Latino; 1 American Indian or Alaska Native, non-Hispanic/Latino; 6 Asian, non-Hispanic/Latino; 2 Two or more races, non-Hispanic/Latino), 3 international. Average age 31. 72 applicants, 88% accepted, 54 enrolled. In 2017, 30 master's, 4 other advanced degrees awarded. *Entrance requirements:* Additional exam requirements/recommendations for international students: Required—TOEFL (minimum score 523 paper-based; 69 iBT); Recommended—IELTS (minimum score 6.5). *Application deadline:* For fall admission, 6/1 for domestic and international students; for spring admission, 11/15 for domestic students, 10/15 for international students; for summer admission, 4/1 for domestic students, 3/30 for international students. Applications are processed on a rolling basis. Application fee: $40. Electronic applications accepted. Tuition and fees vary according to degree level and program. *Financial support:* Fellowships, research assistantships, teaching assistantships, career-related internships or fieldwork, Federal Work-Study, institutionally sponsored loans, scholarships/grants, and unspecified assistantships available. Support available to part-time students. Financial award application deadline: 4/1; financial award applicants required to submit FAFSA. *Unit head:* Dr. Lok C. Lew Yan Voon, Dean of Science and Mathematics, 678-839-5190, Fax: 678-839-5191, E-mail: lokl@westga.edu. *Application contact:* Dr. Toby Ziglar, Assistant Dean of the Graduate School, 678-839-1394, Fax: 678-839-1395, E-mail: graduate@westga.edu.
Website: http://www.westga.edu/cosm

University of Windsor, Faculty of Graduate Studies, Faculty of Science, Department of Biological Sciences, Windsor, ON N9B 3P4, Canada. Offers M Sc, PhD. *Program availability:* Part-time. *Degree requirements:* For master's, thesis; for doctorate, comprehensive exam, thesis/dissertation. *Entrance requirements:* For master's and doctorate, minimum B average. Additional exam requirements/recommendations for international students: Required—TOEFL (minimum score 560 paper-based). Electronic applications accepted. *Faculty research:* Great Lakes Institute: aquatic ecotoxicology, regulation and development of the olfactory system, mating system evolution, signal transduction, aquatic ecology.

University of Wisconsin–La Crosse, College of Science and Health, Department of Biology, La Crosse, WI 54601-3742. Offers aquatic sciences (MS); biology (MS); cellular and molecular biology (MS); clinical microbiology (MS); microbiology (MS); nurse anesthesia (MS); physiology (MS). *Accreditation:* AANA/CANAEP. *Program availability:* Part-time. *Students:* 11 full-time (2 women), 29 part-time (14 women); includes 1 minority (Two or more races, non-Hispanic/Latino). Average age 30. 67 applicants, 28% accepted, 18 enrolled. In 2017, 24 master's awarded. *Degree requirements:* For master's, comprehensive exam, thesis. *Entrance requirements:* For master's, GRE General Test, minimum GPA of 2.85. Additional exam requirements/recommendations for international students: Required—TOEFL (minimum score 550 paper-based; 79 iBT). *Application deadline:* For fall admission, 2/1 priority date for domestic and international students; for spring admission, 1/4 priority date for domestic and international students. Applications are processed on a rolling basis. Electronic applications accepted. *Financial support:* Research assistantships with partial tuition reimbursements, Federal Work-Study, scholarships/grants, health care benefits, and tuition waivers (partial) available. Support available to part-time students. Financial award application deadline: 3/15; financial award applicants required to submit FAFSA. *Unit head:* Dr. Mark Sandheinrich, Department Chair, 608-785-8261, E-mail: msandheinrich@uwlax.edu. *Application contact:* Brandon Schaller, Senior Graduate Student Status Examiner, 608-785-8941, E-mail: admissions@uwlax.edu.
Website: http://uwlax.edu/biology/

University of Wisconsin–Madison, School of Medicine and Public Health, Medical Scientist Training Program, Madison, WI 53705-2221. Offers MD/PhD. *Accreditation:* LCME/AMA. *Financial support:* In 2017–18, 73 students received support. *Unit head:* Dr. Anna Huttenlocher, Director, 608-265-4642, Fax: 608-262-8418, E-mail: huttenlocher@wisc.edu. *Application contact:* Nichole Monzon, Program Co-Administrator, 608-262-6321, E-mail: nichole.monzon@wisc.edu.
Website: http://mstp.med.wisc.edu/

University of Wisconsin–Milwaukee, Graduate School, College of Engineering and Applied Science, Biomedical and Health Informatics Program, Milwaukee, WI 53201-0413. Offers health information systems (PhD); health services management and policy (PhD); knowledge based systems (PhD); medical imaging and instrumentation (PhD); public health informatics (PhD). *Students:* 8 full-time (3 women), 14 part-time (6 women); includes 3 minority (2 Black or African American, non-Hispanic/Latino; 1 Asian, non-Hispanic/Latino), 9 international. Average age 37. 18 applicants, 56% accepted, 4 enrolled. *Degree requirements:* For doctorate, comprehensive exam, thesis/dissertation. *Entrance requirements:* For doctorate, GRE, GMAT or MCAT. Additional exam requirements/recommendations for international students: Required—TOEFL (minimum score 600 paper-based; 79 iBT), IELTS (minimum score 6.5). Application fee: $56 ($96 for international students). Electronic applications accepted. *Financial support:* Fellowships, research assistantships, teaching assistantships, and project assistantships available. *Unit head:* Devendra Misra, PhD, Chair, 414-229-3327, E-mail: misra@uwm.edu. *Application contact:* Betty Warras, Engineering and Computer Science Graduate Programs, 414-229-6169, E-mail: ceas-graduate@uwm.edu.
Website: http://uwm.edu/engineering/academics-2/departments/biomedical-engineering/

University of Wisconsin–Milwaukee, Graduate School, College of Health Sciences, Department of Biomedical Sciences, Milwaukee, WI 53201-0413. Offers MS. *Accreditation:* APTA. *Students:* 7 full-time (6 women), 5 part-time (4 women); includes 2 minority (1 Black or African American, non-Hispanic/Latino; 1 Asian, non-Hispanic/Latino), 2 international. Average age 29. 28 applicants, 43% accepted, 7 enrolled. In 2017, 1 master's awarded. *Entrance requirements:* Additional exam requirements/

recommendations for international students: Required—TOEFL (minimum score 550 paper-based; 79 iBT), IELTS (minimum score 6.5). *Financial support:* Fellowships, research assistantships, teaching assistantships, and project assistantships available. *Unit head:* Raymond Fleming, PhD, Department Chair, 414-229-3980, E-mail: mundo@uwm.edu. *Application contact:* Dean T. Nardelli, PhD, Graduate Program Coordinator, 414-229-2645, Fax: 414-229-2619, E-mail: nardelld@uwm.edu.
Website: http://uwm.edu/healthsciences/academics/biomedical-sciences/

University of Wisconsin–Milwaukee, Graduate School, College of Health Sciences, Program in Health Sciences, Milwaukee, WI 53201-0413. Offers health sciences (PhD), including diagnostic and biomedical sciences, disability and rehabilitation, health administration and policy, human movement sciences, population health. *Students:* 17 full-time (10 women), 7 part-time (4 women); includes 6 minority (1 Black or African American, non-Hispanic/Latino; 3 Asian, non-Hispanic/Latino; 2 Two or more races, non-Hispanic/Latino), 11 international. Average age 33. 7 applicants, 43% accepted, 3 enrolled. In 2017, 1 doctorate awarded. *Degree requirements:* For doctorate, comprehensive exam, thesis/dissertation. *Entrance requirements:* For doctorate, GRE. Additional exam requirements/recommendations for international students: Required—TOEFL (minimum score 600 paper-based), IELTS (minimum score 6.5). Application fee: $56 ($96 for international students). *Financial support:* Fellowships, research assistantships, teaching assistantships, and project assistantships available. *Application contact:* Susan Cashin, PhD, Assistant Dean, 414-229-3303, E-mail: scashin@uwm.edu.
Website: http://uwm.edu/healthsciences/academics/phd-health-sciences/

University of Wisconsin–Milwaukee, Graduate School, College of Letters and Science, Department of Biological Sciences, Milwaukee, WI 53201-0413. Offers cellular and molecular biology (MS, PhD); microbiology (MS, PhD). *Students:* 58 full-time (35 women), 11 part-time (8 women); includes 7 minority (1 Black or African American, non-Hispanic/Latino; 5 Asian, non-Hispanic/Latino; 1 Two or more races, non-Hispanic/Latino), 17 international. Average age 29. 78 applicants, 55% accepted, 29 enrolled. *Degree requirements:* For master's, thesis; for doctorate, thesis/dissertation, 1 foreign language or data analysis proficiency. *Entrance requirements:* For master's and doctorate, GRE General Test. Additional exam requirements/recommendations for international students: Required—TOEFL (minimum score 550 paper-based; 79 iBT), IELTS (minimum score 6.5). *Application deadline:* For fall admission, 3/1 priority date for domestic students. Application fee: $56 ($96 for international students). Electronic applications accepted. *Financial support:* In 2017–18, 9 research assistantships were awarded; fellowships, teaching assistantships, career-related internships or fieldwork, unspecified assistantships, and project assistantships also available. Support available to part-time students. Financial award application deadline: 4/15; financial award applicants required to submit FAFSA. *Unit head:* R. David Heathcote, Department Chair, 414-229-6471, E-mail: rdh@uwm.edu. *Application contact:* General Information Contact, 414-229-4982, Fax: 414-229-6967, E-mail: gradschool@uwm.edu.
Website: https://uwm.edu/biology/

University of Wisconsin–Oshkosh, Graduate Studies, College of Letters and Science, Department of Biology and Microbiology, Oshkosh, WI 54901. Offers biology (MS), including botany, microbiology, zoology. *Degree requirements:* For master's, comprehensive exam, thesis. *Entrance requirements:* For master's, GRE General Test, minimum GPA of 3.0, BS in biology. Additional exam requirements/recommendations for international students: Required—TOEFL (minimum score 550 paper-based; 79 iBT). Electronic applications accepted.

Utah State University, School of Graduate Studies, College of Science, Department of Biology, Logan, UT 84322. Offers biology (MS, PhD); ecology (MS, PhD). *Program availability:* Part-time. *Degree requirements:* For master's, thesis; for doctorate, thesis/dissertation. *Entrance requirements:* For master's and doctorate, GRE General Test, minimum GPA of 3.0. Additional exam requirements/recommendations for international students: Required—TOEFL (minimum score 575 paper-based). *Faculty research:* Plant, insect, microbial, and animal biology.

Vanderbilt University, Department of Biological Sciences, Nashville, TN 37240-1001. Offers MS, PhD. *Faculty:* 20 full-time (4 women). *Students:* 52 full-time (27 women); includes 10 minority (1 Black or African American, non-Hispanic/Latino; 4 Asian, non-Hispanic/Latino; 3 Hispanic/Latino; 2 Two or more races, non-Hispanic/Latino), 18 international. Average age 27. 89 applicants, 16% accepted, 5 enrolled. In 2017, 6 doctorates awarded. Terminal master's awarded for partial completion of doctoral program. *Degree requirements:* For master's, thesis; for doctorate, thesis/dissertation, final and qualifying exams. *Entrance requirements:* For master's and doctorate, GRE General Test. Additional exam requirements/recommendations for international students: Required—TOEFL (minimum score 570 paper-based; 88 iBT). *Application deadline:* For fall admission, 1/15 for domestic and international students. Electronic applications accepted. *Financial support:* Fellowships with tuition reimbursements, research assistantships with full tuition reimbursements, teaching assistantships with full tuition reimbursements, Federal Work-Study, institutionally sponsored loans, scholarships/grants, traineeships, and health care benefits available. Financial award application deadline: 1/15; financial award applicants required to submit CSS PROFILE or FAFSA. *Faculty research:* Protein structure and function, protein transport, membrane ion channels and receptors, signal transduction, posttranscriptional control of gene expression, DNA replication and recombination, biological clocks, development, neurobiology, vector biology, insect physiology, ecology and evolution, bioinformatics. *Unit head:* Dr. Douglas McMahon, Chair, 615-322-2008, Fax: 615-343-6707, E-mail: douglas.g.mcmahon@vanderbilt.edu. *Application contact:* Donna Webb, Director of Graduate Studies, 615-322-2008.
Website: http://sitemason.vanderbilt.edu/biosci/grad/

Villanova University, Graduate School of Liberal Arts and Sciences, Department of Biology, Villanova, PA 19085-1699. Offers MA, MS. *Program availability:* Part-time, evening/weekend. *Faculty:* 8. *Students:* 33 full-time (16 women), 9 part-time (7 women); includes 7 minority (1 Black or African American, non-Hispanic/Latino; 5 Asian, non-Hispanic/Latino; 1 Hispanic/Latino), 3 international. Average age 27. 25 applicants, 80% accepted, 14 enrolled. In 2017, 25 master's awarded. *Entrance requirements:* For master's, GRE General Test, minimum GPA of 3.0, 3 recommendation letters. *Application deadline:* For fall admission, 3/1 for domestic students, 5/1 for international students; for spring admission, 11/15 for domestic students, 10/15 for international students; for summer admission, 5/1 for domestic students, 4/1 for international students. Applications are processed on a rolling basis. Application fee: $50. Electronic applications accepted. *Financial support:* Scholarships/grants and unspecified assistantships available. Financial award applicants required to submit FAFSA. *Unit head:* Dr. Anil Bamezai, Chair, 610-519-4847, E-mail: anil.bamezai@villanova.edu.
Website: http://www1.villanova.edu/villanova/artsci/biology/academics/graduate.html

Virginia Commonwealth University, Graduate School, College of Humanities and Sciences, Department of Biology, Richmond, VA 23284-9005. Offers MS. *Program availability:* Part-time. *Degree requirements:* For master's, thesis. *Entrance requirements:* For master's, GRE General Test, BS in biology or related field. Additional exam requirements/recommendations for international students: Required—TOEFL (minimum score 600 paper-based; 100 iBT) or IELTS (minimum score 6.5). *Faculty research:* Molecular and cellular biology, terrestrial and aquatic ecology, systematics, physiology and developmental biology.

Virginia Commonwealth University, Graduate School, School of Life Sciences, Richmond, VA 23284-9005. Offers M Env Sc, MS, PhD. *Entrance requirements:* For master's and doctorate, GRE. Additional exam requirements/recommendations for international students: Required—TOEFL (minimum score 600 paper-based; 100 iBT). Electronic applications accepted.

Virginia Commonwealth University, Medical College of Virginia-Professional Programs, School of Medicine, Graduate Programs in Medicine, Richmond, VA 23284-9005. Offers MPH, MS, PhD, Certificate, MD/MPH, MD/PhD. *Program availability:* Part-time. Terminal master's awarded for partial completion of doctoral program. *Degree requirements:* For doctorate, thesis/dissertation, comprehensive oral and written exams. *Entrance requirements:* For doctorate, GRE General Test, MCAT.

Virginia Commonwealth University, Program in Pre-Medical Basic Health Sciences, Richmond, VA 23284-9005. Offers Postbaccalaureate Certificate. *Entrance requirements:* For degree, GRE, MCAT or DAT, course work in organic chemistry, minimum undergraduate GPA of 2.8. Additional exam requirements/recommendations for international students: Required—TOEFL (minimum score 600 paper-based). Electronic applications accepted.

Virginia Polytechnic Institute and State University, Graduate School, College of Science, Blacksburg, VA 24061. Offers biological sciences (MS, PhD); biomedical technology development and management (MS); chemistry (MS, PhD); data analysis and applied statistics (MA); economics (PhD); geosciences (MS, PhD); mathematics (MS, PhD); physics (MS, PhD); psychology (MS, PhD); statistics (MS, PhD). *Faculty:* 321 full-time (103 women). *Students:* 557 full-time (205 women), 39 part-time (18 women); includes 68 minority (13 Black or African American, non-Hispanic/Latino; 1 American Indian or Alaska Native, non-Hispanic/Latino; 14 Asian, non-Hispanic/Latino; 32 Hispanic/Latino; 8 Two or more races, non-Hispanic/Latino), 238 international. Average age 27. 1,060 applicants, 15% accepted, 121 enrolled. In 2017, 75 master's, 89 doctorates awarded. *Degree requirements:* For master's, comprehensive exam (for some programs), thesis (for some programs); for doctorate, comprehensive exam (for some programs), thesis/dissertation (for some programs). *Entrance requirements:* For master's and doctorate, GRE/GMAT. Additional exam requirements/recommendations for international students: Required—TOEFL (minimum score 80 iBT). *Application deadline:* For fall admission, 8/1 for domestic students, 4/1 for international students; for spring admission, 1/1 for domestic students, 9/1 for international students. Applications are processed on a rolling basis. Application fee: $75. Electronic applications accepted. *Expenses:* Tuition, state resident: full-time $15,072; part-time $718.50 per credit hour. Tuition, nonresident: full-time $28,810; part-time $1448.25 per credit hour. *Required fees:* $2741; $502 per semester. Tuition and fees vary according to course load, campus/location and program. *Financial support:* In 2017–18, 2 fellowships with full tuition reimbursements (averaging $12,267 per year), 140 research assistantships with full tuition reimbursements (averaging $23,004 per year), 351 teaching assistantships with full tuition reimbursements (averaging $20,157 per year) were awarded. Financial award application deadline: 3/1; financial award applicants required to submit FAFSA. *Total annual research expenditures:* $24.3 million. *Unit head:* Dr. Sally C. Morton, Dean, 540-231-5422, Fax: 540-231-3380, E-mail: scmorton@vt.edu. *Application contact:* Allison Craft, Executive Assistant, 540-231-6394, Fax: 540-231-3380, E-mail: crafta@vt.edu.
Website: http://www.science.vt.edu/

Virginia State University, College of Graduate Studies, College of Natural and Health Sciences, Department of Biology, Petersburg, VA 23806-0001. Offers MS. *Degree requirements:* For master's, one foreign language, thesis. *Entrance requirements:* For master's, GRE General Test.

Wake Forest University, Graduate School of Arts and Sciences, Department of Biology, Winston-Salem, NC 27109. Offers MS, PhD. *Program availability:* Part-time. *Degree requirements:* For master's, one foreign language, thesis; for doctorate, 2 foreign languages, comprehensive exam, thesis/dissertation. *Entrance requirements:* For master's and doctorate, GRE General Test. Additional exam requirements/recommendations for international students: Required—TOEFL (minimum score 79 iBT). Electronic applications accepted. *Faculty research:* Cell biology, ecology, parasitology, immunology.

Wake Forest University, School of Medicine and Graduate School of Arts and Sciences, Graduate Programs in Medicine, Winston-Salem, NC 27109. Offers MS, PhD, MD/PhD. *Degree requirements:* For master's, thesis; for doctorate, thesis/dissertation. *Entrance requirements:* For master's and doctorate, GRE General Test. Additional exam requirements/recommendations for international students: Required—TOEFL. Electronic applications accepted. *Expenses:* Contact institution. *Faculty research:* Atherosclerosis, cardiovascular physiology, pharmacology, neuroanatomy, endocrinology.

Walla Walla University, Graduate Studies, Department of Biological Sciences, College Place, WA 99324. Offers biology (MS). *Degree requirements:* For master's, thesis. *Entrance requirements:* For master's, GRE General Test, GRE Subject Test, minimum GPA of 2.75, three letters of recommendation, official transcripts. Additional exam requirements/recommendations for international students: Required—TOEFL (minimum score 550 paper-based; 79 iBT). *Application deadline:* Applications are processed on a rolling basis. Application fee: $50. Electronic applications accepted. *Financial support:* Teaching assistantships with full tuition reimbursements and Federal Work-Study available. Financial award application deadline: 4/30; financial award applicants required to submit FAFSA. *Faculty research:* Marine biology, plant development, neurobiology, animal physiology, behavior. *Unit head:* David Lindsey, Chair, 509-527-2602, E-mail: david.lindsey@wallawalla.edu. *Application contact:* Dr. Joan Redd, Director of Graduate Program, 509-527-2482, E-mail: joan.redd@wallawalla.edu.
Website: https://wallawalla.edu/academics/areas-of-study/undergraduate-programs/biological-sciences/

Washington State University, College of Arts and Sciences, School of Biological Sciences, Pullman, WA 99164-4236. Offers MS, PhD. Programs are offered at the Pullman campus. *Degree requirements:* For master's, comprehensive exam (for some programs), thesis, oral exam; for doctorate, comprehensive exam, thesis/dissertation, oral exam. *Entrance requirements:* For master's and doctorate, GRE General Test, GRE Subject Test (recommended), three letters of recommendation, official transcripts from each university-level school attended, minimum GPA of 3.0. Additional exam requirements/recommendations for international students: Required—TOEFL, IELTS.

Washington University in St. Louis, The Graduate School, Division of Biology and Biomedical Sciences, St. Louis, MO 63130-4899. Offers biochemistry (PhD); computational and molecular biophysics (PhD); computational and systems biology (PhD); developmental, regenerative, and stem cell biology (PhD); evolution, ecology and population biology (PhD), including ecology, environmental biology, evolutionary biology, genetics; human and statistical genetics (PhD); immunology (PhD); molecular cell biology (PhD); molecular genetics and genomics (PhD); molecular microbiology and microbial pathogenesis (PhD); neurosciences (PhD); plant and microbial biosciences (PhD); MD/PhD. *Degree requirements:* For doctorate, thesis/dissertation. *Entrance requirements:* For doctorate, GRE General Test, GRE Subject Test. Additional exam requirements/recommendations for international students: Required—TOEFL. Electronic applications accepted.

Biological and Biomedical Sciences—General

Wayne State University, College of Liberal Arts and Sciences, Department of Biological Sciences, Detroit, MI 48202. Offers biological sciences (MA, MS, PhD); molecular biotechnology (MS). PhD and MS programs admit for fall only. *Faculty:* 24. *Students:* 48 full-time (25 women), 4 part-time (2 women); includes 2 minority (1 Black or African American, non-Hispanic/Latino; 1 Two or more races, non-Hispanic/Latino), 25 international. Average age 29. 200 applicants, 84% accepted, 11 enrolled. In 2017, 9 master's, 11 doctorates awarded. *Degree requirements:* For master's, thesis (for some programs); for doctorate, thesis/dissertation. *Entrance requirements:* For master's, GRE (for MS applicants), minimum GPA of 3.0; adequate preparation in biological sciences and supporting courses in chemistry, physics and mathematics; curriculum vitae; personal statement; three letters of recommendation (two for MA); for doctorate, GRE, curriculum vitae, statement of goals and career objectives, three letters of reference, bachelor's or master's degree in biological or other science. Additional exam requirements/recommendations for international students: Required—TOEFL (minimum score 550 paper-based; 79 iBT), TWE (minimum score 5.5), Michigan English Language Assessment Battery (minimum score 85); Recommended—IELTS (minimum score 6.5). Application fee: $50. Electronic applications accepted. *Expenses:* Tuition, state resident: full-time $10,224; part-time $638.98 per credit hour. Tuition, nonresident: full-time $22,145; part-time $1384.04 per credit hour. Tuition and fees vary according to course load and program. *Financial support:* In 2017–18, 48 students received support, including 3 fellowships with tuition reimbursements available (averaging $16,000 per year), 11 research assistantships with tuition reimbursements available (averaging $20,094 per year), 37 teaching assistantships with tuition reimbursements available (averaging $19,946 per year); scholarships/grants and unspecified assistantships also available. Financial award applicants required to submit FAFSA. *Faculty research:* Cell biology and cytogenetics, mitochondrial function and aging, genomic and developmental evolution, intra- and inter-cellular signaling, community and landscape ecology and environmental degradation, transcription and chromatin remodeling, microbiology and virology. *Unit head:* Dr. David Njus, Professor and Chair, 313-577-3105, E-mail: dnjus@wayne.edu. *Application contact:* Rose Mary Priest, Graduate Secretary, 313-577-6818, E-mail: rpriest@wayne.edu.
Website: http://clas.wayne.edu/Biology/

Weill Cornell Medicine, Weill Cornell Graduate School of Medical Sciences, New York, NY 10065. Offers MS, PhD. Terminal master's awarded for partial completion of doctoral program. *Degree requirements:* For master's, comprehensive exam, thesis (for some programs); for doctorate, thesis/dissertation, final exam. *Entrance requirements:* For doctorate, GRE General Test. Additional exam requirements/recommendations for international students: Required—TOEFL. Electronic applications accepted. *Expenses:* Contact institution.

Weill Cornell Medicine, Weill Cornell/Rockefeller/Sloan-Kettering Tri-Institutional MD-PhD Program, New York, NY 10065. Offers MD/PhD. Offered jointly with The Rockefeller University and Sloan-Kettering Institute. Electronic applications accepted. *Expenses:* Contact institution. *Faculty research:* Neuroscience, pharmacology, immunology, structural biology, genetics.

Wesleyan University, Graduate Studies, Department of Biology, Middletown, CT 06459. Offers cell and developmental biology (PhD); evolution and ecology (PhD); genetics and genomics (PhD), including bioinformatics; neurobiology and behavior (PhD). Terminal master's awarded for partial completion of doctoral program. *Degree requirements:* For doctorate, comprehensive exam, thesis/dissertation, public seminar. *Entrance requirements:* For doctorate, GRE, official transcripts, three recommendation letters, essay. Additional exam requirements/recommendations for international students: Required—TOEFL. *Application deadline:* For fall admission, 1/15 for domestic and international students. Application fee: $0. Electronic applications accepted. *Financial support:* Stipends available. *Faculty research:* Evolution and ecology, neurobiology and behavior, cell and developmental biology, genetics, genomics and bioinformatics. *Unit head:* Dr. Ann Burke, Chair/Professor, 860-685-3518, E-mail: acburke@wesleyan.edu. *Application contact:* Diane Meredith, Administrative Assistant IV, 860-685-2157, E-mail: dmeredith@wesleyan.edu.
Website: http://www.wesleyan.edu/bio/

West Chester University of Pennsylvania, College of the Sciences and Mathematics, Department of Biology, West Chester, PA 19383. Offers MS, Teaching Certificate. *Program availability:* Part-time, evening/weekend. *Students:* 7 full-time (all women), 11 part-time (7 women); includes 2 minority (both Black or African American, non-Hispanic/Latino), 1 international. Average age 29. 12 applicants, 50% accepted, 1 enrolled. In 2017, 10 master's, 1 other advanced degree awarded. *Degree requirements:* For master's, comprehensive exam (for some programs), thesis (for some programs). *Entrance requirements:* For master's, two letters of reference. Additional exam requirements/recommendations for international students: Required—TOEFL or IELTS. *Application deadline:* For fall admission, 5/15 for international students; for spring admission, 10/15 for international students. Applications are processed on a rolling basis. Application fee: $50. Electronic applications accepted. *Expenses:* Tuition, state resident: full-time $9000; part-time $500 per credit. Tuition, nonresident: full-time $13,500; part-time $750 per credit. *Required fees:* $2959; $149.79 per credit. *Financial support:* Scholarships/grants and unspecified assistantships available. Financial award application deadline: 2/15; financial award applicants required to submit FAFSA. *Faculty research:* Medical microbiology, molecular genetics and physiology of living systems, mammalian biomechanics, invertebrate and vertebrate animal systems, aquatic and terrestrial ecology. *Unit head:* Dr. Giovanni Casotti, Department Chair, 610-436-2538, E-mail: gcasotti@wcupa.edu. *Application contact:* Dr. Anne Boettger, Graduate Coordinator, 610-430-4601, E-mail: aboettger@wcupa.edu.
Website: http://bio.wcupa.edu/biology/index.php

Western Carolina University, Graduate School, College of Arts and Sciences, Department of Biology, Cullowhee, NC 28723. Offers MS. *Program availability:* Part-time. *Students:* 28. *Degree requirements:* For master's, thesis. *Entrance requirements:* For master's, GRE General Test, appropriate undergraduate degree, 3 letters of recommendation, statement of research interest, including the names of two faculty whose research is of interest. Additional exam requirements/recommendations for international students: Required—TOEFL (minimum score 550 paper-based, 79 iBT) or IELTS (6.5). *Application deadline:* For fall admission, 4/15 priority date for domestic and international students; for spring admission, 11/15 priority date for domestic students, 10/15 priority date for international students. Applications are processed on a rolling basis. Application fee: $65. Electronic applications accepted. *Expenses:* $10,000 per year, in-state full-time; $20,308 per year out-of-state full-time. *Financial support:* In 2017–18, 1 research assistantship with full and partial tuition reimbursement (averaging $12,500 per year), 23 teaching assistantships with full and partial tuition reimbursements (averaging $12,500 per year) were awarded; career-related internships or fieldwork, institutionally sponsored loans, scholarships/grants, and unspecified assistantships also available. Financial award application deadline: 4/15; financial award applicants required to submit FAFSA. *Faculty research:* Pathogen interactions, gene expression, plant community ecology, restoration ecology, ornithology, herpetology. *Unit head:* Dr. Seán O'Connell, Department Head, E-mail: soconnell@email.wcu.edu. *Application contact:* Bobbi Smith, E-mail: bobbismith@wcu.edu.
Website: http://www.wcu.edu/as/biology/index.html

Western Illinois University, School of Graduate Studies, College of Arts and Sciences, Department of Biological Sciences, Macomb, IL 61455-1390. Offers biology (MS); environmental GIS (Certificate); zoo and aquarium studies (Certificate). *Program availability:* Part-time. *Students:* 43 full-time (24 women), 24 part-time (14 women); includes 5 minority (1 Black or African American, non-Hispanic/Latino; 2 Hispanic/Latino; 2 Two or more races, non-Hispanic/Latino), 21 international. Average age 28. 20 applicants, 90% accepted, 12 enrolled. In 2017, 22 master's awarded. *Degree requirements:* For master's, thesis or alternative. *Entrance requirements:* Additional exam requirements/recommendations for international students: Required—TOEFL (minimum score 550 paper-based; 80 iBT); Recommended—IELTS. *Application deadline:* Applications are processed on a rolling basis. Application fee: $30. Electronic applications accepted. *Financial support:* In 2017–18, 13 research assistantships with full tuition reimbursements (averaging $7,544 per year), 19 teaching assistantships with full tuition reimbursements (averaging $8,688 per year) were awarded; unspecified assistantships also available. Financial award applicants required to submit FAFSA. *Unit head:* Dr. Richard Musser, Chairperson, 309-298-1546. *Application contact:* Dr. Nancy Parsons, Associate Provost and Director of Graduate Studies, 309-298-1806, Fax: 309-298-2345, E-mail: grad-office@wiu.edu.
Website: http://wiu.edu/biology

Western Kentucky University, Graduate Studies, Ogden College of Science and Engineering, Department of Biology, Bowling Green, KY 42101. Offers MS. *Program availability:* Online learning. *Degree requirements:* For master's, comprehensive exam, thesis optional, research tool. *Entrance requirements:* For master's, GRE General Test, minimum GPA of 2.75. Additional exam requirements/recommendations for international students: Required—TOEFL (minimum score 555 paper-based; 79 iBT). *Faculty research:* Phytoremediation, culturing of salt water organisms, PCR-based standards, biological monitoring (water) bioremediation, genetic diversity.

Western Michigan University, Graduate College, College of Arts and Sciences, Department of Biological Sciences, Kalamazoo, MI 49008. Offers MS, PhD. *Degree requirements:* For master's, thesis; for doctorate, thesis/dissertation.

Western Michigan University, Graduate College, College of Arts and Sciences, Department of Interdisciplinary Arts and Sciences, Kalamazoo, MI 49008. Offers science education (MA, PhD), including biological sciences (PhD), chemistry (PhD), geosciences (PhD), physical geography (PhD), physics (PhD), science education (PhD). *Degree requirements:* For doctorate, thesis/dissertation.

Western University of Health Sciences, Graduate College of Biomedical Sciences, Master of Science in Biomedical Sciences Program, Pomona, CA 91766-1854. Offers MS. *Faculty:* 6 full-time (0 women), 2 part-time/adjunct (1 woman). *Students:* 25 full-time (13 women), 1 part-time (0 women); includes 17 minority (2 Black or African American, non-Hispanic/Latino; 1 American Indian or Alaska Native, non-Hispanic/Latino; 8 Asian, non-Hispanic/Latino; 3 Hispanic/Latino; 3 Two or more races, non-Hispanic/Latino), 1 international. Average age 26. 64 applicants, 36% accepted, 20 enrolled. In 2017, 3 master's awarded. *Degree requirements:* For master's, comprehensive exam (for some programs), thesis. *Entrance requirements:* For master's, GRE, MCAT, or DAT, minimum overall GPA of 3.0; letters of recommendation; personal statement; resume; BS in pharmacy, chemistry, biology or related scientific area. Additional exam requirements/recommendations for international students: Required—TOEFL (minimum score 92 iBT). *Application deadline:* For fall admission, 11/1 for domestic and international students; for spring admission, 6/1 for domestic and international students. Application fee: $50. Electronic applications accepted. *Expenses:* $807 per unit. *Financial support:* In 2017–18, 8 students received support. Scholarships/grants available. Financial award application deadline: 3/2; financial award applicants required to submit FAFSA. *Unit head:* Dr. Guru Betageri, Associate Dean, Graduate College of Biomedical Sciences, 909-469-5682, E-mail: gbetageri@westernu.edu. *Application contact:* Kathryn Ford, Director of Admission, 909-469-5335, Fax: 909-469-5570, E-mail: admissions@westernu.edu.
Website: https://www.westernu.edu/biomedical-sciences/biomedical-sciences-academics/biomedical-sciences-msbs/

Western University of Health Sciences, Graduate College of Biomedical Sciences, Master of Science in Medical Sciences Program, Pomona, CA 91766-1854. Offers MS. *Faculty:* 1 (woman) full-time. *Students:* 30 full-time (16 women); includes 29 minority (6 Black or African American, non-Hispanic/Latino; 1 American Indian or Alaska Native, non-Hispanic/Latino; 8 Asian, non-Hispanic/Latino; 10 Hispanic/Latino; 4 Two or more races, non-Hispanic/Latino). Average age 27. 254 applicants, 12% accepted, 28 enrolled. In 2017, 30 master's awarded. *Degree requirements:* For master's, thesis (for some programs). *Entrance requirements:* For master's, GRE, MCAT, OAT, or DAT, minimum overall GPA of 2.5; letters of recommendation; personal statement; resume; transcripts; bachelor's degree. Additional exam requirements/recommendations for international students: Required—TOEFL (minimum score 89 iBT). *Application deadline:* For fall admission, 2/1 for domestic and international students. Applications are processed on a rolling basis. Application fee: $50. Electronic applications accepted. *Expenses:* Contact institution. *Financial support:* In 2017–18, 27 students received support. Scholarships/grants available. Financial award application deadline: 3/2; financial award applicants required to submit FAFSA. *Faculty research:* Mechanisms implicated in long-term synaptic potentiation and depression in hippocampus and other brain regions; the development and evaluation of liposomal and proliposomal drug delivery systems; the cellular and molecular mechanisms of Alzheimer's disease; the molecular events of inflammation and their relationship to disease processes such as periodontal disease and oral cancer. *Unit head:* Marcos Villa, Director, Master of Medical Sciences Program, Fax: 909-469-5577, E-mail: mvilla@westernu.edu. *Application contact:* Kathryn Ford, Director of Admission, 909-469-5335, Fax: 909-469-5570, E-mail: admissions@westernu.edu.
Website: http://prospective.westernu.edu/medical-sciences/welcome-4/

Western Washington University, Graduate School, College of Sciences and Technology, Department of Biology, Bellingham, WA 98225-5996. Offers MS. *Program availability:* Part-time. *Degree requirements:* For master's, thesis. *Entrance requirements:* For master's, GRE General Test, GRE Subject Test (biology), minimum GPA of 3.0 in last 60 semester hours or last 90 quarter hours. Additional exam requirements/recommendations for international students: Required—TOEFL (minimum score 567 paper-based). Electronic applications accepted. *Faculty research:* Organismal biology, ecology and evolutionary biology, marine biology, cell and molecular biology, developmental biology, larval ecology, microzoo planton, symbiosis.

West Liberty University, College of Sciences, West Liberty, WV 26074. Offers biology (MA, MS); biomedical science (MA); physician assistant studies (MS); zoo science (MA, MS). Tuition and fees vary according to course load and program. *Unit head:* Dr. Karen Kettler, Interim Dean, E-mail: kkettler@westliberty.edu. *Application contact:* Sara Sweeney, Director, Office of Graduate Studies, 304-336-8545, E-mail: sara.sweeney@westliberty.edu.
Website: http://westliberty.edu/college-of-sciences/

West Texas A&M University, College of Agriculture and Natural Sciences, Department of Life, Earth and Environmental Sciences, Program in Biology, Canyon, TX 79015. Offers MS. *Program availability:* Part-time. *Degree requirements:* For master's, comprehensive exam, thesis optional. *Entrance requirements:* For master's, GRE General Test. Additional exam requirements/recommendations for international students: Required—TOEFL (minimum score 550 paper-based). Electronic applications accepted. *Faculty research:* Scorpions, kangaroo mice, seed anatomy with light and scanning electron microscope.

West Virginia University, Eberly College of Arts and Sciences, Morgantown, WV 26506. Offers biology (MS, PhD); chemistry (MS, PhD); communication studies (MA, PhD); computational statistics (PhD); creative writing (MFA); English (MA, PhD); forensic and investigative science (MS); forensic science (PhD); geography (MA); geology (MA, PhD); history (MA, PhD); legal studies (MLS); math (MS); physics (MS, PhD); political science (MA, PhD); professional writing and editing (MA); psychology (MA); public administration (MPA); social work (MSW); sociology (MA, PhD); statistics (MS). *Program availability:* Part-time, evening/weekend, online learning. *Students:* 831 full-time (437 women), 236 part-time (142 women); includes 112 minority (35 Black or African American, non-Hispanic/Latino; 15 Asian, non-Hispanic/Latino; 29 Hispanic/Latino; 33 Two or more races, non-Hispanic/Latino), 235 international. Terminal master's awarded for partial completion of doctoral program. *Degree requirements:* For master's, thesis (for some programs); for doctorate, comprehensive exam, thesis/dissertation. *Entrance requirements:* For master's and doctorate, GRE. Additional exam requirements/recommendations for international students: Required—TOEFL (minimum score 600 paper-based); Recommended—TWE. *Application deadline:* For spring admission, 2/15 priority date for domestic and international students. Applications are processed on a rolling basis. Application fee: $45. Electronic applications accepted. *Expenses:* Tuition, state resident: full-time $9450. Tuition, nonresident: full-time $24,390. *Financial support:* Fellowships with full tuition reimbursements, research assistantships with full tuition reimbursements, teaching assistantships with full tuition reimbursements, career-related internships or fieldwork, Federal Work-Study, institutionally sponsored loans, scholarships/grants, health care benefits, tuition waivers (full and partial), unspecified assistantships, and administrative assistantships available. Financial award application deadline: 2/1; financial award applicants required to submit FAFSA. *Faculty research:* Humanities, social sciences, life science, physical sciences, mathematics. *Unit head:* Dr. Mary Ellen Mazey, Dean, 304-293-4611, Fax: 304-293-6858, E-mail: mary.mazey@mail.wvu.edu. *Application contact:* Dr. Fred L. King, Associate Dean for Graduate Studies, 304-293-4611 Ext. 5205, Fax: 304-293-6858, E-mail: fred.king@mail.wvu.edu.
Website: http://www.as.wvu.edu/

West Virginia University, School of Medicine, Morgantown, WV 26506-9600. Offers biochemistry and molecular biology (PhD); biomedical science (MS); cancer cell biology (PhD); cellular and integrative physiology (PhD); exercise physiology (MS, PhD); health sciences (MS); immunology (PhD); medicine (MD); occupational therapy (MOT); pathologists assistant (MHS); physical therapy (DPT). *Program availability:* Part-time, evening/weekend. *Students:* 781 full-time (440 women), 25 part-time (13 women); includes 140 minority (15 Black or African American, non-Hispanic/Latino; 1 American Indian or Alaska Native, non-Hispanic/Latino; 68 Asian, non-Hispanic/Latino; 37 Hispanic/Latino; 1 Native Hawaiian or other Pacific Islander, non-Hispanic/Latino; 18 Two or more races, non-Hispanic/Latino), 19 international. *Entrance requirements:* Additional exam requirements/recommendations for international students: Required—TOEFL. *Application deadline:* Applications are processed on a rolling basis. Application fee: $60. Electronic applications accepted. *Expenses:* Contact institution. *Financial support:* Fellowships, research assistantships, teaching assistantships, career-related internships or fieldwork, Federal Work-Study, institutionally sponsored loans, health care benefits, tuition waivers (full and partial), and administrative assistantships available. Financial award applicants required to submit FAFSA. *Unit head:* Dr. Clay Marsh, Executive Dean, 304-293-6607, Fax: 304-293-6627, E-mail: clay.marsh@hsc.wvu.edu. *Application contact:* Lisa M. Salati, Assistant Vice President, Graduate Education, 304-293-7759, Fax: 304-293-3080, E-mail: lsalati@hsc.wvu.edu.
Website: https://medicine.hsc.wvu.edu

Wichita State University, Graduate School, Fairmount College of Liberal Arts and Sciences, Department of Biological Sciences, Wichita, KS 67260. Offers MS. *Program availability:* Part-time. *Students:* 25 (15 women). In 2017, 10 master's awarded. *Application deadline:* For fall admission, 3/1 for domestic and international students; for spring admission, 10/1 for domestic students, 8/1 for international students. Application fee: $50 ($65 for international students). *Unit head:* Dr. William J. Hendry, III, Chair, 316-978-3111, Fax: 316-978-3772, E-mail: william.hendry@wichita.edu. *Application contact:* Jordan Oleson, Admissions Coordinator, 316-978-3095, E-mail: jordan.oleson@wichita.edu.
Website: http://www.wichita.edu/biology

Wilfrid Laurier University, Faculty of Graduate and Postdoctoral Studies, Faculty of Science, Department of Biology, Waterloo, ON N2L 3C5, Canada. Offers integrative biology (M Sc). *Degree requirements:* For master's, thesis. *Entrance requirements:* For master's, honours BA in last two years of undergraduate studies with a minimum B average. Additional exam requirements/recommendations for international students: Required—TOEFL (minimum score 89 iBT). Electronic applications accepted. *Faculty research:* Genetic/development, anatomy/physiology, ecology/environment, evolution.

William Paterson University of New Jersey, College of Science and Health, Wayne, NJ 07470-8420. Offers adult gerontology nurse practitioner (Certificate); biology (MS); biotechnology (MS); communication disorders (MS); exercise and sport studies (MS); materials chemistry (MS); nurse practitioner (Certificate); nursing (MSN); nursing education (Certificate); nursing practice (DNP); school nurse (Certificate). *Program availability:* Part-time. *Faculty:* 29 full-time (15 women), 25 part-time/adjunct (24 women). *Students:* 66 full-time (56 women), 197 part-time (163 women); includes 104 minority (15 Black or African American, non-Hispanic/Latino; 45 Asian, non-Hispanic/Latino; 38 Hispanic/Latino; 6 Two or more races, non-Hispanic/Latino), 3 international. Average age 33. 387 applicants, 34% accepted, 77 enrolled. In 2017, 87 master's, 5 doctorates awarded. *Degree requirements:* For master's, comprehensive exam (for some programs), thesis (for some programs), non-thesis internship/practicum (for some programs). *Entrance requirements:* For master's, GRE/MAT, minimum GPA of 3.0; 2-3 letters of recommendation; personal statement; work experience (for some programs); for doctorate, GRE/MAT, minimum GPA of 3.3; work experience; 3 letters of recommendation; interview; master's degree in nursing. Additional exam requirements/recommendations for international students: Required—TOEFL (minimum score 550 paper-based; 79 iBT), IELTS (minimum score 6). *Application deadline:* For fall admission, 6/1 for domestic students, 3/1 for international students; for spring admission, 11/1 for domestic students, 10/1 for international students. Applications are processed on a rolling basis. Application fee: $50. Electronic applications accepted. *Expenses:* Tuition, state resident: full-time $13,920; part-time $6264 per year. Tuition, nonresident: full-time $21,700; part-time $9765 per year. *Required fees:* $80; $36 per year. Tuition and fees vary according to course load, degree level and program. *Financial support:* In 2017–18, 9,000 students received support. Career-related internships or fieldwork, Federal Work-Study, scholarships/grants, and unspecified assistantships available. Support available to part-time students. Financial award application deadline: 3/15; financial award applicants required to submit FAFSA. *Faculty research:* Behaviors of American long-eared bats, postpartum fatigue, methodologies for coating carbon nano-tubes, paleoclimatology, and pre-linguistic gestures in children with language disorders. *Total annual research expenditures:* $291,600. *Unit head:* Dr. Venkat Sharma, Dean, 973-720-2194, Fax: 973-720-3414, E-mail: sharmav@wpunj.edu. *Application contact:* Christina Aiello, Assistant Director, Graduate Admissions, 973-720-2506, Fax: 973-720-2035, E-mail: aielloc@wpunj.edu.
Website: http://www.wpunj.edu/cosh

Winthrop University, College of Arts and Sciences, Department of Biology, Rock Hill, SC 29733. Offers MS. *Program availability:* Part-time. *Students:* 3 full-time (1 woman), 10 part-time (2 women); includes 2 minority (1 Black or African American, non-Hispanic/Latino; 1 Hispanic/Latino). Average age 26. In 2017, 10 master's awarded. *Degree requirements:* For master's, thesis optional. *Entrance requirements:* For master's, GRE General Test. Additional exam requirements/recommendations for international students: Required—TOEFL (minimum score 550 paper-based; 79 iBT). *Application deadline:* For fall admission, 7/15 priority date for domestic students; for spring admission, 12/1 for domestic students. Applications are processed on a rolling basis. Application fee: $50. Electronic applications accepted. *Financial support:* Research assistantships with full tuition reimbursements, Federal Work-Study, scholarships/grants, and unspecified assistantships available. Support available to part-time students. Financial award application deadline: 2/1; financial award applicants required to submit FAFSA. *Faculty research:* Bone biology, bone biomechanics; development of the visual system; cancer research, prostate cancer metastasis; new monkey species in rainforest in Peru. *Unit head:* Dr. Dwight Dimaculangan, Department Chair, 803-323-2111, Fax: 803-323-2246, E-mail: dimaculangad@winthrop.edu. *Application contact:* 800-411-7041, Fax: 803-323-2292, E-mail: gradschool@winthrop.edu.
Website: http://www.winthrop.edu/graduate-studies/biology.htm

Worcester Polytechnic Institute, Graduate Admissions, Department of Biology and Biotechnology, Worcester, MA 01609-2280. Offers biology and biotechnology (MS); biotechnology (PhD). *Program availability:* Part-time, blended/hybrid learning. *Faculty:* 10 full-time (6 women), 1 part-time/adjunct (0 women). *Students:* 22 full-time (11 women), 19 part-time (11 women); includes 4 minority (1 Black or African American, non-Hispanic/Latino; 2 Asian, non-Hispanic/Latino; 1 Hispanic/Latino), 6 international. Average age 28. 85 applicants, 47% accepted, 26 enrolled. In 2017, 1 doctorate awarded. Terminal master's awarded for partial completion of doctoral program. *Degree requirements:* For master's, thesis; for doctorate, comprehensive exam, thesis/dissertation, qualifying exam. *Entrance requirements:* For master's and doctorate, GRE General Test, 3 letters of recommendation, statement of purpose. Additional exam requirements/recommendations for international students: Required—TOEFL (minimum score 563 paper-based; 84 iBT), IELTS (minimum score 7). *Application deadline:* For fall admission, 1/1 priority date for domestic and international students. Application fee: $70. Electronic applications accepted. *Expenses: Tuition:* Full-time $26,226; part-time $1457 per credit. *Required fees:* $60; $30 per credit. One-time fee: $15. Tuition and fees vary according to course load. *Financial support:* Fellowships, research assistantships, teaching assistantships, career-related internships or fieldwork, institutionally sponsored loans, scholarships/grants, and unspecified assistantships available. Financial award application deadline: 1/1. *Unit head:* Dr. Joseph Duffy, Head, 508-831-4111, Fax: 508-831-5936, E-mail: jduffy@wpi.edu. *Application contact:* Dr. Reeta Rao, Graduate Coordinator, 508-831-5538, Fax: 508-831-5936, E-mail: rpr@wpi.edu.
Website: https://www.wpi.edu/academics/departments/biology-biotechnology

Wright State University, Graduate School, College of Science and Mathematics, Department of Biological Sciences, Dayton, OH 45435. Offers biological sciences (MS). *Degree requirements:* For master's, thesis optional. *Entrance requirements:* Additional exam requirements/recommendations for international students: Required—TOEFL.

Wright State University, Graduate School, College of Science and Mathematics and Boonshoft School of Medicine, Program in Biomedical Sciences, Dayton, OH 45435. Offers PhD. *Degree requirements:* For doctorate, thesis/dissertation. *Entrance requirements:* For doctorate, GRE General Test. Additional exam requirements/recommendations for international students: Required—TOEFL.

Yale University, Yale School of Medicine and Graduate School of Arts and Sciences, Combined Program in Biological and Biomedical Sciences (BBS), New Haven, CT 06520. Offers PhD, MD/PhD. *Degree requirements:* For doctorate, thesis/dissertation. *Entrance requirements:* For doctorate, GRE General Test. Additional exam requirements/recommendations for international students: Required—TOEFL. Electronic applications accepted. *Expenses:* Contact institution.

York University, Faculty of Graduate Studies, Faculty of Science, Program in Biology, Toronto, ON M3J 1P3, Canada. Offers M Sc, PhD. *Program availability:* Part-time, evening/weekend. *Degree requirements:* For master's, thesis or alternative; for doctorate, comprehensive exam, thesis/dissertation, preliminary exam. Electronic applications accepted.

Youngstown State University, Graduate School, College of Science, Technology, Engineering and Mathematics, Department of Biological Sciences, Youngstown, OH 44555-0001. Offers environmental biology (MS); molecular biology, microbiology, and genetic (MS); physiology and anatomy (MS). *Program availability:* Part-time. *Degree requirements:* For master's, comprehensive exam, thesis, oral review. *Entrance requirements:* For master's, GRE General Test, minimum GPA of 2.7. Additional exam requirements/recommendations for international students: Required—TOEFL. *Faculty research:* Cell biology, neurophysiology, molecular biology, neurobiology, gene regulation.

CALIFORNIA POLYTECHNIC STATE UNIVERSITY

Master's of Science in Biological Sciences

CAL POLY
Graduate Education

★ For more information, visit http://petersons.to/calpolystateubiologicalsciences

Program of Study

The Masters of Science in Biological Science program is designed to prepare students for many types of biological work that require advanced training beyond the bachelor's degree. The program offers an M.S. in Biological Sciences along with a specialization in regenerative medicine. Both programs are designed to strengthen the student's academic understanding and improve competence for fields that require advanced training beyond the bachelor's degree. Students who graduate with a master's in Biological Sciences from Cal Poly often pursue graduate work at the doctoral level or obtain professional employment in one of the following fields: environmental consulting, teaching, research (e.g., lab manager, research specialist), biotechnology, and related industries.

The specialization in regenerative medicine offers candidates a year of training in place of the thesis as a culminating experience, students are required to complete a non-traditional Comprehensive Exam that includes a 9-month internship at a stem cell research laboratory, a quarter-long project course at Cal Poly, a written report of their internship research, a written report of their quarter-long project course, and an oral presentation of their internship research. This degree prepares candidates to go into industry at laboratories conducting research in regenerative medicine and stem cells, or to pursue a further advanced degree such as a doctorate.

Research Opportunities

California Polytechnic State University is a thesis-based program that gives students strong research experience under the direct leadership of their faculty supervisor. As a result, they graduate with the skills to perform these tasks: 1) critically evaluate and apply scientific research, 2) gather, organize, analyze, and present planning information, and transform information into knowledge for action. Our faculty performs applied research and train students while creating solutions to biological issues and problems using technology that's at the growing interface between biology, medicine, science, and engineering.

Cal Poly's Center for Coastal Marine Sciences (CCMS) promotes basic and applied studies of coastal marine systems. Through the Center, faculty conduct applied research addressing environmental concerns and fostering hands-on learning among Cal Poly students through discovery and outreach. CCMS's facility was donated to the university by Unocal (now Chevron Corporation) in 2001, and the pier has been developed into a premiere research facility for faculty and graduate students. Now, roughly 1,500 students come to the pier each year as part of classes or research activities.

CCMS provides the only marine laboratory facility between Santa Barbara and Monterey; some of the nation's most beautiful and least-impacted coastline. The territory offers a wide diversity of marine habitats, from rocky intertidal zones to sandy coastline to estuarine communities and kelp forest communities. All are in close (1 km) proximity to each other and the CCMS Cal Poly Pier facility. Through research partnerships with major corporations, local laboratories dedicated to biotechnology, and cooperative learning experiences that involve students from around the world, Cal Poly is building momentum toward being a regional powerhouse in biotechnology.

Financial Aid

Graduate students may qualify for federal loans, emergency loans, state grants, scholarships, and veteran's benefits. Students may also pursue loans from private lenders, employer tuition remission programs, and scholarships from private sources.

Cost of Study

For the 2017–18 academic year, tuition for the biological science M.S. programs was $3,622 per term for California residents. Nonresidents must add $264 per enrolled unit. The most current information on tuition and fees is available at https://afd.calpoly.edu/fees/.

Living and Housing Costs

Graduate students can live in campus apartments complete with a full kitchen, private bathrooms, and the option of private or shared bedrooms. Costs for a University apartment per academic year range from $5,770 for an apartment with a double suite bedroom to $9,014 for an apartment with a private bedroom. There are also many opportunities for off-campus housing.

Location

California Polytechnic State University is located in San Luis Obispo, California. According to Colleges in California, its campus is one of the most beautiful in the state. The University is situated in an area known for its mild climate, natural beauty, and outdoor recreational options. Biking, hiking, and sailing are just some of the activities students can enjoy most of the year.

The University

California Polytechnic State University fosters scholarship, service, and teaching in a Learn-by-Doing environment. The application of theory to practice, active-learning methods, and field and laboratory work form the core of this academic approach. The University offers approximately 21,300 students nearly 190 bachelor's, master's, minor, and credential programs. This large offering enables students to create programs of study that reflect their academic and career interests.

California Polytechnic State University's commitment to providing high quality education earns it top honors. In its 2017 guidebook, *U.S. News & World Report* named it the best public, master's-level university in the west. This is the 24th consecutive year that the university has received this honor. The publisher also ranked it ninth among the best universities in the western region.

Faculty

Graduate faculty members in the Biological Sciences Department are committed to helping their students succeed. They integrate theory, research, and practice to provide extensive knowledge and training. Students have an opportunity to form close working relationships with accomplished faculty like Gita R. Kolluru who studies the costs and benefits of sexually selected displays; aggressive intermale interactions; costs of mating and resulting trade-offs; evolution in poeciliid fishes, especially the Cuban species Girardinus metallicus; phenotypic plasticity and geographic variation in mating tactics. And Sean Lema who studies environmental endocrinology; behavioral ecology of marine and freshwater fishes; evolution of developmental and behavioral plasticity; endocrine disruption by chemical pollutants; integration of phenotypic plasticity into new approaches to conservation.

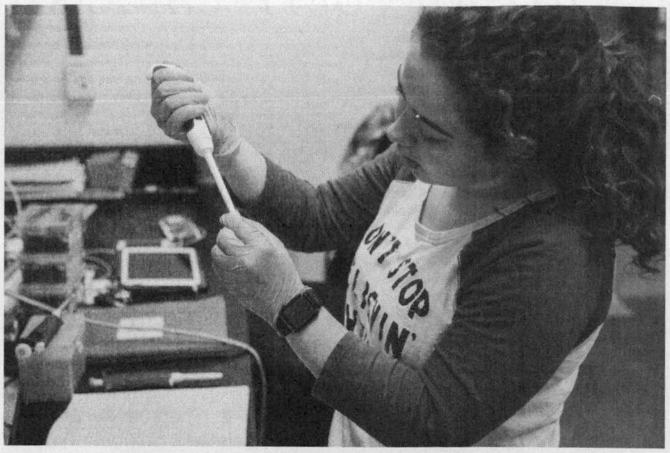

Applying

Most applicants with undergraduate degrees in biology or chemistry are eligible to apply for the M.S. program. Applicants with other undergraduate degrees are also eligible to apply but may require prerequisite course work.

All applicants must submit a statement of purpose; 3 letters of reference; and GRE scores. For applicants with degrees from outside the U.S., all of the above applies. In addition, the applicant's international credentials must be evaluated by AACRAO, ACEI, WES or IERF; proficiency in English must be demonstrated by taking TOEFL (Test of English as a Foreign Language) within the last 2 years with an Internet score of 80 or greater or ELTS (International English Language Testing System) must be taken within 2 years with a score of 6.5 or greater. TOFEL or ELTS is required to issue an I20 visa.

Candidates are strongly encouraged to submit by mid-January. As a relatively small, non-cohort program, it is important that candidates connect with the graduate coordinator, discuss potential areas of research, include these considerations in their statement of interest, and submit applications early. Applications are accepted through the online system Cal State Apply. The filing periods are listed at https://admissions.calpoly.edu/applicants/graduate/deadlines.html and all applicants are responsible for using the University's established applicant checklist for meeting admission deadlines. More information is available at grad.calpoly.edu

Correspondence and Information

California Polytechnic State University
Biological Sciences Department
1 Grand Avenue
San Luis Obispo, California 93407
Phone: 805-756-2616
E-mail: biosci@calpoly.edu
Website: https://bio.calpoly.edu

COLUMBIA UNIVERSITY

Graduate School of Arts and Sciences
Department of Biological Sciences

Program of Study

The Department offers training leading to a Ph.D. in cellular, molecular, developmental, computational, evolutionary, and structural biology as well as genetics, biophysics, and neurobiology. The graduate program provides each student with a strong background in contemporary biology and an in-depth knowledge of one or more of the above areas, with emphasis on interdisciplinary training. All students take a set of core courses together, promoting cohesion and inter-disciplinary exchanges. The specific nature and scheduling of further elective courses are guided by consultation with the graduate student advisers, taking into account the background and specific research interests of the student. An important aspect of this coursework is to provide a constructive and interesting setting to develop advanced skills, including the ability to analyze critically the contemporary research literature and to present such analyses effectively through oral and written presentations. Students acquire additional training in these skills through participation in Departmental seminars and journal clubs, as well as through presentation and defense of original research proposals towards the end of the second year of graduate study.

Students engage in research training right away through laboratory "rotations." Students may choose laboratories in the Department of Biological Sciences on Columbia's main Morningside Heights Campus or any of more than thirty other laboratories at Columbia's Health Sciences Campus carefully selected to join our training program. To inform incoming students of research opportunities, faculty members discuss ongoing research projects with them in a series of "pre-research" seminars held in the first semester of the first year. Students engage in at least two, but normally three laboratory rotations during their first year in order to identify a laboratory for their dissertation research. The choice of a dissertation laboratory is made after consultation between the student and potential faculty dissertation sponsors. Each student is then guided in their future research progress by a Ph.D. Advisory Committee made up of the student's sponsor and at least two other faculty members.

Research Facilities

The core space for the Department of Biological Sciences is the Sherman Fairchild Center for the Life Sciences. The building provides nearly 78,000 square feet of space for the Department's laboratories, as well as extensive shared instrument facilities, including microscopy, X-ray diffraction, fluorescence-activated cell sorting (FACS), real-time PCR analysis, mass spectrometry, infrared scanning, and phosphorimaging, as well as housing and care of research animals. In addition, several Biological Science laboratories are located in the nearby recently constructed Northwest Corner Interdisciplinary Science Building and Mind, Brain, and Behavior Building.

Financial Aid

All accepted students receive generous stipends, complete tuition exemption, and medical insurance. Special fellowships with larger stipends are also available (e.g., to members of minority groups or for students carrying out research in specialized topics).

Cost of Study

Tuition and fees are paid for all graduate students accepted into the Department.

Living and Housing Costs

Most students live in University-owned, subsidized apartments within easy walking distance of the laboratories. In addition, both the Morningside and Health Sciences Campuses are easily reached by public transportation from all areas of the city.

Student Group

There are about 110 graduate students and 70 postdoctoral fellows in the Department.

Location

New York is the cultural center of the country and offers unrivaled opportunities for attending concerts, operas, plays, and sporting events, for visiting outstanding museums, and for varied, affordable dining. Many excellent beaches, ski slopes, and state and national parks are within reasonable driving distance.

The University and the Department

Columbia was established as King's College in 1754 and has grown into one of the major universities of the world. The Department is located on the beautiful main campus in Morningside Heights, which combines the advantages of an urban setting and a peaceful college-town atmosphere.

Applying

Undergraduate training in one of the natural or physical sciences is recommended, but successful students also come from computer science or engineering backgrounds. It is desirable for students to have had at least one year of calculus, as well as courses in organic and physical chemistry, physics, genetics, biochemistry, and cell biology. The Graduate Record Examinations (GRE) is required, as is the Test of English as a Foreign Language (TOEFL) for international applicants whose native language is not English and who do not hold an undergraduate degree from a U.S. college. The GRE Subject Test in biology, biochemistry, chemistry, computer science, or physics is recommended but not required. Completed applications should be returned by January 1 for admission to the fall semester. Applications will be reviewed in the order received, so those submitting complete applications earlier have a better chance of being invited for an interview. Application forms and additional information can be obtained from the Department's website.

Columbia University is an Equal Opportunity/Affirmative Action institution.

Correspondence and Information

Graduate Student Adviser
Department of Biological Sciences
Columbia University
1212 Amsterdam Avenue, Mail Code 2402
Sherman Fairchild Center, Room 600
New York, New York 10027
United States
Phone: 212-854-2313
Fax: 212-865-8246
E-mail: biology@columbia.edu
Website: http://biology.columbia.edu

THE FACULTY AND THEIR RESEARCH

Peter Andolfatto, Professor; Ph.D., University of Chicago, 1999. Constraints on adaptation revealed by the convergent evolution of toxin insensitivity.

J. Chloë Bulinski, Professor; Ph.D., Wisconsin, 1980. Dynamics and functions of the cytoskeleton during chondrogenic differentiation, motility, and cell-cycle progression.

Harmen Bussemaker, Professor; Ph.D., Utrecht (Netherlands), 1995. Data-driven modeling of transcriptional and posttranscriptional networks based on biophysical principles.

Martin Chalfie, Professor; Ph.D., Harvard, 1977; Member, National Academy of Sciences and Nobel Laureate in Chemistry 2008. Developmental genetics of identified nerve cells in *Caenorhabditis elegans;* genetic analysis of cell differentiation, mechanosensory transduction, synapse specification, and aging.

Lawrence A. Chasin, Professor; Ph.D., MIT, 1967. Pre-mRNA splicing in cultured mammalian cells.

Lars Dietrich, Assistant Professor, Ph.D., Heidelberg (Germany), 2004. Bacterial models for biological shape and pattern formation.

Julio Fernandez, Professor; Ph.D., Berkeley, 1982. Study of the cellular events that lead to the release of histamine or catecholamine-containing secretory granules from single, isolated mast cells or chromaffin cells; analysis of single-protein elasticity by atomic force microscopy (AFM).

Stuart Firestein, Professor; Ph.D., Berkeley, 1988. Cellular and molecular physiology of transduction; coding and neuronal regeneration in the vertebrate olfactory system.

Joachim Frank, Professor and Howard Hughes Medical Institute Investigator; Ph.D., Munich Technical, 1970; Member, National Academy of Sciences. Cryoelectron microscopy and three-dimensional reconstruction for the study of the mechanism of protein biosynthesis.

Columbia University

Iva Greenwald, Professor and Howard Hughes Medical Institute Investigator; Ph.D., MIT, 1982; Member, National Academy of Sciences. Development and cell-cell interactions.

Tulle Hazelrigg, Professor; Ph.D., Indiana, 1982. mRNA localization in *Drosophila* oocytes.

Oliver Hobert, Professor and Howard Hughes Medical Institute Investigator; Ph.D., Max Planck Institute for Biochemistry, Martinsried, Germany, 1995. Nervous system development and function.

John F. Hunt, Professor; Ph.D., Yale, 1993. Structural genomics and biophysical studies of the molecular mechanism of transmembrane transport.

Songtao Jia, Associate Professor; Ph.D., UCLA, 2003. Epigenetic regulation of the genome.

Marko Jovanovic, Assistant Professor; Ph.D., Zurich, 2010. Regulation of protein production dynamics: RNA binding proteins and the ribosome code.

Daniel D. Kalderon, Professor; Ph.D., London, 1984. Molecular mechanisms of cellular interactions mediated by cAMP-dependent protein kinase (PKA) in *Drosophila;* roles of PKA in hedgehog signaling and in generating anterior/posterior polarity in oocytes.

Darcy B. Kelley, Professor and Howard Hughes Medical Institute Professor; Ph.D., Rockefeller, 1975. Sexual differentiation of the nervous system; molecular analyses of androgen-regulated development in neurons and muscle; neuroethology of vocal communication; evolution of the nuclear receptor family.

Laura Landweber, Professor; Ph.D., Harvard, 1993. Molecular evolution and RNA-mediated epigenetic inheritance.

James L. Manley, Professor; Ph.D., SUNY at Stony Brook, 1976. Regulation of mRNA synthesis in animal cells; biochemical and genetic analysis of mechanisms and control of mRNA transcription, splicing, and polyadenylation; developmental control of gene expression.

Carol L. Prives, Professor; Ph.D., McGill, 1968; Member, National Academy of Sciences and National Institute of Medicine. Structure and function of the p53 tumor suppressor protein and p53 family members; studies on cell cycle and apoptosis; stress-activated signaling and control of proteolysis.

Ron Prywes, Professor; Ph.D., MIT, 1984. Normal and cancerous mechanisms of regulation of cellular proliferation and gene expression; signal transduction and activation of transcription factors; activation of transcription by the ER stress/unfolded protein response.

Molly Przeworski, Professor; Ph.D., Chicago, 2000. Population genetics, evolutionary genetics, meiotic recombination.

Ozgur Sahin, Associate Professor of Biological Sciences and Physics; Ph.D., Stanford, 2005. Mechanical investigations of biological systems for energy, environment, and biological research.

Guy Sella, Associate Professor; Ph.D., Tel Aviv (Israel), 2001. Evolutionary genetics of adaptation, disease risk and other quantitative traits.

Brent Stockwell, Professor and Howard Hughes Medical Institute Investigator; Ph.D., Harvard, 1997. Diagramming disease networks with chemical and biological tools.

Simon Tavare, Professor; Ph.D., University of Sheffield, UK, 1979. Cancer genomics; evolutionary approaches to cancer; lineage tracing; statistical bioinformatics; computational biology; population genetics, coalescent theory; stochastic computation, approximate Bayesian computation, data science; statistical inference in molecular biology, human genetics, molecular evolution, paleontology; tracking from videos; probabilistic combinatorics.

Raju Tomer, Assistant Professor; Ph.D. European Molecular Biology Laboratory, 2010. Developing and applying molecular, optical, and data analytic methods for multi-scale understanding of complex biological systems.

Liang Tong, Professor; Ph.D., Berkeley, 1989. Structural biology of proteins involved in human diseases (obesity, diabetes, cancer); structural biology of proteins involved in pre-mRNA 3'-end processing.

Alexander A. Tzagoloff, Professor of Biological Sciences; Ph.D., Columbia, 1962. Energy-coupling mechanisms; structure of membrane enzymes; biogenesis of mitochondria; genetics of mitochondria in yeast.

Jian Yang, Professor; Ph.D., Washington (Seattle), 1991. Structure and function of ion channels; molecular mechanisms of ion channel regulation and localization.

Rafael Yuste, Professor and Howard Hughes Medical Institute Investigator; M.D., Madrid, 1987; Ph.D., Rockefeller, 1992. Development and function of the cortical microcircuitry.

Additional Faculty Sponsors for Ph.D. Research

Cory Abate-Shen, Urology, Medicine, Systems Biology, and Pathology and Cell Biology. Computational and preclinical analyses of mouse models of prostate and bladder cancer.

Dimitris Anastassiou, Electrical Engineering. Data mining of large biological datasets—cancer research.

Richard Axel, Biochemistry and Molecular Biophysics/Pathology and Cell Biology; Howard Hughes Medical Institute Investigator and Nobel Laureate in Physiology or Medicine 2004; Member, National Academy of Sciences. Central and peripheral organization of the olfactory system.

Richard J. Baer, Pathology and Cell Biology. The pathogenesis of hereditary breast cancer.

Uttiya Basu, Microbiology and Immunology. RNA surveillance, noncoding RNA processing and DNA alteration events during development and immunity.

Andrea Califano, Biomedical Informatics. Study of gene regulatory and signaling networks in mammalian cellular contexts using computational methods.

Julie C. Canman, Pathology and Cell Biology. Molecular mechanisms of cell division.

Virginia Cornish, Chemistry. Development of in vivo selection strategies for evolving proteins with novel catalytic properties.

Franklin D. Costantini, Genetics and Development. Genetics of kidney development in the mouse; cellular and genetic basis of epithelial branching morphogenesis.

Riccardo Dalla-Favera, Genetics and Development, and Microbiology and Immunology. Molecular genetics of cancer; molecular pathogenesis of lymphoma and leukemia.

Jonathan E. Dworkin, Microbiology and Immunology. Bacterial signaling and interactions with the host.

Jean Gautier, Genetics and Development/Institute for Cancer Genetics. Cell cycle and cell death during early development.

Ruben L. Gonzalez Jr., Chemistry. Single molecule biophysics.

Eric C. Greene, Biochemistry and Molecular Biophysics; Howard Hughes Medical Institute Investigator. Molecular mechanisms of DNA recombination and repair; single-molecule fluorescence microscopy and other biochemical approaches.

Lloyd Greene, Pathology and Cell Biology. Mechanisms of neuronal differentiation and degeneration and their regulation by external growth factors.

Wesley Grueber, Physiology and Cellular Biophysics/Neuroscience. Molecular basis of nervous system development and function in *Drosophila*.

Wei Gu, Pathology and Cell Biology. P53 in tumor suppression and aging.

René Hen, Pharmacology. Serotonin receptors and behavior.

Wayne Hendrickson, Biochemistry and Molecular Biophysics; Howard Hughes Medical Institute Investigator; Member, National Academy of Sciences. Macromolecular structure; X-ray crystallography.

Laura Johnston, Genetics and Development. Control of growth and cell division during development.

Eric Kandel, Physiology and Cellular Biophysics/Psychiatry/Biochemistry and Molecular Biophysics; Howard Hughes Medical Institute Investigator and Nobel Laureate in Physiology or Medicine 2000; Member, National Academy of Sciences. Cell and molecular mechanisms of associative and nonassociative learning.

Stavroula Kousteni, Physiology and Cellular Biophysics. Skeletal functions in metabolism and hematopoiesis.

Stavros Lomvardas, Biochemistry and Molecular Biophysics and Neuroscience. When we understand how diversity works with olfactory receptor neurons, it affects not just our understanding of the senses, but how it shapes human behavior and development as a whole.

Richard Mann, Biochemistry and Molecular Biophysics. Transcriptional control.

Ann McDermott, Chemistry/Biological Sciences/Chemical Engineering; Member, National Academy of Sciences. Solid-state NMR of enzyme active sites and model systems.

Arthur G. Palmer, Biochemistry and Molecular Biophysics. Biomolecular dynamics, structure, and function; NMR spectroscopy.

Liam Paninski, Statistics. Statistical analysis of neural and imaging data.

Emmanuelle Passegue, Genetics and Development.

Itsik Pe'er, Computer Science. Novel computational methods in human genetics.

Rodney Rothstein, Genetics and Development. Yeast genetics; mechanisms of genetic recombination; control of genome stability; functional genomics.

Christian Schindler, Microbiology/Medicine. JAK-STAT signaling and immune response.

Michael M. Shen, Medicine/Genetics and Development/Urology/Systems Biology. Molecular mechanisms of pattern formation and cellular differentiation during mouse embryogenesis; organogenesis and regeneration of the prostate gland; mouse models of prostate cancer.

Michele M Shirasu-Hiza, Genetics and Development. How specific circadian-regulated physiological functions (such as innate immunity, metabolism, and sleep) contribute to health and disease using Drosophila melanogaster.

Steve Siegelbaum, Pharmacology; Howard Hughes Medical Institute Investigator. Molecular studies of ion channel structure and function; synaptic transmission and plasticity in the mammalian brain.

Gary Struhl, Genetics and Development; Howard Hughes Medical Institute Investigator; Member, National Academy of Sciences. Developmental genetics in *Drosophila.*

Lorraine Symington, Microbiology. Homologous recombination in the yeast *Saccharomyces cerevisiae.*

Richard Vallee, Pathology and Cell Biology. Motor proteins in axonal transport, brain developmental disease, and synaptic function.

Hynek Wichterle, Pathology and Cell Biology/ Neuroscience. The use of stem cells to study the development and function of the nervous system.

Charles Zuker, Biochemistry and Molecular Biophysics/Neuroscience. Signal processing, information transfer, and coding mechanisms in sensory systems.

IRELL & MANELLA GRADUATE SCHOOL OF BIOLOGICAL SCIENCES

City of Hope National Medical Center
Beckman Research Institute

IRELL AND MANELLA GRADUATE SCHOOL OF BIOLOGICAL SCIENCES

Programs of Study

The mission of the City of Hope Graduate School of Biological Sciences is to train students to be outstanding research scientists in chemical, molecular, and cellular biology. Graduates of this program are awarded the degree of Doctor of Philosophy in biological sciences and are equipped to address fundamental questions in the life sciences and biomedicine for careers in academia, industry, and government. The time spent in the program is devoted to full-time study and research. During the first year, the student completes the core curriculum and three laboratory rotations (eight to ten weeks each). The core curriculum contains biochemistry, molecular biology, cell biology, and biostatistics/bioinformatics. After the first year, the student prepares and orally defends a research proposal based on an original topic not related to previous work conducted by the student. In the second year the student prepares and defends a research proposal based on their actual thesis topic. Two additional Advanced Topics courses are required after the first year and students are required to take a literature-based journal club every year after the first year. Students also participate in courses on scientific communication and on the responsible conduct of research. After successfully completing the core curriculum and research proposal, students concentrate the majority of their time on their individual dissertation laboratory research project. The written thesis/dissertation must be presented by the student for examination by 3 members of the City of Hope staff and 1 qualified member from an outside institution.

Research Facilities

City of Hope is a premier medical center, one of sixty-nine National Cancer Institute–designated Comprehensive Cancer Centers. The Beckman Research Institute launched the biotech industry by creating the first human recombinant gene products, Insulin and growth hormone, which are now used by millions of people worldwide. State-of-the-art facilities include mass spectrometry, NMR, molecular modeling, cell sorting, DNA sequencing, molecular pathology, scanning and transmission electron microscopy, confocal microscopy, and molecular imaging. The Lee Graff Medical and Scientific Library allows access to the latest biomedical information via its journal and book collection, document delivery, interlibrary loans, and searches of online databases.

Financial Aid

All students in the Graduate School receive a fellowship of $33,000 per year as well as paid health and dental insurance.

Cost of Study

There are no tuition charges. A student services fee of $150 per year is the student's only financial obligation to City of Hope.

Living and Housing Costs

The School has limited, low-cost housing available. Living in student housing provides easy access to campus resources and a connection to the vibrant campus community. Additional housing is available within the immediate area at an average cost of $700 to $1,000 per month.

Student Group

The Graduate School faculty consists of 112 of City of Hope's investigators. Eighty-two graduate students were working toward the Ph.D. degree in biological sciences in 2017–18.

Student Outcomes

Graduates have gone on to work as postdoctoral fellows at California Institute of Technology; Harvard University; Scripps Research Institute; Stanford University; University of California, Los Angeles; University of California, San Diego; University of California, Irvine; Genentech; University of Southern California; and Washington University in St. Louis. Graduates have also found positions with Wyeth-Ayerst Research; Allergan, Inc.; and the U.S. Biodefense and its subsidiary, Stem Cell Research Institute of California, Inc.

Location

City of Hope is located 25 miles northeast of downtown Los Angeles, minutes away from Pasadena and close to beaches, mountains, and many recreational and cultural activities.

The National Medical Center and The Beckman Research Institute

City of Hope was founded in 1913, initially as a tuberculosis sanatorium. Research programs were initiated in 1951, and, in 1983, the Beckman Research Institute of City of Hope was established with support from the Arnold and Mabel Beckman Foundation. The Institute comprises basic science research groups within the Divisions of Biology, Immunology, Molecular Medicine, and Neurosciences, among others.

Applying

The deadline for application is January 1 for classes starting in August. Applying early is advisable. Candidates must submit transcripts, three letters of recommendation, and take the Graduate Record Examination (General Test required, Subject Test recommended). For further information and an application, students should contact the School at the address listed in this description.

Correspondence and Information

City of Hope
Irell & Manella Graduate School of Biological Sciences
1500 East Duarte Road
Duarte, California 91010
United States
Phone: 877-715-GRAD or 626-256-4723
Fax: 626-471-3901
E-mail: gradschool@coh.org
Website: http://www.cityofhope.org/gradschool

THE FACULTY AND THEIR RESEARCH

Professors

Karen S. Aboody, M.D. Neural stem cells—therapeutic applications.
David K. Ann, Ph.D. Signal transduction, metabolism, genome integrity, tumorigenesis and progression.
Behnam Badie, M.D., FACS. Development of minimally invasive techniques for treatment of benign and malignant brain tumors.
Michael E. Barish, Ph.D. Physiological and imaging studies of brain tumors.
Andrea Bild, Ph.D. Matching biological basis of disease to treatment strategies for translational research.
Edouard M. Cantin, Ph.D. Herpes simplex virus infections in the nervous system.
Nadia Carlesso, M.D., Ph.D. Biology of leukemia development and relapse.
Wing-Chun (John) Chan, M.D. The functional genomics of lymphoma.
Saswati Chatterjee, Ph.D. Adeno-associated virus vectors for stem cell gene therapy.
Jianjun Chen, Ph.D. Function, mechanism and therapeutic potentials of RNA/DNA epigenetics in cancer.
Shiuan Chen, Ph.D. Hormones and cancer.
Yuan Chen, Ph.D. Ubiquitin-like modifications.
Warren Chow, M.D. Cell signaling and cancer.
Don J. Diamond, Ph.D. Translational research in cancer vaccines.
Richard W. Ermel, D.V.M., M.P.V.M., Ph.D. Comparative medicine.

Irell & Manella Graduate School of Biological Sciences

Yuman Fong, M.D., D.Sc. (Hon). Targeting cancer using genetically modified viruses.
Stephen J. Forman, M.D., FACP. T-Cell immunotherapy for treatment of cancer.
David Horne, Ph.D. Developing natural products as novel anti-cancer agents.
Susanta Hui, Ph.D. Molecular imaging and theragnostics.
Keiichi Itakura, Ph.D. Functions of Mrf-1 and Mrf-2.
Michael Kahn, Ph.D. Identify and validate pharmacologic tools.
Markus Kalkum, Dr. Rer. Nat. (Ph.D.). Emerging infectious diseases, vaccines, and advanced diagnostics.
Rick A. Kittles, Ph.D. The biological and socio-cultural context of cancer disparities.
Larry W. Kwak, M.D., Ph.D. Hematologic malignancies and stem cell transplantation institute, Toni Stephenson Lymphoma Center.
Mark LaBarge, Ph.D. The cell and tissue biology of aging and cancer susceptibility.
Peter P. Lee, Ph.D. The impact of cancer on immune function.
Ren-Jang Lin, Ph.D. RNA splicing, microRNA, and gene screening.
Linda Malkas, Ph.D. The selective targeting of cancer cells.
Guido Marcucci, M.D. Acute myeloid leukemia and hematologic malignancies.
Jeannine S. McCune, Pharm.D. Making cancer drugs work better through precision medicine.
Marcia M. Miller, Ph.D. Molecular immunogenetics.
Kevin V. Morris, Ph.D. Center for gene therapy.
Markus Muschen, M.D., Ph.D. Genetic target discovery in B cell leukemia and lymphoma.
Rama Natarajan, Ph.D. Diabetic vascular complications.
Susan Neuhausen, Ph.D. Genetic epidemiology of complex diseases.
Timothy R. O'Connor, Ph.D. DNA repair.
Arthur D. Riggs, Ph.D. Epigenetics, chromatin structure, and gene regulation.
Bart O. Roep, Ph.D. , M.D. Translating cause to cure of type 1 diabetes.
Steven T. Rosen, M.D. Developing novel therapies for treatment of hematologic malignancies.
John J. Rossi, Ph.D. The biology and applications of small RNAs.
Paul M. Salvaterra, Ph.D. Modeling Alzheimer-type neurodegeneration.
Victoria Seewaldt, M.D. Early detection of biologically aggressive cancers.
Binghui Shen, Ph.D. DNA replication, repair, and apoptosis nucleases in genome stability and cancer.
Yanhong Shi, Ph.D. Stem cell–based disease modeling and therapeutic development.
John E. Shively, Ph.D. Structure, function, and regulation of carcinoembryonic antigen genes.
Steven S. Smith, Ph.D. Cancer epigenetics.
Cy A. Stein, M.D, Ph.D. Cellular delivery of therapeutic oligonucleotides.
Zijie (ZJ) Sun, M.D., Ph.D. Transcriptional regulation, cell signaling, and hormone action in oncogenesis and development.
Zuoming Sun, Ph.D. Mechanisms regulating T cell-mediated immunity.
John Termini, Ph.D. Mutagenesis and carcinogenesis.
Debbie C. Thurmond, Ph.D. Insulin action and insulin secretion dysfunction in diabetes.
Nagarajan Vaidehi, Ph.D. Predicting protein structure and dynamics for drug discovery.
Jeffrey N. Weitzel, M.D. Genetic predisposition to cancer.
John C. Williams, Ph.D. Structural biology and biophysics.
Anna Wu, Ph.D., Engineering antibodies for cancer targeting.
Jiing-Kuan Yee, Ph.D. Promote cell differentiation from human pluripotent stem cells.
Hua Yu, Ph.D. Stat 3: from basic discoveries to the clinic.
Xiaochun Yu, M.D., Ph.D. DNA damage response, epigenetic modifications and their roles in tumorigenesis.
John A. Zaia, M.D. Anti-HIV/AIDS gene therapy.

Associate and Assistant Professors

Adam M. Bailis, Ph.D. Homologous recombination, genome stability, and the development of targeted cancer therapeutics.
Jacob Berlin, Ph.D. Nanoparticles for the diagnosis and treatment of cancer.
Mark Boldin, M.D., Ph.D. Control of mammalian hematopoiesis, immunity, and cancer by regulatory RNAs.
Christine Brown, Ph.D. Developing Chimeric Antigen Receptor T Cells for malignant brain tumors.
John Burnett, Ph.D. Development of gene and RNA therapies for acquired diseases and genetic disorders.
Angelo Cardoso, M.D., Ph.D. Leukemia cells and the bone marrow microenvironment.
Daniela Castanotto, Ph.D. Therapeutic targeting of cancer genes using small modified nucleic acids.
Ammar Chaudhry, M.D. Integration of advanced imaging, radiobiogenomics, and artificial intelligence-machine learning to develop precision imaging.
Ching-Cheng Chen, Ph.D. Cellular and molecular characterization of the hematopoietic niche.
Chun-Wei David Chen, Ph.D. High throughput genetic screens, epigenetic mechanisms in leukemia and cancers.
Mike Y. Chen, M.D., Ph.D. CBX mediated epigenetic control of glioblastoma epithelial to mesenchymal cell transition.
WenYong Chen, Ph.D. Epigenetics, cancer, and aging.
Zhen (Jen) Chen, B.Med., Ph.D. Non-coding RNA in epigenetic control and endothelial stress responses.
Jessica Clague DeHart, Ph.D., M.P.H. Identifying molecular mechanisms of exercise for cancer prevention.
Thanh Dellinger, M.D. Innovative gene therapy for ovarian cancer.
Sangeetha Dhawan, Ph.D. Epigenetic regulation of beta-cells in health and diabetes developmental and regenerative biology.
Mingye Feng, Ph.D. Macrophage-mediated tumor immunosurveillance in cancer development and metastasis.
Patrick Fueger, Ph.D. Restoration of glucose homeostasis by fortifying functional beta cell mass.
Carlotta A. Glackin, Ph.D. Understanding gene regulation from stem cells.
Robert Hickey, Ph.D. Identification and clinical translation of molecular signatures of disease.
Wendong Huang, Ph.D. Metabolic regulation, diabetes, and cancer.
Janice M. Huss, Ph.D. The role of orphan nuclear receptors in cardiac and skeletal muscle biology.
Rahul Jandial, M.D, Ph.D. Brain metastatic cancer.
Lei Jiang, Ph.D. Metabolic alteration in diabetes and cancer.
Jeremy Jones, Ph.D. Translational research in urologic oncology.
Tijana Jovanovic-Talisman, Ph.D. Super-resolution imaging in drug discovery.
Marcin Kortylewski, Ph.D. Immune cells as targets for cancer therapy.
Hsun Teresa Ku, Ph.D. Pancreatic stem cells.
Ya-Huei Kuo, Ph.D. Molecular genetics of hematopoietic stem cells and leukemia stem cells.
Keane Lai, M.D. Liver cancer and pancreatic cancer.
Yilun Liu, Ph.D. Human RECQ helicases in aging and cancer prevention.
Qiang Lu, Ph.D. Understanding the mechanisms that control self-renewal and differentiation of neural progenitor/stem cells.
Ke Ma, M.D., Ph.D. Circadian clock control of metabolic tissue growth and function.
Edwin R. Manuel, Ph.D. Methods to enhance anti-tumor responses.
Edward M. Newman, Ph.D. Biochemical pharmacology of anti-metabolites.
Vu Ngo, Ph.D. Molecular targets in lymphoid malignancies.
Javier Gordon Ogembo, Ph.D. Understanding the biology of oncogenic viruses.
Flavia Pichiorri, Ph.D. Molecular pathogenesis of multiple myeloma.
Christiane Querfeld, M.D., Ph.D. Identifying tumor microenvironment in cutaneous lymphoma.
Helena Reijonen, Ph.D. Autoimmunity in type 1 diabetes.
Russell Rockne, Ph.D. Mathematical oncology.
Andrei S. Rodin, Ph.D. Computational biology, large data, and molecular evolution.
Dustin E. Schones, Ph.D. Epigenetics and genomics.
Ben Hung-Ping Shih, Ph.D. Stem cell biology and organogenesis.
Christopher Sistrunk, Ph.D. Biomarker development for cancer initiation.
Jeremy M. Stark, Ph.D. Factors and pathways that influence mammalian chromosomal stability.
Timothy W. Synold, Pharm.D. Pharmacokinetics and pharmacodynamics of anti-cancer drugs.
Leo Wang, M.D., Ph.D. Functional proteomics of blood and immune cells.
Qiong (Annabel) Wang, Ph.D. Adipose tissue remodeling in health and disease.
Yanzhong (Frankie) Yang, M.D., Ph.D. Epigenetic regulation of gene expression and genome stability.
Defu Zeng, M.D. Transplantation immune tolerance.

THE ROCKEFELLER UNIVERSITY

Graduate Programs

Programs of Study

Graduate education leading to the Ph.D. is offered to outstanding students regarded as potential leaders in their scientific fields. The University's research covers a wide range of biomedical and related sciences, including chemical and structural biology; genetics and genomics; immunology, virology, and microbiology; medical sciences, systems physiology and human genetics; molecular and cell biology; neurosciences and behavior; organismal biology, evolution, ethology, and ecology; physical, mathematical, and computational biology; and stem cells, development, regeneration, and aging, as summarized by the faculty list in this description. Students work closely with a faculty of active scientists and are encouraged to learn through a combination of course work, tutorial guidance, and apprenticeship in research laboratories. Graduate Fellows spend the first two years engaged in a flexible combination of courses geared toward academic qualification while conducting research in laboratories pertaining to their area of scientific interest. They choose a laboratory for thesis research by the end of the first year and devote their remaining time to pursuit of significant experimental or theoretical research, culminating in a dissertation and thesis defense. Students can spend full time in research; there are no teaching or other service obligations.

The faculties of the Rockefeller University, Weill Cornell Medical College, and the Sloan Kettering Institute collaborate in offering a combined M.D./Ph.D. program in the biomedical sciences to about 135 students. This program, conducted on the adjacent campuses of these three institutions in New York City, normally requires six or seven years of study and leads to an M.D. degree conferred by Weill Cornell Medical College and a Ph.D. degree conferred by either the Rockefeller University, the Weill Cornell Graduate School, or the Gerstner Sloan Kettering Graduate School, depending upon the organizational affiliation of the student's adviser.

Research Facilities

The Rockefeller University supports its 81 laboratories with strong, centralized scientific facilities, providing convenient access to key technologies and services. These include centralized resource centers devoted to bioimaging, cryo-electron microscopy, high-performance computing, genomics, precision fabrication, high-throughput screening, flow cytometry, and more. Rockefeller scientists are also supported by dedicated administration, which includes specialists in information technology, laboratory safety, technology transfer, grants management, and public affairs. The university's physical infrastructure, set on a 15-acre Manhattan campus, includes 481,000 square feet of lab space, along with faculty and administrative offices, event facilities and housing.

Financial Aid

Each student accepted into the Ph.D. program receives a stipend ($40,500 in 2018–19) that is adequate to meet all living expenses. Students also receive an annual budget of $1,500 that can be used for travel, books and journals, computer purchases, and lab supplies.

Cost of Study

The University provides full remission of all tuition and fees for all accepted students.

Living and Housing Costs

On-campus housing is available for all students at subsidized rates. The stipend is designed to cover the cost of food, housing, and other basic living expenses. Students may elect to live off campus, but rents in the vicinity are very high.

Student Group

There are 220 graduate students, of whom 179 are enrolled in the Ph.D. program and 41 in the Ph.D. phase of the combined M.D./Ph.D. program. It is the policy of the Rockefeller University to support equality of educational opportunity. No individual is denied admission to the University or otherwise discriminated against with respect to any program of the University because of creed, color, national or ethnic origin, race, sex, or disability.

Student Outcomes

Graduates of the Rockefeller University have excelled in their professions. Two graduates have been awarded the Nobel Prize, and 31 graduates are members of the National Academy of Sciences. Most Ph.D. graduates move to postdoctoral positions at academic and research centers and subsequently have careers in academics, biotechnology, and the pharmaceutical industry. A few have pursued careers in medicine, law, and business. Almost all M.D./Ph.D. graduates first complete residencies in medical specialties, and most become medical scientists at major academic and medical research centers.

Location

The University is situated between 62nd and 68th streets in Manhattan, overlooking the East River. Despite its central metropolitan location, the 15-acre campus has a distinctive nonurban character, featuring gardens, picnic areas, fountains, and a tennis court. In addition to administrative and residential buildings, there are seven large laboratory buildings and a forty-bed hospital that serves as a clinical research center. Immediate neighbors are New York Presbyterian, Weill Cornell Medical College, and the Sloan-Kettering Institute for Cancer Research. The wide range of institutions in New York City affords unlimited opportunities in research specialties, library facilities, and cultural resources.

The University

The Rockefeller University is dedicated to benefiting humankind through scientific research and its application. Founded in 1901 by John D. Rockefeller as the Rockefeller Institute for Medical Research, it rapidly became a source of major scientific innovation in treating and preventing human disease. Since 1954, the institute has extended its function by offering graduate work at the doctoral level to a select group of qualified students.

Laboratories, rather than departments, are the fundamental units of the University. The absence of departmental barriers between laboratories encourages interdisciplinary, problem-oriented approaches to research and facilitates intellectual interaction and collaboration. The collegial atmosphere fosters independence and initiative in students. In addition to the 220 doctoral students, there are 266 postdoctoral associates and fellows and a faculty of 81 full, associate, and assistant professors on campus who head laboratories.

Applying

Applications for the M.D./Ph.D. program must be completed by October 24; those for the Ph.D. program must be completed by December 1. Applicants are required to submit a personal statement describing research experience and goals as well as reasons for pursuing graduate study at The Rockefeller University. Also required are official transcripts and at least three letters of recommendation. Official GRE General and Subject Test scores are optional. MCAT scores are required for the M.D./Ph.D. program. Further information about each program and details on application procedures may be obtained from the programs' respective websites. This information is also available on the University website, from which application forms and instructions can be downloaded (https://graduateapplication.rockefeller.edu).

Correspondence and Information

Kristen E. Cullen, M.A.
Graduate Admissions Administrator and Registrar
The David Rockefeller Graduate Program
The Rockefeller University
1230 York Avenue, Box 177
New York, New York 10065
Phone: 212-327-8086
E-mail: phd@rockefeller.edu
Website: http://graduate.rockefeller.edu
https://www.facebook.com/rockefelleruniversity
https://twitter.com/rockefelleruniv

LABORATORY HEADS AND THEIR RESEARCH

C. David Allis, Ph.D. (Chromatin Biology and Epigenetics). Studies the role of DNA packaging proteins in gene expression and DNA replication and repair.

Gregory Alushin, Ph.D. (Biophysics). Using cryo-electron microscopy to determine how molecules change their structure in response to pushing or pulling forces.

Cori Bargmann, Ph.D. (Neural Circuits and Behavior). Studies the relationship between genes, neural circuits and behavior in *C. elegans*.

Paul Bieniasz, Ph.D. (Retrovirology) Studies the biology and evolution of retroviruses, including HIV, and genetics of host-virus interactions.

Kivanc Birsoy, Ph.D. (Cancer Cell Metabolism). Investigating cellular metabolism with an emphasis on cancer and metabolic disorders.

Sean Brady, Ph.D. (Genetically Encoded Small Molecules). Discovers and characterizes new small molecules from microbial sources.

Jan L. Breslow, M.D. (Biochemical Genetics and Metabolism). Investigates the genetic basis of atherosclerotic disease.

Ali Brivanlou, Ph.D. (Stem Cell Biology and Molecular Embryology).Researches the molecular events and cellular interactions that establish cell fate in vertebrate embryogenesis.

Jean-Laurent Casanova, M.D., Ph.D. (Human Genetics of Infectious Diseases). Researches the genetic basis of pediatric infectious diseases.

Brian T. Chait, D.Phil. (Mass Spectrometry and Gaseous Ion Chemistry). Uses mass spectrometry as a tool for studying biomolecules and protein interactions.

Jue Chen, Ph.D. (Membrane Biology and Biophysics). Combines structural and function techniques to study ABC membrane transporter proteins in health and disease.

Nam-Hai Chua, Ph.D. (Plant Molecular Biology). Studies molecular signaling pathways involved in plants' response to stress, light and infection.

Joel Cohen, Ph.D., Dr.P.H. (Populations). Studies interactions among groups of living beings in order to develop concepts helpful for understanding populations.

Paul Cohen, M.D., Ph.D. (Molecular Metabolism). Investigates the molecular basis for metabolic disease related to obesity.

Barry Coller, M.D. (Blood and Vascular Biology). Investigates the role of blood platelets and the mechanisms of blood cell adhesion in vascular disease.

Frederick P. Cross, Ph.D. (Cell Cycle Genetics). Investigates the molecular basis of cell cycle control.

Robert B. Darnell, M.D., Ph.D. (Molecular Neuro-Oncology). Works to understand human autoimmune responses to cancer and neurologic disease.

The Rockefeller University

Seth Darst, Ph.D. (Molecular Biophysics). Investigates the structure, function and regulation of the bacterial transcription machinery.
Titia de Lange, Ph.D. (Cell Biology and Genetics). Studies how telomeres protect chromosome ends from the DNA damage response.
Mitchell J. Feigenbaum, Ph.D. (Mathematical Physics). Develops mathematical descriptions and predictions of natural events that exhibit erratic behavior.
Vincent A. Fischetti, Ph.D. (Bacterial Pathogenesis and Immunology). Investigates bacterial infectious disease and the use of phage enzymes to block infection.
Winrich Freiwald, Ph.D. (Neural Systems). Researches the neural processes of object recognition and attention.
Jeffrey M. Friedman, M.D., Ph.D. (Molecular Genetics). Studies the molecular mechanisms that regulate food intake and body weight.
Elaine Fuchs, Ph.D. (Mammalian Cell Biology and Development). Investigates molecular mechanisms of skin stem cells, how they make and repair tissues, and how cancers develop.
Hinonori Funabiki, Ph.D. (Chromosome and Cell Biology). Studies signaling events in chromosome segregation in mitosis.
David C. Gadsby, Ph.D. (Cardiac and Membrane Physiology). Works to understand how ion transport proteins function in cells.
Charles D. Gilbert, M.D., Ph.D. (Neurobiology). Studies neural mechanisms of visual perception, learning and memory.
Konstantin A. Goulianos, Ph.D. (Experimental High-Energy Physics). Studies interactions among basic constituents of matter in order to explore the evolution and fate of the universe.
Paul Greengard, Ph.D. (Molecular and Cellular Neuroscience). Researches the molecular basis of communication between neurons in the mammalian brain.
Howard C. Hang, Ph.D. (Chemical Biology and Microbial Pathogenesis). Develops chemical tools for the study of microbe-host interaction.
Mary E. Hatten, Ph.D. (Developmental Neurobiology). Investigates mechanisms of neuronal differentiation and migration during embryonic development.
Nathaniel Heintz, Ph.D. (Molecular Biology). Investigates histological and functional aspects of the mammalian brain in health and disease.
David D. Ho, M.D. (Dynamics of HIV/SIV Replication). Pursues the development of drugs and vaccines to prevent HIV transmission.
A. James Hudspeth, M.D., Ph.D. (Sensory Neuroscience). Studies neural mechanisms of hearing and pursues treatments for hearing loss.
Erich Jarvis, Ph.D. (Neurobiology). Studies the mechanisms behind vocal learning, with an emphasis on the molecules that guide neuronal connections from motor learning pathways to vocal neurons.
Tarun Kapoor, Ph.D. (Chemistry and Cell Biology). Investigates molecular and physical mechanisms of cell division.
Sebastian Klinge, Ph.D. (Protein and Nucleic Acid Chemistry). Studies the structure and function of macromolecular complexes involved in eukaryotic ribosome assembly.
Bruce W. Knight Jr. (Biophysics). Develops mathematical descriptions of the nerve networks involved in visual perception.
Mary Jeanne Kreek, M.D. (Biology of Addictive Diseases). Investigates the genetic basis of, and novel treatments for, addictive diseases.
Daniel Kronauer, Ph.D. (Insect Social Evolution). Studies evolution in insect societies at the level of the gene, individual, and colony.
James G. Krueger, M.D., Ph.D. (Investigative Dermatology). Uses psoriasis as a model to investigate the pathogenesis of inflammatory disease and autoimmunity.
Stanislas Leibler, Ph.D. (Living Matter). Conducts quantitative analyses of microbial systems on cellular and population levels.
Albert J. Libchaber, Ph.D. (Experimental Condensed-Matter Physics). Applies mathematical models to biological systems at organismal, cellular, and molecular levels.
Shixin Liu, Ph.D. (Nanoscale Biophysics and Biochemistry). Investigates the interactions between biological machines, such as the transcription and translation apparatuses in bacteria.
Roderick MacKinnon, M.D. (Molecular Neurobiology and Biophysics). Studies principles underlying electricity in biology, particularly the passage of ions across cell membranes.
Marcelo Magnasco, Ph.D. (Mathematical Physics). Creates computational and mathematical models to describe neurophysiological systems and living organisms.
Gaby Maimon, Ph.D. (Integrative Brain Function). Studies electrical activity and computation underlying behavior in *Drosophila*.
Luciano Marraffini, Ph.D. (Bacteriology). Investigates the exchange of genetic material among bacteria.
Bruce S. McEwen, Ph.D. (Neuroendocrinology). Studies molecular mechanisms underlying effects of stress and sex hormones on the brain.
Daniel Mucida, Ph.D. (Mucosal Immunology). Investigates mechanisms of immune activity and tolerance in intestinal mucosa.
Fernando Nottebohm, Ph.D. (Animal Behavior). Investigates the biology of vocal learning and neuronal replacement in songbirds.
Michel C. Nussenzweig, M.D., Ph.D. (Molecular Immunology). Studies molecular aspects of adaptive and innate immune responses.
Michael O'Donnell, Ph.D. (DNA Replication). Studies molecular mechanisms of DNA replication, recombination, and repair.
Donald W. Pfaff, Ph.D. (Neurobiology and Behavior). Studies steroid hormone effects on nerve cells regulating specific natural behaviors and overall CNS arousal.
Priya Rajasethupathy, Ph.D. (Neurobiology). Investigates genetic and circuit level mechanisms that underlie disturbances in memory processing.
Jeffrey V. Ravetch, M.D., Ph.D. (Molecular Genetics and Immunology). Investigates mechanisms of the functional diversity of antibodies in host defense and immunotherapy.
George N. Reeke Jr., Ph.D. (Biological Modeling). Uses computational modeling to understand complex biological or neurological functions.
Charles Rice, Ph.D. (Virology). Investigates mechanisms of hepatitis C virus infection and replication.
Viviana Risca, Ph.D. (Biophysics). Uses sequencing, microscopy, and computation to study the dynamic three-dimensional organization of eukaryotic genomes.
Jeremy Rock, Ph.D. (Host-Pathogen Biology). Studies the biology of *Mycobacterium tuberculosis* infection.
Robert G. Roeder, Ph.D. (Biochemistry and Molecular Biology). Studies the proteins and enzymes that execute and regulate gene transcription.
Michael P. Rout, Ph.D. (Cellular and Structural Cell Biology). Researches the structure of nuclear pore complexes and their role in oncogenic and developmental defects.
Vanessa Ruta, Ph.D. (Neurophysiology and Behavior).Investigates neural circuits that underlie innate and learned behaviors.
Thomas P. Sakmar, M.D. (Chemical Biology and Signal Transduction).Conducts biological and chemical Investigations of G protein coupled receptors.
Shai Shaham, Ph.D. (Developmental Genetics). Investigates the role of glial cells in nervous system development and function.
Amy Shyer, Ph.D. (Multicellular mechanics and Tissue Morphogenesis). Studies the mechanical forces and molecular cues that guide tissue formation in the developing vertebrate embryo.
Eric Siggia, Ph.D. (Theoretical Condensed-Matter Physics). Uses bioinformatics to study regulatory patterns in gene expression.
Sanford M. Simon, Ph.D. (Cellular Biophysics). Uses imaging techniques and other biophysical tools to study single events in biological systems.
Agata Smogorzewska, M.D., Ph.D. (Genome Maintenance). Uses Fanconia anemia as a backdrop to investigate DNA repair mechanisms in aging and cancer.
Hermann Steller, Ph.D. (Apoptosis and Cancer Biology). Investigates signaling pathways underlying apoptosis.
Sidney Strickland, Ph.D. (Neurobiology and Genetics). Investigates neurovascular dysfunction in Alzheimer's disease and hemorrhagic stroke.
Alexander Tarakhovsky, M.D., Ph.D. (Immune Cell Epigenetics and Signaling). Investigates the epigenetic control of immune gene expression.
Sohail Tavazoie, M.D., Ph.D. (Systems Cancer Biology). Uses a variety of laboratory and clinical approaches to study the processes of cancer metastasis.
Alexander Tomasz, Ph.D. (Microbiology and Infectious Diseases). Tracks and studies mechanisms of bacterial antibiotic resistance.
Thomas Tuschl, Ph.D. (RNA Molecular Biology). Investigates gene regulatory mechanisms triggered by double-stranded RNA and RNA-binding proteins.
Alipasha Vaziri, Ph.D. (Neurotechnology and Biophysics). Develops and applies new optical imaging techniques with the goal of creating functional images of neural circuits.
Gabriel Victora, Ph.D. (Lymphocyte Dynamics). Investigates the molecular mechanisms behind the immune response.
Leslie Vosshall, Ph.D. (Neurogenetics and Behavior). Investigates how odor stimuli are processed and perceived.
Thomas Walz, Ph.D. (Structural Biology). Using cryo-electron microscopy to understand how the protein structure of membranes enables them to perform their functions.
Michael W. Young, Ph.D. (Genetics). Investigates the genetic regulation of biological clocks that underlie many activities of living organisms.
Li Zhao, Ph.D. (Evolutionary Biology). Using CRISPR-Cas 9 genome editing to investigate the biological function of de novo genes; Investigates the role of natural selection in the origin of genes.

SAINT LOUIS UNIVERSITY

School of Medicine
Graduate Programs in the Biomedical Sciences

★ For more information, visit http://petersons.to/stlouisumed

Programs of Study

Saint Louis University (SLU) is committed to teaching both the science and the art of medicine. The Saint Louis University School of Medicine also offers several graduate programs in biomedical sciences. Students apply to a core program. Upon acceptance, they begin a year of multidisciplinary coursework and four formal laboratory rotations that lead to the selection of a graduate adviser and entry into one of four distinct Ph.D. programs. Matriculating students spend the first academic year in a Core Curriculum that surveys the broad basics of the biomedical sciences and spend afternoons in laboratory rotations where they gain hands-on experience and find their future mentor. Direct entry into the second year of the individual departmental programs is an option for advanced students.

The Ph.D. degree requires 36 credit hours of coursework and 12 credit hours toward the successful completion and defense of an original research dissertation.

Biochemistry and Molecular Biology: This program allows students to explore research in as many as four different disciplines during their first year of graduate training with interdisciplinary lecture courses, small group discussions, and a colloquium series. Courses during the first year of study focus on the basic biochemical, molecular, cellular, and organismal aspects of the biomedical sciences. This prepares students for more intensive, individualized instruction in biochemistry and molecular biology. Students then select a Ph.D. mentor in a specific program and continue their training. Each year, 10¬15 highly qualified candidates with bachelor's degrees are accepted into this multidisciplinary Ph.D. program.

Molecular Microbiology and Immunology: This program focuses on molecular and cellular virology and immunology with the goal of preparing students for a career in academic science or biotechnology. Areas of research emphasis include cell and molecular biology, virology, and immunology. Participants are prepared to become technically skilled and thoughtful scientists.

Pathology: SLU's Department of Pathology offers a graduate doctoral program in molecular pathobiology—the cellular and biochemical study of disease. Students acquire the academic background and practical laboratory skills they will need in a future career. They have opportunities and exposure to technical skills and research expertise through research collaborations faculty maintain with colleagues in the academic and industrial community. As both a basic science and clinical department, SLU's pathology faculty has diverse interests and expertise, from the bench to the bedside. The department stresses close interactions among students, their mentors, and the graduate steering committee to foster intellectual and scientific growth.

Pharmacology and Physiology: This comprehensive program in pharmacological and physiological science is designed to help students develop laboratory research competence, including proficiency in quantitative methods of biology, physiology, and pharmacology. All classes have morning schedules, leaving the afternoons and evenings free for research. Coursework is followed by a preliminary examination that takes the form of the specific aims and research strategies sections of an NIH R01 application. Students will then complete two to three years of graduate work devoted almost exclusively to research related to their dissertation project. Successful completion of a written thesis, and public and private oral defenses are required for graduation. The program is completed in five years, on average.

Research Facilities

The approximately 70 faculty members in the programs of biochemistry and molecular biology, molecular microbiology and immunology, pharmacological and physiological sciences, pathology and the Institute for Molecular Virology provide an almost unlimited variety of research project topics for students. Students have access to some of the most leading-edge facilities and resources anywhere.

The Edward A. Doisy Research Center, a 206,000-square-foot health, science, and research building is the anchor facility. It is the centerpiece of the university's plan to upgrade its facilities and also helps form the eastern anchor of CORTEX, a public-private economic initiative promoting the development of a nationally recognized life-sciences industry in the urban corridor between SLU and Washington University. Additional laboratory space is housed in the School of Medicine's Doisy and Schwitalla Halls. Core facilities available include: comparative medicine, protein core, genomics core, high performance core, X-ray facilities, NMR facility, lipidomics core, and a state-of-the art microscopy core. (https://www.slu.edu/medicine/pathology/microscopy-histology-core.php).

Financial Aid

All graduate students in good academic standing have tuition and health insurance provided at no cost. An annual stipend (currently $30,000) is provided as well. Financial support is guaranteed to students in good academic standing for a period of five years.

Cost of Study

Students must pay a small University Activities Fee that gains them access to the gymnasium facilities. Paid parking is available as an elective.

Living and Housing Costs

Housing is not available for graduate students on the Medical Center campus and most students live a short drive from the research facilities.

Expatistan.com ranks St. Louis as the 70th most expensive large city in North America out of 103 analyzed, reflecting reasonable rents and cost of consumables. Rental apartments and houses can be found in reasonable proximity to the research facilities for between $600 and $1,000 per month. Less expensive apartments can be found in safe neighborhoods within a 20-minute drive from the campus.

Student Outcomes

The Graduate Programs in the Biomedical Sciences have recorded an 85–90 percent graduation rate over the past fifteen years. Most graduating students seek postdoctoral fellowships, but there has been a trend in recent years for immediate, full-time employment in what have been considered "alternative careers." The St. Louis area boasts numerous biotech and pharmaceutical corporations providing abundant employment opportunities and several local universities and colleges recruit SLU graduates for full-time teaching positions. The Graduate Programs in the Biomedical Sciences have recorded an 85–90 percent graduation rate over the past fifteen years. Most graduating students seek postdoctoral fellowships, but there has been a trend in recent years for immediate, full-time employment in what have been considered "alternative careers." The St. Louis area boasts numerous biotech and pharmaceutical corporations providing abundant employment opportunities and several local universities and colleges recruit SLU graduates for full-time teaching positions.

Location

Rich in history, the St. Louis region boasts a low cost of living, a strong sense of community, an emphasis on culture, a multitude of family-friendly activities and a convenient Midwest location. Technology, financial and major health care corporations are just some of the industries calling St. Louis home, with job opportunities available in almost every field.

Ranked one of the most affordable cities in the U.S., St. Louis also offers a wealth of attractions, parks, events, professional sports, and the arts. Walkable neighborhoods throughout the city are filled with unique restaurants, stores, and places to live.

The Graduate Programs in the Biomedical Sciences at SLU are housed on the Medical Center campus, which includes the School of Medicine, the Nursing School, the Doisy College of Health Sciences, and the Center for Advanced Dental Education. The Medical Campus is located in Midtown St. Louis on Grand Boulevard across from the SSM Health Cardinal Glennon Children's Hospital and the SSM Health Saint Louis University Hospital.

The University and the School

Saint Louis University is home to more than 100 graduate programs, including 15 that are ranked among the top 50 in the nation by *U.S. News and World Report*. The University is a private Roman Catholic institution that welcomes students of all religious, ethnic, and demographic backgrounds. A four-year, research university, SLU was founded in 1818 as the first university west of the Mississippi. Graduate and medical programs were established in 1832 and 1836, respectively, also the first in history west of the Mississippi River.

The School of Medicine offers students a comprehensive education that incorporates disease prevention and treatment with compassionate care delivered in a team setting. Students and trainees are also involved in scientific studies so they are trained in the latest disease management techniques. Saint Louis University provides an impressive scope of teaching, research, and clinical care that makes its postgraduate training an invaluable preparation for the practice of private or academic medicine. More than 580 practicing physicians and scientists bring years of specialized training and experience to the campus.

Applying

Prospective students apply initially to the Core Graduate Program in the Biomedical Sciences (https://www.slu.edu/medicine/medical-education/graduate-programs/index.php). Students should possess an above-average GPA, sufficient GRE scores and sufficient TOEFL scores (for international students).

Applications requirements include the official application form and fee, transcripts, three letters of recommendation, GRE G scores (GRE S optional), resume, an interview, and a professional goal statement.

Screening of applicants begins the December preceding the academic year of enrollment. During the months of February, March, and April, highly qualified candidates are invited, at the University's expense, to come to St. Louis for interviews and to acquaint themselves with the area, the University, and the graduate program in biomedical sciences.

Offers of admission into the program are generally made shortly after the interviews are complete. Acceptance of the offer of admission into the program by the applicant is expected no later than April 15. Late applications are considered on a space-available basis.

More specific details and additional information regarding application to the graduate programs in biomedical sciences is available at https://www.slu.edu/medicine/medical-education/graduate-programs/biochemistry-molecular-biology/biochemistry-and-molecular-biology-phd.php.

The Faculty and Their Research

Biochemistry and Molecular Biology (http://biochem.slu.edu/)

Areas of Research: Structural biology, RNA and DNA processing, neurodegenerative disease, gene therapy, transcriptional regulation, gene editing, diseases of the vascular system

Enrico Di Cera M.D., Alice A. Doisy Professor and Chairman
Yuna Ayala, Ph.D., Assistant Professor
Angel Baldan, Ph.D., Associate Professor
Yie-Hwa Chang, Ph.D., Associate Professor
Maureen Donlin, Ph.D., Research Professor
Dale Dorsett, Ph.D., Professor
Joel Eisenberg, Ph.D., Professor
David Ford, Ph.D., Professor
Susana Gonzalo, Ph.D., Associate Professor
Thomasz Heyduk, Ph.D., Professor
Sergey Korolev, Ph.D., Associate Professor
Nicola Pozzi, Ph.D., Assistant Professor
Dorota Skowyra, Ph.D., Associate Professor
Fran Sverdrup, Ph.D., Associate Professor
Alessandro Vindigni, Ph.D., Professor
Francis Yap, Ph.D., Associate Professor

Molecular Microbiology and Immunology (https://www.slu.edu/medicine/medical-education/graduate-programs/molecular-microbiology-immunology/index.php)

Areas of Research: Virology, Immunology, inflammatory disease, retroviruses, dendritic cell function, hepatitis viruses, tumor specific T cells, cancer, adenoviruses

William S.M. Wold, Ph.D., Professor and Chairman
Rajeev Aurora, Ph.D., Associate Professor
James D. Brien, Ph.D., Assistant Professor
Govindaswamy Chinnadurai, Ph.D., Professor
Richard J. DiPaolo, Ph.D., Professor
Duane P. Grandgenett, Ph.D., Professor
David Griggs, Ph.D., Associate Professor
Daniel Hawiger, M.D., Ph.D., Associate Professor
Lynda A. Morrison, Ph.D., Professor
Amelia K. Pinto, Ph.D., Assistant Professor
John E. Tavis, Ph.D., Professor
Ryan Teague, Ph.D., Associate Professor

Pathology (https://www.slu.edu/medicine/pathology/index.php)

Areas of Research: Liver disease, tumor immunology, imaging, breast cancer, heart disease, sepsis

Carole Vogler, M.D., Professor and Chairwoman
Anping Chen, Ph.D., Associate Professor
Grant Kolar, M.D. Ph.D., Assistant Professor
Jacki Kornbluth, Ph.D., Professor
Jane McHowat, Ph.D., Professor
Nancy Phillips, M.D., Professor
Ratna Ray, Ph.D., Professor

Pharmacology and Physiology (https://www.slu.edu/medicine/medical-education/graduate-programs/pharmacology-physiology/index.php)

Areas of Research: Neuroscience, endocrinology and metabolism, pain biology, chemical biology, developmental biology, diabetes, heart disease, autonomic function, cancer, cellular biology, G protein-coupled receptors

Mark M. Voigt Ph.D., Professor and Interim Chair
Michael Ariel, Ph.D. Professor
Joseph Baldassare, Ph.D., Professor
Andrew A. Butler, Ph.D., Professor
Anutosh Chakraborty, Ph.D., Associate Professor
John C. Chrivia, Ph.D., Professor
Jane Cox, Ph.D., Assistant Research Professor
Ian de Vera, Ph.D., Assistant Professor
Terrance Egan, Ph.D., Professor
Colin A. Flaveny, Ph.D., Assistant Professor
Mark M. Knuepfer, Ph.D., Professor
Andrew Lechner, Ph.D., Professor
Heather Macarthur, Ph.D., Associate Professor
Daniela Salvemini, Ph.D., Professor
Willis K. Samson, Ph.D., D.Sc., Professor
John K. Walker, Ph.D., Assistant Professor
Gina L.C. Yosten, Ph.D., Assistant Professor
Daniel S. Zahm, Ph.D., Professor
Jinsong Zhang, Ph.D., Associate Professor

UNIVERSITY OF CALIFORNIA, SAN DIEGO

UC San Diego

Division of Biological Sciences
Program in Biology

★ For more information, visit http:/petersons.to/uc-sandiego_biosci

Programs of Study

The University of California, San Diego (UC San Diego), Division of Biological Sciences, in association with the Salk Institute for Biological Studies, offers a program of graduate studies leading to the Ph.D. degree in biology. The program provides an extraordinary setting for highly motivated students interested in training with distinguished faculty members. The major areas of faculty research are biochemistry and biophysics; bioinformatics; cell and developmental biology; ecology, behavior, and evolution; genetics; immunology, virology, and cancer biology; molecular biology; neurobiology; plant molecular biology; plant systems biology; quantitative biology; quantitative biology; and signal transduction.

The goal of the program is to enable highly talented individuals to develop the skills and experience necessary to become successful world-class scientists. The program includes training in writing research papers and grant applications, presentation of lectures, the ethical conduct of research, and professional skill development to enhance career options. These skills allow graduates to pursue a broad range of careers that involve the use of science to increase the quality of life everywhere.

The educational philosophy of the Biological Sciences doctoral program is to provide a supportive and stimulating environment for highly talented individuals to develop skills and experience necessary to become research leaders in academic and biotechnology, biomedical, or pharmaceutical industries. The program recognizes that graduate students have various career goals and that training and advising requires a broad range of information. Ph.D.'s graduating from the program will have sought after skills and experiences suited to a broad range of career paths, ranging from faculty positions at research universities and teaching colleges through positions in private industry to leadership roles in science communication and policy.

Students must complete the course requirements for one of the program's curricular tracks. Most course work is completed during the first year. All incoming doctoral students take Graduate Boot Camp and Graduate School Fundamentals courses during their first quarter.

Lectures in molecular biology, cell biology, and genetics that provide an advanced foundation in these fundamental disciplines are complemented by small group discussions with faculty moderators focused on the critical evaluation of the primary scientific literature. Flexibility for each student to pursue individual interests during the first year is provided not only through laboratory rotations, but also through elective courses. Once the core course load is completed, students are encouraged to take other courses that enhance their education and research experience.

Building synergies with special and often interdisciplinary training programs is a hallmark of the Ph.D. program. These programs help students develop a broad set of research and professional skills and create vibrant intellectual communities.

Research Facilities

Students have access to more than 100 modern and fully equipped research laboratories in the Division of Biological Sciences and the Salk Institute. The division is also associated with three organized research groups: the Center for Molecular Genetics, the Kavli Institute for Brain and Mind, and the San Diego Center for Molecular Agriculture. Campus research facilities and tools include the San Diego Supercomputer Center; the Biomedical Genomics Microarray Center; the Protein Sequencing Facility; the Biomolecular Mass Spectrometry Facility; a DNA sequencer; and confocal, electron, and photon microscopes. The campus also houses the $115-million San Diego Consortium for Regenerative Medicine facility dedicated to stem cell research.

Biology faculty head several campuswide interdisciplinary initiatives that include other on-campus and off-campus units. These centers create critical research mass well-suited to tackle big research challenges and to jointly propose innovative solutions. Other facilities where students may be involved with research efforts include the Biomedical Genomics Laboratory, the Center for Circadian Biology, the Center for Neural Circuits and Behavior, the California Center for Algae Biotechnology, the San Diego Center for systems Biology, the UC San Diego Natural Reserve system, the UC San Diego Stem Cell Initiative, and Food & Fuel for the 21st Century.

Financial Aid

The Division of Biological Sciences supports all Ph.D. students with an annual stipend. The stipend is funded by federal and state grants and private sources. The stipend is provided in the form of research and teaching assistantships, fellowships, and NIH training grant appointments. International students receive the same level of support as domestic students.

The Program will pay only 1 year of nonresident tuition for U.S. citizens who are non-California residents. It is the responsibility of the nonresident student to become an official resident of the State of California by the end of their first year in order to be exempt from out-of-state tuition in subsequent years.

Students are expected to apply for extramural predoctoral fellowships such as those offered by the National Science Foundation, Ford Foundation, etc., in addition to those administered by the University. If the student is successful and receives funding outside of UC San Diego in the form of a fellowship (e.g., AHA, NIH, Merck, Ford Foundation, home country) that provides stipend and/or fee support, the student may be eligible for a bonus of up to $3,000 above the standard biology graduate stipend.

Housing

All full-time graduate students are eligible for Associated Residential Community Housing. More information is available at http://hdh.ucsd.edu/arch/pages/FAQ.html. Students may also choose to seek their own off-campus housing.

The Faculty

The Division of Biological Science's outstanding faculty and research programs attract the best and brightest students, who want to learn from researchers working at the cutting edge of their respective fields. This concentration of many of the best scientific minds in the world creates truly invaluable learning opportunities for students, providing a scientific breadth and diversity that is tremendously beneficial to their education. A complete listing of faculty members and their areas of research is available online at http://biology.ucsd.edu/publicinfo/dwc?action=faculty_research_list.

Location

UC San Diego and the Salk Institute are located on the Torrey Pines Mesa, along the San Diego coast, overlooking the Pacific Ocean. The campus is also an easy drive from several mountain and desert locales. Along with San Diego's dry, temperate climate, UC San Diego is ideally situated to offer its students year-round outdoor recreational opportunities. The area also shares a rich heritage with its neighbor, Mexico, and supports many cultural events.

The Torrey Pines Mesa is the setting of a world-class scientific and research community as well. This community includes the UC San Diego School of Medicine, the Scripps Institution of Oceanography, the Scripps Research Institute, the Neurosciences Institute, the La Jolla Institute for Allergy and Immunology, the Burnham Institute for Medical Research, the Sidney Kimmel Cancer Center, and hundreds of biotechnology research firms.

The University

UC San Diego is one of the nation's most accomplished research universities, widely acknowledged for its local impact, national influence, and global reach. A leader in climate science research, UC San Diego is one of the greenest universities in the U.S. and works with communities, governments, businesses, and organizations to promote sustainability solutions throughout the region and the world.

With a majestic view of the Pacific Ocean, this distinctively beautiful campus is both a magnet and a catalyst for acclaimed institutes and Nobel laureates. The University's award-winning scholars are experts at the forefront of their fields, with an impressive track record for achieving scientific, medical, and technological breakthroughs. Renowned for its collaborative, diverse, and cross-disciplinary ethos that transcends traditional boundaries in science, arts, and the humanities, UC San Diego attracts like-minded faculty and staff members and stellar students.

Applying

Admission to UC San Diego's Ph.D. program in Biology is highly competitive with only 35–40 students joining the doctoral program each year. New students are admitted for fall quarter only. Competitive applicants must demonstrate excellent undergraduate training in the biological sciences and a strong commitment to research.

Students with exceptional achievement and diverse backgrounds are encouraged to apply. UCSD does not discriminate on the basis of nationality, race, socioeconomic status, sexual orientation, sex, citizenship or disability.

Approximately 30 percent of each incoming class consists of international students. As such, qualified international applicants are also encouraged to apply.

Prospective students should use the UCSD Application for Graduation Admission online. In addition to the application forms, applicants must submit a copy of their GRE test scores, 3 letters of recommendation, a copy of their most recent academic transcripts, and a statement of purpose. It is recommended that applications be submitted well before the deadline to be considered for on-campus interviews.

Applications are processed in order in which they are submitted. Screening of applications will begin in late November. Applications are evaluated by the Admissions Committee (which is comprised of representatives from both the faculty and graduate students) November through January. Important factors in the evaluation of an application include: the nature and quality of the applicant's undergraduate degree program; past academic performance; preparation in the physical sciences and mathematics; previous laboratory and/or field research experience; statement of purpose; letters of recommendation; scores on the Graduate Record Exam; and scores on the English Proficiency Exams (international applicants only).

Selected applicants will be invited to visit the campus and participate in faculty interviews in January/February. The interviews consist of meetings with both faculty and graduate students, as well as the opportunity to visit the UCSD campus and the surrounding research community. Based on the results of the interviews, offers of admission in most cases will be made before the end of February. All applicants will be notified of the Division's decision no later than March 15.

Correspondence and Information

Dr. Jens Lykke-Andersen, Graduate Director
Division of Biological Sciences
University of California, San Diego
9500 Gilman Drive
La Jolla, California 92093
United States
Phone: 858-534-2580
E-mail: biogradprog@ucsd.edu
Website: https://biology.ucsd.edu/education/grad/phd/index.html

Section 2
Anatomy

This section contains a directory of institutions offering graduate work in anatomy. Additional information about programs listed in the directory may be obtained by writing directly to the dean of a graduate school or chair of a department at the address given in the directory.

For programs offering related work, see also in this book *Allied Health; Biomedical Sciences; Cell, Molecular, and Structural Biology; Dentistry and Dental Sciences; Genetics, Developmental Biology, and Reproductive Biology; Neuroscience and Neurobiology; Pathology and Pathobiology; Physiology; Veterinary Medicine and Sciences;* and *Zoology*. In another guide in this series:

Graduate Programs in the Humanities, Arts & Social Sciences

See *Sociology, Anthropology, and Archaeology*

CONTENTS

Program Directory

Anatomy

Albert Einstein College of Medicine, Graduate Programs in the Biomedical Sciences, Department of Anatomy and Structural Biology, Bronx, NY 10461. Offers anatomy (PhD); MD/PhD. *Degree requirements:* For doctorate, thesis/dissertation. *Entrance requirements:* For doctorate, GRE General Test. Additional exam requirements/recommendations for international students: Required—TOEFL. *Application deadline:* For fall admission, 1/15 for domestic students. Application fee: $0. Electronic applications accepted. *Financial support:* Fellowships available. *Faculty research:* Cell motility, cell membranes and membrane-cytoskeletal interactions as applied to processing of pancreatic hormones, mechanisms of secretion. *Unit head:* Dr. John S. Condeelis, Co-Chair, 718-678-1126. *Application contact:* Sheila Cleeton, Executive Director and Registrar, Einstein Graduate Division, 718-430-2128, Fax: 718-430-8655, E-mail: sheila.cleeton@einstein.yu.edu.
Website: http://www.einstein.yu.edu/departments/anatomy-structural-biology/

Augusta University, Program in Cellular Biology and Anatomy, Augusta, GA 30912. Offers PhD. *Degree requirements:* For doctorate, comprehensive exam, thesis/dissertation. *Entrance requirements:* For doctorate, GRE General Test. Additional exam requirements/recommendations for international students: Required—TOEFL (minimum score 550 paper-based; 79 iBT). *Faculty research:* Eye disease, developmental biology, cell injury and death, stroke and neurotoxicity, diabetic complications.

Barry University, School of Podiatric Medicine, Program in Anatomy, Miami Shores, FL 33161-6695. Offers MS. *Entrance requirements:* For master's, GRE.

Boston University, College of Health and Rehabilitation Sciences: Sargent College, Department of Health Sciences, Programs in Human Physiology, Boston, MA 02215. Offers MS, PhD. *Faculty:* 10 full-time (9 women), 5 part-time/adjunct (2 women). *Students:* 8 full-time (5 women), 7 part-time (5 women); includes 2 minority (1 Asian, non-Hispanic/Latino; 1 Hispanic/Latino), 4 international. Average age 24. 49 applicants, 51% accepted, 11 enrolled. In 2017, 10 master's, 3 doctorates awarded. Terminal master's awarded for partial completion of doctoral program. *Degree requirements:* For master's, thesis or alternative; for doctorate, comprehensive exam, thesis/dissertation. *Entrance requirements:* For master's, GRE General Test, minimum GPA of 3.0; for doctorate, GRE General Test. Additional exam requirements/recommendations for international students: Required—TOEFL (minimum score 550 paper-based; 84 iBT). *Application deadline:* For fall admission, 1/15 priority date for domestic and international students. Applications are processed on a rolling basis. Application fee: $95. Electronic applications accepted. *Financial support:* In 2017–18, 9 students received support, including 2 research assistantships with full tuition reimbursements available (averaging $22,000 per year); career-related internships or fieldwork, Federal Work-Study, institutionally sponsored loans, and scholarships/grants also available. Support available to part-time students. Financial award application deadline: 1/15; financial award applicants required to submit FAFSA. *Faculty research:* Skeletal muscle, neural systems, smooth muscle, muscular dystrophy. *Total annual research expenditures:* $3.3 million. *Unit head:* Dr. Paula Quatromoni, Chair, 617-353-5797, Fax: 617-353-7567, E-mail: paulaq@bu.edu. *Application contact:* Sharon Sankey, Assistant Dean, Student Services, 617-353-2713, Fax: 617-353-7500, E-mail: ssankey@bu.edu.

Boston University, School of Medicine, Division of Graduate Medical Sciences, Department of Anatomy and Neurobiology, Boston, MA 02118. Offers MA, PhD, MD/PhD. *Program availability:* Part-time. Terminal master's awarded for partial completion of doctoral program. *Degree requirements:* For master's, thesis; for doctorate, thesis/dissertation. *Application deadline:* For fall admission, 1/15 for domestic students; for spring admission, 10/15 for domestic students. *Unit head:* Dr. Mark Moss, Chairman, 617-638-4200, Fax: 617-638-4216. *Application contact:* GMS Admissions Office, 617-638-5255, E-mail: askgms@bu.edu.
Website: http://www.bumc.bu.edu/anatneuro/

Case Western Reserve University, School of Medicine and School of Graduate Studies, Graduate Programs in Medicine, Department of Anatomy, Cleveland, OH 44106. Offers applied anatomy (MS); MD/MS. *Program availability:* Part-time. *Degree requirements:* For master's, comprehensive exam, thesis (for some programs). *Entrance requirements:* For master's, GRE General Test. Additional exam requirements/recommendations for international students: Required—TOEFL. *Expenses: Tuition:* Full-time $43,854; part-time $1827 per credit hour. *Required fees:* $50; $50 per credit hour. Tuition and fees vary according to course load and program. *Faculty research:* Hypoxia, cell injury, biochemical aberration occurrences in ischemic tissue, human functional morphology, evolutionary morphology.

Columbia University, College of Physicians and Surgeons, Department of Anatomy and Cell Biology, New York, NY 10032. Offers anatomy (M Phil, MA, PhD); anatomy and cell biology (PhD); MD/PhD. Only candidates for the PhD are admitted. Terminal master's awarded for partial completion of doctoral program. *Degree requirements:* For doctorate, thesis/dissertation, oral exam. *Entrance requirements:* For master's and doctorate, GRE General Test. Additional exam requirements/recommendations for international students: Required—TOEFL. *Expenses: Tuition:* Full-time $44,864; part-time $1704 per credit. *Required fees:* $2370 per semester. One-time fee: $105. *Faculty research:* Protein sorting, membrane biophysics, muscle energetics, neuroendocrinology, developmental biology, cytoskeleton, transcription factors.

Creighton University, School of Medicine and Graduate School, Graduate Programs in Medicine, Program in Clinical Anatomy, Omaha, NE 68178-0001. Offers MS. *Degree requirements:* For master's, comprehensive exam, thesis or alternative. *Entrance requirements:* For master's, GRE, MCAT or DAT. Additional exam requirements/recommendations for international students: Required—TOEFL. Electronic applications accepted. Part-time tuition and fees vary according to course load, degree level, campus/location and program. *Faculty research:* Neural crest cell migration; ontogenetic and phylogenetic nervous system development; skeletal biology.

Dalhousie University, Faculty of Graduate Studies and Faculty of Medicine, Graduate Programs in Medicine, Department of Anatomy and Neurobiology, Halifax, NS B3H 4R2, Canada. Offers M Sc, PhD. *Degree requirements:* For master's, thesis; for doctorate, thesis/dissertation. *Entrance requirements:* For master's and doctorate, GRE (recommended), minimum A- average. Additional exam requirements/recommendations for international students: Required—1 of 5 approved tests: TOEFL, IELTS, CANTEST, CAEL, Michigan English Language Assessment Battery. Electronic applications accepted. *Faculty research:* Neuroscience histology, cell biology, neuroendocrinology, evolutionary biology.

Des Moines University, College of Osteopathic Medicine, Program in Anatomy, Des Moines, IA 50312-4104. Offers MS.

Duke University, Graduate School, Department of Evolutionary Anthropology, Durham, NC 27708. Offers cellular and molecular biology (PhD); gross anatomy and physical anthropology (PhD), including comparative morphology of human and non-human primates, primate social behavior, vertebrate paleontology; neuroanatomy (PhD). *Degree requirements:* For doctorate, one foreign language, thesis/dissertation. *Entrance requirements:* For doctorate, GRE General Test. Additional exam requirements/recommendations for international students: Required—TOEFL (minimum score 577 paper-based; 90 iBT) or IELTS (minimum score 7). Electronic applications accepted.

D'Youville College, Program in Anatomy, Buffalo, NY 14201-1084. Offers MS.

East Tennessee State University, Quillen College of Medicine, Department of Biomedical Sciences, Johnson City, TN 37614. Offers anatomy (PhD); biochemistry (PhD); microbiology (PhD); pharmaceutical sciences (PhD); pharmacology (PhD); physiology (PhD); quantitative biosciences (PhD). In 2017, 5 doctorates awarded. *Degree requirements:* For doctorate, comprehensive exam, thesis/dissertation, comprehensive qualifying exam; one-year residency. *Entrance requirements:* For doctorate, GRE General Test, GRE Subject Test, 3 letters of recommendation, minimum of 60 credit hours beyond the baccalaureate degree. Additional exam requirements/recommendations for international students: Required—TOEFL (minimum score 550 paper-based; 79 iBT). *Application deadline:* For fall admission, 6/1 priority date for domestic students, 4/29 for international students; for spring admission, 11/1 for domestic students, 9/29 for international students; for summer admission, 3/15 for domestic students, 2/1 for international students. Applications are processed on a rolling basis. Application fee: $55 ($65 for international students). Electronic applications accepted. *Expenses:* Contact institution. *Financial support:* Research assistantships with full tuition reimbursements, career-related internships or fieldwork, institutionally sponsored loans, scholarships/grants, and unspecified assistantships available. Financial award application deadline: 7/1; financial award applicants required to submit FAFSA. *Faculty research:* Cardiovascular, infectious disease, neurosciences, cancer, immunology. *Unit head:* Theo Hagg, Chair, 423-439-6294, Fax: 423-439-2140, E-mail: haggt1@etsu.edu. *Application contact:* Theo Hagg, Chair, 423-439-6294, Fax: 423-439-2140, E-mail: haggt1@etsu.edu.
Website: http://www.etsu.edu/com/dbms/

Howard University, Graduate School, Department of Anatomy, Washington, DC 20059-0002. Offers MS, PhD. *Degree requirements:* For master's, comprehensive exam, thesis, teaching experience; for doctorate, comprehensive exam, thesis/dissertation, teaching experience. *Entrance requirements:* For master's and doctorate, GRE General Test, minimum GPA of 3.0. Additional exam requirements/recommendations for international students: Required—TOEFL (minimum score 550 paper-based). Electronic applications accepted. *Faculty research:* Neural control of function, mammalian evolution and paleontology, cellular differentiation, cellular and neuronal communication, development, cell biology, molecular biology, anatomy.

Indiana University–Purdue University Indianapolis, Indiana University School of Medicine, Department of Anatomy and Cell Biology, Indianapolis, IN 46202. Offers MS, PhD, MD/PhD. *Degree requirements:* For master's, thesis or alternative; for doctorate, thesis/dissertation. *Entrance requirements:* For master's and doctorate, GRE General Test. Additional exam requirements/recommendations for international students: Required—TOEFL. Electronic applications accepted. *Expenses:* Contact institution. *Faculty research:* Neurobiology, musculoskeletal biology, renal biology, anatomy education.

Johns Hopkins University, School of Medicine, Graduate Programs in Medicine, Center for Functional Anatomy and Evolution, Baltimore, MD 21287. Offers PhD. *Faculty:* 6 full-time (2 women). *Students:* 10 full-time (9 women); includes 1 minority (Hispanic/Latino), 1 international. Average age 28. 18 applicants, 11% accepted, 2 enrolled. In 2017, 1 doctorate awarded. *Degree requirements:* For doctorate, comprehensive exam, thesis/dissertation, oral exams. *Entrance requirements:* For doctorate, GRE. Additional exam requirements/recommendations for international students: Required—TOEFL. *Application deadline:* For fall admission, 1/10 for domestic and international students. Application fee: $85. Electronic applications accepted. *Financial support:* Fellowships, teaching assistantships, career-related internships or fieldwork, institutionally sponsored loans, health care benefits, and tuition waivers (full) available. *Faculty research:* Vertebrate evolution, functional anatomy, primate evolution, vertebrate paleobiology, vertebrate morphology. *Unit head:* Dr. Christopher B. Ruff, Director, 410-955-7126, Fax: 410-614-9030, E-mail: cbruff@jhmi.edu. *Application contact:* Catherine L. Will, Coordinator, Graduate Student Affairs, 410-614-3385, E-mail: grad_study@som.adm.jhu.edu.

Liberty University, School of Health Sciences, Lynchburg, VA 24515. Offers anatomy and cell biology (PhD); biomedical sciences (MS); epidemiology (MPH); exercise science (MS), including clinical, community physical activity, human performance, nutrition; global health (MPH); health promotion (MPH); medical sciences (MA), including biopsychology, business management, health informatics, molecular medicine, public health; nutrition (MPH). *Program availability:* Part-time, online learning. *Students:* 542 full-time (394 women), 696 part-time (541 women); includes 402 minority (286 Black or African American, non-Hispanic/Latino; 10 American Indian or Alaska Native, non-Hispanic/Latino; 34 Asian, non-Hispanic/Latino; 46 Hispanic/Latino; 1 Native Hawaiian or other Pacific Islander, non-Hispanic/Latino; 25 Two or more races, non-Hispanic/Latino), 59 international. Average age 32. 1,592 applicants, 40% accepted, 297 enrolled. In 2017, 204 master's awarded. *Degree requirements:* For master's, thesis (for some programs); for doctorate, thesis/dissertation. *Entrance requirements:* For doctorate, MAT or GRE, minimum GPA of 3.25 in master's program, 2-3 recommendations, writing samples (for some programs), letter of intent, professional vitae. Additional exam requirements/recommendations for international students: Required—TOEFL (minimum score 600 paper-based; 100 iBT). Application fee: $50. *Financial support:* Applicants required to submit FAFSA. *Unit head:* Dr. Ralph Linstra, Dean. *Application contact:* Jay Bridge, Director of Admissions, 800-424-9595, Fax: 800-628-7977, E-mail: gradadmissions@liberty.edu.

Loma Linda University, School of Medicine, Programs in Pathology and Human Anatomy, Loma Linda, CA 92350. Offers human anatomy (PhD); pathology (PhD). *Accreditation:* NAACLS. *Program availability:* Part-time. Terminal master's awarded for partial completion of doctoral program. *Degree requirements:* For doctorate, 2 foreign languages, thesis/dissertation. *Entrance requirements:* For doctorate, GRE General Test. Additional exam requirements/recommendations for international students: Required—TOEFL (minimum score 550 paper-based). *Faculty research:* Neuroendocrine system, histochemistry and image analysis, effect of age and diabetes on PNS, electron microscopy, histology.

Louisiana State University Health Sciences Center, School of Graduate Studies in New Orleans, Department of Cell Biology and Anatomy, New Orleans, LA 70112-2223. Offers cell biology and anatomy (PhD), including clinical anatomy, development, cell, and neurobiology; MD/PhD. *Faculty:* 17 full-time (2 women). *Students:* 5 full-time (3 women), 1 (woman) part-time; includes 1 minority (Asian, non-Hispanic/Latino). 1

applicant. *Degree requirements:* For doctorate, comprehensive exam, thesis/ dissertation. *Entrance requirements:* For doctorate, GRE General Test, minimum undergraduate GPA of 3.0. Additional exam requirements/recommendations for international students: Recommended—TOEFL, IELTS. *Application deadline:* For fall admission, 3/1 priority date for domestic students, 3/1 for international students. Applications are processed on a rolling basis. Application fee: $30. *Expenses:* Tuition, state resident: full-time $11,835; part-time $518 per hour. Tuition, nonresident: full-time $24,108; part-time $1079 per hour. *Required fees:* $1254; $55 per hour. *Financial support:* In 2017–18, 6 students received support. Unspecified assistantships available. Financial award application deadline: 4/1. *Faculty research:* Visual system organization, neural development, plasticity of sensory systems, information processing through the nervous system, visuomotor integration. *Total annual research expenditures:* $900,000. *Unit head:* Dr. Samuel McClugage, Head, 504-568-4011, Fax: 504-568-2165, E-mail: smcclu@lsuhsc.edu. *Application contact:* Dr. R. John Cork, Graduate Coordinator and Professor, 504-568-7177, E-mail: jcork@lsuhsc.edu.
Website: http://www.medschool.lsuhsc.edu/cell_biology/

Louisiana State University Health Sciences Center at Shreveport, Department of Cellular Biology and Anatomy, Shreveport, LA 71130-3932. Offers MS, PhD, MD/PhD. Terminal master's awarded for partial completion of doctoral program. *Degree requirements:* For master's, thesis; for doctorate, thesis/dissertation. *Entrance requirements:* For master's and doctorate, GRE General Test. Additional exam requirements/recommendations for international students: Required—TOEFL. *Faculty research:* Cancer biology, redox biology, neurosciences, immunobiology, cardiovascular sciences.

McGill University, Faculty of Graduate and Postdoctoral Studies, Faculty of Medicine, Department of Anatomy and Cell Biology, Montréal, QC H3A 2T5, Canada. Offers M Sc, PhD.

New York Academy of Art, Master of Fine Arts Program, New York, NY 10013-2911. Offers anatomy (MFA); drawing (MFA); fine arts (MFA), including anatomy; painting (MFA); printmaking (MFA); sculpture (MFA). *Accreditation:* NASAD. *Faculty:* 5 full-time (1 woman), 31 part-time/adjunct (13 women). *Students:* 109 full-time (67 women); includes 19 minority (3 Black or African American, non-Hispanic/Latino; 2 American Indian or Alaska Native, non-Hispanic/Latino; 4 Asian, non-Hispanic/Latino; 8 Hispanic/ Latino; 1 Native Hawaiian or other Pacific Islander, non-Hispanic/Latino; 1 Two or more races, non-Hispanic/Latino), 33 international. Average age 30. 161 applicants, 57% accepted, 60 enrolled. In 2017, 56 master's awarded. *Degree requirements:* For master's, thesis. *Entrance requirements:* For master's, portfolio, essay, two letters of recommendation, curriculum vitae or resume, official undergraduate transcripts. Additional exam requirements/recommendations for international students: Required—TOEFL (minimum score 550 paper-based; 80 iBT), IELTS (minimum score 6.5). *Application deadline:* For fall admission, 1/17 priority date for domestic and international students. Application fee: $80. Electronic applications accepted. Application fee is waived when completed online. *Expenses:* $37,436 annual tuition, $1,500 annual mandatory fees. *Financial support:* In 2017–18, 88 students received support, including 3 fellowships (averaging $10,000 per year); career-related internships or fieldwork, Federal Work-Study, and scholarships/grants also available. Financial award application deadline: 4/15; financial award applicants required to submit FAFSA. *Faculty research:* Drawing, painting, sculpture, anatomy, printmaking. *Total annual research expenditures:* $27,000. *Unit head:* David Kratz, President, 212-966-0300. *Application contact:* Katie Hemmer, Director of Admissions/Registrar, 212-842-5961, E-mail: khemmer@ nyaa.edu.
Website: http://www.nyaa.edu/

New York Chiropractic College, Program in Clinical Anatomy, Seneca Falls, NY 13148-0800. Offers MS. *Degree requirements:* For master's, thesis. *Entrance requirements:* For master's, minimum GPA of 3.0, DC, bachelor's degree or equivalent. Electronic applications accepted. *Faculty research:* Bone histology, biomechanics, craniofacial growth and anatomy, skeletal morphology.

New York Chiropractic College, Program in Human Anatomy and Physiology Instruction, Seneca Falls, NY 13148-0800. Offers MS. *Program availability:* Online learning.

The Ohio State University, College of Medicine, School of Health and Rehabilitation Sciences, Program in Anatomy, Columbus, OH 43210. Offers MS, PhD. *Students:* 28 (20 women). Average age 28. In 2017, 8 master's awarded. Terminal master's awarded for partial completion of doctoral program. *Degree requirements:* For master's, thesis (for some programs); for doctorate, thesis/dissertation. *Entrance requirements:* For master's and doctorate, GRE General Test (suggested minimum score in 50th percentile). Additional exam requirements/recommendations for international students: Required—TOEFL (minimum score 600 paper-based; 100 iBT), Michigan English Language Assessment Battery (minimum score 86); Recommended—IELTS (minimum score 8). *Application deadline:* For fall admission, 12/1 priority date for domestic students, 11/1 priority date for international students. Applications are processed on a rolling basis. Application fee: $60 ($70 for international students). Electronic applications accepted. *Financial support:* Fellowships with tuition reimbursements, research assistantships with tuition reimbursements, teaching assistantships with tuition reimbursements, and Federal Work-Study available. Financial award application deadline: 1/10. *Faculty research:* Cell biology, biomechanical trauma, computer-assisted instruction. *Unit head:* Dr. Deborah S. Larsen, Dean and Director, 614-292-5645, E-mail: larsen.64@osu.edu. *Application contact:* Graduate and Professional Admissions, 614-292-9444, Fax: 614-292-3895, E-mail: gpadmissions@osu.edu.
Website: http://medicine.osu.edu/hrs/anatomy

Palmer College of Chiropractic, Division of Graduate Studies, Davenport, IA 52803-5287. Offers clinical research (MS). *Program availability:* Part-time. *Degree requirements:* For master's, 2 mentored practicum projects. *Entrance requirements:* For master's, GRE General Test, minimum GPA of 2.5, bachelor's and doctoral-level health professions degrees. Additional exam requirements/recommendations for international students: Required—TOEFL. Electronic applications accepted. *Expenses:* Contact institution. *Faculty research:* Chiropractic clinical research.

Penn State Hershey Medical Center, College of Medicine, Graduate School Programs in the Biomedical Sciences, Program in Anatomy, Hershey, PA 17033. Offers MS, PhD, MD/PhD. *Students:* 15 full-time (10 women). 21 applicants, 24% accepted, 5 enrolled. In 2017, 2 master's, 1 doctorate awarded. Terminal master's awarded for partial completion of doctoral program. *Degree requirements:* For master's, thesis or alternative; for doctorate, comprehensive exam, thesis/dissertation. *Entrance requirements:* For master's and doctorate, GRE General Test or MCAT, minimum GPA of 3.0. Additional exam requirements/recommendations for international students: Required—TOEFL (minimum score 81 iBT). *Application deadline:* For fall admission, 1/1 for domestic and international students. Applications are processed on a rolling basis. Application fee: $65. Electronic applications accepted. *Financial support:* In 2017–18, research assistantships with full tuition reimbursements (averaging $27,802 per year) were awarded; fellowships with full tuition reimbursements, scholarships/grants, health care benefits, and unspecified assistantships also available. Financial award applicants required to submit FAFSA. *Faculty research:* Developmental biology, stem cell, cancer-basic science and clinical application, wound healing, angiogenesis. *Unit head:* Dr. Patricia J. McLaughlin, Program Director, 717-531-1045, E-mail: anat-grad-hmc@ psu.edu. *Application contact:* Kristin E. Smith, Director of Graduate Admissions, 717-531-1045, E-mail: kec17@psu.edu.
Website: http://med.psu.edu

Purdue University, School of Veterinary Medicine and Graduate School, Graduate Programs in Veterinary Medicine, Department of Basic Medical Sciences, West Lafayette, IN 47907. Offers anatomy (MS, PhD); pharmacology (MS, PhD); physiology (MS, PhD). *Program availability:* Part-time. Terminal master's awarded for partial completion of doctoral program. *Degree requirements:* For master's, thesis; for doctorate, thesis/dissertation. *Entrance requirements:* For master's and doctorate, GRE General Test. Additional exam requirements/recommendations for international students: Required—TOEFL. Electronic applications accepted. *Faculty research:* Development and regeneration, tissue injury and shock, biomedical engineering, ovarian function, bone and cartilage biology, cell and molecular biology.

Queen's University at Kingston, School of Graduate Studies, Faculty of Health Sciences, Department of Anatomy and Cell Biology, Kingston, ON K7L 3N6, Canada. Offers biology of reproduction (M Sc, PhD); cancer (M Sc, PhD); cardiovascular pathophysiology (M Sc, PhD); cell and molecular biology (M Sc, PhD); drug metabolism (M Sc, PhD); endocrinology (M Sc, PhD); motor control (M Sc, PhD); neural regeneration (M Sc, PhD); neurophysiology (M Sc, PhD). *Program availability:* Part-time. *Degree requirements:* For master's, thesis; for doctorate, one foreign language, comprehensive exam, thesis/dissertation. *Entrance requirements:* Additional exam requirements/recommendations for international students: Required—TOEFL. Electronic applications accepted. *Faculty research:* Human kinetics, neuroscience, reproductive biology, cardiovascular.

Rosalind Franklin University of Medicine and Science, School of Graduate and Postdoctoral Studies - Interdisciplinary Graduate Program in Biomedical Sciences, Department of Cell Biology and Anatomy, North Chicago, IL 60064-3095. Offers PhD, MD/PhD. Terminal master's awarded for partial completion of doctoral program. *Degree requirements:* For doctorate, comprehensive exam, thesis/dissertation, original research project. *Entrance requirements:* For doctorate, GRE General Test, minimum GPA of 3.0. Additional exam requirements/recommendations for international students: Required—TOEFL, TWE. *Faculty research:* Neuroscience, molecular biology.

Rush University, Graduate College, Division of Anatomy and Cell Biology, Chicago, IL 60612-3832. Offers MS, PhD, MD/MS, MD/PhD. Terminal master's awarded for partial completion of doctoral program. *Degree requirements:* For master's, thesis; for doctorate, comprehensive exam, thesis/dissertation, preliminary exam, dissertation proposal. *Entrance requirements:* For master's, GRE General Test, minimum GPA of 3.0, bachelor's degree in biology or chemistry (preferred), interview; for doctorate, GRE General Test, minimum GPA of 3.0, interview. Additional exam requirements/ recommendations for international students: Required—TOEFL. Electronic applications accepted. *Faculty research:* Incontinence following vaginal distension, knee replacement, biomimetric materials, injured spinal motoneurons, implant fixation.

Saint Louis University, Graduate Programs, School of Medicine, Graduate Programs in Biomedical Sciences and Graduate Programs, Center for Anatomical Science and Education, St. Louis, MO 63103. Offers anatomy (MS-R, PhD). *Degree requirements:* For master's, comprehensive exam, thesis; for doctorate, comprehensive exam, thesis/ dissertation, departmental qualifying exams. *Entrance requirements:* For master's, GRE General Test, letters of recommendation, resume; for doctorate, GRE General Test, letters of recommendation, resumé, goal statement, transcripts. Additional exam requirements/recommendations for international students: Required—TOEFL (minimum score 525 paper-based). *Faculty research:* Neurodegenerative diseases, cerebellar cortical circuitry, neurogenesis, evolutionary anatomy.

State University of New York Upstate Medical University, College of Graduate Studies, Program in Cell and Developmental Biology, Syracuse, NY 13210. Offers anatomy (MS, PhD); MD/PhD. Terminal master's awarded for partial completion of doctoral program. *Degree requirements:* For master's, thesis; for doctorate, comprehensive exam, thesis/dissertation. *Entrance requirements:* For master's, GRE General Test, interview; for doctorate, GRE General Test, telephone interview. Additional exam requirements/recommendations for international students: Required—TOEFL. Electronic applications accepted. *Faculty research:* Cancer, disorders of the nervous system, infectious diseases, diabetes/metabolic disorders/cardiovascular diseases.

Stony Brook University, State University of New York, Stony Brook Medicine, School of Medicine and Graduate School, Graduate Programs in Medicine, Department of Anatomical Sciences, Stony Brook, NY 11794. Offers PhD. *Faculty:* 12 full-time (6 women), 1 part-time/adjunct (0 women). *Students:* 1 (woman) full-time, 2 part-time (1 woman). Average age 25. 9 applicants, 22% accepted, 1 enrolled. In 2017, 2 doctorates awarded. *Degree requirements:* For doctorate, comprehensive exam, thesis/ dissertation. *Entrance requirements:* For doctorate, GRE General Test, GRE Subject Test, BA in life sciences, minimum GPA of 3.0. Additional exam requirements/ recommendations for international students: Required—TOEFL. *Application deadline:* For fall admission, 1/15 for domestic students; for spring admission, 10/1 for domestic students. Application fee: $100. *Expenses:* Contact institution. *Financial support:* In 2017–18, 1 fellowship, 1 research assistantship were awarded; teaching assistantships and Federal Work-Study also available. Financial award application deadline: 3/15. *Faculty research:* Anatomy, bioimaging, paleontology, paleobiology, anatomical systems or sites. *Total annual research expenditures:* $333,012. *Unit head:* Dr. Randall Susman, Chair, 631-444-3125, Fax: 631-444-3947, E-mail: randall.susman@stonybrook.edu. *Application contact:* Christine Johnson, Coordinator, 631-444-3114, Fax: 631-444-3947, E-mail: christine.johnson@stonybrook.edu.
Website: http://www.anat.stonybrook.edu/

Universidad Central del Caribe, School of Medicine, Program in Biomedical Sciences, Bayamón, PR 00960-6032. Offers anatomy and cell biology (MA, MS); biochemistry (MS); biomedical sciences (MA); cellular and molecular biology (PhD); microbiology and immunology (MA, MS); pharmacology (MS); physiology (MS).

Universidad de Ciencias Medicas, Graduate Programs, San Jose, Costa Rica. Offers dermatology (SP); family health (MS); health service center administration (MHA); human anatomy (MS); medical and surgery (MD); occupational medicine (MS); pharmacy (Pharm D). *Program availability:* Part-time. *Degree requirements:* For master's, thesis; for doctorate and SP, comprehensive exam. *Entrance requirements:* For master's, MD or bachelor's degree; for doctorate, admissions test; for SP, admissions test, MD.

Université Laval, Faculty of Medicine, Post-Professional Programs in Medical Studies, Québec, QC G1K 7P4, Canada. Offers anatomy–pathology (DESS); anesthesiology (DESS); cardiology (DESS); care of older people (Diploma); clinical research (DESS); community health (DESS); dermatology (DESS); diagnostic radiology (DESS); emergency medicine (Diploma); family medicine (DESS); general surgery (DESS); geriatrics (DESS); hematology (DESS); internal medicine (DESS); maternal and fetal medicine (Diploma); medical biochemistry (DESS); medical microbiology and infectious diseases (DESS); medical oncology (DESS); nephrology (DESS); neurology (DESS); neurosurgery (DESS); obstetrics and gynecology (DESS); ophthalmology (DESS); orthopedic surgery (DESS);

oto-rhino-laryngology (DESS); palliative medicine (Diploma); pediatrics (DESS); plastic surgery (DESS); psychiatry (DESS); pulmonary medicine (DESS); radiology–oncology (DESS); thoracic surgery (DESS); urology (DESS). *Degree requirements:* For other advanced degree, comprehensive exam. *Entrance requirements:* For degree, knowledge of French. Electronic applications accepted.

University at Buffalo, the State University of New York, Graduate School, Jacobs School of Medicine and Biomedical Sciences, Graduate Programs in Medicine and Biomedical Sciences, Department of Pathology and Anatomical Sciences, Buffalo, NY 14203. Offers anatomical sciences (MA, PhD); computational cell biology, anatomy, and pathology (PhD); pathology (MA, PhD). *Program availability:* Part-time. *Faculty:* 17 full-time (4 women). *Students:* 14 full-time (3 women); includes 2 minority (1 American Indian or Alaska Native, non-Hispanic/Latino; 1 Asian, non-Hispanic/Latino), 1 international. Average age 29. 26 applicants, 27% accepted, 6 enrolled. In 2017, 2 master's, 2 doctorates awarded. *Degree requirements:* For master's, thesis; for doctorate, comprehensive exam, thesis/dissertation. *Entrance requirements:* For master's, GRE, MCAT or DAT, 2 letters of recommendation; for doctorate, GRE, MCAT, or DAT, 3 letters of recommendation. Additional exam requirements/recommendations for international students: Required—TOEFL (minimum score 600 paper-based; 100 iBT). *Application deadline:* For fall admission, 5/1 priority date for domestic students, 3/1 priority date for international students. Applications are processed on a rolling basis. Application fee: $85. Electronic applications accepted. *Expenses:* Contact institution. *Financial support:* In 2017–18, 7 students received support, including 1 research assistantship with full tuition reimbursement available (averaging $24,900 per year), 1 teaching assistantship with full tuition reimbursement available (averaging $24,900 per year); Federal Work-Study, health care benefits, and unspecified assistantships also available. Financial award application deadline: 2/1; financial award applicants required to submit FAFSA. *Faculty research:* Immunopathology-immunobiology, experimental hypertension, neuromuscular disease, molecular pathology, cell motility and cytoskeleton. *Total annual research expenditures:* $138,370. *Unit head:* Dr. John E. Tomaszewski, Department Chair, 716-829-2846, Fax: 716-829-2911, E-mail: johntoma@buffalo.edu. *Application contact:* Lannette M. Garcia, Graduate Program Coordinator, 716-829-5204, Fax: 716-829-2911, E-mail: ubpathad@buffalo.edu.
Website: http://medicine.buffalo.edu/departments/pathology.html

University of California, Irvine, School of Medicine and Francisco J. Ayala School of Biological Sciences, Department of Anatomy and Neurobiology, Irvine, CA 92697. Offers biological sciences (MS, PhD); MD/PhD. *Faculty:* 26 full-time (13 women), 2 part-time/adjunct (1 woman). *Students:* 13 full-time (7 women), 3 part-time (2 women); includes 5 minority (all Asian, non-Hispanic/Latino), 2 international. Average age 27. In 2017, 8 doctorates awarded. *Entrance requirements:* For master's and doctorate, GRE General Test, GRE Subject Test. Additional exam requirements/recommendations for international students: Required—TOEFL (minimum score 550 paper-based). *Application deadline:* For fall admission, 1/15 priority date for domestic students, 1/15 for international students. Applications are processed on a rolling basis. Application fee: $105 ($125 for international students). Electronic applications accepted. *Financial support:* Fellowships, research assistantships with full tuition reimbursements, teaching assistantships, institutionally sponsored loans, traineeships, health care benefits, and unspecified assistantships available. Financial award application deadline: 3/1; financial award applicants required to submit FAFSA. *Faculty research:* Neurotransmitter immunocytochemistry, intracellular physiology, molecular neurobiology, forebrain organization and development, structure and function of sensory and motor systems. *Unit head:* Prof. Christine Gall, Interim Chair, 949-824-8652, Fax: 949-824-1255, E-mail: cmgall@uci.edu. *Application contact:* David Lyon, Director of Graduate Studies, 949-824-0447, E-mail: dclyon@uci.edu.

University of California, Los Angeles, David Geffen School of Medicine and Graduate Division, Graduate Programs in Medicine, Department of Neurobiology, Los Angeles, CA 90095. Offers MS, PhD. Terminal master's awarded for partial completion of doctoral program. *Degree requirements:* For master's, comprehensive exam; for doctorate, thesis/dissertation, oral and written qualifying exams; 2 quarters of teaching experience. *Entrance requirements:* For doctorate, GRE General Test; GRE Subject Test, bachelor's degree; minimum undergraduate GPA of 3.0 (or its equivalent if letter grade system not used). Additional exam requirements/recommendations for international students: Required—TOEFL. Electronic applications accepted.

University of Chicago, Division of the Biological Sciences, Department of Organismal Biology and Anatomy, Chicago, IL 60637. Offers integrative biology (PhD). *Faculty:* 20. *Students:* 20 full-time (13 women). 28 applicants, 21% accepted, 4 enrolled. In 2017, 6 doctorates awarded. *Degree requirements:* For doctorate, thesis/dissertation, ethics class, 2 teaching assistantships, preliminary examinations. *Entrance requirements:* For doctorate, GRE General Test, transcripts, statement of purpose, 3 letters of recommendation. Additional exam requirements/recommendations for international students: Required—TOEFL (minimum score 600 paper-based; 104 iBT), IELTS (minimum score 7). *Application deadline:* For fall admission, 12/1 for domestic and international students. Application fee: $90. Electronic applications accepted. *Financial support:* In 2017–18, 12 students received support, including fellowships with full tuition reimbursements available (averaging $31,000 per year), research assistantships with full tuition reimbursements available (averaging $31,000 per year); institutionally sponsored loans, scholarships/grants, traineeships, and health care benefits also available. Financial award application deadline: 12/1. *Faculty research:* Evolution and development, behavioral neurobiology, comparative biomechanics, vertebrate paleontology, integrative neuromechanics. *Unit head:* Dr. Robert Ho, Chair, E-mail: rkh@uchicago.edu. *Application contact:* Audrey Aronowsky, Graduate Research, Education, and Outreach Manager, 773-702-3891, E-mail: aronowsky@uchicago.edu.
Website: http://pondside.uchicago.edu/oba/

University of Colorado Denver, School of Medicine, Program in Cell Biology, Stem Cells, and Development, Aurora, CO 80045. Offers cell biology, stem cells, and developmental biology (PhD); modern human anatomy (MS). In 2017, 1 doctorate awarded. *Degree requirements:* For doctorate, comprehensive exam, thesis/dissertation, at least 30 credit hours of coursework and 30 credit hours of thesis research; laboratory rotations. *Entrance requirements:* For doctorate, GRE, minimum GPA of 3.0; 3 letters of reference; prerequisite coursework in organic chemistry, biology, biochemistry, physics and calculus; research experience (highly recommended). Additional exam requirements/recommendations for international students: Required—TOEFL (minimum score 550 paper-based; 80 iBT). Application fee: $0. *Faculty research:* Development and repair of the vertebrate nervous system; molecular, genetic and developmental mechanisms involved in the patterning of the early spinal cord (neural plate) during vertebrate embryogenesis; structural analysis of protein glycosylation using NMR and mass spectrometry; small RNAs and post-transcriptional gene regulation during nematode gametogenesis and early development; diabetes-mediated changes in cardiovascular gene expression and functional exercise capacity. *Unit head:* Dr. Bruce Appel, Director, 303-724-3465, E-mail: bruce.appel@ucdenver.edu. *Application contact:* Kenton Owsley, Program Administrator, 303-724-3468, Fax: 303-724-3420, E-mail: kenton.owsley@ucdenver.edu.
Website: http://www.ucdenver.edu/academics/colleges/medicalschool/programs/CSD/Pages/CSD.aspx

University of Connecticut Health Center, Graduate School, Programs in Biomedical Sciences, Program in Skeletal Biology and Regeneration, Farmington, CT 06030. Offers PhD, DMD/PhD, MD/PhD. *Degree requirements:* For doctorate, comprehensive exam, thesis/dissertation. *Entrance requirements:* For doctorate, GRE General Test. Additional exam requirements/recommendations for international students: Required—TOEFL (minimum score 600 paper-based). Electronic applications accepted. *Faculty research:* Skeletal development and patterning, bone biology, connective tissue biology, neurophysiology of taste and smell, microbiological aspects of caries.

University of Guelph, Ontario Veterinary College and Graduate Studies, Graduate Programs in Veterinary Sciences, Department of Biomedical Sciences, Guelph, ON N1G 2W1, Canada. Offers morphology (M Sc, DV Sc, PhD); neuroscience (M Sc, DV Sc, PhD); pharmacology (M Sc, DV Sc, PhD); physiology (M Sc, DV Sc, PhD); toxicology (M Sc, DV Sc, PhD). *Program availability:* Part-time. *Degree requirements:* For master's, thesis; for doctorate, comprehensive exam, thesis/dissertation. *Entrance requirements:* For master's, honors B Sc, minimum 75% average in last 20 courses; for doctorate, M Sc with thesis from accredited institution. Additional exam requirements/recommendations for international students: Required—TOEFL (minimum score 550 paper-based; 89 iBT). Electronic applications accepted. *Faculty research:* Cellular morphology; endocrine, vascular and reproductive physiology; clinical pharmacology; veterinary toxicology; developmental biology, neuroscience.

University of Illinois at Chicago, College of Medicine and Graduate College, Graduate Programs in Medicine, Department of Anatomy and Cell Biology, Chicago, IL 60607. Offers MS, MD/PhD. *Degree requirements:* For master's, preliminary oral examination, dissertation and oral defense. *Entrance requirements:* For master's, GRE General Test, minimum GPA of 2.75, 3 letters of recommendation. Additional exam requirements/recommendations for international students: Required—TOEFL (minimum score 550 paper-based). Electronic applications accepted. *Faculty research:* Synapses, axonal transport, neurodegenerative diseases.

The University of Iowa, Roy J. and Lucille A. Carver College of Medicine and Graduate College, Graduate Programs in Medicine, Department of Anatomy and Cell Biology, Iowa City, IA 52242-1316. Offers PhD. *Degree requirements:* For doctorate, comprehensive exam, thesis/dissertation. *Entrance requirements:* For doctorate, GRE General Test, minimum GPA of 3.0. Additional exam requirements/recommendations for international students: Required—TOEFL (minimum score 600 paper-based; 100 iBT). Electronic applications accepted. *Faculty research:* Biology of differentiation and transformation, developmental and vascular cell biology, neurobiology.

The University of Kansas, University of Kansas Medical Center, School of Medicine, Department of Anatomy and Cell Biology, Kansas City, KS 66160. Offers MS, PhD, MD/PhD. *Faculty:* 29. *Students:* 11 full-time (6 women), 5 international. Average age 28. 1 applicant, 100% accepted, 1 enrolled. In 2017, 2 doctorates awarded. Terminal master's awarded for partial completion of doctoral program. *Degree requirements:* For master's, thesis; for doctorate, comprehensive exam, thesis/dissertation. *Entrance requirements:* For master's and doctorate, GRE. Additional exam requirements/recommendations for international students: Required—TOEFL. *Application deadline:* For fall admission, 1/15 priority date for domestic students. Applications are processed on a rolling basis. Application fee: $0. Electronic applications accepted. *Financial support:* In 2017–18, 16 research assistantships with full tuition reimbursements (averaging $24,500 per year), 3 teaching assistantships with full tuition reimbursements (averaging $24,500 per year) were awarded; fellowships, institutionally sponsored loans, scholarships/grants, health care benefits, and unspecified assistantships also available. Financial award application deadline: 3/1; financial award applicants required to submit FAFSA. *Faculty research:* Development of the synapse and neuromuscular junction, pain perception and diabetic neuropathies, cardiovascular and kidney development, reproductive immunology, post-fertilization signaling events. *Total annual research expenditures:* $6.8 million. *Unit head:* Dr. Dale R. Abrahamson, Chairman, 913-588-0702, Fax: 913-588-2710, E-mail: dabrahamson@kumc.edu. *Application contact:* Dr. Julie A. Christianson, Assistant Professor, 913-945-6430, Fax: 913-588-5677, E-mail: jchristianson@kumc.edu.
Website: http://www.kumc.edu/school-of-medicine/anatomy-and-cell-biology.html

University of Kentucky, Graduate School, Graduate School Programs from the College of Medicine, Program in Anatomy and Neurobiology, Lexington, KY 40506-0032. Offers PhD. *Degree requirements:* For doctorate, comprehensive exam, thesis/dissertation. *Entrance requirements:* For doctorate, GRE General Test, minimum undergraduate GPA of 2.75. Additional exam requirements/recommendations for international students: Required—TOEFL (minimum score 550 paper-based). Electronic applications accepted. *Faculty research:* Neuroendocrinology, developmental neurobiology, neurotrophic substances, neural plasticity and trauma, neurobiology of aging.

University of Louisville, School of Medicine, Department of Anatomical Sciences and Neurobiology, Louisville, KY 40292-0001. Offers MS, PhD, MD/PhD. *Faculty:* 19 full-time (5 women), 2 part-time/adjunct (0 women). *Students:* 27 full-time (11 women), 9 part-time (4 women); includes 4 minority (1 Asian, non-Hispanic/Latino; 2 Hispanic/Latino; 1 Two or more races, non-Hispanic/Latino), 1 international. Average age 28. 28 applicants, 54% accepted, 10 enrolled. In 2017, 2 doctorates awarded. Terminal master's awarded for partial completion of doctoral program. *Degree requirements:* For master's, thesis; for doctorate, comprehensive exam, thesis/dissertation. *Entrance requirements:* For master's and doctorate, GRE General Test (minimum score of 1000 verbal and quantitative), minimum GPA of 3.0. Additional exam requirements/recommendations for international students: Required—TOEFL. *Application deadline:* Applications are processed on a rolling basis. Application fee: $65. Electronic applications accepted. *Expenses:* Tuition, state resident: full-time $12,246; part-time $681 per credit hour. Tuition, nonresident: full-time $25,486; part-time $1417 per credit hour. *Required fees:* $196. Tuition and fees vary according to course load, program and reciprocity agreements. *Financial support:* Fellowships with full tuition reimbursements and health care benefits available. Financial award application deadline: 4/15. *Faculty research:* Human adult neural stem cells, development and plasticity of the nervous system, organization of the dorsal thalamus, electrophysiology/neuroanatomy of central neurons mediating control of reproductive and pelvic organs, normal neural mechanisms and plasticity following injury and/or chronic pain, differentiation and regeneration of motor neurons and oligodendrocytes. *Total annual research expenditures:* $3.3 million. *Unit head:* Dr. William Guido, Chair, 502-852-6227, Fax: 502-852-6228, E-mail: w0guid01@gwise.louisville.edu. *Application contact:* Dr. Charles Hubscher, Director of Graduate Studies, 502-852-3058, Fax: 502-852-6228, E-mail: chhub01@louisville.edu.
Website: http://louisville.edu/medicine/departments/anatomy

University of Manitoba, Max Rady College of Medicine and Faculty of Graduate Studies, Graduate Programs in Medicine, Department of Human Anatomy and Cell Science, Winnipeg, MB R3T 2N2, Canada. Offers M Sc, PhD. *Degree requirements:* For master's, thesis; for doctorate, one foreign language, thesis/dissertation.

University of Mississippi Medical Center, School of Graduate Studies in the Health Sciences, Department of Anatomy, Jackson, MS 39216-4505. Offers clinical anatomy (MS, PhD); MD/PhD. *Degree requirements:* For doctorate, comprehensive exam, thesis/dissertation, first authored publication. *Entrance requirements:* For doctorate, GRE General Test, minimum GPA of 3.0, personal statement. Additional exam requirements/

recommendations for international students: Required—TOEFL. *Faculty research:* Systems neuroscience with emphasis on motor and sensory, cell biology with emphasis on cell-matrix interactions, development of cardiovascular system, biology of glial cells.

University of Missouri, School of Medicine and Office of Research and Graduate Studies, Graduate Programs in Medicine, Department of Pathology and Anatomical Sciences, Columbia, MO 65211. Offers MS, PhD. *Entrance requirements:* For master's, GRE (minimum Verbal and Analytical score of 1250), letters of recommendation, minimum GPA of 3.5. Additional exam requirements/recommendations for international students: Required—TOEFL. Electronic applications accepted. *Expenses:* Tuition, state resident: full-time $6480. Tuition, nonresident: full-time $17,744. *Required fees:* $1108. Tuition and fees vary according to course load, campus/location and program. *Unit head:* Dr. Lester Layfield, Chair. *Application contact:* Dr. Lester Layfield, Chair.
Website: http://pathology-anatomy.missouri.edu/

University of Nebraska Medical Center, Interdisciplinary Graduate Program in Biomedical Sciences, Department of Genetics, Cell Biology and Anatomy, Omaha, NE 68198-5805. Offers genetics, cell biology and anatomy (PhD); medical anatomy (MS); molecular genetics and cell biology (MS). Terminal master's awarded for partial completion of doctoral program. *Degree requirements:* For master's, comprehensive exam, thesis (for some programs); for doctorate, comprehensive exam, thesis/dissertation. *Entrance requirements:* For master's, GRE General Test (MCAT or DAT acceptable for MS in medical anatomy); for doctorate, GRE General Test. Additional exam requirements/recommendations for international students: Required—TOEFL (minimum score 550 paper-based; 80 iBT). Electronic applications accepted. *Expenses:* Contact institution. *Faculty research:* Hematology, immunology, developmental biology, genetics cancer biology, neuroscience.

University of North Texas Health Science Center at Fort Worth, Graduate School of Biomedical Sciences, Fort Worth, TX 76107-2699. Offers biochemistry and cancer biology (MS, PhD); biotechnology (MS); cell biology, immunology and microbiology (MS, PhD); clinical research management (MS); forensic genetics (MS); genetics (MS, PhD); integrative physiology (MS, PhD); medical sciences (MS); pharmaceutical sciences and pharmacotherapy (MS, PhD); pharmacology and neuroscience (MS, PhD); structural anatomy and rehabilitation sciences (MS, PhD); DO/MS; DO/PhD. Terminal master's awarded for partial completion of doctoral program. *Degree requirements:* For master's, thesis; for doctorate, thesis/dissertation. *Entrance requirements:* For master's and doctorate, GRE General Test. Additional exam requirements/recommendations for international students: Required—TOEFL. *Expenses:* Contact institution. *Faculty research:* Alzheimer's disease, aging, eye diseases, cancer, cardiovascular disease.

University of Prince Edward Island, Atlantic Veterinary College, Graduate Program in Veterinary Medicine, Charlottetown, PE C1A 4P3, Canada. Offers anatomy (M Sc, PhD); bacteriology (M Sc, PhD); clinical pharmacology (M Sc, PhD); clinical sciences (M Sc, PhD); epidemiology (M Sc, PhD), including reproduction; fish health (M Sc, PhD); food animal nutrition (M Sc, PhD); immunology (M Sc, PhD); microanatomy (M Sc, PhD); parasitology (M Sc, PhD); pathology (M Sc, PhD); pharmacology (M Sc, PhD); physiology (M Sc, PhD); toxicology (M Sc, PhD); veterinary science (M Vet Sc); virology (M Sc, PhD). *Program availability:* Part-time. *Degree requirements:* For master's, thesis; for doctorate, thesis/dissertation. *Entrance requirements:* For master's, DVM, B Sc honors degree, or equivalent; for doctorate, M Sc. Additional exam requirements/recommendations for international students: Required—TOEFL (minimum score 550 paper-based; 80 iBT). *Expenses:* Contact institution. *Faculty research:* Animal health management, infectious diseases, fin fish and shellfish health, basic biomedical sciences, ecosystem health.

University of Puerto Rico–Medical Sciences Campus, School of Medicine, Biomedical Sciences Graduate Program, Department of Anatomy and Neurobiology, San Juan, PR 00936-5067. Offers anatomy (MS, PhD). *Degree requirements:* For master's, one foreign language, comprehensive exam, thesis; for doctorate, one foreign language, comprehensive exam, thesis/dissertation. *Entrance requirements:* For master's and doctorate, GRE General Test, GRE Subject Test, interview, minimum GPA of 3.0, 3 letters of recommendation. Electronic applications accepted. *Faculty research:* Neurobiology, primatology, visual system, muscle structure.

University of Rochester, School of Medicine and Dentistry, Graduate Programs in Medicine and Dentistry, Department of Neurobiology and Anatomy, Programs in Neurobiology and Anatomy, Rochester, NY 14627. Offers PhD, MD/MS. *Degree requirements:* For doctorate, thesis/dissertation, qualifying exam. *Entrance requirements:* For doctorate, GRE General Test.

University of Saskatchewan, College of Medicine, Department of Anatomy and Cell Biology, Saskatoon, SK S7N 5A2, Canada. Offers M Sc, PhD. *Degree requirements:* For master's, thesis; for doctorate, thesis/dissertation. *Entrance requirements:* Additional exam requirements/recommendations for international students: Required—TOEFL.

University of Saskatchewan, Western College of Veterinary Medicine and College of Graduate Studies and Research, Graduate Programs in Veterinary Medicine, Department of Veterinary Biomedical Sciences, Saskatoon, SK S7N 5A2, Canada. Offers veterinary anatomy (M Sc); veterinary biomedical sciences (M Vet Sc); veterinary physiological sciences (M Sc, PhD). *Degree requirements:* For master's, thesis; for doctorate, comprehensive exam (for some programs), thesis/dissertation. *Entrance requirements:* Additional exam requirements/recommendations for international students: Required—TOEFL (minimum score 80 iBT); Recommended—IELTS (minimum score 6.5). Electronic applications accepted. *Faculty research:* Toxicology, animal reproduction, pharmacology, chloride channels, pulmonary pathobiology.

University of South Florida, Morsani College of Medicine and College of Graduate Studies, Graduate Programs in Medical Sciences, Tampa, FL 33620-9951. Offers advanced athletic training (MS); athletic training (MS); bioinformatics and computational biology (MSBCB); biotechnology (MSB); health informatics (MSHI); medical sciences (MSMS, PhD), including aging and neuroscience (MSMS), allergy, immunology and infectious disease (PhD), anatomy, biochemistry and molecular biology, clinical and translational research, health science (MSMS), interdisciplinary medical sciences (MSMS), medical microbiology and immunology (MSMS), metabolic and nutritional medicine (MSMS), microbiology and immunology (PhD), molecular medicine, molecular pharmacology and physiology (PhD), neuroscience (PhD), pathology and cell biology (PhD), women's health (MSMS). *Students:* 372 full-time (212 women), 216 part-time (142 women); includes 257 minority (78 Black or African American, non-Hispanic/Latino; 1 American Indian or Alaska Native, non-Hispanic/Latino; 79 Asian, non-Hispanic/Latino; 84 Hispanic/Latino; 15 Two or more races, non-Hispanic/Latino), 62 international. Average age 28. 1,048 applicants, 46% accepted, 309 enrolled. In 2017, 351 master's, 56 doctorates awarded. Terminal master's awarded for partial completion of doctoral program. *Degree requirements:* For master's, comprehensive exam, thesis; for doctorate, comprehensive exam, thesis/dissertation. *Entrance requirements:* For master's, GRE General Test or GMAT, bachelor's degree or equivalent from regionally-accredited university with minimum GPA of 3.0 in upper-division sciences coursework; prerequisites in general biology, general chemistry, general physics, organic chemistry, quantitative analysis, and integral and differential calculus; for doctorate, GRE General Test, bachelor's degree from regionally-accredited university with minimum GPA of 3.0 in upper-division sciences coursework; 3 letters of recommendation; personal interview; 1-2 page personal statement; prerequisites in biology, chemistry, physics, organic chemistry, quantitative analysis, and integral/differential calculus. Additional exam requirements/recommendations for international students: Required—TOEFL (minimum score 550 paper-based; 79 iBT) or IELTS (minimum score 6.5). *Application deadline:* For fall admission, 2/1 priority date for domestic students, 2/1 for international students. Application fee: $30. Electronic applications accepted. *Expenses:* Contact institution. *Financial support:* In 2017–18, 109 students received support. *Faculty research:* Anatomy, biochemistry, cancer biology, cardiovascular disease, cell biology, immunology, microbiology, molecular biology, neuroscience, pharmacology, physiology. *Total annual research expenditures:* $45.3 million. *Unit head:* Dr. Michael Barber, Professor/Associate Dean for Graduate and Postdoctoral Affairs, 813-974-9908, Fax: 813-974-4317, E-mail: mbarber@health.usf.edu. *Application contact:* Dr. Eric Bennett, Graduate Director, PhD Program in Medical Sciences, 813-974-1545, Fax: 813-974-4317, E-mail: esbennet@health.usf.edu.
Website: http://health.usf.edu/nocms/medicine/graduatestudies/

The University of Tennessee, Graduate School, College of Agricultural Sciences and Natural Resources, Department of Animal Science, Knoxville, TN 37996. Offers animal anatomy (PhD); breeding (MS, PhD); management (MS, PhD); nutrition (MS, PhD); physiology (MS, PhD). *Program availability:* Part-time. *Degree requirements:* For master's, thesis; for doctorate, thesis/dissertation. *Entrance requirements:* For master's and doctorate, GRE General Test, minimum GPA of 2.7. Additional exam requirements/recommendations for international students: Required—TOEFL. Electronic applications accepted.

University of Utah, School of Medicine and Graduate School, Graduate Programs in Medicine, Department of Neurobiology and Anatomy, Salt Lake City, UT 84112-1107. Offers PhD. *Program availability:* Part-time. Terminal master's awarded for partial completion of doctoral program. *Degree requirements:* For doctorate, comprehensive exam, thesis/dissertation. *Entrance requirements:* For doctorate, GRE General Test. Additional exam requirements/recommendations for international students: Required—TOEFL. *Faculty research:* Neuroscience, neuroanatomy, developmental neurobiology, neurogenetics.

The University of Western Ontario, Faculty of Graduate Studies, Biosciences Division, Department of Anatomy and Cell Biology, London, ON N6A 5B8, Canada. Offers anatomy and cell biology (M Sc, PhD); clinical anatomy (M Sc). *Degree requirements:* For master's, thesis; for doctorate, comprehensive exam, thesis/dissertation. *Entrance requirements:* For master's, honors degree or equivalent in biological sciences; for doctorate, master's degree. Additional exam requirements/recommendations for international students: Required—TOEFL. *Faculty research:* Cell and molecular biology, developmental biology, neuroscience, immunobiology and cancer.

Virginia Commonwealth University, Medical College of Virginia-Professional Programs, School of Medicine, Graduate Programs in Medicine, Department of Anatomy and Neurobiology, Richmond, VA 23284-9005. Offers MS. *Degree requirements:* For master's, thesis. *Entrance requirements:* For master's, GRE, MCAT or DAT. Electronic applications accepted.

Wake Forest University, School of Medicine and Graduate School of Arts and Sciences, Graduate Programs in Medicine, Department of Neurobiology and Anatomy, Winston-Salem, NC 27109. Offers PhD, MD/PhD. *Degree requirements:* For doctorate, thesis/dissertation. *Entrance requirements:* For doctorate, GRE General Test. Additional exam requirements/recommendations for international students: Required—TOEFL. Electronic applications accepted. *Faculty research:* Sensory neurobiology, reproductive endocrinology, regulatory processes in cell biology.

Wayne State University, School of Medicine, Office of Biomedical Graduate Programs, Detroit, MI 48202. Offers anatomy and cell biology (MS, PhD); basic medical sciences (MS); biochemistry and molecular biology (MS, PhD); cancer biology (MS, PhD); clinical and translational science (Graduate Certificate); family medicine and public health sciences (MPH, Graduate Certificate), including public health practice; genetic counseling (MS); immunology and microbiology (MS, PhD); medical physics (MS, PhD, Graduate Certificate); medical research (MS); molecular medicine and genomics (MS, PhD), including molecular genetics and genomics; pathology (PhD); pharmacology (MS, PhD); physiology (MS, PhD), including physiology, reproductive sciences (PhD); psychiatry and behavioral neurosciences (PhD), including translational neuroscience; MD/MPH; MD/PhD; MPH/MA; MSW/MPH. *Program availability:* Part-time, evening/weekend. *Students:* 268 full-time (152 women), 117 part-time (59 women); includes 108 minority (19 Black or African American, non-Hispanic/Latino; 1 American Indian or Alaska Native, non-Hispanic/Latino; 62 Asian, non-Hispanic/Latino; 9 Hispanic/Latino; 17 Two or more races, non-Hispanic/Latino), 48 international. Average age 26. 1,133 applicants, 21% accepted, 151 enrolled. In 2017, 70 master's, 25 doctorates, 10 other advanced degrees awarded. Terminal master's awarded for partial completion of doctoral program. *Degree requirements:* For master's, thesis (for some programs); for doctorate, thesis/dissertation. *Entrance requirements:* For master's, doctorate, and Graduate Certificate, GRE. Additional exam requirements/recommendations for international students: Required—TOEFL (minimum score 550 paper-based; 100 iBT), Michigan English Language Assessment Battery (minimum score 85); Recommended—IELTS (minimum score 6.5), TWE (minimum score 5.5). *Application deadline:* For fall admission, 2/1 for domestic and international students. Applications are processed on a rolling basis. Application fee: $50. Electronic applications accepted. *Expenses:* Contact institution. *Financial support:* In 2017–18, 177 students received support, including 64 fellowships with full tuition reimbursements available (averaging $24,388 per year), 79 research assistantships with full tuition reimbursements available (averaging $26,894 per year); scholarships/grants, traineeships, and health care benefits also available. *Faculty research:* Cancer biology, neurosciences, vision sciences, molecular biology, pathology, physiology, pharmacology, public health, medical physics. *Unit head:* Dr. Daniel A. Walz, Associate Dean for Biomedical Graduate Programs, 313-577-1455, Fax: 313-577-8796, E-mail: gradprogs@med.wayne.edu.
Website: https://www.med.wayne.edu/biomedical-graduate-programs/

Wright State University, Graduate School, College of Science and Mathematics, Department of Neuroscience, Cell Biology, and Physiology, Dayton, OH 45435. Offers anatomy (MS); physiology and neuroscience (MS). *Degree requirements:* For master's, thesis optional. *Entrance requirements:* Additional exam requirements/recommendations for international students: Required—TOEFL. *Faculty research:* Reproductive cell biology, neurobiology of pain, neurohistochemistry.

Youngstown State University, Graduate School, College of Science, Technology, Engineering and Mathematics, Department of Biological Sciences, Youngstown, OH 44555-0001. Offers environmental biology (MS); molecular biology, microbiology, and genetic (MS); physiology and anatomy (MS). *Program availability:* Part-time. *Degree requirements:* For master's, comprehensive exam, thesis, oral review. *Entrance requirements:* For master's, GRE General Test, minimum GPA of 2.7. Additional exam requirements/recommendations for international students: Required—TOEFL. *Faculty research:* Cell biology, neurophysiology, molecular biology, neurobiology, gene regulation.

Section 3
Biochemistry

This section contains a directory of institutions offering graduate work in biochemistry, followed by an in-depth entry submitted by an institution that chose to prepare a detailed program description. Additional information about programs listed in the directory but not augmented by an in-depth entry may be obtained by writing directly to the dean of a graduate school or chair of a department at the address given in the directory.

For programs offering related work, see also in this book *Allied Health; Biological and Biomedical Sciences; Biophysics; Botany and Plant Biology; Cell, Molecular, and Structural Biology; Genetics, Developmental Biology, and Reproductive Biology; Microbiological Sciences; Neuroscience and Neurobiology; Nutrition; Pathology and Pathobiology; Pharmacology and Toxicology; Pharmacy and Pharmaceutical Sciences;* and *Physiology.* In the other guides in this series:

Graduate Programs in the Physical Sciences, Mathematics, Agricultural Sciences, the Environment & Natural Resources

See *Agricultural and Food Sciences, Chemistry,* and *Physics*

Graduate Programs in Engineering & Applied Sciences

See *Agricultural Engineering and Bioengineering, Biomedical Engineering and Biotechnology, Chemical Engineering,* and *Materials Sciences and Engineering*

CONTENTS

Biochemistry

Albert Einstein College of Medicine, Graduate Programs in the Biomedical Sciences, Department of Biochemistry, Bronx, NY 10461. Offers PhD, MD/PhD. *Degree requirements:* For doctorate, thesis/dissertation. *Entrance requirements:* For doctorate, GRE General Test. Additional exam requirements/recommendations for international students: Required—TOEFL. *Application deadline:* For fall admission, 1/15 for domestic students. Application fee: $0. *Financial support:* Fellowships available. *Faculty research:* Biochemical mechanisms, enzymology, protein chemistry, bio-organic chemistry, molecular genetics. *Unit head:* Dr. Steven C. Almo, Chair, 718-430-2746. *Application contact:* Sheila Cleeton, Executive Director and Registrar, Einstein Graduate Division, 718-430-2128, Fax: 718-430-8655, E-mail: sheila.cleeton@einstein.yu.edu.
Website: http://www.einstein.yu.edu/departments/biochemistry/

American University of Beirut, Graduate Programs, Faculty of Medicine, Beirut, Lebanon. Offers biochemistry (MS); biomedical engineering (MS); biomedical sciences (PhD); health research (MS); human morphology (MS); medicine (MD); microbiology and immunology (MS); neuroscience (MS); orthodontics (clinical) (MS); pharmacology and therapeutics (MS); physiology (MS). *Program availability:* Part-time. *Faculty:* 335 full-time (117 women), 54 part-time/adjunct (5 women). *Students:* 513 full-time (274 women). Average age 23. 527 applicants, 47% accepted, 169 enrolled. In 2017, 18 master's, 98 doctorates awarded. *Degree requirements:* For master's, one foreign language, comprehensive exam, thesis (for some programs); for doctorate, one foreign language, comprehensive exam, thesis/dissertation. *Entrance requirements:* For doctorate, MCAT (for MD); GRE (for PhD). Additional exam requirements/recommendations for international students: Required—TOEFL (minimum score 600 paper-based; 100 iBT), IELTS (minimum score 7.5). *Application deadline:* Applications are processed on a rolling basis. Application fee: $75. Electronic applications accepted. *Expenses:* Contact institution. *Financial support:* In 2017–18, 302 students received support. Fellowships, research assistantships, teaching assistantships, institutionally sponsored loans, scholarships/grants, tuition waivers, and unspecified assistantships available. *Unit head:* Dr. Mohamed Sayegh, Dean, 961-1-135000 Ext. 4700, Fax: 961-1-744489, E-mail: msayegh@aub.edu.lb. *Application contact:* Dr. Salim Kanaan, Director, Admission's Office, 961-1-350000 Ext. 2594, Fax: 961-1-750775, E-mail: sk00@aub.edu.lb.

Arizona State University at the Tempe campus, College of Liberal Arts and Sciences, Department of Chemistry and Biochemistry, Tempe, AZ 85287-1604. Offers biochemistry (MS, PhD); chemistry (MS, PhD); nanoscience (PSM). Terminal master's awarded for partial completion of doctoral program. *Degree requirements:* For master's, thesis, interactive Program of Study (iPOS) submitted before completing 50 percent of required credit hours; for doctorate, comprehensive exam, thesis/dissertation, interactive Program of Study (iPOS) submitted before completing 50 percent of required credit hours. *Entrance requirements:* For master's and doctorate, GRE, minimum GPA of 3.0 or equivalent in last 2 years of work leading to bachelor's degree. Additional exam requirements/recommendations for international students: Required—TOEFL, IELTS, or PTE. Electronic applications accepted.

Auburn University, Graduate School, College of Sciences and Mathematics, Department of Chemistry and Biochemistry, Auburn University, AL 36849. Offers analytical chemistry (MS, PhD); biochemistry (MS, PhD); inorganic chemistry (MS); organic chemistry (PhD); physical chemistry (MS, PhD). *Program availability:* Part-time. *Faculty:* 30 full-time (6 women), 4 part-time/adjunct (2 women). *Students:* 56 full-time (18 women), 32 part-time (20 women); includes 8 minority (5 Black or African American, non-Hispanic/Latino; 1 Asian, non-Hispanic/Latino; 1 Hispanic/Latino; 1 Two or more races, non-Hispanic/Latino), 50 international. Average age 28. 49 applicants, 69% accepted, 23 enrolled. In 2017, 6 master's, 8 doctorates awarded. *Degree requirements:* For master's, thesis (for some programs); for doctorate, thesis/dissertation, oral and written exams. *Entrance requirements:* For master's and doctorate, GRE General Test. *Application deadline:* Applications are processed on a rolling basis. Application fee: $50 ($60 for international students). Electronic applications accepted. *Expenses:* Tuition, state resident: full-time $10,974; part-time $519 per credit hour. Tuition, nonresident: full-time $29,658; part-time $1557 per credit hour. *Required fees:* $816 per semester. Tuition and fees vary according to degree level and program. *Financial support:* Fellowships, research assistantships, and teaching assistantships available. Financial award application deadline: 3/15; financial award applicants required to submit FAFSA. *Unit head:* Dr. Curtis Shannon, Chair, 334-844-4043, Fax: 334-844-4043. *Application contact:* Dr. George Flowers, Dean of the Graduate School, 334-844-2125.
Website: http://www.auburn.edu/cosam/departments/chemistry/

Augusta University, Program in Biochemistry and Cancer Biology, Augusta, GA 30912. Offers PhD. *Degree requirements:* For doctorate, comprehensive exam, thesis/dissertation. *Entrance requirements:* For doctorate, GRE General Test. Additional exam requirements/recommendations for international students: Required—TOEFL (minimum score 550 paper-based; 79 iBT). Electronic applications accepted. *Faculty research:* Molecular oncology and biomarkers; immunology, inflammation and tolerance; signaling and angiogenesis.

Baylor College of Medicine, Graduate School of Biomedical Sciences, Department of Biochemistry and Molecular Biology, Houston, TX 77030-3498. Offers PhD, MD/PhD. *Degree requirements:* For doctorate, thesis/dissertation, public defense. *Entrance requirements:* For doctorate, GRE General Test, GRE Subject Test (strongly recommended), minimum GPA of 3.0. Additional exam requirements/recommendations for international students: Required—TOEFL. Electronic applications accepted. *Faculty research:* DNA repair, homologous recombination, gene therapy, trinucleotide repeat diseases, retinitis pigmentosa.

Baylor College of Medicine, Graduate School of Biomedical Sciences, Interdepartmental Program in Cell and Molecular Biology, Houston, TX 77030-3498. Offers biochemistry (PhD); cell and molecular biology (PhD); genetics (PhD); human genetics (PhD); immunology (PhD); microbiology (PhD); virology (PhD); MD/PhD. *Degree requirements:* For doctorate, thesis/dissertation, public defense. *Entrance requirements:* For doctorate, GRE General Test, GRE Subject Test (strongly recommended), minimum GPA of 3.0. Additional exam requirements/recommendations for international students: Required—TOEFL. Electronic applications accepted. *Faculty research:* Molecular and cellular biology; cancer, aging and stem cells; genomics and proteomics; microbiome, molecular microbiology; infectious disease, immunology and translational research.

Baylor University, Graduate School, College of Arts and Sciences, Department of Chemistry and Biochemistry, Waco, TX 76798. Offers biochemistry (MS, PhD); chemistry (MS, PhD). *Faculty:* 18 full-time (2 women). *Students:* 72 full-time (24 women), 2 part-time (1 woman); includes 12 minority (3 Black or African American, non-Hispanic/Latino; 2 Asian, non-Hispanic/Latino; 3 Hispanic/Latino; 4 Two or more races, non-Hispanic/Latino), 14 international. Average age 25. 80 applicants, 46% accepted, 16 enrolled. In 2017, 5 master's, 8 doctorates awarded. Terminal master's awarded for partial completion of doctoral program. *Degree requirements:* For master's, thesis or alternative; for doctorate, comprehensive exam, thesis/dissertation. *Entrance requirements:* For doctorate, GRE General Test, transcripts, 3 letters of recommendation, personal statement. Additional exam requirements/recommendations for international students: Required—TOEFL (minimum score 90 iBT). *Application deadline:* For fall admission, 2/15 for domestic and international students. Applications are processed on a rolling basis. Application fee: $50. Electronic applications accepted. *Expenses:* Contact institution. *Financial support:* In 2017–18, 42 students received support, including 6 research assistantships with full tuition reimbursements available (averaging $23,000 per year), 36 teaching assistantships with full tuition reimbursements available (averaging $23,000 per year); tuition waivers (full) also available. Financial award application deadline: 1/15. *Faculty research:* Total synthesis, proteomics, computational materials, enzymology. *Total annual research expenditures:* $2.7 million. *Unit head:* Dr. Michael Trakselis, Director of Graduate Affairs, 254-710-2581, E-mail: michael_trakselis@baylor.edu. *Application contact:* Dr. Kevin Shuford, Director of Graduate Recruiting, 254-710-2576, E-mail: kevin_shuford@baylor.edu.
Website: http://www.baylor.edu/chemistry/

Boston College, Graduate School of Arts and Sciences, Department of Chemistry, Chestnut Hill, MA 02467-3800. Offers biochemistry (PhD); inorganic chemistry (PhD); organic chemistry (PhD); physical chemistry (PhD); science education (MST). *Degree requirements:* For doctorate, thesis/dissertation, qualifying exam. *Entrance requirements:* For doctorate, GRE General Test, GRE Subject Test. Additional exam requirements/recommendations for international students: Required—TOEFL (minimum score 600 paper-based; 100 iBT), IELTS (minimum score 8). Electronic applications accepted. *Faculty research:* Organic and organometallic chemistry, chemical biology and biochemistry, physical and theoretical chemistry, inorganic chemistry.

Boston University, Graduate School of Arts and Sciences, Molecular Biology, Cell Biology, and Biochemistry Program (MCBB), Boston, MA 02215. Offers MA, PhD. *Students:* 35 full-time (17 women), 5 part-time (2 women); includes 10 minority (2 Black or African American, non-Hispanic/Latino; 2 Asian, non-Hispanic/Latino; 4 Hispanic/Latino; 2 Two or more races, non-Hispanic/Latino), 12 international. Average age 27. 150 applicants, 20% accepted, 9 enrolled. In 2017, 3 master's, 4 doctorates awarded. Terminal master's awarded for partial completion of doctoral program. *Degree requirements:* For master's, thesis (for some programs); for doctorate, comprehensive exam, thesis/dissertation, teaching requirement. *Entrance requirements:* For master's and doctorate, GRE General Test, 3 letters of recommendation, transcripts, personal statement. Additional exam requirements/recommendations for international students: Required—TOEFL (minimum score 550 paper-based; 84 iBT). *Application deadline:* For fall admission, 12/5 for domestic and international students. Application fee: $95. Electronic applications accepted. *Financial support:* In 2017–18, 35 students received support, including 4 fellowships with full tuition reimbursements available (averaging $22,000 per year), 12 research assistantships with full tuition reimbursements available (averaging $22,000 per year), 16 teaching assistantships with full tuition reimbursements available (averaging $22,000 per year); Federal Work-Study, scholarships/grants, traineeships, and health care benefits also available. Financial award application deadline: 12/5; financial award applicants required to submit FAFSA. *Unit head:* Dr. Ulla Hansen, Director, 617-353-2432, Fax: 617-353-6340, E-mail: uhansen@bu.edu. *Application contact:* Christina Honeycutt, Academic Administrator, 617-353-2432, Fax: 617-353-6340, E-mail: cjhoney@bu.edu.
Website: http://www.bu.edu/mcbb/

Bradley University, The Graduate School, College of Liberal Arts and Sciences, Mund-Lagowski Department of Chemistry and Biochemistry, Peoria, IL 61625-0002. Offers biochemistry (MS); chemistry (MS). *Program availability:* Part-time, evening/weekend. *Degree requirements:* For master's, comprehensive exam, thesis. *Entrance requirements:* Additional exam requirements/recommendations for international students: Required—TOEFL (minimum score 550 paper-based; 79 iBT), IELTS (minimum score 6.5). Electronic applications accepted.

Brandeis University, Graduate School of Arts and Sciences, Program in Biochemistry and Biophysics, Waltham, MA 02454-9110. Offers biochemistry and biophysics (MS, PhD); quantitative biology (PhD). *Faculty:* 11 full-time (5 women). *Students:* 35 full-time (14 women); includes 8 minority (4 Asian, non-Hispanic/Latino; 2 Hispanic/Latino; 2 Two or more races, non-Hispanic/Latino), 6 international. Average age 27. 77 applicants, 25% accepted, 16 enrolled. In 2017, 1 master's, 6 doctorates awarded. Terminal master's awarded for partial completion of doctoral program. *Degree requirements:* For master's, thesis; for doctorate, thesis/dissertation, qualifying exams. *Entrance requirements:* For master's, GRE General Test, resume, letters of recommendation, statement of purpose, transcripts; for doctorate, GRE General Test, resume, letters of recommendation, statement of purpose, transcripts, list of previous research experience. Additional exam requirements/recommendations for international students: Required—PTE (minimum score 68), TOEFL (minimum score 600 paper-based, 100 iBT) or IELTS (7). *Application deadline:* For fall admission, 12/1 priority date for domestic students. Applications are processed on a rolling basis. Application fee: $75. Electronic applications accepted. *Expenses: Tuition:* Full-time $48,720. *Required fees:* $88. Tuition and fees vary according to course load, degree level, program and student level. *Financial support:* In 2017–18, 39 students received support, including 17 fellowships with full tuition reimbursements available (averaging $33,000 per year), 21 research assistantships with full tuition reimbursements available (averaging $33,000 per year); Federal Work-Study, scholarships/grants, health care benefits, and tuition waivers (partial) also available. Financial award application deadline: 4/15; financial award applicants required to submit FAFSA. *Faculty research:* Macromolecular chemistry, structure and function, biochemistry, biophysics, biological macromolecules. *Unit head:* Dr. Dagmar Ringe, Director of Graduate Studies, 781-736-4902, E-mail: scigradoffice@brandeis.edu. *Application contact:* Rachel Krebs, Department Administrator, 781-736-2352, E-mail: scigradoffice@brandeis.edu.
Website: http://www.brandeis.edu/gsas/programs/bio.html

Brigham Young University, Graduate Studies, College of Physical and Mathematical Sciences, Department of Chemistry and Biochemistry, Provo, UT 84602. Offers biochemistry (MS, PhD); chemistry (MS, PhD). *Faculty:* 37 full-time (5 women), 13 part-time/adjunct (5 women). *Students:* 95 full-time (34 women); includes 6 minority (1 Black or African American, non-Hispanic/Latino; 2 Hispanic/Latino; 3 Two or more races, non-Hispanic/Latino), 53 international. Average age 29. 63 applicants, 71% accepted, 30 enrolled. In 2017, 6 master's, 13 doctorates awarded. *Degree requirements:* For master's, thesis; for doctorate, thesis/dissertation, qualifying exam. *Entrance requirements:* For master's and doctorate, GRE General Test, minimum GPA of 3.0. Additional exam requirements/recommendations for international students: Required—TOEFL (minimum score 580 paper-based; 85 iBT), IELTS (minimum score 7).

Application deadline: For fall admission, 2/1 priority date for domestic and international students. Applications are processed on a rolling basis. Application fee: $50. Electronic applications accepted. *Expenses:* $9,720. *Financial support:* In 2017–18, 91 students received support, including 20 fellowships with full tuition reimbursements available (averaging $26,000 per year), 36 research assistantships with full tuition reimbursements available (averaging $26,000 per year), 34 teaching assistantships with full tuition reimbursements available (averaging $26,000 per year); scholarships/grants and supplementary awards also available. Financial award application deadline: 2/1. *Faculty research:* Separation science, molecular recognition, organic synthesis and biomedical application, biochemistry and molecular biology, molecular spectroscopy. *Total annual research expenditures:* $5.3 million. *Unit head:* Dr. David V. Dearden, Chair, 801-422-2355, Fax: 801-422-0153, E-mail: david_dearden@byu.edu. *Application contact:* Dr. Ken A. Christensen, Graduate Coordinator, 801-422-0249, Fax: 801-422-0153, E-mail: kenc@chem.byu.edu.
Website: http://www.chem.byu.edu/

Brown University, Graduate School, Division of Biology and Medicine, Department of Molecular Biology, Cell Biology, and Biochemistry, Providence, RI 02912. Offers MA, PhD. *Program availability:* Part-time. Terminal master's awarded for partial completion of doctoral program. *Degree requirements:* For master's, thesis (for some programs); for doctorate, one foreign language, thesis/dissertation, preliminary exam. *Entrance requirements:* For master's and doctorate, GRE General Test, GRE Subject Test. Additional exam requirements/recommendations for international students: Required—TOEFL. Electronic applications accepted. *Faculty research:* Molecular genetics, gene regulation.

California Institute of Technology, Division of Biology and Division of Chemistry and Chemical Engineering, Biochemistry and Molecular Biophysics Graduate Option, Pasadena, CA 91125-0001. Offers PhD. *Degree requirements:* For doctorate, thesis/dissertation, qualifying exam. *Entrance requirements:* For doctorate, GRE General Test. Additional exam requirements/recommendations for international students: Required—TOEFL. Electronic applications accepted.

California Institute of Technology, Division of Chemistry and Chemical Engineering, Pasadena, CA 91125-0001. Offers biochemistry and molecular biophysics (MS, PhD); chemical engineering (MS, PhD); chemistry (MS, PhD). *Faculty:* 42 full-time (10 women). *Students:* 295 full-time (115 women); includes 79 minority (3 Black or African American, non-Hispanic/Latino; 41 Asian, non-Hispanic/Latino; 21 Hispanic/Latino; 14 Two or more races, non-Hispanic/Latino), 80 international. Average age 25. 638 applicants, 23% accepted, 43 enrolled. In 2017, 14 master's, 59 doctorates awarded. Terminal master's awarded for partial completion of doctoral program. *Degree requirements:* For master's, thesis; for doctorate, thesis/dissertation. *Entrance requirements:* For doctorate, GRE, BS. Additional exam requirements/recommendations for international students: Required—TOEFL; Recommended—IELTS, TWE. *Application deadline:* For fall admission, 12/15 for domestic and international students. Application fee: $100. Electronic applications accepted. *Expenses:* $48,111 tuition, $1,674 mandatory fees. *Financial support:* In 2017–18, 309 students received support, including fellowships (averaging $33,000 per year), research assistantships (averaging $25,900 per year), teaching assistantships (averaging $5,100 per year); Federal Work-Study, institutionally sponsored loans, scholarships/grants, traineeships, health care benefits, and unspecified assistantships also available. Financial award application deadline: 12/15. *Faculty research:* Biochemistry and molecular biophysics; inorganic, structural, and electrochemistry; organic chemistry and chemical biology; physical, theoretical, and chemical physics; chemical engineering. *Unit head:* Prof. Jacqueline K. Barton, Chair, Division of Chemistry and Chemical Engineering, 626-395-3646, Fax: 626-395-6948, E-mail: jkbarton@caltech.edu. *Application contact:* Natalie Gilmore, Graduate Office, 626-395-3812, Fax: 626-577-9246, E-mail: ngilmore@its.caltech.edu.
Website: http://www.cce.caltech.edu/

California Polytechnic State University, San Luis Obispo, College of Science and Mathematics, Department of Chemistry and Biochemistry, San Luis Obispo, CA 93407. Offers polymers and coating science (MS). *Program availability:* Part-time. *Faculty:* 4 full-time (0 women). *Students:* 3 full-time (1 woman), 4 part-time (1 woman); includes 5 minority (3 Asian, non-Hispanic/Latino; 2 Hispanic/Latino), 1 international. Average age 23. 13 applicants, 38% accepted, 4 enrolled. In 2017, 6 master's awarded. *Degree requirements:* For master's, comprehensive exam (for some programs), thesis (for some programs). *Entrance requirements:* For master's, GRE. Additional exam requirements/recommendations for international students: Required—TOEFL (minimum score 80 iBT). *Application deadline:* For fall admission, 4/1 for domestic and international students. Applications are processed on a rolling basis. Application fee: $55. Electronic applications accepted. *Expenses:* Tuition, state resident: full-time $7176; part-time $4164 per year. *Required fees:* $3690; $3219 per year. $1073 per trimester. *Financial support:* Fellowships, research assistantships, career-related internships or fieldwork, Federal Work-Study, and scholarships/grants available. Support available to part-time students. Financial award application deadline: 3/2; financial award applicants required to submit FAFSA. *Faculty research:* Polymer physical chemistry and analysis, polymer synthesis, coatings formulation. *Unit head:* Dr. Raymond Fernando, Graduate Coordinator, 805-756-2395, E-mail: rhfernan@calpoly.edu.
Website: http://www.chemistry.calpoly.edu/

California State University, East Bay, Office of Graduate Studies, College of Science, Department of Chemistry and Biochemistry, Hayward, CA 94542-3000. Offers biochemistry (MS). *Faculty:* 10 full-time (5 women), 14 part-time/adjunct (5 women). *Students:* 7 full-time (4 women), 14 part-time (8 women); includes 17 minority (3 Black or African American, non-Hispanic/Latino; 5 Asian, non-Hispanic/Latino; 3 Hispanic/Latino; 3 Native Hawaiian or other Pacific Islander, non-Hispanic/Latino; 3 Two or more races, non-Hispanic/Latino). Average age 30. 15 applicants, 73% accepted, 6 enrolled. In 2017, 8 master's awarded. *Degree requirements:* For master's, comprehensive exam or thesis. *Entrance requirements:* For master's, minimum GPA of 2.6 in field during previous 2 years of course work. Additional exam requirements/recommendations for international students: Required—TOEFL (minimum score 550 paper-based). *Application deadline:* For fall admission, 6/1 for domestic and international students. Application fee: $55. Electronic applications accepted. *Financial support:* Fellowships, career-related internships or fieldwork, Federal Work-Study, institutionally sponsored loans, and scholarships/grants available. Support available to part-time students. Financial award application deadline: 3/2; financial award applicants required to submit FAFSA. *Unit head:* Dr. Ann McPartland, Chair, 510-885-3452, Fax: 510-885-4675, E-mail: ann.mcpartland@csueastbay.edu. *Application contact:* Prof. Chul Kim, Chemistry Graduate Advisor, 510-885-3490, Fax: 510-885-4675, E-mail: chul.kim@csueastbay.edu.
Website: http://www20.csueastbay.edu/csci/departments/chemistry

California State University, Long Beach, Graduate Studies, College of Natural Sciences and Mathematics, Department of Chemistry and Biochemistry, Long Beach, CA 90840. Offers biochemistry (MS); chemistry (MS). *Program availability:* Part-time. *Degree requirements:* For master's, thesis, departmental qualifying exam. Electronic applications accepted. *Faculty research:* Enzymology, organic synthesis, molecular modeling, environmental chemistry, reaction kinetics.

California State University, Los Angeles, Graduate Studies, College of Natural and Social Sciences, Department of Chemistry and Biochemistry, Los Angeles, CA 90032-8530. Offers analytical chemistry (MS). *Program availability:* Part-time, evening/weekend. *Degree requirements:* For master's, one foreign language, comprehensive exam or thesis. *Entrance requirements:* Additional exam requirements/recommendations for international students: Required—TOEFL. *Faculty research:* Intercalation of heavy metal, carborane chemistry, conductive polymers and fabrics, titanium reagents, computer modeling and synthesis.

California State University, Northridge, Graduate Studies, College of Science and Mathematics, Department of Chemistry and Biochemistry, Northridge, CA 91330. Offers biochemistry (MS); chemistry (MS), including chemistry, environmental chemistry. *Students:* 2 full-time (0 women), 33 part-time (7 women); includes 17 minority (2 Black or African American, non-Hispanic/Latino; 4 Asian, non-Hispanic/Latino; 11 Hispanic/Latino), 1 international. Average age 28. 43 applicants, 30% accepted, 7 enrolled. In 2017, 4 master's awarded. *Degree requirements:* For master's, thesis. *Entrance requirements:* For master's, GRE General Test or minimum GPA of 3.0. Additional exam requirements/recommendations for international students: Required—TOEFL. *Application deadline:* For fall admission, 11/30 for domestic students. Application fee: $55. Electronic applications accepted. *Financial support:* Teaching assistantships available. Support available to part-time students. Financial award application deadline: 3/1. *Unit head:* Eric Kelson, Chair, 818-677-3381.
Website: http://www.csun.edu/chemistry/

California State University, Sacramento, College of Natural Sciences and Mathematics, Department of Chemistry, Sacramento, CA 95819. Offers biochemistry (MS); chemistry (MS). *Program availability:* Part-time. *Students:* 2 full-time (both women), 27 part-time (11 women); includes 13 minority (1 American Indian or Alaska Native, non-Hispanic/Latino; 8 Asian, non-Hispanic/Latino; 4 Hispanic/Latino). Average age 28. 30 applicants, 47% accepted, 12 enrolled. In 2017, 1 master's awarded. *Degree requirements:* For master's, thesis or project; qualifying exam; writing proficiency exam. *Entrance requirements:* For master's, minimum GPA of 2.5 during previous 2 years of course work, BA in chemistry or equivalent. Additional exam requirements/recommendations for international students: Required—TOEFL (minimum score 550 paper-based; 80 iBT); Recommended—IELTS, TSE. *Application deadline:* For fall admission, 3/1 for domestic and international students. Applications are processed on a rolling basis. Application fee: $55. Electronic applications accepted. *Expenses:* Contact institution. *Financial support:* Career-related internships or fieldwork, Federal Work-Study, and scholarships/grants available. Support available to part-time students. Financial award application deadline: 3/1; financial award applicants required to submit FAFSA. *Unit head:* Dr. Linda Roberts, Chair, 916-278-6684, Fax: 916-278-4986, E-mail: robertslm@csus.edu. *Application contact:* Jose Martinez, Graduate Admissions Supervisor, 916-278-7871, E-mail: martinj@skymail.csus.edu.
Website: http://www.csus.edu/chem

Carnegie Mellon University, Mellon College of Science, Department of Biological Sciences, Pittsburgh, PA 15213-3891. Offers biochemistry (PhD); biophysics (PhD); cell and developmental biology (PhD); computational biology (MS, PhD); genetics (PhD); molecular biology (PhD); neuroscience (PhD); structural biology (PhD). *Degree requirements:* For doctorate, comprehensive exam, thesis/dissertation. *Entrance requirements:* For doctorate, GRE General Test, GRE Subject Test, interview. Electronic applications accepted. *Faculty research:* Genetic structure, function, and regulation; protein structure and function; biological membranes; biological spectroscopy.

Carnegie Mellon University, Mellon College of Science, Department of Chemistry, Pittsburgh, PA 15213-3891. Offers atmospheric chemistry (PhD); bioinorganic chemistry (PhD); bioorganic chemistry and chemical biology (PhD); biophysical chemistry (PhD); catalysis (PhD); green and environmental chemistry (PhD); materials and nanoscience (PhD); renewable energy (PhD); sensors, probes, and imaging (PhD); spectroscopy and single molecule analysis (PhD); theoretical and computational chemistry (PhD). *Program availability:* Part-time. Terminal master's awarded for partial completion of doctoral program. *Degree requirements:* For doctorate, thesis/dissertation, departmental qualifying and oral exams, teaching experience. *Entrance requirements:* For doctorate, GRE General Test, GRE Subject Test. Additional exam requirements/recommendations for international students: Required—TOEFL. Electronic applications accepted. *Faculty research:* Physical and theoretical chemistry, chemical synthesis, biophysical/bioinorganic chemistry.

Case Western Reserve University, School of Medicine and School of Graduate Studies, Graduate Programs in Medicine, Department of Biochemistry, Cleveland, OH 44106. Offers biochemistry (MS, PhD); JD/MS. *Program availability:* Part-time. Terminal master's awarded for partial completion of doctoral program. *Degree requirements:* For master's, thesis (for some programs); for doctorate, thesis/dissertation. *Entrance requirements:* For master's and doctorate, GRE General Test. Additional exam requirements/recommendations for international students: Required—TOEFL. Electronic applications accepted. *Expenses: Tuition:* Full-time $43,854; part-time $1827 per credit hour. *Required fees:* $50; $50 per credit hour. Tuition and fees vary according to course load and program. *Faculty research:* Regulation of metabolism, regulation of gene expression and protein synthesis, cell biology, molecular biology, structural biology.

City College of the City University of New York, Graduate School, Division of Science, Department of Chemistry, Program in Biochemistry, New York, NY 10031-9198. Offers MS, PhD. PhD program offered jointly with Graduate School and University Center of the City University of New York. Terminal master's awarded for partial completion of doctoral program. *Degree requirements:* For doctorate, one foreign language, thesis/dissertation. *Entrance requirements:* For doctorate, GRE. Additional exam requirements/recommendations for international students: Required—TOEFL (minimum score 550 paper-based; 79 iBT). Electronic applications accepted. *Faculty research:* Fatty acid metabolism, lectins, gene structure.

Clark University, Graduate School, Gustav H. Carlson School of Chemistry, Worcester, MA 01610-1477. Offers biochemistry (PhD); chemistry (PhD). *Faculty:* 9 full-time (1 woman). *Students:* 10 full-time (3 women); includes 3 minority (2 Asian, non-Hispanic/Latino; 1 Hispanic/Latino), 6 international. Average age 27. 75 applicants, 23% accepted, 10 enrolled. Terminal master's awarded for partial completion of doctoral program. *Degree requirements:* For doctorate, one foreign language, thesis/dissertation. *Entrance requirements:* For doctorate, GRE General Test. Additional exam requirements/recommendations for international students: Required—TOEFL (minimum score 575 paper-based; 90 iBT), IELTS (minimum score 6.5). *Application deadline:* For fall admission, 1/15 priority date for domestic students. Application fee: $75. Electronic applications accepted. *Financial support:* Fellowships, research assistantships, teaching assistantships, and tuition waivers (full) available. *Faculty research:* Nuclear chemistry, molecular biology simulation, NMR studies, biochemistry, protein folding mechanisms. *Unit head:* Dr. Shuanghong Huo, 508-793-7533, E-mail: shuo@clarku.edu. *Application contact:* Rene Baril, Managerial Secretary, 508-793-7130, Fax: 528-793-7117, E-mail: mbaril@clarku.edu.
Website: http://www.clarku.edu/departments/chemistry/

Colorado State University, College of Natural Sciences, Department of Biochemistry and Molecular Biology, Fort Collins, CO 80523-1870. Offers MS, PhD. *Faculty:* 26 full-time (10

women), 4 part-time/adjunct (3 women). *Students:* 17 full-time (2 women), 26 part-time (14 women); includes 3 minority (2 Asian, non-Hispanic/Latino; 1 Hispanic/Latino), 8 international. Average age 26. 35 applicants, 37% accepted, 11 enrolled. In 2017, 4 master's, 5 doctorates awarded. Terminal master's awarded for partial completion of doctoral program. *Degree requirements:* For master's, comprehensive exam, thesis optional; for doctorate, comprehensive exam, thesis/dissertation, preliminary exam. *Entrance requirements:* For master's, minimum GPA of 3.0, personal statement; for doctorate, GRE, BS/BA with minimum GPA of 3.0, statement of purpose, research interests. Additional exam requirements/recommendations for international students: Required—TOEFL (minimum score 550 paper-based; 50 iBT). *Application deadline:* For fall admission, 1/1 priority date for domestic and international students. Application fee: $60 ($70 for international students). Electronic applications accepted. *Expenses:* Tuition, state resident: full-time $9917. Tuition, nonresident: full-time $24,312. *Required fees:* $2284. Tuition and fees vary according to course load and program. *Financial support:* In 2017–18, 35 students received support, including 31 research assistantships with full and partial tuition reimbursements available (averaging $27,625 per year), 9 teaching assistantships with full and partial tuition reimbursements available (averaging $21,921 per year); fellowships with full and partial tuition reimbursements available, career-related internships or fieldwork, scholarships/grants, and health care benefits also available. *Faculty research:* Genome architecture and function; molecular basis for cancer; cellular trafficking and human disease; drug screening and design; synthetic biology. *Total annual research expenditures:* $5.5 million. *Unit head:* Dr. Laurie A. Stargell, Chair/Professor, 970-491-0569, Fax: 970-491-0494, E-mail: laurie.stargell@colostate.edu. *Application contact:* Kristen DeQuasie, Graduate Program Assistant, 970-491-5566, Fax: 970-491-0494, E-mail: kristen.dequasie@colostate.edu.
Website: http://www.bmb.colostate.edu/

Colorado State University–Pueblo, College of Science and Mathematics, Pueblo, CO 81001-4901. Offers applied natural science (MS), including biochemistry, biology, chemistry. *Program availability:* Part-time, evening/weekend. *Degree requirements:* For master's, comprehensive exam (for some programs), thesis (for some programs), internship report (if non-thesis). *Entrance requirements:* For master's, GRE General Test (minimum score 1000), 2 letters of reference, minimum GPA of 3.0. Additional exam requirements/recommendations for international students: Required—TOEFL (minimum score 500 paper-based), IELTS (minimum score 5). *Faculty research:* Fungal cell walls, molecular biology, bioactive materials synthesis, atomic force microscopy-surface chemistry, nanoscience.

Columbia University, College of Physicians and Surgeons, Department of Biochemistry and Molecular Biophysics, New York, NY 10032. Offers biochemistry and molecular biophysics (M Phil, PhD); biophysics (PhD); MD/PhD. Only candidates for the PhD are admitted. *Degree requirements:* For doctorate, one foreign language, thesis/dissertation. *Entrance requirements:* For master's and doctorate, GRE General Test. Additional exam requirements/recommendations for international students: Required—TOEFL. *Expenses: Tuition:* Full-time $44,864; part-time $1704 per credit. *Required fees:* $2370 per semester. One-time fee: $105.

Cornell University, Graduate School, Graduate Fields of Agriculture and Life Sciences, Field of Biochemistry, Molecular and Cell Biology, Ithaca, NY 14853. Offers biochemistry (PhD); biophysics (PhD); cell biology (PhD); molecular biology (PhD). *Degree requirements:* For doctorate, comprehensive exam, thesis/dissertation, 2 semesters of teaching experience. *Entrance requirements:* For doctorate, GRE General Test, GRE Subject Test (biology, chemistry, physics, biochemistry, cell and molecular biology), 3 letters of recommendation. Additional exam requirements/recommendations for international students: Required—TOEFL (minimum score 600 paper-based; 77 iBT). Electronic applications accepted. *Faculty research:* Biophysics, structural biology.

Cornell University, Graduate School, Graduate Fields of Agriculture and Life Sciences, Field of Plant Biology, Ithaca, NY 14853. Offers cytology (MS, PhD); paleobotany (MS, PhD); plant biochemistry (MS, PhD); plant cell biology (MS, PhD); plant ecology (MS, PhD); plant molecular biology (MS, PhD); plant morphology, anatomy and biomechanics (MS, PhD); plant physiology (MS, PhD); systematic botany (MS, PhD). *Degree requirements:* For doctorate, comprehensive exam, thesis/dissertation. *Entrance requirements:* For doctorate, GRE General Test, GRE Subject Test in biology (recommended), 3 letters of recommendation. Additional exam requirements/recommendations for international students: Required—TOEFL (minimum score 610 paper-based; 77 iBT). Electronic applications accepted. *Faculty research:* Plant cell biology/cytology; plant molecular biology; plant morphology/anatomy/biomechanics; plant physiology, systematic botany, paleobotany; plant ecology, ethnobotany, plant biochemistry, photosynthesis.

Cornell University, Graduate School, Graduate Fields of Arts and Sciences, Field of Chemistry and Chemical Biology, Ithaca, NY 14853. Offers analytical chemistry (PhD); bio-organic chemistry (PhD); biophysical chemistry (PhD); chemical biology (PhD); chemical physics (PhD); inorganic chemistry (PhD); materials chemistry (PhD); organic chemistry (PhD); organometallic chemistry (PhD); physical chemistry (PhD); polymer chemistry (PhD); theoretical chemistry (PhD). *Degree requirements:* For doctorate, comprehensive exam, thesis/dissertation. *Entrance requirements:* For doctorate, GRE General Test, GRE Subject Test (chemistry), 3 letters of recommendation. Additional exam requirements/recommendations for international students: Required—TOEFL (minimum score 600 paper-based; 77 iBT). Electronic applications accepted. *Faculty research:* Analytical, organic, inorganic, physical, materials, chemical biology.

Dalhousie University, Faculty of Medicine, Department of Biochemistry and Molecular Biology, Halifax, NS B3H 4R2, Canada. Offers M Sc, PhD. *Degree requirements:* For master's, thesis, demonstrating/teaching experience, oral defense, seminar; for doctorate, comprehensive exam, thesis/dissertation, demonstrating/teaching experience, oral defense, seminar, 2 short grant proposals in year 3. *Entrance requirements:* For master's and doctorate, GRE. Additional exam requirements/recommendations for international students: Required—1 of 5 approved tests: TOEFL, IELTS, CANTEST, CAEL, Michigan English Language Assessment Battery. Electronic applications accepted. *Expenses:* Contact institution. *Faculty research:* Gene expression and cell regulation; lipids, lipoproteins, and membranes; molecular evolution; proteins, molecular cell biology and molecular genetics; structure, function, and metabolism of biomolecules.

Dartmouth College, Graduate Program in Molecular and Cellular Biology, Department of Biochemistry, Hanover, NH 03755. Offers PhD, MBA/PhD, MD/PhD. *Faculty:* 15 full-time (2 women). *Students:* 38 full-time (15 women); includes 8 minority (2 Asian, non-Hispanic/Latino; 4 Hispanic/Latino; 2 Two or more races, non-Hispanic/Latino), 7 international. Average age 27. In 2017, 6 doctorates awarded. *Entrance requirements:* For doctorate, GRE General Test, letters of recommendation, minimum GPA of 3.0. *Application deadline:* For fall admission, 12/8 for domestic students. Application fee: $75. Electronic applications accepted. *Financial support:* Fellowships and health care benefits available. *Unit head:* Dr. Charles Barlowe, Chair and Professor, 603-650-6156, E-mail: biochemistry@dartmouth.edu. *Application contact:* Janet Cheney, Program Coordinator, 603-650-1612, E-mail: mcb@dartmouth.edu.
Website: http://dms.dartmouth.edu/biochem/

Dartmouth College, School of Graduate and Advanced Studies, Department of Chemistry, Hanover, NH 03755. Offers biophysical chemistry (MS); chemistry (PhD). *Faculty:* 17 full-time (4 women), 1 (woman) part-time/adjunct. *Students:* 41 full-time (13 women); includes 8 minority (1 American Indian or Alaska Native, non-Hispanic/Latino; 3 Asian, non-Hispanic/Latino; 4 Two or more races, non-Hispanic/Latino), 12 international. Average age 26. 96 applicants, 23% accepted, 10 enrolled. In 2017, 3 master's, 5 doctorates awarded. *Entrance requirements:* For doctorate, GRE General Test, GRE Subject Test. Additional exam requirements/recommendations for international students: Required—TOEFL. *Application deadline:* For fall admission, 1/10 for domestic students. Application fee: $0. Electronic applications accepted. *Financial support:* Fellowships, research assistantships, teaching assistantships, institutionally sponsored loans, scholarships/grants, traineeships, tuition waivers (full), and unspecified assistantships available. Financial award application deadline: 4/1; financial award applicants required to submit CSS PROFILE or FAFSA. *Faculty research:* Organic and polymer synthesis, bioinorganic chemistry, magnetic resonance parameters. *Unit head:* Dr. Dean E. Wilcox, Chair, 603-646-2501. *Application contact:* Phyllis Ford, Administrative Assistant, 603-646-2501, E-mail: phyllis.p.ford@dartmouth.edu.
Website: http://www.dartmouth.edu/~chem/

Drexel University, College of Medicine, Biomedical Graduate Programs, Program in Biochemistry, Philadelphia, PA 19104-2875. Offers MS, PhD, MD/PhD. *Program availability:* Part-time. Terminal master's awarded for partial completion of doctoral program. *Degree requirements:* For master's, comprehensive exam, thesis; for doctorate, thesis/dissertation, qualifying exam. *Entrance requirements:* For master's, GRE General Test, minimum GPA of 2.75; for doctorate, GRE General Test, minimum GPA of 3.0. Additional exam requirements/recommendations for international students: Required—TOEFL. Electronic applications accepted.

Duke University, Graduate School, Department of Biochemistry, Durham, NC 27710. Offers crystallography of macromolecules (PhD); enzyme mechanisms (PhD); lipid biochemistry (PhD); membrane structure and function (PhD); molecular genetics (PhD); neurochemistry (PhD); nucleic acid structure and function (PhD); protein structure and function (PhD). *Degree requirements:* For doctorate, thesis/dissertation. *Entrance requirements:* For doctorate, GRE General Test, GRE Subject Test (recommended). Additional exam requirements/recommendations for international students: Required—TOEFL (minimum score 577 paper-based; 90 iBT) or IELTS (minimum score 7). Electronic applications accepted.

Eastern New Mexico University, Graduate School, College of Liberal Arts and Sciences, Department of Physical Sciences, Portales, NM 88130. Offers chemistry (MS), including analytical chemistry, biochemistry, organic chemistry, physical chemistry. *Program availability:* Part-time. *Degree requirements:* For master's, thesis optional, seminar, oral and written comprehensive exams. *Entrance requirements:* For master's, ACS placement examination, minimum GPA of 3.0; 2 letters of recommendation; personal statement of career goals; bachelor's degree with minimum of one year each of general, organic, and analytical chemistry. Additional exam requirements/recommendations for international students: Required—TOEFL (minimum score 550 paper-based; 79 iBT), IELTS (minimum score 6). *Application deadline:* For fall admission, 7/20 priority date for domestic students, 6/20 priority date for international students; for spring admission, 12/15 priority date for domestic students, 11/15 priority date for international students. Applications are processed on a rolling basis. Application fee: $10. Electronic applications accepted. *Financial support:* Application deadline: 3/1; applicants required to submit FAFSA. *Faculty research:* Synfuel, electrochemistry, protein chemistry. *Unit head:* Dr. Juacho Yan, Graduate Coordinator, 575-562-2494, Fax: 575-562-2192, E-mail: juacho.yan@enmu.edu. *Application contact:* Sharon Potter, Department Secretary, Biology and Physical Sciences, 575-562-2174, Fax: 575-562-2192, E-mail: sharon.potter@enmu.edu.
Website: https://www.enmu.edu/academics/colleges-departments/college-liberal-arts-sciences/department-of-physical-sciences

East Tennessee State University, Quillen College of Medicine, Department of Biomedical Sciences, Johnson City, TN 37614. Offers anatomy (PhD); biochemistry (PhD); microbiology (PhD); pharmaceutical sciences (PhD); pharmacology (PhD); physiology (PhD); quantitative biosciences (PhD). In 2017, 5 doctorates awarded. *Degree requirements:* For doctorate, comprehensive exam, thesis/dissertation, comprehensive qualifying exam; one-year residency. *Entrance requirements:* For doctorate, GRE General Test, GRE Subject Test, 3 letters of recommendation, minimum of 60 credit hours beyond the baccalaureate degree. Additional exam requirements/recommendations for international students: Required—TOEFL (minimum score 550 paper-based; 79 iBT). *Application deadline:* For fall admission, 6/1 priority date for domestic students, 4/29 for international students; for spring admission, 11/1 for domestic students, 9/29 for international students; for summer admission, 3/15 for domestic students, 2/1 for international students. Applications are processed on a rolling basis. Application fee: $55 ($65 for international students). Electronic applications accepted. *Expenses:* Contact institution. *Financial support:* Research assistantships with full tuition reimbursements, career-related internships or fieldwork, institutionally sponsored loans, scholarships/grants, and unspecified assistantships available. Financial award application deadline: 7/1; financial award applicants required to submit FAFSA. *Faculty research:* Cardiovascular, infectious disease, neurosciences, cancer, immunology. *Unit head:* Theo Hagg, Chair, 423-439-6294, Fax: 423-439-2140, E-mail: haggt1@etsu.edu. *Application contact:* Theo Hagg, Chair, 423-439-6294, Fax: 423-439-2140, E-mail: haggt1@etsu.edu.
Website: http://www.etsu.edu/com/dbms/

Emory University, Laney Graduate School, Division of Biological and Biomedical Sciences, Program in Biochemistry, Cell and Developmental Biology, Atlanta, GA 30322. Offers PhD. *Degree requirements:* For doctorate, comprehensive exam, thesis/dissertation. *Entrance requirements:* For doctorate, GRE General Test, minimum GPA of 3.0 in science course work (recommended). Additional exam requirements/recommendations for international students: Required—TOEFL. Electronic applications accepted. *Faculty research:* Signal transduction, molecular biology, enzymes and cofactors, receptor and ion channel function, membrane biology.

Florida Institute of Technology, College of Science, Program in Biochemistry, Melbourne, FL 32901-6975. Offers MS. *Program availability:* Part-time. *Students:* Average age 28. 32 applicants, 63% accepted, 2 enrolled. In 2017, 3 master's awarded. *Degree requirements:* For master's, comprehensive exam (for some programs), thesis optional, research proposal, oral examination in defense of the thesis, or final program examination and research project, 30 credit hours. *Entrance requirements:* For master's, GRE General Test (recommended), undergraduate degree in biochemistry, chemistry, or related area. Additional exam requirements/recommendations for international students: Required—TOEFL (minimum score 550 paper-based; 79 iBT). *Application deadline:* For fall admission, 4/4 for international students; for spring admission, 9/30 for international students. Applications are processed on a rolling basis. Electronic applications accepted. *Expenses: Tuition:* Part-time $1241 per credit hour. Part-time tuition and fees vary according to campus/location. *Financial support:* Applicants required to submit FAFSA. *Faculty research:* Energy storage applications, marine and organic chemistry, stereochemistry, medicinal chemistry, environmental chemistry. *Unit head:* Dr. Michael Freund, Department Head, 321-674-7153, E-mail: msfreund@fit.edu. *Application contact:* Cheryl A. Brown, Associate Director of Graduate Admissions, 321-674-7581, Fax: 321-723-9468, E-mail: cbrown@fit.edu.
Website: http://www.fit.edu/programs/

Florida State University, The Graduate School, College of Arts and Sciences, Department of Chemistry and Biochemistry, Tallahassee, FL 32306-4390. Offers

analytical chemistry (MS, PhD); biochemistry (MS, PhD); inorganic chemistry (MS, PhD); materials chemistry (PhD); organic chemistry (MS, PhD); physical chemistry (MS, PhD). *Faculty:* 27 full-time (4 women). *Students:* 160 full-time (52 women), 4 part-time (1 woman); includes 79 minority (9 Black or African American, non-Hispanic/Latino; 46 Asian, non-Hispanic/Latino; 8 Hispanic/Latino; 2 Native Hawaiian or other Pacific Islander, non-Hispanic/Latino; 14 Two or more races, non-Hispanic/Latino). Average age 25. 172 applicants, 52% accepted, 38 enrolled. In 2017, 32 master's, 16 doctorates awarded. Terminal master's awarded for partial completion of doctoral program. *Degree requirements:* For master's, thesis (for some programs); for doctorate, thesis/dissertation. *Entrance requirements:* For master's and doctorate, GRE General Test (minimum scores: 150 verbal, 151 quantitative), minimum upper-division GPA of 3.1 in undergraduate course work. Additional exam requirements/recommendations for international students: Required—TOEFL (minimum score 80 iBT). *Application deadline:* For fall admission, 12/15 priority date for domestic and international students. Application fee: $30. Electronic applications accepted. *Financial support:* In 2017–18, 157 students received support, including 4 fellowships with full tuition reimbursements available (averaging $23,800 per year), 60 research assistantships with full tuition reimbursements available (averaging $23,800 per year), 94 teaching assistantships with full tuition reimbursements available (averaging $23,800 per year). Financial award application deadline: 12/15; financial award applicants required to submit FAFSA. *Faculty research:* Bioanalytical chemistry, separations, microfluidics, petroleomics; materials chemistry, solid state materials, magnets, polymers, catalysts, advanced spectroscopic methods, NMR and EPR, ultrafast, Raman, and mass spectrometry; organic synthesis, natural products, photochemistry, and supramolecular chemistry; biochemistry, structural biology, metabolomics, and anticancer drugs; nanochemistry, applications in energy, sustainability, biology, and technology development; radiochemistry. *Total annual research expenditures:* $4.9 million. *Unit head:* Dr. Geoffrey Strouse, Chairman, 850-644-1244, Fax: 850-644-8281, E-mail: gradinfo@chem.fsu.edu. *Application contact:* Dr. Wei Yang, Associate Chair for Graduate Studies, 850-645-6884, Fax: 850-644-8281, E-mail: gradinfo@chem.fsu.edu.
Website: http://www.chem.fsu.edu/

Florida State University, The Graduate School, College of Arts and Sciences, Department of Scientific Computing, Tallahassee, FL 32306-4120. Offers computational science (MS, PhD), including atmospheric science (PhD), biochemistry (PhD), biological science (PhD), computational science (PhD), geological science (PhD), materials science (PhD), physics (PhD). *Program availability:* Part-time. *Faculty:* 12 full-time (2 women). *Students:* 37 full-time (6 women), 3 part-time (1 woman); includes 14 minority (9 Asian, non-Hispanic/Latino; 1 Hispanic/Latino; 4 Two or more races, non-Hispanic/Latino). Average age 27. 43 applicants, 23% accepted, 9 enrolled. In 2017, 5 master's, 5 doctorates awarded. Terminal master's awarded for partial completion of doctoral program. *Degree requirements:* For master's, thesis (for some programs); for doctorate, comprehensive exam, thesis/dissertation. *Entrance requirements:* For master's and doctorate, GRE General Test, knowledge of at least one object-oriented computing language, 3 letters of recommendation, resume, statement of purpose. Additional exam requirements/recommendations for international students: Required—TOEFL (minimum score 550 paper-based; 80 iBT). *Application deadline:* For fall admission, 1/15 for domestic and international students. Applications are processed on a rolling basis. Application fee: $30. Electronic applications accepted. *Financial support:* In 2017–18, 32 students received support, including 10 research assistantships with full tuition reimbursements available (averaging $26,670 per year), 23 teaching assistantships with full tuition reimbursements available (averaging $23,000 per year); scholarships/grants, health care benefits, tuition waivers (full), and unspecified assistantships also available. Financial award application deadline: 1/15. *Faculty research:* Morphometrics, mathematical and systems biology, mining proteomic and metabolic data, computational materials research, computational fluid dynamics, astrophysics, deep learning, computational neuroscience. *Total annual research expenditures:* $500,000. *Unit head:* Dr. Gordon Erlebacher, Chair, 850-644-7024, E-mail: gerlebacher@fsu.edu. *Application contact:* David Amwake, Administrative Specialist, 850-644-2273, Fax: 850-644-0098, E-mail: damwake@fsu.edu.
Website: http://www.sc.fsu.edu

George Mason University, College of Science, Department of Chemistry and Biochemistry, Fairfax, VA 22030. Offers chemistry (MS); chemistry and biochemistry (PhD). *Faculty:* 15 full-time (4 women), 11 part-time/adjunct (4 women). *Students:* 20 full-time (11 women), 29 part-time (18 women); includes 17 minority (6 Black or African American, non-Hispanic/Latino; 7 Asian, non-Hispanic/Latino; 2 Hispanic/Latino; 2 Two or more races, non-Hispanic/Latino), 5 international. Average age 31. 39 applicants, 72% accepted, 13 enrolled. In 2017, 8 master's, 5 doctorates awarded. *Degree requirements:* For master's, comprehensive exam (for some programs), thesis (for some programs); for doctorate, comprehensive exam, thesis/dissertation, exit seminar. *Entrance requirements:* For doctorate, GRE, BS or MS in chemistry or related discipline. Additional exam requirements/recommendations for international students: Required—TOEFL (minimum score 575 paper-based; 88 iBT), IELTS (minimum score 6.5), PTE (minimum score 59). Application fee: $75 ($80 for international students). Electronic applications accepted. *Expenses:* Tuition, state resident: full-time $11,228; part-time $459.50 per credit. Tuition, nonresident: full-time $30,932; part-time $1280.50 per credit. *Required fees:* $3252; $135.50 per credit. Part-time tuition and fees vary according to course load and program. *Financial support:* In 2017–18, 21 students received support, including 3 research assistantships with tuition reimbursements available (averaging $19,333 per year), 18 teaching assistantships with tuition reimbursements available (averaging $16,077 per year); career-related internships or fieldwork, Federal Work-Study, scholarships/grants, unspecified assistantships, and health care benefits (for full-time research or teaching assistantship recipients) also available. Support available to part-time students. Financial award application deadline: 3/1; financial award applicants required to submit FAFSA. *Faculty research:* Nanomaterials; metabolomics; aquatic and environmental chemistry, biodegradation; antimicrobial, peptides; synthetic and medicinal chemistry, drug discovery. *Total annual research expenditures:* $827,939. *Unit head:* Gerald Weatherspoon, Chair, 703-993-1456, Fax: 703-993-1055, E-mail: grobert1@gmu.edu. *Application contact:* Robert Honeychuck, Graduate Coordinator and Associate Professor, 703-993-1076, Fax: 703-993-1055, E-mail: rhoneych@gmu.edu.
Website: http://chemistry.gmu.edu/

Georgetown University, Graduate School of Arts and Sciences, Department of Biochemistry and Molecular and Cellular Biology, Washington, DC 20057. Offers MS, PhD. *Degree requirements:* For doctorate, comprehensive exam, thesis/dissertation. *Entrance requirements:* For doctorate, GRE General Test. Additional exam requirements/recommendations for international students: Required—TOEFL.

Georgetown University, Graduate School of Arts and Sciences, Department of Chemistry, Washington, DC 20057. Offers analytical chemistry (PhD); biochemistry (PhD); computational chemistry (PhD); inorganic chemistry (PhD); materials chemistry (PhD); organic chemistry (PhD); theoretical chemistry (PhD). Terminal master's awarded for partial completion of doctoral program. *Degree requirements:* For doctorate, comprehensive exam, thesis/dissertation. *Entrance requirements:* For doctorate, GRE General Test. Additional exam requirements/recommendations for international students: Required—TOEFL.

The George Washington University, Columbian College of Arts and Sciences, Institute for Biomedical Sciences, Program in Biochemistry and Systems Biology, Washington, DC 20037. Offers PhD. *Students:* 1 (woman) full-time, 7 part-time (2 women); includes 3 minority (2 Asian, non-Hispanic/Latino; 1 Two or more races, non-Hispanic/Latino), 2 international. Average age 32. 1 applicant. In 2017, 2 doctorates awarded. Terminal master's awarded for partial completion of doctoral program. *Degree requirements:* For doctorate, thesis/dissertation, general exam. *Entrance requirements:* For doctorate, GRE General Test, interview, minimum GPA of 3.0. Additional exam requirements/recommendations for international students: Required—TOEFL (minimum score 600 paper-based). *Application deadline:* For fall admission, 12/15 priority date for domestic and international students; for spring admission, 10/1 priority date for domestic and international students. Applications are processed on a rolling basis. Application fee: $75. Electronic applications accepted. *Expenses: Tuition:* Full-time $28,800; part-time $1655 per credit hour. *Required fees:* $45; $2.75 per credit hour. *Financial support:* In 2017–18, 3 students received support. Fellowships, Federal Work-Study, institutionally sponsored loans, and tuition waivers available. Financial award application deadline: 2/1. *Unit head:* Dr. Eric Hoffman, Director, 202-476-6029, E-mail: ehoffman@cnmcresearch.org. *Application contact:* Information Contact, 202-994-7120, Fax: 202-994-6100, E-mail: genetics@gwu.edu.
Website: http://smhs.gwu.edu/

Georgia State University, College of Arts and Sciences, Department of Biology, Program in Molecular Genetics and Biochemistry, Atlanta, GA 30302-3083. Offers bioinformatics (MS); molecular genetics and biochemistry (MS, PhD). *Program availability:* Part-time. Terminal master's awarded for partial completion of doctoral program. *Entrance requirements:* For master's and doctorate, GRE. *Application deadline:* Applications are processed on a rolling basis. Application fee: $50. Electronic applications accepted. *Expenses:* Tuition, state resident: full-time $7020. Tuition, nonresident: full-time $22,518. *Required fees:* $2128. Tuition and fees vary according to degree level and program. *Financial support:* Fellowships and research assistantships available. Financial award application deadline: 12/3. *Faculty research:* Gene regulation, microbial pathogenesis, molecular transport, protein modeling, viral pathogenesis. *Unit head:* Dr. Charles Derby, Director of Graduate Studies, 404-413-5393, Fax: 404-413-5446, E-mail: cderby@gsu.edu.
Website: http://biology.gsu.edu/

Georgia State University, College of Arts and Sciences, Department of Chemistry, Atlanta, GA 30302-3083. Offers analytical chemistry (MS, PhD); biochemistry (MS, PhD); bioinformatics (MS, PhD); biophysical chemistry (PhD); computational chemistry (MS, PhD); geochemistry (PhD); organic/medicinal chemistry (MS, PhD); physical chemistry (MS). PhD in geochemistry offered jointly with Department of Geosciences. *Program availability:* Part-time. *Faculty:* 41 full-time (17 women). *Students:* 155 full-time (57 women), 11 part-time (4 women); includes 40 minority (18 Black or African American, non-Hispanic/Latino; 10 Asian, non-Hispanic/Latino; 5 Hispanic/Latino; 7 Two or more races, non-Hispanic/Latino), 81 international. Average age 28. 84 applicants, 46% accepted, 26 enrolled. In 2017, 39 master's, 12 doctorates awarded. Terminal master's awarded for partial completion of doctoral program. *Degree requirements:* For master's, one foreign language, comprehensive exam (for some programs), thesis (for some programs); for doctorate, one foreign language, comprehensive exam, thesis/dissertation. *Entrance requirements:* For master's and doctorate, GRE. *Application deadline:* For fall admission, 7/1 priority date for domestic and international students; for winter admission, 11/15 priority date for domestic and international students; for spring admission, 4/15 priority date for domestic and international students. Applications are processed on a rolling basis. Application fee: $50. Electronic applications accepted. *Expenses:* Tuition, state resident: full-time $7020. Tuition, nonresident: full-time $22,518. *Required fees:* $2128. Tuition and fees vary according to degree level and program. *Financial support:* Fellowships with full tuition reimbursements, research assistantships with full tuition reimbursements, and teaching assistantships with full tuition reimbursements available. Financial award applicants required to submit FAFSA. *Faculty research:* Analytical chemistry, biological/biochemistry, biophysical/computational chemistry, chemical education, organic/medicinal chemistry. *Unit head:* Dr. Peng George Wang, Department Chair, 404-413-3591, Fax: 404-413-5505, E-mail: pwang11@gsu.edu.
Website: http://chemistry.gsu.edu/

The Graduate Center, City University of New York, Graduate Studies, Program in Biochemistry, New York, NY 10016-4039. Offers PhD. *Faculty:* 22 full-time (6 women). *Students:* 96 full-time (40 women); includes 18 minority (3 Black or African American, non-Hispanic/Latino; 11 Asian, non-Hispanic/Latino; 4 Hispanic/Latino), 44 international. Average age 32. 44 applicants, 70% accepted, 23 enrolled. In 2017, 7 doctorates awarded. *Degree requirements:* For doctorate, thesis/dissertation, field experience. *Entrance requirements:* For doctorate, GRE General Test. Additional exam requirements/recommendations for international students: Required—TOEFL. *Application deadline:* For fall admission, 1/1 for domestic students; for spring admission, 11/1 for domestic students. Application fee: $125. Electronic applications accepted. *Financial support:* In 2017–18, 56 students received support, including 61 fellowships, 2 teaching assistantships; research assistantships, career-related internships or fieldwork, Federal Work-Study, institutionally sponsored loans, and tuition waivers (full and partial) also available. Financial award application deadline: 4/15; financial award applicants required to submit FAFSA. *Unit head:* Richard S. Magliozzo, Executive Officer, 212-817-8086, Fax: 212-817-1503, E-mail: rmagliozzo@gc.cuny.edu. *Application contact:* Les Gribben, Director of Admissions, 212-817-7470, Fax: 212-817-1624, E-mail: lgribben@gc.cuny.edu.

Harvard University, Graduate School of Arts and Sciences, Department of Chemistry and Chemical Biology, Cambridge, MA 02138. Offers biochemical chemistry (PhD); inorganic chemistry (PhD); organic chemistry (PhD); physical chemistry (PhD). *Degree requirements:* For doctorate, thesis/dissertation, cumulative exams. *Entrance requirements:* For doctorate, GRE General Test, GRE Subject Test. Additional exam requirements/recommendations for international students: Required—TOEFL.

Harvard University, Graduate School of Arts and Sciences, Division of Medical Sciences, Boston, MA 02115. Offers biological chemistry and molecular pharmacology (PhD); cell biology (PhD); genetics (PhD); microbiology and molecular genetics (PhD); pathology (PhD), including experimental pathology. *Degree requirements:* For doctorate, thesis/dissertation. *Entrance requirements:* For doctorate, GRE General Test, GRE Subject Test. Additional exam requirements/recommendations for international students: Required—TOEFL.

Howard University, College of Medicine, Department of Biochemistry and Molecular Biology, Washington, DC 20059-0002. Offers biochemistry and molecular biology (PhD); biotechnology (MS); MD/PhD. *Program availability:* Part-time. *Degree requirements:* For master's, externship; for doctorate, comprehensive exam, thesis/dissertation. *Entrance requirements:* For master's and doctorate, GRE General Test, minimum GPA of 3.0. *Faculty research:* Cellular and molecular biology of olfaction, gene regulation and expression, enzymology, NMR spectroscopy of molecular structure, hormone regulation/metabolism.

Howard University, Graduate School, Department of Chemistry, Washington, DC 20059-0002. Offers analytical chemistry (MS, PhD); atmospheric (MS, PhD);

biochemistry (MS, PhD); environmental (MS, PhD); inorganic chemistry (MS, PhD); organic chemistry (MS, PhD); physical chemistry (MS, PhD). Terminal master's awarded for partial completion of doctoral program. *Degree requirements:* For master's, comprehensive exam, thesis, teaching experience; for doctorate, comprehensive exam, thesis/dissertation, teaching experience. *Entrance requirements:* For master's, GRE General Test, minimum GPA of 2.7; for doctorate, GRE General Test, minimum GPA of 3.0. Additional exam requirements/recommendations for international students: Required—TOEFL. Electronic applications accepted. *Faculty research:* Synthetic organics, materials, natural products, mass spectrometry.

Hunter College of the City University of New York, Graduate School, School of Arts and Sciences, Department of Chemistry, Program in Biochemistry, New York, NY 10065-5085. Offers MA, PhD. *Program availability:* Part-time. *Degree requirements:* For master's, comprehensive exam or thesis. *Entrance requirements:* For master's, GRE General Test, 1 year of course work in chemistry, quantitative analysis, organic chemistry, physical chemistry, biology, biochemistry lecture and laboratory. Additional exam requirements/recommendations for international students: Required—TOEFL. *Faculty research:* Protein/nucleic acid interactions, physical properties of iron-sulfur proteins, neurotransmitter receptors and ion channels, Drosophila melanogaster, requirements of DNA synthesis, oncogenes.

Illinois Institute of Technology, Graduate College, College of Science, Department of Biology, Chicago, IL 60616. Offers applied life sciences (MS); biochemistry (MS); biology (MS, PhD); cell and molecular biology (MS); microbiology (MS); molecular biochemistry and biophysics (MS, PhD). *Program availability:* Part-time, evening/weekend, online learning. Terminal master's awarded for partial completion of doctoral program. *Degree requirements:* For master's, comprehensive exam, thesis (for some programs); for doctorate, comprehensive exam, thesis/dissertation. *Entrance requirements:* For master's, GRE General Test (minimum score 300 Quantitative and Verbal, 2.5 Analytical Writing), minimum undergraduate GPA of 3.0; for doctorate, GRE General Test (minimum score 310 Quantitative and Verbal, 3.0 Analytical Writing); GRE Subject Test (strongly recommended), minimum undergraduate GPA of 3.0. Additional exam requirements/recommendations for international students: Required—TOEFL (minimum score 550 paper-based; 80 iBT). Electronic applications accepted. *Faculty research:* Macromolecular crystallography, insect immunity and basic cell biology, improvement of bacterial strains for enhanced biodesulfurization of petroleum, programmed cell death in cancer cells.

Illinois State University, Graduate School, College of Arts and Sciences, School of Biological Sciences, Normal, IL 61790. Offers animal behavior (MS); bacteriology (MS); biochemistry (MS); biological sciences (MS); biology (PhD); biophysics (MS); biotechnology (MS); botany (MS, PhD); cell biology (MS); conservation biology (MS); developmental biology (MS); ecology (MS, PhD); entomology (MS); evolutionary biology (MS); genetics (MS, PhD); immunology (MS); microbiology (MS, PhD); molecular biology (MS); molecular genetics (MS); neurobiology (MS); neuroscience (MS); parasitology (MS); physiology (MS, PhD); plant biology (MS); plant molecular biology (MS); plant sciences (MS); structural biology (MS); zoology (MS, PhD). *Program availability:* Part-time. *Degree requirements:* For master's, thesis or alternative; for doctorate, variable foreign language requirement, thesis/dissertation, 2 terms of residency. *Entrance requirements:* For master's, GRE General Test, minimum GPA of 2.6 in last 60 hours of course work; for doctorate, GRE General Test. *Faculty research:* Redoc balance and drug development in schistosoma mansoni, control of the growth of listeria monocytogenes at low temperature, regulation of cell expansion and microtubule function by SPRI, CRUI: physiology and fitness consequences of different life history phenotypes.

Indiana University Bloomington, University Graduate School, College of Arts and Sciences, Biochemistry Graduate Program, Bloomington, IN 47405. Offers PhD. *Degree requirements:* For doctorate, comprehensive exam, thesis/dissertation. *Entrance requirements:* For doctorate, GRE. Additional exam requirements/recommendations for international students: Required—TOEFL (minimum score 550 paper-based; 79 iBT), Test of English Proficiency for International Associate Instructor Candidates (TEPAIC). *Faculty research:* Chromosome replication and repair, receptor medicated signal transduction, microbial biochemistry, viral assembly, structural biology, chemical biology, cellular and medicinal biochemistry, plant biochemistry.

Indiana University Bloomington, University Graduate School, College of Arts and Sciences, Department of Chemistry, Bloomington, IN 47405. Offers analytical chemistry (PhD); chemical biology (PhD); chemistry (MAT); inorganic chemistry (PhD); materials chemistry (PhD); organic chemistry (PhD); physical chemistry (PhD); MSES/MS. Terminal master's awarded for partial completion of doctoral program. *Degree requirements:* For master's, thesis; for doctorate, thesis/dissertation. *Entrance requirements:* For master's and doctorate, GRE General Test, GRE Subject Test. Additional exam requirements/recommendations for international students: Required—TOEFL. Electronic applications accepted. *Faculty research:* Synthesis of complex natural products, organic reaction mechanisms, organic electrochemistry, transitive-metal chemistry, solid-state and surface chemistry.

Indiana University–Purdue University Indianapolis, Indiana University School of Medicine, Department of Biochemistry and Molecular Biology, Indianapolis, IN 46202. Offers MS, PhD, MD/MS, MD/PhD. Terminal master's awarded for partial completion of doctoral program. *Degree requirements:* For master's, thesis; for doctorate, thesis/dissertation. *Entrance requirements:* For master's and doctorate, GRE General Test, GRE Subject Test (recommended), previous course work in organic chemistry. Additional exam requirements/recommendations for international students: Required—TOEFL. Electronic applications accepted. *Faculty research:* Metabolic regulation, enzymology, peptide and protein chemistry, cell biology, signal transduction.

Indiana University–Purdue University Indianapolis, School of Science, Department of Chemistry and Chemical Biology, Indianapolis, IN 46202. Offers MS, PhD, MD/PhD. MD/PhD offered jointly with Indiana University School of Medicine and Purdue University. *Program availability:* Part-time, evening/weekend. Terminal master's awarded for partial completion of doctoral program. *Degree requirements:* For master's, thesis (for some programs); for doctorate, comprehensive exam, thesis/dissertation. *Entrance requirements:* For master's and doctorate, minimum GPA of 3.0. Additional exam requirements/recommendations for international students: Required—TOEFL (minimum score 106 iBT). Electronic applications accepted. *Faculty research:* Analytical, biological, inorganic, organic, and physical chemistry.

Irell & Manella Graduate School of Biological Sciences, Graduate Program, Duarte, CA 91010. Offers brain metastatic cancer (PhD); cancer and stem cell metabolism (PhD); cancer biology (PhD); cancer biology and developmental therapeutics (PhD); cell biology (PhD); chemical biology (PhD); chromosomal break repair (PhD); diabetes and pancreatic progenitor cell biology (PhD); DNA repair and cancer biology (PhD); germline epigenetic remodeling and endocrine disruptors (PhD); hematology and hematopoietic cell transplantation (PhD); hematology and immunology (PhD); inflammation and cancer (PhD); micrornas and gene regulation in cardiovascular disease (PhD); mixed chimrism for reversal of autoimmunity (PhD); molecular and cellular biology (PhD); molecular biology and genetics (PhD); nanoparticle mediated twist1 silencing in metastatic cancer (PhD); neuro-oncology and stem cell biology (PhD); neuroscience (PhD); RNA directed therapies for HIV-1 (PhD); small RNA-induced transcriptional gene activation (PhD); stem cell regulation by the microenvironment (PhD); translational oncology and pharmaceutical sciences (PhD); tumor biology (PhD). *Degree requirements:* For doctorate, comprehensive exam, thesis/dissertation, qualifying exams, two advanced courses. *Entrance requirements:* For doctorate, GRE General Test; GRE Subject Test (recommended), 2 years of course work in chemistry (general and organic); 1 year of course work each in biochemistry, general biology, and general physics; 2 semesters of course work in mathematics; significant research laboratory experience. Additional exam requirements/recommendations for international students: Required—TOEFL. Electronic applications accepted. *Faculty research:* Cancer biology, diabetes, stem cell biology, neuroscience, immunology.

See Display on page 65 and Close-Up on page 109.

Johns Hopkins University, Bloomberg School of Public Health, Department of Biochemistry and Molecular Biology, Baltimore, MD 21205. Offers MHS, Sc M, PhD. *Program availability:* Part-time. *Students:* Average age 25. 186 applicants, 53% accepted, 59 enrolled. *Degree requirements:* For master's, thesis; for doctorate, comprehensive exam, thesis/dissertation, oral and written exams. *Entrance requirements:* For master's, MCAT or GRE, 3 letters of recommendation, curriculum vitae; for doctorate, GRE General Test, 3 letters of recommendation, curriculum vitae. *Application deadline:* For fall admission, 12/1 for domestic students. Application fee: $135. Electronic applications accepted. *Financial support:* Fellowships, research assistantships, teaching assistantships, Federal Work-Study, institutionally sponsored loans, scholarships/grants, health care benefits, and stipends available. *Faculty research:* DNA replication, repair, structure, carcinogenesis, protein structure, enzyme catalysts, reproductive biology. *Unit head:* Dr. Michael Matunis, Interim Chair, 410-955-3671, Fax: 410-955-2926, E-mail: bmb@jhsph.edu. *Application contact:* Sharon Gaston, Senior Academic Program Administrator, 410-955-3672, Fax: 410-955-2926, E-mail: bmb@jhsph.edu.
Website: http://www.jhsph.edu/dept/bmb/

Johns Hopkins University, National Institutes of Health Sponsored Programs, Baltimore, MD 21218. Offers biology (PhD), including biochemistry, biophysics, cell biology, developmental biology, genetic biology, molecular biology; cell, molecular, and developmental biology and biophysics (PhD). *Degree requirements:* For doctorate, comprehensive exam, thesis/dissertation. *Entrance requirements:* For doctorate, GRE General Test. Additional exam requirements/recommendations for international students: Required—TOEFL (minimum score 600 paper-based), TWE. Electronic applications accepted. *Faculty research:* Protein and nucleic acid biochemistry and biophysical chemistry, molecular biology and development.

Johns Hopkins University, School of Medicine, Graduate Programs in Medicine, Department of Biological Chemistry, Baltimore, MD 21205. Offers PhD. *Degree requirements:* For doctorate, thesis/dissertation. *Entrance requirements:* For doctorate, GRE General Test. Additional exam requirements/recommendations for international students: Required—TOEFL. Electronic applications accepted. *Faculty research:* Cell adhesion, genetics, signal transduction and RNA metabolism, enzyme structure and function, gene expression.

Johns Hopkins University, School of Medicine, Graduate Programs in Medicine, Program in Biochemistry, Cellular and Molecular Biology, Baltimore, MD 21205. Offers PhD. *Degree requirements:* For doctorate, comprehensive exam, thesis/dissertation. *Entrance requirements:* For doctorate, GRE General Test. Additional exam requirements/recommendations for international students: Required—TOEFL. Electronic applications accepted. *Faculty research:* Developmental biology, genomics/proteomics, protein targeting, signal transduction, structural biology.

Kansas State University, Graduate School, College of Arts and Sciences, Department of Biochemistry and Molecular Biophysics, Manhattan, KS 66506. Offers MS, PhD. *Degree requirements:* For master's, thesis; for doctorate, thesis/dissertation, preliminary exam. *Entrance requirements:* For master's, GRE General Test, minimum GPA of 3.0 for junior and senior year; for doctorate, GRE General Test, minimum undergraduate GPA of 3.0 or an excellent postgraduate record. Additional exam requirements/recommendations for international students: Required—TOEFL (minimum score 550 paper-based; 79 iBT). Electronic applications accepted. *Faculty research:* Protein structure/function, insect biochemistry, computational biochemistry, molecular mechanisms in cancer, membrane and lipids biochemistry, infectious disease and cell division.

Kennesaw State University, College of Science and Mathematics, Program in Chemical Sciences, Kennesaw, GA 30144. Offers biochemistry (MS); chemistry (MS). *Degree requirements:* For master's, thesis. *Entrance requirements:* For master's, GRE. Additional exam requirements/recommendations for international students: Required—TOEFL (minimum score 550 paper-based; 80 iBT), IELTS (minimum score 6.5). *Application deadline:* For fall admission, 4/1 for domestic and international students. Application fee: $60. Electronic applications accepted. *Financial support:* Teaching assistantships with full tuition reimbursements and unspecified assistantships available. Financial award application deadline: 4/1; financial award applicants required to submit FAFSA. *Unit head:* Dr. Chris Dockery, Assistant Department Chair, 470-578-2047, E-mail: mscb@kennesaw.edu. *Application contact:* Admissions Counselor, 470-578-4377, Fax: 470-578-9172, E-mail: ksugrad@kennesaw.edu.
Website: http://csm.kennesaw.edu/chemistry-biochemistry/programs/mscb.php

Laurentian University, School of Graduate Studies and Research, Programme in Chemistry and Biochemistry, Sudbury, ON P3E 2C6, Canada. Offers analytical chemistry (M Sc); biochemistry (M Sc); environmental chemistry (M Sc); organic chemistry (M Sc); physical/theoretical chemistry (M Sc). *Program availability:* Part-time. *Degree requirements:* For master's, thesis or alternative. *Entrance requirements:* For master's, honors degree with minimum second class. *Faculty research:* Cell cycle checkpoints, kinetic modeling, toxicology to metal stress, quantum chemistry, biogeochemistry metal speciation.

Lehigh University, College of Arts and Sciences, Department of Biological Sciences, Bethlehem, PA 18015. Offers biochemistry (PhD); cell and molecular biology (PhD); integrative biology (PhD); molecular biology (MS). *Program availability:* 100% online. *Faculty:* 18 full-time (8 women). *Students:* 38 full-time (20 women), 21 part-time (15 women); includes 12 minority (2 Black or African American, non-Hispanic/Latino; 1 American Indian or Alaska Native, non-Hispanic/Latino; 1 Asian, non-Hispanic/Latino; 6 Hispanic/Latino; 2 Two or more races, non-Hispanic/Latino), 10 international. Average age 28. 33 applicants, 42% accepted, 4 enrolled. In 2017, 8 master's, 4 doctorates awarded. Terminal master's awarded for partial completion of doctoral program. *Degree requirements:* For master's, thesis optional; for doctorate, comprehensive exam, thesis/dissertation. *Entrance requirements:* For doctorate, GRE General Test. Additional exam requirements/recommendations for international students: Required—TOEFL (minimum score 85 iBT). *Application deadline:* For fall admission, 7/15 for domestic and international students; for spring admission, 12/1 for domestic and international students; for summer admission, 4/30 for domestic and international students. Application fee: $75. Electronic applications accepted. *Expenses:* $1,460 per credit. *Financial support:* In 2017–18, 39 students received support, including 8 fellowships with full tuition reimbursements available (averaging $27,600 per year), 17 research

assistantships with full tuition reimbursements available (averaging $27,600 per year), 23 teaching assistantships with full tuition reimbursements available (averaging $27,600 per year); health care benefits and tuition waivers also available. Financial award application deadline: 12/1; financial award applicants required to submit CSS PROFILE or FAFSA. *Faculty research:* Gene expression, cytoskeleton and cell structure, cell cycle and growth regulation, neuroscience, animal behavior, microbiology. *Total annual research expenditures:* $1.8 million. *Unit head:* Dr. Linda Lowe-Krentz, Chairperson, 610-758-5084, Fax: 610-758-4004, E-mail: lljO@lehigh.edu. *Application contact:* Dr. Amber Rice, Graduate Coordinator, 610-758-5509, Fax: 610-758-4004, E-mail: amr511@lehigh.edu.
Website: http://www.lehigh.edu/~inbios/

Loma Linda University, School of Medicine, Programs in Biochemistry and Microbiology, Loma Linda, CA 92350. Offers biochemistry (MS, PhD); microbiology (PhD). *Program availability:* Part-time. *Degree requirements:* For master's, thesis or alternative; for doctorate, thesis/dissertation. *Entrance requirements:* For master's and doctorate, GRE General Test. Additional exam requirements/recommendations for international students: Required—TOEFL (minimum score 550 paper-based). *Faculty research:* Physical chemistry of macromolecules, biochemistry of endocrine system, biochemical mechanism of bone volume regulation.

Louisiana State University and Agricultural & Mechanical College, Graduate School, College of Science, Department of Biological Sciences, Baton Rouge, LA 70803. Offers biochemistry (MS, PhD); biological science (MS, PhD); science (MNS). *Faculty:* 57 full-time (12 women). *Students:* 123 full-time (54 women), 3 part-time (1 woman); includes 20 minority (7 Black or African American, non-Hispanic/Latino; 4 Asian, non-Hispanic/Latino; 7 Hispanic/Latino; 2 Two or more races, non-Hispanic/Latino), 46 international. Average age 29. 70 applicants, 24% accepted, 17 enrolled. In 2017, 1 master's, 18 doctorates awarded. *Financial support:* In 2017–18, 10 fellowships (averaging $37,093 per year), 15 research assistantships (averaging $24,248 per year), 94 teaching assistantships (averaging $22,610 per year) were awarded. *Total annual research expenditures:* $8.6 million.

Louisiana State University Health Sciences Center at Shreveport, Department of Biochemistry and Molecular Biology, Shreveport, LA 71130-3932. Offers MS, PhD, MD/PhD. *Degree requirements:* For master's, thesis; for doctorate, thesis/dissertation. *Entrance requirements:* For master's and doctorate, GRE General Test. Additional exam requirements/recommendations for international students: Required—TOEFL (minimum score 100 iBT), IELTS (minimum score 7). Electronic applications accepted. *Expenses:* Contact institution. *Faculty research:* Yeast genetics, prostate cancer, cell biology, mTOR signaling, Parkinson's Disease, transcriptional mechanisms, chromatin, DNA repair and damage response, protein synthesis, neuroscience, diabetes, cell cycle regulation, tRNA synthetases, stress response, glucose transporters, transmigration and wound repair.

Loyola University Chicago, Graduate School, Integrated Program in Biomedical Sciences, Maywood, IL 60141. Offers biochemistry and molecular biology (MS, PhD); cell and molecular physiology (MS, PhD); infectious disease and immunology (MS); integrative cell biology (MS, PhD); microbiology and immunology (MS, PhD); molecular pharmacology and therapeutics (MS, PhD); neuroscience (MS, PhD). *Faculty:* 84 full-time (32 women). *Students:* 126 full-time (65 women), 1 (woman) part-time; includes 36 minority (5 Black or African American, non-Hispanic/Latino; 14 Asian, non-Hispanic/Latino; 14 Hispanic/Latino; 3 Two or more races, non-Hispanic/Latino), 13 international. Average age 26. 748 applicants, 34% accepted, 124 enrolled. In 2017, 41 master's, 18 doctorates awarded. *Degree requirements:* For master's, thesis; for doctorate, comprehensive exam, thesis/dissertation. *Entrance requirements:* For doctorate, GRE. Additional exam requirements/recommendations for international students: Required—TOEFL (minimum score 94 iBT), IELTS (minimum score 7.5). *Application deadline:* For fall admission, 2/7 for domestic students. Applications are processed on a rolling basis. Electronic applications accepted. *Expenses:* Contact institution. *Financial support:* In 2017–18, 20 students received support. Schmitt Fellowships and yearly tuition scholarships (averaging $25,032) available. Financial award application deadline: 6/15; financial award applicants required to submit FAFSA. *Unit head:* Dr. Leanne L. Cribbs, Associate Dean, Graduate Education, 708-327-2817, Fax: 708-216-8216, E-mail: lcribbs@luc.edu. *Application contact:* Margarita Quesada, Graduate Program Secretary, 708-216-3532, Fax: 708-216-8216, E-mail: mquesad@luc.edu.
Website: http://ssom.luc.edu/graduate_school/degree-programs/ipbsphd/

Massachusetts Institute of Technology, School of Science, Department of Biology, Cambridge, MA 02139. Offers biochemistry (PhD); biological oceanography (PhD); biology (PhD); biophysical chemistry and molecular structure (PhD); cell biology (PhD); computational and systems biology (PhD); developmental biology (PhD); genetics (PhD); immunology (PhD); microbiology (PhD); molecular biology (PhD); neurobiology (PhD). *Degree requirements:* For doctorate, comprehensive exam, thesis/dissertation, teaching assistantship during two semesters. *Entrance requirements:* For doctorate, GRE General Test. Additional exam requirements/recommendations for international students: Required—TOEFL, IELTS. Electronic applications accepted. *Faculty research:* Cellular, developmental and molecular (plant and animal) biology; biochemistry, bioengineering, biophysics and structural biology; classical and molecular genetics, stem cell and epigenetics; immunology and microbiology; cancer biology, molecular medicine, neurobiology and human disease; computational and systems biology.

Massachusetts Institute of Technology, School of Science, Department of Chemistry, Cambridge, MA 02139. Offers biological chemistry (PhD); inorganic chemistry (PhD); organic chemistry (PhD); physical chemistry (PhD). *Degree requirements:* For doctorate, comprehensive exam, thesis/dissertation, teaching assistantship during two semesters. *Entrance requirements:* For doctorate, GRE General Test. Additional exam requirements/recommendations for international students: Required—TOEFL, IELTS. Electronic applications accepted. *Faculty research:* Synthetic organic and organometallic chemistry including catalysis; biological chemistry including bioorganic chemistry; physical chemistry including chemical dynamics, theoretical chemistry and biophysical chemistry; inorganic chemistry including synthesis, catalysis, bioinorganic and physical inorganic chemistry; materials chemistry including surface science, nanoscience and polymers.

Mayo Clinic Graduate School of Biomedical Sciences, Program in Biochemistry and Molecular Biology, Rochester, MN 55905. Offers MS, PhD. *Faculty:* 104 full-time (16 women). *Students:* 42 full-time (21 women); includes 20 minority (2 Black or African American, non-Hispanic/Latino; 11 Asian, non-Hispanic/Latino; 6 Hispanic/Latino; 1 Native Hawaiian or other Pacific Islander, non-Hispanic/Latino). 51 applicants, 18% accepted, 7 enrolled. Terminal master's awarded for partial completion of doctoral program. *Degree requirements:* For master's, thesis; for doctorate, comprehensive exam, thesis/dissertation, oral defense of dissertation, qualifying oral and written exam. *Entrance requirements:* For doctorate, GRE, 1 year of chemistry, biology, calculus, and physics. Additional exam requirements/recommendations for international students: Required—TOEFL. *Application deadline:* For fall admission, 12/1 for domestic and international students. Application fee: $50. Electronic applications accepted. *Financial support:* Fellowships with full tuition reimbursements available. *Faculty research:* Gene structure and function, membranes and receptors/cytoskeleton, oncogenes and growth factors, protein structure and function, steroid hormonal action. *Unit head:* Dr. David J. Katzmann, Director, 507-284-3320, E-mail: katzmann.david@mayo.edu. *Application contact:* Sarah E Giese, Admissions Coordinator, 507-538-1160, E-mail: phd.training@mayo.edu.
Website: http://www.mayo.edu/mgs/

McGill University, Faculty of Graduate and Postdoctoral Studies, Faculty of Medicine, Department of Biochemistry, Montréal, QC H3A 2T5, Canada. Offers M Sc, PhD.

McGill University, Faculty of Graduate and Postdoctoral Studies, Faculty of Science, Department of Chemistry, Montréal, QC H3A 2T5, Canada. Offers chemical biology (M Sc, PhD); chemistry (M Sc, PhD).

McMaster University, Faculty of Health Sciences, Department of Biochemistry and Biomedical Sciences, Hamilton, ON L8S 4M2, Canada. Offers M Sc, PhD. Terminal master's awarded for partial completion of doctoral program. *Degree requirements:* For master's, thesis; for doctorate, comprehensive exam, thesis/dissertation. *Entrance requirements:* For master's and doctorate, minimum B+ average. Additional exam requirements/recommendations for international students: Required—TOEFL (minimum score 550 paper-based). *Faculty research:* Molecular and cell biology, biomolecular structure and function, molecular pharmacology and toxicology.

Medical College of Wisconsin, Graduate School, Department of Biochemistry, Milwaukee, WI 53226-0509. Offers PhD, MD/PhD. *Degree requirements:* For doctorate, comprehensive exam, thesis/dissertation. *Entrance requirements:* For doctorate, GRE, official transcripts, three letters of recommendation. Additional exam requirements/recommendations for international students: Required—TOEFL. *Application deadline:* For fall admission, 1/15 for domestic and international students. Applications are processed on a rolling basis. Application fee: $50. *Financial support:* Fellowships, research assistantships, career-related internships or fieldwork, and institutionally sponsored loans available. Financial award application deadline: 2/15; financial award applicants required to submit CSS PROFILE or FAFSA. *Faculty research:* Enzymology, macromolecular structure and synthesis, nucleic acids, molecular and cell biology. *Unit head:* Dr. John Corbett, Chair, 414-955-8768, Fax: 414-955-6555, E-mail: jcorbett@mcw.edu. *Application contact:* Recruitment Office, 414-955-4402, Fax: 414-955-6555, E-mail: gradschoolrecruit@mcw.edu.
Website: http://www.mcw.edu/biochemistry.htm

Medical University of South Carolina, College of Graduate Studies, Department of Biochemistry and Molecular Biology, Charleston, SC 29425. Offers MS, PhD, MD/PhD. Terminal master's awarded for partial completion of doctoral program. *Degree requirements:* For master's, thesis, oral exam/thesis defense; for doctorate, thesis/dissertation, oral and written exams/dissertation defense. *Entrance requirements:* For master's, GRE General Test; for doctorate, GRE General Test, interview, minimum GPA of 3.0. Additional exam requirements/recommendations for international students: Required—TOEFL (minimum score 600 paper-based; 100 iBT). Electronic applications accepted. *Faculty research:* Lipid biochemistry, DNA replication, nucleic acids, protein structure.

Meharry Medical College, School of Graduate Studies, Program in Biomedical Sciences, Biochemistry and Cancer Biology Emphasis, Nashville, TN 37208-9989. Offers PhD, MD/PhD. *Degree requirements:* For doctorate, comprehensive exam, thesis/dissertation. *Entrance requirements:* For doctorate, GRE. *Faculty research:* Regulation of metabolism, enzymology, signal transduction, physical biochemistry.

Memorial University of Newfoundland, School of Graduate Studies, Department of Biochemistry, St. John's, NL A1C 5S7, Canada. Offers biochemistry (M Sc, PhD); food science (M Sc, PhD). *Program availability:* Part-time. *Degree requirements:* For master's, thesis; for doctorate, comprehensive exam, thesis/dissertation, oral defense of thesis. *Entrance requirements:* For master's, 2nd class degree in related field; for doctorate, M Sc. Electronic applications accepted. *Faculty research:* Toxicology, cell and molecular biology, food engineering, marine biotechnology, lipid biology.

Miami University, College of Arts and Science, Department of Chemistry and Biochemistry, Oxford, OH 45056. Offers MS, PhD. *Students:* 56 full-time (23 women), 1 (woman) part-time; includes 4 minority (3 Black or African American, non-Hispanic/Latino; 1 Hispanic/Latino), 29 international. Average age 27. In 2017, 4 master's, 6 doctorates awarded. *Expenses:* Tuition, state resident: full-time $13,812; part-time $575 per credit hour. Tuition, nonresident: full-time $30,860; part-time $1286 per credit hour. *Unit head:* Dr. Michael Crowder, Professor and Chair, 513-529-7274, E-mail: crowdemw@miamioh.edu. *Application contact:* Dr. David Tierney, Professor, 513-529-3731, E-mail: tiernedl@miamioh.edu.
Website: http://www.miamioh.edu/cas/academics/departments/chemistry-biochemistry/

Michigan State University, College of Human Medicine and The Graduate School, Graduate Programs in Human Medicine, East Lansing, MI 48824. Offers biochemistry and molecular biology (MS, PhD); epidemiology (MS, PhD); microbiology (MS); microbiology and molecular genetics (PhD); pharmacology and toxicology (MS, PhD); physiology (MS, PhD); public health (MPH). *Entrance requirements:* Additional exam requirements/recommendations for international students: Required—TOEFL.

Michigan State University, College of Osteopathic Medicine and The Graduate School, Graduate Studies in Osteopathic Medicine, East Lansing, MI 48824. Offers biochemistry and molecular biology (MS, PhD); microbiology (MS); microbiology and molecular genetics (PhD); pharmacology and toxicology (MS, PhD), including integrative pharmacology (MS), pharmacology and toxicology, pharmacology and toxicology-environmental toxicology (PhD); physiology (MS, PhD).

Michigan State University, The Graduate School, College of Agriculture and Natural Resources, MSU-DOE Plant Research Laboratory, East Lansing, MI 48824. Offers biochemistry and molecular biology (PhD); cellular and molecular biology (PhD); crop and soil sciences (PhD); genetics (PhD); microbiology and molecular genetics (PhD); plant biology (PhD); plant physiology (PhD). Offered jointly with the Department of Energy. *Degree requirements:* For doctorate, comprehensive exam, thesis/dissertation, laboratory rotation, defense of dissertation. *Entrance requirements:* For doctorate, GRE General Test, acceptance into one of the affiliated department programs; 3 letters of recommendation; bachelor's degree or equivalent in life sciences, chemistry, biochemistry, or biophysics; research experience. Electronic applications accepted. *Faculty research:* Role of hormones in the regulation of plant development and physiology, molecular mechanisms associated with signal recognition, development and application of genetic methods and materials, protein routing and function.

Michigan State University, The Graduate School, College of Natural Science and Graduate Programs in Human Medicine and Graduate Studies in Osteopathic Medicine, Department of Biochemistry and Molecular Biology, East Lansing, MI 48824. Offers biochemistry and molecular biology (MS, PhD); biochemistry and molecular biology/environmental toxicology (PhD). *Entrance requirements:* Additional exam requirements/recommendations for international students: Required—TOEFL. Electronic applications accepted.

Michigan Technological University, Graduate School, Interdisciplinary Programs, Houghton, MI 49931. Offers atmospheric sciences (PhD); automotive systems and controls (Graduate Certificate); biochemistry and molecular biology (PhD); computational science and engineering (PhD); data science (MS, Graduate Certificate); engineering-environmental (PhD); international profile (Graduate Certificate);

nanotechnology (Graduate Certificate); sustainability (Graduate Certificate); sustainable water resources systems (Graduate Certificate). *Program availability:* Part-time. *Faculty:* 115 full-time (26 women), 9 part-time/adjunct (2 women). *Students:* 58 full-time (18 women), 17 part-time (5 women). Average age 28. 508 applicants, 28% accepted, 27 enrolled. In 2017, 10 master's, 7 doctorates, 11 other advanced degrees awarded. Terminal master's awarded for partial completion of doctoral program. *Degree requirements:* For master's, comprehensive exam (for some programs), thesis (for some programs); for doctorate, comprehensive exam, thesis/dissertation. *Entrance requirements:* For master's, doctorate, and Graduate Certificate, GRE, statement of purpose, personal statement, official transcripts, 2-3 letters of recommendation. Additional exam requirements/recommendations for international students: Required—TOEFL or IELTS. *Application deadline:* Applications are processed on a rolling basis. Electronic applications accepted. *Expenses:* Tuition, state resident: full-time $17,100; part-time $950 per credit. Tuition, nonresident: full-time $17,100; part-time $950 per credit. *Required fees:* $248; $124 per term. Tuition and fees vary according to course load and program. *Financial support:* In 2017–18, 67 students received support, including 9 fellowships with tuition reimbursements available (averaging $15,790 per year), 17 research assistantships with tuition reimbursements available (averaging $15,790 per year), 7 teaching assistantships with tuition reimbursements available (averaging $15,790 per year); career-related internships or fieldwork, Federal Work-Study, scholarships/grants, health care benefits, unspecified assistantships, and cooperative program also available. Financial award applicants required to submit FAFSA. *Faculty research:* Big data, atmospheric sciences, bioinformatics and systems biology, molecular dynamics, environmental studies. *Unit head:* Dr. Pushpalatha Murthy, Dean of the Graduate School/Associate Provost for Graduate Education, 906-487-3007, Fax: 906-487-2284, E-mail: ppmurthy@mtu.edu. *Application contact:* Carol T. Wingerson, Administrative Aide, 906-487-2328, Fax: 906-487-2284, E-mail: gradadms@mtu.edu.

Mississippi College, Graduate School, College of Arts and Sciences, School of Science and Mathematics, Department of Chemistry and Biochemistry, Clinton, MS 39058. Offers MCS, MS. *Program availability:* Part-time. *Degree requirements:* For master's, comprehensive exam, thesis (for some programs). *Entrance requirements:* For master's, GRE. Additional exam requirements/recommendations for international students: Recommended—TOEFL, IELTS. Electronic applications accepted.

Mississippi State University, College of Agriculture and Life Sciences, Department of Biochemistry, Molecular Biology, Entomology and Plant Pathology, Mississippi State, MS 39762. Offers biochemistry (MS, PhD); entomology (MS, PhD); plant pathology (MS, PhD). *Faculty:* 37 full-time (7 women). *Students:* 45 full-time (23 women), 8 part-time (5 women); includes 4 minority (2 Black or African American, non-Hispanic/Latino; 2 Hispanic/Latino), 12 international. Average age 29. 22 applicants, 23% accepted, 3 enrolled. In 2017, 9 master's, 6 doctorates awarded. Terminal master's awarded for partial completion of doctoral program. *Degree requirements:* For master's, thesis (for some programs), final oral exam; for doctorate, thesis/dissertation, preliminary oral and written exam. *Entrance requirements:* For master's, GRE General Test, minimum GPA of 2.75; for doctorate, GRE. Additional exam requirements/recommendations for international students: Required—TOEFL (minimum score 500 paper-based; 61 iBT); Recommended—IELTS (minimum score 5.5). *Application deadline:* For fall admission, 7/1 for domestic students, 5/1 for international students; for spring admission, 11/1 for domestic students, 9/1 for international students. Applications are processed on a rolling basis. Application fee: $60 ($80 for international students). Electronic applications accepted. *Expenses:* Tuition, state resident: full-time $8318; part-time $462.12 per credit hour. Tuition, nonresident: full-time $22,358; part-time $1242.12 per credit hour. *Required fees:* $110; $12.24 per credit hour. $6.12 per semester. *Financial support:* In 2017–18, 37 research assistantships with full tuition reimbursements (averaging $16,567 per year) were awarded; Federal Work-Study, institutionally sponsored loans, and unspecified assistantships also available. Financial award application deadline: 4/1; financial award applicants required to submit FAFSA. *Faculty research:* Fish nutrition, plant and animal molecular biology, plant biochemistry, enzymology, lipid metabolism, chromatin, cell wall synthesis in rice, a model grass bioenergy species and the source of rice Stover residues using reverse genetic and functional genomic and proteomic approaches. *Unit head:* Dr. Jeffrey Dean, Professor and Head, 662-325-2640, Fax: 662-325-8664, E-mail: jd1891@msstate.edu. *Application contact:* Marina Hunt, Admissions and Enrollment Assistant, 662-325-5188, E-mail: mhunt@grad.msstate.edu.
Website: http://www.biochemistry.msstate.edu

Montana State University, The Graduate School, College of Letters and Science, Department of Chemistry and Biochemistry, Bozeman, MT 59717. Offers biochemistry (MS, PhD); chemistry (MS, PhD). *Program availability:* Part-time. *Degree requirements:* For master's, comprehensive exam, thesis (for some programs); for doctorate, comprehensive exam, thesis/dissertation. *Entrance requirements:* For master's and doctorate, GRE General Test, transcripts, letter of recommendation. Additional exam requirements/recommendations for international students: Required—TOEFL (minimum score 550 paper-based). Electronic applications accepted. *Faculty research:* Proteomics, nano-materials chemistry, computational chemistry, optical spectroscopy, photochemistry.

Montclair State University, The Graduate School, College of Science and Mathematics, Program in Pharmaceutical Biochemistry, Montclair, NJ 07043-1624. Offers MS. *Program availability:* Part-time, evening/weekend. *Entrance requirements:* For master's, GRE General Test, 24 undergraduate credits in chemistry, 2 letters of recommendation, essay. Electronic applications accepted. *Faculty research:* Enzyme kinetics, enzyme expression, pharmaceutical biochemistry, medicinal chemistry, biophysical chemistry.

Mount Allison University, Department of Chemistry and Biochemistry, Sackville, NB E4L 1E4, Canada. Offers chemistry (M Sc). *Degree requirements:* For master's, thesis. *Entrance requirements:* For master's, honors degree in chemistry. Full-time tuition and fees vary according to campus/location and student level. *Financial support:* Fellowships and research assistantships available. *Faculty research:* Organometallic and main group chemistry; medicinal, bio-organic, and bio-inorganic chemistry; materials chemistry; surface chemistry; environmental chemistry; nuclear resonance spectroscopy; green chemistry. *Unit head:* Andrew Grant, Head, 506-364-2361, E-mail: agrant@mta.edu.

New York Medical College, Graduate School of Basic Medical Sciences, Valhalla, NY 10595. Offers biochemistry and molecular biology (MS, PhD); cell biology (MS, PhD); microbiology and immunology (MS, PhD); pathology (MS, PhD); pharmacology (MS, PhD); physiology (MS, PhD); MD/PhD. *Program availability:* Part-time, evening/weekend. *Faculty:* 70 full-time (17 women), 25 part-time/adjunct (9 women). *Students:* 116 full-time (63 women), 25 part-time (11 women); includes 65 minority (17 Black or African American, non-Hispanic/Latino; 1 American Indian or Alaska Native, non-Hispanic/Latino; 23 Asian, non-Hispanic/Latino; 21 Hispanic/Latino; 3 Two or more races, non-Hispanic/Latino), 27 international. Average age 27. 273 applicants, 56% accepted, 59 enrolled. In 2017, 32 master's, 3 doctorates awarded. *Degree requirements:* For master's, thesis; for doctorate, comprehensive exam, thesis/dissertation. *Entrance requirements:* For master's, GRE General Test, MCAT, or DAT; for doctorate, GRE General Test. Additional exam requirements/recommendations for international students: Required—TOEFL. *Application deadline:* For fall admission, 7/1 priority date for domestic students, 5/1 priority date for international students; for spring admission, 12/1 priority date for domestic students, 9/15 priority date for international students. Applications are processed on a rolling basis. Application fee: $75 ($100 for international students). Electronic applications accepted. *Expenses:* $1,125 per credit, $655 fees. *Financial support:* Fellowships, research assistantships, Federal Work-Study, institutionally sponsored loans, scholarships/grants, tuition waivers, and health benefits (for PhD candidates only) available. Support available to part-time students. Financial award application deadline: 4/30; financial award applicants required to submit FAFSA. *Faculty research:* Cardiovascular science, infectious diseases, neuroscience, cancer, cell signaling. *Unit head:* Dr. Francis L. Belloni, Dean, 914-594-4110, Fax: 914-594-4944, E-mail: francis_belloni@nymc.edu. *Application contact:* Valerie Romeo-Messana, Director of Admissions, 914-594-4110, Fax: 914-594-4944, E-mail: v_romeomessana@nymc.edu.
Website: https://www.nymc.edu/graduate-school-of-basic-medical-sciences-gsbms/gsbms-academics/

North Carolina State University, Graduate School, College of Agriculture and Life Sciences, Department of Biochemistry, Raleigh, NC 27695. Offers PhD. *Degree requirements:* For doctorate, thesis/dissertation. *Entrance requirements:* For doctorate, GRE General Test. Additional exam requirements/recommendations for international students: Required—TOEFL. Electronic applications accepted. *Faculty research:* Regulation of gene expression, structure and function of proteins and nucleic acids, molecular biology, high-field NMR, bioinorganic chemistry.

North Dakota State University, College of Graduate and Interdisciplinary Studies, College of Science and Mathematics, Department of Chemistry and Biochemistry, Program in Biochemistry, Fargo, ND 58102. Offers MS, PhD. *Program availability:* Part-time. *Entrance requirements:* Additional exam requirements/recommendations for international students: Required—TOEFL (minimum score 550 paper-based). *Application deadline:* For fall admission, 3/1 priority date for domestic and international students; for spring admission, 9/1 priority date for domestic and international students. Applications are processed on a rolling basis. Application fee: $35. Electronic applications accepted. *Expenses:* Tuition, state resident: full-time $4323; part-time $360.21 per credit. Tuition, nonresident: full-time $6484; part-time $540.31 per credit. *Required fees:* $668; $55.70 per credit. Part-time tuition and fees vary according to degree level, program and reciprocity agreements. *Financial support:* Application deadline: 4/15. *Unit head:* Mukund P. Sibi, Graduate Admissions Director, 701-231-8694, Fax: 701-231-8831, E-mail: mukund.sibi@ndsu.edu. *Application contact:* Elizabeth Worth, Marketing, Recruitment, and Public Relations Coordinator, 701-231-8476, Fax: 701-231-6524, E-mail: elizabeth.worth@ndsu.edu.

Northern Illinois University, Graduate School, College of Liberal Arts and Sciences, Department of Chemistry and Biochemistry, De Kalb, IL 60115-2854. Offers MS, PhD. *Faculty:* 16 full-time (1 woman), 3 part-time/adjunct (1 woman). *Students:* 31 full-time (12 women), 7 part-time (3 women); includes 5 minority (2 Black or African American, non-Hispanic/Latino; 3 Hispanic/Latino), 12 international. Average age 31. 22 applicants, 77% accepted, 5 enrolled. In 2017, 6 master's, 7 doctorates awarded. Terminal master's awarded for partial completion of doctoral program. *Degree requirements:* For master's, comprehensive exam, thesis optional, research seminar; for doctorate, one foreign language, thesis/dissertation, candidacy exam, dissertation defense, research seminar. *Entrance requirements:* For master's, GRE General Test, bachelor's degree in mathematics or science, minimum GPA of 2.75; for doctorate, GRE General Test, bachelor's degree in mathematics or science; minimum undergraduate GPA of 2.75, 3.2 graduate. Additional exam requirements/recommendations for international students: Required—TOEFL (minimum score 550 paper-based). *Application deadline:* For fall admission, 6/1 for domestic students, 5/1 for international students; for spring admission, 11/1 for domestic students, 10/1 for international students. Applications are processed on a rolling basis. Application fee: $40. Electronic applications accepted. *Financial support:* In 2017–18, 10 research assistantships with full tuition reimbursements, 33 teaching assistantships with full tuition reimbursements were awarded; fellowships with full tuition reimbursements, career-related internships or fieldwork, Federal Work-Study, scholarships/grants, tuition waivers (full), and unspecified assistantships also available. Support available to part-time students. Financial award applicants required to submit FAFSA. *Faculty research:* Viscoelastic properties of polymers, lig and buding tocytochrome coxidases, computational inorganic chemistry, chemistry of organosilanes. *Unit head:* Dr. Ralph Wheeler, Chair, 815-753-1181, Fax: 815-753-4802, E-mail: rwheeler@niu.edu. *Application contact:* Graduate School Office, 815-753-0395, E-mail: gradsch@niu.edu.
Website: http://www.chembio.niu.edu/

Northwestern University, The Graduate School, Interdisciplinary Biological Sciences Program (IBiS), Evanston, IL 60208. Offers biochemistry (PhD); bioengineering and biotechnology (PhD); biotechnology (PhD); cell and molecular biology (PhD); developmental and systems biology (PhD); nanotechnology (PhD); neurobiology (PhD); structural biology and biophysics (PhD). *Degree requirements:* For doctorate, thesis/dissertation, qualifying exam. *Entrance requirements:* For doctorate, GRE General Test. Additional exam requirements/recommendations for international students: Required—TOEFL (minimum score 600 paper-based). Electronic applications accepted. *Faculty research:* Biophysics/structural biology, cell/molecular biology, synthetic biology, developmental systems biology, chemical biology/nanotechnology.

The Ohio State University, Graduate School, College of Arts and Sciences, Division of Natural and Mathematical Sciences, Biochemistry Program, Columbus, OH 43210. Offers PhD. *Students:* 72 full-time (33 women), 13 international. Average age 26. In 2017, 2 doctorates awarded. Terminal master's awarded for partial completion of doctoral program. *Entrance requirements:* For doctorate, GRE General Test. Additional exam requirements/recommendations for international students: Required—TOEFL (minimum score 620 paper-based; 105 iBT); Recommended—IELTS (minimum score 8). *Application deadline:* For fall admission, 12/15 priority date for domestic students, 12/1 priority date for international students. Applications are processed on a rolling basis. Application fee: $60 ($70 for international students). Electronic applications accepted. *Financial support:* Fellowships, research assistantships, and teaching assistantships available. *Unit head:* Dr. Jane Jackman, Program Director, 614-247-8097, Fax: 614-292-6511, E-mail: jackman.14@osu.edu. *Application contact:* Graduate and Professional Admissions, 614-292-9444, Fax: 614-292-3895, E-mail: gpadmissions@osu.edu.
Website: http://osbp.osu.edu/

The Ohio State University, Graduate School, College of Arts and Sciences, Division of Natural and Mathematical Sciences, Department of Chemistry and Biochemistry, Columbus, OH 43210. Offers biochemistry (MS); chemistry (MS, PhD). *Faculty:* 48. *Students:* 229 (95 women); includes 24 minority (7 Black or African American, non-Hispanic/Latino; 7 Asian, non-Hispanic/Latino; 10 Hispanic/Latino), 101 international. Average age 26. In 2017, 20 master's, 42 doctorates awarded. *Entrance requirements:* For master's and doctorate, GRE General Test. Additional exam requirements/recommendations for international students: Required—TOEFL (minimum score 550 paper-based; 79 iBT), Michigan English Language Assessment Battery (minimum score 82); Recommended—IELTS (minimum score 7). *Application deadline:* For fall admission, 12/15 for domestic and international students. Applications are processed on a rolling basis. Application fee: $60 ($70 for international students). Electronic applications

accepted. *Financial support:* Fellowships, research assistantships, teaching assistantships, Federal Work-Study, and institutionally sponsored loans available. Support available to part-time students. *Unit head:* Dr. Susan V. Olesik, Chair, 614-292-0733, E-mail: chair@chemistry.ohio-state.edu. *Application contact:* Graduate and Professional Admissions, 614-292-9444, Fax: 614-292-3895, E-mail: gpadmissions@osu.edu.
Website: https://chemistry.osu.edu/

Ohio University, Graduate College, College of Arts and Sciences, Department of Chemistry and Biochemistry, Athens, OH 45701-2979. Offers MS, PhD. *Degree requirements:* For master's, comprehensive exam, thesis, exam; for doctorate, comprehensive exam, thesis/dissertation, exam. *Entrance requirements:* For master's and doctorate, GRE. Additional exam requirements/recommendations for international students: Required—TOEFL (minimum score 550 paper-based; 80 iBT) or IELTS (minimum score 6.5). Electronic applications accepted. *Faculty research:* Materials, RNA, synthesis, carbohydrate, mass spectrometry.

Oklahoma State University, College of Agricultural Science and Natural Resources, Department of Biochemistry and Molecular Biology, Stillwater, OK 74078. Offers MS, PhD. *Faculty:* 20 full-time (8 women). *Students:* 7 full-time (4 women), 13 part-time (5 women); includes 3 minority (1 Asian, non-Hispanic/Latino; 2 Hispanic/Latino), 7 international. Average age 30. 19 applicants, 16% accepted, 3 enrolled. In 2017, 4 master's, 3 doctorates awarded. *Entrance requirements:* For master's and doctorate, GRE or GMAT. Additional exam requirements/recommendations for international students: Required—TOEFL (minimum score 550 paper-based; 79 iBT). *Application deadline:* For fall admission, 3/1 priority date for international students; for spring admission, 8/1 priority date for international students. Applications are processed on a rolling basis. Application fee: $40 ($75 for international students). Electronic applications accepted. *Expenses:* Tuition, state resident: full-time $4019; part-time $2679.60 per year. Tuition, nonresident: full-time $15,286; part-time $10,190.40 per year. *Required fees:* $2129; $1419 per unit. Tuition and fees vary according to program. *Financial support:* Research assistantships, teaching assistantships, career-related internships or fieldwork, Federal Work-Study, scholarships/grants, health care benefits, tuition waivers (partial), and unspecified assistantships available. Support available to part-time students. Financial award application deadline: 3/1; financial award applicants required to submit FAFSA. *Unit head:* Dr. John Gustafson, Department Head, 405-744-6189, Fax: 405-744-7799, E-mail: john.gustafson@okstate.edu.
Website: http://biochemistry.okstate.edu/

Old Dominion University, College of Sciences, Program in Chemistry, Norfolk, VA 23529. Offers analytical chemistry (MS, PhD); biochemistry (MS, PhD); environmental chemistry (MS, PhD); inorganic chemistry (MS, PhD); organic chemistry (MS, PhD); physical chemistry (MS, PhD). *Program availability:* Part-time. *Faculty:* 18 full-time (5 women). *Students:* 36 full-time (18 women), 9 part-time (5 women); includes 6 minority (3 Black or African American, non-Hispanic/Latino; 1 Hispanic/Latino; 2 Two or more races, non-Hispanic/Latino), 21 international. Average age 28. 37 applicants, 35% accepted, 8 enrolled. In 2017, 3 master's, 4 doctorates awarded. Terminal master's awarded for partial completion of doctoral program. *Degree requirements:* For master's, comprehensive exam, thesis (for some programs); for doctorate, comprehensive exam, thesis/dissertation. *Entrance requirements:* For master's and doctorate, GRE General Test, minimum GPA of 3.0 in major, 2.5 overall, transcripts, essay, three letters of recommendation, resume. Additional exam requirements/recommendations for international students: Required—TOEFL (minimum score 84 iBT). *Application deadline:* For fall admission, 7/1 for domestic students, 1/15 for international students; for spring admission, 11/1 for domestic students, 8/15 for international students. Applications are processed on a rolling basis. Application fee: $50. Electronic applications accepted. *Expenses:* Contact institution. *Financial support:* In 2017–18, 45 students received support, including 2 fellowships with full tuition reimbursements available (averaging $18,000 per year), 16 research assistantships with full tuition reimbursements available (averaging $18,000 per year), 26 teaching assistantships with full tuition reimbursements available (averaging $18,000 per year); career-related internships or fieldwork, institutionally sponsored loans, scholarships/grants, health care benefits, and unspecified assistantships also available. Financial award application deadline: 2/15; financial award applicants required to submit FAFSA. *Faculty research:* Biogeochemistry, materials chemistry, computational chemistry, organic chemistry, biofuels. *Total annual research expenditures:* $2.6 million. *Unit head:* Dr. John R. Donat, Graduate Program Director, 757-683-4098, Fax: 757-683-4628, E-mail: chemgpd@odu.edu. *Application contact:* Kristi Rehrauer, Graduate Program Assistant, 757-683-6979, Fax: 757-683-4628, E-mail: krehraue@odu.edu.

Oregon Health & Science University, School of Medicine, Graduate Programs in Medicine, Department of Environmental and Biomolecular Systems, Portland, OR 97239-3098. Offers biochemistry and molecular biology (MS, PhD); environmental science and engineering (MS, PhD). *Program availability:* Part-time. *Faculty:* 13 full-time (4 women). *Students:* 7 full-time (6 women), 2 part-time (0 women); includes 1 minority (American Indian or Alaska Native, non-Hispanic/Latino). Average age 32. In 2017, 7 master's, 3 doctorates awarded. Terminal master's awarded for partial completion of doctoral program. *Degree requirements:* For master's, thesis (for some programs); for doctorate, comprehensive exam, thesis/dissertation, qualifying exam. *Entrance requirements:* For master's and doctorate, GRE General Test (minimum scores: 153 Verbal/148 Quantitative/4.5 Analytical) or MCAT (for some programs). *Application deadline:* For fall admission, 7/15 for domestic students, 5/15 for international students; for winter admission, 10/15 for domestic students, 9/15 for international students; for spring admission, 1/15 for domestic students, 12/15 for international students. Applications are processed on a rolling basis. Application fee: $70. Electronic applications accepted. *Financial support:* Health care benefits and full-tuition and stipends (for PhD students) available. Financial award application deadline: 3/1; financial award applicants required to submit FAFSA. *Faculty research:* Metalloprotein biochemistry, molecular microbiology, environmental microbiology, environmental chemistry, biogeochemistry. *Unit head:* Dr. Michiko Nakano, Program Director. *Application contact:* E-mail: somgrad@ohsu.edu.

Oregon Health & Science University, School of Medicine, Graduate Programs in Medicine, Program in Molecular and Cellular Biosciences, Department of Biochemistry and Molecular Biology, Portland, OR 97239-3098. Offers PhD. *Faculty:* 12 full-time (3 women), 21 part-time/adjunct (3 women). *Students:* 7 full-time (2 women); includes 1 minority (Hispanic/Latino), 1 international. Average age 27. In 2017, 1 doctorate awarded. *Degree requirements:* For doctorate, comprehensive exam, thesis/dissertation, qualifying exam. *Entrance requirements:* For doctorate, GRE General Test (minimum scores: 153 Verbal/148 Quantitative/4.5 Analytical). *Application deadline:* For fall admission, 12/1 for domestic and international students. Application fee: $70. Electronic applications accepted. *Financial support:* Health care benefits, tuition waivers (full), and full-tuition and stipends (for PhD students) available. Financial award application deadline: 3/1; financial award applicants required to submit FAFSA. *Faculty research:* Leishmania, parasites, structure and function of G proteins, cystic fibrosis, genomic instability, biology of ion channels. *Unit head:* Dr. Ujwal Shinde, Program Director, E-mail: somgrad@ohsu.edu. *Application contact:* Lola Bichler, Administrative Coordinator, E-mail: somgrad@ohsu.edu.
Website: http://www.ohsu.edu/som-biochem/

Oregon State University, College of Agricultural Sciences, Program in Food Science and Technology, Corvallis, OR 97331. Offers brewing (MS, PhD); enology (MS, PhD); flavor chemistry (MS, PhD); food and seafood processing (MS, PhD); food chemistry/biochemistry (MS, PhD); food engineering (MS, PhD); food microbiology/biotechnology (MS, PhD); sensory evaluation (MS, PhD). *Entrance requirements:* For master's and doctorate, GRE (minimum Verbal and Quantitative scores of 300), minimum GPA of 3.0 in last 90 hours. Additional exam requirements/recommendations for international students: Required—TOEFL (minimum score 80 iBT), IELTS (minimum score 6.5). *Application deadline:* For fall admission, 4/1 for international students; for winter admission, 7/1 for international students; for spring admission, 10/1 for international students; for summer admission, 1/1 for international students. Application fee: $75 ($85 for international students). *Application contact:* Holly Templeton, Food Science and Technology Advisor, 541-737-6486, E-mail: holly.templeton@oregonstate.edu.
Website: http://oregonstate.edu/foodsci/graduate-program

Oregon State University, College of Science, Program in Biochemistry and Biophysics, Corvallis, OR 97331. Offers MA, MS, PhD. Terminal master's awarded for partial completion of doctoral program. *Degree requirements:* For master's, thesis optional; for doctorate, thesis/dissertation, exams. *Entrance requirements:* For master's and doctorate, GRE, minimum GPA of 3.0. Additional exam requirements/recommendations for international students: Required—TOEFL (minimum score 600 paper-based; 100 iBT), IELTS (minimum score 7). *Application deadline:* For fall admission, 12/15 priority date for domestic and international students. Application fee: $75 ($85 for international students). Electronic applications accepted. *Financial support:* Application deadline: 12/15. *Faculty research:* DNA and deoxyribonucleotide metabolism, cell growth control, receptors and membranes, protein structure and function. *Unit head:* Dina Stoneman, Graduate Program Coordinator, 541-737-4511, E-mail: bboffice@oregonstate.edu.
Website: http://biochem.science.oregonstate.edu/

Oregon State University, Interdisciplinary/Institutional Programs, Program in Environmental Sciences, Corvallis, OR 97331. Offers biogeochemistry (MA, MS, PSM, PhD); ecology (MA, MS, PSM, PhD); environmental education (MA, MS, PhD); quantitative analysis (PSM); social science (MA, MS, PSM, PhD); water resources (MA, MS, PhD). *Program availability:* Part-time. *Degree requirements:* For master's, variable foreign language requirement, thesis; for doctorate, thesis/dissertation. *Entrance requirements:* For master's and doctorate, GRE. Additional exam requirements/recommendations for international students: Required—TOEFL (minimum score 80 iBT), IELTS (minimum score 6.5). *Application deadline:* For fall admission, 1/15 priority date for domestic and international students. Application fee: $75 ($85 for international students). *Unit head:* Dr. Carolyn Fonyo Boggess, Interim Director, 541-760-4196, E-mail: carolyn.fonyo@oregonstate.edu. *Application contact:* Dr. Carolyn Fonyo Boggess, Interim Director, 541-760-4196, E-mail: carolyn.fonyo@oregonstate.edu.
Website: http://gradschool.oregonstate.edu/environmental-sciences-graduate-program-esgp

Pace University, Dyson College of Arts and Sciences, Program in Biochemistry and Molecular Biology, New York, NY 10038. Offers MS. *Program availability:* Part-time, evening/weekend. *Students:* 11 full-time (9 women), 3 part-time (2 women); includes 6 minority (2 Black or African American, non-Hispanic/Latino; 1 Asian, non-Hispanic/Latino; 2 Hispanic/Latino; 1 Two or more races, non-Hispanic/Latino), 2 international. Average age 23. In 2017, 3 master's awarded. *Degree requirements:* For master's, thesis. *Entrance requirements:* For master's, official transcripts, two letters of recommendation, personal statement. Additional exam requirements/recommendations for international students: Required—TOEFL (minimum score 88 iBT), IELTS (minimum score 7) or PTE (minimum score 60). *Application deadline:* For fall admission, 4/15 priority date for domestic students. Applications are processed on a rolling basis. Application fee: $70. Electronic applications accepted. *Financial support:* Research assistantships and scholarships/grants available. Financial award application deadline: 2/15; financial award applicants required to submit FAFSA. *Unit head:* Dr. Nigel Yarlett, Director, MS in Biochemistry and Molecular Biology, 212-346-1853, E-mail: nyarlett@pace.edu. *Application contact:* Susan Ford-Goldschein, Director of Admissions, 212-346-1531, Fax: 212-346-1585, E-mail: graduateadmission@pace.edu.
Website: http://www.pace.edu/dyson/programs/ms-biochemistry-molecular-biology-nyc

Penn State Hershey Medical Center, College of Medicine, Graduate School Programs in the Biomedical Sciences, Graduate Program in Biomedical Sciences, Hershey, PA 17033. Offers biochemistry and molecular genetics (MS, PhD); biomedical sciences (MS, PhD); cellular and integrative physiology (MS, PhD); translational therapeutics (MS, PhD); virology and immunology (MS, PhD); MD/PhD; PhD/MBA. *Students:* 103 full-time (58 women); includes 25 minority (5 Black or African American, non-Hispanic/Latino; 12 Asian, non-Hispanic/Latino; 7 Hispanic/Latino; 1 Native Hawaiian or other Pacific Islander, non-Hispanic/Latino), 28 international. 250 applicants, 22% accepted, 19 enrolled. In 2017, 4 master's, 1 doctorate awarded. Terminal master's awarded for partial completion of doctoral program. *Degree requirements:* For master's, thesis; for doctorate, comprehensive exam, thesis/dissertation, candidacy exam. *Entrance requirements:* For doctorate, GRE General Test. Additional exam requirements/recommendations for international students: Required—TOEFL (minimum score 550 paper-based; 81 iBT). *Application deadline:* For fall admission, 1/1 for domestic and international students. Applications are processed on a rolling basis. Application fee: $65. Electronic applications accepted. *Financial support:* In 2017–18, 103 students received support, including research assistantships with full tuition reimbursements available (averaging $27,802 per year); fellowships, scholarships/grants, traineeships, health care benefits, and unspecified assistantships also available. *Unit head:* Dr. Ralph L. Keil, Chair, 717-531-8595, Fax: 717-531-0786, E-mail: rlk9@psu.edu. *Application contact:* Kristin E. Smith, Director of Graduate Admissions, 717-531-1045, Fax: 717-531-0786, E-mail: kec17@psu.edu.
Website: http://med.psu.edu/bms

Penn State University Park, Graduate School, Eberly College of Science, Department of Biochemistry and Molecular Biology, University Park, PA 16802. Offers biochemistry, microbiology, and molecular biology (MS, PhD); biotechnology (MBIOT). *Unit head:* Dr. Douglas R. Cavener, Dean, 814-865-9591, Fax: 814-865-3634. *Application contact:* Lori Hawn, Director, Graduate Student Services, 814-865-1795, Fax: 814-863-4627, E-mail: l-gswww@lists.psu.edu.
Website: http://bmb.psu.edu/

Purdue University, College of Pharmacy and Graduate School, Graduate Programs in Pharmacy and Pharmacal Sciences, Department of Medicinal Chemistry and Molecular Pharmacology, West Lafayette, IN 47907. Offers biophysical and computational chemistry (PhD); cancer research (PhD); immunology and infectious disease (PhD); medicinal biochemistry and molecular biology (PhD); medicinal chemistry and chemical biology (PhD); molecular pharmacology (PhD); neuropharmacology, neurodegeneration, and neurotoxicity (PhD); systems biology and functional genomics (PhD). *Faculty:* 26 full-time (5 women). *Students:* 52 full-time (22 women), 3 part-time (all women); includes 4 minority (1 Black or African American, non-Hispanic/Latino; 2 Asian, non-Hispanic/Latino; 1 Hispanic/Latino), 29 international. Average age 26. 151 applicants, 19% accepted, 13 enrolled. In 2017, 18 doctorates awarded. *Degree requirements:* For doctorate, thesis/dissertation. *Entrance requirements:* For doctorate, GRE General Test; GRE Subject Test in biology, biochemistry, and chemistry (recommended), minimum undergraduate GPA of 3.0. Additional exam requirements/

recommendations for international students: Required—TOEFL (minimum score 550 paper-based; 77 iBT); Recommended—TWE. *Application deadline:* For fall admission, 2/1 for domestic and international students. Applications are processed on a rolling basis. Application fee: $60 ($75 for international students). Electronic applications accepted. *Financial support:* Fellowships, research assistantships, teaching assistantships, and traineeships available. Support available to part-time students. Financial award applicants required to submit FAFSA. *Faculty research:* Drug design and development, cancer research, drug synthesis and analysis, chemical pharmacology, environmental toxicology. *Unit head:* Zhong-Yin Zhang, Head, 765-494-1403, E-mail: zhang-yn@purdue.edu. *Application contact:* Delayne Graham, Graduate Contact, 765-494-1362, E-mail: dkgraham@purdue.edu.

Purdue University, Graduate School, College of Agriculture, Department of Biochemistry, West Lafayette, IN 47907. Offers MS, PhD. *Faculty:* 22 full-time (7 women). *Students:* 42 full-time (25 women), 2 part-time (0 women); includes 4 minority (1 Black or African American, non-Hispanic/Latino; 2 Asian, non-Hispanic/Latino; 1 Two or more races, non-Hispanic/Latino), 19 international. Average age 27. 53 applicants, 34% accepted, 6 enrolled. In 2017, 1 master's, 6 doctorates awarded. Terminal master's awarded for partial completion of doctoral program. *Degree requirements:* For doctorate, thesis/dissertation, preliminary and qualifying exams. *Entrance requirements:* For doctorate, GRE General Test, minimum undergraduate GPA of 3.0 or equivalent. Additional exam requirements/recommendations for international students: Required—TOEFL (minimum score 600 paper-based; 77 iBT). *Application deadline:* For fall admission, 1/15 priority date for domestic and international students; for spring admission, 9/30 for domestic and international students. Applications are processed on a rolling basis. Application fee: $60 ($75 for international students). Electronic applications accepted. *Financial support:* Fellowships, research assistantships, and teaching assistantships available. Support available to part-time students. Financial award application deadline: 4/15; financial award applicants required to submit FAFSA. *Faculty research:* Molecular biology and post-translational modifications of neuropeptides, membrane transport proteins. *Unit head:* Andrew Mesecar, Head of the Graduate Program, 765-494-1607, E-mail: amesecar@purdue.edu. *Application contact:* Traci Jordan, Graduate Contact for Admissions, 765-496-7232, E-mail: tljordan@purdue.edu.
Website: https://ag.purdue.edu/biochem

Purdue University, Graduate School, PULSe - Purdue University Life Sciences Program, West Lafayette, IN 47907. Offers biomolecular structure and biophysics (PhD); biotechnology (PhD); chemical biology (PhD); chromatin and regulation of gene expression (PhD); integrative neuroscience (PhD); integrative plant sciences (PhD); membrane biology (PhD); microbiology (PhD); molecular evolutionary and cancer biology (PhD); molecular evolutionary genetics (PhD); molecular virology (PhD). *Students:* 60 full-time (29 women); includes 6 minority (4 Hispanic/Latino; 2 Two or more races, non-Hispanic/Latino), 36 international. Average age 25. 127 applicants, 39% accepted, 25 enrolled. *Entrance requirements:* For doctorate, GRE, minimum undergraduate GPA of 3.0. Additional exam requirements/recommendations for international students: Required—TOEFL (minimum score 550 paper-based; 77 iBT). *Application deadline:* For fall admission, 1/15 priority date for domestic and international students. Applications are processed on a rolling basis. Application fee: $60 ($75 for international students). Electronic applications accepted. *Financial support:* In 2017–18, research assistantships with tuition reimbursements (averaging $22,500 per year), teaching assistantships with tuition reimbursements (averaging $22,500 per year) were awarded. *Unit head:* Dr. Jason R. Cannon, Head of the Graduate Program, 765-494-0794, E-mail: cannonjr@purdue.edu. *Application contact:* Lindsey Springer, Graduate Contact for Admissions, 765-496-9667, E-mail: lbcampbe@purdue.edu.
Website: http://www.gradschool.purdue.edu/pulse

Queen's University at Kingston, School of Graduate Studies, Faculty of Health Sciences, Department of Biochemistry, Kingston, ON K7L 3N6, Canada. Offers M Sc, PhD. *Program availability:* Part-time. *Degree requirements:* For master's, thesis, research proposal; for doctorate, comprehensive exam, thesis/dissertation, research proposal. *Entrance requirements:* For master's, GRE (if undergraduate degree is not from a Canadian University); for doctorate, GRE required if undergraduate degree is not from a Canadian University. Additional exam requirements/recommendations for international students: Required—TOEFL (minimum score 580 paper-based). Electronic applications accepted. *Faculty research:* Gene expression, protein structure, enzyme activity, signal transduction.

Rensselaer Polytechnic Institute, Graduate School, School of Science, Program in Biochemistry and Biophysics, Troy, NY 12180-3590. Offers MS, PhD. *Faculty:* 21 full-time (8 women), 2 part-time/adjunct (1 woman). *Students:* 21 full-time (12 women), 1 (woman) part-time; includes 4 minority (3 Asian, non-Hispanic/Latino; 1 Hispanic/Latino), 2 international. Average age 26. 37 applicants, 30% accepted, 4 enrolled. In 2017, 2 doctorates awarded. Terminal master's awarded for partial completion of doctoral program. *Degree requirements:* For master's, thesis optional; for doctorate, comprehensive exam, thesis/dissertation. *Entrance requirements:* For master's and doctorate, GRE. Additional exam requirements/recommendations for international students: Required—TOEFL (minimum score 600 paper-based; 100 iBT), IELTS (minimum score 7), PTE (minimum score 68). *Application deadline:* For fall admission, 1/1 priority date for domestic and international students; for spring admission, 8/15 priority date for domestic and international students. Applications are processed on a rolling basis. Application fee: $75. Electronic applications accepted. *Expenses: Tuition:* Full-time $52,550; part-time $2125 per credit hour. *Required fees:* $2890. *Financial support:* In 2017–18, research assistantships (averaging $23,000 per year), teaching assistantships (averaging $23,000 per year) were awarded; fellowships also available. Financial award application deadline: 1/1. *Faculty research:* Biochemistry; bioinformatics; biophysics; cancer biology; computational biology; molecular, cell, and developmental biology; neuroscience; protein folding; stem cells; structural biology. *Total annual research expenditures:* $2.1 million. *Unit head:* Dr. Cathy Royer, Graduate Program Director, 518-276-3796, E-mail: royerc@rpi.edu.
Website: https://science.rpi.edu/biology

Rice University, Graduate Programs, Wiess School of Natural Sciences, Department of Biochemistry and Cell Biology, Houston, TX 77251-1892. Offers MA, PhD. Terminal master's awarded for partial completion of doctoral program. *Degree requirements:* For master's, thesis; for doctorate, thesis/dissertation. *Entrance requirements:* For master's and doctorate, GRE. Additional exam requirements/recommendations for international students: Required—TOEFL (minimum score 600 paper-based; 90 iBT). Electronic applications accepted. *Expenses:* Contact institution. *Faculty research:* Steroid metabolism, protein structure NMR, biophysics, cell growth and movement.

Rosalind Franklin University of Medicine and Science, School of Graduate and Postdoctoral Studies - Interdisciplinary Graduate Program in Biomedical Sciences, Department of Biochemistry and Molecular Biology, North Chicago, IL 60064-3095. Offers PhD, MD/PhD. Terminal master's awarded for partial completion of doctoral program. *Degree requirements:* For doctorate, comprehensive exam, thesis/dissertation. *Entrance requirements:* For doctorate, GRE General Test, minimum GPA of 3.0. Additional exam requirements/recommendations for international students: Required—TOEFL, TWE. Electronic applications accepted. *Faculty research:* Structure of control enzymes, extracellular matrix, glucose metabolism, gene expression, ATP synthesis.

Rush University, Graduate College, Division of Biochemistry, Chicago, IL 60612-3832. Offers MS, PhD, MD/PhD. *Degree requirements:* For doctorate, thesis/dissertation, preliminary exam. *Entrance requirements:* For doctorate, GRE General Test. Additional exam requirements/recommendations for international students: Required—TOEFL. Electronic applications accepted. *Faculty research:* Biochemistry of extracellular matrix, connective tissue biosynthesis and degradation, molecular biology of connective tissue components, cartilage, arthritis.

Rutgers University–Newark, Graduate School of Biomedical Sciences, Department of Biochemistry and Molecular Biology, Newark, NJ 07107. Offers MS, PhD. *Degree requirements:* For master's, thesis; for doctorate, thesis/dissertation, qualifying exam. *Entrance requirements:* For master's and doctorate, GRE General Test. Additional exam requirements/recommendations for international students: Required—TOEFL. Electronic applications accepted.

Rutgers University–Newark, Graduate School, Program in Chemistry, Newark, NJ 07102. Offers analytical chemistry (MS, PhD); biochemistry (MS, PhD); inorganic chemistry (MS, PhD); organic chemistry (MS, PhD); physical chemistry (MS, PhD). *Program availability:* Part-time, evening/weekend. Terminal master's awarded for partial completion of doctoral program. *Degree requirements:* For master's, thesis optional, cumulative exams; for doctorate, thesis/dissertation, exams, research proposal. *Entrance requirements:* For master's and doctorate, GRE General Test, minimum undergraduate B average. Additional exam requirements/recommendations for international students: Required—TOEFL. Electronic applications accepted. *Faculty research:* Medicinal chemistry, natural products, isotope effects, biophysics and biorganic approaches to enzyme mechanisms, organic and organometallic synthesis.

Rutgers University–New Brunswick, Graduate School-New Brunswick, Department of Chemistry and Chemical Biology, Piscataway, NJ 08854-8097. Offers biological chemistry (MS, PhD); inorganic chemistry (MS, PhD); organic chemistry (MS, PhD); physical chemistry (MS, PhD). *Program availability:* Part-time, evening/weekend. Terminal master's awarded for partial completion of doctoral program. *Degree requirements:* For master's, thesis or alternative, exam; for doctorate, thesis/dissertation, 1 year residency. *Entrance requirements:* For master's and doctorate, GRE General Test, GRE Subject Test. Additional exam requirements/recommendations for international students: Required—TOEFL. Electronic applications accepted. *Faculty research:* Biophysical organic/bioorganic, inorganic/bioinorganic, theoretical, and solid-state/surface chemistry.

Rutgers University–New Brunswick, Graduate School-New Brunswick, Programs in the Molecular Biosciences, Piscataway, NJ 08854-8097. Offers biochemistry (PhD); cell and developmental biology (MS, PhD); microbiology and molecular genetics (MS, PhD), including applied microbiology, clinical microbiology, computational molecular biology (PhD), immunology, microbial biochemistry, molecular genetics, virology. MS, PhD offered jointly with University of Medicine and Dentistry of New Jersey.

Rutgers University–New Brunswick, Graduate School of Biomedical Sciences, Program in Biochemistry, Piscataway, NJ 08854-5635. Offers MS, PhD, MD/PhD. PhD, MS offered jointly with Rutgers, The State University of New Jersey, New Brunswick. Terminal master's awarded for partial completion of doctoral program. *Degree requirements:* For master's, thesis, qualifying exam; for doctorate, thesis/dissertation, qualifying exam. *Entrance requirements:* For master's and doctorate, GRE General Test. Additional exam requirements/recommendations for international students: Required—TOEFL. Electronic applications accepted. *Faculty research:* Signal transduction, regulation of RNA, polymerase II transcribed genes, developmental gene expression.

Saint Louis University, Graduate Programs, School of Medicine, Graduate Programs in Biomedical Sciences and Graduate Programs, Department of Biochemistry and Molecular Biology, St. Louis, MO 63103. Offers PhD. *Degree requirements:* For doctorate, comprehensive exam, thesis/dissertation, departmental qualifying exams. *Entrance requirements:* For doctorate, GRE General Test, GRE Subject Test (optional), letters of recommendation, resume, interview. Additional exam requirements/recommendations for international students: Required—TOEFL (minimum score 525 paper-based). Electronic applications accepted. *Faculty research:* Transcription, chromatin modification and regulation of gene expression; structure/function of proteins and enzymes, including x-ray crystallography; inflammatory mediators in pathenogenesis of diabetes and arteriosclerosis; cellular signaling in response to growth factors, opiates and angiogenic mediators; genomics and proteomics of Cryptococcus neoformans.

San Diego State University, Graduate and Research Affairs, College of Sciences, Department of Chemistry and Biochemistry, San Diego, CA 92182. Offers MA, MS, PhD. PhD offered jointly with University of California, San Diego. Terminal master's awarded for partial completion of doctoral program. *Degree requirements:* For doctorate, thesis/dissertation. *Entrance requirements:* For master's, GRE General Test, bachelor's degree in related field, 3 letters of reference; for doctorate, GRE General Test, GRE Subject Test. Additional exam requirements/recommendations for international students: Required—TOEFL. Electronic applications accepted. *Faculty research:* Nonlinear, laser, and electrochemistry; surface reaction dynamics; catalysis, synthesis, and organometallics; proteins, enzymology, and gene expression regulation.

San Francisco State University, Division of Graduate Studies, College of Science and Engineering, Department of Chemistry and Biochemistry, San Francisco, CA 94132-1722. Offers biochemistry (MS); chemistry (MS). *Program availability:* Part-time. *Application deadline:* Applications are processed on a rolling basis. Electronic applications accepted. *Unit head:* Dr. Teaster Baird, Jr., Chair, 415-338-1288, Fax: 415-338-2384, E-mail: tbaird@sfsu.edu. *Application contact:* Dr. Andrew Ichimura, Graduate Coordinator, 415-405-0721, Fax: 415-338-2384, E-mail: ichimura@sfsu.edu.
Website: http://www.chembiochem.sfsu.edu/0home/0layout.php

Seton Hall University, College of Arts and Sciences, Department of Chemistry and Biochemistry, South Orange, NJ 07079-2697. Offers analytical chemistry (MS, PhD); biochemistry (MS, PhD); chemistry (MS); inorganic chemistry (MS, PhD); organic chemistry (MS, PhD); physical chemistry (MS, PhD). *Program availability:* Part-time, evening/weekend. Terminal master's awarded for partial completion of doctoral program. *Degree requirements:* For master's, thesis optional; for doctorate, comprehensive exam, thesis/dissertation. *Entrance requirements:* Additional exam requirements/recommendations for international students: Required—TOEFL. Electronic applications accepted. *Faculty research:* DNA metal reactions; chromatography; bioinorganic, biophysical, organometallic, polymer chemistry; heterogeneous catalyst; synthetic organic and carbohydrate chemistry.

Simon Fraser University, Office of Graduate Studies and Postdoctoral Fellows, Faculty of Science, Department of Molecular Biology and Biochemistry, Burnaby, BC V5A 1S6, Canada. Offers bioinformatics (Graduate Diploma); molecular biology and biochemistry (M Sc, PhD). *Degree requirements:* For master's, thesis; for doctorate, thesis/dissertation; for Graduate Diploma, practicum. *Entrance requirements:* For master's, minimum GPA of 3.0 (on scale of 4.33) or 3.33 based on last 60 credits of undergraduate courses; for doctorate, minimum GPA of 3.5; for Graduate Diploma, minimum GPA of 2.5 (on scale of 4.33) or 2.67 based on last 60 credits of undergraduate courses. Additional exam requirements/recommendations for international students: Recommended—TOEFL (minimum score 580 paper-based; 100 iBT), IELTS (minimum score 7.5), TWE (minimum score 5). Electronic applications accepted. *Faculty research:* Genomics and bioinformatics, cell and developmental biology, structural biology/biochemistry, immunology, nucleic acid function.

Sonoma State University, School of Science and Technology, Department of Biology, Rohnert Park, CA 94928. Offers biochemistry (MA). *Program availability:* Part-time. *Degree requirements:* For master's, thesis or alternative, oral exam. *Entrance requirements:* For master's, GRE General Test, GRE Subject Test, minimum GPA of 3.0. Additional exam requirements/recommendations for international students: Required—TOEFL (minimum score 500 paper-based). *Application deadline:* For fall admission, 11/30 for domestic students. Applications are processed on a rolling basis. Application fee: $55. *Financial support:* Fellowships, research assistantships, teaching assistantships, career-related internships or fieldwork, Federal Work-Study, and tuition waivers (full) available. Financial award application deadline: 3/2; financial award applicants required to submit FAFSA. *Faculty research:* Plant physiology, comparative physiology, community ecology, restoration ecology, marine ecology, conservation genetics, primate behavior, behavioral ecology, developmental biology, plant and animal systematics. *Unit head:* Dr. Richard Whitkus, Department Chair, 707-664-2303, E-mail: whitkus@sonoma.edu. *Application contact:* Dr. Derek Girman, Graduate Adviser, 707-664-3055, E-mail: girman@sonoma.edu.
Website: http://www.sonoma.edu/biology/

Southern Illinois University Carbondale, Graduate School, College of Science, Department of Chemistry and Biochemistry, Carbondale, IL 62901-4701. Offers MS, PhD. *Program availability:* Part-time. Terminal master's awarded for partial completion of doctoral program. *Degree requirements:* For master's, one foreign language, thesis; for doctorate, variable foreign language requirement, thesis/dissertation. *Entrance requirements:* For master's, GRE, minimum GPA of 2.7; for doctorate, GRE General Test, minimum GPA of 3.25. Additional exam requirements/recommendations for international students: Required—TOEFL. *Faculty research:* Materials, separations, computational chemistry, synthetics.

Southern Illinois University Carbondale, Graduate School, College of Science, Program in Molecular Biology, Microbiology, and Biochemistry, Carbondale, IL 62901-4701. Offers MS, PhD. *Degree requirements:* For master's, thesis; for doctorate, thesis/dissertation. *Entrance requirements:* For master's, GRE, minimum GPA of 2.7; for doctorate, GRE, minimum GPA of 3.25. Additional exam requirements/recommendations for international students: Required—TOEFL. *Faculty research:* Prokaryotic gene regulation and expression; eukaryotic gene regulation; microbial, phylogenetic, and metabolic diversity; immune responses to tumors, pathogens, and autoantigens; protein folding and structure.

Southern University and Agricultural and Mechanical College, Graduate School, College of Sciences, Department of Chemistry, Baton Rouge, LA 70813. Offers analytical chemistry (MS); biochemistry (MS); environmental sciences (MS); inorganic chemistry (MS); organic chemistry (MS); physical chemistry (MS). *Degree requirements:* For master's, thesis. *Entrance requirements:* For master's, GMAT or GRE General Test. Additional exam requirements/recommendations for international students: Required—TOEFL (minimum score 525 paper-based). *Faculty research:* Synthesis of macrocyclic ligands, latex accelerators, anticancer drugs, biosensors, absorption isotheums, isolation of specific enzymes from plants.

Stanford University, School of Medicine, Graduate Programs in Medicine, Department of Biochemistry, Stanford, CA 94305-2004. Offers PhD. *Degree requirements:* For doctorate, thesis/dissertation. *Entrance requirements:* For doctorate, GRE General Test, GRE Subject Test (biology or chemistry). Additional exam requirements/recommendations for international students: Required—TOEFL. Electronic applications accepted. *Expenses: Tuition:* Full-time $48,987; part-time $10,620 per quarter. One-time fee: $400. Tuition and fees vary according to program. *Faculty research:* DNA replication, recombination, and gene regulation; methods of isolating, analyzing, and altering genes and genomes; protein structure, protein folding, and protein processing; protein targeting and transport in the cell; intercellular signaling.

Stanford University, School of Medicine, Graduate Programs in Medicine, Department of Chemical and Systems Biology, Stanford, CA 94305-2004. Offers PhD. *Degree requirements:* For doctorate, thesis/dissertation, qualifying examination. *Entrance requirements:* For doctorate, GRE General Test, GRE Subject Test. Additional exam requirements/recommendations for international students: Required—TOEFL. Electronic applications accepted. *Expenses: Tuition:* Full-time $48,987; part-time $10,620 per quarter. One-time fee: $400. Tuition and fees vary according to program. *Faculty research:* Action of drugs such as epinephrine, cell differentiation and development, microsomal enzymes, neuropeptide gene expression.

State University of New York College of Environmental Science and Forestry, Department of Chemistry, Syracuse, NY 13210-2779. Offers biochemistry (MPS, MS, PhD); environmental chemistry (MPS, MS, PhD); organic chemistry of natural products (MPS, MS, PhD); polymer chemistry (MPS, MS, PhD). *Program availability:* Part-time. *Faculty:* 15 full-time (2 women), 1 part-time/adjunct (0 women). *Students:* 30 full-time (12 women), 7 part-time (5 women); includes 2 minority (1 Black or African American, non-Hispanic/Latino; 1 Asian, non-Hispanic/Latino), 13 international. Average age 27. 44 applicants, 50% accepted, 6 enrolled. In 2017, 3 master's, 3 doctorates awarded. Terminal master's awarded for partial completion of doctoral program. *Degree requirements:* For master's, thesis; for doctorate, comprehensive exam, thesis/dissertation. *Entrance requirements:* For master's and doctorate, GRE General Test, GRE Subject Test, minimum GPA of 3.0. Additional exam requirements/recommendations for international students: Required—TOEFL (minimum score 550 paper-based; 80 iBT), IELTS (minimum score 6). *Application deadline:* For fall admission, 2/1 priority date for domestic and international students; for spring admission, 11/1 priority date for domestic and international students. Applications are processed on a rolling basis. Application fee: $60. Electronic applications accepted. *Expenses:* Tuition, state resident: full-time $10,870; part-time $453 per credit. Tuition, nonresident: full-time $22,210; part-time $925 per credit. *Required fees:* $1435; $70.85 per credit. One-time fee: $25 full-time. Part-time tuition and fees vary according to course load. *Financial support:* In 2017–18, 8 students received support. Unspecified assistantships available. Financial award application deadline: 6/30; financial award applicants required to submit FAFSA. *Faculty research:* Polymer chemistry, biochemistry, environmental chemistry, natural products chemistry. *Total annual research expenditures:* $1.5 million. *Unit head:* Prof. Ivan Gitsov, Chair, 315-470-6851, Fax: 315-470-6856, E-mail: igivanov@syr.edu. *Application contact:* Scott Shannon, Associate Provost for Instruction/Dean of the Graduate School, 315-470-6599, Fax: 315-470-6978, E-mail: sshannon@esf.edu.
Website: http://www.esf.edu/chemistry

State University of New York Upstate Medical University, College of Graduate Studies, Program in Biochemistry and Molecular Biology, Syracuse, NY 13210. Offers biochemistry (MS); biochemistry and molecular biology (PhD); MD/PhD. Terminal master's awarded for partial completion of doctoral program. *Degree requirements:* For master's, thesis; for doctorate, comprehensive exam, thesis/dissertation. *Entrance requirements:* For master's, GRE General Test, interview; for doctorate, GRE General Test, telephone interview. Additional exam requirements/recommendations for international students: Required—TOEFL. Electronic applications accepted. *Faculty research:* Enzymology, membrane structure and functions, developmental biochemistry.

Stevens Institute of Technology, Graduate School, Charles V. Schaefer Jr. School of Engineering and Science, Department of Chemistry, Chemical Biology and Biomedical Engineering, Program in Chemical Biology, Hoboken, NJ 07030. Offers MS, PhD, Certificate. *Program availability:* Part-time, evening/weekend. *Students:* 27 full-time (11 women), 2 part-time (1 woman); includes 1 minority (Black or African American, non-Hispanic/Latino), 19 international. Average age 27. 57 applicants, 33% accepted, 8 enrolled. In 2017, 9 master's, 2 doctorates awarded. *Degree requirements:* For master's, thesis optional, minimum B average in major field and overall; for doctorate, comprehensive exam (for some programs), thesis/dissertation; for Certificate, minimum B average. *Entrance requirements:* Additional exam requirements/recommendations for international students: Required—TOEFL (minimum score 74 iBT), IELTS (minimum score 6). *Application deadline:* For fall admission, 7/1 for domestic students, 4/15 for international students; for spring admission, 12/1 for domestic and international students. Applications are processed on a rolling basis. Application fee: $60. Electronic applications accepted. *Expenses: Tuition:* Full-time $34,494; part-time $1554 per credit. *Required fees:* $291 per semester. *Financial support:* Fellowships, research assistantships, teaching assistantships, career-related internships or fieldwork, Federal Work-Study, scholarships/grants, and unspecified assistantships available. Financial award application deadline: 2/15; financial award applicants required to submit FAFSA. *Unit head:* Patricia Muisener, Program Director, 201-216-3715, Fax: 201-216-8240, E-mail: patricia.muisener@stevens.edu. *Application contact:* Graduate Admissions, 888-783-8367, Fax: 888-511-1306, E-mail: graduate@stevens.edu.

Stony Brook University, State University of New York, Graduate School, College of Arts and Sciences, Department of Biochemistry and Cell Biology, Biochemistry and Cell Biology Program, Stony Brook, NY 11794. Offers MS. *Program availability:* Part-time. *Students:* 17 full-time (7 women), 5 part-time (3 women); includes 7 minority (1 Black or African American, non-Hispanic/Latino; 3 Asian, non-Hispanic/Latino; 2 Hispanic/Latino; 1 Two or more races, non-Hispanic/Latino), 5 international. 59 applicants, 59% accepted, 12 enrolled. In 2017, 12 master's awarded. *Degree requirements:* For master's, thesis. *Entrance requirements:* For master's, three letters of recommendation, BS or BA in a life science related field with minimum B average, personal statement. Additional exam requirements/recommendations for international students: Required—TOEFL (minimum score 550 paper-based; 90 iBT). *Application deadline:* For fall admission, 1/15 for domestic students; for summer admission, 10/1 for domestic students. Applications are processed on a rolling basis. Application fee: $100. Electronic applications accepted. *Expenses:* Contact institution. *Financial support:* In 2017–18, 1 research assistantship was awarded. *Unit head:* Prof. Aaron Neiman, Chair, 631-632-8550, Fax: 631-632-8575, E-mail: aaron.neiman@stonybrook.edu. *Application contact:* Pam Wolfskill, Coordinator, 631-632-8585, Fax: 631-632-8575, E-mail: carol.juliano@stonybrook.edu.
Website: https://www.stonybrook.edu/commcms/biochem/education/graduate/biochemistry-and-cell-biology-ms

Stony Brook University, State University of New York, Graduate School, College of Arts and Sciences, Department of Biochemistry and Cell Biology, Molecular and Cellular Biology Program, Stony Brook, NY 11794. Offers biochemistry and molecular biology (PhD); biological sciences (MA); immunology and pathology (PhD); molecular and cellular biology (PhD). *Students:* 63 full-time (35 women); includes 12 minority (3 Black or African American, non-Hispanic/Latino; 6 Asian, non-Hispanic/Latino; 3 Hispanic/Latino), 35 international. Average age 28. 131 applicants, 25% accepted, 11 enrolled. In 2017, 12 doctorates awarded. *Degree requirements:* For doctorate, comprehensive exam, thesis/dissertation, teaching experience. *Entrance requirements:* For doctorate, GRE General Test, GRE Subject Test. Additional exam requirements/recommendations for international students: Required—TOEFL. *Application deadline:* For fall admission, 1/15 for domestic students; for spring admission, 10/1 for domestic students. Application fee: $100. Electronic applications accepted. *Expenses:* Contact institution. *Financial support:* In 2017–18, 4 fellowships, 29 research assistantships, 12 teaching assistantships were awarded; Federal Work-Study also available. *Unit head:* Prof. Aaron Neiman, Chair, 631-632-8550, Fax: 631-632-8575, E-mail: aaron.neiman@stonybrook.edu. *Application contact:* Amy Saas, Graduate Program Administrator, 631-632-8613, Fax: 631-632-9730, E-mail: mcbgraduateprogram@stonybrook.edu.
Website: https://www.stonybrook.edu/mcb/

Stony Brook University, State University of New York, Graduate School, College of Arts and Sciences, Department of Biochemistry and Cell Biology, Program in Biochemistry and Structural Biology, Stony Brook, NY 11794. Offers PhD. *Students:* 32 full-time (19 women); includes 4 minority (2 Black or African American, non-Hispanic/Latino; 1 Asian, non-Hispanic/Latino; 1 Hispanic/Latino), 6 international. Average age 27. 35 applicants, 46% accepted, 4 enrolled. In 2017, 7 doctorates awarded. *Degree requirements:* For doctorate, thesis/dissertation. *Entrance requirements:* For doctorate, GRE. Additional exam requirements/recommendations for international students: Required—TOEFL (minimum score 90 iBT). *Application deadline:* For fall admission, 1/15 for domestic students; for spring admission, 10/1 for domestic students. Application fee: $100. *Expenses:* Contact institution. *Financial support:* In 2017–18, 2 fellowships, 17 research assistantships, 6 teaching assistantships were awarded. *Unit head:* Prof. Aaron Neiman, Chair, 631-632-8550, Fax: 631-632-8575, E-mail: aaron.neiman@stonybrook.edu. *Application contact:* Amy Saas, Graduate Program Administrator, 631-632-8613, Fax: 631-632-9730, E-mail: amy.saas@stonybrook.edu.
Website: https://www.stonybrook.edu/bsb/

Texas A&M University, College of Agriculture and Life Sciences, Department of Biochemistry and Biophysics, College Station, TX 77843. Offers biochemistry (MS, PhD). *Faculty:* 46. *Students:* 140 full-time (59 women), 3 part-time (1 woman); includes 15 minority (1 Black or African American, non-Hispanic/Latino; 3 Asian, non-Hispanic/Latino; 9 Hispanic/Latino; 1 Native Hawaiian or other Pacific Islander, non-Hispanic/Latino; 1 Two or more races, non-Hispanic/Latino), 68 international. Average age 28. 121 applicants, 21% accepted, 25 enrolled. In 2017, 7 master's, 21 doctorates awarded. *Entrance requirements:* For master's and doctorate, GRE General Test. Additional exam requirements/recommendations for international students: Required—TOEFL (minimum score 550 paper-based; 80 iBT), IELTS (minimum score 6), PTE (minimum score 53). *Application deadline:* For fall admission, 2/1 priority date for domestic students, 12/1 priority date for international students. Applications are processed on a rolling basis. Application fee: $50 ($90 for international students). Electronic applications accepted. *Expenses:* Contact institution. *Financial support:* In 2017–18, 141 students received support, including 6 fellowships with tuition reimbursements available (averaging $20,116 per year), 103 research assistantships with tuition reimbursements available (averaging $13,102 per year), 52 teaching assistantships with tuition reimbursements available (averaging $11,759 per year); career-related internships or fieldwork, institutionally sponsored loans, scholarships/grants, traineeships, health care benefits, tuition waivers (full and partial), and unspecified assistantships also available. Support available to part-time students. Financial award application deadline: 3/15; financial award applicants required to submit FAFSA. *Faculty research:* Enzymology, gene expression, protein structure, plant biochemistry. *Unit head:* Dr. Gregory D. Reinhart,

Department Head, 979-862-5032, Fax: 979-845-9274, E-mail: gdr@tamu.edu. *Application contact:* Rafael Almanzar, Graduate Advisor, 979-845-1779, Fax: 979-845-9274, E-mail: r.almanzar1@tamu.edu.
Website: http://biochemistry.tamu.edu/

Texas Christian University, College of Science and Engineering, Department of Chemistry and Biochemistry, Fort Worth, TX 76129. Offers MA, MS, PhD. *Program availability:* Part-time. *Faculty:* 12 full-time (2 women). *Students:* 21 full-time (15 women), 1 part-time (0 women); includes 4 minority (1 Asian, non-Hispanic/Latino; 2 Hispanic/Latino; 1 Two or more races, non-Hispanic/Latino), 9 international. Average age 27. 21 applicants, 48% accepted, 6 enrolled. In 2017, 3 master's, 4 doctorates awarded. Terminal master's awarded for partial completion of doctoral program. *Degree requirements:* For master's, thesis; for doctorate, thesis/dissertation, literature seminar, cumulative exams, research progress report, independent research proposal, teaching of undergraduate labs. *Entrance requirements:* For master's and doctorate, GRE General Test. Additional exam requirements/recommendations for international students: Required—TOEFL (minimum score 80 iBT). *Application deadline:* For fall admission, 2/1 for domestic and international students; for spring admission, 9/1 for domestic and international students. Applications are processed on a rolling basis. Application fee: $60. Electronic applications accepted. *Financial support:* In 2017–18, 18 students received support, including 18 fellowships with full tuition reimbursements available (averaging $21,000 per year); scholarships/grants, traineeships, health care benefits, tuition waivers, and unspecified assistantships also available. Support available to part-time students. Financial award application deadline: 2/1. *Faculty research:* Bioinorganic chemistry, materials chemistry, protein folding, aggregation and transport phenomena, synthetic methodology and total synthesis, synthetic switches for sensing applications, electronic structure approximations, polymer chemistry, science education, protein modification, ribozymes. *Total annual research expenditures:* $300,000. *Unit head:* Dr. Eric Simanek, Chair/Professor, 817-257-5355, Fax: 817-257-5851, E-mail: e.simanek@tcu.edu. *Application contact:* Dr. Benjamin G. Janesko, Director of Graduate Studies/Associate Professor, 817-257-6202, Fax: 817-257-5851, E-mail: b.janesko@tcu.edu.
Website: http://www.chm.tcu.edu/

Texas State University, The Graduate College, College of Science and Engineering, Program in Biochemistry, San Marcos, TX 78666. Offers MS. *Program availability:* Part-time. *Faculty:* 9 full-time (4 women). *Students:* 10 full-time (6 women), 6 part-time (3 women); includes 11 minority (all Hispanic/Latino). Average age 25. 24 applicants, 54% accepted, 3 enrolled. In 2017, 14 master's awarded. *Degree requirements:* For master's, comprehensive exam, thesis. *Entrance requirements:* For master's, GRE (minimum preferred score of 300), baccalaureate degree in chemistry, biochemistry or closely-related field from regionally-accredited university with minimum GPA of 3.0 on last 60 undergraduate semester hours, 2 letters of recommendation, statement of purpose discussing career goals and undergraduate experiences. Additional exam requirements/recommendations for international students: Required—TOEFL (minimum score 550 paper-based; 78 iBT), IELTS (minimum score 6.5). *Application deadline:* For fall admission, 2/1 priority date for domestic and international students; for spring admission, 10/1 for domestic and international students. Applications are processed on a rolling basis. Application fee: $40 ($90 for international students). Electronic applications accepted. *Expenses:* Tuition, state resident: full-time $7868; part-time $3934 per semester. Tuition, nonresident: full-time $17,828; part-time $8914 per semester. *Required fees:* $2092; $1435 per semester. Tuition and fees vary according to course load. *Financial support:* In 2017–18, 10 students received support, including 10 research assistantships (averaging $17,525 per year), 5 teaching assistantships (averaging $13,500 per year); Federal Work-Study, institutionally sponsored loans, scholarships/grants, health care benefits, and unspecified assistantships also available. Support available to part-time students. Financial award application deadline: 3/1; financial award applicants required to submit FAFSA. *Faculty research:* Chemo-preventive approach to cancer exploiting presumptive link between genomic, a vertebrate model system for characterization of RNA binding proteins, hypoxis-derived treatment for advanced lung cancer, rearrangements of dialkynyazoles, quantitative description of phosphorylation effects on disordered protein structure, mode of action-amaryllidaceae alkaloid lycorine-promising anticancer agent, structure-function of the epithelial sodium channel (ENaC). *Total annual research expenditures:* $495,797. *Unit head:* Dr. Chad Booth, Graduate Advisor, 512-245-8789, Fax: 512-245-2374, E-mail: cb31@txstate.edu. *Application contact:* Dr. Andrea Golato, Dean of Graduate School, 512-245-2581, Fax: 512-245-8365, E-mail: gradcollege@txstate.edu.
Website: http://www.gradcollege.txstate.edu/programs/biochemistry.html

Thomas Jefferson University, Jefferson College of Biomedical Sciences, PhD Program in Biochemistry and Molecular Pharmacology, Philadelphia, PA 19107. Offers PhD. *Faculty:* 57 full-time (12 women). *Students:* 20 full-time (11 women); includes 2 minority (1 Black or African American, non-Hispanic/Latino; 1 Asian, non-Hispanic/Latino), 3 international. In 2017, 7 doctorates awarded. *Degree requirements:* For doctorate, comprehensive exam, thesis/dissertation. *Entrance requirements:* For doctorate, GRE General Test or MCAT, minimum GPA of 3.2. Additional exam requirements/recommendations for international students: Required—TOEFL, IELTS (minimum score 7). *Application deadline:* For fall admission, 12/1 priority date for domestic and international students. Applications are processed on a rolling basis. Application fee: $60. Electronic applications accepted. *Financial support:* In 2017–18, 20 students received support, including 20 fellowships with full tuition reimbursements available (averaging $62,653 per year); Federal Work-Study, institutionally sponsored loans, scholarships/grants, traineeships, health care benefits, and stipends also available. Financial award application deadline: 5/1; financial award applicants required to submit FAFSA. *Faculty research:* Signal transduction and molecular genetics, translational biochemistry, human mitochondrial genetics, molecular biology of protein-RNA interaction, mammalian mitochondrial biogenesis and function. *Unit head:* Dr. Michael J. Root, MD, Program Director, 215-503-4564, Fax: 215-923-2117, E-mail: michael.root@jefferson.edu. *Application contact:* Marc E. Stearns, Senior Associate Director of Admissions, 215-503-0155, Fax: 215-503-3433, E-mail: jgsbs-info@jefferson.edu.
Website: http://www.jefferson.edu/university/biomedical-sciences/degrees-programs/phd-programs/biochemistry-pharmacology.html

Tufts University, Sackler School of Graduate Biomedical Sciences, Cell, Molecular, and Developmental Biology Program, Medford, MA 02155. Offers cancer biology (PhD); developmental and regenerative biology (PhD); molecular and cellular medicine (PhD); structural and chemical biology (PhD). Terminal master's awarded for partial completion of doctoral program. *Degree requirements:* For doctorate, comprehensive exam, thesis/dissertation. *Entrance requirements:* For doctorate, GRE General Test, 3 letters of reference, resume, personal statement. Electronic applications accepted. *Expenses: Tuition:* Full-time $49,892. *Required fees:* $874. Full-time tuition and fees vary according to degree level, program and student level. Part-time tuition and fees vary according to course load. *Faculty research:* Reproduction and hormone action, control of gene expression, cell-matrix and cell-cell interactions, growth control and tumorigenesis, cytoskeleton and contractile proteins.

Tulane University, School of Medicine and School of Liberal Arts, Graduate Programs in Biomedical Sciences, Department of Biochemistry and Molecular Biology, New Orleans, LA 70118-5669. Offers MS. MS and PhD offered through the Graduate School. *Degree requirements:* For master's, thesis. *Entrance requirements:* For master's, GRE General Test, GRE Subject Test, minimum B average in undergraduate course work. Additional exam requirements/recommendations for international students: Required—TOEFL. Electronic applications accepted. *Expenses: Tuition:* Full-time $50,920; part-time $2829 per credit hour. *Required fees:* $2040; $44.50 per credit hour. $580 per term. Tuition and fees vary according to course load, degree level and program. *Faculty research:* Nucleic acid chemistry, complex carbohydrates biochemistry.

Universidad Central del Caribe, School of Medicine, Program in Biomedical Sciences, Bayamón, PR 00960-6032. Offers anatomy and cell biology (MA, MS); biochemistry (MS); biomedical sciences (MA); cellular and molecular biology (PhD); microbiology and immunology (MA, MS); pharmacology (MS); physiology (MS).

Université de Moncton, Faculty of Sciences, Department of Chemistry and Biochemistry, Moncton, NB E1A 3E9, Canada. Offers biochemistry (M Sc); chemistry (M Sc). *Program availability:* Part-time. *Degree requirements:* For master's, one foreign language, thesis. *Entrance requirements:* For master's, minimum GPA of 3.0. Electronic applications accepted. *Faculty research:* Environmental contaminants, natural products synthesis, nutraceutical, organic catalysis, molecular biology of cancer.

Université de Montréal, Faculty of Medicine, Department of Biochemistry, Montréal, QC H3C 3J7, Canada. Offers biochemistry (M Sc, PhD); clinical biochemistry (DEPD). Terminal master's awarded for partial completion of doctoral program. *Degree requirements:* For master's, thesis; for doctorate, thesis/dissertation, general exam. *Entrance requirements:* For master's and doctorate, proficiency in French, knowledge of English; for DEPD, proficiency in French. Electronic applications accepted.

Université de Sherbrooke, Faculty of Medicine and Health Sciences, Graduate Programs in Medicine, Department of Biochemistry, Sherbrooke, QC J1H 5N4, Canada. Offers M Sc, PhD. Terminal master's awarded for partial completion of doctoral program. *Degree requirements:* For master's, thesis; for doctorate, thesis/dissertation. Electronic applications accepted. *Faculty research:* RNA structure-function, chromatin and gene expression, genetic diseases.

Université Laval, Faculty of Medicine, Post-Professional Programs in Medical Studies, Québec, QC G1K 7P4, Canada. Offers anatomy–pathology (DESS); anesthesiology (DESS); cardiology (DESS); care of older people (Diploma); clinical research (DESS); community health (DESS); dermatology (DESS); diagnostic radiology (DESS); emergency medicine (Diploma); family medicine (DESS); general surgery (DESS); geriatrics (DESS); hematology (DESS); internal medicine (DESS); maternal and fetal medicine (Diploma); medical biochemistry (DESS); medical microbiology and infectious diseases (DESS); medical oncology (DESS); nephrology (DESS); neurology (DESS); neurosurgery (DESS); obstetrics and gynecology (DESS); ophthalmology (DESS); orthopedic surgery (DESS); oto-rhino-laryngology (DESS); palliative medicine (Diploma); pediatrics (DESS); plastic surgery (DESS); psychiatry (DESS); pulmonary medicine (DESS); radiology–oncology (DESS); thoracic surgery (DESS); urology (DESS). *Degree requirements:* For other advanced degree, comprehensive exam. *Entrance requirements:* For degree, knowledge of French. Electronic applications accepted.

Université Laval, Faculty of Sciences and Engineering, Department of Biochemistry and Microbiology, Programs in Biochemistry, Québec, QC G1K 7P4, Canada. Offers M Sc, PhD. Terminal master's awarded for partial completion of doctoral program. *Degree requirements:* For master's, thesis; for doctorate, comprehensive exam, thesis/dissertation. *Entrance requirements:* For master's and doctorate, knowledge of French, comprehension of written English. Electronic applications accepted.

University at Buffalo, the State University of New York, Graduate School, Jacobs School of Medicine and Biomedical Sciences, Graduate Programs in Medicine and Biomedical Sciences, Department of Biochemistry, Buffalo, NY 14203. Offers MA, PhD. *Faculty:* 24 full-time (8 women), 1 (woman) part-time/adjunct. *Students:* 28 full-time (12 women); includes 4 minority (1 Black or African American, non-Hispanic/Latino; 1 American Indian or Alaska Native, non-Hispanic/Latino; 2 Hispanic/Latino), 8 international. Average age 25. 10 applicants, 60% accepted, 3 enrolled. In 2017, 2 master's, 6 doctorates awarded. Terminal master's awarded for partial completion of doctoral program. *Degree requirements:* For master's, thesis optional; for doctorate, comprehensive exam, thesis/dissertation. *Entrance requirements:* For master's, GRE General Test; for doctorate, GRE General Test, 3 letters of recommendation. Additional exam requirements/recommendations for international students: Required—TOEFL (minimum score 79 iBT), IELTS. *Application deadline:* For fall admission, 2/1 priority date for domestic and international students. Applications are processed on a rolling basis. Application fee: $85. Electronic applications accepted. *Expenses:* $13,384 resident tuition and fees, $24,724 non-resident tuition and fees. *Financial support:* In 2017–18, 22 students received support, including 1 fellowship with full tuition reimbursement available (averaging $27,000 per year), 21 research assistantships with full tuition reimbursements available (averaging $27,000 per year); scholarships/grants, health care benefits, and unspecified assistantships also available. Financial award application deadline: 2/1; financial award applicants required to submit FAFSA. *Faculty research:* Gene expression, proteins and metalloenzymes, biochemical endocrinology. *Total annual research expenditures:* $3.5 million. *Unit head:* Dr. Mark R. O'Brian, Chair, 716-829-3200, Fax: 716-829-2725, E-mail: mrobrian@buffalo.edu. *Application contact:* Dr. Lee Ann Sinha, Director of Graduate Studies, 716-881-7995, Fax: 716-829-2725, E-mail: leesinha@buffalo.edu.
Website: http://www.smbs.buffalo.edu/bch/

The University of Alabama at Birmingham, Joint Health Sciences, Biochemistry, Structural, and Stem Cell Biology Theme, Birmingham, AL 35294. Offers PhD. *Faculty:* 370. *Students:* 40 full-time (16 women); includes 15 minority (3 Black or African American, non-Hispanic/Latino; 1 American Indian or Alaska Native, non-Hispanic/Latino; 7 Asian, non-Hispanic/Latino; 4 Hispanic/Latino). Average age 26. 30 applicants, 33% accepted, 7 enrolled. In 2017, 5 doctorates awarded. *Degree requirements:* For doctorate, comprehensive exam, thesis/dissertation. *Entrance requirements:* For doctorate, personal statement, resume or curriculum vitae, letters of recommendation, research experience, interview. Additional exam requirements/recommendations for international students: Required—TOEFL (minimum score 80 iBT), IELTS (minimum score 6.5). *Application deadline:* For fall admission, 12/31 for domestic and international students. Applications are processed on a rolling basis. Electronic applications accepted. *Financial support:* In 2017–18, fellowships with full tuition reimbursements (averaging $29,000 per year), research assistantships with full tuition reimbursements (averaging $30,000 per year) were awarded; health care benefits also available. *Unit head:* Dr. Thomas Ryan, Theme Director, 205-996-2175, E-mail: tryan@uab.edu. *Application contact:* Alyssa Zasada, Admissions Manager for Graduate Biomedical Sciences, 205-934-3857, E-mail: grad-gbs@uab.edu.
Website: http://www.uab.edu/gbs/home/themes/bssb

University of Alaska Fairbanks, College of Natural Sciences and Mathematics, Department of Chemistry and Biochemistry, Fairbanks, AK 99775-6160. Offers biochemistry and neuroscience (PhD); chemistry (MA, MS), including chemistry (MS);

environmental chemistry (PhD). *Program availability:* Part-time. *Degree requirements:* For master's, comprehensive exam, thesis (for some programs), oral defense of project or thesis; for doctorate, comprehensive exam, thesis/dissertation, oral defense of dissertation. *Entrance requirements:* For master's, GRE General Test (for MS), bachelor's degree from accredited institution with minimum cumulative undergraduate and major GPA of 3.0; for doctorate, GRE General Test, minimum cumulative GPA of 3.0. Additional exam requirements/recommendations for international students: Required—TOEFL (minimum score 550 paper-based; 79 iBT), TWE. Electronic applications accepted. *Faculty research:* Atmospheric aerosols, cold adaptation, hibernation and neuroprotection, liganogated ion channels, arctic contaminants.

University of Alberta, Faculty of Medicine and Dentistry and Faculty of Graduate Studies and Research, Graduate Programs in Medicine, Department of Biochemistry, Edmonton, AB T6G 2E1, Canada. Offers M Sc, PhD. Terminal master's awarded for partial completion of doctoral program. *Degree requirements:* For master's, thesis; for doctorate, thesis/dissertation. *Entrance requirements:* For master's and doctorate, minimum GPA of 3.3. Additional exam requirements/recommendations for international students: Required—TOEFL (minimum score 550 paper-based). *Faculty research:* Proteins, nucleic acids, membranes, regulation of gene expression, receptors.

The University of Arizona, College of Science, Biochemistry and Molecular and Cellular Biology Program, Tucson, AZ 85721. Offers PhD. *Program availability:* Evening/weekend. *Degree requirements:* For doctorate, thesis/dissertation. *Entrance requirements:* For doctorate, 3 letters of recommendation, statement of purpose. Additional exam requirements/recommendations for international students: Required—TOEFL (minimum score 600 paper-based; 90 iBT), IELTS (minimum score 7). Electronic applications accepted. *Faculty research:* Plant molecular biology, cellular and molecular aspects of development, genetics of bacteria and lower eukaryotes.

The University of Arizona, College of Science, Department of Chemistry and Biochemistry, Tucson, AZ 85721. Offers biochemistry (PhD); chemistry (MA, MS, PhD). *Program availability:* Part-time. *Degree requirements:* For doctorate, comprehensive exam, thesis/dissertation. *Entrance requirements:* For doctorate, GRE General Test, 3 letters of recommendation, statement of purpose. Additional exam requirements/recommendations for international students: Required—TOEFL (minimum score 550 paper-based; 79 iBT). Electronic applications accepted. *Faculty research:* Analytical, inorganic, organic, physical chemistry, biological chemistry.

University of Arkansas for Medical Sciences, Graduate School, Little Rock, AR 72205. Offers biochemistry and molecular biology (MS, PhD); bioinformatics (MS, PhD); cellular physiology and molecular biophysics (MS, PhD); clinical nutrition (MS); interdisciplinary biomedical sciences (MS, PhD, Certificate); interdisciplinary toxicology (MS); microbiology and immunology (PhD); neurobiology and developmental sciences (PhD); pharmacology (PhD); MD/PhD. Bioinformatics programs hosted jointly with the University of Arkansas at Little Rock. *Program availability:* Part-time. Terminal master's awarded for partial completion of doctoral program. *Degree requirements:* For master's, comprehensive exam (for some programs), thesis (for some programs); for doctorate, thesis/dissertation. *Entrance requirements:* For master's and doctorate, GRE. Additional exam requirements/recommendations for international students: Required—TOEFL. Electronic applications accepted. *Expenses:* Contact institution.

The University of British Columbia, Faculty of Medicine, Department of Biochemistry and Molecular Biology, Vancouver, BC V6T 1Z3, Canada. Offers M Sc, PhD. *Degree requirements:* For master's, thesis; for doctorate, comprehensive exam, thesis/dissertation. *Entrance requirements:* For master's, first class B Sc; for doctorate, master's or first class honors bachelor's degree in biochemistry. Additional exam requirements/recommendations for international students: Required—TOEFL (minimum score 625 paper-based). Electronic applications accepted. *Expenses:* Contact institution. *Faculty research:* Membrane biochemistry, protein structure/function, signal transduction, biochemistry.

University of Calgary, Cumming School of Medicine and Faculty of Graduate Studies, Department of Biochemistry and Molecular Biology, Calgary, AB T2N 1N4, Canada. Offers M Sc, PhD. *Degree requirements:* For master's, thesis; for doctorate, thesis/dissertation, candidacy exam. *Entrance requirements:* For master's and doctorate, GRE General Test, minimum GPA of 3.2. Additional exam requirements/recommendations for international students: Required—TOEFL. Electronic applications accepted. *Faculty research:* Molecular and developmental genetics; molecular biology of disease; genomics, proteomics and bioinformatics; cell signaling and structure.

University of California, Berkeley, Graduate Division, Group in Comparative Biochemistry, Berkeley, CA 94720-1500. Offers PhD. *Degree requirements:* For doctorate, thesis/dissertation, qualifying exam. *Entrance requirements:* For doctorate, GRE General Test, GRE Subject Test, minimum GPA of 3.0, 3 letters of recommendation. Additional exam requirements/recommendations for international students: Required—TOEFL. Electronic applications accepted.

University of California, Davis, Graduate Studies, Graduate Group in Biochemistry and Molecular Biology, Davis, CA 95616. Offers MS, PhD. Terminal master's awarded for partial completion of doctoral program. *Degree requirements:* For master's, comprehensive exam (for some programs), thesis (for some programs); for doctorate, thesis/dissertation. *Entrance requirements:* For master's and doctorate, GRE General Test, GRE Subject Test. Additional exam requirements/recommendations for international students: Required—TOEFL (minimum score 550 paper-based). Electronic applications accepted. *Faculty research:* Gene expression, protein structure, molecular virology, protein synthesis, enzymology, membrane transport and structural biology.

University of California, Irvine, Francisco J. Ayala School of Biological Sciences, Department of Molecular Biology and Biochemistry, Irvine, CA 92697. Offers biological science (MS); biological sciences (PhD); biotechnology (MS); biotechnology management (MS); MD/PhD. *Students:* 43 full-time (20 women), 1 part-time (0 women); includes 15 minority (1 Black or African American, non-Hispanic/Latino; 7 Asian, non-Hispanic/Latino; 7 Hispanic/Latino), 4 international. Average age 29. 1 applicant, 100% accepted, 1 enrolled. In 2017, 5 master's, 14 doctorates awarded. *Entrance requirements:* For master's, GRE, minimum GPA of 3.0; for doctorate, GRE General Test, GRE Subject Test, minimum GPA of 3.0. Additional exam requirements/recommendations for international students: Required—TOEFL (minimum score 550 paper-based). *Application deadline:* For fall admission, 12/15 priority date for domestic students, 12/15 for international students. Applications are processed on a rolling basis. Application fee: $105 ($125 for international students). Electronic applications accepted. *Financial support:* Fellowships, research assistantships with full tuition reimbursements, teaching assistantships, institutionally sponsored loans, traineeships, health care benefits, and unspecified assistantships available. Financial award application deadline: 3/1; financial award applicants required to submit FAFSA. *Faculty research:* Structure and synthesis of nucleic acids and proteins, regulation, virology, biochemical genetics, gene organization. *Unit head:* Prof. Christopher Hughes, Chair, 949-824-8771, Fax: 949-824-8551, E-mail: cchughes@uci.edu. *Application contact:* Morgan Oldham, Student Affairs Assistant, 949-826-6034, Fax: 949-824-8551, E-mail: morgano@uci.edu.
Website: http://www.bio.uci.edu/

University of California, Irvine, Francisco J. Ayala School of Biological Sciences and School of Medicine, Interdisciplinary Graduate Program in Cellular and Molecular Biosciences, Irvine, CA 92697. Offers PhD. *Students:* 40 full-time (20 women); includes 19 minority (9 Asian, non-Hispanic/Latino; 6 Hispanic/Latino; 4 Two or more races, non-Hispanic/Latino), 4 international. Average age 25. 371 applicants, 23% accepted, 38 enrolled. *Degree requirements:* For doctorate, thesis/dissertation, teaching assignment, preliminary exam. *Entrance requirements:* For doctorate, GRE General Test, three letters of recommendation, interview. Additional exam requirements/recommendations for international students: Required—TOEFL or IELTS. *Application deadline:* For fall admission, 12/8 for domestic and international students. Application fee: $105 ($125 for international students). Electronic applications accepted. *Expenses:* Contact institution. *Financial support:* Fellowships with full tuition reimbursements, institutionally sponsored loans, scholarships/grants, tuition waivers (full), unspecified assistantships, and stipends available. Financial award application deadline: 1/1; financial award applicants required to submit FAFSA. *Faculty research:* Cellular biochemistry; gene structure and expression; protein structure, function, and design; molecular genetics; pathogenesis and inherited disease. *Unit head:* Melanie Cocco, Director, 949-824-4487, Fax: 949-824-1965, E-mail: mcocco@uci.edu. *Application contact:* Renee Frigo, Administrator, 949-824-8145, Fax: 949-824-1965, E-mail: rfrigo@uci.edu.
Website: http://cmb.uci.edu/

University of California, Irvine, School of Medicine and Francisco J. Ayala School of Biological Sciences, Department of Biological Chemistry, Irvine, CA 92697. Offers biological sciences (MS, PhD). *Students:* 19 full-time (9 women); includes 10 minority (3 Black or African American, non-Hispanic/Latino; 5 Asian, non-Hispanic/Latino; 2 Hispanic/Latino), 3 international. Average age 28. In 2017, 6 doctorates awarded. *Entrance requirements:* For master's, minimum GPA of 3.0; for doctorate, GRE General Test, GRE Subject Test, minimum GPA of 3.0. Additional exam requirements/recommendations for international students: Required—TOEFL (minimum score 550 paper-based). *Application deadline:* For fall admission, 1/15 priority date for domestic students, 1/15 for international students. Application fee: $105 ($125 for international students). Electronic applications accepted. *Financial support:* Fellowships, research assistantships with full tuition reimbursements, teaching assistantships, institutionally sponsored loans, traineeships, health care benefits, and unspecified assistantships available. Financial award application deadline: 3/1; financial award applicants required to submit FAFSA. *Faculty research:* RNA splicing, mammalian chromosomal organization, membrane-hormone interactions, regulation of protein synthesis, molecular genetics of metabolic processes. *Unit head:* Peter Kaiser, Chair/Professor, 949-824-9442, Fax: 949-824-2688, E-mail: pkaiser@uci.edu. *Application contact:* Andrew Komoto, Graduate Coordinator, 949-824-6051, Fax: 949-824-2688, E-mail: akomoto@uci.edu.
Website: http://www.bio.uci.edu/

University of California, Los Angeles, David Geffen School of Medicine and Graduate Division, Graduate Programs in Medicine, Department of Biological Chemistry, Los Angeles, CA 90095. Offers MS, PhD. Terminal master's awarded for partial completion of doctoral program. *Degree requirements:* For master's, comprehensive exam or thesis; for doctorate, thesis/dissertation, oral and written qualifying exams; 2 quarters of teaching experience. *Entrance requirements:* For master's and doctorate, GRE General Test, bachelor's degree; minimum undergraduate GPA of 3.0 (or its equivalent if letter grade system not used). Additional exam requirements/recommendations for international students: Required—TOEFL. Electronic applications accepted.

University of California, Los Angeles, Graduate Division, College of Letters and Science, Department of Chemistry and Biochemistry, Program in Biochemistry and Molecular Biology, Los Angeles, CA 90095. Offers MS, PhD. Terminal master's awarded for partial completion of doctoral program. *Degree requirements:* For master's, comprehensive exam or thesis; for doctorate, thesis/dissertation, oral and written qualifying exams; 3 quarters of teaching experience. *Entrance requirements:* For doctorate, GRE General Test, GRE Subject Test (recommended), bachelor's degree; minimum undergraduate GPA of 3.0 (or its equivalent if letter grade system not used). Additional exam requirements/recommendations for international students: Required—TOEFL. Electronic applications accepted.

University of California, Los Angeles, Graduate Division, College of Letters and Science and David Geffen School of Medicine, UCLA ACCESS to Programs in the Molecular, Cellular and Integrative Life Sciences, Los Angeles, CA 90095. Offers biochemistry and molecular biology (PhD); biological chemistry (PhD); cellular and molecular pathology (PhD); human genetics (PhD); microbiology, immunology, and molecular genetics (PhD); molecular biology (PhD); molecular toxicology (PhD); molecular, cellular and integrative physiology (PhD); neurobiology (PhD); oral biology (PhD); physiology (PhD). *Degree requirements:* For doctorate, thesis/dissertation, oral and written qualifying exams. *Entrance requirements:* For doctorate, GRE General Test, bachelor's degree; minimum undergraduate GPA of 3.0 (or its equivalent if letter grade system not used). Additional exam requirements/recommendations for international students: Required—TOEFL. Electronic applications accepted.

University of California, Merced, Graduate Division, School of Natural Sciences, Merced, CA 95343. Offers applied mathematics (MS, PhD); chemistry and chemical biology (MS, PhD); physics (MS, PhD); quantitative and systems biology (MS, PhD). *Faculty:* 71 full-time (27 women). *Students:* 208 full-time (75 women); includes 71 minority (5 Black or African American, non-Hispanic/Latino; 24 Asian, non-Hispanic/Latino; 33 Hispanic/Latino; 1 Native Hawaiian or other Pacific Islander, non-Hispanic/Latino; 8 Two or more races, non-Hispanic/Latino), 52 international. Average age 28. 293 applicants, 45% accepted, 51 enrolled. In 2017, 9 master's, 18 doctorates awarded. Terminal master's awarded for partial completion of doctoral program. *Degree requirements:* For master's, variable foreign language requirement, comprehensive exam, thesis or alternative; for doctorate, variable foreign language requirement, comprehensive exam, thesis/dissertation. *Entrance requirements:* For master's and doctorate, GRE. Additional exam requirements/recommendations for international students: Required—TOEFL (minimum score 550 paper-based; 80 iBT); Recommended—IELTS (minimum score 7). *Application deadline:* For fall admission, 1/15 for domestic and international students. Application fee: $90 ($110 for international students). Electronic applications accepted. *Expenses:* Tuition, state resident: full-time $11,502; part-time $5751 per semester. Tuition, nonresident: full-time $26,604; part-time $13,302 per semester. *Required fees:* $564 per semester. *Financial support:* In 2017–18, 170 students received support, including 19 fellowships with full tuition reimbursements available (averaging $23,832 per year), 32 research assistantships with full tuition reimbursements available (averaging $16,429 per year), 148 teaching assistantships with full tuition reimbursements available (averaging $16,038 per year); scholarships/grants, traineeships, and health care benefits also available. Financial award application deadline: 1/15. *Faculty research:* Computational science, soft matter physics, applied math, environmental and biological systems, biological and materials chemistry. *Total annual research expenditures:* $4.2 million. *Unit head:* Dr. Elizabeth Dumont, Dean, 209-228-4487, Fax: 209-228-4060, E-mail: edumont@ucmerced.edu. *Application contact:* Tsu Ya, Director of Graduate Admissions and Academic Services, 209-228-4521, Fax: 209-228-6906, E-mail: tya@ucmerced.edu.

Biochemistry

University of California, Riverside, Graduate Division, Department of Biochemistry and Molecular Biology, Riverside, CA 92521-0102. Offers MS, PhD. *Program availability:* Part-time. *Faculty:* 51 full-time (16 women). Terminal master's awarded for partial completion of doctoral program. *Degree requirements:* For master's, comprehensive exam (for some programs), thesis (for some programs), comprehensive exam or thesis; for doctorate, comprehensive exam, thesis/dissertation, 2 quarters of teaching experience, written exam, oral qualifying exam. *Entrance requirements:* For master's, GRE General Test, minimum GPA of 3.0; for doctorate, GRE General Test, minimum GPA of 3.25. Additional exam requirements/recommendations for international students: Required—TOEFL (minimum score 550 paper-based, 80 iBT) or IELTS. *Application deadline:* For fall admission, 1/5 priority date for domestic and international students; for winter admission, 11/15 for domestic students, 9/1 for international students; for spring admission, 3/1 for domestic students, 12/1 for international students. Application fee: $80 ($100 for international students). Electronic applications accepted. *Expenses:* Tuition, state resident: full-time $5746. Tuition, nonresident: full-time $10,780. Tuition and fees vary according to campus/location and program. *Financial support:* Fellowships with full tuition reimbursements, research assistantships with full tuition reimbursements, teaching assistantships with full tuition reimbursements, career-related internships or fieldwork, institutionally sponsored loans, scholarships/grants, health care benefits, and unspecified assistantships available. Financial award application deadline: 1/5; financial award applicants required to submit FAFSA. *Faculty research:* Structural biology and molecular biophysics, signal transduction, plant biochemistry and molecular biology, gene expression and metabolic regulation, molecular toxicology and pathogenesis. *Application contact:* Julio Sosa, E-mail: biochem@ucr.edu.
Website: http://www.biochemistry.ucr.edu/

University of California, San Diego, Graduate Division, Department of Chemistry and Biochemistry, La Jolla, CA 92093. Offers chemistry (MS, PhD). PhD offered jointly with San Diego State University. *Students:* 281 full-time (107 women), 2 part-time (1 woman). 673 applicants, 35% accepted, 78 enrolled. In 2017, 58 master's, 38 doctorates awarded. *Degree requirements:* For master's, comprehensive exam (for some programs), thesis (for some programs); for doctorate, comprehensive exam, thesis/dissertation. *Entrance requirements:* For master's, GRE General Test, MS Thesis Agreement Form, letters of recommendation, statement of purpose; for doctorate, GRE General Test, GRE Subject Test, letters of recommendation, statement of purpose. Additional exam requirements/recommendations for international students: Required—TOEFL (minimum score 550 paper-based; 80 iBT), IELTS (minimum score 7), PTE (minimum score 65). *Application deadline:* For fall admission, 3/17 for domestic students. Application fee: $105 ($125 for international students). Electronic applications accepted. *Financial support:* Fellowships, research assistantships, teaching assistantships, scholarships/grants, and traineeships available. Financial award applicants required to submit FAFSA. *Faculty research:* Analytical and atmospheric chemistry, biochemistry and biophysics, cellular and systems biochemistry, chemical biology, inorganic chemistry, organic chemistry, physical chemistry, quantitative biology, structural biology, theoretical and computational chemistry. *Unit head:* Edward Dennis, Chair, 858-534-3055, E-mail: edennis@ucsd.edu. *Application contact:* Jeff Rances, Admissions Coordinator, 858-534-9728, Fax: 858-534-7687, E-mail: chemgradinfo@ucsd.edu.
Website: http://chemistry.ucsd.edu

University of California, San Francisco, Graduate Division and School of Medicine, Tetrad Graduate Program, Biochemistry and Molecular Biology Track, San Francisco, CA 94143. Offers PhD, MD/PhD. *Degree requirements:* For doctorate, thesis/dissertation. *Entrance requirements:* For doctorate, GRE General Test, GRE Subject Test. Additional exam requirements/recommendations for international students: Required—TOEFL. *Expenses:* Contact institution. *Faculty research:* Structural biology, genetics, cell biology, cell physiology, metabolism.

University of California, San Francisco, School of Pharmacy and Graduate Division, Chemistry and Chemical Biology Graduate Program, San Francisco, CA 94143. Offers PhD. *Degree requirements:* For doctorate, thesis/dissertation. *Entrance requirements:* For doctorate, GRE General Test, minimum GPA of 3.0, bachelor's degree. Additional exam requirements/recommendations for international students: Required—TOEFL (minimum score 550 paper-based; 80 iBT). Electronic applications accepted. *Faculty research:* Macromolecular structure function and dynamics, computational chemistry and biology, biological chemistry and synthetic biology, chemical biology and molecular design, nanomolecular design.

University of California, Santa Barbara, Graduate Division, College of Letters and Sciences, Division of Mathematics, Life, and Physical Sciences, Interdepartmental Graduate Program in Biomolecular Science and Engineering, Santa Barbara, CA 93106-2014. Offers biochemistry and molecular biology (PhD), including biochemistry and molecular biology, biophysics and bioengineering. Terminal master's awarded for partial completion of doctoral program. *Degree requirements:* For doctorate, thesis/dissertation. *Entrance requirements:* For doctorate, GRE General Test. Additional exam requirements/recommendations for international students: Required—TOEFL (minimum score 630 paper-based; 109 iBT), IELTS (minimum score 7). Electronic applications accepted. *Faculty research:* Biochemistry and molecular biology, biophysics, biomaterials, bioengineering, systems biology.

University of California, Santa Cruz, Division of Graduate Studies, Division of Physical and Biological Sciences, Department of Chemistry and Biochemistry, Santa Cruz, CA 95064. Offers MS, PhD. *Degree requirements:* For master's, thesis optional; for doctorate, one foreign language, thesis/dissertation, qualifying exam. *Entrance requirements:* For master's and doctorate, GRE General Test, GRE Subject Test. Additional exam requirements/recommendations for international students: Required—TOEFL (minimum score 570 paper-based; 89 iBT); Recommended—IELTS (minimum score 8). Electronic applications accepted. *Faculty research:* Marine chemistry; biochemistry; inorganic, organic, and physical chemistry.

University of Cincinnati, Graduate School, College of Medicine, Graduate Programs in Biomedical Sciences, Department of Molecular Genetics, Biochemistry and Microbiology, Cincinnati, OH 45221. Offers MS, PhD. Terminal master's awarded for partial completion of doctoral program. *Degree requirements:* For master's, thesis or alternative; for doctorate, thesis/dissertation, qualifying exam. *Entrance requirements:* For master's and doctorate, GRE General Test. Additional exam requirements/recommendations for international students: Required—TOEFL (minimum score 600 paper-based; 100 iBT), TWE. Electronic applications accepted. *Expenses: Tuition, area resident:* Full-time $14,468. Tuition, state resident: full-time $14,968; part-time $754 per credit hour. Tuition, nonresident: full-time $24,210; part-time $1311 per credit hour. *International tuition:* $26,460 full-time. *Required fees:* $3958; $84 per credit hour. One-time fee: $85 full-time. Tuition and fees vary according to course load, degree level and program. *Faculty research:* Cancer biology and developmental genetics, gene regulation and chromosome structure, microbiology and pathogenic mechanisms, structural biology, membrane biochemistry and signal transduction.

University of Cincinnati, Graduate School, McMicken College of Arts and Sciences, Department of Chemistry, Cincinnati, OH 45221. Offers analytical chemistry (MS, PhD); biochemistry (MS, PhD); inorganic chemistry (MS, PhD); organic chemistry (MS, PhD); physical chemistry (MS, PhD); polymer chemistry (MS, PhD); sensors (PhD). *Program availability:* Part-time, evening/weekend. Terminal master's awarded for partial completion of doctoral program. *Degree requirements:* For master's, thesis optional; for doctorate, comprehensive exam, thesis/dissertation. *Entrance requirements:* For master's and doctorate, GRE General Test. Additional exam requirements/recommendations for international students: Required—TOEFL (minimum score 580 paper-based). Electronic applications accepted. *Expenses: Tuition, area resident:* Full-time $14,468. Tuition, state resident: full-time $14,968; part-time $754 per credit hour. Tuition, nonresident: full-time $24,210; part-time $1311 per credit hour. *International tuition:* $26,460 full-time. *Required fees:* $3958; $84 per credit hour. One-time fee: $85 full-time. Tuition and fees vary according to course load, degree level and program. *Faculty research:* Biomedical chemistry, laser chemistry, surface science, chemical sensors, synthesis.

University of Colorado Boulder, Graduate School, College of Arts and Sciences, Department of Chemistry and Biochemistry, Boulder, CO 80309. Offers MS, PhD. *Faculty:* 49 full-time (12 women). *Students:* 230 full-time (85 women), 1 part-time (0 women); includes 56 minority (15 Black or African American, non-Hispanic/Latino; 12 Asian, non-Hispanic/Latino; 21 Hispanic/Latino; 8 Two or more races, non-Hispanic/Latino), 41 international. Average age 26. 602 applicants, 24% accepted, 43 enrolled. In 2017, 5 master's, 22 doctorates awarded. Terminal master's awarded for partial completion of doctoral program. *Degree requirements:* For master's, comprehensive exam or thesis; for doctorate, comprehensive exam, thesis/dissertation, cumulative exam. *Entrance requirements:* For master's, GRE General Test, GRE Subject Test, minimum undergraduate GPA of 2.75; for doctorate, GRE General Test, GRE Subject Test, minimum GPA of 3.0. *Application deadline:* For fall admission, 1/10 for domestic students; for spring admission, 12/15 for domestic students. Applications are processed on a rolling basis. Application fee: $60 ($80 for international students). Electronic applications accepted. Application fee is waived when completed online. *Financial support:* In 2017–18, 600 students received support, including 103 fellowships (averaging $12,229 per year), 122 research assistantships with full and partial tuition reimbursements available (averaging $35,439 per year), 97 teaching assistantships with full and partial tuition reimbursements available (averaging $24,684 per year); institutionally sponsored loans, scholarships/grants, health care benefits, and unspecified assistantships also available. Financial award application deadline: 2/15; financial award applicants required to submit FAFSA. *Faculty research:* Physical chemistry; biochemistry; biochemistry: proteins; catalysis/kinetics; analytical chemistry. *Total annual research expenditures:* $21.6 million. *Application contact:* E-mail: chemgrad@colorado.edu.
Website: http://chem.colorado.edu

University of Colorado Denver, School of Medicine, Biochemistry Program, Aurora, CO 80045. Offers biochemistry (PhD); biochemistry and molecular genetics (PhD). *Students:* 20 applicants, 25% accepted, 4 enrolled. In 2017, 2 doctorates awarded. *Degree requirements:* For doctorate, comprehensive exam, thesis/dissertation, 30 credit hours each of coursework and thesis research. *Entrance requirements:* For doctorate, GRE, minimum of three letters of recommendation from qualified referees. Additional exam requirements/recommendations for international students: Required—TOEFL (minimum score 550 paper-based; 80 iBT). *Application deadline:* For fall admission, 12/1 for domestic students. Applications are processed on a rolling basis. Application fee: $50 ($75 for international students). Electronic applications accepted. *Faculty research:* DNA damage, cancer and neurodegeneration, molecular mechanisms of pro-MRNA splicing, yeast RNA polymerases, DNA replication. *Unit head:* Dr. Mark Johnston, Professor and Chair, 303-724-3203, Fax: 303-724-3215, E-mail: mark.johnston@ucdenver.edu. *Application contact:* Sue Brozowski, Department Contact, 303-724-3202, Fax: 303-724-3215, E-mail: sue.brozowski@ucdenver.edu.
Website: http://www.ucdenver.edu/academics/colleges/medicalschool/departments/biochemistry/Pages/Home.aspx

University of Connecticut Health Center, Graduate School, Programs in Biomedical Sciences, Graduate Program in Molecular Biology and Biochemistry, Farmington, CT 06030. Offers PhD, DMD/PhD, MD/PhD. *Degree requirements:* For doctorate, comprehensive exam, thesis/dissertation. *Entrance requirements:* For doctorate, GRE General Test. Additional exam requirements/recommendations for international students: Required—TOEFL (minimum score 600 paper-based). Electronic applications accepted. *Faculty research:* Molecular biology, structural biology, protein biochemistry, microbial physiology and pathogenesis.

University of Dayton, Department of Chemistry and Biochemistry, Dayton, OH 45469. Offers MS. *Program availability:* Part-time. *Faculty:* 11 full-time (2 women). *Students:* 5 full-time (4 women), 1 international. Average age 25. 56 applicants, 14% accepted. In 2017, 3 master's awarded. *Degree requirements:* For master's, thesis, 30 credit hours. *Entrance requirements:* For master's, BS in chemistry or closely-related discipline. Additional exam requirements/recommendations for international students: Required—TOEFL (minimum score 550 paper-based; 80 iBT), GRE; Recommended—IELTS. *Application deadline:* For fall admission, 5/15 priority date for domestic and international students; for winter admission, 7/1 priority date for international students; for spring admission, 11/1 priority date for international students. Application fee: $0 ($50 for international students). Electronic applications accepted. Tuition and fees vary according to degree level and program. *Financial support:* In 2017–18, 4 teaching assistantships with full tuition reimbursements (averaging $13,600 per year) were awarded; fellowships, research assistantships, and institutionally sponsored loans also available. Financial award application deadline: 5/15; financial award applicants required to submit FAFSA. *Faculty research:* DNA reactive metals, antibiotic efflux inhibitors, flame retardants, medicinal chiral phosphates, supramolecular chemistry. *Total annual research expenditures:* $225,000. *Unit head:* Dr. David Johnson, Chair, 937-229-2631, E-mail: djohnson1@udayton.edu. *Application contact:* Dr. Kevin Church, Graduate Program Director, 937-229-2659, E-mail: kchurch1@udayton.edu.
Website: https://www.udayton.edu/artssciences/academics/chemistry/welcome/index.php

University of Delaware, College of Arts and Sciences, Department of Chemistry and Biochemistry, Newark, DE 19716. Offers biochemistry (MA, MS, PhD); chemistry (MA, MS, PhD). *Program availability:* Part-time. Terminal master's awarded for partial completion of doctoral program. *Degree requirements:* For master's, one foreign language, thesis (for some programs); for doctorate, one foreign language, thesis/dissertation, cumulative exam. *Entrance requirements:* For master's and doctorate, GRE General Test. Additional exam requirements/recommendations for international students: Required—TOEFL (minimum score 600 paper-based). Electronic applications accepted. *Faculty research:* Micro-organisms, bone, cancer metastosis, developmental biology, cell biology, molecular biology.

University of Florida, College of Medicine and Graduate School, Interdisciplinary Program in Biomedical Sciences, Concentration in Biochemistry and Molecular Biology, Gainesville, FL 32611. Offers PhD. *Degree requirements:* For doctorate, thesis/dissertation. *Entrance requirements:* For doctorate, GRE General Test, minimum GPA of 3.0, biochemistry before enrollment. Additional exam requirements/recommendations for international students: Required—TOEFL. Electronic applications accepted. *Faculty research:* Gene expression, metabolic regulation, structural biology, enzyme mechanism, membrane transporters.

University of Georgia, Franklin College of Arts and Sciences, Department of Biochemistry and Molecular Biology, Athens, GA 30602. Offers MS, PhD. *Degree requirements:* For master's, one foreign language, thesis; for doctorate, one foreign language, thesis/dissertation. *Entrance requirements:* For master's and doctorate, GRE General Test. Additional exam requirements/recommendations for international students: Required—TOEFL. Electronic applications accepted.

University of Guelph, Graduate Studies, College of Biological Science, Department of Molecular and Cellular Biology, Guelph, ON N1G 2W1, Canada. Offers biochemistry (M Sc, PhD); biophysics (M Sc, PhD); botany (M Sc, PhD); microbiology (M Sc, PhD); molecular biology and genetics (M Sc, PhD). *Degree requirements:* For master's, thesis, research proposal; for doctorate, comprehensive exam, thesis/dissertation, research proposal. *Entrance requirements:* For master's, minimum B-average during previous 2 years of coursework; for doctorate, minimum A-average. Additional exam requirements/recommendations for international students: Required—TOEFL (minimum score 550 paper-based), IELTS (minimum score 6.5). Electronic applications accepted. *Faculty research:* Physiology, structure, genetics, and ecology of microbes; virology and microbial technology.

University of Guelph, Graduate Studies, College of Physical and Engineering Science, Guelph-Waterloo Centre for Graduate Work in Chemistry and Biochemistry, Guelph, ON N1G 2W1, Canada. Offers M Sc, PhD. M Sc, PhD offered jointly with University of Waterloo. *Program availability:* Part-time. *Degree requirements:* For master's, thesis; for doctorate, thesis/dissertation. *Faculty research:* Inorganic, analytical, biological, physical/theoretical, polymer, and organic chemistry.

University of Houston, College of Natural Sciences and Mathematics, Department of Biology and Biochemistry, Houston, TX 77204. Offers biochemistry (MA, PhD); biology (MA). Terminal master's awarded for partial completion of doctoral program. *Degree requirements:* For master's, comprehensive exam (for some programs), thesis optional; for doctorate, comprehensive exam (for some programs), thesis/dissertation. *Entrance requirements:* For master's and doctorate, GRE. Additional exam requirements/recommendations for international students: Required—TOEFL (minimum score 550 paper-based; 79 iBT), IELTS (minimum score 6.5). Electronic applications accepted. *Faculty research:* Cell and molecular biology, ecology and evolution, biochemical and biophysical sciences, chemical biology.

University of Idaho, College of Graduate Studies, College of Science, Department of Biological Sciences, Moscow, ID 83844. Offers biology (MS, PhD); microbiology, molecular biology and biochemistry (PhD). *Faculty:* 19 full-time (6 women). *Students:* 22. Average age 28. In 2017, 2 master's, 6 doctorates awarded. *Degree requirements:* For doctorate, thesis/dissertation. *Entrance requirements:* For master's and doctorate, GRE, minimum GPA of 3.0. Additional exam requirements/recommendations for international students: Required—TOEFL (minimum score 79 iBT). *Application deadline:* For fall admission, 8/1 for domestic students; for spring admission, 12/15 for domestic students. Applications are processed on a rolling basis. Application fee: $60. Electronic applications accepted. *Expenses:* Tuition, state resident: full-time $6722; part-time $430 per credit hour. Tuition, nonresident: full-time $23,046; part-time $1337 per credit hour. *Required fees:* $2142; $63 per credit hour. *Financial support:* Research assistantships and teaching assistantships available. Financial award applicants required to submit FAFSA. *Faculty research:* Animal behavior development, germ cell development, intraflagellar transport, molecular mechanisms, molecular chaperones. *Unit head:* Dr. James J. Nagler, Chair, 208-885-6280, E-mail: biosci@uidaho.edu. *Application contact:* Sean Scoggin, Graduate Recruitment Coordinator, 208-885-4723, Fax: 208-885-4406, E-mail: graduateadmissions@uidaho.edu.
Website: https://www.uidaho.edu/sci/biology

University of Illinois at Chicago, College of Medicine and Graduate College, Graduate Programs in Medicine, Department of Biochemistry and Molecular Genetics, Chicago, IL 60607-7128. Offers PhD, MD/PhD. Terminal master's awarded for partial completion of doctoral program. *Degree requirements:* For doctorate, thesis/dissertation. *Entrance requirements:* For doctorate, GRE General Test. Additional exam requirements/recommendations for international students: Required—TOEFL. Electronic applications accepted. *Faculty research:* Signal transduction, cell cycle regulation, membrane biology, regulation of gene function and development, protein and nucleic acid structure and function, cancer biology.

University of Illinois at Urbana–Champaign, Graduate College, College of Liberal Arts and Sciences, School of Chemical Sciences, Champaign, IL 61820. Offers MA, MS, PhD, MS/JD, MS/MBA. *Expenses:* Contact institution.

University of Illinois at Urbana–Champaign, Graduate College, College of Liberal Arts and Sciences, School of Molecular and Cellular Biology, Department of Biochemistry, Champaign, IL 61820. Offers MS, PhD.

The University of Iowa, Roy J. and Lucille A. Carver College of Medicine and Graduate College, Graduate Programs in Medicine, Department of Biochemistry, Iowa City, IA 52242. Offers MS, PhD, MD/PhD. Terminal master's awarded for partial completion of doctoral program. *Degree requirements:* For master's, thesis; for doctorate, comprehensive exam, thesis/dissertation. *Entrance requirements:* For master's, GRE General Test. Additional exam requirements/recommendations for international students: Required—TOEFL (minimum score 600 paper-based; 100 iBT). Electronic applications accepted. *Faculty research:* Regulation of gene expression, protein structure, membrane structure/function, DNA structure and replication.

The University of Kansas, Graduate Studies, College of Liberal Arts and Sciences, Department of Molecular Biosciences, Lawrence, KS 66044. Offers biochemistry and biophysics (PhD); microbiology (PhD); molecular, cellular, and developmental biology (PhD). *Program availability:* Part-time. *Students:* 57 full-time (38 women); includes 8 minority (1 Black or African American, non-Hispanic/Latino; 2 Asian, non-Hispanic/Latino; 3 Hispanic/Latino; 2 Two or more races, non-Hispanic/Latino), 27 international. Average age 27. 73 applicants, 33% accepted, 8 enrolled. In 2017, 6 doctorates awarded. Terminal master's awarded for partial completion of doctoral program. *Entrance requirements:* For doctorate, GRE General Test, 1-page statement of research interests and goals, 1-2 page curriculum vitae or resume, official transcript, 3 recommendation letters. Additional exam requirements/recommendations for international students: Required—TOEFL or IELTS. *Application deadline:* For fall admission, 12/1 for domestic and international students. Application fee: $65 ($85 for international students). Electronic applications accepted. *Financial support:* Fellowships, research assistantships, teaching assistantships, scholarships/grants, health care benefits, and unspecified assistantships available. Financial award application deadline: 12/1. *Faculty research:* Structure and function of proteins, genetics of organism development, molecular genetics, neurophysiology, molecular virology and pathogenics, developmental biology, cell biology. *Unit head:* Susan M. Egan, Chair, 785-864-4294, E-mail: sme@ku.edu. *Application contact:* John Connolly, Graduate Admissions Contact, 785-864-4311, E-mail: jconnolly@ku.edu.
Website: http://www.molecularbiosciences.ku.edu/

The University of Kansas, University of Kansas Medical Center, School of Medicine, Department of Biochemistry and Molecular Biology, Kansas City, KS 66160. Offers PhD, MD/PhD. *Faculty:* 19. *Students:* 11 full-time (5 women); includes 1 minority (Black or African American, non-Hispanic/Latino), 1 international. Average age 28. In 2017, 2 doctorates awarded. Terminal master's awarded for partial completion of doctoral program. *Degree requirements:* For doctorate, thesis/dissertation, comprehensive oral and written exam. *Entrance requirements:* For doctorate, GRE. Additional exam requirements/recommendations for international students: Required—TOEFL. *Application deadline:* For fall admission, 12/1 for domestic and international students. Applications are processed on a rolling basis. Application fee: $60. Electronic applications accepted. Application fee is waived when completed online. *Financial support:* In 2017–18, 3 research assistantships with partial tuition reimbursements, 4 teaching assistantships with partial tuition reimbursements were awarded; fellowships, traineeships, health care benefits, and unspecified assistantships also available. Financial award application deadline: 3/1; financial award applicants required to submit FAFSA. *Faculty research:* Determination of protein structure, underlying bases for interaction of proteins with their target, mapping allosteric circuiting within proteins, mechanism of action of transcription factors, renal signal transduction. *Total annual research expenditures:* $2.5 million. *Unit head:* Dr. Gerald M. Carlson, Chairman, 913-588-7005, Fax: 913-588-9896, E-mail: gcarlson@kumc.edu. *Application contact:* Dr. Liskin Swint-Kruse, Professor, 913-588-0399, Fax: 913-588-9896, E-mail: lswint-kruse@kumc.edu.
Website: http://www.kumc.edu/school-of-medicine/biochemistry-and-molecular-biology.html

University of Kentucky, Graduate School, Graduate School Programs from the College of Medicine, Program in Molecular and Cellular Biochemistry, Lexington, KY 40506-0032. Offers PhD, MD/PhD. *Degree requirements:* For doctorate, comprehensive exam, thesis/dissertation. *Entrance requirements:* For doctorate, GRE General Test, minimum undergraduate GPA of 2.75. Additional exam requirements/recommendations for international students: Required—TOEFL (minimum score 550 paper-based). Electronic applications accepted.

University of Lethbridge, School of Graduate Studies, Lethbridge, AB T1K 3M4, Canada. Offers addictions counseling (M Sc); agricultural biotechnology (M Sc); agricultural studies (M Sc, MA); anthropology (MA); archaeology (M Sc, MA); art (MA, MFA); biochemistry (M Sc); biological sciences (M Sc); biomolecular science (PhD); biosystems and biodiversity (PhD); Canadian studies (MA); chemistry (M Sc); computer science (M Sc); computer science and geographical information science (M Sc); counseling (MC); counseling psychology (M Ed); dramatic arts (MA); earth, space, and physical science (PhD); economics (MA); education (MA, PhD); educational leadership (M Ed); English (MA); environmental science (M Sc); evolution and behavior (PhD); exercise science (M Sc); French (MA); French/German (MA); French/Spanish (MA); general education (M Ed); geography (M Sc, MA); German (MA); health sciences (M Sc); individualized multidisciplinary (M Sc, MA); kinesiology (M Sc, MA); management (M Sc), including accounting, finance, human resource management and labor relations, information systems, international management, marketing, policy and strategy; mathematics (M Sc); music (M Mus, MA); Native American studies (MA); neuroscience (M Sc, PhD); new media (MA, MFA); nursing (M Sc, MN); philosophy (MA); physics (M Sc); political science (MA); psychology (M Sc, MA); religious studies (MA); sociology (MA); theatre and dramatic arts (MFA); theoretical and computational science (PhD); urban and regional studies (MA); women and gender studies (MA). *Program availability:* Part-time, evening/weekend. *Degree requirements:* For master's, thesis (for some programs); for doctorate, comprehensive exam, thesis/dissertation. *Entrance requirements:* For master's, GMAT (for M Sc in management), bachelor's degree in related field, minimum GPA of 3.0 during previous 20 graded semester courses, 2 years' teaching or related experience (M Ed); for doctorate, master's degree, minimum graduate GPA of 3.5. Additional exam requirements/recommendations for international students: Required—TOEFL (minimum score 580 paper-based; 93 iBT). Electronic applications accepted. *Faculty research:* Movement and brain plasticity, gibberellin physiology, photosynthesis, carbon cycling, molecular properties of main-group ring components.

University of Louisville, Graduate School, College of Arts and Sciences, Department of Chemistry, Louisville, KY 40292-0001. Offers analytical chemistry (MS, PhD); biochemistry (MS, PhD); chemical physics (PhD); inorganic chemistry (MS, PhD); organic chemistry (MS, PhD); physical chemistry (MS, PhD). *Faculty:* 25 full-time (9 women), 3 part-time/adjunct (2 women). *Students:* 28 full-time (12 women), 25 part-time (6 women); includes 6 minority (2 Black or African American, non-Hispanic/Latino; 2 Asian, non-Hispanic/Latino; 1 Hispanic/Latino; 1 Two or more races, non-Hispanic/Latino), 35 international. Average age 31. 57 applicants, 28% accepted, 12 enrolled. In 2017, 1 master's, 1 doctorate awarded. Terminal master's awarded for partial completion of doctoral program. *Degree requirements:* For master's, thesis (for some programs), literature seminar; for doctorate, thesis/dissertation (for some programs), literature seminar, cumulative exams, research proposal. *Entrance requirements:* For master's and doctorate, GRE General Test, official transcripts, recommendation letters (minimum of 2), personal statement. Additional exam requirements/recommendations for international students: Required—TOEFL (minimum score 550 paper-based; 79 iBT); Recommended—IELTS (minimum score 6.5). *Application deadline:* For fall admission, 1/15 priority date for domestic and international students; for spring admission, 9/15 priority date for domestic and international students. Application fee: $65. Electronic applications accepted. *Expenses:* Tuition, state resident: full-time $12,246; part-time $681 per credit hour. Tuition, nonresident: full-time $25,486; part-time $1417 per credit hour. *Required fees:* $196. Tuition and fees vary according to course load, program and reciprocity agreements. *Financial support:* In 2017–18, 2 fellowships with full tuition reimbursements (averaging $23,000 per year), 10 research assistantships with full tuition reimbursements (averaging $23,000 per year), 39 teaching assistantships with full tuition reimbursements (averaging $23,000 per year) were awarded; scholarships/grants, health care benefits, and unspecified assistantships also available. Financial award application deadline: 1/15. *Faculty research:* Solid state chemistry, chemical synthesis, nanoparticle research, green chemistry, spectroscopic studies, computational chemistry, catalysis. *Total annual research expenditures:* $1.4 million. *Unit head:* Dr. Craig Grapperhaus, Professor, 502-852-8148, Fax: 502-852-8149, E-mail: craig.grapperhaus@louisville.edu. *Application contact:* Sherry Nalley, Graduate Program Assistant, 502-852-6798, Fax: 502-852-6536, E-mail: sherry.nalley@louisville.edu.
Website: http://louisville.edu/chemistry

University of Louisville, School of Medicine, Department of Biochemistry and Molecular Genetics, Louisville, KY 40292-0001. Offers MS, PhD, MD/PhD. *Faculty:* 12 full-time (3 women), 2 part-time/adjunct (1 woman). *Students:* 21 full-time (11 women), 5 part-time (2 women); includes 2 minority (1 Asian, non-Hispanic/Latino; 1 Hispanic/Latino), 5 international. Average age 28. 27 applicants, 26% accepted, 7 enrolled. In 2017, 1 master's, 1 doctorate awarded. Terminal master's awarded for partial completion of doctoral program. *Degree requirements:* For master's, thesis (for some programs); for doctorate, comprehensive exam, thesis/dissertation. *Entrance requirements:* For master's and doctorate, GRE General Test (minimum score of 1000 verbal and quantitative), minimum GPA of 3.0. Additional exam requirements/recommendations for international students: Required—TOEFL, IELTS. *Application deadline:* For fall admission, 12/15 priority date for domestic and international students. Applications are processed on a rolling basis. Application fee: $65. Electronic applications accepted. *Expenses:* Tuition, state resident: full-time $12,246; part-time

$681 per credit hour. Tuition, nonresident: full-time $25,486; part-time $1417 per credit hour. *Required fees:* $196. Tuition and fees vary according to course load, program and reciprocity agreements. *Financial support:* In 2017–18, 5 fellowships with full tuition reimbursements (averaging $25,000 per year) were awarded; health care benefits also available. Financial award application deadline: 1/15. *Faculty research:* Genetics, metabolism in cancer biology and diabetes, lipid molecular signaling, protein trafficking, bioinformatics. *Total annual research expenditures:* $2.1 million. *Unit head:* Dr. Ronald Gregg, Professor and Department Chair, 502-852-5217, Fax: 502-852-4112, E-mail: rggreg02@louisville.edu. *Application contact:* Dr. Brian Clem, Assistant Professor, E-mail: bmggrad@louisville.edu.

The University of Manchester, School of Biological Sciences, Manchester, United Kingdom. Offers adaptive organismal biology (M Phil, PhD); animal biology (M Phil, PhD); biochemistry (M Phil, PhD); bioinformatics (M Phil, PhD); biomolecular sciences (M Phil, PhD); biotechnology (M Phil, PhD); cell biology (M Phil, PhD); cell matrix research (M Phil, PhD); channels and transporters (M Phil, PhD); developmental biology (M Phil, PhD); environmental biology (M Phil, PhD); evolutionary biology (M Phil, PhD); gene expression (M Phil, PhD); genetics (M Phil, PhD); history of science, technology and medicine (M Phil, PhD); immunology (M Phil, PhD); integrative neurobiology and behavior (M Phil, PhD); membrane trafficking (M Phil, PhD); microbiology (M Phil, PhD); molecular and cellular neuroscience (M Phil, PhD); molecular biology (M Phil, PhD); molecular cancer studies (M Phil, PhD); neuroscience (M Phil, PhD); ophthalmology (M Phil, PhD); optometry (M Phil, PhD); organelle function (M Phil, PhD); pharmacology (M Phil, PhD); physiology (M Phil, PhD); plant sciences (M Phil, PhD); stem cell research (M Phil, PhD); structural biology (M Phil, PhD); systems neuroscience (M Phil, PhD); toxicology (M Phil, PhD).

The University of Manchester, School of Chemistry, Manchester, United Kingdom. Offers biological chemistry (PhD); chemistry (M Ent, M Phil, M Sc, D Ent, PhD); inorganic chemistry (PhD); materials chemistry (PhD); nanoscience (PhD); nuclear fission (PhD); organic chemistry (PhD); physical chemistry (PhD); theoretical chemistry (PhD).

University of Manitoba, Max Rady College of Medicine and Faculty of Graduate Studies, Graduate Programs in Medicine, Department of Biochemistry and Medical Genetics, Winnipeg, MB R3T 2N2, Canada. Offers biochemistry and medical genetics (M Sc, PhD); genetic counseling (M Sc). Terminal master's awarded for partial completion of doctoral program. *Degree requirements:* For master's, thesis; for doctorate, thesis/dissertation. *Faculty research:* Cancer, gene expression, membrane lipids, metabolic control, genetic diseases.

University of Maryland, Baltimore, Graduate School, Graduate Program in Life Sciences, Program in Biochemistry and Molecular Biology, Baltimore, MD 21201. Offers biochemistry (MS, PhD); MD/PhD. *Students:* 26 full-time (15 women), 4 part-time (3 women); includes 9 minority (4 Black or African American, non-Hispanic/Latino; 3 Asian, non-Hispanic/Latino; 2 Hispanic/Latino), 5 international. Average age 27. 35 applicants, 34% accepted, 4 enrolled. In 2017, 3 master's, 6 doctorates awarded. *Degree requirements:* For doctorate, comprehensive exam, thesis/dissertation. *Entrance requirements:* For master's and doctorate, GRE General Test, minimum GPA of 3.0, curriculum vitae, essay, 3 letters of recommendation. Additional exam requirements/recommendations for international students: Required—TOEFL (minimum score 80 iBT); Recommended—IELTS (minimum score 7). *Application deadline:* For fall admission, 1/15 for domestic and international students. Application fee: $75. Electronic applications accepted. *Expenses:* Tuition, state resident: full-time $13,990; part-time $661 per credit. Tuition, nonresident: full-time $30,484; part-time $1310 per credit. *Required fees:* $1894; $94 per credit. $415 per semester. Part-time tuition and fees vary according to course load, degree level and program. *Financial support:* In 2017–18, research assistantships with full tuition reimbursements (averaging $26,000 per year) were awarded; fellowships, health care benefits, and unspecified assistantships also available. Financial award application deadline: 3/1; financial award applicants required to submit FAFSA. *Faculty research:* Membrane transport, hormonal regulation, protein structure, molecular virology. *Unit head:* Dr. Gerald Wilson, Professor/Director, 410-706-8904. *Application contact:* Kiriaki Cozmo, Program Coordinator, 410-706-7340, Fax: 410-706-8297, E-mail: kicozmo@som.umaryland.edu.
Website: http://medschool.umaryland.edu/biochemistry/

University of Maryland, College Park, Academic Affairs, College of Computer, Mathematical and Natural Sciences, Department of Chemistry and Biochemistry, Biochemistry Program, College Park, MD 20742. Offers MS, PhD. *Program availability:* Part-time, evening/weekend. Terminal master's awarded for partial completion of doctoral program. *Degree requirements:* For master's, thesis or alternative; for doctorate, thesis/dissertation, 2 seminar presentations, oral exam. *Entrance requirements:* For master's and doctorate, GRE General Test, GRE Subject Test (recommended), minimum GPA of 3.0, 3 letters of recommendation. Additional exam requirements/recommendations for international students: Required—TOEFL. Electronic applications accepted. *Faculty research:* Analytical biochemistry, immunochemistry, drug metabolism, biosynthesis of proteins, mass spectrometry.

University of Massachusetts Amherst, Graduate School, College of Natural Sciences, Department of Biochemistry and Molecular Biology, Amherst, MA 01003. Offers MS, PhD. *Program availability:* Part-time. Terminal master's awarded for partial completion of doctoral program. *Degree requirements:* For master's, thesis or alternative; for doctorate, comprehensive exam, thesis/dissertation. *Entrance requirements:* Additional exam requirements/recommendations for international students: Required—TOEFL (minimum score 550 paper-based; 80 iBT), IELTS (minimum score 6.5). Electronic applications accepted.

University of Massachusetts Amherst, Graduate School, Interdisciplinary Programs, Program in Molecular and Cellular Biology, Amherst, MA 01003. Offers biological chemistry and molecular biophysics (PhD); biomedicine (PhD); cellular and developmental biology (PhD). *Program availability:* Part-time. Terminal master's awarded for partial completion of doctoral program. *Degree requirements:* For doctorate, comprehensive exam, thesis/dissertation. *Entrance requirements:* For doctorate, GRE General Test. Additional exam requirements/recommendations for international students: Required—TOEFL (minimum score 550 paper-based; 80 iBT), IELTS (minimum score 6.5). Electronic applications accepted.

University of Massachusetts Amherst, Graduate School, Interdisciplinary Programs, Program in Plant Biology, Amherst, MA 01003. Offers biochemistry and metabolism (MS, PhD); cell biology and physiology (MS, PhD); environmental, ecological and integrative biology (MS, PhD); genetics and evolution (MS, PhD). *Degree requirements:* For master's, thesis; for doctorate, 2 foreign languages, comprehensive exam, thesis/dissertation. *Entrance requirements:* For master's and doctorate, GRE General Test. Additional exam requirements/recommendations for international students: Required—TOEFL (minimum score 550 paper-based; 80 iBT), IELTS (minimum score 6.5). Electronic applications accepted.

University of Massachusetts Dartmouth, Graduate School, College of Arts and Sciences, Department of Chemistry and Biochemistry, North Dartmouth, MA 02747-2300. Offers chemistry (MS, PhD). *Program availability:* Part-time. *Faculty:* 19 full-time (7 women), 4 part-time/adjunct (1 woman). *Students:* 21 full-time (11 women), 12 part-time (5 women); includes 1 minority (Asian, non-Hispanic/Latino), 17 international. Average age 28. 30 applicants, 70% accepted, 11 enrolled. In 2017, 6 master's awarded. *Degree requirements:* For master's, thesis or project; for doctorate, comprehensive exam, thesis/dissertation. *Entrance requirements:* For master's, GRE (recommended), statement of purpose (minimum of 300 words), resume, official transcripts, 2 letters of recommendation (3 recommended); for doctorate, GRE, statement of purpose (minimum of 300 words), resume, official transcripts, 2 letters of recommendation (3 recommended). Additional exam requirements/recommendations for international students: Required—TOEFL (minimum score 550 paper-based; 79 iBT), IELTS (minimum score 6.5). *Application deadline:* For fall admission, 2/15 priority date for domestic students, 1/15 priority date for international students; for spring admission, 11/1 priority date for domestic students, 10/1 priority date for international students. Application fee: $60. Electronic applications accepted. *Expenses:* Tuition, state resident: full-time $15,449; part-time $643.71 per credit. Tuition, nonresident: full-time $27,880; part-time $1161.67 per credit. *Required fees:* $405; $25.88 per credit. Tuition and fees vary according to course load and reciprocity agreements. *Financial support:* In 2017–18, 4 fellowships (averaging $16,500 per year), 3 research assistantships (averaging $11,667 per year), 19 teaching assistantships (averaging $11,850 per year) were awarded; tuition waivers (full and partial), unspecified assistantships, and instructional assistantships, dissertation writing support also available. Support available to part-time students. Financial award application deadline: 3/1; financial award applicants required to submit FAFSA. *Faculty research:* Molecular imaging probes for iron and reactive oxygen species detection in living systems, self-assembly of peptide nanotubes, host-guest complexes, mechanical and optical properties of carbon nanotubes, cellular antioxidant chemistry. *Total annual research expenditures:* $949,000. *Unit head:* Yuegang Zuo, Graduate Program Director, Chemistry, 508-999-8959, E-mail: yzuo@umassd.edu. *Application contact:* Steven Briggs, Director of Marketing and Recruitment for Graduate Studies, 508-999-8604, Fax: 508-999-8183, E-mail: graduate@umassd.edu.
Website: http://www.umassd.edu/cas/chemistry

University of Massachusetts Lowell, College of Sciences, Department of Chemistry, Lowell, MA 01854. Offers analytical chemistry (PhD); biochemistry (PhD); chemistry (MS, PhD); environmental studies (PhD); green chemistry (PhD); inorganic chemistry (PhD); organic chemistry (PhD); polymer science (MS). Terminal master's awarded for partial completion of doctoral program. *Degree requirements:* For master's, thesis; for doctorate, 2 foreign languages, thesis/dissertation. *Entrance requirements:* For master's and doctorate, GRE General Test. Electronic applications accepted.

University of Massachusetts Medical School, Graduate School of Biomedical Sciences, Worcester, MA 01655-0115. Offers biomedical sciences (PhD), including biochemistry and molecular pharmacology, bioinformatics and computational biology, cancer biology, immunology and microbiology, interdisciplinary, neuroscience, translational science; biomedical sciences (millennium program) (PhD); clinical and population health research (PhD); clinical investigation (MS). *Faculty:* 1,316 full-time (526 women), 357 part-time/adjunct (229 women). *Students:* 347 full-time (180 women); includes 61 minority (10 Black or African American, non-Hispanic/Latino; 1 American Indian or Alaska Native, non-Hispanic/Latino; 35 Asian, non-Hispanic/Latino; 15 Hispanic/Latino), 130 international. Average age 29. 608 applicants, 28% accepted, 54 enrolled. In 2017, 6 master's, 51 doctorates awarded. Terminal master's awarded for partial completion of doctoral program. *Degree requirements:* For master's, comprehensive exam, thesis; for doctorate, comprehensive exam, thesis/dissertation. *Entrance requirements:* For master's, MD, PhD, DVM, or PharmD; for doctorate, GRE General Test, bachelor's degree. Additional exam requirements/recommendations for international students: Required—TOEFL (minimum score 90 iBT) or IELTS (minimum score 7.0). *Application deadline:* For fall admission, 12/15 for domestic and international students. Applications are processed on a rolling basis. Application fee: $80. Electronic applications accepted. Application fee is waived when completed online. *Expenses:* $14,883 in-state tuition and mandatory fees; $31,486 out-of-state. *Financial support:* In 2017–18, 15 fellowships with partial tuition reimbursements (averaging $29,000 per year), 296 research assistantships with full tuition reimbursements (averaging $31,212 per year) were awarded; institutionally sponsored loans and scholarships/grants also available. Financial award application deadline: 5/15. *Faculty research:* RNA biology, molecular/cell/developmental/metabolic biology, bioinformatics and computational biology, clinical/translational research, infectious disease and immunology. *Total annual research expenditures:* $279 million. *Unit head:* Dr. Mary Ellen Lane, Dean, 508-856-4018, E-mail: maryellen.lane@umassmed.edu. *Application contact:* Dr. Kendall Knight, Assistant Vice Provost for Admissions, 508-856-5628, Fax: 508-856-3659, E-mail: kendall.knight@umassmed.edu.
Website: http://www.umassmed.edu/gsbs/

University of Miami, Graduate School, Miller School of Medicine, Graduate Programs in Medicine, Department of Biochemistry and Molecular Biology, Coral Gables, FL 33124. Offers PhD, MD/PhD. *Degree requirements:* For doctorate, comprehensive exam, thesis/dissertation, proposition exams. *Faculty research:* Macromolecule metabolism, molecular genetics, protein folding and 3-D structure, regulation of gene expression and enzyme function, signal transduction and developmental biology.

University of Michigan, Rackham Graduate School, College of Literature, Science, and the Arts, Department of Chemistry, Ann Arbor, MI 48109-1055. Offers analytical chemistry (PhD); chemical biology (PhD); chemical sciences (MS); inorganic chemistry (PhD); materials chemistry (PhD); organic chemistry (PhD); physical chemistry (PhD). *Program availability:* Part-time. *Faculty:* 40 full-time (14 women), 7 part-time/adjunct (3 women). *Students:* 262 full-time (112 women), 4 part-time (all women); includes 44 minority (11 Black or African American, non-Hispanic/Latino; 11 Asian, non-Hispanic/Latino; 19 Hispanic/Latino; 1 Native Hawaiian or other Pacific Islander, non-Hispanic/Latino; 2 Two or more races, non-Hispanic/Latino), 61 international. 535 applicants, 31% accepted, 54 enrolled. In 2017, 62 master's, 33 doctorates awarded. *Degree requirements:* For doctorate, comprehensive exam, thesis/dissertation, oral defense of dissertation, organic cumulative proficiency exams. *Entrance requirements:* For master's, bachelor's degree, 3 letters of recommendation, personal statement; for doctorate, GRE General Test, bachelor's degree, 3 letters of recommendation, personal statement, curriculum vitae/resume. Additional exam requirements/recommendations for international students: Required—TOEFL (minimum score 560 paper-based; 84 iBT) or IELTS. *Application deadline:* For fall admission, 12/15 for domestic and international students. Application fee: $0 ($90 for international students). Electronic applications accepted. *Expenses:* Tuition, state resident: full-time $22,368; part-time $1201 per credit hour. Tuition, nonresident: full-time $45,156; part-time $2467 per credit hour. *Required fees:* $376 per term. Tuition and fees vary according to course load, degree level and program. *Financial support:* In 2017–18, 259 students received support, including 61 fellowships with full tuition reimbursements available (averaging $30,650 per year), 78 research assistantships with full tuition reimbursements available (averaging $30,650 per year), 119 teaching assistantships with full tuition reimbursements available (averaging $30,650 per year); career-related internships or fieldwork, Federal Work-Study, scholarships/grants, traineeships, health care benefits, tuition waivers (full), and unspecified assistantships also available. *Faculty research:* Biological catalysis, protein engineering, chemical sensors, de novo metalloprotein design, supramolecular architecture. *Total annual research expenditures:* $19.6 million.

Unit head: Dr. Robert Kennedy, Professor of Chemistry/Chair, 734-763-9681, Fax: 734-647-4847. *Application contact:* Elizabeth Oxford, Graduate Program Coordinator, 734-764-7278, Fax: 734-647-4865, E-mail: chemadmissions@umich.edu.
Website: http://www.lsa.umich.edu/chem/

University of Michigan, Rackham Graduate School, Program in Biomedical Sciences (PIBS), Department of Biological Chemistry, Ann Arbor, MI 48109. Offers MS, PhD. *Faculty:* 32 full-time (8 women), 2 part-time/adjunct (0 women). *Students:* 35 full-time (14 women); includes 8 minority (1 Black or African American, non-Hispanic/Latino; 4 Asian, non-Hispanic/Latino; 2 Hispanic/Latino; 1 Two or more races, non-Hispanic/Latino), 4 international. Average age 26. 140 applicants, 22% accepted, 17 enrolled. In 2017, 10 master's, 6 doctorates awarded. Terminal master's awarded for partial completion of doctoral program. *Degree requirements:* For master's, written thesis (for research track); literature analysis project (for course track); for doctorate, comprehensive exam, thesis/dissertation, oral defense, written thesis. *Entrance requirements:* For master's, 3 letters of recommendation, undergraduate transcripts, bachelor's degree, research experience; for doctorate, 3 letters of recommendation, undergraduate transcripts, bachelor's degree, significance research experience. Additional exam requirements/recommendations for international students: Required—TOEFL (minimum score 84 iBT). *Application deadline:* For fall admission, 12/1 for domestic and international students. Application fee: $75 ($90 for international students). Electronic applications accepted. *Expenses:* $22,414 full-time in-state, $45,248 out-of-state. *Financial support:* In 2017–18, 2 students received support, including 2 fellowships with full tuition reimbursements available (averaging $30,600 per year), 21 research assistantships with full tuition reimbursements available (averaging $30,600 per year), 8 teaching assistantships with tuition reimbursements available; traineeships, health care benefits, tuition waivers (full), and unspecified assistantships also available. *Faculty research:* Biochemical signaling, structural enzymology, protein processing and folding, regulation of gene expression. *Total annual research expenditures:* $5.4 million. *Unit head:* Sherry Cogswell, Chief Department Administrator, 734-763-0185, Fax: 734-763-4581, E-mail: shercogs@umich.edu. *Application contact:* Elizabeth L. Goodwin, Graduate Program Manager, 734-764-8594, Fax: 734-763-4581, E-mail: egoodwin@umich.edu.
Website: http://www.biochem.med.umich.edu/

University of Michigan, Rackham Graduate School, Program in Chemical Biology, Ann Arbor, MI 48109. Offers cancer chemical biology (MS); chemical biology (PhD). *Program availability:* Part-time. *Faculty:* 57 full-time (19 women). *Students:* 70 full-time (29 women), 4 part-time ([illegible] women); includes [illegible] minority ([illegible] Black or African American, non-Hispanic/Latino; 8 Asian, non-Hispanic/Latino; 6 Hispanic/Latino), 12 international. 115 applicants, 57% accepted, 29 enrolled. In 2017, 16 master's, 11 doctorates awarded. *Degree requirements:* For doctorate, thesis/dissertation. *Entrance requirements:* Additional exam requirements/recommendations for international students: Required—TOEFL (minimum score 600 paper-based; 102 iBT). *Application deadline:* For fall admission, 12/15 priority date for domestic and international students. Applications are processed on a rolling basis. Application fee: $75 ($90 for international students). Electronic applications accepted. *Expenses:* Tuition, state resident: full-time $22,368; part-time $1201 per credit hour. Tuition, nonresident: full-time $45,156; part-time $2467 per credit hour. *Required fees:* $376 per term. Tuition and fees vary according to course load, degree level and program. *Financial support:* In 2017–18, 60 students received support, including fellowships with full tuition reimbursements available (averaging $30,600 per year), research assistantships with full tuition reimbursements available (averaging $30,600 per year); career-related internships or fieldwork, scholarships/grants, traineeships, health care benefits, and unspecified assistantships also available. *Faculty research:* Chemical genetics, structural enzymology, signal transduction, biological catalysis, biomolecular structure, function and recognition. *Unit head:* Prof. Anna Mapp, Program Director, 734-763-7175, Fax: 734-615-1252, E-mail: chemicalbiology@umich.edu. *Application contact:* Admissions Office, 734-764-8129, E-mail: rackadmis@umich.edu.
Website: http://www.chembio.umich.edu/

University of Minnesota, Duluth, Graduate School, Swenson College of Science and Engineering, Department of Chemistry and Biochemistry, Duluth, MN 55812-2496. Offers MS. *Program availability:* Part-time. *Degree requirements:* For master's, thesis. *Entrance requirements:* For master's, bachelor's degree in chemistry, minimum GPA of 3.0. Additional exam requirements/recommendations for international students: Required—TOEFL (minimum score 550 paper-based; 79 iBT), IELTS (minimum score 6.5). *Faculty research:* Physical, inorganic, organic, and analytical chemistry; biochemistry and molecular biology.

University of Minnesota, Duluth, Medical School, Department of Biochemistry, Molecular Biology and Biophysics, Duluth, MN 55812-2496. Offers biochemistry, molecular biology and biophysics (MS); biology and biophysics (PhD); social, administrative, and clinical pharmacy (MS, PhD); toxicology (MS, PhD). Terminal master's awarded for partial completion of doctoral program. *Degree requirements:* For master's, comprehensive exam, thesis; for doctorate, comprehensive exam, thesis/dissertation. *Entrance requirements:* For master's and doctorate, GRE General Test. Additional exam requirements/recommendations for international students: Required—TOEFL. Electronic applications accepted. *Faculty research:* Intestinal cancer biology; hepatotoxins and mitochondriopathies; toxicology; cell cycle regulation in stem cells; neurobiology of brain development, trace metal function and blood-brain barrier; hibernation biology.

University of Minnesota, Twin Cities Campus, Graduate School, College of Biological Sciences, Biochemistry, Molecular Biology and Biophysics Graduate Program, Minneapolis, MN 55455-0213. Offers PhD. *Degree requirements:* For doctorate, thesis/dissertation. *Entrance requirements:* For doctorate, GRE, 3 letters of recommendation, more than 1 semester of laboratory experience. Additional exam requirements/recommendations for international students: Required—TOEFL (minimum score 625 paper-based; 108 iBT with writing subsection 25 and reading subsection 25) or IELTS (minimum score 7). Electronic applications accepted. *Faculty research:* Microbial biochemistry, biotechnology, molecular biology, regulatory biochemistry, structural biology and biophysics, physical biochemistry, enzymology, physiological chemistry.

University of Mississippi Medical Center, School of Graduate Studies in the Health Sciences, Department of Biochemistry, Jackson, MS 39216-4505. Offers PhD, MD/PhD. *Degree requirements:* For doctorate, thesis/dissertation, first authored publication. *Entrance requirements:* For doctorate, GRE General Test, minimum GPA of 3.0. Additional exam requirements/recommendations for international students: Required—TOEFL. *Faculty research:* Structural biology, regulation of gene expression, enzymology of redox reactions, mechanism of anti cancer drugs, function of nuclear substructure.

University of Missouri, Office of Research and Graduate Studies, College of Agriculture, Food and Natural Resources, Department of Biochemistry, Columbia, MO 65211. Offers MS, PhD, PhD/MD. Terminal master's awarded for partial completion of doctoral program. *Entrance requirements:* For master's and doctorate, GRE, minimum GPA of 3.0; undergraduate research; 3 letters of reference; 500-word personal statement. *Expenses:* Tuition, state resident: full-time $6480. Tuition, nonresident: full-time $17,744. *Required fees:* $1108. Tuition and fees vary according to course load, campus/location and program. *Financial support:* Fellowships, research assistantships, teaching assistantships, institutionally sponsored loans, scholarships/grants, health care benefits, and unspecified assistantships available. Support available to part-time students. *Faculty research:* Gene expression; molecular medicine; plant sciences; receptors and signaling; macromolecular synthesis, assembly and localization; structural and chemical biology; proteomics, genomics and combinatorial chemistry; enzymology, nutrition and metabolism.
Website: http://biochem.missouri.edu/grad-program/index.php

University of Missouri–Kansas City, School of Biological Sciences, Program in Molecular Biology and Biochemistry, Kansas City, MO 64110-2499. Offers PhD. Offered through the School of Graduate Studies. *Degree requirements:* For doctorate, comprehensive exam, thesis/dissertation. *Entrance requirements:* For doctorate, GRE General Test, bachelor's degree in chemistry, biology, or a related discipline; minimum GPA of 3.0. Additional exam requirements/recommendations for international students: Required—TOEFL (minimum score 550 paper-based; 80 iBT).

University of Missouri–St. Louis, College of Arts and Sciences, Department of Chemistry and Biochemistry, St. Louis, MO 63121. Offers biochemistry and biotechnology (MS); chemistry (MS, PhD). *Program availability:* Part-time, evening/weekend. *Faculty:* 22 full-time (3 women), 2 part-time/adjunct (1 woman). *Students:* 35 full-time (13 women), 13 part-time (2 women); includes 4 minority (1 Black or African American, non-Hispanic/Latino; 1 Asian, non-Hispanic/Latino; 1 Native Hawaiian or other Pacific Islander, non-Hispanic/Latino; 1 Two or more races, non-Hispanic/Latino), 25 international. 22 applicants, 59% accepted, 5 enrolled. Terminal master's awarded for partial completion of doctoral program. *Degree requirements:* For master's, thesis optional; for doctorate, thesis/dissertation. *Entrance requirements:* For master's, 2 letters of recommendation; for doctorate, GRE General Test, 3 letters of recommendation. Additional exam requirements/recommendations for international students: Required—TOEFL (minimum score 550 paper-based; 79 iBT), IELTS (minimum score 6.5). *Application deadline:* For fall admission, 7/1 priority date for domestic and international students; for spring admission, 12/1 priority date for domestic and international students. Applications are processed on a rolling basis. Application fee: $50 ($40 for international students). Electronic applications accepted. *Expenses:* Tuition, state resident: part-time $476.50 per credit hour. Tuition, nonresident: part-time $1169.70 per credit hour. *Financial support:* Fellowships with tuition reimbursements, research assistantships with tuition reimbursements, and teaching assistantships with tuition reimbursements available. *Faculty research:* Metallaborane chemistry, serum transferrin chemistry, natural products chemistry, organic synthesis. *Unit head:* Cynthia Dupureur, Chair, 314-516-4392, Fax: 314-516-5342, E-mail: cdup@umsl.edu. *Application contact:* Graduate Admissions, 314-516-5458, Fax: 314-516-6996, E-mail: gradadm@umsl.edu.
Website: http://www.umsl.edu/chemistry/

University of Montana, Graduate School, College of Humanities and Sciences, Division of Biological Sciences, Program in Cellular, Molecular and Microbial Biology, Missoula, MT 59812. Offers cellular and developmental biology (PhD); microbial evolution and ecology (PhD); microbiology and immunology (PhD); molecular biology and biochemistry (PhD). Terminal master's awarded for partial completion of doctoral program. *Degree requirements:* For doctorate, variable foreign language requirement, thesis/dissertation. *Entrance requirements:* For doctorate, GRE General Test. *Faculty research:* Ribosome structure, medical microbiology/pathogenesis, microbial ecology/environmental microbiology.

University of Nebraska–Lincoln, Graduate College, College of Agricultural Sciences and Natural Resources and College of Arts and Sciences, Department of Biochemistry, Lincoln, NE 68588. Offers MS, PhD. Terminal master's awarded for partial completion of doctoral program. *Degree requirements:* For master's, thesis optional; for doctorate, comprehensive exam, thesis/dissertation. *Entrance requirements:* For master's and doctorate, GRE General Test, GRE Subject Test. Additional exam requirements/recommendations for international students: Required—TOEFL (minimum score 550 paper-based). Electronic applications accepted. *Faculty research:* Molecular genetics, enzymology, photosynthesis, molecular virology, structural biology.

University of Nebraska–Lincoln, Graduate College, College of Arts and Sciences, Department of Chemistry, Lincoln, NE 68588. Offers analytical chemistry (PhD); biochemistry (PhD); chemistry (MS); inorganic chemistry (PhD); materials chemistry (PhD); organic chemistry (PhD); physical chemistry (PhD). *Degree requirements:* For master's, one foreign language, thesis optional, departmental qualifying exam; for doctorate, one foreign language, comprehensive exam, thesis/dissertation, departmental qualifying exams. *Entrance requirements:* For master's and doctorate, GRE. Additional exam requirements/recommendations for international students: Required—TOEFL (minimum score 550 paper-based). Electronic applications accepted. *Faculty research:* Bioorganic and bioinorganic chemistry, biophysical and bioanalytical chemistry, structure-function of DNA and proteins, organometallics, mass spectrometry.

University of Nebraska Medical Center, Interdisciplinary Graduate Program in Biomedical Sciences, Department of Biochemistry and Molecular Biology, Omaha, NE 68198-5870. Offers MS. *Faculty:* 27 full-time (8 women). *Students:* 45 full-time (26 women); includes 4 minority (3 Asian, non-Hispanic/Latino; 1 Two or more races, non-Hispanic/Latino), 21 international. Average age 28. 13 applicants, 85% accepted, 9 enrolled. Terminal master's awarded for partial completion of doctoral program. *Degree requirements:* For master's, comprehensive exam, thesis. *Entrance requirements:* For master's, GRE General Test. Additional exam requirements/recommendations for international students: Required—TOEFL (minimum score 550 paper-based). *Application deadline:* For fall admission, 6/1 for domestic students, 4/1 for international students; for spring admission, 8/1 for domestic and international students; for summer admission, 1/1 for domestic and international students. Application fee: $45. Electronic applications accepted. Application fee is waived when completed online. *Expenses:* Tuition, state resident: full-time $8451; part-time $4225 per semester. Tuition, nonresident: full-time $24,219; part-time $11,295 per semester. *Required fees:* $589; $117 per term. *Financial support:* In 2017–18, 13 students received support, including 4 fellowships with full tuition reimbursements available (averaging $23,100 per year), 7 research assistantships with full tuition reimbursements available (averaging $23,100 per year); scholarships/grants, health care benefits, and unspecified assistantships also available. Financial award application deadline: 2/15; financial award applicants required to submit FAFSA. *Faculty research:* Biochemistry and molecular biology, including DNA replication, gene regulation, cell-cell communications, structural biology, receptor endocytosis and protein trafficking, nutrition, enzymology, endocrinology, and metabolism (protein, lipid, and carbohydrate). *Total annual research expenditures:* $4.2 million. *Unit head:* Dr. Kaustubh Datta, Chairman, Graduate Committee, 402-559-7404, Fax: 402-559-6650, E-mail: kaustubh.datta@unmc.edu. *Application contact:* Karen Hankins, Office Associate, 402-559-4417, E-mail: karen.hankins@unmc.edu.
Website: http://www.unmc.edu/biochemistry/

University of Nevada, Las Vegas, Graduate College, College of Sciences, Department of Chemistry and Biochemistry, Las Vegas, NV 89154-4003. Offers biochemistry (MS); chemistry (MS, PhD); radio chemistry (PhD). *Program availability:* Part-time. *Faculty:* 15 full-time (2 women). *Students:* 36 full-time (18 women), 9 part-time (5 women); includes 9 minority (2 Black or African American, non-Hispanic/Latino; 3 Asian, non-Hispanic/Latino; 3 Hispanic/Latino; 1 Two or more races, non-Hispanic/Latino), 4 international.

Biochemistry

Average age 31. 41 applicants, 37% accepted, 7 enrolled. In 2017, 3 master's, 5 doctorates awarded. Terminal master's awarded for partial completion of doctoral program. *Degree requirements:* For master's, thesis, departmental seminar; for doctorate, comprehensive exam (for some programs), thesis/dissertation, oral exam. *Entrance requirements:* For master's, GRE General Test, bachelor's degree; 2 letters of recommendation; for doctorate, GRE General Test, bachelor's degree/master's degree with minimum GPA of 3.0; statement of interest; 3 letters of recommendation. Additional exam requirements/recommendations for international students: Required—TOEFL (minimum score 550 paper-based; 80 iBT), IELTS (minimum score 7). *Application deadline:* For fall admission, 2/1 for domestic students; for spring admission, 10/1 for domestic students. Application fee: $60 ($95 for international students). Electronic applications accepted. *Expenses:* Contact institution. *Financial support:* In 2017–18, 34 students received support, including 14 research assistantships with full and partial tuition reimbursements available (averaging $20,391 per year), 20 teaching assistantships with full and partial tuition reimbursements available (averaging $25,310 per year); institutionally sponsored loans, scholarships/grants, health care benefits, and unspecified assistantships also available. Financial award application deadline: 3/15; financial award applicants required to submit FAFSA. *Faculty research:* Material science, biochemistry, chemical education, physical chemistry and theoretical computation, analytical and organic chemistry. *Total annual research expenditures:* $2.6 million. *Unit head:* Dr. Spencer Steinberg, Chair, 702-895-3599, Fax: 702-895-4072, E-mail: spencer.steinberg@unlv.edu. *Application contact:* Dr. Kathleen Robins, Graduate Coordinator, 702-895-4304, Fax: 702-895-4072, E-mail: kathy@physics.unlv.edu.
Website: http://www.unlv.edu/chemistry

University of Nevada, Reno, Graduate School, College of Agriculture, Biotechnology and Natural Resources, Program in Biochemistry, Reno, NV 89557. Offers MS, PhD. Terminal master's awarded for partial completion of doctoral program. *Degree requirements:* For master's, thesis; for doctorate, thesis/dissertation. *Entrance requirements:* For master's, GRE General Test, minimum GPA of 2.75; for doctorate, GRE General Test, minimum GPA of 3.0. Additional exam requirements/recommendations for international students: Required—TOEFL (minimum score 500 paper-based; 61 iBT), IELTS (minimum score 6). Electronic applications accepted. *Faculty research:* Cancer research, insect biochemistry, plant biochemistry, enzymology.

University of New Hampshire, Graduate School, College of Life Sciences and Agriculture, Department of Molecular, Cellular and Biomedical Sciences, Program in Biochemistry, Durham, NH 03824. Offers MS, PhD. *Program availability:* Part-time. *Students:* 15 full-time (5 women), 5 part-time (2 women); includes 1 minority (Two or more races, non-Hispanic/Latino), 6 international. Average age 29. 23 applicants, 43% accepted, 7 enrolled. In 2017, 2 master's awarded. Terminal master's awarded for partial completion of doctoral program. *Entrance requirements:* For master's and doctorate, GRE General Test. Additional exam requirements/recommendations for international students: Required—TOEFL (minimum score 550 paper-based; 80 iBT). *Application deadline:* For fall admission, 1/15 for domestic students. Application fee: $65. Electronic applications accepted. *Financial support:* In 2017–18, 17 students received support, including 1 fellowship, 6 research assistantships, 10 teaching assistantships; career-related internships or fieldwork, Federal Work-Study, scholarships/grants, and tuition waivers (full and partial) also available. Support available to part-time students. Financial award application deadline: 2/15. *Faculty research:* General areas of molecular biology, cellular biology, and biochemistry, with specific research programs in eukaryotic gene regulation; reproductive physiology; molecular population genetics; macromolecular interactions; cell signaling pathways in cancer and leukemia; evolution of eukaryotic genomes; glycobiology; protein kinases and phosphatases in plant signaling; mass spectrometry-based proteomics; chromatin biology; DNA repair mechanisms; etiology of vascular disease; sensory transduction. *Unit head:* Rick Cote, Chair, 603-862-2458. *Application contact:* Paul Boisselle, Administrative Assistant, 603-862-4818, E-mail: paul.boisselle@unh.edu.
Website: http://colsa.unh.edu/mcbs/grad/biochemistry/

University of New Mexico, Graduate Studies, Health Sciences Center, Program in Biomedical Sciences, Albuquerque, NM 87131-5196. Offers biochemistry and molecular biology (MS, PhD); cell biology and physiology (MS, PhD); molecular genetics and microbiology (MS, PhD); neuroscience (MS, PhD); pathology (MS, PhD); toxicology (MS, PhD). *Program availability:* Part-time. *Students:* Average age 29. 61 applicants, 16% accepted, 10 enrolled. In 2017, 11 master's, 14 doctorates awarded. Terminal master's awarded for partial completion of doctoral program. *Degree requirements:* For master's, thesis; for doctorate, comprehensive exam, thesis/dissertation, qualifying exam at the end of year 1/core curriculum. *Entrance requirements:* For master's and doctorate, GRE General Test, minimum undergraduate GPA of 3.0. Additional exam requirements/recommendations for international students: Required—TOEFL. *Application deadline:* For fall admission, 3/1 priority date for domestic and international students. Applications are processed on a rolling basis. Application fee: $50. Electronic applications accepted. *Financial support:* Fellowships, research assistantships with full tuition reimbursements, teaching assistantships, career-related internships or fieldwork, Federal Work-Study, institutionally sponsored loans, scholarships/grants, traineeships, health care benefits, and unspecified assistantships available. Financial award application deadline: 1/1; financial award applicants required to submit FAFSA. *Faculty research:* Infectious disease/immunity, cancer biology, cardiovascular and metabolic diseases, brain and behavioral illness, environmental health. *Unit head:* Dr. Helen J. Hathaway, Program Director, 505-272-1887, Fax: 505-272-2412, E-mail: hhathaway@salud.unm.edu. *Application contact:* Mary Fenton, Admissions Coordinator, 505-272-1887, Fax: 505-272-2412, E-mail: mfenton@salud.unm.edu.

The University of North Carolina at Chapel Hill, School of Medicine and Graduate School, Graduate Programs in Medicine, Department of Biochemistry and Biophysics, Chapel Hill, NC 27599. Offers MS, PhD. Terminal master's awarded for partial completion of doctoral program. *Degree requirements:* For master's, comprehensive exam, thesis; for doctorate, comprehensive exam, thesis/dissertation. *Entrance requirements:* For master's and doctorate, GRE General Test, GRE Subject Test (recommended), minimum GPA of 3.0. Additional exam requirements/recommendations for international students: Required—TOEFL. Electronic applications accepted.

The University of North Carolina at Greensboro, Graduate School, College of Arts and Sciences, Department of Chemistry and Biochemistry, Greensboro, NC 27412-5001. Offers biochemistry (MS); chemistry (MS). *Degree requirements:* For master's, one foreign language, thesis. *Entrance requirements:* For master's, GRE General Test. Additional exam requirements/recommendations for international students: Required—TOEFL. Electronic applications accepted. *Faculty research:* Synthesis of novel cyclopentadienes, molybdenum hydroxylase-cata ladder polymers, vinyl silicones.

University of North Texas, Robert B. Toulouse School of Graduate Studies, Denton, TX 76203-5459. Offers accounting (MS); applied anthropology (MA, MS); applied behavior analysis (Certificate); applied geography (MA); applied technology and performance improvement (M Ed, MS); art education (MA); art history (MA); art museum education (Certificate); arts leadership (Certificate); audiology (Au D); behavior analysis (MS); behavioral science (PhD); biochemistry and molecular biology (MS); biology (MA, MS); biomedical engineering (MS); business analysis (MS); chemistry (MS); clinical health psychology (PhD); communication studies (MA, MS); computer engineering (MS); computer science (MS); counseling (M Ed, MS), including clinical mental health counseling (MS), college and university counseling, elementary school counseling, secondary school counseling; creative writing (MA); criminal justice (MS); curriculum and instruction (M Ed); decision sciences (MBA); design (MA, MFA), including fashion design (MFA), innovation studies, interior design (MFA); early childhood studies (MS); economics (MS); educational leadership (M Ed, Ed D); educational psychology (MS, PhD), including family studies (MS), gifted and talented (MS), human development (MS), learning and cognition (MS), research, measurement and evaluation (MS); electrical engineering (MS); emergency management (MPA); engineering technology (MS); English (MA); English as a second language (MA); environmental science (MS); finance (MBA, MS); financial management (MPA); French (MA); health services management (MBA); higher education (M Ed, Ed D); history (MA, MS); hospitality management (MS); human resources management (MPA); information science (MS); information systems (PhD); information technologies (MBA); interdisciplinary studies (MA, MS); international studies (MA); international sustainable tourism (MS); jazz studies (MM); journalism (MA, MJ, Graduate Certificate), including interactive and virtual digital communication (Graduate Certificate), narrative journalism (Graduate Certificate), public relations (Graduate Certificate); kinesiology (MS); linguistics (MA); local government management (MPA); logistics (PhD); logistics and supply chain management (MBA); long-term care, senior housing, and aging services (MA); management (PhD); marketing (MBA); mathematics (MA, MS); mechanical and energy engineering (MS, PhD); music (MA), including ethnomusicology, music theory, musicology, performance; music composition (PhD); music education (MM Ed, PhD); nonprofit management (MPA); operations and supply chain management (MBA); performance (MM, DMA); philosophy (MA); political science (MA); professional and technical communication (MA); radio, television and film (MA, MFA); rehabilitation counseling (Certificate); sociology (MA); Spanish (MA); special education (M Ed); speech-language pathology (MA); strategic management (MBA); studio art (MFA); teaching (M Ed); MBA/MS. *Program availability:* Part-time, evening/weekend, online learning. Terminal master's awarded for partial completion of doctoral program. *Degree requirements:* For master's, variable foreign language requirement, comprehensive exam (for some programs), thesis (for some programs); for doctorate, variable foreign language requirement, comprehensive exam (for some programs), thesis/dissertation; for other advanced degree, variable foreign language requirement, comprehensive exam (for some programs). *Entrance requirements:* For master's and doctorate, GRE, GMAT. Additional exam requirements/recommendations for international students: Required—TOEFL (minimum score 550 paper-based; 79 iBT). Electronic applications accepted.

University of North Texas Health Science Center at Fort Worth, Graduate School of Biomedical Sciences, Fort Worth, TX 76107-2699. Offers biochemistry and cancer biology (MS, PhD); biotechnology (MS); cell biology, immunology and microbiology (MS, PhD); clinical research management (MS); forensic genetics (MS); genetics (MS, PhD); integrative physiology (MS, PhD); medical sciences (MS); pharmaceutical sciences and pharmacotherapy (MS, PhD); pharmacology and neuroscience (MS, PhD); structural anatomy and rehabilitation sciences (MS, PhD); DO/MS; DO/PhD. Terminal master's awarded for partial completion of doctoral program. *Degree requirements:* For master's, thesis; for doctorate, thesis/dissertation. *Entrance requirements:* For master's and doctorate, GRE General Test. Additional exam requirements/recommendations for international students: Required—TOEFL. *Expenses:* Contact institution. *Faculty research:* Alzheimer's disease, aging, eye diseases, cancer, cardiovascular disease.

University of Notre Dame, Graduate School, College of Science, Department of Chemistry and Biochemistry, Notre Dame, IN 46556. Offers biochemistry (MS, PhD); inorganic chemistry (MS, PhD); organic chemistry (MS, PhD); physical chemistry (MS, PhD). Terminal master's awarded for partial completion of doctoral program. *Degree requirements:* For master's, comprehensive exam, thesis; for doctorate, thesis/dissertation, qualifying exam. *Entrance requirements:* For master's and doctorate, GRE General Test, GRE Subject Test (strongly recommended). Additional exam requirements/recommendations for international students: Required—TOEFL (minimum score 600 paper-based; 80 iBT). Electronic applications accepted. *Faculty research:* Reaction design and mechanistic studies; reactive intermediates; synthesis, structure and reactivity of organometallic cluster complexes and biologically active natural products; bioorganic chemistry; enzymology.

University of Oklahoma, College of Arts and Sciences, Department of Chemistry and Biochemistry, Norman, OK 73019. Offers chemistry (MS, PhD), including analytical chemistry, biochemistry, chemical education, inorganic chemistry, inter-and/or multidisciplinary, organic chemistry, physical chemistry, structural biology. *Program availability:* Part-time. *Faculty:* 32 full-time (11 women). *Students:* 69 full-time (29 women), 42 part-time (17 women); includes 14 minority (1 Black or African American, non-Hispanic/Latino; 1 American Indian or Alaska Native, non-Hispanic/Latino; 6 Asian, non-Hispanic/Latino; 4 Hispanic/Latino; 2 Two or more races, non-Hispanic/Latino), 43 international. Average age 26. 91 applicants, 31% accepted, 23 enrolled. In 2017, 11 master's, 7 doctorates awarded. Terminal master's awarded for partial completion of doctoral program. *Degree requirements:* For master's, comprehensive exam (for some programs), thesis (for some programs); for doctorate, comprehensive exam, thesis/dissertation, general exam. *Entrance requirements:* For master's and doctorate, GRE. Additional exam requirements/recommendations for international students: Required—TOEFL (minimum score 79 iBT) or IELTS (minimum score 6.5). *Application deadline:* For fall admission, 3/31 priority date for domestic and international students; for spring admission, 9/1 priority date for domestic and international students. Application fee: $50 ($100 for international students). Electronic applications accepted. *Expenses:* Tuition, state resident: full-time $5119; part-time $213.30 per credit hour. Tuition, nonresident: full-time $19,778; part-time $824.10 per credit hour. *Required fees:* $3458; $133.55 per credit hour. $126.50 per semester. *Financial support:* In 2017–18, 104 students received support, including 34 research assistantships with full tuition reimbursements available (averaging $17,396 per year), 75 teaching assistantships with full tuition reimbursements available (averaging $16,734 per year); institutionally sponsored loans, scholarships/grants, health care benefits, unspecified assistantships, and full tuition with qualifying graduate assistantship also available. Support available to part-time students. Financial award application deadline: 6/1; financial award applicants required to submit FAFSA. *Faculty research:* Structural biology, solid state materials, natural products, membrane biochemistry, bioanalysis. *Total annual research expenditures:* $7.6 million. *Unit head:* Dr. Ronald L. Halterman, Professor and Chair, 405-325-4812, Fax: 405-325-6111, E-mail: rhalterman@ou.edu. *Application contact:* Carol Jones, Operations Manager, 405-325-4811, Fax: 405-325-6111, E-mail: caroljones@ou.edu.
Website: http://www.ou.edu/cas/chemistry

University of Oklahoma, College of Arts and Sciences and School of Aerospace and Mechanical Engineering and Department of Chemistry and Biochemistry, Program in Cellular and Behavioral Neurobiology, Norman, OK 73019. Offers cellular and behavioral neurobiology (PhD), including biology, chemistry and biochemistry, psychology. *Students:* 5 full-time (2 women), 1 (woman) part-time, 1 international. Average age 27. 8 applicants, 13% accepted, 1 enrolled. In 2017, 1 doctorate awarded. *Degree requirements:* For doctorate, comprehensive exam, thesis/dissertation, 2-3 lab rotations plus requirements of particular home department to which student applies.

Entrance requirements: For doctorate, GRE General Test; GRE Subject Test in chemistry (recommended for applicants to chemistry and biochemistry), transcripts, 3 letters of recommendation, personal statement; publications (for psychology). Additional exam requirements/recommendations for international students: Required—TOEFL (minimum score 79 iBT) or IELTS (minimum score 6.5). Application fee: $50 ($100 for international students). Electronic applications accepted. *Expenses:* Tuition, state resident: full-time $5119; part-time $213.30 per credit hour. Tuition, nonresident: full-time $19,778; part-time $824.10 per credit hour. *Required fees:* $3458; $133.55 per credit hour. $126.50 per semester. *Financial support:* In 2017–18, 5 students received support. Fellowships with full tuition reimbursements available, research assistantships with full tuition reimbursements available, teaching assistantships with full tuition reimbursements available, scholarships/grants, health care benefits, and unspecified assistantships available. Financial award application deadline: 6/1; financial award applicants required to submit FAFSA. *Faculty research:* Behavioral neurobiology, cellular neurobiology, molecular neurobiology, developmental neurobiology, cell signaling. *Unit head:* Dr. Ari Berkowitz, Director, Graduate Program, 405-325-3492, Fax: 405-325-6202, E-mail: ari@ou.edu.
Website: http://www.ou.edu/cbn

University of Oklahoma Health Sciences Center, College of Medicine and Graduate College, Graduate Programs in Medicine, Department of Biochemistry and Molecular Biology, Oklahoma City, OK 73190. Offers biochemistry (MS, PhD); molecular biology (MS, PhD). *Program availability:* Part-time. Terminal master's awarded for partial completion of doctoral program. *Degree requirements:* For master's, thesis; for doctorate, thesis/dissertation. *Entrance requirements:* For master's, GRE General Test, 2 letters of recommendation; for doctorate, GRE General Test, 3 letters of recommendation. Additional exam requirements/recommendations for international students: Required—TOEFL. *Faculty research:* Gene expression, regulation of transcription, enzyme evolution, melanogenesis, signal transduction.

University of Oregon, Graduate School, College of Arts and Sciences, Department of Chemistry, Eugene, OR 97403. Offers biochemistry (MA, MS, PhD); chemistry (MA, MS, PhD). Terminal master's awarded for partial completion of doctoral program. *Degree requirements:* For doctorate, thesis/dissertation. *Entrance requirements:* For master's and doctorate, GRE General Test, minimum GPA of 3.0. Additional exam requirements/recommendations for international students: Required—TOEFL. *Faculty research:* Organic chemistry, organometallic chemistry, inorganic chemistry, physical chemistry, materials science, biochemistry, chemical physics, molecular or cell biology.

University of Ottawa, Faculty of Graduate and Postdoctoral Studies, Faculty of Medicine, Department of Biochemistry, Microbiology and Immunology, Ottawa, ON K1N 6N5, Canada. Offers biochemistry (M Sc, PhD); microbiology and immunology (M Sc, PhD). *Degree requirements:* For master's, thesis; for doctorate, comprehensive exam, thesis/dissertation, seminar. *Entrance requirements:* For master's, honors degree or equivalent, minimum B average; for doctorate, master's degree, minimum B+ average. Electronic applications accepted. *Faculty research:* General biochemistry, molecular biology, microbiology, host biology, nutrition and metabolism.

University of Pennsylvania, Perelman School of Medicine, Biomedical Graduate Studies, Graduate Group in Biochemistry and Molecular Biophysics, Philadelphia, PA 19104. Offers PhD, MD/PhD, VMD/PhD. *Faculty:* 103. *Students:* 89 full-time (50 women); includes 34 minority (2 Black or African American, non-Hispanic/Latino; 10 Asian, non-Hispanic/Latino; 20 Hispanic/Latino; 2 Two or more races, non-Hispanic/Latino), 7 international. 108 applicants, 32% accepted, 14 enrolled. In 2017, 20 doctorates awarded. *Degree requirements:* For doctorate, thesis/dissertation. *Entrance requirements:* Additional exam requirements/recommendations for international students: Required—TOEFL. *Application deadline:* For fall admission, 12/1 priority date for domestic students, 12/1 for international students. Applications are processed on a rolling basis. Application fee: $80. *Financial support:* Fellowships, research assistantships, teaching assistantships, and tuition waivers available. *Faculty research:* Biochemistry of cell differentiation, tissue culture, intermediary metabolism, structure of proteins and nucleic acids, biochemical genetics. *Unit head:* Dr. Kim Sharp, Chairperson, 215-573-3506. *Application contact:* Kelli McKenna, Coordinator, 215-898-4639.
Website: http://www.med.upenn.edu/bmbgrad/

University of Puerto Rico–Medical Sciences Campus, School of Medicine, Biomedical Sciences Graduate Program, Department of Biochemistry, San Juan, PR 00936-5067. Offers MS, PhD. *Degree requirements:* For master's, thesis; for doctorate, comprehensive exam, thesis/dissertation. *Entrance requirements:* For master's and doctorate, GRE General Test, GRE Subject Test, interview, minimum GPA of 3.0. Electronic applications accepted. *Faculty research:* Genetics, cell and molecular biology, cancer biology, protein structure/function, glycosilation of proteins.

University of Regina, Faculty of Graduate Studies and Research, Faculty of Science, Department of Chemistry and Biochemistry, Regina, SK S4S 0A2, Canada. Offers biophysics of biological interfaces (M Sc, PhD); computational chemistry (M Sc, PhD); environmental analytical chemistry (M Sc, PhD); enzymology/chemical biology (M Sc, PhD); inorganic/organometallic chemistry (M Sc, PhD); signal transduction and mechanisms of cancer cell regulation (M Sc, PhD); supramolecular organic photochemistry and photophysics (M Sc, PhD); synthetic organic chemistry (M Sc, PhD). *Faculty:* 11 full-time (3 women), 4 part-time/adjunct (0 women). *Students:* 14 full-time (7 women), 3 part-time (0 women). 38 applicants, 11% accepted. In 2017, 1 doctorate awarded. *Degree requirements:* For master's, thesis; for doctorate, thesis/dissertation. *Entrance requirements:* Additional exam requirements/recommendations for international students: Required—TOEFL (minimum score 580 paper-based; 80 iBT), IELTS (minimum score 6.5), PTE (minimum score 59). *Application deadline:* Applications are processed on a rolling basis. Application fee: $100. Electronic applications accepted. *Expenses:* CAD$10,681 per year (for M Sc); CAD$9,930 per year (for PhD). *Financial support:* In 2017–18, fellowships (averaging $6,444 per year), teaching assistantships (averaging $2,562 per year) were awarded; research assistantships and scholarships/grants also available. Financial award application deadline: 6/15. *Faculty research:* Asymmetric synthesis and methodology, theoretical and computational chemistry, biophysical biochemistry, analytical and environmental chemistry, chemical biology. *Unit head:* Dr. Renata Raina-Fulton, Department Head, 306-585-4012, Fax: 306-337-2409, E-mail: renata.raina@uregina.ca. *Application contact:* Dr. Brian Sterenberg, Graduate Program Coordinator, 306-585-4106, Fax: 306-337-2409, E-mail: brian.sterenberg@uregina.ca.
Website: http://www.uregina.ca/science/chem-biochem/

University of Rhode Island, Graduate School, College of the Environment and Life Sciences, Department of Cell and Molecular Biology, Kingston, RI 02881. Offers biochemistry (MS, PhD); clinical laboratory sciences (MS), including biotechnology, clinical laboratory science, cytopathology; microbiology (MS, PhD); molecular genetics (MS, PhD). *Program availability:* Part-time. *Faculty:* 14 full-time (6 women). *Students:* 17 full-time (9 women), 19 part-time (15 women); includes 9 minority (2 Black or African American, non-Hispanic/Latino; 4 Asian, non-Hispanic/Latino; 2 Hispanic/Latino; 1 Two or more races, non-Hispanic/Latino), 10 international. 26 applicants, 62% accepted, 6 enrolled. In 2017, 17 master's awarded. *Entrance requirements:* Additional exam requirements/recommendations for international students: Required—TOEFL. *Application deadline:* For fall admission, 1/15 for domestic and international students. Application fee: $65. Electronic applications accepted. *Expenses:* Tuition, state resident: full-time $12,706; part-time $786 per credit. Tuition, nonresident: full-time $25,216; part-time $1401 per credit. *Required fees:* $1598; $45 per credit. One-time fee: $30 part-time. *Financial support:* In 2017–18, 4 teaching assistantships with full tuition reimbursements (averaging $12,698 per year) were awarded; traineeships also available. Financial award application deadline: 1/15; financial award applicants required to submit FAFSA. *Unit head:* Dr. Gongqing Sun, Chair and Professor, 401-874-5937, Fax: 401-874-2202, E-mail: gsun@mail.uri.edu. *Application contact:* Bethany Jenkins, Professor, 401-874-7551, E-mail: bjenkins@uri.edu.
Website: https://web.uri.edu/cmb/

University of Rochester, School of Medicine and Dentistry, Graduate Programs in Medicine and Dentistry, Department of Biochemistry and Biophysics, Programs in Biochemistry, Rochester, NY 14627. Offers biochemistry and molecular biology (PhD). Terminal master's awarded for partial completion of doctoral program. *Degree requirements:* For doctorate, thesis/dissertation, qualifying exam. *Entrance requirements:* For doctorate, GRE General Test.

University of Saint Joseph, Department of Chemistry, West Hartford, CT 06117-2700. Offers biochemistry (MS); chemistry (MS). *Program availability:* Part-time, evening/weekend, online learning. *Degree requirements:* For master's, comprehensive exam, thesis optional. *Entrance requirements:* For master's, 2 letters of recommendation, official undergraduate transcript. *Application deadline:* Applications are processed on a rolling basis. Application fee: $50. Electronic applications accepted. Application fee is waived when completed online. *Financial support:* Career-related internships or fieldwork and unspecified assistantships available. Support available to part-time students. Financial award applicants required to submit FAFSA. *Unit head:* Dr. Ellen Anderson, Chair, 860-231-5239, E-mail: eanderson@usj.edu.
Website: https://www.usj.edu/academics/schools/sasbe/chemistry/

University of Saskatchewan, College of Medicine, Department of Biochemistry, Saskatoon, SK S7N 5A2, Canada. Offers M Sc, PhD. *Degree requirements:* For master's, thesis; for doctorate, thesis/dissertation. *Entrance requirements:* Additional exam requirements/recommendations for international students: Required—TOEFL.

The University of Scranton, College of Arts and Sciences, Department of Chemistry, Program in Biochemistry, Scranton, PA 18510. Offers MS. *Program availability:* Part-time, evening/weekend. *Degree requirements:* For master's, comprehensive exam (for some programs), thesis (for some programs), capstone experience. *Entrance requirements:* For master's, minimum GPA of 3.0, three letters of reference. Additional exam requirements/recommendations for international students: Required—TOEFL (minimum score 500 paper-based; 80 iBT), IELTS (minimum score 6.5). Electronic applications accepted.

University of South Carolina, The Graduate School, College of Arts and Sciences, Department of Chemistry and Biochemistry, Columbia, SC 29208. Offers IMA, MAT, MS, PhD. IMA and MAT offered in cooperation with the College of Education. *Program availability:* Part-time. Terminal master's awarded for partial completion of doctoral program. *Degree requirements:* For master's, comprehensive exam, thesis; for doctorate, comprehensive exam, thesis/dissertation. *Entrance requirements:* For master's and doctorate, GRE General Test. Additional exam requirements/recommendations for international students: Required—TOEFL. Electronic applications accepted. *Faculty research:* Spectroscopy, crystallography, organic and organometallic synthesis, analytical chemistry, materials.

University of Southern California, Keck School of Medicine and Graduate School, Graduate Programs in Medicine, Department of Biochemistry and Molecular Biology, Los Angeles, CA 90033. Offers MS. *Program availability:* Part-time. *Faculty:* 22 full-time (4 women). *Students:* 31 full-time (20 women); includes 25 minority (all Asian, non-Hispanic/Latino). Average age 24. 77 applicants, 52% accepted, 14 enrolled. In 2017, 17 master's awarded. Terminal master's awarded for partial completion of doctoral program. *Degree requirements:* For master's, thesis. *Entrance requirements:* For master's, GRE General Test, minimum GPA of 3.0. Additional exam requirements/recommendations for international students: Required—TOEFL (minimum score 600 paper-based; 100 iBT), IELTS. *Application deadline:* For fall admission, 4/1 priority date for domestic and international students. Applications are processed on a rolling basis. Application fee: $90. Electronic applications accepted. *Expenses:* Contact institution. *Financial support:* Application deadline: 5/4; applicants required to submit CSS PROFILE or FAFSA. *Faculty research:* Molecular genetics, gene expression, membrane biochemistry, metabolic regulation, cancer biology. *Total annual research expenditures:* $7.4 million. *Unit head:* Dr. Peggy R. Farnham, Chair, 323-442-8015, E-mail: peggy.farnham@med.usc.edu. *Application contact:* Janet Stoeckert, Administrative Director, Basic Science Departments, 323-442-3568, Fax: 323-442-1610, E-mail: janet.stoeckert@usc.edu.
Website: http://keck.usc.edu/en/Education/Academic_Department_and_Divisions/Department_of_Biochemistry_and_Molecular_Biology.aspx

University of Southern Mississippi, College of Science and Technology, Department of Chemistry and Biochemistry, Hattiesburg, MS 39406-0001. Offers MS, PhD. *Students:* 4 full-time (0 women). 16 applicants, 56% accepted, 4 enrolled. *Degree requirements:* For master's, comprehensive exam, thesis; for doctorate, comprehensive exam, thesis/dissertation. *Entrance requirements:* For master's, GRE General Test, minimum GPA of 2.75 in last 60 hours; for doctorate, GRE General Test, minimum GPA of 3.5. Additional exam requirements/recommendations for international students: Required—TOEFL, IELTS. *Application deadline:* For fall admission, 3/1 priority date for domestic students, 3/1 for international students. Applications are processed on a rolling basis. Application fee: $60. *Expenses:* Tuition, state resident: full-time $3830. *Financial support:* Fellowships, research assistantships with full tuition reimbursements, teaching assistantships with full tuition reimbursements, Federal Work-Study, institutionally sponsored loans, scholarships/grants, health care benefits, and unspecified assistantships available. Support available to part-time students. Financial award application deadline: 3/15; financial award applicants required to submit FAFSA. *Faculty research:* Plant biochemistry, photo chemistry, polymer chemistry, x-ray analysis, enzyme chemistry. *Unit head:* Dr. Vijay Rangachari, Chair, 601-266-4701, Fax: 601-266-6075.
Website: https://www.usm.edu/chemistry-biochemistry

The University of Tennessee, Graduate School, College of Arts and Sciences, Department of Biochemistry, Cellular and Molecular Biology, Knoxville, TN 37996. Offers MS, PhD. Terminal master's awarded for partial completion of doctoral program. *Degree requirements:* For master's, thesis; for doctorate, thesis/dissertation. *Entrance requirements:* For master's and doctorate, GRE General Test, minimum GPA of 2.7. Additional exam requirements/recommendations for international students: Required—TOEFL. Electronic applications accepted.

The University of Texas at Austin, Graduate School, College of Natural Sciences, Department of Chemistry and Biochemistry, Program in Biochemistry, Austin, TX 78712-1111. Offers PhD. *Entrance requirements:* For doctorate, GRE General Test.

The University of Texas at Dallas, School of Natural Sciences and Mathematics, Department of Chemistry and Biochemistry, Richardson, TX 75080. Offers MS, PhD.

Biochemistry

Program availability: Part-time, evening/weekend. *Faculty:* 22 full-time (5 women). *Students:* 98 full-time (51 women), 5 part-time (2 women); includes 25 minority (4 Black or African American, non-Hispanic/Latino; 11 Asian, non-Hispanic/Latino; 10 Hispanic/Latino), 54 international. Average age 28. 154 applicants, 14% accepted, 21 enrolled. In 2017, 4 master's, 13 doctorates awarded. *Degree requirements:* For master's, thesis or internship; for doctorate, comprehensive exam, thesis/dissertation, research practica. *Entrance requirements:* For master's and doctorate, GRE General Test, minimum GPA of 3.0 in upper-level course work in field. Additional exam requirements/recommendations for international students: Required—TOEFL (minimum score 600 paper-based). *Application deadline:* For fall admission, 7/15 for domestic students, 5/1 priority date for international students; for spring admission, 11/15 for domestic students, 9/1 priority date for international students. Applications are processed on a rolling basis. Application fee: $50 ($100 for international students). Electronic applications accepted. *Expenses:* Tuition, state resident: full-time $12,916; part-time $718 per credit hour. Tuition, nonresident: full-time $25,252; part-time $1403 per credit hour. *Financial support:* In 2017–18, 97 students received support, including 43 research assistantships with partial tuition reimbursements available (averaging $24,300 per year), 55 teaching assistantships with partial tuition reimbursements available (averaging $17,280 per year); fellowships, career-related internships or fieldwork, Federal Work-Study, institutionally sponsored loans, scholarships/grants, and unspecified assistantships also available. Support available to part-time students. Financial award application deadline: 4/30; financial award applicants required to submit FAFSA. *Faculty research:* Advanced nano-materials; novel MRI agents; peptidomimetics to treat diabetes; semiconducting polymers for organic electronics; macrocyclic receptors for catalysis, medicine, materials science; electroactive polymers. *Unit head:* Dr. Ken Balkus, Department Head, 972-883-2901, Fax: 972-883-2925, E-mail: chemistry@utdallas.edu.
Website: http://www.utdallas.edu/chemistry/

The University of Texas at El Paso, Graduate School, College of Science, Department of Chemistry and Biochemistry, El Paso, TX 79968-0001. Offers MS, PhD. *Program availability:* Part-time, evening/weekend. *Degree requirements:* For master's, thesis; for doctorate, thesis/dissertation. *Entrance requirements:* For master's, GRE, minimum GPA of 3.0; for doctorate, GRE, letters of recommendation. Additional exam requirements/recommendations for international students: Required—TOEFL; Recommended—IELTS. *Application deadline:* For fall admission, 8/1 priority date for domestic students, 3/1 for international students; for spring admission, 11/1 priority date for domestic students, 9/1 for international students. Applications are processed on a rolling basis. Application fee: $45 ($80 for international students). Electronic applications accepted. *Financial support:* Fellowships with partial tuition reimbursements, research assistantships with partial tuition reimbursements, teaching assistantships with partial tuition reimbursements, institutionally sponsored loans, scholarships/grants, health care benefits, tuition waivers (partial), and unspecified assistantships available. Support available to part-time students. Financial award application deadline: 3/15; financial award applicants required to submit FAFSA.
Website: http://science.utep.edu/chemistry/

The University of Texas Health Science Center at Houston, MD Anderson UTHealth Graduate School, Houston, TX 77225-0036. Offers biochemistry and cell biology (PhD); biomedical sciences (MS); cancer biology (PhD); genetic counseling (MS); genetics and epigenetics (PhD); immunology (PhD); medical physics (MS, PhD); microbiology and infectious diseases (PhD); neuroscience (PhD); quantitative sciences (PhD); therapeutics and pharmacology (PhD); MD/PhD. Terminal master's awarded for partial completion of doctoral program. *Degree requirements:* For master's, thesis; for doctorate, thesis/dissertation. *Entrance requirements:* For master's and doctorate, GRE General Test. Additional exam requirements/recommendations for international students: Required—TOEFL. Electronic applications accepted. *Faculty research:* Biomedical sciences.

The University of Texas Health Science Center at San Antonio, Graduate School of Biomedical Sciences, Department of Biochemistry, San Antonio, TX 78229. Offers MS, PhD. *Degree requirements:* For master's, thesis; for doctorate, comprehensive exam, thesis/dissertation.

The University of Texas Medical Branch, Graduate School of Biomedical Sciences, Program in Biochemistry and Molecular Biology, Galveston, TX 77555. Offers biochemistry (PhD); bioinformatics (PhD); biophysics (PhD); cell biology (PhD); computational biology (PhD); structural biology (PhD). *Degree requirements:* For doctorate, thesis/dissertation. *Entrance requirements:* Additional exam requirements/recommendations for international students: Required—TOEFL (minimum score 550 paper-based). Electronic applications accepted.

The University of Texas Southwestern Medical Center, Southwestern Graduate School of Biomedical Sciences, Division of Basic Science, Program in Biological Chemistry, Dallas, TX 75390. Offers PhD. *Degree requirements:* For doctorate, thesis/dissertation, qualifying exam. *Entrance requirements:* For doctorate, GRE General Test, minimum GPA of 3.0. Additional exam requirements/recommendations for international students: Required—TOEFL. Electronic applications accepted. *Faculty research:* Regulation of gene expression, protein trafficking, molecular neurobiology, protein structure and function, metabolic regulation.

University of the Sciences, Program in Chemistry, Biochemistry and Pharmacognosy, Philadelphia, PA 19104-4495. Offers biochemistry (MS, PhD); chemistry (MS, PhD); pharmacognosy (MS, PhD). *Program availability:* Part-time. *Degree requirements:* For master's, thesis, qualifying exams; for doctorate, comprehensive exam, thesis/dissertation, qualifying exams. *Entrance requirements:* For master's and doctorate, GRE General Test, GRE Subject Test. Additional exam requirements/recommendations for international students: Required—TOEFL, TWE. *Expenses:* Contact institution.

The University of Toledo, College of Graduate Studies, College of Natural Sciences and Mathematics, Department of Chemistry, Toledo, OH 43606-3390. Offers analytical chemistry (MS, PhD); biological chemistry (MS, PhD); inorganic chemistry (MS, PhD); organic chemistry (MS, PhD); physical chemistry (MS, PhD). *Program availability:* Part-time. *Degree requirements:* For master's, thesis or alternative; for doctorate, thesis/dissertation. *Entrance requirements:* For master's and doctorate, GRE General Test, GRE Subject Test, minimum cumulative point-hour ratio of 2.7 for all previous academic work, three letters of recommendation, statement of purpose, transcripts from all prior institutions attended. Additional exam requirements/recommendations for international students: Required—TOEFL (minimum score 550 paper-based; 80 iBT). Electronic applications accepted. *Faculty research:* Enzymology, materials chemistry, crystallography, theoretical chemistry.

The University of Toledo, College of Graduate Studies, College of Pharmacy and Pharmaceutical Sciences, Program in Medicinal and Biological Chemistry, Toledo, OH 43606-3390. Offers MS, PhD. Terminal master's awarded for partial completion of doctoral program. *Degree requirements:* For master's, thesis; for doctorate, thesis/dissertation. *Entrance requirements:* For master's and doctorate, GRE General Test. Additional exam requirements/recommendations for international students: Required—TOEFL (minimum score 550 paper-based; 80 iBT). Electronic applications accepted. *Faculty research:* Neuroscience, molecular modeling, immunotoxicology, organic synthesis, peptide biochemistry.

University of Toronto, Faculty of Medicine, Department of Biochemistry, Toronto, ON M5S 1A1, Canada. Offers M Sc, PhD. *Degree requirements:* For master's, thesis, oral examination of thesis; for doctorate, thesis/dissertation, oral defense of thesis. *Entrance requirements:* For master's, B Sc in biochemistry or molecular biology, minimum B+ average, letters of reference. Additional exam requirements/recommendations for international students: Required—TOEFL (minimum score 580 paper-based; 93 iBT), TWE (minimum score 5). Electronic applications accepted.

The University of Tulsa, Graduate School, College of Engineering and Natural Sciences, Department of Chemistry and Biochemistry, Tulsa, OK 74104-3189. Offers biochemistry (MS); chemistry (MS, PhD). *Program availability:* Part-time. *Faculty:* 15 full-time (2 women), 4 part-time/adjunct (3 women). *Students:* 11 full-time (4 women), 8 part-time (4 women); includes 1 minority (American Indian or Alaska Native, non-Hispanic/Latino), 7 international. Average age 30. 26 applicants, 23% accepted, 3 enrolled. In 2017, 1 doctorate awarded. Terminal master's awarded for partial completion of doctoral program. *Degree requirements:* For master's, thesis optional; for doctorate, comprehensive exam, thesis/dissertation. *Entrance requirements:* For master's, GRE General Test. Additional exam requirements/recommendations for international students: Required—TOEFL (minimum score 550 paper-based; 80 iBT), IELTS (minimum score 6). *Application deadline:* Applications are processed on a rolling basis. Application fee: $55. Electronic applications accepted. *Expenses: Tuition:* Full-time $22,230. *Required fees:* $2000. Tuition and fees vary according to course load and program. *Financial support:* In 2017–18, 16 students received support, including 11 fellowships with full tuition reimbursements available (averaging $3,081 per year), 22 research assistantships with full tuition reimbursements available (averaging $3,787 per year), 9 teaching assistantships with full tuition reimbursements available (averaging $11,269 per year); career-related internships or fieldwork, Federal Work-Study, scholarships/grants, health care benefits, and unspecified assistantships also available. Support available to part-time students. Financial award application deadline: 2/1. *Unit head:* Dr. Dale C. Teeters, Chairperson and Advisor, 918-631-2515, Fax: 918-631-3404, E-mail: dale-teeters@utulsa.edu. *Application contact:* Dr. Syed Hussaini, Graduate School, 918-631-3520, Fax: 918-631-3404, E-mail: syed-hussaini@utulsa.edu.
Website: http://engineering.utulsa.edu/academics/chemistry-and-biochemistry/

University of Utah, School of Medicine and Graduate School, Graduate Programs in Medicine, Department of Biochemistry, Salt Lake City, UT 84112-1107. Offers MS, PhD. Terminal master's awarded for partial completion of doctoral program. *Degree requirements:* For master's, thesis; for doctorate, thesis/dissertation. *Entrance requirements:* For doctorate, GRE Subject Test, minimum GPA of 3.0. Additional exam requirements/recommendations for international students: Required—TOEFL. Electronic applications accepted. *Faculty research:* Protein structure and function, nucleic acid structure and function, nucleic acid enzymology, RNA modification, protein turnover.

University of Vermont, The Robert Larner, MD College of Medicine and Graduate College, Graduate Programs in Medicine, Department of Biochemistry, Burlington, VT 05405. Offers MS, PhD. *Students:* 2 (1 woman). 4 applicants, 25% accepted, 1 enrolled. In 2017, 1 master's awarded. *Degree requirements:* For master's, thesis; for doctorate, thesis/dissertation. *Entrance requirements:* For master's and doctorate, GRE General Test. Additional exam requirements/recommendations for international students: Required—TOEFL (minimum score 550 paper-based, 90 iBT) or IELTS (6.5). *Application deadline:* For fall admission, 12/1 for domestic and international students. Application fee: $65. Electronic applications accepted. *Expenses:* Tuition, state resident: full-time $11,628; part-time $646 per credit. Tuition, nonresident: full-time $29,340; part-time $1630 per credit. *Required fees:* $1994; $10 per credit. Tuition and fees vary according to course load and program. *Financial support:* In 2017–18, 1 research assistantship with full tuition reimbursement (averaging $27,300 per year) was awarded; fellowships, teaching assistantships, and analytical assistantships also available. Financial award application deadline: 3/1. *Faculty research:* Endocrinology, protein chemistry, cell-surface signaling. *Unit head:* Dr. Robert Kelm, Coordinator, 802-656-2220, E-mail: robert.kelm@uvm.edu.
Website: http://www.med.uvm.edu/biochemistry/grad

University of Victoria, Faculty of Graduate Studies, Faculty of Science, Department of Biochemistry and Microbiology, Victoria, BC V8W 2Y2, Canada. Offers biochemistry (M Sc, PhD); microbiology (M Sc, PhD). *Degree requirements:* For master's, thesis, seminar; for doctorate, thesis/dissertation, seminar, candidacy exam. *Entrance requirements:* For master's, GRE General Test, minimum B+ average; for doctorate, GRE General Test, minimum B+ average, M Sc. Additional exam requirements/recommendations for international students: Required—TOEFL (minimum score 600 paper-based). Electronic applications accepted. *Faculty research:* Molecular pathogenesis, prokaryotic, eukaryotic, macromolecular interactions, microbial surfaces, virology, molecular genetics.

University of Virginia, School of Medicine, Department of Biochemistry and Molecular Genetics, Charlottesville, VA 22903. Offers biochemistry (PhD); MD/PhD. *Faculty:* 20 full-time (2 women), 1 part-time/adjunct (0 women). *Students:* 30 full-time (15 women); includes 5 minority (2 Asian, non-Hispanic/Latino; 1 Hispanic/Latino; 2 Two or more races, non-Hispanic/Latino), 5 international. Average age 27. In 2017, 5 doctorates awarded. *Degree requirements:* For doctorate, thesis/dissertation, written research proposal and defense. *Entrance requirements:* For doctorate, GRE General Test, 3 letters of recommendation. Additional exam requirements/recommendations for international students: Recommended—TOEFL (minimum score 630 paper-based; 90 iBT). Application fee: $60. Electronic applications accepted. *Financial support:* Fellowships, health care benefits, and tuition waivers (full) available. Financial award applicants required to submit FAFSA. *Unit head:* Anindya Dutta, Chair, 434-924-1940, Fax: 434-924-5069, E-mail: ad8q@virginia.edu. *Application contact:* Biomedical Sciences Graduate Studies, E-mail: bims@virginia.edu.
Website: http://www.virginia.edu/bmg/

University of Washington, Graduate School, School of Medicine, Graduate Programs in Medicine, Department of Biochemistry, Seattle, WA 98195. Offers PhD. *Degree requirements:* For doctorate, thesis/dissertation. *Entrance requirements:* For doctorate, GRE General Test, GRE Subject Test (biology, chemistry, biochemistry, or cell and molecular biology), minimum GPA of 3.0. Additional exam requirements/recommendations for international students: Required—TOEFL. Electronic applications accepted. *Faculty research:* Blood coagulation, structure and function of enzymes, fertilization events, interaction of plants with bacteria, protein structure.

University of Waterloo, Graduate Studies, Faculty of Science, Guelph-Waterloo Centre for Graduate Work in Chemistry and Biochemistry, Waterloo, ON N2L 3G1, Canada. Offers M Sc, PhD. M Sc, PhD offered jointly with University of Guelph. *Program availability:* Part-time. *Degree requirements:* For master's and doctorate, project or thesis. *Entrance requirements:* For master's, GRE, honors degree, minimum B average; for doctorate, GRE, master's degree, minimum B average. Additional exam requirements/recommendations for international students: Required—TOEFL, IELTS, PTE. Electronic applications accepted. *Faculty research:* Polymer, physical, inorganic, organic, and theoretical chemistry.

The University of Western Ontario, Faculty of Graduate Studies, Biosciences Division, Department of Biochemistry, London, ON N6A 5B8, Canada. Offers M Sc, PhD. *Degree requirements:* For master's, thesis; for doctorate, thesis/dissertation. *Entrance requirements:* For master's, minimum B+ average in last 2 years of undergraduate study; for doctorate, M Sc or an external scholarship winner.

University of Windsor, Faculty of Graduate Studies, Faculty of Science, Department of Chemistry and Biochemistry, Windsor, ON N9B 3P4, Canada. Offers M Sc, PhD. *Program availability:* Part-time. *Degree requirements:* For master's, thesis; for doctorate, comprehensive exam, thesis/dissertation. *Entrance requirements:* For master's and doctorate, minimum B average. Additional exam requirements/recommendations for international students: Required—TOEFL (minimum score 560 paper-based). Electronic applications accepted. *Faculty research:* Molecular biology/recombinant DNA techniques (PCR, cloning mutagenesis), No/02 detectors, western immunoblotting and detection, CD/NMR protein/peptide structure determination, confocal/electron microscopes.

University of Wisconsin–Madison, Graduate School, College of Agricultural and Life Sciences, Department of Biochemistry, Madison, WI 53706. Offers PhD. Terminal master's awarded for partial completion of doctoral program. *Degree requirements:* For doctorate, thesis/dissertation. *Entrance requirements:* For doctorate, GRE General Test, GRE Subject Test (recommended). Additional exam requirements/recommendations for international students: Required—TOEFL. Electronic applications accepted. *Faculty research:* Molecular structure of vitamins and hormones, enzymology, NMR spectroscopy, protein structure, molecular genetics.

University of Wisconsin–Madison, Graduate School, College of Agricultural and Life Sciences, Integrated Program in Biochemistry, Madison, WI 53706. Offers MS, PhD.
Website: https://ipib.wisc.edu/

University of Wisconsin–Milwaukee, Graduate School, College of Letters and Science, Department of Chemistry and Biochemistry, Milwaukee, WI 53201-0413. Offers MS, PhD. *Students:* 62 full-time (20 women), 17 part-time (7 women); includes 7 minority (4 Asian, non-Hispanic/Latino; 3 Two or more races, non-Hispanic/Latino), 35 international. Average age 30. 71 applicants, 28% accepted, 12 enrolled. In 2017, 8 doctorates awarded. *Degree requirements:* For master's, thesis or alternative; for doctorate, thesis/dissertation. *Entrance requirements:* For doctorate, GRE General Test. Additional exam requirements/recommendations for international students: Required—TOEFL (minimum score 600 paper-based; 79 iBT), IELTS (minimum score 6.5). *Application deadline:* For fall admission, 1/1 priority date for domestic students; for spring admission, 9/1 for domestic students. Application fee: $56 ($96 for international students). Electronic applications accepted. *Financial support:* In 2017–18, 3 fellowships, 30 research assistantships, 46 teaching assistantships were awarded; career-related internships or fieldwork, unspecified assistantships, and project assistantships also available. Support available to part-time students. Financial award application deadline: 4/15; financial award applicants required to submit FAFSA. *Faculty research:* Analytical chemistry, biochemistry, inorganic chemistry, organic chemistry, physical chemistry. *Unit head:* Peter Geissinger, Department Chair, 414-229-4098, E-mail: geissing@uwm.edu. *Application contact:* General Information Contact, 414-229-4982, Fax: 414-229-6967, E-mail: gradschool@uwm.edu.
Website: https://uwm.edu/chemistry/

Utah State University, School of Graduate Studies, College of Science, Department of Chemistry and Biochemistry, Logan, UT 84322. Offers biochemistry (MS, PhD); chemistry (MS, PhD). *Program availability:* Part-time. Terminal master's awarded for partial completion of doctoral program. *Degree requirements:* For master's, thesis, oral and written exams; for doctorate, thesis/dissertation, oral and written exams. *Entrance requirements:* For master's and doctorate, GRE General Test, minimum GPA of 3.0. Additional exam requirements/recommendations for international students: Required—TOEFL. *Faculty research:* Analytical, inorganic, organic, and physical chemistry; iron in asbestos chemistry and carcinogenicity; dicopper complexes; photothermal spectrometry; metal molecule clusters.

Vanderbilt University, School of Medicine, Department of Biochemistry, Nashville, TN 37240-1001. Offers MS, PhD, MD/PhD. *Faculty:* 21 full-time (3 women). *Students:* 33 full-time (18 women); includes 10 minority (3 Black or African American, non-Hispanic/Latino; 1 Asian, non-Hispanic/Latino; 5 Hispanic/Latino; 1 Two or more races, non-Hispanic/Latino), 4 international. Average age 27. In 2017, 1 master's, 7 doctorates awarded. Terminal master's awarded for partial completion of doctoral program. *Degree requirements:* For master's, thesis; for doctorate, thesis/dissertation, preliminary, qualifying, and final exams. *Entrance requirements:* For master's, GRE General Test; for doctorate, GRE General Test, GRE Subject Test (recommended). Additional exam requirements/recommendations for international students: Required—TOEFL (minimum score 570 paper-based; 88 iBT). *Application deadline:* For fall admission, 1/15 for domestic and international students. Application fee: $0. Electronic applications accepted. *Financial support:* Fellowships with full tuition reimbursements, research assistantships with full tuition reimbursements, Federal Work-Study, institutionally sponsored loans, scholarships/grants, traineeships, and tuition waivers (partial) available. Financial award application deadline: 1/15; financial award applicants required to submit CSS PROFILE or FAFSA. *Faculty research:* Protein chemistry, carcinogenesis, metabolism, toxicology, receptors and signaling, DNA recognition and transcription. *Unit head:* Dr. John York, Chair, 615-322-3315, Fax: 615-322-4349. *Application contact:* Charles Sanders, Director of Graduate Studies, 615-322-3315, E-mail: chuck.sanders@vanderbilt.edu.
Website: https://medschool.vanderbilt.edu/biochemistry/

Vanderbilt University, School of Medicine, Program in Chemical and Physical Biology, Nashville, TN 37240-1001. Offers PhD. *Students:* 41 full-time (14 women); includes 9 minority (1 Black or African American, non-Hispanic/Latino; 1 Asian, non-Hispanic/Latino; 7 Hispanic/Latino), 6 international. Average age 28. In 2017, 5 doctorates awarded. *Degree requirements:* For doctorate, comprehensive exam, thesis/dissertation, dissertation defense. *Entrance requirements:* For doctorate, GRE, 3 letters of recommendation, official transcripts. Additional exam requirements/recommendations for international students: Required—TOEFL. *Application deadline:* For fall admission, 1/15 priority date for domestic students, 1/15 for international students. Applications are processed on a rolling basis. Application fee: $0. Electronic applications accepted. *Financial support:* Fellowships with full tuition reimbursements, traineeships, health care benefits, and tuition waivers (full) available. *Faculty research:* Mathematical modeling, enzyme kinetics, structural biology, genomics, proteomics and mass spectrometry. *Unit head:* Dr. Bruce Damon, Director of Graduate Studies, 615-322-4235, Fax: 615-343-0490, E-mail: bruce.damon@vanderbilt.edu. *Application contact:* Patricia Mueller, Coordinator, 615-322-8727, E-mail: patricia.l.mueller@vanderbilt.edu.

Virginia Commonwealth University, Medical College of Virginia-Professional Programs, School of Medicine, Graduate Programs in Medicine, Department of Biochemistry and Molecular Biology, Richmond, VA 23284-9005. Offers MS, PhD, MD/PhD. *Degree requirements:* For master's, thesis; for doctorate, thesis/dissertation, comprehensive oral and written exams. *Entrance requirements:* For master's and doctorate, GRE, MCAT or DAT. Electronic applications accepted. *Faculty research:* Molecular biology, peptide/protein chemistry, neurochemistry, enzyme mechanisms, macromolecular structure determination.

Virginia Polytechnic Institute and State University, Graduate School, College of Agriculture and Life Sciences, Blacksburg, VA 24061. Offers agricultural and applied economics (MS, PhD); agricultural and life sciences (MS); agriculture, leadership, and community education (MS, PhD); animal and poultry science (MS, PhD); biochemistry (MS, PhD); crop and soil environmental sciences (MS, PhD); dairy science (MS, PhD); entomology (MS, PhD); food science and technology (MS, PhD); horticulture (PhD); human nutrition, foods and exercise (MS, PhD); plant pathology, physiology, and weed science (MS, PhD). *Faculty:* 241 full-time (73 women), 1 (woman) part-time/adjunct. *Students:* 379 full-time (221 women), 126 part-time (75 women); includes 64 minority (21 Black or African American, non-Hispanic/Latino; 15 Asian, non-Hispanic/Latino; 14 Hispanic/Latino; 14 Two or more races, non-Hispanic/Latino), 119 international. Average age 29. 357 applicants, 46% accepted, 118 enrolled. In 2017, 105 master's, 54 doctorates awarded. *Degree requirements:* For master's, comprehensive exam (for some programs), thesis (for some programs); for doctorate, comprehensive exam (for some programs), thesis/dissertation (for some programs). *Entrance requirements:* For master's and doctorate, GRE/GMAT. Additional exam requirements/recommendations for international students: Required—TOEFL (minimum score 80 iBT). *Application deadline:* For fall admission, 8/1 for domestic students, 4/1 for international students; for spring admission, 1/1 for domestic students, 9/1 for international students. Applications are processed on a rolling basis. Application fee: $75. Electronic applications accepted. *Expenses:* Tuition, state resident: full-time $15,072; part-time $718.50 per credit hour. Tuition, nonresident: full-time $28,810; part-time $1448.25 per credit hour. *Required fees:* $2741; $502 per semester. Tuition and fees vary according to course load, campus/location and program. *Financial support:* In 2017–18, 232 research assistantships with full tuition reimbursements (averaging $21,852 per year), 94 teaching assistantships with full tuition reimbursements (averaging $21,643 per year) were awarded. Financial award application deadline: 3/1; financial award applicants required to submit FAFSA. *Total annual research expenditures:* $44.3 million. *Unit head:* Dr. Alan L. Grant, Dean, 540-231-4152, Fax: 540-231-4163, E-mail: algrant@vt.edu. *Application contact:* Crystal Tawney, Administrative Assistant, 540-231-4152, Fax: 540-231-4163, E-mail: cdtawney@vt.edu.
Website: http://www.cals.vt.edu/

Wake Forest University, School of Medicine and Graduate School of Arts and Sciences, Graduate Programs in Medicine, Department of Biochemistry, Winston-Salem, NC 27109. Offers PhD, MD/PhD. *Degree requirements:* For doctorate, thesis/dissertation. *Entrance requirements:* For doctorate, GRE General Test. Additional exam requirements/recommendations for international students: Required—TOEFL. Electronic applications accepted. *Faculty research:* Biomembranes, cancer, biophysics.

Washington State University, College of Veterinary Medicine, Molecular Biosciences Graduate Program, Pullman, WA 99164-7520. Offers molecular biosciences (MS, PhD), including genetics (PhD). *Faculty:* 26 full-time (9 women), 27 part-time/adjunct (4 women). *Students:* 36 full-time (23 women); includes 10 minority (2 Asian, non-Hispanic/Latino; 6 Hispanic/Latino; 2 Two or more races, non-Hispanic/Latino), 1 international. Average age 27. 76 applicants, 22% accepted, 6 enrolled. In 2017, 1 master's, 10 doctorates awarded. Terminal master's awarded for partial completion of doctoral program. *Degree requirements:* For master's, thesis (for some programs), oral defense; for doctorate, comprehensive exam, thesis/dissertation, oral defense. *Entrance requirements:* For master's and doctorate, GRE General Test, minimum GPA of 3.0. Additional exam requirements/recommendations for international students: Required—TOEFL (minimum score 600 paper-based; 100 iBT). *Application deadline:* For fall admission, 12/15 priority date for domestic and international students. Application fee: $75. Electronic applications accepted. *Expenses:* Contact institution. *Financial support:* In 2017–18, 36 students received support, including 6 fellowships with full tuition reimbursements available (averaging $25,911 per year), 12 research assistantships with full tuition reimbursements available (averaging $25,911 per year), 18 teaching assistantships with full tuition reimbursements available (averaging $25,911 per year); scholarships/grants, traineeships, and health care benefits also available. Financial award application deadline: 4/15. *Faculty research:* Bacterial pathogenesis, microbial metabolism, DNA repair, reproductive biology, cytoskeleton, molecular cell biology, biochemistry, signal transduction, protein export. *Total annual research expenditures:* $4.3 million. *Unit head:* Dr. Jonathan Jones, Director, 509-335-8724, Fax: 509-335-9688, E-mail: jcr.jones@vetmed.wsu.edu. *Application contact:* Tami Breske, Graduate Academic Coordinator, 509-335-4318, E-mail: tbreske@vetmed.wsu.edu.
Website: http://www.smb.wsu.edu

Washington University in St. Louis, The Graduate School, Division of Biology and Biomedical Sciences, Program in Biochemistry, St. Louis, MO 63130-4899. Offers PhD. *Degree requirements:* For doctorate, thesis/dissertation. *Entrance requirements:* For doctorate, GRE General Test, GRE Subject Test. Additional exam requirements/recommendations for international students: Required—TOEFL. Electronic applications accepted. *Faculty research:* Metabolic regulation, signal transduction, receptors, membrane channels and transporters, membrane structure and dynamics, membrane trafficking, cholesterol and lipid metabolism, nucleic acid-protein structure interactions and function, DNA replication and repair, recombination, transcription, translation, enzyme kinetics, cancer biology, cell cycle regulation, apoptosis, cell motility, cytoskeleton, cell division, extracellular matrix, vascular biology, aging, senescence, telomere biology.

Wayne State University, School of Medicine, Office of Biomedical Graduate Programs, Detroit, MI 48202. Offers anatomy and cell biology (MS, PhD); basic medical sciences (MS); biochemistry and molecular biology (MS, PhD); cancer biology (MS, PhD); clinical and translational science (Graduate Certificate); family medicine and public health sciences (MPH, Graduate Certificate), including public health practice; genetic counseling (MS); immunology and microbiology (MS, PhD); medical physics (MS, PhD, Graduate Certificate); medical research (MS); molecular medicine and genomics (MS, PhD), including molecular genetics and genomics; pathology (PhD); pharmacology (MS, PhD); physiology (MS, PhD), including physiology, reproductive sciences (PhD); psychiatry and behavioral neurosciences (PhD), including translational neuroscience; MD/MPH; MD/PhD; MPH/MA; MSW/MPH. *Program availability:* Part-time, evening/weekend. *Students:* 268 full-time (152 women), 117 part-time (59 women); includes 108 minority (19 Black or African American, non-Hispanic/Latino; 1 American Indian or Alaska Native, non-Hispanic/Latino; 62 Asian, non-Hispanic/Latino; 9 Hispanic/Latino; 17 Two or more races, non-Hispanic/Latino), 48 international. Average age 26. 1,133 applicants, 21% accepted, 151 enrolled. In 2017, 70 master's, 25 doctorates, 10 other advanced degrees awarded. Terminal master's awarded for partial completion of doctoral program. *Degree requirements:* For master's, thesis (for some programs); for doctorate, thesis/dissertation. *Entrance requirements:* For master's, doctorate, and Graduate Certificate, GRE. Additional exam requirements/recommendations for international students: Required—TOEFL (minimum score 550 paper-based; 100 iBT), Michigan English Language Assessment Battery (minimum score 85); Recommended—IELTS (minimum score 6.5), TWE (minimum score 5.5). *Application deadline:* For fall admission, 2/1 for domestic and international students. Applications are processed on a rolling basis. Application fee: $50. Electronic applications accepted. *Expenses:* Contact institution. *Financial support:* In 2017–18, 177 students received support, including 64 fellowships with full tuition reimbursements available (averaging $24,388 per year), 79 research assistantships with full tuition reimbursements available (averaging $26,894

per year); scholarships/grants, traineeships, and health care benefits also available. *Faculty research:* Cancer biology, neurosciences, vision sciences, molecular biology, pathology, physiology, pharmacology, public health, medical physics. *Unit head:* Dr. Daniel A. Walz, Associate Dean for Biomedical Graduate Programs, 313-577-1455, Fax: 313-577-8796, E-mail: gradprogs@med.wayne.edu.
Website: https://www.med.wayne.edu/biomedical-graduate-programs/

Weill Cornell Medicine, Weill Cornell Graduate School of Medical Sciences, Biochemistry, Cell and Molecular Biology Allied Program, New York, NY 10065. Offers MS, PhD. Terminal master's awarded for partial completion of doctoral program. *Degree requirements:* For master's, comprehensive exam; for doctorate, thesis/dissertation, final exam. *Entrance requirements:* For doctorate, GRE General Test, background in genetics, molecular biology, chemistry, or biochemistry. Additional exam requirements/recommendations for international students: Required—TOEFL. Electronic applications accepted. *Faculty research:* Molecular structure determination, protein structure, gene structure, stem cell biology, control of gene expression, DNA replication, chromosome maintenance, RNA biosynthesis.

Weill Cornell Medicine, Weill Cornell Graduate School of Medical Sciences, Cornell/Rockefeller/Sloan Kettering Tri-Institutional PhD Program in Chemical Biology, New York, NY 10065. Offers PhD. Program offered jointly with The Rockefeller University and Sloan Kettering Institute. *Degree requirements:* For doctorate, comprehensive exam, thesis/dissertation. *Entrance requirements:* For doctorate, GRE General Test; GRE Subject Test in chemistry (recommended), 3 letters of recommendation. Additional exam requirements/recommendations for international students: Required—TOEFL (minimum score 600 paper-based; 90 iBT). Electronic applications accepted. *Faculty research:* Bioreactive small molecules, macromolecular structure and function, chemical cell biology, biotechnology, computational chemistry.

Wesleyan University, Graduate Studies, Department of Chemistry, Middletown, CT 06459. Offers biochemistry (PhD); chemical physics (PhD); inorganic chemistry (PhD); organic chemistry (PhD); physical chemistry (PhD); theoretical chemistry (PhD). *Faculty:* 11 full-time (3 women), 1 part-time/adjunct (0 women). *Students:* 21 full-time (14 women), 2 part-time (0 women); includes 6 minority (2 Asian, non-Hispanic/Latino; 4 Hispanic/Latino), 4 international. Average age 25. In 2017, 4 doctorates awarded. Terminal master's awarded for partial completion of doctoral program. *Degree requirements:* For doctorate, thesis/dissertation. *Entrance requirements:* For doctorate, GRE General Test, 3 recommendations. Additional exam requirements/recommendations for international students: Required—TOEFL, IELTS. *Application deadline:* 1/1 for domestic and international students; for summer admission, 1/1 for domestic and international students. Application fee: $0. Electronic applications accepted. *Financial support:* In 2017–18, 15 students received support, including 4 research assistantships with full tuition reimbursements available, 13 teaching assistantships with full tuition reimbursements available; institutionally sponsored loans and health care benefits also available. Financial award application deadline: 4/30. *Faculty research:* The synthesis of noble metal and noble metal alloy nanoparticles with well-defined shapes and catalytically-active high-energy surfaces; inorganic chemistry; materials science; scanning electron microscopy (SEM);transition organometallic complexes. *Unit head:* T. David Westmoreland, Chair, 860-685-2743, E-mail: westmoreland@wesleyan.edu. *Application contact:* Holly King, Administrative Assistant/Graduate Program Coordinator, 860-685-2572, Fax: 860-685-2211, E-mail: chemistry@wesleyan.edu.
Website: http://www.wesleyan.edu/chem/

Wesleyan University, Graduate Studies, Department of Molecular Biology and Biochemistry, Middletown, CT 06459. Offers molecular biology and biochemistry (PhD); molecular biophysics (PhD). *Faculty:* 8 full-time (3 women), 2 part-time/adjunct (both women). *Students:* 16 full-time (10 women); includes 4 minority (2 Asian, non-Hispanic/Latino; 1 Hispanic/Latino; 1 Two or more races, non-Hispanic/Latino), 7 international. Average age 24. 24 applicants, 25% accepted, 3 enrolled. In 2017, 2 doctorates awarded. Terminal master's awarded for partial completion of doctoral program. *Degree requirements:* For doctorate, comprehensive exam, thesis/dissertation. *Entrance requirements:* For doctorate, GRE General Test, GRE Subject Test. Additional exam requirements/recommendations for international students: Required—TOEFL. *Application deadline:* For fall admission, 1/15 for domestic and international students. Application fee: $0. Electronic applications accepted. *Financial support:* In 2017–18, 9 teaching assistantships with full tuition reimbursements were awarded; research assistantships with full tuition reimbursements and institutionally sponsored loans also available. Financial award application deadline: 4/15. *Faculty research:* The olfactory system and new frontiers in genome research, chromosome structure and gene expression, gene co-regulation, crystallographic and spectroscopic analysis, DNA replication and repair. *Unit head:* Amy MacQueen, Chair, 860-685-2561, E-mail: amacqueen@wesleyan.edu. *Application contact:* Anika Dane, Administrative Assistant, 860-685-2404, E-mail: adane@wesleyan.edu.
Website: http://www.wesleyan.edu/mbb/

West Virginia University, School of Medicine, Morgantown, WV 26506-9600. Offers biochemistry and molecular biology (PhD); biomedical science (MS); cancer cell biology (PhD); cellular and integrative physiology (PhD); exercise physiology (MS, PhD); health sciences (MS); immunology (PhD); medicine (MD); occupational therapy (MOT); pathologists assistant (MHS); physical therapy (DPT). *Program availability:* Part-time, evening/weekend. *Students:* 781 full-time (440 women), 25 part-time (13 women); includes 140 minority (15 Black or African American, non-Hispanic/Latino; 1 American Indian or Alaska Native, non-Hispanic/Latino; 68 Asian, non-Hispanic/Latino; 37 Hispanic/Latino; 1 Native Hawaiian or other Pacific Islander, non-Hispanic/Latino; 18 Two or more races, non-Hispanic/Latino), 19 international. *Entrance requirements:* Additional exam requirements/recommendations for international students: Required—TOEFL. *Application deadline:* Applications are processed on a rolling basis. Application fee: $60. Electronic applications accepted. *Expenses:* Contact institution. *Financial support:* Fellowships, research assistantships, teaching assistantships, career-related internships or fieldwork, Federal Work-Study, institutionally sponsored loans, health care benefits, tuition waivers (full and partial), and administrative assistantships available. Financial award applicants required to submit FAFSA. *Unit head:* Dr. Clay Marsh, Executive Dean, 304-293-6607, Fax: 304-293-6627, E-mail: clay.marsh@hsc.wvu.edu. *Application contact:* Lisa M. Salati, Assistant Vice President, Graduate Education, 304-293-7759, Fax: 304-293-3080, E-mail: lsalati@hsc.wvu.edu.
Website: https://medicine.hsc.wvu.edu

Worcester Polytechnic Institute, Graduate Admissions, Department of Chemistry and Biochemistry, Worcester, MA 01609-2280. Offers biochemistry (MS, PhD); chemistry (MS, PhD). *Program availability:* Part-time, evening/weekend. *Faculty:* 10 full-time (4 women). *Students:* 22 full-time (11 women), 3 part-time (1 woman); includes 1 minority (Black or African American, non-Hispanic/Latino), 6 international. Average age 27. 29 applicants, 52% accepted, 7 enrolled. In 2017, 1 master's awarded. *Degree requirements:* For doctorate, comprehensive exam, thesis/dissertation. *Entrance requirements:* For master's and doctorate, GRE General Test, 3 letters of recommendation, statement of purpose. Additional exam requirements/recommendations for international students: Required—TOEFL (minimum score 563 paper-based; 84 iBT), IELTS (minimum score 7). *Application deadline:* For fall admission, 1/1 priority date for domestic and international students; for spring admission, 10/1 priority date for domestic and international students. Applications are processed on a rolling basis. Application fee: $70. Electronic applications accepted. *Expenses: Tuition:* Full-time $26,226; part-time $1457 per credit. *Required fees:* $60; $30 per credit. One-time fee: $15. Tuition and fees vary according to course load. *Financial support:* Fellowships, research assistantships, teaching assistantships, career-related internships or fieldwork, institutionally sponsored loans, scholarships/grants, and unspecified assistantships available. Financial award application deadline: 1/1. *Unit head:* Dr. Arne Gericke, Department Head, 508-831-5371, Fax: 508-831-5933, E-mail: agericke@wpi.edu. *Application contact:* Dr. Anita Mattson, Graduate Coordinator, 508-831-5371, Fax: 508-831-5933, E-mail: aemattson@wpi.edu.
Website: https://www.wpi.edu/academics/departments/chemistry-biochemistry

Wright State University, Graduate School, College of Science and Mathematics, Department of Biochemistry and Molecular Biology, Dayton, OH 45435. Offers MS. *Degree requirements:* For master's, thesis. *Entrance requirements:* Additional exam requirements/recommendations for international students: Required—TOEFL. *Faculty research:* Regulation of gene expression, macromolecular structural function, NMR imaging, visual biochemistry.

Yale University, Graduate School of Arts and Sciences, Department of Geology and Geophysics, New Haven, CT 06520. Offers biogeochemistry (PhD); climate dynamics (PhD); geochemistry (PhD); geophysics (PhD); meteorology (PhD); oceanography (PhD); paleontology (PhD); paleooceanography (PhD); petrology (PhD); tectonics (PhD). *Degree requirements:* For doctorate, thesis/dissertation. *Entrance requirements:* For doctorate, GRE General Test. Additional exam requirements/recommendations for international students: Required—TOEFL.

Yale University, Graduate School of Arts and Sciences, Department of Molecular Biophysics and Biochemistry, New Haven, CT 06520. Offers PhD. *Degree requirements:* For doctorate, thesis/dissertation. *Entrance requirements:* For doctorate, GRE General Test, GRE Subject Test.

Yale University, Graduate School of Arts and Sciences, Department of Molecular, Cellular, and Developmental Biology, Program in Biochemistry, Molecular Biology and Chemical Biology, New Haven, CT 06520. Offers PhD. *Degree requirements:* For doctorate, thesis/dissertation. *Entrance requirements:* For doctorate, GRE General Test, GRE Subject Test.

Yale University, Yale School of Medicine and Graduate School of Arts and Sciences, Combined Program in Biological and Biomedical Sciences (BBS), Molecular Biophysics and Biochemistry Track, New Haven, CT 06520. Offers PhD, MD/PhD. *Degree requirements:* For doctorate, thesis/dissertation. *Entrance requirements:* For doctorate, GRE General Test. Additional exam requirements/recommendations for international students: Required—TOEFL. Electronic applications accepted.

Youngstown State University, Graduate School, College of Science, Technology, Engineering and Mathematics, Department of Chemistry, Youngstown, OH 44555-0001. Offers analytical chemistry (MS); biochemistry (MS); chemistry education (MS); inorganic chemistry (MS); organic chemistry (MS); physical chemistry (MS). *Program availability:* Part-time. *Degree requirements:* For master's, thesis. *Entrance requirements:* For master's, bachelor's degree in chemistry, minimum GPA of 2.7. Additional exam requirements/recommendations for international students: Required—TOEFL. *Faculty research:* Analysis of antioxidants, chromatography, defects and disorder in crystalline oxides, hydrogen bonding, novel organic and organometallic materials.

Section 4
Biophysics

This section contains a directory of institutions offering graduate work in biophysics, followed by an in-depth entry submitted by an institution that chose to prepare a detailed program description. Additional information about programs listed in the directory but not augmented by an in-depth entry may be obtained by writing directly to the dean of a graduate school or chair of a department at the address given in the directory.

For programs offering related work, see also in this book *Allied Health; Biochemistry; Biological and Biomedical Sciences; Cell, Molecular, and Structural Biology; Optometry and Vision Sciences; Neuroscience and Neurobiology; Physiology;* and *Public Health.* In the other guides in this series:

Graduate Programs in the Physical Sciences, Mathematics, Agricultural Sciences, the Environment & Natural Resources
See *Chemistry* and *Physics*

Graduate Programs in Engineering & Applied Sciences
See *Agricultural Engineering and Bioengineering* and *Biomedical Engineering and Biotechnology*

CONTENTS

Program Directories

Featured School: Display and Close-Up

Biophysics

Albert Einstein College of Medicine, Graduate Programs in the Biomedical Sciences, Department of Physiology and Biophysics, Bronx, NY 10461. Offers PhD, MD/PhD. *Degree requirements:* For doctorate, thesis/dissertation. *Entrance requirements:* For doctorate, GRE General Test. Additional exam requirements/recommendations for international students: Required—TOEFL. *Application deadline:* For fall admission, 1/15 for domestic students. Application fee: $0. *Financial support:* Fellowships available. *Faculty research:* Biophysical and biochemical basis of body function at the subcellular, cellular, organ, and whole-body level. *Unit head:* Dr. Denis M. Rousseau, Chairperson, 718-430-3592. *Application contact:* Sheila Cleeton, Executive Director and Registrar, Einstein Graduate Division, 718-430-2128, Fax: 718-430-8655, E-mail: sheila.cleeton@einstein.yu.edu.
Website: http://www.einstein.yu.edu/departments/physiology-biophysics/

Baylor College of Medicine, Graduate School of Biomedical Sciences, Department of Molecular Physiology and Biophysics, Houston, TX 77030-3498. Offers cardiovascular sciences (PhD); molecular physiology and biophysics (PhD); MD/PhD. *Degree requirements:* For doctorate, thesis/dissertation, public defense. *Entrance requirements:* For doctorate, GRE General Test, GRE Subject Test (strongly recommended), minimum GPA of 3.0. Additional exam requirements/recommendations for international students: Required—TOEFL. Electronic applications accepted. *Faculty research:* Cardiovascular disease; skeletal muscle disease (myasthenia gravis, muscular dystrophy, malignant hyperthermia, central core disease); cancer; Alzheimer's disease; developmental diseases of the nervous system, eye and heart; diabetes; motor neuron disease (amyotrophic lateral sclerosis and spinal muscular atrophy); asthma; autoimmune diseases.

Boston University, School of Medicine, Division of Graduate Medical Sciences, Department of Physiology and Biophysics, Boston, MA 02118. Offers MA, PhD, MD/PhD. *Program availability:* Part-time. Terminal master's awarded for partial completion of doctoral program. *Degree requirements:* For master's, thesis; for doctorate, thesis/dissertation. *Application deadline:* For fall admission, 1/15 for domestic students; for spring admission, 10/15 for domestic students. *Faculty research:* X-ray scattering, NMR spectroscopy, protein crystallography, structural electron. *Unit head:* Dr. David Atkinson, Chairman, 617-638-4015, Fax: 617-638-4041, E-mail: atkinson@bu.edu. *Application contact:* GMS Admissions Office, 617-638-5255, E-mail: askgms@bu.edu.
Website: http://www.bumc.bu.edu/phys-biophys/

Brandeis University, Graduate School of Arts and Sciences, Program in Biochemistry and Biophysics, Waltham, MA 02454-9110. Offers biochemistry and biophysics (MS, PhD); quantitative biology (PhD). *Faculty:* 11 full-time (5 women). *Students:* 35 full-time (14 women); includes 8 minority (4 Asian, non-Hispanic/Latino; 2 Hispanic/Latino; 2 Two or more races, non-Hispanic/Latino), 6 international. Average age 27. 77 applicants, 25% accepted, 16 enrolled. In 2017, 1 master's, 6 doctorates awarded. Terminal master's awarded for partial completion of doctoral program. *Degree requirements:* For master's, thesis; for doctorate, thesis/dissertation, qualifying exams. *Entrance requirements:* For master's, GRE General Test, resume, letters of recommendation, statement of purpose, transcripts; for doctorate, GRE General Test, resume, letters of recommendation, statement of purpose, transcripts, list of previous research experience. Additional exam requirements/recommendations for international students: Required—PTE (minimum score 68), TOEFL (minimum score 600 paper-based, 100 iBT) or IELTS (7). *Application deadline:* For fall admission, 12/1 priority date for domestic students. Applications are processed on a rolling basis. Application fee: $75. Electronic applications accepted. *Expenses: Tuition:* Full-time $48,720. *Required fees:* $88. Tuition and fees vary according to course load, degree level, program and student level. *Financial support:* In 2017–18, 39 students received support, including 17 fellowships with full tuition reimbursements available (averaging $33,000 per year), 21 research assistantships with full tuition reimbursements available (averaging $33,000 per year); Federal Work-Study, scholarships/grants, health care benefits, and tuition waivers (partial) also available. Financial award application deadline: 4/15; financial award applicants required to submit FAFSA. *Faculty research:* Macromolecular chemistry, structure and function, biochemistry, biophysics, biological macromolecules. *Unit head:* Dr. Dagmar Ringe, Director of Graduate Studies, 781-736-4902, E-mail: scigradoffice@brandeis.edu. *Application contact:* Rachel Krebs, Department Administrator, 781-736-2352, E-mail: scigradoffice@brandeis.edu.
Website: http://www.brandeis.edu/gsas/programs/bio.html

California Institute of Technology, Division of Biology, Program in Cell Biology and Biophysics, Pasadena, CA 91125-0001. Offers PhD. *Degree requirements:* For doctorate, thesis/dissertation, qualifying exam. *Entrance requirements:* For doctorate, GRE General Test.

Carnegie Mellon University, Mellon College of Science, Department of Biological Sciences, Pittsburgh, PA 15213-3891. Offers biochemistry (PhD); biophysics (PhD); cell and developmental biology (PhD); computational biology (MS, PhD); genetics (PhD); molecular biology (PhD); neuroscience (PhD); structural biology (PhD). *Degree requirements:* For doctorate, comprehensive exam, thesis/dissertation. *Entrance requirements:* For doctorate, GRE General Test, GRE Subject Test, interview. Electronic applications accepted. *Faculty research:* Genetic structure, function, and regulation; protein structure and function; biological membranes; biological spectroscopy.

Case Western Reserve University, School of Medicine and School of Graduate Studies, Graduate Programs in Medicine, Department of Physiology and Biophysics, Cleveland, OH 44106. Offers medical physiology (MS); physiology and biophysics (PhD); MD/PhD. Terminal master's awarded for partial completion of doctoral program. *Degree requirements:* For master's, thesis; for doctorate, thesis/dissertation. *Entrance requirements:* For master's, GRE General Test, minimum GPA of 3.28; for doctorate, GRE General Test, minimum GPA of 3.6. Additional exam requirements/recommendations for international students: Required—TOEFL. Electronic applications accepted. *Expenses: Tuition:* Full-time $43,854; part-time $1827 per credit hour. *Required fees:* $50; $50 per credit hour. Tuition and fees vary according to course load and program. *Faculty research:* Cardiovascular physiology, calcium metabolism, epithelial cell biology.

Columbia University, College of Physicians and Surgeons, Department of Biochemistry and Molecular Biophysics, New York, NY 10032. Offers biochemistry and molecular biophysics (M Phil, PhD); biophysics (PhD); MD/PhD. Only candidates for the PhD are admitted. *Degree requirements:* For doctorate, one foreign language, thesis/dissertation. *Entrance requirements:* For master's and doctorate, GRE General Test. Additional exam requirements/recommendations for international students: Required—TOEFL. *Expenses: Tuition:* Full-time $44,864; part-time $1704 per credit. *Required fees:* $2370 per semester. One-time fee: $105.

Columbia University, College of Physicians and Surgeons, Department of Physiology and Cellular Biophysics, New York, NY 10032. Offers M Phil, MA, PhD, MD/PhD. Only candidates for the PhD are admitted. Terminal master's awarded for partial completion of doctoral program. *Degree requirements:* For doctorate, thesis/dissertation. *Entrance requirements:* For master's and doctorate, GRE General Test. Additional exam requirements/recommendations for international students: Required—TOEFL. *Expenses: Tuition:* Full-time $44,864; part-time $1704 per credit. *Required fees:* $2370 per semester. One-time fee: $105. *Faculty research:* Membrane physiology, cellular biology, cardiovascular physiology, neurophysiology.

Columbia University, College of Physicians and Surgeons, Integrated Program in Cellular, Molecular, Structural and Genetic Studies, New York, NY 10032. Offers PhD. Terminal master's awarded for partial completion of doctoral program. *Degree requirements:* For doctorate, thesis/dissertation. *Entrance requirements:* For doctorate, GRE General Test, GRE Subject Test. Additional exam requirements/recommendations for international students: Required—TOEFL. *Expenses:* Contact institution. *Faculty research:* Transcription, macromolecular sorting, gene expression during development, cellular interaction.

Cornell University, Graduate School, Graduate Fields of Agriculture and Life Sciences, Field of Biochemistry, Molecular and Cell Biology, Ithaca, NY 14853. Offers biochemistry (PhD); biophysics (PhD); cell biology (PhD); molecular biology (PhD). *Degree requirements:* For doctorate, comprehensive exam, thesis/dissertation, 2 semesters of teaching experience. *Entrance requirements:* For doctorate, GRE General Test, GRE Subject Test (biology, chemistry, physics, biochemistry, cell and molecular biology), 3 letters of recommendation. Additional exam requirements/recommendations for international students: Required—TOEFL (minimum score 600 paper-based; 77 iBT). Electronic applications accepted. *Faculty research:* Biophysics, structural biology.

Cornell University, Graduate School, Graduate Fields of Agriculture and Life Sciences, Field of Biophysics, Ithaca, NY 14853. Offers PhD. *Degree requirements:* For doctorate, comprehensive exam, thesis/dissertation. *Entrance requirements:* For doctorate, GRE General Test, GRE Subject Test (physics or chemistry preferred), 3 letters of recommendation. Additional exam requirements/recommendations for international students: Required—TOEFL (minimum score 550 paper-based; 77 iBT). Electronic applications accepted. *Faculty research:* Protein structure and function, biomolecular and cellular function, membrane biophysics, signal transduction, computational biology.

Dalhousie University, Faculty of Medicine, Department of Physiology and Biophysics, Halifax, NS B3H 1X5, Canada. Offers M Sc, PhD, M Sc/PhD. *Degree requirements:* For master's, thesis; for doctorate, thesis/dissertation. *Entrance requirements:* For master's and doctorate, GRE Subject Test (for international students). Additional exam requirements/recommendations for international students: Required—1 of 5 approved tests: TOEFL, IELTS, CANTEST, CAEL, Michigan English Language Assessment Battery. Electronic applications accepted. *Faculty research:* Computer modeling, reproductive and endocrine physiology, cardiovascular physiology, neurophysiology, membrane biophysics.

East Carolina University, Graduate School, Thomas Harriot College of Arts and Sciences, Department of Physics, Greenville, NC 27858-4353. Offers applied physics (MS); biomedical physics (PhD); health physics (MS); medical physics (MS). *Program availability:* Part-time. *Students:* 39 full-time (10 women), 8 part-time (2 women); includes 11 minority (4 Black or African American, non-Hispanic/Latino; 4 Asian, non-Hispanic/Latino; 2 Hispanic/Latino; 1 Two or more races, non-Hispanic/Latino), 5 international. Average age 29. 37 applicants, 70% accepted, 16 enrolled. In 2017, 4 master's, 1 doctorate awarded. *Degree requirements:* For master's, comprehensive exam; for doctorate, comprehensive exam, thesis/dissertation. *Entrance requirements:* For master's and doctorate, GRE General Test. Additional exam requirements/recommendations for international students: Recommended—TOEFL (minimum score 78 iBT), IELTS (minimum score 6.5). *Application deadline:* For fall admission, 3/1 priority date for domestic and international students. Applications are processed on a rolling basis. Application fee: $75. Electronic applications accepted. *Expenses:* Tuition, state resident: full-time $4749; part-time $297 per credit hour. Tuition, nonresident: full-time $17,898; part-time $1119 per credit hour. *Required fees:* $2691; $224 per credit hour. Part-time tuition and fees vary according to course load and program. *Financial support:* Research assistantships with partial tuition reimbursements, teaching assistantships with partial tuition reimbursements, and Federal Work-Study available. Support available to part-time students. Financial award application deadline: 3/1. *Faculty research:* Health and medical physics, biological and biomedical physics, radiological physics, acoustics and bioacoustics, theoretical and computational physics. *Unit head:* Dr. Jefferson Shinpaugh, Chair, 252-328-1852, E-mail: shinpaughj@ecu.edu. *Application contact:* Dean of Graduate School, 252-328-6012, Fax: 252-328-6071, E-mail: gradschool@ecu.edu.
Website: http://www.ecu.edu/cs-cas/physics/

Emory University, Laney Graduate School, Department of Physics, Atlanta, GA 30322-1100. Offers biophysics (PhD); experimental condensed matter physics (PhD); theoretical and computational statistical physics (PhD); MS/PhD. *Degree requirements:* For doctorate, thesis/dissertation, qualifier proposal. *Entrance requirements:* For doctorate, GRE General Test, minimum GPA of 3.0. Additional exam requirements/recommendations for international students: Required—TOEFL (minimum score 600 paper-based). Electronic applications accepted. *Faculty research:* Experimental studies of the structure and function of metalloproteins, soft condensed matter, granular materials, biophotonics and fluorescence correlation spectroscopy, single molecule studies of DNA-protein systems.

Harvard University, Graduate School of Arts and Sciences, Committee on Biophysics, Cambridge, MA 02138. Offers PhD. *Degree requirements:* For doctorate, thesis/dissertation, exam, qualifying paper. *Entrance requirements:* For doctorate, GRE General Test, GRE Subject Test (recommended). Additional exam requirements/recommendations for international students: Required—TOEFL. *Faculty research:* Structural molecular biology, cell and membrane biophysics, molecular genetics, physical biochemistry, mathematical biophysics.

See Display on the next page and Close-Up on page 153.

Howard University, Graduate School, Department of Physiology and Biophysics, Washington, DC 20059-0002. Offers biophysics (PhD); physiology (PhD). *Degree requirements:* For doctorate, comprehensive exam, thesis/dissertation. *Entrance requirements:* For doctorate, GRE General Test, minimum B average in field. *Faculty research:* Cardiovascular physiology, pulmonary physiology, renal physiology, neurophysiology, endocrinology.

Illinois State University, Graduate School, College of Arts and Sciences, School of Biological Sciences, Normal, IL 61790. Offers animal behavior (MS); bacteriology (MS); biochemistry (MS); biological sciences (MS); biology (PhD); biophysics (MS); biotechnology (MS); botany (MS, PhD); cell biology (MS); conservation biology (MS); developmental biology (MS); ecology (MS, PhD); entomology (MS); evolutionary biology (MS); genetics (MS, PhD); immunology (MS); microbiology (MS, PhD); molecular biology (MS); molecular genetics (MS); neurobiology (MS); neuroscience (MS); parasitology (MS); physiology (MS, PhD); plant biology (MS); plant molecular biology (MS); plant sciences (MS); structural biology (MS); zoology (MS, PhD). *Program availability:* Part-time. *Degree requirements:* For master's, thesis or alternative; for doctorate, variable foreign language requirement, thesis/dissertation, 2 terms of residency. *Entrance requirements:* For master's, GRE General Test, minimum GPA of 2.6 in last 60 hours of course work; for doctorate, GRE General Test. *Faculty research:* Redoc balance and drug development in schistosoma mansoni, control of the growth of listeria monocytogenes at low temperature, regulation of cell expansion and microtubule function by SPRI, CRUI: physiology and fitness consequences of different life history phenotypes.

Iowa State University of Science and Technology, Program in Biophysics, Ames, IA 50011. Offers MS, PhD. *Entrance requirements:* For master's, GRE. Additional exam requirements/recommendations for international students: Required—TOEFL (minimum score 550 paper-based; 79 iBT), IELTS (minimum score 6.5). Electronic applications accepted.

Johns Hopkins University, National Institutes of Health Sponsored Programs, Baltimore, MD 21218. Offers biology (PhD), including biochemistry, biophysics, cell biology, developmental biology, genetic biology, molecular biology; cell, molecular, and developmental biology and biophysics (PhD). *Degree requirements:* For doctorate, comprehensive exam, thesis/dissertation. *Entrance requirements:* For doctorate, GRE General Test. Additional exam requirements/recommendations for international students: Required—TOEFL (minimum score 600 paper-based), TWE. Electronic applications accepted. *Faculty research:* Protein and nucleic acid biochemistry and biophysical chemistry, molecular biology and development.

Johns Hopkins University, Zanvyl Krieger School of Arts and Sciences, Thomas C. Jenkins Department of Biophysics, Baltimore, MD 21218. Offers PhD. *Faculty:* 11 full-time (5 women). *Students:* 61 full-time (18 women); includes 14 minority (7 Asian, non-Hispanic/Latino; 6 Hispanic/Latino; 1 Two or more races, non-Hispanic/Latino), 4 international. Average age 26. 56 applicants, 36% accepted, 8 enrolled. In 2017, 9 doctorates awarded. *Degree requirements:* For doctorate, comprehensive exam, thesis/dissertation. *Entrance requirements:* For doctorate, GRE General Test. Additional exam requirements/recommendations for international students: Required—TOEFL (minimum score 600 paper-based), IELTS; Recommended—TWE. *Application deadline:* For fall admission, 12/5 for domestic and international students. Application fee: $75. Electronic applications accepted. *Financial support:* In 2017–18, fellowships with full tuition reimbursements (averaging $29,218 per year), research assistantships (averaging $31,626 per year) were awarded; scholarships/grants, traineeships, and health care benefits also available. Financial award application deadline: 4/15. *Faculty research:* Application of thermodynamics and kinetics, NMR spectroscopy, X-ray crystallography and computational methods to examine the function and structural and physical properties of proteins and nucleic acids. *Unit head:* Dr. Bertrand Garcia-Moreno, Professor and Department Chair, 410-516-7245, Fax: 410-516-4118, E-mail: bertrand@jhu.edu. *Application contact:* Nicole M. Goode, Coordinator, Graduate Admissions, 410-516-5197, Fax: 410-516-4118, E-mail: ngoode@jhu.edu.
Website: http://biophysics.jhu.edu/

Northwestern University, The Graduate School, Interdisciplinary Biological Sciences Program (IBiS), Evanston, IL 60208. Offers biochemistry (PhD); bioengineering and biotechnology (PhD); biotechnology (PhD); cell and molecular biology (PhD); developmental and systems biology (PhD); nanotechnology (PhD); neurobiology (PhD); structural biology and biophysics (PhD). *Degree requirements:* For doctorate, thesis/dissertation, qualifying exam. *Entrance requirements:* For doctorate, GRE General Test. Additional exam requirements/recommendations for international students: Required—TOEFL (minimum score 600 paper-based). Electronic applications accepted. *Faculty research:* Biophysics/structural biology, cell/molecular biology, synthetic biology, developmental systems biology, chemical biology/nanotechnology.

The Ohio State University, Graduate School, College of Arts and Sciences, Division of Natural and Mathematical Sciences, Program in Biophysics, Columbus, OH 43210. Offers MS, PhD. *Students:* 31 full-time (9 women), 1 (woman) part-time, 9 international. Average age 27. In 2017, 6 master's, 7 doctorates awarded. *Entrance requirements:* For master's and doctorate, GRE General Test (minimum 50th percentile on each section). Additional exam requirements/recommendations for international students: Required—TOEFL (minimum score 600 paper-based; 100 iBT), Michigan English Language Assessment Battery (minimum score 86); Recommended—IELTS (minimum score 8). *Application deadline:* For fall admission, 12/13 priority date for domestic students, 11/30 priority date for international students; for spring admission, 12/14 for domestic students, 11/12 for international students; for summer admission, 5/15 for domestic students, 4/14 for international students. Applications are processed on a rolling basis. Application fee: $60 ($70 for international students). Electronic applications accepted. *Financial support:* Fellowships, research assistantships, teaching assistantships, Federal Work-Study, and institutionally sponsored loans available. Support available to part-time students. *Unit head:* Dr. Jeffrey Kuret, Professor, Department of Molecular and Cellular Biochemistry, 614-688-5899, E-mail: kuret.3@osu.edu. *Application contact:* Brigid Graham, Program Administrator, 614-292-5626, Fax: 614-292-4466, E-mail: biophysics@osu.edu.
Website: http://biophysics.osu.edu/

Oregon State University, College of Science, Program in Biochemistry and Biophysics, Corvallis, OR 97331. Offers MA, MS, PhD. Terminal master's awarded for partial completion of doctoral program. *Degree requirements:* For master's, thesis optional; for doctorate, thesis/dissertation, exams. *Entrance requirements:* For master's and doctorate, GRE, minimum GPA of 3.0. Additional exam requirements/recommendations for international students: Required—TOEFL (minimum score 600 paper-based; 100 iBT), IELTS (minimum score 7). *Application deadline:* For fall admission, 12/15 priority date for domestic and international students. Application fee: $75 ($85 for international students). Electronic applications accepted. *Financial support:* Application deadline: 12/15. *Faculty research:* DNA and deoxyribonucleotide metabolism, cell growth control, receptors and membranes, protein structure and function. *Unit head:* Dina Stoneman, Graduate Program Coordinator, 541-737-4511, E-mail: bboffice@oregonstate.edu.
Website: http://biochem.science.oregonstate.edu/

Purdue University, Graduate School, College of Science, Department of Biological Sciences, West Lafayette, IN 47907. Offers biochemistry (PhD); biophysics (PhD); cell and developmental biology (PhD); ecology, evolutionary and population biology (MS, PhD), including ecology, evolutionary biology, population biology; genetics (MS, PhD); microbiology (MS, PhD); molecular biology (PhD); neurobiology (MS, PhD); plant physiology (PhD). *Faculty:* 42 full-time (13 women), 3 part-time/adjunct (0 women). *Students:* 115 full-time (58 women), 6 part-time (4 women); includes 17 minority (1 Black or African American, non-Hispanic/Latino; 6 Asian, non-Hispanic/Latino; 9 Hispanic/Latino; 1 Two or more races, non-Hispanic/Latino), 60 international. Average age 27.

Biophysics

165 applicants, 12% accepted, 15 enrolled. In 2017, 5 master's, 16 doctorates awarded. Terminal master's awarded for partial completion of doctoral program. *Degree requirements:* For master's, thesis (for some programs); for doctorate, thesis/dissertation, seminars, teaching experience. *Entrance requirements:* For master's, GRE General Test (minimum analytical writing score of 3.5), minimum undergraduate GPA of 3.0; for doctorate, GRE General Test (minimum analytical writing score of 3.5), minimum undergraduate GPA of 3.5. Additional exam requirements/recommendations for international students: Required—TOEFL minimum score 600 paper-based; 107 iBT (for MS), 80 iBT (for PhD). *Application deadline:* For fall admission, 12/7 for domestic and international students. Applications are processed on a rolling basis. Application fee: $60 ($75 for international students). Electronic applications accepted. *Financial support:* Fellowships, research assistantships, and teaching assistantships available. Support available to part-time students. Financial award application deadline: 2/15; financial award applicants required to submit FAFSA. *Unit head:* Stephen Konieczny, Head, 765-494-4407, E-mail: sfk@purdue.edu. *Application contact:* Georgina E. Rupp, Graduate Coordinator, 765-494-8142, E-mail: ruppg@purdue.edu.
Website: http://www.bio.purdue.edu/

Purdue University, Graduate School, PULSe - Purdue University Life Sciences Program, West Lafayette, IN 47907. Offers biomolecular structure and biophysics (PhD); biotechnology (PhD); chemical biology (PhD); chromatin and regulation of gene expression (PhD); integrative neuroscience (PhD); integrative plant sciences (PhD); membrane biology (PhD); microbiology (PhD); molecular evolutionary and cancer biology (PhD); molecular evolutionary genetics (PhD); molecular virology (PhD). *Students:* 60 full-time (29 women); includes 6 minority (4 Hispanic/Latino; 2 Two or more races, non-Hispanic/Latino), 36 international. Average age 25. 127 applicants, 39% accepted, 25 enrolled. *Entrance requirements:* For doctorate, GRE, minimum undergraduate GPA of 3.0. Additional exam requirements/recommendations for international students: Required—TOEFL (minimum score 550 paper-based; 77 iBT). *Application deadline:* For fall admission, 1/15 priority date for domestic and international students. Applications are processed on a rolling basis. Application fee: $60 ($75 for international students). Electronic applications accepted. *Financial support:* In 2017–18, research assistantships with tuition reimbursements (averaging $22,500 per year), teaching assistantships with tuition reimbursements (averaging $22,500 per year) were awarded. *Unit head:* Dr. Jason R. Cannon, Head of the Graduate Program, 765-494-0794, E-mail: cannonjr@purdue.edu. *Application contact:* Lindsey Springer, Graduate Contact for Admissions, 765-496-9667, E-mail: lbcampbe@purdue.edu.
Website: http://www.gradschool.purdue.edu/pulse

Rensselaer Polytechnic Institute, Graduate School, School of Science, Program in Biochemistry and Biophysics, Troy, NY 12180-3590. Offers MS, PhD. *Faculty:* 21 full-time (8 women), 2 part-time/adjunct (1 woman). *Students:* 21 full-time (12 women), 1 (woman) part-time; includes 4 minority (3 Asian, non-Hispanic/Latino; 1 Hispanic/Latino), 2 international. Average age 26. 37 applicants, 30% accepted, 4 enrolled. In 2017, 2 doctorates awarded. Terminal master's awarded for partial completion of doctoral program. *Degree requirements:* For master's, thesis optional; for doctorate, comprehensive exam, thesis/dissertation. *Entrance requirements:* For master's and doctorate, GRE. Additional exam requirements/recommendations for international students: Required—TOEFL (minimum score 600 paper-based; 100 iBT), IELTS (minimum score 7), PTE (minimum score 68). *Application deadline:* For fall admission, 1/1 priority date for domestic and international students; for spring admission, 8/15 priority date for domestic and international students. Applications are processed on a rolling basis. Application fee: $75. Electronic applications accepted. *Expenses: Tuition:* Full-time $52,550; part-time $2125 per credit hour. *Required fees:* $2890. *Financial support:* In 2017–18, research assistantships (averaging $23,000 per year), teaching assistantships (averaging $23,000 per year) were awarded; fellowships also available. Financial award application deadline: 1/1. *Faculty research:* Biochemistry; bioinformatics; biophysics; cancer biology; computational biology; molecular, cell, and developmental biology; neuroscience; protein folding; stem cells; structural biology. *Total annual research expenditures:* $2.1 million. *Unit head:* Dr. Cathy Royer, Graduate Program Director, 518-276-3796, E-mail: royerc@rpi.edu.
Website: https://science.rpi.edu/biology

Rosalind Franklin University of Medicine and Science, School of Graduate and Postdoctoral Studies - Interdisciplinary Graduate Program in Biomedical Sciences, Department of Physiology and Biophysics, North Chicago, IL 60064-3095. Offers MS, PhD, MD/PhD. Terminal master's awarded for partial completion of doctoral program. *Degree requirements:* For master's, comprehensive exam, thesis; for doctorate, comprehensive exam, thesis/dissertation. *Entrance requirements:* For master's and doctorate, GRE General Test. Additional exam requirements/recommendations for international students: Required—TOEFL, TWE. *Faculty research:* Membrane transport, mechanisms of cellular regulation, brain metabolism, peptide metabolism.

Stanford University, School of Humanities and Sciences, Program in Biophysics, Stanford, CA 94305-2004. Offers PhD. *Degree requirements:* For doctorate, thesis/dissertation, oral exam. *Entrance requirements:* For doctorate, GRE General Test, GRE Subject Test. Additional exam requirements/recommendations for international students: Required—TOEFL. Electronic applications accepted. *Expenses: Tuition:* Full-time $48,987; part-time $10,620 per quarter. One-time fee: $400. Tuition and fees vary according to program.

Stony Brook University, State University of New York, Stony Brook Medicine, School of Medicine and Graduate School, Graduate Programs in Medicine, Department of Physiology and Biophysics, Stony Brook, NY 11794. Offers PhD. *Faculty:* 12 full-time (4 women), 1 part-time/adjunct (0 women). *Students:* 31 full-time (6 women); includes 14 minority (3 Black or African American, non-Hispanic/Latino; 4 Asian, non-Hispanic/Latino; 7 Hispanic/Latino), 1 international. Average age 23. 5 applicants. In 2017, 2 doctorates awarded. *Degree requirements:* For doctorate, comprehensive exam, thesis/dissertation. *Entrance requirements:* For doctorate, GRE General Test, GRE Subject Test, BS in related field, minimum GPA of 3.0, recommendation. Additional exam requirements/recommendations for international students: Required—TOEFL (minimum score 550 paper-based). *Application deadline:* For fall admission, 1/15 for domestic students; for spring admission, 10/1 for domestic students. Application fee: $100. *Expenses:* Contact institution. *Financial support:* In 2017–18, 1 research assistantship was awarded; fellowships, teaching assistantships, and Federal Work-Study also available. Financial award application deadline: 3/15. *Faculty research:* Biophysics, human physiology, ion channels, physiology, signal transduction. *Total annual research expenditures:* $3.8 million. *Unit head:* Dr. Todd Miller, Chair, 631-444-3533, Fax: 631-444-3432, E-mail: todd.miller@stonybrook.edu. *Application contact:* Odalis Hernandez, Coordinator, 631-444-3057, Fax: 631-444-9749, E-mail: odalis.hernandez@stonybrook.edu.
Website: https://medicine.stonybrookmedicine.edu/pnb

Texas Christian University, College of Science and Engineering, Department of Physics and Astronomy, Fort Worth, TX 76129. Offers physics (MA, MS, PhD), including astrophysics (PhD), biophysics (PhD); PhD/MBA. *Program availability:* Part-time. *Faculty:* 7 full-time (2 women). *Students:* 17 full-time (7 women); includes 3 minority (1 Black or African American, non-Hispanic/Latino; 2 Hispanic/Latino), 7 international. Average age 29. 25 applicants, 20% accepted, 3 enrolled. In 2017, 2 master's, 3 doctorates awarded. Terminal master's awarded for partial completion of doctoral program. *Degree requirements:* For master's, one foreign language, comprehensive exam, thesis or alternative; for doctorate, comprehensive exam, thesis/dissertation. *Entrance requirements:* For master's and doctorate, GRE. Additional exam requirements/recommendations for international students: Required—TOEFL (minimum score 550 paper-based; 80 iBT), IELTS (minimum score 6.5). *Application deadline:* For fall admission, 2/1 for domestic and international students; for spring admission, 9/1 for domestic and international students. Applications are processed on a rolling basis. Application fee: $60. Electronic applications accepted. *Expenses:* Contact institution. *Financial support:* In 2017–18, 14 students received support, including 1 research assistantship with full tuition reimbursement available (averaging $23,000 per year), 13 teaching assistantships with full tuition reimbursements available (averaging $20,500 per year); scholarships/grants and unspecified assistantships also available. Financial award application deadline: 2/1. *Faculty research:* Nanomaterials, computer simulations of biophysical processes, nonlinear dynamics, studies of galaxy evolution using stars and gas, spectroscopy and fluorescence of biomolecules. *Total annual research expenditures:* $265,000. *Unit head:* Dr. Yuri M. Strzhemechny, Associate Professor/Chair, 817-257-5793, Fax: 817-257-7742, E-mail: y.strzhemechny@tcu.edu. *Application contact:* Dr. Peter M. Frinchaboy, III, Associate Professor, 817-257-6387, Fax: 817-257-7742, E-mail: p.frinchaboy@tcu.edu.
Website: http://physics.tcu.edu/

Université de Sherbrooke, Faculty of Medicine and Health Sciences, Graduate Programs in Medicine, Department of Physiology and Biophysics, Sherbrooke, QC J1H 5N4, Canada. Offers M Sc, PhD. Terminal master's awarded for partial completion of doctoral program. *Degree requirements:* For master's, thesis; for doctorate, thesis/dissertation. Electronic applications accepted. *Faculty research:* Ion channels, neurological basis of pain, insulin resistance, obesity.

Université du Québec à Trois-Rivières, Graduate Programs, Program in Biophysics and Cellular Biology, Trois-Rivières, QC G9A 5H7, Canada. Offers M Sc, PhD. *Program availability:* Part-time. *Degree requirements:* For master's, thesis; for doctorate, thesis/dissertation. *Entrance requirements:* For master's, appropriate bachelor's degree, proficiency in French; for doctorate, appropriate master's degree, proficiency in French.

University at Buffalo, the State University of New York, Graduate School, Graduate Programs in Cancer Research and Biomedical Sciences at Roswell Park Cancer Institute, Department of Molecular and Cellular Biophysics and Biochemistry at Roswell Park Cancer Institute, Buffalo, NY 14260. Offers PhD. *Faculty:* 21 full-time (3 women). *Students:* 16 full-time (11 women); includes 2 minority (1 Black or African American, non-Hispanic/Latino; 1 Asian, non-Hispanic/Latino), 5 international. 14 applicants, 43% accepted, 4 enrolled. In 2017, 9 doctorates awarded. *Degree requirements:* For doctorate, comprehensive exam, thesis/dissertation, oral defense of dissertation. *Entrance requirements:* For doctorate, GRE General Test. Additional exam requirements/recommendations for international students: Required—TOEFL (minimum score 79 iBT). *Application deadline:* For fall admission, 1/5 priority date for domestic and international students. Application fee: $75. Electronic applications accepted. *Financial support:* In 2017–18, 17 students received support, including 17 research assistantships with full tuition reimbursements available (averaging $27,000 per year); scholarships/grants, health care benefits, and unspecified assistantships also available. Financial award application deadline: 1/5. *Faculty research:* MRI research, structural and function of biomolecules, photodynamic therapy, DNA damage and repair, heat-shock proteins and vaccine research. *Unit head:* Dr. Eugene Kandel, Director of Graduate Studies, 716-845-3530, E-mail: eugene.kandel@roswellpark.org. *Application contact:* Dr. Norman J. Karin, Associate Dean, 716-845-2339, Fax: 716-845-8178, E-mail: norman.karin@roswellpark.edu.
Website: http://www.roswellpark.edu/education/phd-programs/molecular-cellular-biophysics-and-biochemistry

University at Buffalo, the State University of New York, Graduate School, Jacobs School of Medicine and Biomedical Sciences, Graduate Programs in Medicine and Biomedical Sciences, Department of Physiology and Biophysics, Buffalo, NY 14203. Offers biophysics (MS, PhD); physiology (MA, PhD). *Faculty:* 17 full-time (4 women). *Students:* 6 full-time (1 woman); includes 4 minority (1 Black or African American, non-Hispanic/Latino; 3 Asian, non-Hispanic/Latino). Average age 27. 13 applicants, 23% accepted, 2 enrolled. In 2017, 2 master's, 3 doctorates awarded. Terminal master's awarded for partial completion of doctoral program. *Degree requirements:* For master's, comprehensive exam, thesis or alternative, oral exam, project; for doctorate, comprehensive exam, thesis/dissertation, oral and written qualifying exam or 2 research proposals. *Entrance requirements:* For master's, GRE General Test, unofficial transcripts, 3 letters of recommendation, personal statement, curriculum vitae; for doctorate, GRE General Test or MCAT, unofficial transcripts, 3 letters of recommendation, personal statement, curriculum vitae. Additional exam requirements/recommendations for international students: Required—TOEFL (minimum score 550 paper-based; 79 iBT). *Application deadline:* Applications are processed on a rolling basis. Application fee: $85. Electronic applications accepted. *Expenses:* Contact institution. *Financial support:* In 2017–18, 1 research assistantship with full tuition reimbursement (averaging $27,000 per year) was awarded; health care benefits also available. Financial award applicants required to submit FAFSA. *Faculty research:* Neurosciences, ion channels, cardiac physiology, renal/epithelial transport, cardiopulmonary exercise. *Total annual research expenditures:* $2.7 million. *Unit head:* Dr. Perry M. Hogan, Chair, 716-829-2738, Fax: 716-829-2344, E-mail: phogan@buffalo.edu. *Application contact:* Kara M. Rickicki, Graduate Programs Coordinator, 716-829-2417, Fax: 716-829-2344, E-mail: rickicki@buffalo.edu.
Website: https://medicine.buffalo.edu/departments/physiology.html

University of California, Berkeley, Graduate Division, College of Letters and Science, Group in Biophysics, Berkeley, CA 94720-1500. Offers PhD. *Degree requirements:* For doctorate, thesis/dissertation, qualifying exam. *Entrance requirements:* For doctorate, GRE General Test, minimum GPA of 3.0, 3 letters of recommendation. Electronic applications accepted.

University of California, Davis, Graduate Studies, Graduate Group in Biophysics, Davis, CA 95616. Offers MS, PhD. *Degree requirements:* For doctorate, thesis/dissertation. *Entrance requirements:* For master's and doctorate, GRE General Test, GRE Subject Test. Additional exam requirements/recommendations for international students: Required—TOEFL (minimum score 550 paper-based). Electronic applications accepted. *Faculty research:* Molecular structure, protein structure/function relationships, spectroscopy.

University of California, Irvine, School of Medicine and Francisco J. Ayala School of Biological Sciences, Department of Physiology and Biophysics, Irvine, CA 92697. Offers biological sciences (PhD); MD/PhD. *Students:* 14 full-time (6 women), 1 part-time (0 women); includes 7 minority (1 American Indian or Alaska Native, non-Hispanic/Latino; 4 Asian, non-Hispanic/Latino; 2 Hispanic/Latino), 4 international. Average age 29. In 2017, 3 doctorates awarded. *Entrance requirements:* For doctorate, GRE General Test, GRE Subject Test, minimum GPA of 3.0. Additional exam requirements/recommendations for international students: Required—TOEFL (minimum score 550 paper-based). *Application deadline:* For fall admission, 1/15 priority date for domestic students, 1/15 for international students. Application fee: $105 ($125 for international students). Electronic

applications accepted. *Financial support:* Fellowships, research assistantships with full tuition reimbursements, teaching assistantships, institutionally sponsored loans, traineeships, health care benefits, and unspecified assistantships available. Financial award application deadline: 3/1; financial award applicants required to submit FAFSA. *Faculty research:* Membrane physiology, exercise physiology, regulation of hormone biosynthesis and action, endocrinology, ion channels and signal transduction. *Unit head:* Prof. Michael Cahalan, Chair, 949-824-7776, Fax: 949-824-3143, E-mail: mcahalan@ucl.edu. *Application contact:* Janita Parpana, Chief Administrative Officer, 949-824-6833, Fax: 949-824-8540, E-mail: jparpana@uci.edu.
Website: http://www.physiology.uci.edu/

University of California, San Diego, Graduate Division, Department of Physics, La Jolla, CA 92093. Offers biophysics (PhD); computational neuroscience (PhD); computational science (PhD); multi-scale biology (PhD); physics (MS, PhD); quantitative biology (PhD). *Students:* 149 full-time (28 women). 514 applicants, 20% accepted, 28 enrolled. In 2017, 8 master's, 20 doctorates awarded. *Degree requirements:* For doctorate, comprehensive exam, thesis/dissertation, 1-quarter teaching assistantship. *Entrance requirements:* For doctorate, GRE General Test, GRE Subject Test, statement of purpose, three letters of reference. Additional exam requirements/recommendations for international students: Required—TOEFL (minimum score 550 paper-based; 80 iBT), IELTS (minimum score 7). *Application deadline:* For fall admission, 12/20 for domestic students. Application fee: $105 ($125 for international students). Electronic applications accepted. *Financial support:* Fellowships, research assistantships, teaching assistantships, scholarships/grants, and unspecified assistantships available. Financial award applicants required to submit FAFSA. *Faculty research:* Astrophysics/astronomy, biological physics, condensed matter/material science, elementary particles, plasma physics. *Unit head:* Benjamin Grinstein, Chair, 858-534-6857, E-mail: chair@physics.ucsd.edu. *Application contact:* Saixious Dominguez-Kilday, Graduate Admissions Coordinator, 858-534-3293, E-mail: skilday@physics.ucsd.edu.
Website: http://physics.ucsd.edu/

University of California, San Francisco, School of Pharmacy and School of Medicine, Program in Biophysics, San Francisco, CA 94143. Offers PhD. *Degree requirements:* For doctorate, thesis/dissertation. *Entrance requirements:* For doctorate, GRE General Test; GRE Subject Test (recommended), bachelor's degree with minimum GPA of 3.0. Additional exam requirements/recommendations for international students: Required—TOEFL. Electronic applications accepted. *Faculty research:* Structural biology, proteomics and genomics, biophysical approaches to cell biology, complex biological systems, computational and theoretical biophysics, membrane biophysics, protein engineering and synthetic biology.

University of California, Santa Barbara, Graduate Division, College of Letters and Sciences, Division of Mathematics, Life, and Physical Sciences, Interdepartmental Graduate Program in Biomolecular Science and Engineering, Santa Barbara, CA 93106-2014. Offers biochemistry and molecular biology (PhD), including biochemistry and molecular biology, biophysics and bioengineering. Terminal master's awarded for partial completion of doctoral program. *Degree requirements:* For doctorate, thesis/dissertation. *Entrance requirements:* For doctorate, GRE General Test. Additional exam requirements/recommendations for international students: Required—TOEFL (minimum score 630 paper-based; 109 iBT), IELTS (minimum score 7). Electronic applications accepted. *Faculty research:* Biochemistry and molecular biology, biophysics, biomaterials, bioengineering, systems biology.

University of Chicago, Division of the Physical Sciences, Graduate Program in Biophysical Sciences, Chicago, IL 60637. Offers PhD. *Students:* 33 full-time (7 women); includes 9 minority (5 Asian, non-Hispanic/Latino; 3 Hispanic/Latino; 1 Two or more races, non-Hispanic/Latino), 6 international. Average age 26. 98 applicants, 20% accepted, 6 enrolled. In 2017, 4 doctorates awarded. *Degree requirements:* For doctorate, comprehensive exam, thesis/dissertation, ethics class, 2 teaching assistantships. *Entrance requirements:* For doctorate, GRE General Test, research statement, 3 letters of recommendation, transcripts for all previous degrees and institutions attended. Additional exam requirements/recommendations for international students: Required—TOEFL (minimum score 600 paper-based; 104 iBT), IELTS (minimum score 7). *Application deadline:* For fall admission, 12/4 for domestic and international students. Application fee: $90. Electronic applications accepted. *Financial support:* In 2017–18, 8 students received support, including 14 fellowships with full tuition reimbursements available (averaging $29,053 per year), 10 research assistantships with full tuition reimbursements available (averaging $29,053 per year); teaching assistantships, institutionally sponsored loans, scholarships/grants, traineeships, health care benefits, and unspecified assistantships also available. Financial award application deadline: 12/4. *Faculty research:* Physical probes of biological systems, ultrafast dynamics and nonequilibrium theory of biological systems, computational simulation of large-scale biodynamics, protein design and protein-lipid interactions, epigenetics and genomics. *Unit head:* Dr. Tobin Sosnick, Director, 773-218-5950, E-mail: biophysics@uchicago.edu. *Application contact:* Michele Wittels, Administrator, 773-834-7456, E-mail: biophysics@uchicago.edu.
Website: http://biophysics.uchicago.edu/

University of Cincinnati, Graduate School, College of Medicine, Graduate Programs in Biomedical Sciences, Department of Pharmacology and Cell Biophysics, Cincinnati, OH 45221. Offers cell biophysics (PhD); pharmacology (PhD). *Degree requirements:* For doctorate, thesis/dissertation, qualifying exam. *Entrance requirements:* For doctorate, GRE General Test. Additional exam requirements/recommendations for international students: Required—TOEFL. Electronic applications accepted. *Expenses: Tuition, area resident:* Full-time $14,468. Tuition, state resident: full-time $14,968; part-time $754 per credit hour. Tuition, nonresident: full-time $24,210; part-time $1311 per credit hour. *International tuition:* $26,460 full-time. *Required fees:* $3958; $84 per credit hour. One-time fee: $85 full-time. Tuition and fees vary according to course load, degree level and program. *Faculty research:* Lipoprotein research, enzyme regulation, electrophysiology, gene actuation.

University of Colorado Denver, School of Medicine, Graduate Program in Genetic Counseling, Aurora, CO 80045. Offers biophysics and genetics (MS). *Students:* 12 full-time (11 women), 1 (woman) part-time. Average age 25. 141 applicants, 5% accepted, 6 enrolled. In 2017, 4 master's awarded. *Degree requirements:* For master's, 44 core semester hours, project or thesis. *Entrance requirements:* For master's, GRE, minimum undergraduate GPA of 3.0; 4 letters of recommendation; prerequisite coursework in biology, general chemistry, general biochemistry, general genetics, and general psychology; experience in counseling and laboratory settings and strong understanding of genetic counseling field (highly recommended). Additional exam requirements/recommendations for international students: Required—TOEFL (minimum score 570 paper-based; 89 iBT). *Application deadline:* For fall admission, 1/1 for domestic students, 12/1 for international students. Application fee: $50 ($75 for international students). Electronic applications accepted. *Faculty research:* Psychosocial aspects of genetic counseling, clinical cytogenetics and molecular genetics, human inborn errors of metabolism, congenital malformations and disorders of the newborn, cancer genetics and genetic counseling. *Application contact:* Kenton Owsley, Program Administrator, 303-724-3468, E-mail: somadmin@ucdenver.edu.
Website: http://www.ucdenver.edu/academics/colleges/Graduate-School/academic-programs/genetic-counseling/Pages/default.aspx

University of Connecticut, Graduate School, College of Liberal Arts and Sciences, Department of Molecular and Cell Biology, Storrs, CT 06269. Offers applied genomics (PSM); cell and developmental biology (MS, PhD); genetics and genomics (MS, PhD); microbial systems analysis (PSM); microbiology (MS, PhD); structural biology, biochemistry and biophysics (MS, PhD). Terminal master's awarded for partial completion of doctoral program. *Degree requirements:* For master's, comprehensive exam; for doctorate, thesis/dissertation. *Entrance requirements:* For master's and doctorate, GRE General Test, GRE Subject Test. Additional exam requirements/recommendations for international students: Required—TOEFL (minimum score 550 paper-based). Electronic applications accepted.

University of Guelph, Graduate Studies, Biophysics Interdepartmental Group, Guelph, ON N1G 2W1, Canada. Offers M Sc, PhD. *Degree requirements:* For master's, thesis; for doctorate, comprehensive exam, thesis/dissertation. *Entrance requirements:* For master's, minimum B average during previous 2 years of course work; for doctorate, minimum B+ average. Additional exam requirements/recommendations for international students: Required—TOEFL (minimum score 550 paper-based). Electronic applications accepted. *Faculty research:* Molecular, cellular, structural, and computational biophysics.

University of Guelph, Graduate Studies, College of Biological Science, Department of Molecular and Cellular Biology, Guelph, ON N1G 2W1, Canada. Offers biochemistry (M Sc, PhD); biophysics (M Sc, PhD); botany (M Sc, PhD); microbiology (M Sc, PhD); molecular biology and genetics (M Sc, PhD). *Degree requirements:* For master's, thesis, research proposal; for doctorate, comprehensive exam, thesis/dissertation, research proposal. *Entrance requirements:* For master's, minimum B-average during previous 2 years of coursework; for doctorate, minimum A-average. Additional exam requirements/recommendations for international students: Required—TOEFL (minimum score 550 paper-based), IELTS (minimum score 6.5). Electronic applications accepted. *Faculty research:* Physiology, structure, genetics, and ecology of microbes; virology and microbial technology.

University of Illinois at Chicago, College of Medicine and Graduate College, Graduate Programs in Medicine, Department of Physiology and Biophysics, Chicago, IL 60607-7128. Offers MS, PhD. Terminal master's awarded for partial completion of doctoral program. *Degree requirements:* For master's, thesis; for doctorate, thesis/dissertation. *Entrance requirements:* For master's and doctorate, GRE General Test. Additional exam requirements/recommendations for international students: Required—TOEFL. Electronic applications accepted. *Faculty research:* Neuroscience, endocrinology and reproduction, cell physiology, exercise physiology, NMR, cardiovascular physiology and metabolism, cytoskeleton and vascular biology, gastrointestinal and epithelial cell biology, reproductive and endocrine sciences.

University of Illinois at Urbana–Champaign, Graduate College, College of Liberal Arts and Sciences, School of Molecular and Cellular Biology, Center for Biophysics and Computational Biology, Champaign, IL 61820. Offers MS, PhD.

The University of Iowa, Roy J. and Lucille A. Carver College of Medicine and Graduate College, Graduate Programs in Medicine, Department of Molecular Physiology and Biophysics, Iowa City, IA 52242. Offers MS, PhD. *Degree requirements:* For master's, comprehensive exam; for doctorate, comprehensive exam, thesis/dissertation. *Entrance requirements:* For master's, GRE General Test; for doctorate, GRE. Additional exam requirements/recommendations for international students: Required—TOEFL. Electronic applications accepted. *Faculty research:* Cellular and molecular endocrinology, membrane structure and function, cardiac cell electrophysiology, regulation of gene expression, neurophysiology.

The University of Kansas, Graduate Studies, College of Liberal Arts and Sciences, Department of Molecular Biosciences, Lawrence, KS 66044. Offers biochemistry and biophysics (PhD); microbiology (PhD); molecular, cellular, and developmental biology (PhD). *Program availability:* Part-time. *Students:* 57 full-time (38 women); includes 8 minority (1 Black or African American, non-Hispanic/Latino; 2 Asian, non-Hispanic/Latino; 3 Hispanic/Latino; 2 Two or more races, non-Hispanic/Latino), 27 international. Average age 27. 73 applicants, 33% accepted, 8 enrolled. In 2017, 6 doctorates awarded. Terminal master's awarded for partial completion of doctoral program. *Entrance requirements:* For doctorate, GRE General Test, 1-page statement of research interests and goals, 1-2 page curriculum vitae or resume, official transcript, 3 recommendation letters. Additional exam requirements/recommendations for international students: Required—TOEFL or IELTS. *Application deadline:* For fall admission, 12/1 for domestic and international students. Application fee: $65 ($85 for international students). Electronic applications accepted. *Financial support:* Fellowships, research assistantships, teaching assistantships, scholarships/grants, health care benefits, and unspecified assistantships available. Financial award application deadline: 12/1. *Faculty research:* Structure and function of proteins, genetics of organism development, molecular genetics, neurophysiology, molecular virology and pathogenics, developmental biology, cell biology. *Unit head:* Susan M. Egan, Chair, 785-864-4294, E-mail: sme@ku.edu. *Application contact:* John Connolly, Graduate Admissions Contact, 785-864-4311, E-mail: jconnolly@ku.edu.
Website: http://www.molecularbiosciences.ku.edu/

The University of Manchester, School of Physics and Astronomy, Manchester, United Kingdom. Offers astronomy and astrophysics (M Sc, PhD); biological physics (M Sc, PhD); condensed matter physics (M Sc, PhD); nonlinear and liquid crystals physics (M Sc, PhD); nuclear physics (M Sc, PhD); particle physics (M Sc, PhD); photon physics (M Sc, PhD); physics (M Sc, PhD); theoretical physics (M Sc, PhD).

University of Maryland, College Park, Academic Affairs, College of Computer, Mathematical and Natural Sciences, Department of Biology, PhD Program in Biological Sciences, College Park, MD 20742. Offers behavior, ecology, evolution, and systematics (PhD); computational biology, bioinformatics, and genomics (PhD); molecular and cellular biology (PhD); physiological systems (PhD). *Degree requirements:* For doctorate, comprehensive exam, thesis/dissertation, thesis work presentation in seminar. *Entrance requirements:* For doctorate, GRE General Test; GRE Subject Test in biology (recommended), academic transcripts, statement of purpose/research interests, 3 letters of recommendation. Additional exam requirements/recommendations for international students: Required—TOEFL. Electronic applications accepted.

University of Maryland, College Park, Academic Affairs, College of Computer, Mathematical and Natural Sciences, Institute for Physical Science and Technology, Program in Biophysics, College Park, MD 20742. Offers PhD.

University of Miami, Graduate School, Miller School of Medicine, Graduate Programs in Medicine, Department of Physiology and Biophysics, Coral Gables, FL 33124. Offers PhD, MD/PhD. *Degree requirements:* For doctorate, thesis/dissertation, qualifying exam. *Entrance requirements:* For doctorate, GRE General Test, minimum GPA of 3.0 in sciences. Additional exam requirements/recommendations for international students: Required—TOEFL. *Faculty research:* Cell and membrane physiology, cell-to-cell communication, molecular neurobiology, neuroimmunology, neural development.

University of Michigan, Rackham Graduate School, College of Literature, Science, and the Arts, Department of Biophysics, Ann Arbor, MI 48109. Offers PhD. *Faculty:* 42

full-time (12 women). *Students:* 33 full-time (11 women); includes 5 minority (2 Black or African American, non-Hispanic/Latino; 2 Asian, non-Hispanic/Latino; 1 Hispanic/Latino), 5 international. Average age 22. 59 applicants, 32% accepted, 3 enrolled. In 2017, 5 doctorates awarded. *Degree requirements:* For doctorate, thesis/dissertation, preliminary exam, oral defense of dissertation. *Entrance requirements:* Additional exam requirements/recommendations for international students: Required—TOEFL (minimum score 84 iBT). *Application deadline:* For fall admission, 12/6 for domestic and international students. Application fee: $75 ($90 for international students). Electronic applications accepted. Application fee is waived when completed online. *Expenses:* Tuition, state resident: full-time $22,368; part-time $1201 per credit hour. Tuition, nonresident: full-time $45,156; part-time $2467 per credit hour. *Required fees:* $376 per term. Tuition and fees vary according to course load, degree level and program. *Financial support:* In 2017–18, 10 fellowships with full tuition reimbursements (averaging $29,025 per year), 10 research assistantships with full tuition reimbursements (averaging $29,025 per year), 7 teaching assistantships with full tuition reimbursements (averaging $29,025 per year) were awarded; scholarships/grants, traineeships, health care benefits, and unspecified assistantships also available. Financial award application deadline: 3/15. *Faculty research:* Structural biology, computational biophysics, physical chemistry, cellular biophysics, membrane biophysics. *Unit head:* Dr. Charles Brooks, III, Program Director, 734-764-1146, E-mail: brookscl@umich.edu. *Application contact:* Sara Grosky, Student Services Administrator, 734-763-6722, E-mail: saramin@umich.edu.
Website: https://www.lsa.umich.edu/biophysics

University of Minnesota, Duluth, Medical School, Department of Biochemistry, Molecular Biology and Biophysics, Duluth, MN 55812-2496. Offers biochemistry, molecular biology and biophysics (MS); biology and biophysics (PhD); social, administrative, and clinical pharmacy (MS, PhD); toxicology (MS, PhD). Terminal master's awarded for partial completion of doctoral program. *Degree requirements:* For master's, comprehensive exam, thesis; for doctorate, comprehensive exam, thesis/dissertation. *Entrance requirements:* For master's and doctorate, GRE General Test. Additional exam requirements/recommendations for international students: Required—TOEFL. Electronic applications accepted. *Faculty research:* Intestinal cancer biology; hepatotoxins and mitochondriopathies; toxicology; cell cycle regulation in stem cells; neurobiology of brain development, trace metal function and blood-brain barrier; hibernation biology.

University of Minnesota, Twin Cities Campus, Graduate School, College of Biological Sciences, Biochemistry, Molecular Biology and Biophysics Graduate Program, Minneapolis, MN 55455-0213. Offers PhD. *Degree requirements:* For doctorate, thesis/dissertation. *Entrance requirements:* For doctorate, GRE, 3 letters of recommendation, more than 1 semester of laboratory experience. Additional exam requirements/recommendations for international students: Required—TOEFL (minimum score 625 paper-based; 108 iBT with writing subsection 25 and reading subsection 25) or IELTS (minimum score 7). Electronic applications accepted. *Faculty research:* Microbial biochemistry, biotechnology, molecular biology, regulatory biochemistry, structural biology and biophysics, physical biochemistry, enzymology, physiological chemistry.

University of Minnesota, Twin Cities Campus, Graduate School, Program in Biophysical Sciences and Medical Physics, Minneapolis, MN 55455-0213. Offers MS, PhD. *Program availability:* Part-time. *Degree requirements:* For master's, thesis optional, research paper, oral exam; for doctorate, thesis/dissertation, oral/written preliminary exam, oral final exam. *Faculty research:* Theoretical biophysics, radiological physics, cellular and molecular biophysics.

University of Mississippi Medical Center, School of Graduate Studies in the Health Sciences, Department of Physiology and Biophysics, Jackson, MS 39216-4505. Offers PhD, MD/PhD. *Degree requirements:* For doctorate, thesis/dissertation, first authored publication. *Entrance requirements:* For doctorate, GRE General Test, minimum GPA of 3.0. *Faculty research:* Cardiovascular, renal, endocrine, and cellular neurophysiology; molecular physiology.

University of Missouri–Kansas City, School of Biological Sciences, Program in Cell Biology and Biophysics, Kansas City, MO 64110-2499. Offers PhD. Offered through the School of Graduate Studies. *Degree requirements:* For doctorate, comprehensive exam, thesis/dissertation. *Entrance requirements:* For doctorate, GRE General Test, bachelor's degree in chemistry, biology or related field; minimum GPA of 3.0. Additional exam requirements/recommendations for international students: Required—TOEFL (minimum score 550 paper-based; 80 iBT). Electronic applications accepted.

The University of North Carolina at Chapel Hill, School of Medicine and Graduate School, Graduate Programs in Medicine, Department of Biochemistry and Biophysics, Chapel Hill, NC 27599. Offers MS, PhD. Terminal master's awarded for partial completion of doctoral program. *Degree requirements:* For master's, comprehensive exam, thesis; for doctorate, comprehensive exam, thesis/dissertation. *Entrance requirements:* For master's and doctorate, GRE General Test, GRE Subject Test (recommended), minimum GPA of 3.0. Additional exam requirements/recommendations for international students: Required—TOEFL. Electronic applications accepted.

University of Regina, Faculty of Graduate Studies and Research, Faculty of Science, Department of Chemistry and Biochemistry, Regina, SK S4S 0A2, Canada. Offers biophysics of biological interfaces (M Sc, PhD); computational chemistry (M Sc, PhD); environmental analytical chemistry (M Sc, PhD); enzymology/chemical biology (M Sc, PhD); inorganic/organometallic chemistry (M Sc, PhD); signal transduction and mechanisms of cancer cell regulation (M Sc, PhD); supramolecular organic photochemistry and photophysics (M Sc, PhD); synthetic organic chemistry (M Sc, PhD). *Faculty:* 11 full-time (3 women), 4 part-time/adjunct (0 women). *Students:* 14 full-time (7 women), 3 part-time (0 women). 38 applicants, 11% accepted. In 2017, 1 doctorate awarded. *Degree requirements:* For master's, thesis; for doctorate, thesis/dissertation. *Entrance requirements:* Additional exam requirements/recommendations for international students: Required—TOEFL (minimum score 580 paper-based; 80 iBT), IELTS (minimum score 6.5), PTE (minimum score 59). *Application deadline:* Applications are processed on a rolling basis. Application fee: $100. Electronic applications accepted. *Expenses:* CAD$10,681 per year (for M Sc); CAD$9,930 per year (for PhD). *Financial support:* In 2017–18, fellowships (averaging $6,444 per year), teaching assistantships (averaging $2,562 per year) were awarded; research assistantships and scholarships/grants also available. Financial award application deadline: 6/15. *Faculty research:* Asymmetric synthesis and methodology, theoretical and computational chemistry, biophysical biochemistry, analytical and environmental chemistry, chemical biology. *Unit head:* Dr. Renata Raina-Fulton, Department Head, 306-585-4012, Fax: 306-337-2409, E-mail: renata.raina@uregina.ca. *Application contact:* Dr. Brian Sterenberg, Graduate Program Coordinator, 306-585-4106, Fax: 306-337-2409, E-mail: brian.sterenberg@uregina.ca.
Website: http://www.uregina.ca/science/chem-biochem/

University of Rochester, School of Medicine and Dentistry, Graduate Programs in Medicine and Dentistry, Department of Biochemistry and Biophysics, Programs in Biophysics, Rochester, NY 14627. Offers biophysics, structural and computational biology (PhD). Terminal master's awarded for partial completion of doctoral program. *Degree requirements:* For doctorate, thesis/dissertation, qualifying exam. *Entrance requirements:* For doctorate, GRE General Test.

University of Southern California, Keck School of Medicine and Graduate School, Graduate Programs in Medicine, Department of Physiology and Biophysics, Los Angeles, CA 90089. Offers MS. *Program availability:* Part-time. *Faculty:* 13 full-time (2 women). *Students:* 3 full-time (all women), 1 part-time (0 women); includes 2 minority (1 Asian, non-Hispanic/Latino; 1 Hispanic/Latino). Average age 23. 7 applicants, 43% accepted, 2 enrolled. In 2017, 2 master's awarded. *Degree requirements:* For master's, thesis optional. *Entrance requirements:* For master's, GRE General Test, minimum GPA of 3.0. Additional exam requirements/recommendations for international students: Required—TOEFL (minimum score 600 paper-based; 100 iBT). *Application deadline:* For fall admission, 12/1 priority date for domestic and international students. Applications are processed on a rolling basis. Application fee: $85. Electronic applications accepted. *Expenses:* Contact institution. *Financial support:* Application deadline: 4/15; applicants required to submit FAFSA. *Faculty research:* Endocrinology and metabolism, neurophysiology, mathematical modeling, cell transport, autoimmunity and cancer immunotherapy. *Unit head:* Dr. Berislav Zlokovic, Chair, 323-442-2566, Fax: 323-442-2230, E-mail: zlokovic@usc.edu. *Application contact:* Monica Pan, Student Services Advisor, 323-442-0230, Fax: 323-442-1610, E-mail: monicap@med.usc.edu.

University of Southern California, Keck School of Medicine, Program in Medical Biophysics, Los Angeles, CA 90033. Offers PhD. *Faculty:* 23 full-time (6 women). *Students:* 4 full-time (3 women); includes 1 minority (Hispanic/Latino), 1 international. Average age 24. 4 applicants, 100% accepted, 4 enrolled. *Degree requirements:* For doctorate, comprehensive exam, thesis/dissertation. *Entrance requirements:* For doctorate, GRE, minimum GPA of 3.5. Additional exam requirements/recommendations for international students: Required—TOEFL (minimum score 600 paper-based; 100 iBT), IELTS (minimum score 7), PTE. *Application deadline:* For fall admission, 12/1 priority date for domestic and international students. Application fee: $90. Electronic applications accepted. *Financial support:* In 2017–18, 4 students received support, including 1 fellowship with full tuition reimbursement available (averaging $33,000 per year), 3 research assistantships with full tuition reimbursements available (averaging $33,000 per year); institutionally sponsored loans, scholarships/grants, traineeships, health care benefits, and unspecified assistantships also available. Financial award application deadline: 4/15; financial award applicants required to submit CSS PROFILE or FAFSA. *Unit head:* Dr. Ralf Langen, Director, 323-442-1475, Fax: 323-442-1199, E-mail: langen@med.usc.edu. *Application contact:* Dr. Joyce Perez, Manager of Student Programs, 323-442-1645, Fax: 323-442-1199, E-mail: jpperez@med.usc.edu.
Website: https://keck.usc.edu/pibbs/phd-programs/medical-biophysics

The University of Texas Medical Branch, Graduate School of Biomedical Sciences, Program in Biochemistry and Molecular Biology, Galveston, TX 77555. Offers biochemistry (PhD); bioinformatics (PhD); biophysics (PhD); cell biology (PhD); computational biology (PhD); structural biology (PhD). *Degree requirements:* For doctorate, thesis/dissertation. *Entrance requirements:* Additional exam requirements/recommendations for international students: Required—TOEFL (minimum score 550 paper-based). Electronic applications accepted.

University of Toronto, Faculty of Medicine, Department of Medical Biophysics, Toronto, ON M5S 1A1, Canada. Offers M Sc, PhD. *Degree requirements:* For master's, thesis; for doctorate, thesis/dissertation. *Entrance requirements:* For master's and doctorate, resume, 2 letters of reference. Additional exam requirements/recommendations for international students: Required—TOEFL (minimum score 620 paper-based), TWE (minimum score 5). Electronic applications accepted.

University of Virginia, School of Medicine, Department of Molecular Physiology and Biological Physics, Charlottesville, VA 22903. Offers biological and physical sciences (MS); physiology (PhD); MD/PhD. *Faculty:* 26 full-time (6 women), 1 part-time/adjunct (0 women). *Students:* 3 full-time (1 woman); includes 1 minority (Hispanic/Latino). Average age 28. In 2017, 17 master's, 1 doctorate awarded. *Entrance requirements:* For doctorate, GRE General Test, GRE Subject Test. Additional exam requirements/recommendations for international students: Required—TOEFL. *Application deadline:* For fall admission, 2/15 for domestic and international students. Applications are processed on a rolling basis. Application fee: $60. Electronic applications accepted. *Financial support:* Fellowships, research assistantships, and teaching assistantships available. Financial award applicants required to submit FAFSA. *Unit head:* Dr. Mark Yeager, Chair, 434-924-5108, Fax: 434-982-1616, E-mail: my3r@virginia.edu. *Application contact:* Director of Graduate Studies, E-mail: physiograd@virginia.edu.
Website: http://www.healthsystem.virginia.edu/internet/physio/

University of Virginia, School of Medicine, Interdisciplinary Program in Biophysics, Charlottesville, VA 22908. Offers PhD. *Students:* 14 full-time (6 women), 1 (woman) part-time; includes 2 minority (1 Asian, non-Hispanic/Latino; 1 Hispanic/Latino), 6 international. Average age 28. In 2017, 3 doctorates awarded. *Degree requirements:* For doctorate, thesis/dissertation, research proposal, oral defense. *Entrance requirements:* For doctorate, GRE General Test, GRE Subject Test (recommended), 2 or more letters of recommendation. Additional exam requirements/recommendations for international students: Required—TOEFL. *Application deadline:* For fall admission, 4/15 for domestic and international students. Applications are processed on a rolling basis. Application fee: $60. Electronic applications accepted. *Financial support:* Fellowships with full tuition reimbursements, research assistantships with full tuition reimbursements, teaching assistantships with full tuition reimbursements, and tuition waivers (full) available. Financial award application deadline: 1/15; financial award applicants required to submit FAFSA. *Faculty research:* Structural biology and structural genomics, structural biology of membrane proteins and membrane biophysics, spectroscopy and thermodynamics of macromolecular interactions, high resolution imaging and cell biophysics. *Unit head:* Dr. Robert K. Nakamoto, Director of the Biophysics Program, 434-982-0279, E-mail: rkn3c@virginia.edu. *Application contact:* Carrie Walker, Graduate Programs Coordinator, 434-924-1744, E-mail: caw9g@virginia.edu.
Website: http://www.medicine.virginia.edu/education/phd/scbb-new-biophysics/welcome-to-biophysics-at-uva.html

University of Washington, Graduate School, School of Medicine, Graduate Programs in Medicine, Department of Physiology and Biophysics, Seattle, WA 98195. Offers PhD. *Degree requirements:* For doctorate, thesis/dissertation. *Entrance requirements:* For doctorate, GRE General Test. Additional exam requirements/recommendations for international students: Required—TOEFL (minimum score 580 paper-based; 70 iBT). *Faculty research:* Membrane and cell biophysics, neuroendocrinology, cardiovascular and respiratory physiology, systems neurophysiology and behavior, molecular physiology.

The University of Western Ontario, Faculty of Graduate Studies, Biosciences Division, Department of Medical Biophysics, London, ON N6A 5B8, Canada. Offers M Sc, PhD. *Degree requirements:* For master's, thesis; for doctorate, thesis/dissertation. *Entrance requirements:* Additional exam requirements/recommendations for international students: Required—TOEFL. *Faculty research:* Haemodynamics and cardiovascular biomechanics, microcirculation, orthopedic biomechanics, radiobiology, medical imaging.

University of Wisconsin–Madison, Graduate School, Program in Biophysics, Madison, WI 53706. Offers PhD. *Degree requirements:* For doctorate, comprehensive exam, thesis/dissertation. *Entrance requirements:* For doctorate, GRE General Test, minimum GPA of 3.0. Additional exam requirements/recommendations for international students: Required—TOEFL (minimum score 580 paper-based; 92 iBT). Electronic applications accepted. *Faculty research:* NMR spectroscopy, high-speed automated DNA sequencing, x-ray crystallography, neuronal signaling and exocytosis, protein structure.

Vanderbilt University, School of Medicine, Department of Molecular Physiology and Biophysics, Nashville, TN 37240-1001. Offers MS, PhD, MD/PhD. *Faculty:* 26 full-time (3 women). *Students:* 27 full-time (15 women); includes 7 minority (2 Black or African American, non-Hispanic/Latino; 2 Asian, non-Hispanic/Latino; 3 Hispanic/Latino). Average age 27. In 2017, 9 doctorates awarded. *Degree requirements:* For doctorate, comprehensive exam, thesis/dissertation, preliminary, qualifying, and final exams. *Entrance requirements:* For doctorate, GRE General Test, GRE Subject Test (recommended). Additional exam requirements/recommendations for international students: Required—TOEFL (minimum score 570 paper-based; 88 iBT). *Application deadline:* For fall admission, 1/15 for domestic and international students. Application fee: $0. Electronic applications accepted. *Financial support:* Fellowships with full tuition reimbursements, research assistantships with full tuition reimbursements, Federal Work-Study, institutionally sponsored loans, scholarships/grants, traineeships, health care benefits, and tuition waivers (partial) available. Financial award application deadline: 1/15; financial award applicants required to submit CSS PROFILE or FAFSA. *Faculty research:* Biophysics, cell signaling and gene regulation, human genetics, diabetes and obesity, neuroscience. *Unit head:* Dr. Roger Cone, Acting Chair, 615-322-7000, Fax: 615-343-0490, E-mail: roger.cone@vanderbilt.edu. *Application contact:* Richard O'Brien, Director of Graduate Studies, 615-322-7000, E-mail: richard.obrien@vanderbilt.edu.
Website: http://www.mc.vanderbilt.edu/root/vumc.php?site-MPB

Vanderbilt University, School of Medicine, Program in Chemical and Physical Biology, Nashville, TN 37240-1001. Offers PhD. *Students:* 41 full-time (14 women); includes 9 minority (1 Black or African American, non-Hispanic/Latino; 1 Asian, non-Hispanic/Latino; 7 Hispanic/Latino), 6 international. Average age 28. In 2017, 5 doctorates awarded. *Degree requirements:* For doctorate, comprehensive exam, thesis/dissertation, dissertation defense. *Entrance requirements:* For doctorate, GRE, 3 letters of recommendation, official transcripts. Additional exam requirements/recommendations for international students: Required—TOEFL. *Application deadline:* For fall admission, 1/15 priority date for domestic students, 1/15 for international students. Applications are processed on a rolling basis. Application fee: $0. Electronic applications accepted. *Financial support:* Fellowships with full tuition reimbursements, traineeships, health care benefits, and tuition waivers (full) available. *Faculty research:* Mathematical modeling, enzyme kinetics, structural biology, genomics, proteomics and mass spectrometry. *Unit head:* Dr. Bruce Damon, Director of Graduate Studies, 615-322-4235, Fax: 615-343-0490, E-mail: bruce.damon@vanderbilt.edu. *Application contact:* Patricia Mueller, Coordinator, 615-322-8727, E-mail: patricia.l.mueller@vanderbilt.edu.

Washington State University, College of Veterinary Medicine, Molecular Biosciences Graduate Program, Pullman, WA 99164-7520. Offers molecular biosciences (MS, PhD), including genetics (PhD). *Faculty:* 26 full-time (9 women), 27 part-time/adjunct (4 women). *Students:* 36 full-time (23 women); includes 10 minority (2 Asian, non-Hispanic/Latino; 6 Hispanic/Latino; 2 Two or more races, non-Hispanic/Latino), 1 international. Average age 27. 76 applicants, 22% accepted, 6 enrolled. In 2017, 1 master's, 10 doctorates awarded. Terminal master's awarded for partial completion of doctoral program. *Degree requirements:* For master's, thesis (for some programs), oral defense; for doctorate, comprehensive exam, thesis/dissertation, oral defense. *Entrance requirements:* For master's and doctorate, GRE General Test, minimum GPA of 3.0. Additional exam requirements/recommendations for international students: Required—TOEFL (minimum score 600 paper-based; 100 iBT). *Application deadline:* For fall admission, 12/15 priority date for domestic and international students. Application fee: $75. Electronic applications accepted. *Expenses:* Contact institution. *Financial support:* In 2017–18, 36 students received support, including 6 fellowships with full tuition reimbursements available (averaging $25,911 per year), 12 research assistantships with full tuition reimbursements available (averaging $25,911 per year), 18 teaching assistantships with full tuition reimbursements available (averaging $25,911 per year); scholarships/grants, traineeships, and health care benefits also available. Financial award application deadline: 4/15. *Faculty research:* Bacterial pathogenesis, microbial metabolism, DNA repair, reproductive biology, cytoskeleton, molecular cell biology, biochemistry, signal transduction, protein export. *Total annual research expenditures:* $4.3 million. *Unit head:* Dr. Jonathan Jones, Director, 509-335-8724, Fax: 509-335-9688, E-mail: jcr.jones@vetmed.wsu.edu. *Application contact:* Tami Breske, Graduate Academic Coordinator, 509-335-4318, E-mail: tbreske@vetmed.wsu.edu.
Website: http://www.smb.wsu.edu

Weill Cornell Medicine, Weill Cornell Graduate School of Medical Sciences, Physiology, Biophysics and Systems Biology Program, New York, NY 10065. Offers MS, PhD. Terminal master's awarded for partial completion of doctoral program. *Degree requirements:* For master's, comprehensive exam; for doctorate, thesis/dissertation, final exam. *Entrance requirements:* For doctorate, GRE General Test, introductory courses in biology, inorganic and organic chemistry, physics, and mathematics. Additional exam requirements/recommendations for international students: Required—TOEFL. *Faculty research:* Receptor-mediated regulation of cell function, molecular properties of channels or receptors, bioinformatics, mathematical modeling.

Yale University, Graduate School of Arts and Sciences, Department of Molecular Biophysics and Biochemistry, New Haven, CT 06520. Offers PhD. *Degree requirements:* For doctorate, thesis/dissertation. *Entrance requirements:* For doctorate, GRE General Test, GRE Subject Test.

Molecular Biophysics

Baylor College of Medicine, Graduate School of Biomedical Sciences, Program in Structural and Computational Biology and Molecular Biophysics, Houston, TX 77030-3498. Offers PhD, MD/PhD. MD/PhD offered jointly with Rice University and University of Houston. *Degree requirements:* For doctorate, thesis/dissertation, public defense. *Entrance requirements:* For doctorate, GRE General Test, GRE Subject Test (strongly recommended), minimum GPA of 3.0. Additional exam requirements/recommendations for international students: Required—TOEFL. Electronic applications accepted. *Faculty research:* Computational biology, structural biology, biophysics.

California Institute of Technology, Division of Biology and Division of Chemistry and Chemical Engineering, Biochemistry and Molecular Biophysics Graduate Option, Pasadena, CA 91125-0001. Offers PhD. *Degree requirements:* For doctorate, thesis/dissertation, qualifying exam. *Entrance requirements:* For doctorate, GRE General Test. Additional exam requirements/recommendations for international students: Required—TOEFL. Electronic applications accepted.

California Institute of Technology, Division of Chemistry and Chemical Engineering, Pasadena, CA 91125-0001. Offers biochemistry and molecular biophysics (MS, PhD); chemical engineering (MS, PhD); chemistry (MS, PhD). *Faculty:* 42 full-time (10 women). *Students:* 295 full-time (115 women); includes 79 minority (3 Black or African American, non-Hispanic/Latino; 41 Asian, non-Hispanic/Latino; 21 Hispanic/Latino; 14 Two or more races, non-Hispanic/Latino), 80 international. Average age 25. 638 applicants, 23% accepted, 43 enrolled. In 2017, 14 master's, 59 doctorates awarded. Terminal master's awarded for partial completion of doctoral program. *Degree requirements:* For master's, thesis; for doctorate, thesis/dissertation. *Entrance requirements:* For doctorate, GRE, BS. Additional exam requirements/recommendations for international students: Required—TOEFL; Recommended—IELTS, TWE. *Application deadline:* For fall admission, 12/15 for domestic and international students. Application fee: $100. Electronic applications accepted. *Expenses:* $48,111 tuition, $1,674 mandatory fees. *Financial support:* In 2017–18, 309 students received support, including fellowships (averaging $33,000 per year), research assistantships (averaging $25,900 per year), teaching assistantships (averaging $5,100 per year); Federal Work-Study, institutionally sponsored loans, scholarships/grants, traineeships, health care benefits, and unspecified assistantships also available. Financial award application deadline: 12/15. *Faculty research:* Biochemistry and molecular biophysics; inorganic, structural, and electrochemistry; organic chemistry and chemical biology; physical, theoretical, and chemical physics; chemical engineering. *Unit head:* Prof. Jacqueline K. Barton, Chair, Division of Chemistry and Chemical Engineering, 626-395-3646, Fax: 626-395-6948, E-mail: jkbarton@caltech.edu. *Application contact:* Natalie Gilmore, Graduate Office, 626-395-3812, Fax: 626-577-9246, E-mail: ngilmore@its.caltech.edu.
Website: http://www.cce.caltech.edu/

Carnegie Mellon University, Mellon College of Science, Joint Pitt + CMU Molecular Biophysics and Structural Biology Graduate Program, Pittsburgh, PA 15213-3891. Offers PhD. Program offered jointly with University of Pittsburgh. *Degree requirements:* For doctorate, comprehensive exam, thesis/dissertation. *Entrance requirements:* For doctorate, GRE General Test. Additional exam requirements/recommendations for international students: Required—TOEFL (minimum score 600 paper-based; 100 iBT), IELTS (minimum score 7). Electronic applications accepted. *Faculty research:* Structural biology, protein dynamics and folding, computational biophysics, molecular informatics, membrane biophysics and ion channels, NMR, x-ray crystallography cryaelectron microscopy.

Duke University, Graduate School, University Program in Structural Biology and Biophysics, Durham, NC 27710. Offers Certificate. Students must be enrolled in a participating PhD program (biochemistry, cell biology, chemistry, molecular genetics, neurobiology, pharmacology). *Entrance requirements:* For degree, GRE General Test. Additional exam requirements/recommendations for international students: Required—TOEFL (minimum score 577 paper-based; 90 iBT) or IELTS (minimum score 7).

Florida State University, The Graduate School, College of Arts and Sciences, Program in Molecular Biophysics, Tallahassee, FL 32306. Offers structural biology (PhD). *Faculty:* 32 full-time (6 women). *Students:* 18 full-time (6 women); includes 1 minority (Hispanic/Latino), 9 international. Average age 27. 23 applicants, 48% accepted, 4 enrolled. In 2017, 4 doctorates awarded. *Degree requirements:* For doctorate, comprehensive exam, thesis/dissertation, teaching 1 term in professor's major department. *Entrance requirements:* For doctorate, GRE General Test (minimum score 153 Verbal portion, 154 Quantitative portion). Additional exam requirements/recommendations for international students: Required—TOEFL (minimum score 550 paper-based; 90 iBT), IELTS (minimum score 6.5). *Application deadline:* For fall admission, 12/15 for domestic and international students. Application fee: $30. Electronic applications accepted. *Expenses:* Contact institution. *Financial support:* In 2017–18, 17 students received support, including 4 fellowships with partial tuition reimbursements available (averaging $34,000 per year), 15 research assistantships with partial tuition reimbursements available (averaging $24,200 per year), 2 teaching assistantships with partial tuition reimbursements available (averaging $24,200 per year); scholarships/grants, health care benefits, tuition waivers (partial), and unspecified assistantships also available. Financial award application deadline: 12/15; financial award applicants required to submit FAFSA. *Faculty research:* Protein and nucleic acid structure and function, membrane protein structure, computational biophysics, 3-D image reconstruction. *Unit head:* Dr. Hong Li, Director, 850-644-6785, Fax: 850-644-7244, E-mail: hli4@fsu.edu. *Application contact:* Jana Sefcikova, Academic Coordinator, Graduate Programs, 850-644-1012, Fax: 850-644-7244, E-mail: jsefcikova@fsu.edu.
Website: http://biophysics.fsu.edu/

Illinois Institute of Technology, Graduate College, College of Science, Department of Biology, Chicago, IL 60616. Offers applied life sciences (MS); biochemistry (MS); biology (MS, PhD); cell and molecular biology (MS); microbiology (MS); molecular biochemistry and biophysics (MS, PhD). *Program availability:* Part-time, evening/weekend, online learning. Terminal master's awarded for partial completion of doctoral program. *Degree requirements:* For master's, comprehensive exam, thesis (for some programs); for doctorate, comprehensive exam, thesis/dissertation. *Entrance requirements:* For master's, GRE General Test (minimum score 300 Quantitative and Verbal, 2.5 Analytical Writing), minimum undergraduate GPA of 3.0; for doctorate, GRE General Test (minimum score 310 Quantitative and Verbal, 3.0 Analytical Writing); GRE Subject Test (strongly recommended), minimum undergraduate GPA of 3.0. Additional exam requirements/recommendations for international students: Required—TOEFL (minimum score 550 paper-based; 80 iBT). Electronic applications accepted. *Faculty research:* Macromolecular crystallography, insect immunity and basic cell biology, improvement of bacterial strains for enhanced biodesulfurization of petroleum, programmed cell death in cancer cells.

Johns Hopkins University, Zanvyl Krieger School of Arts and Sciences, Program in Cell, Molecular, Developmental Biology, and Biophysics, Baltimore, MD 21218. Offers PhD. Terminal master's awarded for partial completion of doctoral program. *Degree requirements:* For doctorate, comprehensive exam, thesis/dissertation. *Entrance requirements:* For doctorate, GRE General Test. Additional exam requirements/recommendations for international students: Required—TOEFL (minimum score 600 paper-based), IELTS, TWE. Electronic applications accepted. *Faculty research:* Cell biology, molecular biology and development, biochemistry, developmental biology, biophysics, genetics.

Rutgers University–New Brunswick, Graduate School-New Brunswick, BioMaPS Institute for Quantitative Biology, Piscataway, NJ 08854-8097. Offers computational biology and molecular biophysics (PhD). *Degree requirements:* For doctorate, comprehensive exam, thesis/dissertation. *Entrance requirements:* For doctorate, GRE. Additional exam requirements/recommendations for international students: Required—TOEFL. Electronic applications accepted. *Faculty research:* Structural biology, systems biology, bioinformatics, translational medicine, genomics.

University at Buffalo, the State University of New York, Graduate School, Graduate Programs in Cancer Research and Biomedical Sciences at Roswell Park Cancer Institute, Buffalo, NY 14260. Offers cancer pathology and prevention (PhD); cellular and molecular biology (PhD); immunology (PhD); interdisciplinary natural sciences (MS); molecular and cellular biophysics and biochemistry (PhD); molecular pharmacology and cancer therapeutics (PhD). *Faculty:* 128 full time (35 women). *Students:* 15 full-time (10 women); includes 1 minority (Two or more races, non-Hispanic/Latino), 6 international. 186 applicants, 25% accepted, 28 enrolled. In 2017, 15 master's, 11 doctorates awarded. Terminal master's awarded for partial completion of doctoral program. *Degree requirements:* For master's, thesis, oral defense of thesis; for doctorate, comprehensive exam, thesis/dissertation, oral defense of dissertation. *Entrance requirements:* For master's and doctorate, GRE General Test. Additional exam requirements/recommendations for international students: Required—TOEFL (minimum score 79 iBT). *Application deadline:* For fall admission, 1/5 priority date for domestic and international students. Application fee: $75. Electronic applications accepted. *Financial support:* In 2017–18, 91 students received support, including 91 research assistantships with full tuition reimbursements available (averaging $27,000 per year); scholarships/grants, health care benefits, and unspecified assistantships also available. Financial award application deadline: 1/5. *Faculty research:* Basic and biomedical cancer research, cell and molecular biology, biophysics, drug design, immunology, genetics, experimental pathology, biochemistry, molecular pharmacology, cancer therapeutics. *Application contact:* Dr. Norman J. Karin, Associate Dean, 716-845-2339, Fax: 716-845-8178, E-mail: norman.karin@roswellpark.edu.
Website: http://www.roswellpark.edu/education

University of Arkansas for Medical Sciences, Graduate School, Little Rock, AR 72205. Offers biochemistry and molecular biology (MS, PhD); bioinformatics (MS, PhD); cellular physiology and molecular biophysics (MS, PhD); clinical nutrition (MS); interdisciplinary biomedical sciences (MS, PhD, Certificate); interdisciplinary toxicology (MS); microbiology and immunology (PhD); neurobiology and developmental sciences (PhD); pharmacology (PhD); MD/PhD. Bioinformatics programs hosted jointly with the University of Arkansas at Little Rock. *Program availability:* Part-time. Terminal master's awarded for partial completion of doctoral program. *Degree requirements:* For master's, comprehensive exam (for some programs), thesis (for some programs); for doctorate, thesis/dissertation. *Entrance requirements:* For master's and doctorate, GRE. Additional exam requirements/recommendations for international students: Required—TOEFL. Electronic applications accepted. *Expenses:* Contact institution.

University of Chicago, Division of the Biological Sciences, Biochemistry and Molecular Biology Department, Chicago, IL 60637. Offers PhD, MD/PhD. *Students:* 24 full-time (13 women). 65 applicants, 35% accepted, 5 enrolled. In 2017, 8 doctorates awarded. *Degree requirements:* For doctorate, thesis/dissertation, ethics class, 2 teaching assistantships. *Entrance requirements:* For doctorate, GRE General Test, transcripts, statement of purpose, 3 letters of recommendation. Additional exam requirements/recommendations for international students: Required—TOEFL (minimum score 600 paper-based; 104 iBT), IELTS (minimum score 7). *Application deadline:* For fall admission, 12/1 for domestic and international students. Application fee: $90. Electronic applications accepted. *Financial support:* In 2017–18, 26 students received support, including fellowships with full tuition reimbursements available (averaging $31,000 per year), research assistantships with full tuition reimbursements available (averaging $31,000 per year); institutionally sponsored loans, scholarships/grants, traineeships, and health care benefits also available. Financial award application deadline: 12/1. *Faculty research:* Molecular biology, gene expression, and DNA-protein interactions; membrane biochemistry, molecular endocrinology, and transmembrane signaling; enzyme mechanisms, physical biochemistry, and structural biology. *Total annual research expenditures:* $5 million. *Unit head:* Dr. Tobin Sosnick, Chair, E-mail: trsosnic@uchicago.edu. *Application contact:* Lisa Anderson, Graduate Student Administrator, 773-834-3586, Fax: 773-702-0439, E-mail: landerso@bsd.uchicago.edu.
Website: http://bmb.uchospitals.edu/

University of Massachusetts Amherst, Graduate School, Interdisciplinary Programs, Program in Molecular and Cellular Biology, Amherst, MA 01003. Offers biological chemistry and molecular biophysics (PhD); biomedicine (PhD); cellular and developmental biology (PhD). *Program availability:* Part-time. Terminal master's awarded for partial completion of doctoral program. *Degree requirements:* For doctorate, comprehensive exam, thesis/dissertation. *Entrance requirements:* For doctorate, GRE General Test. Additional exam requirements/recommendations for international students: Required—TOEFL (minimum score 550 paper-based; 80 iBT), IELTS (minimum score 6.5). Electronic applications accepted.

University of Pennsylvania, Perelman School of Medicine, Biomedical Graduate Studies, Graduate Group in Biochemistry and Molecular Biophysics, Philadelphia, PA 19104. Offers PhD, MD/PhD, VMD/PhD. *Faculty:* 103. *Students:* 89 full-time (50 women); includes 34 minority (2 Black or African American, non-Hispanic/Latino; 10 Asian, non-Hispanic/Latino; 20 Hispanic/Latino; 2 Two or more races, non-Hispanic/Latino), 7 international. 108 applicants, 32% accepted, 14 enrolled. In 2017, 20 doctorates awarded. *Degree requirements:* For doctorate, thesis/dissertation. *Entrance requirements:* Additional exam requirements/recommendations for international students: Required—TOEFL. *Application deadline:* For fall admission, 12/1 priority date for domestic students, 12/1 for international students. Applications are processed on a rolling basis. Application fee: $80. *Financial support:* Fellowships, research assistantships, teaching assistantships, and tuition waivers available. *Faculty research:* Biochemistry of cell differentiation, tissue culture, intermediary metabolism, structure of proteins and nucleic acids, biochemical genetics. *Unit head:* Dr. Kim Sharp, Chairperson, 215-573-3506. *Application contact:* Kelli McKenna, Coordinator, 215-898-4639.
Website: http://www.med.upenn.edu/bmbgrad/

University of Pittsburgh, School of Medicine, Graduate Programs in Medicine and Kenneth P. Dietrich School of Arts and Sciences, Molecular Biophysics and Structural Biology Graduate Program, Pittsburgh, PA 15260. Offers PhD. Program jointly offered with Carnegie Mellon University. *Faculty:* 21 full-time (5 women). *Students:* 10 full-time (5 women), 2 international. Average age 29. 40 applicants, 35% accepted, 5 enrolled. In 2017, 2 doctorates awarded. *Degree requirements:* For doctorate, comprehensive exam, thesis/dissertation. *Entrance requirements:* For doctorate, GRE General Test. Additional exam requirements/recommendations for international students: Required—TOEFL (minimum score 600 paper-based; 100 iBT), IELTS (minimum score 7). *Application deadline:* For fall admission, 1/15 priority date for domestic and international students. Application fee: $50. Electronic applications accepted. *Expenses:* $26,782 full-time resident per academic year, $42,006 non-resident. *Financial support:* In 2017–18, 10 students received support, including 5 research assistantships with full tuition reimbursements available (averaging $29,500 per year); traineeships also available. *Faculty research:* Structure and dynamics of membrane proteins, principles of protein structure and dynamics, macromolecular recognition, gene regulation and signaling, virus structure and nano-machinery. *Unit head:* Dr. James Conway, Director, 412-383-9847, Fax: 412-648-1077, E-mail: mbsbinfo@medschool.pitt.edu. *Application contact:* Lauren Zielinski, Student Affairs Specialist, 412-383-7866, Fax: 412-648-1077, E-mail: mbsbinfo@medschool.pitt.edu.
Website: http://www.mbsb.pitt.edu

The University of Texas Medical Branch, Graduate School of Biomedical Sciences, Molecular Biophysics Educational Track, Galveston, TX 77555. Offers PhD.

The University of Texas Southwestern Medical Center, Southwestern Graduate School of Biomedical Sciences, Division of Basic Science, Program in Molecular Biophysics, Dallas, TX 75390. Offers PhD. *Degree requirements:* For doctorate, thesis/dissertation, qualifying exam. *Entrance requirements:* For doctorate, GRE General Test, minimum GPA of 3.0. Additional exam requirements/recommendations for international students: Required—TOEFL. Electronic applications accepted. *Faculty research:* Optical spectroscopy, x-ray crystallography, protein chemistry, ion channels, contractile and cytoskeletal proteins.

Washington University in St. Louis, The Graduate School, Division of Biology and Biomedical Sciences, Program in Computational and Molecular Biophysics, St. Louis, MO 63130-4899. Offers PhD. *Degree requirements:* For doctorate, thesis/dissertation. *Entrance requirements:* For doctorate, GRE General Test, GRE Subject Test. Additional exam requirements/recommendations for international students: Required—TOEFL. Electronic applications accepted. *Faculty research:* Structural biology, protein and nucleic acid kinetics and thermodynamics, single-molecule enzymology, motor proteins, biophysical pathogenesis, protein design, nanoscience, ion channels and lipid membranes, computational biophysics.

Wesleyan University, Graduate Studies, Department of Molecular Biology and Biochemistry, Middletown, CT 06459. Offers molecular biology and biochemistry (PhD); molecular biophysics (PhD). *Faculty:* 8 full-time (3 women), 2 part-time/adjunct (both women). *Students:* 16 full-time (10 women); includes 4 minority (2 Asian, non-Hispanic/Latino; 1 Hispanic/Latino; 1 Two or more races, non-Hispanic/Latino), 7 international. Average age 24. 24 applicants, 25% accepted, 3 enrolled. In 2017, 2 doctorates awarded. Terminal master's awarded for partial completion of doctoral program. *Degree requirements:* For doctorate, comprehensive exam, thesis/dissertation. *Entrance requirements:* For doctorate, GRE General Test, GRE Subject Test. Additional exam requirements/recommendations for international students: Required—TOEFL. *Application deadline:* For fall admission, 1/15 for domestic and international students. Application fee: $0. Electronic applications accepted. *Financial support:* In 2017–18, 9 teaching assistantships with full tuition reimbursements were awarded; research assistantships with full tuition reimbursements and institutionally sponsored loans also available. Financial award application deadline: 4/15. *Faculty research:* The olfactory system and new frontiers in genome research, chromosome structure and gene expression, gene co-regulation, crystallographic and spectroscopic analysis, DNA replication and repair. *Unit head:* Amy MacQueen, Chair, 860-685-2561, E-mail: amacqueen@wesleyan.edu. *Application contact:* Anika Dane, Administrative Assistant, 860-685-2404, E-mail: adane@wesleyan.edu.
Website: http://www.wesleyan.edu/mbb/

Yale University, Yale School of Medicine and Graduate School of Arts and Sciences, Combined Program in Biological and Biomedical Sciences (BBS), Molecular Biophysics and Biochemistry Track, New Haven, CT 06520. Offers PhD, MD/PhD. *Degree requirements:* For doctorate, thesis/dissertation. *Entrance requirements:* For doctorate, GRE General Test. Additional exam requirements/recommendations for international students: Required—TOEFL. Electronic applications accepted.

Radiation Biology

Georgetown University, Graduate School of Arts and Sciences, Department of Health Physics and Radiation Protection, Washington, DC 20057. Offers health physics (MS); nuclear nonproliferation (MS). *Degree requirements:* For master's, thesis. *Entrance requirements:* Additional exam requirements/recommendations for international students: Required—TOEFL.

Université de Sherbrooke, Faculty of Medicine and Health Sciences, Graduate Programs in Medicine, Program in Radiobiology, Sherbrooke, QC J1H 5N4, Canada. Offers M Sc, PhD. Terminal master's awarded for partial completion of doctoral program. *Degree requirements:* For master's, thesis; for doctorate, thesis/dissertation. Electronic applications accepted. *Faculty research:* DNA repair, physiochemical actions of radiation, radiopharmacy, phototherapy, imaging.

The University of Iowa, Roy J. and Lucille A. Carver College of Medicine and Graduate College, Graduate Programs in Medicine, Program in Free Radical and Radiation Biology, Iowa City, IA 52242-1316. Offers MS. *Program availability:* Part-time. *Degree requirements:* For master's, thesis. *Entrance requirements:* For master's, GRE. Additional exam requirements/recommendations for international students: Required—TOEFL. *Faculty research:* Radiation injury and cellular repair, cell proliferation kinetics, free radical biology, tumor control, positron emission tomography (PET) imaging, electron paramagnetic resonance (EPR).

University of Oklahoma Health Sciences Center, College of Medicine and Graduate College, Graduate Programs in Medicine, Department of Radiological Sciences, Oklahoma City, OK 73190. Offers medical radiation physics (MS, PhD), including diagnostic radiology, nuclear medicine, radiation therapy, ultrasound. *Program availability:* Part-time. Terminal master's awarded for partial completion of doctoral program. *Degree requirements:* For master's, thesis; for doctorate, thesis/dissertation. *Entrance requirements:* For master's, GRE General Test; for doctorate, GRE General Test, 3 letters of recommendation. Additional exam requirements/recommendations for international students: Required—TOEFL. *Faculty research:* Monte Carlo applications in radiation therapy, observer-performed studies in diagnostic radiology, error analysis in gated cardiac nuclear medicine studies, nuclear medicine absorbed fraction determinations.

HARVARD UNIVERSITY

Biophysics Program

Program of Study

The Committee on Higher Degrees in Biophysics offers a program of study leading to the Ph.D. degree. The committee comprises senior representatives of the Departments of Chemistry and Chemical Biology, Physics, and Molecular and Cellular Biology; the School of Engineering and Applied Sciences; and the Division of Medical Sciences. Students receive sufficient training in physics, biology, and chemistry to enable them to apply the concepts and methods of the physical sciences to the solution of biological problems.

An initial goal of the Biophysics Program is to provide an introduction through courses and seminars to several of the diverse areas of biophysics, such as structural molecular biology, cell and membrane biophysics, neurobiology, molecular genetics, physical biochemistry, and theoretical biophysics. The program is flexible, and special effort has been devoted to minimizing course work and other formal requirements. Students engage in several research rotations during their first two years. The qualifying examination is taken at the end of the second year to determine admission to candidacy. Students undertake dissertation research as early as possible in the field and subject of their choice. Opportunities for dissertation research are available in a number of special fields. The Ph.D. requires not less than three years devoted to advanced studies, including dissertation research and the dissertation. The Committee on Higher Degrees in Biophysics anticipates that it takes an average of five years, with the maximum being six years, to complete this program.

Research Facilities

Many more of the University's modern research facilities are available to the biophysics student because of the interdepartmental nature of the program. Research programs may be pursued in the Departments of Chemistry and Chemical Biology, Molecular and Cellular Biology, Applied Physics, and Engineering Sciences in Cambridge as well as in the Departments of Biological Chemistry and Molecular Pharmacology, Genetics, Microbiology, Neurobiology, and Cell Biology in the Harvard Medical School Division of Medical Sciences. Research may also be pursued in the Harvard School of Public Health, the Dana Farber Cancer Institute, Children's Hospital, Massachusetts General Hospital, Beth Israel Hospital, and more than ten other Harvard-affiliated institutions located throughout the cities.

Financial Aid

In 2018–19, all graduate students receive a stipend ($38,376 for twelve months) and full tuition and health fees ($50,926). A semester of teaching is required in the second year. Students are strongly encouraged to apply for fellowships from such sources as the National Science Foundation, the NDSEG, the Hertz Foundation, and the Ford Foundation. Full-time Ph.D. candidates in good academic standing are guaranteed full financial support through their sixth year of study or throughout their academic program if less than six years.

Cost of Study

Tuition and health fees for the 2018–19 academic year are $50,926. After two years in residence, students are eligible for a reduced rate (currently $16,604).

Living and Housing Costs

Accommodations in graduate residence halls are available at rents ranging from $6,872 to $10,794 per academic year. In addition, there are approximately 1,500 apartments available for graduate students in Harvard-owned buildings. Applications may be obtained from the Harvard University Housing Office, which also maintains a list of available private rooms, houses, and apartments in the vicinity.

Student Group

On average, the program enrolls roughly 54 students annually. Currently, 17 women and 8 international students are enrolled in the program. Biophysics students intermingle in both their research and their social life with graduate students from the many other departments where research in the biophysical sciences is carried out.

Location

The Biophysics Program maintains a dual-campus orientation in the neighboring cities of Cambridge and Boston. Their proximity provides for a wide range of academic, cultural, extracurricular, and recreational opportunities, and the large numbers of theaters, museums, libraries, and universities contribute to enrich the scientific and cultural life of students. Because New England is compact in area, it is easy to reach countryside, mountains, and seacoast for winter and summer sports or just for a change of scenery.

The University

Established in 1636 in the Massachusetts Bay Colony, Harvard has grown to become a complex of many facilities whose educational vitality, social commitment, and level of cultural achievement contribute to make the University a leader in the academic world. Comprising more than 15,000 students and 3,000 faculty members, Harvard appeals to self-directed, resourceful students of diverse beliefs and backgrounds.

Applying

Students must apply by December 1, 2018, to be considered for admission in September 2019. Scores on the General Test of the Graduate Record Examinations are suggested and GRE Subject Tests are recommended. Due to the early application deadline, applicants should plan to take any GRE test no later than October to ensure that original scores are received by December 1. Information about Graduate School fellowships and scholarships, admission procedures, and graduate study at Harvard may be obtained by writing to the Admissions Office.

Correspondence and Information

For information on the program:
Harvard Biophysics Program
Building C2, Room 122
Harvard Medical School Campus
240 Longwood Avenue
Boston, Massachusetts 02115
United States
E-mail: biophys@fas.harvard.edu
Website: http://biophysics.fas.harvard.edu

For application forms for admission and financial aid (applications accepted online only):
Admissions Office
Graduate School of Arts and Sciences
Holyoke Center
Harvard University
1350 Massachusetts Avenue
Cambridge, Massachusetts 02138
United States
E-mail: admiss@fas.harvard.edu
Website: http://www.gsas.harvard.edu

THE FACULTY AND THEIR RESEARCH

The following faculty members accept students for degree work in biophysics (this is a partial listing and the faculty are constantly being updated and added to). Dissertation research with other faculty members is possible by arrangement.

Jonathan Abraham, M.D., Ph.D., Assistant Professor of Microbiology and Immunobiology. Molecular level studies of highly lethal human diseases.

Mark L. Andermann, Ph.D., Assistant Professor of Medicine. Cognitive networks mediating hunger-dependent attention to food cues.

Haribabu Arthanari, Ph.D. Assistant Professor of Biological Chemistry and Molecular Pharmacology. Therapeutic targeting of protein-protein interactions.

John Assad, Ph.D., Professor of Neurobiology. Mechanisms of visual processing in the visual cortex of awake behaving monkeys.

Frederick M. Ausubel, Ph.D., Professor of Genetics. Molecular biology of microbial pathogenesis in plants and animals.

Brian J. Bacskai, M.D., Ph.D., Professor of Neurology. Using multi-photon microscopy to address fundamental questions in Alzheimer's disease research.

Stephen C. Blacklow, M.D., Ph.D., Gustavus Adolphus Pfeiffer Professor of Biological Chemistry and Molecular Pharmacology. Molecular basis for specificity in protein folding and protein-protein interactions.

Martha L. Bulyk, Ph.D., Professor of Medicine and Pathology. Computational methods; genomic and proteomic technologies in the study of DNA-protein interactions.

James J. Chou, Ph.D., Associate Professor of Biological Chemistry and Molecular Pharmacology. NMR spectroscopy on membrane-associated proteins and peptides.

George McDonald Church, Ph.D., Professor of Genetics. Human and microbial functional genomics; genotyping; gene expression regulatory network models.

Lee Stirling Churchman, Ph.D., Assistant Professor of Genetics. Regulation of the RNA polymerase motor mechanism in vivo.

Adam E. Cohen, Ph.D., Professor of Chemistry and Chemical Biology and of Physics. Analysis of structure and function of nicotinic acetylcholine receptors.

Harvard University

Jonathan B. Cohen, Ph.D., Professor of Neurobiology. Structure and function of ligand-gated ion channels.
David P. Corey, Ph.D., Professor of Neurobiology. Ion channels in neural cell membranes.
Benjamin de Bivort, Ph.D., Associate Professor of Organismic and Evolutionary Biology. Characterizing the molecular, neural circuit, and ecological underpinnings of behavioral diversity in the fruit fly.
Vladimir Denic, Ph.D., Professor of Molecular and Cellular Biology. Structural diversification of very long-chain fatty acids.
Michael M. Desai, Ph.D., Professor of Organismic and Evolutionary Biology and of Physics. Theoretical and experimental approaches to study genetic variation within populations.
Jan Drugowitsch, Ph.D., Assistant Professor of Neurobiology. Statistical neuronal computations underlying complex decisions and behavior.
Michael J. Eck, M.D., Ph.D., Professor of Biological Chemistry and Molecular Pharmacology. Structural studies of proteins involved in signal transduction pathways.
Florian Engert, Ph.D., Professor of Molecular and Cellular Biology. Synaptic plasticity and neuronal networks.
Conor L. Evans, Ph.D., Assistant Professor of Dermatology. Development and application of optical detection, treatment, and monitoring approaches targeting major human diseases.
Ethan C. Garner, Ph.D., Associate Professor of Molecular and Cellular Biology. Organization, structure, and dynamics of the prokaryotic cytoplasm.
Rachelle Gaudet, Ph.D., Professor of Molecular and Cellular Biology. Structural studies of the stereochemistry of signaling and transport through biological membranes.
David E. Golan, M.D., Ph.D., Professor of Biological Chemistry and Molecular Pharmacology and of Medicine. Membrane dynamics; membrane structure; cellular adhesion.
Jeffrey Wade Harper, Ph.D. Professor of Cell Biology. Interaction and quantitative proteomics to understand signaling networks in the ubiquitin system.
Stephen C. Harrison, Ph.D., Professor of Biological Chemistry and Molecular Pharmacology. Structure of viruses and viral membranes; protein-DNA interactions; structural aspects of signal transduction and membrane traffic; X-ray diffraction.
Lene V. Hau, Ph.D., Mallinckrodt Professor of Physics and Applied Physics. Light-matter interactions, nanoscience, and molecular and synthetic biology.
James M. Hogle, Ph.D., Professor of Biological Chemistry and Molecular Pharmacology. Structure and function of viruses and virus-related proteins; X-ray crystallography.
Sun Hur, Ph.D., Associate Professor of Biological Chemistry and Molecular Pharmacology. Principles of self versus nonself RNA discrimination by the immune system.
Donald E. Ingber, M.D., Ph.D., Professor of Bioengineering and Judah Folkman Professor of Vascular Biology. Research in integrin signaling, cytoskeleton, and control of angiogenesis.
Tomas Kirchhausen, Ph.D., Professor of Cell Biology. Molecular mechanisms of membrane traffic; X-ray crystallography; chemical genetics.
Nancy Kleckner, Ph.D., Herchel Smith Professor of Molecular Biology. Chromosome metabolism in bacteria and yeast.
Gabriel Kreiman, Ph.D., Associate Professor of Neurology. Transcriptional regulatory circuits and neuronal circuits in visual recognition.
Andrew C. Kruse, Ph.D., Associate Professor of Biological Chemistry and Molecular Pharmacology. Studying the molecular basis of cell signaling through biochemical and biophysical techniques.
Galit Lahav, Ph.D., Professor of Systems Biology. Dynamics of network motifs in single living human cells.
Maria K. Lehtinen, Ph.D., Assistant Professor of Pathology. Cerebrospinal fluid-based signaling during brain development and in disease.
Maofu Liao, Ph.D., Assistant Professor of Cell Biology. High-resolution cryo-electron microscopy (Cryo-EM) to study structure and function of membrane proteins and DNA-Protein machines.
David R. Liu, Ph.D., Professor of Chemistry and Chemical Biology. Organic chemistry and chemical biology.
Jun S. Liu, Ph.D., Professor of Statistics. Stochastic processes, probability theory, and statistical inference.
Joseph J. Loparo, Ph.D., Associate Professor of Biological Chemistry and Molecular Pharmacology. Developing novel single-molecule methods to study multiprotein complexes.
Jarrod Marto, Ph.D., Associate Professor of Biological Chemistry and Molecular Pharmacology. Quantitative proteomics of cancer progression.
Keith W. Miller, Ph.D., Mallinckrodt Professor of Pharmacology, Department of Anesthesia. Molecular mechanisms of regulatory conformation changes and drug action on membrane receptors and channels, using rapid kinetics, time-resolved photolabeling, and spectroscopy (EPR, fluorescence, NMR); characterization of lipid-protein interactions in membrane proteins.
Leonid A. Mirny, Ph.D., Professor of Medical Engineering and Science, and of Physics. Three dimensional organization of chromosomes; Evolutionary dynamics of cancer. Timothy Mitchison, Ph.D., Hasib Sabbagh Professor of Systems Biology. Cytoskeleton dynamics; mechanism of mitosis and cell locomotion; small-molecule inhibitors.
Danesh Moazed, Ph.D., Professor of Cell Biology. Studies on the assembly and stable propagation of epigenetic chromatin domains.
Andrew W. Murray, Ph.D., Herchel Smith Professor of Molecular Genetics. Regulation of mitosis.
Venkatesh N. Murthy, Ph.D., Professor of Molecular and Cellular Biology. Mechanisms of synaptic transmission and plasticity.
Daniel J. Needleman, Ph.D., Professor of Applied Physics and Professor of Molecular and Cellular Biology. Physics of macromolecular assemblies and subcellular organization.
Bence P. Olveczky, Ph.D., Professor of Organismic and Evolutionary Biology. Neurobiology of vocal learning.
David Pellman, M.D., Professor of Cell Biology. The mechanics and regulation of mitosis.
Mara Prentiss, Ph.D., Professor of Physics. Exploitation of optical manipulation to measure adhesion properties, including virus cell binding.
Sharad Ramanathan, Ph.D., Professor of Molecular and Cellular Biology. Decision-making in cells and organisms.
Tom A. Rapoport, Ph.D., Professor of Cell Biology. Mechanism of how proteins are transported across the endoplasmic reticulum membrane.
Gary Ruvkun, Ph.D., Professor of Genetics. Genetic control of developmental timing, neurogenesis, and neural function.
Bernardo L. Sabatini, Ph.D., Professor of Neurobiology. Regulation of synaptic transmission and dendritic function in the mammalian brain.
Aravinthan D. T. Samuel, Ph.D., Professor of Physics. Topics in biophysics, neurobiology, and animal behavior.
Stuart L. Schreiber, Ph.D., Morris Loeb Professor of Chemistry and Chemical Biology. Forward and reverse chemical genetics: using small molecules to explore biology.
Brian Seed, Ph.D., Professor of Genetics. Genetic analysis of signal transduction in the immune system.
Eugene Shakhnovich, Ph.D., Professor of Chemistry and Chemical Biology. Theory and experiments in protein folding and design; theory of molecular evolution; rational drug design and physical chemistry of protein-ligand interactions; theory of complex systems.
Sichen Susan Shao, Ph.D., Assistant Professor of Cell Biology. Regulation of protein biosynthesis and quality control.
William Shih, Ph.D., Professor of Biological Chemistry and Molecular Pharmacology. Biomolecular nanotechnology.
Steven E. Shoelson, M.D., Ph.D., Professor of Medicine. Structural and cellular biology of insulin signal transduction, insulin, resistance, diabetes, and obesity.
Pamela Silver, Ph.D., Professor of Systems Biology. Nucleocytoplasmic transport; RNA-protein interactions; protein methylation; cell-based small-molecule screens.
Poitrek Sliz, Ph.D., Associate Professor of Biological Chemistry and Molecular Pharmacology. Using structural biology and computing as robust tools to dissect mechanisms of disease.
Timothy A. Springer, Ph.D., Latham Family Professor of Pathology. Molecular biology of immune cell interactions.
Hanno Steen, Ph.D., Associate Professor of Pathology. Cell cycle studies using mass spectrometric and proteomic technology.
Radhika Subramanian, Ph.D., Assistant Professor of Molecular Biology, Department of Genetics. Assembling complex cytoskeletal architectures from simple building blocks.
Shamil R. Sunyaev, Ph.D., Professor of Computational Genomics, Division of Genetics. Population genetic variation and genomic divergence, with a focus on protein coding regions.
Jack W. Szostak, Ph.D., Professor of Genetics. Directed evolution; information content and molecular function; self-replicating systems.
Naoshige Uchida, Ph.D., Professor of Molecular and Cellular Biology. Sensory information in neuronal processes.
Gerhard Wagner, Ph.D., Elkan Blout Professor of Biological Chemistry and Molecular Pharmacology. Protein and nucleic acid structure, interaction, and mobility; NMR spectroscopy.
John R. Wakeley, Ph.D., Professor of Organismic and Evolutionary Biology. Theoretical population genetics.
Johannes C. Walter, Ph.D., Professor of Biological Chemistry and Molecular Pharmacology. Maintenance of genome stability in S phase.
George M. Whitesides, Ph.D., Mallinckrodt Professor of Chemistry. Molecular pharmacology; biosurface chemistry; virology.
Wesley P. Wong, Ph.D., Assistant Professor of Biological Chemistry and Molecular Pharmacology. Understanding physical basis of how biological systems work at the nanoscale, focused on the role of mechanical force.
Hao Wu, Ph.D., Asa and Patricia Springer Professor of Structural Biology. Elucidating the molecular mechanism of signal transduction by immune receptors.
Kai Wucherpfennig, M.D., Ph.D., Professor of Neurology. Basic mechanisms of T cell mediated autoimmune diseases.
Xiaoliang Sunney Xie, Ph.D., Mallinckrodt Professor of Chemistry and Chemical Biology. Single-molecule spectroscopy and dynamics; molecular interaction and chemical dynamics in biological systems.
Gary Yellen, Ph.D., Professor of Neurobiology. Molecular physiology of ion channels: functional motions, drug interactions, and electrophysiological mechanisms.
Peng Yin, Ph.D., Professor of Systems Biology. Biomolecular engineering and synthetic biology.
Xaiowei Zhuang, Ph.D., Professor of Chemistry and Chemical Biology and of Physics. Single-molecule biophysics.

Section 5
Botany and Plant Biology

This section contains a directory of institutions offering graduate work in botany and plant biology. Additional information about programs listed in the directory may be obtained by writing directly to the dean of a graduate school or chair of a department at the address given in the directory.

For programs offering related work, see also in this book *Biochemistry; Biological and Biomedical Sciences; Cell, Molecular, and Structural Biology; Ecology, Environmental Biology, and Evolutionary Biology; Entomology; Genetics, Developmental Biology, and Reproductive Biology;* and *Microbiological Sciences.* In the other guides in this series:

Graduate Programs in the Humanities, Arts & Social Sciences
See *Architecture (Landscape Architecture)* and *Economics (Agricultural Economics and Agribusiness)*

Graduate Programs in the Physical Sciences, Mathematics, Agricultural Sciences, the Environment & Natural Resources
See *Agricultural and Food Sciences*

Graduate Programs in Engineering & Applied Sciences
See *Agricultural Engineering* and *Bioengineering*

CONTENTS

Program Directories

Botany

Auburn University, Graduate School, College of Sciences and Mathematics, Department of Biological Sciences, Auburn University, AL 36849. Offers botany (MS); zoology (MS). *Faculty:* 37 full-time (16 women), 1 (woman) part-time/adjunct. *Students:* 42 full-time (19 women), 65 part-time (43 women); includes 15 minority (8 Black or African American, non-Hispanic/Latino; 1 Asian, non-Hispanic/Latino; 2 Hispanic/Latino; 4 Two or more races, non-Hispanic/Latino), 15 international. Average age 27. 83 applicants, 41% accepted, 23 enrolled. In 2017, 22 master's, 7 doctorates awarded. *Entrance requirements:* For master's and doctorate, GRE General Test. Additional exam requirements/recommendations for international students: Required—TOEFL. Application fee: $50 ($60 for international students). Electronic applications accepted. *Expenses:* Tuition, state resident: full-time $10,974; part-time $519 per credit hour. Tuition, nonresident: full-time $29,658; part-time $1557 per credit hour. *Required fees:* $816 per semester. Tuition and fees vary according to degree level and program. *Financial support:* Research assistantships and teaching assistantships available. Financial award applicants required to submit FAFSA. *Unit head:* Dr. Jason E. Bond, Chair, 334-844-3906, Fax: 334-844-1645. *Application contact:* Dr. George Flowers, Dean of the Graduate School, 334-844-2125.

Central Washington University, School of Graduate Studies and Research, College of the Sciences, Department of Biological Sciences, Ellensburg, WA 98926. Offers botany (MS); microbiology and parasitology (MS); stream ecology and fisheries (MS); terrestrial ecology (MS). *Program availability:* Part-time. *Entrance requirements:* For master's, GRE General Test, minimum GPA of 3.0. Additional exam requirements/ recommendations for international students: Required—TOEFL (minimum score 550 paper-based; 79 iBT). *Application deadline:* For fall admission, 2/1 priority date for domestic students; for winter admission, 10/1 for domestic students; for spring admission, 1/1 for domestic students. Applications are processed on a rolling basis. Application fee: $50. Electronic applications accepted. *Financial support:* Application deadline: 3/1; applicants required to submit FAFSA. *Unit head:* Dr. Kristina A. Ernest, Graduate Coordinator, 509-963-2805, E-mail: kristina.ernest@cwu.edu. *Application contact:* Justine Eason, Admissions Program Coordinator, 509-963-3103, Fax: 509-963-1799, E-mail: masters@cwu.edu.

Claremont Graduate University, Graduate Programs, Program in Botany, Claremont, CA 91711-6160. Offers MS, PhD. *Program availability:* Part-time. Terminal master's awarded for partial completion of doctoral program. *Entrance requirements:* For master's and doctorate, GRE General Test. Additional exam requirements/ recommendations for international students: Required—TOEFL (minimum score 75 iBT). Electronic applications accepted.

Colorado State University, College of Natural Sciences, Department of Biology, Fort Collins, CO 80523-1878. Offers botany (MS, PhD). *Faculty:* 32 full-time (13 women), 8 part-time/adjunct (5 women). *Students:* 16 full-time (9 women), 20 part-time (8 women); includes 3 minority (1 Asian, non-Hispanic/Latino; 2 Hispanic/Latino), 4 international. Average age 30. 28 applicants, 36% accepted, 7 enrolled. In 2017, 6 master's, 3 doctorates awarded. Terminal master's awarded for partial completion of doctoral program. *Degree requirements:* For master's, thesis, defense; for doctorate, comprehensive exam, thesis/dissertation. *Entrance requirements:* For master's and doctorate, transcripts, minimum GPA of 3.0; recommendation letters. Additional exam requirements/recommendations for international students: Required—TOEFL (minimum score 550 paper-based; 80 iBT), IELTS (minimum score 6.5). *Application deadline:* For fall admission, 1/1 for domestic and international students; for spring admission, 10/1 for domestic and international students. Application fee: $60 ($70 for international students). Electronic applications accepted. *Expenses:* Tuition, state resident: full-time $9917. Tuition, nonresident: full-time $24,312. *Required fees:* $2284. Tuition and fees vary according to course load and program. *Financial support:* In 2017–18, 80 students received support, including 15 research assistantships with full and partial tuition reimbursements available (averaging $20,524 per year), 69 teaching assistantships with full and partial tuition reimbursements available (averaging $18,656 per year); fellowships with full and partial tuition reimbursements available, career-related internships or fieldwork, health care benefits, and unspecified assistantships also available. Financial award applicants required to submit FAFSA. *Faculty research:* Cell and molecular biology, organismal biology, ecology and evolutionary biology. *Total annual research expenditures:* $7 million. *Unit head:* Dr. Michael F. Antolin, Department Chair and Professor, 970-491-7011, Fax: 970-491-0649, E-mail: michael.antolin@colostate.edu. *Application contact:* Dorothy Ramirez, Graduate Coordinator, 970-491-1923, Fax: 970-491-0649, E-mail: dramirez@colostate.edu.
Website: http://www.biology.colostate.edu/

Dalhousie University, Faculty of Agriculture, Halifax, NS B3H 4R2, Canada. Offers agriculture (M Sc), including air quality, animal behavior, animal molecular genetics, animal nutrition, animal technology, aquaculture, botany, crop management, crop physiology, ecology, environmental microbiology, food science, horticulture, nutrient management, pest management, physiology, plant biotechnology, plant pathology, soil chemistry, soil fertility, waste management and composting, water quality. *Program availability:* Part-time. *Degree requirements:* For master's, thesis, ATC Exam Teaching Assistantship. *Entrance requirements:* For master's, honors B Sc, minimum GPA of 3.0. Additional exam requirements/recommendations for international students: Required—TOEFL (minimum score 580 paper-based; 92 iBT), IELTS, Michigan English Language Assessment Battery, CanTEST, CAEL. *Faculty research:* Bio-product development, organic agriculture, nutrient management, air and water quality, agricultural biotechnology.

Emporia State University, Department of Biological Sciences, Emporia, KS 66801-5415. Offers botany (MS); environmental biology (MS); forensic science (MS); general biology (MS); microbial and cellular biology (MS); zoology (MS). *Program availability:* Part-time. *Faculty:* 13 full-time (3 women), 1 part-time/adjunct (0 women). *Students:* 20 full-time (11 women), 15 part-time (3 women); includes 3 minority (2 Hispanic/Latino; 1 Two or more races, non-Hispanic/Latino), 17 international. 17 applicants, 59% accepted, 8 enrolled. In 2017, 21 master's awarded. *Degree requirements:* For master's, comprehensive exam or thesis. *Entrance requirements:* For master's, GRE, appropriate undergraduate degree, interview, letters of reference. Additional exam requirements/ recommendations for international students: Required—TOEFL (minimum score 520 paper-based; 68 iBT). *Application deadline:* For fall admission, 8/15 priority date for domestic students. Applications are processed on a rolling basis. Application fee: $30 ($75 for international students). Electronic applications accepted. *Expenses:* Tuition, state resident: full-time $6084; part-time $253.50 per credit hour. Tuition, nonresident: full-time $18,924; part-time $788.50 per credit hour. *Required fees:* $1943; $80.95 per credit hour. Tuition and fees vary according to campus/location. *Financial support:* In 2017–18, 7 research assistantships with full tuition reimbursements (averaging $9,747 per year), 15 teaching assistantships with full tuition reimbursements (averaging $7,499 per year) were awarded; career-related internships or fieldwork, Federal Work-Study, institutionally sponsored loans, health care benefits, and unspecified assistantships also available. Financial award application deadline: 3/15; financial award applicants required to submit FAFSA. *Faculty research:* Fisheries, range, and wildlife management; aquatic, plant, grassland, vertebrate, and invertebrate ecology; mammalian and plant systematics, taxonomy, and evolution; immunology, virology, and molecular biology. *Unit head:* Dr. Tim Burnett, Interim Chair, 620-341-5910, Fax: 620-341-5608, E-mail: tburnett@emporia.edu.
Website: http://www.emporia.edu/info/degrees-courses/grad/biology

Illinois State University, Graduate School, College of Arts and Sciences, School of Biological Sciences, Normal, IL 61790. Offers animal behavior (MS); bacteriology (MS); biochemistry (MS); biological sciences (MS); biology (PhD); biophysics (MS); biotechnology (MS); botany (MS, PhD); cell biology (MS); conservation biology (MS); developmental biology (MS); ecology (MS, PhD); entomology (MS); evolutionary biology (MS); genetics (MS, PhD); immunology (MS); microbiology (MS, PhD); molecular biology (MS); molecular genetics (MS); neurobiology (MS); neuroscience (MS); parasitology (MS); physiology (MS, PhD); plant biology (MS); plant molecular biology (MS); plant sciences (MS); structural biology (MS); zoology (MS, PhD). *Program availability:* Part-time. *Degree requirements:* For master's, thesis or alternative; for doctorate, variable foreign language requirement, thesis/dissertation, 2 terms of residency. *Entrance requirements:* For master's, GRE General Test, minimum GPA of 2.6 in last 60 hours of course work; for doctorate, GRE General Test. *Faculty research:* Redoc balance and drug development in schistosoma mansoni, control of the growth of listeria monocytogenes at low temperature, regulation of cell expansion and microtubule function by SPRI, CRUI: physiology and fitness consequences of different life history phenotypes.

Kent State University, College of Arts and Sciences, Department of Biological Sciences, Kent, OH 44242-0001. Offers biological sciences (MA, MS, PhD), including botany (MS, PhD), cell biology (MS, PhD), ecology (MS, PhD), physiology (MS, PhD). *Program availability:* Part-time. *Faculty:* 28 full-time (10 women), 3 part-time/adjunct (2 women). *Students:* 55 full-time (37 women), 10 part-time (6 women); includes 6 minority (3 Black or African American, non-Hispanic/Latino; 1 Asian, non-Hispanic/Latino; 2 Two or more races, non-Hispanic/Latino), 12 international. Average age 28. 27 applicants, 56% accepted, 11 enrolled. In 2017, 4 master's, 6 doctorates awarded. Terminal master's awarded for partial completion of doctoral program. *Degree requirements:* For master's, thesis (for some programs), departmental seminar presentation about research (for MS); for doctorate, thesis/dissertation, departmental seminar presentation about research, admitted to doctoral candidacy following written and oral candidacy. *Entrance requirements:* For master's, GRE, minimum GPA of 3.0, official transcripts, goal statement, three letters of recommendation, list of up to five potential faculty advisors, undergraduate coursework roughly equivalent to a biology minor; for doctorate, GRE, official transcripts, goal statement, three letters of recommendation, list of up to five potential faculty advisors, baccalaureate degree with strong background in biology and related subjects such as chemistry and mathematics. Additional exam requirements/recommendations for international students: Required—TOEFL (minimum score 587 paper-based, 94 iBT), Michigan English Language Assessment Battery (minimum score 82), IELTS (7.0), or PTE (65). *Application deadline:* For fall admission, 12/15 for domestic students, 12/5 for international students. Applications are processed on a rolling basis. Application fee: $45 ($70 for international students). Electronic applications accepted. *Expenses:* Tuition, state resident: full-time $11,310; part-time $515 per credit hour. Tuition, nonresident: full-time $20,396; part-time $928 per credit hour. *International tuition:* $18,544 full-time. *Financial support:* Research assistantships with full tuition reimbursements, teaching assistantships with full tuition reimbursements, Federal Work-Study, scholarships/grants, and unspecified assistantships available. Financial award application deadline: 12/15. *Unit head:* Dr. James L. Blank, Dean, 330-672-2650, E-mail: jblank@kent.edu. *Application contact:* Dr. Heather K. Caldwell, Associate Professor and Graduate Coordinator, 330-672-3636, E-mail: hcaldwel@kent.edu.
Website: http://www.kent.edu/biology

North Carolina State University, Graduate School, College of Agriculture and Life Sciences, Department of Plant Biology, Raleigh, NC 27695. Offers MS, PhD. *Program availability:* Part-time. Terminal master's awarded for partial completion of doctoral program. *Degree requirements:* For master's, thesis (for some programs); for doctorate, thesis/dissertation. *Entrance requirements:* For master's and doctorate, GRE. Additional exam requirements/recommendations for international students: Required—TOEFL. Electronic applications accepted. *Faculty research:* Plant molecular and cell biology, aquatic ecology, community ecology, restoration, systematics plant pathogen and environmental interactions.

North Dakota State University, College of Graduate and Interdisciplinary Studies, College of Science and Mathematics, Department of Biological Sciences, Fargo, ND 58102. Offers biology (MS); botany (MS, PhD); zoology (MS, PhD). *Entrance requirements:* For master's and doctorate, GRE General Test. Additional exam requirements/recommendations for international students: Required—TOEFL. *Application deadline:* For fall admission, 1/15 for domestic students. Applications are processed on a rolling basis. Application fee: $35. Electronic applications accepted. *Expenses:* Tuition, state resident: full-time $4323; part-time $360.21 per credit. Tuition, nonresident: full-time $6484; part-time $540.31 per credit. *Required fees:* $668; $55.70 per credit. Part-time tuition and fees vary according to degree level, program and reciprocity agreements. *Financial support:* Application deadline: 4/15; applicants required to submit FAFSA. *Faculty research:* Comparative endocrinology, physiology, behavioral ecology, plant cell biology, aquatic biology. *Unit head:* Dr. Katie Reindl, Graduate Coordinator, 701-231-7087, E-mail: katie.reindl@ndsu.edu. *Application contact:* Elizabeth Worth, Marketing, Recruitment, and Public Relations Coordinator, 701-231-8476, Fax: 701-231-6524, E-mail: elizabeth.worth@ndsu.edu.
Website: http://www.ndsu.edu/biology/

Oklahoma State University, College of Arts and Sciences, Department of Plant Biology, Ecology, and Evolution, Stillwater, OK 74078. Offers botany (MS); environmental science (PhD). *Faculty:* 15 full-time (5 women). *Students:* 2 full-time (0 women), 11 part-time (7 women), 3 international. Average age 30. 3 applicants, 67% accepted, 2 enrolled. *Entrance requirements:* For master's and doctorate, GRE or GMAT. Additional exam requirements/recommendations for international students: Required—TOEFL (minimum score 550 paper-based; 79 iBT). *Application deadline:* For fall admission, 3/1 priority date for international students; for spring admission, 8/1 priority date for international students. Applications are processed on a rolling basis. Application fee: $40 ($75 for international students). Electronic applications accepted. *Expenses:* Tuition, state resident: full-time $4019; part-time $2679.60 per year. Tuition, nonresident: full-time $15,286; part-time $10,190.40 per year. *Required fees:* $2129; $1419 per unit. Tuition and fees vary according to program. *Financial support:*

Research assistantships, teaching assistantships, career-related internships or fieldwork, Federal Work-Study, scholarships/grants, health care benefits, tuition waivers (partial), and unspecified assistantships available. Support available to part-time students. Financial award application deadline: 3/1; financial award applicants required to submit FAFSA. *Faculty research:* Ethnobotany, developmental genetics of Arabidopsis, biological roles of plasmodesmata, community ecology and biodiversity, nutrient cycling in grassland ecosystems. *Unit head:* Dr. Thomas Wikle, Interim Department Head, 405-744-7978, Fax: 405-744-7074, E-mail: twikle@okstate.edu.
Website: http://plantbio.okstate.edu

Oregon State University, College of Agricultural Sciences, Program in Botany and Plant Pathology, Corvallis, OR 97331. Offers applied systematics (MS); ecology (MS, PhD); genetics (MS, PhD); genomics and computational biology (MS, PhD); molecular and cellular biology (MS, PhD); mycology (MS, PhD); plant pathology (MS, PhD); plant physiology (MS, PhD). *Entrance requirements:* For master's and doctorate, GRE. *Application deadline:* For fall admission, 12/1 for domestic and international students. Application fee: $75 ($85 for international students). *Financial support:* Application deadline: 12/1. *Unit head:* John Fowler, Chair of Graduate Studies, E-mail: fowlerj@science.oregonstate.edu.
Website: http://bpp.oregonstate.edu/

Purdue University, Graduate School, College of Agriculture, Department of Botany and Plant Pathology, West Lafayette, IN 47907. Offers MS, PhD. *Program availability:* Part-time. *Faculty:* 28 full-time (10 women), 1 part-time/adjunct (0 women). *Students:* 50 full-time (20 women), 6 part-time (0 women); includes 8 minority (1 Black or African American, non-Hispanic/Latino; 1 American Indian or Alaska Native, non-Hispanic/Latino; 2 Asian, non-Hispanic/Latino; 4 Hispanic/Latino), 25 international. Average age 27. 34 applicants, 18% accepted, 6 enrolled. In 2017, 5 master's, 4 doctorates awarded. Terminal master's awarded for partial completion of doctoral program. *Degree requirements:* For master's, thesis; for doctorate, thesis/dissertation. *Entrance requirements:* For master's, GRE General Test, minimum undergraduate GPA of 3.0 or equivalent; for doctorate, GRE, minimum undergraduate GPA of 3.0 or equivalent. Additional exam requirements/recommendations for international students: Required—TOEFL (minimum score 550 paper-based; 77 iBT); Recommended—TWE. *Application deadline:* For fall admission, 4/15 priority date for domestic and international students; for spring admission, 12/15 for domestic students, 9/15 for international students; for summer admission, 4/15 for domestic students, 2/15 for international students. Applications are processed on a rolling basis. Application fee: $60 ($75 for international students). Electronic applications accepted. *Financial support:* In 2017 [illegible] students received support. Fellowships with full tuition reimbursements available, research assistantships with full tuition reimbursements available, teaching assistantships with full tuition reimbursements available, and career-related internships or fieldwork available. Support available to part-time students. Financial award application deadline: 3/1; financial award applicants required to submit FAFSA. *Faculty research:* Biotechnology, plant growth, weed control, crop improvement, plant physiology. *Unit head:* Christopher Staiger, Head of the Graduate Program, 765-494-4615, E-mail: staiger@purdue.edu. *Application contact:* Tyson J. McFall, Graduate Contact, 765-494-0352, E-mail: tjmcfall@purdue.edu.
Website: https://ag.purdue.edu/btny

The University of British Columbia, Faculty of Science, Department of Botany, Vancouver, BC V6T 1Z4, Canada. Offers M Sc, PhD. *Degree requirements:* For master's, thesis; for doctorate, comprehensive exam, thesis/dissertation. *Entrance requirements:* Additional exam requirements/recommendations for international students: Required—TOEFL. Electronic applications accepted. *Expenses:* Contact institution. *Faculty research:* Plant ecology, evolution and systematics, cell and developmental biology, plant physiology/biochemistry, genetics.

University of California, Riverside, Graduate Division, Department of Botany and Plant Sciences, Riverside, CA 92521-0102. Offers plant biology (MS, PhD), including plant cell, molecular, and developmental biology (PhD), plant ecology (PhD), plant genetics (PhD). *Program availability:* Part-time. Terminal master's awarded for partial completion of doctoral program. *Degree requirements:* For master's, comprehensive exams or thesis; for doctorate, thesis/dissertation, qualifying exams. *Entrance requirements:* For master's and doctorate, GRE General Test, minimum GPA of 3.2. Additional exam requirements/recommendations for international students: Required—TOEFL (minimum score 550 paper-based, 80 iBT) or IELTS. *Application deadline:* For fall admission, 12/1 for domestic and international students; for winter admission, 11/15 for domestic students, 9/1 for international students; for spring admission, 3/1 for domestic students, 12/1 for international students. Application fee: $80 ($100 for international students). Electronic applications accepted. *Expenses:* Tuition, state resident: full-time $5746. Tuition, nonresident: full-time $10,780. Tuition and fees vary according to campus/location and program. *Financial support:* Fellowships with tuition reimbursements, research assistantships with tuition reimbursements, teaching assistantships with tuition reimbursements, career-related internships or fieldwork, Federal Work-Study, institutionally sponsored loans, scholarships/grants, health care benefits, tuition waivers (full and partial), and unspecified assistantships available. Financial award applicants required to submit FAFSA. *Faculty research:* Agricultural plant biology; biochemistry and physiology; cellular, molecular and developmental biology; ecology, evolution, systematics and ethnobotany; genetics, genomics and bioinformatics. *Unit head:* Dr. Patricia Springer, Chair. *Application contact:* Laura McGeehan, Graduate Student Services Advisor, 800-735-0717, E-mail: plantbio@ucr.edu.
Website: http://www.plantbiology.ucr.edu/

University of Connecticut, Graduate School, College of Liberal Arts and Sciences, Department of Ecology and Evolutionary Biology, Storrs, CT 06269. Offers botany (MS, PhD). Terminal master's awarded for partial completion of doctoral program. *Degree requirements:* For master's, comprehensive exam; for doctorate, thesis/dissertation. *Entrance requirements:* For master's and doctorate, GRE General Test, GRE Subject Test. Additional exam requirements/recommendations for international students: Required—TOEFL (minimum score 550 paper-based). Electronic applications accepted.

University of Florida, Graduate School, College of Liberal Arts and Sciences, Department of Biology, Gainesville, FL 32611. Offers botany (MS, MST, PhD), including botany, tropical conservation and development, wetland sciences; zoology (MS, MST, PhD), including animal molecular and cellular biology (PhD), tropical conservation and development, wetland sciences, zoology. *Degree requirements:* For master's, comprehensive exam (for some programs), thesis; for doctorate, comprehensive exam, thesis/dissertation. *Entrance requirements:* For master's and doctorate, GRE General Test, minimum GPA of 3.0. Additional exam requirements/recommendations for international students: Required—TOEFL (minimum score 550 paper-based; 80 iBT), IELTS (minimum score 6). Electronic applications accepted. *Faculty research:* Ecology of natural populations, plant and animal genome evolution, biodiversity, plant biology, behavior.

University of Guelph, Graduate Studies, College of Biological Science, Department of Integrative Biology, Botany and Zoology, Guelph, ON N1G 2W1, Canada. Offers botany (M Sc, PhD); zoology (M Sc, PhD). *Program availability:* Part-time. *Degree requirements:* For master's, thesis, research proposal; for doctorate, thesis/dissertation, research proposal, qualifying exam. *Entrance requirements:* For master's, minimum B average during previous 2 years of course work. Additional exam requirements/recommendations for international students: Required—TOEFL (minimum score 550 paper-based), IELTS (minimum score 6.5). Electronic applications accepted. *Faculty research:* Aquatic science, environmental physiology, parasitology, wildlife biology, management.

University of Guelph, Graduate Studies, College of Biological Science, Department of Molecular and Cellular Biology, Guelph, ON N1G 2W1, Canada. Offers biochemistry (M Sc, PhD); biophysics (M Sc, PhD); botany (M Sc, PhD); microbiology (M Sc, PhD); molecular biology and genetics (M Sc, PhD). *Degree requirements:* For master's, thesis, research proposal; for doctorate, comprehensive exam, thesis/dissertation, research proposal. *Entrance requirements:* For master's, minimum B-average during previous 2 years of coursework; for doctorate, minimum A-average. Additional exam requirements/recommendations for international students: Required—TOEFL (minimum score 550 paper-based), IELTS (minimum score 6.5). Electronic applications accepted. *Faculty research:* Physiology, structure, genetics, and ecology of microbes; virology and microbial technology.

University of Hawaii at Manoa, Office of Graduate Education, College of Natural Sciences, Department of Botany, Honolulu, HI 96822. Offers MS, PhD. *Program availability:* Part-time. Terminal master's awarded for partial completion of doctoral program. *Degree requirements:* For master's, one foreign language, thesis optional, presentation; for doctorate, one foreign language, comprehensive exam, thesis/dissertation, presentation. *Entrance requirements:* For master's and doctorate, GRE General Test, GRE Subject Test (biology). Additional exam requirements/recommendations for international students: Required—TOEFL (minimum score 540 paper-based; 76 iBT), IELTS (minimum score 5). *Faculty research:* Plant ecology, evolution, systematics, conservation biology, ethnobotany.

University of Maine, Graduate School, College of Natural Sciences, Forestry, and Agriculture, School of Biology and Ecology, Orono, ME 04469. Offers biological sciences (PhD); botany and plant pathology (MS); entomology (MS); zoology (MS, PhD). *Program availability:* Part-time. *Faculty:* 30 full-time (16 women), 2 part-time/adjunct (1 woman). *Students:* 61 full-time (40 women), 22 part-time (11 women); includes 7 minority (1 American Indian or Alaska Native, non-Hispanic/Latino; 3 Asian, non-Hispanic/Latino; 3 Hispanic/Latino), 14 international. Average age 30. 69 applicants, 87% accepted, 28 enrolled. In 2017, 7 master's, 9 doctorates awarded. Terminal master's awarded for partial completion of doctoral program. *Degree requirements:* For master's, thesis (for some programs); for doctorate, comprehensive exam, thesis/dissertation. *Entrance requirements:* For master's and doctorate, GRE General Test. Additional exam requirements/recommendations for international students: Required—TOEFL (minimum score 80 iBT), IELTS (minimum score 6.5). *Application deadline:* For fall admission, 2/1 priority date for domestic students. Applications are processed on a rolling basis. Application fee: $65. Electronic applications accepted. *Expenses:* Tuition, state resident: full-time $7722; part-time $429 per credit hour. Tuition, nonresident: full-time $25,146; part-time $1397 per credit hour. *Required fees:* $1162; $581 per credit hour. *Financial support:* In 2017–18, 92 students received support, including 2 fellowships with full tuition reimbursements available (averaging $25,000 per year), 47 research assistantships with full tuition reimbursements available (averaging $19,800 per year), 32 teaching assistantships with full tuition reimbursements available (averaging $15,200 per year); career-related internships or fieldwork, Federal Work-Study, institutionally sponsored loans, tuition waivers (full and partial), and unspecified assistantships also available. Financial award application deadline: 3/1. *Faculty research:* Ecology and evolution (aquatic, terrestrial, paleo); development and genetics; biomedical research; ecophysiology and stress; invasion ecology and pest management. *Total annual research expenditures:* $3.1 million. *Unit head:* Dr. Andrei Alyokhin, Director, 207-581-2977, Fax: 207-581-2537. *Application contact:* Scott G. Delcourt, Assistant Vice President for Graduate Studies and Senior Associate Dean, 207-581-3291, Fax: 207-581-3232, E-mail: graduate@maine.edu.
Website: http://sbe.umaine.edu/

University of Manitoba, Faculty of Graduate Studies, Faculty of Science, Department of Biological Sciences, Winnipeg, MB R3T 2N2, Canada. Offers botany (M Sc, PhD); ecology (M Sc, PhD); zoology (M Sc, PhD).

The University of North Carolina at Chapel Hill, Graduate School, College of Arts and Sciences, Department of Biology, Chapel Hill, NC 27599. Offers botany (MA, MS, PhD); cell biology, development, and physiology (MA, MS, PhD); cell motility and cytoskeleton (PhD); ecology and behavior (MA, MS, PhD); genetics and molecular biology (MA, MS, PhD); morphology, systematics, and evolution (MA, MS, PhD). Terminal master's awarded for partial completion of doctoral program. *Degree requirements:* For master's, comprehensive exam, thesis (for some programs); for doctorate, comprehensive exam, thesis/dissertation. *Entrance requirements:* For master's, GRE General Test, GRE Subject Test, 2 semesters of calculus or statistics; 2 semesters of physics, organic chemistry; 3 semesters of biology; for doctorate, GRE General Test, GRE Subject Test, 2 semesters calculus or statistics, 2 semesters physics, organic chemistry, 3 semesters of biology. Additional exam requirements/recommendations for international students: Required—TOEFL (minimum score 550 paper-based). Electronic applications accepted. *Faculty research:* Gene expression, biomechanics, yeast genetics, plant ecology, plant molecular biology.

University of Wisconsin–Madison, Graduate School, College of Letters and Science, Department of Botany, Madison, WI 53706-1380. Offers MS, PhD. *Program availability:* Part-time. Terminal master's awarded for partial completion of doctoral program. *Degree requirements:* For master's, thesis; for doctorate, one foreign language, thesis/dissertation. *Entrance requirements:* For master's and doctorate, GRE General Test. Electronic applications accepted. *Faculty research:* Taxonomy and systematics; ecology; structural botany; physiological, cellular, and molecular biology.

University of Wisconsin–Oshkosh, Graduate Studies, College of Letters and Science, Department of Biology and Microbiology, Oshkosh, WI 54901. Offers biology (MS), including botany, microbiology, zoology. *Degree requirements:* For master's, comprehensive exam, thesis. *Entrance requirements:* For master's, GRE General Test, minimum GPA of 3.0, BS in biology. Additional exam requirements/recommendations for international students: Required—TOEFL (minimum score 550 paper-based; 79 iBT). Electronic applications accepted.

University of Wyoming, College of Arts and Sciences, Department of Botany, Laramie, WY 82071. Offers botany (MS, PhD); botany/water resources (MS). *Program availability:* Part-time. Terminal master's awarded for partial completion of doctoral program. *Degree requirements:* For master's, thesis; for doctorate, thesis/dissertation. *Entrance requirements:* For master's and doctorate, GRE General Test, minimum GPA of 3.0. Additional exam requirements/recommendations for international students: Required—TOEFL. Electronic applications accepted. *Faculty research:* Ecology, systematics, physiology, mycology, genetics.

Plant Biology

Arizona State University at the Tempe campus, College of Liberal Arts and Sciences, School of Life Sciences, Tempe, AZ 85287-4601. Offers animal behavior (PhD); applied ethics (biomedical and health ethics) (MA); biology (MS, PhD), including biology, biology and society, complex adaptive systems science (PhD), plant biology and conservation (MS); environmental life sciences (PhD); evolutionary biology (PhD); history and philosophy of science (PhD); human and social dimensions of science and technology (PhD); microbiology (PhD); molecular and cellular biology (PhD); neuroscience (PhD). Terminal master's awarded for partial completion of doctoral program. *Degree requirements:* For master's, thesis (for some programs), interactive Program of Study (iPOS) submitted before completing 50 percent of required credit hours; for doctorate, variable foreign language requirement, comprehensive exam, thesis/dissertation, interactive Program of Study (iPOS) submitted before completing 50 percent of required credit hours. *Entrance requirements:* For master's and doctorate, GRE, minimum GPA of 3.0 or equivalent in last 2 years of work leading to bachelor's degree. Additional exam requirements/recommendations for international students: Required—TOEFL (minimum score 600 paper-based; 100 iBT). Electronic applications accepted.

Clemson University, Graduate School, College of Agriculture, Forestry and Life Sciences, Department of Plant and Environmental Sciences, Clemson, SC 29634. Offers entomology (MS, PhD); plant and environmental sciences (MS, PhD). *Program availability:* Part-time. *Faculty:* 38 full-time (11 women). *Students:* 79 full-time (29 women), 15 part-time (0 women); includes 5 minority (2 Black or African American, non-Hispanic/Latino; 1 Asian, non-Hispanic/Latino; 2 Two or more races, non-Hispanic/Latino), 32 international. Average age 30. 36 applicants, 89% accepted, 17 enrolled. In 2017, 12 master's, 3 doctorates awarded. *Degree requirements:* For master's, thesis; for doctorate, comprehensive exam, thesis/dissertation. *Entrance requirements:* For master's and doctorate, GRE General Test, unofficial transcripts, letters of recommendation. Additional exam requirements/recommendations for international students: Required—TOEFL (minimum score 80 iBT), IELTS (minimum score 6.5), PTE (minimum score 54). *Application deadline:* Applications are processed on a rolling basis. Application fee: $80 ($90 for international students). Electronic applications accepted. *Expenses:* $5,174 per semester full-time resident, $9,714 per semester full-time non-resident, $511 per credit hour part-time resident, $1,017 per credit hour part-time non-resident; $741 per credit hour online; other fees may apply per session. *Financial support:* In 2017–18, 67 students received support, including 9 fellowships with partial tuition reimbursements available (averaging $8,833 per year), 42 research assistantships with partial tuition reimbursements available (averaging $19,811 per year), 13 teaching assistantships with partial tuition reimbursements available (averaging $22,607 per year); unspecified assistantships also available. Financial award application deadline: 2/15. *Faculty research:* Agronomy, horticulture, plant pathology, plant physiology, entomology. *Total annual research expenditures:* $4.1 million. *Unit head:* Dr. Matthew Turnbull, Interim Department Chair, 864-656-4964, E-mail: turnbul@clemson.edu. *Application contact:* Dr. Guido Schnabel, Graduate Program Coordinator, 864-656-6705, E-mail: schnabel@clemson.edu.
Website: http://www.clemson.edu/cafls/departments/plant-environmental-sciences/index.html

Cornell University, Graduate School, Graduate Fields of Agriculture and Life Sciences, Field of Plant Biology, Ithaca, NY 14853. Offers cytology (MS, PhD); paleobotany (MS, PhD); plant biochemistry (MS, PhD); plant cell biology (MS, PhD); plant ecology (MS, PhD); plant molecular biology (MS, PhD); plant morphology, anatomy and biomechanics (MS, PhD); plant physiology (MS, PhD); systematic botany (MS, PhD). *Degree requirements:* For doctorate, comprehensive exam, thesis/dissertation. *Entrance requirements:* For doctorate, GRE General Test, GRE Subject Test in biology (recommended), 3 letters of recommendation. Additional exam requirements/recommendations for international students: Required—TOEFL (minimum score 610 paper-based; 77 iBT). Electronic applications accepted. *Faculty research:* Plant cell biology/cytology; plant molecular biology; plant morphology/anatomy/biomechanics; plant physiology, systematic botany, paleobotany; plant ecology, ethnobotany, plant biochemistry, photosynthesis.

Illinois State University, Graduate School, College of Arts and Sciences, School of Biological Sciences, Normal, IL 61790. Offers animal behavior (MS); bacteriology (MS); biochemistry (MS); biological sciences (MS); biology (PhD); biophysics (MS); biotechnology (MS); botany (MS, PhD); cell biology (MS); conservation biology (MS); developmental biology (MS); ecology (MS, PhD); entomology (MS); evolutionary biology (MS); genetics (MS, PhD); immunology (MS); microbiology (MS, PhD); molecular biology (MS); molecular genetics (MS); neurobiology (MS); neuroscience (MS); parasitology (MS); physiology (MS, PhD); plant biology (MS); plant molecular biology (MS); plant sciences (MS); structural biology (MS); zoology (MS, PhD). *Program availability:* Part-time. *Degree requirements:* For master's, thesis or alternative; for doctorate, variable foreign language requirement, thesis/dissertation, 2 terms of residency. *Entrance requirements:* For master's, GRE General Test, minimum GPA of 2.6 in last 60 hours of course work; for doctorate, GRE General Test. *Faculty research:* Redoc balance and drug development in schistosoma mansoni, control of the growth of listeria monocytogenes at low temperature, regulation of cell expansion and microtubule function by SPRI, CRUI: physiology and fitness consequences of different life history phenotypes.

Indiana University Bloomington, University Graduate School, College of Arts and Sciences, Department of Biology, Bloomington, IN 47405. Offers biology teaching (MAT); biotechnology (MA); evolution, ecology, and behavior (MA, PhD); genetics (PhD); microbiology (MA, PhD); molecular, cellular, and developmental biology (PhD); plant sciences (MA, PhD); zoology (MA, PhD). Terminal master's awarded for partial completion of doctoral program. *Degree requirements:* For master's, thesis, oral defense; for doctorate, thesis/dissertation, oral defense. *Entrance requirements:* For master's and doctorate, GRE General Test. Additional exam requirements/recommendations for international students: Required—TOEFL (minimum score 100 iBT). Electronic applications accepted. *Faculty research:* Evolution, ecology and behavior; microbiology; molecular biology and genetics; plant biology.

Iowa State University of Science and Technology, Program in Plant Biology, Ames, IA 50011. Offers MS, PhD. *Degree requirements:* For master's, thesis; for doctorate, thesis/dissertation. *Entrance requirements:* For master's and doctorate, GRE General Test. Additional exam requirements/recommendations for international students: Required—TOEFL (minimum score 550 paper-based; 79 iBT), IELTS (minimum score 6.5). Electronic applications accepted.

Michigan State University, The Graduate School, College of Agriculture and Natural Resources, MSU-DOE Plant Research Laboratory, East Lansing, MI 48824. Offers biochemistry and molecular biology (PhD); cellular and molecular biology (PhD); crop and soil sciences (PhD); genetics (PhD); microbiology and molecular genetics (PhD); plant biology (PhD); plant physiology (PhD). Offered jointly with the Department of Energy. *Degree requirements:* For doctorate, comprehensive exam, thesis/dissertation, laboratory rotation, defense of dissertation. *Entrance requirements:* For doctorate, GRE General Test, acceptance into one of the affiliated department programs; 3 letters of recommendation; bachelor's degree or equivalent in life sciences, chemistry, biochemistry, or biophysics; research experience. Electronic applications accepted. *Faculty research:* Role of hormones in the regulation of plant development and physiology, molecular mechanisms associated with signal recognition, development and application of genetic methods and materials, protein routing and function.

Michigan State University, The Graduate School, College of Natural Science and College of Agriculture and Natural Resources, Department of Plant Biology, East Lansing, MI 48824. Offers plant biology (MS, PhD); plant breeding, genetics and biotechnology - plant biology (MS, PhD). *Entrance requirements:* Additional exam requirements/recommendations for international students: Required—TOEFL. Electronic applications accepted. *Faculty research:* Physiological, molecular, and biochemical mechanisms; systematics; inheritance; ecology and geohistory.

New York University, Graduate School of Arts and Science, Department of Biology, New York, NY 10012-1019. Offers biology (PhD); biomedical journalism (MS); cancer and molecular biology (PhD); computational biology (PhD); computers in biological research (MS); developmental genetics (PhD); general biology (MS); immunology and microbiology (PhD); molecular genetics (PhD); neurobiology (PhD); oral biology (MS); plant biology (PhD); recombinant DNA technology (MS); MS/MBA. *Program availability:* Part-time. *Students:* Average age 27. 394 applicants, 56% accepted, 77 enrolled. In 2017, 68 master's, 9 doctorates awarded. Terminal master's awarded for partial completion of doctoral program. *Degree requirements:* For master's, thesis or alternative, qualifying paper; for doctorate, comprehensive exam, thesis/dissertation. *Entrance requirements:* For master's and doctorate, GRE General Test. Additional exam requirements/recommendations for international students: Required—TOEFL. *Application deadline:* For fall admission, 12/1 priority date for domestic students, 12/1 for international students. Application fee: $100. *Expenses: Tuition:* Full-time $41,352; part-time $19,968 per year. *Required fees:* $2496; $1628 per unit. $814 per term. Tuition and fees vary according to course load and program. *Financial support:* Fellowships, research assistantships, teaching assistantships, career-related internships or fieldwork, Federal Work-Study, institutionally sponsored loans, scholarships/grants, health care benefits, and unspecified assistantships available. Financial award application deadline: 12/1; financial award applicants required to submit FAFSA. *Faculty research:* Genomics, molecular and cell biology, development and molecular genetics, molecular evolution of plants and animals. *Unit head:* Stephen Small, Chair, 212-998-8200, Fax: 212-995-4015, E-mail: biology.admissions@nyu.edu. *Application contact:* Ken Birnbaum, Director of Graduate Studies, PhD Programs, 212-998-8200, Fax: 212-995-4015, E-mail: biology.admissions@nyu.edu.
Website: http://biology.as.nyu.edu/

North Carolina State University, Graduate School, College of Agriculture and Life Sciences, Department of Plant Biology, Raleigh, NC 27695. Offers MS, PhD. *Program availability:* Part-time. Terminal master's awarded for partial completion of doctoral program. *Degree requirements:* For master's, thesis (for some programs); for doctorate, thesis/dissertation. *Entrance requirements:* For master's and doctorate, GRE. Additional exam requirements/recommendations for international students: Required—TOEFL. Electronic applications accepted. *Faculty research:* Plant molecular and cell biology, aquatic ecology, community ecology, restoration, systematics plant pathogen and environmental interactions.

Northwestern University, The Graduate School, Judd A. and Marjorie Weinberg College of Arts and Sciences, Program in Plant Biology and Conservation, Evanston, IL 60208. Offers MA, PhD. Program held jointly with Chicago Botanic Garden.

Ohio University, Graduate College, College of Arts and Sciences, Department of Environmental and Plant Biology, Athens, OH 45701-2979. Offers MS, PhD. *Program availability:* Part-time. *Degree requirements:* For master's, thesis, 2 terms of teaching experience; for doctorate, comprehensive exam, thesis/dissertation, 2 terms of teaching experience. *Entrance requirements:* For master's, GRE General Test, minimum GPA of 3.0; for doctorate, GRE General Test, minimum GPA of 3.2. Additional exam requirements/recommendations for international students: Required—TOEFL (minimum score 620 paper-based; 105 iBT) or IELTS (minimum score 7.5). Electronic applications accepted. *Faculty research:* Eastern deciduous forest ecology, evolutionary developmental plant biology, phylogenetic systematics, plant cell wall biotechnology.

Oklahoma State University, College of Arts and Sciences, Department of Plant Biology, Ecology, and Evolution, Stillwater, OK 74078. Offers botany (MS); environmental science (PhD). *Faculty:* 15 full-time (5 women). *Students:* 2 full-time (0 women), 11 part-time (7 women), 3 international. Average age 30. 3 applicants, 67% accepted, 2 enrolled. *Entrance requirements:* For master's and doctorate, GRE or GMAT. Additional exam requirements/recommendations for international students: Required—TOEFL (minimum score 550 paper-based; 79 iBT). *Application deadline:* For fall admission, 3/1 priority date for international students; for spring admission, 8/1 priority date for international students. Applications are processed on a rolling basis. Application fee: $40 ($75 for international students). Electronic applications accepted. *Expenses:* Tuition, state resident: full-time $4019; part-time $2679.60 per year. Tuition, nonresident: full-time $15,286; part-time $10,190.40 per year. *Required fees:* $2129; $1419 per unit. Tuition and fees vary according to program. *Financial support:* Research assistantships, teaching assistantships, career-related internships or fieldwork, Federal Work-Study, scholarships/grants, health care benefits, tuition waivers (partial), and unspecified assistantships available. Support available to part-time students. Financial award application deadline: 3/1; financial award applicants required to submit FAFSA. *Faculty research:* Ethnobotany, developmental genetics of Arabidopsis, biological roles of plasmodesmata, community ecology and biodiversity, nutrient cycling in grassland ecosystems. *Unit head:* Dr. Thomas Wikle, Interim Department Head, 405-744-7978, Fax: 405-744-7074, E-mail: twikle@okstate.edu.
Website: http://plantbio.okstate.edu

Penn State University Park, Graduate School, Intercollege Graduate Programs, Intercollege Graduate Program in Plant Biology, University Park, PA 16802. Offers MS, PhD. *Unit head:* Dr. Regina Vasilatos-Younken, Dean, 814-865-2516, Fax: 814-863-4627. *Application contact:* Lori Hawn, Director, Graduate Student Services, 814-865-1795, Fax: 814-863-4627, E-mail: l-gswww@lists.psu.edu.
Website: http://www.huck.psu.edu/content/graduate-programs/plant-biology

Rutgers University–New Brunswick, Graduate School-New Brunswick, Program in Plant Biology, Piscataway, NJ 08854-8097. Offers horticulture and plant technology (MS, PhD); molecular and cellular biology (MS, PhD); organismal and population biology (MS, PhD); plant pathology (MS, PhD). *Program availability:* Part-time. Terminal master's awarded for partial completion of doctoral program. *Degree requirements:* For master's, comprehensive exam, thesis or alternative; for doctorate, comprehensive exam, thesis/dissertation. *Entrance requirements:* For master's and doctorate, GRE General Test, GRE Subject Test (recommended). Additional exam requirements/recommendations for international students: Required—TOEFL (minimum score 600 paper-based). Electronic applications accepted. *Faculty research:* Molecular biology and biochemistry of plants, plant development and genomics, plant protection, plant improvement, plant management of horticultural and field crops.

Southern Illinois University Carbondale, Graduate School, College of Science, Department of Plant Biology, Carbondale, IL 62901-4701. Offers MS, PhD. *Degree requirements:* For master's, thesis; for doctorate, one foreign language, thesis/dissertation. *Entrance requirements:* For master's, GRE General Test, minimum GPA of 2.7; for doctorate, GRE General Test, minimum GPA of 3.25. Additional exam requirements/recommendations for international students: Required—TOEFL (minimum score 80 iBT). *Faculty research:* Algal toxins, ethnobotany, community and wetland ecology, morphogenesis, systematics and evolution.

Université Laval, Faculty of Agricultural and Food Sciences, Program in Plant Biology, Québec, QC G1K 7P4, Canada. Offers M Sc, PhD. Terminal master's awarded for partial completion of doctoral program. *Degree requirements:* For master's, thesis (for some programs); for doctorate, comprehensive exam, thesis/dissertation. *Entrance requirements:* For master's and doctorate, knowledge of French and English. Electronic applications accepted.

University of Alberta, Faculty of Graduate Studies and Research, Department of Biological Sciences, Edmonton, AB T6G 2E1, Canada. Offers environmental biology and ecology (M Sc, PhD); microbiology and biotechnology (M Sc, PhD); molecular biology and genetics (M Sc, PhD); physiology and cell biology (M Sc, PhD); plant biology (M Sc, PhD); systematics and evolution (M Sc, PhD). Terminal master's awarded for partial completion of doctoral program. *Degree requirements:* For master's, thesis; for doctorate, thesis/dissertation. *Entrance requirements:* Additional exam requirements/recommendations for international students: Required—TOEFL.

University of California, Berkeley, Graduate Division, College of Natural Resources, Department of Plant and Microbial Biology, Berkeley, CA 94720-1500. Offers microbiology (PhD); plant biology (PhD). *Degree requirements:* For doctorate, thesis/dissertation, qualifying exam, seminar presentation. *Entrance requirements:* For doctorate, GRE General Test, minimum GPA of 3.0, 3 letters of recommendation. Electronic applications accepted. *Faculty research:* Development, molecular biology, genetics, microbial biology, mycology.

University of California, Davis, Graduate Studies, Graduate Group in Plant Biology, Davis, CA 95616. Offers MS, PhD. *Degree requirements:* For master's, comprehensive exam (for some programs), thesis (for some programs); for doctorate, thesis/dissertation. *Entrance requirements:* For master's, GRE General Test, GRE Subject Test (biology), minimum GPA of 3.0; for doctorate, GRE General Test, GRE Subject Test (biology). Additional exam requirements/recommendations for international students: Required—TOEFL (minimum score 550 paper-based). Electronic applications accepted. *Faculty research:* Cell and molecular biology, ecology, systematics and evolution, integrative plant and crop physiology, plant development and structure.

University of California, Riverside, Graduate Division, Department of Botany and Plant Sciences, Riverside, CA 92521-0102. Offers plant biology (MS, PhD), including plant cell, molecular, and developmental biology (PhD), plant ecology (PhD), plant genetics (PhD). *Program availability:* Part-time. Terminal master's awarded for partial completion of doctoral program. *Degree requirements:* For master's, comprehensive exams or thesis; for doctorate, thesis/dissertation, qualifying exams. *Entrance requirements:* For master's and doctorate, GRE General Test, minimum GPA of 3.2. Additional exam requirements/recommendations for international students: Required—TOEFL (minimum score 550 paper-based, 80 iBT) or IELTS. *Application deadline:* For fall admission, 12/1 for domestic and international students; for winter admission, 11/15 for domestic students, 9/1 for international students; for spring admission, 3/1 for domestic students, 12/1 for international students. Application fee: $80 ($100 for international students). Electronic applications accepted. *Expenses:* Tuition, state resident: full-time $5746. Tuition, nonresident: full-time $10,780. Tuition and fees vary according to campus/location and program. *Financial support:* Fellowships with tuition reimbursements, research assistantships with tuition reimbursements, teaching assistantships with tuition reimbursements, career-related internships or fieldwork, Federal Work-Study, institutionally sponsored loans, scholarships/grants, health care benefits, tuition waivers (full and partial), and unspecified assistantships available. Financial award applicants required to submit FAFSA. *Faculty research:* Agricultural plant biology; biochemistry and physiology; cellular, molecular and developmental biology; ecology, evolution, systematics and ethnobotany; genetics, genomics and bioinformatics. *Unit head:* Dr. Patricia Springer, Chair. *Application contact:* Laura McGeehan, Graduate Student Services Advisor, 800-735-0717, E-mail: plantbio@ucr.edu.
Website: http://www.plantbiology.ucr.edu/

University of Florida, Graduate School, College of Agricultural and Life Sciences and College of Liberal Arts and Sciences, Program in Plant Molecular and Cellular Biology, Gainesville, FL 32611. Offers plant molecular and cellular biology (MS, PhD), including toxicology (PhD). *Degree requirements:* For master's, thesis; for doctorate, comprehensive exam, thesis/dissertation, first author peer-reviewed publication. *Entrance requirements:* For master's and doctorate, GRE General Test, minimum GPA of 3.0. Additional exam requirements/recommendations for international students: Required—TOEFL (minimum score 550 paper-based; 80 iBT), IELTS (minimum score 6). Electronic applications accepted. *Faculty research:* The understanding of molecular and cellular mechanisms that mediate plant development, adaptation, and evolution including bioinformatics, genomics, proteomics, genetics, biochemistry, breeding, physiology and molecular and cellular biology.

University of Georgia, Franklin College of Arts and Sciences, Department of Plant Biology, Athens, GA 30602. Offers MS, PhD. *Degree requirements:* For master's, thesis; for doctorate, one foreign language, thesis/dissertation. *Entrance requirements:* For master's and doctorate, GRE General Test. Electronic applications accepted.

University of Illinois at Urbana–Champaign, Graduate College, College of Liberal Arts and Sciences, School of Integrative Biology, Department of Plant Biology, Champaign, IL 61820. Offers plant biology (MS, PhD); plant biotechnology (PSM).

University of Maryland, College Park, Academic Affairs, College of Computer, Mathematical and Natural Sciences, Department of Cell Biology and Molecular Genetics, College Park, MD 20742. Offers cell biology and molecular genetics (MS, PhD); molecular and cellular biology (PhD); plant biology (MS, PhD). *Program availability:* Part-time, evening/weekend. Terminal master's awarded for partial completion of doctoral program. *Degree requirements:* For master's, thesis; for doctorate, thesis/dissertation. *Entrance requirements:* For master's, GRE General Test, minimum GPA of 3.0, 3 letters of recommendation; for doctorate, GRE General Test. Additional exam requirements/recommendations for international students: Required—TOEFL. Electronic applications accepted. *Faculty research:* Cytoskeletal activity, membrane biology, cell division, genetics and genomics, virology.

University of Massachusetts Amherst, Graduate School, Interdisciplinary Programs, Program in Plant Biology, Amherst, MA 01003. Offers biochemistry and metabolism (MS, PhD); cell biology and physiology (MS, PhD); environmental, ecological and integrative biology (MS, PhD); genetics and evolution (MS, PhD). *Degree requirements:* For master's, thesis; for doctorate, 2 foreign languages, comprehensive exam, thesis/dissertation. *Entrance requirements:* For master's and doctorate, GRE General Test. Additional exam requirements/recommendations for international students: Required—TOEFL (minimum score 550 paper-based; 80 iBT), IELTS (minimum score 6.5). Electronic applications accepted.

University of Minnesota, Twin Cities Campus, Graduate School, College of Biological Sciences, Program in Plant Biological Sciences, Minneapolis, MN 55455-0213. Offers MS, PhD. *Program availability:* Part-time. Terminal master's awarded for partial completion of doctoral program. *Degree requirements:* For master's, thesis or alternative; for doctorate, thesis/dissertation, written and oral preliminary exams. *Entrance requirements:* For master's and doctorate, GRE General Test. Additional exam requirements/recommendations for international students: Required—TOEFL. Electronic applications accepted. *Faculty research:* Cell and molecular biology; plant physiology; plant structure, diversity, and development; ecology, systematics, evolution and genomics.

University of Oklahoma, College of Arts and Sciences, Department of Microbiology and Plant Biology, Program in Plant Biology, Norman, OK 73019. Offers ecology and evolutionary biology (PhD); plant biology (MS, PhD). *Students:* 6 full-time (4 women), 10 part-time (4 women); includes 2 minority (1 American Indian or Alaska Native, non-Hispanic/Latino; 1 Asian, non-Hispanic/Latino), 4 international. Average age 30. 10 applicants, 50% accepted, 5 enrolled. In 2017, 2 master's, 2 doctorates awarded. Terminal master's awarded for partial completion of doctoral program. *Degree requirements:* For master's, thesis; for doctorate, comprehensive exam, thesis/dissertation. *Entrance requirements:* For master's and doctorate, GRE, 3 recommendation letters, letter of intent, bachelor's degree. Additional exam requirements/recommendations for international students: Required—TOEFL (minimum score 80 iBT) or IELTS (minimum score 6.5). *Application deadline:* For fall admission, 3/1 for domestic and international students; for spring admission, 9/1 for domestic and international students; for summer admission, 9/1 for domestic and international students. Application fee: $50 ($100 for international students). Electronic applications accepted. *Expenses:* Tuition, state resident: full-time $5119; part-time $213.30 per credit hour. Tuition, nonresident: full-time $19,778; part-time $824.10 per credit hour. *Required fees:* $3458; $133.55 per credit hour. $126.50 per semester. *Financial support:* In 2017–18, 13 students received support. Research assistantships with full and partial tuition reimbursements available, teaching assistantships with full and partial tuition reimbursements available, Federal Work-Study, institutionally sponsored loans, scholarships/grants, health care benefits, and unspecified assistantships available. Support available to part-time students. Financial award application deadline: 6/1; financial award applicants required to submit FAFSA. *Faculty research:* Ecology, evolution, and systematics of plants; molecular biology of plant stress and reproduction; global change biology and ecosystem modeling; plant structure and development; science education. *Unit head:* Dr. Anne K. Dunn, Department Chair/Associate Professor of Microbiology, 405-325-4321, E-mail: akdunn@ou.edu. *Application contact:* Elizabeth Karr, Graduate Liaison/Associate Professor of Microbiology, 405-325-5133, E-mail: lizkarr@ou.edu.
Website: http://mpbio.ou.edu

The University of Texas at Austin, Graduate School, College of Natural Sciences, School of Biological Sciences, Program in Plant Biology, Austin, TX 78712-1111. Offers MA, PhD. *Entrance requirements:* For master's and doctorate, GRE General Test, minimum GPA of 3.0. Additional exam requirements/recommendations for international students: Required—TOEFL. Electronic applications accepted. *Faculty research:* Systematics, plant molecular biology, psychology, coology, ovolution.

University of Vermont, Graduate College, College of Agriculture and Life Sciences, Field Naturalist Program, Burlington, VT 05405. Offers plant biology (MS), including field naturalist. *Faculty:* 2 full-time (1 woman), 11 part-time/adjunct (3 women). *Students:* 8 (5 women). 6 applicants, 17% accepted, 1 enrolled. In 2017, 4 master's awarded. *Degree requirements:* For master's, thesis, final exam, project. *Entrance requirements:* For master's, GRE General Test, interview. Additional exam requirements/recommendations for international students: Required—TOEFL (minimum score 550 paper-based, 90 iBT) or IELTS (6.5). *Application deadline:* For fall admission, 2/15 for domestic and international students. Application fee: $65. Electronic applications accepted. *Expenses:* Tuition, state resident: full-time $11,628; part-time $646 per credit. Tuition, nonresident: full-time $29,340; part-time $1630 per credit. *Required fees:* $1994; $10 per credit. Tuition and fees vary according to course load and program. *Financial support:* In 2017–18, 8 students received support, including 8 teaching assistantships with full tuition reimbursements available (averaging $12,000 per year); fellowships, research assistantships, scholarships/grants, and health care benefits also available. Financial award application deadline: 3/1. *Faculty research:* Integrative field science, environmental problem-solving. *Unit head:* Dr. Jeffrey Hughes, Director, 802-656-2930. *Application contact:* Lillian Reade, Coordinator, 802-656-2930, Fax: 802-656-0440, E-mail: lillian.reade@uvm.edu.
Website: http://www.uvm.edu/~fntrlst/

University of Vermont, Graduate College, College of Agriculture and Life Sciences, Program in Plant Biology, Burlington, VT 05405. Offers plant biology (MS, PhD). *Students:* 14 (9 women); includes 1 minority (Asian, non-Hispanic/Latino), 5 international. 24 applicants, 38% accepted, 6 enrolled. In 2017, 1 doctorate awarded. *Entrance requirements:* For master's and doctorate, GRE. Additional exam requirements/recommendations for international students: Required—TOEFL (minimum score 550 paper-based, 100 iBT) or IELTS (7). *Application deadline:* For fall admission, 12/1 for domestic and international students. Application fee: $65. Electronic applications accepted. *Expenses:* Tuition, state resident: full-time $11,628; part-time $646 per credit. Tuition, nonresident: full-time $29,340; part-time $1630 per credit. *Required fees:* $1994; $10 per credit. Tuition and fees vary according to course load and program. *Financial support:* In 2017–18, 14 students received support, including 1 research assistantship with full tuition reimbursement available (averaging $27,000 per year), 13 teaching assistantships with full tuition reimbursements available (averaging $27,000 per year); health care benefits also available. Financial award application deadline: 12/1. *Unit head:* Dr. Jill Preston, 802-656-0434, E-mail: jill.preston@uvm.edu.
Website: http://www.uvm.edu/~plantbio/grad.php

Washington University in St. Louis, The Graduate School, Division of Biology and Biomedical Sciences, Program in Plant and Microbial Biosciences, St. Louis, MO 63130-4899. Offers PhD. *Degree requirements:* For doctorate, thesis/dissertation. *Entrance requirements:* For doctorate, GRE General Test, GRE Subject Test. Additional exam requirements/recommendations for international students: Required—TOEFL. Electronic applications accepted. *Faculty research:* Cell biology; development; physiology, signaling, development, metabolic regulation, photosynthesis, bioenergy, protein structure-function, synthetic biology, biogeochemistry, environmental microbiology, ecology, population genetics and molecular evolution.

Yale University, Graduate School of Arts and Sciences, Department of Molecular, Cellular, and Developmental Biology, Program in Plant Sciences, New Haven, CT 06520. Offers PhD. *Degree requirements:* For doctorate, thesis/dissertation. *Entrance requirements:* For doctorate, GRE General Test, GRE Subject Test.

Plant Molecular Biology

Cornell University, Graduate School, Graduate Fields of Agriculture and Life Sciences, Field of Plant Biology, Ithaca, NY 14853. Offers cytology (MS, PhD); paleobotany (MS, PhD); plant biochemistry (MS, PhD); plant cell biology (MS, PhD); plant ecology (MS, PhD); plant molecular biology (MS, PhD); plant morphology, anatomy and biomechanics (MS, PhD); plant physiology (MS, PhD); systematic botany (MS, PhD). *Degree requirements:* For doctorate, comprehensive exam, thesis/dissertation. *Entrance requirements:* For doctorate, GRE General Test, GRE Subject Test in biology (recommended), 3 letters of recommendation. Additional exam requirements/recommendations for international students: Required—TOEFL (minimum score 610 paper-based; 77 iBT). Electronic applications accepted. *Faculty research:* Plant cell biology/cytology; plant molecular biology; plant morphology/anatomy/biomechanics; plant physiology, systematic botany, paleobotany; plant ecology, ethnobotany, plant biochemistry, photosynthesis.

Illinois State University, Graduate School, College of Arts and Sciences, School of Biological Sciences, Normal, IL 61790. Offers animal behavior (MS); bacteriology (MS); biochemistry (MS); biological sciences (MS); biology (PhD); biophysics (MS); biotechnology (MS); botany (MS, PhD); cell biology (MS); conservation biology (MS); developmental biology (MS); ecology (MS, PhD); entomology (MS); evolutionary biology (MS); genetics (MS, PhD); immunology (MS); microbiology (MS, PhD); molecular biology (MS); molecular genetics (MS); neurobiology (MS); neuroscience (MS); parasitology (MS); physiology (MS, PhD); plant biology (MS); plant molecular biology (MS); plant sciences (MS); structural biology (MS); zoology (MS, PhD). *Program availability:* Part-time. *Degree requirements:* For master's, thesis or alternative; for doctorate, variable foreign language requirement, thesis/dissertation, 2 terms of residency. *Entrance requirements:* For master's, GRE General Test, minimum GPA of 2.6 in last 60 hours of course work; for doctorate, GRE General Test. *Faculty research:* Redoc balance and drug development in schistosoma mansoni, control of the growth of listeria monocytogenes at low temperature, regulation of cell expansion and microtubule function by SPRI, CRUI: physiology and fitness consequences of different life history phenotypes.

Oregon State University, Interdisciplinary/Institutional Programs, Program in Molecular and Cellular Biology, Corvallis, OR 97331. Offers bioinformatics (PhD); biotechnology (PhD); genome biology (PhD); molecular virology (PhD); plant molecular biology (PhD). *Degree requirements:* For doctorate, thesis/dissertation, oral and written qualifying exams. *Entrance requirements:* For doctorate, GRE. Additional exam requirements/recommendations for international students: Required—TOEFL (minimum score 80 iBT), IELTS (minimum score 6.5). *Application deadline:* For fall admission, 8/1 for domestic students, 4/1 for international students; for winter admission, 12/1 for domestic students, 7/1 for international students; for spring admission, 2/1 for domestic students, 10/1 for international students; for summer admission, 5/1 for domestic students, 1/1 for international students. Application fee: $75 ($85 for international students). *Financial support:* Application deadline: 1/1. *Unit head:* Dr. Kristin Carroll, Assistant Director, Molecular and Cellular Biology Program, 541-737-5259, E-mail: kirstin.carroll@oregonstate.edu. *Application contact:* Dr. Kristin Carroll, Assistant Director, Molecular and Cellular Biology Program, 541-737-5259, E-mail: kirstin.carroll@oregonstate.edu.
Website: http://gradschool.oregonstate.edu/molecular-and-cellular-biology-graduate-program

Rutgers University–New Brunswick, Graduate School-New Brunswick, Program in Plant Biology, Piscataway, NJ 08854-8097. Offers horticulture and plant technology (MS, PhD); molecular and cellular biology (MS, PhD); organismal and population biology (MS, PhD); plant pathology (MS, PhD). *Program availability:* Part-time. Terminal master's awarded for partial completion of doctoral program. *Degree requirements:* For master's, comprehensive exam, thesis or alternative; for doctorate, comprehensive exam, thesis/dissertation. *Entrance requirements:* For master's and doctorate, GRE General Test, GRE Subject Test (recommended). Additional exam requirements/recommendations for international students: Required—TOEFL (minimum score 600 paper-based). Electronic applications accepted. *Faculty research:* Molecular biology and biochemistry of plants, plant development and genomics, plant protection, plant improvement, plant management of horticultural and field crops.

University of California, Riverside, Graduate Division, Department of Botany and Plant Sciences, Riverside, CA 92521-0102. Offers plant biology (MS, PhD), including plant cell, molecular, and developmental biology (PhD), plant ecology (PhD), plant genetics (PhD). *Program availability:* Part-time. Terminal master's awarded for partial completion of doctoral program. *Degree requirements:* For master's, comprehensive exams or thesis; for doctorate, thesis/dissertation, qualifying exams. *Entrance requirements:* For master's and doctorate, GRE General Test, minimum GPA of 3.2. Additional exam requirements/recommendations for international students: Required—TOEFL (minimum score 550 paper-based, 80 iBT) or IELTS. *Application deadline:* For fall admission, 12/1 for domestic and international students; for winter admission, 11/15 for domestic students, 9/1 for international students; for spring admission, 3/1 for domestic students, 12/1 for international students. Application fee: $80 ($100 for international students). Electronic applications accepted. *Expenses:* Tuition, state resident: full-time $5746. Tuition, nonresident: full-time $10,780. Tuition and fees vary according to campus/location and program. *Financial support:* Fellowships with tuition reimbursements, research assistantships with tuition reimbursements, teaching assistantships with tuition reimbursements, career-related internships or fieldwork, Federal Work-Study, institutionally sponsored loans, scholarships/grants, health care benefits, tuition waivers (full and partial), and unspecified assistantships available. Financial award applicants required to submit FAFSA. *Faculty research:* Agricultural plant biology; biochemistry and physiology; cellular, molecular and developmental biology; ecology, evolution, systematics and ethnobotany; genetics, genomics and bioinformatics. *Unit head:* Dr. Patricia Springer, Chair. *Application contact:* Laura McGeehan, Graduate Student Services Advisor, 800-735-0717, E-mail: plantbio@ucr.edu.
Website: http://www.plantbiology.ucr.edu/

University of Florida, Graduate School, College of Agricultural and Life Sciences and College of Liberal Arts and Sciences, Program in Plant Molecular and Cellular Biology, Gainesville, FL 32611. Offers plant molecular and cellular biology (MS, PhD), including toxicology (PhD). *Degree requirements:* For master's, thesis; for doctorate, comprehensive exam, thesis/dissertation, first author peer-reviewed publication. *Entrance requirements:* For master's and doctorate, GRE General Test, minimum GPA of 3.0. Additional exam requirements/recommendations for international students: Required—TOEFL (minimum score 550 paper-based; 80 iBT), IELTS (minimum score 6). Electronic applications accepted. *Faculty research:* The understanding of molecular and cellular mechanisms that mediate plant development, adaptation, and evolution including bioinformatics, genomics, proteomics, genetics, biochemistry, breeding, physiology and molecular and cellular biology.

University of Massachusetts Amherst, Graduate School, Interdisciplinary Programs, Program in Plant Biology, Amherst, MA 01003. Offers biochemistry and metabolism (MS, PhD); cell biology and physiology (MS, PhD); environmental, ecological and integrative biology (MS, PhD); genetics and evolution (MS, PhD). *Degree requirements:* For master's, thesis; for doctorate, 2 foreign languages, comprehensive exam, thesis/dissertation. *Entrance requirements:* For master's and doctorate, GRE General Test. Additional exam requirements/recommendations for international students: Required—TOEFL (minimum score 550 paper-based; 80 iBT), IELTS (minimum score 6.5). Electronic applications accepted.

Plant Pathology

Auburn University, Graduate School, College of Agriculture, Department of Entomology and Plant Pathology, Auburn University, AL 36849. Offers entomology (M Ag, MS); plant pathology (M Ag, MS, PhD). *Program availability:* Part-time. *Faculty:* 18 full-time (7 women). *Students:* 30 full-time (18 women), 14 part-time (4 women); includes 1 minority (Black or African American, non-Hispanic/Latino), 26 international. Average age 27. 23 applicants, 52% accepted, 11 enrolled. In 2017, 11 master's, 5 doctorates awarded. *Degree requirements:* For master's, thesis (for some programs); for doctorate, one foreign language, thesis/dissertation. *Entrance requirements:* For master's, GRE General Test; for doctorate, GRE General Test, GRE Subject Test, master's degree with thesis. *Application deadline:* Applications are processed on a rolling basis. Application fee: $50 ($60 for international students). Electronic applications accepted. *Expenses:* Tuition, state resident: full-time $10,974; part-time $519 per credit hour. Tuition, nonresident: full-time $29,658; part-time $1557 per credit hour. *Required fees:* $816 per semester. Tuition and fees vary according to degree level and program. *Financial support:* Research assistantships, teaching assistantships, and Federal Work-Study available. Support available to part-time students. Financial award application deadline: 3/15; financial award applicants required to submit FAFSA. *Faculty research:* Pest management, biological control, systematics, medical entomology. *Unit head:* Dr. Nannan Liu, Chair, 334-844-4266. *Application contact:* Dr. George Flowers, Dean of the Graduate School, 334-844-2125.

Colorado State University, College of Agricultural Sciences, Department of Bioagricultural Sciences and Pest Management, Fort Collins, CO 80523-1177. Offers entomology (MS, PhD); pest management (MS); plant pathology (MS, PhD); weed science (MS, PhD). *Faculty:* 24 full-time (9 women), 2 part-time/adjunct (1 woman). *Students:* 21 full-time (10 women), 20 part-time (14 women); includes 5 minority (1 Asian, non-Hispanic/Latino; 2 Hispanic/Latino; 2 Two or more races, non-Hispanic/Latino), 10 international. Average age 28. 22 applicants, 36% accepted, 7 enrolled. In 2017, 5 master's, 2 doctorates awarded. Terminal master's awarded for partial completion of doctoral program. *Degree requirements:* For master's, thesis; for doctorate, thesis/dissertation. *Entrance requirements:* For master's and doctorate, minimum GPA of 3.0, three letters of recommendation, essay, transcripts, short essay outlining experience and career goals. Additional exam requirements/recommendations for international students: Required—TOEFL (minimum score 550 paper-based). *Application deadline:* For fall admission, 1/15 priority date for domestic and international students; for spring admission, 9/1 priority date for domestic and international students. Application fee: $60 ($70 for international students). Electronic applications accepted. *Expenses:* Tuition, state resident: full-time $9917. Tuition, nonresident: full-time $24,312. *Required fees:* $2284. Tuition and fees vary according to course load and program. *Financial support:* In 2017–18, 29 research assistantships with partial tuition reimbursements (averaging $19,578 per year), 8 teaching assistantships with partial tuition reimbursements (averaging $17,978 per year) were awarded; fellowships with partial tuition reimbursements and scholarships/grants also available. Financial award application deadline: 1/15. *Faculty research:* Genomics and molecular biology, ecology and genetics, ecology and evolution of pest organisms, herbicide resistant weeds. *Total annual research expenditures:* $3.3 million. *Unit head:* Dr. Amy Charkowski, Department Head and Professor, 970-491-8586, E-mail: amy.charkowski@colostate.edu. *Application contact:* Janet Dill, Graduate Student Coordinator, 970-491-0402, Fax: 970-491-3862, E-mail: janet.dill@colostate.edu.
Website: http://bspm.agsci.colostate.edu/

Cornell University, Graduate School, Graduate Fields of Agriculture and Life Sciences, Field of Plant Pathology and Plant-Microbe Biology, Ithaca, NY 14853. Offers fungal and oomycete biology (MPS, MS, PhD); plant microbe pathology (MPS, MS, PhD); plant pathology (MPS, MS, PhD). *Degree requirements:* For master's, thesis (MS), project paper (MPS); for doctorate, comprehensive exam, thesis/dissertation. *Entrance requirements:* For master's and doctorate, GRE General Test, GRE Subject Test (biology recommended), 3 letters of recommendation. Additional exam requirements/recommendations for international students: Required—TOEFL (minimum score 550 paper-based; 77 iBT). Electronic applications accepted. *Faculty research:* Plant pathology; mycology; molecular plant pathology; plant disease epidemiology, ecological and environmental plant pathology; plant disease epidemiology and simulation modeling.

Dalhousie University, Faculty of Agriculture, Halifax, NS B3H 4R2, Canada. Offers agriculture (M Sc), including air quality, animal behavior, animal molecular genetics, animal nutrition, animal technology, aquaculture, botany, crop management, crop physiology, ecology, environmental microbiology, food science, horticulture, nutrient management, pest management, physiology, plant biotechnology, plant pathology, soil chemistry, soil fertility, waste management and composting, water quality. *Program* *availability:* Part-time. *Degree requirements:* For master's, thesis, ATC Exam Teaching Assistantship. *Entrance requirements:* For master's, honors B Sc, minimum GPA of 3.0. Additional exam requirements/recommendations for international students: Required—TOEFL (minimum score 580 paper-based; 92 iBT), IELTS, Michigan English Language Assessment Battery, CanTEST, CAEL. *Faculty research:* Bio-product development, organic agriculture, nutrient management, air and water quality, agricultural biotechnology.

Iowa State University of Science and Technology, Department of Plant Pathology, Ames, IA 50011. Offers MS, PhD. *Entrance requirements:* For master's and doctorate, GRE General Test, resume. Additional exam requirements/recommendations for international students: Required—TOEFL (minimum score 550 paper-based; 79 iBT), IELTS (minimum score 6.5). Electronic applications accepted.

Kansas State University, Graduate School, College of Agriculture, Department of Plant Pathology, Manhattan, KS 66506. Offers genetics (MS, PhD); plant pathology (MS, PhD). Terminal master's awarded for partial completion of doctoral program. *Degree requirements:* For master's, thesis, oral exam; for doctorate, thesis/dissertation, preliminary exams, oral exam. *Entrance requirements:* For master's and doctorate, minimum undergraduate GPA of 3.0. Additional exam requirements/recommendations for international students: Required—TOEFL (minimum score 550 paper-based; 79 iBT). Electronic applications accepted. *Faculty research:* Applied microbiology, microbial genetics, microbial ecology/epidemiology, integrated pest management, plant genetics/genomics/molecular biology, genetics.

Louisiana State University and Agricultural & Mechanical College, Graduate School, College of Agriculture, Department of Plant Pathology and Crop Physiology, Baton Rouge, LA 70803. Offers plant health (MS, PhD). *Faculty:* 17 full-time (0 women). *Students:* 22 full-time (8 women), 2 part-time (1 woman), 16 international. Average age 31. 6 applicants, 33% accepted, 2 enrolled. In 2017, 5 master's, 3 doctorates awarded. *Financial support:* In 2017–18, 20 research assistantships (averaging $20,929 per year) were awarded. *Total annual research expenditures:* $1,844.

Michigan State University, The Graduate School, College of Agriculture and Natural Resources and College of Natural Science, Department of Plant Pathology, East Lansing, MI 48824. Offers MS, PhD. *Entrance requirements:* Additional exam requirements/recommendations for international students: Required—TOEFL.

Montana State University, The Graduate School, College of Agriculture, Department of Plant Sciences and Plant Pathology, Bozeman, MT 59717. Offers plant pathology (MS); plant sciences (MS, PhD), including plant genetics (PhD), plant pathology (PhD). *Program availability:* Part-time. *Degree requirements:* For master's, comprehensive exam; for doctorate, comprehensive exam, thesis/dissertation. *Entrance requirements:* For master's, GRE General Test, minimum GPA of 3.0; for doctorate, GRE General Test. Additional exam requirements/recommendations for international students: Required—TOEFL (minimum score 550 paper-based). Electronic applications accepted. *Faculty research:* Plant genetics, plant metabolism, plant microbe interactions, plant pathology, entomology research.

New Mexico State University, College of Agricultural, Consumer and Environmental Sciences, Department of Entomology, Plant Pathology and Weed Science, Las Cruces, NM 88003-8001. Offers MS. *Program availability:* Part-time. *Faculty:* 10 full-time (1 woman). *Students:* 13 full-time (7 women), 4 part-time (1 woman); includes 8 minority (1 American Indian or Alaska Native, non-Hispanic/Latino; 7 Hispanic/Latino), 4 international. Average age 25. 9 applicants, 44% accepted, 4 enrolled. In 2017, 5 master's awarded. *Degree requirements:* For master's, comprehensive exam, thesis. *Entrance requirements:* For master's, GRE General Test. Additional exam requirements/recommendations for international students: Required—TOEFL (minimum score 550 paper-based; 79 iBT), IELTS (minimum score 6.5). *Application deadline:* For fall admission, 7/1 priority date for domestic students; for spring admission, 11/1 priority date for domestic students. Applications are processed on a rolling basis. Application fee: $40 ($50 for international students). Electronic applications accepted. *Expenses:* Tuition, state resident: full-time $4390. Tuition, nonresident: full-time $15,309. *Required fees:* $853. *Financial support:* In 2017–18, 16 students received support, including 11 research assistantships (averaging $20,678 per year), 4 teaching assistantships (averaging $17,386 per year); career-related internships or fieldwork, Federal Work-Study, scholarships/grants, traineeships, health care benefits, and unspecified assistantships also available. Support available to part-time students. Financial award application deadline: 3/1. *Faculty research:* Entomology, nematology, plant pathology, weed science, plant genetics, environmental science. *Total annual research expenditures:* $2.5 million. *Unit head:* Dr. Gerald K. Sims, Department Head, 575-646-3225, Fax: 575-646-8087, E-mail: gksims@nmsu.edu. *Application contact:* Belinda Williams, 575-646-3225, Fax: 575-646-8087.
Website: http://eppws.nmsu.edu/

North Carolina State University, Graduate School, College of Agriculture and Life Sciences, Department of Plant Pathology, Raleigh, NC 27695. Offers MS, PhD. Terminal master's awarded for partial completion of doctoral program. *Degree requirements:* For master's, thesis (for some programs); for doctorate, thesis/dissertation. *Entrance requirements:* For master's and doctorate, GRE. Additional exam requirements/recommendations for international students: Required—TOEFL. Electronic applications accepted. *Faculty research:* Microbe-plant interactions, biology of plant pathogens, pathogen evaluation, host-plant resistance, genomics.

North Dakota State University, College of Graduate and Interdisciplinary Studies, College of Agriculture, Food Systems, and Natural Resources, Department of Plant Pathology, Fargo, ND 58102. Offers MS, PhD. *Program availability:* Part-time. *Entrance requirements:* Additional exam requirements/recommendations for international students: Required—TOEFL (minimum score 550 paper-based; 79 iBT). *Application deadline:* For fall admission, 5/1 for international students; for winter admission, 8/1 for international students. Applications are processed on a rolling basis. Application fee: $35. Electronic applications accepted. *Expenses:* Tuition, state resident: full-time $4323; part-time $360.21 per credit. Tuition, nonresident: full-time $6484; part-time $540.31 per credit. *Required fees:* $668; $55.70 per credit. Part-time tuition and fees vary according to degree level, program and reciprocity agreements. *Financial support:* Application deadline: 4/15. *Faculty research:* Electron microscopy, disease physiology, molecular biology, genetic resistance, tissue culture. *Unit head:* Dr. Jack B. Rasmussen, Department Chair, 701-231-7058, Fax: 701-231-7851, E-mail: jack.rasmussen@ndsu.edu. *Application contact:* Elizabeth Worth, Marketing, Recruitment, and Public Relations Coordinator, 701-231-8476, Fax: 701-231-6524, E-mail: elizabeth.worth@ndsu.edu.
Website: http://www.ag.ndsu.edu/plantpath/

The Ohio State University, Graduate School, College of Food, Agricultural, and Environmental Sciences, Department of Plant Pathology, Columbus, OH 43210. Offers MPHM, MS, PhD. MPHM offered jointly with Department of Entomology. *Faculty:* 8. *Students:* 48 full-time (27 women), 13 part-time (5 women), 28 international. Average age 28. In 2017, 13 master's, 5 doctorates awarded. *Entrance requirements:* For master's and doctorate, GRE General Test. Additional exam requirements/recommendations for international students: Required—TOEFL (minimum score 550 paper-based; 79 iBT), Michigan English Language Assessment Battery (minimum score 82); Recommended—IELTS (minimum score 7). *Application deadline:* For fall admission, 12/13 priority date for domestic students, 11/30 priority date for international students; for spring admission, 10/17 for domestic students, 9/1 for international students; for summer admission, 2/13 for domestic students, 1/31 for international students. Applications are processed on a rolling basis. Application fee: $60 ($70 for international students). Electronic applications accepted. *Financial support:* Fellowships, research assistantships, teaching assistantships, Federal Work-Study, and institutionally sponsored loans available. Support available to part-time students. *Unit head:* Dr. Laurence Madden, Acting Chair, 330-263-3839, E-mail: madden.1@osu.edu. *Application contact:* Graduate and Professional Admissions, 614-292-9444, Fax: 614-292-3895, E-mail: gpadmissions@osu.edu.
Website: http://plantpath.osu.edu/

Oklahoma State University, College of Agricultural Science and Natural Resources, Department of Entomology and Plant Pathology, Stillwater, OK 74078. Offers entomology (PhD); entomology and plant pathology (MS). *Faculty:* 26 full-time (7 women). *Students:* 4 full-time (3 women), 28 part-time (16 women); includes 3 minority (1 American Indian or Alaska Native, non-Hispanic/Latino; 2 Hispanic/Latino), 13 international. Average age 29. 11 applicants, 45% accepted, 5 enrolled. In 2017, 7 master's, 6 doctorates awarded. *Entrance requirements:* For master's and doctorate, GRE or GMAT. Additional exam requirements/recommendations for international students: Required—TOEFL (minimum score 550 paper-based; 79 iBT). *Application deadline:* For fall admission, 3/1 priority date for international students; for spring admission, 8/1 priority date for international students. Applications are processed on a rolling basis. Application fee: $40 ($75 for international students). Electronic applications accepted. *Expenses:* Tuition, state resident: full-time $4019; part-time $2679.60 per year. Tuition, nonresident: full-time $15,286; part-time $10,190.40 per year. *Required fees:* $2129; $1419 per unit. Tuition and fees vary according to program. *Financial support:* Research assistantships, teaching assistantships, career-related internships or fieldwork, Federal Work-Study, scholarships/grants, health care benefits, tuition waivers (partial), and unspecified assistantships available. Support available to part-time students. Financial award application deadline: 3/1; financial award applicants required to submit FAFSA. *Unit head:* Dr. Phillip Mulder, Jr., Department Head, 405-744-5527, Fax: 405-744-6039, E-mail: phil.mulder@okstate.edu. *Application contact:* Dr. Bob Hunger, Graduate Coordinator, 405-744-9958, Fax: 405-744-6039, E-mail: bob.hunger@okstate.edu.
Website: http://entoplp.okstate.edu/

Oregon State University, College of Agricultural Sciences, Program in Botany and Plant Pathology, Corvallis, OR 97331. Offers applied systematics (MS); ecology (MS, PhD); genetics (MS, PhD); genomics and computational biology (MS, PhD); molecular and cellular biology (MS, PhD); mycology (MS, PhD); plant pathology (MS, PhD); plant physiology (MS, PhD). *Entrance requirements:* For master's and doctorate, GRE. *Application deadline:* For fall admission, 12/1 for domestic and international students. Application fee: $75 ($85 for international students). *Financial support:* Application deadline: 12/1. *Unit head:* John Fowler, Chair of Graduate Studies, E-mail: fowlerj@science.oregonstate.edu.
Website: http://bpp.oregonstate.edu/

Penn State University Park, Graduate School, College of Agricultural Sciences, Department of Plant Pathology and Environmental Microbiology, University Park, PA 16802. Offers plant pathology (MS, PhD). *Unit head:* Dr. Richard T. Roush, Dean, 814-865-2541, Fax: 814-865-3103. *Application contact:* Lori Hawn, Director, Graduate Student Services, 814-865-1795, Fax: 814-863-4627, E-mail: l-gswww@lists.psu.edu.
Website: http://plantpath.psu.edu/

Purdue University, Graduate School, College of Agriculture, Department of Botany and Plant Pathology, West Lafayette, IN 47907. Offers MS, PhD. *Program availability:* Part-time. *Faculty:* 28 full-time (10 women), 1 part-time/adjunct (0 women). *Students:* 50 full-time (20 women), 6 part-time (0 women); includes 8 minority (1 Black or African American, non-Hispanic/Latino; 1 American Indian or Alaska Native, non-Hispanic/Latino; 2 Asian, non-Hispanic/Latino; 4 Hispanic/Latino), 25 international. Average age 27. 34 applicants, 18% accepted, 6 enrolled. In 2017, 5 master's, 4 doctorates awarded. Terminal master's awarded for partial completion of doctoral program. *Degree requirements:* For master's, thesis; for doctorate, thesis/dissertation. *Entrance requirements:* For master's, GRE General Test, minimum undergraduate GPA of 3.0 or equivalent; for doctorate, GRE, minimum undergraduate GPA of 3.0 or equivalent. Additional exam requirements/recommendations for international students: Required—TOEFL (minimum score 550 paper-based; 77 iBT); Recommended—TWE. *Application deadline:* For fall admission, 4/15 priority date for domestic and international students; for spring admission, 12/15 for domestic students, 9/15 for international students; for summer admission, 4/15 for domestic students, 2/15 for international students. Applications are processed on a rolling basis. Application fee: $60 ($75 for international students). Electronic applications accepted. *Financial support:* In 2017–18, 30 students received support. Fellowships with full tuition reimbursements available, research assistantships with full tuition reimbursements available, teaching assistantships with full tuition reimbursements available, and career-related internships or fieldwork available. Support available to part-time students. Financial award application deadline: 3/1; financial award applicants required to submit FAFSA. *Faculty research:* Biotechnology, plant growth, weed control, crop improvement, plant physiology. *Unit head:* Christopher Staiger, Head of the Graduate Program, 765-494-4615, E-mail: staiger@purdue.edu. *Application contact:* Tyson J. McFall, Graduate Contact, 765-494-0352, E-mail: tjmcfall@purdue.edu.
Website: https://ag.purdue.edu/btny

Rutgers University–New Brunswick, Graduate School-New Brunswick, Program in Plant Biology, Piscataway, NJ 08854-8097. Offers horticulture and plant technology (MS, PhD); molecular and cellular biology (MS, PhD); organismal and population biology (MS, PhD); plant pathology (MS, PhD). *Program availability:* Part-time. Terminal master's awarded for partial completion of doctoral program. *Degree requirements:* For master's, comprehensive exam, thesis or alternative; for doctorate, comprehensive exam, thesis/dissertation. *Entrance requirements:* For master's and doctorate, GRE General Test, GRE Subject Test (recommended). Additional exam requirements/recommendations for international students: Required—TOEFL (minimum score 600 paper-based). Electronic applications accepted. *Faculty research:* Molecular biology and biochemistry of plants, plant development and genomics, plant protection, plant improvement, plant management of horticultural and field crops.

State University of New York College of Environmental Science and Forestry, Department of Environmental and Forest Biology, Syracuse, NY 13210-2779. Offers applied ecology (MPS); chemical ecology (MPS, MS, PhD); conservation biology (MPS, MS, PhD); ecology (MPS, MS, PhD); entomology (MPS, MS, PhD); environmental interpretation (MPS, MS, PhD); environmental physiology (MPS, MS, PhD); fish and wildlife biology and management (MPS, MS, PhD); forest pathology and mycology (MPS, MS, PhD); plant biotechnology (MPS); plant science and biotechnology (MPS, MS, PhD). *Program availability:* Part-time. *Faculty:* 30 full-time (10 women), 4 part-time/adjunct (3 women). *Students:* 117 full-time (65 women), 18 part-time (6 women); includes 8 minority (6 American Indian or Alaska Native, non-Hispanic/Latino; 1 Asian, non-Hispanic/Latino; 1 Hispanic/Latino), 23 international. Average age 30. 84

applicants, 52% accepted, 31 enrolled. In 2017, 30 master's, 3 doctorates awarded. Terminal master's awarded for partial completion of doctoral program. *Degree requirements:* For master's, thesis (for some programs), capstone seminar; for doctorate, comprehensive exam, thesis/dissertation, capstone seminar. *Entrance requirements:* For master's and doctorate, GRE General Test, minimum GPA of 3.0. Additional exam requirements/recommendations for international students: Required—TOEFL (minimum score 550 paper-based; 80 iBT), IELTS (minimum score 6). *Application deadline:* For fall admission, 2/1 priority date for domestic and international students; for spring admission, 11/1 priority date for domestic and international students. Applications are processed on a rolling basis. Application fee: $60. Electronic applications accepted. *Expenses:* Tuition, state resident: full-time $10,870; part-time $453 per credit. Tuition, nonresident: full-time $22,210; part-time $925 per credit. *Required fees:* $1435; $70.85 per credit. One-time fee: $25 full-time. Part-time tuition and fees vary according to course load. *Financial support:* In 2017–18, 42 students received support. Unspecified assistantships available. Financial award application deadline: 6/30; financial award applicants required to submit FAFSA. *Faculty research:* Ecology, conservation biology, fish and wildlife biology and management, plant science, entomology. *Total annual research expenditures:* $5.3 million. *Unit head:* Dr. Neil H. Ringler, Chair, 315-470-6803, Fax: 315-470-6934, E-mail: nhringle@esf.edu. *Application contact:* Scott Shannon, Associate Provost for Instruction/Dean of the Graduate School, 315-470-6599, E-mail: esfgrad@esf.edu.
Website: http://www.esf.edu/efb/grad/default.asp

Texas A&M University, College of Agriculture and Life Sciences, Department of Plant Pathology and Microbiology, College Station, TX 77843. Offers plant pathology (MS, PhD). *Program availability:* Part-time, blended/hybrid learning. *Faculty:* 15. *Students:* 31 full-time (9 women), 3 part-time (1 woman); includes 7 minority (2 Black or African American, non-Hispanic/Latino; 3 Asian, non-Hispanic/Latino; 1 Hispanic/Latino; 1 Two or more races, non-Hispanic/Latino), 11 international. Average age 27. 13 applicants, 100% accepted, 7 enrolled. In 2017, 2 master's, 3 doctorates awarded. *Degree requirements:* For master's, comprehensive exam (for some programs), thesis; for doctorate, comprehensive exam, thesis/dissertation. *Entrance requirements:* For master's and doctorate, GRE General Test, letters of recommendation, BS/BA in biological sciences. Additional exam requirements/recommendations for international students: Required—TOEFL (minimum score 550 paper-based; 80 iBT), IELTS (minimum score 6), PTE (minimum score 53). *Application deadline:* Applications are processed on a rolling basis. Application fee: $50 ($90 for international students). Electronic applications accepted. *Expenses:* Contact institution. *Financial support:* In 2017–18, 31 students received support, including 3 fellowships with tuition reimbursements available (averaging $19,800 per year), 18 research assistantships with tuition reimbursements available (averaging $11,735 per year), 13 teaching assistantships with tuition reimbursements available (averaging $12,546 per year); career-related internships or fieldwork, institutionally sponsored loans, scholarships/grants, traineeships, health care benefits, tuition waivers (full and partial), and unspecified assistantships also available. Support available to part-time students. Financial award application deadline: 3/15; financial award applicants required to submit FAFSA. *Faculty research:* Plant disease control, population biology of plant pathogens, disease epidemiology, molecular genetics of host/parasite interactions. *Unit head:* Dr. Leland S. Pierson, III, Professor and Department Head, 979-845-8288, Fax: 979-845-6483, E-mail: lspierson@tamu.edu. *Application contact:* Dr. Heather H. Wilkinson, Associate Department Head for Academics, 979-845-1491, E-mail: h-wilkinson@tamu.edu.
Website: http://plantpathology.tamu.edu/

The University of Arizona, College of Agriculture and Life Sciences, School of Plant Sciences, Program in Plant Pathology, Tucson, AZ 85721. Offers MS, PhD. *Program availability:* Part-time. *Degree requirements:* For master's, thesis optional; for doctorate, thesis/dissertation. *Entrance requirements:* For master's, GRE (recommended), minimum GPA of 3.0, academic resume, 3 letters of recommendation; for doctorate, GRE (recommended), minimum GPA of 3.0, academic resume, statement of purpose, 3 letters of recommendation. Additional exam requirements/recommendations for international students: Required—TOEFL (minimum score 550 paper-based; 79 iBT). Electronic applications accepted. *Faculty research:* Fungal molecular biology, ecology of soil-borne plant pathogens, plant virology, plant bacteriology, plant/pathogen interactions.

University of Arkansas, Graduate School, Dale Bumpers College of Agricultural, Food and Life Sciences, Department of Plant Pathology, Fayetteville, AR 72701. Offers MS. In 2017, 3 master's awarded. *Degree requirements:* For master's, thesis. *Application deadline:* For fall admission, 8/1 for domestic students, 4/1 for international students; for spring admission, 12/1 for domestic students, 10/1 for international students; for summer admission, 4/15 for domestic students, 3/1 for international students. Applications are processed on a rolling basis. Application fee: $60. Electronic applications accepted. *Expenses:* Tuition, state resident: full-time $3782. Tuition, nonresident: full-time $10,238. *Financial support:* In 2017–18, 10 research assistantships were awarded; fellowships, teaching assistantships, career-related internships or fieldwork, and Federal Work-Study also available. Support available to part-time students. Financial award application deadline: 4/1; financial award applicants required to submit FAFSA. *Unit head:* Dr. Terry Kirkpatrick, Department Head, 479-575-2490, E-mail: kirkpatr@uark.edu. *Application contact:* Ken Korth, Professor, 479-575-2445, E-mail: kkorth@uark.edu.
Website: https://plant-pathology.uark.edu/

University of California, Davis, Graduate Studies, Program in Plant Pathology, Davis, CA 95616. Offers MS, PhD. Terminal master's awarded for partial completion of doctoral program. *Degree requirements:* For master's, comprehensive exam (for some programs), thesis (for some programs); for doctorate, thesis/dissertation. *Entrance requirements:* For master's and doctorate, GRE General Test. Additional exam requirements/recommendations for international students: Required—TOEFL (minimum score 550 paper-based). Electronic applications accepted. *Faculty research:* Soil microbiology; diagnosis etiology and control of plant diseases; genomics and molecular biology of plant microbe interactions; biotechnology, ecology of plant pathogens and epidemiology of diseases in agricultural and native ecosystems.

University of California, Riverside, Graduate Division, Department of Plant Pathology, Riverside, CA 92521-0102. Offers MS, PhD. Terminal master's awarded for partial completion of doctoral program. *Degree requirements:* For master's, comprehensive exams or thesis; for doctorate, thesis/dissertation, qualifying exams. *Entrance requirements:* For master's and doctorate, GRE General Test (minimum score 1100 or approximately 300 on new scoring scale), minimum GPA of 3.2. Additional exam requirements/recommendations for international students: Required—TOEFL (minimum score 550 paper-based; 80 iBT). Electronic applications accepted. *Expenses:* Tuition, state resident: full-time $5746. Tuition, nonresident: full-time $10,780. Tuition and fees vary according to campus/location and program. *Faculty research:* Host-pathogen interactions, biological control and integrated approaches to disease management, fungicide behavior, molecular genetics.

University of Florida, Graduate School, College of Agricultural and Life Sciences, Department of Plant Pathology, Gainesville, FL 32611. Offers plant pathology (MS, PhD), including toxicology (PhD). *Program availability:* Part-time. Terminal master's awarded for partial completion of doctoral program. *Degree requirements:* For master's, comprehensive exam (for some programs), thesis optional; for doctorate, comprehensive exam, thesis/dissertation. *Entrance requirements:* For master's and doctorate, GRE General Test, minimum GPA of 3.0. Additional exam requirements/recommendations for international students: Required—TOEFL (minimum score 550 paper-based; 80 iBT), IELTS (minimum score 6). Electronic applications accepted. *Faculty research:* Epidemiology, molecular biology of host-parasite interactions, bacteriology, virology, post-harvest diseases.

University of Georgia, College of Agricultural and Environmental Sciences, Department of Plant Pathology, Athens, GA 30602. Offers MS, PhD. *Degree requirements:* For master's, thesis (MS); for doctorate, one foreign language, thesis/dissertation. *Entrance requirements:* For master's and doctorate, GRE General Test. Electronic applications accepted.

University of Guelph, Graduate Studies, Ontario Agricultural College, Department of Environmental Biology, Guelph, ON N1G 2W1, Canada. Offers entomology (M Sc, PhD); environmental microbiology and biotechnology (M Sc, PhD); environmental toxicology (M Sc, PhD); plant and forest systems (M Sc, PhD); plant pathology (M Sc, PhD). *Program availability:* Part-time. *Degree requirements:* For master's, thesis; for doctorate, comprehensive exam, thesis/dissertation. *Entrance requirements:* For master's, minimum 75% average during previous 2 years of course work; for doctorate, minimum 75% average. Additional exam requirements/recommendations for international students: Required—TOEFL or IELTS. Electronic applications accepted. *Faculty research:* Entomology, environmental microbiology and biotechnology, environmental toxicology, forest ecology, plant pathology.

University of Hawaii at Manoa, Office of Graduate Education, College of Tropical Agriculture and Human Resources, Department of Plant and Environmental Protection Sciences, Program in Tropical Plant Pathology, Honolulu, HI 96822. Offers MS, PhD. *Program availability:* Part-time. *Degree requirements:* For master's, thesis optional; for doctorate, comprehensive exam, thesis/dissertation. *Entrance requirements:* For master's and doctorate, GRE General Test. Additional exam requirements/recommendations for international students: Required—TOEFL (minimum score 540 paper-based; 76 iBT), IELTS (minimum score 5).

University of Idaho, College of Graduate Studies, College of Agricultural and Life Sciences, Department of Entomology, Plant Pathology and Nematology, Moscow, ID 83844. Offers plant science (MS). *Faculty:* 8 full-time. *Students:* 15. Average age 31. *Entrance requirements:* For master's and doctorate, GRE General Test, minimum GPA of 3.0. Additional exam requirements/recommendations for international students: Required—TOEFL (minimum score 550 paper-based; 79 iBT). *Application deadline:* For fall admission, 7/1 for domestic students; for spring admission, 11/1 for domestic students. Applications are processed on a rolling basis. Application fee: $60. Electronic applications accepted. *Expenses:* Tuition, state resident: full-time $6722; part-time $430 per credit hour. Tuition, nonresident: full-time $23,046; part-time $1337 per credit hour. *Required fees:* $2142; $63 per credit hour. *Financial support:* Research assistantships and teaching assistantships available. Financial award applicants required to submit FAFSA. *Faculty research:* Seed potato production, wheat production, insect pests, plant pathogens. *Unit head:* Dr. Paul McDaniel, Department Head, 208-885-6274, Fax: 208-885-7760, E-mail: pses@uidaho.edu. *Application contact:* Sean Scoggin, Graduate Recruitment Coordinator, 208-885-4001, Fax: 208-885-4406, E-mail: graduateadmissions@uidaho.edu.
Website: http://www.uidaho.edu/cals/entomology-plant-pathology-and-nematology

University of Kentucky, Graduate School, College of Agriculture, Food and Environment, Program in Plant Pathology, Lexington, KY 40506-0032. Offers MS, PhD. *Degree requirements:* For master's, comprehensive exam, thesis; for doctorate, comprehensive exam, thesis/dissertation. *Entrance requirements:* For master's, GRE General Test, minimum undergraduate GPA of 2.75; for doctorate, GRE General Test, minimum graduate GPA of 3.0. Additional exam requirements/recommendations for international students: Required—TOEFL (minimum score 550 paper-based). Electronic applications accepted. *Faculty research:* Molecular biology of viruses and fungi, biochemistry and physiology of disease resistance, plant transformation, disease ecology, forest pathology.

University of Maine, Graduate School, College of Natural Sciences, Forestry, and Agriculture, School of Biology and Ecology, Orono, ME 04469. Offers biological sciences (PhD); botany and plant pathology (MS); entomology (MS); zoology (MS, PhD). *Program availability:* Part-time. *Faculty:* 30 full-time (16 women), 2 part-time/adjunct (1 woman). *Students:* 61 full-time (40 women), 22 part-time (11 women); includes 7 minority (1 American Indian or Alaska Native, non-Hispanic/Latino; 3 Asian, non-Hispanic/Latino; 3 Hispanic/Latino), 14 international. Average age 30. 69 applicants, 87% accepted, 28 enrolled. In 2017, 7 master's, 9 doctorates awarded. Terminal master's awarded for partial completion of doctoral program. *Degree requirements:* For master's, thesis (for some programs); for doctorate, comprehensive exam, thesis/dissertation. *Entrance requirements:* For master's and doctorate, GRE General Test. Additional exam requirements/recommendations for international students: Required—TOEFL (minimum score 80 iBT), IELTS (minimum score 6.5). *Application deadline:* For fall admission, 2/1 priority date for domestic students. Applications are processed on a rolling basis. Application fee: $65. Electronic applications accepted. *Expenses:* Tuition, state resident: full-time $7722; part-time $429 per credit hour. Tuition, nonresident: full-time $25,146; part-time $1397 per credit hour. *Required fees:* $1162; $581 per credit hour. *Financial support:* In 2017–18, 92 students received support, including 2 fellowships with full tuition reimbursements available (averaging $25,000 per year), 47 research assistantships with full tuition reimbursements available (averaging $19,800 per year), 32 teaching assistantships with full tuition reimbursements available (averaging $15,200 per year); career-related internships or fieldwork, Federal Work-Study, institutionally sponsored loans, tuition waivers (full and partial), and unspecified assistantships also available. Financial award application deadline: 3/1. *Faculty research:* Ecology and evolution (aquatic, terrestrial, paleo); development and genetics; biomedical research; ecophysiology and stress; invasion ecology and pest management. *Total annual research expenditures:* $3.1 million. *Unit head:* Dr. Andrei Aloykhin, Director, 207-581-2977, Fax: 207-581-2537. *Application contact:* Scott G. Delcourt, Assistant Vice President for Graduate Studies and Senior Associate Dean, 207-581-3291, Fax: 207-581-3232, E-mail: graduate@maine.edu.
Website: http://sbe.umaine.edu/

University of Minnesota, Twin Cities Campus, Graduate School, College of Food, Agricultural and Natural Resource Sciences, Department of Plant Pathology, St. Paul, MN 55108. Offers MS, PhD. *Program availability:* Part-time. *Faculty:* 17 full-time (7 women), 10 part-time/adjunct (3 women). *Students:* 20 full-time (10 women), 5 part-time (3 women), 8 international. 30 applicants. In 2017, 3 master's, 2 doctorates awarded. Terminal master's awarded for partial completion of doctoral program. *Degree requirements:* For master's, comprehensive exam, thesis; for doctorate, comprehensive exam, thesis/dissertation. *Entrance requirements:* For master's and doctorate, GRE General Test. Additional exam requirements/recommendations for international students: Required—TOEFL (minimum score 550 paper-based; 79 iBT), IELTS

(minimum score 6.5). *Application deadline:* For fall admission, 12/1 priority date for domestic and international students. Applications are processed on a rolling basis. Application fee: $75 ($95 for international students). Electronic applications accepted. *Financial support:* In 2017–18, fellowships with full tuition reimbursements (averaging $40,000 per year), research assistantships with full and partial tuition reimbursements (averaging $40,000 per year) were awarded; career-related internships or fieldwork, scholarships/grants, traineeships, health care benefits, and unspecified assistantships also available. Support available to part-time students. Financial award application deadline: 12/1. *Faculty research:* Plant disease management, disease resistance, product deterioration, international agriculture, molecular biology. *Unit head:* Dr. James Bradeen, Department Head, 612-625-9736, E-mail: jbradeen@umn.edu. *Application contact:* Dr. Dean Malvick, Director of Graduate Studies, 612-625-5282, E-mail: dmalvick@umn.edu.
Website: http://plpa.cfans.umn.edu/

The University of Tennessee, Graduate School, College of Agricultural Sciences and Natural Resources, Department of Entomology and Plant Pathology, Knoxville, TN 37996. Offers entomology (MS, PhD); integrated pest management and bioactive natural products (PhD); plant pathology (MS, PhD). *Program availability:* Part-time. *Degree requirements:* For master's, thesis, seminar. *Entrance requirements:* For master's, GRE General Test, minimum GPA of 2.7, 3 reference letters, letter of intent; for doctorate, GRE General Test, minimum GPA of 2.7, 3 reference letters, letter of intent, proposed dissertation research. Additional exam requirements/recommendations for international students: Required—TOEFL. Electronic applications accepted.

University of Vermont, Graduate College, College of Agriculture and Life Sciences, Department of Plant and Soil Science, Burlington, VT 05405. Offers agroecology (Graduate Certificate); plant and soil science (MS, PhD), including agroecology, agronomy (MS), ecological landscape design, entomology, horticulture (MS), plant pathology (MS), soil science. *Students:* 27 (15 women), 5 international. 23 applicants, 39% accepted, 7 enrolled. In 2017, 3 master's, 2 doctorates awarded. *Degree requirements:* For master's, thesis; for doctorate, one foreign language, thesis/dissertation. *Entrance requirements:* For master's and doctorate, GRE General Test. Additional exam requirements/recommendations for international students: Required—TOEFL (minimum score 550 paper-based; 90 iBT), IELTS (minimum score 6.5). *Application deadline:* For fall admission, 1/15 for domestic students, 2/15 for international students. Application fee: $65. Electronic applications accepted. *Expenses:* Tuition, state resident: full-time $11,628; part-time $646 per credit. Tuition, nonresident: full-time $29,340; part-time $1630 per credit. *Required fees:* $1994; $10 per credit. Tuition and fees vary according to course load and program. *Financial support:* In 2017–18, 18 students received support, including 10 research assistantships with full tuition reimbursements available (averaging $25,500 per year), 8 teaching assistantships with full tuition reimbursements available (averaging $23,500 per year); fellowships, scholarships/grants, and health care benefits also available. Financial award application deadline: 1/15. *Faculty research:* Soil chemistry, plant nutrition. *Unit head:* Dr. Josef Gorres, Coordinator, 802-656-2630, E-mail: josef.gorres@uvm.edu.
Website: http://www.uvm.edu/~pss/?Page=grad_intro.html&SM=grad_prog_menu.html

University of Wisconsin–Madison, Graduate School, College of Agricultural and Life Sciences, Department of Plant Pathology, Madison, WI 53706-1380. Offers MS, PhD. *Program availability:* Part-time. Terminal master's awarded for partial completion of doctoral program. *Degree requirements:* For master's, thesis; for doctorate, thesis/dissertation. *Entrance requirements:* For master's and doctorate, GRE. Additional exam requirements/recommendations for international students: Required—TOEFL. Electronic applications accepted. *Faculty research:* Plant disease, plant health, plant-microbe interactions, plant disease management, biological control.

Virginia Polytechnic Institute and State University, Graduate School, College of Agriculture and Life Sciences, Blacksburg, VA 24061. Offers agricultural and applied economics (MS, PhD); agricultural and life sciences (MS); agriculture, leadership, and community education (MS, PhD); animal and poultry science (MS, PhD); biochemistry (MS, PhD); crop and soil environmental sciences (MS, PhD); dairy science (MS, PhD); entomology (MS, PhD); food science and technology (MS, PhD); horticulture (PhD); human nutrition, foods and exercise (MS, PhD); plant pathology, physiology, and weed science (MS, PhD). *Faculty:* 241 full-time (73 women), 1 (woman) part-time/adjunct. *Students:* 379 full-time (221 women), 126 part-time (75 women); includes 64 minority (21 Black or African American, non-Hispanic/Latino; 15 Asian, non-Hispanic/Latino; 14 Hispanic/Latino; 14 Two or more races, non-Hispanic/Latino), 119 international. Average age 29. 357 applicants, 46% accepted, 118 enrolled. In 2017, 105 master's, 54 doctorates awarded. *Degree requirements:* For master's, comprehensive exam (for some programs), thesis (for some programs); for doctorate, comprehensive exam (for some programs), thesis/dissertation (for some programs). *Entrance requirements:* For master's and doctorate, GRE/GMAT. Additional exam requirements/recommendations for international students: Required—TOEFL (minimum score 80 iBT). *Application deadline:* For fall admission, 8/1 for domestic students, 4/1 for international students; for spring admission, 1/1 for domestic students, 9/1 for international students. Applications are processed on a rolling basis. Application fee: $75. Electronic applications accepted. *Expenses:* Tuition, state resident: full-time $15,072; part-time $718.50 per credit hour. Tuition, nonresident: full-time $28,810; part-time $1448.25 per credit hour. *Required fees:* $2741; $502 per semester. Tuition and fees vary according to course load, campus/location and program. *Financial support:* In 2017–18, 232 research assistantships with full tuition reimbursements (averaging $21,852 per year), 94 teaching assistantships with full tuition reimbursements (averaging $21,643 per year) were awarded. Financial award application deadline: 3/1; financial award applicants required to submit FAFSA. *Total annual research expenditures:* $44.3 million. *Unit head:* Dr. Alan L. Grant, Dean, 540-231-4152, Fax: 540-231-4163, E-mail: algrant@vt.edu. *Application contact:* Crystal Tawney, Administrative Assistant, 540-231-4152, Fax: 540-231-4163, E-mail: cdtawney@vt.edu.
Website: http://www.cals.vt.edu/

Washington State University, College of Agricultural, Human, and Natural Resource Sciences, Department of Plant Pathology, Pullman, WA 99164. Offers MS, PhD. Programs offered at the Pullman campus. Terminal master's awarded for partial completion of doctoral program. *Degree requirements:* For master's, comprehensive exam (for some programs), thesis (for some programs), oral exam; for doctorate, comprehensive exam, thesis/dissertation, oral exam. *Entrance requirements:* For master's and doctorate, GRE, statement of purpose. Additional exam requirements/recommendations for international students: Required—TOEFL (minimum score 550 paper-based), IELTS. Electronic applications accepted. *Faculty research:* Biology of fungi, bacteria, and viruses; diseases of plants; genetics of fungi, bacteria, and viruses.

West Virginia University, Davis College of Agriculture, Forestry and Consumer Sciences, Morgantown, WV 26506. Offers agricultural and extension education (MS, PhD); agriculture and resource management (MS); agriculture, natural resources and design (M Agr); agronomy (MS); animal and food science (PhD); animal physiology (MS); applied and environmental microbiology (MS); design and merchandising (MS); entomology (MS); forest resource science (PhD); forestry (MSF); genetics and developmental biology (MS, PhD); horticulture (MS); human and community development (PhD); landscape architecture (MLA); natural resource economics (PhD); nutritional and food science (MS); plant and soil science (PhD); plant pathology (MS); recreation, parks and tourism resources (MS); reproductive physiology (MS, PhD); wildlife and fisheries resources (PhD). *Program availability:* Part-time. *Students:* 200 full-time (97 women), 53 part-time (32 women); includes 27 minority (6 Black or African American, non-Hispanic/Latino; 1 American Indian or Alaska Native, non-Hispanic/Latino; 4 Asian, non-Hispanic/Latino; 11 Hispanic/Latino; 5 Two or more races, non-Hispanic/Latino), 67 international. *Degree requirements:* For master's, thesis; for doctorate, thesis/dissertation. *Entrance requirements:* Additional exam requirements/recommendations for international students: Required—TOEFL (minimum score 550 paper-based). *Application deadline:* For fall admission, 6/1 priority date for domestic students, 6/1 for international students; for spring admission, 1/5 for domestic and international students. Applications are processed on a rolling basis. Application fee: $60. Electronic applications accepted. *Expenses:* Tuition, state resident: full-time $9450. Tuition, nonresident: full-time $24,390. *Financial support:* Fellowships, research assistantships, teaching assistantships, career-related internships or fieldwork, Federal Work-Study, institutionally sponsored loans, tuition waivers (full and partial), and unspecified assistantships available. Financial award application deadline: 2/1; financial award applicants required to submit FAFSA. *Faculty research:* Reproductive physiology, soil and water quality, human nutrition, aquaculture, wildlife management. *Unit head:* Dr. Dan J. Robison, Dean, 304-293-2395, Fax: 304-293-3740, E-mail: dan.robison@mail.wvu.edu. *Application contact:* Dr. Dennis K. Smith, Associate Dean, 304-293-2275, Fax: 304-293-3740, E-mail: denny.smith@mail.wvu.edu.
Website: https://www.davis.wvu.edu

Plant Physiology

Cornell University, Graduate School, Graduate Fields of Agriculture and Life Sciences, Field of Plant Biology, Ithaca, NY 14853. Offers cytology (MS, PhD); paleobotany (MS, PhD); plant biochemistry (MS, PhD); plant cell biology (MS, PhD); plant ecology (MS, PhD); plant molecular biology (MS, PhD); plant morphology, anatomy and biomechanics (MS, PhD); plant physiology (MS, PhD); systematic botany (MS, PhD). *Degree requirements:* For doctorate, comprehensive exam, thesis/dissertation. *Entrance requirements:* For doctorate, GRE General Test, GRE Subject Test in biology (recommended), 3 letters of recommendation. Additional exam requirements/recommendations for international students: Required—TOEFL (minimum score 610 paper-based; 77 iBT). Electronic applications accepted. *Faculty research:* Plant cell biology/cytology; plant molecular biology; plant morphology/anatomy/biomechanics; plant physiology, systematic botany, paleobotany; plant ecology, ethnobotany, plant biochemistry, photosynthesis.

Dalhousie University, Faculty of Agriculture, Halifax, NS B3H 4R2, Canada. Offers agriculture (M Sc), including air quality, animal behavior, animal molecular genetics, animal nutrition, animal technology, aquaculture, botany, crop management, crop physiology, ecology, environmental microbiology, food science, horticulture, nutrient management, pest management, physiology, plant biotechnology, plant pathology, soil chemistry, soil fertility, waste management and composting, water quality. *Program availability:* Part-time. *Degree requirements:* For master's, thesis, ATC Exam Teaching Assistantship. *Entrance requirements:* For master's, honors B Sc, minimum GPA of 3.0. Additional exam requirements/recommendations for international students: Required—TOEFL (minimum score 580 paper-based; 92 iBT), IELTS, Michigan English Language Assessment Battery, CanTEST, CAEL. *Faculty research:* Bio-product development, organic agriculture, nutrient management, air and water quality, agricultural biotechnology.

Oregon State University, College of Agricultural Sciences, Program in Botany and Plant Pathology, Corvallis, OR 97331. Offers applied systematics (MS); ecology (MS, PhD); genetics (MS, PhD); genomics and computational biology (MS, PhD); molecular and cellular biology (MS, PhD); mycology (MS, PhD); plant pathology (MS, PhD); plant physiology (MS, PhD). *Entrance requirements:* For master's and doctorate, GRE. *Application deadline:* For fall admission, 12/1 for domestic and international students. Application fee: $75 ($85 for international students). *Financial support:* Application deadline: 12/1. *Unit head:* John Fowler, Chair of Graduate Studies, E-mail: fowlerj@science.oregonstate.edu.
Website: http://bpp.oregonstate.edu/

Purdue University, Graduate School, College of Science, Department of Biological Sciences, West Lafayette, IN 47907. Offers biochemistry (PhD); biophysics (PhD); cell and developmental biology (PhD); ecology, evolutionary and population biology (MS, PhD), including ecology, evolutionary biology, population biology; genetics (MS, PhD); microbiology (MS, PhD); molecular biology (PhD); neurobiology (MS, PhD); plant physiology (PhD). *Faculty:* 42 full-time (13 women), 3 part-time/adjunct (0 women). *Students:* 115 full-time (58 women), 6 part-time (4 women); includes 17 minority (1 Black or African American, non-Hispanic/Latino; 6 Asian, non-Hispanic/Latino; 9 Hispanic/Latino; 1 Two or more races, non-Hispanic/Latino), 60 international. Average age 27. 165 applicants, 12% accepted, 15 enrolled. In 2017, 5 master's, 16 doctorates awarded. Terminal master's awarded for partial completion of doctoral program. *Degree requirements:* For master's, thesis (for some programs); for doctorate, thesis/dissertation, seminars, teaching experience. *Entrance requirements:* For master's, GRE General Test (minimum analytical writing score of 3.5), minimum undergraduate GPA of 3.0; for doctorate, GRE General Test (minimum analytical writing score of 3.5), minimum undergraduate GPA of 3.5. Additional exam requirements/recommendations for international students: Required—TOEFL minimum score 600 paper-based; 107 iBT (for MS), 80 iBT (for PhD). *Application deadline:* For fall admission, 12/7 for domestic and international students. Applications are processed on a rolling basis. Application fee: $60 ($75 for international students). Electronic applications accepted. *Financial support:* Fellowships, research assistantships, and teaching assistantships available. Support available to part-time students. Financial award application deadline: 2/15; financial award applicants required to submit FAFSA. *Unit head:* Stephen Konieczny, Head, 765-494-4407, E-mail: sfk@purdue.edu. *Application contact:* Georgina E. Rupp, Graduate

Plant Physiology

Coordinator, 765-494-8142, E-mail: ruppg@purdue.edu.
Website: http://www.bio.purdue.edu/

University of Manitoba, Faculty of Graduate Studies, Faculty of Agricultural and Food Sciences, Department of Plant Science, Winnipeg, MB R3T 2N2, Canada. Offers agronomy and plant protection (M Sc, PhD); horticulture (M Sc, PhD); plant breeding and genetics (M Sc, PhD); plant physiology-biochemistry (M Sc, PhD). *Degree requirements:* For master's, thesis; for doctorate, one foreign language, thesis/dissertation.

University of Massachusetts Amherst, Graduate School, Interdisciplinary Programs, Program in Plant Biology, Amherst, MA 01003. Offers biochemistry and metabolism (MS, PhD); cell biology and physiology (MS, PhD); environmental, ecological and integrative biology (MS, PhD); genetics and evolution (MS, PhD). *Degree requirements:* For master's, thesis; for doctorate, 2 foreign languages, comprehensive exam, thesis/dissertation. *Entrance requirements:* For master's and doctorate, GRE General Test. Additional exam requirements/recommendations for international students: Required—TOEFL (minimum score 550 paper-based; 80 iBT), IELTS (minimum score 6.5). Electronic applications accepted.

The University of Tennessee, Graduate School, College of Arts and Sciences, Program in Life Sciences, Knoxville, TN 37996. Offers genome science and technology (MS, PhD); plant physiology and genetics (MS, PhD). *Degree requirements:* For doctorate, one foreign language, thesis/dissertation. *Entrance requirements:* For master's and doctorate, GRE General Test, minimum GPA of 2.7. Additional exam requirements/recommendations for international students: Required—TOEFL. Electronic applications accepted.

Virginia Polytechnic Institute and State University, Graduate School, College of Agriculture and Life Sciences, Blacksburg, VA 24061. Offers agricultural and applied economics (MS, PhD); agricultural and life sciences (MS); agriculture, leadership, and community education (MS, PhD); animal and poultry science (MS, PhD); biochemistry (MS, PhD); crop and soil environmental sciences (MS, PhD); dairy science (MS, PhD); entomology (MS, PhD); food science and technology (MS, PhD); horticulture (PhD); human nutrition, foods and exercise (MS, PhD); plant pathology, physiology, and weed science (MS, PhD). *Faculty:* 241 full-time (73 women), 1 (woman) part-time/adjunct. *Students:* 379 full-time (221 women), 126 part-time (75 women); includes 64 minority (21 Black or African American, non-Hispanic/Latino; 15 Asian, non-Hispanic/Latino; 14 Hispanic/Latino; 14 Two or more races, non-Hispanic/Latino), 119 international. Average age 29. 357 applicants, 46% accepted, 118 enrolled. In 2017, 105 master's, 54 doctorates awarded. *Degree requirements:* For master's, comprehensive exam (for some programs), thesis (for some programs); for doctorate, comprehensive exam (for some programs), thesis/dissertation (for some programs). *Entrance requirements:* For master's and doctorate, GRE/GMAT. Additional exam requirements/recommendations for international students: Required—TOEFL (minimum score 80 iBT). *Application deadline:* For fall admission, 8/1 for domestic students, 4/1 for international students; for spring admission, 1/1 for domestic students, 9/1 for international students. Applications are processed on a rolling basis. Application fee: $75. Electronic applications accepted. *Expenses:* Tuition, state resident: full-time $15,072; part-time $718.50 per credit hour. Tuition, nonresident: full-time $28,810; part-time $1448.25 per credit hour. *Required fees:* $2741; $502 per semester. Tuition and fees vary according to course load, campus/location and program. *Financial support:* In 2017–18, 232 research assistantships with full tuition reimbursements (averaging $21,852 per year), 94 teaching assistantships with full tuition reimbursements (averaging $21,643 per year) were awarded. Financial award application deadline: 3/1; financial award applicants required to submit FAFSA. *Total annual research expenditures:* $44.3 million. *Unit head:* Dr. Alan L. Grant, Dean, 540-231-4152, Fax: 540-231-4163, E-mail: algrant@vt.edu. *Application contact:* Crystal Tawney, Administrative Assistant, 540-231-4152, Fax: 540-231-4163, E-mail: cdtawney@vt.edu.
Website: http://www.cals.vt.edu/

Section 6
Cell, Molecular, and Structural Biology

This section contains a directory of institutions offering graduate work in cell, molecular, and structural biology, followed by in-depth entries submitted by institutions that chose to prepare detailed program descriptions. Additional information about programs listed in the directory but not augmented by an in-depth entry may be obtained by writing directly to the dean of a graduate school or chair of a department at the address given in the directory.

For programs offering related work, see also in this book *Anatomy; Biochemistry; Biological and Biomedical Sciences; Biophysics; Botany and Plant Biology; Genetics, Developmental Biology, and Reproductive Biology; Microbiological Sciences; Pathology and Pathobiology; Pharmacology and Toxicology; Pharmacy and Pharmaceutical Sciences; Physiology;* and *Veterinary Medicine and Sciences.* In the other guides in this series:

Graduate Programs in the Physical Sciences, Mathematics, Agricultural Sciences, the Environment & Natural Resources

See *Chemistry*

Graduate Programs in Engineering & Applied Sciences

See *Agricultural Engineering and Bioengineering* and *Biomedical Engineering and Biotechnology*

CONTENTS

Program Directories

Featured Schools: Displays and Close-Ups

See also:

Cancer Biology/Oncology

Augusta University, Program in Biochemistry and Cancer Biology, Augusta, GA 30912. Offers PhD. *Degree requirements:* For doctorate, comprehensive exam, thesis/dissertation. *Entrance requirements:* For doctorate, GRE General Test. Additional exam requirements/recommendations for international students: Required—TOEFL (minimum score 550 paper-based; 79 IBT). Electronic applications accepted. *Faculty research:* Molecular oncology and biomarkers; immunology, inflammation and tolerance; signaling and angiogenesis.

Baylor College of Medicine, Graduate School of Biomedical Sciences, Program in Translational Biology and Molecular Medicine, Houston, TX 77030-3498. Offers PhD. *Degree requirements:* For doctorate, thesis/dissertation, public defense. *Entrance requirements:* For doctorate, GRE, minimum GPA of 3.0. Additional exam requirements/recommendations for international students: Required—TOEFL. Electronic applications accepted. *Faculty research:* Molecular medicine, translational biology, human disease biology and therapy.

Case Western Reserve University, School of Medicine and School of Graduate Studies, Graduate Programs in Medicine, Cancer Biology Training Program, Cleveland, OH 44106. Offers PhD, MD/PhD. *Degree requirements:* For doctorate, comprehensive exam, thesis/dissertation. *Entrance requirements:* For doctorate, GRE. Additional exam requirements/recommendations for international students: Required—TOEFL (minimum score 550 paper-based). *Expenses: Tuition:* Full-time $43,854; part-time $1827 per credit hour. *Required fees:* $50; $50 per credit hour. Tuition and fees vary according to course load and program.

Duke University, Graduate School, University Program in Molecular Cancer Biology, Durham, NC 27710. Offers PhD. *Degree requirements:* For doctorate, thesis/dissertation. *Entrance requirements:* For doctorate, GRE General Test, GRE Subject Test in biology or biochemistry, cell and molecular biology (recommended). Additional exam requirements/recommendations for international students: Required—TOEFL (minimum score 577 paper-based; 90 iBT) or IELTS (minimum score 7). Electronic applications accepted.

Emory University, Laney Graduate School, Division of Biological and Biomedical Sciences, Program in Cancer Biology, Atlanta, GA 30322. Offers PhD. *Degree requirements:* For doctorate, comprehensive exam, thesis/dissertation. *Entrance requirements:* For doctorate, GRE General Test, minimum GPA of 3.0 in science course work (recommended). Additional exam requirements/recommendations for international students: Required—TOEFL. Electronic applications accepted. *Expenses:* Contact institution. *Faculty research:* Basic and translational cancer research, molecular and cellular biology, genetics and epigenetics, signal transduction, genetic engineering and nanotechnologies.

Gerstner Sloan Kettering Graduate School of Biomedical Sciences, Program in Cancer Biology, New York, NY 10021. Offers PhD. *Faculty:* 126 full-time (25 women). *Students:* 70 full-time (28 women); includes 11 minority (1 Black or African American, non-Hispanic/Latino; 5 Asian, non-Hispanic/Latino; 5 Hispanic/Latino), 29 international. 228 applicants, 17% accepted, 14 enrolled. In 2017, 7 doctorates awarded. *Degree requirements:* For doctorate, thesis/dissertation. *Entrance requirements:* For doctorate, GRE, transcripts, three letters of recommendation. Additional exam requirements/recommendations for international students: Required—TOEFL. *Application deadline:* For fall admission, 12/1 for domestic and international students. Electronic applications accepted. *Financial support:* In 2017–18, 70 students received support. Teaching assistantships and fellowship package including stipend ($38,655), full-tuition scholarship, first-year allowance, and comprehensive medical and dental insurance available. *Faculty research:* Structural biology, computational biology, genomics, immunology, chemical biology. *Unit head:* Linda Burnley, Associate Dean, 646-888-6639, E-mail: burnleyl@sloankettering.edu. *Application contact:* Main Office, 646-888-6639, Fax: 646-422-2351, E-mail: gradstudies@sloankettering.edu.

See Display below and Close-Up on page 207.

Grand Valley State University, College of Health Professions, Medical Dosimetry Program, Allendale, MI 49401-9403. Offers MS. *Program availability:* Part-time. *Students:* 15 full-time (8 women), 2 part-time (1 woman); includes 4 minority (all Asian, non-Hispanic/Latino). Average age 28. 26 applicants, 81% accepted, 15 enrolled. In 2017, 10 master's awarded. *Degree requirements:* For master's, project or thesis. *Entrance requirements:* For master's, minimum GPA of 3.0, resume, personal statement, 2 letters of recommendation, 16 hours of volunteer or paid health care experience or 2-3 hours of job shadow. Additional exam requirements/recommendations for international students: Required—TOEFL (minimum iBT score of 80), IELTS (6.5), or Michigan English Language Assessment Battery (77). *Application deadline:* For fall admission, 3/1 for domestic students. Application fee: $30. Electronic applications accepted. *Expenses:* $657 per credit hour. *Financial support:* Fellowships available. *Unit head:* Dr. Scott Green, Director, 616-331-5752, Fax: 616-331-5632, E-mail: greensc@gvsu.edu. *Application contact:* Darlene Zwart, Student Services Coordinator, 616-331-3958, E-mail: zwartda@gvsu.edu.
Website: http://www.gvsu.edu/grad/dosimetry/

Irell & Manella Graduate School of Biological Sciences, Graduate Program, Duarte, CA 91010. Offers brain metastatic cancer (PhD); cancer and stem cell metabolism (PhD); cancer biology (PhD); cancer biology and developmental therapeutics (PhD); cell biology (PhD); chemical biology (PhD); chromosomal break repair (PhD); diabetes and pancreatic progenitor cell biology (PhD); DNA repair and cancer biology (PhD); germline epigenetic remodeling and endocrine disruptors (PhD); hematology and hematopoietic cell transplantation (PhD); hematology and immunology (PhD); inflammation and cancer (PhD); micrornas and gene regulation in cardiovascular disease (PhD); mixed chimrism for reversal of autoimmunity (PhD); molecular and cellular biology (PhD); molecular biology and genetics (PhD); nanoparticle mediated twist1 silencing in metastatic cancer (PhD); neuro-oncology and stem cell biology (PhD); neuroscience (PhD); RNA directed therapies for HIV-1 (PhD); small RNA-induced transcriptional gene activation (PhD); stem cell regulation by the microenvironment (PhD); translational oncology and pharmaceutical sciences (PhD); tumor biology (PhD). *Degree requirements:* For doctorate, comprehensive exam, thesis/dissertation, qualifying exams, two advanced courses. *Entrance requirements:* For doctorate, GRE General Test; GRE Subject Test (recommended), 2 years of course work in chemistry (general and organic); 1 year of course work each in biochemistry, general biology, and general physics; 2 semesters of course work in mathematics; significant research laboratory experience. Additional exam requirements/recommendations for international students: Required—TOEFL. Electronic applications accepted. *Faculty research:* Cancer biology, diabetes, stem cell biology, neuroscience, immunology.

See Display on page 65 and Close-Up on page 109.

McMaster University, Faculty of Health Sciences and School of Graduate Studies, Program in Medical Sciences, Genetics and Cancer Area, Hamilton, ON L8S 4M2, Canada. Offers M Sc, PhD, MD/PhD. *Degree requirements:* For master's, thesis; for doctorate, comprehensive exam, thesis/dissertation. *Entrance requirements:* For master's, honors B Sc, B+ average in related field; for doctorate, M Sc, minimum B+ average, students with proven research experience and an A average may be admitted with a B Sc degree. Additional exam requirements/recommendations for international students: Required—TOEFL (minimum score 580 paper-based; 92 iBT).

Medical University of South Carolina, College of Graduate Studies, Program in Molecular and Cellular Biology and Pathobiology, Charleston, SC 29425. Offers cancer biology (PhD); cardiovascular biology (PhD); cardiovascular imaging (PhD); cell regulation (PhD); craniofacial biology (PhD); genetics and development (PhD); marine biomedicine (PhD); DMD/PhD; MD/PhD. *Degree requirements:* For doctorate, thesis/dissertation, oral and written exams. *Entrance requirements:* For doctorate, GRE General Test, interview, minimum GPA of 3.0. Additional exam requirements/recommendations for international students: Required—TOEFL (minimum score 600 paper-based; 100 iBT). Electronic applications accepted.

Meharry Medical College, School of Graduate Studies, Program in Biomedical Sciences, Biochemistry and Cancer Biology Emphasis, Nashville, TN 37208-9989. Offers PhD, MD/PhD. *Degree requirements:* For doctorate, comprehensive exam, thesis/dissertation. *Entrance requirements:* For doctorate, GRE. *Faculty research:* Regulation of metabolism, enzymology, signal transduction, physical biochemistry.

Memorial University of Newfoundland, Faculty of Medicine and School of Graduate Studies, Graduate Programs in Medicine, Division of Biomedical Sciences, St. John's, NL A1C 5S7, Canada. Offers cancer (M Sc, PhD); cardiovascular (M Sc, PhD); immunology (M Sc, PhD); neuroscience (M Sc, PhD). *Program availability:* Part-time. *Degree requirements:* For master's, thesis; for doctorate, comprehensive exam, thesis/dissertation, oral defense of thesis. *Entrance requirements:* For master's, MD or B Sc; for doctorate, MD or M Sc. Additional exam requirements/recommendations for international students: Required—TOEFL. *Faculty research:* Neuroscience, immunology, cardiovascular, and cancer.

New York University, Graduate School of Arts and Science, Department of Biology, New York, NY 10012-1019. Offers biology (PhD); biomedical journalism (MS); cancer and molecular biology (PhD); computational biology (PhD); computers in biological research (MS); developmental genetics (PhD); general biology (MS); immunology and microbiology (PhD); molecular genetics (PhD); neurobiology (PhD); oral biology (MS); plant biology (PhD); recombinant DNA technology (MS); MS/MBA. *Program availability:* Part-time. *Students:* Average age 27. 394 applicants, 56% accepted, 77 enrolled. In 2017, 68 master's, 9 doctorates awarded. Terminal master's awarded for partial completion of doctoral program. *Degree requirements:* For master's, thesis or alternative, qualifying paper; for doctorate, comprehensive exam, thesis/dissertation. *Entrance requirements:* For master's and doctorate, GRE General Test. Additional exam requirements/recommendations for international students: Required—TOEFL. *Application deadline:* For fall admission, 12/1 priority date for domestic students, 12/1 for international students. Application fee: $100. *Expenses: Tuition:* Full-time $41,352; part-time $19,968 per year. *Required fees:* $2496; $1628 per unit. $814 per term. Tuition and fees vary according to course load and program. *Financial support:* Fellowships, research assistantships, teaching assistantships, career-related internships or fieldwork, Federal Work-Study, institutionally sponsored loans, scholarships/grants, health care benefits, and unspecified assistantships available. Financial award application deadline: 12/1; financial award applicants required to submit FAFSA. *Faculty research:* Genomics, molecular and cell biology, development and molecular genetics, molecular evolution of plants and animals. *Unit head:* Stephen Small, Chair, 212-998-8200, Fax: 212-995-4015, E-mail: biology.admissions@nyu.edu. *Application contact:* Ken Birnbaum, Director of Graduate Studies, PhD Programs, 212-998-8200, Fax: 212-995-4015, E-mail: biology.admissions@nyu.edu.
Website: http://biology.as.nyu.edu/

New York University, School of Medicine and Graduate School of Arts and Science, Sackler Institute of Graduate Biomedical Sciences, New York, NY 10016. Offers biomedical imaging and technology (PhD); biostatistics (PhD); cellular and molecular biology (PhD); developmental genetics (PhD); epidemiology (PhD); genome integrity (PhD); immunology and inflammation (PhD); microbiology (PhD); molecular biophysics (PhD); molecular oncology and tumor immunology (PhD); molecular pharmacology (PhD); neuroscience and physiology (PhD), including immunology, molecular oncology; stem cell biology (PhD); systems and computational biomedicine (PhD); MD/PhD. *Faculty:* 207 full-time (51 women). *Students:* 236 full-time (138 women), 1 part-time (0 women); includes 68 minority (13 Black or African American, non-Hispanic/Latino; 26 Asian, non-Hispanic/Latino; 28 Hispanic/Latino; 1 Native Hawaiian or other Pacific Islander, non-Hispanic/Latino), 79 international. Average age 27. 761 applicants, 18% accepted, 59 enrolled. In 2017, 35 doctorates awarded. *Degree requirements:* For doctorate, comprehensive exam, thesis/dissertation, qualifying exam; thesis defense. *Entrance requirements:* For doctorate, GRE. Additional exam requirements/recommendations for international students: Required—TOEFL, IELTS. *Application deadline:* For fall admission, 12/1 for domestic and international students. Applications are processed on a rolling basis. Application fee: $100. Electronic applications accepted. Application fee is waived when completed online. *Expenses:* Contact institution. *Financial support:* Health care benefits, tuition waivers (full), and unspecified assistantships available. *Faculty research:* Biomedical sciences. *Unit head:* Dr. Naoko Tanese, Associate Dean for Biomedical Sciences/Director, Sackler Institute, 212-263-8945, E-mail: naoko.tanese@nyumc.org. *Application contact:* Jessica Dong, Program Manager, 212-263-5648, E-mail: sackler-info@nyumc.org.
Website: https://med.nyu.edu/research/sackler-institute-graduate-biomedical-sciences/

Oregon Health & Science University, School of Medicine, Graduate Programs in Medicine, Program in Molecular and Cellular Biosciences, Cancer Biology Program, Portland, OR 97239-3098. Offers PhD. *Faculty:* 55 part-time/adjunct (17 women). *Students:* 10 full-time (5 women); includes 1 minority (Asian, non-Hispanic/Latino), 3 international. Average age 28. In 2017, 6 doctorates awarded. *Degree requirements:* For doctorate, comprehensive exam, thesis/dissertation, qualifying exam. *Entrance requirements:* For doctorate, GRE General Test (minimum scores: 158 Verbal/148 Quantitative/4.5 Analytical). *Application deadline:* For fall admission, 12/1 for domestic and international students. Application fee: $70. Electronic applications accepted. *Financial support:* Health care benefits and full-tuition and stipends (for PhD students) available. Financial award application deadline: 3/1; financial award applicants required to submit FAFSA. *Faculty research:* Signal transduction, apoptosis, carcinogenesis, genome integrity, tumor micro-environment. *Unit head:* Dr. Matthew Thayer, Program Director, E-mail: somgrad@ohsu.edu. *Application contact:* Lola Bichler, Program Coordinator, E-mail: somgrad@ohsu.edu.
Website: http://www.ohsu.edu/cancerbio

Purdue University, Graduate School, PULSe - Purdue University Life Sciences Program, West Lafayette, IN 47907. Offers biomolecular structure and biophysics (PhD); biotechnology (PhD); chemical biology (PhD); chromatin and regulation of gene expression (PhD); integrative neuroscience (PhD); integrative plant sciences (PhD); membrane biology (PhD); microbiology (PhD); molecular evolutionary and cancer biology (PhD); molecular evolutionary genetics (PhD); molecular virology (PhD). *Students:* 60 full-time (29 women); includes 6 minority (4 Hispanic/Latino; 2 Two or more races, non-Hispanic/Latino), 36 international. Average age 25. 127 applicants, 39% accepted, 25 enrolled. *Entrance requirements:* For doctorate, GRE, minimum undergraduate GPA of 3.0. Additional exam requirements/recommendations for international students: Required—TOEFL (minimum score 550 paper-based; 77 iBT). *Application deadline:* For fall admission, 1/15 priority date for domestic and international students. Applications are processed on a rolling basis. Application fee: $60 ($75 for international students). Electronic applications accepted. *Financial support:* In 2017–18, research assistantships with tuition reimbursements (averaging $22,500 per year), teaching assistantships with tuition reimbursements (averaging $22,500 per year) were awarded. *Unit head:* Dr. Jason R. Cannon, Head of the Graduate Program, 765-494-0794, E-mail: cannonjr@purdue.edu. *Application contact:* Lindsey Springer, Graduate Contact for Admissions, 765-496-9667, E-mail: lbcampbe@purdue.edu.
Website: http://www.gradschool.purdue.edu/pulse

Queen's University at Kingston, School of Graduate Studies, Faculty of Health Sciences, Department of Anatomy and Cell Biology, Kingston, ON K7L 3N6, Canada. Offers biology of reproduction (M Sc, PhD); cancer (M Sc, PhD); cardiovascular pathophysiology (M Sc, PhD); cell and molecular biology (M Sc, PhD); drug metabolism (M Sc, PhD); endocrinology (M Sc, PhD); motor control (M Sc, PhD); neural regeneration (M Sc, PhD); neurophysiology (M Sc, PhD). *Program availability:* Part-time. *Degree requirements:* For master's, thesis; for doctorate, one foreign language, comprehensive exam, thesis/dissertation. *Entrance requirements:* Additional exam requirements/recommendations for international students: Required—TOEFL. Electronic applications accepted. *Faculty research:* Human kinetics, neuroscience, reproductive biology, cardiovascular.

Rutgers University–Newark, Graduate School of Biomedical Sciences, Newark, NJ 07107. Offers biodefense (Certificate); biomedical engineering (PhD); biomedical sciences (multidisciplinary) (PhD); cellular biology, neuroscience and physiology (PhD), including neuroscience, physiology, biophysics, cardiovascular biology, molecular pharmacology, stem cell biology; infection, immunity and inflammation (PhD), including immunology, infectious disease, microbiology, oral biology; molecular biology, genetics and cancer (PhD), including biochemistry, molecular genetics, cancer biology, radiation biology, bioinformatics; neuroscience (Certificate); pharmacological sciences (Certificate); stem cell (Certificate); DMD/PhD; MD/PhD. PhD in biomedical engineering offered jointly with New Jersey Institute of Technology. *Program availability:* Part-time, evening/weekend. Terminal master's awarded for partial completion of doctoral program. *Degree requirements:* For doctorate, thesis/dissertation, qualifying exam. *Entrance requirements:* For doctorate, GRE General Test. Additional exam requirements/recommendations for international students: Required—TOEFL. Electronic applications accepted.

Rutgers University–New Brunswick, Graduate School-New Brunswick, Program in Endocrinology and Animal Biosciences, Piscataway, NJ 08854-8097. Offers MS, PhD. Terminal master's awarded for partial completion of doctoral program. *Degree requirements:* For master's, thesis; for doctorate, comprehensive exam, thesis/dissertation. *Entrance requirements:* For master's and doctorate, GRE General Test. Additional exam requirements/recommendations for international students: Required—TOEFL. Electronic applications accepted. *Faculty research:* Comparative and behavioral endocrinology, epigenetic regulation of the endocrine system, exercise physiology and immunology, fetal and neonatal developmental programming, mammary gland biology and breast cancer, neuroendocrinology and alcohol studies, reproductive and developmental toxicology.

Saint Francis University, Cancer Care Program, Loretto, PA 15940-0600. Offers MS. *Faculty:* 10 full-time (5 women). *Students:* 10 full-time (2 women), 1 (woman) part-time; includes 1 minority (Asian, non-Hispanic/Latino). Average age 23. *Application deadline:* Applications are processed on a rolling basis. Application fee: $35. Electronic applications accepted. *Expenses:* Contact institution. *Financial support:* Applicants required to submit FAFSA. *Unit head:* Dr. Stephen LoRusso, Coordinator, 814-472-3853, E-mail: slorusso@francis.edu. *Application contact:* Dr. Peter Raymond Skoner, Associate Provost, 814-472-3085, Fax: 814-472-3365, E-mail: pskoner@francis.edu.
Website: https://www.francis.edu/master-of-cancer-care/

Thomas Jefferson University, Jefferson College of Biomedical Sciences, PhD Program in Genetics, Genomics and Cancer Biology, Philadelphia, PA 19107. Offers PhD. *Faculty:* 41 full-time (12 women). *Students:* 16 full-time (9 women); includes 1 minority (Hispanic/Latino), 2 international. In 2017, 5 doctorates awarded. *Degree requirements:* For doctorate, comprehensive exam, thesis/dissertation. *Entrance requirements:* For doctorate, GRE General Test, minimum GPA of 3.2. Additional exam requirements/recommendations for international students: Required—TOEFL, IELTS (minimum score 7). *Application deadline:* For fall admission, 12/1 priority date for domestic and international students. Applications are processed on a rolling basis. Application fee: $60. Electronic applications accepted. *Financial support:* In 2017–18, 16 students received support, including 16 fellowships with full tuition reimbursements available (averaging $62,653 per year); Federal Work-Study, institutionally sponsored loans, scholarships/grants, traineeships, health care benefits, and stipends also available. Financial award application deadline: 5/1; financial award applicants required to submit FAFSA. *Faculty research:* Functional genomics, cancer susceptibility, cell cycle, regulation oncogenes and tumor suppressor genes, genetics of neoplastic disease. *Unit head:* Dr. Lucia Languino, Program Director, 215-503-3442, E-mail: lucia.languino@jefferson.edu. *Application contact:* Marc E. Stearns, Senior Associate Director of Admissions, 215-503-0155, Fax: 215-503-3433, E-mail: jgsbs-info@jefferson.edu.
Website: http://www.jefferson.edu/university/biomedical-sciences/degrees-programs/phd-programs/genetics.html

Tufts University, Sackler School of Graduate Biomedical Sciences, Cell, Molecular, and Developmental Biology Program, Medford, MA 02155. Offers cancer biology (PhD); developmental and regenerative biology (PhD); molecular and cellular medicine (PhD); structural and chemical biology (PhD). Terminal master's awarded for partial completion of doctoral program. *Degree requirements:* For doctorate, comprehensive exam, thesis/dissertation. *Entrance requirements:* For doctorate, GRE General Test, 3 letters of reference, resume, personal statement. Electronic applications accepted. *Expenses: Tuition:* Full-time $49,892. *Required fees:* $874. Full-time tuition and fees vary according to degree level, program and student level. Part-time tuition and fees vary according to course load. *Faculty research:* Reproduction and hormone action, control of gene expression, cell-matrix and cell-cell interactions, growth control and tumorigenesis, cytoskeleton and contractile proteins.

Université Laval, Faculty of Medicine, Post-Professional Programs in Medical Studies, Québec, QC G1K 7P4, Canada. Offers anatomy–pathology (DESS); anesthesiology (DESS); cardiology (DESS); care of older people (Diploma); clinical research (DESS); community health (DESS); dermatology (DESS); diagnostic radiology (DESS); emergency medicine (Diploma); family medicine (DESS); general surgery (DESS); geriatrics (DESS); hematology (DESS); internal medicine (DESS); maternal and fetal medicine (Diploma); medical biochemistry (DESS); medical microbiology and infectious diseases (DESS); medical oncology (DESS); nephrology (DESS); neurology (DESS); neurosurgery (DESS);

obstetrics and gynecology (DESS); ophthalmology (DESS); orthopedic surgery (DESS); oto-rhino-laryngology (DESS); palliative medicine (Diploma); pediatrics (DESS); plastic surgery (DESS); psychiatry (DESS); pulmonary medicine (DESS); radiology–oncology (DESS); thoracic surgery (DESS); urology (DESS). *Degree requirements:* For other advanced degree, comprehensive exam. *Entrance requirements:* For degree, knowledge of French. Electronic applications accepted.

University at Buffalo, the State University of New York, Graduate School, Graduate Programs in Cancer Research and Biomedical Sciences at Roswell Park Cancer Institute, Interdisciplinary Master of Science Program at Roswell Park Cancer Institute, Buffalo, NY 14260. Offers MS. *Program availability:* Part-time. *Faculty:* 118 full-time (35 women). *Students:* 5 full-time (3 women), 5 international. 15 applicants, 47% accepted, 5 enrolled. In 2017, 17 master's awarded. *Degree requirements:* For master's, thesis, oral defense of thesis based on research project. *Entrance requirements:* For master's, GRE General Test. Additional exam requirements/recommendations for international students: Required—TOEFL (minimum score 79 iBT). *Application deadline:* For fall admission, 3/1 priority date for domestic and international students. Application fee: $75. Electronic applications accepted. *Faculty research:* Biochemistry, oncology, pathology, biophysics, pharmacology, molecular biology, cellular biology, genetics, bioinformatics, immunology, therapeutic development, epidemiology. *Application contact:* Dr. Norman J. Karin, Associate Dean, 716-845-2339, Fax: 716-845-8178, E-mail: norman.karin@roswellpark.edu.
Website: http://www.roswellpark.edu/education/interdisciplinary-masters

The University of Alabama at Birmingham, Joint Health Sciences, Cancer Biology Theme, Birmingham, AL 35294. Offers PhD. *Faculty:* 370. *Students:* 42 full-time (28 women); includes 20 minority (5 Black or African American, non-Hispanic/Latino; 13 Asian, non-Hispanic/Latino; 2 Hispanic/Latino). Average age 27. 43 applicants, 23% accepted, 5 enrolled. In 2017, 6 doctorates awarded. *Degree requirements:* For doctorate, comprehensive exam, thesis/dissertation. *Entrance requirements:* For doctorate, personal statement, resume or curriculum vitae, letters of recommendation, research experience, interview. Additional exam requirements/recommendations for international students: Required—TOEFL (minimum score 80 iBT), IELTS (minimum score 6.5). *Application deadline:* For fall admission, 12/31 for domestic and international students. Applications are processed on a rolling basis. Electronic applications accepted. *Financial support:* In 2017–18, fellowships with full tuition reimbursements (averaging $29,000 per year), research assistantships with full tuition reimbursements (averaging $30,000 per year) were awarded; health care benefits also available. *Unit head:* Dr. Lalita Shevde-Samant, Theme Director, 205-975-6261, E-mail: lsamant@uab.edu. *Application contact:* Alyssa Zasada, Admissions Manager for Graduate Biomedical Sciences, 205-934-3857, E-mail: grad-gbs@uab.edu.
Website: http://www.uab.edu/gbs/home/themes/cancer

University of Alberta, Faculty of Medicine and Dentistry and Faculty of Graduate Studies and Research, Graduate Programs in Medicine, Department of Oncology, Edmonton, AB T6G 2E1, Canada. Offers M Sc, PhD. Terminal master's awarded for partial completion of doctoral program. *Degree requirements:* For master's, thesis; for doctorate, thesis/dissertation. *Entrance requirements:* For master's and doctorate, minimum GPA of 7.0 on a 9.0 scale, B SC. Additional exam requirements/recommendations for international students: Required—TOEFL (minimum score 600 paper-based). Electronic applications accepted. *Faculty research:* Experimental oncology, radiation oncology, medical physics, medical oncology.

The University of Arizona, Graduate Interdisciplinary Programs, Graduate Interdisciplinary Program in Cancer Biology, Tucson, AZ 85721. Offers PhD. *Degree requirements:* For doctorate, comprehensive exam, thesis/dissertation. *Entrance requirements:* For doctorate, GRE General Test, 3 letters of recommendation. Additional exam requirements/recommendations for international students: Required—TOEFL (minimum score 550 paper-based; 79 iBT). Electronic applications accepted. *Faculty research:* Differential gene expression, DNA-protein cross linking, cell growth regulation steroid, receptor proteins.

University of Calgary, Cumming School of Medicine and Faculty of Graduate Studies, Medical Science Graduate Program, Calgary, AB T2N 1N4, Canada. Offers cancer biology (M Sc, PhD); critical care medicine (M Sc, PhD); joint injury and arthritis (M Sc, PhD); molecular and medical genetics (M Sc, PhD); mountain medicine and high altitude physiology (M Sc, PhD); pathologists' assistant (M Sc, PhD). *Degree requirements:* For master's, thesis; for doctorate, thesis/dissertation, candidacy exam. *Entrance requirements:* For master's, minimum undergraduate GPA of 3.2; for doctorate, minimum graduate GPA of 3.2. Additional exam requirements/recommendations for international students: Required—TOEFL (minimum score 600 paper-based). Electronic applications accepted. *Faculty research:* Cancer biology, immunology, joint injury and arthritis, medical education, population genomics.

University of Chicago, Division of the Biological Sciences, Committee on Cancer Biology, Chicago, IL 60637. Offers PhD. *Students:* 38 full-time (21 women); includes 8 minority (6 Asian, non-Hispanic/Latino; 1 Hispanic/Latino; 1 Two or more races, non-Hispanic/Latino), 12 international. Average age 26. 144 applicants, 9% accepted, 6 enrolled. In 2017, 3 doctorates awarded. *Degree requirements:* For doctorate, thesis/dissertation, ethics class, 2 teaching assistantships, preliminary exam. *Entrance requirements:* For doctorate, GRE General Test, transcripts, statement of purpose, 3 letters of recommendation. Additional exam requirements/recommendations for international students: Required—TOEFL (minimum score 600 paper-based; 104 iBT), IELTS (minimum score 7). *Application deadline:* For fall admission, 12/1 for domestic and international students. Application fee: $90. Electronic applications accepted. *Financial support:* In 2017–18, 25 students received support, including research assistantships with full tuition reimbursements available (averaging $31,000 per year); fellowships, institutionally sponsored loans, and traineeships also available. Financial award application deadline: 12/1. *Faculty research:* Cancer genetics, apoptosis, signal transduction, tumor biology, cell cycle regulation. *Total annual research expenditures:* $58 million. *Unit head:* Kay Macleod, Chair, 773-834-8309, E-mail: kmacleod@uchicago.edu. *Application contact:* Administrative Director, 773-834-3899, E-mail: biomed@bsd.uchicago.edu.
Website: http://biomedsciences.uchicago.edu/page/committee-cancer-biology

University of Cincinnati, Graduate School, College of Medicine, Graduate Programs in Biomedical Sciences, Cancer and Cell Biology Graduate Program, Cincinnati, OH 45267. Offers PhD. *Faculty:* 50 full-time (17 women). *Students:* 28 full-time (17 women); includes 7 minority (3 Black or African American, non-Hispanic/Latino; 3 Hispanic/Latino; 1 Native Hawaiian or other Pacific Islander, non-Hispanic/Latino), 8 international. Average age 26. 50 applicants, 12% accepted, 4 enrolled. In 2017, 4 doctorates awarded. *Degree requirements:* For doctorate, thesis/dissertation, qualifying exam. *Entrance requirements:* For doctorate, GRE or MCAT, baccalaureate degree; strong background in biology, chemistry, and/or physics and mathematics; minimum overall GPA of 3.0; curriculum vitae or resume; transcripts; essay; letters of recommendation. Additional exam requirements/recommendations for international students: Required—TOEFL (minimum score 600 paper-based; 100 iBT), IELTS (minimum score 7), PTE (minimum score 68). *Application deadline:* For fall admission, 1/14 priority date for domestic and international students. Applications are processed on a rolling basis. Application fee: $65 ($70 for international students). Electronic applications accepted. *Expenses:* Tuition, stipend, and student health insurance covered by the program. *Financial support:* In 2017–18, 7 fellowships with full tuition reimbursements (averaging $23,000 per year), 28 research assistantships with full tuition reimbursements (averaging $29,000 per year) were awarded; health care benefits, unspecified assistantships, and stipends also available. Support available to part-time students. Financial award application deadline: 4/15. *Faculty research:* Cancer biology, cell and molecular biology, breast cancer, pancreatic cancer, drug discovery. *Unit head:* Dr. Susan Waltz, Program Director, 513-558-8675, E-mail: susan.waltz@uc.edu. *Application contact:* Emily Spinks, Program Manager, 513-558-7379, E-mail: cellcoordinator@uc.edu.
Website: https://www.med.uc.edu/cancerbiology/graduate

University of Colorado Denver, School of Medicine, Program in Cancer Biology, Aurora, CO 80045. Offers PhD. In 2017, 7 doctorates awarded. *Degree requirements:* For doctorate, comprehensive exam, thesis/dissertation, 3 laboratory rotations. *Entrance requirements:* For doctorate, GRE General Test, interview, minimum undergraduate GPA of 3.0. Additional exam requirements/recommendations for international students: Required—TOEFL (minimum score 550 paper-based; 80 iBT). Application fee: $0. *Faculty research:* Signal transduction by tyrosine kinases, estrogen and progesterone receptors in breast cancer, mechanism of mitochondrial DNA replication in the mammalian cell. *Unit head:* Dr. Mary Reyland, Director, Cancer Biology Program, 303-724-4572, E-mail: mary.reyland@ucdenver.edu. *Application contact:* Sabrena Heilman, Program Administrator, 303-724-3245, E-mail: sabrena.heilman@ucdenver.edu.
Website: http://www.ucdenver.edu/academics/colleges/Graduate-School/academic-programs/cancerbiology/Pages/cancerbiologyprogram.aspx

University of Delaware, College of Arts and Sciences, Department of Biological Sciences, Newark, DE 19716. Offers biotechnology (MS); cancer biology (MS, PhD); cell and extracellular matrix biology (MS, PhD); cell and systems physiology (MS, PhD); developmental biology (MS, PhD); ecology and evolution (MS, PhD); microbiology (MS, PhD); molecular biology and genetics (MS, PhD). Terminal master's awarded for partial completion of doctoral program. *Degree requirements:* For master's, thesis, preliminary exam; for doctorate, comprehensive exam, thesis/dissertation, preliminary exam. *Entrance requirements:* For master's and doctorate, GRE General Test. Additional exam requirements/recommendations for international students: Required—TOEFL (minimum score 600 paper-based); Recommended—TWE. Electronic applications accepted. *Faculty research:* Microorganisms, bone, cancer metastasis, developmental biology, cell biology, DNA.

The University of Kansas, University of Kansas Medical Center, School of Medicine, Graduate Programs in Cancer Biology, Kansas City, KS 66160. Offers MS, PhD. *Faculty:* 8. *Students:* 8 full-time (4 women), 1 part-time (0 women), 1 international. Average age 27. 10 applicants, 40% accepted. *Degree requirements:* For master's, thesis; for doctorate, comprehensive exam, thesis/dissertation. *Entrance requirements:* For master's and doctorate, GRE. Additional exam requirements/recommendations for international students: Required—TOEFL or IELTS. *Application deadline:* For fall admission, 12/1 priority date for domestic and international students. Applications are processed on a rolling basis. Application fee: $60. Electronic applications accepted. *Financial support:* In 2017–18, 2 fellowships with full tuition reimbursements (averaging $28,000 per year), 2 research assistantships with full tuition reimbursements (averaging $24,000 per year) were awarded. Financial award application deadline: 3/1; financial award applicants required to submit FAFSA. *Faculty research:* Cancer genetics, mechanisms of metastasis, tumor microenvironment, GI cancers (colon, pancreatic, liver), sarcomas, cancer chemoprevention, chemotherapy, radiotherapy, drug resistance, breast cancer, tumor immunology. *Total annual research expenditures:* $1.7 million. *Unit head:* Dr. Danny R. Welch, Chair, 913-945-7739.
Website: http://www.kumc.edu/school-of-medicine/cancer-biology.html

The University of Manchester, School of Biological Sciences, Manchester, United Kingdom. Offers adaptive organismal biology (M Phil, PhD); animal biology (M Phil, PhD); biochemistry (M Phil, PhD); bioinformatics (M Phil, PhD); biomolecular sciences (M Phil, PhD); biotechnology (M Phil, PhD); cell biology (M Phil, PhD); cell matrix research (M Phil, PhD); channels and transporters (M Phil, PhD); developmental biology (M Phil, PhD); environmental biology (M Phil, PhD); evolutionary biology (M Phil, PhD); gene expression (M Phil, PhD); genetics (M Phil, PhD); history of science, technology and medicine (M Phil, PhD); immunology (M Phil, PhD); integrative neurobiology and behavior (M Phil, PhD); membrane trafficking (M Phil, PhD); microbiology (M Phil, PhD); molecular and cellular neuroscience (M Phil, PhD); molecular biology (M Phil, PhD); molecular cancer studies (M Phil, PhD); neuroscience (M Phil, PhD); ophthalmology (M Phil, PhD); optometry (M Phil, PhD); organelle function (M Phil, PhD); pharmacology (M Phil, PhD); physiology (M Phil, PhD); plant sciences (M Phil, PhD); stem cell research (M Phil, PhD); structural biology (M Phil, PhD); systems neuroscience (M Phil, PhD); toxicology (M Phil, PhD).

The University of Manchester, School of Dentistry, Manchester, United Kingdom. Offers basic dental sciences (cancer studies) (M Phil, PhD); basic dental sciences (molecular genetics) (M Phil, PhD); basic dental sciences (stem cell biology) (M Phil, PhD); biomaterials sciences and dental technology (M Phil, PhD); dental public health/community dentistry (M Phil, PhD); dental science (clinical) (PhD); endodontology (M Phil, PhD); fixed and removable prosthodontics (M Phil, PhD); operative dentistry (M Phil, PhD); oral and maxillofacial surgery (M Phil, PhD); oral radiology (M Phil, PhD); orthodontics (M Phil, PhD); restorative dentistry (M Phil, PhD).

University of Manitoba, Faculty of Graduate Studies, College of Nursing, Winnipeg, MB R3T 2N2, Canada. Offers cancer nursing (MN); nursing (MN). *Degree requirements:* For master's, thesis.

University of Maryland, Baltimore, Graduate School, Graduate Program in Life Sciences, Program in Molecular Medicine, Baltimore, MD 21201. Offers cancer biology (PhD); cell and molecular physiology (PhD); human genetics and genomic medicine (PhD); molecular toxicology and pharmacology (PhD); MD/PhD. *Students:* 62 full-time (35 women), 2 part-time (0 women); includes 21 minority (7 Black or African American, non-Hispanic/Latino; 8 Asian, non-Hispanic/Latino; 4 Hispanic/Latino; 2 Two or more races, non-Hispanic/Latino), 4 international. Average age 27. 89 applicants, 30% accepted, 3 enrolled. In 2017, 13 doctorates awarded. *Degree requirements:* For doctorate, comprehensive exam, thesis/dissertation. *Entrance requirements:* For doctorate, GRE, minimum GPA of 3.0, curriculum vitae, essay, 3 letters of recommendation. Additional exam requirements/recommendations for international students: Required—TOEFL (minimum score 80 iBT); Recommended—IELTS (minimum score 7). *Application deadline:* For fall admission, 12/1 priority date for domestic students, 1/15 for international students. Application fee: $75. Electronic applications accepted. *Expenses:* Tuition, state resident: full-time $13,990; part-time $661 per credit. Tuition, nonresident: full-time $30,484; part-time $1310 per credit. *Required fees:* $1894; $94 per credit. $415 per semester. Part-time tuition and fees vary according to course load, degree level and program. *Financial support:* In 2017–18, research assistantships with partial tuition reimbursements (averaging $26,000 per year) were awarded; fellowships and health care benefits also available. Financial award application deadline: 3/1; financial award applicants required to submit FAFSA. *Unit head:* Dr. Toni Antalis, Director, 410-706-8222, E-mail: tantalis@som.umaryland.edu. *Application contact:* Marcina Garner, Program Coordinator, 410-706-6044, Fax: 410-706-6040, E-mail: mgarner@som.umaryland.edu.
Website: http://molecularmedicine.umaryland.edu

University of Massachusetts Medical School, Graduate School of Biomedical Sciences, Worcester, MA 01655-0115. Offers biomedical sciences (PhD), including biochemistry and molecular pharmacology, bioinformatics and computational biology, cancer biology, immunology and microbiology, interdisciplinary, neuroscience, translational science; biomedical sciences (millennium program) (PhD); clinical and population health research (PhD); clinical investigation (MS). *Faculty:* 1,316 full-time (526 women), 357 part-time/adjunct (229 women). *Students:* 347 full-time (180 women); includes 61 minority (10 Black or African American, non-Hispanic/Latino; 1 American Indian or Alaska Native, non-Hispanic/Latino; 35 Asian, non-Hispanic/Latino; 15 Hispanic/Latino), 130 international. Average age 29. 608 applicants, 28% accepted, 54 enrolled. In 2017, 6 master's, 51 doctorates awarded. Terminal master's awarded for partial completion of doctoral program. *Degree requirements:* For master's, comprehensive exam, thesis; for doctorate, comprehensive exam, thesis/dissertation. *Entrance requirements:* For master's, MD, PhD, DVM, or PharmD; for doctorate, GRE General Test, bachelor's degree. Additional exam requirements/recommendations for international students: Required—TOEFL (minimum score 90 iBT) or IELTS (minimum score 7.0). *Application deadline:* For fall admission, 12/15 for domestic and international students. Applications are processed on a rolling basis. Application fee: $80. Electronic applications accepted. Application fee is waived when completed online. *Expenses:* $14,883 in-state tuition and mandatory fees; $31,486 out-of-state. *Financial support:* In 2017–18, 15 fellowships with partial tuition reimbursements (averaging $29,000 per year), 296 research assistantships with full tuition reimbursements (averaging $31,212 per year) were awarded; institutionally sponsored loans and scholarships/grants also available. Financial award application deadline: 5/15. *Faculty research:* RNA biology, molecular/cell/developmental/metabolic biology, bioinformatics and computational biology, clinical/translational research, infectious disease and immunology. *Total annual research expenditures:* $279 million. *Unit head:* Dr. Mary Ellen Lane, Dean, 508-856-4018, E-mail: maryellen.lane@umassmed.edu. *Application contact:* Dr. Kendall Knight, Assistant Vice Provost for Admissions, 508-856-5628, Fax: 508-856-3659, E-mail: kendall.knight@umassmed.edu.
Website: http://www.umassmed.edu/gsbs/

University of Miami, Graduate School, Miller School of Medicine, Program in Cancer Biology, Coral Gables, FL 33124. Offers PhD, MD/PhD.

University of Michigan, Rackham Graduate School, Program in Biomedical Sciences (PIBS), Doctoral Program in Cancer Biology, Ann Arbor, MI 48109. Offers PhD. *Faculty:* 40 full-time (11 women). *Students:* 16 full-time (10 women); includes 8 minority (1 American Indian or Alaska Native, non-Hispanic/Latino; 3 Asian, non-Hispanic/Latino; 3 Hispanic/Latino; 1 Two or more races, non-Hispanic/Latino). Average age 27. 128 applicants, 9% accepted, 6 enrolled. In 2017, 3 doctorates awarded. *Degree requirements:* For doctorate, thesis/dissertation, preliminary examination, oral defense of dissertation. *Entrance requirements:* For doctorate, GRE General Test, three letters of recommendation, research experience, personal and research statements. Additional exam requirements/recommendations for international students: Required—TOEFL (minimum score 84 iBT). *Application deadline:* For fall admission, 12/1 for domestic students. Application fee: $75. Electronic applications accepted. *Expenses:* $45,576 per year. *Financial support:* In 2017–18, 16 students received support, including 8 fellowships with full tuition reimbursements available (averaging $30,600 per year), 8 research assistantships with full tuition reimbursements available (averaging $30,600 per year); scholarships/grants, health care benefits, tuition waivers (full), and unspecified assistantships also available. Financial award application deadline: 12/1. *Faculty research:* Tumor immunology, viral oncogenesis, cell biology, genetics, epidemiology, pathology, bioinformatics, cancer biology, cancer genetics, cancer immunology and hematopoiesis, developmental therapeutics, translational and clinical research, cancer epidemiology and prevention. *Total annual research expenditures:* $1.6 million. *Unit head:* Dr. Elizabeth Lawlor, Professor of Pediatric Oncology/Associate Director for Education and Training, UM Comprehensive Cancer Center/Director, Cancer Biology Program, 734-615-4814, Fax: 734-764-9017, E-mail: elawlor@umich.edu. *Application contact:* Michelle S. Melis, Director of Student Life, Programs in Biomedical Sciences (PIBS), 734-615-6538, Fax: 734-647-7022, E-mail: msmtegan@umich.edu.
Website: http://cancerbio.medicine.umich.edu/

University of Michigan, Rackham Graduate School, Program in Chemical Biology, Ann Arbor, MI 48109. Offers cancer chemical biology (MS); chemical biology (PhD). *Program availability:* Part-time. *Faculty:* 57 full-time (19 women). *Students:* 70 full-time (29 women), 4 part-time (3 women); includes 23 minority (9 Black or African American, non-Hispanic/Latino; 8 Asian, non-Hispanic/Latino; 6 Hispanic/Latino), 12 international. 115 applicants, 57% accepted, 29 enrolled. In 2017, 16 master's, 11 doctorates awarded. *Degree requirements:* For doctorate, thesis/dissertation. *Entrance requirements:* Additional exam requirements/recommendations for international students: Required—TOEFL (minimum score 600 paper-based; 102 iBT). *Application deadline:* For fall admission, 12/15 priority date for domestic and international students. Applications are processed on a rolling basis. Application fee: $75 ($90 for international students). Electronic applications accepted. *Expenses:* Tuition, state resident: full-time $22,368; part-time $1201 per credit hour. Tuition, nonresident: full-time $45,156; part-time $2467 per credit hour. *Required fees:* $376 per term. Tuition and fees vary according to course load, degree level and program. *Financial support:* In 2017–18, 60 students received support, including fellowships with full tuition reimbursements available (averaging $30,600 per year), research assistantships with full tuition reimbursements available (averaging $30,600 per year); career-related internships or fieldwork, scholarships/grants, traineeships, health care benefits, and unspecified assistantships also available. *Faculty research:* Chemical genetics, structural enzymology, signal transduction, biological catalysis, biomolecular structure, function and recognition. *Unit head:* Prof. Anna Mapp, Program Director, 734-763-7175, Fax: 734-615-1252, E-mail: chemicalbiology@umich.edu. *Application contact:* Admissions Office, 734-764-8129, E-mail: rackadmis@umich.edu.
Website: http://www.chembio.umich.edu/

University of Minnesota, Twin Cities Campus, Graduate School, PhD Program in Microbiology, Immunology and Cancer Biology, Minneapolis, MN 55455-0213. Offers PhD. *Degree requirements:* For doctorate, thesis/dissertation. *Entrance requirements:* For doctorate, GRE General Test. Additional exam requirements/recommendations for international students: Required—TOEFL (minimum score 600 paper-based). Electronic applications accepted. *Faculty research:* Virology, microbiology, cancer biology, immunology.

University of Nebraska Medical Center, Interdisciplinary Graduate Program in Biomedical Sciences, Cancer Research Doctoral Program, Omaha, NE 68198-6805. Offers PhD. *Faculty:* 71 full-time (20 women). *Students:* 30 full-time (17 women); includes 3 minority (1 Black or African American, non-Hispanic/Latino; 2 Asian, non-Hispanic/Latino), 6 international. Average age 27. 22 applicants, 14% accepted, 3 enrolled. In 2017, 8 doctorates awarded. Terminal master's awarded for partial completion of doctoral program. *Degree requirements:* For doctorate, comprehensive exam, thesis/dissertation. *Entrance requirements:* For doctorate, GRE, 3 letters of reference; course work in chemistry, biology, physics and mathematics. Additional exam requirements/recommendations for international students: Required—TOEFL (minimum score 550 paper-based; 95 iBT). *Application deadline:* For fall admission, 6/1 for domestic students, 4/1 for international students; for spring admission, 11/1 for domestic students, 10/1 for international students; for summer admission, 4/1 for domestic students, 2/1 for international students. Applications are processed on a rolling basis. Application fee: $60. Electronic applications accepted. *Expenses:* Tuition, state resident: full-time $8451; part-time $4225 per semester. Tuition, nonresident: full-time $24,219; part-time $11,295 per semester. *Required fees:* $589; $117 per term. *Financial support:* In 2017–18, 30 students received support, including 11 fellowships with full tuition reimbursements available (averaging $23,400 per year), 22 research assistantships with full tuition reimbursements available (averaging $26,500 per year); unspecified assistantships also available. *Faculty research:* Cancer genetics, cancer development and metastasis, cell signaling, tumor immunology, molecular therapies for cancer. *Unit head:* Dr. Joyce Solheim, Graduate Committee Chair, 402-559-4539, Fax: 402-559-8270, E-mail: jsolheim@unmc.edu. *Application contact:* Misty Pocwierz-Gaines, Cancer Research Doctoral Program Coordinator, 402-559-4092, E-mail: misty.pocwierz@unmc.edu.
Website: http://www.unmc.edu/eppley/education/crgp.html

University of North Texas Health Science Center at Fort Worth, Graduate School of Biomedical Sciences, Fort Worth, TX 76107-2699. Offers biochemistry and cancer biology (MS, PhD); biotechnology (MS); cell biology, immunology and microbiology (MS, PhD); clinical research management (MS); forensic genetics (MS); genetics (MS, PhD); integrative physiology (MS, PhD); medical sciences (MS); pharmaceutical sciences and pharmacotherapy (MS, PhD); pharmacology and neuroscience (MS, PhD); structural anatomy and rehabilitation sciences (MS, PhD); DO/MS; DO/PhD. Terminal master's awarded for partial completion of doctoral program. *Degree requirements:* For master's, thesis; for doctorate, thesis/dissertation. *Entrance requirements:* For master's and doctorate, GRE General Test. Additional exam requirements/recommendations for international students: Required—TOEFL. *Expenses:* Contact institution. *Faculty research:* Alzheimer's disease, aging, eye diseases, cancer, cardiovascular disease.

University of Pennsylvania, Perelman School of Medicine, Biomedical Graduate Studies, Graduate Group in Cell and Molecular Biology, Philadelphia, PA 19104. Offers cancer biology (PhD); cell biology, physiology, and metabolism (PhD); developmental stem cell regenerative biology (PhD); gene therapy and vaccines (PhD); genetics and gene regulation (PhD); microbiology, virology, and parasitology (PhD); MD/PhD; VMD/PhD. *Faculty:* 363. *Students:* 343 full-time (197 women); includes 114 minority (7 Black or African American, non-Hispanic/Latino; 51 Asian, non-Hispanic/Latino; 41 Hispanic/Latino; 15 Two or more races, non-Hispanic/Latino), 50 international. 588 applicants, 22% accepted, 61 enrolled. In 2017, 61 doctorates awarded. *Degree requirements:* For doctorate, thesis/dissertation. *Entrance requirements:* For doctorate, GRE General Test. Additional exam requirements/recommendations for international students: Required—TOEFL. *Application deadline:* For fall admission, 12/1 priority date for domestic and international students. Applications are processed on a rolling basis. Application fee: $80. Electronic applications accepted. *Financial support:* In 2017–18, 339 students received support. Fellowships, research assistantships, teaching assistantships, and tuition waivers available. *Unit head:* Dr. Daniel Kessler, Graduate Group Chair, 215-898-1478. *Application contact:* Meagan Schofer, Coordinator, 215-898-1478.
Website: http://www.med.upenn.edu/camb/

University of Regina, Faculty of Graduate Studies and Research, Faculty of Science, Department of Chemistry and Biochemistry, Regina, SK S4S 0A2, Canada. Offers biophysics of biological interfaces (M Sc, PhD); computational chemistry (M Sc, PhD); environmental analytical chemistry (M Sc, PhD); enzymology/chemical biology (M Sc, PhD); inorganic/organometallic chemistry (M Sc, PhD); signal transduction and mechanisms of cancer cell regulation (M Sc, PhD); supramolecular organic photochemistry and photophysics (M Sc, PhD); synthetic organic chemistry (M Sc, PhD). *Faculty:* 11 full-time (3 women), 4 part-time/adjunct (0 women). *Students:* 14 full-time (7 women), 3 part-time (0 women). 38 applicants, 11% accepted. In 2017, 1 doctorate awarded. *Degree requirements:* For master's, thesis; for doctorate, thesis/dissertation. *Entrance requirements:* Additional exam requirements/recommendations for international students: Required—TOEFL (minimum score 580 paper-based; 80 iBT), IELTS (minimum score 6.5), PTE (minimum score 59). *Application deadline:* Applications are processed on a rolling basis. Application fee: $100. Electronic applications accepted. *Expenses:* CAD$10,681 per year (for M Sc); CAD$9,930 per year (for PhD). *Financial support:* In 2017–18, fellowships (averaging $6,444 per year), teaching assistantships (averaging $2,562 per year) were awarded; research assistantships and scholarships/grants also available. Financial award application deadline: 6/15. *Faculty research:* Asymmetric synthesis and methodology, theoretical and computational chemistry, biophysical biochemistry, analytical and environmental chemistry, chemical biology. *Unit head:* Dr. Renata Raina-Fulton, Department Head, 306-585-4012, Fax: 306-337-2409, E-mail: renata.raina@uregina.ca. *Application contact:* Dr. Brian Sterenberg, Graduate Program Coordinator, 306-585-4106, Fax: 306-337-2409, E-mail: brian.sterenberg@uregina.ca.
Website: http://www.uregina.ca/science/chem-biochem/

University of Southern California, Keck School of Medicine, Program in Cancer Biology and Genomics, Los Angeles, CA 90033. Offers PhD. *Faculty:* 43 full-time (10 women). *Students:* 22 full-time (15 women); includes 7 minority (4 Asian, non-Hispanic/Latino; 2 Hispanic/Latino; 1 Two or more races, non-Hispanic/Latino), 10 international. Average age 28. 7 applicants, 100% accepted, 7 enrolled. *Degree requirements:* For doctorate, comprehensive exam, thesis/dissertation. *Entrance requirements:* For doctorate, GRE, minimum GPA of 3.0. Additional exam requirements/recommendations for international students: Required—TOEFL (minimum score 600 paper-based; 100 iBT), IELTS (minimum score 7), PTE. *Application deadline:* For fall admission, 12/1 priority date for domestic and international students. Application fee: $90. Electronic applications accepted. *Financial support:* In 2017–18, 22 students received support, including 3 fellowships with full tuition reimbursements available (averaging $33,000 per year), 7 research assistantships with full tuition reimbursements available (averaging $33,000 per year); institutionally sponsored loans, scholarships/grants, traineeships, health care benefits, and unspecified assistantships also available. Financial award application deadline: 4/15; financial award applicants required to submit CSS PROFILE or FAFSA. *Unit head:* Dr. Baruch Frenkel, Director, 323-442-1475, Fax: 323-442-1199, E-mail: frenkel@med.usc.edu. *Application contact:* Dr. Joyce Perez, Manager of Student Programs, 323-442-1645, Fax: 323-442-1199, E-mail: jpperez@med.usc.edu.
Website: http://pibbs.usc.edu/research-and-programs/phd-programs/

University of South Florida, College of Arts and Sciences, Department of Cell Biology, Microbiology, and Molecular Biology, Tampa, FL 33620-9951. Offers biology (MS), including cell biology, microbiology and molecular biology; cancer biology (PhD); cancer chemical biology (PhD); cancer immunology and immunotherapy (PhD); cell and molecular biology (PhD); microbiology (MS). *Faculty:* 19 full-time (6 women). *Students:* 81 full-time (55 women), 4 part-time (2 women); includes 12 minority (1 Black or African American, non-Hispanic/Latino; 2 Asian, non-Hispanic/Latino; 5 Hispanic/Latino; 4 Two or more races, non-Hispanic/Latino), 29 international. Average age 27. 159 applicants, 18% accepted, 23 enrolled. In 2017, 21 master's, 10 doctorates awarded. *Degree requirements:* For master's, thesis or alternative; for doctorate, comprehensive exam, thesis/dissertation. *Entrance requirements:* For master's and doctorate, GRE General

Test, minimum GPA of 3.0, extensive background in biology or chemistry. Additional exam requirements/recommendations for international students: Required—TOEFL (minimum score 570 paper-based; 79 iBT) or IELTS (minimum score 6.5). *Application deadline:* For fall admission, 11/30 priority date for domestic and international students; for spring admission, 7/1 priority date for domestic students, 7/1 for international students. Application fee: $30. *Financial support:* In 2017–18, 10 students received support. Career-related internships or fieldwork, health care benefits, and unspecified assistantships available. Financial award application deadline: 4/1. *Faculty research:* Cell biology, microbiology and molecular biology: basic and applied science in bacterial pathogenesis, genome integrity and mechanisms of aging, structural and computational biology; cancer biology: immunology, cancer control, signal transduction, drug discovery, genomics. *Total annual research expenditures:* $1.8 million. *Unit head:* Dr. James Garey, Professor/Chair, 813-974-7103, Fax: 813-974-1614, E-mail: garey@usf.edu. *Application contact:* Dr. Kenneth Wright, Associate Professor of Cancer Biology, H. Lee Moffitt Cancer Center and Research Institute, 813-745-3918, Fax: 813-974-1614, E-mail: ken.wright@moffitt.org.
Website: http://biology.usf.edu/cmmb/

The University of Texas Health Science Center at Houston, MD Anderson UTHealth Graduate School, Houston, TX 77225-0036. Offers biochemistry and cell biology (PhD); biomedical sciences (MS); cancer biology (PhD); genetic counseling (MS); genetics and epigenetics (PhD); immunology (PhD); medical physics (MS, PhD); microbiology and infectious diseases (PhD); neuroscience (PhD); quantitative sciences (PhD); therapeutics and pharmacology (PhD); MD/PhD. Terminal master's awarded for partial completion of doctoral program. *Degree requirements:* For master's, thesis; for doctorate, thesis/dissertation. *Entrance requirements:* For master's and doctorate, GRE General Test. Additional exam requirements/recommendations for international students: Required—TOEFL. Electronic applications accepted. *Faculty research:* Biomedical sciences.

The University of Texas Southwestern Medical Center, Southwestern Graduate School of Biomedical Sciences, Division of Basic Science, Program in Cancer Biology, Dallas, TX 75390. Offers PhD. *Degree requirements:* For doctorate, thesis/dissertation, qualifying examination.

University of the District of Columbia, College of Arts and Sciences, Program in Cancer Biology, Prevention and Control, Washington, DC 20008-1175. Offers MS. Program offered in partnership with Lombardi Comprehensive Cancer Center at Georgetown University.

The University of Toledo, College of Graduate Studies, College of Medicine and Life Sciences, Department of Biochemistry and Cancer Biology, Toledo, OH 43606-3390. Offers cancer biology (MSBS, PhD); MD/MSBS; MD/PhD. Terminal master's awarded for partial completion of doctoral program. *Degree requirements:* For master's, thesis, qualifying exam; for doctorate, thesis/dissertation, qualifying exam. *Entrance requirements:* For master's and doctorate, GRE, minimum undergraduate GPA of 3.0, three letters of recommendation, statement of purpose, transcripts from all prior institutions attended; resume. Additional exam requirements/recommendations for international students: Required—TOEFL (minimum score 550 paper-based; 80 iBT). Electronic applications accepted.

University of Utah, School of Medicine and Graduate School, Graduate Programs in Medicine, Department of Oncological Sciences, Salt Lake City, UT 84112-1107. Offers M Phil, MS, PhD. Terminal master's awarded for partial completion of doctoral program. *Degree requirements:* For master's, thesis (for some programs); for doctorate, thesis/dissertation. *Entrance requirements:* For master's and doctorate, GRE General Test, GRE Subject Test, minimum GPA of 3.0. Additional exam requirements/recommendations for international students: Required—TOEFL. *Faculty research:* Molecular basis of cell growth and differences, regulation of gene expression, biochemical mechanics of DNA replication, molecular biology and biochemistry of signal transduction, somatic cell genetics.

University of Wisconsin–La Crosse, College of Science and Health, Department of Health Professions, Program in Medical Dosimetry, La Crosse, WI 54601-3742. Offers MS. *Program availability:* Online learning. *Students:* 60 full-time (37 women), 1 part-time (0 women); includes 10 minority (4 Asian, non-Hispanic/Latino; 3 Hispanic/Latino; 3 Two or more races, non-Hispanic/Latino). Average age 32. 58 applicants, 59% accepted, 34 enrolled. In 2017, 21 master's awarded. *Entrance requirements:* For master's, American Registry of Radiologic Technologists test, Medical Dosimetrist Certification Board Exam. Additional exam requirements/recommendations for international students: Required—TOEFL (minimum score 600 paper-based; 100 iBT). *Application deadline:* For fall admission, 12/1 priority date for domestic students, 11/1 priority date for international students. Application fee: $50. Electronic applications accepted. *Expenses:* Contact institution. *Financial support:* Federal Work-Study and scholarships/grants available. Support available to part-time students. Financial award applicants required to submit FAFSA. *Unit head:* Nishele Lenards, Program Director, 608-785-8470, E-mail: nlenards@uwlax.edu. *Application contact:* Brandon Schaller, Senior Graduate Student Status Examiner, 608-785-8941, E-mail: admissions@uwlax.edu.
Website: http://www.uwlax.edu/md/

University of Wisconsin–Madison, School of Medicine and Public Health, Cancer Biology Graduate Program, Madison, WI 53706. Offers PhD. *Faculty:* 51 full-time (15 women). *Students:* 28 full-time (14 women); includes 7 minority (2 Asian, non-Hispanic/Latino; 4 Hispanic/Latino; 1 Two or more races, non-Hispanic/Latino), 7 international. Average age 27. 135 applicants, 14% accepted, 4 enrolled. In 2017, 4 doctorates awarded. *Degree requirements:* For doctorate, comprehensive exam, thesis/dissertation. *Entrance requirements:* For doctorate, GRE General Test. Additional exam requirements/recommendations for international students: Required—TOEFL (minimum score 580 paper-based; 92 iBT). *Application deadline:* For fall admission, 12/1 priority date for domestic and international students. Application fee: $75. Electronic applications accepted. *Financial support:* In 2017–18, 28 students received support, including fellowships with full tuition reimbursements available (averaging $28,000 per year), research assistantships with full tuition reimbursements available (averaging $2,800 per year); teaching assistantships, scholarships/grants, traineeships, and health care benefits also available. Financial award application deadline: 12/1. *Faculty research:* Cancer genetics, tumor virology, chemical carcinogenesis, signal transduction, cell cycle. *Total annual research expenditures:* $18 million. *Unit head:* Dr. Paul F. Lambert, Director, 608-262-8533, Fax: 608-262-2824, E-mail: lambert@oncology.wisc.edu. *Application contact:* Jenny M. Schroeder, Administrative Program Manager, 608-262-4682, Fax: 608-262-2824, E-mail: jmschroeder2@oncology.wisc.edu.
Website: http://www.cancerbiology.wisc.edu/

Wake Forest University, School of Medicine and Graduate School of Arts and Sciences, Graduate Programs in Medicine, Department of Cancer Biology, Winston-Salem, NC 27109. Offers PhD, MD/PhD. *Degree requirements:* For doctorate, thesis/dissertation. *Entrance requirements:* For doctorate, GRE General Test. Additional exam requirements/recommendations for international students: Required—TOEFL. Electronic applications accepted. *Faculty research:* Cancer research, mechanisms of carcinogenesis, signal transduction and regulation of cell growth.

Wayne State University, School of Medicine, Office of Biomedical Graduate Programs, Detroit, MI 48202. Offers anatomy and cell biology (MS, PhD); basic medical sciences (MS); biochemistry and molecular biology (MS, PhD); cancer biology (MS, PhD); clinical and translational science (Graduate Certificate); family medicine and public health sciences (MPH, Graduate Certificate), including public health practice; genetic counseling (MS); immunology and microbiology (MS, PhD); medical physics (MS, PhD, Graduate Certificate); medical research (MS); molecular medicine and genomics (MS, PhD), including molecular genetics and genomics; pathology (PhD); pharmacology (MS, PhD); physiology (MS, PhD), including physiology, reproductive sciences (PhD); psychiatry and behavioral neurosciences (PhD), including translational neuroscience; MD/MPH; MD/PhD; MPH/MA; MSW/MPH. *Program availability:* Part-time, evening/weekend. *Students:* 268 full-time (152 women), 117 part-time (59 women); includes 108 minority (19 Black or African American, non-Hispanic/Latino; 1 American Indian or Alaska Native, non-Hispanic/Latino; 62 Asian, non-Hispanic/Latino; 9 Hispanic/Latino; 17 Two or more races, non-Hispanic/Latino), 48 international. Average age 26. 1,133 applicants, 21% accepted, 151 enrolled. In 2017, 70 master's, 25 doctorates, 10 other advanced degrees awarded. Terminal master's awarded for partial completion of doctoral program. *Degree requirements:* For master's, thesis (for some programs); for doctorate, thesis/dissertation. *Entrance requirements:* For master's, doctorate, and Graduate Certificate, GRE. Additional exam requirements/recommendations for international students: Required—TOEFL (minimum score 550 paper-based; 100 iBT), Michigan English Language Assessment Battery (minimum score 85); Recommended—IELTS (minimum score 6.5), TWE (minimum score 5.5). *Application deadline:* For fall admission, 2/1 for domestic and international students. Applications are processed on a rolling basis. Application fee: $50. Electronic applications accepted. *Expenses:* Contact institution. *Financial support:* In 2017–18, 177 students received support, including 64 fellowships with full tuition reimbursements available (averaging $24,388 per year), 79 research assistantships with full tuition reimbursements available (averaging $26,894 per year); scholarships/grants, traineeships, and health care benefits also available. *Faculty research:* Cancer biology, neurosciences, vision sciences, molecular biology, pathology, physiology, pharmacology, public health, medical physics. *Unit head:* Dr. Daniel A. Walz, Associate Dean for Biomedical Graduate Programs, 313-577-1455, Fax: 313-577-8796, E-mail: gradprogs@med.wayne.edu.
Website: https://www.med.wayne.edu/biomedical-graduate-programs/

West Virginia University, School of Medicine, Morgantown, WV 26506-9600. Offers biochemistry and molecular biology (PhD); biomedical science (MS); cancer cell biology (PhD); cellular and integrative physiology (PhD); exercise physiology (MS, PhD); health sciences (MS); immunology (PhD); medicine (MD); occupational therapy (MOT); pathologists assistant (MHS); physical therapy (DPT). *Program availability:* Part-time, evening/weekend. *Students:* 781 full-time (440 women), 25 part-time (13 women); includes 140 minority (15 Black or African American, non-Hispanic/Latino; 1 American Indian or Alaska Native, non-Hispanic/Latino; 68 Asian, non-Hispanic/Latino; 37 Hispanic/Latino; 1 Native Hawaiian or other Pacific Islander, non-Hispanic/Latino; 18 Two or more races, non-Hispanic/Latino), 19 international. *Entrance requirements:* Additional exam requirements/recommendations for international students: Required—TOEFL. *Application deadline:* Applications are processed on a rolling basis. Application fee: $60. Electronic applications accepted. *Expenses:* Contact institution. *Financial support:* Fellowships, research assistantships, teaching assistantships, career-related internships or fieldwork, Federal Work-Study, institutionally sponsored loans, health care benefits, tuition waivers (full and partial), and administrative assistantships available. Financial award applicants required to submit FAFSA. *Unit head:* Dr. Clay Marsh, Executive Dean, 304-293-6607, Fax: 304-293-6627, E-mail: clay.marsh@hsc.wvu.edu. *Application contact:* Lisa M. Salati, Assistant Vice President, Graduate Education, 304-293-7759, Fax: 304-293-3080, E-mail: lsalati@hsc.wvu.edu.
Website: https://medicine.hsc.wvu.edu

Cell Biology

Albany College of Pharmacy and Health Sciences, School of Arts and Sciences, Albany, NY 12208. Offers clinical laboratory sciences (MS); cytotechnology and molecular cytology (MS); health outcomes research (MS); molecular biosciences (MS). *Degree requirements:* For master's, thesis. *Entrance requirements:* For master's, GRE, minimum GPA of 3.0. Additional exam requirements/recommendations for international students: Required—TOEFL (minimum score 84 iBT). Electronic applications accepted.

Albany Medical College, Center for Cell Biology and Cancer Research, Albany, NY 12208-3479. Offers MS, PhD. *Program availability:* Part-time. Terminal master's awarded for partial completion of doctoral program. *Degree requirements:* For master's, thesis; for doctorate, comprehensive exam, thesis/dissertation. *Entrance requirements:* For master's and doctorate, GRE General Test, all transcripts, letters of recommendation. Additional exam requirements/recommendations for international students: Required—TOEFL. *Faculty research:* Cancer cell biology, tissue remodeling, signal transduction, gene regulation, cell adhesion, angiogenesis.

Albert Einstein College of Medicine, Graduate Programs in the Biomedical Sciences, Department of Cell Biology, Bronx, NY 10461. Offers PhD, MD/PhD. *Degree requirements:* For doctorate, thesis/dissertation. *Entrance requirements:* For doctorate, GRE General Test. Additional exam requirements/recommendations for international students: Required—TOEFL. *Application deadline:* For fall admission, 1/15 for domestic students. Application fee: $0. *Financial support:* Fellowships available. *Faculty research:* Molecular and genetic basis of gene expression in animal cells; expression of differentiated traits of albumin, hemoglobin, myosin, and immunoglobin. *Unit head:* Dr. Art Skoultchi, Chairman, 718-430-2169. *Application contact:* Sheila Cleeton, Executive Director and Registrar, Einstein Graduate Division, 718-430-2128, Fax: 718-430-8655, E-mail: sheila.cleeton@einstein.yu.edu.
Website: http://www.einstein.yu.edu/departments/cell-biology/

American University of Beirut, Graduate Programs, Faculty of Arts and Sciences, 1107 2020, Lebanon. Offers anthropology (MA); Arab and Middle Eastern history (PhD);

Arabic language and literature (MA, PhD); archaeology (MA); art history and curating (MA); biology (MS); cell and molecular biology (PhD); chemistry (MS); clinical psychology (MA); computational sciences (MS); computer science (MS); economics (MA); education (MA), including administration and policy studies, elementary education, mathematics education, psychology school guidance, psychology test and measurements, science education, teaching English as a foreign language; English language (MA); English literature (MA); environmental policy planning (MS); financial economics (MAFE); general psychology (MA); geology (MS); history (MA), Islamic studies (MA); mathematics (MS); media studies (MA); Middle East studies (MA); philosophy (MA); physics (MS); political studies (MA); public administration (MA); public policy and international affairs (MA); sociology (MA); theoretical physics (PhD). *Program availability:* Part-time. *Faculty:* 108 full-time (36 women), 5 part-time/adjunct (4 women). *Students:* 251 full-time (180 women), 233 part-time (172 women). Average age 26. 425 applicants, 65% accepted, 121 enrolled. In 2017, 47 master's, 2 doctorates awarded. *Degree requirements:* For master's, one foreign language, comprehensive exam, thesis (for some programs), project; for doctorate, one foreign language, comprehensive exam, thesis/dissertation. *Entrance requirements:* For master's, GRE General Test (for some programs); for doctorate, GRE General Test (GRE Subject Test for theoretical physics). Additional exam requirements/recommendations for international students: Required—TOEFL (minimum score 583 paper-based; 97 iBT), IELTS (minimum score 7). *Application deadline:* For fall admission, 2/8 for domestic students; for spring admission, 11/3 for domestic students. Application fee: $50. Electronic applications accepted. *Expenses:* Contact institution. *Financial support:* In 2017–18, 29 fellowships, 40 research assistantships were awarded; teaching assistantships, scholarships/grants, tuition waivers (full and partial), and unspecified assistantships also available. Financial award application deadline: 4/4. *Unit head:* Dr. Nadia Maria El Cheikh, Dean, Faculty of Arts and Sciences, 961-1-374374 Ext. 3800, Fax: 961-1-744461, E-mail: nmcheikh@aub.edu.lb. *Application contact:* Rima Rassi, Graduate Studies Officer, 961-1-350000 Ext. 3833, Fax: 961-1-744461, E-mail: rr46@aub.edu.lb.
Website: http://www.aub.edu.lb/fas/pages/default.aspx

Appalachian State University, Cratis D. Williams Graduate School, Department of Biology, Boone, NC 28608. Offers cell and molecular biology (MS). *Program availability:* Part-time. *Degree requirements:* For master's, comprehensive exam, thesis. *Entrance requirements:* For master's, GRE General Test, 3 letters of recommendation. Additional exam requirements/recommendations for international students: Required—TOEFL (minimum score 570 paper-based; 79 iBT), IELTS (minimum score 6.5). Electronic applications accepted. *Faculty research:* Aquatic and terrestrial ecology, animal and plant physiology, behavior and systematics, immunology and cell biology, molecular biology and microbiology.

Arizona State University at the Tempe campus, College of Liberal Arts and Sciences, School of Life Sciences, Tempe, AZ 85287-4601. Offers animal behavior (PhD); applied ethics (biomedical and health ethics) (MA); biology (MS, PhD), including biology, biology and society, complex adaptive systems science (PhD), plant biology and conservation (MS); environmental life sciences (PhD); evolutionary biology (PhD); history and philosophy of science (PhD); human and social dimensions of science and technology (PhD); microbiology (PhD); molecular and cellular biology (PhD); neuroscience (PhD). Terminal master's awarded for partial completion of doctoral program. *Degree requirements:* For master's, thesis (for some programs), interactive Program of Study (iPOS) submitted before completing 50 percent of required credit hours; for doctorate, variable foreign language requirement, comprehensive exam, thesis/dissertation, interactive Program of Study (iPOS) submitted before completing 50 percent of required credit hours. *Entrance requirements:* For master's and doctorate, GRE, minimum GPA of 3.0 or equivalent in last 2 years of work leading to bachelor's degree. Additional exam requirements/recommendations for international students: Required—TOEFL (minimum score 600 paper-based; 100 iBT). Electronic applications accepted.

Auburn University, Graduate School, Interdepartmental Programs, Auburn University, AL 36849. Offers applied economics (PhD); cell and molecular biology (PhD); real estate development (MRED); sociology and rural sociology (MA, MS). *Program availability:* Part-time. *Students:* 31 full-time (18 women), 44 part-time (11 women); includes 16 minority (9 Black or African American, non-Hispanic/Latino; 1 Asian, non-Hispanic/Latino; 5 Hispanic/Latino; 1 Two or more races, non-Hispanic/Latino), 17 international. Average age 34. 63 applicants, 71% accepted, 33 enrolled. In 2017, 18 master's, 9 doctorates awarded. *Entrance requirements:* For master's, GRE General Test. *Application deadline:* Applications are processed on a rolling basis. Application fee: $50 ($60 for international students). Electronic applications accepted. *Expenses:* Tuition, state resident: full-time $10,974; part-time $519 per credit hour. Tuition, nonresident: full-time $29,658; part-time $1557 per credit hour. *Required fees:* $816 per semester. Tuition and fees vary according to degree level and program. *Financial support:* Fellowships, research assistantships, teaching assistantships, and Federal Work-Study available. Support available to part-time students. Financial award application deadline: 3/15; financial award applicants required to submit FAFSA. *Application contact:* Dr. George Flowers, Dean of the Graduate School, 334-844-2125.

Augusta University, Program in Cellular Biology and Anatomy, Augusta, GA 30912. Offers PhD. *Degree requirements:* For doctorate, comprehensive exam, thesis/dissertation. *Entrance requirements:* For doctorate, GRE General Test. Additional exam requirements/recommendations for international students: Required—TOEFL (minimum score 550 paper-based; 79 iBT). *Faculty research:* Eye disease, developmental biology, cell injury and death, stroke and neurotoxicity, diabetic complications.

Baylor College of Medicine, Graduate School of Biomedical Sciences, Department of Molecular and Cellular Biology, Houston, TX 77030-3498. Offers PhD, MD/PhD. *Degree requirements:* For doctorate, thesis/dissertation, public defense, qualifying exam. *Entrance requirements:* For doctorate, GRE General Test, GRE Subject Test (strongly recommended), minimum GPA of 3.0. Additional exam requirements/recommendations for international students: Required—TOEFL. Electronic applications accepted. *Faculty research:* Hormone action, development, cancer, gene therapy, neurobiology.

Baylor College of Medicine, Graduate School of Biomedical Sciences, Interdepartmental Program in Cell and Molecular Biology, Houston, TX 77030-3498. Offers biochemistry (PhD); cell and molecular biology (PhD); genetics (PhD); human genetics (PhD); immunology (PhD); microbiology (PhD); virology (PhD); MD/PhD. *Degree requirements:* For doctorate, thesis/dissertation, public defense. *Entrance requirements:* For doctorate, GRE General Test, GRE Subject Test (strongly recommended), minimum GPA of 3.0. Additional exam requirements/recommendations for international students: Required—TOEFL. Electronic applications accepted. *Faculty research:* Molecular and cellular biology; cancer, aging and stem cells; genomics and proteomics; microbiome, molecular microbiology; infectious disease, immunology and translational research.

Boston University, Graduate School of Arts and Sciences, Molecular Biology, Cell Biology, and Biochemistry Program (MCBB), Boston, MA 02215. Offers MA, PhD. *Students:* 35 full-time (17 women), 5 part-time (2 women); includes 10 minority (2 Black or African American, non-Hispanic/Latino; 2 Asian, non-Hispanic/Latino; 4 Hispanic/Latino; 2 Two or more races, non-Hispanic/Latino), 12 international. Average age 27. 150 applicants, 20% accepted, 9 enrolled. In 2017, 3 master's, 4 doctorates awarded. Terminal master's awarded for partial completion of doctoral program. *Degree requirements:* For master's, thesis (for some programs); for doctorate, comprehensive exam, thesis/dissertation, teaching requirement. *Entrance requirements:* For master's and doctorate, GRE General Test, 3 letters of recommendation, transcripts, personal statement. Additional exam requirements/recommendations for international students: Required—TOEFL (minimum score 550 paper-based; 84 iBT). *Application deadline:* For fall admission, 12/5 for domestic and international students. Application fee: $95. Electronic applications accepted. *Financial support:* In 2017–18, 35 students received support, including 4 fellowships with full tuition reimbursements available (averaging $22,000 per year), 12 research assistantships with full tuition reimbursements available (averaging $22,000 per year), 16 teaching assistantships with full tuition reimbursements available (averaging $22,000 per year); Federal Work-Study, scholarships/grants, traineeships, and health care benefits also available. Financial award application deadline: 12/5; financial award applicants required to submit FAFSA. *Unit head:* Dr. Ulla Hansen, Director, 617-353-2432, Fax: 617-353-6340, E-mail: uhansen@bu.edu. *Application contact:* Christina Honeycutt, Academic Administrator, 617-353-2432, Fax: 617-353-6340, E-mail: cjhoney@bu.edu.
Website: http://www.bu.edu/mcbb/

Boston University, School of Medicine, Division of Graduate Medical Sciences, Department of Biochemistry, Boston, MA 02118. Offers MA, PhD, MD/PhD. *Program availability:* Part-time. Terminal master's awarded for partial completion of doctoral program. *Degree requirements:* For master's, thesis or alternative; for doctorate, thesis/dissertation. *Application deadline:* For fall admission, 1/15 for domestic students; for spring admission, 10/15 for domestic students. *Unit head:* Dr. David A. Harris, Chair, 617-638-5090. *Application contact:* GMS Admissions Office, 617-638-5255, E-mail: askgms@bu.edu.
Website: http://www.bumc.bu.edu/biochemistry/

Boston University, School of Medicine, Division of Graduate Medical Sciences, Program in Cell and Molecular Biology, Boston, MA 02118. Offers PhD. *Degree requirements:* For doctorate, thesis/dissertation. *Application deadline:* For fall admission, 1/15 for domestic students; for spring admission, 10/15 for domestic students. *Financial support:* Scholarships/grants and traineeships available. Financial award applicants required to submit FAFSA. *Unit head:* Dr. Vickery Trinkaus-Randall, Director, 617-638-6099, Fax: 617-638-5337, E-mail: vickery@bu.edu. *Application contact:* GMS Admissions Office, 617-638-5255, E-mail: askgms@bu.edu.
Website: http://www.bumc.bu.edu/cmbio/

Brandeis University, Graduate School of Arts and Sciences, Program in Molecular and Cell Biology, Waltham, MA 02454-9110. Offers genetics (PhD); microbiology (PhD); molecular and cell biology (MS, PhD); molecular biology (PhD); neurobiology (PhD); quantitative biology (PhD). *Faculty:* 27 full-time (13 women), 3 part-time/adjunct (2 women). *Students:* 47 full-time (29 women), 2 part-time (1 woman); includes 10 minority (1 American Indian or Alaska Native, non-Hispanic/Latino; 2 Asian, non-Hispanic/Latino; 6 Hispanic/Latino; 1 Two or more races, non-Hispanic/Latino), 11 international. Average age 27. 138 applicants, 25% accepted, 18 enrolled. In 2017, 11 master's, 8 doctorates awarded. Terminal master's awarded for partial completion of doctoral program. *Degree requirements:* For master's, thesis optional, research project, research lab, or project lab; for doctorate, comprehensive exam, thesis/dissertation, journal clubs; research seminar; colloquia; qualifying exam. *Entrance requirements:* For master's, GRE General Test, transcripts, resume, letters of recommendation, statement of purpose; for doctorate, GRE General Test, transcripts, resume, letters of recommendation, statement of purpose, list of previous research experience. Additional exam requirements/recommendations for international students: Required—PTE (minimum score 68), TOEFL (minimum score 600 paper-based, 100 iBT) or IELTS (7). *Application deadline:* For fall admission, 12/1 priority date for domestic students; for spring admission, 11/15 for domestic students, 10/15 for international students. Applications are processed on a rolling basis. Application fee: $75. Electronic applications accepted. *Expenses: Tuition:* Full-time $48,720. *Required fees:* $88. Tuition and fees vary according to course load, degree level, program and student level. *Financial support:* In 2017–18, 46 students received support, including 20 fellowships with full tuition reimbursements available (averaging $33,000 per year), 19 research assistantships with full tuition reimbursements available (averaging $33,000 per year); scholarships/grants and tuition waivers (partial) also available. Financial award application deadline: 4/15; financial award applicants required to submit FAFSA. *Faculty research:* Molecular biology, genetics and development; structural and cell biology; neurobiology. *Unit head:* Dr. James Haber, Co-Chair, 781-736-2462, E-mail: haber@brandeis.edu. *Application contact:* Jena Pitman-Leung, Department Administrator, 781-736-2352, E-mail: scigradoffice@brandeis.edu.
Website: http://www.brandeis.edu/gsas/programs/mcbio.html

Brown University, Graduate School, Division of Biology and Medicine, Department of Molecular Biology, Cell Biology, and Biochemistry, Providence, RI 02912. Offers MA, PhD. *Program availability:* Part-time. Terminal master's awarded for partial completion of doctoral program. *Degree requirements:* For master's, thesis (for some programs); for doctorate, one foreign language, thesis/dissertation, preliminary exam. *Entrance requirements:* For master's and doctorate, GRE General Test, GRE Subject Test. Additional exam requirements/recommendations for international students: Required—TOEFL. Electronic applications accepted. *Faculty research:* Molecular genetics, gene regulation.

California Institute of Technology, Division of Biology, Program in Cell Biology and Biophysics, Pasadena, CA 91125-0001. Offers PhD. *Degree requirements:* For doctorate, thesis/dissertation, qualifying exam. *Entrance requirements:* For doctorate, GRE General Test.

California State University, Sacramento, College of Natural Sciences and Mathematics, Department of Biological Sciences, Sacramento, CA 95819. Offers biological conservation (MS); molecular and cellular biology (MS); stem cell (MA). *Program availability:* Part-time. *Students:* 25 full-time (15 women), 26 part-time (14 women); includes 11 minority (2 Black or African American, non-Hispanic/Latino; 1 American Indian or Alaska Native, non-Hispanic/Latino; 8 Asian, non-Hispanic/Latino), 1 international. Average age 29. 82 applicants, 29% accepted, 18 enrolled. In 2017, 11 master's awarded. *Degree requirements:* For master's, thesis or project; writing proficiency exam. *Entrance requirements:* For master's, GRE, bachelor's degree in biology or equivalent; minimum GPA of 2.75 in all biology courses, 3.0 in all upper-division biology courses. Additional exam requirements/recommendations for international students: Required—TOEFL (minimum score 550 paper-based; 80 iBT); Recommended—IELTS, TSE. *Application deadline:* For fall admission, 2/1 for domestic and international students. Applications are processed on a rolling basis. Application fee: $55. Electronic applications accepted. *Expenses:* Contact institution. *Financial support:* Teaching assistantships, career-related internships or fieldwork, Federal Work-Study, and scholarships/grants available. Support available to part-time students. Financial award application deadline: 3/1; financial award applicants required to submit FAFSA. *Unit head:* Dr. Shannon Datwyler, Chair, 916-278-6535, Fax: 916-278-6993, E-mail: datwyler@csus.edu. *Application contact:* Jose Martinez, Graduate Admissions Supervisor, 916-278-7871, E-mail: martinj@skymail.csus.edu.
Website: http://www.csus.edu/bios

Cell Biology

Carnegie Mellon University, Mellon College of Science, Department of Biological Sciences, Pittsburgh, PA 15213-3891. Offers biochemistry (PhD); biophysics (PhD); cell and developmental biology (PhD); computational biology (MS, PhD); genetics (PhD); molecular biology (PhD); neuroscience (PhD); structural biology (PhD). *Degree requirements:* For doctorate, comprehensive exam, thesis/dissertation. *Entrance requirements:* For doctorate, GRE General Test, GRE Subject Test, interview. Electronic applications accepted. *Faculty research:* Genetic structure, function, and regulation; protein structure and function; biological membranes; biological spectroscopy.

Case Western Reserve University, School of Medicine and School of Graduate Studies, Graduate Programs in Medicine, Department of Molecular Biology and Microbiology, Program in Cell Biology, Cleveland, OH 44106. Offers PhD. *Degree requirements:* For doctorate, thesis/dissertation. *Entrance requirements:* For doctorate, GRE General Test, GRE Subject Test, previous course work in biochemistry. Additional exam requirements/recommendations for international students: Required—TOEFL. Electronic applications accepted. *Expenses: Tuition:* Full-time $43,854; part-time $1827 per credit hour. *Required fees:* $50; $50 per credit hour. Tuition and fees vary according to course load and program. *Faculty research:* Macromolecular transport, membrane traffic, signal transduction, nuclear organization, lipid metabolism.

The Catholic University of America, School of Arts and Sciences, Department of Biology, Washington, DC 20064. Offers biotechnology (MS); cell and microbial biology (MS, PhD), including cell biology; clinical laboratory science (MS, PhD); MSLS/MS. MSLS/MS offered jointly with Department of Library and Information Science. *Program availability:* Part-time. *Faculty:* 10 full-time (4 women), 7 part-time/adjunct (1 woman). *Students:* 24 full-time (18 women), 43 part-time (20 women); includes 7 minority (2 Black or African American, non-Hispanic/Latino; 3 Asian, non-Hispanic/Latino; 2 Two or more races, non-Hispanic/Latino), 48 international. Average age 31. 56 applicants, 61% accepted, 18 enrolled. In 2017, 7 master's, 1 doctorate awarded. Terminal master's awarded for partial completion of doctoral program. *Degree requirements:* For master's and doctorate, comprehensive exam. *Entrance requirements:* For master's and doctorate, GRE General Test, GRE Subject Test, statement of purpose, official copies of academic transcripts, three letters of recommendation. Additional exam requirements/recommendations for international students: Required—TOEFL (minimum score 550 paper-based; 80 iBT). *Application deadline:* For fall admission, 7/15 priority date for domestic students, 7/1 for international students; for spring admission, 11/15 priority date for domestic students, 11/1 for international students. Applications are processed on a rolling basis. Application fee: $55. Electronic applications accepted. *Expenses:* Contact institution. *Financial support:* Fellowships, research assistantships, teaching assistantships, Federal Work-Study, scholarships/grants, tuition waivers (full and partial), and unspecified assistantships available. Financial award application deadline: 2/1; financial award applicants required to submit FAFSA. *Faculty research:* Virus structure and assembly, hepatic and epithelial cell biology, drug resistance and genome stabilization in yeast, biophysics of ion-conductive nanostructures, eukaryotic gene regulation, cancer and vaccine research. *Total annual research expenditures:* $1.7 million. *Unit head:* Dr. Venigalla Rao, Chair, 202-319-5271, Fax: 202-319-5721, E-mail: rao@cua.edu. *Application contact:* Dr. Steven Brown, Director of Graduate Admissions, 202-319-5057, Fax: 202-319-6533, E-mail: cua-admissions@cua.edu.
Website: http://biology.cua.edu/

Columbia University, College of Physicians and Surgeons, Department of Anatomy and Cell Biology, New York, NY 10032. Offers anatomy (M Phil, MA, PhD); anatomy and cell biology (PhD); MD/PhD. Only candidates for the PhD are admitted. Terminal master's awarded for partial completion of doctoral program. *Degree requirements:* For doctorate, thesis/dissertation, oral exam. *Entrance requirements:* For master's and doctorate, GRE General Test. Additional exam requirements/recommendations for international students: Required—TOEFL. *Expenses: Tuition:* Full-time $44,864; part-time $1704 per credit. *Required fees:* $2370 per semester. One-time fee: $105. *Faculty research:* Protein sorting, membrane biophysics, muscle energetics, neuroendocrinology, developmental biology, cytoskeleton, transcription factors.

Columbia University, College of Physicians and Surgeons, Integrated Program in Cellular, Molecular, Structural and Genetic Studies, New York, NY 10032. Offers PhD. Terminal master's awarded for partial completion of doctoral program. *Degree requirements:* For doctorate, thesis/dissertation. *Entrance requirements:* For doctorate, GRE General Test, GRE Subject Test. Additional exam requirements/recommendations for international students: Required—TOEFL. *Expenses:* Contact institution. *Faculty research:* Transcription, macromolecular sorting, gene expression during development, cellular interaction.

Cornell University, Graduate School, Graduate Fields of Agriculture and Life Sciences, Field of Biochemistry, Molecular and Cell Biology, Ithaca, NY 14853. Offers biochemistry (PhD); biophysics (PhD); cell biology (PhD); molecular biology (PhD). *Degree requirements:* For doctorate, comprehensive exam, thesis/dissertation, 2 semesters of teaching experience. *Entrance requirements:* For doctorate, GRE General Test, GRE Subject Test (biology, chemistry, physics, biochemistry, cell and molecular biology), 3 letters of recommendation. Additional exam requirements/recommendations for international students: Required—TOEFL (minimum score 600 paper-based; 77 iBT). Electronic applications accepted. *Faculty research:* Biophysics, structural biology.

Cornell University, Graduate School, Graduate Fields of Agriculture and Life Sciences, Field of Computational Biology, Ithaca, NY 14853. Offers computational behavioral biology (PhD); computational biology (PhD); computational cell biology (PhD); computational ecology (PhD); computational genetics (PhD); computational macromolecular biology (PhD); computational organismal biology (PhD). *Degree requirements:* For doctorate, comprehensive exam, thesis/dissertation, 2 semesters of teaching experience. *Entrance requirements:* For doctorate, GRE General Test, GRE Subject Test (biology), 2 letters of recommendation. Additional exam requirements/recommendations for international students: Required—TOEFL (minimum score 550 paper-based; 77 iBT). Electronic applications accepted. *Faculty research:* Computational behavioral biology, computational biology, computational cell biology, computational ecology, computational genetics, computational macromolecular biology, computational organismal biology.

Dartmouth College, Graduate Program in Molecular and Cellular Biology, Hanover, NH 03755. Offers PhD, MBA/PhD, MD/PhD. *Faculty:* 70 full-time (16 women), 6 part-time/adjunct (3 women). *Students:* 62 full-time (28 women); includes 12 minority (2 Asian, non-Hispanic/Latino; 9 Hispanic/Latino; 1 Two or more races, non-Hispanic/Latino), 22 international. Average age 26. 161 applicants, 38% accepted, 30 enrolled. In 2017, 9 doctorates awarded. *Entrance requirements:* For doctorate, GRE General Test, letters of recommendation, minimum GPA of 3.0. *Application deadline:* For fall admission, 12/8 for domestic students. Applications are processed on a rolling basis. Application fee: $75. Electronic applications accepted. *Financial support:* Fellowships and health care benefits available. *Unit head:* Dr. Patrick J. Dolph, Vice Chair, 603-650-1092, E-mail: mcb@dartmouth.edu. *Application contact:* Janet Cheney, Program Coordinator, 603-650-1612, E-mail: mcb@dartmouth.edu.
Website: http://dms.dartmouth.edu/mcb/

Drexel University, College of Medicine, Biomedical Graduate Programs, Interdisciplinary Program in Molecular and Cell Biology and Genetics, Philadelphia, PA 19104-2875. Offers MS, PhD, MD/PhD. Terminal master's awarded for partial completion of doctoral program. *Degree requirements:* For master's, comprehensive exam, thesis; for doctorate, thesis/dissertation, qualifying exam. *Entrance requirements:* For master's, GRE General Test, minimum GPA of 2.75; for doctorate, GRE General Test, minimum GPA of 3.0. Additional exam requirements/recommendations for international students: Required—TOEFL. Electronic applications accepted. *Faculty research:* Molecular anatomy, biochemistry, medical biotechnology, molecular pathology, microbiology and immunology.

Duke University, Graduate School, Department of Cell Biology, Durham, NC 27710. Offers PhD. *Degree requirements:* For doctorate, thesis/dissertation. *Entrance requirements:* For doctorate, GRE General Test, GRE Subject Test in biology, chemistry, cell and molecular biology (recommended). Additional exam requirements/recommendations for international students: Required—TOEFL (minimum score 577 paper-based; 90 iBT) or IELTS (minimum score 7). Electronic applications accepted.

Duke University, Graduate School, Department of Evolutionary Anthropology, Durham, NC 27708. Offers cellular and molecular biology (PhD); gross anatomy and physical anthropology (PhD), including comparative morphology of human and non-human primates, primate social behavior, vertebrate paleontology; neuroanatomy (PhD). *Degree requirements:* For doctorate, one foreign language, thesis/dissertation. *Entrance requirements:* For doctorate, GRE General Test. Additional exam requirements/recommendations for international students: Required—TOEFL (minimum score 577 paper-based; 90 iBT) or IELTS (minimum score 7). Electronic applications accepted.

Duke University, Graduate School, Program in Cell and Molecular Biology, Durham, NC 27710. Offers Certificate. Students must be enrolled in a participating PhD program (biology, cell biology, immunology, molecular genetics, neurobiology, pathology, pharmacology). *Entrance requirements:* Additional exam requirements/recommendations for international students: Required—TOEFL (minimum score 577 paper-based; 90 iBT) or IELTS (minimum score 7). Electronic applications accepted.

Emory University, Laney Graduate School, Division of Biological and Biomedical Sciences, Program in Biochemistry, Cell and Developmental Biology, Atlanta, GA 30322. Offers PhD. *Degree requirements:* For doctorate, comprehensive exam, thesis/dissertation. *Entrance requirements:* For doctorate, GRE General Test, minimum GPA of 3.0 in science course work (recommended). Additional exam requirements/recommendations for international students: Required—TOEFL. Electronic applications accepted. *Faculty research:* Signal transduction, molecular biology, enzymes and cofactors, receptor and ion channel function, membrane biology.

Emporia State University, Department of Biological Sciences, Emporia, KS 66801-5415. Offers botany (MS); environmental biology (MS); forensic science (MS); general biology (MS); microbial and cellular biology (MS); zoology (MS). *Program availability:* Part-time. *Faculty:* 13 full-time (3 women), 1 part-time/adjunct (0 women). *Students:* 20 full-time (11 women), 15 part-time (3 women); includes 3 minority (2 Hispanic/Latino; 1 Two or more races, non-Hispanic/Latino), 17 international. 17 applicants, 59% accepted, 8 enrolled. In 2017, 21 master's awarded. *Degree requirements:* For master's, comprehensive exam or thesis. *Entrance requirements:* For master's, GRE, appropriate undergraduate degree, interview, letters of reference. Additional exam requirements/recommendations for international students: Required—TOEFL (minimum score 520 paper-based; 68 iBT). *Application deadline:* For fall admission, 8/15 priority date for domestic students. Applications are processed on a rolling basis. Application fee: $30 ($75 for international students). Electronic applications accepted. *Expenses:* Tuition, state resident: full-time $6084; part-time $253.50 per credit hour. Tuition, nonresident: full-time $18,924; part-time $788.50 per credit hour. *Required fees:* $1943; $80.95 per credit hour. Tuition and fees vary according to campus/location. *Financial support:* In 2017–18, 7 research assistantships with full tuition reimbursements (averaging $9,747 per year), 15 teaching assistantships with full tuition reimbursements (averaging $7,499 per year) were awarded; career-related internships or fieldwork, Federal Work-Study, institutionally sponsored loans, health care benefits, and unspecified assistantships also available. Financial award application deadline: 3/15; financial award applicants required to submit FAFSA. *Faculty research:* Fisheries, range, and wildlife management; aquatic, plant, grassland, vertebrate, and invertebrate ecology; mammalian and plant systematics, taxonomy, and evolution; immunology, virology, and molecular biology. *Unit head:* Dr. Tim Burnett, Interim Chair, 620-341-5910, Fax: 620-341-5608, E-mail: tburnett@emporia.edu.
Website: http://www.emporia.edu/info/degrees-courses/grad/biology

Florida Institute of Technology, College of Science, Program in Biological Sciences, Melbourne, FL 32901-6975. Offers biological science (PhD); biotechnology (MS); cell and molecular biology (MS); ecology (MS); marine biology (MS). *Program availability:* Part-time. *Students:* Average age 26. 230 applicants, 24% accepted, 21 enrolled. In 2017, 27 master's, 3 doctorates awarded. *Degree requirements:* For master's, thesis (for some programs), research, seminar, internship, or summer lab; for doctorate, comprehensive exam, thesis/dissertation, dissertations seminar, publications. *Entrance requirements:* For master's, GRE General Test, 3 letters of recommendation; statement of objectives; bachelor's degree in biology, chemistry, biochemistry or equivalent; for doctorate, GRE General Test, resume, 3 letters of recommendation, minimum GPA of 3.2, statement of objectives. Additional exam requirements/recommendations for international students: Required—TOEFL (minimum score 550 paper-based; 79 iBT). *Application deadline:* For fall admission, 3/1 for domestic students, 4/1 for international students; for spring admission, 9/1 for domestic and international students. Applications are processed on a rolling basis. Electronic applications accepted. *Expenses: Tuition:* Part-time $1241 per credit hour. Part-time tuition and fees vary according to campus/location. *Financial support:* Career-related internships or fieldwork, institutionally sponsored loans, tuition waivers (partial), unspecified assistantships, and tuition remissions available. Support available to part-time students. Financial award application deadline: 3/1; financial award applicants required to submit FAFSA. *Faculty research:* Initiation of protein synthesis in eukaryotic cells, fixation of radioactive carbon, changes in DNA molecule, endangered or threatened avian and mammalian species, hydro acoustics and feeding preference of the West Indian manatee. *Unit head:* Dr. Richard B. Aronson, Department Head, 321-674-8034, Fax: 321-674-7238, E-mail: raronson@fit.edu. *Application contact:* Cheryl A. Brown, Associate Director of Graduate Admissions, 321-674-7581, Fax: 321-723-9468, E-mail: cbrown@fit.edu.
Website: http://cos.fit.edu/biology/

Florida State University, The Graduate School, College of Arts and Sciences, Department of Biological Science, Specialization in Cell and Molecular Biology, Tallahassee, FL 32306-4295. Offers MS, PhD. *Faculty:* 24 full-time (6 women). *Students:* 52 full-time (29 women); includes 2 minority (1 Black or African American, non-Hispanic/Latino; 1 Two or more races, non-Hispanic/Latino), 24 international. Average age 29. 52 applicants, 31% accepted, 9 enrolled. In 2017, 1 master's, 4 doctorates awarded. Terminal master's awarded for partial completion of doctoral program. *Degree requirements:* For master's, comprehensive exam (for some programs), thesis, teaching experience, seminar presentation; for doctorate, comprehensive exam, thesis/dissertation, teaching experience; seminar presentation. *Entrance requirements:* For master's and doctorate, GRE General Test, minimum

upper-division GPA of 3.0. Additional exam requirements/recommendations for international students: Required—TOEFL (minimum score 600 paper-based; 92 iBT). *Application deadline:* For fall admission, 12/1 for domestic and international students. Application fee: $30. Electronic applications accepted. *Financial support:* In 2017–18, 52 students received support, including 2 fellowships with full tuition reimbursements available (averaging $30,000 per year), 12 research assistantships with full tuition reimbursements available (averaging $23,800 per year), 38 teaching assistantships with full tuition reimbursements available (averaging $23,800 per year); scholarships/grants and unspecified assistantships also available. Financial award application deadline: 12/1; financial award applicants required to submit FAFSA. *Faculty research:* Molecular biology; genetics and genomics; developmental biology and gene expression; cell structure, function, and motility; chromatin structure and function; biophysical and structural biology. *Unit head:* Dr. Thomas A. Houpt, Professor and Associate Chair, 850-644-4783, Fax: 850-644-8447, E-mail: houpt@bio.fsu.edu. *Application contact:* Jessica Webber, Coordinator, Graduate Affairs, 850-644-3023, Fax: 850-644-8447, E-mail: gradinfo@bio.fsu.edu.
Website: http://www.bio.fsu.edu/cmb/

Georgia State University, College of Arts and Sciences, Department of Biology, Program in Cellular and Molecular Biology and Physiology, Atlanta, GA 30302-3083. Offers bioinformatics (MS); cellular and molecular biology and physiology (MS, PhD). *Program availability:* Part-time. Terminal master's awarded for partial completion of doctoral program. *Entrance requirements:* For master's and doctorate, GRE. *Application deadline:* Applications are processed on a rolling basis. Application fee: $50. Electronic applications accepted. *Expenses:* Tuition, state resident: full-time $7020. Tuition, nonresident: full-time $22,518. *Required fees:* $2128. Tuition and fees vary according to degree level and program. *Financial support:* Fellowships and research assistantships available. Financial award application deadline: 12/3. *Faculty research:* Membrane transport, viral infection, molecular immunology, protein modeling, gene regulation. *Unit head:* Dr. Charles Derby, Director of Graduate Studies, 404-413-5393, Fax: 404-413-5446, E-mail: cderby@gsu.edu.
Website: http://biology.gsu.edu/

Grand Valley State University, College of Liberal Arts and Sciences, Program in Cell and Molecular Biology, Allendale, MI 49401-9403. Offers MS. *Faculty:* 8 full-time (5 women). *Students:* 16 full-time (13 women), 18 part-time (8 women); includes 3 minority (2 Black or African American, non-Hispanic/Latino; 1 Asian, non-Hispanic/Latino), 13 international. Average age 26. 30 applicants, 70% accepted, 13 enrolled. In 2017, 15 master's awarded. *Degree requirements:* For master's, thesis or internship. *Entrance requirements:* For master's, GRE, minimum GPA of 3.0, resume or curriculum vitae, personal statement, minimum of 2 letters of recommendation, interview. Additional exam requirements/recommendations for international students: Required—TOEFL (minimum iBT score of 80), IELTS (6.5), or Michigan English Language Assessment Battery (77). *Application deadline:* Applications are processed on a rolling basis. Application fee: $30. Electronic applications accepted. *Expenses:* $657 per credit hour. *Financial support:* In 2017–18, 17 students received support, including 1 fellowship, 12 research assistantships with full and partial tuition reimbursements available (averaging $4,000 per year); unspecified assistantships also available. *Faculty research:* Plant cell biology, plant development, cell/signal integration. *Unit head:* Dr. Mark Staves, Department Chair, 616-331-2473, Fax: 616-331-3446, E-mail: stavesm@gvsu.edu. *Application contact:* Dr. Tim Born, PSM Coordinator/Student Recruiting Contact, 616-331-8643, Fax: 616-331-6770, E-mail: bornt@gvsu.edu.

Harvard University, Graduate School of Arts and Sciences, Department of Molecular and Cellular Biology, Cambridge, MA 02138. Offers PhD. *Degree requirements:* For doctorate, thesis/dissertation, oral exam. *Entrance requirements:* For doctorate, GRE General Test, GRE Subject Test (recommended). Additional exam requirements/recommendations for international students: Required—TOEFL.

Harvard University, Graduate School of Arts and Sciences, Division of Medical Sciences, Boston, MA 02115. Offers biological chemistry and molecular pharmacology (PhD); cell biology (PhD); genetics (PhD); microbiology and molecular genetics (PhD); pathology (PhD), including experimental pathology. *Degree requirements:* For doctorate, thesis/dissertation. *Entrance requirements:* For doctorate, GRE General Test, GRE Subject Test. Additional exam requirements/recommendations for international students: Required—TOEFL.

Illinois Institute of Technology, Graduate College, College of Science, Department of Biology, Chicago, IL 60616. Offers applied life sciences (MS); biochemistry (MS); biology (MS, PhD); cell and molecular biology (MS); microbiology (MS); molecular biochemistry and biophysics (MS, PhD). *Program availability:* Part-time, evening/weekend, online learning. Terminal master's awarded for partial completion of doctoral program. *Degree requirements:* For master's, comprehensive exam, thesis (for some programs); for doctorate, comprehensive exam, thesis/dissertation. *Entrance requirements:* For master's, GRE General Test (minimum score 300 Quantitative and Verbal, 2.5 Analytical Writing), minimum undergraduate GPA of 3.0; for doctorate, GRE General Test (minimum score 310 Quantitative and Verbal, 3.0 Analytical Writing); GRE Subject Test (strongly recommended), minimum undergraduate GPA of 3.0. Additional exam requirements/recommendations for international students: Required—TOEFL (minimum score 550 paper-based; 80 iBT). Electronic applications accepted. *Faculty research:* Macromolecular crystallography, insect immunity and basic cell biology, improvement of bacterial strains for enhanced biodesulfurization of petroleum, programmed cell death in cancer cells.

Illinois State University, Graduate School, College of Arts and Sciences, School of Biological Sciences, Normal, IL 61790. Offers animal behavior (MS); bacteriology (MS); biochemistry (MS); biological sciences (MS); biology (PhD); biophysics (MS); biotechnology (MS); botany (MS, PhD); cell biology (MS); conservation biology (MS); developmental biology (MS); ecology (MS, PhD); entomology (MS); evolutionary biology (MS); genetics (MS, PhD); immunology (MS); microbiology (MS, PhD); molecular biology (MS); molecular genetics (MS); neurobiology (MS); neuroscience (MS); parasitology (MS); physiology (MS, PhD); plant biology (MS); plant molecular biology (MS); plant sciences (MS); structural biology (MS); zoology (MS, PhD). *Program availability:* Part-time. *Degree requirements:* For master's, thesis or alternative; for doctorate, variable foreign language requirement, thesis/dissertation, 2 terms of residency. *Entrance requirements:* For master's, GRE General Test, minimum GPA of 2.6 in last 60 hours of course work; for doctorate, GRE General Test. *Faculty research:* Redoc balance and drug development in schistosoma mansoni, control of the growth of listeria monocytogenes at low temperature, regulation of cell expansion and microtubule function by SPRI, CRUI: physiology and fitness consequences of different life history phenotypes.

Indiana State University, College of Graduate and Professional Studies, College of Arts and Sciences, Department of Biology, Terre Haute, IN 47809. Offers cellular and molecular biology (PhD); ecology, systematics and evolution (PhD); life sciences (MS); physiology (PhD); science education (MS). *Degree requirements:* For master's, thesis optional; for doctorate, comprehensive exam, thesis/dissertation. *Entrance requirements:* For master's and doctorate, GRE General Test. Electronic applications accepted.

Indiana University Bloomington, University Graduate School, College of Arts and Sciences, Department of Biology, Bloomington, IN 47405. Offers biology teaching (MAT); biotechnology (MA); evolution, ecology, and behavior (MA, PhD); genetics (PhD); microbiology (MA, PhD); molecular, cellular, and developmental biology (PhD); plant sciences (MA, PhD); zoology (MA, PhD). Terminal master's awarded for partial completion of doctoral program. *Degree requirements:* For master's, thesis, oral defense; for doctorate, thesis/dissertation, oral defense. *Entrance requirements:* For master's and doctorate, GRE General Test. Additional exam requirements/recommendations for international students: Required—TOEFL (minimum score 100 iBT). Electronic applications accepted. *Faculty research:* Evolution, ecology and behavior; microbiology; molecular biology and genetics; plant biology.

Indiana University–Purdue University Indianapolis, Indiana University School of Medicine, Department of Anatomy and Cell Biology, Indianapolis, IN 46202. Offers MS, PhD, MD/PhD. *Degree requirements:* For master's, thesis or alternative; for doctorate, thesis/dissertation. *Entrance requirements:* For master's and doctorate, GRE General Test. Additional exam requirements/recommendations for international students: Required—TOEFL. Electronic applications accepted. *Expenses:* Contact institution. *Faculty research:* Neurobiology, musculoskeletal biology, renal biology, anatomy education.

Iowa State University of Science and Technology, Program in Molecular, Cellular, and Developmental Biology, Ames, IA 50011. Offers MS, PhD. *Entrance requirements:* For master's and doctorate, GRE General Test. Additional exam requirements/recommendations for international students: Required—TOEFL (minimum score 580 paper-based; 85 iBT), IELTS (minimum score 7). Electronic applications accepted.

Irell & Manella Graduate School of Biological Sciences, Graduate Program, Duarte, CA 91010. Offers brain metastatic cancer (PhD); cancer and stem cell metabolism (PhD); cancer biology (PhD); cancer biology and developmental therapeutics (PhD); cell biology (PhD); chemical biology (PhD); chromosomal break repair (PhD); diabetes and pancreatic progenitor cell biology (PhD); DNA repair and cancer biology (PhD); germline epigenetic remodeling and endocrine disruptors (PhD); hematology and hematopoietic cell transplantation (PhD); hematology and immunology (PhD); inflammation and cancer (PhD); micrornas and gene regulation in cardiovascular disease (PhD); mixed chimrism for reversal of autoimmunity (PhD); molecular and cellular biology (PhD); molecular biology and genetics (PhD); nanoparticle mediated twist1 silencing in metastatic cancer (PhD); neuro-oncology and stem cell biology (PhD); neuroscience (PhD); RNA directed therapies for HIV-1 (PhD); small RNA-induced transcriptional gene activation (PhD); stem cell regulation by the microenvironment (PhD); translational oncology and pharmaceutical sciences (PhD); tumor biology (PhD). *Degree requirements:* For doctorate, comprehensive exam, thesis/dissertation, qualifying exams, two advanced courses. *Entrance requirements:* For doctorate, GRE General Test; GRE Subject Test (recommended), 2 years of course work in chemistry (general and organic); 1 year of course work each in biochemistry, general biology, and general physics; 2 semesters of course work in mathematics; significant research laboratory experience. Additional exam requirements/recommendations for international students: Required—TOEFL. Electronic applications accepted. *Faculty research:* Cancer biology, diabetes, stem cell biology, neuroscience, immunology.

See Display on page 65 and Close-Up on page 109.

Johns Hopkins University, National Institutes of Health Sponsored Programs, Baltimore, MD 21218. Offers biology (PhD), including biochemistry, biophysics, cell biology, developmental biology, genetic biology, molecular biology; cell, molecular, and developmental biology and biophysics (PhD). *Degree requirements:* For doctorate, comprehensive exam, thesis/dissertation. *Entrance requirements:* For doctorate, GRE General Test. Additional exam requirements/recommendations for international students: Required—TOEFL (minimum score 600 paper-based), TWE. Electronic applications accepted. *Faculty research:* Protein and nucleic acid biochemistry and biophysical chemistry, molecular biology and development.

Johns Hopkins University, School of Medicine, Graduate Programs in Medicine, Graduate Program in Cellular and Molecular Medicine, Baltimore, MD 21287. Offers PhD. *Faculty:* 125 full-time (38 women). *Students:* 113 full-time (72 women); includes 35 minority (4 Black or African American, non-Hispanic/Latino; 2 American Indian or Alaska Native, non-Hispanic/Latino; 17 Asian, non-Hispanic/Latino; 9 Hispanic/Latino; 3 Two or more races, non-Hispanic/Latino), 19 international. Average age 27. 265 applicants, 17% accepted, 21 enrolled. In 2017, 19 doctorates awarded. *Degree requirements:* For doctorate, comprehensive exam, thesis/dissertation, oral exam, thesis defense. *Entrance requirements:* For doctorate, GRE. *Application deadline:* For winter admission, 12/8 for domestic students. Application fee: $110. Electronic applications accepted. *Expenses:* Contact institution. *Financial support:* In 2017–18, 124 students received support, including 3 fellowships with tuition reimbursements available (averaging $31,936 per year); scholarships/grants, health care benefits, and tuition waivers (full) also available. *Faculty research:* Cancer, cardiovascular, cell biology, immunology, neuroscience, genetics of human disease. *Unit head:* Dr. Rajini Rao, Director, 410-955-4732, Fax: 410-614-7294, E-mail: rrao@jhmi.edu. *Application contact:* Leslie Lichter-Mason, Admissions Administrator, 410-614-0391, Fax: 410-614-7294, E-mail: llichte2@jhmi.edu.
Website: http://cmm.jhmi.edu

Johns Hopkins University, School of Medicine, Graduate Programs in Medicine, Program in Biochemistry, Cellular and Molecular Biology, Baltimore, MD 21205. Offers PhD. *Degree requirements:* For doctorate, comprehensive exam, thesis/dissertation. *Entrance requirements:* For doctorate, GRE General Test. Additional exam requirements/recommendations for international students: Required—TOEFL. Electronic applications accepted. *Faculty research:* Developmental biology, genomics/proteomics, protein targeting, signal transduction, structural biology.

Johns Hopkins University, Zanvyl Krieger School of Arts and Sciences, Program in Cell, Molecular, Developmental Biology, and Biophysics, Baltimore, MD 21218. Offers PhD. Terminal master's awarded for partial completion of doctoral program. *Degree requirements:* For doctorate, comprehensive exam, thesis/dissertation. *Entrance requirements:* For doctorate, GRE General Test. Additional exam requirements/recommendations for international students: Required—TOEFL (minimum score 600 paper-based), IELTS, TWE. Electronic applications accepted. *Faculty research:* Cell biology, molecular biology and development, biochemistry, developmental biology, biophysics, genetics.

Kent State University, College of Arts and Sciences, Department of Biological Sciences, Kent, OH 44242-0001. Offers biological sciences (MA, MS, PhD), including botany (MS, PhD), cell biology (MS, PhD), ecology (MS, PhD), physiology (MS, PhD). *Program availability:* Part-time. *Faculty:* 28 full-time (10 women), 3 part-time/adjunct (2 women). *Students:* 55 full-time (37 women), 10 part-time (6 women); includes 6 minority (3 Black or African American, non-Hispanic/Latino; 1 Asian, non-Hispanic/Latino; 2 Two or more races, non-Hispanic/Latino), 12 international. Average age 28. 27 applicants, 56% accepted, 11 enrolled. In 2017, 4 master's, 6 doctorates awarded. Terminal master's awarded for partial completion of doctoral program. *Degree requirements:* For master's, thesis (for some programs), departmental seminar presentation about research (for MS); for doctorate, thesis/dissertation, departmental seminar presentation

about research, admitted to doctoral candidacy following written and oral candidacy. *Entrance requirements:* For master's, GRE, minimum GPA of 3.0, official transcripts, goal statement, three letters of recommendation, list of up to five potential faculty advisors, undergraduate coursework roughly equivalent to a biology minor; for doctorate, GRE, official transcripts, goal statement, three letters of recommendation, list of up to five potential faculty advisors, baccalaureate degree with strong background in biology and related subjects such as chemistry and mathematics. Additional exam requirements/recommendations for international students: Required—TOEFL (minimum score 587 paper-based, 94 iBT), Michigan English Language Assessment Battery (minimum score 82), IELTS (7.0), or PTE (65). *Application deadline:* For fall admission, 12/15 for domestic students, 12/5 for international students. Applications are processed on a rolling basis. Application fee: $45 ($70 for international students). Electronic applications accepted. *Expenses:* Tuition, state resident: full-time $11,310; part-time $515 per credit hour. Tuition, nonresident: full-time $20,396; part-time $928 per credit hour. *International tuition:* $18,544 full-time. *Financial support:* Research assistantships with full tuition reimbursements, teaching assistantships with full tuition reimbursements, Federal Work-Study, scholarships/grants, and unspecified assistantships available. Financial award application deadline: 12/15. *Unit head:* Dr. James L. Blank, Dean, 330-672-2650, E-mail: jblank@kent.edu. *Application contact:* Dr. Heather K. Caldwell, Associate Professor and Graduate Coordinator, 330-672-3636, E-mail: hcaldwel@kent.edu.
Website: http://www.kent.edu/biology

Kent State University, College of Arts and Sciences, School of Biomedical Sciences, Kent, OH 44242-0001. Offers biological anthropology (PhD); biomedical mathematics (MS, PhD); cellular and molecular biology (MS, PhD), including cellular biology and structures, molecular biology and genetics; neurosciences (MS, PhD); pharmacology (MS, PhD); physiology (MS, PhD). *Faculty:* 22 full-time (9 women), 3 part-time/adjunct (1 woman). *Students:* 75 full-time (46 women); includes 8 minority (1 Black or African American, non-Hispanic/Latino; 3 Asian, non-Hispanic/Latino; 2 Hispanic/Latino; 2 Two or more races, non-Hispanic/Latino), 25 international. Average age 28. 70 applicants, 23% accepted, 13 enrolled. In 2017, 23 master's, 5 doctorates awarded. Terminal master's awarded for partial completion of doctoral program. *Degree requirements:* For master's, thesis; for doctorate, comprehensive exam, thesis/dissertation. *Entrance requirements:* For master's, GRE, bachelor's degree, transcripts, minimum GPA of 3.0, goal statement, three letters of recommendation, academic preparation adequate to perform graduate work in the desired field; for doctorate, GRE, master's degree, minimum GPA of 3.0, transcripts, goal statement, three letters of recommendation. Additional exam requirements/recommendations for international students: Required—TOEFL (minimum score 600 paper-based, 100 iBT), Michigan English Language Assessment Battery (minimum score 85), IELTS (minimum score 7.0) or PTE (minimum score 68). *Application deadline:* For fall admission, 1/1 for domestic and international students. Applications are processed on a rolling basis. Application fee: $45 ($70 for international students). Electronic applications accepted. *Expenses:* Tuition, state resident: full-time $11,310; part-time $515 per credit hour. Tuition, nonresident: full-time $20,396; part-time $928 per credit hour. *International tuition:* $18,544 full-time. *Financial support:* Research assistantships with full tuition reimbursements, teaching assistantships, and unspecified assistantships available. Financial award application deadline: 1/1. *Unit head:* Dr. Ernest J. Freeman, Director, School of Biomedical Sciences, 330-672-2363, E-mail: efreema2@kent.edu.
Website: http://www.kent.edu/biomedical/

Lehigh University, College of Arts and Sciences, Department of Biological Sciences, Bethlehem, PA 18015. Offers biochemistry (PhD); cell and molecular biology (PhD); integrative biology (PhD); molecular biology (MS). *Program availability:* 100% online. *Faculty:* 18 full-time (8 women). *Students:* 38 full-time (20 women), 21 part-time (15 women); includes 12 minority (2 Black or African American, non-Hispanic/Latino; 1 American Indian or Alaska Native, non-Hispanic/Latino; 1 Asian, non-Hispanic/Latino; 6 Hispanic/Latino; 2 Two or more races, non-Hispanic/Latino), 10 international. Average age 28. 33 applicants, 42% accepted, 4 enrolled. In 2017, 8 master's, 4 doctorates awarded. Terminal master's awarded for partial completion of doctoral program. *Degree requirements:* For master's, thesis optional; for doctorate, comprehensive exam, thesis/dissertation. *Entrance requirements:* For doctorate, GRE General Test. Additional exam requirements/recommendations for international students: Required—TOEFL (minimum score 85 iBT). *Application deadline:* For fall admission, 7/15 for domestic and international students; for spring admission, 12/1 for domestic and international students; for summer admission, 4/30 for domestic and international students. Application fee: $75. Electronic applications accepted. *Expenses:* $1,460 per credit. *Financial support:* In 2017–18, 39 students received support, including 8 fellowships with full tuition reimbursements available (averaging $27,600 per year), 17 research assistantships with full tuition reimbursements available (averaging $27,600 per year), 23 teaching assistantships with full tuition reimbursements available (averaging $27,600 per year); health care benefits and tuition waivers also available. Financial award application deadline: 12/1; financial award applicants required to submit CSS PROFILE or FAFSA. *Faculty research:* Gene expression, cytoskeleton and cell structure, cell cycle and growth regulation, neuroscience, animal behavior, microbiology. *Total annual research expenditures:* $1.8 million. *Unit head:* Dr. Linda Lowe-Krentz, Chairperson, 610-758-5084, Fax: 610-758-4004, E-mail: lij0@lehigh.edu. *Application contact:* Dr. Amber Rice, Graduate Coordinator, 610-758-5509, Fax: 610-758-4004, E-mail: amr511@lehigh.edu.
Website: http://www.lehigh.edu/~inbios/

Liberty University, School of Health Sciences, Lynchburg, VA 24515. Offers anatomy and cell biology (PhD); biomedical sciences (MS); epidemiology (MPH); exercise science (MS), including clinical, community physical activity, human performance, nutrition; global health (MPH); health promotion (MPH); medical sciences (MA), including biopsychology, business management, health informatics, molecular medicine, public health; nutrition (MPH). *Program availability:* Part-time, online learning. *Students:* 542 full-time (394 women), 696 part-time (541 women); includes 402 minority (286 Black or African American, non-Hispanic/Latino; 10 American Indian or Alaska Native, non-Hispanic/Latino; 34 Asian, non-Hispanic/Latino; 46 Hispanic/Latino; 1 Native Hawaiian or other Pacific Islander, non-Hispanic/Latino; 25 Two or more races, non-Hispanic/Latino), 59 international. Average age 32. 1,592 applicants, 40% accepted, 297 enrolled. In 2017, 204 master's awarded. *Degree requirements:* For master's, thesis (for some programs); for doctorate, thesis/dissertation. *Entrance requirements:* For doctorate, MAT or GRE, minimum GPA of 3.25 in master's program, 2-3 recommendations, writing samples (for some programs), letter of intent, professional vitae. Additional exam requirements/recommendations for international students: Required—TOEFL (minimum score 600 paper-based; 100 iBT). Application fee: $50. *Financial support:* Applicants required to submit FAFSA. *Unit head:* Dr. Ralph Linstra, Dean. *Application contact:* Jay Bridge, Director of Admissions, 800-424-9595, Fax: 800-628-7977, E-mail: gradadmissions@liberty.edu.

Louisiana State University Health Sciences Center, School of Graduate Studies in New Orleans, Department of Cell Biology and Anatomy, New Orleans, LA 70112-2223. Offers cell biology and anatomy (PhD), including clinical anatomy, development, cell, and neurobiology; MD/PhD. *Faculty:* 17 full-time (2 women). *Students:* 5 full-time (3 women), 1 (woman) part-time; includes 1 minority (Asian, non-Hispanic/Latino). 1 applicant. *Degree requirements:* For doctorate, comprehensive exam, thesis/dissertation. *Entrance requirements:* For doctorate, GRE General Test, minimum undergraduate GPA of 3.0. Additional exam requirements/recommendations for international students: Recommended—TOEFL, IELTS. *Application deadline:* For fall admission, 3/1 priority date for domestic students, 3/1 for international students. Applications are processed on a rolling basis. Application fee: $30. *Expenses:* Tuition, state resident: full-time $11,835; part-time $518 per hour. Tuition, nonresident: full-time $24,108; part-time $1079 per hour. *Required fees:* $1254; $55 per hour. *Financial support:* In 2017–18, 6 students received support. Unspecified assistantships available. Financial award application deadline: 4/1. *Faculty research:* Visual system organization, neural development, plasticity of sensory systems, information processing through the nervous system, visuomotor integration. *Total annual research expenditures:* $900,000. *Unit head:* Dr. Samuel McClugage, Head, 504-568-4011, Fax: 504-568-2165, E-mail: smcclu@lsuhsc.edu. *Application contact:* Dr. R. John Cork, Graduate Coordinator and Professor, 504-568-7177, E-mail: jcork@lsuhsc.edu.
Website: http://www.medschool.lsuhsc.edu/cell_biology/

Louisiana State University Health Sciences Center at Shreveport, Department of Cellular Biology and Anatomy, Shreveport, LA 71130-3932. Offers MS, PhD, MD/PhD. Terminal master's awarded for partial completion of doctoral program. *Degree requirements:* For master's, thesis; for doctorate, thesis/dissertation. *Entrance requirements:* For master's and doctorate, GRE General Test. Additional exam requirements/recommendations for international students: Required—TOEFL. *Faculty research:* Cancer biology, redox biology, neurosciences, immunobiology, cardiovascular sciences.

Loyola University Chicago, Graduate School, Integrated Program in Biomedical Sciences, Maywood, IL 60141. Offers biochemistry and molecular biology (MS, PhD); cell and molecular physiology (MS, PhD); infectious disease and immunology (MS); integrative cell biology (MS, PhD); microbiology and immunology (MS, PhD); molecular pharmacology and therapeutics (MS, PhD); neuroscience (MS, PhD). *Faculty:* 84 full-time (32 women). *Students:* 126 full-time (65 women), 1 (woman) part-time; includes 36 minority (5 Black or African American, non-Hispanic/Latino; 14 Asian, non-Hispanic/Latino; 14 Hispanic/Latino; 3 Two or more races, non-Hispanic/Latino), 13 international. Average age 26. 748 applicants, 34% accepted, 124 enrolled. In 2017, 41 master's, 18 doctorates awarded. *Degree requirements:* For master's, thesis; for doctorate, comprehensive exam, thesis/dissertation. *Entrance requirements:* For doctorate, GRE. Additional exam requirements/recommendations for international students: Required—TOEFL (minimum score 94 iBT), IELTS (minimum score 7.5). *Application deadline:* For fall admission, 2/7 for domestic students. Applications are processed on a rolling basis. Electronic applications accepted. *Expenses:* Contact institution. *Financial support:* In 2017–18, 20 students received support. Schmitt Fellowships and yearly tuition scholarships (averaging $25,032) available. Financial award application deadline: 6/15; financial award applicants required to submit FAFSA. *Unit head:* Dr. Leanne L. Cribbs, Associate Dean, Graduate Education, 708-327-2817, Fax: 708-216-8216, E-mail: lcribbs@luc.edu. *Application contact:* Margarita Quesada, Graduate Program Secretary, 708-216-3532, Fax: 708-216-8216, E-mail: mquesad@luc.edu.
Website: http://ssom.luc.edu/graduate_school/degree-programs/ipbsphd/

Marquette University, Graduate School, College of Arts and Sciences, Department of Biology, Milwaukee, WI 53201-1881. Offers cell biology (MS, PhD); developmental biology (MS, PhD); ecology (MS, PhD); epithelial physiology (MS, PhD); genetics (MS, PhD); microbiology (MS, PhD); molecular biology (MS, PhD); muscle and exercise physiology (MS, PhD); neuroscience (PhD). Terminal master's awarded for partial completion of doctoral program. *Degree requirements:* For master's, comprehensive exam, thesis, 1 year of teaching experience or equivalent; for doctorate, thesis/dissertation, 1 year of teaching experience or equivalent, qualifying exam. *Entrance requirements:* For master's and doctorate, GRE General Test, GRE Subject Test, official transcripts from all current and previous colleges/universities except Marquette, statement of professional goals and aspirations, three letters of recommendation. Additional exam requirements/recommendations for international students: Required—TOEFL (minimum score 530 paper-based). Electronic applications accepted. *Faculty research:* Neurobiology, neuroendocrinology, epithelial physiology, neuropeptide interactions, synaptic transmission.

Massachusetts Institute of Technology, School of Science, Department of Biology, Cambridge, MA 02139. Offers biochemistry (PhD); biological oceanography (PhD); biology (PhD); biophysical chemistry and molecular structure (PhD); cell biology (PhD); computational and systems biology (PhD); developmental biology (PhD); genetics (PhD); immunology (PhD); microbiology (PhD); molecular biology (PhD); neurobiology (PhD). *Degree requirements:* For doctorate, comprehensive exam, thesis/dissertation, teaching assistantship during two semesters. *Entrance requirements:* For doctorate, GRE General Test. Additional exam requirements/recommendations for international students: Required—TOEFL, IELTS. Electronic applications accepted. *Faculty research:* Cellular, developmental and molecular (plant and animal) biology; biochemistry, bioengineering, biophysics and structural biology; classical and molecular genetics, stem cell and epigenetics; immunology and microbiology; cancer biology, molecular medicine, neurobiology and human disease; computational and systems biology.

McGill University, Faculty of Graduate and Postdoctoral Studies, Faculty of Medicine, Department of Anatomy and Cell Biology, Montréal, QC H3A 2T5, Canada. Offers M Sc, PhD.

McMaster University, Faculty of Health Sciences and School of Graduate Studies, Program in Medical Sciences, Metabolism and Nutrition Area, Hamilton, ON L8S 4M2, Canada. Offers M Sc, PhD, MD/PhD. *Degree requirements:* For master's, thesis; for doctorate, comprehensive exam, thesis/dissertation. *Entrance requirements:* For master's, honors B Sc, B+ average in related field; for doctorate, M Sc, minimum B+ average, students with proven research experience and an A average may be admitted with a B Sc degree. Additional exam requirements/recommendations for international students: Required—TOEFL (minimum score 580 paper-based; 92 iBT).

Medical University of South Carolina, College of Graduate Studies, Program in Molecular and Cellular Biology and Pathobiology, Charleston, SC 29425. Offers cancer biology (PhD); cardiovascular biology (PhD); cardiovascular imaging (PhD); cell regulation (PhD); craniofacial biology (PhD); genetics and development (PhD); marine biomedicine (PhD); DMD/PhD; MD/PhD. *Degree requirements:* For doctorate, thesis/dissertation, oral and written exams. *Entrance requirements:* For doctorate, GRE General Test, interview, minimum GPA of 3.0. Additional exam requirements/recommendations for international students: Required—TOEFL (minimum score 600 paper-based; 100 iBT). Electronic applications accepted.

Michigan State University, The Graduate School, College of Agriculture and Natural Resources, MSU-DOE Plant Research Laboratory, East Lansing, MI 48824. Offers biochemistry and molecular biology (PhD); cellular and molecular biology (PhD); crop and soil sciences (PhD); genetics (PhD); microbiology and molecular genetics (PhD); plant biology (PhD); plant physiology (PhD). Offered jointly with the Department of Energy. *Degree requirements:* For doctorate, comprehensive exam, thesis/dissertation, laboratory rotation, defense of dissertation. *Entrance requirements:* For doctorate, GRE General Test, acceptance into one of the affiliated department programs; 3 letters of recommendation; bachelor's degree or equivalent in life sciences, chemistry, biochemistry, or biophysics; research experience. Electronic applications accepted. *Faculty research:* Role of hormones in the regulation of plant development and physiology, molecular mechanisms associated with signal recognition, development and application of genetic methods and materials, protein routing and function.

Michigan State University, The Graduate School, College of Natural Science, Program in Cell and Molecular Biology, East Lansing, MI 48824. Offers cell and molecular biology (MS, PhD); cell and molecular biology/environmental toxicology (PhD). *Entrance requirements:* Additional exam requirements/recommendations for international students: Required—TOEFL. Electronic applications accepted.

Missouri State University, Graduate College, College of Health and Human Services, Department of Biomedical Sciences, Program in Cell and Molecular Biology, Springfield, MO 65897. Offers MS. *Program availability:* Part-time. *Faculty:* 28 full-time (18 women), 5 part-time/adjunct (3 women). *Students:* 6 full-time (3 women), 5 part-time (1 woman); includes 2 minority (1 Black or African American, non-Hispanic/Latino; 1 Hispanic/Latino). Average age 24. 7 applicants, 43% accepted, 3 enrolled. In 2017, 2 master's awarded. *Degree requirements:* For master's, thesis or alternative, oral and written exams. *Entrance requirements:* For master's, GRE General Test, 2 semesters of course work in organic chemistry and physics, 1 semester of course work in calculus, minimum GPA of 3.0 in last 60 hours of course work. Additional exam requirements/recommendations for international students: Required—TOEFL (minimum score 550 paper-based; 79 iBT), IELTS (minimum score 6). *Application deadline:* For fall admission, 7/20 priority date for domestic students, 5/1 for international students; for spring admission, 12/20 priority date for domestic students, 9/1 for international students. Applications are processed on a rolling basis. Application fee: $35 ($50 for international students). Electronic applications accepted. *Expenses:* Tuition, state resident: full-time $2915; part-time $2021 per credit hour. Tuition, nonresident: full-time $5354; part-time $3647 per credit hour. *International tuition:* $11,992 full-time. *Required fees:* $173; $173 per credit hour. Tuition and fees vary according to class time, course level, course load, degree level, campus/location and program. *Financial support:* In 2017–18, 11 research assistantships (averaging $8,772 per year) were awarded; career-related internships or fieldwork, Federal Work-Study, institutionally sponsored loans, scholarships/grants, and unspecified assistantships also available. Support available to part-time students. Financial award application deadline: 3/31; financial award applicants required to submit FAFSA. *Faculty research:* Extracellular matrix membrane protein, P2 nucleotide receptors, double stranded RNA viruses. *Unit head:* Dr. Scott Zimmerman, Program Director, 417-836-5478, Fax: 417-836-5588, E-mail: scottzimmerman@missouristate.edu. *Application contact:* Stephanie Praschan, Director, Graduate Enrollment Management, 417-836-5330, Fax: 417-836-6200, E-mail: stephaniepraschan@missouristate.edu.
Website: http://www.missouristate.edu/bms/CMB/

New York Medical College, Graduate School of Basic Medical Sciences, Valhalla, NY 10595. Offers biochemistry and molecular biology (MS, PhD); cell biology (MS, PhD); microbiology and immunology (MS, PhD); pathology (MS, PhD); pharmacology (MS, PhD); physiology (MS, PhD); MD/PhD. *Program availability:* Part-time, evening/weekend. *Faculty:* 70 full-time (17 women), 25 part-time/adjunct (9 women). *Students:* 116 full-time (63 women), 25 part-time (11 women); includes 65 minority (17 Black or African American, non-Hispanic/Latino; 1 American Indian or Alaska Native, non-Hispanic/Latino; 23 Asian, non-Hispanic/Latino; 21 Hispanic/Latino; 3 Two or more races, non-Hispanic/Latino), 27 international. Average age 27. 273 applicants, 56% accepted, 59 enrolled. In 2017, 32 master's, 3 doctorates awarded. *Degree requirements:* For master's, thesis; for doctorate, comprehensive exam, thesis/dissertation. *Entrance requirements:* For master's, GRE General Test, MCAT, or DAT; for doctorate, GRE General Test. Additional exam requirements/recommendations for international students: Required—TOEFL. *Application deadline:* For fall admission, 7/1 priority date for domestic students, 5/1 priority date for international students; for spring admission, 12/1 priority date for domestic students, 9/15 priority date for international students. Applications are processed on a rolling basis. Application fee: $75 ($100 for international students). Electronic applications accepted. *Expenses:* $1,125 per credit, $655 fees. *Financial support:* Fellowships, research assistantships, Federal Work-Study, institutionally sponsored loans, scholarships/grants, tuition waivers, and health benefits (for PhD candidates only) available. Support available to part-time students. Financial award application deadline: 4/30; financial award applicants required to submit FAFSA. *Faculty research:* Cardiovascular science, infectious diseases, neuroscience, cancer, cell signaling. *Unit head:* Dr. Francis L. Belloni, Dean, 914-594-4110, Fax: 914-594-4944, E-mail: francis_belloni@nymc.edu. *Application contact:* Valerie Romeo-Messana, Director of Admissions, 914-594-4110, Fax: 914-594-4944, E-mail: v_romeomessana@nymc.edu.
Website: https://www.nymc.edu/graduate-school-of-basic-medical-sciences-gsbms/gsbms-academics/

New York University, School of Medicine and Graduate School of Arts and Science, Sackler Institute of Graduate Biomedical Sciences, New York, NY 10016. Offers biomedical imaging and technology (PhD); biostatistics (PhD); cellular and molecular biology (PhD); developmental genetics (PhD); epidemiology (PhD); genome integrity (PhD); immunology and inflammation (PhD); microbiology (PhD); molecular biophysics (PhD); molecular oncology and tumor immunology (PhD); molecular pharmacology (PhD); neuroscience and physiology (PhD), including immunology, molecular oncology; stem cell biology (PhD); systems and computational biomedicine (PhD); MD/PhD. *Faculty:* 207 full-time (51 women). *Students:* 236 full-time (138 women), 1 part-time (0 women); includes 68 minority (13 Black or African American, non-Hispanic/Latino; 26 Asian, non-Hispanic/Latino; 28 Hispanic/Latino; 1 Native Hawaiian or other Pacific Islander, non-Hispanic/Latino), 79 international. Average age 27. 761 applicants, 18% accepted, 59 enrolled. In 2017, 35 doctorates awarded. *Degree requirements:* For doctorate, comprehensive exam, thesis/dissertation, qualifying exam; thesis defense. *Entrance requirements:* For doctorate, GRE. Additional exam requirements/recommendations for international students: Required—TOEFL, IELTS. *Application deadline:* For fall admission, 12/1 for domestic and international students. Applications are processed on a rolling basis. Application fee: $100. Electronic applications accepted. Application fee is waived when completed online. *Expenses:* Contact institution. *Financial support:* Health care benefits, tuition waivers (full), and unspecified assistantships available. *Faculty research:* Biomedical sciences. *Unit head:* Dr. Naoko Tanese, Associate Dean for Biomedical Sciences/Director, Sackler Institute, 212-263-8945, E-mail: naoko.tanese@nyumc.org. *Application contact:* Jessica Dong, Program Manager, 212-263-5648, E-mail: sackler-info@nyumc.org.
Website: https://med.nyu.edu/research/sackler-institute-graduate-biomedical-sciences/

North Carolina State University, College of Veterinary Medicine, Program in Comparative Biomedical Sciences, Raleigh, NC 27695. Offers cell biology (MS, PhD); infectious disease (MS, PhD); pathology (MS, PhD); pharmacology (MS, PhD); population medicine (MS, PhD). *Program availability:* Part-time. *Degree requirements:* For master's, thesis; for doctorate, thesis/dissertation. *Entrance requirements:* For master's and doctorate, GRE General Test. Additional exam requirements/recommendations for international students: Required—TOEFL (minimum score 550 paper-based). Electronic applications accepted. *Expenses:* Contact institution. *Faculty research:* Infectious diseases, cell biology, pharmacology and toxicology, genomics, pathology and population medicine.

North Dakota State University, College of Graduate and Interdisciplinary Studies, Interdisciplinary Program in Cellular and Molecular Biology, Fargo, ND 58102. Offers PhD. *Degree requirements:* For doctorate, thesis/dissertation. *Entrance requirements:* Additional exam requirements/recommendations for international students: Required—TOEFL. *Application deadline:* Applications are processed on a rolling basis. Electronic applications accepted. *Expenses:* Tuition, state resident: full-time $4323; part-time $360.21 per credit. Tuition, nonresident: full-time $6484; part-time $540.31 per credit. *Required fees:* $668; $55.70 per credit. Part-time tuition and fees vary according to degree level, program and reciprocity agreements. *Financial support:* Fellowships, research assistantships, teaching assistantships, and unspecified assistantships available. *Unit head:* Dr. Jane Schuh, Director, 701-231-7841, E-mail: jane.schuh@ndsu.edu.
Website: http://www.ndsu.edu/cellularmolecularbiology/

Northeastern Illinois University, College of Graduate Studies and Research, College of Arts and Sciences, Program in Biology, Chicago, IL 60625. Offers biology (MS), including cell biology, ecology, molecular biology, organismal biology. *Program availability:* Part-time, evening/weekend. *Degree requirements:* For master's, comprehensive exam, thesis optional. *Entrance requirements:* For master's, minimum GPA of 2.75. Additional exam requirements/recommendations for international students: Required—TOEFL (minimum score 550 paper-based; 79 iBT). *Application deadline:* For fall admission, 4/1 priority date for domestic students; for spring admission, 8/15 for domestic students. Applications are processed on a rolling basis. Application fee: $30. Electronic applications accepted. *Expenses:* Tuition, state resident: full-time $7274; part-time $404.11 per credit hour. Tuition, nonresident: full-time $14,548; part-time $808.23 per credit hour. *Required fees:* $1284. *Financial support:* Applicants required to submit FAFSA. *Faculty research:* Paleoecology and freshwater biology, protein biosynthesis and targeting, microbial growth and physiology, molecular biology of antibody production, reptilian neurobiology. *Unit head:* Dr. John Kasmer, Department Chair, 773-442-5717, E-mail: j-kasmer@neiu.edu. *Application contact:* Martha Narvaez, Graduate Admission Representative, 773-442-6006, E-mail: m-narvaez@neiu.edu.

Northwestern University, The Graduate School, Interdisciplinary Biological Sciences Program (IBiS), Evanston, IL 60208. Offers biochemistry (PhD); bioengineering and biotechnology (PhD); biotechnology (PhD); cell and molecular biology (PhD); developmental and systems biology (PhD); nanotechnology (PhD); neurobiology (PhD); structural biology and biophysics (PhD). *Degree requirements:* For doctorate, thesis/dissertation, qualifying exam. *Entrance requirements:* For doctorate, GRE General Test. Additional exam requirements/recommendations for international students: Required—TOEFL (minimum score 600 paper-based). Electronic applications accepted. *Faculty research:* Biophysics/structural biology, cell/molecular biology, synthetic biology, developmental systems biology, chemical biology/nanotechnology.

The Ohio State University, Graduate School, College of Arts and Sciences, Division of Natural and Mathematical Sciences, Department of Molecular Genetics, Columbus, OH 43210. Offers cell and developmental biology (MS, PhD); genetics (MS, PhD); molecular biology (MS, PhD). *Faculty:* 30. *Students:* 34 full-time (16 women), 13 international. Average age 26. In 2017, 6 doctorates awarded. *Entrance requirements:* For doctorate, GRE General Test, GRE Subject Test in biology or chemistry (recommended). Additional exam requirements/recommendations for international students: Required—TOEFL (minimum score 550 paper-based; 79 iBT), Michigan English Language Assessment Battery (minimum score 82); Recommended—IELTS (minimum score 7). *Application deadline:* For fall admission, 12/13 priority date for domestic students, 11/30 priority date for international students; for spring admission, 3/1 for domestic students, 2/1 for international students. Applications are processed on a rolling basis. Application fee: $60 ($70 for international students). Electronic applications accepted. *Financial support:* Fellowships, research assistantships, teaching assistantships, Federal Work-Study, and institutionally sponsored loans available. Support available to part-time students. *Unit head:* Dr. Mark Seeger, Chair, 614-292-5106, E-mail: seeger.9@osu.edu. *Application contact:* Graduate and Professional Admissions, 614-292-9444, Fax: 614-292-3895, E-mail: gpadmissions@osu.edu.
Website: https://molgen.osu.edu/

The Ohio State University, Graduate School, College of Arts and Sciences, Division of Natural and Mathematical Sciences, Program in Molecular, Cellular and Developmental Biology, Columbus, OH 43210. Offers MS, PhD. *Students:* 87 full-time (44 women); includes 6 minority (all Asian, non-Hispanic/Latino), 30 international. Average age 26. In 2017, 3 master's, 18 doctorates awarded. Terminal master's awarded for partial completion of doctoral program. *Entrance requirements:* For doctorate, GRE General Test, GRE Subject Test in any science (desired, preferably biology or chemistry, biochemistry or cell and molecular biology). Additional exam requirements/recommendations for international students: Required—TOEFL (minimum score 600 paper-based; 85 iBT); Recommended—IELTS (minimum score 8). *Application deadline:* For fall admission, 12/13 priority date for domestic students, 11/30 priority date for international students; for spring admission, 3/1 for domestic students, 2/1 for international students. Applications are processed on a rolling basis. Application fee: $60 ($70 for international students). Electronic applications accepted. *Financial support:* Fellowships, research assistantships, and teaching assistantships available. *Unit head:* Dr. Dawn Chandler, Co-Director, 614-722-5597, E-mail: chandler.135@osu.edu. *Application contact:* Graduate and Professional Admissions, 614-292-9444, Fax: 614-292-3895, E-mail: gpadmissions@osu.edu.
Website: http://mcdb.osu.edu/

Ohio University, Graduate College, College of Arts and Sciences, Department of Biological Sciences, Athens, OH 45701-2979. Offers biological sciences (MS, PhD); cell biology and physiology (MS, PhD); ecology and evolutionary biology (MS, PhD); exercise physiology and muscle biology (MS, PhD); microbiology (MS, PhD); neuroscience (MS, PhD). Terminal master's awarded for partial completion of doctoral program. *Degree requirements:* For master's, comprehensive exam, thesis, 1 quarter of teaching experience; for doctorate, comprehensive exam, thesis/dissertation, 2 quarters of teaching experience. *Entrance requirements:* For master's, GRE General Test, names of three faculty members whose research interests most closely match the applicant's interest; for doctorate, GRE General Test, essay concerning prior training, research interest and career goals, plus names of three faculty members whose research interests most closely match the applicant's interest. Additional exam requirements/recommendations for international students: Required—TOEFL (minimum score 620 paper-based; 105 iBT) or IELTS (minimum score 7.5). Electronic applications accepted. *Faculty research:* Ecology and evolutionary biology, exercise physiology and muscle biology, neurobiology, cell biology, physiology.

Ohio University, Graduate College, College of Arts and Sciences, Interdisciplinary Graduate Program in Molecular and Cellular Biology, Athens, OH 45701-2979. Offers PhD. *Degree requirements:* For doctorate, comprehensive exam, thesis/dissertation, research proposal, teaching experience. *Entrance requirements:* For doctorate, GRE General Test. Additional exam requirements/recommendations for international students: Required—TOEFL (minimum score 620 paper-based; 105 iBT); Recommended—TWE. Electronic applications accepted. *Faculty research:* Animal biotechnology, plant molecular biology RNA, immunology, cellular genetics, biochemistry of signal transduction, cancer research, membrane transport, bioinformatics, bioengineering, chemical biology and drug discovery, diabetes, microbiology, neuroscience.

Cell Biology

Oregon Health & Science University, School of Medicine, Graduate Programs in Medicine, Program in Molecular and Cellular Biosciences, Cell and Developmental Biology Graduate Program, Portland, OR 97239-3098. Offers PhD. *Faculty:* 11 full-time (6 women), 38 part-time/adjunct (6 women). *Students:* 9 full-time (4 women); includes 2 minority (both Asian, non-Hispanic/Latino), 1 international. Average age 28. *Degree requirements:* For doctorate, comprehensive exam, thesis/dissertation, qualifying exam. *Entrance requirements:* For doctorate, GRE General Test (minimum scores: 153 Verbal/148 Quantitative/4.5 Analytical) or MCAT. *Application deadline:* For fall admission, 12/1 for domestic and international students. Application fee: $70. *Financial support:* Health care benefits, tuition waivers (full), and full-tuition and stipends available. Financial award application deadline: 3/1; financial award applicants required to submit FAFSA. *Faculty research:* Biosynthesis, intracellular trafficking, and function of essential cellular components; signal transduction and developmental regulation of gene expression; regulation of cell proliferation, growth, and motility; mechanisms of morphogenesis and differentiation; mechanisms controlling the onset, progression, and dissemination of cancer. *Unit head:* Dr. Philip Copenhaver, Program Director, E-mail: somgrad@ohsu.edu. *Application contact:* Lola Bichler, Program Coordinator, E-mail: somgrad@ohsu.edu.
Website: http://www.ohsu.edu/xd/education/schools/school-of-medicine/departments/basic-science-departments/cell-and-developmental-biology/graduate-program/CDB-

Oregon State University, College of Agricultural Sciences, Program in Botany and Plant Pathology, Corvallis, OR 97331. Offers applied systematics (MS); ecology (MS, PhD); genetics (MS, PhD); genomics and computational biology (MS, PhD); molecular and cellular biology (MS, PhD); mycology (MS, PhD); plant pathology (MS, PhD); plant physiology (MS, PhD). *Entrance requirements:* For master's and doctorate, GRE. *Application deadline:* For fall admission, 12/1 for domestic and international students. Application fee: $75 ($85 for international students). *Financial support:* Application deadline: 12/1. *Unit head:* John Fowler, Chair of Graduate Studies, E-mail: fowlerj@science.oregonstate.edu.
Website: http://bpp.oregonstate.edu/

Oregon State University, Interdisciplinary/Institutional Programs, Program in Molecular and Cellular Biology, Corvallis, OR 97331. Offers bioinformatics (PhD); biotechnology (PhD); genome biology (PhD); molecular virology (PhD); plant molecular biology (PhD). *Degree requirements:* For doctorate, thesis/dissertation, oral and written qualifying exams. *Entrance requirements:* For doctorate, GRE. Additional exam requirements/recommendations for international students: Required—TOEFL (minimum score 80 iBT), IELTS (minimum score 6.5). *Application deadline:* For fall admission, 8/1 for domestic students, 4/1 for international students; for winter admission, 12/1 for domestic students, 7/1 for international students; for spring admission, 2/1 for domestic students, 10/1 for international students; for summer admission, 5/1 for domestic students, 1/1 for international students. Application fee: $75 ($85 for international students). *Financial support:* Application deadline: 1/1. *Unit head:* Dr. Kristin Carroll, Assistant Director, Molecular and Cellular Biology Program, 541-737-5259, E-mail: kirstin.carroll@oregonstate.edu. *Application contact:* Dr. Kristin Carroll, Assistant Director, Molecular and Cellular Biology Program, 541-737-5259, E-mail: kirstin.carroll@oregonstate.edu.
Website: http://gradschool.oregonstate.edu/molecular-and-cellular-biology-graduate-program

Penn State Hershey Medical Center, College of Medicine, Graduate School Programs in the Biomedical Sciences, Huck Institutes of the Life Sciences, Intercollege Graduate Program in Molecular Cellular and Integrative Biosciences, Hershey, PA 17033. Offers cell and developmental biology (PhD); molecular medicine (PhD); molecular toxicology (PhD); neurobiology (PhD). *Students:* 3 full-time (2 women); includes 2 minority (both Asian, non-Hispanic/Latino). 2 applicants, 100% accepted, 2 enrolled. In 2017, 1 doctorate awarded. *Degree requirements:* For doctorate, comprehensive exam, thesis/dissertation, oral exam. *Entrance requirements:* For doctorate, GRE, minimum GPA of 3.0. Additional exam requirements/recommendations for international students: Required—TOEFL (minimum score 500 paper-based). *Application deadline:* For fall admission, 1/31 priority date for domestic students, 2/1 priority date for international students. Applications are processed on a rolling basis. Application fee: $65. Electronic applications accepted. *Financial support:* In 2017–18, research assistantships with full tuition reimbursements (averaging $26,196 per year) were awarded; fellowships with full tuition reimbursements, career-related internships or fieldwork, Federal Work-Study, scholarships/grants, health care benefits, and unspecified assistantships also available. Financial award applicants required to submit FAFSA. *Faculty research:* Vascular biology, molecular toxicology, chemical biology, immune system, pathophysiological basis of human disease. *Unit head:* Dr. Peter Hudson, Director, 814-865-6057, E-mail: pjh18@psu.edu. *Application contact:* Kathy Shuey, Administrative Assistant, 717-531-8982, Fax: 717-531-0786, E-mail: grad-hmc@psu.edu.
Website: http://www.huck.psu.edu/education/molecular-cellular-and-integrative-biosciences

Penn State University Park, Graduate School, Intercollege Graduate Programs, Program in Molecular, Cellular, and Integrative Biosciences, University Park, PA 16802. Offers MS, PhD. *Unit head:* Dr. Regina Vasilatos-Younken, Dean, 814-865-2516, Fax: 814-863-4627. *Application contact:* Lori Hawn, Director, Graduate Student Services, 814-865-1795, Fax: 814-863-4627, E-mail: l-gswww@lists.psu.edu.
Website: http://www.huck.psu.edu/content/graduate-programs/molecular-cellular-and-integrative-biosciences

Purdue University, Graduate School, College of Science, Department of Biological Sciences, West Lafayette, IN 47907. Offers biochemistry (PhD); biophysics (PhD); cell and developmental biology (PhD); ecology, evolutionary and population biology (MS, PhD), including ecology, evolutionary biology, population biology; genetics (MS, PhD); microbiology (MS, PhD); molecular biology (PhD); neurobiology (MS, PhD); plant physiology (PhD). *Faculty:* 42 full-time (13 women), 3 part-time/adjunct (0 women). *Students:* 115 full-time (58 women), 6 part-time (4 women); includes 17 minority (1 Black or African American, non-Hispanic/Latino; 6 Asian, non-Hispanic/Latino; 9 Hispanic/Latino; 1 Two or more races, non-Hispanic/Latino), 60 international. Average age 27. 165 applicants, 12% accepted, 15 enrolled. In 2017, 5 master's, 16 doctorates awarded. Terminal master's awarded for partial completion of doctoral program. *Degree requirements:* For master's, thesis (for some programs); for doctorate, thesis/dissertation, seminars, teaching experience. *Entrance requirements:* For master's, GRE General Test (minimum analytical writing score of 3.5), minimum undergraduate GPA of 3.0; for doctorate, GRE General Test (minimum analytical writing score of 3.5), minimum undergraduate GPA of 3.5. Additional exam requirements/recommendations for international students: Required—TOEFL minimum score 600 paper-based; 107 iBT (for MS), 80 iBT (for PhD). *Application deadline:* For fall admission, 12/7 for domestic and international students. Applications are processed on a rolling basis. Application fee: $60 ($75 for international students). Electronic applications accepted. *Financial support:* Fellowships, research assistantships, and teaching assistantships available. Support available to part-time students. Financial award application deadline: 2/15; financial award applicants required to submit FAFSA. *Unit head:* Stephen Konieczny, Head, 765-494-4407, E-mail: sfk@purdue.edu. *Application contact:* Georgina E. Rupp, Graduate Coordinator, 765-494-8142, E-mail: ruppg@purdue.edu.
Website: http://www.bio.purdue.edu/

Queen's University at Kingston, School of Graduate Studies, Faculty of Health Sciences, Department of Anatomy and Cell Biology, Kingston, ON K7L 3N6, Canada. Offers biology of reproduction (M Sc, PhD); cancer (M Sc, PhD); cardiovascular pathophysiology (M Sc, PhD); cell and molecular biology (M Sc, PhD); drug metabolism (M Sc, PhD); endocrinology (M Sc, PhD); motor control (M Sc, PhD); neural regeneration (M Sc, PhD); neurophysiology (M Sc, PhD). *Program availability:* Part-time. *Degree requirements:* For master's, thesis; for doctorate, one foreign language, comprehensive exam, thesis/dissertation. *Entrance requirements:* Additional exam requirements/recommendations for international students: Required—TOEFL. Electronic applications accepted. *Faculty research:* Human kinetics, neuroscience, reproductive biology, cardiovascular.

Quinnipiac University, College of Arts and Sciences, Program in Molecular and Cell Biology, Hamden, CT 06518-1940. Offers MS. *Program availability:* Part-time, evening/weekend. *Faculty:* 9 full-time (5 women), 1 part-time/adjunct (0 women). *Students:* 17 full-time (11 women), 9 part-time (5 women); includes 4 minority (2 Black or African American, non-Hispanic/Latino; 2 Hispanic/Latino), 4 international. 52 applicants, 58% accepted, 10 enrolled. In 2017, 14 master's awarded. *Degree requirements:* For master's, thesis optional. *Entrance requirements:* For master's, bachelor's degree in biological, medical, or health sciences. Additional exam requirements/recommendations for international students: Required—TOEFL (minimum score 575 paper-based; 90 iBT), IELTS (minimum score 6.5). *Application deadline:* For fall admission, 7/30 priority date for domestic students, 4/30 priority date for international students; for spring admission, 12/15 priority date for domestic students, 9/30 priority date for international students. Applications are processed on a rolling basis. Application fee: $45. Electronic applications accepted. *Financial support:* Federal Work-Study, scholarships/grants, and unspecified assistantships available. Financial award application deadline: 6/1; financial award applicants required to submit FAFSA. *Unit head:* Dr. Lise Thomas, Director, 203-582-8497, E-mail: graduate@qu.edu. *Application contact:* Office of Graduate Admissions, 800-462-1944, Fax: 203-582-3443, E-mail: graduate@qu.edu.
Website: http://www.qu.edu/gradmolecular

Rice University, Graduate Programs, Wiess School of Natural Sciences, Department of Biochemistry and Cell Biology, Houston, TX 77251-1892. Offers MA, PhD. Terminal master's awarded for partial completion of doctoral program. *Degree requirements:* For master's, thesis; for doctorate, thesis/dissertation. *Entrance requirements:* For master's and doctorate, GRE. Additional exam requirements/recommendations for international students: Required—TOEFL (minimum score 600 paper-based; 90 iBT). Electronic applications accepted. *Expenses:* Contact institution. *Faculty research:* Steroid metabolism, protein structure NMR, biophysics, cell growth and movement.

Rosalind Franklin University of Medicine and Science, School of Graduate and Postdoctoral Studies - Interdisciplinary Graduate Program in Biomedical Sciences, Department of Cell Biology and Anatomy, North Chicago, IL 60064-3095. Offers PhD, MD/PhD. Terminal master's awarded for partial completion of doctoral program. *Degree requirements:* For doctorate, comprehensive exam, thesis/dissertation, original research project. *Entrance requirements:* For doctorate, GRE General Test, minimum GPA of 3.0. Additional exam requirements/recommendations for international students: Required—TOEFL, TWE. *Faculty research:* Neuroscience, molecular biology.

Rush University, Graduate College, Division of Anatomy and Cell Biology, Chicago, IL 60612-3832. Offers MS, PhD, MD/MS, MD/PhD. Terminal master's awarded for partial completion of doctoral program. *Degree requirements:* For master's, thesis; for doctorate, comprehensive exam, thesis/dissertation, preliminary exam, dissertation proposal. *Entrance requirements:* For master's, GRE General Test, minimum GPA of 3.0, bachelor's degree in biology or chemistry (preferred), interview; for doctorate, GRE General Test, minimum GPA of 3.0, interview. Additional exam requirements/recommendations for international students: Required—TOEFL. Electronic applications accepted. *Faculty research:* Incontinence following vaginal distension, knee replacement, biomimetric materials, injured spinal motoneurons, implant fixation.

Rutgers University–Newark, Graduate School of Biomedical Sciences, Department of Cell Biology and Molecular Medicine, Newark, NJ 07107. Offers PhD. *Degree requirements:* For doctorate, thesis/dissertation, qualifying exam. *Entrance requirements:* For doctorate, GRE General Test. Additional exam requirements/recommendations for international students: Required—TOEFL. Electronic applications accepted.

Rutgers University–New Brunswick, Graduate School-New Brunswick, Programs in the Molecular Biosciences, Program in Cell and Developmental Biology, Piscataway, NJ 08854-8097. Offers MS, PhD. MS, PhD offered jointly with University of Medicine and Dentistry of New Jersey. *Program availability:* Part-time. Terminal master's awarded for partial completion of doctoral program. *Degree requirements:* For master's, thesis; for doctorate, thesis/dissertation, written qualifying exam. *Entrance requirements:* For master's, GRE General Test; for doctorate, GRE General Test, GRE Subject Test (recommended), minimum GPA of 3.0. Additional exam requirements/recommendations for international students: Required—TOEFL. Electronic applications accepted. *Faculty research:* Signal transduction and regulation of gene expression, developmental biology, cellular biology, developmental genetics, neurobiology.

San Diego State University, Graduate and Research Affairs, College of Sciences, Department of Biology, San Diego, CA 92182. Offers biology (MA, MS), including ecology (MS), molecular biology (MS), physiology (MS), systematics/evolution (MS); cell and molecular biology (PhD); ecology (MS, PhD); microbiology (MS). Terminal master's awarded for partial completion of doctoral program. *Degree requirements:* For master's, thesis; for doctorate, thesis/dissertation. *Entrance requirements:* For master's, GRE General Test, GRE Subject Test, resume or curriculum vitae, 2 letters of recommendation. Additional exam requirements/recommendations for international students: Required—TOEFL. Electronic applications accepted.

San Diego State University, Graduate and Research Affairs, College of Sciences, Molecular Biology Institute, Program in Cell and Molecular Biology, San Diego, CA 92182. Offers PhD. Program offered jointly with University of California, San Diego. *Degree requirements:* For doctorate, thesis/dissertation, oral comprehensive qualifying exam. *Entrance requirements:* For doctorate, GRE General Test, GRE Subject Test, resumé or curriculum vitae, 3 letters of recommendation. Electronic applications accepted. *Faculty research:* Structure/dynamics of protein kinesis, chromatin structure and DNA methylation membrane biochemistry, secretory protein targeting, molecular biology of cardiac myocytes.

San Francisco State University, Division of Graduate Studies, College of Science and Engineering, Department of Biology, Program in Cell and Molecular Biology, San Francisco, CA 94132-1722. Offers MS. *Application deadline:* Applications are processed on a rolling basis. *Unit head:* Dr. Diana Chu, Program Coordinator, 415-405-3487, Fax: 415-338-2295, E-mail: chud@sfsu.edu.
Website: http://biology.sfsu.edu/programs/graduate

Southern Methodist University, Dedman College of Humanities and Sciences, Department of Biological Sciences, Dallas, TX 75275. Offers molecular and cellular biology (MA, MS, PhD). Terminal master's awarded for partial completion of doctoral program. *Degree requirements:* For master's, thesis (for MS), oral exam; for doctorate, thesis/dissertation, qualifying exam. *Entrance requirements:* For master's, GRE General

Test (minimum score 1200), minimum GPA of 3.0; for doctorate, GRE General Test (minimum score: 1200), minimum GPA of 3.0. Additional exam requirements/recommendations for international students: Required—TOEFL (minimum score 550 paper-based). *Application deadline:* For fall admission, 2/1 priority date for domestic and international students; for spring admission, 11/30 priority date for domestic and international students. Applications are processed on a rolling basis. Application fee: $60. Electronic applications accepted. *Financial support:* Applicants required to submit FAFSA. *Faculty research:* Free radicals and aging, protein structure, chromatin structure, signal processes, retroviral pathogenesis. *Unit head:* Dr. Robert Harrod, Advisor for Graduate Studies, 214-768-3864, E-mail: rharrod@smu.edu. *Application contact:* Dr. Pia Vogel, Graduate Advisor, 214-768-1790, Fax: 214-768-3955, E-mail: pvogel@smu.edu.
Website: http://smu.edu/biology/Graduate.asp

State University of New York Downstate Medical Center, School of Graduate Studies, Program in Molecular and Cellular Biology, Brooklyn, NY 11203-2098. Offers PhD, MD/PhD. Affiliation with a particular PhD degree-granting program is deferred to the second year. *Degree requirements:* For doctorate, comprehensive exam, thesis/dissertation. *Entrance requirements:* For doctorate, GRE General Test. Additional exam requirements/recommendations for international students: Recommended—TOEFL. *Faculty research:* Mechanism of gene regulation, molecular virology.

State University of New York Upstate Medical University, College of Graduate Studies, Program in Cell and Developmental Biology, Syracuse, NY 13210. Offers anatomy (MS, PhD); MD/PhD. Terminal master's awarded for partial completion of doctoral program. *Degree requirements:* For master's, thesis; for doctorate, comprehensive exam, thesis/dissertation. *Entrance requirements:* For master's, GRE General Test, interview; for doctorate, GRE General Test, telephone interview. Additional exam requirements/recommendations for international students: Required—TOEFL. Electronic applications accepted. *Faculty research:* Cancer, disorders of the nervous system, infectious diseases, diabetes/metabolic disorders/cardiovascular diseases.

Stony Brook University, State University of New York, Graduate School, College of Arts and Sciences, Department of Biochemistry and Cell Biology, Biochemistry and Cell Biology Program, Stony Brook, NY 11794. Offers MS. *Program availability:* Part-time. *Students:* 17 full-time (7 women), 5 part-time (3 women); includes 7 minority (1 Black or African American, non-Hispanic/Latino; 3 Asian, non-Hispanic/Latino; 2 Hispanic/Latino; 1 Two or more races, non-Hispanic/Latino), 5 international. 55 applicants, 60% accepted, 12 enrolled. In 2017, 12 master's awarded. *Degree requirements:* For master's, thesis. *Entrance requirements:* For master's, three letters of recommendation, BS or BA in a life science related field with minimum B average, personal statement. Additional exam requirements/recommendations for international students: Required—TOEFL (minimum score 550 paper-based; 90 iBT). *Application deadline:* For fall admission, 1/15 for domestic students; for summer admission, 10/1 for domestic students. Applications are processed on a rolling basis. Application fee: $100. Electronic applications accepted. *Expenses:* Contact institution. *Financial support:* In 2017–18, 1 research assistantship was awarded. *Unit head:* Prof. Aaron Neiman, Chair, 631-632-8550, Fax: 631-632-8575, E-mail: aaron.neiman@stonybrook.edu. *Application contact:* Pam Wolfskill, Coordinator, 631-632-8585, Fax: 631-632-8575, E-mail: carol.juliano@stonybrook.edu.
Website: https://www.stonybrook.edu/commcms/biochem/education/graduate/biochemistry-and-cell-biology-ms

Stony Brook University, State University of New York, Graduate School, College of Arts and Sciences, Department of Biochemistry and Cell Biology, Molecular and Cellular Biology Program, Stony Brook, NY 11794. Offers biochemistry and molecular biology (PhD); biological sciences (MA); immunology and pathology (PhD); molecular and cellular biology (PhD). *Students:* 63 full-time (35 women); includes 12 minority (3 Black or African American, non-Hispanic/Latino; 6 Asian, non-Hispanic/Latino; 3 Hispanic/Latino), 35 international. Average age 28. 131 applicants, 25% accepted, 11 enrolled. In 2017, 12 doctorates awarded. *Degree requirements:* For doctorate, comprehensive exam, thesis/dissertation, teaching experience. *Entrance requirements:* For doctorate, GRE General Test, GRE Subject Test. Additional exam requirements/recommendations for international students: Required—TOEFL. *Application deadline:* For fall admission, 1/15 for domestic students; for spring admission, 10/1 for domestic students. Application fee: $100. Electronic applications accepted. *Expenses:* Contact institution. *Financial support:* In 2017–18, 4 fellowships, 29 research assistantships, 12 teaching assistantships were awarded; Federal Work-Study also available. *Unit head:* Prof. Aaron Neiman, Chair, 631-632-8550, Fax: 631-632-8575, E-mail: aaron.neiman@stonybrook.edu. *Application contact:* Amy Saas, Graduate Program Administrator, 631-632-8613, Fax: 631-632-9730, E-mail: mcbgraduateprogram@stonybrook.edu.
Website: https://www.stonybrook.edu/mcb/

Texas Tech University Health Sciences Center, Graduate School of Biomedical Sciences, Program in Biomedical Sciences, Lubbock, TX 79430. Offers MS, PhD, MD/PhD, MS/PhD. Terminal master's awarded for partial completion of doctoral program. *Degree requirements:* For master's, comprehensive exam, thesis; for doctorate, comprehensive exam, thesis/dissertation. *Entrance requirements:* For master's and doctorate, GRE General Test, minimum GPA of 3.0. Additional exam requirements/recommendations for international students: Required—TOEFL (minimum score 550 paper-based). Electronic applications accepted. *Faculty research:* Biochemical endocrinology, neurobiology, molecular biology, reproductive biology, biology of developing systems.

Thomas Jefferson University, Jefferson College of Biomedical Sciences, MS Program in Cell and Developmental Biology, Philadelphia, PA 19107. Offers MS. *Program availability:* Part-time, evening/weekend. *Faculty:* 43 full-time (16 women), 28 part-time/adjunct (9 women). *Students:* 12 part-time (5 women); includes 1 minority (Asian, non-Hispanic/Latino), 2 international. 14 applicants, 93% accepted, 6 enrolled. In 2017, 9 master's awarded. *Degree requirements:* For master's, thesis, clerkship. *Entrance requirements:* For master's, GRE General Test or MCAT, minimum GPA of 3.0. Additional exam requirements/recommendations for international students: Required—TOEFL, IELTS (minimum score 7). *Application deadline:* For fall admission, 8/1 priority date for domestic students, 3/1 priority date for international students; for winter admission, 12/1 priority date for domestic students, 6/1 priority date for international students; for spring admission, 4/1 priority date for domestic students. Applications are processed on a rolling basis. Application fee: $50. Electronic applications accepted. *Financial support:* Federal Work-Study and institutionally sponsored loans available. Support available to part-time students. Financial award application deadline: 5/1; financial award applicants required to submit FAFSA. *Faculty research:* Developmental biology, cell biology, planning and management, drug development. *Unit head:* Dr. Gerald B. Grunwald, Dean and Program Director, 215-503-4191, Fax: 215-503-6690, E-mail: gerald.grunwald@jefferson.edu. *Application contact:* Marc E. Stearns, Senior Associate Director of Admissions, 215-503-0155, Fax: 215-503-3433, E-mail: jgsbs-info@jefferson.edu.
Website: http://www.jefferson.edu/university/biomedical-sciences/degrees-programs/master-programs/cell-developmental-biology.html

Thomas Jefferson University, Jefferson College of Biomedical Sciences, PhD Program in Cell Biology and Regenerative Medicine, Philadelphia, PA 19107. Offers PhD. *Faculty:* 57 full-time (15 women). *Students:* 20 full-time (15 women); includes 3 minority (2 Asian, non-Hispanic/Latino; 1 Hispanic/Latino), 6 international. In 2017, 7 doctorates awarded. *Degree requirements:* For doctorate, comprehensive exam, thesis/dissertation. *Entrance requirements:* For doctorate, GRE General Test, minimum GPA of 3.2. Additional exam requirements/recommendations for international students: Required—TOEFL (minimum score 100 iBT), IELTS (minimum score 7). *Application deadline:* For fall admission, 12/1 priority date for domestic and international students. Applications are processed on a rolling basis. Application fee: $60. Electronic applications accepted. *Financial support:* In 2017–18, 20 fellowships with full tuition reimbursements (averaging $62,653 per year) were awarded; Federal Work-Study, institutionally sponsored loans, scholarships/grants, traineeships, health care benefits, and stipends also available. Financial award application deadline: 5/1; financial award applicants required to submit FAFSA. *Unit head:* Dr. Nancy J. Philp, Program Director, 215-503-7854, E-mail: nancy.philp@jefferson.edu. *Application contact:* Marc E. Stearns, Senior Associate Director of Admissions, 215-503-0155, Fax: 215-503-3433, E-mail: jgsbs-info@jefferson.edu.
Website: http://www.jefferson.edu/university/biomedical-sciences/degrees-programs/phd-programs/cell-biology.html

Tufts University, Sackler School of Graduate Biomedical Sciences, Cell, Molecular, and Developmental Biology Program, Medford, MA 02155. Offers cancer biology (PhD); developmental and regenerative biology (PhD); molecular and cellular medicine (PhD); structural and chemical biology (PhD). Terminal master's awarded for partial completion of doctoral program. *Degree requirements:* For doctorate, comprehensive exam, thesis/dissertation. *Entrance requirements:* For doctorate, GRE General Test, 3 letters of reference, resume, personal statement. Electronic applications accepted. *Expenses: Tuition:* Full-time $49,892. *Required fees:* $874. Full-time tuition and fees vary according to degree level, program and student level. Part-time tuition and fees vary according to course load. *Faculty research:* Reproduction and hormone action, control of gene expression, cell-matrix and cell-cell interactions, growth control and tumorigenesis, cytoskeleton and contractile proteins.

Tulane University, School of Medicine and School of Liberal Arts, Graduate Programs in Biomedical Sciences, Department of Structural and Cellular Biology, New Orleans, LA 70118-5669. Offers MS, PhD, MD/PhD. MS and PhD offered through the Graduate School. *Degree requirements:* For master's, one foreign language, thesis; for doctorate, 2 foreign languages, thesis/dissertation. *Entrance requirements:* For master's, GRE General Test, minimum B average in undergraduate course work; for doctorate, GRE General Test. Additional exam requirements/recommendations for international students: Required—TOEFL. Electronic applications accepted. *Expenses: Tuition:* Full-time $50,920; part-time $2829 per credit hour. *Required fees:* $2040; $44.50 per credit hour. $580 per term. Tuition and fees vary according to course load, degree level and program. *Faculty research:* Reproductive endocrinology, visual neuroscience, neural response to altered hormones.

Tulane University, School of Medicine and School of Liberal Arts, Graduate Programs in Biomedical Sciences, Interdisciplinary Graduate Program in Molecular and Cellular Biology, New Orleans, LA 70118-5669. Offers PhD, MD/PhD. PhD offered through the Graduate School. *Degree requirements:* For doctorate, thesis/dissertation. *Entrance requirements:* For doctorate, GRE General Test, GRE Subject Test. Additional exam requirements/recommendations for international students: Required—TOEFL. Electronic applications accepted. *Expenses: Tuition:* Full-time $50,920; part-time $2829 per credit hour. *Required fees:* $2040; $44.50 per credit hour. $580 per term. Tuition and fees vary according to course load, degree level and program. *Faculty research:* Developmental biology, neuroscience, virology.

Tulane University, School of Science and Engineering, Department of Cell and Molecular Biology, New Orleans, LA 70118-5669. Offers MS, PhD. Terminal master's awarded for partial completion of doctoral program. *Degree requirements:* For doctorate, thesis/dissertation. *Entrance requirements:* For master's, GRE General Test, minimum B average in undergraduate course work; for doctorate, GRE General Test. Additional exam requirements/recommendations for international students: Required—TOEFL. Electronic applications accepted. *Expenses: Tuition:* Full-time $50,920; part-time $2829 per credit hour. *Required fees:* $2040; $44.50 per credit hour. $580 per term. Tuition and fees vary according to course load, degree level and program.

Uniformed Services University of the Health Sciences, F. Edward Hebert School of Medicine, Graduate Programs in the Biomedical Sciences and Public Health, Graduate Program in Molecular and Cell Biology, Bethesda, MD 20814-4799. Offers MS, PhD. *Degree requirements:* For doctorate, comprehensive exam, thesis/dissertation, qualifying exam. *Entrance requirements:* For doctorate, GRE General Test, minimum GPA of 3.0. Electronic applications accepted. *Faculty research:* Immunology, biochemistry, cancer biology, stem cell biology.

See Display on page 194 and Close-Up on page 209.

Universidad Central del Caribe, School of Medicine, Program in Biomedical Sciences, Bayamón, PR 00960-6032. Offers anatomy and cell biology (MA, MS); biochemistry (MS); biomedical sciences (MA); cellular and molecular biology (PhD); microbiology and immunology (MA, MS); pharmacology (MS); physiology (MS).

Université de Montréal, Faculty of Medicine, Department of Pathology and Cellular Biology, Montréal, QC H3C 3J7, Canada. Offers M Sc, PhD. Terminal master's awarded for partial completion of doctoral program. *Degree requirements:* For master's, thesis; for doctorate, thesis/dissertation, general exam. *Entrance requirements:* For master's and doctorate, proficiency in French, knowledge of English. Electronic applications accepted. *Faculty research:* Immunopathology, cardiovascular pathology, oncogenetics, cellular neurocytology, muscular dystrophy.

Université de Sherbrooke, Faculty of Medicine and Health Sciences, Graduate Programs in Medicine, Department of Anatomy and Cell Biology, Sherbrooke, QC J1H 5N4, Canada. Offers cell biology (M Sc, PhD). Terminal master's awarded for partial completion of doctoral program. *Degree requirements:* For master's, thesis; for doctorate, thesis/dissertation. Electronic applications accepted. *Faculty research:* Biology of the gut epithelium, signal transduction, gene expression and differentiation, intestinal inflammation, vascular and skeletal muscle cell biology.

Université Laval, Faculty of Medicine, Graduate Programs in Medicine, Programs in Cellular and Molecular Biology, Québec, QC G1K 7P4, Canada. Offers M Sc, PhD. Terminal master's awarded for partial completion of doctoral program. *Degree requirements:* For master's, thesis; for doctorate, comprehensive exam, thesis/dissertation. *Entrance requirements:* For master's and doctorate, knowledge of French, comprehension of written English. Electronic applications accepted. *Faculty research:* Oral bacterial metabolism, sugar transport.

University at Buffalo, the State University of New York, Graduate School, Graduate Programs in Cancer Research and Biomedical Sciences at Roswell Park Cancer Institute, Department of Cellular and Molecular Biology at Roswell Park Cancer Institute, Buffalo, NY 14260. Offers PhD. *Faculty:* 25 full-time (4 women). *Students:* 12 full-time (7 women), 2 international. 48 applicants, 29% accepted, 2 enrolled. In 2017, 6 doctorates

awarded. *Degree requirements:* For doctorate, comprehensive exam, thesis/dissertation, oral defense of dissertation. *Entrance requirements:* For doctorate, GRE General Test. Additional exam requirements/recommendations for international students: Required—TOEFL (minimum score 79 iBT). *Application deadline:* For fall admission, 1/5 priority date for domestic and international students. Application fee: $75. Electronic applications accepted. *Financial support:* In 2017–18, 21 students received support, including 21 research assistantships with full tuition reimbursements available (averaging $27,000 per year); scholarships/grants, health care benefits, and unspecified assistantships also available. Financial award application deadline: 1/5. *Faculty research:* Cancer genetics, chromatin structure and replication, regulation of transcription, human gene mapping, genetic and structural approaches to regulation of gene expression. *Unit head:* Dr. Dominic J. Smiraglia, Director of Graduate Studies, 716-845-1347, Fax: 716-845-1698, E-mail: dominic.smiraglia@roswellpark.org. *Application contact:* Dr. Norman J. Karin, Associate Dean, 716-845-2339, Fax: 716-845-8178, E-mail: norman.karin@roswellpark.edu.
Website: http://www.roswellpark.edu/education/phd-programs/cellular-molecular-biology

University at Buffalo, the State University of New York, Graduate School, Jacobs School of Medicine and Biomedical Sciences, Graduate Programs in Medicine and Biomedical Sciences, Department of Pathology and Anatomical Sciences, Buffalo, NY 14203. Offers anatomical sciences (MA, PhD); computational cell biology, anatomy, and pathology (PhD); pathology (MA, PhD). *Program availability:* Part-time. *Faculty:* 17 full-time (4 women). *Students:* 14 full-time (3 women); includes 2 minority (1 American Indian or Alaska Native, non-Hispanic/Latino; 1 Asian, non-Hispanic/Latino), 1 international. Average age 29. 26 applicants, 27% accepted, 6 enrolled. In 2017, 2 master's, 2 doctorates awarded. *Degree requirements:* For master's, thesis; for doctorate, comprehensive exam, thesis/dissertation. *Entrance requirements:* For master's, GRE, MCAT or DAT, 2 letters of recommendation; for doctorate, GRE, MCAT, or DAT, 3 letters of recommendation. Additional exam requirements/recommendations for international students: Required—TOEFL (minimum score 600 paper-based; 100 iBT). *Application deadline:* For fall admission, 5/1 priority date for domestic students, 3/1 priority date for international students. Applications are processed on a rolling basis. Application fee: $85. Electronic applications accepted. *Expenses:* Contact institution. *Financial support:* In 2017–18, 7 students received support, including 1 research assistantship with full tuition reimbursement available (averaging $24,900 per year), 1 teaching assistantship with full tuition reimbursement available (averaging $24,900 per year); Federal Work-Study, health care benefits, and unspecified assistantships also available. Financial award application deadline: 2/1; financial award applicants required to submit FAFSA. *Faculty research:* Immunopathology-immunobiology, experimental hypertension, neuromuscular disease, molecular pathology, cell motility and cytoskeleton. *Total annual research expenditures:* $138,370. *Unit head:* Dr. John E. Tomaszewski, Department Chair, 716-829-2846, Fax: 716-829-2911, E-mail: johntoma@buffalo.edu. *Application contact:* Lannette M. Garcia, Graduate Program Coordinator, 716-829-5204, Fax: 716-829-2911, E-mail: ubpathad@buffalo.edu.
Website: http://medicine.buffalo.edu/departments/pathology.html

The University of Alabama at Birmingham, Joint Health Sciences, Biochemistry, Structural, and Stem Cell Biology Theme, Birmingham, AL 35294. Offers PhD. *Faculty:* 370. *Students:* 40 full-time (16 women); includes 15 minority (3 Black or African American, non-Hispanic/Latino; 1 American Indian or Alaska Native, non-Hispanic/Latino; 7 Asian, non-Hispanic/Latino; 4 Hispanic/Latino). Average age 26. 30 applicants, 33% accepted, 7 enrolled. In 2017, 5 doctorates awarded. *Degree requirements:* For doctorate, comprehensive exam, thesis/dissertation. *Entrance requirements:* For doctorate, personal statement, resume or curriculum vitae, letters of recommendation, research experience, interview. Additional exam requirements/recommendations for international students: Required—TOEFL (minimum score 80 iBT), IELTS (minimum score 6.5). *Application deadline:* For fall admission, 12/31 for domestic and international students. Applications are processed on a rolling basis. Electronic applications accepted. *Financial support:* In 2017–18, fellowships with full tuition reimbursements (averaging $29,000 per year), research assistantships with full tuition reimbursements (averaging $30,000 per year) were awarded; health care benefits also available. *Unit head:* Dr. Thomas Ryan, Theme Director, 205-996-2175, E-mail: tryan@uab.edu. *Application contact:* Alyssa Zasada, Admissions Manager for Graduate Biomedical Sciences, 205-934-3857, E-mail: grad-gbs@uab.edu.
Website: http://www.uab.edu/gbs/home/themes/bssb

The University of Alabama at Birmingham, Joint Health Sciences, Cell, Molecular, and Developmental Biology Theme, Birmingham, AL 35294. Offers PhD. *Faculty:* 370. *Students:* 50 full-time (28 women); includes 17 minority (6 Black or African American, non-Hispanic/Latino; 8 Asian, non-Hispanic/Latino; 2 Hispanic/Latino; 1 Two or more races, non-Hispanic/Latino). Average age 27. 32 applicants, 28% accepted, 3 enrolled. In 2017, 7 doctorates awarded. *Degree requirements:* For doctorate, comprehensive exam, thesis/dissertation. *Entrance requirements:* For doctorate, personal statement, resume or curriculum vitae, letters of recommendation, research experience, interview. Additional exam requirements/recommendations for international students: Required—TOEFL (minimum score 80 iBT), IELTS (minimum score 6.5). *Application deadline:* For fall admission, 12/31 for domestic and international students. Applications are processed on a rolling basis. Electronic applications accepted. *Financial support:* In 2017–18, fellowships with full tuition reimbursements (averaging $29,000 per year), research assistantships with full tuition reimbursements (averaging $30,000 per year) were awarded; health care benefits also available. *Unit head:* Dr. Alecia K. Gross, Theme Director, 205-975-8396, E-mail: agross@uab.edu. *Application contact:* Alyssa Zasada, Admissions Manager for Graduate Biomedical Sciences, 205-934-3857, E-mail: grad-gbs@uab.edu.
Website: http://www.uab.edu/gbs/home/themes/cmdb

University of Alberta, Faculty of Graduate Studies and Research, Department of Biological Sciences, Edmonton, AB T6G 2E1, Canada. Offers environmental biology and ecology (M Sc, PhD); microbiology and biotechnology (M Sc, PhD); molecular biology and genetics (M Sc, PhD); physiology and cell biology (M Sc, PhD); plant biology (M Sc, PhD); systematics and evolution (M Sc, PhD). Terminal master's awarded for partial completion of doctoral program. *Degree requirements:* For master's, thesis; for doctorate, thesis/dissertation. *Entrance requirements:* Additional exam requirements/recommendations for international students: Required—TOEFL.

University of Alberta, Faculty of Medicine and Dentistry and Faculty of Graduate Studies and Research, Graduate Programs in Medicine, Department of Cell Biology, Edmonton, AB T6G 2E1, Canada. Offers cell and molecular biology (M Sc, PhD). Terminal master's awarded for partial completion of doctoral program. *Degree requirements:* For master's, thesis; for doctorate, thesis/dissertation. *Entrance requirements:* For master's and doctorate, 3 letters of reference, curriculum vitae. Additional exam requirements/recommendations for international students: Required—TOEFL (minimum score 600 paper-based). *Faculty research:* Protein targeting, membrane trafficking, signal transduction, cell growth and division, cell-cell interaction and development.

The University of Arizona, College of Science, Biochemistry and Molecular and Cellular Biology Program, Tucson, AZ 85721. Offers PhD. *Program availability:* Evening/weekend. *Degree requirements:* For doctorate, thesis/dissertation. *Entrance requirements:* For doctorate, 3 letters of recommendation, statement of purpose. Additional exam requirements/recommendations for international students: Required—TOEFL (minimum score 600 paper-based; 90 iBT), IELTS (minimum score 7). Electronic applications accepted. *Faculty research:* Plant molecular biology, cellular and molecular aspects of development, genetics of bacteria and lower eukaryotes.

University of Arkansas, Graduate School, Interdisciplinary Program in Cell and Molecular Biology, Fayetteville, AR 72701. Offers MS, PhD. In 2017, 11 master's, 4 doctorates awarded. *Degree requirements:* For doctorate, thesis/dissertation. *Application deadline:* For fall admission, 8/1 for domestic students, 4/1 for international students; for spring admission, 12/1 for domestic students, 10/1 for international students; for summer admission, 4/15 for domestic students, 3/1 for international students. Applications are processed on a rolling basis. Application fee: $60. Electronic applications accepted. *Expenses:* Tuition, state resident: full-time $3782. Tuition, nonresident: full-time $10,238. *Financial support:* In 2017–18, 31 research assistantships, 12 teaching assistantships were awarded; fellowships with tuition reimbursements also available. Financial award application deadline: 4/1; financial award applicants required to submit FAFSA. *Unit head:* Dr. Douglas Rhoads, Program Director, 479-575-4010, Fax: 479-575-5908, E-mail: drhoads@uark.edu. *Application contact:* Adnan Alrubaye, Program Associate Director, 479-575-3251, Fax: 479-575-4010, E-mail: aakhalaf@uark.edu.
Website: https://cell.uark.edu/

The University of British Columbia, Faculty of Medicine, Department of Cellular and Physiological Sciences, Vancouver, BC V6T 1Z3, Canada. Offers bioinformatics (M Sc, PhD); cell and developmental biology (M Sc, PhD); genome science and technology (M Sc, PhD); neuroscience (M Sc, PhD). *Degree requirements:* For master's, thesis, oral defense; for doctorate, comprehensive exam, thesis/dissertation, oral defense. *Entrance requirements:* For master's, minimum overall B+ average in third- and fourth-year courses; for doctorate, minimum overall B+ average in master's degree (or equivalent) from approved institution with clear evidence of research ability or potential. Additional exam requirements/recommendations for international students: Required—TOEFL, IELTS. *Expenses:* Contact institution.

University of California, Berkeley, Graduate Division, College of Letters and Science, Department of Molecular and Cell Biology, Berkeley, CA 94720-1500. Offers PhD. *Degree requirements:* For doctorate, comprehensive exam, thesis/dissertation, qualifying exam, 2 semesters of teaching. *Entrance requirements:* For doctorate, GRE General Test, GRE Subject Test (recommended), minimum GPA of 3.0. Additional exam requirements/recommendations for international students: Required—TOEFL (minimum score 570 paper-based; 68 iBT), IELTS (minimum score 7). Electronic applications accepted. *Faculty research:* Biochemistry, biophysics and structural biology; cell and developmental biology; genetics, genomics and development; immunology and pathogenesis; neurobiology.

University of California, Davis, Graduate Studies, Graduate Group in Cell and Developmental Biology, Davis, CA 95616. Offers MS, PhD. *Degree requirements:* For master's, comprehensive exam (for some programs), thesis (for some programs); for doctorate, thesis/dissertation. *Entrance requirements:* For doctorate, GRE General Test, GRE Subject Test. Additional exam requirements/recommendations for international students: Required—TOEFL (minimum score 550 paper-based). Electronic applications accepted. *Faculty research:* Molecular basis of cell function and development.

University of California, Irvine, Francisco J. Ayala School of Biological Sciences, Department of Developmental and Cell Biology, Irvine, CA 92697. Offers biological sciences (MS, PhD). *Students:* 39 full-time (25 women); includes 20 minority (1 Black or African American, non-Hispanic/Latino; 1 American Indian or Alaska Native, non-Hispanic/Latino; 10 Asian, non-Hispanic/Latino; 8 Hispanic/Latino), 4 international. Average age 28. 2 applicants, 100% accepted, 2 enrolled. In 2017, 8 master's, 12 doctorates awarded. *Entrance requirements:* For master's and doctorate, GRE General Test, GRE Subject Test, minimum GPA of 3.0. Additional exam requirements/recommendations for international students: Required—TOEFL (minimum score 550 paper-based). *Application deadline:* For fall admission, 12/15 priority date for domestic and international students. Application fee: $105 ($125 for international students). Electronic applications accepted. *Financial support:* Fellowships, research assistantships with full tuition reimbursements, teaching assistantships, institutionally sponsored loans, traineeships, health care benefits, and unspecified assistantships available. Financial award application deadline: 3/1; financial award applicants required to submit FAFSA. *Faculty research:* Genetics and development, oncogene signaling pathways, gene regulation, tissue regeneration and molecular genetics. *Unit head:* Prof. Thomas F. Schilling, Chair, 949-824-4562, Fax: 949-824-1105, E-mail: dkodowd@uci.edu. *Application contact:* Prof. Aimee Edinger, Graduate Advisor, 949-824-1921, Fax: 949-824-4709, E-mail: aedinger@uci.edu.
Website: http://devcell.bio.uci.edu/

University of California, Irvine, Francisco J. Ayala School of Biological Sciences and School of Medicine, Interdisciplinary Graduate Program in Cellular and Molecular Biosciences, Irvine, CA 92697. Offers PhD. *Students:* 40 full-time (20 women); includes 19 minority (9 Asian, non-Hispanic/Latino; 6 Hispanic/Latino; 4 Two or more races, non-Hispanic/Latino), 4 international. Average age 25. 371 applicants, 23% accepted, 38 enrolled. *Degree requirements:* For doctorate, thesis/dissertation, teaching assignment, preliminary exam. *Entrance requirements:* For doctorate, GRE General Test, three letters of recommendation, interview. Additional exam requirements/recommendations for international students: Required—TOEFL or IELTS. *Application deadline:* For fall admission, 12/8 for domestic and international students. Application fee: $105 ($125 for international students). Electronic applications accepted. *Expenses:* Contact institution. *Financial support:* Fellowships with full tuition reimbursements, institutionally sponsored loans, scholarships/grants, tuition waivers (full), unspecified assistantships, and stipends available. Financial award application deadline: 1/1; financial award applicants required to submit FAFSA. *Faculty research:* Cellular biochemistry; gene structure and expression; protein structure, function, and design; molecular genetics; pathogenesis and inherited disease. *Unit head:* Melanie Cocco, Director, 949-824-4487, Fax: 949-824-1965, E-mail: mcocco@uci.edu. *Application contact:* Renee Frigo, Administrator, 949-824-8145, Fax: 949-824-1965, E-mail: rfrigo@uci.edu.
Website: http://cmb.uci.edu/

University of California, Los Angeles, David Geffen School of Medicine and Graduate Division, Graduate Programs in Medicine, Department of Neurobiology, Los Angeles, CA 90095. Offers MS, PhD. Terminal master's awarded for partial completion of doctoral program. *Degree requirements:* For master's, comprehensive exam; for doctorate, thesis/dissertation, oral and written qualifying exams; 2 quarters of teaching experience. *Entrance requirements:* For doctorate, GRE General Test; GRE Subject Test, bachelor's degree; minimum undergraduate GPA of 3.0 (or its equivalent if letter grade system not used). Additional exam requirements/recommendations for international students: Required—TOEFL. Electronic applications accepted.

University of California, Los Angeles, Graduate Division, College of Letters and Science, Department of Molecular, Cell and Developmental Biology, Los Angeles, CA 90095. Offers MA, PhD. Terminal master's awarded for partial completion of doctoral program. *Degree requirements:* For master's, comprehensive exam, thesis; for doctorate, thesis/dissertation, oral and written qualifying exams; 2 quarters of teaching experience. *Entrance requirements:* For doctorate, GRE General Test. Additional exam requirements/recommendations for international students: Required—TOEFL. Electronic applications accepted.

University of California, Los Angeles, Graduate Division, College of Letters and Science and David Geffen School of Medicine, UCLA ACCESS to Programs in the Molecular, Cellular and Integrative Life Sciences, Los Angeles, CA 90095. Offers biochemistry and molecular biology (PhD); biological chemistry (PhD); cellular and molecular pathology (PhD); human genetics (PhD); microbiology, immunology, and molecular genetics (PhD); molecular biology (PhD); molecular toxicology (PhD); molecular, cellular and integrative physiology (PhD); neurobiology (PhD); oral biology (PhD); physiology (PhD). *Degree requirements:* For doctorate, thesis/dissertation, oral and written qualifying exams. *Entrance requirements:* For doctorate, GRE General Test, bachelor's degree; minimum undergraduate GPA of 3.0 (or its equivalent if letter grade system not used). Additional exam requirements/recommendations for international students: Required—TOEFL. Electronic applications accepted.

University of California, Riverside, Graduate Division, Program in Cell, Molecular, and Developmental Biology, Riverside, CA 92521-0102. Offers MS, PhD. Terminal master's awarded for partial completion of doctoral program. *Degree requirements:* For master's, thesis, oral defense of thesis; for doctorate, thesis/dissertation, oral defense of thesis, qualifying exams, 2 quarters of teaching experience. *Entrance requirements:* For master's and doctorate, GRE General Test, minimum GPA of 3.2. Additional exam requirements/recommendations for international students: Required—TOEFL (minimum score 550 paper-based; 80 iBT). Electronic applications accepted. *Expenses:* Tuition, state resident: full-time $5746. Tuition, nonresident: full-time $10,780. Tuition and fees vary according to campus/location and program.

University of California, San Francisco, Graduate Division and School of Medicine, Tetrad Graduate Program, Cell Biology Track, San Francisco, CA 94143. Offers PhD, MD/PhD. *Degree requirements:* For doctorate, thesis/dissertation. *Entrance requirements:* For doctorate, GRE General Test, GRE Subject Test. Additional exam requirements/recommendations for international students: Required—TOEFL. *Expenses:* Contact institution.

University of California, Santa Barbara, Graduate Division, College of Letters and Sciences, Division of Mathematics, Life, and Physical Sciences, Department of Molecular, Cellular, and Developmental Biology, Santa Barbara, CA 93106-9625. Offers MA, PhD, MA/PhD. Terminal master's awarded for partial completion of doctoral program. *Degree requirements:* For master's, comprehensive exam (for some programs), thesis (for some programs); for doctorate, comprehensive exam, thesis/dissertation. *Entrance requirements:* For master's and doctorate, GRE General Test, 3 letters of recommendation, statement of purpose, personal achievements/contributions statement, resume/curriculum vitae, transcripts for post-secondary institutions attended. Additional exam requirements/recommendations for international students: Required—TOEFL (minimum score 550 paper-based; 80 iBT), IELTS (minimum score 7). Electronic applications accepted. *Faculty research:* Microbiology, neurobiology (including stem cell research), developmental, virology, cell biology.

University of California, Santa Cruz, Division of Graduate Studies, Division of Physical and Biological Sciences, Program in Molecular, Cellular, and Developmental Biology, Santa Cruz, CA 95064. Offers MA, PhD. Terminal master's awarded for partial completion of doctoral program. *Degree requirements:* For master's, thesis; for doctorate, thesis/dissertation, qualifying exam. *Entrance requirements:* For master's and doctorate, GRE General Test, 3 letters of recommendation, interview. Additional exam requirements/recommendations for international students: Required—TOEFL (minimum score 550 paper-based; 83 iBT); Recommended—IELTS (minimum score 8). Electronic applications accepted. *Faculty research:* RNA biology, chromatin and chromosome biology, neurobiology, stem cell biology and differentiation, cell structure and function.

University of Chicago, Division of the Biological Sciences, Program in Cell and Molecular Biology, Chicago, IL 60637. Offers PhD. *Faculty:* 24. *Students:* 27 full-time (9 women); includes 10 minority (2 Black or African American, non-Hispanic/Latino; 1 American Indian or Alaska Native, non-Hispanic/Latino; 2 Asian, non-Hispanic/Latino; 4 Hispanic/Latino; 1 Two or more races, non-Hispanic/Latino), 5 international. Average age 27. 75 applicants, 24% accepted, 6 enrolled. In 2017, 6 doctorates awarded. *Degree requirements:* For doctorate, thesis/dissertation, ethics class, 2 teaching assistantships. *Entrance requirements:* For doctorate, GRE General Test, transcripts, statement of purpose, 3 letters of recommendation. Additional exam requirements/recommendations for international students: Required—TOEFL (minimum score 600 paper-based; 104 iBT), IELTS (minimum score 7). *Application deadline:* For fall admission, 12/1 for domestic and international students. Application fee: $90. Electronic applications accepted. *Financial support:* In 2017–18, 28 students received support, including fellowships with full tuition reimbursements available (averaging $31,000 per year), research assistantships with full tuition reimbursements available (averaging $31,000 per year); institutionally sponsored loans, scholarships/grants, traineeships, and health care benefits also available. Financial award application deadline: 12/1. *Faculty research:* Regulation of cell division; formation of organelles; dynamics of cell and tissue behavior; genome inheritance and expression; cytoskeleton function in organizing cellular processes. *Total annual research expenditures:* $8 million. *Unit head:* David Kovar, Chair, E-mail: drkovar@uchicago.edu. *Application contact:* Kristine Gaston, Graduate Program Director, 773-702-8037, E-mail: kristine@bsd.uchicago.edu.
Website: http://cellmolbio.bsd.uchicago.edu/

University of Cincinnati, Graduate School, College of Medicine, Graduate Programs in Biomedical Sciences, Cancer and Cell Biology Graduate Program, Cincinnati, OH 45267. Offers PhD. *Faculty:* 50 full-time (17 women). *Students:* 28 full-time (17 women); includes 7 minority (3 Black or African American, non-Hispanic/Latino; 3 Hispanic/Latino; 1 Native Hawaiian or other Pacific Islander, non-Hispanic/Latino), 8 international. Average age 26. 50 applicants, 12% accepted, 4 enrolled. In 2017, 4 doctorates awarded. *Degree requirements:* For doctorate, thesis/dissertation, qualifying exam. *Entrance requirements:* For doctorate, GRE or MCAT, baccalaureate degree; strong background in biology, chemistry, and/or physics and mathematics; minimum overall GPA of 3.0; curriculum vitae or resume; transcripts; essay; letters of recommendation. Additional exam requirements/recommendations for international students: Required—TOEFL (minimum score 600 paper-based; 100 iBT), IELTS (minimum score 7), PTE (minimum score 68). *Application deadline:* For fall admission, 1/14 priority date for domestic and international students. Applications are processed on a rolling basis. Application fee: $65 ($70 for international students). Electronic applications accepted. *Expenses:* Tuition, stipend, and student health insurance covered by the program. *Financial support:* In 2017–18, 7 fellowships with full tuition reimbursements (averaging $23,000 per year), 28 research assistantships with full tuition reimbursements (averaging $29,000 per year) were awarded; health care benefits, unspecified assistantships, and stipends also available. Support available to part-time students. Financial award application deadline: 4/15. *Faculty research:* Cancer biology, cell and molecular biology, breast cancer, pancreatic cancer, drug discovery. *Unit head:* Dr. Susan Waltz, Program Director, 513-558-8675, E-mail: susan.waltz@uc.edu. *Application contact:* Emily Spinks, Program Manager, 513-558-7379, E-mail: cellcoordinator@uc.edu.
Website: https://www.med.uc.edu/cancerbiology/graduate

University of Colorado Boulder, Graduate School, College of Arts and Sciences, Department of Molecular, Cellular, and Developmental Biology, Boulder, CO 80309. Offers cellular structure and function (MA, PhD); developmental biology (PhD); molecular biology (PhD). *Faculty:* 29 full-time (10 women). *Students:* 51 full-time (26 women), 4 part-time (1 woman); includes 8 minority (3 Asian, non-Hispanic/Latino; 4 Hispanic/Latino; 1 Two or more races, non-Hispanic/Latino), 10 international. Average age 27. 345 applicants, 9% accepted, 12 enrolled. In 2017, 10 doctorates awarded. Terminal master's awarded for partial completion of doctoral program. *Degree requirements:* For master's, comprehensive exam, thesis or alternative; for doctorate, comprehensive exam, thesis/dissertation. *Entrance requirements:* For master's, GRE General Test, GRE Subject Test, minimum undergraduate GPA of 3.0; for doctorate, GRE General Test, GRE Subject Test. *Application deadline:* For fall admission, 12/1 for domestic students; for spring admission, 12/1 for domestic students. Application fee: $60 ($80 for international students). Electronic applications accepted. Application fee is waived when completed online. *Financial support:* In 2017–18, 158 students received support, including 48 fellowships (averaging $12,292 per year), 38 research assistantships with full and partial tuition reimbursements available (averaging $34,642 per year), 10 teaching assistantships with full and partial tuition reimbursements available (averaging $30,525 per year); institutionally sponsored loans, scholarships/grants, health care benefits, and unspecified assistantships also available. Financial award application deadline: 2/15; financial award applicants required to submit FAFSA. *Faculty research:* Molecular biology; cellular biology; genetics; developmental biology; biochemistry: proteins. *Total annual research expenditures:* $15.3 million. *Application contact:* E-mail: mcdbgrad@colorado.edu.
Website: http://mcdb.colorado.edu/graduate

University of Colorado Denver, School of Medicine, Program in Cell Biology, Stem Cells, and Development, Aurora, CO 80045. Offers cell biology, stem cells, and developmental biology (PhD); modern human anatomy (MS). In 2017, 1 doctorate awarded. *Degree requirements:* For doctorate, comprehensive exam, thesis/dissertation, at least 30 credit hours of coursework and 30 credit hours of thesis research; laboratory rotations. *Entrance requirements:* For doctorate, GRE, minimum GPA of 3.0; 3 letters of reference; prerequisite coursework in organic chemistry, biology, biochemistry, physics and calculus; research experience (highly recommended). Additional exam requirements/recommendations for international students: Required—TOEFL (minimum score 550 paper-based; 80 iBT). Application fee: $0. *Faculty research:* Development and repair of the vertebrate nervous system; molecular, genetic and developmental mechanisms involved in the patterning of the early spinal cord (neural plate) during vertebrate embryogenesis; structural analysis of protein glycosylation using NMR and mass spectrometry; small RNAs and post-transcriptional gene regulation during nematode gametogenesis and early development; diabetes-mediated changes in cardiovascular gene expression and functional exercise capacity. *Unit head:* Dr. Bruce Appel, Director, 303-724-3465, E-mail: bruce.appel@ucdenver.edu. *Application contact:* Kenton Owsley, Program Administrator, 303-724-3468, Fax: 303-724-3420, E-mail: kenton.owsley@ucdenver.edu.
Website: http://www.ucdenver.edu/academics/colleges/medicalschool/programs/CSD/Pages/CSD.aspx

University of Connecticut, Graduate School, College of Liberal Arts and Sciences, Department of Molecular and Cell Biology, Storrs, CT 06269. Offers applied genomics (PSM); cell and developmental biology (MS, PhD); genetics and genomics (MS, PhD); microbial systems analysis (PSM); microbiology (MS, PhD); structural biology, biochemistry and biophysics (MS, PhD). Terminal master's awarded for partial completion of doctoral program. *Degree requirements:* For master's, comprehensive exam; for doctorate, thesis/dissertation. *Entrance requirements:* For master's and doctorate, GRE General Test, GRE Subject Test. Additional exam requirements/recommendations for international students: Required—TOEFL (minimum score 550 paper-based). Electronic applications accepted.

University of Connecticut Health Center, Graduate School, Graduate Program in Cell Analysis and Modeling, Farmington, CT 06030. Offers PhD. *Degree requirements:* For doctorate, comprehensive exam, thesis/dissertation. *Entrance requirements:* For doctorate, GRE General Test. Additional exam requirements/recommendations for international students: Required—TOEFL (minimum score 600 paper-based). Electronic applications accepted.

University of Connecticut Health Center, Graduate School, Programs in Biomedical Sciences, Graduate Program in Cell Biology, Farmington, CT 06030. Offers PhD, DMD/PhD, MD/PhD. *Degree requirements:* For doctorate, comprehensive exam, thesis/dissertation. *Entrance requirements:* For doctorate, GRE General Test. Additional exam requirements/recommendations for international students: Required—TOEFL (minimum score 600 paper-based). Electronic applications accepted. *Faculty research:* Vascular biology, computational biology, cytoskeleton and molecular motors, reproductive biology, signal transduction.

University of Delaware, College of Arts and Sciences, Department of Biological Sciences, Newark, DE 19716. Offers biotechnology (MS); cancer biology (MS, PhD); cell and extracellular matrix biology (MS, PhD); cell and systems physiology (MS, PhD); developmental biology (MS, PhD); ecology and evolution (MS, PhD); microbiology (MS, PhD); molecular biology and genetics (MS, PhD). Terminal master's awarded for partial completion of doctoral program. *Degree requirements:* For master's, thesis, preliminary exam; for doctorate, comprehensive exam, thesis/dissertation, preliminary exam. *Entrance requirements:* For master's and doctorate, GRE General Test. Additional exam requirements/recommendations for international students: Required—TOEFL (minimum score 600 paper-based); Recommended—TWE. Electronic applications accepted. *Faculty research:* Microorganisms, bone, cancer metastasis, developmental biology, cell biology, DNA.

University of Denver, Division of Natural Sciences and Mathematics, Department of Biological Sciences, Denver, CO 80208. Offers biology, ecology and evolution (MS, PhD); biomedical sciences (PSM); cell and molecular biology (MS, PhD). *Program availability:* Part-time. *Students:* Average age 25. 71 applicants, 44% accepted, 18 enrolled. In 2017, 7 master's, 3 doctorates awarded. Terminal master's awarded for partial completion of doctoral program. *Degree requirements:* For master's, comprehensive exam (for some programs), thesis; for doctorate, one foreign language, comprehensive exam (for some programs), thesis/dissertation. *Entrance requirements:* For master's and doctorate, GRE General Test, bachelor's degree in biology or related field, transcripts, personal statement, three letters of recommendation. Additional exam requirements/recommendations for international students: Required—TOEFL (minimum score 550 paper-based; 80 iBT). *Application deadline:* For fall admission, 1/1 priority date for domestic and international students. Applications are processed on a rolling basis. Application fee: $65. Electronic applications accepted. *Expenses:* Contact institution. *Financial support:* In 2017–18, 35 students received support, including 5 research assistantships with tuition reimbursements available (averaging $18,667 per year), 14 teaching assistantships with tuition reimbursements available (averaging $18,095 per year); Federal Work-Study, institutionally sponsored loans, scholarships/grants, and unspecified assistantships also available. Support available to part-time students. Financial award application deadline: 2/15; financial award applicants required to submit FAFSA. *Faculty research:* Molecular biology, cell biology, neurobiology,

ecology, molecular evolution. *Unit head:* Dr. Joseph Angleson, Associate Professor and Chair, 303-871-3463, Fax: 303-871-3471, E-mail: jangleso@du.edu. *Application contact:* Randi Flageolle, Assistant to the Chair, 303-871-3457, Fax: 303-871-3471, E-mail: rflageol@du.edu.
Website: http://www.du.edu/nsm/departments/biologicalsciences

University of Florida, College of Medicine and Graduate School, Interdisciplinary Program in Biomedical Sciences, Concentration in Molecular Cell Biology, Gainesville, FL 32611. Offers PhD. *Degree requirements:* For doctorate, thesis/dissertation. *Entrance requirements:* For doctorate, GRE General Test, minimum GPA of 3.0, biochemistry before enrollment. Additional exam requirements/recommendations for international students: Required—TOEFL, IELTS. Electronic applications accepted.

University of Florida, Graduate School, College of Agricultural and Life Sciences, Department of Animal Sciences, Interdisciplinary Concentration in Animal Molecular and Cellular Biology, Gainesville, FL 32611. Offers MS, PhD. *Entrance requirements:* For master's and doctorate, GRE General Test, minimum GPA of 3.0. Additional exam requirements/recommendations for international students: Required—TOEFL (minimum score 550 paper-based; 80 iBT), IELTS (minimum score 6). Electronic applications accepted.

University of Florida, Graduate School, College of Agricultural and Life Sciences, Department of Microbiology and Cell Science, Gainesville, FL 32611. Offers microbiology and cell science (MS, PhD), including medical microbiology and biochemistry (MS), toxicology (PhD). *Degree requirements:* For master's, comprehensive exam, thesis (for some programs); for doctorate, comprehensive exam, thesis/dissertation. *Entrance requirements:* For master's and doctorate, GRE General Test, minimum GPA of 3.0. Additional exam requirements/recommendations for international students: Required—TOEFL (minimum score 550 paper-based; 80 iBT), IELTS (minimum score 6). Electronic applications accepted. *Faculty research:* Biomass conversion, membrane and cell wall chemistry, plant biochemistry and genetics.

University of Florida, Graduate School, College of Liberal Arts and Sciences, Department of Biology, Gainesville, FL 32611. Offers botany (MS, MST, PhD), including botany, tropical conservation and development, wetland sciences; zoology (MS, MST, PhD), including animal molecular and cellular biology (PhD), tropical conservation and development, wetland sciences, zoology. *Degree requirements:* For master's, comprehensive exam (for some programs), thesis; for doctorate, comprehensive exam, thesis/dissertation. *Entrance requirements:* For master's and doctorate, GRE General Test, minimum GPA of 3.0. Additional exam requirements/recommendations for international students: Required—TOEFL (minimum score 550 paper-based; 80 iBT), IELTS (minimum score 6). Electronic applications accepted. *Faculty research:* Ecology of natural populations, plant and animal genome evolution, biodiversity, plant biology, behavior.

University of Georgia, Franklin College of Arts and Sciences, Department of Cellular Biology, Athens, GA 30602. Offers MS, PhD. *Degree requirements:* For master's, thesis; for doctorate, one foreign language, thesis/dissertation. *Entrance requirements:* For master's and doctorate, GRE General Test. Electronic applications accepted.

University of Guelph, Graduate Studies, College of Biological Science, Department of Molecular and Cellular Biology, Guelph, ON N1G 2W1, Canada. Offers biochemistry (M Sc, PhD); biophysics (M Sc, PhD); botany (M Sc, PhD); microbiology (M Sc, PhD); molecular biology and genetics (M Sc, PhD). *Degree requirements:* For master's, thesis, research proposal; for doctorate, comprehensive exam, thesis/dissertation, research proposal. *Entrance requirements:* For master's, minimum B-average during previous 2 years of coursework; for doctorate, minimum A-average. Additional exam requirements/recommendations for international students: Required—TOEFL (minimum score 550 paper-based), IELTS (minimum score 6.5). Electronic applications accepted. *Faculty research:* Physiology, structure, genetics, and ecology of microbes; virology and microbial technology.

University of Illinois at Chicago, College of Medicine and Graduate College, Graduate Programs in Medicine, Department of Anatomy and Cell Biology, Chicago, IL 60607. Offers MS, MD/PhD. *Degree requirements:* For master's, preliminary oral examination, dissertation and oral defense. *Entrance requirements:* For master's, GRE General Test, minimum GPA of 2.75, 3 letters of recommendation. Additional exam requirements/recommendations for international students: Required—TOEFL (minimum score 550 paper-based). Electronic applications accepted. *Faculty research:* Synapses, axonal transport, neurodegenerative diseases.

University of Illinois at Chicago, Program in Neuroscience, Chicago, IL 60607. Offers cellular and systems neuroscience and cell biology (PhD); neuroscience (MS).

University of Illinois at Urbana–Champaign, Graduate College, College of Liberal Arts and Sciences, School of Molecular and Cellular Biology, Department of Cell and Developmental Biology, Champaign, IL 61820. Offers PhD.

The University of Iowa, Graduate College, College of Liberal Arts and Sciences, Department of Biology, Iowa City, IA 52242-1324. Offers biology (MS, PhD); cell and developmental biology (MS, PhD); evolution (MS, PhD); genetics (MS, PhD); neurobiology (MS, PhD). Terminal master's awarded for partial completion of doctoral program. *Degree requirements:* For master's, thesis optional, exam; for doctorate, comprehensive exam, thesis/dissertation. *Entrance requirements:* For master's and doctorate, GRE General Test, minimum GPA of 3.0. Additional exam requirements/recommendations for international students: Required—TOEFL (minimum score 600 paper-based; 100 iBT). Electronic applications accepted. *Faculty research:* Neurobiology, evolutionary biology, genetics, cell and developmental biology.

The University of Iowa, Graduate College, Program in Molecular and Cellular Biology, Iowa City, IA 52242-1316. Offers PhD. *Degree requirements:* For doctorate, comprehensive exam, thesis/dissertation. *Entrance requirements:* For doctorate, GRE General Test, minimum GPA of 3.0. Additional exam requirements/recommendations for international students: Required—TOEFL (minimum score 600 paper-based; 100 iBT). Electronic applications accepted. *Faculty research:* Regulation of gene expression, inherited human genetic diseases, signal transduction mechanisms, structural biology and function.

The University of Iowa, Roy J. and Lucille A. Carver College of Medicine and Graduate College, Graduate Programs in Medicine, Department of Anatomy and Cell Biology, Iowa City, IA 52242-1316. Offers PhD. *Degree requirements:* For doctorate, comprehensive exam, thesis/dissertation. *Entrance requirements:* For doctorate, GRE General Test, minimum GPA of 3.0. Additional exam requirements/recommendations for international students: Required—TOEFL (minimum score 600 paper-based; 100 iBT). Electronic applications accepted. *Faculty research:* Biology of differentiation and transformation, developmental and vascular cell biology, neurobiology.

The University of Kansas, Graduate Studies, College of Liberal Arts and Sciences, Department of Molecular Biosciences, Lawrence, KS 66044. Offers biochemistry and biophysics (PhD); microbiology (PhD); molecular, cellular, and developmental biology (PhD). *Program availability:* Part-time. *Students:* 57 full-time (38 women); includes 8 minority (1 Black or African American, non-Hispanic/Latino; 2 Asian, non-Hispanic/Latino; 3 Hispanic/Latino; 2 Two or more races, non-Hispanic/Latino), 27 international. Average age 27. 73 applicants, 33% accepted, 8 enrolled. In 2017, 6 doctorates awarded. Terminal master's awarded for partial completion of doctoral program. *Entrance requirements:* For doctorate, GRE General Test, 1-page statement of research interests and goals, 1-2 page curriculum vitae or resume, official transcript, 3 recommendation letters. Additional exam requirements/recommendations for international students: Required—TOEFL or IELTS. *Application deadline:* For fall admission, 12/1 for domestic and international students. Application fee: $65 ($85 for international students). Electronic applications accepted. *Financial support:* Fellowships, research assistantships, teaching assistantships, scholarships/grants, health care benefits, and unspecified assistantships available. Financial award application deadline: 12/1. *Faculty research:* Structure and function of proteins, genetics of organism development, molecular genetics, neurophysiology, molecular virology and pathogenics, developmental biology, cell biology. *Unit head:* Susan M. Egan, Chair, 785-864-4294, E-mail: sme@ku.edu. *Application contact:* John Connolly, Graduate Admissions Contact, 785-864-4311, E-mail: jconnolly@ku.edu.
Website: http://www.molecularbiosciences.ku.edu/

The University of Kansas, University of Kansas Medical Center, School of Medicine, Department of Anatomy and Cell Biology, Kansas City, KS 66160. Offers MS, PhD, MD/PhD. *Faculty:* 29. *Students:* 11 full-time (6 women), 5 international. Average age 28. 1 applicant, 100% accepted, 1 enrolled. In 2017, 2 doctorates awarded. Terminal master's awarded for partial completion of doctoral program. *Degree requirements:* For master's, thesis; for doctorate, comprehensive exam, thesis/dissertation. *Entrance requirements:* For master's and doctorate, GRE. Additional exam requirements/recommendations for international students: Required—TOEFL. *Application deadline:* For fall admission, 1/15 priority date for domestic students. Applications are processed on a rolling basis. Application fee: $0. Electronic applications accepted. *Financial support:* In 2017–18, 16 research assistantships with full tuition reimbursements (averaging $24,500 per year), 3 teaching assistantships with full tuition reimbursements (averaging $24,500 per year) were awarded; fellowships, institutionally sponsored loans, scholarships/grants, health care benefits, and unspecified assistantships also available. Financial award application deadline: 3/1; financial award applicants required to submit FAFSA. *Faculty research:* Development of the synapse and neuromuscular junction, pain perception and diabetic neuropathies, cardiovascular and kidney development, reproductive immunology, post-fertilization signaling events. *Total annual research expenditures:* $6.8 million. *Unit head:* Dr. Dale R. Abrahamson, Chairman, 913-588-0702, Fax: 913-588-2710, E-mail: dabrahamson@kumc.edu. *Application contact:* Dr. Julie A. Christianson, Assistant Professor, 913-945-6430, Fax: 913-588-5677, E-mail: jchristianson@kumc.edu.
Website: http://www.kumc.edu/school-of-medicine/anatomy-and-cell-biology.html

The University of Manchester, School of Biological Sciences, Manchester, United Kingdom. Offers adaptive organismal biology (M Phil, PhD); animal biology (M Phil, PhD); biochemistry (M Phil, PhD); bioinformatics (M Phil, PhD); biomolecular sciences (M Phil, PhD); biotechnology (M Phil, PhD); cell biology (M Phil, PhD); cell matrix research (M Phil, PhD); channels and transporters (M Phil, PhD); developmental biology (M Phil, PhD); environmental biology (M Phil, PhD); evolutionary biology (M Phil, PhD); gene expression (M Phil, PhD); genetics (M Phil, PhD); history of science, technology and medicine (M Phil, PhD); immunology (M Phil, PhD); integrative neurobiology and behavior (M Phil, PhD); membrane trafficking (M Phil, PhD); microbiology (M Phil, PhD); molecular and cellular neuroscience (M Phil, PhD); molecular biology (M Phil, PhD); molecular cancer studies (M Phil, PhD); neuroscience (M Phil, PhD); ophthalmology (M Phil, PhD); optometry (M Phil, PhD); organelle function (M Phil, PhD); pharmacology (M Phil, PhD); physiology (M Phil, PhD); plant sciences (M Phil, PhD); stem cell research (M Phil, PhD); structural biology (M Phil, PhD); systems neuroscience (M Phil, PhD); toxicology (M Phil, PhD).

University of Maryland, Baltimore, Graduate School, Graduate Program in Life Sciences, Program in Cellular and Molecular Biomedical Science, Baltimore, MD 21201. Offers MS. *Program availability:* Part-time. *Students:* 15 full-time (12 women), 8 part-time (5 women); includes 7 minority (4 Black or African American, non-Hispanic/Latino; 2 Asian, non-Hispanic/Latino; 1 Hispanic/Latino), 8 international. Average age 28. 41 applicants, 61% accepted, 5 enrolled. In 2017, 9 master's awarded. *Degree requirements:* For master's, thesis (for some programs). *Entrance requirements:* For master's, GRE General Test, minimum GPA of 3.0, curriculum vitae, essay, 3 letters of recommendation. Additional exam requirements/recommendations for international students: Required—TOEFL (minimum score 80 iBT); Recommended—IELTS (minimum score 7). *Application deadline:* For fall admission, 4/15 priority date for domestic students, 1/15 for international students. Application fee: $75. Electronic applications accepted. *Expenses:* Tuition, state resident: full-time $13,990; part-time $661 per credit. Tuition, nonresident: full-time $30,484; part-time $1310 per credit. *Required fees:* $1894; $94 per credit. $415 per semester. Part-time tuition and fees vary according to course load, degree level and program. *Financial support:* Fellowships, Federal Work-Study, and unspecified assistantships available. Financial award application deadline: 3/1; financial award applicants required to submit FAFSA. *Unit head:* Dr. Dudley Strickland, Director, Graduate Program in Life Sciences, 410-706-8010. *Application contact:* Keith T. Brooks, Assistant Dean, 410-706-7131, Fax: 410-706-3473, E-mail: kbrooks@umaryland.edu.

University of Maryland, Baltimore, Graduate School, Graduate Program in Life Sciences, Program in Molecular Medicine, Baltimore, MD 21201. Offers cancer biology (PhD); cell and molecular physiology (PhD); human genetics and genomic medicine (PhD); molecular toxicology and pharmacology (PhD); MD/PhD. *Students:* 62 full-time (35 women), 2 part-time (0 women); includes 21 minority (7 Black or African American, non-Hispanic/Latino; 8 Asian, non-Hispanic/Latino; 4 Hispanic/Latino; 2 Two or more races, non-Hispanic/Latino), 4 international. Average age 27. 89 applicants, 30% accepted, 3 enrolled. In 2017, 13 doctorates awarded. *Degree requirements:* For doctorate, comprehensive exam, thesis/dissertation. *Entrance requirements:* For doctorate, GRE, minimum GPA of 3.0, curriculum vitae, essay, 3 letters of recommendation. Additional exam requirements/recommendations for international students: Required—TOEFL (minimum score 80 iBT); Recommended—IELTS (minimum score 7). *Application deadline:* For fall admission, 12/1 priority date for domestic students, 1/15 for international students. Application fee: $75. Electronic applications accepted. *Expenses:* Tuition, state resident: full-time $13,990; part-time $661 per credit. Tuition, nonresident: full-time $30,484; part-time $1310 per credit. *Required fees:* $1894; $94 per credit. $415 per semester. Part-time tuition and fees vary according to course load, degree level and program. *Financial support:* In 2017–18, research assistantships with partial tuition reimbursements (averaging $26,000 per year) were awarded; fellowships and health care benefits also available. Financial award application deadline: 3/1; financial award applicants required to submit FAFSA. *Unit head:* Dr. Toni Antalis, Director, 410-706-8222, E-mail: tantalis@som.umaryland.edu. *Application contact:* Marcina Garner, Program Coordinator, 410-706-6044, Fax: 410-706-6040, E-mail: mgarner@som.umaryland.edu.
Website: http://molecularmedicine.umaryland.edu

University of Maryland, Baltimore County, The Graduate School, College of Natural and Mathematical Sciences, Department of Biological Sciences, Program in Molecular and Cell Biology, Baltimore, MD 21250. Offers PhD. *Faculty:* 26 full-time (11 women). *Students:* 2 full-time (both women), 1 international. Average age 23. 25 applicants, 44% accepted, 2 enrolled. In 2017, 1 doctorate awarded. *Degree requirements:* For

doctorate, thesis/dissertation. *Entrance requirements:* For doctorate, GRE General Test, GRE Subject Test, minimum GPA of 3.0. Additional exam requirements/recommendations for international students: Required—TOEFL (minimum score 80 iBT), IELTS (minimum score 6.5). *Application deadline:* For fall admission, 4/15 priority date for domestic and international students. Application fee: $50. Electronic applications accepted. *Expenses: Required fees:* $132. *Financial support:* In 2017–18, 2 students received support, including 1 research assistantship with full tuition reimbursement available (averaging $24,600 per year), 1 teaching assistantship with full tuition reimbursement available (averaging $24,600 per year); unspecified assistantships also available. *Unit head:* Dr. Michelle Starz-Gaiano, Director, 410-455-2217, Fax: 410-455-3875, E-mail: biograd@umbc.edu. *Application contact:* Brandy Darcey, Graduate Program Coordinator, 410-4553669, E-mail: bdarcey@umbc.edu.
Website: http://biology.umbc.edu/grad/graduate-programs/mocb/

University of Maryland, College Park, Academic Affairs, College of Computer, Mathematical and Natural Sciences, Department of Biology, PhD Program in Biological Sciences, College Park, MD 20742. Offers behavior, ecology, evolution, and systematics (PhD); computational biology, bioinformatics, and genomics (PhD); molecular and cellular biology (PhD); physiological systems (PhD). *Degree requirements:* For doctorate, comprehensive exam, thesis/dissertation, thesis work presentation in seminar. *Entrance requirements:* For doctorate, GRE General Test; GRE Subject Test in biology (recommended), academic transcripts, statement of purpose/research interests, 3 letters of recommendation. Additional exam requirements/recommendations for international students: Required—TOEFL. Electronic applications accepted.

University of Maryland, College Park, Academic Affairs, College of Computer, Mathematical and Natural Sciences, Department of Cell Biology and Molecular Genetics, Program in Cell Biology and Molecular Genetics, College Park, MD 20742. Offers MS, PhD. *Degree requirements:* For master's, thesis; for doctorate, thesis/dissertation, exams. *Faculty research:* Cytoskeletal activity, membrane biology, cell division, genetics and genomics, virology.

University of Maryland, College Park, Academic Affairs, College of Computer, Mathematical and Natural Sciences, Department of Cell Biology and Molecular Genetics, Program in Molecular and Cellular Biology, College Park, MD 20742. Offers PhD. *Program availability:* Part-time, evening/weekend. *Degree requirements:* For doctorate, thesis/dissertation, exam, public service. *Faculty research:* Monoclonal antibody production, oligonucleotide synthesis, macromolular processing, signal transduction, developmental biology.

University of Massachusetts Amherst, Graduate School, Interdisciplinary Programs, Program in Molecular and Cellular Biology, Amherst, MA 01003. Offers biological chemistry and molecular biophysics (PhD); biomedicine (PhD); cellular and developmental biology (PhD). *Program availability:* Part-time. Terminal master's awarded for partial completion of doctoral program. *Degree requirements:* For doctorate, comprehensive exam, thesis/dissertation. *Entrance requirements:* For doctorate, GRE General Test. Additional exam requirements/recommendations for international students: Required—TOEFL (minimum score 550 paper-based; 80 iBT), IELTS (minimum score 6.5). Electronic applications accepted.

University of Massachusetts Amherst, Graduate School, Interdisciplinary Programs, Program in Plant Biology, Amherst, MA 01003. Offers biochemistry and metabolism (MS, PhD); cell biology and physiology (MS, PhD); environmental, ecological and integrative biology (MS, PhD); genetics and evolution (MS, PhD). *Degree requirements:* For master's, thesis; for doctorate, 2 foreign languages, comprehensive exam, thesis/dissertation. *Entrance requirements:* For master's and doctorate, GRE General Test. Additional exam requirements/recommendations for international students: Required—TOEFL (minimum score 550 paper-based; 80 iBT), IELTS (minimum score 6.5). Electronic applications accepted.

University of Miami, Graduate School, Miller School of Medicine, Graduate Programs in Medicine, Department of Cell Biology and Anatomy, Coral Gables, FL 33124. Offers molecular cell and developmental biology (PhD); MD/PhD. *Degree requirements:* For doctorate, thesis/dissertation. *Entrance requirements:* For doctorate, GRE General Test, GRE Subject Test. Additional exam requirements/recommendations for international students: Required—TOEFL. Electronic applications accepted.

University of Michigan, Rackham Graduate School, College of Literature, Science, and the Arts, Department of Molecular, Cellular, and Developmental Biology, Ann Arbor, MI 48109. Offers MS, PhD. *Program availability:* Part-time. *Faculty:* 37 full-time (12 women). *Students:* 85 full-time (51 women); includes 10 minority (2 Black or African American, non-Hispanic/Latino; 2 Asian, non-Hispanic/Latino; 6 Hispanic/Latino), 44 international. Average age 26. 139 applicants, 27% accepted, 23 enrolled. In 2017, 6 master's, 10 doctorates awarded. Terminal master's awarded for partial completion of doctoral program. *Degree requirements:* For master's, thesis (for some programs), 24 credits with at least 16 in molecular, cellular, and developmental biology and 4 in a cognate field; for doctorate, comprehensive exam, thesis/dissertation, preliminary exam, oral defense. *Entrance requirements:* Additional exam requirements/recommendations for international students: Required—TOEFL (minimum score 560 paper-based; 83 iBT). *Application deadline:* For fall admission, 12/15 for domestic and international students; for winter admission, 11/1 for domestic and international students; for spring admission, 4/1 for domestic and international students. Application fee: $75 ($90 for international students). Electronic applications accepted. *Expenses:* $11,184 in-state; $22,578 out of state; $5,954 candidacy. *Financial support:* In 2017–18, 65 students received support, including 23 fellowships with full tuition reimbursements available (averaging $30,600 per year), 32 research assistantships with full tuition reimbursements available (averaging $30,600 per year), 21 teaching assistantships with full tuition reimbursements available (averaging $30,600 per year); traineeships and health care benefits also available. Financial award application deadline: 12/15. *Faculty research:* Cell biology, microbiology, neurobiology and physiology, developmental biology and plant molecular biology. *Total annual research expenditures:* $8.9 million. *Unit head:* Dr. Robert J. Denver, Department Chair, 734-764-7476, Fax: 734-615-6337, E-mail: rdenver@umich.edu. *Application contact:* Mary Carr, Graduate Coordinator, 734-615-1635, Fax: 734-764-0884, E-mail: carrmm@umich.edu.
Website: http://www.mcdb.lsa.umich.edu

University of Michigan, Rackham Graduate School, Program in Biomedical Sciences (PIBS), Department of Cell and Developmental Biology, Ann Arbor, MI 48109. Offers PhD. *Faculty:* 21 full-time (10 women). *Students:* 21 full-time (11 women); includes 14 minority (1 Black or African American, non-Hispanic/Latino; 10 Asian, non-Hispanic/Latino; 3 Hispanic/Latino). Average age 29. 57 applicants, 18% accepted, 6 enrolled. In 2017, 5 doctorates awarded. *Degree requirements:* For doctorate, thesis/dissertation, oral defense of dissertation, preliminary exam. *Entrance requirements:* For doctorate, GRE General Test, 3 letters of recommendation, research experience. Additional exam requirements/recommendations for international students: Required—TOEFL (minimum score 84 iBT). *Application deadline:* For fall admission, 12/1 for domestic and international students. Application fee: $75 ($90 for international students). Electronic applications accepted. *Expenses:* Tuition, state resident: full-time $22,368; part-time $1201 per credit hour. Tuition, nonresident: full-time $45,156; part-time $2467 per credit hour. *Required fees:* $376 per term. Tuition and fees vary according to course load, degree level and program. *Financial support:* In 2017–18, fellowships (averaging $29,025 per year) were awarded; scholarships/grants, health care benefits, tuition waivers (full), and unspecified assistantships also available. Financial award application deadline: 12/1. *Faculty research:* Cell signaling, stem cells, organogenesis, cell biology, developmental genetics. *Total annual research expenditures:* $5.8 million. *Unit head:* Dr. Pierre A. Coulombe, Professor and Chair, 734-615-7509, Fax: 734-763-1166, E-mail: coulombe@umich.edu. *Application contact:* Michelle S. Melis, Director of Student Life, 734-615-6538, Fax: 734-647-7022, E-mail: msmtegan@umich.edu.
Website: http://cdb.med.umich.edu/

University of Michigan, Rackham Graduate School, Program in Biomedical Sciences (PIBS), Interdisciplinary Program in Cellular and Molecular Biology, Ann Arbor, MI 48109. Offers PhD. *Faculty:* 166 part-time/adjunct (43 women). *Students:* 52 full-time (35 women); includes 17 minority (1 Black or African American, non-Hispanic/Latino; 9 Asian, non-Hispanic/Latino; 5 Hispanic/Latino; 2 Two or more races, non-Hispanic/Latino). Average age 27. 71 applicants, 49% accepted, 7 enrolled. In 2017, 27 doctorates awarded. *Degree requirements:* For doctorate, comprehensive exam, thesis/dissertation, preliminary exam; oral defense of dissertation. *Entrance requirements:* For doctorate, GRE General Test. Additional exam requirements/recommendations for international students: Required—TOEFL (minimum score 560 paper-based; 84 iBT), IELTS (minimum score 6.5), Michigan English Language Assessment Battery. *Application deadline:* For fall admission, 12/1 for domestic students. Application fee: $75 ($90 for international students). Electronic applications accepted. *Expenses:* Contact institution. *Financial support:* In 2017–18, 52 students received support, including 36 fellowships with full tuition reimbursements available (averaging $30,600 per year), 3 research assistantships with full tuition reimbursements available (averaging $30,600 per year), 13 teaching assistantships with full tuition reimbursements available (averaging $30,600 per year); scholarships/grants, traineeships, and health care benefits also available. *Faculty research:* Cell and systems biology, cell physiology, biochemistry, genetics/gene regulation, genomics/proteomics, computational biology, microbial pathogenesis, immunology, development, aging, neurobiology, molecular mechanisms of disease, cancer biology. *Total annual research expenditures:* $20 million. *Unit head:* Dr. Robert S. Fuller, Director, 734-936-9764, Fax: 734-763-7799, E-mail: bfuller@umich.edu. *Application contact:* Patricia Ocelnik, Program Administrator, 734-764-5428, Fax: 734-647-7022, E-mail: cmbgrad@umich.edu.
Website: http://cmb.medicine.umich.edu

University of Minnesota, Twin Cities Campus, Graduate School, Program in Molecular, Cellular, Developmental Biology and Genetics, Minneapolis, MN 55455-0213. Offers genetic counseling (MS); molecular, cellular, developmental biology and genetics (PhD). Terminal master's awarded for partial completion of doctoral program. *Degree requirements:* For master's, thesis optional; for doctorate, thesis/dissertation. *Entrance requirements:* For master's and doctorate, GRE General Test. Additional exam requirements/recommendations for international students: Required—TOEFL (minimum score 625 paper-based; 80 iBT). Electronic applications accepted. *Faculty research:* Membrane receptors and membrane transport, cell interactions, cytoskeleton and cell mobility, regulation of gene expression, plant cell and molecular biology.

University of Minnesota, Twin Cities Campus, Graduate School, Stem Cell Biology Graduate Program, Minneapolis, MN 55455-3007. Offers MS. *Degree requirements:* For master's, thesis. *Entrance requirements:* For master's, GRE, BS, BA, or foreign equivalent in biological sciences or related field; minimum undergraduate GPA of 3.2. Additional exam requirements/recommendations for international students: Required—TOEFL (minimum score 580 paper-based, with a minimum score of 4 in the TWE, or 94 Internet-based, with a minimum score of 22 on each of the reading and listening, 26 on the speaking, and 26 on the writing section. *Faculty research:* Stem cell and developmental biology; embryonic stem cells; iPS cells; muscle satellite cells; hematopoietic stem cells; neuronal stem cells; cardiovascular, kidney and limb development; regenerating systems.

University of Missouri–Kansas City, School of Biological Sciences, Program in Cell Biology and Biophysics, Kansas City, MO 64110-2499. Offers PhD. Offered through the School of Graduate Studies. *Degree requirements:* For doctorate, comprehensive exam, thesis/dissertation. *Entrance requirements:* For doctorate, GRE General Test, bachelor's degree in chemistry, biology or related field; minimum GPA of 3.0. Additional exam requirements/recommendations for international students: Required—TOEFL (minimum score 550 paper-based; 80 iBT). Electronic applications accepted.

University of Montana, Graduate School, College of Humanities and Sciences, Division of Biological Sciences, Program in Cellular, Molecular and Microbial Biology, Missoula, MT 59812. Offers cellular and developmental biology (PhD); microbial evolution and ecology (PhD); microbiology and immunology (PhD); molecular biology and biochemistry (PhD). Terminal master's awarded for partial completion of doctoral program. *Degree requirements:* For doctorate, variable foreign language requirement, thesis/dissertation. *Entrance requirements:* For doctorate, GRE General Test. *Faculty research:* Ribosome structure, medical microbiology/pathogenesis, microbial ecology/environmental microbiology.

University of Nebraska Medical Center, Interdisciplinary Graduate Program in Biomedical Sciences, Department of Genetics, Cell Biology and Anatomy, Omaha, NE 68198-5805. Offers genetics, cell biology and anatomy (PhD); medical anatomy (MS); molecular genetics and cell biology (MS). Terminal master's awarded for partial completion of doctoral program. *Degree requirements:* For master's, comprehensive exam, thesis (for some programs); for doctorate, comprehensive exam, thesis/dissertation. *Entrance requirements:* For master's, GRE General Test (MCAT or DAT acceptable for MS in medical anatomy); for doctorate, GRE General Test. Additional exam requirements/recommendations for international students: Required—TOEFL (minimum score 550 paper-based; 80 iBT). Electronic applications accepted. *Expenses:* Contact institution. *Faculty research:* Hematology, immunology, developmental biology, genetics cancer biology, neuroscience.

University of Nevada, Reno, Graduate School, Interdisciplinary Program in Cell and Molecular Biology, Reno, NV 89557. Offers MS, PhD. Terminal master's awarded for partial completion of doctoral program. *Degree requirements:* For master's, thesis; for doctorate, thesis/dissertation. *Entrance requirements:* For master's, GRE Subject Test (recommended), minimum GPA of 2.75; for doctorate, GRE Subject Test (recommended), minimum GPA of 3.0. Additional exam requirements/recommendations for international students: Required—TOEFL (minimum score 500 paper-based; 61 iBT), IELTS (minimum score 6). Electronic applications accepted. *Faculty research:* Cellular biology, biophysics, cancer, microbiology, insect biochemistry.

University of New Haven, Graduate School, College of Arts and Sciences, Program in Cellular and Molecular Biology, West Haven, CT 06516. Offers MS. *Program availability:* Part-time, evening/weekend. *Faculty:* 10 full-time (5 women), 8 part-time/adjunct (4 women). *Students:* 39 full-time (21 women), 8 part-time (6 women); includes 10 minority (5 Black or African American, non-Hispanic/Latino; 2 Asian, non-Hispanic/Latino; 2 Hispanic/Latino; 1 Two or more races, non-Hispanic/Latino), 10 international. Average age 26. 56 applicants, 91% accepted, 22 enrolled. In 2017, 24 master's awarded. *Entrance requirements:* Additional exam requirements/recommendations for

international students: Required—TOEFL (minimum score 80 iBT), IELTS, PTE. *Application deadline:* Applications are processed on a rolling basis. Application fee: $50. Electronic applications accepted. Application fee is waived when completed online. *Expenses: Tuition:* Full-time $16,020; part-time $890 per credit hour. *Required fees:* $220; $90 per term. *Financial support:* Research assistantships with partial tuition reimbursements, teaching assistantships with partial tuition reimbursements, Federal Work-Study, scholarships/grants, and unspecified assistantships available. Support available to part-time students. Financial award application deadline: 5/1; financial award applicants required to submit FAFSA. *Unit head:* Dr. Christina Zito, Assistant Professor, 203-479-4299, E-mail: czito@newhaven.edu.
Website: http://www.newhaven.edu/4724/

University of New Mexico, Graduate Studies, Health Sciences Center, Program in Biomedical Sciences, Albuquerque, NM 87131-5196. Offers biochemistry and molecular biology (MS, PhD); cell biology and physiology (MS, PhD); molecular genetics and microbiology (MS, PhD); neuroscience (MS, PhD); pathology (MS, PhD); toxicology (MS, PhD). *Program availability:* Part-time. *Students:* Average age 29. 61 applicants, 16% accepted, 10 enrolled. In 2017, 11 master's, 14 doctorates awarded. Terminal master's awarded for partial completion of doctoral program. *Degree requirements:* For master's, thesis; for doctorate, comprehensive exam, thesis/dissertation, qualifying exam at the end of year 1/core curriculum. *Entrance requirements:* For master's and doctorate, GRE General Test, minimum undergraduate GPA of 3.0. Additional exam requirements/recommendations for international students: Required—TOEFL. *Application deadline:* For fall admission, 3/1 priority date for domestic and international students. Applications are processed on a rolling basis. Application fee: $50. Electronic applications accepted. *Financial support:* Fellowships, research assistantships with full tuition reimbursements, teaching assistantships, career-related internships or fieldwork, Federal Work-Study, institutionally sponsored loans, scholarships/grants, traineeships, health care benefits, and unspecified assistantships available. Financial award application deadline: 1/1; financial award applicants required to submit FAFSA. *Faculty research:* Infectious disease/immunity, cancer biology, cardiovascular and metabolic diseases, brain and behavioral illness, environmental health. *Unit head:* Dr. Helen J. Hathaway, Program Director, 505-272-1887, Fax: 505-272-2412, E-mail: hhathaway@salud.unm.edu. *Application contact:* Mary Fenton, Admissions Coordinator, 505-272-1887, Fax: 505-272-2412, E-mail: mfenton@salud.unm.edu.

The University of North Carolina at Chapel Hill, Graduate School, College of Arts and Sciences, Department of Biology, Chapel Hill, NC 27599. Offers botany (MA, MS, PhD); cell biology, development, and physiology (MA, MS, PhD); cell motility and cytoskeleton (PhD); ecology and behavior (MA, MS, PhD); genetics and molecular biology (MA, MS, PhD); morphology, systematics, and evolution (MA, MS, PhD). Terminal master's awarded for partial completion of doctoral program. *Degree requirements:* For master's, comprehensive exam, thesis (for some programs); for doctorate, comprehensive exam, thesis/dissertation. *Entrance requirements:* For master's, GRE General Test, GRE Subject Test, 2 semesters of calculus or statistics; 2 semesters of physics, organic chemistry; 3 semesters of biology; for doctorate, GRE General Test, GRE Subject Test, 2 semesters calculus or statistics, 2 semesters physics, organic chemistry, 3 semesters of biology. Additional exam requirements/recommendations for international students: Required—TOEFL (minimum score 550 paper-based). Electronic applications accepted. *Faculty research:* Gene expression, biomechanics, yeast genetics, plant ecology, plant molecular biology.

The University of North Carolina at Chapel Hill, School of Medicine and Graduate School, Graduate Programs in Medicine, Department of Cell and Developmental Biology, Chapel Hill, NC 27599. Offers PhD. *Degree requirements:* For doctorate, comprehensive exam, thesis/dissertation. *Entrance requirements:* For doctorate, GRE General Test, GRE Subject Test. Electronic applications accepted. *Faculty research:* Cell adhesion, motility and cytoskeleton; molecular analysis of signal transduction; development biology and toxicology; reproductive biology; cell and molecular imaging.

University of Notre Dame, Graduate School, College of Science, Department of Biological Sciences, Notre Dame, IN 46556. Offers aquatic ecology, evolution and environmental biology (MS, PhD); cellular and molecular biology (MS, PhD); genetics (MS, PhD); physiology (MS, PhD); vector biology and parasitology (MS, PhD). Terminal master's awarded for partial completion of doctoral program. *Degree requirements:* For master's, comprehensive exam, thesis; for doctorate, comprehensive exam, thesis/dissertation, candidacy exam. *Entrance requirements:* For master's and doctorate, GRE General Test. Additional exam requirements/recommendations for international students: Required—TOEFL (minimum score 600 paper-based; 80 iBT). Electronic applications accepted. *Faculty research:* Tropical disease, molecular genetics, neurobiology, evolutionary biology, aquatic biology.

University of Oklahoma Health Sciences Center, College of Medicine and Graduate College, Graduate Programs in Medicine, Department of Cell Biology, Oklahoma City, OK 73190. Offers MS, PhD. *Degree requirements:* For master's, thesis; for doctorate, thesis/dissertation. *Entrance requirements:* For doctorate, GRE General Test, GRE Subject Test, 3 letters of recommendation. Additional exam requirements/recommendations for international students: Required—TOEFL. *Faculty research:* Neurobiology, reproductive, neuronal plasticity, extracellular matrix, neuroendocrinology.

University of Ottawa, Faculty of Graduate and Postdoctoral Studies, Faculty of Medicine, Department of Cellular and Molecular Medicine, Ottawa, ON K1H 8M5, Canada. Offers M Sc, PhD. *Degree requirements:* For master's, thesis, seminar; for doctorate, comprehensive exam, thesis/dissertation, seminar. *Entrance requirements:* For master's, honors degree or equivalent, minimum B average; for doctorate, master's degree, minimum B+ average. Electronic applications accepted. *Faculty research:* Physiology, pharmacology, growth and development.

University of Pennsylvania, Perelman School of Medicine, Biomedical Graduate Studies, Graduate Group in Cell and Molecular Biology, Philadelphia, PA 19104. Offers cancer biology (PhD); cell biology, physiology, and metabolism (PhD); developmental stem cell regenerative biology (PhD); gene therapy and vaccines (PhD); genetics and gene regulation (PhD); microbiology, virology, and parasitology (PhD); MD/PhD; VMD/PhD. *Faculty:* 363. *Students:* 343 full-time (197 women); includes 114 minority (7 Black or African American, non-Hispanic/Latino; 51 Asian, non-Hispanic/Latino; 41 Hispanic/Latino; 15 Two or more races, non-Hispanic/Latino), 50 international. 588 applicants, 22% accepted, 61 enrolled. In 2017, 61 doctorates awarded. *Degree requirements:* For doctorate, thesis/dissertation. *Entrance requirements:* For doctorate, GRE General Test. Additional exam requirements/recommendations for international students: Required—TOEFL. *Application deadline:* For fall admission, 12/1 priority date for domestic and international students. Applications are processed on a rolling basis. Application fee: $80. Electronic applications accepted. *Financial support:* In 2017–18, 339 students received support. Fellowships, research assistantships, teaching assistantships, and tuition waivers available. *Unit head:* Dr. Daniel Kessler, Graduate Group Chair, 215-898-1478. *Application contact:* Meagan Schofer, Coordinator, 215-898-1478.
Website: http://www.med.upenn.edu/camb/

University of Pittsburgh, Kenneth P. Dietrich School of Arts and Sciences, Department of Biological Sciences, Program in Molecular, Cellular, and Developmental Biology, Pittsburgh, PA 15260. Offers PhD. *Program availability:* Part-time, online learning. *Faculty:* 23 full-time (6 women). *Students:* 38 full-time (20 women); includes 2 minority (1 Black or African American, non-Hispanic/Latino; 1 Asian, non-Hispanic/Latino), 7 international. Average age 23. In 2017, 5 doctorates awarded. *Degree requirements:* For doctorate, comprehensive exam, thesis/dissertation, completion of research integrity module. *Entrance requirements:* For doctorate, GRE General Test, GRE Subject Test. Additional exam requirements/recommendations for international students: Required—TOEFL (minimum score 90 iBT). *Application deadline:* Applications are processed on a rolling basis. Application fee: $0. Electronic applications accepted. *Financial support:* In 2017–18, 23 fellowships with full tuition reimbursements (averaging $34,776 per year), 63 research assistantships with full tuition reimbursements (averaging $28,800 per year), 20 teaching assistantships with full tuition reimbursements (averaging $28,250 per year) were awarded; Federal Work-Study, traineeships, health care benefits, and tuition waivers also available. *Unit head:* Dr. Karen M. Arndt, Professor, 412-624-6963, Fax: 412-624-4349, E-mail: arndt@pitt.edu. *Application contact:* Cathleen M. Barr, Graduate Administrator, 412-624-4268, Fax: 412-624-4349, E-mail: cbarr@pitt.edu.
Website: http://www.biology.pitt.edu

University of Pittsburgh, School of Medicine, Graduate Programs in Medicine, Cell Biology and Molecular Physiology Graduate Program, Pittsburgh, PA 15260. Offers PhD. *Faculty:* 46 full-time (11 women). *Students:* 6 full-time (5 women). Average age 26. 350 applicants, 21% accepted, 16 enrolled. In 2017, 2 doctorates awarded. *Degree requirements:* For doctorate, comprehensive exam, thesis/dissertation. *Entrance requirements:* For doctorate, GRE General Test, minimum GPA of 3.2, 3 letters of recommendation, official transcripts, baccalaureate degree. Additional exam requirements/recommendations for international students: Required—TOEFL (minimum score 600 paper-based; 100 iBT), IELTS (minimum score 7). *Application deadline:* For fall admission, 12/1 priority date for domestic and international students. Application fee: $50. Electronic applications accepted. *Expenses:* $26,782 in-state, $42,006 out-of-state. *Financial support:* In 2017–18, 6 students received support, including 1 research assistantship with full tuition reimbursement available (averaging $29,500 per year), 4 teaching assistantships with full tuition reimbursements available (averaging $29,500 per year); traineeships also available. *Faculty research:* Genetic disorders of ion channels, regulation of gene expression development, membrane traffic of proteins and lipids, reproductive biology, signal transduction in diabetes and metabolism. *Unit head:* Dr. Michael Butterworth, Program Director, 412-383-8591, E-mail: michael7@pitt.edu. *Application contact:* Carol Williams, Admissions and Recruiting Manager, 412-648-9003, Fax: 412-648-1077, E-mail: gradstudies@medschool.pitt.edu.
Website: http://www.gradbiomed.pitt.edu

University of Puerto Rico–Río Piedras, College of Natural Sciences, Department of Biology, San Juan, PR 00931-3300. Offers ecology/systematics (MS, PhD); evolution/genetics (MS, PhD); molecular/cellular biology (MS, PhD); neuroscience (MS, PhD). *Program availability:* Part-time. *Degree requirements:* For master's, one foreign language, comprehensive exam, thesis; for doctorate, one foreign language, comprehensive exam, thesis/dissertation. *Entrance requirements:* For master's, GRE Subject Test, interview, minimum GPA of 3.0, letter of recommendation; for doctorate, GRE Subject Test, interview, master's degree, minimum GPA of 3.0, letter of recommendation. *Faculty research:* Environmental, poblational and systematic biology.

University of Rhode Island, Graduate School, College of the Environment and Life Sciences, Department of Biological Sciences, Kingston, RI 02881. Offers cell and molecular biology (MS, PhD); earth and environmental sciences (MS, PhD); ecology and ecosystem sciences (MS, PhD); evolutionary and marine biology (MS, PhD); sustainable agriculture and food systems (MS, PhD). *Program availability:* Part-time. *Faculty:* 18 full-time (10 women). *Students:* 99 full-time (56 women), 16 part-time (12 women); includes 10 minority (4 Black or African American, non-Hispanic/Latino; 3 Asian, non-Hispanic/Latino; 2 Hispanic/Latino; 1 Two or more races, non-Hispanic/Latino), 21 international. 151 applicants, 22% accepted, 26 enrolled. In 2017, 18 master's, 9 doctorates awarded. *Entrance requirements:* Additional exam requirements/recommendations for international students: Required—TOEFL. *Application deadline:* For fall admission, 1/15 for domestic and international students. Application fee: $65. Electronic applications accepted. *Expenses:* Tuition, state resident: full-time $12,706; part-time $786 per credit. Tuition, nonresident: full-time $25,216; part-time $1401 per credit. *Required fees:* $1598; $45 per credit. One-time fee: $30 part-time. *Financial support:* In 2017–18, 4 research assistantships with tuition reimbursements (averaging $12,698 per year) were awarded. Financial award application deadline: 1/15; financial award applicants required to submit FAFSA. *Faculty research:* Physiological constraints on predators in the Antarctic, effects of CO_2 absorption in salt water particularly as it impacts pteropods. *Unit head:* Dr. Evan Preisser, Chair, 401-874-2120, E-mail: preisser@uri.edu.
Website: http://web.uri.edu/bio/

University of Rhode Island, Graduate School, College of the Environment and Life Sciences, Department of Cell and Molecular Biology, Kingston, RI 02881. Offers biochemistry (MS, PhD); clinical laboratory sciences (MS), including biotechnology, clinical laboratory science, cytopathology; microbiology (MS, PhD); molecular genetics (MS, PhD). *Program availability:* Part-time. *Faculty:* 14 full-time (6 women). *Students:* 17 full-time (9 women), 19 part-time (15 women); includes 9 minority (2 Black or African American, non-Hispanic/Latino; 4 Asian, non-Hispanic/Latino; 2 Hispanic/Latino; 1 Two or more races, non-Hispanic/Latino), 10 international. 26 applicants, 62% accepted, 6 enrolled. In 2017, 17 master's awarded. *Entrance requirements:* Additional exam requirements/recommendations for international students: Required—TOEFL. *Application deadline:* For fall admission, 1/15 for domestic and international students. Application fee: $65. Electronic applications accepted. *Expenses:* Tuition, state resident: full-time $12,706; part-time $786 per credit. Tuition, nonresident: full-time $25,216; part-time $1401 per credit. *Required fees:* $1598; $45 per credit. One-time fee: $30 part-time. *Financial support:* In 2017–18, 4 teaching assistantships with tuition reimbursements (averaging $12,698 per year) were awarded; traineeships also available. Financial award application deadline: 1/15; financial award applicants required to submit FAFSA. *Unit head:* Dr. Gongqing Sun, Chair and Professor, 401-874-5937, Fax: 401-874-2202, E-mail: gsun@mail.uri.edu. *Application contact:* Bethany Jenkins, Professor, 401-874-7551, E-mail: bjenkins@uri.edu.
Website: https://web.uri.edu/cmb/

University of Saskatchewan, College of Medicine, Department of Anatomy and Cell Biology, Saskatoon, SK S7N 5A2, Canada. Offers M Sc, PhD. *Degree requirements:* For master's, thesis; for doctorate, thesis/dissertation. *Entrance requirements:* Additional exam requirements/recommendations for international students: Required—TOEFL.

University of South Carolina, The Graduate School, College of Arts and Sciences, Department of Biological Sciences, Graduate Training Program in Molecular, Cellular, and Developmental Biology, Columbia, SC 29208. Offers MS, PhD. *Degree requirements:* For master's, one foreign language, thesis; for doctorate, one foreign language, thesis/dissertation. *Entrance requirements:* For master's and doctorate, GRE General Test, minimum GPA of 3.0 in science. Electronic applications accepted. *Faculty research:* Marine ecology, population and evolutionary biology, molecular biology and genetics, development.

University of South Dakota, Graduate School, Sanford School of Medicine and Graduate School, Biomedical Sciences Graduate Program, Cellular and Molecular Biology Group, Vermillion, SD 57069. Offers MS, PhD. Terminal master's awarded for partial completion of doctoral program. *Degree requirements:* For master's, thesis; for doctorate, comprehensive exam, thesis/dissertation. *Entrance requirements:* For master's and doctorate, GRE General Test, GRE Subject Test, minimum GPA of 3.0. Additional exam requirements/recommendations for international students: Required—TOEFL (minimum score 550 paper-based; 80 iBT), IELTS (minimum score 6). *Application deadline:* For fall admission, 4/15 priority date for domestic students, 3/15 for international students. Applications are processed on a rolling basis. Application fee: $35. Electronic applications accepted. *Expenses:* Contact institution. *Financial support:* In 2017–18, 10 students received support. Fellowships with partial tuition reimbursements available and research assistantships with partial tuition reimbursements available available. Financial award application deadline: 4/15; financial award applicants required to submit FAFSA. *Faculty research:* Molecular aspects of protein and DNA, neurochemistry and energy transduction, gene regulation, cellular development. *Unit head:* 605-658-6322, Fax: 605-677-6381, E-mail: biomed@usd.edu. *Application contact:* Graduate School, 605-658-6140, Fax: 605-677-6118, E-mail: grad@usd.edu.
Website: http://www.usd.edu/medicine/basic-biomedical-sciences

University of Southern California, Keck School of Medicine and Graduate School, Graduate Programs in Medicine, Master of Science Program in Stem Cell Biology and Regenerative Medicine, Los Angeles, CA 90033. Offers MS. *Program availability:* Part-time. *Faculty:* 7 full-time (1 woman). *Students:* 26 full-time (13 women), 11 part-time (7 women); includes 23 minority (1 Black or African American, non-Hispanic/Latino; 21 Asian, non-Hispanic/Latino; 1 Hispanic/Latino). Average age 23. 104 applicants, 54% accepted, 37 enrolled. In 2017, 26 master's awarded. *Entrance requirements:* For master's, GRE, MCAT, or DAT. Additional exam requirements/recommendations for international students: Required—TOEFL (minimum score 90 iBT), IELTS (minimum score 6.5). *Application deadline:* For fall admission, 4/30 for domestic and international students. Applications are processed on a rolling basis. Application fee: $58. Electronic applications accepted. *Faculty research:* Developmental and stem cell biology, regeneration of pancreatic beta cells, genetic factors in neurodegenerative disease, stem cell self-renewal and differentiation, etiology of congenital cardiovascular defects. *Unit head:* Dr. Henry Sucov, Program Director, 323-442-2563, Fax: 323-442-2230, E-mail: sucov@usc.edu. *Application contact:* Salinah Smith, Program Assistant, 323-865-1266, Fax: 323-442-8067, E-mail: salinah.smith@med.usc.edu.
Website: http://scrm.usc.edu/

University of Southern California, Keck School of Medicine, Program in Development, Stem Cell and Regenerative Medicine, Los Angeles, CA 90033. Offers PhD. *Faculty:* 36 full-time (15 women). *Students:* 38 full-time (15 women); includes 6 minority (4 Asian, non-Hispanic/Latino; 1 Hispanic/Latino; 1 Two or more races, non-Hispanic/Latino), 18 international. Average age 26. 11 applicants, 100% accepted, 11 enrolled. *Degree requirements:* For doctorate, comprehensive exam, thesis/dissertation. *Entrance requirements:* For doctorate, GRE, minimum GPA of 3.5. Additional exam requirements/recommendations for international students: Required—TOEFL (minimum score 600 paper-based; 100 iBT), IELTS (minimum score 7), PTE. *Application deadline:* For fall admission, 12/1 priority date for domestic and international students. Application fee: $90. Electronic applications accepted. *Financial support:* In 2017–18, 38 students received support, including 13 fellowships with full tuition reimbursements available (averaging $33,000 per year), 25 research assistantships with full tuition reimbursements available (averaging $33,000 per year); institutionally sponsored loans, scholarships/grants, traineeships, health care benefits, and unspecified assistantships also available. Financial award application deadline: 4/15; financial award applicants required to submit CSS PROFILE or FAFSA. *Unit head:* Dr. Gage Crump, Director, 323-442-1475, Fax: 323-442-1199, E-mail: gcrump@med.usc.edu. *Application contact:* Dr. Joyce Perez, Manager of Student Programs, 323-442-1645, Fax: 323-442-1199, E-mail: jpperez@med.usc.edu.
Website: http://keck.usc.edu/pibbs/phd-programs/development-stem-cell-and-regenerative-medicine

University of South Florida, College of Arts and Sciences, Department of Cell Biology, Microbiology, and Molecular Biology, Tampa, FL 33620-9951. Offers biology (MS), including cell biology, microbiology and molecular biology; cancer biology (PhD); cancer chemical biology (PhD); cancer immunology and immunotherapy (PhD); cell and molecular biology (PhD); microbiology (MS). *Faculty:* 19 full-time (6 women). *Students:* 81 full-time (55 women), 4 part-time (2 women); includes 12 minority (1 Black or African American, non-Hispanic/Latino; 2 Asian, non-Hispanic/Latino; 5 Hispanic/Latino; 4 Two or more races, non-Hispanic/Latino), 29 international. Average age 27. 159 applicants, 18% accepted, 23 enrolled. In 2017, 21 master's, 10 doctorates awarded. *Degree requirements:* For master's, thesis or alternative; for doctorate, comprehensive exam, thesis/dissertation. *Entrance requirements:* For master's and doctorate, GRE General Test, minimum GPA of 3.0, extensive background in biology or chemistry. Additional exam requirements/recommendations for international students: Required—TOEFL (minimum score 570 paper-based; 79 iBT) or IELTS (minimum score 6.5). *Application deadline:* For fall admission, 11/30 priority date for domestic and international students; for spring admission, 7/1 priority date for domestic students, 7/1 for international students. Application fee: $30. *Financial support:* In 2017–18, 10 students received support. Career-related internships or fieldwork, health care benefits, and unspecified assistantships available. Financial award application deadline: 4/1. *Faculty research:* Cell biology, microbiology and molecular biology: basic and applied science in bacterial pathogenesis, genome integrity and mechanisms of aging, structural and computational biology; cancer biology: immunology, cancer control, signal transduction, drug discovery, genomics. *Total annual research expenditures:* $1.8 million. *Unit head:* Dr. James Garey, Professor/Chair, 813-974-7103, Fax: 813-974-1614, E-mail: garey@usf.edu. *Application contact:* Dr. Kenneth Wright, Associate Professor of Cancer Biology, H. Lee Moffitt Cancer Center and Research Institute, 813-745-3918, Fax: 813-974-1614, E-mail: ken.wright@moffitt.org.
Website: http://biology.usf.edu/cmmb/

University of South Florida, Morsani College of Medicine and College of Graduate Studies, Graduate Programs in Medical Sciences, Tampa, FL 33620-9951. Offers advanced athletic training (MS); athletic training (MS); bioinformatics and computational biology (MSBCB); biotechnology (MSB); health informatics (MSHI); medical sciences (MSMS, PhD), including aging and neuroscience (MSMS), allergy, immunology and infectious disease (PhD), anatomy, biochemistry and molecular biology, clinical and translational research, health science (MSMS), interdisciplinary medical sciences (MSMS), medical microbiology and immunology (MSMS), metabolic and nutritional medicine (MSMS), microbiology and immunology (PhD), molecular medicine, molecular pharmacology and physiology (PhD), neuroscience (PhD), pathology and cell biology (PhD), women's health (MSMS). *Students:* 372 full-time (212 women), 216 part-time (142 women); includes 257 minority (78 Black or African American, non-Hispanic/Latino; 1 American Indian or Alaska Native, non-Hispanic/Latino; 79 Asian, non-Hispanic/Latino; 84 Hispanic/Latino; 15 Two or more races, non-Hispanic/Latino), 62 international. Average age 28. 1,048 applicants, 46% accepted, 309 enrolled. In 2017, 351 master's, 56 doctorates awarded. Terminal master's awarded for partial completion of doctoral program. *Degree requirements:* For master's, comprehensive exam, thesis; for doctorate, comprehensive exam, thesis/dissertation. *Entrance requirements:* For master's, GRE General Test or GMAT, bachelor's degree or equivalent from regionally-accredited university with minimum GPA of 3.0 in upper-division sciences coursework; prerequisites in general biology, general chemistry, general physics, organic chemistry, quantitative analysis, and integral and differential calculus; for doctorate, GRE General Test, bachelor's degree from regionally-accredited university with minimum GPA of 3.0 in upper-division sciences coursework; 3 letters of recommendation; personal interview; 1-2 page personal statement; prerequisites in biology, chemistry, physics, organic chemistry, quantitative analysis, and integral/differential calculus. Additional exam requirements/recommendations for international students: Required—TOEFL (minimum score 550 paper-based; 79 iBT) or IELTS (minimum score 6.5). *Application deadline:* For fall admission, 2/1 priority date for domestic students, 2/1 for international students. Application fee: $30. Electronic applications accepted. *Expenses:* Contact institution. *Financial support:* In 2017–18, 109 students received support. *Faculty research:* Anatomy, biochemistry, cancer biology, cardiovascular disease, cell biology, immunology, microbiology, molecular biology, neuroscience, pharmacology, physiology. *Total annual research expenditures:* $45.3 million. *Unit head:* Dr. Michael Barber, Professor/Associate Dean for Graduate and Postdoctoral Affairs, 813-974-9908, Fax: 813-974-4317, E-mail: mbarber@health.usf.edu. *Application contact:* Dr. Eric Bennett, Graduate Director, PhD Program in Medical Sciences, 813-974-1545, Fax: 813-974-4317, E-mail: esbennet@health.usf.edu.
Website: http://health.usf.edu/nocms/medicine/graduatestudies/

The University of Texas at Austin, Graduate School, Institute for Cellular and Molecular Biology, Austin, TX 78712-1111. Offers PhD.

The University of Texas at Dallas, School of Natural Sciences and Mathematics, Department of Biological Sciences, Richardson, TX 75080. Offers bioinformatics and computational biology (MS); biotechnology (MS); molecular and cell biology (MS, PhD). *Program availability:* Part-time, evening/weekend. *Faculty:* 22 full-time (4 women), 3 part-time/adjunct (2 women). *Students:* 107 full-time (64 women), 26 part-time (11 women); includes 24 minority (3 Black or African American, non-Hispanic/Latino; 12 Asian, non-Hispanic/Latino; 5 Hispanic/Latino; 4 Two or more races, non-Hispanic/Latino), 76 international. Average age 27. 307 applicants, 23% accepted, 45 enrolled. In 2017, 37 master's, 9 doctorates awarded. *Degree requirements:* For master's, thesis optional; for doctorate, thesis/dissertation, publishable paper. *Entrance requirements:* For master's and doctorate, GRE (minimum combined score of 1000 on verbal and quantitative). Additional exam requirements/recommendations for international students: Required—TOEFL (minimum score 550 paper-based; 80 iBT). *Application deadline:* For fall admission, 7/15 for domestic students, 5/1 priority date for international students; for spring admission, 11/15 for domestic students, 9/1 priority date for international students. Applications are processed on a rolling basis. Application fee: $50 ($100 for international students). Electronic applications accepted. *Expenses:* Tuition, state resident: full-time $12,916; part-time $718 per credit hour. Tuition, nonresident: full-time $25,252; part-time $1403 per credit hour. *Financial support:* In 2017–18, 78 students received support, including 14 research assistantships with partial tuition reimbursements available (averaging $25,380 per year), 59 teaching assistantships with partial tuition reimbursements available (averaging $17,265 per year); fellowships with partial tuition reimbursements available, career-related internships or fieldwork, Federal Work-Study, institutionally sponsored loans, scholarships/grants, and unspecified assistantships also available. Support available to part-time students. Financial award application deadline: 4/30; financial award applicants required to submit FAFSA. *Faculty research:* Role of mitochondria in neurodegenerative diseases, protein-DNA interactions in site-specific recombination, eukaryotic gene expression, bio-nanotechnology, sickle cell research. *Unit head:* Dr. Stephen Spiro, Department Head, 972-883-6032, Fax: 972-883-4551, E-mail: stephen.spiro@utdallas.edu. *Application contact:* Dr. Lawrence Reitzer, Graduate Advisor, 972-883-2502, Fax: 972-883-4551, E-mail: reitzer@utdallas.edu.
Website: http://www.utdallas.edu/biology/

The University of Texas at San Antonio, College of Sciences, Department of Biology, San Antonio, TX 78249-0617. Offers biology (MS); biotechnology (MS); cell and molecular biology (PhD); neurobiology (PhD). *Faculty:* 37 full-time (10 women), 1 part-time/adjunct (0 women). *Students:* 111 full-time (64 women), 50 part-time (25 women); includes 76 minority (5 Black or African American, non-Hispanic/Latino; 1 American Indian or Alaska Native, non-Hispanic/Latino; 11 Asian, non-Hispanic/Latino; 55 Hispanic/Latino; 1 Native Hawaiian or other Pacific Islander, non-Hispanic/Latino; 3 Two or more races, non-Hispanic/Latino), 30 international. Average age 27. 153 applicants, 55% accepted, 57 enrolled. In 2017, 17 master's, 3 doctorates awarded. Terminal master's awarded for partial completion of doctoral program. *Degree requirements:* For master's, comprehensive exam, thesis or alternative; for doctorate, comprehensive exam, thesis/dissertation. *Entrance requirements:* For master's, GRE General Test, bachelor's degree with 18 credit hours in field of study or in another appropriate field of study; for doctorate, GRE General Test, 3 letters of recommendation, statement of purpose, resume. Additional exam requirements/recommendations for international students: Required—TOEFL (minimum score 500 paper-based; 100 iBT), IELTS (minimum score 5). *Application deadline:* For fall admission, 6/15 for domestic students, 3/1 for international students; for spring admission, 10/15 for domestic students, 9/15 for international students. Application fee: $50 ($90 for international students). Electronic applications accepted. *Expenses:* Tuition, state resident: full-time $5495. Tuition, nonresident: full-time $21,938. *Required fees:* $1915. Tuition and fees vary according to program. *Faculty research:* Development of human and veterinary vaccines against a fungal disease, mammalian germ cells and stem cells, dopamine neuron physiology and addiction, plant biochemistry, dendritic computation and synaptic plasticity. *Total annual research expenditures:* $9.1 million. *Unit head:* Dr. Garry Sunter, Chair, 210-458-5479, E-mail: garry.sunter@utsa.edu.
Website: http://bio.utsa.edu/

The University of Texas Health Science Center at Houston, MD Anderson UTHealth Graduate School, Houston, TX 77225-0036. Offers biochemistry and cell biology (PhD); biomedical sciences (MS); cancer biology (PhD); genetic counseling (MS); genetics and epigenetics (PhD); immunology (PhD); medical physics (MS, PhD); microbiology and infectious diseases (PhD); neuroscience (PhD); quantitative sciences (PhD); therapeutics and pharmacology (PhD); MD/PhD. Terminal master's awarded for partial completion of doctoral program. *Degree requirements:* For master's, thesis; for doctorate, thesis/dissertation. *Entrance requirements:* For master's and doctorate, GRE General Test. Additional exam requirements/recommendations for international students: Required—TOEFL. Electronic applications accepted. *Faculty research:* Biomedical sciences.

The University of Texas Health Science Center at San Antonio, Graduate School of Biomedical Sciences, Department of Cellular and Structural Biology, San Antonio, TX 78229-3900. Offers MS, PhD. *Degree requirements:* For master's, thesis; for doctorate, comprehensive exam, thesis/dissertation.

The University of Texas Medical Branch, Graduate School of Biomedical Sciences, Program in Biochemistry and Molecular Biology, Galveston, TX 77555. Offers biochemistry (PhD); bioinformatics (PhD); biophysics (PhD); cell biology (PhD);

computational biology (PhD); structural biology (PhD). *Degree requirements:* For doctorate, thesis/dissertation. *Entrance requirements:* Additional exam requirements/recommendations for international students: Required—TOEFL (minimum score 550 paper-based). Electronic applications accepted.

The University of Texas Medical Branch, Graduate School of Biomedical Sciences, Program in Cell Biology, Galveston, TX 77555. Offers MS, PhD. *Degree requirements:* For doctorate, thesis/dissertation. *Entrance requirements:* For doctorate, GRE General Test. Additional exam requirements/recommendations for international students: Required—TOEFL (minimum score 550 paper-based). Electronic applications accepted.

The University of Texas Southwestern Medical Center, Southwestern Graduate School of Biomedical Sciences, Division of Basic Science, Program in Cell Regulation, Dallas, TX 75390. Offers PhD. *Degree requirements:* For doctorate, thesis/dissertation, qualifying exam. *Entrance requirements:* For doctorate, GRE General Test, minimum GPA of 3.0. Additional exam requirements/recommendations for international students: Required—TOEFL. Electronic applications accepted. *Faculty research:* Molecular and cellular approaches to regulatory biology, receptor-effector coupling, membrane structure, function, and assembly.

University of the Sciences, Program in Cell Biology and Biotechnology, Philadelphia, PA 19104-4495. Offers MS. *Program availability:* Part-time, evening/weekend. *Degree requirements:* For master's, thesis optional. *Entrance requirements:* For master's, GRE General Test. Additional exam requirements/recommendations for international students: Required—TOEFL, TWE. *Expenses:* Contact institution.

University of Toronto, School of Graduate Studies, Faculty of Arts and Science, Department of Cell and Systems Biology, Toronto, ON M5S 1A1, Canada. Offers M Sc, PhD. *Degree requirements:* For master's, thesis, thesis defense; for doctorate, thesis/dissertation, thesis defense, oral thesis examination. *Entrance requirements:* For master's, minimum B+ average in final year, B overall, 3 letters of reference. Additional exam requirements/recommendations for international students: Required—TOEFL (minimum score 580 paper-based; 93 iBT), TWE (minimum score 5). Electronic applications accepted.

University of Vermont, Graduate College, Cross-College Interdisciplinary Program, Cellular, Molecular and Biomedical Sciences Program, Burlington, VT 05405. Offers PhD. *Students:* 48 (26 women). Average age 29. 74 applicants, 35% accepted, 9 enrolled. In 2017, 6 doctorates awarded. *Degree requirements:* For doctorate, thesis/dissertation. *Entrance requirements:* For doctorate, GRE General Test. Additional exam requirements/recommendations for international students: Required—TOEFL (minimum score 550 paper-based; 100 iBT), IELTS (minimum score 7). *Application deadline:* For fall admission, 12/1 for domestic and international students. Application fee: $65. Electronic applications accepted. *Expenses:* Tuition, state resident: full-time $11,628; part-time $646 per credit. Tuition, nonresident: full-time $29,340; part-time $1630 per credit. *Required fees:* $1994; $10 per credit. Tuition and fees vary according to course load and program. *Financial support:* In 2017–18, 16 research assistantships with full tuition reimbursements (averaging $28,000 per year), 33 teaching assistantships with full tuition reimbursements (averaging $28,000 per year) were awarded; fellowships and career-related internships or fieldwork also available. Financial award application deadline: 3/1. *Faculty research:* Cancer biology and genome stability, genomics and computational biology, immunology and microbial pathogenesis, stem cell and developmental biology, lung and cardiovascular biology. *Unit head:* Dr. Matthew Poynter, Director, 802-656-8045, E-mail: cmb@uvm.edu. *Application contact:* Jessica Lalime, Administrator, 802-656-9673, E-mail: cmb@uvm.edu.
Website: https://www.uvm.edu/cmb

University of Virginia, School of Medicine, Department of Cell Biology, Charlottesville, VA 22903. Offers PhD, MD/PhD. *Faculty:* 17 full-time (7 women). *Students:* 11 full-time (7 women); includes 4 minority (3 Black or African American, non-Hispanic/Latino; 1 American Indian or Alaska Native, non-Hispanic/Latino), 3 international. Average age 28. In 2017, 1 doctorate awarded. *Degree requirements:* For doctorate, one foreign language, thesis/dissertation. *Entrance requirements:* For doctorate, GRE General Test, GRE Subject Test (recommended), 2 letters of recommendation. Additional exam requirements/recommendations for international students: Required—TOEFL. *Application deadline:* For fall admission, 4/15 for domestic and international students. Applications are processed on a rolling basis. Application fee: $60. Electronic applications accepted. *Financial support:* Application deadline: 1/15; applicants required to submit FAFSA. *Unit head:* Dr. Douglas DeSimone, Chairman, 434-924-9430, E-mail: dwd3m@virginia.edu. *Application contact:* Biomedical Sciences Graduate Study, E-mail: bims@virginia.edu.
Website: http://www.medicine.virginia.edu/basic-science/departments/cell-biology

University of Washington, Graduate School, School of Medicine, Graduate Programs in Medicine, Program in Molecular and Cellular Biology, Seattle, WA 98195. Offers PhD. Offered in partnership with Fred Hutchinson Cancer Research Center, Seattle Biomedical Research Center, and Institute for Systems Biology. *Degree requirements:* For doctorate, thesis/dissertation. *Entrance requirements:* For doctorate, GRE General Test. Additional exam requirements/recommendations for international students: Required—TOEFL. Electronic applications accepted.

The University of Western Ontario, Faculty of Graduate Studies, Biosciences Division, Department of Anatomy and Cell Biology, London, ON N6A 5B8, Canada. Offers anatomy and cell biology (M Sc, PhD); clinical anatomy (M Sc). *Degree requirements:* For master's, thesis; for doctorate, comprehensive exam, thesis/dissertation. *Entrance requirements:* For master's, honors degree or equivalent in biological sciences; for doctorate, master's degree. Additional exam requirements/recommendations for international students: Required—TOEFL. *Faculty research:* Cell and molecular biology, developmental biology, neuroscience, immunobiology and cancer.

University of Wisconsin–La Crosse, College of Science and Health, Department of Biology, La Crosse, WI 54601-3742. Offers aquatic sciences (MS); biology (MS); cellular and molecular biology (MS); clinical microbiology (MS); microbiology (MS); nurse anesthesia (MS); physiology (MS). *Accreditation:* AANA/CANAEP. *Program availability:* Part-time. *Students:* 11 full-time (2 women), 29 part-time (14 women); includes 1 minority (Two or more races, non-Hispanic/Latino). Average age 30. 67 applicants, 28% accepted, 18 enrolled. In 2017, 24 master's awarded. *Degree requirements:* For master's, comprehensive exam, thesis. *Entrance requirements:* For master's, GRE General Test, minimum GPA of 2.85. Additional exam requirements/recommendations for international students: Required—TOEFL (minimum score 550 paper-based; 79 iBT). *Application deadline:* For fall admission, 2/1 priority date for domestic and international students; for spring admission, 1/4 priority date for domestic and international students. Applications are processed on a rolling basis. Electronic applications accepted. *Financial support:* Research assistantships with partial tuition reimbursements, Federal Work-Study, scholarships/grants, health care benefits, and tuition waivers (partial) available. Support available to part-time students. Financial award application deadline: 3/15; financial award applicants required to submit FAFSA. *Unit head:* Dr. Mark Sandheinrich, Department Chair, 608-785-8261, E-mail: msandheinrich@uwlax.edu. *Application contact:* Brandon Schaller, Senior Graduate Student Status Examiner, 608-785-8941, E-mail: admissions@uwlax.edu.
Website: http://uwlax.edu/biology/

University of Wisconsin–Madison, Graduate School, Program in Cellular and Molecular Biology, Madison, WI 53706-1596. Offers PhD. *Faculty:* 186 full-time (66 women). *Students:* 80 full-time (39 women); includes 7 minority (1 Black or African American, non-Hispanic/Latino; 1 Asian, non-Hispanic/Latino; 3 Hispanic/Latino; 2 Native Hawaiian or other Pacific Islander, non-Hispanic/Latino), 20 international. Average age 27. 334 applicants, 15% accepted, 14 enrolled. In 2017, 15 doctorates awarded. *Degree requirements:* For doctorate, comprehensive exam, thesis/dissertation. *Entrance requirements:* For doctorate, GRE General Test, GRE Subject Test (recommended), minimum GPA of 3.0, lab experience. Additional exam requirements/recommendations for international students: Required—TOEFL (minimum score 580 paper-based; 92 iBT). *Application deadline:* For fall admission, 12/1 for domestic and international students. Application fee: $75 ($81 for international students). Electronic applications accepted. *Financial support:* In 2017–18, 66 students received support. Fellowships with full tuition reimbursements available, research assistantships with full tuition reimbursements available, teaching assistantships, traineeships, health care benefits, and unspecified assistantships available. *Faculty research:* Virology, cancer biology, transcriptional mechanisms, developmental biology, immunology. *Unit head:* Dr. David Wassarman, Graduate Program Chair, 608-262-3203. *Application contact:* CMB Office, 608-262-3203, E-mail: cmb@bocklabs.wisc.edu.
Website: http://www.cmb.wisc.edu/

University of Wisconsin–Milwaukee, Graduate School, College of Letters and Science, Department of Biological Sciences, Milwaukee, WI 53201-0413. Offers cellular and molecular biology (MS, PhD); microbiology (MS, PhD). *Students:* 58 full-time (35 women), 11 part-time (8 women); includes 7 minority (1 Black or African American, non-Hispanic/Latino; 5 Asian, non-Hispanic/Latino; 1 Two or more races, non-Hispanic/Latino), 17 international. Average age 29. 78 applicants, 55% accepted, 29 enrolled. *Degree requirements:* For master's, thesis; for doctorate, thesis/dissertation, 1 foreign language or data analysis proficiency. *Entrance requirements:* For master's and doctorate, GRE General Test. Additional exam requirements/recommendations for international students: Required—TOEFL (minimum score 550 paper-based; 79 iBT), IELTS (minimum score 6.5). *Application deadline:* For fall admission, 3/1 priority date for domestic students. Application fee: $56 ($96 for international students). Electronic applications accepted. *Financial support:* In 2017–18, 9 research assistantships were awarded; fellowships, teaching assistantships, career-related internships or fieldwork, unspecified assistantships, and project assistantships also available. Support available to part-time students. Financial award application deadline: 4/15; financial award applicants required to submit FAFSA. *Unit head:* R. David Heathcote, Department Chair, 414-229-6471, E-mail: rdh@uwm.edu. *Application contact:* General Information Contact, 414-229-4982, Fax: 414-229-6967, E-mail: gradschool@uwm.edu.
Website: https://uwm.edu/biology/

University of Wyoming, Graduate Program in Molecular and Cellular Life Sciences, Laramie, WY 82071. Offers PhD. *Degree requirements:* For doctorate, thesis/dissertation, four eight-week laboratory rotations, comprehensive basic practical exam, two-part qualifying exam, seminars, symposium.

Vanderbilt University, School of Medicine, Department of Cell and Developmental Biology, Nashville, TN 37240-1001. Offers MS, PhD, MD/PhD. *Faculty:* 23 full-time (9 women). *Students:* 57 full-time (40 women); includes 11 minority (3 Black or African American, non-Hispanic/Latino; 2 Asian, non-Hispanic/Latino; 3 Hispanic/Latino; 1 Native Hawaiian or other Pacific Islander, non-Hispanic/Latino; 2 Two or more races, non-Hispanic/Latino), 11 international. Average age 27. In 2017, 1 master's, 13 doctorates awarded. Terminal master's awarded for partial completion of doctoral program. *Degree requirements:* For master's, thesis or alternative; for doctorate, thesis/dissertation, preliminary, qualifying, and final exams. *Entrance requirements:* For master's, GRE General Test; for doctorate, GRE General Test, GRE Subject Test (recommended). Additional exam requirements/recommendations for international students: Required—TOEFL (minimum score 570 paper-based; 88 iBT). *Application deadline:* For fall admission, 1/15 for domestic and international students. Application fee: $0. Electronic applications accepted. *Financial support:* Fellowships with tuition reimbursements, research assistantships with tuition reimbursements, career-related internships or fieldwork, Federal Work-Study, institutionally sponsored loans, scholarships/grants, traineeships, health care benefits, and tuition waivers (partial) available. Financial award application deadline: 1/15; financial award applicants required to submit CSS PROFILE or FAFSA. *Faculty research:* Cancer biology, cell cycle regulation, cell signaling, cytoskeletal biology, developmental biology, neurobiology, proteomics, stem cell biology, structural biology, reproductive biology, trafficking and transport, medical education and gross anatomy. *Unit head:* Dr. Steve Hann, Director of Graduate Studies, 615-322-2134, Fax: 615-343-4539, E-mail: steve.hann@vanderbilt.edu. *Application contact:* Kristi Hargrove, Coordinator, 615-322-2294, Fax: 615-343-4539, E-mail: kristi.l.hargrove@vanderbilt.edu.
Website: http://www.mc.vanderbilt.edu/cdb/

Washington University in St. Louis, The Graduate School, Division of Biology and Biomedical Sciences, Program in Molecular Cell Biology, St. Louis, MO 63130-4899. Offers PhD. *Degree requirements:* For doctorate, thesis/dissertation. *Entrance requirements:* For doctorate, GRE General Test, GRE Subject Test. Additional exam requirements/recommendations for international students: Required—TOEFL. Electronic applications accepted. *Faculty research:* Cell adhesion, protein trafficking and organelle biogenesis, cell cycle, receptors, signal transduction, gene expression, metabolism, cytoskeleton and motility, membrane excitability, molecular basis of diseases.

Wayne State University, School of Medicine, Office of Biomedical Graduate Programs, Detroit, MI 48202. Offers anatomy and cell biology (MS, PhD); basic medical sciences (MS); biochemistry and molecular biology (MS, PhD); cancer biology (MS, PhD); clinical and translational science (Graduate Certificate); family medicine and public health sciences (MPH, Graduate Certificate), including public health practice; genetic counseling (MS); immunology and microbiology (MS, PhD); medical physics (MS, PhD, Graduate Certificate); medical research (MS); molecular medicine and genomics (MS, PhD), including molecular genetics and genomics; pathology (PhD); pharmacology (MS, PhD); physiology (MS, PhD), including physiology, reproductive sciences (PhD); psychiatry and behavioral neurosciences (PhD), including translational neuroscience; MD/MPH; MD/PhD; MPH/MA; MSW/MPH. *Program availability:* Part-time, evening/weekend. *Students:* 268 full-time (152 women), 117 part-time (59 women); includes 108 minority (19 Black or African American, non-Hispanic/Latino; 1 American Indian or Alaska Native, non-Hispanic/Latino; 62 Asian, non-Hispanic/Latino; 9 Hispanic/Latino; 17 Two or more races, non-Hispanic/Latino), 48 international. Average age 26. 1,133 applicants, 21% accepted, 151 enrolled. In 2017, 70 master's, 25 doctorates, 10 other advanced degrees awarded. Terminal master's awarded for partial completion of doctoral program. *Degree requirements:* For master's, thesis (for some programs); for doctorate, thesis/dissertation. *Entrance requirements:* For master's, doctorate, and Graduate Certificate, GRE. Additional exam requirements/recommendations for international students: Required—TOEFL (minimum score 550 paper-based; 100 iBT), Michigan English Language Assessment Battery (minimum score 85); Recommended—IELTS (minimum score 6.5), TWE (minimum score 5.5). *Application deadline:* For fall admission, 2/1 for domestic and international students. Applications are processed on a rolling basis. Application fee: $50. Electronic applications accepted. *Expenses:* Contact institution. *Financial support:* In 2017–18, 177 students received support, including 64 fellowships with full tuition reimbursements available (averaging $24,388 per year), 79

research assistantships with full tuition reimbursements available (averaging $26,894 per year); scholarships/grants, traineeships, and health care benefits also available. *Faculty research:* Cancer biology, neurosciences, vision sciences, molecular biology, pathology, physiology, pharmacology, public health, medical physics. *Unit head:* Dr. Daniel A. Walz, Associate Dean for Biomedical Graduate Programs, 313-577-1455, Fax: 313-577-8796, E-mail: gradprogs@med.wayne.edu.
Website: https://www.med.wayne.edu/biomedical-graduate-programs/

Weill Cornell Medicine, Weill Cornell Graduate School of Medical Sciences, Biochemistry, Cell and Molecular Biology Allied Program, New York, NY 10065. Offers MS, PhD. Terminal master's awarded for partial completion of doctoral program. *Degree requirements:* For master's, comprehensive exam; for doctorate, thesis/dissertation, final exam. *Entrance requirements:* For doctorate, GRE General Test, background in genetics, molecular biology, chemistry, or biochemistry. Additional exam requirements/recommendations for international students: Required—TOEFL. Electronic applications accepted. *Faculty research:* Molecular structure determination, protein structure, gene structure, stem cell biology, control of gene expression, DNA replication, chromosome maintenance, RNA biosynthesis.

Wesleyan University, Graduate Studies, Department of Biology, Middletown, CT 06459. Offers cell and developmental biology (PhD); evolution and ecology (PhD); genetics and genomics (PhD), including bioinformatics; neurobiology and behavior (PhD). Terminal master's awarded for partial completion of doctoral program. *Degree requirements:* For doctorate, comprehensive exam, thesis/dissertation, public seminar. *Entrance requirements:* For doctorate, GRE, official transcripts, three recommendation letters, essay. Additional exam requirements/recommendations for international students: Required—TOEFL. *Application deadline:* For fall admission, 1/15 for domestic and international students. Application fee: $0. Electronic applications accepted. *Financial support:* Stipends available. *Faculty research:* Evolution and ecology, neurobiology and behavior, cell and developmental biology, genetics, genomics and bioinformatics. *Unit head:* Dr. Ann Burke, Chair/Professor, 860-685-3518, E-mail: acburke@wesleyan.edu. *Application contact:* Diane Meredith, Administrative Assistant IV, 860-685-2157, E-mail: dmeredith@wesleyan.edu.
Website: http://www.wesleyan.edu/bio/

Yale University, Graduate School of Arts and Sciences, Department of Cell Biology, New Haven, CT 06520. Offers PhD. *Degree requirements:* For doctorate, thesis/dissertation. *Entrance requirements:* For doctorate, GRE General Test. *Expenses:* Contact institution.

Yale University, Graduate School of Arts and Sciences, Department of Molecular, Cellular, and Developmental Biology, Program in Cellular and Developmental Biology, New Haven, CT 06520. Offers PhD. *Degree requirements:* For doctorate, thesis/dissertation. *Entrance requirements:* For doctorate, GRE General Test, GRE Subject Test.

Yale University, Yale School of Medicine and Graduate School of Arts and Sciences, Combined Program in Biological and Biomedical Sciences (BBS), Molecular Cell Biology, Genetics, and Development Track, New Haven, CT 06520. Offers PhD, MD/PhD. *Entrance requirements:* Additional exam requirements/recommendations for international students: Required—TOEFL.

Molecular Biology

Albany College of Pharmacy and Health Sciences, School of Arts and Sciences, Albany, NY 12208. Offers clinical laboratory sciences (MS); cytotechnology and molecular cytology (MS); health outcomes research (MS); molecular biosciences (MS). *Degree requirements:* For master's, thesis. *Entrance requirements:* For master's, GRE, minimum GPA of 3.0. Additional exam requirements/recommendations for international students: Required—TOEFL (minimum score 84 iBT). Electronic applications accepted.

Albany Medical College, Center for Cell Biology and Cancer Research, Albany, NY 12208-3479. Offers MS, PhD. *Program availability:* Part-time. Terminal master's awarded for partial completion of doctoral program. *Degree requirements:* For master's, thesis; for doctorate, comprehensive exam, thesis/dissertation. *Entrance requirements:* For master's and doctorate, GRE General Test, all transcripts, letters of recommendation. Additional exam requirements/recommendations for international students: Required—TOEFL. *Faculty research:* Cancer cell biology, tissue remodeling, signal transduction, gene regulation, cell adhesion, angiogenesis.

Albert Einstein College of Medicine, Graduate Programs in the Biomedical Sciences, Department of Developmental and Molecular Biology, Bronx, NY 10461. Offers PhD, MD/PhD. *Degree requirements:* For doctorate, thesis/dissertation. *Entrance requirements:* For doctorate, GRE General Test. Additional exam requirements/recommendations for international students: Required—TOEFL. *Application deadline:* For fall admission, 1/15 for domestic students. Application fee: $0. *Financial support:* Fellowships available. *Faculty research:* DNA, RNA, and protein synthesis in prokaryotes and eukaryotes; chemical and enzymatic alteration of RNA; glycoproteins. *Unit head:* Dr. Liang Zhu, Interim Chair, 718-430-3320. *Application contact:* Sheila Cleeton, Executive Director and Registrar, Einstein Graduate Division, 718-430-2128, Fax: 718-430-8655, E-mail: sheila.cleeton@einstein.yu.edu.
Website: http://www.einstein.yu.edu/departments/developmental-molecular-biology/

American University of Beirut, Graduate Programs, Faculty of Arts and Sciences, 1107 2020, Lebanon. Offers anthropology (MA); Arab and Middle Eastern history (PhD); Arabic language and literature (MA, PhD); archaeology (MA); art history and curating (MA); biology (MS); cell and molecular biology (PhD); chemistry (MS); clinical psychology (MA); computational sciences (MS); computer science (MS); economics (MA); education (MA), including administration and policy studies, elementary education, mathematics education, psychology school guidance, psychology test and measurements, science education, teaching English as a foreign language; English language (MA); English literature (MA); environmental policy planning (MS); financial economics (MAFE); general psychology (MA); geology (MS); history (MA); Islamic studies (MA); mathematics (MS); media studies (MA); Middle East studies (MA); philosophy (MA); physics (MS); political studies (MA); public administration (MA); public policy and international affairs (MA); sociology (MA); theoretical physics (PhD). *Program availability:* Part-time. *Faculty:* 108 full-time (36 women), 5 part-time/adjunct (4 women). *Students:* 251 full-time (180 women), 233 part-time (172 women). Average age 26. 425 applicants, 65% accepted, 121 enrolled. In 2017, 47 master's, 2 doctorates awarded. *Degree requirements:* For master's, one foreign language, comprehensive exam, thesis (for some programs), project; for doctorate, one foreign language, comprehensive exam, thesis/dissertation. *Entrance requirements:* For master's, GRE General Test (for some programs); for doctorate, GRE General Test (GRE Subject Test for theoretical physics). Additional exam requirements/recommendations for international students: Required—TOEFL (minimum score 583 paper-based; 97 iBT), IELTS (minimum score 7). *Application deadline:* For fall admission, 2/8 for domestic students; for spring admission, 11/3 for domestic students. Application fee: $50. Electronic applications accepted. *Expenses:* Contact institution. *Financial support:* In 2017–18, 29 fellowships, 40 research assistantships were awarded; teaching assistantships, scholarships/grants, tuition waivers (full and partial), and unspecified assistantships also available. Financial award application deadline: 4/4. *Unit head:* Dr. Nadia Maria El Cheikh, Dean, Faculty of Arts and Sciences, 961-1-374374 Ext. 3800, Fax: 961-1-744461, E-mail: nmcheikh@aub.edu.lb. *Application contact:* Rima Rassi, Graduate Studies Officer, 961-1-350000 Ext. 3833, Fax: 961-1-744461, E-mail: rr46@aub.edu.lb.
Website: http://www.aub.edu.lb/fas/pages/default.aspx

Appalachian State University, Cratis D. Williams Graduate School, Department of Biology, Boone, NC 28608. Offers cell and molecular biology (MS). *Program availability:* Part-time. *Degree requirements:* For master's, comprehensive exam, thesis. *Entrance requirements:* For master's, GRE General Test, 3 letters of recommendation. Additional exam requirements/recommendations for international students: Required—TOEFL (minimum score 570 paper-based; 79 iBT), IELTS (minimum score 6.5). Electronic applications accepted. *Faculty research:* Aquatic and terrestrial ecology, animal and plant physiology, behavior and systematics, immunology and cell biology, molecular biology and microbiology.

Arizona State University at the Tempe campus, College of Liberal Arts and Sciences, School of Life Sciences, Tempe, AZ 85287-4601. Offers animal behavior (PhD); applied ethics (biomedical and health ethics) (MA); biology (MS, PhD), including biology, biology and society, complex adaptive systems science (PhD), plant biology and conservation (MS); environmental life sciences (PhD); evolutionary biology (PhD); history and philosophy of science (PhD); human and social dimensions of science and technology (PhD); microbiology (PhD); molecular and cellular biology (PhD); neuroscience (PhD). Terminal master's awarded for partial completion of doctoral program. *Degree requirements:* For master's, thesis (for some programs), interactive Program of Study (iPOS) submitted before completing 50 percent of required credit hours; for doctorate, variable foreign language requirement, comprehensive exam, thesis/dissertation, interactive Program of Study (iPOS) submitted before completing 50 percent of required credit hours. *Entrance requirements:* For master's and doctorate, GRE, minimum GPA of 3.0 or equivalent in last 2 years of work leading to bachelor's degree. Additional exam requirements/recommendations for international students: Required—TOEFL (minimum score 600 paper-based; 100 iBT). Electronic applications accepted.

Arkansas State University, Graduate School, College of Sciences and Mathematics, Program in Molecular Biosciences, State University, AR 72467. Offers molecular biosciences (MS, PhD). *Program availability:* Part-time. *Degree requirements:* For master's, comprehensive exam, thesis; for doctorate, comprehensive exam, thesis/dissertation. *Entrance requirements:* For master's, GRE, appropriate bachelor's degree, official transcripts, immunization records, letters of reference, autobiography; for doctorate, GRE, appropriate bachelor's or master's degree, interview, letters of recommendation, official transcripts, personal statement, immunization records. Additional exam requirements/recommendations for international students: Required—TOEFL (minimum score 550 paper-based; 79 iBT), IELTS (minimum score 6), PTE (minimum score 56). Electronic applications accepted.

Auburn University, Graduate School, Interdepartmental Programs, Auburn University, AL 36849. Offers applied economics (PhD); cell and molecular biology (PhD); real estate development (MRED); sociology and rural sociology (MA, MS). *Program availability:* Part-time. *Students:* 31 full-time (18 women), 44 part-time (11 women); includes 16 minority (9 Black or African American, non-Hispanic/Latino; 1 Asian, non-Hispanic/Latino; 5 Hispanic/Latino; 1 Two or more races, non-Hispanic/Latino), 17 international. Average age 34. 63 applicants, 71% accepted, 33 enrolled. In 2017, 18 master's, 9 doctorates awarded. *Entrance requirements:* For master's, GRE General Test. *Application deadline:* Applications are processed on a rolling basis. Application fee: $50 ($60 for international students). Electronic applications accepted. *Expenses:* Tuition, state resident: full-time $10,974; part-time $519 per credit hour. Tuition, nonresident: full-time $29,658; part-time $1557 per credit hour. *Required fees:* $816 per semester. Tuition and fees vary according to degree level and program. *Financial support:* Fellowships, research assistantships, teaching assistantships, and Federal Work-Study available. Support available to part-time students. Financial award application deadline: 3/15; financial award applicants required to submit FAFSA. *Application contact:* Dr. George Flowers, Dean of the Graduate School, 334-844-2125.

Baylor College of Medicine, Graduate School of Biomedical Sciences, Department of Biochemistry and Molecular Biology, Houston, TX 77030-3498. Offers PhD, MD/PhD. *Degree requirements:* For doctorate, thesis/dissertation, public defense. *Entrance requirements:* For doctorate, GRE General Test, GRE Subject Test (strongly recommended), minimum GPA of 3.0. Additional exam requirements/recommendations for international students: Required—TOEFL. Electronic applications accepted. *Faculty research:* DNA repair, homologous recombination, gene therapy, trinucleotide repeat diseases, retinitis pigmentosa.

Baylor College of Medicine, Graduate School of Biomedical Sciences, Department of Molecular and Cellular Biology, Houston, TX 77030-3498. Offers PhD, MD/PhD. *Degree requirements:* For doctorate, thesis/dissertation, public defense, qualifying exam. *Entrance requirements:* For doctorate, GRE General Test, GRE Subject Test (strongly recommended), minimum GPA of 3.0. Additional exam requirements/recommendations for international students: Required—TOEFL. Electronic applications accepted. *Faculty research:* Hormone action, development, cancer, gene therapy, neurobiology.

Baylor College of Medicine, Graduate School of Biomedical Sciences, Interdepartmental Program in Cell and Molecular Biology, Houston, TX 77030-3498. Offers biochemistry (PhD); cell and molecular biology (PhD); genetics (PhD); human genetics (PhD); immunology (PhD); microbiology (PhD); virology (PhD); MD/PhD. *Degree requirements:* For doctorate, thesis/dissertation, public defense. *Entrance requirements:* For doctorate, GRE General Test, GRE Subject Test (strongly recommended), minimum GPA of 3.0. Additional exam requirements/recommendations for international students: Required—TOEFL. Electronic applications accepted. *Faculty research:* Molecular and cellular biology; cancer, aging and stem cells; genomics and proteomics; microbiome, molecular microbiology; infectious disease, immunology and translational research.

Molecular Biology

Boise State University, College of Arts and Sciences, Department of Biological Sciences, Boise, ID 83725-0399. Offers biology (MA, MS); biomolecular sciences (PhD); raptor biology (MS). *Program availability:* Part-time. *Faculty:* 26. *Students:* 51 full-time (23 women), 10 part-time (5 women); includes 7 minority (1 Black or African American, non-Hispanic/Latino; 1 American Indian or Alaska Native, non-Hispanic/Latino; 1 Asian, non-Hispanic/Latino; 3 Hispanic/Latino; 1 Native Hawaiian or other Pacific Islander, non-Hispanic/Latino), 6 international. Average age 30. 45 applicants, 27% accepted, 10 enrolled. In 2017, 13 master's awarded. *Degree requirements:* For master's, thesis. *Entrance requirements:* For master's, GRE General Test, minimum GPA of 3.0. Additional exam requirements/recommendations for international students: Required—TOEFL (minimum score 550 paper-based; 80 iBT), IELTS (minimum score 6). *Application deadline:* For fall admission, 1/15 for domestic and international students; for spring admission, 10/1 for domestic and international students. Application fee: $65 ($95 for international students). Electronic applications accepted. *Expenses:* Tuition, state resident: full-time $6471; part-time $390 per credit. Tuition, nonresident: full-time $21,787; part-time $685 per credit. *Required fees:* $2283; $100 per term. Part-time tuition and fees vary according to course load and program. *Financial support:* Research assistantships, teaching assistantships, institutionally sponsored loans, and unspecified assistantships available. Financial award application deadline: 1/15; financial award applicants required to submit FAFSA. *Faculty research:* Soil and stream microbial ecology, avian ecology. *Unit head:* Dr. Kevin Feris, Chair, 208-426-4267, E-mail: kevinferis@boisestate.edu. *Application contact:* Dr. Ian Roberts, Graduate Coordinator, 208-426-3208, E-mail: iroberts@boisestate.edu.
Website: http://biology.boisestate.edu/graduate-programs/

Boston University, Graduate School of Arts and Sciences, Molecular Biology, Cell Biology, and Biochemistry Program (MCBB), Boston, MA 02215. Offers MA, PhD. *Students:* 35 full-time (17 women), 5 part-time (2 women); includes 10 minority (2 Black or African American, non-Hispanic/Latino; 2 Asian, non-Hispanic/Latino; 4 Hispanic/Latino; 2 Two or more races, non-Hispanic/Latino), 12 international. Average age 27. 150 applicants, 20% accepted, 9 enrolled. In 2017, 3 master's, 4 doctorates awarded. Terminal master's awarded for partial completion of doctoral program. *Degree requirements:* For master's, thesis (for some programs); for doctorate, comprehensive exam, thesis/dissertation, teaching requirement. *Entrance requirements:* For master's and doctorate, GRE General Test, 3 letters of recommendation, transcripts, personal statement. Additional exam requirements/recommendations for international students: Required—TOEFL (minimum score 550 paper-based; 84 iBT). *Application deadline:* For fall admission, 12/5 for domestic and international students. Application fee: $95. Electronic applications accepted. *Financial support:* In 2017–18, 35 students received support, including 4 fellowships with full tuition reimbursements available (averaging $22,000 per year), 12 research assistantships with full tuition reimbursements available (averaging $22,000 per year), 16 teaching assistantships with full tuition reimbursements available (averaging $22,000 per year); Federal Work-Study, scholarships/grants, traineeships, and health care benefits also available. Financial award application deadline: 12/5; financial award applicants required to submit FAFSA. *Unit head:* Dr. Ulla Hansen, Director, 617-353-2432, Fax: 617-353-6340, E-mail: uhansen@bu.edu. *Application contact:* Christina Honeycutt, Academic Administrator, 617-353-2432, Fax: 617-353-6340, E-mail: cjhoney@bu.edu.
Website: http://www.bu.edu/mcbb/

Boston University, School of Medicine, Division of Graduate Medical Sciences, Department of Biochemistry, Boston, MA 02118. Offers MA, PhD, MD/PhD. *Program availability:* Part-time. Terminal master's awarded for partial completion of doctoral program. *Degree requirements:* For master's, thesis or alternative; for doctorate, thesis/dissertation. *Application deadline:* For fall admission, 1/15 for domestic students; for spring admission, 10/15 for domestic students. *Unit head:* Dr. David A. Harris, Chair, 617-638-5090. *Application contact:* GMS Admissions Office, 617-638-5255, E-mail: askgms@bu.edu.
Website: http://www.bumc.bu.edu/biochemistry/

Boston University, School of Medicine, Division of Graduate Medical Sciences, Program in Cell and Molecular Biology, Boston, MA 02118. Offers PhD. *Degree requirements:* For doctorate, thesis/dissertation. *Application deadline:* For fall admission, 1/15 for domestic students; for spring admission, 10/15 for domestic students. *Financial support:* Scholarships/grants and traineeships available. Financial award applicants required to submit FAFSA. *Unit head:* Dr. Vickery Trinkaus-Randall, Director, 617-638-6099, Fax: 617-638-5337, E-mail: vickery@bu.edu. *Application contact:* GMS Admissions Office, 617-638-5255, E-mail: askgms@bu.edu.
Website: http://www.bumc.bu.edu/cmbio/

Brandeis University, Graduate School of Arts and Sciences, Program in Molecular and Cell Biology, Waltham, MA 02454-9110. Offers genetics (PhD); microbiology (PhD); molecular and cell biology (MS, PhD); molecular biology (PhD); neurobiology (PhD); quantitative biology (PhD). *Faculty:* 27 full-time (13 women), 3 part-time/adjunct (2 women). *Students:* 47 full-time (29 women), 2 part-time (1 woman); includes 10 minority (1 American Indian or Alaska Native, non-Hispanic/Latino; 2 Asian, non-Hispanic/Latino; 6 Hispanic/Latino; 1 Two or more races, non-Hispanic/Latino), 11 international. Average age 27. 138 applicants, 25% accepted, 18 enrolled. In 2017, 11 master's, 8 doctorates awarded. Terminal master's awarded for partial completion of doctoral program. *Degree requirements:* For master's, thesis optional, research project, research lab, or project lab; for doctorate, comprehensive exam, thesis/dissertation, journal clubs; research seminar; colloquia; qualifying exam. *Entrance requirements:* For master's, GRE General Test, transcripts, resume, letters of recommendation, statement of purpose; for doctorate, GRE General Test, transcripts, resume, letters of recommendation, statement of purpose, list of previous research experience. Additional exam requirements/recommendations for international students: Required—PTE (minimum score 68), TOEFL (minimum score 600 paper-based, 100 iBT) or IELTS (7). *Application deadline:* For fall admission, 12/1 priority date for domestic students; for spring admission, 11/15 for domestic students, 10/15 for international students. Applications are processed on a rolling basis. Application fee: $75. Electronic applications accepted. *Expenses: Tuition:* Full-time $48,720. *Required fees:* $88. Tuition and fees vary according to course load, degree level, program and student level. *Financial support:* In 2017–18, 46 students received support, including 20 fellowships with full tuition reimbursements available (averaging $33,000 per year), 19 research assistantships with full tuition reimbursements available (averaging $33,000 per year); scholarships/grants and tuition waivers (partial) also available. Financial award application deadline: 4/15; financial award applicants required to submit FAFSA. *Faculty research:* Molecular biology, genetics and development; structural and cell biology; neurobiology. *Unit head:* Dr. James Haber, Co-Chair, 781-736-2462, E-mail: haber@brandeis.edu. *Application contact:* Jena Pitman-Leung, Department Administrator, 781-736-2352, E-mail: scigradoffice@brandeis.edu.
Website: http://www.brandeis.edu/gsas/programs/mcbio.html

Brigham Young University, Graduate Studies, College of Life Sciences, Department of Microbiology and Molecular Biology, Provo, UT 84602. Offers MS, PhD. *Faculty:* 19 full-time (4 women), 6 part-time/adjunct (5 women). *Students:* 8 full-time (6 women), 31 part-time (14 women); includes 9 minority (4 Asian, non-Hispanic/Latino; 4 Hispanic/Latino; 1 Native Hawaiian or other Pacific Islander, non-Hispanic/Latino). Average age 28. 12 applicants, 83% accepted, 7 enrolled. In 2017, 6 master's, 2 doctorates awarded. Terminal master's awarded for partial completion of doctoral program. *Degree requirements:* For master's, comprehensive exam, thesis; for doctorate, comprehensive exam, thesis/dissertation. *Entrance requirements:* For master's, GRE General Test, minimum GPA of 3.0 during previous 2 years; for doctorate, GRE General Test, minimum GPA of 3.0. Additional exam requirements/recommendations for international students: Required—TOEFL (minimum score 580 paper-based; 85 iBT), IELTS (minimum score 7). *Application deadline:* For fall admission, 1/15 for domestic and international students. Application fee: $50. Electronic applications accepted. *Expenses:* $2,730 per semester for members of the Church of Jesus Christ of Latter-day Saints; $5,460 per semester for those who are not members of the Church. *Financial support:* In 2017–18, 18 students received support, including 17 research assistantships with full tuition reimbursements available (averaging $22,500 per year); institutionally sponsored loans, scholarships/grants, health care benefits, and unspecified assistantships also available. Financial award application deadline: 3/1; financial award applicants required to submit FAFSA. *Faculty research:* Immunobiology, molecular genetics, molecular virology, cancer biology, pathogenic and environmental microbiology. *Total annual research expenditures:* $523,825. *Unit head:* Dr. Richard Robison, Chair, 801-422-2416, Fax: 801-422-0004, E-mail: richard_robison@byu.edu. *Application contact:* Dr. Joel Griffitts, Graduate Coordinator, 801-422-7997, Fax: 801-422-0004, E-mail: joelg@byu.edu.
Website: http://mmbio.byu.edu/

Brown University, Graduate School, Division of Biology and Medicine, Department of Molecular Biology, Cell Biology, and Biochemistry, Providence, RI 02912. Offers MA, PhD. *Program availability:* Part-time. Terminal master's awarded for partial completion of doctoral program. *Degree requirements:* For master's, thesis (for some programs); for doctorate, one foreign language, thesis/dissertation, preliminary exam. *Entrance requirements:* For master's and doctorate, GRE General Test, GRE Subject Test. Additional exam requirements/recommendations for international students: Required—TOEFL. Electronic applications accepted. *Faculty research:* Molecular genetics, gene regulation.

California Institute of Technology, Division of Biology, Program in Molecular Biology, Pasadena, CA 91125-0001. Offers PhD. *Degree requirements:* For doctorate, thesis/dissertation, qualifying exam. *Entrance requirements:* For doctorate, GRE General Test.

California State University, Sacramento, College of Natural Sciences and Mathematics, Department of Biological Sciences, Sacramento, CA 95819. Offers biological conservation (MS); molecular and cellular biology (MS); stem cell (MA). *Program availability:* Part-time. *Students:* 25 full-time (15 women), 26 part-time (14 women); includes 11 minority (2 Black or African American, non-Hispanic/Latino; 1 American Indian or Alaska Native, non-Hispanic/Latino; 8 Asian, non-Hispanic/Latino), 1 international. Average age 29. 82 applicants, 29% accepted, 18 enrolled. In 2017, 11 master's awarded. *Degree requirements:* For master's, thesis or project; writing proficiency exam. *Entrance requirements:* For master's, GRE, bachelor's degree in biology or equivalent; minimum GPA of 2.75 in all biology courses, 3.0 in all upper-division biology courses. Additional exam requirements/recommendations for international students: Required—TOEFL (minimum score 550 paper-based; 80 iBT); Recommended—IELTS, TSE. *Application deadline:* For fall admission, 2/1 for domestic and international students. Applications are processed on a rolling basis. Application fee: $55. Electronic applications accepted. *Expenses:* Contact institution. *Financial support:* Teaching assistantships, career-related internships or fieldwork, Federal Work-Study, and scholarships/grants available. Support available to part-time students. Financial award application deadline: 3/1; financial award applicants required to submit FAFSA. *Unit head:* Dr. Shannon Datwyler, Chair, 916-278-6535, Fax: 916-278-6993, E-mail: datwyler@csus.edu. *Application contact:* Jose Martinez, Graduate Admissions Supervisor, 916-278-7871, E-mail: martinj@skymail.csus.edu.
Website: http://www.csus.edu/bios

Carnegie Mellon University, Mellon College of Science, Department of Biological Sciences, Pittsburgh, PA 15213-3891. Offers biochemistry (PhD); biophysics (PhD); cell and developmental biology (PhD); computational biology (MS, PhD); genetics (PhD); molecular biology (PhD); neuroscience (PhD); structural biology (PhD). *Degree requirements:* For doctorate, comprehensive exam, thesis/dissertation. *Entrance requirements:* For doctorate, GRE General Test, GRE Subject Test, interview. Electronic applications accepted. *Faculty research:* Genetic structure, function, and regulation; protein structure and function; biological membranes; biological spectroscopy.

Case Western Reserve University, School of Medicine and School of Graduate Studies, Graduate Programs in Medicine, Department of Molecular Biology and Microbiology, Cleveland, OH 44106-4960. Offers cell biology (PhD); molecular biology (PhD); molecular virology (PhD); MD/PhD. Students are admitted to an integrated Biomedical Sciences Training Program involving 11 basic science programs at Case Western Reserve University. *Degree requirements:* For doctorate, thesis/dissertation. *Entrance requirements:* For doctorate, GRE General Test, GRE Subject Test. Additional exam requirements/recommendations for international students: Required—TOEFL. Electronic applications accepted. *Expenses: Tuition:* Full-time $43,854; part-time $1827 per credit hour. *Required fees:* $50; $50 per credit hour. Tuition and fees vary according to course load and program. *Faculty research:* Gene expression in eukaryotic and prokaryotic systems; microbial physiology; intracellular transport and signaling; mechanisms of oncogenesis; molecular mechanisms of RNA processing, editing, and catalysis.

Central Connecticut State University, School of Graduate Studies, School of Engineering, Science and Technology, Department of Biomolecular Sciences, New Britain, CT 06050-4010. Offers MS, Certificate. *Program availability:* Part-time, evening/weekend. *Faculty:* 8 full-time (2 women). *Students:* 22 full-time (10 women), 29 part-time (19 women); includes 22 minority (10 Black or African American, non-Hispanic/Latino; 8 Asian, non-Hispanic/Latino; 4 Hispanic/Latino), 1 international. Average age 28. 40 applicants, 73% accepted, 19 enrolled. In 2017, 13 master's, 3 other advanced degrees awarded. *Degree requirements:* For master's, comprehensive exam, thesis or alternative; for Certificate, qualifying exam. *Entrance requirements:* For master's, minimum undergraduate GPA of 2.7, essay; for Certificate, essay. Additional exam requirements/recommendations for international students: Required—TOEFL (minimum score 550 paper-based; 79 iBT); Recommended—IELTS (minimum score 6.5). *Application deadline:* For fall admission, 8/1 for domestic students, 5/1 for international students; for spring admission, 11/1 for domestic and international students. Applications are processed on a rolling basis. Application fee: $50. Electronic applications accepted. *Expenses: Tuition, area resident:* Full-time $6757. Tuition, state resident: full-time $9750; part-time $374 per credit. Tuition, nonresident: full-time $18,102; part-time $374 per credit. *Required fees:* $4635; $255 per credit. *Financial support:* In 2017–18, 13 students received support. Career-related internships or fieldwork, Federal Work-Study, scholarships/grants, and unspecified assistantships available. Support available to part-time students. Financial award application deadline: 3/1; financial award applicants required to submit FAFSA. *Unit head:* Dr. Kathy Martin, Chair, 860-832-3560, E-mail: martink@ccsu.edu. *Application contact:* Patricia Gardner, Associate Director of Graduate Studies, 860-832-2350, Fax: 860-832-2362.
Website: http://www.ccsu.edu/bms/

Clemson University, Graduate School, College of Science, Department of Genetics and Biochemistry, Clemson, SC 29634. Offers biochemistry and molecular biology (PhD); genetics (PhD). *Faculty:* 24 full-time (12 women). *Students:* 49 full-time (22 women); includes 3 minority (all Hispanic/Latino), 20 international. Average age 26. 54 applicants, 41% accepted, 16 enrolled. In 2017, 11 doctorates awarded. *Degree requirements:* For doctorate, comprehensive exam, thesis/dissertation. *Entrance requirements:* For doctorate, GRE General Test, unofficial transcripts, letters of recommendation. Additional exam requirements/recommendations for international students: Required—TOEFL (minimum score 80 iBT), IELTS (minimum score 6.5), PTE (minimum score 54). *Application deadline:* For fall admission, 1/1 for domestic and international students; for spring admission, 9/1 for domestic and international students. Applications are processed on a rolling basis. Application fee: $80 ($90 for international students). Electronic applications accepted. *Expenses:* $5,174 per semester full-time resident, $9,714 per semester full-time non-resident, $511 per credit hour part-time resident, $1,017 per credit hour part-time non-resident; $741 per credit hour online; other fees may apply per session. *Financial support:* In 2017–18, 41 students received support, including 7 fellowships with partial tuition reimbursements available (averaging $10,000 per year), 14 research assistantships with partial tuition reimbursements available (averaging $24,786 per year), 20 teaching assistantships with partial tuition reimbursements available (averaging $26,200 per year). Financial award application deadline: 1/1. *Faculty research:* Animal genetics, genomics and bioinformatics, microbial pathogenesis, plant genetics and biochemistry, cell and developmental biology. *Total annual research expenditures:* $1.2 million. *Unit head:* Dr. William Marcotte, Jr., Department Chair, 864-656-3586, E-mail: marcotw@clemson.edu. *Application contact:* Dr. Hong Luo, Graduate Program Coordinator, 864-656-1746, E-mail: hluo@clemson.edu.
Website: https://www.clemson.edu/science/departments/genetics-biochemistry/

Columbia University, College of Physicians and Surgeons, Integrated Program in Cellular, Molecular, Structural and Genetic Studies, New York, NY 10032. Offers PhD. Terminal master's awarded for partial completion of doctoral program. *Degree requirements:* For doctorate, thesis/dissertation. *Entrance requirements:* For doctorate, GRE General Test, GRE Subject Test. Additional exam requirements/recommendations for international students: Required—TOEFL. *Expenses:* Contact institution. *Faculty research:* Transcription, macromolecular sorting, gene expression during development, cellular interaction.

Cornell University, Graduate School, Graduate Fields of Agriculture and Life Sciences, Field of Biochemistry, Molecular and Cell Biology, Ithaca, NY 14853. Offers biochemistry (PhD); biophysics (PhD); cell biology (PhD); molecular biology (PhD). *Degree requirements:* For doctorate, comprehensive exam, thesis/dissertation, 2 semesters of teaching experience. *Entrance requirements:* For doctorate, GRE General Test, GRE Subject Test (biology, chemistry, physics, biochemistry, cell and molecular biology), 3 letters of recommendation. Additional exam requirements/recommendations for international students: Required—TOEFL (minimum score 600 paper-based; 77 iBT). Electronic applications accepted. *Faculty research:* Biophysics, structural biology.

Cornell University, Graduate School, Graduate Fields of Agriculture and Life Sciences and Graduate Fields of Human Ecology, Field of Nutrition, Ithaca, NY 14853. Offers animal nutrition (MPS, PhD); community nutrition (MPS, PhD); human nutrition (MPS, PhD); international nutrition (MPS, PhD); molecular biochemistry (MPS, PhD). *Degree requirements:* For master's, thesis (MS), project papers (MPS); for doctorate, comprehensive exam, thesis/dissertation. *Entrance requirements:* For master's and doctorate, GRE General Test, previous course work in organic chemistry (with laboratory) and biochemistry; 2 letters of recommendation. Additional exam requirements/recommendations for international students: Required—TOEFL (minimum score 550 paper-based; 77 iBT). Electronic applications accepted. *Faculty research:* Nutritional biochemistry, experimental human and animal nutrition, international nutrition, community nutrition.

Dartmouth College, Graduate Program in Molecular and Cellular Biology, Hanover, NH 03755. Offers PhD, MBA/PhD, MD/PhD. *Faculty:* 70 full-time (16 women), 6 part-time/adjunct (3 women). *Students:* 62 full-time (28 women); includes 12 minority (2 Asian, non-Hispanic/Latino; 9 Hispanic/Latino; 1 Two or more races, non-Hispanic/Latino), 22 international. Average age 26. 161 applicants, 38% accepted, 30 enrolled. In 2017, 9 doctorates awarded. *Entrance requirements:* For doctorate, GRE General Test, letters of recommendation, minimum GPA of 3.0. *Application deadline:* For fall admission, 12/8 for domestic students. Applications are processed on a rolling basis. Application fee: $75. Electronic applications accepted. *Financial support:* Fellowships and health care benefits available. *Unit head:* Dr. Patrick J. Dolph, Vice Chair, 603-650-1092, E-mail: mcb@dartmouth.edu. *Application contact:* Janet Cheney, Program Coordinator, 603-650-1612, E-mail: mcb@dartmouth.edu.
Website: http://dms.dartmouth.edu/mcb/

Drexel University, College of Medicine, Biomedical Graduate Programs, Interdisciplinary Program in Molecular and Cell Biology and Genetics, Philadelphia, PA 19104-2875. Offers MS, PhD, MD/PhD. Terminal master's awarded for partial completion of doctoral program. *Degree requirements:* For master's, comprehensive exam, thesis; for doctorate, thesis/dissertation, qualifying exam. *Entrance requirements:* For master's, GRE General Test, minimum GPA of 2.75; for doctorate, GRE General Test, minimum GPA of 3.0. Additional exam requirements/recommendations for international students: Required—TOEFL. Electronic applications accepted. *Faculty research:* Molecular anatomy, biochemistry, medical biotechnology, molecular pathology, microbiology and immunology.

Duke University, Graduate School, Department of Evolutionary Anthropology, Durham, NC 27708. Offers cellular and molecular biology (PhD); gross anatomy and physical anthropology (PhD), including comparative morphology of human and non-human primates, primate social behavior, vertebrate paleontology; neuroanatomy (PhD). *Degree requirements:* For doctorate, one foreign language, thesis/dissertation. *Entrance requirements:* For doctorate, GRE General Test. Additional exam requirements/recommendations for international students: Required—TOEFL (minimum score 577 paper-based; 90 iBT) or IELTS (minimum score 7). Electronic applications accepted.

Duke University, Graduate School, Program in Cell and Molecular Biology, Durham, NC 27710. Offers Certificate. Students must be enrolled in a participating PhD program (biology, cell biology, immunology, molecular genetics, neurobiology, pathology, pharmacology). *Entrance requirements:* Additional exam requirements/recommendations for international students: Required—TOEFL (minimum score 577 paper-based; 90 iBT) or IELTS (minimum score 7). Electronic applications accepted.

East Carolina University, Graduate School, Thomas Harriot College of Arts and Sciences, Department of Biology, Greenville, NC 27858-4353. Offers biology (MS); molecular biology and biotechnology (MS). *Program availability:* Part-time. *Students:* 39 full-time (24 women), 16 part-time (8 women); includes 8 minority (5 Black or African American, non-Hispanic/Latino; 2 Asian, non-Hispanic/Latino; 1 Two or more races, non-Hispanic/Latino). Average age 26. 52 applicants, 54% accepted, 17 enrolled. In 2017, 8 master's awarded. *Degree requirements:* For master's, comprehensive exam, thesis. *Entrance requirements:* For master's, GRE General Test, GRE Subject Test. Additional exam requirements/recommendations for international students: Recommended—TOEFL, IELTS. *Application deadline:* For fall admission, 6/1 priority date for domestic students, 3/1 priority date for international students; for spring admission, 10/15 priority date for domestic students. Applications are processed on a rolling basis. Application fee: $75. Electronic applications accepted. *Expenses:* Tuition, state resident: full-time $4749; part-time $297 per credit hour. Tuition, nonresident: full-time $17,898; part-time $1119 per credit hour. *Required fees:* $2691; $224 per credit hour. Part-time tuition and fees vary according to course load and program. *Financial support:* Fellowships with partial tuition reimbursements, research assistantships with partial tuition reimbursements, teaching assistantships with partial tuition reimbursements, career-related internships or fieldwork, Federal Work-Study, scholarships/grants, and unspecified assistantships available. Support available to part-time students. Financial award application deadline: 3/1. *Faculty research:* Biotechnology, biochemistry, bioinformatics, microbiology, cell biology. *Unit head:* Dr. Jeff McKinnon, Chair, 252-328-6718, E-mail: mckinnonj@ecu.edu. *Application contact:* Dean of Graduate School, 252-328-6012, Fax: 252-328-6071, E-mail: gradschool@ecu.edu.
Website: http://www.ecu.edu/cs-cas/biology/

Emory University, Laney Graduate School, Division of Biological and Biomedical Sciences, Program in Genetics and Molecular Biology, Atlanta, GA 30322-1100. Offers PhD. *Degree requirements:* For doctorate, comprehensive exam, thesis/dissertation. *Entrance requirements:* For doctorate, GRE General Test, minimum GPA of 3.0 in science course work (recommended). Additional exam requirements/recommendations for international students: Required—TOEFL. Electronic applications accepted. *Faculty research:* Gene regulation, genetic combination, developmental regulation.

Florida Institute of Technology, College of Science, Program in Biological Sciences, Melbourne, FL 32901-6975. Offers biological science (PhD); biotechnology (MS); cell and molecular biology (MS); ecology (MS); marine biology (MS). *Program availability:* Part-time. *Students:* Average age 26. 230 applicants, 24% accepted, 21 enrolled. In 2017, 27 master's, 3 doctorates awarded. *Degree requirements:* For master's, thesis (for some programs), research, seminar, internship, or summer lab; for doctorate, comprehensive exam, thesis/dissertation, dissertations seminar, publications. *Entrance requirements:* For master's, GRE General Test, 3 letters of recommendation; statement of objectives; bachelor's degree in biology, chemistry, biochemistry or equivalent; for doctorate, GRE General Test, resume, 3 letters of recommendation, minimum GPA of 3.2, statement of objectives. Additional exam requirements/recommendations for international students: Required—TOEFL (minimum score 550 paper-based; 79 iBT). *Application deadline:* For fall admission, 3/1 for domestic students, 4/1 for international students; for spring admission, 9/1 for domestic and international students. Applications are processed on a rolling basis. Electronic applications accepted. *Expenses: Tuition:* Part-time $1241 per credit hour. Part-time tuition and fees vary according to campus/location. *Financial support:* Career-related internships or fieldwork, institutionally sponsored loans, tuition waivers (partial), unspecified assistantships, and tuition remissions available. Support available to part-time students. Financial award application deadline: 3/1; financial award applicants required to submit FAFSA. *Faculty research:* Initiation of protein synthesis in eukaryotic cells, fixation of radioactive carbon, changes in DNA molecule, endangered or threatened avian and mammalian species, hydro acoustics and feeding preference of the West Indian manatee. *Unit head:* Dr. Richard B. Aronson, Department Head, 321-674-8034, Fax: 321-674-7238, E-mail: raronson@fit.edu. *Application contact:* Cheryl A. Brown, Associate Director of Graduate Admissions, 321-674-7581, Fax: 321-723-9468, E-mail: cbrown@fit.edu.
Website: http://cos.fit.edu/biology/

Florida State University, The Graduate School, College of Arts and Sciences, Department of Biological Science, Specialization in Cell and Molecular Biology, Tallahassee, FL 32306-4295. Offers MS, PhD. *Faculty:* 24 full-time (6 women). *Students:* 52 full-time (29 women); includes 2 minority (1 Black or African American, non-Hispanic/Latino; 1 Two or more races, non-Hispanic/Latino), 24 international. Average age 29. 52 applicants, 31% accepted, 9 enrolled. In 2017, 1 master's, 4 doctorates awarded. Terminal master's awarded for partial completion of doctoral program. *Degree requirements:* For master's, comprehensive exam (for some programs), thesis, teaching experience, seminar presentation; for doctorate, comprehensive exam, thesis/dissertation, teaching experience; seminar presentation. *Entrance requirements:* For master's and doctorate, GRE General Test, minimum upper-division GPA of 3.0. Additional exam requirements/recommendations for international students: Required—TOEFL (minimum score 600 paper-based; 92 iBT). *Application deadline:* For fall admission, 12/1 for domestic and international students. Application fee: $30. Electronic applications accepted. *Financial support:* In 2017–18, 52 students received support, including 2 fellowships with full tuition reimbursements available (averaging $30,000 per year), 12 research assistantships with full tuition reimbursements available (averaging $23,800 per year), 38 teaching assistantships with full tuition reimbursements available (averaging $23,800 per year); scholarships/grants and unspecified assistantships also available. Financial award application deadline: 12/1; financial award applicants required to submit FAFSA. *Faculty research:* Molecular biology; genetics and genomics; developmental biology and gene expression; cell structure, function, and motility; chromatin structure and function; biophysical and structural biology. *Unit head:* Dr. Thomas A. Houpt, Professor and Associate Chair, 850-644-4783, Fax: 850-644-8447, E-mail: houpt@bio.fsu.edu. *Application contact:* Jessica Webber, Coordinator, Graduate Affairs, 850-644-3023, Fax: 850-644-8447, E-mail: gradinfo@bio.fsu.edu.
Website: http://www.bio.fsu.edu/cmb/

Georgetown University, Graduate School of Arts and Sciences, Department of Biochemistry and Molecular and Cellular Biology, Washington, DC 20057. Offers MS, PhD. *Degree requirements:* For doctorate, comprehensive exam, thesis/dissertation. *Entrance requirements:* For doctorate, GRE General Test. Additional exam requirements/recommendations for international students: Required—TOEFL.

Georgia State University, College of Arts and Sciences, Department of Biology, Program in Cellular and Molecular Biology and Physiology, Atlanta, GA 30302-3083. Offers bioinformatics (MS); cellular and molecular biology and physiology (MS, PhD). *Program availability:* Part-time. Terminal master's awarded for partial completion of doctoral program. *Entrance requirements:* For master's and doctorate, GRE. *Application deadline:* Applications are processed on a rolling basis. Application fee: $50. Electronic applications accepted. *Expenses:* Tuition, state resident: full-time $7020. Tuition, nonresident: full-time $22,518. *Required fees:* $2128. Tuition and fees vary according to degree level and program. *Financial support:* Fellowships and research assistantships available. Financial award application deadline: 12/3. *Faculty research:* Membrane transport, viral infection, molecular immunology, protein modeling, gene regulation. *Unit head:* Dr. Charles Derby, Director of Graduate Studies, 404-413-5393, Fax: 404-413-5446, E-mail: cderby@gsu.edu.
Website: http://biology.gsu.edu/

Grand Valley State University, College of Liberal Arts and Sciences, Program in Cell and Molecular Biology, Allendale, MI 49401-9403. Offers MS. *Faculty:* 8 full-time (5 women). *Students:* 16 full-time (13 women), 18 part-time (8 women); includes 3 minority (2 Black or African American, non-Hispanic/Latino; 1 Asian, non-Hispanic/Latino), 13 international. Average age 26. 30 applicants, 73% accepted, 12 enrolled. In 2017, 15 master's awarded. *Degree requirements:* For master's, thesis or internship. *Entrance requirements:* For master's, GRE, minimum GPA of 3.0, resume or curriculum vitae, personal statement, minimum of 2 letters of recommendation, interview. Additional exam requirements/recommendations for international students: Required—TOEFL (minimum iBT score of 80), IELTS (6.5), or Michigan English Language Assessment Battery (77). *Application deadline:* Applications are processed on a rolling basis. Application fee: $30. Electronic applications accepted. *Expenses:* $657 per credit hour. *Financial support:* In 2017–18, 17 students received support, including 1 fellowship, 12 research assistantships with full and partial tuition reimbursements available (averaging $4,000 per year); unspecified assistantships also available. *Faculty research:* Plant cell biology, plant development, cell/signal integration. *Unit head:* Dr. Mark Staves, Department Chair, 616-331-2473, Fax: 616-331-3446, E-mail: stavesm@gvsu.edu. *Application contact:* Dr. Tim Born, PSM Coordinator/Student Recruiting Contact, 616-331-8643, Fax: 616-331-6770, E-mail: bornt@gvsu.edu.

Harvard University, Graduate School of Arts and Sciences, Department of Molecular and Cellular Biology, Cambridge, MA 02138. Offers PhD. *Degree requirements:* For doctorate, thesis/dissertation, oral exam. *Entrance requirements:* For doctorate, GRE General Test, GRE Subject Test (recommended). Additional exam requirements/recommendations for international students: Required—TOEFL.

Harvard University, Graduate School of Arts and Sciences, Program in Chemical Biology, Cambridge, MA 02138. Offers PhD.

Hood College, Graduate School, Program in Biomedical Science, Frederick, MD 21701-8575. Offers biomedical science (MS), including biotechnology/molecular biology, microbiology/immunology/virology. *Program availability:* Part-time, evening/weekend. *Faculty:* 5 full-time (3 women), 1 (woman) part-time/adjunct. *Students:* 13 full-time (6 women), 73 part-time (39 women); includes 21 minority (12 Black or African American, non-Hispanic/Latino; 6 Asian, non-Hispanic/Latino; 2 Hispanic/Latino; 1 Two or more races, non-Hispanic/Latino), 6 international. Average age 30. 24 applicants, 92% accepted, 14 enrolled. In 2017, 13 master's awarded. *Degree requirements:* For master's, thesis or alternative. *Entrance requirements:* For master's, bachelor's degree in biology; minimum GPA of 3.0; undergraduate course work in cell biology, chemistry, organic chemistry, and genetics. Additional exam requirements/recommendations for international students: Required—TOEFL (minimum score 575 paper-based; 89 iBT), IELTS (minimum score 6). *Application deadline:* For fall admission, 8/15 priority date for domestic students, 8/5 for international students; for spring admission, 12/1 priority date for domestic students, 12/1 for international students; for summer admission, 5/1 priority date for domestic students, 4/15 for international students. Applications are processed on a rolling basis. Application fee: $35. Electronic applications accepted. *Expenses:* $500 per credit plus $110 comprehensive fee per semester, plus any applicable lab fees by course. *Financial support:* Research assistantships with full tuition reimbursements, tuition waivers (partial), and unspecified assistantships available. Financial award applicants required to submit FAFSA. *Faculty research:* Molecular signaling in cell tumor initiation, biomedical ethics, genetic and biochemical approaches to study regulation of gene expression. *Unit head:* Dr. April M. Boulton, Dean of the Graduate School, 301-696-3600, E-mail: gofurther@hood.edu. *Application contact:* Larbi Bricha, Assistant Director of Graduate Admissions, 301-696-3600, E-mail: gofurther@hood.edu.
Website: http://www.hood.edu/graduate

Howard University, College of Medicine, Department of Biochemistry and Molecular Biology, Washington, DC 20059-0002. Offers biochemistry and molecular biology (PhD); biotechnology (MS); MD/PhD. *Program availability:* Part-time. *Degree requirements:* For master's, externship; for doctorate, comprehensive exam, thesis/dissertation. *Entrance requirements:* For master's and doctorate, GRE General Test, minimum GPA of 3.0. *Faculty research:* Cellular and molecular biology of olfaction, gene regulation and expression, enzymology, NMR spectroscopy of molecular structure, hormone regulation/metabolism.

Illinois Institute of Technology, Graduate College, College of Science, Department of Biology, Chicago, IL 60616. Offers applied life sciences (MS); biochemistry (MS); biology (MS, PhD); cell and molecular biology (MS); microbiology (MS); molecular biochemistry and biophysics (MS, PhD). *Program availability:* Part-time, evening/weekend, online learning. Terminal master's awarded for partial completion of doctoral program. *Degree requirements:* For master's, comprehensive exam, thesis (for some programs); for doctorate, comprehensive exam, thesis/dissertation. *Entrance requirements:* For master's, GRE General Test (minimum score 300 Quantitative and Verbal, 2.5 Analytical Writing), minimum undergraduate GPA of 3.0; for doctorate, GRE General Test (minimum score 310 Quantitative and Verbal, 3.0 Analytical Writing); GRE Subject Test (strongly recommended), minimum undergraduate GPA of 3.0. Additional exam requirements/recommendations for international students: Required—TOEFL (minimum score 550 paper-based; 80 iBT). Electronic applications accepted. *Faculty research:* Macromolecular crystallography, insect immunity and basic cell biology, improvement of bacterial strains for enhanced biodesulfurization of petroleum, programmed cell death in cancer cells.

Illinois State University, Graduate School, College of Arts and Sciences, School of Biological Sciences, Normal, IL 61790. Offers animal behavior (MS); bacteriology (MS); biochemistry (MS); biological sciences (MS); biology (PhD); biophysics (MS); biotechnology (MS); botany (MS, PhD); cell biology (MS); conservation biology (MS); developmental biology (MS); ecology (MS, PhD); entomology (MS); evolutionary biology (MS); genetics (MS, PhD); immunology (MS); microbiology (MS, PhD); molecular biology (MS); molecular genetics (MS); neurobiology (MS); neuroscience (MS); parasitology (MS); physiology (MS, PhD); plant biology (MS); plant molecular biology (MS); plant sciences (MS); structural biology (MS); zoology (MS, PhD). *Program availability:* Part-time. *Degree requirements:* For master's, thesis or alternative; for doctorate, variable foreign language requirement, thesis/dissertation, 2 terms of residency. *Entrance requirements:* For master's, GRE General Test, minimum GPA of 2.6 in last 60 hours of course work; for doctorate, GRE General Test. *Faculty research:* Redoc balance and drug development in schistosoma mansoni, control of the growth of listeria monocytogenes at low temperature, regulation of cell expansion and microtubule function by SPRI, CRUI: physiology and fitness consequences of different life history phenotypes.

Indiana State University, College of Graduate and Professional Studies, College of Arts and Sciences, Department of Biology, Terre Haute, IN 47809. Offers cellular and molecular biology (PhD); ecology, systematics and evolution (PhD); life sciences (MS); physiology (PhD); science education (MS). *Degree requirements:* For master's, thesis optional; for doctorate, comprehensive exam, thesis/dissertation. *Entrance requirements:* For master's and doctorate, GRE General Test. Electronic applications accepted.

Indiana University Bloomington, University Graduate School, College of Arts and Sciences, Department of Biology, Bloomington, IN 47405. Offers biology teaching (MAT); biotechnology (MA); evolution, ecology, and behavior (MA, PhD); genetics (PhD); microbiology (MA, PhD); molecular, cellular, and developmental biology (PhD); plant sciences (MA, PhD); zoology (MA, PhD). Terminal master's awarded for partial completion of doctoral program. *Degree requirements:* For master's, thesis, oral defense; for doctorate, thesis/dissertation, oral defense. *Entrance requirements:* For master's and doctorate, GRE General Test. Additional exam requirements/recommendations for international students: Required—TOEFL (minimum score 100 iBT). Electronic applications accepted. *Faculty research:* Evolution, ecology and behavior; microbiology; molecular biology and genetics; plant biology.

Indiana University–Purdue University Indianapolis, Indiana University School of Medicine, Department of Biochemistry and Molecular Biology, Indianapolis, IN 46202. Offers MS, PhD, MD/MS, MD/PhD. Terminal master's awarded for partial completion of doctoral program. *Degree requirements:* For master's, thesis; for doctorate, thesis/dissertation. *Entrance requirements:* For master's and doctorate, GRE General Test, GRE Subject Test (recommended), previous course work in organic chemistry. Additional exam requirements/recommendations for international students: Required—TOEFL. Electronic applications accepted. *Faculty research:* Metabolic regulation, enzymology, peptide and protein chemistry, cell biology, signal transduction.

Inter American University of Puerto Rico, Metropolitan Campus, Graduate Programs, Program in Medical Technology, San Juan, PR 00919-1293. Offers administration of clinical laboratories (MS); molecular microbiology (MS). *Accreditation:* NAACLS. *Program availability:* Part-time. *Degree requirements:* For master's, comprehensive exam. *Entrance requirements:* For master's, BS in medical technology, minimum GPA of 2.5. Electronic applications accepted.

Iowa State University of Science and Technology, Bioinformatics and Computational Biology Program, Ames, IA 50011. Offers MS, PhD. *Degree requirements:* For doctorate, thesis/dissertation. *Entrance requirements:* For master's and doctorate, GRE General Test. Additional exam requirements/recommendations for international students: Recommended—TOEFL, IELTS. Electronic applications accepted. *Faculty research:* Functional and structural genomics, genome evolution, macromolecular structure and function, mathematical biology and biological statistics, metabolic and developmental networks.

Iowa State University of Science and Technology, Program in Molecular, Cellular, and Developmental Biology, Ames, IA 50011. Offers MS, PhD. *Entrance requirements:* For master's and doctorate, GRE General Test. Additional exam requirements/recommendations for international students: Required—TOEFL (minimum score 580 paper-based; 85 iBT), IELTS (minimum score 7). Electronic applications accepted.

Irell & Manella Graduate School of Biological Sciences, Graduate Program, Duarte, CA 91010. Offers brain metastatic cancer (PhD); cancer and stem cell metabolism (PhD); cancer biology (PhD); cancer biology and developmental therapeutics (PhD); cell biology (PhD); chemical biology (PhD); chromosomal break repair (PhD); diabetes and pancreatic progenitor cell biology (PhD); DNA repair and cancer biology (PhD); germline epigenetic remodeling and endocrine disruptors (PhD); hematology and hematopoietic cell transplantation (PhD); hematology and immunology (PhD); inflammation and cancer (PhD); micrornas and gene regulation in cardiovascular disease (PhD); mixed chimrism for reversal of autoimmunity (PhD); molecular and cellular biology (PhD); molecular biology and genetics (PhD); nanoparticle mediated twist1 silencing in metastatic cancer (PhD); neuro-oncology and stem cell biology (PhD); neuroscience (PhD); RNA directed therapies for HIV-1 (PhD); small RNA-induced transcriptional gene activation (PhD); stem cell regulation by the microenvironment (PhD); translational oncology and pharmaceutical sciences (PhD); tumor biology (PhD). *Degree requirements:* For doctorate, comprehensive exam, thesis/dissertation, qualifying exams, two advanced courses. *Entrance requirements:* For doctorate, GRE General Test; GRE Subject Test (recommended), 2 years of course work in chemistry (general and organic); 1 year of course work each in biochemistry, general biology, and general physics; 2 semesters of course work in mathematics; significant research laboratory experience. Additional exam requirements/recommendations for international students: Required—TOEFL. Electronic applications accepted. *Faculty research:* Cancer biology, diabetes, stem cell biology, neuroscience, immunology.

See Display on page 65 and Close-Up on page 109.

Johns Hopkins University, Bloomberg School of Public Health, Department of Biochemistry and Molecular Biology, Baltimore, MD 21205. Offers MHS, Sc M, PhD. *Program availability:* Part-time. *Students:* Average age 25. 186 applicants, 53% accepted, 59 enrolled. *Degree requirements:* For master's, thesis; for doctorate, comprehensive exam, thesis/dissertation, oral and written exams. *Entrance requirements:* For master's, MCAT or GRE, 3 letters of recommendation, curriculum vitae; for doctorate, GRE General Test, 3 letters of recommendation, curriculum vitae. *Application deadline:* For fall admission, 12/1 for domestic students. Application fee: $135. Electronic applications accepted. *Financial support:* Fellowships, research assistantships, teaching assistantships, Federal Work-Study, institutionally sponsored loans, scholarships/grants, health care benefits, and stipends available. *Faculty research:* DNA replication, repair, structure, carcinogenesis, protein structure, enzyme catalysts, reproductive biology. *Unit head:* Dr. Michael Matunis, Interim Chair, 410-955-3671, Fax: 410-955-2926, E-mail: bmb@jhsph.edu. *Application contact:* Sharon Gaston, Senior Academic Program Administrator, 410-955-3672, Fax: 410-955-2926, E-mail: bmb@jhsph.edu.
Website: http://www.jhsph.edu/dept/bmb/

Johns Hopkins University, National Institutes of Health Sponsored Programs, Baltimore, MD 21218. Offers biology (PhD), including biochemistry, biophysics, cell biology, developmental biology, genetic biology, molecular biology; cell, molecular, and developmental biology and biophysics (PhD). *Degree requirements:* For doctorate, comprehensive exam, thesis/dissertation. *Entrance requirements:* For doctorate, GRE General Test. Additional exam requirements/recommendations for international students: Required—TOEFL (minimum score 600 paper-based), TWE. Electronic applications accepted. *Faculty research:* Protein and nucleic acid biochemistry and biophysical chemistry, molecular biology and development.

Johns Hopkins University, School of Medicine, Graduate Programs in Medicine, Department of Pharmacology and Molecular Sciences, Baltimore, MD 21205. Offers PhD. *Degree requirements:* For doctorate, comprehensive exam, thesis/dissertation, departmental seminar. *Entrance requirements:* For doctorate, GRE General Test. Additional exam requirements/recommendations for international students: Required—TOEFL. Electronic applications accepted.

Johns Hopkins University, School of Medicine, Graduate Programs in Medicine, Program in Biochemistry, Cellular and Molecular Biology, Baltimore, MD 21205. Offers PhD. *Degree requirements:* For doctorate, comprehensive exam, thesis/dissertation. *Entrance requirements:* For doctorate, GRE General Test. Additional exam requirements/recommendations for international students: Required—TOEFL. Electronic applications accepted. *Faculty research:* Developmental biology, genomics/proteomics, protein targeting, signal transduction, structural biology.

Kent State University, College of Arts and Sciences, School of Biomedical Sciences, Kent, OH 44242-0001. Offers biological anthropology (PhD); biomedical mathematics (MS, PhD); cellular and molecular biology (MS, PhD), including cellular biology and structures, molecular biology and genetics; neurosciences (MS, PhD); pharmacology (MS, PhD); physiology (MS, PhD). *Faculty:* 22 full-time (9 women), 3 part-time/adjunct (1 woman). *Students:* 75 full-time (46 women); includes 8 minority (1 Black or African American, non-Hispanic/Latino; 3 Asian, non-Hispanic/Latino; 2 Hispanic/Latino; 2 Two

or more races, non-Hispanic/Latino), 25 international. Average age 28. 70 applicants, 23% accepted, 13 enrolled. In 2017, 23 master's, 5 doctorates awarded. Terminal master's awarded for partial completion of doctoral program. *Degree requirements:* For master's, thesis; for doctorate, comprehensive exam, thesis/dissertation. *Entrance requirements:* For master's, GRE, bachelor's degree, transcripts, minimum GPA of 3.0, goal statement, three letters of recommendation, academic preparation adequate to perform graduate work in the desired field; for doctorate, GRE, master's degree, minimum GPA of 3.0, transcripts, goal statement, three letters of recommendation. Additional exam requirements/recommendations for international students: Required—TOEFL (minimum score 600 paper-based, 100 iBT), Michigan English Language Assessment Battery (minimum score 85), IELTS (minimum score 7.0) or PTE (minimum score 68). *Application deadline:* For fall admission, 1/1 for domestic and international students. Applications are processed on a rolling basis. Application fee: $45 ($70 for international students). Electronic applications accepted. *Expenses:* Tuition, state resident: full-time $11,310; part-time $515 per credit hour. Tuition, nonresident: full-time $20,396; part-time $928 per credit hour. *International tuition:* $18,544 full-time. *Financial support:* Research assistantships with full tuition reimbursements, teaching assistantships, and unspecified assistantships available. Financial award application deadline: 1/1. *Unit head:* Dr. Ernest J. Freeman, Director, School of Biomedical Sciences, 330-672-2363, E-mail: efreema2@kent.edu.
Website: http://www.kent.edu/biomedical/

Lehigh University, College of Arts and Sciences, Department of Biological Sciences, Bethlehem, PA 18015. Offers biochemistry (PhD); cell and molecular biology (PhD); integrative biology (PhD); molecular biology (MS). *Program availability:* 100% online. *Faculty:* 18 full-time (8 women). *Students:* 38 full-time (20 women), 21 part-time (15 women); includes 12 minority (2 Black or African American, non-Hispanic/Latino; 1 American Indian or Alaska Native, non-Hispanic/Latino; 1 Asian, non-Hispanic/Latino; 6 Hispanic/Latino; 2 Two or more races, non-Hispanic/Latino), 10 international. Average age 28. 33 applicants, 42% accepted, 4 enrolled. In 2017, 8 master's, 4 doctorates awarded. Terminal master's awarded for partial completion of doctoral program. *Degree requirements:* For master's, thesis optional; for doctorate, comprehensive exam, thesis/dissertation. *Entrance requirements:* For doctorate, GRE General Test. Additional exam requirements/recommendations for international students: Required—TOEFL (minimum score 85 iBT). *Application deadline:* For fall admission, 7/15 for domestic and international students; for spring admission, 12/1 for domestic and international students; for summer admission, 4/30 for domestic and international students. Application fee: $75. Electronic applications accepted. *Expenses:* $1,460 per credit. *Financial support:* In 2017–18, 39 students received support, including 8 fellowships with full tuition reimbursements available (averaging $27,600 per year), 17 research assistantships with full tuition reimbursements available (averaging $27,600 per year), 23 teaching assistantships with full tuition reimbursements available (averaging $27,600 per year); health care benefits and tuition waivers also available. Financial award application deadline: 12/1; financial award applicants required to submit CSS PROFILE or FAFSA. *Faculty research:* Gene expression, cytoskeleton and cell structure, cell cycle and growth regulation, neuroscience, animal behavior, microbiology. *Total annual research expenditures:* $1.8 million. *Unit head:* Dr. Linda Lowe-Krentz, Chairperson, 610-758-5084, Fax: 610-758-4004, E-mail: lij0@lehigh.edu. *Application contact:* Dr. Amber Rice, Graduate Coordinator, 610-758-5509, Fax: 610-758-4004, E-mail: amr511@lehigh.edu.
Website: http://www.lehigh.edu/~inbios/

Lipscomb University, Program in Biomolecular Science, Nashville, TN 37204-3951. Offers human disease (MS); laboratory research (MS). *Program availability:* Part-time, evening/weekend. *Faculty:* 6 full-time (4 women). *Students:* 31 full-time (15 women); includes 10 minority (6 Black or African American, non-Hispanic/Latino; 2 Asian, non-Hispanic/Latino; 2 Hispanic/Latino). Average age 26. 67 applicants, 51% accepted, 11 enrolled. In 2017, 23 master's awarded. *Degree requirements:* For master's, capstone project. *Entrance requirements:* For master's, GRE (minimum score of 300/1000 on prior scoring system), MCAT (minimum score of 24), DAT (minimum score of 17), BS in related field, transcripts, minimum undergraduate GPA of 3.0, 2 letters of recommendation, resume. Additional exam requirements/recommendations for international students: Required—TOEFL (minimum score 570 paper-based). *Application deadline:* For fall admission, 8/1 for domestic students; for winter admission, 12/14 for domestic students; for spring admission, 5/14 for domestic students. Applications are processed on a rolling basis. Application fee: $50 ($75 for international students). Electronic applications accepted. *Expenses:* Contact institution. *Financial support:* Unspecified assistantships available. Financial award applicants required to submit FAFSA. *Unit head:* Dr. Kent Gallaher, Director, 615-966-5721, E-mail: kent.gallaher@lipscomb.edu. *Application contact:* Tina Fulford, Administrative Assistant, 615-966-5330, E-mail: tina.fulford@lipscomb.edu.
Website: http://www.lipscomb.edu/biology/Graduate-Program

Louisiana State University Health Sciences Center at Shreveport, Department of Biochemistry and Molecular Biology, Shreveport, LA 71130-3932. Offers MS, PhD, MD/PhD. *Degree requirements:* For master's, thesis; for doctorate, thesis/dissertation. *Entrance requirements:* For master's and doctorate, GRE General Test. Additional exam requirements/recommendations for international students: Required—TOEFL (minimum score 100 iBT), IELTS (minimum score 7). Electronic applications accepted. *Expenses:* Contact institution. *Faculty research:* Yeast genetics, prostate cancer, cell biology, mTOR signaling, Parkinson's Disease, transcriptional mechanisms, chromatin, DNA repair and damage response, protein synthesis, neuroscience, diabetes, cell cycle regulation, tRNA synthetases, stress response, glucose transporters, transmigration and wound repair.

Louisiana Tech University, Graduate School, College of Applied and Natural Sciences, Ruston, LA 71272. Offers biology (MS); dietetics (Graduate Certificate); health informatics (MHI); molecular science and nanotechnology (MS, PhD). *Program availability:* Part-time. *Faculty:* 56 full-time (31 women), 10 part-time/adjunct (4 women). *Students:* 75 full-time (49 women), 32 part-time (23 women); includes 32 minority (19 Black or African American, non-Hispanic/Latino; 4 Asian, non-Hispanic/Latino; 8 Hispanic/Latino; 1 Two or more races, non-Hispanic/Latino), 9 international. Average age 29. 46 applicants, 67% accepted, 10 enrolled. In 2017, 36 master's, 1 doctorate, 15 other advanced degrees awarded. *Degree requirements:* For master's, comprehensive exam (for some programs), thesis (for some programs); for doctorate, comprehensive exam, thesis/dissertation. *Entrance requirements:* For master's and doctorate, GRE General Test, transcript with bachelor's degree awarded; for Graduate Certificate, transcript with bachelor's degree awarded. Additional exam requirements/recommendations for international students: Required—TOEFL (minimum score 550 paper-based; 80 iBT), IELTS (minimum score 6.5). *Application deadline:* For fall admission, 8/1 priority date for domestic students, 6/1 for international students; for winter admission, 11/1 priority date for domestic students, 9/1 for international students; for spring admission, 2/1 priority date for domestic students, 12/1 for international students; for summer admission, 5/1 priority date for domestic students, 3/1 for international students. Applications are processed on a rolling basis. Application fee: $40. Electronic applications accepted. *Expenses:* Tuition, state resident: full-time $5146. Tuition, nonresident: full-time $10,147. *International tuition:* $10,267 full-time. *Required fees:* $2273. *Financial support:* In 2017–18, 19 students received support, including 19 research assistantships with partial tuition reimbursements available (averaging $8,817 per year); career-related internships or fieldwork, Federal Work-Study, scholarships/grants, and unspecified assistantships also available. Financial award application deadline: 2/1. *Faculty research:* Developmentally appropriate practices in early childhood education, maternal and child nutrition, nutrition and cardiovascular disease, and early intervention for infants and toddlers; research in cell and molecular biology; health promotion in emerging adults, insulin pump use, forensic nursing, qualitative research, empathy in nursing students, civility in nursing education, and STI education; gene expression data analysis and data mining, knowledge discovery for health related data. *Unit head:* Dr. Gary A. Kennedy, Dean, 318-257-4287, Fax: 318-257-5060, E-mail: kennedy@latech.edu.
Website: http://ans.latech.edu/

Loyola University Chicago, Graduate School, Integrated Program in Biomedical Sciences, Maywood, IL 60141. Offers biochemistry and molecular biology (MS, PhD); cell and molecular physiology (MS, PhD); infectious disease and immunology (MS); integrative cell biology (MS, PhD); microbiology and immunology (MS, PhD); molecular pharmacology and therapeutics (MS, PhD); neuroscience (MS, PhD). *Faculty:* 84 full-time (32 women). *Students:* 126 full-time (65 women), 1 (woman) part-time; includes 36 minority (5 Black or African American, non-Hispanic/Latino; 14 Asian, non-Hispanic/Latino; 14 Hispanic/Latino; 3 Two or more races, non-Hispanic/Latino), 13 international. Average age 26. 748 applicants, 34% accepted, 124 enrolled. In 2017, 41 master's, 18 doctorates awarded. *Degree requirements:* For master's, thesis; for doctorate, comprehensive exam, thesis/dissertation. *Entrance requirements:* For doctorate, GRE. Additional exam requirements/recommendations for international students: Required—TOEFL (minimum score 94 iBT), IELTS (minimum score 7.5). *Application deadline:* For fall admission, 2/7 for domestic students. Applications are processed on a rolling basis. Electronic applications accepted. *Expenses:* Contact institution. *Financial support:* In 2017–18, 20 students received support. Schmitt Fellowships and yearly tuition scholarships (averaging $25,032) available. Financial award application deadline: 6/15; financial award applicants required to submit FAFSA. *Unit head:* Dr. Leanne L. Cribbs, Associate Dean, Graduate Education, 708-327-2817, Fax: 708-216-8216, E-mail: lcribbs@luc.edu. *Application contact:* Margarita Quesada, Graduate Program Secretary, 708-216-3532, Fax: 708-216-8216, E-mail: mquesad@luc.edu.
Website: http://ssom.luc.edu/graduate_school/degree-programs/ipbsphd/

Marquette University, Graduate School, College of Arts and Sciences, Department of Biology, Milwaukee, WI 53201-1881. Offers cell biology (MS, PhD); developmental biology (MS, PhD); ecology (MS, PhD); epithelial physiology (MS, PhD); genetics (MS, PhD); microbiology (MS, PhD); molecular biology (MS, PhD); muscle and exercise physiology (MS, PhD); neuroscience (PhD). Terminal master's awarded for partial completion of doctoral program. *Degree requirements:* For master's, comprehensive exam, thesis, 1 year of teaching experience or equivalent; for doctorate, thesis/dissertation, 1 year of teaching experience or equivalent, qualifying exam. *Entrance requirements:* For master's and doctorate, GRE General Test, GRE Subject Test, official transcripts from all current and previous colleges/universities except Marquette, statement of professional goals and aspirations, three letters of recommendation. Additional exam requirements/recommendations for international students: Required—TOEFL (minimum score 530 paper-based). Electronic applications accepted. *Faculty research:* Neurobiology, neuroendocrinology, epithelial physiology, neuropeptide interactions, synaptic transmission.

Massachusetts Institute of Technology, School of Engineering, Department of Electrical Engineering and Computer Science, Cambridge, MA 02139. Offers computer science (PhD, Sc D, ECS); computer science and engineering (PhD, Sc D); computer science and molecular biology (M Eng); electrical engineering (PhD, Sc D, EE); electrical engineering and computer science (M Eng, SM, PhD, Sc D); SM/MBA. *Degree requirements:* For master's and other advanced degree, thesis; for doctorate, comprehensive exam, thesis/dissertation. *Entrance requirements:* Additional exam requirements/recommendations for international students: Required—TOEFL, IELTS. Electronic applications accepted. *Faculty research:* Information systems, circuits, biomedical sciences and engineering, computer science: artificial intelligence, systems, theory.

Massachusetts Institute of Technology, School of Science, Department of Biology, Cambridge, MA 02139. Offers biochemistry (PhD); biological oceanography (PhD); biology (PhD); biophysical chemistry and molecular structure (PhD); cell biology (PhD); computational and systems biology (PhD); developmental biology (PhD); genetics (PhD); immunology (PhD); microbiology (PhD); molecular biology (PhD); neurobiology (PhD). *Degree requirements:* For doctorate, comprehensive exam, thesis/dissertation, teaching assistantship during two semesters. *Entrance requirements:* For doctorate, GRE General Test. Additional exam requirements/recommendations for international students: Required—TOEFL, IELTS. Electronic applications accepted. *Faculty research:* Cellular, developmental and molecular (plant and animal) biology; biochemistry, bioengineering, biophysics and structural biology; classical and molecular genetics, stem cell and epigenetics; immunology and microbiology; cancer biology, molecular medicine, neurobiology and human disease; computational and systems biology.

Mayo Clinic Graduate School of Biomedical Sciences, Program in Biochemistry and Molecular Biology, Rochester, MN 55905. Offers MS, PhD. *Faculty:* 104 full-time (16 women). *Students:* 42 full-time (21 women); includes 20 minority (2 Black or African American, non-Hispanic/Latino; 11 Asian, non-Hispanic/Latino; 6 Hispanic/Latino; 1 Native Hawaiian or other Pacific Islander, non-Hispanic/Latino). 51 applicants, 18% accepted, 7 enrolled. Terminal master's awarded for partial completion of doctoral program. *Degree requirements:* For master's, thesis; for doctorate, comprehensive exam, thesis/dissertation, oral defense of dissertation, qualifying oral and written exam. *Entrance requirements:* For doctorate, GRE, 1 year of chemistry, biology, calculus, and physics. Additional exam requirements/recommendations for international students: Required—TOEFL. *Application deadline:* For fall admission, 12/1 for domestic and international students. Application fee: $50. Electronic applications accepted. *Financial support:* Fellowships with full tuition reimbursements available. *Faculty research:* Gene structure and function, membranes and receptors/cytoskeleton, oncogenes and growth factors, protein structure and function, steroid hormonal action. *Unit head:* Dr. David J. Katzmann, Director, 507-284-3320, E-mail: katzmann.david@mayo.edu. *Application contact:* Sarah E Giese, Admissions Coordinator, 507-538-1160, E-mail: phd.training@mayo.edu.
Website: http://www.mayo.edu/mgs/

McMaster University, Faculty of Health Sciences and School of Graduate Studies, Program in Medical Sciences, Hamilton, ON L8S 4M2, Canada. Offers blood and vascular (M Sc, PhD); genetics and cancer (M Sc, PhD); immunity and infection (M Sc, PhD); metabolism and nutrition (M Sc, PhD); neurosciences and behavioral sciences (M Sc, PhD); physiology/pharmacology (M Sc, PhD); MD/PhD. *Degree requirements:* For master's, thesis; for doctorate, comprehensive exam, thesis/dissertation. *Entrance requirements:* For master's, honors B Sc, B+ average in related field; for doctorate, M Sc, minimum B+ average. Additional exam requirements/recommendations for international students: Required—TOEFL (minimum score 580 paper-based; 92 iBT).

Medical University of South Carolina, College of Graduate Studies, Department of Biochemistry and Molecular Biology, Charleston, SC 29425. Offers MS, PhD, MD/PhD.

Molecular Biology

Terminal master's awarded for partial completion of doctoral program. *Degree requirements:* For master's, thesis, oral exam/thesis defense; for doctorate, thesis/dissertation, oral and written exams/dissertation defense. *Entrance requirements:* For master's, GRE General Test; for doctorate, GRE General Test, interview, minimum GPA of 3.0. Additional exam requirements/recommendations for international students: Required—TOEFL (minimum score 600 paper-based; 100 iBT). Electronic applications accepted. *Faculty research:* Lipid biochemistry, DNA replication, nucleic acids, protein structure.

Medical University of South Carolina, College of Graduate Studies, Program in Molecular and Cellular Biology and Pathobiology, Charleston, SC 29425. Offers cancer biology (PhD); cardiovascular biology (PhD); cardiovascular imaging (PhD); cell regulation (PhD); craniofacial biology (PhD); genetics and development (PhD); marine biomedicine (PhD); DMD/PhD; MD/PhD. *Degree requirements:* For doctorate, thesis/dissertation, oral and written exams. *Entrance requirements:* For doctorate, GRE General Test, interview, minimum GPA of 3.0. Additional exam requirements/recommendations for international students: Required—TOEFL (minimum score 600 paper-based; 100 iBT). Electronic applications accepted.

Michigan State University, The Graduate School, College of Agriculture and Natural Resources, MSU-DOE Plant Research Laboratory, East Lansing, MI 48824. Offers biochemistry and molecular biology (PhD); cellular and molecular biology (PhD); crop and soil sciences (PhD); genetics (PhD); microbiology and molecular genetics (PhD); plant biology (PhD); plant physiology (PhD). Offered jointly with the Department of Energy. *Degree requirements:* For doctorate, comprehensive exam, thesis/dissertation, laboratory rotation, defense of dissertation. *Entrance requirements:* For doctorate, GRE General Test, acceptance into one of the affiliated department programs; 3 letters of recommendation; bachelor's degree or equivalent in life sciences, chemistry, biochemistry, or biophysics; research experience. Electronic applications accepted. *Faculty research:* Role of hormones in the regulation of plant development and physiology, molecular mechanisms associated with signal recognition, development and application of genetic methods and materials, protein routing and function.

Michigan State University, The Graduate School, College of Natural Science and Graduate Programs in Human Medicine and Graduate Studies in Osteopathic Medicine, Department of Biochemistry and Molecular Biology, East Lansing, MI 48824. Offers biochemistry and molecular biology (MS, PhD); biochemistry and molecular biology/environmental toxicology (PhD). *Entrance requirements:* Additional exam requirements/recommendations for international students: Required—TOEFL. Electronic applications accepted.

Michigan State University, The Graduate School, College of Natural Science, Program in Cell and Molecular Biology, East Lansing, MI 48824. Offers cell and molecular biology (MS, PhD); cell and molecular biology/environmental toxicology (PhD). *Entrance requirements:* Additional exam requirements/recommendations for international students: Required—TOEFL. Electronic applications accepted.

Michigan Technological University, Graduate School, Interdisciplinary Programs, Houghton, MI 49931. Offers atmospheric sciences (PhD); automotive systems and controls (Graduate Certificate); biochemistry and molecular biology (PhD); computational science and engineering (PhD); data science (MS, Graduate Certificate); engineering-environmental (PhD); international profile (Graduate Certificate); nanotechnology (Graduate Certificate); sustainability (Graduate Certificate); sustainable water resources systems (Graduate Certificate). *Program availability:* Part-time. *Faculty:* 115 full-time (26 women), 9 part-time/adjunct (2 women). *Students:* 58 full-time (18 women), 17 part-time (5 women). Average age 28. 508 applicants, 28% accepted, 27 enrolled. In 2017, 10 master's, 7 doctorates, 11 other advanced degrees awarded. Terminal master's awarded for partial completion of doctoral program. *Degree requirements:* For master's, comprehensive exam (for some programs), thesis (for some programs); for doctorate, comprehensive exam, thesis/dissertation. *Entrance requirements:* For master's, doctorate, and Graduate Certificate, GRE, statement of purpose, personal statement, official transcripts, 2-3 letters of recommendation. Additional exam requirements/recommendations for international students: Required—TOEFL or IELTS. *Application deadline:* Applications are processed on a rolling basis. Electronic applications accepted. *Expenses:* Tuition, state resident: full-time $17,100; part-time $950 per credit. Tuition, nonresident: full-time $17,100; part-time $950 per credit. *Required fees:* $248; $124 per term. Tuition and fees vary according to course load and program. *Financial support:* In 2017–18, 67 students received support, including 9 fellowships with tuition reimbursements available (averaging $15,790 per year), 17 research assistantships with tuition reimbursements available (averaging $15,790 per year), 7 teaching assistantships with tuition reimbursements available (averaging $15,790 per year); career-related internships or fieldwork, Federal Work-Study, scholarships/grants, health care benefits, unspecified assistantships, and cooperative program also available. Financial award applicants required to submit FAFSA. *Faculty research:* Big data, atmospheric sciences, bioinformatics and systems biology, molecular dynamics, environmental studies. *Unit head:* Dr. Pushpalatha Murthy, Dean of the Graduate School/Associate Provost for Graduate Education, 906-487-3007, Fax: 906-487-2284, E-mail: ppmurthy@mtu.edu. *Application contact:* Carol T. Wingerson, Administrative Aide, 906-487-2328, Fax: 906-487-2284, E-mail: gradadms@mtu.edu.

Middle Tennessee State University, College of Graduate Studies, College of Basic and Applied Sciences, Interdisciplinary Program in Molecular Biosciences, Murfreesboro, TN 37132. Offers PhD. *Degree requirements:* For doctorate, comprehensive exam, thesis/dissertation. *Entrance requirements:* For doctorate, GRE. Additional exam requirements/recommendations for international students: Required—TOEFL (minimum score 525 paper-based; 71 iBT) or IELTS (minimum score 6). Electronic applications accepted.

Mississippi State University, College of Agriculture and Life Sciences, Department of Biochemistry, Molecular Biology, Entomology and Plant Pathology, Mississippi State, MS 39762. Offers biochemistry (MS, PhD); entomology (MS, PhD); plant pathology (MS, PhD). *Faculty:* 37 full-time (7 women). *Students:* 45 full-time (23 women), 8 part-time (5 women); includes 4 minority (2 Black or African American, non-Hispanic/Latino; 2 Hispanic/Latino), 12 international. Average age 29. 22 applicants, 23% accepted, 3 enrolled. In 2017, 9 master's, 6 doctorates awarded. Terminal master's awarded for partial completion of doctoral program. *Degree requirements:* For master's, thesis (for some programs), final oral exam; for doctorate, thesis/dissertation, preliminary oral and written exam. *Entrance requirements:* For master's, GRE General Test, minimum GPA of 2.75; for doctorate, GRE. Additional exam requirements/recommendations for international students: Required—TOEFL (minimum score 500 paper-based; 61 iBT); Recommended—IELTS (minimum score 5.5). *Application deadline:* For fall admission, 7/1 for domestic students, 5/1 for international students; for spring admission, 11/1 for domestic students, 9/1 for international students. Applications are processed on a rolling basis. Application fee: $60 ($80 for international students). Electronic applications accepted. *Expenses:* Tuition, state resident: full-time $8318; part-time $462.12 per credit hour. Tuition, nonresident: full-time $22,358; part-time $1242.12 per credit hour. *Required fees:* $110; $12.24 per credit hour. $6.12 per semester. *Financial support:* In 2017–18, 37 research assistantships with full tuition reimbursements (averaging $16,567 per year) were awarded; Federal Work-Study, institutionally sponsored loans, and unspecified assistantships also available. Financial award application deadline: 4/1; financial award applicants required to submit FAFSA. *Faculty research:* Fish nutrition, plant and animal molecular biology, plant biochemistry, enzymology, lipid metabolism, chromatin, cell wall synthesis in rice, a model grass bioenergy species and the source of rice Stover residues using reverse genetic and functional genomic and proteomic approaches. *Unit head:* Dr. Jeffrey Dean, Professor and Head, 662-325-2640, Fax: 662-325-8664, E-mail: jd1891@msstate.edu. *Application contact:* Marina Hunt, Admissions and Enrollment Assistant, 662-325-5188, E-mail: mhunt@grad.msstate.edu.
Website: http://www.biochemistry.msstate.edu

Missouri State University, Graduate College, College of Health and Human Services, Department of Biomedical Sciences, Program in Cell and Molecular Biology, Springfield, MO 65897. Offers MS. *Program availability:* Part-time. *Faculty:* 28 full-time (18 women), 5 part-time/adjunct (3 women). *Students:* 6 full-time (3 women), 5 part-time (1 woman); includes 2 minority (1 Black or African American, non-Hispanic/Latino; 1 Hispanic/Latino). Average age 24. 7 applicants, 43% accepted, 3 enrolled. In 2017, 2 master's awarded. *Degree requirements:* For master's, thesis or alternative, oral and written exams. *Entrance requirements:* For master's, GRE General Test, 2 semesters of course work in organic chemistry and physics, 1 semester of course work in calculus, minimum GPA of 3.0 in last 60 hours of course work. Additional exam requirements/recommendations for international students: Required—TOEFL (minimum score 550 paper-based; 79 iBT), IELTS (minimum score 6). *Application deadline:* For fall admission, 7/20 priority date for domestic students, 5/1 for international students; for spring admission, 12/20 priority date for domestic students, 9/1 for international students. Applications are processed on a rolling basis. Application fee: $35 ($50 for international students). Electronic applications accepted. *Expenses:* Tuition, state resident: full-time $2915; part-time $2021 per credit hour. Tuition, nonresident: full-time $5354; part-time $3647 per credit hour. *International tuition:* $11,992 full-time. *Required fees:* $173; $173 per credit hour. Tuition and fees vary according to class time, course level, course load, degree level, campus/location and program. *Financial support:* In 2017–18, 11 research assistantships (averaging $8,772 per year) were awarded; career-related internships or fieldwork, Federal Work-Study, institutionally sponsored loans, scholarships/grants, and unspecified assistantships also available. Support available to part-time students. Financial award application deadline: 3/31; financial award applicants required to submit FAFSA. *Faculty research:* Extracellular matrix membrane protein, P2 nucleotide receptors, double stranded RNA viruses. *Unit head:* Dr. Scott Zimmerman, Program Director, 417-836-5478, Fax: 417-836-5588, E-mail: scottzimmerman@missouristate.edu. *Application contact:* Stephanie Praschan, Director, Graduate Enrollment Management, 417-836-5330, Fax: 417-836-6200, E-mail: stephaniepraschan@missouristate.edu.
Website: http://www.missouristate.edu/bms/CMB/

Montclair State University, The Graduate School, College of Science and Mathematics, Molecular Biology Certificate Program, Montclair, NJ 07043-1624. Offers Certificate. *Degree requirements:* For Certificate, thesis optional.

Montclair State University, The Graduate School, College of Science and Mathematics, MS Program in Molecular Biology, Montclair, NJ 07043-1624. Offers MS. *Degree requirements:* For master's, thesis optional.

New Mexico State University, Graduate School, Program in Molecular Biology, Las Cruces, NM 88003. Offers MS, PhD. *Program availability:* Part-time. *Faculty:* 2 full-time (both women). *Students:* 11 full-time (9 women), 2 part-time (both women), 10 international. Average age 30. 15 applicants, 53% accepted, 2 enrolled. In 2017, 1 doctorate awarded. *Entrance requirements:* For master's and doctorate, GRE General Test, minimum GPA of 3.3. Additional exam requirements/recommendations for international students: Required—TOEFL (minimum score 550 paper-based; 79 iBT), IELTS (minimum score 6.5). *Application deadline:* For fall admission, 12/15 for domestic and international students; for spring admission, 10/15 for domestic and international students. Applications are processed on a rolling basis. Application fee: $40 ($50 for international students). Electronic applications accepted. *Expenses:* Tuition, state resident: full-time $4390. Tuition, nonresident: full-time $15,309. *Required fees:* $853. *Financial support:* In 2017–18, 13 students received support, including 3 fellowships (averaging $4,390 per year), 1 research assistantship (averaging $21,000 per year), 5 teaching assistantships (averaging $17,530 per year); career-related internships or fieldwork, Federal Work-Study, scholarships/grants, health care benefits, and unspecified assistantships also available. Financial award application deadline: 3/1. *Unit head:* 575-646-3437, Fax: 575-646-8087, E-mail: nancyt@nmsu.edu. *Application contact:* Nancy Treffler-McDow, Administrative Assistant, 575-646-3437, Fax: 575-646-8087, E-mail: nancyt@nmsu.edu.
Website: http://molb.research.nmsu.edu

New York Medical College, Graduate School of Basic Medical Sciences, Valhalla, NY 10595. Offers biochemistry and molecular biology (MS, PhD); cell biology (MS, PhD); microbiology and immunology (MS, PhD); pathology (MS, PhD); pharmacology (MS, PhD); physiology (MS, PhD); MD/PhD. *Program availability:* Part-time, evening/weekend. *Faculty:* 70 full-time (17 women), 25 part-time/adjunct (9 women). *Students:* 116 full-time (63 women), 25 part-time (11 women); includes 65 minority (17 Black or African American, non-Hispanic/Latino; 1 American Indian or Alaska Native, non-Hispanic/Latino; 23 Asian, non-Hispanic/Latino; 21 Hispanic/Latino; 3 Two or more races, non-Hispanic/Latino), 27 international. Average age 27. 273 applicants, 56% accepted, 59 enrolled. In 2017, 32 master's, 3 doctorates awarded. *Degree requirements:* For master's, thesis; for doctorate, comprehensive exam, thesis/dissertation. *Entrance requirements:* For master's, GRE General Test, MCAT, or DAT; for doctorate, GRE General Test. Additional exam requirements/recommendations for international students: Required—TOEFL. *Application deadline:* For fall admission, 7/1 priority date for domestic students, 5/1 priority date for international students; for spring admission, 12/1 priority date for domestic students, 9/15 priority date for international students. Applications are processed on a rolling basis. Application fee: $75 ($100 for international students). Electronic applications accepted. *Expenses:* $1,125 per credit, $655 fees. *Financial support:* Fellowships, research assistantships, Federal Work-Study, institutionally sponsored loans, scholarships/grants, tuition waivers, and health benefits (for PhD candidates only) available. Support available to part-time students. Financial award application deadline: 4/30; financial award applicants required to submit FAFSA. *Faculty research:* Cardiovascular science, infectious diseases, neuroscience, cancer, cell signaling. *Unit head:* Dr. Francis L. Belloni, Dean, 914-594-4110, Fax: 914-594-4944, E-mail: francis_belloni@nymc.edu. *Application contact:* Valerie Romeo-Messana, Director of Admissions, 914-594-4110, Fax: 914-594-4944, E-mail: v_romeomessana@nymc.edu.
Website: https://www.nymc.edu/graduate-school-of-basic-medical-sciences-gsbms/gsbms-academics/

New York University, Graduate School of Arts and Science, Department of Biology, New York, NY 10012-1019. Offers biology (PhD); biomedical journalism (MS); cancer and molecular biology (PhD); computational biology (PhD); computers in biological research (MS); developmental genetics (PhD); general biology (MS); immunology and microbiology (PhD); molecular genetics (PhD); neurobiology (PhD); oral biology (MS); plant biology (PhD); recombinant DNA technology (MS); MS/MBA. *Program availability:* Part-time. *Students:* Average age 27. 394 applicants, 56% accepted, 77 enrolled. In

2017, 68 master's, 9 doctorates awarded. Terminal master's awarded for partial completion of doctoral program. *Degree requirements:* For master's, thesis or alternative, qualifying paper; for doctorate, comprehensive exam, thesis/dissertation. *Entrance requirements:* For master's and doctorate, GRE General Test. Additional exam requirements/recommendations for international students: Required—TOEFL. *Application deadline:* For fall admission, 12/1 priority date for domestic students, 12/1 for international students. Application fee: $100. *Expenses: Tuition:* Full-time $41,352; part-time $19,968 per year. *Required fees:* $2496; $1628 per unit. $814 per term. Tuition and fees vary according to course load and program. *Financial support:* Fellowships, research assistantships, teaching assistantships, career-related internships or fieldwork, Federal Work-Study, institutionally sponsored loans, scholarships/grants, health care benefits, and unspecified assistantships available. Financial award application deadline: 12/1; financial award applicants required to submit FAFSA. *Faculty research:* Genomics, molecular and cell biology, development and molecular genetics, molecular evolution of plants and animals. *Unit head:* Stephen Small, Chair, 212-998-8200, Fax: 212-995-4015, E-mail: biology.admissions@nyu.edu. *Application contact:* Ken Birnbaum, Director of Graduate Studies, PhD Programs, 212-998-8200, Fax: 212-995-4015, E-mail: biology.admissions@nyu.edu.
Website: http://biology.as.nyu.edu/

New York University, School of Medicine and Graduate School of Arts and Science, Sackler Institute of Graduate Biomedical Sciences, New York, NY 10016. Offers biomedical imaging and technology (PhD); biostatistics (PhD); cellular and molecular biology (PhD); developmental genetics (PhD); epidemiology (PhD); genome integrity (PhD); immunology and inflammation (PhD); microbiology (PhD); molecular biophysics (PhD); molecular oncology and tumor immunology (PhD); molecular pharmacology (PhD); neuroscience and physiology (PhD), including immunology, molecular oncology; stem cell biology (PhD); systems and computational biomedicine (PhD); MD/PhD. *Faculty:* 207 full-time (51 women). *Students:* 236 full-time (138 women), 1 part-time (0 women); includes 68 minority (13 Black or African American, non-Hispanic/Latino; 26 Asian, non-Hispanic/Latino; 28 Hispanic/Latino; 1 Native Hawaiian or other Pacific Islander, non-Hispanic/Latino), 79 international. Average age 27. 761 applicants, 18% accepted, 59 enrolled. In 2017, 35 doctorates awarded. *Degree requirements:* For doctorate, comprehensive exam, thesis/dissertation, qualifying exam; thesis defense. *Entrance requirements:* For doctorate, GRE. Additional exam requirements/recommendations for international students: Required—TOEFL, IELTS. *Application deadline:* For fall admission, 12/1 for domestic and international students. Applications are processed on a rolling basis. Application fee: $100. Electronic applications accepted. Application fee is waived when completed online. *Expenses:* Contact institution. *Financial support:* Health care benefits, tuition waivers (full), and unspecified assistantships available. *Faculty research:* Biomedical sciences. *Unit head:* Dr. Naoko Tanese, Associate Dean for Biomedical Sciences/Director, Sackler Institute, 212-263-8945, E-mail: naoko.tanese@nyumc.org. *Application contact:* Jessica Dong, Program Manager, 212-263-5648, E-mail: sackler-info@nyumc.org.
Website: https://med.nyu.edu/research/sackler-institute-graduate-biomedical-sciences/

North Dakota State University, College of Graduate and Interdisciplinary Studies, Interdisciplinary Program in Cellular and Molecular Biology, Fargo, ND 58102. Offers PhD. *Degree requirements:* For doctorate, thesis/dissertation. *Entrance requirements:* Additional exam requirements/recommendations for international students: Required—TOEFL. *Application deadline:* Applications are processed on a rolling basis. Electronic applications accepted. *Expenses:* Tuition, state resident: full-time $4323; part-time $360.21 per credit. Tuition, nonresident: full-time $6484; part-time $540.31 per credit. *Required fees:* $668; $55.70 per credit. Part-time tuition and fees vary according to degree level, program and reciprocity agreements. *Financial support:* Fellowships, research assistantships, teaching assistantships, and unspecified assistantships available. *Unit head:* Dr. Jane Schuh, Director, 701-231-7841, E-mail: jane.schuh@ndsu.edu.
Website: http://www.ndsu.edu/cellularmolecularbiology/

Northeastern Illinois University, College of Graduate Studies and Research, College of Arts and Sciences, Program in Biology, Chicago, IL 60625. Offers biology (MS), including cell biology, ecology, molecular biology, organismal biology. *Program availability:* Part-time, evening/weekend. *Degree requirements:* For master's, comprehensive exam, thesis optional. *Entrance requirements:* For master's, minimum GPA of 2.75. Additional exam requirements/recommendations for international students: Required—TOEFL (minimum score 550 paper-based; 79 iBT). *Application deadline:* For fall admission, 4/1 priority date for domestic students; for spring admission, 8/15 for domestic students. Applications are processed on a rolling basis. Application fee: $30. Electronic applications accepted. *Expenses:* Tuition, state resident: full-time $7274; part-time $404.11 per credit hour. Tuition, nonresident: full-time $14,548; part-time $808.23 per credit hour. *Required fees:* $1284. *Financial support:* Applicants required to submit FAFSA. *Faculty research:* Paleoecology and freshwater biology, protein biosynthesis and targeting, microbial growth and physiology, molecular biology of antibody production, reptilian neurobiology. *Unit head:* Dr. John Kasmer, Department Chair, 773-442-5717, E-mail: j-kasmer@neiu.edu. *Application contact:* Martha Narvaez, Graduate Admission Representative, 773-442-6006, E-mail: m-narvaez@neiu.edu.

Northwestern University, The Graduate School, Interdisciplinary Biological Sciences Program (IBiS), Evanston, IL 60208. Offers biochemistry (PhD); bioengineering and biotechnology (PhD); biotechnology (PhD); cell and molecular biology (PhD); developmental and systems biology (PhD); nanotechnology (PhD); neurobiology (PhD); structural biology and biophysics (PhD). *Degree requirements:* For doctorate, thesis/dissertation, qualifying exam. *Entrance requirements:* For doctorate, GRE General Test. Additional exam requirements/recommendations for international students: Required—TOEFL (minimum score 600 paper-based). Electronic applications accepted. *Faculty research:* Biophysics/structural biology, cell/molecular biology, synthetic biology, developmental systems biology, chemical biology/nanotechnology.

The Ohio State University, Graduate School, College of Arts and Sciences, Division of Natural and Mathematical Sciences, Department of Molecular Genetics, Columbus, OH 43210. Offers cell and developmental biology (MS, PhD); genetics (MS, PhD); molecular biology (MS, PhD). *Faculty:* 30. *Students:* 34 full-time (16 women), 13 international. Average age 26. In 2017, 6 doctorates awarded. *Entrance requirements:* For doctorate, GRE General Test, GRE Subject Test in biology or chemistry (recommended). Additional exam requirements/recommendations for international students: Required—TOEFL (minimum score 550 paper-based; 79 iBT), Michigan English Language Assessment Battery (minimum score 82); Recommended—IELTS (minimum score 7). *Application deadline:* For fall admission, 12/13 priority date for domestic students, 11/30 priority date for international students; for spring admission, 3/1 for domestic students, 2/1 for international students. Applications are processed on a rolling basis. Application fee: $60 ($70 for international students). Electronic applications accepted. *Financial support:* Fellowships, research assistantships, teaching assistantships, Federal Work-Study, and institutionally sponsored loans available. Support available to part-time students. *Unit head:* Dr. Mark Seeger, Chair, 614-292-5106, E-mail: seeger.9@osu.edu. *Application contact:* Graduate and Professional Admissions, 614-292-9444, Fax: 614-292-3895, E-mail: gpadmissions@osu.edu.
Website: https://molgen.osu.edu/

The Ohio State University, Graduate School, College of Arts and Sciences, Division of Natural and Mathematical Sciences, Program in Molecular, Cellular and Developmental Biology, Columbus, OH 43210. Offers MS, PhD. *Students:* 87 full-time (44 women); includes 6 minority (all Asian, non-Hispanic/Latino), 30 international. Average age 26. In 2017, 3 master's, 18 doctorates awarded. Terminal master's awarded for partial completion of doctoral program. *Entrance requirements:* For doctorate, GRE General Test, GRE Subject Test in any science (desired, preferably biology or chemistry, biochemistry or cell and molecular biology). Additional exam requirements/recommendations for international students: Required—TOEFL (minimum score 600 paper-based; 85 iBT); Recommended—IELTS (minimum score 8). *Application deadline:* For fall admission, 12/13 priority date for domestic students, 11/30 priority date for international students; for spring admission, 3/1 for domestic students, 2/1 for international students. Applications are processed on a rolling basis. Application fee: $60 ($70 for international students). Electronic applications accepted. *Financial support:* Fellowships, research assistantships, and teaching assistantships available. *Unit head:* Dr. Dawn Chandler, Co-Director, 614-722-5597, E-mail: chandler.135@osu.edu. *Application contact:* Graduate and Professional Admissions, 614-292-9444, Fax: 614-292-3895, E-mail: gpadmissions@osu.edu.
Website: http://mcdb.osu.edu/

Ohio University, Graduate College, College of Arts and Sciences, Interdisciplinary Graduate Program in Molecular and Cellular Biology, Athens, OH 45701-2979. Offers PhD. *Degree requirements:* For doctorate, comprehensive exam, thesis/dissertation, research proposal, teaching experience. *Entrance requirements:* For doctorate, GRE General Test. Additional exam requirements/recommendations for international students: Required—TOEFL (minimum score 620 paper-based; 105 iBT); Recommended—TWE. Electronic applications accepted. *Faculty research:* Animal biotechnology, plant molecular biology RNA, immunology, cellular genetics, biochemistry of signal transduction, cancer research, membrane transport, bioinformatics, bioengineering, chemical biology and drug discovery, diabetes, microbiology, neuroscience.

Oklahoma State University, College of Agricultural Science and Natural Resources, Department of Biochemistry and Molecular Biology, Stillwater, OK 74078. Offers MS, PhD. *Faculty:* 20 full-time (8 women). *Students:* 7 full-time (4 women), 13 part-time (5 women); includes 3 minority (1 Asian, non-Hispanic/Latino; 2 Hispanic/Latino), 7 international. Average age 30. 19 applicants, 16% accepted, 3 enrolled. In 2017, 4 master's, 3 doctorates awarded. *Entrance requirements:* For master's and doctorate, GRE or GMAT. Additional exam requirements/recommendations for international students: Required—TOEFL (minimum score 550 paper-based; 79 iBT). *Application deadline:* For fall admission, 3/1 priority date for international students; for spring admission, 8/1 priority date for international students. Applications are processed on a rolling basis. Application fee: $40 ($75 for international students). Electronic applications accepted. *Expenses:* Tuition, state resident: full-time $4019; part-time $2679.60 per year. Tuition, nonresident: full-time $15,286; part-time $10,190.40 per year. *Required fees:* $2129; $1419 per unit. Tuition and fees vary according to program. *Financial support:* Research assistantships, teaching assistantships, career-related internships or fieldwork, Federal Work-Study, scholarships/grants, health care benefits, tuition waivers (partial), and unspecified assistantships available. Support available to part-time students. Financial award application deadline: 3/1; financial award applicants required to submit FAFSA. *Unit head:* Dr. John Gustafson, Department Head, 405-744-6189, Fax: 405-744-7799, E-mail: john.gustafson@okstate.edu.
Website: http://biochemistry.okstate.edu/

Oregon Health & Science University, School of Medicine, Graduate Programs in Medicine, Department of Environmental and Biomolecular Systems, Portland, OR 97239-3098. Offers biochemistry and molecular biology (MS, PhD); environmental science and engineering (MS, PhD). *Program availability:* Part-time. *Faculty:* 13 full-time (4 women). *Students:* 7 full-time (6 women), 2 part-time (0 women); includes 1 minority (American Indian or Alaska Native, non-Hispanic/Latino). Average age 32. In 2017, 7 master's, 3 doctorates awarded. Terminal master's awarded for partial completion of doctoral program. *Degree requirements:* For master's, thesis (for some programs); for doctorate, comprehensive exam, thesis/dissertation, qualifying exam. *Entrance requirements:* For master's and doctorate, GRE General Test (minimum scores: 153 Verbal/148 Quantitative/4.5 Analytical) or MCAT (for some programs). *Application deadline:* For fall admission, 7/15 for domestic students, 5/15 for international students; for winter admission, 10/15 for domestic students, 9/15 for international students; for spring admission, 1/15 for domestic students, 12/15 for international students. Applications are processed on a rolling basis. Application fee: $70. Electronic applications accepted. *Financial support:* Health care benefits and full-tuition and stipends (for PhD students) available. Financial award application deadline: 3/1; financial award applicants required to submit FAFSA. *Faculty research:* Metalloprotein biochemistry, molecular microbiology, environmental microbiology, environmental chemistry, biogeochemistry. *Unit head:* Dr. Michiko Nakano, Program Director. *Application contact:* E-mail: somgrad@ohsu.edu.

Oregon Health & Science University, School of Medicine, Graduate Programs in Medicine, Program in Molecular and Cellular Biosciences, Department of Biochemistry and Molecular Biology, Portland, OR 97239-3098. Offers PhD. *Faculty:* 12 full-time (3 women), 21 part-time/adjunct (3 women). *Students:* 7 full-time (2 women); includes 1 minority (Hispanic/Latino), 1 international. Average age 27. In 2017, 1 doctorate awarded. *Degree requirements:* For doctorate, comprehensive exam, thesis/dissertation, qualifying exam. *Entrance requirements:* For doctorate, GRE General Test (minimum scores: 153 Verbal/148 Quantitative/4.5 Analytical). *Application deadline:* For fall admission, 12/1 for domestic and international students. Application fee: $70. Electronic applications accepted. *Financial support:* Health care benefits, tuition waivers (full), and full-tuition and stipends (for PhD students) available. Financial award application deadline: 3/1; financial award applicants required to submit FAFSA. *Faculty research:* Leishmania, parasites, structure and function of G proteins, cystic fibrosis, genomic instability, biology of ion channels. *Unit head:* Dr. Ujwal Shinde, Program Director, E-mail: somgrad@ohsu.edu. *Application contact:* Lola Bichler, Administrative Coordinator, E-mail: somgrad@ohsu.edu.
Website: http://www.ohsu.edu/som-biochem/

Oregon State University, College of Agricultural Sciences, Program in Botany and Plant Pathology, Corvallis, OR 97331. Offers applied systematics (MS); ecology (MS, PhD); genetics (MS, PhD); genomics and computational biology (MS, PhD); molecular and cellular biology (MS, PhD); mycology (MS, PhD); plant pathology (MS, PhD); plant physiology (MS, PhD). *Entrance requirements:* For master's and doctorate, GRE. *Application deadline:* For fall admission, 12/1 for domestic and international students. Application fee: $75 ($85 for international students). *Financial support:* Application deadline: 12/1. *Unit head:* John Fowler, Chair of Graduate Studies, E-mail: fowlerj@science.oregonstate.edu.
Website: http://bpp.oregonstate.edu/

Oregon State University, Interdisciplinary/Institutional Programs, Program in Molecular and Cellular Biology, Corvallis, OR 97331. Offers bioinformatics (PhD); biotechnology (PhD); genome biology (PhD); molecular virology (PhD); plant molecular biology (PhD). *Degree requirements:* For doctorate, thesis/dissertation, oral and written qualifying

exams. *Entrance requirements:* For doctorate, GRE. Additional exam requirements/recommendations for international students: Required—TOEFL (minimum score 80 iBT), IELTS (minimum score 6.5). *Application deadline:* For fall admission, 8/1 for domestic students, 4/1 for international students; for winter admission, 12/1 for domestic students, 7/1 for international students; for spring admission, 2/1 for domestic students, 10/1 for international students; for summer admission, 5/1 for domestic students, 1/1 for international students. Application fee: $75 ($85 for international students). *Financial support:* Application deadline: 1/1. *Unit head:* Dr. Kristin Carroll, Assistant Director, Molecular and Cellular Biology Program, 541-737-5259, E-mail: kirstin.carroll@oregonstate.edu. *Application contact:* Dr. Kristin Carroll, Assistant Director, Molecular and Cellular Biology Program, 541-737-5259, E-mail: kirstin.carroll@oregonstate.edu.
Website: http://gradschool.oregonstate.edu/molecular-and-cellular-biology-graduate-program

Pace University, Dyson College of Arts and Sciences, Program in Biochemistry and Molecular Biology, New York, NY 10038. Offers MS. *Program availability:* Part-time, evening/weekend. *Students:* 11 full-time (9 women), 3 part-time (2 women); includes 6 minority (2 Black or African American, non-Hispanic/Latino; 1 Asian, non-Hispanic/Latino; 2 Hispanic/Latino; 1 Two or more races, non-Hispanic/Latino), 2 international. Average age 23. In 2017, 3 master's awarded. *Degree requirements:* For master's, thesis. *Entrance requirements:* For master's, official transcripts, two letters of recommendation, personal statement. Additional exam requirements/recommendations for international students: Required—TOEFL (minimum score 88 iBT), IELTS (minimum score 7) or PTE (minimum score 60). *Application deadline:* For fall admission, 4/15 priority date for domestic students. Applications are processed on a rolling basis. Application fee: $70. Electronic applications accepted. *Financial support:* Research assistantships and scholarships/grants available. Financial award application deadline: 2/15; financial award applicants required to submit FAFSA. *Unit head:* Dr. Nigel Yarlett, Director, MS in Biochemistry and Molecular Biology, 212-346-1853, E-mail: nyarlett@pace.edu. *Application contact:* Susan Ford-Goldschein, Director of Admissions, 212-346-1531, Fax: 212-346-1585, E-mail: graduateadmission@pace.edu.
Website: http://www.pace.edu/dyson/programs/ms-biochemistry-molecular-biology-nyc

Penn State University Park, Graduate School, Eberly College of Science, Department of Biochemistry and Molecular Biology, University Park, PA 16802. Offers biochemistry, microbiology, and molecular biology (MS, PhD); biotechnology (MBIOT). *Unit head:* Dr. Douglas R. Cavener, Dean, 814-865-9591, Fax: 814-865-3634. *Application contact:* Lori Hawn, Director, Graduate Student Services, 814-865-1795, Fax: 814-863-4627, E-mail: l-gswww@lists.psu.edu.
Website: http://bmb.psu.edu/

Penn State University Park, Graduate School, Intercollege Graduate Programs, Program in Molecular, Cellular, and Integrative Biosciences, University Park, PA 16802. Offers MS, PhD. *Unit head:* Dr. Regina Vasilatos-Younken, Dean, 814-865-2516, Fax: 814-863-4627. *Application contact:* Lori Hawn, Director, Graduate Student Services, 814-865-1795, Fax: 814-863-4627, E-mail: l-gswww@lists.psu.edu.
Website: http://www.huck.psu.edu/content/graduate-programs/molecular-cellular-and-integrative-biosciences

Princeton University, Graduate School, Department of Molecular Biology, Princeton, NJ 08544-1019. Offers PhD. *Degree requirements:* For doctorate, thesis/dissertation. *Entrance requirements:* For doctorate, GRE General Test. Additional exam requirements/recommendations for international students: Required—TOEFL (minimum score 600 paper-based). Electronic applications accepted. *Faculty research:* Genetics, virology, biochemistry.

Purdue University, College of Pharmacy and Graduate School, Graduate Programs in Pharmacy and Pharmacal Sciences, Department of Medicinal Chemistry and Molecular Pharmacology, West Lafayette, IN 47907. Offers biophysical and computational chemistry (PhD); cancer research (PhD); immunology and infectious disease (PhD); medicinal biochemistry and molecular biology (PhD); medicinal chemistry and chemical biology (PhD); molecular pharmacology (PhD); neuropharmacology, neurodegeneration, and neurotoxicity (PhD); systems biology and functional genomics (PhD). *Faculty:* 26 full-time (5 women). *Students:* 52 full-time (22 women), 3 part-time (all women); includes 4 minority (1 Black or African American, non-Hispanic/Latino; 2 Asian, non-Hispanic/Latino; 1 Hispanic/Latino), 29 international. Average age 26. 151 applicants, 19% accepted, 13 enrolled. In 2017, 18 doctorates awarded. *Degree requirements:* For doctorate, thesis/dissertation. *Entrance requirements:* For doctorate, GRE General Test; GRE Subject Test in biology, biochemistry, and chemistry (recommended), minimum undergraduate GPA of 3.0. Additional exam requirements/recommendations for international students: Required—TOEFL (minimum score 550 paper-based; 77 iBT); Recommended—TWE. *Application deadline:* For fall admission, 2/1 for domestic and international students. Applications are processed on a rolling basis. Application fee: $60 ($75 for international students). Electronic applications accepted. *Financial support:* Fellowships, research assistantships, teaching assistantships, and traineeships available. Support available to part-time students. Financial award applicants required to submit FAFSA. *Faculty research:* Drug design and development, cancer research, drug synthesis and analysis, chemical pharmacology, environmental toxicology. *Unit head:* Zhong-Yin Zhang, Head, 765-494-1403, E-mail: zhang-yn@purdue.edu. *Application contact:* Delayne Graham, Graduate Contact, 765-494-1362, E-mail: dkgraham@purdue.edu.

Purdue University, Graduate School, College of Science, Department of Biological Sciences, West Lafayette, IN 47907. Offers biochemistry (PhD); biophysics (PhD); cell and developmental biology (PhD); ecology, evolutionary and population biology (MS, PhD), including ecology, evolutionary biology, population biology; genetics (MS, PhD); microbiology (MS, PhD); molecular biology (PhD); neurobiology (MS, PhD); plant physiology (PhD). *Faculty:* 42 full-time (13 women), 3 part-time/adjunct (0 women). *Students:* 115 full-time (58 women), 6 part-time (4 women); includes 17 minority (1 Black or African American, non-Hispanic/Latino; 6 Asian, non-Hispanic/Latino; 9 Hispanic/Latino; 1 Two or more races, non-Hispanic/Latino), 60 international. Average age 27. 165 applicants, 12% accepted, 15 enrolled. In 2017, 5 master's, 16 doctorates awarded. Terminal master's awarded for partial completion of doctoral program. *Degree requirements:* For master's, thesis (for some programs); for doctorate, thesis/dissertation, seminars, teaching experience. *Entrance requirements:* For master's, GRE General Test (minimum analytical writing score of 3.5), minimum undergraduate GPA of 3.0; for doctorate, GRE General Test (minimum analytical writing score of 3.5), minimum undergraduate GPA of 3.5. Additional exam requirements/recommendations for international students: Required—TOEFL minimum score 600 paper-based; 107 iBT (for MS), 80 iBT (for PhD). *Application deadline:* For fall admission, 12/7 for domestic and international students. Applications are processed on a rolling basis. Application fee: $60 ($75 for international students). Electronic applications accepted. *Financial support:* Fellowships, research assistantships, and teaching assistantships available. Support available to part-time students. Financial award application deadline: 2/15; financial award applicants required to submit FAFSA. *Unit head:* Stephen Konieczny, Head, 765-494-4407, E-mail: sfk@purdue.edu. *Application contact:* Georgina E. Rupp, Graduate Coordinator, 765-494-8142, E-mail: ruppg@purdue.edu.
Website: http://www.bio.purdue.edu/

Purdue University, Graduate School, PULSe - Purdue University Life Sciences Program, West Lafayette, IN 47907. Offers biomolecular structure and biophysics (PhD); biotechnology (PhD); chemical biology (PhD); chromatin and regulation of gene expression (PhD); integrative neuroscience (PhD); integrative plant sciences (PhD); membrane biology (PhD); microbiology (PhD); molecular evolutionary and cancer biology (PhD); molecular evolutionary genetics (PhD); molecular virology (PhD). *Students:* 60 full-time (29 women); includes 6 minority (4 Hispanic/Latino; 2 Two or more races, non-Hispanic/Latino), 36 international. Average age 25. 127 applicants, 39% accepted, 25 enrolled. *Entrance requirements:* For doctorate, GRE, minimum undergraduate GPA of 3.0. Additional exam requirements/recommendations for international students: Required—TOEFL (minimum score 550 paper-based; 77 iBT). *Application deadline:* For fall admission, 1/15 priority date for domestic and international students. Applications are processed on a rolling basis. Application fee: $60 ($75 for international students). Electronic applications accepted. *Financial support:* In 2017–18, research assistantships with tuition reimbursements (averaging $22,500 per year), teaching assistantships with tuition reimbursements (averaging $22,500 per year) were awarded. *Unit head:* Dr. Jason R. Cannon, Head of the Graduate Program, 765-494-0794, E-mail: cannonjr@purdue.edu. *Application contact:* Lindsey Springer, Graduate Contact for Admissions, 765-496-9667, E-mail: lbcampbe@purdue.edu.
Website: http://www.gradschool.purdue.edu/pulse

Queen's University at Kingston, School of Graduate Studies, Faculty of Health Sciences, Department of Anatomy and Cell Biology, Kingston, ON K7L 3N6, Canada. Offers biology of reproduction (M Sc, PhD); cancer (M Sc, PhD); cardiovascular pathophysiology (M Sc, PhD); cell and molecular biology (M Sc, PhD); drug metabolism (M Sc, PhD); endocrinology (M Sc, PhD); motor control (M Sc, PhD); neural regeneration (M Sc, PhD); neurophysiology (M Sc, PhD). *Program availability:* Part-time. *Degree requirements:* For master's, thesis; for doctorate, one foreign language, comprehensive exam, thesis/dissertation. *Entrance requirements:* Additional exam requirements/recommendations for international students: Required—TOEFL. Electronic applications accepted. *Faculty research:* Human kinetics, neuroscience, reproductive biology, cardiovascular.

Quinnipiac University, College of Arts and Sciences, Program in Molecular and Cell Biology, Hamden, CT 06518-1940. Offers MS. *Program availability:* Part-time, evening/weekend. *Faculty:* 9 full-time (5 women), 1 part-time/adjunct (0 women). *Students:* 17 full-time (11 women), 9 part-time (5 women); includes 4 minority (2 Black or African American, non-Hispanic/Latino; 2 Hispanic/Latino), 4 international. 52 applicants, 58% accepted, 10 enrolled. In 2017, 14 master's awarded. *Degree requirements:* For master's, thesis optional. *Entrance requirements:* For master's, bachelor's degree in biological, medical, or health sciences. Additional exam requirements/recommendations for international students: Required—TOEFL (minimum score 575 paper-based; 90 iBT), IELTS (minimum score 6.5). *Application deadline:* For fall admission, 7/30 priority date for domestic students, 4/30 priority date for international students; for spring admission, 12/15 priority date for domestic students, 9/30 priority date for international students. Applications are processed on a rolling basis. Application fee: $45. Electronic applications accepted. *Financial support:* Federal Work-Study, scholarships/grants, and unspecified assistantships available. Financial award application deadline: 6/1; financial award applicants required to submit FAFSA. *Unit head:* Dr. Lise Thomas, Director, 203-582-8497, E-mail: graduate@qu.edu. *Application contact:* Office of Graduate Admissions, 800-462-1944, Fax: 203-582-3443, E-mail: graduate@qu.edu.
Website: http://www.qu.edu/gradmolecular

Rosalind Franklin University of Medicine and Science, School of Graduate and Postdoctoral Studies - Interdisciplinary Graduate Program in Biomedical Sciences, Department of Biochemistry and Molecular Biology, North Chicago, IL 60064-3095. Offers PhD, MD/PhD. Terminal master's awarded for partial completion of doctoral program. *Degree requirements:* For doctorate, comprehensive exam, thesis/dissertation. *Entrance requirements:* For doctorate, GRE General Test, minimum GPA of 3.0. Additional exam requirements/recommendations for international students: Required—TOEFL, TWE. Electronic applications accepted. *Faculty research:* Structure of control enzymes, extracellular matrix, glucose metabolism, gene expression, ATP synthesis.

Rutgers University–Newark, Graduate School of Biomedical Sciences, Department of Biochemistry and Molecular Biology, Newark, NJ 07107. Offers MS, PhD. *Degree requirements:* For master's, thesis; for doctorate, thesis/dissertation, qualifying exam. *Entrance requirements:* For master's and doctorate, GRE General Test. Additional exam requirements/recommendations for international students: Required—TOEFL. Electronic applications accepted.

Rutgers University–New Brunswick, Graduate School-New Brunswick, Programs in the Molecular Biosciences, Piscataway, NJ 08854-8097. Offers biochemistry (PhD); cell and developmental biology (MS, PhD); microbiology and molecular genetics (MS, PhD), including applied microbiology, clinical microbiology, computational molecular biology (PhD), immunology, microbial biochemistry, molecular genetics, virology. MS, PhD offered jointly with University of Medicine and Dentistry of New Jersey.

Rutgers University–New Brunswick, Graduate School of Biomedical Sciences, Piscataway, NJ 08854-5635. Offers biochemistry and molecular biology (MS, PhD); biomedical engineering (MS, PhD); biomedical science (MS); cellular and molecular pharmacology (MS, PhD); clinical and translational science (MS); environmental sciences/exposure assessment (PhD); molecular genetics, microbiology and immunology (MS, PhD); neuroscience (MS, PhD); physiology and integrative biology (MS, PhD); toxicology (PhD); MD/PhD. Terminal master's awarded for partial completion of doctoral program. *Degree requirements:* For master's, thesis (for some programs), ethics training; for doctorate, comprehensive exam, thesis/dissertation, ethics training. *Entrance requirements:* For master's, GRE General Test, MCAT, DAT; for doctorate, GRE General Test. Additional exam requirements/recommendations for international students: Required—TOEFL. Electronic applications accepted.

Sacred Heart University, Graduate Programs, College of Arts and Sciences, Department of Chemistry, Fairfield, CT 06825. Offers bioinformatics (MS); chemistry (MS); molecular biology (MS). *Program availability:* Part-time, evening/weekend. *Faculty:* 5 full-time (1 woman), 1 part-time/adjunct (0 women). *Students:* 26 full-time (14 women), 15 part-time (10 women); includes 4 minority (2 Black or African American, non-Hispanic/Latino; 2 Hispanic/Latino), 30 international. Average age 26. 33 applicants, 94% accepted, 8 enrolled. In 2017, 27 master's awarded. *Degree requirements:* For master's, thesis optional. *Entrance requirements:* For master's, bachelor's degree in related area (natural science with a heavy concentration in chemistry), minimum GPA of 2.75. Additional exam requirements/recommendations for international students: Required—TOEFL (minimum score 570 paper-based, 80 iBT), TWE, or IELTS (6.5); Recommended—TSE. *Application deadline:* For fall admission, 9/1 priority date for domestic students; for spring admission, 1/1 priority date for domestic students. Applications are processed on a rolling basis. Application fee: $75. Electronic applications accepted. *Expenses:* $850 per credit part-time; $8,500 per semester full-time; $50 per semester part-time fee; $115 per semester full-time registration fee, $40 per semester library fee, $25 per semester graduate student fee. *Financial support:* Unspecified assistantships available. Financial award applicants required to submit FAFSA. *Unit head:* Dr. Eid Alkhatib, Chair, 203-365-7546, E-mail: alkhatibe@

sacredheart.edu. *Application contact:* Pam Pillo, Executive Director of Graduate Admissions, 203-365-7619, Fax: 203-365-4732, E-mail: gradstudies@sacredheart.edu.
Website: http://www.sacredheart.edu/academics/collegeofartssciences/academicdepartments/chemistry/graduatedegreesandcertificates/

Saint Louis University, Graduate Programs, School of Medicine, Graduate Programs in Biomedical Sciences and Graduate Programs, Department of Biochemistry and Molecular Biology, St. Louis, MO 63103. Offers PhD. *Degree requirements:* For doctorate, comprehensive exam, thesis/dissertation, departmental qualifying exams. *Entrance requirements:* For doctorate, GRE General Test, GRE Subject Test (optional), letters of recommendation, resume, interview. Additional exam requirements/recommendations for international students: Required—TOEFL (minimum score 525 paper-based). Electronic applications accepted. *Faculty research:* Transcription, chromatin modification and regulation of gene expression; structure/function of proteins and enzymes, including x-ray crystallography; inflammatory mediators in pathenogenesis of diabetes and arteriosclerosis; cellular signaling in response to growth factors, opiates and angiogenic mediators; genomics and proteomics of Cryptococcus neoformans.

San Diego State University, Graduate and Research Affairs, College of Sciences, Department of Biology, San Diego, CA 92182. Offers biology (MA, MS), including ecology (MS), molecular biology (MS), physiology (MS), systematics/evolution (MS); cell and molecular biology (PhD); ecology (MS, PhD); microbiology (MS). Terminal master's awarded for partial completion of doctoral program. *Degree requirements:* For master's, thesis; for doctorate, thesis/dissertation. *Entrance requirements:* For master's, GRE General Test, GRE Subject Test, resume or curriculum vitae, 2 letters of recommendation. Additional exam requirements/recommendations for international students: Required—TOEFL. Electronic applications accepted.

San Diego State University, Graduate and Research Affairs, College of Sciences, Molecular Biology Institute, Program in Cell and Molecular Biology, San Diego, CA 92182. Offers PhD. Program offered jointly with University of California, San Diego. *Degree requirements:* For doctorate, thesis/dissertation, oral comprehensive qualifying exam. *Entrance requirements:* For doctorate, GRE General Test, GRE Subject Test, resumé or curriculum vitae, 3 letters of recommendation. Electronic applications accepted. *Faculty research:* Structure/dynamics of protein kinesis, chromatin structure and DNA methylation membrane biochemistry, secretory protein targeting, molecular biology of cardiac myocytes.

San Francisco State University, Division of Graduate Studies, College of Science and Engineering, Department of Biology, Program in Cell and Molecular Biology, San Francisco, CA 94132-1722. Offers MS. *Application deadline:* Applications are processed on a rolling basis. *Unit head:* Dr. Diana Chu, Program Coordinator, 415-405-3487, Fax: 415-338-2295, E-mail: chud@sfsu.edu.
Website: http://biology.sfsu.edu/programs/graduate

San Jose State University, Graduate Studies and Research, College of Science, San Jose, CA 95192-0099. Offers bioinformatics (MS); biological sciences (MA, MS), including ecology and evolution (MS), molecular biology and microbiology (MS), physiology (MS); biotechnology (MBT); chemistry (MA, MS); computer science (MS); geology (MS); marine science (MS); mathematics (MA, MS), including mathematics education (MA); medical products development management (MS); meteorology (MS); physics (MS), including computational physics, modern optics, physics; statistics (MS). MS in marine science offered through Moss Landing Marine Labs. *Program availability:* Part-time. *Faculty:* 78 full-time (27 women), 25 part-time/adjunct (13 women). *Students:* 154 full-time (76 women), 212 part-time (102 women); includes 135 minority (4 Black or African American, non-Hispanic/Latino; 78 Asian, non-Hispanic/Latino; 27 Hispanic/Latino; 1 Native Hawaiian or other Pacific Islander, non-Hispanic/Latino; 25 Two or more races, non-Hispanic/Latino), 135 international. Average age 28. 1,156 applicants, 26% accepted, 179 enrolled. In 2017, 196 master's awarded. *Degree requirements:* For master's, comprehensive exam (for some programs), thesis (for some programs), directed reading, colloquium, project, writing project, statistical consulting. *Entrance requirements:* Additional exam requirements/recommendations for international students: Required—TOEFL (minimum score 550 paper-based; 80 iBT), IELTS (minimum score 6.5), TWE, PTE (minimum score 53). *Application deadline:* For fall admission, 2/1 for domestic and international students. Applications are processed on a rolling basis. Application fee: $55. Electronic applications accepted. *Expenses:* Tuition, state resident: full-time $7176. Tuition, nonresident: full-time $16,680. Tuition and fees vary according to course load and program. *Financial support:* Fellowships, research assistantships, career-related internships or fieldwork, Federal Work-Study, scholarships/grants, traineeships, tuition waivers (full and partial), and unspecified assistantships available. Support available to part-time students. Financial award application deadline: 4/28; financial award applicants required to submit FAFSA. *Unit head:* Dr. Michael Kaufman, Dean, 408-924-4800, Fax: 408-924-4815, E-mail: michael.kaufman@sjsu.edu.
Website: http://www.sjsu.edu/science/

Seton Hall University, College of Arts and Sciences, Department of Biological Sciences, South Orange, NJ 07079-2697. Offers biology (MS); biology/business administration (MS); microbiology (MS); molecular bioscience (PhD); molecular bioscience/neuroscience (PhD). *Program availability:* Part-time, evening/weekend. *Degree requirements:* For master's, thesis optional; for doctorate, comprehensive exam, thesis/dissertation. *Entrance requirements:* For master's, GRE or undergraduate degree (BS in biological sciences) with minimum GPA of 3.0 from accredited U.S. institution; for doctorate, GRE. Additional exam requirements/recommendations for international students: Required—TOEFL. Electronic applications accepted. *Faculty research:* Neurobiology, genetics, immunology, molecular biology, cellular physiology, toxicology, microbiology, bioinformatics.

Simon Fraser University, Office of Graduate Studies and Postdoctoral Fellows, Faculty of Science, Department of Molecular Biology and Biochemistry, Burnaby, BC V5A 1S6, Canada. Offers bioinformatics (Graduate Diploma); molecular biology and biochemistry (M Sc, PhD). *Degree requirements:* For master's, thesis; for doctorate, thesis/dissertation; for Graduate Diploma, practicum. *Entrance requirements:* For master's, minimum GPA of 3.0 (on scale of 4.33) or 3.33 based on last 60 credits of undergraduate courses; for doctorate, minimum GPA of 3.5; for Graduate Diploma, minimum GPA of 2.5 (on scale of 4.33) or 2.67 based on last 60 credits of undergraduate courses. Additional exam requirements/recommendations for international students: Recommended—TOEFL (minimum score 580 paper-based; 100 iBT), IELTS (minimum score 7.5), TWE (minimum score 5). Electronic applications accepted. *Faculty research:* Genomics and bioinformatics, cell and developmental biology, structural biology/biochemistry, immunology, nucleic acid function.

Southern Illinois University Carbondale, Graduate School, College of Science, Program in Molecular Biology, Microbiology, and Biochemistry, Carbondale, IL 62901-4701. Offers MS, PhD. *Degree requirements:* For master's, thesis; for doctorate, thesis/dissertation. *Entrance requirements:* For master's, GRE, minimum GPA of 2.7; for doctorate, GRE, minimum GPA of 3.25. Additional exam requirements/recommendations for international students: Required—TOEFL. *Faculty research:* Prokaryotic gene regulation and expression; eukaryotic gene regulation; microbial, phylogenetic, and metabolic diversity; immune responses to tumors, pathogens, and autoantigens; protein folding and structure.

Southern Methodist University, Dedman College of Humanities and Sciences, Department of Biological Sciences, Dallas, TX 75275. Offers molecular and cellular biology (MA, MS, PhD). Terminal master's awarded for partial completion of doctoral program. *Degree requirements:* For master's, thesis (for MS), oral exam; for doctorate, thesis/dissertation, qualifying exam. *Entrance requirements:* For master's, GRE General Test (minimum score 1200), minimum GPA of 3.0; for doctorate, GRE General Test (minimum score: 1200), minimum GPA of 3.0. Additional exam requirements/recommendations for international students: Required—TOEFL (minimum score 550 paper-based). *Application deadline:* For fall admission, 2/1 priority date for domestic and international students; for spring admission, 11/30 priority date for domestic and international students. Applications are processed on a rolling basis. Application fee: $60. Electronic applications accepted. *Financial support:* Applicants required to submit FAFSA. *Faculty research:* Free radicals and aging, protein structure, chromatin structure, signal processes, retroviral pathogenesis. *Unit head:* Dr. Robert Harrod, Advisor for Graduate Studies, 214-768-3864, E-mail: rharrod@smu.edu. *Application contact:* Dr. Pia Vogel, Graduate Advisor, 214-768-1790, Fax: 214-768-3955, E-mail: pvogel@smu.edu.
Website: http://smu.edu/biology/Graduate.asp

State University of New York Downstate Medical Center, School of Graduate Studies, Program in Molecular and Cellular Biology, Brooklyn, NY 11203-2098. Offers PhD, MD/PhD. Affiliation with a particular PhD degree-granting program is deferred to the second year. *Degree requirements:* For doctorate, comprehensive exam, thesis/dissertation. *Entrance requirements:* For doctorate, GRE General Test. Additional exam requirements/recommendations for international students: Recommended—TOEFL. *Faculty research:* Mechanism of gene regulation, molecular virology.

State University of New York Upstate Medical University, College of Graduate Studies, Program in Biochemistry and Molecular Biology, Syracuse, NY 13210. Offers biochemistry (MS); biochemistry and molecular biology (PhD); MD/PhD. Terminal master's awarded for partial completion of doctoral program. *Degree requirements:* For master's, thesis; for doctorate, comprehensive exam, thesis/dissertation. *Entrance requirements:* For master's, GRE General Test, interview; for doctorate, GRE General Test, telephone interview. Additional exam requirements/recommendations for international students: Required—TOEFL. Electronic applications accepted. *Faculty research:* Enzymology, membrane structure and functions, developmental biochemistry.

Stony Brook University, State University of New York, Graduate School, College of Arts and Sciences, Department of Biochemistry and Cell Biology, Molecular and Cellular Biology Program, Stony Brook, NY 11794. Offers biochemistry and molecular biology (PhD); biological sciences (MA); immunology and pathology (PhD); molecular and cellular biology (PhD). *Students:* 63 full-time (35 women); includes 12 minority (3 Black or African American, non-Hispanic/Latino; 6 Asian, non-Hispanic/Latino; 3 Hispanic/Latino), 35 international. Average age 28. 131 applicants, 25% accepted, 11 enrolled. In 2017, 12 doctorates awarded. *Degree requirements:* For doctorate, comprehensive exam, thesis/dissertation, teaching experience. *Entrance requirements:* For doctorate, GRE General Test, GRE Subject Test. Additional exam requirements/recommendations for international students: Required—TOEFL. *Application deadline:* For fall admission, 1/15 for domestic students; for spring admission, 10/1 for domestic students. Application fee: $100. Electronic applications accepted. *Expenses:* Contact institution. *Financial support:* In 2017–18, 4 fellowships, 29 research assistantships, 12 teaching assistantships were awarded; Federal Work-Study also available. *Unit head:* Prof. Aaron Neiman, Chair, 631-632-8550, Fax: 631-632-8575, E-mail: aaron.neiman@stonybrook.edu. *Application contact:* Amy Saas, Graduate Program Administrator, 631-632-8613, Fax: 631-632-9730, E-mail: mcbgraduateprogram@stonybrook.edu.
Website: https://www.stonybrook.edu/mcb/

Texas Woman's University, Graduate School, College of Arts and Sciences, Department of Biology, Denton, TX 76204. Offers biology (MS); molecular biology (PhD). PhD in molecular biology offered through cooperative program of the Federation of North Texas Area Universities (The University of North Texas, Texas Woman's University, and Texas A&M Commerce). *Program availability:* Part-time. *Faculty:* 15 full-time (10 women), 1 part-time/adjunct (0 women). *Students:* 1 full-time (0 women), 40 part-time (29 women); includes 5 minority (1 Black or African American, non-Hispanic/Latino; 2 Asian, non-Hispanic/Latino; 1 Hispanic/Latino; 1 Two or more races, non-Hispanic/Latino), 22 international. Average age 33. 19 applicants, 53% accepted, 2 enrolled. In 2017, 3 doctorates awarded. Terminal master's awarded for partial completion of doctoral program. *Degree requirements:* For master's, comprehensive exam, thesis (for some programs), professional paper or thesis; for doctorate, comprehensive exam, thesis/dissertation, 1-year residency. *Entrance requirements:* For master's, GRE General Test (preferred minimum score 148 [425 old version] verbal, 140 [425 old version] quantitative), 3 letters of reference; letter of interest; for doctorate, GRE General Test (preferred minimum score 153 [500 old version] verbal, 144 [500 old version] quantitative), 3 letters of reference, letter of interest. Additional exam requirements/recommendations for international students: Required—TOEFL (minimum score 550 paper-based; 79 iBT); Recommended—IELTS (minimum score 6.5), TSE (minimum score 53). *Application deadline:* For fall admission, 3/1 priority date for domestic and international students; for spring admission, 11/1 priority date for domestic students, 7/1 priority date for international students; for summer admission, 5/1 priority date for domestic students, 2/1 priority date for international students. Applications are processed on a rolling basis. Application fee: $50 ($75 for international students). Electronic applications accepted. *Expenses:* $7,520 per year full-time in-state; $16,820 per year full-time out-of-state. *Financial support:* In 2017–18, 15 students received support, including 1 research assistantship (averaging $31,488 per year), 15 teaching assistantships (averaging $29,092 per year); career-related internships or fieldwork, institutionally sponsored loans, scholarships/grants, traineeships, health care benefits, and unspecified assistantships also available. Support available to part-time students. Financial award application deadline: 3/1; financial award applicants required to submit FAFSA. *Faculty research:* Electron microscopy, protein degradation, sensory neuroscience, transcription regulation, virus: host interactions. *Unit head:* Dr. Ron Hovis, Interim Chair, 940-898-2351, Fax: 940-898-2382, E-mail: biology@twu.edu. *Application contact:* Korie Hawkins, Associate Director of Admissions, Graduate Recruitment, 940-898-3188, Fax: 940-898-3081, E-mail: admissions@twu.edu.
Website: http://www.twu.edu/biology

Tufts University, Sackler School of Graduate Biomedical Sciences, Cell, Molecular, and Developmental Biology Program, Medford, MA 02155. Offers cancer biology (PhD); developmental and regenerative biology (PhD); molecular and cellular medicine (PhD); structural and chemical biology (PhD). Terminal master's awarded for partial completion of doctoral program. *Degree requirements:* For doctorate, comprehensive exam, thesis/dissertation. *Entrance requirements:* For doctorate, GRE General Test, 3 letters of reference, resume, personal statement. Electronic applications accepted. *Expenses: Tuition:* Full-time $49,892. *Required fees:* $874. Full-time tuition and fees vary according to degree level, program and student level. Part-time tuition and fees vary according to course load. *Faculty research:* Reproduction and hormone action, control of gene expression, cell-matrix and cell-cell interactions, growth control and tumorigenesis, cytoskeleton and contractile proteins.

Molecular Biology

Tufts University, Sackler School of Graduate Biomedical Sciences, Molecular Microbiology Program, Medford, MA 02155. Offers medically-oriented research in graduate education (PhD); molecular microbiology (PhD). Terminal master's awarded for partial completion of doctoral program. *Degree requirements:* For doctorate, comprehensive exam, thesis/dissertation. *Entrance requirements:* For doctorate, GRE General Test, 3 letters of reference, resume, personal statement. Electronic applications accepted. *Expenses: Tuition:* Full-time $49,892. *Required fees:* $874. Full-time tuition and fees vary according to degree level, program and student level. Part-time tuition and fees vary according to course load. *Faculty research:* Mechanisms of gene regulation, interactions of microorganisms and viruses with host cells, infection response.

Tulane University, School of Medicine and School of Liberal Arts, Graduate Programs in Biomedical Sciences, Interdisciplinary Graduate Program in Molecular and Cellular Biology, New Orleans, LA 70118-5669. Offers PhD, MD/PhD. PhD offered through the Graduate School. *Degree requirements:* For doctorate, thesis/dissertation. *Entrance requirements:* For doctorate, GRE General Test, GRE Subject Test. Additional exam requirements/recommendations for international students: Required—TOEFL. Electronic applications accepted. *Expenses: Tuition:* Full-time $50,920; part-time $2829 per credit hour. *Required fees:* $2040; $44.50 per credit hour. $580 per term. Tuition and fees vary according to course load, degree level and program. *Faculty research:* Developmental biology, neuroscience, virology.

Tulane University, School of Science and Engineering, Department of Cell and Molecular Biology, New Orleans, LA 70118-5669. Offers MS, PhD. Terminal master's awarded for partial completion of doctoral program. *Degree requirements:* For doctorate, thesis/dissertation. *Entrance requirements:* For master's, GRE General Test, minimum B average in undergraduate course work; for doctorate, GRE General Test. Additional exam requirements/recommendations for international students: Required—TOEFL. Electronic applications accepted. *Expenses: Tuition:* Full-time $50,920; part-time $2829 per credit hour. *Required fees:* $2040; $44.50 per credit hour. $580 per term. Tuition and fees vary according to course load, degree level and program.

Uniformed Services University of the Health Sciences, F. Edward Hebert School of Medicine, Graduate Programs in the Biomedical Sciences and Public Health, Graduate Program in Molecular and Cell Biology, Bethesda, MD 20814-4799. Offers MS, PhD. *Degree requirements:* For doctorate, comprehensive exam, thesis/dissertation, qualifying exam. *Entrance requirements:* For doctorate, GRE General Test, minimum GPA of 3.0. Electronic applications accepted. *Faculty research:* Immunology, biochemistry, cancer biology, stem cell biology.

See Display below and Close-Up on page 209.

Universidad Central del Caribe, School of Medicine, Program in Biomedical Sciences, Bayamón, PR 00960-6032. Offers anatomy and cell biology (MA, MS); biochemistry (MS); biomedical sciences (MA); cellular and molecular biology (PhD); microbiology and immunology (MA, MS); pharmacology (MS); physiology (MS).

Université de Montréal, Faculty of Medicine, Program in Molecular Biology, Montréal, QC H3C 3J7, Canada. Offers M Sc, PhD. Terminal master's awarded for partial completion of doctoral program. *Degree requirements:* For master's, thesis; for doctorate, thesis/dissertation, general exam. *Entrance requirements:* For master's and doctorate, proficiency in French, knowledge of English. Electronic applications accepted. *Faculty research:* Protein interactions, intracellular signaling, development and differentiation, hematopoiesis, stem cells.

Université Laval, Faculty of Medicine, Graduate Programs in Medicine, Programs in Cellular and Molecular Biology, Québec, QC G1K 7P4, Canada. Offers M Sc, PhD. Terminal master's awarded for partial completion of doctoral program. *Degree requirements:* For master's, thesis; for doctorate, comprehensive exam, thesis/dissertation. *Entrance requirements:* For master's and doctorate, knowledge of French, comprehension of written English. Electronic applications accepted. *Faculty research:* Oral bacterial metabolism, sugar transport.

University at Buffalo, the State University of New York, Graduate School, Graduate Programs in Cancer Research and Biomedical Sciences at Roswell Park Cancer Institute, Department of Cellular and Molecular Biology at Roswell Park Cancer Institute, Buffalo, NY 14260. Offers PhD. *Faculty:* 25 full-time (4 women). *Students:* 12 full-time (7 women), 2 international. 48 applicants, 29% accepted, 2 enrolled. In 2017, 6 doctorates awarded. *Degree requirements:* For doctorate, comprehensive exam, thesis/dissertation, oral defense of dissertation. *Entrance requirements:* For doctorate, GRE General Test. Additional exam requirements/recommendations for international students: Required—TOEFL (minimum score 79 iBT). *Application deadline:* For fall admission, 1/5 priority date for domestic and international students. Application fee: $75. Electronic applications accepted. *Financial support:* In 2017–18, 21 students received support, including 21 research assistantships with full tuition reimbursements available (averaging $27,000 per year); scholarships/grants, health care benefits, and unspecified assistantships also available. Financial award application deadline: 1/5. *Faculty research:* Cancer genetics, chromatin structure and replication, regulation of transcription, human gene mapping, genetic and structural approaches to regulation of gene expression. *Unit head:* Dr. Dominic J. Smiraglia, Director of Graduate Studies, 716-845-1347, Fax: 716-845-1698, E-mail: dominic.smiraglia@roswellpark.org. *Application contact:* Dr. Norman J. Karin, Associate Dean, 716-845-2339, Fax: 716-845-8178, E-mail: norman.karin@roswellpark.edu.
Website: http://www.roswellpark.edu/education/phd-programs/cellular-molecular-biology

The University of Alabama at Birmingham, Joint Health Sciences, Cell, Molecular, and Developmental Biology Theme, Birmingham, AL 35294. Offers PhD. *Faculty:* 370. *Students:* 50 full-time (28 women); includes 17 minority (6 Black or African American, non-Hispanic/Latino; 8 Asian, non-Hispanic/Latino; 2 Hispanic/Latino; 1 Two or more races, non-Hispanic/Latino). Average age 27. 32 applicants, 28% accepted, 3 enrolled. In 2017, 7 doctorates awarded. *Degree requirements:* For doctorate, comprehensive exam, thesis/dissertation. *Entrance requirements:* For doctorate, personal statement, resume or curriculum vitae, letters of recommendation, research experience, interview. Additional exam requirements/recommendations for international students: Required—TOEFL (minimum score 80 iBT), IELTS (minimum score 6.5). *Application deadline:* For fall admission, 12/31 for domestic and international students. Applications are processed on a rolling basis. Electronic applications accepted. *Financial support:* In 2017–18, fellowships with full tuition reimbursements (averaging $29,000 per year), research assistantships with full tuition reimbursements (averaging $30,000 per year) were awarded; health care benefits also available. *Unit head:* Dr. Alecia K. Gross, Theme Director, 205-975-8396, E-mail: agross@uab.edu. *Application contact:* Alyssa Zasada, Admissions Manager for Graduate Biomedical Sciences, 205-934-3857, E-mail: grad-gbs@uab.edu.
Website: http://www.uab.edu/gbs/home/themes/cmdb

University of Alberta, Faculty of Graduate Studies and Research, Department of Biological Sciences, Edmonton, AB T6G 2E1, Canada. Offers environmental biology and ecology (M Sc, PhD); microbiology and biotechnology (M Sc, PhD); molecular biology and genetics (M Sc, PhD); physiology and cell biology (M Sc, PhD); plant biology (M Sc, PhD); systematics and evolution (M Sc, PhD). Terminal master's awarded for partial completion of doctoral program. *Degree requirements:* For master's, thesis; for doctorate, thesis/dissertation. *Entrance requirements:* Additional exam requirements/recommendations for international students: Required—TOEFL.

University of Alberta, Faculty of Medicine and Dentistry and Faculty of Graduate Studies and Research, Graduate Programs in Medicine, Department of Cell Biology, Edmonton, AB T6G 2E1, Canada. Offers cell and molecular biology (M Sc, PhD). Terminal master's awarded for partial completion of doctoral program. *Degree requirements:* For master's, thesis; for doctorate, thesis/dissertation. *Entrance requirements:* For master's and doctorate, 3 letters of reference, curriculum vitae. Additional exam requirements/recommendations for international students: Required—TOEFL (minimum score 600 paper-based). *Faculty research:* Protein targeting, membrane trafficking, signal transduction, cell growth and division, cell-cell interaction and development.

The University of Arizona, College of Science, Biochemistry and Molecular and Cellular Biology Program, Tucson, AZ 85721. Offers PhD. *Program availability:* Evening/weekend. *Degree requirements:* For doctorate, thesis/dissertation. *Entrance requirements:* For doctorate, 3 letters of recommendation, statement of purpose. Additional exam requirements/recommendations for international students: Required—TOEFL (minimum score 600 paper-based; 90 iBT), IELTS (minimum score 7). Electronic applications accepted. *Faculty research:* Plant molecular biology, cellular and molecular aspects of development, genetics of bacteria and lower eukaryotes.

University of Arkansas, Graduate School, Interdisciplinary Program in Cell and Molecular Biology, Fayetteville, AR 72701. Offers MS, PhD. In 2017, 11 master's, 4 doctorates awarded. *Degree requirements:* For doctorate, thesis/dissertation. *Application deadline:* For fall admission, 8/1 for domestic students, 4/1 for international students; for spring admission, 12/1 for domestic students, 10/1 for international students; for summer admission, 4/15 for domestic students, 3/1 for international students. Applications are processed on a rolling basis. Application fee: $60. Electronic applications accepted. *Expenses:* Tuition, state resident: full-time $3782. Tuition, nonresident: full-time $10,238. *Financial support:* In 2017–18, 31 research assistantships, 12 teaching assistantships were awarded; fellowships with tuition reimbursements also available. Financial award application deadline: 4/1; financial award applicants required to submit FAFSA. *Unit head:* Dr. Douglas Rhoads, Program Director, 479-575-4010, Fax: 479-575-5908, E-mail: drhoads@uark.edu. *Application contact:* Adnan Alrubaye, Program Associate Director, 479-575-3251, Fax: 479-575-4010, E-mail: aakhalaf@uark.edu.
Website: https://cell.uark.edu/

University of Arkansas for Medical Sciences, Graduate School, Little Rock, AR 72205. Offers biochemistry and molecular biology (MS, PhD); bioinformatics (MS, PhD); cellular physiology and molecular biophysics (MS, PhD); clinical nutrition (MS); interdisciplinary biomedical sciences (MS, PhD, Certificate); interdisciplinary toxicology (MS); microbiology and immunology (PhD); neurobiology and developmental sciences (PhD); pharmacology (PhD); MD/PhD. Bioinformatics programs hosted jointly with the University of Arkansas at Little Rock. *Program availability:* Part-time. Terminal master's awarded for partial completion of doctoral program. *Degree requirements:* For master's, comprehensive exam (for some programs), thesis (for some programs); for doctorate, thesis/dissertation. *Entrance requirements:* For master's and doctorate, GRE. Additional exam requirements/recommendations for international students: Required—TOEFL. Electronic applications accepted. *Expenses:* Contact institution.

The University of British Columbia, Faculty of Medicine, Department of Biochemistry and Molecular Biology, Vancouver, BC V6T 1Z3, Canada. Offers M Sc, PhD. *Degree requirements:* For master's, thesis; for doctorate, comprehensive exam, thesis/dissertation. *Entrance requirements:* For master's, first class B Sc; for doctorate, master's or first class honors bachelor's degree in biochemistry. Additional exam requirements/recommendations for international students: Required—TOEFL (minimum score 625 paper-based). Electronic applications accepted. *Expenses:* Contact institution. *Faculty research:* Membrane biochemistry, protein structure/function, signal transduction, biochemistry.

University of Calgary, Cumming School of Medicine and Faculty of Graduate Studies, Department of Biochemistry and Molecular Biology, Calgary, AB T2N 1N4, Canada. Offers M Sc, PhD. *Degree requirements:* For master's, thesis; for doctorate, thesis/dissertation, candidacy exam. *Entrance requirements:* For master's and doctorate, GRE General Test, minimum GPA of 3.2. Additional exam requirements/recommendations for international students: Required—TOEFL. Electronic applications accepted. *Faculty research:* Molecular and developmental genetics; molecular biology of disease; genomics, proteomics and bioinformatics; cell signaling and structure.

University of California, Berkeley, Graduate Division, College of Letters and Science, Department of Molecular and Cell Biology, Berkeley, CA 94720-1500. Offers PhD. *Degree requirements:* For doctorate, comprehensive exam, thesis/dissertation, qualifying exam, 2 semesters of teaching. *Entrance requirements:* For doctorate, GRE General Test, GRE Subject Test (recommended), minimum GPA of 3.0. Additional exam requirements/recommendations for international students: Required—TOEFL (minimum score 570 paper-based; 68 iBT), IELTS (minimum score 7). Electronic applications accepted. *Faculty research:* Biochemistry, biophysics and structural biology; cell and developmental biology; genetics, genomics and development; immunology and pathogenesis; neurobiology.

University of California, Davis, Graduate Studies, Graduate Group in Biochemistry and Molecular Biology, Davis, CA 95616. Offers MS, PhD. Terminal master's awarded for partial completion of doctoral program. *Degree requirements:* For master's, comprehensive exam (for some programs), thesis (for some programs); for doctorate, thesis/dissertation. *Entrance requirements:* For master's and doctorate, GRE General Test, GRE Subject Test. Additional exam requirements/recommendations for international students: Required—TOEFL (minimum score 550 paper-based). Electronic applications accepted. *Faculty research:* Gene expression, protein structure, molecular virology, protein synthesis, enzymology, membrane transport and structural biology.

University of California, Irvine, Francisco J. Ayala School of Biological Sciences, Department of Molecular Biology and Biochemistry, Irvine, CA 92697. Offers biological science (MS); biological sciences (PhD); biotechnology (MS); biotechnology management (MS); MD/PhD. *Students:* 43 full-time (20 women), 1 part-time (0 women); includes 15 minority (1 Black or African American, non-Hispanic/Latino; 7 Asian, non-Hispanic/Latino; 7 Hispanic/Latino), 4 international. Average age 29. 1 applicant, 100% accepted, 1 enrolled. In 2017, 5 master's, 14 doctorates awarded. *Entrance requirements:* For master's, GRE, minimum GPA of 3.0; for doctorate, GRE General Test, GRE Subject Test, minimum GPA of 3.0. Additional exam requirements/recommendations for international students: Required—TOEFL (minimum score 550 paper-based). *Application deadline:* For fall admission, 12/15 priority date for domestic students, 12/15 for international students. Applications are processed on a rolling basis. Application fee: $105 ($125 for international students). Electronic applications accepted. *Financial support:* Fellowships, research assistantships with full tuition reimbursements, teaching assistantships, institutionally sponsored loans, traineeships, health care benefits, and unspecified assistantships available. Financial award application deadline: 3/1; financial award applicants required to submit FAFSA. *Faculty research:* Structure and synthesis of nucleic acids and proteins, regulation, virology, biochemical genetics, gene organization. *Unit head:* Prof. Christopher Hughes, Chair, 949-824-8771, Fax: 949-824-8551, E-mail: cchughes@uci.edu. *Application contact:* Morgan Oldham, Student Affairs Assistant, 949-826-6034, Fax: 949-824-8551, E-mail: morgano@uci.edu.
Website: http://www.bio.uci.edu/

University of California, Irvine, Francisco J. Ayala School of Biological Sciences and School of Medicine, Interdisciplinary Graduate Program in Cellular and Molecular Biosciences, Irvine, CA 92697. Offers PhD. *Students:* 40 full-time (20 women); includes 19 minority (9 Asian, non-Hispanic/Latino; 6 Hispanic/Latino; 4 Two or more races, non-Hispanic/Latino), 4 international. Average age 25. 371 applicants, 23% accepted, 38 enrolled. *Degree requirements:* For doctorate, thesis/dissertation, teaching assignment, preliminary exam. *Entrance requirements:* For doctorate, GRE General Test, three letters of recommendation, interview. Additional exam requirements/recommendations for international students: Required—TOEFL or IELTS. *Application deadline:* For fall admission, 12/8 for domestic and international students. Application fee: $105 ($125 for international students). Electronic applications accepted. *Expenses:* Contact institution. *Financial support:* Fellowships with full tuition reimbursements, institutionally sponsored loans, scholarships/grants, tuition waivers (full), unspecified assistantships, and stipends available. Financial award application deadline: 1/1; financial award applicants required to submit FAFSA. *Faculty research:* Cellular biochemistry; gene structure and expression; protein structure, function, and design; molecular genetics; pathogenesis and inherited disease. *Unit head:* Melanie Cocco, Director, 949-824-4487, Fax: 949-824-1965, E-mail: mcocco@uci.edu. *Application contact:* Renee Frigo, Administrator, 949-824-8145, Fax: 949-824-1965, E-mail: rfrigo@uci.edu.
Website: http://cmb.uci.edu/

University of California, Los Angeles, Graduate Division, College of Letters and Science, Department of Chemistry and Biochemistry, Program in Biochemistry and Molecular Biology, Los Angeles, CA 90095. Offers MS, PhD. Terminal master's awarded for partial completion of doctoral program. *Degree requirements:* For master's, comprehensive exam or thesis; for doctorate, thesis/dissertation, oral and written qualifying exams; 3 quarters of teaching experience. *Entrance requirements:* For doctorate, GRE General Test, GRE Subject Test (recommended), bachelor's degree; minimum undergraduate GPA of 3.0 (or its equivalent if letter grade system not used). Additional exam requirements/recommendations for international students: Required—TOEFL. Electronic applications accepted.

University of California, Los Angeles, Graduate Division, College of Letters and Science, Department of Molecular, Cell and Developmental Biology, Los Angeles, CA 90095. Offers MA, PhD. Terminal master's awarded for partial completion of doctoral program. *Degree requirements:* For master's, comprehensive exam, thesis; for doctorate, thesis/dissertation, oral and written qualifying exams; 2 quarters of teaching experience. *Entrance requirements:* For doctorate, GRE General Test. Additional exam requirements/recommendations for international students: Required—TOEFL. Electronic applications accepted.

University of California, Los Angeles, Graduate Division, College of Letters and Science, Program in Molecular Biology, Los Angeles, CA 90095. Offers PhD, MD/PhD. *Degree requirements:* For doctorate, thesis/dissertation, oral and written qualifying exams. *Entrance requirements:* For doctorate, GRE General Test; GRE Subject Test (biochemistry, chemistry, biology, or physics), bachelor's degree; minimum undergraduate GPA of 3.0 (or its equivalent if letter grade system not used). Additional exam requirements/recommendations for international students: Required—TOEFL. Electronic applications accepted.

University of California, Los Angeles, Graduate Division, College of Letters and Science and David Geffen School of Medicine, UCLA ACCESS to Programs in the Molecular, Cellular and Integrative Life Sciences, Los Angeles, CA 90095. Offers biochemistry and molecular biology (PhD); biological chemistry (PhD); cellular and molecular pathology (PhD); human genetics (PhD); microbiology, immunology, and molecular genetics (PhD); molecular biology (PhD); molecular toxicology (PhD); molecular, cellular and integrative physiology (PhD); neurobiology (PhD); oral biology (PhD); physiology (PhD). *Degree requirements:* For doctorate, thesis/dissertation, oral and written qualifying exams. *Entrance requirements:* For doctorate, GRE General Test, bachelor's degree; minimum undergraduate GPA of 3.0 (or its equivalent if letter grade system not used). Additional exam requirements/recommendations for international students: Required—TOEFL. Electronic applications accepted.

University of California, Riverside, Graduate Division, Department of Biochemistry and Molecular Biology, Riverside, CA 92521-0102. Offers MS, PhD. *Program availability:* Part-time. *Faculty:* 51 full-time (16 women). Terminal master's awarded for partial completion of doctoral program. *Degree requirements:* For master's, comprehensive exam (for some programs), thesis (for some programs), comprehensive exam or thesis; for doctorate, comprehensive exam, thesis/dissertation, 2 quarters of teaching experience, written exam, oral qualifying exam. *Entrance requirements:* For master's, GRE General Test, minimum GPA of 3.0; for doctorate, GRE General Test, minimum GPA of 3.25. Additional exam requirements/recommendations for international students: Required—TOEFL (minimum score 550 paper-based, 80 iBT) or IELTS. *Application deadline:* For fall admission, 1/5 priority date for domestic and international students; for winter admission, 11/15 for domestic students, 9/1 for international students; for spring admission, 3/1 for domestic students, 12/1 for international students. Application fee: $80 ($100 for international students). Electronic applications accepted. *Expenses:* Tuition, state resident: full-time $5746. Tuition, nonresident: full-time $10,780. Tuition and fees vary according to campus/location and program. *Financial support:* Fellowships with full tuition reimbursements, research assistantships with full tuition reimbursements, teaching assistantships with full tuition reimbursements, career-related internships or fieldwork, institutionally sponsored loans, scholarships/grants, health care benefits, and unspecified assistantships available. Financial award application deadline: 1/5; financial award applicants required to submit FAFSA. *Faculty research:* Structural biology and molecular biophysics, signal transduction, plant biochemistry and molecular biology, gene expression and metabolic regulation, molecular toxicology and pathogenesis. *Application contact:* Julio Sosa, E-mail: biochem@ucr.edu.
Website: http://www.biochemistry.ucr.edu/

University of California, Riverside, Graduate Division, Program in Cell, Molecular, and Developmental Biology, Riverside, CA 92521-0102. Offers MS, PhD. Terminal master's awarded for partial completion of doctoral program. *Degree requirements:* For master's, thesis, oral defense of thesis; for doctorate, thesis/dissertation, oral defense of thesis, qualifying exams, 2 quarters of teaching experience. *Entrance requirements:* For master's and doctorate, GRE General Test, minimum GPA of 3.2. Additional exam requirements/recommendations for international students: Required—TOEFL (minimum score 550 paper-based; 80 iBT). Electronic applications accepted. *Expenses:* Tuition, state resident: full-time $5746. Tuition, nonresident: full-time $10,780. Tuition and fees vary according to campus/location and program.

University of California, San Francisco, Graduate Division and School of Medicine, Tetrad Graduate Program, Biochemistry and Molecular Biology Track, San Francisco, CA 94143. Offers PhD, MD/PhD. *Degree requirements:* For doctorate, thesis/dissertation. *Entrance requirements:* For doctorate, GRE General Test, GRE Subject Test. Additional exam requirements/recommendations for international students: Required—TOEFL. *Expenses:* Contact institution. *Faculty research:* Structural biology, genetics, cell biology, cell physiology, metabolism.

Molecular Biology

University of California, Santa Barbara, Graduate Division, College of Letters and Sciences, Division of Mathematics, Life, and Physical Sciences, Department of Molecular, Cellular, and Developmental Biology, Santa Barbara, CA 93106-9625. Offers MA, PhD, MA/PhD. Terminal master's awarded for partial completion of doctoral program. *Degree requirements:* For master's, comprehensive exam (for some programs), thesis (for some programs); for doctorate, comprehensive exam, thesis/dissertation. *Entrance requirements:* For master's and doctorate, GRE General Test, 3 letters of recommendation, statement of purpose, personal achievements/contributions statement, resume/curriculum vitae, transcripts for post-secondary institutions attended. Additional exam requirements/recommendations for international students: Required—TOEFL (minimum score 550 paper-based; 80 iBT), IELTS (minimum score 7). Electronic applications accepted. *Faculty research:* Microbiology, neurobiology (including stem cell research), developmental, virology, cell biology.

University of California, Santa Barbara, Graduate Division, College of Letters and Sciences, Division of Mathematics, Life, and Physical Sciences, Interdepartmental Graduate Program in Biomolecular Science and Engineering, Santa Barbara, CA 93106-2014. Offers biochemistry and molecular biology (PhD), including biochemistry and molecular biology, biophysics and bioengineering. Terminal master's awarded for partial completion of doctoral program. *Degree requirements:* For doctorate, thesis/dissertation. *Entrance requirements:* For doctorate, GRE General Test. Additional exam requirements/recommendations for international students: Required—TOEFL (minimum score 630 paper-based; 109 iBT), IELTS (minimum score 7). Electronic applications accepted. *Faculty research:* Biochemistry and molecular biology, biophysics, biomaterials, bioengineering, systems biology.

University of California, Santa Cruz, Division of Graduate Studies, Division of Physical and Biological Sciences, Program in Molecular, Cellular, and Developmental Biology, Santa Cruz, CA 95064. Offers MA, PhD. Terminal master's awarded for partial completion of doctoral program. *Degree requirements:* For master's, thesis; for doctorate, thesis/dissertation, qualifying exam. *Entrance requirements:* For master's and doctorate, GRE General Test, 3 letters of recommendation, interview. Additional exam requirements/recommendations for international students: Required—TOEFL (minimum score 550 paper-based; 83 iBT); Recommended—IELTS (minimum score 8). Electronic applications accepted. *Faculty research:* RNA biology, chromatin and chromosome biology, neurobiology, stem cell biology and differentiation, cell structure and function.

University of Chicago, Division of the Biological Sciences, Program in Cell and Molecular Biology, Chicago, IL 60637. Offers PhD. *Faculty:* 24. *Students:* 27 full-time (9 women); includes 10 minority (2 Black or African American, non-Hispanic/Latino; 1 American Indian or Alaska Native, non-Hispanic/Latino; 2 Asian, non-Hispanic/Latino; 4 Hispanic/Latino; 1 Two or more races, non-Hispanic/Latino), 5 international. Average age 27. 75 applicants, 24% accepted, 6 enrolled. In 2017, 6 doctorates awarded. *Degree requirements:* For doctorate, thesis/dissertation, ethics class, 2 teaching assistantships. *Entrance requirements:* For doctorate, GRE General Test, transcripts, statement of purpose, 3 letters of recommendation. Additional exam requirements/recommendations for international students: Required—TOEFL (minimum score 600 paper-based; 104 iBT), IELTS (minimum score 7). *Application deadline:* For fall admission, 12/1 for domestic and international students. Application fee: $90. Electronic applications accepted. *Financial support:* In 2017–18, 28 students received support, including fellowships with full tuition reimbursements available (averaging $31,000 per year), research assistantships with full tuition reimbursements available (averaging $31,000 per year); institutionally sponsored loans, scholarships/grants, traineeships, and health care benefits also available. Financial award application deadline: 12/1. *Faculty research:* Regulation of cell division; formation of organelles; dynamics of cell and tissue behavior; genome inheritance and expression; cytoskeleton function in organizing cellular processes. *Total annual research expenditures:* $8 million. *Unit head:* David Kovar, Chair, E-mail: drkovar@uchicago.edu. *Application contact:* Kristine Gaston, Graduate Program Director, 773-702-8037, E-mail: kristine@bsd.uchicago.edu.
Website: http://cellmolbio.bsd.uchicago.edu/

University of Cincinnati, Graduate School, College of Medicine, Graduate Programs in Biomedical Sciences, Department of Environmental Health, Programs in Environmental Genetics and Molecular Toxicology, Cincinnati, OH 45221. Offers MS, PhD. *Degree requirements:* For doctorate, thesis/dissertation. *Entrance requirements:* For master's, GRE, minimum GPA of 3.0, 3 letters of recommendation. Additional exam requirements/recommendations for international students: Required—TOEFL (minimum score 520 paper-based). *Expenses: Tuition, area resident:* Full-time $14,468. Tuition, state resident: full-time $14,968; part-time $754 per credit hour. Tuition, nonresident: full-time $24,210; part-time $1311 per credit hour. *International tuition:* $26,460 full-time. *Required fees:* $3958; $84 per credit hour. One-time fee: $85 full-time. Tuition and fees vary according to course load, degree level and program.

University of Cincinnati, Graduate School, College of Medicine, Graduate Programs in Biomedical Sciences, Department of Molecular Genetics, Biochemistry and Microbiology, Cincinnati, OH 45221. Offers MS, PhD. Terminal master's awarded for partial completion of doctoral program. *Degree requirements:* For master's, thesis or alternative; for doctorate, thesis/dissertation, qualifying exam. *Entrance requirements:* For master's and doctorate, GRE General Test. Additional exam requirements/recommendations for international students: Required—TOEFL (minimum score 600 paper-based; 100 iBT), TWE. Electronic applications accepted. *Expenses: Tuition, area resident:* Full-time $14,468. Tuition, state resident: full-time $14,968; part-time $754 per credit hour. Tuition, nonresident: full-time $24,210; part-time $1311 per credit hour. *International tuition:* $26,460 full-time. *Required fees:* $3958; $84 per credit hour. One-time fee: $85 full-time. Tuition and fees vary according to course load, degree level and program. *Faculty research:* Cancer biology and developmental genetics, gene regulation and chromosome structure, microbiology and pathogenic mechanisms, structural biology, membrane biochemistry and signal transduction.

University of Cincinnati, Graduate School, College of Medicine, Graduate Programs in Biomedical Sciences, Department of Pediatrics, Program in Molecular and Developmental Biology, Cincinnati, OH 45221. Offers PhD. *Degree requirements:* For doctorate, thesis/dissertation, qualifying exam. *Entrance requirements:* For doctorate, GRE General Test, minimum GPA of 3.2. Additional exam requirements/recommendations for international students: Required—TOEFL (minimum score 520 paper-based). Electronic applications accepted. *Expenses: Tuition, area resident:* Full-time $14,468. Tuition, state resident: full-time $14,968; part-time $754 per credit hour. Tuition, nonresident: full-time $24,210; part-time $1311 per credit hour. *International tuition:* $26,460 full-time. *Required fees:* $3958; $84 per credit hour. One-time fee: $85 full-time. Tuition and fees vary according to course load, degree level and program. *Faculty research:* Cancer biology, cardiovascular biology, developmental biology, human genetics, gene therapy, genomics and bioinformatics, immunobiology, molecular medicine, neuroscience, pulmonary biology, reproductive biology, stem cell biology.

University of Colorado Boulder, Graduate School, College of Arts and Sciences, Department of Molecular, Cellular, and Developmental Biology, Boulder, CO 80309. Offers cellular structure and function (MA, PhD); developmental biology (PhD); molecular biology (PhD). *Faculty:* 29 full-time (10 women). *Students:* 51 full-time (26 women), 4 part-time (1 woman); includes 8 minority (3 Asian, non-Hispanic/Latino; 4 Hispanic/Latino; 1 Two or more races, non-Hispanic/Latino), 10 international. Average age 27. 345 applicants, 9% accepted, 12 enrolled. In 2017, 10 doctorates awarded. Terminal master's awarded for partial completion of doctoral program. *Degree requirements:* For master's, comprehensive exam, thesis or alternative; for doctorate, comprehensive exam, thesis/dissertation. *Entrance requirements:* For master's, GRE General Test, GRE Subject Test, minimum undergraduate GPA of 3.0; for doctorate, GRE General Test, GRE Subject Test. *Application deadline:* For fall admission, 12/1 for domestic students; for spring admission, 12/1 for domestic students. Application fee: $60 ($80 for international students). Electronic applications accepted. Application fee is waived when completed online. *Financial support:* In 2017–18, 158 students received support, including 48 fellowships (averaging $12,292 per year), 38 research assistantships with full and partial tuition reimbursements available (averaging $34,642 per year), 10 teaching assistantships with full and partial tuition reimbursements available (averaging $30,525 per year); institutionally sponsored loans, scholarships/grants, health care benefits, and unspecified assistantships also available. Financial award application deadline: 2/15; financial award applicants required to submit FAFSA. *Faculty research:* Molecular biology; cellular biology; genetics; developmental biology; biochemistry: proteins. *Total annual research expenditures:* $15.3 million. *Application contact:* E-mail: mcdbgrad@colorado.edu.
Website: http://mcdb.colorado.edu/graduate

University of Colorado Denver, School of Medicine, Program in Molecular Biology, Aurora, CO 80045. Offers biomolecular structure (PhD). *Students:* 52 applicants, 12% accepted, 5 enrolled. In 2017, 9 doctorates awarded. *Degree requirements:* For doctorate, comprehensive exam, thesis/dissertation, 2 years of structured didactic courses, 2-3 years of research, laboratory work, thesis project. *Entrance requirements:* For doctorate, GRE, organic chemistry (2 semesters, including 1 semester of laboratory), biology, general physics, college-level mathematics through calculus, three letters of reference. Additional exam requirements/recommendations for international students: Required—TOEFL (minimum score 550 paper-based; 80 iBT). *Application deadline:* For fall admission, 12/1 for domestic students, 11/1 for international students. Application fee: $50 ($75 for international students). Electronic applications accepted. *Financial support:* Unspecified assistantships available. *Faculty research:* Gene transcription, RNA processing, chromosome dynamics, DNA damage and repair, chromatin assembly. *Unit head:* Dr. Mark Johnston, Chair, 303-724-3203, E-mail: mark.johnston@ucdenver.edu. *Application contact:* Sabrena Heilman, Program Administrator, 303-724-3245, E-mail: sabrena.heilman@ucdenver.edu.
Website: http://www.ucdenver.edu/academics/colleges/medicalschool/programs/Molbio/Pages/MolecularBiology.aspx

University of Colorado Denver, School of Medicine, Program in Pharmacology, Aurora, CO 80206. Offers bioinformatics (PhD); biomolecular structure (PhD). *Students:* 26 full-time (12 women); includes 7 minority (2 Asian, non-Hispanic/Latino; 4 Hispanic/Latino; 1 Two or more races, non-Hispanic/Latino), 2 international. Average age 27. 28 applicants, 14% accepted, 4 enrolled. In 2017, 3 doctorates awarded. *Degree requirements:* For doctorate, comprehensive exam, thesis/dissertation, major seminar, 3 research rotations in the first year, 30 hours each of course work and thesis. *Entrance requirements:* For doctorate, GRE General Test, three letters of recommendation, personal statement. Additional exam requirements/recommendations for international students: Required—TOEFL (minimum score 550 paper-based; 80 iBT). *Application deadline:* For fall admission, 12/15 for domestic students, 11/15 for international students. Application fee: $50 ($75 for international students). Electronic applications accepted. *Financial support:* Fellowships, research assistantships, teaching assistantships, institutionally sponsored loans, scholarships/grants, traineeships, health care benefits, tuition waivers (full), and unspecified assistantships available. *Faculty research:* Cancer biology, drugs of abuse, neuroscience, signal transduction, structural biology. *Unit head:* Dr. Andrew Thorburn, Interim Chair, 303-724-3290, Fax: 303-724-3663, E-mail: andrew.thorburn@ucdenver.edu. *Application contact:* Elizabeth Bowen, Graduate Program Coordinator, 303-724-3565, E-mail: elizabeth.bowen@ucdenver.edu.
Website: http://www.ucdenver.edu/academics/colleges/medicalschool/departments/Pharmacology/Pages/Pharmacology.aspx

University of Connecticut, Graduate School, College of Liberal Arts and Sciences, Department of Molecular and Cell Biology, Storrs, CT 06269. Offers applied genomics (PSM); cell and developmental biology (MS, PhD); genetics and genomics (MS, PhD); microbial systems analysis (PSM); microbiology (MS, PhD); structural biology, biochemistry and biophysics (MS, PhD). Terminal master's awarded for partial completion of doctoral program. *Degree requirements:* For master's, comprehensive exam; for doctorate, thesis/dissertation. *Entrance requirements:* For master's and doctorate, GRE General Test, GRE Subject Test. Additional exam requirements/recommendations for international students: Required—TOEFL (minimum score 550 paper-based). Electronic applications accepted.

University of Connecticut Health Center, Graduate School, Programs in Biomedical Sciences, Graduate Program in Molecular Biology and Biochemistry, Farmington, CT 06030. Offers PhD, DMD/PhD, MD/PhD. *Degree requirements:* For doctorate, comprehensive exam, thesis/dissertation. *Entrance requirements:* For doctorate, GRE General Test. Additional exam requirements/recommendations for international students: Required—TOEFL (minimum score 600 paper-based). Electronic applications accepted. *Faculty research:* Molecular biology, structural biology, protein biochemistry, microbial physiology and pathogenesis.

University of Delaware, College of Arts and Sciences, Department of Biological Sciences, Newark, DE 19716. Offers biotechnology (MS); cancer biology (MS, PhD); cell and extracellular matrix biology (MS, PhD); cell and systems physiology (MS, PhD); developmental biology (MS, PhD); ecology and evolution (MS, PhD); microbiology (MS, PhD); molecular biology and genetics (MS, PhD). Terminal master's awarded for partial completion of doctoral program. *Degree requirements:* For master's, thesis, preliminary exam; for doctorate, comprehensive exam, thesis/dissertation, preliminary exam. *Entrance requirements:* For master's and doctorate, GRE General Test. Additional exam requirements/recommendations for international students: Required—TOEFL (minimum score 600 paper-based); Recommended—TWE. Electronic applications accepted. *Faculty research:* Microorganisms, bone, cancer metastasis, developmental biology, cell biology, DNA.

University of Denver, Division of Natural Sciences and Mathematics, Department of Biological Sciences, Denver, CO 80208. Offers biology, ecology and evolution (MS, PhD); biomedical sciences (PSM); cell and molecular biology (MS, PhD). *Program availability:* Part-time. *Students:* Average age 25. 71 applicants, 44% accepted, 18 enrolled. In 2017, 7 master's, 3 doctorates awarded. Terminal master's awarded for partial completion of doctoral program. *Degree requirements:* For master's, comprehensive exam (for some programs), thesis; for doctorate, one foreign language, comprehensive exam (for some programs), thesis/dissertation. *Entrance requirements:* For master's and doctorate, GRE General Test, bachelor's degree in biology or related field, transcripts, personal statement, three letters of recommendation. Additional exam requirements/recommendations for international students: Required—TOEFL (minimum score 550 paper-based; 80 iBT). *Application deadline:* For fall admission, 1/1 priority date for domestic and international students. Applications are processed on a rolling basis. Application fee: $65. Electronic applications accepted. *Expenses:* Contact

institution. *Financial support:* In 2017–18, 35 students received support, including 5 research assistantships with tuition reimbursements available (averaging $18,667 per year), 14 teaching assistantships with tuition reimbursements available (averaging $18,095 per year); Federal Work-Study, institutionally sponsored loans, scholarships/grants, and unspecified assistantships also available. Support available to part-time students. Financial award application deadline: 2/15; financial award applicants required to submit FAFSA. *Faculty research:* Molecular biology, cell biology, neurobiology, ecology, molecular evolution. *Unit head:* Dr. Joseph Angleson, Associate Professor and Chair, 303-871-3463, Fax: 303-871-3471, E-mail: jangleso@du.edu. *Application contact:* Randi Flageolle, Assistant to the Chair, 303-871-3457, Fax: 303-871-3471, E-mail: rflageol@du.edu.
Website: http://www.du.edu/nsm/departments/biologicalsciences

University of Florida, College of Medicine and Graduate School, Interdisciplinary Program in Biomedical Sciences, Concentration in Biochemistry and Molecular Biology, Gainesville, FL 32611. Offers PhD. *Degree requirements:* For doctorate, thesis/dissertation. *Entrance requirements:* For doctorate, GRE General Test, minimum GPA of 3.0, biochemistry before enrollment. Additional exam requirements/recommendations for international students: Required—TOEFL. Electronic applications accepted. *Faculty research:* Gene expression, metabolic regulation, structural biology, enzyme mechanism, membrane transporters.

University of Florida, Graduate School, College of Agricultural and Life Sciences, Department of Animal Sciences, Interdisciplinary Concentration in Animal Molecular and Cellular Biology, Gainesville, FL 32611. Offers MS, PhD. *Entrance requirements:* For master's and doctorate, GRE General Test, minimum GPA of 3.0. Additional exam requirements/recommendations for international students: Required—TOEFL (minimum score 550 paper-based; 80 iBT), IELTS (minimum score 6). Electronic applications accepted.

University of Florida, Graduate School, College of Liberal Arts and Sciences, Department of Biology, Gainesville, FL 32611. Offers botany (MS, MST, PhD), including botany, tropical conservation and development, wetland sciences; zoology (MS, MST, PhD), including animal molecular and cellular biology (PhD), tropical conservation and development, wetland sciences, zoology. *Degree requirements:* For master's, comprehensive exam (for some programs), thesis; for doctorate, comprehensive exam, thesis/dissertation. *Entrance requirements:* For master's and doctorate, GRE General Test, minimum GPA of 3.0. Additional exam requirements/recommendations for international students: Required—TOEFL (minimum score 550 paper-based; 80 iBT), IELTS (minimum score 6). Electronic applications accepted. *Faculty research:* Ecology of natural populations, plant and animal genome evolution, biodiversity, plant biology, behavior.

University of Georgia, Franklin College of Arts and Sciences, Department of Biochemistry and Molecular Biology, Athens, GA 30602. Offers MS, PhD. *Degree requirements:* For master's, one foreign language, thesis; for doctorate, one foreign language, thesis/dissertation. *Entrance requirements:* For master's and doctorate, GRE General Test. Additional exam requirements/recommendations for international students: Required—TOEFL. Electronic applications accepted.

University of Guelph, Graduate Studies, College of Biological Science, Department of Molecular and Cellular Biology, Guelph, ON N1G 2W1, Canada. Offers biochemistry (M Sc, PhD); biophysics (M Sc, PhD); botany (M Sc, PhD); microbiology (M Sc, PhD); molecular biology and genetics (M Sc, PhD). *Degree requirements:* For master's, thesis, research proposal; for doctorate, comprehensive exam, thesis/dissertation, research proposal. *Entrance requirements:* For master's, minimum B-average during previous 2 years of coursework; for doctorate, minimum A-average. Additional exam requirements/recommendations for international students: Required—TOEFL (minimum score 550 paper-based), IELTS (minimum score 6.5). Electronic applications accepted. *Faculty research:* Physiology, structure, genetics, and ecology of microbes; virology and microbial technology.

University of Hawaii at Manoa, John A. Burns School of Medicine, Program in Cell and Molecular Biology, Honolulu, HI 96813. Offers MS, PhD. *Program availability:* Part-time. Terminal master's awarded for partial completion of doctoral program. *Degree requirements:* For master's, thesis optional; for doctorate, comprehensive exam, thesis/dissertation. *Entrance requirements:* For master's and doctorate, GRE General Test, minimum GPA of 3.0. Additional exam requirements/recommendations for international students: Required—TOEFL (minimum score 500 paper-based; 61 iBT), IELTS (minimum score 5).

University of Hawaii at Manoa, Office of Graduate Education, College of Tropical Agriculture and Human Resources, Department of Molecular Biosciences and Bioengineering, Honolulu, HI 96822. Offers bioengineering (MS); molecular bioscience and bioengineering (MS); molecular biosciences and bioengineering (PhD). *Program availability:* Part-time. *Degree requirements:* For master's, thesis optional; for doctorate, comprehensive exam, thesis/dissertation. *Entrance requirements:* For master's and doctorate, GRE General Test. Additional exam requirements/recommendations for international students: Required—TOEFL (minimum score 550 paper-based; 79 iBT), IELTS (minimum score 5). *Faculty research:* Mechanization, agricultural systems, waste management, water management, cell culture.

University of Illinois at Chicago, College of Medicine and Graduate College, Graduate Programs in Medicine, Department of Biochemistry and Molecular Genetics, Chicago, IL 60607-7128. Offers PhD, MD/PhD. Terminal master's awarded for partial completion of doctoral program. *Degree requirements:* For doctorate, thesis/dissertation. *Entrance requirements:* For doctorate, GRE General Test. Additional exam requirements/recommendations for international students: Required—TOEFL. Electronic applications accepted. *Faculty research:* Signal transduction, cell cycle regulation, membrane biology, regulation of gene function and development, protein and nucleic acid structure and function, cancer biology.

The University of Iowa, Graduate College, Program in Molecular and Cellular Biology, Iowa City, IA 52242-1316. Offers PhD. *Degree requirements:* For doctorate, comprehensive exam, thesis/dissertation. *Entrance requirements:* For doctorate, GRE General Test, minimum GPA of 3.0. Additional exam requirements/recommendations for international students: Required—TOEFL (minimum score 600 paper-based; 100 iBT). Electronic applications accepted. *Faculty research:* Regulation of gene expression, inherited human genetic diseases, signal transduction mechanisms, structural biology and function.

The University of Kansas, Graduate Studies, College of Liberal Arts and Sciences, Department of Molecular Biosciences, Lawrence, KS 66044. Offers biochemistry and biophysics (PhD); microbiology (PhD); molecular, cellular, and developmental biology (PhD). *Program availability:* Part-time. *Students:* 57 full-time (38 women); includes 8 minority (1 Black or African American, non-Hispanic/Latino; 2 Asian, non-Hispanic/Latino; 3 Hispanic/Latino; 2 Two or more races, non-Hispanic/Latino), 27 international. Average age 27. 73 applicants, 33% accepted, 8 enrolled. In 2017, 6 doctorates awarded. Terminal master's awarded for partial completion of doctoral program. *Entrance requirements:* For doctorate, GRE General Test, 1-page statement of research interests and goals, 1-2 page curriculum vitae or resume, official transcript, 3 recommendation letters. Additional exam requirements/recommendations for international students: Required—TOEFL or IELTS. *Application deadline:* For fall admission, 12/1 for domestic and international students. Application fee: $65 ($85 for international students). Electronic applications accepted. *Financial support:* Fellowships, research assistantships, teaching assistantships, scholarships/grants, health care benefits, and unspecified assistantships available. Financial award application deadline: 12/1. *Faculty research:* Structure and function of proteins, genetics of organism development, molecular genetics, neurophysiology, molecular virology and pathogenics, developmental biology, cell biology. *Unit head:* Susan M. Egan, Chair, 785-864-4294, E-mail: sme@ku.edu. *Application contact:* John Connolly, Graduate Admissions Contact, 785-864-4311, E-mail: jconnolly@ku.edu.
Website: http://www.molecularbiosciences.ku.edu/

The University of Kansas, University of Kansas Medical Center, School of Medicine, Department of Biochemistry and Molecular Biology, Kansas City, KS 66160. Offers PhD, MD/PhD. *Faculty:* 19. *Students:* 11 full-time (5 women); includes 1 minority (Black or African American, non-Hispanic/Latino), 1 international. Average age 28. In 2017, 2 doctorates awarded. Terminal master's awarded for partial completion of doctoral program. *Degree requirements:* For doctorate, thesis/dissertation, comprehensive oral and written exam. *Entrance requirements:* For doctorate, GRE. Additional exam requirements/recommendations for international students: Required—TOEFL. *Application deadline:* For fall admission, 12/1 for domestic and international students. Applications are processed on a rolling basis. Application fee: $60. Electronic applications accepted. Application fee is waived when completed online. *Financial support:* In 2017–18, 3 research assistantships with partial tuition reimbursements, 4 teaching assistantships with partial tuition reimbursements were awarded; fellowships, traineeships, health care benefits, and unspecified assistantships also available. Financial award application deadline: 3/1; financial award applicants required to submit FAFSA. *Faculty research:* Determination of protein structure, underlying bases for interaction of proteins with their target, mapping allosteric circuiting within proteins, mechanism of action of transcription factors, renal signal transduction. *Total annual research expenditures:* $2.5 million. *Unit head:* Dr. Gerald M. Carlson, Chairman, 913-588-7005, Fax: 913-588-9896, E-mail: gcarlson@kumc.edu. *Application contact:* Dr. Liskin Swint-Kruse, Professor, 913-588-0399, Fax: 913-588-9896, E-mail: lswint-kruse@kumc.edu.
Website: http://www.kumc.edu/school-of-medicine/biochemistry-and-molecular-biology.html

University of Lethbridge, School of Graduate Studies, Lethbridge, AB T1K 3M4, Canada. Offers addictions counseling (M Sc); agricultural biotechnology (M Sc); agricultural studies (M Sc, MA); anthropology (MA); archaeology (M Sc, MA); art (MA, MFA); biochemistry (M Sc); biological sciences (M Sc); biomolecular science (PhD); biosystems and biodiversity (PhD); Canadian studies (MA); chemistry (M Sc); computer science (M Sc); computer science and geographical information science (M Sc); counseling (MC); counseling psychology (M Ed); dramatic arts (MA); earth, space, and physical science (PhD); economics (MA); education (MA, PhD); educational leadership (M Ed); English (MA); environmental science (M Sc); evolution and behavior (PhD); exercise science (M Sc); French (MA); French/German (MA); French/Spanish (MA); general education (M Ed); geography (M Sc, MA); German (MA); health sciences (M Sc); individualized multidisciplinary (M Sc, MA); kinesiology (M Sc, MA); management (M Sc), including accounting, finance, human resource management and labor relations, information systems, international management, marketing, policy and strategy; mathematics (M Sc); music (M Mus, MA); Native American studies (MA); neuroscience (M Sc, PhD); new media (MA, MFA); nursing (M Sc, MN); philosophy (MA); physics (M Sc); political science (MA); psychology (M Sc, MA); religious studies (MA); sociology (MA); theatre and dramatic arts (MFA); theoretical and computational science (PhD); urban and regional studies (MA); women and gender studies (MA). *Program availability:* Part-time, evening/weekend. *Degree requirements:* For master's, thesis (for some programs); for doctorate, comprehensive exam, thesis/dissertation. *Entrance requirements:* For master's, GMAT (for M Sc in management), bachelor's degree in related field, minimum GPA of 3.0 during previous 20 graded semester courses, 2 years' teaching or related experience (M Ed); for doctorate, master's degree, minimum graduate GPA of 3.5. Additional exam requirements/recommendations for international students: Required—TOEFL (minimum score 580 paper-based; 93 iBT). Electronic applications accepted. *Faculty research:* Movement and brain plasticity, gibberellin physiology, photosynthesis, carbon cycling, molecular properties of main-group ring components.

University of Maine, Graduate School, College of Natural Sciences, Forestry, and Agriculture, Department of Molecular and Biomedical Sciences, Orono, ME 04469. Offers microbiology (PhD). *Faculty:* 11 full-time (5 women), 7 part-time/adjunct (3 women). *Students:* 18 full-time (10 women), 5 part-time (4 women); includes 2 minority (both Asian, non-Hispanic/Latino), 5 international. Average age 29. 25 applicants, 28% accepted, 6 enrolled. In 2017, 3 master's, 2 doctorates awarded. *Degree requirements:* For master's, thesis (for some programs); for doctorate, comprehensive exam, thesis/dissertation. *Entrance requirements:* For master's and doctorate, GRE General Test. Additional exam requirements/recommendations for international students: Required—TOEFL (minimum score 580 paper-based; 92 iBT), IELTS (minimum score 7). *Application deadline:* For fall admission, 1/15 for domestic and international students; for spring admission, 9/15 for domestic and international students. Applications are processed on a rolling basis. Application fee: $65. Electronic applications accepted. *Expenses:* Tuition, state resident: full-time $7722; part-time $429 per credit hour. Tuition, nonresident: full-time $25,146; part-time $1397 per credit hour. *Required fees:* $1162; $581 per credit hour. *Financial support:* In 2017–18, 19 students received support, including 1 fellowship with full tuition reimbursement available (averaging $23,100 per year), 7 research assistantships with full tuition reimbursements available (averaging $23,300 per year), 11 teaching assistantships with full tuition reimbursements available (averaging $21,700 per year); tuition waivers (full and partial) also available. Financial award application deadline: 3/1. *Faculty research:* Immunology and microbiology, bioinformatics, molecular and cellular toxicology, zebrafish, signal transduction, protein biochemistry. *Total annual research expenditures:* $1.6 million. *Unit head:* Dr. Robert Gundersen, Chair, 207-581-2802, Fax: 207-581-2801. *Application contact:* Scott G. Delcourt, Assistant Vice President for Graduate Studies and Senior Associate Dean, 207-581-3291, Fax: 207-581-3232, E-mail: graduate@maine.edu.
Website: http://umaine.edu/biomed/

The University of Manchester, School of Biological Sciences, Manchester, United Kingdom. Offers adaptive organismal biology (M Phil, PhD); animal biology (M Phil, PhD); biochemistry (M Phil, PhD); bioinformatics (M Phil, PhD); biomolecular sciences (M Phil, PhD); biotechnology (M Phil, PhD); cell biology (M Phil, PhD); cell matrix research (M Phil, PhD); channels and transporters (M Phil, PhD); developmental biology (M Phil, PhD); environmental biology (M Phil, PhD); evolutionary biology (M Phil, PhD); gene expression (M Phil, PhD); genetics (M Phil, PhD); history of science, technology and medicine (M Phil, PhD); immunology (M Phil, PhD); integrative neurobiology and behavior (M Phil, PhD); membrane trafficking (M Phil, PhD); microbiology (M Phil, PhD); molecular and cellular neuroscience (M Phil, PhD); molecular biology (M Phil, PhD); molecular cancer studies (M Phil, PhD); neuroscience (M Phil, PhD); ophthalmology (M Phil, PhD); optometry (M Phil, PhD); organelle function (M Phil, PhD); pharmacology (M Phil, PhD); physiology (M Phil, PhD); plant sciences (M Phil, PhD); stem cell research (M Phil, PhD); structural biology (M Phil, PhD); systems neuroscience (M Phil, PhD); toxicology (M Phil, PhD).

Molecular Biology

The University of Manchester, School of Dentistry, Manchester, United Kingdom. Offers basic dental sciences (cancer studies) (M Phil, PhD); basic dental sciences (molecular genetics) (M Phil, PhD); basic dental sciences (stem cell biology) (M Phil, PhD); biomaterials sciences and dental technology (M Phil, PhD); dental public health/community dentistry (M Phil, PhD); dental science (clinical) (PhD); endodontology (M Phil, PhD); fixed and removable prosthodontics (M Phil, PhD); operative dentistry (M Phil, PhD); oral and maxillofacial surgery (M Phil, PhD); oral radiology (M Phil, PhD); orthodontics (M Phil, PhD); restorative dentistry (M Phil, PhD).

University of Maryland, Baltimore, Graduate School, Graduate Program in Life Sciences, Program in Biochemistry and Molecular Biology, Baltimore, MD 21201. Offers biochemistry (MS, PhD); MD/PhD. *Students:* 26 full-time (15 women), 4 part-time (3 women); includes 9 minority (4 Black or African American, non-Hispanic/Latino; 3 Asian, non-Hispanic/Latino; 2 Hispanic/Latino), 5 international. Average age 27. 35 applicants, 34% accepted, 4 enrolled. In 2017, 3 master's, 6 doctorates awarded. *Degree requirements:* For doctorate, comprehensive exam, thesis/dissertation. *Entrance requirements:* For master's and doctorate, GRE General Test, minimum GPA of 3.0, curriculum vitae, essay, 3 letters of recommendation. Additional exam requirements/recommendations for international students: Required—TOEFL (minimum score 80 iBT); Recommended—IELTS (minimum score 7). *Application deadline:* For fall admission, 1/15 for domestic and international students. Application fee: $75. Electronic applications accepted. *Expenses:* Tuition, state resident: full-time $13,990; part-time $661 per credit. Tuition, nonresident: full-time $30,484; part-time $1310 per credit. *Required fees:* $1894; $94 per credit. $415 per semester. Part-time tuition and fees vary according to course load, degree level and program. *Financial support:* In 2017–18, research assistantships with full tuition reimbursements (averaging $26,000 per year) were awarded; fellowships, health care benefits, and unspecified assistantships also available. Financial award application deadline: 3/1; financial award applicants required to submit FAFSA. *Faculty research:* Membrane transport, hormonal regulation, protein structure, molecular virology. *Unit head:* Dr. Gerald Wilson, Professor/Director, 410-706-8904. *Application contact:* Kiriaki Cozmo, Program Coordinator, 410-706-7340, Fax: 410-706-8297, E-mail: kicozmo@som.umaryland.edu.
Website: http://medschool.umaryland.edu/biochemistry/

University of Maryland, Baltimore, Graduate School, Graduate Program in Life Sciences, Program in Cellular and Molecular Biomedical Science, Baltimore, MD 21201. Offers MS. *Program availability:* Part-time. *Students:* 15 full-time (12 women), 8 part-time (5 women); includes 7 minority (4 Black or African American, non-Hispanic/Latino; 2 Asian, non-Hispanic/Latino; 1 Hispanic/Latino), 8 international. Average age 28. 41 applicants, 61% accepted, 5 enrolled. In 2017, 9 master's awarded. *Degree requirements:* For master's, thesis (for some programs). *Entrance requirements:* For master's, GRE General Test, minimum GPA of 3.0, curriculum vitae, essay, 3 letters of recommendation. Additional exam requirements/recommendations for international students: Required—TOEFL (minimum score 80 iBT); Recommended—IELTS (minimum score 7). *Application deadline:* For fall admission, 4/15 priority date for domestic students, 1/15 for international students. Application fee: $75. Electronic applications accepted. *Expenses:* Tuition, state resident: full-time $13,990; part-time $661 per credit. Tuition, nonresident: full-time $30,484; part-time $1310 per credit. *Required fees:* $1894; $94 per credit. $415 per semester. Part-time tuition and fees vary according to course load, degree level and program. *Financial support:* Fellowships, Federal Work-Study, and unspecified assistantships available. Financial award application deadline: 3/1; financial award applicants required to submit FAFSA. *Unit head:* Dr. Dudley Strickland, Director, Graduate Program in Life Sciences, 410-706-8010. *Application contact:* Keith T. Brooks, Assistant Dean, 410-706-7131, Fax: 410-706-3473, E-mail: kbrooks@umaryland.edu.

University of Maryland, Baltimore, Graduate School, Graduate Program in Life Sciences, Program in Molecular Medicine, Baltimore, MD 21201. Offers cancer biology (PhD); cell and molecular physiology (PhD); human genetics and genomic medicine (PhD); molecular toxicology and pharmacology (PhD); MD/PhD. *Students:* 62 full-time (35 women), 2 part-time (0 women); includes 21 minority (7 Black or African American, non-Hispanic/Latino; 8 Asian, non-Hispanic/Latino; 4 Hispanic/Latino; 2 Two or more races, non-Hispanic/Latino), 4 international. Average age 27. 89 applicants, 30% accepted, 3 enrolled. In 2017, 13 doctorates awarded. *Degree requirements:* For doctorate, comprehensive exam, thesis/dissertation. *Entrance requirements:* For doctorate, GRE, minimum GPA of 3.0, curriculum vitae, essay, 3 letters of recommendation. Additional exam requirements/recommendations for international students: Required—TOEFL (minimum score 80 iBT); Recommended—IELTS (minimum score 7). *Application deadline:* For fall admission, 12/1 priority date for domestic students, 1/15 for international students. Application fee: $75. Electronic applications accepted. *Expenses:* Tuition, state resident: full-time $13,990; part-time $661 per credit. Tuition, nonresident: full-time $30,484; part-time $1310 per credit. *Required fees:* $1894; $94 per credit. $415 per semester. Part-time tuition and fees vary according to course load, degree level and program. *Financial support:* In 2017–18, research assistantships with partial tuition reimbursements (averaging $26,000 per year) were awarded; fellowships and health care benefits also available. Financial award application deadline: 3/1; financial award applicants required to submit FAFSA. *Unit head:* Dr. Toni Antalis, Director, 410-706-8222, E-mail: tantalis@som.umaryland.edu. *Application contact:* Marcina Garner, Program Coordinator, 410-706-6044, Fax: 410-706-6040, E-mail: mgarner@som.umaryland.edu.
Website: http://molecularmedicine.umaryland.edu

University of Maryland, Baltimore County, The Graduate School, College of Natural and Mathematical Sciences, Department of Biological Sciences, Program in Applied Molecular Biology, Baltimore, MD 21250. Offers MS. *Faculty:* 26 full-time (11 women). *Students:* 6 full-time (3 women), 2 part-time (1 woman); includes 1 minority (Asian, non-Hispanic/Latino), 1 international. Average age 27. 25 applicants, 44% accepted, 8 enrolled. In 2017, 7 master's awarded. *Entrance requirements:* For master's, GRE General Test, GRE Subject Test (recommended), minimum GPA of 3.0. Additional exam requirements/recommendations for international students: Required—TOEFL (minimum score 600 paper-based; 80 iBT), IELTS (minimum score 6.5). *Application deadline:* For fall admission, 2/1 priority date for domestic and international students. Applications are processed on a rolling basis. Application fee: $50. Electronic applications accepted. *Expenses: Required fees:* $132. *Financial support:* Applicants required to submit FAFSA. *Faculty research:* Structure-function of RNA, genetics and molecular biology, biological chemistry. *Unit head:* Dr. Michelle Starz-Gaiano, Director, Applied Molecular Biology Graduate Program, 410-455-2217, Fax: 410-455-3875, E-mail: biograd@umbc.edu. *Application contact:* Brandy Darcey, Graduate Program Coordinator, 410-455-3669, Fax: 410-455-3875, E-mail: bdarcey@umbc.edu.
Website: http://biology.umbc.edu/grad/graduate-programs/apmb/

University of Maryland, Baltimore County, The Graduate School, College of Natural and Mathematical Sciences, Department of Biological Sciences, Program in Molecular and Cell Biology, Baltimore, MD 21250. Offers PhD. *Faculty:* 26 full-time (11 women). *Students:* 2 full-time (both women), 1 international. Average age 23. 25 applicants, 44% accepted, 2 enrolled. In 2017, 1 doctorate awarded. *Degree requirements:* For doctorate, thesis/dissertation. *Entrance requirements:* For doctorate, GRE General Test, GRE Subject Test, minimum GPA of 3.0. Additional exam requirements/recommendations for international students: Required—TOEFL (minimum score 80 iBT), IELTS (minimum score 6.5). *Application deadline:* For fall admission, 4/15 priority date for domestic and international students. Application fee: $50. Electronic applications accepted. *Expenses: Required fees:* $132. *Financial support:* In 2017–18, 2 students received support, including 1 research assistantship with full tuition reimbursement available (averaging $24,600 per year), 1 teaching assistantship with full tuition reimbursement available (averaging $24,600 per year); unspecified assistantships also available. *Unit head:* Dr. Michelle Starz-Gaiano, Director, 410-455-2217, Fax: 410-455-3875, E-mail: biograd@umbc.edu. *Application contact:* Brandy Darcey, Graduate Program Coordinator, 410-4553669, E-mail: bdarcey@umbc.edu.
Website: http://biology.umbc.edu/grad/graduate-programs/mocb/

University of Maryland, College Park, Academic Affairs, College of Computer, Mathematical and Natural Sciences, Department of Biology, PhD Program in Biological Sciences, College Park, MD 20742. Offers behavior, ecology, evolution, and systematics (PhD); computational biology, bioinformatics, and genomics (PhD); molecular and cellular biology (PhD); physiological systems (PhD). *Degree requirements:* For doctorate, comprehensive exam, thesis/dissertation, thesis work presentation in seminar. *Entrance requirements:* For doctorate, GRE General Test; GRE Subject Test in biology (recommended), academic transcripts, statement of purpose/research interests, 3 letters of recommendation. Additional exam requirements/recommendations for international students: Required—TOEFL. Electronic applications accepted.

University of Maryland, College Park, Academic Affairs, College of Computer, Mathematical and Natural Sciences, Department of Cell Biology and Molecular Genetics, Program in Molecular and Cellular Biology, College Park, MD 20742. Offers PhD. *Program availability:* Part-time, evening/weekend. *Degree requirements:* For doctorate, thesis/dissertation, exam, public service. *Faculty research:* Monoclonal antibody production, oligonucleotide synthesis, macronolular processing, signal transduction, developmental biology.

University of Miami, Graduate School, Miller School of Medicine, Graduate Programs in Medicine, Department of Biochemistry and Molecular Biology, Coral Gables, FL 33124. Offers PhD, MD/PhD. *Degree requirements:* For doctorate, comprehensive exam, thesis/dissertation, proposition exams. *Faculty research:* Macromolecule metabolism, molecular genetics, protein folding and 3-D structure, regulation of gene expression and enzyme function, signal transduction and developmental biology.

University of Miami, Graduate School, Miller School of Medicine, Graduate Programs in Medicine, Department of Cell Biology and Anatomy, Coral Gables, FL 33124. Offers molecular cell and developmental biology (PhD); MD/PhD. *Degree requirements:* For doctorate, thesis/dissertation. *Entrance requirements:* For doctorate, GRE General Test, GRE Subject Test. Additional exam requirements/recommendations for international students: Required—TOEFL. Electronic applications accepted.

University of Michigan, Rackham Graduate School, College of Literature, Science, and the Arts, Department of Molecular, Cellular, and Developmental Biology, Ann Arbor, MI 48109. Offers MS, PhD. *Program availability:* Part-time. *Faculty:* 37 full-time (12 women). *Students:* 85 full-time (51 women); includes 10 minority (2 Black or African American, non-Hispanic/Latino; 2 Asian, non-Hispanic/Latino; 6 Hispanic/Latino), 44 international. Average age 26. 139 applicants, 27% accepted, 23 enrolled. In 2017, 6 master's, 10 doctorates awarded. Terminal master's awarded for partial completion of doctoral program. *Degree requirements:* For master's, thesis (for some programs), 24 credits with at least 16 in molecular, cellular, and developmental biology and 4 in a cognate field; for doctorate, comprehensive exam, thesis/dissertation, preliminary exam, oral defense. *Entrance requirements:* Additional exam requirements/recommendations for international students: Required—TOEFL (minimum score 560 paper-based; 83 iBT). *Application deadline:* For fall admission, 12/15 for domestic and international students; for winter admission, 11/1 for domestic and international students; for spring admission, 4/1 for domestic students. Application fee: $75 ($90 for international students). Electronic applications accepted. *Expenses:* $11,184 in-state; $22,578 out of state; $5,954 candidacy. *Financial support:* In 2017–18, 65 students received support, including 23 fellowships with full tuition reimbursements available (averaging $30,600 per year), 32 research assistantships with full tuition reimbursements available (averaging $30,600 per year), 21 teaching assistantships with full tuition reimbursements available (averaging $30,600 per year); traineeships and health care benefits also available. Financial award application deadline: 12/15. *Faculty research:* Cell biology, microbiology, neurobiology and physiology, developmental biology and plant molecular biology. *Total annual research expenditures:* $8.9 million. *Unit head:* Dr. Robert J. Denver, Department Chair, 734-764-7476, Fax: 734-615-6337, E-mail: rdenver@umich.edu. *Application contact:* Mary Carr, Graduate Coordinator, 734-615-1635, Fax: 734-764-0884, E-mail: carrmm@umich.edu.
Website: http://www.mcdb.lsa.umich.edu

University of Michigan, Rackham Graduate School, Program in Biomedical Sciences (PIBS), Interdisciplinary Program in Cellular and Molecular Biology, Ann Arbor, MI 48109. Offers PhD. *Faculty:* 166 part-time/adjunct (43 women). *Students:* 52 full-time (35 women); includes 17 minority (1 Black or African American, non-Hispanic/Latino; 9 Asian, non-Hispanic/Latino; 5 Hispanic/Latino; 2 Two or more races, non-Hispanic/Latino). Average age 27. 71 applicants, 49% accepted, 7 enrolled. In 2017, 27 doctorates awarded. *Degree requirements:* For doctorate, comprehensive exam, thesis/dissertation, preliminary exam; oral defense of dissertation. *Entrance requirements:* For doctorate, GRE General Test. Additional exam requirements/recommendations for international students: Required—TOEFL (minimum score 560 paper-based; 84 iBT), IELTS (minimum score 6.5), Michigan English Language Assessment Battery. *Application deadline:* For fall admission, 12/1 for domestic students. Application fee: $75 ($90 for international students). Electronic applications accepted. *Expenses:* Contact institution. *Financial support:* In 2017–18, 52 students received support, including 36 fellowships with full tuition reimbursements available (averaging $30,600 per year), 3 research assistantships with full tuition reimbursements available (averaging $30,600 per year), 13 teaching assistantships with full tuition reimbursements available (averaging $30,600 per year); scholarships/grants, traineeships, and health care benefits also available. *Faculty research:* Cell and systems biology, cell physiology, biochemistry, genetics/gene regulation, genomics/proteomics, computational biology, microbial pathogenesis, immunology, development, aging, neurobiology, molecular mechanisms of disease, cancer biology. *Total annual research expenditures:* $20 million. *Unit head:* Dr. Robert S. Fuller, Director, 734-936-9764, Fax: 734-763-7799, E-mail: bfuller@umich.edu. *Application contact:* Patricia Ocelnik, Program Administrator, 734-764-5428, Fax: 734-647-7022, E-mail: cmbgrad@umich.edu.
Website: http://cmb.medicine.umich.edu

University of Minnesota, Duluth, Medical School, Department of Biochemistry, Molecular Biology and Biophysics, Duluth, MN 55812-2496. Offers biochemistry, molecular biology and biophysics (MS); biology and biophysics (PhD); social, administrative, and clinical pharmacy (MS, PhD); toxicology (MS, PhD). Terminal master's awarded for partial completion of doctoral program. *Degree requirements:* For master's, comprehensive exam, thesis; for doctorate, comprehensive exam, thesis/dissertation. *Entrance requirements:* For master's and doctorate, GRE General Test. Additional exam requirements/recommendations for international students: Required—

TOEFL. Electronic applications accepted. *Faculty research:* Intestinal cancer biology; hepatotoxins and mitochondriopathies; toxicology; cell cycle regulation in stem cells; neurobiology of brain development, trace metal function and blood-brain barrier; hibernation biology.

University of Minnesota, Twin Cities Campus, Graduate School, College of Biological Sciences, Biochemistry, Molecular Biology and Biophysics Graduate Program, Minneapolis, MN 55455-0213. Offers PhD. *Degree requirements:* For doctorate, thesis/dissertation. *Entrance requirements:* For doctorate, GRE, 3 letters of recommendation, more than 1 semester of laboratory experience. Additional exam requirements/recommendations for international students: Required—TOEFL (minimum score 625 paper-based; 108 iBT with writing subsection 25 and reading subsection 25) or IELTS (minimum score 7). Electronic applications accepted. *Faculty research:* Microbial biochemistry, biotechnology, molecular biology, regulatory biochemistry, structural biology and biophysics, physical biochemistry, enzymology, physiological chemistry.

University of Minnesota, Twin Cities Campus, Graduate School, Program in Molecular, Cellular, Developmental Biology and Genetics, Minneapolis, MN 55455-0213. Offers genetic counseling (MS); molecular, cellular, developmental biology and genetics (PhD). Terminal master's awarded for partial completion of doctoral program. *Degree requirements:* For master's, thesis optional; for doctorate, thesis/dissertation. *Entrance requirements:* For master's and doctorate, GRE General Test. Additional exam requirements/recommendations for international students: Required—TOEFL (minimum score 625 paper-based; 80 iBT). Electronic applications accepted. *Faculty research:* Membrane receptors and membrane transport, cell interactions, cytoskeleton and cell mobility, regulation of gene expression, plant cell and molecular biology.

University of Missouri–Kansas City, School of Biological Sciences, Program in Molecular Biology and Biochemistry, Kansas City, MO 64110-2499. Offers PhD. Offered through the School of Graduate Studies. *Degree requirements:* For doctorate, comprehensive exam, thesis/dissertation. *Entrance requirements:* For doctorate, GRE General Test, bachelor's degree in chemistry, biology, or a related discipline; minimum GPA of 3.0. Additional exam requirements/recommendations for international students: Required—TOEFL (minimum score 550 paper-based; 80 iBT).

University of Montana, Graduate School, College of Humanities and Sciences, Division of Biological Sciences, Program in Cellular, Molecular and Microbial Biology, Missoula, MT 59812. Offers cellular and developmental biology (PhD); microbial evolution and ecology (PhD); microbiology and immunology (PhD); molecular biology and biochemistry (PhD). Terminal master's awarded for partial completion of doctoral program. *Degree requirements:* For doctorate, variable foreign language requirement, thesis/dissertation. *Entrance requirements:* For doctorate, GRE General Test. *Faculty research:* Ribosome structure, medical microbiology/pathogenesis, microbial ecology/environmental microbiology.

University of Nebraska Medical Center, Interdisciplinary Graduate Program in Biomedical Sciences, Department of Biochemistry and Molecular Biology, Omaha, NE 68198-5870. Offers MS. *Faculty:* 27 full-time (8 women). *Students:* 45 full-time (26 women); includes 4 minority (3 Asian, non-Hispanic/Latino; 1 Two or more races, non-Hispanic/Latino), 21 international. Average age 28. 13 applicants, 85% accepted, 9 enrolled. Terminal master's awarded for partial completion of doctoral program. *Degree requirements:* For master's, comprehensive exam, thesis. *Entrance requirements:* For master's, GRE General Test. Additional exam requirements/recommendations for international students: Required—TOEFL (minimum score 550 paper-based). *Application deadline:* For fall admission, 6/1 for domestic students, 4/1 for international students; for spring admission, 8/1 for domestic and international students; for summer admission, 1/1 for domestic and international students. Application fee: $45. Electronic applications accepted. Application fee is waived when completed online. *Expenses:* Tuition, state resident: full-time $8451; part-time $4225 per semester. Tuition, nonresident: full-time $24,219; part-time $11,295 per semester. *Required fees:* $589; $117 per term. *Financial support:* In 2017–18, 13 students received support, including 4 fellowships with full tuition reimbursements available (averaging $23,100 per year), 7 research assistantships with full tuition reimbursements available (averaging $23,100 per year); scholarships/grants, health care benefits, and unspecified assistantships also available. Financial award application deadline: 2/15; financial award applicants required to submit FAFSA. *Faculty research:* Biochemistry and molecular biology, including DNA replication, gene regulation, cell-cell communications, structural biology, receptor endocytosis and protein trafficking, nutrition, enzymology, endocrinology, and metabolism (protein, lipid, and carbohydrate). *Total annual research expenditures:* $4.2 million. *Unit head:* Dr. Kaustubh Datta, Chairman, Graduate Committee, 402-559-7404, Fax: 402-559-6650, E-mail: kaustubh.datta@unmc.edu. *Application contact:* Karen Hankins, Office Associate, 402-559-4417, E-mail: karen.hankins@unmc.edu.
Website: http://www.unmc.edu/biochemistry/

University of Nevada, Reno, Graduate School, Interdisciplinary Program in Cell and Molecular Biology, Reno, NV 89557. Offers MS, PhD. Terminal master's awarded for partial completion of doctoral program. *Degree requirements:* For master's, thesis; for doctorate, thesis/dissertation. *Entrance requirements:* For master's, GRE Subject Test (recommended), minimum GPA of 2.75; for doctorate, GRE Subject Test (recommended), minimum GPA of 3.0. Additional exam requirements/recommendations for international students: Required—TOEFL (minimum score 500 paper-based; 61 iBT), IELTS (minimum score 6). Electronic applications accepted. *Faculty research:* Cellular biology, biophysics, cancer, microbiology, insect biochemistry.

University of New Haven, Graduate School, College of Arts and Sciences, Program in Cellular and Molecular Biology, West Haven, CT 06516. Offers MS. *Program availability:* Part-time, evening/weekend. *Faculty:* 10 full-time (5 women), 8 part-time/adjunct (4 women). *Students:* 39 full-time (21 women), 8 part-time (6 women); includes 10 minority (5 Black or African American, non-Hispanic/Latino; 2 Asian, non-Hispanic/Latino; 2 Hispanic/Latino; 1 Two or more races, non-Hispanic/Latino), 10 international. Average age 26. 56 applicants, 91% accepted, 22 enrolled. In 2017, 24 master's awarded. *Entrance requirements:* Additional exam requirements/recommendations for international students: Required—TOEFL (minimum score 80 iBT), IELTS, PTE. *Application deadline:* Applications are processed on a rolling basis. Application fee: $50. Electronic applications accepted. Application fee is waived when completed online. *Expenses: Tuition:* Full-time $16,020; part-time $890 per credit hour. *Required fees:* $220; $90 per term. *Financial support:* Research assistantships with partial tuition reimbursements, teaching assistantships with partial tuition reimbursements, Federal Work-Study, scholarships/grants, and unspecified assistantships available. Support available to part-time students. Financial award application deadline: 5/1; financial award applicants required to submit FAFSA. *Unit head:* Dr. Christina Zito, Assistant Professor, 203-479-4299, E-mail: czito@newhaven.edu.
Website: http://www.newhaven.edu/4724/

University of New Mexico, Graduate Studies, Health Sciences Center, Program in Biomedical Sciences, Albuquerque, NM 87131-5196. Offers biochemistry and molecular biology (MS, PhD); cell biology and physiology (MS, PhD); molecular genetics and microbiology (MS, PhD); neuroscience (MS, PhD); pathology (MS, PhD); toxicology (MS, PhD). *Program availability:* Part-time. *Students:* Average age 29. 61 applicants, 16% accepted, 10 enrolled. In 2017, 11 master's, 14 doctorates awarded. Terminal master's awarded for partial completion of doctoral program. *Degree requirements:* For master's, thesis; for doctorate, comprehensive exam, thesis/dissertation, qualifying exam at the end of year 1/core curriculum. *Entrance requirements:* For master's and doctorate, GRE General Test, minimum undergraduate GPA of 3.0. Additional exam requirements/recommendations for international students: Required—TOEFL. *Application deadline:* For fall admission, 3/1 priority date for domestic and international students. Applications are processed on a rolling basis. Application fee: $50. Electronic applications accepted. *Financial support:* Fellowships, research assistantships with full tuition reimbursements, teaching assistantships, career-related internships or fieldwork, Federal Work-Study, institutionally sponsored loans, scholarships/grants, traineeships, health care benefits, and unspecified assistantships available. Financial award application deadline: 1/1; financial award applicants required to submit FAFSA. *Faculty research:* Infectious disease/immunity, cancer biology, cardiovascular and metabolic diseases, brain and behavioral illness, environmental health. *Unit head:* Dr. Helen J. Hathaway, Program Director, 505-272-1887, Fax: 505-272-2412, E-mail: hhathaway@salud.unm.edu. *Application contact:* Mary Fenton, Admissions Coordinator, 505-272-1887, Fax: 505-272-2412, E-mail: mfenton@salud.unm.edu.

The University of North Carolina at Chapel Hill, Graduate School, College of Arts and Sciences, Department of Biology, Chapel Hill, NC 27599. Offers botany (MA, MS, PhD); cell biology, development, and physiology (MA, MS, PhD); cell motility and cytoskeleton (PhD); ecology and behavior (MA, MS, PhD); genetics and molecular biology (MA, MS, PhD); morphology, systematics, and evolution (MA, MS, PhD). Terminal master's awarded for partial completion of doctoral program. *Degree requirements:* For master's, comprehensive exam, thesis (for some programs); for doctorate, comprehensive exam, thesis/dissertation. *Entrance requirements:* For master's, GRE General Test, GRE Subject Test, 2 semesters of calculus or statistics; 2 semesters of physics, organic chemistry; 3 semesters of biology; for doctorate, GRE General Test, GRE Subject Test, 2 semesters calculus or statistics, 2 semesters physics, organic chemistry, 3 semesters of biology. Additional exam requirements/recommendations for international students: Required—TOEFL (minimum score 550 paper-based). Electronic applications accepted. *Faculty research:* Gene expression, biomechanics, yeast genetics, plant ecology, plant molecular biology.

The University of North Carolina at Chapel Hill, School of Medicine and Graduate School, Graduate Programs in Medicine, Curriculum in Genetics and Molecular Biology, Chapel Hill, NC 27599. Offers MS, PhD. *Degree requirements:* For doctorate, comprehensive exam, thesis/dissertation. *Entrance requirements:* For doctorate, GRE, minimum GPA of 3.0. Additional exam requirements/recommendations for international students: Required—TOEFL. Electronic applications accepted. *Faculty research:* Telomere replication and germline immortality, experimental evolution in microorganisms, genetic vulnerabilities in tumor genomes, genetics of cell cycle control during Drosophila development, mammalian genetics.

University of North Texas, Robert B. Toulouse School of Graduate Studies, Denton, TX 76203-5459. Offers accounting (MS); applied anthropology (MA, MS); applied behavior analysis (Certificate); applied geography (MA); applied technology and performance improvement (M Ed, MS); art education (MA); art history (MA); art museum education (Certificate); arts leadership (Certificate); audiology (Au D); behavior analysis (MS); behavioral science (PhD); biochemistry and molecular biology (MS); biology (MA, MS); biomedical engineering (MS); business analysis (MS); chemistry (MS); clinical health psychology (PhD); communication studies (MA, MS); computer engineering (MS); computer science (MS); counseling (M Ed, MS), including clinical mental health counseling (MS), college and university counseling, elementary school counseling, secondary school counseling; creative writing (MA); criminal justice (MS); curriculum and instruction (M Ed); decision sciences (MBA); design (MA, MFA), including fashion design (MFA), innovation studies, interior design (MFA); early childhood studies (MS), economics (MS); educational leadership (M Ed, Ed D); educational psychology (MS, PhD), including family studies (MS), gifted and talented (MS), human development (MS), learning and cognition (MS), research, measurement and evaluation (MS); electrical engineering (MS); emergency management (MPA); engineering technology (MS); English (MA); English as a second language (MA); environmental science (MS); finance (MBA, MS); financial management (MPA); French (MA); health services management (MBA); higher education (M Ed, Ed D); history (MA, MS); hospitality management (MS); human resources management (MPA); information science (MS); information systems (PhD); information technologies (MBA); interdisciplinary studies (MA, MS); international studies (MA); international sustainable tourism (MS); jazz studies (MM); journalism (MA, MJ, Graduate Certificate), including interactive and virtual digital communication (Graduate Certificate), narrative journalism (Graduate Certificate), public relations (Graduate Certificate); kinesiology (MS); linguistics (MA); local government management (MPA); logistics (PhD); logistics and supply chain management (MBA); long-term care, senior housing, and aging services (MA); management (PhD); marketing (MBA); mathematics (MA, MS); mechanical and energy engineering (MS, PhD); music (MA), including ethnomusicology, music theory, musicology, performance; music composition (PhD); music education (MM Ed, PhD); nonprofit management (MPA); operations and supply chain management (MBA); performance (MM, DMA); philosophy (MA); political science (MA); professional and technical communication (MA); radio, television and film (MA, MFA); rehabilitation counseling (Certificate); sociology (MA); Spanish (MA); special education (M Ed); speech-language pathology (MA); strategic management (MBA); studio art (MFA); teaching (M Ed); MBA/MS. *Program availability:* Part-time, evening/weekend, online learning. Terminal master's awarded for partial completion of doctoral program. *Degree requirements:* For master's, variable foreign language requirement, comprehensive exam (for some programs), thesis (for some programs); for doctorate, variable foreign language requirement, comprehensive exam (for some programs), thesis/dissertation; for other advanced degree, variable foreign language requirement, comprehensive exam (for some programs). *Entrance requirements:* For master's and doctorate, GRE, GMAT. Additional exam requirements/recommendations for international students: Required—TOEFL (minimum score 550 paper-based; 79 iBT). Electronic applications accepted.

University of Notre Dame, Graduate School, College of Science, Department of Biological Sciences, Notre Dame, IN 46556. Offers aquatic ecology, evolution and environmental biology (MS, PhD); cellular and molecular biology (MS, PhD); genetics (MS, PhD); physiology (MS, PhD); vector biology and parasitology (MS, PhD). Terminal master's awarded for partial completion of doctoral program. *Degree requirements:* For master's, comprehensive exam, thesis; for doctorate, comprehensive exam, thesis/dissertation, candidacy exam. *Entrance requirements:* For master's and doctorate, GRE General Test. Additional exam requirements/recommendations for international students: Required—TOEFL (minimum score 600 paper-based; 80 iBT). Electronic applications accepted. *Faculty research:* Tropical disease, molecular genetics, neurobiology, evolutionary biology, aquatic biology.

University of Oklahoma Health Sciences Center, College of Medicine and Graduate College, Graduate Programs in Medicine, Department of Biochemistry and Molecular Biology, Oklahoma City, OK 73190. Offers biochemistry (MS, PhD); molecular biology (MS, PhD). *Program availability:* Part-time. Terminal master's awarded for partial completion of doctoral program. *Degree requirements:* For master's, thesis; for doctorate, thesis/dissertation. *Entrance requirements:* For master's, GRE General Test,

2 letters of recommendation; for doctorate, GRE General Test, 3 letters of recommendation. Additional exam requirements/recommendations for international students: Required—TOEFL. *Faculty research:* Gene expression, regulation of transcription, enzyme evolution, melanogenesis, signal transduction.

University of Oregon, Graduate School, College of Arts and Sciences, Department of Biology, Eugene, OR 97403. Offers ecology and evolution (MA, MS, PhD); marine biology (MA, MS, PhD); molecular, cellular and genetic biology (PhD); neuroscience and development (PhD). Terminal master's awarded for partial completion of doctoral program. *Degree requirements:* For master's, thesis (for some programs); for doctorate, thesis/dissertation. *Entrance requirements:* For master's and doctorate, GRE General Test, minimum GPA of 3.2. Additional exam requirements/recommendations for international students: Required—TOEFL. *Faculty research:* Developmental neurobiology; evolution, population biology, and quantitative genetics; regulation of gene expression; biochemistry of marine organisms.

University of Ottawa, Faculty of Graduate and Postdoctoral Studies, Faculty of Medicine, Department of Cellular and Molecular Medicine, Ottawa, ON K1H 8M5, Canada. Offers M Sc, PhD. *Degree requirements:* For master's, thesis, seminar; for doctorate, comprehensive exam, thesis/dissertation, seminar. *Entrance requirements:* For master's, honors degree or equivalent, minimum B average; for doctorate, master's degree, minimum B+ average. Electronic applications accepted. *Faculty research:* Physiology, pharmacology, growth and development.

University of Pennsylvania, Perelman School of Medicine, Biomedical Graduate Studies, Graduate Group in Cell and Molecular Biology, Philadelphia, PA 19104. Offers cancer biology (PhD); cell biology, physiology, and metabolism (PhD); developmental stem cell regenerative biology (PhD); gene therapy and vaccines (PhD); genetics and gene regulation (PhD); microbiology, virology, and parasitology (PhD); MD/PhD; VMD/PhD. *Faculty:* 363. *Students:* 343 full-time (197 women); includes 114 minority (7 Black or African American, non-Hispanic/Latino; 51 Asian, non-Hispanic/Latino; 41 Hispanic/Latino; 15 Two or more races, non-Hispanic/Latino), 50 international. 588 applicants, 22% accepted, 61 enrolled. In 2017, 61 doctorates awarded. *Degree requirements:* For doctorate, thesis/dissertation. *Entrance requirements:* For doctorate, GRE General Test. Additional exam requirements/recommendations for international students: Required—TOEFL. *Application deadline:* For fall admission, 12/1 priority date for domestic and international students. Applications are processed on a rolling basis. Application fee: $80. Electronic applications accepted. *Financial support:* In 2017–18, 339 students received support. Fellowships, research assistantships, teaching assistantships, and tuition waivers available. *Unit head:* Dr. Daniel Kessler, Graduate Group Chair, 215-898-1478. *Application contact:* Meagan Schofer, Coordinator, 215-898-1478.
Website: http://www.med.upenn.edu/camb/

University of Pittsburgh, Kenneth P. Dietrich School of Arts and Sciences, Department of Biological Sciences, Program in Molecular, Cellular, and Developmental Biology, Pittsburgh, PA 15260. Offers PhD. *Program availability:* Part-time, online learning. *Faculty:* 23 full-time (6 women). *Students:* 38 full-time (20 women); includes 2 minority (1 Black or African American, non-Hispanic/Latino; 1 Asian, non-Hispanic/Latino), 7 international. Average age 23. In 2017, 5 doctorates awarded. *Degree requirements:* For doctorate, comprehensive exam, thesis/dissertation, completion of research integrity module. *Entrance requirements:* For doctorate, GRE General Test, GRE Subject Test. Additional exam requirements/recommendations for international students: Required—TOEFL (minimum score 90 iBT). *Application deadline:* Applications are processed on a rolling basis. Application fee: $0. Electronic applications accepted. *Financial support:* In 2017–18, 23 fellowships with full tuition reimbursements (averaging $34,776 per year), 63 research assistantships with full tuition reimbursements (averaging $28,800 per year), 20 teaching assistantships with full tuition reimbursements (averaging $28,250 per year) were awarded; Federal Work-Study, traineeships, health care benefits, and tuition waivers also available. *Unit head:* Dr. Karen M. Arndt, Professor, 412-624-6963, Fax: 412-624-4349, E-mail: arndt@pitt.edu. *Application contact:* Cathleen M. Barr, Graduate Administrator, 412-624-4268, Fax: 412-624-4349, E-mail: cbarr@pitt.edu.
Website: http://www.biology.pitt.edu

University of Puerto Rico–Río Piedras, College of Natural Sciences, Department of Biology, San Juan, PR 00931-3300. Offers ecology/systematics (MS, PhD); evolution/genetics (MS, PhD); molecular/cellular biology (MS, PhD); neuroscience (MS, PhD). *Program availability:* Part-time. *Degree requirements:* For master's, one foreign language, comprehensive exam, thesis; for doctorate, one foreign language, comprehensive exam, thesis/dissertation. *Entrance requirements:* For master's, GRE Subject Test, interview, minimum GPA of 3.0, letter of recommendation; for doctorate, GRE Subject Test, interview, master's degree, minimum GPA of 3.0, letter of recommendation. *Faculty research:* Environmental, poblational and systematic biology.

University of Rhode Island, Graduate School, College of the Environment and Life Sciences, Department of Biological Sciences, Kingston, RI 02881. Offers cell and molecular biology (MS, PhD); earth and environmental sciences (MS, PhD); ecology and ecosystem sciences (MS, PhD); evolutionary and marine biology (MS, PhD); sustainable agriculture and food systems (MS, PhD). *Program availability:* Part-time. *Faculty:* 18 full-time (10 women). *Students:* 99 full-time (56 women), 16 part-time (12 women); includes 10 minority (4 Black or African American, non-Hispanic/Latino; 3 Asian, non-Hispanic/Latino; 2 Hispanic/Latino; 1 Two or more races, non-Hispanic/Latino), 21 international. 151 applicants, 22% accepted, 26 enrolled. In 2017, 18 master's, 9 doctorates awarded. *Entrance requirements:* Additional exam requirements/recommendations for international students: Required—TOEFL. *Application deadline:* For fall admission, 1/15 for domestic and international students. Application fee: $65. Electronic applications accepted. *Expenses:* Tuition, state resident: full-time $12,706; part-time $786 per credit. Tuition, nonresident: full-time $25,216; part-time $1401 per credit. *Required fees:* $1598; $45 per credit. One-time fee: $30 part-time. *Financial support:* In 2017–18, 4 research assistantships with tuition reimbursements (averaging $12,698 per year) were awarded. Financial award application deadline: 1/15; financial award applicants required to submit FAFSA. *Faculty research:* Physiological constraints on predators in the Antarctic, effects of CO2 absorption in salt water particularly as it impacts pteropods. *Unit head:* Dr. Evan Preisser, Chair, 401-874-2120, E-mail: preisser@uri.edu.
Website: http://web.uri.edu/bio/

University of Rhode Island, Graduate School, College of the Environment and Life Sciences, Department of Cell and Molecular Biology, Kingston, RI 02881. Offers biochemistry (MS, PhD); clinical laboratory sciences (MS), including biotechnology, clinical laboratory science, cytopathology; microbiology (MS, PhD); molecular genetics (MS, PhD). *Program availability:* Part-time. *Faculty:* 14 full-time (6 women). *Students:* 17 full-time (9 women), 19 part-time (15 women); includes 9 minority (2 Black or African American, non-Hispanic/Latino; 4 Asian, non-Hispanic/Latino; 2 Hispanic/Latino; 1 Two or more races, non-Hispanic/Latino), 10 international. 26 applicants, 62% accepted, 6 enrolled. In 2017, 17 master's awarded. *Entrance requirements:* Additional exam requirements/recommendations for international students: Required—TOEFL. *Application deadline:* For fall admission, 1/15 for domestic and international students. Application fee: $65. Electronic applications accepted. *Expenses:* Tuition, state resident: full-time $12,706; part-time $786 per credit. Tuition, nonresident: full-time $25,216; part-time $1401 per credit. *Required fees:* $1598; $45 per credit. One-time fee: $30 part-time. *Financial support:* In 2017–18, 4 teaching assistantships with tuition reimbursements (averaging $12,698 per year) were awarded; traineeships also available. Financial award application deadline: 1/15; financial award applicants required to submit FAFSA. *Unit head:* Dr. Gongqing Sun, Chair and Professor, 401-874-5937, Fax: 401-874-2202, E-mail: gsun@mail.uri.edu. *Application contact:* Bethany Jenkins, Professor, 401-874-7551, E-mail: bjenkins@uri.edu.
Website: https://web.uri.edu/cmb/

University of Rochester, School of Arts and Sciences, Department of Biology, Rochester, NY 14627. Offers biology (MS); ecology, genetics, and genomics (PhD); molecular, cellular, and developmental biology evolution (PhD). *Faculty:* 21 full-time (6 women). *Students:* 42 full-time (17 women), 4 part-time (all women); includes 6 minority (1 Asian, non-Hispanic/Latino; 3 Hispanic/Latino; 2 Two or more races, non-Hispanic/Latino), 22 international. Average age 27. 119 applicants, 22% accepted, 11 enrolled. In 2017, 6 master's, 5 doctorates awarded. Terminal master's awarded for partial completion of doctoral program. *Degree requirements:* For master's, comprehensive exam (for some programs), thesis (for some programs); for doctorate, thesis/dissertation, qualifying exam. *Entrance requirements:* For master's and doctorate, GRE General Test, GRE Subject Test (highly recommended), personal statement, transcripts, three letters of recommendation. Additional exam requirements/recommendations for international students: Required—TOEFL. *Application deadline:* For fall admission, 1/2 for domestic and international students. Application fee: $60. Electronic applications accepted. *Expenses:* $1,596 per credit hour. *Financial support:* In 2017–18, 36 students received support, including 1 fellowship (averaging $23,000 per year), 20 research assistantships (averaging $28,000 per year), 15 teaching assistantships (averaging $28,000 per year); health care benefits and tuition waivers (full) also available. Financial award application deadline: 1/1. *Faculty research:* Evolution, ecology, genetics, cellular biology, molecular biology. *Total annual research expenditures:* $6.7 million. *Unit head:* Michael Welte, Professor and Chair, 585-276-3897, E-mail: michael.welte@rochester.edu. *Application contact:* Cynthia Landry, Administrative Assistant, 585-275-7991, E-mail: cynthia.landry@rochester.edu.
Website: https://www.sas.rochester.edu/bio/graduate/index.html

University of Rochester, School of Medicine and Dentistry, Graduate Programs in Medicine and Dentistry, Department of Biochemistry and Biophysics, Programs in Biochemistry, Rochester, NY 14627. Offers biochemistry and molecular biology (PhD). Terminal master's awarded for partial completion of doctoral program. *Degree requirements:* For doctorate, thesis/dissertation, qualifying exam. *Entrance requirements:* For doctorate, GRE General Test.

University of South Carolina, The Graduate School, College of Arts and Sciences, Department of Biological Sciences, Graduate Training Program in Molecular, Cellular, and Developmental Biology, Columbia, SC 29208. Offers MS, PhD. *Degree requirements:* For master's, one foreign language, thesis; for doctorate, one foreign language, thesis/dissertation. *Entrance requirements:* For master's and doctorate, GRE General Test, minimum GPA of 3.0 in science. Electronic applications accepted. *Faculty research:* Marine ecology, population and evolutionary biology, molecular biology and genetics, development.

University of South Dakota, Graduate School, Sanford School of Medicine and Graduate School, Biomedical Sciences Graduate Program, Cellular and Molecular Biology Group, Vermillion, SD 57069. Offers MS, PhD. Terminal master's awarded for partial completion of doctoral program. *Degree requirements:* For master's, thesis; for doctorate, comprehensive exam, thesis/dissertation. *Entrance requirements:* For master's and doctorate, GRE General Test, GRE Subject Test, minimum GPA of 3.0. Additional exam requirements/recommendations for international students: Required—TOEFL (minimum score 550 paper-based; 80 iBT), IELTS (minimum score 6). *Application deadline:* For fall admission, 4/15 priority date for domestic students, 3/15 for international students. Applications are processed on a rolling basis. Application fee: $35. Electronic applications accepted. *Expenses:* Contact institution. *Financial support:* In 2017–18, 10 students received support. Fellowships with partial tuition reimbursements available and research assistantships with partial tuition reimbursements available available. Financial award application deadline: 4/15; financial award applicants required to submit FAFSA. *Faculty research:* Molecular aspects of protein and DNA, neurochemistry and energy transduction, gene regulation, cellular development. *Unit head:* 605-658-6322, Fax: 605-677-6381, E-mail: biomed@usd.edu. *Application contact:* Graduate School, 605-658-6140, Fax: 605-677-6118, E-mail: grad@usd.edu.
Website: http://www.usd.edu/medicine/basic-biomedical-sciences

University of Southern California, Graduate School, Dana and David Dornsife College of Letters, Arts and Sciences, Department of Biological Sciences, Program in Molecular and Computational Biology, Los Angeles, CA 90089. Offers computational biology and bioinformatics (PhD); molecular biology (PhD). *Degree requirements:* For doctorate, comprehensive exam, thesis/dissertation, qualifying examination, dissertation defense. *Entrance requirements:* For doctorate, GRE, 3 letters of recommendation, personal statement, resume, minimum GPA of 3.0. Additional exam requirements/recommendations for international students: Required—TOEFL (minimum score 600 paper-based; 100 iBT). Electronic applications accepted. *Faculty research:* Biochemistry and molecular biology; genomics; computational biology and bioinformatics; cell and developmental biology, and genetics; DNA replication and repair, and cancer biology.

University of Southern California, Keck School of Medicine and Graduate School, Graduate Programs in Medicine, Department of Biochemistry and Molecular Biology, Los Angeles, CA 90033. Offers MS. *Program availability:* Part-time. *Faculty:* 22 full-time (4 women). *Students:* 31 full-time (20 women); includes 25 minority (all Asian, non-Hispanic/Latino). Average age 24. 77 applicants, 52% accepted, 14 enrolled. In 2017, 17 master's awarded. Terminal master's awarded for partial completion of doctoral program. *Degree requirements:* For master's, thesis. *Entrance requirements:* For master's, GRE General Test, minimum GPA of 3.0. Additional exam requirements/recommendations for international students: Required—TOEFL (minimum score 600 paper-based; 100 iBT), IELTS. *Application deadline:* For fall admission, 4/1 priority date for domestic and international students. Applications are processed on a rolling basis. Application fee: $90. Electronic applications accepted. *Expenses:* Contact institution. *Financial support:* Application deadline: 5/4; applicants required to submit CSS PROFILE or FAFSA. *Faculty research:* Molecular genetics, gene expression, membrane biochemistry, metabolic regulation, cancer biology. *Total annual research expenditures:* $7.4 million. *Unit head:* Dr. Peggy R. Farnham, Chair, 323-442-8015, E-mail: peggy.farnham@med.usc.edu. *Application contact:* Janet Stoeckert, Administrative Director, Basic Science Departments, 323-442-3568, Fax: 323-442-1610, E-mail: janet.stoeckert@usc.edu.
Website: http://keck.usc.edu/en/Education/Academic_Department_and_Divisions/Department_of_Biochemistry_and_Molecular_Biology.aspx

University of Southern Maine, College of Science, Technology, and Health, Program in Applied Medical Sciences, Portland, ME 04103. Offers MS. *Program availability:* Part-time. *Degree requirements:* For master's, thesis. *Entrance requirements:* For master's, GRE General Test, minimum GPA of 3.0. Additional exam requirements/recommendations for international students: Required—TOEFL. Electronic applications accepted. *Faculty research:* Cancer biology, toxicology, environmental health, epidemiology, autoimmune disease, immunology, infectious disease, virology.

University of South Florida, College of Arts and Sciences, Department of Cell Biology, Microbiology, and Molecular Biology, Tampa, FL 33620-9951. Offers biology (MS), including cell biology, microbiology and molecular biology; cancer biology (PhD); cancer chemical biology (PhD); cancer immunology and immunotherapy (PhD); cell and molecular biology (PhD); microbiology (MS). *Faculty:* 19 full-time (6 women). *Students:* 81 full-time (55 women), 4 part-time (2 women); includes 12 minority (1 Black or African American, non-Hispanic/Latino; 2 Asian, non-Hispanic/Latino; 5 Hispanic/Latino; 4 Two or more races, non-Hispanic/Latino), 29 international. Average age 27. 159 applicants, 18% accepted, 23 enrolled. In 2017, 21 master's, 10 doctorates awarded. *Degree requirements:* For master's, thesis or alternative; for doctorate, comprehensive exam, thesis/dissertation. *Entrance requirements:* For master's and doctorate, GRE General Test, minimum GPA of 3.0, extensive background in biology or chemistry. Additional exam requirements/recommendations for international students: Required—TOEFL (minimum score 570 paper-based; 79 iBT) or IELTS (minimum score 6.5). *Application deadline:* For fall admission, 11/30 priority date for domestic and international students; for spring admission, 7/1 priority date for domestic students, 7/1 for international students. Application fee: $30. *Financial support:* In 2017–18, 10 students received support. Career-related internships or fieldwork, health care benefits, and unspecified assistantships available. Financial award application deadline: 4/1. *Faculty research:* Cell biology, microbiology and molecular biology: basic and applied science in bacterial pathogenesis, genome integrity and mechanisms of aging, structural and computational biology; cancer biology: immunology, cancer control, signal transduction, drug discovery, genomics. *Total annual research expenditures:* $1.8 million. *Unit head:* Dr. James Garey, Professor/Chair, 813-974-7103, Fax: 813-974-1614, E-mail: garey@usf.edu. *Application contact:* Dr. Kenneth Wright, Associate Professor of Cancer Biology, H. Lee Moffitt Cancer Center and Research Institute, 813-745-3918, Fax: 813-974-1614, E-mail: ken.wright@moffitt.org.
Website: http://biology.usf.edu/cmmb/

University of South Florida, Morsani College of Medicine and College of Graduate Studies, Graduate Programs in Medical Sciences, Tampa, FL 33620-9951. Offers advanced athletic training (MS); athletic training (MS); bioinformatics and computational biology (MSBCB); biotechnology (MSB); health informatics (MSHI); medical sciences (MSMS, PhD), including aging and neuroscience (MSMS), allergy, immunology and infectious disease (PhD), anatomy, biochemistry and molecular biology, clinical and translational research, health science (MSMS), interdisciplinary medical sciences (MSMS), medical microbiology and immunology (MSMS), metabolic and nutritional medicine (MSMS), microbiology and immunology (PhD), molecular medicine, molecular pharmacology and physiology (PhD), neuroscience (PhD), pathology and cell biology (PhD), women's health (MSMS). *Students:* 372 full-time (212 women), 216 part-time (142 women); includes 257 minority (78 Black or African American, non-Hispanic/Latino; 1 American Indian or Alaska Native, non-Hispanic/Latino; 79 Asian, non-Hispanic/Latino; 84 Hispanic/Latino; 15 Two or more races, non-Hispanic/Latino), 62 international. Average age 28. 1,048 applicants, 46% accepted, 309 enrolled. In 2017, 351 master's, 56 doctorates awarded. Terminal master's awarded for partial completion of doctoral program. *Degree requirements:* For master's, comprehensive exam, thesis; for doctorate, comprehensive exam, thesis/dissertation. *Entrance requirements:* For master's, GRE General Test or GMAT, bachelor's degree or equivalent from regionally-accredited university with minimum GPA of 3.0 in upper-division sciences coursework; prerequisites in general biology, general chemistry, general physics, organic chemistry, quantitative analysis, and integral and differential calculus; for doctorate, GRE General Test, bachelor's degree from regionally-accredited university with minimum GPA of 3.0 in upper-division sciences coursework; 3 letters of recommendation; personal interview; 1-2 page personal statement; prerequisites in biology, chemistry, physics, organic chemistry, quantitative analysis, and integral/differential calculus. Additional exam requirements/recommendations for international students: Required—TOEFL (minimum score 550 paper-based; 79 iBT) or IELTS (minimum score 6.5). *Application deadline:* For fall admission, 2/1 priority date for domestic students, 2/1 for international students. Application fee: $30. Electronic applications accepted. *Expenses:* Contact institution. *Financial support:* In 2017–18, 109 students received support. *Faculty research:* Anatomy, biochemistry, cancer biology, cardiovascular disease, cell biology, immunology, microbiology, molecular biology, neuroscience, pharmacology, physiology. *Total annual research expenditures:* $45.3 million. *Unit head:* Dr. Michael Barber, Professor/Associate Dean for Graduate and Postdoctoral Affairs, 813-974-9908, Fax: 813-974-4317, E-mail: mbarber@health.usf.edu. *Application contact:* Dr. Eric Bennett, Graduate Director, PhD Program in Medical Sciences, 813-974-1545, Fax: 813-974-4317, E-mail: esbennet@health.usf.edu.
Website: http://health.usf.edu/nocms/medicine/graduatestudies/

The University of Texas at Austin, Graduate School, Institute for Cellular and Molecular Biology, Austin, TX 78712-1111. Offers PhD.

The University of Texas at Dallas, School of Natural Sciences and Mathematics, Department of Biological Sciences, Richardson, TX 75080. Offers bioinformatics and computational biology (MS); biotechnology (MS); molecular and cell biology (MS, PhD). *Program availability:* Part-time, evening/weekend. *Faculty:* 22 full-time (4 women), 3 part-time/adjunct (2 women). *Students:* 107 full-time (64 women), 26 part-time (11 women); includes 24 minority (3 Black or African American, non-Hispanic/Latino; 12 Asian, non-Hispanic/Latino; 5 Hispanic/Latino; 4 Two or more races, non-Hispanic/Latino), 76 international. Average age 27. 307 applicants, 23% accepted, 45 enrolled. In 2017, 37 master's, 9 doctorates awarded. *Degree requirements:* For master's, thesis optional; for doctorate, thesis/dissertation, publishable paper. *Entrance requirements:* For master's and doctorate, GRE (minimum combined score of 1000 on verbal and quantitative). Additional exam requirements/recommendations for international students: Required—TOEFL (minimum score 550 paper-based; 80 iBT). *Application deadline:* For fall admission, 7/15 for domestic students, 5/1 priority date for international students; for spring admission, 11/15 for domestic students, 9/1 priority date for international students. Applications are processed on a rolling basis. Application fee: $50 ($100 for international students). Electronic applications accepted. *Expenses:* Tuition, state resident: full-time $12,916; part-time $718 per credit hour. Tuition, nonresident: full-time $25,252; part-time $1403 per credit hour. *Financial support:* In 2017–18, 78 students received support, including 14 research assistantships with partial tuition reimbursements available (averaging $25,380 per year), 59 teaching assistantships with partial tuition reimbursements available (averaging $17,265 per year); fellowships with partial tuition reimbursements available, career-related internships or fieldwork, Federal Work-Study, institutionally sponsored loans, scholarships/grants, and unspecified assistantships also available. Support available to part-time students. Financial award application deadline: 4/30; financial award applicants required to submit FAFSA. *Faculty research:* Role of mitochondria in neurodegenerative diseases, protein-DNA interactions in site-specific recombination, eukaryotic gene expression, bio-nanotechnology, sickle cell research. *Unit head:* Dr. Stephen Spiro, Department Head, 972-883-6032, Fax: 972-883-4551, E-mail: stephen.spiro@utdallas.edu. *Application contact:* Dr. Lawrence Reitzer, Graduate Advisor, 972-883-2502, Fax: 972-883-4551, E-mail: reitzer@utdallas.edu.
Website: http://www.utdallas.edu/biology/

The University of Texas at San Antonio, College of Sciences, Department of Biology, San Antonio, TX 78249-0617. Offers biology (MS); biotechnology (MS); cell and molecular biology (PhD); neurobiology (PhD). *Faculty:* 37 full-time (10 women), 1 part-time/adjunct (0 women). *Students:* 111 full-time (64 women), 50 part-time (25 women); includes 76 minority (5 Black or African American, non-Hispanic/Latino; 1 American Indian or Alaska Native, non-Hispanic/Latino; 11 Asian, non-Hispanic/Latino; 55 Hispanic/Latino; 1 Native Hawaiian or other Pacific Islander, non-Hispanic/Latino; 3 Two or more races, non-Hispanic/Latino), 30 international. Average age 27. 153 applicants, 55% accepted, 57 enrolled. In 2017, 17 master's, 3 doctorates awarded. Terminal master's awarded for partial completion of doctoral program. *Degree requirements:* For master's, comprehensive exam, thesis or alternative; for doctorate, comprehensive exam, thesis/dissertation. *Entrance requirements:* For master's, GRE General Test, bachelor's degree with 18 credit hours in field of study or in another appropriate field of study; for doctorate, GRE General Test, 3 letters of recommendation, statement of purpose, resume. Additional exam requirements/recommendations for international students: Required—TOEFL (minimum score 500 paper-based; 100 iBT), IELTS (minimum score 5). *Application deadline:* For fall admission, 6/15 for domestic students, 3/1 for international students; for spring admission, 10/15 for domestic students, 9/15 for international students. Application fee: $50 ($90 for international students). Electronic applications accepted. *Expenses:* Tuition, state resident: full-time $5495. Tuition, nonresident: full-time $21,938. *Required fees:* $1915. Tuition and fees vary according to program. *Faculty research:* Development of human and veterinary vaccines against a fungal disease, mammalian germ cells and stem cells, dopamine neuron physiology and addiction, plant biochemistry, dendritic computation and synaptic plasticity. *Total annual research expenditures:* $9.1 million. *Unit head:* Dr. Garry Sunter, Chair, 210-458-5479, E-mail: garry.sunter@utsa.edu.
Website: http://bio.utsa.edu/

University of Utah, School of Medicine, Program in Molecular Biology, Salt Lake City, UT 84132. Offers PhD. *Degree requirements:* For doctorate, thesis/dissertation, preliminary exams. *Entrance requirements:* For doctorate, GRE General Test, personal statement, transcripts, letters of recommendation. Additional exam requirements/recommendations for international students: Required—TOEFL (minimum score 500 paper-based; 60 iBT). Electronic applications accepted. *Faculty research:* Biochemistry/structural biology; cancer/cell biology; genetics; developmental biology; gene expression; microbiology/immunology and neurobiology.

University of Vermont, Graduate College, Cross-College Interdisciplinary Program, Cellular, Molecular and Biomedical Sciences Program, Burlington, VT 05405. Offers PhD. *Students:* 48 (26 women). Average age 29. 74 applicants, 35% accepted, 9 enrolled. In 2017, 9 doctorates awarded. *Degree requirements:* For doctorate, thesis/dissertation. *Entrance requirements:* For doctorate, GRE General Test. Additional exam requirements/recommendations for international students: Required—TOEFL (minimum score 550 paper-based; 100 iBT), IELTS (minimum score 7). *Application deadline:* For fall admission, 12/1 for domestic and international students. Application fee: $65. Electronic applications accepted. *Expenses:* Tuition, state resident: full-time $11,628; part-time $646 per credit. Tuition, nonresident: full-time $29,340; part-time $1630 per credit. *Required fees:* $1994; $10 per credit. Tuition and fees vary according to course load and program. *Financial support:* In 2017–18, 16 research assistantships with full tuition reimbursements (averaging $28,000 per year), 33 teaching assistantships with full tuition reimbursements (averaging $28,000 per year) were awarded; fellowships and career-related internships or fieldwork also available. Financial award application deadline: 3/1. *Faculty research:* Cancer biology and genome stability, genomics and computational biology, immunology and microbial pathogenesis, stem cell and developmental biology, lung and cardiovascular biology. *Unit head:* Dr. Matthew Poynter, Director, 802-656-8045, E-mail: cmb@uvm.edu. *Application contact:* Jessica Lalime, Administrator, 802-656-9673, E-mail: cmb@uvm.edu.
Website: https://www.uvm.edu/cmb

University of Washington, Graduate School, School of Medicine, Graduate Programs in Medicine, Program in Molecular and Cellular Biology, Seattle, WA 98195. Offers PhD. Offered in partnership with Fred Hutchinson Cancer Research Center, Seattle Biomedical Research Center, and Institute for Systems Biology. *Degree requirements:* For doctorate, thesis/dissertation. *Entrance requirements:* For doctorate, GRE General Test. Additional exam requirements/recommendations for international students: Required—TOEFL. Electronic applications accepted.

University of Wisconsin–La Crosse, College of Science and Health, Department of Biology, La Crosse, WI 54601-3742. Offers aquatic sciences (MS); biology (MS); cellular and molecular biology (MS); clinical microbiology (MS); microbiology (MS); nurse anesthesia (MS); physiology (MS). *Accreditation:* AANA/CANAEP. *Program availability:* Part-time. *Students:* 11 full-time (2 women), 29 part-time (14 women); includes 1 minority (Two or more races, non-Hispanic/Latino). Average age 30. 67 applicants, 28% accepted, 18 enrolled. In 2017, 24 master's awarded. *Degree requirements:* For master's, comprehensive exam, thesis. *Entrance requirements:* For master's, GRE General Test, minimum GPA of 2.85. Additional exam requirements/recommendations for international students: Required—TOEFL (minimum score 550 paper-based; 79 iBT). *Application deadline:* For fall admission, 2/1 priority date for domestic and international students; for spring admission, 1/4 priority date for domestic and international students. Applications are processed on a rolling basis. Electronic applications accepted. *Financial support:* Research assistantships with partial tuition reimbursements, Federal Work-Study, scholarships/grants, health care benefits, and tuition waivers (partial) available. Support available to part-time students. Financial award application deadline: 3/15; financial award applicants required to submit FAFSA. *Unit head:* Dr. Mark Sandheinrich, Department Chair, 608-785-8261, E-mail: msandheinrich@uwlax.edu. *Application contact:* Brandon Schaller, Senior Graduate Student Status Examiner, 608-785-8941, E-mail: admissions@uwlax.edu.
Website: http://uwlax.edu/biology/

University of Wisconsin–Madison, Graduate School, Program in Cellular and Molecular Biology, Madison, WI 53706-1596. Offers PhD. *Faculty:* 186 full-time (66 women). *Students:* 80 full-time (39 women); includes 7 minority (1 Black or African American, non-Hispanic/Latino; 1 Asian, non-Hispanic/Latino; 3 Hispanic/Latino; 2 Native Hawaiian or other Pacific Islander, non-Hispanic/Latino), 20 international. Average age 27. 334 applicants, 15% accepted, 14 enrolled. In 2017, 15 doctorates awarded. *Degree requirements:* For doctorate, comprehensive exam, thesis/dissertation. *Entrance requirements:* For doctorate, GRE General Test, GRE Subject Test (recommended), minimum GPA of 3.0, lab experience. Additional exam requirements/recommendations for international students: Required—TOEFL (minimum score 580 paper-based; 92 iBT). *Application deadline:* For fall admission, 12/1 for domestic and international students. Application fee: $75 ($81 for international students). Electronic applications accepted. *Financial support:* In 2017–18, 66 students received support. Fellowships with full tuition reimbursements available, research assistantships with full tuition reimbursements available, teaching assistantships, traineeships, health care benefits, and unspecified assistantships available. *Faculty research:* Virology, cancer biology, transcriptional mechanisms, developmental biology, immunology. *Unit head:* Dr. David Wassarman, Graduate Program Chair, 608-262-3203. *Application contact:* CMB Office, 608-262-3203, E-mail: cmb@bocklabs.wisc.edu.
Website: http://www.cmb.wisc.edu/

University of Wisconsin–Milwaukee, Graduate School, College of Letters and Science, Department of Biological Sciences, Milwaukee, WI 53201-0413. Offers cellular and molecular biology (MS, PhD); microbiology (MS, PhD). *Students:* 58 full-time (35 women), 11 part-time (8 women); includes 7 minority (1 Black or African American, non-Hispanic/Latino; 5 Asian, non-Hispanic/Latino; 1 Two or more races, non-Hispanic/Latino), 17 international. Average age 29. 78 applicants, 55% accepted, 29 enrolled. *Degree requirements:* For master's, thesis; for doctorate, thesis/dissertation, 1 foreign language or data analysis proficiency. *Entrance requirements:* For master's and doctorate, GRE General Test. Additional exam requirements/recommendations for international students: Required—TOEFL (minimum score 550 paper-based; 79 iBT), IELTS (minimum score 6.5). *Application deadline:* For fall admission, 3/1 priority date for domestic students. Application fee: $56 ($96 for international students). Electronic applications accepted. *Financial support:* In 2017–18, 9 research assistantships were awarded; fellowships, teaching assistantships, career-related internships or fieldwork, unspecified assistantships, and project assistantships also available. Support available to part-time students. Financial award application deadline: 4/15; financial award applicants required to submit FAFSA. *Unit head:* R. David Heathcote, Department Chair, 414-229-6471, E-mail: rdh@uwm.edu. *Application contact:* General Information Contact, 414-229-4982, Fax: 414-229-6967, E-mail: gradschool@uwm.edu.
Website: https://uwm.edu/biology/

University of Wisconsin–Parkside, College of Natural and Health Sciences, Program in Applied Molecular Biology, Kenosha, WI 53141. Offers MSBS. *Program availability:* Part-time. *Faculty:* 7 full-time (2 women). *Students:* 9 full-time (4 women); includes 1 minority (Hispanic/Latino). Average age 25. 1 applicant, 100% accepted, 1 enrolled. In 2017, 4 master's awarded. *Degree requirements:* For master's, thesis. *Entrance requirements:* For master's, GRE General Test, BS or BA from regionally-accredited institution; minimum GPA of 3.0; 2 semesters each of general chemistry, organic chemistry, introduction to biology with laboratory, and physics; 1 semester each of genetics, biochemistry, molecular biology, and calculus. Additional exam requirements/recommendations for international students: Required—TOEFL (minimum score 525 paper-based; 71 iBT). *Application deadline:* Applications are processed on a rolling basis. Application fee: $56. Electronic applications accepted. *Financial support:* Application deadline: 7/1. *Faculty research:* Enzyme kinetics, bacterial stress responses, RNA stability, proteomic analysis, genomic analysis. *Unit head:* Dr. Bryan Lewis, Interim Associate Dean, 262-595-2327, Fax: 262-595-2056, E-mail: lewisb@uwp.edu. *Application contact:* Dr. Bryan Lewis, Interim Associate Dean, 262-595-2327, Fax: 262-595-2056, E-mail: lewisb@uwp.edu.
Website: https://www.uwp.edu/learn/programs/appliedmolecbio.cfm

University of Wyoming, College of Agriculture and Natural Resources, Department of Molecular Biology, Laramie, WY 82071. Offers MA, MS, PhD. Terminal master's awarded for partial completion of doctoral program. *Degree requirements:* For master's, comprehensive exam (for some programs), thesis; for doctorate, comprehensive exam, thesis/dissertation. *Entrance requirements:* For master's and doctorate, GRE General Test, GRE Subject Test (recommended), minimum GPA of 3.0. Additional exam requirements/recommendations for international students: Required—TOEFL. Electronic applications accepted. *Faculty research:* Protein structure/function, developmental regulation, yeast genetics, bacterial pathogenesis.

University of Wyoming, Graduate Program in Molecular and Cellular Life Sciences, Laramie, WY 82071. Offers PhD. *Degree requirements:* For doctorate, thesis/dissertation, four eight-week laboratory rotations, comprehensive basic practical exam, two-part qualifying exam, seminars, symposium.

Vanderbilt University, School of Medicine, Department of Molecular Physiology and Biophysics, Nashville, TN 37240-1001. Offers MS, PhD, MD/PhD. *Faculty:* 26 full-time (3 women). *Students:* 27 full-time (15 women); includes 7 minority (2 Black or African American, non-Hispanic/Latino; 2 Asian, non-Hispanic/Latino; 3 Hispanic/Latino). Average age 27. In 2017, 9 doctorates awarded. *Degree requirements:* For doctorate, comprehensive exam, thesis/dissertation, preliminary, qualifying, and final exams. *Entrance requirements:* For doctorate, GRE General Test, GRE Subject Test (recommended). Additional exam requirements/recommendations for international students: Required—TOEFL (minimum score 570 paper-based; 88 iBT). *Application deadline:* For fall admission, 1/15 for domestic and international students. Application fee: $0. Electronic applications accepted. *Financial support:* Fellowships with full tuition reimbursements, research assistantships with full tuition reimbursements, Federal Work-Study, institutionally sponsored loans, scholarships/grants, traineeships, health care benefits, and tuition waivers (partial) available. Financial award application deadline: 1/15; financial award applicants required to submit CSS PROFILE or FAFSA. *Faculty research:* Biophysics, cell signaling and gene regulation, human genetics, diabetes and obesity, neuroscience. *Unit head:* Dr. Roger Cone, Acting Chair, 615-322-7000, Fax: 615-343-0490, E-mail: roger.cone@vanderbilt.edu. *Application contact:* Richard O'Brien, Director of Graduate Studies, 615-322-7000, E-mail: richard.obrien@vanderbilt.edu.
Website: http://www.mc.vanderbilt.edu/root/vumc.php?site-MPB

Virginia Commonwealth University, Medical College of Virginia-Professional Programs, School of Medicine, Graduate Programs in Medicine, Department of Biochemistry and Molecular Biology, Richmond, VA 23284-9005. Offers MS, PhD, MD/PhD. *Degree requirements:* For master's, thesis; for doctorate, thesis/dissertation, comprehensive oral and written exams. *Entrance requirements:* For master's and doctorate, GRE, MCAT or DAT. Electronic applications accepted. *Faculty research:* Molecular biology, peptide/protein chemistry, neurochemistry, enzyme mechanisms, macromolecular structure determination.

Virginia Commonwealth University, Medical College of Virginia-Professional Programs, School of Medicine, Graduate Programs in Medicine, Department of Physiology and Biophysics, Richmond, VA 23284-9005. Offers molecular biology and genetics (MS); physical therapy (PhD); physiology (MS, PhD); MD/PhD. Terminal master's awarded for partial completion of doctoral program. *Degree requirements:* For master's, thesis; for doctorate, thesis/dissertation, comprehensive oral and written exams. *Entrance requirements:* For master's, GRE General Test, MCAT, or DAT; for doctorate, GRE, MCAT or DAT. Additional exam requirements/recommendations for international students: Required—TOEFL (minimum score 600 paper-based; 100 iBT). Electronic applications accepted.

Washington University in St. Louis, The Graduate School, Division of Biology and Biomedical Sciences, Program in Molecular Cell Biology, St. Louis, MO 63130-4899. Offers PhD. *Degree requirements:* For doctorate, thesis/dissertation. *Entrance requirements:* For doctorate, GRE General Test, GRE Subject Test. Additional exam requirements/recommendations for international students: Required—TOEFL. Electronic applications accepted. *Faculty research:* Cell adhesion, protein trafficking and organelle biogenesis, cell cycle, receptors, signal transduction, gene expression, metabolism, cytoskeleton and motility, membrane excitability, molecular basis of diseases.

Wayne State University, School of Medicine, Office of Biomedical Graduate Programs, Detroit, MI 48202. Offers anatomy and cell biology (MS, PhD); basic medical sciences (MS); biochemistry and molecular biology (MS, PhD); cancer biology (MS, PhD); clinical and translational science (Graduate Certificate); family medicine and public health sciences (MPH, Graduate Certificate), including public health practice; genetic counseling (MS); immunology and microbiology (MS, PhD); medical physics (MS, PhD, Graduate Certificate); medical research (MS); molecular medicine and genomics (MS, PhD), including molecular genetics and genomics; pathology (PhD); pharmacology (MS, PhD); physiology (MS, PhD), including physiology, reproductive sciences (PhD); psychiatry and behavioral neurosciences (PhD), including translational neuroscience; MD/MPH; MD/PhD; MPH/MA; MSW/MPH. *Program availability:* Part-time, evening/weekend. *Students:* 268 full-time (152 women), 117 part-time (59 women); includes 108 minority (19 Black or African American, non-Hispanic/Latino; 1 American Indian or Alaska Native, non-Hispanic/Latino; 62 Asian, non-Hispanic/Latino; 9 Hispanic/Latino; 17 Two or more races, non-Hispanic/Latino), 48 international. Average age 26. 1,133 applicants, 21% accepted, 151 enrolled. In 2017, 70 master's, 25 doctorates, 10 other advanced degrees awarded. Terminal master's awarded for partial completion of doctoral program. *Degree requirements:* For master's, thesis (for some programs); for doctorate, thesis/dissertation. *Entrance requirements:* For master's, doctorate, and Graduate Certificate, GRE. Additional exam requirements/recommendations for international students: Required—TOEFL (minimum score 550 paper-based; 100 iBT), Michigan English Language Assessment Battery (minimum score 85); Recommended—IELTS (minimum score 6.5), TWE (minimum score 5.5). *Application deadline:* For fall admission, 2/1 for domestic and international students. Applications are processed on a rolling basis. Application fee: $50. Electronic applications accepted. *Expenses:* Contact institution. *Financial support:* In 2017–18, 177 students received support, including 64 fellowships with full tuition reimbursements available (averaging $24,388 per year), 79 research assistantships with full tuition reimbursements available (averaging $26,894 per year); scholarships/grants, traineeships, and health care benefits also available. *Faculty research:* Cancer biology, neurosciences, vision sciences, molecular biology, pathology, physiology, pharmacology, public health, medical physics. *Unit head:* Dr. Daniel A. Walz, Associate Dean for Biomedical Graduate Programs, 313-577-1455, Fax: 313-577-8796, E-mail: gradprogs@med.wayne.edu.
Website: https://www.med.wayne.edu/biomedical-graduate-programs/

Weill Cornell Medicine, Weill Cornell Graduate School of Medical Sciences, Biochemistry, Cell and Molecular Biology Allied Program, New York, NY 10065. Offers MS, PhD. Terminal master's awarded for partial completion of doctoral program. *Degree requirements:* For master's, comprehensive exam; for doctorate, thesis/dissertation, final exam. *Entrance requirements:* For doctorate, GRE General Test, background in genetics, molecular biology, chemistry, or biochemistry. Additional exam requirements/recommendations for international students: Required—TOEFL. Electronic applications accepted. *Faculty research:* Molecular structure determination, protein structure, gene structure, stem cell biology, control of gene expression, DNA replication, chromosome maintenance, RNA biosynthesis.

Wesleyan University, Graduate Studies, Department of Molecular Biology and Biochemistry, Middletown, CT 06459. Offers molecular biology and biochemistry (PhD); molecular biophysics (PhD). *Faculty:* 8 full-time (3 women), 2 part-time/adjunct (both women). *Students:* 16 full-time (10 women); includes 4 minority (2 Asian, non-Hispanic/Latino; 1 Hispanic/Latino; 1 Two or more races, non-Hispanic/Latino), 7 international. Average age 24. 24 applicants, 25% accepted, 3 enrolled. In 2017, 2 doctorates awarded. Terminal master's awarded for partial completion of doctoral program. *Degree requirements:* For doctorate, comprehensive exam, thesis/dissertation. *Entrance requirements:* For doctorate, GRE General Test, GRE Subject Test. Additional exam requirements/recommendations for international students: Required—TOEFL. *Application deadline:* For fall admission, 1/15 for domestic and international students. Application fee: $0. Electronic applications accepted. *Financial support:* In 2017–18, 9 teaching assistantships with full tuition reimbursements were awarded; research assistantships with full tuition reimbursements and institutionally sponsored loans also available. Financial award application deadline: 4/15. *Faculty research:* The olfactory system and new frontiers in genome research, chromosome structure and gene expression, gene co-regulation, crystallographic and spectroscopic analysis, DNA replication and repair. *Unit head:* Amy MacQueen, Chair, 860-685-2561, E-mail: amacqueen@wesleyan.edu. *Application contact:* Anika Dane, Administrative Assistant, 860-685-2404, E-mail: adane@wesleyan.edu.
Website: http://www.wesleyan.edu/mbb/

West Virginia University, School of Medicine, Morgantown, WV 26506-9600. Offers biochemistry and molecular biology (PhD); biomedical science (MS); cancer cell biology (PhD); cellular and integrative physiology (PhD); exercise physiology (MS, PhD); health sciences (MS); immunology (PhD); medicine (MD); occupational therapy (MOT); pathologists assistant (MHS); physical therapy (DPT). *Program availability:* Part-time, evening/weekend. *Students:* 781 full-time (440 women), 25 part-time (13 women); includes 140 minority (15 Black or African American, non-Hispanic/Latino; 1 American Indian or Alaska Native, non-Hispanic/Latino; 68 Asian, non-Hispanic/Latino; 37 Hispanic/Latino; 1 Native Hawaiian or other Pacific Islander, non-Hispanic/Latino; 18 Two or more races, non-Hispanic/Latino), 19 international. *Entrance requirements:* Additional exam requirements/recommendations for international students: Required—TOEFL. *Application deadline:* Applications are processed on a rolling basis. Application fee: $60. Electronic applications accepted. *Expenses:* Contact institution. *Financial support:* Fellowships, research assistantships, teaching assistantships, career-related internships or fieldwork, Federal Work-Study, institutionally sponsored loans, health care benefits, tuition waivers (full and partial), and administrative assistantships available. Financial award applicants required to submit FAFSA. *Unit head:* Dr. Clay Marsh, Executive Dean, 304-293-6607, Fax: 304-293-6627, E-mail: clay.marsh@hsc.wvu.edu. *Application contact:* Lisa M. Salati, Assistant Vice President, Graduate Education, 304-293-7759, Fax: 304-293-3080, E-mail: lsalati@hsc.wvu.edu.
Website: https://medicine.hsc.wvu.edu

Wright State University, Graduate School, College of Science and Mathematics, Department of Biochemistry and Molecular Biology, Dayton, OH 45435. Offers MS. *Degree requirements:* For master's, thesis. *Entrance requirements:* Additional exam requirements/recommendations for international students: Required—TOEFL. *Faculty research:* Regulation of gene expression, macromolecular structural function, NMR imaging, visual biochemistry.

Yale University, Graduate School of Arts and Sciences, Department of Molecular, Cellular, and Developmental Biology, Program in Biochemistry, Molecular Biology and Chemical Biology, New Haven, CT 06520. Offers PhD. *Degree requirements:* For doctorate, thesis/dissertation. *Entrance requirements:* For doctorate, GRE General Test, GRE Subject Test.

Yale University, Yale School of Medicine and Graduate School of Arts and Sciences, Combined Program in Biological and Biomedical Sciences (BBS), Molecular Cell Biology, Genetics, and Development Track, New Haven, CT 06520. Offers PhD, MD/PhD. *Entrance requirements:* Additional exam requirements/recommendations for international students: Required—TOEFL.

Youngstown State University, Graduate School, College of Science, Technology, Engineering and Mathematics, Department of Biological Sciences, Youngstown, OH 44555-0001. Offers environmental biology (MS); molecular biology, microbiology, and genetic (MS); physiology and anatomy (MS). *Program availability:* Part-time. *Degree requirements:* For master's, comprehensive exam, thesis, oral review. *Entrance requirements:* For master's, GRE General Test, minimum GPA of 2.7. Additional exam requirements/recommendations for international students: Required—TOEFL. *Faculty research:* Cell biology, neurophysiology, molecular biology, neurobiology, gene regulation.

Molecular Medicine

Augusta University, Program in Molecular Medicine, Augusta, GA 30912. Offers PhD. *Degree requirements:* For doctorate, comprehensive exam, thesis/dissertation. *Entrance requirements:* For doctorate, GRE General Test. Additional exam requirements/recommendations for international students: Required—TOEFL (minimum score 550 paper-based; 79 iBT). Electronic applications accepted. *Faculty research:* Developmental neurobiology, cancer, regenerative medicine, molecular chaperones, molecular immunology.

Baylor College of Medicine, Graduate School of Biomedical Sciences, Program in Translational Biology and Molecular Medicine, Houston, TX 77030-3498. Offers PhD. *Degree requirements:* For doctorate, thesis/dissertation, public defense. *Entrance requirements:* For doctorate, GRE, minimum GPA of 3.0. Additional exam requirements/recommendations for international students: Required—TOEFL. Electronic applications accepted. *Faculty research:* Molecular medicine, translational biology, human disease biology and therapy.

Boston University, School of Medicine, Division of Graduate Medical Sciences, Program in Molecular and Translational Medicine, Boston, MA 02215. Offers PhD, MD/PhD. *Degree requirements:* For doctorate, thesis/dissertation. *Application deadline:* For fall admission, 1/15 for domestic students; for spring admission, 10/15 for domestic students. *Unit head:* Dr. Matt Jones, Director, 617-638-4860, E-mail: mattj@bu.edu. *Application contact:* GMS Admissions Office, 617-638-5255, E-mail: askgms@bu.edu.
Website: http://www.bumc.bu.edu/gpmm

Case Western Reserve University, School of Medicine and School of Graduate Studies, Graduate Programs in Medicine, Cleveland Clinic Lerner Research Institute–Molecular Medicine PhD Program, Cleveland, OH 44106. Offers PhD. *Degree requirements:* For doctorate, comprehensive exam, thesis/dissertation, seminar. *Entrance requirements:* For doctorate, GRE, 3 letters of reference, prior research experience, interview. Additional exam requirements/recommendations for international students: Required—TOEFL (minimum score 577 paper-based; 90 iBT); Recommended—IELTS (minimum score 7). Electronic applications accepted. *Expenses: Tuition:* Full-time $43,854; part-time $1827 per credit hour. *Required fees:* $50; $50 per credit hour. Tuition and fees vary according to course load and program. *Faculty research:* Cancer, cardiovascular disease, neuroscience, molecular biology, genetics.

Cleveland State University, College of Graduate Studies, College of Sciences and Health Professions, Department of Chemistry, Cleveland, OH 44115. Offers clinical chemistry (PhD), including cellular and molecular medicine, clinical/bioanalytical chemistry (PhD); organic chemistry (MS); physical chemistry (MS). *Program availability:* Part-time, evening/weekend. *Faculty:* 17 full-time (3 women). *Students:* 50 full-time (26 women), 22 part-time (12 women); includes 3 minority (2 Black or African American, non-Hispanic/Latino; 1 Asian, non-Hispanic/Latino), 40 international. Average age 30. 63 applicants, 63% accepted, 11 enrolled. In 2017, 6 master's, 12 doctorates awarded. *Entrance requirements:* For master's and doctorate, GRE General Test. Additional exam requirements/recommendations for international students: Required—TOEFL (minimum score 550 paper-based; 78 iBT). *Application deadline:* Applications are processed on a rolling basis. Application fee: $40. Electronic applications accepted. *Financial support:* In 2017–18, 44 students received support. Fellowships, research assistantships, teaching assistantships, scholarships/grants, and unspecified assistantships available. Financial award application deadline: 1/15. *Faculty research:* Bioanalytical techniques and molecular diagnostics, glycoproteomics and antithrombotic agents, drug discovery and innovation, analytical pharmacology, inflammatory disease research. *Total annual research expenditures:* $3 million. *Unit head:* Dr. David W. Ball, Chair, 216-687-2467, Fax: 216-687-9298, E-mail: d.ball@csuohio.edu. *Application contact:* Richelle P. Emery, Administrative Coordinator, 216-687-2457, Fax: 216-687-9298, E-mail: r.emery@csuohio.edu.
Website: http://www.csuohio.edu/sciences/chemistry

Dartmouth College, Program in Experimental and Molecular Medicine, Hanover, NH 03755. Offers MBA/PhD, MD/PhD. *Faculty:* 35 full-time (6 women), 15 part-time/adjunct (6 women). *Students:* 44 full-time (26 women); includes 8 minority (5 Asian, non-Hispanic/Latino; 3 Hispanic/Latino), 4 international. Average age 26. 72 applicants, 25% accepted, 5 enrolled. *Entrance requirements:* Additional exam requirements/recommendations for international students: Required—TOEFL (minimum score 620 paper-based; 105 iBT). *Application deadline:* For fall admission, 1/1 for domestic and international students. Application fee: $75. Electronic applications accepted. *Financial support:* Fellowships and health care benefits available. *Faculty research:* Biomedical physiology and immunotherapy, cancer biology and molecular therapeutics, molecular pharmacology toxicology and experimental therapeutics, neuroscience. *Unit head:* Dr. Michael Spinella, Director, 603-650-1126, Fax: 603-650-4932. *Application contact:* Gail Egner, Program Administrator, 603-650-4933, Fax: 603-650-4932, E-mail: gail.p.egner@dartmouth.edu.
Website: http://geiselmed.dartmouth.edu/pemm/

Drexel University, College of Medicine, Biomedical Graduate Programs, Molecular Medicine Program, Philadelphia, PA 19104-2875. Offers MS.

Elmezzi Graduate School of Molecular Medicine, Graduate Program, Manhasset, NY 11030. Offers PhD. *Faculty:* 41 full-time (13 women). *Students:* 8 full-time (2 women); includes 2 minority (both Asian, non-Hispanic/Latino). Average age 30. *Degree requirements:* For doctorate, comprehensive exam, thesis/dissertation. *Entrance requirements:* For doctorate, MCAT or GRE, MD or equivalent, current curriculum vitae, official transcripts, three letters of recommendation, interview. *Application deadline:* Applications are processed on a rolling basis. Application fee: $100. *Financial support:* Fellowships with full tuition reimbursements, health care benefits, and tuition waivers (full) available. *Faculty research:* Cardiopulmonary disease, cancer, inflammation, genetics of complex disorders, cytokine biology. *Unit head:* Dr. Bettie M. Steinberg, Provost, 516-562-1159, Fax: 516-562-1022, E-mail: bsteinbe@lij.edu. *Application contact:* Emilia C. Hristis, Education Coordinator, 516-562-3405, Fax: 516-562-1022, E-mail: ehristis@nshs.edu.
Website: http://www.feinsteininstitute.org/education/the-elmezzi-graduate-school-of-molecular-medicine/

The George Washington University, Columbian College of Arts and Sciences, Institute for Biomedical Sciences, Program in Molecular Medicine, Washington, DC 20037. Offers molecular and cellular oncology (PhD); neurosciences (PhD); pharmacology and physiology (PhD). *Students:* 7 full-time (5 women), 22 part-time (16 women); includes 8 minority (2 Black or African American, non-Hispanic/Latino; 5 American Indian or Alaska Native, non-Hispanic/Latino; 1 Hispanic/Latino), 4 international. Average age 29. In 2017, 4 doctorates awarded. *Degree requirements:* For doctorate, comprehensive exam, thesis/dissertation, general exams. *Entrance requirements:* For doctorate, GRE General Test, interview, minimum GPA of 3.0. Additional exam requirements/recommendations for international students: Required—TOEFL (minimum score 600 paper-based). *Application deadline:* For fall admission, 12/15 priority date for domestic and international students. Applications are processed on a rolling basis. Application fee: $75. Electronic applications accepted. *Expenses: Tuition:* Full-time $28,800; part-time $1655 per credit hour. *Required fees:* $45; $2.75 per credit hour. *Financial support:* In 2017–18, 10 students received support. Fellowships with tuition reimbursements available, Federal Work-Study, institutionally sponsored loans, and tuition waivers available. Financial award application deadline: 2/1. *Unit head:* Dr. Norman Lee, Director, 202-994-2179, E-mail: nhlee@gwu.edu. *Application contact:* 202-994-2179, Fax: 202-994-0967, E-mail: gwibs@gwu.edu.
Website: http://smhs.gwu.edu/ibs/program/introduction-molecular-medicine-program

Hofstra University, Donald and Barbara Zucker School of Medicine at Hofstra/Northwell, Hempstead, NY 11549. Offers medicine (MD); molecular basis of medicine (PhD); MD/MPH; MD/PhD. *Accreditation:* LCME/AMA. *Faculty:* 19 full-time (13 women), 15 part-time/adjunct (7 women). *Students:* 417 full-time (196 women); includes 181 minority (20 Black or African American, non-Hispanic/Latino; 90 Asian, non-Hispanic/Latino; 56 Hispanic/Latino; 5 Native Hawaiian or other Pacific Islander, non-Hispanic/Latino; 10 Two or more races, non-Hispanic/Latino), 1 international. Average age 25. 6,088 applicants, 6% accepted, 100 enrolled. In 2017, 75 doctorates awarded. *Entrance requirements:* For doctorate, MCAT. Additional exam requirements/recommendations for international students: Required—TOEFL (for PhD students only). *Application deadline:* For fall admission, 12/1 priority date for domestic students. Application fee: $100. Electronic applications accepted. *Expenses:* $24,720 per term. *Financial support:* In 2017–18, 298 students received support, including 288 fellowships with full and partial tuition reimbursements available (averaging $24,461 per year), research assistantships with full and partial tuition reimbursements available (averaging $6,075 per year); career-related internships or fieldwork, Federal Work-Study, institutionally sponsored loans, scholarships/grants, tuition waivers (full and partial), and unspecified assistantships also available. Support available to part-time students. Financial award applicants required to submit FAFSA. *Faculty research:* Bioelectric medicine; immunology and inflammation; neuroscience; cancer biology; health services/outcomes. *Unit head:* Dr. Lawrence Smith, Dean, 516-463-7517, Fax: 516-463-7540, E-mail: lawrence.smith@hofstra.edu. *Application contact:* Sunil Samuel, Assistant Vice President of Admissions, 516-463-4723, Fax: 516-463-4664.
Website: http://medicine.hofstra.edu/index.html

Johns Hopkins University, School of Medicine, Graduate Programs in Medicine, Graduate Program in Cellular and Molecular Medicine, Baltimore, MD 21287. Offers PhD. *Faculty:* 125 full-time (38 women). *Students:* 113 full-time (72 women); includes 35 minority (4 Black or African American, non-Hispanic/Latino; 2 American Indian or Alaska Native, non-Hispanic/Latino; 17 Asian, non-Hispanic/Latino; 9 Hispanic/Latino; 3 Two or more races, non-Hispanic/Latino), 19 international. Average age 27. 265 applicants, 17% accepted, 21 enrolled. In 2017, 19 doctorates awarded. *Degree requirements:* For doctorate, comprehensive exam, thesis/dissertation, oral exam, thesis defense. *Entrance requirements:* For doctorate, GRE. *Application deadline:* For winter admission, 12/8 for domestic students. Application fee: $110. Electronic applications accepted. *Expenses:* Contact institution. *Financial support:* In 2017–18, 124 students received support, including 3 fellowships with tuition reimbursements available (averaging $31,936 per year), scholarships/grants, health care benefits, and tuition waivers (full) also available. *Faculty research:* Cancer, cardiovascular, cell biology, immunology, neuroscience, genetics of human disease. *Unit head:* Dr. Rajini Rao, Director, 410-955-4732, Fax: 410-614-7294, E-mail: rrao@jhmi.edu. *Application contact:* Leslie Lichter-Mason, Admissions Administrator, 410-614-0391, Fax: 410-614-7294, E-mail: llichte2@jhmi.edu.
Website: http://cmm.jhmi.edu

Liberty University, School of Health Sciences, Lynchburg, VA 24515. Offers anatomy and cell biology (PhD); biomedical sciences (MS); epidemiology (MPH); exercise science (MS), including clinical, community physical activity, human performance, nutrition; global health (MPH); health promotion (MPH); medical sciences (MA), including biopsychology, business management, health informatics, molecular medicine, public health; nutrition (MPH). *Program availability:* Part-time, online learning. *Students:* 542 full-time (394 women), 696 part-time (541 women); includes 402 minority (286 Black or African American, non-Hispanic/Latino; 10 American Indian or Alaska Native, non-Hispanic/Latino; 34 Asian, non-Hispanic/Latino; 46 Hispanic/Latino; 1 Native Hawaiian or other Pacific Islander, non-Hispanic/Latino; 25 Two or more races, non-Hispanic/Latino), 59 international. Average age 32. 1,592 applicants, 40% accepted, 297 enrolled. In 2017, 204 master's awarded. *Degree requirements:* For master's, thesis (for some programs); for doctorate, thesis/dissertation. *Entrance requirements:* For doctorate, MAT or GRE, minimum GPA of 3.25 in master's program, 2-3 recommendations, writing samples (for some programs), letter of intent, professional vitae. Additional exam requirements/recommendations for international students: Required—TOEFL (minimum score 600 paper-based; 100 iBT). Application fee: $50. *Financial support:* Applicants required to submit FAFSA. *Unit head:* Dr. Ralph Linstra, Dean. *Application contact:* Jay Bridge, Director of Admissions, 800-424-9595, Fax: 800-628-7977, E-mail: gradadmissions@liberty.edu.

Oregon Health & Science University, School of Medicine, Graduate Programs in Medicine, Department of Environmental and Biomolecular Systems, Portland, OR 97239-3098. Offers biochemistry and molecular biology (MS, PhD); environmental science and engineering (MS, PhD). *Program availability:* Part-time. *Faculty:* 13 full-time (4 women). *Students:* 7 full-time (6 women), 2 part-time (0 women); includes 1 minority (American Indian or Alaska Native, non-Hispanic/Latino). Average age 32. In 2017, 7 master's, 3 doctorates awarded. Terminal master's awarded for partial completion of doctoral program. *Degree requirements:* For master's, thesis (for some programs); for doctorate, comprehensive exam, thesis/dissertation, qualifying exam. *Entrance requirements:* For master's and doctorate, GRE General Test (minimum scores: 153 Verbal/148 Quantitative/4.5 Analytical) or MCAT (for some programs). *Application deadline:* For fall admission, 7/15 for domestic students, 5/15 for international students; for winter admission, 10/15 for domestic students, 9/15 for international students; for spring admission, 1/15 for domestic students, 12/15 for international students. Applications are processed on a rolling basis. Application fee: $70. Electronic applications accepted. *Financial support:* Health care benefits and full-tuition and stipends (for PhD students) available. Financial award application deadline: 3/1; financial award applicants required to submit FAFSA. *Faculty research:* Metalloprotein biochemistry, molecular microbiology, environmental microbiology, environmental chemistry, biogeochemistry. *Unit head:* Dr. Michiko Nakano, Program Director. *Application contact:* E-mail: somgrad@ohsu.edu.

Penn State Hershey Medical Center, College of Medicine, Graduate School Programs in the Biomedical Sciences, Huck Institutes of the Life Sciences, Intercollege Graduate

Molecular Medicine

Program in Molecular Cellular and Integrative Biosciences, Hershey, PA 17033. Offers cell and developmental biology (PhD); molecular medicine (PhD); molecular toxicology (PhD); neurobiology (PhD). *Students:* 3 full-time (2 women); includes 2 minority (both Asian, non-Hispanic/Latino). 2 applicants, 100% accepted, 2 enrolled. In 2017, 1 doctorate awarded. *Degree requirements:* For doctorate, comprehensive exam, thesis/dissertation, oral exam. *Entrance requirements:* For doctorate, GRE, minimum GPA of 3.0. Additional exam requirements/recommendations for international students: Required—TOEFL (minimum score 500 paper-based). *Application deadline:* For fall admission, 1/31 priority date for domestic students, 2/1 priority date for international students. Applications are processed on a rolling basis. Application fee: $65. Electronic applications accepted. *Financial support:* In 2017–18, research assistantships with full tuition reimbursements (averaging $26,196 per year) were awarded; fellowships with full tuition reimbursements, career-related internships or fieldwork, Federal Work-Study, scholarships/grants, health care benefits, and unspecified assistantships also available. Financial award applicants required to submit FAFSA. *Faculty research:* Vascular biology, molecular toxicology, chemical biology, immune system, pathophysiological basis of human disease. *Unit head:* Dr. Peter Hudson, Director, 814-865-6057, E-mail: pjh18@psu.edu. *Application contact:* Kathy Shuey, Administrative Assistant, 717-531-8982, Fax: 717-531-0786, E-mail: grad-hmc@psu.edu.
Website: http://www.huck.psu.edu/education/molecular-cellular-and-integrative-biosciences

Queen's University at Kingston, School of Graduate Studies, Faculty of Health Sciences, Department of Pathology and Molecular Medicine, Kingston, ON K7L 3N6, Canada. Offers M Sc, PhD. *Program availability:* Part-time. *Degree requirements:* For master's, thesis; for doctorate, comprehensive exam, thesis/dissertation. *Entrance requirements:* Additional exam requirements/recommendations for international students: Required—TOEFL. *Faculty research:* Immunopathology, cancer biology, immunology and metastases, cell differentiation, blood coagulation.

Rutgers University–Newark, Graduate School of Biomedical Sciences, Department of Cell Biology and Molecular Medicine, Newark, NJ 07107. Offers PhD. *Degree requirements:* For doctorate, thesis/dissertation, qualifying exam. *Entrance requirements:* For doctorate, GRE General Test. Additional exam requirements/recommendations for international students: Required—TOEFL. Electronic applications accepted.

Tufts University, Sackler School of Graduate Biomedical Sciences, Cell, Molecular, and Developmental Biology Program, Medford, MA 02155. Offers cancer biology (PhD); developmental and regenerative biology (PhD); molecular and cellular medicine (PhD); structural and chemical biology (PhD). Terminal master's awarded for partial completion of doctoral program. *Degree requirements:* For doctorate, comprehensive exam, thesis/dissertation. *Entrance requirements:* For doctorate, GRE General Test, 3 letters of reference, resume, personal statement. Electronic applications accepted. *Expenses: Tuition:* Full-time $49,892. *Required fees:* $874. Full-time tuition and fees vary according to degree level, program and student level. Part-time tuition and fees vary according to course load. *Faculty research:* Reproduction and hormone action, control of gene expression, cell-matrix and cell-cell interactions, growth control and tumorigenesis, cytoskeleton and contractile proteins.

The University of Alabama at Birmingham, Joint Health Sciences, Pathobiology and Molecular Medicine Theme, Birmingham, AL 35294. Offers PhD. *Faculty:* 370. *Students:* 37 full-time (24 women); includes 15 minority (6 Black or African American, non-Hispanic/Latino; 5 Asian, non-Hispanic/Latino; 4 Hispanic/Latino). Average age 28. 30 applicants, 27% accepted, 6 enrolled. In 2017, 9 doctorates awarded. *Degree requirements:* For doctorate, comprehensive exam, thesis/dissertation. *Entrance requirements:* For doctorate, personal statement, resume or curriculum vitae, letters of recommendation, research experience, interview. Additional exam requirements/recommendations for international students: Required—TOEFL (minimum score 80 iBT), IELTS (minimum score 6.5). *Application deadline:* For fall admission, 12/31 for domestic and international students. Applications are processed on a rolling basis. Electronic applications accepted. *Financial support:* In 2017–18, fellowships with full tuition reimbursements (averaging $29,000 per year), research assistantships with full tuition reimbursements (averaging $30,000 per year) were awarded; health care benefits also available. *Unit head:* Dr. Yabing Chen, Theme Director, 205-996-6293, E-mail: ybchen@uab.edu. *Application contact:* Alyssa Zasada, Admissions Manager for Graduate Biomedical Sciences, 205-934-3857, E-mail: grad-gbs@uab.edu.
Website: http://www.uab.edu/gbs/home/themes/pbmm

The University of Arizona, College of Medicine, Department of Cellular and Molecular Medicine, Tucson, AZ 85721. Offers MS, PhD. *Degree requirements:* For doctorate, comprehensive exam. *Entrance requirements:* Additional exam requirements/recommendations for international students: Required—TOEFL, IELTS. Electronic applications accepted. *Faculty research:* Heart and vascular development, neural development, cellular toxicology, immunobiology, cell biology and cancer biology.

University of Cincinnati, Graduate School, College of Medicine, Graduate Programs in Biomedical Sciences, Program in Pathobiology and Molecular Medicine, Cincinnati, OH 45267-0529. Offers pathology (PhD), including anatomic pathology, laboratory medicine, pathobiology and molecular medicine. *Degree requirements:* For doctorate, thesis/dissertation, qualifying exam. *Entrance requirements:* For doctorate, GRE General Test. Additional exam requirements/recommendations for international students: Required—TOEFL. Electronic applications accepted. *Expenses: Tuition, area resident:* Full-time $14,468. Tuition, state resident: full-time $14,968; part-time $754 per credit hour. Tuition, nonresident: full-time $24,210; part-time $1311 per credit hour. *International tuition:* $26,460 full-time. *Required fees:* $3958; $84 per credit hour. One-time fee: $85 full-time. Tuition and fees vary according to course load, degree level and program. *Faculty research:* Cardiovascular and lipid disorders, digestive and kidney disease, endocrine and metabolic disorders, hematologic and oncogenic, immunology and infectious disease.

University of Maryland, Baltimore, Graduate School, Graduate Program in Life Sciences, Program in Molecular Medicine, Baltimore, MD 21201. Offers cancer biology (PhD); cell and molecular physiology (PhD); human genetics and genomic medicine (PhD); molecular toxicology and pharmacology (PhD); MD/PhD. *Students:* 62 full-time (35 women), 2 part-time (0 women); includes 21 minority (7 Black or African American, non-Hispanic/Latino; 8 Asian, non-Hispanic/Latino; 4 Hispanic/Latino; 2 Two or more races, non-Hispanic/Latino), 4 international. Average age 27. 89 applicants, 30% accepted, 3 enrolled. In 2017, 13 doctorates awarded. *Degree requirements:* For doctorate, comprehensive exam, thesis/dissertation. *Entrance requirements:* For doctorate, GRE, minimum GPA of 3.0, curriculum vitae, essay, 3 letters of recommendation. Additional exam requirements/recommendations for international students: Required—TOEFL (minimum score 80 iBT); Recommended—IELTS (minimum score 7). *Application deadline:* For fall admission, 12/1 priority date for domestic students, 1/15 for international students. Application fee: $75. Electronic applications accepted. *Expenses:* Tuition, state resident: full-time $13,990; part-time $661 per credit. Tuition, nonresident: full-time $30,484; part-time $1310 per credit. *Required fees:* $1894; $94 per credit. $415 per semester. Part-time tuition and fees vary according to course load, degree level and program. *Financial support:* In 2017–18, research assistantships with partial tuition reimbursements (averaging $26,000 per year) were awarded; fellowships and health care benefits also available. Financial award application deadline: 3/1; financial award applicants required to submit FAFSA. *Unit head:* Dr. Toni Antalis, Director, 410-706-8222, E-mail: tantalis@som.umaryland.edu. *Application contact:* Marcina Garner, Program Coordinator, 410-706-6044, Fax: 410-706-6040, E-mail: mgarner@som.umaryland.edu.
Website: http://molecularmedicine.umaryland.edu

University of Nebraska Medical Center, Interdisciplinary Graduate Program in Biomedical Sciences, Integrative Physiology and Molecular Medicine Doctoral Program, Omaha, NE 68198-5850. Offers PhD. *Program availability:* Part-time. *Faculty:* 12 full-time (2 women). *Students:* 2 full-time (both women), both international. Average age 29. 3 applicants, 33% accepted, 1 enrolled. *Degree requirements:* For doctorate, comprehensive exam, thesis/dissertation, at least one first-author research publication. *Entrance requirements:* For doctorate, GRE General Test or MCAT, course work in biology, chemistry, mathematics, and physics; minimum GPA of 3.25. Additional exam requirements/recommendations for international students: Required—TOEFL (minimum score 600 paper-based; 95 iBT), IELTS (minimum score 7). *Application deadline:* For fall admission, 6/1 for domestic students, 4/1 for international students. Applications are processed on a rolling basis. Electronic applications accepted. *Expenses:* Tuition, state resident: full-time $8451; part-time $4225 per semester. Tuition, nonresident: full-time $24,219; part-time $11,295 per semester. *Required fees:* $589; $117 per term. *Financial support:* In 2017–18, 2 research assistantships with full tuition reimbursements (averaging $26,500 per year) were awarded; fellowships, scholarships/grants, health care benefits, and unspecified assistantships also available. Support available to part-time students. Financial award application deadline: 2/1; financial award applicants required to submit FAFSA. *Faculty research:* Cardiovascular, neuroscience, renal physiology and pathophysiology, cardiopulmonary and renal consequences of heart failure, free radical biology, reproductive endocrinology, inflammation. *Total annual research expenditures:* $4.1 million. *Unit head:* Dr. Pamela K. Carmines, Vice Chair for Graduate Education, Department of Cellular and Integrative Physiology, 402-559-9343, Fax: 402-559-4438, E-mail: pcarmines@unmc.edu. *Application contact:* Kim Kavan, Office Associate, 402-559-4426, E-mail: kimberly.kavan@unmc.edu.
Website: https://www.unmc.edu/physiology/education/ipmmprogram/index.html

University of South Florida, Morsani College of Medicine and College of Graduate Studies, Graduate Programs in Medical Sciences, Tampa, FL 33620-9951. Offers advanced athletic training (MS); athletic training (MS); bioinformatics and computational biology (MSBCB); biotechnology (MSB); health informatics (MSHI); medical sciences (MSMS, PhD), including aging and neuroscience (MSMS), allergy, immunology and infectious disease (PhD), anatomy, biochemistry and molecular biology, clinical and translational research, health science (MSMS), interdisciplinary medical sciences (MSMS), medical microbiology and immunology (MSMS), metabolic and nutritional medicine (MSMS), microbiology and immunology (PhD), molecular medicine, molecular pharmacology and physiology (PhD), neuroscience (PhD), pathology and cell biology (PhD), women's health (MSMS). *Students:* 372 full-time (212 women), 216 part-time (142 women); includes 257 minority (78 Black or African American, non-Hispanic/Latino; 1 American Indian or Alaska Native, non-Hispanic/Latino; 79 Asian, non-Hispanic/Latino; 84 Hispanic/Latino; 15 Two or more races, non-Hispanic/Latino), 62 international. Average age 28. 1,048 applicants, 46% accepted, 309 enrolled. In 2017, 351 master's, 56 doctorates awarded. Terminal master's awarded for partial completion of doctoral program. *Degree requirements:* For master's, comprehensive exam, thesis; for doctorate, comprehensive exam, thesis/dissertation. *Entrance requirements:* For master's, GRE General Test or GMAT, bachelor's degree or equivalent from regionally-accredited university with minimum GPA of 3.0 in upper-division sciences coursework; prerequisites in general biology, general chemistry, general physics, organic chemistry, quantitative analysis, and integral and differential calculus; for doctorate, GRE General Test, bachelor's degree from regionally-accredited university with minimum GPA of 3.0 in upper-division sciences coursework; 3 letters of recommendation; personal interview; 1-2 page personal statement; prerequisites in biology, chemistry, physics, organic chemistry, quantitative analysis, and integral/differential calculus. Additional exam requirements/recommendations for international students: Required—TOEFL (minimum score 550 paper-based; 79 iBT) or IELTS (minimum score 6.5). *Application deadline:* For fall admission, 2/1 priority date for domestic students, 2/1 for international students. Application fee: $30. Electronic applications accepted. *Expenses:* Contact institution. *Financial support:* In 2017–18, 109 students received support. *Faculty research:* Anatomy, biochemistry, cancer biology, cardiovascular disease, cell biology, immunology, microbiology, molecular biology, neuroscience, pharmacology, physiology. *Total annual research expenditures:* $45.3 million. *Unit head:* Dr. Michael Barber, Professor/Associate Dean for Graduate and Postdoctoral Affairs, 813-974-9908, Fax: 813-974-4317, E-mail: mbarber@health.usf.edu. *Application contact:* Dr. Eric Bennett, Graduate Director, PhD Program in Medical Sciences, 813-974-1545, Fax: 813-974-4317, E-mail: esbennet@health.usf.edu.
Website: http://health.usf.edu/nocms/medicine/graduatestudies/

The University of Texas Health Science Center at San Antonio, Graduate School of Biomedical Sciences, Department of Molecular Medicine, San Antonio, TX 78245-3207. Offers MS, PhD. Terminal master's awarded for partial completion of doctoral program. *Degree requirements:* For master's, comprehensive exam, thesis; for doctorate, comprehensive exam, thesis/dissertation.

Wake Forest University, School of Medicine and Graduate School of Arts and Sciences, Graduate Programs in Medicine, Program in Molecular Medicine, Winston-Salem, NC 27109. Offers MS, PhD, MD/PhD. *Degree requirements:* For master's, thesis; for doctorate, thesis/dissertation. *Entrance requirements:* For master's and doctorate, GRE General Test. Additional exam requirements/recommendations for international students: Required—TOEFL. Electronic applications accepted. *Faculty research:* Human biology and disease, scientific basis of medicine, cellular and molecular mechanisms of health and disease.

Wayne State University, School of Medicine, Office of Biomedical Graduate Programs, Detroit, MI 48202. Offers anatomy and cell biology (MS, PhD); basic medical sciences (MS); biochemistry and molecular biology (MS, PhD); cancer biology (MS, PhD); clinical and translational science (Graduate Certificate); family medicine and public health sciences (MPH, Graduate Certificate), including public health practice; genetic counseling (MS); immunology and microbiology (MS, PhD); medical physics (MS, PhD, Graduate Certificate); medical research (MS); molecular medicine and genomics (MS, PhD), including molecular genetics and genomics; pathology (PhD); pharmacology (MS, PhD); physiology (MS, PhD), including physiology, reproductive sciences (PhD); psychiatry and behavioral neurosciences (PhD), including translational neuroscience; MD/MPH; MD/PhD; MPH/MA; MSW/MPH. *Program availability:* Part-time, evening/weekend. *Students:* 268 full-time (152 women), 117 part-time (59 women); includes 108 minority (19 Black or African American, non-Hispanic/Latino; 1 American Indian or Alaska Native, non-Hispanic/Latino; 62 Asian, non-Hispanic/Latino; 9 Hispanic/Latino; 17 Two or more races, non-Hispanic/Latino), 48 international. Average age 26. 1,133 applicants, 21% accepted, 151 enrolled. In 2017, 70 master's, 25 doctorates, 10 other advanced degrees awarded. Terminal master's awarded for partial completion of doctoral program. *Degree requirements:* For master's, thesis (for some programs); for doctorate, thesis/dissertation. *Entrance requirements:* For master's, doctorate, and

Graduate Certificate, GRE. Additional exam requirements/recommendations for international students: Required—TOEFL (minimum score 550 paper-based; 100 iBT), Michigan English Language Assessment Battery (minimum score 85); Recommended—IELTS (minimum score 6.5), TWE (minimum score 5.5). *Application deadline:* For fall admission, 2/1 for domestic and international students. Applications are processed on a rolling basis. Application fee: $50. Electronic applications accepted. *Expenses:* Contact institution. *Financial support:* In 2017–18, 177 students received support, including 64 fellowships with full tuition reimbursements available (averaging $24,388 per year), 79 research assistantships with full tuition reimbursements available (averaging $26,894 per year); scholarships/grants, traineeships, and health care benefits also available. *Faculty research:* Cancer biology, neurosciences, vision sciences, molecular biology, pathology, physiology, pharmacology, public health, medical physics. *Unit head:* Dr. Daniel A. Walz, Associate Dean for Biomedical Graduate Programs, 313-577-1455, Fax: 313-577-8796, E-mail: gradprogs@med.wayne.edu.
Website: https://www.med.wayne.edu/biomedical-graduate-programs/

Yale University, Yale School of Medicine and Graduate School of Arts and Sciences, Combined Program in Biological and Biomedical Sciences (BBS), Pharmacological Sciences and Molecular Medicine Track, New Haven, CT 06520. Offers PhD, MD/PhD. *Degree requirements:* For doctorate, thesis/dissertation. *Entrance requirements:* For doctorate, GRE General Test. Additional exam requirements/recommendations for international students: Required—TOEFL. Electronic applications accepted.

Structural Biology

Albert Einstein College of Medicine, Graduate Programs in the Biomedical Sciences, Department of Anatomy and Structural Biology, Bronx, NY 10461. Offers anatomy (PhD); MD/PhD. *Degree requirements:* For doctorate, thesis/dissertation. *Entrance requirements:* For doctorate, GRE General Test. Additional exam requirements/recommendations for international students: Required—TOEFL. *Application deadline:* For fall admission, 1/15 for domestic students. Application fee: $0. Electronic applications accepted. *Financial support:* Fellowships available. *Faculty research:* Cell motility, cell membranes and membrane-cytoskeletal interactions as applied to processing of pancreatic hormones, mechanisms of secretion. *Unit head:* Dr. John S. Condeelis, Co-Chair, 718-678-1126. *Application contact:* Sheila Cleeton, Executive Director and Registrar, Einstein Graduate Division, 718-430-2128, Fax: 718-430-8655, E-mail: sheila.cleeton@einstein.yu.edu.
Website: http://www.einstein.yu.edu/departments/anatomy-structural-biology/

Baylor College of Medicine, Graduate School of Biomedical Sciences, Program in Structural and Computational Biology and Molecular Biophysics, Houston, TX 77030-3498. Offers PhD, MD/PhD. MD/PhD offered jointly with Rice University and University of Houston. *Degree requirements:* For doctorate, thesis/dissertation, public defense. *Entrance requirements:* For doctorate, GRE General Test, GRE Subject Test (strongly recommended), minimum GPA of 3.0. Additional exam requirements/recommendations for international students: Required—TOEFL. Electronic applications accepted. *Faculty research:* Computational biology, structural biology, biophysics.

Carnegie Mellon University, Mellon College of Science, Department of Biological Sciences, Pittsburgh, PA 15213-3891. Offers biochemistry (PhD); biophysics (PhD); cell and developmental biology (PhD); computational biology (MS, PhD); genetics (PhD); molecular biology (PhD); neuroscience (PhD); structural biology (PhD). *Degree requirements:* For doctorate, comprehensive exam, thesis/dissertation. *Entrance requirements:* For doctorate, GRE General Test, GRE Subject Test, interview. Electronic applications accepted. *Faculty research:* Genetic structure, function, and regulation; protein structure and function; biological membranes; biological spectroscopy.

Carnegie Mellon University, Mellon College of Science, Joint Pitt + CMU Molecular Biophysics and Structural Biology Graduate Program, Pittsburgh, PA 15213-3891. Offers PhD. Program offered jointly with University of Pittsburgh. *Degree requirements:* For doctorate, comprehensive exam, thesis/dissertation. *Entrance requirements:* For doctorate, GRE General Test. Additional exam requirements/recommendations for international students: Required—TOEFL (minimum score 600 paper-based; 100 iBT), IELTS (minimum score 7). Electronic applications accepted. *Faculty research:* Structural biology, protein dynamics and folding, computational biophysics, molecular informatics, membrane biophysics and ion channels, NMR, x-ray crystallography cryaelectron microscopy.

Columbia University, College of Physicians and Surgeons, Integrated Program in Cellular, Molecular, Structural and Genetic Studies, New York, NY 10032. Offers PhD. Terminal master's awarded for partial completion of doctoral program. *Degree requirements:* For doctorate, thesis/dissertation. *Entrance requirements:* For doctorate, GRE General Test, GRE Subject Test. Additional exam requirements/recommendations for international students: Required—TOEFL. *Expenses:* Contact institution. *Faculty research:* Transcription, macromolecular sorting, gene expression during development, cellular interaction.

Duke University, Graduate School, University Program in Structural Biology and Biophysics, Durham, NC 27710. Offers Certificate. Students must be enrolled in a participating PhD program (biochemistry, cell biology, chemistry, molecular genetics, neurobiology, pharmacology). *Entrance requirements:* For degree, GRE General Test. Additional exam requirements/recommendations for international students: Required—TOEFL (minimum score 577 paper-based; 90 iBT) or IELTS (minimum score 7).

Florida State University, The Graduate School, College of Arts and Sciences, Program in Molecular Biophysics, Tallahassee, FL 32306. Offers structural biology (PhD). *Faculty:* 32 full-time (6 women). *Students:* 18 full-time (6 women); includes 1 minority (Hispanic/Latino), 9 international. Average age 27. 23 applicants, 48% accepted, 4 enrolled. In 2017, 4 doctorates awarded. *Degree requirements:* For doctorate, comprehensive exam, thesis/dissertation, teaching 1 term in professor's major department. *Entrance requirements:* For doctorate, GRE General Test (minimum score 153 Verbal portion, 154 Quantitative portion). Additional exam requirements/recommendations for international students: Required—TOEFL (minimum score 550 paper-based; 90 iBT), IELTS (minimum score 6.5). *Application deadline:* For fall admission, 12/15 for domestic and international students. Application fee: $30. Electronic applications accepted. *Expenses:* Contact institution. *Financial support:* In 2017–18, 17 students received support, including 4 fellowships with partial tuition reimbursements available (averaging $34,000 per year), 15 research assistantships with partial tuition reimbursements available (averaging $24,200 per year), 2 teaching assistantships with partial tuition reimbursements available (averaging $24,200 per year); scholarships/grants, health care benefits, tuition waivers (partial), and unspecified assistantships also available. Financial award application deadline: 12/15; financial award applicants required to submit FAFSA. *Faculty research:* Protein and nucleic acid structure and function, membrane protein structure, computational biophysics, 3-D image reconstruction. *Unit head:* Dr. Hong Li, Director, 850-644-6785, Fax: 850-644-7244, E-mail: hli4@fsu.edu. *Application contact:* Jana Sefcikova, Academic Coordinator, Graduate Programs, 850-644-1012, Fax: 850-644-7244, E-mail: jsefcikova@fsu.edu.
Website: http://biophysics.fsu.edu/

Illinois State University, Graduate School, College of Arts and Sciences, School of Biological Sciences, Normal, IL 61790. Offers animal behavior (MS); bacteriology (MS); biochemistry (MS); biological sciences (MS); biology (PhD); biophysics (MS); biotechnology (MS); botany (MS, PhD); cell biology (MS); conservation biology (MS); developmental biology (MS); ecology (MS, PhD); entomology (MS); evolutionary biology (MS); genetics (MS, PhD); immunology (MS); microbiology (MS, PhD); molecular biology (MS); molecular genetics (MS); neurobiology (MS); neuroscience (MS); parasitology (MS); physiology (MS, PhD); plant biology (MS); plant molecular biology (MS); plant sciences (MS); structural biology (MS); zoology (MS, PhD). *Program availability:* Part-time. *Degree requirements:* For master's, thesis or alternative; for doctorate, variable foreign language requirement, thesis/dissertation, 2 terms of residency. *Entrance requirements:* For master's, GRE General Test, minimum GPA of 2.6 in last 60 hours of course work; for doctorate, GRE General Test. *Faculty research:* Redoc balance and drug development in schistosoma mansoni, control of the growth of listeria monocytogenes at low temperature, regulation of cell expansion and microtubule function by SPRI, CRUI: physiology and fitness consequences of different life history phenotypes.

Iowa State University of Science and Technology, Bioinformatics and Computational Biology Program, Ames, IA 50011. Offers MS, PhD. *Degree requirements:* For doctorate, thesis/dissertation. *Entrance requirements:* For master's and doctorate, GRE General Test. Additional exam requirements/recommendations for international students: Recommended—TOEFL, IELTS. Electronic applications accepted. *Faculty research:* Functional and structural genomics, genome evolution, macromolecular structure and function, mathematical biology and biological statistics, metabolic and developmental networks.

Massachusetts Institute of Technology, School of Science, Department of Biology, Cambridge, MA 02139. Offers biochemistry (PhD); biological oceanography (PhD); biology (PhD); biophysical chemistry and molecular structure (PhD); cell biology (PhD); computational and systems biology (PhD); developmental biology (PhD); genetics (PhD); immunology (PhD); microbiology (PhD); molecular biology (PhD); neurobiology (PhD). *Degree requirements:* For doctorate, comprehensive exam, thesis/dissertation, teaching assistantship during two semesters. *Entrance requirements:* For doctorate, GRE General Test. Additional exam requirements/recommendations for international students: Required—TOEFL, IELTS. Electronic applications accepted. *Faculty research:* Cellular, developmental and molecular (plant and animal) biology; biochemistry, bioengineering, biophysics and structural biology; classical and molecular genetics, stem cell and epigenetics; immunology and microbiology; cancer biology, molecular medicine, neurobiology and human disease; computational and systems biology.

Michigan State University, The Graduate School, College of Natural Science, Quantitative Biology Program, East Lansing, MI 48824. Offers PhD.

New York University, School of Medicine and Graduate School of Arts and Science, Sackler Institute of Graduate Biomedical Sciences, New York, NY 10016. Offers biomedical imaging and technology (PhD); biostatistics (PhD); cellular and molecular biology (PhD); developmental genetics (PhD); epidemiology (PhD); genome integrity (PhD); immunology and inflammation (PhD); microbiology (PhD); molecular biophysics (PhD); molecular oncology and tumor immunology (PhD); molecular pharmacology (PhD); neuroscience and physiology (PhD), including immunology, molecular oncology; stem cell biology (PhD); systems and computational biomedicine (PhD); MD/PhD. *Faculty:* 207 full-time (51 women). *Students:* 236 full-time (138 women), 1 part-time (0 women); includes 68 minority (13 Black or African American, non-Hispanic/Latino; 26 Asian, non-Hispanic/Latino; 28 Hispanic/Latino; 1 Native Hawaiian or other Pacific Islander, non-Hispanic/Latino), 79 international. Average age 27. 761 applicants, 18% accepted, 59 enrolled. In 2017, 35 doctorates awarded. *Degree requirements:* For doctorate, comprehensive exam, thesis/dissertation, qualifying exam; thesis defense. *Entrance requirements:* For doctorate, GRE. Additional exam requirements/recommendations for international students: Required—TOEFL, IELTS. *Application deadline:* For fall admission, 12/1 for domestic and international students. Applications are processed on a rolling basis. Application fee: $100. Electronic applications accepted. Application fee is waived when completed online. *Expenses:* Contact institution. *Financial support:* Health care benefits, tuition waivers (full), and unspecified assistantships available. *Faculty research:* Biomedical sciences. *Unit head:* Dr. Naoko Tanese, Associate Dean for Biomedical Sciences/Director, Sackler Institute, 212-263-8945, E-mail: naoko.tanese@nyumc.org. *Application contact:* Jessica Dong, Program Manager, 212-263-5648, E-mail: sackler-info@nyumc.org.
Website: https://med.nyu.edu/research/sackler-institute-graduate-biomedical-sciences/

Northwestern University, The Graduate School, Interdisciplinary Biological Sciences Program (IBiS), Evanston, IL 60208. Offers biochemistry (PhD); bioengineering and biotechnology (PhD); biotechnology (PhD); cell and molecular biology (PhD); developmental and systems biology (PhD); nanotechnology (PhD); neurobiology (PhD); structural biology and biophysics (PhD). *Degree requirements:* For doctorate, thesis/dissertation, qualifying exam. *Entrance requirements:* For doctorate, GRE General Test. Additional exam requirements/recommendations for international students: Required—TOEFL (minimum score 600 paper-based). Electronic applications accepted. *Faculty research:* Biophysics/structural biology, cell/molecular biology, synthetic biology, developmental systems biology, chemical biology/nanotechnology.

Stanford University, School of Medicine, Graduate Programs in Medicine, Department of Structural Biology, Stanford, CA 94305-2004. Offers PhD. *Degree requirements:* For doctorate, thesis/dissertation. *Entrance requirements:* For doctorate, GRE General Test, GRE Subject Test. Additional exam requirements/recommendations for international students: Required—TOEFL. Electronic applications accepted. *Expenses: Tuition:* Full-time $48,987; part-time $10,620 per quarter. One-time fee: $400. Tuition and fees vary according to program.

Stony Brook University, State University of New York, Graduate School, College of Arts and Sciences, Department of Biochemistry and Cell Biology, Program in Biochemistry and Structural Biology, Stony Brook, NY 11794. Offers PhD. *Students:* 32

full-time (19 women); includes 4 minority (2 Black or African American, non-Hispanic/Latino; 1 Asian, non-Hispanic/Latino; 1 Hispanic/Latino), 6 international. Average age 27. 35 applicants, 46% accepted, 4 enrolled. In 2017, 7 doctorates awarded. *Degree requirements:* For doctorate, thesis/dissertation. *Entrance requirements:* For doctorate, GRE. Additional exam requirements/recommendations for international students: Required—TOEFL (minimum score 90 iBT). *Application deadline:* For fall admission, 1/15 for domestic students; for spring admission, 10/1 for domestic students. Application fee: $100. *Expenses:* Contact institution. *Financial support:* In 2017–18, 2 fellowships, 17 research assistantships, 6 teaching assistantships were awarded. *Unit head:* Prof. Aaron Neiman, Chair, 631-632-8550, Fax: 631-632-8575, E-mail: aaron.neiman@stonybrook.edu. *Application contact:* Amy Saas, Graduate Program Administrator, 631-632-8613, Fax: 631-632-9730, E-mail: amy.saas@stonybrook.edu.
Website: https://www.stonybrook.edu/bsb/

Tufts University, Sackler School of Graduate Biomedical Sciences, Cell, Molecular, and Developmental Biology Program, Medford, MA 02155. Offers cancer biology (PhD); developmental and regenerative biology (PhD); molecular and cellular medicine (PhD); structural and chemical biology (PhD). Terminal master's awarded for partial completion of doctoral program. *Degree requirements:* For doctorate, comprehensive exam, thesis/dissertation. *Entrance requirements:* For doctorate, GRE General Test, 3 letters of reference, resume, personal statement. Electronic applications accepted. *Expenses: Tuition:* Full-time $49,892. *Required fees:* $874. Full-time tuition and fees vary according to degree level, program and student level. Part-time tuition and fees vary according to course load. *Faculty research:* Reproduction and hormone action, control of gene expression, cell-matrix and cell-cell interactions, growth control and tumorigenesis, cytoskeleton and contractile proteins.

Tulane University, School of Medicine and School of Liberal Arts, Graduate Programs in Biomedical Sciences, Department of Structural and Cellular Biology, New Orleans, LA 70118-5669. Offers MS, PhD, MD/PhD. MS and PhD offered through the Graduate School. *Degree requirements:* For master's, one foreign language, thesis; for doctorate, 2 foreign languages, thesis/dissertation. *Entrance requirements:* For master's, GRE General Test, minimum B average in undergraduate course work; for doctorate, GRE General Test. Additional exam requirements/recommendations for international students: Required—TOEFL. Electronic applications accepted. *Expenses: Tuition:* Full-time $50,920; part-time $2829 per credit hour. *Required fees:* $2040; $44.50 per credit hour. $580 per term. Tuition and fees vary according to course load, degree level and program. *Faculty research:* Reproductive endocrinology, visual neuroscience, neural response to altered hormones.

University at Buffalo, the State University of New York, Graduate School, Jacobs School of Medicine and Biomedical Sciences, Graduate Programs in Medicine and Biomedical Sciences, Department of Structural Biology, Buffalo, NY 14203. Offers MS, PhD. *Faculty:* 2 full-time (0 women), 5 part-time/adjunct (1 woman). *Students:* 2 full-time (0 women). Average age 27. Terminal master's awarded for partial completion of doctoral program. *Degree requirements:* For master's, comprehensive exam, thesis; for doctorate, comprehensive exam, thesis/dissertation. *Entrance requirements:* For master's, BS or BA in science, engineering, or math; for doctorate, GRE General Test, BS or BA in science, engineering, or math. Additional exam requirements/recommendations for international students: Required—TOEFL (minimum score 600 paper-based; 100 iBT). *Application deadline:* For fall admission, 2/1 priority date for domestic and international students. Applications are processed on a rolling basis. Application fee: $50. Electronic applications accepted. *Financial support:* Application deadline: 2/1; applicants required to submit FAFSA. *Faculty research:* Infectious disease, membrane proteins, X-ray crystallography, enzymology, fatty acid metabolism. *Total annual research expenditures:* $4.5 million. *Unit head:* Dr. Michael G. Malkowski, Chair/Professor, 716-898-8624, Fax: 716-898-8660, E-mail: mgm22@buffalo.edu. *Application contact:* Elizabeth A. White, Administrative Director, 716-829-3399, Fax: 716-829-2437, E-mail: bethw@buffalo.edu.
Website: http://mikemalkowski.wordpress.com

The University of Alabama at Birmingham, Joint Health Sciences, Biochemistry, Structural, and Stem Cell Biology Theme, Birmingham, AL 35294. Offers PhD. *Faculty:* 370. *Students:* 40 full-time (16 women); includes 15 minority (3 Black or African American, non-Hispanic/Latino; 1 American Indian or Alaska Native, non-Hispanic/Latino; 7 Asian, non-Hispanic/Latino; 4 Hispanic/Latino). Average age 26. 30 applicants, 33% accepted, 7 enrolled. In 2017, 5 doctorates awarded. *Degree requirements:* For doctorate, comprehensive exam, thesis/dissertation. *Entrance requirements:* For doctorate, personal statement, resume or curriculum vitae, letters of recommendation, research experience, interview. Additional exam requirements/recommendations for international students: Required—TOEFL (minimum score 80 iBT), IELTS (minimum score 6.5). *Application deadline:* For fall admission, 12/31 for domestic and international students. Applications are processed on a rolling basis. Electronic applications accepted. *Financial support:* In 2017–18, fellowships with full tuition reimbursements (averaging $29,000 per year), research assistantships with full tuition reimbursements (averaging $30,000 per year) were awarded; health care benefits also available. *Unit head:* Dr. Thomas Ryan, Theme Director, 205-996-2175, E-mail: tryan@uab.edu. *Application contact:* Alyssa Zasada, Admissions Manager for Graduate Biomedical Sciences, 205-934-3857, E-mail: grad-gbs@uab.edu.
Website: http://www.uab.edu/gbs/home/themes/bssb

University of Connecticut, Graduate School, College of Liberal Arts and Sciences, Department of Molecular and Cell Biology, Storrs, CT 06269. Offers applied genomics (PSM); cell and developmental biology (MS, PhD); genetics and genomics (MS, PhD); microbial systems analysis (PSM); microbiology (MS, PhD); structural biology, biochemistry and biophysics (MS, PhD). Terminal master's awarded for partial completion of doctoral program. *Degree requirements:* For master's, comprehensive exam; for doctorate, thesis/dissertation. *Entrance requirements:* For master's and doctorate, GRE General Test, GRE Subject Test. Additional exam requirements/recommendations for international students: Required—TOEFL (minimum score 550 paper-based). Electronic applications accepted.

The University of Manchester, School of Biological Sciences, Manchester, United Kingdom. Offers adaptive organismal biology (M Phil, PhD); animal biology (M Phil, PhD); biochemistry (M Phil, PhD); bioinformatics (M Phil, PhD); biomolecular sciences (M Phil, PhD); biotechnology (M Phil, PhD); cell biology (M Phil, PhD); cell matrix research (M Phil, PhD); channels and transporters (M Phil, PhD); developmental biology (M Phil, PhD); environmental biology (M Phil, PhD); evolutionary biology (M Phil, PhD); gene expression (M Phil, PhD); genetics (M Phil, PhD); history of science, technology and medicine (M Phil, PhD); immunology (M Phil, PhD); integrative neurobiology and behavior (M Phil, PhD); membrane trafficking (M Phil, PhD); microbiology (M Phil, PhD); molecular and cellular neuroscience (M Phil, PhD); molecular biology (M Phil, PhD); molecular cancer studies (M Phil, PhD); neuroscience (M Phil, PhD); ophthalmology (M Phil, PhD); optometry (M Phil, PhD); organelle function (M Phil, PhD); pharmacology (M Phil, PhD); physiology (M Phil, PhD); plant sciences (M Phil, PhD); stem cell research (M Phil, PhD); structural biology (M Phil, PhD); systems neuroscience (M Phil, PhD); toxicology (M Phil, PhD).

University of Minnesota, Twin Cities Campus, Graduate School, College of Biological Sciences, Biochemistry, Molecular Biology and Biophysics Graduate Program, Minneapolis, MN 55455-0213. Offers PhD. *Degree requirements:* For doctorate, thesis/dissertation. *Entrance requirements:* For doctorate, GRE, 3 letters of recommendation, more than 1 semester of laboratory experience. Additional exam requirements/recommendations for international students: Required—TOEFL (minimum score 625 paper-based; 108 iBT with writing subsection 25 and reading subsection 25) or IELTS (minimum score 7). Electronic applications accepted. *Faculty research:* Microbial biochemistry, biotechnology, molecular biology, regulatory biochemistry, structural biology and biophysics, physical biochemistry, enzymology, physiological chemistry.

University of Oklahoma, College of Arts and Sciences, Department of Chemistry and Biochemistry, Norman, OK 73019. Offers chemistry (MS, PhD), including analytical chemistry, biochemistry, chemical education, inorganic chemistry, inter-and/or multidisciplinary, organic chemistry, physical chemistry, structural biology. *Program availability:* Part-time. *Faculty:* 32 full-time (11 women). *Students:* 69 full-time (29 women), 42 part-time (17 women); includes 14 minority (1 Black or African American, non-Hispanic/Latino; 1 American Indian or Alaska Native, non-Hispanic/Latino; 6 Asian, non-Hispanic/Latino; 4 Hispanic/Latino; 2 Two or more races, non-Hispanic/Latino), 43 international. Average age 26. 91 applicants, 31% accepted, 23 enrolled. In 2017, 11 master's, 7 doctorates awarded. Terminal master's awarded for partial completion of doctoral program. *Degree requirements:* For master's, comprehensive exam (for some programs), thesis (for some programs); for doctorate, comprehensive exam, thesis/dissertation, general exam. *Entrance requirements:* For master's and doctorate, GRE. Additional exam requirements/recommendations for international students: Required—TOEFL (minimum score 79 iBT) or IELTS (minimum score 6.5). *Application deadline:* For fall admission, 3/31 priority date for domestic and international students; for spring admission, 9/1 priority date for domestic and international students. Application fee: $50 ($100 for international students). Electronic applications accepted. *Expenses:* Tuition, state resident: full-time $5119; part-time $213.30 per credit hour. Tuition, nonresident: full-time $19,778; part-time $824.10 per credit hour. *Required fees:* $3458; $133.55 per credit hour. $126.50 per semester. *Financial support:* In 2017–18, 104 students received support, including 34 research assistantships with full tuition reimbursements available (averaging $17,396 per year), 75 teaching assistantships with full tuition reimbursements available (averaging $16,734 per year); institutionally sponsored loans, scholarships/grants, health care benefits, unspecified assistantships, and full tuition with qualifying graduate assistantship also available. Support available to part-time students. Financial award application deadline: 6/1; financial award applicants required to submit FAFSA. *Faculty research:* Structural biology, solid state materials, natural products, membrane biochemistry, bioanalysis. *Total annual research expenditures:* $7.6 million. *Unit head:* Dr. Ronald L. Halterman, Professor and Chair, 405-325-4812, Fax: 405-325-6111, E-mail: rhalterman@ou.edu. *Application contact:* Carol Jones, Operations Manager, 405-325-4811, Fax: 405-325-6111, E-mail: caroljones@ou.edu.
Website: http://www.ou.edu/cas/chemistry

University of Pittsburgh, School of Medicine, Graduate Programs in Medicine and Kenneth P. Dietrich School of Arts and Sciences, Molecular Biophysics and Structural Biology Graduate Program, Pittsburgh, PA 15260. Offers PhD. Program jointly offered with Carnegie Mellon University. *Faculty:* 21 full-time (5 women). *Students:* 10 full-time (5 women), 2 international. Average age 29. 40 applicants, 35% accepted, 5 enrolled. In 2017, 2 doctorates awarded. *Degree requirements:* For doctorate, comprehensive exam, thesis/dissertation. *Entrance requirements:* For doctorate, GRE General Test. Additional exam requirements/recommendations for international students: Required—TOEFL (minimum score 600 paper-based; 100 iBT), IELTS (minimum score 7). *Application deadline:* For fall admission, 1/15 priority date for domestic and international students. Application fee: $50. Electronic applications accepted. *Expenses:* $26,782 full-time resident per academic year, $42,006 non-resident. *Financial support:* In 2017–18, 10 students received support, including 5 research assistantships with full tuition reimbursements available (averaging $29,500 per year); traineeships also available. *Faculty research:* Structure and dynamics of membrane proteins, principles of protein structure and dynamics, macromolecular recognition, gene regulation and signaling, virus structure and nano-machinery. *Unit head:* Dr. James Conway, Director, 412-383-9847, Fax: 412-648-1077, E-mail: mbsbinfo@medschool.pitt.edu. *Application contact:* Lauren Zielinski, Student Affairs Specialist, 412-383-7866, Fax: 412-648-1077, E-mail: mbsbinfo@medschool.pitt.edu.
Website: http://www.mbsb.pitt.edu

University of Rochester, School of Medicine and Dentistry, Graduate Programs in Medicine and Dentistry, Department of Biochemistry and Biophysics, Programs in Biophysics, Rochester, NY 14627. Offers biophysics, structural and computational biology (PhD). Terminal master's awarded for partial completion of doctoral program. *Degree requirements:* For doctorate, thesis/dissertation, qualifying exam. *Entrance requirements:* For doctorate, GRE General Test.

The University of Texas Health Science Center at San Antonio, Graduate School of Biomedical Sciences, Department of Cellular and Structural Biology, San Antonio, TX 78229-3900. Offers MS, PhD. *Degree requirements:* For master's, thesis; for doctorate, comprehensive exam, thesis/dissertation.

The University of Texas Medical Branch, Graduate School of Biomedical Sciences, Program in Biochemistry and Molecular Biology, Galveston, TX 77555. Offers biochemistry (PhD); bioinformatics (PhD); biophysics (PhD); cell biology (PhD); computational biology (PhD); structural biology (PhD). *Degree requirements:* For doctorate, thesis/dissertation. *Entrance requirements:* Additional exam requirements/recommendations for international students: Required—TOEFL (minimum score 550 paper-based). Electronic applications accepted.

University of Washington, Graduate School, School of Medicine, Graduate Programs in Medicine, Department of Biological Structure, Seattle, WA 98195. Offers PhD. *Degree requirements:* For doctorate, thesis/dissertation. *Faculty research:* Cellular and developmental biology, experimental immunology and hematology, molecular structure and molecular biology, neurobiology, x-rays.

Weill Cornell Medicine, Weill Cornell Graduate School of Medical Sciences, Biochemistry, Cell and Molecular Biology Allied Program, New York, NY 10065. Offers MS, PhD. Terminal master's awarded for partial completion of doctoral program. *Degree requirements:* For master's, comprehensive exam; for doctorate, thesis/dissertation, final exam. *Entrance requirements:* For doctorate, GRE General Test, background in genetics, molecular biology, chemistry, or biochemistry. Additional exam requirements/recommendations for international students: Required—TOEFL. Electronic applications accepted. *Faculty research:* Molecular structure determination, protein structure, gene structure, stem cell biology, control of gene expression, DNA replication, chromosome maintenance, RNA biosynthesis.

GERSTNER SLOAN KETTERING GRADUATE SCHOOL OF BIOMEDICAL SCIENCES

Ph.D. in Cancer Biology Program

Gerstner Sloan Kettering
Graduate School of Biomedical Sciences
Memorial Sloan Kettering Cancer Center

Program of Study

The Louis V. Gerstner, Jr. Graduate School of Biomedical Sciences, Memorial Sloan Kettering Cancer Center offers a doctoral program that trains laboratory scientists to work in research areas directly applicable to human disease and, in particular, cancer.

The unique curriculum integrates Memorial Sloan Kettering's basic science and clinical arms to maximize the potential of future basic scientists to improve human health.

During the first year, students complete a core course that introduces recent findings in relevant topics through didactic lecture and discussion of research papers. A practicum in biostatistics and computational biology is offered in the fall and spring semesters. Students will also complete three 5-week laboratory rotations, with each one culminating in an oral presentation of their findings; three visits with clinicians; course work in logic and critical analysis; and two semesters of the President's Research Seminar Series Journal Club, which introduces students to the published works of world-renowned speakers.

After completing the didactic portion of their education in the first year, students focus full time on thesis research. Students are expected to present a written and oral thesis proposal by March 31 of the second year. Following successful completion of the Thesis Proposal Exam (TPE), students are advanced to candidacy. Continuing throughout their graduate programs, students take part in the Current Topics Journal Club, together with the Graduate Student Seminar, in which students present their own research.

Students also have the option of selecting a clinical mentor who directs the student in participating in hospital-based academic activities such as grand rounds and conferences with pathology and disease management teams.

Research Facilities

Memorial Sloan Kettering's research space totals approximately 575,000 square feet, with many cutting-edge laboratories and facilities housed within the Rockefeller Research Laboratories building and the Zuckerman Research Center, a building with open, spacious floors designed to encourage collaboration.

There are dozens of research core facilities that serve both basic and clinical research needs, offering state-of-the-art instruments and technical staff support to graduate students. The Memorial Sloan Kettering Cancer Center library subscribes to a full range of science, medical, and healthcare resources. Students have access to an array of published literature, with the majority of these titles available electronically. The library's website provides access to an extensive collection of resources, including an online catalog, databases, electronic books, and electronic journals.

Financial Aid

All matriculated students receive a fellowship package that includes an annual stipend ($39,815 for 2018–19); a first-year allowance to be used for books, journals, and other school expenses; a scholarship that covers the full cost of tuition and fees; comprehensive medical, dental, and vision insurance; a laptop computer; relocation costs (up to $500); and paid membership in the New York Academy of Sciences.

Eligible students may also apply for individual funding from agencies such as the National Institutes of Health and the National Science Foundation. Recipients of one of these fellowships receive an additional stipend of $5,000 per year during the award period from the school; this is in addition to any supplement necessary to bring the stipend to the common level. Travel awards are given to students who present a poster or a short talk at a scientific meeting.

Living and Housing Costs

Affordable housing in proximity to the research buildings is provided to all Gerstner Sloan Kettering students. Housing units are located in family-oriented neighborhoods on or near Manhattan's Upper East Side. Students who have spouses or significant others can apply for family units. The housing contract runs for the student's duration of study and is automatically renewed each year based on academic progress.

Student Group

Currently there are 73 full-time students (53 percent men, 47 percent women), with 11 percent minority and 42 percent international. Applicants are expected to hold an undergraduate degree from an accredited institution and have significant basic science research experience. College-level coursework in the following areas is required: biology, chemistry, physics, organic chemistry, mathematics, and biochemistry.

Student Outcomes

Graduates of the program are expected to enter into careers as researchers, scientists, and educators in excellent laboratories, hospitals, medical schools, and research institutions throughout the country and around the world.

Location

The campus is located on Manhattan's Upper East Side, home to some of New York City's best shopping and dining. Several world-famous museums are within walking distance, and Central Park is a few blocks away. New York also offers theater, live music, outdoor recreation, and cultural attractions such as the Metropolitan Museum of Art, all accessible by public transportation.

Gerstner Sloan Kettering Graduate School of Biomedical Sciences

The Faculty

Information regarding the faculty members is available online at: http://www.sloankettering.edu/research/faculty.

The Graduate School

The Louis V. Gerstner, Jr. Graduate School of Biomedical Sciences, Memorial Sloan Kettering Cancer Center, offers the next generation of basic scientists an intensive Ph.D. program to study the biological sciences through the lens of cancer.

The Gerstner Sloan Kettering Graduate School of Biomedical Sciences is accredited by the New York State Board of Regents and the Commissioner of Education, located at 89 Washington Avenue, Albany, New York 12234; phone: 518-474-3852.

Cancer Biology, HEGIS code: 0499.00 has been approved by the New York State Education Department as the official program offered by GSK. This program has been registered and is listed on the Department's Inventory of Registered Programs: http://www.nysed.gov/heds/IRPSL1.html

The school can award two graduate degrees: Master of Science (M.S.), program code: 29204, and Doctor of Philosophy (PhD.), program code: 29205.

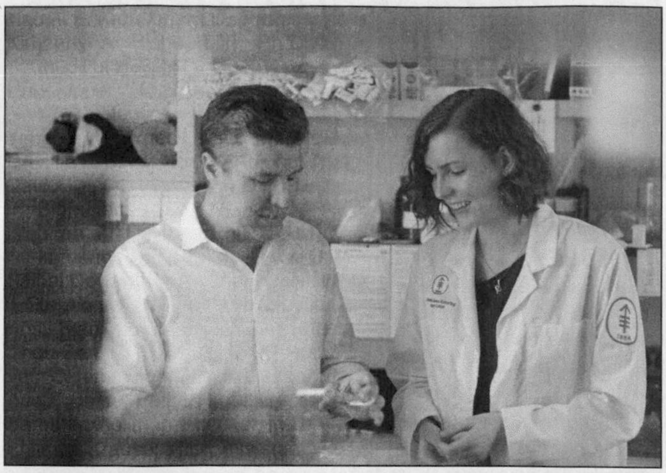

Dr. Michael Overholtzer with Michelle Reigman in the laboratory.

The Louis V. Gerstner, Jr. Graduate School of Biomedical Sciences, Memorial Sloan Kettering Cancer Center offers a doctoral program that trains laboratory scientists to work in research areas directly applicable to human disease, and in particular, cancer.

Applying

Prospective students must submit the online application, official transcripts from all colleges previously attended, and three letters of recommendation from advisers and/or research mentors. Submission of General and Advanced Subject Graduate Record Examination (GRE) scores is optional and not required for admission. Official scores for the Test of English as a Foreign Language (TOEFL) exams are required for applicants who do not speak English as their first language (can be waived for those who earned their undergraduate degrees in the United States). An in-person interview is requested from those applicants being seriously considered for admission, but the requirement may be waived if geographical constraints are overwhelming and may be substituted with video interviews. There is currently no application fee. The deadline to apply is December 1, and interviews take place the following January.

Correspondence and Information

Gerstner Sloan Kettering Graduate School of Biomedical Sciences
Memorial Sloan Kettering Cancer Center
1275 York Avenue, Box 441
New York, New York 10065
Phone: 646-888-6639
Fax: 646-422-2351
E-mail: gradstudies@sloankettering.edu
Website: http://www.sloankettering.edu

UNIFORMED SERVICES UNIVERSITY OF THE HEALTH SCIENCES

F. Edward Hébert School of Medicine Graduate Program in Molecular and Cell Biology

Program of Study

The program of study is designed for full-time students who wish to obtain a Ph.D. degree in the area of molecular and cell biology. This interdepartmental graduate program, which includes faculty members from both basic and clinical departments, offers research expertise in a wide range of areas, including bacteriology, immunology, genetics, biochemistry, regulation of gene expression, and cancer biology. The program includes core courses in molecular and cell biology that provide necessary knowledge for modern biomedical research, as well as advanced electives in areas of faculty expertise. The first-year curriculum includes courses in biochemistry, cell biology, experimental methodology, genetics, and immunology. During the first summer, students participate in laboratory rotations in two laboratories of their choice, leading to the choice of a mentor for their doctoral research. The second-year curriculum offers advanced elective courses in a variety of disciplines, including biochemistry, cell biology, immunology, molecular endocrinology, and virology, and marks the transition from classwork to original laboratory research. Throughout their graduate experience, students participate in journal clubs designed to foster interaction across disciplines and to develop the critical skills needed for data presentation and analysis. A year-round seminar series brings renowned scientists to the Uniformed Services University of the Health Sciences (USUHS) to share their results and to meet with students and faculty members. Students may also take advantage of seminars hosted by other programs and departments as well as those presented at the National Institutes of Health. Completion of the research project and preparation and successful defense of a written dissertation leads to the degree of Doctor of Philosophy.

Research Facilities

The University possesses outstanding facilities for research in molecular and cell biology. Well-equipped laboratories and extramurally funded faculty members provide an outstanding environment in which to pursue state-of-the-art research. Shared equipment in a modern biomedical instrumentation core facility includes oligonucleotide and peptide synthesizers and sequencers; a variety of imaging equipment, including laser confocal and electron microscopes; fluorescent-activated cell sorters; and an ACAS workstation. A recently added proteomics facility contains both MADLI-TOF and ESI tandem mass spectrometers. All offices, laboratories, and the Learning Resource Center are equipped with high-speed Internet connectivity and have access to an extensive online journal collection.

Financial Aid

USUHS provides an attractive package of financial support that is administered as a federal salary. This salary is available on a competitive basis to all civilian graduate students. Salaries are made on an annual basis and are renewable for up to three years. For the 2018 academic year, salaries offered for graduate students were $44,981 per year. In addition to this base support, health insurance and transit benefits are provided if needed.

Cost of Study

Graduate students are **not** required to pay tuition. Civilian graduate students do **not** incur any obligation to the United States government for service after completion of their graduate training programs. Active-duty military personnel incur an obligation for additional military service by Department of Defense regulations that govern sponsored graduate education. Students are required to maintain health insurance.

Living and Housing Costs

The University does not have housing for graduate students. However, there is an abundant supply of rental housing in the area. Living costs in the greater Washington, D.C., area are comparable to those of other East Coast metropolitan areas.

Student Group

The first graduate students in the interdisciplinary Graduate Program in Molecular and Cell Biology at USUHS were admitted in 1995. Over the last decade, the Graduate Program in Molecular and Cell Biology has grown significantly; 25 students are currently enrolled. More than 45 Ph.D. degrees in molecular and cell biology have been awarded over the past eighteen years.

Location

Metropolitan Washington has a population of about 5 million residents in the District of Columbia and the surrounding areas of Maryland and Virginia. The region is a center of education and research and is home to five major universities, four medical schools, the National Library of Medicine and the National Institutes of Health (next to the USUHS campus), Walter Reed National Military Medical Center, the Armed Forces Institute of Pathology, the Library of Congress, the Smithsonian Institution, the National Bureau of Standards, and many other private and government research centers. Many cultural advantages of the area include the theater, a major symphony orchestra, major-league sports, and world-famous museums. The Metro subway system has a station near campus and provides a convenient connection from the University to museums and cultural attractions of downtown Washington. The University is within easy distance of three major airports: Baltimore Washington International, Reagan International, and Dulles International. Both Reagan and Dulles International airports are accessible from the University via metro subway. For outdoor activities, the Blue Ridge Mountains, the Chesapeake Bay, and the Atlantic coast beaches are all within a few hours' drive.

The University

USUHS is located just outside Washington, D.C., in Bethesda, Maryland. The campus is situated on an attractive, wooded site at the Walter Reed National Military Medical Center and is close to several major federal health research facilities. Through various affiliation agreements, these institutes provide additional resources to enhance the educational experience of graduate students at USUHS.

Applying

Both civilians and military personnel are eligible to apply for graduate study at USUHS. Before matriculation, each applicant must complete a baccalaureate degree that includes college-level courses in biology, inorganic chemistry, mathematics, organic chemistry, and physics. Advanced courses in biology, chemistry, or related fields, such as biochemistry, cell biology, genetics, immunology, microbiology, molecular biology, and physical chemistry, are desirable but not essential. Each applicant must complete an online application at https://registrar.usuhs.edu. Active-duty military personnel must obtain the approval and sponsorship of their parent military department in addition to acceptance from USUHS. USUHS subscribes fully to the policy of equal educational opportunity and selects students on a competitive basis without regard to race, sex, creed, or national origin. Students may apply online at https://registrar.usuhs.edu or https://www.usuhs.edu/graded/prospectivestudents. Completed applications must be received before December 1 for matriculation in August. Applications received between December 2 and June 1 may be considered if space is available.

Correspondence and Information

For an application and information about the program, contact:

Dr. Mary Lou Cutler, Director
Graduate Program in Molecular and Cell Biology
Uniformed Services University of the Health Sciences
4301 Jones Bridge Road
Bethesda, Maryland 20814
United States
Phone: 301-295-3642
Fax: 301-295-1996
E-mail: mary.cutler@usuhs.edu
Website: http://www.usuhs.edu/mcb/

Tina Finley
Administrative Officer
Uniformed Services University of the Health Sciences
4301 Jones Bridge Road
Bethesda, Maryland 20814
United States
Phone: 301-295-3642
E-mail: netina.finley@usuhs.edu

THE FACULTY AND THEIR RESEARCH

Regina C. Armstrong, Professor and Director of Translational Research, Center for Neuroscience and Regenerative Medicine; Ph.D., University of North Carolina at Chapel Hill, 1987. Cellular and molecular mechanisms of neural stem/progenitor cell development and regeneration in demyelinating diseases and brain injury models.

Roopa Biswas, Assistant Professor, Ph.D. Ohio State, 1997. Mechanisms of regulation of inflammation; https://www.usuhs.edu/apg/faculty.

Christopher C. Broder, Professor and Director; Ph.D., Florida, 1989. Virus-host cell interactions, vaccines, and therapeutics; *Henipaviruses*; filoviruses; Australian bat *Lyssavirus*.

Teodor Brumeanu, Professor; M.D., Carol Davila (Romania), 1978. Medicine.

Barrington G. Burnett, Assistant Professor; Ph.D., Pennsylvania, 2005. The ubiquitin-proteasome system in neuronal maintenance and neurodegeneration.

Thomas P. Conrads, Professor, Ph.D., Ohio State, 1999. Discovery and validation of genomic, proteomic, and small molecule biomarkers and surrogates for enhanced cancer patient management through improved early detection, patient stratification, and monitoring for therapeutic efficacy, outcome, and recurrence.

Rachel Cox, Assistant Professor, Ph.D., North Carolina at Chapel Hill, 1998. Mitochondrial dynamics and inheritance during development. *Dis. Model Mech.* 2(9/10):490–9, 2009.

Mary Lou Cutler, Professor and Director; Ph.D., Drexel (Hahnemann), 1980. Role of molecules that suppress transformation by the Ras oncogene; adhesion signal transduction and human carcinogenesis. *Cell Adhes. Migrat.* 9:1–6, 2015; *Exp. Cell Res.* 330:358–70, 2015; *Cell Communication and Signaling* 7:279–93, 2013; *Eur. J. Cell Biol.* 87:721–34, 2008; *J. Cell. Physiol.* 214:38–46, 2007; *BMC Cell Biol.* 7:34, 2006;.

Clifton Dalgard, Associate Professor; Core Director, The American Genome Center; Ph.D., C.L.S., Uniformed Services University of the Health Sciences, 2005. Identification of a small molecule that selectively inhibits ERG-positive cancer cell growth, *Canc. Res.* 78(13), 2018.

Michael Daly, Professor; Ph.D., London, 1988. Pathology.

Thomas N. Darling, Professor; M.D./Ph.D., Duke, 1990. mTOR signaling pathway in skin regeneration and disease. *eLife* 6:e23202, 2017; *J. Am. Acad. Dermatol.*

153:660–5, 2017; *J. Clin. Invest.* 127:349–64, 2017; *J. Investig. Dermatol.* 136:535–8, 2016; *Hum. Mol. Genet.* 23:2023–9, 2014.

Stephen Davies, Assistant Professor; Ph.D., Cornell. Microbiology.

Thomas A. Davis, Professor, Deputy Vice Chair of Research; Ph.D., George Washington University, 1993. Traumatic injury, wound healing, heteropic ossification, allograft transplantation, tolerance induction. *Stem Cells Transl. Med.* 3:1–7, 2014; *Clin. Orthop. Relat. Res.* 473:2831–9.,2015; *Shock 44 Suppl.* 1:123–8.

Regina Day, Professor; Ph.D., Tufts, 1995. Mechanisms of normal tissue repair and mechanisms of fibrotic remodeling, especially radiation. *Mol. Biol. Cell* 21:4240–50, 2010; *Mol. Biol. Cell* 24:2088–07, 2013; *Mol. Pharmacol.* 85:898–908, 2014.

Saibal Dey, Professor and Vice Chair, Department of Biochemistry; Ph.D., Wayne State (Michigan), 1994. Allosteric modulation of the human multidrug transporter P-glycoprotein (MDR1 or ABCB1), which confers multidrug resistance in cancer cells and alters bioavailability of many anticancer and antimicrobial agents. *Biochemistry* 51:2852–66, 2012; *J. Biol. Chem.* 281(16):10699–777, 2006; *Biochemistry* 45:2739–51, 2006; *J. Biol. Chem.* 278(20):18132–9, 2003.

Albert Dobi, Associate Director, Basic Science Research Program, Center for Prostate Disease Research; Research Assistant Professor of Surgery and Molecular/Cell Biology, Department of Surgery; Ph.D., University of Szeged (Hungary). Mechanisms of prostate tumorigenesis. *Nat. Rev. Urol.* 15:125–31, 2018; *Canc. Res.* 78:3659–71, 2018; *Mol. Canc. Res.* 15:1308–17, 2017; *E-Biomedicine (Lancet)* 2:1957–64, 2015.

Martin Doughty, Associate Professor, Department of Anatomy, Physiology, and Genetics; Ph.D. Optimizing induced pluripotent stem cells (iPSCs) for cell replacement therapy to treat traumatic brain injury (TBI); identifying transcriptional programs that function in cerebellar neurogenesis and pattern formation.

Yang Du, Associate Professor; Ph.D., Texas Tech, 2000. Leukemia development mechanisms. *Nat. Genet.* 45:942–6, 2013; *Leumekia* 30:200–8, 2016; *Oncotarget* 7:86300–12, 2016.

J. Stephen Dumler, Professor, M.D.; University of Maryland, Baltimore, 1985. Vector-borne diseases, especially tick-transmitted rickettsiae; mechanisms of disease, epigenetics of microbe-host interactions; immunopathology; vascular permeability.

Teresa M. Dunn, Professor; Ph.D., Brandeis, 1984. Sphingolipid synthesis and function. *J. Biol. Chem.* 277:11481–8, 2002 and 277:10194–200, 2002; *Mol. Cell Biol.* 21:109–25, 2001; *Methods Enzymol.* 312:317–30, 2000.

Gabriela S. Dveksler, Professor; Ph.D., Uniformed Services University of the Health Sciences, 1991. Roles of placentally-derived pregnancy specific glycoproteins in immunomodulation and angiogenesis. *Mucosal Immunology* 7:348–58, 2014; *J. Biol. Chem.* 290:4422–31, 2015.

Ying-Hong Feng, Associate Professor; Ph.D., Oxford, 1993. Pharmacology.

Thomas P. Flagg, Ph.D., Assistant Professor, Maryland, Baltimore, 2001. Cardiac ATP-sensitive potassium channel structure and function.

Kristi L. Frank, Assistant Professor; Ph.D., Mayo Clinic College of Medicine, 2007. Mechanisms of biofilm formation by Gram-positive pathogens; prevention and treatment of biofilm infections.

Zygmund Galdzicki, Professor; Ph.D., Wroclaw (Poland), 1982. Neurophysiological and molecular mechanisms underlying functional brain deficits following repetitive traumatic brain injury; exposure to high altitude and sleep deprivation, with particular emphasis on neuronal network activity, brain vasculature, and microglial function.

Chou Zen Giam, Professor; Ph.D., UConn Health Center, 1983. Human T-cell leukemia viruses and Kaposi's sarcoma herpesvirus; NF-kappa B regulation; genomic instability and senescence; viral oncogenesis. *PLoS Pathogens* 11:e1005102, 2015; *Oncogene* doi:10.1038/onc.2013.567, 2014; *PLoS Pathogens* 7:e1002025, 2011.

David A. Grahame, Professor; Ph.D., Ohio State, 1984. Metalloenzyme structure and function in bacteria and archaea. *Biochemistry* 52:1705–16, 2013; *J. Biol. Chem.* 285(20):15450–63, 2010.

Sergey Iordanskiy, Assistant Professor; Ph.D., Moscow State (Russia), 1994. Endogenous retroviruses and retroelements in inflammatory response, including radiation-induced inflammation; exosomes in intercellular communications under stress conditions and in cell pathogenesis. *J. Biol. Chem.* 292(28):11682–701, 2017; *J. Biol. Chem.* 291(3):1251–66, 2016.

Ann E. Jerse, Associate Professor; Ph.D., Maryland, Baltimore, 1991. Estradiol-treated female mice as surrogate hosts for *Neisseria gonorrhoeae* genital-tract infections. *Front. Microbio.* 2:107, 2011, doi: 10.3389/fmicb.2011.00107.

Sharon L. Juliano, Professor; Ph.D., Pennsylvania, 1982. Mechanisms of development and plasticity in the cerebral cortex, with particular emphasis on the migration of neurons into the cortical plate; factors maintaining the function and morphology of radial glia and Cajal-Retzius cells.

Robert Kortum, Assistant Professor; M.D., Ph.D. Nebraska, 2006. Identification of therapeutic targets in Ras-driven cancers.

Prasanna Satpute-Krishnan, Assistant Professor; Ph.D., Brown, 2007. Protein quality control and trafficking in the secretory pathway.

Jason Lees, Assistant Professor; Ph.D., Iowa, 2004. T cell trafficking and lesion development in neuroinflammation.

Joseph Mattapallil, Associate Professor; Ph.D., California, Davis, 1997. Molecular and cellular mechanisms of retrovirus (HIV and SIV) and *Falvivirus* (Zika and Dengue) pathogenesis using nonhuman primate models. *Sci. Rep.* 7(1):10498, 2017; *Cell. Immunol.* 310:156–64, 2016; *J. Immunol. Res.* 15:673815, 2015; *J. Virol.* 8995:2972–8, 2015; *Clin. Vaccine Immunol.* 21(11):1469–73, 2014; *Curr. HIV Res.* 2014; *PLos One* 9(5):e98060; *J. Virol.* 87(12):7093–101, 2013.

Anthony T. Maurelli, Professor; Ph.D., Alabama at Birmingham, 1983. Molecular genetics of bacterial pathogens; molecular biology and pathogenesis of the intracellular pathogens *Shigella* and *Chlamydia*. *Nature* 506:507–10, 2014; *BMC Genom.* 11:272, 2010; *mBio* 2:e00051-11, 2011.

Ernest Maynard, Assistant Professor; Ph.D., Texas A&M, 2001. Zinc binding to the HCCH motif of HIV-1 virion infectivity factor induces a conformational change that mediates protein-protein interactions. *Proc. Natl. Acad. Sci. U.S.A.* 103:18475–80, 2006.

Joseph T. McCabe, Professor and Vice Chair; Ph.D., CUNY Graduate Center, 1983. Diazoxide, as a postconditioning and delayed preconditioner trigger, increases HSP25 and HSP70 in the central nervous system following combined cerebral stroke and hemorrhagic shock. *J. Neurotrauma* 24(3):532–46. 2007.

D. Scott Merrell, Professor; Ph.D., Tufts, 2001. *H. pylori*, gene regulation; gastric cancer; role of the microbiome in health and disease; MRSA and skin and soft tissue infections; copper resistance in *Acinetobacter baumannii*. *Sci. Rep.* 7(1):11057, 2017, doi: 10.1038/s41598-017-11382-y.

Alexandra C. Miller, Assistant Professor; Ph.D., SUNY, 1986. Low dose radiation and heavy metal exposure induced late effects: mechanisms and prevention. Development of models to study radiation late effects. *Rev. Environ. Health* 29(3):25–34, 2013.

Edward Mitre, Assistant Professor; M.D., Johns Hopkins, 1995. Immune modulation by parasitic helminthes; www.usuhs.mil/mic/mitre.html.

Galina Petukhova, Associate Professor, Ph.D., Shemyakin & Ovchinnikov Institute of Bioorganic Chemistry, Moscow, 1994. Molecular mechanisms of genetic recombination in mammals. *Nature* 472:375–78, 2011.

Harvey Pollard, Professor and Chair; Ph.D., 1969, M.D., 1973, Chicago. Differential regulation of inflammation by inflammatory mediators in cystic fibrosis lung epithelial cells. *J. Interferon Cytokine Res.* 33:121–9, 2013.

Jeremy Rotty, Assistant Professor; Ph.D., Johns Hopkins, 2011. Leukocyte migration, with particular emphasis on extracellular matrix sensing by macrophages. Major approaches in the lab include using mice as an in vivo system to directly image endogenous macrophages as they respond to physiological and pathological cues, and in vitro studies using microfluidic chambers to investigate macrophage motility in 2-D and 3-D in vitro. *Dev. Cell* 42(5):498–513, 2017; *Dev. Cell* 32(1):54–67, 2015; *Nat. Rev. Mol. Cell Biol.* 14(1):7–12, 2013.

Brian C. Schaefer, Professor; Ph.D., Harvard, 1995. Mechanisms of leukocyte activation, particularly regulation of cytoplasmic signals to NF-kappaB; role of immune response in neurotropic viral infections; regulation of macrophage survival and function; macrophage role in anti-tumor immunity; imaging, biochemical, and cellular approaches to elucidate signal transduction mechanisms. *Brain Behav. Immun.* 61:96–109, 2017; *Science Signaling* 7:ra45, 2014; *Immunity* 36:947–58, 2012

David Scott, Professor; Ph.D., Yale. Regulation of the immune response; CAR therapy; immune tolerance; hemophilia; autoimmunity. *Blood* 125:1107. PMID: 25498909; *Blood* 129: 238–45; *Mol. Ther.* 18:1527–35, PMID; 20485267; *Sci. Transl. Med.* 2015 Feb. 18;7(275):275ra21. PMID 25696000, 2015.

Frank Shewmaker, Assistant Professor; Ph.D., Tulane. Prions, amyloid, and protein aggregation, especially in relation to neurodegenerative disease.

Vijay K. Singh, Professor; Ph.D. Central Drug Research Institute (India), 1983. Mechanism of radiation injury and advanced development of promising radiation countermeasures for acute radiation syndrome. *Sci. Rep.* 7:9777, 2017; *Sci. Transl. Med.* 9:eaal2408, 2017; *Radiat. Res.* 185:285–98, 2016; *PLoS One* 10:e0135388, 2015; *Int. J. Radiat. Biol.* 91:690–702, 2015.

Clifford M. Snapper, Professor; M.D., Albany Medical College, 1981. In vivo regulation of protein- and polysaccharide-specific humoral immunity to extracellular bacteria and development of antibacterial and antiviral vaccines. *Vaccine* 34(34):4050–5, 2016. *Vaccine* 31(30):3039–45, 2013.

Andrew Snow, Associate Professor; Ph.D., Stanford, 2005. Molecular control of human lymphocyte homeostasis via antigen receptor signaling and apoptosis; dysregulation of lymphocyte homeostasis in monogenic immune disorders. *Front. Immunol.* 8:913, 2017, *Nat. Genet.* 49:1192–1201, 2017; *J. Immunol.* 198: 147–155, 2017; *Sci. Trans. Med.* 8:321ra7, 2016.

Shiv Srivastava, Professor and Co-Director, Center for Prostate Disease Research, Department of Surgery; Ph.D., Indian Institute of Technology (New Delhi), 1980. Prostate cancer molecular biology/translational research. *Canc. Res.* 78:3659–71, 2018; *Nat. Rev. Urol.* 15:125–31, 2018; *Sci. Rep.* 7:1109, 2017; *E-Biomedicine (Lancet)*, 2:1957–64, 2015.

Tharun Sundaresan, Associate Professor; Ph.D., Centre for Cellular and Molecular Biology (India), 1995. Mechanism of eukaryotic mRNA decay, with particular focus on the role of Lsm1-7-Pat1 complex. *RNA* 20:1465—75, 2014; *Int. Rev. Cell Mol. Biol.* 272:149–89, 2009.

Viqar Syed, Associate Professor; Ph.D., Karolinska Institute (Stockholm). Understanding the process of carcinogenesis and developing novel therapeutic strategies for cancer prevention. *Gynecol. Oncol.* 140:503–11, 2016; *J. Cell. Biochem.* 117:1279–87, 2016; *Oncotarget* 7:69733–48, 2016; *Oncotarget* 7:77576–90, 2016; *Oncotarget* 8:113583–97, 2017.

Aviva Symes, Professor; Ph.D., University College (London), 1990. Neuroinflammation, neurogenesis, and therapeutics after traumatic brain injury. *Brain* 138:3299–315, 2015; *Amer. J. Pathol.* 185:2641–52, 2015.

Geeta Upadhyay; Ph.D., SG Postgraduate Institute of Medical Sciences, (India), 2003. *Proc. Natl. Acad. Sci. U.S.A.* 108:7820–5, 2011, PMID: 21518866; *Canc. Res.* 76:3376–86, 2016, PMID: 27197181; *Oncotarget* 7:11165–93, 2016, PMID: 26862846.

Charles S. Via, Professor; M.D., Virginia, 1973. The role of T cells in lupus and in graft-versus-host disease. *J. Immunol.* 190(9):4562–72, 2013.

Shuishu Wang, Assistant Professor, Ph.D., Purdue, 1999. Structural basis of DNA sequence recognition by the response regulator PhoP in *Mycobacterium tuberculosis*. *ACS Omega* 2,3509–17, 2017; *FEBS Open Bio.* 7, 1196–207, 2017; *Sci. Rep.* 6, 24442, 2016.

Kim Williamson, Professor; Ph.D. *Annu. Rev. Microbiol.* DOI:10.1146/annurev-micro-090817–062712, 2018; *Malaria Journal* 16:254.DOI:10.1186/s12936-017-1896-7, 2017.

T. John Wu, Professor; Ph.D., Texas A&M, 1991. Molecular and cellular neuroendocrinology of reproduction and stress. *Endocrinology* 159(6):2363–75, 2018; *Front.Endocrinol* 9:45, 2018; *Neurosci. Lett.* 640:53–9, 2017; *Endocrine* 49(2):470–8, 2015; *New Engl. J. Med.* 371:2363–74, 2014.

Xin Xiang, Professor; Ph.D., University of Medicine and Dentistry of New Jersey, 1991. HookA is a novel dynein-early endosome linker critical for cargo movement in vivo. *J. Cell Biol.* 204:1009–26, 2014.

Section 7
Computational, Systems, and Translational Biology

This section contains a directory of institutions offering graduate work in computational, systems, and translational biology. Additional information about programs listed in the directory may be obtained by writing directly to the dean of a graduate school or chair of a department at the address given in the directory.

CONTENTS

Program Directories

Featured School: Display and Close-Up

Computational Biology

Albert Einstein College of Medicine, Graduate Programs in the Biomedical Sciences, Department of Systems and Computational Biology, Bronx, NY 10461. Offers PhD. *Unit head:* Karen L. Goldman, Administrator, 718-678-1250, Fax: 718-678-1018. *Application contact:* Salvatore Calabro, Director of Graduate Admissions, 718-430-2345, Fax: 718-430-8655, E-mail: phd@einstein.yu.edu.
Website: http://www.einstein.yu.edu/departments/systems-computational-biology/

Baylor College of Medicine, Graduate School of Biomedical Sciences, Program in Structural and Computational Biology and Molecular Biophysics, Houston, TX 77030-3498. Offers PhD, MD/PhD. MD/PhD offered jointly with Rice University and University of Houston. *Degree requirements:* For doctorate, thesis/dissertation, public defense. *Entrance requirements:* For doctorate, GRE General Test, GRE Subject Test (strongly recommended), minimum GPA of 3.0. Additional exam requirements/recommendations for international students: Required—TOEFL. Electronic applications accepted. *Faculty research:* Computational biology, structural biology, biophysics.

Carnegie Mellon University, Joint CMU-Pitt PhD Program in Computational Biology, Pittsburgh, PA 15213-3891. Offers PhD.

Carnegie Mellon University, Mellon College of Science, Department of Biological Sciences, Program in Computational Biology, Pittsburgh, PA 15213-3891. Offers MS. *Entrance requirements:* For master's, GRE General Test, GRE Subject Test, interview.

Claremont Graduate University, Graduate Programs, Institute of Mathematical Sciences, Claremont, CA 91711-6160. Offers computational and systems biology (PhD); computational mathematics and numerical analysis (MA, MS); computational science (PhD); engineering and industrial applied mathematics (PhD); mathematics (PhD); operations research and statistics (MA, MS); physical applied mathematics (MA, MS); pure mathematics (MA, MS); scientific computing (MA, MS); systems and control theory (MA, MS). PhD programs offered jointly with San Diego State University and California State University, Long Beach. *Program availability:* Part-time. Terminal master's awarded for partial completion of doctoral program. *Entrance requirements:* For master's and doctorate, GRE General Test. Additional exam requirements/recommendations for international students: Required—TOEFL (minimum score 75 iBT). Electronic applications accepted.

The College of William and Mary, Faculty of Arts and Sciences, Department of Applied Science, Williamsburg, VA 23185. Offers accelerator science (PhD); applied mathematics (PhD); applied mechanics (PhD); applied robotics (PhD); applied science (MS); atmospheric and environmental science (PhD); computational neuroscience (PhD); interface, thin film and surface science (PhD); lasers and optics (PhD); magnetic resonance (PhD); materials science and engineering (PhD); mathematical and computational biology (PhD); medical imaging (PhD); nanotechnology (PhD); neuroscience (PhD); non-destructive evaluation (PhD); polymer chemistry (PhD); remote sensing (PhD). *Program availability:* Part-time. *Faculty:* 11 full-time (3 women). *Students:* 30 full-time (11 women), 3 part-time (0 women); includes 6 minority (2 Black or African American, non-Hispanic/Latino; 1 Asian, non-Hispanic/Latino; 2 Hispanic/Latino; 1 Two or more races, non-Hispanic/Latino), 13 international. Average age 27. 34 applicants, 47% accepted, 10 enrolled. In 2017, 5 doctorates awarded. Terminal master's awarded for partial completion of doctoral program. *Degree requirements:* For master's, comprehensive exam, thesis; for doctorate, comprehensive exam, thesis/dissertation, 4 core courses. *Entrance requirements:* For master's and doctorate, GRE General Test, GRE Subject Test. Additional exam requirements/recommendations for international students: Required—TOEFL, IELTS. *Application deadline:* For fall admission, 2/1 priority date for domestic students, 2/1 for international students; for spring admission, 10/5 priority date for domestic students, 10/5 for international students. Applications are processed on a rolling basis. Application fee: $50. Electronic applications accepted. *Expenses:* Contact institution. *Financial support:* In 2017–18, 8 students received support, including 27 research assistantships (averaging $26,000 per year), 1 teaching assistantship (averaging $9,500 per year); fellowships, scholarships/grants, health care benefits, tuition waivers (full), and unspecified assistantships also available. Financial award application deadline: 4/15; financial award applicants required to submit FAFSA. *Faculty research:* Computational biology, non-destructive evaluation, neurophysiology, laser spectroscopy, nanotechnology. *Total annual research expenditures:* $536,220. *Unit head:* Dr. Christopher Del Negro, Chair, 757-221-7808, Fax: 757-221-2050, E-mail: cadeln@wm.edu. *Application contact:* Lianne Rios Ashburne, Graduate Program Coordinator, 757-221-2563, Fax: 757-221-2050, E-mail: lrashburne@wm.edu.
Website: http://www.wm.edu/as/appliedscience

Cornell University, Graduate School, Graduate Fields of Agriculture and Life Sciences, Field of Computational Biology, Ithaca, NY 14853. Offers computational behavioral biology (PhD); computational biology (PhD); computational cell biology (PhD); computational ecology (PhD); computational genetics (PhD); computational macromolecular biology (PhD); computational organismal biology (PhD). *Degree requirements:* For doctorate, comprehensive exam, thesis/dissertation, 2 semesters of teaching experience. *Entrance requirements:* For doctorate, GRE General Test, GRE Subject Test (biology), 2 letters of recommendation. Additional exam requirements/recommendations for international students: Required—TOEFL (minimum score 550 paper-based; 77 iBT). Electronic applications accepted. *Faculty research:* Computational behavioral biology, computational biology, computational cell biology, computational ecology, computational genetics, computational macromolecular biology, computational organismal biology.

Duke University, Graduate School, Department of Computational Biology and Bioinformatics, Durham, NC 27708. Offers PhD, Certificate. *Degree requirements:* For doctorate, thesis/dissertation. *Entrance requirements:* For doctorate, GRE General Test. Additional exam requirements/recommendations for international students: Required—TOEFL (minimum score 577 paper-based; 90 iBT) or IELTS (minimum score 7). Electronic applications accepted.

George Mason University, College of Science, School of Systems Biology, Manassas, VA 20110. Offers bioinformatics and computational biology (MS, PhD, Certificate); bioinformatics management (MS, PSM); biology (MS); biosciences (PhD); personalized medicine (Certificate). *Faculty:* 12 full-time (4 women), 2 part-time/adjunct (0 women). *Students:* 107 full-time (54 women), 89 part-time (44 women); includes 64 minority (6 Black or African American, non-Hispanic/Latino; 35 Asian, non-Hispanic/Latino; 14 Hispanic/Latino; 9 Two or more races, non-Hispanic/Latino), 37 international. Average age 31. 141 applicants, 79% accepted, 64 enrolled. In 2017, 27 master's, 8 doctorates, 4 other advanced degrees awarded. *Degree requirements:* For master's, comprehensive exam (for some programs), research project or thesis; for doctorate, comprehensive exam, thesis/dissertation. *Entrance requirements:* For master's, GRE, resume; 3 letters of recommendation; expanded goals statement; 2 copies of official transcripts; bachelor's degree in related field with minimum GPA of 3.0 in last 60 hours; for doctorate, GRE, self-assessment form; resume; 3 letters of recommendation; expanded goals statement; 2 copies of official transcripts; bachelor's degree in related field with minimum GPA of 3.0 in last 60 hours; for Certificate, resume; 2 copies of official transcripts. Additional exam requirements/recommendations for international students: Required—TOEFL (minimum score 575 paper-based; 88 iBT), IELTS (minimum score 6.5), PTE (minimum score 59). Application fee: $75 ($80 for international students). Electronic applications accepted. *Expenses:* Tuition, state resident: full-time $11,228; part-time $459.50 per credit. Tuition, nonresident: full-time $30,932; part-time $1280.50 per credit. *Required fees:* $3252; $135.50 per credit. Part-time tuition and fees vary according to course load and program. *Financial support:* In 2017–18, 51 students received support, including 15 fellowships (averaging $3,902 per year), 14 research assistantships with tuition reimbursements available (averaging $16,679 per year), 38 teaching assistantships with tuition reimbursements available (averaging $15,754 per year); career-related internships or fieldwork, Federal Work-Study, scholarships/grants, unspecified assistantships, and health care benefits (for full-time research or teaching assistantship recipients) also available. Support available to part-time students. Financial award application deadline: 3/1; financial award applicants required to submit FAFSA. *Faculty research:* Functional genomics of chronic human diseases, ecology of vector-borne infectious diseases, neurogenetics, molecular biology, computational modeling, proteomics, chronic metabolic diseases, nanotechnology. *Total annual research expenditures:* $766,416. *Unit head:* Dr. Iosif Vaisman, Director, 703-993-8431, Fax: 703-993-8976, E-mail: ivaisman@gmu.edu. *Application contact:* Diane St. Germain, Graduate Student Services Coordinator, 703-993-4263, Fax: 703-993-8976, E-mail: dstgerma@gmu.edu.
Website: http://ssb.gmu.edu/

Harvard University, Harvard T.H. Chan School of Public Health, Master of Science Program in Computational Biology and Quantitative Genetics, Cambridge, MA 02138. Offers SM. Offered jointly by the Department of Biostatistics and the Department of Epidemiology. *Students:* 21 full-time (16 women), 3 part-time (1 woman); includes 5 minority (all Asian, non-Hispanic/Latino), 16 international. Average age 29. 41 applicants, 51% accepted, 13 enrolled. In 2017, 12 master's awarded. *Entrance requirements:* For master's, GRE. Additional exam requirements/recommendations for international students: Recommended—TOEFL (minimum score 600 paper-based; 100 iBT), IELTS (minimum score 7). *Application deadline:* For fall admission, 12/1 for domestic and international students. Application fee: $120. Electronic applications accepted. *Financial support:* Application deadline: 2/15; applicants required to submit FAFSA. *Unit head:* Dr. John Quackenbush, Director, 617-582-8163. *Application contact:* Vincent W. James, Director of Admissions, 617-432-1031, Fax: 617-432-7080, E-mail: admissions@hsph.harvard.edu.
Website: http://www.hsph.harvard.edu/sm-computational-biology/

Iowa State University of Science and Technology, Bioinformatics and Computational Biology Program, Ames, IA 50011. Offers MS, PhD. *Degree requirements:* For doctorate, thesis/dissertation. *Entrance requirements:* For master's and doctorate, GRE General Test. Additional exam requirements/recommendations for international students: Recommended—TOEFL, IELTS. Electronic applications accepted. *Faculty research:* Functional and structural genomics, genome evolution, macromolecular structure and function, mathematical biology and biological statistics, metabolic and developmental networks.

Lewis University, College of Arts and Sciences, Program in Data Science, Romeoville, IL 60446. Offers computational biology and bioinformatics (MS); computer science (MS). *Program availability:* Part-time, evening/weekend, 100% online, blended/hybrid learning. *Students:* 18 full-time (6 women), 97 part-time (24 women); includes 34 minority (9 Black or African American, non-Hispanic/Latino; 6 Asian, non-Hispanic/Latino; 10 Hispanic/Latino; 1 Native Hawaiian or other Pacific Islander, non-Hispanic/Latino; 8 Two or more races, non-Hispanic/Latino), 5 international. Average age 35. *Entrance requirements:* For master's, bachelor's degree, undergraduate coursework in calculus, minimum undergraduate GPA of 3.0, resume, statement of purpose, two letters of recommendation. Additional exam requirements/recommendations for international students: Required—TOEFL (minimum score 550 paper-based; 79 iBT), IELTS (minimum score 6). *Application deadline:* For fall admission, 5/1 priority date for international students; for winter admission, 11/1 priority date for international students. Applications are processed on a rolling basis. Application fee: $40. Electronic applications accepted. Application fee is waived when completed online. Tuition and fees vary according to program. *Financial support:* Federal Work-Study available. Financial award application deadline: 5/1; financial award applicants required to submit FAFSA. *Unit head:* Dr. Piotr Szczurek, Director, 815-588-7083, E-mail: szczurpi@lewisu.edu. *Application contact:* Linda Campbell, Graduate Admissions Counselor, 815-836-5610, E-mail: grad@lewisu.edu.
Website: http://www.lewisu.edu/academics/data-science/index.htm

Massachusetts Institute of Technology, School of Engineering and School of Science, Program in Computational and Systems Biology, Cambridge, MA 02139. Offers PhD. *Degree requirements:* For doctorate, comprehensive exam, thesis/dissertation, teaching assistantship during one semester; training in the ethical conduct of research. *Entrance requirements:* For doctorate, GRE General Test. Additional exam requirements/recommendations for international students: Required—TOEFL, IELTS. Electronic applications accepted. *Faculty research:* Computational biology and bioinformatics, biological design and synthetic biology, gene and protein networks, systems biology of cancer, nano-biology and microsystems.

Massachusetts Institute of Technology, School of Science, Department of Biology, Cambridge, MA 02139. Offers biochemistry (PhD); biological oceanography (PhD); biology (PhD); biophysical chemistry and molecular structure (PhD); cell biology (PhD); computational and systems biology (PhD); developmental biology (PhD); genetics (PhD); immunology (PhD); microbiology (PhD); molecular biology (PhD); neurobiology (PhD). *Degree requirements:* For doctorate, comprehensive exam, thesis/dissertation, teaching assistantship during two semesters. *Entrance requirements:* For doctorate, GRE General Test. Additional exam requirements/recommendations for international students: Required—TOEFL, IELTS. Electronic applications accepted. *Faculty research:* Cellular, developmental and molecular (plant and animal) biology; biochemistry, bioengineering, biophysics and structural biology; classical and molecular genetics, stem cell and epigenetics; immunology and microbiology; cancer biology, molecular medicine, neurobiology and human disease; computational and systems biology.

New York University, Graduate School of Arts and Science, Department of Biology, Program in Computational Biology, New York, NY 10012-1019. Offers PhD. *Students:* Average age 29. In 2017, 3 doctorates awarded. *Entrance requirements:* For doctorate, GRE. Additional exam requirements/recommendations for international students: Required—TOEFL. *Application deadline:* For fall admission, 12/1 for domestic and international students. Application fee: $100. *Expenses: Tuition:* Full-time $41,352; part-time $19,968 per year. *Required fees:* $2496; $1628 per unit. $814 per term. Tuition and fees vary according to course load and program. *Financial support:* Fellowships, research assistantships, teaching assistantships, Federal Work-Study, institutionally sponsored loans, scholarships/grants, health care benefits, and unspecified assistantships available. Financial award application deadline: 12/1. *Unit head:* Daniel Tranchina, Co-Director, 212-998-4856, Fax: 212-995-4121, E-mail: biology@nyu.edu. *Application contact:* Mike Shelley, Co-Director, 212-998-4856, Fax: 212-995-4121, E-mail: biology@nyu.edu.

Oregon Health & Science University, School of Medicine, Graduate Programs in Medicine, Department of Medical Informatics and Clinical Epidemiology, Portland, OR 97239-3098. Offers bioinformatics and computational biology (MS, PhD); clinical informatics (MBI, MS, PhD, Certificate); health information management (Certificate). *Program availability:* Part-time, online learning. *Faculty:* 12 full-time (6 women), 15 part-time/adjunct (7 women). *Students:* 23 full-time (7 women), 78 part-time (26 women); includes 25 minority (1 Black or African American, non-Hispanic/Latino; 18 Asian, non-Hispanic/Latino; 2 Hispanic/Latino; 4 Two or more races, non-Hispanic/Latino), 10 international. Average age 37. 63 applicants, 83% accepted, 33 enrolled. In 2017, 40 master's, 3 doctorates awarded. Terminal master's awarded for partial completion of doctoral program. *Degree requirements:* For master's, thesis or capstone project; for doctorate, comprehensive exam, thesis/dissertation, qualifying exam. *Entrance requirements:* For master's and doctorate, GRE General Test (minimum scores: 153 Verbal/148 Quantitative/4.5 Analytical), coursework in computer programming, human anatomy and physiology. *Application deadline:* For fall admission, 12/1 for domestic students; for winter admission, 11/1 for domestic students; for spring admission, 2/1 for domestic students. Applications are processed on a rolling basis. Application fee: $70. Electronic applications accepted. *Expenses:* Contact institution. *Financial support:* Fellowships with full tuition reimbursements, research assistantships, Federal Work-Study, scholarships/grants, health care benefits, and full-tuition and stipends (for PhD students) available. Financial award application deadline: 3/1; financial award applicants required to submit FAFSA. *Faculty research:* Clinical informatics, computational biology, health information management, genomics, data analytics. *Unit head:* Dr. William Hersh, Program Director, E-mail: somgrad@ohsu.edu. *Application contact:* Lauren Ludwig, Administrative Coordinator, E-mail: informat@ohsu.edu.
Website: http://www.ohsu.edu/dmice/

Oregon State University, College of Agricultural Sciences, Program in Botany and Plant Pathology, Corvallis, OR 97331. Offers applied systematics (MS); ecology (MS, PhD); genetics (MS, PhD); genomics and computational biology (MS, PhD); molecular and cellular biology (MS, PhD); mycology (MS, PhD); plant pathology (MS, PhD); plant physiology (MS, PhD). *Entrance requirements:* For master's and doctorate, GRE. *Application deadline:* For fall admission, 12/1 for domestic and international students. Application fee: $75 ($85 for international students). *Financial support:* Application deadline: 12/1. *Unit head:* John Fowler, Chair of Graduate Studies, E-mail: fowlerj@science.oregonstate.edu.
Website: http://bpp.oregonstate.edu/

Oregon State University, College of Engineering, Program in Bioengineering, Corvallis, OR 97331. Offers biomaterials (M Eng, MS, PhD); biomedical devices and instrumentation (M Eng, MS, PhD); human performance engineering (M Eng, MS, PhD); medical imaging (M Eng, MS, PhD); systems and computational biology (M Eng, MS, PhD). Electronic applications accepted. *Expenses:* Contact institution. *Faculty research:* Biomaterials, biomedical devices and instrumentation, human performance engineering, medical imaging, systems and computational biology. *Unit head:* Anita Hughes, Graduate Program Coordinator, E-mail: anita.hughes@oregonstate.edu.

Princeton University, Graduate School, Department of Molecular Biology, Princeton, NJ 08544-1019. Offers PhD. *Degree requirements:* For doctorate, thesis/dissertation. *Entrance requirements:* For doctorate, GRE General Test. Additional exam requirements/recommendations for international students: Required—TOEFL (minimum score 600 paper-based). Electronic applications accepted. *Faculty research:* Genetics, virology, biochemistry.

Rutgers University–Camden, Graduate School of Arts and Sciences, Program in Computational and Integrative Biology, Camden, NJ 08102-1401. Offers MS, PhD. *Degree requirements:* For doctorate, original research, oral defense. *Entrance requirements:* For master's and doctorate, GRE General Test; GRE Subject Test (recommended), transcripts, personal statement, three letters of recommendation. Additional exam requirements/recommendations for international students: Required—TOEFL. Electronic applications accepted.

Rutgers University–Newark, Graduate School, Program in Computational Biology, Newark, NJ 07102. Offers MS. Program offered jointly with New Jersey Institute of Technology. *Entrance requirements:* For master's, GRE, minimum undergraduate B average. Additional exam requirements/recommendations for international students: Required—TOEFL.

Rutgers University–New Brunswick, Graduate School-New Brunswick, BioMaPS Institute for Quantitative Biology, Piscataway, NJ 08854-8097. Offers computational biology and molecular biophysics (PhD). *Degree requirements:* For doctorate, comprehensive exam, thesis/dissertation. *Entrance requirements:* For doctorate, GRE. Additional exam requirements/recommendations for international students: Required—TOEFL. Electronic applications accepted. *Faculty research:* Structural biology, systems biology, bioinformatics, translational medicine, genomics.

Saint Louis University, Graduate Programs, College of Arts and Sciences, Department of Computer Science, St. Louis, MO 63103. Offers bioinformatics and computational biology (MS); computer science (MS); software engineering (MS). MS in bioinformatics and computational biology offered in coordination with Departments of Biology, Chemistry, and Mathematics and Statistics).

University of California, Irvine, Francisco J. Ayala School of Biological Sciences, Program in Mathematical, Computational and Systems Biology, Irvine, CA 92697. Offers PhD. *Students:* 32 full-time (12 women); includes 7 minority (5 Asian, non-Hispanic/Latino; 2 Hispanic/Latino), 12 international. Average age 26. 102 applicants, 31% accepted, 11 enrolled. Application fee: $105 ($125 for international students). *Unit head:* Prof. John Lowengrub, Director, 949-824-8456, Fax: 949-824-7993, E-mail: jlowengr@uci.edu. *Application contact:* Aracely Dean, Assistant Administrative Analyst, 949-824-4120, Fax: 949-824-6444, E-mail: mcsb@uci.edu.
Website: http://mcsb.bio.uci.edu/

University of Colorado Denver, College of Liberal Arts and Sciences, Department of Mathematical and Statistical Sciences, Denver, CO 80217. Offers applied mathematics (MS, PhD), including applied mathematics, applied probability (MS), applied statistics (MS), computational biology (PhD), computational mathematics (PhD), discrete mathematics, finite geometry (PhD), mathematics education (PhD), mathematics of engineering and science (MS), numerical analysis, operations research (MS), optimization and operations research (PhD), probability (PhD), statistics (PhD). *Program availability:* Part-time. *Students:* Average age 32. 88 applicants, 66% accepted, 12 enrolled. In 2017, 13 master's, 2 doctorates awarded. *Degree requirements:* For master's, comprehensive exam, thesis optional, 30 hours of course work with minimum GPA of 3.0; for doctorate, comprehensive exam, thesis/dissertation, 42 hours of course work with minimum GPA of 3.25. *Entrance requirements:* For master's, GRE General Test; GRE Subject Test in math (recommended), 30 hours of course work in mathematics (24 of which must be upper-division mathematics), bachelor's degree with minimum GPA of 3.0; for doctorate, GRE General Test; GRE Subject Test in math (recommended), 30 hours of course work in mathematics (24 of which must be upper-division mathematics), master's degree with minimum GPA of 3.25. Additional exam requirements/recommendations for international students: Required—TOEFL (minimum score 537 paper-based; 75 iBT); Recommended—IELTS (minimum score 6.5). *Application deadline:* For fall admission, 4/1 for domestic and international students; for spring admission, 10/1 for domestic and international students; for summer admission, 4/1 for domestic and international students. Application fee: $50 ($75 for international students). Electronic applications accepted. *Financial support:* In 2017–18, 35 students received support. Fellowships with partial tuition reimbursements available, research assistantships with full tuition reimbursements available, teaching assistantships with full tuition reimbursements available, Federal Work-Study, institutionally sponsored loans, scholarships/grants, and traineeships available. Financial award application deadline: 4/1; financial award applicants required to submit FAFSA. *Faculty research:* Computational mathematics, computational biology, discrete mathematics and geometry, probability and statistics, optimization. *Unit head:* Dr. Michael Ferrara, Graduate Chair, 303-315-1705, E-mail: michael.ferrara@ucdenver.edu. *Application contact:* Julie Blunck, Program Assistant, 303-315-1743, E-mail: julie.blunck@ucdenver.edu.
Website: http://www.ucdenver.edu/academics/colleges/CLAS/Departments/math/Pages/MathStats.aspx

University of Colorado Denver, School of Medicine, Program in Computational Bioscience, Aurora, CO 80045-0511. Offers PhD. *Program availability:* Part-time. *Students:* 13 full-time (9 women), 1 (woman) part-time; includes 2 minority (both Two or more races, non-Hispanic/Latino), 2 international. Average age 29. 16 applicants, 25% accepted, 3 enrolled. In 2017, 5 doctorates awarded. *Degree requirements:* For doctorate, comprehensive exam, thesis/dissertation, minimum of 30 semester credit hours each of course work and dissertation research. *Entrance requirements:* For doctorate, GRE General Test, GRE Subject Test in computer science (recommended), demonstrated adequate computational and biological backgrounds, interviews. Additional exam requirements/recommendations for international students: Required—TOEFL (minimum score 550 paper-based; 80 iBT). *Application deadline:* For fall admission, 12/1 for domestic students, 11/1 for international students. Application fee: $50 ($75 for international students). Electronic applications accepted. *Faculty research:* Physical simulations of biological macromolecules and their dynamics, gene expression array analysis and interpretation of expression data, natural language processing in the biomedical literature, metabolic and signaling pathway analysis, evolutionary reconstruction and disease gene finding. *Unit head:* Dr. Larry Hunter, Director, 303-724-3574, E-mail: larry.hunter@ucdenver.edu. *Application contact:* Elizabeth Wethington, Administrative Coordinator, 303-724-7280, Fax: 303-724-6881, E-mail: elizabeth.wethington@ucdenver.edu.
Website: http://compbio.ucdenver.edu/

University of Idaho, College of Graduate Studies, College of Science, Department of Bioinformatics and Computational Biology, Moscow, ID 83844. Offers MS, PhD. *Faculty:* 16 full-time (5 women). *Students:* 21. Average age 29. In 2017, 1 master's, 3 doctorates awarded. *Degree requirements:* For master's, thesis; for doctorate, thesis/dissertation. *Entrance requirements:* For master's, GRE, minimum GPA of 3.0. Additional exam requirements/recommendations for international students: Required—TOEFL (minimum score 100 iBT). *Application deadline:* For fall admission, 8/1 for domestic students; for spring admission, 12/15 for domestic students. Applications are processed on a rolling basis. Application fee: $60. Electronic applications accepted. *Expenses:* Tuition, state resident: full-time $6722; part-time $430 per credit hour. Tuition, nonresident: full-time $23,046; part-time $1337 per credit hour. *Required fees:* $2142; $63 per credit hour. *Financial support:* Applicants required to submit FAFSA. *Unit head:* Dr. Eva Top, Director, 208-885-6010, E-mail: bcb@uidaho.edu. *Application contact:* Sean Scoggin, Graduate Recruitment Coordinator, 208-885-4723, Fax: 208-885-4406, E-mail: graduateadmissions@uidaho.edu.
Website: http://www.uidaho.edu/cogs/bcb

University of Illinois at Urbana–Champaign, Graduate College, College of Liberal Arts and Sciences, School of Molecular and Cellular Biology, Center for Biophysics and Computational Biology, Champaign, IL 61820. Offers MS, PhD.

The University of Iowa, Graduate College, Program in Informatics, Iowa City, IA 52242-1316. Offers bioinformatics (MS, PhD); bioinformatics and computational biology (Certificate); geoinformatics (MS, PhD, Certificate); health informatics (MS, PhD, Certificate); information science (MS, PhD, Certificate). *Degree requirements:* For master's, thesis optional; for doctorate, comprehensive exam, thesis/dissertation. *Entrance requirements:* For master's and doctorate, GRE General Test, minimum GPA of 3.0. Additional exam requirements/recommendations for international students: Required—TOEFL (minimum score 550 paper-based; 81 iBT). Electronic applications accepted.

The University of Kansas, Graduate Studies, College of Liberal Arts and Sciences, Department of Computational Biology, Lawrence, KS 66045. Offers PhD. *Students:* 15 full-time (6 women); includes 3 minority (1 Black or African American, non-Hispanic/Latino; 2 Asian, non-Hispanic/Latino), 5 international. Average age 30. 16 applicants, 19% accepted, 2 enrolled. In 2017, 1 doctorate awarded. *Entrance requirements:* For doctorate, GRE, official transcripts of all undergraduate and graduate study completed, three letters of recommendation received directly from the persons writing them, resume or curriculum vitae, personal statement. Additional exam requirements/recommendations for international students: Required—TOEFL. *Application deadline:* For fall admission, 6/1 for domestic and international students. Application fee: $65 ($85 for international students). Electronic applications accepted. *Financial support:* Research assistantships, teaching assistantships, scholarships/grants, and unspecified assistantships available. *Faculty research:* Life sciences, computational modeling tools, community-wide activities in bioinformatics, education for the new generation of researchers. *Unit head:* Illya Vakser, Director, 785-864-1057, E-mail: vakser@ku.edu. *Application contact:* Debbie Douglass-Metsker, Office Manager, 785-864-1057, E-mail: douglass@ku.edu.
Website: http://www.bioinformatics.ku.edu/

University of Maryland, College Park, Academic Affairs, College of Computer, Mathematical and Natural Sciences, Department of Biology, PhD Program in Biological Sciences, College Park, MD 20742. Offers behavior, ecology, evolution, and systematics (PhD); computational biology, bioinformatics, and genomics (PhD); molecular and cellular biology (PhD); physiological systems (PhD). *Degree requirements:* For doctorate, comprehensive exam, thesis/dissertation, thesis work presentation in seminar. *Entrance requirements:* For doctorate, GRE General Test; GRE Subject Test in biology (recommended), academic transcripts, statement of purpose/research interests, 3 letters of recommendation. Additional exam requirements/recommendations for international students: Required—TOEFL. Electronic applications accepted.

Computational Biology

University of Massachusetts Medical School, Graduate School of Biomedical Sciences, Worcester, MA 01655-0115. Offers biomedical sciences (PhD), including biochemistry and molecular pharmacology, bioinformatics and computational biology, cancer biology, immunology and microbiology, interdisciplinary, neuroscience, translational science; biomedical sciences (millennium program) (PhD); clinical and population health research (PhD); clinical investigation (MS). *Faculty:* 1,316 full-time (526 women), 357 part-time/adjunct (229 women). *Students:* 347 full-time (180 women); includes 61 minority (10 Black or African American, non-Hispanic/Latino; 1 American Indian or Alaska Native, non-Hispanic/Latino; 35 Asian, non-Hispanic/Latino; 15 Hispanic/Latino), 130 international. Average age 29. 608 applicants, 28% accepted, 54 enrolled. In 2017, 6 master's, 51 doctorates awarded. Terminal master's awarded for partial completion of doctoral program. *Degree requirements:* For master's, comprehensive exam, thesis; for doctorate, comprehensive exam, thesis/dissertation. *Entrance requirements:* For master's, MD, PhD, DVM, or PharmD; for doctorate, GRE General Test, bachelor's degree. Additional exam requirements/recommendations for international students: Required—TOEFL (minimum score 90 iBT) or IELTS (minimum score 7.0). *Application deadline:* For fall admission, 12/15 for domestic and international students. Applications are processed on a rolling basis. Application fee: $80. Electronic applications accepted. Application fee is waived when completed online. *Expenses:* $14,883 in-state tuition and mandatory fees; $31,486 out-of-state. *Financial support:* In 2017–18, 15 fellowships with partial tuition reimbursements (averaging $29,000 per year), 296 research assistantships with full tuition reimbursements (averaging $31,212 per year) were awarded; institutionally sponsored loans and scholarships/grants also available. Financial award application deadline: 5/15. *Faculty research:* RNA biology, molecular/cell/developmental/metabolic biology, bioinformatics and computational biology, clinical/translational research, infectious disease and immunology. *Total annual research expenditures:* $279 million. *Unit head:* Dr. Mary Ellen Lane, Dean, 508-856-4018, E-mail: maryellen.lane@umassmed.edu. *Application contact:* Dr. Kendall Knight, Assistant Vice Provost for Admissions, 508-856-5628, Fax: 508-856-3659, E-mail: kendall.knight@umassmed.edu.
Website: http://www.umassmed.edu/gsbs/

University of Minnesota Rochester, Graduate Programs, Rochester, MN 55904. Offers bioinformatics and computational biology (MS, PhD); business administration (MBA); occupational therapy (MOT).

The University of North Carolina at Chapel Hill, School of Medicine and Graduate School, Graduate Programs in Medicine, Curriculum in Bioinformatics and Computational Biology, Chapel Hill, NC 27599. Offers PhD. *Degree requirements:* For doctorate, comprehensive exam, thesis/dissertation. *Entrance requirements:* For doctorate, GRE, minimum GPA of 3.0. Additional exam requirements/recommendations for international students: Required—TOEFL. Electronic applications accepted. *Faculty research:* Protein folding, design and evolution and molecular biophysics of disease; mathematical modeling of signaling pathways and regulatory networks; bioinformatics, medical informatics, user interface design; statistical genetics and genetic epidemiology datamining, classification and clustering analysis of gene-expression data.

University of Pennsylvania, Perelman School of Medicine, Biomedical Graduate Studies, Graduate Group in Genomics and Computational Biology, Philadelphia, PA 19104. Offers PhD, MD/PhD, VMD/PhD. *Faculty:* 83. *Students:* 43 full-time (16 women); includes 17 minority (1 Black or African American, non-Hispanic/Latino; 13 Asian, non-Hispanic/Latino; 1 Hispanic/Latino; 2 Two or more races, non-Hispanic/Latino), 7 international. 102 applicants, 22% accepted, 9 enrolled. In 2017, 7 doctorates awarded. *Degree requirements:* For doctorate, thesis/dissertation. *Entrance requirements:* For doctorate, GRE. Additional exam requirements/recommendations for international students: Required—TOEFL. *Application deadline:* For fall admission, 12/1 priority date for domestic students, 12/1 for international students. Applications are processed on a rolling basis. Application fee: $80. *Financial support:* In 2017–18, 40 students received support. Fellowships, research assistantships, teaching assistantships, and tuition waivers available. *Unit head:* Dr. Li-San Wang, Chairperson, 215-746-7015. *Application contact:* Maureen Kirsch, Graduate Coordinator, 215-746-2807.
Website: http://www.med.upenn.edu/gcb/

University of Pittsburgh, School of Medicine, Computational Biology Program, Pittsburgh, PA 15260. Offers PhD. Program jointly offered with Carnegie Mellon University. *Faculty:* 29 full-time (7 women), 65 part-time/adjunct (14 women). *Students:* 48 full-time (18 women); includes 32 minority (1 Black or African American, non-Hispanic/Latino; 28 Asian, non-Hispanic/Latino; 3 Hispanic/Latino). Average age 26. 197 applicants, 25% accepted. In 2017, 5 doctorates awarded. Terminal master's awarded for partial completion of doctoral program. *Degree requirements:* For doctorate, comprehensive exam, thesis/dissertation, 72 credits of academic work. *Entrance requirements:* For doctorate, GRE General Test, 3 letters of recommendation, statement of purpose, transcripts, curriculum vitae. Additional exam requirements/recommendations for international students: Required—TOEFL (minimum score 600 paper-based; 100 iBT), IELTS (minimum score 7). *Application deadline:* For fall admission, 12/1 for domestic and international students. Application fee: $75. Electronic applications accepted. *Financial support:* In 2017–18, 48 students received support. Health care benefits and stipends (averaging $29,500 annually) available. *Faculty research:* Big data and scalable machine learning, bioimage informatics, cellular and systems modeling, computational genomics, computational structural biology. *Unit head:* Dr. James R. Faeder, Director, 412-648-8171, Fax: 412-648-3163, E-mail: faeder@pitt.edu. *Application contact:* Kelly Gentille, Educational Programs Coordinator, 412-648-8107, Fax: 412-648-3163, E-mail: kmg120@pitt.edu.
Website: http://www.compbio.pitt.edu/

University of Rochester, School of Medicine and Dentistry, Graduate Programs in Medicine and Dentistry, Department of Biochemistry and Biophysics, Programs in Biophysics, Rochester, NY 14627. Offers biophysics, structural and computational biology (PhD). Terminal master's awarded for partial completion of doctoral program. *Degree requirements:* For doctorate, thesis/dissertation, qualifying exam. *Entrance requirements:* For doctorate, GRE General Test.

University of Southern California, Graduate School, Dana and David Dornsife College of Letters, Arts and Sciences, Department of Biological Sciences, Program in Molecular and Computational Biology, Los Angeles, CA 90089. Offers computational biology and bioinformatics (PhD); molecular biology (PhD). *Degree requirements:* For doctorate, comprehensive exam, thesis/dissertation, qualifying examination, dissertation defense. *Entrance requirements:* For doctorate, GRE, 3 letters of recommendation, personal statement, resume, minimum GPA of 3.0. Additional exam requirements/recommendations for international students: Required—TOEFL (minimum score 600 paper-based; 100 iBT). Electronic applications accepted. *Faculty research:* Biochemistry and molecular biology; genomics; computational biology and bioinformatics; cell and developmental biology, and genetics; DNA replication and repair, and cancer biology.

University of South Florida, Morsani College of Medicine and College of Graduate Studies, Graduate Programs in Medical Sciences, Tampa, FL 33620-9951. Offers advanced athletic training (MS); athletic training (MS); bioinformatics and computational biology (MSBCB); biotechnology (MSB); health informatics (MSHI); medical sciences (MSMS, PhD), including aging and neuroscience (MSMS), allergy, immunology and infectious disease (PhD), anatomy, biochemistry and molecular biology, clinical and translational research, health science (MSMS), interdisciplinary medical sciences (MSMS), medical microbiology and immunology (MSMS), metabolic and nutritional medicine (MSMS), microbiology and immunology (PhD), molecular medicine, molecular pharmacology and physiology (PhD), neuroscience (PhD), pathology and cell biology (PhD), women's health (MSMS). *Students:* 372 full-time (212 women), 216 part-time (142 women); includes 257 minority (78 Black or African American, non-Hispanic/Latino; 1 American Indian or Alaska Native, non-Hispanic/Latino; 79 Asian, non-Hispanic/Latino; 84 Hispanic/Latino; 15 Two or more races, non-Hispanic/Latino), 62 international. Average age 28. 1,048 applicants, 46% accepted, 309 enrolled. In 2017, 351 master's, 56 doctorates awarded. Terminal master's awarded for partial completion of doctoral program. *Degree requirements:* For master's, comprehensive exam, thesis; for doctorate, comprehensive exam, thesis/dissertation. *Entrance requirements:* For master's, GRE General Test or GMAT, bachelor's degree or equivalent from regionally-accredited university with minimum GPA of 3.0 in upper-division sciences coursework; prerequisites in general biology, general chemistry, general physics, organic chemistry, quantitative analysis, and integral and differential calculus; for doctorate, GRE General Test, bachelor's degree from regionally-accredited university with minimum GPA of 3.0 in upper-division sciences coursework; 3 letters of recommendation; personal interview; 1-2 page personal statement; prerequisites in biology, chemistry, physics, organic chemistry, quantitative analysis, and integral/differential calculus. Additional exam requirements/recommendations for international students: Required—TOEFL (minimum score 550 paper-based; 79 iBT) or IELTS (minimum score 6.5). *Application deadline:* For fall admission, 2/1 priority date for domestic students, 2/1 for international students. Application fee: $30. Electronic applications accepted. *Expenses:* Contact institution. *Financial support:* In 2017–18, 109 students received support. *Faculty research:* Anatomy, biochemistry, cancer biology, cardiovascular disease, cell biology, immunology, microbiology, molecular biology, neuroscience, pharmacology, physiology. *Total annual research expenditures:* $45.3 million. *Unit head:* Dr. Michael Barber, Professor/Associate Dean for Graduate and Postdoctoral Affairs, 813-974-9908, Fax: 813-974-4317, E-mail: mbarber@health.usf.edu. *Application contact:* Dr. Eric Bennett, Graduate Director, PhD Program in Medical Sciences, 813-974-1545, Fax: 813-974-4317, E-mail: esbennet@health.usf.edu.
Website: http://health.usf.edu/nocms/medicine/graduatestudies/

The University of Texas Medical Branch, Graduate School of Biomedical Sciences, Program in Biochemistry and Molecular Biology, Galveston, TX 77555. Offers biochemistry (PhD); bioinformatics (PhD); biophysics (PhD); cell biology (PhD); computational biology (PhD); structural biology (PhD). *Degree requirements:* For doctorate, thesis/dissertation. *Entrance requirements:* Additional exam requirements/recommendations for international students: Required—TOEFL (minimum score 550 paper-based). Electronic applications accepted.

University of Wyoming, Graduate Program in Molecular and Cellular Life Sciences, Laramie, WY 82071. Offers PhD. *Degree requirements:* For doctorate, thesis/dissertation, four eight-week laboratory rotations, comprehensive basic practical exam, two-part qualifying exam, seminars, symposium.

Washington University in St. Louis, The Graduate School, Division of Biology and Biomedical Sciences, Program in Computational and Systems Biology, St. Louis, MO 63130-4899. Offers PhD. *Degree requirements:* For doctorate, thesis/dissertation. *Entrance requirements:* For doctorate, GRE General Test, GRE Subject Test. Additional exam requirements/recommendations for international students: Required—TOEFL. Electronic applications accepted. *Faculty research:* Systems biology, genomics, sequence analysis, regulatory networks, synthetic biology, metagenomics, metabolomics, proteomics, epigenomics, transcriptomics, lipidomics, single cell dynamics, high-throughput technology development, applied math and mathematical models of biological processes, computational biology, comparative genomics, personalized medicine, genome engineering, machine learning, big data science, next generation sequencing and its applications, bioinformatics.

Wayne State University, College of Engineering, Department of Computer Science, Detroit, MI 48202. Offers computer science (MS, PhD), including bioinformatics and computational biology (PhD); data science and business analytics (MS). Application deadline for PhD is February 17. *Faculty:* 19. *Students:* 96 full-time (40 women), 28 part-time (6 women); includes 11 minority (2 Black or African American, non-Hispanic/Latino; 7 Asian, non-Hispanic/Latino; 2 Two or more races, non-Hispanic/Latino), 86 international. Average age 29. 283 applicants, 31% accepted, 19 enrolled. In 2017, 58 master's, 6 doctorates awarded. *Degree requirements:* For master's, thesis (for some programs), practicum (for MS in data science and business analytics); for doctorate, thesis/dissertation. *Entrance requirements:* For master's, GRE (GMAT accepted for MS in data science and business analytics), minimum GPA of 3.0, three letters of recommendation, adequate preparation in computer science and mathematics courses, personal statement, resume (for MS in data science and business analytics); for doctorate, GRE, bachelor's or master's degree in computer science or related field; minimum GPA of 3.3 in most recent degree; three letters of recommendation; personal statement; adequate preparation in computer science and mathematics courses. Additional exam requirements/recommendations for international students: Required—TOEFL (minimum score 550 paper-based; 79 iBT), TWE (minimum score 5.5); Recommended—IELTS (minimum score 6.5). *Application deadline:* For fall admission, 6/1 priority date for domestic students, 5/1 priority date for international students; for winter admission, 10/1 priority date for domestic students, 9/1 priority date for international students; for spring admission, 2/1 priority date for domestic students, 1/2 priority date for international students. Applications are processed on a rolling basis. Application fee: $50. Electronic applications accepted. *Expenses:* Contact institution. *Financial support:* In 2017–18, 68 students received support, including 5 fellowships with tuition reimbursements available (averaging $17,200 per year), 14 research assistantships with tuition reimbursements available (averaging $19,553 per year), 31 teaching assistantships with tuition reimbursements available (averaging $19,560 per year); scholarships/grants, health care benefits, and unspecified assistantships also available. Financial award application deadline: 2/17; financial award applicants required to submit FAFSA. *Faculty research:* Software engineering, databases, bioinformatics, artificial intelligence, networking, distributed and parallel computing, security, graphics, visualizations. *Total annual research expenditures:* $1.1 million. *Unit head:* Dr. Loren Schwiebert, Chair, 313-577-5474, E-mail: loren@wayne.edu. *Application contact:* Areej Salaymeh, Graduate Advisor, 313-577-2477, E-mail: csgradadvisor@cs.wayne.edu.
Website: http://engineering.wayne.edu/cs/

Weill Cornell Medicine, Weill Cornell Graduate School of Medical Sciences, Cornell/Weill Cornell/Sloan Kettering Tri-Institutional PhD Program in Computational Biology and Medicine, New York, NY 10065. Offers PhD. Terminal master's awarded for partial completion of doctoral program. *Degree requirements:* For doctorate, comprehensive exam, thesis/dissertation. *Entrance requirements:* For doctorate, GRE General Test, three letters of recommendation. Additional exam requirements/recommendations for international students: Required—TOEFL. Electronic applications accepted. *Faculty research:* Computational genomics and gene regulation, quantitative and systems biology, cancer biology and genomics, structural biology and biophysics, computational neuroscience.

Worcester Polytechnic Institute, Graduate Admissions, Program in Bioinformatics and Computational Biology, Worcester, MA 01609-2280. Offers MS, PhD. *Program availability:* Evening/weekend. *Students:* 13 full-time (6 women), 8 international. Average age 27. 31 applicants, 55% accepted, 6 enrolled. In 2017, 1 master's awarded. *Entrance requirements:* For master's and doctorate, GRE, 3 letters of recommendation, statement of purpose. Additional exam requirements/recommendations for international students: Required—TOEFL (minimum score 563 paper-based; 84 iBT), IELTS (minimum score 7). *Application deadline:* For fall admission, 1/1 priority date for domestic and international students; for spring admission, 10/1 priority date for domestic and international students. Applications are processed on a rolling basis. Application fee: $70. Electronic applications accepted. *Expenses: Tuition:* Full-time $26,226; part-time $1457 per credit. *Required fees:* $60; $30 per credit. One-time fee: $15. Tuition and fees vary according to course load. *Financial support:* Fellowships, research assistantships, teaching assistantships, and career-related internships or fieldwork available. Financial award application deadline: 1/1. *Unit head:* Dmitry Korkin, Professor, 508-831-5543, Fax: 508-831-5936, E-mail: dkorkin@wpi.edu. *Application contact:* Barbara Milanese, Administrative Assistant, 508-831-5543, Fax: 508-831-5936, E-mail: milanese@wpi.edu.
Website: https://www.wpi.edu/academics/departments/bioinformatics-computational-biology

Yale University, Yale School of Medicine and Graduate School of Arts and Sciences, Combined Program in Biological and Biomedical Sciences (BBS), Computational Biology and Bioinformatics Track, New Haven, CT 06520. Offers PhD, MD/PhD. *Entrance requirements:* Additional exam requirements/recommendations for international students: Required—TOEFL.

Systems Biology

Albert Einstein College of Medicine, Graduate Programs in the Biomedical Sciences, Department of Systems and Computational Biology, Bronx, NY 10461. Offers PhD. *Unit head:* Karen L. Goldman, Administrator, 718-678-1250, Fax: 718-678-1018. *Application contact:* Salvatore Calabro, Director of Graduate Admissions, 718-430-2345, Fax: 718-430-8655, E-mail: phd@einstein.yu.edu.
Website: http://www.einstein.yu.edu/departments/systems-computational-biology/

George Mason University, College of Science, School of Systems Biology, Manassas, VA 20110. Offers bioinformatics and computational biology (MS, PhD, Certificate); bioinformatics management (MS, PSM); biology (MS); biosciences (PhD); personalized medicine (Certificate). *Faculty:* 12 full-time (4 women), 2 part-time/adjunct (0 women). *Students:* 107 full-time (54 women), 89 part-time (44 women); includes 64 minority (6 Black or African American, non-Hispanic/Latino; 35 Asian, non-Hispanic/Latino; 14 Hispanic/Latino; 9 Two or more races, non-Hispanic/Latino), 37 international. Average age 31. 141 applicants, 79% accepted, 64 enrolled. In 2017, 27 master's, 0 doctorates, 4 other advanced degrees awarded. *Degree requirements:* For master's, comprehensive exam (for some programs), research project or thesis; for doctorate, comprehensive exam, thesis/dissertation. *Entrance requirements:* For master's, GRE, resume; 3 letters of recommendation; expanded goals statement; 2 copies of official transcripts; bachelor's degree in related field with minimum GPA of 3.0 in last 60 hours; for doctorate, GRE, self-assessment form; resume; 3 letters of recommendation; expanded goals statement; 2 copies of official transcripts; bachelor's degree in related field with minimum GPA of 3.0 in last 60 hours; for Certificate, resume; 2 copies of official transcripts. Additional exam requirements/recommendations for international students: Required—TOEFL (minimum score 575 paper-based; 88 iBT), IELTS (minimum score 6.5), PTE (minimum score 59). Application fee: $75 ($80 for international students). Electronic applications accepted. *Expenses:* Tuition, state resident: full-time $11,228; part-time $459.50 per credit. Tuition, nonresident: full-time $30,932; part-time $1280.50 per credit. *Required fees:* $3252; $135.50 per credit. Part-time tuition and fees vary according to course load and program. *Financial support:* In 2017–18, 51 students received support, including 15 fellowships (averaging $3,902 per year), 14 research assistantships with tuition reimbursements available (averaging $16,679 per year), 38 teaching assistantships with tuition reimbursements available (averaging $15,754 per year); career-related internships or fieldwork, Federal Work-Study, scholarships/grants, unspecified assistantships, and health care benefits (for full-time research or teaching assistantship recipients) also available. Support available to part-time students. Financial award application deadline: 3/1; financial award applicants required to submit FAFSA. *Faculty research:* Functional genomics of chronic human diseases, ecology of vector-borne infectious diseases, neurogenetics, molecular biology, computational modeling, proteomics, chronic metabolic diseases, nanotechnology. *Total annual research expenditures:* $766,416. *Unit head:* Dr. Iosif Vaisman, Director, 703-993-8431, Fax: 703-993-8976, E-mail: ivaisman@gmu.edu. *Application contact:* Diane St. Germain, Graduate Student Services Coordinator, 703-993-4263, Fax: 703-993-8976, E-mail: dstgerma@gmu.edu.
Website: http://ssb.gmu.edu/

The George Washington University, Columbian College of Arts and Sciences, Institute for Biomedical Sciences, Program in Biochemistry and Systems Biology, Washington, DC 20037. Offers PhD. *Students:* 1 (woman) full-time, 7 part-time (2 women); includes 3 minority (2 Asian, non-Hispanic/Latino; 1 Two or more races, non-Hispanic/Latino), 2 international. Average age 32. 1 applicant. In 2017, 2 doctorates awarded. Terminal master's awarded for partial completion of doctoral program. *Degree requirements:* For doctorate, thesis/dissertation, general exam. *Entrance requirements:* For doctorate, GRE General Test, interview, minimum GPA of 3.0. Additional exam requirements/recommendations for international students: Required—TOEFL (minimum score 600 paper-based). *Application deadline:* For fall admission, 12/15 priority date for domestic and international students; for spring admission, 10/1 priority date for domestic and international students. Applications are processed on a rolling basis. Application fee: $75. Electronic applications accepted. *Expenses: Tuition:* Full-time $28,800; part-time $1655 per credit hour. *Required fees:* $45; $2.75 per credit hour. *Financial support:* In 2017–18, 3 students received support. Fellowships, Federal Work-Study, institutionally sponsored loans, and tuition waivers available. Financial award application deadline: 2/1. *Unit head:* Dr. Eric Hoffman, Director, 202-476-6029, E-mail: ehoffman@cnmcresearch.org. *Application contact:* Information Contact, 202-994-7120, Fax: 202-994-6100, E-mail: genetics@gwu.edu.
Website: http://smhs.gwu.edu/

Harvard University, Graduate School of Arts and Sciences, Department of Systems Biology, Cambridge, MA 02138. Offers PhD. *Degree requirements:* For doctorate, thesis/dissertation, lab rotation, qualifying examination. *Entrance requirements:* For doctorate, GRE. Additional exam requirements/recommendations for international students: Required—TOEFL. Electronic applications accepted.

Massachusetts Institute of Technology, School of Engineering and School of Science, Program in Computational and Systems Biology, Cambridge, MA 02139. Offers PhD. *Degree requirements:* For doctorate, comprehensive exam, thesis/dissertation, teaching assistantship during one semester; training in the ethical conduct of research. *Entrance requirements:* For doctorate, GRE General Test. Additional exam requirements/recommendations for international students: Required—TOEFL, IELTS. Electronic applications accepted. *Faculty research:* Computational biology and bioinformatics, biological design and synthetic biology, gene and protein networks, systems biology of cancer, nano-biology and microsystems.

Michigan State University, The Graduate School, College of Natural Science, Quantitative Biology Program, East Lansing, MI 48824. Offers PhD.

Northwestern University, The Graduate School, Interdisciplinary Biological Sciences Program (IBiS), Evanston, IL 60208. Offers biochemistry (PhD); bioengineering and biotechnology (PhD); biotechnology (PhD); cell and molecular biology (PhD); developmental and systems biology (PhD); nanotechnology (PhD); neurobiology (PhD); structural biology and biophysics (PhD). *Degree requirements:* For doctorate, thesis/dissertation, qualifying exam. *Entrance requirements:* For doctorate, GRE General Test. Additional exam requirements/recommendations for international students: Required—TOEFL (minimum score 600 paper-based). Electronic applications accepted. *Faculty research:* Biophysics/structural biology, cell/molecular biology, synthetic biology, developmental systems biology, chemical biology/nanotechnology.

Oregon State University, College of Engineering, Program in Bioengineering, Corvallis, OR 97331. Offers biomaterials (M Eng, MS, PhD); biomedical devices and instrumentation (M Eng, MS, PhD); human performance engineering (M Eng, MS, PhD); medical imaging (M Eng, MS, PhD); systems and computational biology (M Eng, MS, PhD). Electronic applications accepted. *Expenses:* Contact institution. *Faculty research:* Biomaterials, biomedical devices and instrumentation, human performance engineering, medical imaging, systems and computational biology. *Unit head:* Anita Hughes, Graduate Program Coordinator, E-mail: anita.hughes@oregonstate.edu.

Purdue University, College of Pharmacy and Graduate School, Graduate Programs in Pharmacy and Pharmacal Sciences, Department of Medicinal Chemistry and Molecular Pharmacology, West Lafayette, IN 47907. Offers biophysical and computational chemistry (PhD); cancer research (PhD); immunology and infectious disease (PhD); medicinal biochemistry and molecular biology (PhD); medicinal chemistry and chemical biology (PhD); molecular pharmacology (PhD); neuropharmacology, neurodegeneration, and neurotoxicity (PhD); systems biology and functional genomics (PhD). *Faculty:* 26 full-time (5 women). *Students:* 52 full-time (22 women), 3 part-time (all women); includes 4 minority (1 Black or African American, non-Hispanic/Latino; 2 Asian, non-Hispanic/Latino; 1 Hispanic/Latino), 29 international. Average age 26. 151 applicants, 19% accepted, 13 enrolled. In 2017, 18 doctorates awarded. *Degree requirements:* For doctorate, thesis/dissertation. *Entrance requirements:* For doctorate, GRE General Test; GRE Subject Test in biology, biochemistry, and chemistry (recommended), minimum undergraduate GPA of 3.0. Additional exam requirements/recommendations for international students: Required—TOEFL (minimum score 550 paper-based; 77 iBT); Recommended—TWE. *Application deadline:* For fall admission, 2/1 for domestic and international students. Applications are processed on a rolling basis. Application fee: $60 ($75 for international students). Electronic applications accepted. *Financial support:* Fellowships, research assistantships, teaching assistantships, and traineeships available. Support available to part-time students. Financial award applicants required to submit FAFSA. *Faculty research:* Drug design and development, cancer research, drug synthesis and analysis, chemical pharmacology, environmental toxicology. *Unit head:* Zhong-Yin Zhang, Head, 765-494-1403, E-mail: zhang-yn@purdue.edu. *Application contact:* Delayne Graham, Graduate Contact, 765-494-1362, E-mail: dkgraham@purdue.edu.

Rutgers University–New Brunswick, Graduate School-New Brunswick, BioMaPS Institute for Quantitative Biology, Piscataway, NJ 08854-8097. Offers computational biology and molecular biophysics (PhD). *Degree requirements:* For doctorate, comprehensive exam, thesis/dissertation. *Entrance requirements:* For doctorate, GRE. Additional exam requirements/recommendations for international students: Required—TOEFL. Electronic applications accepted. *Faculty research:* Structural biology, systems biology, bioinformatics, translational medicine, genomics.

Stanford University, School of Medicine, Graduate Programs in Medicine, Department of Chemical and Systems Biology, Stanford, CA 94305-2004. Offers PhD. *Degree requirements:* For doctorate, thesis/dissertation, qualifying examination. *Entrance requirements:* For doctorate, GRE General Test, GRE Subject Test. Additional exam requirements/recommendations for international students: Required—TOEFL. Electronic applications accepted. *Expenses: Tuition:* Full-time $48,987; part-time $10,620 per quarter. One-time fee: $400. Tuition and fees vary according to program. *Faculty research:* Action of drugs such as epinephrine, cell differentiation and development, microsomal enzymes, neuropeptide gene expression.

University of California, Irvine, Francisco J. Ayala School of Biological Sciences, Program in Mathematical, Computational and Systems Biology, Irvine, CA 92697. Offers PhD. *Students:* 32 full-time (12 women); includes 7 minority (5 Asian, non-Hispanic/Latino; 2 Hispanic/Latino), 12 international. Average age 26. 102 applicants, 31% accepted, 11 enrolled. Application fee: $105 ($125 for international students). *Unit head:* Prof. John Lowengrub, Director, 949-824-8456, Fax: 949-824-7993, E-mail: jlowengr@uci.edu. *Application contact:* Aracely Dean, Assistant Administrative Analyst, 949-824-4120, Fax: 949-824-6444, E-mail: mcsb@uci.edu.
Website: http://mcsb.bio.uci.edu/

University of California, Merced, Graduate Division, School of Natural Sciences, Merced, CA 95343. Offers applied mathematics (MS, PhD); chemistry and chemical biology (MS, PhD); physics (MS, PhD); quantitative and systems biology (MS, PhD). *Faculty:* 71 full-time (27 women). *Students:* 208 full-time (75 women); includes 71 minority (5 Black or African American, non-Hispanic/Latino; 24 Asian, non-Hispanic/Latino; 33 Hispanic/Latino; 1 Native Hawaiian or other Pacific Islander, non-Hispanic/Latino; 8 Two or more races, non-Hispanic/Latino), 52 international. Average age 28. 293 applicants, 45% accepted, 51 enrolled. In 2017, 9 master's, 18 doctorates awarded. Terminal master's awarded for partial completion of doctoral program. *Degree requirements:* For master's, variable foreign language requirement, comprehensive exam, thesis or alternative; for doctorate, variable foreign language requirement, comprehensive exam, thesis/dissertation. *Entrance requirements:* For master's and doctorate, GRE. Additional exam requirements/recommendations for international students: Required—TOEFL (minimum score 550 paper-based; 80 iBT); Recommended—IELTS (minimum score 7). *Application deadline:* For fall admission, 1/15 for domestic and international students. Application fee: $90 ($110 for international students). Electronic applications accepted. *Expenses:* Tuition, state resident: full-time $11,502; part-time $5751 per semester. Tuition, nonresident: full-time $26,604; part-time $13,302 per semester. *Required fees:* $564 per semester. *Financial support:* In 2017–18, 170 students received support, including 19 fellowships with full tuition reimbursements available (averaging $23,832 per year), 32 research assistantships with full tuition reimbursements available (averaging $16,429 per year), 148 teaching assistantships with full tuition reimbursements available (averaging $16,038 per year); scholarships/grants, traineeships, and health care benefits also available. Financial award application deadline: 1/15. *Faculty research:* Computational science, soft matter physics, applied math, environmental and biological systems, biological and materials chemistry. *Total annual research expenditures:* $4.2 million. *Unit head:* Dr. Elizabeth Dumont, Dean, 209-228-4060, E-mail: edumont@ucmerced.edu. *Application contact:* Tsu Ya, Director of Graduate Admissions and Academic Services, 209-228-4521, Fax: 209-228-6906, E-mail: tya@ucmerced.edu.

★ **University of California, San Diego,** Graduate Division, Program in Bioinformatics and Systems Biology, La Jolla, CA 92093. Offers PhD. *Students:* 72 full-time (20 women). 262 applicants, 16% accepted, 17 enrolled. In 2017, 8 doctorates awarded. *Degree requirements:* For doctorate, comprehensive exam, thesis/dissertation, two quarters as teaching assistant. *Entrance requirements:* For doctorate, GRE General Test. Additional exam requirements/recommendations for international students: Required—TOEFL (minimum score 550 paper-based; 80 iBT), IELTS (minimum score 7). *Application deadline:* For fall admission, 12/19 for domestic students. Application fee: $105 ($125 for international students). Electronic applications accepted. *Financial support:* Fellowships, research assistantships, teaching assistantships, scholarships/grants, and traineeships available. Financial award applicants required to submit FAFSA. *Faculty research:* Quantitative foundations of computational biology, structural bioinformatics and systems pharmacology, proteomics and metabolomics, epigenomics and gene expression control, genetic and molecular networks. *Unit head:* Vineet Bafna, Director, 858-822-4978, E-mail: vbafna@ucsd.edu. *Application contact:* Kelly Thorpe, Graduate Coordinator, 858-534-7538, E-mail: bioinfo@ucsd.edu.
Website: http://bioinformatics.ucsd.edu/

See Display below and Close-Up on page 219.

University of Chicago, Division of the Biological Sciences, Committee on Genetics, Genomics and Systems Biology, Chicago, IL 60637. Offers PhD. *Students:* 32 full-time (17 women); includes 8 minority (1 Black or African American, non-Hispanic/Latino; 4 Asian, non-Hispanic/Latino; 1 Hispanic/Latino; 1 Native Hawaiian or other Pacific Islander, non-Hispanic/Latino; 1 Two or more races, non-Hispanic/Latino), 9 international. Average age 26. 76 applicants, 25% accepted, 9 enrolled. In 2017, 4 doctorates awarded. *Degree requirements:* For doctorate, thesis/dissertation, ethics class, 2 teaching assistantships, preliminary exam. *Entrance requirements:* For doctorate, GRE General Test, transcripts, statement of purpose, 3 letters of recommendation. Additional exam requirements/recommendations for international students: Required—TOEFL (minimum score 600 paper-based; 104 iBT), IELTS (minimum score 7). *Application deadline:* For fall admission, 12/1 for domestic and international students. Application fee: $90. Electronic applications accepted. *Financial support:* In 2017–18, 21 students received support, including fellowships with full tuition reimbursements available (averaging $31,000 per year), research assistantships with full tuition reimbursements available (averaging $31,000 per year); institutionally sponsored loans, scholarships/grants, traineeships, and health care benefits also available. Financial award application deadline: 12/1. *Faculty research:* Molecular genetics, developmental genetics, population genetics, human genetics, computational biology. *Unit head:* Yoav Gilad, PhD, Chair, E-mail: bsdadmissions@uchicago.edu. *Application contact:* Sue Levison, Administrator, 773-702-2464, Fax: 773-702-2464, E-mail: committee-on-genetics@uchicago.edu.

University of Cincinnati, Graduate School, College of Medicine, Systems Biology and Physiology Graduate Program, Cincinnati, OH 45267-0576. Offers PhD. *Entrance requirements:* Additional exam requirements/recommendations for international students: Required—TOEFL (minimum score 100 iBT) or IELTS (minimum score 6.5). *Expenses: Tuition, area resident:* Full-time $14,468. Tuition, state resident: full-time $14,968; part-time $754 per credit hour. Tuition, nonresident: full-time $24,210; part-time $1311 per credit hour. *International tuition:* $26,460 full-time. *Required fees:* $3958; $84 per credit hour. One-time fee: $85 full-time. Tuition and fees vary according to course load, degree level and program. *Faculty research:* Gastrointestinal physiology, systems biology, transmembrane ion transport, muscle physiology, neurophysiology.

University of Colorado Denver, College of Liberal Arts and Sciences, Department of Integrative Biology, Denver, CO 80217. Offers biology (MS); integrative and systems biology (PhD). *Program availability:* Part-time. *Faculty:* 21 full-time (7 women), 2 part-time/adjunct (both women). *Students:* 29 full-time (17 women), 13 part-time (5 women); includes 8 minority (2 Asian, non-Hispanic/Latino; 3 Hispanic/Latino; 1 Native Hawaiian or other Pacific Islander, non-Hispanic/Latino; 2 Two or more races, non-Hispanic/Latino), 1 international. Average age 29. 38 applicants, 34% accepted, 13 enrolled. In 2017, 9 master's awarded. *Degree requirements:* For master's, comprehensive exam, thesis, 30-32 credit hours; for doctorate, comprehensive exam, thesis/dissertation. *Entrance requirements:* For master's, GRE General Test (minimum score in 50th percentile in each section), BA/BS from accredited institution awarded within the last 10 years; minimum undergraduate GPA of 3.0; prerequisite courses: 1 year each of general biology and general chemistry; 1 semester each of general genetics, general ecology, and cell biology; and a structure/function course; for doctorate, GRE, minimum undergraduate GPA of 3.2, three letters of recommendation, official transcripts from all universities and colleges attended. Additional exam requirements/recommendations for international students: Required—TOEFL (minimum score 537 paper-based; 75 iBT); Recommended—IELTS (minimum score 6.5). *Application deadline:* For fall admission, 1/15 for domestic and international students. Application fee: $50 ($75 for international students). Electronic applications accepted. *Financial support:* In 2017–18, 27 students received support. Fellowships, research assistantships, teaching assistantships, Federal Work-Study, institutionally sponsored loans, scholarships/grants, and traineeships available. Financial award application deadline: 4/1; financial award applicants required to submit FAFSA. *Faculty research:* Molecular developmental biology; quantitative ecology, biogeography, and population dynamics; environmental signaling and endocrine disruption; speciation, the evolution of reproductive isolation, and hybrid zones; evolutionary, behavioral, and conservation ecology. *Unit head:* Dr. John Swallow, Chair, 303-556-6154, E-mail: john.swallow@ucdenver.edu. *Application contact:* Dr. Michael Wunder, Graduate Advisor, 303-556-8870, E-mail: michael.wunder@ucdenver.edu.
Website: http://www.ucdenver.edu/academics/colleges/CLAS/Departments/biology/Programs/MasterofScience/Pages/BiologyMasterOfScience.aspx

University of Pittsburgh, School of Medicine, Computational Biology Program, Pittsburgh, PA 15260. Offers PhD. Program jointly offered with Carnegie Mellon University. *Faculty:* 29 full-time (7 women), 65 part-time/adjunct (14 women). *Students:* 48 full-time (18 women); includes 32 minority (1 Black or African American, non-Hispanic/Latino; 28 Asian, non-Hispanic/Latino; 3 Hispanic/Latino). Average age 26. 197 applicants, 25% accepted. In 2017, 5 doctorates awarded. Terminal master's awarded

for partial completion of doctoral program. *Degree requirements:* For doctorate, comprehensive exam, thesis/dissertation, 72 credits of academic work. *Entrance requirements:* For doctorate, GRE General Test, 3 letters of recommendation, statement of purpose, transcripts, curriculum vitae. Additional exam requirements/ recommendations for international students: Required—TOEFL (minimum score 600 paper-based; 100 iBT), IELTS (minimum score 7). *Application deadline:* For fall admission, 12/1 for domestic and international students. Application fee: $75. Electronic applications accepted. *Financial support:* In 2017–18, 48 students received support. Health care benefits and stipends (averaging $29,500 annually) available. *Faculty research:* Big data and scalable machine learning, bioimage informatics, cellular and systems modeling, computational genomics, computational structural biology. *Unit head:* Dr. James R. Faeder, Director, 412-648-8171, Fax: 412-648-3163, E-mail: faeder@pitt.edu. *Application contact:* Kelly Gentille, Educational Programs Coordinator, 412-648-8107, Fax: 412-648-3163, E-mail: kmg120@pitt.edu.
Website: http://www.compbio.pitt.edu/

University of Pittsburgh, School of Medicine, Graduate Programs in Medicine and Kenneth P. Dietrich School of Arts and Sciences, Integrative Systems Biology Graduate Program, Pittsburgh, PA 15260. Offers PhD. *Faculty:* 66 full-time (15 women). *Students:* 17 full-time (6 women); includes 1 minority (Black or African American, non-Hispanic/ Latino), 4 international. Average age 26. 32 applicants, 47% accepted, 5 enrolled. *Degree requirements:* For doctorate, comprehensive exam, thesis/dissertation. *Entrance requirements:* For doctorate, GRE, minimum GPA of 3.7, 3 letters of recommendation, baccalaureate degree in natural or physical science or engineering program, personal statement. Additional exam requirements/recommendations for international students: Required—TOEFL (minimum score 700 paper-based; 100 iBT), IELTS (minimum score 7). *Application deadline:* For fall admission, 1/1 priority date for domestic and international students. Application fee: $50. Electronic applications accepted. *Expenses:* $26,782 in-state, $42,006 out-of-state. *Financial support:* In 2017–18, 17 students received support. Traineeships available. *Faculty research:* Developmental biology; genomics; computational biology; systems biology; structural biology. *Unit head:* Dr. Neil Hukriede, Program Director, 412-648-9918, E-mail: hukriede@pitt.edu. *Application contact:* Shari Murphy, Program Coordinator, 412-692-9907, E-mail: sas101@pitt.edu.
Website: http://www.isb.pitt.edu

University of Toronto, School of Graduate Studies, Faculty of Arts and Science, Department of Cell and Systems Biology, Toronto, ON M5S 1A1, Canada. Offers M Sc, PhD. *Degree requirements:* For master's, thesis, thesis defense; for doctorate, thesis/ dissertation, thesis defense, oral thesis examination. *Entrance requirements:* For master's, minimum B+ average in final year, B overall, 3 letters of reference. Additional exam requirements/recommendations for international students: Required—TOEFL (minimum score 580 paper-based; 93 iBT), TWE (minimum score 5). Electronic applications accepted.

Virginia Commonwealth University, Graduate School, School of Life Sciences, Doctoral Program in Integrative Life Sciences, Richmond, VA 23284-9005. Offers PhD. *Entrance requirements:* For doctorate, GRE, minimum GPA of 3.0 in last 60 credits of undergraduate work or in graduate degree, 3 letters of recommendation. Additional exam requirements/recommendations for international students: Required—TOEFL (minimum score 600 paper-based; 100 iBT). Electronic applications accepted.

Washington University in St. Louis, The Graduate School, Division of Biology and Biomedical Sciences, Program in Computational and Systems Biology, St. Louis, MO 63130-4899. Offers PhD. *Degree requirements:* For doctorate, thesis/dissertation. *Entrance requirements:* For doctorate, GRE General Test, GRE Subject Test. Additional exam requirements/recommendations for international students: Required—TOEFL. Electronic applications accepted. *Faculty research:* Systems biology, genomics, sequence analysis, regulatory networks, synthetic biology, metagenomics, metabolomics, proteomics, epigenomics, transcriptomics, lipidomics, single cell dynamics, high-throughput technology development, applied math and mathematical models of biological processes, computational biology, comparative genomics, personalized medicine, genome engineering, machine learning, big data science, next generation sequencing and its applications, bioinformatics.

Weill Cornell Medicine, Weill Cornell Graduate School of Medical Sciences, Physiology, Biophysics and Systems Biology Program, New York, NY 10065. Offers MS, PhD. Terminal master's awarded for partial completion of doctoral program. *Degree requirements:* For master's, comprehensive exam; for doctorate, thesis/dissertation, final exam. *Entrance requirements:* For doctorate, GRE General Test, introductory courses in biology, inorganic and organic chemistry, physics, and mathematics. Additional exam requirements/recommendations for international students: Required—TOEFL. *Faculty research:* Receptor-mediated regulation of cell function, molecular properties of channels or receptors, bioinformatics, mathematical modeling.

Translational Biology

Baylor College of Medicine, Graduate School of Biomedical Sciences, Program in Translational Biology and Molecular Medicine, Houston, TX 77030-3498. Offers PhD. *Degree requirements:* For doctorate, thesis/dissertation, public defense. *Entrance requirements:* For doctorate, GRE, minimum GPA of 3.0. Additional exam requirements/ recommendations for international students: Required—TOEFL. Electronic applications accepted. *Faculty research:* Molecular medicine, translational biology, human disease biology and therapy.

Boston University, School of Medicine, Division of Graduate Medical Sciences, Program in Molecular and Translational Medicine, Boston, MA 02215. Offers PhD, MD/ PhD. *Degree requirements:* For doctorate, thesis/dissertation. *Application deadline:* For fall admission, 1/15 for domestic students; for spring admission, 10/15 for domestic students. *Unit head:* Dr. Matt Jones, Director, 617-638-4860, E-mail: mattj@bu.edu. *Application contact:* GMS Admissions Office, 617-638-5255, E-mail: askgms@bu.edu.
Website: http://www.bumc.bu.edu/gpmm

Cedars-Sinai Medical Center, Graduate Programs, Los Angeles, CA 90048. Offers biomedical and translational sciences (PhD); magnetic resonance in medicine (MS). *Faculty:* 60 full-time (15 women). *Students:* 40 full-time (26 women); includes 12 minority (2 Black or African American, non-Hispanic/Latino; 4 Asian, non-Hispanic/Latino; 4 Hispanic/Latino; 2 Native Hawaiian or other Pacific Islander, non-Hispanic/Latino). Average age 29. 55 applicants, 15% accepted, 8 enrolled. *Degree requirements:* For doctorate, comprehensive exam, thesis/dissertation. *Entrance requirements:* For doctorate, GRE, 3 letters of recommendation. Additional exam requirements/ recommendations for international students: Required—TOEFL (minimum score 550 paper-based; 80 iBT), IELTS (minimum score 6.5). *Application deadline:* For fall admission, 1/31 for domestic students. Application fee: $35. Electronic applications accepted. *Financial support:* Health care benefits and annual stipends (averaging $36,000) available. *Faculty research:* Regenerative medicine, immunology and host-pathogen interactions, cancer biology, genomics, tissue fibrosis and repair, neurosciences, metabolism, heart biology. *Total annual research expenditures:* $36 million. *Application contact:* Emma Yates Casler, Program Coordinator, 310-423-8294, E-mail: yatese@cshs.org.
Website: https://www.cedars-sinai.edu/Education/Graduate-Research-Education/

Rutgers University–New Brunswick, Graduate School of Biomedical Sciences, Program in Clinical and Translational Science, Piscataway, NJ 08854-8097. Offers MS. *Program availability:* Part-time. *Degree requirements:* For master's, thesis.

University of California, Irvine, School of Medicine, Program in Biomedical and Translational Science, Irvine, CA 92697. Offers MS. *Students:* 14 full-time (9 women), 1 part-time (0 women); includes 6 minority (1 Black or African American, non-Hispanic/ Latino; 4 Asian, non-Hispanic/Latino; 1 Hispanic/Latino), 6 international. Average age 30. 34 applicants, 56% accepted, 13 enrolled. In 2017, 10 master's awarded. *Entrance requirements:* For master's, curriculum vitae. *Application deadline:* For fall admission, 1/ 15 priority date for domestic students. Application fee: $105 ($125 for international students). *Unit head:* Dr. Sherrie Kaplan, Director, 949-824-0095.
Website: http://www.som.uci.edu/bats/education/ms-degree.asp

The University of Iowa, Graduate College, Program in Translational Biomedicine, Iowa City, IA 52242-1316. Offers MS, PhD. Terminal master's awarded for partial completion of doctoral program. *Degree requirements:* For master's, comprehensive exam; for doctorate, comprehensive exam, thesis/dissertation. *Entrance requirements:* For master's and doctorate, minimum GPA of 3.0. Additional exam requirements/ recommendations for international students: Required—TOEFL (minimum score 550 paper-based; 81 iBT). Electronic applications accepted.

University of Massachusetts Medical School, Graduate School of Biomedical Sciences, Worcester, MA 01655-0115. Offers biomedical sciences (PhD), including biochemistry and molecular pharmacology, bioinformatics and computational biology, cancer biology, immunology and microbiology, interdisciplinary, neuroscience, translational science; biomedical sciences (millennium program) (PhD); clinical and population health research (PhD); clinical investigation (MS). *Faculty:* 1,316 full-time (526 women), 357 part-time/adjunct (229 women). *Students:* 347 full-time (180 women); includes 61 minority (10 Black or African American, non-Hispanic/Latino; 1 American Indian or Alaska Native, non-Hispanic/Latino; 35 Asian, non-Hispanic/Latino; 15 Hispanic/Latino), 130 international. Average age 29. 608 applicants, 28% accepted, 54 enrolled. In 2017, 6 master's, 51 doctorates awarded. Terminal master's awarded for partial completion of doctoral program. *Degree requirements:* For master's, comprehensive exam, thesis; for doctorate, comprehensive exam, thesis/dissertation. *Entrance requirements:* For master's, MD, PhD, DVM, or PharmD; for doctorate, GRE General Test, bachelor's degree. Additional exam requirements/recommendations for international students: Required—TOEFL (minimum score 90 iBT) or IELTS (minimum score 7.0). *Application deadline:* For fall admission, 12/15 for domestic and international students. Applications are processed on a rolling basis. Application fee: $80. Electronic applications accepted. Application fee is waived when completed online. *Expenses:* $14,883 in-state tuition and mandatory fees; $31,486 out-of-state. *Financial support:* In 2017–18, 15 fellowships with partial tuition reimbursements (averaging $29,000 per year), 296 research assistantships with full tuition reimbursements (averaging $31,212 per year) were awarded; institutionally sponsored loans and scholarships/grants also available. Financial award application deadline: 5/15. *Faculty research:* RNA biology, molecular/cell/developmental/metabolic biology, bioinformatics and computational biology, clinical/translational research, infectious disease and immunology. *Total annual research expenditures:* $279 million. *Unit head:* Dr. Mary Ellen Lane, Dean, 508-856-4018, E-mail: maryellen.lane@umassmed.edu. *Application contact:* Dr. Kendall Knight, Assistant Vice Provost for Admissions, 508-856-5628, Fax: 508-856-3659, E-mail: kendall.knight@umassmed.edu.
Website: http://www.umassmed.edu/gsbs/

The University of Texas at San Antonio, Joint PhD Program in Translational Science, San Antonio, TX 78249-0617. Offers PhD. Program offered in partnership with The University of Texas Health Science Center at San Antonio, The University of Texas at Austin, and The University of Texas Health Science Center at Houston. *Program availability:* Part-time. *Students:* 1 full-time (0 women), 7 part-time (4 women); includes 4 minority (all Hispanic/Latino), 1 international. Average age 37. *Degree requirements:* For doctorate, comprehensive exam, thesis/dissertation. *Entrance requirements:* For doctorate, GRE General Test, official transcripts, copy of U.S. medical license/ certificate, criminal background check, resume or curriculum vitae, 3 letters of recommendation, statement of purpose. Additional exam requirements/ recommendations for international students: Required—TOEFL (minimum score 565 paper-based; 86 iBT), IELTS (minimum score 6.5). *Application deadline:* For fall admission, 11/1 for domestic and international students. Application fee: $50 ($90 for international students). Electronic applications accepted. *Expenses:* Contact institution. *Financial support:* In 2017–18, 1 student received support. Research assistantships, teaching assistantships, scholarships/grants, and unspecified assistantships available. *Faculty research:* Community-acquired methicillin-resistant staphylococcus (CA-MRSA); epigenetic changes in cancer genomes; occupational injury and prevention; addiction science; inflammation, tissue injury, and regeneration. *Unit head:* Dr. Chris Frei, Program Director, 210-567-8355, Fax: 210-564-4301, E-mail: freic@uthscsa.edu. *Application contact:* Susan Stappenbeck, Senior Project Coordinator, 210-567-8094, E-mail: stappenbeck@uthscsa.edu.
Website: http://iims.uthscsa.edu/ed_trans_sci_phd.html

The University of Texas Medical Branch, Graduate School of Biomedical Sciences, Program in Human Pathophysiology and Translational Medicine, Galveston, TX 77555. Offers MS, PhD. *Degree requirements:* For master's, thesis or alternative; for doctorate, thesis/dissertation. *Entrance requirements:* For master's and doctorate, GRE General Test. Additional exam requirements/recommendations for international students: Required—TOEFL (minimum score 550 paper-based). Electronic applications accepted.

UNIVERSITY OF CALIFORNIA, SAN DIEGO

UC San Diego
Bioinformatics and Systems Biology

Bioinformatics and Systems Biology Program

★ For more information, visit http://petersons.to/uc-sandiego_bioinformatics

Program of Study

There is an enormous need for trained professionals who are experts in biology, biomedicine, and computing. The Bioinformatics and Systems Biology Graduate Program at University of California, San Diego (UCSD), founded in 2001 by Professor Shankar Subramaniam, addresses this need. It includes five schools and divisions on the UC San Diego campus: the Jacobs School of Engineering (bioengineering, computer science and engineering, and nanoengineering), the Division of Biological Sciences (molecular biology, cell and developmental biology, neurobiology, ecology/behavior/evolution), the Division of Physical Sciences (chemistry and biochemistry, physics, and mathematics), the School of Medicine, and the Skaggs School of Pharmacy and Pharmaceutical Sciences. The graduate program is supported by the respective schools, divisions, and departments as well as by a substantial NIH Training Grant and more than fifty associated faculty.

The Bioinformatics and Systems Biology Graduate Program is organized around two disciplinary tracks that have distinct, yet overlapping, faculty and curricular requirements: Bioinformatics and Systems Biology (BISB) and Biomedical Informatics (BMI). Students indicate their interest in one track, but are able to request a switch at any time during their study. For each track there are four required core courses (generally completed within the first year) and 16 units to be chosen from a list of elective fields to be completed within the first two years. The core curriculum ensures that every student within the program has the same knowledge basis in key areas of bioinformatics, systems biology, and biomedical informatics. The electives are intended to provide students with in-depth courses related to their own research interests.

In addition, students must also take the colloquium for their track; one of two ethics courses; the Research Rotation requirement; research units with their dissertation advisor after joining a lab; and two quarters as a teaching assistant.

Research Facilities

UC San Diego recently ranked fifth in the nation for annual federal research and development spending. The University excels in both traditional scholarly disciplines and fields that cross these disciplines, such as neuroscience, nanoscience, and climate science.

UC San Diego researchers consistently earn international acclaim. They include Nobel and Pulitzer prize winners, members of the National Academies, and recipients of MacArthur Foundation "genius grants."

The Jacobs School of Engineering ranks seventh in the nation and 23rd in the world according to a *U.S. News & World Report* best global universities ranking, published October 2015. With $162 million in federal, state, and industry research support in FY15, the Jacobs School of Engineering ranks ninth in the nation for research expenditures per faculty member (*U.S. News & World Report*, published March 2016), reflecting UC San Diego's leadership as a research university.

The UC San Diego Library, ranked among the nation's top public academic libraries, plays a critical role in advancing and supporting the university's research, teaching, patient care, and public service missions. The world-renowned research for which UC San Diego is known starts at the UC San Diego Library, which provides the foundation of knowledge needed to advance cutting-edge discoveries in a wide range of disciplines.

Financial Aid

All U.S. citizens and residents admitted into the Ph.D. program are supported by a financial support package to cover tuition and fees (determined by the Graduate Division), as well as a stipend (set by the program; $32,000 as of October 1, 2016) that covers living expenses, so long as they are in good academic standing with university and program requirements.

Living and Housing costs

UCSD has several options for on-campus living; additional details are available on the Associated Rental Community Housing (ARCH) website, http://hdh.ucsd.edu/arch/pages/. Those looking for off-campus housing can find more information at http://offcampushousing.ucsd.edu/.

Student Group

The University's diverse student population is drawn from the best and brightest worldwide. With over 500 student organizations, there is something for everyone. The Graduate Bioinformatics Council (GBIC) represents the students of the Bioinformatics and System Biology Ph.D. program.

Student Outcomes

There is enormous demand from academia, industry, and government for trained professionals in bioinformatics and biomedical informatics. A report from the Working Group on Data and Informatics to the NIH Advisory Committee to the Director recognized the shortage of biomedical scientists with appropriate computing expertise and called for strong NIH support of cross-disciplinary education and training. Academic institutions in health sciences, the healthcare industry, and government institutions are seeking highly skilled individuals who can manage and analyze large amounts of data, and who can connect discoveries at different biological scales (from molecular to individual to population levels).

Location

The university's main campus is located near the Pacific Ocean on 1,200 acres of coastal woodland in La Jolla, California. About a 25-minute drive to downtown, and hour trip to Tijuana, Mexico, UCSD is not far from any fun destination.

The University

The University of California, San Diego is a student-centered, research-focused, service-oriented public institution that provides opportunity for all. Recognized as one of the top 15 research universities worldwide, a culture of collaboration sparks discoveries that advance society and drive economic impact. UCSD is home to over 500 student organizations, and six colleges. UCSD sponsors 23 intercollegiate men's and women's sports at the NCAA Division II level. The Tritons compete primarily in California Collegiate Athletic Association, widely regarded as the premiere conference for D-II athletics.

Applying

Admission review will be on a competitive basis based on the applicants' undergraduate track record, Graduate Record Examination General Test (GRE) scores, and other scholastic achievements. Special attention will be given to the quantitative and analytical section scores of the GRE and the formal education in quantitative methods. The applications will be screened and evaluated by the Admissions Committee with input from program faculty. Applicants must apply online at https://gradapply.ucsd.edu/ and must submit a completed UC San Diego Application for Graduate Admission.

Correspondence and Information

Bioinformatics and Systems Biology Graduate Coordinator
Powell-Focht Bioengineering Hall
University of California, San Diego
9500 Gilman Drive MC 0419
La Jolla, California 92093-0419
United States
Phone: 858-822-4948
E-mail: bioinfo@ucsd.edu
Website: http://bioinformatics.ucsd.edu

THE FACULTY AND THEIR RESEARCH

Bioinformatics and Systems Biology Research Areas

Ruben Abagyan, Professor, School of Pharmacy.
Vineet Bafna, Professor, Computer Science and Engineering, Graduate and Undergraduate, Program Director Bioinformatics.
Nuno Bandeira, Assistant Professor, Computer Science and Engineering.
Vikas Bansal, Assistant Professor, Pediatrics.
Steve Briggs, Professor, Biological Sciences.
Hannah Carter, Assistant Professor of Medicine, School of Medicine.
Pieter Dorrestein, Assistant Professor, School of Pharmacy.

University of California, San Diego

Joseph Ecker, Professor, Biological Sciences.
Charles Elkan, Professor, Computer Science and Engineering.
Ronald M. Evans, Professor and Director, Salk Institute for Biological Studies.
Kelly Frazer, Professor, Pediatrics.
Yoav Freund, Professor, Computer Science and Engineering.
Terry Gaasterland, Professor and Director of Scripps Genome Center, Marine Biology Research Division.
Kyle Gaulton, Assistant Professor, Pediatrics.
Michael Gilson, Professor, School of Pharmacy.
Christopher Glass, Professor, Cellular and Molecular Medicine.
Joseph Gleeson, Professor/HHMI Investigator, Neurosciences (School of Medicine).
Lawrence Goldstein, Professor, Cellular and Molecular Medicine.
Nan Hao, Assistant Professor, Biological Sciences.
Jeff Hasty, Associate Professor, Biological Sciences.
Michael Holst, Professor, Mathematics.
Vivian Hook, Professor, School of Pharmacy.
Xiaohua Huang, Assistant Professor, Bioengineering.
Terence Hwa, Professor, Physics Professor, Biological Sciences.
Lilia Iakoucheva, Associate Professor, Psychiatry.
Trey Ideker, Professor, School of Medicine.
Suckjoon Jun, Assistant Professor, Physics Assistant Professor, Biological Sciences.
Amy Kiger, Assistant Professor, Biological Sciences.
Rob Knight, Professor, Pediatrics.
Richard Kolodner, Professor, School of Medicine.
Julie Law, Assistant Professor, Salk Institute for Biological Studies.
Nathan E. Lewis, Assistant Professor, Pediatrics.
Prashant Mali, Assistant Professor, Bioengineering.
Andrew McCammon, Professor, Chemistry and Biochemistry.
Andrew McCulloch, Professor, Bioengineering.
Graham McVicker, Assistant Professor, Salk Institute for Biological Studies.
Jill Mesirov, Professor, School of Medicine Associate Vice Chancellor, Computational Health Sciences, Professor of Medicine, Division of Medical Genetics.
Christian Metallo, Assistant Professor, Bioengineering.
Siavash Mirarab, Assistant Professor, Electrical and Computer Engineering.
Eran Mukamel, Assistant Professor, Cognitive Science.
Saket Navlakha, Assistant Professor, Salk Institute for Biological Studies.
Lucila Ohno-Machado, Professor, Division of Biomedical Informatics.
Bernhard Palsson, Professor, Bioengineering.
Pavel Pevzner, Professor and Ronald R Taylor Chair, Computer Science and Engineering.
Anjana Rao, Adjunct Professor, Pharmacology.
Bing Ren, Professor, Cellular and Molecular Medicine Graduate Program Associate Director, Bioinformatics.
Doug Richman, Professor, Pathology.
Scott Rifkin, Assistant Professor, Biological Sciences.
Michael Rosenfeld, Professor, School of Medicine.
Debashis Sahoo, Assistant Professor, Pediatrics.
Nicholas Schork, Professor, Scripps Research Institute.
Julian Schroeder, Professor, Biological Sciences.
Dorothy Sears, Associate Professor, School of Medicine.
Jonathan Sebat, Chief, Beyster Center for Molecular Genomics of Neuropsychiatric Diseases; Associate Professor of Psychiatry and Cellular & Molecular Medicine, Cellular and Molecular Medicine.
Shankar Subramaniam, Professor, Bioengineering.
Gurol Suel, Associate Professor, Biological Sciences.
Palmer Taylor, Professor and Dean, School of Pharmacy.
Susan Taylor, Professor, Chemistry and Biochemistry.
Glenn Tesler Associate Professor, Mathematics.
Roger Tsien, Professor, Pharmacology.
Inder Verma, Adjunct Professor, Biological Sciences.
Yingxiao (Peter) Wang, Associate Professor, Bioengineering.
Wei Wang, Professor, Chemistry and Biochemistry.
Joel Wertheim, Assistant Professor of Medicine, Division of Infectious Diseases, School of Medicine.
Ruth Williams, Professor, Mathematics.
Christopher Woelk, Assistant Professor; Dir., Genomics Core, CFAR, School of Medicine.
Roy Wollman, Assistant Professor, Chemistry and Biochemistry.
Ronghui (Lily) Xu, Professor, Mathematics.
Gene Yeo, Professor, Cellular and Molecular Medicine.
Kun Zhang, Associate Professor, Bioengineering.
Sheng Zhong, Associate Professor, Bioengineering.

Biomedical Informatics Research Areas

Predictive Modeling and Personalized Medicine

Olivier Harismendy
Chun-Nan Hsu
Lucila Ohno-Machado
Gene Yeo

Privacy Technology, Data Sharing, and Big Data Analytics

Charles Elkan
Yoav Freundm
Lucila Ohno-Machado
Staal Vinterbo
Gene Yeo

Data Models and Knowledge Representation

Chun-Nan Hsu
Hyeon-eui Kim

Decision Support Systems

Robert El-Kareh

Biomedical Natural Language Processing

Charles ElkanChun-Nan Hsu

Bioinformatics Applications in Human Disease

Olivier Harismendy
Lilia Iakoucheva
Dorothy Sears
Christopher Woelk
Gene Yeo, Professor
Jason Young, Assistant Professor

Section 8
Ecology, Environmental Biology, and Evolutionary Biology

This section contains a directory of institutions offering graduate work in ecology, environmental biology. Additional information about programs listed in the directory may be obtained by writing directly to the dean of a graduate school or chair of a department at the address given in the directory.

For programs offering related work, see also in this book *Biological and Biomedical Sciences; Botany and Plant Biology; Entomology; Genetics, Developmental Biology, and Reproductive Biology; Microbiological Sciences; Pharmacology and Toxicology; Public Health;* and *Zoology.* In the other guides in this series:

Graduate Programs in the Humanities, Arts & Social Sciences

See *Sociology, Anthropology, and Archaeology*

Graduate Programs in the Physical Sciences, Mathematics, Agricultural Sciences, the Environment & Natural Resources

See *Agricultural and Food Sciences, Geosciences, Marine Sciences and Oceanography,* and *Mathematical Sciences*

Graduate Programs in Engineering & Applied Sciences

See *Civil and Environmental Engineering, Management of Engineering and Technology,* and *Ocean Engineering*

CONTENTS

Program Directories

Conservation Biology

Antioch University New England, Graduate School, Department of Environmental Studies, Program in Conservation Biology, Keene, NH 03431-3552. Offers MS. *Degree requirements:* For master's, thesis or project. *Entrance requirements:* For master's, resume, 3 letters of recommendation. Additional exam requirements/recommendations for international students: Required—TOEFL (minimum score 550 paper-based). Electronic applications accepted.

Arizona State University at the Tempe campus, College of Liberal Arts and Sciences, School of Life Sciences, Tempe, AZ 85287-4601. Offers animal behavior (PhD); applied ethics (biomedical and health ethics) (MA); biology (MS, PhD), including biology, biology and society, complex adaptive systems science (PhD), plant biology and conservation (MS); environmental life sciences (PhD); evolutionary biology (PhD); history and philosophy of science (PhD); human and social dimensions of science and technology (PhD); microbiology (PhD); molecular and cellular biology (PhD); neuroscience (PhD). Terminal master's awarded for partial completion of doctoral program. *Degree requirements:* For master's, thesis (for some programs), interactive Program of Study (iPOS) submitted before completing 50 percent of required credit hours; for doctorate, variable foreign language requirement, comprehensive exam, thesis/dissertation, interactive Program of Study (iPOS) submitted before completing 50 percent of required credit hours. *Entrance requirements:* For master's and doctorate, GRE, minimum GPA of 3.0 or equivalent in last 2 years of work leading to bachelor's degree. Additional exam requirements/recommendations for international students: Required—TOEFL (minimum score 600 paper-based; 100 iBT). Electronic applications accepted.

California State University, Sacramento, College of Natural Sciences and Mathematics, Department of Biological Sciences, Sacramento, CA 95819. Offers biological conservation (MS); molecular and cellular biology (MS); stem cell (MA). *Program availability:* Part-time. *Students:* 25 full-time (15 women), 26 part-time (14 women); includes 11 minority (2 Black or African American, non-Hispanic/Latino; 1 American Indian or Alaska Native, non-Hispanic/Latino; 8 Asian, non-Hispanic/Latino), 1 international. Average age 29. 82 applicants, 29% accepted, 18 enrolled. In 2017, 11 master's awarded. *Degree requirements:* For master's, thesis or project; writing proficiency exam. *Entrance requirements:* For master's, GRE, bachelor's degree in biology or equivalent; minimum GPA of 2.75 in all biology courses, 3.0 in all upper-division biology courses. Additional exam requirements/recommendations for international students: Required—TOEFL (minimum score 550 paper-based; 80 iBT); Recommended—IELTS, TSE. *Application deadline:* For fall admission, 2/1 for domestic and international students. Applications are processed on a rolling basis. Application fee: $55. Electronic applications accepted. *Expenses:* Contact institution. *Financial support:* Teaching assistantships, career-related internships or fieldwork, Federal Work-Study, and scholarships/grants available. Support available to part-time students. Financial award application deadline: 3/1; financial award applicants required to submit FAFSA. *Unit head:* Dr. Shannon Datwyler, Chair, 916-278-6535, Fax: 916-278-6993, E-mail: datwyler@csus.edu. *Application contact:* Jose Martinez, Graduate Admissions Supervisor, 916-278-7871, E-mail: martinj@skymail.csus.edu.
Website: http://www.csus.edu/bios

California State University, Stanislaus, College of Natural Sciences, MS Program in Ecology and Sustainability, Turlock, CA 95382. Offers ecological conservation (MS). *Program availability:* Part-time. *Degree requirements:* For master's, thesis. *Entrance requirements:* For master's, GRE, minimum GPA of 3.0, 3 letters of recommendation, personal statement. Additional exam requirements/recommendations for international students: Required—TOEFL (minimum score 550 paper-based). Electronic applications accepted.

Central Michigan University, College of Graduate Studies, College of Science and Technology, Department of Biology, Mount Pleasant, MI 48859. Offers biology (MS); conservation biology (MS). *Program availability:* Part-time. *Degree requirements:* For master's, thesis or alternative. *Entrance requirements:* For master's, GRE, bachelor's degree with a major in biological science, minimum GPA of 3.0. Electronic applications accepted. *Faculty research:* Conservation biology, morphology and taxonomy of aquatic plants, molecular biology and genetics, microbials and invertebrate ecology, vertebrates.

Colorado State University, Warner College of Natural Resources, Department of Fish, Wildlife, and Conservation Biology, Fort Collins, CO 80523-1474. Offers MFWCB, MS, PhD. *Program availability:* 100% online. *Faculty:* 12 full-time (4 women), 4 part-time/adjunct (0 women). *Students:* 9 full-time (5 women), 32 part-time (14 women); includes 4 minority (3 Hispanic/Latino; 1 Two or more races, non-Hispanic/Latino), 1 international. Average age 31. 49 applicants, 35% accepted, 16 enrolled. In 2017, 4 master's, 2 doctorates awarded. *Degree requirements:* For master's, comprehensive exam, thesis (for some programs); for doctorate, comprehensive exam, thesis/dissertation. *Entrance requirements:* For master's, GRE, minimum cumulative undergraduate GPA of 3.0; faculty advisor; statement of purpose; related degree; 2 years of relevant employment (for online program); for doctorate, GRE, minimum cumulative undergraduate GPA of 3.0; faculty advisor; statement of purpose; related degree. Additional exam requirements/recommendations for international students: Required—TOEFL (minimum score 550 paper-based; 79 iBT), IELTS (minimum score 6.5). *Application deadline:* Applications are processed on a rolling basis. Application fee: $60 ($70 for international students). Electronic applications accepted. *Expenses:* $705 per credit hour (for online MFWCB). *Financial support:* In 2017–18, 18 research assistantships (averaging $24,220 per year), 7 teaching assistantships (averaging $14,256 per year) were awarded; career-related internships or fieldwork and unspecified assistantships also available. *Faculty research:* Impacts and management of exotics; endangered species management; capture-mark-recapture methods; conservation and management of aquatic ecosystems; wildlife disease ecology. *Total annual research expenditures:* $2.6 million. *Unit head:* Dr. Kenneth Wilson, Department Head, 970-491-5020, Fax: 970-491-5091, E-mail: kenneth.wilson@colostate.edu. *Application contact:* Kim Samsel, Assistant to Department Head, 970-491-5020, Fax: 970-491-5091, E-mail: kim.samsel@colostate.edu.
Website: http://warnercnr.colostate.edu/fwcb-home/

Columbia University, Graduate School of Arts and Sciences, New York, NY 10027. Offers African-American studies (MA); American studies (MA); anthropology (MA, PhD); art history and archaeology (MA, PhD); astronomy (PhD); biological sciences (PhD); biotechnology (MA); chemical physics (PhD); chemistry (PhD); classical studies (MA, PhD); classics (MA, PhD); climate and society (MA); conservation biology (MA); earth and environmental sciences (PhD); East Asia: regional studies (MA); East Asian languages and cultures (MA, PhD); ecology, evolution and environmental biology (MA), including conservation biology; ecology, evolution, and environmental biology (PhD), including ecology and evolutionary biology, evolutionary primatology; economics (MA, PhD); English and comparative literature (MA, PhD); French and Romance philology (MA, PhD); Germanic languages (MA, PhD); global French studies (MA); global thought (MA); Hispanic cultural studies (MA); history (PhD); history and literature (MA); human rights studies (MA); Islamic studies (MA); Italian (MA, PhD); Japanese pedagogy (MA); Jewish studies (MA); Latin America and the Caribbean: regional studies (MA); Latin American and Iberian cultures (PhD); mathematics (MA, PhD), including finance (MA); medieval and Renaissance studies (MA); Middle Eastern, South Asian, and African studies (MA, PhD); modern art: critical and curatorial studies (MA); modern European studies (MA); museum anthropology (MA); music (DMA, PhD); oral history (MA); philosophical foundations of physics (MA); philosophy (MA, PhD); physics (PhD); political science (MA, PhD); psychology (PhD); quantitative methods in the social sciences (MA); religion (MA, PhD); Russia, Eurasia and East Europe: regional studies (MA); Russian translation (MA); Slavic cultures (MA); Slavic languages (MA, PhD); sociology (MA, PhD); South Asian studies (MA); statistics (MA, PhD); theatre (PhD). Dual-degree programs require admission to both Graduate School of Arts and Sciences and another Columbia school. *Program availability:* Part-time. Terminal master's awarded for partial completion of doctoral program. *Degree requirements:* For master's, variable foreign language requirement, comprehensive exam (for some programs), thesis (for some programs); for doctorate, variable foreign language requirement, comprehensive exam (for some programs), thesis/dissertation. *Entrance requirements:* For master's and doctorate, GRE General Test, GRE Subject Test (for some programs). Additional exam requirements/recommendations for international students: Required—TOEFL, IELTS. Electronic applications accepted. *Expenses: Tuition:* Full-time $44,864; part-time $1704 per credit. *Required fees:* $2370 per semester. One-time fee: $105.

Cornell University, Graduate School, Graduate Fields of Agriculture and Life Sciences, Field of Natural Resources, Ithaca, NY 14853. Offers community-based natural resources management (MS, PhD); conservation biology (MS, PhD); ecosystem biology and biogeochemistry (MPS, MS, PhD); environmental management (MPS); fishery and aquatic science (MPS, MS, PhD); forest science (MPS, MS, PhD); human dimensions of natural resources management (MPS, MS, PhD); policy and institutional analysis (MS, PhD); program development and evaluation (MPS, MS, PhD); quantitative ecology (MS, PhD); wildlife science (MPS, MS, PhD). *Degree requirements:* For master's, thesis (MS), project paper (MPS); for doctorate, comprehensive exam, thesis/dissertation. *Entrance requirements:* For master's and doctorate, GRE General Test, 2 letters of recommendation. Additional exam requirements/recommendations for international students: Required—TOEFL (minimum score 550 paper-based; 77 iBT). Electronic applications accepted. *Faculty research:* Ecosystem-level dynamics, systems modeling, conservation biology/management, resource management's human dimensions, biogeochemistry.

Florida Institute of Technology, College of Science, Program in Conservation Technology, Melbourne, FL 32901-6975. Offers MS. *Program availability:* Part-time. *Students:* Average age 35. 6 applicants, 50% accepted. In 2017, 4 master's awarded. *Entrance requirements:* For master's, GRE General Test, 3 letters of recommendation, statement of objectives. Additional exam requirements/recommendations for international students: Required—TOEFL (minimum score 550 paper-based; 79 iBT). *Application deadline:* Applications are processed on a rolling basis. Electronic applications accepted. *Expenses: Tuition:* Part-time $1241 per credit hour. Part-time tuition and fees vary according to campus/location. *Financial support:* Applicants required to submit FAFSA. *Unit head:* Dr. Richard B. Aronson, Department Head, 321-674-8034, Fax: 321-674-7238, E-mail: raronson@fit.edu. *Application contact:* Cheryl A. Brown, Associate Director of Graduate Admissions, 321-674-7581, Fax: 321-723-9468, E-mail: cbrown@fit.edu.
Website: http://www.fit.edu/programs/

Fordham University, Graduate School of Arts and Sciences, Department of Biological Sciences, New York, NY 10458. Offers biological sciences (MS, PhD); conservation biology (Graduate Certificate). *Program availability:* Part-time, evening/weekend. *Faculty:* 18 full-time (2 women). *Students:* 46 full-time (30 women); includes 4 minority (1 Asian, non-Hispanic/Latino; 3 Hispanic/Latino), 9 international. Average age 29. 64 applicants, 50% accepted, 15 enrolled. In 2017, 7 master's, 5 doctorates, 3 other advanced degrees awarded. Terminal master's awarded for partial completion of doctoral program. *Degree requirements:* For master's, one foreign language, comprehensive exam, thesis optional; for doctorate, one foreign language, comprehensive exam, thesis/dissertation. *Entrance requirements:* For master's and doctorate, GRE General Test, GRE Subject Test (recommended). Additional exam requirements/recommendations for international students: Required—TOEFL (minimum score 550 paper-based). *Application deadline:* For fall admission, 1/4 priority date for domestic students; for spring admission, 11/1 for domestic students. Application fee: $70. Electronic applications accepted. *Financial support:* In 2017–18, 28 students received support, including 4 fellowships with tuition reimbursements available (averaging $31,000 per year), 42 teaching assistantships with tuition reimbursements available (averaging $29,270 per year); Federal Work-Study, institutionally sponsored loans, scholarships/grants, tuition waivers (full and partial), and unspecified assistantships also available. Support available to part-time students. Financial award application deadline: 1/4; financial award applicants required to submit FAFSA. *Faculty research:* Avian ecology, behavioral ecology, and conservation biology; plant, community and ecosystem responses to invasive organisms; neurobiology and ion channel disorders; biochemical, physiological and morphological basis of pattern formation; behavioral, physiological and biochemical adaptations of mammals to extreme environments; evolutionary ecology, functional morphology and ichthyology; genotypic response to biogeographic and anthropogenic factors; community-based sustainable resource use. *Total annual research expenditures:* $1.5 million. *Unit head:* Dr. James Lewis, Chair, 718-817-3642, Fax: 718-817-3645, E-mail: jdlewis@fordham.edu. *Application contact:* Travis Strattion, Interim Director of Graduate Admissions, 718-817-4417, Fax: 718-817-3566, E-mail: tstrattion@fordham.edu.

Frostburg State University, College of Liberal Arts and Sciences, Department of Biology, Program in Applied Ecology and Conservation Biology, Frostburg, MD 21532. Offers MS. *Faculty:* 10. *Students:* 8 full-time (7 women), 6 part-time (4 women). Average age 28. 18 applicants, 61% accepted, 4 enrolled. In 2017, 4 master's awarded. *Degree requirements:* For master's, thesis. *Entrance requirements:* For master's, GRE General Test, resume. Additional exam requirements/recommendations for international students: Required—TOEFL. *Application deadline:* For fall admission, 7/15 priority date for domestic students. Applications are processed on a rolling basis. Application fee: $45. Electronic applications accepted. *Expenses:* Tuition, state resident: part-time $433 per credit hour. Tuition, nonresident: part-time $557 per credit hour. *Required fees:* $121 per credit hour. $27 per term. *Financial support:* In 2017–18, 8 research assistantships with full tuition reimbursements (averaging $5,000 per year) were awarded; career-related internships or fieldwork and Federal Work-Study also available. Financial award application deadline: 4/1; financial award applicants required to submit FAFSA. *Faculty research:* Forest ecology, microbiology of man-made wetlands, invertebrate zoology and entomology, wildlife and carnivore ecology, aquatic pollution ecology. *Unit head:* Dr. Sunshine Brosi, Coordinator, 301-687-4213, E-mail: slbrosi@frostburg.edu. *Application contact:* Vickie Mazer, Director, Graduate Services, 301-687-7053, Fax: 301-687-4597, E-mail: vmmazer@frostburg.edu.

Illinois State University, Graduate School, College of Arts and Sciences, School of Biological Sciences, Normal, IL 61790. Offers animal behavior (MS); bacteriology (MS); biochemistry (MS); biological sciences (MS); biology (PhD); biophysics (MS); biotechnology (MS); botany (MS, PhD); cell biology (MS); conservation biology (MS); developmental biology (MS); ecology (MS, PhD); entomology (MS); evolutionary biology (MS); genetics (MS, PhD); immunology (MS); microbiology (MS, PhD); molecular biology (MS); molecular genetics (MS); neurobiology (MS); neuroscience (MS); parasitology (MS); physiology (MS, PhD); plant biology (MS); plant molecular biology (MS); plant sciences (MS); structural biology (MS); zoology (MS, PhD). *Program availability:* Part-time. *Degree requirements:* For master's, thesis or alternative; for doctorate, variable foreign language requirement, thesis/dissertation, 2 terms of residency. *Entrance requirements:* For master's, GRE General Test, minimum GPA of 2.6 in last 60 hours of course work; for doctorate, GRE General Test. *Faculty research:* Redoc balance and drug development in schistosoma mansoni, control of the growth of listeria monocytogenes at low temperature, regulation of cell expansion and microtubule function by SPRI, CRUI: physiology and fitness consequences of different life history phenotypes.

North Dakota State University, College of Graduate and Interdisciplinary Studies, Interdisciplinary Program in Environmental and Conservation Sciences, Fargo, ND 58102. Offers MS, PhD. *Entrance requirements:* Additional exam requirements/recommendations for international students: Required—TOEFL. *Expenses:* Tuition, state resident: full-time $4323; part-time $360.21 per credit. Tuition, nonresident: full-time $6484; part-time $540.31 per credit. *Required fees:* $668; $55.70 per credit. Part-time tuition and fees vary according to degree level, program and reciprocity agreements. *Unit head:* Eakalak Khan, Director, 701-231-7717, Fax: 701-231-6185, E-mail: eakalak.khan@ndsu.edu. *Application contact:* Madonna Fitzgerald, Academic Assistant, 701-231-6456, E-mail: madonna.fitzgerald@ndsu.edu.
Website: http://www.ndsu.edu/ecs/

Oregon State University, College of Agricultural Sciences, Program in Fisheries Science, Corvallis, OR 97331. Offers aquaculture (MS); conservation biology (MS, PhD); fish genetics (MS, PhD); ichthyology (MS, PhD); limnology (MS, PhD); parasites and diseases (MS, PhD); physiology and ecology of marine and freshwater fishes (MS, PhD); stream ecology (MS, PhD); toxicology (MS, PhD); water pollution biology (MS, PhD). *Program availability:* Part-time. *Entrance requirements:* For master's and doctorate, GRE, minimum GPA of 3.0 in last 90 hours. Additional exam requirements/recommendations for international students: Required—TOEFL (minimum score 80 iBT), IELTS (minimum score 6.5). *Application deadline:* For fall admission, 5/1 for domestic students, 4/1 for international students. Application fee: $75 ($85 for international students). *Faculty research:* Fisheries ecology, fish toxicology, stream ecology, quantitative analyses of marine and freshwater fish populations. *Unit head:* Dr. Selina Heppell, Department Head/Professor of Fisheries, 541-737-9039, Fax: 541-737-3590, E-mail: selina.heppell@oregonstate.edu. *Application contact:* Dr. Selina Heppell, Department Head/Professor of Fisheries, 541-737-9039, Fax: 541-737-3590, E-mail: selina.heppell@oregonstate.edu.
Website: http://fw.oregonstate.edu/content/graduate

State University of New York College of Environmental Science and Forestry, Department of Environmental and Forest Biology, Syracuse, NY 13210-2779. Offers applied ecology (MPS); chemical ecology (MPS, MS, PhD); conservation biology (MPS, MS, PhD); ecology (MPS, MS, PhD); entomology (MPS, MS, PhD); environmental interpretation (MPS, MS, PhD); environmental physiology (MPS, MS, PhD); fish and wildlife biology and management (MPS, MS, PhD); forest pathology and mycology (MPS, MS, PhD); plant biotechnology (MPS); plant science and biotechnology (MPS, MS, PhD). *Program availability:* Part-time. *Faculty:* 30 full-time (10 women), 4 part-time/adjunct (3 women). *Students:* 117 full-time (65 women), 18 part-time (6 women); includes 8 minority (6 American Indian or Alaska Native, non-Hispanic/Latino; 1 Asian, non-Hispanic/Latino; 1 Hispanic/Latino), 23 international. Average age 30. 84 applicants, 52% accepted, 31 enrolled. In 2017, 30 master's, 3 doctorates awarded. Terminal master's awarded for partial completion of doctoral program. *Degree requirements:* For master's, thesis (for some programs), capstone seminar; for doctorate, comprehensive exam, thesis/dissertation, capstone seminar. *Entrance requirements:* For master's and doctorate, GRE General Test, minimum GPA of 3.0. Additional exam requirements/recommendations for international students: Required—TOEFL (minimum score 550 paper-based; 80 iBT), IELTS (minimum score 6). *Application deadline:* For fall admission, 2/1 priority date for domestic and international students; for spring admission, 11/1 priority date for domestic and international students. Applications are processed on a rolling basis. Application fee: $60. Electronic applications accepted. *Expenses:* Tuition, state resident: full-time $10,870; part-time $453 per credit. Tuition, nonresident: full-time $22,210; part-time $925 per credit. *Required fees:* $1435; $70.85 per credit. One-time fee: $25 full-time. Part-time tuition and fees vary according to course load. *Financial support:* In 2017–18, 42 students received support. Unspecified assistantships available. Financial award application deadline: 6/30; financial award applicants required to submit FAFSA. *Faculty research:* Ecology, conservation biology, fish and wildlife biology and management, plant science, entomology. *Total annual research expenditures:* $5.3 million. *Unit head:* Dr. Neil H. Ringler, Chair, 315-470-6803, Fax: 315-470-6934, E-mail: nhringle@esf.edu. *Application contact:* Scott Shannon, Associate Provost for Instruction/Dean of the Graduate School, 315-470-6599, E-mail: esfgrad@esf.edu.
Website: http://www.esf.edu/efb/grad/default.asp

Texas State University, The Graduate College, College of Science and Engineering, Program in Population and Conservation Biology, San Marcos, TX 78666. Offers MS. *Faculty:* 7 full-time (1 woman). *Students:* 6 full-time (4 women), 6 part-time (4 women); includes 2 minority (both Hispanic/Latino). Average age 29. 3 applicants, 33% accepted. In 2017, 3 master's awarded. *Degree requirements:* For master's, comprehensive exam, thesis. *Entrance requirements:* For master's, GRE (minimum recommended score in at least the 50th percentile on both the verbal and quantitative portions), baccalaureate degree in biology or related discipline from regionally-accredited university with minimum GPA of 3.0 on last 60 undergraduate semester hours, statement of purpose, current curriculum vitae, 3 letters of recommendation, letter of intent to mentor from faculty member of Biology Department. Additional exam requirements/recommendations for international students: Required—TOEFL (minimum score 550 paper-based; 78 iBT), IELTS (minimum score 6.5). *Application deadline:* For fall admission, 2/1 priority date for domestic and international students; for spring admission, 10/15 for domestic students, 10/1 for international students; for summer admission, 4/15 for domestic students, 3/15 for international students. Applications are processed on a rolling basis. Application fee: $40 ($90 for international students). Electronic applications accepted. *Expenses:* Tuition, state resident: full-time $7868; part-time $3934 per semester. Tuition, nonresident: full-time $17,828; part-time $8914 per semester. *Required fees:* $2092; $1435 per semester. Tuition and fees vary according to course load. *Financial support:* In 2017–18, 7 students received support, including 10 teaching assistantships (averaging $13,621 per year); research assistantships, Federal Work-Study, institutionally sponsored loans, scholarships/grants, health care benefits, and unspecified assistantships also available. Support available to part-time students. Financial award application deadline: 3/1; financial award applicants required to submit FAFSA. *Faculty research:* A unique window into the ecology of cretaceous forests, ESA compliance and avoidance monitoring during construction and maintenance, natural hybridization in central Texas Berbers, evaluating the effectiveness of freshwater mussel mitigation strategies, movement patterns and habitat use of the Rio Grande Cooter within lotic ecosystem, divergent selection and reproductive isolation in Louisiana Iris, characterization of epigenetic factors and their regulatory roles, endangered species research. *Total annual research expenditures:* $929,046. *Unit head:* Dr. Noland Martin, Graduate Advisor, 512-245-3317, E-mail: nm14@txstate.edu. *Application contact:* Dr. Andrea Golato, Dean of the Graduate School, 512-245-2581, Fax: 512-245-8365, E-mail: jw02@swt.edu.
Website: http://www.bio.txstate.edu/Graduate-Programs/M.S.PopulationConservationBiology.html

Tropical Agriculture Research and Higher Education Center, Graduate School, Turrialba, Costa Rica. Offers agribusiness management (MS); agroforestry systems (PhD); development practices (MS); ecological agriculture (MS); environmental socioeconomics (MS); forestry in tropical and subtropical zones (PhD); integrated watershed management (MS); international sustainable tourism (MS); management and conservation of tropical rainforests and biodiversity (MS); tropical agriculture (PhD); tropical agroforestry (MS). *Entrance requirements:* For master's, GRE, 2 years of related professional experience, letters of recommendation; for doctorate, GRE, 4 letters of recommendation, letter of support from employing organization, master's degree in agronomy, biological sciences, forestry, natural resources or related field. Additional exam requirements/recommendations for international students: Required—TOEFL (minimum score 550 paper-based). Electronic applications accepted. *Faculty research:* Biodiversity in fragmented landscapes, ecosystem management, integrated pest management, environmental livestock production, biotechnology carbon balances in diverse land uses.

University of Alberta, Faculty of Graduate Studies and Research, Department of Renewable Resources, Edmonton, AB T6G 2E1, Canada. Offers agroforestry (M Ag, M Sc, MF); conservation biology (M Sc, PhD); forest biology and management (M Sc, PhD); land reclamation and remediation (M Sc, PhD); protected areas and wildlands management (M Sc, PhD); soil science (M Ag, M Sc, PhD); water and land resources (M Ag, M Sc, PhD); wildlife ecology and management (M Sc, PhD); MBA/M Ag; MBA/MF. *Program availability:* Part-time. *Degree requirements:* For master's, thesis (for some programs); for doctorate, comprehensive exam, thesis/dissertation. *Entrance requirements:* For master's, minimum 2 years of relevant professional experiences, minimum GPA of 3.0; for doctorate, minimum GPA of 3.0. Additional exam requirements/recommendations for international students: Required—TOEFL (minimum score 550 paper-based). Electronic applications accepted. *Faculty research:* Natural and managed landscapes.

University of Central Florida, College of Sciences, Department of Biology, Orlando, FL 32816. Offers biology (MS); conservation biology (PhD). *Program availability:* Part-time, evening/weekend. *Students:* 57 full-time (24 women), 9 part-time (5 women); includes 8 minority (1 Black or African American, non-Hispanic/Latino; 3 Asian, non-Hispanic/Latino; 3 Hispanic/Latino; 1 Two or more races, non-Hispanic/Latino), 10 international. Average age 28. 58 applicants, 41% accepted, 15 enrolled. In 2017, 15 master's, 4 doctorates awarded. *Degree requirements:* For master's, comprehensive exam, thesis or alternative, field exam. *Entrance requirements:* For master's, GRE General Test, minimum GPA of 3.0 in last 60 hours, letters of recommendation, resume, personal/professional statement; for doctorate, GRE General Test, letters of recommendation, resume, personal/professional statement. Additional exam requirements/recommendations for international students: Required—TOEFL. *Application deadline:* For fall admission, 1/15 priority date for domestic students. Application fee: $30. Electronic applications accepted. *Expenses:* Tuition, state resident: part-time $288.16 per credit hour. Tuition, nonresident: part-time $1073.31 per credit hour. Tuition and fees vary according to program. *Financial support:* In 2017–18, 53 students received support, including 17 fellowships with partial tuition reimbursements available (averaging $9,459 per year), 6 research assistantships with partial tuition reimbursements available (averaging $8,536 per year), 46 teaching assistantships with partial tuition reimbursements available (averaging $12,428 per year); career-related internships or fieldwork, Federal Work-Study, institutionally sponsored loans, health care benefits, tuition waivers (partial), and unspecified assistantships also available. Financial award application deadline: 3/1; financial award applicants required to submit FAFSA. *Unit head:* Dr. Graham Worthy, Chair, 407-823-2141, Fax: 407-823-5769, E-mail: graham.worthy@ucf.edu. *Application contact:* Associate Director, Graduate Admissions, 407-823-2766, Fax: 407-823-6442, E-mail: gradadmissions@ucf.edu.
Website: http://biology.cos.ucf.edu/

University of Hawaii at Hilo, Program in Tropical Conservation Biology and Environmental Science, Hilo, HI 96720-4091. Offers MS. *Entrance requirements:* Additional exam requirements/recommendations for international students: Required—TOEFL, IELTS. Electronic applications accepted.

University of Illinois at Urbana–Champaign, Graduate College, College of Liberal Arts and Sciences, School of Integrative Biology, Program in Ecology, Evolution and Conservation Biology, Champaign, IL 61820. Offers MS, PhD.

University of Maryland, College Park, Academic Affairs, College of Computer, Mathematical and Natural Sciences, Department of Biology, Program in Sustainable Development and Conservation Biology, College Park, MD 20742. Offers MS. *Program availability:* Part-time, evening/weekend. *Degree requirements:* For master's, internship, scholarly paper. *Entrance requirements:* For master's, GRE General Test, minimum GPA of 3.0, 3 letters of recommendation. Electronic applications accepted. *Faculty research:* Biodiversity, global change, conservation.

University of Minnesota, Twin Cities Campus, Graduate School, College of Food, Agricultural and Natural Resource Sciences, Program in Conservation Biology, Minneapolis, MN 55455-0213. Offers MS, PhD. *Program availability:* Part-time. Terminal master's awarded for partial completion of doctoral program. *Degree requirements:* For master's, comprehensive exam, thesis; for doctorate, comprehensive exam, thesis/dissertation. *Entrance requirements:* For master's and doctorate, GRE, advanced ecology course. Additional exam requirements/recommendations for international students: Required—TOEFL (minimum score 550 paper-based; 79 iBT), IELTS (minimum score 6.5). Electronic applications accepted. *Faculty research:* Wildlife conservation, fisheries and aquatic biology, invasive species, human dimensions, GIS, restoration ecology.

University of Nevada, Reno, Graduate School, Interdisciplinary Program in Ecology, Evolution, and Conservation Biology, Reno, NV 89557. Offers PhD. Offered through the College of Arts and Science, the M. C. Fleischmann College of Agriculture, and the Desert Research Institute. *Degree requirements:* For doctorate, thesis/dissertation. *Entrance requirements:* For doctorate, GRE General Test, GRE Subject Test, minimum GPA of 3.0. Additional exam requirements/recommendations for international students:

Required—TOEFL (minimum score 500 paper-based; 61 iBT), IELTS (minimum score 6). Electronic applications accepted. *Faculty research:* Population biology, behavioral ecology, plant response to climate change, conservation of endangered species, restoration of natural ecosystems.

University of New Hampshire, Graduate School, College of Life Sciences and Agriculture, Department of Natural Resources and the Environment, Durham, NH 03824. Offers environmental conservation (MS); environmental economics (MS); forestry (MS); natural resources (MS); resource administration and management (MS); soil and water resource management (MS); wildlife and conservation biology (MS). *Program availability:* Part-time. *Students:* 21 full-time (11 women), 28 part-time (12 women); includes 2 minority (1 Hispanic/Latino; 1 Two or more races, non-Hispanic/Latino), 2 international. Average age 28. 47 applicants, 40% accepted, 17 enrolled. In 2017, 10 master's awarded. *Entrance requirements:* For master's, GRE General Test. Additional exam requirements/recommendations for international students: Required—TOEFL (minimum score 550 paper-based; 80 iBT). *Application deadline:* For fall admission, 2/15 priority date for domestic students, 4/1 for international students; for spring admission, 12/1 for domestic students. Application fee: $65. Electronic applications accepted. *Financial support:* In 2017–18, 36 students received support, including 13 research assistantships, 19 teaching assistantships; fellowships, career-related internships or fieldwork, Federal Work-Study, scholarships/grants, and tuition waivers (full and partial) also available. Support available to part-time students. Financial award application deadline: 2/15. *Unit head:* Peter Pekins, Chair, 603-862-1017, E-mail: natural.resources@unh.edu. *Application contact:* Wendy Rose, Administrative Assistant, 603-862-3933, E-mail: natural.resources@unh.edu.
Website: http://colsa.unh.edu/nren

The University of West Alabama, School of Graduate Studies, College of Natural Sciences and Mathematics, Program in Conservation Biology, Livingston, AL 35470. Offers MS. *Program availability:* Part-time, evening/weekend, 100% online. *Faculty:* 8 full-time (1 woman), 2 part-time/adjunct (0 women). *Students:* 14 (10 women); includes 1 minority (Two or more races, non-Hispanic/Latino). Average age 29. 5 applicants, 100% accepted, 5 enrolled. In 2017, 8 master's awarded. *Degree requirements:* For master's, thesis optional. *Entrance requirements:* For master's, GRE, bachelor's degree with minimum GPA of 2.5, official transcripts, statement of purpose, three academic references. Additional exam requirements/recommendations for international students: Required—TOEFL (minimum score 500 paper-based; 61 iBT). *Application deadline:* Applications are processed on a rolling basis. Application fee: $40. Electronic applications accepted. *Expenses:* Tuition, state resident: part-time $371 per credit hour. Tuition, nonresident: part-time $742 per credit hour. *Required fees:* $130 per semester. *Financial support:* In 2017–18, 5 teaching assistantships (averaging $7,344 per year) were awarded; Federal Work-Study, scholarships/grants, and unspecified assistantships also available. Support available to part-time students. Financial award application deadline: 3/1; financial award applicants required to submit FAFSA. *Unit head:* Dr. John McCall, Dean, 205-652-3412, Fax: 205-652-3831, E-mail: jmccall@uwa.edu.
Website: http://www.uwa.edu/nsm/

University of Wisconsin–Madison, Graduate School, Gaylord Nelson Institute for Environmental Studies, Environmental Conservation Program, Madison, WI 53706-1380. Offers MS. *Degree requirements:* For master's, thesis or alternative, spring/summer leadership (internship) experience. *Entrance requirements:* For master's, GRE General Test (recommended for potential scholarship consideration). Additional exam requirements/recommendations for international students: Required—TOEFL (minimum score 550 paper-based, 80 iBT) or IELTS (6.5). Electronic applications accepted. *Expenses:* Contact institution. *Faculty research:* Geographic information systems, forestry, wildlife ecology, agroecology, landscape architecture, sociology, rural sociology, plant ecology, biodiversity, sustainability, sustainable development, conservation biology, conservation planning/management, land tenure.

University of Wisconsin–Stout, Graduate School, College of Science, Technology, Engineering and Mathematics, Program in Conservation Biology, Menomonie, WI 54751. Offers PSM. *Program availability:* Online learning.

Ecology

Baylor University, Graduate School, College of Arts and Sciences, The Institute of Ecological, Earth and Environmental Sciences, Waco, TX 76798. Offers PhD. *Faculty:* 24 full-time (4 women). *Students:* 5 full-time (1 woman); includes 2 minority (1 Asian, non-Hispanic/Latino; 1 Hispanic/Latino), 2 international. Average age 25. 8 applicants, 25% accepted, 1 enrolled. In 2017, 1 doctorate awarded. *Degree requirements:* For doctorate, comprehensive exam, thesis/dissertation. *Entrance requirements:* For doctorate, GRE. Additional exam requirements/recommendations for international students: Required—TOEFL (minimum score 550 paper-based; 80 iBT); Recommended—IELTS (minimum score 6.5). *Application deadline:* For fall admission, 2/15 priority date for domestic and international students. Application fee: $40. Electronic applications accepted. *Expenses:* Contact institution. *Financial support:* In 2017–18, 5 students received support, including 5 research assistantships with full and partial tuition reimbursements available (averaging $22,000 per year), 5 teaching assistantships with full and partial tuition reimbursements available (averaging $22,000 per year); scholarships/grants, health care benefits, tuition waivers (partial), and unspecified assistantships also available. Financial award application deadline: 2/15. *Faculty research:* Ecosystem processes, environmental toxicology and risk assessment, biogeochemical cycling, chemical fate and transport, conservation management. *Unit head:* Dr. Joe C. Yelderman, Jr., Director, 254-710-2224, E-mail: joe_yelderman@baylor.edu. *Application contact:* Shannon Koehler, Office Manager, 254-710-2224, Fax: 254-710-2298, E-mail: shannon_koehler@baylor.edu.
Website: http://www.baylor.edu/TIEEES/

Brown University, Graduate School, Division of Biology and Medicine, Department of Ecology and Evolutionary Biology, Providence, RI 02912. Offers PhD. *Degree requirements:* For doctorate, thesis/dissertation, preliminary exam. *Entrance requirements:* For doctorate, GRE General Test, GRE Subject Test. Additional exam requirements/recommendations for international students: Required—TOEFL. Electronic applications accepted. *Faculty research:* Marine ecology, behavioral ecology, population genetics, evolutionary morphology, plant ecology.

California Institute of Integral Studies, School of Consciousness and Transformation, San Francisco, CA 94103. Offers anthropology and social change (MA, PhD); Asian philosophies and cultures (MA); creative inquiry/interdisciplinary arts (MFA); East-West psychology (MA, PhD); integral and transpersonal psychology (PhD); philosophy and religion (PhD), including ecology, spirituality, and religion, philosophy, cosmology, and consciousness, women's spirituality; philosophy, cosmology, and consciousness (Certificate); transformative leadership (MA); transformative studies (PhD); women, gender, spirituality and social justice (MA); writing and consciousness (MFA). *Program availability:* Part-time, evening/weekend, 100% online, blended/hybrid learning. *Students:* 392 full-time (265 women), 141 part-time (98 women); includes 145 minority (40 Black or African American, non-Hispanic/Latino; 1 American Indian or Alaska Native, non-Hispanic/Latino; 19 Asian, non-Hispanic/Latino; 54 Hispanic/Latino; 31 Two or more races, non-Hispanic/Latino), 61 international. Average age 43. 212 applicants, 96% accepted, 153 enrolled. In 2017, 49 master's, 36 doctorates awarded. Terminal master's awarded for partial completion of doctoral program. *Degree requirements:* For master's, thesis optional; for doctorate, comprehensive exam, thesis/dissertation, 1 foreign language (for Asian philosophies and cultures). *Entrance requirements:* For master's, minimum GPA of 3.0, letters of recommendation, writing sample; for doctorate, master's degree, minimum GPA of 3.0, letters of recommendation, writing sample. Additional exam requirements/recommendations for international students: Required—TOEFL. *Application deadline:* For fall admission, 2/1 priority date for domestic and international students; for spring admission, 10/15 priority date for domestic and international students. Applications are processed on a rolling basis. Application fee: $65. Electronic applications accepted. *Expenses:* $21,400 tuition and fees (for MA); $28,390 (for MFA); $24,658 (for PhD). *Financial support:* Fellowships, research assistantships, teaching assistantships, career-related internships or fieldwork, Federal Work-Study, and scholarships/grants available. Support available to part-time students. Financial award application deadline: 4/15; financial award applicants required to submit FAFSA. *Faculty research:* Ecology and sustainability, philosophy and religion, East-West psychology, integrative health, social and cultural anthropology, transformative leadership. *Unit head:* Kathy Littles, Academic Dean, 415-575-6100, E-mail: klittles@ciis.edu. *Application contact:* Ellen Durst, Director of Admissions, 415-575-6100, Fax: 415-575-1268, E-mail: admissions@ciis.edu.
Website: http://www.ciis.edu/

California State University, Stanislaus, College of Natural Sciences, MS Program in Ecology and Sustainability, Turlock, CA 95382. Offers ecological conservation (MS). *Program availability:* Part-time. *Degree requirements:* For master's, thesis. *Entrance requirements:* For master's, GRE, minimum GPA of 3.0, 3 letters of recommendation, personal statement. Additional exam requirements/recommendations for international students: Required—TOEFL (minimum score 550 paper-based). Electronic applications accepted.

Central Washington University, School of Graduate Studies and Research, College of the Sciences, Department of Biological Sciences, Ellensburg, WA 98926. Offers botany (MS); microbiology and parasitology (MS); stream ecology and fisheries (MS); terrestrial ecology (MS). *Program availability:* Part-time. *Entrance requirements:* For master's, GRE General Test, minimum GPA of 3.0. Additional exam requirements/recommendations for international students: Required—TOEFL (minimum score 550 paper-based; 79 iBT). *Application deadline:* For fall admission, 2/1 priority date for domestic students; for winter admission, 10/1 for domestic students; for spring admission, 1/1 for domestic students. Applications are processed on a rolling basis. Application fee: $50. Electronic applications accepted. *Financial support:* Application deadline: 3/1; applicants required to submit FAFSA. *Unit head:* Dr. Kristina A. Ernest, Graduate Coordinator, 509-963-2805, E-mail: kristina.ernest@cwu.edu. *Application contact:* Justine Eason, Admissions Program Coordinator, 509-963-3103, Fax: 509-963-1799, E-mail: masters@cwu.edu.

Columbia University, Graduate School of Arts and Sciences, New York, NY 10027. Offers African-American studies (MA); American studies (MA); anthropology (MA, PhD); art history and archaeology (MA, PhD); astronomy (PhD); biological sciences (PhD); biotechnology (MA); chemical physics (PhD); chemistry (PhD); classical studies (MA, PhD); classics (MA, PhD); climate and society (MA); conservation biology (MA); earth and environmental sciences (PhD); East Asia: regional studies (MA); East Asian languages and cultures (MA, PhD); ecology, evolution and environmental biology (MA), including conservation biology; ecology, evolution, and environmental biology (PhD), including ecology and evolutionary biology, evolutionary primatology; economics (MA, PhD); English and comparative literature (MA, PhD); French and Romance philology (MA, PhD); Germanic languages (MA, PhD); global French studies (MA); global thought (MA); Hispanic cultural studies (MA); history (PhD); history and literature (MA); human rights studies (MA); Islamic studies (MA); Italian (MA, PhD); Japanese pedagogy (MA); Jewish studies (MA); Latin America and the Caribbean: regional studies (MA); Latin American and Iberian cultures (PhD); mathematics (MA, PhD), including finance (MA); medieval and Renaissance studies (MA); Middle Eastern, South Asian, and African studies (MA, PhD); modern art: critical and curatorial studies (MA); modern European studies (MA); museum anthropology (MA); music (DMA, PhD); oral history (MA); philosophical foundations of physics (MA); philosophy (MA, PhD); physics (PhD); political science (MA, PhD); psychology (PhD); quantitative methods in the social sciences (MA); religion (MA, PhD); Russia, Eurasia and East Europe: regional studies (MA); Russian translation (MA); Slavic cultures (MA); Slavic languages (MA, PhD); sociology (MA, PhD); South Asian studies (MA); statistics (MA, PhD); theatre (PhD). Dual-degree programs require admission to both Graduate School of Arts and Sciences and another Columbia school. *Program availability:* Part-time. Terminal master's awarded for partial completion of doctoral program. *Degree requirements:* For master's, variable foreign language requirement, comprehensive exam (for some programs), thesis (for some programs); for doctorate, variable foreign language requirement, comprehensive exam (for some programs), thesis/dissertation. *Entrance requirements:* For master's and doctorate, GRE General Test, GRE Subject Test (for some programs). Additional exam requirements/recommendations for international students: Required—TOEFL, IELTS. Electronic applications accepted. *Expenses: Tuition:* Full-time $44,864; part-time $1704 per credit. *Required fees:* $2370 per semester. One-time fee: $105.

Cornell University, Graduate School, Graduate Fields of Agriculture and Life Sciences, Field of Computational Biology, Ithaca, NY 14853. Offers computational behavioral biology (PhD); computational biology (PhD); computational cell biology (PhD); computational ecology (PhD); computational genetics (PhD); computational macromolecular biology (PhD); computational organismal biology (PhD). *Degree requirements:* For doctorate, comprehensive exam, thesis/dissertation, 2 semesters of teaching experience. *Entrance requirements:* For doctorate, GRE General Test, GRE Subject Test (biology), 2 letters of recommendation. Additional exam requirements/recommendations for international students: Required—TOEFL (minimum score 550 paper-based; 77 iBT). Electronic applications accepted. *Faculty research:* Computational behavioral biology, computational biology, computational cell biology, computational ecology, computational genetics, computational macromolecular biology, computational organismal biology.

Cornell University, Graduate School, Graduate Fields of Agriculture and Life Sciences, Field of Ecology and Evolutionary Biology, Ithaca, NY 14853. Offers ecology (PhD), including animal ecology, applied ecology, biogeochemistry, community and ecosystem ecology, limnology, oceanography, physiological ecology, plant ecology, population ecology, theoretical ecology, vertebrate zoology; evolutionary biology (PhD), including ecological genetics, paleobiology, population biology, systematics. *Degree requirements:* For doctorate, comprehensive exam, thesis/dissertation, 2 semesters of teaching experience. *Entrance requirements:* For doctorate, GRE General Test, GRE Subject Test (biology), 2 letters of recommendation. Additional exam requirements/recommendations for international students: Required—TOEFL (minimum score 550 paper-based; 77 iBT). Electronic applications accepted. *Faculty research:* Population and organismal biology, population and evolutionary genetics, systematics and macroevolution, biochemistry, conservation biology.

Cornell University, Graduate School, Graduate Fields of Agriculture and Life Sciences, Field of Horticulture, Ithaca, NY 14853. Offers breeding of horticultural crops (MPS); horticultural crop management systems (MPS); human-plant interactions (MPS, PhD); physiology and ecology of horticultural crops (MPS, MS, PhD). *Degree requirements:* For master's, thesis (MS); for doctorate, comprehensive exam, thesis/dissertation. *Entrance requirements:* For master's and doctorate, GRE General Test, 3 letters of recommendation. Additional exam requirements/recommendations for international students: Required—TOEFL (minimum score 550 paper-based; 77 iBT). Electronic applications accepted. *Faculty research:* Plant selection/plant materials, greenhouse management, greenhouse crop production, urban landscape management, turfgrass management.

Cornell University, Graduate School, Graduate Fields of Agriculture and Life Sciences, Field of Natural Resources, Ithaca, NY 14853. Offers community-based natural resources management (MS, PhD); conservation biology (MS, PhD); ecosystem biology and biogeochemistry (MPS, MS, PhD); environmental management (MPS); fishery and aquatic science (MPS, MS, PhD); forest science (MPS, MS, PhD); human dimensions of natural resources management (MPS, MS, PhD); policy and institutional analysis (MS, PhD); program development and evaluation (MPS, MS, PhD); quantitative ecology (MS, PhD); wildlife science (MPS, MS, PhD). *Degree requirements:* For master's, thesis (MS), project paper (MPS); for doctorate, comprehensive exam, thesis/dissertation. *Entrance requirements:* For master's and doctorate, GRE General Test, 2 letters of recommendation. Additional exam requirements/recommendations for international students: Required—TOEFL (minimum score 550 paper-based; 77 iBT). Electronic applications accepted. *Faculty research:* Ecosystem-level dynamics, systems modeling, conservation biology/management, resource management's human dimensions, biogeochemistry.

Dalhousie University, Faculty of Agriculture, Halifax, NS B3H 4R2, Canada. Offers agriculture (M Sc), including air quality, animal behavior, animal molecular genetics, animal nutrition, animal technology, aquaculture, botany, crop management, crop physiology, ecology, environmental microbiology, food science, horticulture, nutrient management, pest management, physiology, plant biotechnology, plant pathology, soil chemistry, soil fertility, waste management and composting, water quality. *Program availability:* Part-time. *Degree requirements:* For master's, thesis, ATC Exam Teaching Assistantship. *Entrance requirements:* For master's, honors B Sc, minimum GPA of 3.0. Additional exam requirements/recommendations for international students: Required—TOEFL (minimum score 580 paper-based; 92 iBT), IELTS, Michigan English Language Assessment Battery, CanTEST, CAEL. *Faculty research:* Bio-product development, organic agriculture, nutrient management, air and water quality, agricultural biotechnology.

Dartmouth College, School of Graduate and Advanced Studies, Program in Ecology, Evolution, Ecosystems, and Society, Hanover, NH 03755. Offers ecology and evolutionary biology (PhD); sustainability, ecosystems, and environment (PhD). *Faculty:* 9 full-time (5 women). *Students:* 22 full-time (14 women); includes 1 minority (Hispanic/Latino), 3 international. Average age 28. 40 applicants, 15% accepted, 3 enrolled. In 2017, 1 doctorate awarded. *Entrance requirements:* For doctorate, GRE General Test, GRE Subject Test in biology (highly recommended). Additional exam requirements/recommendations for international students: Required—TOEFL. *Application deadline:* For fall admission, 12/1 for domestic students. Electronic applications accepted. *Financial support:* Fellowships, research assistantships, teaching assistantships, institutionally sponsored loans, traineeships, and unspecified assistantships available. Financial award applicants required to submit FAFSA. *Unit head:* Dr. Mathew Ayres, Chair, 603-646-2788. *Application contact:* Amy Layne, Administrative Assistant, 603-646-3847.
Website: http://sites.dartmouth.edu/EEES/

Duke University, Graduate School, Department of Ecology, Durham, NC 27708-0329. Offers PhD, Certificate. *Degree requirements:* For doctorate, thesis/dissertation. *Entrance requirements:* For doctorate, GRE General Test. Additional exam requirements/recommendations for international students: Required—TOEFL (minimum score 577 paper-based; 90 iBT) or IELTS (minimum score 7). Electronic applications accepted.

Eastern Kentucky University, The Graduate School, College of Arts and Sciences, Department of Biological Sciences, Richmond, KY 40475-3102. Offers biological sciences (MS); ecology (MS). *Program availability:* Part-time. *Degree requirements:* For master's, thesis. *Entrance requirements:* For master's, GRE General Test, minimum GPA of 2.5. *Faculty research:* Systematics, ecology, and biodiversity; animal behavior; protein structure and molecular genetics; biomonitoring and aquatic toxicology; pathogenesis of microbes and parasites.

Emory University, Laney Graduate School, Division of Biological and Biomedical Sciences, Program in Population Biology, Ecology and Evolution, Atlanta, GA 30322-1100. Offers PhD. *Degree requirements:* For doctorate, comprehensive exam, thesis/dissertation. *Entrance requirements:* For doctorate, GRE General Test, minimum GPA of 3.0 in science course work (recommended). Additional exam requirements/recommendations for international students: Required—TOEFL. Electronic applications accepted. *Faculty research:* Evolution of microbes, infectious disease, the immune system, genetic disease in humans, evolution of behavior.

Florida Institute of Technology, College of Science, Program in Biological Sciences, Melbourne, FL 32901-6975. Offers biological science (PhD); biotechnology (MS); cell and molecular biology (MS); ecology (MS); marine biology (MS). *Program availability:* Part-time. *Students:* Average age 26. 230 applicants, 24% accepted, 21 enrolled. In 2017, 27 master's, 3 doctorates awarded. *Degree requirements:* For master's, thesis (for some programs), research, seminar, internship, or summer lab; for doctorate, comprehensive exam, thesis/dissertation, dissertations seminar, publications. *Entrance requirements:* For master's, GRE General Test, 3 letters of recommendation; statement of objectives; bachelor's degree in biology, chemistry, biochemistry or equivalent; for doctorate, GRE General Test, resume, 3 letters of recommendation, minimum GPA of 3.2, statement of objectives. Additional exam requirements/recommendations for international students: Required—TOEFL (minimum score 550 paper-based; 79 iBT). *Application deadline:* For fall admission, 3/1 for domestic students, 4/1 for international students; for spring admission, 9/1 for domestic and international students. Applications are processed on a rolling basis. Electronic applications accepted. *Expenses: Tuition:* Part-time $1241 per credit hour. Part-time tuition and fees vary according to campus/location. *Financial support:* Career-related internships or fieldwork, institutionally sponsored loans, tuition waivers (partial), unspecified assistantships, and tuition remissions available. Support available to part-time students. Financial award application deadline: 3/1; financial award applicants required to submit FAFSA. *Faculty research:* Initiation of protein synthesis in eukaryotic cells, fixation of radioactive carbon, changes in DNA molecule, endangered or threatened avian and mammalian species, hydro acoustics and feeding preference of the West Indian manatee. *Unit head:* Dr. Richard B. Aronson, Department Head, 321-674-8034, Fax: 321-674-7238, E-mail: raronson@fit.edu. *Application contact:* Cheryl A. Brown, Associate Director of Graduate Admissions, 321-674-7581, Fax: 321-723-9468, E-mail: cbrown@fit.edu.
Website: http://cos.fit.edu/biology/

Florida State University, The Graduate School, College of Arts and Sciences, Department of Biological Science, Specialization in Ecology and Evolutionary Biology, Tallahassee, FL 32306-4295. Offers MS, PhD. *Faculty:* 23 full-time (9 women). *Students:* 50 full-time (25 women); includes 5 minority (2 Black or African American, non-Hispanic/Latino; 1 Native Hawaiian or other Pacific Islander, non-Hispanic/Latino; 2 Two or more races, non-Hispanic/Latino). Average age 29. 93 applicants, 18% accepted, 12 enrolled. In 2017, 4 master's, 5 doctorates awarded. Terminal master's awarded for partial completion of doctoral program. *Degree requirements:* For master's, comprehensive exam (for some programs), thesis, teaching experience, seminar presentation; for doctorate, comprehensive exam, thesis/dissertation, teaching experience; seminar presentation. *Entrance requirements:* For master's and doctorate, GRE General Test, minimum upper-division GPA of 3.0. Additional exam requirements/recommendations for international students: Required—TOEFL (minimum score 600 paper-based; 92 iBT). *Application deadline:* For fall admission, 12/1 for domestic and international students. Application fee: $30. Electronic applications accepted. *Financial support:* In 2017–18, 53 students received support, including 5 fellowships with tuition reimbursements available (averaging $30,000 per year), 11 research assistantships with full tuition reimbursements available (averaging $21,500 per year), 37 teaching assistantships with full tuition reimbursements available (averaging $21,500 per year); scholarships/grants and unspecified assistantships also available. Financial award application deadline: 12/1; financial award applicants required to submit FAFSA. *Faculty research:* Ecology and conservation biology; evolution; marine biology; phylogeny and systematics; theoretical, computational and mathematical biology. *Unit head:* Dr. Thomas A. Houpt, Professor and Associate Chair, 850-644-4783, Fax: 850-644-8447, E-mail: houpt@bio.fsu.edu. *Application contact:* Jessica Webber, Coordinator, Graduate Affairs, 850-644-3023, Fax: 850-644-9829, E-mail: gradinfo@bio.fsu.edu.
Website: http://www.bio.fsu.edu/

Frostburg State University, College of Liberal Arts and Sciences, Department of Biology, Program in Applied Ecology and Conservation Biology, Frostburg, MD 21532. Offers MS. *Faculty:* 10. *Students:* 8 full-time (7 women), 6 part-time (4 women). Average age 28. 18 applicants, 61% accepted, 4 enrolled. In 2017, 4 master's awarded. *Degree requirements:* For master's, thesis. *Entrance requirements:* For master's, GRE General Test, resume. Additional exam requirements/recommendations for international students: Required—TOEFL. *Application deadline:* For fall admission, 7/15 priority date for domestic students. Applications are processed on a rolling basis. Application fee: $45. Electronic applications accepted. *Expenses:* Tuition, state resident: part-time $433 per credit hour. Tuition, nonresident: part-time $557 per credit hour. *Required fees:* $121 per credit hour. $27 per term. *Financial support:* In 2017–18, 8 research assistantships with full tuition reimbursements (averaging $5,000 per year) were awarded; career-related internships or fieldwork and Federal Work-Study also available. Financial award application deadline: 4/1; financial award applicants required to submit FAFSA. *Faculty research:* Forest ecology, microbiology of man-made wetlands, invertebrate zoology and entomology, wildlife and carnivore ecology, aquatic pollution ecology. *Unit head:* Dr. Sunshine Brosi, Coordinator, 301-687-4213, E-mail: slbrosi@frostburg.edu. *Application contact:* Vickie Mazer, Director, Graduate Services, 301-687-7053, Fax: 301-687-4597, E-mail: vmmazer@frostburg.edu.

George Mason University, College of Science, Department of Environmental Science and Policy, Fairfax, VA 22030. Offers environmental science and policy (MS, PhD), including aquatic ecology (MS), conservation science and policy (MS), earth surface processes and environmental geochemistry (MS), environmental biocomplexity (MS), environmental management (MS), environmental science and policy (MS), environmental science communication (MS). *Faculty:* 23 full-time (10 women), 7 part-time/adjunct (2 women). *Students:* 48 full-time (33 women), 62 part-time (37 women); includes 13 minority (3 Black or African American, non-Hispanic/Latino; 8 Asian, non-Hispanic/Latino; 2 Hispanic/Latino), 6 international. Average age 34. 46 applicants, 80% accepted, 22 enrolled. In 2017, 14 master's, 13 doctorates awarded. *Degree requirements:* For master's, variable foreign language requirement, comprehensive exam (for some programs), thesis (for some programs); for doctorate, variable foreign language requirement, comprehensive exam, thesis/dissertation. *Entrance requirements:* For master's, GRE, BA or BS; for doctorate, GRE, advanced degree or equivalent research experience. Additional exam requirements/recommendations for international students: Required—TOEFL (minimum score 575 paper-based; 88 iBT), IELTS (minimum score 6.5), PTE (minimum score 59). Application fee: $75 ($80 for international students). Electronic applications accepted. *Expenses:* Tuition, state resident: full-time $11,228; part-time $459.50 per credit. Tuition, nonresident: full-time $30,932; part-time $1280.50 per credit. *Required fees:* $3252; $135.50 per credit. Part-time tuition and fees vary according to course load and program. *Financial support:* In 2017–18, 40 students received support, including 1 fellowship, 5 research assistantships with tuition reimbursements available (averaging $21,000 per year), 35 teaching assistantships with tuition reimbursements available (averaging $15,428 per year); career-related internships or fieldwork, Federal Work-Study, scholarships/grants, unspecified assistantships, and health care benefits (for full-time research or teaching assistantship recipients) also available. Support available to part-time students. Financial award application deadline: 3/1; financial award applicants required to submit FAFSA. *Faculty research:* Conservation of species and ecosystems; water and watersheds; one health and sustainability; climate change; interdisciplinary (including natural and social science). *Total annual research expenditures:* $300,156. *Unit head:* Dr. Alonso Aguirre, Chair, 703-993-7590, E-mail: aaguirr3@gmu.edu. *Application contact:* Sharon Bloomquist, Graduate Program Coordinator, 703-993-3187, Fax: 703-993-1066, E-mail: sbloomqu@gmu.edu.
Website: http://esp.gmu.edu/

Illinois State University, Graduate School, College of Arts and Sciences, School of Biological Sciences, Normal, IL 61790. Offers animal behavior (MS); bacteriology (MS); biochemistry (MS); biological sciences (MS); biology (PhD); biophysics (MS); biotechnology (MS); botany (MS, PhD); cell biology (MS); conservation biology (MS); developmental biology (MS); ecology (MS, PhD); entomology (MS); evolutionary biology (MS); genetics (MS, PhD); immunology (MS); microbiology (MS, PhD); molecular biology (MS); molecular genetics (MS); neurobiology (MS); neuroscience (MS); parasitology (MS); physiology (MS, PhD); plant biology (MS); plant molecular biology (MS); plant sciences (MS); structural biology (MS); zoology (MS, PhD). *Program availability:* Part-time. *Degree requirements:* For master's, thesis or alternative; for doctorate, variable foreign language requirement, thesis/dissertation, 2 terms of residency. *Entrance requirements:* For master's, GRE General Test, minimum GPA of 2.6 in last 60 hours of course work; for doctorate, GRE General Test. *Faculty research:* Redoc balance and drug development in schistosoma mansoni, control of the growth of listeria monocytogenes at low temperature, regulation of cell expansion and microtubule function by SPRI, CRUI: physiology and fitness consequences of different life history phenotypes.

Indiana State University, College of Graduate and Professional Studies, College of Arts and Sciences, Department of Biology, Terre Haute, IN 47809. Offers cellular and molecular biology (PhD); ecology, systematics and evolution (PhD); life sciences (MS); physiology (PhD); science education (MS). *Degree requirements:* For master's, thesis optional; for doctorate, comprehensive exam, thesis/dissertation. *Entrance requirements:* For master's and doctorate, GRE General Test. Electronic applications accepted.

Indiana University Bloomington, School of Public and Environmental Affairs, Environmental Science Programs, Bloomington, IN 47405. Offers applied ecology (MSES); energy (MSES); environmental chemistry, toxicology, and risk assessment (MSES); environmental science (PhD); hazardous materials management (Certificate); specialized environmental science (MSES); water resources (MSES); JD/MSES; MSES/MA; MSES/MPA; MSES/MS. *Program availability:* Part-time. Terminal master's awarded for partial completion of doctoral program. *Degree requirements:* For master's, capstone or thesis; internship; for doctorate, comprehensive exam, thesis/dissertation. *Entrance requirements:* For master's, GRE General Test or GMAT, official transcripts, 3 letters of recommendation, resume, personal statement; for doctorate, GRE General Test or LSAT, official transcripts, 3 letters of recommendation, resume or curriculum vitae, statement of purpose. Additional exam requirements/recommendations for international students: Required—TOEFL (minimum score 600 paper-based; 96 iBT); Recommended—IELTS (minimum score 7). Electronic applications accepted. *Faculty research:* Applied ecology, bio-geochemistry, toxicology, wetlands ecology, environmental microbiology, forest ecology, environmental chemistry.

Indiana University Bloomington, University Graduate School, College of Arts and Sciences, Department of Biology, Bloomington, IN 47405. Offers biology teaching (MAT); biotechnology (MA); evolution, ecology, and behavior (MA, PhD); genetics (PhD); microbiology (MA, PhD); molecular, cellular, and developmental biology (PhD); plant sciences (MA, PhD); zoology (MA, PhD). Terminal master's awarded for partial completion of doctoral program. *Degree requirements:* For master's, thesis, oral defense; for doctorate, thesis/dissertation, oral defense. *Entrance requirements:* For master's and doctorate, GRE General Test. Additional exam requirements/recommendations for international students: Required—TOEFL (minimum score 100 iBT). Electronic applications accepted. *Faculty research:* Evolution, ecology and behavior; microbiology; molecular biology and genetics; plant biology.

Inter American University of Puerto Rico, Bayamón Campus, Graduate School, Bayamón, PR 00957. Offers biology (MS), including environmental sciences and ecology, molecular biotechnology; electrical engineering (ME), including control system, potence system; human resources (MBA); mechanical engineering (ME, MS), including aerospace, energy. *Program availability:* Part-time, evening/weekend. *Faculty:* 12 full-time (2 women), 3 part-time/adjunct (2 women). *Students:* 6 full-time (5 women), 99 part-time (62 women); includes 104 minority (1 Black or African American, non-Hispanic/Latino; 103 Hispanic/Latino). Average age 29. 46 applicants, 98% accepted, 34 enrolled. In 2017, 29 master's awarded. *Degree requirements:* For master's, comprehensive exam, research project. *Entrance requirements:* For master's, EXADEP, GRE General Test, letters of recommendation. *Application deadline:* For fall admission, 7/1 for domestic students, 5/1 priority date for international students; for winter admission, 11/15 priority date for domestic and international students; for spring admission, 2/15 priority date for domestic and international students. Application fee: $31. *Unit head:* Dr. Carlos J. Olivares, Acting Chancellor, 787-279-1200 Ext. 2295, Fax: 787-279-2205, E-mail: colivares@bayamon.inter.edu. *Application contact:* Aurelis Báez, Director of Student Services, 787-279-1912 Ext. 2017, Fax: 787-279-2205, E-mail: abaez@bayamon.inter.edu.

Iowa State University of Science and Technology, Program in Ecology and Evolutionary Biology, Ames, IA 50011. Offers MS, PhD. *Degree requirements:* For master's, thesis or alternative; for doctorate, thesis/dissertation. *Entrance requirements:* For master's and doctorate, GRE General Test. Additional exam requirements/recommendations for international students: Required—TOEFL (minimum score 550 paper-based; 79 iBT), IELTS (minimum score 6.5). Electronic applications accepted. *Faculty research:* Landscape ecology, aquatic and method ecology, physiological ecology, population genetics and evolution, systematics.

Kent State University, College of Arts and Sciences, Department of Biological Sciences, Kent, OH 44242-0001. Offers biological sciences (MA, MS, PhD), including botany (MS, PhD), cell biology (MS, PhD), ecology (MS, PhD), physiology (MS, PhD). *Program availability:* Part-time. *Faculty:* 28 full-time (10 women), 3 part-time/adjunct (2 women). *Students:* 55 full-time (37 women), 10 part-time (6 women); includes 6 minority (3 Black or African American, non-Hispanic/Latino; 1 Asian, non-Hispanic/Latino; 2 Two or more races, non-Hispanic/Latino), 12 international. Average age 28. 27 applicants, 56% accepted, 11 enrolled. In 2017, 4 master's, 6 doctorates awarded. Terminal master's awarded for partial completion of doctoral program. *Degree requirements:* For master's, thesis (for some programs), departmental seminar presentation about research (for MS); for doctorate, thesis/dissertation, departmental seminar presentation about research, admitted to doctoral candidacy following written and oral candidacy. *Entrance requirements:* For master's, GRE, minimum GPA of 3.0, official transcripts, goal statement, three letters of recommendation, list of up to five potential faculty advisors, undergraduate coursework roughly equivalent to a biology minor; for doctorate, GRE, official transcripts, goal statement, three letters of recommendation, list of up to five potential faculty advisors, baccalaureate degree with strong background in biology and related subjects such as chemistry and mathematics. Additional exam requirements/recommendations for international students: Required—TOEFL (minimum score 587 paper-based, 94 iBT), Michigan English Language Assessment Battery (minimum score 82), IELTS (7.0), or PTE (65). *Application deadline:* For fall admission, 12/15 for domestic students, 12/5 for international students. Applications are processed on a rolling basis. Application fee: $45 ($70 for international students). Electronic applications accepted. *Expenses:* Tuition, state resident: full-time $11,310; part-time $515 per credit hour. Tuition, nonresident: full-time $20,396; part-time $928 per credit hour. *International tuition:* $18,544 full-time. *Financial support:* Research assistantships with full tuition reimbursements, teaching assistantships with full tuition reimbursements, Federal Work-Study, scholarships/grants, and unspecified assistantships available. Financial award application deadline: 12/15. *Unit head:* Dr. James L. Blank, Dean, 330-672-2650, E-mail: jblank@kent.edu. *Application contact:* Dr. Heather K. Caldwell, Associate Professor and Graduate Coordinator, 330-672-3636, E-mail: hcaldwel@kent.edu.
Website: http://www.kent.edu/biology

Laurentian University, School of Graduate Studies and Research, Programme in Biology, Sudbury, ON P3E 2C6, Canada. Offers biology (M Sc); boreal ecology (PhD). *Program availability:* Part-time. *Degree requirements:* For master's, thesis. *Entrance requirements:* For master's, honors degree with second class or better. *Faculty research:* Recovery of acid-stressed lakes, effects of climate change, origin and maintenance of biocomplexity, radionuclide dynamics, cytogenetic studies of plants.

Lesley University, Graduate School of Education, Cambridge, MA 02138-2790. Offers arts, community, and education (M Ed); autism studies (Certificate); curriculum and instruction (M Ed, CAGS); early childhood education (M Ed); ecological teaching and learning (MS); educational studies (PhD), including adult learning, educational leadership, individually designed; elementary education (M Ed); emergent technologies for educators (Certificate); ESLArts: language learning through the arts (M Ed); high school education (M Ed); individually designed (M Ed); integrated teaching through the arts (M Ed); literacy for K-8 classroom teachers (M Ed); mathematics education (M Ed); middle school education (M Ed); moderate disabilities (M Ed); online learning (Certificate); reading (CAGS); science in education (M Ed); severe disabilities (M Ed); special needs (CAGS); specialist teacher of reading (M Ed); teacher of visual art (M Ed); technology in education (M Ed, CAGS). *Accreditation:* TEAC. *Program availability:* Part-time, evening/weekend, online learning. *Degree requirements:* For master's, practicum; for doctorate, thesis/dissertation. *Entrance requirements:* For master's, Massachusetts Tests for Educator Licensure (MTEL), transcripts, statement of purpose, recommendations; interview (for special education); for doctorate, GRE General Test, transcripts, statement of purpose, recommendations, interview, master's degree, resume; for other advanced degree, interview, master's degree. Additional exam requirements/recommendations for international students: Required—TOEFL (minimum score 550 paper-based; 80 iBT). Electronic applications accepted. *Faculty research:* Assessment in literacy, mathematics and science; autism spectrum disorders; instructional technology and online learning; multicultural education and English language learners.

Marquette University, Graduate School, College of Arts and Sciences, Department of Biology, Milwaukee, WI 53201-1881. Offers cell biology (MS, PhD); developmental biology (MS, PhD); ecology (MS, PhD); epithelial physiology (MS, PhD); genetics (MS, PhD); microbiology (MS, PhD); molecular biology (MS, PhD); muscle and exercise physiology (MS, PhD); neuroscience (PhD). Terminal master's awarded for partial completion of doctoral program. *Degree requirements:* For master's, comprehensive exam, thesis, 1 year of teaching experience or equivalent; for doctorate, thesis/dissertation, 1 year of teaching experience or equivalent, qualifying exam. *Entrance requirements:* For master's and doctorate, GRE General Test, GRE Subject Test, official transcripts from all current and previous colleges/universities except Marquette, statement of professional goals and aspirations, three letters of recommendation. Additional exam requirements/recommendations for international students: Required—TOEFL (minimum score 530 paper-based). Electronic applications accepted. *Faculty research:* Neurobiology, neuroendocrinology, epithelial physiology, neuropeptide interactions, synaptic transmission.

Michigan State University, The Graduate School, College of Natural Science, Interdepartmental Program in Ecology, Evolutionary Biology and Behavior, East Lansing, MI 48824. Offers PhD. *Entrance requirements:* Additional exam requirements/recommendations for international students: Required—TOEFL. Electronic applications accepted.

Michigan Technological University, Graduate School, School of Forest Resources and Environmental Science, Houghton, MI 49931. Offers applied ecology (MS); applied ecology and environment sciences (MS); forest molecular genetics and biotechnology (MS, PhD); forest resources and environmental science (MF, MGIS); forest science (PhD); forestry ecology and management (MS). *Accreditation:* SAF. *Program availability:* Part-time. *Faculty:* 37 full-time (8 women), 19 part-time/adjunct (4 women). *Students:* 44 full-time (15 women), 15 part-time (6 women); includes 3 minority (1 Black or African American, non-Hispanic/Latino; 2 Two or more races, non-Hispanic/Latino), 15 international. Average age 30. 125 applicants, 22% accepted, 19 enrolled. In 2017, 26 master's, 3 doctorates awarded. Terminal master's awarded for partial completion of doctoral program. *Degree requirements:* For master's, thesis (for some programs), comprehensive exam (for non-research degrees); for doctorate, comprehensive exam, thesis/dissertation. *Entrance requirements:* For master's and doctorate, GRE, statement of purpose, personal statement, official transcripts, 3 letters of recommendation, resume/curriculum vitae. Additional exam requirements/recommendations for international students: Required—TOEFL (recommended minimum score 79 iBT) or IELTS (recommended minimum score of 6.5). *Application deadline:* Applications are processed on a rolling basis. Electronic applications accepted. *Expenses:* Tuition, state resident: full-time $17,100; part-time $950 per credit. Tuition, nonresident: full-time $17,100; part-time $950 per credit. *Required fees:* $248; $124 per term. Tuition and fees vary according to course load and program. *Financial support:* In 2017–18, 34 students received support, including 4 fellowships with tuition reimbursements available (averaging $15,790 per year), 17 research assistantships with tuition reimbursements available (averaging $15,790 per year), 7 teaching assistantships with tuition reimbursements available (averaging $15,790 per year); career-related internships or fieldwork, Federal Work-Study, scholarships/grants, health care benefits, unspecified assistantships, and cooperative program also available. Financial award applicants required to submit FAFSA. *Faculty research:* Forestry, wildlife ecology and management; natural resources, applied ecology and environmental science; biotechnology and molecular genetics; forest biomaterials; geospatial science and technology. *Total annual research expenditures:* $3.6 million. *Unit head:* Dr. Terry Sharik, Dean, 906-487-2352, Fax: 906-487-2915, E-mail: tlsharik@mtu.edu. *Application contact:* Dr. Andrew J. Storer, Associate Dean, 906-487-3470, Fax: 906-487-2915, E-mail: storer@mtu.edu.
Website: http://www.mtu.edu/forest/

Montana State University, The Graduate School, College of Letters and Science, Department of Ecology, Bozeman, MT 59717. Offers ecological and environmental statistics (MS); ecology and environmental sciences (PhD); fish and wildlife biology (PhD); fish and wildlife management (MS). *Program availability:* Part-time. *Degree requirements:* For master's, comprehensive exam, thesis (for some programs); for doctorate, comprehensive exam, thesis/dissertation. *Entrance requirements:* For master's and doctorate, GRE, minimum GPA of 3.0, letters of recommendation, essay. Additional exam requirements/recommendations for international students: Required—TOEFL (minimum score 550 paper-based). Electronic applications accepted. *Faculty research:* Community ecology, population ecology, land-use effects, management and conservation, environmental modeling.

Montclair State University, The Graduate School, College of Science and Mathematics, Program in Biology, Montclair, NJ 07043-1624. Offers biological science/education (MS); biology (MS); ecology and evolution (MS); physiology (MS).

Naropa University, Graduate Programs, Program in Ecopsychology, Boulder, CO 80302-6697. Offers MA. *Program availability:* Part-time, blended/hybrid learning. *Faculty:* 2 full-time (1 woman). *Students:* 9 full-time (7 women), 11 part-time (7 women); includes 2 minority (both Hispanic/Latino), 3 international. Average age 36. 14 applicants, 86% accepted, 9 enrolled. In 2017, 8 master's awarded. *Degree requirements:* For master's, thesis, service learning. *Entrance requirements:* For master's, curriculum vitae/resume with pertinent academic, employment and volunteer activities; 2 letters of recommendation; transcripts; letter of interest. Additional exam requirements/recommendations for international students: Required—TOEFL (minimum score 550 paper-based; 80 iBT). *Application deadline:* For fall admission, 1/15 priority date for domestic and international students. Applications are processed on a rolling basis. Application fee: $60. Electronic

applications accepted. *Expenses:* $995 per credit. *Financial support:* In 2017–18, 11 students received support. Career-related internships or fieldwork, Federal Work-Study, scholarships/grants, tuition waivers (partial), and unspecified assistantships available. Support available to part-time students. Financial award application deadline: 3/1; financial award applicants required to submit FAFSA. *Unit head:* Dr. Tina Fields, Chair, Ecopsychology, 303-245-4654, E-mail: tfields@naropa.edu. *Application contact:* Office of Admissions, 303-546-3572, Fax: 303-546-3583, E-mail: admissions@naropa.edu.
Website: http://www.naropa.edu/academics/masters/ecopsychology/index.php

Northeastern Illinois University, College of Graduate Studies and Research, College of Arts and Sciences, Program in Biology, Chicago, IL 60625. Offers biology (MS), including cell biology, ecology, molecular biology, organismal biology. *Program availability:* Part-time, evening/weekend. *Degree requirements:* For master's, comprehensive exam, thesis optional. *Entrance requirements:* For master's, minimum GPA of 2.75. Additional exam requirements/recommendations for international students: Required—TOEFL (minimum score 550 paper-based; 79 iBT). *Application deadline:* For fall admission, 4/1 priority date for domestic students; for spring admission, 8/15 for domestic students. Applications are processed on a rolling basis. Application fee: $30. Electronic applications accepted. *Expenses:* Tuition, state resident: full-time $7274; part-time $404.11 per credit hour. Tuition, nonresident: full-time $14,548; part-time $808.23 per credit hour. *Required fees:* $1284. *Financial support:* Applicants required to submit FAFSA. *Faculty research:* Paleoecology and freshwater biology, protein biosynthesis and targeting, microbial growth and physiology, molecular biology of antibody production, reptilian neurobiology. *Unit head:* Dr. John Kasmer, Department Chair, 773-442-5717, E-mail: j-kasmer@neiu.edu. *Application contact:* Martha Narvaez, Graduate Admission Representative, 773-442-6006, E-mail: m-narvaez@neiu.edu.

The Ohio State University, Graduate School, College of Arts and Sciences, Division of Natural and Mathematical Sciences, Department of Evolution, Ecology, and Organismal Biology, Columbus, OH 43210. Offers MS, PhD. *Faculty:* 23. *Students:* 57 full-time (25 women), 6 international. Average age 28. In 2017, 4 master's, 9 doctorates awarded. *Entrance requirements:* For master's and doctorate, GRE General Test. Additional exam requirements/recommendations for international students: Required—TOEFL (minimum score 550 paper-based; 79 iBT), Michigan English Language Assessment Battery (minimum score 86); Recommended—IELTS (minimum score 7). *Application deadline:* For fall admission, 12/1 priority date for domestic students, 11/30 priority date for international students. Applications are processed on a rolling basis. Application fee: $60 ($70 for international students). Electronic applications accepted. *Financial support:* Fellowships, research assistantships, teaching assistantships, Federal Work Study, and institutionally sponsored loans available. Support available to part-time students. *Unit head:* Dr. John Freudenstein, Chair and Professor, 614-688-0363, E-mail: freudenstein.1@osu.edu. *Application contact:* Graduate and Professional Admissions, 614-292-9444, Fax: 614-292-3895, E-mail: gpadmissions@osu.edu.
Website: http://eeob.osu.edu/

The Ohio State University, Graduate School, College of Food, Agricultural, and Environmental Sciences, School of Environment and Natural Resources, Columbus, OH 43210. Offers ecological restoration (MS, PhD); ecosystem science (MS, PhD); environment and natural resources (MENR); environmental social sciences (MS, PhD); fisheries and wildlife science (MS, PhD); forest science (MS, PhD); rural sociology (MS, PhD); soil science (MS, PhD). *Faculty:* 37. *Students:* 86 full-time (53 women), 8 part-time (4 women), 7 international. Average age 29. In 2017, 34 master's, 7 doctorates awarded. *Entrance requirements:* For master's and doctorate, GRE. Additional exam requirements/recommendations for international students: Required—TOEFL (minimum score 550 paper-based; 79 iBT), Michigan English Language Assessment Battery (minimum score 82); Recommended—IELTS (minimum score 7). *Application deadline:* For fall admission, 1/1 priority date for domestic students, 12/15 priority date for international students; for spring admission, 11/1 for domestic students, 9/15 for international students. Applications are processed on a rolling basis. Application fee: $60 ($70 for international students). Electronic applications accepted. *Financial support:* Fellowships, research assistantships, teaching assistantships, health care benefits, and unspecified assistantships available. *Unit head:* Dr. Jeff S. Sharp, Director, 614-292-9410, E-mail: sharp.123@osu.edu. *Application contact:* Graduate and Professional Admissions, 614-292-9444, Fax: 614-292-3895, E-mail: gpadmissions@osu.edu.
Website: http://senr.osu.edu/

Ohio University, Graduate College, College of Arts and Sciences, Department of Biological Sciences, Athens, OH 45701-2979. Offers biological sciences (MS, PhD); cell biology and physiology (MS, PhD); ecology and evolutionary biology (MS, PhD); exercise physiology and muscle biology (MS, PhD); microbiology (MS, PhD); neuroscience (MS, PhD). Terminal master's awarded for partial completion of doctoral program. *Degree requirements:* For master's, comprehensive exam, thesis, 1 quarter of teaching experience; for doctorate, comprehensive exam, thesis/dissertation, 2 quarters of teaching experience. *Entrance requirements:* For master's, GRE General Test, names of three faculty members whose research interests most closely match the applicant's interest; for doctorate, GRE General Test, essay concerning prior training, research interest and career goals, plus names of three faculty members whose research interests most closely match the applicant's interest. Additional exam requirements/recommendations for international students: Required—TOEFL (minimum score 620 paper-based; 105 iBT) or IELTS (minimum score 7.5). Electronic applications accepted. *Faculty research:* Ecology and evolutionary biology, exercise physiology and muscle biology, neurobiology, cell biology, physiology.

Oklahoma State University, College of Arts and Sciences, Department of Plant Biology, Ecology, and Evolution, Stillwater, OK 74078. Offers botany (MS); environmental science (PhD). *Faculty:* 15 full-time (5 women). *Students:* 2 full-time (0 women), 11 part-time (7 women), 3 international. Average age 30. 3 applicants, 67% accepted, 2 enrolled. *Entrance requirements:* For master's and doctorate, GRE or GMAT. Additional exam requirements/recommendations for international students: Required—TOEFL (minimum score 550 paper-based; 79 iBT). *Application deadline:* For fall admission, 3/1 priority date for international students; for spring admission, 8/1 priority date for international students. Applications are processed on a rolling basis. Application fee: $40 ($75 for international students). Electronic applications accepted. *Expenses:* Tuition, state resident: full-time $4019; part-time $2679.60 per year. Tuition, nonresident: full-time $15,286; part-time $10,190.40 per year. *Required fees:* $2129; $1419 per unit. Tuition and fees vary according to program. *Financial support:* Research assistantships, teaching assistantships, career-related internships or fieldwork, Federal Work-Study, scholarships/grants, health care benefits, tuition waivers (partial), and unspecified assistantships available. Support available to part-time students. Financial award application deadline: 3/1; financial award applicants required to submit FAFSA. *Faculty research:* Ethnobotany, developmental genetics of Arabidopsis, biological roles of plasmodesmata, community ecology and biodiversity, nutrient cycling in grassland ecosystems. *Unit head:* Dr. Thomas Wikle, Interim Department Head, 405-744-7978, Fax: 405-744-7074, E-mail: twikle@okstate.edu.
Website: http://plantbio.okstate.edu

Old Dominion University, College of Sciences, Program in Ecological Sciences, Norfolk, VA 23529. Offers PhD. *Faculty:* 12 full-time (5 women), 41 part-time/adjunct (7 women). *Students:* 7 full-time (5 women), 9 part-time (6 women), 1 international. Average age 30. 8 applicants, 50% accepted, 4 enrolled. In 2017, 1 doctorate awarded. *Degree requirements:* For doctorate, one foreign language, comprehensive exam, thesis/dissertation. *Entrance requirements:* For doctorate, GRE General Test, 3 letters of recommendation. Additional exam requirements/recommendations for international students: Required—TOEFL (minimum score 550 paper-based; 79 iBT). *Application deadline:* For fall admission, 2/1 priority date for domestic and international students. Applications are processed on a rolling basis. Application fee: $50. Electronic applications accepted. *Expenses:* Tuition, state resident: full-time $8928; part-time $496 per credit. Tuition, nonresident: full-time $22,482; part-time $1249 per credit. *Required fees:* $66 per semester. *Financial support:* In 2017–18, 12 students received support, including 3 fellowships with full tuition reimbursements available (averaging $17,000 per year), 4 research assistantships with full tuition reimbursements available (averaging $15,750 per year), 9 teaching assistantships with full tuition reimbursements available (averaging $15,000 per year); scholarships/grants also available. Financial award application deadline: 2/15; financial award applicants required to submit FAFSA. *Faculty research:* Marine ecology, physiological ecology, ecology of infectious diseases, ecological and evolutionary processes, molecular genetics. *Total annual research expenditures:* $2 million. *Unit head:* Dr. Holly Gaff, Graduate Program Director, 757-683-6903, Fax: 757-683-5283, E-mail: hgaff@odu.edu. *Application contact:* William Heffelfinger, Director of Graduate Admissions, 757-683-5554, Fax: 757-683-3255, E-mail: gradadmit@odu.edu.
Website: http://www.odu.edu/academics/programs/doctoral/ecological-sciences

Oregon State University, College of Agricultural Sciences, Program in Botany and Plant Pathology, Corvallis, OR 97331. Offers applied systematics (MS); ecology (MS, PhD); genetics (MS, PhD); genomics and computational biology (MS, PhD); molecular and cellular biology (MS, PhD); mycology (MS, PhD); plant pathology (MS, PhD); plant physiology (MS, PhD). *Entrance requirements:* For master's and doctorate, GRE. *Application deadline:* For fall admission, 12/1 for domestic and international students. Application fee: $75 ($85 for international students). *Financial support:* Application deadline: 12/1. *Unit head:* John Fowler, Chair of Graduate Studies, E-mail: fowlerj@science.oregonstate.edu.
Website: http://bpp.oregonstate.edu/

Oregon State University, Interdisciplinary/Institutional Programs, Program in Environmental Sciences, Corvallis, OR 97331. Offers biogeochemistry (MA, MS, PSM, PhD); ecology (MA, MS, PSM, PhD); environmental education (MA, MS, PhD); quantitative analysis (PSM); social science (MA, MS, PSM, PhD); water resources (MA, MS, PhD). *Program availability:* Part-time. *Degree requirements:* For master's, variable foreign language requirement, thesis; for doctorate, thesis/dissertation. *Entrance requirements:* For master's and doctorate, GRE. Additional exam requirements/recommendations for international students: Required—TOEFL (minimum score 80 iBT), IELTS (minimum score 6.5). *Application deadline:* For fall admission, 1/15 priority date for domestic and international students. Application fee: $75 ($85 for international students). *Unit head:* Dr. Carolyn Fonyo Boggess, Interim Director, 541-760-4196, E-mail: carolyn.fonyo@oregonstate.edu. *Application contact:* Dr. Carolyn Fonyo Boggess, Interim Director, 541-760-4196, E-mail: carolyn.fonyo@oregonstate.edu.
Website: http://gradschool.oregonstate.edu/environmental-sciences-graduate-program-esgp

Penn State University Park, Graduate School, Intercollege Graduate Programs, Intercollege Graduate Program in Ecology, University Park, PA 16802. Offers MS, PhD. *Unit head:* Dr. Regina Vasilatos-Younken, Dean, 814-865-2516, Fax: 814-863-4627. *Application contact:* Lori Hawn, Director, Graduate Student Services, 814-865-1795, Fax: 814-863-4627, E-mail: l-gswww@lists.psu.edu.
Website: http://huck.psu.edu/content/graduate-programs/ecology

Princeton University, Graduate School, Department of Ecology and Evolutionary Biology, Princeton, NJ 08544-1019. Offers PhD. *Degree requirements:* For doctorate, thesis/dissertation. *Entrance requirements:* For doctorate, GRE General Test, GRE Subject Test. Additional exam requirements/recommendations for international students: Required—TOEFL (minimum score 600 paper-based). Electronic applications accepted.

Purdue University, College of Engineering, Division of Environmental and Ecological Engineering, West Lafayette, IN 47907. Offers MS, PhD. *Faculty:* 59. *Students:* 41. In 2017, 3 master's awarded. *Degree requirements:* For master's, thesis optional; for doctorate, thesis/dissertation. *Entrance requirements:* For master's and doctorate, GRE, minimum GPA of 3.0. *Application deadline:* For fall admission, 12/15 for domestic and international students. Application fee: $60 ($75 for international students). *Financial support:* Fellowships with full and partial tuition reimbursements, research assistantships with full and partial tuition reimbursements, teaching assistantships with full and partial tuition reimbursements, career-related internships or fieldwork, scholarships/grants, health care benefits, and unspecified assistantships available. Financial award applicants required to submit FAFSA. *Faculty research:* Water quality engineering, sustainable energy systems and impacts, greening the built environment, air quality engineering, watershed engineering and management, environmental remediation, life cycle engineering, reducing impacts of chemicals and materials. *Unit head:* Dr. John W. Sutherland, Professor/Head of Environmental and Ecological Engineering, 765-496-9697, E-mail: jwsuther@purdue.edu. *Application contact:* Patricia Finney, Graduate Administrative Assistant, 765-496-0545, E-mail: eee@purdue.edu.
Website: https://engineering.purdue.edu/EEE

Purdue University, Graduate School, College of Agriculture, Department of Forestry and Natural Resources, West Lafayette, IN 47907. Offers fisheries and aquatic sciences (MS, MSF, PhD); forest biology (MS, MSF, PhD); natural resource social science (MS, PhD); natural resources social science (MSF); quantitative ecology (MS, MSF, PhD); wildlife science (MS, MSF, PhD); wood products and wood products manufacturing (MS, MSF, PhD). *Faculty:* 27 full-time (5 women), 1 part-time/adjunct (0 women). *Students:* 61 full-time (35 women), 9 part-time (3 women); includes 5 minority (1 American Indian or Alaska Native, non-Hispanic/Latino; 3 Hispanic/Latino; 1 Two or more races, non-Hispanic/Latino), 16 international. Average age 28. 44 applicants, 34% accepted, 15 enrolled. In 2017, 12 master's, 7 doctorates awarded. *Degree requirements:* For master's, thesis; for doctorate, thesis/dissertation. *Entrance requirements:* For master's and doctorate, GRE General Test (minimum score: verbal 50th percentile; quantitative 50th percentile; analytical writing 4.0), minimum undergraduate GPA of 3.2 or equivalent. Additional exam requirements/recommendations for international students: Required—TOEFL (minimum score 550 paper-based; 77 iBT). *Application deadline:* For fall admission, 1/5 for domestic students, 1/15 for international students; for spring admission, 9/15 for domestic and international students. Applications are processed on a rolling basis. Application fee: $60 ($75 for international students). Electronic applications accepted. *Financial support:* In 2017–18, 10 research assistantships (averaging $15,259 per year) were awarded; fellowships, teaching assistantships, career-related internships or fieldwork, and scholarships/grants also available. Support available to part-time students. Financial award application deadline: 1/5; financial award applicants required to submit FAFSA. *Faculty research:* Wildlife management, forest management, forest ecology, forest soils, limnology. *Unit head:* Robert G. Wagner, Head of the Graduate Program, 765-494-3590, E-mail: rgwagner@purdue.edu. *Application contact:* Christine Hofmeyer, Graduate Contact, 765-494-3572, E-mail: chofmeye@purdue.edu.
Website: https://ag.purdue.edu/fnr

Ecology

Purdue University, Graduate School, College of Science, Department of Biological Sciences, West Lafayette, IN 47907. Offers biochemistry (PhD); biophysics (PhD); cell and developmental biology (PhD); ecology, evolutionary and population biology (MS, PhD), including ecology, evolutionary biology, population biology; genetics (MS, PhD); microbiology (MS, PhD); molecular biology (PhD); neurobiology (MS, PhD); plant physiology (PhD). *Faculty:* 42 full-time (13 women), 3 part-time/adjunct (0 women). *Students:* 115 full-time (58 women), 6 part-time (4 women); includes 17 minority (1 Black or African American, non-Hispanic/Latino; 6 Asian, non-Hispanic/Latino; 9 Hispanic/Latino; 1 Two or more races, non-Hispanic/Latino), 60 international. Average age 27. 165 applicants, 12% accepted, 15 enrolled. In 2017, 5 master's, 16 doctorates awarded. Terminal master's awarded for partial completion of doctoral program. *Degree requirements:* For master's, thesis (for some programs); for doctorate, thesis/dissertation, seminars, teaching experience. *Entrance requirements:* For master's, GRE General Test (minimum analytical writing score of 3.5), minimum undergraduate GPA of 3.0; for doctorate, GRE General Test (minimum analytical writing score of 3.5), minimum undergraduate GPA of 3.5. Additional exam requirements/recommendations for international students: Required—TOEFL minimum score 600 paper-based; 107 iBT (for MS), 80 iBT (for PhD). *Application deadline:* For fall admission, 12/7 for domestic and international students. Applications are processed on a rolling basis. Application fee: $60 ($75 for international students). Electronic applications accepted. *Financial support:* Fellowships, research assistantships, and teaching assistantships available. Support available to part-time students. Financial award application deadline: 2/15; financial award applicants required to submit FAFSA. *Unit head:* Stephen Konieczny, Head, 765-494-4407, E-mail: sfk@purdue.edu. *Application contact:* Georgina E. Rupp, Graduate Coordinator, 765-494-8142, E-mail: ruppg@purdue.edu.
Website: http://www.bio.purdue.edu/

Purdue University, Graduate School, Interdisciplinary Graduate Program in Ecological Sciences and Engineering, West Lafayette, IN 47907. Offers MS, PhD. *Students:* 44 full-time (19 women), 4 part-time (all women); includes 13 minority (4 Black or African American, non-Hispanic/Latino; 1 American Indian or Alaska Native, non-Hispanic/Latino; 3 Asian, non-Hispanic/Latino; 2 Hispanic/Latino; 3 Two or more races, non-Hispanic/Latino), 18 international. Average age 27. 37 applicants, 49% accepted, 12 enrolled. *Degree requirements:* For master's, thesis optional; for doctorate, thesis/dissertation, written and oral preliminary exam. *Entrance requirements:* For master's and doctorate, GRE (minimum old score Verbal and Quantitative combined 1200, new score 300; Analytical Writing 4.0), previous research or environmental project experience; minimum GPA of 3.3. Additional exam requirements/recommendations for international students: Required—TOEFL (minimum score 550 paper-based; 77 iBT), IELTS (minimum score 6.5); Recommended—TWE. *Application deadline:* For fall admission, 12/15 for domestic and international students. Applications are processed on a rolling basis. Application fee: $65 ($70 for international students). Electronic applications accepted. *Financial support:* Fellowships and research assistantships available. *Unit head:* Dr. Linda S. Lee, Head of the Graduate Program, 765-494-8612, E-mail: lslee@purdue.edu. *Application contact:* Deirdre Carmicheal, Graduate Contact, 765-494-0379, E-mail: dnolan@purdue.edu.
Website: http://www.gradschool.purdue.edu/ese/

Rice University, Graduate Programs, Wiess School of Natural Sciences, Department of Ecology and Evolutionary Biology, Houston, TX 77251-1892. Offers MA, MS, PhD. Terminal master's awarded for partial completion of doctoral program. *Degree requirements:* For master's, comprehensive exam (for some programs), thesis (for some programs); for doctorate, comprehensive exam, thesis/dissertation. *Entrance requirements:* For master's and doctorate, GRE General Test, GRE Subject Test. Additional exam requirements/recommendations for international students: Required—TOEFL (minimum score 600 paper-based; 90 iBT). Electronic applications accepted. *Faculty research:* Trace gas emissions, wetlands, biology, community ecology of forests and grasslands, conservation biology specialization.

Rutgers University–New Brunswick, Graduate School-New Brunswick, Program in Ecology and Evolution, Piscataway, NJ 08854-8097. Offers MS, PhD. *Program availability:* Part-time. Terminal master's awarded for partial completion of doctoral program. *Degree requirements:* For master's, comprehensive exam; for doctorate, comprehensive exam, thesis/dissertation. *Entrance requirements:* For master's and doctorate, GRE General Test, minimum GPA of 3.0. Additional exam requirements/recommendations for international students: Required—TOEFL (minimum score 550 paper-based). Electronic applications accepted. *Faculty research:* Population and community ecology, population genetics, evolutionary biology, conservation biology, ecosystem ecology.

San Diego State University, Graduate and Research Affairs, College of Sciences, Department of Biology, Program in Ecology, San Diego, CA 92182. Offers MS, PhD. PhD offered jointly with University of California, Davis. *Degree requirements:* For master's, thesis; for doctorate, thesis/dissertation. *Entrance requirements:* For master's, GRE General Test, resumé or curriculum vitae, 2 letters of recommendation; for doctorate, GRE General Test, GRE Subject Test, resume or curriculum vitae, 3 letters of recommendation. Electronic applications accepted. *Faculty research:* Conservation and restoration ecology, coastal and marine ecology, global change and ecosystem ecology.

San Francisco State University, Division of Graduate Studies, College of Science and Engineering, Department of Biology, Program in Ecology, Evolution, and Conservation Biology, San Francisco, CA 94132-1722. Offers MS. *Application deadline:* Applications are processed on a rolling basis. *Unit head:* Dr. Andrew Zink, Acting Coordinator, 415-405-2761, Fax: 415-338-2295, E-mail: zink@sfsu.edu.
Website: http://biology.sfsu.edu/graduate/ecology-evolution-and-conservation-biology-eecb-0

San Jose State University, Graduate Studies and Research, College of Science, San Jose, CA 95192-0099. Offers bioinformatics (MS); biological sciences (MA, MS), including ecology and evolution (MS), molecular biology and microbiology (MS), physiology (MS); biotechnology (MBT); chemistry (MA, MS); computer science (MS); geology (MS); marine science (MS); mathematics (MA, MS), including mathematics education (MA); medical products development management (MS); meteorology (MS); physics (MS), including computational physics, modern optics, physics; statistics (MS). MS in marine science offered through Moss Landing Marine Labs. *Program availability:* Part-time. *Faculty:* 78 full-time (27 women), 25 part-time/adjunct (13 women). *Students:* 154 full-time (76 women), 212 part-time (102 women); includes 135 minority (4 Black or African American, non-Hispanic/Latino; 78 Asian, non-Hispanic/Latino; 27 Hispanic/Latino; 1 Native Hawaiian or other Pacific Islander, non-Hispanic/Latino; 25 Two or more races, non-Hispanic/Latino), 135 international. Average age 28. 1,156 applicants, 26% accepted, 179 enrolled. In 2017, 196 master's awarded. *Degree requirements:* For master's, comprehensive exam (for some programs), thesis (for some programs), directed reading, colloquium, project, writing project, statistical consulting. *Entrance requirements:* Additional exam requirements/recommendations for international students: Required—TOEFL (minimum score 550 paper-based; 80 iBT), IELTS (minimum score 6.5), TWE, PTE (minimum score 53). *Application deadline:* For fall admission, 2/1 for domestic and international students. Applications are processed on a rolling basis. Application fee: $55. Electronic applications accepted. *Expenses:* Tuition, state resident: full-time $7176. Tuition, nonresident: full-time $16,680. Tuition and fees vary according to course load and program. *Financial support:* Fellowships, research assistantships, career-related internships or fieldwork, Federal Work-Study, scholarships/grants, traineeships, tuition waivers (full and partial), and unspecified assistantships available. Support available to part-time students. Financial award application deadline: 4/28; financial award applicants required to submit FAFSA. *Unit head:* Dr. Michael Kaufman, Dean, 408-924-4800, Fax: 408-924-4815, E-mail: michael.kaufman@sjsu.edu.
Website: http://www.sjsu.edu/science/

Stanford University, School of Humanities and Sciences, Department of Anthropology, Stanford, CA 94305-2004. Offers anthropology (MA); archaeology (PhD); culture and society (PhD); ecology and environment (PhD). Terminal master's awarded for partial completion of doctoral program. *Degree requirements:* For master's, thesis; for doctorate, one foreign language, thesis/dissertation. *Entrance requirements:* For master's and doctorate, GRE General Test. Additional exam requirements/recommendations for international students: Required—TOEFL. Electronic applications accepted. *Expenses: Tuition:* Full-time $48,987; part-time $10,620 per quarter. One-time fee: $400. Tuition and fees vary according to program.

State University of New York College of Environmental Science and Forestry, Department of Environmental and Forest Biology, Syracuse, NY 13210-2779. Offers applied ecology (MPS); chemical ecology (MPS, MS, PhD); conservation biology (MPS, MS, PhD); ecology (MPS, MS, PhD); entomology (MPS, MS, PhD); environmental interpretation (MPS, MS, PhD); environmental physiology (MPS, MS, PhD); fish and wildlife biology and management (MPS, MS, PhD); forest pathology and mycology (MPS, MS, PhD); plant biotechnology (MPS); plant science and biotechnology (MPS, MS, PhD). *Program availability:* Part-time. *Faculty:* 30 full-time (10 women), 4 part-time/adjunct (3 women). *Students:* 117 full-time (65 women), 18 part-time (6 women); includes 8 minority (6 American Indian or Alaska Native, non-Hispanic/Latino; 1 Asian, non-Hispanic/Latino; 1 Hispanic/Latino), 23 international. Average age 30. 84 applicants, 52% accepted, 31 enrolled. In 2017, 30 master's, 3 doctorates awarded. Terminal master's awarded for partial completion of doctoral program. *Degree requirements:* For master's, thesis (for some programs), capstone seminar; for doctorate, comprehensive exam, thesis/dissertation, capstone seminar. *Entrance requirements:* For master's and doctorate, GRE General Test, minimum GPA of 3.0. Additional exam requirements/recommendations for international students: Required—TOEFL (minimum score 550 paper-based; 80 iBT), IELTS (minimum score 6). *Application deadline:* For fall admission, 2/1 priority date for domestic and international students; for spring admission, 11/1 priority date for domestic and international students. Applications are processed on a rolling basis. Application fee: $60. Electronic applications accepted. *Expenses:* Tuition, state resident: full-time $10,870; part-time $453 per credit. Tuition, nonresident: full-time $22,210; part-time $925 per credit. *Required fees:* $1435; $70.85 per credit. One-time fee: $25 full-time. Part-time tuition and fees vary according to course load. *Financial support:* In 2017–18, 42 students received support. Unspecified assistantships available. Financial award application deadline: 6/30; financial award applicants required to submit FAFSA. *Faculty research:* Ecology, conservation biology, fish and wildlife biology and management, plant science, entomology. *Total annual research expenditures:* $5.3 million. *Unit head:* Dr. Neil H. Ringler, Chair, 315-470-6803, Fax: 315-470-6934, E-mail: nhringle@esf.edu. *Application contact:* Scott Shannon, Associate Provost for Instruction/Dean of the Graduate School, 315-470-6599, E-mail: esfgrad@esf.edu.
Website: http://www.esf.edu/efb/grad/default.asp

State University of New York College of Environmental Science and Forestry, Department of Forest and Natural Resources Management, Syracuse, NY 13210-2779. Offers ecology and ecosystems (MPS, MS, PhD); economics, governance and human dimensions (MPS, MS, PhD); forest and natural resources management (MPS, MS, PhD); forest resources management (MF); monitoring, analysis and modeling (MPS, MS, PhD). *Accreditation:* SAF. *Program availability:* Part-time. *Faculty:* 33 full-time (8 women), 7 part-time/adjunct (0 women). *Students:* 48 full-time (24 women), 7 part-time (2 women); includes 4 minority (1 American Indian or Alaska Native, non-Hispanic/Latino; 1 Asian, non-Hispanic/Latino; 2 Hispanic/Latino), 18 international. Average age 31. 43 applicants, 79% accepted, 14 enrolled. In 2017, 21 master's, 1 doctorate awarded. Terminal master's awarded for partial completion of doctoral program. *Degree requirements:* For master's, thesis (for some programs); for doctorate, comprehensive exam, thesis/dissertation. *Entrance requirements:* For master's and doctorate, GRE General Test, minimum GPA of 3.0. Additional exam requirements/recommendations for international students: Required—TOEFL (minimum score 550 paper-based; 80 iBT), IELTS (minimum score 6). *Application deadline:* For fall admission, 2/1 priority date for domestic and international students; for spring admission, 11/1 priority date for domestic and international students. Applications are processed on a rolling basis. Application fee: $60. *Expenses:* Tuition, state resident: full-time $10,870; part-time $453 per credit. Tuition, nonresident: full-time $22,210; part-time $925 per credit. *Required fees:* $1435; $70.85 per credit. One-time fee: $25 full-time. Part-time tuition and fees vary according to course load. *Financial support:* In 2017–18, 20 students received support. Unspecified assistantships available. Financial award application deadline: 6/30; financial award applicants required to submit FAFSA. *Faculty research:* Silviculture recreation management, tree improvement, operations management, economics. *Total annual research expenditures:* $3.6 million. *Unit head:* Dr. Robert Malmsheimer, Interim Chair, 315-470-6909, Fax: 315-470-6535, E-mail: rwmalmsh@esf.edu. *Application contact:* Scott Shannon, Associate Provost for Instruction/Dean of the Graduate School, 315-470-6599, Fax: 315-470-6978, E-mail: esfgrad@esf.edu.
Website: http://www.esf.edu/fnrm/

Stony Brook University, State University of New York, Graduate School, College of Arts and Sciences, Department of Ecology and Evolution, Stony Brook, NY 11794. Offers applied ecology (MA); ecology and evolution (PhD). *Faculty:* 16 full-time (5 women), 1 part-time/adjunct (0 women). *Students:* 42 full-time (19 women), 1 part-time (0 women); includes 2 minority (both Asian, non-Hispanic/Latino), 12 international. Average age 28. 31 applicants, 42% accepted, 8 enrolled. In 2017, 3 doctorates awarded. *Degree requirements:* For doctorate, one foreign language, comprehensive exam, thesis/dissertation, teaching experience. *Entrance requirements:* For doctorate, GRE General Test, GRE Subject Test. Additional exam requirements/recommendations for international students: Required—TOEFL. *Application deadline:* For fall admission, 1/15 for domestic students; for spring admission, 10/1 for domestic students. Application fee: $100. Electronic applications accepted. *Expenses:* Contact institution. *Financial support:* In 2017–18, 7 fellowships, 3 research assistantships, 24 teaching assistantships were awarded; Federal Work-Study also available. *Faculty research:* Ecology, ecology and population, evolution, biodiversity, environmental conservation. *Total annual research expenditures:* $1.6 million. *Unit head:* Dr. Robert W. Thacker, Chair, 631-632-8590, E-mail: robert.thacker@stonybrook.edu. *Application contact:* Melissa Cohen, Coordinator, 631-246-8604, Fax: 631-632-7626, E-mail: melissa.j.cohen@stonybrook.edu.
Website: http://life.bio.sunysb.edu/ee/

Tulane University, School of Science and Engineering, Department of Ecology and Evolutionary Biology, New Orleans, LA 70118-5669. Offers MS, PhD. Terminal master's awarded for partial completion of doctoral program. *Degree requirements:* For master's, thesis or alternative; for doctorate, thesis/dissertation. *Entrance requirements:* For master's, GRE General Test, minimum B average in undergraduate course work; for doctorate, GRE General Test. Additional exam requirements/recommendations for international students: Required—TOEFL. Electronic applications accepted. *Expenses: Tuition:* Full-time $50,920; part-time $2829 per credit hour. *Required fees:* $2040; $44.50 per credit hour. $580 per term. Tuition and fees vary according to course load, degree level and program. *Faculty research:* Ichthyology, plant systematics, crustacean endocrinology, ecotoxicology, ornithology.

Universidad Nacional Pedro Henriquez Urena, Graduate School, Santo Domingo, Dominican Republic. Offers agricultural diversity (MS), including horticultural/fruit production, tropical animal production; conservation of monuments and cultural assets (M Arch); ecology and environment (MS); environmental engineering (MEE); international relations (MA); natural resource management (MS); political science (MA); project optimization (MPM); project feasibility (MPM); project management (MPM); sanitation engineering (ME); science for teachers (MS); tropical Caribbean architecture (M Arch).

University at Buffalo, the State University of New York, Graduate School, College of Arts and Sciences, Program in Evolution, Ecology and Behavior, Buffalo, NY 14260. Offers MS, PhD, Certificate. *Faculty:* 16 full-time (7 women), 5 part-time/adjunct (2 women). *Students:* 17 full-time (13 women), 2 international. Average age 25. 14 applicants, 7% accepted, 1 enrolled. In 2017, 9 master's awarded. Terminal master's awarded for partial completion of doctoral program. *Degree requirements:* For master's, project; for doctorate, comprehensive exam, thesis/dissertation. *Entrance requirements:* For master's, GRE, minimum undergraduate GPA of 3.0; for doctorate, GRE, minimum GPA of 3.0. Additional exam requirements/recommendations for international students: Required—TOEFL (minimum score 550 paper-based; 79 iBT). *Application deadline:* For fall admission, 1/15 priority date for domestic and international students. Applications are processed on a rolling basis. Application fee: $75. Electronic applications accepted. *Financial support:* In 2017–18, 3 fellowships with full tuition reimbursements, 1 research assistantship with full tuition reimbursement, 5 teaching assistantships with full tuition reimbursements were awarded; Federal Work-Study, scholarships/grants, health care benefits, and unspecified assistantships also available. Financial award application deadline: 1/15; financial award applicants required to submit FAFSA. *Faculty research:* Coral reef ecology, evolution and ecology of aquatic invertebrates, animal communication, paleobiology, primate behavior. *Unit head:* Dr. Howard Lasker, Program Director, 716-645-4870, E-mail: ub-evb@buffalo.edu.
Website: http://www.evolutionecologybehavior.buffalo.edu/

University at Buffalo, the State University of New York, Graduate School, School of Architecture and Planning, Department of Architecture, Buffalo, NY 14260. Offers architecture (M Arch); ecological practices (MS Arch); M Arch/MBA; M Arch/MFA; M Arch/MUP. *Program availability:* Part-time. *Faculty:* 34 full-time (11 women), 11 part-time/adjunct (5 women). *Students:* 104 full-time (46 women), 10 part-time (4 women); includes 26 minority (12 Black or African American, non-Hispanic/Latino; 3 Asian, non-Hispanic/Latino; 8 Hispanic/Latino; 3 Two or more races, non-Hispanic/Latino), 21 international. Average age 25. 215 applicants, 27% accepted, 32 enrolled. In 2017, 61 master's awarded. *Degree requirements:* For master's, thesis or alternative, project, portfolio. *Entrance requirements:* For master's, GRE, portfolio, three letters of recommendation, transcripts, personal statement. Additional exam requirements/recommendations for international students: Required—TOEFL (minimum score 79 iBT), IELTS (minimum score 6.5). *Application deadline:* For fall admission, 1/1 priority date for domestic and international students. Application fee: $75. Electronic applications accepted. *Expenses:* $16,292 (for M Arch); $13,382 (for MS). *Financial support:* In 2017–18, 75 students received support, including 6 fellowships with full tuition reimbursements available (averaging $15,000 per year), 2 research assistantships with partial tuition reimbursements available (averaging $14,967 per year), 43 teaching assistantships with partial tuition reimbursements available (averaging $4,900 per year); career-related internships or fieldwork, Federal Work-Study, scholarships/grants, health care benefits, and unspecified assistantships also available. Financial award application deadline: 3/1; financial award applicants required to submit FAFSA. *Faculty research:* Ecological practices, inclusive design, material culture, situated technologies, urban design. *Total annual research expenditures:* $2.5 million. *Unit head:* Prof. Omar Khan, Chair, 716-829-3486, Fax: 716-829-3256, E-mail: omar.khan@buffalo.edu. *Application contact:* Debra Eggebrecht, Assistant to the Chair, 716-829-3486, Fax: 716-829-3256, E-mail: dle2@buffalo.edu.
Website: http://www.ap.buffalo.edu/architecture/

University of Alberta, Faculty of Graduate Studies and Research, Department of Biological Sciences, Edmonton, AB T6G 2E1, Canada. Offers environmental biology and ecology (M Sc, PhD); microbiology and biotechnology (M Sc, PhD); molecular biology and genetics (M Sc, PhD); physiology and cell biology (M Sc, PhD); plant biology (M Sc, PhD); systematics and evolution (M Sc, PhD). Terminal master's awarded for partial completion of doctoral program. *Degree requirements:* For master's, thesis; for doctorate, thesis/dissertation. *Entrance requirements:* Additional exam requirements/recommendations for international students: Required—TOEFL.

The University of Arizona, College of Science, Department of Ecology and Evolutionary Biology, Tucson, AZ 85721. Offers MS, PhD. Terminal master's awarded for partial completion of doctoral program. *Degree requirements:* For master's, thesis optional; for doctorate, one foreign language, comprehensive exam, thesis/dissertation. *Entrance requirements:* For master's, GRE General Test, GRE Subject Test, statement of purpose, curriculum vitae, 3 letters of recommendation; for doctorate, GRE General Test, GRE Subject Test, curriculum vitae, 3 letters of recommendation. Additional exam requirements/recommendations for international students: Required—TOEFL (minimum score 550 paper-based; 79 iBT). *Faculty research:* Biological diversity, evolutionary history, evolutionary mechanisms, community structure.

University of California, Davis, Graduate Studies, Graduate Group in Ecology, Davis, CA 95616. Offers MS, PhD. PhD offered jointly with San Diego State University. *Degree requirements:* For master's, comprehensive exam (for some programs), thesis (for some programs); for doctorate, thesis/dissertation. *Entrance requirements:* For master's and doctorate, GRE General Test. Additional exam requirements/recommendations for international students: Required—TOEFL (minimum score 550 paper-based). Electronic applications accepted. *Faculty research:* Agricultural conservation, physiological restoration, environmental policy, ecotoxicology.

University of California, Irvine, Francisco J. Ayala School of Biological Sciences, Department of Ecology and Evolutionary Biology, Irvine, CA 92697. Offers biological sciences (MS, PhD). *Students:* 55 full-time (30 women); includes 23 minority (2 Asian, non-Hispanic/Latino; 17 Hispanic/Latino; 4 Two or more races, non-Hispanic/Latino), 1 international. Average age 29. 68 applicants, 31% accepted, 8 enrolled. In 2017, 7 master's, 10 doctorates awarded. *Entrance requirements:* For master's and doctorate, GRE General Test, GRE Subject Test, minimum GPA of 3.0. Additional exam requirements/recommendations for international students: Required—TOEFL (minimum score 550 paper-based). *Application deadline:* For fall admission, 1/15 priority date for domestic students, 1/15 for international students. Applications are processed on a rolling basis. Application fee: $105 ($125 for international students). Electronic applications accepted. *Financial support:* Fellowships, research assistantships with full tuition reimbursements, teaching assistantships, career-related internships or fieldwork, institutionally sponsored loans, traineeships, health care benefits, and unspecified assistantships available. Financial award application deadline: 3/1; financial award applicants required to submit FAFSA. *Faculty research:* Ecological energetics, quantitative genetics, life history evolution, plant-herbivore and plant-pollinator interactions, molecular evolution. *Unit head:* Laurence D. Mueller, Professor/Department Chair, 949-824-4744, Fax: 949-824-2181, E-mail: ldmuelle@uci.edu. *Application contact:* Pam McDonald, Student Affairs Coordinator, 949-824-4743, Fax: 949-824-2181, E-mail: pmcdonal@uci.edu.
Website: http://ecoevo.bio.uci.edu/

University of California, Los Angeles, Graduate Division, College of Letters and Science, Department of Ecology and Evolutionary Biology, Los Angeles, CA 90095. Offers MA, PhD. Terminal master's awarded for partial completion of doctoral program. *Degree requirements:* For master's, comprehensive exam or thesis; for doctorate, thesis/dissertation, oral and written qualifying exams; 3 quarters of teaching experience. *Entrance requirements:* For master's and doctorate, GRE General Test, GRE Subject Test (biology), bachelor's degree; minimum undergraduate GPA of 3.0 (or its equivalent if letter grade system not used). Additional exam requirements/recommendations for international students: Required—TOEFL. Electronic applications accepted.

University of California, Santa Barbara, Graduate Division, College of Letters and Sciences, Division of Mathematics, Life, and Physical Sciences, Department of Ecology, Evolution, and Marine Biology, Santa Barbara, CA 93106-9620. Offers MA, PhD, MA/PhD. *Degree requirements:* For master's, comprehensive exam (for some programs), thesis (for some programs); for doctorate, comprehensive exam, thesis/dissertation. *Entrance requirements:* For master's and doctorate, GRE General Test. Additional exam requirements/recommendations for international students: Required—TOEFL (minimum score 550 paper-based; 80 iBT), IELTS. Electronic applications accepted. *Faculty research:* Community ecology, evolution, marine biology, population genetics, stream ecology.

University of California, Santa Cruz, Division of Graduate Studies, Division of Physical and Biological Sciences, Department of Ecology and Evolutionary Biology, Santa Cruz, CA 95064. Offers MA, PhD. *Degree requirements:* For master's, thesis; for doctorate, comprehensive exam, thesis/dissertation. *Entrance requirements:* For master's and doctorate, GRE General Test, GRE Subject Test, 3 letters of recommendation. Additional exam requirements/recommendations for international students: Required—TOEFL (minimum score 550 paper-based; 83 iBT); Recommended—IELTS (minimum score 8). Electronic applications accepted. *Faculty research:* Population and community ecology, evolutionary biology, physiology and behavior (marine and terrestrial), systematics and biodiversity.

University of Chicago, Division of the Biological Sciences, Department of Ecology and Evolution, Chicago, IL 60637. Offers PhD. *Faculty:* 23. *Students:* 27 full-time (9 women); includes 4 minority (2 Asian, non-Hispanic/Latino; 2 Hispanic/Latino), 9 international. Average age 27. 46 applicants, 20% accepted, 5 enrolled. In 2017, 7 doctorates awarded. *Degree requirements:* For doctorate, comprehensive exam, thesis/dissertation, ethics class, 2 teaching assistantships. *Entrance requirements:* For doctorate, GRE General Test, transcripts, statement of purpose, 3 letters of recommendation. Additional exam requirements/recommendations for international students: Required—TOEFL (minimum score 600 paper-based; 104 iBT), IELTS (minimum score 7). *Application deadline:* For fall admission, 12/1 for domestic and international students. Application fee: $90. Electronic applications accepted. *Financial support:* In 2017–18, 22 students received support, including fellowships with full tuition reimbursements available (averaging $31,000 per year), research assistantships with full tuition reimbursements available (averaging $31,000 per year); institutionally sponsored loans, scholarships/grants, traineeships, and health care benefits also available. Financial award application deadline: 12/1. *Faculty research:* Genetic variation and evolution, animal behavior, ecology, mechanisms of speciation. *Unit head:* Dr. Joy Bergelson, Chair, E-mail: jbergels@uchicago.edu. *Application contact:* Audrey Aronowsky, Graduate Research, Education, and Outreach Manager, 773-702-3891, E-mail: aronowsky@uchicago.edu.
Website: http://pondside.uchicago.edu/ee/

University of Colorado Boulder, Graduate School, College of Arts and Sciences, Department of Ecology and Evolutionary Biology, Boulder, CO 80309. Offers population biology (MA). *Faculty:* 34 full-time (14 women). *Students:* 73 full-time (41 women), 2 part-time (both women); includes 11 minority (1 Black or African American, non-Hispanic/Latino; 5 Hispanic/Latino; 5 Two or more races, non-Hispanic/Latino), 7 international. Average age 29. 152 applicants, 22% accepted, 20 enrolled. In 2017, 5 master's, 14 doctorates awarded. Terminal master's awarded for partial completion of doctoral program. *Degree requirements:* For master's, comprehensive exam, thesis or alternative; for doctorate, comprehensive exam, thesis/dissertation. *Entrance requirements:* For master's, GRE General Test, GRE Subject Test, minimum undergraduate GPA of 3.0; for doctorate, GRE General Test, GRE Subject Test. *Application deadline:* For fall admission, 12/1 for domestic students; for spring admission, 12/1 for domestic students. Application fee: $60 ($80 for international students). Electronic applications accepted. Application fee is waived when completed online. *Financial support:* In 2017–18, 171 students received support, including 31 fellowships (averaging $16,364 per year), 12 research assistantships with full and partial tuition reimbursements available (averaging $39,779 per year), 51 teaching assistantships with full and partial tuition reimbursements available (averaging $26,113 per year); institutionally sponsored loans, scholarships/grants, health care benefits, and unspecified assistantships also available. Financial award application deadline: 2/15; financial award applicants required to submit FAFSA. *Faculty research:* Ecology; evolutionary biology; biological sciences; genetics; conservation biology. *Total annual research expenditures:* $5.2 million. *Application contact:* E-mail: ebiograd@colorado.edu.
Website: http://ebio.colorado.edu

University of Colorado Denver, College of Liberal Arts and Sciences, Department of Geography and Environmental Sciences, Denver, CO 80217. Offers environmental sciences (MS), including air quality, ecosystems, environmental health, geospatial analysis, hazardous waste, water quality. *Program availability:* Part-time, evening/weekend. *Faculty:* 13 full-time (4 women), 5 part-time/adjunct (2 women). *Students:* 58 applicants, 76% accepted, 21 enrolled. In 2017, 17 master's awarded. *Degree requirements:* For master's, thesis or alternative, 30 credits including 21 of core requirements and 9 of environmental science electives. *Entrance requirements:* For master's, GRE General Test, BA in one of the natural/physical sciences or engineering (or equivalent background); prerequisite coursework in calculus and physics (one semester each); general chemistry with lab and general biology with lab (two semesters each); three letters of recommendation. Additional exam requirements/recommendations for international students: Required—TOEFL (minimum score 537 paper-based; 75 iBT); Recommended—IELTS (minimum score 6.5). *Application deadline:* For fall admission, 1/20 for domestic and international students; for spring admission, 10/1 for domestic and international students. Application fee: $50 ($75 for international students). Electronic applications accepted. *Faculty research:* Air quality, environmental health, ecosystems, hazardous waste, water quality, geospatial analysis and environmental science education.

Ecology

Unit head: Anne Chinn, Director of MS in Environmental Sciences Program, 303-556-3958, E-mail: ges@ucdenver.edu. *Application contact:* Sue Eddleman, Program Assistant, 303-352-3698, E-mail: sue.eddleman@ucdenver.edu.
Website: http://www.ucdenver.edu/academics/colleges/CLAS/Departments/ges/Programs/MasterofScience/Pages/MasterofScience.aspx

University of Connecticut, Graduate School, College of Liberal Arts and Sciences, Department of Psychology, Storrs, CT 06269. Offers behavioral neuroscience (PhD); biopsychology (PhD); clinical psychology (MA, PhD); cognition and instruction (PhD); developmental psychology (MA, PhD); ecological psychology (PhD); experimental psychology (PhD); general psychology (MA, PhD); industrial/organizational psychology (PhD); language and cognition (PhD); neuroscience (PhD); social psychology (MA, PhD). *Accreditation:* APA. Terminal master's awarded for partial completion of doctoral program. *Degree requirements:* For master's, comprehensive exam; for doctorate, thesis/dissertation. *Entrance requirements:* For master's and doctorate, GRE General Test, GRE Subject Test. Additional exam requirements/recommendations for international students: Required—TOEFL (minimum score 550 paper-based). Electronic applications accepted.

University of Delaware, College of Agriculture and Natural Resources, Department of Entomology and Wildlife Ecology, Newark, DE 19716. Offers entomology and applied ecology (MS, PhD), including avian ecology, evolution and taxonomy, insect biological control, insect ecology and behavior (MS), insect genetics, pest management, plant-insect interactions, wildlife ecology and management. *Program availability:* Part-time. *Degree requirements:* For master's, comprehensive exam, thesis, oral exam, seminar; for doctorate, comprehensive exam, thesis/dissertation, qualifying exam, seminar. *Entrance requirements:* For master's, GRE General Test, minimum GPA of 3.0 in field, 2.8 overall; for doctorate, GRE General Test, GRE Subject Test (biology), minimum GPA of 3.0 in field, 2.8 overall. Additional exam requirements/recommendations for international students: Required—TOEFL. Electronic applications accepted. *Faculty research:* Ecology and evolution of plant-insect interactions, ecology of wildlife conservation management, habitat restoration, biological control, applied ecosystem management.

University of Delaware, College of Arts and Sciences, Department of Biological Sciences, Newark, DE 19716. Offers biotechnology (MS); cancer biology (MS, PhD); cell and extracellular matrix biology (MS, PhD); cell and systems physiology (MS, PhD); developmental biology (MS, PhD); ecology and evolution (MS, PhD); microbiology (MS, PhD); molecular biology and genetics (MS, PhD). Terminal master's awarded for partial completion of doctoral program. *Degree requirements:* For master's, thesis, preliminary exam; for doctorate, comprehensive exam, thesis/dissertation, preliminary exam. *Entrance requirements:* For master's and doctorate, GRE General Test. Additional exam requirements/recommendations for international students: Required—TOEFL (minimum score 600 paper-based); Recommended—TWE. Electronic applications accepted. *Faculty research:* Microorganisms, bone, cancer metastasis, developmental biology, cell biology, DNA.

University of Denver, Division of Natural Sciences and Mathematics, Department of Biological Sciences, Denver, CO 80208. Offers biology, ecology and evolution (MS, PhD); biomedical sciences (PSM); cell and molecular biology (MS, PhD). *Program availability:* Part-time. *Students:* Average age 25. 71 applicants, 44% accepted, 18 enrolled. In 2017, 7 master's, 3 doctorates awarded. Terminal master's awarded for partial completion of doctoral program. *Degree requirements:* For master's, comprehensive exam (for some programs), thesis; for doctorate, one foreign language, comprehensive exam (for some programs), thesis/dissertation. *Entrance requirements:* For master's and doctorate, GRE General Test, bachelor's degree in biology or related field, transcripts, personal statement, three letters of recommendation. Additional exam requirements/recommendations for international students: Required—TOEFL (minimum score 550 paper-based; 80 iBT). *Application deadline:* For fall admission, 1/1 priority date for domestic and international students. Applications are processed on a rolling basis. Application fee: $65. Electronic applications accepted. *Expenses:* Contact institution. *Financial support:* In 2017–18, 35 students received support, including 5 research assistantships with tuition reimbursements available (averaging $18,667 per year), 14 teaching assistantships with tuition reimbursements available (averaging $18,095 per year); Federal Work-Study, institutionally sponsored loans, scholarships/grants, and unspecified assistantships also available. Support available to part-time students. Financial award application deadline: 2/15; financial award applicants required to submit FAFSA. *Faculty research:* Molecular biology, cell biology, neurobiology, ecology, molecular evolution. *Unit head:* Dr. Joseph Angleson, Associate Professor and Chair, 303-871-3463, Fax: 303-871-3471, E-mail: jangleso@du.edu. *Application contact:* Randi Flageolle, Assistant to the Chair, 303-871-3457, Fax: 303-871-3471, E-mail: rflageol@du.edu.
Website: http://www.du.edu/nsm/departments/biologicalsciences

University of Florida, Graduate School, College of Agricultural and Life Sciences, Department of Wildlife Ecology and Conservation, Gainesville, FL 32611. Offers environmental education and communications (Certificate); wildlife ecology and conservation (MS, PhD), including geographic information systems, tropical conservation and development, wetland sciences. *Degree requirements:* For master's, comprehensive exam, thesis optional; for doctorate, comprehensive exam, thesis/dissertation. *Entrance requirements:* For master's and doctorate, GRE General Test (minimum 34th percentile for Quantitative), minimum GPA of 3.3. Additional exam requirements/recommendations for international students: Required—TOEFL (minimum score 550 paper-based; 80 iBT), IELTS (minimum score 6). Electronic applications accepted. *Faculty research:* Conservation biology, spatial ecology, wildlife conservation and management, wetlands ecology and conservation, human dimensions in wildlife conservation.

University of Florida, Graduate School, School of Natural Resources and Environment, Gainesville, FL 32611. Offers interdisciplinary ecology (MS, PhD). *Degree requirements:* For master's, comprehensive exam, thesis; for doctorate, comprehensive exam, thesis/dissertation. *Entrance requirements:* For master's and doctorate, GRE General Test, minimum GPA of 3.0. Additional exam requirements/recommendations for international students: Required—TOEFL (minimum score 550 paper-based; 80 iBT), IELTS (minimum score 6). Electronic applications accepted. *Faculty research:* Natural sciences, social sciences, sustainability studies, research design and methods.

University of Georgia, Eugene P. Odum School of Ecology, Athens, GA 30602. Offers conservation ecology and sustainable development (MS); ecology (PhD). *Degree requirements:* For master's, thesis; for doctorate, one foreign language, thesis/dissertation. *Entrance requirements:* For master's and doctorate, GRE General Test. Electronic applications accepted.

University of Guelph, Graduate Studies, College of Biological Science, Department of Integrative Biology, Botany and Zoology, Guelph, ON N1G 2W1, Canada. Offers botany (M Sc, PhD); zoology (M Sc, PhD). *Program availability:* Part-time. *Degree requirements:* For master's, thesis, research proposal; for doctorate, thesis/dissertation, research proposal, qualifying exam. *Entrance requirements:* For master's, minimum B average during previous 2 years of course work. Additional exam requirements/recommendations for international students: Required—TOEFL (minimum score 550 paper-based), IELTS (minimum score 6.5). Electronic applications accepted. *Faculty research:* Aquatic science, environmental physiology, parasitology, wildlife biology, management.

University of Illinois at Urbana–Champaign, Graduate College, College of Liberal Arts and Sciences, School of Integrative Biology, Department of Animal Biology, Champaign, IL 61820. Offers animal biology (ecology, ethology and evolution) (MS, PhD).

University of Illinois at Urbana–Champaign, Graduate College, College of Liberal Arts and Sciences, School of Integrative Biology, Program in Ecology, Evolution and Conservation Biology, Champaign, IL 61820. Offers MS, PhD.

The University of Kansas, Graduate Studies, College of Liberal Arts and Sciences, Department of Ecology and Evolutionary Biology, Lawrence, KS 66045. Offers MA, PhD. *Program availability:* Part-time. *Students:* 70 full-time (33 women), 3 part-time (0 women); includes 6 minority (1 Black or African American, non-Hispanic/Latino; 1 Hispanic/Latino; 4 Two or more races, non-Hispanic/Latino), 23 international. Average age 29. 65 applicants, 40% accepted, 20 enrolled. In 2017, 8 master's, 8 doctorates awarded. Terminal master's awarded for partial completion of doctoral program. *Degree requirements:* For master's, comprehensive exam, thesis (for some programs), 30-36 credits, thesis presentation; for doctorate, comprehensive exam, thesis/dissertation, residency, final exam, dissertation defense. *Entrance requirements:* For master's and doctorate, GRE General Test, curriculum vitae, personal statement, three letters of recommendation, official transcripts. Additional exam requirements/recommendations for international students: Required—TOEFL or IELTS. *Application deadline:* For fall admission, 12/1 for domestic and international students. Application fee: $65 ($85 for international students). Electronic applications accepted. *Financial support:* Fellowships, research assistantships, teaching assistantships, scholarships/grants, traineeships, health care benefits, and unspecified assistantships available. Financial award application deadline: 12/1. *Faculty research:* Ecology and global change, diversity and macroevolution, evolutionary mechanisms, systematics/phylogenetic, biogeography. *Unit head:* Dr. Christopher Haufler, Chair, 785-864-3255, E-mail: vulgare@ku.edu. *Application contact:* Aagje Ashe, Graduate Coordinator, 785-864-2362, Fax: 785-864-5860, E-mail: a4ashe@ku.edu.
Website: http://eeb.ku.edu/

The University of Manchester, School of Biological Sciences, Manchester, United Kingdom. Offers adaptive organismal biology (M Phil, PhD); animal biology (M Phil, PhD); biochemistry (M Phil, PhD); bioinformatics (M Phil, PhD); biomolecular sciences (M Phil, PhD); biotechnology (M Phil, PhD); cell biology (M Phil, PhD); cell matrix research (M Phil, PhD); channels and transporters (M Phil, PhD); developmental biology (M Phil, PhD); environmental biology (M Phil, PhD); evolutionary biology (M Phil, PhD); gene expression (M Phil, PhD); genetics (M Phil, PhD); history of science, technology and medicine (M Phil, PhD); immunology (M Phil, PhD); integrative neurobiology and behavior (M Phil, PhD); membrane trafficking (M Phil, PhD); microbiology (M Phil, PhD); molecular and cellular neuroscience (M Phil, PhD); molecular biology (M Phil, PhD); molecular cancer studies (M Phil, PhD); neuroscience (M Phil, PhD); ophthalmology (M Phil, PhD); optometry (M Phil, PhD); organelle function (M Phil, PhD); pharmacology (M Phil, PhD); physiology (M Phil, PhD); plant sciences (M Phil, PhD); stem cell research (M Phil, PhD); structural biology (M Phil, PhD); systems neuroscience (M Phil, PhD); toxicology (M Phil, PhD).

University of Manitoba, Faculty of Graduate Studies, Faculty of Science, Department of Biological Sciences, Winnipeg, MB R3T 2N2, Canada. Offers botany (M Sc, PhD); ecology (M Sc, PhD); zoology (M Sc, PhD).

University of Maryland, College Park, Academic Affairs, College of Computer, Mathematical and Natural Sciences, Department of Biology, Behavior, Ecology, Evolution, and Systematics Program, College Park, MD 20742. Offers MS, PhD. *Degree requirements:* For master's, thesis, oral defense, seminar; for doctorate, thesis/dissertation, exam, 4 seminars. *Entrance requirements:* For master's and doctorate, GRE General Test, GRE Subject Test (biology), 3 letters of recommendation. Additional exam requirements/recommendations for international students: Required—TOEFL. *Faculty research:* Animal behavior, biostatistics, ecology, evolution, neurothology.

University of Maryland, College Park, Academic Affairs, College of Computer, Mathematical and Natural Sciences, Department of Biology, PhD Program in Biological Sciences, College Park, MD 20742. Offers behavior, ecology, evolution, and systematics (PhD); computational biology, bioinformatics, and genomics (PhD); molecular and cellular biology (PhD); physiological systems (PhD). *Degree requirements:* For doctorate, comprehensive exam, thesis/dissertation, thesis work presentation in seminar. *Entrance requirements:* For doctorate, GRE General Test; GRE Subject Test in biology (recommended), academic transcripts, statement of purpose/research interests, 3 letters of recommendation. Additional exam requirements/recommendations for international students: Required—TOEFL. Electronic applications accepted.

University of Michigan, Rackham Graduate School, College of Literature, Science, and the Arts, Department of Ecology and Evolutionary Biology, Ann Arbor, MI 48109. Offers MS, PhD. *Faculty:* 51 full-time (18 women). *Students:* 80 full-time (44 women); includes 38 minority (5 Black or African American, non-Hispanic/Latino; 1 American Indian or Alaska Native, non-Hispanic/Latino; 5 Asian, non-Hispanic/Latino; 15 Hispanic/Latino; 1 Native Hawaiian or other Pacific Islander, non-Hispanic/Latino; 11 Two or more races, non-Hispanic/Latino), 15 international. Average age 27. 147 applicants, 20% accepted, 20 enrolled. In 2017, 13 master's, 6 doctorates awarded. Terminal master's awarded for partial completion of doctoral program. *Degree requirements:* For master's, thesis (for some programs); for doctorate, comprehensive exam, thesis/dissertation, 2 semesters of teaching. *Entrance requirements:* For master's and doctorate, GRE. Additional exam requirements/recommendations for international students: Required—TOEFL (minimum score 84 iBT). *Application deadline:* For fall admission, 12/1 priority date for domestic and international students. Application fee: $75 ($90 for international students). Electronic applications accepted. *Expenses:* $21,673. *Financial support:* In 2017–18, 80 students received support, including 35 fellowships with full tuition reimbursements available (averaging $27,399 per year), 11 research assistantships with full tuition reimbursements available (averaging $27,399 per year), 36 teaching assistantships with full tuition reimbursements available (averaging $27,399 per year); scholarships/grants, traineeships, health care benefits, and unspecified assistantships also available. *Faculty research:* Population and community ecology, ecosystem ecology and biogeochemistry, global change biology, evolution of behavior, evolutionary genetics, phylogenetics and phylogeography. *Total annual research expenditures:* $5.1 million. *Unit head:* Dr. Diarmaid O' Foighil, Chair, 734-615-4912, Fax: 734-763-0544. *Application contact:* Kati Ellis, Graduate Program Assistant and Recruiter, 734-764-1443, Fax: 734-763-0544, E-mail: eeb.gradcoord@umich.edu.
Website: http://lsa.umich.edu/eeb/

University of Michigan, School for Environment and Sustainability, Program in Natural Resources and Environment, Ann Arbor, MI 48109. Offers behavior, education and communication (MS); conservation ecology (MS); environmental informatics (MS); environmental justice (MS); environmental policy and planning (MS); natural resources and environment (PhD); sustainable systems (MS); MS/JD; MS/MBA; MS/MPH; MS/MPP; MS/MSE; MS/MURP. Terminal master's awarded for partial completion of doctoral program. *Degree requirements:* For master's, practicum or group project; for doctorate, comprehensive exam, thesis/dissertation, oral defense of dissertation, preliminary exam. *Entrance requirements:* For master's, GRE General Test; for doctorate, GRE

General Test, master's degree. Additional exam requirements/recommendations for international students: Required—TOEFL (minimum score 560 paper-based; 84 iBT), IELTS (minimum score 6.5). Electronic applications accepted. *Expenses:* Tuition, state resident: full-time $22,368; part-time $1201 per credit hour. Tuition, nonresident: full-time $45,156; part-time $2467 per credit hour. *Required fees:* $376 per term. Tuition and fees vary according to course load, degree level and program. *Faculty research:* Ecological science, social sciences, and sustainable systems.

University of Minnesota, Twin Cities Campus, Graduate School, College of Biological Sciences, Department of Ecology, Evolution, and Behavior, St. Paul, MN 55418. Offers MS, PhD. Terminal master's awarded for partial completion of doctoral program. *Degree requirements:* For master's, comprehensive exam, thesis or projects; for doctorate, comprehensive exam, thesis/dissertation. *Entrance requirements:* For master's and doctorate, GRE General Test, minimum GPA of 3.0. Additional exam requirements/recommendations for international students: Required—TOEFL (minimum score 550 paper-based; 79 iBT), Michigan English Language Assessment Battery. Electronic applications accepted. *Faculty research:* Behavioral ecology, community ecology, community genetics, ecosystem and global change, evolution and systematics.

University of Missouri, Office of Research and Graduate Studies, College of Arts and Science, Division of Biological Sciences, Columbia, MO 65211. Offers evolutionary biology and ecology (MA, PhD). Terminal master's awarded for partial completion of doctoral program. *Entrance requirements:* For master's and doctorate, GRE General Test (minimum score 1200 verbal and quantitative), minimum GPA of 3.0. Additional exam requirements/recommendations for international students: Required—TOEFL. *Expenses:* Tuition, state resident: full-time $6480. Tuition, nonresident: full-time $17,744. *Required fees:* $1108. Tuition and fees vary according to course load, campus/location and program. *Financial support:* Fellowships, research assistantships, teaching assistantships, institutionally sponsored loans, traineeships, health care benefits, and unspecified assistantships available.
Website: http://biology.missouri.edu/graduate-studies/

University of Montana, Graduate School, College of Forestry and Conservation, Missoula, MT 59812. Offers fish and wildlife biology (PhD); forest and conservation sciences (PhD); forestry (MS); recreation management (MS); resource conservation (MS); systems ecology (MS, PhD); wildlife biology (MS). *Degree requirements:* For doctorate, thesis/dissertation. *Entrance requirements:* For master's and doctorate, GRE General Test. Additional exam requirements/recommendations for international students: Required—TOEFL (minimum score 575 paper-based).

University of Montana, Graduate School, College of Humanities and Sciences, Division of Biological Sciences, Interdisciplinary Program in Systems Ecology, Missoula, MT 59812. Offers MS, PhD.

University of Montana, Graduate School, College of Humanities and Sciences, Division of Biological Sciences, Program in Organismal Biology and Ecology, Missoula, MT 59812. Offers MS, PhD. Terminal master's awarded for partial completion of doctoral program. *Degree requirements:* For master's, one foreign language, thesis; for doctorate, 2 foreign languages, thesis/dissertation. *Entrance requirements:* For master's and doctorate, GRE General Test. *Faculty research:* Conservation biology, ecology and behavior, evolutionary genetics, avian biology.

University of Nevada, Reno, Graduate School, Interdisciplinary Program in Ecology, Evolution, and Conservation Biology, Reno, NV 89557. Offers PhD. Offered through the College of Arts and Science, the M. C. Fleischmann College of Agriculture, and the Desert Research Institute. *Degree requirements:* For doctorate, thesis/dissertation. *Entrance requirements:* For doctorate, GRE General Test, GRE Subject Test, minimum GPA of 3.0. Additional exam requirements/recommendations for international students: Required—TOEFL (minimum score 500 paper-based; 61 iBT), IELTS (minimum score 6). Electronic applications accepted. *Faculty research:* Population biology, behavioral ecology, plant response to climate change, conservation of endangered species, restoration of natural ecosystems.

University of New Haven, Graduate School, College of Arts and Sciences, Program in Environmental Science, West Haven, CT 06516. Offers environmental ecology (MS); environmental geoscience (MS); environmental health and management (MS); environmental science (MS); geographical information systems (MS). *Program availability:* Part-time, evening/weekend. *Students:* 27 full-time (17 women), 8 part-time (3 women); includes 3 minority (2 Black or African American, non-Hispanic/Latino; 1 Hispanic/Latino), 6 international. Average age 25. 46 applicants, 87% accepted, 19 enrolled. In 2017, 11 master's awarded. *Entrance requirements:* Additional exam requirements/recommendations for international students: Required—TOEFL (minimum score 80 iBT), IELTS, PTE. *Application deadline:* Applications are processed on a rolling basis. Application fee: $50. Electronic applications accepted. Application fee is waived when completed online. *Expenses: Tuition:* Full-time $16,020; part-time $890 per credit hour. *Required fees:* $220; $90 per term. *Financial support:* Research assistantships with partial tuition reimbursements, teaching assistantships with partial tuition reimbursements, Federal Work-Study, scholarships/grants, and unspecified assistantships available. Support available to part-time students. Financial award applicants required to submit FAFSA. *Unit head:* Dr. Roman Zajac, Coordinator, 203-932-7114, E-mail: rzajac@newhaven.edu. *Application contact:* Michelle Mason, Director of Graduate Enrollment, 203-932-7067, E-mail: mmason@newhaven.edu.
Website: http://www.newhaven.edu/4728/

The University of North Carolina at Chapel Hill, Graduate School, College of Arts and Sciences, Curriculum in Ecology, Chapel Hill, NC 27599. Offers MA, MS, PhD. *Degree requirements:* For master's, comprehensive exam, thesis (for some programs), oral defense of thesis; for doctorate, comprehensive exam, thesis/dissertation, oral exams, oral defense of dissertation. *Entrance requirements:* For master's and doctorate, GRE General Test. Additional exam requirements/recommendations for international students: Required—TOEFL (minimum score 550 paper-based). Electronic applications accepted. *Faculty research:* Community and population ecology and ecosystems, human ecology, landscape ecology, conservation ecology, marine ecology.

The University of North Carolina at Chapel Hill, Graduate School, College of Arts and Sciences, Department of Biology, Chapel Hill, NC 27599. Offers botany (MA, MS, PhD); cell biology, development, and physiology (MA, MS, PhD); cell motility and cytoskeleton (PhD); ecology and behavior (MA, MS, PhD); genetics and molecular biology (MA, MS, PhD); morphology, systematics, and evolution (MA, MS, PhD). Terminal master's awarded for partial completion of doctoral program. *Degree requirements:* For master's, comprehensive exam, thesis (for some programs); for doctorate, comprehensive exam, thesis/dissertation. *Entrance requirements:* For master's, GRE General Test, GRE Subject Test, 2 semesters of calculus or statistics; 2 semesters of physics, organic chemistry; 3 semesters of biology; for doctorate, GRE General Test, GRE Subject Test, 2 semesters calculus or statistics, 2 semesters physics, organic chemistry, 3 semesters of biology. Additional exam requirements/recommendations for international students: Required—TOEFL (minimum score 550 paper-based). Electronic applications accepted. *Faculty research:* Gene expression, biomechanics, yeast genetics, plant ecology, plant molecular biology.

University of Notre Dame, Graduate School, College of Science, Department of Biological Sciences, Notre Dame, IN 46556. Offers aquatic ecology, evolution and environmental biology (MS, PhD); cellular and molecular biology (MS, PhD); genetics (MS, PhD); physiology (MS, PhD); vector biology and parasitology (MS, PhD). Terminal master's awarded for partial completion of doctoral program. *Degree requirements:* For master's, comprehensive exam, thesis; for doctorate, comprehensive exam, thesis/dissertation, candidacy exam. *Entrance requirements:* For master's and doctorate, GRE General Test. Additional exam requirements/recommendations for international students: Required—TOEFL (minimum score 600 paper-based; 80 iBT). Electronic applications accepted. *Faculty research:* Tropical disease, molecular genetics, neurobiology, evolutionary biology, aquatic biology.

University of Oklahoma, College of Arts and Sciences, Department of Biology, Norman, OK 73019. Offers biology (MS, PhD); cellular and behavioral neurobiology (PhD), including biology; ecology and evolutionary biology (PhD), including biology. *Faculty:* 38 full-time (10 women), 1 (woman) part-time/adjunct. *Students:* 13 full-time (4 women), 9 part-time (6 women); includes 5 minority (2 Asian, non-Hispanic/Latino; 2 Hispanic/Latino; 1 Two or more races, non-Hispanic/Latino), 5 international. Average age 28. 27 applicants, 15% accepted, 4 enrolled. In 2017, 6 master's awarded. *Degree requirements:* For master's, thesis, course in biostatistics; for doctorate, comprehensive exam, thesis/dissertation, course in biostatistics, 2 semesters as teaching assistant. *Entrance requirements:* For master's and doctorate, GRE General Test, transcripts, 3 letters of recommendation, personal statement, curriculum vitae. Additional exam requirements/recommendations for international students: Required—TOEFL (minimum score 79 iBT) or IELTS (minimum score 6.5). *Application deadline:* For fall admission, 12/15 priority date for domestic and international students. Application fee: $50 ($100 for international students). Electronic applications accepted. *Expenses:* Tuition, state resident: full-time $5119; part-time $213.30 per credit hour. Tuition, nonresident: full-time $19,778; part-time $824.10 per credit hour. *Required fees:* $3458; $133.55 per credit hour. $126.50 per semester. *Financial support:* In 2017–18, 19 students received support, including 10 fellowships with full tuition reimbursements available (averaging $3,257 per year), 6 research assistantships with full tuition reimbursements available (averaging $15,419 per year), 38 teaching assistantships with full tuition reimbursements available (averaging $16,413 per year); scholarships/grants and assistantships (with tuition waivers and health insurance) also available. Financial award application deadline: 6/1; financial award applicants required to submit FAFSA. *Faculty research:* Geographical ecology, biology of behavior, cellular and behavioral neurobiology, evolutionary and molecular genetics; evolution of development. *Total annual research expenditures:* $1.2 million. *Unit head:* Dr. Richard Broughton, Professor and Chair, 405-325-6200, Fax: 405-325-6202, E-mail: biology@ou.edu. *Application contact:* Dianna Wilson, Academic Counselor, 405-325-9139, Fax: 405-325-6202, E-mail: biologygrad@ou.edu.
Website: http://www.ou.edu/cas/biology

University of Oklahoma, College of Arts and Sciences, Department of Microbiology and Plant Biology, Program in Plant Biology, Norman, OK 73019. Offers ecology and evolutionary biology (PhD); plant biology (MS, PhD). *Students:* 6 full-time (4 women), 10 part-time (4 women); includes 2 minority (1 American Indian or Alaska Native, non-Hispanic/Latino; 1 Asian, non-Hispanic/Latino), 4 international. Average age 30. 10 applicants, 50% accepted, 5 enrolled. In 2017, 2 master's, 2 doctorates awarded. Terminal master's awarded for partial completion of doctoral program. *Degree requirements:* For master's, thesis; for doctorate, comprehensive exam, thesis/dissertation. *Entrance requirements:* For master's and doctorate, GRE, 3 recommendation letters, letter of intent, bachelor's degree. Additional exam requirements/recommendations for international students: Required—TOEFL (minimum score 80 iBT) or IELTS (minimum score 6.5). *Application deadline:* For fall admission, 3/1 for domestic and international students; for spring admission, 9/1 for domestic and international students; for summer admission, 9/1 for domestic and international students. Application fee: $50 ($100 for international students). Electronic applications accepted. *Expenses:* Tuition, state resident: full-time $5119; part-time $213.30 per credit hour. Tuition, nonresident: full-time $19,778; part-time $824.10 per credit hour. *Required fees:* $3458; $133.55 per credit hour. $126.50 per semester. *Financial support:* In 2017–18, 13 students received support. Research assistantships with full and partial tuition reimbursements available, teaching assistantships with full and partial tuition reimbursements available, Federal Work-Study, institutionally sponsored loans, scholarships/grants, health care benefits, and unspecified assistantships available. Support available to part-time students. Financial award application deadline: 6/1; financial award applicants required to submit FAFSA. *Faculty research:* Ecology, evolution, and systematics of plants; molecular biology of plant stress and reproduction; global change biology and ecosystem modeling; plant structure and development; science education. *Unit head:* Dr. Anne K. Dunn, Department Chair/Associate Professor of Microbiology, 405-325-4321, E-mail: akdunn@ou.edu. *Application contact:* Elizabeth Karr, Graduate Liaison/Associate Professor of Microbiology, 405-325-5133, E-mail: lizkarr@ou.edu.
Website: http://mpbio.ou.edu

University of Oklahoma, College of Arts and Sciences, Program in Ecology and Evolutionary Biology, Norman, OK 73019. Offers PhD. *Students:* 23 full-time (12 women), 13 part-time (7 women); includes 5 minority (2 Black or African American, non-Hispanic/Latino; 1 Asian, non-Hispanic/Latino; 2 Hispanic/Latino), 7 international. Average age 28. 19 applicants, 42% accepted, 8 enrolled. In 2017, 8 doctorates awarded. *Degree requirements:* For doctorate, comprehensive exam, thesis/dissertation, course in biostatistics; 2 semesters as a teaching assistant. *Entrance requirements:* For doctorate, GRE General Test, transcripts, 3 letters of recommendation, personal statement, curriculum vitae. Additional exam requirements/recommendations for international students: Required—TOEFL (minimum score 79 iBT) or IELTS (minimum score 6.5). *Application deadline:* For fall admission, 12/15 priority date for domestic students, 12/15 for international students. Application fee: $50 ($100 for international students). Electronic applications accepted. *Expenses:* Tuition, state resident: full-time $5119; part-time $213.30 per credit hour. Tuition, nonresident: full-time $19,778; part-time $824.10 per credit hour. *Required fees:* $3458; $133.55 per credit hour. $126.50 per semester. *Financial support:* In 2017–18, 38 students received support. Fellowships, research assistantships with full tuition reimbursements available, teaching assistantships with full tuition reimbursements available, scholarships/grants, and assistantships (with tuition waivers and health insurance) available. Financial award application deadline: 6/1; financial award applicants required to submit FAFSA. *Faculty research:* Geographical ecology, global change biology, evolutionary biology, phylogenetics, ecosystem ecology. *Unit head:* Dr. Michael Kaspari, Professor, 405-325-3371, Fax: 405-325-6202, E-mail: mkaspari@ou.edu. *Application contact:* Dianna Wilson, Academic Counselor, 405-325-9139, Fax: 405-325-6202, E-mail: biologygrad@ou.edu.
Website: http://www.ou.edu/eeb

University of Oregon, Graduate School, College of Arts and Sciences, Department of Biology, Eugene, OR 97403. Offers ecology and evolution (MA, MS, PhD); marine biology (MA, MS, PhD); molecular, cellular and genetic biology (PhD); neuroscience and development (PhD). Terminal master's awarded for partial completion of doctoral program. *Degree requirements:* For master's, thesis (for some programs); for doctorate, thesis/dissertation. *Entrance requirements:* For master's and doctorate, GRE General Test, minimum GPA of 3.2. Additional exam requirements/recommendations for international students: Required—TOEFL. *Faculty research:* Developmental neurobiology; evolution, population biology, and quantitative genetics; regulation of gene expression; biochemistry of marine organisms.

Ecology

University of Pittsburgh, Kenneth P. Dietrich School of Arts and Sciences, Department of Biological Sciences, Program in Ecology and Evolution, Pittsburgh, PA 15260. Offers PhD. *Program availability:* Part-time, online learning. *Faculty:* 6 full-time (2 women). *Students:* 13 full-time (12 women); includes 1 minority (Hispanic/Latino), 2 international. Average age 23. In 2017, 1 doctorate awarded. *Degree requirements:* For doctorate, comprehensive exam, thesis/dissertation, completion of research integrity module. *Entrance requirements:* For doctorate, GRE General Test, GRE Subject Test. Additional exam requirements/recommendations for international students: Required—TOEFL (minimum score 90 iBT). *Application deadline:* Applications are processed on a rolling basis. Application fee: $0. Electronic applications accepted. *Financial support:* In 2017–18, 11 fellowships with full tuition reimbursements (averaging $34,776 per year), 9 research assistantships with full tuition reimbursements (averaging $28,800 per year), 14 teaching assistantships with full tuition reimbursements (averaging $28,535 per year) were awarded; Federal Work-Study, traineeships, health care benefits, and tuition waivers also available. *Unit head:* Dr. Karen M. Arndt, Professor, 412-624-6963, Fax: 412-624-4349, E-mail: arndt@pitt.edu. *Application contact:* Cathleen M. Barr, Graduate Administrator, 412-624-4268, Fax: 412-624-4349, E-mail: cbarr@pitt.edu.
Website: http://www.biology.pitt.edu

University of Puerto Rico–Río Piedras, College of Natural Sciences, Department of Biology, San Juan, PR 00931-3300. Offers ecology/systematics (MS, PhD); evolution/genetics (MS, PhD); molecular/cellular biology (MS, PhD); neuroscience (MS, PhD). *Program availability:* Part-time. *Degree requirements:* For master's, one foreign language, comprehensive exam, thesis; for doctorate, one foreign language, comprehensive exam, thesis/dissertation. *Entrance requirements:* For master's, GRE Subject Test, interview, minimum GPA of 3.0, letter of recommendation; for doctorate, GRE Subject Test, interview, master's degree, minimum GPA of 3.0, letter of recommendation. *Faculty research:* Environmental, poblational and systematic biology.

University of Rhode Island, Graduate School, College of the Environment and Life Sciences, Department of Biological Sciences, Kingston, RI 02881. Offers cell and molecular biology (MS, PhD); earth and environmental sciences (MS, PhD); ecology and ecosystem sciences (MS, PhD); evolutionary and marine biology (MS, PhD); sustainable agriculture and food systems (MS, PhD). *Program availability:* Part-time. *Faculty:* 18 full-time (10 women). *Students:* 99 full-time (56 women), 16 part-time (12 women); includes 10 minority (4 Black or African American, non-Hispanic/Latino; 3 Asian, non-Hispanic/Latino; 2 Hispanic/Latino; 1 Two or more races, non-Hispanic/Latino), 21 international. 151 applicants, 22% accepted, 26 enrolled. In 2017, 18 master's, 9 doctorates awarded. *Entrance requirements:* Additional exam requirements/recommendations for international students: Required—TOEFL. *Application deadline:* For fall admission, 1/15 for domestic and international students. Application fee: $65. Electronic applications accepted. *Expenses:* Tuition, state resident: full-time $12,706; part-time $786 per credit. Tuition, nonresident: full-time $25,216; part-time $1401 per credit. *Required fees:* $1598; $45 per credit. One-time fee: $30 part-time. *Financial support:* In 2017–18, 4 research assistantships with tuition reimbursements (averaging $12,698 per year) were awarded. Financial award application deadline: 1/15; financial award applicants required to submit FAFSA. *Faculty research:* Physiological constraints on predators in the Antarctic, effects of CO2 absorption in salt water particularly as it impacts pteropods. *Unit head:* Dr. Evan Preisser, Chair, 401-874-2120, E-mail: preisser@uri.edu.
Website: http://web.uri.edu/bio/

University of Rochester, School of Arts and Sciences, Department of Biology, Rochester, NY 14627. Offers biology (MS); ecology, genetics, and genomics (PhD); molecular, cellular, and developmental biology evolution (PhD). *Faculty:* 21 full-time (6 women). *Students:* 42 full-time (17 women), 4 part-time (all women); includes 6 minority (1 Asian, non-Hispanic/Latino; 3 Hispanic/Latino; 2 Two or more races, non-Hispanic/Latino), 22 international. Average age 27. 119 applicants, 22% accepted, 11 enrolled. In 2017, 6 master's, 5 doctorates awarded. Terminal master's awarded for partial completion of doctoral program. *Degree requirements:* For master's, comprehensive exam (for some programs), thesis (for some programs); for doctorate, thesis/dissertation, qualifying exam. *Entrance requirements:* For master's and doctorate, GRE General Test, GRE Subject Test (highly recommended), personal statement, transcripts, three letters of recommendation. Additional exam requirements/recommendations for international students: Required—TOEFL. *Application deadline:* For fall admission, 1/2 for domestic and international students. Application fee: $60. Electronic applications accepted. *Expenses:* $1,596 per credit hour. *Financial support:* In 2017–18, 36 students received support, including 1 fellowship (averaging $23,000 per year), 20 research assistantships (averaging $28,000 per year), 15 teaching assistantships (averaging $28,000 per year); health care benefits and tuition waivers (full) also available. Financial award application deadline: 1/1. *Faculty research:* Evolution, ecology, genetics, cellular biology, molecular biology. *Total annual research expenditures:* $6.7 million. *Unit head:* Michael Welte, Professor and Chair, 585-276-3897, E-mail: michael.welte@rochester.edu. *Application contact:* Cynthia Landry, Administrative Assistant, 585-275-7991, E-mail: cynthia.landry@rochester.edu.
Website: https://www.sas.rochester.edu/bio/graduate/index.html

University of South Carolina, The Graduate School, College of Arts and Sciences, Department of Biological Sciences, Graduate Training Program in Ecology, Evolution, and Organismal Biology, Columbia, SC 29208. Offers MS, PhD. *Degree requirements:* For master's, one foreign language, comprehensive exam, thesis; for doctorate, one foreign language, comprehensive exam, thesis/dissertation. *Entrance requirements:* For master's and doctorate, GRE General Test, minimum GPA of 3.0 in science. Additional exam requirements/recommendations for international students: Required—TOEFL (minimum score 570 paper-based). Electronic applications accepted.

University of South Florida, College of Arts and Sciences, Department of Integrative Biology, Tampa, FL 33620-9951. Offers biology (MS), including ecology and evolution (MS, PhD), environmental and ecological microbiology (MS, PhD), physiology and morphology (MS, PhD); integrative biology (PhD), including ecology and evolution (MS, PhD), environmental and ecological microbiology (MS, PhD), physiology and morphology (MS, PhD). *Program availability:* Part-time. *Faculty:* 14 full-time (5 women). *Students:* 21 full-time (11 women), 1 (woman) part-time; includes 1 minority (Asian, non-Hispanic/Latino), 2 international. Average age 30. 35 applicants, 17% accepted, 5 enrolled. In 2017, 7 master's, 5 doctorates awarded. *Degree requirements:* For master's, comprehensive exam, thesis (for some programs); for doctorate, comprehensive exam, thesis/dissertation. *Entrance requirements:* For master's and doctorate, GRE General Test, minimum GPA of 3.0 in last 60 hours of BS. *Application deadline:* For fall admission, 11/30 priority date for domestic and international students; for spring admission, 7/1 priority date for domestic and international students. Application fee: $30. Electronic applications accepted. *Financial support:* In 2017–18, 7 students received support. Research assistantships, teaching assistantships, and unspecified assistantships available. Financial award application deadline: 6/30; financial award applicants required to submit FAFSA. *Faculty research:* Marine ecology, ecosystem responses to urbanization, biomechanical and physiological mechanisms of animal movement, population biology and conservation, microbial ecology and public health microbiology, natural diversity of parasites and herbivores; ecosystems, vertebrates, disturbance ecology, functional and ecological morphology of feeding in fishes, rare amphibians and reptiles, genomics in ecological experiments, ecotoxicology, global carbon cycle, plant-animal interactions. *Total annual research expenditures:* $1.9 million. *Unit head:* Dr. Valerie Harwood, Professor and Chair, 813-974-1524, Fax: 813-974-3263, E-mail: vharwood@usf.edu. *Application contact:* Dr. Stephen Deban, Associate Professor and Graduate Program Director, 813-974-2242, E-mail: sdeban@usf.edu.
Website: http://biology.usf.edu/ib/grad/

The University of Tennessee, Graduate School, College of Arts and Sciences, Department of Ecology and Evolutionary Biology, Knoxville, TN 37996. Offers behavior (MS, PhD); ecology (MS, PhD); evolutionary biology (MS, PhD). *Program availability:* Part-time. *Degree requirements:* For master's, thesis; for doctorate, thesis/dissertation. *Entrance requirements:* For master's and doctorate, GRE General Test, minimum GPA of 2.7. Additional exam requirements/recommendations for international students: Required—TOEFL. Electronic applications accepted.

The University of Tennessee, Graduate School, College of Arts and Sciences, Department of Mathematics, Knoxville, TN 37996. Offers applied mathematics (MS); mathematical ecology (PhD); mathematics (M Math, MS, PhD). *Program availability:* Part-time. *Degree requirements:* For master's, thesis or alternative; for doctorate, one foreign language, thesis/dissertation. *Entrance requirements:* For master's and doctorate, minimum GPA of 2.7. Additional exam requirements/recommendations for international students: Required—TOEFL. Electronic applications accepted.

The University of Texas at Austin, Graduate School, College of Natural Sciences, School of Biological Sciences, Program in Ecology, Evolution and Behavior, Austin, TX 78712-1111. Offers PhD. *Entrance requirements:* For doctorate, GRE General Test. Additional exam requirements/recommendations for international students: Required—TOEFL. Electronic applications accepted.

The University of Texas at San Antonio, College of Sciences, Department of Environmental Science and Ecology, San Antonio, TX 78249-0617. Offers MS. *Students:* 15 full-time (10 women), 16 part-time (12 women); includes 13 minority (2 Black or African American, non-Hispanic/Latino; 9 Hispanic/Latino; 1 Native Hawaiian or other Pacific Islander, non-Hispanic/Latino; 1 Two or more races, non-Hispanic/Latino), 4 international. Average age 28. 12 applicants, 67% accepted, 5 enrolled. In 2017, 17 master's awarded. *Entrance requirements:* For master's, GRE, bachelor's degree in biology, ecology, environmental science, chemistry, geology, engineering, or some other related scientific discipline; one semester each of general statistics, organic chemistry, and environmental science or ecology; undergraduate transcripts; resume; two recommendation letters; statement of purpose. Additional exam requirements/recommendations for international students: Required—TOEFL (minimum score 550 paper-based; 79 iBT), IELTS (minimum score 6.5). *Application deadline:* For fall admission, 6/15 for domestic students, 3/1 for international students; for spring admission, 10/15 for domestic students, 9/15 for international students. Application fee: $50 ($90 for international students). Electronic applications accepted. *Expenses:* Tuition, state resident: full-time $5495. Tuition, nonresident: full-time $21,938. *Required fees:* $1915. Tuition and fees vary according to program. *Faculty research:* Conservation biology, environmental chemistry and toxicology, freshwater ecology, natural resource policy and administration, river restoration. *Total annual research expenditures:* $25,256. *Unit head:* Dr. Janis Bush, Chair, 210-458-5660, E-mail: janis.bush@utsa.edu. *Application contact:* Monica Rodriguez, Director of Graduate Admissions, 210-458-4331, Fax: 210-458-4332, E-mail: graduate.admissions@utsa.edu.
Website: http://www.utsa.edu/ecology/EnvSci/

The University of Toledo, College of Graduate Studies, College of Natural Sciences and Mathematics, Department of Environmental Sciences, Toledo, OH 43606-3390. Offers biology (MS, PhD), including ecology; geology (MS), including earth surface processes. *Program availability:* Part-time. *Degree requirements:* For master's, thesis or alternative. *Entrance requirements:* For master's, GRE General Test, minimum cumulative point-hour ratio of 2.7 for all previous academic work, three letters of recommendation, statement of purpose, transcripts from all prior institutions attended. Additional exam requirements/recommendations for international students: Required—TOEFL (minimum score 550 paper-based; 80 iBT). Electronic applications accepted. *Faculty research:* Environmental geochemistry, geophysics, petrology and mineralogy, paleontology, geohydrology.

University of Toronto, School of Graduate Studies, Faculty of Arts and Science, Department of Ecology and Evolutionary Biology, Toronto, ON M5S 1A1, Canada. Offers M Sc, PhD. *Degree requirements:* For master's, thesis, thesis defense; for doctorate, thesis/dissertation, thesis defense. *Entrance requirements:* For master's, minimum B average in last 2 years; knowledge of physics, chemistry, and biology. Additional exam requirements/recommendations for international students: Required—TOEFL (minimum score 580 paper-based; 93 iBT), TWE (minimum score 5). Electronic applications accepted.

University of Washington, Graduate School, College of the Environment, School of Environmental and Forest Sciences, Seattle, WA 98195. Offers bioresource science and engineering (MS, PhD); environmental horticulture (MEH); forest ecology (MS, PhD); forest management (MFR); forest soils (MS, PhD); restoration ecology (MS, PhD); restoration ecology and environmental horticulture (MS, PhD); social sciences (MS, PhD); sustainable resource management (MS, PhD); wildlife science (MS, PhD); MFR/MAIS; MPA/MS. *Accreditation:* SAF. *Program availability:* Part-time. *Degree requirements:* For master's, thesis; for doctorate, comprehensive exam, thesis/dissertation. *Entrance requirements:* For master's and doctorate, GRE, minimum GPA of 3.0. Additional exam requirements/recommendations for international students: Required—TOEFL. Electronic applications accepted. *Faculty research:* Ecosystem analysis, silviculture and forest protection, paper science and engineering, environmental horticulture and urban forestry, natural resource policy and economics, restoration ecology and environment horticulture, conservation, human dimensions, wildlife, bioresource science and engineering.

University of Wisconsin–Madison, Graduate School, College of Agricultural and Life Sciences, Agroecology Program, Madison, WI 53706-1380. Offers MS. *Degree requirements:* For master's, thesis (for some programs). *Entrance requirements:* For master's, GRE. Additional exam requirements/recommendations for international students: Required—TOEFL (minimum score 580 paper-based; 92 iBT), IELTS (minimum score 7). Electronic applications accepted. *Faculty research:* Multifunctional landscape, socio-ecological systems, participatory solutions to environmental problems.

University of Wyoming, Program in Ecology, Laramie, WY 82071. Offers MS, PhD. *Entrance requirements:* For master's and doctorate, GRE.

Utah State University, School of Graduate Studies, College of Science, Department of Biology, Logan, UT 84322. Offers biology (MS, PhD); ecology (MS, PhD). *Program availability:* Part-time. *Degree requirements:* For master's, thesis; for doctorate, thesis/dissertation. *Entrance requirements:* For master's and doctorate, GRE General Test, minimum GPA of 3.0. Additional exam requirements/recommendations for international students: Required—TOEFL (minimum score 575 paper-based). *Faculty research:* Plant, insect, microbial, and animal biology.

Utah State University, School of Graduate Studies, S.J. and Jessie E. Quinney College of Natural Resources, Department of Environment and Society, Logan, UT 84322.

Offers bioregional planning (MS); geography (MA, MS); human dimensions of ecosystem science and management (MS, PhD); recreation resource management (MS, PhD). *Degree requirements:* For master's, comprehensive exam, thesis (for some programs). *Entrance requirements:* For master's and doctorate, GRE General Test, minimum GPA of 3.0. Additional exam requirements/recommendations for international students: Required—TOEFL. Electronic applications accepted. *Faculty research:* Geographic information systems/geographic and environmental education, bioregional planning, natural resource and environmental policy, outdoor recreation and tourism, natural resource and environmental management.

Utah State University, School of Graduate Studies, S.J. and Jessie E. Quinney College of Natural Resources, Department of Watershed Sciences, Logan, UT 84322. Offers ecology (MS, PhD); fisheries biology (MS, PhD); watershed science (MS, PhD). *Degree requirements:* For master's, thesis (for some programs); for doctorate, thesis/dissertation. *Entrance requirements:* For master's and doctorate, GRE General Test, minimum GPA of 3.2. Additional exam requirements/recommendations for international students: Required—TOEFL. Electronic applications accepted. *Faculty research:* Behavior, population ecology, habitat, conservation biology, restoration, aquatic ecology, fisheries management, fluvial geomorphology, remote sensing, conservation biology.

Utah State University, School of Graduate Studies, S.J. and Jessie E. Quinney College of Natural Resources, Department of Wildland Resources, Logan, UT 84322. Offers ecology (MS, PhD); forestry (MS, PhD); range science (MS, PhD); wildlife biology (MS, PhD). *Program availability:* Part-time. *Degree requirements:* For master's, thesis; for doctorate, comprehensive exam, thesis/dissertation. *Entrance requirements:* For master's and doctorate, GRE General Test, minimum GPA of 3.0. Additional exam requirements/recommendations for international students: Required—TOEFL. *Faculty research:* Range plant ecophysiology, plant community ecology, ruminant nutrition, population ecology.

Washington University in St. Louis, The Graduate School, Division of Biology and Biomedical Sciences, Program in Evolution, Ecology and Population Biology, St. Louis, MO 63130-4899. Offers ecology (PhD). *Degree requirements:* For doctorate, thesis/dissertation. *Entrance requirements:* For doctorate, GRE General Test, GRE Subject Test. Additional exam requirements/recommendations for international students: Required—TOEFL. Electronic applications accepted. *Faculty research:* Population ecology, community ecology, plant and animal evolution; microbial evolution, evolution of behavior, phylogenetics, systematics, theoretical and experimental population genetics.

Wesleyan University, Graduate Studies, Department of Biology, Middletown, CT 06459. Offers cell and developmental biology (PhD); evolution and ecology (PhD); genetics and genomics (PhD), including bioinformatics; neurobiology and behavior (PhD). Terminal master's awarded for partial completion of doctoral program. *Degree requirements:* For doctorate, comprehensive exam, thesis/dissertation, public seminar. *Entrance requirements:* For doctorate, GRE, official transcripts, three recommendation letters, essay. Additional exam requirements/recommendations for international students: Required—TOEFL. *Application deadline:* For fall admission, 1/15 for domestic and international students. Application fee: $0. Electronic applications accepted. *Financial support:* Stipends available. *Faculty research:* Evolution and ecology, neurobiology and behavior, cell and developmental biology, genetics, genomics and bioinformatics. *Unit head:* Dr. Ann Burke, Chair/Professor, 860-685-3518, E-mail: acburke@wesleyan.edu. *Application contact:* Diane Meredith, Administrative Assistant IV, 860-685-2157, E-mail: dmeredith@wesleyan.edu.
Website: http://www.wesleyan.edu/bio/

Western Illinois University, School of Graduate Studies, College of Arts and Sciences, Program in Environmental Science: Large River Ecosystems, Macomb, IL 61455-1390. Offers PhD. *Students:* 4 full-time (3 women), 2 part-time (both women), 1 international. Average age 37. 3 applicants, 33% accepted. *Degree requirements:* For doctorate, thesis/dissertation. *Entrance requirements:* For doctorate, GRE, three letters of recommendation, official transcripts, statement of research intent, curriculum vitae. Additional exam requirements/recommendations for international students: Required—TOEFL. *Application deadline:* Applications are processed on a rolling basis. Application fee: $30. *Financial support:* In 2017–18, 4 students received support, including 1 research assistantship with full tuition reimbursement available (averaging $7,544 per year), 3 teaching assistantships with full tuition reimbursements available (averaging $8,688 per year). *Unit head:* Dr. Roger Viadero, Director, Institute for Environmental Sciences, 309-298-2040. *Application contact:* Dr. Nancy Parsons, Associate Provost and Director of Graduate Studies, 309-298-1806, Fax: 309-298-2345, E-mail: grad-office@wiu.edu.
Website: http://wiu.edu/graduate_studies/programs_of_study/environsci_profile.php

Yale University, Graduate School of Arts and Sciences, Department of Ecology and Evolutionary Biology, New Haven, CT 06520. Offers PhD. *Entrance requirements:* For doctorate, GRE General Test, GRE Subject Test (biology).

Environmental Biology

Baylor University, Graduate School, College of Arts and Sciences, Department of Biology, Waco, TX 76798. Offers biology (MA, MS, PhD); environmental biology (MS); limnology (MS). *Program availability:* Part-time. *Faculty:* 13 full-time (3 women). *Students:* 47 full-time (24 women), 2 part-time (1 woman); includes 7 minority (2 Black or African American, non-Hispanic/Latino; 1 Asian, non-Hispanic/Latino; 1 Hispanic/Latino; 3 Two or more races, non-Hispanic/Latino), 6 international. In 2017, 6 master's awarded. *Degree requirements:* For master's, thesis (for some programs); for doctorate, thesis/dissertation. *Entrance requirements:* For master's and doctorate, GRE General Test. Additional exam requirements/recommendations for international students: Required—TOEFL. *Application deadline:* For fall admission, 2/15 priority date for domestic and international students. Applications are processed on a rolling basis. Application fee: $25. *Financial support:* Research assistantships with full and partial tuition reimbursements, teaching assistantships with full and partial tuition reimbursements, career-related internships or fieldwork, Federal Work-Study, institutionally sponsored loans, and tuition waivers (full and partial) available. Support available to part-time students. Financial award application deadline: 2/28. *Faculty research:* Terrestrial ecology, aquatic ecology, genetics. *Unit head:* Dr. Ryan King, Graduate Program Director, 254-710-2150, Fax: 254-710-2969, E-mail: ryan_s_king@baylor.edu. *Application contact:* Tamara Lehmann, Academic Support Associate, 254-710-2578, Fax: 254-710-2969, E-mail: tamara_lehmann@baylor.edu.
Website: http://www.baylor.edu/biology/

Chatham University, Program in Biology, Pittsburgh, PA 15232-2826. Offers environmental biology (MS); human biology (MS). *Program availability:* Part-time. *Faculty:* 1 full-time (0 women), 2 part-time/adjunct (1 woman). *Students:* 51 full-time (39 women), 9 part-time (6 women); includes 23 minority (10 Black or African American, non-Hispanic/Latino; 1 American Indian or Alaska Native, non-Hispanic/Latino; 9 Asian, non-Hispanic/Latino; 3 Hispanic/Latino), 5 international. Average age 25. 180 applicants, 60% accepted, 39 enrolled. In 2017, 52 master's awarded. *Degree requirements:* For master's, thesis optional. *Entrance requirements:* For master's, 3 letters of recommendation. Additional exam requirements/recommendations for international students: Required—TOEFL (minimum score 600 paper-based; 100 iBT), IELTS (minimum score 7), TWE. *Application deadline:* For fall admission, 4/1 priority date for domestic and international students; for spring admission, 11/1 priority date for domestic students, 10/1 priority date for international students. Applications are processed on a rolling basis. Application fee: $45. Electronic applications accepted. Application fee is waived when completed online. *Expenses: Tuition:* Full-time $16,740; part-time $930 per credit. *Required fees:* $486; $27 per credit. $243 per semester. *Financial support:* Applicants required to submit FAFSA. *Faculty research:* Molecular evolution of iron homeostasis, characteristics of soil bacterial communities, gene flow through seed movement, role of gonadotropins in spermatogonial proliferation, phosphatide/inositol metabolism in epithelial cells. *Unit head:* Dr. Lisa Lambert, Director, 412-365-1217, E-mail: lambert@chatham.edu. *Application contact:* Ashlee Bartko, Senior Assistant Director of Graduate Admission, 412-365-1115, Fax: 412-365-1609, E-mail: gradadmissions@chatham.edu.
Website: http://www.chatham.edu/departments/sciences/graduate/biology

Dalhousie University, Faculty of Agriculture, Halifax, NS B3H 4R2, Canada. Offers agriculture (M Sc), including air quality, animal behavior, animal molecular genetics, animal nutrition, animal technology, aquaculture, botany, crop management, crop physiology, ecology, environmental microbiology, food science, horticulture, nutrient management, pest management, physiology, plant biotechnology, plant pathology, soil chemistry, soil fertility, waste management and composting, water quality. *Program availability:* Part-time. *Degree requirements:* For master's, thesis, ATC Exam Teaching Assistantship. *Entrance requirements:* For master's, honors B Sc, minimum GPA of 3.0. Additional exam requirements/recommendations for international students: Required—TOEFL (minimum score 580 paper-based; 92 iBT), IELTS, Michigan English Language Assessment Battery, CanTEST, CAEL. *Faculty research:* Bio-product development, organic agriculture, nutrient management, air and water quality, agricultural biotechnology.

Dartmouth College, School of Graduate and Advanced Studies, Program in Ecology, Evolution, Ecosystems, and Society, Hanover, NH 03755. Offers ecology and evolutionary biology (PhD); sustainability, ecosystems, and environment (PhD). *Faculty:* 9 full-time (5 women). *Students:* 22 full-time (14 women); includes 1 minority (Hispanic/Latino), 3 international. Average age 28. 40 applicants, 15% accepted, 3 enrolled. In 2017, 1 doctorate awarded. *Entrance requirements:* For doctorate, GRE General Test, GRE Subject Test in biology (highly recommended). Additional exam requirements/recommendations for international students: Required—TOEFL. *Application deadline:* For fall admission, 12/1 for domestic students. Electronic applications accepted. *Financial support:* Fellowships, research assistantships, teaching assistantships, institutionally sponsored loans, traineeships, and unspecified assistantships available. Financial award applicants required to submit FAFSA. *Unit head:* Dr. Mathew Ayres, Chair, 603-646-2788. *Application contact:* Amy Layne, Administrative Assistant, 603-646-3847.
Website: http://sites.dartmouth.edu/EEES/

Emporia State University, Department of Biological Sciences, Emporia, KS 66801-5415. Offers botany (MS); environmental biology (MS); forensic science (MS); general biology (MS); microbial and cellular biology (MS); zoology (MS). *Program availability:* Part-time. *Faculty:* 13 full-time (3 women), 1 part-time/adjunct (0 women). *Students:* 20 full-time (11 women), 15 part-time (3 women); includes 3 minority (2 Hispanic/Latino; 1 Two or more races, non-Hispanic/Latino), 17 international. 17 applicants, 59% accepted, 8 enrolled. In 2017, 21 master's awarded. *Degree requirements:* For master's, comprehensive exam or thesis. *Entrance requirements:* For master's, GRE, appropriate undergraduate degree, interview, letters of reference. Additional exam requirements/recommendations for international students: Required—TOEFL (minimum score 520 paper-based; 68 iBT). *Application deadline:* For fall admission, 8/15 priority date for domestic students. Applications are processed on a rolling basis. Application fee: $30 ($75 for international students). Electronic applications accepted. *Expenses:* Tuition, state resident: full-time $6084; part-time $253.50 per credit hour. Tuition, nonresident: full-time $18,924; part-time $788.50 per credit hour. *Required fees:* $1943; $80.95 per credit hour. Tuition and fees vary according to campus/location. *Financial support:* In 2017–18, 7 research assistantships with full tuition reimbursements (averaging $9,747 per year), 15 teaching assistantships with full tuition reimbursements (averaging $7,499 per year) were awarded; career-related internships or fieldwork, Federal Work-Study, institutionally sponsored loans, health care benefits, and unspecified assistantships also available. Financial award application deadline: 3/15; financial award applicants required to submit FAFSA. *Faculty research:* Fisheries, range, and wildlife management; aquatic, plant, grassland, vertebrate, and invertebrate ecology; mammalian and plant systematics, taxonomy, and evolution; immunology, virology, and molecular biology. *Unit head:* Dr. Tim Burnett, Interim Chair, 620-341-5910, Fax: 620-341-5608, E-mail: tburnett@emporia.edu.
Website: http://www.emporia.edu/info/degrees-courses/grad/biology

Georgia State University, College of Arts and Sciences, Department of Biology, Program in Applied and Environmental Microbiology, Atlanta, GA 30302-3083. Offers applied and environmental microbiology (MS, PhD); bioinformatics (MS). *Program availability:* Part-time. Terminal master's awarded for partial completion of doctoral program. *Degree requirements:* For master's, comprehensive exam (for some programs), thesis optional; for doctorate, comprehensive exam, thesis/dissertation. *Entrance requirements:* For master's and doctorate, GRE. *Application deadline:* For fall admission, 7/1 priority date for domestic students, 6/1 priority date for international students; for spring admission, 11/15 priority date for domestic students, 10/15 priority date for international students. Applications are processed on a rolling basis. Application fee: $50. Electronic applications accepted. *Expenses:* Tuition, state resident: full-time $7020. Tuition, nonresident: full-time $22,518. *Required fees:* $2128. Tuition and fees vary according to degree level and program. *Financial support:* In 2017–18, fellowships with full tuition reimbursements (averaging $22,000 per year), research assistantships with full tuition reimbursements (averaging $20,000 per year) were awarded. Financial award application deadline: 12/3. *Faculty research:* Bioremediation, biofilms, indoor air quality control, environmental toxicology, product biosynthesis. *Unit head:* Dr. Charles Derby, Director of Graduate Studies, 404-413-5393, Fax: 404-413-5446, E-mail: cderby@gsu.edu.
Website: http://biology.gsu.edu/

Governors State University, College of Arts and Sciences, Program in Environmental Biology, University Park, IL 60484. Offers MS. *Program availability:* Part-time. *Faculty:*

41 full-time (14 women), 45 part-time/adjunct (18 women). *Students:* 2 full-time (0 women), 14 part-time (7 women); includes 5 minority (2 Black or African American, non-Hispanic/Latino; 1 Asian, non-Hispanic/Latino; 2 Hispanic/Latino), 1 international. Average age 32. 11 applicants, 55% accepted, 4 enrolled. In 2017, 1 master's awarded. *Application deadline:* For fall admission, 4/1 for domestic students. Applications are processed on a rolling basis. Application fee: $50. Electronic applications accepted. *Expenses:* Tuition, state resident: full-time $8472; part-time $353 per credit hour. Tuition, nonresident: full-time $16,944; part-time $706 per credit hour. *Required fees:* $1824; $76 per credit hour. $38 per term. Tuition and fees vary according to course load, degree level and program. *Financial support:* Application deadline: 5/1; applicants required to submit FAFSA. *Unit head:* Steve Shih, Chair, Division of Science, Mathematics, and Technology, 708-534-5000 Ext. 4547, E-mail: sshih@govst.edu.

Hampton University, School of Science, Department of Biological Sciences, Hampton, VA 23668. Offers biology (MS); environmental science (MS). *Program availability:* Part-time. *Students:* 1 (woman) full-time, 1 (woman) part-time; both minorities (both Black or African American, non-Hispanic/Latino). Average age 24. 7 applicants. In 2017, 2 master's awarded. *Degree requirements:* For master's, comprehensive exam (for some programs), thesis optional. *Entrance requirements:* For master's, GRE General Test. *Application deadline:* For fall admission, 6/1 priority date for domestic students, 6/1 for international students; for spring admission, 11/1 priority date for domestic students, 11/1 for international students; for summer admission, 4/1 priority date for domestic students, 2/1 priority date for international students. Applications are processed on a rolling basis. Application fee: $35. Electronic applications accepted. *Expenses:* *Tuition:* Full-time $22,630; part-time $575 per semester hour. *Required fees:* $70. Tuition and fees vary according to program. *Financial support:* Fellowships, research assistantships, teaching assistantships, career-related internships or fieldwork, Federal Work-Study, institutionally sponsored loans, scholarships/grants, and stipends available. Support available to part-time students. Financial award application deadline: 6/30; financial award applicants required to submit FAFSA. *Faculty research:* Molecular mechanisms responsible for initiation, promotion, and progression of breast, colon, prostate, thyroid, and skin cancers; isolation and characterization of bacteria in natural and contaminated environments and study of probable uses in biocontrol, diabetes, and hypertension. *Unit head:* Dr. Jermel Watkins, Chair, 757-727-5267, E-mail: jermel.watkins@hamptonu.edu.

Hood College, Graduate School, Program in Environmental Biology, Frederick, MD 21701-8575. Offers environmental biology (MS); geographic information systems (Certificate). *Program availability:* Part-time, evening/weekend. *Faculty:* 2 full-time (1 woman), 3 part-time/adjunct (2 women). *Students:* 4 full-time (3 women), 35 part-time (25 women); includes 8 minority (2 Black or African American, non-Hispanic/Latino; 2 Asian, non-Hispanic/Latino; 2 Hispanic/Latino; 2 Two or more races, non-Hispanic/Latino), 2 international. Average age 30. 16 applicants, 81% accepted, 7 enrolled. In 2017, 12 master's, 7 other advanced degrees awarded. *Degree requirements:* For master's, thesis or alternative. *Entrance requirements:* For master's, minimum GPA of 2.75, 1 year of undergraduate biology and chemistry, 1 semester of mathematics, essay. Additional exam requirements/recommendations for international students: Required—TOEFL (minimum score 575 paper-based; 89 iBT), IELTS (minimum score 6.5). *Application deadline:* For fall admission, 8/15 priority date for domestic students, 8/5 for international students; for spring admission, 12/1 priority date for domestic students, 12/1 for international students; for summer admission, 5/1 for domestic students, 4/15 for international students. Applications are processed on a rolling basis. Application fee: $35. Electronic applications accepted. *Expenses:* $465 per credit plus $110 comprehensive fee per semester. *Financial support:* Research assistantships with full tuition reimbursements, tuition waivers (partial), and unspecified assistantships available. Financial award applicants required to submit FAFSA. *Unit head:* Dr. April M. Boulton, Dean of the Graduate School, 301-696-3600, E-mail: gofurther@hood.edu. *Application contact:* Jan Marcus, Assistant Director of Graduate Admissions, 301-696-3600, E-mail: gofurther@hood.edu.
Website: http://www.hood.edu/graduate

Massachusetts Institute of Technology, School of Engineering, Department of Civil and Environmental Engineering, Cambridge, MA 02139. Offers biological oceanography (PhD, Sc D); chemical oceanography (PhD, Sc D); civil and environmental engineering (M Eng, SM, PhD, Sc D); civil and environmental systems (PhD, Sc D); civil engineering (PhD, Sc D, CE); civil engineering and computation (PhD); coastal engineering (PhD, Sc D); construction engineering and management (PhD, Sc D); environmental biology (PhD, Sc D); environmental chemistry (PhD, Sc D); environmental engineering (PhD, Sc D); environmental engineering and computation (PhD); environmental fluid mechanics (PhD, Sc D); geotechnical and geoenvironmental engineering (PhD, Sc D); hydrology (PhD, Sc D); information technology (PhD, Sc D); oceanographic engineering (PhD, Sc D); structures and materials (PhD, Sc D); transportation (PhD, Sc D); SM/MBA. *Degree requirements:* For master's, thesis; for doctorate, comprehensive exam, thesis/dissertation; for CE, comprehensive exam, thesis. *Entrance requirements:* For master's, doctorate, and CE, GRE General Test. Additional exam requirements/recommendations for international students: Required—TOEFL, IELTS. Electronic applications accepted. *Faculty research:* Environmental chemistry, environmental fluid mechanics and coastal engineering, environmental microbiology, geotechnical engineering and geomechanics, hydrology and hydro climatology, infrastructure systems, mechanics of materials and structures, transportation systems.

Missouri University of Science and Technology, Department of Biological Sciences, Rolla, MO 65409. Offers applied and environmental biology (MS). *Faculty:* 10 full-time (3 women). *Students:* 10 full-time (6 women), 6 part-time (5 women); includes 1 minority (Hispanic/Latino), 6 international. Average age 28. 19 applicants, 68% accepted, 7 enrolled. In 2017, 8 master's awarded. *Entrance requirements:* For master's, GRE (minimum score 600 quantitative, 4 writing). Additional exam requirements/recommendations for international students: Required—TOEFL (minimum score 570 paper-based). Application fee: $50. *Expenses:* Tuition, state resident: full-time $7391; part-time $3696 per year. Tuition, nonresident: full-time $21,712; part-time $10,857 per year. *Required fees:* $728; $564 per unit. Tuition and fees vary according to course load. *Financial support:* In 2017–18, 6 research assistantships (averaging $1,810 per year), 1 teaching assistantship (averaging $1,814 per year) were awarded; institutionally sponsored loans and unspecified assistantships also available. *Total annual research expenditures:* $306,173. *Unit head:* Dr. David Duvernell, Chair, 573-341-6988, Fax: 573-341-4821, E-mail: duvernelld@mst.edu. *Application contact:* Debbie Schwertz, Admissions Coordinator, 573-341-6013, Fax: 573-341-6271, E-mail: schwertz@mst.edu.
Website: http://biosci.mst.edu/

Morgan State University, School of Graduate Studies, School of Computer, Mathematical, and Natural Sciences, Department of Biology, Program in Bioenvironmental Science, Baltimore, MD 21251. Offers PhD. *Degree requirements:* For doctorate, comprehensive exam, thesis/dissertation, oral defense of dissertation. *Entrance requirements:* For doctorate, GRE General Test, GRE Subject Test (biology, chemistry, or related science), bachelor's or master's degree in biology, chemistry, physics or related field; minimum GPA of 3.0. Additional exam requirements/recommendations for international students: Required—TOEFL (minimum score 550 paper-based). *Application deadline:* For fall admission, 2/1 priority date for domestic students; for spring admission, 10/1 priority date for domestic students. Applications are processed on a rolling basis. Application fee: $0. *Expenses:* Tuition, state resident: part-time $433 per credit. Tuition, nonresident: part-time $851 per credit. *Required fees:* $81.50 per credit. *Financial support:* Application deadline: 2/1. *Unit head:* Chunlei Fan, Program Coordinator, 443-885-5933, E-mail: chunlei.fan@morgan.edu. *Application contact:* Dr. Dean Campbell, Graduate Recruitment Specialist, 443-885-3185, Fax: 443-885-8226, E-mail: dean.campbell@morgan.edu.

Nicholls State University, Graduate Studies, College of Arts and Sciences, Department of Biological Sciences, Thibodaux, LA 70310. Offers marine and environmental biology (MS). *Program availability:* Part-time. *Degree requirements:* For master's, comprehensive exam, thesis. *Entrance requirements:* For master's, GRE. Additional exam requirements/recommendations for international students: Required—TOEFL (minimum score 600 paper-based). *Faculty research:* Bioremediation, ecology, public health, biotechnology, physiology.

Ohio University, Graduate College, College of Arts and Sciences, Department of Environmental and Plant Biology, Athens, OH 45701-2979. Offers MS, PhD. *Program availability:* Part-time. *Degree requirements:* For master's, thesis, 2 terms of teaching experience; for doctorate, comprehensive exam, thesis/dissertation, 2 terms of teaching experience. *Entrance requirements:* For master's, GRE General Test, minimum GPA of 3.0; for doctorate, GRE General Test, minimum GPA of 3.2. Additional exam requirements/recommendations for international students: Required—TOEFL (minimum score 620 paper-based; 105 iBT) or IELTS (minimum score 7.5). Electronic applications accepted. *Faculty research:* Eastern deciduous forest ecology, evolutionary developmental plant biology, phylogenetic systematics, plant cell wall biotechnology.

Oregon State University, College of Science, Program in Microbiology, Corvallis, OR 97331. Offers environmental microbiology (MA, MS, PhD); food microbiology (MA, MS, PhD); genomics (MA, MS, PhD); immunology (MA, MS, PhD); microbial ecology (MA, MS, PhD); microbial evolution (MA, MS, PhD); parasitology (MA, MS, PhD); pathogenic microbiology (MA, MS, PhD); virology (MA). Terminal master's awarded for partial completion of doctoral program. *Entrance requirements:* For master's and doctorate, GRE. Additional exam requirements/recommendations for international students: Required—TOEFL (minimum score 600 paper-based; 100 iBT). *Application deadline:* For fall admission, 1/1 for domestic and international students. Application fee: $75 ($85 for international students). *Financial support:* Application deadline: 1/15. *Faculty research:* Genetics, physiology, biotechnology, pathogenic microbiology, plant virology. *Unit head:* Dr. Jerri Bartholomew, Professor and Department Head, 541-737-1834, E-mail: barthol j@science.oregonstate.edu. *Application contact:* Kim Halsey, Graduate Admissions Committee Chair, 541-737-1831, E-mail: kim.halsey@oregonstate.edu.
Website: http://microbiology.science.oregonstate.edu/

Regis University, Regis College, Denver, CO 80221-1099. Offers biomedical sciences (MS); developmental practice (MDP); education (MA); environmental biology (MS). *Accreditation:* TEAC. *Program availability:* Part-time. *Degree requirements:* For master's, thesis (for some programs), capstone presentation. *Entrance requirements:* For master's, official transcript reflecting baccalaureate degree awarded from U.S.-based regionally-accredited college or university. Additional exam requirements/recommendations for international students: Required—TOEFL (minimum score 550 paper-based; 82 iBT). Electronic applications accepted. *Expenses:* Contact institution.

Rutgers University–New Brunswick, Graduate School-New Brunswick, Department of Environmental Sciences, Piscataway, NJ 08854-8097. Offers air pollution and resources (MS, PhD); aquatic biology (MS, PhD); aquatic chemistry (MS, PhD); atmospheric science (MS, PhD); chemistry and physics of aerosol and hydrosol systems (MS, PhD); environmental chemistry (MS, PhD); environmental microbiology (MS, PhD); environmental toxicology (PhD); exposure assessment (PhD); fate and effects of pollutants (MS, PhD); pollution prevention and control (MS, PhD); water and wastewater treatment (MS, PhD); water resources (MS, PhD). Terminal master's awarded for partial completion of doctoral program. *Degree requirements:* For master's, comprehensive exam, thesis or alternative, oral final exam; for doctorate, comprehensive exam, thesis/dissertation, thesis defense, qualifying exam. *Entrance requirements:* For master's and doctorate, GRE General Test. Additional exam requirements/recommendations for international students: Required—TOEFL. Electronic applications accepted. *Faculty research:* Biological waste treatment; contaminant fate and transport; air, soil and water quality.

State University of New York College of Environmental Science and Forestry, Department of Environmental and Forest Biology, Syracuse, NY 13210-2779. Offers applied ecology (MPS); chemical ecology (MPS, MS, PhD); conservation biology (MPS, MS, PhD); ecology (MPS, MS, PhD); entomology (MPS, MS, PhD); environmental interpretation (MPS, MS, PhD); environmental physiology (MPS, MS, PhD); fish and wildlife biology and management (MPS, MS, PhD); forest pathology and mycology (MPS, MS, PhD); plant biotechnology (MPS); plant science and biotechnology (MPS, MS, PhD). *Program availability:* Part-time. *Faculty:* 30 full-time (10 women), 4 part-time/adjunct (3 women). *Students:* 117 full-time (65 women), 18 part-time (6 women); includes 8 minority (6 American Indian or Alaska Native, non-Hispanic/Latino; 1 Asian, non-Hispanic/Latino; 1 Hispanic/Latino), 23 international. Average age 30. 84 applicants, 52% accepted, 31 enrolled. In 2017, 30 master's, 3 doctorates awarded. Terminal master's awarded for partial completion of doctoral program. *Degree requirements:* For master's, thesis (for some programs), capstone seminar; for doctorate, comprehensive exam, thesis/dissertation, capstone seminar. *Entrance requirements:* For master's and doctorate, GRE General Test, minimum GPA of 3.0. Additional exam requirements/recommendations for international students: Required—TOEFL (minimum score 550 paper-based; 80 iBT), IELTS (minimum score 6). *Application deadline:* For fall admission, 2/1 priority date for domestic and international students; for spring admission, 11/1 priority date for domestic and international students. Applications are processed on a rolling basis. Application fee: $60. Electronic applications accepted. *Expenses:* Tuition, state resident: full-time $10,870; part-time $453 per credit. Tuition, nonresident: full-time $22,210; part-time $925 per credit. *Required fees:* $1435; $70.85 per credit. One-time fee: $25 full-time. Part-time tuition and fees vary according to course load. *Financial support:* In 2017–18, 42 students received support. Unspecified assistantships available. Financial award application deadline: 6/30; financial award applicants required to submit FAFSA. *Faculty research:* Ecology, conservation biology, fish and wildlife biology and management, plant science, entomology. *Total annual research expenditures:* $5.3 million. *Unit head:* Dr. Neil H. Ringler, Chair, 315-470-6803, Fax: 315-470-6934, E-mail: nhringle@esf.edu. *Application contact:* Scott Shannon, Associate Provost for Instruction/Dean of the Graduate School, 315-470-6599, E-mail: esfgrad@esf.edu.
Website: http://www.esf.edu/efb/grad/default.asp

Universidad del Turabo, Graduate Programs, Programs in Science and Technology, Gurabo, PR 00778-3030. Offers environmental analysis (MSE), including environmental chemistry; environmental management (MSE), including pollution management; environmental science (D Sc), including environmental biology. *Entrance requirements:* For master's, GRE, EXADEP, GMAT, interview, official transcript, essay, recommendation letters; for doctorate, GRE, EXADEP, GMAT, official transcript, recommendation letters, essay, curriculum vitae, interview. Electronic applications accepted.

University of Alberta, Faculty of Graduate Studies and Research, Department of Biological Sciences, Edmonton, AB T6G 2E1, Canada. Offers environmental biology and ecology (M Sc, PhD); microbiology and biotechnology (M Sc, PhD); molecular biology and genetics (M Sc, PhD); physiology and cell biology (M Sc, PhD); plant biology (M Sc, PhD); systematics and evolution (M Sc, PhD). Terminal master's awarded for partial completion of doctoral program. *Degree requirements:* For master's, thesis; for doctorate, thesis/dissertation. *Entrance requirements:* Additional exam requirements/recommendations for international students: Required—TOEFL.

University of California, Santa Cruz, Division of Graduate Studies, Division of Physical and Biological Sciences, Environmental Toxicology Department, Santa Cruz, CA 95064. Offers MS, PhD. Terminal master's awarded for partial completion of doctoral program. *Degree requirements:* For master's, comprehensive exam, thesis; for doctorate, thesis/dissertation, qualifying exams. *Entrance requirements:* For master's and doctorate, GRE. Additional exam requirements/recommendations for international students: Required—TOEFL (minimum score 550 paper-based; 83 iBT); Recommended—IELTS (minimum score 8). Electronic applications accepted. *Faculty research:* Molecular mechanisms of reactive DNA methylation toxicity, anthropogenic perturbations of biogeochemical cycles, anaerobic microbiology and biotransformation of pollutants and toxic metals, organismal responses and therapeutic treatment of toxins, microbiology, molecular genetics, genomics.

University of Guelph, Graduate Studies, Ontario Agricultural College, Department of Environmental Biology, Guelph, ON N1G 2W1, Canada. Offers entomology (M Sc, PhD); environmental microbiology and biotechnology (M Sc, PhD); environmental toxicology (M Sc, PhD); plant and forest systems (M Sc, PhD); plant pathology (M Sc, PhD). *Program availability:* Part-time. *Degree requirements:* For master's, thesis; for doctorate, comprehensive exam, thesis/dissertation. *Entrance requirements:* For master's, minimum 75% average during previous 2 years of course work; for doctorate, minimum 75% average. Additional exam requirements/recommendations for international students: Required—TOEFL or IELTS. Electronic applications accepted. *Faculty research:* Entomology, environmental microbiology and biotechnology, environmental toxicology, forest ecology, plant pathology.

University of Louisiana at Lafayette, College of Sciences, Department of Biology, Lafayette, LA 70504. Offers biology (MS); environmental and evolutionary biology (PhD). Terminal master's awarded for partial completion of doctoral program. *Degree requirements:* For master's, thesis; for doctorate, 2 foreign languages, comprehensive exam, thesis/dissertation. *Entrance requirements:* For master's, GRE General Test, minimum GPA of 2.75; for doctorate, GRE General Test, GRE Subject Test, minimum GPA of 3.0. Additional exam requirements/recommendations for international students: Required—TOEFL (minimum score 550 paper-based). *Application deadline:* For fall admission, 5/15 for domestic and international students; for spring admission, 10/1 for domestic and international students. Applications are processed on a rolling basis. Application fee: $25 ($30 for international students). Electronic applications accepted. *Financial support:* Application deadline: 5/1. *Faculty research:* Structure and ultrastructure, system biology, ecology, processes, environmental physiology. *Unit head:* Dr. Scott France, Graduate Admissions Chair, 337-482-6320, E-mail: france@louisiana.edu. *Application contact:* Dr. Paul Leberg, Graduate Coordinator, 337-482-6750, Fax: 337-482-5834, E-mail: leberg@louisiana.edu.

University of Louisville, Graduate School, College of Arts and Sciences, Department of Biology, Louisville, KY 40292-0001. Offers biology (MS); environmental biology (PhD). *Program availability:* Part-time. *Faculty:* 25 full-time (9 women), 6 part-time/adjunct (3 women). *Students:* 38 full-time (17 women), 7 part-time (4 women); includes 9 minority (1 Asian, non-Hispanic/Latino; 4 Hispanic/Latino; 4 Two or more races, non-Hispanic/Latino), 11 international. Average age 29. 32 applicants, 50% accepted, 13 enrolled. In 2017, 6 master's, 1 doctorate awarded. Terminal master's awarded for partial completion of doctoral program. *Degree requirements:* For master's, comprehensive exam, thesis (for some programs); for doctorate, comprehensive exam, thesis/dissertation. *Entrance requirements:* For master's, GRE, MCAT, or DAT; for doctorate, GRE. Additional exam requirements/recommendations for international students: Required—TOEFL (minimum score 550 paper-based; 83 iBT), IELTS (minimum score 6.5). *Application deadline:* For fall admission, 1/15 priority date for domestic and international students; for spring admission, 12/1 for domestic and international students; for summer admission, 4/15 for domestic and international students. Applications are processed on a rolling basis. Application fee: $65. Electronic applications accepted. *Expenses:* Tuition, state resident: full-time $12,246; part-time $681 per credit hour. Tuition, nonresident: full-time $25,486; part-time $1417 per credit hour. *Required fees:* $196. Tuition and fees vary according to course load, program and reciprocity agreements. *Financial support:* In 2017–18, 2 fellowships with full tuition reimbursements (averaging $22,000 per year), 2 research assistantships with full tuition reimbursements (averaging $22,000 per year), 24 teaching assistantships with full tuition reimbursements (averaging $22,000 per year) were awarded; unspecified assistantships also available. Financial award application deadline: 1/15. *Faculty research:* Molecular, microbiology, ecology, animal behavior, evolution. *Total annual research expenditures:* $744,439. *Unit head:* Dr. Ronald Fell, Chair, 502-852-6771, Fax: 502-852-0725, E-mail: rdfell@louisville.edu. *Application contact:* Latonia Craig, Director of Graduate Recruitment and Diversity Retention, 502-852-5207, E-mail: gradadm@louisville.edu.
Website: http://louisville.edu/biology

The University of Manchester, School of Biological Sciences, Manchester, United Kingdom. Offers adaptive organismal biology (M Phil, PhD); animal biology (M Phil, PhD); biochemistry (M Phil, PhD); bioinformatics (M Phil, PhD); biomolecular sciences (M Phil, PhD); biotechnology (M Phil, PhD); cell biology (M Phil, PhD); cell matrix research (M Phil, PhD); channels and transporters (M Phil, PhD); developmental biology (M Phil, PhD); environmental biology (M Phil, PhD); evolutionary biology (M Phil, PhD); gene expression (M Phil, PhD); genetics (M Phil, PhD); history of science, technology and medicine (M Phil, PhD); immunology (M Phil, PhD); integrative neurobiology and behavior (M Phil, PhD); membrane trafficking (M Phil, PhD); microbiology (M Phil, PhD); molecular and cellular neuroscience (M Phil, PhD); molecular biology (M Phil, PhD); molecular cancer studies (M Phil, PhD); neuroscience (M Phil, PhD); ophthalmology (M Phil, PhD); optometry (M Phil, PhD); organelle function (M Phil, PhD); pharmacology (M Phil, PhD); physiology (M Phil, PhD); plant sciences (M Phil, PhD); stem cell research (M Phil, PhD); structural biology (M Phil, PhD); systems neuroscience (M Phil, PhD); toxicology (M Phil, PhD).

University of Massachusetts Amherst, Graduate School, College of Natural Sciences, Department of Environmental Conservation, Amherst, MA 01003. Offers building systems (MS, PhD); environmental policy and human dimensions (MS, PhD); forest resources (MS, PhD); sustainability science (MS); water, wetlands and watersheds (MS, PhD); wildlife and fisheries conservation (MS, PhD). *Program availability:* Part-time. Terminal master's awarded for partial completion of doctoral program. *Degree requirements:* For master's, thesis or alternative; for doctorate, comprehensive exam, thesis/dissertation. *Entrance requirements:* For master's and doctorate, GRE General Test. Additional exam requirements/recommendations for international students: Required—TOEFL (minimum score 550 paper-based; 80 iBT), IELTS (minimum score 6.5). Electronic applications accepted.

University of Southern California, Graduate School, Dana and David Dornsife College of Letters, Arts and Sciences, Department of Biological Sciences, Program in Marine Biology and Biological Oceanography, Los Angeles, CA 90089. Offers marine and environmental biology (MS); marine biology and biological oceanography (PhD). Terminal master's awarded for partial completion of doctoral program. *Degree requirements:* For master's, research paper; for doctorate, comprehensive exam, thesis/dissertation, qualifying examination, dissertation defense. *Entrance requirements:* For master's and doctorate, GRE, 3 letters of recommendation, personal statement, resume, minimum GPA of 3.0. Additional exam requirements/recommendations for international students: Required—TOEFL (minimum score 600 paper-based; 100 iBT). Electronic applications accepted. *Faculty research:* Microbial ecology, biogeochemistry, and geobiology; biodiversity and molecular ecology; integrative organismal biology; conservation biology; marine genomics.

University of South Florida, College of Arts and Sciences, Department of Integrative Biology, Tampa, FL 33620-9951. Offers biology (MS), including ecology and evolution (MS, PhD), environmental and ecological microbiology (MS, PhD), physiology and morphology (MS, PhD); integrative biology (PhD), including ecology and evolution (MS, PhD), environmental and ecological microbiology (MS, PhD), physiology and morphology (MS, PhD). *Program availability:* Part-time. *Faculty:* 14 full-time (5 women). *Students:* 21 full-time (11 women), 1 (woman) part-time; includes 1 minority (Asian, non-Hispanic/Latino), 2 international. Average age 30. 35 applicants, 17% accepted, 5 enrolled. In 2017, 7 master's, 5 doctorates awarded. *Degree requirements:* For master's, comprehensive exam, thesis (for some programs); for doctorate, comprehensive exam, thesis/dissertation. *Entrance requirements:* For master's and doctorate, GRE General Test, minimum GPA of 3.0 in last 60 hours of BS. *Application deadline:* For fall admission, 11/30 priority date for domestic and international students; for spring admission, 7/1 priority date for domestic and international students. Application fee: $30. Electronic applications accepted. *Financial support:* In 2017–18, 7 students received support. Research assistantships, teaching assistantships, and unspecified assistantships available. Financial award application deadline: 6/30; financial award applicants required to submit FAFSA. *Faculty research:* Marine ecology, ecosystem responses to urbanization, biomechanical and physiological mechanisms of animal movement, population biology and conservation, microbial ecology and public health microbiology, natural diversity of parasites and herbivores; ecosystems, vertebrates, disturbance ecology, functional and ecological morphology of feeding in fishes, rare amphibians and reptiles, genomics in ecological experiments, ecotoxicology, global carbon cycle, plant-animal interactions. *Total annual research expenditures:* $1.9 million. *Unit head:* Dr. Valerie Harwood, Professor and Chair, 813-974-1524, Fax: 813-974-3263, E-mail: vharwood@usf.edu. *Application contact:* Dr. Stephen Deban, Associate Professor and Graduate Program Director, 813-974-2242, E-mail: sdeban@usf.edu.
Website: http://biology.usf.edu/ib/grad/

University of Wisconsin–Madison, School of Medicine and Public Health, Molecular and Environmental Toxicology Graduate Program, Madison, WI 53706. Offers MS, PhD. *Application contact:* Mark Marohl, Graduate Program Coordinator, 608-263-4580, E-mail: mdmarohl@wisc.edu.
Website: http://www.med.wisc.edu/metc/

Washington University in St. Louis, The Graduate School, Division of Biology and Biomedical Sciences, St. Louis, MO 63130-4899. Offers biochemistry (PhD); computational and molecular biophysics (PhD); computational and systems biology (PhD); developmental, regenerative, and stem cell biology (PhD); evolution, ecology and population biology (PhD), including ecology, environmental biology, evolutionary biology, genetics; human and statistical genetics (PhD); immunology (PhD); molecular cell biology (PhD); molecular genetics and genomics (PhD); molecular microbiology and microbial pathogenesis (PhD); neurosciences (PhD); plant and microbial biosciences (PhD); MD/PhD. *Degree requirements:* For doctorate, thesis/dissertation. *Entrance requirements:* For doctorate, GRE General Test, GRE Subject Test. Additional exam requirements/recommendations for international students: Required—TOEFL. Electronic applications accepted.

Youngstown State University, Graduate School, College of Science, Technology, Engineering and Mathematics, Department of Biological Sciences, Youngstown, OH 44555-0001. Offers environmental biology (MS); molecular biology, microbiology, and genetic (MS); physiology and anatomy (MS). *Program availability:* Part-time. *Degree requirements:* For master's, comprehensive exam, thesis, oral review. *Entrance requirements:* For master's, GRE General Test, minimum GPA of 2.7. Additional exam requirements/recommendations for international students: Required—TOEFL. *Faculty research:* Cell biology, neurophysiology, molecular biology, neurobiology, gene regulation.

Evolutionary Biology

Arizona State University at the Tempe campus, College of Liberal Arts and Sciences, School of Life Sciences, Tempe, AZ 85287-4601. Offers animal behavior (PhD); applied ethics (biomedical and health ethics) (MA); biology (MS, PhD), including biology, biology and society, complex adaptive systems science (PhD), plant biology and conservation (MS); environmental life sciences (PhD); evolutionary biology (PhD); history and philosophy of science (PhD); human and social dimensions of science and technology (PhD); microbiology (PhD); molecular and cellular biology (PhD); neuroscience (PhD). Terminal master's awarded for partial completion of doctoral program. *Degree requirements:* For master's, thesis (for some programs), interactive Program of Study (iPOS) submitted before completing 50 percent of required credit hours; for doctorate, variable foreign language requirement, comprehensive exam, thesis/dissertation, interactive Program of Study (iPOS) submitted before completing 50 percent of required credit hours. *Entrance requirements:* For master's and doctorate, GRE, minimum GPA of 3.0 or equivalent in last 2 years of work leading to bachelor's degree. Additional exam requirements/recommendations for international students: Required—TOEFL (minimum score 600 paper-based; 100 iBT). Electronic applications accepted.

Evolutionary Biology

Brown University, Graduate School, Division of Biology and Medicine, Department of Ecology and Evolutionary Biology, Providence, RI 02912. Offers PhD. *Degree requirements:* For doctorate, thesis/dissertation, preliminary exam. *Entrance requirements:* For doctorate, GRE General Test, GRE Subject Test. Additional exam requirements/recommendations for international students: Required—TOEFL. Electronic applications accepted. *Faculty research:* Marine ecology, behavioral ecology, population genetics, evolutionary morphology, plant ecology.

Columbia University, Graduate School of Arts and Sciences, New York, NY 10027. Offers African-American studies (MA); American studies (MA); anthropology (MA, PhD); art history and archaeology (MA, PhD); astronomy (PhD); biological sciences (PhD); biotechnology (MA); chemical physics (PhD); chemistry (PhD); classical studies (MA, PhD); classics (MA, PhD); climate and society (MA); conservation biology (MA); earth and environmental sciences (PhD); East Asia: regional studies (MA); East Asian languages and cultures (MA, PhD); ecology, evolution and environmental biology (MA), including conservation biology; ecology, evolution, and environmental biology (PhD), including ecology and evolutionary biology, evolutionary primatology; economics (MA, PhD); English and comparative literature (MA, PhD); French and Romance philology (MA, PhD); Germanic languages (MA, PhD); global French studies (MA); global thought (MA); Hispanic cultural studies (MA); history (PhD); history and literature (MA); human rights studies (MA); Islamic studies (MA); Italian (MA, PhD); Japanese pedagogy (MA); Jewish studies (MA); Latin America and the Caribbean: regional studies (MA); Latin American and Iberian cultures (PhD); mathematics (MA, PhD), including finance (MA); medieval and Renaissance studies (MA); Middle Eastern, South Asian, and African studies (MA, PhD); modern art: critical and curatorial studies (MA); modern European studies (MA); museum anthropology (MA); music (DMA, PhD); oral history (MA); philosophical foundations of physics (MA); philosophy (MA, PhD); physics (PhD); political science (MA, PhD); psychology (PhD); quantitative methods in the social sciences (MA); religion (MA, PhD); Russia, Eurasia and East Europe: regional studies (MA); Russian translation (MA); Slavic cultures (MA); Slavic languages (MA, PhD); sociology (MA, PhD); South Asian studies (MA); statistics (MA, PhD); theatre (PhD). Dual-degree programs require admission to both Graduate School of Arts and Sciences and another Columbia school. *Program availability:* Part-time. Terminal master's awarded for partial completion of doctoral program. *Degree requirements:* For master's, variable foreign language requirement, comprehensive exam (for some programs), thesis (for some programs); for doctorate, variable foreign language requirement, comprehensive exam (for some programs), thesis/dissertation. *Entrance requirements:* For master's and doctorate, GRE General Test, GRE Subject Test (for some programs). Additional exam requirements/recommendations for international students: Required—TOEFL, IELTS. Electronic applications accepted. *Expenses: Tuition:* Full-time $44,864; part-time $1704 per credit. *Required fees:* $2370 per semester. One-time fee: $105.

Cornell University, Graduate School, Graduate Fields of Agriculture and Life Sciences, Field of Ecology and Evolutionary Biology, Ithaca, NY 14853. Offers ecology (PhD), including animal ecology, applied ecology, biogeochemistry, community and ecosystem ecology, limnology, oceanography, physiological ecology, plant ecology, population ecology, theoretical ecology, vertebrate zoology; evolutionary biology (PhD), including ecological genetics, paleobiology, population biology, systematics. *Degree requirements:* For doctorate, comprehensive exam, thesis/dissertation, 2 semesters of teaching experience. *Entrance requirements:* For doctorate, GRE General Test, GRE Subject Test (biology), 2 letters of recommendation. Additional exam requirements/recommendations for international students: Required—TOEFL (minimum score 550 paper-based; 77 iBT). Electronic applications accepted. *Faculty research:* Population and organismal biology, population and evolutionary genetics, systematics and macroevolution, biochemistry, conservation biology.

Dartmouth College, School of Graduate and Advanced Studies, Program in Ecology, Evolution, Ecosystems, and Society, Hanover, NH 03755. Offers ecology and evolutionary biology (PhD); sustainability, ecosystems, and environment (PhD). *Faculty:* 9 full-time (5 women). *Students:* 22 full-time (14 women); includes 1 minority (Hispanic/Latino), 3 international. Average age 28. 40 applicants, 15% accepted, 3 enrolled. In 2017, 1 doctorate awarded. *Entrance requirements:* For doctorate, GRE General Test, GRE Subject Test in biology (highly recommended). Additional exam requirements/recommendations for international students: Required—TOEFL. *Application deadline:* For fall admission, 12/1 for domestic students. Electronic applications accepted. *Financial support:* Fellowships, research assistantships, teaching assistantships, institutionally sponsored loans, traineeships, and unspecified assistantships available. Financial award applicants required to submit FAFSA. *Unit head:* Dr. Mathew Ayres, Chair, 603-646-2788. *Application contact:* Amy Layne, Administrative Assistant, 603-646-3847.
Website: http://sites.dartmouth.edu/EEES/

Emory University, Laney Graduate School, Division of Biological and Biomedical Sciences, Program in Population Biology, Ecology and Evolution, Atlanta, GA 30322-1100. Offers PhD. *Degree requirements:* For doctorate, comprehensive exam, thesis/dissertation. *Entrance requirements:* For doctorate, GRE General Test, minimum GPA of 3.0 in science course work (recommended). Additional exam requirements/recommendations for international students: Required—TOEFL. Electronic applications accepted. *Faculty research:* Evolution of microbes, infectious disease, the immune system, genetic disease in humans, evolution of behavior.

Florida State University, The Graduate School, College of Arts and Sciences, Department of Biological Science, Specialization in Ecology and Evolutionary Biology, Tallahassee, FL 32306-4295. Offers MS, PhD. *Faculty:* 23 full-time (9 women). *Students:* 50 full-time (25 women); includes 5 minority (2 Black or African American, non-Hispanic/Latino; 1 Native Hawaiian or other Pacific Islander, non-Hispanic/Latino; 2 Two or more races, non-Hispanic/Latino). Average age 29. 93 applicants, 18% accepted, 12 enrolled. In 2017, 4 master's, 5 doctorates awarded. Terminal master's awarded for partial completion of doctoral program. *Degree requirements:* For master's, comprehensive exam (for some programs), thesis, teaching experience, seminar presentation; for doctorate, comprehensive exam, thesis/dissertation, teaching experience; seminar presentation. *Entrance requirements:* For master's and doctorate, GRE General Test, minimum upper-division GPA of 3.0. Additional exam requirements/recommendations for international students: Required—TOEFL (minimum score 600 paper-based; 92 iBT). *Application deadline:* For fall admission, 12/1 for domestic and international students. Application fee: $30. Electronic applications accepted. *Financial support:* In 2017–18, 53 students received support, including 5 fellowships with tuition reimbursements available (averaging $30,000 per year), 11 research assistantships with full tuition reimbursements available (averaging $21,500 per year), 37 teaching assistantships with full tuition reimbursements available (averaging $21,500 per year); scholarships/grants and unspecified assistantships also available. Financial award application deadline: 12/1; financial award applicants required to submit FAFSA. *Faculty research:* Ecology and conservation biology; evolution; marine biology; phylogeny and systematics; theoretical, computational and mathematical biology. *Unit head:* Dr. Thomas A. Houpt, Professor and Associate Chair, 850-644-4783, Fax: 850-644-8447, E-mail: houpt@bio.fsu.edu. *Application contact:* Jessica Webber, Coordinator, Graduate Affairs, 850-644-3023, Fax: 850-644-9829, E-mail: gradinfo@bio.fsu.edu.
Website: http://www.bio.fsu.edu/

Harvard University, Graduate School of Arts and Sciences, Department of Organismic and Evolutionary Biology, Cambridge, MA 02138. Offers biology (PhD). *Degree requirements:* For doctorate, 2 foreign languages, public presentation of thesis research, exam. *Entrance requirements:* For doctorate, GRE General Test, GRE Subject Test (recommended), 7 courses in biology, chemistry, physics, mathematics, computer science, or geology. Additional exam requirements/recommendations for international students: Required—TOEFL.

Illinois State University, Graduate School, College of Arts and Sciences, School of Biological Sciences, Normal, IL 61790. Offers animal behavior (MS); bacteriology (MS); biochemistry (MS); biological sciences (MS); biology (PhD); biophysics (MS); biotechnology (MS); botany (MS, PhD); cell biology (MS); conservation biology (MS); developmental biology (MS); ecology (MS, PhD); entomology (MS); evolutionary biology (MS); genetics (MS, PhD); immunology (MS); microbiology (MS, PhD); molecular biology (MS); molecular genetics (MS); neurobiology (MS); neuroscience (MS); parasitology (MS); physiology (MS, PhD); plant biology (MS); plant molecular biology (MS); plant sciences (MS); structural biology (MS); zoology (MS, PhD). *Program availability:* Part-time. *Degree requirements:* For master's, thesis or alternative; for doctorate, variable foreign language requirement, thesis/dissertation, 2 terms of residency. *Entrance requirements:* For master's, GRE General Test, minimum GPA of 2.6 in last 60 hours of course work; for doctorate, GRE General Test. *Faculty research:* Redoc balance and drug development in schistosoma mansoni, control of the growth of listeria monocytogenes at low temperature, regulation of cell expansion and microtubule function by SPRI, CRUI: physiology and fitness consequences of different life history phenotypes.

Indiana State University, College of Graduate and Professional Studies, College of Arts and Sciences, Department of Biology, Terre Haute, IN 47809. Offers cellular and molecular biology (PhD); ecology, systematics and evolution (PhD); life sciences (MS); physiology (PhD); science education (MS). *Degree requirements:* For master's, thesis optional; for doctorate, comprehensive exam, thesis/dissertation. *Entrance requirements:* For master's and doctorate, GRE General Test. Electronic applications accepted.

Indiana University Bloomington, University Graduate School, College of Arts and Sciences, Department of Biology, Bloomington, IN 47405. Offers biology teaching (MAT); biotechnology (MA); evolution, ecology, and behavior (MA, PhD); genetics (PhD); microbiology (MA, PhD); molecular, cellular, and developmental biology (PhD); plant sciences (MA, PhD); zoology (MA, PhD). Terminal master's awarded for partial completion of doctoral program. *Degree requirements:* For master's, thesis, oral defense; for doctorate, thesis/dissertation, oral defense. *Entrance requirements:* For master's and doctorate, GRE General Test. Additional exam requirements/recommendations for international students: Required—TOEFL (minimum score 100 iBT). Electronic applications accepted. *Faculty research:* Evolution, ecology and behavior; microbiology; molecular biology and genetics; plant biology.

Iowa State University of Science and Technology, Program in Ecology and Evolutionary Biology, Ames, IA 50011. Offers MS, PhD. *Degree requirements:* For master's, thesis or alternative; for doctorate, thesis/dissertation. *Entrance requirements:* For master's and doctorate, GRE General Test. Additional exam requirements/recommendations for international students: Required—TOEFL (minimum score 550 paper-based; 79 iBT), IELTS (minimum score 6.5). Electronic applications accepted. *Faculty research:* Landscape ecology, aquatic and method ecology, physiological ecology, population genetics and evolution, systematics.

Johns Hopkins University, School of Medicine, Graduate Programs in Medicine, Center for Functional Anatomy and Evolution, Baltimore, MD 21287. Offers PhD. *Faculty:* 6 full-time (2 women). *Students:* 10 full-time (9 women); includes 1 minority (Hispanic/Latino), 1 international. Average age 28. 18 applicants, 11% accepted, 2 enrolled. In 2017, 1 doctorate awarded. *Degree requirements:* For doctorate, comprehensive exam, thesis/dissertation, oral exams. *Entrance requirements:* For doctorate, GRE. Additional exam requirements/recommendations for international students: Required—TOEFL. *Application deadline:* For fall admission, 1/10 for domestic and international students. Application fee: $85. Electronic applications accepted. *Financial support:* Fellowships, teaching assistantships, career-related internships or fieldwork, institutionally sponsored loans, health care benefits, and tuition waivers (full) available. *Faculty research:* Vertebrate evolution, functional anatomy, primate evolution, vertebrate paleobiology, vertebrate morphology. *Unit head:* Dr. Christopher B. Ruff, Director, 410-955-7126, Fax: 410-614-9030, E-mail: cbruff@jhmi.edu. *Application contact:* Catherine L. Will, Coordinator, Graduate Student Affairs, 410-614-3385, E-mail: grad_study@som.adm.jhu.edu.

Michigan State University, The Graduate School, College of Natural Science, Interdepartmental Program in Ecology, Evolutionary Biology and Behavior, East Lansing, MI 48824. Offers PhD. *Entrance requirements:* Additional exam requirements/recommendations for international students: Required—TOEFL. Electronic applications accepted.

Montclair State University, The Graduate School, College of Science and Mathematics, Program in Biology, Montclair, NJ 07043-1624. Offers biological science/education (MS); biology (MS); ecology and evolution (MS); physiology (MS).

The Ohio State University, Graduate School, College of Arts and Sciences, Division of Natural and Mathematical Sciences, Department of Evolution, Ecology, and Organismal Biology, Columbus, OH 43210. Offers MS, PhD. *Faculty:* 23. *Students:* 57 full-time (25 women), 6 international. Average age 28. In 2017, 4 master's, 9 doctorates awarded. *Entrance requirements:* For master's and doctorate, GRE General Test. Additional exam requirements/recommendations for international students: Required—TOEFL (minimum score 550 paper-based; 79 iBT), Michigan English Language Assessment Battery (minimum score 86); Recommended—IELTS (minimum score 7). *Application deadline:* For fall admission, 12/1 priority date for domestic students, 11/30 priority date for international students. Applications are processed on a rolling basis. Application fee: $60 ($70 for international students). Electronic applications accepted. *Financial support:* Fellowships, research assistantships, teaching assistantships, Federal Work-Study, and institutionally sponsored loans available. Support available to part-time students. *Unit head:* Dr. John Freudenstein, Chair and Professor, 614-688-0363, E-mail: freudenstein.1@osu.edu. *Application contact:* Graduate and Professional Admissions, 614-292-9444, Fax: 614-292-3895, E-mail: gpadmissions@osu.edu.
Website: http://eeob.osu.edu/

Ohio University, Graduate College, College of Arts and Sciences, Department of Biological Sciences, Athens, OH 45701-2979. Offers biological sciences (MS, PhD); cell biology and physiology (MS, PhD); ecology and evolutionary biology (MS, PhD); exercise physiology and muscle biology (MS, PhD); microbiology (MS, PhD); neuroscience (MS, PhD). Terminal master's awarded for partial completion of doctoral program. *Degree requirements:* For master's, comprehensive exam, thesis, 1 quarter of teaching experience; for doctorate, comprehensive exam, thesis/dissertation, 2 quarters of teaching experience. *Entrance requirements:* For master's, GRE General Test, names of three faculty members whose research interests most closely match the applicant's interest; for doctorate, GRE General Test, essay concerning prior training, research interest and career goals, plus names of three faculty members whose research interests most closely match the applicant's interest. Additional exam requirements/recommendations for international students: Required—TOEFL (minimum score 620 paper-based; 105 iBT) or IELTS (minimum score 7.5). Electronic applications accepted. *Faculty research:* Ecology and evolutionary biology, exercise physiology and muscle biology, neurobiology, cell biology, physiology.

Oklahoma State University, College of Arts and Sciences, Department of Plant Biology, Ecology, and Evolution, Stillwater, OK 74078. Offers botany (MS); environmental science (PhD). *Faculty:* 15 full-time (5 women). *Students:* 2 full-time (0 women), 11 part-time (7 women), 3 international. Average age 30. 3 applicants, 67% accepted, 2 enrolled. *Entrance requirements:* For master's and doctorate, GRE or GMAT. Additional exam requirements/recommendations for international students: Required—TOEFL (minimum score 550 paper-based; 79 iBT). *Application deadline:* For fall admission, 3/1 priority date for international students; for spring admission, 8/1 priority date for international students. Applications are processed on a rolling basis. Application fee: $40 ($75 for international students). Electronic applications accepted. *Expenses:* Tuition, state resident: full-time $4019; part-time $2679.60 per year. Tuition, nonresident: full-time $15,286; part-time $10,190.40 per year. *Required fees:* $2129; $1419 per unit. Tuition and fees vary according to program. *Financial support:* Research assistantships, teaching assistantships, career-related internships or fieldwork, Federal Work-Study, scholarships/grants, health care benefits, tuition waivers (partial), and unspecified assistantships available. Support available to part-time students. Financial award application deadline: 3/1; financial award applicants required to submit FAFSA. *Faculty research:* Ethnobotany, developmental genetics of Arabidopsis, biological roles of plasmodesmata, community ecology and biodiversity, nutrient cycling in grassland ecosystems. *Unit head:* Dr. Thomas Wikle, Interim Department Head, 405-744-7978, Fax: 405-744-7074, E-mail: twikle@okstate.edu.
Website: http://plantbio.okstate.edu

Princeton University, Graduate School, Department of Ecology and Evolutionary Biology, Princeton, NJ 08544-1019. Offers PhD. *Degree requirements:* For doctorate, thesis/dissertation. *Entrance requirements:* For doctorate, GRE General Test, GRE Subject Test. Additional exam requirements/recommendations for international students: Required—TOEFL (minimum score 600 paper-based). Electronic applications accepted.

Purdue University, Graduate School, College of Science, Department of Biological Sciences, West Lafayette, IN 47907. Offers biochemistry (PhD); biophysics (PhD); cell and developmental biology (PhD); ecology, evolutionary and population biology (MS, PhD), including ecology, evolutionary biology, population biology; genetics (MS, PhD); microbiology (MS, PhD); molecular biology (PhD); neurobiology (MS, PhD), plant physiology (PhD). *Faculty:* 42 full-time (13 women), 3 part-time/adjunct (0 women). *Students:* 115 full-time (58 women), 6 part-time (4 women); includes 17 minority (1 Black or African American, non-Hispanic/Latino; 6 Asian, non-Hispanic/Latino; 9 Hispanic/Latino; 1 Two or more races, non-Hispanic/Latino), 60 international. Average age 27. 165 applicants, 12% accepted, 15 enrolled. In 2017, 5 master's, 16 doctorates awarded. Terminal master's awarded for partial completion of doctoral program. *Degree requirements:* For master's, thesis (for some programs); for doctorate, thesis/dissertation, seminars, teaching experience. *Entrance requirements:* For master's, GRE General Test (minimum analytical writing score of 3.5), minimum undergraduate GPA of 3.0; for doctorate, GRE General Test (minimum analytical writing score of 3.5), minimum undergraduate GPA of 3.5. Additional exam requirements/recommendations for international students: Required—TOEFL minimum score 600 paper-based; 107 iBT (for MS), 80 iBT (for PhD). *Application deadline:* For fall admission, 12/7 for domestic and international students. Applications are processed on a rolling basis. Application fee: $60 ($75 for international students). Electronic applications accepted. *Financial support:* Fellowships, research assistantships, and teaching assistantships available. Support available to part-time students. Financial award application deadline: 2/15; financial award applicants required to submit FAFSA. *Unit head:* Stephen Konieczny, Head, 765-494-4407, E-mail: sfk@purdue.edu. *Application contact:* Georgina E. Rupp, Graduate Coordinator, 765-494-8142, E-mail: ruppg@purdue.edu.
Website: http://www.bio.purdue.edu/

Purdue University, Graduate School, PULSe - Purdue University Life Sciences Program, West Lafayette, IN 47907. Offers biomolecular structure and biophysics (PhD); biotechnology (PhD); chemical biology (PhD); chromatin and regulation of gene expression (PhD); integrative neuroscience (PhD); integrative plant sciences (PhD); membrane biology (PhD); microbiology (PhD); molecular evolutionary and cancer biology (PhD); molecular evolutionary genetics (PhD); molecular virology (PhD). *Students:* 60 full-time (29 women); includes 6 minority (4 Hispanic/Latino; 2 Two or more races, non-Hispanic/Latino), 36 international. Average age 25. 127 applicants, 39% accepted, 25 enrolled. *Entrance requirements:* For doctorate, GRE, minimum undergraduate GPA of 3.0. Additional exam requirements/recommendations for international students: Required—TOEFL (minimum score 550 paper-based; 77 iBT). *Application deadline:* For fall admission, 1/15 priority date for domestic and international students. Applications are processed on a rolling basis. Application fee: $60 ($75 for international students). Electronic applications accepted. *Financial support:* In 2017–18, research assistantships with tuition reimbursements (averaging $22,500 per year), teaching assistantships with tuition reimbursements (averaging $22,500 per year) were awarded. *Unit head:* Dr. Jason R. Cannon, Head of the Graduate Program, 765-494-0794, E-mail: cannonjr@purdue.edu. *Application contact:* Lindsey Springer, Graduate Contact for Admissions, 765-496-9667, E-mail: lbcampbe@purdue.edu.
Website: http://www.gradschool.purdue.edu/pulse

Rice University, Graduate Programs, Wiess School of Natural Sciences, Department of Ecology and Evolutionary Biology, Houston, TX 77251-1892. Offers MA, MS, PhD. Terminal master's awarded for partial completion of doctoral program. *Degree requirements:* For master's, comprehensive exam (for some programs), thesis (for some programs); for doctorate, comprehensive exam, thesis/dissertation. *Entrance requirements:* For master's and doctorate, GRE General Test, GRE Subject Test. Additional exam requirements/recommendations for international students: Required—TOEFL (minimum score 600 paper-based; 90 iBT). Electronic applications accepted. *Faculty research:* Trace gas emissions, wetlands, biology, community ecology of forests and grasslands, conservation biology specialization.

Rutgers University–New Brunswick, Graduate School-New Brunswick, Program in Ecology and Evolution, Piscataway, NJ 08854-8097. Offers MS, PhD. *Program availability:* Part-time. Terminal master's awarded for partial completion of doctoral program. *Degree requirements:* For master's, comprehensive exam; for doctorate, comprehensive exam, thesis/dissertation. *Entrance requirements:* For master's and doctorate, GRE General Test, minimum GPA of 3.0. Additional exam requirements/recommendations for international students: Required—TOEFL (minimum score 550 paper-based). Electronic applications accepted. *Faculty research:* Population and community ecology, population genetics, evolutionary biology, conservation biology, ecosystem ecology.

Rutgers University–New Brunswick, Graduate School-New Brunswick, Program in Plant Biology, Piscataway, NJ 08854-8097. Offers horticulture and plant technology (MS, PhD); molecular and cellular biology (MS, PhD); organismal and population biology (MS, PhD); plant pathology (MS, PhD). *Program availability:* Part-time. Terminal master's awarded for partial completion of doctoral program. *Degree requirements:* For master's, comprehensive exam, thesis or alternative; for doctorate, comprehensive exam, thesis/dissertation. *Entrance requirements:* For master's and doctorate, GRE General Test, GRE Subject Test (recommended). Additional exam requirements/recommendations for international students: Required—TOEFL (minimum score 600 paper-based). Electronic applications accepted. *Faculty research:* Molecular biology and biochemistry of plants, plant development and genomics, plant protection, plant improvement, plant management of horticultural and field crops.

Stony Brook University, State University of New York, Graduate School, College of Arts and Sciences, Department of Ecology and Evolution, Stony Brook, NY 11794. Offers applied ecology (MA); ecology and evolution (PhD). *Faculty:* 16 full-time (5 women), 1 part-time/adjunct (0 women). *Students:* 42 full-time (19 women), 1 part-time (0 women); includes 2 minority (both Asian, non-Hispanic/Latino), 12 international. Average age 28. 31 applicants, 42% accepted, 8 enrolled. In 2017, 3 doctorates awarded. *Degree requirements:* For doctorate, one foreign language, comprehensive exam, thesis/dissertation, teaching experience. *Entrance requirements:* For doctorate, GRE General Test, GRE Subject Test. Additional exam requirements/recommendations for international students: Required—TOEFL. *Application deadline:* For fall admission, 1/15 for domestic students; for spring admission, 10/1 for domestic students. Application fee: $100. Electronic applications accepted. *Expenses:* Contact institution. *Financial support:* In 2017–18, 7 fellowships, 3 research assistantships, 24 teaching assistantships were awarded; Federal Work-Study also available. *Faculty research:* Ecology, ecology and population, evolution, biodiversity, environmental conservation. *Total annual research expenditures:* $1.6 million. *Unit head:* Dr. Robert W. Thacker, Chair, 631-632-8590, E-mail: robert.thacker@stonybrook.edu. *Application contact:* Melissa Cohen, Coordinator, 631-246-8604, Fax: 631-632-7626, E-mail: melissa.j.cohen@stonybrook.edu.
Website: http://life.bio.sunysb.edu/ee/

Tulane University, School of Science and Engineering, Department of Ecology and Evolutionary Biology, New Orleans, LA 70118-5669. Offers MS, PhD. Terminal master's awarded for partial completion of doctoral program. *Degree requirements:* For master's, thesis or alternative; for doctorate, thesis/dissertation. *Entrance requirements:* For master's, GRE General Test, minimum B average in undergraduate course work; for doctorate, GRE General Test. Additional exam requirements/recommendations for international students: Required—TOEFL. Electronic applications accepted. *Expenses: Tuition:* Full-time $50,920; part-time $2829 per credit hour. *Required fees:* $2040; $44.50 per credit hour. $580 per term. Tuition and fees vary according to course load, degree level and program. *Faculty research:* Ichthyology, plant systematics, crustacean endocrinology, ecotoxicology, ornithology.

University at Buffalo, the State University of New York, Graduate School, College of Arts and Sciences, Program in Evolution, Ecology and Behavior, Buffalo, NY 14260. Offers MS, PhD, Certificate. *Faculty:* 16 full-time (7 women), 5 part-time/adjunct (2 women). *Students:* 17 full-time (13 women), 2 international. Average age 25. 14 applicants, 7% accepted, 1 enrolled. In 2017, 9 master's awarded. Terminal master's awarded for partial completion of doctoral program. *Degree requirements:* For master's, project; for doctorate, comprehensive exam, thesis/dissertation. *Entrance requirements:* For master's, GRE, minimum undergraduate GPA of 3.0; for doctorate, GRE, minimum GPA of 3.0. Additional exam requirements/recommendations for international students: Required—TOEFL (minimum score 550 paper-based; 79 iBT). *Application deadline:* For fall admission, 1/15 priority date for domestic and international students. Applications are processed on a rolling basis. Application fee: $75. Electronic applications accepted. *Financial support:* In 2017–18, 3 fellowships with full tuition reimbursements, 1 research assistantship with full tuition reimbursement, 5 teaching assistantships with full tuition reimbursements were awarded; Federal Work-Study, scholarships/grants, health care benefits, and unspecified assistantships also available. Financial award application deadline: 1/15; financial award applicants required to submit FAFSA. *Faculty research:* Coral reef ecology, evolution and ecology of aquatic invertebrates, animal communication, paleobiology, primate behavior. *Unit head:* Dr. Howard Lasker, Program Director, 716-645-4870, E-mail: ub-evb@buffalo.edu.
Website: http://www.evolutionecologybehavior.buffalo.edu/

University of Alberta, Faculty of Graduate Studies and Research, Department of Biological Sciences, Edmonton, AB T6G 2E1, Canada. Offers environmental biology and ecology (M Sc, PhD); microbiology and biotechnology (M Sc, PhD); molecular biology and genetics (M Sc, PhD); physiology and cell biology (M Sc, PhD); plant biology (M Sc, PhD); systematics and evolution (M Sc, PhD). Terminal master's awarded for partial completion of doctoral program. *Degree requirements:* For master's, thesis; for doctorate, thesis/dissertation. *Entrance requirements:* Additional exam requirements/recommendations for international students: Required—TOEFL.

The University of Arizona, College of Science, Department of Ecology and Evolutionary Biology, Tucson, AZ 85721. Offers MS, PhD. Terminal master's awarded for partial completion of doctoral program. *Degree requirements:* For master's, thesis optional; for doctorate, one foreign language, comprehensive exam, thesis/dissertation. *Entrance requirements:* For master's, GRE General Test, GRE Subject Test, statement of purpose, curriculum vitae, 3 letters of recommendation; for doctorate, GRE General Test, GRE Subject Test, curriculum vitae, 3 letters of recommendation. Additional exam requirements/recommendations for international students: Required—TOEFL (minimum score 550 paper-based; 79 iBT). *Faculty research:* Biological diversity, evolutionary history, evolutionary mechanisms, community structure.

University of California, Davis, Graduate Studies, Graduate Group in Population Biology, Davis, CA 95616. Offers PhD. *Degree requirements:* For doctorate, thesis/dissertation. *Entrance requirements:* For doctorate, GRE General Test, GRE Subject Test. Additional exam requirements/recommendations for international students: Required—TOEFL (minimum score 550 paper-based). Electronic applications accepted. *Faculty research:* Population ecology, population genetics, systematics, evolution, community ecology.

University of California, Irvine, Francisco J. Ayala School of Biological Sciences, Department of Ecology and Evolutionary Biology, Irvine, CA 92697. Offers biological sciences (MS, PhD). *Students:* 55 full-time (30 women); includes 23 minority (2 Asian, non-Hispanic/Latino; 17 Hispanic/Latino; 4 Two or more races, non-Hispanic/Latino), 1 international. Average age 29. 68 applicants, 31% accepted, 8 enrolled. In 2017, 7 master's, 10 doctorates awarded. *Entrance requirements:* For master's and doctorate, GRE General Test, GRE Subject Test, minimum GPA of 3.0. Additional exam requirements/recommendations for international students: Required—TOEFL (minimum score 550 paper-based). *Application deadline:* For fall admission, 1/15 priority date for domestic students, 1/15 for international students. Applications are processed on a rolling basis. Application fee: $105 ($125 for international students). Electronic applications accepted. *Financial support:* Fellowships, research assistantships with full tuition reimbursements, teaching assistantships, career-related internships or fieldwork, institutionally sponsored loans, traineeships, health care benefits, and unspecified assistantships available. Financial award application deadline: 3/1; financial award applicants required to submit FAFSA. *Faculty research:* Ecological energetics, quantitative genetics, life history evolution, plant-herbivore and plant-pollinator interactions, molecular evolution. *Unit head:* Laurence D. Mueller, Professor/Department Chair, 949-824-4744, Fax: 949-824-2181, E-mail: ldmuelle@uci.edu. *Application contact:* Pam McDonald, Student Affairs Coordinator, 949-824-4743, Fax: 949-824-2181, E-mail: pmcdonal@uci.edu.
Website: http://ecoevo.bio.uci.edu/

Evolutionary Biology

University of California, Los Angeles, Graduate Division, College of Letters and Science, Department of Ecology and Evolutionary Biology, Los Angeles, CA 90095. Offers MA, PhD. Terminal master's awarded for partial completion of doctoral program. *Degree requirements:* For master's, comprehensive exam or thesis; for doctorate, thesis/dissertation, oral and written qualifying exams; 3 quarters of teaching experience. *Entrance requirements:* For master's and doctorate, GRE General Test, GRE Subject Test (biology), bachelor's degree; minimum undergraduate GPA of 3.0 (or its equivalent if letter grade system not used). Additional exam requirements/recommendations for international students: Required—TOEFL. Electronic applications accepted.

University of California, Riverside, Graduate Division, Department of Evolution, Ecology, and Organismal Biology, Riverside, CA 92521-0102. Offers evolution, ecology and organismal biology (MS, PhD). *Faculty:* 40 full-time (14 women). Terminal master's awarded for partial completion of doctoral program. *Degree requirements:* For master's, thesis, oral defense of thesis; for doctorate, comprehensive exam, thesis/dissertation, 3 quarters of teaching experience, qualifying exams. *Entrance requirements:* For master's and doctorate, GRE General Test, minimum GPA of 3.2. Additional exam requirements/recommendations for international students: Required—TOEFL (minimum score 550 paper-based, 80 iBT) or IELTS; Recommended—TWE. *Application deadline:* For fall admission, 1/5 priority date for domestic and international students; for winter admission, 11/15 for domestic students, 9/1 for international students; for spring admission, 3/1 for domestic students, 12/1 for international students. Application fee: $80 ($100 for international students). Electronic applications accepted. *Expenses:* Tuition, state resident: full-time $5746. Tuition, nonresident: full-time $10,780. Tuition and fees vary according to campus/location and program. *Financial support:* Fellowships, research assistantships, teaching assistantships, career-related internships or fieldwork, Federal Work-Study, institutionally sponsored loans, scholarships/grants, tuition waivers (full and partial), and unspecified assistantships available. Financial award application deadline: 1/5; financial award applicants required to submit FAFSA. *Faculty research:* Ecology, evolutionary biology, physiology, quantitative genetics, conservation biology, systems biology. *Unit head:* Dr. Helen Regan, Department Chair, E-mail: helen.regan@ucr.edu. *Application contact:* Dawn Loyola, Director of Graduate Student Advising, 800-735-0717, E-mail: eeobgrad@ucr.edu.
Website: http://www.biology.ucr.edu/

University of California, Santa Barbara, Graduate Division, College of Letters and Sciences, Division of Mathematics, Life, and Physical Sciences, Department of Ecology, Evolution, and Marine Biology, Santa Barbara, CA 93106-9620. Offers MA, PhD, MA/PhD. *Degree requirements:* For master's, comprehensive exam (for some programs), thesis (for some programs); for doctorate, comprehensive exam, thesis/dissertation. *Entrance requirements:* For master's and doctorate, GRE General Test. Additional exam requirements/recommendations for international students: Required—TOEFL (minimum score 550 paper-based; 80 iBT), IELTS. Electronic applications accepted. *Faculty research:* Community ecology, evolution, marine biology, population genetics, stream ecology.

University of California, Santa Cruz, Division of Graduate Studies, Division of Physical and Biological Sciences, Department of Ecology and Evolutionary Biology, Santa Cruz, CA 95064. Offers MA, PhD. *Degree requirements:* For master's, thesis; for doctorate, comprehensive exam, thesis/dissertation. *Entrance requirements:* For master's and doctorate, GRE General Test, GRE Subject Test, 3 letters of recommendation. Additional exam requirements/recommendations for international students: Required—TOEFL (minimum score 550 paper-based; 83 iBT); Recommended—IELTS (minimum score 8). Electronic applications accepted. *Faculty research:* Population and community ecology, evolutionary biology, physiology and behavior (marine and terrestrial), systematics and biodiversity.

University of Chicago, Division of the Biological Sciences, Committee on Evolutionary Biology, Chicago, IL 60637. Offers PhD. *Students:* 29 full-time (14 women); includes 12 minority (2 Black or African American, non-Hispanic/Latino; 1 Asian, non-Hispanic/Latino; 7 Hispanic/Latino; 2 Two or more races, non-Hispanic/Latino), 2 international. Average age 28. 46 applicants, 15% accepted, 6 enrolled. In 2017, 4 doctorates awarded. Terminal master's awarded for partial completion of doctoral program. *Degree requirements:* For doctorate, thesis/dissertation, ethics class, 2 teaching assistantships. *Entrance requirements:* For doctorate, GRE General Test, transcripts, statement of purpose, 3 letters of recommendation. Additional exam requirements/recommendations for international students: Required—TOEFL (minimum score 600 paper-based; 104 iBT), IELTS (minimum score 7). *Application deadline:* For fall admission, 12/1 for domestic and international students. Application fee: $90. Electronic applications accepted. *Financial support:* In 2017–18, 29 students received support, including fellowships with full tuition reimbursements available (averaging $31,000 per year), research assistantships with full tuition reimbursements available (averaging $31,000 per year); institutionally sponsored loans, scholarships/grants, traineeships, and health care benefits also available. Financial award application deadline: 12/1. *Faculty research:* Systematics and evolutionary theory, genetics, functional morphology and physiology, behavior, ecology and biogeography. *Unit head:* Dr. Michael Coates, Chair, 773-834-8417, Fax: 773-702-4699, E-mail: bsdadmissions@uchicago.edu. *Application contact:* Carolyn Johnson, Graduate Administrative Director, 773-702-9474, Fax: 773-702-4699, E-mail: csjohnso@uchicago.edu.
Website: http://evbio.uchicago.edu/

University of Colorado Boulder, Graduate School, College of Arts and Sciences, Department of Ecology and Evolutionary Biology, Boulder, CO 80309. Offers population biology (MA). *Faculty:* 34 full-time (14 women). *Students:* 73 full-time (41 women), 2 part-time (both women); includes 11 minority (1 Black or African American, non-Hispanic/Latino; 5 Hispanic/Latino; 5 Two or more races, non-Hispanic/Latino), 7 international. Average age 29. 152 applicants, 22% accepted, 20 enrolled. In 2017, 5 master's, 14 doctorates awarded. Terminal master's awarded for partial completion of doctoral program. *Degree requirements:* For master's, comprehensive exam, thesis or alternative; for doctorate, comprehensive exam, thesis/dissertation. *Entrance requirements:* For master's, GRE General Test, GRE Subject Test, minimum undergraduate GPA of 3.0; for doctorate, GRE General Test, GRE Subject Test. *Application deadline:* For fall admission, 12/1 for domestic students; for spring admission, 12/1 for domestic students. Application fee: $60 ($80 for international students). Electronic applications accepted. Application fee is waived when completed online. *Financial support:* In 2017–18, 171 students received support, including 31 fellowships (averaging $16,364 per year), 12 research assistantships with full and partial tuition reimbursements available (averaging $39,779 per year), 51 teaching assistantships with full and partial tuition reimbursements available (averaging $26,113 per year); institutionally sponsored loans, scholarships/grants, health care benefits, and unspecified assistantships also available. Financial award application deadline: 2/15; financial award applicants required to submit FAFSA. *Faculty research:* Ecology; evolutionary biology; biological sciences; genetics; conservation biology. *Total annual research expenditures:* $5.2 million. *Application contact:* E-mail: ebiograd@colorado.edu.
Website: http://ebio.colorado.edu

University of Delaware, College of Arts and Sciences, Department of Biological Sciences, Newark, DE 19716. Offers biotechnology (MS); cancer biology (MS, PhD); cell and extracellular matrix biology (MS, PhD); cell and systems physiology (MS, PhD); developmental biology (MS, PhD); ecology and evolution (MS, PhD); microbiology (MS, PhD); molecular biology and genetics (MS, PhD). Terminal master's awarded for partial completion of doctoral program. *Degree requirements:* For master's, thesis, preliminary exam; for doctorate, comprehensive exam, thesis/dissertation, preliminary exam. *Entrance requirements:* For master's and doctorate, GRE General Test. Additional exam requirements/recommendations for international students: Required—TOEFL (minimum score 600 paper-based); Recommended—TWE. Electronic applications accepted. *Faculty research:* Microorganisms, bone, cancer metastasis, developmental biology, cell biology, DNA.

University of Denver, Division of Natural Sciences and Mathematics, Department of Biological Sciences, Denver, CO 80208. Offers biology, ecology and evolution (MS, PhD); biomedical sciences (PSM); cell and molecular biology (MS, PhD). *Program availability:* Part-time. *Students:* Average age 25. 71 applicants, 44% accepted, 18 enrolled. In 2017, 7 master's, 3 doctorates awarded. Terminal master's awarded for partial completion of doctoral program. *Degree requirements:* For master's, comprehensive exam (for some programs), thesis; for doctorate, one foreign language, comprehensive exam (for some programs), thesis/dissertation. *Entrance requirements:* For master's and doctorate, GRE General Test, bachelor's degree in biology or related field, transcripts, personal statement, three letters of recommendation. Additional exam requirements/recommendations for international students: Required—TOEFL (minimum score 550 paper-based; 80 iBT). *Application deadline:* For fall admission, 1/1 priority date for domestic and international students. Applications are processed on a rolling basis. Application fee: $65. Electronic applications accepted. *Expenses:* Contact institution. *Financial support:* In 2017–18, 35 students received support, including 5 research assistantships with tuition reimbursements available (averaging $18,667 per year), 14 teaching assistantships with tuition reimbursements available (averaging $18,095 per year); Federal Work-Study, institutionally sponsored loans, scholarships/grants, and unspecified assistantships also available. Support available to part-time students. Financial award application deadline: 2/15; financial award applicants required to submit FAFSA. *Faculty research:* Molecular biology, cell biology, neurobiology, ecology, molecular evolution. *Unit head:* Dr. Joseph Angleson, Associate Professor and Chair, 303-871-3463, Fax: 303-871-3471, E-mail: jangleso@du.edu. *Application contact:* Randi Flageolle, Assistant to the Chair, 303-871-3457, Fax: 303-871-3471, E-mail: rflageol@du.edu.
Website: http://www.du.edu/nsm/departments/biologicalsciences

University of Guelph, Graduate Studies, College of Biological Science, Department of Integrative Biology, Botany and Zoology, Guelph, ON N1G 2W1, Canada. Offers botany (M Sc, PhD); zoology (M Sc, PhD). *Program availability:* Part-time. *Degree requirements:* For master's, thesis, research proposal; for doctorate, thesis/dissertation, research proposal, qualifying exam. *Entrance requirements:* For master's, minimum B average during previous 2 years of course work. Additional exam requirements/recommendations for international students: Required—TOEFL (minimum score 550 paper-based), IELTS (minimum score 6.5). Electronic applications accepted. *Faculty research:* Aquatic science, environmental physiology, parasitology, wildlife biology, management.

University of Illinois at Urbana–Champaign, Graduate College, College of Liberal Arts and Sciences, School of Integrative Biology, Department of Animal Biology, Champaign, IL 61820. Offers animal biology (ecology, ethology and evolution) (MS, PhD).

University of Illinois at Urbana–Champaign, Graduate College, College of Liberal Arts and Sciences, School of Integrative Biology, Program in Ecology, Evolution and Conservation Biology, Champaign, IL 61820. Offers MS, PhD.

The University of Iowa, Graduate College, College of Liberal Arts and Sciences, Department of Biology, Iowa City, IA 52242-1324. Offers biology (MS, PhD); cell and developmental biology (MS, PhD); evolution (MS, PhD); genetics (MS, PhD); neurobiology (MS, PhD). Terminal master's awarded for partial completion of doctoral program. *Degree requirements:* For master's, thesis optional, exam; for doctorate, comprehensive exam, thesis/dissertation. *Entrance requirements:* For master's and doctorate, GRE General Test, minimum GPA of 3.0. Additional exam requirements/recommendations for international students: Required—TOEFL (minimum score 600 paper-based; 100 iBT). Electronic applications accepted. *Faculty research:* Neurobiology, evolutionary biology, genetics, cell and developmental biology.

The University of Kansas, Graduate Studies, College of Liberal Arts and Sciences, Department of Ecology and Evolutionary Biology, Lawrence, KS 66045. Offers MA, PhD. *Program availability:* Part-time. *Students:* 70 full-time (33 women), 3 part-time (0 women); includes 6 minority (1 Black or African American, non-Hispanic/Latino; 1 Hispanic/Latino; 4 Two or more races, non-Hispanic/Latino), 23 international. Average age 29. 65 applicants, 40% accepted, 20 enrolled. In 2017, 8 master's, 8 doctorates awarded. Terminal master's awarded for partial completion of doctoral program. *Degree requirements:* For master's, comprehensive exam, thesis (for some programs), 30-36 credits, thesis presentation; for doctorate, comprehensive exam, thesis/dissertation, residency, final exam, dissertation defense. *Entrance requirements:* For master's and doctorate, GRE General Test, curriculum vitae, personal statement, three letters of recommendation, official transcripts. Additional exam requirements/recommendations for international students: Required—TOEFL or IELTS. *Application deadline:* For fall admission, 12/1 for domestic and international students. Application fee: $65 ($85 for international students). Electronic applications accepted. *Financial support:* Fellowships, research assistantships, teaching assistantships, scholarships/grants, traineeships, health care benefits, and unspecified assistantships available. Financial award application deadline: 12/1. *Faculty research:* Ecology and global change, diversity and macroevolution, evolutionary mechanisms, systematics/phylogenetic, biogeography. *Unit head:* Dr. Christopher Haufler, Chair, 785-864-3255, E-mail: vulgare@ku.edu. *Application contact:* Aagje Ashe, Graduate Coordinator, 785-864-2362, Fax: 785-864-5860, E-mail: a4ashe@ku.edu.
Website: http://eeb.ku.edu/

University of Louisiana at Lafayette, College of Sciences, Department of Biology, Lafayette, LA 70504. Offers biology (MS); environmental and evolutionary biology (PhD). Terminal master's awarded for partial completion of doctoral program. *Degree requirements:* For master's, thesis; for doctorate, 2 foreign languages, comprehensive exam, thesis/dissertation. *Entrance requirements:* For master's, GRE General Test, minimum GPA of 2.75; for doctorate, GRE General Test, GRE Subject Test, minimum GPA of 3.0. Additional exam requirements/recommendations for international students: Required—TOEFL (minimum score 550 paper-based). *Application deadline:* For fall admission, 5/15 for domestic and international students; for spring admission, 10/1 for domestic and international students. Applications are processed on a rolling basis. Application fee: $25 ($30 for international students). Electronic applications accepted. *Financial support:* Application deadline: 5/1. *Faculty research:* Structure and ultrastructure, system biology, ecology, processes, environmental physiology. *Unit head:* Dr. Scott France, Graduate Admissions Chair, 337-482-6320, E-mail: france@louisiana.edu. *Application contact:* Dr. Paul Leberg, Graduate Coordinator, 337-482-6750, Fax: 337-482-5834, E-mail: leberg@louisiana.edu.

The University of Manchester, School of Biological Sciences, Manchester, United Kingdom. Offers adaptive organismal biology (M Phil, PhD); animal biology (M Phil, PhD); biochemistry (M Phil, PhD); bioinformatics (M Phil, PhD); biomolecular sciences (M Phil, PhD); biotechnology (M Phil, PhD); cell biology (M Phil, PhD); cell matrix research (M Phil, PhD); channels and transporters (M Phil, PhD); developmental biology (M Phil, PhD); environmental biology (M Phil, PhD); evolutionary biology (M Phil, PhD); gene expression (M Phil, PhD); genetics (M Phil, PhD); history of science, technology and medicine (M Phil, PhD); immunology (M Phil, PhD); integrative neurobiology and behavior (M Phil, PhD); membrane trafficking (M Phil, PhD); microbiology (M Phil, PhD); molecular and cellular neuroscience (M Phil, PhD); molecular biology (M Phil, PhD); molecular cancer studies (M Phil, PhD); neuroscience (M Phil, PhD); ophthalmology (M Phil, PhD); optometry (M Phil, PhD); organelle function (M Phil, PhD); pharmacology (M Phil, PhD); physiology (M Phil, PhD); plant sciences (M Phil, PhD); stem cell research (M Phil, PhD); structural biology (M Phil, PhD); systems neuroscience (M Phil, PhD); toxicology (M Phil, PhD).

University of Maryland, College Park, Academic Affairs, College of Computer, Mathematical and Natural Sciences, Department of Biology, Behavior, Ecology, Evolution, and Systematics Program, College Park, MD 20742. Offers MS, PhD. *Degree requirements:* For master's, thesis, oral defense, seminar; for doctorate, thesis/dissertation, exam, 4 seminars. *Entrance requirements:* For master's and doctorate, GRE General Test, GRE Subject Test (biology), 3 letters of recommendation. Additional exam requirements/recommendations for international students: Required—TOEFL. *Faculty research:* Animal behavior, biostatistics, ecology, evolution, neurothology.

University of Maryland, College Park, Academic Affairs, College of Computer, Mathematical and Natural Sciences, Department of Biology, PhD Program in Biological Sciences, College Park, MD 20742. Offers behavior, ecology, evolution, and systematics (PhD); computational biology, bioinformatics, and genomics (PhD); molecular and cellular biology (PhD); physiological systems (PhD). *Degree requirements:* For doctorate, comprehensive exam, thesis/dissertation, thesis work presentation in seminar. *Entrance requirements:* For doctorate, GRE General Test; GRE Subject Test in biology (recommended), academic transcripts, statement of purpose/research interests, 3 letters of recommendation. Additional exam requirements/recommendations for international students: Required—TOEFL. Electronic applications accepted.

University of Massachusetts Amherst, Graduate School, Interdisciplinary Programs, Program in Organismic and Evolutionary Biology, Amherst, MA 01003. Offers MS, PhD. *Program availability:* Part-time. Terminal master's awarded for partial completion of doctoral program. *Degree requirements:* For master's, thesis or alternative; for doctorate, comprehensive exam, thesis/dissertation. *Entrance requirements:* For master's and doctorate, GRE General Test, 3 letters of recommendation. Additional exam requirements/recommendations for international students: Required—TOEFL (minimum score 550 paper-based; 80 iBT), IELTS (minimum score 6.5). Electronic applications accepted.

University of Massachusetts Amherst, Graduate School, Interdisciplinary Programs, Program in Plant Biology, Amherst, MA 01003. Offers biochemistry and metabolism (MS, PhD); cell biology and physiology (MS, PhD); environmental, ecological and integrative biology (MS, PhD); genetics and evolution (MS, PhD). *Degree requirements:* For master's, thesis; for doctorate, 2 foreign languages, comprehensive exam, thesis/dissertation. *Entrance requirements:* For master's and doctorate, GRE General Test. Additional exam requirements/recommendations for international students: Required—TOEFL (minimum score 550 paper-based; 80 iBT), IELTS (minimum score 6.5). Electronic applications accepted.

University of Miami, Graduate School, College of Arts and Sciences, Department of Biology, Coral Gables, FL 33124. Offers biology (MS, PhD); genetics and evolution (MS, PhD). Terminal master's awarded for partial completion of doctoral program. *Degree requirements:* For master's, comprehensive exam (for some programs), thesis (for some programs); for doctorate, thesis/dissertation, oral and written qualifying exam. *Entrance requirements:* For master's, GRE General Test, 3 letters of recommendation, research papers; for doctorate, GRE General Test, 3 letters of recommendation, research papers, sponsor letter. Additional exam requirements/recommendations for international students: Required—TOEFL (minimum score 550 paper-based; 59 iBT). Electronic applications accepted. *Faculty research:* Neuroscience to ethology; plants, vertebrates and mycorrhizae; phylogenies, life histories and species interactions; molecular biology, gene expression and populations; cells, auditory neurons and vertebrate locomotion.

University of Michigan, Rackham Graduate School, College of Literature, Science, and the Arts, Department of Ecology and Evolutionary Biology, Ann Arbor, MI 48109. Offers MS, PhD. *Faculty:* 51 full-time (18 women). *Students:* 80 full-time (44 women); includes 38 minority (5 Black or African American, non-Hispanic/Latino; 1 American Indian or Alaska Native, non-Hispanic/Latino; 5 Asian, non-Hispanic/Latino; 15 Hispanic/Latino; 1 Native Hawaiian or other Pacific Islander, non-Hispanic/Latino; 11 Two or more races, non-Hispanic/Latino), 15 international. Average age 27. 147 applicants, 20% accepted, 20 enrolled. In 2017, 13 master's, 6 doctorates awarded. Terminal master's awarded for partial completion of doctoral program. *Degree requirements:* For master's, thesis (for some programs); for doctorate, comprehensive exam, thesis/dissertation, 2 semesters of teaching. *Entrance requirements:* For master's and doctorate, GRE. Additional exam requirements/recommendations for international students: Required—TOEFL (minimum score 84 iBT). *Application deadline:* For fall admission, 12/1 priority date for domestic and international students. Application fee: $75 ($90 for international students). Electronic applications accepted. *Expenses:* $21,673. *Financial support:* In 2017–18, 80 students received support, including 35 fellowships with full tuition reimbursements available (averaging $27,399 per year), 11 research assistantships with full tuition reimbursements available (averaging $27,399 per year), 36 teaching assistantships with full tuition reimbursements available (averaging $27,399 per year); scholarships/grants, traineeships, health care benefits, and unspecified assistantships also available. *Faculty research:* Population and community ecology, ecosystem ecology and biogeochemistry, global change biology, evolution of behavior, evolutionary genetics, phylogenetics and phylogeography. *Total annual research expenditures:* $5.1 million. *Unit head:* Dr. Diarmaid O' Foighil, Chair, 734-615-4912, Fax: 734-763-0544. *Application contact:* Kati Ellis, Graduate Program Assistant and Recruiter, 734-764-1443, Fax: 734-763-0544, E-mail: eeb.gradcoord@umich.edu.
Website: http://lsa.umich.edu/eeb/

University of Minnesota, Twin Cities Campus, Graduate School, College of Biological Sciences, Department of Ecology, Evolution, and Behavior, St. Paul, MN 55418. Offers MS, PhD. Terminal master's awarded for partial completion of doctoral program. *Degree requirements:* For master's, comprehensive exam, thesis or projects; for doctorate, comprehensive exam, thesis/dissertation. *Entrance requirements:* For master's and doctorate, GRE General Test, minimum GPA of 3.0. Additional exam requirements/recommendations for international students: Required—TOEFL (minimum score 550 paper-based; 79 iBT), Michigan English Language Assessment Battery. Electronic applications accepted. *Faculty research:* Behavioral ecology, community ecology, community genetics, ecosystem and global change, evolution and systematics.

University of Missouri, Office of Research and Graduate Studies, College of Arts and Science, Division of Biological Sciences, Columbia, MO 65211. Offers evolutionary biology and ecology (MA, PhD). Terminal master's awarded for partial completion of doctoral program. *Entrance requirements:* For master's and doctorate, GRE General Test (minimum score 1200 verbal and quantitative), minimum GPA of 3.0. Additional exam requirements/recommendations for international students: Required—TOEFL. *Expenses:* Tuition, state resident: full-time $6480. Tuition, nonresident: full-time $17,744. *Required fees:* $1108. Tuition and fees vary according to course load, campus/location and program. *Financial support:* Fellowships, research assistantships, teaching assistantships, institutionally sponsored loans, traineeships, health care benefits, and unspecified assistantships available.
Website: http://biology.missouri.edu/graduate-studies/

University of Nevada, Reno, Graduate School, Interdisciplinary Program in Ecology, Evolution, and Conservation Biology, Reno, NV 89557. Offers PhD. Offered through the College of Arts and Science, the M. C. Fleischmann College of Agriculture, and the Desert Research Institute. *Degree requirements:* For doctorate, thesis/dissertation. *Entrance requirements:* For doctorate, GRE General Test, GRE Subject Test, minimum GPA of 3.0. Additional exam requirements/recommendations for international students: Required—TOEFL (minimum score 500 paper-based; 61 iBT), IELTS (minimum score 6). Electronic applications accepted. *Faculty research:* Population biology, behavioral ecology, plant response to climate change, conservation of endangered species, restoration of natural ecosystems.

University of New Hampshire, Graduate School, College of Life Sciences and Agriculture, Department of Molecular, Cellular and Biomedical Sciences, Program in Molecular and Evolutionary Systems Biology, Durham, NH 03824. Offers PhD. *Program availability:* Part-time. *Students:* 6 full-time (2 women), 1 (woman) part-time, 2 international. Average age 29. 9 applicants, 56% accepted, 1 enrolled. *Entrance requirements:* For doctorate, GRE General Test. Additional exam requirements/recommendations for international students: Required—TOEFL (minimum score 550 paper-based; 80 iBT). *Application deadline:* For fall admission, 1/15 for domestic and international students. Application fee: $65. Electronic applications accepted. *Financial support:* In 2017–18, 7 students received support, including 4 research assistantships, 3 teaching assistantships; Federal Work-Study, scholarships/grants, and tuition waivers (full and partial) also available. Support available to part-time students. Financial award application deadline: 2/15. *Unit head:* Rick Cote, Chair, 603-862-2458. *Application contact:* Paul Boisselle, Administrative Assistant, 603-862-4814, E-mail: paul.boisselle@unh.edu.
Website: http://colsa.unh.edu/mcbs/mesb/mesb-phd

The University of North Carolina at Chapel Hill, Graduate School, College of Arts and Sciences, Department of Biology, Chapel Hill, NC 27599. Offers botany (MA, MS, PhD); cell biology, development, and physiology (MA, MS, PhD); cell motility and cytoskeleton (PhD); ecology and behavior (MA, MS, PhD); genetics and molecular biology (MA, MS, PhD); morphology, systematics, and evolution (MA, MS, PhD). Terminal master's awarded for partial completion of doctoral program. *Degree requirements:* For master's, comprehensive exam, thesis (for some programs); for doctorate, comprehensive exam, thesis/dissertation. *Entrance requirements:* For master's, GRE General Test, GRE Subject Test, 2 semesters of calculus or statistics; 2 semesters of physics, organic chemistry; 3 semesters of biology; for doctorate, GRE General Test, GRE Subject Test, 2 semesters calculus or statistics, 2 semesters physics, organic chemistry, 3 semesters of biology. Additional exam requirements/recommendations for international students: Required—TOEFL (minimum score 550 paper-based). Electronic applications accepted. *Faculty research:* Gene expression, biomechanics, yeast genetics, plant ecology, plant molecular biology.

University of Notre Dame, Graduate School, College of Science, Department of Biological Sciences, Notre Dame, IN 46556. Offers aquatic ecology, evolution and environmental biology (MS, PhD); cellular and molecular biology (MS, PhD); genetics (MS, PhD); physiology (MS, PhD); vector biology and parasitology (MS, PhD). Terminal master's awarded for partial completion of doctoral program. *Degree requirements:* For master's, comprehensive exam, thesis; for doctorate, comprehensive exam, thesis/dissertation, candidacy exam. *Entrance requirements:* For master's and doctorate, GRE General Test. Additional exam requirements/recommendations for international students: Required—TOEFL (minimum score 600 paper-based; 80 iBT). Electronic applications accepted. *Faculty research:* Tropical disease, molecular genetics, neurobiology, evolutionary biology, aquatic biology.

University of Oklahoma, College of Arts and Sciences, Department of Biology, Norman, OK 73019. Offers biology (MS, PhD); cellular and behavioral neurobiology (PhD), including biology; ecology and evolutionary biology (PhD), including biology. *Faculty:* 38 full-time (10 women), 1 (woman) part-time/adjunct. *Students:* 13 full-time (4 women), 9 part-time (6 women); includes 5 minority (2 Asian, non-Hispanic/Latino; 2 Hispanic/Latino; 1 Two or more races, non-Hispanic/Latino), 5 international. Average age 28. 27 applicants, 15% accepted, 4 enrolled. In 2017, 6 master's awarded. *Degree requirements:* For master's, thesis, course in biostatistics; for doctorate, comprehensive exam, thesis/dissertation, course in biostatistics, 2 semesters as teaching assistant. *Entrance requirements:* For master's and doctorate, GRE General Test, transcripts, 3 letters of recommendation, personal statement, curriculum vitae. Additional exam requirements/recommendations for international students: Required—TOEFL (minimum score 79 iBT) or IELTS (minimum score 6.5). *Application deadline:* For fall admission, 12/15 priority date for domestic and international students. Application fee: $50 ($100 for international students). Electronic applications accepted. *Expenses:* Tuition, state resident: full-time $5119; part-time $213.30 per credit hour. Tuition, nonresident: full-time $19,778; part-time $824.10 per credit hour. *Required fees:* $3458; $133.55 per credit hour. $126.50 per semester. *Financial support:* In 2017–18, 19 students received support, including 10 fellowships with full tuition reimbursements available (averaging $3,257 per year), 6 research assistantships with full tuition reimbursements available (averaging $15,419 per year), 38 teaching assistantships with full tuition reimbursements available (averaging $16,413 per year); scholarships/grants and assistantships (with tuition waivers and health insurance) also available. Financial award application deadline: 6/1; financial award applicants required to submit FAFSA. *Faculty research:* Geographical ecology, biology of behavior, cellular and behavioral neurobiology, evolutionary and molecular genetics; evolution of development. *Total annual research expenditures:* $1.2 million. *Unit head:* Dr. Richard Broughton, Professor and Chair, 405-325-6200, Fax: 405-325-6202, E-mail: biology@ou.edu. *Application contact:* Dianna Wilson, Academic Counselor, 405-325-9139, Fax: 405-325-6202, E-mail: biologygrad@ou.edu.
Website: http://www.ou.edu/cas/biology

University of Oklahoma, College of Arts and Sciences, Department of Microbiology and Plant Biology, Program in Plant Biology, Norman, OK 73019. Offers ecology and evolutionary biology (PhD); plant biology (MS, PhD). *Students:* 6 full-time (4 women), 10 part-time (4 women); includes 2 minority (1 American Indian or Alaska Native, non-Hispanic/Latino; 1 Asian, non-Hispanic/Latino), 4 international. Average age 30. 10 applicants, 50% accepted, 5 enrolled. In 2017, 2 master's, 2 doctorates awarded. Terminal master's awarded for partial completion of doctoral program. *Degree requirements:* For master's, thesis; for doctorate, comprehensive exam, thesis/

dissertation. *Entrance requirements:* For master's and doctorate, GRE, 3 recommendation letters, letter of intent, bachelor's degree. Additional exam requirements/recommendations for international students: Required—TOEFL (minimum score 80 iBT) or IELTS (minimum score 6.5). *Application deadline:* For fall admission, 3/1 for domestic and international students; for spring admission, 9/1 for domestic and international students; for summer admission, 9/1 for domestic and international students. Application fee: $50 ($100 for international students). Electronic applications accepted. *Expenses:* Tuition, state resident: full-time $5119; part-time $213.30 per credit hour. Tuition, nonresident: full-time $19,778; part-time $824.10 per credit hour. *Required fees:* $3458; $133.55 per credit hour. $126.50 per semester. *Financial support:* In 2017–18, 13 students received support. Research assistantships with full and partial tuition reimbursements available, teaching assistantships with full and partial tuition reimbursements available, Federal Work-Study, institutionally sponsored loans, scholarships/grants, health care benefits, and unspecified assistantships available. Support available to part-time students. Financial award application deadline: 6/1; financial award applicants required to submit FAFSA. *Faculty research:* Ecology, evolution, and systematics of plants; molecular biology of plant stress and reproduction; global change biology and ecosystem modeling; plant structure and development; science education. *Unit head:* Dr. Anne K. Dunn, Department Chair/Associate Professor of Microbiology, 405-325-4321, E-mail: akdunn@ou.edu. *Application contact:* Elizabeth Karr, Graduate Liaison/Associate Professor of Microbiology, 405-325-5133, E-mail: lizkarr@ou.edu.
Website: http://mpbio.ou.edu

University of Oklahoma, College of Arts and Sciences, Program in Ecology and Evolutionary Biology, Norman, OK 73019. Offers PhD. *Students:* 23 full-time (12 women), 13 part-time (7 women); includes 5 minority (2 Black or African American, non-Hispanic/Latino; 1 Asian, non-Hispanic/Latino; 2 Hispanic/Latino), 7 international. Average age 28. 19 applicants, 42% accepted, 8 enrolled. In 2017, 8 doctorates awarded. *Degree requirements:* For doctorate, comprehensive exam, thesis/dissertation, course in biostatistics; 2 semesters as a teaching assistant. *Entrance requirements:* For doctorate, GRE General Test, transcripts, 3 letters of recommendation, personal statement, curriculum vitae. Additional exam requirements/recommendations for international students: Required—TOEFL (minimum score 79 iBT) or IELTS (minimum score 6.5). *Application deadline:* For fall admission, 12/15 priority date for domestic students, 12/15 for international students. Application fee: $50 ($100 for international students). Electronic applications accepted. *Expenses:* Tuition, state resident: full-time $5119; part-time $213.30 per credit hour. Tuition, nonresident: full-time $19,778; part-time $824.10 per credit hour. *Required fees:* $3458; $133.55 per credit hour. $126.50 per semester. *Financial support:* In 2017–18, 38 students received support. Fellowships, research assistantships with full tuition reimbursements available, teaching assistantships with full tuition reimbursements available, scholarships/grants, and assistantships (with tuition waivers and health insurance) available. Financial award application deadline: 6/1; financial award applicants required to submit FAFSA. *Faculty research:* Geographical ecology, global change biology, evolutionary biology, phylogenetics, ecosystem ecology. *Unit head:* Dr. Michael Kaspari, Professor, 405-325-3371, Fax: 405-325-6202, E-mail: mkaspari@ou.edu. *Application contact:* Dianna Wilson, Academic Counselor, 405-325-9139, Fax: 405-325-6202, E-mail: biologygrad@ou.edu.
Website: http://www.ou.edu/eeb

University of Oregon, Graduate School, College of Arts and Sciences, Department of Biology, Eugene, OR 97403. Offers ecology and evolution (MA, MS, PhD); marine biology (MA, MS, PhD); molecular, cellular and genetic biology (PhD); neuroscience and development (PhD). Terminal master's awarded for partial completion of doctoral program. *Degree requirements:* For master's, thesis (for some programs); for doctorate, thesis/dissertation. *Entrance requirements:* For master's and doctorate, GRE General Test, minimum GPA of 3.2. Additional exam requirements/recommendations for international students: Required—TOEFL. *Faculty research:* Developmental neurobiology; evolution, population biology, and quantitative genetics; regulation of gene expression; biochemistry of marine organisms.

University of Pittsburgh, Kenneth P. Dietrich School of Arts and Sciences, Department of Biological Sciences, Program in Ecology and Evolution, Pittsburgh, PA 15260. Offers PhD. *Program availability:* Part-time, online learning. *Faculty:* 6 full-time (2 women). *Students:* 13 full-time (12 women); includes 1 minority (Hispanic/Latino), 2 international. Average age 23. In 2017, 1 doctorate awarded. *Degree requirements:* For doctorate, comprehensive exam, thesis/dissertation, completion of research integrity module. *Entrance requirements:* For doctorate, GRE General Test, GRE Subject Test. Additional exam requirements/recommendations for international students: Required—TOEFL (minimum score 90 iBT). *Application deadline:* Applications are processed on a rolling basis. Application fee: $0. Electronic applications accepted. *Financial support:* In 2017–18, 11 fellowships with full tuition reimbursements (averaging $34,776 per year), 9 research assistantships with full tuition reimbursements (averaging $28,800 per year), 14 teaching assistantships with full tuition reimbursements (averaging $28,535 per year) were awarded; Federal Work-Study, traineeships, health care benefits, and tuition waivers also available. *Unit head:* Dr. Karen M. Arndt, Professor, 412-624-6963, Fax: 412-624-4349, E-mail: arndt@pitt.edu. *Application contact:* Cathleen M. Barr, Graduate Administrator, 412-624-4268, Fax: 412-624-4349, E-mail: cbarr@pitt.edu.
Website: http://www.biology.pitt.edu

University of Puerto Rico–Río Piedras, College of Natural Sciences, Department of Biology, San Juan, PR 00931-3300. Offers ecology/systematics (MS, PhD); evolution/genetics (MS, PhD); molecular/cellular biology (MS, PhD); neuroscience (MS, PhD). *Program availability:* Part-time. *Degree requirements:* For master's, one foreign language, comprehensive exam, thesis; for doctorate, one foreign language, comprehensive exam, thesis/dissertation. *Entrance requirements:* For master's, GRE Subject Test, interview, minimum GPA of 3.0, letter of recommendation; for doctorate, GRE Subject Test, interview, master's degree, minimum GPA of 3.0, letter of recommendation. *Faculty research:* Environmental, poblational and systematic biology.

University of Rhode Island, Graduate School, College of the Environment and Life Sciences, Department of Biological Sciences, Kingston, RI 02881. Offers cell and molecular biology (MS, PhD); earth and environmental sciences (MS, PhD); ecology and ecosystem sciences (MS, PhD); evolutionary and marine biology (MS, PhD); sustainable agriculture and food systems (MS, PhD). *Program availability:* Part-time. *Faculty:* 18 full-time (10 women). *Students:* 99 full-time (56 women), 16 part-time (12 women); includes 10 minority (4 Black or African American, non-Hispanic/Latino; 3 Asian, non-Hispanic/Latino; 2 Hispanic/Latino; 1 Two or more races, non-Hispanic/Latino), 21 international. 151 applicants, 22% accepted, 26 enrolled. In 2017, 18 master's, 9 doctorates awarded. *Entrance requirements:* Additional exam requirements/recommendations for international students: Required—TOEFL. *Application deadline:* For fall admission, 1/15 for domestic and international students. Application fee: $65. Electronic applications accepted. *Expenses:* Tuition, state resident: full-time $12,706; part-time $786 per credit. Tuition, nonresident: full-time $25,216; part-time $1401 per credit. *Required fees:* $1598; $45 per credit. One-time fee: $30 part-time. *Financial support:* In 2017–18, 4 research assistantships with tuition reimbursements (averaging $12,698 per year) were awarded. Financial award application deadline: 1/15; financial award applicants required to submit FAFSA. *Faculty research:* Physiological constraints on predators in the Antarctic, effects of CO_2 absorption in salt water particularly as it impacts pteropods. *Unit head:* Dr. Evan Preisser, Chair, 401-874-2120, E-mail: preisser@uri.edu.
Website: http://web.uri.edu/bio/

University of South Carolina, The Graduate School, College of Arts and Sciences, Department of Biological Sciences, Graduate Training Program in Ecology, Evolution, and Organismal Biology, Columbia, SC 29208. Offers MS, PhD. *Degree requirements:* For master's, one foreign language, comprehensive exam, thesis; for doctorate, one foreign language, comprehensive exam, thesis/dissertation. *Entrance requirements:* For master's and doctorate, GRE General Test, minimum GPA of 3.0 in science. Additional exam requirements/recommendations for international students: Required—TOEFL (minimum score 570 paper-based). Electronic applications accepted.

University of Southern California, Graduate School, Dana and David Dornsife College of Letters, Arts and Sciences, Department of Biological Sciences, Program in Integrative and Evolutionary Biology, Los Angeles, CA 90089. Offers PhD. M.S. in Biology is a terminal degree only. Terminal master's awarded for partial completion of doctoral program. *Degree requirements:* For doctorate, comprehensive exam, thesis/dissertation, qualifying examination, dissertation defense. *Entrance requirements:* For doctorate, GRE, 3 letters of recommendation, personal statement, resume, minimum GPA of 3.0. Additional exam requirements/recommendations for international students: Required—TOEFL (minimum score 600 paper-based; 100 iBT). Electronic applications accepted. *Faculty research:* Organisms and their interaction with the environment, evolution and life history, integration of the control and dynamics of physiological processes, biomechanics and rehabilitation engineering, primate behavior and ecology.

University of South Florida, College of Arts and Sciences, Department of Integrative Biology, Tampa, FL 33620-9951. Offers biology (MS), including ecology and evolution (MS, PhD), environmental and ecological microbiology (MS, PhD), physiology and morphology (MS, PhD); integrative biology (PhD), including ecology and evolution (MS, PhD), environmental and ecological microbiology (MS, PhD), physiology and morphology (MS, PhD). *Program availability:* Part-time. *Faculty:* 14 full-time (5 women). *Students:* 21 full-time (11 women), 1 (woman) part-time; includes 1 minority (Asian, non-Hispanic/Latino), 2 international. Average age 30. 35 applicants, 17% accepted, 5 enrolled. In 2017, 7 master's, 5 doctorates awarded. *Degree requirements:* For master's, comprehensive exam, thesis (for some programs); for doctorate, comprehensive exam, thesis/dissertation. *Entrance requirements:* For master's and doctorate, GRE General Test, minimum GPA of 3.0 in last 60 hours of BS. *Application deadline:* For fall admission, 11/30 priority date for domestic and international students; for spring admission, 7/1 priority date for domestic and international students. Application fee: $30. Electronic applications accepted. *Financial support:* In 2017–18, 7 students received support. Research assistantships, teaching assistantships, and unspecified assistantships available. Financial award application deadline: 6/30; financial award applicants required to submit FAFSA. *Faculty research:* Marine ecology, ecosystem responses to urbanization, biomechanical and physiological mechanisms of animal movement, population biology and conservation, microbial ecology and public health microbiology, natural diversity of parasites and herbivores; ecosystems, vertebrates, disturbance ecology, functional and ecological morphology of feeding in fishes, rare amphibians and reptiles, genomics in ecological experiments, ecotoxicology, global carbon cycle, plant-animal interactions. *Total annual research expenditures:* $1.9 million. *Unit head:* Dr. Valerie Harwood, Professor and Chair, 813-974-1524, Fax: 813-974-3263, E-mail: vharwood@usf.edu. *Application contact:* Dr. Stephen Deban, Associate Professor and Graduate Program Director, 813-974-2242, E-mail: sdeban@usf.edu.
Website: http://biology.usf.edu/ib/grad/

The University of Tennessee, Graduate School, College of Arts and Sciences, Department of Ecology and Evolutionary Biology, Knoxville, TN 37996. Offers behavior (MS, PhD); ecology (MS, PhD); evolutionary biology (MS, PhD). *Program availability:* Part-time. *Degree requirements:* For master's, thesis; for doctorate, thesis/dissertation. *Entrance requirements:* For master's and doctorate, GRE General Test, minimum GPA of 2.7. Additional exam requirements/recommendations for international students: Required—TOEFL. Electronic applications accepted.

The University of Texas at Austin, Graduate School, College of Natural Sciences, School of Biological Sciences, Program in Ecology, Evolution and Behavior, Austin, TX 78712-1111. Offers PhD. *Entrance requirements:* For doctorate, GRE General Test. Additional exam requirements/recommendations for international students: Required—TOEFL. Electronic applications accepted.

University of Toronto, School of Graduate Studies, Faculty of Arts and Science, Department of Ecology and Evolutionary Biology, Toronto, ON M5S 1A1, Canada. Offers M Sc, PhD. *Degree requirements:* For master's, thesis, thesis defense; for doctorate, thesis/dissertation, thesis defense. *Entrance requirements:* For master's, minimum B average in last 2 years; knowledge of physics, chemistry, and biology. Additional exam requirements/recommendations for international students: Required—TOEFL (minimum score 580 paper-based; 93 iBT), TWE (minimum score 5). Electronic applications accepted.

Washington University in St. Louis, The Graduate School, Division of Biology and Biomedical Sciences, Program in Evolution, Ecology and Population Biology, St. Louis, MO 63130-4899. Offers ecology (PhD). *Degree requirements:* For doctorate, thesis/dissertation. *Entrance requirements:* For doctorate, GRE General Test, GRE Subject Test. Additional exam requirements/recommendations for international students: Required—TOEFL. Electronic applications accepted. *Faculty research:* Population ecology, community ecology, plant and animal evolution; microbial evolution, evolution of behavior, phylogenetics, systematics, theoretical and experimental population genetics.

Wesleyan University, Graduate Studies, Department of Biology, Middletown, CT 06459. Offers cell and developmental biology (PhD); evolution and ecology (PhD); genetics and genomics (PhD), including bioinformatics; neurobiology and behavior (PhD). Terminal master's awarded for partial completion of doctoral program. *Degree requirements:* For doctorate, comprehensive exam, thesis/dissertation, public seminar. *Entrance requirements:* For doctorate, GRE, official transcripts, three recommendation letters, essay. Additional exam requirements/recommendations for international students: Required—TOEFL. *Application deadline:* For fall admission, 1/15 for domestic and international students. Application fee: $0. Electronic applications accepted. *Financial support:* Stipends available. *Faculty research:* Evolution and ecology, neurobiology and behavior, cell and developmental biology, genetics, genomics and bioinformatics. *Unit head:* Dr. Ann Burke, Chair/Professor, 860-685-3518, E-mail: acburke@wesleyan.edu. *Application contact:* Diane Meredith, Administrative Assistant IV, 860-685-2157, E-mail: dmeredith@wesleyan.edu.
Website: http://www.wesleyan.edu/bio/

Yale University, Graduate School of Arts and Sciences, Department of Ecology and Evolutionary Biology, New Haven, CT 06520. Offers PhD. *Entrance requirements:* For doctorate, GRE General Test, GRE Subject Test (biology).

Section 9
Entomology

This section contains a directory of institutions offering graduate work in entomology. Additional information about programs listed in the directory may be obtained by writing directly to the dean of a graduate school or chair of a department at the address given in the directory.

For programs offering related work, see also in this book *Biochemistry; Biological and Biomedical Sciences; Botany and Plant Biology; Ecology, Environmental Biology, and Evolutionary Biology; Genetics, Developmental Biology, and Reproductive Biology; Microbiological Sciences; Physiology;* and *Zoology*. In the other guides in this series:

Graduate Programs in the Humanities, Arts & Social Sciences

See *Economics (Agricultural Economics and Agribusiness)*

Graduate Programs in the Physical Sciences, Mathematics, Agricultural Sciences, the Environment & Natural Resources

See *Agricultural and Food Sciences* and *Environmental Sciences and Management*

Graduate Programs in Engineering & Applied Sciences

See *Agricultural Engineering* and *Bioengineering*

CONTENTS

Entomology

Auburn University, Graduate School, College of Agriculture, Department of Entomology and Plant Pathology, Auburn University, AL 36849. Offers entomology (M Ag, MS); plant pathology (M Ag, MS, PhD). *Program availability:* Part-time. *Faculty:* 18 full-time (7 women). *Students:* 30 full-time (18 women), 14 part-time (4 women); includes 1 minority (Black or African American, non-Hispanic/Latino), 26 international. Average age 27. 23 applicants, 52% accepted, 11 enrolled. In 2017, 11 master's, 5 doctorates awarded. *Degree requirements:* For master's, thesis (for some programs); for doctorate, one foreign language, thesis/dissertation. *Entrance requirements:* For master's, GRE General Test; for doctorate, GRE General Test, GRE Subject Test, master's degree with thesis. *Application deadline:* Applications are processed on a rolling basis. Application fee: $50 ($60 for international students). Electronic applications accepted. *Expenses:* Tuition, state resident: full-time $10,974; part-time $519 per credit hour. Tuition, nonresident: full-time $29,658; part-time $1557 per credit hour. *Required fees:* $816 per semester. Tuition and fees vary according to degree level and program. *Financial support:* Research assistantships, teaching assistantships, and Federal Work-Study available. Support available to part-time students. Financial award application deadline: 3/15; financial award applicants required to submit FAFSA. *Faculty research:* Pest management, biological control, systematics, medical entomology. *Unit head:* Dr. Nannan Liu, Chair, 334-844-4266. *Application contact:* Dr. George Flowers, Dean of the Graduate School, 334-844-2125.

Clemson University, Graduate School, College of Agriculture, Forestry and Life Sciences, Department of Plant and Environmental Sciences, Clemson, SC 29634. Offers entomology (MS, PhD); plant and environmental sciences (MS, PhD). *Program availability:* Part-time. *Faculty:* 38 full-time (11 women). *Students:* 79 full-time (29 women), 15 part-time (0 women); includes 5 minority (2 Black or African American, non-Hispanic/Latino; 1 Asian, non-Hispanic/Latino; 2 Two or more races, non-Hispanic/Latino), 32 international. Average age 30. 36 applicants, 89% accepted, 17 enrolled. In 2017, 12 master's, 3 doctorates awarded. *Degree requirements:* For master's, thesis; for doctorate, comprehensive exam, thesis/dissertation. *Entrance requirements:* For master's and doctorate, GRE General Test, unofficial transcripts, letters of recommendation. Additional exam requirements/recommendations for international students: Required—TOEFL (minimum score 80 iBT), IELTS (minimum score 6.5), PTE (minimum score 54). *Application deadline:* Applications are processed on a rolling basis. Application fee: $80 ($90 for international students). Electronic applications accepted. *Expenses:* $5,174 per semester full-time resident, $9,714 per semester full-time non-resident, $511 per credit hour part-time resident, $1,017 per credit hour part-time non-resident; $741 per credit hour online; other fees may apply per session. *Financial support:* In 2017–18, 67 students received support, including 9 fellowships with partial tuition reimbursements available (averaging $8,833 per year), 42 research assistantships with partial tuition reimbursements available (averaging $19,811 per year), 13 teaching assistantships with partial tuition reimbursements available (averaging $22,607 per year); unspecified assistantships also available. Financial award application deadline: 2/15. *Faculty research:* Agronomy, horticulture, plant pathology, plant physiology, entomology. *Total annual research expenditures:* $4.1 million. *Unit head:* Dr. Matthew Turnbull, Interim Department Chair, 864-656-4964, E-mail: turnbul@clemson.edu. *Application contact:* Dr. Guido Schnabel, Graduate Program Coordinator, 864-656-6705, E-mail: schnabel@clemson.edu.
Website: http://www.clemson.edu/cafls/departments/plant-environmental-sciences/index.html

Colorado State University, College of Agricultural Sciences, Department of Bioagricultural Sciences and Pest Management, Fort Collins, CO 80523-1177. Offers entomology (MS, PhD); pest management (MS); plant pathology (MS, PhD); weed science (MS, PhD). *Faculty:* 24 full-time (9 women), 2 part-time/adjunct (1 woman). *Students:* 21 full-time (10 women), 20 part-time (14 women); includes 5 minority (1 Asian, non-Hispanic/Latino; 2 Hispanic/Latino; 2 Two or more races, non-Hispanic/Latino), 10 international. Average age 28. 22 applicants, 36% accepted, 7 enrolled. In 2017, 5 master's, 2 doctorates awarded. Terminal master's awarded for partial completion of doctoral program. *Degree requirements:* For master's, thesis; for doctorate, thesis/dissertation. *Entrance requirements:* For master's and doctorate, minimum GPA of 3.0, three letters of recommendation, essay, transcripts, short essay outlining experience and career goals. Additional exam requirements/recommendations for international students: Required—TOEFL (minimum score 550 paper-based). *Application deadline:* For fall admission, 1/15 priority date for domestic and international students; for spring admission, 9/1 priority date for domestic and international students. Application fee: $60 ($70 for international students). Electronic applications accepted. *Expenses:* Tuition, state resident: full-time $9917. Tuition, nonresident: full-time $24,312. *Required fees:* $2284. Tuition and fees vary according to course load and program. *Financial support:* In 2017–18, 29 research assistantships with partial tuition reimbursements (averaging $19,578 per year), 8 teaching assistantships with partial tuition reimbursements (averaging $17,978 per year) were awarded; fellowships with partial tuition reimbursements and scholarships/grants also available. Financial award application deadline: 1/15. *Faculty research:* Genomics and molecular biology, ecology and genetics, ecology and evolution of pest organisms, herbicide resistant weeds. *Total annual research expenditures:* $3.3 million. *Unit head:* Dr. Amy Charkowski, Department Head and Professor, 970-491-8586, E-mail: amy.charkowski@colostate.edu. *Application contact:* Janet Dill, Graduate Student Coordinator, 970-491-0402, Fax: 970-491-3862, E-mail: janet.dill@colostate.edu.
Website: http://bspm.agsci.colostate.edu/

Cornell University, Graduate School, Graduate Fields of Agriculture and Life Sciences, Field of Entomology, Ithaca, NY 14853. Offers acarology (MS, PhD); apiculture (MS, PhD); applied entomology (MS, PhD); aquatic entomology (MS, PhD); biological control (MS, PhD); insect behavior (MS, PhD); insect biochemistry (MS, PhD); insect ecology (MS, PhD); insect genetics (MS, PhD); insect morphology (MS, PhD); insect pathology (MS, PhD); insect physiology (MS, PhD); insect systematics (MS, PhD); insect toxicology and insecticide chemistry (MS, PhD); integrated pest management (MS, PhD); medical and veterinary entomology (MS, PhD). *Degree requirements:* For master's, thesis; for doctorate, comprehensive exam, thesis/dissertation. *Entrance requirements:* For master's and doctorate, GRE General Test, GRE Subject Test (biology), 3 letters of recommendation. Additional exam requirements/recommendations for international students: Required—TOEFL (minimum score 550 paper-based; 77 iBT). Electronic applications accepted. *Faculty research:* Systematics and biodiversity, integrated pest management, pathology and biological control, toxicology and physiology, ecology and behavior.

Illinois State University, Graduate School, College of Arts and Sciences, School of Biological Sciences, Normal, IL 61790. Offers animal behavior (MS); bacteriology (MS); biochemistry (MS); biological sciences (MS); biology (PhD); biophysics (MS); biotechnology (MS); botany (MS, PhD); cell biology (MS); conservation biology (MS); developmental biology (MS); ecology (MS, PhD); entomology (MS); evolutionary biology (MS); genetics (MS, PhD); immunology (MS); microbiology (MS, PhD); molecular biology (MS); molecular genetics (MS); neurobiology (MS); neuroscience (MS); parasitology (MS); physiology (MS, PhD); plant biology (MS); plant molecular biology (MS); plant sciences (MS); structural biology (MS); zoology (MS, PhD). *Program availability:* Part-time. *Degree requirements:* For master's, thesis or alternative; for doctorate, variable foreign language requirement, thesis/dissertation, 2 terms of residency. *Entrance requirements:* For master's, GRE General Test, minimum GPA of 2.6 in last 60 hours of course work; for doctorate, GRE General Test. *Faculty research:* Redoc balance and drug development in schistosoma mansoni, control of the growth of listeria monocytogenes at low temperature, regulation of cell expansion and microtubule function by SPRI, CRUI: physiology and fitness consequences of different life history phenotypes.

Iowa State University of Science and Technology, Department of Entomology, Ames, IA 50011. Offers MS, PhD. *Degree requirements:* For master's, thesis; for doctorate, thesis/dissertation. *Entrance requirements:* For master's and doctorate, GRE General Test, GRE Subject Test (biology). Additional exam requirements/recommendations for international students: Required—TOEFL (minimum score 550 paper-based; 79 iBT), IELTS (minimum score 6.5). Electronic applications accepted.

Kansas State University, Graduate School, College of Agriculture, Department of Entomology, Manhattan, KS 66506. Offers MS, PhD. *Degree requirements:* For master's, thesis, oral exam; for doctorate, comprehensive exam, thesis/dissertation, written and oral exams. *Entrance requirements:* Additional exam requirements/recommendations for international students: Required—TOEFL (minimum score 550 paper-based; 79 iBT). Electronic applications accepted. *Faculty research:* Molecular genetics, biologically-based pest management, host plant resistance, ecological genomics, stored product entomology.

Louisiana State University and Agricultural & Mechanical College, Graduate School, College of Agriculture, Department of Entomology, Baton Rouge, LA 70803. Offers MS, PhD. *Faculty:* 15 full-time (3 women). *Students:* 32 full-time (16 women), 4 part-time (2 women); includes 4 minority (1 Black or African American, non-Hispanic/Latino; 1 Asian, non-Hispanic/Latino; 2 Hispanic/Latino), 16 international. Average age 28. 28 applicants, 43% accepted, 11 enrolled. In 2017, 9 master's, 1 doctorate awarded. *Financial support:* In 2017–18, 30 research assistantships (averaging $21,550 per year), 1 teaching assistantship (averaging $22,000 per year) were awarded. *Total annual research expenditures:* $3,460.

McGill University, Faculty of Graduate and Postdoctoral Studies, Faculty of Agricultural and Environmental Sciences, Department of Natural Resource Sciences, Montréal, QC H3A 2T5, Canada. Offers entomology (M Sc, PhD); environmental assessment (M Sc); forest science (M Sc, PhD); microbiology (M Sc, PhD); micrometeorology (M Sc, PhD); neotropical environment (M Sc, PhD); soil science (M Sc, PhD); wildlife biology (M Sc, PhD).

Michigan State University, The Graduate School, College of Agriculture and Natural Resources and College of Natural Science, Department of Entomology, East Lansing, MI 48824. Offers entomology (MS, PhD); integrated pest management (MS). *Entrance requirements:* Additional exam requirements/recommendations for international students: Required—TOEFL (minimum score 550 paper-based), Michigan State University ELT (minimum score 85), Michigan English Language Assessment Battery (minimum score 83). Electronic applications accepted.

New Mexico State University, College of Agricultural, Consumer and Environmental Sciences, Department of Entomology, Plant Pathology and Weed Science, Las Cruces, NM 88003-8001. Offers MS. *Program availability:* Part-time. *Faculty:* 10 full-time (1 woman). *Students:* 13 full-time (7 women), 4 part-time (1 woman); includes 8 minority (1 American Indian or Alaska Native, non-Hispanic/Latino; 7 Hispanic/Latino), 4 international. Average age 25. 9 applicants, 44% accepted, 4 enrolled. In 2017, 5 master's awarded. *Degree requirements:* For master's, comprehensive exam, thesis. *Entrance requirements:* For master's, GRE General Test. Additional exam requirements/recommendations for international students: Required—TOEFL (minimum score 550 paper-based; 79 iBT), IELTS (minimum score 6.5). *Application deadline:* For fall admission, 7/1 priority date for domestic students; for spring admission, 11/1 priority date for domestic students. Applications are processed on a rolling basis. Application fee: $40 ($50 for international students). Electronic applications accepted. *Expenses:* Tuition, state resident: full-time $4390. Tuition, nonresident: full-time $15,309. *Required fees:* $853. *Financial support:* In 2017–18, 16 students received support, including 11 research assistantships (averaging $20,678 per year), 4 teaching assistantships (averaging $17,386 per year); career-related internships or fieldwork, Federal Work-Study, scholarships/grants, traineeships, health care benefits, and unspecified assistantships also available. Support available to part-time students. Financial award application deadline: 3/1. *Faculty research:* Entomology, nematology, plant pathology, weed science, plant genetics, environmental science. *Total annual research expenditures:* $2.5 million. *Unit head:* Dr. Gerald K. Sims, Department Head, 575-646-3225, Fax: 575-646-8087, E-mail: gksims@nmsu.edu. *Application contact:* Belinda Williams, 575-646-3225, Fax: 575-646-8087.
Website: http://eppws.nmsu.edu/

North Carolina State University, Graduate School, College of Agriculture and Life Sciences, Department of Entomology, Raleigh, NC 27695. Offers MS, PhD. Terminal master's awarded for partial completion of doctoral program. *Degree requirements:* For master's, thesis (for some programs); for doctorate, thesis/dissertation. *Entrance requirements:* For master's and doctorate, GRE General Test. Electronic applications accepted. *Faculty research:* Physiology, biocontrol, ecology, forest entomology, apiculture.

North Dakota State University, College of Graduate and Interdisciplinary Studies, College of Agriculture, Food Systems, and Natural Resources, Department of Entomology, Fargo, ND 58102. Offers MS, PhD. *Program availability:* Part-time. *Degree requirements:* For master's, thesis; for doctorate, comprehensive exam, thesis/dissertation. *Entrance requirements:* For master's and doctorate, minimum GPA of 3.0. Additional exam requirements/recommendations for international students: Required—TOEFL (minimum score 550 paper-based; 79 iBT). *Application deadline:* For fall admission, 5/1 for international students; for winter admission, 8/1 for international students. Application fee: $35. Electronic applications accepted. *Expenses:* Tuition, state resident: full-time $4323; part-time $360.21 per credit. Tuition, nonresident: full-time $6484; part-time $540.31 per credit. *Required fees:* $668; $55.70 per credit. Part-time tuition and fees vary according to degree level, program and reciprocity agreements. *Financial support:* Application deadline: 4/15. *Faculty research:* Insect systematics, conservation biology, integrated pest management, insect behavior, insect biology. *Unit head:* Jason Harmon, Program Leader, 701-231-5083, Fax: 701-231-8557, E-mail: jason.harmon@ndsu.edu. *Application contact:* Jason Harmon, Program Leader, 701-231-5083, Fax: 701-231-8557, E-mail: jason.harmon@ndsu.edu.
Website: http://www.ndsu.edu/entomology/

The Ohio State University, Graduate School, College of Food, Agricultural, and Environmental Sciences, Department of Entomology, Columbus, OH 43210. Offers MPHM, MS, PhD. MPHM offered jointly with Department of Plant Pathology. *Faculty:* 6. *Students:* 20 full-time (10 women). Average age 27. In 2017, 4 master's, 5 doctorates awarded. *Degree requirements:* For master's, variable foreign language requirement, thesis optional; for doctorate, variable foreign language requirement, thesis/dissertation. *Entrance requirements:* For master's and doctorate, GRE General Test. Additional exam requirements/recommendations for international students: Required—TOEFL (minimum score 550 paper-based; 79 iBT), Michigan English Language Assessment Battery (minimum score 82); Recommended—IELTS (minimum score 7). *Application deadline:* For fall admission, 12/15 priority date for domestic students, 11/30 priority date for international students; for spring admission, 12/12 for domestic students, 11/10 for international students; for summer admission, 4/10 for domestic students, 3/13 for international students. Applications are processed on a rolling basis. Application fee: $60 ($70 for international students). Electronic applications accepted. *Financial support:* Fellowships with tuition reimbursements, research assistantships with tuition reimbursements, teaching assistantships with tuition reimbursements, Federal Work-Study, and institutionally sponsored loans available. Support available to part-time students. *Faculty research:* Acarology, insect systematics, soil ecology, integrated pest management, chemical ecology. *Unit head:* Dr. Carol Anelli, Professor and Interim Chair, 614-292-9325, E-mail: anelli.7@osu.edu. *Application contact:* Graduate and Professional Admissions, 614-292-9444, Fax: 614-292-3895, E-mail: gpadmissions@osu.edu.
Website: http://entomology.osu.edu/

Oklahoma State University, College of Agricultural Science and Natural Resources, Department of Entomology and Plant Pathology, Stillwater, OK 74078. Offers entomology (PhD); entomology and plant pathology (MS). *Faculty:* 26 full-time (7 women). *Students:* 4 full-time (3 women), 28 part-time (16 women); includes 3 minority (1 American Indian or Alaska Native, non-Hispanic/Latino; 2 Hispanic/Latino), 13 international. Average age 29. 11 applicants, 45% accepted, 5 enrolled. In 2017, 7 master's, 6 doctorates awarded. *Entrance requirements:* For master's and doctorate, GRE or GMAT. Additional exam requirements/recommendations for international students: Required—TOEFL (minimum score 550 paper-based; 79 iBT). *Application deadline:* For fall admission, 3/1 priority date for international students; for spring admission, 8/1 priority date for international students. Applications are processed on a rolling basis. Application fee: $40 ($75 for international students). Electronic applications accepted. *Expenses:* Tuition, state resident: full-time $4019; part-time $2679.60 per year. Tuition, nonresident: full-time $15,286; part-time $10,190.40 per year. *Required fees:* $2129; $1419 per unit. Tuition and fees vary according to program. *Financial support:* Research assistantships, teaching assistantships, career-related internships or fieldwork, Federal Work-Study, scholarships/grants, health care benefits, tuition waivers (partial), and unspecified assistantships available. Support available to part-time students. Financial award application deadline: 3/1; financial award applicants required to submit FAFSA. *Unit head:* Dr. Phillip Mulder, Jr., Department Head, 405-744-5527, Fax: 405-744-6039, E-mail: phil.mulder@okstate.edu. *Application contact:* Dr. Bob Hunger, Graduate Coordinator, 405-744-9958, Fax: 405-744-6039, E-mail: bob.hunger@okstate.edu.
Website: http://entoplp.okstate.edu/

Penn State University Park, Graduate School, College of Agricultural Sciences, Department of Entomology, University Park, PA 16802. Offers MS, PhD. *Unit head:* Dr. Richard T. Roush, Dean, 814-865-2541, Fax: 814-865-3103. *Application contact:* Lori Hawn, Director, Graduate Student Services, 814-865-1795, Fax: 814-863-4627, E-mail: l-gswww@lists.psu.edu.
Website: http://ento.psu.edu/

Purdue University, Graduate School, College of Agriculture, Department of Entomology, West Lafayette, IN 47907. Offers MS, PhD. *Program availability:* Part-time. *Faculty:* 25 full-time (3 women), 2 part-time/adjunct (0 women). *Students:* 35 full-time (15 women), 4 part-time (all women); includes 7 minority (1 Black or African American, non-Hispanic/Latino; 1 Asian, non-Hispanic/Latino; 1 Hispanic/Latino; 4 Two or more races, non-Hispanic/Latino), 8 international. Average age 29. 21 applicants, 43% accepted, 7 enrolled. In 2017, 5 master's, 4 doctorates awarded. *Degree requirements:* For master's, thesis (for some programs), seminar; for doctorate, thesis/dissertation, seminar. *Entrance requirements:* For master's, GRE General Test, minimum undergraduate GPA of 3.0 or equivalent; for doctorate, GRE, minimum undergraduate GPA of 3.0 or equivalent; master's degree (highly recommended). Additional exam requirements/recommendations for international students: Required—TOEFL (minimum score 550 paper-based; 77 iBT). *Application deadline:* For fall admission, 7/1 priority date for domestic students, 3/15 for international students; for spring admission, 11/1 for domestic students, 8/15 for international students. Applications are processed on a rolling basis. Application fee: $60 ($75 for international students). Electronic applications accepted. *Financial support:* Fellowships with tuition reimbursements, research assistantships with tuition reimbursements, teaching assistantships with tuition reimbursements, and career-related internships or fieldwork available. Support available to part-time students. Financial award application deadline: 3/1; financial award applicants required to submit FAFSA. *Faculty research:* Insect biochemistry, nematology, aquatic diptera, behavioral ecology, insect physiology. *Unit head:* Stephen Cameron, Head, 765-494-4554, E-mail: cameros@purdue.edu. *Application contact:* Amanda L. Wilson, Graduate Contact, 765-494-9061, E-mail: apendle@purdue.edu.
Website: https://ag.purdue.edu/entm

Rutgers University–New Brunswick, Graduate School-New Brunswick, Program in Entomology, Piscataway, NJ 08854-8097. Offers MS, PhD. *Degree requirements:* For master's, thesis or alternative; for doctorate, thesis/dissertation. *Entrance requirements:* For master's and doctorate, GRE General Test, GRE Subject Test (recommended). Additional exam requirements/recommendations for international students: Required—TOEFL. Electronic applications accepted. *Faculty research:* Insect toxicology, biolorial control, pathology, IPM and ecology, insect systematics.

Simon Fraser University, Office of Graduate Studies and Postdoctoral Fellows, Faculty of Science, Department of Biological Sciences, Burnaby, BC V5A 1S6, Canada. Offers bioinformatics (Graduate Diploma); biological sciences (M Sc, PhD); environmental toxicology (MET); pest management (MPM). *Degree requirements:* For master's, thesis; for doctorate, thesis/dissertation, candidacy exam; for Graduate Diploma, practicum. *Entrance requirements:* For master's, minimum GPA of 3.0 (on scale of 4.33) or 3.33 based on last 60 credits of undergraduate courses; for doctorate, minimum GPA of 3.5 (on scale of 4.33); for Graduate Diploma, minimum GPA of 2.5 (on scale of 4.33) or 2.67 based on last 60 credits of undergraduate courses. Additional exam requirements/recommendations for international students: Recommended—TOEFL (minimum score 580 paper-based; 93 iBT), IELTS (minimum score 7), TWE (minimum score 5). Electronic applications accepted. *Faculty research:* Cell biology, wildlife ecology, environmental and evolutionary physiology, environmental toxicology, pest management.

State University of New York College of Environmental Science and Forestry, Department of Environmental and Forest Biology, Syracuse, NY 13210-2779. Offers applied ecology (MPS); chemical ecology (MPS, MS, PhD); conservation biology (MPS, MS, PhD); ecology (MPS, MS, PhD); entomology (MPS, MS, PhD); environmental interpretation (MPS, MS, PhD); environmental physiology (MPS, MS, PhD); fish and wildlife biology and management (MPS, MS, PhD); forest pathology and mycology (MPS, MS, PhD); plant biotechnology (MPS); plant science and biotechnology (MPS, MS, PhD). *Program availability:* Part-time. *Faculty:* 30 full-time (10 women), 4 part-time/adjunct (3 women). *Students:* 117 full-time (65 women), 18 part-time (6 women); includes 8 minority (6 American Indian or Alaska Native, non-Hispanic/Latino; 1 Asian, non-Hispanic/Latino; 1 Hispanic/Latino), 23 international. Average age 30. 84 applicants, 52% accepted, 31 enrolled. In 2017, 30 master's, 3 doctorates awarded. Terminal master's awarded for partial completion of doctoral program. *Degree requirements:* For master's, thesis (for some programs), capstone seminar; for doctorate, comprehensive exam, thesis/dissertation, capstone seminar. *Entrance requirements:* For master's and doctorate, GRE General Test, minimum GPA of 3.0. Additional exam requirements/recommendations for international students: Required—TOEFL (minimum score 550 paper-based; 80 iBT), IELTS (minimum score 6). *Application deadline:* For fall admission, 2/1 priority date for domestic and international students; for spring admission, 11/1 priority date for domestic and international students. Applications are processed on a rolling basis. Application fee: $60. Electronic applications accepted. *Expenses:* Tuition, state resident: full-time $10,870; part-time $453 per credit. Tuition, nonresident: full-time $22,210; part-time $925 per credit. *Required fees:* $1435; $70.85 per credit. One-time fee: $25 full-time. Part-time tuition and fees vary according to course load. *Financial support:* In 2017–18, 42 students received support. Unspecified assistantships available. Financial award application deadline: 6/30; financial award applicants required to submit FAFSA. *Faculty research:* Ecology, conservation biology, fish and wildlife biology and management, plant science, entomology. *Total annual research expenditures:* $5.3 million. *Unit head:* Dr. Neil H. Ringler, Chair, 315-470-6803, Fax: 315-470-6934, E-mail: nhringle@esf.edu. *Application contact:* Scott Shannon, Associate Provost for Instruction/Dean of the Graduate School, 315-470-6599, E-mail: esfgrad@esf.edu.
Website: http://www.esf.edu/efb/grad/default.asp

Texas A&M University, College of Agriculture and Life Sciences, Department of Entomology, College Station, TX 77843. Offers MS, PhD. *Faculty:* 24. *Students:* 76 full-time (40 women), 9 part-time (2 women); includes 22 minority (3 Black or African American, non-Hispanic/Latino; 6 Asian, non-Hispanic/Latino; 10 Hispanic/Latino; 3 Two or more races, non-Hispanic/Latino), 20 international. Average age 29. 30 applicants, 77% accepted, 20 enrolled. In 2017, 8 master's, 10 doctorates awarded. *Degree requirements:* For master's, comprehensive exam, thesis (for some programs); for doctorate, comprehensive exam, thesis/dissertation. *Entrance requirements:* For master's and doctorate, GRE General Test. Additional exam requirements/recommendations for international students: Required—TOEFL (minimum score 550 paper-based; 80 iBT), IELTS (minimum score 6), PTE (minimum score 53). *Application deadline:* For fall admission, 6/1 priority date for domestic students; for spring admission, 11/1 for domestic students; for summer admission, 3/1 for domestic students. Applications are processed on a rolling basis. Application fee: $50 ($90 for international students). Electronic applications accepted. *Expenses:* Contact institution. *Financial support:* In 2017–18, 77 students received support, including 12 fellowships with tuition reimbursements available (averaging $31,147 per year), 50 research assistantships with tuition reimbursements available (averaging $11,366 per year), 32 teaching assistantships with tuition reimbursements available (averaging $10,977 per year); career-related internships or fieldwork, institutionally sponsored loans, scholarships/grants, traineeships, health care benefits, tuition waivers (full and partial), and unspecified assistantships also available. Support available to part-time students. Financial award application deadline: 3/15; financial award applicants required to submit FAFSA. *Faculty research:* Biology, biological control, integrated pest management, systematics, host plant resistance. *Unit head:* Dr. David Ragsdale, Head, 979-845-2510, Fax: 979-845-6305, E-mail: dragsdale@tamu.edu. *Application contact:* Rebecca Hapes, Senior Academic Advisor II, 979-845-9733, E-mail: rhapes@tamu.edu.
Website: http://entomology.tamu.edu

The University of Arizona, Graduate Interdisciplinary Programs, Graduate Interdisciplinary Program in Entomology and Insect Science, Tucson, AZ 85721. Offers MS, PhD. *Program availability:* Part-time. *Degree requirements:* For master's, thesis; for doctorate, comprehensive exam, thesis/dissertation. *Entrance requirements:* For master's, GRE General Test, GRE Subject Test, minimum GPA of 3.0, 3 letters of recommendation; for doctorate, GRE General Test, GRE Subject Test, minimum GPA of 3.0, 3 letters of recommendation, statement of purpose. Additional exam requirements/recommendations for international students: Required—TOEFL (minimum score 550 paper-based). *Faculty research:* Toxicology and physiology, plant/insect relations, vector biology, insect pest management, chemical ecology.

University of Arkansas, Graduate School, Dale Bumpers College of Agricultural, Food and Life Sciences, Department of Entomology, Fayetteville, AR 72701. Offers MS, PhD. In 2017, 6 master's, 5 doctorates awarded. *Degree requirements:* For master's, thesis; for doctorate, one foreign language, thesis/dissertation. *Entrance requirements:* For master's, GRE, minimum GPA of 3.0; for doctorate, GRE, minimum GPA of 3.25. *Application deadline:* For fall admission, 8/1 for domestic students, 4/1 for international students; for spring admission, 12/1 for domestic students, 10/1 for international students; for summer admission, 4/15 for domestic students, 3/1 for international students. Applications are processed on a rolling basis. Application fee: $60. Electronic applications accepted. *Expenses:* Tuition, state resident: full-time $3782. Tuition, nonresident: full-time $10,238. *Financial support:* In 2017–18, 19 research assistantships were awarded; fellowships with tuition reimbursements, teaching assistantships, career-related internships or fieldwork, and Federal Work-Study also available. Support available to part-time students. Financial award application deadline: 4/1; financial award applicants required to submit FAFSA. *Faculty research:* Integrated pest management, insect virology, insect taxonomy. *Unit head:* Dr. Terry Kirkpatrick, Interim Department Head, 479-575-2490, E-mail: kirkpatr@uark.edu.
Website: https://entomology.uark.edu/index.php

University of California, Davis, Graduate Studies, Graduate Group in Integrated Pest Management, Davis, CA 95616. Offers MS. *Degree requirements:* For master's, comprehensive exam (for some programs), thesis (for some programs). *Entrance requirements:* For master's, GRE General Test, GRE Subject Test (biology), minimum GPA of 3.0. Additional exam requirements/recommendations for international students: Required—TOEFL (minimum score 550 paper-based). Electronic applications accepted.

University of California, Davis, Graduate Studies, Program in Entomology, Davis, CA 95616. Offers MS, PhD. Terminal master's awarded for partial completion of doctoral program. *Degree requirements:* For master's, comprehensive exam (for some programs), thesis (for some programs); for doctorate, thesis/dissertation. *Entrance requirements:* For master's and doctorate, GRE General Test, GRE Subject Test (biology). Additional exam requirements/recommendations for international students: Required—TOEFL (minimum score 550 paper-based). Electronic applications accepted. *Faculty research:* Bee biology, biological control, systematics, medical/veterinary entomology, pest management.

University of California, Riverside, Graduate Division, Department of Entomology, Riverside, CA 92521-0102. Offers MS, PhD. *Program availability:* Part-time. Terminal master's awarded for partial completion of doctoral program. *Degree requirements:* For master's, thesis; for doctorate, thesis/dissertation, qualifying exams. *Entrance requirements:* For master's and doctorate, GRE General Test, minimum GPA of 3.2. Additional exam requirements/recommendations for international students: Required—TOEFL (minimum score 550 paper-based; 80 iBT) or IELTS. Electronic applications accepted. *Expenses:* Tuition, state resident: full-time $5746. Tuition, nonresident: full-time $10,780. Tuition and fees vary according to campus/location and program. *Faculty research:* Agricultural, urban, medical, and veterinary entomology; biological control; chemical ecology; insect pathogens; novel toxicants.

University of Delaware, College of Agriculture and Natural Resources, Department of Entomology and Wildlife Ecology, Newark, DE 19716. Offers entomology and applied ecology (MS, PhD), including avian ecology, evolution and taxonomy, insect biological control, insect ecology and behavior (MS), insect genetics, pest management, plant-insect interactions, wildlife ecology and management. *Program availability:* Part-time. *Degree requirements:* For master's, comprehensive exam, thesis, oral exam, seminar; for doctorate, comprehensive exam, thesis/dissertation, qualifying exam, seminar. *Entrance requirements:* For master's, GRE General Test, minimum GPA of 3.0 in field, 2.8 overall; for doctorate, GRE General Test, GRE Subject Test (biology), minimum GPA of 3.0 in field, 2.8 overall. Additional exam requirements/recommendations for international students: Required—TOEFL. Electronic applications accepted. *Faculty research:* Ecology and evolution of plant-insect interactions, ecology of wildlife conservation management, habitat restoration, biological control, applied ecosystem management.

University of Georgia, College of Agricultural and Environmental Sciences, Department of Entomology, Athens, GA 30602. Offers entomology (MS, PhD). *Degree requirements:* For master's, thesis (MS); for doctorate, one foreign language, thesis/dissertation. *Entrance requirements:* For master's and doctorate, GRE General Test. Electronic applications accepted. *Faculty research:* Apiculture, acarology, aquatic and soil biology, ecology, systematics.

University of Guelph, Graduate Studies, Ontario Agricultural College, Department of Environmental Biology, Guelph, ON N1G 2W1, Canada. Offers entomology (M Sc, PhD); environmental microbiology and biotechnology (M Sc, PhD); environmental toxicology (M Sc, PhD); plant and forest systems (M Sc, PhD); plant pathology (M Sc, PhD). *Program availability:* Part-time. *Degree requirements:* For master's, thesis; for doctorate, comprehensive exam, thesis/dissertation. *Entrance requirements:* For master's, minimum 75% average during previous 2 years of course work; for doctorate, minimum 75% average. Additional exam requirements/recommendations for international students: Required—TOEFL or IELTS. Electronic applications accepted. *Faculty research:* Entomology, environmental microbiology and biotechnology, environmental toxicology, forest ecology, plant pathology.

University of Hawaii at Manoa, Office of Graduate Education, College of Tropical Agriculture and Human Resources, Department of Plant and Environmental Protection Sciences, Program in Entomology, Honolulu, HI 96822. Offers MS, PhD. *Program availability:* Part-time. *Degree requirements:* For master's, thesis optional; for doctorate, comprehensive exam, thesis/dissertation. *Entrance requirements:* For master's and doctorate, GRE General Test, GRE Subject Test (biology). Additional exam requirements/recommendations for international students: Required—TOEFL (minimum score 500 paper-based; 61 iBT), IELTS (minimum score 5). *Faculty research:* Integrated pest management, biological control, urban entomology, medical/forensic entomology resistance.

University of Idaho, College of Graduate Studies, College of Agricultural and Life Sciences, Department of Entomology, Plant Pathology and Nematology, Moscow, ID 83844. Offers plant science (MS). *Faculty:* 8 full-time. *Students:* 15. Average age 31. *Entrance requirements:* For master's and doctorate, GRE General Test, minimum GPA of 3.0. Additional exam requirements/recommendations for international students: Required—TOEFL (minimum score 550 paper-based; 79 iBT). *Application deadline:* For fall admission, 7/1 for domestic students; for spring admission, 11/1 for domestic students. Applications are processed on a rolling basis. Application fee: $60. Electronic applications accepted. *Expenses:* Tuition, state resident: full-time $6722; part-time $430 per credit hour. Tuition, nonresident: full-time $23,046; part-time $1337 per credit hour. *Required fees:* $2142; $63 per credit hour. *Financial support:* Research assistantships and teaching assistantships available. Financial award applicants required to submit FAFSA. *Faculty research:* Seed potato production, wheat production, insect pests, plant pathogens. *Unit head:* Dr. Paul McDaniel, Department Head, 208-885-6274, Fax: 208-885-7760, E-mail: pses@uidaho.edu. *Application contact:* Sean Scoggin, Graduate Recruitment Coordinator, 208-885-4001, Fax: 208-885-4406, E-mail: graduateadmissions@uidaho.edu.
Website: http://www.uidaho.edu/cals/entomology-plant-pathology-and-nematology

University of Illinois at Urbana–Champaign, Graduate College, College of Liberal Arts and Sciences, School of Integrative Biology, Department of Entomology, Champaign, IL 61820. Offers MS, PhD. Terminal master's awarded for partial completion of doctoral program.

University of Kentucky, Graduate School, College of Agriculture, Food and Environment, Program in Entomology, Lexington, KY 40506-0032. Offers MS, PhD. *Degree requirements:* For master's, comprehensive exam, thesis optional; for doctorate, comprehensive exam, thesis/dissertation. *Entrance requirements:* For master's, GRE General Test, minimum undergraduate GPA of 2.75; for doctorate, GRE General Test, minimum graduate GPA of 3.0. Additional exam requirements/recommendations for international students: Required—TOEFL (minimum score 550 paper-based). Electronic applications accepted. *Faculty research:* Applied entomology, behavior, insect biology and ecology, biological control, insect physiology and molecular biology.

University of Maine, Graduate School, College of Natural Sciences, Forestry, and Agriculture, School of Biology and Ecology, Orono, ME 04469. Offers biological sciences (PhD); botany and plant pathology (MS); entomology (MS); zoology (MS, PhD). *Program availability:* Part-time. *Faculty:* 30 full-time (16 women), 2 part-time/adjunct (1 woman). *Students:* 61 full-time (40 women), 22 part-time (11 women); includes 7 minority (1 American Indian or Alaska Native, non-Hispanic/Latino; 3 Asian, non-Hispanic/Latino; 3 Hispanic/Latino), 14 international. Average age 30. 69 applicants, 87% accepted, 28 enrolled. In 2017, 7 master's, 9 doctorates awarded. Terminal master's awarded for partial completion of doctoral program. *Degree requirements:* For master's, thesis (for some programs); for doctorate, comprehensive exam, thesis/dissertation. *Entrance requirements:* For master's and doctorate, GRE General Test. Additional exam requirements/recommendations for international students: Required—TOEFL (minimum score 80 iBT), IELTS (minimum score 6.5). *Application deadline:* For fall admission, 2/1 priority date for domestic students. Applications are processed on a rolling basis. Application fee: $65. Electronic applications accepted. *Expenses:* Tuition, state resident: full-time $7722; part-time $429 per credit hour. Tuition, nonresident: full-time $25,146; part-time $1397 per credit hour. *Required fees:* $1162; $581 per credit hour. *Financial support:* In 2017–18, 92 students received support, including 2 fellowships with full tuition reimbursements available (averaging $25,000 per year), 47 research assistantships with full tuition reimbursements available (averaging $19,800 per year), 32 teaching assistantships with full tuition reimbursements available (averaging $15,200 per year); career-related internships or fieldwork, Federal Work-Study, institutionally sponsored loans, tuition waivers (full and partial), and unspecified assistantships also available. Financial award application deadline: 3/1. *Faculty research:* Ecology and evolution (aquatic, terrestrial, paleo); development and genetics; biomedical research; ecophysiology and stress; invasion ecology and pest management. *Total annual research expenditures:* $3.1 million. *Unit head:* Dr. Andrei Aloykhin, Director, 207-581-2977, Fax: 207-581-2537. *Application contact:* Scott G. Delcourt, Assistant Vice President for Graduate Studies and Senior Associate Dean, 207-581-3291, Fax: 207-581-3232, E-mail: graduate@maine.edu.
Website: http://sbe.umaine.edu/

University of Manitoba, Faculty of Graduate Studies, Faculty of Agricultural and Food Sciences, Department of Entomology, Winnipeg, MB R3T 2N2, Canada. Offers M Sc, PhD. *Degree requirements:* For master's, thesis; for doctorate, one foreign language, thesis/dissertation.

University of Maryland, College Park, Academic Affairs, College of Computer, Mathematical and Natural Sciences, Department of Entomology, College Park, MD 20742. Offers MS, PhD. *Program availability:* Part-time, evening/weekend. Terminal master's awarded for partial completion of doctoral program. *Degree requirements:* For master's, thesis; for doctorate, thesis/dissertation, oral qualifying exam. *Entrance requirements:* For master's and doctorate, GRE General Test, minimum GPA of 3.0, 3 letters of recommendation. Electronic applications accepted. *Faculty research:* Pest management, biosystematics, physiology and morphology, toxicology.

University of Minnesota, Twin Cities Campus, Graduate School, College of Food, Agricultural and Natural Resource Sciences, Entomology Graduate Program, Saint Paul, MN 55108. Offers MS, PhD. *Program availability:* Part-time. Terminal master's awarded for partial completion of doctoral program. *Degree requirements:* For master's, comprehensive exam, thesis; for doctorate, comprehensive exam, thesis/dissertation. *Entrance requirements:* For master's, GRE, minimum undergraduate GPA of 3.0; for doctorate, GRE, minimum undergraduate GPA of 3.0, graduate 3.5. Additional exam requirements/recommendations for international students: Required—TOEFL (minimum score 550 paper-based; 79 iBT), IELTS (minimum score 6.5). Electronic applications accepted. *Faculty research:* Behavior, ecology, molecular genetics, physiology, systematics and taxonomy.

University of Nebraska–Lincoln, Graduate College, College of Agricultural Sciences and Natural Resources, Department of Entomology, Lincoln, NE 68588. Offers MS, PhD. *Program availability:* Online learning. *Degree requirements:* For master's, thesis optional; for doctorate, comprehensive exam, thesis/dissertation. *Entrance requirements:* For master's and doctorate, GRE General Test. Additional exam requirements/recommendations for international students: Required—TOEFL (minimum score 550 paper-based). Electronic applications accepted. *Faculty research:* Ecology and behavior, insect-plant interactions, integrated pest management, genetics, urban entomology.

The University of Tennessee, Graduate School, College of Agricultural Sciences and Natural Resources, Department of Entomology and Plant Pathology, Knoxville, TN 37996. Offers entomology (MS, PhD); integrated pest management and bioactive natural products (PhD); plant pathology (MS, PhD). *Program availability:* Part-time. *Degree requirements:* For master's, thesis, seminar. *Entrance requirements:* For master's, GRE General Test, minimum GPA of 2.7, 3 reference letters, letter of intent; for doctorate, GRE General Test, minimum GPA of 2.7, 3 reference letters, letter of intent, proposed dissertation research. Additional exam requirements/recommendations for international students: Required—TOEFL. Electronic applications accepted.

University of Vermont, Graduate College, College of Agriculture and Life Sciences, Department of Plant and Soil Science, Burlington, VT 05405. Offers agroecology (Graduate Certificate); plant and soil science (MS, PhD), including agroecology, agronomy (MS), ecological landscape design, entomology, horticulture (MS), plant pathology (MS), soil science. *Students:* 27 (15 women), 5 international. 23 applicants, 39% accepted, 7 enrolled. In 2017, 3 master's, 2 doctorates awarded. *Degree requirements:* For master's, thesis; for doctorate, one foreign language, thesis/dissertation. *Entrance requirements:* For master's and doctorate, GRE General Test. Additional exam requirements/recommendations for international students: Required—TOEFL (minimum score 550 paper-based; 90 iBT), IELTS (minimum score 6.5). *Application deadline:* For fall admission, 1/15 for domestic students, 2/15 for international students. Application fee: $65. Electronic applications accepted. *Expenses:* Tuition, state resident: full-time $11,628; part-time $646 per credit. Tuition, nonresident: full-time $29,340; part-time $1630 per credit. *Required fees:* $1994; $10 per credit. Tuition and fees vary according to course load and program. *Financial support:* In 2017–18, 18 students received support, including 10 research assistantships with full tuition reimbursements available (averaging $25,500 per year), 8 teaching assistantships with full tuition reimbursements available (averaging $23,500 per year); fellowships, scholarships/grants, and health care benefits also available. Financial award application deadline: 1/15. *Faculty research:* Soil chemistry, plant nutrition. *Unit head:* Dr. Josef Gorres, Coordinator, 802-656-2630, E-mail: josef.gorres@uvm.edu.
Website: http://www.uvm.edu/~pss/?Page=grad_intro.html&SM=grad_prog_menu.html

University of Wisconsin–Madison, Graduate School, College of Agricultural and Life Sciences, Department of Entomology, Madison, WI 53706-1380. Offers MS, PhD. *Degree requirements:* For master's, thesis; for doctorate, thesis/dissertation. *Entrance requirements:* For master's and doctorate, GRE General Test, minimum GPA of 3.0. Additional exam requirements/recommendations for international students: Required—TOEFL. Electronic applications accepted. *Faculty research:* Ecology, biocontrol, molecular.

University of Wyoming, College of Agriculture and Natural Resources, Department of Renewable Resources, Program in Entomology, Laramie, WY 82071. Offers MS, PhD. *Degree requirements:* For master's, thesis; for doctorate, thesis/dissertation. *Entrance requirements:* For master's and doctorate, GRE General Test, minimum GPA of 3.0. Additional exam requirements/recommendations for international students: Required—TOEFL. Electronic applications accepted. *Faculty research:* Insect pest management, taxonomy, biocontrol of weeds, forest insects, insects affecting humans and animals.

Virginia Polytechnic Institute and State University, Graduate School, College of Agriculture and Life Sciences, Blacksburg, VA 24061. Offers agricultural and applied economics (MS, PhD); agricultural and life sciences (MS); agriculture, leadership, and community education (MS, PhD); animal and poultry science (MS, PhD); biochemistry (MS, PhD); crop and soil environmental sciences (MS, PhD); dairy science (MS, PhD); entomology (MS, PhD); food science and technology (MS, PhD); horticulture (PhD); human nutrition, foods and exercise (MS, PhD); plant pathology, physiology, and weed science (MS, PhD). *Faculty:* 241 full-time (73 women), 1 (woman) part-time/adjunct. *Students:* 379 full-time (221 women), 126 part-time (75 women); includes 64 minority (21 Black or African American, non-Hispanic/Latino; 15 Asian, non-Hispanic/Latino; 14 Hispanic/Latino; 14 Two or more races, non-Hispanic/Latino), 119 international. Average age 29. 357 applicants, 46% accepted, 118 enrolled. In 2017, 105 master's, 54 doctorates awarded. *Degree requirements:* For master's, comprehensive exam (for some programs), thesis (for some programs); for doctorate, comprehensive exam (for

some programs), thesis/dissertation (for some programs). *Entrance requirements:* For master's and doctorate, GRE/GMAT. Additional exam requirements/recommendations for international students: Required—TOEFL (minimum score 80 iBT). *Application deadline:* For fall admission, 8/1 for domestic students, 4/1 for international students; for spring admission, 1/1 for domestic students, 9/1 for international students. Applications are processed on a rolling basis. Application fee: $75. Electronic applications accepted. *Expenses:* Tuition, state resident: full-time $15,072; part-time $718.50 per credit hour. Tuition, nonresident: full-time $20,810; part-time $1148.25 per credit hour. *Required fees:* $2741; $502 per semester. Tuition and fees vary according to course load, campus/location and program. *Financial support:* In 2017–18, 232 research assistantships with full tuition reimbursements (averaging $21,852 per year), 94 teaching assistantships with full tuition reimbursements (averaging $21,643 per year) were awarded. Financial award application deadline: 3/1; financial award applicants required to submit FAFSA. *Total annual research expenditures:* $44.3 million. *Unit head:* Dr. Alan L. Grant, Dean, 540-231-4152, Fax: 540-231-4163, E-mail: algrant@vt.edu. *Application contact:* Crystal Tawney, Administrative Assistant, 540-231-4152, Fax: 540-231-4163, E-mail: cdtawney@vt.edu.
Website: http://www.cals.vt.edu/

Washington State University, College of Agricultural, Human, and Natural Resource Sciences, Department of Entomology, Pullman, WA 99164. Offers MS, PhD. Programs offered at the Pullman campus. Terminal master's awarded for partial completion of doctoral program. *Degree requirements:* For master's, comprehensive exam, thesis, oral exam; for doctorate, comprehensive exam, thesis/dissertation, oral exam, written exam. *Entrance requirements:* For master's, GRE General Test, GRE Subject Test in advanced biology (recommended), undergraduate degree in biology, ecology or related area; minimum GPA of 3.0; 3 letters of recommendation; for doctorate, GRE General Test, MS in entomology, biology, ecology or related area; minimum GPA of 3.0; 3 letters of recommendation. Additional exam requirements/recommendations for international students: Required—TOEFL (minimum score 550 paper-based), IELTS. Electronic applications accepted. *Faculty research:* Apiculture, biological control of arthropods, integrated pest management, ecology, physiology and systematics of insects.

West Virginia University, Davis College of Agriculture, Forestry and Consumer Sciences, Morgantown, WV 26506. Offers agricultural and extension education (MS, PhD); agriculture and resource management (MS); agriculture, natural resources and design (M Agr); agronomy (MS); animal and food science (PhD); animal physiology (MS); applied and environmental microbiology (MS); design and merchandising (MS); entomology (MS); forest resource science (PhD); forestry (MSF); genetics and developmental biology (MS, PhD); horticulture (MS); human and community development (PhD); landscape architecture (MLA); natural resource economics (PhD); nutritional and food science (MS); plant and soil science (PhD); plant pathology (MS); recreation, parks and tourism resources (MS); reproductive physiology (MS, PhD); wildlife and fisheries resources (PhD). *Program availability:* Part-time. *Students:* 200 full-time (97 women), 53 part-time (32 women); includes 27 minority (6 Black or African American, non-Hispanic/Latino; 1 American Indian or Alaska Native, non-Hispanic/Latino; 4 Asian, non-Hispanic/Latino; 11 Hispanic/Latino; 5 Two or more races, non-Hispanic/Latino), 67 international. *Degree requirements:* For master's, thesis; for doctorate, thesis/dissertation. *Entrance requirements:* Additional exam requirements/recommendations for international students: Required—TOEFL (minimum score 550 paper-based). *Application deadline:* For fall admission, 6/1 priority date for domestic students, 6/1 for international students; for spring admission, 1/5 for domestic and international students. Applications are processed on a rolling basis. Application fee: $60. Electronic applications accepted. *Expenses:* Tuition, state resident: full-time $9450. Tuition, nonresident: full-time $24,390. *Financial support:* Fellowships, research assistantships, teaching assistantships, career-related internships or fieldwork, Federal Work-Study, institutionally sponsored loans, tuition waivers (full and partial), and unspecified assistantships available. Financial award application deadline: 2/1; financial award applicants required to submit FAFSA. *Faculty research:* Reproductive physiology, soil and water quality, human nutrition, aquaculture, wildlife management. *Unit head:* Dr. Dan J. Robison, Dean, 304-293-2395, Fax: 304-293-3740, E-mail: dan.robison@mail.wvu.edu. *Application contact:* Dr. Dennis K. Smith, Associate Dean, 304-293-2275, Fax: 304-293-3740, E-mail: denny.smith@mail.wvu.edu.
Website: https://www.davis.wvu.edu

Section 10
Genetics, Developmental Biology, and Reproductive Biology

This section contains a directory of institutions offering graduate work in genetics, developmental biology, and reproductive biology, followed by in-depth entries submitted by institutions that chose to prepare detailed program descriptions. Additional information about programs listed in the directory but not augmented by an in-depth entry may be obtained by writing directly to the dean of a graduate school or chair of a department at the address given in the directory.

For programs offering related work, see also all other sections of this book. In the other guides in this series:

Graduate Programs in the Physical Sciences, Mathematics, Agricultural Sciences, the Environment & Natural Resources

See *Agricultural and Food Sciences, Chemistry,* and *Environmental Sciences and Management*

Graduate Programs in Engineering & Applied Sciences

See *Agricultural Engineering and Bioengineering* and *Biomedical Engineering and Biotechnology*

CONTENTS

Program Directories

Featured School: Display and Close-Up

See:

Developmental Biology

Albert Einstein College of Medicine, Graduate Programs in the Biomedical Sciences, Department of Developmental and Molecular Biology, Bronx, NY 10461. Offers PhD, MD/PhD. *Degree requirements:* For doctorate, thesis/dissertation. *Entrance requirements:* For doctorate, GRE General Test. Additional exam requirements/recommendations for international students: Required—TOEFL. *Application deadline:* For fall admission, 1/15 for domestic students. Application fee: $0. *Financial support:* Fellowships available. *Faculty research:* DNA, RNA, and protein synthesis in prokaryotes and eukaryotes; chemical and enzymatic alteration of RNA; glycoproteins. *Unit head:* Dr. Liang Zhu, Interim Chair, 718-430-3320. *Application contact:* Sheila Cleeton, Executive Director and Registrar, Einstein Graduate Division, 718-430-2128, Fax: 718-430-8655, E-mail: sheila.cleeton@einstein.yu.edu.
Website: http://www.einstein.yu.edu/departments/developmental-molecular-biology/

Baylor College of Medicine, Graduate School of Biomedical Sciences, Program in Developmental Biology, Houston, TX 77030-3498. Offers PhD, MD/PhD. *Degree requirements:* For doctorate, thesis/dissertation, public defense. *Entrance requirements:* For doctorate, GRE General Test, GRE Subject Test (strongly recommended), minimum GPA of 3.0. Additional exam requirements/recommendations for international students: Required—TOEFL. Electronic applications accepted. *Faculty research:* Stem cells, cancer, neurobiology, organogenesis, genetics of model organisms.

Brigham Young University, Graduate Studies, College of Life Sciences, Department of Physiology and Developmental Biology, Provo, UT 84602. Offers neuroscience (MS, PhD); physiology and developmental biology (MS, PhD). *Program availability:* Part-time. *Faculty:* 19 full-time (1 woman), 4 part-time/adjunct (3 women). *Students:* 33 full-time (16 women); includes 6 minority (5 Asian, non-Hispanic/Latino; 1 Hispanic/Latino). Average age 30. 14 applicants, 43% accepted, 3 enrolled. In 2017, 6 master's, 4 doctorates awarded. Terminal master's awarded for partial completion of doctoral program. *Degree requirements:* For master's, thesis, oral exam; for doctorate, comprehensive exam, thesis/dissertation. *Entrance requirements:* For master's, GRE General Test, MCAT, or DAT, minimum GPA of 3.0 during previous 2 years; for doctorate, GRE General Test, minimum GPA of 3.0 overall. Additional exam requirements/recommendations for international students: Required—TOEFL (minimum score 580 paper-based; 85 iBT); Recommended—IELTS. *Application deadline:* For fall admission, 2/1 priority date for domestic and international students; for winter admission, 9/10 priority date for domestic students, 9/10 for international students; for spring admission, 2/1 for domestic and international students; for summer admission, 2/1 for domestic and international students. Application fee: $50. Electronic applications accepted. *Expenses:* $6,880 full-time first year for members of the Church of Jesus Christ of Latter-day Saints; $13,760 for those who are not members of the Church; $405 per credit for additional years. *Financial support:* In 2017–18, 33 students received support, including 1 fellowship with partial tuition reimbursement available (averaging $15,000 per year), 16 research assistantships with full tuition reimbursements available (averaging $15,500 per year), 18 teaching assistantships with partial tuition reimbursements available (averaging $14,900 per year); career-related internships or fieldwork, institutionally sponsored loans, scholarships/grants, tuition waivers (full and partial), unspecified assistantships, and tuition awards also available. Financial award application deadline: 2/1. *Faculty research:* Sex differentiation of the brain, exercise physiology, developmental biology, membrane biophysics, neuroscience, heart differentiation/birth defects. *Total annual research expenditures:* $435,024. *Unit head:* Dr. Dixon J. Woodbury, Chair, 801-422-7562, Fax: 801-422-0004, E-mail: dixon_woodbury@byu.edu. *Application contact:* Connie L. Provost, Graduate Program Manager, 801-422-3706, Fax: 801-422-0004, E-mail: connie_provost@byu.edu.
Website: http://pdbio.byu.edu

California Institute of Technology, Division of Biology, Program in Developmental Biology, Pasadena, CA 91125-0001. Offers PhD. *Degree requirements:* For doctorate, thesis/dissertation, qualifying exam. *Entrance requirements:* For doctorate, GRE General Test.

California State University, Sacramento, College of Natural Sciences and Mathematics, Department of Biological Sciences, Sacramento, CA 95819. Offers biological conservation (MS); molecular and cellular biology (MS); stem cell (MA). *Program availability:* Part-time. *Students:* 25 full-time (15 women), 26 part-time (14 women); includes 11 minority (2 Black or African American, non-Hispanic/Latino; 1 American Indian or Alaska Native, non-Hispanic/Latino; 8 Asian, non-Hispanic/Latino), 1 international. Average age 29. 82 applicants, 29% accepted, 18 enrolled. In 2017, 11 master's awarded. *Degree requirements:* For master's, thesis or project; writing proficiency exam. *Entrance requirements:* For master's, GRE, bachelor's degree in biology or equivalent; minimum GPA of 2.75 in all biology courses, 3.0 in all upper-division biology courses. Additional exam requirements/recommendations for international students: Required—TOEFL (minimum score 550 paper-based; 80 iBT); Recommended—IELTS, TSE. *Application deadline:* For fall admission, 2/1 for domestic and international students. Applications are processed on a rolling basis. Application fee: $55. Electronic applications accepted. *Expenses:* Contact institution. *Financial support:* Teaching assistantships, career-related internships or fieldwork, Federal Work-Study, and scholarships/grants available. Support available to part-time students. Financial award application deadline: 3/1; financial award applicants required to submit FAFSA. *Unit head:* Dr. Shannon Datwyler, Chair, 916-278-6535, Fax: 916-278-6993, E-mail: datwyler@csus.edu. *Application contact:* Jose Martinez, Graduate Admissions Supervisor, 916-278-7871, E-mail: martinj@skymail.csus.edu.
Website: http://www.csus.edu/bios

Carnegie Mellon University, Mellon College of Science, Department of Biological Sciences, Pittsburgh, PA 15213-3891. Offers biochemistry (PhD); biophysics (PhD); cell and developmental biology (PhD); computational biology (MS, PhD); genetics (PhD); molecular biology (PhD); neuroscience (PhD); structural biology (PhD). *Degree requirements:* For doctorate, comprehensive exam, thesis/dissertation. *Entrance requirements:* For doctorate, GRE General Test, GRE Subject Test, interview. Electronic applications accepted. *Faculty research:* Genetic structure, function, and regulation; protein structure and function; biological membranes; biological spectroscopy.

Columbia University, College of Physicians and Surgeons, Department of Genetics and Development, New York, NY 10032. Offers genetics (M Phil, MA, PhD); MD/PhD. Only candidates for the PhD are admitted. Terminal master's awarded for partial completion of doctoral program. *Degree requirements:* For doctorate, thesis/dissertation. *Entrance requirements:* For master's and doctorate, GRE General Test. Additional exam requirements/recommendations for international students: Required—TOEFL. *Expenses: Tuition:* Full-time $44,864; part-time $1704 per credit. *Required fees:* $2370 per semester. One-time fee: $105. *Faculty research:* Mammalian cell differentiation and meiosis, developmental genetics, yeast and human genetics, chromosome structure, molecular and cellular biology.

Cornell University, Graduate School, Graduate Fields of Agriculture and Life Sciences, Field of Genetics, Genomics and Development, Ithaca, NY 14853. Offers developmental biology (PhD); genetics (PhD); genomics (PhD). *Degree requirements:* For doctorate, comprehensive exam, thesis/dissertation, 2 semesters of teaching experience. *Entrance requirements:* For doctorate, GRE General Test, GRE Subject Test in biology or biochemistry (recommended), 2 letters of recommendation. Additional exam requirements/recommendations for international students: Required—TOEFL (minimum score 550 paper-based; 77 iBT). Electronic applications accepted. *Faculty research:* Molecular and general genetics, developmental biology and developmental genetics, evolution and population genetics, plant genetics, microbial genetics.

Duke University, Graduate School, Program in Developmental and Stem Cell Biology, Durham, NC 27710. Offers Certificate. *Entrance requirements:* For degree, GRE General Test. Additional exam requirements/recommendations for international students: Required—TOEFL (minimum score 577 paper-based; 90 iBT) or IELTS (minimum score 7).

Emory University, Laney Graduate School, Division of Biological and Biomedical Sciences, Program in Biochemistry, Cell and Developmental Biology, Atlanta, GA 30322. Offers PhD. *Degree requirements:* For doctorate, comprehensive exam, thesis/dissertation. *Entrance requirements:* For doctorate, GRE General Test, minimum GPA of 3.0 in science course work (recommended). Additional exam requirements/recommendations for international students: Required—TOEFL. Electronic applications accepted. *Faculty research:* Signal transduction, molecular biology, enzymes and cofactors, receptor and ion channel function, membrane biology.

Illinois State University, Graduate School, College of Arts and Sciences, School of Biological Sciences, Normal, IL 61790. Offers animal behavior (MS); bacteriology (MS); biochemistry (MS); biological sciences (MS); biology (PhD); biophysics (MS); biotechnology (MS); botany (MS, PhD); cell biology (MS); conservation biology (MS); developmental biology (MS); ecology (MS, PhD); entomology (MS); evolutionary biology (MS); genetics (MS, PhD); immunology (MS); microbiology (MS, PhD); molecular biology (MS); molecular genetics (MS); neurobiology (MS); neuroscience (MS); parasitology (MS); physiology (MS, PhD); plant biology (MS); plant molecular biology (MS); plant sciences (MS); structural biology (MS); zoology (MS, PhD). *Program availability:* Part-time. *Degree requirements:* For master's, thesis or alternative; for doctorate, variable foreign language requirement, thesis/dissertation, 2 terms of residency. *Entrance requirements:* For master's, GRE General Test, minimum GPA of 2.6 in last 60 hours of course work; for doctorate, GRE General Test. *Faculty research:* Redoc balance and drug development in schistosoma mansoni, control of the growth of listeria monocytogenes at low temperature, regulation of cell expansion and microtubule function by SPRI, CRUI: physiology and fitness consequences of different life history phenotypes.

Iowa State University of Science and Technology, Program in Molecular, Cellular, and Developmental Biology, Ames, IA 50011. Offers MS, PhD. *Entrance requirements:* For master's and doctorate, GRE General Test. Additional exam requirements/recommendations for international students: Required—TOEFL (minimum score 580 paper-based; 85 iBT), IELTS (minimum score 7). Electronic applications accepted.

Irell & Manella Graduate School of Biological Sciences, Graduate Program, Duarte, CA 91010. Offers brain metastatic cancer (PhD); cancer and stem cell metabolism (PhD); cancer biology (PhD); cancer biology and developmental therapeutics (PhD); cell biology (PhD); chemical biology (PhD); chromosomal break repair (PhD); diabetes and pancreatic progenitor cell biology (PhD); DNA repair and cancer biology (PhD); germline epigenetic remodeling and endocrine disruptors (PhD); hematology and hematopoietic cell transplantation (PhD); hematology and immunology (PhD); inflammation and cancer (PhD); micrornas and gene regulation in cardiovascular disease (PhD); mixed chimrism for reversal of autoimmunity (PhD); molecular and cellular biology (PhD); molecular biology and genetics (PhD); nanoparticle mediated twist1 silencing in metastatic cancer (PhD); neuro-oncology and stem cell biology (PhD); neuroscience (PhD); RNA directed therapies for HIV-1 (PhD); small RNA-induced transcriptional gene activation (PhD); stem cell regulation by the microenvironment (PhD); translational oncology and pharmaceutical sciences (PhD); tumor biology (PhD). *Degree requirements:* For doctorate, comprehensive exam, thesis/dissertation, qualifying exams, two advanced courses. *Entrance requirements:* For doctorate, GRE General Test; GRE Subject Test (recommended), 2 years of course work in chemistry (general and organic); 1 year of course work each in biochemistry, general biology, and general physics; 2 semesters of course work in mathematics; significant research laboratory experience. Additional exam requirements/recommendations for international students: Required—TOEFL. Electronic applications accepted. *Faculty research:* Cancer biology, diabetes, stem cell biology, neuroscience, immunology.

See Display on page 65 and Close-Up on page 109.

Johns Hopkins University, National Institutes of Health Sponsored Programs, Baltimore, MD 21218. Offers biology (PhD), including biochemistry, biophysics, cell biology, developmental biology, genetic biology, molecular biology; cell, molecular, and developmental biology and biophysics (PhD). *Degree requirements:* For doctorate, comprehensive exam, thesis/dissertation. *Entrance requirements:* For doctorate, GRE General Test. Additional exam requirements/recommendations for international students: Required—TOEFL (minimum score 600 paper-based), TWE. Electronic applications accepted. *Faculty research:* Protein and nucleic acid biochemistry and biophysical chemistry, molecular biology and development.

Johns Hopkins University, Zanvyl Krieger School of Arts and Sciences, Program in Cell, Molecular, Developmental Biology, and Biophysics, Baltimore, MD 21218. Offers PhD. Terminal master's awarded for partial completion of doctoral program. *Degree requirements:* For doctorate, comprehensive exam, thesis/dissertation. *Entrance requirements:* For doctorate, GRE General Test. Additional exam requirements/recommendations for international students: Required—TOEFL (minimum score 600 paper-based), IELTS, TWE. Electronic applications accepted. *Faculty research:* Cell biology, molecular biology and development, biochemistry, developmental biology, biophysics, genetics.

Louisiana State University Health Sciences Center, School of Graduate Studies in New Orleans, Department of Cell Biology and Anatomy, New Orleans, LA 70112-2223. Offers cell biology and anatomy (PhD), including clinical anatomy, development, cell, and neurobiology; MD/PhD. *Faculty:* 17 full-time (2 women). *Students:* 5 full-time (3 women), 1 (woman) part-time; includes 1 minority (Asian, non-Hispanic/Latino). 1 applicant. *Degree requirements:* For doctorate, comprehensive exam, thesis/dissertation. *Entrance requirements:* For doctorate, GRE General Test, minimum

undergraduate GPA of 3.0. Additional exam requirements/recommendations for international students: Recommended—TOEFL, IELTS. *Application deadline:* For fall admission, 3/1 priority date for domestic students, 3/1 for international students. Applications are processed on a rolling basis. Application fee: $30. *Expenses:* Tuition, state resident: full-time $11,835; part-time $518 per hour. Tuition, nonresident: full-time $24,108; part-time $1079 per hour. *Required fees:* $1254; $55 per hour. *Financial support:* In 2017–18, 6 students received support. Unspecified assistantships available. Financial award application deadline: 4/1. *Faculty research:* Visual system organization, neural development, plasticity of sensory systems, information processing through the nervous system, visuomotor integration. *Total annual research expenditures:* $900,000. *Unit head:* Dr. Samuel McClugage, Head, 504-568-4011, Fax: 504-568-2165, E-mail: smcclu@lsuhsc.edu. *Application contact:* Dr. R. John Cork, Graduate Coordinator and Professor, 504-568-7177, E-mail: jcork@lsuhsc.edu.
Website: http://www.medschool.lsuhsc.edu/cell_biology/

Marquette University, Graduate School, College of Arts and Sciences, Department of Biology, Milwaukee, WI 53201-1881. Offers cell biology (MS, PhD); developmental biology (MS, PhD); ecology (MS, PhD); epithelial physiology (MS, PhD); genetics (MS, PhD); microbiology (MS, PhD); molecular biology (MS, PhD); muscle and exercise physiology (MS, PhD); neuroscience (PhD). Terminal master's awarded for partial completion of doctoral program. *Degree requirements:* For master's, comprehensive exam, thesis, 1 year of teaching experience or equivalent; for doctorate, thesis/dissertation, 1 year of teaching experience or equivalent, qualifying exam. *Entrance requirements:* For master's and doctorate, GRE General Test, GRE Subject Test, official transcripts from all current and previous colleges/universities except Marquette, statement of professional goals and aspirations, three letters of recommendation. Additional exam requirements/recommendations for international students: Required—TOEFL (minimum score 530 paper-based). Electronic applications accepted. *Faculty research:* Neurobiology, neuroendocrinology, epithelial physiology, neuropeptide interactions, synaptic transmission.

Massachusetts Institute of Technology, School of Science, Department of Biology, Cambridge, MA 02139. Offers biochemistry (PhD); biological oceanography (PhD); biology (PhD); biophysical chemistry and molecular structure (PhD); cell biology (PhD); computational and systems biology (PhD); developmental biology (PhD); genetics (PhD); immunology (PhD); microbiology (PhD); molecular biology (PhD); neurobiology (PhD). *Degree requirements:* For doctorate, comprehensive exam, thesis/dissertation, teaching assistantship during two semesters. *Entrance requirements:* For doctorate, GRE General Test. Additional exam requirements/recommendations for international students: Required—TOEFL, IELTS. Electronic applications accepted. *Faculty research:* Cellular, developmental and molecular (plant and animal) biology; biochemistry, bioengineering, biophysics and structural biology; classical and molecular genetics, stem cell and epigenetics; immunology and microbiology; cancer biology, molecular medicine, neurobiology and human disease; computational and systems biology.

Medical University of South Carolina, College of Graduate Studies, Program in Molecular and Cellular Biology and Pathobiology, Charleston, SC 29425. Offers cancer biology (PhD); cardiovascular biology (PhD); cardiovascular imaging (PhD); cell regulation (PhD); craniofacial biology (PhD); genetics and development (PhD); marine biomedicine (PhD); DMD/PhD; MD/PhD. *Degree requirements:* For doctorate, thesis/dissertation, oral and written exams. *Entrance requirements:* For doctorate, GRE General Test, interview, minimum GPA of 3.0. Additional exam requirements/recommendations for international students: Required—TOEFL (minimum score 600 paper-based; 100 iBT). Electronic applications accepted.

New York University, Graduate School of Arts and Science, Department of Biology, New York, NY 10012-1019. Offers biology (PhD); biomedical journalism (MS); cancer and molecular biology (PhD); computational biology (PhD); computers in biological research (MS); developmental genetics (PhD); general biology (MS); immunology and microbiology (PhD); molecular genetics (PhD); neurobiology (PhD); oral biology (MS); plant biology (PhD); recombinant DNA technology (MS); MS/MBA. *Program availability:* Part-time. *Students:* Average age 27. 394 applicants, 56% accepted, 77 enrolled. In 2017, 68 master's, 9 doctorates awarded. Terminal master's awarded for partial completion of doctoral program. *Degree requirements:* For master's, thesis or alternative, qualifying paper; for doctorate, comprehensive exam, thesis/dissertation. *Entrance requirements:* For master's and doctorate, GRE General Test. Additional exam requirements/recommendations for international students: Required—TOEFL. *Application deadline:* For fall admission, 12/1 priority date for domestic students, 12/1 for international students. Application fee: $100. *Expenses: Tuition:* Full-time $41,352; part-time $19,968 per year. *Required fees:* $2496; $1628 per unit. $814 per term. Tuition and fees vary according to course load and program. *Financial support:* Fellowships, research assistantships, teaching assistantships, career-related internships or fieldwork, Federal Work-Study, institutionally sponsored loans, scholarships/grants, health care benefits, and unspecified assistantships available. Financial award application deadline: 12/1; financial award applicants required to submit FAFSA. *Faculty research:* Genomics, molecular and cell biology, development and molecular genetics, molecular evolution of plants and animals. *Unit head:* Stephen Small, Chair, 212-998-8200, Fax: 212-995-4015, E-mail: biology.admissions@nyu.edu. *Application contact:* Ken Birnbaum, Director of Graduate Studies, PhD Programs, 212-998-8200, Fax: 212-995-4015, E-mail: biology.admissions@nyu.edu.
Website: http://biology.as.nyu.edu/

New York University, School of Medicine and Graduate School of Arts and Science, Sackler Institute of Graduate Biomedical Sciences, New York, NY 10016. Offers biomedical imaging and technology (PhD); biostatistics (PhD); cellular and molecular biology (PhD); developmental genetics (PhD); epidemiology (PhD); genome integrity (PhD); immunology and inflammation (PhD); microbiology (PhD); molecular biophysics (PhD); molecular oncology and tumor immunology (PhD); molecular pharmacology (PhD); neuroscience and physiology (PhD), including immunology, molecular oncology; stem cell biology (PhD); systems and computational biomedicine (PhD); MD/PhD. *Faculty:* 207 full-time (51 women). *Students:* 236 full-time (138 women), 1 part-time (0 women); includes 68 minority (13 Black or African American, non-Hispanic/Latino; 26 Asian, non-Hispanic/Latino; 28 Hispanic/Latino; 1 Native Hawaiian or other Pacific Islander, non-Hispanic/Latino), 79 international. Average age 27. 761 applicants, 18% accepted, 59 enrolled. In 2017, 35 doctorates awarded. *Degree requirements:* For doctorate, comprehensive exam, thesis/dissertation, qualifying exam; thesis defense. *Entrance requirements:* For doctorate, GRE. Additional exam requirements/recommendations for international students: Required—TOEFL, IELTS. *Application deadline:* For fall admission, 12/1 for domestic and international students. Applications are processed on a rolling basis. Application fee: $100. Electronic applications accepted. Application fee is waived when completed online. *Expenses:* Contact institution. *Financial support:* Health care benefits, tuition waivers (full), and unspecified assistantships available. *Faculty research:* Biomedical sciences. *Unit head:* Dr. Naoko Tanese, Associate Dean for Biomedical Sciences/Director, Sackler Institute, 212-263-8945, E-mail: naoko.tanese@nyumc.org. *Application contact:* Jessica Dong, Program Manager, 212-263-5648, E-mail: sackler-info@nyumc.org.
Website: https://med.nyu.edu/research/sackler-institute-graduate-biomedical-sciences/

Northwestern University, The Graduate School, Interdisciplinary Biological Sciences Program (IBiS), Evanston, IL 60208. Offers biochemistry (PhD); bioengineering and biotechnology (PhD); biotechnology (PhD); cell and molecular biology (PhD); developmental and systems biology (PhD); nanotechnology (PhD); neurobiology (PhD); structural biology and biophysics (PhD). *Degree requirements:* For doctorate, thesis/dissertation, qualifying exam. *Entrance requirements:* For doctorate, GRE General Test. Additional exam requirements/recommendations for international students: Required—TOEFL (minimum score 600 paper-based). Electronic applications accepted. *Faculty research:* Biophysics/structural biology, cell/molecular biology, synthetic biology, developmental systems biology, chemical biology/nanotechnology.

The Ohio State University, Graduate School, College of Arts and Sciences, Division of Natural and Mathematical Sciences, Department of Molecular Genetics, Columbus, OH 43210. Offers cell and developmental biology (MS, PhD); genetics (MS, PhD); molecular biology (MS, PhD). *Faculty:* 30. *Students:* 34 full-time (16 women), 13 international. Average age 26. In 2017, 6 doctorates awarded. *Entrance requirements:* For doctorate, GRE General Test, GRE Subject Test in biology or chemistry (recommended). Additional exam requirements/recommendations for international students: Required—TOEFL (minimum score 550 paper-based; 79 iBT), Michigan English Language Assessment Battery (minimum score 82); Recommended—IELTS (minimum score 7). *Application deadline:* For fall admission, 12/13 priority date for domestic students, 11/30 priority date for international students; for spring admission, 3/1 for domestic students, 2/1 for international students. Applications are processed on a rolling basis. Application fee: $60 ($70 for international students). Electronic applications accepted. *Financial support:* Fellowships, research assistantships, teaching assistantships, Federal Work-Study, and institutionally sponsored loans available. Support available to part-time students. *Unit head:* Dr. Mark Seeger, Chair, 614-292-5106, E-mail: seeger.9@osu.edu. *Application contact:* Graduate and Professional Admissions, 614-292-9444, Fax: 614-292-3895, E-mail: gpadmissions@osu.edu.
Website: https://molgen.osu.edu/

The Ohio State University, Graduate School, College of Arts and Sciences, Division of Natural and Mathematical Sciences, Program in Molecular, Cellular and Developmental Biology, Columbus, OH 43210. Offers MS, PhD. *Students:* 87 full-time (44 women); includes 6 minority (all Asian, non-Hispanic/Latino), 30 international. Average age 26. In 2017, 3 master's, 18 doctorates awarded. Terminal master's awarded for partial completion of doctoral program. *Entrance requirements:* For doctorate, GRE General Test, GRE Subject Test in any science (desired, preferably biology or chemistry, biochemistry or cell and molecular biology). Additional exam requirements/recommendations for international students: Required—TOEFL (minimum score 600 paper-based; 85 iBT), Recommended—IELTS (minimum score 8). *Application deadline:* For fall admission, 12/13 priority date for domestic students, 11/30 priority date for international students; for spring admission, 3/1 for domestic students, 2/1 for international students. Applications are processed on a rolling basis. Application fee: $60 ($70 for international students). Electronic applications accepted. *Financial support:* Fellowships, research assistantships, and teaching assistantships available. *Unit head:* Dr. Dawn Chandler, Co-Director, 614-722-5597, E-mail: chandler.135@osu.edu. *Application contact:* Graduate and Professional Admissions, 614-292-9444, Fax: 614-292-3895, E-mail: gpadmissions@osu.edu.
Website: http://mcdb.osu.edu/

Oregon Health & Science University, School of Medicine, Graduate Programs in Medicine, Program in Molecular and Cellular Biosciences, Cell and Developmental Biology Graduate Program, Portland, OR 97239-3098. Offers PhD. *Faculty:* 11 full-time (6 women), 38 part-time/adjunct (6 women). *Students:* 9 full-time (4 women); includes 2 minority (both Asian, non-Hispanic/Latino), 1 international. Average age 28. *Degree requirements:* For doctorate, comprehensive exam, thesis/dissertation, qualifying exam. *Entrance requirements:* For doctorate, GRE General Test (minimum scores: 153 Verbal/148 Quantitative/4.5 Analytical) or MCAT. *Application deadline:* For fall admission, 12/1 for domestic and international students. Application fee: $70. *Financial support:* Health care benefits, tuition waivers (full), and full-tuition and stipends available. Financial award application deadline: 3/1; financial award applicants required to submit FAFSA. *Faculty research:* Biosynthesis, intracellular trafficking, and function of essential cellular components; signal transduction and developmental regulation of gene expression; regulation of cell proliferation, growth, and motility; mechanisms of morphogenesis and differentiation; mechanisms controlling the onset, progression, and dissemination of cancer. *Unit head:* Dr. Philip Copenhaver, Program Director, E-mail: somgrad@ohsu.edu. *Application contact:* Lola Bichler, Program Coordinator, E-mail: somgrad@ohsu.edu.
Website: http://www.ohsu.edu/xd/education/schools/school-of-medicine/departments/basic-science-departments/cell-and-developmental-biology/graduate-program/CDB-

Penn State Hershey Medical Center, College of Medicine, Graduate School Programs in the Biomedical Sciences, Huck Institutes of the Life Sciences, Intercollege Graduate Program in Molecular Cellular and Integrative Biosciences, Hershey, PA 17033. Offers cell and developmental biology (PhD); molecular medicine (PhD); molecular toxicology (PhD); neurobiology (PhD). *Students:* 3 full-time (2 women); includes 2 minority (both Asian, non-Hispanic/Latino). 2 applicants, 100% accepted, 2 enrolled. In 2017, 1 doctorate awarded. *Degree requirements:* For doctorate, comprehensive exam, thesis/dissertation, oral exam. *Entrance requirements:* For doctorate, GRE, minimum GPA of 3.0. Additional exam requirements/recommendations for international students: Required—TOEFL (minimum score 500 paper-based). *Application deadline:* For fall admission, 1/31 priority date for domestic students, 2/1 priority date for international students. Applications are processed on a rolling basis. Application fee: $65. Electronic applications accepted. *Financial support:* In 2017–18, research assistantships with full tuition reimbursements (averaging $26,196 per year) were awarded; fellowships with full tuition reimbursements, career-related internships or fieldwork, Federal Work-Study, scholarships/grants, health care benefits, and unspecified assistantships also available. Financial award applicants required to submit FAFSA. *Faculty research:* Vascular biology, molecular toxicology, chemical biology, immune system, pathophysiological basis of human disease. *Unit head:* Dr. Peter Hudson, Director, 814-865-6057, E-mail: pjh18@psu.edu. *Application contact:* Kathy Shuey, Administrative Assistant, 717-531-8982, Fax: 717-531-0786, E-mail: grad-hmc@psu.edu.
Website: http://www.huck.psu.edu/education/molecular-cellular-and-integrative-biosciences

Purdue University, Graduate School, College of Science, Department of Biological Sciences, West Lafayette, IN 47907. Offers biochemistry (PhD); biophysics (PhD); cell and developmental biology (PhD); ecology, evolutionary and population biology (MS, PhD), including ecology, evolutionary biology, population biology; genetics (MS, PhD); microbiology (MS, PhD); molecular biology (PhD); neurobiology (MS, PhD); plant physiology (PhD). *Faculty:* 42 full-time (13 women), 3 part-time/adjunct (0 women). *Students:* 115 full-time (58 women), 6 part-time (4 women); includes 17 minority (1 Black or African American, non-Hispanic/Latino; 6 Asian, non-Hispanic/Latino; 9 Hispanic/Latino; 1 Two or more races, non-Hispanic/Latino), 60 international. Average age 27. 165 applicants, 12% accepted, 15 enrolled. In 2017, 5 master's, 16 doctorates awarded. Terminal master's awarded for partial completion of doctoral program. *Degree requirements:* For master's, thesis (for some programs); for doctorate, thesis/dissertation, seminars, teaching experience. *Entrance requirements:* For master's, GRE General Test (minimum analytical writing score of 3.5), minimum undergraduate GPA of 3.0; for doctorate, GRE General Test (minimum analytical writing score of 3.5), minimum

undergraduate GPA of 3.5. Additional exam requirements/recommendations for international students: Required—TOEFL minimum score 600 paper-based; 107 iBT (for MS), 80 iBT (for PhD). *Application deadline:* For fall admission, 12/7 for domestic and international students. Applications are processed on a rolling basis. Application fee: $60 ($75 for international students). Electronic applications accepted. *Financial support:* Fellowships, research assistantships, and teaching assistantships available. Support available to part-time students. Financial award application deadline: 2/15; financial award applicants required to submit FAFSA. *Unit head:* Stephen Konieczny, Head, 765-494-4407, E-mail: sfk@purdue.edu. *Application contact:* Georgina E. Rupp, Graduate Coordinator, 765-494-8142, E-mail: ruppg@purdue.edu.
Website: http://www.bio.purdue.edu/

Rutgers University–Newark, Graduate School of Biomedical Sciences, Newark, NJ 07107. Offers biodefense (Certificate); biomedical engineering (PhD); biomedical sciences (multidisciplinary) (PhD); cellular biology, neuroscience and physiology (PhD), including neuroscience, physiology, biophysics, cardiovascular biology, molecular pharmacology, stem cell biology; infection, immunity and inflammation (PhD), including immunology, infectious disease, microbiology, oral biology; molecular biology, genetics and cancer (PhD), including biochemistry, molecular genetics, cancer biology, radiation biology, bioinformatics; neuroscience (Certificate); pharmacological sciences (Certificate); stem cell (Certificate); DMD/PhD; MD/PhD. PhD in biomedical engineering offered jointly with New Jersey Institute of Technology. *Program availability:* Part-time, evening/weekend. Terminal master's awarded for partial completion of doctoral program. *Degree requirements:* For doctorate, thesis/dissertation, qualifying exam. *Entrance requirements:* For doctorate, GRE General Test. Additional exam requirements/recommendations for international students: Required—TOEFL. Electronic applications accepted.

Rutgers University–New Brunswick, Graduate School-New Brunswick, Programs in the Molecular Biosciences, Program in Cell and Developmental Biology, Piscataway, NJ 08854-8097. Offers MS, PhD. MS, PhD offered jointly with University of Medicine and Dentistry of New Jersey. *Program availability:* Part-time. Terminal master's awarded for partial completion of doctoral program. *Degree requirements:* For master's, thesis; for doctorate, thesis/dissertation, written qualifying exam. *Entrance requirements:* For master's, GRE General Test; for doctorate, GRE General Test, GRE Subject Test (recommended), minimum GPA of 3.0. Additional exam requirements/recommendations for international students: Required—TOEFL. Electronic applications accepted. *Faculty research:* Signal transduction and regulation of gene expression, developmental biology, cellular biology, developmental genetics, neurobiology.

San Francisco State University, Division of Graduate Studies, College of Science and Engineering, Department of Biology, Professional Science Master's Program, San Francisco, CA 94132-1722. Offers biotechnology (PSM); stem cell science (PSM). *Unit head:* Dr. Lily Chen, Director, 415-338-6763, Fax: 415-338-2295, E-mail: lilychen@sfsu.edu. *Application contact:* Dr. Linda H. Chen, Associate Director and Program Coordinator, 415-338-1696, Fax: 415-338-2295, E-mail: psm@sfsu.edu.
Website: http://psm.sfsu.edu/

Stanford University, School of Medicine, Graduate Programs in Medicine, Department of Developmental Biology, Stanford, CA 94305-2004. Offers MS, PhD. *Degree requirements:* For doctorate, thesis/dissertation, qualifying examination. *Entrance requirements:* For doctorate, GRE General Test, GRE Subject Test. Additional exam requirements/recommendations for international students: Required—TOEFL. Electronic applications accepted. *Expenses: Tuition:* Full-time $48,987; part-time $10,620 per quarter. One-time fee: $400. Tuition and fees vary according to program. *Faculty research:* Mammalian embryology; developmental genetics with particular emphasis on microbial systems; &ITDictyostelium&RO, &ITDrosophila&RO, the nematode, and the mouse.

Stony Brook University, State University of New York, Graduate School, College of Arts and Sciences, Department of Biochemistry and Cell Biology, Stony Brook, NY 11794. Offers biochemistry and cell biology (MS); biochemistry and structural biology (PhD); molecular and cellular biology (MA, PhD), including biochemistry and molecular biology (PhD), biological sciences (MA), cellular and developmental biology (PhD), immunology and pathology (PhD), molecular and cellular biology (PhD). *Faculty:* 18 full-time (5 women). *Students:* 112 full-time (61 women), 5 part-time (3 women); includes 23 minority (6 Black or African American, non-Hispanic/Latino; 10 Asian, non-Hispanic/Latino; 6 Hispanic/Latino; 1 Two or more races, non-Hispanic/Latino), 56 international. Average age 27. 225 applicants, 37% accepted, 27 enrolled. In 2017, 12 master's, 19 doctorates awarded. *Degree requirements:* For doctorate, comprehensive exam, thesis/dissertation, teaching experience. *Entrance requirements:* For doctorate, GRE General Test, GRE Subject Test. Additional exam requirements/recommendations for international students: Required—TOEFL (minimum score 90 iBT). *Application deadline:* For fall admission, 1/15 for domestic students; for spring admission, 10/15 for domestic students. Application fee: $100. *Expenses:* Contact institution. *Financial support:* In 2017–18, 6 fellowships, 47 research assistantships, 18 teaching assistantships were awarded; Federal Work-Study also available. *Faculty research:* Bioimaging, cell signaling, cell biology, biochemistry, pathogenesis. *Total annual research expenditures:* $6.6 million. *Unit head:* Prof. Aaron Neiman, Chair, 631-632-1543, Fax: 631-632-8575, E-mail: aaron.neiman@stonybrook.edu. *Application contact:* Pam Wolfskill, Coordinator, 631-632-8585, Fax: 631-632-9730, E-mail: pamela.wolfskill@stonybrook.edu.
Website: http://www.sunysb.edu/biochem/

Thomas Jefferson University, Jefferson College of Biomedical Sciences, MS Program in Cell and Developmental Biology, Philadelphia, PA 19107. Offers MS. *Program availability:* Part-time, evening/weekend. *Faculty:* 43 full-time (16 women), 28 part-time/adjunct (9 women). *Students:* 12 part-time (5 women); includes 1 minority (Asian, non-Hispanic/Latino), 2 international. 14 applicants, 93% accepted, 6 enrolled. In 2017, 9 master's awarded. *Degree requirements:* For master's, thesis, clerkship. *Entrance requirements:* For master's, GRE General Test or MCAT, minimum GPA of 3.0. Additional exam requirements/recommendations for international students: Required—TOEFL, IELTS (minimum score 7). *Application deadline:* For fall admission, 8/1 priority date for domestic students, 3/1 priority date for international students; for winter admission, 12/1 priority date for domestic students, 6/1 priority date for international students; for spring admission, 4/1 priority date for domestic students. Applications are processed on a rolling basis. Application fee: $50. Electronic applications accepted. *Financial support:* Federal Work-Study and institutionally sponsored loans available. Support available to part-time students. Financial award application deadline: 5/1; financial award applicants required to submit FAFSA. *Faculty research:* Developmental biology, cell biology, planning and management, drug development. *Unit head:* Dr. Gerald B. Grunwald, Dean and Program Director, 215-503-4191, Fax: 215-503-6690, E-mail: gerald.grunwald@jefferson.edu. *Application contact:* Marc E. Stearns, Senior Associate Director of Admissions, 215-503-0155, Fax: 215-503-3433, E-mail: jgsbs-info@jefferson.edu.
Website: http://www.jefferson.edu/university/biomedical-sciences/degrees-programs/master-programs/cell-developmental-biology.html

Tufts University, Sackler School of Graduate Biomedical Sciences, Cell, Molecular, and Developmental Biology Program, Medford, MA 02155. Offers cancer biology (PhD); developmental and regenerative biology (PhD); molecular and cellular medicine (PhD); structural and chemical biology (PhD). Terminal master's awarded for partial completion of doctoral program. *Degree requirements:* For doctorate, comprehensive exam, thesis/dissertation. *Entrance requirements:* For doctorate, GRE General Test, 3 letters of reference, resume, personal statement. Electronic applications accepted. *Expenses: Tuition:* Full-time $49,892. *Required fees:* $874. Full-time tuition and fees vary according to degree level, program and student level. Part-time tuition and fees vary according to course load. *Faculty research:* Reproduction and hormone action, control of gene expression, cell-matrix and cell-cell interactions, growth control and tumorigenesis, cytoskeleton and contractile proteins.

The University of Alabama at Birmingham, Joint Health Sciences, Cell, Molecular, and Developmental Biology Theme, Birmingham, AL 35294. Offers PhD. *Faculty:* 370. *Students:* 50 full-time (28 women); includes 17 minority (6 Black or African American, non-Hispanic/Latino; 8 Asian, non-Hispanic/Latino; 2 Hispanic/Latino; 1 Two or more races, non-Hispanic/Latino). Average age 27. 32 applicants, 28% accepted, 3 enrolled. In 2017, 7 doctorates awarded. *Degree requirements:* For doctorate, comprehensive exam, thesis/dissertation. *Entrance requirements:* For doctorate, personal statement, resume or curriculum vitae, letters of recommendation, research experience, interview. Additional exam requirements/recommendations for international students: Required—TOEFL (minimum score 80 iBT), IELTS (minimum score 6.5). *Application deadline:* For fall admission, 12/31 for domestic and international students. Applications are processed on a rolling basis. Electronic applications accepted. *Financial support:* In 2017–18, fellowships with full tuition reimbursements (averaging $29,000 per year), research assistantships with full tuition reimbursements (averaging $30,000 per year) were awarded; health care benefits also available. *Unit head:* Dr. Alecia K. Gross, Theme Director, 205-975-8396, E-mail: agross@uab.edu. *Application contact:* Alyssa Zasada, Admissions Manager for Graduate Biomedical Sciences, 205-934-3857, E-mail: grad-gbs@uab.edu.
Website: http://www.uab.edu/gbs/home/themes/cmdb

The University of British Columbia, Faculty of Medicine, Department of Cellular and Physiological Sciences, Vancouver, BC V6T 1Z3, Canada. Offers bioinformatics (M Sc, PhD); cell and developmental biology (M Sc, PhD); genome science and technology (M Sc, PhD); neuroscience (M Sc, PhD). *Degree requirements:* For master's, thesis, oral defense; for doctorate, comprehensive exam, thesis/dissertation, oral defense. *Entrance requirements:* For master's, minimum overall B+ average in third- and fourth-year courses; for doctorate, minimum overall B+ average in master's degree (or equivalent) from approved institution with clear evidence of research ability or potential. Additional exam requirements/recommendations for international students: Required—TOEFL, IELTS. *Expenses:* Contact institution.

University of California, Davis, Graduate Studies, Graduate Group in Cell and Developmental Biology, Davis, CA 95616. Offers MS, PhD. *Degree requirements:* For master's, comprehensive exam (for some programs), thesis (for some programs); for doctorate, thesis/dissertation. *Entrance requirements:* For doctorate, GRE General Test, GRE Subject Test. Additional exam requirements/recommendations for international students: Required—TOEFL (minimum score 550 paper-based). Electronic applications accepted. *Faculty research:* Molecular basis of cell function and development.

University of California, Irvine, Francisco J. Ayala School of Biological Sciences, Department of Developmental and Cell Biology, Irvine, CA 92697. Offers biological sciences (MS, PhD). *Students:* 39 full-time (25 women); includes 20 minority (1 Black or African American, non-Hispanic/Latino; 1 American Indian or Alaska Native, non-Hispanic/Latino; 10 Asian, non-Hispanic/Latino; 8 Hispanic/Latino), 4 international. Average age 28. 2 applicants, 100% accepted, 2 enrolled. In 2017, 8 master's, 12 doctorates awarded. *Entrance requirements:* For master's and doctorate, GRE General Test, GRE Subject Test, minimum GPA of 3.0. Additional exam requirements/recommendations for international students: Required—TOEFL (minimum score 550 paper-based). *Application deadline:* For fall admission, 12/15 priority date for domestic and international students. Application fee: $105 ($125 for international students). Electronic applications accepted. *Financial support:* Fellowships, research assistantships with full tuition reimbursements, teaching assistantships, institutionally sponsored loans, traineeships, health care benefits, and unspecified assistantships available. Financial award application deadline: 3/1; financial award applicants required to submit FAFSA. *Faculty research:* Genetics and development, oncogene signaling pathways, gene regulation, tissue regeneration and molecular genetics. *Unit head:* Prof. Thomas F. Schilling, Chair, 949-824-4562, Fax: 949-824-1105, E-mail: dkodowd@uci.edu. *Application contact:* Prof. Aimee Edinger, Graduate Advisor, 949-824-1921, Fax: 949-824-4709, E-mail: aedinger@uci.edu.
Website: http://devcell.bio.uci.edu/

University of California, Los Angeles, Graduate Division, College of Letters and Science, Department of Molecular, Cell and Developmental Biology, Los Angeles, CA 90095. Offers MA, PhD. Terminal master's awarded for partial completion of doctoral program. *Degree requirements:* For master's, comprehensive exam, thesis; for doctorate, thesis/dissertation, oral and written qualifying exams; 2 quarters of teaching experience. *Entrance requirements:* For doctorate, GRE General Test. Additional exam requirements/recommendations for international students: Required—TOEFL. Electronic applications accepted.

University of California, Riverside, Graduate Division, Program in Cell, Molecular, and Developmental Biology, Riverside, CA 92521-0102. Offers MS, PhD. Terminal master's awarded for partial completion of doctoral program. *Degree requirements:* For master's, thesis, oral defense of thesis; for doctorate, thesis/dissertation, oral defense of thesis, qualifying exams, 2 quarters of teaching experience. *Entrance requirements:* For master's and doctorate, GRE General Test, minimum GPA of 3.2. Additional exam requirements/recommendations for international students: Required—TOEFL (minimum score 550 paper-based; 80 iBT). Electronic applications accepted. *Expenses:* Tuition, state resident: full-time $5746. Tuition, nonresident: full-time $10,780. Tuition and fees vary according to campus/location and program.

University of California, San Francisco, Graduate Division and School of Medicine, Tetrad Graduate Program, San Francisco, CA 94143. Offers biochemistry and molecular biology (PhD); cell biology (PhD); developmental biology (PhD); genetics (PhD); MD/PhD. *Degree requirements:* For doctorate, thesis/dissertation. *Entrance requirements:* For doctorate, GRE General Test, GRE Subject Test. Additional exam requirements/recommendations for international students: Required—TOEFL. *Expenses:* Contact institution.

University of California, Santa Barbara, Graduate Division, College of Letters and Sciences, Division of Mathematics, Life, and Physical Sciences, Department of Molecular, Cellular, and Developmental Biology, Santa Barbara, CA 93106-9625. Offers MA, PhD, MA/PhD. Terminal master's awarded for partial completion of doctoral program. *Degree requirements:* For master's, comprehensive exam (for some programs), thesis (for some programs); for doctorate, comprehensive exam, thesis/dissertation. *Entrance requirements:* For master's and doctorate, GRE General Test, 3 letters of recommendation, statement of purpose, personal achievements/contributions statement, resume/curriculum vitae, transcripts for post-secondary institutions attended. Additional exam requirements/recommendations for international students: Required—TOEFL (minimum score 550 paper-based; 80 iBT), IELTS (minimum score 7). Electronic applications accepted. *Faculty research:* Microbiology, neurobiology (including stem cell research), developmental, virology, cell biology.

University of California, Santa Cruz, Division of Graduate Studies, Division of Physical and Biological Sciences, Program in Molecular, Cellular, and Developmental Biology, Santa Cruz, CA 95064. Offers MA, PhD. Terminal master's awarded for partial completion of doctoral program. *Degree requirements:* For master's, thesis; for doctorate, thesis/dissertation, qualifying exam. *Entrance requirements:* For master's and doctorate, GRE General Test, 3 letters of recommendation, interview. Additional exam requirements/recommendations for international students: Required—TOEFL (minimum score 550 paper-based; 83 iBT), Recommended—IELTS (minimum score 8). Electronic applications accepted. *Faculty research:* RNA biology, chromatin and chromosome biology, neurobiology, stem cell biology and differentiation, cell structure and function.

University of Chicago, Division of the Biological Sciences, Committee on Development, Regeneration, and Stem Cell Biology, Chicago, IL 60637-1513. Offers PhD. *Students:* 23 full-time (9 women). 50 applicants, 22% accepted, 4 enrolled. In 2017, 3 doctorates awarded. *Degree requirements:* For doctorate, thesis/dissertation, ethics class, 2 teaching assistantships, preliminary exams. *Entrance requirements:* For doctorate, GRE General Test, transcripts, statement of purpose, 3 letters of recommendation. Additional exam requirements/recommendations for international students: Required—TOEFL (minimum score 600 paper-based; 104 iBT), IELTS (minimum score 7). *Application deadline:* For fall admission, 12/1 for domestic and international students. Application fee: $90. Electronic applications accepted. *Financial support:* In 2017–18, 16 students received support, including fellowships with full tuition reimbursements available (averaging $31,000 per year), research assistantships with full tuition reimbursements available (averaging $31,000 per year); institutionally sponsored loans, scholarships/grants, traineeships, and health care benefits also available. Financial award application deadline: 12/1. *Faculty research:* Stem cells and regeneration, developmental genetics, regulatory mechanisms in development and disease, cellular basis of development. *Unit head:* Ilaria Rebay, Chair, 773-702-8037, E-mail: bsdadmissions@uchicago.edu. *Application contact:* Kristine Gaston, Graduate Program Director, 773-702-8037, E-mail: kristine@bsd.uchicago.edu.
Website: http://devbio.bsd.uchicago.edu/

University of Cincinnati, Graduate School, College of Medicine, Graduate Programs in Biomedical Sciences, Department of Pediatrics, Program in Molecular and Developmental Biology, Cincinnati, OH 45221. Offers PhD. *Degree requirements:* For doctorate, thesis/dissertation, qualifying exam. *Entrance requirements:* For doctorate, GRE General Test, minimum GPA of 3.2. Additional exam requirements/recommendations for international students: Required—TOEFL (minimum score 520 paper-based). Electronic applications accepted. *Expenses: Tuition, area resident:* Full-time $14,468. Tuition, state resident: full-time $14,968; part-time $754 per credit hour. Tuition, nonresident: full-time $24,210; part-time $1311 per credit hour. *International tuition:* $26,460 full-time. *Required fees:* $3958; $84 per credit hour. One-time fee: $85 full-time. Tuition and fees vary according to course load, degree level and program. *Faculty research:* Cancer biology, cardiovascular biology, developmental biology, human genetics, gene therapy, genomics and bioinformatics, immunobiology, molecular medicine, neuroscience, pulmonary biology, reproductive biology, stem cell biology.

University of Colorado Boulder, Graduate School, College of Arts and Sciences, Department of Molecular, Cellular, and Developmental Biology, Boulder, CO 80309. Offers cellular structure and function (MA, PhD); developmental biology (PhD); molecular biology (PhD). *Faculty:* 29 full-time (10 women). *Students:* 51 full-time (26 women), 4 part-time (1 woman); includes 8 minority (3 Asian, non-Hispanic/Latino; 4 Hispanic/Latino; 1 Two or more races, non-Hispanic/Latino), 10 international. Average age 27. 345 applicants, 9% accepted, 12 enrolled. In 2017, 10 doctorates awarded. Terminal master's awarded for partial completion of doctoral program. *Degree requirements:* For master's, comprehensive exam, thesis or alternative; for doctorate, comprehensive exam, thesis/dissertation. *Entrance requirements:* For master's, GRE General Test, GRE Subject Test, minimum undergraduate GPA of 3.0; for doctorate, GRE General Test, GRE Subject Test. *Application deadline:* For fall admission, 12/1 for domestic students; for spring admission, 12/1 for domestic students. Application fee: $60 ($80 for international students). Electronic applications accepted. Application fee is waived when completed online. *Financial support:* In 2017–18, 158 students received support, including 48 fellowships (averaging $12,292 per year), 38 research assistantships with full and partial tuition reimbursements available (averaging $34,642 per year), 10 teaching assistantships with full and partial tuition reimbursements available (averaging $30,525 per year); institutionally sponsored loans, scholarships/grants, health care benefits, and unspecified assistantships also available. Financial award application deadline: 2/15; financial award applicants required to submit FAFSA. *Faculty research:* Molecular biology; cellular biology; genetics; developmental biology; biochemistry: proteins. *Total annual research expenditures:* $15.3 million. *Application contact:* E-mail: mcdbgrad@colorado.edu.
Website: http://mcdb.colorado.edu/graduate

University of Colorado Denver, School of Medicine, Program in Cell Biology, Stem Cells, and Development, Aurora, CO 80045. Offers cell biology, stem cells, and developmental biology (PhD); modern human anatomy (MS). In 2017, 1 doctorate awarded. *Degree requirements:* For doctorate, comprehensive exam, thesis/dissertation, at least 30 credit hours of coursework and 30 credit hours of thesis research; laboratory rotations. *Entrance requirements:* For doctorate, GRE, minimum GPA of 3.0; 3 letters of reference; prerequisite coursework in organic chemistry, biology, biochemistry, physics and calculus; research experience (highly recommended). Additional exam requirements/recommendations for international students: Required—TOEFL (minimum score 550 paper-based; 80 iBT). Application fee: $0. *Faculty research:* Development and repair of the vertebrate nervous system; molecular, genetic and developmental mechanisms involved in the patterning of the early spinal cord (neural plate) during vertebrate embryogenesis; structural analysis of protein glycosylation using NMR and mass spectrometry; small RNAs and post-transcriptional gene regulation during nematode gametogenesis and early development; diabetes-mediated changes in cardiovascular gene expression and functional exercise capacity. *Unit head:* Dr. Bruce Appel, Director, 303-724-3465, E-mail: bruce.appel@ucdenver.edu. *Application contact:* Kenton Owsley, Program Administrator, 303-724-3468, Fax: 303-724-3420, E-mail: kenton.owsley@ucdenver.edu.
Website: http://www.ucdenver.edu/academics/colleges/medicalschool/programs/CSD/Pages/CSD.aspx

University of Connecticut, Graduate School, College of Liberal Arts and Sciences, Department of Molecular and Cell Biology, Storrs, CT 06269. Offers applied genomics (PSM); cell and developmental biology (MS, PhD); genetics and genomics (MS, PhD); microbial systems analysis (PSM); microbiology (MS, PhD); structural biology, biochemistry and biophysics (MS, PhD). Terminal master's awarded for partial completion of doctoral program. *Degree requirements:* For master's, comprehensive exam; for doctorate, thesis/dissertation. *Entrance requirements:* For master's and doctorate, GRE General Test, GRE Subject Test. Additional exam requirements/recommendations for international students: Required—TOEFL (minimum score 550 paper-based). Electronic applications accepted.

University of Connecticut Health Center, Graduate School, Programs in Biomedical Sciences, Program in Genetics and Developmental Biology, Farmington, CT 06030. Offers PhD, DMD/PhD, MD/PhD. *Degree requirements:* For doctorate, comprehensive exam, thesis/dissertation. *Entrance requirements:* For doctorate, GRE General Test, GRE Subject Test. Additional exam requirements/recommendations for international students: Required—TOEFL (minimum score 600 paper-based). Electronic applications accepted. *Faculty research:* Developmental biology, genomic imprinting, RNA biology, RNA alternative splicing, human embryonic stem cells.

University of Delaware, College of Arts and Sciences, Department of Biological Sciences, Newark, DE 19716. Offers biotechnology (MS); cancer biology (MS, PhD); cell and extracellular matrix biology (MS, PhD); cell and systems physiology (MS, PhD); developmental biology (MS, PhD); ecology and evolution (MS, PhD); microbiology (MS, PhD); molecular biology and genetics (MS, PhD). Terminal master's awarded for partial completion of doctoral program. *Degree requirements:* For master's, thesis, preliminary exam; for doctorate, comprehensive exam, thesis/dissertation, preliminary exam. *Entrance requirements:* For master's and doctorate, GRE General Test. Additional exam requirements/recommendations for international students: Required—TOEFL (minimum score 600 paper-based); Recommended—TWE. Electronic applications accepted. *Faculty research:* Microorganisms, bone, cancer metastasis, developmental biology, cell biology, DNA.

University of Hawaii at Manoa, John A. Burns School of Medicine, Program in Developmental and Reproductive Biology, Honolulu, HI 96813. Offers MS, PhD. *Program availability:* Part-time. *Degree requirements:* For doctorate, thesis/dissertation. *Entrance requirements:* For doctorate, GRE General Test, GRE Subject Test. Additional exam requirements/recommendations for international students: Recommended—TOEFL (minimum score 560 paper-based), IELTS (minimum score 5). *Faculty research:* Biology of gametes and fertilization, reproductive endocrinology.

University of Illinois at Urbana–Champaign, Graduate College, College of Liberal Arts and Sciences, School of Molecular and Cellular Biology, Department of Cell and Developmental Biology, Champaign, IL 61820. Offers PhD.

The University of Kansas, Graduate Studies, College of Liberal Arts and Sciences, Department of Molecular Biosciences, Lawrence, KS 66044. Offers biochemistry and biophysics (PhD); microbiology (PhD); molecular, cellular, and developmental biology (PhD). *Program availability:* Part-time. *Students:* 57 full-time (38 women); includes 8 minority (1 Black or African American, non-Hispanic/Latino; 2 Asian, non-Hispanic/Latino; 3 Hispanic/Latino; 2 Two or more races, non-Hispanic/Latino), 27 international. Average age 27. 73 applicants, 33% accepted, 8 enrolled. In 2017, 6 doctorates awarded. Terminal master's awarded for partial completion of doctoral program. *Entrance requirements:* For doctorate, GRE General Test, 1-page statement of research interests and goals, 1-2 page curriculum vitae or resume, official transcript, 3 recommendation letters. Additional exam requirements/recommendations for international students: Required—TOEFL or IELTS. *Application deadline:* For fall admission, 12/1 for domestic and international students. Application fee: $65 ($85 for international students). Electronic applications accepted. *Financial support:* Fellowships, research assistantships, teaching assistantships, scholarships/grants, health care benefits, and unspecified assistantships available. Financial award application deadline: 12/1. *Faculty research:* Structure and function of proteins, genetics of organism development, molecular genetics, neurophysiology, molecular virology and pathogenics, developmental biology, cell biology. *Unit head:* Susan M. Egan, Chair, 785-864-4294, E-mail: sme@ku.edu. *Application contact:* John Connolly, Graduate Admissions Contact, 785-864-4311, E-mail: jconnolly@ku.edu.
Website: http://www.molecularbiosciences.ku.edu/

The University of Manchester, School of Biological Sciences, Manchester, United Kingdom. Offers adaptive organismal biology (M Phil, PhD); animal biology (M Phil, PhD); biochemistry (M Phil, PhD); bioinformatics (M Phil, PhD); biomolecular sciences (M Phil, PhD); biotechnology (M Phil, PhD); cell biology (M Phil, PhD); cell matrix research (M Phil, PhD); channels and transporters (M Phil, PhD); developmental biology (M Phil, PhD); environmental biology (M Phil, PhD); evolutionary biology (M Phil, PhD); gene expression (M Phil, PhD); genetics (M Phil, PhD); history of science, technology and medicine (M Phil, PhD); immunology (M Phil, PhD); integrative neurobiology and behavior (M Phil, PhD); membrane trafficking (M Phil, PhD); microbiology (M Phil, PhD); molecular and cellular neuroscience (M Phil, PhD); molecular biology (M Phil, PhD); molecular cancer studies (M Phil, PhD); neuroscience (M Phil, PhD); ophthalmology (M Phil, PhD); optometry (M Phil, PhD); organelle function (M Phil, PhD); pharmacology (M Phil, PhD); physiology (M Phil, PhD); plant sciences (M Phil, PhD); stem cell research (M Phil, PhD); structural biology (M Phil, PhD); systems neuroscience (M Phil, PhD); toxicology (M Phil, PhD).

The University of Manchester, School of Dentistry, Manchester, United Kingdom. Offers basic dental sciences (cancer studies) (M Phil, PhD); basic dental sciences (molecular genetics) (M Phil, PhD); basic dental sciences (stem cell biology) (M Phil, PhD); biomaterials sciences and dental technology (M Phil, PhD); dental public health/community dentistry (M Phil, PhD); dental science (clinical) (PhD); endodontology (M Phil, PhD); fixed and removable prosthodontics (M Phil, PhD); operative dentistry (M Phil, PhD); oral and maxillofacial surgery (M Phil, PhD); oral radiology (M Phil, PhD); orthodontics (M Phil, PhD); restorative dentistry (M Phil, PhD).

University of Massachusetts Amherst, Graduate School, Interdisciplinary Programs, Program in Molecular and Cellular Biology, Amherst, MA 01003. Offers biological chemistry and molecular biophysics (PhD); biomedicine (PhD); cellular and developmental biology (PhD). *Program availability:* Part-time. Terminal master's awarded for partial completion of doctoral program. *Degree requirements:* For doctorate, comprehensive exam, thesis/dissertation. *Entrance requirements:* For doctorate, GRE General Test. Additional exam requirements/recommendations for international students: Required—TOEFL (minimum score 550 paper-based; 80 iBT), IELTS (minimum score 6.5). Electronic applications accepted.

University of Miami, Graduate School, Miller School of Medicine, Graduate Programs in Medicine, Department of Cell Biology and Anatomy, Coral Gables, FL 33124. Offers molecular cell and developmental biology (PhD); MD/PhD. *Degree requirements:* For doctorate, thesis/dissertation. *Entrance requirements:* For doctorate, GRE General Test, GRE Subject Test. Additional exam requirements/recommendations for international students: Required—TOEFL. Electronic applications accepted.

University of Michigan, Rackham Graduate School, College of Literature, Science, and the Arts, Department of Molecular, Cellular, and Developmental Biology, Ann Arbor, MI 48109. Offers MS, PhD. *Program availability:* Part-time. *Faculty:* 37 full-time (12 women). *Students:* 85 full-time (51 women); includes 10 minority (2 Black or African American, non-Hispanic/Latino; 2 Asian, non-Hispanic/Latino; 6 Hispanic/Latino), 44 international. Average age 26. 139 applicants, 27% accepted, 23 enrolled. In 2017, 6 master's, 10 doctorates awarded. Terminal master's awarded for partial completion of doctoral program. *Degree requirements:* For master's, thesis (for some programs), 24 credits with at least 16 in molecular, cellular, and developmental biology and 4 in a cognate field; for doctorate, comprehensive exam, thesis/dissertation, preliminary exam, oral defense. *Entrance requirements:* Additional exam requirements/recommendations for international students: Required—TOEFL (minimum score 560 paper-based; 83 iBT). *Application deadline:* For fall admission, 12/15 for domestic and international students; for winter admission, 11/1 for domestic and international students; for spring admission, 4/1 for domestic and international students. Application fee: $75 ($90 for international

students). Electronic applications accepted. *Expenses:* $11,184 in-state; $22,578 out of state; $5,954 candidacy. *Financial support:* In 2017–18, 65 students received support, including 23 fellowships with full tuition reimbursements available (averaging $30,600 per year), 32 research assistantships with full tuition reimbursements available (averaging $30,600 per year), 21 teaching assistantships with full tuition reimbursements available (averaging $30,600 per year); traineeships and health care benefits also available. Financial award application deadline: 12/15. *Faculty research:* Cell biology, microbiology, neurobiology and physiology, developmental biology and plant molecular biology. *Total annual research expenditures:* $8.9 million. *Unit head:* Dr. Robert J. Denver, Department Chair, 734-764-7476, Fax: 734-615-6337, E-mail: rdenver@umich.edu. *Application contact:* Mary Carr, Graduate Coordinator, 734-615-1635, Fax: 734-764-0884, E-mail: carrmm@umich.edu.
Website: http://www.mcdb.lsa.umich.edu

University of Michigan, Rackham Graduate School, Program in Biomedical Sciences (PIBS), Department of Cell and Developmental Biology, Ann Arbor, MI 48109. Offers PhD. *Faculty:* 21 full-time (10 women). *Students:* 21 full-time (11 women); includes 14 minority (1 Black or African American, non-Hispanic/Latino; 10 Asian, non-Hispanic/Latino; 3 Hispanic/Latino). Average age 29. 57 applicants, 18% accepted, 6 enrolled. In 2017, 5 doctorates awarded. *Degree requirements:* For doctorate, thesis/dissertation, oral defense of dissertation, preliminary exam. *Entrance requirements:* For doctorate, GRE General Test, 3 letters of recommendation, research experience. Additional exam requirements/recommendations for international students: Required—TOEFL (minimum score 84 iBT). *Application deadline:* For fall admission, 12/1 for domestic and international students. Application fee: $75 ($90 for international students). Electronic applications accepted. *Expenses:* Tuition, state resident: full-time $22,368; part-time $1201 per credit hour. Tuition, nonresident: full-time $45,156; part-time $2467 per credit hour. *Required fees:* $376 per term. Tuition and fees vary according to course load, degree level and program. *Financial support:* In 2017–18, fellowships (averaging $29,025 per year) were awarded; scholarships/grants, health care benefits, tuition waivers (full), and unspecified assistantships also available. Financial award application deadline: 12/1. *Faculty research:* Cell signaling, stem cells, organogenesis, cell biology, developmental genetics. *Total annual research expenditures:* $5.8 million. *Unit head:* Dr. Pierre A. Coulombe, Professor and Chair, 734-615-7509, Fax: 734-763-1166, E-mail: coulombe@umich.edu. *Application contact:* Michelle S. Melis, Director of Student Life, 734-615-6538, Fax: 734-647-7022, E-mail: msmtegan@umich.edu.
Website: http://cdb.med.umich.edu/

University of Minnesota, Twin Cities Campus, Graduate School, Program in Molecular, Cellular, Developmental Biology and Genetics, Minneapolis, MN 55455-0213. Offers genetic counseling (MS); molecular, cellular, developmental biology and genetics (PhD). Terminal master's awarded for partial completion of doctoral program. *Degree requirements:* For master's, thesis optional; for doctorate, thesis/dissertation. *Entrance requirements:* For master's and doctorate, GRE General Test. Additional exam requirements/recommendations for international students: Required—TOEFL (minimum score 625 paper-based; 80 iBT). Electronic applications accepted. *Faculty research:* Membrane receptors and membrane transport, cell interactions, cytoskeleton and cell mobility, regulation of gene expression, plant cell and molecular biology.

University of Montana, Graduate School, College of Humanities and Sciences, Division of Biological Sciences, Program in Cellular, Molecular and Microbial Biology, Missoula, MT 59812. Offers cellular and developmental biology (PhD); microbial evolution and ecology (PhD); microbiology and immunology (PhD); molecular biology and biochemistry (PhD). Terminal master's awarded for partial completion of doctoral program. *Degree requirements:* For doctorate, variable foreign language requirement, thesis/dissertation. *Entrance requirements:* For doctorate, GRE General Test. *Faculty research:* Ribosome structure, medical microbiology/pathogenesis, microbial ecology/ environmental microbiology.

The University of North Carolina at Chapel Hill, Graduate School, College of Arts and Sciences, Department of Biology, Chapel Hill, NC 27599. Offers botany (MA, MS, PhD); cell biology, development, and physiology (MA, MS, PhD); cell motility and cytoskeleton (PhD); ecology and behavior (MA, MS, PhD); genetics and molecular biology (MA, MS, PhD); morphology, systematics, and evolution (MA, MS, PhD). Terminal master's awarded for partial completion of doctoral program. *Degree requirements:* For master's, comprehensive exam, thesis (for some programs); for doctorate, comprehensive exam, thesis/dissertation. *Entrance requirements:* For master's, GRE General Test, GRE Subject Test, 2 semesters of calculus or statistics; 2 semesters of physics, organic chemistry; 3 semesters of biology; for doctorate, GRE General Test, GRE Subject Test, 2 semesters calculus or statistics, 2 semesters physics, organic chemistry, 3 semesters of biology. Additional exam requirements/recommendations for international students: Required—TOEFL (minimum score 550 paper-based). Electronic applications accepted. *Faculty research:* Gene expression, biomechanics, yeast genetics, plant ecology, plant molecular biology.

The University of North Carolina at Chapel Hill, School of Medicine and Graduate School, Graduate Programs in Medicine, Department of Cell and Developmental Biology, Chapel Hill, NC 27599. Offers PhD. *Degree requirements:* For doctorate, comprehensive exam, thesis/dissertation. *Entrance requirements:* For doctorate, GRE General Test, GRE Subject Test. Electronic applications accepted. *Faculty research:* Cell adhesion, motility and cytoskeleton; molecular analysis of signal transduction; development biology and toxicology; reproductive biology; cell and molecular imaging.

University of Pennsylvania, Perelman School of Medicine, Biomedical Graduate Studies, Graduate Group in Cell and Molecular Biology, Philadelphia, PA 19104. Offers cancer biology (PhD); cell biology, physiology, and metabolism (PhD); developmental stem cell regenerative biology (PhD); gene therapy and vaccines (PhD); genetics and gene regulation (PhD); microbiology, virology, and parasitology (PhD); MD/PhD; VMD/PhD. *Faculty:* 363. *Students:* 343 full-time (197 women); includes 114 minority (7 Black or African American, non-Hispanic/Latino; 51 Asian, non-Hispanic/Latino; 41 Hispanic/Latino; 15 Two or more races, non-Hispanic/Latino), 50 international. 588 applicants, 22% accepted, 61 enrolled. In 2017, 61 doctorates awarded. *Degree requirements:* For doctorate, thesis/dissertation. *Entrance requirements:* For doctorate, GRE General Test. Additional exam requirements/recommendations for international students: Required—TOEFL. *Application deadline:* For fall admission, 12/1 priority date for domestic and international students. Applications are processed on a rolling basis. Application fee: $80. Electronic applications accepted. *Financial support:* In 2017–18, 339 students received support. Fellowships, research assistantships, teaching assistantships, and tuition waivers available. *Unit head:* Dr. Daniel Kessler, Graduate Group Chair, 215-898-1478. *Application contact:* Meagan Schofer, Coordinator, 215-898-1478.
Website: http://www.med.upenn.edu/camb/

University of Pittsburgh, Kenneth P. Dietrich School of Arts and Sciences, Department of Biological Sciences, Program in Molecular, Cellular, and Developmental Biology, Pittsburgh, PA 15260. Offers PhD. *Program availability:* Part-time, online learning. *Faculty:* 23 full-time (6 women). *Students:* 38 full-time (20 women); includes 2 minority (1 Black or African American, non-Hispanic/Latino; 1 Asian, non-Hispanic/Latino), 7 international. Average age 23. In 2017, 5 doctorates awarded. *Degree requirements:* For doctorate, comprehensive exam, thesis/dissertation, completion of research integrity module. *Entrance requirements:* For doctorate, GRE General Test, GRE Subject Test. Additional exam requirements/recommendations for international students: Required—TOEFL (minimum score 90 iBT). *Application deadline:* Applications are processed on a rolling basis. Application fee: $0. Electronic applications accepted. *Financial support:* In 2017–18, 23 fellowships with full tuition reimbursements (averaging $34,776 per year), 63 research assistantships with full tuition reimbursements (averaging $28,800 per year), 20 teaching assistantships with full tuition reimbursements (averaging $28,250 per year) were awarded; Federal Work-Study, traineeships, health care benefits, and tuition waivers also available. *Unit head:* Dr. Karen M. Arndt, Professor, 412-624-6963, Fax: 412-624-4349, E-mail: arndt@pitt.edu. *Application contact:* Cathleen M. Barr, Graduate Administrator, 412-624-4268, Fax: 412-624-4349, E-mail: cbarr@pitt.edu.
Website: http://www.biology.pitt.edu

University of Pittsburgh, School of Medicine, Graduate Programs in Medicine, Molecular Genetics and Developmental Biology Graduate Program, Pittsburgh, PA 15260. Offers PhD. *Faculty:* 54 full-time (15 women). *Students:* 12 full-time (9 women); includes 2 minority (1 Black or African American, non-Hispanic/Latino; 1 Two or more races, non-Hispanic/Latino), 3 international. Average age 28. 350 applicants, 21% accepted, 12 enrolled. In 2017, 1 doctorate awarded. *Degree requirements:* For doctorate, comprehensive exam, thesis/dissertation. *Entrance requirements:* For doctorate, GRE General Test, minimum GPA of 3.2, 3 letters of recommendation, official transcripts, baccalaureate degree. Additional exam requirements/recommendations for international students: Required—TOEFL (minimum score 600 paper-based; 100 iBT), IELTS (minimum score 7). *Application deadline:* For fall admission, 12/1 priority date for domestic and international students. Application fee: $50. Electronic applications accepted. *Financial support:* In 2017–18, 8 students received support, including 2 fellowships with full tuition reimbursements available (averaging $29,500 per year), 2 research assistantships with full tuition reimbursements available (averaging $29,500 per year); teaching assistantships, traineeships, and tuition waivers also available. *Faculty research:* Developmental biology, regenerative medicine, molecular genetics, stem cell biology, reproductive biology. *Unit head:* Dr. Michael Tsang, Director, 412-648-3248, E-mail: tsang@pitt.edu. *Application contact:* Carol Williams, Admissions and Recruiting Manager, 412-648-8957, Fax: 412-648-1077, E-mail: gradstudies@medschool.pitt.edu.
Website: http://www.gradbiomed.pitt.edu/

University of South Carolina, The Graduate School, College of Arts and Sciences, Department of Biological Sciences, Graduate Training Program in Molecular, Cellular, and Developmental Biology, Columbia, SC 29208. Offers MS, PhD. *Degree requirements:* For master's, one foreign language, thesis; for doctorate, one foreign language, thesis/dissertation. *Entrance requirements:* For master's and doctorate, GRE General Test, minimum GPA of 3.0 in science. Electronic applications accepted. *Faculty research:* Marine ecology, population and evolutionary biology, molecular biology and genetics, development.

University of Southern California, Keck School of Medicine, Program in Development, Stem Cell and Regenerative Medicine, Los Angeles, CA 90033. Offers PhD. *Faculty:* 36 full-time (15 women). *Students:* 38 full-time (15 women); includes 6 minority (4 Asian, non-Hispanic/Latino; 1 Hispanic/Latino; 1 Two or more races, non-Hispanic/Latino), 18 international. Average age 26. 11 applicants, 100% accepted, 11 enrolled. *Degree requirements:* For doctorate, comprehensive exam, thesis/dissertation. *Entrance requirements:* For doctorate, GRE, minimum GPA of 3.5. Additional exam requirements/ recommendations for international students: Required—TOEFL (minimum score 600 paper-based; 100 iBT), IELTS (minimum score 7), PTE. *Application deadline:* For fall admission, 12/1 priority date for domestic and international students. Application fee: $90. Electronic applications accepted. *Financial support:* In 2017–18, 38 students received support, including 13 fellowships with full tuition reimbursements available (averaging $33,000 per year), 25 research assistantships with full tuition reimbursements available (averaging $33,000 per year); institutionally sponsored loans, scholarships/grants, traineeships, health care benefits, and unspecified assistantships also available. Financial award application deadline: 4/15; financial award applicants required to submit CSS PROFILE or FAFSA. *Unit head:* Dr. Gage Crump, Director, 323-442-1475, Fax: 323-442-1199, E-mail: gcrump@med.usc.edu. *Application contact:* Dr. Joyce Perez, Manager of Student Programs, 323-442-1645, Fax: 323-442-1199, E-mail: jpperez@med.usc.edu.
Website: http://keck.usc.edu/pibbs/phd-programs/development-stem-cell-and-regenerative-medicine

The University of Texas Southwestern Medical Center, Southwestern Graduate School of Biomedical Sciences, Division of Basic Science, Program in Genetics and Development, Dallas, TX 75390. Offers PhD. *Degree requirements:* For doctorate, thesis/dissertation, qualifying exam. *Entrance requirements:* For doctorate, GRE General Test, minimum GPA of 3.0. Additional exam requirements/recommendations for international students: Required—TOEFL. Electronic applications accepted. *Faculty research:* Human molecular genetics, chromosome structure, gene regulation, molecular biology, gene expression.

Vanderbilt University, School of Medicine, Department of Cell and Developmental Biology, Nashville, TN 37240-1001. Offers MS, PhD, MD/PhD. *Faculty:* 23 full-time (9 women). *Students:* 57 full-time (40 women); includes 11 minority (3 Black or African American, non-Hispanic/Latino; 2 Asian, non-Hispanic/Latino; 3 Hispanic/Latino; 1 Native Hawaiian or other Pacific Islander, non-Hispanic/Latino; 2 Two or more races, non-Hispanic/Latino), 11 international. Average age 27. In 2017, 1 master's, 13 doctorates awarded. Terminal master's awarded for partial completion of doctoral program. *Degree requirements:* For master's, thesis or alternative; for doctorate, thesis/ dissertation, preliminary, qualifying, and final exams. *Entrance requirements:* For master's, GRE General Test; for doctorate, GRE General Test, GRE Subject Test (recommended). Additional exam requirements/recommendations for international students: Required—TOEFL (minimum score 570 paper-based; 88 iBT). *Application deadline:* For fall admission, 1/15 for domestic and international students. Application fee: $0. Electronic applications accepted. *Financial support:* Fellowships with tuition reimbursements, research assistantships with tuition reimbursements, career-related internships or fieldwork, Federal Work-Study, institutionally sponsored loans, scholarships/grants, traineeships, health care benefits, and tuition waivers (partial) available. Financial award application deadline: 1/15; financial award applicants required to submit CSS PROFILE or FAFSA. *Faculty research:* Cancer biology, cell cycle regulation, cell signaling, cytoskeletal biology, developmental biology, neurobiology, proteomics, stem cell biology, structural biology, reproductive biology, trafficking and transport, medical education and gross anatomy. *Unit head:* Dr. Steve Hann, Director of Graduate Studies, 615-322-2134, Fax: 615-343-4539, E-mail: steve.hann@vanderbilt.edu. *Application contact:* Kristi Hargrove, Coordinator, 615-322-2294, Fax: 615-343-4539, E-mail: kristi.l.hargrove@vanderbilt.edu.
Website: http://www.mc.vanderbilt.edu/cdb/

Washington University in St. Louis, The Graduate School, Division of Biology and Biomedical Sciences, Program in Developmental, Regenerative, and Stem Cell Biology, St. Louis, MO 63130-4899. Offers PhD. *Degree requirements:* For doctorate, thesis/ dissertation. *Entrance requirements:* For doctorate, GRE General Test, GRE Subject Test. Additional exam requirements/recommendations for international students: Required—TOEFL. Electronic applications accepted. *Faculty research:* Development, stem cell biology, regenerative biology, cell reprogramming, cell biology, genetics, cell signaling, the biology of cancer, epigenetics, circadian rhythms, systems biology.

Wesleyan University, Graduate Studies, Department of Biology, Middletown, CT 06459. Offers cell and developmental biology (PhD); evolution and ecology (PhD); genetics and genomics (PhD), including bioinformatics; neurobiology and behavior (PhD). Terminal master's awarded for partial completion of doctoral program. *Degree requirements:* For doctorate, comprehensive exam, thesis/dissertation, public seminar. *Entrance requirements:* For doctorate, GRE, official transcripts, three recommendation letters, essay. Additional exam requirements/recommendations for international students: Required—TOEFL. *Application deadline:* For fall admission, 1/15 for domestic and international students. Application fee: $0. Electronic applications accepted. *Financial support:* Stipends available. *Faculty research:* Evolution and ecology, neurobiology and behavior, cell and developmental biology, genetics, genomics and bioinformatics. *Unit head:* Dr. Ann Burke, Chair/Professor, 860-685-3518, E-mail: acburke@wesleyan.edu. *Application contact:* Diane Meredith, Administrative Assistant IV, 860-685-2157, E-mail: dmeredith@wesleyan.edu.
Website: http://www.wesleyan.edu/bio/

West Virginia University, Davis College of Agriculture, Forestry and Consumer Sciences, Morgantown, WV 26506. Offers agricultural and extension education (MS, PhD); agriculture and resource management (MS); agriculture, natural resources and design (M Agr); agronomy (MS); animal and food science (PhD); animal physiology (MS); applied and environmental microbiology (MS); design and merchandising (MS); entomology (MS); forest resource science (PhD); forestry (MSF); genetics and developmental biology (MS, PhD); horticulture (MS); human and community development (PhD); landscape architecture (MLA); natural resource economics (PhD); nutritional and food science (MS); plant and soil science (PhD); plant pathology (MS); recreation, parks and tourism resources (MS); reproductive physiology (MS, PhD); wildlife and fisheries resources (PhD). *Program availability:* Part-time. *Students:* 200 full-time (97 women), 53 part-time (32 women); includes 27 minority (6 Black or African American, non-Hispanic/Latino; 1 American Indian or Alaska Native, non-Hispanic/Latino; 4 Asian, non-Hispanic/Latino; 11 Hispanic/Latino; 5 Two or more races, non-Hispanic/Latino), 67 international. *Degree requirements:* For master's, thesis; for doctorate, thesis/dissertation. *Entrance requirements:* Additional exam requirements/recommendations for international students: Required—TOEFL (minimum score 550 paper-based). *Application deadline:* For fall admission, 6/1 priority date for domestic students, 6/1 for international students; for spring admission, 1/5 for domestic and international students. Applications are processed on a rolling basis. Application fee: $60. Electronic applications accepted. *Expenses:* Tuition, state resident: full-time $9450. Tuition, nonresident: full-time $24,390. *Financial support:* Fellowships, research assistantships, teaching assistantships, career-related internships or fieldwork, Federal Work-Study, institutionally sponsored loans, tuition waivers (full and partial), and unspecified assistantships available. Financial award application deadline: 2/1; financial award applicants required to submit FAFSA. *Faculty research:* Reproductive physiology, soil and water quality, human nutrition, aquaculture, wildlife management. *Unit head:* Dr. Dan J. Robison, Dean, 304-293-2395, Fax: 304-293-3740, E-mail: dan.robison@mail.wvu.edu. *Application contact:* Dr. Dennis K. Smith, Associate Dean, 304-293-2275, Fax: 304-293-3740, E-mail: denny.smith@mail.wvu.edu.
Website: https://www.davis.wvu.edu

Yale University, Graduate School of Arts and Sciences, Department of Molecular, Cellular, and Developmental Biology, New Haven, CT 06520. Offers biochemistry, molecular biology and chemical biology (PhD); cellular and developmental biology (PhD); genetics (PhD); neurobiology (PhD); plant sciences (PhD). *Degree requirements:* For doctorate, thesis/dissertation. *Entrance requirements:* For doctorate, GRE General Test, GRE Subject Test.

Genetics

Albert Einstein College of Medicine, Graduate Programs in the Biomedical Sciences, Department of Genetics, Bronx, NY 10461. Offers computational genetics (PhD); molecular genetics (PhD); translational genetics (PhD); MD/PhD. *Degree requirements:* For doctorate, thesis/dissertation. *Entrance requirements:* For doctorate, GRE General Test. Additional exam requirements/recommendations for international students: Required—TOEFL. *Application deadline:* For fall admission, 1/15 for domestic students. Application fee: $0. *Financial support:* Fellowships available. *Faculty research:* Neurologic genetics in &ITDrosophila&RO, biochemical genetics of yeast, developmental genetics in the mouse. *Unit head:* Dr. Jan Vijg, Chair, 718-678-1151. *Application contact:* Sheila Cleeton, Executive Director and Registrar, Einstein Graduate Division, 718-430-2128, Fax: 718-430-8655, E-mail: sheila.cleeton@einstein.yu.edu.
Website: http://www.einstein.yu.edu/departments/genetics/

Baylor College of Medicine, Graduate School of Biomedical Sciences, Department of Molecular and Human Genetics, Houston, TX 77030-3498. Offers PhD, MD/PhD. *Degree requirements:* For doctorate, thesis/dissertation, public defense. *Entrance requirements:* For doctorate, GRE General Test, GRE Subject Test (strongly recommended), minimum GPA of 3.0. Additional exam requirements/recommendations for international students: Required—TOEFL. Electronic applications accepted. *Faculty research:* Human genetics, genome biology, epigenetics, gene therapy, model organisms.

Baylor College of Medicine, Graduate School of Biomedical Sciences, Interdepartmental Program in Cell and Molecular Biology, Houston, TX 77030-3498. Offers biochemistry (PhD); cell and molecular biology (PhD); genetics (PhD); human genetics (PhD); immunology (PhD); microbiology (PhD); virology (PhD); MD/PhD. *Degree requirements:* For doctorate, thesis/dissertation, public defense. *Entrance requirements:* For doctorate, GRE General Test, GRE Subject Test (strongly recommended), minimum GPA of 3.0. Additional exam requirements/recommendations for international students: Required—TOEFL. Electronic applications accepted. *Faculty research:* Molecular and cellular biology; cancer, aging and stem cells; genomics and proteomics; microbiome, molecular microbiology; infectious disease, immunology and translational research.

Baylor College of Medicine, Graduate School of Biomedical Sciences, Program in Translational Biology and Molecular Medicine, Houston, TX 77030-3498. Offers PhD. *Degree requirements:* For doctorate, thesis/dissertation, public defense. *Entrance requirements:* For doctorate, GRE, minimum GPA of 3.0. Additional exam requirements/recommendations for international students: Required—TOEFL. Electronic applications accepted. *Faculty research:* Molecular medicine, translational biology, human disease biology and therapy.

Boston University, School of Medicine, Division of Graduate Medical Sciences, Program in Genetics and Genomics, Boston, MA 02215. Offers PhD. *Degree requirements:* For doctorate, thesis/dissertation. *Application deadline:* For fall admission, 1/15 for domestic students; for spring admission, 10/15 for domestic students. *Unit head:* Dr. Yuriy Alekseyev, Director, 617-414-1369, E-mail: yurik@bu.edu. *Application contact:* GMS Admissions Office, 617-638-5255, E-mail: askgms@bu.edu.
Website: http://www.bumc.bu.edu/gpgg/graduate-program/

Brandeis University, Graduate School of Arts and Sciences, Program in Molecular and Cell Biology, Waltham, MA 02454-9110. Offers genetics (PhD); microbiology (PhD); molecular and cell biology (MS, PhD); molecular biology (PhD); neurobiology (PhD); quantitative biology (PhD). *Faculty:* 27 full-time (13 women), 3 part-time/adjunct (2 women). *Students:* 47 full-time (29 women), 2 part-time (1 woman); includes 10 minority (1 American Indian or Alaska Native, non-Hispanic/Latino; 2 Asian, non-Hispanic/Latino; 6 Hispanic/Latino; 1 Two or more races, non-Hispanic/Latino), 11 international. Average age 27. 138 applicants, 25% accepted, 18 enrolled. In 2017, 11 master's, 8 doctorates awarded. Terminal master's awarded for partial completion of doctoral program. *Degree requirements:* For master's, thesis optional, research project, research lab, or project lab; for doctorate, comprehensive exam, thesis/dissertation, journal clubs; research seminar; colloquia; qualifying exam. *Entrance requirements:* For master's, GRE General Test, transcripts, resume, letters of recommendation, statement of purpose; for doctorate, GRE General Test, transcripts, resume, letters of recommendation, statement of purpose, list of previous research experience. Additional exam requirements/recommendations for international students: Required—PTE (minimum score 68), TOEFL (minimum score 600 paper-based, 100 iBT) or IELTS (7). *Application deadline:* For fall admission, 12/1 priority date for domestic students; for spring admission, 11/15 for domestic students, 10/15 for international students. Applications are processed on a rolling basis. Application fee: $75. Electronic applications accepted. *Expenses: Tuition:* Full-time $48,720. *Required fees:* $88. Tuition and fees vary according to course load, degree level, program and student level. *Financial support:* In 2017–18, 46 students received support, including 20 fellowships with full tuition reimbursements available (averaging $33,000 per year), 19 research assistantships with full tuition reimbursements available (averaging $33,000 per year); scholarships/grants and tuition waivers (partial) also available. Financial award application deadline: 4/15; financial award applicants required to submit FAFSA. *Faculty research:* Molecular biology, genetics and development; structural and cell biology; neurobiology. *Unit head:* Dr. James Haber, Co-Chair, 781-736-2462, E-mail: haber@brandeis.edu. *Application contact:* Jena Pitman-Leung, Department Administrator, 781-736-2352, E-mail: scigradoffice@brandeis.edu.
Website: http://www.brandeis.edu/gsas/programs/mcbio.html

California Institute of Technology, Division of Biology, Program in Genetics, Pasadena, CA 91125-0001. Offers PhD. *Degree requirements:* For doctorate, thesis/dissertation, qualifying exam. *Entrance requirements:* For doctorate, GRE General Test.

Carnegie Mellon University, Mellon College of Science, Department of Biological Sciences, Pittsburgh, PA 15213-3891. Offers biochemistry (PhD); biophysics (PhD); cell and developmental biology (PhD); computational biology (MS, PhD); genetics (PhD); molecular biology (PhD); neuroscience (PhD); structural biology (PhD). *Degree requirements:* For doctorate, comprehensive exam, thesis/dissertation. *Entrance requirements:* For doctorate, GRE General Test, GRE Subject Test, interview. Electronic applications accepted. *Faculty research:* Genetic structure, function, and regulation; protein structure and function; biological membranes; biological spectroscopy.

Clemson University, Graduate School, College of Behavioral, Social and Health Sciences, School of Nursing, Clemson, SC 29634. Offers clinical and translational research (PhD); global health (Certificate), including low resource countries; healthcare genetics (PhD); nursing (MS, DNP), including adult/gerontology nurse practitioner (MS), family nurse practitioner (MS). *Accreditation:* AACN. *Program availability:* Part-time, 100% online, blended/hybrid learning. *Faculty:* 37 full-time (35 women). *Students:* 130 full-time (118 women), 195 part-time (170 women); includes 50 minority (23 Black or African American, non-Hispanic/Latino; 5 Asian, non-Hispanic/Latino; 16 Hispanic/Latino; 6 Two or more races, non-Hispanic/Latino), 14 international. Average age 34. 71 applicants, 66% accepted, 33 enrolled. In 2017, 88 master's, 2 doctorates, 10 other advanced degrees awarded. *Degree requirements:* For master's, comprehensive exam, thesis or alternative; for doctorate, comprehensive exam, thesis/dissertation. *Entrance requirements:* For master's, GRE General Test, South Carolina RN license, unofficial transcripts, resume, letters of recommendation; for doctorate, GRE General Test, unofficial transcripts, MS/MA thesis or publications, curriculum vitae, statement of career goals, letters of recommendation. Additional exam requirements/recommendations for international students: Required—TOEFL (minimum score 80 iBT), IELTS (minimum score 6.5), PTE (minimum score 54). *Application deadline:* For fall admission, 3/1 priority date for domestic and international students; for spring admission, 10/1 priority date for domestic and international students. Application fee: $80 ($90 for international students). Electronic applications accepted. *Expenses:* Contact institution. *Financial support:* In 2017–18, 41 students received support, including 46 teaching assistantships with partial tuition reimbursements available (averaging $4,919 per year); career-related internships or fieldwork and unspecified assistantships also available. Financial award application deadline: 3/1. *Faculty research:* Breast cancer, healthcare, genetics, international healthcare, educational innovation and technology. *Total annual research expenditures:* $371,674. *Unit head:* Dr. Kathleen Valentine, Director and Associate College Dean, 864-656-4758, E-mail: klvalen@clemson.edu. *Application contact:* Dr. Stephanie Davis, Graduate Studies Coordinator, 864-656-2588, E-mail: stephad@clemson.edu.
Website: http://www.clemson.edu/cbshs/departments/nursing/

Clemson University, Graduate School, College of Science, Department of Genetics and Biochemistry, Clemson, SC 29634. Offers biochemistry and molecular biology (PhD); genetics (PhD). *Faculty:* 24 full-time (12 women). *Students:* 49 full-time (22 women); includes 3 minority (all Hispanic/Latino), 20 international. Average age 26. 54 applicants, 41% accepted, 16 enrolled. In 2017, 11 doctorates awarded. *Degree requirements:* For doctorate, comprehensive exam, thesis/dissertation. *Entrance requirements:* For doctorate, GRE General Test, unofficial transcripts, letters of recommendation. Additional exam requirements/recommendations for international students: Required—TOEFL (minimum score 80 iBT), IELTS (minimum score 6.5), PTE (minimum score 54). *Application deadline:* For fall admission, 1/1 for domestic and international students; for spring admission, 9/1 for domestic and international students. Applications are processed on a rolling basis. Application fee: $80 ($90 for international students). Electronic applications accepted. *Expenses:* $5,174 per semester full-time resident, $9,714 per

semester full-time non-resident, $511 per credit hour part-time resident, $1,017 per credit hour part-time non-resident; $741 per credit hour online; other fees may apply per session. *Financial support:* In 2017–18, 41 students received support, including 7 fellowships with partial tuition reimbursements available (averaging $10,000 per year), 14 research assistantships with partial tuition reimbursements available (averaging $24,786 per year), 20 teaching assistantships with partial tuition reimbursements available (averaging $26,200 per year). Financial award application deadline: 1/1. *Faculty research:* Animal genetics, genomics and bioinformatics, microbial pathogenesis, plant genetics and biochemistry, cell and developmental biology. *Total annual research expenditures:* $1.2 million. *Unit head:* Dr. William Marcotte, Jr., Department Chair, 864-656-3586, E-mail: marcotw@clemson.edu. *Application contact:* Dr. Hong Luo, Graduate Program Coordinator, 864-656-1746, E-mail: hluo@clemson.edu.
Website: https://www.clemson.edu/science/departments/genetics-biochemistry/

Columbia University, College of Physicians and Surgeons, Department of Genetics and Development, New York, NY 10032. Offers genetics (M Phil, MA, PhD); MD/PhD. Only candidates for the PhD are admitted. Terminal master's awarded for partial completion of doctoral program. *Degree requirements:* For doctorate, thesis/dissertation. *Entrance requirements:* For master's and doctorate, GRE General Test. Additional exam requirements/recommendations for international students: Required—TOEFL. *Expenses: Tuition:* Full-time $44,864; part-time $1704 per credit. *Required fees:* $2370 per semester. One-time fee: $105. *Faculty research:* Mammalian cell differentiation and meiosis, developmental genetics, yeast and human genetics, chromosome structure, molecular and cellular biology.

Columbia University, College of Physicians and Surgeons, Integrated Program in Cellular, Molecular, Structural and Genetic Studies, New York, NY 10032. Offers PhD. Terminal master's awarded for partial completion of doctoral program. *Degree requirements:* For doctorate, thesis/dissertation. *Entrance requirements:* For doctorate, GRE General Test, GRE Subject Test. Additional exam requirements/recommendations for international students: Required—TOEFL. *Expenses:* Contact institution. *Faculty research:* Transcription, macromolecular sorting, gene expression during development, cellular interaction.

Cornell University, Graduate School, Graduate Fields of Agriculture and Life Sciences, Field of Computational Biology, Ithaca, NY 14853. Offers computational behavioral biology (PhD); computational biology (PhD); computational cell biology (PhD); computational ecology (PhD); computational genetics (PhD); computational macromolecular biology (PhD); computational organismal biology (PhD). *Degree requirements:* For doctorate, comprehensive exam, thesis/dissertation, 2 semesters of teaching experience. *Entrance requirements:* For doctorate, GRE General Test, GRE Subject Test (biology), 2 letters of recommendation. Additional exam requirements/recommendations for international students: Required—TOEFL (minimum score 550 paper-based; 77 iBT). Electronic applications accepted. *Faculty research:* Computational behavioral biology, computational biology, computational cell biology, computational ecology, computational genetics, computational macromolecular biology, computational organismal biology.

Cornell University, Graduate School, Graduate Fields of Agriculture and Life Sciences, Field of Genetics, Genomics and Development, Ithaca, NY 14853. Offers developmental biology (PhD); genetics (PhD); genomics (PhD). *Degree requirements:* For doctorate, comprehensive exam, thesis/dissertation, 2 semesters of teaching experience. *Entrance requirements:* For doctorate, GRE General Test, GRE Subject Test in biology or biochemistry (recommended), 2 letters of recommendation. Additional exam requirements/recommendations for international students: Required—TOEFL (minimum score 550 paper-based; 77 iBT). Electronic applications accepted. *Faculty research:* Molecular and general genetics, developmental biology and developmental genetics, evolution and population genetics, plant genetics, microbial genetics.

Dartmouth College, Graduate Program in Molecular and Cellular Biology, Department of Genetics, Hanover, NH 03755. Offers PhD, MBA/PhD, MD/PhD. In 2017, 8 doctorates awarded. *Entrance requirements:* For doctorate, GRE General Test, letters of recommendation, minimum GPA of 3.0. *Application deadline:* For fall admission, 12/8 for domestic students. Application fee: $75. Electronic applications accepted. *Financial support:* Fellowships and health care benefits available. *Unit head:* Dr. Jay C. Dunlap, Chair and Professor, 603-650-1108, E-mail: genetics@dartmouth.edu. *Application contact:* Janet Cheney, Program Coordinator, 603-650-1612, E-mail: mcb@dartmouth.edu.
Website: http://www.dartmouth.edu/~genetics/

Drexel University, College of Medicine, Biomedical Graduate Programs, Interdisciplinary Program in Molecular and Cell Biology and Genetics, Philadelphia, PA 19104-2875. Offers MS, PhD, MD/PhD. Terminal master's awarded for partial completion of doctoral program. *Degree requirements:* For master's, comprehensive exam, thesis; for doctorate, thesis/dissertation, qualifying exam. *Entrance requirements:* For master's, GRE General Test, minimum GPA of 2.75; for doctorate, GRE General Test, minimum GPA of 3.0. Additional exam requirements/recommendations for international students: Required—TOEFL. Electronic applications accepted. *Faculty research:* Molecular anatomy, biochemistry, medical biotechnology, molecular pathology, microbiology and immunology.

Duke University, Graduate School, Department of Biochemistry, Durham, NC 27710. Offers crystallography of macromolecules (PhD); enzyme mechanisms (PhD); lipid biochemistry (PhD); membrane structure and function (PhD); molecular genetics (PhD); neurochemistry (PhD); nucleic acid structure and function (PhD); protein structure and function (PhD). *Degree requirements:* For doctorate, thesis/dissertation. *Entrance requirements:* For doctorate, GRE General Test, GRE Subject Test (recommended). Additional exam requirements/recommendations for international students: Required—TOEFL (minimum score 577 paper-based; 90 iBT) or IELTS (minimum score 7). Electronic applications accepted.

Duke University, Graduate School, University Program in Genetics and Genomics, Durham, NC 27710. Offers PhD. *Degree requirements:* For doctorate, variable foreign language requirement, thesis/dissertation. *Entrance requirements:* For doctorate, GRE General Test. Additional exam requirements/recommendations for international students: Required—TOEFL (minimum score 577 paper-based; 90 iBT) or IELTS (minimum score 7).

Emory University, Laney Graduate School, Division of Biological and Biomedical Sciences, Program in Genetics and Molecular Biology, Atlanta, GA 30322-1100. Offers PhD. *Degree requirements:* For doctorate, comprehensive exam, thesis/dissertation. *Entrance requirements:* For doctorate, GRE General Test, minimum GPA of 3.0 in science course work (recommended). Additional exam requirements/recommendations for international students: Required—TOEFL. Electronic applications accepted. *Faculty research:* Gene regulation, genetic combination, developmental regulation.

Harvard University, Graduate School of Arts and Sciences, Division of Medical Sciences, Boston, MA 02115. Offers biological chemistry and molecular pharmacology (PhD); cell biology (PhD); genetics (PhD); microbiology and molecular genetics (PhD); pathology (PhD), including experimental pathology. *Degree requirements:* For doctorate, thesis/dissertation. *Entrance requirements:* For doctorate, GRE General Test, GRE Subject Test. Additional exam requirements/recommendations for international students: Required—TOEFL.

Harvard University, Harvard T.H. Chan School of Public Health, Master of Science Program in Computational Biology and Quantitative Genetics, Cambridge, MA 02138. Offers SM. Offered jointly by the Department of Biostatistics and the Department of Epidemiology. *Students:* 21 full-time (16 women), 3 part-time (1 woman); includes 5 minority (all Asian, non-Hispanic/Latino), 16 international. Average age 29. 41 applicants, 51% accepted, 13 enrolled. In 2017, 12 master's awarded. *Entrance requirements:* For master's, GRE. Additional exam requirements/recommendations for international students: Recommended—TOEFL (minimum score 600 paper-based; 100 iBT), IELTS (minimum score 7). *Application deadline:* For fall admission, 12/1 for domestic and international students. Application fee: $120. Electronic applications accepted. *Financial support:* Application deadline: 2/15; applicants required to submit FAFSA. *Unit head:* Dr. John Quackenbush, Director, 617-582-8163. *Application contact:* Vincent W. James, Director of Admissions, 617-432-1031, Fax: 617-432-7080, E-mail: admissions@hsph.harvard.edu.
Website: http://www.hsph.harvard.edu/sm-computational-biology/

Illinois State University, Graduate School, College of Arts and Sciences, School of Biological Sciences, Normal, IL 61790. Offers animal behavior (MS); bacteriology (MS); biochemistry (MS); biological sciences (MS); biology (PhD); biophysics (MS); biotechnology (MS); botany (MS, PhD); cell biology (MS); conservation biology (MS); developmental biology (MS); ecology (MS, PhD); entomology (MS); evolutionary biology (MS); genetics (MS, PhD); immunology (MS); microbiology (MS, PhD); molecular biology (MS); molecular genetics (MS); neurobiology (MS); neuroscience (MS); parasitology (MS); physiology (MS, PhD); plant biology (MS); plant molecular biology (MS); plant sciences (MS); structural biology (MS); zoology (MS, PhD). *Program availability:* Part-time. *Degree requirements:* For master's, thesis or alternative; for doctorate, variable foreign language requirement, thesis/dissertation, 2 terms of residency. *Entrance requirements:* For master's, GRE General Test, minimum GPA of 2.6 in last 60 hours of course work; for doctorate, GRE General Test. *Faculty research:* Redoc balance and drug development in schistosoma mansoni, control of the growth of listeria monocytogenes at low temperature, regulation of cell expansion and microtubule function by SPRI, CRUI: physiology and fitness consequences of different life history phenotypes.

Indiana University Bloomington, University Graduate School, College of Arts and Sciences, Department of Biology, Bloomington, IN 47405. Offers biology teaching (MAT); biotechnology (MA); evolution, ecology, and behavior (MA, PhD); genetics (PhD); microbiology (MA, PhD); molecular, cellular, and developmental biology (PhD); plant sciences (MA, PhD); zoology (MA, PhD). Terminal master's awarded for partial completion of doctoral program. *Degree requirements:* For master's, thesis, oral defense; for doctorate, thesis/dissertation, oral defense. *Entrance requirements:* For master's and doctorate, GRE General Test. Additional exam requirements/recommendations for international students: Required—TOEFL (minimum score 100 iBT). Electronic applications accepted. *Faculty research:* Evolution, ecology and behavior; microbiology; molecular biology and genetics; plant biology.

Iowa State University of Science and Technology, Bioinformatics and Computational Biology Program, Ames, IA 50011. Offers MS, PhD. *Degree requirements:* For doctorate, thesis/dissertation. *Entrance requirements:* For master's and doctorate, GRE General Test. Additional exam requirements/recommendations for international students: Recommended—TOEFL, IELTS. Electronic applications accepted. *Faculty research:* Functional and structural genomics, genome evolution, macromolecular structure and function, mathematical biology and biological statistics, metabolic and developmental networks.

Iowa State University of Science and Technology, Program in Genetics, Ames, IA 50011. Offers MS, PhD. *Entrance requirements:* For master's and doctorate, GRE General Test. Additional exam requirements/recommendations for international students: Required—TOEFL (minimum score 550 paper-based; 79 iBT), IELTS (minimum score 6.5). Electronic applications accepted.

Irell & Manella Graduate School of Biological Sciences, Graduate Program, Duarte, CA 91010. Offers brain metastatic cancer (PhD); cancer and stem cell metabolism (PhD); cancer biology (PhD); cancer biology and developmental therapeutics (PhD); cell biology (PhD); chemical biology (PhD); chromosomal break repair (PhD); diabetes and pancreatic progenitor cell biology (PhD); DNA repair and cancer biology (PhD); germline epigenetic remodeling and endocrine disruptors (PhD); hematology and hematopoietic cell transplantation (PhD); hematology and immunology (PhD); inflammation and cancer (PhD); micrornas and gene regulation in cardiovascular disease (PhD); mixed chimrism for reversal of autoimmunity (PhD); molecular and cellular biology (PhD); molecular biology and genetics (PhD); nanoparticle mediated twist1 silencing in metastatic cancer (PhD); neuro-oncology and stem cell biology (PhD); neuroscience (PhD); RNA directed therapies for HIV-1 (PhD); small RNA-induced transcriptional gene activation (PhD); stem cell regulation by the microenvironment (PhD); translational oncology and pharmaceutical sciences (PhD); tumor biology (PhD). *Degree requirements:* For doctorate, comprehensive exam, thesis/dissertation, qualifying exams, two advanced courses. *Entrance requirements:* For doctorate, GRE General Test; GRE Subject Test (recommended), 2 years of course work in chemistry (general and organic); 1 year of course work each in biochemistry, general biology, and general physics; 2 semesters of course work in mathematics; significant research laboratory experience. Additional exam requirements/recommendations for international students: Required—TOEFL. Electronic applications accepted. *Faculty research:* Cancer biology, diabetes, stem cell biology, neuroscience, immunology.

See Display on page 65 and Close-Up on page 109.

Johns Hopkins University, Bloomberg School of Public Health, Department of Epidemiology, Baltimore, MD 21205. Offers cancer epidemiology (MHS, Sc M, PhD, Sc D); cardiovascular disease and clinical epidemiology (MHS, Sc M, PhD, Sc D); clinical trials (PhD, Sc D); clinical trials and evidence synthesis (MHS, Sc M, PhD, Sc D); environmental epidemiology (MHS, Sc M, PhD, Sc D); epidemiology of aging (MHS, Sc M, PhD, Sc D); general epidemiology and methodology (MHS, Sc M); genetic epidemiology (MHS, Sc M, PhD, Sc D); infectious disease epidemiology (MHS, Sc M, PhD, Sc D). *Students:* 160 full-time (111 women), 14 part-time (9 women); includes 44 minority (9 Black or African American, non-Hispanic/Latino; 1 American Indian or Alaska Native, non-Hispanic/Latino; 20 Asian, non-Hispanic/Latino; 9 Hispanic/Latino; 1 Native Hawaiian or other Pacific Islander, non-Hispanic/Latino; 4 Two or more races, non-Hispanic/Latino), 64 international. Average age 29. 408 applicants, 29% accepted, 61 enrolled. In 2017, 36 master's, 16 doctorates awarded. *Degree requirements:* For master's, comprehensive exam, thesis, 1-year full-time residency; for doctorate, comprehensive exam, thesis/dissertation, 2 years' full-time residency, oral and written exams, student teaching. *Entrance requirements:* For master's, GRE General Test or MCAT, 3 letters of recommendation, curriculum vitae; for doctorate, GRE General Test, minimum 1 year of work experience, 3 letters of recommendation, curriculum vitae, academic records from all schools. Additional exam requirements/recommendations for international students: Required—TOEFL (minimum score 100 iBT), IELTS (minimum score 7.5). *Application deadline:* Applications are processed on a rolling basis. Application fee: $135. Electronic applications accepted. *Financial support:* Fellowships, Federal Work-Study, institutionally sponsored loans, scholarships/grants, traineeships, and stipends available. Support available to part-time students. Financial award

application deadline: 3/15. *Faculty research:* Cancer and congenital malformations, nutritional epidemiology, AIDS, tuberculosis, cardiovascular disease, risk assessment. *Unit head:* Dr. David D. Celentano, Chair, 410-955-3286, Fax: 410-955-0863. *Application contact:* Frances S. Burman, Academic Program Manager, 410-955-3926, Fax: 410-955-0863, E-mail: fburman@jhsph.edu.
Website: http://www.jhsph.edu/dept/epi/index.html

Johns Hopkins University, National Institutes of Health Sponsored Programs, Baltimore, MD 21218. Offers biology (PhD), including biochemistry, biophysics, cell biology, developmental biology, genetic biology, molecular biology; cell, molecular, and developmental biology and biophysics (PhD). *Degree requirements:* For doctorate, comprehensive exam, thesis/dissertation. *Entrance requirements:* For doctorate, GRE General Test. Additional exam requirements/recommendations for international students: Required—TOEFL (minimum score 600 paper-based), TWE. Electronic applications accepted. *Faculty research:* Protein and nucleic acid biochemistry and biophysical chemistry, molecular biology and development.

Kansas State University, Graduate School, College of Agriculture, Department of Animal Sciences and Industry, Manhattan, KS 66506. Offers genetics (MS, PhD); meat science (MS, PhD); monogastric nutrition (MS, PhD); physiology (MS, PhD); ruminant nutrition (MS, PhD). *Degree requirements:* For master's, comprehensive exam, thesis, oral exam; for doctorate, comprehensive exam, thesis/dissertation, preliminary exams. *Entrance requirements:* Additional exam requirements/recommendations for international students: Required—TOEFL (minimum score 550 paper-based; 79 iBT). Electronic applications accepted. *Faculty research:* Animal nutrition, animal physiology, meat science, animal genetics.

Kansas State University, Graduate School, College of Agriculture, Department of Plant Pathology, Manhattan, KS 66506. Offers genetics (MS, PhD); plant pathology (MS, PhD). Terminal master's awarded for partial completion of doctoral program. *Degree requirements:* For master's, thesis, oral exam; for doctorate, thesis/dissertation, preliminary exams, oral exam. *Entrance requirements:* For master's and doctorate, minimum undergraduate GPA of 3.0. Additional exam requirements/recommendations for international students: Required—TOEFL (minimum score 550 paper-based; 79 iBT). Electronic applications accepted. *Faculty research:* Applied microbiology, microbial genetics, microbial ecology/epidemiology, integrated pest management, plant genetics/genomics/molecular biology, genetics.

Kent State University, College of Arts and Sciences, School of Biomedical Sciences, Kent, OH 44242-0001. Offers biological anthropology (PhD); biomedical mathematics (MS, PhD); cellular and molecular biology (MS, PhD), including cellular biology and structures, molecular biology and genetics; neurosciences (MS, PhD); pharmacology (MS, PhD); physiology (MS, PhD). *Faculty:* 22 full-time (9 women), 3 part-time/adjunct (1 woman). *Students:* 75 full-time (46 women); includes 8 minority (1 Black or African American, non-Hispanic/Latino; 3 Asian, non-Hispanic/Latino; 2 Hispanic/Latino; 2 Two or more races, non-Hispanic/Latino), 25 international. Average age 28. 70 applicants, 23% accepted, 13 enrolled. In 2017, 23 master's, 5 doctorates awarded. Terminal master's awarded for partial completion of doctoral program. *Degree requirements:* For master's, thesis; for doctorate, comprehensive exam, thesis/dissertation. *Entrance requirements:* For master's, GRE, bachelor's degree, transcripts, minimum GPA of 3.0, goal statement, three letters of recommendation, academic preparation adequate to perform graduate work in the desired field; for doctorate, GRE, master's degree, minimum GPA of 3.0, transcripts, goal statement, three letters of recommendation. Additional exam requirements/recommendations for international students: Required—TOEFL (minimum score 600 paper-based, 100 iBT), Michigan English Language Assessment Battery (minimum score 85), IELTS (minimum score 7.0) or PTE (minimum score 68). *Application deadline:* For fall admission, 1/1 for domestic and international students. Applications are processed on a rolling basis. Application fee: $45 ($70 for international students). Electronic applications accepted. *Expenses:* Tuition, state resident: full-time $11,310; part-time $515 per credit hour. Tuition, nonresident: full-time $20,396; part-time $928 per credit hour. *International tuition:* $18,544 full-time. *Financial support:* Research assistantships with full tuition reimbursements, teaching assistantships, and unspecified assistantships available. Financial award application deadline: 1/1. *Unit head:* Dr. Ernest J. Freeman, Director, School of Biomedical Sciences, 330-672-2363, E-mail: efreema2@kent.edu.
Website: http://www.kent.edu/biomedical/

Marquette University, Graduate School, College of Arts and Sciences, Department of Biology, Milwaukee, WI 53201-1881. Offers cell biology (MS, PhD); developmental biology (MS, PhD); ecology (MS, PhD); epithelial physiology (MS, PhD); genetics (MS, PhD); microbiology (MS, PhD); molecular biology (MS, PhD); muscle and exercise physiology (MS, PhD); neuroscience (PhD). Terminal master's awarded for partial completion of doctoral program. *Degree requirements:* For master's, comprehensive exam, thesis, 1 year of teaching experience or equivalent; for doctorate, thesis/dissertation, 1 year of teaching experience or equivalent, qualifying exam. *Entrance requirements:* For master's and doctorate, GRE General Test, GRE Subject Test, official transcripts from all current and previous colleges/universities except Marquette, statement of professional goals and aspirations, three letters of recommendation. Additional exam requirements/recommendations for international students: Required—TOEFL (minimum score 530 paper-based). Electronic applications accepted. *Faculty research:* Neurobiology, neuroendocrinology, epithelial physiology, neuropeptide interactions, synaptic transmission.

Massachusetts Institute of Technology, School of Science, Department of Biology, Cambridge, MA 02139. Offers biochemistry (PhD); biological oceanography (PhD); biology (PhD); biophysical chemistry and molecular structure (PhD); cell biology (PhD); computational and systems biology (PhD); developmental biology (PhD); genetics (PhD); immunology (PhD); microbiology (PhD); molecular biology (PhD); neurobiology (PhD). *Degree requirements:* For doctorate, comprehensive exam, thesis/dissertation, teaching assistantship during two semesters. *Entrance requirements:* For doctorate, GRE General Test. Additional exam requirements/recommendations for international students: Required—TOEFL, IELTS. Electronic applications accepted. *Faculty research:* Cellular, developmental and molecular (plant and animal) biology; biochemistry, bioengineering, biophysics and structural biology; classical and molecular genetics, stem cell and epigenetics; immunology and microbiology; cancer biology, molecular medicine, neurobiology and human disease; computational and systems biology.

Mayo Clinic Graduate School of Biomedical Sciences, Program in Virology and Gene Therapy, Rochester, MN 55905. Offers PhD. *Faculty:* 12 full-time (4 women). *Students:* 17 full-time (6 women); includes 4 minority (3 Asian, non-Hispanic/Latino; 1 Hispanic/Latino). 24 applicants, 25% accepted, 3 enrolled. *Degree requirements:* For doctorate, comprehensive exam, thesis/dissertation. *Entrance requirements:* Additional exam requirements/recommendations for international students: Required—TOEFL. *Application deadline:* For fall admission, 12/1 for domestic and international students. Application fee: $50. Electronic applications accepted. *Financial support:* Fellowships available. *Faculty research:* Virology, viral vectors, gene therapy, cancer immunotherapy, vaccine development. *Unit head:* Dr. Michael Barry, Director, 507-538-1188, E-mail: barry.michael@mayo.edu. *Application contact:* Sarah E. Giese, Admissions Coordinator, 507-538-1160, E-mail: phd.training@mayo.edu.
Website: http://www.mayo.edu/mayo-clinic-graduate-school-of-biomedical-sciences/programs/phd/tracks/virology-and-gene-therapy

McMaster University, Faculty of Health Sciences and School of Graduate Studies, Program in Medical Sciences, Genetics and Cancer Area, Hamilton, ON L8S 4M2, Canada. Offers M Sc, PhD, MD/PhD. *Degree requirements:* For master's, thesis; for doctorate, comprehensive exam, thesis/dissertation. *Entrance requirements:* For master's, honors B Sc, B+ average in related field; for doctorate, M Sc, minimum B+ average, students with proven research experience and an A average may be admitted with a B Sc degree. Additional exam requirements/recommendations for international students: Required—TOEFL (minimum score 580 paper-based; 92 iBT).

Medical University of South Carolina, College of Graduate Studies, Program in Molecular and Cellular Biology and Pathobiology, Charleston, SC 29425. Offers cancer biology (PhD); cardiovascular biology (PhD); cardiovascular imaging (PhD); cell regulation (PhD); craniofacial biology (PhD); genetics and development (PhD); marine biomedicine (PhD); DMD/PhD; MD/PhD. *Degree requirements:* For doctorate, thesis/dissertation, oral and written exams. *Entrance requirements:* For doctorate, GRE General Test, interview, minimum GPA of 3.0. Additional exam requirements/recommendations for international students: Required—TOEFL (minimum score 600 paper-based; 100 iBT). Electronic applications accepted.

Michigan State University, College of Veterinary Medicine and The Graduate School, Graduate Programs in Veterinary Medicine and College of Natural Science, Department of Microbiology and Molecular Genetics, East Lansing, MI 48824. Offers industrial microbiology (MS, PhD); microbiology (MS, PhD); microbiology and molecular genetics (MS, PhD); microbiology–environmental toxicology (PhD). *Entrance requirements:* For master's, GRE General Test. Additional exam requirements/recommendations for international students: Required—TOEFL (minimum score 550 paper-based), Michigan State University ELT (minimum score 85), Michigan English Language Assessment Battery (minimum score 83). Electronic applications accepted.

Michigan State University, The Graduate School, College of Agriculture and Natural Resources, MSU-DOE Plant Research Laboratory, East Lansing, MI 48824. Offers biochemistry and molecular biology (PhD); cellular and molecular biology (PhD); crop and soil sciences (PhD); genetics (PhD); microbiology and molecular genetics (PhD); plant biology (PhD); plant physiology (PhD). Offered jointly with the Department of Energy. *Degree requirements:* For doctorate, comprehensive exam, thesis/dissertation, laboratory rotation, defense of dissertation. *Entrance requirements:* For doctorate, GRE General Test, acceptance into one of the affiliated department programs; 3 letters of recommendation; bachelor's degree or equivalent in life sciences, chemistry, biochemistry, or biophysics; research experience. Electronic applications accepted. *Faculty research:* Role of hormones in the regulation of plant development and physiology, molecular mechanisms associated with signal recognition, development and application of genetic methods and materials, protein routing and function.

Michigan State University, The Graduate School, College of Natural Science, Program in Genetics, East Lansing, MI 48824. Offers genetics (MS, PhD); genetics–environmental toxicology (PhD). *Entrance requirements:* Additional exam requirements/recommendations for international students: Required—TOEFL. Electronic applications accepted.

Mississippi State University, College of Agriculture and Life Sciences, Department of Animal and Dairy Sciences, Mississippi State, MS 39762. Offers agricultural life sciences (MS), including animal physiology (MS, PhD), genetics (MS, PhD); agricultural science (PhD), including animal dairy sciences, animal nutrition (MS, PhD); agriculture (MS), including animal nutrition (MS, PhD), animal science; life sciences (PhD), including animal physiology (MS, PhD), genetics (MS, PhD). *Faculty:* 19 full-time (6 women). *Students:* 20 full-time (12 women), 6 part-time (2 women); includes 2 minority (1 Black or African American, non-Hispanic/Latino; 1 American Indian or Alaska Native, non-Hispanic/Latino), 7 international. Average age 27. 21 applicants, 33% accepted, 5 enrolled. In 2017, 5 master's, 3 doctorates awarded. *Degree requirements:* For master's, comprehensive exam (for some programs), thesis, written proposal of intended research area; for doctorate, comprehensive exam, thesis/dissertation, written proposal of intended research area. *Entrance requirements:* For master's, GRE General Test, minimum GPA of 3.0; for doctorate, GRE General Test. Additional exam requirements/recommendations for international students: Required—TOEFL (minimum score 575 paper-based; 84 iBT), IELTS (minimum score 7). *Application deadline:* For fall admission, 7/1 for domestic students, 5/1 for international students; for spring admission, 11/1 for domestic students, 9/1 for international students. Applications are processed on a rolling basis. Application fee: $60 ($80 for international students). Electronic applications accepted. *Expenses:* Tuition, state resident: full-time $8318; part-time $462.12 per credit hour. Tuition, nonresident: full-time $22,358; part-time $1242.12 per credit hour. *Required fees:* $110; $12.24 per credit hour. $6.12 per semester. *Financial support:* In 2017–18, 15 research assistantships (averaging $13,571 per year) were awarded; Federal Work-Study, institutionally sponsored loans, and unspecified assistantships also available. Financial award application deadline: 4/1; financial award applicants required to submit FAFSA. *Faculty research:* Ecology and population dynamics, physiology, biochemistry and behavior, systematics. *Unit head:* Dr. John Blanton, Professor and Head, 662-325-2935, Fax: 662-325-8873, E-mail: jblanton@ads.msstate.edu. *Application contact:* Marina Hunt, Admissions and Enrollment Assistant, 662-325-5188, E-mail: mhunt@grad.msstate.edu.
Website: http://www.ads.msstate.edu/

New York University, Graduate School of Arts and Science, Department of Biology, New York, NY 10012-1019. Offers biology (PhD); biomedical journalism (MS); cancer and molecular biology (PhD); computational biology (PhD); computers in biological research (MS); developmental genetics (PhD); general biology (MS); immunology and microbiology (PhD); molecular genetics (PhD); neurobiology (PhD); oral biology (MS); plant biology (PhD); recombinant DNA technology (MS); MS/MBA. *Program availability:* Part-time. *Students:* Average age 27. 394 applicants, 56% accepted, 77 enrolled. In 2017, 68 master's, 9 doctorates awarded. Terminal master's awarded for partial completion of doctoral program. *Degree requirements:* For master's, thesis or alternative, qualifying paper; for doctorate, comprehensive exam, thesis/dissertation. *Entrance requirements:* For master's and doctorate, GRE General Test. Additional exam requirements/recommendations for international students: Required—TOEFL. *Application deadline:* For fall admission, 12/1 priority date for domestic students, 12/1 for international students. Application fee: $100. *Expenses: Tuition:* Full-time $41,352; part-time $19,968 per year. *Required fees:* $2496; $1628 per unit. $814 per term. Tuition and fees vary according to course load and program. *Financial support:* Fellowships, research assistantships, teaching assistantships, career-related internships or fieldwork, Federal Work-Study, institutionally sponsored loans, scholarships/grants, health care benefits, and unspecified assistantships available. Financial award application deadline: 12/1; financial award applicants required to submit FAFSA. *Faculty research:* Genomics, molecular and cell biology, development and molecular genetics, molecular evolution of plants and animals. *Unit head:* Stephen Small, Chair, 212-998-8200, Fax: 212-995-4015, E-mail: biology.admissions@nyu.edu. *Application contact:* Ken Birnbaum, Director of Graduate Studies, PhD Programs, 212-998-8200, Fax: 212-995-4015, E-mail: biology.admissions@nyu.edu.
Website: http://biology.as.nyu.edu/

North Carolina State University, Graduate School, College of Agriculture and Life Sciences, Department of Genetics, Raleigh, NC 27695. Offers MG, MS, PhD. Terminal master's awarded for partial completion of doctoral program. *Degree requirements:* For master's, thesis (for some programs); for doctorate, thesis/dissertation. *Entrance requirements:* For master's and doctorate, GRE General Test, minimum GPA of 3.0. Electronic applications accepted. *Faculty research:* Population and quantitative genetics, plant molecular genetics, developmental genetics.

The Ohio State University, Graduate School, College of Arts and Sciences, Division of Natural and Mathematical Sciences, Department of Molecular Genetics, Columbus, OH 43210. Offers cell and developmental biology (MS, PhD); genetics (MS, PhD); molecular biology (MS, PhD). *Faculty:* 30. *Students:* 34 full-time (16 women), 13 international. Average age 26. In 2017, 6 doctorates awarded. *Entrance requirements:* For doctorate, GRE General Test, GRE Subject Test in biology or chemistry (recommended). Additional exam requirements/recommendations for international students: Required—TOEFL (minimum score 550 paper-based; 79 iBT), Michigan English Language Assessment Battery (minimum score 82); Recommended—IELTS (minimum score 7). *Application deadline:* For fall admission, 12/13 priority date for domestic students, 11/30 priority date for international students; for spring admission, 3/1 for domestic students, 2/1 for international students. Applications are processed on a rolling basis. Application fee: $60 ($70 for international students). Electronic applications accepted. *Financial support:* Fellowships, research assistantships, teaching assistantships, Federal Work-Study, and institutionally sponsored loans available. Support available to part-time students. *Unit head:* Dr. Mark Seeger, Chair, 614-292-5106, E-mail: seeger.9@osu.edu. *Application contact:* Graduate and Professional Admissions, 614-292-9444, Fax: 614-292-3895, E-mail: gpadmissions@osu.edu.
Website: https://molgen.osu.edu/

Oregon Health & Science University, School of Medicine, Graduate Programs in Medicine, Program in Molecular and Cellular Biosciences, Department of Molecular and Medical Genetics, Portland, OR 97239-3098. Offers PhD. *Faculty:* 15 full-time (6 women), 30 part-time/adjunct (12 women). *Students:* 9 full-time (5 women); includes 1 minority (Black or African American, non-Hispanic/Latino), 1 international. Average age 29. In 2017, 1 doctorate awarded. Terminal master's awarded for partial completion of doctoral program. *Degree requirements:* For doctorate, comprehensive exam, thesis/dissertation. *Entrance requirements:* For doctorate, GRE General Test (minimum scores: 153 Verbal/148 Quantitative/4.5 Analytical) or MCAT (for some programs). *Application deadline:* For fall admission, 12/1 for domestic and international students. Application fee: $70. Electronic applications accepted. *Financial support:* Health care benefits and full-tuition and stipends (for PhD students) available. Financial award application deadline: 3/1; financial award applicants required to submit FAFSA. *Faculty research:* Human molecular genetics and cytogenetics, neurogenomics, epigenetics/epigenomics, cancer genetics, biochemical genetics, gene therapy. *Unit head:* Dr. Amanda McCullough, Program Director, E-mail: somgrad@oshsu.edu. *Application contact:* Brandi Colbert, Program Coordinator, E-mail: somgrad@ohsu.edu.
Website: http://www.ohsu.edu/xd/education/schools/school-of-medicine/departments/basic-science-departments/molecular-and-medical-genetics/index.cfm

Oregon State University, College of Agricultural Sciences, Program in Botany and Plant Pathology, Corvallis, OR 97331. Offers applied systematics (MS); ecology (MS, PhD); genetics (MS, PhD); genomics and computational biology (MS, PhD); molecular and cellular biology (MS, PhD); mycology (MS, PhD); plant pathology (MS, PhD); plant physiology (MS, PhD). *Entrance requirements:* For master's and doctorate, GRE. *Application deadline:* For fall admission, 12/1 for domestic and international students. Application fee: $75 ($85 for international students). *Financial support:* Application deadline: 12/1. *Unit head:* John Fowler, Chair of Graduate Studies, E-mail: fowlerj@science.oregonstate.edu.
Website: http://bpp.oregonstate.edu/

Oregon State University, College of Agricultural Sciences, Program in Horticulture, Corvallis, OR 97331. Offers breeding, genetics, and biotechnology (MS, PhD); community and landscape horticultural systems (MS, PhD); sustainable crop production (MS, PhD). *Degree requirements:* For master's, thesis (for some programs); for doctorate, thesis/dissertation. *Entrance requirements:* For master's and doctorate, GRE General Test, minimum GPA of 3.0 in last 90 hours. Additional exam requirements/recommendations for international students: Required—TOEFL (minimum score 80 iBT), IELTS (minimum score 6.5). *Application deadline:* For fall admission, 4/1 for international students; for winter admission, 7/1 for international students; for spring admission, 10/1 for international students; for summer admission, 1/1 for international students. Application fee: $75 ($85 for international students). *Application contact:* John Lambrinos, Horticulture Advisor, 541-737-3484, E-mail: lambrinj@hort.oregonstate.edu.
Website: http://horticulture.oregonstate.edu/content/graduate-students

Purdue University, Graduate School, College of Science, Department of Biological Sciences, West Lafayette, IN 47907. Offers biochemistry (PhD); biophysics (PhD); cell and developmental biology (PhD); ecology, evolutionary and population biology (MS, PhD), including ecology, evolutionary biology, population biology; genetics (MS, PhD); microbiology (MS, PhD); molecular biology (PhD); neurobiology (MS, PhD); plant physiology (PhD). *Faculty:* 42 full-time (13 women), 3 part-time/adjunct (0 women). *Students:* 115 full-time (58 women), 6 part-time (4 women); includes 17 minority (1 Black or African American, non-Hispanic/Latino; 6 Asian, non-Hispanic/Latino; 9 Hispanic/Latino; 1 Two or more races, non-Hispanic/Latino), 60 international. Average age 27. 165 applicants, 12% accepted, 15 enrolled. In 2017, 5 master's, 16 doctorates awarded. Terminal master's awarded for partial completion of doctoral program. *Degree requirements:* For master's, thesis (for some programs); for doctorate, thesis/dissertation, seminars, teaching experience. *Entrance requirements:* For master's, GRE General Test (minimum analytical writing score of 3.5), minimum undergraduate GPA of 3.0; for doctorate, GRE General Test (minimum analytical writing score of 3.5), minimum undergraduate GPA of 3.5. Additional exam requirements/recommendations for international students: Required—TOEFL minimum score 600 paper-based; 107 iBT (for MS), 80 iBT (for PhD). *Application deadline:* For fall admission, 12/7 for domestic and international students. Applications are processed on a rolling basis. Application fee: $60 ($75 for international students). Electronic applications accepted. *Financial support:* Fellowships, research assistantships, and teaching assistantships available. Support available to part-time students. Financial award application deadline: 2/15; financial award applicants required to submit FAFSA. *Unit head:* Stephen Konieczny, Head, 765-494-4407, E-mail: sfk@purdue.edu. *Application contact:* Georgina E. Rupp, Graduate Coordinator, 765-494-8142, E-mail: ruppg@purdue.edu.
Website: http://www.bio.purdue.edu/

Purdue University, Graduate School, PULSe - Purdue University Life Sciences Program, West Lafayette, IN 47907. Offers biomolecular structure and biophysics (PhD); biotechnology (PhD); chemical biology (PhD); chromatin and regulation of gene expression (PhD); integrative neuroscience (PhD); integrative plant sciences (PhD); membrane biology (PhD); microbiology (PhD); molecular evolutionary and cancer biology (PhD); molecular evolutionary genetics (PhD); molecular virology (PhD). *Students:* 60 full-time (29 women); includes 6 minority (4 Hispanic/Latino; 2 Two or more races, non-Hispanic/Latino), 36 international. Average age 25. 127 applicants, 39% accepted, 25 enrolled. *Entrance requirements:* For doctorate, GRE, minimum undergraduate GPA of 3.0. Additional exam requirements/recommendations for international students: Required—TOEFL (minimum score 550 paper-based; 77 iBT). *Application deadline:* For fall admission, 1/15 priority date for domestic and international students. Applications are processed on a rolling basis. Application fee: $60 ($75 for international students). Electronic applications accepted. *Financial support:* In 2017–18, research assistantships with tuition reimbursements (averaging $22,500 per year), teaching assistantships with tuition reimbursements (averaging $22,500 per year) were awarded. *Unit head:* Dr. Jason R. Cannon, Head of the Graduate Program, 765-494-0794, E-mail: cannonjr@purdue.edu. *Application contact:* Lindsey Springer, Graduate Contact for Admissions, 765-496-9667, E-mail: lbcampbe@purdue.edu.
Website: http://www.gradschool.purdue.edu/pulse

Rutgers University–New Brunswick, Graduate School-New Brunswick, Programs in the Molecular Biosciences, Piscataway, NJ 08854-8097. Offers biochemistry (PhD); cell and developmental biology (MS, PhD); microbiology and molecular genetics (MS, PhD), including applied microbiology, clinical microbiology, computational molecular biology (PhD), immunology, microbial biochemistry, molecular genetics, virology. MS, PhD offered jointly with University of Medicine and Dentistry of New Jersey.

Stanford University, School of Medicine, Graduate Programs in Medicine, Department of Genetics, Stanford, CA 94305-2004. Offers genetics (PhD). *Degree requirements:* For doctorate, thesis/dissertation, qualifying examination, teaching requirement. *Entrance requirements:* For doctorate, GRE General Test, GRE Subject Test. Additional exam requirements/recommendations for international students: Required—TOEFL. Electronic applications accepted. *Expenses: Tuition:* Full-time $48,987; part-time $10,620 per quarter. One-time fee: $400. Tuition and fees vary according to program. *Faculty research:* Molecular biology of DNA replication in human cells, analysis of existing and search for new DNA polymorphisms in humans, molecular genetics of prokaryotic and eukaryotic genetic elements, proteins in DNA replication.

Stony Brook University, State University of New York, Graduate School, College of Arts and Sciences, Graduate Program in Genetics, Stony Brook, NY 11794. Offers PhD. *Students:* 33 full-time (13 women), 1 (woman) part-time; includes 9 minority (4 Asian, non-Hispanic/Latino; 3 Hispanic/Latino; 2 Two or more races, non-Hispanic/Latino), 11 international. Average age 27. 53 applicants, 26% accepted, 8 enrolled. In 2017, 6 doctorates awarded. *Degree requirements:* For doctorate, comprehensive exam, thesis/dissertation, teaching experience. *Entrance requirements:* For doctorate, GRE General Test, GRE Subject Test. Additional exam requirements/recommendations for international students: Required—TOEFL (minimum score 90 iBT). *Application deadline:* For fall admission, 1/15 for domestic students; for spring admission, 10/1 for domestic students. Application fee: $100. *Expenses:* Contact institution. *Financial support:* In 2017–18, 9 fellowships, 8 research assistantships, 6 teaching assistantships were awarded; Federal Work-Study also available. *Faculty research:* Gene structure, gene regulation, genetics. *Unit head:* Dr. Martha B. Furie, Program Director, 631-632-4232, Fax: 631-632-4294, E-mail: martha.furie@stonybrook.edu. *Application contact:* Jennifer Jokinen, Coordinator, 631-632-8812, Fax: 631-632-9797, E-mail: jennifer.jokinen@stonybrook.edu.
Website: http://life.bio.sunysb.edu/gen/

Thomas Jefferson University, Jefferson College of Biomedical Sciences, PhD Program in Genetics, Genomics and Cancer Biology, Philadelphia, PA 19107. Offers PhD. *Faculty:* 41 full-time (12 women). *Students:* 16 full-time (9 women); includes 1 minority (Hispanic/Latino), 2 international. In 2017, 5 doctorates awarded. *Degree requirements:* For doctorate, comprehensive exam, thesis/dissertation. *Entrance requirements:* For doctorate, GRE General Test, minimum GPA of 3.2. Additional exam requirements/recommendations for international students: Required—TOEFL, IELTS (minimum score 7). *Application deadline:* For fall admission, 12/1 priority date for domestic and international students. Applications are processed on a rolling basis. Application fee: $60. Electronic applications accepted. *Financial support:* In 2017–18, 16 students received support, including 16 fellowships with full tuition reimbursements available (averaging $62,653 per year); Federal Work-Study, institutionally sponsored loans, scholarships/grants, traineeships, health care benefits, and stipends also available. Financial award application deadline: 5/1; financial award applicants required to submit FAFSA. *Faculty research:* Functional genomics, cancer susceptibility, cell cycle, regulation oncogenes and tumor suppressor genes, genetics of neoplastic disease. *Unit head:* Dr. Lucia Languino, Program Director, 215-503-3442, E-mail: lucia.languino@jefferson.edu. *Application contact:* Marc E. Stearns, Senior Associate Director of Admissions, 215-503-0155, Fax: 215-503-3433, E-mail: jgsbs-info@jefferson.edu.
Website: http://www.jefferson.edu/university/biomedical-sciences/degrees-programs/phd-programs/genetics.html

Tufts University, Sackler School of Graduate Biomedical Sciences, Genetics Program, Medford, MA 02155. Offers genetics (PhD); mammalian genetics (PhD). Terminal master's awarded for partial completion of doctoral program. *Degree requirements:* For doctorate, comprehensive exam, thesis/dissertation. *Entrance requirements:* For doctorate, GRE General Test, 3 letters of reference, resume, personal statement. Electronic applications accepted. *Expenses: Tuition:* Full-time $49,892. *Required fees:* $874. Full-time tuition and fees vary according to degree level, program and student level. Part-time tuition and fees vary according to course load. *Faculty research:* Cancer genetics, developmental and neurogenetics, microbial and yeast genetics, the genetics of bacterial and viral pathogens, Drosophila genetics, human genetics and gene discovery.

Université de Montréal, Faculty of Medicine, Program in Medical Genetics, Montréal, QC H3C 3J7, Canada. Offers DESS.

Université du Québec à Chicoutimi, Graduate Programs, Program in Experimental Medicine, Chicoutimi, QC G7H 2B1, Canada. Offers genetics (M Sc). *Degree requirements:* For master's, thesis. *Entrance requirements:* For master's, appropriate bachelor's degree, proficiency in French.

University at Buffalo, the State University of New York, Graduate School, Jacobs School of Medicine and Biomedical Sciences, Graduate Programs in Medicine and Biomedical Sciences, Program in Genetics, Genomics and Bioinformatics, Buffalo, NY 14260. Offers MS, PhD, MD/PhD. *Faculty:* 59 full-time (16 women). *Students:* 13 full-time (6 women); includes 4 minority (all Asian, non-Hispanic/Latino). Average age 25. 22 applicants, 64% accepted, 5 enrolled. In 2017, 3 master's awarded. Terminal master's awarded for partial completion of doctoral program. *Degree requirements:* For master's, thesis or alternative; for doctorate, thesis/dissertation. *Entrance requirements:* For master's and doctorate, GRE. Additional exam requirements/recommendations for international students: Required—TOEFL (minimum score 100 iBT); Recommended—IELTS (minimum score 6.5). *Application deadline:* For fall admission, 3/1 for domestic and international students. Application fee: $85. Electronic applications accepted. *Expenses:* Contact institution. *Faculty research:* Human and medical genetics and genomics, developmental genomics and genetics, microbial genetics and pathogenesis, bioinformatics. *Unit head:* Dr. Richard Gronostajski, Director, 716-829-3471, Fax: 716-849-6655, E-mail: rgron@buffalo.edu. *Application contact:* Renad Aref, Program Administrator, 716-881-8209, Fax: 716-849-6655, E-mail: raaref@buffalo.edu.
Website: http://medicine.buffalo.edu/education/ggb.html

The University of Alabama at Birmingham, Joint Health Sciences, Genetics, Genomics, and Bioinformatics Theme, Birmingham, AL 35294. Offers PhD. *Faculty:*

370. *Students:* 37 full-time (23 women); includes 8 minority (3 Black or African American, non-Hispanic/Latino; 4 Asian, non-Hispanic/Latino; 1 Two or more races, non-Hispanic/Latino). Average age 27. 27 applicants, 33% accepted, 3 enrolled. In 2017, 4 doctorates awarded. *Degree requirements:* For doctorate, comprehensive exam, thesis/dissertation. *Entrance requirements:* For doctorate, personal statement, resume or curriculum vitae, letters of recommendation, research experience, interview. Additional exam requirements/recommendations for international students: Required—TOEFL (minimum score 80 iBT), IELTS (minimum score 6.5). *Application deadline:* For fall admission, 12/31 for domestic and international students. Applications are processed on a rolling basis. Electronic applications accepted. *Financial support:* In 2017–18, fellowships with full tuition reimbursements (averaging $29,000 per year), research assistantships with full tuition reimbursements (averaging $30,000 per year) were awarded; health care benefits also available. *Unit head:* Dr. Kevin Dybvig, Theme Director, 205-934-9327, E-mail: dybvig@uab.edu. *Application contact:* Alyssa Zasada, Admissions Manager for Graduate Biomedical Sciences, 205-934-3857, E-mail: grad-gbs@uab.edu.
Website: http://www.uab.edu/gbs/home/themes/ggb

University of Alberta, Faculty of Graduate Studies and Research, Department of Biological Sciences, Edmonton, AB T6G 2E1, Canada. Offers environmental biology and ecology (M Sc, PhD); microbiology and biotechnology (M Sc, PhD); molecular biology and genetics (M Sc, PhD); physiology and cell biology (M Sc, PhD); plant biology (M Sc, PhD); systematics and evolution (M Sc, PhD). Terminal master's awarded for partial completion of doctoral program. *Degree requirements:* For master's, thesis; for doctorate, thesis/dissertation. *Entrance requirements:* Additional exam requirements/recommendations for international students: Required—TOEFL.

University of Alberta, Faculty of Medicine and Dentistry and Faculty of Graduate Studies and Research, Graduate Programs in Medicine, Department of Medical Genetics, Edmonton, AB T6G 2E1, Canada. Offers M Sc, PhD. *Degree requirements:* For master's, comprehensive exam, thesis; for doctorate, comprehensive exam, thesis/dissertation. *Entrance requirements:* For master's and doctorate, minimum GPA of 3.2. *Faculty research:* Clinical and molecular cytogenetics, ocular genetics, Prader-Willi syndrome, genomic instability, developmental genetics.

The University of Arizona, Graduate Interdisciplinary Programs, Graduate Interdisciplinary Program in Genetics, Tucson, AZ 85719. Offers MS, PhD. Terminal master's awarded for partial completion of doctoral program. *Degree requirements:* For master's, thesis; for doctorate, one foreign language, comprehensive exam, thesis/dissertation. *Entrance requirements:* For master's, GRE General Test, 3 letters of recommendation; for doctorate, GRE General Test, statement of purpose, 3 letters of recommendation. Additional exam requirements/recommendations for international students: Required—TOEFL (minimum score 550 paper-based; 79 iBT). Electronic applications accepted. *Faculty research:* Cancer research; DNA repair; plant and animal cytogenetics; molecular, population, and ecological genetics.

The University of British Columbia, Faculty of Medicine, Department of Medical Genetics, Medical Genetics Graduate Program, Vancouver, BC V6T 1Z1, Canada. Offers M Sc, PhD. *Degree requirements:* For master's, thesis, 18 credits of coursework; for doctorate, comprehensive exam, thesis/dissertation, 18 credits of coursework. Electronic applications accepted. *Expenses:* Contact institution.

University of Calgary, Cumming School of Medicine and Faculty of Graduate Studies, Medical Science Graduate Program, Calgary, AB T2N 1N4, Canada. Offers cancer biology (M Sc, PhD); critical care medicine (M Sc, PhD); joint injury and arthritis (M Sc, PhD); molecular and medical genetics (M Sc, PhD); mountain medicine and high altitude physiology (M Sc, PhD); pathologists' assistant (M Sc, PhD). *Degree requirements:* For master's, thesis; for doctorate, thesis/dissertation, candidacy exam. *Entrance requirements:* For master's, minimum undergraduate GPA of 3.2; for doctorate, minimum graduate GPA of 3.2. Additional exam requirements/recommendations for international students: Required—TOEFL (minimum score 600 paper-based). Electronic applications accepted. *Faculty research:* Cancer biology, immunology, joint injury and arthritis, medical education, population genomics.

University of California, Davis, Graduate Studies, Graduate Group in Genetics, Davis, CA 95616. Offers MS, PhD. Terminal master's awarded for partial completion of doctoral program. *Degree requirements:* For master's, comprehensive exam (for some programs), thesis (for some programs); for doctorate, thesis/dissertation. *Entrance requirements:* For master's and doctorate, GRE General Test, GRE Subject Test. Additional exam requirements/recommendations for international students: Required—TOEFL (minimum score 550 paper-based). Electronic applications accepted. *Faculty research:* Molecular, quantitative, and developmental genetics; cytogenetics; plant breeding.

University of California, Irvine, Francisco J. Ayala School of Biological Sciences and School of Medicine, Interdisciplinary Graduate Program in Cellular and Molecular Biosciences, Irvine, CA 92697. Offers PhD. *Students:* 40 full-time (20 women); includes 19 minority (9 Asian, non-Hispanic/Latino; 6 Hispanic/Latino; 4 Two or more races, non-Hispanic/Latino), 4 international. Average age 25. 371 applicants, 23% accepted, 38 enrolled. *Degree requirements:* For doctorate, thesis/dissertation, teaching assignment, preliminary exam. *Entrance requirements:* For doctorate, GRE General Test, three letters of recommendation, interview. Additional exam requirements/recommendations for international students: Required—TOEFL or IELTS. *Application deadline:* For fall admission, 12/8 for domestic and international students. Application fee: $105 ($125 for international students). Electronic applications accepted. *Expenses:* Contact institution. *Financial support:* Fellowships with full tuition reimbursements, institutionally sponsored loans, scholarships/grants, tuition waivers (full), unspecified assistantships, and stipends available. Financial award application deadline: 1/1; financial award applicants required to submit FAFSA. *Faculty research:* Cellular biochemistry; gene structure and expression; protein structure, function, and design; molecular genetics; pathogenesis and inherited disease. *Unit head:* Melanie Cocco, Director, 949-824-4487, Fax: 949-824-1965, E-mail: mcocco@uci.edu. *Application contact:* Renee Frigo, Administrator, 949-824-8145, Fax: 949-824-1965, E-mail: rfrigo@uci.edu.
Website: http://cmb.uci.edu/

University of California, Riverside, Graduate Division, Graduate Program in Genetics, Genomics, and Bioinformatics, Riverside, CA 92521-0102. Offers PhD. *Degree requirements:* For doctorate, thesis/dissertation, qualifying exams, teaching experience. *Entrance requirements:* For doctorate, GRE General Test, minimum GPA of 3.2. Additional exam requirements/recommendations for international students: Required—TOEFL (minimum score 550 paper-based, 80 iBT) or IELTS. *Application deadline:* For fall admission, 12/1 priority date for domestic and international students; for winter admission, 11/15 for domestic students, 9/1 for international students; for spring admission, 3/1 for domestic students, 12/1 for international students. Application fee: $85 ($100 for international students). Electronic applications accepted. *Expenses:* Tuition, state resident: full-time $5746. Tuition, nonresident: full-time $10,780. Tuition and fees vary according to campus/location and program. *Financial support:* Fellowships with tuition reimbursements, research assistantships with tuition reimbursements, teaching assistantships with tuition reimbursements, career-related internships or fieldwork, Federal Work-Study, institutionally sponsored loans, health care benefits, tuition waivers (full and partial), and unspecified assistantships available. Financial award applicants required to submit FAFSA. *Faculty research:* Molecular genetics, evolution and population genetics, genomics and bioinformatics. *Application contact:* Julio Sosa, E-mail: ggb@ucr.edu.
Website: http://ggb.ucr.edu/

University of California, San Francisco, Graduate Division and School of Medicine, Tetrad Graduate Program, Genetics Track, San Francisco, CA 94143. Offers PhD, MD/PhD. *Degree requirements:* For doctorate, thesis/dissertation. *Entrance requirements:* For doctorate, GRE General Test, GRE Subject Test. Additional exam requirements/recommendations for international students: Required—TOEFL. *Expenses:* Contact institution. *Faculty research:* Gene expression; chromosome structure and mechanics; medical, somatic cell, and radiation genetics.

University of Chicago, Division of the Biological Sciences, Committee on Genetics, Genomics and Systems Biology, Chicago, IL 60637. Offers PhD. *Students:* 32 full-time (17 women); includes 8 minority (1 Black or African American, non-Hispanic/Latino; 4 Asian, non-Hispanic/Latino; 1 Hispanic/Latino; 1 Native Hawaiian or other Pacific Islander, non-Hispanic/Latino; 1 Two or more races, non-Hispanic/Latino), 9 international. Average age 26. 76 applicants, 25% accepted, 9 enrolled. In 2017, 4 doctorates awarded. *Degree requirements:* For doctorate, thesis/dissertation, ethics class, 2 teaching assistantships, preliminary exam. *Entrance requirements:* For doctorate, GRE General Test, transcripts, statement of purpose, 3 letters of recommendation. Additional exam requirements/recommendations for international students: Required—TOEFL (minimum score 600 paper-based; 104 iBT), IELTS (minimum score 7). *Application deadline:* For fall admission, 12/1 for domestic and international students. Application fee: $90. Electronic applications accepted. *Financial support:* In 2017–18, 21 students received support, including fellowships with full tuition reimbursements available (averaging $31,000 per year), research assistantships with full tuition reimbursements available (averaging $31,000 per year); institutionally sponsored loans, scholarships/grants, traineeships, and health care benefits also available. Financial award application deadline: 12/1. *Faculty research:* Molecular genetics, developmental genetics, population genetics, human genetics, computational biology. *Unit head:* Yoav Gilad, PhD, Chair, E-mail: bsdadmissions@uchicago.edu. *Application contact:* Sue Levison, Administrator, 773-702-2464, Fax: 773-702-2464, E-mail: committee-on-genetics@uchicago.edu.

University of Colorado Denver, School of Medicine, Program in Human Medical Genetics and Genomics, Aurora, CO 80206. Offers PhD. *Students:* 10 full-time (6 women); includes 4 minority (1 Asian, non-Hispanic/Latino; 3 Hispanic/Latino), 1 international. Average age 27. 47 applicants, 2% accepted, 1 enrolled. In 2017, 4 doctorates awarded. *Degree requirements:* For doctorate, comprehensive exam, thesis/dissertation, at least 30 semester hours in course work (rotations and research courses taken prior to the completion of the comprehensive examination) and 30 semester hours of thesis/didactic credits prior to defending. *Entrance requirements:* For doctorate, GRE General Test (minimum combined score of 1205), minimum GPA of 3.0, 4 letters of recommendation; prerequisite courses in biology, chemistry (general and organic), physics, genetics, calculus, and statistics (recommended). Additional exam requirements/recommendations for international students: Required—TOEFL (minimum score 570 paper-based; 80 iBT). *Application deadline:* For fall admission, 12/1 for domestic students, 1/1 priority date for international students. Application fee: $50 ($75 for international students). Electronic applications accepted. *Financial support:* Fellowships, research assistantships, teaching assistantships, Federal Work-Study, institutionally sponsored loans, scholarships/grants, traineeships, health care benefits, and unspecified assistantships available. *Faculty research:* Mapping, discovery, and function of disease genes affecting skin and craniofacial development and autoimmunity; genetics of colon cancer; clinical proteomics; biochemical markers of disease, including cancer; modeling human genetic diseases with patient-derived induced pluripotent stem cells; cell cycle control of DNA replication and mutagenesis in yeast and human cancer cells; mechanisms of cancer chemoprevention. *Unit head:* Dr. Richard A. Spritz, Director, 303-724-3107, E-mail: richard.spritz@ucdenver.edu. *Application contact:* Maia Evans, Program Administrator, 303-724-3102, Fax: 303-724-3100, E-mail: adama.evans@ucdenver.edu.
Website: http://www.ucdenver.edu/academics/colleges/medicalschool/programs/HumanMedicalGenetics/Pages/Genetics.aspx

University of Connecticut, Graduate School, College of Liberal Arts and Sciences, Department of Molecular and Cell Biology, Storrs, CT 06269. Offers applied genomics (PSM); cell and developmental biology (MS, PhD); genetics and genomics (MS, PhD); microbial systems analysis (PSM); microbiology (MS, PhD); structural biology, biochemistry and biophysics (MS, PhD). Terminal master's awarded for partial completion of doctoral program. *Degree requirements:* For master's, comprehensive exam; for doctorate, thesis/dissertation. *Entrance requirements:* For master's and doctorate, GRE General Test, GRE Subject Test. Additional exam requirements/recommendations for international students: Required—TOEFL (minimum score 550 paper-based). Electronic applications accepted.

University of Connecticut Health Center, Graduate School, Programs in Biomedical Sciences, Program in Genetics and Developmental Biology, Farmington, CT 06030. Offers PhD, DMD/PhD, MD/PhD. *Degree requirements:* For doctorate, comprehensive exam, thesis/dissertation. *Entrance requirements:* For doctorate, GRE General Test, GRE Subject Test. Additional exam requirements/recommendations for international students: Required—TOEFL (minimum score 600 paper-based). Electronic applications accepted. *Faculty research:* Developmental biology, genomic imprinting, RNA biology, RNA alternative splicing, human embryonic stem cells.

University of Delaware, College of Arts and Sciences, Department of Biological Sciences, Newark, DE 19716. Offers biotechnology (MS); cancer biology (MS, PhD); cell and extracellular matrix biology (MS, PhD); cell and systems physiology (MS, PhD); developmental biology (MS, PhD); ecology and evolution (MS, PhD); microbiology (MS, PhD); molecular biology and genetics (MS, PhD). Terminal master's awarded for partial completion of doctoral program. *Degree requirements:* For master's, thesis, preliminary exam; for doctorate, comprehensive exam, thesis/dissertation, preliminary exam. *Entrance requirements:* For master's and doctorate, GRE General Test. Additional exam requirements/recommendations for international students: Required—TOEFL (minimum score 600 paper-based); Recommended—TWE. Electronic applications accepted. *Faculty research:* Microorganisms, bone, cancer metastasis, developmental biology, cell biology, DNA.

University of Florida, College of Medicine and Graduate School, Interdisciplinary Program in Biomedical Sciences, Concentration in Genetics, Gainesville, FL 32611. Offers PhD. *Degree requirements:* For doctorate, thesis/dissertation. *Entrance requirements:* For doctorate, GRE General Test, minimum GPA of 3.0, biochemistry before enrollment. Additional exam requirements/recommendations for international students: Required—TOEFL, IELTS. Electronic applications accepted.

University of Georgia, College of Agricultural and Environmental Sciences, Institute of Plant Breeding, Genetics and Genomics, Athens, GA 30602. Offers MS, PhD.

University of Georgia, Franklin College of Arts and Sciences, Department of Genetics, Athens, GA 30602. Offers MS, PhD. Terminal master's awarded for partial completion of doctoral program. *Degree requirements:* For master's, thesis; for doctorate, comprehensive exam, thesis/dissertation. *Entrance requirements:* For master's and doctorate, GRE General Test. Additional exam requirements/recommendations for international students: Required—TOEFL. Electronic applications accepted.

University of Hawaii at Manoa, John A. Burns School of Medicine, Program in Cell and Molecular Biology, Honolulu, HI 96813. Offers MS, PhD. *Program availability:* Part-time. Terminal master's awarded for partial completion of doctoral program. *Degree requirements:* For master's, thesis optional; for doctorate, comprehensive exam, thesis/dissertation. *Entrance requirements:* For master's and doctorate, GRE General Test, minimum GPA of 3.0. Additional exam requirements/recommendations for international students: Required—TOEFL (minimum score 500 paper-based; 61 iBT), IELTS (minimum score 5).

University of Illinois at Chicago, College of Medicine and Graduate College, Graduate Programs in Medicine, Department of Biochemistry and Molecular Genetics, Chicago, IL 60607-7128. Offers PhD, MD/PhD. Terminal master's awarded for partial completion of doctoral program. *Degree requirements:* For doctorate, thesis/dissertation. *Entrance requirements:* For doctorate, GRE General Test. Additional exam requirements/recommendations for international students: Required—TOEFL. Electronic applications accepted. *Faculty research:* Signal transduction, cell cycle regulation, membrane biology, regulation of gene function and development, protein and nucleic acid structure and function, cancer biology.

The University of Iowa, Graduate College, College of Liberal Arts and Sciences, Department of Biology, Iowa City, IA 52242-1324. Offers biology (MS, PhD); cell and developmental biology (MS, PhD); evolution (MS, PhD); genetics (MS, PhD); neurobiology (MS, PhD). Terminal master's awarded for partial completion of doctoral program. *Degree requirements:* For master's, thesis optional, exam; for doctorate, comprehensive exam, thesis/dissertation. *Entrance requirements:* For master's and doctorate, GRE General Test, minimum GPA of 3.0. Additional exam requirements/recommendations for international students: Required—TOEFL (minimum score 600 paper-based; 100 iBT). Electronic applications accepted. *Faculty research:* Neurobiology, evolutionary biology, genetics, cell and developmental biology.

The University of Iowa, Graduate College, Program in Genetics, Iowa City, IA 52242-1316. Offers PhD. *Degree requirements:* For doctorate, comprehensive exam, thesis/dissertation. *Entrance requirements:* For doctorate, GRE General Test, minimum GPA of 3.0. Additional exam requirements/recommendations for international students: Required—TOEFL (minimum score 600 paper-based; 100 iBT). Electronic applications accepted. *Expenses:* Contact institution. *Faculty research:* Developmental genetics, eukaryotic gene expression, human genetics, molecular and biochemical genetics, evolutionary genetics.

The University of Iowa, Roy J. and Lucille A. Carver College of Medicine and Graduate College, Graduate Programs in Medicine, Department of Microbiology, Iowa City, IA 52242-1316. Offers general microbiology and microbial physiology (MS, PhD); immunology (MS, PhD); microbial genetics (MS, PhD); pathogenic bacteriology (MS, PhD); virology (MS, PhD). *Degree requirements:* For master's, thesis; for doctorate, comprehensive exam, thesis/dissertation. *Entrance requirements:* For master's and doctorate, GRE General Test. Additional exam requirements/recommendations for international students: Required—TOEFL (minimum score 600 paper-based). Electronic applications accepted. *Faculty research:* Gene regulation, processing and transport of HIV, retroviral pathogenesis, biodegradation, biofilm.

The University of Manchester, School of Biological Sciences, Manchester, United Kingdom. Offers adaptive organismal biology (M Phil, PhD); animal biology (M Phil, PhD); biochemistry (M Phil, PhD); bioinformatics (M Phil, PhD); biomolecular sciences (M Phil, PhD); biotechnology (M Phil, PhD); cell biology (M Phil, PhD); cell matrix research (M Phil, PhD); channels and transporters (M Phil, PhD); developmental biology (M Phil, PhD); environmental biology (M Phil, PhD); evolutionary biology (M Phil, PhD); gene expression (M Phil, PhD); genetics (M Phil, PhD); history of science, technology and medicine (M Phil, PhD); immunology (M Phil, PhD); integrative neurobiology and behavior (M Phil, PhD); membrane trafficking (M Phil, PhD); microbiology (M Phil, PhD); molecular and cellular neuroscience (M Phil, PhD); molecular biology (M Phil, PhD); molecular cancer studies (M Phil, PhD); neuroscience (M Phil, PhD); ophthalmology (M Phil, PhD); optometry (M Phil, PhD); organelle function (M Phil, PhD); pharmacology (M Phil, PhD); physiology (M Phil, PhD); plant sciences (M Phil, PhD); stem cell research (M Phil, PhD); structural biology (M Phil, PhD); systems neuroscience (M Phil, PhD); toxicology (M Phil, PhD).

University of Massachusetts Amherst, Graduate School, Interdisciplinary Programs, Program in Plant Biology, Amherst, MA 01003. Offers biochemistry and metabolism (MS, PhD); cell biology and physiology (MS, PhD); environmental, ecological and integrative biology (MS, PhD); genetics and evolution (MS, PhD). *Degree requirements:* For master's, thesis; for doctorate, 2 foreign languages, comprehensive exam, thesis/dissertation. *Entrance requirements:* For master's and doctorate, GRE General Test. Additional exam requirements/recommendations for international students: Required—TOEFL (minimum score 550 paper-based; 80 iBT), IELTS (minimum score 6.5). Electronic applications accepted.

University of Miami, Graduate School, College of Arts and Sciences, Department of Biology, Coral Gables, FL 33124. Offers biology (MS, PhD); genetics and evolution (MS, PhD). Terminal master's awarded for partial completion of doctoral program. *Degree requirements:* For master's, comprehensive exam (for some programs), thesis (for some programs); for doctorate, thesis/dissertation, oral and written qualifying exam. *Entrance requirements:* For master's, GRE General Test, 3 letters of recommendation, research papers; for doctorate, GRE General Test, 3 letters of recommendation, research papers, sponsor letter. Additional exam requirements/recommendations for international students: Required—TOEFL (minimum score 550 paper-based; 59 iBT). Electronic applications accepted. *Faculty research:* Neuroscience to ethology; plants, vertebrates and mycorrhizae; phylogenies, life histories and species interactions; molecular biology, gene expression and populations; cells, auditory neurons and vertebrate locomotion.

University of Minnesota, Twin Cities Campus, Graduate School, Program in Molecular, Cellular, Developmental Biology and Genetics, Minneapolis, MN 55455-0213. Offers genetic counseling (MS); molecular, cellular, developmental biology and genetics (PhD). Terminal master's awarded for partial completion of doctoral program. *Degree requirements:* For master's, thesis optional; for doctorate, thesis/dissertation. *Entrance requirements:* For master's and doctorate, GRE General Test. Additional exam requirements/recommendations for international students: Required—TOEFL (minimum score 625 paper-based; 80 iBT). Electronic applications accepted. *Faculty research:* Membrane receptors and membrane transport, cell interactions, cytoskeleton and cell mobility, regulation of gene expression, plant cell and molecular biology.

University of Nebraska Medical Center, Interdisciplinary Graduate Program in Biomedical Sciences, Department of Genetics, Cell Biology and Anatomy, Omaha, NE 68198-5805. Offers genetics, cell biology and anatomy (PhD); medical anatomy (MS); molecular genetics and cell biology (MS). Terminal master's awarded for partial completion of doctoral program. *Degree requirements:* For master's, comprehensive exam, thesis (for some programs); for doctorate, comprehensive exam, thesis/dissertation. *Entrance requirements:* For master's, GRE General Test (MCAT or DAT acceptable for MS in medical anatomy); for doctorate, GRE General Test. Additional exam requirements/recommendations for international students: Required—TOEFL (minimum score 550 paper-based; 80 iBT). Electronic applications accepted. *Expenses:* Contact institution. *Faculty research:* Hematology, immunology, developmental biology, genetics cancer biology, neuroscience.

University of New Hampshire, Graduate School, College of Life Sciences and Agriculture, Department of Molecular, Cellular and Biomedical Sciences, Program in Genetics, Durham, NH 03824. Offers MS, PhD. *Program availability:* Part-time. *Students:* 11 full-time (7 women), 8 part-time (6 women); includes 3 minority (all Hispanic/Latino), 3 international. Average age 27. 19 applicants, 53% accepted, 9 enrolled. In 2017, 3 master's, 3 doctorates awarded. *Entrance requirements:* For master's and doctorate, GRE General Test, GRE Subject Test. Additional exam requirements/recommendations for international students: Required—TOEFL (minimum score 550 paper-based; 80 iBT). *Application deadline:* For fall admission, 1/15 for domestic and international students. Application fee: $65. Electronic applications accepted. *Financial support:* In 2017–18, 17 students received support, including 3 research assistantships, 14 teaching assistantships; fellowships, career-related internships or fieldwork, Federal Work-Study, and scholarships/grants also available. Support available to part-time students. Financial award application deadline: 2/15. *Unit head:* Rick Cote, Chair, 603-862-2458. *Application contact:* Paul Boisselle, Administrative Assistant, 603-862-4818, E-mail: genetics.dept@unh.edu.
Website: http://colsa.unh.edu/mcbs/genetics-graduate-programs/

University of New Mexico, Graduate Studies, Health Sciences Center, Program in Biomedical Sciences, Albuquerque, NM 87131-5196. Offers biochemistry and molecular biology (MS, PhD); cell biology and physiology (MS, PhD); molecular genetics and microbiology (MS, PhD); neuroscience (MS, PhD); pathology (MS, PhD); toxicology (MS, PhD). *Program availability:* Part-time. *Students:* Average age 29. 61 applicants, 16% accepted, 10 enrolled. In 2017, 11 master's, 14 doctorates awarded. Terminal master's awarded for partial completion of doctoral program. *Degree requirements:* For master's, thesis; for doctorate, comprehensive exam, thesis/dissertation, qualifying exam at the end of year 1/core curriculum. *Entrance requirements:* For master's and doctorate, GRE General Test, minimum undergraduate GPA of 3.0. Additional exam requirements/recommendations for international students: Required—TOEFL. *Application deadline:* For fall admission, 3/1 priority date for domestic and international students. Applications are processed on a rolling basis. Application fee: $50. Electronic applications accepted. *Financial support:* Fellowships, research assistantships with full tuition reimbursements, teaching assistantships, career-related internships or fieldwork, Federal Work-Study, institutionally sponsored loans, scholarships/grants, traineeships, health care benefits, and unspecified assistantships available. Financial award application deadline: 1/1; financial award applicants required to submit FAFSA. *Faculty research:* Infectious disease/immunity, cancer biology, cardiovascular and metabolic diseases, brain and behavioral illness, environmental health. *Unit head:* Dr. Helen J. Hathaway, Program Director, 505-272-1887, Fax: 505-272-2412, E-mail: hhathaway@salud.unm.edu. *Application contact:* Mary Fenton, Admissions Coordinator, 505-272-1887, Fax: 505-272-2412, E-mail: mfenton@salud.unm.edu.

The University of North Carolina at Chapel Hill, Graduate School, College of Arts and Sciences, Department of Biology, Chapel Hill, NC 27599. Offers botany (MA, MS, PhD); cell biology, development, and physiology (MA, MS, PhD); cell motility and cytoskeleton (PhD); ecology and behavior (MA, MS, PhD); genetics and molecular biology (MA, MS, PhD); morphology, systematics, and evolution (MA, MS, PhD). Terminal master's awarded for partial completion of doctoral program. *Degree requirements:* For master's, comprehensive exam, thesis (for some programs); for doctorate, comprehensive exam, thesis/dissertation. *Entrance requirements:* For master's, GRE General Test, GRE Subject Test, 2 semesters of calculus or statistics; 2 semesters of physics, organic chemistry; 3 semesters of biology; for doctorate, GRE General Test, GRE Subject Test, 2 semesters calculus or statistics, 2 semesters physics, organic chemistry, 3 semesters of biology. Additional exam requirements/recommendations for international students: Required—TOEFL (minimum score 550 paper-based). Electronic applications accepted. *Faculty research:* Gene expression, biomechanics, yeast genetics, plant ecology, plant molecular biology.

The University of North Carolina at Chapel Hill, School of Medicine and Graduate School, Graduate Programs in Medicine, Curriculum in Genetics and Molecular Biology, Chapel Hill, NC 27599. Offers MS, PhD. *Degree requirements:* For doctorate, comprehensive exam, thesis/dissertation. *Entrance requirements:* For doctorate, GRE, minimum GPA of 3.0. Additional exam requirements/recommendations for international students: Required—TOEFL. Electronic applications accepted. *Faculty research:* Telomere replication and germline immortality, experimental evolution in microorganisms, genetic vulnerabilities in tumor genomes, genetics of cell cycle control during Drosophila development, mammalian genetics.

University of North Dakota, Graduate School, College of Arts and Sciences, Department of Biology, Grand Forks, ND 58202. Offers biology (MS); fisheries/wildlife (PhD); genetics (PhD); zoology (PhD). Terminal master's awarded for partial completion of doctoral program. *Degree requirements:* For master's, thesis, final exam; for doctorate, comprehensive exam, thesis/dissertation, final exam. *Entrance requirements:* For master's, GRE General Test, GRE Subject Test, minimum GPA of 3.0; for doctorate, GRE General Test, GRE Subject Test, minimum GPA of 3.5. Additional exam requirements/recommendations for international students: Required—TOEFL (minimum score 550 paper-based; 79 iBT), IELTS (minimum score 6.5). Electronic applications accepted. *Faculty research:* Population biology, wildlife ecology, RNA processing, hormonal control of behavior.

University of North Texas Health Science Center at Fort Worth, Graduate School of Biomedical Sciences, Fort Worth, TX 76107-2699. Offers biochemistry and cancer biology (MS, PhD); biotechnology (MS); cell biology, immunology and microbiology (MS, PhD); clinical research management (MS); forensic genetics (MS); genetics (MS, PhD); integrative physiology (MS, PhD); medical sciences (MS); pharmaceutical sciences and pharmacotherapy (MS, PhD); pharmacology and neuroscience (MS, PhD); structural anatomy and rehabilitation sciences (MS, PhD); DO/MS; DO/PhD. Terminal master's awarded for partial completion of doctoral program. *Degree requirements:* For master's, thesis; for doctorate, thesis/dissertation. *Entrance requirements:* For master's and doctorate, GRE General Test. Additional exam requirements/recommendations for international students: Required—TOEFL. *Expenses:* Contact institution. *Faculty research:* Alzheimer's disease, aging, eye diseases, cancer, cardiovascular disease.

University of Notre Dame, Graduate School, College of Science, Department of Biological Sciences, Notre Dame, IN 46556. Offers aquatic ecology, evolution and environmental biology (MS, PhD); cellular and molecular biology (MS, PhD); genetics (MS, PhD); physiology (MS, PhD); vector biology and parasitology (MS, PhD). Terminal master's awarded for partial completion of doctoral program. *Degree requirements:* For master's, comprehensive exam, thesis; for doctorate, comprehensive exam, thesis/dissertation, candidacy exam. *Entrance requirements:* For master's and doctorate, GRE General Test. Additional exam requirements/recommendations for international students: Required—TOEFL (minimum score 600 paper-based; 80 iBT). Electronic applications accepted. *Faculty research:* Tropical disease, molecular genetics, neurobiology, evolutionary biology, aquatic biology.

University of Oregon, Graduate School, College of Arts and Sciences, Department of Biology, Eugene, OR 97403. Offers ecology and evolution (MA, MS, PhD); marine biology (MA, MS, PhD); molecular, cellular and genetic biology (PhD); neuroscience and development (PhD). Terminal master's awarded for partial completion of doctoral program. *Degree requirements:* For master's, thesis (for some programs); for doctorate, thesis/dissertation. *Entrance requirements:* For master's and doctorate, GRE General Test, minimum GPA of 3.2. Additional exam requirements/recommendations for international students: Required—TOEFL. *Faculty research:* Developmental neurobiology; evolution, population biology, and quantitative genetics; regulation of gene expression; biochemistry of marine organisms.

University of Pennsylvania, Perelman School of Medicine, Biomedical Graduate Studies, Graduate Group in Cell and Molecular Biology, Philadelphia, PA 19104. Offers cancer biology (PhD); cell biology, physiology, and metabolism (PhD); developmental stem cell regenerative biology (PhD); gene therapy and vaccines (PhD); genetics and gene regulation (PhD); microbiology, virology, and parasitology (PhD); MD/PhD; VMD/PhD. *Faculty:* 363. *Students:* 343 full-time (197 women); includes 114 minority (7 Black or African American, non-Hispanic/Latino; 51 Asian, non-Hispanic/Latino; 41 Hispanic/Latino; 15 Two or more races, non-Hispanic/Latino), 50 international. 588 applicants, 22% accepted, 61 enrolled. In 2017, 61 doctorates awarded. *Degree requirements:* For doctorate, thesis/dissertation. *Entrance requirements:* For doctorate, GRE General Test. Additional exam requirements/recommendations for international students: Required—TOEFL. *Application deadline:* For fall admission, 12/1 priority date for domestic and international students. Applications are processed on a rolling basis. Application fee: $80. Electronic applications accepted. *Financial support:* In 2017–18, 339 students received support. Fellowships, research assistantships, teaching assistantships, and tuition waivers available. *Unit head:* Dr. Daniel Kessler, Graduate Group Chair, 215-898-1478. *Application contact:* Meagan Schofer, Coordinator, 215-898-1478.
Website: http://www.med.upenn.edu/camb/

University of Puerto Rico–Río Piedras, College of Natural Sciences, Department of Biology, San Juan, PR 00931-3300. Offers ecology/systematics (MS, PhD); evolution/genetics (MS, PhD); molecular/cellular biology (MS, PhD); neuroscience (MS, PhD). *Program availability:* Part-time. *Degree requirements:* For master's, one foreign language, comprehensive exam, thesis; for doctorate, one foreign language, comprehensive exam, thesis/dissertation. *Entrance requirements:* For master's, GRE Subject Test, interview, minimum GPA of 3.0, letter of recommendation; for doctorate, GRE Subject Test, interview, master's degree, minimum GPA of 3.0, letter of recommendation. *Faculty research:* Environmental, poblational and systematic biology.

University of Rochester, School of Arts and Sciences, Department of Biology, Rochester, NY 14627. Offers biology (MS); ecology, genetics, and genomics (PhD); molecular, cellular, and developmental biology evolution (PhD). *Faculty:* 21 full-time (6 women). *Students:* 42 full-time (17 women), 4 part-time (all women); includes 6 minority (1 Asian, non-Hispanic/Latino; 3 Hispanic/Latino; 2 Two or more races, non-Hispanic/Latino), 22 international. Average age 27. 119 applicants, 22% accepted, 11 enrolled. In 2017, 6 master's, 5 doctorates awarded. Terminal master's awarded for partial completion of doctoral program. *Degree requirements:* For master's, comprehensive exam (for some programs), thesis (for some programs); for doctorate, thesis/dissertation, qualifying exam. *Entrance requirements:* For master's and doctorate, GRE General Test, GRE Subject Test (highly recommended), personal statement, transcripts, three letters of recommendation. Additional exam requirements/recommendations for international students: Required—TOEFL. *Application deadline:* For fall admission, 1/2 for domestic and international students. Application fee: $60. Electronic applications accepted. *Expenses:* $1,596 per credit hour. *Financial support:* In 2017–18, 36 students received support, including 1 fellowship (averaging $23,000 per year), 20 research assistantships (averaging $28,000 per year), 15 teaching assistantships (averaging $28,000 per year); health care benefits and tuition waivers (full) also available. Financial award application deadline: 1/1. *Faculty research:* Evolution, ecology, genetics, cellular biology, molecular biology. *Total annual research expenditures:* $6.7 million. *Unit head:* Michael Welte, Professor and Chair, 585-276-3897, E-mail: michael.welte@rochester.edu. *Application contact:* Cynthia Landry, Administrative Assistant, 585-275-7991, E-mail: cynthia.landry@rochester.edu.
Website: https://www.sas.rochester.edu/bio/graduate/index.html

University of Rochester, School of Medicine and Dentistry, Graduate Programs in Medicine and Dentistry, Department of Biomedical Genetics, Rochester, NY 14627. Offers genetics, genomics and development (PhD). *Degree requirements:* For doctorate, thesis/dissertation, qualifying exam. *Entrance requirements:* For doctorate, GRE General Test.

The University of Tennessee, Graduate School, College of Arts and Sciences, Program in Life Sciences, Knoxville, TN 37996. Offers genome science and technology (MS, PhD); plant physiology and genetics (MS, PhD). *Degree requirements:* For doctorate, one foreign language, thesis/dissertation. *Entrance requirements:* For master's and doctorate, GRE General Test, minimum GPA of 2.7. Additional exam requirements/recommendations for international students: Required—TOEFL. Electronic applications accepted.

The University of Texas Health Science Center at Houston, MD Anderson UTHealth Graduate School, Houston, TX 77225-0036. Offers biochemistry and cell biology (PhD); biomedical sciences (MS); cancer biology (PhD); genetic counseling (MS); genetics and epigenetics (PhD); immunology (PhD); medical physics (MS, PhD); microbiology and infectious diseases (PhD); neuroscience (PhD); quantitative sciences (PhD); therapeutics and pharmacology (PhD); MD/PhD. Terminal master's awarded for partial completion of doctoral program. *Degree requirements:* For master's, thesis; for doctorate, thesis/dissertation. *Entrance requirements:* For master's and doctorate, GRE General Test. Additional exam requirements/recommendations for international students: Required—TOEFL. Electronic applications accepted. *Faculty research:* Biomedical sciences.

The University of Texas MD Anderson Cancer Center, School of Health Professions, Houston, TX 77030. Offers diagnostic genetics (MS). *Degree requirements:* For master's, successful defense of a written applied research project. *Entrance requirements:* For master's, bachelor's degree, minimum GPA of 3.0, clinical certification, three reference letters, personal interview. Additional exam requirements/recommendations for international students: Required—TOEFL.

The University of Texas Southwestern Medical Center, Southwestern Graduate School of Biomedical Sciences, Division of Basic Science, Program in Genetics and Development, Dallas, TX 75390. Offers PhD. *Degree requirements:* For doctorate, thesis/dissertation, qualifying exam. *Entrance requirements:* For doctorate, GRE General Test, minimum GPA of 3.0. Additional exam requirements/recommendations for international students: Required—TOEFL. Electronic applications accepted. *Faculty research:* Human molecular genetics, chromosome structure, gene regulation, molecular biology, gene expression.

University of Washington, Graduate School, School of Public Health, Institute for Public Health Genetics, Seattle, WA 98195. Offers genetic epidemiology (MS); public health genetics (MPH, PhD, Graduate Certificate). *Program availability:* Part-time, evening/weekend, online learning. *Students:* 10 full-time (8 women), 1 (woman) part-time; includes 2 minority (both Asian, non-Hispanic/Latino). Average age 31. 21 applicants, 33% accepted, 4 enrolled. In 2017, 2 doctorates awarded. Terminal master's awarded for partial completion of doctoral program. Electronic applications accepted. *Financial support:* Research assistantships and teaching assistantships available. *Unit head:* Dr. Bruce S. Weir, Director of the Institute for Public Health Genetics, 206-221-7947, E-mail: bsweir@uw.edu. *Application contact:* Grecia Alejandra Garcia Luga, Graduate Student Adviser and Curriculum Coordinator, 206-616-9286.
Website: http://iphg.biostat.washington.edu/

University of Wisconsin–Madison, Graduate School, College of Agricultural and Life Sciences and Graduate Programs in Medicine, Department of Genetics, Madison, WI 53706-1380. Offers genetic counseling (MS); genetics (PhD). *Degree requirements:* For doctorate, thesis/dissertation.

University of Wyoming, Graduate Program in Molecular and Cellular Life Sciences, Laramie, WY 82071. Offers PhD. *Degree requirements:* For doctorate, thesis/dissertation, four eight-week laboratory rotations, comprehensive basic practical exam, two-part qualifying exam, seminars, symposium.

Van Andel Institute Graduate School, PhD Program, Grand Rapids, MI 49503. Offers cell and molecular genetics (PhD). *Faculty:* 37 full-time (10 women). *Students:* 27 full-time (19 women); includes 6 minority (1 Black or African American, non-Hispanic/Latino; 4 Asian, non-Hispanic/Latino; 1 Hispanic/Latino). Average age 24. *Degree requirements:* For doctorate, comprehensive exam, thesis/dissertation. *Entrance requirements:* For doctorate, GRE, personal statement, 3 letters of recommendation, official transcripts from all institutions attended, sample of scientific writing (research paper). Additional exam requirements/recommendations for international students: Required—TOEFL. *Application deadline:* For fall admission, 12/1 for domestic and international students. Applications are processed on a rolling basis. Electronic applications accepted. *Expenses:* Contact institution. *Financial support:* Fellowships and health care benefits available. *Faculty research:* Epigenetics, neurodegenerative science, cancer and cell biology. *Unit head:* Steve Triezenberg, President and Dean, 616-234-5708, Fax: 616-234-5709, E-mail: steve.triezenberg@vai.org. *Application contact:* Christy Mayo, Enrollment and Records Administrator, 616-234-5722, Fax: 616-234-5709, E-mail: christy.mayo@vai.org.

Virginia Polytechnic Institute and State University, Graduate School, Intercollege, Blacksburg, VA 24061. Offers genetics, bioinformatics, and computational biology (PhD); information technology (MIT); macromolecular science and engineering (MS, PhD); translational biology, medicine, and health (PhD). *Students:* 167 full-time (86 women), 776 part-time (279 women); includes 253 minority (60 Black or African American, non-Hispanic/Latino; 113 Asian, non-Hispanic/Latino; 41 Hispanic/Latino; 1 Native Hawaiian or other Pacific Islander, non-Hispanic/Latino; 37 Two or more races, non-Hispanic/Latino), 81 international. Average age 33. 664 applicants, 65% accepted, 304 enrolled. In 2017, 93 master's, 13 doctorates awarded. *Degree requirements:* For master's, comprehensive exam (for some programs), thesis (for some programs); for doctorate, comprehensive exam (for some programs), thesis/dissertation (for some programs). *Entrance requirements:* For master's and doctorate, GRE/GMAT. Additional exam requirements/recommendations for international students: Required—TOEFL (minimum score 80 iBT). *Application deadline:* For fall admission, 8/1 for domestic students, 4/1 for international students; for spring admission, 1/1 for domestic students, 9/1 for international students. Applications are processed on a rolling basis. Application fee: $75. Electronic applications accepted. *Expenses:* Tuition, state resident: full-time $15,072; part-time $718.50 per credit hour. Tuition, nonresident: full-time $28,810; part-time $1448.25 per credit hour. *Required fees:* $2741; $502 per semester. Tuition and fees vary according to course load, campus/location and program. *Financial support:* In 2017–18, 39 fellowships with full and partial tuition reimbursements (averaging $17,696 per year), 119 research assistantships with full tuition reimbursements (averaging $24,500 per year), 20 teaching assistantships with full tuition reimbursements (averaging $24,663 per year) were awarded. Financial award application deadline: 3/1; financial award applicants required to submit FAFSA. *Unit head:* Dr. Karen P. DePauw, Vice President and Dean for Graduate Education, 540-231-7581, Fax: 540-231-1670, E-mail: kpdepauw@vt.edu.

Washington State University, College of Veterinary Medicine, Molecular Biosciences Graduate Program, Pullman, WA 99164-7520. Offers molecular biosciences (MS, PhD), including genetics (PhD). *Faculty:* 26 full-time (9 women), 27 part-time/adjunct (4 women). *Students:* 36 full-time (23 women); includes 10 minority (2 Asian, non-Hispanic/Latino; 6 Hispanic/Latino; 2 Two or more races, non-Hispanic/Latino), 1 international. Average age 27. 76 applicants, 22% accepted, 6 enrolled. In 2017, 1 master's, 10 doctorates awarded. Terminal master's awarded for partial completion of doctoral program. *Degree requirements:* For master's, thesis (for some programs), oral defense; for doctorate, comprehensive exam, thesis/dissertation, oral defense. *Entrance requirements:* For master's and doctorate, GRE General Test, minimum GPA of 3.0. Additional exam requirements/recommendations for international students: Required—TOEFL (minimum score 600 paper-based; 100 iBT). *Application deadline:* For fall admission, 12/15 priority date for domestic and international students. Application fee: $75. Electronic applications accepted. *Expenses:* Contact institution. *Financial support:* In 2017–18, 36 students received support, including 6 fellowships with full tuition reimbursements available (averaging $25,911 per year), 12 research assistantships with full tuition reimbursements available (averaging $25,911 per year), 18 teaching assistantships with full tuition reimbursements available (averaging $25,911 per year); scholarships/grants, traineeships, and health care benefits also available. Financial award application deadline: 4/15. *Faculty research:* Bacterial pathogenesis, microbial metabolism, DNA repair, reproductive biology, cytoskeleton, molecular cell biology, biochemistry, signal transduction, protein export. *Total annual research expenditures:* $4.3 million. *Unit head:* Dr. Jonathan Jones, Director, 509-335-8724, Fax: 509-335-9688, E-mail: jcr.jones@vetmed.wsu.edu. *Application contact:* Tami Breske, Graduate Academic Coordinator, 509-335-4318, E-mail: tbreske@vetmed.wsu.edu.
Website: http://www.smb.wsu.edu

Washington University in St. Louis, The Graduate School, Division of Biology and Biomedical Sciences, St. Louis, MO 63130-4899. Offers biochemistry (PhD); computational and molecular biophysics (PhD); computational and systems biology (PhD); developmental, regenerative, and stem cell biology (PhD); evolution, ecology and population biology (PhD), including ecology, environmental biology, evolutionary biology, genetics; human and statistical genetics (PhD); immunology (PhD); molecular cell biology (PhD); molecular genetics and genomics (PhD); molecular microbiology and microbial pathogenesis (PhD); neurosciences (PhD); plant and microbial biosciences (PhD); MD/PhD. *Degree requirements:* For doctorate, thesis/dissertation. *Entrance requirements:* For doctorate, GRE General Test, GRE Subject Test. Additional exam requirements/recommendations for international students: Required—TOEFL. Electronic applications accepted.

Washington University in St. Louis, School of Medicine, Program in Clinical Investigation, St. Louis, MO 63130-4899. Offers clinical investigation (MS), including bioethics, entrepreneurship, genetics/genomics, translational medicine. *Program availability:* Part-time, evening/weekend. *Degree requirements:* For master's, thesis. *Entrance requirements:* For master's, doctoral-level degree or in process of obtaining doctoral-level degree. Electronic applications accepted. *Faculty research:* Anesthesiology, infectious diseases, neurology, obstetrics and gynecology, orthopedic surgery.

Wesleyan University, Graduate Studies, Department of Biology, Middletown, CT 06459. Offers cell and developmental biology (PhD); evolution and ecology (PhD); genetics and genomics (PhD), including bioinformatics; neurobiology and behavior (PhD). Terminal master's awarded for partial completion of doctoral program. *Degree requirements:* For doctorate, comprehensive exam, thesis/dissertation, public seminar. *Entrance requirements:* For doctorate, GRE, official transcripts, three recommendation letters, essay. Additional exam requirements/recommendations for international students: Required—TOEFL. *Application deadline:* For fall admission, 1/15 for domestic and international students. Application fee: $0. Electronic applications accepted. *Financial support:* Stipends available. *Faculty research:* Evolution and ecology, neurobiology and behavior, cell and developmental biology, genetics, genomics and bioinformatics. *Unit head:* Dr. Ann Burke, Chair/Professor, 860-685-3518, E-mail: acburke@wesleyan.edu. *Application contact:* Diane Meredith, Administrative Assistant IV, 860-685-2157, E-mail: dmeredith@wesleyan.edu.
Website: http://www.wesleyan.edu/bio/

West Virginia University, Davis College of Agriculture, Forestry and Consumer Sciences, Morgantown, WV 26506. Offers agricultural and extension education (MS, PhD); agriculture and resource management (MS); agriculture, natural resources and design (M Agr); agronomy (MS); animal and food science (PhD); animal physiology (MS); applied and environmental microbiology (MS); design and merchandising (MS); entomology (MS); forest resource science (PhD); forestry (MSF); genetics and developmental biology (MS, PhD); horticulture (MS); human and community development (PhD); landscape architecture (MLA); natural resource economics (PhD); nutritional and food science (MS); plant and soil science (PhD); plant pathology (MS); recreation, parks and tourism resources (MS); reproductive physiology (MS, PhD); wildlife and fisheries resources (PhD). *Program availability:* Part-time. *Students:* 200 full-time (97 women), 53 part-time (32 women); includes 27 minority (6 Black or African American, non-Hispanic/Latino; 1 American Indian or Alaska Native, non-Hispanic/Latino; 4 Asian, non-Hispanic/Latino; 11 Hispanic/Latino; 5 Two or more races, non-Hispanic/Latino), 67 international. *Degree requirements:* For master's, thesis; for doctorate, thesis/dissertation. *Entrance requirements:* Additional exam requirements/recommendations for international students: Required—TOEFL (minimum score 550 paper-based). *Application deadline:* For fall admission, 6/1 priority date for domestic students, 6/1 for international students; for spring admission, 1/5 for domestic and international students. Applications are processed on a rolling basis. Application fee: $60. Electronic applications accepted. *Expenses:* Tuition, state resident: full-time $9450. Tuition, nonresident: full-time $24,390. *Financial support:* Fellowships, research assistantships, teaching assistantships, career-related internships or fieldwork, Federal Work-Study, institutionally sponsored loans, tuition waivers (full and partial), and unspecified assistantships available. Financial award application deadline: 2/1; financial award applicants required to submit FAFSA. *Faculty research:* Reproductive physiology, soil and water quality, human nutrition, aquaculture, wildlife management. *Unit head:* Dr. Dan J. Robison, Dean, 304-293-2395, Fax: 304-293-3740, E-mail: dan.robison@mail.wvu.edu. *Application contact:* Dr. Dennis K. Smith, Associate Dean, 304-293-2275, Fax: 304-293-3740, E-mail: denny.smith@mail.wvu.edu.
Website: https://www.davis.wvu.edu

Yale University, Graduate School of Arts and Sciences, Department of Genetics, New Haven, CT 06520. Offers PhD, MD/PhD. *Degree requirements:* For doctorate, thesis/dissertation. *Entrance requirements:* For doctorate, GRE General Test, GRE Subject Test.

Yale University, Graduate School of Arts and Sciences, Department of Molecular, Cellular, and Developmental Biology, Program in Genetics, New Haven, CT 06520. Offers PhD. *Degree requirements:* For doctorate, thesis/dissertation. *Entrance requirements:* For doctorate, GRE General Test, GRE Subject Test.

Yale University, Yale School of Medicine and Graduate School of Arts and Sciences, Combined Program in Biological and Biomedical Sciences (BBS), Molecular Cell Biology, Genetics, and Development Track, New Haven, CT 06520. Offers PhD, MD/PhD. *Entrance requirements:* Additional exam requirements/recommendations for international students: Required—TOEFL.

Genomic Sciences

Albert Einstein College of Medicine, Graduate Programs in the Biomedical Sciences, Department of Genetics, Bronx, NY 10461. Offers computational genetics (PhD); molecular genetics (PhD); translational genetics (PhD); MD/PhD. *Degree requirements:* For doctorate, thesis/dissertation. *Entrance requirements:* For doctorate, GRE General Test. Additional exam requirements/recommendations for international students: Required—TOEFL. *Application deadline:* For fall admission, 1/15 for domestic students. Application fee: $0. *Financial support:* Fellowships available. *Faculty research:* Neurologic genetics in &ITDrosophila&RO, biochemical genetics of yeast, developmental genetics in the mouse. *Unit head:* Dr. Jan Vijg, Chair, 718-678-1151. *Application contact:* Sheila Cleeton, Executive Director and Registrar, Einstein Graduate Division, 718-430-2128, Fax: 718-430-8655, E-mail: sheila.cleeton@einstein.yu.edu.
Website: http://www.einstein.yu.edu/departments/genetics/

Augusta University, Program in Genomic Medicine, Augusta, GA 30912. Offers PhD. *Degree requirements:* For doctorate, comprehensive exam, thesis/dissertation. *Entrance requirements:* For doctorate, GRE General Test. Additional exam requirements/recommendations for international students: Required—TOEFL (minimum score 550 paper-based; 79 iBT). Electronic applications accepted. *Faculty research:* Genetic and genomic basis of diseases (diabetes, cancer, autoimmunity), development of diagnostic markers, bioinformatics, computational biology.

Black Hills State University, Graduate Studies, Program in Integrative Genomics, Spearfish, SD 57799. Offers MS. *Entrance requirements:* Additional exam requirements/recommendations for international students: Required—TOEFL (minimum score 500 paper-based; 60 iBT).

Boston University, School of Medicine, Division of Graduate Medical Sciences, Program in Genetics and Genomics, Boston, MA 02215. Offers PhD. *Degree requirements:* For doctorate, thesis/dissertation. *Application deadline:* For fall admission, 1/15 for domestic students; for spring admission, 10/15 for domestic students. *Unit head:* Dr. Yuriy Alekseyev, Director, 617-414-1369, E-mail: yurik@bu.edu. *Application contact:* GMS Admissions Office, 617-638-5255, E-mail: askgms@bu.edu.
Website: http://www.bumc.bu.edu/gpgg/graduate-program/

Case Western Reserve University, School of Medicine and School of Graduate Studies, Graduate Programs in Medicine, Department of Genetics and Genome Sciences, Cleveland, OH 44106. Offers genetic counseling (MS); genetics and genome sciences (PhD); MD/PhD. Terminal master's awarded for partial completion of doctoral program. *Degree requirements:* For master's, thesis; for doctorate, comprehensive exam, thesis/dissertation. *Entrance requirements:* For master's, GRE General Test; for doctorate, GRE General Test, GRE Subject Test. Additional exam requirements/recommendations for international students: Required—TOEFL. *Expenses: Tuition:* Full-time $43,854; part-time $1827 per credit hour. *Required fees:* $50; $50 per credit hour. Tuition and fees vary according to course load and program. *Faculty research:* Eukaryotic genetics, regulation of gene expression, chromosome structure and function.

Concordia University, School of Graduate Studies, Faculty of Arts and Science, Department of Biology, Montréal, QC H3G 1M8, Canada. Offers biology (M Sc, PhD); biotechnology and genomics (Diploma). *Degree requirements:* For master's, thesis; for doctorate, thesis/dissertation, pedagogical training. *Entrance requirements:* For master's, honors degree in biology; for doctorate, M Sc in life science. *Faculty research:* Cell biology, animal physiology, ecology, microbiology/molecular biology, plant physiology/biochemistry and biotechnology.

Cornell University, Graduate School, Graduate Fields of Agriculture and Life Sciences, Field of Genetics, Genomics and Development, Ithaca, NY 14853. Offers developmental biology (PhD); genetics (PhD); genomics (PhD). *Degree requirements:* For doctorate, comprehensive exam, thesis/dissertation, 2 semesters of teaching experience. *Entrance requirements:* For doctorate, GRE General Test, GRE Subject Test in biology or biochemistry (recommended), 2 letters of recommendation. Additional exam requirements/recommendations for international students: Required—TOEFL (minimum score 550 paper-based; 77 iBT). Electronic applications accepted. *Faculty research:* Molecular and general genetics, developmental biology and developmental genetics, evolution and population genetics, plant genetics, microbial genetics.

Duke University, Graduate School, University Program in Genetics and Genomics, Durham, NC 27710. Offers PhD. *Degree requirements:* For doctorate, variable foreign language requirement, thesis/dissertation. *Entrance requirements:* For doctorate, GRE General Test. Additional exam requirements/recommendations for international students: Required—TOEFL (minimum score 577 paper-based; 90 iBT) or IELTS (minimum score 7).

Manchester University, Master of Science in Pharmacogenomics Program, Fort Wayne, IN 46845. Offers MS. *Program availability:* Part-time, 100% online, blended/hybrid learning. *Faculty:* 9 full-time (4 women). *Students:* 2 full-time (both women), 1 (woman) part-time; includes 1 minority (Asian, non-Hispanic/Latino). Average age 23. 18 applicants, 22% accepted, 3 enrolled. *Degree requirements:* For master's, minimum cumulative GPA of 3.0 at end of third semester; completion of all required didactic and clinical courses with grade of C or better. *Entrance requirements:* For master's, minimum of a bachelor's degree (chemistry, biology, medical technician, etc.); minimum GPA of 3.0 (preferred), science 2.7; official transcripts from all undergraduate and graduate schools attended; 2 letters of reference submitted on the applicant's behalf. *Application deadline:* Applications are processed on a rolling basis. Application fee: $25. Electronic applications accepted. *Expenses:* Contact institution. *Faculty research:* Genetic variation of pharmacogenes in a Burmese population of northeast Indiana, pharmacogene inheritance in specific populations of northeast Indiana, interprofessional education in pharmacogenomic, state-wide benchmarking of pharmacy student education in pharmacogenomics, transplant pharmacogenomics. *Unit head:* Dr. Dave F. Kisor, Director, 260-470-2747, E-mail: dfkisor@manchester.edu. *Application contact:* Greg Hetrick, Director of Student Services, 260-470-2656, E-mail: gbhetrick@manchester.edu.
Website: https://www.manchester.edu/academics/colleges/college-of-pharmacy-natural-health-sciences/academic-programs/masters

Massachusetts Institute of Technology, School of Engineering, Harvard-MIT Health Sciences and Technology Program, Cambridge, MA 02139. Offers health sciences and technology (SM, PhD, Sc D), including bioastronautics (PhD, Sc D), bioinformatics and integrative genomics (PhD, Sc D), medical engineering and medical physics (PhD, Sc D), speech and hearing bioscience and technology (PhD, Sc D). Terminal master's awarded for partial completion of doctoral program. *Degree requirements:* For doctorate, comprehensive exam, thesis/dissertation. *Entrance requirements:* For doctorate, GRE General Test. Additional exam requirements/recommendations for international students: Required—TOEFL, IELTS. Electronic applications accepted. *Faculty research:* Biomedical imaging, drug delivery, medical devices, medical diagnostics, regenerative biomedical technologies.

New York University, School of Medicine and Graduate School of Arts and Science, Sackler Institute of Graduate Biomedical Sciences, New York, NY 10016. Offers biomedical imaging and technology (PhD); biostatistics (PhD); cellular and molecular biology (PhD); developmental genetics (PhD); epidemiology (PhD); genome integrity (PhD); immunology and inflammation (PhD); microbiology (PhD); molecular biophysics (PhD); molecular oncology and tumor immunology (PhD); molecular pharmacology (PhD); neuroscience and physiology (PhD), including immunology, molecular oncology; stem cell biology (PhD); systems and computational biomedicine (PhD); MD/PhD. *Faculty:* 207 full-time (51 women). *Students:* 236 full-time (138 women), 1 part-time (0 women); includes 68 minority (13 Black or African American, non-Hispanic/Latino; 26 Asian, non-Hispanic/Latino; 28 Hispanic/Latino; 1 Native Hawaiian or other Pacific Islander, non-Hispanic/Latino), 79 international. Average age 27. 761 applicants, 18% accepted, 59 enrolled. In 2017, 35 doctorates awarded. *Degree requirements:* For doctorate, comprehensive exam, thesis/dissertation, qualifying exam; thesis defense. *Entrance requirements:* For doctorate, GRE. Additional exam requirements/recommendations for international students: Required—TOEFL, IELTS. *Application deadline:* For fall admission, 12/1 for domestic and international students. Applications are processed on a rolling basis. Application fee: $100. Electronic applications accepted. Application fee is waived when completed online. *Expenses:* Contact institution. *Financial support:* Health care benefits, tuition waivers (full), and unspecified assistantships available. *Faculty research:* Biomedical sciences. *Unit head:* Dr. Naoko Tanese, Associate Dean for Biomedical Sciences/Director, Sackler Institute, 212-263-8945, E-mail: naoko.tanese@nyumc.org. *Application contact:* Jessica Dong, Program Manager, 212-263-5648, E-mail: sackler-info@nyumc.org.
Website: https://med.nyu.edu/research/sackler-institute-graduate-biomedical-sciences/

North Carolina State University, Graduate School, College of Agriculture and Life Sciences, Graduate Program in Genomic Sciences, Raleigh, NC 27695. Offers MS, PhD.

North Carolina State University, Graduate School, College of Agriculture and Life Sciences, Program in Functional Genomics, Raleigh, NC 27695. Offers MFG, MS, PhD. *Degree requirements:* For master's, thesis (for some programs); for doctorate, thesis/dissertation. *Entrance requirements:* For master's and doctorate, GRE, minimum B average. Additional exam requirements/recommendations for international students: Required—TOEFL. Electronic applications accepted. *Faculty research:* Genome structure, genome expression, molecular evolution, nucleic acid structure/function, proteomics.

North Dakota State University, College of Graduate and Interdisciplinary Studies, Interdisciplinary Program in Genomics and Bioinformatics, Fargo, ND 58102. Offers MS, PhD. *Program availability:* Part-time. *Degree requirements:* For master's, thesis; for doctorate, comprehensive exam, thesis/dissertation. *Entrance requirements:* For master's and doctorate, minimum GPA of 3.0. Additional exam requirements/recommendations for international students: Required—TOEFL. *Application deadline:* Applications are processed on a rolling basis. Electronic applications accepted. *Expenses:* Tuition, state resident: full-time $4323; part-time $360.21 per credit. Tuition, nonresident: full-time $6484; part-time $540.31 per credit. *Required fees:* $668; $55.70 per credit. Part-time tuition and fees vary according to degree level, program and reciprocity agreements. *Financial support:* Research assistantships with full tuition reimbursements and unspecified assistantships available. *Unit head:* Dr. Phillip E. McClean, Director, 701-231-8443, Fax: 701-231-8474. *Application contact:* Elizabeth Worth, Marketing, Recruitment, and Public Relations Coordinator, 701-231-8476, Fax: 701-231-6524, E-mail: elizabeth.worth@ndsu.edu.

Oregon State University, College of Agricultural Sciences, Program in Botany and Plant Pathology, Corvallis, OR 97331. Offers applied systematics (MS); ecology (MS, PhD); genetics (MS, PhD); genomics and computational biology (MS, PhD); molecular and cellular biology (MS, PhD); mycology (MS, PhD); plant pathology (MS, PhD); plant physiology (MS, PhD). *Entrance requirements:* For master's and doctorate, GRE. *Application deadline:* For fall admission, 12/1 for domestic and international students. Application fee: $75 ($85 for international students). *Financial support:* Application deadline: 12/1. *Unit head:* John Fowler, Chair of Graduate Studies, E-mail: fowlerj@science.oregonstate.edu.
Website: http://bpp.oregonstate.edu/

Oregon State University, College of Science, Program in Microbiology, Corvallis, OR 97331. Offers environmental microbiology (MA, MS, PhD); food microbiology (MA, MS, PhD); genomics (MA, MS, PhD); immunology (MA, MS, PhD); microbial ecology (MA, MS, PhD); microbial evolution (MA, MS, PhD); parasitology (MA, MS, PhD); pathogenic microbiology (MA, MS, PhD); virology (MA). Terminal master's awarded for partial completion of doctoral program. *Entrance requirements:* For master's and doctorate, GRE. Additional exam requirements/recommendations for international students: Required—TOEFL (minimum score 600 paper-based; 100 iBT). *Application deadline:* For fall admission, 1/1 for domestic and international students. Application fee: $75 ($85 for international students). *Financial support:* Application deadline: 1/15. *Faculty research:* Genetics, physiology, biotechnology, pathogenic microbiology, plant virology. *Unit head:* Dr. Jerri Bartholomew, Professor and Department Head, 541-737-1834, E-mail: barthol j@science.oregonstate.edu. *Application contact:* Kim Halsey, Graduate Admissions Committee Chair, 541-737-1831, E-mail: kim.halsey@oregonstate.edu.
Website: http://microbiology.science.oregonstate.edu/

Penn State Hershey Medical Center, College of Medicine, Graduate School Programs in the Biomedical Sciences, Huck Institutes of the Life Sciences, Intercollege Graduate Program in Bioinformatics and Genomics, Hershey, PA 17033-2360. Program also offered at University Park location. *Unit head:* Dr. Peter Hudson, Director, 814-865-6057. *Application contact:* Kathy Shuey, Administrative Assistant, 717-531-8082, Fax: 717-531-0786, E-mail: grad-hmc@psu.edu.
Website: https://www.huck.psu.edu/content/graduate-programs/bioinformatics-and-genomics

Purdue University, College of Pharmacy and Graduate School, Graduate Programs in Pharmacy and Pharmacal Sciences, Department of Medicinal Chemistry and Molecular Pharmacology, West Lafayette, IN 47907. Offers biophysical and computational chemistry (PhD); cancer research (PhD); immunology and infectious disease (PhD); medicinal biochemistry and molecular biology (PhD); medicinal chemistry and chemical biology (PhD); molecular pharmacology (PhD); neuropharmacology, neurodegeneration, and neurotoxicity (PhD); systems biology and functional genomics (PhD). *Faculty:* 26 full-time (5 women). *Students:* 52 full-time (22 women), 3 part-time (all women); includes 4 minority (1 Black or African American, non-Hispanic/Latino; 2 Asian, non-Hispanic/Latino; 1 Hispanic/Latino), 29 international. Average age 26. 151 applicants, 19% accepted, 13 enrolled. In 2017, 18 doctorates awarded. *Degree requirements:* For doctorate, thesis/dissertation. *Entrance requirements:* For doctorate, GRE General Test; GRE Subject Test in biology, biochemistry, and chemistry (recommended), minimum undergraduate GPA of 3.0. Additional exam requirements/recommendations for international students: Required—TOEFL (minimum score 550 paper-based; 77 iBT); Recommended—TWE. *Application deadline:* For fall admission, 2/1 for domestic and international students. Applications are processed on a rolling basis. Application fee: $60 ($75 for international students). Electronic applications accepted. *Financial support:* Fellowships, research assistantships, teaching assistantships, and traineeships available. Support available to part-time students. Financial award applicants required to submit FAFSA. *Faculty research:* Drug design and development, cancer research, drug synthesis and analysis, chemical pharmacology, environmental toxicology. *Unit head:* Zhong-Yin Zhang, Head, 765-494-1403, E-mail: zhang-yn@purdue.edu. *Application contact:* Delayne Graham, Graduate Contact, 765-494-1362, E-mail: dkgraham@purdue.edu.

Thomas Jefferson University, Jefferson College of Biomedical Sciences, PhD Program in Genetics, Genomics and Cancer Biology, Philadelphia, PA 19107. Offers PhD. *Faculty:* 41 full-time (12 women). *Students:* 16 full-time (9 women); includes 1 minority (Hispanic/Latino), 2 international. In 2017, 5 doctorates awarded. *Degree requirements:* For doctorate, comprehensive exam, thesis/dissertation. *Entrance requirements:* For doctorate, GRE General Test, minimum GPA of 3.2. Additional exam requirements/recommendations for international students: Required—TOEFL, IELTS (minimum score 7). *Application deadline:* For fall admission, 12/1 priority date for domestic and international students. Applications are processed on a rolling basis. Application fee: $60. Electronic applications accepted. *Financial support:* In 2017–18, 16 students received support, including 16 fellowships with full tuition reimbursements available (averaging $62,653 per year); Federal Work-Study, institutionally sponsored loans, scholarships/grants, traineeships, health care benefits, and stipends also available. Financial award application deadline: 5/1; financial award applicants required to submit FAFSA. *Faculty research:* Functional genomics, cancer susceptibility, cell cycle, regulation oncogenes and tumor suppressor genes, genetics of neoplastic disease. *Unit head:* Dr. Lucia Languino, Program Director, 215-503-3442, E-mail: lucia.languino@jefferson.edu. *Application contact:* Marc E. Stearns, Senior Associate Director of Admissions, 215-503-0155, Fax: 215-503-3433, E-mail: jgsbs-info@jefferson.edu.
Website: http://www.jefferson.edu/university/biomedical-sciences/degrees-programs/phd-programs/genetics.html

University at Buffalo, the State University of New York, Graduate School, Jacobs School of Medicine and Biomedical Sciences, Graduate Programs in Medicine and Biomedical Sciences, Program in Genetics, Genomics and Bioinformatics, Buffalo, NY 14260. Offers MS, PhD, MD/PhD. *Faculty:* 59 full-time (16 women). *Students:* 13 full-time (6 women); includes 4 minority (all Asian, non-Hispanic/Latino). Average age 25. 22 applicants, 64% accepted, 5 enrolled. In 2017, 3 master's awarded. Terminal master's awarded for partial completion of doctoral program. *Degree requirements:* For master's, thesis or alternative; for doctorate, thesis/dissertation. *Entrance requirements:* For master's and doctorate, GRE. Additional exam requirements/recommendations for international students: Required—TOEFL (minimum score 100 iBT); Recommended—IELTS (minimum score 6.5). *Application deadline:* For fall admission, 3/1 for domestic and international students. Application fee: $85. Electronic applications accepted. *Expenses:* Contact institution. *Faculty research:* Human and medical genetics and genomics, developmental genomics and genetics, microbial genetics and pathogenesis, bioinformatics. *Unit head:* Dr. Richard Gronostajski, Director, 716-829-3471, Fax: 716-849-6655, E-mail: rgron@buffalo.edu. *Application contact:* Renad Aref, Program Administrator, 716-881-8209, Fax: 716-849-6655, E-mail: raaref@buffalo.edu.
Website: http://medicine.buffalo.edu/education/ggb.html

The University of Alabama at Birmingham, Joint Health Sciences, Genetics, Genomics, and Bioinformatics Theme, Birmingham, AL 35294. Offers PhD. *Faculty:* 370. *Students:* 37 full-time (23 women); includes 8 minority (3 Black or African American, non-Hispanic/Latino; 4 Asian, non-Hispanic/Latino; 1 Two or more races, non-Hispanic/Latino). Average age 27. 27 applicants, 33% accepted, 3 enrolled. In 2017, 4 doctorates awarded. *Degree requirements:* For doctorate, comprehensive exam, thesis/dissertation. *Entrance requirements:* For doctorate, personal statement, resume or curriculum vitae, letters of recommendation, research experience, interview. Additional exam requirements/recommendations for international students: Required—TOEFL (minimum score 80 iBT), IELTS (minimum score 6.5). *Application deadline:* For fall admission, 12/31 for domestic and international students. Applications are processed on a rolling basis. Electronic applications accepted. *Financial support:* In 2017–18, fellowships with full tuition reimbursements (averaging $29,000 per year), research assistantships with full tuition reimbursements (averaging $30,000 per year) were awarded; health care benefits also available. *Unit head:* Dr. Kevin Dybvig, Theme Director, 205-934-9327, E-mail: dybvig@uab.edu. *Application contact:* Alyssa Zasada, Admissions Manager for Graduate Biomedical Sciences, 205-934-3857, E-mail: grad-gbs@uab.edu.
Website: http://www.uab.edu/gbs/home/themes/ggb

University of California, Riverside, Graduate Division, Graduate Program in Genetics, Genomics, and Bioinformatics, Riverside, CA 92521-0102. Offers PhD. *Degree requirements:* For doctorate, thesis/dissertation, qualifying exams, teaching experience. *Entrance requirements:* For doctorate, GRE General Test, minimum GPA of 3.2. Additional exam requirements/recommendations for international students: Required—TOEFL (minimum score 550 paper-based, 80 iBT) or IELTS. *Application deadline:* For fall admission, 12/1 priority date for domestic and international students; for winter admission, 11/15 for domestic students, 9/1 for international students; for spring admission, 3/1 for domestic students, 12/1 for international students. Application fee: $85 ($100 for international students). Electronic applications accepted. *Expenses:* Tuition, state resident: full-time $5746. Tuition, nonresident: full-time $10,780. Tuition and fees vary according to campus/location and program. *Financial support:* Fellowships with tuition reimbursements, research assistantships with tuition reimbursements, teaching assistantships with tuition reimbursements, career-related internships or fieldwork, Federal Work-Study, institutionally sponsored loans, health care benefits, tuition waivers (full and partial), and unspecified assistantships available. Financial award applicants required to submit FAFSA. *Faculty research:* Molecular genetics, evolution and population genetics, genomics and bioinformatics. *Application contact:* Julio Sosa, E-mail: ggb@ucr.edu.
Website: http://ggb.ucr.edu/

University of California, San Francisco, School of Pharmacy and Graduate Division, Pharmaceutical Sciences and Pharmacogenomics Program, San Francisco, CA 94158-0775. Offers PhD. *Degree requirements:* For doctorate, comprehensive exam, thesis/dissertation. *Entrance requirements:* For doctorate, GRE General Test, bachelor's degree, 3 letters of recommendation, personal statement. Additional exam requirements/recommendations for international students: Required—TOEFL. Electronic applications accepted. *Faculty research:* Drug development sciences, molecular pharmacology, therapeutic bioengineering, pharmacogenomics and functional genomics, quantitative and systems pharmacology, computational genomics.

University of Chicago, Division of the Biological Sciences, Committee on Genetics, Genomics and Systems Biology, Chicago, IL 60637. Offers PhD. *Students:* 32 full-time (17 women); includes 8 minority (1 Black or African American, non-Hispanic/Latino; 4 Asian, non-Hispanic/Latino; 1 Hispanic/Latino; 1 Native Hawaiian or other Pacific Islander, non-Hispanic/Latino; 1 Two or more races, non-Hispanic/Latino), 9 international. Average age 26. 76 applicants, 25% accepted, 9 enrolled. In 2017, 4 doctorates awarded. *Degree requirements:* For doctorate, thesis/dissertation, ethics class, 2 teaching assistantships, preliminary exam. *Entrance requirements:* For doctorate, GRE General Test, transcripts, statement of purpose, 3 letters of recommendation. Additional exam requirements/recommendations for international students: Required—TOEFL (minimum score 600 paper-based; 104 iBT), IELTS (minimum score 7). *Application deadline:* For fall admission, 12/1 for domestic and international students. Application fee: $90. Electronic applications accepted. *Financial support:* In 2017–18, 21 students received support, including fellowships with full tuition reimbursements available (averaging $31,000 per year), research assistantships with full tuition reimbursements available (averaging $31,000 per year); institutionally sponsored loans, scholarships/grants, traineeships, and health care benefits also available. Financial award application deadline: 12/1. *Faculty research:* Molecular genetics, developmental genetics, population genetics, human genetics, computational biology. *Unit head:* Yoav Gilad, PhD, Chair, E-mail: bsdadmissions@uchicago.edu. *Application contact:* Sue Levison, Administrator, 773-702-2464, Fax: 773-702-2464, E-mail: committee-on-genetics@uchicago.edu.

University of Cincinnati, Graduate School, College of Medicine, Graduate Programs in Biomedical Sciences, Department of Environmental Health, Programs in Environmental Genetics and Molecular Toxicology, Cincinnati, OH 45221. Offers MS, PhD. *Degree requirements:* For doctorate, thesis/dissertation. *Entrance requirements:* For master's, GRE, minimum GPA of 3.0, 3 letters of recommendation. Additional exam requirements/recommendations for international students: Required—TOEFL (minimum score 520 paper-based). *Expenses: Tuition, area resident:* Full-time $14,468. Tuition, state resident: full-time $14,968; part-time $754 per credit hour. Tuition, nonresident: full-time $24,210; part-time $1311 per credit hour. *International tuition:* $26,460 full-time. *Required fees:* $3958; $84 per credit hour. One-time fee: $85 full-time. Tuition and fees vary according to course load, degree level and program.

University of Colorado Denver, School of Medicine, Program in Human Medical Genetics and Genomics, Aurora, CO 80206. Offers PhD. *Students:* 10 full-time (6 women); includes 4 minority (1 Asian, non-Hispanic/Latino; 3 Hispanic/Latino), 1 international. Average age 27. 47 applicants, 2% accepted, 1 enrolled. In 2017, 4

doctorates awarded. *Degree requirements:* For doctorate, comprehensive exam, thesis/dissertation, at least 30 semester hours in course work (rotations and research courses taken prior to the completion of the comprehensive examination) and 30 semester hours of thesis/didactic credits prior to defending. *Entrance requirements:* For doctorate, GRE General Test (minimum combined score of 1205), minimum GPA of 3.0, 4 letters of recommendation; prerequisite courses in biology, chemistry (general and organic), physics, genetics, calculus, and statistics (recommended). Additional exam requirements/recommendations for international students: Required—TOEFL (minimum score 570 paper-based; 80 iBT). *Application deadline:* For fall admission, 12/1 for domestic students, 1/1 priority date for international students. Application fee: $50 ($75 for international students). Electronic applications accepted. *Financial support:* Fellowships, research assistantships, teaching assistantships, Federal Work-Study, institutionally sponsored loans, scholarships/grants, traineeships, health care benefits, and unspecified assistantships available. *Faculty research:* Mapping, discovery, and function of disease genes affecting skin and craniofacial development and autoimmunity; genetics of colon cancer; clinical proteomics; biochemical markers of disease, including cancer; modeling human genetic diseases with patient-derived induced pluripotent stem cells; cell cycle control of DNA replication and mutagenesis in yeast and human cancer cells; mechanisms of cancer chemoprevention. *Unit head:* Dr. Richard A. Spritz, Director, 303-724-3107, E-mail: richard.spritz@ucdenver.edu. *Application contact:* Maia Evans, Program Administrator, 303-724-3102, Fax: 303-724-3100, E-mail: adama.evans@ucdenver.edu.
Website: http://www.ucdenver.edu/academics/colleges/medicalschool/programs/HumanMedicalGenetics/Pages/Genetics.aspx

University of Connecticut, Graduate School, College of Liberal Arts and Sciences, Department of Molecular and Cell Biology, Storrs, CT 06269. Offers applied genomics (PSM); cell and developmental biology (MS, PhD); genetics and genomics (MS, PhD); microbial systems analysis (PSM); microbiology (MS, PhD); structural biology, biochemistry and biophysics (MS, PhD). Terminal master's awarded for partial completion of doctoral program. *Degree requirements:* For master's, comprehensive exam; for doctorate, thesis/dissertation. *Entrance requirements:* For master's and doctorate, GRE General Test, GRE Subject Test. Additional exam requirements/recommendations for international students: Required—TOEFL (minimum score 550 paper-based). Electronic applications accepted.

University of Georgia, College of Agricultural and Environmental Sciences, Institute of Plant Breeding, Genetics and Genomics, Athens, GA 30602. Offers MS, PhD.

University of Maryland, Baltimore, School of Medicine, Department of Epidemiology and Public Health, Baltimore, MD 21201. Offers biostatistics (MS); clinical research (MS); epidemiology and preventive medicine (MPH, MS, PhD); gerontology (PhD); human genetics and genomic medicine (MS, PhD); molecular epidemiology (MS, PhD); toxicology (MS, PhD); JD/MS; MD/PhD; MS/PhD. *Accreditation:* CEPH. *Program availability:* Part-time. *Students:* 88 full-time (72 women), 53 part-time (38 women); includes 51 minority (21 Black or African American, non-Hispanic/Latino; 20 Asian, non-Hispanic/Latino; 7 Hispanic/Latino; 3 Two or more races, non-Hispanic/Latino), 29 international. Average age 30. In 2017, 24 master's, 14 doctorates awarded. *Degree requirements:* For doctorate, comprehensive exam, thesis/dissertation. *Entrance requirements:* For master's and doctorate, GRE General Test. Additional exam requirements/recommendations for international students: Required—TOEFL (minimum score 550 paper-based; 80 iBT); Recommended—IELTS (minimum score 7). *Application deadline:* For fall admission, 1/15 for domestic and international students. Application fee: $75. Electronic applications accepted. *Expenses:* Contact institution. *Financial support:* In 2017–18, research assistantships with partial tuition reimbursements (averaging $26,000 per year) were awarded; fellowships, Federal Work-Study, scholarships/grants, and unspecified assistantships also available. Financial award application deadline: 3/1; financial award applicants required to submit FAFSA. *Unit head:* Dr. Laura Hungerford, Program Director, 410-706-8492, Fax: 410-706-4225. *Application contact:* Jessica Kelley, Program Coordinator, 410-706-8492, Fax: 410-706-4225, E-mail: jkelley@som.umaryland.edu.
Website: http://lifesciences.umaryland.edu/epidemiology/

University of Maryland, College Park, Academic Affairs, College of Computer, Mathematical and Natural Sciences, Department of Biology, PhD Program in Biological Sciences, College Park, MD 20742. Offers behavior, ecology, evolution, and systematics (PhD); computational biology, bioinformatics, and genomics (PhD); molecular and cellular biology (PhD); physiological systems (PhD). *Degree requirements:* For doctorate, comprehensive exam, thesis/dissertation, thesis work presentation in seminar. *Entrance requirements:* For doctorate, GRE General Test; GRE Subject Test in biology (recommended), academic transcripts, statement of purpose/research interests, 3 letters of recommendation. Additional exam requirements/recommendations for international students: Required—TOEFL. Electronic applications accepted.

University of Pennsylvania, Perelman School of Medicine, Biomedical Graduate Studies, Graduate Group in Genomics and Computational Biology, Philadelphia, PA 19104. Offers PhD, MD/PhD, VMD/PhD. *Faculty:* 83. *Students:* 43 full-time (16 women); includes 17 minority (1 Black or African American, non-Hispanic/Latino; 13 Asian, non-Hispanic/Latino; 1 Hispanic/Latino; 2 Two or more races, non-Hispanic/Latino), 7 international. 102 applicants, 22% accepted, 9 enrolled. In 2017, 7 doctorates awarded. *Degree requirements:* For doctorate, thesis/dissertation. *Entrance requirements:* For doctorate, GRE. Additional exam requirements/recommendations for international students: Required—TOEFL. *Application deadline:* For fall admission, 12/1 priority date for domestic students, 12/1 for international students. Applications are processed on a rolling basis. Application fee: $80. *Financial support:* In 2017–18, 40 students received support. Fellowships, research assistantships, teaching assistantships, and tuition waivers available. *Unit head:* Dr. Li-San Wang, Chairperson, 215-746-7015. *Application contact:* Maureen Kirsch, Graduate Coordinator, 215-746-2807.
Website: http://www.med.upenn.edu/gcb/

University of Rochester, School of Medicine and Dentistry, Graduate Programs in Medicine and Dentistry, Department of Biomedical Genetics, Rochester, NY 14627. Offers genetics, genomics and development (PhD). *Degree requirements:* For doctorate, thesis/dissertation, qualifying exam. *Entrance requirements:* For doctorate, GRE General Test.

University of Southern California, Keck School of Medicine, Program in Cancer Biology and Genomics, Los Angeles, CA 90033. Offers PhD. *Faculty:* 43 full-time (10 women). *Students:* 22 full-time (15 women); includes 7 minority (4 Asian, non-Hispanic/Latino; 2 Hispanic/Latino; 1 Two or more races, non-Hispanic/Latino), 10 international. Average age 28. 7 applicants, 100% accepted, 7 enrolled. *Degree requirements:* For doctorate, comprehensive exam, thesis/dissertation. *Entrance requirements:* For doctorate, GRE, minimum GPA of 3.0. Additional exam requirements/recommendations for international students: Required—TOEFL (minimum score 600 paper-based; 100 iBT), IELTS (minimum score 7), PTE. *Application deadline:* For fall admission, 12/1 priority date for domestic and international students. Application fee: $90. Electronic applications accepted. *Financial support:* In 2017–18, 22 students received support, including 3 fellowships with full tuition reimbursements available (averaging $33,000 per year), 7 research assistantships with full tuition reimbursements available (averaging $33,000 per year); institutionally sponsored loans, scholarships/grants, traineeships, health care benefits, and unspecified assistantships also available. Financial award application deadline: 4/15; financial award applicants required to submit CSS PROFILE or FAFSA. *Unit head:* Dr. Baruch Frenkel, Director, 323-442-1475, Fax: 323-442-1199, E-mail: frenkel@med.usc.edu. *Application contact:* Dr. Joyce Perez, Manager of Student Programs, 323-442-1645, Fax: 323-442-1199, E-mail: jpperez@med.usc.edu.
Website: http://pibbs.usc.edu/research-and-programs/phd-programs/

The University of Tennessee, Graduate School, College of Arts and Sciences, Program in Life Sciences, Knoxville, TN 37996. Offers genome science and technology (MS, PhD); plant physiology and genetics (MS, PhD). *Degree requirements:* For doctorate, one foreign language, thesis/dissertation. *Entrance requirements:* For master's and doctorate, GRE General Test, minimum GPA of 2.7. Additional exam requirements/recommendations for international students: Required—TOEFL. Electronic applications accepted.

The University of Tennessee–Oak Ridge National Laboratory, Graduate Program in Genome Science and Technology, Knoxville, TN 37966. Offers life sciences (MS, PhD). *Degree requirements:* For master's, thesis; for doctorate, comprehensive exam, thesis/dissertation. *Entrance requirements:* For master's and doctorate, GRE General Test. Additional exam requirements/recommendations for international students: Required—TOEFL. Electronic applications accepted. *Faculty research:* Genetics/genomics, structural biology/proteomics, computational biology/bioinformatics, bioanalytical technologies.

The University of Texas Health Science Center at Houston, School of Public Health, Houston, TX 77030. Offers behavioral science (PhD); biostatistics (MPH, MS, PhD); environmental health (MPH); epidemiology (MPH, MS, PhD); general public health (Certificate); genomics and bioinformatics (Certificate); health disparities (Certificate); health promotion/health education (MPH, Dr PH); healthcare management (Certificate); management, policy and community health (MPH, Dr PH, PhD); maternal and child health (Certificate); public health informatics (Certificate); DDS/MPH; JD/MPH; MBA/MPH; MD/MPH; MGPS/MPH; MP Aff/MPH; MS/MPH; MSN/MPH; MSW/MPH; PhD/MPH. Specific programs are offered at each of our six campuses in Texas (Austin, Brownsville, Dallas, El Paso, Houston, and San Antonio). *Accreditation:* CEPH. *Program availability:* Part-time. *Faculty:* 140 full-time (74 women), 23 part-time/adjunct (14 women). *Students:* 604 full-time (446 women), 534 part-time (384 women); includes 504 minority (106 Black or African American, non-Hispanic/Latino; 177 Asian, non-Hispanic/Latino; 88 Hispanic/Latino; 1 Native Hawaiian or other Pacific Islander, non-Hispanic/Latino; 132 Two or more races, non-Hispanic/Latino). Average age 31. 1,425 applicants, 58% accepted, 423 enrolled. In 2017, 315 master's, 68 doctorates awarded. *Degree requirements:* For master's, thesis (for some programs); for doctorate, comprehensive exam, thesis/dissertation. *Entrance requirements:* For master's and doctorate, GRE General Test. Additional exam requirements/recommendations for international students: Required—TOEFL (minimum score 600 paper-based, 100 iBT) or IELTS (7.5). *Application deadline:* For fall admission, 3/1 for domestic and international students; for spring admission, 10/1 for domestic and international students; for summer admission, 3/1 for domestic students. Applications are processed on a rolling basis. Application fee: $135. Electronic applications accepted. *Expenses:* $233 per semester credit hour resident tuition, $980 per semester credit hour non-resident tuition. *Financial support:* Fellowships, research assistantships, teaching assistantships, career-related internships or fieldwork, institutionally sponsored loans, scholarships/grants, traineeships, health care benefits, and unspecified assistantships available. Support available to part-time students. Financial award application deadline: 5/5; financial award applicants required to submit FAFSA. *Faculty research:* Chronic and infectious disease epidemiology; health promotion and health education; applied and theoretical biostatistics; healthcare management, policy and economics; environmental and occupational health. *Total annual research expenditures:* $47.8 million. *Unit head:* Dr. Susan Emery, Senior Associate Dean of Academic and Research Affairs. *Application contact:* Elvis Parada, Manager of Admissions and Recruitment, 713-500-9028, Fax: 713-500-9068, E-mail: elvis.a.parada@uth.tmc.edu.
Website: https://sph.uth.edu

The University of Toledo, College of Graduate Studies, College of Medicine and Life Sciences, Interdepartmental Programs, Toledo, OH 43606-3390. Offers bioinformatics and proteomics/genomics (MSBS); biomarkers and bioinformatics (Certificate); biomarkers and diagnostics (PSM); human donation sciences (MSBS); medical sciences (MSBS); MD/MSBS. *Degree requirements:* For master's, thesis or alternative. *Entrance requirements:* For master's, GRE, minimum undergraduate GPA of 3.0, three letters of recommendation, statement of purpose, transcripts from all prior institutions attended, resume; for Certificate, minimum undergraduate GPA of 3.0, three letters of recommendation, statement of purpose, transcripts from all prior institutions attended, resume. Additional exam requirements/recommendations for international students: Required—TOEFL (minimum score 550 paper-based; 80 iBT). Electronic applications accepted.

University of Washington, Graduate School, School of Medicine, Graduate Programs in Medicine, Department of Genome Sciences, Seattle, WA 98195. Offers PhD. *Degree requirements:* For doctorate, thesis/dissertation, general exam. *Entrance requirements:* For doctorate, GRE General Test, minimum GPA of 3.0. Additional exam requirements/recommendations for international students: Required—TOEFL. Electronic applications accepted. *Faculty research:* Model organism genetics, human and medical genetics, genomics and proteomics, computational biology.

Wake Forest University, School of Medicine and Graduate School of Arts and Sciences, Graduate Programs in Medicine, Molecular Genetics and Genomics Program, Winston-Salem, NC 27109. Offers PhD, MD/PhD. *Degree requirements:* For doctorate, thesis/dissertation. *Entrance requirements:* For doctorate, GRE General Test. Additional exam requirements/recommendations for international students: Required—TOEFL. Electronic applications accepted. *Faculty research:* Control of gene expression, molecular pathogenesis, protein biosynthesis, cell development, clinical cytogenetics.

Washington University in St. Louis, School of Medicine, Program in Clinical Investigation, St. Louis, MO 63130-4899. Offers clinical investigation (MS), including bioethics, entrepreneurship, genetics/genomics, translational medicine. *Program availability:* Part-time, evening/weekend. *Degree requirements:* For master's, thesis. *Entrance requirements:* For master's, doctoral-level degree or in process of obtaining doctoral-level degree. Electronic applications accepted. *Faculty research:* Anesthesiology, infectious diseases, neurology, obstetrics and gynecology, orthopedic surgery.

Wayne State University, School of Medicine, Office of Biomedical Graduate Programs, Detroit, MI 48202. Offers anatomy and cell biology (MS, PhD); basic medical sciences (MS); biochemistry and molecular biology (MS, PhD); cancer biology (MS, PhD); clinical and translational science (Graduate Certificate); family medicine and public health sciences (MPH, Graduate Certificate), including public health practice; genetic counseling (MS); immunology and microbiology (MS, PhD); medical physics (MS, PhD, Graduate Certificate); medical research (MS); molecular medicine and genomics (MS, PhD), including molecular genetics and genomics; pathology (PhD); pharmacology (MS, PhD); physiology (MS, PhD), including physiology, reproductive sciences (PhD); psychiatry and behavioral neurosciences (PhD), including translational neuroscience; MD/MPH; MD/PhD; MPH/MA; MSW/MPH. *Program availability:* Part-time, evening/weekend. *Students:* 268 full-time (152 women), 117 part-time (59 women); includes 108

minority (19 Black or African American, non-Hispanic/Latino; 1 American Indian or Alaska Native, non-Hispanic/Latino; 62 Asian, non-Hispanic/Latino; 9 Hispanic/Latino; 17 Two or more races, non-Hispanic/Latino), 48 international. Average age 26. 1,133 applicants, 21% accepted, 151 enrolled. In 2017, 70 master's, 25 doctorates, 10 other advanced degrees awarded. Terminal master's awarded for partial completion of doctoral program. *Degree requirements:* For master's, thesis (for some programs); for doctorate, thesis/dissertation. *Entrance requirements:* For master's, doctorate, and Graduate Certificate, GRE. Additional exam requirements/recommendations for international students: Required—TOEFL (minimum score 550 paper-based; 100 iBT), Michigan English Language Assessment Battery (minimum score 85); Recommended—IELTS (minimum score 6.5), TWE (minimum score 5.5). *Application deadline:* For fall admission, 2/1 for domestic and international students. Applications are processed on a rolling basis. Application fee: $50. Electronic applications accepted. *Expenses:* Contact institution. *Financial support:* In 2017–18, 177 students received support, including 64 fellowships with full tuition reimbursements available (averaging $24,388 per year), 79 research assistantships with full tuition reimbursements available (averaging $26,894 per year); scholarships/grants, traineeships, and health care benefits also available. *Faculty research:* Cancer biology, neurosciences, vision sciences, molecular biology, pathology, physiology, pharmacology, public health, medical physics. *Unit head:* Dr. Daniel A. Walz, Associate Dean for Biomedical Graduate Programs, 313-577-1455, Fax: 313-577-8796, E-mail: gradprogs@med.wayne.edu.
Website: https://www.med.wayne.edu/biomedical-graduate-programs/

Wesleyan University, Graduate Studies, Department of Biology, Middletown, CT 06459. Offers cell and developmental biology (PhD); evolution and ecology (PhD); genetics and genomics (PhD), including bioinformatics; neurobiology and behavior (PhD). Terminal master's awarded for partial completion of doctoral program. *Degree requirements:* For doctorate, comprehensive exam, thesis/dissertation, public seminar. *Entrance requirements:* For doctorate, GRE, official transcripts, three recommendation letters, essay. Additional exam requirements/recommendations for international students: Required—TOEFL. *Application deadline:* For fall admission, 1/15 for domestic and international students. Application fee: $0. Electronic applications accepted. *Financial support:* Stipends available. *Faculty research:* Evolution and ecology, neurobiology and behavior, cell and developmental biology, genetics, genomics and bioinformatics. *Unit head:* Dr. Ann Burke, Chair/Professor, 860-685-3518, E-mail: acburke@wesleyan.edu. *Application contact:* Diane Meredith, Administrative Assistant IV, 860-685-2157, E-mail: dmeredith@wesleyan.edu.
Website: http://www.wesleyan.edu/bio/

Yale University, Yale School of Medicine and Graduate School of Arts and Sciences, Combined Program in Biological and Biomedical Sciences (BBS), Computational Biology and Bioinformatics Track, New Haven, CT 06520. Offers PhD, MD/PhD. *Entrance requirements:* Additional exam requirements/recommendations for international students: Required—TOEFL.

Human Genetics

Baylor College of Medicine, Graduate School of Biomedical Sciences, Department of Molecular and Human Genetics, Houston, TX 77030-3498. Offers PhD, MD/PhD. *Degree requirements:* For doctorate, thesis/dissertation, public defense. *Entrance requirements:* For doctorate, GRE General Test, GRE Subject Test (strongly recommended), minimum GPA of 3.0. Additional exam requirements/recommendations for international students: Required—TOEFL. Electronic applications accepted. *Faculty research:* Human genetics, genome biology, epigenetics, gene therapy, model organisms.

Baylor College of Medicine, Graduate School of Biomedical Sciences, Interdepartmental Program in Cell and Molecular Biology, Houston, TX 77030-3498. Offers biochemistry (PhD); cell and molecular biology (PhD); genetics (PhD); human genetics (PhD); immunology (PhD); microbiology (PhD); virology (PhD); MD/PhD. *Degree requirements:* For doctorate, thesis/dissertation, public defense. *Entrance requirements:* For doctorate, GRE General Test, GRE Subject Test (strongly recommended), minimum GPA of 3.0. Additional exam requirements/recommendations for international students: Required—TOEFL. Electronic applications accepted. *Faculty research:* Molecular and cellular biology; cancer, aging and stem cells; genomics and proteomics; microbiome, molecular microbiology; infectious disease, immunology and translational research.

Case Western Reserve University, School of Medicine and School of Graduate Studies, Graduate Programs in Medicine, Department of Genetics and Genome Sciences, Cleveland, OH 44106. Offers genetic counseling (MS); genetics and genome sciences (PhD); MD/PhD. Terminal master's awarded for partial completion of doctoral program. *Degree requirements:* For master's, thesis; for doctorate, comprehensive exam, thesis/dissertation. *Entrance requirements:* For master's, GRE General Test; for doctorate, GRE General Test, GRE Subject Test. Additional exam requirements/recommendations for international students: Required—TOEFL. *Expenses: Tuition:* Full-time $43,854; part-time $1827 per credit hour. *Required fees:* $50; $50 per credit hour. Tuition and fees vary according to course load and program. *Faculty research:* Eukaryotic genetics, regulation of gene expression, chromosome structure and function.

Emory University, School of Medicine, Programs in Allied Health Professions, Genetic Counseling Training Program, Atlanta, GA 30322. Offers MM Sc. *Degree requirements:* For master's, thesis, capstone project. *Entrance requirements:* For master's, GRE General Test, minimum GPA of 3.0; prerequisites: genetics, statistics, psychology, and biochemistry. Additional exam requirements/recommendations for international students: Required—TOEFL. *Faculty research:* Cancer genetics, lysosomal storage disease, carrier screening, public health genomics, genetic counseling, psychology, molecular genetics.

Louisiana State University Health Sciences Center, School of Graduate Studies in New Orleans, Department of Human Genetics, New Orleans, LA 70112-2223. Offers PhD, MD/PhD. *Faculty:* 10 full-time (4 women). *Students:* 5 full-time (all women); includes 2 minority (1 Black or African American, non-Hispanic/Latino; 1 Asian, non-Hispanic/Latino). Average age 26. 2 applicants. In 2017, 1 doctorate awarded. Terminal master's awarded for partial completion of doctoral program. *Degree requirements:* For doctorate, comprehensive exam, thesis/dissertation. *Entrance requirements:* For doctorate, GRE General Test. Additional exam requirements/recommendations for international students: Recommended—TOEFL, IELTS. *Application deadline:* For fall admission, 4/1 priority date for domestic students, 4/1 for international students. Applications are processed on a rolling basis. Application fee: $30. *Expenses:* Tuition, state resident: full-time $11,835; part-time $518 per hour. Tuition, nonresident: full-time $24,108; part-time $1079 per hour. *Required fees:* $1254; $55 per hour. *Financial support:* Unspecified assistantships available. Financial award application deadline: 4/1. *Faculty research:* Genetic epidemiology, segregation and linkage analysis, gene mapping. *Unit head:* Dr. Lucio Miele, Professor and Head, 504-568-6150. *Application contact:* Dr. Diptasri Mandal, Graduate Coordinator, 504-568-6156, Fax: 504-568-8500, E-mail: dmanda@lsuhsc.edu.
Website: http://www.medschool.lsuhsc.edu/genetics/

McGill University, Faculty of Graduate and Postdoctoral Studies, Faculty of Medicine, Department of Human Genetics, Montréal, QC H3A 2T5, Canada. Offers genetic counseling (M Sc); human genetics (M Sc, PhD).

Memorial University of Newfoundland, Faculty of Medicine and School of Graduate Studies, Graduate Programs in Medicine, Division of Human Genetics, St. John's, NL A1C 5S7, Canada. Offers M Sc, PhD, MD/PhD. *Program availability:* Part-time. *Degree requirements:* For master's, thesis; for doctorate, comprehensive exam, thesis/dissertation, oral defense of thesis. *Entrance requirements:* For master's, MD or B Sc; for doctorate, MD or M Sc. Additional exam requirements/recommendations for international students: Required—TOEFL. *Faculty research:* Cancer genetics, gene mapping, medical genetics, birth defects, population genetics.

Sarah Lawrence College, Graduate Studies, Joan H. Marks Graduate Program in Human Genetics, Bronxville, NY 10708-5999. Offers MS. *Program availability:* Part-time. *Degree requirements:* For master's, thesis, fieldwork. *Entrance requirements:* For master's, previous course work in biology, chemistry, developmental biology, genetics, probability and statistics. Additional exam requirements/recommendations for international students: Required—TOEFL (minimum score 600 paper-based). Electronic applications accepted. *Expenses:* Contact institution.

Thomas Jefferson University, Jefferson College of Biomedical Sciences, MS Program in Human Genetics and Genetic Counseling, Philadelphia, PA 19107. Offers MS. *Faculty:* 1 (woman) full-time, 6 part-time/adjunct (all women). *Students:* 6 full-time (all women); includes 1 minority (Hispanic/Latino). 36 applicants, 17% accepted, 6 enrolled. *Entrance requirements:* For master's, BA, personal statement, official transcripts, recommendation letters. Additional exam requirements/recommendations for international students: Required—TOEFL, IELTS (minimum score 7). *Application deadline:* For fall admission, 3/15 for domestic students. Applications are processed on a rolling basis. Application fee: $50. Electronic applications accepted. *Financial support:* Federal Work-Study and institutionally sponsored loans available. Support available to part-time students. Financial award application deadline: 5/1; financial award applicants required to submit FAFSA. *Unit head:* Dr. Rachael Brandt, Program Director, E-mail: rachael.brandt@jefferson.edu. *Application contact:* Marc E. Stearns, Senior Associate Director of Admissions, 215-503-0155, Fax: 215-503-3433, E-mail: jgsbs-info@jefferson.edu.

Tulane University, School of Medicine and School of Liberal Arts, Graduate Programs in Biomedical Sciences, Program in Human Genetics, New Orleans, LA 70118-5669. Offers MS. MS and PhD offered through the Graduate School. *Degree requirements:* For master's, thesis. *Entrance requirements:* For master's, GRE, MCAT. Additional exam requirements/recommendations for international students: Required—TOEFL. Electronic applications accepted. *Expenses: Tuition:* Full-time $50,920; part-time $2829 per credit hour. *Required fees:* $2040; $44.50 per credit hour. $580 per term. Tuition and fees vary according to course load, degree level and program. *Faculty research:* Inborn errors of metabolism, DNA methylation, gene therapy.

University of California, Los Angeles, David Geffen School of Medicine and Graduate Division, Graduate Programs in Medicine, Department of Human Genetics, Los Angeles, CA 90095. Offers MS, PhD. *Degree requirements:* For master's, thesis; for doctorate, thesis/dissertation, written and oral qualifying examination; 2 quarters of teaching experience. *Entrance requirements:* For master's and doctorate, GRE General Test; GRE Subject Test (recommended), bachelor's degree; minimum undergraduate GPA of 3.0 (or its equivalent if letter grade system not used). Additional exam requirements/recommendations for international students: Required—TOEFL. Electronic applications accepted.

University of California, Los Angeles, Graduate Division, College of Letters and Science and David Geffen School of Medicine, UCLA ACCESS to Programs in the Molecular, Cellular and Integrative Life Sciences, Los Angeles, CA 90095. Offers biochemistry and molecular biology (PhD); biological chemistry (PhD); cellular and molecular pathology (PhD); human genetics (PhD); microbiology, immunology, and molecular genetics (PhD); molecular biology (PhD); molecular toxicology (PhD); molecular, cellular and integrative physiology (PhD); neurobiology (PhD); oral biology (PhD); physiology (PhD). *Degree requirements:* For doctorate, thesis/dissertation, oral and written qualifying exams. *Entrance requirements:* For doctorate, GRE General Test, bachelor's degree; minimum undergraduate GPA of 3.0 (or its equivalent if letter grade system not used). Additional exam requirements/recommendations for international students: Required—TOEFL. Electronic applications accepted.

University of Chicago, Division of the Biological Sciences, Department of Human Genetics, Chicago, IL 60637. Offers PhD. *Faculty:* 28. *Students:* 16 full-time (7 women). 45 applicants, 22% accepted, 4 enrolled. In 2017, 5 doctorates awarded. *Degree requirements:* For doctorate, comprehensive exam, thesis/dissertation, ethics class, 2 teaching assistantships. *Entrance requirements:* For doctorate, GRE General Test, transcripts, statement of purpose, 3 letters of recommendation. Additional exam requirements/recommendations for international students: Required—TOEFL (minimum score 600 paper-based; 104 iBT), IELTS (minimum score 7). *Application deadline:* For fall admission, 12/1 for domestic and international students. Application fee: $90. Electronic applications accepted. *Financial support:* In 2017–18, 21 students received support, including fellowships with full tuition reimbursements available (averaging $31,000 per year), research assistantships with full tuition reimbursements available (averaging $31,000 per year); institutionally sponsored loans, scholarships/grants, traineeships, and health care benefits also available. Financial award application deadline: 12/1. *Faculty research:* Population and evolutionary genetics; systems biology; epigenetics and stem cell genetics; genomics of gene regulation; animal models of human disease. *Unit head:* Dr. Carole Ober, Chair, E-mail: bsdadmissions@uchicago.edu. *Application contact:* Candice Lewis, Graduate Education Administrator, 773-834-6864, E-mail: cllewis@uchicago.edu.
Website: http://genes.uchicago.edu/

University of Manitoba, Max Rady College of Medicine and Faculty of Graduate Studies, Graduate Programs in Medicine, Department of Biochemistry and Medical Genetics, Winnipeg, MB R3T 2N2, Canada. Offers biochemistry and medical genetics (M Sc, PhD); genetic counseling (M Sc). Terminal master's awarded for partial completion of doctoral program. *Degree requirements:* For master's, thesis; for doctorate, thesis/dissertation. *Faculty research:* Cancer, gene expression, membrane lipids, metabolic control, genetic diseases.

University of Maryland, Baltimore, School of Medicine, Department of Epidemiology and Public Health, Baltimore, MD 21201. Offers biostatistics (MS); clinical research (MS); epidemiology and preventive medicine (MPH, MS, PhD); gerontology (PhD); human genetics and genomic medicine (MS, PhD); molecular epidemiology (MS, PhD); toxicology (MS, PhD); JD/MS; MD/PhD; MS/PhD. *Accreditation:* CEPH. *Program availability:* Part-time. *Students:* 88 full-time (72 women), 53 part-time (38 women); includes 51 minority (21 Black or African American, non-Hispanic/Latino; 20 Asian, non-Hispanic/Latino; 7 Hispanic/Latino; 3 Two or more races, non-Hispanic/Latino), 29 international. Average age 30. In 2017, 24 master's, 14 doctorates awarded. *Degree requirements:* For doctorate, comprehensive exam, thesis/dissertation. *Entrance requirements:* For master's and doctorate, GRE General Test. Additional exam requirements/recommendations for international students: Required—TOEFL (minimum score 550 paper-based; 80 iBT); Recommended—IELTS (minimum score 7). *Application deadline:* For fall admission, 1/15 for domestic and international students. Application fee: $75. Electronic applications accepted. *Expenses:* Contact institution. *Financial support:* In 2017–18, research assistantships with partial tuition reimbursements (averaging $26,000 per year) were awarded; fellowships, Federal Work-Study, scholarships/grants, and unspecified assistantships also available. Financial award application deadline: 3/1; financial award applicants required to submit FAFSA. *Unit head:* Dr. Laura Hungerford, Program Director, 410-706-8492, Fax: 410-706-4225. *Application contact:* Jessica Kelley, Program Coordinator, 410-706-8492, Fax: 410-706-4225, E-mail: jkelley@som.umaryland.edu.
Website: http://lifesciences.umaryland.edu/epidemiology/

University of Michigan, Rackham Graduate School, Program in Biomedical Sciences (PIBS), Department of Human Genetics, Ann Arbor, MI 48109. Offers genetic counseling (MS); human genetics (MS, PhD). *Faculty:* 39 full-time (16 women). *Students:* 44 full-time (34 women); includes 5 minority (2 Asian, non-Hispanic/Latino; 1 Hispanic/Latino; 2 Two or more races, non-Hispanic/Latino), 5 international. Average age 29. 257 applicants, 15% accepted, 16 enrolled. In 2017, 12 master's, 3 doctorates awarded. Terminal master's awarded for partial completion of doctoral program. *Degree requirements:* For master's, thesis optional, research project (for MS in genetic counseling); for doctorate, thesis/dissertation, oral preliminary exam, oral defense of dissertation. *Entrance requirements:* For master's, GRE General Test, bachelor's degree; 3 letters of recommendation; advocacy experience (for the MS in genetic counseling); for doctorate, bachelor's degree; 3 letters of recommendation. Additional exam requirements/recommendations for international students: Required—TOEFL (minimum score 84 iBT). Application fee: $75 ($90 for international students). Electronic applications accepted. *Expenses:* $22,742 resident full-time; $45,576 non-resident full-time. *Financial support:* In 2017–18, 42 students received support, including 33 fellowships with tuition reimbursements available, 7 research assistantships with full tuition reimbursements available (averaging $30,600 per year), 7 teaching assistantships with full tuition reimbursements available (averaging $30,600 per year); Federal Work-Study, scholarships/grants, traineeships, and health care benefits also available. Financial award application deadline: 4/30; financial award applicants required to submit CSS PROFILE or FAFSA. *Faculty research:* Molecular and developmental genetics, genetics of Mendelian and complex human disease, genome biology, statistical and population genetics, epigenetics. *Total annual research expenditures:* $5.6 million. *Unit head:* Jeffery R. Holden, Chief Department Administrator, 734-764-6361, Fax: 734-763-3784, E-mail: jholden@umich.edu. *Application contact:* Molly G. Martin, Student Services Coordinator, 734-764-5490, Fax: 734-763-3784, E-mail: mollymu@umich.edu.
Website: http://www.hg.med.umich.edu/

University of Pennsylvania, Perelman School of Medicine, Center for Clinical Epidemiology and Biostatistics, Philadelphia, PA 19104. Offers clinical epidemiology (MSCE), including bioethics, clinical trials, human genetics, patient centered outcome research, pharmacoepidemiology. *Program availability:* Part-time. *Faculty:* 102 full-time (49 women), 69 part-time/adjunct (25 women). *Students:* 92 full-time (61 women), 3 part-time (2 women); includes 35 minority (11 Black or African American, non-Hispanic/Latino; 18 Asian, non-Hispanic/Latino; 6 Hispanic/Latino). Average age 35. 45 applicants, 87% accepted, 30 enrolled. In 2017, 23 master's awarded. *Degree requirements:* For master's, comprehensive exam, thesis. *Entrance requirements:* For master's, GRE General Test or MCAT, advanced degree, clinical experience. Additional exam requirements/recommendations for international students: Required—TOEFL. *Application deadline:* For fall admission, 12/1 priority date for domestic students, 12/1 for international students. Application fee: $0. Electronic applications accepted. *Expenses:* Contact institution. *Financial support:* In 2017–18, 50 students received support, including 50 fellowships with tuition reimbursements available (averaging $45,500 per year); research assistantships, teaching assistantships, and tuition waivers also available. Financial award application deadline: 12/1. *Faculty research:* Patient-centered outcomes, pharmacoepidemiology, women's health, cancer epidemiology, genetic epidemiology. *Total annual research expenditures:* $38.7 million. *Unit head:* Dr. Harold I. Feldman, Director, 215-573-0901, E-mail: hfeldman@mail.med.upenn.edu. *Application contact:* Jennifer Kuklinski, Program Coordinator, 215-573-2382, E-mail: jkuklins@mail.med.upenn.edu.
Website: http://www.cceb.med.upenn.edu/

University of Pittsburgh, Graduate School of Public Health, Department of Human Genetics, Pittsburgh, PA 15261. Offers genetic counseling (MS); human genetics (MS, PhD); public health genetics (MPH, Certificate); MD/PhD; MS/MPH. *Program availability:* Part-time. *Faculty:* 19. *Students:* 59 full-time (48 women), 13 part-time (all women); includes 8 minority (2 Black or African American, non-Hispanic/Latino; 1 Asian, non-Hispanic/Latino; 2 Hispanic/Latino; 1 Native Hawaiian or other Pacific Islander, non-Hispanic/Latino; 2 Two or more races, non-Hispanic/Latino), 16 international. Average age 27. 226 applicants, 35% accepted, 27 enrolled. *Degree requirements:* For master's, thesis, final paper; comprehensive exam and thesis defense (for MS); for doctorate, comprehensive exam, thesis/dissertation, qualifying examination. *Entrance requirements:* For master's and doctorate, GRE General Test (above the 70th percentile for the verbal and quantitative tests), previous course work in biochemistry and behavioral or social sciences (recommended); bachelor's degree in a discipline related to the biological or behavioral sciences from accredited college or university with minimum GPA of 3.0, introductory courses in genetics and calculus. Additional exam requirements/recommendations for international students: Required—TOEFL (minimum score 550 paper-based, 80 iBT) or IELTS (minimum score 6.5); GRE. *Application deadline:* For fall admission, 4/15 priority date for domestic students, 3/15 priority date for international students; for spring admission, 10/15 priority date for domestic students, 8/1 priority date for international students. Applications are processed on a rolling basis. Application fee: $135. Electronic applications accepted. *Expenses:* $13,068 full-time in-state tuition per term, $21,696 out-of-state. *Financial support:* Fellowships, research assistantships, teaching assistantships, career-related internships or fieldwork, institutionally sponsored loans, scholarships/grants, traineeships, health care benefits, tuition waivers, and unspecified assistantships available. Support available to part-time students. Financial award applicants required to submit CSS PROFILE or FAFSA. *Faculty research:* Search for Alzheimer's disease gene, genetics, factors of oral health, cellular Samoan variant, connections of brain imaging and dementia. *Total annual research expenditures:* $3.9 million. *Unit head:* Dr. Eleanor Feingold, Acting Chair, 412-648-3353, Fax: 412-624-3020. *Application contact:* Jennifer Heinemann, Department Administrator, 412-624-1560, Fax: 412-624-3020, E-mail: jdh150@pitt.edu.
Website: http://www.publichealth.pitt.edu/hugen

University of Utah, School of Medicine and Graduate School, Graduate Programs in Medicine, Department of Human Genetics, Salt Lake City, UT 84112-1107. Offers MS, PhD. Terminal master's awarded for partial completion of doctoral program. *Degree requirements:* For master's, comprehensive exam, thesis optional; for doctorate, comprehensive exam, thesis/dissertation. Electronic applications accepted. *Faculty research:* RNA metabolism, drosophilia genetics, mouse genetics, protein synthesis.

Vanderbilt University, Program in Human Genetics, Nashville, TN 37240-1001. Offers PhD. *Faculty:* 31 full-time (9 women). *Students:* 10 full-time (5 women); includes 2 minority (both Asian, non-Hispanic/Latino), 2 international. Average age 26. In 2017, 3 doctorates awarded. *Degree requirements:* For doctorate, comprehensive exam, thesis/dissertation. *Entrance requirements:* For doctorate, GRE General Test. Additional exam requirements/recommendations for international students: Required—TOEFL (minimum score 570 paper-based; 88 iBT). *Application deadline:* For fall admission, 1/15 for domestic and international students. Application fee: $0. Electronic applications accepted. *Financial support:* Fellowships, research assistantships, Federal Work-Study, institutionally sponsored loans, traineeships, and health care benefits available. Financial award application deadline: 1/15; financial award applicants required to submit CSS PROFILE or FAFSA. *Faculty research:* Disease gene discovery, computational genomics, translational genetics. *Unit head:* Dr. Nancy Cox, Director, 615-343-8555, Fax: 615-322-1453, E-mail: nancy.j.cox@vanderbilt.edu. *Application contact:* David Samuels, Director of Graduate Studies, 615-343-8555, E-mail: david.c.samuels@vanderbilt.edu.
Website: https://medschool.vanderbilt.edu/igp/human-genetics

Virginia Commonwealth University, Medical College of Virginia-Professional Programs, School of Medicine, Graduate Programs in Medicine, Department of Human and Molecular Genetics, Richmond, VA 23284-9005. Offers genetic counseling (MS); human genetics (PhD); MD/PhD. *Degree requirements:* For master's, thesis; for doctorate, thesis/dissertation, comprehensive oral and written exams. *Entrance requirements:* For master's, GRE; for doctorate, GRE General Test. Additional exam requirements/recommendations for international students: Required—TOEFL (minimum score 600 paper-based; 100 iBT). Electronic applications accepted. *Faculty research:* Genetic epidemiology, biochemical genetics, quantitative genetics, human cytogenetics, molecular genetics.

Washington University in St. Louis, The Graduate School, Division of Biology and Biomedical Sciences, Program in Human and Statistical Genetics, St. Louis, MO 63130-4899. Offers PhD. *Degree requirements:* For doctorate, thesis/dissertation. *Entrance requirements:* For doctorate, GRE General Test, GRE Subject Test. Additional exam requirements/recommendations for international students: Required—TOEFL. Electronic applications accepted. *Faculty research:* Human genetics, statistical genetics, functional genomics, molecular genetics, Mendelian disease, complex disease, human disease models, systems biology.

Molecular Genetics

Albert Einstein College of Medicine, Graduate Programs in the Biomedical Sciences, Department of Genetics, Bronx, NY 10461. Offers computational genetics (PhD); molecular genetics (PhD); translational genetics (PhD); MD/PhD. *Degree requirements:* For doctorate, thesis/dissertation. *Entrance requirements:* For doctorate, GRE General Test. Additional exam requirements/recommendations for international students: Required—TOEFL. *Application deadline:* For fall admission, 1/15 for domestic students. Application fee: $0. *Financial support:* Fellowships available. *Faculty research:* Neurologic genetics in &ITDrosophila&RO, biochemical genetics of yeast, developmental genetics in the mouse. *Unit head:* Dr. Jan Vijg, Chair, 718-678-1151. *Application contact:* Sheila Cleeton, Executive Director and Registrar, Einstein Graduate Division, 718-430-2128, Fax: 718-430-8655, E-mail: sheila.cleeton@einstein.yu.edu.
Website: http://www.einstein.yu.edu/departments/genetics/

Duke University, Graduate School, Department of Molecular Genetics and Microbiology, Durham, NC 27710. Offers PhD. *Degree requirements:* For doctorate, thesis/dissertation. *Entrance requirements:* For doctorate, GRE General Test, GRE Subject Test in biology, chemistry, or biochemistry, cell and molecular biology (recommended). Additional exam requirements/recommendations for international students: Required—TOEFL (minimum score 577 paper-based; 90 iBT) or IELTS (minimum score 7). Electronic applications accepted.

Emory University, Laney Graduate School, Division of Biological and Biomedical Sciences, Program in Microbiology and Molecular Genetics, Atlanta, GA 30322-1100. Offers PhD. *Degree requirements:* For doctorate, comprehensive exam, thesis/dissertation. *Entrance requirements:* For doctorate, GRE General Test, minimum GPA of 3.0 in science course work (recommended). Additional exam requirements/recommendations for international students: Required—TOEFL. Electronic applications accepted. *Faculty research:* Bacterial genetics and physiology, microbial development, molecular biology of viruses and bacterial pathogens, DNA recombination.

Georgia State University, College of Arts and Sciences, Department of Biology, Program in Molecular Genetics and Biochemistry, Atlanta, GA 30302-3083. Offers bioinformatics (MS); molecular genetics and biochemistry (MS, PhD). *Program*

availability: Part-time. Terminal master's awarded for partial completion of doctoral program. *Entrance requirements:* For master's and doctorate, GRE. *Application deadline:* Applications are processed on a rolling basis. Application fee: $50. Electronic applications accepted. *Expenses:* Tuition, state resident: full-time $7020. Tuition, nonresident: full-time $22,518. *Required fees:* $2128. Tuition and fees vary according to degree level and program. *Financial support:* Fellowships and research assistantships available. Financial award application deadline: 12/3. *Faculty research:* Gene regulation, microbial pathogenesis, molecular transport, protein modeling, viral pathogenesis. *Unit head:* Dr. Charles Derby, Director of Graduate Studies, 404-413-5393, Fax: 404-413-5446, E-mail: cderby@gsu.edu.
Website: http://biology.gsu.edu/

Harvard University, Graduate School of Arts and Sciences, Division of Medical Sciences, Boston, MA 02115. Offers biological chemistry and molecular pharmacology (PhD); cell biology (PhD); genetics (PhD); microbiology and molecular genetics (PhD); pathology (PhD), including experimental pathology. *Degree requirements:* For doctorate, thesis/dissertation. *Entrance requirements:* For doctorate, GRE General Test, GRE Subject Test. Additional exam requirements/recommendations for international students: Required—TOEFL.

Illinois State University, Graduate School, College of Arts and Sciences, School of Biological Sciences, Normal, IL 61790. Offers animal behavior (MS); bacteriology (MS); biochemistry (MS); biological sciences (MS); biology (PhD); biophysics (MS); biotechnology (MS); botany (MS, PhD); cell biology (MS); conservation biology (MS); developmental biology (MS); ecology (MS, PhD); entomology (MS); evolutionary biology (MS); genetics (MS, PhD); immunology (MS); microbiology (MS, PhD); molecular biology (MS); molecular genetics (MS); neurobiology (MS); neuroscience (MS); parasitology (MS); physiology (MS, PhD); plant biology (MS); plant molecular biology (MS); plant sciences (MS); structural biology (MS); zoology (MS, PhD). *Program availability:* Part-time. *Degree requirements:* For master's, thesis or alternative; for doctorate, variable foreign language requirement, thesis/dissertation, 2 terms of residency. *Entrance requirements:* For master's, GRE General Test, minimum GPA of 2.6 in last 60 hours of course work; for doctorate, GRE General Test. *Faculty research:* Redoc balance and drug development in schistosoma mansoni, control of the growth of listeria monocytogenes at low temperature, regulation of cell expansion and microtubule function by SPRI, CRUI: physiology and fitness consequences of different life history phenotypes.

Indiana University–Purdue University Indianapolis, Indiana University School of Medicine, Department of Medical and Molecular Genetics, Indianapolis, IN 46202. Offers genetic counseling (MS), medical and molecular genetics (MS, PhD); MD/MS; MD/PhD. *Program availability:* Part-time. Terminal master's awarded for partial completion of doctoral program. *Degree requirements:* For master's, thesis optional; for doctorate, thesis/dissertation, research ethics. *Entrance requirements:* For master's and doctorate, GRE General Test, minimum GPA of 3.0. Additional exam requirements/recommendations for international students: Required—TOEFL (minimum score 79 iBT), IELTS (minimum score 6.5). *Expenses:* Contact institution. *Faculty research:* Twins, human gene mapping, chromosomes and malignancy, clinical genetics.

Iowa State University of Science and Technology, Program in Animal Breeding and Genetics, Ames, IA 50011. Offers animal breeding and genetics (MS); immunogenetics (PhD); molecular genetics (PhD); quantitative genetics (PhD). *Entrance requirements:* For master's and doctorate, GRE. Additional exam requirements/recommendations for international students: Required—TOEFL (minimum score 550 paper-based; 80 iBT), IELTS (minimum score 6.5). Electronic applications accepted.

Michigan State University, College of Human Medicine and The Graduate School, Graduate Programs in Human Medicine, East Lansing, MI 48824. Offers biochemistry and molecular biology (MS, PhD); epidemiology (MS, PhD); microbiology (MS); microbiology and molecular genetics (PhD); pharmacology and toxicology (MS, PhD); physiology (MS, PhD); public health (MPH). *Entrance requirements:* Additional exam requirements/recommendations for international students: Required—TOEFL.

Michigan State University, College of Osteopathic Medicine and The Graduate School, Graduate Studies in Osteopathic Medicine, East Lansing, MI 48824. Offers biochemistry and molecular biology (MS, PhD); microbiology (MS); microbiology and molecular genetics (PhD); pharmacology and toxicology (MS, PhD), including integrative pharmacology (MS), pharmacology and toxicology, pharmacology and toxicology-environmental toxicology (PhD); physiology (MS, PhD).

New York University, Graduate School of Arts and Science, Department of Biology, New York, NY 10012-1019. Offers biology (PhD); biomedical journalism (MS); cancer and molecular biology (PhD); computational biology (PhD); computers in biological research (MS); developmental genetics (PhD); general biology (MS); immunology and microbiology (PhD); molecular genetics (PhD); neurobiology (PhD); oral biology (MS); plant biology (PhD); recombinant DNA technology (MS); MS/MBA. *Program availability:* Part-time. *Students:* Average age 27. 394 applicants, 56% accepted, 77 enrolled. In 2017, 68 master's, 9 doctorates awarded. Terminal master's awarded for partial completion of doctoral program. *Degree requirements:* For master's, thesis or alternative, qualifying paper; for doctorate, comprehensive exam, thesis/dissertation. *Entrance requirements:* For master's and doctorate, GRE General Test. Additional exam requirements/recommendations for international students: Required—TOEFL. *Application deadline:* For fall admission, 12/1 priority date for domestic students, 12/1 for international students. Application fee: $100. *Expenses: Tuition:* Full-time $41,352; part-time $19,968 per year. *Required fees:* $2496; $1628 per unit. $814 per term. Tuition and fees vary according to course load and program. *Financial support:* Fellowships, research assistantships, teaching assistantships, career-related internships or fieldwork, Federal Work-Study, institutionally sponsored loans, scholarships/grants, health care benefits, and unspecified assistantships available. Financial award application deadline: 12/1; financial award applicants required to submit FAFSA. *Faculty research:* Genomics, molecular and cell biology, development and molecular genetics, molecular evolution of plants and animals. *Unit head:* Stephen Small, Chair, 212-998-8200, Fax: 212-995-4015, E-mail: biology.admissions@nyu.edu. *Application contact:* Ken Birnbaum, Director of Graduate Studies, PhD Programs, 212-998-8200, Fax: 212-995-4015, E-mail: biology.admissions@nyu.edu.
Website: http://biology.as.nyu.edu/

Northern Michigan University, Office of Graduate Education and Research, College of Health Sciences and Professional Studies, School of Clinical Sciences, Marquette, MI 49855-5301. Offers clinical molecular genetics (MS). *Program availability:* Part-time. *Degree requirements:* For master's, thesis or project to be presented as a seminar at the conclusion of the program. *Entrance requirements:* For master's, minimum undergraduate GPA of 3.0; bachelor's degree in clinical laboratory science or biology; laboratory experience; statement of intent that includes lab skills and experiences along with reason for pursuing this degree; 3 letters of recommendation (instructors or professional references). Additional exam requirements/recommendations for international students: Required—TOEFL (minimum score 550 paper-based; 79 iBT), IELTS (minimum score 6.5). *Application deadline:* For fall admission, 7/1 for domestic students. Applications are processed on a rolling basis. Application fee: $50. Electronic applications accepted. *Expenses:* Tuition, state resident: full-time $9417; part-time $542 per credit hour. Tuition, nonresident: full-time $12,873; part-time $758 per credit hour. Tuition and fees vary according to course load, degree level and program. *Financial support:* Federal Work-Study, scholarships/grants, and unspecified assistantships available. Support available to part-time students. Financial award application deadline: 3/1; financial award applicants required to submit FAFSA. *Unit head:* Paul Mann, Associate Dean/Director, 906-227-2338, E-mail: pmann@nmu.edu. *Application contact:* Paul Mann, Associate Dean/Director, 906-227-2338, E-mail: pmann@nmu.edu.
Website: http://www.nmu.edu/clinicalsciences/

The Ohio State University, Graduate School, College of Arts and Sciences, Division of Natural and Mathematical Sciences, Department of Molecular Genetics, Columbus, OH 43210. Offers cell and developmental biology (MS, PhD); genetics (MS, PhD); molecular biology (MS, PhD). *Faculty:* 30. *Students:* 34 full-time (16 women), 13 international. Average age 26. In 2017, 6 doctorates awarded. *Entrance requirements:* For doctorate, GRE General Test, GRE Subject Test in biology or chemistry (recommended). Additional exam requirements/recommendations for international students: Required—TOEFL (minimum score 550 paper-based; 79 iBT), Michigan English Language Assessment Battery (minimum score 82); Recommended—IELTS (minimum score 7). *Application deadline:* For fall admission, 12/13 priority date for domestic students, 11/30 priority date for international students; for spring admission, 3/1 for domestic students, 2/1 for international students. Applications are processed on a rolling basis. Application fee: $60 ($70 for international students). Electronic applications accepted. *Financial support:* Fellowships, research assistantships, teaching assistantships, Federal Work-Study, and institutionally sponsored loans available. Support available to part-time students. *Unit head:* Dr. Mark Seeger, Chair, 614-292-5106, E-mail: seeger.9@osu.edu. *Application contact:* Graduate and Professional Admissions, 614-292-9444, Fax: 614-292-3895, E-mail: gpadmissions@osu.edu.
Website: https://molgen.osu.edu/

Oklahoma State University, College of Arts and Sciences, Department of Microbiology and Molecular Genetics, Stillwater, OK 74078. Offers MS, PhD. *Faculty:* 17 full-time (4 women). *Students:* 12 full-time (5 women), 19 part-time (11 women); includes 6 minority (2 Hispanic/Latino; 4 Two or more races, non-Hispanic/Latino), 15 international. Average age 29. 35 applicants, 37% accepted, 13 enrolled. In 2017, 4 master's, 1 doctorate awarded. *Entrance requirements:* For master's and doctorate, GRE General Test. Additional exam requirements/recommendations for international students: Required—TOEFL (minimum score 550 paper-based; 79 iBT). *Application deadline:* For fall admission, 3/1 priority date for international students; for spring admission, 8/1 priority date for international students. Applications are processed on a rolling basis. Application fee: $40 ($75 for international students). Electronic applications accepted. *Expenses:* Tuition, state resident: full-time $4019; part-time $2679.00 per year. Tuition, nonresident: full-time $15,286; part-time $10,190.40 per year. *Required fees:* $2129; $1419 per unit. Tuition and fees vary according to program. *Financial support:* Research assistantships, teaching assistantships, career-related internships or fieldwork, Federal Work-Study, scholarships/grants, health care benefits, tuition waivers (partial), and unspecified assistantships available. Support available to part-time students. Financial award application deadline: 3/1; financial award applicants required to submit FAFSA. *Faculty research:* Bioinformatics, genomics-genetics, virology, environmental microbiology, development-molecular mechanisms. *Unit head:* Dr. Tyrrell Conway, Professor and Department Head, 405-744-6243, Fax: 405-744-6790, E-mail: tconway@okstate.edu.
Website: http://microbiology.okstate.edu

Penn State Hershey Medical Center, College of Medicine, Graduate School Programs in the Biomedical Sciences, Graduate Program in Biomedical Sciences, Hershey, PA 17033. Offers biochemistry and molecular genetics (MS, PhD); biomedical sciences (MS, PhD); cellular and integrative physiology (MS, PhD); translational therapeutics (MS, PhD); virology and immunology (MS, PhD); MD/PhD; PhD/MBA. *Students:* 103 full-time (58 women); includes 25 minority (5 Black or African American, non-Hispanic/Latino; 12 Asian, non-Hispanic/Latino; 7 Hispanic/Latino; 1 Native Hawaiian or other Pacific Islander, non-Hispanic/Latino), 28 international. 250 applicants, 22% accepted, 19 enrolled. In 2017, 4 master's, 1 doctorate awarded. Terminal master's awarded for partial completion of doctoral program. *Degree requirements:* For master's, thesis; for doctorate, comprehensive exam, thesis/dissertation, candidacy exam. *Entrance requirements:* For doctorate, GRE General Test. Additional exam requirements/recommendations for international students: Required—TOEFL (minimum score 550 paper-based; 81 iBT). *Application deadline:* For fall admission, 1/1 for domestic and international students. Applications are processed on a rolling basis. Application fee: $65. Electronic applications accepted. *Financial support:* In 2017–18, 103 students received support, including research assistantships with full tuition reimbursements available (averaging $27,802 per year); fellowships, scholarships/grants, traineeships, health care benefits, and unspecified assistantships also available. *Unit head:* Dr. Ralph L. Keil, Chair, 717-531-8595, Fax: 717-531-0786, E-mail: rlk9@psu.edu. *Application contact:* Kristin E. Smith, Director of Graduate Admissions, 717-531-1045, Fax: 717-531-0786, E-mail: kec17@psu.edu.
Website: http://med.psu.edu/bms

Rutgers University–Newark, Graduate School of Biomedical Sciences, Department of Microbiology and Molecular Genetics, Newark, NJ 07107. Offers PhD. *Degree requirements:* For doctorate, thesis/dissertation, qualifying exam. *Entrance requirements:* For doctorate, GRE General Test. Additional exam requirements/recommendations for international students: Required—TOEFL. Electronic applications accepted. *Faculty research:* Molecular genetics of yeast, mutagenesis and carcinogenesis of DNA, bacterial protein synthesis, mammalian cell genetics, adenovirus gene expression.

Rutgers University–New Brunswick, Graduate School-New Brunswick, Programs in the Molecular Biosciences, Piscataway, NJ 08854-8097. Offers biochemistry (PhD); cell and developmental biology (MS, PhD); microbiology and molecular genetics (MS, PhD), including applied microbiology, clinical microbiology, computational molecular biology (PhD), immunology, microbial biochemistry, molecular genetics, virology. MS, PhD offered jointly with University of Medicine and Dentistry of New Jersey.

Rutgers University–New Brunswick, Graduate School of Biomedical Sciences, Program in Microbiology and Molecular Genetics, Piscataway, NJ 08854-5635. Offers MS, PhD, MD/PhD. Terminal master's awarded for partial completion of doctoral program. *Degree requirements:* For master's, thesis, qualifying exam; for doctorate, thesis/dissertation, qualifying exam. *Entrance requirements:* For master's and doctorate, GRE General Test. Additional exam requirements/recommendations for international students: Required—TOEFL. Electronic applications accepted. *Faculty research:* Interferon, receptors, retrovirus evolution, Arbo virus/host cell interactions.

Stony Brook University, State University of New York, Stony Brook Medicine, School of Medicine and Graduate School, Graduate Programs in Medicine, Department of Molecular Genetics and Microbiology, Stony Brook, NY 11794. Offers PhD. *Faculty:* 16 full-time (4 women), 3 part-time/adjunct (1 woman). *Students:* 23 full-time (6 women); includes 6 minority (2 Asian, non-Hispanic/Latino; 4 Hispanic/Latino), 4 international. Average age 26. 56 applicants, 25% accepted, 4 enrolled. In 2017, 2 doctorates awarded. *Degree requirements:* For doctorate, comprehensive exam, thesis/dissertation. *Entrance requirements:* For doctorate, GRE General Test, GRE Subject Test, undergraduate training in biochemistry, genetics, and cell biology;

recommendations; personal statement. Additional exam requirements/recommendations for international students: Required—TOEFL (minimum score 550 paper-based; 90 iBT). *Application deadline:* For fall admission, 1/15 for domestic students; for spring admission, 10/1 for domestic students. Application fee: $100. *Expenses:* Contact institution. *Financial support:* In 2017–18, 8 fellowships, 10 research assistantships were awarded; teaching assistantships and Federal Work-Study also available. Financial award application deadline: 3/15. *Faculty research:* Bioimaging, infectious diseases or agents, pathogenesis, viral studies (virology), genetics. *Total annual research expenditures:* $8.8 million. *Unit head:* Dr. David G. Thanassi, Interim Chair, 631-632-4549, Fax: 631-632-9797, E-mail: david.thanassi@stonybrook.edu. *Application contact:* Jennifer Jokinen, Program Coordinator, 631-632-8812, Fax: 631-632-9797, E-mail: jennifer.jokinen@stonybrook.edu.
Website: http://www.mgm.stonybrook.edu/index.shtml

University of Calgary, Cumming School of Medicine and Faculty of Graduate Studies, Medical Science Graduate Program, Calgary, AB T2N 1N4, Canada. Offers cancer biology (M Sc, PhD); critical care medicine (M Sc, PhD); joint injury and arthritis (M Sc, PhD); molecular and medical genetics (M Sc, PhD); mountain medicine and high altitude physiology (M Sc, PhD); pathologists' assistant (M Sc, PhD). *Degree requirements:* For master's, thesis; for doctorate, thesis/dissertation, candidacy exam. *Entrance requirements:* For master's, minimum undergraduate GPA of 3.2; for doctorate, minimum graduate GPA of 3.2. Additional exam requirements/recommendations for international students: Required—TOEFL (minimum score 600 paper-based). Electronic applications accepted. *Faculty research:* Cancer biology, immunology, joint injury and arthritis, medical education, population genomics.

University of California, Irvine, School of Medicine and Francisco J. Ayala School of Biological Sciences, Department of Microbiology and Molecular Genetics, Irvine, CA 92697. Offers biological sciences (MS, PhD); MD/PhD. *Students:* 15 full-time (8 women), 2 part-time (both women); includes 8 minority (1 Black or African American, non-Hispanic/Latino; 1 American Indian or Alaska Native, non-Hispanic/Latino; 3 Asian, non-Hispanic/Latino; 3 Hispanic/Latino). Average age 30. In 2017, 2 doctorates awarded. *Entrance requirements:* For doctorate, GRE General Test, GRE Subject Test, minimum GPA of 3.0. Additional exam requirements/recommendations for international students: Required—TOEFL (minimum score 550 paper-based). *Application deadline:* For fall admission, 12/15 priority date for domestic students, 12/15 for international students. Application fee: $105 ($125 for international students). Electronic applications accepted. *Financial support:* Fellowships, research assistantships with full tuition reimbursements, teaching assistantships, institutionally sponsored loans, traineeships, health care benefits, and unspecified assistantships available. Financial award applicants required to submit FAFSA. *Faculty research:* Molecular biology and genetics of viruses, bacteria, and yeast; immune response; molecular biology of cultured animal cells; genetic basis of cancer; genetics and physiology of infectious agents. *Unit head:* Rozanne M. Sandri-Goldin, Chair, 949-824-7570, Fax: 949-824-8598, E-mail: rmsandri@uci.edu. *Application contact:* Janet Horwitz, Graduate Student Coordinator, 949-824-7669, E-mail: horwitz@uci.edu.
Website: http://www.microbiology.uci.edu/graduate-students.asp

University of California, Los Angeles, David Geffen School of Medicine and Graduate Division, Graduate Programs in Medicine, Department of Microbiology, Immunology and Molecular Genetics, Los Angeles, CA 90095. Offers MS, PhD. *Degree requirements:* For master's, thesis; for doctorate, thesis/dissertation, oral and written qualifying exams; 2 quarters of teaching experience. *Entrance requirements:* For master's and doctorate, GRE General Test, bachelor's degree; minimum undergraduate GPA of 3.0 (or its equivalent if letter grade system not used). Additional exam requirements/recommendations for international students: Required—TOEFL. Electronic applications accepted.

University of Cincinnati, Graduate School, College of Medicine, Graduate Programs in Biomedical Sciences, Department of Molecular Genetics, Biochemistry and Microbiology, Cincinnati, OH 45221. Offers MS, PhD. Terminal master's awarded for partial completion of doctoral program. *Degree requirements:* For master's, thesis or alternative; for doctorate, thesis/dissertation, qualifying exam. *Entrance requirements:* For master's and doctorate, GRE General Test. Additional exam requirements/recommendations for international students: Required—TOEFL (minimum score 600 paper-based; 100 iBT), TWE. Electronic applications accepted. *Expenses: Tuition, area resident:* Full-time $14,468. Tuition, state resident: full-time $14,968; part-time $754 per credit hour. Tuition, nonresident: full-time $24,210; part-time $1311 per credit hour. *International tuition:* $26,460 full-time. *Required fees:* $3958; $84 per credit hour. One-time fee: $85 full-time. Tuition and fees vary according to course load, degree level and program. *Faculty research:* Cancer biology and developmental genetics, gene regulation and chromosome structure, microbiology and pathogenic mechanisms, structural biology, membrane biochemistry and signal transduction.

University of Colorado Denver, School of Medicine, Biochemistry Program, Aurora, CO 80045. Offers biochemistry (PhD); biochemistry and molecular genetics (PhD). *Students:* 20 applicants, 25% accepted, 4 enrolled. In 2017, 2 doctorates awarded. *Degree requirements:* For doctorate, comprehensive exam, thesis/dissertation, 30 credit hours each of coursework and thesis research. *Entrance requirements:* For doctorate, GRE, minimum of three letters of recommendation from qualified referees. Additional exam requirements/recommendations for international students: Required—TOEFL (minimum score 550 paper-based; 80 iBT). *Application deadline:* For fall admission, 12/1 for domestic students. Applications are processed on a rolling basis. Application fee: $50 ($75 for international students). Electronic applications accepted. *Faculty research:* DNA damage, cancer and neurodegeneration, molecular mechanisms of pro-MRNA splicing, yeast RNA polymerases, DNA replication. *Unit head:* Dr. Mark Johnston, Professor and Chair, 303-724-3203, Fax: 303-724-3215, E-mail: mark.johnston@ucdenver.edu. *Application contact:* Sue Brozowski, Department Contact, 303-724-3202, Fax: 303-724-3215, E-mail: sue.brozowski@ucdenver.edu.
Website: http://www.ucdenver.edu/academics/colleges/medicalschool/departments/biochemistry/Pages/Home.aspx

University of Florida, College of Medicine, Department of Molecular Genetics and Microbiology, Gainesville, FL 32610-0266. Offers MS. Terminal master's awarded for partial completion of doctoral program. *Degree requirements:* For master's, thesis. *Entrance requirements:* For master's, GRE General Test, minimum GPA of 3.0. Additional exam requirements/recommendations for international students: Required—TOEFL, IELTS. Electronic applications accepted.

University of Guelph, Graduate Studies, College of Biological Science, Department of Molecular and Cellular Biology, Guelph, ON N1G 2W1, Canada. Offers biochemistry (M Sc, PhD); biophysics (M Sc, PhD); botany (M Sc, PhD); microbiology (M Sc, PhD); molecular biology and genetics (M Sc, PhD). *Degree requirements:* For master's, thesis, research proposal; for doctorate, comprehensive exam, thesis/dissertation, research proposal. *Entrance requirements:* For master's, minimum B-average during previous 2 years of coursework; for doctorate, minimum A-average. Additional exam requirements/recommendations for international students: Required—TOEFL (minimum score 550 paper-based), IELTS (minimum score 6.5). Electronic applications accepted. *Faculty research:* Physiology, structure, genetics, and ecology of microbes; virology and microbial technology.

University of Illinois at Chicago, College of Medicine and Graduate College, Graduate Programs in Medicine, Department of Biochemistry and Molecular Genetics, Chicago, IL 60607-7128. Offers PhD, MD/PhD. Terminal master's awarded for partial completion of doctoral program. *Degree requirements:* For doctorate, thesis/dissertation. *Entrance requirements:* For doctorate, GRE General Test. Additional exam requirements/recommendations for international students: Required—TOEFL. Electronic applications accepted. *Faculty research:* Signal transduction, cell cycle regulation, membrane biology, regulation of gene function and development, protein and nucleic acid structure and function, cancer biology.

University of Louisville, School of Medicine, Department of Biochemistry and Molecular Genetics, Louisville, KY 40292-0001. Offers MS, PhD, MD/PhD. *Faculty:* 12 full-time (3 women), 2 part-time/adjunct (1 woman). *Students:* 21 full-time (11 women), 5 part-time (2 women); includes 2 minority (1 Asian, non-Hispanic/Latino; 1 Hispanic/Latino), 5 international. Average age 28. 27 applicants, 26% accepted, 7 enrolled. In 2017, 1 master's, 1 doctorate awarded. Terminal master's awarded for partial completion of doctoral program. *Degree requirements:* For master's, thesis (for some programs); for doctorate, comprehensive exam, thesis/dissertation. *Entrance requirements:* For master's and doctorate, GRE General Test (minimum score of 1000 verbal and quantitative), minimum GPA of 3.0. Additional exam requirements/recommendations for international students: Required—TOEFL, IELTS. *Application deadline:* For fall admission, 12/15 priority date for domestic and international students. Applications are processed on a rolling basis. Application fee: $65. Electronic applications accepted. *Expenses:* Tuition, state resident: full-time $12,246; part-time $681 per credit hour. Tuition, nonresident: full-time $25,486; part-time $1417 per credit hour. *Required fees:* $196. Tuition and fees vary according to course load, program and reciprocity agreements. *Financial support:* In 2017–18, 5 fellowships with full tuition reimbursements (averaging $25,000 per year) were awarded; health care benefits also available. Financial award application deadline: 1/15. *Faculty research:* Genetics, metabolism in cancer biology and diabetes, lipid molecular signaling, protein trafficking, bioinformatics. *Total annual research expenditures:* $2.1 million. *Unit head:* Dr. Ronald Gregg, Professor and Department Chair, 502-852-5217, Fax: 502-852-4112, E-mail: rggreg02@louisville.edu. *Application contact:* Dr. Brian Clem, Assistant Professor, E-mail: bmggrad@louisville.edu.

The University of Manchester, School of Biological Sciences, Manchester, United Kingdom. Offers adaptive organismal biology (M Phil, PhD); animal biology (M Phil, PhD); biochemistry (M Phil, PhD); bioinformatics (M Phil, PhD); biomolecular sciences (M Phil, PhD); biotechnology (M Phil, PhD); cell biology (M Phil, PhD); cell matrix research (M Phil, PhD); channels and transporters (M Phil, PhD); developmental biology (M Phil, PhD); environmental biology (M Phil, PhD); evolutionary biology (M Phil, PhD); gene expression (M Phil, PhD); genetics (M Phil, PhD); history of science, technology and medicine (M Phil, PhD); immunology (M Phil, PhD); integrative neurobiology and behavior (M Phil, PhD); membrane trafficking (M Phil, PhD); microbiology (M Phil, PhD); molecular and cellular neuroscience (M Phil, PhD); molecular biology (M Phil, PhD); molecular cancer studies (M Phil, PhD); neuroscience (M Phil, PhD); ophthalmology (M Phil, PhD); optometry (M Phil, PhD); organelle function (M Phil, PhD); pharmacology (M Phil, PhD); physiology (M Phil, PhD); plant sciences (M Phil, PhD); stem cell research (M Phil, PhD); structural biology (M Phil, PhD); systems neuroscience (M Phil, PhD); toxicology (M Phil, PhD).

University of Maryland, College Park, Academic Affairs, College of Computer, Mathematical and Natural Sciences, Department of Cell Biology and Molecular Genetics, Program in Cell Biology and Molecular Genetics, College Park, MD 20742. Offers MS, PhD. *Degree requirements:* For master's, thesis; for doctorate, thesis/dissertation, exams. *Faculty research:* Cytoskeletal activity, membrane biology, cell division, genetics and genomics, virology.

University of Nebraska Medical Center, Interdisciplinary Graduate Program in Biomedical Sciences, Department of Genetics, Cell Biology and Anatomy, Omaha, NE 68198-5805. Offers genetics, cell biology and anatomy (PhD); medical anatomy (MS); molecular genetics and cell biology (MS). Terminal master's awarded for partial completion of doctoral program. *Degree requirements:* For master's, comprehensive exam, thesis (for some programs); for doctorate, comprehensive exam, thesis/dissertation. *Entrance requirements:* For master's, GRE General Test (MCAT or DAT acceptable for MS in medical anatomy); for doctorate, GRE General Test. Additional exam requirements/recommendations for international students: Required—TOEFL (minimum score 550 paper-based; 80 iBT). Electronic applications accepted. *Expenses:* Contact institution. *Faculty research:* Hematology, immunology, developmental biology, genetics cancer biology, neuroscience.

University of Pittsburgh, School of Medicine, Graduate Programs in Medicine, Molecular Genetics and Developmental Biology Graduate Program, Pittsburgh, PA 15260. Offers PhD. *Faculty:* 54 full-time (15 women). *Students:* 12 full-time (9 women); includes 2 minority (1 Black or African American, non-Hispanic/Latino; 1 Two or more races, non-Hispanic/Latino), 3 international. Average age 28. 350 applicants, 21% accepted, 12 enrolled. In 2017, 1 doctorate awarded. *Degree requirements:* For doctorate, comprehensive exam, thesis/dissertation. *Entrance requirements:* For doctorate, GRE General Test, minimum GPA of 3.2, 3 letters of recommendation, official transcripts, baccalaureate degree. Additional exam requirements/recommendations for international students: Required—TOEFL (minimum score 600 paper-based; 100 iBT), IELTS (minimum score 7). *Application deadline:* For fall admission, 12/1 priority date for domestic and international students. Application fee: $50. Electronic applications accepted. *Financial support:* In 2017–18, 8 students received support, including 2 fellowships with full tuition reimbursements available (averaging $29,500 per year), 2 research assistantships with full tuition reimbursements available (averaging $29,500 per year); teaching assistantships, traineeships, and tuition waivers also available. *Faculty research:* Developmental biology, regenerative medicine, molecular genetics, stem cell biology, reproductive biology. *Unit head:* Dr. Michael Tsang, Director, 412-648-3248, E-mail: tsang@pitt.edu. *Application contact:* Carol Williams, Admissions and Recruiting Manager, 412-648-8957, Fax: 412-648-1077, E-mail: gradstudies@medschool.pitt.edu.
Website: http://www.gradbiomed.pitt.edu/

University of Rhode Island, Graduate School, College of the Environment and Life Sciences, Department of Cell and Molecular Biology, Kingston, RI 02881. Offers biochemistry (MS, PhD); clinical laboratory sciences (MS), including biotechnology, clinical laboratory science, cytopathology; microbiology (MS, PhD); molecular genetics (MS, PhD). *Program availability:* Part-time. *Faculty:* 14 full-time (6 women). *Students:* 17 full-time (9 women), 19 part-time (15 women); includes 9 minority (2 Black or African American, non-Hispanic/Latino; 4 Asian, non-Hispanic/Latino; 2 Hispanic/Latino; 1 Two or more races, non-Hispanic/Latino), 10 international. 26 applicants, 62% accepted, 6 enrolled. In 2017, 17 master's awarded. *Entrance requirements:* Additional exam requirements/recommendations for international students: Required—TOEFL. *Application deadline:* For fall admission, 1/15 for domestic and international students. Application fee: $65. Electronic applications accepted. *Expenses:* Tuition, state resident: full-time $12,706; part-time $786 per credit. Tuition, nonresident: full-time $25,216; part-time $1401 per credit. *Required fees:* $1598; $45 per credit. One-time fee: $30 part-time. *Financial support:* In 2017–18, 4 teaching assistantships with tuition

reimbursements (averaging $12,698 per year) were awarded; traineeships also available. Financial award application deadline: 1/15; financial award applicants required to submit FAFSA. *Unit head:* Dr. Gongqing Sun, Chair and Professor, 401-874-5937, Fax: 401-874-2202, E-mail: gsun@mail.uri.edu. *Application contact:* Bethany Jenkins, Professor, 401-874-7551, E-mail: bjenkins@uri.edu.
Website: https://web.uri.edu/cmb/

University of Toronto, Faculty of Medicine, Department of Molecular Genetics, Toronto, ON M5S 1A1, Canada. Offers genetic counseling (M Sc); molecular genetics (M Sc, PhD). *Degree requirements:* For master's, thesis; for doctorate, thesis/dissertation. *Entrance requirements:* For master's, B Sc or equivalent; for doctorate, M Sc or equivalent, minimum B+ average. Additional exam requirements/recommendations for international students: Required—TOEFL, IELTS (minimum score 7), Michigan English Language Assessment Battery (minimum score 85), or COPE (minimum score 4). Electronic applications accepted. *Faculty research:* Structural biology, developmental genetics, molecular medicine, genetic counseling.

University of Virginia, School of Medicine, Department of Biochemistry and Molecular Genetics, Charlottesville, VA 22903. Offers biochemistry (PhD); MD/PhD. *Faculty:* 20 full-time (2 women), 1 part-time/adjunct (0 women). *Students:* 30 full-time (15 women); includes 5 minority (2 Asian, non-Hispanic/Latino; 1 Hispanic/Latino; 2 Two or more races, non-Hispanic/Latino), 5 international. Average age 27. In 2017, 5 doctorates awarded. *Degree requirements:* For doctorate, thesis/dissertation, written research proposal and defense. *Entrance requirements:* For doctorate, GRE General Test, 3 letters of recommendation. Additional exam requirements/recommendations for international students: Recommended—TOEFL (minimum score 630 paper-based; 90 iBT). Application fee: $60. Electronic applications accepted. *Financial support:* Fellowships, health care benefits, and tuition waivers (full) available. Financial award applicants required to submit FAFSA. *Unit head:* Anindya Dutta, Chair, 434-924-1940, Fax: 434-924-5069, E-mail: ad8q@virginia.edu. *Application contact:* Biomedical Sciences Graduate Studies, E-mail: bims@virginia.edu.
Website: http://www.virginia.edu/bmg/

Van Andel Institute Graduate School, PhD Program, Grand Rapids, MI 49503. Offers cell and molecular genetics (PhD). *Faculty:* 37 full-time (10 women). *Students:* 27 full-time (19 women); includes 6 minority (1 Black or African American, non-Hispanic/Latino; 4 Asian, non-Hispanic/Latino; 1 Hispanic/Latino). Average age 24. *Degree requirements:* For doctorate, comprehensive exam, thesis/dissertation. *Entrance requirements:* For doctorate, GRE, personal statement, 3 letters of recommendation, official transcripts from all institutions attended, sample of scientific writing (research paper). Additional exam requirements/recommendations for international students: Required—TOEFL. *Application deadline:* For fall admission, 12/1 for domestic and international students. Applications are processed on a rolling basis. Electronic applications accepted. *Expenses:* Contact institution. *Financial support:* Fellowships and health care benefits available. *Faculty research:* Epigenetics, neurodegenerative science, cancer and cell biology. *Unit head:* Steve Triezenberg, President and Dean, 616-234-5708, Fax: 616-234-5709, E-mail: steve.triezenberg@vai.org. *Application contact:* Christy Mayo, Enrollment and Records Administrator, 616-234-5722, Fax: 616-234-5709, E-mail: christy.mayo@vai.org.

Virginia Commonwealth University, Medical College of Virginia-Professional Programs, School of Medicine, Graduate Programs in Medicine, Department of Physiology and Biophysics, Richmond, VA 23284-9005. Offers molecular biology and genetics (MS); physical therapy (PhD); physiology (MS, PhD); MD/PhD. Terminal master's awarded for partial completion of doctoral program. *Degree requirements:* For master's, thesis; for doctorate, thesis/dissertation, comprehensive oral and written exams. *Entrance requirements:* For master's, GRE General Test, MCAT, or DAT; for doctorate, GRE, MCAT or DAT. Additional exam requirements/recommendations for international students: Required—TOEFL (minimum score 600 paper-based; 100 iBT). Electronic applications accepted.

Wake Forest University, School of Medicine and Graduate School of Arts and Sciences, Graduate Programs in Medicine, Molecular Genetics and Genomics Program, Winston-Salem, NC 27109. Offers PhD, MD/PhD. *Degree requirements:* For doctorate, thesis/dissertation. *Entrance requirements:* For doctorate, GRE General Test. Additional exam requirements/recommendations for international students: Required—TOEFL. Electronic applications accepted. *Faculty research:* Control of gene expression, molecular pathogenesis, protein biosynthesis, cell development, clinical cytogenetics.

Washington University in St. Louis, The Graduate School, Division of Biology and Biomedical Sciences, Program in Molecular Genetics and Genomics, St. Louis, MO 63130-4899. Offers PhD. *Degree requirements:* For doctorate, thesis/dissertation. *Entrance requirements:* For doctorate, GRE General Test, GRE Subject Test. Additional exam requirements/recommendations for international students: Required—TOEFL. Electronic applications accepted. *Faculty research:* Genetics, genetic basis of disease, genomics, epigenetics, genetic engineering, genome editing, model organism genetics, development, cell biology, molecular biology, complex traits, bioinformatics, systems biology.

Wayne State University, School of Medicine, Office of Biomedical Graduate Programs, Detroit, MI 48202. Offers anatomy and cell biology (MS, PhD); basic medical sciences (MS); biochemistry and molecular biology (MS, PhD); cancer biology (MS, PhD); clinical and translational science (Graduate Certificate); family medicine and public health sciences (MPH, Graduate Certificate), including public health practice; genetic counseling (MS); immunology and microbiology (MS, PhD); medical physics (MS, PhD, Graduate Certificate); medical research (MS); molecular medicine and genomics (MS, PhD), including molecular genetics and genomics; pathology (PhD); pharmacology (MS, PhD); physiology (MS, PhD), including physiology, reproductive sciences (PhD); psychiatry and behavioral neurosciences (PhD), including translational neuroscience; MD/MPH; MD/PhD; MPH/MA; MSW/MPH. *Program availability:* Part-time, evening/weekend. *Students:* 268 full-time (152 women), 117 part-time (59 women); includes 108 minority (19 Black or African American, non-Hispanic/Latino; 1 American Indian or Alaska Native, non-Hispanic/Latino; 62 Asian, non-Hispanic/Latino; 9 Hispanic/Latino; 17 Two or more races, non-Hispanic/Latino), 48 international. Average age 26. 1,133 applicants, 21% accepted, 151 enrolled. In 2017, 70 master's, 25 doctorates, 10 other advanced degrees awarded. Terminal master's awarded for partial completion of doctoral program. *Degree requirements:* For master's, thesis (for some programs); for doctorate, thesis/dissertation. *Entrance requirements:* For master's, doctorate, and Graduate Certificate, GRE. Additional exam requirements/recommendations for international students: Required—TOEFL (minimum score 550 paper-based; 100 iBT), Michigan English Language Assessment Battery (minimum score 85); Recommended—IELTS (minimum score 6.5), TWE (minimum score 5.5). *Application deadline:* For fall admission, 2/1 for domestic and international students. Applications are processed on a rolling basis. Application fee: $50. Electronic applications accepted. *Expenses:* Contact institution. *Financial support:* In 2017–18, 177 students received support, including 64 fellowships with full tuition reimbursements available (averaging $24,388 per year), 79 research assistantships with full tuition reimbursements available (averaging $26,894 per year); scholarships/grants, traineeships, and health care benefits also available. *Faculty research:* Cancer biology, neurosciences, vision sciences, molecular biology, pathology, physiology, pharmacology, public health, medical physics. *Unit head:* Dr. Daniel A. Walz, Associate Dean for Biomedical Graduate Programs, 313-577-1455, Fax: 313-577-8796, E-mail: gradprogs@med.wayne.edu.
Website: https://www.med.wayne.edu/biomedical-graduate-programs/

Reproductive Biology

Eastern Virginia Medical School, Master's Program in Clinical Embryology and Andrology, Norfolk, VA 23501-1980. Offers MS. *Program availability:* Online learning. *Entrance requirements:* Additional exam requirements/recommendations for international students: Required—TOEFL (minimum score 550 paper-based; 80 iBT). Electronic applications accepted. *Expenses:* Contact institution.

Queen's University at Kingston, School of Graduate Studies, Faculty of Health Sciences, Department of Anatomy and Cell Biology, Kingston, ON K7L 3N6, Canada. Offers biology of reproduction (M Sc, PhD); cancer (M Sc, PhD); cardiovascular pathophysiology (M Sc, PhD); cell and molecular biology (M Sc, PhD); drug metabolism (M Sc, PhD); endocrinology (M Sc, PhD); motor control (M Sc, PhD); neural regeneration (M Sc, PhD); neurophysiology (M Sc, PhD). *Program availability:* Part-time. *Degree requirements:* For master's, thesis; for doctorate, one foreign language, comprehensive exam, thesis/dissertation. *Entrance requirements:* Additional exam requirements/recommendations for international students: Required—TOEFL. Electronic applications accepted. *Faculty research:* Human kinetics, neuroscience, reproductive biology, cardiovascular.

Rutgers University–New Brunswick, Graduate School-New Brunswick, Program in Endocrinology and Animal Biosciences, Piscataway, NJ 08854-8097. Offers MS, PhD. Terminal master's awarded for partial completion of doctoral program. *Degree requirements:* For master's, thesis; for doctorate, comprehensive exam, thesis/dissertation. *Entrance requirements:* For master's and doctorate, GRE General Test. Additional exam requirements/recommendations for international students: Required—TOEFL. Electronic applications accepted. *Faculty research:* Comparative and behavioral endocrinology, epigenetic regulation of the endocrine system, exercise physiology and immunology, fetal and neonatal developmental programming, mammary gland biology and breast cancer, neuroendocrinology and alcohol studies, reproductive and developmental toxicology.

Tufts University, Cummings School of Veterinary Medicine, North Grafton, MA 01536. Offers animals and public policy (MS); biomedical sciences (PhD), including digestive diseases, infectious diseases, neuroscience and reproductive biology, pathology; conservation medicine (MS); veterinary medicine (DVM); DVM/MPH; DVM/MS. *Accreditation:* AVMA (one or more programs are accredited). *Degree requirements:* For master's, thesis (for some programs); for doctorate, comprehensive exam, thesis/dissertation (for some programs). *Entrance requirements:* For master's and doctorate, GRE General Test. Additional exam requirements/recommendations for international students: Required—TOEFL or IELTS. Electronic applications accepted. *Expenses:* Contact institution. *Faculty research:* Oncology, veterinary ethics, international veterinary medicine, veterinary genomics, pathogenesis of Clostridium difficile, wildlife fertility control.

The University of British Columbia, Faculty of Medicine, Department of Obstetrics and Gynecology, Program in Reproductive and Developmental Sciences, Vancouver, BC V6H 3N1, Canada. Offers M Sc, PhD. *Program availability:* Part-time. Terminal master's awarded for partial completion of doctoral program. *Degree requirements:* For master's, thesis; for doctorate, thesis/dissertation. *Entrance requirements:* For master's, B Sc or equivalent, MD, DVM, DDS; for doctorate, B Sc with first class honors, M Sc, MD, DVM, DDS. Additional exam requirements/recommendations for international students: Required—TOEFL, IELTS. Electronic applications accepted. *Expenses:* Contact institution. *Faculty research:* Reproductive and placental endocrinology; immunology of reproductive, fertilization, and embryonic development; perinatal metabolism; neonatal development.

University of Hawaii at Manoa, John A. Burns School of Medicine, Program in Developmental and Reproductive Biology, Honolulu, HI 96813. Offers MS, PhD. *Program availability:* Part-time. *Degree requirements:* For doctorate, thesis/dissertation. *Entrance requirements:* For doctorate, GRE General Test, GRE Subject Test. Additional exam requirements/recommendations for international students: Recommended—TOEFL (minimum score 560 paper-based), IELTS (minimum score 5). *Faculty research:* Biology of gametes and fertilization, reproductive endocrinology.

University of Saskatchewan, College of Medicine, Department of Obstetrics, Gynecology and Reproductive Services, Saskatoon, SK S7N 5A2, Canada. Offers M Sc, PhD. *Degree requirements:* For master's, thesis; for doctorate, thesis/dissertation. *Entrance requirements:* Additional exam requirements/recommendations for international students: Required—TOEFL.

University of Wyoming, College of Agriculture and Natural Resources, Department of Animal Sciences, Program in Reproductive Biology, Laramie, WY 82071. Offers MS, PhD. *Degree requirements:* For master's, thesis; for doctorate, thesis/dissertation. *Entrance requirements:* For master's, GRE General Test, minimum GPA of 3.0; for doctorate, GRE General Test, minimum GPA of 3.0 or MS degree. Additional exam requirements/recommendations for international students: Required—TOEFL. *Faculty research:* Fetal programming, chemical suppression, ovaria function, genetics.

Section 11
Marine Biology

This section contains a directory of institutions offering graduate work in marine biology. Additional information about programs listed in the directory may be obtained by writing directly to the dean of a graduate school or chair of a department at the address given in the directory.

For programs offering related work, see also in this book *Biological and Biomedical Sciences* and *Zoology.* In another guide in this series:

Graduate Programs in the Physical Sciences, Mathematics, Agricultural Sciences, the Environment & Natural Resources

See *Marine Sciences and Oceanography*

CONTENTS

Program Directory

Marine Biology

College of Charleston, Graduate School, School of Sciences and Mathematics, Program in Marine Biology, Charleston, SC 29412. Offers MS. *Degree requirements:* For master's, comprehensive exam, thesis. *Entrance requirements:* For master's, GRE General Test, 3 letters of recommendation. Additional exam requirements/recommendations for international students: Required—TOEFL (minimum score 81 iBT). Electronic applications accepted. *Faculty research:* Ecology, environmental physiology, marine genomics, bioinformatics, toxicology, cell biology, population biology, fisheries science, animal physiology, biodiversity, estuarine ecology, evolution and systematics, microbial processes, plant physiology, immunology.

Florida Institute of Technology, College of Science, Program in Biological Sciences, Melbourne, FL 32901-6975. Offers biological science (PhD); biotechnology (MS); cell and molecular biology (MS); ecology (MS); marine biology (MS). *Program availability:* Part-time. *Students:* Average age 26. 230 applicants, 24% accepted, 21 enrolled. In 2017, 27 master's, 3 doctorates awarded. *Degree requirements:* For master's, thesis (for some programs), research, seminar, internship, or summer lab; for doctorate, comprehensive exam, thesis/dissertation, dissertations seminar, publications. *Entrance requirements:* For master's, GRE General Test, 3 letters of recommendation; statement of objectives; bachelor's degree in biology, chemistry, biochemistry or equivalent; for doctorate, GRE General Test, resume, 3 letters of recommendation, minimum GPA of 3.2, statement of objectives. Additional exam requirements/recommendations for international students: Required—TOEFL (minimum score 550 paper-based; 79 iBT). *Application deadline:* For fall admission, 3/1 for domestic students, 4/1 for international students; for spring admission, 9/1 for domestic and international students. Applications are processed on a rolling basis. Electronic applications accepted. *Expenses: Tuition:* Part-time $1241 per credit hour. Part-time tuition and fees vary according to campus/location. *Financial support:* Career-related internships or fieldwork, institutionally sponsored loans, tuition waivers (partial), unspecified assistantships, and tuition remissions available. Support available to part-time students. Financial award application deadline: 3/1; financial award applicants required to submit FAFSA. *Faculty research:* Initiation of protein synthesis in eukaryotic cells, fixation of radioactive carbon, changes in DNA molecule, endangered or threatened avian and mammalian species, hydro acoustics and feeding preference of the West Indian manatee. *Unit head:* Dr. Richard B. Aronson, Department Head, 321-674-8034, Fax: 321-674-7238, E-mail: raronson@fit.edu. *Application contact:* Cheryl A. Brown, Associate Director of Graduate Admissions, 321-674-7581, Fax: 321-723-9468, E-mail: cbrown@fit.edu.
Website: http://cos.fit.edu/biology/

Montclair State University, The Graduate School, College of Science and Mathematics, Program in Marine Biology and Coastal Sciences, Montclair, NJ 07043-1624. Offers MS. *Degree requirements:* For master's, thesis.

Nicholls State University, Graduate Studies, College of Arts and Sciences, Department of Biological Sciences, Thibodaux, LA 70310. Offers marine and environmental biology (MS). *Program availability:* Part-time. *Degree requirements:* For master's, comprehensive exam, thesis. *Entrance requirements:* For master's, GRE. Additional exam requirements/recommendations for international students: Required—TOEFL (minimum score 600 paper-based). *Faculty research:* Bioremediation, ecology, public health, biotechnology, physiology.

Northeastern University, College of Science, Boston, MA 02115-5096. Offers applied mathematics (MS); bioinformatics (MS); biology (PhD); biotechnology (MS); chemistry and chemical biology (MS, PhD); environmental science and policy (MS); marine and environmental sciences (PhD); marine biology (MS); mathematics (MS, PhD); operations research (MSOR); physics (MS, PhD); psychology (PhD). *Program availability:* Part-time. Terminal master's awarded for partial completion of doctoral program. *Degree requirements:* For master's, comprehensive exam (for some programs), thesis; for doctorate, comprehensive exam (for some programs), thesis/dissertation. *Entrance requirements:* For master's, GRE General Test. *Application deadline:* Applications are processed on a rolling basis. Application fee: $75. Electronic applications accepted. *Expenses:* Contact institution. *Financial support:* Fellowships with tuition reimbursements, research assistantships with tuition reimbursements, teaching assistantships with tuition reimbursements, career-related internships or fieldwork, scholarships/grants, health care benefits, tuition waivers (full and partial), and unspecified assistantships available. Support available to part-time students. Financial award applicants required to submit FAFSA. *Unit head:* Dr. Kenneth Henderson, Dean, 617-373-5089, E-mail: k.henderson@northeastern.edu. *Application contact:* Graduate Student Services, 617-373-4275, E-mail: gradcos@northeastern.edu.
Website: https://cos.northeastern.edu/

Nova Southeastern University, Halmos College of Natural Sciences and Oceanography, Fort Lauderdale, FL 33314-7796. Offers biological sciences (MS), including health studies; marine biology and oceanography (PhD), including marine biology, oceanography. *Program availability:* Part-time, evening/weekend, blended/hybrid learning. *Faculty:* 17 full-time (3 women), 22 part-time/adjunct (11 women). *Students:* 29 full-time (18 women), 149 part-time (93 women); includes 29 minority (5 Black or African American, non-Hispanic/Latino; 6 Asian, non-Hispanic/Latino; 12 Hispanic/Latino; 6 Two or more races, non-Hispanic/Latino), 5 international. Average age 30. 78 applicants, 73% accepted, 34 enrolled. In 2017, 46 master's, 1 doctorate awarded. *Degree requirements:* For master's, thesis; for doctorate, comprehensive exam, thesis/dissertation, departmental qualifying exam. *Entrance requirements:* For master's, GRE General Test, 3 letters of recommendation; BS/BA in natural science (for marine biology program); BS/BA in biology (for biological sciences program); minor in the natural sciences or equivalent (for coastal zone management and marine environmental sciences); for doctorate, GRE General Test, master's degree. Additional exam requirements/recommendations for international students: Required—TOEFL (minimum score 550 paper-based); Recommended—IELTS. *Application deadline:* Applications are processed on a rolling basis. Application fee: $50. Electronic applications accepted. *Expenses:* Contact institution. *Financial support:* In 2017–18, 101 students received support, including 6 fellowships with full and partial tuition reimbursements available (averaging $25,000 per year), 40 research assistantships with full and partial tuition reimbursements available (averaging $20,000 per year), 8 teaching assistantships with tuition reimbursements available (averaging $15,000 per year); career-related internships or fieldwork, Federal Work-Study, scholarships/grants, health care benefits, tuition waivers (full and partial), and unspecified assistantships also available. Support available to part-time students. Financial award application deadline: 4/15; financial award applicants required to submit FAFSA. *Faculty research:* Physical and biological oceanography, molecular and microbiology, ecology and evolution, coral reefs, marine ecosystems. *Total annual research expenditures:* $5 million. *Unit head:* Dr. Richard Dodge, Dean, 954-262-3600, Fax: 954-262-4020, E-mail: dodge@nsu.nova.edu. *Application contact:* Dr. Bernhard Riegl, Chair, Department of Marine and Environmental Sciences, 954-262-3600, Fax: 954-262-4020, E-mail: rieglb@nova.edu.
Website: http://cnso.nova.edu

Princeton University, Graduate School, Department of Geosciences, Princeton, NJ 08544-1019. Offers atmospheric and oceanic sciences (PhD); geosciences (PhD); ocean sciences and marine biology (PhD). *Degree requirements:* For doctorate, one foreign language, thesis/dissertation. *Entrance requirements:* For doctorate, GRE General Test. Additional exam requirements/recommendations for international students: Required—TOEFL (minimum score 600 paper-based). Electronic applications accepted. *Faculty research:* Biogeochemistry, climate science, earth history, regional geology and tectonics, solid–earth geophysics.

Rutgers University–New Brunswick, Graduate School-New Brunswick, Department of Environmental Sciences, Piscataway, NJ 08854-8097. Offers air pollution and resources (MS, PhD); aquatic biology (MS, PhD); aquatic chemistry (MS, PhD); atmospheric science (MS, PhD); chemistry and physics of aerosol and hydrosol systems (MS, PhD); environmental chemistry (MS, PhD); environmental microbiology (MS, PhD); environmental toxicology (PhD); exposure assessment (PhD); fate and effects of pollutants (MS, PhD); pollution prevention and control (MS, PhD); water and wastewater treatment (MS, PhD); water resources (MS, PhD). Terminal master's awarded for partial completion of doctoral program. *Degree requirements:* For master's, comprehensive exam, thesis or alternative, oral final exam; for doctorate, comprehensive exam, thesis/dissertation, thesis defense, qualifying exam. *Entrance requirements:* For master's and doctorate, GRE General Test. Additional exam requirements/recommendations for international students: Required—TOEFL. Electronic applications accepted. *Faculty research:* Biological waste treatment; contaminant fate and transport; air, soil and water quality.

San Francisco State University, Division of Graduate Studies, College of Science and Engineering, Department of Biology, Program in Marine Biology, San Francisco, CA 94132-1722. Offers MS. *Unit head:* Dr. Karen Crow, Program Coordinator, 415-405-2760, Fax: 415-338-2295, E-mail: crow@sfsu.edu. *Application contact:* Dr. Jonathon Stillman, Graduate Advisor, 415-338-3790, Fax: 415-338-2295, E-mail: stillmaj@sfsu.edu.
Website: http://biology.sfsu.edu/graduate/marine_biology

Texas A&M University, Galveston Campus, Department of Marine Biology, College Station, TX 77843. Offers MS, PhD. *Faculty:* 18. *Students:* 55 full-time (33 women), 5 part-time (3 women); includes 9 minority (2 Black or African American, non-Hispanic/Latino; 1 Asian, non-Hispanic/Latino; 5 Hispanic/Latino; 1 Two or more races, non-Hispanic/Latino), 7 international. Average age 29. 33 applicants, 73% accepted, 15 enrolled. In 2017, 8 master's, 1 doctorate awarded. Terminal master's awarded for partial completion of doctoral program. *Degree requirements:* For master's, comprehensive exam (for some programs), thesis (for some programs); for doctorate, comprehensive exam, thesis/dissertation. *Entrance requirements:* For master's and doctorate, GRE. Additional exam requirements/recommendations for international students: Required—TOEFL (minimum score 550 paper-based; 80 iBT), IELTS (minimum score 6). *Application deadline:* For fall admission, 5/1 for domestic and international students; for spring admission, 10/1 for domestic and international students. Application fee: $50. Electronic applications accepted. *Expenses:* Contact institution. *Financial support:* In 2017–18, 56 students received support, including 1 fellowship (averaging $51,000 per year), 27 research assistantships (averaging $8,939 per year), 39 teaching assistantships (averaging $10,675 per year); scholarships/grants, health care benefits, and unspecified assistantships also available. Financial award application deadline: 3/1; financial award applicants required to submit FAFSA. *Faculty research:* Fisheries, coastal and wetland ecologies, phytoplankton, marine mammals, seafood safety, marine invertebrates and marine biospeleology. *Unit head:* Dr. John Schwarz, Professor/Chair of Marine Biology Interdisciplinary Program, 409-740-4428, E-mail: schwarzj@tamug.edu. *Application contact:* Nicole Kinslow, Director of Graduate Studies, 409-740-4937, Fax: 409-740-4754, E-mail: kinslown@tamug.edu.
Website: http://www.tamug.edu/marb/

Texas A&M University–Corpus Christi, College of Graduate Studies, College of Science and Engineering, Corpus Christi, TX 78412. Offers biology (MS, PhD); chemistry (MS); coastal and marine system science (MS, PhD); computer science (MS); environmental science (MS); fisheries and mariculture (MS); geospatial computing sciences (PhD); geospatial surveying engineering (MS); marine biology (MS, PhD); mathematics (MS). *Program availability:* Part-time, evening/weekend. *Faculty:* 94 full-time (17 women), 63 part-time/adjunct (21 women). *Students:* 201 full-time (102 women), 56 part-time (28 women); includes 33 minority (3 Black or African American, non-Hispanic/Latino; 3 American Indian or Alaska Native, non-Hispanic/Latino; 5 Asian, non-Hispanic/Latino; 20 Hispanic/Latino; 2 Two or more races, non-Hispanic/Latino), 84 international. Average age 29. 245 applicants, 56% accepted, 82 enrolled. In 2017, 73 master's, 5 doctorates awarded. *Degree requirements:* For master's, comprehensive exam, thesis. *Entrance requirements:* For master's, GRE General Test. Additional exam requirements/recommendations for international students: Required—TOEFL (minimum score 550 paper-based; 69 iBT), IELTS (minimum score 6.5). *Application deadline:* For fall admission, 7/15 priority date for domestic students, 5/1 priority date for international students; for spring admission, 11/15 priority date for domestic students, 9/1 priority date for international students. Applications are processed on a rolling basis. Application fee: $50 ($70 for international students). Electronic applications accepted. *Expenses:* Tuition, state resident: full-time $3568; part-time $198.24 per credit hour. Tuition, nonresident: full-time $11,038; part-time $613.24 per credit hour. *Required fees:* $2129; $1422.58 per semester. Tuition and fees vary according to program. *Financial support:* Research assistantships, teaching assistantships, career-related internships or fieldwork, Federal Work-Study, institutionally sponsored loans, scholarships/grants, health care benefits, and unspecified assistantships available. Support available to part-time students. Financial award application deadline: 3/15; financial award applicants required to submit FAFSA. *Unit head:* Dr. Frank Pezold, Dean, 361-825-2349, E-mail: frank.pezold@tamucc.edu. *Application contact:* Graduate Admissions Coordinator, 361-825-2177, Fax: 361-825-2755, E-mail: gradweb@tamucc.edu.
Website: http://www.sci.tamucc.edu/

Texas State University, The Graduate College, College of Science and Engineering, Program in Aquatic Resources, San Marcos, TX 78666. Offers MS, PhD. *Faculty:* 6 full-time (2 women), 1 part-time/adjunct (0 women). *Students:* 45 full-time (23 women), 11 part-time (9 women); includes 13 minority (2 Black or African American, non-Hispanic/Latino; 2 Asian, non-Hispanic/Latino; 7 Hispanic/Latino; 2 Two or more races, non-Hispanic/Latino), 9 international. Average age 31. 18 applicants, 56% accepted, 7 enrolled. In 2017, 10 master's, 1 doctorate awarded. *Degree requirements:* For master's, comprehensive exam, thesis, 3 seminars; for doctorate, comprehensive exam, thesis/dissertation. *Entrance requirements:* For master's, GRE General Test (minimum recommended score in at least the 50th percentile on both the verbal and quantitative portions), baccalaureate degree in biology or related discipline from regionally-accredited university with minimum GPA of 3.0 on last 60 undergraduate semester hours; intent to

mentor letter from biology faculty member; resume; statement of purpose describing professional aspirations and academic goals; 3 letters of recommendation; for doctorate, GRE (recommended score in at least the 60th percentile on both the verbal and quantitative portions), baccalaureate degree from regionally-accredited university; master's degree in biology, chemistry, engineering, geology, or related natural science field with minimum GPA of 3.25; resume; statement of purpose with aspirations and goals; 3 letters of recommendation. Additional exam requirements/recommendations for international students: Required—TOEFL (minimum score 550 paper-based, 78 iBT), IELTS (minimum score 6.5). *Application deadline:* For fall admission, 1/15 priority date for domestic and international students; for spring admission, 8/15 for domestic students, 8/1 for international students; for summer admission, 4/15 for domestic students, 3/15 for international students. Applications are processed on a rolling basis. Application fee: $40 ($90 for international students). Electronic applications accepted. *Expenses:* Tuition, state resident: full-time $7868; part-time $3934 per semester. Tuition, nonresident: full-time $17,828; part-time $8914 per semester. *Required fees:* $2092; $1435 per semester. Tuition and fees vary according to course load. *Financial support:* In 2017–18, 11 students received support, including 17 research assistantships (averaging $24,943 per year), 29 teaching assistantships (averaging $21,937 per year); Federal Work-Study, institutionally sponsored loans, scholarships/grants, health care benefits, and unspecified assistantships also available. Support available to part-time students. Financial award application deadline: 3/1; financial award applicants required to submit FAFSA. *Faculty research:* Endangered species research in freshwater mussels, Brazos basin instream flow validation, ecological indicators and habitat characterization in the Colorado and Lavaca Rivers, carryover Comal Springs Riffle Beetle Habitat Connectivity study, state of Texas interagency cooperation contract for endangered species research, endangered species research projects for the prairie chub, applied environmental research and biological monitoring of Comal and San Marcos Springs Systems. *Total annual research expenditures:* $1 million. *Unit head:* Dr. Michael Clay Green, PhD Advisor, 512-245-8037, Fax: 512-245-8713, E-mail: mg54@txstate.edu. *Application contact:* Dr. Andrea Golato, Dean of the Graduate School, 512-245-2581, Fax: 512-245-8365, E-mail: jw02@swt.edu.
Website: http://www.bio.txstate.edu/Graduate-Programs.html/

University of Alaska Fairbanks, College of Fisheries and Ocean Sciences, Program in Marine Sciences and Limnology, Fairbanks, AK 99775-7220. Offers marine biology (MS, PhD); oceanography (MS, PhD). *Program availability:* Part-time. *Degree requirements:* For master's, comprehensive exam, thesis, oral defense of thesis; for doctorate, comprehensive exam, thesis/dissertation, oral defense of dissertation. *Entrance requirements:* For master's, GRE General Test, bachelor's degree from accredited institution with minimum cumulative undergraduate and major GPA of 3.0; for doctorate, GRE General Test, minimum cumulative GPA of 3.0. Additional exam requirements/recommendations for international students: Required—TOEFL (minimum score 550 paper-based; 79 iBT), IELTS (minimum score 6.5). Electronic applications accepted.

University of California, Santa Barbara, Graduate Division, College of Letters and Sciences, Division of Mathematics, Life, and Physical Sciences, Department of Ecology, Evolution, and Marine Biology, Santa Barbara, CA 93106-9620. Offers MA, PhD, MA/PhD. *Degree requirements:* For master's, comprehensive exam (for some programs), thesis (for some programs); for doctorate, comprehensive exam, thesis/dissertation. *Entrance requirements:* For master's and doctorate, GRE General Test. Additional exam requirements/recommendations for international students: Required—TOEFL (minimum score 550 paper-based; 80 iBT), IELTS. Electronic applications accepted. *Faculty research:* Community ecology, evolution, marine biology, population genetics, stream ecology.

University of Guam, Office of Graduate Studies, College of Natural and Applied Sciences, Program in Biology, Mangilao, GU 96923. Offers tropical marine biology (MS). *Degree requirements:* For master's, comprehensive exam, thesis. *Entrance requirements:* For master's, GRE General Test, GRE Subject Test. Additional exam requirements/recommendations for international students: Required—TOEFL. *Faculty research:* Maintenance and ecology of coral reefs.

University of Hawaii at Hilo, Program in Tropical Conservation Biology and Environmental Science, Hilo, HI 96720-4091. Offers MS. *Entrance requirements:* Additional exam requirements/recommendations for international students: Required—TOEFL, IELTS. Electronic applications accepted.

University of Hawaii at Manoa, Office of Graduate Education, School of Ocean and Earth Science and Technology, Program in Marine Biology, Honolulu, HI 96822. Offers MS, PhD. Offered in conjunction with the College of Natural Sciences. *Degree requirements:* For master's, thesis, research project; for doctorate, thesis/dissertation, research project. *Entrance requirements:* For master's and doctorate, GRE. Additional exam requirements/recommendations for international students: Required—TOEFL. *Expenses:* Contact institution. *Faculty research:* Ecology, ichthyology, behavior of marine animals, developmental biology.

University of Massachusetts Dartmouth, Graduate School, College of Arts and Sciences, Department of Biology, North Dartmouth, MA 02747-2300. Offers biology (MS); integrative biology (PhD); marine biology (MS). *Program availability:* Part-time. *Faculty:* 19 full-time (9 women), 1 (woman) part-time/adjunct. *Students:* 15 full-time (11 women), 6 part-time (3 women); includes 4 minority (2 Asian, non-Hispanic/Latino; 1 Hispanic/Latino; 1 Two or more races, non-Hispanic/Latino), 1 international. Average age 26. 25 applicants, 52% accepted, 7 enrolled. In 2017, 6 master's awarded. *Degree requirements:* For master's, thesis; for doctorate, comprehensive exam, thesis/dissertation. *Entrance requirements:* For master's and doctorate, GRE, statement of purpose (minimum of 300 words), resume, official transcripts, 3 letters of recommendation. Additional exam requirements/recommendations for international students: Required—TOEFL (minimum score 550 paper-based; 79 iBT), IELTS (minimum score 6.5). *Application deadline:* For fall admission, 1/15 priority date for domestic students, 12/15 priority date for international students. Application fee: $60. Electronic applications accepted. *Expenses:* Tuition, state resident: full-time $15,449; part-time $643.71 per credit. Tuition, nonresident: full-time $27,880; part-time $1161.67 per credit. *Required fees:* $405; $25.88 per credit. Tuition and fees vary according to course load and reciprocity agreements. *Financial support:* In 2017–18, 7 research assistantships (averaging $16,027 per year), 10 teaching assistantships (averaging $18,375 per year) were awarded; tuition waivers (full), unspecified assistantships, and instructional assistantships also available. Support available to part-time students. Financial award application deadline: 3/1; financial award applicants required to submit FAFSA. *Faculty research:* Quality of the antibody for pathogen recognition, evolution of social systems, mechanism of cell polarization, transmission of apicomplexan infection in Atlantic sea scallops, antibody mediated protection. *Total annual research expenditures:* $2.1 million. *Unit head:* Whitney Hable, Graduate Program Director, Biology/Marine Biology, 508-999-8206, E-mail: whable@umassd.edu. *Application contact:* Steven Briggs, Director of Marketing and Recruitment for Graduate Studies, 508-999-8604, Fax: 508-999-8183, E-mail: graduate@umassd.edu.
Website: http://www.umassd.edu/cas/biology

University of Miami, Graduate School, Rosenstiel School of Marine and Atmospheric Science, Division of Marine Biology and Fisheries, Coral Gables, FL 33124. Offers MA, MS, PhD. Terminal master's awarded for partial completion of doctoral program. *Degree requirements:* For master's, comprehensive exam, thesis; for doctorate, comprehensive exam, thesis/dissertation. *Entrance requirements:* For master's and doctorate, GRE General Test. Additional exam requirements/recommendations for international students: Required—TOEFL (minimum score 550 paper-based). Electronic applications accepted. *Faculty research:* Biochemistry, physiology, plankton, coral, biology.

University of New Hampshire, Graduate School, College of Life Sciences and Agriculture, Department of Biological Sciences, Durham, NH 03824. Offers integrative and organismal biology (MS, PhD); marine biology (MS, PhD). *Program availability:* Part-time. *Students:* 11 full-time (7 women), 25 part-time (19 women); includes 2 minority (both Two or more races, non-Hispanic/Latino), 2 international. Average age 26. 42 applicants, 21% accepted, 6 enrolled. In 2017, 2 master's awarded. *Entrance requirements:* For master's and doctorate, GRE General Test. Additional exam requirements/recommendations for international students: Required—TOEFL (minimum score 550 paper-based; 80 iBT). *Application deadline:* For fall admission, 3/15 for domestic and international students; for spring admission, 12/1 for domestic students. Application fee: $65. Electronic applications accepted. *Financial support:* In 2017–18, 32 students received support, including 11 research assistantships, 21 teaching assistantships; fellowships also available. Financial award application deadline: 2/15. *Unit head:* Don Chandler, Chair, 603-862-1735. *Application contact:* Diane Lavalliere, Senior Academic and Student Support Assistant, 603-862-2100, E-mail: diane.lavalliere@unh.edu.
Website: http://www.colsa.unh.edu/dbs

The University of North Carolina Wilmington, College of Arts and Sciences, Department of Biology and Marine Biology, Wilmington, NC 28403-3297. Offers biology (MS); marine biology (MS, PhD). *Program availability:* Part-time. *Faculty:* 39 full-time (12 women), 2 part-time/adjunct (0 women). *Students:* 4 full-time (3 women), 71 part-time (44 women); includes 7 minority (1 Black or African American, non-Hispanic/Latino; 3 Asian, non-Hispanic/Latino; 2 Hispanic/Latino; 1 Two or more races, non-Hispanic/Latino), 2 international. Average age 29. 72 applicants, 31% accepted, 22 enrolled. In 2017, 16 master's, 2 doctorates awarded. *Degree requirements:* For master's, comprehensive exam, thesis; for doctorate, comprehensive exam, thesis/dissertation. *Entrance requirements:* For master's, GRE General Test, 3 recommendations, research interests form and statement, resume or curriculum vitae, baccalaureate degree from biology-related field; for doctorate, GRE General Test, 3 recommendations, resume or curriculum vitae, summary of MS thesis research, statement of PhD research interests, copies of publications, master's degree or BS and 1 year of completed work in the MS in biology program. Additional exam requirements/recommendations for international students: Required—TOEFL (minimum score 550 paper-based; 79 iBT), IELTS (minimum score 6.5). *Application deadline:* For fall admission, 6/15 for domestic students; for spring admission, 11/30 for domestic students. Applications are processed on a rolling basis. Application fee: $75. Electronic applications accepted. *Expenses:* Tuition, state resident: full-time $4626; part-time $226.76 per credit hour. Tuition, nonresident: full-time $17,834; part-time $874.22 per credit hour. *Required fees:* $2124. Tuition and fees vary according to program. *Financial support:* Research assistantships with tuition reimbursements, teaching assistantships with tuition reimbursements, and scholarships/grants available. Support available to part-time students. Financial award application deadline: 1/1; financial award applicants required to submit FAFSA. *Faculty research:* Ecology, physiology, cell and molecular biology, systematics, biomechanics. *Unit head:* Dr. Heather Koopman, Chair, 910-962-7199, E-mail: koopmanh@uncw.edu. *Application contact:* Dr. Stephen Kinsey, Graduate Coordinator, 910-962-7398, Fax: 910-962-4066, E-mail: kinseys@uncw.edu.
Website: http://www.uncw.edu/bio/graduate.html

University of Oregon, Graduate School, College of Arts and Sciences, Department of Biology, Eugene, OR 97403. Offers ecology and evolution (MA, MS, PhD); marine biology (MA, MS, PhD); molecular, cellular and genetic biology (PhD); neuroscience and development (PhD). Terminal master's awarded for partial completion of doctoral program. *Degree requirements:* For master's, thesis (for some programs); for doctorate, thesis/dissertation. *Entrance requirements:* For master's and doctorate, GRE General Test, minimum GPA of 3.2. Additional exam requirements/recommendations for international students: Required—TOEFL. *Faculty research:* Developmental neurobiology; evolution, population biology, and quantitative genetics; regulation of gene expression; biochemistry of marine organisms.

University of Rhode Island, Graduate School, College of the Environment and Life Sciences, Department of Biological Sciences, Kingston, RI 02881. Offers cell and molecular biology (MS, PhD); earth and environmental sciences (MS, PhD); ecology and ecosystem sciences (MS, PhD); evolutionary and marine biology (MS, PhD); sustainable agriculture and food systems (MS, PhD). *Program availability:* Part-time. *Faculty:* 18 full-time (10 women). *Students:* 99 full-time (56 women), 16 part-time (12 women); includes 10 minority (4 Black or African American, non-Hispanic/Latino; 3 Asian, non-Hispanic/Latino; 2 Hispanic/Latino; 1 Two or more races, non-Hispanic/Latino), 21 international. 151 applicants, 22% accepted, 26 enrolled. In 2017, 18 master's, 9 doctorates awarded. *Entrance requirements:* Additional exam requirements/recommendations for international students: Required—TOEFL. *Application deadline:* For fall admission, 1/15 for domestic and international students. Application fee: $65. Electronic applications accepted. *Expenses:* Tuition, state resident: full-time $12,706; part-time $786 per credit. Tuition, nonresident: full-time $25,216; part-time $1401 per credit. *Required fees:* $1598; $45 per credit. One-time fee: $30 part-time. *Financial support:* In 2017–18, 4 research assistantships with tuition reimbursements (averaging $12,698 per year) were awarded. Financial award application deadline: 1/15; financial award applicants required to submit FAFSA. *Faculty research:* Physiological constraints on predators in the Antarctic, effects of CO2 absorption in salt water particularly as it impacts pteropods. *Unit head:* Dr. Evan Preisser, Chair, 401-874-2120, E-mail: preisser@uri.edu.
Website: http://web.uri.edu/bio/

University of Southern California, Graduate School, Dana and David Dornsife College of Letters, Arts and Sciences, Department of Biological Sciences, Program in Marine Biology and Biological Oceanography, Los Angeles, CA 90089. Offers marine and environmental biology (MS); marine biology and biological oceanography (PhD). Terminal master's awarded for partial completion of doctoral program. *Degree requirements:* For master's, research paper; for doctorate, comprehensive exam, thesis/dissertation, qualifying examination, dissertation defense. *Entrance requirements:* For master's and doctorate, GRE, 3 letters of recommendation, personal statement, resume, minimum GPA of 3.0. Additional exam requirements/recommendations for international students: Required—TOEFL (minimum score 600 paper-based; 100 iBT). Electronic applications accepted. *Faculty research:* Microbial ecology, biogeochemistry, and geobiology; biodiversity and molecular ecology; integrative organismal biology; conservation biology; marine genomics.

Western Illinois University, School of Graduate Studies, College of Arts and Sciences, Department of Biological Sciences, Macomb, IL 61455-1390. Offers biology (MS); environmental GIS (Certificate); zoo and aquarium studies (Certificate). *Program availability:* Part-time. *Students:* 43 full-time (24 women), 24 part-time (14 women); includes 5 minority (1 Black or African American, non-Hispanic/Latino; 2 Hispanic/Latino; 2 Two or more races, non-Hispanic/Latino), 21 international. Average age 28. 20 applicants, 90% accepted, 12 enrolled. In 2017, 22 master's awarded. *Degree requirements:* For master's, thesis or alternative. *Entrance requirements:* Additional exam requirements/recommendations for international students: Required—TOEFL (minimum score 550 paper-based; 80 iBT); Recommended—IELTS. *Application*

Marine Biology

deadline: Applications are processed on a rolling basis. Application fee: $30. Electronic applications accepted. *Financial support:* In 2017–18, 13 research assistantships with full tuition reimbursements (averaging $7,544 per year), 19 teaching assistantships with full tuition reimbursements (averaging $8,688 per year) were awarded; unspecified assistantships also available. Financial award applicants required to submit FAFSA. *Unit head:* Dr. Richard Musser, Chairperson, 309-298-1546. *Application contact:* Dr. Nancy Parsons, Associate Provost and Director of Graduate Studies, 309-298-1806, Fax: 309-298-2345, E-mail: grad-office@wiu.edu.
Website: http://wiu.edu/biology

Woods Hole Oceanographic Institution, MIT/WHOI Joint Program in Oceanography/Applied Ocean Science and Engineering, Woods Hole, MA 02543-1541. Offers applied ocean science and engineering (PhD); biological oceanography (PhD); chemical oceanography (PhD); marine geology and geophysics (PhD); physical oceanography (PhD). Program offered jointly with Massachusetts Institute of Technology. *Degree requirements:* For doctorate, thesis/dissertation. *Entrance requirements:* For doctorate, GRE General Test. Additional exam requirements/recommendations for international students: Required—TOEFL or IELTS. Electronic applications accepted.

Section 12
Microbiological Sciences

This section contains a directory of institutions offering graduate work in microbiological sciences, followed by in-depth entries submitted by institutions that chose to prepare detailed program descriptions. Additional information about programs listed in the directory but not augmented by an in-depth entry may be obtained by writing directly to the dean of a graduate school or chair of a department at the address given in the directory.

For programs offering related work, see also in this book *Allied Health; Biochemistry; Biological and Biomedical Sciences; Botany and Plant Biology; Cell, Molecular, and Structural Biology; Dentistry and Dental Sciences; Ecology, Environmental Biology, and Evolutionary Biology; Entomology; Genetics, Developmental Biology, and Reproductive Biology; Parasitology; Pathology and Pathobiology; Pharmacy and Pharmaceutical Sciences; Public Health; Physiology; Veterinary Medicine and Sciences;* and *Zoology*. In the other guides in this series:

Graduate Programs in the Physical Sciences, Mathematics, Agricultural Sciences, the Environment & Natural Resources
See *Agricultural and Food Sciences* and *Chemistry*

Graduate Programs in Engineering & Applied Sciences
See *Agricultural Engineering and Bioengineering* and *Biomedical Engineering and Biotechnology*

CONTENTS

Program Directories

Featured Schools: Displays and Close-Ups

See also:

Bacteriology

Illinois State University, Graduate School, College of Arts and Sciences, School of Biological Sciences, Normal, IL 61790. Offers animal behavior (MS); bacteriology (MS); biochemistry (MS); biological sciences (MS); biology (PhD); biophysics (MS); biotechnology (MS); botany (MS, PhD); cell biology (MS); conservation biology (MS); developmental biology (MS); ecology (MS, PhD); entomology (MS); evolutionary biology (MS); genetics (MS, PhD); immunology (MS); microbiology (MS, PhD); molecular biology (MS); molecular genetics (MS); neurobiology (MS); neuroscience (MS); parasitology (MS); physiology (MS, PhD); plant biology (MS); plant molecular biology (MS); plant sciences (MS); structural biology (MS); zoology (MS, PhD). *Program availability:* Part-time. *Degree requirements:* For master's, thesis or alternative; for doctorate, variable foreign language requirement, thesis/dissertation, 2 terms of residency. *Entrance requirements:* For master's, GRE General Test, minimum GPA of 2.6 in last 60 hours of course work; for doctorate, GRE General Test. *Faculty research:* Redoc balance and drug development in schistosoma mansoni, control of the growth of listeria monocytogenes at low temperature, regulation of cell expansion and microtubule function by SPRI, CRUI: physiology and fitness consequences of different life history phenotypes.

The University of Iowa, Roy J. and Lucille A. Carver College of Medicine and Graduate College, Graduate Programs in Medicine, Department of Microbiology, Iowa City, IA 52242-1316. Offers general microbiology and microbial physiology (MS, PhD); immunology (MS, PhD); microbial genetics (MS, PhD); pathogenic bacteriology (MS, PhD); virology (MS, PhD). *Degree requirements:* For master's, thesis; for doctorate, comprehensive exam, thesis/dissertation. *Entrance requirements:* For master's and doctorate, GRE General Test. Additional exam requirements/recommendations for international students: Required—TOEFL (minimum score 600 paper-based). Electronic applications accepted. *Faculty research:* Gene regulation, processing and transport of HIV, retroviral pathogenesis, biodegradation, biofilm.

University of Prince Edward Island, Atlantic Veterinary College, Graduate Program in Veterinary Medicine, Charlottetown, PE C1A 4P3, Canada. Offers anatomy (M Sc, PhD); bacteriology (M Sc, PhD); clinical pharmacology (M Sc, PhD); clinical sciences (M Sc, PhD); epidemiology (M Sc, PhD), including reproduction; fish health (M Sc, PhD); food animal nutrition (M Sc, PhD); immunology (M Sc, PhD); microanatomy (M Sc, PhD); parasitology (M Sc, PhD); pathology (M Sc, PhD); pharmacology (M Sc, PhD); physiology (M Sc, PhD); toxicology (M Sc, PhD); veterinary science (M Vet Sc); virology (M Sc, PhD). *Program availability:* Part-time. *Degree requirements:* For master's, thesis; for doctorate, thesis/dissertation. *Entrance requirements:* For master's, DVM, B Sc honors degree, or equivalent; for doctorate, M Sc. Additional exam requirements/recommendations for international students: Required—TOEFL (minimum score 550 paper-based; 80 iBT). *Expenses:* Contact institution. *Faculty research:* Animal health management, infectious diseases, fin fish and shellfish health, basic biomedical sciences, ecosystem health.

University of Wisconsin–Madison, Graduate School, College of Agricultural and Life Sciences, Department of Bacteriology, Madison, WI 53706-1380. Offers MS. *Program availability:* Part-time. *Entrance requirements:* Additional exam requirements/recommendations for international students: Required—TOEFL. Electronic applications accepted. *Faculty research:* Microbial physiology, gene regulation, microbial ecology, plant-microbe interactions, symbiosis.

Immunology

Albany Medical College, Center for Immunology and Microbial Disease, Albany, NY 12208-3479. Offers MS, PhD. *Program availability:* Part-time. Terminal master's awarded for partial completion of doctoral program. *Degree requirements:* For master's, thesis; for doctorate, comprehensive exam, thesis/dissertation, oral qualifying exam, written preliminary exam, 1 published paper-peer review. *Entrance requirements:* For master's, GRE General Test, all transcripts, letters of recommendation; for doctorate, GRE General Test, letters of recommendation. Additional exam requirements/recommendations for international students: Required—TOEFL. *Faculty research:* Microbial and viral pathogenesis, cancer development and cell transformation, biochemical and genetic mechanisms responsible for human disease.

Albert Einstein College of Medicine, Graduate Programs in the Biomedical Sciences, Department of Microbiology and Immunology, Bronx, NY 10461. Offers PhD, MD/PhD. *Degree requirements:* For doctorate, thesis/dissertation. *Entrance requirements:* For doctorate, GRE General Test. Additional exam requirements/recommendations for international students: Required—TOEFL. *Application deadline:* For fall admission, 1/15 for domestic students. Application fee: $0. *Financial support:* Fellowships available. *Faculty research:* Nature of histocompatibility antigens, lymphoid cell receptors, regulation of immune responses and mechanisms of resistance to infection. *Unit head:* Dr. Steven Porcelli, Chair, 718-430-2811, E-mail: steven.porcelli@einstein.yu.edu. *Application contact:* Salvatore Calabro, Director of Graduate Admissions, 718-430-2345, Fax: 718-430-8655, E-mail: phd@einstein.yu.edu.
Website: http://www.einstein.yu.edu/departments/microbiology-immunology/

American University of Beirut, Graduate Programs, Faculty of Medicine, Beirut, Lebanon. Offers biochemistry (MS); biomedical engineering (MS); biomedical sciences (PhD); health research (MS); human morphology (MS); medicine (MD); microbiology and immunology (MS); neuroscience (MS); orthodontics (clinical) (MS); pharmacology and therapeutics (MS); physiology (MS). *Program availability:* Part-time. *Faculty:* 335 full-time (117 women), 54 part-time/adjunct (5 women). *Students:* 513 full-time (274 women). Average age 23. 527 applicants, 47% accepted, 169 enrolled. In 2017, 18 master's, 98 doctorates awarded. *Degree requirements:* For master's, one foreign language, comprehensive exam, thesis (for some programs); for doctorate, one foreign language, comprehensive exam, thesis/dissertation. *Entrance requirements:* For doctorate, MCAT (for MD); GRE (for PhD). Additional exam requirements/recommendations for international students: Required—TOEFL (minimum score 600 paper-based; 100 iBT), IELTS (minimum score 7.5). *Application deadline:* Applications are processed on a rolling basis. Application fee: $75. Electronic applications accepted. *Expenses:* Contact institution. *Financial support:* In 2017–18, 302 students received support. Fellowships, research assistantships, teaching assistantships, institutionally sponsored loans, scholarships/grants, tuition waivers, and unspecified assistantships available. *Unit head:* Dr. Mohamed Sayegh, Dean, 961-1-135000 Ext. 4700, Fax: 961-1-744489, E-mail: msayegh@aub.edu.lb. *Application contact:* Dr. Salim Kanaan, Director, Admission's Office, 961-1-350000 Ext. 2594, Fax: 961-1-750775, E-mail: sk00@aub.edu.lb.

Baylor College of Medicine, Graduate School of Biomedical Sciences, Department of Immunology, Houston, TX 77030-3498. Offers PhD, MD/PhD. *Degree requirements:* For doctorate, thesis/dissertation, public defense. *Entrance requirements:* For doctorate, GRE General Test, GRE Subject Test (strongly recommended), minimum GPA of 3.0. Additional exam requirements/recommendations for international students: Required—TOEFL. Electronic applications accepted. *Faculty research:* MHC expression, inflammation and allergy, germinal center biology, HIV pathogenesis, immune responses to gene therapy.

Baylor College of Medicine, Graduate School of Biomedical Sciences, Interdepartmental Program in Cell and Molecular Biology, Houston, TX 77030-3498. Offers biochemistry (PhD); cell and molecular biology (PhD); genetics (PhD); human genetics (PhD); immunology (PhD); microbiology (PhD); virology (PhD); MD/PhD. *Degree requirements:* For doctorate, thesis/dissertation, public defense. *Entrance requirements:* For doctorate, GRE General Test, GRE Subject Test (strongly recommended), minimum GPA of 3.0. Additional exam requirements/recommendations for international students: Required—TOEFL. Electronic applications accepted. *Faculty research:* Molecular and cellular biology; cancer, aging and stem cells; genomics and proteomics; microbiome, molecular microbiology; infectious disease, immunology and translational research.

Boston University, School of Medicine, Division of Graduate Medical Sciences, Immunology Training Program, Boston, MA 02215. Offers PhD, MD/PhD. *Degree requirements:* For doctorate, thesis/dissertation. *Application deadline:* For fall admission, 1/15 for domestic students; for spring admission, 10/15 for domestic students. *Unit head:* Dr. Tom Kepler, Director, 617-638-6464, E-mail: itp@bu.edu. *Application contact:* GMS Admissions Office, 617-638-5255, E-mail: askgms@bu.edu.
Website: http://www.bumc.bu.edu/immunology/

California Institute of Technology, Division of Biology, Program in Immunology, Pasadena, CA 91125-0001. Offers PhD. *Degree requirements:* For doctorate, thesis/dissertation, qualifying exam. *Entrance requirements:* For doctorate, GRE General Test.

Case Western Reserve University, School of Medicine and School of Graduate Studies, Graduate Programs in Medicine, Immunology Training Program, Cleveland, OH 44106. Offers PhD, MD/PhD. *Degree requirements:* For doctorate, comprehensive exam, thesis/dissertation. *Entrance requirements:* For doctorate, GRE General Test, GRE Subject Test. Additional exam requirements/recommendations for international students: Required—TOEFL (minimum score 550 paper-based). Electronic applications accepted. *Expenses: Tuition:* Full-time $43,854; part-time $1827 per credit hour. *Required fees:* $50; $50 per credit hour. Tuition and fees vary according to course load and program. *Faculty research:* Immunology, immunopathology, immunochemistry, infectious diseases.

Colorado State University, College of Veterinary Medicine and Biomedical Sciences, Department of Microbiology, Immunology and Pathology, Fort Collins, CO 80523-1682. Offers microbiology, immunology and pathology (MS, PhD); pathology (PhD). *Faculty:* 76 full-time (35 women), 11 part-time/adjunct (7 women). *Students:* 73 full-time (52 women), 36 part-time (29 women); includes 18 minority (2 Black or African American, non-Hispanic/Latino; 1 American Indian or Alaska Native, non-Hispanic/Latino; 7 Asian, non-Hispanic/Latino; 6 Hispanic/Latino; 2 Two or more races, non-Hispanic/Latino), 7 international. Average age 29. 200 applicants, 32% accepted, 54 enrolled. In 2017, 43 master's, 12 doctorates awarded. Terminal master's awarded for partial completion of doctoral program. *Degree requirements:* For master's, comprehensive exam (for some programs), thesis (for some programs); for doctorate, comprehensive exam, thesis/dissertation. *Entrance requirements:* For master's and doctorate, GRE General Test or MCAT, minimum GPA of 3.0; written statement; transcripts; resume/curriculum vitae; three recommendations. Additional exam requirements/recommendations for international students: Required—TOEFL (minimum score 550 paper-based; 80 iBT), IELTS (minimum score 6.5). *Application deadline:* For fall admission, 4/1 for domestic and international students; for spring admission, 12/15 for domestic and international students. Application fee: $60 ($70 for international students). Electronic applications accepted. *Expenses:* $120 per credit hour. *Financial support:* In 2017–18, 20 research assistantships with full and partial tuition reimbursements (averaging $24,368 per year), 6 teaching assistantships with full and partial tuition reimbursements (averaging $17,883 per year) were awarded; fellowships with full and partial tuition reimbursements and health care benefits also available. Financial award application deadline: 12/15. *Faculty research:* Bacteriology, immunology, prion biology, vector biology, virology. *Total annual research expenditures:* $20.9 million. *Unit head:* Dr. Mark Zabel, Associate Department Head for Graduate Education, 970-491-1455, E-mail: mark.zabel@colostate.edu. *Application contact:* Heidi Runge, Academic Support Coordinator for Graduate Studies, 970-491-1630, Fax: 970-491-1815, E-mail: heidi.runge@colostate.edu.
Website: http://csu-cvmbs.colostate.edu/academics/mip/graduate/Pages/microbiology-immunology-professional-masters.aspx

Creighton University, School of Medicine and Graduate School, Graduate Programs in Medicine, Omaha, NE 68178-0001. Offers biomedical sciences (MS, PhD); clinical anatomy (MS); medical microbiology and immunology (MS, PhD); pharmacology (MS, PhD), including pharmaceutical sciences (MS), pharmacology; MD/PhD; Pharm D/MS. Terminal master's awarded for partial completion of doctoral program. *Degree requirements:* For master's, thesis; for doctorate, thesis/dissertation. *Entrance requirements:* For master's and doctorate, GRE General Test. Additional exam requirements/recommendations for international students: Required—TOEFL (minimum score 550 paper-based; 80 iBT). Electronic applications accepted. *Expenses:* Contact institution. *Faculty research:* Molecular biology and gene transfection, infectious disease, antimicrobial agents and chemotherapy, virology, pharmacological secretion.

Dalhousie University, Faculty of Medicine, Department of Microbiology and Immunology, Halifax, NS B3H 4R2, Canada. Offers M Sc, PhD. *Degree requirements:* For master's, thesis; for doctorate, comprehensive exam, thesis/dissertation. *Entrance requirements:* For master's, GRE General Test, honors B Sc; for doctorate, GRE General Test, honors B Sc in microbiology, M Sc in discipline or transfer after 1 year in master's program. Additional exam requirements/recommendations for international students: Required—1 of 5 approved tests: TOEFL, IELTS, CANTEST, CAEL, Michigan English Language Assessment Battery. Electronic applications accepted. *Faculty research:* Virology, molecular genetics, pathogenesis, bacteriology, immunology.

Dartmouth College, Graduate Program in Molecular and Cellular Biology, Department of Microbiology and Immunology, Program in Immunology, Hanover, NH 03755. Offers PhD, MBA/PhD, MD/PhD. *Entrance requirements:* For doctorate, GRE, letters of recommendation. *Application deadline:* For fall admission, 12/8 for domestic students. Application fee: $75. Electronic applications accepted. *Financial support:* Fellowships and health care benefits available. *Faculty research:* Tumor immunotherapy, cell and molecular biology of connective tissue degradation in rheumatoid arthritis and cancer, immunology and immunotherapy of tumors of the central nervous system, transcriptional regulation of hematopoiesis and leukemia, bacterial pathogenesis. *Unit head:* Dr. William R. Green, Chair, 603-650-4919, Fax: 603-650-6223, E-mail: immunology@dartmouth.edu. *Application contact:* Marcia L. Ingalls, Administrative Assistant, 603-650-4919, Fax: 603-650-6223, E-mail: immunology@dartmouth.edu.
Website: https://geiselmed.dartmouth.edu/immuno/

Drexel University, College of Medicine, Biomedical Graduate Programs, Program in Microbiology and Immunology, Philadelphia, PA 19104-2875. Offers MS, PhD, MD/PhD. Terminal master's awarded for partial completion of doctoral program. *Degree requirements:* For master's, comprehensive exam, thesis; for doctorate, thesis/dissertation, qualifying exam. *Entrance requirements:* For master's, GRE General Test, minimum GPA of 2.75; for doctorate, GRE General Test, minimum GPA of 3.0. Additional exam requirements/recommendations for international students: Required—TOEFL. Electronic applications accepted. *Faculty research:* Immunology of malarial parasites, virology, bacteriology, molecular biology, parasitology.

Duke University, Graduate School, Department of Immunology, Durham, NC 27710. Offers PhD. *Degree requirements:* For doctorate, thesis/dissertation. *Entrance requirements:* For doctorate, GRE General Test, GRE Subject Test in biology or biochemistry, cell and molecular biology (strongly recommended). Additional exam requirements/recommendations for international students: Required—TOEFL (minimum score 577 paper-based; 90 iBT) or IELTS (minimum score 7). Electronic applications accepted.

Emory University, Laney Graduate School, Division of Biological and Biomedical Sciences, Program in Immunology and Molecular Pathogenesis, Atlanta, GA 30322-1100. Offers PhD. *Degree requirements:* For doctorate, comprehensive exam, thesis/dissertation. *Entrance requirements:* For doctorate, GRE General Test, minimum GPA of 3.0 in science course work (recommended). Additional exam requirements/recommendations for international students: Required—TOEFL. Electronic applications accepted. *Faculty research:* Transplantation immunology, autoimmunity, microbial pathogenesis.

Georgetown University, Graduate School of Arts and Sciences, Department of Microbiology and Immunology, Washington, DC 20057. Offers biohazardous threat agents and emerging infectious diseases (MS); biomedical science policy and advocacy (MS); general microbiology and immunology (MS); global infectious diseases (PhD); microbiology and immunology (PhD). *Program availability:* Part-time. *Degree requirements:* For master's, 30 credit hours of coursework, for doctorate, comprehensive exam, thesis/dissertation. *Entrance requirements:* For master's, GRE General Test, 3 letters of reference, bachelor's degree in related field; for doctorate, GRE General Test, 3 letters of reference, MS/BS in related field. Additional exam requirements/recommendations for international students: Required—TOEFL (minimum score 505 paper-based). Electronic applications accepted. *Faculty research:* Pathogenesis and basic biology of the fungus Candida albicans, molecular biology of viral immunopathological mechanisms in Multiple Sclerosis.

The George Washington University, Columbian College of Arts and Sciences, Institute for Biomedical Sciences, Program in Microbiology and Immunology, Washington, DC 20037. Offers PhD. *Students:* 6 full-time (4 women), 9 part-time (1 woman); includes 4 minority (3 Asian, non-Hispanic/Latino; 1 Hispanic/Latino), 2 international. Average age 28. In 2017, 6 doctorates awarded. *Degree requirements:* For doctorate, thesis/dissertation. *Entrance requirements:* For doctorate, GRE General Test, minimum GPA of 3.0. Additional exam requirements/recommendations for international students: Required—TOEFL (minimum score 600 paper-based). *Application deadline:* For fall admission, 12/15 priority date for domestic and international students. Applications are processed on a rolling basis. Application fee: $75. Electronic applications accepted. *Expenses: Tuition:* Full-time $28,800; part-time $1655 per credit hour. *Required fees:* $45; $2.75 per credit hour. *Financial support:* In 2017–18, 10 students received support. Fellowships with tuition reimbursements available and tuition waivers available. *Unit head:* Dr. David Leitenberg, Director, 202-994-9475, Fax: 202-994-2913, E-mail: dleit@gwu.edu. *Application contact:* Information Contact, 202-994-3532, Fax: 202-994-2913, E-mail: mitm@gwu.edu.
Website: http://smhs.gwu.edu/microbiology/

Hood College, Graduate School, Program in Biomedical Science, Frederick, MD 21701-8575. Offers biomedical science (MS), including biotechnology/molecular biology, microbiology/immunology/virology. *Program availability:* Part-time, evening/weekend. *Faculty:* 5 full-time (3 women), 1 (woman) part-time/adjunct. *Students:* 13 full-time (6 women), 73 part-time (39 women); includes 21 minority (12 Black or African American, non-Hispanic/Latino; 6 Asian, non-Hispanic/Latino; 2 Hispanic/Latino; 1 Two or more races, non-Hispanic/Latino), 6 international. Average age 30. 24 applicants, 92% accepted, 14 enrolled. In 2017, 13 master's awarded. *Degree requirements:* For master's, thesis or alternative. *Entrance requirements:* For master's, bachelor's degree in biology; minimum GPA of 3.0; undergraduate course work in cell biology, chemistry, organic chemistry, and genetics. Additional exam requirements/recommendations for international students: Required—TOEFL (minimum score 575 paper-based; 89 iBT), IELTS (minimum score 6). *Application deadline:* For fall admission, 8/15 priority date for domestic students, 8/5 for international students; for spring admission, 12/1 priority date for domestic students, 12/1 for international students; for summer admission, 5/1 priority date for domestic students, 4/15 for international students. Applications are processed on a rolling basis. Application fee: $35. Electronic applications accepted. *Expenses:* $500 per credit plus $110 comprehensive fee per semester, plus any applicable lab fees by course. *Financial support:* Research assistantships with full tuition reimbursements, tuition waivers (partial), and unspecified assistantships available. Financial award applicants required to submit FAFSA. *Faculty research:* Molecular signaling in cell tumor initiation, biomedical ethics, genetic and biochemical approaches to study regulation of gene expression. *Unit head:* Dr. April M. Boulton, Dean of the Graduate School, 301-696-3600, E-mail: gofurther@hood.edu. *Application contact:* Larbi Bricha, Assistant Director of Graduate Admissions, 301-696-3600, E-mail: gofurther@hood.edu.
Website: http://www.hood.edu/graduate

Illinois State University, Graduate School, College of Arts and Sciences, School of Biological Sciences, Normal, IL 61790. Offers animal behavior (MS); bacteriology (MS); biochemistry (MS); biological sciences (MS); biology (PhD); biophysics (MS); biotechnology (MS); botany (MS, PhD); cell biology (MS); conservation biology (MS); developmental biology (MS); ecology (MS, PhD); entomology (MS); evolutionary biology (MS); genetics (MS, PhD); immunology (MS); microbiology (MS, PhD); molecular biology (MS); molecular genetics (MS); neurobiology (MS); neuroscience (MS); parasitology (MS); physiology (MS, PhD); plant biology (MS); plant molecular biology (MS); plant sciences (MS); structural biology (MS); zoology (MS, PhD). *Program availability:* Part-time. *Degree requirements:* For master's, thesis or alternative; for doctorate, variable foreign language requirement, thesis/dissertation, 2 terms of residency. *Entrance requirements:* For master's, GRE General Test, minimum GPA of 2.6 in last 60 hours of course work; for doctorate, GRE General Test. *Faculty research:* Redoc balance and drug development in schistosoma mansoni, control of the growth of listeria monocytogenes at low temperature, regulation of cell expansion and microtubule function by SPRI, CRUI: physiology and fitness consequences of different life history phenotypes.

Indiana University–Purdue University Indianapolis, Indiana University School of Medicine, Department of Microbiology and Immunology, Indianapolis, IN 46202. Offers MS, PhD, MD/MS, MD/PhD. Terminal master's awarded for partial completion of doctoral program. *Degree requirements:* For master's, thesis; for doctorate, thesis/dissertation. *Entrance requirements:* For master's and doctorate, GRE General Test, previous course work in calculus, cell biology, chemistry, genetics, physics, and biochemistry. *Faculty research:* Host-parasite interactions, molecular biology, cellular and molecular immunology and hematology, viral and bacterial pathogenesis, cancer research.

Iowa State University of Science and Technology, Program in Immunobiology, Ames, IA 50011. Offers MS, PhD. *Entrance requirements:* For master's and doctorate, GRE General Test, resume. Additional exam requirements/recommendations for international students: Required—TOEFL (minimum score 600 paper-based; 85 iBT), IELTS (minimum score 7). Electronic applications accepted. *Faculty research:* Immunogenetics, cellular and molecular immunology, infectious disease, neuroimmunology.

Irell & Manella Graduate School of Biological Sciences, Graduate Program, Duarte, CA 91010. Offers brain metastatic cancer (PhD); cancer and stem cell metabolism (PhD); cancer biology (PhD); cancer biology and developmental therapeutics (PhD); cell biology (PhD); chemical biology (PhD); chromosomal break repair (PhD); diabetes and pancreatic progenitor cell biology (PhD); DNA repair and cancer biology (PhD); germline epigenetic remodeling and endocrine disruptors (PhD); hematology and hematopoietic cell transplantation (PhD); hematology and immunology (PhD); inflammation and cancer (PhD); micrornas and gene regulation in cardiovascular disease (PhD); mixed chimrism for reversal of autoimmunity (PhD); molecular and cellular biology (PhD); molecular biology and genetics (PhD); nanoparticle mediated twist1 silencing in metastatic cancer (PhD); neuro-oncology and stem cell biology (PhD); neuroscience (PhD); RNA directed therapies for HIV-1 (PhD); small RNA-induced transcriptional gene activation (PhD); stem cell regulation by the microenvironment (PhD); translational oncology and pharmaceutical sciences (PhD); tumor biology (PhD). *Degree requirements:* For doctorate, comprehensive exam, thesis/dissertation, qualifying exams, two advanced courses. *Entrance requirements:* For doctorate, GRE General Test; GRE Subject Test (recommended), 2 years of course work in chemistry (general and organic); 1 year of course work each in biochemistry, general biology, and general physics; 2 semesters of course work in mathematics; significant research laboratory experience. Additional exam requirements/recommendations for international students: Required—TOEFL. Electronic applications accepted. *Faculty research:* Cancer biology, diabetes, stem cell biology, neuroscience, immunology.

See Display on page 65 and Close-Up on page 109.

Johns Hopkins University, Bloomberg School of Public Health, W. Harry Feinstone Department of Molecular Microbiology and Immunology, Baltimore, MD 21218. Offers MHS, Sc M, PhD. *Degree requirements:* For master's, comprehensive exam, thesis (for some programs), essay, written exams; for doctorate, comprehensive exam, thesis/dissertation, 1-year full-time residency, oral and written exams. *Entrance requirements:* For master's, GRE General Test or MCAT, 3 letters of recommendation, curriculum vitae; for doctorate, GRE General Test, 3 letters of recommendation, transcripts, curriculum vitae. Additional exam requirements/recommendations for international students: Required—TOEFL (minimum score 600 paper-based). Electronic applications accepted. *Faculty research:* Immunology, virology, bacteriology, parasitology, vector biology, disease ecology, pathogenesis of infectious disease, immune responses to infectious agents, vector-borne and tropical diseases, biochemistry and molecular biology of infectious agents, population genetics of insect vectors, genetic regulation and immune responses in insect vectors, vaccine development, hormonal effects on pathogenesis and immune responses.

Johns Hopkins University, School of Medicine, Graduate Programs in Medicine, Immunology Program, Baltimore, MD 21218. Offers PhD. *Degree requirements:* For doctorate, comprehensive exam, thesis/dissertation, oral exam, final thesis seminar. *Entrance requirements:* For doctorate, GRE General Test, 2 letters of recommendation. Additional exam requirements/recommendations for international students: Required—TOEFL (minimum score 550 paper-based). Electronic applications accepted. *Faculty research:* HIV immunity, tumor immunity, major histocompatibility complex, transplantation, genetics of antibodies and T-cell receptors; immune response to infectious agents; antigen recognition; immune regulation; autoimmune diseases; immune cell signaling.

London Metropolitan University, Graduate Programs, London, United Kingdom. Offers applied psychology (M Sc); architecture (MA); biomedical science (M Sc); blood science (M Sc); cancer pharmacology (M Sc); computer networking and cyber security (M Sc); computing and information systems (M Sc); conference interpreting (MA); counter-terrorism studies (M Sc); creative, digital and professional writing (MA); crime, violence and prevention (M Sc); criminology (M Sc); curating contemporary art (MA); data analytics (M Sc); digital media (MA); early childhood studies (MA); education (MA, Ed D); financial services law, regulation and compliance (LL M); food science (M Sc); forensic psychology (M Sc); health and social care management and policy (M Sc); human nutrition (M Sc); human resource management (MA); human rights and international conflict (MA); information technology (M Sc); intelligence and security studies (M Sc); international oil, gas and energy law (LL M); international relations (MA); interpreting (MA); learning and teaching in higher education (MA); legal practice (LL M); media and entertainment law (LL M); organizational and consumer psychology (M Sc); psychological therapy (M Sc); psychology of mental health (M Sc); public health (M Sc); public policy and management (MPA); security studies (M Sc); social work (M Sc); spatial planning and urban design (MA); sports therapy (M Sc); supporting older children and young people with dyslexia (MA); teaching languages (MA), including Arabic, English; translation (MA); woman and child abuse (MA).

Louisiana State University Health Sciences Center, School of Graduate Studies in New Orleans, Department of Microbiology, Immunology, and Parasitology, New

Orleans, LA 70112-1393. Offers microbiology and immunology (PhD); MD/PhD. *Faculty:* 22 full-time (5 women). *Students:* 10 full-time (6 women). Average age 26. 15 applicants, 27% accepted, 4 enrolled. In 2017, 4 doctorates awarded. *Degree requirements:* For doctorate, comprehensive exam, thesis/dissertation, preliminary exam, qualifying exam. *Entrance requirements:* For doctorate, GRE General Test. Additional exam requirements/recommendations for international students: Recommended—TOEFL, IELTS. *Application deadline:* For fall admission, 4/1 for domestic and international students. Applications are processed on a rolling basis. Application fee: $30. *Expenses:* Tuition, state resident: full-time $11,835; part-time $518 per hour. Tuition, nonresident: full-time $24,108; part-time $1079 per hour. *Required fees:* $1254; $55 per hour. *Financial support:* Unspecified assistantships available. Financial award application deadline: 4/15. *Faculty research:* Microbial physiology, animal virology, vaccine development, AIDS drug studies, pathogenic mechanisms, molecular immunology. *Unit head:* Dr. Alistair Ramsay, Professor and Head, 504-568-4062, Fax: 504-568-2918, E-mail: aramsa@lsuhsc.edu. *Application contact:* Dr. Doug Johnston, Assistant Professor, E-mail: mipapp@lsuhsc.edu.
Website: http://www.medschool.lsuhsc.edu/microbiology/

Louisiana State University Health Sciences Center at Shreveport, Department of Microbiology and Immunology, Shreveport, LA 71130-3932. Offers MS, PhD, MD/PhD. Terminal master's awarded for partial completion of doctoral program. *Degree requirements:* For master's, comprehensive exam, thesis; for doctorate, comprehensive exam, thesis/dissertation, research proposal. *Entrance requirements:* For master's and doctorate, GRE General Test. Additional exam requirements/recommendations for international students: Required—TOEFL. Electronic applications accepted. *Expenses:* Contact institution. *Faculty research:* Infectious disease, molecular bacteriology, pathogenesis, molecular virology and immunology.

Loyola University Chicago, Graduate School, Integrated Program in Biomedical Sciences, Maywood, IL 60141. Offers biochemistry and molecular biology (MS, PhD); cell and molecular physiology (MS, PhD); infectious disease and immunology (MS); integrative cell biology (MS, PhD); microbiology and immunology (MS, PhD); molecular pharmacology and therapeutics (MS, PhD); neuroscience (MS, PhD). *Faculty:* 84 full-time (32 women). *Students:* 126 full-time (65 women), 1 (woman) part-time; includes 36 minority (5 Black or African American, non-Hispanic/Latino; 14 Asian, non-Hispanic/Latino; 14 Hispanic/Latino; 3 Two or more races, non-Hispanic/Latino), 13 international. Average age 26. 748 applicants, 34% accepted, 124 enrolled. In 2017, 41 master's, 18 doctorates awarded. *Degree requirements:* For master's, thesis; for doctorate, comprehensive exam, thesis/dissertation. *Entrance requirements:* For doctorate, GRE. Additional exam requirements/recommendations for international students: Required—TOEFL (minimum score 94 iBT), IELTS (minimum score 7.5). *Application deadline:* For fall admission, 2/7 for domestic students. Applications are processed on a rolling basis. Electronic applications accepted. *Expenses:* Contact institution. *Financial support:* In 2017–18, 20 students received support. Schmitt Fellowships and yearly tuition scholarships (averaging $25,032) available. Financial award application deadline: 6/15; financial award applicants required to submit FAFSA. *Unit head:* Dr. Leanne L. Cribbs, Associate Dean, Graduate Education, 708-327-2817, Fax: 708-216-8216, E-mail: lcribbs@luc.edu. *Application contact:* Margarita Quesada, Graduate Program Secretary, 708-216-3532, Fax: 708-216-8216, E-mail: mquesad@luc.edu.
Website: http://ssom.luc.edu/graduate_school/degree-programs/ipbsphd/

Massachusetts Institute of Technology, School of Science, Department of Biology, Cambridge, MA 02139. Offers biochemistry (PhD); biological oceanography (PhD); biology (PhD); biophysical chemistry and molecular structure (PhD); cell biology (PhD); computational and systems biology (PhD); developmental biology (PhD); genetics (PhD); immunology (PhD); microbiology (PhD); molecular biology (PhD); neurobiology (PhD). *Degree requirements:* For doctorate, comprehensive exam, thesis/dissertation, teaching assistantship during two semesters. *Entrance requirements:* For doctorate, GRE General Test. Additional exam requirements/recommendations for international students: Required—TOEFL, IELTS. Electronic applications accepted. *Faculty research:* Cellular, developmental and molecular (plant and animal) biology; biochemistry, bioengineering, biophysics and structural biology; classical and molecular genetics, stem cell and epigenetics; immunology and microbiology; cancer biology, molecular medicine, neurobiology and human disease; computational and systems biology.

Mayo Clinic Graduate School of Biomedical Sciences, Program in Immunology, Rochester, MN 55905. Offers PhD. *Faculty:* 27 full-time (7 women). *Students:* 31 full-time (16 women); includes 6 minority (1 American Indian or Alaska Native, non-Hispanic/Latino; 3 Asian, non-Hispanic/Latino; 2 Hispanic/Latino). 38 applicants, 45% accepted, 8 enrolled. Terminal master's awarded for partial completion of doctoral program. *Degree requirements:* For doctorate, comprehensive exam, thesis/dissertation, oral defense of dissertation, qualifying oral and written exam. *Entrance requirements:* For doctorate, GRE, 1 year of chemistry, biology, calculus, and physics. Additional exam requirements/recommendations for international students: Required—TOEFL. *Application deadline:* For fall admission, 12/1 for domestic and international students. Application fee: $50. Electronic applications accepted. *Financial support:* Fellowships with full tuition reimbursements available. *Faculty research:* Immunogenetics, autoimmunity, receptor signal transduction, T lymphocyte activation, transplantation, vaccines and immune-based therapies. *Unit head:* Dr. Karen Hedin, Director, 507-284-2713, E-mail: hedin.karen@mayo.edu. *Application contact:* Sarah E Giese, Admissions Coordinator, 507-538-1160, E-mail: phd.training@mayo.edu.
Website: http://www.mayo.edu/mgs/

McGill University, Faculty of Graduate and Postdoctoral Studies, Faculty of Medicine, Department of Microbiology and Immunology, Montréal, QC H3A 2T5, Canada. Offers M Sc, M Sc A, PhD.

McMaster University, Faculty of Health Sciences and School of Graduate Studies, Program in Medical Sciences, Immunity and Infection Area, Hamilton, ON L8S 4M2, Canada. Offers M Sc, PhD, MD/PhD. *Degree requirements:* For master's, thesis; for doctorate, comprehensive exam, thesis/dissertation. *Entrance requirements:* For master's, honors B Sc, B+ average in related field; for doctorate, M Sc, minimum B+ average, students with proven research experience and an A average may be admitted with a B Sc degree. Additional exam requirements/recommendations for international students: Required—TOEFL (minimum score 580 paper-based; 92 iBT).

Medical University of South Carolina, College of Graduate Studies, Department of Microbiology and Immunology, Charleston, SC 29425. Offers MS, PhD, DMD/PhD, MD/PhD. Terminal master's awarded for partial completion of doctoral program. *Degree requirements:* For master's, thesis; for doctorate, thesis/dissertation, oral and written exams. *Entrance requirements:* For master's, GRE General Test, MCAT, or DAT, minimum GPA of 3.0; for doctorate, GRE General Test, interview, minimum GPA of 3.0, research experience. Additional exam requirements/recommendations for international students: Required—TOEFL (minimum score 600 paper-based; 100 iBT). Electronic applications accepted. *Faculty research:* Inmate and adaptive immunology, gene therapy/vector development, vaccinology, proteomics of biowarfare agents, bacterial and fungal pathogenesis.

Meharry Medical College, School of Graduate Studies, Program in Biomedical Sciences, Microbiology and Immunology Emphasis, Nashville, TN 37208-9989. Offers PhD, MD/PhD. *Degree requirements:* For doctorate, comprehensive exam, thesis/dissertation. *Entrance requirements:* For doctorate, GRE General Test, GRE Subject Test, undergraduate degree in related science. *Faculty research:* Microbial and bacterial pathogenesis, viral transcription, immune response to viruses and parasites.

Memorial University of Newfoundland, Faculty of Medicine and School of Graduate Studies, Graduate Programs in Medicine, Division of Biomedical Sciences, St. John's, NL A1C 5S7, Canada. Offers cancer (M Sc, PhD); cardiovascular (M Sc, PhD); immunology (M Sc, PhD); neuroscience (M Sc, PhD). *Program availability:* Part-time. *Degree requirements:* For master's, thesis; for doctorate, comprehensive exam, thesis/dissertation, oral defense of thesis. *Entrance requirements:* For master's, MD or B Sc; for doctorate, MD or M Sc. Additional exam requirements/recommendations for international students: Required—TOEFL. *Faculty research:* Neuroscience, immunology, cardiovascular, and cancer.

Montana State University, The Graduate School, College of Agriculture, Department of Immunology and Infectious Diseases, Bozeman, MT 59717. Offers MS, PhD. *Program availability:* Part-time. *Degree requirements:* For master's, comprehensive exam; for doctorate, comprehensive exam, thesis/dissertation. *Entrance requirements:* For master's and doctorate, GRE General Test. Additional exam requirements/recommendations for international students: Required—TOEFL (minimum score 550 paper-based). Electronic applications accepted. *Faculty research:* Immunology, mechanisms of infectious disease pathogenesis, mechanisms of host defense, lymphocyte development, host-pathogen interactions.

New York Medical College, Graduate School of Basic Medical Sciences, Valhalla, NY 10595. Offers biochemistry and molecular biology (MS, PhD); cell biology (MS, PhD); microbiology and immunology (MS, PhD); pathology (MS, PhD); pharmacology (MS, PhD); physiology (MS, PhD); MD/PhD. *Program availability:* Part-time, evening/weekend. *Faculty:* 70 full-time (17 women), 25 part-time/adjunct (9 women). *Students:* 116 full-time (63 women), 25 part-time (11 women); includes 65 minority (17 Black or African American, non-Hispanic/Latino; 1 American Indian or Alaska Native, non-Hispanic/Latino; 23 Asian, non-Hispanic/Latino; 21 Hispanic/Latino; 3 Two or more races, non-Hispanic/Latino), 27 international. Average age 27. 273 applicants, 56% accepted, 59 enrolled. In 2017, 32 master's, 3 doctorates awarded. *Degree requirements:* For master's, thesis; for doctorate, comprehensive exam, thesis/dissertation. *Entrance requirements:* For master's, GRE General Test, MCAT, or DAT; for doctorate, GRE General Test. Additional exam requirements/recommendations for international students: Required—TOEFL. *Application deadline:* For fall admission, 7/1 priority date for domestic students, 5/1 priority date for international students; for spring admission, 12/1 priority date for domestic students, 9/15 priority date for international students. Applications are processed on a rolling basis. Application fee: $75 ($100 for international students). Electronic applications accepted. *Expenses:* $1,125 per credit, $655 fees. *Financial support:* Fellowships, research assistantships, Federal Work-Study, institutionally sponsored loans, scholarships/grants, tuition waivers, and health benefits (for PhD candidates only) available. Support available to part-time students. Financial award application deadline: 4/30; financial award applicants required to submit FAFSA. *Faculty research:* Cardiovascular science, infectious diseases, neuroscience, cancer, cell signaling. *Unit head:* Dr. Francis L. Belloni, Dean, 914-594-4110, Fax: 914-594-4944, E-mail: francis_belloni@nymc.edu. *Application contact:* Valerie Romeo-Messana, Director of Admissions, 914-594-4110, Fax: 914-594-4944, E-mail: v_romeomessana@nymc.edu.
Website: https://www.nymc.edu/graduate-school-of-basic-medical-sciences-gsbms/gsbms-academics/

New York University, Graduate School of Arts and Science, Department of Biology, New York, NY 10012-1019. Offers biology (PhD); biomedical journalism (MS); cancer and molecular biology (PhD); computational biology (PhD); computers in biological research (MS); developmental genetics (PhD); general biology (MS); immunology and microbiology (PhD); molecular genetics (PhD); neurobiology (PhD); oral biology (MS); plant biology (PhD); recombinant DNA technology (MS); MS/MBA. *Program availability:* Part-time. *Students:* Average age 27. 394 applicants, 56% accepted, 77 enrolled. In 2017, 68 master's, 9 doctorates awarded. Terminal master's awarded for partial completion of doctoral program. *Degree requirements:* For master's, thesis or alternative, qualifying paper; for doctorate, comprehensive exam, thesis/dissertation. *Entrance requirements:* For master's and doctorate, GRE General Test. Additional exam requirements/recommendations for international students: Required—TOEFL. *Application deadline:* For fall admission, 12/1 priority date for domestic students, 12/1 for international students. Application fee: $100. *Expenses: Tuition:* Full-time $41,352; part-time $19,968 per year. *Required fees:* $2496; $1628 per unit. $814 per term. Tuition and fees vary according to course load and program. *Financial support:* Fellowships, research assistantships, teaching assistantships, career-related internships or fieldwork, Federal Work-Study, institutionally sponsored loans, scholarships/grants, health care benefits, and unspecified assistantships available. Financial award application deadline: 12/1; financial award applicants required to submit FAFSA. *Faculty research:* Genomics, molecular and cell biology, development and molecular genetics, molecular evolution of plants and animals. *Unit head:* Stephen Small, Chair, 212-998-8200, Fax: 212-995-4015, E-mail: biology.admissions@nyu.edu. *Application contact:* Ken Birnbaum, Director of Graduate Studies, PhD Programs, 212-998-8200, Fax: 212-995-4015, E-mail: biology.admissions@nyu.edu.
Website: http://biology.as.nyu.edu/

New York University, School of Medicine and Graduate School of Arts and Science, Sackler Institute of Graduate Biomedical Sciences, New York, NY 10016. Offers biomedical imaging and technology (PhD); biostatistics (PhD); cellular and molecular biology (PhD); developmental genetics (PhD); epidemiology (PhD); genome integrity (PhD); immunology and inflammation (PhD); microbiology (PhD); molecular biophysics (PhD); molecular oncology and tumor immunology (PhD); molecular pharmacology (PhD); neuroscience and physiology (PhD), including immunology, molecular oncology; stem cell biology (PhD); systems and computational biomedicine (PhD); MD/PhD. *Faculty:* 207 full-time (51 women). *Students:* 236 full-time (138 women), 1 part-time (0 women); includes 68 minority (13 Black or African American, non-Hispanic/Latino; 26 Asian, non-Hispanic/Latino; 28 Hispanic/Latino; 1 Native Hawaiian or other Pacific Islander, non-Hispanic/Latino), 79 international. Average age 27. 761 applicants, 18% accepted, 59 enrolled. In 2017, 35 doctorates awarded. *Degree requirements:* For doctorate, comprehensive exam, thesis/dissertation, qualifying exam; thesis defense. *Entrance requirements:* For doctorate, GRE. Additional exam requirements/recommendations for international students: Required—TOEFL, IELTS. *Application deadline:* For fall admission, 12/1 for domestic and international students. Applications are processed on a rolling basis. Application fee: $100. Electronic applications accepted. Application fee is waived when completed online. *Expenses:* Contact institution. *Financial support:* Health care benefits, tuition waivers (full), and unspecified assistantships available. *Faculty research:* Biomedical sciences. *Unit head:* Dr. Naoko Tanese, Associate Dean for Biomedical Sciences/Director, Sackler Institute, 212-263-8945, E-mail: naoko.tanese@nyumc.org. *Application contact:* Jessica Dong, Program Manager, 212-263-5648, E-mail: sackler-info@nyumc.org.
Website: https://med.nyu.edu/research/sackler-institute-graduate-biomedical-sciences/

Old Dominion University, College of Sciences, Master of Science in Biology Program, Norfolk, VA 23529. Offers biology (MS); microbiology and immunology (MS). *Program availability:* Part-time. *Faculty:* 22 full-time (4 women), 22 part-time/adjunct (2 women). *Students:* 18 full-time (11 women), 15 part-time (11 women); includes 4 minority (2 Black or African American, non-Hispanic/Latino; 2 Asian, non-Hispanic/Latino). Average age 28. 28 applicants, 25% accepted, 6 enrolled. In 2017, 10 master's awarded. *Degree requirements:* For master's, comprehensive exam, thesis optional, 31 credits. *Entrance requirements:* For master's, GRE General Test, MCAT, minimum GPA of 3.0. Additional exam requirements/recommendations for international students: Required—TOEFL (minimum score 550 paper-based; 79 iBT). *Application deadline:* For fall admission, 2/1 priority date for domestic and international students; for winter admission, 6/1 priority date for domestic and international students; for spring admission, 10/1 priority date for domestic and international students. Application fee: $50. Electronic applications accepted. *Expenses:* Tuition, state resident: full-time $8928; part-time $496 per credit. Tuition, nonresident: full-time $22,482; part-time $1249 per credit. *Required fees:* $66 per semester. *Financial support:* In 2017–18, 11 students received support, including 2 fellowships (averaging $6,575 per year), 10 research assistantships with partial tuition reimbursements available (averaging $15,000 per year), 9 teaching assistantships with partial tuition reimbursements available (averaging $15,000 per year); career-related internships or fieldwork and scholarships/grants also available. Support available to part-time students. Financial award application deadline: 2/1; financial award applicants required to submit FAFSA. *Faculty research:* Ecology and systematics of vertebrates, marine biology, molecular and cellular microbiology and immunology, vector-borne diseases, human and ecological physiology. *Total annual research expenditures:* $2 million. *Unit head:* Dr. Robert Ratzlaff, Graduate Program Director, 757-683-4361, Fax: 757-683-5283, E-mail: biolgpd@odu.edu. *Application contact:* William Heffelfinger, Director of Graduate Admissions, 757-683-5554, Fax: 757-683-3255, E-mail: gradadmit@odu.edu.
Website: http://sci.odu.edu/biology/academics/bio-ms.shtml

Oregon Health & Science University, School of Medicine, Graduate Programs in Medicine, Program in Molecular and Cellular Biosciences, Department of Molecular Microbiology and Immunology, Portland, OR 97239-3098. Offers PhD. *Faculty:* 28 full-time (8 women), 21 part-time/adjunct (6 women). *Students:* 12 full-time (7 women); includes 2 minority (1 Asian, non-Hispanic/Latino; 1 Two or more races, non-Hispanic/Latino). Average age 28. In 2017, 4 doctorates awarded. Terminal master's awarded for partial completion of doctoral program. *Degree requirements:* For doctorate, comprehensive exam, thesis/dissertation, qualifying exam. *Entrance requirements:* For doctorate, GRE General Test (minimum scores: 153 Verbal/148 Quantitative/4.5 Analytical) or MCAT (for some programs). *Application deadline:* For fall admission, 12/1 for domestic and international students. Application fee: $70. Electronic applications accepted. *Financial support:* Health care benefits, tuition waivers (full), and full-tuition and stipends available. Financial award application deadline: 3/1; financial award applicants required to submit FAFSA. *Faculty research:* Molecular biology of bacterial and viral pathogens, cellular and humoral immunology, molecular biology of microbes. *Unit head:* Dr. Georgiana Purdy, Program Director, E-mail: mmi@ohsu.edu. *Application contact:* Brandi Colbert, Program Coordinator, E-mail: mmi@ohsu.edu.
Website: http://www.ohsu.edu/microbiology

Oregon State University, College of Science, Program in Microbiology, Corvallis, OR 97331. Offers environmental microbiology (MA, MS, PhD); food microbiology (MA, MS, PhD); genomics (MA, MS, PhD); immunology (MA, MS, PhD); microbial ecology (MA, MS, PhD); microbial evolution (MA, MS, PhD); parasitology (MA, MS, PhD); pathogenic microbiology (MA, MS, PhD); virology (MA). Terminal master's awarded for partial completion of doctoral program. *Entrance requirements:* For master's and doctorate, GRE. Additional exam requirements/recommendations for international students: Required—TOEFL (minimum score 600 paper-based; 100 iBT). *Application deadline:* For fall admission, 1/1 for domestic and international students. Application fee: $75 ($85 for international students). *Financial support:* Application deadline: 1/15. *Faculty research:* Genetics, physiology, biotechnology, pathogenic microbiology, plant virology. *Unit head:* Dr. Jerri Bartholomew, Professor and Department Head, 541-737-1834, E-mail: bartholj@science.oregonstate.edu. *Application contact:* Kim Halsey, Graduate Admissions Committee Chair, 541-737-1831, E-mail: kim.halsey@oregonstate.edu.
Website: http://microbiology.science.oregonstate.edu/

Penn State Hershey Medical Center, College of Medicine, Graduate School Programs in the Biomedical Sciences, Graduate Program in Biomedical Sciences, Hershey, PA 17033. Offers biochemistry and molecular genetics (MS, PhD); biomedical sciences (MS, PhD); cellular and integrative physiology (MS, PhD); translational therapeutics (MS, PhD); virology and immunology (MS, PhD); MD/PhD; PhD/MBA. *Students:* 103 full-time (58 women); includes 25 minority (5 Black or African American, non-Hispanic/Latino; 12 Asian, non-Hispanic/Latino; 7 Hispanic/Latino; 1 Native Hawaiian or other Pacific Islander, non-Hispanic/Latino), 28 international. 250 applicants, 22% accepted, 19 enrolled. In 2017, 4 master's, 1 doctorate awarded. Terminal master's awarded for partial completion of doctoral program. *Degree requirements:* For master's, thesis; for doctorate, comprehensive exam, thesis/dissertation, candidacy exam. *Entrance requirements:* For doctorate, GRE General Test. Additional exam requirements/recommendations for international students: Required—TOEFL (minimum score 550 paper-based; 81 iBT). *Application deadline:* For fall admission, 1/1 for domestic and international students. Applications are processed on a rolling basis. Application fee: $65. Electronic applications accepted. *Financial support:* In 2017–18, 103 students received support, including research assistantships with full tuition reimbursements available (averaging $27,802 per year); fellowships, scholarships/grants, traineeships, health care benefits, and unspecified assistantships also available. *Unit head:* Dr. Ralph L. Keil, Chair, 717-531-8595, Fax: 717-531-0786, E-mail: rlk9@psu.edu. *Application contact:* Kristin E. Smith, Director of Graduate Admissions, 717-531-1045, Fax: 717-531-0786, E-mail: kec17@psu.edu.
Website: http://med.psu.edu/bms

Purdue University, College of Pharmacy and Graduate School, Graduate Programs in Pharmacy and Pharmacal Sciences, Department of Medicinal Chemistry and Molecular Pharmacology, West Lafayette, IN 47907. Offers biophysical and computational chemistry (PhD); cancer research (PhD); immunology and infectious disease (PhD); medicinal biochemistry and molecular biology (PhD); medicinal chemistry and chemical biology (PhD); molecular pharmacology (PhD); neuropharmacology, neurodegeneration, and neurotoxicity (PhD); systems biology and functional genomics (PhD). *Faculty:* 26 full-time (5 women). *Students:* 52 full-time (22 women), 3 part-time (all women); includes 4 minority (1 Black or African American, non-Hispanic/Latino; 2 Asian, non-Hispanic/Latino; 1 Hispanic/Latino), 29 international. Average age 26. 151 applicants, 19% accepted, 13 enrolled. In 2017, 18 doctorates awarded. *Degree requirements:* For doctorate, thesis/dissertation. *Entrance requirements:* For doctorate, GRE General Test; GRE Subject Test in biology, biochemistry, and chemistry (recommended), minimum undergraduate GPA of 3.0. Additional exam requirements/recommendations for international students: Required—TOEFL (minimum score 550 paper-based; 77 iBT); Recommended—TWE. *Application deadline:* For fall admission, 2/1 for domestic and international students. Applications are processed on a rolling basis. Application fee: $60 ($75 for international students). Electronic applications accepted. *Financial support:* Fellowships, research assistantships, teaching assistantships, and traineeships available. Support available to part-time students. Financial award applicants required to submit FAFSA. *Faculty research:* Drug design and development, cancer research, drug synthesis and analysis, chemical pharmacology, environmental toxicology. *Unit head:* Zhong-Yin Zhang, Head, 765-494-1403, E-mail: zhang-yn@purdue.edu. *Application contact:* Delayne Graham, Graduate Contact, 765-494-1362, E-mail: dkgraham@purdue.edu.

Purdue University, School of Veterinary Medicine and Graduate School, Graduate Programs in Veterinary Medicine, Department of Comparative Pathobiology, West Lafayette, IN 47907-2027. Offers comparative epidemiology and public health (MS); comparative epidemiology and public heath (PhD); comparative microbiology and immunology (MS, PhD); comparative pathobiology (MS, PhD); interdisciplinary studies (PhD), including microbial pathogenesis, molecular signaling and cancer biology, molecular virology; lab animal medicine (MS); veterinary anatomic pathology (MS); veterinary clinical pathology (MS). Terminal master's awarded for partial completion of doctoral program. *Degree requirements:* For master's, thesis (for some programs); for doctorate, thesis/dissertation. *Entrance requirements:* For master's and doctorate, GRE General Test. Additional exam requirements/recommendations for international students: Required—TOEFL (minimum score 575 paper-based), IELTS (minimum score 6.5), TWE (minimum score 4). Electronic applications accepted.

Queen's University at Kingston, School of Graduate Studies, Faculty of Health Sciences, Department of Microbiology and Immunology, Kingston, ON K7L 3N6, Canada. Offers M Sc, PhD. *Program availability:* Part-time. *Degree requirements:* For master's, thesis; for doctorate, comprehensive exam, thesis/dissertation. *Entrance requirements:* For master's and doctorate, minimum B+ average. Additional exam requirements/recommendations for international students: Required—TOEFL (minimum score 600 paper-based). Electronic applications accepted. *Faculty research:* Bacteriology, virology, immunology, education in microbiology and immunology, microbial pathogenesis.

Rosalind Franklin University of Medicine and Science, School of Graduate and Postdoctoral Studies - Interdisciplinary Graduate Program in Biomedical Sciences, Department of Microbiology and Immunology, North Chicago, IL 60064-3095. Offers PhD, MD/PhD. Terminal master's awarded for partial completion of doctoral program. *Degree requirements:* For doctorate, comprehensive exam, thesis/dissertation. *Entrance requirements:* For doctorate, GRE General Test. Additional exam requirements/recommendations for international students: Required—TOEFL, TWE. *Faculty research:* Molecular biology, parasitology, virology.

Rush University, Graduate College, Division of Immunology and Microbiology, Program in Immunology/Microbiology, Chicago, IL 60612-3832. Offers immunology (MS, PhD), virology (MS, PhD), MD/PhD. *Program availability:* Part-time. Terminal master's awarded for partial completion of doctoral program. *Degree requirements:* For master's, thesis; for doctorate, thesis/dissertation, comprehensive preliminary exam. *Entrance requirements:* For master's, GRE General Test; for doctorate, GRE General Test, interview, minimum GPA of 3.0. Additional exam requirements/recommendations for international students: Required—TOEFL. Electronic applications accepted. *Faculty research:* Human genetics, autoimmunity, tumor biology, complement, HIV immunopathology genesis.

Rutgers University–Newark, Graduate School of Biomedical Sciences, Program in Molecular Pathology and Immunology, Newark, NJ 07107. Offers PhD. *Accreditation:* NAACLS. *Entrance requirements:* Additional exam requirements/recommendations for international students: Required—TOEFL. Electronic applications accepted.

Rutgers University–New Brunswick, Graduate School-New Brunswick, Programs in the Molecular Biosciences, Piscataway, NJ 08854-8097. Offers biochemistry (PhD); cell and developmental biology (MS, PhD); microbiology and molecular genetics (MS, PhD), including applied microbiology, clinical microbiology, computational molecular biology (PhD), immunology, microbial biochemistry, molecular genetics, virology. MS, PhD offered jointly with University of Medicine and Dentistry of New Jersey.

Saint Louis University, Graduate Programs, School of Medicine, Graduate Programs in Biomedical Sciences, Department of Molecular Microbiology and Immunology, St. Louis, MO 63103. Offers PhD. *Degree requirements:* For doctorate, comprehensive exam, thesis/dissertation, qualifying exams. *Entrance requirements:* For doctorate, GRE General Test (GRE Subject Test optional), letters of recommendation, resume, interview. Additional exam requirements/recommendations for international students: Required—TOEFL (minimum score 525 paper-based). Electronic applications accepted. *Faculty research:* Pathogenesis of hepatitis C virus, herperviruses, pox viruses, rheumatoid arthritis, antiviral drugs and vaccines in biodefense, cancer gene therapy, virology and immunology.

Stanford University, School of Medicine, Graduate Programs in Medicine, Department of Microbiology and Immunology, Stanford, CA 94305-2004. Offers PhD. *Degree requirements:* For doctorate, comprehensive exam, thesis/dissertation, 2 quarter teaching assistantship. *Entrance requirements:* For doctorate, GRE General Test, GRE Subject Test (biology or biochemistry). Additional exam requirements/recommendations for international students: Required—TOEFL. Electronic applications accepted. *Expenses: Tuition:* Full-time $48,987; part-time $10,620 per quarter. One-time fee: $400. Tuition and fees vary according to program. *Faculty research:* Molecular pathogenesis of bacteria viruses and parasites, immune system function, autoimmunity, molecular biology.

State University of New York Upstate Medical University, College of Graduate Studies, Program in Microbiology and Immunology, Syracuse, NY 13210. Offers microbiology (MS); microbiology and immunology (PhD); MD/PhD. Terminal master's awarded for partial completion of doctoral program. *Degree requirements:* For master's, thesis; for doctorate, comprehensive exam, thesis/dissertation. *Entrance requirements:* For master's, GRE General Test, interview; for doctorate, GRE General Test, telephone interview. Additional exam requirements/recommendations for international students: Required—TOEFL. Electronic applications accepted. *Faculty research:* Cancer, disorders of the nervous system, infectious diseases, diabetes/metabolic disorders/cardiovascular diseases.

Stony Brook University, State University of New York, Graduate School, College of Arts and Sciences, Department of Biochemistry and Cell Biology, Molecular and Cellular Biology Program, Stony Brook, NY 11794. Offers biochemistry and molecular biology (PhD); biological sciences (MA); immunology and pathology (PhD); molecular and cellular biology (PhD). *Students:* 63 full-time (35 women); includes 12 minority (3 Black or African American, non-Hispanic/Latino; 6 Asian, non-Hispanic/Latino; 3 Hispanic/Latino), 35 international. Average age 28. 131 applicants, 25% accepted, 11 enrolled. In 2017, 12 doctorates awarded. *Degree requirements:* For doctorate, comprehensive exam, thesis/dissertation, teaching experience. *Entrance requirements:* For doctorate, GRE General Test, GRE Subject Test. Additional exam requirements/recommendations for international students: Required—TOEFL. *Application deadline:* For fall admission, 1/15 for domestic students; for spring admission, 10/1 for domestic students. Application fee: $100. Electronic applications accepted. *Expenses:* Contact institution. *Financial support:* In 2017–18, 4 fellowships, 29 research assistantships, 12 teaching assistantships were awarded; Federal Work-Study also available. *Unit head:* Prof. Aaron Neiman, Chair, 631-632-8550, Fax: 631-632-8575, E-mail: aaron.neiman@stonybrook.edu. *Application contact:* Amy Saas, Graduate Program Administrator, 631-632-8613, Fax: 631-632-9730, E-mail: mcbgraduateprogram@stonybrook.edu.
Website: https://www.stonybrook.edu/mcb/

Immunology

Thomas Jefferson University, Jefferson College of Biomedical Sciences, PhD Program in Immunology and Microbial Pathogenesis, Philadelphia, PA 19107. Offers PhD. *Faculty:* 31 full-time (5 women). *Students:* 11 full-time (6 women); includes 3 minority (2 Asian, non-Hispanic/Latino; 1 Hispanic/Latino), 2 international. Average age 28. In 2017, 5 doctorates awarded. *Degree requirements:* For doctorate, comprehensive exam, thesis/dissertation. *Entrance requirements:* For doctorate, GRE General Test, minimum GPA of 3.2. Additional exam requirements/recommendations for international students: Required—TOEFL, IELTS (minimum score 7). *Application deadline:* For fall admission, 12/1 priority date for domestic and international students. Applications are processed on a rolling basis. Application fee: $60. Electronic applications accepted. *Financial support:* In 2017–18, 16 students received support, including 11 fellowships with full tuition reimbursements available (averaging $62,653 per year); Federal Work-Study, institutionally sponsored loans, scholarships/grants, traineeships, health care benefits, and stipends also available. Financial award application deadline: 5/1; financial award applicants required to submit FAFSA. *Unit head:* Dr. Jianke Zhang, Program Director, 215-503-4559, E-mail: jianke.zhang@jefferson.edu. *Application contact:* Marc E. Stearns, Senior Associate Director of Admissions, 215-503-0155, Fax: 215-503-3433, E-mail: jgsbs-info@jefferson.edu.
Website: http://www.jefferson.edu/university/biomedical-sciences/degrees-programs/phd-programs/immunology.html

Tufts University, Sackler School of Graduate Biomedical Sciences, Immunology Program, Medford, MA 02155. Offers PhD. Terminal master's awarded for partial completion of doctoral program. *Degree requirements:* For doctorate, comprehensive exam, thesis/dissertation. *Entrance requirements:* For doctorate, GRE General Test, 3 letters of reference, resume, personal statement. Electronic applications accepted. *Expenses: Tuition:* Full-time $49,892. *Required fees:* $874. Full-time tuition and fees vary according to degree level, program and student level. Part-time tuition and fees vary according to course load. *Faculty research:* Genetic regulation of the ontogeny and activation of lymphocytes, mechanisms of antigen-receptor gene rearrangement, biology and molecular biology of negative selection (tolerance) of B and T cells, activation signal pathways, gene expression and the biochemistry of apoptosis.

Tulane University, School of Medicine and School of Liberal Arts, Graduate Programs in Biomedical Sciences, Department of Microbiology and Immunology, New Orleans, LA 70118-5669. Offers MS. MS and PhD offered through the Graduate School. *Degree requirements:* For master's, thesis. *Entrance requirements:* For master's, GRE General Test, minimum B average in undergraduate course work. Additional exam requirements/recommendations for international students: Required—TOEFL. Electronic applications accepted. *Expenses: Tuition:* Full-time $50,920; part-time $2829 per credit hour. *Required fees:* $2040; $44.50 per credit hour. $580 per term. Tuition and fees vary according to course load, degree level and program. *Faculty research:* Vaccine development, viral pathogenesis, molecular virology, bacterial pathogenesis, fungal pathogenesis.

Uniformed Services University of the Health Sciences, F. Edward Hebert School of Medicine, Graduate Programs in the Biomedical Sciences and Public Health, Graduate Program in Emerging Infectious Diseases, Bethesda, MD 20814-4799. Offers PhD. *Degree requirements:* For doctorate, comprehensive exam, thesis/dissertation, qualifying exam. *Entrance requirements:* For doctorate, GRE General Test. Electronic applications accepted. *Faculty research:* Pathogenesis, host response, and epidemiology of infectious diseases.

See Display on page 284 and Close-Up on page 303.

Universidad Central del Caribe, School of Medicine, Program in Biomedical Sciences, Bayamón, PR 00960-6032. Offers anatomy and cell biology (MA, MS); biochemistry (MS); biomedical sciences (MA); cellular and molecular biology (PhD); microbiology and immunology (MA, MS); pharmacology (MS); physiology (MS).

Université de Montréal, Faculty of Medicine, Department of Microbiology and Immunology, Montréal, QC H3C 3J7, Canada. Offers M Sc, PhD. Programs offered jointly with Faculty of Veterinary Medicine and Université du Québec, Institut Armand-Frappier. Terminal master's awarded for partial completion of doctoral program. *Degree requirements:* For master's, thesis; for doctorate, thesis/dissertation, general exam. *Entrance requirements:* For master's and doctorate, proficiency in French, knowledge of English. Electronic applications accepted.

Université de Montréal, Faculty of Veterinary Medicine, Program in Virology and Immunology, Montréal, QC H3C 3J7, Canada. Offers PhD. Program offered jointly with Université du Québec, Institut Armand-Frappier. *Degree requirements:* For doctorate, thesis/dissertation, general exam. *Entrance requirements:* For doctorate, proficiency in French, knowledge of English. Electronic applications accepted.

Université de Sherbrooke, Faculty of Medicine and Health Sciences, Graduate Programs in Medicine, Program in Immunology, Sherbrooke, QC J1H 5N4, Canada. Offers M Sc, PhD. Electronic applications accepted. *Faculty research:* Cytokine receptor signal transduction, lipid mediators and inflammation, TGFbeta convertases.

Université du Québec, Institut National de la Recherche Scientifique, Graduate Programs, INRS - Institut Armand-Frappier, Laval, QC G1K 9A9, Canada. Offers applied microbiology (M Sc); biology (PhD); experimental health sciences (M Sc); virology and immunology (M Sc, PhD). *Program availability:* Part-time. *Faculty:* 48 full-time. *Students:* 149 full-time (89 women), 18 part-time (11 women), 86 international. Average age 30. 29 applicants, 93% accepted, 25 enrolled. In 2017, 16 master's, 13 doctorates awarded. *Degree requirements:* For master's, thesis; for doctorate, thesis/dissertation. *Entrance requirements:* For master's, appropriate bachelor's degree, proficiency in French; for doctorate, appropriate master's degree, proficiency in French. *Application deadline:* For fall admission, 3/30 for domestic and international students; for winter admission, 11/1 for domestic and international students; for spring admission, 3/1 for domestic and international students. Application fee: $45 Canadian dollars. Electronic applications accepted. *Financial support:* In 2017–18, fellowships (averaging $16,500 per year) were awarded; research assistantships also available. *Faculty research:* Immunity, infection and cancer; toxicology and environmental biotechnology; molecular pharmacochemistry. *Unit head:* Pierre Talbot, Director, 450-687-5010 Ext. 4300, Fax: 450-686-5501, E-mail: pierre.talbot@iaf.inrs.ca. *Application contact:* Sylvie Richard, Registrar, 418-654-2518, Fax: 418-654-3858, E-mail: sylvie.richard@adm.inrs.ca.
Website: http://www.iaf.inrs.ca

Université Laval, Faculty of Medicine, Graduate Programs in Medicine, Programs in Microbiology-Immunology, Québec, QC G1K 7P4, Canada. Offers M Sc, PhD. Terminal master's awarded for partial completion of doctoral program. *Degree requirements:* For master's, thesis; for doctorate, comprehensive exam, thesis/dissertation. *Entrance requirements:* For master's and doctorate, knowledge of French, comprehension of written English. Electronic applications accepted.

University at Buffalo, the State University of New York, Graduate School, Graduate Programs in Cancer Research and Biomedical Sciences at Roswell Park Cancer Institute, Department of Immunology at Roswell Park Cancer Institute, Buffalo, NY 14260. Offers PhD. *Faculty:* 22 full-time (7 women). *Students:* 23 full-time (14 women); includes 3 minority (2 Black or African American, non-Hispanic/Latino; 1 Two or more races, non-Hispanic/Latino), 5 international. 41 applicants, 24% accepted, 3 enrolled. *Degree requirements:* For doctorate, comprehensive exam, thesis/dissertation, oral defense of dissertation. *Entrance requirements:* For doctorate, GRE General Test. Additional exam requirements/recommendations for international students: Required—TOEFL (minimum score 79 iBT). *Application deadline:* For fall admission, 1/5 priority date for domestic and international students. Application fee: $75. Electronic applications accepted. *Financial support:* In 2017–18, 23 students received support, including 23 research assistantships with full tuition reimbursements available (averaging $27,000 per year); scholarships/grants, health care benefits, and unspecified assistantships also available. Financial award application deadline: 1/5. *Faculty research:* Immunochemistry, immunobiology, molecular immunology, hybridoma studies, recombinant DNA studies. *Unit head:* Dr. Kelvin Lee, Chair, 716-845-4106, Fax: 716-845-2993, E-mail: kelvin.lee@roswellpark.org. *Application contact:* Dr. Norman J. Karin, Associate Dean, 716-845-4630, Fax: 716-845-8178, E-mail: norman.karin@roswellpark.edu.
Website: http://www.roswellpark.edu/education/phd-programs/immunology

University at Buffalo, the State University of New York, Graduate School, Jacobs School of Medicine and Biomedical Sciences, Graduate Programs in Medicine and Biomedical Sciences, Department of Microbiology and Immunology, Buffalo, NY 14203. Offers MS, PhD. *Program availability:* Part-time. *Faculty:* 17 full-time (6 women), 2 part-time/adjunct (0 women). *Students:* 16 full-time (9 women), 5 part-time (4 women); includes 5 minority (2 Black or African American, non-Hispanic/Latino; 1 American Indian or Alaska Native, non-Hispanic/Latino; 2 Asian, non-Hispanic/Latino). Average age 26. 39 applicants, 46% accepted, 7 enrolled. In 2017, 2 master's, 3 doctorates awarded. Terminal master's awarded for partial completion of doctoral program. *Degree requirements:* For master's, comprehensive exam, thesis or alternative; for doctorate, thesis/dissertation, departmental qualifying exam. *Entrance requirements:* For master's and doctorate, GRE General Test, 3 letters of recommendation, personal statement, curriculum vitae/resume, transcripts. Additional exam requirements/recommendations for international students: Required—TOEFL (minimum score 79 iBT) or IELTS (minimum score 6.5). *Application deadline:* For fall admission, 4/1 priority date for international students. Applications are processed on a rolling basis. Application fee: $85. Electronic applications accepted. *Expenses:* $621 per credit hour resident tuition and fees; $1,093 per credit hour nonresident tuition and fees. *Financial support:* In 2017–18, 15 students received support, including 2 fellowships with full tuition reimbursements available (averaging $24,000 per year), 12 research assistantships with full tuition reimbursements available (averaging $27,000 per year), 2 teaching assistantships (averaging $5,333 per year); health care benefits and unspecified assistantships also available. Financial award application deadline: 2/1; financial award applicants required to submit FAFSA. *Faculty research:* Bacteriology, immunology, parasitology, virology, mycology. *Total annual research expenditures:* $5.4 million. *Unit head:* Dr. James Bangs, Chair/Professor, 716-829-2907, Fax: 716-829-2158. *Application contact:* Dr. Ira Blader, Director of Graduate Studies, 716-829-5809, Fax: 716-829-2158.
Website: http://medicine.buffalo.edu/departments/micro.html

The University of Alabama at Birmingham, Joint Health Sciences, Immunology Theme, Birmingham, AL 35294. Offers PhD. *Faculty:* 370. *Students:* 43 full-time (18 women); includes 18 minority (4 Black or African American, non-Hispanic/Latino; 10 Asian, non-Hispanic/Latino; 4 Hispanic/Latino). Average age 27. 44 applicants, 25% accepted, 7 enrolled. In 2017, 8 doctorates awarded. *Degree requirements:* For doctorate, comprehensive exam, thesis/dissertation. *Entrance requirements:* For doctorate, personal statement, resume or curriculum vitae, letters of recommendation, research experience, interview. Additional exam requirements/recommendations for international students: Required—TOEFL (minimum score 80 iBT), IELTS (minimum score 6.5). *Application deadline:* For fall admission, 12/31 for domestic and international students. Applications are processed on a rolling basis. Electronic applications accepted. *Financial support:* In 2017–18, fellowships with full tuition reimbursements (averaging $29,000 per year), research assistantships with full tuition reimbursements (averaging $30,000 per year) were awarded; health care benefits also available. *Unit head:* Dr. Louis Justement, Theme Director, 205-934-1429, E-mail: lbjust@uab.edu. *Application contact:* Alyssa Zasada, Admissions Manager for Graduate Biomedical Sciences, 205-934-3857, E-mail: grad-gbs@uab.edu.
Website: http://www.uab.edu/gbs/home/themes/imm

University of Alberta, Faculty of Medicine and Dentistry and Faculty of Graduate Studies and Research, Graduate Programs in Medicine, Department of Medical Microbiology and Immunology, Edmonton, AB T6G 2E1, Canada. Offers M Sc, PhD. Terminal master's awarded for partial completion of doctoral program. *Degree requirements:* For master's, thesis; for doctorate, thesis/dissertation. *Entrance requirements:* For master's and doctorate, minimum GPA of 3.3. Additional exam requirements/recommendations for international students: Required—TOEFL (minimum score 600 paper-based; 96 iBT). *Faculty research:* Cellular and reproductive immunology, microbial pathogenesis, mechanisms of antibiotic resistance, molecular biology of mammalian viruses, antiviral chemotherapy.

The University of Arizona, College of Medicine, Department of Immunobiology, Tucson, AZ 85721. Offers PhD. *Degree requirements:* For doctorate, thesis/dissertation. *Entrance requirements:* For doctorate, GRE General Test, minimum GPA of 3.0. *Faculty research:* Environmental and pathogenic microbiology, molecular biology.

University of Arkansas for Medical Sciences, Graduate School, Little Rock, AR 72205. Offers biochemistry and molecular biology (MS, PhD); bioinformatics (MS, PhD); cellular physiology and molecular biophysics (MS, PhD); clinical nutrition (MS); interdisciplinary biomedical sciences (MS, PhD, Certificate); interdisciplinary toxicology (MS); microbiology and immunology (PhD); neurobiology and developmental sciences (PhD); pharmacology (PhD); MD/PhD. Bioinformatics programs hosted jointly with the University of Arkansas at Little Rock. *Program availability:* Part-time. Terminal master's awarded for partial completion of doctoral program. *Degree requirements:* For master's, comprehensive exam (for some programs), thesis (for some programs); for doctorate, thesis/dissertation. *Entrance requirements:* For master's and doctorate, GRE. Additional exam requirements/recommendations for international students: Required—TOEFL. Electronic applications accepted. *Expenses:* Contact institution.

The University of British Columbia, Faculty of Science, Department of Microbiology and Immunology, Vancouver, BC V6T 1Z3, Canada. Offers M Sc, PhD. *Degree requirements:* For master's, thesis; for doctorate, comprehensive exam, thesis/dissertation. *Entrance requirements:* For master's and doctorate, GRE General Test. Additional exam requirements/recommendations for international students: Required—TOEFL. Electronic applications accepted. *Expenses:* Contact institution. *Faculty research:* Bacterial genetics, metabolism, pathogenic bacteriology, virology.

University of Calgary, Cumming School of Medicine and Faculty of Graduate Studies, Department of Microbiology, Immunology and Infectious Diseases, Calgary, AB T2N 1N4, Canada. Offers M Sc, PhD. *Degree requirements:* For master's, thesis, oral thesis exam; for doctorate, thesis/dissertation, candidacy exam, oral thesis exam. *Entrance requirements:* For master's and doctorate, minimum GPA of 3.2. Additional exam requirements/recommendations for international students: Required—TOEFL (minimum score 580 paper-based). Electronic applications accepted. *Faculty research:* Bacteriology, virology, parasitology, immunology.

University of California, Berkeley, Graduate Division, School of Public Health, Group in Infectious Diseases and Immunity, Berkeley, CA 94720-1500. Offers PhD. *Entrance requirements:* For doctorate, GRE General Test, minimum GPA of 3.0, 3 letters of recommendation. Electronic applications accepted.

University of California, Davis, Graduate Studies, Graduate Group in Immunology, Davis, CA 95616. Offers MS, PhD. Terminal master's awarded for partial completion of doctoral program. *Degree requirements:* For master's, comprehensive exam (for some programs), thesis (for some programs); for doctorate, thesis/dissertation. *Entrance requirements:* For master's and doctorate, GRE General Test. Additional exam requirements/recommendations for international students: Required—TOEFL (minimum score 550 paper-based). Electronic applications accepted. *Faculty research:* Immune regulation in autoimmunity, immunopathology, immunotoxicology, tumor immunology, avian immunology.

University of California, Los Angeles, David Geffen School of Medicine and Graduate Division, Graduate Programs in Medicine, Department of Microbiology, Immunology and Molecular Genetics, Los Angeles, CA 90095. Offers MS, PhD. *Degree requirements:* For master's, thesis; for doctorate, thesis/dissertation, oral and written qualifying exams; 2 quarters of teaching experience. *Entrance requirements:* For master's and doctorate, GRE General Test, bachelor's degree; minimum undergraduate GPA of 3.0 (or its equivalent if letter grade system not used). Additional exam requirements/recommendations for international students: Required—TOEFL. Electronic applications accepted.

University of California, Los Angeles, Graduate Division, College of Letters and Science and David Geffen School of Medicine, UCLA ACCESS to Programs in the Molecular, Cellular and Integrative Life Sciences, Los Angeles, CA 90095. Offers biochemistry and molecular biology (PhD); biological chemistry (PhD); cellular and molecular pathology (PhD); human genetics (PhD); microbiology, immunology, and molecular genetics (PhD); molecular biology (PhD); molecular toxicology (PhD); molecular, cellular and integrative physiology (PhD); neurobiology (PhD); oral biology (PhD); physiology (PhD). *Degree requirements:* For doctorate, thesis/dissertation, oral and written qualifying exams. *Entrance requirements:* For doctorate, GRE General Test, bachelor's degree; minimum undergraduate GPA of 3.0 (or its equivalent if letter grade system not used). Additional exam requirements/recommendations for international students: Required—TOEFL. Electronic applications accepted.

University of Chicago, Division of the Biological Sciences, Committee on Immunology, Chicago, IL 60637. Offers PhD. *Students:* 38 full-time (16 women); includes 10 minority (3 Black or African American, non-Hispanic/Latino; 5 Asian, non-Hispanic/Latino; 1 Hispanic/Latino; 1 Two or more races, non-Hispanic/Latino), 2 international. Average age 27. 108 applicants, 14% accepted, 6 enrolled. In 2017, 5 doctorates awarded. *Degree requirements:* For doctorate, thesis/dissertation, ethics class, 2 teaching assistantships, preliminary exams. *Entrance requirements:* For doctorate, GRE General Test, transcripts, statement of purpose, 3 letters of recommendation. Additional exam requirements/recommendations for international students: Required—TOEFL (minimum score 600 paper-based; 104 iBT), IELTS (minimum score 7). *Application deadline:* For fall admission, 12/1 for domestic and international students. Application fee: $90. Electronic applications accepted. *Financial support:* In 2017–18, 27 students received support, including 10 fellowships with full tuition reimbursements available (averaging $31,000 per year), 16 research assistantships with full tuition reimbursements available (averaging $31,000 per year); institutionally sponsored loans, scholarships/grants, traineeships, and health care benefits also available. Financial award application deadline: 12/1. *Faculty research:* Molecular immunology, transplantation, auto immunology, neuroimmunology, tumor immunology. *Total annual research expenditures:* $15 million. *Unit head:* Dr. Alexander Chervonsky, Chair, 773-702-1371, E-mail: bsdadmissions@uchicago.edu. *Application contact:* Lisa Abston-Leftridge, PhD, Administrative Director, 773-834-3899, E-mail: labstonleftridge@bsd.uchicago.edu.
Website: http://biomedsciences.uchicago.edu/page/committee-immunology-0

University of Cincinnati, Graduate School, College of Medicine, Graduate Programs in Biomedical Sciences, Department of Pediatrics, Cincinnati, OH 45221. Offers immunobiology (PhD); molecular and developmental biology (PhD). *Degree requirements:* For doctorate, thesis/dissertation, qualifying exam. *Entrance requirements:* For doctorate, GRE General Test, minimum GPA of 3.0. Additional exam requirements/recommendations for international students: Required—TOEFL (minimum score 600 paper-based; 100 iBT). Electronic applications accepted. *Expenses: Tuition, area resident:* Full-time $14,468. Tuition, state resident: full-time $14,968; part-time $754 per credit hour. Tuition, nonresident: full-time $24,210; part-time $1311 per credit hour. *International tuition:* $26,460 full-time. *Required fees:* $3958; $84 per credit hour. One-time fee: $85 full-time. Tuition and fees vary according to course load, degree level and program. *Faculty research:* Pulmonary biology, molecular cardiovascular, developmental biology, cancer biology, genetics.

University of Cincinnati, Graduate School, College of Medicine, Graduate Programs in Biomedical Sciences, Immunology Graduate Program, Cincinnati, OH 45229. Offers MS, PhD. *Program availability:* Part-time. *Degree requirements:* For master's, seminar, thesis with oral defense; for doctorate, seminar, dissertation with oral defense, written and oral candidacy exams. *Entrance requirements:* For master's, GRE, bachelor's degree in biology-related field or bachelor's degree in any field and work experience in biology-related field; for doctorate, GRE, bachelor's degree in biology-related field. Additional exam requirements/recommendations for international students: Required—TOEFL (minimum score 100 iBT). Electronic applications accepted. *Expenses: Tuition, area resident:* Full-time $14,468. Tuition, state resident: full-time $14,968; part-time $754 per credit hour. Tuition, nonresident: full-time $24,210; part-time $1311 per credit hour. *International tuition:* $26,460 full-time. *Required fees:* $3958; $84 per credit hour. One-time fee: $85 full-time. Tuition and fees vary according to course load, degree level and program. *Faculty research:* Allergy and asthma, cancer, organ transplantation, immunodeficiences: Lupus and AIDS, diabetes.

University of Colorado Denver, School of Medicine, Integrated Department of Immunology, Aurora, CO 80206. Offers PhD. *Students:* 37 full-time (17 women), 1 (woman) part-time; includes 7 minority (3 Asian, non-Hispanic/Latino; 2 Hispanic/Latino; 2 Two or more races, non-Hispanic/Latino). Average age 28. 69 applicants, 7% accepted, 5 enrolled. In 2017, 11 doctorates awarded. *Degree requirements:* For doctorate, thesis/dissertation, 30 credit hours of formal course work, three laboratory rotations, oral comprehensive examination, 30 credit hours of dissertation research, final defense of the dissertation. *Entrance requirements:* For doctorate, GRE, letters of recommendation, statement of purpose, interview. Additional exam requirements/recommendations for international students: Required—TOEFL (minimum score 550 paper-based; 89 iBT). *Application deadline:* For fall admission, 12/1 for domestic students, 11/1 for international students. Application fee: $50 ($75 for international students). Electronic applications accepted. *Faculty research:* Gene regulation, immune signaling, apoptosis, stem cells, vaccines. *Unit head:* Dr. John Cambier, Professor/Chairman, 303-724-8663, E-mail: john.cambier@ucdenver.edu. *Application contact:* Elizabeth Wethington, LEAD Program Administrator, 303-724-7280, E-mail: elizabeth.wethington@ucdenver.edu.
Website: http://www.ucdenver.edu/academics/colleges/medicalschool/departments/ImmunologyMicrobiology/gradprogram/immugradprog/Pages/ImmuGradHome.aspx

University of Colorado Denver, School of Medicine, Program in Microbiology, Aurora, CO 80206. Offers microbiology (PhD); microbiology and immunology (PhD). In 2017, 3 doctorates awarded. *Entrance requirements:* For doctorate, GRE, three letters of reference, two copies of official transcripts, minimum GPA of 3.0. Application fee: $0. *Faculty research:* Molecular mechanisms of picornavirus replication, mechanisms of papovavirus assembly, human immune response in multiple sclerosis. *Unit head:* Dr. John Cambier, Chair, 303-724-8663, E-mail: john.cambier@ucdenver.edu. *Application contact:* Elizabeth Wethington, Program Administrator, 303-724-7280, E-mail: elizabeth.wethington@ucdenver.edu.
Website: http://www.ucdenver.edu/academics/colleges/medicalschool/departments/ImmunologyMicrobiology/Pages/welcome.aspx

University of Connecticut Health Center, Graduate School, Programs in Biomedical Sciences, Graduate Program in Immunology, Farmington, CT 06030. Offers PhD, DMD/PhD, MD/PhD. *Degree requirements:* For doctorate, comprehensive exam, thesis/dissertation. *Entrance requirements:* For doctorate, GRE General Test. Additional exam requirements/recommendations for international students: Required—TOEFL (minimum score 600 paper-based). Electronic applications accepted. *Faculty research:* Developmental immunology, T-cell immunity, lymphoid cell development, tolerance and tumor immunity, leukocyte chemotaxis.

University of Florida, College of Medicine and Graduate School, Interdisciplinary Program in Biomedical Sciences, Concentration in Immunology and Microbiology, Gainesville, FL 32611. Offers PhD. *Degree requirements:* For doctorate, thesis/dissertation. *Entrance requirements:* For doctorate, GRE General Test, minimum GPA of 3.0, biochemistry before enrollment. Additional exam requirements/recommendations for international students: Required—TOEFL. Electronic applications accepted.

University of Guelph, Ontario Veterinary College and Graduate Studies, Graduate Programs in Veterinary Sciences, Department of Pathobiology, Guelph, ON N1G 2W1, Canada. Offers anatomic pathology (DV Sc, Diploma); clinical pathology (Diploma); comparative pathology (M Sc, PhD); immunology (M Sc, PhD); laboratory animal science (DV Sc); pathology (M Sc, PhD, Diploma); veterinary infectious diseases (M Sc, PhD); zoo animal/wildlife medicine (DV Sc). *Degree requirements:* For master's, thesis; for doctorate, thesis/dissertation. *Entrance requirements:* For master's, DVM with B average or an honours degree in biological sciences; for doctorate, DVM or MSC degree, minimum B+ average. Additional exam requirements/recommendations for international students: Required—TOEFL (minimum score 550 paper-based). *Faculty research:* Pathogenesis; diseases of animals, wildlife, fish, and laboratory animals; parasitology; immunology; veterinary infectious diseases; laboratory animal science.

University of Illinois at Chicago, College of Medicine and Graduate College, Graduate Programs in Medicine, Department of Microbiology and Immunology, Chicago, IL 60607-7128. Offers PhD, MD/PhD. *Degree requirements:* For doctorate, thesis/dissertation. *Entrance requirements:* For doctorate, GRE General Test, minimum GPA of 2.75. Additional exam requirements/recommendations for international students: Required—TOEFL. *Faculty research:* Class I major histocompatibility complex molecules; proteins such as azurin with the immunoglobulin folds; T cell immunobiology relevant to disease pathogenesis, immunotherapeutics and vaccines for HIV/AIDS, tuberculosis, AIDS-related tuberculosis, and malaria, plague and smallpox; intracellular bacterial pathogen Listeria monocytogenes; virus infection.

The University of Iowa, Graduate College, Program in Immunology, Iowa City, IA 52242-1316. Offers PhD. *Degree requirements:* For doctorate, comprehensive exam, thesis/dissertation. *Entrance requirements:* For doctorate, GRE General Test, minimum GPA of 3.0. Additional exam requirements/recommendations for international students: Required—TOEFL (minimum score 600 paper-based; 100 iBT). Electronic applications accepted.

The University of Iowa, Roy J. and Lucille A. Carver College of Medicine and Graduate College, Graduate Programs in Medicine, Department of Microbiology, Iowa City, IA 52242-1316. Offers general microbiology and microbial physiology (MS, PhD); immunology (MS, PhD); microbial genetics (MS, PhD); pathogenic bacteriology (MS, PhD); virology (MS, PhD). *Degree requirements:* For master's, thesis; for doctorate, comprehensive exam, thesis/dissertation. *Entrance requirements:* For master's and doctorate, GRE General Test. Additional exam requirements/recommendations for international students: Required—TOEFL (minimum score 600 paper-based). Electronic applications accepted. *Faculty research:* Gene regulation, processing and transport of HIV, retroviral pathogenesis, biodegradation, biofilm.

University of Kentucky, Graduate School, Graduate School Programs from the College of Medicine, Program in Microbiology and Immunology, Lexington, KY 40506-0032. Offers PhD. *Degree requirements:* For doctorate, comprehensive exam, thesis/dissertation. *Entrance requirements:* For doctorate, GRE General Test, minimum undergraduate GPA of 2.75. Additional exam requirements/recommendations for international students: Required—TOEFL (minimum score 550 paper-based). Electronic applications accepted.

University of Louisville, School of Medicine, Department of Microbiology and Immunology, Louisville, KY 40292-0001. Offers MS, PhD, MD/PhD. *Program availability:* Part-time. *Students:* 34 full-time (20 women), 6 part-time (5 women); includes 7 minority (2 Black or African American, non-Hispanic/Latino; 1 Hispanic/Latino; 4 Two or more races, non-Hispanic/Latino), 10 international. Average age 29. 36 applicants, 25% accepted, 8 enrolled. Terminal master's awarded for partial completion of doctoral program. *Degree requirements:* For master's, comprehensive exam, thesis or alternative; for doctorate, comprehensive exam, thesis/dissertation. *Entrance requirements:* For master's and doctorate, GRE General Test (minimum score of 300 verbal and quantitative), minimum GPA of 3.0; 1 year of course work in biology and organic chemistry; 1 semester of course work in introductory calculus and biochemistry. Additional exam requirements/recommendations for international students: Required—TOEFL (minimum score 550 paper-based; 79 iBT), IELTS (minimum score 6.5). *Application deadline:* For fall admission, 3/1 priority date for domestic and international students. Applications are processed on a rolling basis. Application fee: $65. Electronic applications accepted. *Expenses:* Tuition, state resident: full-time $12,246; part-time $681 per credit hour. Tuition, nonresident: full-time $25,486; part-time $1417 per credit hour. *Required fees:* $196. Tuition and fees vary according to course load, program and reciprocity agreements. *Financial support:* In 2017–18, fellowships with full tuition reimbursements (averaging $25,500 per year), research assistantships with full tuition reimbursements (averaging $25,500 per year) were awarded; health care benefits also available. Financial award application deadline: 3/1. *Faculty research:* Biodefense/emerging infectious diseases; autoimmune disease and basic immune mechanisms; bacterial and viral pathogenesis; vaccines; tumor immunity. *Total annual research expenditures:* $4.7 million. *Unit head:* Dr. Nejat Egilmez, Chair, 502-852-5351, Fax: 502-852-7531, E-mail: nejat.egilmez@louisville.edu. *Application contact:* Carolyn Burton, Graduate Program Coordinator, 502-852-6208, Fax: 502-852-7531, E-mail: cmburt01@louisville.edu.
Website: http://louisville.edu/medicine/departments/microbiology

The University of Manchester, School of Biological Sciences, Manchester, United Kingdom. Offers adaptive organismal biology (M Phil, PhD); animal biology (M Phil, PhD); biochemistry (M Phil, PhD); bioinformatics (M Phil, PhD); biomolecular sciences

(M Phil, PhD); biotechnology (M Phil, PhD); cell biology (M Phil, PhD); cell matrix research (M Phil, PhD); channels and transporters (M Phil, PhD); developmental biology (M Phil, PhD); environmental biology (M Phil, PhD); evolutionary biology (M Phil, PhD); gene expression (M Phil, PhD); genetics (M Phil, PhD); history of science, technology and medicine (M Phil, PhD); immunology (M Phil, PhD); integrative neurobiology and behavior (M Phil, PhD); membrane trafficking (M Phil, PhD); microbiology (M Phil, PhD); molecular and cellular neuroscience (M Phil, PhD); molecular biology (M Phil, PhD); molecular cancer studies (M Phil, PhD); neuroscience (M Phil, PhD); ophthalmology (M Phil, PhD); optometry (M Phil, PhD); organelle function (M Phil, PhD); pharmacology (M Phil, PhD); physiology (M Phil, PhD); plant sciences (M Phil, PhD); stem cell research (M Phil, PhD); structural biology (M Phil, PhD); systems neuroscience (M Phil, PhD); toxicology (M Phil, PhD).

University of Manitoba, Max Rady College of Medicine and Faculty of Graduate Studies, Graduate Programs in Medicine, Department of Immunology, Winnipeg, MB R3T 2N2, Canada. Offers M Sc, PhD. Terminal master's awarded for partial completion of doctoral program. *Degree requirements:* For master's, thesis; for doctorate, one foreign language, thesis/dissertation. *Faculty research:* Immediate hypersensitivity, regulation of the immune response, natural immunity, cytokines, inflammation.

University of Maryland, Baltimore, Graduate School, Graduate Program in Life Sciences, Program in Molecular Microbiology and Immunology, Baltimore, MD 21201. Offers PhD, MD/PhD. *Students:* 42 full-time (22 women); includes 13 minority (5 Black or African American, non-Hispanic/Latino; 4 Asian, non-Hispanic/Latino; 1 Hispanic/Latino; 3 Two or more races, non-Hispanic/Latino), 2 international. Average age 28. 101 applicants, 11% accepted, 3 enrolled. In 2017, 11 doctorates awarded. *Degree requirements:* For doctorate, comprehensive exam, thesis/dissertation. *Entrance requirements:* For doctorate, GRE General Test, minimum GPA of 3.0, curriculum vitae, essay, 3 letters of recommendation. Additional exam requirements/recommendations for international students: Required—TOEFL (minimum score 80 iBT); Recommended—IELTS (minimum score 7). *Application deadline:* For fall admission, 1/15 for domestic and international students. Application fee: $75. Electronic applications accepted. *Expenses:* Tuition, state resident: full-time $13,990; part-time $661 per credit. Tuition, nonresident: full-time $30,484; part-time $1310 per credit. *Required fees:* $1894; $94 per credit. $415 per semester. Part-time tuition and fees vary according to course load, degree level and program. *Financial support:* In 2017–18, research assistantships with partial tuition reimbursements (averaging $26,000 per year) were awarded; fellowships and health care benefits also available. Financial award application deadline: 3/1; financial award applicants required to submit FAFSA. *Unit head:* Dr. Brett Hassel, Director, 410-706-2344, E-mail: bhassel@som.umaryland.edu. *Application contact:* June Green, Program Coordinator, 410-706-7126, Fax: 410-706-2129, E-mail: jgreen@umaryland.edu.
Website: http://lifesciences.umaryland.edu/microbiology/

University of Massachusetts Medical School, Graduate School of Biomedical Sciences, Worcester, MA 01655-0115. Offers biomedical sciences (PhD), including biochemistry and molecular pharmacology, bioinformatics and computational biology, cancer biology, immunology and microbiology, interdisciplinary, neuroscience, translational science; biomedical sciences (millennium program) (PhD); clinical and population health research (PhD); clinical investigation (MS). *Faculty:* 1,316 full-time (526 women), 357 part-time/adjunct (229 women). *Students:* 347 full-time (180 women); includes 61 minority (10 Black or African American, non-Hispanic/Latino; 1 American Indian or Alaska Native, non-Hispanic/Latino; 35 Asian, non-Hispanic/Latino; 15 Hispanic/Latino), 130 international. Average age 29. 608 applicants, 28% accepted, 54 enrolled. In 2017, 6 master's, 51 doctorates awarded. Terminal master's awarded for partial completion of doctoral program. *Degree requirements:* For master's, comprehensive exam, thesis; for doctorate, comprehensive exam, thesis/dissertation. *Entrance requirements:* For master's, MD, PhD, DVM, or PharmD; for doctorate, GRE General Test, bachelor's degree. Additional exam requirements/recommendations for international students: Required—TOEFL (minimum score 90 iBT) or IELTS (minimum score 7.0). *Application deadline:* For fall admission, 12/15 for domestic and international students. Applications are processed on a rolling basis. Application fee: $80. Electronic applications accepted. Application fee is waived when completed online. *Expenses:* $14,883 in-state tuition and mandatory fees; $31,486 out-of-state. *Financial support:* In 2017–18, 15 fellowships with partial tuition reimbursements (averaging $29,000 per year), 296 research assistantships with full tuition reimbursements (averaging $31,212 per year) were awarded; institutionally sponsored loans and scholarships/grants also available. Financial award application deadline: 5/15. *Faculty research:* RNA biology, molecular/cell/developmental/metabolic biology, bioinformatics and computational biology, clinical/translational research, infectious disease and immunology. *Total annual research expenditures:* $279 million. *Unit head:* Dr. Mary Ellen Lane, Dean, 508-856-4018, E-mail: maryellen.lane@umassmed.edu. *Application contact:* Dr. Kendall Knight, Assistant Vice Provost for Admissions, 508-856-5628, Fax: 508-856-3659, E-mail: kendall.knight@umassmed.edu.
Website: http://www.umassmed.edu/gsbs/

University of Miami, Graduate School, Miller School of Medicine, Graduate Programs in Medicine, Department of Microbiology and Immunology, Coral Gables, FL 33124. Offers PhD, MD/PhD. *Degree requirements:* For doctorate, thesis/dissertation, oral and written qualifying exams. *Entrance requirements:* For doctorate, GRE General Test. Additional exam requirements/recommendations for international students: Required—TOEFL. Electronic applications accepted. *Faculty research:* Cellular and molecular immunology, molecular and pathogenic virology, pathogenic bacteriology and gene therapy of cancer.

University of Michigan, Rackham Graduate School, Program in Biomedical Sciences (PIBS), Department of Microbiology and Immunology, Ann Arbor, MI 48109-5620. Offers MS, PhD. *Program availability:* Part-time. *Faculty:* 25 full-time (14 women), 15 part-time/adjunct (4 women). *Students:* 40 full-time (21 women), 3 part-time (2 women); includes 6 minority (2 Black or African American, non-Hispanic/Latino; 3 Asian, non-Hispanic/Latino; 1 Hispanic/Latino), 2 international. Average age 27. 147 applicants, 10% accepted, 7 enrolled. In 2017, 4 master's, 9 doctorates awarded. Terminal master's awarded for partial completion of doctoral program. *Degree requirements:* For master's, thesis optional; for doctorate, comprehensive exam, thesis/dissertation, oral defense of dissertation, preliminary exam. *Entrance requirements:* For master's and doctorate, GRE General Test. Additional exam requirements/recommendations for international students: Required—TOEFL (minimum score 600 paper-based; 84 iBT), TWE. *Application deadline:* For fall admission, 12/1 for domestic and international students. Application fee: $75. Electronic applications accepted. *Expenses:* Tuition, state resident: full-time $22,368; part-time $1201 per credit hour. Tuition, nonresident: full-time $45,156; part-time $2467 per credit hour. *Required fees:* $376 per term. Tuition and fees vary according to course load, degree level and program. *Financial support:* In 2017–18, 15 fellowships with full tuition reimbursements (averaging $28,500 per year), 20 research assistantships with full tuition reimbursements (averaging $28,500 per year) were awarded; scholarships/grants, health care benefits, and tuition waivers (full) also available. Financial award application deadline: 5/15. *Faculty research:* Mechanisms by which viruses, bacteria, fungi, and parasites elicit pathogenesis in the infected host; viral pathogens; bacterial pathogens; eukaryotic pathogens; innate immunity; adaptive immunity cell biology of infection. *Total annual research expenditures:* $10.2 million. *Unit head:* Dr. Harry L. T. Mobley, Chair, 734-764-1466, Fax: 734-764-3562, E-mail: hmobley@umich.edu. *Application contact:* Heidi Thompson, Senior Student Administrative Assistant, 734-763-3532, Fax: 734-764-3562, E-mail: heiditho@umich.edu.
Website: http://www.med.umich.edu/microbio/

University of Michigan, Rackham Graduate School, Program in Biomedical Sciences (PIBS), Program in Immunology, Ann Arbor, MI 48109-0619. Offers PhD. *Faculty:* 67 full-time (21 women). *Students:* 21 full-time (10 women); includes 11 minority (2 Black or African American, non-Hispanic/Latino; 5 Asian, non-Hispanic/Latino; 3 Hispanic/Latino; 1 Native Hawaiian or other Pacific Islander, non-Hispanic/Latino). Average age 28. 97 applicants, 12% accepted, 6 enrolled. In 2017, 4 doctorates awarded. *Degree requirements:* For doctorate, thesis/dissertation, oral defense of dissertation, preliminary exam. *Entrance requirements:* For doctorate, GRE General Test, 3 letters of recommendation, research experience, personal statement. Additional exam requirements/recommendations for international students: Required—TOEFL (minimum score 84 iBT). *Application deadline:* For fall admission, 12/1 for domestic students. Application fee: $75. Electronic applications accepted. *Expenses:* $45,576 per year. *Financial support:* In 2017–18, 24 students received support, including 14 fellowships with full tuition reimbursements available (averaging $30,600 per year), 6 research assistantships with full tuition reimbursements available (averaging $30,600 per year); scholarships/grants, health care benefits, tuition waivers (full), and unspecified assistantships also available. Financial award application deadline: 12/1. *Faculty research:* Cytokine networks, T and B cell activation, autoimmunity, antigen processing/presentation, cell signaling, cytokine production, regulation of immune cell differentiation, and the link between innate and acquired immunity. *Total annual research expenditures:* $2.1 million. *Unit head:* Dr. Bethany Moore, Professor of Internal Medicine, Microbiology and Immunology/Graduate Program in Immunology Director, 734-647-8378, Fax: 734-615-2331, E-mail: bmoore@umich.edu. *Application contact:* Michelle S. Melis, Director of Student Life, 734-615-6538, Fax: 734-647-7022, E-mail: msmtegan@umich.edu.
Website: http://immunology.medicine.umich.edu/

University of Minnesota, Duluth, Medical School, Microbiology, Immunology and Molecular Pathobiology Section, Duluth, MN 55812-2496. Offers MS, PhD. MS, PhD offered jointly with University of Minnesota, Twin Cities Campus. Terminal master's awarded for partial completion of doctoral program. *Degree requirements:* For master's, thesis, final oral exam; for doctorate, thesis/dissertation, final exam, oral and written preliminary exams. *Entrance requirements:* For master's and doctorate, GRE General Test. Additional exam requirements/recommendations for international students: Required—TOEFL. *Faculty research:* Immunomodulation, molecular diagnosis of rabies, cytokines, cancer immunology, cytomegalovirus infection.

University of Minnesota, Twin Cities Campus, Graduate School, PhD Program in Microbiology, Immunology and Cancer Biology, Minneapolis, MN 55455-0213. Offers PhD. *Degree requirements:* For doctorate, thesis/dissertation. *Entrance requirements:* For doctorate, GRE General Test. Additional exam requirements/recommendations for international students: Required—TOEFL (minimum score 600 paper-based). Electronic applications accepted. *Faculty research:* Virology, microbiology, cancer biology, immunology.

University of Missouri, School of Medicine and Office of Research and Graduate Studies, Graduate Programs in Medicine, Department of Molecular Microbiology and Immunology, Columbia, MO 65211. Offers PhD. Terminal master's awarded for partial completion of doctoral program. *Degree requirements:* For doctorate, thesis/dissertation. *Entrance requirements:* For doctorate, GRE General Test, minimum GPA of 3.0. Additional exam requirements/recommendations for international students: Required—TOEFL. *Expenses:* Tuition, state resident: full-time $6480. Tuition, nonresident: full-time $17,744. *Required fees:* $1108. Tuition and fees vary according to course load, campus/location and program. *Financial support:* Fellowships, research assistantships, teaching assistantships, institutionally sponsored loans, scholarships/grants, traineeships, health care benefits, and unspecified assistantships available. Support available to part-time students. *Unit head:* Dr. Donald H. Burke-Aguero, Interim Chair. *Application contact:* Dr. Donald H. Burke-Aguero, Interim Chair.
Website: http://medicine.missouri.edu/education/phd.html

University of Montana, Graduate School, College of Humanities and Sciences, Division of Biological Sciences, Program in Cellular, Molecular and Microbial Biology, Missoula, MT 59812. Offers cellular and developmental biology (PhD); microbial evolution and ecology (PhD); microbiology and immunology (PhD); molecular biology and biochemistry (PhD). Terminal master's awarded for partial completion of doctoral program. *Degree requirements:* For doctorate, variable foreign language requirement, thesis/dissertation. *Entrance requirements:* For doctorate, GRE General Test. *Faculty research:* Ribosome structure, medical microbiology/pathogenesis, microbial ecology/environmental microbiology.

University of Nebraska Medical Center, Interdisciplinary Graduate Program in Biomedical Sciences, Immunology, Pathology and Infectious Disease Graduate Program, Omaha, NE 68198-5900. Offers MS, PhD. *Program availability:* Part-time. *Faculty:* 84 full-time (26 women). *Students:* 41 full-time (27 women), 4 part-time (3 women); includes 5 minority (1 Black or African American, non-Hispanic/Latino; 1 American Indian or Alaska Native, non-Hispanic/Latino; 3 Asian, non-Hispanic/Latino), 21 international. Average age 28. 21 applicants, 38% accepted, 7 enrolled. In 2017, 4 master's, 2 doctorates awarded. Terminal master's awarded for partial completion of doctoral program. *Degree requirements:* For master's, comprehensive exam, thesis; for doctorate, comprehensive exam, thesis/dissertation. *Entrance requirements:* For master's, previous course work in biology, chemistry, mathematics, and physics; for doctorate, GRE General Test, previous course work in biology, chemistry, mathematics, and physics. Additional exam requirements/recommendations for international students: Required—TOEFL (minimum score 550 paper-based; 90 iBT), IELTS (minimum score 6.5). *Application deadline:* For fall admission, 4/1 for domestic and international students; for spring admission, 10/1 for domestic and international students; for summer admission, 3/1 for domestic students, 1/1 for international students. Applications are processed on a rolling basis. Application fee: $60. Electronic applications accepted. *Expenses:* Tuition, state resident: full-time $8451; part-time $4225 per semester. Tuition, nonresident: full-time $24,219; part-time $11,295 per semester. *Required fees:* $589; $117 per term. *Financial support:* In 2017–18, 5 students received support, including 2 fellowships with full tuition reimbursements available (averaging $24,000 per year), 3 research assistantships with full tuition reimbursements available (averaging $24,000 per year); scholarships/grants, health care benefits, and unspecified assistantships also available. Financial award application deadline: 3/1; financial award applicants required to submit FAFSA. *Faculty research:* Infectious diseases, cancer biology, immunobiology, molecular virology, molecular genetics. *Unit head:* Dr. Rakesh K. Singh, Chair, Graduate Committee, 402-559-9949, Fax: 402-559-5900, E-mail: rsingh@unmc.edu. *Application contact:* Tuire Cechin, Graduate Program Coordinator, 402-559-4042, Fax: 402-559-5900, E-mail: tcechin@unmc.edu.
Website: http://www.unmc.edu/pathology/

The University of North Carolina at Chapel Hill, School of Medicine and Graduate School, Graduate Programs in Medicine, Department of Microbiology and Immunology, Chapel Hill, NC 27599-7290. Offers immunology (MS, PhD); microbiology (MS, PhD). Terminal master's awarded for partial completion of doctoral program. *Degree requirements:* For master's, comprehensive exam, thesis; for doctorate, comprehensive exam, thesis/dissertation. *Entrance requirements:* For master's and doctorate, GRE General Test, minimum GPA of 3.0. Electronic applications accepted. *Faculty research:* HIV pathogenesis, immune response, t-cell mediated autoimmunity, alpha-viruses, bacterial chemotaxis, francisella tularensis, pertussis, Mycobacterium tuberculosis, Burkholderia, Dengue virus.

University of North Texas Health Science Center at Fort Worth, Graduate School of Biomedical Sciences, Fort Worth, TX 76107-2699. Offers biochemistry and cancer biology (MS, PhD); biotechnology (MS); cell biology, immunology and microbiology (MS, PhD); clinical research management (MS); forensic genetics (MS); genetics (MS, PhD); integrative physiology (MS, PhD); medical sciences (MS); pharmaceutical sciences and pharmacotherapy (MS, PhD); pharmacology and neuroscience (MS, PhD); structural anatomy and rehabilitation sciences (MS, PhD); DO/MS; DO/PhD. Terminal master's awarded for partial completion of doctoral program. *Degree requirements:* For master's, thesis; for doctorate, thesis/dissertation. *Entrance requirements:* For master's and doctorate, GRE General Test. Additional exam requirements/recommendations for international students: Required—TOEFL. *Expenses:* Contact institution. *Faculty research:* Alzheimer's disease, aging, eye diseases, cancer, cardiovascular disease.

University of Oklahoma Health Sciences Center, College of Medicine and Graduate College, Graduate Programs in Medicine, Department of Microbiology and Immunology, Oklahoma City, OK 73190. Offers immunology (MS, PhD); microbiology (MS, PhD). *Program availability:* Part-time. Terminal master's awarded for partial completion of doctoral program. *Degree requirements:* For master's, thesis or alternative; for doctorate, one foreign language, thesis/dissertation. *Entrance requirements:* For doctorate, GRE General Test, 3 letters of recommendation. Additional exam requirements/recommendations for international students: Required—TOEFL. *Faculty research:* Molecular genetics, pathogenesis, streptococcal infections, gram-positive virulence, monoclonal antibodies.

University of Ottawa, Faculty of Graduate and Postdoctoral Studies, Faculty of Medicine, Department of Biochemistry, Microbiology and Immunology, Ottawa, ON K1N 6N5, Canada. Offers biochemistry (M Sc, PhD); microbiology and immunology (M Sc, PhD). *Degree requirements:* For master's, thesis; for doctorate, comprehensive exam, thesis/dissertation, seminar. *Entrance requirements:* For master's, honors degree or equivalent, minimum B average; for doctorate, master's degree, minimum B+ average. Electronic applications accepted. *Faculty research:* General biochemistry, molecular biology, microbiology, host biology, nutrition and metabolism.

University of Pennsylvania, Perelman School of Medicine, Biomedical Graduate Studies, Graduate Group in Immunology, Philadelphia, PA 19104. Offers PhD, MD/PhD, VMD/PhD. *Faculty:* 123. *Students:* 63 full-time (31 women); includes 27 minority (1 Black or African American, non-Hispanic/Latino; 14 Asian, non-Hispanic/Latino; 4 Hispanic/Latino; 8 Two or more races, non-Hispanic/Latino), 1 international. 144 applicants, 13% accepted, 6 enrolled. In 2017, 9 doctorates awarded. *Degree requirements:* For doctorate, thesis/dissertation. *Entrance requirements:* For doctorate, GRE General Test, undergraduate major in natural or physical science. Additional exam requirements/recommendations for international students: Required—TOEFL. *Application deadline:* For fall admission, 12/1 for domestic and international students. Applications are processed on a rolling basis. Application fee: $80. Electronic applications accepted. *Financial support:* In 2017–18, 55 students received support. Fellowships, research assistantships, teaching assistantships, and tuition waivers available. *Faculty research:* Immunology structure and function, cell surface receptors, lymphocyte functional transplantation immunology, cellular immunology, molecular biology of immunoglobulins. *Unit head:* Dr. David Allman, Chair, 215-746-5547. *Application contact:* Mary Taylor, Graduate Coordinator, 215-573-4394.
Website: http://www.med.upenn.edu/immun/

University of Pittsburgh, School of Medicine, Graduate Programs in Medicine, Microbiology and Immunology Program, Pittsburgh, PA 15260. Offers PhD. *Faculty:* 90 full-time (29 women). *Students:* 58 full-time (33 women); includes 12 minority (5 Black or African American, non-Hispanic/Latino; 5 Asian, non-Hispanic/Latino; 2 Hispanic/Latino), 9 international. Average age 26. 350 applicants, 21% accepted, 16 enrolled. *Degree requirements:* For doctorate, comprehensive exam, thesis/dissertation, 34 course credits, 38 dissertation credits, published paper. *Entrance requirements:* For doctorate, GRE General Test. Additional exam requirements/recommendations for international students: Required—TOEFL (minimum score 600 paper-based; 100 iBT), IELTS (minimum score 7). *Application deadline:* For fall admission, 12/1 priority date for domestic and international students. Application fee: $50. Electronic applications accepted. *Expenses:* $26,782 in-state, $42,006 out-of-state. *Financial support:* In 2017–18, 46 students received support, including 10 research assistantships with full tuition reimbursements available (averaging $29,500 per year); traineeships also available. *Unit head:* Dr. Robert Binder, Director, 412-383-7722, Fax: 412-383-8906, E-mail: rjb42@pitt.edu. *Application contact:* Kristen Digiacomo, Coordinator, 412-624-5981, E-mail: kmd78@pitt.edu.
Website: http://www.pmi.pitt.edu

University of Prince Edward Island, Atlantic Veterinary College, Graduate Program in Veterinary Medicine, Charlottetown, PE C1A 4P3, Canada. Offers anatomy (M Sc, PhD); bacteriology (M Sc, PhD); clinical pharmacology (M Sc, PhD); clinical sciences (M Sc, PhD); epidemiology (M Sc, PhD), including reproduction; fish health (M Sc, PhD); food animal nutrition (M Sc, PhD); immunology (M Sc, PhD); microanatomy (M Sc, PhD); parasitology (M Sc, PhD); pathology (M Sc, PhD); pharmacology (M Sc, PhD); physiology (M Sc, PhD); toxicology (M Sc, PhD); veterinary science (M Vet Sc); virology (M Sc, PhD). *Program availability:* Part-time. *Degree requirements:* For master's, thesis; for doctorate, thesis/dissertation. *Entrance requirements:* For master's, DVM, B Sc honors degree, or equivalent; for doctorate, M Sc. Additional exam requirements/recommendations for international students: Required—TOEFL (minimum score 550 paper-based; 80 iBT). *Expenses:* Contact institution. *Faculty research:* Animal health management, infectious diseases, fin fish and shellfish health, basic biomedical sciences, ecosystem health.

University of Rochester, School of Medicine and Dentistry, Graduate Programs in Medicine and Dentistry, Department of Microbiology and Immunology, Program in Microbiology and Immunology, Rochester, NY 14627. Offers MS, PhD.

University of Saskatchewan, College of Medicine, Department of Microbiology and Immunology, Saskatoon, SK S7N 5A2, Canada. Offers M Sc, PhD. *Degree requirements:* For master's, thesis; for doctorate, thesis/dissertation. *Entrance requirements:* Additional exam requirements/recommendations for international students: Required—TOEFL.

University of South Dakota, Graduate School, Sanford School of Medicine and Graduate School, Biomedical Sciences Graduate Program, Molecular Microbiology and Immunology Group, Vermillion, SD 57069. Offers MS, PhD. Terminal master's awarded for partial completion of doctoral program. *Degree requirements:* For master's, thesis; for doctorate, comprehensive exam, thesis/dissertation. *Entrance requirements:* For master's and doctorate, GRE General Test, minimum GPA of 3.0. Additional exam requirements/recommendations for international students: Required—TOEFL (minimum score 550 paper-based; 80 iBT), IELTS (minimum score 6). *Application deadline:* For fall admission, 4/15 priority date for domestic students, 3/15 for international students. Applications are processed on a rolling basis. Application fee: $35. Electronic applications accepted. *Expenses:* Contact institution. *Financial support:* In 2017–18, 6 students received support. Fellowships with partial tuition reimbursements available, research assistantships with partial tuition reimbursements available, and unspecified assistantships available. Financial award application deadline: 4/15; financial award applicants required to submit FAFSA. *Faculty research:* Structure-function membranes, plasmids, immunology, virology, pathogenesis. *Total annual research expenditures:* $325,000. *Unit head:* 605-658-6322, Fax: 605-677-6381, E-mail: biomed@usd.edu. *Application contact:* Graduate School, 605-658-6140, Fax: 605-677-6118.

University of Southern California, Keck School of Medicine and Graduate School, Graduate Programs in Medicine, Department of Molecular Microbiology and Immunology, Los Angeles, CA 90033. Offers MS. *Program availability:* Part-time. *Faculty:* 21 full-time (4 women), 1 (woman) part-time/adjunct. *Students:* 28 full-time (13 women), 1 (woman) part-time; includes 5 minority (4 Asian, non-Hispanic/Latino; 1 Hispanic/Latino), 20 international. Average age 24. 45 applicants, 62% accepted, 16 enrolled. In 2017, 8 master's awarded. Terminal master's awarded for partial completion of doctoral program. *Degree requirements:* For master's, comprehensive exam (for some programs), thesis optional. *Entrance requirements:* For master's, GRE General Test (Verbal and Quantitative), minimum GPA of 3.0. Additional exam requirements/recommendations for international students: Required—TOEFL (minimum score 100 iBT), IELTS (minimum score 6.5). *Application deadline:* For fall admission, 6/1 for domestic students, 5/1 for international students; for spring admission, 11/1 for domestic students, 10/1 for international students. Applications are processed on a rolling basis. Application fee: $90. Electronic applications accepted. *Expenses:* Contact institution. *Financial support:* Career-related internships or fieldwork, Federal Work-Study, institutionally sponsored loans, scholarships/grants, and health care benefits available. Financial award application deadline: 3/1; financial award applicants required to submit FAFSA. *Faculty research:* Animal virology, microbial genetics, molecular and cellular immunology, cellular differentiation control of protein synthesis, HIV. *Unit head:* Dr. Axel H. Schonthal, Associate Professor/Program Chairman, 323-442-1730, Fax: 323-442-1721, E-mail: schontha@usc.edu. *Application contact:* Silvina V. Campos, Administrative Assistant II, 323-442-1713, Fax: 323-442-1721, E-mail: scampos@usc.edu.
Website: http://keck.usc.edu/molecular-microbiology-and-immunology/

University of Southern Maine, College of Science, Technology, and Health, Program in Applied Medical Sciences, Portland, ME 04103. Offers MS. *Program availability:* Part-time. *Degree requirements:* For master's, thesis. *Entrance requirements:* For master's, GRE General Test, minimum GPA of 3.0. Additional exam requirements/recommendations for international students: Required—TOEFL. Electronic applications accepted. *Faculty research:* Cancer biology, toxicology, environmental health, epidemiology, autoimmune disease, immunology, infectious disease, virology.

University of South Florida, Morsani College of Medicine and College of Graduate Studies, Graduate Programs in Medical Sciences, Tampa, FL 33620-9951. Offers advanced athletic training (MS); athletic training (MS); bioinformatics and computational biology (MSBCB); biotechnology (MSB); health informatics (MSHI); medical sciences (MSMS, PhD), including aging and neuroscience (MSMS), allergy, immunology and infectious disease (PhD), anatomy, biochemistry and molecular biology, clinical and translational research, health science (MSMS), interdisciplinary medical sciences (MSMS), medical microbiology and immunology (MSMS), metabolic and nutritional medicine (MSMS), microbiology and immunology (PhD), molecular medicine, molecular pharmacology and physiology (PhD), neuroscience (PhD), pathology and cell biology (PhD), women's health (MSMS). *Students:* 372 full-time (212 women), 216 part-time (142 women); includes 257 minority (78 Black or African American, non-Hispanic/Latino; 1 American Indian or Alaska Native, non-Hispanic/Latino; 79 Asian, non-Hispanic/Latino; 84 Hispanic/Latino; 15 Two or more races, non-Hispanic/Latino), 62 international. Average age 28. 1,048 applicants, 46% accepted, 309 enrolled. In 2017, 351 master's, 56 doctorates awarded. Terminal master's awarded for partial completion of doctoral program. *Degree requirements:* For master's, comprehensive exam, thesis; for doctorate, comprehensive exam, thesis/dissertation. *Entrance requirements:* For master's, GRE General Test or GMAT, bachelor's degree or equivalent from regionally-accredited university with minimum GPA of 3.0 in upper-division sciences coursework; prerequisites in general biology, general chemistry, general physics, organic chemistry, quantitative analysis, and integral and differential calculus; for doctorate, GRE General Test, bachelor's degree from regionally-accredited university with minimum GPA of 3.0 in upper-division sciences coursework; 3 letters of recommendation; personal interview; 1-2 page personal statement; prerequisites in biology, chemistry, physics, organic chemistry, quantitative analysis, and integral/differential calculus. Additional exam requirements/recommendations for international students: Required—TOEFL (minimum score 550 paper-based; 79 iBT) or IELTS (minimum score 6.5). *Application deadline:* For fall admission, 2/1 priority date for domestic students, 2/1 for international students. Application fee: $30. Electronic applications accepted. *Expenses:* Contact institution. *Financial support:* In 2017–18, 109 students received support. *Faculty research:* Anatomy, biochemistry, cancer biology, cardiovascular disease, cell biology, immunology, microbiology, molecular biology, neuroscience, pharmacology, physiology. *Total annual research expenditures:* $45.3 million. *Unit head:* Dr. Michael Barber, Professor/Associate Dean for Graduate and Postdoctoral Affairs, 813-974-9908, Fax: 813-974-4317, E-mail: mbarber@health.usf.edu. *Application contact:* Dr. Eric Bennett, Graduate Director, PhD Program in Medical Sciences, 813-974-1545, Fax: 813-974-4317, E-mail: esbennet@health.usf.edu.
Website: http://health.usf.edu/nocms/medicine/graduatestudies/

The University of Texas Health Science Center at Houston, MD Anderson UTHealth Graduate School, Houston, TX 77225-0036. Offers biochemistry and cell biology (PhD); biomedical sciences (MS); cancer biology (PhD); genetic counseling (MS); genetics and epigenetics (PhD); immunology (PhD); medical physics (MS, PhD); microbiology and infectious diseases (PhD); neuroscience (PhD); quantitative sciences (PhD); therapeutics and pharmacology (PhD); MD/PhD. Terminal master's awarded for partial completion of doctoral program. *Degree requirements:* For master's, thesis; for doctorate, thesis/dissertation. *Entrance requirements:* For master's and doctorate, GRE General Test. Additional exam requirements/recommendations for international students: Required—TOEFL. Electronic applications accepted. *Faculty research:* Biomedical sciences.

The University of Texas Health Science Center at San Antonio, Graduate School of Biomedical Sciences, Department of Microbiology and Immunology, San Antonio, TX 78229-3900. Offers MS, PhD. *Degree requirements:* For master's, thesis; for doctorate, comprehensive exam, thesis/dissertation.

The University of Texas Medical Branch, Graduate School of Biomedical Sciences, Program in Microbiology and Immunology, Galveston, TX 77555. Offers MS, PhD. Terminal master's awarded for partial completion of doctoral program. *Degree* *requirements:* For master's, thesis or alternative; for doctorate, thesis/dissertation. *Entrance requirements:* For doctorate, GRE General Test, minimum GPA of 3.0. Additional exam requirements/recommendations for international students: Required—TOEFL (minimum score 550 paper-based). Electronic applications accepted.

The University of Texas Southwestern Medical Center, Southwestern Graduate School of Biomedical Sciences, Division of Basic Science, Program in Immunology, Dallas, TX 75390. Offers PhD. *Degree requirements:* For doctorate, thesis/dissertation, qualifying exam. *Entrance requirements:* For doctorate, GRE General Test, minimum GPA of 3.0. Additional exam requirements/recommendations for international students: Required—TOEFL. Electronic applications accepted. *Faculty research:* Antibody diversity and idiotype, cytotoxic effector mechanisms, natural killer cells, biology of immunoglobulins, oncogenes.

The University of Toledo, College of Graduate Studies, College of Medicine and Life Sciences, Department of Medical Microbiology and Immunology, Toledo, OH 43606-3390. Offers infection, immunity, and transplantation (MSBS, PhD); MD/MSBS; MD/PhD. Terminal master's awarded for partial completion of doctoral program. *Degree requirements:* For master's, thesis, qualifying exam; for doctorate, thesis/dissertation, qualifying exam. *Entrance requirements:* For master's and doctorate, GRE, minimum undergraduate GPA of 3.0, three letters of recommendation, statement of purpose, transcripts from all prior institutions attended, resume. Additional exam requirements/recommendations for international students: Required—TOEFL (minimum score 550 paper-based; 80 iBT). Electronic applications accepted.

University of Toronto, Faculty of Medicine, Department of Immunology, Toronto, ON M5S 1A1, Canada. Offers M Sc, PhD, MD/PhD. *Degree requirements:* For master's, thesis, thesis defense; for doctorate, thesis/dissertation, thesis defense. *Entrance requirements:* For master's, resume, 3 letters of reference. Additional exam requirements/recommendations for international students: Required—TOEFL (minimum score 580 paper-based; 93 iBT), TWE (minimum score 5). Electronic applications accepted.

University of Washington, Graduate School, School of Medicine, Graduate Programs in Medicine, Department of Immunology, Seattle, WA 98109-8059. Offers PhD. *Degree requirements:* For doctorate, thesis/dissertation, 1st-authored paper, accepted for publication. *Entrance requirements:* For doctorate, GRE General Test, BA or BS in related field. Additional exam requirements/recommendations for international students: Required—TOEFL (minimum score 600 paper-based; 100 iBT). Electronic applications accepted. *Faculty research:* Molecular and cellular immunology, regulation of lymphocyte differentiation and responses, genetics of immune recognition genetics and pathogenesis of autoimmune diseases, signal transduction.

The University of Western Ontario, Faculty of Graduate Studies, Biosciences Division, Department of Microbiology and Immunology, London, ON N6A 5B8, Canada. Offers M Sc, PhD. *Degree requirements:* For master's, thesis, oral and written exam; for doctorate, thesis/dissertation, oral and written exam. *Entrance requirements:* For master's, honors degree or equivalent in microbiology, immunology, or other biological science; minimum B average; for doctorate, M Sc in microbiology and immunology. Additional exam requirements/recommendations for international students: Required—TOEFL. *Faculty research:* Virology, molecular pathogenesis, cellular immunology, molecular biology.

Vanderbilt University, School of Medicine, Department of Microbiology and Immunology, Nashville, TN 37240-1001. Offers MS, PhD, MD/PhD. *Faculty:* 36 full-time (9 women). *Students:* 52 full-time (30 women); includes 13 minority (2 Black or African American, non-Hispanic/Latino; 1 American Indian or Alaska Native, non-Hispanic/Latino; 3 Asian, non-Hispanic/Latino; 3 Hispanic/Latino; 4 Two or more races, non-Hispanic/Latino), 4 international. Average age 27. In 2017, 15 doctorates awarded. Terminal master's awarded for partial completion of doctoral program. *Degree requirements:* For master's, thesis; for doctorate, thesis/dissertation, final and qualifying exams. *Entrance requirements:* For master's and doctorate, GRE General Test, GRE Subject Test (recommended). Additional exam requirements/recommendations for international students: Required—TOEFL (minimum score 570 paper-based; 88 iBT). *Application deadline:* For fall admission, 1/15 for domestic and international students. Application fee: $0. Electronic applications accepted. *Financial support:* Fellowships with full tuition reimbursements, research assistantships with full tuition reimbursements, Federal Work-Study, institutionally sponsored loans, scholarships/grants, traineeships, health care benefits, and tuition waivers (partial) available. Financial award application deadline: 1/15; financial award applicants required to submit CSS PROFILE or FAFSA. *Faculty research:* Cellular and molecular microbiology, viruses, genes, cancer, molecular pathogenesis of microbial diseases, immunobiology. *Unit head:* Dr. Roger Cone, Acting Chair, 615-322-7000, Fax: 615-322-5551, E-mail: roger.cone@vanderbilt.edu. *Application contact:* Jay Jerome, Director of Graduate Studies, 615-322-2123, E-mail: jay.jerome@vanderbilt.edu.
Website: http://www.mc.vanderbilt.edu/root/vumc.php?site-vmcpathology

Vanderbilt University, School of Medicine, Department of Molecular Pathology and Immunology, Nashville, TN 37240-1001. Offers PhD, MD/PhD. *Faculty:* 32 full-time (10 women). *Students:* 14 full-time (8 women); includes 3 minority (1 American Indian or Alaska Native, non-Hispanic/Latino; 1 Hispanic/Latino; 1 Two or more races, non-Hispanic/Latino), 2 international. Average age 29. In 2017, 2 doctorates awarded. *Degree requirements:* For doctorate, thesis/dissertation, qualifying and final exams. *Entrance requirements:* For doctorate, GRE General Test. Additional exam requirements/recommendations for international students: Required—TOEFL (minimum score 570 paper-based; 88 iBT). *Application deadline:* For fall admission, 1/15 for domestic and international students. Application fee: $0. Electronic applications accepted. *Financial support:* Fellowships with full tuition reimbursements, research assistantships with full tuition reimbursements, Federal Work-Study, institutionally sponsored loans, traineeships, health care benefits, and tuition waivers (partial) available. Financial award application deadline: 1/15; financial award applicants required to submit CSS PROFILE or FAFSA. *Faculty research:* Vascular biology and biochemistry, tumor pathology, the immune response, inflammation and repair, the biology of the extracellular matrix in response to disease processes, the pathogenesis of infectious agents, the regulation of gene expression in disease. *Unit head:* Lorie Franklin, Administrative Assistant/Assistant Director of Graduate Studies, 615-343-8324, Fax: 615-322-0576, E-mail: lorie.franklin@vanderbilt.edu. *Application contact:* Walter B. Bieschke, Program Coordinator for Graduate Admissions, 615-342-0236, E-mail: vandygrad@vanderbilt.edu.
Website: https://medschool.vanderbilt.edu/igp/molecular-pathology-immunology

Virginia Commonwealth University, Medical College of Virginia-Professional Programs, School of Medicine, Graduate Programs in Medicine, Department of Microbiology and Immunology, Richmond, VA 23284-9005. Offers microbiology and immunology (MS, PhD); MD/PhD. *Degree requirements:* For master's, thesis; for doctorate, thesis/dissertation, comprehensive oral and written exams. *Entrance requirements:* For master's and doctorate, GRE General Test or MCAT. Additional exam requirements/recommendations for international students: Required—TOEFL (minimum score 600 paper-based; 100 iBT). Electronic applications accepted. *Faculty research:* Microbial physiology and genetics, molecular biology, crystallography of biological molecules, antibiotics and chemotherapy, membrane transport.

Wake Forest University, School of Medicine and Graduate School of Arts and Sciences, Graduate Programs in Medicine, Department of Microbiology and Immunology, Winston-Salem, NC 27109. Offers PhD, MD/PhD. *Degree requirements:* For doctorate, thesis/dissertation. *Entrance requirements:* For doctorate, GRE General Test. Additional exam requirements/recommendations for international students: Required—TOEFL. Electronic applications accepted. *Faculty research:* Molecular immunology, bacterial pathogenesis and molecular genetics, viral pathogenesis, regulation of mRNA metabolism, leukocyte biology.

Washington State University, College of Veterinary Medicine, Paul G. Allen School for Global Animal Health, Pullman, WA 99164. Offers immunology and infectious diseases (MS, PhD). *Faculty:* 38 full-time (13 women), 10 part-time/adjunct (5 women). *Students:* 19 full-time (8 women); includes 4 minority (1 Asian, non-Hispanic/Latino; 3 Hispanic/Latino), 4 international. 8 applicants, 100% accepted, 8 enrolled. In 2017, 3 doctorates awarded. Terminal master's awarded for partial completion of doctoral program. *Degree requirements:* For master's, thesis, oral exam; for doctorate, thesis/dissertation, oral exam. *Entrance requirements:* For master's and doctorate, minimum GPA of 3.0. Additional exam requirements/recommendations for international students: Required—TOEFL (minimum score 550 paper-based, 80 iBT), IELTS (7.0), or Michigan English Language Assessment Battery. *Application deadline:* Applications are processed on a rolling basis. Application fee: $75. Electronic applications accepted. *Financial support:* In 2017–18, 19 students received support, including 5 fellowships with full tuition reimbursements available, 14 research assistantships; teaching assistantships, institutionally sponsored loans, scholarships/grants, traineeships, health care benefits, and unspecified assistantships also available. Financial award application deadline: 3/1. *Faculty research:* Immunology, infectious disease, virology, disease surveillance, vaccine development. *Total annual research expenditures:* $6.8 million. *Unit head:* Dr. Thomas Kawula, Director, Paul G. Allen School for Global Animal Health, 509-335-5861, Fax: 509-335-6328, E-mail: tom.kawula@vetmed.wsu.edu. *Application contact:* Sue Zumwalt, Administrative Manager, 509-335-6027, Fax: 509-335-8529, E-mail: szumwalt@wsu.edu.
Website: http://globalhealth.wsu.edu/

Washington State University, College of Veterinary Medicine, Program in Immunology and Infectious Diseases, Pullman, WA 99164-7040. Offers MS, PhD. *Faculty:* 38 full-time (13 women), 10 part-time/adjunct (5 women). *Students:* 34 full-time (26 women); includes 5 minority (1 Black or African American, non-Hispanic/Latino; 3 Asian, non-Hispanic/Latino; 1 Hispanic/Latino), 11 international. Average age 31. 45 applicants, 29% accepted, 8 enrolled. In 2017, 2 master's, 1 doctorate awarded. Terminal master's awarded for partial completion of doctoral program. *Degree requirements:* For master's, thesis, oral exam; for doctorate, thesis/dissertation, oral exam. *Entrance requirements:* For master's and doctorate, minimum GPA of 3.0. Additional exam requirements/recommendations for international students: Required—TOEFL (minimum score 550 paper-based; 80 iBT). *Application deadline:* Applications are processed on a rolling basis. Application fee: $75. Electronic applications accepted. *Financial support:* In 2017–18, 31 students received support, including 5 fellowships, 26 research assistantships, 2 teaching assistantships; institutionally sponsored loans, scholarships/grants, traineeships, and unspecified assistantships also available. Financial award application deadline: 3/1; financial award applicants required to submit FAFSA. *Faculty research:* Microbial pathogenesis, veterinary and wildlife parasitology, laboratory animal pathology, immune responses to infectious diseases. *Unit head:* Dr. Robert H. Mealey, Chair, 509-335-6030, Fax: 509-335-8529, E-mail: rmealey@wsu.edu. *Application contact:* Sue Zumwalt, Graduate Coordinator, 509-335-6027, Fax: 509-335-8529, E-mail: szumwalt@wsu.edu.
Website: http://vmp.vetmed.wsu.edu/graduate-programs

Washington University in St. Louis, The Graduate School, Division of Biology and Biomedical Sciences, Program in Immunology, St. Louis, MO 63130-4899. Offers PhD. *Degree requirements:* For doctorate, thesis/dissertation. *Entrance requirements:* For doctorate, GRE General Test, GRE Subject Test. Additional exam requirements/recommendations for international students: Required—TOEFL. Electronic applications accepted. *Faculty research:* Cellular immunology, molecular immunology, lineage development, autoimmunity, cancer immunotherapy, transcription factors, epigenomics, mucosal immunity, innate immunity, bacterial, viral, and parasite immunity, immune evasion, antigen processing and presentation, dendritic cells, T cell signaling, antigen receptor diversification.

Wayne State University, School of Medicine, Office of Biomedical Graduate Programs, Detroit, MI 48202. Offers anatomy and cell biology (MS, PhD); basic medical sciences (MS); biochemistry and molecular biology (MS, PhD); cancer biology (MS, PhD); clinical and translational science (Graduate Certificate); family medicine and public health sciences (MPH, Graduate Certificate), including public health practice; genetic counseling (MS); immunology and microbiology (MS, PhD); medical physics (MS, PhD, Graduate Certificate); medical research (MS); molecular medicine and genomics (MS, PhD), including molecular genetics and genomics; pathology (PhD); pharmacology (MS, PhD); physiology (MS, PhD), including physiology, reproductive sciences (PhD); psychiatry and behavioral neurosciences (PhD), including translational neuroscience; MD/MPH; MD/PhD; MPH/MA; MSW/MPH. *Program availability:* Part-time, evening/weekend. *Students:* 268 full-time (152 women), 117 part-time (59 women); includes 108 minority (19 Black or African American, non-Hispanic/Latino; 1 American Indian or Alaska Native, non-Hispanic/Latino; 62 Asian, non-Hispanic/Latino; 9 Hispanic/Latino; 17 Two or more races, non-Hispanic/Latino), 48 international. Average age 26. 1,133 applicants, 21% accepted, 151 enrolled. In 2017, 70 master's, 25 doctorates, 10 other advanced degrees awarded. Terminal master's awarded for partial completion of doctoral program. *Degree requirements:* For master's, thesis (for some programs); for doctorate, thesis/dissertation. *Entrance requirements:* For master's, doctorate, and Graduate Certificate, GRE. Additional exam requirements/recommendations for international students: Required—TOEFL (minimum score 550 paper-based; 100 iBT), Michigan English Language Assessment Battery (minimum score 85); Recommended—IELTS (minimum score 6.5), TWE (minimum score 5.5). *Application deadline:* For fall admission, 2/1 for domestic and international students. Applications are processed on a rolling basis. Application fee: $50. Electronic applications accepted. *Expenses:* Contact institution. *Financial support:* In 2017–18, 177 students received support, including 64 fellowships with full tuition reimbursements available (averaging $24,388 per year), 79 research assistantships with full tuition reimbursements available (averaging $26,894 per year); scholarships/grants, traineeships, and health care benefits also available. *Faculty research:* Cancer biology, neurosciences, vision sciences, molecular biology, pathology, physiology, pharmacology, public health, medical physics. *Unit head:* Dr. Daniel A. Walz, Associate Dean for Biomedical Graduate Programs, 313-577-1455, Fax: 313-577-8796, E-mail: gradprogs@med.wayne.edu.
Website: https://www.med.wayne.edu/biomedical-graduate-programs/

Weill Cornell Medicine, Weill Cornell Graduate School of Medical Sciences, Immunology and Microbial Pathogenesis Program, New York, NY 10065. Offers immunology (MS, PhD), including immunology, microbiology, pathology. Terminal master's awarded for partial completion of doctoral program. *Degree requirements:* For master's, comprehensive exam; for doctorate, thesis/dissertation, final exam. *Entrance requirements:* For doctorate, GRE General Test, laboratory research experience, course work in biological sciences. Additional exam requirements/recommendations for international students: Required—TOEFL. Electronic applications accepted. *Faculty research:* Microbial immunity, tumor immunology, lymphocyte and leukocyte biology, auto immunity, stem cell/bone marrow transplantation.

West Virginia University, School of Medicine, Morgantown, WV 26506-9600. Offers biochemistry and molecular biology (PhD); biomedical science (MS); cancer cell biology (PhD); cellular and integrative physiology (PhD); exercise physiology (MS, PhD); health sciences (MS); immunology (PhD); medicine (MD); occupational therapy (MOT); pathologists assistant (MHS); physical therapy (DPT). *Program availability:* Part-time, evening/weekend. *Students:* 781 full-time (440 women), 25 part-time (13 women); includes 140 minority (15 Black or African American, non-Hispanic/Latino; 1 American Indian or Alaska Native, non-Hispanic/Latino; 68 Asian, non-Hispanic/Latino; 37 Hispanic/Latino; 1 Native Hawaiian or other Pacific Islander, non-Hispanic/Latino; 18 Two or more races, non-Hispanic/Latino), 19 international. *Entrance requirements:* Additional exam requirements/recommendations for international students: Required—TOEFL. *Application deadline:* Applications are processed on a rolling basis. Application fee: $60. Electronic applications accepted. *Expenses:* Contact institution. *Financial support:* Fellowships, research assistantships, teaching assistantships, career-related internships or fieldwork, Federal Work-Study, institutionally sponsored loans, health care benefits, tuition waivers (full and partial), and administrative assistantships available. Financial award applicants required to submit FAFSA. *Unit head:* Dr. Clay Marsh, Executive Dean, 304-293-6607, Fax: 304-293-6627, E-mail: clay.marsh@hsc.wvu.edu. *Application contact:* Lisa M. Salati, Assistant Vice President, Graduate Education, 304-293-7759, Fax: 304-293-3080, E-mail: lsalati@hsc.wvu.edu.
Website: https://medicine.hsc.wvu.edu

Wright State University, Graduate School, College of Science and Mathematics, Program in Microbiology and Immunology, Dayton, OH 45435. Offers MS. *Program availability:* Part-time. *Degree requirements:* For master's, thesis. *Entrance requirements:* Additional exam requirements/recommendations for international students: Required—TOEFL. *Faculty research:* Reproductive immunology, viral pathogenesis, virus-host cell interactions.

Yale University, Graduate School of Arts and Sciences, Department of Immunobiology, New Haven, CT 06520. Offers PhD. *Degree requirements:* For doctorate, thesis/dissertation. *Entrance requirements:* For doctorate, GRE General Test.

Yale University, Yale School of Medicine and Graduate School of Arts and Sciences, Combined Program in Biological and Biomedical Sciences (BBS), Immunology Track, New Haven, CT 06520. Offers PhD, MD/PhD. *Degree requirements:* For doctorate, thesis/dissertation. *Entrance requirements:* For doctorate, GRE General Test. Additional exam requirements/recommendations for international students: Required—TOEFL. Electronic applications accepted.

Infectious Diseases

Georgetown University, Graduate School of Arts and Sciences, Department of Microbiology and Immunology, Washington, DC 20057. Offers biohazardous threat agents and emerging infectious diseases (MS); biomedical science policy and advocacy (MS); general microbiology and immunology (MS); global infectious diseases (PhD); microbiology and immunology (PhD). *Program availability:* Part-time. *Degree requirements:* For master's, 30 credit hours of coursework; for doctorate, comprehensive exam, thesis/dissertation. *Entrance requirements:* For master's, GRE General Test, 3 letters of reference, bachelor's degree in related field; for doctorate, GRE General Test, 3 letters of reference, MS/BS in related field. Additional exam requirements/recommendations for international students: Required—TOEFL (minimum score 505 paper-based). Electronic applications accepted. *Faculty research:* Pathogenesis and basic biology of the fungus Candida albicans, molecular biology of viral immunopathological mechanisms in Multiple Sclerosis.

The George Washington University, Milken Institute School of Public Health, Department of Epidemiology and Biostatistics, Washington, DC 20052. Offers biostatistics (MPH); epidemiology (MPH); microbiology and emerging infectious diseases (MSPH). *Students:* 75 full-time (58 women), 78 part-time (62 women); includes 62 minority (14 Black or African American, non-Hispanic/Latino; 32 Asian, non-Hispanic/Latino; 12 Hispanic/Latino; 1 Native Hawaiian or other Pacific Islander, non-Hispanic/Latino; 3 Two or more races, non-Hispanic/Latino), 14 international. Average age 28. 521 applicants, 59% accepted, 48 enrolled. In 2017, 51 master's awarded. *Entrance requirements:* For master's, GMAT, GRE General Test, or MCAT. Additional exam requirements/recommendations for international students: Required—TOEFL. *Application deadline:* For fall admission, 4/15 priority date for domestic students, 4/15 for international students; for spring admission, 11/1 for domestic and international students. Applications are processed on a rolling basis. Application fee: $75. *Expenses: Tuition:* Full-time $28,800; part-time $1655 per credit hour. *Required fees:* $45; $2.75 per credit hour. *Financial support:* In 2017–18, 6 students received support. Tuition waivers available. Financial award application deadline: 2/15. *Unit head:* Dr. Alan E. Greenberg, Chair, 202-994-0612, E-mail: aeg1@gwu.edu. *Application contact:* Jane Smith, Director of Admissions, 202-994-0248, Fax: 202-994-1860, E-mail: sphhsinfo@gwumc.edu.

The George Washington University, School of Medicine and Health Sciences, Health Sciences Programs, Washington, DC 20052. Offers clinical practice management (MSHS); clinical research administration (MSHS); emergency services management (MSHS); end-of-life care (MSHS); immunohematology (MSHS); immunohematology and biotechnology (MSHS); physical therapy (DPT); physician assistant (MSHS). *Program availability:* Online learning. *Faculty:* 31 full-time (23 women), 4 part-time/adjunct (2 women). *Students:* 304 full-time (233 women), 321 part-time (248 women); includes 212 minority (70 Black or African American, non-Hispanic/Latino; 1 American Indian or Alaska Native, non-Hispanic/Latino; 64 Asian, non-Hispanic/Latino; 59 Hispanic/Latino; 3 Native Hawaiian or other Pacific Islander, non-Hispanic/Latino; 15 Two or more races, non-Hispanic/Latino), 18 international. Average age 33. 2,366 applicants, 19% accepted, 246 enrolled. In 2017, 159 master's, 49 doctorates, 2 other advanced degrees awarded. *Entrance requirements:* Additional exam requirements/recommendations for international students: Required—TOEFL (minimum score 550 paper-based). *Application deadline:* Applications are processed on a rolling basis. Application fee: $75. *Expenses:* Contact institution. *Unit head:* Jean E. Johnson, Senior Associate Dean, 202-994-3725, E-mail: jejohns@gwu.edu. *Application contact:* Joke Ogundiran, Director of Admission, 202-994-1668, Fax: 202-994-0870, E-mail: jokeogun@gwu.edu.

Johns Hopkins University, Bloomberg School of Public Health, Department of Epidemiology, Baltimore, MD 21205. Offers cancer epidemiology (MHS, Sc M, PhD, Sc D); cardiovascular disease and clinical epidemiology (MHS, Sc M, PhD, Sc D); clinical trials (PhD, Sc D); clinical trials and evidence synthesis (MHS, Sc M, PhD, Sc D); environmental epidemiology (MHS, Sc M, PhD, Sc D); epidemiology of aging (MHS, Sc M, PhD, Sc D); general epidemiology and methodology (MHS, Sc M); genetic epidemiology (MHS, Sc M, PhD, Sc D); infectious disease epidemiology (MHS, Sc M, PhD, Sc D). *Students:* 160 full-time (111 women), 14 part-time (9 women); includes 41 minority (9 Black or African American, non-Hispanic/Latino; 1 American Indian or Alaska Native, non-Hispanic/Latino; 20 Asian, non-Hispanic/Latino; 9 Hispanic/Latino; 1 Native Hawaiian or other Pacific Islander, non-Hispanic/Latino; 4 Two or more races, non-Hispanic/Latino), 64 international. Average age 29. 408 applicants, 29% accepted, 61 enrolled. In 2017, 36 master's, 16 doctorates awarded. *Degree requirements:* For master's, comprehensive exam, thesis, 1-year full-time residency; for doctorate, comprehensive exam, thesis/dissertation, 2 years' full-time residency, oral and written exams, student teaching. *Entrance requirements:* For master's, GRE General Test or MCAT, 3 letters of recommendation, curriculum vitae; for doctorate, GRE General Test, minimum 1 year of work experience, 3 letters of recommendation, curriculum vitae, academic records from all schools. Additional exam requirements/recommendations for international students: Required—TOEFL (minimum score 100 iBT), IELTS (minimum score 7.5). *Application deadline:* Applications are processed on a rolling basis. Application fee: $135. Electronic applications accepted. *Financial support:* Fellowships, Federal Work-Study, institutionally sponsored loans, scholarships/grants, traineeships, and stipends available. Support available to part-time students. Financial award application deadline: 3/15. *Faculty research:* Cancer and congenital malformations, nutritional epidemiology, AIDS, tuberculosis, cardiovascular disease, risk assessment. *Unit head:* Dr. David D. Celentano, Chair, 410-955-3286, Fax: 410-955-0863. *Application contact:* Frances O. Burman, Academic Program Manager, 410-955-3926, Fax: 410-955-0863, E-mail: fburman@jhsph.edu.
Website: http://www.jhsph.edu/dept/epi/index.html

Loyola University Chicago, Graduate School, Integrated Program in Biomedical Sciences, Maywood, IL 60141. Offers biochemistry and molecular biology (MS, PhD); cell and molecular physiology (MS, PhD); infectious disease and immunology (MS); integrative cell biology (MS, PhD); microbiology and immunology (MS, PhD); molecular pharmacology and therapeutics (MS, PhD); neuroscience (MS, PhD). *Faculty:* 84 full-time (32 women). *Students:* 126 full-time (65 women), 1 (woman) part-time; includes 36 minority (5 Black or African American, non-Hispanic/Latino; 14 Asian, non-Hispanic/Latino; 14 Hispanic/Latino; 3 Two or more races, non-Hispanic/Latino), 13 international. Average age 26. 748 applicants, 34% accepted, 124 enrolled. In 2017, 41 master's, 18 doctorates awarded. *Degree requirements:* For master's, thesis; for doctorate, comprehensive exam, thesis/dissertation. *Entrance requirements:* For doctorate, GRE. Additional exam requirements/recommendations for international students: Required—TOEFL (minimum score 94 iBT), IELTS (minimum score 7.5). *Application deadline:* For fall admission, 2/7 for domestic students. Applications are processed on a rolling basis. Electronic applications accepted. *Expenses:* Contact institution. *Financial support:* In 2017–18, 20 students received support. Schmitt Fellowships and yearly tuition scholarships (averaging $25,032) available. Financial award application deadline: 6/15; financial award applicants required to submit FAFSA. *Unit head:* Dr. Leanne L. Cribbs, Associate Dean, Graduate Education, 708-327-2817, Fax: 708-216-8216, E-mail: lcribbs@luc.edu. *Application contact:* Margarita Quesada, Graduate Program Secretary, 708-216-3532, Fax: 708-216-8216, E-mail: mquesad@luc.edu.
Website: http://ssom.luc.edu/graduate_school/degree-programs/ipbsphd/

Loyola University Chicago, Graduate School, Marcella Niehoff School of Nursing, Maywood, IL 60141. Offers adult clinical nurse specialist (MSN, Certificate); adult nurse practitioner (Certificate); dietetics (MS); family nurse practitioner (Certificate); family, adult, and women's health nurse practitioner (MSN); health systems leadership (MSN); healthcare quality using education in safety and technology (DNP); infection prevention (MSN, DNP); nursing science (PhD); women's health clinical nurse specialist (Certificate). *Accreditation:* AACN. *Program availability:* Part-time, blended/hybrid learning. *Faculty:* 24 full-time (22 women), 21 part-time/adjunct (19 women). *Students:* 188 full-time (178 women), 222 part-time (208 women); includes 105 minority (23 Black or African American, non-Hispanic/Latino; 40 Asian, non-Hispanic/Latino; 30 Hispanic/Latino; 2 Native Hawaiian or other Pacific Islander, non-Hispanic/Latino; 10 Two or more races, non-Hispanic/Latino), 4 international. Average age 36. 197 applicants, 55% accepted, 80 enrolled. In 2017, 94 master's, 17 doctorates, 26 other advanced degrees awarded. *Degree requirements:* For master's, comprehensive exam; for doctorate, thesis/dissertation, qualifying examination (for PhD); capstone project (for DNP). *Entrance requirements:* For master's, BSN, minimum nursing GPA of 3.0, Illinois RN license, 3 letters of recommendation, 1000 hours of experience in area of specialty prior to starting clinical rotations, personal statement; for doctorate, BSN or MSN, minimum GPA of 3.0, professional nursing license, 3 letters of recommendation, personal statement. Additional exam requirements/recommendations for international students: Required—TOEFL (minimum score 550 paper-based; 79 iBT), IELTS (minimum score 6.5). *Application deadline:* For fall admission, 6/1 priority date for domestic and international students; for spring admission, 11/15 priority date for domestic and international students; for summer admission, 3/15 priority date for domestic and international students. Applications are processed on a rolling basis. Application fee: $50. Electronic applications accepted. Application fee is waived when completed online. *Expenses:* Contact institution. *Financial support:* In 2017–18, 10 students received support, including 3 research assistantships with full tuition reimbursements available (averaging $18,000 per year), 1 teaching assistantship with full tuition reimbursement available (averaging $18,000 per year); scholarships/grants, unspecified assistantships, and nurse faculty loan program also available. Financial award application deadline: 5/1; financial award applicants required to submit FAFSA. *Faculty research:* Epigenetics and social determinants of health; women's health; vitamin D; health equity; interprofessional education; prevention and self-management of chronic disease; body mass in oncology patients. *Total annual research expenditures:* $1.4 million. *Unit head:* Dr. Vickie Keough, Dean, 708-216-5448, Fax: 708-216-9555, E-mail: vkeough@luc.edu. *Application contact:* Toni Topalova, Enrollment Advisor, 708-216-3751, Fax: 708-216-9555, E-mail: atopalova@luc.edu.
Website: http://www.luc.edu/nursing/

Montana State University, The Graduate School, College of Agriculture, Department of Immunology and Infectious Diseases, Bozeman, MT 59717. Offers MS, PhD. *Program availability:* Part-time. *Degree requirements:* For master's, comprehensive exam; for doctorate, comprehensive exam, thesis/dissertation. *Entrance requirements:* For master's and doctorate, GRE General Test. Additional exam requirements/ recommendations for international students: Required—TOEFL (minimum score 550 paper-based). Electronic applications accepted. *Faculty research:* Immunology, mechanisms of infectious disease pathogenesis, mechanisms of host defense, lymphocyte development, host-pathogen interactions.

North Carolina State University, College of Veterinary Medicine, Program in Comparative Biomedical Sciences, Raleigh, NC 27695. Offers cell biology (MS, PhD); infectious disease (MS, PhD); pathology (MS, PhD); pharmacology (MS, PhD); population medicine (MS, PhD). *Program availability:* Part-time. *Degree requirements:* For master's, thesis; for doctorate, thesis/dissertation. *Entrance requirements:* For master's and doctorate, GRE General Test. Additional exam requirements/ recommendations for international students: Required—TOEFL (minimum score 550 paper-based). Electronic applications accepted. *Expenses:* Contact institution. *Faculty research:* Infectious diseases, cell biology, pharmacology and toxicology, genomics, pathology and population medicine.

North Dakota State University, College of Graduate and Interdisciplinary Studies, College of Health Professions, Department of Public Health, Fargo, ND 58102. Offers American Indian public health (MPH); community health sciences (MPH); management of infectious diseases (MPH); Pharm D/MPH. *Accreditation:* CEPH. *Program availability:* Online learning. *Expenses:* Tuition, state resident: full-time $4323; part-time $360.21 per credit. Tuition, nonresident: full-time $6484; part-time $540.31 per credit. *Required fees:* $668; $55.70 per credit. Part-time tuition and fees vary according to degree level, program and reciprocity agreements. *Unit head:* Stefanie Meyer, Program Coordinator, 701-231-6549, E-mail: stefanie.meyer@ndsu.edu. *Application contact:* Stefanie Meyer, Program Coordinator, 701-231-6549, E-mail: stefanie.meyer@ndsu.edu.
Website: http://www.ndsu.edu/publichealth/

See Display on page 781 and Close-Up on page 845.

Rutgers University–Newark, Graduate School of Biomedical Sciences, Newark, NJ 07107. Offers biodefense (Certificate); biomedical engineering (PhD); biomedical sciences (multidisciplinary) (PhD); cellular biology, neuroscience and physiology (PhD), including neuroscience, physiology, biophysics, cardiovascular biology, molecular pharmacology, stem cell biology; infection, immunity and inflammation (PhD), including immunology, infectious disease, microbiology, oral biology; molecular biology, genetics and cancer (PhD), including biochemistry, molecular genetics, cancer biology, radiation biology, bioinformatics; neuroscience (Certificate); pharmacological sciences (Certificate); stem cell (Certificate); DMD/PhD; MD/PhD. PhD in biomedical engineering offered jointly with New Jersey Institute of Technology. *Program availability:* Part-time, evening/weekend. Terminal master's awarded for partial completion of doctoral program. *Degree requirements:* For doctorate, thesis/dissertation, qualifying exam. *Entrance requirements:* For doctorate, GRE General Test. Additional exam requirements/recommendations for international students: Required—TOEFL. Electronic applications accepted.

Thomas Jefferson University, Jefferson College of Biomedical Sciences, Certificate Program in Infectious Disease Control, Philadelphia, PA 19107. Offers Certificate. *Program availability:* Part-time. *Faculty:* 43 full-time (16 women), 28 part-time/adjunct (9 women). *Students:* 7 part-time (4 women); includes 1 minority (Black or African American, non-Hispanic/Latino). 7 applicants, 100% accepted, 4 enrolled. In 2017, 2 Certificates awarded. *Entrance requirements:* For degree, GRE General Test (recommended). Additional exam requirements/recommendations for international students: Required—TOEFL, IELTS (minimum score 7). *Application deadline:* For fall admission, 8/1 priority date for domestic students, 3/1 priority date for international students; for winter admission, 12/1 priority date for domestic students, 6/1 priority date for international students; for spring admission, 4/1 priority date for domestic students. Applications are processed on a rolling basis. Application fee: $50. *Financial support:* Federal Work-Study and institutionally sponsored loans available. Support available to part-time students. Financial award application deadline: 5/1; financial award applicants required to submit FAFSA. *Unit head:* Dr. James P. McGettigan, Program Director, 215-503-4629, Fax: 215-503-5393. *Application contact:* Marc E. Stearns, Senior Associate Director of Admissions, 215-503-0155, Fax: 215-503-3433, E-mail: jgsbs-info@jefferson.edu.
Website: http://www.jefferson.edu/university/biomedical-sciences/degrees-programs/graduate-certificate.html

Tufts University, Cummings School of Veterinary Medicine, North Grafton, MA 01536. Offers animals and public policy (MS); biomedical sciences (PhD), including digestive diseases, infectious diseases, neuroscience and reproductive biology, pathology; conservation medicine (MS); veterinary medicine (DVM); DVM/MPH; DVM/MS. *Accreditation:* AVMA (one or more programs are accredited). *Degree requirements:* For master's, thesis (for some programs); for doctorate, comprehensive exam, thesis/ dissertation (for some programs). *Entrance requirements:* For master's and doctorate, GRE General Test. Additional exam requirements/recommendations for international students: Required—TOEFL or IELTS. Electronic applications accepted. *Expenses:* Contact institution. *Faculty research:* Oncology, veterinary ethics, international veterinary medicine, veterinary genomics, pathogenesis of Clostridium difficile, wildlife fertility control.

Uniformed Services University of the Health Sciences, F. Edward Hebert School of Medicine, Graduate Programs in the Biomedical Sciences and Public Health, Graduate Program in Emerging Infectious Diseases, Bethesda, MD 20814-4799. Offers PhD. *Degree requirements:* For doctorate, comprehensive exam, thesis/dissertation, qualifying exam. *Entrance requirements:* For doctorate, GRE General Test. Electronic applications accepted. *Faculty research:* Pathogenesis, host response, and epidemiology of infectious diseases.

See Display below and Close-Up on page 303.

Université Laval, Faculty of Medicine, Post-Professional Programs in Medical Studies, Québec, QC G1K 7P4, Canada. Offers anatomy–pathology (DESS); anesthesiology (DESS); cardiology (DESS); care of older people (Diploma); clinical research (DESS); community health (DESS); dermatology (DESS); diagnostic radiology (DESS); emergency medicine (Diploma); family medicine (DESS); general surgery (DESS); geriatrics (DESS); hematology (DESS); internal medicine (DESS); maternal and fetal medicine (Diploma); medical biochemistry (DESS); medical microbiology and infectious diseases (DESS); medical oncology (DESS); nephrology (DESS); neurology (DESS); neurosurgery (DESS); obstetrics and gynecology (DESS); ophthalmology (DESS); orthopedic surgery (DESS); oto-rhino-laryngology (DESS); palliative medicine (Diploma); pediatrics (DESS); plastic surgery (DESS); psychiatry (DESS); pulmonary medicine (DESS); radiology–oncology (DESS); thoracic surgery (DESS); urology (DESS). *Degree requirements:* For other advanced degree, comprehensive exam. *Entrance requirements:* For degree, knowledge of French. Electronic applications accepted.

The University of British Columbia, Faculty of Medicine, Experimental Medicine Program, Vancouver, BC V5Z 1M9, Canada. Offers M Sc, PhD. *Degree requirements:* For master's, thesis; for doctorate, comprehensive exam, thesis/dissertation. *Entrance requirements:* For master's, minimum GPA of 75% or B+ standing, B Sc or MD; for doctorate, minimum GPA of 75% or B+ standing, M Sc. Additional exam requirements/ recommendations for international students: Required—TOEFL (minimum score 590 paper-based, 96 iBT), IELTS (minimum score 7.0) or Michigan English Language Assessment Battery (minimum score 84). Electronic applications accepted. *Expenses:* Contact institution. *Faculty research:* Infectious diseases, respiratory medicine, genetics, pediatrics, oncology and signal transduction.

University of Calgary, Cumming School of Medicine and Faculty of Graduate Studies, Department of Microbiology, Immunology and Infectious Diseases, Calgary, AB T2N 1N4, Canada. Offers M Sc, PhD. *Degree requirements:* For master's, thesis, oral thesis exam; for doctorate, thesis/dissertation, candidacy exam, oral thesis exam. *Entrance requirements:* For master's and doctorate, minimum GPA of 3.2. Additional exam requirements/recommendations for international students: Required—TOEFL (minimum score 580 paper-based). Electronic applications accepted. *Faculty research:* Bacteriology, virology, parasitology, immunology.

University of California, Berkeley, Graduate Division, School of Public Health, Group in Epidemiology, Berkeley, CA 94720-1500. Offers epidemiology (MS, PhD); infectious diseases (PhD). *Degree requirements:* For master's, comprehensive exam; for doctorate, thesis/dissertation, oral and written exam. *Entrance requirements:* For master's, GRE General Test, minimum GPA of 3.0; MD, DDS, DVM, or PhD in biomedical science (MPH); for doctorate, GRE General Test, minimum GPA of 3.0. Electronic applications accepted.

University of California, Berkeley, Graduate Division, School of Public Health, Group in Infectious Diseases and Immunity, Berkeley, CA 94720-1500. Offers PhD. *Entrance requirements:* For doctorate, GRE General Test, minimum GPA of 3.0, 3 letters of recommendation. Electronic applications accepted.

University of Georgia, College of Veterinary Medicine, Department of Infectious Diseases, Athens, GA 30602. Offers PhD. *Degree requirements:* For doctorate, one foreign language, thesis/dissertation. *Entrance requirements:* For doctorate, GRE General Test. Electronic applications accepted.

University of Guelph, Ontario Veterinary College and Graduate Studies, Graduate Programs in Veterinary Sciences, Department of Pathobiology, Guelph, ON N1G 2W1, Canada. Offers anatomic pathology (DV Sc, Diploma); clinical pathology (Diploma); comparative pathology (M Sc, PhD); immunology (M Sc, PhD); laboratory animal science (DV Sc); pathology (M Sc, PhD, Diploma); veterinary infectious diseases (M Sc, PhD); zoo animal/wildlife medicine (DV Sc). *Degree requirements:* For master's, thesis; for doctorate, thesis/dissertation. *Entrance requirements:* For master's, DVM with B average or an honours degree in biological sciences; for doctorate, DVM or MSC degree, minimum B+ average. Additional exam requirements/recommendations for international students: Required—TOEFL (minimum score 550 paper-based). *Faculty research:* Pathogenesis; diseases of animals, wildlife, fish, and laboratory animals; parasitology; immunology; veterinary infectious diseases; laboratory animal science.

University of Manitoba, Max Rady College of Medicine and Faculty of Graduate Studies, Graduate Programs in Medicine, Department of Medical Microbiology and Infectious Diseases, Winnipeg, MB R3T 2N2, Canada. Offers M Sc, PhD. *Program availability:* Part-time. Terminal master's awarded for partial completion of doctoral program. *Degree requirements:* For master's, thesis; for doctorate, one foreign language, thesis/dissertation. *Entrance requirements:* For master's and doctorate, minimum GPA of 3.0. Electronic applications accepted. *Faculty research:* HIV, bacterial adhesion, sexually transmitted diseases, virus structure/function and assembly.

University of Minnesota, Twin Cities Campus, School of Public Health, Division of Environmental Health Sciences, Area in Environmental Infectious Diseases, Minneapolis, MN 55455-0213. Offers MPH, MS, PhD. *Degree requirements:* For doctorate, thesis/dissertation. *Entrance requirements:* For master's and doctorate, GRE General Test. Electronic applications accepted.

University of Nebraska Medical Center, Interdisciplinary Graduate Program in Biomedical Sciences, Immunology, Pathology and Infectious Disease Graduate Program, Omaha, NE 68198-5900. Offers MS, PhD. *Program availability:* Part-time. *Faculty:* 84 full-time (26 women). *Students:* 41 full-time (27 women), 4 part-time (3 women); includes 5 minority (1 Black or African American, non-Hispanic/Latino; 1 American Indian or Alaska Native, non-Hispanic/Latino; 3 Asian, non-Hispanic/Latino), 21 international. Average age 28. 21 applicants, 38% accepted, 7 enrolled. In 2017, 4 master's, 2 doctorates awarded. Terminal master's awarded for partial completion of doctoral program. *Degree requirements:* For master's, comprehensive exam, thesis; for doctorate, comprehensive exam, thesis/dissertation. *Entrance requirements:* For master's, previous course work in biology, chemistry, mathematics, and physics; for doctorate, GRE General Test, previous course work in biology, chemistry, mathematics, and physics. Additional exam requirements/recommendations for international students: Required—TOEFL (minimum score 550 paper-based; 90 iBT), IELTS (minimum score 6.5). *Application deadline:* For fall admission, 4/1 for domestic and international students; for spring admission, 10/1 for domestic and international students; for summer admission, 3/1 for domestic students, 1/1 for international students. Applications are processed on a rolling basis. Application fee: $60. Electronic applications accepted. *Expenses:* Tuition, state resident: full-time $8451; part-time $4225 per semester. Tuition, nonresident: full-time $24,219; part-time $11,295 per semester. *Required fees:* $589; $117 per term. *Financial support:* In 2017–18, 5 students received support, including 2 fellowships with full tuition reimbursements available (averaging $24,000 per year), 3 research assistantships with full tuition reimbursements available (averaging $24,000 per year); scholarships/grants, health care benefits, and unspecified assistantships also available. Financial award application deadline: 3/1; financial award applicants required to submit FAFSA. *Faculty research:* Infectious diseases, cancer biology, immunobiology, molecular virology, molecular genetics. *Unit head:* Dr. Rakesh K. Singh, Chair, Graduate Committee, 402-559-9949, Fax: 402-559-5900, E-mail: rsingh@unmc.edu. *Application contact:* Tuire Cechin, Graduate Program Coordinator, 402-559-4042, Fax: 402-559-5900, E-mail: tcechin@unmc.edu.
Website: http://www.unmc.edu/pathology/

University of Pittsburgh, Graduate School of Public Health, Department of Infectious Diseases and Microbiology, Pittsburgh, PA 15261. Offers infectious diseases and microbiology (MS, PhD); management, intervention, and community practice (MPH); pathogenesis, eradication, and laboratory practice (MPH). *Program availability:* Part-time. *Faculty:* 21 full-time (7 women), 5 part-time/adjunct (2 women). *Students:* 55 full-time (34 women), 19 part-time (12 women); includes 17 minority (2 Black or African American, non-Hispanic/Latino; 8 Asian, non-Hispanic/Latino; 1 Hispanic/Latino; 6 Two or more races, non-Hispanic/Latino), 8 international. Average age 26. 152 applicants, 51% accepted, 27 enrolled. In 2017, 34 master's, 2 doctorates awarded. Terminal master's awarded for partial completion of doctoral program. *Degree requirements:* For master's, thesis, comprehensive exam (for MS); for doctorate, comprehensive exam, thesis/dissertation, preliminary exam, dissertation defense. *Entrance requirements:* For master's, GRE General Test, MCAT, or DAT, minimum GPA of 3.0, 6 credits of behavioral science; for doctorate, GRE General Test, MCAT, DAT, minimum GPA of 3.0; research experience; knowledge of biology or microbiology, chemistry, and algebra. Additional exam requirements/recommendations for international students: Required—TOEFL (minimum score 550 paper-based, 80 iBT) or IELTS (minimum score 6.5). *Application deadline:* For fall admission, 1/15 priority date for domestic students, 3/15 priority date for international students. Applications are processed on a rolling basis. Application fee: $135. Electronic applications accepted. *Expenses:* $26,136 per year in-state tuition, $43,392 out-of-state, $850 fees. *Financial support:* In 2017–18, 38 students received support, including 19 research assistantships with full tuition reimbursements available; fellowships, teaching assistantships, scholarships/grants, and tuition waivers (full) also available. Financial award applicants required to submit FAFSA. *Faculty research:* Development of HIV vaccines, complications of antiretroviral therapy, emerging infections, herpes viruses. *Unit head:* Robin Tierno, Department Administrator, 412-624-3105, Fax: 412-624-4953, E-mail: rtierno@pitt.edu. *Application contact:* Abby Kincaid, Student Services Coordinator, 412-624-3331, E-mail: abbykincaid@pitt.edu.
Website: http://www.publichealth.pitt.edu/idm

University of South Florida, Morsani College of Medicine and College of Graduate Studies, Graduate Programs in Medical Sciences, Tampa, FL 33620-9951. Offers advanced athletic training (MS); athletic training (MS); bioinformatics and computational biology (MSBCB); biotechnology (MSB); health informatics (MSHI); medical sciences (MSMS, PhD), including aging and neuroscience (MSMS), allergy, immunology and infectious disease (PhD), anatomy, biochemistry and molecular biology, clinical and translational research, health science (MSMS), interdisciplinary medical sciences (MSMS), medical microbiology and immunology (MSMS), metabolic and nutritional medicine (MSMS), microbiology and immunology (PhD), molecular medicine, molecular pharmacology and physiology (PhD), neuroscience (PhD), pathology and cell biology (PhD), women's health (MSMS). *Students:* 372 full-time (212 women), 216 part-time (142 women); includes 257 minority (78 Black or African American, non-Hispanic/Latino; 1 American Indian or Alaska Native, non-Hispanic/Latino; 79 Asian, non-Hispanic/Latino; 84 Hispanic/Latino; 15 Two or more races, non-Hispanic/Latino), 62 international. Average age 28. 1,048 applicants, 46% accepted, 309 enrolled. In 2017, 351 master's, 56 doctorates awarded. Terminal master's awarded for partial completion of doctoral program. *Degree requirements:* For master's, comprehensive exam, thesis; for doctorate, comprehensive exam, thesis/dissertation. *Entrance requirements:* For master's, GRE General Test or GMAT, bachelor's degree or equivalent from regionally-accredited university with minimum GPA of 3.0 in upper-division sciences coursework; prerequisites in general biology, general chemistry, general physics, organic chemistry, quantitative analysis, and integral and differential calculus; for doctorate, GRE General Test, bachelor's degree from regionally-accredited university with minimum GPA of 3.0 in upper-division sciences coursework; 3 letters of recommendation; personal interview; 1-2 page personal statement; prerequisites in biology, chemistry, physics, organic chemistry, quantitative analysis, and integral/differential calculus. Additional exam requirements/recommendations for international students: Required—TOEFL (minimum score 550 paper-based; 79 iBT) or IELTS (minimum score 6.5). *Application deadline:* For fall admission, 2/1 priority date for domestic students, 2/1 for international students. Application fee: $30. Electronic applications accepted. *Expenses:* Contact institution. *Financial support:* In 2017–18, 109 students received support. *Faculty research:* Anatomy, biochemistry, cancer biology, cardiovascular disease, cell biology, immunology, microbiology, molecular biology, neuroscience, pharmacology, physiology. *Total annual research expenditures:* $45.3 million. *Unit head:* Dr. Michael Barber, Professor/Associate Dean for Graduate and Postdoctoral Affairs, 813-974-9908, Fax: 813-974-4317, E-mail: mbarber@health.usf.edu. *Application contact:* Dr. Eric Bennett, Graduate Director, PhD Program in Medical Sciences, 813-974-1545, Fax: 813-974-4317, E-mail: esbennet@health.usf.edu.
Website: http://health.usf.edu/nocms/medicine/graduatestudies/

The University of Texas Health Science Center at Houston, MD Anderson UTHealth Graduate School, Houston, TX 77225-0036. Offers biochemistry and cell biology (PhD); biomedical sciences (MS); cancer biology (PhD); genetic counseling (MS); genetics and epigenetics (PhD); immunology (PhD); medical physics (MS, PhD); microbiology and infectious diseases (PhD); neuroscience (PhD); quantitative sciences (PhD); therapeutics and pharmacology (PhD); MD/PhD. Terminal master's awarded for partial completion of doctoral program. *Degree requirements:* For master's, thesis; for doctorate, thesis/dissertation. *Entrance requirements:* For master's and doctorate, GRE General Test. Additional exam requirements/recommendations for international students: Required—TOEFL. Electronic applications accepted. *Faculty research:* Biomedical sciences.

Washington State University, College of Veterinary Medicine, Program in Immunology and Infectious Diseases, Pullman, WA 99164-7040. Offers MS, PhD. *Faculty:* 38 full-time (13 women), 10 part-time/adjunct (5 women). *Students:* 34 full-time (26 women); includes 5 minority (1 Black or African American, non-Hispanic/Latino; 3 Asian, non-Hispanic/Latino; 1 Hispanic/Latino), 11 international. Average age 31. 45 applicants, 29% accepted, 8 enrolled. In 2017, 2 master's, 1 doctorate awarded. Terminal master's awarded for partial completion of doctoral program. *Degree requirements:* For master's, thesis, oral exam; for doctorate, thesis/dissertation, oral exam. *Entrance requirements:* For master's and doctorate, minimum GPA of 3.0. Additional exam requirements/recommendations for international students: Required—TOEFL (minimum score 550 paper-based; 80 iBT). *Application deadline:* Applications are processed on a rolling basis. Application fee: $75. Electronic applications accepted. *Financial support:* In 2017–18, 31 students received support, including 5 fellowships, 26 research assistantships, 2 teaching assistantships; institutionally sponsored loans, scholarships/grants, traineeships, and unspecified assistantships also available. Financial award application deadline: 3/1; financial award applicants required to submit FAFSA. *Faculty research:* Microbial pathogenesis, veterinary and wildlife parasitology, laboratory animal pathology, immune responses to infectious diseases. *Unit head:* Dr. Robert H. Mealey, Chair, 509-335-6030, Fax: 509-335-8529, E-mail: rmealey@wsu.edu. *Application contact:* Sue Zumwalt, Graduate Coordinator, 509-335-6027, Fax: 509-335-8529, E-mail: szumwalt@wsu.edu.
Website: http://vmp.vetmed.wsu.edu/graduate-programs

Yale University, Yale School of Medicine and Graduate School of Arts and Sciences, Combined Program in Biological and Biomedical Sciences (BBS), Microbiology Track, New Haven, CT 06520. Offers PhD, MD/PhD. *Degree requirements:* For doctorate, thesis/dissertation. *Entrance requirements:* For doctorate, GRE General Test, GRE Subject Test. Additional exam requirements/recommendations for international students: Required—TOEFL. Electronic applications accepted.

Medical Microbiology

The Citadel, The Military College of South Carolina, Citadel Graduate College, School of Humanities and Social Sciences, Department of History, Charleston, SC 29409. Offers history (MA); history and teaching content (Graduate Certificate). Program offered jointly with The Graduate School of the College of Charleston. *Program availability:* Part-time, evening/weekend. *Degree requirements:* For master's, variable foreign language requirement, thesis optional. *Entrance requirements:* For master's, GRE (minimum verbal score of 152) taken within the last 5 years, minimum undergraduate GPA of 2.5 (3.0 in major); 3 letters of recommendation; evidence of ability to conduct research and present findings; at least 15 hours of history course work; for Graduate Certificate, no more than 2 page letter of intent that answers specific questions listed on the Department of History website and academic course catalog; 3 references familiar with work; baccalaureate degree in specified fields. Additional exam requirements/recommendations for international students: Required—TOEFL (minimum score 550 paper-based). Electronic applications accepted. *Expenses:* Tuition, state resident: part-time $587 per credit hour. Tuition, nonresident: part-time $988 per credit hour. *Required fees:* $90 per term.

Creighton University, School of Medicine and Graduate School, Graduate Programs in Medicine, Omaha, NE 68178-0001. Offers biomedical sciences (MS, PhD); clinical anatomy (MS); medical microbiology and immunology (MS, PhD); pharmacology (MS, PhD), including pharmaceutical sciences (MS), pharmacology; MD/PhD; Pharm D/MS. Terminal master's awarded for partial completion of doctoral program. *Degree requirements:* For master's, thesis; for doctorate, thesis/dissertation. *Entrance requirements:* For master's and doctorate, GRE General Test. Additional exam requirements/recommendations for international students: Required—TOEFL (minimum score 550 paper-based; 80 iBT). Electronic applications accepted. *Expenses:* Contact institution. *Faculty research:* Molecular biology and gene transfection, infectious disease, antimicrobial agents and chemotherapy, virology, pharmacological secretion.

HEC Montreal, School of Business Administration, Doctoral Program in Administration, Montréal, QC H3T 2A7, Canada. Offers accounting (PhD); applied economics (PhD); data science (PhD); finance (PhD); financial engineering (PhD); information technology (PhD); international business (PhD); logistics and operations management (PhD); management science (PhD); management, strategy and organizations (PhD); marketing (PhD); organizational behaviour and human resources (PhD). Program offered jointly with Concordia University, McGill University, and Universite du Quebec a Montreal. *Accreditation:* AACSB. *Students:* 114 full-time (47 women). 78 applicants, 42% accepted, 24 enrolled. In 2017, 23 doctorates awarded. *Entrance requirements:* For doctorate, TAGE MAGE, GMAT, or GRE, master's degree in administration or related field. *Application deadline:* For fall admission, 1/15 for domestic and international students. Application fee: $88 ($187 for international students). Electronic applications accepted. *Expenses:* Tuition, state resident: full-time $2869 Canadian dollars; part-time $79.70 Canadian dollars per credit. Tuition, nonresident: full-time $8883 Canadian dollars; part-time $246.76 Canadian dollars per credit. *International tuition:* $19,648 Canadian dollars full-time. *Required fees:* $41.20 Canadian dollars per credit. $67.94 Canadian dollars per term. Tuition and fees vary according to degree level and program. *Financial support:* Research assistantships, teaching assistantships, and scholarships/grants available. Financial award application deadline: 9/2. *Faculty research:* Art management, business policy, entrepreneurship, new technologies, transportation. *Unit head:* Jacques Robert, Director, 514-340-6853, E-mail: jacques.robert@hec.ca. *Application contact:* Julie Bilodeau, PhD Program Analyst, 514-340-6151, Fax: 514-340-6411, E-mail: analyste.phd@hec.ca.
Website: http://www.hec.ca/en/programs/phd/index.html

Idaho State University, Office of Graduate Studies, College of Science and Engineering, Department of Biological Sciences, Pocatello, ID 83209-8007. Offers biology (MNS, MS, DA, PhD); clinical laboratory science (MS); microbiology (MS). *Accreditation:* NAACLS. *Program availability:* Part-time. *Degree requirements:* For master's, comprehensive exam, thesis; for doctorate, comprehensive exam, thesis/dissertation, 9 credits of internship (for DA). *Entrance requirements:* For master's, GRE General Test, minimum GPA of 3.0 in all upper division classes; for doctorate, GRE General Test, GRE Subject Test (biology), diagnostic exam (DA), minimum GPA of 3.0 in all upper division classes. Additional exam requirements/recommendations for international students: Required—TOEFL (minimum score 550 paper-based; 80 iBT). Electronic applications accepted. *Faculty research:* Ecology, plant and animal physiology, plant and animal developmental biology, immunology, molecular biology, bioinfomatics.

Rutgers University–New Brunswick, Graduate School-New Brunswick, Programs in the Molecular Biosciences, Piscataway, NJ 08854-8097. Offers biochemistry (PhD); cell and developmental biology (MS, PhD); microbiology and molecular genetics (MS, PhD), including applied microbiology, clinical microbiology, computational molecular biology (PhD), immunology, microbial biochemistry, molecular genetics, virology. MS, PhD offered jointly with University of Medicine and Dentistry of New Jersey.

Université du Québec, Institut National de la Recherche Scientifique, Graduate Programs, INRS - Institut Armand-Frappier, Laval, QC G1K 9A9, Canada. Offers applied microbiology (M Sc); biology (PhD); experimental health sciences (M Sc); virology and immunology (M Sc, PhD). *Program availability:* Part-time. *Faculty:* 48 full-time. *Students:* 149 full-time (89 women), 18 part-time (11 women), 86 international. Average age 30. 29 applicants, 93% accepted, 25 enrolled. In 2017, 16 master's, 13 doctorates awarded. *Degree requirements:* For master's, thesis; for doctorate, thesis/dissertation. *Entrance requirements:* For master's, appropriate bachelor's degree, proficiency in French; for doctorate, appropriate master's degree, proficiency in French. *Application deadline:* For fall admission, 3/30 for domestic and international students; for winter admission, 11/1 for domestic and international students; for spring admission, 3/1 for domestic and international students. Application fee: $45 Canadian dollars. Electronic applications accepted. *Financial support:* In 2017–18, fellowships (averaging $16,500 per year) were awarded; research assistantships also available. *Faculty research:* Immunity, infection and cancer; toxicology and environmental biotechnology; molecular pharmacochemistry. *Unit head:* Pierre Talbot, Director, 450-687-5010 Ext. 4300, Fax: 450-686-5501, E-mail: pierre.talbot@iaf.inrs.ca. *Application contact:* Sylvie Richard, Registrar, 418-654-2518, Fax: 418-654-3858, E-mail: sylvie.richard@adm.inrs.ca.
Website: http://www.iaf.inrs.ca

University of Alberta, Faculty of Medicine and Dentistry and Faculty of Graduate Studies and Research, Graduate Programs in Medicine, Department of Medical Microbiology and Immunology, Edmonton, AB T6G 2E1, Canada. Offers M Sc, PhD. Terminal master's awarded for partial completion of doctoral program. *Degree requirements:* For master's, thesis; for doctorate, thesis/dissertation. *Entrance requirements:* For master's and doctorate, minimum GPA of 3.3. Additional exam requirements/recommendations for international students: Required—TOEFL (minimum score 600 paper-based; 96 iBT). *Faculty research:* Cellular and reproductive immunology, microbial pathogenesis, mechanisms of antibiotic resistance, molecular biology of mammalian viruses, antiviral chemotherapy.

University of Hawaii at Manoa, John A. Burns School of Medicine and Office of Graduate Education, Graduate Programs in Biomedical Sciences, Department of Tropical Medicine, Medical Microbiology and Pharmacology, Honolulu, HI 96822. Offers tropical medicine (MS, PhD). *Program availability:* Part-time. Terminal master's awarded for partial completion of doctoral program. *Degree requirements:* For master's, thesis optional; for doctorate, comprehensive exam, thesis/dissertation. *Entrance requirements:* For master's and doctorate, GRE General Test. Additional exam requirements/recommendations for international students: Required—TOEFL (minimum score 580 paper-based; 92 iBT), IELTS (minimum score 5). *Faculty research:* Immunological studies of dengue, malaria, Kawasaki's disease, lupus erythematosus, rheumatoid disease.

University of Manitoba, Max Rady College of Medicine and Faculty of Graduate Studies, Graduate Programs in Medicine, Department of Medical Microbiology and Infectious Diseases, Winnipeg, MB R3T 2N2, Canada. Offers M Sc, PhD. *Program availability:* Part-time. Terminal master's awarded for partial completion of doctoral program. *Degree requirements:* For master's, thesis; for doctorate, one foreign language, thesis/dissertation. *Entrance requirements:* For master's and doctorate, minimum GPA of 3.0. Electronic applications accepted. *Faculty research:* HIV, bacterial adhesion, sexually transmitted diseases, virus structure/function and assembly.

University of Minnesota, Duluth, Medical School, Microbiology, Immunology and Molecular Pathobiology Section, Duluth, MN 55812-2496. Offers MS, PhD. MS, PhD offered jointly with University of Minnesota, Twin Cities Campus. Terminal master's awarded for partial completion of doctoral program. *Degree requirements:* For master's, thesis, final oral exam; for doctorate, thesis/dissertation, final exam, oral and written preliminary exams. *Entrance requirements:* For master's and doctorate, GRE General Test. Additional exam requirements/recommendations for international students: Required—TOEFL. *Faculty research:* Immunomodulation, molecular diagnosis of rabies, cytokines, cancer immunology, cytomegalovirus infection.

University of Southern California, Keck School of Medicine, Program in Medical Biology, Los Angeles, CA 90033. Offers PhD. *Faculty:* 46 full-time (13 women). *Students:* 28 full-time (18 women); includes 5 minority (3 Asian, non-Hispanic/Latino; 1 Hispanic/Latino; 1 Two or more races, non-Hispanic/Latino), 14 international. Average age 26. 15 applicants, 100% accepted, 15 enrolled. *Degree requirements:* For doctorate, comprehensive exam, thesis/dissertation. *Entrance requirements:* For doctorate, GRE, minimum GPA of 3.5. Additional exam requirements/recommendations for international students: Required—TOEFL (minimum score 600 paper-based; 100 iBT), IELTS (minimum score 7), PTE. *Application deadline:* For fall admission, 12/1 priority date for domestic and international students. Application fee: $90. Electronic applications accepted. *Financial support:* In 2017–18, 28 students received support, including 1 fellowship with full tuition reimbursement available (averaging $33,000 per year), 24 research assistantships with full tuition reimbursements available (averaging $33,000 per year), 3 teaching assistantships with full tuition reimbursements available (averaging $33,000 per year); institutionally sponsored loans, scholarships/grants, traineeships, health care benefits, and unspecified assistantships also available. Financial award application deadline: 4/15; financial award applicants required to submit CSS PROFILE or FAFSA. *Unit head:* Dr. Martin Kast, Director, 323-442-1645, Fax: 323-442-1199, E-mail: mkast@usc.edu. *Application contact:* Dr. Joyce Perez, Manager of Student Programs, 323-442-1645, Fax: 323-442-1199, E-mail: jpperez@med.usc.edu.
Website: http://pibbs.usc.edu/research-and-programs/phd-programs/

University of South Florida, Morsani College of Medicine and College of Graduate Studies, Graduate Programs in Medical Sciences, Tampa, FL 33620-9951. Offers advanced athletic training (MS); athletic training (MS); bioinformatics and computational biology (MSBCB); biotechnology (MSB); health informatics (MSHI); medical sciences (MSMS, PhD), including aging and neuroscience (MSMS), allergy, immunology and infectious disease (PhD), anatomy, biochemistry and molecular biology, clinical and translational research, health science (MSMS), interdisciplinary medical sciences (MSMS), medical microbiology and immunology (MSMS), metabolic and nutritional medicine (MSMS), microbiology and immunology (PhD), molecular medicine, molecular pharmacology and physiology (PhD), neuroscience (PhD), pathology and cell biology (PhD), women's health (MSMS). *Students:* 372 full-time (212 women), 216 part-time (142 women); includes 257 minority (78 Black or African American, non-Hispanic/Latino; 1 American Indian or Alaska Native, non-Hispanic/Latino; 79 Asian, non-Hispanic/Latino; 84 Hispanic/Latino; 15 Two or more races, non-Hispanic/Latino), 62 international. Average age 28. 1,048 applicants, 46% accepted, 309 enrolled. In 2017, 351 master's, 56 doctorates awarded. Terminal master's awarded for partial completion of doctoral program. *Degree requirements:* For master's, comprehensive exam, thesis; for doctorate, comprehensive exam, thesis/dissertation. *Entrance requirements:* For master's, GRE General Test or GMAT, bachelor's degree or equivalent from regionally-accredited university with minimum GPA of 3.0 in upper-division sciences coursework; prerequisites in general biology, general chemistry, general physics, organic chemistry, quantitative analysis, and integral and differential calculus; for doctorate, GRE General Test, bachelor's degree from regionally-accredited university with minimum GPA of 3.0 in upper-division sciences coursework; 3 letters of recommendation; personal interview; 1-2 page personal statement; prerequisites in biology, chemistry, physics, organic chemistry, quantitative analysis, and integral/differential calculus. Additional exam requirements/recommendations for international students: Required—TOEFL (minimum score 550 paper-based; 79 iBT) or IELTS (minimum score 6.5). *Application deadline:* For fall admission, 2/1 priority date for domestic students, 2/1 for international students. Application fee: $30. Electronic applications accepted. *Expenses:* Contact institution. *Financial support:* In 2017–18, 109 students received support. *Faculty research:* Anatomy, biochemistry, cancer biology, cardiovascular disease, cell biology, immunology, microbiology, molecular biology, neuroscience, pharmacology, physiology. *Total annual research expenditures:* $45.3 million. *Unit head:* Dr. Michael Barber, Professor/Associate Dean for Graduate and Postdoctoral Affairs, 813-974-9908, Fax: 813-974-4317, E-mail: mbarber@health.usf.edu. *Application contact:* Dr. Eric Bennett, Graduate Director, PhD Program in Medical Sciences, 813-974-1545, Fax: 813-974-4317, E-mail: esbennet@health.usf.edu.
Website: http://health.usf.edu/nocms/medicine/graduatestudies/

University of Wisconsin–La Crosse, College of Science and Health, Department of Biology, La Crosse, WI 54601-3742. Offers aquatic sciences (MS); biology (MS); cellular and molecular biology (MS); clinical microbiology (MS); microbiology (MS); nurse anesthesia (MS); physiology (MS). *Accreditation:* AANA/CANAEP. *Program availability:* Part-time. *Students:* 11 full-time (2 women), 29 part-time (14 women); includes 1 minority (Two or more races, non-Hispanic/Latino). Average age 30. 67 applicants, 28% accepted, 18 enrolled. In 2017, 24 master's awarded. *Degree requirements:* For master's, comprehensive exam, thesis. *Entrance requirements:* For master's, GRE General Test, minimum GPA of 2.85. Additional exam requirements/recommendations

for international students: Required—TOEFL (minimum score 550 paper-based; 79 iBT). *Application deadline:* For fall admission, 2/1 priority date for domestic and international students; for spring admission, 1/4 priority date for domestic and international students. Applications are processed on a rolling basis. Electronic applications accepted. *Financial support:* Research assistantships with partial tuition reimbursements, Federal Work-Study, scholarships/grants, health care benefits, and tuition waivers (partial) available. Support available to part-time students. Financial award application deadline: 3/15; financial award applicants required to submit FAFSA. *Unit head:* Dr. Mark Sandheinrich, Department Chair, 608-785-8261, E-mail: msandheinrich@uwlax.edu. *Application contact:* Brandon Schaller, Senior Graduate Student Status Examiner, 608-785-8941, E-mail: admissions@uwlax.edu.
Website: http://uwlax.edu/biology/

University of Wisconsin–La Crosse, College of Science and Health, Department of Microbiology, La Crosse, WI 54601-3742. Offers clinical microbiology (MS); microbiology (MS). *Students:* 11 full-time (4 women), 13 part-time (8 women); includes 2 minority (1 Asian, non-Hispanic/Latino; 1 Hispanic/Latino), 1 international. Average age 26. 12 applicants, 92% accepted, 7 enrolled. In 2017, 4 master's awarded. *Unit head:* Michael Hoffman, Chair/Program Director, 608-785-6984, E-mail: mhoffman@uwlax.edu.
Website: http://www.uwlax.edu/microbiology/

University of Wisconsin–Madison, Graduate School, College of Agricultural and Life Sciences and College of Agricultural and Life Sciences, Microbiology Doctoral Training Program, Madison, WI 53706. Offers PhD.
Website: http://www.microbiology.wisc.edu/

Microbiology

Alabama State University, College of Science, Mathematics and Technology, Department of Biological Sciences, Montgomery, AL 36101-0271. Offers biology (MS); microbiology (PhD). *Faculty:* 13 full-time (4 women), 7 part-time/adjunct (4 women). *Students:* 12 full-time (9 women), 21 part-time (11 women); includes 25 minority (23 Black or African American, non-Hispanic/Latino; 1 Asian, non-Hispanic/Latino; 1 Two or more races, non-Hispanic/Latino), 2 international. Average age 22. 11 applicants, 91% accepted, 5 enrolled. In 2017, 2 doctorates awarded. *Degree requirements:* For master's, one foreign language, comprehensive exam, thesis; for doctorate, 3 foreign languages, thesis/dissertation. *Entrance requirements:* For master's, GRE General Test, GRE Subject Test, writing competency test. Additional exam requirements/recommendations for international students: Required—TOEFL (minimum score 500 paper-based). *Application deadline:* For fall admission, 4/15 for domestic and international students; for spring admission, 11/15 for domestic and international students; for summer admission, 3/15 for domestic and international students. Applications are processed on a rolling basis. Application fee: $25. Electronic applications accepted. *Expenses:* Tuition, state resident: part-time $412 per credit hour. Tuition, nonresident: part-time $824 per credit hour. *Required fees:* $685 per semester. *Financial support:* Research assistantships and scholarships/grants available. Financial award application deadline: 6/30; financial award applicants required to submit FAFSA. *Faculty research:* Salmonella pseudomonas, cancer cells. *Unit head:* Dr. Boakai K. Robertson, Chair, 334-229-4467, Fax: 334-229-1007, E-mail: bkrobertson@alasu.edu. *Application contact:* Dr. William Person, Dean of Graduate Studies, 334-229-4274, Fax: 334-229-4928, E-mail: wperson@alasu.edu.
Website: http://www.alasu.edu/academics/colleges—departments/science-mathematics-technology/biological-sciences-department/index.aspx

Albany Medical College, Center for Immunology and Microbial Disease, Albany, NY 12208-3479. Offers MS, PhD. *Program availability:* Part-time. Terminal master's awarded for partial completion of doctoral program. *Degree requirements:* For master's, thesis; for doctorate, comprehensive exam, thesis/dissertation, oral qualifying exam, written preliminary exam, 1 published paper-peer review. *Entrance requirements:* For master's, GRE General Test, all transcripts, letters of recommendation; for doctorate, GRE General Test, letters of recommendation. Additional exam requirements/recommendations for international students: Required—TOEFL. *Faculty research:* Microbial and viral pathogenesis, cancer development and cell transformation, biochemical and genetic mechanisms responsible for human disease.

Albert Einstein College of Medicine, Graduate Programs in the Biomedical Sciences, Department of Microbiology and Immunology, Bronx, NY 10461. Offers PhD, MD/PhD. *Degree requirements:* For doctorate, thesis/dissertation. *Entrance requirements:* For doctorate, GRE General Test. Additional exam requirements/recommendations for international students: Required—TOEFL. *Application deadline:* For fall admission, 1/15 for domestic students. Application fee: $0. *Financial support:* Fellowships available. *Faculty research:* Nature of histocompatibility antigens, lymphoid cell receptors, regulation of immune responses and mechanisms of resistance to infection. *Unit head:* Dr. Steven Porcelli, Chair, 718-430-2811, E-mail: steven.porcelli@einstein.yu.edu. *Application contact:* Salvatore Calabro, Director of Graduate Admissions, 718-430-2345, Fax: 718-430-8655, E-mail: phd@einstein.yu.edu.
Website: http://www.einstein.yu.edu/departments/microbiology-immunology/

American University of Beirut, Graduate Programs, Faculty of Medicine, Beirut, Lebanon. Offers biochemistry (MS); biomedical engineering (MS); biomedical sciences (PhD); health research (MS); human morphology (MS); medicine (MD); microbiology and immunology (MS); neuroscience (MS); orthodontics (clinical) (MS); pharmacology and therapeutics (MS); physiology (MS). *Program availability:* Part-time. *Faculty:* 335 full-time (117 women), 54 part-time/adjunct (5 women). *Students:* 513 full-time (274 women). Average age 23. 527 applicants, 47% accepted, 169 enrolled. In 2017, 18 master's, 98 doctorates awarded. *Degree requirements:* For master's, one foreign language, comprehensive exam, thesis (for some programs); for doctorate, one foreign language, comprehensive exam, thesis/dissertation. *Entrance requirements:* For doctorate, MCAT (for MD); GRE (for PhD). Additional exam requirements/recommendations for international students: Required—TOEFL (minimum score 600 paper-based; 100 iBT), IELTS (minimum score 7.5). *Application deadline:* Applications are processed on a rolling basis. Application fee: $75. Electronic applications accepted. *Expenses:* Contact institution. *Financial support:* In 2017–18, 302 students received support. Fellowships, research assistantships, teaching assistantships, institutionally sponsored loans, scholarships/grants, tuition waivers, and unspecified assistantships available. *Unit head:* Dr. Mohamed Sayegh, Dean, 961-1-135000 Ext. 4700, Fax: 961-1-744489, E-mail: msayegh@aub.edu.lb. *Application contact:* Dr. Salim Kanaan, Director, Admission's Office, 961-1-350000 Ext. 2594, Fax: 961-1-750775, E-mail: sk00@aub.edu.lb.

Arizona State University at the Tempe campus, College of Liberal Arts and Sciences, School of Life Sciences, Tempe, AZ 85287-4601. Offers animal behavior (PhD); applied ethics (biomedical and health ethics) (MA); biology (MS, PhD), including biology, biology and society, complex adaptive systems science (PhD), plant biology and conservation (MS); environmental life sciences (PhD); evolutionary biology (PhD); history and philosophy of science (PhD); human and social dimensions of science and technology (PhD); microbiology (PhD); molecular and cellular biology (PhD); neuroscience (PhD). Terminal master's awarded for partial completion of doctoral program. *Degree requirements:* For master's, thesis (for some programs), interactive Program of Study (iPOS) submitted before completing 50 percent of required credit hours; for doctorate, variable foreign language requirement, comprehensive exam, thesis/dissertation, interactive Program of Study (iPOS) submitted before completing 50 percent of required credit hours. *Entrance requirements:* For master's and doctorate, GRE, minimum GPA of 3.0 or equivalent in last 2 years of work leading to bachelor's degree. Additional exam requirements/recommendations for international students: Required—TOEFL (minimum score 600 paper-based; 100 iBT). Electronic applications accepted.

Baylor College of Medicine, Graduate School of Biomedical Sciences, Department of Molecular Virology and Microbiology, Houston, TX 77030-3498. Offers PhD, MD/PhD. *Degree requirements:* For doctorate, thesis/dissertation, public defense. *Entrance requirements:* For doctorate, GRE General Test, GRE Subject Test (strongly recommended), minimum GPA of 3.0. Additional exam requirements/recommendations for international students: Required—TOEFL. Electronic applications accepted. *Faculty research:* Microbiology, viral molecular biology, bacterial molecular biology, microbial pathogenesis, microbial genomics.

Baylor College of Medicine, Graduate School of Biomedical Sciences, Interdepartmental Program in Cell and Molecular Biology, Houston, TX 77030-3498. Offers biochemistry (PhD); cell and molecular biology (PhD); genetics (PhD); human genetics (PhD); immunology (PhD); microbiology (PhD); virology (PhD); MD/PhD. *Degree requirements:* For doctorate, thesis/dissertation, public defense. *Entrance requirements:* For doctorate, GRE General Test, GRE Subject Test (strongly recommended), minimum GPA of 3.0. Additional exam requirements/recommendations for international students: Required—TOEFL. Electronic applications accepted. *Faculty research:* Molecular and cellular biology; cancer, aging and stem cells; genomics and proteomics; microbiome, molecular microbiology; infectious disease, immunology and translational research.

Boston University, School of Medicine, Division of Graduate Medical Sciences, Department of Microbiology, Boston, MA 02118. Offers PhD, MD/PhD. Terminal master's awarded for partial completion of doctoral program. *Degree requirements:* For doctorate, comprehensive exam, thesis/dissertation. *Entrance requirements:* Additional exam requirements/recommendations for international students: Required—TOEFL. *Application deadline:* For fall admission, 1/15 for domestic students; for spring admission, 10/15 for domestic students. *Unit head:* Dr. Ronald B. Corley, Chairman, 617-638-4284, Fax: 617-638-4286, E-mail: rbcorley@bu.edu. *Application contact:* GMS Admissions Office, 617-638-5255, E-mail: askgms@bu.edu.
Website: http://www.bumc.bu.edu/microbiology/

Brandeis University, Graduate School of Arts and Sciences, Program in Molecular and Cell Biology, Waltham, MA 02454-9110. Offers genetics (PhD); microbiology (PhD); molecular and cell biology (MS, PhD); molecular biology (PhD); neurobiology (PhD); quantitative biology (PhD). *Faculty:* 27 full-time (13 women), 3 part-time/adjunct (2 women). *Students:* 47 full-time (29 women), 2 part-time (1 woman); includes 10 minority (1 American Indian or Alaska Native, non-Hispanic/Latino; 2 Asian, non-Hispanic/Latino; 6 Hispanic/Latino; 1 Two or more races, non-Hispanic/Latino), 11 international. Average age 27. 138 applicants, 25% accepted, 18 enrolled. In 2017, 11 master's, 8 doctorates awarded. Terminal master's awarded for partial completion of doctoral program. *Degree requirements:* For master's, thesis optional, research project, research lab, or project lab; for doctorate, comprehensive exam, thesis/dissertation, journal clubs; research seminar; colloquia; qualifying exam. *Entrance requirements:* For master's, GRE General Test, transcripts, resume, letters of recommendation, statement of purpose; for doctorate, GRE General Test, transcripts, resume, letters of recommendation, statement of purpose, list of previous research experience. Additional exam requirements/recommendations for international students: Required—PTE (minimum score 68), TOEFL (minimum score 600 paper-based, 100 iBT) or IELTS (7). *Application deadline:* For fall admission, 12/1 priority date for domestic students; for spring admission, 11/15 for domestic students, 10/15 for international students. Applications are processed on a rolling basis. Application fee: $75. Electronic applications accepted. *Expenses: Tuition:* Full-time $48,720. *Required fees:* $88. Tuition and fees vary according to course load, degree level, program and student level. *Financial support:* In 2017–18, 46 students received support, including 20 fellowships with full tuition reimbursements available (averaging $33,000 per year), 19 research assistantships with full tuition reimbursements available (averaging $33,000 per year); scholarships/grants and tuition waivers (partial) also available. Financial award application deadline: 4/15; financial award applicants required to submit FAFSA. *Faculty research:* Molecular biology, genetics and development; structural and cell biology; neurobiology. *Unit head:* Dr. James Haber, Co-Chair, 781-736-2462, E-mail: haber@brandeis.edu. *Application contact:* Jena Pitman-Leung, Department Administrator, 781-736-2352, E-mail: scigradoffice@brandeis.edu.
Website: http://www.brandeis.edu/gsas/programs/mcbio.html

Brigham Young University, Graduate Studies, College of Life Sciences, Department of Microbiology and Molecular Biology, Provo, UT 84602. Offers MS, PhD. *Faculty:* 19 full-time (4 women), 6 part-time/adjunct (5 women). *Students:* 8 full-time (6 women), 31 part-time (14 women); includes 9 minority (4 Asian, non-Hispanic/Latino; 4 Hispanic/Latino; 1 Native Hawaiian or other Pacific Islander, non-Hispanic/Latino). Average age 28. 12 applicants, 83% accepted, 7 enrolled. In 2017, 6 master's, 2 doctorates awarded. Terminal master's awarded for partial completion of doctoral program. *Degree requirements:* For master's, comprehensive exam, thesis; for doctorate, comprehensive exam, thesis/dissertation. *Entrance requirements:* For master's, GRE General Test, minimum GPA of 3.0 during previous 2 years; for doctorate, GRE General Test, minimum GPA of 3.0. Additional exam requirements/recommendations for international students: Required—TOEFL (minimum score 580 paper-based; 85 iBT), IELTS (minimum score 7). *Application deadline:* For fall admission, 1/15 for domestic and international students. Application fee: $50. Electronic applications accepted. *Expenses:* $2,730 per semester for members of the Church of Jesus Christ of Latter-day Saints; $5,460 per semester for those who are not members of the Church. *Financial support:* In 2017–18, 18 students received support, including 17 research assistantships with full

tuition reimbursements available (averaging $22,500 per year); institutionally sponsored loans, scholarships/grants, health care benefits, and unspecified assistantships also available. Financial award application deadline: 3/1; financial award applicants required to submit FAFSA. *Faculty research:* Immunobiology, molecular genetics, molecular virology, cancer biology, pathogenic and environmental microbiology. *Total annual research expenditures:* $523,825. *Unit head:* Dr. Richard Robison, Chair, 801-422-2416, Fax: 801-422-0004, E-mail: richard_robison@byu.edu. *Application contact:* Dr. Joel Griffitts, Graduate Coordinator, 801-422-7997, Fax: 801-422-0004, E-mail: joelg@byu.edu.
Website: http://mmbio.byu.edu/

California State University, Long Beach, Graduate Studies, College of Natural Sciences and Mathematics, Department of Biological Sciences, Long Beach, CA 90840. Offers biology (MS); microbiology (MS). *Program availability:* Part-time. *Entrance requirements:* For master's, GRE Subject Test, minimum GPA of 3.0. Electronic applications accepted.

Case Western Reserve University, School of Medicine and School of Graduate Studies, Graduate Programs in Medicine, Department of Molecular Biology and Microbiology, Cleveland, OH 44106-4960. Offers cell biology (PhD); molecular biology (PhD); molecular virology (PhD); MD/PhD. Students are admitted to an integrated Biomedical Sciences Training Program involving 11 basic science programs at Case Western Reserve University. *Degree requirements:* For doctorate, thesis/dissertation. *Entrance requirements:* For doctorate, GRE General Test, GRE Subject Test. Additional exam requirements/recommendations for international students: Required—TOEFL. Electronic applications accepted. *Expenses: Tuition:* Full-time $43,854; part-time $1827 per credit hour. *Required fees:* $50; $50 per credit hour. Tuition and fees vary according to course load and program. *Faculty research:* Gene expression in eukaryotic and prokaryotic systems; microbial physiology; intracellular transport and signaling; mechanisms of oncogenesis; molecular mechanisms of RNA processing, editing, and catalysis.

The Catholic University of America, School of Arts and Sciences, Department of Biology, Washington, DC 20064. Offers biotechnology (MS); cell and microbial biology (MS, PhD), including cell biology; clinical laboratory science (MS, PhD); MSLS/MS. MSLS/MS offered jointly with Department of Library and Information Science. *Program availability:* Part-time. *Faculty:* 10 full-time (4 women), 7 part-time/adjunct (1 woman). *Students:* 24 full-time (18 women), 43 part-time (20 women); includes 7 minority (2 Black or African American, non-Hispanic/Latino; 3 Asian, non-Hispanic/Latino; 2 Two or more races, non-Hispanic/Latino), 48 international. Average age 31. 56 applicants, 61% accepted, 18 enrolled. In 2017, 7 master's, 1 doctorate awarded. Terminal master's awarded for partial completion of doctoral program. *Degree requirements:* For master's and doctorate, comprehensive exam. *Entrance requirements:* For master's and doctorate, GRE General Test, GRE Subject Test, statement of purpose, official copies of academic transcripts, three letters of recommendation. Additional exam requirements/recommendations for international students: Required—TOEFL (minimum score 550 paper-based; 80 iBT). *Application deadline:* For fall admission, 7/15 priority date for domestic students, 7/1 for international students; for spring admission, 11/15 priority date for domestic students, 11/1 for international students. Applications are processed on a rolling basis. Application fee: $55. Electronic applications accepted. *Expenses:* Contact institution. *Financial support:* Fellowships, research assistantships, teaching assistantships, Federal Work-Study, scholarships/grants, tuition waivers (full and partial), and unspecified assistantships available. Financial award application deadline: 2/1; financial award applicants required to submit FAFSA. *Faculty research:* Virus structure and assembly, hepatic and epithelial cell biology, drug resistance and genome stabilization in yeast, biophysics of ion-conductive nanostructures, eukaryotic gene regulation, cancer and vaccine research. *Total annual research expenditures:* $1.7 million. *Unit head:* Dr. Venigalla Rao, Chair, 202-319-5271, Fax: 202-319-5721, E-mail: rao@cua.edu. *Application contact:* Dr. Steven Brown, Director of Graduate Admissions, 202-319-5057, Fax: 202-319-6533, E-mail: cua-admissions@cua.edu.
Website: http://biology.cua.edu/

Central Washington University, School of Graduate Studies and Research, College of the Sciences, Department of Biological Sciences, Ellensburg, WA 98926. Offers botany (MS); microbiology and parasitology (MS); stream ecology and fisheries (MS); terrestrial ecology (MS). *Program availability:* Part-time. *Entrance requirements:* For master's, GRE General Test, minimum GPA of 3.0. Additional exam requirements/recommendations for international students: Required—TOEFL (minimum score 550 paper-based; 79 iBT). *Application deadline:* For fall admission, 2/1 priority date for domestic students; for winter admission, 10/1 for domestic students; for spring admission, 1/1 for domestic students. Applications are processed on a rolling basis. Application fee: $50. Electronic applications accepted. *Financial support:* Application deadline: 3/1; applicants required to submit FAFSA. *Unit head:* Dr. Kristina A. Ernest, Graduate Coordinator, 509-963-2805, E-mail: kristina.ernest@cwu.edu. *Application contact:* Justine Eason, Admissions Program Coordinator, 509-963-3103, Fax: 509-963-1799, E-mail: masters@cwu.edu.

Clemson University, Graduate School, College of Science, Department of Biological Sciences, Clemson, SC 29634. Offers biological sciences (MS, PhD); biological sciences for science educators (MBS); environmental toxicology (MS, PhD); microbiology (MS, PhD). *Program availability:* Part-time, 100% online. *Faculty:* 46 full-time (15 women), 9 part-time/adjunct (4 women). *Students:* 136 full-time (86 women), 546 part-time (386 women); includes 76 minority (26 Black or African American, non-Hispanic/Latino; 2 American Indian or Alaska Native, non-Hispanic/Latino; 10 Asian, non-Hispanic/Latino; 20 Hispanic/Latino; 18 Two or more races, non-Hispanic/Latino), 34 international. Average age 35. 245 applicants, 75% accepted, 143 enrolled. In 2017, 182 master's, 12 doctorates awarded. *Degree requirements:* For master's, comprehensive exam (for some programs), thesis (for some programs); for doctorate, comprehensive exam, thesis/dissertation. *Entrance requirements:* For master's and doctorate, GRE General Test, unofficial transcripts, letters of recommendation. Additional exam requirements/recommendations for international students: Required—TOEFL (minimum score 100 iBT), IELTS (minimum score 7.5), PTE (minimum score 72). *Application deadline:* For fall admission, 1/5 for domestic and international students. Application fee: $80 ($90 for international students). Electronic applications accepted. *Expenses:* $5,174 per semester full-time resident, $9,714 per semester full-time non-resident, $511 per credit hour part-time resident, $1,017 per credit hour part-time non-resident; $741 per credit hour online; other fees may apply per session. *Financial support:* In 2017–18, 47 students received support, including 2 fellowships with partial tuition reimbursements available (averaging $17,000 per year), 8 research assistantships with partial tuition reimbursements available (averaging $23,063 per year), 37 teaching assistantships with partial tuition reimbursements available (averaging $21,662 per year). Financial award application deadline: 1/5. *Faculty research:* Microbiology, cell and developmental biology, evolutionary biology, ecology, molecular biology. *Total annual research expenditures:* $1.5 million. *Unit head:* Dr. Robert Cohen, Department Chair, 864-656-1112, Fax: 864-656-0435, E-mail: rscohen@clemson.edu. *Application contact:* Jay Lyn Martin, Student Services Program Coordinator, 864-656-3587, Fax: 864-656-0435, E-mail: jaylyn@clemson.edu.
Website: http://www.clemson.edu/science/departments/biosci/

Colorado State University, College of Veterinary Medicine and Biomedical Sciences, Department of Microbiology, Immunology and Pathology, Fort Collins, CO 80523-1682. Offers microbiology, immunology and pathology (MS, PhD); pathology (PhD). *Faculty:* 76 full-time (35 women), 11 part-time/adjunct (7 women). *Students:* 73 full-time (52 women), 36 part-time (29 women); includes 18 minority (2 Black or African American, non-Hispanic/Latino; 1 American Indian or Alaska Native, non-Hispanic/Latino; 7 Asian, non-Hispanic/Latino; 6 Hispanic/Latino; 2 Two or more races, non-Hispanic/Latino), 7 international. Average age 29. 200 applicants, 32% accepted, 54 enrolled. In 2017, 43 master's, 12 doctorates awarded. Terminal master's awarded for partial completion of doctoral program. *Degree requirements:* For master's, comprehensive exam (for some programs), thesis (for some programs); for doctorate, comprehensive exam, thesis/dissertation. *Entrance requirements:* For master's and doctorate, GRE General Test or MCAT, minimum GPA of 3.0; written statement; transcripts; resume/curriculum vitae; three recommendations. Additional exam requirements/recommendations for international students: Required—TOEFL (minimum score 550 paper-based; 80 iBT), IELTS (minimum score 6.5). *Application deadline:* For fall admission, 4/1 for domestic and international students; for spring admission, 12/15 for domestic and international students. Application fee: $60 ($70 for international students). Electronic applications accepted. *Expenses:* $120 per credit hour. *Financial support:* In 2017–18, 20 research assistantships with full and partial tuition reimbursements (averaging $24,368 per year), 6 teaching assistantships with full and partial tuition reimbursements (averaging $17,883 per year) were awarded; fellowships with full and partial tuition reimbursements and health care benefits also available. Financial award application deadline: 12/15. *Faculty research:* Bacteriology, immunology, prion biology, vector biology, virology. *Total annual research expenditures:* $20.9 million. *Unit head:* Dr. Mark Zabel, Associate Department Head for Graduate Education, 970-491-1455, E-mail: mark.zabel@colostate.edu. *Application contact:* Heidi Runge, Academic Support Coordinator for Graduate Studies, 970-491-1630, Fax: 970-491-1815, E-mail: heidi.runge@colostate.edu.
Website: http://csu-cvmbs.colostate.edu/academics/mip/graduate/Pages/microbiology-immunology-professional-masters.aspx

Columbia University, College of Physicians and Surgeons, Department of Microbiology, New York, NY 10032. Offers biomedical sciences (M Phil, MA, PhD); MD/PhD. Only candidates for the PhD are admitted. Terminal master's awarded for partial completion of doctoral program. *Degree requirements:* For doctorate, thesis/dissertation. *Entrance requirements:* For master's, GRE General Test; for doctorate, GRE. Additional exam requirements/recommendations for international students: Required—TOEFL. *Expenses: Tuition:* Full-time $44,864; part-time $1704 per credit. *Required fees:* $2370 per semester. One-time fee: $105. *Faculty research:* Prokaryotic molecular biology, immunology, virology, yeast molecular genetics, regulation of gene expression.

Cornell University, Graduate School, Graduate Fields of Agriculture and Life Sciences, Field of Microbiology, Ithaca, NY 14853. Offers PhD. *Degree requirements:* For doctorate, comprehensive exam, thesis/dissertation, 2 semesters of teaching experience. *Entrance requirements:* For doctorate, GRE General Test, 3 letters of recommendation. Additional exam requirements/recommendations for international students: Required—TOEFL (minimum score 550 paper-based; 77 iBT). Electronic applications accepted. *Faculty research:* Microbial diversity, molecular biology, biotechnology, microbial ecology, phytobacteriology.

Dalhousie University, Faculty of Medicine, Department of Microbiology and Immunology, Halifax, NS B3H 4R2, Canada. Offers M Sc, PhD. *Degree requirements:* For master's, thesis; for doctorate, comprehensive exam, thesis/dissertation. *Entrance requirements:* For master's, GRE General Test, honors B Sc; for doctorate, GRE General Test, honors B Sc in microbiology, M Sc in discipline or transfer after 1 year in master's program. Additional exam requirements/recommendations for international students: Required—1 of 5 approved tests: TOEFL, IELTS, CANTEST, CAEL, Michigan English Language Assessment Battery. Electronic applications accepted. *Faculty research:* Virology, molecular genetics, pathogenesis, bacteriology, immunology.

Dartmouth College, Graduate Program in Molecular and Cellular Biology, Department of Microbiology and Immunology, Program in Microbiology and Molecular Pathogenesis, Hanover, NH 03755. Offers PhD, MBA/PhD, MD/PhD. *Application deadline:* For fall admission, 12/8 for domestic students. Application fee: $75. Electronic applications accepted. *Financial support:* Fellowships and health care benefits available. *Unit head:* Dr. William R. Green, Chair, 603-650-8607, Fax: 603-650-6223. *Application contact:* Janet Cheney, Program Administrator, 608-650-1612, Fax: 608-650-6223.
Website: https://www.dartmouth.edu/~m2p2/

Drexel University, College of Medicine, Biomedical Graduate Programs, Program in Microbiology and Immunology, Philadelphia, PA 19104-2875. Offers MS, PhD, MD/PhD. Terminal master's awarded for partial completion of doctoral program. *Degree requirements:* For master's, comprehensive exam, thesis; for doctorate, thesis/dissertation, qualifying exam. *Entrance requirements:* For master's, GRE General Test, minimum GPA of 2.75; for doctorate, GRE General Test, minimum GPA of 3.0. Additional exam requirements/recommendations for international students: Required—TOEFL. Electronic applications accepted. *Faculty research:* Immunology of malarial parasites, virology, bacteriology, molecular biology, parasitology.

Duke University, Graduate School, Department of Molecular Genetics and Microbiology, Durham, NC 27710. Offers PhD. *Degree requirements:* For doctorate, thesis/dissertation. *Entrance requirements:* For doctorate, GRE General Test, GRE Subject Test in biology, chemistry, or biochemistry, cell and molecular biology (recommended). Additional exam requirements/recommendations for international students: Required—TOEFL (minimum score 577 paper-based; 90 iBT) or IELTS (minimum score 7). Electronic applications accepted.

East Tennessee State University, Quillen College of Medicine, Department of Biomedical Sciences, Johnson City, TN 37614. Offers anatomy (PhD); biochemistry (PhD); microbiology (PhD); pharmaceutical sciences (PhD); pharmacology (PhD); physiology (PhD); quantitative biosciences (PhD). In 2017, 5 doctorates awarded. *Degree requirements:* For doctorate, comprehensive exam, thesis/dissertation, comprehensive qualifying exam; one-year residency. *Entrance requirements:* For doctorate, GRE General Test, GRE Subject Test, 3 letters of recommendation, minimum of 60 credit hours beyond the baccalaureate degree. Additional exam requirements/recommendations for international students: Required—TOEFL (minimum score 550 paper-based; 79 iBT). *Application deadline:* For fall admission, 6/1 priority date for domestic students, 4/29 for international students; for spring admission, 11/1 for domestic students, 9/29 for international students; for summer admission, 3/15 for domestic students, 2/1 for international students. Applications are processed on a rolling basis. Application fee: $55 ($65 for international students). Electronic applications accepted. *Expenses:* Contact institution. *Financial support:* Research assistantships with full tuition reimbursements, career-related internships or fieldwork, institutionally sponsored loans, scholarships/grants, and unspecified assistantships available. Financial award application deadline: 7/1; financial award applicants required to submit FAFSA. *Faculty research:* Cardiovascular, infectious disease, neurosciences, cancer, immunology. *Unit head:* Theo Hagg, Chair, 423-439-6294, Fax: 423-439-2140, E-mail: haggt1@etsu.edu. *Application contact:* Theo Hagg, Chair, 423-439-6294, Fax: 423-439-2140, E-mail: haggt1@etsu.edu.
Website: http://www.etsu.edu/com/dbms/

East Tennessee State University, School of Graduate Studies, College of Arts and Sciences, Department of Biological Sciences, Johnson City, TN 37614. Offers biology (MS); biomedical sciences (MS); microbiology (MS). *Degree requirements:* For master's, comprehensive exam, thesis. *Entrance requirements:* For master's, GRE General Test or GRE Subject Test, minimum GPA of 3.0, undergraduate degree in life or physical sciences, two letters of recommendation; course in calculus and/or course in probability and statistics (recommended). Additional exam requirements/recommendations for international students: Required—TOEFL (minimum score 550 paper-based; 79 iBT). *Application deadline:* For fall admission, 6/1 for domestic students, 4/29 for international students; for spring admission, 11/1 for domestic students, 9/29 for international students; for summer admission, 3/15 for domestic students, 2/1 for international students. Application fee: $55 ($65 for international students). Electronic applications accepted. *Financial support:* Teaching assistantships with full tuition reimbursements, institutionally sponsored loans, scholarships/grants, and unspecified assistantships available. Financial award application deadline: 7/1; financial award applicants required to submit FAFSA. *Faculty research:* Neuroethology, chronobiology, molecular biology, behavioral ecology, systematics, paleo botany. *Unit head:* Dr. Joseph Bidwell, Chair, 423-439-4329, Fax: 423-439-5958, E-mail: bidwell@etsu.edu. *Application contact:* Dr. Joseph Bidwell, Chair, 423-439-4329, Fax: 423-439-5958, E-mail: bidwell@etsu.edu.
Website: http://www.etsu.edu/cas/biology/

Emory University, Laney Graduate School, Division of Biological and Biomedical Sciences, Program in Microbiology and Molecular Genetics, Atlanta, GA 30322-1100. Offers PhD. *Degree requirements:* For doctorate, comprehensive exam, thesis/dissertation. *Entrance requirements:* For doctorate, GRE General Test, minimum GPA of 3.0 in science course work (recommended). Additional exam requirements/recommendations for international students: Required—TOEFL. Electronic applications accepted. *Faculty research:* Bacterial genetics and physiology, microbial development, molecular biology of viruses and bacterial pathogens, DNA recombination.

Emporia State University, Department of Biological Sciences, Emporia, KS 66801-5415. Offers botany (MS); environmental biology (MS); forensic science (MS); general biology (MS); microbial and cellular biology (MS); zoology (MS). *Program availability:* Part-time. *Faculty:* 13 full-time (3 women), 1 part-time/adjunct (0 women). *Students:* 20 full-time (11 women), 15 part-time (3 women); includes 3 minority (2 Hispanic/Latino; 1 Two or more races, non-Hispanic/Latino), 17 international. 17 applicants, 59% accepted, 8 enrolled. In 2017, 21 master's awarded. *Degree requirements:* For master's, comprehensive exam or thesis. *Entrance requirements:* For master's, GRE, appropriate undergraduate degree, interview, letters of reference. Additional exam requirements/recommendations for international students: Required—TOEFL (minimum score 520 paper-based; 68 iBT). *Application deadline:* For fall admission, 8/15 priority date for domestic students. Applications are processed on a rolling basis. Application fee: $30 ($75 for international students). Electronic applications accepted. *Expenses:* Tuition, state resident: full-time $6084; part-time $253.50 per credit hour. Tuition, nonresident: full-time $18,924; part-time $788.50 per credit hour. *Required fees:* $1943; $80.95 per credit hour. Tuition and fees vary according to campus/location. *Financial support:* In 2017–18, 7 research assistantships with full tuition reimbursements (averaging $9,747 per year), 15 teaching assistantships with full tuition reimbursements (averaging $7,499 per year) were awarded; career-related internships or fieldwork, Federal Work-Study, institutionally sponsored loans, health care benefits, and unspecified assistantships also available. Financial award application deadline: 3/15; financial award applicants required to submit FAFSA. *Faculty research:* Fisheries, range, and wildlife management; aquatic, plant, grassland, vertebrate, and invertebrate ecology; mammalian and plant systematics, taxonomy, and evolution; immunology, virology, and molecular biology. *Unit head:* Dr. Tim Burnett, Interim Chair, 620-341-5910, Fax: 620-341-5608, E-mail: tburnett@emporia.edu.
Website: http://www.emporia.edu/info/degrees-courses/grad/biology

Georgetown University, Graduate School of Arts and Sciences, Department of Microbiology and Immunology, Washington, DC 20057. Offers biohazardous threat agents and emerging infectious diseases (MS); biomedical science policy and advocacy (MS); general microbiology and immunology (MS); global infectious diseases (PhD); microbiology and immunology (PhD). *Program availability:* Part-time. *Degree requirements:* For master's, 30 credit hours of coursework; for doctorate, comprehensive exam, thesis/dissertation. *Entrance requirements:* For master's, GRE General Test, 3 letters of reference, bachelor's degree in related field; for doctorate, GRE General Test, 3 letters of reference, MS/BS in related field. Additional exam requirements/recommendations for international students: Required—TOEFL (minimum score 505 paper-based). Electronic applications accepted. *Faculty research:* Pathogenesis and basic biology of the fungus Candida albicans, molecular biology of viral immunopathological mechanisms in Multiple Sclerosis.

The George Washington University, Columbian College of Arts and Sciences, Institute for Biomedical Sciences, Program in Microbiology and Immunology, Washington, DC 20037. Offers PhD. *Students:* 6 full-time (4 women), 9 part-time (1 woman); includes 4 minority (3 Asian, non-Hispanic/Latino; 1 Hispanic/Latino), 2 international. Average age 28. In 2017, 6 doctorates awarded. *Degree requirements:* For doctorate, thesis/dissertation. *Entrance requirements:* For doctorate, GRE General Test, minimum GPA of 3.0. Additional exam requirements/recommendations for international students: Required—TOEFL (minimum score 600 paper-based). *Application deadline:* For fall admission, 12/15 priority date for domestic and international students. Applications are processed on a rolling basis. Application fee: $75. Electronic applications accepted. *Expenses: Tuition:* Full-time $28,800; part-time $1655 per credit hour. *Required fees:* $45; $2.75 per credit hour. *Financial support:* In 2017–18, 10 students received support. Fellowships with tuition reimbursements available and tuition waivers available. *Unit head:* Dr. David Leitenberg, Director, 202-994-9475, Fax: 202-994-2913, E-mail: dleit@gwu.edu. *Application contact:* Information Contact, 202-994-3532, Fax: 202-994-2913, E-mail: mitm@gwu.edu.
Website: http://smhs.gwu.edu/microbiology/

The George Washington University, Milken Institute School of Public Health, Department of Epidemiology and Biostatistics, Washington, DC 20052. Offers biostatistics (MPH); epidemiology (MPH); microbiology and emerging infectious diseases (MSPH). *Students:* 75 full-time (58 women), 78 part-time (62 women); includes 62 minority (14 Black or African American, non-Hispanic/Latino; 32 Asian, non-Hispanic/Latino; 12 Hispanic/Latino; 1 Native Hawaiian or other Pacific Islander, non-Hispanic/Latino; 3 Two or more races, non-Hispanic/Latino), 14 international. Average age 28. 521 applicants, 59% accepted, 48 enrolled. In 2017, 51 master's awarded. *Entrance requirements:* For master's, GMAT, GRE General Test, or MCAT. Additional exam requirements/recommendations for international students: Required—TOEFL. *Application deadline:* For fall admission, 4/15 priority date for domestic students, 4/15 for international students; for spring admission, 11/1 for domestic and international students. Applications are processed on a rolling basis. Application fee: $75. *Expenses: Tuition:* Full-time $28,800; part-time $1655 per credit hour. *Required fees:* $45; $2.75 per credit hour. *Financial support:* In 2017–18, 6 students received support. Tuition waivers available. Financial award application deadline: 2/15. *Unit head:* Dr. Alan E. Greenberg, Chair, 202-994-0612, E-mail: aeg1@gwu.edu. *Application contact:* Jane Smith, Director of Admissions, 202-994-0248, Fax: 202-994-1860, E-mail: sphhsinfo@gwumc.edu.

The George Washington University, School of Medicine and Health Sciences, Health Sciences Programs, Washington, DC 20052. Offers clinical practice management (MSHS); clinical research administration (MSHS); emergency services management (MSHS); end-of-life care (MSHS); immunohematology (MSHS); immunohematology and biotechnology (MSHS); physical therapy (DPT); physician assistant (MSHS). *Program availability:* Online learning. *Faculty:* 31 full-time (23 women), 4 part-time/adjunct (2 women). *Students:* 304 full-time (233 women), 321 part-time (248 women); includes 212 minority (70 Black or African American, non-Hispanic/Latino; 1 American Indian or Alaska Native, non-Hispanic/Latino; 64 Asian, non-Hispanic/Latino; 59 Hispanic/Latino; 3 Native Hawaiian or other Pacific Islander, non-Hispanic/Latino; 15 Two or more races, non-Hispanic/Latino), 18 international. Average age 33. 2,366 applicants, 19% accepted, 246 enrolled. In 2017, 159 master's, 49 doctorates, 2 other advanced degrees awarded. *Entrance requirements:* Additional exam requirements/recommendations for international students: Required—TOEFL (minimum score 550 paper-based). *Application deadline:* Applications are processed on a rolling basis. Application fee: $75. *Expenses:* Contact institution. *Unit head:* Jean E. Johnson, Senior Associate Dean, 202-994-3725, E-mail: jejohns@gwu.edu. *Application contact:* Joke Ogundiran, Director of Admission, 202-994-1668, Fax: 202-994-0870, E-mail: jokeogun@gwu.edu.

Georgia State University, College of Arts and Sciences, Department of Biology, Program in Applied and Environmental Microbiology, Atlanta, GA 30302-3083. Offers applied and environmental microbiology (MS, PhD); bioinformatics (MS). *Program availability:* Part-time. Terminal master's awarded for partial completion of doctoral program. *Degree requirements:* For master's, comprehensive exam (for some programs), thesis optional; for doctorate, comprehensive exam, thesis/dissertation. *Entrance requirements:* For master's and doctorate, GRE. *Application deadline:* For fall admission, 7/1 priority date for domestic students, 6/1 priority date for international students; for spring admission, 11/15 priority date for domestic students, 10/15 priority date for international students. Applications are processed on a rolling basis. Application fee: $50. Electronic applications accepted. *Expenses:* Tuition, state resident: full-time $7020. Tuition, nonresident: full-time $22,518. *Required fees:* $2128. Tuition and fees vary according to degree level and program. *Financial support:* In 2017–18, fellowships with full tuition reimbursements (averaging $22,000 per year), research assistantships with full tuition reimbursements (averaging $20,000 per year) were awarded. Financial award application deadline: 12/3. *Faculty research:* Bioremediation, biofilms, indoor air quality control, environmental toxicology, product biosynthesis. *Unit head:* Dr. Charles Derby, Director of Graduate Studies, 404-413-5393, Fax: 404-413-5446, E-mail: cderby@gsu.edu.
Website: http://biology.gsu.edu/

Harvard University, Graduate School of Arts and Sciences, Division of Medical Sciences, Boston, MA 02115. Offers biological chemistry and molecular pharmacology (PhD); cell biology (PhD); genetics (PhD); microbiology and molecular genetics (PhD); pathology (PhD), including experimental pathology. *Degree requirements:* For doctorate, thesis/dissertation. *Entrance requirements:* For doctorate, GRE General Test, GRE Subject Test. Additional exam requirements/recommendations for international students: Required—TOEFL.

Hood College, Graduate School, Program in Biomedical Science, Frederick, MD 21701-8575. Offers biomedical science (MS), including biotechnology/molecular biology, microbiology/immunology/virology. *Program availability:* Part-time, evening/weekend. *Faculty:* 5 full-time (3 women), 1 (woman) part-time/adjunct. *Students:* 13 full-time (6 women), 73 part-time (39 women); includes 21 minority (12 Black or African American, non-Hispanic/Latino; 6 Asian, non-Hispanic/Latino; 2 Hispanic/Latino; 1 Two or more races, non-Hispanic/Latino), 6 international. Average age 30. 24 applicants, 92% accepted, 14 enrolled. In 2017, 13 master's awarded. *Degree requirements:* For master's, thesis or alternative. *Entrance requirements:* For master's, bachelor's degree in biology; minimum GPA of 3.0; undergraduate course work in cell biology, chemistry, organic chemistry, and genetics. Additional exam requirements/recommendations for international students: Required—TOEFL (minimum score 575 paper-based; 89 iBT), IELTS (minimum score 6). *Application deadline:* For fall admission, 8/15 priority date for domestic students, 8/5 for international students; for spring admission, 12/1 priority date for domestic students, 12/1 for international students; for summer admission, 5/1 priority date for domestic students, 4/15 for international students. Applications are processed on a rolling basis. Application fee: $35. Electronic applications accepted. *Expenses:* $500 per credit plus $110 comprehensive fee per semester, plus any applicable lab fees by course. *Financial support:* Research assistantships with full tuition reimbursements, tuition waivers (partial), and unspecified assistantships available. Financial award applicants required to submit FAFSA. *Faculty research:* Molecular signaling in cell tumor initiation, biomedical ethics, genetic and biochemical approaches to study regulation of gene expression. *Unit head:* Dr. April M. Boulton, Dean of the Graduate School, 301-696-3600, E-mail: gofurther@hood.edu. *Application contact:* Larbi Bricha, Assistant Director of Graduate Admissions, 301-696-3600, E-mail: gofurther@hood.edu.
Website: http://www.hood.edu/graduate

Howard University, College of Medicine, Department of Microbiology, Washington, DC 20059-0002. Offers PhD. *Degree requirements:* For doctorate, one foreign language, comprehensive exam, thesis/dissertation, qualifying exam, teaching experience. *Entrance requirements:* For doctorate, GRE General Test, minimum GPA of 3.0 in sciences. Additional exam requirements/recommendations for international students: Required—TOEFL. *Faculty research:* Immunology, molecular and cellular microbiology, microbial genetics, microbial physiology, pathogenic bacteriology, medical mycology, medical parasitology, virology.

Idaho State University, Office of Graduate Studies, College of Science and Engineering, Department of Biological Sciences, Pocatello, ID 83209-8007. Offers biology (MNS, MS, DA, PhD); clinical laboratory science (MS); microbiology (MS). *Accreditation:* NAACLS. *Program availability:* Part-time. *Degree requirements:* For master's, comprehensive exam, thesis; for doctorate, comprehensive exam, thesis/dissertation, 9 credits of internship (for DA). *Entrance requirements:* For master's, GRE General Test, minimum GPA of 3.0 in all upper division classes; for doctorate, GRE General Test, GRE Subject Test (biology), diagnostic exam (DA), minimum GPA of 3.0 in all upper division classes. Additional exam requirements/recommendations for international students: Required—TOEFL (minimum score 550 paper-based; 80 iBT). Electronic applications accepted. *Faculty research:* Ecology, plant and animal physiology, plant and animal developmental biology, immunology, molecular biology, bioinfomatics.

Illinois Institute of Technology, Graduate College, College of Science, Department of Biology, Chicago, IL 60616. Offers applied life sciences (MS); biochemistry (MS); biology (MS, PhD); cell and molecular biology (MS); microbiology (MS); molecular biochemistry and biophysics (MS, PhD). *Program availability:* Part-time, evening/weekend, online learning. Terminal master's awarded for partial completion of doctoral program. *Degree requirements:* For master's, comprehensive exam, thesis (for some programs); for doctorate, comprehensive exam, thesis/dissertation. *Entrance requirements:* For master's, GRE General Test (minimum score 300 Quantitative and Verbal, 2.5 Analytical Writing), minimum undergraduate GPA of 3.0; for doctorate, GRE General Test (minimum score 310 Quantitative and Verbal, 3.0 Analytical Writing); GRE Subject Test (strongly recommended), minimum undergraduate GPA of 3.0. Additional exam requirements/recommendations for international students: Required—TOEFL (minimum score 550 paper-based; 80 iBT). Electronic applications accepted. *Faculty research:* Macromolecular crystallography, insect immunity and basic cell biology, improvement of bacterial strains for enhanced biodesulfurization of petroleum, programmed cell death in cancer cells.

Illinois State University, Graduate School, College of Arts and Sciences, School of Biological Sciences, Normal, IL 61790. Offers animal behavior (MS); bacteriology (MS); biochemistry (MS); biological sciences (MS); biology (PhD); biophysics (MS); biotechnology (MS); botany (MS, PhD); cell biology (MS); conservation biology (MS); developmental biology (MS); ecology (MS, PhD); entomology (MS); evolutionary biology (MS), genetics (MS, PhD); immunology (MS); microbiology (MS, PhD); molecular biology (MS); molecular genetics (MS); neurobiology (MS); neuroscience (MS); parasitology (MS); physiology (MS, PhD); plant biology (MS); plant molecular biology (MS); plant sciences (MS); structural biology (MS); zoology (MS, PhD). *Program availability:* Part-time. *Degree requirements:* For master's, thesis or alternative; for doctorate, variable foreign language requirement, thesis/dissertation, 2 terms of residency. *Entrance requirements:* For master's, GRE General Test, minimum GPA of 2.6 in last 60 hours of course work; for doctorate, GRE General Test. *Faculty research:* Redoc balance and drug development in schistosoma mansoni, control of the growth of listeria monocytogenes at low temperature, regulation of cell expansion and microtubule function by SPRI, CRUI: physiology and fitness consequences of different life history phenotypes.

Indiana University Bloomington, University Graduate School, College of Arts and Sciences, Department of Biology, Bloomington, IN 47405. Offers biology teaching (MAT); biotechnology (MA); evolution, ecology, and behavior (MA, PhD); genetics (PhD); microbiology (MA, PhD); molecular, cellular, and developmental biology (PhD); plant sciences (MA, PhD); zoology (MA, PhD). Terminal master's awarded for partial completion of doctoral program. *Degree requirements:* For master's, thesis, oral defense; for doctorate, thesis/dissertation, oral defense. *Entrance requirements:* For master's and doctorate, GRE General Test. Additional exam requirements/recommendations for international students: Required—TOEFL (minimum score 100 iBT). Electronic applications accepted. *Faculty research:* Evolution, ecology and behavior; microbiology; molecular biology and genetics; plant biology.

Indiana University–Purdue University Indianapolis, Indiana University School of Medicine, Department of Microbiology and Immunology, Indianapolis, IN 46202. Offers MS, PhD, MD/MS, MD/PhD. Terminal master's awarded for partial completion of doctoral program. *Degree requirements:* For master's, thesis; for doctorate, thesis/dissertation. *Entrance requirements:* For master's and doctorate, GRE General Test, previous course work in calculus, cell biology, chemistry, genetics, physics, and biochemistry. *Faculty research:* Host-parasite interactions, molecular biology, cellular and molecular immunology and hematology, viral and bacterial pathogenesis, cancer research.

Inter American University of Puerto Rico, Metropolitan Campus, Graduate Programs, Program in Medical Technology, San Juan, PR 00919-1293. Offers administration of clinical laboratories (MS); molecular microbiology (MS). *Accreditation:* NAACLS. *Program availability:* Part-time. *Degree requirements:* For master's, comprehensive exam. *Entrance requirements:* For master's, BS in medical technology, minimum GPA of 2.5. Electronic applications accepted.

Iowa State University of Science and Technology, Department of Veterinary Microbiology and Preventive Medicine, Ames, IA 50011. Offers veterinary microbiology (MS, PhD). *Entrance requirements:* For master's and doctorate, GRE General Test. Additional exam requirements/recommendations for international students: Required—TOEFL (minimum score 550 paper-based; 79 iBT), IELTS (minimum score 6.5). Electronic applications accepted. *Faculty research:* Bacteriology, immunology, virology, public health and food safety.

Iowa State University of Science and Technology, Program in Microbiology, Ames, IA 50011. Offers MS, PhD. *Entrance requirements:* For master's and doctorate, GRE General Test. Additional exam requirements/recommendations for international students: Required—TOEFL (minimum score 550 paper-based; 79 iBT), IELTS (minimum score 6.5). Electronic applications accepted.

Johns Hopkins University, Bloomberg School of Public Health, W. Harry Feinstone Department of Molecular Microbiology and Immunology, Baltimore, MD 21218. Offers MHS, Sc M, PhD. *Degree requirements:* For master's, comprehensive exam, thesis (for some programs), essay, written exams; for doctorate, comprehensive exam, thesis/dissertation, 1-year full-time residency, oral and written exams. *Entrance requirements:* For master's, GRE General Test or MCAT, 3 letters of recommendation, curriculum vitae; for doctorate, GRE General Test, 3 letters of recommendation, transcripts, curriculum vitae. Additional exam requirements/recommendations for international students: Required—TOEFL (minimum score 600 paper-based). Electronic applications accepted. *Faculty research:* Immunology, virology, bacteriology, parasitology, vector biology, disease ecology, pathogenesis of infectious disease, immune responses to infectious agents, vector-borne and tropical diseases, biochemistry and molecular biology of infectious agents, population genetics of insect vectors, genetic regulation and immune responses in insect vectors, vaccine development, hormonal effects on pathogenesis and immune responses.

Loma Linda University, School of Medicine, Programs in Biochemistry and Microbiology, Loma Linda, CA 92350. Offers biochemistry (MS, PhD); microbiology (PhD). *Program availability:* Part-time. *Degree requirements:* For master's, thesis or alternative; for doctorate, thesis/dissertation. *Entrance requirements:* For master's and doctorate, GRE General Test. Additional exam requirements/recommendations for international students: Required—TOEFL (minimum score 550 paper-based). *Faculty research:* Physical chemistry of macromolecules, biochemistry of endocrine system, biochemical mechanism of bone volume regulation.

Louisiana State University Health Sciences Center, School of Graduate Studies in New Orleans, Department of Microbiology, Immunology, and Parasitology, New Orleans, LA 70112-1393. Offers microbiology and immunology (PhD); MD/PhD. *Faculty:* 22 full-time (5 women). *Students:* 10 full-time (6 women). Average age 26. 15 applicants, 27% accepted, 4 enrolled. In 2017, 4 doctorates awarded. *Degree requirements:* For doctorate, comprehensive exam, thesis/dissertation, preliminary exam, qualifying exam. *Entrance requirements:* For doctorate, GRE General Test. Additional exam requirements/recommendations for international students: Recommended—TOEFL, IELTS. *Application deadline:* For fall admission, 4/1 for domestic and international students. Applications are processed on a rolling basis. Application fee: $30. *Expenses:* Tuition, state resident: full-time $11,835; part-time $518 per hour. Tuition, nonresident: full-time $24,108; part-time $1079 per hour. *Required fees:* $1254; $55 per hour. *Financial support:* Unspecified assistantships available. Financial award application deadline: 4/15. *Faculty research:* Microbial physiology, animal virology, vaccine development, AIDS drug studies, pathogenic mechanisms, molecular immunology. *Unit head:* Dr. Alistair Ramsay, Professor and Head, 504-568-4062, Fax: 504-568-2918, E-mail: aramsa@lsuhsc.edu. *Application contact:* Dr. Doug Johnston, Assistant Professor, E-mail: mipapp@lsuhsc.edu.
Website: http://www.medschool.lsuhsc.edu/microbiology/

Louisiana State University Health Sciences Center at Shreveport, Department of Microbiology and Immunology, Shreveport, LA 71130-3932. Offers MS, PhD, MD/PhD. Terminal master's awarded for partial completion of doctoral program. *Degree requirements:* For master's, comprehensive exam, thesis; for doctorate, comprehensive exam, thesis/dissertation, research proposal. *Entrance requirements:* For master's and doctorate, GRE General Test. Additional exam requirements/recommendations for international students: Required—TOEFL. Electronic applications accepted. *Expenses:* Contact institution. *Faculty research:* Infectious disease, molecular bacteriology, pathogenesis, molecular virology and immunology.

Loyola University Chicago, Graduate School, Integrated Program in Biomedical Sciences, Maywood, IL 60141. Offers biochemistry and molecular biology (MS, PhD); cell and molecular physiology (MS, PhD); infectious disease and immunology (MS); integrative cell biology (MS, PhD); microbiology and immunology (MS, PhD); molecular pharmacology and therapeutics (MS, PhD); neuroscience (MS, PhD). *Faculty:* 84 full-time (32 women). *Students:* 126 full-time (65 women), 1 (woman) part-time; includes 36 minority (5 Black or African American, non-Hispanic/Latino; 14 Asian, non-Hispanic/Latino; 14 Hispanic/Latino; 3 Two or more races, non-Hispanic/Latino), 13 international. Average age 26. 748 applicants, 34% accepted, 124 enrolled. In 2017, 41 master's, 18 doctorates awarded. *Degree requirements:* For master's, thesis; for doctorate, comprehensive exam, thesis/dissertation. *Entrance requirements:* For doctorate, GRE. Additional exam requirements/recommendations for international students: Required—TOEFL (minimum score 94 iBT), IELTS (minimum score 7.5). *Application deadline:* For fall admission, 2/7 for domestic students. Applications are processed on a rolling basis. Electronic applications accepted. *Expenses:* Contact institution. *Financial support:* In 2017–18, 20 students received support. Schmitt Fellowships and yearly tuition scholarships (averaging $25,032) available. Financial award application deadline: 6/15; financial award applicants required to submit FAFSA. *Unit head:* Dr. Leanne L. Cribbs, Associate Dean, Graduate Education, 708-327-2817, Fax: 708-216-8216, E-mail: lcribbs@luc.edu. *Application contact:* Margarita Quesada, Graduate Program Secretary, 708-216-3532, Fax: 708-216-8216, E-mail: mquesad@luc.edu.
Website: http://ssom.luc.edu/graduate_school/degree-programs/ipbsphd/

Marquette University, Graduate School, College of Arts and Sciences, Department of Biology, Milwaukee, WI 53201-1881. Offers cell biology (MS, PhD); developmental biology (MS, PhD); ecology (MS, PhD); epithelial physiology (MS, PhD); genetics (MS, PhD); microbiology (MS, PhD); molecular biology (MS, PhD); muscle and exercise physiology (MS, PhD); neuroscience (PhD). Terminal master's awarded for partial completion of doctoral program. *Degree requirements:* For master's, comprehensive exam, thesis, 1 year of teaching experience or equivalent; for doctorate, thesis/dissertation, 1 year of teaching experience or equivalent, qualifying exam. *Entrance requirements:* For master's and doctorate, GRE General Test, GRE Subject Test, official transcripts from all current and previous colleges/universities except Marquette, statement of professional goals and aspirations, three letters of recommendation. Additional exam requirements/recommendations for international students: Required—TOEFL (minimum score 530 paper-based). Electronic applications accepted. *Faculty research:* Neurobiology, neuroendocrinology, epithelial physiology, neuropeptide interactions, synaptic transmission.

Massachusetts Institute of Technology, School of Science, Department of Biology, Cambridge, MA 02139. Offers biochemistry (PhD); biological oceanography (PhD); biology (PhD); biophysical chemistry and molecular structure (PhD); cell biology (PhD); computational and systems biology (PhD); developmental biology (PhD); genetics (PhD); immunology (PhD); microbiology (PhD); molecular biology (PhD); neurobiology (PhD). *Degree requirements:* For doctorate, comprehensive exam, thesis/dissertation, teaching assistantship during two semesters. *Entrance requirements:* For doctorate, GRE General Test. Additional exam requirements/recommendations for international students: Required—TOEFL, IELTS. Electronic applications accepted. *Faculty research:* Cellular, developmental and molecular (plant and animal) biology; biochemistry, bioengineering, biophysics and structural biology; classical and molecular genetics, stem cell and epigenetics; immunology and microbiology; cancer biology, molecular medicine, neurobiology and human disease; computational and systems biology.

McGill University, Faculty of Graduate and Postdoctoral Studies, Faculty of Agricultural and Environmental Sciences, Department of Natural Resource Sciences, Montréal, QC H3A 2T5, Canada. Offers entomology (M Sc, PhD); environmental assessment (M Sc); forest science (M Sc, PhD); microbiology (M Sc, PhD); micrometeorology (M Sc, PhD); neotropical environment (M Sc, PhD); soil science (M Sc, PhD); wildlife biology (M Sc, PhD).

McGill University, Faculty of Graduate and Postdoctoral Studies, Faculty of Medicine, Department of Microbiology and Immunology, Montréal, QC H3A 2T5, Canada. Offers M Sc, M Sc A, PhD.

Medical University of South Carolina, College of Graduate Studies, Department of Microbiology and Immunology, Charleston, SC 29425. Offers MS, PhD, DMD/PhD, MD/PhD. Terminal master's awarded for partial completion of doctoral program. *Degree requirements:* For master's, thesis; for doctorate, thesis/dissertation, oral and written exams. *Entrance requirements:* For master's, GRE General Test, MCAT, or DAT, minimum GPA of 3.0; for doctorate, GRE General Test, interview, minimum GPA of 3.0, research experience. Additional exam requirements/recommendations for international students: Required—TOEFL (minimum score 600 paper-based; 100 iBT). Electronic applications accepted. *Faculty research:* Innate and adaptive immunology, gene therapy/vector development, vaccinology, proteomics of biowarfare agents, bacterial and fungal pathogenesis.

Meharry Medical College, School of Graduate Studies, Program in Biomedical Sciences, Microbiology and Immunology Emphasis, Nashville, TN 37208-9989. Offers PhD, MD/PhD. *Degree requirements:* For doctorate, comprehensive exam, thesis/dissertation. *Entrance requirements:* For doctorate, GRE General Test, GRE Subject Test, undergraduate degree in related science. *Faculty research:* Microbial and bacterial pathogenesis, viral transcription, immune response to viruses and parasites.

Miami University, College of Arts and Science, Department of Microbiology, Oxford, OH 45056. Offers MS, PhD. *Students:* 22 full-time (13 women), 1 (woman) part-time; includes 5 minority (3 Asian, non-Hispanic/Latino; 2 Hispanic/Latino), 6 international. Average age 26. In 2017, 6 doctorates awarded. *Expenses:* Tuition, state resident: full-time $13,812; part-time $575 per credit hour. Tuition, nonresident: full-time $30,860; part-time $1286 per credit hour. *Unit head:* Dr. Louis A. Actis, Chair, 513-529-5424, E-mail: actisla@miamioh.edu. *Application contact:* Dr. Mitchell Balish, Associate Professor and Director of Graduate Studies, 513-529-0167, E-mail: balishmf@miamioh.edu.
Website: http://www.miamioh.edu/microbiology

Michigan State University, College of Human Medicine and The Graduate School, Graduate Programs in Human Medicine, East Lansing, MI 48824. Offers biochemistry and molecular biology (MS, PhD); epidemiology (MS, PhD); microbiology (MS); microbiology and molecular genetics (PhD); pharmacology and toxicology (MS, PhD); physiology (MS, PhD); public health (MPH). *Entrance requirements:* Additional exam requirements/recommendations for international students: Required—TOEFL.

Michigan State University, College of Osteopathic Medicine and The Graduate School, Graduate Studies in Osteopathic Medicine, East Lansing, MI 48824. Offers biochemistry and molecular biology (MS, PhD); microbiology (MS); microbiology and molecular genetics (PhD); pharmacology and toxicology (MS, PhD), including integrative pharmacology (MS), pharmacology and toxicology, pharmacology and toxicology-environmental toxicology (PhD); physiology (MS, PhD).

Michigan State University, College of Veterinary Medicine and The Graduate School, Graduate Programs in Veterinary Medicine and College of Natural Science, Department of Microbiology and Molecular Genetics, East Lansing, MI 48824. Offers industrial microbiology (MS, PhD); microbiology (MS, PhD); microbiology and molecular genetics (MS, PhD); microbiology–environmental toxicology (PhD). *Entrance requirements:* For master's, GRE General Test. Additional exam requirements/recommendations for international students: Required—TOEFL (minimum score 550 paper-based), Michigan State University ELT (minimum score 85), Michigan English Language Assessment Battery (minimum score 83). Electronic applications accepted.

Michigan State University, The Graduate School, College of Agriculture and Natural Resources, MSU-DOE Plant Research Laboratory, East Lansing, MI 48824. Offers biochemistry and molecular biology (PhD); cellular and molecular biology (PhD); crop and soil sciences (PhD); genetics (PhD); microbiology and molecular genetics (PhD); plant biology (PhD); plant physiology (PhD). Offered jointly with the Department of Energy. *Degree requirements:* For doctorate, comprehensive exam, thesis/dissertation, laboratory rotation, defense of dissertation. *Entrance requirements:* For doctorate, GRE General Test, acceptance into one of the affiliated department programs; 3 letters of recommendation; bachelor's degree or equivalent in life sciences, chemistry, biochemistry, or biophysics; research experience. Electronic applications accepted. *Faculty research:* Role of hormones in the regulation of plant development and physiology, molecular mechanisms associated with signal recognition, development and application of genetic methods and materials, protein routing and function.

Montana State University, The Graduate School, College of Letters and Science, Department of Microbiology, Bozeman, MT 59717. Offers MS, PhD. *Program availability:* Part-time. *Degree requirements:* For master's, comprehensive exam; for doctorate, comprehensive exam, thesis/dissertation. *Entrance requirements:* For master's and doctorate, GRE General Test. Additional exam requirements/recommendations for international students: Required—TOEFL (minimum score 550 paper-based). Electronic applications accepted. *Faculty research:* Medical microbiology, environmental microbiology, biofilms, immunology, molecular biology and bioinformatics.

New York Medical College, Graduate School of Basic Medical Sciences, Valhalla, NY 10595. Offers biochemistry and molecular biology (MS, PhD); cell biology (MS, PhD); microbiology and immunology (MS, PhD); pathology (MS, PhD); pharmacology (MS, PhD); physiology (MS, PhD); MD/PhD. *Program availability:* Part-time, evening/weekend. *Faculty:* 70 full-time (17 women), 25 part-time/adjunct (9 women). *Students:* 116 full-time (63 women), 25 part-time (11 women); includes 65 minority (17 Black or African American, non-Hispanic/Latino; 1 American Indian or Alaska Native, non-Hispanic/Latino; 23 Asian, non-Hispanic/Latino; 21 Hispanic/Latino; 3 Two or more races, non-Hispanic/Latino), 27 international. Average age 27. 273 applicants, 56% accepted, 59 enrolled. In 2017, 32 master's, 3 doctorates awarded. *Degree requirements:* For master's, thesis; for doctorate, comprehensive exam, thesis/dissertation. *Entrance requirements:* For master's, GRE General Test, MCAT, or DAT; for doctorate, GRE General Test. Additional exam requirements/recommendations for international students: Required—TOEFL. *Application deadline:* For fall admission, 7/1 priority date for domestic students, 5/1 priority date for international students; for spring admission, 12/1 priority date for domestic students, 9/15 priority date for international students. Applications are processed on a rolling basis. Application fee: $75 ($100 for international students). Electronic applications accepted. *Expenses:* $1,125 per credit, $655 fees. *Financial support:* Fellowships, research assistantships, Federal Work-Study, institutionally sponsored loans, scholarships/grants, tuition waivers, and health benefits (for PhD candidates only) available. Support available to part-time students. Financial award application deadline: 4/30; financial award applicants required to submit FAFSA. *Faculty research:* Cardiovascular science, infectious diseases, neuroscience, cancer, cell signaling. *Unit head:* Dr. Francis L. Belloni, Dean, 914-594-4110, Fax: 914-594-4944, E-mail: francis_belloni@nymc.edu. *Application contact:* Valerie Romeo-Messana, Director of Admissions, 914-594-4110, Fax: 914-594-4944, E-mail: v_romeomessana@nymc.edu.
Website: https://www.nymc.edu/graduate-school-of-basic-medical-sciences-gsbms/gsbms-academics/

New York University, Graduate School of Arts and Science, Department of Biology, New York, NY 10012-1019. Offers biology (PhD); biomedical journalism (MS); cancer and molecular biology (PhD); computational biology (PhD); computers in biological research (MS); developmental genetics (PhD); general biology (MS); immunology and microbiology (PhD); molecular genetics (PhD); neurobiology (PhD); oral biology (MS); plant biology (PhD); recombinant DNA technology (MS); MS/MBA. *Program availability:* Part-time. *Students:* Average age 27. 394 applicants, 56% accepted, 77 enrolled. In 2017, 68 master's, 9 doctorates awarded. Terminal master's awarded for partial completion of doctoral program. *Degree requirements:* For master's, thesis or alternative, qualifying paper; for doctorate, comprehensive exam, thesis/dissertation. *Entrance requirements:* For master's and doctorate, GRE General Test. Additional exam requirements/recommendations for international students: Required—TOEFL. *Application deadline:* For fall admission, 12/1 priority date for domestic students, 12/1 for international students. Application fee: $100. *Expenses: Tuition:* Full-time $41,352; part-time $19,968 per year. *Required fees:* $2496; $1628 per unit. $814 per term. Tuition and fees vary according to course load and program. *Financial support:* Fellowships, research assistantships, teaching assistantships, career-related internships or fieldwork, Federal Work-Study, institutionally sponsored loans, scholarships/grants, health care benefits, and unspecified assistantships available. Financial award application deadline: 12/1; financial award applicants required to submit FAFSA. *Faculty research:* Genomics, molecular and cell biology, development and molecular genetics, molecular evolution of plants and animals. *Unit head:* Stephen Small, Chair, 212-998-8200, Fax: 212-995-4015, E-mail: biology.admissions@nyu.edu. *Application contact:* Ken Birnbaum, Director of Graduate Studies, PhD Programs, 212-998-8200, Fax: 212-995-4015, E-mail: biology.admissions@nyu.edu.
Website: http://biology.as.nyu.edu/

New York University, School of Medicine and Graduate School of Arts and Science, Sackler Institute of Graduate Biomedical Sciences, New York, NY 10016. Offers biomedical imaging and technology (PhD); biostatistics (PhD); cellular and molecular biology (PhD); developmental genetics (PhD); epidemiology (PhD); genome integrity (PhD); immunology and inflammation (PhD); microbiology (PhD); molecular biophysics (PhD); molecular oncology and tumor immunology (PhD); molecular pharmacology (PhD); neuroscience and physiology (PhD), including immunology, molecular oncology; stem cell biology (PhD); systems and computational biomedicine (PhD); MD/PhD. *Faculty:* 207 full-time (51 women). *Students:* 236 full-time (138 women), 1 part-time (0 women); includes 68 minority (13 Black or African American, non-Hispanic/Latino; 26 Asian, non-Hispanic/Latino; 28 Hispanic/Latino; 1 Native Hawaiian or other Pacific Islander, non-Hispanic/Latino), 79 international. Average age 27. 761 applicants, 18% accepted, 59 enrolled. In 2017, 35 doctorates awarded. *Degree requirements:* For doctorate, comprehensive exam, thesis/dissertation, qualifying exam; thesis defense. *Entrance requirements:* For doctorate, GRE. Additional exam requirements/recommendations for international students: Required—TOEFL, IELTS. *Application deadline:* For fall admission, 12/1 for domestic and international students. Applications are processed on a rolling basis. Application fee: $100. Electronic applications accepted. Application fee is waived when completed online. *Expenses:* Contact institution. *Financial support:* Health care benefits, tuition waivers (full), and unspecified assistantships available. *Faculty research:* Biomedical sciences. *Unit head:* Dr. Naoko Tanese, Associate Dean for Biomedical Sciences/Director, Sackler Institute, 212-263-8945, E-mail: naoko.tanese@nyumc.org. *Application contact:* Jessica Dong, Program Manager, 212-263-5648, E-mail: sackler-info@nyumc.org.
Website: https://med.nyu.edu/research/sackler-institute-graduate-biomedical-sciences/

North Carolina State University, Graduate School, College of Agriculture and Life Sciences, Department of Microbiology, Program in Microbiology, Raleigh, NC 27695. Offers MS, PhD. *Degree requirements:* For master's, thesis (for some programs); for doctorate, thesis/dissertation. *Entrance requirements:* For master's and doctorate, GRE. Electronic applications accepted.

North Dakota State University, College of Graduate and Interdisciplinary Studies, College of Agriculture, Food Systems, and Natural Resources, Department of Microbiological Sciences, Fargo, ND 58102. Offers microbiology (MS); molecular pathogenesis (PhD). *Program availability:* Part-time. *Degree requirements:* For master's, thesis; for doctorate, thesis/dissertation, oral and written preliminary exams. *Entrance requirements:* For master's and doctorate, GRE. Additional exam requirements/recommendations for international students: Required—TOEFL (minimum score 525 paper-based; 71 iBT). *Application deadline:* For fall admission, 2/15 priority date for domestic students. Applications are processed on a rolling basis. Application fee: $35. *Expenses:* Tuition, state resident: full-time $4323; part-time $360.21 per credit. Tuition, nonresident: full-time $6484; part-time $540.31 per credit. *Required fees:* $668; $55.70 per credit. Part-time tuition and fees vary according to degree level, program and reciprocity agreements. *Financial support:* Application deadline: 4/15. *Faculty research:* Bacterial gene regulation, antibiotic resistance, molecular virology, mechanisms of bacterial pathogenesis, immunology of animals. *Unit head:* Peter Bergholz, Graduate Coordinator, 701-231-5946, E-mail: peter.bergholz@ndsu.edu. *Application contact:* Eugene Berry, Associate Professor, 701-231-7520, Fax: 701-231-7514, E-mail: eugene.berry@ndsu.edu.
Website: http://www.ndsu.edu/micro/

The Ohio State University, Graduate School, College of Arts and Sciences, Division of Natural and Mathematical Sciences, Department of Microbiology, Columbus, OH 43210. Offers MS, PhD. *Faculty:* 21. *Students:* 51 full-time (24 women), 16 international. Average age 26. In 2017, 2 master's, 5 doctorates awarded. Terminal master's awarded for partial completion of doctoral program. *Entrance requirements:* For doctorate, GRE General Test. Additional exam requirements/recommendations for international students: Required—TOEFL (minimum score 600 paper-based; 100 iBT), Michigan English Language Assessment Battery (minimum score 82); Recommended—IELTS (minimum score 8). *Application deadline:* For fall admission, 12/15 priority date for domestic students, 11/30 priority date for international students; for spring admission, 3/1 for domestic students, 2/1 for international students. Applications are processed on a rolling basis. Application fee: $60 ($70 for international students). Electronic applications accepted. *Financial support:* Fellowships, research assistantships, teaching assistantships, Federal Work-Study, and institutionally sponsored loans available. Support available to part-time students. *Unit head:* Dr. Michael Ibba, Chair and Professor, 614-292-2120, E-mail: ibba.1@osu.edu. *Application contact:* Graduate and Professional Admissions, 614-292-9444, Fax: 614-292-3895, E-mail: gpadmissions@osu.edu.
Website: http://microbiology.osu.edu/

Ohio University, Graduate College, College of Arts and Sciences, Department of Biological Sciences, Athens, OH 45701-2979. Offers biological sciences (MS, PhD); cell biology and physiology (MS, PhD); ecology and evolutionary biology (MS, PhD); exercise physiology and muscle biology (MS, PhD); microbiology (MS, PhD); neuroscience (MS, PhD). Terminal master's awarded for partial completion of doctoral program. *Degree requirements:* For master's, comprehensive exam, thesis, 1 quarter of teaching experience; for doctorate, comprehensive exam, thesis/dissertation, 2 quarters of teaching experience. *Entrance requirements:* For master's, GRE General Test, names of three faculty members whose research interests most closely match the applicant's interest; for doctorate, GRE General Test, essay concerning prior training, research interest and career goals, plus names of three faculty members whose research interests most closely match the applicant's interest. Additional exam requirements/recommendations for international students: Required—TOEFL (minimum score 620 paper-based; 105 iBT) or IELTS (minimum score 7.5). Electronic applications accepted. *Faculty research:* Ecology and evolutionary biology, exercise physiology and muscle biology, neurobiology, cell biology, physiology.

Oklahoma State University, College of Arts and Sciences, Department of Microbiology and Molecular Genetics, Stillwater, OK 74078. Offers MS, PhD. *Faculty:* 17 full-time (4 women). *Students:* 12 full-time (5 women), 19 part-time (11 women); includes 6 minority (2 Hispanic/Latino; 4 Two or more races, non-Hispanic/Latino), 15 international. Average age 29. 35 applicants, 37% accepted, 13 enrolled. In 2017, 4 master's, 1 doctorate awarded. *Entrance requirements:* For master's and doctorate, GRE General Test. Additional exam requirements/recommendations for international students: Required—TOEFL (minimum score 550 paper-based; 79 iBT). *Application deadline:* For fall admission, 3/1 priority date for international students; for spring admission, 8/1 priority date for international students. Applications are processed on a rolling basis. Application fee: $40 ($75 for international students). Electronic applications accepted. *Expenses:* Tuition, state resident: full-time $4019; part-time $2679.60 per year. Tuition, nonresident: full-time $15,286; part-time $10,190.40 per year. *Required fees:* $2129; $1419 per unit. Tuition and fees vary according to program. *Financial support:* Research assistantships, teaching assistantships, career-related internships or fieldwork, Federal Work-Study, scholarships/grants, health care benefits, tuition waivers (partial), and unspecified assistantships available. Support available to part-time students. Financial award application deadline: 3/1; financial award applicants required to submit FAFSA. *Faculty research:* Bioinformatics, genomics-genetics, virology, environmental microbiology, development-molecular mechanisms. *Unit head:* Dr. Tyrrell Conway, Professor and Department Head, 405-744-6243, Fax: 405-744-6790, E-mail: tconway@okstate.edu.
Website: http://microbiology.okstate.edu

Old Dominion University, College of Sciences, Master of Science in Biology Program, Norfolk, VA 23529. Offers biology (MS); microbiology and immunology (MS). *Program availability:* Part-time. *Faculty:* 22 full-time (4 women), 22 part-time/adjunct (2 women). *Students:* 18 full-time (11 women), 15 part-time (11 women); includes 4 minority (2 Black or African American, non-Hispanic/Latino; 2 Asian, non-Hispanic/Latino). Average age 28. 28 applicants, 25% accepted, 6 enrolled. In 2017, 10 master's awarded. *Degree requirements:* For master's, comprehensive exam, thesis optional, 31 credits. *Entrance requirements:* For

master's, GRE General Test, MCAT, minimum GPA of 3.0. Additional exam requirements/ recommendations for international students: Required—TOEFL (minimum score 550 paper-based; 79 iBT). *Application deadline:* For fall admission, 2/1 priority date for domestic and international students; for winter admission, 6/1 priority date for domestic and international students; for spring admission, 10/1 priority date for domestic and international students. Application fee: $50. Electronic applications accepted. *Expenses:* Tuition, state resident: full-time $8928; part-time $496 per credit. Tuition, nonresident: full-time $22,482; part-time $1249 per credit. *Required fees:* $66 per semester. *Financial support:* In 2017–18, 11 students received support, including 2 fellowships (averaging $6,575 per year), 10 research assistantships with partial tuition reimbursements available (averaging $15,000 per year), 9 teaching assistantships with partial tuition reimbursements available (averaging $15,000 per year); career-related internships or fieldwork and scholarships/grants also available. Support available to part-time students. Financial award application deadline: 2/1; financial award applicants required to submit FAFSA. *Faculty research:* Ecology and systematics of vertebrates, marine biology, molecular and cellular microbiology and immunology, vector-borne diseases, human and ecological physiology. *Total annual research expenditures:* $2 million. *Unit head:* Dr. Robert Ratzlaff, Graduate Program Director, 757-683-4361, Fax: 757-683-5283, E-mail: biolgpd@odu.edu. *Application contact:* William Heffelfinger, Director of Graduate Admissions, 757-683-5554, Fax: 757-683-3255, E-mail: gradadmit@odu.edu.
Website: http://sci.odu.edu/biology/academics/bio-ms.shtml

Oregon Health & Science University, School of Medicine, Graduate Programs in Medicine, Program in Molecular and Cellular Biosciences, Department of Molecular Microbiology and Immunology, Portland, OR 97239-3098. Offers PhD. *Faculty:* 28 full-time (8 women), 21 part-time/adjunct (6 women). *Students:* 12 full-time (7 women); includes 2 minority (1 Asian, non-Hispanic/Latino; 1 Two or more races, non-Hispanic/Latino). Average age 28. In 2017, 4 doctorates awarded. Terminal master's awarded for partial completion of doctoral program. *Degree requirements:* For doctorate, comprehensive exam, thesis/dissertation, qualifying exam. *Entrance requirements:* For doctorate, GRE General Test (minimum scores: 153 Verbal/148 Quantitative/4.5 Analytical) or MCAT (for some programs). *Application deadline:* For fall admission, 12/1 for domestic and international students. Application fee: $70. Electronic applications accepted. *Financial support:* Health care benefits, tuition waivers (full), and full-tuition and stipends available. Financial award application deadline: 3/1; financial award applicants required to submit FAFSA. *Faculty research:* Molecular biology of bacterial and viral pathogens, cellular and humoral immunology, molecular biology of microbes. *Unit head:* Dr. Georgiana Purdy, Program Director, E-mail: mmi@ohsu.edu. *Application contact:* Brandi Colbert, Program Coordinator, E-mail: mmi@ohsu.edu.
Website: http://www.ohsu.edu/microbiology

Oregon State University, College of Science, Program in Microbiology, Corvallis, OR 97331. Offers environmental microbiology (MA, MS, PhD); food microbiology (MA, MS, PhD); genomics (MA, MS, PhD); immunology (MA, MS, PhD); microbial ecology (MA, MS, PhD); microbial evolution (MA, MS, PhD); parasitology (MA, MS, PhD); pathogenic microbiology (MA, MS, PhD); virology (MA). Terminal master's awarded for partial completion of doctoral program. *Entrance requirements:* For master's and doctorate, GRE. Additional exam requirements/recommendations for international students: Required—TOEFL (minimum score 600 paper-based; 100 iBT). *Application deadline:* For fall admission, 1/1 for domestic and international students. Application fee: $75 ($85 for international students). *Financial support:* Application deadline: 1/15. *Faculty research:* Genetics, physiology, biotechnology, pathogenic microbiology, plant virology. *Unit head:* Dr. Jerri Bartholomew, Professor and Department Head, 541-737-1834, E-mail: bartholj@science.oregonstate.edu. *Application contact:* Kim Halsey, Graduate Admissions Committee Chair, 541-737-1831, E-mail: kim.halsey@oregonstate.edu.
Website: http://microbiology.science.oregonstate.edu/

Purdue University, Graduate School, College of Science, Department of Biological Sciences, West Lafayette, IN 47907. Offers biochemistry (PhD); biophysics (PhD); cell and developmental biology (PhD); ecology, evolutionary and population biology (MS, PhD), including ecology, evolutionary biology, population biology; genetics (MS, PhD); microbiology (MS, PhD); molecular biology (PhD); neurobiology (MS, PhD); plant physiology (PhD). *Faculty:* 42 full-time (13 women), 3 part-time/adjunct (0 women). *Students:* 115 full-time (58 women), 6 part-time (4 women); includes 17 minority (1 Black or African American, non-Hispanic/Latino; 6 Asian, non-Hispanic/Latino; 9 Hispanic/Latino; 1 Two or more races, non-Hispanic/Latino), 60 international. Average age 27. 165 applicants, 12% accepted, 15 enrolled. In 2017, 5 master's, 16 doctorates awarded. Terminal master's awarded for partial completion of doctoral program. *Degree requirements:* For master's, thesis (for some programs); for doctorate, thesis/dissertation, seminars, teaching experience. *Entrance requirements:* For master's, GRE General Test (minimum analytical writing score of 3.5), minimum undergraduate GPA of 3.0; for doctorate, GRE General Test (minimum analytical writing score of 3.5), minimum undergraduate GPA of 3.5. Additional exam requirements/recommendations for international students: Required—TOEFL minimum score 600 paper-based; 107 iBT (for MS), 80 iBT (for PhD). *Application deadline:* For fall admission, 12/7 for domestic and international students. Applications are processed on a rolling basis. Application fee: $60 ($75 for international students). Electronic applications accepted. *Financial support:* Fellowships, research assistantships, and teaching assistantships available. Support available to part-time students. Financial award application deadline: 2/15; financial award applicants required to submit FAFSA. *Unit head:* Stephen Konieczny, Head, 765-494-4407, E-mail: sfk@purdue.edu. *Application contact:* Georgina E. Rupp, Graduate Coordinator, 765-494-8142, E-mail: ruppg@purdue.edu.
Website: http://www.bio.purdue.edu/

Purdue University, Graduate School, PULSe - Purdue University Life Sciences Program, West Lafayette, IN 47907. Offers biomolecular structure and biophysics (PhD); biotechnology (PhD); chemical biology (PhD); chromatin and regulation of gene expression (PhD); integrative neuroscience (PhD); integrative plant sciences (PhD); membrane biology (PhD); microbiology (PhD); molecular evolutionary and cancer biology (PhD); molecular evolutionary genetics (PhD); molecular virology (PhD). *Students:* 60 full-time (29 women); includes 6 minority (4 Hispanic/Latino; 2 Two or more races, non-Hispanic/Latino), 36 international. Average age 25. 127 applicants, 39% accepted, 25 enrolled. *Entrance requirements:* For doctorate, GRE, minimum undergraduate GPA of 3.0. Additional exam requirements/recommendations for international students: Required—TOEFL (minimum score 550 paper-based; 77 iBT). *Application deadline:* For fall admission, 1/15 priority date for domestic and international students. Applications are processed on a rolling basis. Application fee: $60 ($75 for international students). Electronic applications accepted. *Financial support:* In 2017–18, research assistantships with tuition reimbursements (averaging $22,500 per year), teaching assistantships with tuition reimbursements (averaging $22,500 per year) were awarded. *Unit head:* Dr. Jason R. Cannon, Head of the Graduate Program, 765-494-0794, E-mail: cannonjr@purdue.edu. *Application contact:* Lindsey Springer, Graduate Contact for Admissions, 765-496-9667, E-mail: lbcampbe@purdue.edu.
Website: http://www.gradschool.purdue.edu/pulse

Purdue University, School of Veterinary Medicine and Graduate School, Graduate Programs in Veterinary Medicine, Department of Comparative Pathobiology, West Lafayette, IN 47907-2027. Offers comparative epidemiology and public health (MS); comparative epidemiology and public heath (PhD); comparative microbiology and immunology (MS, PhD); comparative pathobiology (MS, PhD); interdisciplinary studies (PhD), including microbial pathogenesis, molecular signaling and cancer biology, molecular virology; lab animal medicine (MS); veterinary anatomic pathology (MS); veterinary clinical pathology (MS). Terminal master's awarded for partial completion of doctoral program. *Degree requirements:* For master's, thesis (for some programs); for doctorate, thesis/dissertation. *Entrance requirements:* For master's and doctorate, GRE General Test. Additional exam requirements/recommendations for international students: Required—TOEFL (minimum score 575 paper-based), IELTS (minimum score 6.5), TWE (minimum score 4). Electronic applications accepted.

Queen's University at Kingston, School of Graduate Studies, Faculty of Health Sciences, Department of Microbiology and Immunology, Kingston, ON K7L 3N6, Canada. Offers M Sc, PhD. *Program availability:* Part-time. *Degree requirements:* For master's, thesis; for doctorate, comprehensive exam, thesis/dissertation. *Entrance requirements:* For master's and doctorate, minimum B+ average. Additional exam requirements/recommendations for international students: Required—TOEFL (minimum score 600 paper-based). Electronic applications accepted. *Faculty research:* Bacteriology, virology, immunology, education in microbiology and immunology, microbial pathogenesis.

Rosalind Franklin University of Medicine and Science, School of Graduate and Postdoctoral Studies - Interdisciplinary Graduate Program in Biomedical Sciences, Department of Microbiology and Immunology, North Chicago, IL 60064-3095. Offers PhD, MD/PhD. Terminal master's awarded for partial completion of doctoral program. *Degree requirements:* For doctorate, comprehensive exam, thesis/dissertation. *Entrance requirements:* For doctorate, GRE General Test. Additional exam requirements/recommendations for international students: Required—TOEFL, TWE. *Faculty research:* Molecular biology, parasitology, virology.

Rush University, Graduate College, Division of Immunology and Microbiology, Chicago, IL 60612-3832. Offers microbiology (PhD); virology (MS, PhD), including immunology, virology; MD/PhD. *Degree requirements:* For doctorate, thesis/dissertation, comprehensive preliminary exam. *Entrance requirements:* For doctorate, GRE General Test, interview, minimum GPA of 3.0. Additional exam requirements/recommendations for international students: Required—TOEFL. *Faculty research:* Immune interactions of cells and membranes, HIV immunopathogenesis, autoimmunity, tumor biology.

Rutgers University–Newark, Graduate School of Biomedical Sciences, Department of Microbiology and Molecular Genetics, Newark, NJ 07107. Offers PhD. *Degree requirements:* For doctorate, thesis/dissertation, qualifying exam. *Entrance requirements:* For doctorate, GRE General Test. Additional exam requirements/recommendations for international students: Required—TOEFL. Electronic applications accepted. *Faculty research:* Molecular genetics of yeast, mutagenesis and carcinogenesis of DNA, bacterial protein synthesis, mammalian cell genetics, adenovirus gene expression.

Rutgers University–New Brunswick, Graduate School-New Brunswick, Programs in the Molecular Biosciences, Piscataway, NJ 08854-8097. Offers biochemistry (PhD); cell and developmental biology (MS, PhD); microbiology and molecular genetics (MS, PhD), including applied microbiology, clinical microbiology, computational molecular biology (PhD), immunology, microbial biochemistry, molecular genetics, virology. MS, PhD offered jointly with University of Medicine and Dentistry of New Jersey.

Rutgers University–New Brunswick, Graduate School of Biomedical Sciences, Program in Microbiology and Molecular Genetics, Piscataway, NJ 08854-5635. Offers MS, PhD, MD/PhD. Terminal master's awarded for partial completion of doctoral program. *Degree requirements:* For master's, thesis, qualifying exam; for doctorate, thesis/dissertation, qualifying exam. *Entrance requirements:* For master's and doctorate, GRE General Test. Additional exam requirements/recommendations for international students: Required—TOEFL. Electronic applications accepted. *Faculty research:* Interferon, receptors, retrovirus evolution, Arbo virus/host cell interactions.

Saint Louis University, Graduate Programs, School of Medicine, Graduate Programs in Biomedical Sciences, Department of Molecular Microbiology and Immunology, St. Louis, MO 63103. Offers PhD. *Degree requirements:* For doctorate, comprehensive exam, thesis/dissertation, qualifying exams. *Entrance requirements:* For doctorate, GRE General Test (GRE Subject Test optional), letters of recommendation, resume, interview. Additional exam requirements/recommendations for international students: Required—TOEFL (minimum score 525 paper-based). Electronic applications accepted. *Faculty research:* Pathogenesis of hepatitis C virus, herperviruses, pox viruses, rheumatoid arthritis, antiviral drugs and vaccines in biodefense, cancer gene therapy, virology and immunology.

San Diego State University, Graduate and Research Affairs, College of Sciences, Department of Biology, Program in Microbiology, San Diego, CA 92182. Offers MS. *Degree requirements:* For master's, thesis, oral exam. *Entrance requirements:* For master's, GRE General Test, GRE Subject Test, resume or curriculum vitae, 2 letters of recommendation. Additional exam requirements/recommendations for international students: Required—TOEFL. Electronic applications accepted.

San Francisco State University, Division of Graduate Studies, College of Science and Engineering, Department of Biology, Program in Microbiology, San Francisco, CA 94132-1722. Offers MS. *Application deadline:* Applications are processed on a rolling basis. *Unit head:* Dr. Diana Chu, Program Coordinator, 415-405-3487, Fax: 415-338-2295, E-mail: chud@sfsu.edu.
Website: http://biology.sfsu.edu/graduate/microbiology

Seton Hall University, College of Arts and Sciences, Department of Biological Sciences, South Orange, NJ 07079-2697. Offers biology (MS); biology/business administration (MS); microbiology (MS); molecular bioscience (PhD); molecular bioscience/neuroscience (PhD). *Program availability:* Part-time, evening/weekend. *Degree requirements:* For master's, thesis optional; for doctorate, comprehensive exam, thesis/dissertation. *Entrance requirements:* For master's, GRE or undergraduate degree (BS in biological sciences) with minimum GPA of 3.0 from accredited U.S. institution; for doctorate, GRE. Additional exam requirements/recommendations for international students: Required—TOEFL. Electronic applications accepted. *Faculty research:* Neurobiology, genetics, immunology, molecular biology, cellular physiology, toxicology, microbiology, bioinformatics.

South Dakota State University, Graduate School, College of Agriculture and Biological Sciences, Department of Biology and Microbiology, Brookings, SD 57007. Offers biological sciences (MS, PhD). *Program availability:* Part-time. *Degree requirements:* For master's, thesis (for some programs), oral exam; for doctorate, comprehensive exam, thesis/dissertation, oral exam. *Entrance requirements:* For master's and doctorate, GRE General Test. Additional exam requirements/recommendations for international students: Required—TOEFL (minimum score 600 paper-based; 100 iBT). *Faculty research:* Ecosystem ecology; plant, animal and microbial genomics; animal infectious disease, microbial bioproducts.

Southern Illinois University Carbondale, Graduate School, College of Science, Program in Molecular Biology, Microbiology, and Biochemistry, Carbondale, IL 62901-4701. Offers MS, PhD. *Degree requirements:* For master's, thesis; for doctorate, thesis/dissertation.

Entrance requirements: For master's, GRE, minimum GPA of 2.7; for doctorate, GRE, minimum GPA of 3.25. Additional exam requirements/recommendations for international students: Required—TOEFL. *Faculty research:* Prokaryotic gene regulation and expression; eukaryotic gene regulation; microbial, phylogenetic, and metabolic diversity; immune responses to tumors, pathogens, and autoantigens; protein folding and structure.

Southwestern Oklahoma State University, College of Professional and Graduate Studies, School of Behavioral Sciences and Education, Specialization in Health Sciences and Microbiology, Weatherford, OK 73096-3098. Offers M Ed.

Stanford University, School of Medicine, Graduate Programs in Medicine, Department of Microbiology and Immunology, Stanford, CA 94305-2004. Offers PhD. *Degree requirements:* For doctorate, comprehensive exam, thesis/dissertation, 2 quarter teaching assistantship. *Entrance requirements:* For doctorate, GRE General Test, GRE Subject Test (biology or biochemistry). Additional exam requirements/recommendations for international students: Required—TOEFL. Electronic applications accepted. *Expenses: Tuition:* Full-time $48,987; part-time $10,620 per quarter. One-time fee: $400. Tuition and fees vary according to program. *Faculty research:* Molecular pathogenesis of bacteria viruses and parasites, immune system function, autoimmunity, molecular biology.

State University of New York Upstate Medical University, College of Graduate Studies, Program in Microbiology and Immunology, Syracuse, NY 13210. Offers microbiology (MS); microbiology and immunology (PhD); MD/PhD. Terminal master's awarded for partial completion of doctoral program. *Degree requirements:* For master's, thesis; for doctorate, comprehensive exam, thesis/dissertation. *Entrance requirements:* For master's, GRE General Test, interview; for doctorate, GRE General Test, telephone interview. Additional exam requirements/recommendations for international students: Required—TOEFL. Electronic applications accepted. *Faculty research:* Cancer, disorders of the nervous system, infectious diseases, diabetes/metabolic disorders/cardiovascular diseases.

Stony Brook University, State University of New York, Stony Brook Medicine, School of Medicine and Graduate School, Graduate Programs in Medicine, Department of Molecular Genetics and Microbiology, Stony Brook, NY 11794. Offers PhD. *Faculty:* 16 full-time (4 women), 3 part-time/adjunct (1 woman). *Students:* 23 full-time (6 women); includes 6 minority (2 Asian, non-Hispanic/Latino; 4 Hispanic/Latino), 4 international. Average age 26. 56 applicants, 25% accepted, 4 enrolled. In 2017, 2 doctorates awarded. *Degree requirements:* For doctorate, comprehensive exam, thesis/dissertation. *Entrance requirements:* For doctorate, GRE General Test, GRE Subject Test, undergraduate training in biochemistry, genetics, and cell biology; recommendations; personal statement. Additional exam requirements/recommendations for international students: Required—TOEFL (minimum score 550 paper-based; 90 iBT). *Application deadline:* For fall admission, 1/15 for domestic students; for spring admission, 10/1 for domestic students. Application fee: $100. *Expenses:* Contact institution. *Financial support:* In 2017–18, 8 fellowships, 10 research assistantships were awarded; teaching assistantships and Federal Work-Study also available. Financial award application deadline: 3/15. *Faculty research:* Bioimaging, infectious diseases or agents, pathogenesis, viral studies (virology), genetics. *Total annual research expenditures:* $8.8 million. *Unit head:* Dr. David G. Thanassi, Interim Chair, 631-632-4549, Fax: 631-632-9797, E-mail: david.thanassi@stonybrook.edu. *Application contact:* Jennifer Jokinen, Program Coordinator, 631-632-8812, Fax: 631-632-9797, E-mail: jennifer.jokinen@stonybrook.edu.
Website: http://www.mgm.stonybrook.edu/index.shtml

Texas A&M University, College of Science, Department of Biology, College Station, TX 77843. Offers biology (MS, PhD); microbiology (MS, PhD). *Faculty:* 39. *Students:* 89 full-time (48 women), 5 part-time (3 women); includes 10 minority (2 Black or African American, non-Hispanic/Latino; 3 Asian, non-Hispanic/Latino; 3 Hispanic/Latino; 2 Two or more races, non-Hispanic/Latino), 40 international. Average age 29. 109 applicants, 28% accepted, 19 enrolled. In 2017, 5 master's, 19 doctorates awarded. *Degree requirements:* For master's, thesis or alternative; for doctorate, comprehensive exam, thesis/dissertation. *Entrance requirements:* For master's and doctorate, GRE General Test. Additional exam requirements/recommendations for international students: Required—TOEFL. *Application deadline:* For fall admission, 12/1 for domestic students. Applications are processed on a rolling basis. Application fee: $50 ($90 for international students). Electronic applications accepted. *Expenses:* Contact institution. *Financial support:* In 2017–18, 87 students received support, including 4 fellowships with tuition reimbursements available (averaging $25,816 per year), 41 research assistantships with tuition reimbursements available (averaging $14,313 per year), 45 teaching assistantships with tuition reimbursements available (averaging $13,974 per year); career-related internships or fieldwork, institutionally sponsored loans, scholarships/grants, traineeships, health care benefits, tuition waivers (full and partial), and unspecified assistantships also available. Support available to part-time students. Financial award application deadline: 4/1; financial award applicants required to submit FAFSA. *Faculty research:* Biological clocks, cell, molecular and developmental biology, ecology and evolutionary biology, genetics and genomics, microbiology. *Unit head:* Dr. Tom McKnight, Department Head, 979-845-3896, Fax: 979-845-2891, E-mail: mcknight@bio.tamu.edu. *Application contact:* Dr. Arne Lekven, Graduate Advisor, 979-458-3461, Fax: 979-845-2891, E-mail: alekven@bio.tamu.edu.
Website: http://www.bio.tamu.edu/index.html

Texas Tech University, Graduate School, College of Arts and Sciences, Department of Biological Sciences, Lubbock, TX 79409-3131. Offers biology (MS, PhD); environmental sustainability and natural resource management (PSM); microbiology (MS); zoology (MS, PhD). *Program availability:* Part-time, blended/hybrid learning. *Faculty:* 44 full-time (16 women). *Students:* 103 full-time (56 women), 13 part-time (5 women); includes 12 minority (2 Black or African American, non-Hispanic/Latino; 2 Asian, non-Hispanic/Latino; 6 Hispanic/Latino; 2 Two or more races, non-Hispanic/Latino), 51 international. Average age 29. 77 applicants, 36% accepted, 17 enrolled. In 2017, 13 master's, 10 doctorates awarded. *Degree requirements:* For master's, comprehensive exam, thesis or alternative; for doctorate, comprehensive exam, thesis/dissertation. *Entrance requirements:* For master's and doctorate, GRE General Test. Additional exam requirements/recommendations for international students: Required—TOEFL (minimum score 550 paper-based; 79 iBT). *Application deadline:* For fall admission, 6/1 priority date for domestic students, 1/15 priority date for international students; for spring admission, 9/1 priority date for domestic students, 6/15 priority date for international students. Applications are processed on a rolling basis. Application fee: $60. Electronic applications accepted. *Expenses:* Contact institution. *Financial support:* In 2017–18, 110 students received support, including 85 fellowships (averaging $1,960 per year), 28 research assistantships (averaging $8,365 per year), 93 teaching assistantships (averaging $15,744 per year); Federal Work-Study and health care benefits also available. Financial award application deadline: 2/15; financial award applicants required to submit FAFSA. *Faculty research:* Biodiversity, genomics and evolution; climate change in arid ecosystems, plant biology and biotechnology; animal communication and behavior; microbiomes, zoonosis and emerging diseases. *Total annual research expenditures:* $1.7 million. *Unit head:* Dr. Ron Chesser, Chair, 806-834-0121, Fax: 806-742-2963, E-mail: ron.chesser@ttu.edu. *Application contact:* Dr. Lou Densmore, Graduate Adviser, 806-834-6479, Fax: 806-742-2963, E-mail: lou.densmore@ttu.edu.
Website: http://www.depts.ttu.edu/biology/

Thomas Jefferson University, Jefferson College of Biomedical Sciences, MS Program in Microbiology, Philadelphia, PA 19107. Offers MS. *Program availability:* Part-time, evening/weekend. *Faculty:* 43 full-time (16 women), 28 part-time/adjunct (9 women). *Students:* 24 part-time (17 women); includes 4 minority (1 Black or African American, non-Hispanic/Latino; 1 American Indian or Alaska Native, non-Hispanic/Latino; 1 Asian, non-Hispanic/Latino; 1 Hispanic/Latino), 3 international. Average age 29. 22 applicants, 45% accepted, 4 enrolled. In 2017, 8 master's awarded. *Degree requirements:* For master's, thesis, clerkship. *Entrance requirements:* For master's, GRE General Test or MCAT, minimum GPA of 3.0. Additional exam requirements/recommendations for international students: Required—TOEFL, IELTS (minimum score 7). *Application deadline:* For fall admission, 8/1 priority date for domestic students, 3/1 priority date for international students; for winter admission, 12/1 priority date for domestic students, 6/1 priority date for international students; for spring admission, 4/1 priority date for domestic students. Applications are processed on a rolling basis. Application fee: $50. Electronic applications accepted. *Financial support:* Federal Work-Study and institutionally sponsored loans available. Support available to part-time students. Financial award application deadline: 5/1; financial award applicants required to submit FAFSA. *Faculty research:* Vaccinology, epidemiology, planning and management, microbiology. *Unit head:* Dr. James P. McGettigan, Program Director, 215-503-4629, Fax: 215-503-5393, E-mail: james.mcgettigan@jefferson.edu. *Application contact:* Marc E. Stearns, Senior Associate Director of Admissions, 215-503-0155, Fax: 215-503-3433, E-mail: jgsbs-info@jefferson.edu.
Website: http://www.jefferson.edu/university/biomedical-sciences/degrees-programs/master-programs/microbiology.html

Thomas Jefferson University, Jefferson College of Biomedical Sciences, PhD Program in Immunology and Microbial Pathogenesis, Philadelphia, PA 19107. Offers PhD. *Faculty:* 31 full-time (5 women). *Students:* 11 full-time (6 women); includes 3 minority (2 Asian, non-Hispanic/Latino; 1 Hispanic/Latino), 2 international. Average age 28. In 2017, 5 doctorates awarded. *Degree requirements:* For doctorate, comprehensive exam, thesis/dissertation. *Entrance requirements:* For doctorate, GRE General Test, minimum GPA of 3.2. Additional exam requirements/recommendations for international students: Required—TOEFL, IELTS (minimum score 7). *Application deadline:* For fall admission, 12/1 priority date for domestic and international students. Applications are processed on a rolling basis. Application fee: $60. Electronic applications accepted. *Financial support:* In 2017–18, 16 students received support, including 11 fellowships with full tuition reimbursements available (averaging $62,653 per year); Federal Work-Study, institutionally sponsored loans, scholarships/grants, traineeships, health care benefits, and stipends also available. Financial award application deadline: 5/1; financial award applicants required to submit FAFSA. *Unit head:* Dr. Jianke Zhang, Program Director, 215-503-4559, E-mail: jianke.zhang@jefferson.edu. *Application contact:* Marc E. Stearns, Senior Associate Director of Admissions, 215-503-0155, Fax: 215-503-3433, E-mail: jgsbs-info@jefferson.edu.
Website: http://www.jefferson.edu/university/biomedical-sciences/degrees-programs/phd-programs/immunology.html

Tufts University, Sackler School of Graduate Biomedical Sciences, Molecular Microbiology Program, Medford, MA 02155. Offers medically-oriented research in graduate education (PhD); molecular microbiology (PhD). Terminal master's awarded for partial completion of doctoral program. *Degree requirements:* For doctorate, comprehensive exam, thesis/dissertation. *Entrance requirements:* For doctorate, GRE General Test, 3 letters of reference, resume, personal statement. Electronic applications accepted. *Expenses: Tuition:* Full-time $49,892. *Required fees:* $874. Full-time tuition and fees vary according to degree level, program and student level. Part-time tuition and fees vary according to course load. *Faculty research:* Mechanisms of gene regulation, interactions of microorganisms and viruses with host cells, infection response.

Tulane University, School of Medicine and School of Liberal Arts, Graduate Programs in Biomedical Sciences, Department of Microbiology and Immunology, New Orleans, LA 70118-5669. Offers MS. MS and PhD offered through the Graduate School. *Degree requirements:* For master's, thesis. *Entrance requirements:* For master's, GRE General Test, minimum B average in undergraduate course work. Additional exam requirements/recommendations for international students: Required—TOEFL. Electronic applications accepted. *Expenses: Tuition:* Full-time $50,920; part-time $2829 per credit hour. *Required fees:* $2040; $44.50 per credit hour. $580 per term. Tuition and fees vary according to course load, degree level and program. *Faculty research:* Vaccine development, viral pathogenesis, molecular virology, bacterial pathogenesis, fungal pathogenesis.

Universidad Central del Caribe, School of Medicine, Program in Biomedical Sciences, Bayamón, PR 00960-6032. Offers anatomy and cell biology (MA, MS); biochemistry (MS); biomedical sciences (MA); cellular and molecular biology (PhD); microbiology and immunology (MA, MS); pharmacology (MS); physiology (MS).

Université de Montréal, Faculty of Medicine, Department of Microbiology and Immunology, Montréal, QC H3C 3J7, Canada. Offers M Sc, PhD. Programs offered jointly with Faculty of Veterinary Medicine and Université du Québec, Institut Armand-Frappier. Terminal master's awarded for partial completion of doctoral program. *Degree requirements:* For master's, thesis; for doctorate, thesis/dissertation, general exam. *Entrance requirements:* For master's and doctorate, proficiency in French, knowledge of English. Electronic applications accepted.

Université de Sherbrooke, Faculty of Medicine and Health Sciences, Graduate Programs in Medicine, Program in Microbiology, Sherbrooke, QC J1H 5N4, Canada. Offers M Sc, PhD. Terminal master's awarded for partial completion of doctoral program. *Degree requirements:* For master's, thesis; for doctorate, thesis/dissertation. Electronic applications accepted. *Faculty research:* Oncogenes, alternative splicing mechanisms, genomics, telomerase, DNA repair, Clostridium difficile, Campylobacter jejuni.

Université du Québec, Institut National de la Recherche Scientifique, Graduate Programs, INRS - Institut Armand-Frappier, Laval, QC G1K 9A9, Canada. Offers applied microbiology (M Sc); biology (PhD); experimental health sciences (M Sc); virology and immunology (M Sc, PhD). *Program availability:* Part-time. *Faculty:* 48 full-time. *Students:* 149 full-time (89 women), 18 part-time (11 women), 86 international. Average age 30. 29 applicants, 93% accepted, 25 enrolled. In 2017, 16 master's, 13 doctorates awarded. *Degree requirements:* For master's, thesis; for doctorate, thesis/dissertation. *Entrance requirements:* For master's, appropriate bachelor's degree, proficiency in French; for doctorate, appropriate master's degree, proficiency in French. *Application deadline:* For fall admission, 3/30 for domestic and international students; for winter admission, 11/1 for domestic and international students; for spring admission, 3/1 for domestic and international students. Application fee: $45 Canadian dollars. Electronic applications accepted. *Financial support:* In 2017–18, fellowships (averaging $16,500 per year) were awarded; research assistantships also available. *Faculty research:* Immunity, infection and cancer; toxicology and environmental biotechnology; molecular pharmacochemistry. *Unit head:* Pierre Talbot, Director, 450-687-5010 Ext. 4300, Fax: 450-686-5501, E-mail: pierre.talbot@iaf.inrs.ca. *Application contact:* Sylvie Richard, Registrar, 418-654-2518, Fax: 418-654-3858, E-mail: sylvie.richard@adm.inrs.ca.
Website: http://www.iaf.inrs.ca

Microbiology

Université Laval, Faculty of Agricultural and Food Sciences, Program in Agricultural Microbiology, Québec, QC G1K 7P4, Canada. Offers agricultural microbiology (M Sc); agro-food microbiology (PhD). Terminal master's awarded for partial completion of doctoral program. *Degree requirements:* For master's, thesis; for doctorate, comprehensive exam, thesis/dissertation. *Entrance requirements:* For master's and doctorate, knowledge of French and English. Electronic applications accepted.

Université Laval, Faculty of Medicine, Graduate Programs in Medicine, Programs in Microbiology-Immunology, Québec, QC G1K 7P4, Canada. Offers M Sc, PhD. Terminal master's awarded for partial completion of doctoral program. *Degree requirements:* For master's, thesis; for doctorate, comprehensive exam, thesis/dissertation. *Entrance requirements:* For master's and doctorate, knowledge of French, comprehension of written English. Electronic applications accepted.

Université Laval, Faculty of Sciences and Engineering, Department of Biochemistry and Microbiology, Programs in Microbiology, Québec, QC G1K 7P4, Canada. Offers M Sc, PhD. Terminal master's awarded for partial completion of doctoral program. *Degree requirements:* For master's, thesis; for doctorate, comprehensive exam, thesis/dissertation. *Entrance requirements:* For master's and doctorate, knowledge of French, comprehension of written English. Electronic applications accepted.

University at Buffalo, the State University of New York, Graduate School, Jacobs School of Medicine and Biomedical Sciences, Graduate Programs in Medicine and Biomedical Sciences, Department of Microbiology and Immunology, Buffalo, NY 14203. Offers MS, PhD. *Program availability:* Part-time. *Faculty:* 17 full-time (6 women), 2 part-time/adjunct (0 women). *Students:* 16 full-time (9 women), 5 part-time (4 women); includes 5 minority (2 Black or African American, non-Hispanic/Latino; 1 American Indian or Alaska Native, non-Hispanic/Latino; 2 Asian, non-Hispanic/Latino). Average age 26. 39 applicants, 46% accepted, 7 enrolled. In 2017, 2 master's, 3 doctorates awarded. Terminal master's awarded for partial completion of doctoral program. *Degree requirements:* For master's, comprehensive exam, thesis or alternative; for doctorate, thesis/dissertation, departmental qualifying exam. *Entrance requirements:* For master's and doctorate, GRE General Test, 3 letters of recommendation, personal statement, curriculum vitae/resume, transcripts. Additional exam requirements/recommendations for international students: Required—TOEFL (minimum score 79 iBT) or IELTS (minimum score 6.5). *Application deadline:* For fall admission, 4/1 priority date for international students. Applications are processed on a rolling basis. Application fee: $85. Electronic applications accepted. *Expenses:* $621 per credit hour resident tuition and fees; $1,093 per credit hour nonresident tuition and fees. *Financial support:* In 2017–18, 15 students received support, including 2 fellowships with full tuition reimbursements available (averaging $24,000 per year), 12 research assistantships with full tuition reimbursements available (averaging $27,000 per year), 2 teaching assistantships (averaging $5,333 per year); health care benefits and unspecified assistantships also available. Financial award application deadline: 2/1; financial award applicants required to submit FAFSA. *Faculty research:* Bacteriology, immunology, parasitology, virology, mycology. *Total annual research expenditures:* $5.4 million. *Unit head:* Dr. James Bangs, Chair/Professor, 716-829-2907, Fax: 716-829-2158. *Application contact:* Dr. Ira Blader, Director of Graduate Studies, 716-829-5809, Fax: 716-829-2158.
Website: http://medicine.buffalo.edu/departments/micro.html

The University of Alabama at Birmingham, Joint Health Sciences, Microbiology Theme, Birmingham, AL 35294. Offers PhD. *Faculty:* 370. *Students:* 39 full-time (21 women); includes 13 minority (2 Black or African American, non-Hispanic/Latino; 1 American Indian or Alaska Native, non-Hispanic/Latino; 10 Asian, non-Hispanic/Latino). Average age 26. 52 applicants, 29% accepted, 5 enrolled. In 2017, 8 doctorates awarded. *Degree requirements:* For doctorate, comprehensive exam, thesis/dissertation. *Entrance requirements:* For doctorate, personal statement, resume or curriculum vitae, letters of recommendation, research experience, interview. Additional exam requirements/recommendations for international students: Required—TOEFL (minimum score 80 iBT), IELTS (minimum score 6.5). *Application deadline:* For fall admission, 12/31 priority date for domestic students, 12/31 for international students. Applications are processed on a rolling basis. Electronic applications accepted. *Financial support:* In 2017–18, fellowships with full tuition reimbursements (averaging $29,000 per year), research assistantships with full tuition reimbursements (averaging $30,000 per year) were awarded; health care benefits also available. *Unit head:* Dr. Janet Yother, Theme Director, 205-934-9531, E-mail: jyother@uab.edu. *Application contact:* Alyssa Zasada, Admissions Manager for Graduate Biomedical Sciences, 205-934-3857, E-mail: grad-gbs@uab.edu.
Website: http://www.uab.edu/gbs/home/themes/mic

University of Alberta, Faculty of Graduate Studies and Research, Department of Biological Sciences, Edmonton, AB T6G 2E1, Canada. Offers environmental biology and ecology (M Sc, PhD); microbiology and biotechnology (M Sc, PhD); molecular biology and genetics (M Sc, PhD); physiology and cell biology (M Sc, PhD); plant biology (M Sc, PhD); systematics and evolution (M Sc, PhD). Terminal master's awarded for partial completion of doctoral program. *Degree requirements:* For master's, thesis; for doctorate, thesis/dissertation. *Entrance requirements:* Additional exam requirements/recommendations for international students: Required—TOEFL.

The University of Arizona, College of Medicine, Department of Immunobiology, Tucson, AZ 85721. Offers PhD. *Degree requirements:* For doctorate, thesis/dissertation. *Entrance requirements:* For doctorate, GRE General Test, minimum GPA of 3.0. *Faculty research:* Environmental and pathogenic microbiology, molecular biology.

University of Arkansas for Medical Sciences, Graduate School, Little Rock, AR 72205. Offers biochemistry and molecular biology (MS, PhD); bioinformatics (MS, PhD); cellular physiology and molecular biophysics (MS, PhD); clinical nutrition (MS); interdisciplinary biomedical sciences (MS, PhD, Certificate); interdisciplinary toxicology (MS); microbiology and immunology (PhD); neurobiology and developmental sciences (PhD); pharmacology (PhD); MD/PhD. Bioinformatics programs hosted jointly with the University of Arkansas at Little Rock. *Program availability:* Part-time. Terminal master's awarded for partial completion of doctoral program. *Degree requirements:* For master's, comprehensive exam (for some programs), thesis (for some programs); for doctorate, thesis/dissertation. *Entrance requirements:* For master's and doctorate, GRE. Additional exam requirements/recommendations for international students: Required—TOEFL. Electronic applications accepted. *Expenses:* Contact institution.

The University of British Columbia, Faculty of Science, Department of Microbiology and Immunology, Vancouver, BC V6T 1Z3, Canada. Offers M Sc, PhD. *Degree requirements:* For master's, thesis; for doctorate, comprehensive exam, thesis/dissertation. *Entrance requirements:* For master's and doctorate, GRE General Test. Additional exam requirements/recommendations for international students: Required—TOEFL. Electronic applications accepted. *Expenses:* Contact institution. *Faculty research:* Bacterial genetics, metabolism, pathogenic bacteriology, virology.

University of Calgary, Cumming School of Medicine and Faculty of Graduate Studies, Department of Microbiology, Immunology and Infectious Diseases, Calgary, AB T2N 1N4, Canada. Offers M Sc, PhD. *Degree requirements:* For master's, thesis, oral thesis exam; for doctorate, thesis/dissertation, candidacy exam, oral thesis exam. *Entrance requirements:* For master's and doctorate, minimum GPA of 3.2. Additional exam requirements/recommendations for international students: Required—TOEFL (minimum score 580 paper-based). Electronic applications accepted. *Faculty research:* Bacteriology, virology, parasitology, immunology.

University of California, Berkeley, Graduate Division, College of Natural Resources, Department of Plant and Microbial Biology, Berkeley, CA 94720-1500. Offers microbiology (PhD); plant biology (PhD). *Degree requirements:* For doctorate, thesis/dissertation, qualifying exam, seminar presentation. *Entrance requirements:* For doctorate, GRE General Test, minimum GPA of 3.0, 3 letters of recommendation. Electronic applications accepted. *Faculty research:* Development, molecular biology, genetics, microbial biology, mycology.

University of California, Davis, Graduate Studies, Graduate Group in Microbiology, Davis, CA 95616. Offers MS, PhD. Terminal master's awarded for partial completion of doctoral program. *Degree requirements:* For master's, thesis; for doctorate, thesis/dissertation. *Entrance requirements:* For master's and doctorate, GRE General Test, minimum GPA of 3.0. Additional exam requirements/recommendations for international students: Required—TOEFL (minimum score 550 paper-based). Electronic applications accepted. *Faculty research:* Microbial physiology and genetics, microbial molecular and cellular biology, microbial ecology, microbial pathogenesis and immunology, urology.

University of California, Irvine, School of Medicine and Francisco J. Ayala School of Biological Sciences, Department of Microbiology and Molecular Genetics, Irvine, CA 92697. Offers biological sciences (MS, PhD); MD/PhD. *Students:* 15 full-time (8 women), 2 part-time (both women); includes 8 minority (1 Black or African American, non-Hispanic/Latino; 1 American Indian or Alaska Native, non-Hispanic/Latino; 3 Asian, non-Hispanic/Latino; 3 Hispanic/Latino). Average age 30. In 2017, 2 doctorates awarded. *Entrance requirements:* For doctorate, GRE General Test, GRE Subject Test, minimum GPA of 3.0. Additional exam requirements/recommendations for international students: Required—TOEFL (minimum score 550 paper-based). *Application deadline:* For fall admission, 12/15 priority date for domestic students, 12/15 for international students. Application fee: $105 ($125 for international students). Electronic applications accepted. *Financial support:* Fellowships, research assistantships with full tuition reimbursements, teaching assistantships, institutionally sponsored loans, traineeships, health care benefits, and unspecified assistantships available. Financial award applicants required to submit FAFSA. *Faculty research:* Molecular biology and genetics of viruses, bacteria, and yeast; immune response; molecular biology of cultured animal cells; genetic basis of cancer; genetics and physiology of infectious agents. *Unit head:* Rozanne M. Sandri-Goldin, Chair, 949-824-7570, Fax: 949-824-8598, E-mail: rmsandri@uci.edu. *Application contact:* Janet Horwitz, Graduate Student Coordinator, 949-824-7669, E-mail: horwitz@uci.edu.
Website: http://www.microbiology.uci.edu/graduate-students.asp

University of California, Los Angeles, David Geffen School of Medicine and Graduate Division, Graduate Programs in Medicine, Department of Microbiology, Immunology and Molecular Genetics, Los Angeles, CA 90095. Offers MS, PhD. *Degree requirements:* For master's, thesis; for doctorate, thesis/dissertation, oral and written qualifying exams; 2 quarters of teaching experience. *Entrance requirements:* For master's and doctorate, GRE General Test, bachelor's degree; minimum undergraduate GPA of 3.0 (or its equivalent if letter grade system not used). Additional exam requirements/recommendations for international students: Required—TOEFL. Electronic applications accepted.

University of California, Riverside, Graduate Division, Program in Microbiology, Riverside, CA 92521-0102. Offers MS, PhD. *Program availability:* Part-time. Terminal master's awarded for partial completion of doctoral program. *Degree requirements:* For master's, thesis; for doctorate, thesis/dissertation, qualifying exams. *Entrance requirements:* For master's and doctorate, GRE General Test, minimum GPA of 3.2. Additional exam requirements/recommendations for international students: Required—TOEFL (minimum score 550 paper-based; 80 iBT). Electronic applications accepted. *Expenses:* Tuition, state resident: full-time $5746. Tuition, nonresident: full-time $10,780. Tuition and fees vary according to campus/location and program. *Faculty research:* Host-pathogen interactions; environmental microbiology; bioremediation; molecular microbiology; microbial genetics, physiology, and pathogenesis.

University of Chicago, Division of the Biological Sciences, Committee on Microbiology, Chicago, IL 60637. Offers PhD. *Students:* 22 full-time (16 women); includes 6 minority (1 Black or African American, non-Hispanic/Latino; 2 Asian, non-Hispanic/Latino; 1 Hispanic/Latino; 2 Two or more races, non-Hispanic/Latino), 4 international. Average age 25. 83 applicants, 14% accepted, 4 enrolled. In 2017, 4 doctorates awarded. *Degree requirements:* For doctorate, thesis/dissertation, ethics class, 2 teaching assistantships. *Entrance requirements:* For doctorate, GRE General Test, transcripts, statement of purpose, 3 letters of recommendation. Additional exam requirements/recommendations for international students: Required—TOEFL (minimum score 600 paper-based; 104 iBT), IELTS (minimum score 7). *Application deadline:* For fall admission, 12/1 for domestic and international students. Application fee: $90. Electronic applications accepted. *Financial support:* In 2017–18, 18 students received support, including fellowships with full tuition reimbursements available (averaging $31,000 per year), research assistantships with full tuition reimbursements available (averaging $31,000 per year); institutionally sponsored loans, scholarships/grants, traineeships, and health care benefits also available. Financial award application deadline: 12/1. *Faculty research:* Pathophysiology of microbial infection, evolutionary ecology of plant-microbe interactions, virology, microbiomes, host-microbe interactions. *Unit head:* Sean Crosson, PhD, Chair, E-mail: biomed@bsd.uchicago.edu. *Application contact:* Lisa Abston-Leftridge, PhD, Administrator, 773-834-3899, E-mail: biomed@bsd.uchicago.edu.
Website: http://biomedsciences.uchicago.edu/page/microbiology

University of Cincinnati, Graduate School, College of Medicine, Graduate Programs in Biomedical Sciences, Department of Molecular Genetics, Biochemistry and Microbiology, Cincinnati, OH 45221. Offers MS, PhD. Terminal master's awarded for partial completion of doctoral program. *Degree requirements:* For master's, thesis or alternative; for doctorate, thesis/dissertation, qualifying exam. *Entrance requirements:* For master's and doctorate, GRE General Test. Additional exam requirements/recommendations for international students: Required—TOEFL (minimum score 600 paper-based; 100 iBT), TWE. Electronic applications accepted. *Expenses: Tuition, area resident:* Full-time $14,468. Tuition, state resident: full-time $14,968; part-time $754 per credit hour. Tuition, nonresident: full-time $24,210; part-time $1311 per credit hour. *International tuition:* $26,460 full-time. *Required fees:* $3958; $84 per credit hour. One-time fee: $85 full-time. Tuition and fees vary according to course load, degree level and program. *Faculty research:* Cancer biology and developmental genetics, gene regulation and chromosome structure, microbiology and pathogenic mechanisms, structural biology, membrane biochemistry and signal transduction.

University of Colorado Denver, School of Medicine, Program in Microbiology, Aurora, CO 80206. Offers microbiology (PhD); microbiology and immunology (PhD). In 2017, 3 doctorates awarded. *Entrance requirements:* For doctorate, GRE, three letters of reference, two copies of official transcripts, minimum GPA of 3.0. Application fee: $0. *Faculty research:* Molecular mechanisms of picornavirus replication, mechanisms of papovavirus assembly, human immune response in multiple sclerosis. *Unit head:* Dr.

John Cambier, Chair, 303-724-8663, E-mail: john.cambier@ucdenver.edu. *Application contact:* Elizabeth Wethington, Program Administrator, 303-724-7280, E-mail: elizabeth.wethington@ucdenver.edu.
Website: http://www.ucdenver.edu/academics/colleges/medicalschool/departments/ImmunologyMicrobiology/Pages/welcome.aspx

University of Connecticut, Graduate School, College of Liberal Arts and Sciences, Department of Molecular and Cell Biology, Storrs, CT 06269. Offers applied genomics (PSM); cell and developmental biology (MS, PhD); genetics and genomics (MS, PhD); microbial systems analysis (PSM); microbiology (MS, PhD); structural biology, biochemistry and biophysics (MS, PhD). Terminal master's awarded for partial completion of doctoral program. *Degree requirements:* For master's, comprehensive exam; for doctorate, thesis/dissertation. *Entrance requirements:* For master's and doctorate, GRE General Test, GRE Subject Test. Additional exam requirements/recommendations for international students: Required—TOEFL (minimum score 550 paper-based). Electronic applications accepted.

University of Delaware, College of Arts and Sciences, Department of Biological Sciences, Newark, DE 19716. Offers biotechnology (MS); cancer biology (MS, PhD); cell and extracellular matrix biology (MS, PhD); cell and systems physiology (MS, PhD); developmental biology (MS, PhD); ecology and evolution (MS, PhD); microbiology (MS, PhD); molecular biology and genetics (MS, PhD). Terminal master's awarded for partial completion of doctoral program. *Degree requirements:* For master's, thesis, preliminary exam; for doctorate, comprehensive exam, thesis/dissertation, preliminary exam. *Entrance requirements:* For master's and doctorate, GRE General Test. Additional exam requirements/recommendations for international students: Required—TOEFL (minimum score 600 paper-based); Recommended—TWE. Electronic applications accepted. *Faculty research:* Microorganisms, bone, cancer metastasis, developmental biology, cell biology, DNA.

University of Florida, College of Medicine, Department of Molecular Genetics and Microbiology, Gainesville, FL 32610-0266. Offers MS. Terminal master's awarded for partial completion of doctoral program. *Degree requirements:* For master's, thesis. *Entrance requirements:* For master's, GRE General Test, minimum GPA of 3.0. Additional exam requirements/recommendations for international students: Required—TOEFL, IELTS. Electronic applications accepted.

University of Florida, College of Medicine and Graduate School, Interdisciplinary Program in Biomedical Sciences, Concentration in Immunology and Microbiology, Gainesville, FL 32611. Offers PhD. *Degree requirements:* For doctorate, thesis/dissertation. *Entrance requirements:* For doctorate, GRE General Test, minimum GPA of 3.0, biochemistry before enrollment. Additional exam requirements/recommendations for international students: Required—TOEFL. Electronic applications accepted.

University of Florida, Graduate School, College of Agricultural and Life Sciences, Department of Microbiology and Cell Science, Gainesville, FL 32611. Offers microbiology and cell science (MS, PhD), including medical microbiology and biochemistry (MS), toxicology (PhD). *Degree requirements:* For master's, comprehensive exam, thesis (for some programs); for doctorate, comprehensive exam, thesis/dissertation. *Entrance requirements:* For master's and doctorate, GRE General Test, minimum GPA of 3.0. Additional exam requirements/recommendations for international students: Required—TOEFL (minimum score 550 paper-based; 80 iBT), IELTS (minimum score 6). Electronic applications accepted. *Faculty research:* Biomass conversion, membrane and cell wall chemistry, plant biochemistry and genetics.

University of Georgia, Franklin College of Arts and Sciences, Department of Microbiology, Athens, GA 30602. Offers MS, PhD. *Degree requirements:* For master's, thesis; for doctorate, one foreign language, thesis/dissertation. *Entrance requirements:* For master's and doctorate, GRE General Test. Additional exam requirements/recommendations for international students: Required—TOEFL (minimum score 560 paper-based). Electronic applications accepted.

University of Guelph, Graduate Studies, College of Biological Science, Department of Molecular and Cellular Biology, Guelph, ON N1G 2W1, Canada. Offers biochemistry (M Sc, PhD); biophysics (M Sc, PhD); botany (M Sc, PhD); microbiology (M Sc, PhD); molecular biology and genetics (M Sc, PhD). *Degree requirements:* For master's, thesis, research proposal; for doctorate, comprehensive exam, thesis/dissertation, research proposal. *Entrance requirements:* For master's, minimum B-average during previous 2 years of coursework; for doctorate, minimum A-average. Additional exam requirements/recommendations for international students: Required—TOEFL (minimum score 550 paper-based), IELTS (minimum score 6.5). Electronic applications accepted. *Faculty research:* Physiology, structure, genetics, and ecology of microbes; virology and microbial technology.

University of Hawaii at Manoa, Office of Graduate Education, College of Natural Sciences, Department of Microbiology, Honolulu, HI 96822. Offers MS, PhD. *Program availability:* Part-time. *Degree requirements:* For master's, thesis optional; for doctorate, comprehensive exam, thesis/dissertation. *Entrance requirements:* For master's and doctorate, GRE General Test. Additional exam requirements/recommendations for international students: Required—TOEFL (minimum score 580 paper-based; 92 iBT), IELTS (minimum score 5). *Faculty research:* Virology, immunology, microbial physiology, medical microbiology, bacterial genetics.

University of Idaho, College of Graduate Studies, College of Science, Department of Biological Sciences, Moscow, ID 83844. Offers biology (MS, PhD); microbiology, molecular biology and biochemistry (PhD). *Faculty:* 19 full-time (6 women). *Students:* 22. Average age 28. In 2017, 2 master's, 6 doctorates awarded. *Degree requirements:* For doctorate, thesis/dissertation. *Entrance requirements:* For master's and doctorate, GRE, minimum GPA of 3.0. Additional exam requirements/recommendations for international students: Required—TOEFL (minimum score 79 iBT). *Application deadline:* For fall admission, 8/1 for domestic students; for spring admission, 12/15 for domestic students. Applications are processed on a rolling basis. Application fee: $60. Electronic applications accepted. *Expenses:* Tuition, state resident: full-time $6722; part-time $430 per credit hour. Tuition, nonresident: full-time $23,046; part-time $1337 per credit hour. *Required fees:* $2142; $63 per credit hour. *Financial support:* Research assistantships and teaching assistantships available. Financial award applicants required to submit FAFSA. *Faculty research:* Animal behavior development, germ cell development, intraflagellar transport, molecular mechanisms, molecular chaperones. *Unit head:* Dr. James J. Nagler, Chair, 208-885-6280, E-mail: biosci@uidaho.edu. *Application contact:* Sean Scoggin, Graduate Recruitment Coordinator, 208-885-4723, Fax: 208-885-4406, E-mail: graduateadmissions@uidaho.edu.
Website: https://www.uidaho.edu/sci/biology

University of Illinois at Chicago, College of Medicine and Graduate College, Graduate Programs in Medicine, Department of Microbiology and Immunology, Chicago, IL 60607-7128. Offers PhD, MD/PhD. *Degree requirements:* For doctorate, thesis/dissertation. *Entrance requirements:* For doctorate, GRE General Test, minimum GPA of 2.75. Additional exam requirements/recommendations for international students: Required—TOEFL. *Faculty research:* Class I major histocompatibility complex molecules; proteins such as azurin with the immunoglobulin folds; T cell immunobiology relevant to disease pathogenesis, immunotherapeutics and vaccines for HIV/AIDS, tuberculosis, AIDS-related tuberculosis, and malaria, plague and smallpox; intracellular bacterial pathogen Listeria monocytogenes; virus infection.

University of Illinois at Urbana–Champaign, Graduate College, College of Liberal Arts and Sciences, School of Molecular and Cellular Biology, Department of Microbiology, Champaign, IL 61820. Offers MS, PhD.

The University of Iowa, Roy J. and Lucille A. Carver College of Medicine and Graduate College, Graduate Programs in Medicine, Department of Microbiology, Iowa City, IA 52242-1316. Offers general microbiology and microbial physiology (MS, PhD); immunology (MS, PhD); microbial genetics (MS, PhD); pathogenic bacteriology (MS, PhD); virology (MS, PhD). *Degree requirements:* For master's, thesis; for doctorate, comprehensive exam, thesis/dissertation. *Entrance requirements:* For master's and doctorate, GRE General Test. Additional exam requirements/recommendations for international students: Required—TOEFL (minimum score 600 paper-based). Electronic applications accepted. *Faculty research:* Gene regulation, processing and transport of HIV, retroviral pathogenesis, biodegradation, biofilm.

The University of Kansas, Graduate Studies, College of Liberal Arts and Sciences, Department of Molecular Biosciences, Lawrence, KS 66044. Offers biochemistry and biophysics (PhD); microbiology (PhD); molecular, cellular, and developmental biology (PhD). *Program availability:* Part-time. *Students:* 57 full-time (38 women); includes 8 minority (1 Black or African American, non-Hispanic/Latino; 2 Asian, non-Hispanic/Latino; 3 Hispanic/Latino; 2 Two or more races, non-Hispanic/Latino), 27 international. Average age 27. 73 applicants, 33% accepted, 8 enrolled. In 2017, 6 doctorates awarded. Terminal master's awarded for partial completion of doctoral program. *Entrance requirements:* For doctorate, GRE General Test, 1-page statement of research interests and goals, 1-2 page curriculum vitae or resume, official transcript, 3 recommendation letters. Additional exam requirements/recommendations for international students: Required—TOEFL or IELTS. *Application deadline:* For fall admission, 12/1 for domestic and international students. Application fee: $65 ($85 for international students). Electronic applications accepted. *Financial support:* Fellowships, research assistantships, teaching assistantships, scholarships/grants, health care benefits, and unspecified assistantships available. Financial award application deadline: 12/1. *Faculty research:* Structure and function of proteins, genetics of organism development, molecular genetics, neurophysiology, molecular virology and pathogenics, developmental biology, cell biology. *Unit head:* Susan M. Egan, Chair, 785-864-4294, E-mail: sme@ku.edu. *Application contact:* John Connolly, Graduate Admissions Contact, 785-864-4311, E-mail: jconnolly@ku.edu.
Website: http://www.molecularbiosciences.ku.edu/

The University of Kansas, University of Kansas Medical Center, School of Medicine, Department of Microbiology, Molecular Genetics and Immunology, Kansas City, KS 66160. Offers MS, PhD, MD/PhD. *Faculty:* 13. *Students:* 15 full-time (7 women), 1 part-time (0 women); includes 2 minority (1 Asian, non-Hispanic/Latino; 1 Two or more races, non-Hispanic/Latino), 6 international. Average age 27. 28 applicants, 7% accepted, 2 enrolled. In 2017, 4 doctorates awarded. Terminal master's awarded for partial completion of doctoral program. *Degree requirements:* For master's, thesis; for doctorate, comprehensive exam, thesis/dissertation. *Entrance requirements:* For master's and doctorate, GRE General Test, B Sc. Additional exam requirements/recommendations for international students: Required—TOEFL or IELTS. *Application deadline:* For fall admission, 1/1 priority date for domestic and international students. Applications are processed on a rolling basis. Application fee: $60. Electronic applications accepted. *Financial support:* Research assistantships with full tuition reimbursements, teaching assistantships with full tuition reimbursements, and unspecified assistantships available. Financial award application deadline: 3/1; financial award applicants required to submit FAFSA. *Faculty research:* Immunology, infectious disease, virology, molecular genetics, bacteriology. *Total annual research expenditures:* $3.9 million. *Unit head:* Dr. Joseph Lutkenhaus, Professor/Chair, 913-588-7054, Fax: 913-588-7295, E-mail: jlutkenh@kumc.edu. *Application contact:* Dr. Jianming Qiu, Microbiology Graduate Program Director, 913-588-4329, Fax: 913-588-7295, E-mail: jqiu@kumc.edu.
Website: http://www.kumc.edu/school-of-medicine/microbiology-molecular-genetics-and-immunology.html

University of Kentucky, Graduate School, Graduate School Programs from the College of Medicine, Program in Microbiology and Immunology, Lexington, KY 40506-0032. Offers PhD. *Degree requirements:* For doctorate, comprehensive exam, thesis/dissertation. *Entrance requirements:* For doctorate, GRE General Test, minimum undergraduate GPA of 2.75. Additional exam requirements/recommendations for international students: Required—TOEFL (minimum score 550 paper-based). Electronic applications accepted.

University of Louisville, School of Medicine, Department of Microbiology and Immunology, Louisville, KY 40292-0001. Offers MS, PhD, MD/PhD. *Program availability:* Part-time. *Students:* 34 full-time (20 women), 6 part-time (5 women); includes 7 minority (2 Black or African American, non-Hispanic/Latino; 1 Hispanic/Latino; 4 Two or more races, non-Hispanic/Latino), 10 international. Average age 29. 36 applicants, 25% accepted, 8 enrolled. Terminal master's awarded for partial completion of doctoral program. *Degree requirements:* For master's, comprehensive exam, thesis or alternative; for doctorate, comprehensive exam, thesis/dissertation. *Entrance requirements:* For master's and doctorate, GRE General Test (minimum score of 300 verbal and quantitative), minimum GPA of 3.0; 1 year of course work in biology and organic chemistry; 1 semester of course work in introductory calculus and biochemistry. Additional exam requirements/recommendations for international students: Required—TOEFL (minimum score 550 paper-based; 79 iBT), IELTS (minimum score 6.5). *Application deadline:* For fall admission, 3/1 priority date for domestic and international students. Applications are processed on a rolling basis. Application fee: $65. Electronic applications accepted. *Expenses:* Tuition, state resident: full-time $12,246; part-time $681 per credit hour. Tuition, nonresident: full-time $25,486; part-time $1417 per credit hour. *Required fees:* $196. Tuition and fees vary according to course load, program and reciprocity agreements. *Financial support:* In 2017–18, fellowships with full tuition reimbursements (averaging $25,500 per year), research assistantships with full tuition reimbursements (averaging $25,500 per year) were awarded; health care benefits also available. Financial award application deadline: 3/1. *Faculty research:* Biodefense/emerging infectious diseases; autoimmune disease and basic immune mechanisms; bacterial and viral pathogenesis; vaccines; tumor immunity. *Total annual research expenditures:* $4.7 million. *Unit head:* Dr. Nejat Egilmez, Chair, 502-852-5351, Fax: 502-852-7531, E-mail: nejat.egilmez@louisville.edu. *Application contact:* Carolyn Burton, Graduate Program Coordinator, 502-852-6208, Fax: 502-852-7531, E-mail: cmburt01@louisville.edu.
Website: http://louisville.edu/medicine/departments/microbiology

University of Maine, Graduate School, College of Natural Sciences, Forestry, and Agriculture, Department of Molecular and Biomedical Sciences, Orono, ME 04469. Offers microbiology (PhD). *Faculty:* 11 full-time (5 women), 7 part-time/adjunct (3 women). *Students:* 18 full-time (10 women), 5 part-time (4 women); includes 2 minority (both Asian, non-Hispanic/Latino), 5 international. Average age 29. 25 applicants, 28% accepted, 6 enrolled. In 2017, 3 master's, 2 doctorates awarded. *Degree requirements:* For master's, thesis (for some programs); for doctorate, comprehensive exam, thesis/dissertation. *Entrance requirements:* For master's and doctorate, GRE General Test. Additional exam requirements/recommendations for international students: Required—

TOEFL (minimum score 580 paper-based; 92 iBT), IELTS (minimum score 7). *Application deadline:* For fall admission, 1/15 for domestic and international students; for spring admission, 9/15 for domestic and international students. Applications are processed on a rolling basis. Application fee: $65. Electronic applications accepted. *Expenses:* Tuition, state resident: full-time $7722; part-time $429 per credit hour. Tuition, nonresident: full-time $25,146; part-time $1397 per credit hour. *Required fees:* $1162; $581 per credit hour. *Financial support:* In 2017–18, 19 students received support, including 1 fellowship with full tuition reimbursement available (averaging $23,100 per year), 7 research assistantships with full tuition reimbursements available (averaging $23,300 per year), 11 teaching assistantships with full tuition reimbursements available (averaging $21,700 per year); tuition waivers (full and partial) also available. Financial award application deadline: 3/1. *Faculty research:* Immunology and microbiology, bioinformatics, molecular and cellular toxicology, zebrafish, signal transduction, protein biochemistry. *Total annual research expenditures:* $1.6 million. *Unit head:* Dr. Robert Gundersen, Chair, 207-581-2802, Fax: 207-581-2801. *Application contact:* Scott G. Delcourt, Assistant Vice President for Graduate Studies and Senior Associate Dean, 207-581-3291, Fax: 207-581-3232, E-mail: graduate@maine.edu.
Website: http://umaine.edu/biomed/

The University of Manchester, School of Biological Sciences, Manchester, United Kingdom. Offers adaptive organismal biology (M Phil, PhD); animal biology (M Phil, PhD); biochemistry (M Phil, PhD); bioinformatics (M Phil, PhD); biomolecular sciences (M Phil, PhD); biotechnology (M Phil, PhD); cell biology (M Phil, PhD); cell matrix research (M Phil, PhD); channels and transporters (M Phil, PhD); developmental biology (M Phil, PhD); environmental biology (M Phil, PhD); evolutionary biology (M Phil, PhD); gene expression (M Phil, PhD); genetics (M Phil, PhD); history of science, technology and medicine (M Phil, PhD); immunology (M Phil, PhD); integrative neurobiology and behavior (M Phil, PhD); membrane trafficking (M Phil, PhD); microbiology (M Phil, PhD); molecular and cellular neuroscience (M Phil, PhD); molecular biology (M Phil, PhD); molecular cancer studies (M Phil, PhD); neuroscience (M Phil, PhD); ophthalmology (M Phil, PhD); optometry (M Phil, PhD); organelle function (M Phil, PhD); pharmacology (M Phil, PhD); physiology (M Phil, PhD); plant sciences (M Phil, PhD); stem cell research (M Phil, PhD); structural biology (M Phil, PhD); systems neuroscience (M Phil, PhD); toxicology (M Phil, PhD).

University of Manitoba, Faculty of Graduate Studies, Faculty of Science, Department of Microbiology, Winnipeg, MB R3T 2N2, Canada. Offers M Sc, PhD. *Degree requirements:* For master's, thesis; for doctorate, one foreign language, thesis/dissertation.

University of Maryland, Baltimore, Graduate School, Graduate Program in Life Sciences, Program in Molecular Microbiology and Immunology, Baltimore, MD 21201. Offers PhD, MD/PhD. *Students:* 42 full-time (22 women); includes 13 minority (5 Black or African American, non-Hispanic/Latino; 4 Asian, non-Hispanic/Latino; 1 Hispanic/Latino; 3 Two or more races, non-Hispanic/Latino), 2 international. Average age 28. 101 applicants, 11% accepted, 3 enrolled. In 2017, 11 doctorates awarded. *Degree requirements:* For doctorate, comprehensive exam, thesis/dissertation. *Entrance requirements:* For doctorate, GRE General Test, minimum GPA of 3.0, curriculum vitae, essay, 3 letters of recommendation. Additional exam requirements/recommendations for international students: Required—TOEFL (minimum score 80 iBT); Recommended—IELTS (minimum score 7). *Application deadline:* For fall admission, 1/15 for domestic and international students. Application fee: $75. Electronic applications accepted. *Expenses:* Tuition, state resident: full-time $13,990; part-time $661 per credit. Tuition, nonresident: full-time $30,484; part-time $1310 per credit. *Required fees:* $1894; $94 per credit. $415 per semester. Part-time tuition and fees vary according to course load, degree level and program. *Financial support:* In 2017–18, research assistantships with partial tuition reimbursements (averaging $26,000 per year) were awarded; fellowships and health care benefits also available. Financial award application deadline: 3/1; financial award applicants required to submit FAFSA. *Unit head:* Dr. Brett Hassel, Director, 410-706-2344, E-mail: bhassel@som.umaryland.edu. *Application contact:* June Green, Program Coordinator, 410-706-7126, Fax: 410-706-2129, E-mail: jgreen@umaryland.edu.
Website: http://lifesciences.umaryland.edu/microbiology/

★ **University of Massachusetts Amherst,** Graduate School, College of Natural Sciences, Department of Microbiology, Amherst, MA 01003. Offers MS, PhD. *Program availability:* Part-time. Terminal master's awarded for partial completion of doctoral program. *Degree requirements:* For master's, thesis or alternative; for doctorate, comprehensive exam, thesis/dissertation. *Entrance requirements:* For master's and doctorate, GRE General Test. Additional exam requirements/recommendations for international students: Required—TOEFL (minimum score 550 paper-based; 80 iBT), IELTS (minimum score 6.5). Electronic applications accepted. *Faculty research:* Microbial physiology, genetics, immunology, parasitology, pathogenic bacteriology.

See Display below and Close-Up on page 305.

University of Massachusetts Medical School, Graduate School of Biomedical Sciences, Worcester, MA 01655-0115. Offers biomedical sciences (PhD), including biochemistry and molecular pharmacology, bioinformatics and computational biology, cancer biology, immunology and microbiology, interdisciplinary, neuroscience, translational science; biomedical sciences (millennium program) (PhD); clinical and population health research (PhD); clinical investigation (MS). *Faculty:* 1,316 full-time (526 women), 357 part-time/adjunct (229 women). *Students:* 347 full-time (180 women); includes 61 minority (10 Black or African American, non-Hispanic/Latino; 1 American Indian or Alaska Native, non-Hispanic/Latino; 35 Asian, non-Hispanic/Latino; 15 Hispanic/Latino), 130 international. Average age 29. 608 applicants, 28% accepted, 54 enrolled. In 2017, 6 master's, 51 doctorates awarded. Terminal master's awarded for partial completion of doctoral program. *Degree requirements:* For master's, comprehensive exam, thesis; for doctorate, comprehensive exam, thesis/dissertation. *Entrance requirements:* For master's, MD, PhD, DVM, or PharmD; for doctorate, GRE General Test, bachelor's degree. Additional exam requirements/recommendations for international students: Required—TOEFL (minimum score 90 iBT) or IELTS (minimum score 7.0). *Application deadline:* For fall admission, 12/15 for domestic and international students. Applications are processed on a rolling basis. Application fee: $80. Electronic applications accepted. Application fee is waived when completed online. *Expenses:* $14,883 in-state tuition and mandatory fees; $31,486 out-of-state. *Financial support:* In 2017–18, 15 fellowships with partial tuition reimbursements (averaging $29,000 per year), 296 research assistantships with full tuition reimbursements (averaging $31,212 per year) were awarded; institutionally sponsored loans and scholarships/grants also available. Financial award application deadline: 5/15. *Faculty research:* RNA biology, molecular/cell/developmental/metabolic biology, bioinformatics and computational biology, clinical/translational research, infectious disease and immunology. *Total annual research expenditures:* $279 million. *Unit head:* Dr. Mary Ellen Lane, Dean, 508-856-4018, E-mail: maryellen.lane@umassmed.edu. *Application contact:* Dr. Kendall Knight, Assistant Vice Provost for Admissions, 508-856-5628, Fax: 508-856-3659, E-mail: kendall.knight@umassmed.edu.
Website: http://www.umassmed.edu/gsbs/

University of Miami, Graduate School, Miller School of Medicine, Graduate Programs in Medicine, Department of Microbiology and Immunology, Coral Gables, FL 33124. Offers PhD, MD/PhD. *Degree requirements:* For doctorate, thesis/dissertation, oral and written qualifying exams. *Entrance requirements:* For doctorate, GRE General Test. Additional exam requirements/recommendations for international students: Required—TOEFL. Electronic applications accepted. *Faculty research:* Cellular and molecular immunology, molecular and pathogenic virology, pathogenic bacteriology and gene therapy of cancer.

University of Michigan, Rackham Graduate School, Program in Biomedical Sciences (PIBS), Department of Microbiology and Immunology, Ann Arbor, MI 48109-5620. Offers MS, PhD. *Program availability:* Part-time. *Faculty:* 25 full-time (14 women), 15 part-time/adjunct (4 women). *Students:* 40 full-time (21 women), 3 part-time (2 women); includes 6 minority (2 Black or African American, non-Hispanic/Latino; 3 Asian, non-Hispanic/Latino; 1 Hispanic/Latino), 2 international. Average age 27. 147 applicants, 10% accepted, 7 enrolled. In 2017, 4 master's, 9 doctorates awarded. Terminal master's awarded for partial completion of doctoral program. *Degree requirements:* For master's, thesis optional; for doctorate, comprehensive exam, thesis/dissertation, oral defense of dissertation, preliminary exam. *Entrance requirements:* For master's and doctorate, GRE General Test. Additional exam requirements/recommendations for international students: Required—TOEFL (minimum score 600 paper-based; 84 iBT), TWE. *Application deadline:* For fall admission, 12/1 for domestic and international students. Application fee: $75. Electronic applications accepted. *Expenses:* Tuition, state resident: full-time $22,368; part-time $1201 per credit hour. Tuition, nonresident: full-time $45,156; part-time $2467 per credit hour. *Required fees:* $376 per term. Tuition and fees vary according to course load, degree level and program. *Financial support:* In 2017–18, 15 fellowships with full tuition reimbursements (averaging $28,500 per year), 20 research assistantships with full tuition reimbursements (averaging $28,500 per year) were awarded; scholarships/grants, health care benefits, and tuition waivers (full) also available. Financial award application deadline: 5/15. *Faculty research:* Mechanisms by which viruses, bacteria, fungi, and parasites elicit pathogenesis in the infected host; viral pathogens; bacterial pathogens; eukaryotic pathogens; innate immunity; adaptive immunity cell biology of infection. *Total annual research expenditures:* $10.2 million. *Unit head:* Dr. Harry L. T. Mobley, Chair, 734-764-1466, Fax: 734-764-3562, E-mail: hmobley@umich.edu. *Application contact:* Heidi Thompson, Senior Student Administrative Assistant, 734-763-3532, Fax: 734-764-3562, E-mail: heiditho@umich.edu.
Website: http://www.med.umich.edu/microbio/

University of Minnesota, Twin Cities Campus, Graduate School, PhD Program in Microbiology, Immunology and Cancer Biology, Minneapolis, MN 55455-0213. Offers PhD. *Degree requirements:* For doctorate, thesis/dissertation. *Entrance requirements:* For doctorate, GRE General Test. Additional exam requirements/recommendations for international students: Required—TOEFL (minimum score 600 paper-based). Electronic applications accepted. *Faculty research:* Virology, microbiology, cancer biology, immunology.

University of Mississippi Medical Center, School of Graduate Studies in the Health Sciences, Department of Microbiology, Jackson, MS 39216-4505. Offers PhD, MD/PhD. *Degree requirements:* For doctorate, comprehensive exam, thesis/dissertation, first authored publication. *Entrance requirements:* For doctorate, GRE General Test (minimum score of 300), minimum GPA of 3.0. Additional exam requirements/recommendations for international students: Recommended—TOEFL (minimum score 550 paper-based; 79 iBT), IELTS (minimum score 6.5), TSE (minimum score 53). Electronic applications accepted. *Faculty research:* Host-pathogen interaction, microbial population genetics, immunology, virology, parasitology.

University of Missouri, School of Medicine and Office of Research and Graduate Studies, Graduate Programs in Medicine, Department of Molecular Microbiology and Immunology, Columbia, MO 65211. Offers PhD. Terminal master's awarded for partial completion of doctoral program. *Degree requirements:* For doctorate, thesis/dissertation. *Entrance requirements:* For doctorate, GRE General Test, minimum GPA of 3.0. Additional exam requirements/recommendations for international students: Required—TOEFL. *Expenses:* Tuition, state resident: full-time $6480. Tuition, nonresident: full-time $17,744. *Required fees:* $1108. Tuition and fees vary according to course load, campus/location and program. *Financial support:* Fellowships, research assistantships, teaching assistantships, institutionally sponsored loans, scholarships/grants, traineeships, health care benefits, and unspecified assistantships available. Support available to part-time students. *Unit head:* Dr. Donald H. Burke-Aguero, Interim Chair. *Application contact:* Dr. Donald H. Burke-Aguero, Interim Chair.
Website: http://medicine.missouri.edu/education/phd.html

University of Montana, Graduate School, College of Humanities and Sciences, Division of Biological Sciences, Program in Cellular, Molecular and Microbial Biology, Missoula, MT 59812. Offers cellular and developmental biology (PhD); microbial evolution and ecology (PhD); microbiology and immunology (PhD); molecular biology and biochemistry (PhD). Terminal master's awarded for partial completion of doctoral program. *Degree requirements:* For doctorate, variable foreign language requirement, thesis/dissertation. *Entrance requirements:* For doctorate, GRE General Test. *Faculty research:* Ribosome structure, medical microbiology/pathogenesis, microbial ecology/environmental microbiology.

University of New Hampshire, Graduate School, College of Life Sciences and Agriculture, Department of Molecular, Cellular and Biomedical Sciences, Program in Microbiology, Durham, NH 03824. Offers MS, PhD. *Program availability:* Part-time. *Students:* 6 full-time (2 women), 6 part-time (3 women); includes 2 minority (1 Hispanic/Latino; 1 Two or more races, non-Hispanic/Latino). Average age 25. 27 applicants, 30% accepted, 4 enrolled. In 2017, 1 master's awarded. Terminal master's awarded for partial completion of doctoral program. *Entrance requirements:* For master's and doctorate, GRE General Test. Additional exam requirements/recommendations for international students: Required—TOEFL (minimum score 550 paper-based; 80 iBT). *Application deadline:* For fall admission, 1/15 for domestic and international students. Application fee: $65. Electronic applications accepted. *Financial support:* In 2017–18, 12 students received support, including 3 research assistantships, 9 teaching assistantships; fellowships, career-related internships or fieldwork, Federal Work-Study, scholarships/grants, and tuition waivers (full and partial) also available. Support available to part-time students. Financial award application deadline: 2/15. *Unit head:* Rick Cote, Chair, 603-862-2458. *Application contact:* Paul Boisselle, Administrative Assistant, 603-862-4814, E-mail: paul.boisselle@unh.edu.
Website: http://colsa.unh.edu/mcbs/microbiology/microbiology-ms

University of New Mexico, Graduate Studies, Health Sciences Center, Program in Biomedical Sciences, Albuquerque, NM 87131-5196. Offers biochemistry and molecular biology (MS, PhD); cell biology and physiology (MS, PhD); molecular genetics and microbiology (MS, PhD); neuroscience (MS, PhD); pathology (MS, PhD); toxicology (MS, PhD). *Program availability:* Part-time. *Students:* Average age 29. 61 applicants, 16% accepted, 10 enrolled. In 2017, 11 master's, 14 doctorates awarded. Terminal master's awarded for partial completion of doctoral program. *Degree requirements:* For master's, thesis; for doctorate, comprehensive exam, thesis/dissertation, qualifying exam at the end of year 1/core curriculum. *Entrance requirements:* For master's and doctorate, GRE General Test, minimum undergraduate GPA of 3.0. Additional exam requirements/recommendations for international students: Required—TOEFL. *Application deadline:* For fall admission, 3/1 priority date for domestic and international students. Applications are processed on a rolling basis. Application fee: $50. Electronic applications accepted. *Financial support:* Fellowships, research assistantships with full tuition reimbursements, teaching assistantships, career-related internships or fieldwork, Federal Work-Study, institutionally sponsored loans, scholarships/grants, traineeships, health care benefits, and unspecified assistantships available. Financial award application deadline: 1/1; financial award applicants required to submit FAFSA. *Faculty research:* Infectious disease/immunity, cancer biology, cardiovascular and metabolic diseases, brain and behavioral illness, environmental health. *Unit head:* Dr. Helen J. Hathaway, Program Director, 505-272-1887, Fax: 505-272-2412, E-mail: hhathaway@salud.unm.edu. *Application contact:* Mary Fenton, Admissions Coordinator, 505-272-1887, Fax: 505-272-2412, E-mail: mfenton@salud.unm.edu.

The University of North Carolina at Chapel Hill, School of Medicine and Graduate School, Graduate Programs in Medicine, Department of Microbiology and Immunology, Chapel Hill, NC 27599-7290. Offers immunology (MS, PhD); microbiology (MS, PhD). Terminal master's awarded for partial completion of doctoral program. *Degree requirements:* For master's, comprehensive exam, thesis; for doctorate, comprehensive exam, thesis/dissertation. *Entrance requirements:* For master's and doctorate, GRE General Test, minimum GPA of 3.0. Electronic applications accepted. *Faculty research:* HIV pathogenesis, immune response, t-cell mediated autoimmunity, alpha-viruses, bacterial chemotaxis, francisella tularensis, pertussis, Mycobacterium tuberculosis, Burkholderia, Dengue virus.

University of North Texas Health Science Center at Fort Worth, Graduate School of Biomedical Sciences, Fort Worth, TX 76107-2699. Offers biochemistry and cancer biology (MS, PhD); biotechnology (MS); cell biology, immunology and microbiology (MS, PhD); clinical research management (MS); forensic genetics (MS); genetics (MS, PhD); integrative physiology (MS, PhD); medical sciences (MS); pharmaceutical sciences and pharmacotherapy (MS, PhD); pharmacology and neuroscience (MS, PhD); structural anatomy and rehabilitation sciences (MS, PhD); DO/MS; DO/PhD. Terminal master's awarded for partial completion of doctoral program. *Degree requirements:* For master's, thesis; for doctorate, thesis/dissertation. *Entrance requirements:* For master's and doctorate, GRE General Test. Additional exam requirements/recommendations for international students: Required—TOEFL. *Expenses:* Contact institution. *Faculty research:* Alzheimer's disease, aging, eye diseases, cancer, cardiovascular disease.

University of Oklahoma, College of Arts and Sciences, Department of Microbiology and Plant Biology, Program in Microbiology, Norman, OK 73019. Offers MS, PhD. *Students:* 8 full-time (4 women), 17 part-time (8 women); includes 7 minority (1 American Indian or Alaska Native, non-Hispanic/Latino; 2 Asian, non-Hispanic/Latino; 2 Hispanic/Latino; 2 Two or more races, non-Hispanic/Latino), 8 international. Average age 28. 25 applicants, 20% accepted, 2 enrolled. In 2017, 7 master's, 7 doctorates awarded. Terminal master's awarded for partial completion of doctoral program. *Degree requirements:* For master's, thesis; for doctorate, comprehensive exam, thesis/dissertation. *Entrance requirements:* For master's and doctorate, GRE, 3 recommendation letters, letter of intent, bachelor's degree. Additional exam requirements/recommendations for international students: Required—TOEFL (minimum score 80 iBT) or IELTS (minimum score 6.5). *Application deadline:* For fall admission, 3/1 for domestic and international students; for spring admission, 9/1 for domestic and international students; for summer admission, 9/1 for domestic and international students. Application fee: $50 ($100 for international students). Electronic applications accepted. *Expenses:* Tuition, state resident: full-time $5119; part-time $213.30 per credit hour. Tuition, nonresident: full-time $19,778; part-time $824.10 per credit hour. *Required fees:* $3458; $133.55 per credit hour. $126.50 per semester. *Financial support:* In 2017–18, 21 students received support. Research assistantships with full and partial tuition reimbursements available, teaching assistantships with full and partial tuition reimbursements available, Federal Work-Study, institutionally sponsored loans, scholarships/grants, health care benefits, and unspecified assistantships available. Support available to part-time students. Financial award application deadline: 6/1; financial award applicants required to submit FAFSA. *Faculty research:* Anaerobic microbiology, biodegradation and bioremediation, environmental microbiology and genomics, microbial genetics and molecular biology, microbial stress responses. *Unit head:* Dr. Anne K. Dunn, Department Chair/Associate Professor of Microbiology, 405-325-4321, Fax: 405-325-7619, E-mail: akdunn@ou.edu. *Application contact:* Elizabeth Karr, Graduate Liaison/Associate Professor of Microbiology, 405-325-5133, E-mail: lizkarr@ou.edu.
Website: http://mpbio.ou.edu/

University of Oklahoma Health Sciences Center, College of Medicine and Graduate College, Graduate Programs in Medicine, Department of Microbiology and Immunology, Oklahoma City, OK 73190. Offers immunology (MS, PhD); microbiology (MS, PhD). *Program availability:* Part-time. Terminal master's awarded for partial completion of doctoral program. *Degree requirements:* For master's, thesis or alternative; for doctorate, one foreign language, thesis/dissertation. *Entrance requirements:* For doctorate, GRE General Test, 3 letters of recommendation. Additional exam requirements/recommendations for international students: Required—TOEFL. *Faculty research:* Molecular genetics, pathogenesis, streptococcal infections, gram-positive virulence, monoclonal antibodies.

University of Ottawa, Faculty of Graduate and Postdoctoral Studies, Faculty of Medicine, Department of Biochemistry, Microbiology and Immunology, Ottawa, ON K1N 6N5, Canada. Offers biochemistry (M Sc, PhD); microbiology and immunology (M Sc, PhD). *Degree requirements:* For master's, thesis; for doctorate, comprehensive exam, thesis/dissertation, seminar. *Entrance requirements:* For master's, honors degree or equivalent, minimum B average; for doctorate, master's degree, minimum B+ average. Electronic applications accepted. *Faculty research:* General biochemistry, molecular biology, microbiology, host biology, nutrition and metabolism.

University of Pennsylvania, Perelman School of Medicine, Biomedical Graduate Studies, Graduate Group in Cell and Molecular Biology, Philadelphia, PA 19104. Offers cancer biology (PhD); cell biology, physiology, and metabolism (PhD); developmental stem cell regenerative biology (PhD); gene therapy and vaccines (PhD); genetics and gene regulation (PhD); microbiology, virology, and parasitology (PhD); MD/PhD; VMD/PhD. *Faculty:* 363. *Students:* 343 full-time (197 women); includes 114 minority (7 Black or African American, non-Hispanic/Latino; 51 Asian, non-Hispanic/Latino; 41 Hispanic/Latino; 15 Two or more races, non-Hispanic/Latino), 50 international. 588 applicants, 22% accepted, 61 enrolled. In 2017, 61 doctorates awarded. *Degree requirements:* For doctorate, thesis/dissertation. *Entrance requirements:* For doctorate, GRE General Test. Additional exam requirements/recommendations for international students: Required—TOEFL. *Application deadline:* For fall admission, 12/1 priority date for domestic and international students. Applications are processed on a rolling basis. Application fee: $80. Electronic applications accepted. *Financial support:* In 2017–18, 339 students received support. Fellowships, research assistantships, teaching assistantships, and tuition waivers available. *Unit head:* Dr. Daniel Kessler, Graduate Group Chair, 215-898-1478. *Application contact:* Meagan Schofer, Coordinator, 215-898-1478.
Website: http://www.med.upenn.edu/camb/

University of Pittsburgh, Graduate School of Public Health, Department of Infectious Diseases and Microbiology, Pittsburgh, PA 15261. Offers infectious diseases and microbiology (MS, PhD); management, intervention, and community practice (MPH); pathogenesis, eradication, and laboratory practice (MPH). *Program availability:* Part-time. *Faculty:* 21 full-time (7 women), 5 part-time/adjunct (2 women). *Students:* 55 full-time (34 women), 19 part-time (12 women); includes 17 minority (2 Black or African American, non-Hispanic/Latino; 8 Asian, non-Hispanic/Latino; 1 Hispanic/Latino; 6 Two or more races, non-Hispanic/Latino), 8 international. Average age 26. 152 applicants,

51% accepted, 27 enrolled. In 2017, 34 master's, 2 doctorates awarded. Terminal master's awarded for partial completion of doctoral program. *Degree requirements:* For master's, thesis, comprehensive exam (for MS); for doctorate, comprehensive exam, thesis/dissertation, preliminary exam, dissertation defense. *Entrance requirements:* For master's, GRE General Test, MCAT, or DAT, minimum GPA of 3.0, 6 credits of behavioral science; for doctorate, GRE General Test, MCAT, DAT, minimum GPA of 3.0; research experience; knowledge of biology or microbiology, chemistry, and algebra. Additional exam requirements/recommendations for international students: Required—TOEFL (minimum score 550 paper-based, 80 iBT) or IELTS (minimum score 6.5). *Application deadline:* For fall admission, 1/15 priority date for domestic students, 3/15 priority date for international students. Applications are processed on a rolling basis. Application fee: $135. Electronic applications accepted. *Expenses:* $26,136 per year in-state tuition, $43,392 out-of-state, $850 fees. *Financial support:* In 2017–18, 38 students received support, including 19 research assistantships with full tuition reimbursements available; fellowships, teaching assistantships, scholarships/grants, and tuition waivers (full) also available. Financial award applicants required to submit FAFSA. *Faculty research:* Development of HIV vaccines, complications of antiretroviral therapy, emerging infections, herpes viruses. *Unit head:* Robin Tierno, Department Administrator, 412-624-3105, Fax: 412-624-4953, E-mail: rtierno@pitt.edu. *Application contact:* Abby Kincaid, Student Services Coordinator, 412-624-3331, E-mail: abbykincaid@pitt.edu.
Website: http://www.publichealth.pitt.edu/idm

University of Pittsburgh, School of Medicine, Graduate Programs in Medicine, Microbiology and Immunology Program, Pittsburgh, PA 15260. Offers PhD. *Faculty:* 90 full-time (29 women). *Students:* 58 full-time (33 women); includes 12 minority (5 Black or African American, non-Hispanic/Latino; 5 Asian, non-Hispanic/Latino; 2 Hispanic/Latino), 9 international. Average age 26. 350 applicants, 21% accepted, 16 enrolled. *Degree requirements:* For doctorate, comprehensive exam, thesis/dissertation, 34 course credits, 38 dissertation credits, published paper. *Entrance requirements:* For doctorate, GRE General Test. Additional exam requirements/recommendations for international students: Required—TOEFL (minimum score 600 paper-based; 100 iBT), IELTS (minimum score 7). *Application deadline:* For fall admission, 12/1 priority date for domestic and international students. Application fee: $50. Electronic applications accepted. *Expenses:* $26,782 in-state, $42,006 out-of-state. *Financial support:* In 2017–18, 46 students received support, including 10 research assistantships with full tuition reimbursements available (averaging $29,500 per year); traineeships also available. *Unit head:* Dr. Robert Binder, Director, 412-383-7722, Fax: 412-383-8906, E-mail: rjb42@pitt.edu. *Application contact:* Kristen Digiacomo, Coordinator, 412-624-5981, E-mail: kmd78@pitt.edu.
Website: http://www.pmi.pitt.edu

University of Puerto Rico–Medical Sciences Campus, School of Medicine, Biomedical Sciences Graduate Program, Department of Microbiology and Medical Zoology, San Juan, PR 00936-5067. Offers MS, PhD. *Degree requirements:* For master's, one foreign language, thesis; for doctorate, one foreign language, comprehensive exam, thesis/dissertation. *Entrance requirements:* For master's and doctorate, GRE General Test, GRE Subject Test, interview, minimum GPA of 3.0, 3 letters of recommendation. *Faculty research:* Molecular and general parasitology, immunology, development of viral vaccines and antiviral agents, antibiotic resistance, bacteriology.

University of Rhode Island, Graduate School, College of the Environment and Life Sciences, Department of Cell and Molecular Biology, Kingston, RI 02881. Offers biochemistry (MS, PhD); clinical laboratory sciences (MS), including biotechnology, clinical laboratory science, cytopathology; microbiology (MS, PhD); molecular genetics (MS, PhD). *Program availability:* Part-time. *Faculty:* 14 full-time (6 women). *Students:* 17 full-time (9 women), 19 part-time (15 women); includes 9 minority (2 Black or African American, non-Hispanic/Latino; 4 Asian, non-Hispanic/Latino; 2 Hispanic/Latino; 1 Two or more races, non-Hispanic/Latino), 10 international. 26 applicants, 62% accepted, 6 enrolled. In 2017, 17 master's awarded. *Entrance requirements:* Additional exam requirements/recommendations for international students: Required—TOEFL. *Application deadline:* For fall admission, 1/15 for domestic and international students. Application fee: $65. Electronic applications accepted. *Expenses:* Tuition, state resident: full-time $12,706; part-time $786 per credit. Tuition, nonresident: full-time $25,216; part-time $1401 per credit. *Required fees:* $1598; $45 per credit. One-time fee: $30 part-time. *Financial support:* In 2017–18, 4 teaching assistantships with tuition reimbursements (averaging $12,698 per year) were awarded; traineeships also available. Financial award application deadline: 1/15; financial award applicants required to submit FAFSA. *Unit head:* Dr. Gongqing Sun, Chair and Professor, 401-874-5937, Fax: 401-874-2202, E-mail: gsun@mail.uri.edu. *Application contact:* Bethany Jenkins, Professor, 401-874-7551, E-mail: bjenkins@uri.edu.
Website: https://web.uri.edu/cmb/

University of Rochester, School of Medicine and Dentistry, Graduate Programs in Medicine and Dentistry, Department of Microbiology and Immunology, Program in Medical Microbiology, Rochester, NY 14627. Offers MS, PhD.

University of Rochester, School of Medicine and Dentistry, Graduate Programs in Medicine and Dentistry, Department of Microbiology and Immunology, Program in Microbiology and Immunology, Rochester, NY 14627. Offers MS, PhD.

University of Saskatchewan, College of Medicine, Department of Microbiology and Immunology, Saskatoon, SK S7N 5A2, Canada. Offers M Sc, PhD. *Degree requirements:* For master's, thesis; for doctorate, thesis/dissertation. *Entrance requirements:* Additional exam requirements/recommendations for international students: Required—TOEFL.

University of Saskatchewan, Western College of Veterinary Medicine and College of Graduate Studies and Research, Graduate Programs in Veterinary Medicine, Department of Veterinary Microbiology, Saskatoon, SK S7N 5A2, Canada. Offers M Sc, M Vet Sc, PhD. *Degree requirements:* For master's, thesis; for doctorate, comprehensive exam (for some programs), thesis/dissertation. *Entrance requirements:* Additional exam requirements/recommendations for international students: Required—TOEFL (minimum score 80 iBT) or IELTS (minimum score 6.5). Electronic applications accepted. *Faculty research:* Immunology, vaccinology, epidemiology, virology, parasitology.

University of South Dakota, Graduate School, Sanford School of Medicine and Graduate School, Biomedical Sciences Graduate Program, Molecular Microbiology and Immunology Group, Vermillion, SD 57069. Offers MS, PhD. Terminal master's awarded for partial completion of doctoral program. *Degree requirements:* For master's, thesis; for doctorate, comprehensive exam, thesis/dissertation. *Entrance requirements:* For master's and doctorate, GRE General Test, minimum GPA of 3.0. Additional exam requirements/recommendations for international students: Required—TOEFL (minimum score 550 paper-based; 80 iBT), IELTS (minimum score 6). *Application deadline:* For fall admission, 4/15 priority date for domestic students, 3/15 for international students. Applications are processed on a rolling basis. Application fee: $35. Electronic applications accepted. *Expenses:* Contact institution. *Financial support:* In 2017–18, 6 students received support. Fellowships with partial tuition reimbursements available, research assistantships with partial tuition reimbursements available, and unspecified assistantships available. Financial award application deadline: 4/15; financial award applicants required to submit FAFSA. *Faculty research:* Structure-function membranes, plasmids, immunology, virology, pathogenesis. *Total annual research expenditures:* $325,000. *Unit head:* 605-658-6322, Fax: 605-677-6381, E-mail: biomed@usd.edu. *Application contact:* Graduate School, 605-658-6140, Fax: 605-677-6118.

University of Southern California, Keck School of Medicine and Graduate School, Graduate Programs in Medicine, Department of Molecular Microbiology and Immunology, Los Angeles, CA 90033. Offers MS. *Program availability:* Part-time. *Faculty:* 21 full-time (4 women), 1 (woman) part-time/adjunct. *Students:* 28 full-time (13 women), 1 (woman) part-time; includes 5 minority (4 Asian, non-Hispanic/Latino; 1 Hispanic/Latino), 20 international. Average age 24. 45 applicants, 62% accepted, 16 enrolled. In 2017, 8 master's awarded. Terminal master's awarded for partial completion of doctoral program. *Degree requirements:* For master's, comprehensive exam (for some programs), thesis optional. *Entrance requirements:* For master's, GRE General Test (Verbal and Quantitative), minimum GPA of 3.0. Additional exam requirements/recommendations for international students: Required—TOEFL (minimum score 100 iBT), IELTS (minimum score 6.5). *Application deadline:* For fall admission, 6/1 for domestic students, 5/1 for international students; for spring admission, 11/1 for domestic students, 10/1 for international students. Applications are processed on a rolling basis. Application fee: $90. Electronic applications accepted. *Expenses:* Contact institution. *Financial support:* Career-related internships or fieldwork, Federal Work-Study, institutionally sponsored loans, scholarships/grants, and health care benefits available. Financial award application deadline: 3/1; financial award applicants required to submit FAFSA. *Faculty research:* Animal virology, microbial genetics, molecular and cellular immunology, cellular differentiation control of protein synthesis, HIV. *Unit head:* Dr. Axel H. Schonthal, Associate Professor/Program Chairman, 323-442-1730, Fax: 323-442-1721, E-mail: schontha@usc.edu. *Application contact:* Silvina V. Campos, Administrative Assistant II, 323-442-1713, Fax: 323-442-1721, E-mail: scampos@usc.edu.
Website: http://keck.usc.edu/molecular-microbiology-and-immunology/

University of South Florida, College of Arts and Sciences, Department of Cell Biology, Microbiology, and Molecular Biology, Tampa, FL 33620-9951. Offers biology (MS), including cell biology, microbiology and molecular biology; cancer biology (PhD); cancer chemical biology (PhD); cancer immunology and immunotherapy (PhD); cell and molecular biology (PhD); microbiology (MS). *Faculty:* 19 full-time (6 women). *Students:* 81 full-time (55 women), 4 part-time (2 women); includes 12 minority (1 Black or African American, non-Hispanic/Latino; 2 Asian, non-Hispanic/Latino; 5 Hispanic/Latino; 4 Two or more races, non-Hispanic/Latino), 29 international. Average age 27. 159 applicants, 18% accepted, 23 enrolled. In 2017, 21 master's, 10 doctorates awarded. *Degree requirements:* For master's, thesis or alternative; for doctorate, comprehensive exam, thesis/dissertation. *Entrance requirements:* For master's and doctorate, GRE General Test, minimum GPA of 3.0, extensive background in biology or chemistry. Additional exam requirements/recommendations for international students: Required—TOEFL (minimum score 570 paper-based; 79 iBT) or IELTS (minimum score 6.5). *Application deadline:* For fall admission, 11/30 priority date for domestic and international students; for spring admission, 7/1 priority date for domestic students, 7/1 for international students. Application fee: $30. *Financial support:* In 2017–18, 10 students received support. Career-related internships or fieldwork, health care benefits, and unspecified assistantships available. Financial award application deadline: 4/1. *Faculty research:* Cell biology, microbiology and molecular biology: basic and applied science in bacterial pathogenesis, genome integrity and mechanisms of aging, structural and computational biology; cancer biology: immunology, cancer control, signal transduction, drug discovery, genomics. *Total annual research expenditures:* $1.8 million. *Unit head:* Dr. James Garey, Professor/Chair, 813-974-7103, Fax: 813-974-1614, E-mail: garey@usf.edu. *Application contact:* Dr. Kenneth Wright, Associate Professor of Cancer Biology, H. Lee Moffitt Cancer Center and Research Institute, 813-745-3918, Fax: 813-974-1614, E-mail: ken.wright@moffitt.org.
Website: http://biology.usf.edu/cmmb/

University of South Florida, College of Arts and Sciences, Department of Integrative Biology, Tampa, FL 33620-9951. Offers biology (MS), including ecology and evolution (MS, PhD), environmental and ecological microbiology (MS, PhD), physiology and morphology (MS, PhD); integrative biology (PhD), including ecology and evolution (MS, PhD), environmental and ecological microbiology (MS, PhD), physiology and morphology (MS, PhD). *Program availability:* Part-time. *Faculty:* 14 full-time (5 women). *Students:* 21 full-time (11 women), 1 (woman) part-time; includes 1 minority (Asian, non-Hispanic/Latino), 2 international. Average age 30. 35 applicants, 17% accepted, 5 enrolled. In 2017, 7 master's, 5 doctorates awarded. *Degree requirements:* For master's, comprehensive exam, thesis (for some programs); for doctorate, comprehensive exam, thesis/dissertation. *Entrance requirements:* For master's and doctorate, GRE General Test, minimum GPA of 3.0 in last 60 hours of BS. *Application deadline:* For fall admission, 11/30 priority date for domestic and international students; for spring admission, 7/1 priority date for domestic and international students. Application fee: $30. Electronic applications accepted. *Financial support:* In 2017–18, 7 students received support. Research assistantships, teaching assistantships, and unspecified assistantships available. Financial award application deadline: 6/30; financial award applicants required to submit FAFSA. *Faculty research:* Marine ecology, ecosystem responses to urbanization, biomechanical and physiological mechanisms of animal movement, population biology and conservation, microbial ecology and public health microbiology, natural diversity of parasites and herbivores; ecosystems, vertebrates, disturbance ecology, functional and ecological morphology of feeding in fishes, rare amphibians and reptiles, genomics in ecological experiments, ecotoxicology, global carbon cycle, plant-animal interactions. *Total annual research expenditures:* $1.9 million. *Unit head:* Dr. Valerie Harwood, Professor and Chair, 813-974-1524, Fax: 813-974-3263, E-mail: vharwood@usf.edu. *Application contact:* Dr. Stephen Deban, Associate Professor and Graduate Program Director, 813-974-2242, E-mail: sdeban@usf.edu.
Website: http://biology.usf.edu/ib/grad/

The University of Tennessee, Graduate School, College of Arts and Sciences, Department of Microbiology, Knoxville, TN 37996. Offers MS, PhD. *Program availability:* Part-time. *Degree requirements:* For master's, thesis; for doctorate, thesis/dissertation. *Entrance requirements:* For master's and doctorate, GRE General Test, minimum GPA of 2.7. Additional exam requirements/recommendations for international students: Required—TOEFL. Electronic applications accepted.

The University of Texas at Austin, Graduate School, College of Natural Sciences, School of Biological Sciences, Program in Microbiology, Austin, TX 78712-1111. Offers PhD. *Entrance requirements:* For doctorate, GRE General Test. Electronic applications accepted.

The University of Texas Health Science Center at Houston, MD Anderson UTHealth Graduate School, Houston, TX 77225-0036. Offers biochemistry and cell biology (PhD); biomedical sciences (MS); cancer biology (PhD); genetic counseling (MS); genetics and epigenetics (PhD); immunology (PhD); medical physics (MS, PhD); microbiology and infectious diseases (PhD); neuroscience (PhD); quantitative sciences (PhD);

therapeutics and pharmacology (PhD); MD/PhD. Terminal master's awarded for partial completion of doctoral program. *Degree requirements:* For master's, thesis; for doctorate, thesis/dissertation. *Entrance requirements:* For master's and doctorate, GRE General Test. Additional exam requirements/recommendations for international students: Required—TOEFL. Electronic applications accepted. *Faculty research:* Biomedical sciences.

The University of Texas Health Science Center at San Antonio, Graduate School of Biomedical Sciences, Department of Microbiology and Immunology, San Antonio, TX 78229-3900. Offers MS, PhD. *Degree requirements:* For master's, thesis; for doctorate, comprehensive exam, thesis/dissertation.

The University of Texas Medical Branch, Graduate School of Biomedical Sciences, Program in Microbiology and Immunology, Galveston, TX 77555. Offers MS, PhD. Terminal master's awarded for partial completion of doctoral program. *Degree requirements:* For master's, thesis or alternative; for doctorate, thesis/dissertation. *Entrance requirements:* For doctorate, GRE General Test, minimum GPA of 3.0. Additional exam requirements/recommendations for international students: Required—TOEFL (minimum score 550 paper-based). Electronic applications accepted.

The University of Texas Southwestern Medical Center, Southwestern Graduate School of Biomedical Sciences, Division of Basic Science, Program in Molecular Microbiology, Dallas, TX 75390. Offers PhD. *Degree requirements:* For doctorate, thesis/dissertation, oral and written exams. *Entrance requirements:* For doctorate, GRE General Test, minimum GPA of 3.0. Additional exam requirements/recommendations for international students: Required—TOEFL. Electronic applications accepted. *Faculty research:* Cell and molecular immunology, molecular pathogenesis of infectious disease, virology.

University of Victoria, Faculty of Graduate Studies, Faculty of Science, Department of Biochemistry and Microbiology, Victoria, BC V8W 2Y2, Canada. Offers biochemistry (M Sc, PhD); microbiology (M Sc, PhD). *Degree requirements:* For master's, thesis, seminar; for doctorate, thesis/dissertation, seminar, candidacy exam. *Entrance requirements:* For master's, GRE General Test, minimum B+ average; for doctorate, GRE General Test, minimum B+ average, M Sc. Additional exam requirements/recommendations for international students: Required—TOEFL (minimum score 600 paper-based). Electronic applications accepted. *Faculty research:* Molecular pathogenesis, prokaryotic, eukaryotic, macromolecular interactions, microbial surfaces, virology, molecular genetics.

University of Virginia, School of Medicine, Department of Microbiology, Immunology, and Cancer Biology, Charlottesville, VA 22903. Offers PhD, MD/PhD. *Faculty:* 37 full-time (15 women). *Students:* 52 full-time (35 women); includes 12 minority (3 Black or African American, non-Hispanic/Latino; 3 Asian, non-Hispanic/Latino; 6 Hispanic/Latino), 7 international. Average age 28. In 2017, 12 doctorates awarded. *Degree requirements:* For doctorate, thesis/dissertation. *Entrance requirements:* For doctorate, GRE General Test, 2 or more letters of recommendation. Additional exam requirements/recommendations for international students: Required—TOEFL (minimum score 600 paper-based; 90 iBT). *Application deadline:* For fall admission, 2/1 for domestic and international students. Applications are processed on a rolling basis. Application fee: $60. Electronic applications accepted. *Financial support:* Fellowships, traineeships, and unspecified assistantships available. Financial award applicants required to submit FAFSA. *Faculty research:* Virology, membrane biology and molecular genetics. *Unit head:* Kodi S. Ravichandran, Chair, 434-924-1948, Fax: 434-982-1071, E-mail: kr4h@virginia.edu. *Application contact:* Lucy Pemberton, Director of Graduate Studies, 434-243-6737, Fax: 434-924-1236, E-mail: lfp2n@virginia.edu.
Website: http://www.medicine.virginia.edu/basic-science/departments/microbiology-immunology-and-cancer-biology

University of Washington, Graduate School, School of Medicine, Graduate Programs in Medicine, Department of Microbiology, Seattle, WA 98195. Offers PhD. *Degree requirements:* For doctorate, thesis/dissertation. *Entrance requirements:* For doctorate, GRE General Test, GRE Subject Test (recommended). Electronic applications accepted. *Faculty research:* Bacterial genetics and physiology, mechanisms of bacterial and viral pathogenesis, bacterial-plant interaction.

The University of Western Ontario, Faculty of Graduate Studies, Biosciences Division, Department of Microbiology and Immunology, London, ON N6A 5B8, Canada. Offers M Sc, PhD. *Degree requirements:* For master's, thesis, oral and written exam; for doctorate, thesis/dissertation, oral and written exam. *Entrance requirements:* For master's, honors degree or equivalent in microbiology, immunology, or other biological science; minimum B average; for doctorate, M Sc in microbiology and immunology. Additional exam requirements/recommendations for international students: Required—TOEFL. *Faculty research:* Virology, molecular pathogenesis, cellular immunology, molecular biology.

University of Wisconsin–La Crosse, College of Science and Health, Department of Biology, La Crosse, WI 54601-3742. Offers aquatic sciences (MS); biology (MS); cellular and molecular biology (MS); clinical microbiology (MS); microbiology (MS); nurse anesthesia (MS); physiology (MS). *Accreditation:* AANA/CANAEP. *Program availability:* Part-time. *Students:* 11 full-time (2 women), 29 part-time (14 women); includes 1 minority (Two or more races, non-Hispanic/Latino). Average age 30. 67 applicants, 28% accepted, 18 enrolled. In 2017, 24 master's awarded. *Degree requirements:* For master's, comprehensive exam, thesis. *Entrance requirements:* For master's, GRE General Test, minimum GPA of 2.85. Additional exam requirements/recommendations for international students: Required—TOEFL (minimum score 550 paper-based; 79 iBT). *Application deadline:* For fall admission, 2/1 priority date for domestic and international students; for spring admission, 1/4 priority date for domestic and international students. Applications are processed on a rolling basis. Electronic applications accepted. *Financial support:* Research assistantships with partial tuition reimbursements, Federal Work-Study, scholarships/grants, health care benefits, and tuition waivers (partial) available. Support available to part-time students. Financial award application deadline: 3/15; financial award applicants required to submit FAFSA. *Unit head:* Dr. Mark Sandheinrich, Department Chair, 608-785-8261, E-mail: msandheinrich@uwlax.edu. *Application contact:* Brandon Schaller, Senior Graduate Student Status Examiner, 608-785-8941, E-mail: admissions@uwlax.edu.
Website: http://uwlax.edu/biology/

University of Wisconsin–La Crosse, College of Science and Health, Department of Microbiology, La Crosse, WI 54601-3742. Offers clinical microbiology (MS); microbiology (MS). *Students:* 11 full-time (4 women), 13 part-time (8 women); includes 2 minority (1 Asian, non-Hispanic/Latino; 1 Hispanic/Latino), 1 international. Average age 26. 12 applicants, 92% accepted, 7 enrolled. In 2017, 4 master's awarded. *Unit head:* Michael Hoffman, Chair/Program Director, 608-785-6984, E-mail: mhoffman@uwlax.edu.
Website: http://www.uwlax.edu/microbiology/

University of Wisconsin–Madison, Graduate School, College of Agricultural and Life Sciences and College of Agricultural and Life Sciences, Microbiology Doctoral Training Program, Madison, WI 53706. Offers PhD.
Website: http://www.microbiology.wisc.edu/

University of Wisconsin–Milwaukee, Graduate School, College of Letters and Science, Department of Biological Sciences, Milwaukee, WI 53201-0413. Offers cellular and molecular biology (MS, PhD); microbiology (MS, PhD). *Students:* 58 full-time (35 women), 11 part-time (8 women); includes 7 minority (1 Black or African American, non-Hispanic/Latino; 5 Asian, non-Hispanic/Latino; 1 Two or more races, non-Hispanic/Latino), 17 international. Average age 29. 78 applicants, 55% accepted, 29 enrolled. *Degree requirements:* For master's, thesis; for doctorate, thesis/dissertation, 1 foreign language or data analysis proficiency. *Entrance requirements:* For master's and doctorate, GRE General Test. Additional exam requirements/recommendations for international students: Required—TOEFL (minimum score 550 paper-based; 79 iBT), IELTS (minimum score 6.5). *Application deadline:* For fall admission, 3/1 priority date for domestic students. Application fee: $56 ($96 for international students). Electronic applications accepted. *Financial support:* In 2017–18, 9 research assistantships were awarded; fellowships, teaching assistantships, career-related internships or fieldwork, unspecified assistantships, and project assistantships also available. Support available to part-time students. Financial award application deadline: 4/15; financial award applicants required to submit FAFSA. *Unit head:* R. David Heathcote, Department Chair, 414-229-6471, E-mail: rdh@uwm.edu. *Application contact:* General Information Contact, 414-229-4982, Fax: 414-229-6967, E-mail: gradschool@uwm.edu.
Website: https://uwm.edu/biology/

University of Wisconsin–Oshkosh, Graduate Studies, College of Letters and Science, Department of Biology and Microbiology, Oshkosh, WI 54901. Offers biology (MS), including botany, microbiology, zoology. *Degree requirements:* For master's, comprehensive exam, thesis. *Entrance requirements:* For master's, GRE General Test, minimum GPA of 3.0, BS in biology. Additional exam requirements/recommendations for international students: Required—TOEFL (minimum score 550 paper-based; 79 iBT). Electronic applications accepted.

University of Wyoming, Graduate Program in Molecular and Cellular Life Sciences, Laramie, WY 82071. Offers PhD. *Degree requirements:* For doctorate, thesis/dissertation, four eight-week laboratory rotations, comprehensive basic practical exam, two-part qualifying exam, seminars, symposium.

Vanderbilt University, School of Medicine, Department of Microbiology and Immunology, Nashville, TN 37240-1001. Offers MS, PhD, MD/PhD. *Faculty:* 36 full-time (9 women). *Students:* 52 full-time (30 women); includes 13 minority (2 Black or African American, non-Hispanic/Latino; 1 American Indian or Alaska Native, non-Hispanic/Latino; 3 Asian, non-Hispanic/Latino; 3 Hispanic/Latino; 4 Two or more races, non-Hispanic/Latino), 4 international. Average age 27. In 2017, 15 doctorates awarded. Terminal master's awarded for partial completion of doctoral program. *Degree requirements:* For master's, thesis; for doctorate, thesis/dissertation, final and qualifying exams. *Entrance requirements:* For master's and doctorate, GRE General Test, GRE Subject Test (recommended). Additional exam requirements/recommendations for international students: Required—TOEFL (minimum score 570 paper-based; 88 iBT). *Application deadline:* For fall admission, 1/15 for domestic and international students. Application fee: $0. Electronic applications accepted. *Financial support:* Fellowships with full tuition reimbursements, research assistantships with full tuition reimbursements, Federal Work-Study, institutionally sponsored loans, scholarships/grants, traineeships, health care benefits, and tuition waivers (partial) available. Financial award application deadline: 1/15; financial award applicants required to submit CSS PROFILE or FAFSA. *Faculty research:* Cellular and molecular microbiology, viruses, genes, cancer, molecular pathogenesis of microbial diseases, immunobiology. *Unit head:* Dr. Roger Cone, Acting Chair, 615-322-7000, Fax: 615-322-5551, E-mail: roger.cone@vanderbilt.edu. *Application contact:* Jay Jerome, Director of Graduate Studies, 615-322-2123, E-mail: jay.jerome@vanderbilt.edu.
Website: http://www.mc.vanderbilt.edu/root/vumc.php?site-vmcpathology

Virginia Commonwealth University, Medical College of Virginia-Professional Programs, School of Medicine, Graduate Programs in Medicine, Department of Microbiology and Immunology, Richmond, VA 23284-9005. Offers microbiology and immunology (MS, PhD); MD/PhD. *Degree requirements:* For master's, thesis; for doctorate, thesis/dissertation, comprehensive oral and written exams. *Entrance requirements:* For master's and doctorate, GRE General Test or MCAT. Additional exam requirements/recommendations for international students: Required—TOEFL (minimum score 600 paper-based; 100 iBT). Electronic applications accepted. *Faculty research:* Microbial physiology and genetics, molecular biology, crystallography of biological molecules, antibiotics and chemotherapy, membrane transport.

Wagner College, Division of Graduate Studies, Program in Microbiology, Staten Island, NY 10301-4495. Offers MS. *Program availability:* Part-time, evening/weekend. *Faculty:* 3 full-time (1 woman), 3 part-time/adjunct (all women). *Students:* 12 full-time (7 women), 10 part-time (4 women); includes 6 minority (2 Black or African American, non-Hispanic/Latino; 2 Asian, non-Hispanic/Latino; 2 Hispanic/Latino), 5 international. Average age 25. 19 applicants, 89% accepted, 12 enrolled. In 2017, 12 master's awarded. *Degree requirements:* For master's, comprehensive exam or thesis. *Entrance requirements:* For master's, minimum GPA of 3.0, proficiency in statistics, undergraduate major in biological science or chemistry, undergraduate microbiology course, 16 credits of chemistry including organic chemistry with lab. Additional exam requirements/recommendations for international students: Required—TOEFL (minimum score 550 paper-based; 79 iBT), IELTS (minimum score 6.5). *Application deadline:* For fall admission, 5/1 priority date for domestic students, 3/1 priority date for international students; for spring admission, 12/1 for domestic students, 10/1 for international students. Applications are processed on a rolling basis. Application fee: $60. Electronic applications accepted. *Financial support:* In 2017–18, 12 students received support. Career-related internships or fieldwork, unspecified assistantships, and alumni fellowship grants available. Financial award applicants required to submit FAFSA. *Faculty research:* Listeria monocytogenes pathogenesis, plant extracts as anti-microbial agents, neuroimmunology. *Unit head:* Dr. Christopher Corbo, Director, 718-390-3385, E-mail: ccorbo@wagner.edu. *Application contact:* Patricia Clancy, Assistant Director for Enrollment, 718-420-4464, Fax: 718-390-3105, E-mail: patricia.clancy@wagner.edu.

Wake Forest University, School of Medicine and Graduate School of Arts and Sciences, Graduate Programs in Medicine, Department of Microbiology and Immunology, Winston-Salem, NC 27109. Offers PhD, MD/PhD. *Degree requirements:* For doctorate, thesis/dissertation. *Entrance requirements:* For doctorate, GRE General Test. Additional exam requirements/recommendations for international students: Required—TOEFL. Electronic applications accepted. *Faculty research:* Molecular immunology, bacterial pathogenesis and molecular genetics, viral pathogenesis, regulation of mRNA metabolism, leukocyte biology.

Washington University in St. Louis, The Graduate School, Division of Biology and Biomedical Sciences, Program in Molecular Microbiology and Microbial Pathogenesis, St. Louis, MO 63130-4899. Offers PhD. *Degree requirements:* For doctorate, thesis/dissertation. *Entrance requirements:* For doctorate, GRE General Test, GRE Subject Test. Additional exam requirements/recommendations for international students: Required—TOEFL. Electronic applications accepted. *Faculty research:* Host-pathogen interactions, cellular microbiology, molecular microbiology, microbial pathogenesis, pathogen discovery, emerging infectious diseases, microbial physiology and biochemistry, comparative genomics, gene expression and regulation, microbiome and host interactions, virology, bacteriology, mycology, parasitology.

Microbiology

Wayne State University, School of Medicine, Office of Biomedical Graduate Programs, Detroit, MI 48202. Offers anatomy and cell biology (MS, PhD); basic medical sciences (MS); biochemistry and molecular biology (MS, PhD); cancer biology (MS, PhD); clinical and translational science (Graduate Certificate); family medicine and public health sciences (MPH, Graduate Certificate), including public health practice; genetic counseling (MS); immunology and microbiology (MS, PhD); medical physics (MS, PhD, Graduate Certificate); medical research (MS); molecular medicine and genomics (MS, PhD), including molecular genetics and genomics; pathology (PhD); pharmacology (MS, PhD); physiology (MS, PhD), including physiology, reproductive sciences (PhD); psychiatry and behavioral neurosciences (PhD), including translational neuroscience; MD/MPH; MD/PhD; MPH/MA; MSW/MPH. *Program availability:* Part-time, evening/weekend. *Students:* 268 full-time (152 women), 117 part-time (59 women); includes 108 minority (19 Black or African American, non-Hispanic/Latino; 1 American Indian or Alaska Native, non-Hispanic/Latino; 62 Asian, non-Hispanic/Latino; 9 Hispanic/Latino; 17 Two or more races, non-Hispanic/Latino), 48 international. Average age 26. 1,133 applicants, 21% accepted, 151 enrolled. In 2017, 70 master's, 25 doctorates, 10 other advanced degrees awarded. Terminal master's awarded for partial completion of doctoral program. *Degree requirements:* For master's, thesis (for some programs); for doctorate, thesis/dissertation. *Entrance requirements:* For master's, doctorate, and Graduate Certificate, GRE. Additional exam requirements/recommendations for international students: Required—TOEFL (minimum score 550 paper-based; 100 iBT), Michigan English Language Assessment Battery (minimum score 85); Recommended—IELTS (minimum score 6.5), TWE (minimum score 5.5). *Application deadline:* For fall admission, 2/1 for domestic and international students. Applications are processed on a rolling basis. Application fee: $50. Electronic applications accepted. *Expenses:* Contact institution. *Financial support:* In 2017–18, 177 students received support, including 64 fellowships with full tuition reimbursements available (averaging $24,388 per year), 79 research assistantships with full tuition reimbursements available (averaging $26,894 per year); scholarships/grants, traineeships, and health care benefits also available. *Faculty research:* Cancer biology, neurosciences, vision sciences, molecular biology, pathology, physiology, pharmacology, public health, medical physics. *Unit head:* Dr. Daniel A. Walz, Associate Dean for Biomedical Graduate Programs, 313-577-1455, Fax: 313-577-8796, E-mail: gradprogs@med.wayne.edu.
Website: https://www.med.wayne.edu/biomedical-graduate-programs/

Wright State University, Graduate School, College of Science and Mathematics, Program in Microbiology and Immunology, Dayton, OH 45435. Offers MS. *Program availability:* Part-time. *Degree requirements:* For master's, thesis. *Entrance requirements:* Additional exam requirements/recommendations for international students: Required—TOEFL. *Faculty research:* Reproductive immunology, viral pathogenesis, virus-host cell interactions.

Yale University, Yale School of Medicine and Graduate School of Arts and Sciences, Combined Program in Biological and Biomedical Sciences (BBS), Microbiology Track, New Haven, CT 06520. Offers PhD, MD/PhD. *Degree requirements:* For doctorate, thesis/dissertation. *Entrance requirements:* For doctorate, GRE General Test, GRE Subject Test. Additional exam requirements/recommendations for international students: Required—TOEFL. Electronic applications accepted.

Youngstown State University, Graduate School, College of Science, Technology, Engineering and Mathematics, Department of Biological Sciences, Youngstown, OH 44555-0001. Offers environmental biology (MS); molecular biology, microbiology, and genetic (MS); physiology and anatomy (MS). *Program availability:* Part-time. *Degree requirements:* For master's, comprehensive exam, thesis, oral review. *Entrance requirements:* For master's, GRE General Test, minimum GPA of 2.7. Additional exam requirements/recommendations for international students: Required—TOEFL. *Faculty research:* Cell biology, neurophysiology, molecular biology, neurobiology, gene regulation.

Virology

Baylor College of Medicine, Graduate School of Biomedical Sciences, Department of Molecular Virology and Microbiology, Houston, TX 77030-3498. Offers PhD, MD/PhD. *Degree requirements:* For doctorate, thesis/dissertation, public defense. *Entrance requirements:* For doctorate, GRE General Test, GRE Subject Test (strongly recommended), minimum GPA of 3.0. Additional exam requirements/recommendations for international students: Required—TOEFL. Electronic applications accepted. *Faculty research:* Microbiology, viral molecular biology, bacterial molecular biology, microbial pathogenesis, microbial genomics.

Baylor College of Medicine, Graduate School of Biomedical Sciences, Interdepartmental Program in Cell and Molecular Biology, Houston, TX 77030-3498. Offers biochemistry (PhD); cell and molecular biology (PhD); genetics (PhD); human genetics (PhD); immunology (PhD); microbiology (PhD); virology (PhD); MD/PhD. *Degree requirements:* For doctorate, thesis/dissertation, public defense. *Entrance requirements:* For doctorate, GRE General Test, GRE Subject Test (strongly recommended), minimum GPA of 3.0. Additional exam requirements/recommendations for international students: Required—TOEFL. Electronic applications accepted. *Faculty research:* Molecular and cellular biology; cancer, aging and stem cells; genomics and proteomics; microbiome, molecular microbiology; infectious disease, immunology and translational research.

Case Western Reserve University, School of Medicine and School of Graduate Studies, Graduate Programs in Medicine, Department of Molecular Biology and Microbiology, Program in Molecular Virology, Cleveland, OH 44106. Offers PhD. *Entrance requirements:* Additional exam requirements/recommendations for international students: Required—TOEFL (minimum score 550 paper-based). *Expenses: Tuition:* Full-time $43,854; part-time $1827 per credit hour. *Required fees:* $50; $50 per credit hour. Tuition and fees vary according to course load and program.

Mayo Clinic Graduate School of Biomedical Sciences, Program in Virology and Gene Therapy, Rochester, MN 55905. Offers PhD. *Faculty:* 12 full-time (4 women). *Students:* 17 full-time (6 women); includes 4 minority (3 Asian, non-Hispanic/Latino; 1 Hispanic/Latino). 24 applicants, 25% accepted, 3 enrolled. *Degree requirements:* For doctorate, comprehensive exam, thesis/dissertation. *Entrance requirements:* Additional exam requirements/recommendations for international students: Required—TOEFL. *Application deadline:* For fall admission, 12/1 for domestic and international students. Application fee: $50. Electronic applications accepted. *Financial support:* Fellowships available. *Faculty research:* Virology, viral vectors, gene therapy, cancer immunotherapy, vaccine development. *Unit head:* Dr. Michael Barry, Director, 507-538-1188, E-mail: barry.michael@mayo.edu. *Application contact:* Sarah E. Giese, Admissions Coordinator, 507-538-1160, E-mail: phd.training@mayo.edu.
Website: http://www.mayo.edu/mayo-clinic-graduate-school-of-biomedical-sciences/programs/phd/tracks/virology-and-gene-therapy

McMaster University, Faculty of Health Sciences and School of Graduate Studies, Program in Medical Sciences, Hamilton, ON L8S 4M2, Canada. Offers blood and vascular (M Sc, PhD); genetics and cancer (M Sc, PhD); immunity and infection (M Sc, PhD); metabolism and nutrition (M Sc, PhD); neurosciences and behavioral sciences (M Sc, PhD); physiology/pharmacology (M Sc, PhD); MD/PhD. *Degree requirements:* For master's, thesis; for doctorate, comprehensive exam, thesis/dissertation. *Entrance requirements:* For master's, honors B Sc, B+ average in related field; for doctorate, M Sc, minimum B+ average. Additional exam requirements/recommendations for international students: Required—TOEFL (minimum score 580 paper-based; 92 iBT).

Oregon State University, College of Science, Program in Microbiology, Corvallis, OR 97331. Offers environmental microbiology (MA, MS, PhD); food microbiology (MA, MS, PhD); genomics (MA, MS, PhD); immunology (MA, MS, PhD); microbial ecology (MA, MS, PhD); microbial evolution (MA, MS, PhD); parasitology (MA, MS, PhD); pathogenic microbiology (MA, MS, PhD); virology (MA). Terminal master's awarded for partial completion of doctoral program. *Entrance requirements:* For master's and doctorate, GRE. Additional exam requirements/recommendations for international students: Required—TOEFL (minimum score 600 paper-based; 100 iBT). *Application deadline:* For fall admission, 1/1 for domestic and international students. Application fee: $75 ($85 for international students). *Financial support:* Application deadline: 1/15. *Faculty research:* Genetics, physiology, biotechnology, pathogenic microbiology, plant virology. *Unit head:* Dr. Jerri Bartholomew, Professor and Department Head, 541-737-1834, E-mail: bartholj@science.oregonstate.edu. *Application contact:* Kim Halsey, Graduate Admissions Committee Chair, 541-737-1831, E-mail: kim.halsey@oregonstate.edu.
Website: http://microbiology.science.oregonstate.edu/

Oregon State University, Interdisciplinary/Institutional Programs, Program in Molecular and Cellular Biology, Corvallis, OR 97331. Offers bioinformatics (PhD); biotechnology (PhD); genome biology (PhD); molecular virology (PhD); plant molecular biology (PhD). *Degree requirements:* For doctorate, thesis/dissertation, oral and written qualifying exams. *Entrance requirements:* For doctorate, GRE. Additional exam requirements/recommendations for international students: Required—TOEFL (minimum score 80 iBT), IELTS (minimum score 6.5). *Application deadline:* For fall admission, 8/1 for domestic students, 4/1 for international students; for winter admission, 12/1 for domestic students, 7/1 for international students; for spring admission, 2/1 for domestic students, 10/1 for international students; for summer admission, 5/1 for domestic students, 1/1 for international students. Application fee: $75 ($85 for international students). *Financial support:* Application deadline: 1/1. *Unit head:* Dr. Kristin Carroll, Assistant Director, Molecular and Cellular Biology Program, 541-737-5259, E-mail: kirstin.carroll@oregonstate.edu. *Application contact:* Dr. Kristin Carroll, Assistant Director, Molecular and Cellular Biology Program, 541-737-5259, E-mail: kirstin.carroll@oregonstate.edu.
Website: http://gradschool.oregonstate.edu/molecular-and-cellular-biology-graduate-program

Penn State Hershey Medical Center, College of Medicine, Graduate School Programs in the Biomedical Sciences, Graduate Program in Biomedical Sciences, Hershey, PA 17033. Offers biochemistry and molecular genetics (MS, PhD); biomedical sciences (MS, PhD); cellular and integrative physiology (MS, PhD); translational therapeutics (MS, PhD); virology and immunology (MS, PhD); MD/PhD; PhD/MBA. *Students:* 103 full-time (58 women); includes 25 minority (5 Black or African American, non-Hispanic/Latino; 12 Asian, non-Hispanic/Latino; 7 Hispanic/Latino; 1 Native Hawaiian or other Pacific Islander, non-Hispanic/Latino), 28 international. 250 applicants, 22% accepted, 19 enrolled. In 2017, 4 master's, 1 doctorate awarded. Terminal master's awarded for partial completion of doctoral program. *Degree requirements:* For master's, thesis; for doctorate, comprehensive exam, thesis/dissertation, candidacy exam. *Entrance requirements:* For doctorate, GRE General Test. Additional exam requirements/recommendations for international students: Required—TOEFL (minimum score 550 paper-based; 81 iBT). *Application deadline:* For fall admission, 1/1 for domestic and international students. Applications are processed on a rolling basis. Application fee: $65. Electronic applications accepted. *Financial support:* In 2017–18, 103 students received support, including research assistantships with full tuition reimbursements available (averaging $27,802 per year); fellowships, scholarships/grants, traineeships, health care benefits, and unspecified assistantships also available. *Unit head:* Dr. Ralph L. Keil, Chair, 717-531-8595, Fax: 717-531-0786, E-mail: rlk9@psu.edu. *Application contact:* Kristin E. Smith, Director of Graduate Admissions, 717-531-1045, Fax: 717-531-0786, E-mail: kec17@psu.edu.
Website: http://med.psu.edu/bms

Purdue University, Graduate School, PULSe - Purdue University Life Sciences Program, West Lafayette, IN 47907. Offers biomolecular structure and biophysics (PhD); biotechnology (PhD); chemical biology (PhD); chromatin and regulation of gene expression (PhD); integrative neuroscience (PhD); integrative plant sciences (PhD); membrane biology (PhD); microbiology (PhD); molecular evolutionary and cancer biology (PhD); molecular evolutionary genetics (PhD); molecular virology (PhD). *Students:* 60 full-time (29 women); includes 6 minority (4 Hispanic/Latino; 2 Two or more races, non-Hispanic/Latino), 36 international. Average age 25. 127 applicants, 39% accepted, 25 enrolled. *Entrance requirements:* For doctorate, GRE, minimum undergraduate GPA of 3.0. Additional exam requirements/recommendations for international students: Required—TOEFL (minimum score 550 paper-based; 77 iBT). *Application deadline:* For fall admission, 1/15 priority date for domestic and international students. Applications are processed on a rolling basis. Application fee: $60 ($75 for international students). Electronic applications accepted. *Financial support:* In 2017–18, research assistantships with tuition reimbursements (averaging $22,500 per year), teaching assistantships with tuition reimbursements (averaging $22,500 per year) were awarded. *Unit head:* Dr. Jason R. Cannon, Head of the Graduate Program, 765-494-0794, E-mail: cannonjr@purdue.edu. *Application contact:* Lindsey Springer, Graduate Contact for Admissions, 765-496-9667, E-mail: lbcampbe@purdue.edu.
Website: http://www.gradschool.purdue.edu/pulse

Purdue University, School of Veterinary Medicine and Graduate School, Graduate Programs in Veterinary Medicine, Department of Comparative Pathobiology, West Lafayette, IN 47907-2027. Offers comparative epidemiology and public health (MS); comparative epidemiology and public heath (PhD); comparative microbiology and immunology (MS, PhD); comparative pathobiology (MS, PhD); interdisciplinary studies (PhD), including microbial pathogenesis, molecular signaling and cancer biology, molecular virology; lab animal medicine (MS); veterinary anatomic pathology (MS); veterinary clinical pathology (MS). Terminal master's awarded for partial completion of doctoral program. *Degree requirements:* For master's, thesis (for some programs); for doctorate, thesis/dissertation. *Entrance requirements:* For master's and doctorate, GRE General Test. Additional exam requirements/recommendations for international students: Required—TOEFL (minimum score 575 paper-based), IELTS (minimum score 6.5), TWE (minimum score 4). Electronic applications accepted.

Rush University, Graduate College, Division of Immunology and Microbiology, Program in Immunology/Microbiology, Chicago, IL 60612-3832. Offers immunology (MS, PhD); virology (MS, PhD); MD/PhD. *Program availability:* Part-time. Terminal master's awarded for partial completion of doctoral program. *Degree requirements:* For master's, thesis; for doctorate, thesis/dissertation, comprehensive preliminary exam. *Entrance requirements:* For master's, GRE General Test; for doctorate, GRE General Test, interview, minimum GPA of 3.0. Additional exam requirements/recommendations for international students: Required—TOEFL. Electronic applications accepted. *Faculty research:* Human genetics, autoimmunity, tumor biology, complement, HIV immunopathology genesis.

Rutgers University–New Brunswick, Graduate School-New Brunswick, Programs in the Molecular Biosciences, Piscataway, NJ 08854-8097. Offers biochemistry (PhD); cell and developmental biology (MS, PhD); microbiology and molecular genetics (MS, PhD), including applied microbiology, clinical microbiology, computational molecular biology (PhD), immunology, microbial biochemistry, molecular genetics, virology. MS, PhD offered jointly with University of Medicine and Dentistry of New Jersey.

Université de Montréal, Faculty of Veterinary Medicine, Program in Virology and Immunology, Montréal, QC H3C 3J7, Canada. Offers PhD. Program offered jointly with Université du Québec, Institut Armand-Frappier. *Degree requirements:* For doctorate, thesis/dissertation, general exam. *Entrance requirements:* For doctorate, proficiency in French, knowledge of English. Electronic applications accepted.

Université du Québec, Institut National de la Recherche Scientifique, Graduate Programs, INRS - Institut Armand-Frappier, Laval, QC G1K 9A9, Canada. Offers applied microbiology (M Sc); biology (PhD); experimental health sciences (M Sc); virology and immunology (M Sc, PhD). *Program availability:* Part-time. *Faculty:* 48 full-time. *Students:* 149 full-time (89 women), 18 part-time (11 women), 86 international. Average age 30. 29 applicants, 93% accepted, 25 enrolled. In 2017, 16 master's, 13 doctorates awarded. *Degree requirements:* For master's, thesis; for doctorate, thesis/dissertation. *Entrance requirements:* For master's, appropriate bachelor's degree, proficiency in French; for doctorate, appropriate master's degree, proficiency in French. *Application deadline:* For fall admission, 3/30 for domestic and international students; for winter admission, 11/1 for domestic and international students; for spring admission, 3/1 for domestic and international students. Application fee: $45 Canadian dollars. Electronic applications accepted. *Financial support:* In 2017–18, fellowships (averaging $16,500 per year) were awarded; research assistantships also available. *Faculty research:* Immunity, infection and cancer; toxicology and environmental biotechnology; molecular pharmacochemistry. *Unit head:* Pierre Talbot, Director, 450-687-5010 Ext. 4300, Fax: 450-686-5501, E-mail: pierre.talbot@iaf.inrs.ca. *Application contact:* Sylvie Richard, Registrar, 418-654-2518, Fax: 418-654-3858, E-mail: sylvie.richard@adm.inrs.ca.
Website: http://www.iaf.inrs.ca

The University of Iowa, Roy J. and Lucille A. Carver College of Medicine and Graduate College, Graduate Programs in Medicine, Department of Microbiology, Iowa City, IA 52242-1316. Offers general microbiology and microbial physiology (MS, PhD); immunology (MS, PhD); microbial genetics (MS, PhD); pathogenic bacteriology (MS, PhD); virology (MS, PhD). *Degree requirements:* For master's, thesis; for doctorate, comprehensive exam, thesis/dissertation. *Entrance requirements:* For master's and doctorate, GRE General Test. Additional exam requirements/recommendations for international students: Required—TOEFL (minimum score 600 paper-based). Electronic applications accepted. *Faculty research:* Gene regulation, processing and transport of HIV, retroviral pathogenesis, biodegradation, biofilm.

University of Minnesota, Twin Cities Campus, Graduate School, PhD Program in Microbiology, Immunology and Cancer Biology, Minneapolis, MN 55455-0213. Offers PhD. *Degree requirements:* For doctorate, thesis/dissertation. *Entrance requirements:* For doctorate, GRE General Test. Additional exam requirements/recommendations for international students: Required—TOEFL (minimum score 600 paper-based). Electronic applications accepted. *Faculty research:* Virology, microbiology, cancer biology, immunology.

University of Pennsylvania, Perelman School of Medicine, Biomedical Graduate Studies, Graduate Group in Cell and Molecular Biology, Philadelphia, PA 19104. Offers cancer biology (PhD); cell biology, physiology, and metabolism (PhD); developmental stem cell regenerative biology (PhD); gene therapy and vaccines (PhD); genetics and gene regulation (PhD); microbiology, virology, and parasitology (PhD); MD/PhD; VMD/PhD. *Faculty:* 363. *Students:* 343 full-time (197 women); includes 114 minority (7 Black or African American, non-Hispanic/Latino; 51 Asian, non-Hispanic/Latino; 41 Hispanic/Latino; 15 Two or more races, non-Hispanic/Latino), 50 international. 588 applicants, 22% accepted, 61 enrolled. In 2017, 61 doctorates awarded. *Degree requirements:* For doctorate, thesis/dissertation. *Entrance requirements:* For doctorate, GRE General Test. Additional exam requirements/recommendations for international students: Required—TOEFL. *Application deadline:* For fall admission, 12/1 priority date for domestic and international students. Applications are processed on a rolling basis. Application fee: $80. Electronic applications accepted. *Financial support:* In 2017–18, 339 students received support. Fellowships, research assistantships, teaching assistantships, and tuition waivers available. *Unit head:* Dr. Daniel Kessler, Graduate Group Chair, 215-898-1478. *Application contact:* Meagan Schofer, Coordinator, 215-898-1478.
Website: http://www.med.upenn.edu/camb/

University of Prince Edward Island, Atlantic Veterinary College, Graduate Program in Veterinary Medicine, Charlottetown, PE C1A 4P3, Canada. Offers anatomy (M Sc, PhD); bacteriology (M Sc, PhD); clinical pharmacology (M Sc, PhD); clinical sciences (M Sc, PhD); epidemiology (M Sc, PhD), including reproduction; fish health (M Sc, PhD); food animal nutrition (M Sc, PhD); immunology (M Sc, PhD); microanatomy (M Sc, PhD); parasitology (M Sc, PhD); pathology (M Sc, PhD); pharmacology (M Sc, PhD); physiology (M Sc, PhD); toxicology (M Sc, PhD); veterinary science (M Vet Sc); virology (M Sc, PhD). *Program availability:* Part-time. *Degree requirements:* For master's, thesis; for doctorate, thesis/dissertation. *Entrance requirements:* For master's, DVM, B Sc honors degree, or equivalent; for doctorate, M Sc. Additional exam requirements/recommendations for international students: Required—TOEFL (minimum score 550 paper-based; 80 iBT). *Expenses:* Contact institution. *Faculty research:* Animal health management, infectious diseases, fin fish and shellfish health, basic biomedical sciences, ecosystem health.

Yale University, Yale School of Medicine and Graduate School of Arts and Sciences, Combined Program in Biological and Biomedical Sciences (BBS), Microbiology Track, New Haven, CT 06520. Offers PhD, MD/PhD. *Degree requirements:* For doctorate, thesis/dissertation. *Entrance requirements:* For doctorate, GRE General Test, GRE Subject Test. Additional exam requirements/recommendations for international students: Required—TOEFL. Electronic applications accepted.

UNIFORMED SERVICES UNIVERSITY OF THE HEALTH SCIENCES

F. Edward Hébert School of Medicine
Graduate Program in Emerging Infectious Diseases

Program of Study

One of the missions of the Uniformed Services University of the Health Sciences (USUHS) is to provide both civilians and military students with high-quality training leading to advanced degrees in the biomedical sciences. The Graduate Program in Emerging Infectious Diseases (EID) is designed for applicants who wish to pursue an interdisciplinary program of study leading to the Ph.D. degree and was created for students who are primarily interested in the pathogenesis, host response, and epidemiology of infectious diseases. No M.S. degree program is currently offered. A broadly based core program of formal training is combined with an intensive laboratory research experience in the different disciplines encompassed by the field of infectious diseases. Courses are taught by an interdisciplinary EID faculty who hold primary appointments in the Departments of Microbiology and Immunology, Pathology, Preventive Medicine and Biometrics, Pediatrics, and Medicine. Research training emphasizes modern methods in molecular biology and cell biology, as well as interdisciplinary approaches.

During the first two years, all students are required to complete a series of broadly based core courses and laboratory rotations. Students also select one of two academic tracks in which to focus the remainder of their course work. The two tracks are Microbiology and Immunology, and Preventive Medicine and Biometrics. Advanced coursework is required in each academic track. In addition, each student selects a faculty member with whom he or she would like to carry out a thesis research project. By the end of the second year, the student must complete all requirements for advancement to candidacy for the Ph.D. degree, which includes satisfactory completion of formal course work and passage of the qualifying examination. After advancement to candidacy, the student must complete an original research project and prepare and defend a written dissertation under the supervision of his or her faculty adviser and an advisory committee.

Research Facilities

Each academic department of the University is provided with laboratories for the support of a variety of research projects. Laboratories are available in most areas of study that encompass the interdisciplinary field of emerging infectious diseases, including both basic and medical aspects of bacteriology, bacterial genetics, virology, cellular and molecular immunology, parasitology, pathogenic mechanisms of disease, pathology of infectious disease, and epidemiology of infectious diseases. Resources available to students within the University include real-time PCR, microarray spotters and readers, EPICS, FACSAria and LSRII cell sorters and analyzers, Luminex 100 analyzer, automated oligonucleotide and peptide synthesizers and sequencing, MALDI-TOF Mass Spectrometer, high-resolution electron microscopes, confocal microscopes, a certified central animal facility, and state-of-the-art computer facilities. In addition, a BSL-3 biohazard containment laboratory suite is available. The library/learning resources center subscribes to nearly 3,000 journals (print and online) and maintains several Window and MAC personal computers for use by students, faculty members, and staff members. Biostatisticians serve as a resource for students and faculty members.

Financial Aid

USUHS provides an attractive package of financial support that is administered as a federal salary. This support is available on a competitive basis to all civilian graduate students. Awards are made on an annual basis and are renewable for up to three years. For the 2018–19 academic year, financial support for graduate students is $44,900. In addition to this base support, health insurance and transit benefits are provided, if needed.

Cost of Study

Graduate students in the Emerging Infectious Diseases Program are not required to pay tuition or fees. Civilian students do not incur obligations to the United States government for service after completion of their graduate training programs.

Living and Housing Costs

There is a reasonable supply of affordable rental housing in the area. The University does not have housing for graduate students. Living costs in the greater Washington, D.C., area are comparable to those of other East Coast metropolitan areas.

Student Group

The first full-time graduate students were admitted to the EID program in 2000. There are currently 22 full-time students enrolled in the EID graduate program. The University also has Ph.D. programs in departmentally based basic biomedical sciences, as well as interdisciplinary graduate programs in molecular and cell biology and in neurosciences.

Student Outcomes

Graduates hold faculty, research associate, postdoctoral, science policy, and other positions in universities, medical schools, government, and industrial research institutions. Since 2005, 67 Ph.D.'s have been awarded.

Location

The greater Washington metropolitan area has a population of about 3 million that includes the District of Columbia and the surrounding areas of Maryland and Virginia. The region is a center of education and research and is home to five major universities, four medical schools, and numerous other internationally recognized private and government research centers. In addition, multiple cultural advantages exist in the area and include theaters, a major symphony orchestra, major-league sports, and world-famous museums. The Metro subway system has a station adjacent to the campus and provides a convenient connection from the University to cultural attractions and activities in downtown Washington. The international community in Washington is the source of many diverse cuisines and international cultural events. For a wide variety of outdoor activities, the Blue Ridge Mountains, Chesapeake Bay, and Atlantic coast beaches are all within a 1- to 3-hour drive. Many national and local parks serve the area for weekend hikes, bicycling, and picnics.

The University

USUHS is located just outside Washington, D.C., in Bethesda, Maryland. The campus is situated in an attractive, park-like setting on the grounds of the Walter Reed National Military Medical Center (WRNMMC) and across the street from the National Institutes of Health (NIH). Wooded areas with jogging and biking trails surround the University. NIH and other research institutes in the area provide additional resources to enhance the education experience of graduate students at USUHS. Students can visit the USUHS website at http://www.usuhs.edu/eid.

Uniformed Services University of the Health Sciences

Applying

The Admissions Committee, in consultation with other faculty members, evaluates applications to the program. Each applicant must complete the online application form and have academic transcripts of postsecondary education, and results of the Graduate Record Examinations sent. No GRE Subject Test is required. In addition, three letters of recommendation from individuals familiar with the academic achievements and/or research experience of the applicant are required, as well as a personal statement that expresses the applicant's career objectives. USUHS subscribes fully to the policy of equal educational opportunity and selects students on a competitive basis without regard to race, color, gender, creed, or national origin. Prospective students may apply at https://registrar.usuhs.edu. Completed applications should be received on or before December 1.

Both civilians and military personnel are eligible to apply. Prior to acceptance, each applicant must complete a baccalaureate degree that includes required courses in mathematics, biology, physics, and chemistry (inorganic, organic, and biochemistry). Advanced-level courses in microbiology, molecular biology, genetics, and cell biology are very strongly recommended. All students are expected to have a reasonable level of computer literacy. Active-duty military applicants must obtain the approval and sponsorship of their parent military service, in addition to acceptance into the EID graduate program.

Correspondence and Information

Dr. Christopher C. Broder, Director
Graduate Program in Emerging Infectious Diseases
Uniformed Services University
4301 Jones Bridge Road
Bethesda, Maryland 20814-4755
United States
Phone: 301-295-5749
Fax: 301-295-9145
E-mail: christopher.broder@usuhs.edu
Website: http://www.usuhs.edu/eid

Patricia Grant
Administrative Officer
Graduate Program in Emerging Infectious Diseases
Uniformed Services University
4301 Jones Bridge Road
Bethesda, Maryland 20814-4755
United States
Phone: 301-295-3400
Fax: 301-295-9145
E-mail: patricia.grant@usuhs.edu

THE FACULTY

The interdisciplinary graduate programs at USUHS are superimposed on the departmental structure. Therefore, all faculty members in the interdisciplinary Graduate Program in Emerging Infectious Diseases (EID) have primary appointments in either a basic science or a clinical department and secondary appointments in EID. The faculty is derived primarily from the Departments of Microbiology and Immunology, Pathology, Preventive Medicine and Biometrics, Pediatrics, and Medicine. Thus, the faculty in EID includes the experts in infectious diseases, regardless of department. For additional information, students should visit the USUHS Academic Department website at http://www.usuhs.mil/academic.html. To address e-mail to specific faculty members at USUHS, students should use the first name, a period, the last name, and @usuhs.edu as the address; for example, to send e-mail to John Doe, the address would be john.doe@usuhs.edu.

Naomi E. Aronson, M.D.; Professor, Medicine.
Kimberly A. Bishop-Lilly, Ph.D.; Adjunct Assistant Professor, Navy Medical Research Center.
Christopher C. Broder, Ph.D.; Professor, Microbiology and Immunology.
Timothy H. Burgess, M.D., M.P.H.; Assistant Professor, Medicine.
Drusilla L. Burns, Ph.D.; Adjunct Assistant Professor, CBER, FDA.
David F. Cruess, Ph.D.; Professor, Preventive Medicine and Biometrics.
Stephen J. Davies, Ph.D.; Associate Professor, Microbiology and Immunology.
Saibal Dey, Ph.D.; Adjunct Assistant Professor, Biochemistry.
J. Stephen Dumler, M.D.; Professor, Pathology.
Kristi Frank, Ph.D.; Assistant Professor, Microbiology and Immunology.
Chou-Zen Giam, Ph.D.; Professor, Microbiology and Immunology.
Val G. Hemming, M.D.; Professor, Pediatrics.
Ann E. Jerse, Ph.D.; Professor, Microbiology and Immunology.
Barbara Knollman-Ritschel, M.D.; Professor, Pathology.
Philip R. Krause, M.D.; Assistant Professor, CBER, FDA.
Larry W. Laughlin, M.D., Ph.D.; Professor, Preventive Medicine and Biometrics.
George Liechti, Ph.D.; Assistant Professor, Microbiology and Immunology.
Joseph Mattapallil, Ph.D.; Associate Professor, Microbiology and Immunology.
Angela Melton-Celsa, Ph.D.; Associate Professor, Microbiology and Immunology.
D. Scotty Merrell, Ph.D.; Professor, Microbiology and Immunology.
Eleanor S. Metcalf, Ph.D.; Professor, Microbiology and Immunology.
Nelson L. Michael, M.D., Ph.D.; Adjunct Assistant Professor, Medicine.
Edward Mitre, M.D.; Associate Professor, Microbiology and Immunology.
Jittawadee Murphy, Ph.D.; Assistant Professor, Preventive Medicine and Biometrics.
Martin G. Ottolini, M.D.; Associate Professor, Pediatrics.
Jose Marcelo Ramalho-Ortigao, D.Sc.; Associate Professor, Preventive Medicine and Biometrics.
Allen L. Richards, Ph.D.; Professor, Preventive Medicine and Biometrics.
Brian C. Schaefer, Ph.D.; Associate Professor, Microbiology and Immunology.
David W. Scott, Ph.D.; Professor, Medicine.
Frank P. Shewmaker, Ph.D.; Associate Professor, Pharmacology.
Clifford M. Snapper, M.D.; Professor, Pathology.
Andrew L. Snow, Ph.D.; Assistant Professor, Pharmacology.
V. Ann Stewart, D.V.M., Ph.D.; Professor, Preventive Medicine and Biometrics.
J. Thomas Stocker, M.D.; Professor, Pathology.
Charles Via, M.D.; Assistant Professor, Pathology.
Shuishu Wang, Ph.D.; Assistant Professor, Biochemistry.
Kim Williamson, Ph.D.; Professor, Microbiology and Immunology.

UNIVERSITY OF MASSACHUSETTS AMHERST

Department of Microbiology

★ For more information, visit http://petersons.to/umassmicrobiology

University of Massachusetts Amherst

Programs of Study

The Department of Microbiology at the University of Massachusetts Amherst (UMass) offers programs of graduate study leading to the M.S. and Ph.D. degrees in microbiology. Postdoctoral training is also available. Courses covering various areas in the field of microbiology are offered by the Departmental faculty members, listed in the Faculty and Their Research section.

In the Ph.D. program, formal course work is completed during the first two years. From the start, a large portion of a student's time is dedicated to research. Students actively participate in ongoing research during two 1-semester rotations and then select dissertation problems from the wide spectrum of research areas pursued by the faculty. The following research fields are represented: microbial physiology, genetics, immunology, virology, parasitology, pathogenic bacteriology, fungal pathogenesis, molecular biology, microbial ecology, and environmental microbiology. In the second year, Ph.D. candidates must pass a comprehensive preliminary examination. Degree requirements are completed by submission and defense of a dissertation. There is no foreign language requirement. Completion of the Ph.D. program generally takes four years beyond the bachelor's degree.

Research Facilities

The Department of Microbiology occupies space in the Morrill Science Center, Life Science Laboratories, and Fernald Hall. Laboratories are spacious and well equipped for research and teaching. State-of-the-art equipment necessary for investigation into all aspects of microbiology is available within the Department. The Department's facilities include tissue- and cell-culture laboratories, animal quarters, and various instrument rooms containing preparative and analytical ultracentrifuges, scintillation counters, fermenters, anaerobic chambers, equipment for chromatographic and electrophoretic procedures, photography, and other standard laboratory procedures. Centralized facilities provide state-of-the-art equipment and expertise to support research projects, such as the Light Microscopy Core, Genomics Resource Laboratory, Mass Spectrometry Facility and Flow Cytometry. A full list of core facilities can be found at http://www.umass.edu/ials/core-facilities.

Financial Aid

Financial aid is available in the form of University fellowships and teaching assistantships. Research assistantships are available for advanced graduate students. All assistantships include a waiver of tuition.

Cost of Study

In academic year 2018–19, annual tuition for in-state residents was $2,021 per credit; nonresident tuition was $3,848 per credit. Full-time students register for at least 9 credits per semester. The mandatory fees and tuition assessed for full-time graduate students (9 credits) was $7,891 per semester for in-state residents and $15,422 for nonresidents. Tuition is waived with eligible graduate assistantships. Tuition and fees are subject to change. More information is available in the Bursar's Office fee schedule online at http://www.umass.edu/bursar.

Living and Housing Costs

Graduate student housing is available in several twelve-month campus residence halls through University Housing Services. The University owns and manages unfurnished apartments of various sizes for family housing on or near the campus. Off-campus housing is available; rents vary widely and depend on factors such as size and location. A free bus system connects UMass with all neighboring communities.

Student Group

The Department has approximately 40 graduate and 225 undergraduate students as well as 10 postdoctoral fellows. Enrollment at the Amherst campus is about 29,000, including 6,500 graduate students.

Microbiology graduate students have the option of participating in activities sponsored by the Microbiology Graduate Student Group (MGSG). The group is open to all students pursuing a master's or doctoral degree from the Department of Microbiology at UMass Amherst. The purpose of this organization is (1) fostering student involvement in and communication within the Microbiology program at the University of Massachusetts Amherst, (2) creating an environment for student researchers to present their work and engage in scientific discourse, (3) encouraging participation in scientific conferences, (4) increasing the number of visiting speakers, and (5) promoting student participation in local, state and national American Society for Microbiology activities.

Location

The 1,450-acre campus of the University provides a rich cultural environment in a rural setting. Amherst is situated in the picturesque Pioneer Valley in historic western Massachusetts. The area is renowned for its natural beauty. Green open land framed by the outline of the Holyoke Range, clear streams, country roads, forests, grazing cattle, and shade trees are characteristic of the region. A broad spectrum of cultural activities and extensive recreational facilities are available within the University and at four neighboring colleges—Smith, Amherst, Mount Holyoke, and Hampshire. Opportunities for outdoor winter sports are exceptional. Amherst is 90 miles west of Boston and 175 miles north of New York City, and Cape Cod is a 3½-hour drive away.

The University

The University of Massachusetts is the state university of the Commonwealth of Massachusetts and is the flagship campus of the five-campus UMass system. Departments affiliated with the ten colleges and schools of the University offer a variety of graduate degrees through the Graduate School. The Amherst campus consists of approximately 150 buildings, including the twenty-eight-story W. E. B. DuBois Library, which is the largest at a state-supported institution in New England. The library features more than 5.8 million items and is home to a state-of-the-art learning commons equipped with computer workstations and high-speed network access.

Applying

The secure online application is available on the University of Massachusetts Graduate School website: http://www.umass.edu/gradschool. Prospective students are required to take the Graduate Record Examination. Applications for admission should be received by the Graduate Admissions Office by December 1 for September enrollment. Applications received after this date are considered only if space is available.

Correspondence and Information

Graduate Program Director
Department of Microbiology
Morrill IV, N416
639 North Pleasant Street
University of Massachusetts Amherst
Amherst, Massachusetts 01003-9298
United States
Phone: 413-545-2051
Fax: 413-545-1578
E-mail: microbio-dept@microbio.umass.edu
Website: http://www.micro.umass.edu

THE FACULTY AND THEIR RESEARCH

J. F. Holden, Professor and Department Head; Ph.D., Washington (Seattle). Physiology of hyperthermophilic archaea; geomicrobiology of hydrothermal vents; agricultural waste remediation and bioenergy using thermophiles. *Front. Microbiol.* 9:1550, 2018; *Environ. Microbiol.* 20:949–57, 2018; *Environ. Microbiol. Rep.* 8:196–200, 2016; *Front. Microbiol.* 7:1240, 2016; *Front. Microbiol.* 7:167, 2016; *G-cubed* 17:300–23, 2016.

C. L. Baldwin, Adjunct Professor; Ph.D., Cornell. Cellular responses to bacterial and protozoan pathogens of humans and livestock including *Brucella*, *Leptospira*, *Mycobacteria*, and *Theileria*. *J. Immunol*, 192:6, 2014; *Plos One*. 10.1371/journal.pone.0089357; *BMC Genet.* 13:86.

University of Massachusetts Amherst

J. P. Burand, Professor; Ph.D., Washington State. Biology and molecular biology of insect pathogenic viruses, particularly nonoccluded insect viruses and bee viruses, with emphasis on virus-host interactions that affect the virulence and persistence of these viruses in insects. *J. Insect Sci.* 18:3, 2018 https://doi.org/10.1093/jisesa/iey040; *Viruses* 9(10):307, 2017 https://doi.org/10.3390/v9100307; *J. Invertebr. Pathol.* 143:61–8, 2016 doi:10.1016/j.jip.2016.11.016; *J. Invertebr. Pathol.* 112(S1):S68–74, 2013 http://dx.doi.org/10.1016/j.jip.2012.07.012.

P. Chien, Adjunct Associate Professor; Ph.D., California, San Francisco. Protein degradation during bacterial cell-cycle progression and stress. *Annu. Rev. Genet.* Nov 23;50:423–45, 2016; *Mol. Microbiol.* Dec;102(6):1075–85, 2016; *Cell* Oct 8;163(2):419–31, 2015; *Mol. Cell.* Jul 2;59(1):104–16, 2015.*Proc. Natl. Acad. Sci. Unit. States Am.* Nov 5:110(45):18138–43, 2013; *Cell* 154:623–36, 2013. *Mol. Microbiol.* 88(6):1083–92, 2013; *Mol. Microbiol.* 87(6):1277–89, 2013; *Mol. Cell* 43(4):550–60, 2013; *Structure* 20(7):1223–32, 2012.

K. M. DeAngelis, Associate Professor; Ph.D., Berkeley. Microbial ecology of carbon cycling in soils; microbial feedbacks to climate change; lignocellulosic biofuels. *Global Change Biol.* 24(3):895–905, 2018; *ASM Gen. Ann.* 6(5):e01452-17, 2018; *ASM Gen. Ann.* 6(4):e01451-17, 2018; *PLos One* 12(10), e0186440, 2017; *Science* 358(6359):101–5, 2017; *Trends Microbiol.* 25(10):788–96, 2017.

B. Goodell, Professor. Ph.D., Oregon State. Oxidative redox mechanisms and fungal disease initiation. *Biotechnology for Biofuels*, 10:179, 2017 doi.org/10.1186/s13068-017-0865-2; *Sci. Rep.* 7:41798, 2017 doi:10.1038/srep41798; *Biosci. Biotechnol. Biochem.* 80:12, 2016 doi:10.1080/09168451.2016.1220822; *Appl. Environ. Microbiol.* 82:22 6557–72, 2016 doi:10.1128/AEM.01768-16; *Curr. Opin. Chem. Bio.* 29:108–19 2015; *Science* 333:762 2011 doi:10.1126/science.1205411.

S. Goodwin, Dean, College of Natural Sciences; Ph.D., Wisconsin.

K. L. Griffith, Assistant Professor; Ph.D., Maryland. Cell-cell signaling in bacteria; development of tools for studying regulatory networks. *J. Mol. Bio.* 381:261–75, 2008; *Mol. Microbiol.* 70:1012–25, 2008.

G. Jung, Adjunct Professor; Ph.D., Nebraska. Molecular mechanisms of multidrug resistance (MDR) (MDR) and xenobiotic detoxification in filamentous fungi; impact of soil microbes and nematodes on turf quality and disease suppression; turfgrass disease control and management; tomato breeding. *mBio* 9:e00457-18, 2018; *Phytobiomes* 2:71–81, 2018; *Fungal Genet. Biol.* 115:64–77, 2018; *Appl. Soil Ecol.* 121:161–71, 2018; *Nanotechnology* 28:155101, 2017.

M. M. Klingbeil, Associate Professor and Graduate Program Director; Ph.D., Toledo. Molecular and biochemical parasitology, replication and repair of mitochondrial DNA (kinetoplast DNA) and nuclear DNA replication initiation in African trypanosomes. *Trends Parasitol.* [Epub ahead of print], 2016; *PLos One* 10:e0130998, 2015; *MBio* 6:e02425–14, 2015; *Mol. Microbiol.* 87:196–210, 2013; *Eukaryot. Cell* 11:844–55, 2012; *Mol. Biochem. Parasitol.* 175:68–75, 2011; *Mol. Microbiol.* 75:1414–25, 2010; *Mol. Cell* 5:398–400, 2009; *Eukaryot. Cell* 7:2141–6, 2008; *Science* 309:409–15, 2005; *Proc. Natl. Acad. Sci. U.S.A.* 101:4333–4, 2004; *J. Biol. Chem.* 278:49095–101, 2003; *Mol. Cell* 10:175–86, 2002.

J. M. Lopes, Professor and Associate Dean; Ph.D., South Carolina. Regulation of gene expression in eukaryotes. *Genes, Genomes & Genomics* 4:761–7, 2014; *J. Mol. Biol.* 425:457–65, 2013; *Mol. Microbiol.* 83:395–407, 2012.

D. R. Lovley, Distinguished University Professor; Ph.D., Michigan State. Physiology, ecology, and evolution of anaerobic microorganisms; interspecies and microbe-electrode electron exchange; bioremediation; microbially produced electronic materials. *mBio* 8:e00695–17, 2017; *Ann. Rev. Microbiol.* 71:643–64, 2017; *ISME J.* 11:327–36, 2017; *Small* 12:4481–5, 2016.

Y. S. Morita, Assistant Professor; Ph.D., Johns Hopkins. Biosynthesis of lipids and glycans and the pathogenesis of mycobacterial diseases. *mBio* 9:e01823-17, 2018; *Chemistry* 292:17407–17, 2017; *Proc. Natl. Acad. Sci. Unit. States Am.* 113:5400–5, 2016; *mBio* 4:e00472–512, 2013.

M. Muller, Assistant Professor; Ph.D., Pasteur Institute, Paris, France. Viral manipulation of the host gene expression environment with an emphasis on herpesviruses and regulation of RNA decay. *PLoS Pathogens* 13:e1006593 2017; *PLoS Path.* 12;11(5):e1004899, 2015; *PLoS One* 24;9(3):e92581, 2014; *J. Vis. Exp.* 18;(77):e50404, 2013; *Open J. Virol.* 6:173-89, 2012; *Methods* 58(4):349–59, 2012; *PLoS Path.* 8(6):e1002761, 2012; *Nature Methods* 29;8(12):990–2, 2011.

K. Nüsslein, Professor; Ph.D., Michigan State. Microbial ecology of terrestrial and aquatic environments; relating the stress of environmental influences to community structure and function, with emphasis on understanding interactions among bacterial communities. *Front. Microbiol.* 9:1501 2018; *Mol. Ecol.* 26:1547–56, 2017; *Appl. Soil Ecol.* 107:48–56, 2016; *Front. Microbiol.* 6:1057 & 6:779, 2015; *Soil Biol. Biochem.* 80:1–8, 2015; *The ISME Journal* 8:1548–50, 2014; *Mol. Ecol.* 23:2988–99, 2014; *Appl. Environ. Microbiol.* 80:281–8, 2014; *PNAS* 110:988–93, 2013; *Appl. Microbio. Biotechnol.*, 2013, doi: 10.1007/s00253-013-4963-1; *Front. Extr. Microbiol.* 3:175, 2012; *Bioresource Technology* 123:207–13, 2012; *Appl. Microbiol. Biotechnol.* 2:6, 2012; *Biointerfaces* 87(1):109–15, 2011; *Water Res.* 44:4970–9, 2010; *Curr. Opin. Biotechnol.* 21:339–45, 2010; *Geomicrobiology* 26:9–20, 2009.

S. T. Petsch, Adjunct Associate Professor; Ph.D., Yale. Transport, transformation, and biodegradation of natural organic matter in sediments, soils, and sedimentary rocks. *Geology,* 36:139–42, 2008; *Appl. Environ. Microbiol.* 73:4171–9, 2007; *Geochim. Cosmochim. Acta* 71:4233–50, 2007; *SEPM* 5:5–9, 2007; *Am. J. Sci.* 306:575–615, 2006; *Palaeogeogr. Palaeoclim. Palaeoecol.* 219:157–70, 2005; *Gas Technol. Inst.* GRI-05/0023, 2004; *Am. J. Sci.* 304:234–49, 2004; *Org. Geochem.* 34:731–43, 2003.

S. M. Rich, Professor; Ph.D. California, Irvine. Population genetics and evolution of vectorborne and zoonotic diseases. *Proc. Natl. Acad. Sci. Unit. States Am.* 106:14902–7; *Emerg. Infect. Dis.* 15:585–7; *Gene* 304:65–75; *Proc. Natl. Acad. Sci. Unit. States Am.* 98:15038–43; *J. Clin. Microbiol.* 39:494–7; *Proc. Natl. Acad. Sci. Unit. States Am.* 95:4425–30; *Proc. Natl. Acad. Sci. Unit. States Am.* 94:13040–45; *Insect Mol. Biol.* 6:123–9; *Proc. Natl. Acad. Sci. Unit. States Am.* 92:6284–8.

S. J. Sandler, Professor; Ph.D., California, Berkeley. Molecular genetics of recombination; DNA replication and DNA repair in bacteria. *Mol. Microbiol.* 57:1074, 2005; *Mol. Microbiol.* 53:1343, 2004.

D. A. Sela, Adjunct Assistant Professor; Ph.D., California, Davis. Breast milk interactions with the infant microbiome; nutritional microbiology; comparative microbial genomics. *Evolution, Medicine, and Public Health* PMID: 25835022, 2015; *Am. J. Clin. Nutr.* PMID:24452239, 2014; *Appl. Environ. Microbiol.* PMID:22138995, 2013; *J. Biol. Chem.* PMID:21288901, 2011; *Trends Microbiol.* PMID:20409714, 2010; *Proc. Natl. Acad. Sci. Unit. States Am.* PMID:19033196, 2008.

M. Sloan Siegrist, Assistant Professor; Ph.D., Harvard School of Public Health. Mycobacterial cell envelope; mechanisms by which *Mycobacterium* tuberculosis adapts to the host environment; bacterial cell wall engineering for basic and translational applications. *Cell Reports*, PMID: 25892235, 2015; *FEMS Microbiol. Rev.*, PMID: 25725012, 2014; *Proc. Natl. Acad. Sci. Unit. States Am.*, PMID: 25049412, 2014; *mBio*, PMID: 24803520, 2014; *Proc. Natl. Acad. Sci. Unit. States Am.*, PMID: 24706769, 2014; *ACS Chemical Biology*, PMID: 23240806, 2013; *J. Am. Chem. Soc.*, PMID: 22978752, 2012; *Proc. Natl. Acad. Sci. Unit. States Am.*, PMID: 19846780, 2009.

D. Wang, Adjunct Assistant Professor; Ph.D., Duke. Mechanisms of intracellular symbiosis between eukaryotic legume hosts and nitrogen-fixing bacteria. *Mol. Plant* 4(4):581, 2011; *Science* 327(5969):1126, 2010; *Current Biology* 17(20):1784, 2007.

W. Webley, Associate Professor and Director of Pre-Medical/Pre-Dental Advising; Ph.D., Massachusetts. Immunology and pathogenic bacteriology; understanding the role and mechanism of *Chlamydia* involvement in chronic severe asthma; design and development of a novel multi-subunit vaccine display/delivery system for *Chlamydia;* role of domestic flies in transmission of blinding trachoma. *Respir. Res.* (18)98, 2017; *Lancet Respir. Med.* 4(3), 2016; *Trends* 23(7); 2015; *World Biomedical Frontiers* ISSN:2328-0166, 2014; *PLos One* 8(12), 2013; *Biology of AIDS*, 2nd edition, Kendall/Hunt Publishing; *Vaccine* 30(41):5942–8, 2012; *Plos One* 7(4), 2012; *Resp. Res.* 13(1):32, 2012; *Eur. Respir. J.* 38(4)994–5, 2011; *Respirology* 16(7):1081–7, 2011; *Pediatr. Infect. Dis. J.*, 29(12):1093–8, 2010; *Eur. Respir. J.*, 33:1–8, 2009; *Biology of AIDS,* 2nd ed., Dubuque, Iowa: Kendall/Hunt Publishing Company, 2008; *CHEST* 134(suppl.), 2008; *CHEST* 132(4):607, 2007; *J. Clin. Apheresis* 3, 2006; *BMC Infect. Dis.* 6:23, 2006; *Am. J. Respir. Crit. Care Med.* 171(10):1083–8, 2005; *BMC Infect. Dis.* 4(1):23, 2004 (with Stuart and Norkin); *Curr. Microbiol.* 49(1):13–21, 2004; *Am. J. Respir. Crit. Care Med.* 169(7):A586, 2004; *J. Clin. Apheresis* 18(2), 2003; *Exp. Cell Res.* 287(1):67–78, 2003.

H. Xiao, Adjunct Associate Professor; Ph.D., Wisconsin–Madison. Diet-based strategies for disease prevention; interaction between dietary components and human microbiome; enhancement of biological activity of dietary components by combination regimen; food processing, and nanotechnology; http://www.umass.edu/foodsci/faculty/hang-xiao.

Section 13
Neuroscience and Neurobiology

This section contains a directory of institutions offering graduate work in neuroscience and neurobiology, followed by in-depth entries submitted by institutions that chose to prepare detailed program descriptions. Additional information about programs listed in the directory but not augmented by an in-depth entry may be obtained by writing directly to the dean of a graduate school or chair of a department at the address given in the directory.

For programs offering related work, see also in this book *Anatomy; Biochemistry; Biological and Biomedical Sciences; Biophysics; Cell, Molecular, and Structural Biology; Genetics, Developmental Biology, and Reproductive Biology; Optometry and Vision Sciences; Pathology and Pathobiology; Pharmacology and Toxicology; Physiology;* and *Zoology.* In another guide in this series:

Graduate Programs in the Humanities, Arts & Social Sciences
See *Psychology and Counseling*

CONTENTS

Program Directories

Featured Schools: Displays and Close-Ups

See also:

Biopsychology

American University, College of Arts and Sciences, Department of Psychology, Washington, DC 22016-8062. Offers addiction and addictive behavior (Certificate); behavior, cognition, and neuroscience (PhD); clinical psychology (PhD); psychobiology of healing (Certificate); psychology (MA). *Accreditation:* APA. *Program availability:* Part-time. *Faculty:* 20 full-time (8 women), 9 part-time/adjunct (7 women). *Students:* 80 full-time (68 women), 8 part-time (7 women); includes 15 minority (5 Black or African American, non-Hispanic/Latino; 4 Asian, non-Hispanic/Latino; 5 Hispanic/Latino; 1 Two or more races, non-Hispanic/Latino), 6 international. Average age 28. 461 applicants, 12% accepted, 23 enrolled. In 2017, 24 master's, 11 doctorates awarded. *Degree requirements:* For master's, comprehensive exam, thesis or alternative; for doctorate, comprehensive exam, thesis/dissertation. *Entrance requirements:* For master's, GRE General Test, GRE Subject Test, statement of purpose, transcripts, 2 letters of recommendation; for doctorate, GRE General Test, GRE Subject Test, 3 letters of recommendation, statement of purpose, transcripts, resume. Additional exam requirements/recommendations for international students: Required—TOEFL (minimum score 600 paper-based; 100 iBT). *Application deadline:* For fall admission, 3/1 priority date for domestic students. Application fee: $55. *Expenses:* Contact institution. *Financial support:* Research assistantships, teaching assistantships, institutionally sponsored loans, scholarships/grants, and unspecified assistantships available. Financial award application deadline: 2/1; financial award applicants required to submit FAFSA. *Unit head:* Dr. David Haaga, Department Chair, 202-885-1718, Fax: 202-885-1023, E-mail: ahrens@american.edu. *Application contact:* Jonathan Harper, Associate Director, Graduate Recruitment, 202-885-3622, E-mail: jharper@american.edu.
Website: http://www.american.edu/CAS/Psychology/

Argosy University, Atlanta, Georgia School of Professional Psychology, Atlanta, GA 30328. Offers clinical psychology (MA, Psy D, Postdoctoral Respecialization Certificate), including child and family psychology (Psy D), general adult clinical (Psy D), health psychology (Psy D), neuropsychology/geropsychology (Psy D); community counseling (MA), including marriage and family therapy; counselor education and supervision (Ed D); forensic psychology (MA); industrial organizational psychology (MA); marriage and family therapy (Certificate); sport-exercise psychology (MA). *Accreditation:* APA.

Argosy University, Twin Cities, Minnesota School of Professional Psychology, Eagan, MN 55121. Offers clinical psychology (MA, Psy D), including child and family psychology (Psy D), forensic psychology (Psy D), health and neuropsychology (Psy D), trauma (Psy D); forensic counseling (Post-Graduate Certificate); forensic psychology (MA); industrial organizational psychology (MA); marriage and family therapy (MA, DMFT), including forensic counseling (MA). *Accreditation:* AAMFT; AAMFT/COAMFTE; APA.

Binghamton University, State University of New York, Graduate School, Harpur College of Arts and Sciences, Department of Psychology, Program in Psychology - Behavioral Neuroscience, Binghamton, NY 13902-6000. Offers PhD. *Program availability:* Part-time. *Students:* 16 full-time (8 women), 13 part-time (8 women); includes 8 minority (1 Black or African American, non-Hispanic/Latino; 4 Asian, non-Hispanic/Latino; 2 Hispanic/Latino; 1 Two or more races, non-Hispanic/Latino). Average age 27. 30 applicants, 43% accepted, 6 enrolled. In 2017, 3 doctorates awarded. Terminal master's awarded for partial completion of doctoral program. *Degree requirements:* For doctorate, thesis/dissertation. *Entrance requirements:* For doctorate, GRE General Test. Additional exam requirements/recommendations for international students: Required—TOEFL (minimum score 550 paper-based; 80 iBT). *Application deadline:* For fall admission, 12/15 priority date for domestic and international students. Application fee: $75. Electronic applications accepted. *Financial support:* In 2017–18, 24 students received support, including 3 research assistantships with full tuition reimbursements available (averaging $18,500 per year), 15 teaching assistantships with full tuition reimbursements available (averaging $18,500 per year); career-related internships or fieldwork, Federal Work-Study, institutionally sponsored loans, scholarships/grants, health care benefits, tuition waivers (full and partial), and unspecified assistantships also available. Financial award applicants required to submit FAFSA. *Unit head:* Dr. J. David Jentsch, Program Coordinator, 607-777-4875, E-mail: jjentsch@binghamton.edu. *Application contact:* Ben Balkaya, Assistant Dean and Director, 607-777-2151, Fax: 607-777-2501, E-mail: balkaya@binghamton.edu.

Boston University, School of Medicine, Division of Graduate Medical Sciences, Program in Mental Health Counseling and Behavioral Medicine, Boston, MA 02215. Offers MA. *Faculty research:* HIV/AIDS, trauma, behavioral medicine (obesity, breast cancer), neurosciences, autism, serious mental illness, sports psychology. *Unit head:* Dr. Stephen Brady, Director, 617-414-2320, Fax: 617-414-2323, E-mail: sbrady@bu.edu. *Application contact:* GMS Admissions Office, 617-638-5255, E-mail: askgms@bu.edu.
Website: http://www.bumc.bu.edu/mhbm/

Carnegie Mellon University, Dietrich College of Humanities and Social Sciences, Department of Psychology, Area of Cognitive Neuroscience, Pittsburgh, PA 15213-3891. Offers PhD. *Degree requirements:* For doctorate, comprehensive exam, thesis/dissertation. *Entrance requirements:* For doctorate, GRE General Test. Additional exam requirements/recommendations for international students: Required—TOEFL.

Cornell University, Graduate School, Graduate Fields of Arts and Sciences, Field of Psychology, Ithaca, NY 14853. Offers biopsychology (PhD); human experimental psychology (PhD); personality and social psychology (PhD). *Degree requirements:* For doctorate, comprehensive exam, thesis/dissertation, 2 semesters of teaching experience. *Entrance requirements:* For doctorate, GRE General Test, 3 letters of recommendation. Additional exam requirements/recommendations for international students: Required—TOEFL (minimum score 550 paper-based; 77 iBT). Electronic applications accepted. *Faculty research:* Sensory and perceptual systems, social cognition, cognitive development, quantitative and computational modeling, behavioral neuroscience.

Drexel University, College of Arts and Sciences, Department of Psychology, Philadelphia, PA 19104-2875. Offers clinical psychology (PhD), including clinical psychology, forensic psychology, health psychology, neuropsychology; psychology (MS); JD/PhD. *Accreditation:* APA (one or more programs are accredited). *Degree requirements:* For doctorate, thesis/dissertation, internship. *Entrance requirements:* For doctorate, GRE General Test. Additional exam requirements/recommendations for international students: Required—TOEFL. Electronic applications accepted. *Expenses:* Contact institution. *Faculty research:* Neurosciences, rehabilitation psychology, cognitive science, neurological assessment.

Duke University, Graduate School, Department of Psychology and Neuroscience, Durham, NC 27708. Offers biological psychology (PhD); clinical psychology (PhD); cognitive psychology (PhD); developmental psychology (PhD); experimental psychology (PhD); health psychology (PhD); human social development (PhD); JD/MA. *Accreditation:* APA (one or more programs are accredited). *Degree requirements:* For doctorate, thesis/dissertation. *Entrance requirements:* For doctorate, GRE General Test. Additional exam requirements/recommendations for international students: Required—TOEFL (minimum score 577 paper-based; 90 iBT) or IELTS (minimum score 7). Electronic applications accepted.

Florida State University, The Graduate School, College of Arts and Sciences, Interdisciplinary Program in Neuroscience, Tallahassee, FL 32306. Offers neuroscience (PhD); psychobiology (MS). *Faculty:* 35 full-time (12 women), 2 part-time/adjunct (both women). *Students:* 44 full-time (27 women); includes 5 minority (1 Black or African American, non-Hispanic/Latino; 1 Asian, non-Hispanic/Latino; 1 Hispanic/Latino; 2 Two or more races, non-Hispanic/Latino), 5 international. Average age 26. 50 applicants, 10% accepted, 1 enrolled. In 2017, 5 master's, 6 doctorates awarded. Terminal master's awarded for partial completion of doctoral program. *Degree requirements:* For master's, thesis; for doctorate, comprehensive exam, thesis/dissertation. *Entrance requirements:* For doctorate, GRE General Test (suggested minimum score above 60th percentile on both verbal and quantitative sections), minimum GPA of 3.0, research experience, letters of recommendation. Additional exam requirements/recommendations for international students: Required—TOEFL (minimum score 80 iBT). *Application deadline:* For fall admission, 12/1 for domestic and international students. Application fee: $30. Electronic applications accepted. *Financial support:* In 2017–18, 38 students received support, including 6 fellowships with full tuition reimbursements available (averaging $22,815 per year), 19 research assistantships with full tuition reimbursements available (averaging $23,815 per year), 14 teaching assistantships with full tuition reimbursements available (averaging $22,815 per year); health care benefits also available. Financial award application deadline: 12/1; financial award applicants required to submit FAFSA. *Faculty research:* Sensory processes, neural development and plasticity, ingestive behavior, behavioral and molecular genetics, hormonal control of behavior. *Total annual research expenditures:* $1.8 million. *Unit head:* Dr. Frank Johnson, Director, 850-644-8566, Fax: 850-645-0349, E-mail: johnson@psy.fsu.edu. *Application contact:* Janice Parker, Graduate Program Associate, 850-645-9147, Fax: 850-644-0349, E-mail: info@neuro.fsu.edu.
Website: http://www.neuro.fsu.edu

The Graduate Center, City University of New York, Graduate Studies, Program in Psychology, New York, NY 10016-4039. Offers basic applied neurocognition (PhD); biopsychology (PhD); clinical psychology (PhD); developmental psychology (PhD); environmental psychology (PhD); experimental psychology (PhD); industrial psychology (PhD); learning processes (PhD); neuropsychology (PhD); psychology (PhD); social personality (PhD). *Faculty:* 119 full-time (40 women). *Students:* 428 full-time (308 women); includes 118 minority (31 Black or African American, non-Hispanic/Latino; 31 Asian, non-Hispanic/Latino; 47 Hispanic/Latino; 1 Native Hawaiian or other Pacific Islander, non-Hispanic/Latino; 8 Two or more races, non-Hispanic/Latino), 53 international. Average age 33. 795 applicants, 12% accepted, 56 enrolled. In 2017, 46 doctorates awarded. *Degree requirements:* For doctorate, one foreign language, thesis/dissertation. *Entrance requirements:* For doctorate, GRE General Test. Additional exam requirements/recommendations for international students: Required—TOEFL. *Application deadline:* For fall admission, 12/1 priority date for domestic students. Application fee: $125. Electronic applications accepted. *Financial support:* In 2017–18, 371 students received support, including 340 fellowships, 34 research assistantships, 33 teaching assistantships; career-related internships or fieldwork, Federal Work-Study, institutionally sponsored loans, and tuition waivers (full and partial) also available. Financial award application deadline: 2/1; financial award applicants required to submit FAFSA. *Unit head:* Richard Bodnar, Executive Officer, 212-817-8706, Fax: 212-817-1533, E-mail: rbodnar@gc.cuny.edu. *Application contact:* Les Gribben, Director of Admissions, 212-817-7470, Fax: 212-817-1624, E-mail: lgribben@gc.cuny.edu.

Harvard University, Graduate School of Arts and Sciences, Department of Psychology, Cambridge, MA 02138. Offers psychology (PhD), including behavior and decision analysis, cognition, developmental psychology, experimental psychology, personality, psychobiology, psychopathology; social psychology (PhD). *Accreditation:* APA. *Degree requirements:* For doctorate, thesis/dissertation, general exams. *Entrance requirements:* For doctorate, GRE General Test. Additional exam requirements/recommendations for international students: Required—TOEFL.

Howard University, Graduate School, Department of Psychology, Washington, DC 20059-0002. Offers clinical psychology (PhD); developmental psychology (PhD); experimental psychology (PhD); neuropsychology (PhD); personality psychology (PhD); psychology (MS); social psychology (PhD). *Accreditation:* APA (one or more programs are accredited). *Program availability:* Part-time. *Degree requirements:* For master's, thesis; for doctorate, comprehensive exam, thesis/dissertation, qualifying exam. *Entrance requirements:* For master's, GRE General Test, minimum GPA of 2.5, bachelor's degree in psychology or related field; for doctorate, GRE General Test, minimum GPA of 3.0. *Faculty research:* Personality and psychophysiology, educational and social development of African-American children, child and adult psychopathology.

Liberty University, School of Health Sciences, Lynchburg, VA 24515. Offers anatomy and cell biology (PhD); biomedical sciences (MS); epidemiology (MPH); exercise science (MS), including clinical, community physical activity, human performance, nutrition; global health (MPH); health promotion (MPH); medical sciences (MA), including biopsychology, business management, health informatics, molecular medicine, public health; nutrition (MPH). *Program availability:* Part-time, online learning. *Students:* 542 full-time (394 women), 696 part-time (541 women); includes 402 minority (286 Black or African American, non-Hispanic/Latino; 10 American Indian or Alaska Native, non-Hispanic/Latino; 34 Asian, non-Hispanic/Latino; 46 Hispanic/Latino; 1 Native Hawaiian or other Pacific Islander, non-Hispanic/Latino; 25 Two or more races, non-Hispanic/Latino), 59 international. Average age 32. 1,592 applicants, 40% accepted, 297 enrolled. In 2017, 204 master's awarded. *Degree requirements:* For master's, thesis (for some programs); for doctorate, thesis/dissertation. *Entrance requirements:* For doctorate, MAT or GRE, minimum GPA of 3.25 in master's program, 2-3 recommendations, writing samples (for some programs), letter of intent, professional vitae. Additional exam requirements/recommendations for international students: Required—TOEFL (minimum score 600 paper-based; 100 iBT). Application fee: $50. *Financial support:* Applicants required to submit FAFSA. *Unit head:* Dr. Ralph Linstra, Dean. *Application contact:* Jay Bridge, Director of Admissions, 800-424-9595, Fax: 800-628-7977, E-mail: gradadmissions@liberty.edu.

Louisiana State University and Agricultural & Mechanical College, Graduate School, College of Humanities and Social Sciences, Department of Psychology, Baton Rouge, LA 70803. Offers biological psychology (MA, PhD); clinical psychology (MA, PhD); cognitive psychology (MA, PhD); developmental psychology (MA, PhD); school psychology (MA, PhD). *Accreditation:* APA (one or more programs are accredited). *Faculty:* 29 full-time (11 women). *Students:* 78 full-time (57 women), 18 part-time (14 women); includes 25 minority (8 Black or African American, non-Hispanic/Latino; 5 Asian, non-Hispanic/Latino; 5 Hispanic/Latino; 1 Native Hawaiian or other Pacific Islander, non-Hispanic/Latino; 6 Two or more races, non-Hispanic/Latino), 4 international. Average age 27. 239 applicants, 8% accepted, 18 enrolled. In 2017, 15 master's, 12 doctorates awarded. *Financial support:* In 2017–18, 7 fellowships (averaging $41,483 per year), 9 research assistantships (averaging $19,441 per year), 58 teaching assistantships (averaging $19,688 per year) were awarded. *Total annual research expenditures:* $326,871.

Memorial University of Newfoundland, School of Graduate Studies, Interdisciplinary Program in Cognitive and Behavioral Ecology, St. John's, NL A1C 5S7, Canada. Offers M Sc, PhD. *Degree requirements:* For master's, thesis, public lecture; for doctorate, comprehensive exam, thesis/dissertation, oral defense of dissertation. *Entrance requirements:* For master's, honors degree (minimum 2nd class standing) in related field; for doctorate, master's degree. Electronic applications accepted. *Faculty research:* Seabird feeding ecology, marine mammal and seabird energetics, systems of fish, seabird/seal/fisheries interaction.

Northwestern University, The Graduate School, Judd A. and Marjorie Weinberg College of Arts and Sciences, Department of Psychology, Evanston, IL 60208. Offers brain, behavior and cognition (PhD); clinical psychology (PhD); cognitive psychology (PhD); personality psychology (PhD); social psychology (PhD); JD/PhD. Admissions and degrees offered through The Graduate School. *Accreditation:* APA (one or more programs are accredited). *Program availability:* Part-time. *Degree requirements:* For doctorate, thesis/dissertation. *Entrance requirements:* For doctorate, GRE General Test, GRE Subject Test. Additional exam requirements/recommendations for international students: Required—TOEFL. Electronic applications accepted. *Faculty research:* Memory and higher order cognition, anxiety and depression, effectiveness of psychotherapy, social cognition, molecular basis of memory.

Northwestern University, The Graduate School and Feinberg School of Medicine, Program in Clinical Psychology, Evanston, IL 60208. Offers clinical psychology (PhD), including clinical neuropsychology. Admissions and degree offered through The Graduate School. *Accreditation:* APA. *Degree requirements:* For doctorate, thesis/dissertation, clinical internship. *Entrance requirements:* For doctorate, GRE General Test, GRE Subject Test, minimum GPA of 3.2, course work in psychology. Additional exam requirements/recommendations for international students: Required—TOEFL. *Faculty research:* Cancer and cardiovascular risk reduction, evaluation of mental health services and policy, neuropsychological assessment, outcome of psychotherapy, cognitive therapy, pediatric and clinical child psychology.

Oregon Health & Science University, School of Medicine, Graduate Programs in Medicine, Department of Behavioral Neuroscience, Portland, OR 97239-3098. Offers PhD. *Faculty:* 21 full-time (7 women), 25 part-time/adjunct (9 women). *Students:* 29 full-time (16 women); includes 10 minority (2 Black or African American, non-Hispanic/Latino; 2 Asian, non-Hispanic/Latino; 5 Hispanic/Latino; 1 Two or more races, non-Hispanic/Latino). Average age 29. 109 applicants, 14% accepted, 5 enrolled. In 2017, 2 doctorates awarded. Terminal master's awarded for partial completion of doctoral program. *Degree requirements:* For doctorate, comprehensive exam, thesis/dissertation, qualifying exam. *Entrance requirements:* For doctorate, GRE General Test (minimum scores: 153 Verbal/148 Quantitative/4.5 Analytical), undergraduate coursework in biopsychology and other basic science areas. *Application deadline:* For fall admission, 12/1 for domestic and international students. Application fee: $70. Electronic applications accepted. *Financial support:* Fellowships, research assistantships, health care benefits, tuition waivers (full), and stipends (for PhD students) available. Financial award application deadline: 3/1; financial award applicants required to submit FAFSA. *Faculty research:* Behavioral neuroscience, behavioral genomics, biological basis of drug and alcohol abuse, cognitive neuroscience, neuropharmacology and neuroendocrinology. *Unit head:* Dr. Bita Moghaddam, Program Director. *Application contact:* Kris Thomason, Graduate Program Manager, 503-494-8464, E-mail: somgrad@ohsu.edu.
Website: http://www.ohsu.edu/som-BehNeuro/

Palo Alto University, PGSP-Stanford Psy D Consortium Program, Palo Alto, CA 94304. Offers Psy D. Program offered jointly with Stanford University. *Accreditation:* APA. *Faculty:* 14 full-time (12 women), 61 part-time/adjunct (42 women). *Students:* 167 full-time (140 women), 1 (woman) part-time; includes 56 minority (7 Black or African American, non-Hispanic/Latino; 1 American Indian or Alaska Native, non-Hispanic/Latino; 14 Asian, non-Hispanic/Latino; 15 Hispanic/Latino; 19 Two or more races, non-Hispanic/Latino). Average age 26. 417 applicants, 11% accepted, 30 enrolled. In 2017, 28 doctorates awarded. *Degree requirements:* For doctorate, comprehensive exam, thesis/dissertation, 2000-hour clinical internship. *Entrance requirements:* For doctorate, GRE General Test (minimum overall score 1200); GRE Subject Test in psychology (highly recommended), undergraduate degree in psychology or related area with minimum GPA of 3.3. Additional exam requirements/recommendations for international students: Required—TOEFL, IELTS. *Application deadline:* For fall admission, 12/2 priority date for domestic and international students. Applications are processed on a rolling basis. Application fee: $50. Electronic applications accepted. *Expenses:* Contact institution. *Financial support:* In 2017–18, 95 students received support, including fellowships (averaging $4,000 per year), research assistantships (averaging $1,000 per year), teaching assistantships (averaging $3,000 per year); Federal Work-Study and scholarships/grants also available. Financial award applicants required to submit FAFSA. *Unit head:* Dr. Steve Smith, Co-Director of Clinical Training, PGSP-Stanford Psy D Consortium, E-mail: stevesmith@paloaltou.edu. *Application contact:* Dr. Kimberly Hill, Co-Director of Clinical Training, PGSP-Stanford Psy D Consortium, 650-725-5582, E-mail: khill@paloaltou.edu.
Website: http://www.paloaltou.edu/graduate-programs/pgsp-psyd-stanford-consortium

Penn State University Park, Graduate School, College of Health and Human Development, Department of Biobehavioral Health, University Park, PA 16802. Offers MS, PhD. *Unit head:* Dr. Ann C. Crouter, Dean, 814-865-1420, Fax: 814-865-3282. *Application contact:* Lori Hawn, Director, Graduate Student Services, 814-865-1795, Fax: 814-863-4627, E-mail: l-gswww@lists.psu.edu.
Website: http://bbh.hhdev.psu.edu/

Philadelphia College of Osteopathic Medicine, Graduate and Professional Programs, Department of Psychology, Philadelphia, PA 19131-1694. Offers applied behavior analysis (Certificate); clinical health psychology (Post-Doctoral Certificate); clinical neuropsychology (Post-Doctoral Certificate); clinical psychology (Psy D); educational psychology (PhD); mental health counseling (MS); organizational development and leadership (MS); psychology (Certificate); public health management and administration (MS); school psychology (MS, Psy D, Ed S). *Accreditation:* APA. *Faculty:* 19 full-time (11 women), 122 part-time/adjunct (58 women). *Students:* 487 (335 women); includes 138 minority (89 Black or African American, non-Hispanic/Latino; 4 American Indian or Alaska Native, non-Hispanic/Latino; 11 Asian, non-Hispanic/Latino; 12 Hispanic/Latino; 22 Two or more races, non-Hispanic/Latino). 298 applicants, 44% accepted, 100 enrolled. In 2017, 50 master's, 43 doctorates, 10 other advanced degrees awarded. Terminal master's awarded for partial completion of doctoral program. *Degree requirements:* For master's, comprehensive exam (for some programs), thesis (for some programs); for doctorate, comprehensive exam, thesis/dissertation. *Entrance requirements:* For master's, GRE or MAT, minimum GPA of 3.0; bachelor's degree from regionally-accredited college or university; for doctorate, PRAXIS II (for Psy D in school psychology), minimum undergraduate GPA of 3.0; for other advanced degree, GRE (for Ed S). Additional exam requirements/recommendations for international students: Required—TOEFL (minimum score 79 iBT). *Application deadline:* Applications are processed on a rolling basis. Application fee: $50. Electronic applications accepted. *Financial support:* In 2017–18, 28 teaching assistantships were awarded; Federal Work-Study, institutionally sponsored loans, and scholarships/grants also available. Financial award application deadline: 3/15; financial award applicants required to submit FAFSA. *Faculty research:* Adult and childhood anxiety and ADHD; coping with chronic illness; primary care psychology/integrated health care; applied behavior analysis; psychological, educational, and neuropsychological assessment. *Total annual research expenditures:* $533,489. *Unit head:* Dr. Robert DiTomasso, Chairman, 215-871-6442, Fax: 215-871-6458, E-mail: robertd@pcom.edu. *Application contact:* Johnathan Cox, Associate Director of Admissions, 215-871-6700, Fax: 215-871-6719, E-mail: johnathancox@pcom.edu.

Rutgers University–Newark, Graduate School, Program in Psychology, Newark, NJ 07102. Offers cognitive neuroscience (PhD); cognitive science (PhD); perception (PhD); psychobiology (PhD); social cognition (PhD). *Degree requirements:* For doctorate, comprehensive exam, thesis/dissertation. *Entrance requirements:* For doctorate, GRE General Test, GRE Subject Test, minimum undergraduate B average. Electronic applications accepted. *Faculty research:* Visual perception (luminance, motion), neuroendocrine mechanisms in behavior (reproduction, pain), attachment theory, connectionist modeling of cognition.

Rutgers University–New Brunswick, Graduate School-New Brunswick, Program in Psychology, Piscataway, NJ 08854-8097. Offers behavioral neuroscience (PhD); clinical psychology (PhD); cognitive psychology (PhD); interdisciplinary health psychology (PhD); social psychology (PhD). *Accreditation:* APA. *Degree requirements:* For doctorate, comprehensive exam, thesis/dissertation. *Entrance requirements:* For doctorate, GRE General Test, 3 letters of recommendation. Additional exam requirements/recommendations for international students: Required—TOEFL (minimum score 577 paper-based). Electronic applications accepted. *Faculty research:* Learning and memory, behavioral ecology, hormones and behavior, psychopharmacology, anxiety disorders.

The University of British Columbia, Faculty of Arts and Faculty of Graduate Studies, Department of Psychology, Vancouver, BC V6T 1Z4, Canada. Offers behavioral neuroscience (MA, PhD); clinical psychology (MA, PhD); cognitive science (MA, PhD); developmental psychology (MA, PhD); health psychology (MA, PhD); quantitative methods (MA, PhD); social/personality psychology (MA, PhD). *Accreditation:* APA (one or more programs are accredited). Terminal master's awarded for partial completion of doctoral program. *Degree requirements:* For master's, thesis; for doctorate, comprehensive exam, thesis/dissertation. *Entrance requirements:* For master's and doctorate, GRE General Test. Additional exam requirements/recommendations for international students: Required—TOEFL. Electronic applications accepted. *Expenses:* Contact institution. *Faculty research:* Clinical, developmental, social/personality, cognition, behavioral neuroscience.

University of Connecticut, Graduate School, College of Liberal Arts and Sciences, Department of Psychology, Storrs, CT 06269. Offers behavioral neuroscience (PhD); biopsychology (PhD); clinical psychology (MA, PhD); cognition and instruction (PhD); developmental psychology (MA, PhD); ecological psychology (PhD); experimental psychology (PhD); general psychology (MA, PhD); industrial/organizational psychology (PhD); language and cognition (PhD); neuroscience (PhD); social psychology (MA, PhD). *Accreditation:* APA. Terminal master's awarded for partial completion of doctoral program. *Degree requirements:* For master's, comprehensive exam; for doctorate, thesis/dissertation. *Entrance requirements:* For master's and doctorate, GRE General Test, GRE Subject Test. Additional exam requirements/recommendations for international students: Required—TOEFL (minimum score 550 paper-based). Electronic applications accepted.

University of Michigan, Rackham Graduate School, College of Literature, Science, and the Arts, Department of Psychology, Ann Arbor, MI 48109. Offers biopsychology (PhD); clinical science (PhD); cognition and cognitive neuroscience (PhD); developmental psychology (PhD); personality and social contexts (PhD); social psychology (PhD). *Accreditation:* APA. *Faculty:* 66 full-time (31 women), 28 part-time/adjunct (17 women). *Students:* 148 full-time (113 women); includes 61 minority (13 Black or African American, non-Hispanic/Latino; 1 American Indian or Alaska Native, non-Hispanic/Latino; 12 Asian, non-Hispanic/Latino; 28 Hispanic/Latino; 7 Two or more races, non-Hispanic/Latino), 24 international. Average age 27. 691 applicants, 7% accepted, 35 enrolled. In 2017, 34 doctorates awarded. Terminal master's awarded for partial completion of doctoral program. *Degree requirements:* For doctorate, comprehensive exam, thesis/dissertation, oral defense of dissertation, preliminary exam. *Entrance requirements:* For doctorate, GRE General Test. Additional exam requirements/recommendations for international students: Required—TOEFL. *Application deadline:* For fall admission, 12/1 for domestic and international students. Application fee: $75 ($90 for international students). Electronic applications accepted. *Expenses:* $11,184 in-state, $22,578 out-of-state. *Financial support:* In 2017–18, 90 students received support, including 61 fellowships with full tuition reimbursements available (averaging $26,400 per year), 10 research assistantships with full tuition reimbursements available (averaging $26,400 per year), 89 teaching assistantships with full tuition reimbursements available (averaging $26,400 per year); career-related internships or fieldwork, traineeships, and health care benefits also available. Financial award application deadline: 4/15. *Unit head:* Prof. Patricia Reuter-Lorenz, Department Chair, 734-764-7429. *Application contact:* Sheri M. Circele, Psychology Student Academic Affairs, 734-764-2580, Fax: 734-764-3520, E-mail: psych.saa@umich.edu.
Website: http://www.lsa.umich.edu/psych/

University of Minnesota, Twin Cities Campus, Graduate School, College of Liberal Arts, Department of Psychology, Program in Cognitive and Biological Psychology, Minneapolis, MN 55455-0213. Offers PhD. *Degree requirements:* For doctorate, comprehensive exam, thesis/dissertation. *Entrance requirements:* For doctorate, GRE General Test, GRE Subject Test (recommended), 12 credits of upper-level psychology courses, including a course in statistics or psychological measurement. Additional exam requirements/recommendations for international students: Required—TOEFL (minimum score 550 paper-based; 79 iBT).

University of Nebraska–Lincoln, Graduate College, College of Arts and Sciences, Department of Psychology, Lincoln, NE 68588. Offers biopsychology (PhD); clinical psychology (PhD); cognitive psychology (PhD); developmental psychology (PhD); psychology (MA); social/personality psychology (PhD); JD/MA; JD/PhD. *Accreditation:* APA (one or more programs are accredited). *Degree requirements:* For master's, thesis optional; for doctorate, comprehensive exam, thesis/dissertation. *Entrance requirements:* For master's and doctorate, GRE General Test. Additional exam requirements/recommendations for international students: Required—TOEFL (minimum score 550 paper-based). Electronic applications accepted. *Faculty research:* Law and psychology, rural mental health, chronic mental illness, neuropsychology, child clinical psychology.

The University of North Carolina at Chapel Hill, Graduate School, College of Arts and Sciences, Department of Psychology, Chapel Hill, NC 27599-3270. Offers behavioral neuroscience psychology (PhD); clinical psychology (PhD); cognitive psychology (PhD); developmental psychology (PhD); quantitative psychology (PhD); social psychology (PhD). *Accreditation:* APA. *Degree requirements:* For doctorate, comprehensive exam, thesis/dissertation. *Entrance requirements:* For doctorate, GRE General Test, minimum GPA of 3.0. Additional exam requirements/recommendations for international students: Required—TOEFL (minimum score 550 paper-based; 79 iBT), IELTS (minimum score 7). Electronic applications accepted. *Faculty research:* Expressed emotion, cognitive development, social cognitive neuroscience, human memory personality.

University of Oklahoma Health Sciences Center, College of Medicine and Graduate College, Graduate Programs in Medicine, Department of Psychiatry and Behavioral Sciences, Oklahoma City, OK 73190. Offers biological psychology (MS, PhD). *Degree requirements:* For master's, thesis; for doctorate, thesis/dissertation. *Entrance requirements:* For doctorate, GRE General Test, 3 letters of recommendation. Additional exam requirements/recommendations for international students: Required—TOEFL. *Faculty research:* Behavioral neuroscience, human neuropsychology, psychophysiology, behavioral medicine, health psychology.

University of Oregon, Graduate School, College of Arts and Sciences, Department of Psychology, Eugene, OR 97403. Offers clinical psychology (PhD); cognitive psychology (MA, MS, PhD); developmental psychology (MA, MS, PhD); physiological psychology (MA, MS, PhD); psychology (MA, MS, PhD); social/personality psychology (MA, MS, PhD). *Accreditation:* APA (one or more programs are accredited). Terminal master's awarded for partial completion of doctoral program. *Degree requirements:* For doctorate, thesis/dissertation. *Entrance requirements:* For master's, GRE General Test, minimum GPA of 3.0; for doctorate, GRE General Test. Additional exam requirements/recommendations for international students: Required—TOEFL.

The University of Texas at Austin, Graduate School, The Institute for Neuroscience, Austin, TX 78712-1111. Offers PhD, MD/PhD. Terminal master's awarded for partial completion of doctoral program. *Degree requirements:* For doctorate, thesis/dissertation. *Entrance requirements:* For doctorate, GRE. Electronic applications accepted. *Faculty research:* Cellular/molecular biology, neurobiology, pharmacology, behavioral neuroscience.

University of Windsor, Faculty of Graduate Studies, Faculty of Arts and Social Sciences, Department of Psychology, Windsor, ON N9B 3P4, Canada. Offers adult clinical (MA, PhD); applied social psychology (MA, PhD); child clinical (MA, PhD); clinical neuropsychology (MA, PhD). *Degree requirements:* For master's, thesis; for doctorate, comprehensive exam, thesis/dissertation. *Entrance requirements:* For master's, GRE General Test, GRE Subject Test in psychology, minimum B average; for doctorate, GRE General Test, GRE Subject Test in psychology, master's degree. Additional exam requirements/recommendations for international students: Required—TOEFL (minimum score 600 paper-based). Electronic applications accepted. *Faculty research:* Gambling, suicidology, emotional competence, psychotherapy and trauma.

University of Wisconsin–Madison, Graduate School, College of Letters and Science, Department of Psychology, Program in Biology of Brain and Behavior, Madison, WI 53706-1380. Offers PhD. *Degree requirements:* For doctorate, comprehensive exam, thesis/dissertation. *Entrance requirements:* For doctorate, GRE General Test, minimum undergraduate GPA of 3.0. Additional exam requirements/recommendations for international students: Required—TOEFL. Electronic applications accepted.

Wayne State University, School of Medicine, Office of Biomedical Graduate Programs, Detroit, MI 48202. Offers anatomy and cell biology (MS, PhD); basic medical sciences (MS); biochemistry and molecular biology (MS, PhD); cancer biology (MS, PhD); clinical and translational science (Graduate Certificate); family medicine and public health sciences (MPH, Graduate Certificate), including public health practice; genetic counseling (MS); immunology and microbiology (MS, PhD); medical physics (MS, PhD, Graduate Certificate); medical research (MS); molecular medicine and genomics (MS, PhD), including molecular genetics and genomics; pathology (PhD); pharmacology (MS, PhD); physiology (MS, PhD), including physiology, reproductive sciences (PhD); psychiatry and behavioral neurosciences (PhD), including translational neuroscience; MD/MPH; MD/PhD; MPH/MA; MSW/MPH. *Program availability:* Part-time, evening/weekend. *Students:* 268 full-time (152 women), 117 part-time (59 women); includes 108 minority (19 Black or African American, non-Hispanic/Latino; 1 American Indian or Alaska Native, non-Hispanic/Latino; 62 Asian, non-Hispanic/Latino; 9 Hispanic/Latino; 17 Two or more races, non-Hispanic/Latino), 48 international. Average age 26. 1,133 applicants, 21% accepted, 151 enrolled. In 2017, 70 master's, 25 doctorates, 10 other advanced degrees awarded. Terminal master's awarded for partial completion of doctoral program. *Degree requirements:* For master's, thesis (for some programs); for doctorate, thesis/dissertation. *Entrance requirements:* For master's, doctorate, and Graduate Certificate, GRE. Additional exam requirements/recommendations for international students: Required—TOEFL (minimum score 550 paper-based; 100 iBT), Michigan English Language Assessment Battery (minimum score 85); Recommended—IELTS (minimum score 6.5), TWE (minimum score 5.5). *Application deadline:* For fall admission, 2/1 for domestic and international students. Applications are processed on a rolling basis. Application fee: $50. Electronic applications accepted. *Expenses:* Contact institution. *Financial support:* In 2017–18, 177 students received support, including 64 fellowships with full tuition reimbursements available (averaging $24,388 per year), 79 research assistantships with full tuition reimbursements available (averaging $26,894 per year); scholarships/grants, traineeships, and health care benefits also available. *Faculty research:* Cancer biology, neurosciences, vision sciences, molecular biology, pathology, physiology, pharmacology, public health, medical physics. *Unit head:* Dr. Daniel A. Walz, Associate Dean for Biomedical Graduate Programs, 313-577-1455, Fax: 313-577-8796, E-mail: gradprogs@med.wayne.edu.
Website: https://www.med.wayne.edu/biomedical-graduate-programs/

Neurobiology

Boston University, School of Medicine, Division of Graduate Medical Sciences, Department of Anatomy and Neurobiology, Boston, MA 02118. Offers MA, PhD, MD/PhD. *Program availability:* Part-time. Terminal master's awarded for partial completion of doctoral program. *Degree requirements:* For master's, thesis; for doctorate, thesis/dissertation. *Application deadline:* For fall admission, 1/15 for domestic students; for spring admission, 10/15 for domestic students. *Unit head:* Dr. Mark Moss, Chairman, 617-638-4200, Fax: 617-638-4216. *Application contact:* GMS Admissions Office, 617-638-5255, E-mail: askgms@bu.edu.
Website: http://www.bumc.bu.edu/anatneuro/

Brandeis University, Graduate School of Arts and Sciences, Program in Molecular and Cell Biology, Waltham, MA 02454-9110. Offers genetics (PhD); microbiology (PhD); molecular and cell biology (MS, PhD); molecular biology (PhD); neurobiology (PhD); quantitative biology (PhD). *Faculty:* 27 full-time (13 women), 3 part-time/adjunct (2 women). *Students:* 47 full-time (29 women), 2 part-time (1 woman); includes 10 minority (1 American Indian or Alaska Native, non-Hispanic/Latino; 2 Asian, non-Hispanic/Latino; 6 Hispanic/Latino; 1 Two or more races, non-Hispanic/Latino), 11 international. Average age 27. 138 applicants, 25% accepted, 18 enrolled. In 2017, 11 master's, 8 doctorates awarded. Terminal master's awarded for partial completion of doctoral program. *Degree requirements:* For master's, thesis optional, research project, research lab, or project lab; for doctorate, comprehensive exam, thesis/dissertation, journal clubs; research seminar; colloquia; qualifying exam. *Entrance requirements:* For master's, GRE General Test, transcripts, resume, letters of recommendation, statement of purpose; for doctorate, GRE General Test, transcripts, resume, letters of recommendation, statement of purpose, list of previous research experience. Additional exam requirements/recommendations for international students: Required—PTE (minimum score 68), TOEFL (minimum score 600 paper-based, 100 iBT) or IELTS (7). *Application deadline:* For fall admission, 12/1 priority date for domestic students; for spring admission, 11/15 for domestic students, 10/15 for international students. Applications are processed on a rolling basis. Application fee: $75. Electronic applications accepted. *Expenses: Tuition:* Full-time $48,720. *Required fees:* $88. Tuition and fees vary according to course load, degree level, program and student level. *Financial support:* In 2017–18, 46 students received support, including 20 fellowships with full tuition reimbursements available (averaging $33,000 per year), 19 research assistantships with full tuition reimbursements available (averaging $33,000 per year); scholarships/grants and tuition waivers (partial) also available. Financial award application deadline: 4/15; financial award applicants required to submit FAFSA. *Faculty research:* Molecular biology, genetics and development; structural and cell biology; neurobiology. *Unit head:* Dr. James Haber, Co-Chair, 781-736-2462, E-mail: haber@brandeis.edu. *Application contact:* Jena Pitman-Leung, Department Administrator, 781-736-2352, E-mail: scigradoffice@brandeis.edu.
Website: http://www.brandeis.edu/gsas/programs/mcbio.html

California Institute of Technology, Division of Biology, Program in Neurobiology, Pasadena, CA 91125-0001. Offers PhD. *Degree requirements:* For doctorate, thesis/dissertation, qualifying exam. *Entrance requirements:* For doctorate, GRE General Test.

Carnegie Mellon University, Mellon College of Science, Department of Biological Sciences, Pittsburgh, PA 15213-3891. Offers biochemistry (PhD); biophysics (PhD); cell and developmental biology (PhD); computational biology (MS, PhD); genetics (PhD); molecular biology (PhD); neuroscience (PhD); structural biology (PhD). *Degree requirements:* For doctorate, comprehensive exam, thesis/dissertation. *Entrance requirements:* For doctorate, GRE General Test, GRE Subject Test, interview. Electronic applications accepted. *Faculty research:* Genetic structure, function, and regulation; protein structure and function; biological membranes; biological spectroscopy.

Columbia University, College of Physicians and Surgeons, Program in Neurobiology and Behavior, New York, NY 10032. Offers PhD. Only candidates for the PhD are admitted. *Degree requirements:* For doctorate, thesis/dissertation. *Entrance requirements:* For doctorate, GRE General Test. Additional exam requirements/recommendations for international students: Required—TOEFL. *Expenses:* Contact institution. *Faculty research:* Cellular and molecular mechanisms of neural development, neuropathology, neuropharmacology.

Cornell University, Graduate School, Graduate Fields of Agriculture and Life Sciences, Field of Neurobiology and Behavior, Ithaca, NY 14853. Offers behavioral biology (PhD), including behavioral ecology, chemical ecology, ethology, neuroethology, sociobiology; neurobiology (PhD), including cellular and molecular neurobiology, neuroanatomy, neurochemistry, neuropharmacology, neurophysiology, sensory physiology. *Degree requirements:* For doctorate, comprehensive exam, thesis/dissertation, 1 year of teaching experience, seminar presentation. *Entrance requirements:* For doctorate, GRE General Test, GRE Subject Test (biology), 3 letters of recommendation. Additional exam requirements/recommendations for international students: Required—TOEFL (minimum score 550 paper-based; 77 iBT). Electronic applications accepted. *Faculty research:* Cellular neurobiology and neuropharmacology, integrative neurobiology, social behavior, chemical ecology, neuroethology.

Dalhousie University, Faculty of Graduate Studies and Faculty of Medicine, Graduate Programs in Medicine, Department of Anatomy and Neurobiology, Halifax, NS B3H 4R2, Canada. Offers M Sc, PhD. *Degree requirements:* For master's, thesis; for doctorate, thesis/dissertation. *Entrance requirements:* For master's and doctorate, GRE (recommended), minimum A- average. Additional exam requirements/recommendations for international students: Required—1 of 5 approved tests: TOEFL, IELTS, CANTEST, CAEL, Michigan English Language Assessment Battery. Electronic applications accepted. *Faculty research:* Neuroscience histology, cell biology, neuroendocrinology, evolutionary biology.

Duke University, Graduate School, Department of Evolutionary Anthropology, Durham, NC 27708. Offers cellular and molecular biology (PhD); gross anatomy and physical anthropology (PhD), including comparative morphology of human and non-human primates, primate social behavior, vertebrate paleontology; neuroanatomy (PhD). *Degree requirements:* For doctorate, one foreign language, thesis/dissertation. *Entrance requirements:* For doctorate, GRE General Test. Additional exam requirements/recommendations for international students: Required—TOEFL (minimum score 577 paper-based; 90 iBT) or IELTS (minimum score 7). Electronic applications accepted.

Duke University, Graduate School, Department of Neurobiology, Durham, NC 27710. Offers PhD. *Degree requirements:* For doctorate, variable foreign language requirement, thesis/dissertation. *Entrance requirements:* For doctorate, GRE General Test. Additional exam requirements/recommendations for international students: Required—TOEFL (minimum score 577 paper-based; 90 iBT) or IELTS (minimum score 7). Electronic applications accepted.

Georgia State University, College of Arts and Sciences, Department of Biology, Program in Neurobiology and Behavior, Atlanta, GA 30302-3083. Offers bioinformatics (MS); neurobiology and behavior (MS, PhD). *Program availability:* Part-time. Terminal master's awarded for partial completion of doctoral program. *Entrance requirements:* For master's and doctorate, GRE. *Application deadline:* Applications are processed on a rolling basis. Application fee: $50. Electronic applications accepted. *Expenses:* Tuition, state resident: full-time $7020. Tuition, nonresident: full-time $22,518. *Required fees:* $2128. Tuition and fees vary according to degree level and program. *Financial support:* Fellowships and research assistantships available. Financial award application

deadline: 12/3. *Faculty research:* Behavior, circadian and circa-annual rhythms, developmental genetics, neuroendocrinology, cytoskeletal dynamics. *Unit head:* Dr. Charles Derby, Director of Graduate Studies, 404-413-5393, Fax: 404-413-5446, E-mail: cderby@gsu.edu.
Website: http://biology.gsu.edu/

Harvard University, Graduate School of Arts and Sciences, Program in Neuroscience, Boston, MA 02115. Offers neurobiology (PhD). *Degree requirements:* For doctorate, thesis/dissertation, qualifying exam. *Entrance requirements:* For doctorate, GRE General Test, GRE Subject Test. Additional exam requirements/recommendations for international students: Required—TOEFL. *Faculty research:* Relationship between diseases of the nervous system and basic science.

Illinois State University, Graduate School, College of Arts and Sciences, School of Biological Sciences, Normal, IL 61790. Offers animal behavior (MS); bacteriology (MS); biochemistry (MS); biological sciences (MS); biology (PhD); biophysics (MS); biotechnology (MS); botany (MS, PhD); cell biology (MS); conservation biology (MS); developmental biology (MS); ecology (MS, PhD); entomology (MS); evolutionary biology (MS); genetics (MS, PhD); immunology (MS); microbiology (MS, PhD); molecular biology (MS); molecular genetics (MS); neurobiology (MS); neuroscience (MS); parasitology (MS); physiology (MS, PhD); plant biology (MS); plant molecular biology (MS); plant sciences (MS); structural biology (MS); zoology (MS, PhD). *Program availability:* Part-time. *Degree requirements:* For master's, thesis or alternative; for doctorate, variable foreign language requirement, thesis/dissertation, 2 terms of residency. *Entrance requirements:* For master's, GRE General Test, minimum GPA of 2.6 in last 60 hours of course work; for doctorate, GRE General Test. *Faculty research:* Redoc balance and drug development in schistosoma mansoni, control of the growth of listeria monocytogenes at low temperature, regulation of cell expansion and microtubule function by SPRI, CRUI: physiology and fitness consequences of different life history phenotypes.

Indiana University–Purdue University Indianapolis, Indiana University School of Medicine, Stark Neurosciences Research Institute, Indianapolis, IN 46202. Offers medical neuroscience (PhD). *Degree requirements:* For doctorate, thesis/dissertation. *Entrance requirements:* For doctorate, GRE General Test, previous course work in calculus, organic chemistry, and physics. *Faculty research:* Neurobiology from molecular level to complex behavioral interactions.

Louisiana State University Health Sciences Center, School of Graduate Studies in New Orleans, Department of Cell Biology and Anatomy, New Orleans, LA 70112-2223. Offers cell biology and anatomy (PhD), including clinical anatomy, development, cell, and neurobiology; MD/PhD. *Faculty:* 17 full-time (2 women). *Students:* 6 full-time (0 women), 1 (woman) part-time; includes 1 minority (Asian, non-Hispanic/Latino). 1 applicant. *Degree requirements:* For doctorate, comprehensive exam, thesis/dissertation. *Entrance requirements:* For doctorate, GRE General Test, minimum undergraduate GPA of 3.0. Additional exam requirements/recommendations for international students: Recommended—TOEFL, IELTS. *Application deadline:* For fall admission, 3/1 priority date for domestic students, 3/1 for international students. Applications are processed on a rolling basis. Application fee: $30. *Expenses:* Tuition, state resident: full-time $11,835; part-time $518 per hour. Tuition, nonresident: full-time $24,108; part-time $1079 per hour. *Required fees:* $1254; $55 per hour. *Financial support:* In 2017–18, 6 students received support. Unspecified assistantships available. Financial award application deadline: 4/1. *Faculty research:* Visual system organization, neural development, plasticity of sensory systems, information processing through the nervous system, visuomotor integration. *Total annual research expenditures:* $900,000. *Unit head:* Dr. Samuel McClugage, Head, 504-568-4011, Fax: 504-568-2165, E-mail: smcclu@lsuhsc.edu. *Application contact:* Dr. R. John Cork, Graduate Coordinator and Professor, 504-568-7177, E-mail: jcork@lsuhsc.edu.
Website: http://www.medschool.lsuhsc.edu/cell_biology/

Massachusetts Institute of Technology, School of Science, Department of Biology, Cambridge, MA 02139. Offers biochemistry (PhD); biological oceanography (PhD); biology (PhD); biophysical chemistry and molecular structure (PhD); cell biology (PhD); computational and systems biology (PhD); developmental biology (PhD); genetics (PhD); immunology (PhD); microbiology (PhD); molecular biology (PhD); neurobiology (PhD). *Degree requirements:* For doctorate, comprehensive exam, thesis/dissertation, teaching assistantship during two semesters. *Entrance requirements:* For doctorate, GRE General Test. Additional exam requirements/recommendations for international students: Required—TOEFL, IELTS. Electronic applications accepted. *Faculty research:* Cellular, developmental and molecular (plant and animal) biology; biochemistry, bioengineering, biophysics and structural biology; classical and molecular genetics, stem cell and epigenetics; immunology and microbiology; cancer biology, molecular medicine, neurobiology and human disease; computational and systems biology.

New York University, Graduate School of Arts and Science, Department of Biology, New York, NY 10012-1019. Offers biology (PhD); biomedical journalism (MS); cancer and molecular biology (PhD); computational biology (PhD); computers in biological research (MS); developmental genetics (PhD); general biology (MS); immunology and microbiology (PhD); molecular genetics (PhD); neurobiology (PhD); oral biology (MS); plant biology (PhD); recombinant DNA technology (MS); MS/MBA. *Program availability:* Part-time. *Students:* Average age 27. 394 applicants, 56% accepted, 77 enrolled. In 2017, 68 master's, 9 doctorates awarded. Terminal master's awarded for partial completion of doctoral program. *Degree requirements:* For master's, thesis or alternative, qualifying paper; for doctorate, comprehensive exam, thesis/dissertation. *Entrance requirements:* For master's and doctorate, GRE General Test. Additional exam requirements/recommendations for international students: Required—TOEFL. *Application deadline:* For fall admission, 12/1 priority date for domestic students, 12/1 for international students. Application fee: $100. *Expenses: Tuition:* Full-time $41,352; part-time $19,968 per year. *Required fees:* $2496; $1628 per unit. $814 per term. Tuition and fees vary according to course load and program. *Financial support:* Fellowships, research assistantships, teaching assistantships, career-related internships or fieldwork, Federal Work-Study, institutionally sponsored loans, scholarships/grants, health care benefits, and unspecified assistantships available. Financial award application deadline: 12/1; financial award applicants required to submit FAFSA. *Faculty research:* Genomics, molecular and cell biology, development and molecular genetics, molecular evolution of plants and animals. *Unit head:* Stephen Small, Chair, 212-998-8200, Fax: 212-995-4015, E-mail: biology.admissions@nyu.edu. *Application contact:* Ken Birnbaum, Director of Graduate Studies, PhD Programs, 212-998-8200, Fax: 212-995-4015, E-mail: biology.admissions@nyu.edu.
Website: http://biology.as.nyu.edu/

Northwestern University, The Graduate School, Interdisciplinary Biological Sciences Program (IBiS), Evanston, IL 60208. Offers biochemistry (PhD); bioengineering and biotechnology (PhD); biotechnology (PhD); cell and molecular biology (PhD); developmental and systems biology (PhD); nanotechnology (PhD); neurobiology (PhD); structural biology and biophysics (PhD). *Degree requirements:* For doctorate, thesis/dissertation, qualifying exam. *Entrance requirements:* For doctorate, GRE General Test. Additional exam requirements/recommendations for international students: Required—TOEFL (minimum score 600 paper-based). Electronic applications accepted. *Faculty research:* Biophysics/structural biology, cell/molecular biology, synthetic biology, developmental systems biology, chemical biology/nanotechnology.

Northwestern University, The Graduate School, Judd A. and Marjorie Weinberg College of Arts and Sciences, Department of Neurobiology, Evanston, IL 60208. Offers neurobiology and physiology (MS). Admissions and degrees offered through The Graduate School. *Program availability:* Part-time. *Degree requirements:* For master's, thesis. *Entrance requirements:* For master's, GRE General Test and MCAT (strongly recommended). Additional exam requirements/recommendations for international students: Required—TOEFL. Electronic applications accepted. *Expenses:* Contact institution. *Faculty research:* Sensory neurobiology and neuroendocrinology, reproductive biology, vision physiology and psychophysics, cell and developmental biology.

Penn State Hershey Medical Center, College of Medicine, Graduate School Programs in the Biomedical Sciences, Huck Institutes of the Life Sciences, Intercollege Graduate Program in Molecular Cellular and Integrative Biosciences, Hershey, PA 17033. Offers cell and developmental biology (PhD); molecular medicine (PhD); molecular toxicology (PhD); neurobiology (PhD). *Students:* 3 full-time (2 women); includes 2 minority (both Asian, non-Hispanic/Latino). 2 applicants, 100% accepted, 2 enrolled. In 2017, 1 doctorate awarded. *Degree requirements:* For doctorate, comprehensive exam, thesis/dissertation, oral exam. *Entrance requirements:* For doctorate, GRE, minimum GPA of 3.0. Additional exam requirements/recommendations for international students: Required—TOEFL (minimum score 500 paper-based). *Application deadline:* For fall admission, 1/31 priority date for domestic students, 2/1 priority date for international students. Applications are processed on a rolling basis. Application fee: $65. Electronic applications accepted. *Financial support:* In 2017–18, research assistantships with full tuition reimbursements (averaging $26,196 per year) were awarded; fellowships with full tuition reimbursements, career-related internships or fieldwork, Federal Work-Study, scholarships/grants, health care benefits, and unspecified assistantships also available. Financial award applicants required to submit FAFSA. *Faculty research:* Vascular biology, molecular toxicology, chemical biology, immune system, pathophysiological basis of human disease. *Unit head:* Dr. Peter Hudson, Director, 814-865-6057, E-mail: pjh18@psu.edu. *Application contact:* Kathy Shuey, Administrative Assistant, 717-531-8982, Fax: 717-531-0786, E-mail: grad-hmc@psu.edu.
Website: http://www.huck.psu.edu/education/molecular-cellular-and-integrative-biosciences

Purdue University, Graduate School, College of Science, Department of Biological Sciences, West Lafayette, IN 47907. Offers biochemistry (PhD); biophysics (PhD); cell and developmental biology (PhD); ecology, evolutionary and population biology (MS, PhD), including ecology, evolutionary biology, population biology; genetics (MS, PhD); microbiology (MS, PhD); molecular biology (PhD); neurobiology (MS, PhD); plant physiology (PhD). *Faculty:* 42 full-time (13 women), 3 part-time/adjunct (0 women). *Students:* 115 full-time (58 women), 6 part-time (4 women); includes 17 minority (1 Black or African American, non-Hispanic/Latino; 6 Asian, non-Hispanic/Latino; 9 Hispanic/Latino; 1 Two or more races, non-Hispanic/Latino), 60 international. Average age 27. 165 applicants, 12% accepted, 15 enrolled. In 2017, 5 master's, 16 doctorates awarded. Terminal master's awarded for partial completion of doctoral program. *Degree requirements:* For master's, thesis (for some programs); for doctorate, thesis/dissertation, seminars, teaching experience. *Entrance requirements:* For master's, GRE General Test (minimum analytical writing score of 3.5), minimum undergraduate GPA of 3.0; for doctorate, GRE General Test (minimum analytical writing score of 3.5), minimum undergraduate GPA of 3.5. Additional exam requirements/recommendations for international students: Required—TOEFL minimum score 600 paper-based; 107 iBT (for MS), 80 iBT (for PhD). *Application deadline:* For fall admission, 12/7 for domestic and international students. Applications are processed on a rolling basis. Application fee: $60 ($75 for international students). Electronic applications accepted. *Financial support:* Fellowships, research assistantships, and teaching assistantships available. Support available to part-time students. Financial award application deadline: 2/15; financial award applicants required to submit FAFSA. *Unit head:* Stephen Konieczny, Head, 765-494-4407, E-mail: sfk@purdue.edu. *Application contact:* Georgina E. Rupp, Graduate Coordinator, 765-494-8142, E-mail: ruppg@purdue.edu.
Website: http://www.bio.purdue.edu/

Queen's University at Kingston, School of Graduate Studies, Faculty of Health Sciences, Department of Anatomy and Cell Biology, Kingston, ON K7L 3N6, Canada. Offers biology of reproduction (M Sc, PhD); cancer (M Sc, PhD); cardiovascular pathophysiology (M Sc, PhD); cell and molecular biology (M Sc, PhD); drug metabolism (M Sc, PhD); endocrinology (M Sc, PhD); motor control (M Sc, PhD); neural regeneration (M Sc, PhD); neurophysiology (M Sc, PhD). *Program availability:* Part-time. *Degree requirements:* For master's, thesis; for doctorate, one foreign language, comprehensive exam, thesis/dissertation. *Entrance requirements:* Additional exam requirements/recommendations for international students: Required—TOEFL. Electronic applications accepted. *Faculty research:* Human kinetics, neuroscience, reproductive biology, cardiovascular.

Université Laval, Faculty of Medicine, Graduate Programs in Medicine, Programs in Neurobiology, Québec, QC G1K 7P4, Canada. Offers M Sc, PhD. Terminal master's awarded for partial completion of doctoral program. *Degree requirements:* For master's, thesis; for doctorate, comprehensive exam, thesis/dissertation. *Entrance requirements:* For master's and doctorate, knowledge of French and English. Electronic applications accepted.

University of Arkansas for Medical Sciences, Graduate School, Little Rock, AR 72205. Offers biochemistry and molecular biology (MS, PhD); bioinformatics (MS, PhD); cellular physiology and molecular biophysics (MS, PhD); clinical nutrition (MS); interdisciplinary biomedical sciences (MS, PhD, Certificate); interdisciplinary toxicology (MS); microbiology and immunology (PhD); neurobiology and developmental sciences (PhD); pharmacology (PhD); MD/PhD. Bioinformatics programs hosted jointly with the University of Arkansas at Little Rock. *Program availability:* Part-time. Terminal master's awarded for partial completion of doctoral program. *Degree requirements:* For master's, comprehensive exam (for some programs), thesis (for some programs); for doctorate, thesis/dissertation. *Entrance requirements:* For master's and doctorate, GRE. Additional exam requirements/recommendations for international students: Required—TOEFL. Electronic applications accepted. *Expenses:* Contact institution.

University of California, Irvine, Francisco J. Ayala School of Biological Sciences, Department of Neurobiology and Behavior, Irvine, CA 92697. Offers biological sciences (MS, PhD); MD/PhD. *Students:* 30 full-time (15 women), 2 part-time (1 woman); includes 13 minority (1 Black or African American, non-Hispanic/Latino; 4 Asian, non-Hispanic/Latino; 8 Hispanic/Latino). Average age 28. In 2017, 8 master's, 8 doctorates awarded. *Entrance requirements:* For master's and doctorate, GRE General Test, GRE Subject Test, minimum GPA of 3.0. Additional exam requirements/recommendations for international students: Required—TOEFL (minimum score 550 paper-based). *Application deadline:* For fall admission, 1/15 priority date for domestic students, 1/15 for international students. Applications are processed on a rolling basis. Application fee: $105 ($125 for international students). Electronic applications accepted. *Financial support:* Fellowships, research assistantships with full tuition reimbursements, teaching assistantships, institutionally sponsored loans, traineeships, health care benefits, and unspecified assistantships available. Financial award application deadline: 3/1; financial award applicants required to submit FAFSA. *Faculty research:* Synaptic processes,

neurophysiology, neuroendocrinology, neuroanatomy, molecular neurobiology. *Unit head:* Marcelo A. Wood, Chair, 949-824-6114, Fax: 949-824-2447, E-mail: mwood@uci.edu. *Application contact:* Sally Dabiri, Department Administrator, 949-824-4727, Fax: 949-824-2447, E-mail: sfdabiri@uci.edu.
Website: http://neurobiology.uci.edu/

University of California, Irvine, School of Medicine and Francisco J. Ayala School of Biological Sciences, Department of Anatomy and Neurobiology, Irvine, CA 92697. Offers biological sciences (MS, PhD); MD/PhD. *Faculty:* 26 full-time (13 women), 2 part-time/adjunct (1 woman). *Students:* 13 full-time (7 women), 3 part-time (2 women); includes 5 minority (all Asian, non-Hispanic/Latino), 2 international. Average age 27. In 2017, 8 doctorates awarded. *Entrance requirements:* For master's and doctorate, GRE General Test, GRE Subject Test. Additional exam requirements/recommendations for international students: Required—TOEFL (minimum score 550 paper-based). *Application deadline:* For fall admission, 1/15 priority date for domestic students, 1/15 for international students. Applications are processed on a rolling basis. Application fee: $105 ($125 for international students). Electronic applications accepted. *Financial support:* Fellowships, research assistantships with full tuition reimbursements, teaching assistantships, institutionally sponsored loans, traineeships, health care benefits, and unspecified assistantships available. Financial award application deadline: 3/1; financial award applicants required to submit FAFSA. *Faculty research:* Neurotransmitter immunocytochemistry, intracellular physiology, molecular neurobiology, forebrain organization and development, structure and function of sensory and motor systems. *Unit head:* Prof. Christine Gall, Interim Chair, 949-824-8652, Fax: 949-824-1255, E-mail: cmgall@uci.edu. *Application contact:* David Lyon, Director of Graduate Studies, 949-824-0447, E-mail: dclyon@uci.edu.

University of California, Los Angeles, David Geffen School of Medicine and Graduate Division, Graduate Programs in Medicine, Department of Neurobiology, Los Angeles, CA 90095. Offers MS, PhD. Terminal master's awarded for partial completion of doctoral program. *Degree requirements:* For master's, comprehensive exam; for doctorate, thesis/dissertation, oral and written qualifying exams; 2 quarters of teaching experience. *Entrance requirements:* For doctorate, GRE General Test; GRE Subject Test, bachelor's degree; minimum undergraduate GPA of 3.0 (or its equivalent if letter grade system not used). Additional exam requirements/recommendations for international students: Required—TOEFL. Electronic applications accepted.

University of California, Los Angeles, Graduate Division, College of Letters and Science and David Geffen School of Medicine, UCLA ACCESS to Programs in the Molecular, Cellular and Integrative Life Sciences, Los Angeles, CA 90095. Offers biochemistry and molecular biology (PhD); biological chemistry (PhD); cellular and molecular pathology (PhD); human genetics (PhD); microbiology, immunology, and molecular genetics (PhD); molecular biology (PhD); molecular toxicology (PhD); molecular, cellular and integrative physiology (PhD); neurobiology (PhD); oral biology (PhD); physiology (PhD). *Degree requirements:* For doctorate, thesis/dissertation, oral and written qualifying exams. *Entrance requirements:* For doctorate, GRE General Test, bachelor's degree; minimum undergraduate GPA of 3.0 (or its equivalent if letter grade system not used). Additional exam requirements/recommendations for international students: Required—TOEFL. Electronic applications accepted.

University of Chicago, Division of the Biological Sciences, Program in Neurobiology, Chicago, IL 60637. Offers PhD. *Faculty:* 45 full-time (14 women). *Students:* 30 full-time (18 women); includes 12 minority (2 Black or African American, non-Hispanic/Latino; 5 Asian, non-Hispanic/Latino; 4 Hispanic/Latino; 1 Two or more races, non-Hispanic/Latino), 6 international. Average age 26. 156 applicants, 13% accepted, 5 enrolled. In 2017, 1 doctorate awarded. *Degree requirements:* For doctorate, comprehensive exam, thesis/dissertation, ethics class, 2 teaching assistantships. *Entrance requirements:* For doctorate, GRE General Test, transcripts, statement of purpose, 3 letters of recommendation. Additional exam requirements/recommendations for international students: Required—TOEFL (minimum score 600 paper-based; 104 iBT), IELTS (minimum score 7). *Application deadline:* For fall admission, 12/1 for domestic and international students. Application fee: $90. Electronic applications accepted. *Financial support:* In 2017–18, 27 students received support, including fellowships with full tuition reimbursements available (averaging $31,000 per year), research assistantships with full tuition reimbursements available (averaging $31,000 per year); institutionally sponsored loans, scholarships/grants, traineeships, and health care benefits also available. Financial award application deadline: 12/1. *Faculty research:* Systems neurophysiology; behavioral and cognitive neuroscience; computation and imaging; genetic, developmental, molecular, and cellular neurobiology. *Unit head:* Daniel McGehee, PhD, Chair, E-mail: neurograd@uchicago.edu. *Application contact:* Elena Rizzo, Administrative Director, E-mail: erizzo@uchicago.edu.
Website: http://neuroscience.uchicago.edu/graduate-training/neurobiology-curriculum/

University of Connecticut, Graduate School, College of Liberal Arts and Sciences, Department of Physiology and Neurobiology, Storrs, CT 06269. Offers comparative physiology (MS, PhD). Terminal master's awarded for partial completion of doctoral program. *Degree requirements:* For master's, comprehensive exam; for doctorate, thesis/dissertation. *Entrance requirements:* For master's and doctorate, GRE General Test, GRE Subject Test. Additional exam requirements/recommendations for international students: Required—TOEFL (minimum score 550 paper-based). Electronic applications accepted.

The University of Iowa, Graduate College, College of Liberal Arts and Sciences, Department of Biology, Iowa City, IA 52242-1324. Offers biology (MS, PhD); cell and developmental biology (MS, PhD); evolution (MS, PhD); genetics (MS, PhD); neurobiology (MS, PhD). Terminal master's awarded for partial completion of doctoral program. *Degree requirements:* For master's, thesis optional, exam; for doctorate, comprehensive exam, thesis/dissertation. *Entrance requirements:* For master's and doctorate, GRE General Test, minimum GPA of 3.0. Additional exam requirements/recommendations for international students: Required—TOEFL (minimum score 600 paper-based; 100 iBT). Electronic applications accepted. *Faculty research:* Neurobiology, evolutionary biology, genetics, cell and developmental biology.

University of Kentucky, Graduate School, Graduate School Programs from the College of Medicine, Program in Anatomy and Neurobiology, Lexington, KY 40506-0032. Offers PhD. *Degree requirements:* For doctorate, comprehensive exam, thesis/dissertation. *Entrance requirements:* For doctorate, GRE General Test, minimum undergraduate GPA of 2.75. Additional exam requirements/recommendations for international students: Required—TOEFL (minimum score 550 paper-based). Electronic applications accepted. *Faculty research:* Neuroendocrinology, developmental neurobiology, neurotrophic substances, neural plasticity and trauma, neurobiology of aging.

University of Louisville, School of Medicine, Department of Anatomical Sciences and Neurobiology, Louisville, KY 40292-0001. Offers MS, PhD, MD/PhD. *Faculty:* 19 full-time (5 women), 2 part-time/adjunct (0 women). *Students:* 27 full-time (11 women), 9 part-time (4 women); includes 4 minority (1 Asian, non-Hispanic/Latino; 2 Hispanic/Latino; 1 Two or more races, non-Hispanic/Latino), 1 international. Average age 28. 28 applicants, 54% accepted, 10 enrolled. In 2017, 2 doctorates awarded. Terminal master's awarded for partial completion of doctoral program. *Degree requirements:* For master's, thesis; for doctorate, comprehensive exam, thesis/dissertation. *Entrance requirements:* For master's and doctorate, GRE General Test (minimum score of 1000 verbal and quantitative), minimum GPA of 3.0. Additional exam requirements/recommendations for international students: Required—TOEFL. *Application deadline:* Applications are processed on a rolling basis. Application fee: $65. Electronic applications accepted. *Expenses:* Tuition, state resident: full-time $12,246; part-time $681 per credit hour. Tuition, nonresident: full-time $25,486; part-time $1417 per credit hour. *Required fees:* $196. Tuition and fees vary according to course load, program and reciprocity agreements. *Financial support:* Fellowships with full tuition reimbursements and health care benefits available. Financial award application deadline: 4/15. *Faculty research:* Human adult neural stem cells, development and plasticity of the nervous system, organization of the dorsal thalamus, electrophysiology/neuroanatomy of central neurons mediating control of reproductive and pelvic organs, normal neural mechanisms and plasticity following injury and/or chronic pain, differentiation and regeneration of motor neurons and oligodendrocytes. *Total annual research expenditures:* $3.3 million. *Unit head:* Dr. William Guido, Chair, 502-852-6227, Fax: 502-852-6228, E-mail: w0guid01@gwise.louisville.edu. *Application contact:* Dr. Charles Hubscher, Director of Graduate Studies, 502-852-3058, Fax: 502-852-6228, E-mail: chhub01@louisville.edu.
Website: http://louisville.edu/medicine/departments/anatomy

The University of Manchester, School of Biological Sciences, Manchester, United Kingdom. Offers adaptive organismal biology (M Phil, PhD); animal biology (M Phil, PhD); biochemistry (M Phil, PhD); bioinformatics (M Phil, PhD); biomolecular sciences (M Phil, PhD); biotechnology (M Phil, PhD); cell biology (M Phil, PhD); cell matrix research (M Phil, PhD); channels and transporters (M Phil, PhD); developmental biology (M Phil, PhD); environmental biology (M Phil, PhD); evolutionary biology (M Phil, PhD); gene expression (M Phil, PhD); genetics (M Phil, PhD); history of science, technology and medicine (M Phil, PhD); immunology (M Phil, PhD); integrative neurobiology and behavior (M Phil, PhD); membrane trafficking (M Phil, PhD); microbiology (M Phil, PhD); molecular and cellular neuroscience (M Phil, PhD); molecular biology (M Phil, PhD); molecular cancer studies (M Phil, PhD); neuroscience (M Phil, PhD); ophthalmology (M Phil, PhD); optometry (M Phil, PhD); organelle function (M Phil, PhD); pharmacology (M Phil, PhD); physiology (M Phil, PhD); plant sciences (M Phil, PhD); stem cell research (M Phil, PhD); structural biology (M Phil, PhD); systems neuroscience (M Phil, PhD); toxicology (M Phil, PhD).

University of Maryland, Baltimore, Graduate School, Graduate Program in Life Sciences, Program in Neuroscience, Baltimore, MD 21201. Offers PhD, MD/PhD. *Program availability:* Part-time. *Students:* 41 full-time (19 women), 3 part-time (2 women); includes 11 minority (1 Black or African American, non-Hispanic/Latino; 6 Asian, non-Hispanic/Latino; 2 Hispanic/Latino; 2 Two or more races, non-Hispanic/Latino), 2 international. Average age 28. 99 applicants, 17% accepted, 7 enrolled. In 2017, 8 doctorates awarded. *Degree requirements:* For doctorate, comprehensive exam, thesis/dissertation. *Entrance requirements:* For doctorate, GRE General Test, minimum GPA of 3.0, curriculum vitae, essay, 3 letters of recommendation. Additional exam requirements/recommendations for international students: Required—TOEFL (minimum score 80 iBT); Recommended—IELTS (minimum score 7). *Application deadline:* For fall admission, 12/15 for domestic students, 1/15 for international students. Application fee: $75. Electronic applications accepted. *Expenses:* Tuition, state resident: full-time $13,990; part-time $661 per credit. Tuition, nonresident: full-time $30,484; part-time $1310 per credit. *Required fees:* $1894; $94 per credit. $415 per semester. Part-time tuition and fees vary according to course load, degree level and program. *Financial support:* In 2017–18, research assistantships with partial tuition reimbursements (averaging $26,000 per year) were awarded; fellowships, health care benefits, and unspecified assistantships also available. Financial award application deadline: 3/1; financial award applicants required to submit FAFSA. *Faculty research:* Molecular, biochemical, and cellular pharmacology; membrane biophysics; synaptology; developmental neurobiology. *Unit head:* Dr. Jessica Mong, Director, 410-706-4295, E-mail: jmong@umaryland.edu. *Application contact:* Renee Cockerham, Program Manager, 410-706-4701, Fax: 410-706-4724, E-mail: neurosci@umaryland.edu.
Website: http://lifesciences.umaryland.edu/Neuroscience/

University of Minnesota, Twin Cities Campus, Graduate School, Graduate Program in Neuroscience, Minneapolis, MN 55455-0213. Offers MS, PhD. Terminal master's awarded for partial completion of doctoral program. *Degree requirements:* For master's, thesis; for doctorate, thesis/dissertation. *Entrance requirements:* For doctorate, GRE. Additional exam requirements/recommendations for international students: Required—TOEFL. Electronic applications accepted. *Faculty research:* Cellular and molecular neuroscience, behavioral neuroscience, developmental neuroscience, neurodegenerative diseases, pain, addiction, motor control.

The University of North Carolina at Chapel Hill, School of Medicine and Graduate School, Graduate Programs in Medicine, Curriculum in Neurobiology, Chapel Hill, NC 27599. Offers PhD. *Degree requirements:* For doctorate, comprehensive exam, thesis/dissertation. *Entrance requirements:* For doctorate, GRE General Test, minimum GPA of 3.0. Electronic applications accepted.

University of Oklahoma, College of Arts and Sciences, Department of Biology, Norman, OK 73019. Offers biology (MS, PhD); cellular and behavioral neurobiology (PhD), including biology; ecology and evolutionary biology (PhD), including biology. *Faculty:* 38 full-time (10 women), 1 (woman) part-time/adjunct. *Students:* 13 full-time (4 women), 9 part-time (6 women); includes 5 minority (2 Asian, non-Hispanic/Latino; 2 Hispanic/Latino; 1 Two or more races, non-Hispanic/Latino), 5 international. Average age 28. 27 applicants, 15% accepted, 4 enrolled. In 2017, 6 master's awarded. *Degree requirements:* For master's, thesis, course in biostatistics; for doctorate, comprehensive exam, thesis/dissertation, course in biostatistics, 2 semesters as teaching assistant. *Entrance requirements:* For master's and doctorate, GRE General Test, transcripts, 3 letters of recommendation, personal statement, curriculum vitae. Additional exam requirements/recommendations for international students: Required—TOEFL (minimum score 79 iBT) or IELTS (minimum score 6.5). *Application deadline:* For fall admission, 12/15 priority date for domestic and international students. Application fee: $50 ($100 for international students). Electronic applications accepted. *Expenses:* Tuition, state resident: full-time $5119; part-time $213.30 per credit hour. Tuition, nonresident: full-time $19,778; part-time $824.10 per credit hour. *Required fees:* $3458; $133.55 per credit hour. $126.50 per semester. *Financial support:* In 2017–18, 19 students received support, including 10 fellowships with full tuition reimbursements available (averaging $3,257 per year), 6 research assistantships with full tuition reimbursements available (averaging $15,419 per year), 38 teaching assistantships with full tuition reimbursements available (averaging $16,413 per year); scholarships/grants and assistantships (with tuition waivers and health insurance) also available. Financial award application deadline: 6/1; financial award applicants required to submit FAFSA. *Faculty research:* Geographical ecology, biology of behavior, cellular and behavioral neurobiology, evolutionary and molecular genetics; evolution of development. *Total annual research expenditures:* $1.2 million. *Unit head:* Dr. Richard Broughton, Professor and Chair, 405-325-6200, Fax: 405-325-6202, E-mail: biology@ou.edu. *Application contact:* Dianna Wilson, Academic Counselor, 405-325-9139, Fax: 405-325-6202, E-mail: biologygrad@ou.edu.
Website: http://www.ou.edu/cas/biology

University of Oklahoma, College of Arts and Sciences and School of Aerospace and Mechanical Engineering and Department of Chemistry and Biochemistry, Program in Cellular and Behavioral Neurobiology, Norman, OK 73019. Offers cellular and behavioral neurobiology (PhD), including biology, chemistry and biochemistry, psychology. *Students:* 5 full-time (2 women), 1 (woman) part-time, 1 international. Average age 27. 8 applicants, 13% accepted, 1 enrolled. In 2017, 1 doctorate awarded. *Degree requirements:* For doctorate, comprehensive exam, thesis/dissertation, 2-3 lab rotations plus requirements of particular home department to which student applies. *Entrance requirements:* For doctorate, GRE General Test; GRE Subject Test in chemistry (recommended for applicants to chemistry and biochemistry), transcripts, 3 letters of recommendation, personal statement; publications (for psychology). Additional exam requirements/recommendations for international students: Required—TOEFL (minimum score 79 iBT) or IELTS (minimum score 6.5). Application fee: $50 ($100 for international students). Electronic applications accepted. *Expenses:* Tuition, state resident: full-time $5119; part-time $213.30 per credit hour. Tuition, nonresident: full-time $19,778; part-time $824.10 per credit hour. *Required fees:* $3458; $133.55 per credit hour. $126.50 per semester. *Financial support:* In 2017–18, 5 students received support. Fellowships with full tuition reimbursements available, research assistantships with full tuition reimbursements available, teaching assistantships with full tuition reimbursements available, scholarships/grants, health care benefits, and unspecified assistantships available. Financial award application deadline: 6/1; financial award applicants required to submit FAFSA. *Faculty research:* Behavioral neurobiology, cellular neurobiology, molecular neurobiology, developmental neurobiology, cell signaling. *Unit head:* Dr. Ari Berkowitz, Director, Graduate Program, 405-325-3492, Fax: 405-325-6202, E-mail: ari@ou.edu.
Website: http://www.ou.edu/cbn

University of Rochester, School of Medicine and Dentistry, Graduate Programs in Medicine and Dentistry, Department of Neurobiology and Anatomy, Programs in Neurobiology and Anatomy, Rochester, NY 14627. Offers PhD, MD/MS. *Degree requirements:* For doctorate, thesis/dissertation, qualifying exam. *Entrance requirements:* For doctorate, GRE General Test.

University of Southern California, Graduate School, Dana and David Dornsife College of Letters, Arts and Sciences, Department of Biological Sciences, Program in Neurobiology, Los Angeles, CA 90089. Offers PhD. M.S. is terminal degree only. Terminal master's awarded for partial completion of doctoral program. *Degree requirements:* For doctorate, comprehensive exam, thesis/dissertation, qualifying examination, dissertation defense. *Entrance requirements:* For doctorate, GRE, 3 letters of recommendation, personal statement, resume, minimum GPA of 3.0. Additional exam requirements/recommendations for international students: Required—TOEFL (minimum score 600 paper-based; 100 iBT). Electronic applications accepted. *Faculty research:* Neural basis of emotion and motivation, learning and memory, cell biology and physiology of neuronal signaling, sensory processing, development and aging.

The University of Texas at Austin, Graduate School, The Institute for Neuroscience, Austin, TX 78712-1111. Offers PhD, MD/PhD. Terminal master's awarded for partial completion of doctoral program. *Degree requirements:* For doctorate, thesis/dissertation. *Entrance requirements:* For doctorate, GRE. Electronic applications accepted. *Faculty research:* Cellular/molecular biology, neurobiology, pharmacology, behavioral neuroscience.

The University of Texas at San Antonio, College of Sciences, Department of Biology, San Antonio, TX 78249-0617. Offers biology (MS); biotechnology (MS); cell and molecular biology (PhD); neurobiology (PhD). *Faculty:* 37 full-time (10 women), 1 part-time/adjunct (0 women). *Students:* 111 full-time (64 women), 50 part-time (25 women); includes 76 minority (5 Black or African American, non-Hispanic/Latino; 1 American Indian or Alaska Native, non-Hispanic/Latino; 11 Asian, non-Hispanic/Latino; 55 Hispanic/Latino; 1 Native Hawaiian or other Pacific Islander, non-Hispanic/Latino; 3 Two or more races, non-Hispanic/Latino), 30 international. Average age 27. 153 applicants, 55% accepted, 57 enrolled. In 2017, 17 master's, 3 doctorates awarded. Terminal master's awarded for partial completion of doctoral program. *Degree requirements:* For master's, comprehensive exam, thesis or alternative; for doctorate, comprehensive exam, thesis/dissertation. *Entrance requirements:* For master's, GRE General Test, bachelor's degree with 18 credit hours in field of study or in another appropriate field of study; for doctorate, GRE General Test, 3 letters of recommendation, statement of purpose, resume. Additional exam requirements/recommendations for international students: Required—TOEFL (minimum score 500 paper-based; 100 iBT), IELTS (minimum score 5). *Application deadline:* For fall admission, 6/15 for domestic students, 3/1 for international students; for spring admission, 10/15 for domestic students, 9/15 for international students. Application fee: $50 ($90 for international students). Electronic applications accepted. *Expenses:* Tuition, state resident: full-time $5495. Tuition, nonresident: full-time $21,938. *Required fees:* $1915. Tuition and fees vary according to program. *Faculty research:* Development of human and veterinary vaccines against a fungal disease, mammalian germ cells and stem cells, dopamine neuron physiology and addiction, plant biochemistry, dendritic computation and synaptic plasticity. *Total annual research expenditures:* $9.1 million. *Unit head:* Dr. Garry Sunter, Chair, 210-458-5479, E-mail: garry.sunter@utsa.edu.
Website: http://bio.utsa.edu/

University of Utah, School of Medicine and Graduate School, Graduate Programs in Medicine, Department of Neurobiology and Anatomy, Salt Lake City, UT 84112-1107. Offers PhD. *Program availability:* Part-time. Terminal master's awarded for partial completion of doctoral program. *Degree requirements:* For doctorate, comprehensive exam, thesis/dissertation. *Entrance requirements:* For doctorate, GRE General Test. Additional exam requirements/recommendations for international students: Required—TOEFL. *Faculty research:* Neuroscience, neuroanatomy, developmental neurobiology, neurogenetics.

University of Washington, Graduate School, School of Medicine, Graduate Programs in Medicine, Graduate Program in Neurobiology and Behavior, Seattle, WA 98195. Offers PhD. *Degree requirements:* For doctorate, thesis/dissertation. *Entrance requirements:* For doctorate, GRE. Additional exam requirements/recommendations for international students: Required—TOEFL. Electronic applications accepted. *Faculty research:* Motor, sensory systems, neuroplasticity, animal behavior, neuroendocrinology, computational neuroscience.

Virginia Commonwealth University, Medical College of Virginia-Professional Programs, School of Medicine, Graduate Programs in Medicine, Department of Anatomy and Neurobiology, Richmond, VA 23284-9005. Offers MS. *Degree requirements:* For master's, thesis. *Entrance requirements:* For master's, GRE, MCAT or DAT. Electronic applications accepted.

Wake Forest University, School of Medicine and Graduate School of Arts and Sciences, Graduate Programs in Medicine, Department of Neurobiology and Anatomy, Winston-Salem, NC 27109. Offers PhD, MD/PhD. *Degree requirements:* For doctorate, thesis/dissertation. *Entrance requirements:* For doctorate, GRE General Test. Additional exam requirements/recommendations for international students: Required—TOEFL. Electronic applications accepted. *Faculty research:* Sensory neurobiology, reproductive endocrinology, regulatory processes in cell biology.

Wesleyan University, Graduate Studies, Department of Biology, Middletown, CT 06459. Offers cell and developmental biology (PhD); evolution and ecology (PhD); genetics and genomics (PhD), including bioinformatics; neurobiology and behavior (PhD). Terminal master's awarded for partial completion of doctoral program. *Degree requirements:* For doctorate, comprehensive exam, thesis/dissertation, public seminar. *Entrance requirements:* For doctorate, GRE, official transcripts, three recommendation letters, essay. Additional exam requirements/recommendations for international students: Required—TOEFL. *Application deadline:* For fall admission, 1/15 for domestic and international students. Application fee: $0. Electronic applications accepted. *Financial support:* Stipends available. *Faculty research:* Evolution and ecology, neurobiology and behavior, cell and developmental biology, genetics, genomics and bioinformatics. *Unit head:* Dr. Ann Burke, Chair/Professor, 860-685-3518, E-mail: acburke@wesleyan.edu. *Application contact:* Diane Meredith, Administrative Assistant IV, 860-685-2157, E-mail: dmeredith@wesleyan.edu.
Website: http://www.wesleyan.edu/bio/

Yale University, Graduate School of Arts and Sciences, Department of Molecular, Cellular, and Developmental Biology, Program in Neurobiology, New Haven, CT 06520. Offers PhD. *Degree requirements:* For doctorate, thesis/dissertation. *Entrance requirements:* For doctorate, GRE General Test, GRE Subject Test.

Yale University, Yale School of Medicine and Graduate School of Arts and Sciences, Combined Program in Biological and Biomedical Sciences (BBS), Department of Neurobiology, New Haven, CT 06520. Offers PhD. *Degree requirements:* For doctorate, thesis/dissertation. *Entrance requirements:* For doctorate, GRE General Test, GRE Subject Test.

Neuroscience

Albany Medical College, Center for Neuropharmacology and Neuroscience, Albany, NY 12208-3479. Offers MS, PhD. Terminal master's awarded for partial completion of doctoral program. *Degree requirements:* For master's, thesis; for doctorate, comprehensive exam, thesis/dissertation. *Entrance requirements:* For master's, GRE General Test, all transcripts, letters of recommendation; for doctorate, GRE General Test, letters of recommendation. Additional exam requirements/recommendations for international students: Required—TOEFL. *Faculty research:* Molecular and cellular neuroscience, neuronal development, addiction.

Albert Einstein College of Medicine, Graduate Programs in the Biomedical Sciences, Dominick P. Purpura Department of Neuroscience, Bronx, NY 10461. Offers PhD, MD/PhD. *Degree requirements:* For doctorate, thesis/dissertation, qualifying exam. *Entrance requirements:* For doctorate, GRE General Test. Additional exam requirements/recommendations for international students: Required—TOEFL. *Application deadline:* For fall admission, 1/15 for domestic students. Application fee: $0. *Financial support:* Fellowships available. *Faculty research:* Structure-function relations at chemical and electrical synapses, mechanisms of electrogenesis, analysis of neuronal subsystems. *Unit head:* Dr. Kamran Khodakhah, Chair, 718-430-3794. *Application contact:* Sheila Cleeton, Executive Director and Registrar, Einstein Graduate Division, 718-430-2128, Fax: 718-430-8655, E-mail: sheila.cleeton@einstein.yu.edu.
Website: http://www.einstein.yu.edu/departments/neuroscience/

Alliant International University–San Diego, Shirley M. Hufstedler School of Education, Educational Psychology Programs, San Diego, CA 92131. Offers educational psychology (Psy D); pupil personnel services (Credential); school neuropsychology (Certificate); school psychology (MA); school-based mental health (Certificate). *Program availability:* Part-time. *Degree requirements:* For doctorate, comprehensive exam, thesis/dissertation, internship. *Entrance requirements:* For master's, minimum GPA of 2.5, letters of recommendation; for doctorate, minimum GPA of 3.0, letters of recommendation. Additional exam requirements/recommendations for international students: Required—TOEFL (minimum score 550 paper-based; 80 iBT), TWE (minimum score 5). Electronic applications accepted. *Faculty research:* School-based mental health, pupil personnel services, childhood mood, school-based assessment.

American University, College of Arts and Sciences, Department of Psychology, Washington, DC 22016-8062. Offers addiction and addictive behavior (Certificate); behavior, cognition, and neuroscience (PhD); clinical psychology (PhD); psychobiology of healing (Certificate); psychology (MA). *Accreditation:* APA. *Program availability:* Part-time. *Faculty:* 20 full-time (8 women), 9 part-time/adjunct (7 women). *Students:* 80 full-time (68 women), 8 part-time (7 women); includes 15 minority (5 Black or African American, non-Hispanic/Latino; 4 Asian, non-Hispanic/Latino; 5 Hispanic/Latino; 1 Two or more races, non-Hispanic/Latino), 6 international. Average age 28. 461 applicants, 12% accepted, 23 enrolled. In 2017, 24 master's, 11 doctorates awarded. *Degree requirements:* For master's, comprehensive exam, thesis or alternative; for doctorate, comprehensive exam, thesis/dissertation. *Entrance requirements:* For master's, GRE General Test, GRE Subject Test, statement of purpose, transcripts, 2 letters of recommendation; for doctorate, GRE General Test, GRE Subject Test, 3 letters of recommendation, statement of purpose, transcripts, resume. Additional exam requirements/recommendations for international students: Required—TOEFL (minimum score 600 paper-based; 100 iBT). *Application deadline:* For fall admission, 3/1 priority date for domestic students. Application fee: $55. *Expenses:* Contact institution. *Financial support:* Research assistantships, teaching assistantships, institutionally sponsored loans, scholarships/grants, and unspecified assistantships available. Financial award application deadline: 2/1; financial award applicants required to submit FAFSA. *Unit head:* Dr. David Haaga, Department Chair, 202-885-1718, Fax: 202-885-1023, E-mail: ahrens@american.edu. *Application contact:* Jonathan Harper, Associate Director, Graduate Recruitment, 202-885-3622, E-mail: jharper@american.edu.
Website: http://www.american.edu/CAS/Psychology/

American University of Beirut, Graduate Programs, Faculty of Medicine, Beirut, Lebanon. Offers biochemistry (MS); biomedical engineering (MS); biomedical sciences

(PhD); health research (MS); human morphology (MS); medicine (MD); microbiology and immunology (MS); neuroscience (MS); orthodontics (clinical) (MS); pharmacology and therapeutics (MS); physiology (MS). *Program availability:* Part-time. *Faculty:* 335 full-time (117 women), 54 part-time/adjunct (5 women). *Students:* 513 full-time (274 women). Average age 23. 527 applicants, 47% accepted, 169 enrolled. In 2017, 18 master's, 98 doctorates awarded. *Degree requirements:* For master's, one foreign language, comprehensive exam, thesis (for some programs); for doctorate, one foreign language, comprehensive exam, thesis/dissertation. *Entrance requirements:* For doctorate, MCAT (for MD); GRE (for PhD). Additional exam requirements/recommendations for international students: Required—TOEFL (minimum score 600 paper-based; 100 iBT), IELTS (minimum score 7.5). *Application deadline:* Applications are processed on a rolling basis. Application fee: $75. Electronic applications accepted. *Expenses:* Contact institution. *Financial support:* In 2017–18, 302 students received support. Fellowships, research assistantships, teaching assistantships, institutionally sponsored loans, scholarships/grants, tuition waivers, and unspecified assistantships available. *Unit head:* Dr. Mohamed Sayegh, Dean, 961-1-135000 Ext. 4700, Fax: 961-1-744489, E-mail: msayegh@aub.edu.lb. *Application contact:* Dr. Salim Kanaan, Director, Admission's Office, 961-1-350000 Ext. 2594, Fax: 961-1-750775, E-mail: sk00@aub.edu.lb.

Argosy University, Chicago, Illinois School of Professional Psychology, Doctoral Program in Clinical Psychology, Chicago, IL 60601. Offers child and adolescent psychology (Psy D); client-centered and experiential psychotherapies (Psy D); diversity and multicultural psychology (Psy D); family psychology (Psy D); forensic psychology (Psy D); health psychology (Psy D); neuropsychology (Psy D); organizational consulting (Psy D); psychoanalytic psychology (Psy D); psychology and spirituality (Psy D). *Accreditation:* APA.

Argosy University, Phoenix, Arizona School of Professional Psychology, Program in Clinical Psychology, Phoenix, AZ 85021. Offers clinical psychology (MA); neuropsychology (Psy D); sports-exercise psychology (Psy D).

Argosy University, Phoenix, Arizona School of Professional Psychology, Program in Neuropsychology, Phoenix, AZ 85021. Offers Psy D.

Argosy University, Tampa, Florida School of Professional Psychology, Program in Clinical Psychology, Tampa, FL 33607. Offers clinical psychology (MA, Psy D), including child and adolescent psychology (Psy D), geropsychology (Psy D), marriage/couples and family therapy (Psy D), neuropsychology (Psy D). *Accreditation:* APA.

Arizona State University at the Tempe campus, College of Liberal Arts and Sciences, Department of Psychology, Tempe, AZ 85287-1104. Offers applied behavior analysis (MS); behavioral neuroscience (PhD); clinical psychology (PhD); cognitive science (PhD); developmental psychology (PhD); quantitative psychology (PhD); social psychology (PhD). *Accreditation:* APA. *Degree requirements:* For doctorate, comprehensive exam, thesis/dissertation, interactive Program of Study (iPOS) submitted before completing 50 percent of required credit hours. *Entrance requirements:* For doctorate, GRE General Test, GRE Subject Test, minimum GPA of 3.0 or equivalent in last 2 years of work leading to bachelor's degree. Additional exam requirements/recommendations for international students: Required—TOEFL, IELTS, or PTE. Electronic applications accepted.

Arizona State University at the Tempe campus, College of Liberal Arts and Sciences, School of Life Sciences, Tempe, AZ 85287-4601. Offers animal behavior (PhD); applied ethics (biomedical and health ethics) (MA); biology (MS, PhD), including biology, biology and society, complex adaptive systems science (PhD), plant biology and conservation (MS); environmental life sciences (PhD); evolutionary biology (PhD); history and philosophy of science (PhD); human and social dimensions of science and technology (PhD); microbiology (PhD); molecular and cellular biology (PhD); neuroscience (PhD). Terminal master's awarded for partial completion of doctoral program. *Degree requirements:* For master's, thesis (for some programs), interactive Program of Study (iPOS) submitted before completing 50 percent of required credit hours; for doctorate, variable foreign language requirement, comprehensive exam, thesis/dissertation, interactive Program of Study (iPOS) submitted before completing 50 percent of required credit hours. *Entrance requirements:* For master's and doctorate, GRE, minimum GPA of 3.0 or equivalent in last 2 years of work leading to bachelor's degree. Additional exam requirements/recommendations for international students: Required—TOEFL (minimum score 600 paper-based; 100 iBT). Electronic applications accepted.

Arizona State University at the Tempe campus, Graduate College, Interdisciplinary Graduate Program in Neuroscience, Tempe, AZ 85287-1003. Offers PhD. Terminal master's awarded for partial completion of doctoral program. *Degree requirements:* For doctorate, comprehensive exam, thesis/dissertation, All students must submit an interactive Program of Study (iPOS) before completing 50 percent of the credit hours required for their degree program. A student is not eligible to apply for the Foreign Language Examination (if appl), comprehensive exams, dissertation proposal/prospectus or dissertation defense (if appl) without an approved iPOS. *Entrance requirements:* For doctorate, GRE, GPA of 3.0 or better in the last 2 years of work leading to the bachelor's degree, 3 letters of recommendation, statement of research interests and goals, CV or resume, and the completed Interdisciplinary Neuroscience Academic Record form. Additional exam requirements/recommendations for international students: Required—TOEFL (minimum score 550 paper-based; 80 iBT), IELTS (minimum score 6.5). Electronic applications accepted.

Augusta University, Program in Neuroscience, Augusta, GA 30912. Offers PhD. *Degree requirements:* For doctorate, comprehensive exam, thesis/dissertation. *Entrance requirements:* For doctorate, GRE General Test. Additional exam requirements/recommendations for international students: Required—TOEFL (minimum score 550 paper-based; 79 iBT). Electronic applications accepted. *Faculty research:* Learning and memory, neuronal migration, synapse formation, regeneration, developmental neurobiology, neurodegeneration and neural repair.

Ball State University, Graduate School, Teachers College, Department of Educational Psychology, Muncie, IN 47306. Offers educational psychology (MA, MS), including educational psychology (MA, MS, PhD); educational psychology (PhD), including educational psychology (MA, MS, PhD); gifted and talented education (Certificate); human development and learning (Certificate); instructional design and assessment (Certificate); neuropsychology (Certificate); quantitative psychology (MS); response to intervention (Certificate); school psychology (MA, PhD), including school psychology (MA, PhD, Ed S); school psychology (Ed S), including school psychology (MA, PhD, Ed S). *Program availability:* 100% online. *Faculty:* 24 full-time (15 women), 3 part-time/adjunct (all women). *Students:* 68 full-time (49 women), 122 part-time (106 women); includes 33 minority (16 Black or African American, non-Hispanic/Latino; 4 Asian, non-Hispanic/Latino; 7 Hispanic/Latino; 6 Two or more races, non-Hispanic/Latino), 3 international. Average age 32. 146 applicants, 42% accepted, 47 enrolled. In 2017, 49 master's, 8 doctorates, 20 other advanced degrees awarded. *Degree requirements:* For doctorate, thesis/dissertation; for other advanced degree, thesis. *Entrance requirements:* For master's, GRE General Test, minimum baccalaureate GPA of 2.75 or 3.0 in latter half of baccalaureate, professional goals and self-assessment; for doctorate, GRE General Test, minimum graduate GPA of 3.2; for other advanced degree, GRE General Test. Additional exam requirements/recommendations for international students: Required—TOEFL (minimum score 550 paper-based; 79 iBT), IELTS (minimum score 6.5). *Application deadline:* Applications are processed on a rolling basis. Application fee: $60. Electronic applications accepted. *Financial support:* In 2017–18, 40 students received support, including 29 research assistantships with partial tuition reimbursements available (averaging $12,276 per year), 3 teaching assistantships with partial tuition reimbursements available (averaging $11,167 per year); unspecified assistantships also available. Financial award application deadline: 3/1; financial award applicants required to submit FAFSA. *Unit head:* Dr. Jerell Cassady, Chairperson, 765-285-8503, E-mail: jccassady@bsu.edu. *Application contact:* Dr. Jerrell Cassady, Chairperson, 765-285-8503, Fax: 765-285-5455, E-mail: jccassady@bsu.edu. Website: http://www.bsu.edu/edpsych

Baylor College of Medicine, Graduate School of Biomedical Sciences, Department of Neuroscience, Houston, TX 77030-3498. Offers PhD, MD/PhD. *Degree requirements:* For doctorate, thesis/dissertation, public defense. *Entrance requirements:* For doctorate, GRE General Test, GRE Subject Test (strongly recommended), minimum GPA of 3.0. Additional exam requirements/recommendations for international students: Required—TOEFL. Electronic applications accepted. *Faculty research:* Neurodegenerative, neurodevelopment, neurophysiology, addiction, learning and memory.

Boston University, School of Medicine, Division of Graduate Medical Sciences, Graduate Program for Neuroscience, Boston, MA 02215. Offers PhD. *Degree requirements:* For doctorate, thesis/dissertation. *Unit head:* Dr. Shelley Russek, Director, 617-638-4319, E-mail: srussek@bu.edu. *Application contact:* GMS Admissions Office, 617-638-5255, E-mail: askgms@bu.edu.
Website: http://www.bu.edu/neuro/graduate/

Boston University, School of Medicine, Division of Graduate Medical Sciences, Program in Behavioral Neuroscience, Boston, MA 02215. Offers PhD. *Program availability:* Part-time. *Degree requirements:* For doctorate, thesis/dissertation. *Application deadline:* For fall admission, 1/15 for domestic students; for spring admission, 10/15 for domestic students. *Financial support:* Federal Work-Study, scholarships/grants, and traineeships available. *Unit head:* Dr. Carole Palumbo, Director, 617-638-5255, E-mail: cpalumbo@bu.edu. *Application contact:* GMS Admissions Office, 617-638-5255, E-mail: askgms@bu.edu.
Website: http://www.bumc.bu.edu/busm-bns/

Brandeis University, Graduate School of Arts and Sciences, Department of Psychology, Waltham, MA 02454-9110. Offers brain, body and behavior (PhD); cognitive neuroscience (PhD); general psychology (MA); social/developmental psychology (PhD). *Program availability:* Part-time. *Faculty:* 14 full-time (7 women), 4 part-time/adjunct (3 women). *Students:* 34 full-time (26 women), 4 part-time (2 women); includes 8 minority (5 Asian, non-Hispanic/Latino; 3 Hispanic/Latino), 10 international. Average age 27. 124 applicants, 31% accepted, 15 enrolled. In 2017, 13 master's, 7 doctorates awarded. Terminal master's awarded for partial completion of doctoral program. *Degree requirements:* For master's, thesis or alternative; for doctorate, thesis/dissertation, research reports. *Entrance requirements:* For master's and doctorate, GRE General Test; GRE Subject Test (recommended), letters of recommendation, statement of purpose, transcripts, resume. Additional exam requirements/recommendations for international students: Required—PTE (minimum score 68), TOEFL (minimum score 600 paper-based, 100 iBT) or IELTS (7). *Application deadline:* For fall admission, 12/1 priority date for domestic students. Applications are processed on a rolling basis. Application fee: $75. Electronic applications accepted. *Expenses: Tuition:* Full-time $48,720. *Required fees:* $88. Tuition and fees vary according to course load, degree level, program and student level. *Financial support:* In 2017–18, 40 students received support, including 20 fellowships with full tuition reimbursements available (averaging $24,480 per year), 26 teaching assistantships with partial tuition reimbursements available (averaging $3,200 per year); Federal Work-Study, scholarships/grants, health care benefits, and tuition waivers (partial) also available. Support available to part-time students. Financial award application deadline: 4/15; financial award applicants required to submit FAFSA. *Faculty research:* Brain, body, and behavior across the lifespan; face perception and nonverbal communication; learning and memory; motor control and spatial orientation; neurophysiology of learning and decision making; personality and cognition in adulthood and old age; social, cultural and affective neuroscience; social relations and health physiology; speech comprehension and memory; taste physiology and psychophysics; visual perception. *Unit head:* Dr. Angela Gutchess, Department Chair, 781-736-3303, E-mail: gutchess@brandeis.edu. *Application contact:* Dr. Sarah Lupis, Department Administrator, 781-736-3303, E-mail: slupis@brandeis.edu.
Website: http://www.brandeis.edu/gsas/programs/psychology.html

Brandeis University, Graduate School of Arts and Sciences, Program in Neuroscience, Waltham, MA 02454-9110. Offers neuroscience (MS, PhD); quantitative biology (PhD). *Faculty:* 24 full-time (8 women). *Students:* 65 full-time (34 women); includes 16 minority (2 Black or African American, non-Hispanic/Latino; 1 American Indian or Alaska Native, non-Hispanic/Latino; 4 Asian, non-Hispanic/Latino; 8 Hispanic/Latino; 1 Two or more races, non-Hispanic/Latino), 14 international. Average age 27. 182 applicants, 18% accepted, 19 enrolled. In 2017, 3 master's, 5 doctorates awarded. Terminal master's awarded for partial completion of doctoral program. *Degree requirements:* For master's, thesis optional, research project; for doctorate, comprehensive exam, thesis/dissertation, qualifying exams, teaching experience, journal club, research seminars. *Entrance requirements:* For master's, GRE General Test, transcripts, statement of purpose, resume, letters of recommendation; for doctorate, GRE General Test, transcripts, statement of purpose, resume, letters of recommendation, listing of previous research experience. Additional exam requirements/recommendations for international students: Required—PTE (minimum score 68), TOEFL (minimum score 600 paper-based, 100 iBT) or IELTS (7). *Application deadline:* For fall admission, 12/1 priority date for domestic students. Applications are processed on a rolling basis. Application fee: $75. Electronic applications accepted. *Expenses: Tuition:* Full-time $48,720. *Required fees:* $88. Tuition and fees vary according to course load, degree level, program and student level. *Financial support:* In 2017–18, 62 students received support, including 23 fellowships with full tuition reimbursements available (averaging $33,000 per year), 30 research assistantships with full tuition reimbursements available (averaging $33,000 per year); Federal Work-Study, scholarships/grants, health care benefits, and tuition waivers (partial) also available. Financial award application deadline: 4/15; financial award applicants required to submit FAFSA. *Faculty research:* Behavioral/cognitive neuroscience, cellular and molecular neuroscience, computational neuroscience and systems neuroscience, and developmental neuroscience. *Unit head:* Dr. Avi Rodal, Director of Graduate Studies, 781-736-2459, E-mail: arodal@brandeis.edu. *Application contact:* Jena Pitman-Leung, Academic Administrator, 781-736-2352, E-mail: scigradoffice@brandeis.edu.
Website: http://www.brandeis.edu/gsas/programs/neuroscience.html

Brigham Young University, Graduate Studies, College of Family, Home, and Social Sciences, Department of Psychology, Provo, UT 84602. Offers clinical psychology (PhD); cognitive and behavioral neuroscience (PhD). *Accreditation:* APA. *Faculty:* 31 full-time (8 women), 16 part-time/adjunct (7 women). *Students:* 59 full-time (33 women); includes 7 minority (2 Black or African American, non-Hispanic/Latino; 3 Asian, non-Hispanic/Latino; 1 Hispanic/Latino; 1 Native Hawaiian or other Pacific Islander, non-Hispanic/Latino), 4 international. Average age 29. 49 applicants, 33% accepted, 10

enrolled. In 2017, 11 doctorates awarded. *Degree requirements:* For doctorate, comprehensive exam (for some programs), thesis/dissertation, publishable paper. *Entrance requirements:* For doctorate, GRE General Test, minimum GPA of 3.0. Additional exam requirements/recommendations for international students: Required—TOEFL (minimum score 580 paper-based; 85 iBT). *Application deadline:* For fall admission, 12/1 for domestic and international students. Application fee: $50. Electronic applications accepted. *Expenses:* $10,320 per academic year for members of the Church of Jesus Christ of Latter-day Saints; $20,640 for those who are not members of the Church. *Financial support:* In 2017–18, 41 students received support, including 39 research assistantships with partial tuition reimbursements available (averaging $12,000 per year), 5 teaching assistantships with partial tuition reimbursements available (averaging $12,000 per year); career-related internships or fieldwork, scholarships/grants, tuition waivers (partial), and unspecified assistantships also available. Financial award application deadline: 5/31. *Faculty research:* Psychotherapy process, Alzheimer's disease/dementia, psychology and law, health, psychology, addiction. *Total annual research expenditures:* $711,243. *Unit head:* Dr. Dawson Hedges, Chair, 801-422-6357, Fax: 801-422-0602, E-mail: dawson_hedges@byu.edu. *Application contact:* Leesa D. Scott, Coordinator of Student Programs, 801-422-4560, Fax: 801-422-0602, E-mail: leesa_scott@byu.edu.
Website: http://psychology.byu.edu/

Brigham Young University, Graduate Studies, College of Life Sciences, Department of Physiology and Developmental Biology, Provo, UT 84602. Offers neuroscience (MS, PhD); physiology and developmental biology (MS, PhD). *Program availability:* Part-time. *Faculty:* 19 full-time (1 woman), 4 part-time/adjunct (3 women). *Students:* 33 full-time (16 women); includes 6 minority (5 Asian, non-Hispanic/Latino; 1 Hispanic/Latino). Average age 30. 14 applicants, 43% accepted, 3 enrolled. In 2017, 6 master's, 4 doctorates awarded. Terminal master's awarded for partial completion of doctoral program. *Degree requirements:* For master's, thesis, oral exam; for doctorate, comprehensive exam, thesis/dissertation. *Entrance requirements:* For master's, GRE General Test, MCAT, or DAT, minimum GPA of 3.0 during previous 2 years; for doctorate, GRE General Test, minimum GPA of 3.0 overall. Additional exam requirements/recommendations for international students: Required—TOEFL (minimum score 580 paper-based; 85 iBT); Recommended—IELTS. *Application deadline:* For fall admission, 2/1 priority date for domestic and international students; for winter admission, 9/10 priority date for domestic students, 9/10 for international students; for spring admission, 2/1 for domestic and international students; for summer admission, 2/1 for domestic and international students. Application fee: $50. Electronic applications accepted. *Expenses:* $6,880 full-time first year for members of the Church of Jesus Christ of Latter-day Saints; $13,760 for those who are not members of the Church; $405 per credit for additional years. *Financial support:* In 2017–18, 33 students received support, including 1 fellowship with partial tuition reimbursement available (averaging $15,000 per year), 16 research assistantships with full tuition reimbursements available (averaging $15,500 per year), 18 teaching assistantships with partial tuition reimbursements available (averaging $14,900 per year); career-related internships or fieldwork, institutionally sponsored loans, scholarships/grants, tuition waivers (full and partial), unspecified assistantships, and tuition awards also available. Financial award application deadline: 2/1. *Faculty research:* Sex differentiation of the brain, exercise physiology, developmental biology, membrane biophysics, neuroscience, heart differentiation/birth defects. *Total annual research expenditures:* $435,024. *Unit head:* Dr. Dixon J. Woodbury, Chair, 801-422-7562, Fax: 801-422-0004, E-mail: dixon_woodbury@byu.edu. *Application contact:* Connie L. Provost, Graduate Program Manager, 801-422-3706, Fax: 801-422-0004, E-mail: connie_provost@byu.edu.
Website: http://pdbio.byu.edu

Brock University, Faculty of Graduate Studies, Faculty of Social Sciences, Program in Psychology, St. Catharines, ON L2S 3A1, Canada. Offers behavioral neuroscience (MA, PhD); life span development (MA, PhD); social personality (MA, PhD). *Program availability:* Part-time. *Degree requirements:* For master's, thesis; for doctorate, thesis/dissertation. *Entrance requirements:* For master's, GRE, honors degree; for doctorate, GRE, master's degree. Additional exam requirements/recommendations for international students: Required—TOEFL (minimum score 550 paper-based; 80 iBT), IELTS (minimum score 6.5), TWE (minimum score 4). Electronic applications accepted. *Faculty research:* Social personality, behavioral neuroscience, life-span development.

Brown University, Graduate School, Division of Biology and Medicine, Department of Neuroscience, Providence, RI 02912. Offers PhD. *Degree requirements:* For doctorate, thesis/dissertation, preliminary exam. *Entrance requirements:* For doctorate, GRE General Test, GRE Subject Test. Additional exam requirements/recommendations for international students: Required—TOEFL. Electronic applications accepted. *Faculty research:* Neurophysiology, systems neuroscience, membrane biophysics, neuropharmacology, sensory systems.

Brown University, National Institutes of Health Sponsored Programs, Providence, RI 02912. Offers neuroscience (PhD).

California Institute of Technology, Division of Engineering and Applied Science, Option in Computation and Neural Systems, Pasadena, CA 91125-0001. Offers MS, PhD. Terminal master's awarded for partial completion of doctoral program. *Degree requirements:* For doctorate, thesis/dissertation, qualifying exam. *Entrance requirements:* For doctorate, GRE General Test. *Faculty research:* Biological and artificial computational devices, modeling of sensory processes and learning, theory of collective computation.

Carleton University, Faculty of Graduate Studies, Faculty of Arts and Social Sciences, Department of Psychology, Ottawa, ON K1S 5B6, Canada. Offers neuroscience (M Sc); psychology (MA, PhD). *Program availability:* Part-time. *Degree requirements:* For master's, thesis; for doctorate, comprehensive exam, thesis/dissertation. *Entrance requirements:* For master's, honors degree; for doctorate, GRE, master's degree. Additional exam requirements/recommendations for international students: Required—TOEFL. *Faculty research:* Behavioral neuroscience, social and personality psychology, cognitive/perception, developmental psychology, computer user research and evaluation, forensic psychology, health psychology.

Carnegie Mellon University, Center for the Neural Basis of Cognition, Pittsburgh, PA 15213-3891. Offers PhD.

Case Western Reserve University, School of Medicine and School of Graduate Studies, Graduate Programs in Medicine, Department of Neurosciences, Cleveland, OH 44106. Offers neuroscience (PhD); MD/PhD. Terminal master's awarded for partial completion of doctoral program. *Degree requirements:* For doctorate, thesis/dissertation. *Entrance requirements:* For doctorate, GRE General Test, 3 letters of recommendation. Additional exam requirements/recommendations for international students: Required—TOEFL (minimum score 90 iBT). Electronic applications accepted. *Expenses: Tuition:* Full-time $43,854; part-time $1827 per credit hour. *Required fees:* $50; $50 per credit hour. Tuition and fees vary according to course load and program. *Faculty research:* Neurotropic factors, synapse formation, regeneration, determination of cell fate, cellular neuroscience.

Central Michigan University, College of Graduate Studies, College of Humanities and Social and Behavioral Sciences, Department of Psychology, Program in Neuroscience, Mount Pleasant, MI 48859. Offers MS, PhD. *Degree requirements:* For master's, comprehensive exam, thesis or alternative; for doctorate, thesis/dissertation. *Entrance requirements:* For master's and doctorate, GRE. Electronic applications accepted.

College of Staten Island of the City University of New York, Graduate Programs, Division of Science and Technology, Program in Neuroscience and Developmental Disabilities, Staten Island, NY 10314-6600. Offers MS. *Program availability:* Part-time, evening/weekend. *Faculty:* 8 full-time, 4 part-time/adjunct. *Students:* 23. 23 applicants, 48% accepted, 4 enrolled. In 2017, 3 master's awarded. *Degree requirements:* For master's, comprehensive exam, thesis, 37 credits (31 in courses, 6 in thesis research), oral preliminary exam, thesis defense. *Entrance requirements:* For master's, three letters of recommendation; minimum GPA of 3.0 in undergraduate biology, mathematics, psychology or other science; interview. Additional exam requirements/recommendations for international students: Required—TOEFL (minimum score 550 paper-based; 79 iBT), IELTS (minimum score 6.5). *Application deadline:* For fall admission, 4/25 priority date for domestic and international students; for spring admission, 11/25 priority date for domestic and international students. Applications are processed on a rolling basis. Application fee: $125. Electronic applications accepted. *Expenses:* Tuition, state resident: full-time $10,450; part-time $440 per credit. Tuition, nonresident: full-time $19,320; part-time $440 per credit. *Required fees:* $181.10 per semester. Tuition and fees vary according to program. *Unit head:* Dr. Alejandra Alonso, Graduate Program Coordinator, 718-982-4153, E-mail: alejandra.alonso@csi.cuny.edu. *Application contact:* Sasha Spence, Associate Director for Graduate Admissions, 718-982-2019, Fax: 718-982-2500, E-mail: sasha.spence@csi.cuny.edu.
Website: https://www.csi.cuny.edu/sites/default/files/pdf/admissions/grad/pdf/Neuroscience%20Fact%20Sheet.pdf

The College of William and Mary, Faculty of Arts and Sciences, Department of Applied Science, Williamsburg, VA 23185. Offers accelerator science (PhD); applied mathematics (PhD); applied mechanics (PhD); applied robotics (PhD); applied science (MS); atmospheric and environmental science (PhD); computational neuroscience (PhD); interface, thin film and surface science (PhD); lasers and optics (PhD); magnetic resonance (PhD); materials science and engineering (PhD); mathematical and computational biology (PhD); medical imaging (PhD); nanotechnology (PhD); neuroscience (PhD); non-destructive evaluation (PhD); polymer chemistry (PhD); remote sensing (PhD). *Program availability:* Part-time. *Faculty:* 11 full-time (3 women). *Students:* 30 full-time (11 women), 3 part-time (0 women); includes 6 minority (2 Black or African American, non-Hispanic/Latino; 1 Asian, non-Hispanic/Latino; 2 Hispanic/Latino; 1 Two or more races, non-Hispanic/Latino), 13 international. Average age 27. 34 applicants, 47% accepted, 10 enrolled. In 2017, 5 doctorates awarded. Terminal master's awarded for partial completion of doctoral program. *Degree requirements:* For master's, comprehensive exam, thesis; for doctorate, comprehensive exam, thesis/dissertation, 4 core courses. *Entrance requirements:* For master's and doctorate, GRE General Test, GRE Subject Test. Additional exam requirements/recommendations for international students: Required—TOEFL, IELTS. *Application deadline:* For fall admission, 2/1 priority date for domestic students, 2/1 for international students; for spring admission, 10/5 priority date for domestic students, 10/5 for international students. Applications are processed on a rolling basis. Application fee: $50. Electronic applications accepted. *Expenses:* Contact institution. *Financial support:* In 2017–18, 8 students received support, including 27 research assistantships (averaging $26,000 per year), 1 teaching assistantship (averaging $9,500 per year); fellowships, scholarships/grants, health care benefits, tuition waivers (full), and unspecified assistantships also available. Financial award application deadline: 4/15; financial award applicants required to submit FAFSA. *Faculty research:* Computational biology, non-destructive evaluation, neurophysiology, laser spectroscopy, nanotechnology. *Total annual research expenditures:* $536,220. *Unit head:* Dr. Christopher Del Negro, Chair, 757-221-7808, Fax: 757-221-2050, E-mail: cadeln@wm.edu. *Application contact:* Lianne Rios Ashburne, Graduate Program Coordinator, 757-221-2563, Fax: 757-221-2050, E-mail: lrashburne@wm.edu.
Website: http://www.wm.edu/as/appliedscience

Dalhousie University, Faculty of Graduate Studies, Neuroscience Institute, Halifax, NS B3H 4H7, Canada. Offers M Sc, PhD. *Degree requirements:* For doctorate, thesis/dissertation. *Entrance requirements:* For master's and doctorate, 4 year honors degree or equivalent, minimum A- average. Additional exam requirements/recommendations for international students: Required—1 of 5 approved tests: TOEFL, IELTS, CANTEST, CAEL, Michigan English Language Assessment Battery. Electronic applications accepted. *Faculty research:* Molecular, cellular, systems, behavioral and clinical neuroscience.

Dalhousie University, Faculty of Science, Department of Psychology, Halifax, NS B3H 4R2, Canada. Offers clinical psychology (PhD); psychology (M Sc, PhD); psychology/neuroscience (M Sc, PhD). *Degree requirements:* For master's, thesis; for doctorate, thesis/dissertation. *Entrance requirements:* For doctorate, GRE General Test. Additional exam requirements/recommendations for international students: Required—TOEFL, IELTS, CANTEST, CAEL, or Michigan English Language Assessment Battery. Electronic applications accepted. *Faculty research:* Physiological psychology, psychology of learning, learning and behavior, forensic clinical health psychology, development perception and cognition.

Dartmouth College, School of Graduate and Advanced Studies, Department of Psychological and Brain Sciences, Hanover, NH 03755. Offers cognitive neuroscience (PhD); psychology (PhD). *Faculty:* 28 full-time (8 women), 7 part-time/adjunct (5 women). *Students:* 39 full-time (18 women); includes 5 minority (1 American Indian or Alaska Native, non-Hispanic/Latino; 1 Asian, non-Hispanic/Latino; 3 Hispanic/Latino), 15 international. Average age 28. 94 applicants, 11% accepted, 5 enrolled. In 2017, 3 doctorates awarded. *Degree requirements:* For doctorate, thesis/dissertation. *Entrance requirements:* For doctorate, GRE General Test, GRE Subject Test. Additional exam requirements/recommendations for international students: Required—TOEFL. *Application deadline:* For fall admission, 12/1 for domestic students. Application fee: $50. Electronic applications accepted. *Faculty research:* Behavioral neuroscience, cognitive neuroscience, cognitive science, social/personality psychology. *Unit head:* Dr. David Bucci, Chair, 603-646-3439. *Application contact:* Julia Abraham, Department Administrator, 603-646-2744, E-mail: julia.s.abraham@dartmouth.edu.
Website: http://www.dartmouth.edu/~psych/graduate/

Delaware State University, Graduate Programs, Department of Biological Sciences, Dover, DE 19901-2277. Offers biological sciences (MA, MS); biology education (MS); molecular and cellular neuroscience (MS); neuroscience (PhD). *Program availability:* Part-time, evening/weekend. *Degree requirements:* For master's, thesis (for some programs). *Entrance requirements:* For master's, GRE, minimum GPA of 3.0 in major, 2.75 overall. Additional exam requirements/recommendations for international students: Required—TOEFL (minimum score 550 paper-based). Electronic applications accepted. *Faculty research:* Cell biology, immunology, microbiology, genetics, ecology.

Drexel University, College of Arts and Sciences, Department of Psychology, Clinical Psychology Program, Philadelphia, PA 19104-2875. Offers clinical psychology (PhD); forensic psychology (PhD); health psychology (PhD); neuropsychology (PhD). *Accreditation:* APA. Terminal master's awarded for partial completion of doctoral program. *Degree requirements:* For doctorate, thesis/dissertation, qualifying exam.

Entrance requirements: For doctorate, GRE General Test, GRE Subject Test, minimum GPA of 3.0. Electronic applications accepted. *Expenses:* Contact institution. *Faculty research:* Cognitive behavioral therapy, stress and coping, eating disorders, substance abuse, developmental disabilities.

Drexel University, College of Medicine, Biomedical Graduate Programs, Program in Neuroscience, Philadelphia, PA 19104-2875. Offers MS, PhD, MD/PhD. *Degree requirements:* For doctorate, thesis/dissertation, qualifying exam. *Entrance requirements:* For doctorate, GRE General Test or MCAT, minimum GPA of 2.75. Additional exam requirements/recommendations for international students: Required—TOEFL. Electronic applications accepted. *Faculty research:* Central monoamine systems, drugs of abuse, anatomy/physiology of sensory systems, neurodegenerative disorders and recovery of function, neuromodulation and synaptic plasticity.

Duke University, Graduate School, Cognitive Neuroscience Admitting Program, Durham, NC 27708. Offers PhD, Certificate. PhD offered through one of the participating departments: Neurobiology, Psychology and Neuroscience, Biomedical Engineering, Computer Science, Evolutionary Anthropology, or Philosophy. *Degree requirements:* For doctorate, thesis/dissertation. *Entrance requirements:* For doctorate, GRE General Test. Additional exam requirements/recommendations for international students: Required—TOEFL (minimum score 577 paper-based; 90 iBT) or IELTS (minimum score 7). Electronic applications accepted.

Emory University, Laney Graduate School, Department of Psychology, Atlanta, GA 30322-1100. Offers clinical psychology (PhD); cognition and development (PhD); neuroscience and animal behavior (PhD). *Accreditation:* APA. *Degree requirements:* For doctorate, comprehensive exam, thesis/dissertation. *Entrance requirements:* For doctorate, GRE General Test, minimum GPA of 3.25. Additional exam requirements/recommendations for international students: Required—TOEFL. Electronic applications accepted. *Faculty research:* Neuroscience and animal behavior; adult and child psychopathology, cognition development assessment.

Emory University, Laney Graduate School, Division of Biological and Biomedical Sciences, Program in Neuroscience, Atlanta, GA 30322-1100. Offers PhD. *Degree requirements:* For doctorate, comprehensive exam, thesis/dissertation. *Entrance requirements:* For doctorate, GRE General Test, minimum GPA of 3.0 in science course work (recommended). Additional exam requirements/recommendations for international students: Required—TOEFL. Electronic applications accepted. *Faculty research:* Cell and molecular biology, development, behavior, neurodegenerative disease.

Fielding Graduate University, Graduate Programs, School of Psychology, Post Doctoral Certificate Program in Neuropsychology, Santa Barbara, CA 93105-3814. Offers Post-Doctoral Certificate. *Program availability:* Part-time-only, evening/weekend. *Faculty:* 2 part-time/adjunct (0 women). *Students:* 33 part-time (20 women); includes 7 minority (2 Black or African American, non-Hispanic/Latino; 2 Asian, non-Hispanic/Latino; 3 Hispanic/Latino). Average age 47. 26 applicants, 96% accepted, 13 enrolled. In 2017, 11 Post-Doctoral Certificates awarded. *Entrance requirements:* For degree, PhD, Psy D, or Ed D in psychology; minimum GPA of 3.0; curriculum vitae; psychologist license or certificate; official transcript. *Application deadline:* For fall admission, 8/4 for domestic students. Application fee: $75. Electronic applications accepted. *Expenses:* Contact institution. *Financial support:* Scholarships/grants available. Financial award applicants required to submit FAFSA. *Unit head:* Dr. Gerald Porter, Provost and Senior Vice President, 805-898-2940, E-mail: gporter@fielding.edu. *Application contact:* Enrollment Coordinator, 800-340-1099 Ext. 4098, Fax: 805-687-9793, E-mail: psyadmission@fielding.edu.
Website: http://www.fielding.edu/our-programs/school-of-psychology/postdoctoral-neuropsychology-certificate/

Florida Atlantic University, Charles E. Schmidt College of Science, Center for Complex Systems and Brain Sciences, Boca Raton, FL 33431-0991. Offers PhD. *Faculty:* 1 full-time (0 women). *Students:* 8 full-time (1 woman), 6 part-time (2 women); includes 4 minority (1 Black or African American, non-Hispanic/Latino; 1 Asian, non-Hispanic/Latino; 1 Hispanic/Latino; 1 Two or more races, non-Hispanic/Latino), 2 international. Average age 31. 10 applicants, 10% accepted, 1 enrolled. In 2017, 1 doctorate awarded. *Degree requirements:* For doctorate, thesis/dissertation. *Entrance requirements:* For doctorate, GRE General Test, minimum GPA of 3.0 in last 60 hours of undergraduate course work. Additional exam requirements/recommendations for international students: Required—TOEFL (minimum score 500 paper-based; 61 iBT), IELTS (minimum score 6). *Application deadline:* For fall admission, 1/15 priority date for domestic and international students. Application fee: $30. *Expenses:* Tuition, state resident: full-time $7400; part-time $369.82 per credit. Tuition, nonresident: full-time $20,496; part-time $1042.81 per credit. *Financial support:* Fellowships with full tuition reimbursements, research assistantships with partial tuition reimbursements, teaching assistantships with partial tuition reimbursements, Federal Work-Study, and traineeships available. *Faculty research:* Motor behavior, speech perception, nonlinear dynamics and fractals, behavioral neuroscience, cellular and molecular neuroscience. *Unit head:* Dr. Armin Fuchs, Graduate Coordinator, 561-297-0125, E-mail: fuchs@ccs.fau.edu.
Website: http://www.ccs.fau.edu/

Florida International University, College of Arts, Sciences, and Education, Department of Psychology, Miami, FL 33199. Offers behavioral analysis (MS); clinical science (PhD); cognitive neuroscience (PhD); counseling psychology (MS); developmental science (MS, PhD); legal psychology (MS, PhD); organizational psychology (MS, PhD). Program has fall admissions only. *Accreditation:* APA. *Program availability:* Part-time, evening/weekend. *Faculty:* 45 full-time (28 women), 48 part-time/adjunct (31 women). *Students:* 162 full-time (122 women), 13 part-time (5 women); includes 94 minority (11 Black or African American, non-Hispanic/Latino; 5 Asian, non-Hispanic/Latino; 75 Hispanic/Latino; 3 Two or more races, non-Hispanic/Latino), 12 international. Average age 27. 290 applicants, 21% accepted, 50 enrolled. In 2017, 43 master's, 13 doctorates awarded. Terminal master's awarded for partial completion of doctoral program. *Degree requirements:* For master's, thesis; for doctorate, comprehensive exam, thesis/dissertation. *Entrance requirements:* For master's, GRE General Test, minimum GPA of 3.0, resume, 3 letters of recommendation; for doctorate, GRE General Test, 3 letters of recommendation, resume, letter of intent, two writing samples, minimum GPA of 3.0. Additional exam requirements/recommendations for international students: Required—TOEFL (minimum score 550 paper-based; 80 iBT). *Application deadline:* For fall admission, 12/15 for domestic and international students. Application fee: $30. Electronic applications accepted. *Expenses:* Tuition, state resident: full-time $8912; part-time $446 per credit hour. Tuition, nonresident: full-time $21,393; part-time $992 per credit hour. *Required fees:* $390; $195 per semester. *Financial support:* Institutionally sponsored loans and scholarships/grants available. Financial award application deadline: 3/1. *Faculty research:* Legal psychology, organizational and industrial psychology, child behavior psychology. *Unit head:* Dr. Jeremy Pettit, Interim Chair, 305-348-1671, Fax: 305-348-3646, E-mail: jeremy.pettit@fiu.edu. *Application contact:* Nanett Rojas, Assistant Director, Graduate Admissions, 305-348-7464, Fax: 305-348-7441, E-mail: gradadm@fiu.edu.

Florida State University, College of Medicine, Division of Research and Graduate Programs, Tallahassee, FL 32306-4300. Offers biomedical sciences (PhD); neuroscience (PhD). *Faculty:* 28 full-time (8 women). *Students:* 41 full-time (26 women); includes 10 minority (2 Black or African American, non-Hispanic/Latino; 1 Asian, non-Hispanic/Latino; 1 Hispanic/Latino; 6 Two or more races, non-Hispanic/Latino), 3 international. Average age 27. 30 applicants, 50% accepted, 7 enrolled. In 2017, 6 doctorates awarded. *Degree requirements:* For doctorate, comprehensive exam, thesis/dissertation, seminar. *Entrance requirements:* For doctorate, GRE. Additional exam requirements/recommendations for international students: Required—TOEFL (minimum score 550 paper-based; 80 iBT). *Application deadline:* For fall admission, 12/1 for domestic and international students. Application fee: $30. Electronic applications accepted. *Expenses:* $13,000 per year. *Financial support:* In 2017–18, 39 students received support, including 41 research assistantships with full tuition reimbursements available (averaging $29,900 per year). Financial award application deadline: 12/1; financial award applicants required to submit FAFSA. *Faculty research:* Cell biology and development, neuroscience, stem cell and cell biology, molecular structure and function, genetics and genomics, cardiovascular disease and infectious disease. *Total annual research expenditures:* $24.5 million. *Unit head:* Dr. Jeffrey N. Joyce, Senior Associate Dean for Research and Graduate Programs, 850-644-2190, Fax: 850-644-9399, E-mail: jeffrey.joyce@med.fsu.edu. *Application contact:* Robin Ryan, Academic Program Specialist, 850-645-6420, Fax: 850-644-5781, E-mail: robin.ryan@med.fsu.edu.

Florida State University, The Graduate School, College of Arts and Sciences, Interdisciplinary Program in Neuroscience, Tallahassee, FL 32306. Offers neuroscience (PhD); psychobiology (MS). *Faculty:* 35 full-time (12 women), 2 part-time/adjunct (both women). *Students:* 44 full-time (27 women); includes 5 minority (1 Black or African American, non-Hispanic/Latino; 1 Asian, non-Hispanic/Latino; 1 Hispanic/Latino; 2 Two or more races, non-Hispanic/Latino), 5 international. Average age 26. 50 applicants, 10% accepted, 1 enrolled. In 2017, 5 master's, 6 doctorates awarded. Terminal master's awarded for partial completion of doctoral program. *Degree requirements:* For master's, thesis; for doctorate, comprehensive exam, thesis/dissertation. *Entrance requirements:* For doctorate, GRE General Test (suggested minimum score above 60th percentile on both verbal and quantitative sections), minimum GPA of 3.0, research experience, letters of recommendation. Additional exam requirements/recommendations for international students: Required—TOEFL (minimum score 80 iBT). *Application deadline:* For fall admission, 12/1 for domestic and international students. Application fee: $30. Electronic applications accepted. *Financial support:* In 2017–18, 38 students received support, including 6 fellowships with full tuition reimbursements available (averaging $22,815 per year), 19 research assistantships with full tuition reimbursements available (averaging $23,815 per year), 14 teaching assistantships with full tuition reimbursements available (averaging $22,815 per year); health care benefits also available. Financial award application deadline: 12/1; financial award applicants required to submit FAFSA. *Faculty research:* Sensory processes, neural development and plasticity, ingestive behavior, behavioral and molecular genetics, hormonal control of behavior. *Total annual research expenditures:* $1.8 million. *Unit head:* Dr. Frank Johnson, Director, 850-644-8566, Fax: 850-645-0349, E-mail: johnson@psy.fsu.edu. *Application contact:* Janice Parker, Graduate Program Associate, 850-645-9147, Fax: 850-644-0349, E-mail: info@neuro.fsu.edu.
Website: http://www.neuro.fsu.edu

Gallaudet University, The Graduate School, Washington, DC 20002-3625. Offers American Sign Language/English bilingual early childhood deaf education: birth to 5 (Certificate); audiology (Au D); clinical psychology (PhD); deaf and hard of hearing infants, toddlers, and their families (Certificate); deaf education (MA, Ed S); deaf history (Certificate); deaf studies (Certificate); educating deaf students with disabilities (Certificate); education: teacher preparation (MA), including deaf education, early childhood education and deaf education, elementary education and deaf education, secondary education and deaf education; educational neuroscience (PhD); hearing, speech and language sciences (MS, PhD); international development (MA); interpretation (MA, PhD), including combined interpreting practice and research (MA), interpreting research (MA); linguistics (MA, PhD); mental health counseling (MA); peer mentoring (Certificate); public administration (MPA); school counseling (MA); school psychology (Psy S); sign language teaching (MA); social work (MSW); speech-language pathology (MS). *Program availability:* Part-time. Terminal master's awarded for partial completion of doctoral program. *Degree requirements:* For master's, comprehensive exam (for some programs), thesis optional; for doctorate, comprehensive exam, thesis/dissertation. *Entrance requirements:* For master's and doctorate, GRE General Test or MAT, letters of recommendation, interviews, goals statement, American Sign Language proficiency interview, written English competency. Additional exam requirements/recommendations for international students: Required—TOEFL. Electronic applications accepted. *Faculty research:* Signing math dictionaries, telecommunications access, cancer genetics, linguistics, visual language and visual learning, integrated quantum materials, deaf legal discourse, advance recruitment and retention in geosciences.

George Mason University, College of Humanities and Social Sciences, Department of Psychology, Fairfax, VA 22030. Offers applied developmental psychology (MA, PhD); clinical psychology (PhD); cognitive and behavioral neuroscience (MA, PhD); cognitive neuroscience (Certificate); human factors/applied cognition (MA, PhD, Certificate), including transportation human factors (Certificate), usability (Certificate); industrial/organizational psychology (MA, PhD). *Accreditation:* APA. *Faculty:* 41 full-time (20 women), 5 part-time/adjunct (all women). *Students:* 152 full-time (101 women), 56 part-time (39 women); includes 47 minority (15 Black or African American, non-Hispanic/Latino; 13 Asian, non-Hispanic/Latino; 13 Hispanic/Latino; 1 Native Hawaiian or other Pacific Islander, non-Hispanic/Latino; 5 Two or more races, non-Hispanic/Latino), 12 international. Average age 27. 719 applicants, 19% accepted, 61 enrolled. In 2017, 55 master's, 18 doctorates, 8 other advanced degrees awarded. *Degree requirements:* For master's, comprehensive exam, thesis or practicum research; for doctorate, comprehensive exam, thesis/dissertation, 2nd-year project. *Entrance requirements:* For master's, GRE, 2 official transcripts; goals statement; 15 undergraduate credits in concentration for which the applicant is applying; for doctorate, GRE, 3 letters of recommendation; resume; goals statement; minimum GPA of 3.0 overall for last 60 undergraduate credits, 3.25 in psychology courses; 15 undergraduate credits in concentration for which the applicant is applying; 2 official transcripts; for Certificate, GRE, 2 official transcripts; expanded goals statement; 3 letters of recommendation. Additional exam requirements/recommendations for international students: Required—TOEFL (minimum score 575 paper-based; 88 iBT), IELTS (minimum score 6.5), PTE (minimum score 59). Application fee: $75 ($80 for international students). Electronic applications accepted. *Expenses:* Tuition, state resident: full-time $11,228; part-time $459.50 per credit. Tuition, nonresident: full-time $30,932; part-time $1280.50 per credit. *Required fees:* $3252; $135.50 per credit. Part-time tuition and fees vary according to course load and program. *Financial support:* In 2017–18, 110 students received support, including 6 fellowships (averaging $4,829 per year), 52 research assistantships with tuition reimbursements available (averaging $10,933 per year), 70 teaching assistantships with tuition reimbursements available (averaging $7,703 per year); career-related internships or fieldwork, Federal Work-Study, scholarships/grants, tuition waivers (partial), unspecified assistantships, and health care benefits (for full-time research or teaching assistantship recipients) also available. Support available to part-time students. Financial award application deadline: 3/1; financial award applicants required to submit FAFSA. *Faculty research:* Applied developmental psychology,

biopsychology, clinical psychology, human factors/applied cognition psychology, industrial/organizational psychology, school psychology. *Total annual research expenditures:* $2.6 million. *Unit head:* Reeshad Dalal, Department Chair, 703-993-9487, Fax: 703-993-1359, E-mail: rdalal@gmu.edu. *Application contact:* Michael Hock, Graduate Program Coordinator, 703-993-1548, Fax: 703-993-1359, E-mail: mhock2@gmu.edu.
Website: http://psychology.gmu.edu

George Mason University, College of Science, Program In Neuroscience, Fairfax, VA 22030. Offers PhD. *Faculty:* 24 full-time (6 women), 1 part-time/adjunct (0 women). *Students:* 13 full-time (6 women), 1 part-time (0 women); includes 3 minority (2 Asian, non-Hispanic/Latino; 1 Hispanic/Latino), 4 international. Average age 33. 23 applicants, 17% accepted, 2 enrolled. In 2017, 3 doctorates awarded. *Degree requirements:* For doctorate, comprehensive exam, thesis/dissertation, at least one publication in a refereed journal (print or press). *Entrance requirements:* For doctorate, GRE, bachelor's degree in related field with minimum GPA of 3.25; expanded goals statement; 2 copies of official transcripts; 3 letters of recommendation. Additional exam requirements/recommendations for international students: Required—TOEFL (minimum score 575 paper-based; 88 iBT), IELTS (minimum score 6.5), PTE (minimum score 59). Application fee: $75 ($80 for international students). Electronic applications accepted. *Expenses:* Tuition, state resident: full-time $11,228; part-time $459.50 per credit. Tuition, nonresident: full-time $30,932; part-time $1280.50 per credit. *Required fees:* $3252; $135.50 per credit. Part-time tuition and fees vary according to course load and program. *Financial support:* In 2017–18, 12 students received support, including 11 research assistantships with tuition reimbursements available (averaging $18,735 per year), 2 teaching assistantships with tuition reimbursements available; career-related internships or fieldwork, Federal Work-Study, scholarships/grants, unspecified assistantships, and health care benefits (for full-time research or teaching assistantship recipients) also available. Support available to part-time students. Financial award application deadline: 3/1; financial award applicants required to submit FAFSA. *Faculty research:* Biophysical and biochemical mechanisms of learning and memory; characterization and classification of neuron shape; cellular and molecular mechanisms of nicotinic receptor drug actions; cognitive neuroscience. *Unit head:* Saleet Jafri, Director, 703-993-8420, E-mail: sjafri@gmu.edu. *Application contact:* Avrama L. Blackwell, Director of PhD Program, 703-993-4381, Fax: 703-993-4325, E-mail: avrama@gmu.edu.
Website: http://neuroscience.gmu.edu/

Georgetown University, Graduate School of Arts and Sciences, Department of Psychology, Washington, DC 20057. Offers human development and public policy (PhD); lifespan cognitive neuroscience (PhD); PhD/MPP. PhD/MPP offered jointly with McCourt School of Public Policy. *Faculty:* 13 full-time (9 women). *Students:* 17 full-time (11 women), 3 international. 105 applicants, 5 enrolled. *Degree requirements:* For doctorate, thesis/dissertation, area paper. *Entrance requirements:* For doctorate, GRE General Test, GRE Subject Test. Additional exam requirements/recommendations for international students: Required—TOEFL. *Application deadline:* For fall admission, 12/1 for domestic and international students. Application fee: $50 ($55 for international students). Electronic applications accepted. *Financial support:* In 2017–18, 16 students received support, including 16 teaching assistantships with full tuition reimbursements available (averaging $28,000 per year); research assistantships also available. Financial award application deadline: 2/1; financial award applicants required to submit FAFSA. *Unit head:* Dr. Chandan Vaidya, Chair, 202-687-4274, Fax: 202-687-6050, E-mail: cjv2@georgetown.edu. *Application contact:* Graduate School Admissions Office, 202-687-5568, E-mail: gradmail@georgetown.edu.
Website: https://psychology.georgetown.edu

Georgetown University, Graduate School of Arts and Sciences, Interdisciplinary Program in Neuroscience, Washington, DC 20057. Offers PhD, MD/PhD. *Degree requirements:* For doctorate, thesis/dissertation. *Entrance requirements:* For doctorate, GRE General Test. Additional exam requirements/recommendations for international students: Required—TOEFL.

Georgia State University, College of Arts and Sciences, Department of Psychology, Atlanta, GA 30302-3083. Offers clinical psychology (PhD); cognitive sciences (PhD); community psychology (PhD); developmental psychology (PhD); neuropsychology and behavioral neuroscience (PhD). *Accreditation:* APA. *Faculty:* 40 full-time (26 women). *Students:* 102 full-time (80 women), 4 part-time (all women); includes 26 minority (7 Black or African American, non-Hispanic/Latino; 10 Asian, non-Hispanic/Latino; 4 Hispanic/Latino; 5 Two or more races, non-Hispanic/Latino), 8 international. Average age 27. 450 applicants, 7% accepted, 16 enrolled. In 2017, 21 doctorates awarded. *Entrance requirements:* For doctorate, GRE. Additional exam requirements/recommendations for international students: Required—TOEFL (minimum score 550 paper-based; 80 iBT). *Application deadline:* For fall admission, 12/1 for domestic and international students. Application fee: $50. Electronic applications accepted. *Expenses:* Tuition, state resident: full-time $7020. Tuition, nonresident: full-time $22,518. *Required fees:* $2128. Tuition and fees vary according to degree level and program. *Financial support:* In 2017–18, fellowships with full tuition reimbursements (averaging $19,282 per year), research assistantships with full tuition reimbursements (averaging $5,173 per year), teaching assistantships with full tuition reimbursements (averaging $6,389 per year) were awarded; scholarships/grants, traineeships, health care benefits, and unspecified assistantships also available. Financial award applicants required to submit FAFSA. *Faculty research:* Clinical psychology, developmental psychology, community psychology, neuropsychology and behavioral neuroscience, cognitive sciences. *Unit head:* Dr. Lisa Armistead, Chair, 404-413-6205, Fax: 404-413-6207, E-mail: lparmistead@gsu.edu. *Application contact:* Dr. Lindsey Cohen, Director of Graduate Studies, 404-413-6263, Fax: 404-413-6207, E-mail: llcohen@gsu.edu.

Georgia State University, College of Arts and Sciences, Neuroscience Institute, Atlanta, GA 30302-3083. Offers PhD. *Faculty:* 20 full-time (8 women). *Students:* 55 full-time (31 women), 2 part-time (1 woman); includes 12 minority (2 Black or African American, non-Hispanic/Latino; 4 Asian, non-Hispanic/Latino; 4 Hispanic/Latino; 2 Two or more races, non-Hispanic/Latino), 12 international. Average age 28. 48 applicants, 42% accepted, 12 enrolled. In 2017, 6 doctorates awarded. Terminal master's awarded for partial completion of doctoral program. *Entrance requirements:* For doctorate, GRE. Additional exam requirements/recommendations for international students: Required—TOEFL. *Application deadline:* For fall admission, 12/10 for domestic and international students. Application fee: $50. Electronic applications accepted. *Expenses:* Tuition, state resident: full-time $7020. Tuition, nonresident: full-time $22,518. *Required fees:* $2128. Tuition and fees vary according to degree level and program. *Financial support:* In 2017–18, fellowships (averaging $22,000 per year), research assistantships (averaging $22,000 per year) were awarded. Financial award applicants required to submit FAFSA. *Faculty research:* Neuroendocrinology; computational neuroscience; brain plasticity; neuromodulation of social behavior; neurobiology of learning and memory, drugs of abuse, and motor and sensory systems. *Unit head:* Prof. Walter Wilczynski, Director, 404-413-6307, E-mail: wwilczynski@gsu.edu. *Application contact:* Dr. Laura L. Carruth, Director of Graduate Studies, 404-413-5340, E-mail: lcarruth@gsu.edu.
Website: http://www.neuroscience.gsu.edu/

The Graduate Center, City University of New York, Graduate Studies, Program in Psychology, New York, NY 10016-4039. Offers basic applied neurocognition (PhD); biopsychology (PhD); clinical psychology (PhD); developmental psychology (PhD); environmental psychology (PhD); experimental psychology (PhD); industrial psychology (PhD); learning processes (PhD); neuropsychology (PhD); psychology (PhD); social personality (PhD). *Faculty:* 119 full-time (40 women). *Students:* 428 full-time (308 women); includes 118 minority (31 Black or African American, non-Hispanic/Latino; 31 Asian, non-Hispanic/Latino; 47 Hispanic/Latino; 1 Native Hawaiian or other Pacific Islander, non-Hispanic/Latino; 8 Two or more races, non-Hispanic/Latino), 53 international. Average age 33. 795 applicants, 12% accepted, 56 enrolled. In 2017, 46 doctorates awarded. *Degree requirements:* For doctorate, one foreign language, thesis/dissertation. *Entrance requirements:* For doctorate, GRE General Test. Additional exam requirements/recommendations for international students: Required—TOEFL. *Application deadline:* For fall admission, 12/1 priority date for domestic students. Application fee: $125. Electronic applications accepted. *Financial support:* In 2017–18, 371 students received support, including 340 fellowships, 34 research assistantships, 33 teaching assistantships; career-related internships or fieldwork, Federal Work-Study, institutionally sponsored loans, and tuition waivers (full and partial) also available. Financial award application deadline: 2/1; financial award applicants required to submit FAFSA. *Unit head:* Richard Bodnar, Executive Officer, 212-817-8706, Fax: 212-817-1533, E-mail: rbodnar@gc.cuny.edu. *Application contact:* Les Gribben, Director of Admissions, 212-817-7470, Fax: 212-817-1624, E-mail: lgribben@gc.cuny.edu.

Harvard University, Graduate School of Arts and Sciences, Program in Neuroscience, Boston, MA 02115. Offers neurobiology (PhD). *Degree requirements:* For doctorate, thesis/dissertation, qualifying exam. *Entrance requirements:* For doctorate, GRE General Test, GRE Subject Test. Additional exam requirements/recommendations for international students: Required—TOEFL. *Faculty research:* Relationship between diseases of the nervous system and basic science.

Icahn School of Medicine at Mount Sinai, Graduate School of Biomedical Sciences, New York, NY 10029-6504. Offers biomedical sciences (MS, PhD); clinical research education (MS, PhD); community medicine (MPH); genetic counseling (MS); neurosciences (PhD); MD/PhD. Terminal master's awarded for partial completion of doctoral program. *Degree requirements:* For master's, thesis; for doctorate, comprehensive exam, thesis/dissertation. *Entrance requirements:* For master's, GRE General Test; for doctorate, GRE General Test, GRE Subject Test, 3 years of college pre-med course work. Additional exam requirements/recommendations for international students: Required—TOEFL. Electronic applications accepted. *Faculty research:* Cancer, genetics and genomics, immunology, neuroscience, developmental and stem cell biology, translational research.

Illinois State University, Graduate School, College of Arts and Sciences, School of Biological Sciences, Normal, IL 61790. Offers animal behavior (MS); bacteriology (MS); biochemistry (MS); biological sciences (MS); biology (PhD); biophysics (MS); biotechnology (MS); botany (MS, PhD); cell biology (MS); conservation biology (MS); developmental biology (MS); ecology (MS, PhD); entomology (MS); evolutionary biology (MS); genetics (MS, PhD); immunology (MS); microbiology (MS, PhD); molecular biology (MS); molecular genetics (MS); neurobiology (MS); neuroscience (MS); parasitology (MS); physiology (MS, PhD); plant biology (MS); plant molecular biology (MS); plant sciences (MS); structural biology (MS); zoology (MS, PhD). *Program availability:* Part-time. *Degree requirements:* For master's, thesis or alternative; for doctorate, variable foreign language requirement, thesis/dissertation, 2 terms of residency. *Entrance requirements:* For master's, GRE General Test, minimum GPA of 2.6 in last 60 hours of course work; for doctorate, GRE General Test. *Faculty research:* Redox balance and drug development in schistosoma mansoni, control of the growth of listeria monocytogenes at low temperature, regulation of cell expansion and microtubule function by SPRI, CRUI: physiology and fitness consequences of different life history phenotypes.

Immaculata University, College of Graduate Studies, Department of Psychology, Immaculata, PA 19345. Offers clinical mental health counseling (MA); clinical psychology (Psy D); forensic psychology (Graduate Certificate); integrative psychotherapy (Graduate Certificate); neuropsychology (Graduate Certificate); psychodynamic psychotherapy (Graduate Certificate); psychological testing (Graduate Certificate); school counseling (MA, Graduate Certificate); school psychology (MA). *Accreditation:* APA. *Program availability:* Part-time, evening/weekend. Terminal master's awarded for partial completion of doctoral program. *Degree requirements:* For master's, comprehensive exam, thesis optional; for doctorate, comprehensive exam, thesis/dissertation. *Entrance requirements:* For master's, GRE General Test or MAT, minimum GPA of 3.0; for doctorate, GRE General Test or MAT, minimum GPA of 3.5. Additional exam requirements/recommendations for international students: Required—TOEFL, IELTS. Electronic applications accepted. *Faculty research:* Supervision ethics, psychology of teaching, gender.

Indiana University Bloomington, University Graduate School, College of Arts and Sciences, Department of Psychological and Brain Sciences, Bloomington, IN 47405. Offers clinical science (PhD); cognitive neuroscience (PhD); cognitive psychology (PhD); developmental psychology (PhD); methods of behavior (PhD); molecular systems neuroscience (PhD); social psychology (PhD). *Accreditation:* APA. *Degree requirements:* For doctorate, comprehensive exam, 90 credit hours, 2 advanced statistics/methods courses, 2 written research projects, the teaching of psychology course, teaching 1 semester of undergraduate methods course, qualifying examination, minor or a second major, first-year research seminar course, dissertation defense, written dissertation. *Entrance requirements:* For doctorate, GRE. Additional exam requirements/recommendations for international students: Required—TOEFL (minimum score 550 paper-based; 79 iBT). Electronic applications accepted. *Faculty research:* Clinical science, cognitive neuroscience, cognitive psychology, developmental psychology, mechanisms of behavior, molecular and systems neuroscience, social psychology.

Indiana University Bloomington, University Graduate School, College of Arts and Sciences, Program in Neuroscience, Bloomington, IN 47405. Offers PhD. *Degree requirements:* For doctorate, comprehensive exam, thesis/dissertation, qualifying exam. *Entrance requirements:* For doctorate, GRE, bachelor's degree. Additional exam requirements/recommendations for international students: Required—TOEFL. Electronic applications accepted. *Faculty research:* Cellular and molecular neuroscience, cognitive neuroscience, developmental neuroscience, disorders of the nervous system, sensory and motor processes.

Iowa State University of Science and Technology, Program in Neuroscience, Ames, IA 50011. Offers MS, PhD. *Degree requirements:* For master's, thesis; for doctorate, thesis/dissertation. *Entrance requirements:* For master's and doctorate, GRE General Test, resume. Additional exam requirements/recommendations for international students: Required—TOEFL (minimum score 580 paper-based; 85 iBT), IELTS (minimum score 7). Electronic applications accepted. *Faculty research:* Behavioral pharmacology and immunology, developmental neurobiology, neuroendocrinology, neuroregulatory mechanisms at the cellular level, signal transduction in neurons.

Neuroscience

Irell & Manella Graduate School of Biological Sciences, Graduate Program, Duarte, CA 91010. Offers brain metastatic cancer (PhD); cancer and stem cell metabolism (PhD); cancer biology (PhD); cancer biology and developmental therapeutics (PhD); cell biology (PhD); chemical biology (PhD); chromosomal break repair (PhD); diabetes and pancreatic progenitor cell biology (PhD); DNA repair and cancer biology (PhD); germline epigenetic remodeling and endocrine disruptors (PhD); hematology and hematopoietic cell transplantation (PhD); hematology and immunology (PhD); inflammation and cancer (PhD); micrornas and gene regulation in cardiovascular disease (PhD); mixed chimrism for reversal of autoimmunity (PhD); molecular and cellular biology (PhD); molecular biology and genetics (PhD); nanoparticle mediated twist1 silencing in metastatic cancer (PhD); neuro oncology and stem cell biology (PhD); neuroscience (PhD); RNA directed therapies for HIV-1 (PhD); small RNA-induced transcriptional gene activation (PhD); stem cell regulation by the microenvironment (PhD); translational oncology and pharmaceutical sciences (PhD); tumor biology (PhD). *Degree requirements:* For doctorate, comprehensive exam, thesis/dissertation, qualifying exams, two advanced courses. *Entrance requirements:* For doctorate, GRE General Test; GRE Subject Test (recommended), 2 years of course work in chemistry (general and organic); 1 year of course work each in biochemistry, general biology, and general physics; 2 semesters of course work in mathematics; significant research laboratory experience. Additional exam requirements/recommendations for international students: Required—TOEFL. Electronic applications accepted. *Faculty research:* Cancer biology, diabetes, stem cell biology, neuroscience, immunology.

See Display on page 65 and Close-Up on page 109.

Johns Hopkins University, School of Medicine, Graduate Programs in Medicine, Neuroscience Training Program, Baltimore, MD 21218. Offers PhD. *Degree requirements:* For doctorate, comprehensive exam, thesis/dissertation, thesis defense. *Entrance requirements:* For doctorate, GRE General Test, bachelor's degree in science or mathematics. Additional exam requirements/recommendations for international students: Required—TOEFL. Electronic applications accepted. *Expenses:* Contact institution. *Faculty research:* Neurophysiology, neurochemistry, neuroanatomy, pharmacology, development.

Kent State University, College of Arts and Sciences, School of Biomedical Sciences, Kent, OH 44242-0001. Offers biological anthropology (PhD); biomedical mathematics (MS, PhD); cellular and molecular biology (MS, PhD), including cellular biology and structures, molecular biology and genetics; neurosciences (MS, PhD); pharmacology (MS, PhD); physiology (MS, PhD). *Faculty:* 22 full-time (9 women), 3 part-time/adjunct (1 woman). *Students:* 75 full-time (46 women); includes 8 minority (1 Black or African American, non-Hispanic/Latino; 3 Asian, non-Hispanic/Latino; 2 Hispanic/Latino; 2 Two or more races, non-Hispanic/Latino), 25 international. Average age 28. 70 applicants, 23% accepted, 13 enrolled. In 2017, 23 master's, 5 doctorates awarded. Terminal master's awarded for partial completion of doctoral program. *Degree requirements:* For master's, thesis; for doctorate, comprehensive exam, thesis/dissertation. *Entrance requirements:* For master's, GRE, bachelor's degree, transcripts, minimum GPA of 3.0, goal statement, three letters of recommendation, academic preparation adequate to perform graduate work in the desired field; for doctorate, GRE, master's degree, minimum GPA of 3.0, transcripts, goal statement, three letters of recommendation. Additional exam requirements/recommendations for international students: Required—TOEFL (minimum score 600 paper-based, 100 iBT), Michigan English Language Assessment Battery (minimum score 85), IELTS (minimum score 7.0) or PTE (minimum score 68). *Application deadline:* For fall admission, 1/1 for domestic and international students. Applications are processed on a rolling basis. Application fee: $45 ($70 for international students). Electronic applications accepted. *Expenses:* Tuition, state resident: full-time $11,310; part-time $515 per credit hour. Tuition, nonresident: full-time $20,396; part-time $928 per credit hour. *International tuition:* $18,544 full-time. *Financial support:* Research assistantships with full tuition reimbursements, teaching assistantships, and unspecified assistantships available. Financial award application deadline: 1/1. *Unit head:* Dr. Ernest J. Freeman, Director, School of Biomedical Sciences, 330-672-2363, E-mail: efreema2@kent.edu.
Website: http://www.kent.edu/biomedical/

Louisiana State University Health Sciences Center, School of Graduate Studies in New Orleans, Interdisciplinary Neuroscience Graduate Program, New Orleans, LA 70112-2223. Offers PhD, MD/PhD. *Faculty:* 16 full-time (5 women). *Students:* 6 full-time (4 women); includes 2 minority (1 Asian, non-Hispanic/Latino; 1 Hispanic/Latino), 2 international. Average age 26. 5 applicants, 20% accepted, 1 enrolled. *Degree requirements:* For doctorate, comprehensive exam, thesis/dissertation. *Entrance requirements:* For doctorate, GRE General Test, previous course work in chemistry, mathematics, physics, and computer science. Additional exam requirements/recommendations for international students: Recommended—TOEFL, IELTS. *Application deadline:* For fall admission, 4/1 for domestic and international students. Applications are processed on a rolling basis. Application fee: $30. *Expenses:* Tuition, state resident: full-time $11,835; part-time $518 per hour. Tuition, nonresident: full-time $24,108; part-time $1079 per hour. *Required fees:* $1254; $55 per hour. *Financial support:* Unspecified assistantships available. Financial award application deadline: 8/1. *Faculty research:* Visual system, second messengers, drugs and behavior, signal transduction, plasticity and development. *Unit head:* Dr. Nicolas G. Bazan, Department Head, 504-599-0831, Fax: 504-568-5801. *Application contact:* Dr. Hamilton Farris, Graduate Coordinator, 504-568-4027, Fax: 504-599-0685, E-mail: hfarri@lsuhsc.edu.
Website: http://www.medschool.lsuhsc.edu/neuroscience/grad_program/

Loyola University Chicago, Graduate School, Integrated Program in Biomedical Sciences, Maywood, IL 60141. Offers biochemistry and molecular biology (MS, PhD); cell and molecular physiology (MS, PhD); infectious disease and immunology (MS); integrative cell biology (MS, PhD); microbiology and immunology (MS, PhD); molecular pharmacology and therapeutics (MS, PhD); neuroscience (MS, PhD). *Faculty:* 84 full-time (32 women). *Students:* 126 full-time (65 women), 1 (woman) part-time; includes 36 minority (5 Black or African American, non-Hispanic/Latino; 14 Asian, non-Hispanic/Latino; 14 Hispanic/Latino; 3 Two or more races, non-Hispanic/Latino), 13 international. Average age 26. 748 applicants, 34% accepted, 124 enrolled. In 2017, 41 master's, 18 doctorates awarded. *Degree requirements:* For master's, thesis; for doctorate, comprehensive exam, thesis/dissertation. *Entrance requirements:* For doctorate, GRE. Additional exam requirements/recommendations for international students: Required—TOEFL (minimum score 94 iBT), IELTS (minimum score 7.5). *Application deadline:* For fall admission, 2/7 for domestic students. Applications are processed on a rolling basis. Electronic applications accepted. *Expenses:* Contact institution. *Financial support:* In 2017–18, 20 students received support. Schmitt Fellowships and yearly tuition scholarships (averaging $25,032) available. Financial award application deadline: 6/15; financial award applicants required to submit FAFSA. *Unit head:* Dr. Leanne L. Cribbs, Associate Dean, Graduate Education, 708-327-2817, Fax: 708-216-8216, E-mail: lcribbs@luc.edu. *Application contact:* Margarita Quesada, Graduate Program Secretary, 708-216-3532, Fax: 708-216-8216, E-mail: mquesad@luc.edu.
Website: http://ssom.luc.edu/graduate_school/degree-programs/ipbsphd/

Marquette University, Graduate School, College of Arts and Sciences, Department of Biology, Milwaukee, WI 53201-1881. Offers cell biology (MS, PhD); developmental biology (MS, PhD); ecology (MS, PhD); epithelial physiology (MS, PhD); genetics (MS, PhD); microbiology (MS, PhD); molecular biology (MS, PhD); muscle and exercise physiology (MS, PhD); neuroscience (PhD). Terminal master's awarded for partial completion of doctoral program. *Degree requirements:* For master's, comprehensive exam, thesis, 1 year of teaching experience or equivalent; for doctorate, thesis/dissertation, 1 year of teaching experience or equivalent, qualifying exam. *Entrance requirements:* For master's and doctorate, GRE General Test, GRE Subject Test, official transcripts from all current and previous colleges/universities except Marquette, statement of professional goals and aspirations, three letters of recommendation. Additional exam requirements/recommendations for international students: Required—TOEFL (minimum score 530 paper-based). Electronic applications accepted. *Faculty research:* Neurobiology, neuroendocrinology, epithelial physiology, neuropeptide interactions, synaptic transmission.

Massachusetts Institute of Technology, School of Science, Department of Brain and Cognitive Sciences, Cambridge, MA 02139. Offers cognitive science (PhD); neuroscience (PhD). *Degree requirements:* For doctorate, comprehensive exam, thesis/dissertation. *Entrance requirements:* For doctorate, GRE General Test. Additional exam requirements/recommendations for international students: Required—TOEFL, IELTS. Electronic applications accepted. *Faculty research:* Vision, audition, and other perceptual systems: physiology and computation; learning, memory, and executive control: molecular and systems approaches; sensorimotor systems: physiology and computation; neural and cognitive development and plasticity; language and high-level cognition: learning, acquisition, and computation.

Mayo Clinic Graduate School of Biomedical Sciences, Program in Neuroscience, Rochester, MN 55905. Offers MS, PhD. *Faculty:* 32 full-time (7 women). *Students:* 19 full-time (11 women); includes 6 minority (5 Asian, non-Hispanic/Latino; 1 Hispanic/Latino). 37 applicants, 19% accepted, 3 enrolled. *Degree requirements:* For doctorate, comprehensive exam, thesis/dissertation, oral defense of dissertation, qualifying oral and written exam. *Entrance requirements:* For doctorate, GRE, 1 year of chemistry, biology, calculus, and physics. Additional exam requirements/recommendations for international students: Required—TOEFL. *Application deadline:* For fall admission, 12/1 priority date for domestic students, 12/1 for international students. Application fee: $50. Electronic applications accepted. *Financial support:* Fellowships with full tuition reimbursements available. *Faculty research:* Cholinergic receptor/Alzheimer's; molecular biology, channels, receptors, and mental disease; neuronal cytoskeleton; growth factors; gene regulation; neuroregeneration. *Unit head:* Pamela J. McLean, Director, 904-953-6692, E-mail: mclean.pamela@mayo.edu. *Application contact:* Sarah E. Giese, Admissions Coordinator, 507-538-1160, E-mail: phd.training@mayo.edu.
Website: http://www.mayo.edu/mgs/

McGill University, Faculty of Graduate and Postdoctoral Studies, Faculty of Medicine, Department of Neurology and Neurosurgery, Montréal, QC H3A 2T5, Canada. Offers M Sc, PhD.

McMaster University, Faculty of Health Sciences and School of Graduate Studies, Program in Medical Sciences, Neurosciences and Behavioral Sciences Area, Hamilton, ON L8S 4M2, Canada. Offers M Sc, PhD, MD/PhD. *Degree requirements:* For master's, thesis; for doctorate, comprehensive exam, thesis/dissertation. *Entrance requirements:* For master's, honors B Sc, B+ average in related field; for doctorate, M Sc, minimum B+ average, students with proven research experience and an A average may be admitted with a B Sc degree. Additional exam requirements/recommendations for international students: Required—TOEFL (minimum score 580 paper-based).

Medical College of Wisconsin, Graduate School, Neuroscience Doctoral Program, Milwaukee, WI 53226-0509. Offers PhD, MD/PhD. *Degree requirements:* For doctorate, comprehensive exam, thesis/dissertation. *Entrance requirements:* For doctorate, GRE, official transcripts, three letters of recommendation. Additional exam requirements/recommendations for international students: Required—TOEFL. *Application deadline:* For fall admission, 1/15 for domestic and international students. Applications are processed on a rolling basis. Application fee: $50. *Financial support:* Fellowships, research assistantships, institutionally sponsored loans, scholarships/grants, and annual stipends available. Support available to part-time students. Financial award application deadline: 2/15. *Faculty research:* Neurobiology, development, neuroscience, teratology. *Unit head:* Dr. Cheryl Stucky, Director, 414-955-8373, Fax: 414-955-6555, E-mail: cstucky@mcw.edu. *Application contact:* Recruitment Office, 414-955-4402, Fax: 414-955-6555, E-mail: gradschoolrecruit@mcw.edu.
Website: http://www.mcw.edu/Graduate-School/Programs/Neuroscience-PhD-Program.htm

Medical University of South Carolina, College of Graduate Studies, Department of Neurosciences, Charleston, SC 29425. Offers MS, PhD, DMD/PhD, MD/PhD. Terminal master's awarded for partial completion of doctoral program. *Degree requirements:* For master's, thesis; for doctorate, thesis/dissertation, oral and written exams. *Entrance requirements:* For master's, GRE General Test; for doctorate, GRE General Test, interview, minimum GPA of 3.0. Additional exam requirements/recommendations for international students: Required—TOEFL (minimum score 600 paper-based; 100 iBT). Electronic applications accepted. *Faculty research:* Addiction, aging, movement disorders, membrane physiology, neurotransmission and behavior.

Meharry Medical College, School of Graduate Studies, Program in Biomedical Sciences, Neuroscience Emphasis, Nashville, TN 37208-9989. Offers PhD, MD/PhD. *Degree requirements:* For doctorate, comprehensive exam, thesis/dissertation. *Entrance requirements:* For doctorate, GRE. *Faculty research:* Neurochemistry, pain, smooth muscle tone.

Memorial University of Newfoundland, Faculty of Medicine and School of Graduate Studies, Graduate Programs in Medicine, Division of Biomedical Sciences, St. John's, NL A1C 5S7, Canada. Offers cancer (M Sc, PhD); cardiovascular (M Sc, PhD); immunology (M Sc, PhD); neuroscience (M Sc, PhD). *Program availability:* Part-time. *Degree requirements:* For master's, thesis; for doctorate, comprehensive exam, thesis/dissertation, oral defense of thesis. *Entrance requirements:* For master's, MD or B Sc; for doctorate, MD or M Sc. Additional exam requirements/recommendations for international students: Required—TOEFL. *Faculty research:* Neuroscience, immunology, cardiovascular, and cancer.

Michigan State University, The Graduate School, College of Natural Science, Program in Neuroscience, East Lansing, MI 48824. Offers MS, PhD. *Entrance requirements:* Additional exam requirements/recommendations for international students: Required—TOEFL. Electronic applications accepted.

Montana State University, The Graduate School, College of Letters and Science, Department of Cell Biology and Neuroscience, Bozeman, MT 59717. Offers biological sciences (PhD); neuroscience (MS, PhD). *Program availability:* Part-time. *Degree requirements:* For master's, comprehensive exam; for doctorate, comprehensive exam, thesis/dissertation. *Entrance requirements:* For master's and doctorate, GRE General Test. Additional exam requirements/recommendations for international students: Required—TOEFL (minimum score 550 paper-based). Electronic applications accepted. *Faculty research:* Development of the nervous system, neuronal mechanisms of visual perception, ion channel biophysics, mechanisms of sensory coding, neuroinformatics.

New York University, Graduate School of Arts and Science, Center for Neural Science, New York, NY 10012-1019. Offers PhD. *Faculty:* 15 full-time (3 women). *Students:* 50 full-time (21 women); includes 8 minority (5 Asian, non-Hispanic/Latino; 2 Hispanic/Latino; 1 Two or more races, non-Hispanic/Latino), 14 international. Average age 28. 269 applicants, 9% accepted, 9 enrolled. In 2017, 1 doctorate awarded. *Degree requirements:* For doctorate, one foreign language, thesis/dissertation. *Entrance requirements:* For doctorate, GRE, interview. Additional exam requirements/recommendations for international students: Required—TOEFL. *Application deadline:* For fall admission, 12/1 for domestic and international students. Application fee: $100. *Expenses: Tuition:* Full-time $41,352; part-time $19,968 per year. *Required fees:* $2496; $1628 per unit. $814 per term. Tuition and fees vary according to course load and program. *Financial support:* Fellowships with tuition reimbursements, research assistantships with tuition reimbursements, career-related internships or fieldwork, Federal Work-Study, institutionally sponsored loans, scholarships/grants, health care benefits, and unspecified assistantships available. Financial award application deadline: 12/1; financial award applicants required to submit FAFSA. *Faculty research:* Systems and integrative neuroscience; combining biology, cognition, computation, and theory. *Unit head:* J. Anthony Movshon, Chair, 212-998-7780, Fax: 212-995-4011, E-mail: admissions@cns.nyu.edu. *Application contact:* Michael Hawken, Director of Graduate Studies, 212-998-7780, Fax: 212-995-4011, E-mail: admissions@cns.nyu.edu.
Website: http://www.cns.nyu.edu/

New York University, School of Medicine and Graduate School of Arts and Science, Sackler Institute of Graduate Biomedical Sciences, New York, NY 10016. Offers biomedical imaging and technology (PhD); biostatistics (PhD); cellular and molecular biology (PhD); developmental genetics (PhD); epidemiology (PhD); genome integrity (PhD); immunology and inflammation (PhD); microbiology (PhD); molecular biophysics (PhD); molecular oncology and tumor immunology (PhD); molecular pharmacology (PhD); neuroscience and physiology (PhD), including immunology, molecular oncology; stem cell biology (PhD); systems and computational biomedicine (PhD); MD/PhD. *Faculty:* 207 full-time (51 women). *Students:* 236 full-time (138 women), 1 part-time (0 women); includes 68 minority (13 Black or African American, non-Hispanic/Latino; 26 Asian, non-Hispanic/Latino; 28 Hispanic/Latino; 1 Native Hawaiian or other Pacific Islander, non-Hispanic/Latino), 79 international. Average age 27. 761 applicants, 18% accepted, 59 enrolled. In 2017, 35 doctorates awarded. *Degree requirements:* For doctorate, comprehensive exam, thesis/dissertation, qualifying exam; thesis defense. *Entrance requirements:* For doctorate, GRE. Additional exam requirements/recommendations for international students: Required—TOEFL, IELTS. *Application deadline:* For fall admission, 12/1 for domestic and international students. Applications are processed on a rolling basis. Application fee: $100. Electronic applications accepted. Application fee is waived when completed online. *Expenses:* Contact institution. *Financial support:* Health care benefits, tuition waivers (full), and unspecified assistantships available. *Faculty research:* Biomedical sciences. *Unit head:* Dr. Naoko Tanese, Associate Dean for Biomedical Sciences/Director, Sackler Institute, 212-263-8945, E-mail: naoko.tanese@nyumc.org. *Application contact:* Jessica Dong, Program Manager, 212-263-5648, E-mail: sackler-info@nyumc.org.
Website: https://med.nyu.edu/research/sackler-institute-graduate-biomedical-sciences/

Northwestern University, Feinberg School of Medicine, Department of Physical Therapy and Human Movement Sciences, Chicago, IL 60611-2814. Offers neuroscience (PhD), including movement and rehabilitation science; physical therapy (DPT); DPT/MPH; DPT/PhD. *Accreditation:* APTA. *Degree requirements:* For doctorate, research project. *Entrance requirements:* For doctorate, GRE General Test (for DPT), baccalaureate degree with minimum GPA of 3.0 in required course work (DPT). Additional exam requirements/recommendations for international students: Required—TOEFL (minimum score 100 iBT). *Application deadline:* For fall admission, 10/1 for domestic and international students. Applications are processed on a rolling basis. Electronic applications accepted. *Expenses:* Contact institution. *Financial support:* Institutionally sponsored loans and scholarships/grants available. Financial award application deadline: 3/1; financial award applicants required to submit FAFSA. *Unit head:* Dr. Julius P. A. Dewald, Professor and Chair, 312-908-8160, Fax: 312-908-0741. *Application contact:* Dr. Jane Sullivan, Professor/Assistant Chair for Recruitment and Admissions, 312-908-8160, Fax: 312-908-0741, E-mail: dpt-admissions@northwestern.edu.
Website: http://www.feinberg.northwestern.edu/sites/pthms/

Northwestern University, The Graduate School, Interdepartmental Neuroscience Program, Evanston, IL 60208. Offers PhD. Admissions and degree offered through The Graduate School. *Degree requirements:* For doctorate, thesis/dissertation. *Entrance requirements:* For doctorate, GRE General Test. Additional exam requirements/recommendations for international students: Required—TOEFL. *Faculty research:* Circadian rhythms, synaptic neurotransmissions, cognitive neuroscience, sensory/motor systems, cell biology and structure/function, neurobiology of disease.

The Ohio State University, Graduate School, College of Arts and Sciences, Division of Natural and Mathematical Sciences, Neuroscience Graduate Program, Columbus, OH 43210. Offers PhD. *Students:* 40 full-time (21 women). Average age 26. In 2017, 7 doctorates awarded. *Degree requirements:* For doctorate, comprehensive exam, thesis/dissertation. *Entrance requirements:* For doctorate, GRE General Test, GRE Subject Test in biology, psychology, biochemistry, or cell and molecular biology (recommended). Additional exam requirements/recommendations for international students: Required—TOEFL (minimum score 600 paper-based; 100 iBT); Recommended—IELTS (minimum score 8). *Application deadline:* For fall admission, 12/1 for domestic students, 11/30 for international students. Applications are processed on a rolling basis. Application fee: $60 ($70 for international students). Electronic applications accepted. *Financial support:* Fellowships, research assistantships, and unspecified assistantships available. *Faculty research:* Neurotrauma and disease, behavioral neuroscience, systems neuroscience, stress and neuroimmunology, molecular and cellular neuroscience. *Unit head:* 614-292-2379, E-mail: ngsp@osu.edu. *Application contact:* Neuroscience Graduate Studies Program, 614-292-2379, Fax: 614-292-0490, E-mail: ngsp@osu.edu.
Website: http://www.ngsp.osu.edu/

The Ohio State University, Graduate School, College of Arts and Sciences, Division of Social and Behavioral Sciences, Department of Psychology, Columbus, OH 43210. Offers behavioral neuroscience (PhD); clinical psychology (PhD); cognitive psychology (PhD); developmental psychology (PhD); intellectual and developmental disabilities psychology (PhD); quantitative psychology (PhD); social psychology (PhD). *Accreditation:* APA. *Faculty:* 52. *Students:* 144 full-time (86 women); includes 18 minority (8 Asian, non-Hispanic/Latino; 10 Hispanic/Latino), 28 international. Average age 26. In 2017, 21 doctorates awarded. *Entrance requirements:* For doctorate, GRE General Test. Additional exam requirements/recommendations for international students: Required—TOEFL (minimum score 600 paper-based; 100 iBT); Recommended—IELTS (minimum score 8). *Application deadline:* For fall admission, 12/1 for domestic and international students. Applications are processed on a rolling basis. Application fee: $60 ($70 for international students). Electronic applications accepted. *Financial support:* Fellowships, research assistantships, and teaching assistantships available. *Unit head:* Dr. John Bruno, Chair, 614-292-3038, E-mail: bruno.1@osu.edu. *Application contact:* Graduate and Professional Admissions, 614-292-9444, Fax: 614-292-3895, E-mail: gpadmissions@osu.edu.
Website: http://psychology.osu.edu/

Ohio University, Graduate College, College of Arts and Sciences, Department of Biological Sciences, Athens, OH 45701-2979. Offers biological sciences (MS, PhD); cell biology and physiology (MS, PhD); ecology and evolutionary biology (MS, PhD); exercise physiology and muscle biology (MS, PhD); microbiology (MS, PhD); neuroscience (MS, PhD). Terminal master's awarded for partial completion of doctoral program. *Degree requirements:* For master's, comprehensive exam, thesis, 1 quarter of teaching experience; for doctorate, comprehensive exam, thesis/dissertation, 2 quarters of teaching experience. *Entrance requirements:* For master's, GRE General Test, names of three faculty members whose research interests most closely match the applicant's interest; for doctorate, GRE General Test, essay concerning prior training, research interest and career goals, plus names of three faculty members whose research interests most closely match the applicant's interest. Additional exam requirements/recommendations for international students: Required—TOEFL (minimum score 620 paper-based; 105 iBT) or IELTS (minimum score 7.5). Electronic applications accepted. *Faculty research:* Ecology and evolutionary biology, exercise physiology and muscle biology, neurobiology, cell biology, physiology.

Oregon Health & Science University, School of Medicine, Graduate Programs in Medicine, Department of Behavioral Neuroscience, Portland, OR 97239-3098. Offers PhD. *Faculty:* 21 full-time (7 women), 25 part-time/adjunct (9 women). *Students:* 29 full-time (16 women); includes 10 minority (2 Black or African American, non-Hispanic/Latino; 2 Asian, non-Hispanic/Latino; 5 Hispanic/Latino; 1 Two or more races, non-Hispanic/Latino). Average age 29. 109 applicants, 14% accepted, 5 enrolled. In 2017, 2 doctorates awarded. Terminal master's awarded for partial completion of doctoral program. *Degree requirements:* For doctorate, comprehensive exam, thesis/dissertation, qualifying exam. *Entrance requirements:* For doctorate, GRE General Test (minimum scores: 153 Verbal/148 Quantitative/4.5 Analytical), undergraduate coursework in biopsychology and other basic science areas. *Application deadline:* For fall admission, 12/1 for domestic and international students. Application fee: $70. Electronic applications accepted. *Financial support:* Fellowships, research assistantships, health care benefits, tuition waivers (full), and stipends (for PhD students) available. Financial award application deadline: 3/1; financial award applicants required to submit FAFSA. *Faculty research:* Behavioral neuroscience, behavioral genomics, biological basis of drug and alcohol abuse, cognitive neuroscience, neuropharmacology and neuroendocrinology. *Unit head:* Dr. Bita Moghaddam, Program Director. *Application contact:* Kris Thomason, Graduate Program Manager, 503-494-8464, E-mail: somgrad@ohsu.edu.
Website: http://www.ohsu.edu/som-BehNeuro/

Oregon Health & Science University, School of Medicine, Graduate Programs in Medicine, Neuroscience Graduate Program, Portland, OR 97239-3098. Offers PhD. *Faculty:* 44 full-time (13 women), 105 part-time/adjunct (34 women). *Students:* 46 full-time (23 women); includes 4 minority (1 Black or African American, non-Hispanic/Latino; 1 Asian, non-Hispanic/Latino; 1 Hispanic/Latino; 1 Two or more races, non-Hispanic/Latino), 6 international. Average age 28. 162 applicants, 16% accepted, 9 enrolled. In 2017, 9 doctorates awarded. Terminal master's awarded for partial completion of doctoral program. *Degree requirements:* For doctorate, comprehensive exam, thesis/dissertation, qualifying exam. *Entrance requirements:* For doctorate, GRE General Test (minimum scores: 153 Verbal/148 Quantitative/4.5 Analytical) or MCAT (for some programs). *Application deadline:* For fall admission, 12/1 for domestic and international students. Application fee: $70. Electronic applications accepted. *Financial support:* Scholarships/grants, health care benefits, and full-tuition and stipends (for PhD students) available. Financial award application deadline: 3/1; financial award applicants required to submit FAFSA. *Faculty research:* Development, neurobiology of disease, molecular, systems, behavioral, cellular, biophysics of channels and transporters, gene regulation, neuronal signaling, synapses and circuits, sensory systems, neuroendocrinology, neurobiology of disease. *Unit head:* Dr. Gary Westbrook, Program Director, E-mail: ngp@ohsu.edu. *Application contact:* Liz Lawson-Weber, Program Coordinator, E-mail: ngp@ohsu.edu.
Website: http://www.ohsu.edu/ngp

Penn State Hershey Medical Center, College of Medicine, Graduate School Programs in the Biomedical Sciences, Huck Institutes of the Life Sciences, Intercollege Graduate Program in Neuroscience, Hershey, PA 17033. Offers MS, PhD, MD/PhD. Program also offered at University Park location. *Students:* 20 full-time (11 women); includes 1 minority (Black or African American, non-Hispanic/Latino), 3 international. 50 applicants, 10% accepted, 4 enrolled. Terminal master's awarded for partial completion of doctoral program. *Degree requirements:* For master's, thesis or alternative; for doctorate, comprehensive exam, thesis/dissertation, oral exam. *Entrance requirements:* For master's, GRE General Test; for doctorate, GRE General Test, minimum GPA of 3.0. Additional exam requirements/recommendations for international students: Required—TOEFL (minimum score 81 iBT). *Application deadline:* For fall admission, 1/1 for domestic and international students. Applications are processed on a rolling basis. Application fee: $65. Electronic applications accepted. *Financial support:* In 2017–18, research assistantships with full tuition reimbursements (averaging $27,802 per year) were awarded; fellowships with full tuition reimbursements, health care benefits, and unspecified assistantships also available. *Faculty research:* Behavioral neuroscience, growth factors and neuropeptides, molecular neurobiology and neurogenetics, neuronal aging and brain metabolism, neuronal and glial development. *Unit head:* Dr. Alistair Barber, Program Director, 717-531-6506, Fax: 717-531-0786, E-mail: ajb19@psu.edu. *Application contact:* Kristin E. Smith, Director of Graduate Admissions, 717-531-1045, Fax: 717-531-0786, E-mail: kec17@psu.edu.
Website: http://med.psu.edu

Princeton University, Graduate School, Department of Psychology, Princeton, NJ 08544-1019. Offers neuroscience (PhD); psychology (PhD). *Degree requirements:* For doctorate, thesis/dissertation. *Entrance requirements:* For doctorate, GRE General Test, GRE Subject Test. Additional exam requirements/recommendations for international students: Required—TOEFL (minimum score 550 paper-based). Electronic applications accepted.

Princeton University, Princeton Neuroscience Institute, Princeton, NJ 08544-1019. Offers PhD. Electronic applications accepted.

Purdue University, College of Pharmacy and Graduate School, Graduate Programs in Pharmacy and Pharmacal Sciences, Department of Medicinal Chemistry and Molecular Pharmacology, West Lafayette, IN 47907. Offers biophysical and computational chemistry (PhD); cancer research (PhD); immunology and infectious disease (PhD); medicinal biochemistry and molecular biology (PhD); medicinal chemistry and chemical biology (PhD); molecular pharmacology (PhD); neuropharmacology, neurodegeneration, and neurotoxicity (PhD); systems biology and functional genomics (PhD). *Faculty:* 26 full-time (5 women). *Students:* 52 full-time (22 women), 3 part-time (all women); includes 4 minority (1 Black or African American, non-Hispanic/Latino; 2 Asian, non-Hispanic/Latino; 1 Hispanic/Latino), 29 international. Average age 26. 151 applicants, 19% accepted, 13 enrolled. In 2017, 18 doctorates awarded. *Degree requirements:* For doctorate, thesis/dissertation. *Entrance requirements:* For doctorate, GRE General Test; GRE Subject Test in biology, biochemistry, and chemistry (recommended), minimum undergraduate GPA of 3.0. Additional exam requirements/recommendations for international students: Required—TOEFL (minimum score 550 paper-based; 77 iBT); Recommended—TWE. *Application deadline:* For fall admission, 2/1 for domestic and international students. Applications are processed on a rolling basis. Application fee: $60 ($75 for international students). Electronic applications accepted. *Financial support:* Fellowships, research assistantships, teaching assistantships, and traineeships available. Support available to part-time students. Financial award applicants required to submit FAFSA. *Faculty research:* Drug design and development, cancer research, drug synthesis and analysis, chemical pharmacology, environmental toxicology. *Unit head:* Zhong-Yin Zhang, Head, 765-494-1403, E-mail: zhang-yn@purdue.edu. *Application contact:* Delayne Graham, Graduate Contact, 765-494-1362, E-mail: dkgraham@purdue.edu.

Purdue University, Graduate School, College of Health and Human Sciences, Department of Psychological Sciences, West Lafayette, IN 47907. Offers behavioral neuroscience (PhD); clinical psychology (PhD); cognitive psychology (PhD); industrial/organizational psychology (PhD); mathematical and computational cognitive science (PhD). *Accreditation:* APA. *Faculty:* 46 full-time (18 women), 1 part-time/adjunct (0 women). *Students:* 64 full-time (41 women), 4 part-time (3 women); includes 13 minority (1 Black or African American, non-Hispanic/Latino; 4 Asian, non-Hispanic/Latino; 6 Hispanic/Latino; 2 Two or more races, non-Hispanic/Latino), 12 international. Average age 27. 288 applicants, 8% accepted, 16 enrolled. In 2017, 9 doctorates awarded. Terminal master's awarded for partial completion of doctoral program. *Degree requirements:* For doctorate, thesis/dissertation. *Entrance requirements:* For doctorate, GRE General Test, minimum undergraduate GPA of 3.0 or equivalent. Additional exam requirements/recommendations for international students: Required—TOEFL (minimum score 550 paper-based; 77 iBT); Recommended—TWE. *Application deadline:* For fall admission, 12/3 for domestic and international students. Applications are processed on a rolling basis. Application fee: $60 ($75 for international students). Electronic applications accepted. *Financial support:* Fellowships with partial tuition reimbursements, research assistantships with partial tuition reimbursements, teaching assistantships with partial tuition reimbursements, and career-related internships or fieldwork available. Support available to part-time students. Financial award applicants required to submit FAFSA. *Faculty research:* Career development of women in science, development of friendships during childhood and adolescence, social competence, human information processing. *Unit head:* Dr. David Rollock, Head, 765-494-6061, E-mail: rollock@purdue.edu. *Application contact:* Nancy A. O'Brien, Graduate Contact, 765-494-6067, E-mail: nobrien@psych.pardue.edu.
Website: http://www.psych.purdue.edu/

Purdue University, Graduate School, PULSe - Purdue University Life Sciences Program, West Lafayette, IN 47907. Offers biomolecular structure and biophysics (PhD); biotechnology (PhD); chemical biology (PhD); chromatin and regulation of gene expression (PhD); integrative neuroscience (PhD); integrative plant sciences (PhD); membrane biology (PhD); microbiology (PhD); molecular evolutionary and cancer biology (PhD); molecular evolutionary genetics (PhD); molecular virology (PhD). *Students:* 60 full-time (29 women); includes 6 minority (4 Hispanic/Latino; 2 Two or more races, non-Hispanic/Latino), 36 international. Average age 25. 127 applicants, 39% accepted, 25 enrolled. *Entrance requirements:* For doctorate, GRE, minimum undergraduate GPA of 3.0. Additional exam requirements/recommendations for international students: Required—TOEFL (minimum score 550 paper-based; 77 iBT). *Application deadline:* For fall admission, 1/15 priority date for domestic and international students. Applications are processed on a rolling basis. Application fee: $60 ($75 for international students). Electronic applications accepted. *Financial support:* In 2017–18, research assistantships with tuition reimbursements (averaging $22,500 per year), teaching assistantships with tuition reimbursements (averaging $22,500 per year) were awarded. *Unit head:* Dr. Jason R. Cannon, Head of the Graduate Program, 765-494-0794, E-mail: cannonjr@purdue.edu. *Application contact:* Lindsey Springer, Graduate Contact for Admissions, 765-496-9667, E-mail: lbcampbe@purdue.edu.
Website: http://www.gradschool.purdue.edu/pulse

Queens College of the City University of New York, Mathematics and Natural Sciences Division, Department of Psychology, Queens, NY 11367-1597. Offers applied behavior analysis (MA); behavioral neuroscience (MA); general psychology (MA). *Program availability:* Part-time. *Students:* 2 full-time (1 woman), 99 part-time (78 women); includes 55 minority (10 Black or African American, non-Hispanic/Latino; 1 American Indian or Alaska Native, non-Hispanic/Latino; 11 Asian, non-Hispanic/Latino; 31 Hispanic/Latino; 2 Two or more races, non-Hispanic/Latino), 3 international. Average age 27. *Degree requirements:* For master's, comprehensive exam (for some programs), thesis. *Entrance requirements:* For master's, minimum GPA of 3.0. Additional exam requirements/recommendations for international students: Required—TOEFL, IELTS. *Application deadline:* For fall admission, 4/1 for domestic students; for spring admission, 11/1 for domestic students. Applications are processed on a rolling basis. Application fee: $125. Electronic applications accepted. *Financial support:* Career-related internships or fieldwork, institutionally sponsored loans, and unspecified assistantships available. Financial award application deadline: 4/1; financial award applicants required to submit FAFSA. *Unit head:* Robert Lanson, Chair, 718-997-3200, E-mail: robert.lanson@qc.cuny.edu. *Application contact:* Elizabeth D'Amico-Ramirez, Assistant Director of Graduate Admissions, 718-997-5203, E-mail: elizabeth.damicoramirez@qc.cuny.edu.
Website: http://psychology.qc.cuny.edu/

Queen's University at Kingston, School of Graduate Studies, Faculty of Health Sciences, Department of Anatomy and Cell Biology, Kingston, ON K7L 3N6, Canada. Offers biology of reproduction (M Sc, PhD); cancer (M Sc, PhD); cardiovascular pathophysiology (M Sc, PhD); cell and molecular biology (M Sc, PhD); drug metabolism (M Sc, PhD); endocrinology (M Sc, PhD); motor control (M Sc, PhD); neural regeneration (M Sc, PhD); neurophysiology (M Sc, PhD). *Program availability:* Part-time. *Degree requirements:* For master's, thesis; for doctorate, one foreign language, comprehensive exam, thesis/dissertation. *Entrance requirements:* Additional exam requirements/recommendations for international students: Required—TOEFL. Electronic applications accepted. *Faculty research:* Human kinetics, neuroscience, reproductive biology, cardiovascular.

Rosalind Franklin University of Medicine and Science, School of Graduate and Postdoctoral Studies - Interdisciplinary Graduate Program in Biomedical Sciences, Department of Neuroscience, North Chicago, IL 60064-3095. Offers PhD, MD/PhD. *Degree requirements:* For doctorate, comprehensive exam, thesis/dissertation, original research project. *Entrance requirements:* For doctorate, GRE General Test. Additional exam requirements/recommendations for international students: Required—TOEFL, TWE.

Rush University, Graduate College, Division of Neuroscience, Chicago, IL 60612-3832. Offers MS, PhD. Terminal master's awarded for partial completion of doctoral program. *Degree requirements:* For master's, thesis; for doctorate, thesis/dissertation. *Entrance requirements:* For master's and doctorate, GRE General Test. Additional exam requirements/recommendations for international students: Required—TOEFL. Electronic applications accepted. *Faculty research:* Neurodegenerative disorders, neurobiology of memory, aging, pathology and genetics of Alzheimer's disease.

Rutgers University–Newark, Graduate School of Biomedical Sciences, Program in Integrative Neuroscience, Newark, NJ 07107. Offers PhD. Program offered jointly with Rutgers, The State University of New Jersey, New Brunswick. *Degree requirements:* For doctorate, thesis/dissertation, qualifying exam. *Entrance requirements:* For doctorate, GRE General Test, minimum GPA of 3.5. Additional exam requirements/recommendations for international students: Required—TOEFL. Electronic applications accepted.

Rutgers University–Newark, Graduate School, Program in Psychology, Newark, NJ 07102. Offers cognitive neuroscience (PhD); cognitive science (PhD); perception (PhD); psychobiology (PhD); social cognition (PhD). *Degree requirements:* For doctorate, comprehensive exam, thesis/dissertation. *Entrance requirements:* For doctorate, GRE General Test, GRE Subject Test, minimum undergraduate B average. Electronic applications accepted. *Faculty research:* Visual perception (luminance, motion), neuroendocrine mechanisms in behavior (reproduction, pain), attachment theory, connectionist modeling of cognition.

Rutgers University–New Brunswick, Graduate School-New Brunswick, Program in Endocrinology and Animal Biosciences, Piscataway, NJ 08854-8097. Offers MS, PhD. Terminal master's awarded for partial completion of doctoral program. *Degree requirements:* For master's, thesis; for doctorate, comprehensive exam, thesis/dissertation. *Entrance requirements:* For master's and doctorate, GRE General Test. Additional exam requirements/recommendations for international students: Required—TOEFL. Electronic applications accepted. *Faculty research:* Comparative and behavioral endocrinology, epigenetic regulation of the endocrine system, exercise physiology and immunology, fetal and neonatal developmental programming, mammary gland biology and breast cancer, neuroendocrinology and alcohol studies, reproductive and developmental toxicology.

Rutgers University–New Brunswick, Graduate School of Biomedical Sciences, Program in Neuroscience, Piscataway, NJ 08854-5635. Offers MS, PhD, MD/PhD. *Degree requirements:* For master's, thesis, qualifying exam; for doctorate, thesis/dissertation, qualifying exam. *Entrance requirements:* Additional exam requirements/recommendations for international students: Required—TOEFL. Electronic applications accepted.

Seton Hall University, College of Arts and Sciences, Department of Biological Sciences, South Orange, NJ 07079-2697. Offers biology (MS); biology/business administration (MS); microbiology (MS); molecular bioscience (PhD); molecular bioscience/neuroscience (PhD). *Program availability:* Part-time, evening/weekend. *Degree requirements:* For master's, thesis optional; for doctorate, comprehensive exam, thesis/dissertation. *Entrance requirements:* For master's, GRE or undergraduate degree (BS in biological sciences) with minimum GPA of 3.0 from accredited U.S. institution; for doctorate, GRE. Additional exam requirements/recommendations for international students: Required—TOEFL. Electronic applications accepted. *Faculty research:* Neurobiology, genetics, immunology, molecular biology, cellular physiology, toxicology, microbiology, bioinformatics.

State University of New York Downstate Medical Center, School of Graduate Studies, Program in Neural and Behavioral Science, Brooklyn, NY 11203-2098. Offers PhD, MD/PhD. *Degree requirements:* For doctorate, comprehensive exam, thesis/dissertation. *Entrance requirements:* For doctorate, GRE. Additional exam requirements/recommendations for international students: Recommended—TOEFL. *Faculty research:* Molecular neuroscience, cellular neuroscience, systems neuroscience, behavioral neuroscience, behavior.

State University of New York Upstate Medical University, College of Graduate Studies, Program in Neuroscience, Syracuse, NY 13210. Offers PhD. *Degree requirements:* For doctorate, comprehensive exam, thesis/dissertation. *Entrance requirements:* For doctorate, GRE General Test, telephone interview. Additional exam requirements/recommendations for international students: Required—TOEFL. Electronic applications accepted. *Faculty research:* Cancer, disorders of the nervous system, infectious diseases, diabetes/metabolic disorders/cardiovascular diseases.

Stony Brook University, State University of New York, Graduate School, College of Arts and Sciences, Department of Neurobiology and Behavior, Stony Brook, NY 11794. Offers neuroscience (MS, PhD). *Faculty:* 16 full-time (3 women), 1 part-time/adjunct (0 women). *Students:* 34 full-time (15 women); includes 12 minority (2 Black or African American, non-Hispanic/Latino; 5 Asian, non-Hispanic/Latino; 3 Hispanic/Latino; 2 Two or more races, non-Hispanic/Latino), 7 international. Average age 27. 63 applicants, 30% accepted, 8 enrolled. In 2017, 7 doctorates awarded. *Degree requirements:* For doctorate, comprehensive exam, thesis/dissertation, teaching experience. *Entrance requirements:* For doctorate, GRE General Test, GRE Subject Test, minimum GPA of 3.0. Additional exam requirements/recommendations for international students: Required—TOEFL (minimum score 90 iBT). *Application deadline:* For fall admission, 1/15 for domestic students; for spring admission, 10/1 for domestic students. Application fee: $100. Electronic applications accepted. *Expenses:* Contact institution. *Financial support:* In 2017–18, 8 fellowships, 10 research assistantships, 5 teaching assistantships were awarded; Federal Work-Study also available. *Faculty research:* Cerebral cortex, neurobiology, neurodegenerative diseases, brain, brain disorders, ion channels, synaptic transmission, neocortex, cell signaling, cerebral cortex. *Total annual research expenditures:* $3.9 million. *Unit head:* Dr. Lorna Role, Chair, 631-632-8616, Fax: 631-632-6661, E-mail: lorna.role@stonybrook.edu. *Application contact:* Odalis Hernandez, Coordinator, 631-632-8078, Fax: 631-632-6661, E-mail: odalis.hernandez@stonybrook.edu.
Website: http://medicine.stonybrookmedicine.edu/neurobiology/

Stony Brook University, State University of New York, Graduate School, College of Arts and Sciences, Department of Psychology, Program in Integrative Neuroscience, Stony Brook, NY 11794. Offers PhD. *Students:* 15 full-time (11 women); includes 2 minority (1 Black or African American, non-Hispanic/Latino; 1 Asian, non-Hispanic/Latino), 2 international. Average age 28. 27 applicants, 26% accepted, 4 enrolled. In 2017, 2 doctorates awarded. *Degree requirements:* For doctorate, thesis/dissertation. *Entrance requirements:* For doctorate, GRE General Test, GRE Subject Test. Additional exam requirements/recommendations for international students: Required—TOEFL (minimum score 90 iBT). *Application deadline:* For fall admission, 1/15 for domestic students; for spring admission, 10/1 for domestic students. Application fee: $100. Electronic applications accepted. *Expenses:* Contact institution. *Financial support:* In 2017–18, 2 fellowships, 1 research assistantship, 9 teaching assistantships were awarded. *Unit head:* Dr. Sheri Levy, Chair, 631-632-4355, E-mail: sheri.levy@stonybrook.edu. *Application contact:* Marilynn Wollmuth, Coordinator, 631-632-7855, Fax: 631-632-7876, E-mail: marilyn.wollmuth@stonybrook.edu.
Website: http://www.stonybrook.edu/commcms/psychology/integrative_neuroscience/overview.html

Syracuse University, College of Arts and Sciences, Department of Biology, Syracuse, NY 13244. Offers biology (MS, PhD); neuroscience (PhD). Terminal master's awarded for partial completion of doctoral program. *Degree requirements:* For master's, thesis; for doctorate, thesis/dissertation. *Entrance requirements:* For master's and doctorate, GRE General Test, GRE Subject Test (recommended), BS or BA, at least a minimal background in both physical and biological sciences, three letters of recommendation, personal statement, transcripts. Additional exam requirements/recommendations for international students: Required—TOEFL (minimum score 100 iBT). *Application*

deadline: For fall admission, 12/15 priority date for domestic and international students. Application fee: $75. Electronic applications accepted. *Financial support:* Fellowships with full tuition reimbursements, research assistantships with tuition reimbursements, teaching assistantships with tuition reimbursements, and scholarships/grants available. Financial award application deadline: 12/15; financial award applicants required to submit FAFSA. *Faculty research:* Cell signaling, plant ecosystem ecology, aquatic ecology, genetics and molecular biology of color vision, ion transport by cell membranes. *Unit head:* Dr. Ramesh Raina, Professor, Biology/Department Chair, 315-443-4546, E-mail: raraina@syr.edu. *Application contact:* Lynn Fall, Graduate Program Administrator, 315-443-9154, E-mail: biology@syr.edu.
Website: http://biology.syr.edu/

Teachers College, Columbia University, Department of Biobehavioral Sciences, New York, NY 10027-6696. Offers applied exercise physiology (Ed M, MA, Ed D); communication sciences and disorders (MS, Ed D, PhD); kinesiology (PhD); motor learning and control (Ed M, MA); motor learning/movement science (Ed D); neuroscience and education (MS); physical education (MA, Ed D). *Accreditation:* ASHA. *Program availability:* Part-time, evening/weekend. *Students:* 180 full-time (160 women), 176 part-time (141 women); includes 149 minority (17 Black or African American, non-Hispanic/Latino; 40 Asian, non-Hispanic/Latino; 83 Hispanic/Latino; 9 Two or more races, non-Hispanic/Latino), 30 international. Average age 29. 738 applicants, 41% accepted, 164 enrolled. *Financial support:* Fellowships, teaching assistantships, career-related internships or fieldwork, Federal Work-Study, institutionally sponsored loans, traineeships, and tuition waivers (full and partial) available. Support available to part-time students. *Unit head:* Prof. Carol Garber, Chair, 212-678-3891, E-mail: garber@tc.columbia.edu. *Application contact:* David Estrella, Director of Admissions, 212-678-3305, E-mail: estrella@tc.columbia.edu.
Website: http://www.tc.columbia.edu/biobehavioral-sciences/

Texas Christian University, College of Science and Engineering, Department of Psychology, Fort Worth, TX 76129. Offers developmental trauma (MS); experimental psychology (PhD), including cognition/developmental, learning, neuroscience, social. *Faculty:* 13 full-time (6 women), 2 part-time/adjunct (both women). *Students:* 32 full-time (25 women); includes 5 minority (1 Asian, non-Hispanic/Latino; 2 Hispanic/Latino; 2 Two or more races, non-Hispanic/Latino), 2 international. Average age 26. 50 applicants, 34% accepted, 16 enrolled. In 2017, 8 master's, 2 doctorates awarded. Terminal master's awarded for partial completion of doctoral program. *Degree requirements:* For master's, thesis; for doctorate, thesis/dissertation. *Entrance requirements:* For doctorate, GRE General Test. Additional exam requirements/recommendations for international students: Required—TOEFL. *Application deadline:* For fall admission, 2/1 for domestic and international students. Application fee: $60 ($0 for international students). Electronic applications accepted. *Expenses:* Contact institution. *Financial support:* In 2017–18, 23 students received support, including 23 teaching assistantships with full tuition reimbursements available (averaging $19,750 per year); scholarships/grants also available. Financial award application deadline: 2/1; financial award applicants required to submit FAFSA. *Faculty research:* Neuroscience, human and animal learning, cognition, development, experimental social psychology. *Unit head:* Dr. Mauricio R. Papini, Chair, 817-257-7410, Fax: 817-257-7681, E-mail: m.papini@tcu.edu. *Application contact:* Cindy Hayes, Administrative Assistant, 817-257-7410, Fax: 817-257-7681, E-mail: c.hayes@tcu.edu.
Website: https://psychology.tcu.edu/current-graduate-students/

Thomas Jefferson University, Jefferson College of Biomedical Sciences, PhD Program in Neuroscience, Philadelphia, PA 19107. Offers PhD. Offered jointly with the Farber Institute for Neuroscience. *Faculty:* 31 full-time (10 women). *Students:* 13 full-time (4 women); includes 2 minority (1 Black or African American, non-Hispanic/Latino; 1 Asian, non-Hispanic/Latino), 2 international. In 2017, 1 doctorate awarded. *Degree requirements:* For doctorate, comprehensive exam, thesis/dissertation. *Entrance requirements:* For doctorate, GRE General Test, strong background in the sciences, interview, previous research experience. Additional exam requirements/recommendations for international students: Required—TOEFL, IELTS (minimum score 7). *Application deadline:* For fall admission, 12/1 priority date for domestic and international students. Applications are processed on a rolling basis. Application fee: $60. Electronic applications accepted. *Financial support:* In 2017–18, 13 students received support, including 13 fellowships with full tuition reimbursements available (averaging $62,653 per year); Federal Work-Study, institutionally sponsored loans, scholarships/grants, traineeships, health care benefits, and stipends also available. Financial award application deadline: 5/1; financial award applicants required to submit FAFSA. *Unit head:* Dr. Kyunghee Koh, Program Director, 215-955-5905, E-mail: kyunghee.koh@jefferson.edu. *Application contact:* Marc E. Stearns, Senior Associate Director of Admissions, 215-503-4400, Fax: 215-503-3433, E-mail: jgsbs-info@jefferson.edu.
Website: http://www.jefferson.edu/university/biomedical-sciences/degrees-programs/phd-programs/neuroscience.html

Tufts University, Cummings School of Veterinary Medicine, North Grafton, MA 01536. Offers animals and public policy (MS); biomedical sciences (PhD), including digestive diseases, infectious diseases, neuroscience and reproductive biology, pathology; conservation medicine (MS); veterinary medicine (DVM); DVM/MPH; DVM/MS. *Accreditation:* AVMA (one or more programs are accredited). *Degree requirements:* For master's, thesis (for some programs); for doctorate, comprehensive exam, thesis/dissertation (for some programs). *Entrance requirements:* For master's and doctorate, GRE General Test. Additional exam requirements/recommendations for international students: Required—TOEFL or IELTS. Electronic applications accepted. *Expenses:* Contact institution. *Faculty research:* Oncology, veterinary ethics, international veterinary medicine, veterinary genomics, pathogenesis of Clostridium difficile, wildlife fertility control.

Tufts University, Sackler School of Graduate Biomedical Sciences, Neuroscience Program, Medford, MA 02155. Offers PhD. Terminal master's awarded for partial completion of doctoral program. *Degree requirements:* For doctorate, comprehensive exam, thesis/dissertation. *Entrance requirements:* For doctorate, GRE General Test, 3 letters of reference, personal statement, resume. Electronic applications accepted. *Expenses: Tuition:* Full-time $49,892. *Required fees:* $874. Full-time tuition and fees vary according to degree level, program and student level. Part-time tuition and fees vary according to course load. *Faculty research:* Molecular, cellular, and systems analyses of synapses and circuits and their implications for neurological disease.

Tulane University, School of Medicine and School of Liberal Arts, Graduate Programs in Biomedical Sciences, Program in Neuroscience, New Orleans, LA 70118-5669. Offers MS, PhD, MD/PhD. MS and PhD offered through the Graduate School. *Degree requirements:* For doctorate, thesis/dissertation, qualifying exam. *Entrance requirements:* For doctorate, GRE General Test. Additional exam requirements/recommendations for international students: Required—TOEFL. Electronic applications accepted. *Expenses: Tuition:* Full-time $50,920; part-time $2829 per credit hour. *Required fees:* $2040; $44.50 per credit hour. $580 per term. Tuition and fees vary according to course load, degree level and program. *Faculty research:* Neuroendocrinology, ion channels, neuropeptides.

Tulane University, School of Science and Engineering, Neuroscience Program, New Orleans, LA 70118-5669. Offers MS, PhD. *Expenses: Tuition:* Full-time $50,920; part-time $2829 per credit hour. *Required fees:* $2040; $44.50 per credit hour. $580 per term. Tuition and fees vary according to course load, degree level and program.

Uniformed Services University of the Health Sciences, F. Edward Hebert School of Medicine, Graduate Programs in the Biomedical Sciences and Public Health, Graduate Program in Neuroscience, Bethesda, MD 20814-4799. Offers PhD. *Degree requirements:* For doctorate, comprehensive exam, thesis/dissertation, qualifying exams. *Entrance requirements:* For doctorate, GRE General Test, minimum GPA of 3.0; course work in biology, general chemistry, organic chemistry. Electronic applications accepted. *Faculty research:* Neuronal development and plasticity, molecular neurobiology, environmental adaptations, stress and injury.

See Display on the next page and Close-Up on page 329.

Universidad de Iberoamerica, Graduate School, San Jose, Costa Rica. Offers clinical neuropsychology (PhD); clinical psychology (M Psych); educational psychology (M Psych); forensic psychology (M Psych); hospital management (MHA); intensive care nursing (MN); medicine (MD).

Université de Montréal, Faculty of Medicine, Department of Physiology, Program in Neurological Sciences, Montréal, QC H3C 3J7, Canada. Offers M Sc, PhD. Terminal master's awarded for partial completion of doctoral program. *Degree requirements:* For master's, thesis; for doctorate, thesis/dissertation, general exam. *Entrance requirements:* For master's and doctorate, proficiency in French, knowledge of English. Electronic applications accepted.

University at Albany, State University of New York, College of Arts and Sciences, Department of Psychology, Albany, NY 12222-0001. Offers behavioral neuroscience (PhD); clinical psychology (PhD); cognitive psychology (PhD); industrial/organizational psychology (MA, PhD); social-personality psychology (PhD). *Accreditation:* APA (one or more programs are accredited). *Faculty:* 31 full-time (13 women). *Students:* 63 full-time (42 women), 49 part-time (33 women); includes 25 minority (4 Black or African American, non-Hispanic/Latino; 8 Asian, non-Hispanic/Latino; 4 Hispanic/Latino; 9 Two or more races, non-Hispanic/Latino), 11 international. 295 applicants, 14% accepted, 28 enrolled. In 2017, 13 master's, 5 doctorates awarded. *Degree requirements:* For doctorate, thesis/dissertation. *Entrance requirements:* For doctorate, GRE General Test, GRE Subject Test. Additional exam requirements/recommendations for international students: Required—TOEFL (minimum score 550 paper-based). *Application deadline:* For fall admission, 1/15 for domestic and international students. Application fee: $75. Electronic applications accepted. *Expenses:* Tuition, state resident: full-time $10,870; part-time $453 per credit hour. Tuition, nonresident: full-time $22,210; part-time $925 per credit hour. *Required fees:* $84.68 per credit hour. $508.06 per semester. Part-time tuition and fees vary according to course load and program. *Financial support:* Fellowships, research assistantships, teaching assistantships, and career-related internships or fieldwork available. Financial award application deadline: 2/1. *Unit head:* Christine K. Wagner, Chair, 518-442-4820, Fax: 518-442-4867, E-mail: cwagner@albany.edu. *Application contact:* Michael DeRensis, Director, Graduate Admissions, 518-442-3980, Fax: 518-442-3922, E-mail: graduate@albany.edu.
Website: http://www.albany.edu/psychology/

University at Buffalo, the State University of New York, Graduate School, Jacobs School of Medicine and Biomedical Sciences, Graduate Programs in Medicine and Biomedical Sciences, Neuroscience Program, Buffalo, NY 14260. Offers MS, PhD. *Faculty:* 88 full-time (24 women), 1 part-time/adjunct (0 women). *Students:* 37 full-time (19 women); includes 16 minority (2 Black or African American, non-Hispanic/Latino; 12 Asian, non-Hispanic/Latino; 2 Hispanic/Latino). Average age 25. 57 applicants, 39% accepted, 14 enrolled. In 2017, 8 master's, 6 doctorates awarded. Terminal master's awarded for partial completion of doctoral program. *Degree requirements:* For master's, thesis or project; for doctorate, comprehensive exam, thesis/dissertation. *Entrance requirements:* For master's, GRE General Test, 3 letters of recommendation, transcripts; for doctorate, GRE General Test or MCAT. Additional exam requirements/recommendations for international students: Required—TOEFL (minimum score 550 paper-based; 80 iBT). *Application deadline:* For fall admission, 7/15 priority date for domestic and international students. Applications are processed on a rolling basis. Application fee: $85. Electronic applications accepted. *Expenses:* Contact institution. *Financial support:* In 2017–18, 17 students received support, including 17 research assistantships with full tuition reimbursements available (averaging $27,000 per year); health care benefits also available. Financial award application deadline: 9/1. *Faculty research:* Neural degeneration and regeneration, synapse formation and elimination, glial cell biology, sensory systems, ion channels and receptors. *Total annual research expenditures:* $6 million. *Unit head:* Dr. Malcolm Slaughter, Professor, 716-829-3240, E-mail: mslaught@buffalo.edu. *Application contact:* Kara M. Rickicki, Graduate Programs Coordinator, 716-829-2417, E-mail: kkms@buffalo.edu.
Website: http://wings.buffalo.edu/neuroscience/

The University of Alabama at Birmingham, College of Arts and Sciences, Program in Psychology, Birmingham, AL 35294. Offers behavioral neuroscience (PhD); lifespan developmental psychology (PhD); medical/clinical psychology (PhD); psychology (MA). *Accreditation:* APA (one or more programs are accredited). *Entrance requirements:* For master's and doctorate, GRE General Test, letters of recommendation. Electronic applications accepted. *Faculty research:* Biological basis of behavior structure, function of the nervous system.

The University of Alabama at Birmingham, Joint Health Sciences, Neuroscience Theme, Birmingham, AL 35294. Offers PhD. *Faculty:* 370. *Students:* 37 full-time (26 women); includes 14 minority (4 Black or African American, non-Hispanic/Latino; 6 Asian, non-Hispanic/Latino; 2 Hispanic/Latino; 2 Two or more races, non-Hispanic/Latino). Average age 26. 56 applicants, 20% accepted, 5 enrolled. In 2017, 2 doctorates awarded. *Degree requirements:* For doctorate, comprehensive exam, thesis/dissertation. *Entrance requirements:* For doctorate, personal statement, resume or curriculum vitae, letters of recommendation, research experience, interview. Additional exam requirements/recommendations for international students: Required—TOEFL (minimum score 53 iBT), IELTS (minimum score 6.5). *Application deadline:* For fall admission, 12/31 for domestic and international students. Applications are processed on a rolling basis. Electronic applications accepted. *Financial support:* In 2017–18, fellowships with full tuition reimbursements (averaging $29,000 per year), research assistantships with full tuition reimbursements (averaging $30,000 per year) were awarded; health care benefits also available. *Unit head:* Dr. Karen Gamble, Theme Director, 205-934-4663, E-mail: klgamble@uab.edu. *Application contact:* Alyssa Zasada, Admissions Manager for Graduate Biomedical Sciences, 205-934-3857, E-mail: grad-gbs@uab.edu.
Website: http://www.uab.edu/gbs/home/themes/nesc

University of Alaska Fairbanks, College of Natural Sciences and Mathematics, Department of Chemistry and Biochemistry, Fairbanks, AK 99775-6160. Offers biochemistry and neuroscience (PhD); chemistry (MA, MS), including chemistry (MS); environmental chemistry (PhD). *Program availability:* Part-time. *Degree requirements:* For master's, comprehensive exam, thesis (for some programs), oral defense of project or thesis; for doctorate, comprehensive exam, thesis/dissertation, oral defense of dissertation. *Entrance requirements:* For master's, GRE General Test (for MS), bachelor's degree from accredited institution with minimum cumulative undergraduate and major GPA of 3.0; for doctorate, GRE General Test, minimum cumulative GPA of 3.0. Additional exam requirements/recommendations for international students: Required—TOEFL (minimum score 550 paper-based; 79 iBT), TWE. Electronic applications accepted. *Faculty research:* Atmospheric aerosols, cold adaptation, hibernation and neuroprotection, liganogated ion channels, arctic contaminants.

University of Alberta, Faculty of Medicine and Dentistry and Faculty of Graduate Studies and Research, Graduate Programs in Medicine, Centre for Neuroscience, Edmonton, AB T6G 2E1, Canada. Offers M Sc, PhD. Terminal master's awarded for partial completion of doctoral program. *Degree requirements:* For master's, thesis; for doctorate, thesis/dissertation. *Entrance requirements:* For master's and doctorate, minimum GPA of 3.3. Additional exam requirements/recommendations for international students: Required—TOEFL (minimum score 600 paper-based). Electronic applications accepted. *Faculty research:* Sensory and motor mechanisms, neural growth and regeneration, molecular neurobiology, synaptic mechanisms, behavioral and psychiatric neuroscience.

The University of Arizona, Graduate Interdisciplinary Programs, Graduate Interdisciplinary Program in Neuroscience, Tucson, AZ 85719. Offers PhD. *Degree requirements:* For doctorate, thesis/dissertation. *Entrance requirements:* For doctorate, GRE (minimum score 1100), minimum GPA of 3.5, 3 letters of recommendation. Additional exam requirements/recommendations for international students: Required—TOEFL (minimum score 550 paper-based; 79 iBT). Electronic applications accepted. *Faculty research:* Cognitive neuroscience, developmental neurobiology, speech and hearing, motor control, insect neurobiology.

The University of British Columbia, Faculty of Arts and Faculty of Graduate Studies, Department of Psychology, Vancouver, BC V6T 1Z4, Canada. Offers behavioral neuroscience (MA, PhD); clinical psychology (MA, PhD); cognitive science (MA, PhD); developmental psychology (MA, PhD); health psychology (MA, PhD); quantitative methods (MA, PhD); social/personality psychology (MA, PhD). *Accreditation:* APA (one or more programs are accredited). Terminal master's awarded for partial completion of doctoral program. *Degree requirements:* For master's, thesis; for doctorate, comprehensive exam, thesis/dissertation. *Entrance requirements:* For master's and doctorate, GRE General Test. Additional exam requirements/recommendations for international students: Required—TOEFL. Electronic applications accepted. *Expenses:* Contact institution. *Faculty research:* Clinical, developmental, social/personality, cognition, behavioral neuroscience.

The University of British Columbia, Faculty of Medicine, Department of Cellular and Physiological Sciences, Vancouver, BC V6T 1Z3, Canada. Offers bioinformatics (M Sc, PhD); cell and developmental biology (M Sc, PhD); genome science and technology (M Sc, PhD); neuroscience (M Sc, PhD). *Degree requirements:* For master's, thesis, oral defense; for doctorate, comprehensive exam, thesis/dissertation, oral defense. *Entrance requirements:* For master's, minimum overall B+ average in third- and fourth-year courses; for doctorate, minimum overall B+ average in master's degree (or equivalent) from approved institution with clear evidence of research ability or potential. Additional exam requirements/recommendations for international students: Required—TOEFL, IELTS. *Expenses:* Contact institution.

University of Calgary, Cumming School of Medicine and Faculty of Graduate Studies, Department of Neuroscience, Calgary, AB T2N 1N4, Canada. Offers M Sc, PhD. *Degree requirements:* For master's, thesis, oral thesis exam; for doctorate, thesis/dissertation, candidacy exam, oral thesis exam. *Entrance requirements:* For master's and doctorate, minimum GPA of 3.2 during previous 2 years. Additional exam requirements/recommendations for international students: Required—TOEFL (minimum score 580 paper-based). Electronic applications accepted. *Faculty research:* Cellular pharmacology and neurotoxicology, developmental neurobiology, molecular basis of neurodegenerative diseases, neural systems, ion channels.

University of California, Berkeley, Graduate Division, Neuroscience Graduate Program, Berkeley, CA 94720-3200. Offers PhD. *Degree requirements:* For doctorate, qualifying exam, teaching requirement, research thesis/dissertation. *Entrance requirements:* For doctorate, GRE General Test, minimum GPA of 3.0, 3 letters of recommendation, at least one year of laboratory experience. Additional exam requirements/recommendations for international students: Required—TOEFL or IELTS. Electronic applications accepted. *Faculty research:* Analysis of ion channels, signal transduction mechanisms, and gene regulation; development of neurons, synapses, and circuits; synapse function and plasticity; mechanisms of sensory processing; principles of function of cerebral cortex; neural basis for learning, attention, and sleep; neural basis for human emotion, language, motor control, and other high-level cognitive processes.

University of California, Davis, Graduate Studies, Graduate Group in Neuroscience, Davis, CA 95616. Offers PhD. *Degree requirements:* For doctorate, thesis/dissertation. *Entrance requirements:* For doctorate, GRE General Test, GRE Subject Test. Additional exam requirements/recommendations for international students: Required—TOEFL (minimum score 550 paper-based). Electronic applications accepted. *Faculty research:* Neuroethology, cognitive neurosciences, cortical neurophysics, cellular and molecular neurobiology.

University of California, Irvine, Francisco J. Ayala School of Biological Sciences, Interdepartmental Neuroscience Program, Irvine, CA 92697. Offers PhD. *Students:* 13 full-time (9 women); includes 7 minority (1 Black or African American, non-Hispanic/Latino; 3 Asian, non-Hispanic/Latino; 2 Hispanic/Latino; 1 Two or more races, non-Hispanic/Latino), 1 international. Average age 25. 216 applicants, 15% accepted, 12 enrolled. *Application deadline:* For fall admission, 12/2 for domestic students. Application fee: $105 ($125 for international students). Electronic applications accepted. *Unit head:* Prof. Karina S. Cramer, Director, 949-824-4211, Fax: 949-824-2447, E-mail: cramerk@uci.edu. *Application contact:* Gary R. Roman, Program Administrator, 949-824-6226, Fax: 949-824-4150, E-mail: gary.roman@uci.edu.
Website: http://www.inp.uci.edu/

University of California, Los Angeles, David Geffen School of Medicine and Graduate Division, Graduate Programs in Medicine, Interdepartmental Program in Neuroscience, Los Angeles, CA 90095. Offers PhD. *Degree requirements:* For doctorate, thesis/dissertation, oral and written qualifying exams; 1 quarter of teaching experience. *Entrance requirements:* For doctorate, GRE General Test or MCAT, bachelor's degree; minimum undergraduate GPA of 3.0 (or its equivalent if letter grade system not used). Additional exam requirements/recommendations for international students: Required—TOEFL. Electronic applications accepted.

University of California, Riverside, Graduate Division, Program in Neuroscience, Riverside, CA 92521. Offers PhD. *Degree requirements:* For doctorate, comprehensive exam, thesis/dissertation, 2 quarters of teaching experience, qualifying exams. *Entrance requirements:* For doctorate, GRE General Test, minimum GPA of 3.25. Additional exam requirements/recommendations for international students: Required—TOEFL (minimum score 550 paper-based; 80 iBT); Recommended—IELTS. *Application deadline:* For fall admission, 1/5 priority date for domestic and international students. Application fee: $80 ($100 for international students). Electronic applications accepted. *Expenses:* Tuition, state resident: full-time $5746. Tuition, nonresident: full-time $10,780. Tuition and fees vary according to campus/location and program. *Financial support:* Fellowships with full tuition reimbursements, research assistantships with full tuition reimbursements, teaching assistantships with full tuition reimbursements, institutionally sponsored loans, scholarships/grants, health care benefits, and tuition waivers available. Financial award

application deadline: 1/5. *Faculty research:* Cellular and molecular neuroscience, development and plasticity, systems neuroscience and behavior, computational neuroscience, cognitive neuroscience, medical neuroscience. *Unit head:* Dr. Michael Adams. *Application contact:* Margarita Roman, Student Services Advisor, 951-827-4716, Fax: 951-827-5517, E-mail: margarita.roman@ucr.edu.
Website: http://www.neuro.ucr.edu/

University of California, San Diego, Graduate Division, Department of Physics, La Jolla, CA 92093. Offers biophysics (PhD); computational neuroscience (PhD); computational science (PhD); multi-scale biology (PhD); physics (MS, PhD); quantitative biology (PhD). *Students:* 149 full-time (28 women). 514 applicants, 20% accepted, 28 enrolled. In 2017, 8 master's, 20 doctorates awarded. *Degree requirements:* For doctorate, comprehensive exam, thesis/dissertation, 1-quarter teaching assistantship. *Entrance requirements:* For doctorate, GRE General Test, GRE Subject Test, statement of purpose, three letters of reference. Additional exam requirements/recommendations for international students: Required—TOEFL (minimum score 550 paper-based; 80 iBT), IELTS (minimum score 7). *Application deadline:* For fall admission, 12/20 for domestic students. Application fee: $105 ($125 for international students). Electronic applications accepted. *Financial support:* Fellowships, research assistantships, teaching assistantships, scholarships/grants, and unspecified assistantships available. Financial award applicants required to submit FAFSA. *Faculty research:* Astrophysics/astronomy, biological physics, condensed matter/material science, elementary particles, plasma physics. *Unit head:* Benjamin Grinstein, Chair, 858-534-6857, E-mail: chair@physics.ucsd.edu. *Application contact:* Saixious Dominguez-Kilday, Graduate Admissions Coordinator, 858-534-3293, E-mail: skilday@physics.ucsd.edu.
Website: http://physics.ucsd.edu/

University of California, San Diego, School of Medicine and Graduate Division, Program in Neurosciences, La Jolla, CA 92093. Offers PhD. *Students:* 98 full-time (44 women), 2 part-time (both women). 544 applicants, 10% accepted, 17 enrolled. In 2017, 12 doctorates awarded. *Degree requirements:* For doctorate, comprehensive exam, thesis/dissertation, 1-quarter teaching assistantship, 3 research rotations. *Entrance requirements:* For doctorate, GRE General Test, three letters of recommendation, statement of purpose. Additional exam requirements/recommendations for international students: Required—TOEFL (minimum score 550 paper-based; 80 iBT), IELTS (minimum score 7). *Application deadline:* For fall admission, 12/6 for domestic students. Application fee: $105 ($125 for international students). Electronic applications accepted. *Financial support:* Fellowships, research assistantships, teaching assistantships, scholarships/grants, traineeships, unspecified assistantships, and readerships available. Financial award applicants required to submit FAFSA. *Faculty research:* Cellular and developmental; biochemistry and molecular; cognitive, behavioral and psychopharmacology; clinical; computational; systems. *Unit head:* Timothy Gentner, Chair, 858-822-6763, E-mail: tgentner@ucsd.edu. *Application contact:* Erin Gilbert, Graduate Coordinator, 858-534-3377, E-mail: neurograd@ucsd.edu.
Website: http://neurograd.ucsd.edu

University of California, San Francisco, Graduate Division, Program in Neuroscience, San Francisco, CA 94143. Offers PhD. *Degree requirements:* For doctorate, thesis/dissertation. *Entrance requirements:* For doctorate, GRE General Test or MCAT, official transcripts, two letters of recommendation. Additional exam requirements/recommendations for international students: Required—TOEFL. Electronic applications accepted. *Faculty research:* Molecular neurobiology, synaptic plasticity, mechanisms of motor learning.

University of California, Santa Barbara, Graduate Division, College of Letters and Sciences, Division of Mathematics, Life, and Physical Sciences, Interdepartmental Graduate Program in Dynamical Neuroscience, Santa Barbara, CA 93106-2014. Offers PhD. *Degree requirements:* For doctorate, comprehensive exam, thesis/dissertation. *Entrance requirements:* Additional exam requirements/recommendations for international students: Required—TOEFL. Electronic applications accepted. *Faculty research:* Computational neuroscience, network science, computational vision, neuro imaging, signal processing.

University of Chicago, Division of the Biological Sciences, Program in Computational Neuroscience, Chicago, IL 60637-1513. Offers PhD. *Faculty:* 34. *Students:* 27 full-time (9 women); includes 3 minority (2 Asian, non-Hispanic/Latino; 1 Two or more races, non-Hispanic/Latino), 10 international. Average age 27. 78 applicants, 22% accepted, 5 enrolled. In 2017, 2 doctorates awarded. *Degree requirements:* For doctorate, thesis/dissertation, ethics class, 2 teaching assistantships. *Entrance requirements:* For doctorate, GRE General Test, transcripts, statement of purpose, 3 letters of recommendation. Additional exam requirements/recommendations for international students: Required—TOEFL (minimum score 600 paper-based; 104 iBT), IELTS (minimum score 7). *Application deadline:* For fall admission, 12/1 for domestic and international students. Application fee: $90. Electronic applications accepted. *Financial support:* In 2017–18, 21 students received support, including fellowships with full tuition reimbursements available (averaging $31,000 per year), research assistantships with full tuition reimbursements available (averaging $31,000 per year); institutionally sponsored loans, scholarships/grants, traineeships, and health care benefits also available. Financial award application deadline: 12/1. *Faculty research:* Quantitative and modelling methods; nervous system function; natural behaviors and cognitive processes; design of devices that duplicate behaviors. *Unit head:* Dr. David Freedman, Graduate Program Chair, E-mail: dfreedman@uchicago.edu. *Application contact:* Elena Rizzo, Administrative Director, 773-795-3849, E-mail: erizzo@uchicago.edu.
Website: http://neuroscience.uchicago.edu/graduate-training/computational-neuroscience-curriculum/

University of Cincinnati, Graduate School, Neuroscience Graduate Program, Cincinnati, OH 45267. Offers PhD. *Degree requirements:* For doctorate, thesis/dissertation, qualifying exam. *Entrance requirements:* For doctorate, GRE General Test. Additional exam requirements/recommendations for international students: Required—TOEFL (minimum score 100 iBT), IELTS (minimum score 6.5). Electronic applications accepted. *Expenses: Tuition, area resident:* Full-time $14,468. Tuition, state resident: full-time $14,968; part-time $754 per credit hour. Tuition, nonresident: full-time $24,210; part-time $1311 per credit hour. *International tuition:* $26,460 full-time. *Required fees:* $3958; $84 per credit hour. One-time fee: $85 full-time. Tuition and fees vary according to course load, degree level and program. *Faculty research:* Developmental neurobiology, membrane and channel biophysics, molecular neurobiology, neuroendocrinology, neuronal cell biology.

University of Colorado Denver, School of Medicine, Program in Neuroscience, Aurora, CO 80206. Offers PhD. *Students:* 37 full-time (20 women); includes 7 minority (1 Black or African American, non-Hispanic/Latino; 1 Asian, non-Hispanic/Latino; 2 Hispanic/Latino; 3 Two or more races, non-Hispanic/Latino), 1 international. Average age 27. 88 applicants, 9% accepted, 8 enrolled. In 2017, 7 doctorates awarded. *Degree requirements:* For doctorate, comprehensive exam, thesis/dissertation, structured class schedule each year paired with lab rotations. *Entrance requirements:* For doctorate, GRE, baccalaureate degree in a biological science, chemistry, physics or engineering (recommended); minimum GPA of 3.2. Additional exam requirements/recommendations for international students: Required—TOEFL (minimum score 550 paper-based; 80 iBT). *Application deadline:* For fall admission, 12/1 for domestic students, 11/1 priority date for international students. Application fee: $50 ($75 for international students). Electronic applications accepted. *Financial support:* Fellowships, research assistantships, teaching assistantships, Federal Work-Study, institutionally sponsored loans, scholarships/grants, traineeships, health care benefits, tuition waivers (full), and unspecified assistantships available. *Faculty research:* Neurobiology of olfaction, ion channels, schizophrenia, spinal cord regeneration, neurotransplantation. *Unit head:* Dr. Wendy Macklin, Professor and Chair, 303-724-3426, Fax: 303-724-3420, E-mail: wendy.macklin@ucdenver.edu. *Application contact:* Deanne Sylvester, Program Administrator, 303-724-3120, Fax: 303-724-3121, E-mail: deanne.sylvester@ucdenver.edu.
Website: http://www.ucdenver.edu/academics/colleges/medicalschool/programs/Neuroscience/Pages/Neuroscience.aspx

University of Connecticut, Graduate School, College of Liberal Arts and Sciences, Department of Psychology, Storrs, CT 06269. Offers behavioral neuroscience (PhD); biopsychology (PhD); clinical psychology (MA, PhD); cognition and instruction (PhD); developmental psychology (MA, PhD); ecological psychology (PhD); experimental psychology (PhD); general psychology (MA, PhD); industrial/organizational psychology (PhD); language and cognition (PhD); neuroscience (PhD); social psychology (MA, PhD). *Accreditation:* APA. Terminal master's awarded for partial completion of doctoral program. *Degree requirements:* For master's, comprehensive exam; for doctorate, thesis/dissertation. *Entrance requirements:* For master's and doctorate, GRE General Test, GRE Subject Test. Additional exam requirements/recommendations for international students: Required—TOEFL (minimum score 550 paper-based). Electronic applications accepted.

University of Connecticut Health Center, Graduate School, Programs in Biomedical Sciences, Program in Neuroscience, Farmington, CT 06030. Offers PhD, DMD/PhD, MD/PhD. *Degree requirements:* For doctorate, comprehensive exam, thesis/dissertation. *Entrance requirements:* For doctorate, GRE General Test, interview (recommended). Additional exam requirements/recommendations for international students: Required—TOEFL (minimum score 600 paper-based). Electronic applications accepted. *Faculty research:* Molecular and systems neuroscience, neuroanatomy, neurophysiology, neurochemistry, neuropathology.

University of Delaware, College of Arts and Sciences, Department of Psychology, Newark, DE 19716. Offers behavioral neuroscience (PhD); clinical psychology (PhD); cognitive psychology (PhD); social psychology (PhD). *Accreditation:* APA. *Degree requirements:* For doctorate, thesis/dissertation. *Entrance requirements:* For doctorate, GRE General Test. Additional exam requirements/recommendations for international students: Required—TOEFL (minimum score 600 paper-based). Electronic applications accepted. *Faculty research:* Emotion development, neural and cognitive aspects of memory, neural control of feeding, intergroup relations, social cognition and communication.

University of Florida, College of Medicine and Graduate School, Interdisciplinary Program in Biomedical Sciences, Concentration in Neuroscience, Gainesville, FL 32611. Offers PhD. *Degree requirements:* For doctorate, thesis/dissertation. *Entrance requirements:* For doctorate, GRE General Test, minimum GPA of 3.0, biochemistry before enrollment. Additional exam requirements/recommendations for international students: Required—TOEFL. Electronic applications accepted. *Faculty research:* Neural injury and repair, neurophysiology, neurotoxicology, cellular and molecular neurobiology, neuroimmunology and endocrinology.

University of Georgia, Biomedical and Health Sciences Institute, Athens, GA 30602. Offers neuroscience (PhD). *Entrance requirements:* For doctorate, GRE, official transcripts, 3 letters of recommendation, statement of interest. Additional exam requirements/recommendations for international students: Required—TOEFL.

University of Guelph, Ontario Veterinary College and Graduate Studies, Graduate Programs in Veterinary Sciences, Department of Biomedical Sciences, Guelph, ON N1G 2W1, Canada. Offers morphology (M Sc, DV Sc, PhD); neuroscience (M Sc, DV Sc, PhD); pharmacology (M Sc, DV Sc, PhD); physiology (M Sc, DV Sc, PhD); toxicology (M Sc, DV Sc, PhD). *Program availability:* Part-time. *Degree requirements:* For master's, thesis; for doctorate, comprehensive exam, thesis/dissertation. *Entrance requirements:* For master's, honors B Sc, minimum 75% average in last 20 courses; for doctorate, M Sc with thesis from accredited institution. Additional exam requirements/recommendations for international students: Required—TOEFL (minimum score 550 paper-based; 89 iBT). Electronic applications accepted. *Faculty research:* Cellular morphology; endocrine, vascular and reproductive physiology; clinical pharmacology; veterinary toxicology; developmental biology, neuroscience.

University of Guelph, Ontario Veterinary College and Graduate Studies, Graduate Programs in Veterinary Sciences, Department of Clinical Studies, Guelph, ON N1G 2W1, Canada. Offers anesthesiology (M Sc, DV Sc); cardiology (DV Sc, Diploma); clinical studies (Diploma); dermatology (M Sc); diagnostic imaging (M Sc, DV Sc); emergency/critical care (M Sc, DV Sc, Diploma); medicine (M Sc, DV Sc); neurology (M Sc, DV Sc); ophthalmology (M Sc, DV Sc); surgery (M Sc, DV Sc). *Degree requirements:* For master's, thesis; for doctorate, comprehensive exam, thesis/dissertation. *Entrance requirements:* Additional exam requirements/recommendations for international students: Required—TOEFL (minimum score 550 paper-based), IELTS (minimum score 6.5). Electronic applications accepted. *Faculty research:* Orthopedics, respirology, oncology, exercise physiology, cardiology.

University of Hartford, College of Arts and Sciences, Department of Biology, Program in Neuroscience, West Hartford, CT 06117-1599. Offers MS. *Program availability:* Part-time, evening/weekend. *Degree requirements:* For master's, comprehensive exam, thesis optional, oral exams. *Entrance requirements:* For master's, GRE General Test, GRE Subject Test, MCAT. Additional exam requirements/recommendations for international students: Required—TOEFL (minimum score 550 paper-based). Electronic applications accepted. *Faculty research:* Neurobiology of aging, central actions of neural steroids, neuroendocrine control of reproduction, retinopathies in sharks, plasticity in the central nervous system.

University of Illinois at Chicago, Program in Neuroscience, Chicago, IL 60607. Offers cellular and systems neuroscience and cell biology (PhD); neuroscience (MS).

University of Illinois at Urbana–Champaign, Graduate College, College of Liberal Arts and Sciences, School of Molecular and Cellular Biology, Neuroscience Program, Champaign, IL 61820. Offers PhD.

The University of Iowa, Graduate College, Program in Neuroscience, Iowa City, IA 52242-1316. Offers PhD. *Degree requirements:* For doctorate, comprehensive exam, thesis/dissertation. *Entrance requirements:* For doctorate, GRE General Test, minimum GPA of 3.0. Additional exam requirements/recommendations for international students: Required—TOEFL (minimum score 600 paper-based; 100 iBT). Electronic applications accepted. *Faculty research:* Molecular, cellular, and developmental systems; behavioral neurosciences.

The University of Kansas, Graduate Studies, School of Pharmacy, Program in Neurosciences, Lawrence, KS 66045. Offers MS, PhD. *Program availability:* Part-time. *Students:* 11 full-time (5 women); includes 1 minority (Hispanic/Latino), 1 international. Average age 32. 18 applicants, 11% accepted, 2 enrolled. In 2017, 3 master's, 1

doctorate awarded. *Entrance requirements:* For master's and doctorate, GRE, BA or BS in neuroscience or a related study, three letters of recommendation, personal statement, minimum GPA of 3.0. Additional exam requirements/recommendations for international students: Required—TOEFL. *Application deadline:* For fall admission, 1/15 priority date for domestic and international students. Application fee: $65 ($85 for international students). Electronic applications accepted. *Financial support:* Fellowships, research assistantships, teaching assistantships, and scholarships/grants available. Financial award application deadline: 1/15. *Unit head:* Ruth Anne Atchley, Chair, 785-864-4131, E-mail: ratchley@ku.edu. *Application contact:* Sarah Hoadley, Graduate Admission Contact, 785-864-4002, E-mail: sarahhoadley@ku.edu.
Website: http://www.neuroscience.ku.edu/

The University of Kansas, University of Kansas Medical Center, School of Medicine, Neuroscience Graduate Program, Kansas City, KS 66045-7582. Offers PhD, MD/PhD. *Students:* 8 full-time (3 women); includes 1 minority (Hispanic/Latino), 1 international. Average age 28. In 2017, 2 doctorates awarded. Terminal master's awarded for partial completion of doctoral program. *Degree requirements:* For doctorate, comprehensive exam, thesis/dissertation. *Entrance requirements:* For doctorate, GRE. Additional exam requirements/recommendations for international students: Required—TOEFL. Application fee: $60. Application fee is waived when completed online. *Financial support:* Fellowships with partial tuition reimbursements, research assistantships with full tuition reimbursements, and teaching assistantships with full tuition reimbursements available. Financial award application deadline: 3/1; financial award applicants required to submit FAFSA. *Unit head:* Dr. Doug Wright, Professor, Department of Anatomy and Cell Biology, 913-588-2713, Fax: 913-588-2710, E-mail: dwright@kumc.edu. *Application contact:* Marcia Jones, Director of Graduate Studies, 913-588-1238, Fax: 913-588-5242, E-mail: mjones@kumc.edu.
Website: http://www.kumc.edu/school-of-medicine/neuroscience.html

University of Lethbridge, School of Graduate Studies, Lethbridge, AB T1K 3M4, Canada. Offers addictions counseling (M Sc); agricultural biotechnology (M Sc); agricultural studies (M Sc, MA); anthropology (MA); archaeology (M Sc, MA); art (MA, MFA); biochemistry (M Sc); biological sciences (M Sc); biomolecular science (PhD); biosystems and biodiversity (PhD); Canadian studies (MA); chemistry (M Sc); computer science (M Sc); computer science and geographical information science (M Sc); counseling (MC); counseling psychology (M Ed); dramatic arts (MA); earth, space, and physical science (PhD); economics (MA); education (MA, PhD); educational leadership (M Ed); English (MA); environmental science (M Sc); evolution and behavior (PhD); exercise science (M Sc); French (MA); French/German (MA); French/Spanish (MA); general education (M Ed); geography (M Sc, MA); German (MA); health sciences (M Sc); individualized multidisciplinary (M Sc, MA); kinesiology (M Sc, MA); management (M Sc), including accounting, finance, human resource management and labor relations, information systems, international management, marketing, policy and strategy; mathematics (M Sc); music (M Mus, MA); Native American studies (MA); neuroscience (M Sc, PhD); new media (MA, MFA); nursing (M Sc, MN); philosophy (MA); physics (M Sc); political science (MA); psychology (M Sc, MA); religious studies (MA); sociology (MA); theatre and dramatic arts (MFA); theoretical and computational science (PhD); urban and regional studies (MA); women and gender studies (MA). *Program availability:* Part-time, evening/weekend. *Degree requirements:* For master's, thesis (for some programs); for doctorate, comprehensive exam, thesis/dissertation. *Entrance requirements:* For master's, GMAT (for M Sc in management), bachelor's degree in related field, minimum GPA of 3.0 during previous 20 graded semester courses, 2 years' teaching or related experience (M Ed); for doctorate, master's degree, minimum graduate GPA of 3.5. Additional exam requirements/recommendations for international students: Required—TOEFL (minimum score 580 paper-based; 93 iBT). Electronic applications accepted. *Faculty research:* Movement and brain plasticity, gibberellin physiology, photosynthesis, carbon cycling, molecular properties of main-group ring components.

The University of Manchester, School of Biological Sciences, Manchester, United Kingdom. Offers adaptive organismal biology (M Phil, PhD); animal biology (M Phil, PhD); biochemistry (M Phil, PhD); bioinformatics (M Phil, PhD); biomolecular sciences (M Phil, PhD); biotechnology (M Phil, PhD); cell biology (M Phil, PhD); cell matrix research (M Phil, PhD); channels and transporters (M Phil, PhD); developmental biology (M Phil, PhD); environmental biology (M Phil, PhD); evolutionary biology (M Phil, PhD); gene expression (M Phil, PhD); genetics (M Phil, PhD); history of science, technology and medicine (M Phil, PhD); immunology (M Phil, PhD); integrative neurobiology and behavior (M Phil, PhD); membrane trafficking (M Phil, PhD); microbiology (M Phil, PhD); molecular and cellular neuroscience (M Phil, PhD); molecular biology (M Phil, PhD); molecular cancer studies (M Phil, PhD); neuroscience (M Phil, PhD); ophthalmology (M Phil, PhD); optometry (M Phil, PhD); organelle function (M Phil, PhD); pharmacology (M Phil, PhD); physiology (M Phil, PhD); plant sciences (M Phil, PhD); stem cell research (M Phil, PhD); structural biology (M Phil, PhD); systems neuroscience (M Phil, PhD); toxicology (M Phil, PhD).

University of Maryland, Baltimore, Graduate School, Graduate Program in Life Sciences, Program in Neuroscience, Baltimore, MD 21201. Offers PhD, MD/PhD. *Program availability:* Part-time. *Students:* 41 full-time (19 women), 3 part-time (2 women); includes 11 minority (1 Black or African American, non-Hispanic/Latino; 6 Asian, non-Hispanic/Latino; 2 Hispanic/Latino; 2 Two or more races, non-Hispanic/Latino), 2 international. Average age 28. 99 applicants, 17% accepted, 7 enrolled. In 2017, 8 doctorates awarded. *Degree requirements:* For doctorate, comprehensive exam, thesis/dissertation. *Entrance requirements:* For doctorate, GRE General Test, minimum GPA of 3.0, curriculum vitae, essay, 3 letters of recommendation. Additional exam requirements/recommendations for international students: Required—TOEFL (minimum score 80 iBT); Recommended—IELTS (minimum score 7). *Application deadline:* For fall admission, 12/15 for domestic students, 1/15 for international students. Application fee: $75. Electronic applications accepted. *Expenses:* Tuition, state resident: full-time $13,990; part-time $661 per credit. Tuition, nonresident: full-time $30,484; part-time $1310 per credit. *Required fees:* $1894; $94 per credit. $415 per semester. Part-time tuition and fees vary according to course load, degree level and program. *Financial support:* In 2017–18, research assistantships with partial tuition reimbursements (averaging $26,000 per year) were awarded; fellowships, health care benefits, and unspecified assistantships also available. Financial award application deadline: 3/1; financial award applicants required to submit FAFSA. *Faculty research:* Molecular, biochemical, and cellular pharmacology; membrane biophysics; synaptology; developmental neurobiology. *Unit head:* Dr. Jessica Mong, Director, 410-706-4295, E-mail: jmong@umaryland.edu. *Application contact:* Renee Cockerham, Program Manager, 410-706-4701, Fax: 410-706-4724, E-mail: neurosci@umaryland.edu.
Website: http://lifesciences.umaryland.edu/Neuroscience/

University of Maryland, Baltimore County, The Graduate School, College of Natural and Mathematical Sciences, Department of Biological Sciences, Program in Neuroscience and Cognitive Sciences, Baltimore, MD 21250. Offers PhD. *Faculty:* 6 full-time (3 women). *Students:* 3 full-time (2 women); includes 2 minority (1 Black or African American, non-Hispanic/Latino; 1 Asian, non-Hispanic/Latino). Average age 24. 11 applicants, 27% accepted, 3 enrolled. *Degree requirements:* For doctorate, thesis/dissertation. *Entrance requirements:* For doctorate, GRE General Test, minimum GPA of 3.0. Additional exam requirements/recommendations for international students: Required—TOEFL (minimum score 80 iBT), IELTS (minimum score 6.5). *Application deadline:* For fall admission, 4/15 priority date for domestic and international students. Application fee: $50. Electronic applications accepted. *Expenses: Required fees:* $132. *Financial support:* In 2017–18, 3 students received support, including 1 research assistantship with full tuition reimbursement available (averaging $24,600 per year), 2 teaching assistantships with full tuition reimbursements available (averaging $23,518 per year); health care benefits and unspecified assistantships also available. *Faculty research:* Developmental biology and neural tube defects, vision science, olfactory systems, neurobiological adaptations of animals, conversion of light into a biological signal in vision. *Unit head:* Dr. Michelle Starz-Gaiano, Director, 410-455-2217, Fax: 410-455-3875, E-mail: biograd@umbc.edu. *Application contact:* Brandy Darcey, Graduate Program Coordinator, 410-455-3669, E-mail: bdarcey@umbc.edu.
Website: http://biology.umbc.edu

University of Maryland, College Park, Academic Affairs, College of Behavioral and Social Sciences, Department of Hearing and Speech Sciences, College Park, MD 20742. Offers audiology (MA, PhD); hearing and speech sciences (Au D); language pathology (MA, PhD); neuroscience (PhD); speech (MA, PhD). *Accreditation:* ASHA (one or more programs are accredited). *Degree requirements:* For master's, thesis optional; for doctorate, thesis/dissertation, written and oral exams. *Entrance requirements:* For master's, GRE General Test, minimum GPA of 3.5, 3 letters of recommendation; for doctorate, GRE General Test, minimum GPA of 3.5. Additional exam requirements/recommendations for international students: Required—TOEFL. Electronic applications accepted. *Faculty research:* Speech perception, language acquisition, bilingualism, hearing loss.

University of Maryland, College Park, Academic Affairs, College of Behavioral and Social Sciences, Program in Neurosciences and Cognitive Sciences, College Park, MD 20742. Offers PhD. *Degree requirements:* For doctorate, comprehensive exam, thesis/dissertation. *Entrance requirements:* For doctorate, GRE General Test, 3 letters of recommendation. Additional exam requirements/recommendations for international students: Required—TOEFL. Electronic applications accepted. *Faculty research:* Molecular neurobiology, cognition, neural and behavioral systems language, memory, human development.

University of Massachusetts Amherst, Graduate School, Interdisciplinary Programs, Program in Neuroscience and Behavior, Amherst, MA 01003. Offers animal behavior and learning (PhD); molecular and cellular neuroscience (PhD); neural and behavioral development (PhD); neuroendocrinology (PhD); neuroscience and behavior (MS); sensorimotor, cognitive, and computational neuroscience (PhD). Terminal master's awarded for partial completion of doctoral program. *Degree requirements:* For master's, thesis or alternative; for doctorate, comprehensive exam, thesis/dissertation. *Entrance requirements:* For master's, GRE General Test; for doctorate, GRE General Test; GRE Subject Test in psychology, biology, or mathematics (recommended). Additional exam requirements/recommendations for international students: Required—TOEFL (minimum score 550 paper-based; 80 iBT), IELTS (minimum score 6.5). Electronic applications accepted.

University of Massachusetts Medical School, Graduate School of Biomedical Sciences, Worcester, MA 01655-0115. Offers biomedical sciences (PhD), including biochemistry and molecular pharmacology, bioinformatics and computational biology, cancer biology, immunology and microbiology, interdisciplinary, neuroscience, translational science; biomedical sciences (millennium program) (PhD); clinical and population health research (PhD); clinical investigation (MS). *Faculty:* 1,316 full-time (526 women), 357 part-time/adjunct (229 women). *Students:* 347 full-time (180 women); includes 61 minority (10 Black or African American, non-Hispanic/Latino; 1 American Indian or Alaska Native, non-Hispanic/Latino; 35 Asian, non-Hispanic/Latino; 15 Hispanic/Latino), 130 international. Average age 29. 608 applicants, 28% accepted, 54 enrolled. In 2017, 6 master's, 51 doctorates awarded. Terminal master's awarded for partial completion of doctoral program. *Degree requirements:* For master's, comprehensive exam, thesis; for doctorate, comprehensive exam, thesis/dissertation. *Entrance requirements:* For master's, MD, PhD, DVM, or PharmD; for doctorate, GRE General Test, bachelor's degree. Additional exam requirements/recommendations for international students: Required—TOEFL (minimum score 90 iBT) or IELTS (minimum score 7.0). *Application deadline:* For fall admission, 12/15 for domestic and international students. Applications are processed on a rolling basis. Application fee: $80. Electronic applications accepted. Application fee is waived when completed online. *Expenses:* $14,883 in-state tuition and mandatory fees; $31,486 out-of-state. *Financial support:* In 2017–18, 15 fellowships with partial tuition reimbursements (averaging $29,000 per year), 296 research assistantships with full tuition reimbursements (averaging $31,212 per year) were awarded; institutionally sponsored loans and scholarships/grants also available. Financial award application deadline: 5/15. *Faculty research:* RNA biology, molecular/cell/developmental/metabolic biology, bioinformatics and computational biology, clinical/translational research, infectious disease and immunology. *Total annual research expenditures:* $279 million. *Unit head:* Dr. Mary Ellen Lane, Dean, 508-856-4018, E-mail: maryellen.lane@umassmed.edu. *Application contact:* Dr. Kendall Knight, Assistant Vice Provost for Admissions, 508-856-5628, Fax: 508-856-3659, E-mail: kendall.knight@umassmed.edu.
Website: http://www.umassmed.edu/gsbs/

University of Miami, Graduate School, College of Arts and Sciences, Department of Psychology, Coral Gables, FL 33124. Offers adult clinical (PhD); behavioral neuroscience (PhD); child clinical (PhD); developmental psychology (PhD); health clinical (PhD); psychology (MS). *Accreditation:* APA (one or more programs are accredited). *Degree requirements:* For doctorate, comprehensive exam, thesis/dissertation. *Entrance requirements:* For doctorate, GRE General Test, minimum GPA of 3.5. Additional exam requirements/recommendations for international students: Required—TOEFL. Electronic applications accepted. *Faculty research:* Behavioral factors in cardiovascular disease and cancer adult psychopathology, developmental disabilities, social and emotional development, mechanisms of coping.

University of Miami, Graduate School, Miller School of Medicine, Graduate Programs in Medicine, Neuroscience Program, Coral Gables, FL 33124. Offers PhD, MD/PhD. *Degree requirements:* For doctorate, thesis/dissertation, qualifying exam. *Entrance requirements:* For doctorate, GRE General Test. Additional exam requirements/recommendations for international students: Required—TOEFL (minimum score 550 paper-based). Electronic applications accepted. *Faculty research:* Cellular and molecular biology, transduction, nerve regeneration and embryonic development, membrane biophysics.

University of Michigan, Rackham Graduate School, College of Literature, Science, and the Arts, Department of Psychology, Ann Arbor, MI 48109. Offers biopsychology (PhD); clinical science (PhD); cognition and cognitive neuroscience (PhD); developmental psychology (PhD); personality and social contexts (PhD); social psychology (PhD). *Accreditation:* APA. *Faculty:* 66 full-time (31 women), 28 part-time/adjunct (17 women). *Students:* 148 full-time (113 women); includes 61 minority (13 Black or African American, non-Hispanic/Latino; 1 American Indian or Alaska Native, non-Hispanic/Latino; 12 Asian, non-Hispanic/Latino; 28 Hispanic/Latino; 7 Two or more races, non-Hispanic/Latino), 24 international. Average age 27. 691 applicants, 7%

accepted, 35 enrolled. In 2017, 34 doctorates awarded. Terminal master's awarded for partial completion of doctoral program. *Degree requirements:* For doctorate, comprehensive exam, thesis/dissertation, oral defense of dissertation, preliminary exam. *Entrance requirements:* For doctorate, GRE General Test. Additional exam requirements/recommendations for international students: Required—TOEFL. *Application deadline:* For fall admission, 12/1 for domestic and international students. Application fee: $75 ($90 for international students). Electronic applications accepted. *Expenses:* $11,184 in-state, $22,578 out-of-state. *Financial support:* In 2017–18, 90 students received support, including 61 fellowships with full tuition reimbursements available (averaging $26,400 per year), 10 research assistantships with full tuition reimbursements available (averaging $26,400 per year), 89 teaching assistantships with full tuition reimbursements available (averaging $26,400 per year); career-related internships or fieldwork, traineeships, and health care benefits also available. Financial award application deadline: 4/15. *Unit head:* Prof. Patricia Reuter-Lorenz, Department Chair, 734-764-7429. *Application contact:* Sheri M. Circele, Psychology Student Academic Affairs, 734-764-2580, Fax: 734-764-3520, E-mail: psych.saa@umich.edu.
Website: http://www.lsa.umich.edu/psych/

University of Michigan, Rackham Graduate School, Program in Biomedical Sciences (PIBS), Neuroscience Graduate Program, Ann Arbor, MI 48072-2216. Offers PhD. *Faculty:* 153 full-time (40 women). *Students:* 64 full-time (38 women); includes 24 minority (1 American Indian or Alaska Native, non-Hispanic/Latino; 7 Asian, non-Hispanic/Latino; 16 Hispanic/Latino), 3 international. Average age 27. 204 applicants, 17% accepted, 12 enrolled. In 2017, 18 doctorates awarded. *Degree requirements:* For doctorate, thesis/dissertation, oral defense of dissertation, preliminary exam. *Entrance requirements:* For doctorate, 3 letters of recommendation, research experience. Additional exam requirements/recommendations for international students: Required—TOEFL (minimum score 84 iBT). *Application deadline:* For fall admission, 12/1 for domestic and international students. Application fee: $75 ($90 for international students). Electronic applications accepted. *Expenses:* Tuition, state resident: full-time $22,368; part-time $1201 per credit hour. Tuition, nonresident: full-time $45,156; part-time $2467 per credit hour. *Required fees:* $376 per term. Tuition and fees vary according to course load, degree level and program. *Financial support:* In 2017–18, 64 students received support, including 64 fellowships with full tuition reimbursements available (averaging $30,604 per year); scholarships/grants, tuition waivers (full), and unspecified assistantships also available. Financial award application deadline: 12/1. *Faculty research:* Developmental neurobiology, cellular and molecular neurobiology, cognitive neuroscience, sensory neuroscience, behavioral neuroscience. *Unit head:* Dr. Audrey Seasholtz, Director, 734-763-[illegible], Fax: 734-647-0717, E-mail: aseashol@umich.edu. *Application contact:* Rachel A. Harbach, Student Services Administrator, 734-763-9638, Fax: 734-647-0717, E-mail: rachelfk@umich.edu.
Website: http://neuroscience.med.umich.edu/

University of Michigan–Flint, School of Health Professions and Studies, Program in Physical Therapy, Flint, MI 48502-1950. Offers adult neurology (PhD); neurology (Certificate); orthopedics (PhD, Certificate); pediatrics (PhD, Certificate); physical therapy (DPT). *Accreditation:* APTA. *Program availability:* Part-time, evening/weekend, 100% online. *Faculty:* 16 full-time (12 women), 17 part-time/adjunct (10 women). *Students:* 176 full-time (104 women), 44 part-time (27 women); includes 34 minority (2 Black or African American, non-Hispanic/Latino; 1 American Indian or Alaska Native, non-Hispanic/Latino; 23 Asian, non-Hispanic/Latino; 2 Hispanic/Latino; 6 Two or more races, non-Hispanic/Latino), 16 international. Average age 27. 346 applicants, 38% accepted, 67 enrolled. In 2017, 88 doctorates, 4 other advanced degrees awarded. *Degree requirements:* For doctorate, thesis/dissertation or alternative. *Entrance requirements:* For doctorate, GRE (minimum Verbal score between 340-480; Quantitative 370-710), bachelor's or master's physical therapy degree from regionally-accredited institution, current physical therapy license in the United States or Canada, minimum overall GPA of 3.0 in the physical therapy degree, current CPR certification (depending on program); for Certificate, DPT from accredited institution; current physical therapy license in the United States or Canada; minimum overall GPA of 3.0 in the physical therapy degree; current CPR certification. Additional exam requirements/recommendations for international students: Required—TOEFL (minimum score 84 iBT), IELTS (minimum score 6.5). *Application deadline:* For fall admission, 5/1 for domestic students, 2/1 for international students; for winter admission, 7/31 for domestic students, 4/1 for international students; for spring admission, 3/1 for domestic students, 12/1 for international students. Application fee: $55. Electronic applications accepted. *Expenses:* Contact institution. *Financial support:* Federal Work-Study and unspecified assistantships available. Support available to part-time students. Financial award application deadline: 3/1; financial award applicants required to submit FAFSA. *Faculty research:* Cumulative trauma disorders, oncology rehabilitation, neurological rehabilitation, musculoskeletal rehabilitation, cardiopulmonary rehabilitation. *Unit head:* Dr. Amy Yorke, Department Admissions Chair, 810-762-3373, E-mail: amyorke@umflint.edu. *Application contact:* Frank Fanzone, Senior Administrative Assistant, 810-762-3373, Fax: 810-766-6668, E-mail: ffanzone@umflint.edu.
Website: https://www.umflint.edu/pt

University of Minnesota, Twin Cities Campus, Graduate School, Graduate Program in Neuroscience, Minneapolis, MN 55455-0213. Offers MS, PhD. Terminal master's awarded for partial completion of doctoral program. *Degree requirements:* For master's, thesis; for doctorate, thesis/dissertation. *Entrance requirements:* For doctorate, GRE. Additional exam requirements/recommendations for international students: Required—TOEFL. Electronic applications accepted. *Faculty research:* Cellular and molecular neuroscience, behavioral neuroscience, developmental neuroscience, neurodegenerative diseases, pain, addiction, motor control.

University of Mississippi Medical Center, School of Graduate Studies in the Health Sciences, Program in Neuroscience, Jackson, MS 39216-4505. Offers PhD. *Degree requirements:* For doctorate, comprehensive exam, thesis/dissertation, 1st authored publication. *Entrance requirements:* For doctorate, GRE, BA, BS. Additional exam requirements/recommendations for international students: Required—TOEFL (minimum score 550 paper-based, 79 iBT), IELTS (minimum score 6.5), or PTE (minimum score 53). Electronic applications accepted. *Faculty research:* Neuroendocrinology, drugs of abuse, psychiatric neuroscience, sensory neuroscience, circadian rhythms.

University of Missouri–St. Louis, College of Arts and Sciences, Department of Psychological Sciences, St. Louis, MO 63121. Offers behavioral neuroscience (MA, PhD); clinical psychology (PhD); trauma studies (Certificate). *Accreditation:* APA (one or more programs are accredited). *Program availability:* Evening/weekend. *Students:* 58 full-time (41 women), 17 part-time (11 women); includes 12 minority (4 Black or African American, non-Hispanic/Latino; 4 Asian, non-Hispanic/Latino; 3 Hispanic/Latino; 1 Two or more races, non-Hispanic/Latino), 3 international. 242 applicants, 8% accepted, 16 enrolled. Terminal master's awarded for partial completion of doctoral program. *Degree requirements:* For master's, thesis; for doctorate, thesis/dissertation. *Entrance requirements:* For master's, GRE General Test, 3 letters of recommendation; for doctorate, GRE General Test, GRE Subject Test, 3 letters of recommendation. Additional exam requirements/recommendations for international students: Required—TOEFL (minimum score 550 paper-based; 79 iBT), IELTS (minimum score 6.5). *Application deadline:* For fall admission, 12/15 for domestic and international students. Application fee: $50 ($40 for international students). Electronic applications accepted. *Expenses:* Tuition, state resident: part-time $476.50 per credit hour. Tuition, nonresident: part-time $1169.70 per credit hour. *Financial support:* Fellowships with full tuition reimbursements, research assistantships with tuition reimbursements, teaching assistantships with tuition reimbursements, and scholarships/grants available. Financial award applicants required to submit FAFSA. *Faculty research:* Bereavement and loss, neuroscience, post-traumatic stress disorder, conflict and negotiation, social psychology. *Unit head:* Michael G. Griffin, Chair, 314-516-5391, Fax: 314-516-5392, E-mail: michael_griffin@umsl.edu. *Application contact:* 314-516-5458, Fax: 314-516-6996, E-mail: gradadm@umsl.edu.
Website: http://www.umsl.edu/divisions/artscience/psychology/

University of Montana, Graduate School, College of Health Professions and Biomedical Sciences, Skaggs School of Pharmacy, Department of Biomedical and Pharmaceutical Sciences, Missoula, MT 59812. Offers biomedical sciences (PhD); medicinal chemistry (MS, PhD); molecular and cellular toxicology (MS, PhD); neuroscience (PhD); pharmaceutical sciences (MS). *Accreditation:* ACPE. *Degree requirements:* For master's, oral defense of thesis; for doctorate, research dissertation defense. *Entrance requirements:* For master's and doctorate, GRE General Test. Additional exam requirements/recommendations for international students: Required—TOEFL (minimum score 540 paper-based). Electronic applications accepted. *Faculty research:* Cardiovascular pharmacology, medicinal chemistry, neurosciences, environmental toxicology, pharmacogenetics, cancer.

University of Nebraska Medical Center, Interdisciplinary Graduate Program in Biomedical Sciences, Department of Pharmacology and Experimental Neuroscience, Omaha, NE 68198-5800. Offers PhD. *Faculty:* 26 full-time (8 women), 2 part-time/adjunct (0 women). *Students:* 31 full-time (10 women); includes 1 minority (Black or African American, non-Hispanic/Latino), 11 international. Average age 28. 12 applicants, 42% accepted, 5 enrolled. In 2017, 6 doctorates awarded. Terminal master's awarded for partial completion of doctoral program. *Degree requirements:* For doctorate, comprehensive exam, thesis/dissertation. *Entrance requirements:* For doctorate, GRE General Test. Additional exam requirements/recommendations for international students: Required—TOEFL (minimum score 90 iBT). *Application deadline:* For fall admission, 6/1 for domestic students, 4/1 for international students. Applications are processed on a rolling basis. Application fee: $45. Electronic applications accepted. *Expenses:* Tuition, state resident: full-time $8451; part-time $4225 per semester. Tuition, nonresident: full-time $24,219; part-time $11,295 per semester. *Required fees:* $580; $117 per term. *Financial support:* In 2017–18, 6 students received support, including 6 fellowships with full tuition reimbursements available (averaging $23,400 per year); research assistantships, scholarships/grants, health care benefits, and unspecified assistantships also available. Financial award application deadline: 2/15. *Faculty research:* Neuropharmacology, molecular pharmacology, toxicology, molecular biology, neuroscience. *Unit head:* Dr. Keshore Bidasee, Chair, Graduate Studies, 402-559-9018, Fax: 402-559-7495, E-mail: kbidasee@unmc.edu. *Application contact:* Reed Felderman, Office Administrator, 402-559-4044, Fax: 402-559-7495, E-mail: reed.felderman@unmc.edu.
Website: http://www.unmc.edu/pharmacology/

University of New Mexico, Graduate Studies, College of Arts and Sciences, Program in Psychology, Albuquerque, NM 87131-2039. Offers behavioral neuroscience (PhD); clinical psychology (PhD); cognitive neuroimaging (PhD); developmental psychology (PhD); evolution (PhD); health psychology (PhD); quantitative methodology (PhD). *Accreditation:* APA. *Students:* Average age 30. 227 applicants, 11% accepted, 16 enrolled. In 2017, 10 doctorates awarded. *Degree requirements:* For doctorate, comprehensive exam, thesis/dissertation. *Entrance requirements:* For doctorate, GRE General Test, GRE Subject Test (psychology), minimum GPA of 3.0. Additional exam requirements/recommendations for international students: Required—TOEFL (minimum score 550 paper-based; 79 iBT), IELTS (minimum score 6.5). *Application deadline:* For fall admission, 12/15 priority date for domestic and international students. Applications are processed on a rolling basis. Application fee: $50. Electronic applications accepted. *Financial support:* Fellowships, research assistantships, teaching assistantships, career-related internships or fieldwork, Federal Work-Study, institutionally sponsored loans, scholarships/grants, health care benefits, tuition waivers (partial), and unspecified assistantships available. Financial award application deadline: 3/1; financial award applicants required to submit FAFSA. *Faculty research:* Addiction, cognition, brain and behavior, developmental, evolutionary, functioning neuroimaging, health psychology, learning and memory, neuroscience. *Total annual research expenditures:* $727,970. *Unit head:* Dr. Jane Ellen Smith, Department Chair, 505-277-4121, Fax: 505-277-1394. *Application contact:* Rikk Murphy, Graduate Program Coordinator, 505-277-5009, Fax: 505-277-1394, E-mail: advising@unm.edu.
Website: http://psych.unm.edu

University of New Mexico, Graduate Studies, Health Sciences Center, Program in Biomedical Sciences, Albuquerque, NM 87131-5196. Offers biochemistry and molecular biology (MS, PhD); cell biology and physiology (MS, PhD); molecular genetics and microbiology (MS, PhD); neuroscience (MS, PhD); pathology (MS, PhD); toxicology (MS, PhD). *Program availability:* Part-time. *Students:* Average age 29. 61 applicants, 16% accepted, 10 enrolled. In 2017, 11 master's, 14 doctorates awarded. Terminal master's awarded for partial completion of doctoral program. *Degree requirements:* For master's, thesis; for doctorate, comprehensive exam, thesis/dissertation, qualifying exam at the end of year 1/core curriculum. *Entrance requirements:* For master's and doctorate, GRE General Test, minimum undergraduate GPA of 3.0. Additional exam requirements/recommendations for international students: Required—TOEFL. *Application deadline:* For fall admission, 3/1 priority date for domestic and international students. Applications are processed on a rolling basis. Application fee: $50. Electronic applications accepted. *Financial support:* Fellowships, research assistantships with full tuition reimbursements, teaching assistantships, career-related internships or fieldwork, Federal Work-Study, institutionally sponsored loans, scholarships/grants, traineeships, health care benefits, and unspecified assistantships available. Financial award application deadline: 1/1; financial award applicants required to submit FAFSA. *Faculty research:* Infectious disease/immunity, cancer biology, cardiovascular and metabolic diseases, brain and behavioral illness, environmental health. *Unit head:* Dr. Helen J. Hathaway, Program Director, 505-272-1887, Fax: 505-272-2412, E-mail: hhathaway@salud.unm.edu. *Application contact:* Mary Fenton, Admissions Coordinator, 505-272-1887, Fax: 505-272-2412, E-mail: mfenton@salud.unm.edu.

The University of North Carolina at Chapel Hill, Graduate School, College of Arts and Sciences, Department of Psychology, Chapel Hill, NC 27599-3270. Offers behavioral neuroscience psychology (PhD); clinical psychology (PhD); cognitive psychology (PhD); developmental psychology (PhD); quantitative psychology (PhD); social psychology (PhD). *Accreditation:* APA. *Degree requirements:* For doctorate, comprehensive exam, thesis/dissertation. *Entrance requirements:* For doctorate, GRE General Test, minimum GPA of 3.0. Additional exam requirements/recommendations for international students: Required—TOEFL (minimum score 550 paper-based; 79 iBT), IELTS (minimum score 7). Electronic applications accepted. *Faculty research:* Expressed emotion, cognitive development, social cognitive neuroscience, human memory personality.

Neuroscience

University of North Texas Health Science Center at Fort Worth, Graduate School of Biomedical Sciences, Fort Worth, TX 76107-2699. Offers biochemistry and cancer biology (MS, PhD); biotechnology (MS); cell biology, immunology and microbiology (MS, PhD); clinical research management (MS); forensic genetics (MS); genetics (MS, PhD); integrative physiology (MS, PhD); medical sciences (MS); pharmaceutical sciences and pharmacotherapy (MS, PhD); pharmacology and neuroscience (MS, PhD); structural anatomy and rehabilitation sciences (MS, PhD); DO/MS; DO/PhD. Terminal master's awarded for partial completion of doctoral program. *Degree requirements:* For master's, thesis; for doctorate, thesis/dissertation. *Entrance requirements:* For master's and doctorate, GRE General Test. Additional exam requirements/recommendations for international students: Required—TOEFL. *Expenses:* Contact institution. *Faculty research:* Alzheimer's disease, aging, eye diseases, cancer, cardiovascular disease.

University of Oklahoma Health Sciences Center, College of Medicine and Graduate College, Graduate Programs in Medicine, Department of Neuroscience, Oklahoma City, OK 73190. Offers MS, PhD. *Degree requirements:* For doctorate, thesis/dissertation. *Entrance requirements:* For master's and doctorate, GRE General Test, 3 letters of recommendation. Additional exam requirements/recommendations for international students: Required—TOEFL.

University of Oregon, Graduate School, College of Arts and Sciences, Department of Biology, Eugene, OR 97403. Offers ecology and evolution (MA, MS, PhD); marine biology (MA, MS, PhD); molecular, cellular and genetic biology (PhD); neuroscience and development (PhD). Terminal master's awarded for partial completion of doctoral program. *Degree requirements:* For master's, thesis (for some programs); for doctorate, thesis/dissertation. *Entrance requirements:* For master's and doctorate, GRE General Test, minimum GPA of 3.2. Additional exam requirements/recommendations for international students: Required—TOEFL. *Faculty research:* Developmental neurobiology; evolution, population biology, and quantitative genetics; regulation of gene expression; biochemistry of marine organisms.

University of Pennsylvania, Perelman School of Medicine, Biomedical Graduate Studies, Graduate Group in Neuroscience, Philadelphia, PA 19104. Offers PhD, MD/PhD, VMD/PhD. *Faculty:* 169. *Students:* 121 full-time (68 women); includes 45 minority (2 Black or African American, non-Hispanic/Latino; 19 Asian, non-Hispanic/Latino; 18 Hispanic/Latino; 6 Two or more races, non-Hispanic/Latino), 6 international. 333 applicants, 15% accepted, 22 enrolled. In 2017, 16 doctorates awarded. *Degree requirements:* For doctorate, thesis/dissertation. *Entrance requirements:* For doctorate, GRE General Test. Additional exam requirements/recommendations for international students: Required—TOEFL. *Application deadline:* For fall admission, 12/1 for domestic and international students. Applications are processed on a rolling basis. Application fee: $80. Electronic applications accepted. *Financial support:* In 2017–18, 110 students received support. Fellowships, research assistantships, teaching assistantships, and tuition waivers available. *Faculty research:* Molecular and cellular neuroscience, behavioral neuroscience, developmental neurobiology, systems neuroscience and neurophysiology, neurochemistry. *Unit head:* Dr. Joshua Gold, Chair, 215-746-0028. *Application contact:* Christine Clay, Coordinator, 215-898-8048.
Website: http://www.med.upenn.edu/ngg

University of Pittsburgh, Kenneth P. Dietrich School of Arts and Sciences, Center for Neuroscience, Pittsburgh, PA 15260. Offers PhD. Program held jointly with School of Medicine. *Faculty:* 110 full-time (32 women). *Students:* 46 full-time (27 women); includes 9 minority (1 Black or African American, non-Hispanic/Latino; 4 Asian, non-Hispanic/Latino; 2 Hispanic/Latino; 2 Two or more races, non-Hispanic/Latino), 2 international. Average age 26. 189 applicants, 23% accepted, 12 enrolled. *Degree requirements:* For doctorate, comprehensive exam, thesis/dissertation. *Entrance requirements:* For doctorate, GRE, interview. Additional exam requirements/recommendations for international students: Required—TOEFL (minimum score 100 iBT), IELTS (minimum score 7). *Application deadline:* For fall admission, 12/1 priority date for domestic and international students. Application fee: $50. Electronic applications accepted. *Expenses:* $26,782 resident; $42,006 non-resident. *Financial support:* In 2017–18, 42 students received support, including 19 fellowships with full tuition reimbursements available (averaging $29,500 per year), 15 research assistantships with full tuition reimbursements available (averaging $29,500 per year), 1 teaching assistantship with full tuition reimbursement available (averaging $29,500 per year); traineeships also available. *Faculty research:* Behavioral/systems/cognitive, cell and molecular, development/plasticity/repair, neurobiology of pain. *Unit head:* Dr. Brian Davis, Co-Director, 412-645-9745, Fax: 412-648-1441, E-mail: bmd1@pitt.edu. *Application contact:* Lisa M. Summe, Graduate Program Administrator, 412-383-3260, Fax: 412-648-1441, E-mail: lms232@pitt.edu.
Website: http://cnup.neurobio.pitt.edu/

University of Puerto Rico–Río Piedras, College of Natural Sciences, Department of Biology, San Juan, PR 00931-3300. Offers ecology/systematics (MS, PhD); evolution/genetics (MS, PhD); molecular/cellular biology (MS, PhD); neuroscience (MS, PhD). *Program availability:* Part-time. *Degree requirements:* For master's, one foreign language, comprehensive exam, thesis; for doctorate, one foreign language, comprehensive exam, thesis/dissertation. *Entrance requirements:* For master's, GRE Subject Test, interview, minimum GPA of 3.0, letter of recommendation; for doctorate, GRE Subject Test, interview, master's degree, minimum GPA of 3.0, letter of recommendation. *Faculty research:* Environmental, poblational and systematic biology.

University of Rochester, School of Medicine and Dentistry, Graduate Programs in Medicine and Dentistry, Department of Neurobiology and Anatomy, Interdepartmental Programs in Neuroscience, Rochester, NY 14627. Offers PhD. Terminal master's awarded for partial completion of doctoral program. *Degree requirements:* For doctorate, one foreign language, thesis/dissertation, qualifying exam. *Entrance requirements:* For doctorate, GRE General Test.

University of South Dakota, Graduate School, Sanford School of Medicine and Graduate School, Biomedical Sciences Graduate Program, Program in Neuroscience, Vermillion, SD 57069. Offers MS, PhD. Terminal master's awarded for partial completion of doctoral program. *Degree requirements:* For master's, thesis; for doctorate, comprehensive exam, thesis/dissertation. *Entrance requirements:* For master's and doctorate, GRE General Test, minimum GPA of 3.0. Additional exam requirements/recommendations for international students: Required—TOEFL (minimum score 550 paper-based; 80 iBT), IELTS (minimum score 6). *Application deadline:* For fall admission, 4/15 for domestic students, 3/15 for international students. Applications are processed on a rolling basis. Application fee: $35. Electronic applications accepted. *Expenses:* Contact institution. *Financial support:* Fellowships with partial tuition reimbursements, research assistantships with partial tuition reimbursements, and unspecified assistantships available. Financial award application deadline: 4/15; financial award applicants required to submit FAFSA. *Faculty research:* Central nervous system learning, neural plasticity, respiratory control. *Unit head:* 605-658-6322, Fax: 605-677-6381, E-mail: biomed@usd.edu. *Application contact:* Graduate School, 605-658-6140, Fax: 605-677-6118.
Website: http://www.usd.edu/medicine/basic-biomedical-sciences

University of Southern California, Graduate School, Dana and David Dornsife College of Letters, Arts and Sciences, Program in Neuroscience, Los Angeles, CA 90089. Offers MS, PhD. M.S. degree is terminal degree only. Terminal master's awarded for partial completion of doctoral program. *Degree requirements:* For master's, research paper; for doctorate, comprehensive exam, thesis/dissertation, qualifying examination, dissertation defense. *Entrance requirements:* For doctorate, GRE, 3 letters of recommendation, personal statement, resume. Additional exam requirements/recommendations for international students: Required—TOEFL (minimum score 600 paper-based; 100 iBT). Electronic applications accepted. *Faculty research:* Cellular and molecular neurobiology, behavioral and systems neurobiology, cognitive neuroscience, computation neuroscience and neural engineering, neuroscience of aging.

University of South Florida, College of Arts and Sciences, Department of Psychology, Tampa, FL 33620-9951. Offers psychology (PhD), including clinical psychology, cognition, neuroscience and social psychology, industrial-organizational psychology. *Accreditation:* APA. *Faculty:* 30 full-time (11 women). *Students:* 79 full-time (53 women), 11 part-time (8 women); includes 12 minority (1 Black or African American, non-Hispanic/Latino; 5 Asian, non-Hispanic/Latino; 4 Hispanic/Latino; 2 Two or more races, non-Hispanic/Latino), 7 international. Average age 28. 393 applicants, 3% accepted, 11 enrolled. In 2017, 17 doctorates awarded. *Degree requirements:* For doctorate, comprehensive exam, thesis/dissertation, internship. *Entrance requirements:* For doctorate, GRE General Test, minimum upper-division GPA of 3.4, three letters of recommendation, personal goals statement. Additional exam requirements/recommendations for international students: Required—TOEFL (minimum score 550 paper-based; 79 iBT) or IELTS (minimum score 6.5). *Application deadline:* For fall admission, 12/1 priority date for domestic and international students. Application fee: $30. Electronic applications accepted. *Expenses:* Contact institution. *Financial support:* In 2017–18, 43 students received support, including 18 research assistantships with tuition reimbursements available (averaging $14,727 per year), 57 teaching assistantships with tuition reimbursements available (averaging $14,543 per year); tuition waivers (partial) and unspecified assistantships also available. Financial award applicants required to submit FAFSA. *Faculty research:* Clinical, cognitive, neuroscience, social, and industrial/organizational. *Total annual research expenditures:* $2 million. *Unit head:* Dr. Toru Shimizu, Chairperson, 813-974-0352, Fax: 813-974-4617, E-mail: shimizu@usf.edu. *Application contact:* Dr. Sandra Schneider, Professor and Graduate Program Director, 813-974-0928, E-mail: sandra@usf.edu.
Website: http://psychology.usf.edu/

University of South Florida, Innovative Education, Tampa, FL 33620-9951. Offers adult, career and higher education (Graduate Certificate), including college teaching, leadership in developing human resources, leadership in higher education; Africana studies (Graduate Certificate), including diasporas and health disparities, genocide and human rights; aging studies (Graduate Certificate), including gerontology; art research (Graduate Certificate), including museum studies; business foundations (Graduate Certificate); chemical and biomedical engineering (Graduate Certificate), including materials science and engineering, water, health and sustainability; child and family studies (Graduate Certificate), including positive behavior support; civil and industrial engineering (Graduate Certificate), including transportation systems analysis; community and family health (Graduate Certificate), including maternal and child health, social marketing and public health, violence and injury: prevention and intervention, women's health; criminology (Graduate Certificate), including criminal justice administration; data science for public administration (Graduate Certificate); digital humanities (Graduate Certificate); educational measurement and research (Graduate Certificate), including evaluation; English (Graduate Certificate), including comparative literary studies, creative writing, professional and technical communication; entrepreneurship (Graduate Certificate); environmental health (Graduate Certificate), including safety management; epidemiology and biostatistics (Graduate Certificate), including applied biostatistics, biostatistics, concepts and tools of epidemiology, epidemiology, epidemiology of infectious diseases; geography, environment and planning (Graduate Certificate), including community development, environmental policy and management, geographical information systems; geology (Graduate Certificate), including hydrogeology; global health (Graduate Certificate), including disaster management, global health and Latin American and Caribbean studies, global health practice, humanitarian assistance, infection control; government and international affairs (Graduate Certificate), including Cuban studies, globalization studies; health policy and management (Graduate Certificate), including health management and leadership, public health policy and programs; hearing specialist: early intervention (Graduate Certificate); industrial and management systems engineering (Graduate Certificate), including systems engineering, technology management; information studies (Graduate Certificate), including school library media specialist; information systems/decision sciences (Graduate Certificate), including analytics and business intelligence; instructional technology (Graduate Certificate), including distance education, Florida digital/virtual educator, instructional design, multimedia design, Web design; internal medicine, bioethics and medical humanities (Graduate Certificate), including biomedical ethics; Latin American and Caribbean studies (Graduate Certificate); leadership for coastal resiliency planning (Graduate Certificate); mass communications (Graduate Certificate), including multimedia journalism; mathematics and statistics (Graduate Certificate), including mathematics; medicine (Graduate Certificate), including aging and neuroscience, bioinformatics, biotechnology, brain fitness and memory management, clinical investigation, hand and upper limb rehabilitation, health informatics, health sciences, integrative weight management, intellectual property, medicine and gender, metabolic and nutritional medicine, metabolic cardiology, pharmacy sciences; national and competitive intelligence (Graduate Certificate); nursing (Graduate Certificate), including simulation based academic fellowship in advanced pain management; psychological and social foundations (Graduate Certificate), including career counseling, college teaching, diversity in education, mental health counseling, school counseling; public affairs (Graduate Certificate), including nonprofit management, public management, research administration; public health (Graduate Certificate), including assessing chemical toxicity and public health risks, health equity, pharmacoepidemiology, public health generalist, toxicology, translational research in adolescent behavioral health; public health practices (Graduate Certificate), including planning for healthy communities; rehabilitation and mental health counseling (Graduate Certificate), including integrative mental health care, marriage and family therapy, rehabilitation technology; secondary education (Graduate Certificate), including ESOL, foreign language education: culture and content, foreign language education: professional; social work (Graduate Certificate), including geriatric social work/clinical gerontology; special education (Graduate Certificate), including autism spectrum disorder, disabilities education: severe/profound; world languages (Graduate Certificate), including teaching English as a second language (TESL) or foreign language. *Unit head:* Dr. Cynthia DeLuca, Associate Vice President and Assistant Vice Provost, 813-974-3077, Fax: 813-974-7061, E-mail: deluca@usf.edu. *Application contact:* Owen Hooper, Director, Summer and Alternative Calendar Programs, 813-974-6917, E-mail: hooper@usf.edu.
Website: http://www.usf.edu/innovative-education/

University of South Florida, Morsani College of Medicine and College of Graduate Studies, Graduate Programs in Medical Sciences, Tampa, FL 33620-9951. Offers advanced athletic training (MS); athletic training (MS); bioinformatics and computational biology (MSBCB); biotechnology (MSB); health informatics (MSHI); medical sciences

(MSMS, PhD), including aging and neuroscience (MSMS), allergy, immunology and infectious disease (PhD), anatomy, biochemistry and molecular biology, clinical and translational research, health science (MSMS), interdisciplinary medical sciences (MSMS), medical microbiology and immunology (MSMS), metabolic and nutritional medicine (MSMS), microbiology and immunology (PhD), molecular medicine, molecular pharmacology and physiology (PhD), neuroscience (PhD), pathology and cell biology (PhD), women's health (MSMS). *Students:* 372 full-time (212 women), 216 part-time (142 women); includes 257 minority (78 Black or African American, non Hispanic/Latino; 1 American Indian or Alaska Native, non-Hispanic/Latino; 79 Asian, non-Hispanic/Latino; 84 Hispanic/Latino; 15 Two or more races, non-Hispanic/Latino), 62 international. Average age 28. 1,048 applicants, 46% accepted, 309 enrolled. In 2017, 351 master's, 56 doctorates awarded. Terminal master's awarded for partial completion of doctoral program. *Degree requirements:* For master's, comprehensive exam, thesis; for doctorate, comprehensive exam, thesis/dissertation. *Entrance requirements:* For master's, GRE General Test or GMAT, bachelor's degree or equivalent from regionally-accredited university with minimum GPA of 3.0 in upper-division sciences coursework; prerequisites in general biology, general chemistry, general physics, organic chemistry, quantitative analysis, and integral and differential calculus; for doctorate, GRE General Test, bachelor's degree from regionally-accredited university with minimum GPA of 3.0 in upper-division sciences coursework; 3 letters of recommendation; personal interview; 1-2 page personal statement; prerequisites in biology, chemistry, physics, organic chemistry, quantitative analysis, and integral/differential calculus. Additional exam requirements/recommendations for international students: Required—TOEFL (minimum score 550 paper-based; 79 iBT) or IELTS (minimum score 6.5). *Application deadline:* For fall admission, 2/1 priority date for domestic students, 2/1 for international students. Application fee: $30. Electronic applications accepted. *Expenses:* Contact institution. *Financial support:* In 2017–18, 109 students received support. *Faculty research:* Anatomy, biochemistry, cancer biology, cardiovascular disease, cell biology, immunology, microbiology, molecular biology, neuroscience, pharmacology, physiology. *Total annual research expenditures:* $45.3 million. *Unit head:* Dr. Michael Barber, Professor/Associate Dean for Graduate and Postdoctoral Affairs, 813-974-9908, Fax: 813-974-4317, E-mail: mbarber@health.usf.edu. *Application contact:* Dr. Eric Bennett, Graduate Director, PhD Program in Medical Sciences, 813-974-1545, Fax: 813-974-4317, E-mail: esbennet@health.usf.edu.
Website: http://health.usf.edu/nocms/medicine/graduatestudies/

The University of Texas at Austin, Graduate School, College of Liberal Arts, Department of Psychology, Austin, TX 78712-1111. Offers behavioral neuroscience (PhD); clinical psychology (PhD); cognitive systems (PhD); developmental psychology (PhD); individual differences and evolutionary psychology (PhD); perceptual systems (PhD); social psychology (PhD). *Accreditation:* APA. *Degree requirements:* For doctorate, thesis/dissertation. *Entrance requirements:* For doctorate, GRE General Test. Electronic applications accepted. *Faculty research:* Behavioral neuroscience, sensory neuroscience, evolutionary psychology, cognitive processes in psychopathology, cognitive processes and their development.

The University of Texas at Austin, Graduate School, The Institute for Neuroscience, Austin, TX 78712-1111. Offers PhD, MD/PhD. Terminal master's awarded for partial completion of doctoral program. *Degree requirements:* For doctorate, thesis/dissertation. *Entrance requirements:* For doctorate, GRE. Electronic applications accepted. *Faculty research:* Cellular/molecular biology, neurobiology, pharmacology, behavioral neuroscience.

The University of Texas at Dallas, School of Behavioral and Brain Sciences, Program in Cognition and Neuroscience, Richardson, TX 75080. Offers applied cognition and neuroscience (MS); cognition and neuroscience (PhD). *Program availability:* Part-time, evening/weekend. *Faculty:* 31 full-time (11 women), 1 part-time/adjunct (0 women). *Students:* 186 full-time (101 women), 31 part-time (21 women); includes 65 minority (10 Black or African American, non-Hispanic/Latino; 2 American Indian or Alaska Native, non-Hispanic/Latino; 26 Asian, non-Hispanic/Latino; 19 Hispanic/Latino; 8 Two or more races, non-Hispanic/Latino), 50 international. Average age 27. 193 applicants, 51% accepted, 70 enrolled. In 2017, 76 master's, 15 doctorates awarded. *Degree requirements:* For master's, internship; for doctorate, thesis/dissertation. *Entrance requirements:* For master's and doctorate, GRE General Test, minimum GPA of 3.0 in upper-level coursework in field. Additional exam requirements/recommendations for international students: Required—TOEFL (minimum score 550 paper-based). *Application deadline:* For fall admission, 7/15 for domestic students, 5/1 priority date for international students; for spring admission, 11/15 for domestic students, 9/1 priority date for international students. Applications are processed on a rolling basis. Application fee: $50 ($100 for international students). Electronic applications accepted. *Expenses:* Tuition, state resident: full-time $12,916; part-time $718 per credit hour. Tuition, nonresident: full-time $25,252; part-time $1403 per credit hour. *Financial support:* In 2017–18, 116 students received support, including 32 research assistantships with partial tuition reimbursements available (averaging $29,711 per year), 52 teaching assistantships with partial tuition reimbursements available (averaging $18,873 per year); fellowships, career-related internships or fieldwork, Federal Work-Study, institutionally sponsored loans, scholarships/grants, and unspecified assistantships also available. Support available to part-time students. Financial award application deadline: 4/30; financial award applicants required to submit FAFSA. *Faculty research:* Neural plasticity, neuroimaging, face recognition, cognitive and neurobiological mechanisms of human memory, treatment interventions for semantic memory retrieval problems. *Unit head:* Dr. Francesca Filbey, Area Head, 972-883-3311, Fax: 972-883-3491, E-mail: francesca.filbey@utdallas.edu.
Website: http://www.utdallas.edu/bbs/degrees/cn-degrees/

The University of Texas Health Science Center at Houston, MD Anderson UTHealth Graduate School, Houston, TX 77225-0036. Offers biochemistry and cell biology (PhD); biomedical sciences (MS); cancer biology (PhD); genetic counseling (MS); genetics and epigenetics (PhD); immunology (PhD); medical physics (MS, PhD); microbiology and infectious diseases (PhD); neuroscience (PhD); quantitative sciences (PhD); therapeutics and pharmacology (PhD); MD/PhD. Terminal master's awarded for partial completion of doctoral program. *Degree requirements:* For master's, thesis; for doctorate, thesis/dissertation. *Entrance requirements:* For master's and doctorate, GRE General Test. Additional exam requirements/recommendations for international students: Required—TOEFL. Electronic applications accepted. *Faculty research:* Biomedical sciences.

The University of Texas Health Science Center at San Antonio, Graduate School of Biomedical Sciences, Department of Pharmacology, San Antonio, TX 78229-3900. Offers neuroscience (PhD). *Degree requirements:* For doctorate, comprehensive exam, thesis/dissertation.

The University of Texas Medical Branch, Graduate School of Biomedical Sciences, Program in Neuroscience, Galveston, TX 77555. Offers PhD. *Degree requirements:* For doctorate, thesis/dissertation. *Entrance requirements:* For doctorate, GRE General Test. Additional exam requirements/recommendations for international students: Required—TOEFL (minimum score 550 paper-based). Electronic applications accepted.

The University of Texas Southwestern Medical Center, Southwestern Graduate School of Biomedical Sciences, Division of Basic Science, Program in Neuroscience, Dallas, TX 75390. Offers PhD. *Degree requirements:* For doctorate, thesis/dissertation, qualifying exam. *Entrance requirements:* For doctorate, GRE General Test, minimum GPA of 3.0. Additional exam requirements/recommendations for international students: Required—TOEFL. Electronic applications accepted. *Faculty research:* Ion channels, sensory transduction, membrane excitability and biophysics, synaptic transmission, developmental neurogenetics.

The University of Toledo, College of Graduate Studies, College of Medicine and Life Sciences, Department of Neurosciences, Toledo, OH 43606-3390. Offers MSBS, PhD, MD/MSBS, MD/PhD. Terminal master's awarded for partial completion of doctoral program. *Degree requirements:* For master's, thesis, qualifying exam; for doctorate, thesis/dissertation, qualifying exam. *Entrance requirements:* For master's and doctorate, GRE, minimum undergraduate GPA of 3.0, three letters of recommendation, statement of purpose, transcripts from all prior institutions attended, resume. Additional exam requirements/recommendations for international students: Required—TOEFL (minimum score 550 paper-based; 80 iBT). Electronic applications accepted.

University of Utah, Graduate School, College of Social and Behavioral Science, Department of Psychology, Salt Lake City, UT 84112. Offers clinical psychology (PhD); psychology (PhD), including cognitive neuroscience, developmental psychology, social psychology. *Accreditation:* APA. *Faculty:* 32 full-time (15 women), 11 part-time/adjunct (7 women). *Students:* 53 full-time (36 women), 10 part-time (7 women); includes 10 minority (2 Black or African American, non-Hispanic/Latino; 1 Asian, non-Hispanic/Latino; 4 Hispanic/Latino; 3 Two or more races, non-Hispanic/Latino), 5 international. Average age 26. 295 applicants, 8% accepted, 13 enrolled. In 2017, 11 doctorates awarded. *Entrance requirements:* For doctorate, GRE General Test. Additional exam requirements/recommendations for international students: Required—TOEFL (minimum score 500 paper-based). Application fee: $55 ($65 for international students). Electronic applications accepted. *Expenses:* All admitted students are guaranteed funding and full tuition benefit for four years. *Financial support:* In 2017–18, 51 students received support, including 2 fellowships with full tuition reimbursements available (averaging $17,000 per year), 16 research assistantships with full tuition reimbursements available (averaging $16,800 per year), 30 teaching assistantships with full tuition reimbursements available (averaging $16,800 per year); career-related internships or fieldwork, health care benefits, and unspecified assistantships also available. Financial award application deadline: 4/15; financial award applicants required to submit FAFSA. *Faculty research:* Cognitive neuroscience, health, social cognition, psychopathology, cognitive and social development. *Total annual research expenditures:* $1.9 million. *Unit head:* Dr. Lisa G. Aspinwall, Chair, 801-581-8925, Fax: 801-581-5841, E-mail: lisa.aspinwall@utah.edu. *Application contact:* Nancy Seegmiller, Program Manager, 801-581-8925, Fax: 801-581-5841, E-mail: nancy.seegmiller@psych.utah.edu.
Website: http://www.psych.utah.edu/

University of Utah, School of Medicine and Graduate School, Graduate Programs in Medicine, Program in Neuroscience, Salt Lake City, UT 84112-1107. Offers PhD. *Degree requirements:* For doctorate, thesis/dissertation. *Entrance requirements:* For doctorate, GRE General Test, minimum GPA of 3.0. Additional exam requirements/recommendations for international students: Required—TOEFL (minimum score 500 paper-based); Recommended—TWE (minimum score 6). Electronic applications accepted. *Faculty research:* Brain and behavioral neuroscience, cellular neuroscience, molecular neuroscience, neurobiology of disease, developmental neuroscience.

University of Vermont, Graduate College, Cross-College Interdisciplinary Program, Graduate Program in Neuroscience, Burlington, VT 05405. Offers PhD. *Students:* 26 (14 women); includes 1 minority (Black or African American, non-Hispanic/Latino), 6 international. Average age 28. 35 applicants, 23% accepted, 4 enrolled. In 2017, 1 doctorate awarded. *Degree requirements:* For doctorate, thesis/dissertation. *Entrance requirements:* For doctorate, GRE General Test. Additional exam requirements/recommendations for international students: Required—TOEFL (minimum score 550 paper-based, 100 iBT) or IELTS (7). *Application deadline:* For fall admission, 12/1 for domestic and international students. Application fee: $65. Electronic applications accepted. *Expenses:* Tuition, state resident: full-time $11,628; part-time $646 per credit. Tuition, nonresident: full-time $29,340; part-time $1630 per credit. *Required fees:* $1994; $10 per credit. Tuition and fees vary according to course load and program. *Financial support:* In 2017–18, 26 teaching assistantships with full tuition reimbursements (averaging $28,000 per year) were awarded; research assistantships and health care benefits also available. Financial award application deadline: 3/1. *Unit head:* Dr. Anthony Morielli, Director, 802-656-2230, E-mail: anthony.morielli@uvm.edu. *Application contact:* Carrie Perkins, Program Administrator, 802-656-1178, E-mail: neurogp@uvm.edu.
Website: https://www.uvm.edu/neurosciencegrad

University of Virginia, School of Medicine, Department of Neuroscience, Charlottesville, VA 22903. Offers PhD, MD/PhD. *Faculty:* 12 full-time (3 women). *Students:* 32 full-time (14 women); includes 7 minority (2 Black or African American, non-Hispanic/Latino; 4 Asian, non-Hispanic/Latino; 1 Hispanic/Latino), 2 international. Average age 27. In 2017, 7 doctorates awarded. *Degree requirements:* For doctorate, thesis/dissertation. *Entrance requirements:* For doctorate, GRE General Test, 2 letters of recommendation. Additional exam requirements/recommendations for international students: Required—TOEFL. *Application deadline:* For fall admission, 4/15 for domestic and international students. Applications are processed on a rolling basis. Application fee: $60. Electronic applications accepted. *Financial support:* Application deadline: 1/15; applicants required to submit FAFSA. *Unit head:* Dr. Jonathan Kipnis, Chair, 434-982-3858, Fax: 434-982-4380, E-mail: uva-ngp@virginia.edu. *Application contact:* Biomedical Sciences Graduate Studies, E-mail: bims@virginia.edu.
Website: http://www.medicine.virginia.edu/basic-science/departments/neurosci/home-page

University of Washington, Graduate School, College of Arts and Sciences, Department of Psychology, Seattle, WA 98195. Offers animal behavior (PhD); applied child and adolescent psychology: prevention and treatment (MA); behavioral neuroscience (PhD); clinical psychology (PhD); cognition and perception (PhD); developmental psychology (PhD); quantitative psychology (PhD); social psychology and personality (PhD). *Accreditation:* APA (one or more programs are accredited). *Degree requirements:* For doctorate, thesis/dissertation. *Entrance requirements:* For doctorate, GRE General Test, minimum GPA of 3.0. Electronic applications accepted. *Faculty research:* Addictive behaviors, artificial intelligence, child psychopathology, mechanisms and development of vision, physiology of ingestive behaviors.

The University of Western Ontario, Faculty of Graduate Studies, Biosciences Division, Department of Clinical Neurological Sciences, London, ON N6A 5B8, Canada. Offers M Sc, PhD. Terminal master's awarded for partial completion of doctoral program. *Degree requirements:* For master's, thesis; for doctorate, thesis/dissertation. *Entrance requirements:* For master's, honors degree or equivalent, minimum B+ average; for doctorate, master's degree, minimum B+ average. *Faculty research:* Behavioral neuroscience, neural regeneration and degeneration, visual development, human motor function.

University of Wisconsin–Madison, Graduate School, College of Letters and Science, Department of Psychology, Program in Cognitive Neurosciences, Madison, WI 53706-

1380. Offers PhD. *Degree requirements:* For doctorate, comprehensive exam, thesis/dissertation. *Entrance requirements:* For doctorate, GRE General Test, minimum undergraduate GPA of 3.0. Additional exam requirements/recommendations for international students: Required—TOEFL. Electronic applications accepted.

University of Wisconsin–Madison, School of Medicine and Public Health, Neuroscience Training Program, Madison, WI 53706. Offers PhD, MD/PhD, PhD/JD. *Application contact:* 608-262-4932, E-mail: ntp@mailplus.wisc.edu.
Website: http://ntp.neuroscience.wisc.edu/

Virginia Commonwealth University, Medical College of Virginia-Professional Programs, School of Medicine, Graduate Program in Neuroscience, Richmond, VA 23284-9005. Offers PhD. Program offered with Departments of Anatomy, Biochemistry and Molecular Biophysics, Pharmacology and Toxicology, and Physiology. *Entrance requirements:* For doctorate, GRE or MCAT. Additional exam requirements/recommendations for international students: Required—TOEFL (minimum score 600 paper-based; 100 iBT). Electronic applications accepted.

Virginia Commonwealth University, Medical College of Virginia-Professional Programs, School of Medicine, Graduate Programs in Medicine, Department of Pharmacology and Toxicology, Richmond, VA 23284-9005. Offers neuroscience (PhD); pharmacology (Certificate); pharmacology and toxicology (MS, PhD); MD/PhD. Terminal master's awarded for partial completion of doctoral program. *Degree requirements:* For master's, thesis; for doctorate, thesis/dissertation, comprehensive oral and written exams. *Entrance requirements:* For master's and doctorate, GRE or MCAT. Additional exam requirements/recommendations for international students: Required—TOEFL (minimum score 600 paper-based; 100 iBT). Electronic applications accepted. *Faculty research:* Drug abuse, drug metabolism, pharmacodynamics, peptide synthesis, receptor mechanisms.

Wake Forest University, School of Medicine and Graduate School of Arts and Sciences, Graduate Programs in Medicine, Interdisciplinary Program in Neuroscience, Winston-Salem, NC 27109. Offers PhD, MD/PhD. *Degree requirements:* For doctorate, thesis/dissertation. *Entrance requirements:* For doctorate, GRE General Test. Additional exam requirements/recommendations for international students: Required—TOEFL. Electronic applications accepted. *Faculty research:* Neurobiology of substance abuse, learning and memory, aging, sensory neurobiology, nervous system development.

Washington State University, College of Veterinary Medicine, Program in Neuroscience, Pullman, WA 99164-6520. Offers MS, PhD. *Program availability:* Part-time. *Faculty:* 54 full-time (15 women). *Students:* 22 full-time (11 women); includes 8 minority (5 Asian, non-Hispanic/Latino; 3 Hispanic/Latino). Average age 28. 57 applicants, 14% accepted, 3 enrolled. In 2017, 1 master's, 4 doctorates awarded. Terminal master's awarded for partial completion of doctoral program. *Degree requirements:* For master's, thesis, written exam; for doctorate, thesis/dissertation, written exam, oral exam. *Entrance requirements:* For master's and doctorate, GRE General Test, minimum GPA of 3.0. Additional exam requirements/recommendations for international students: Required—TOEFL (minimum score 550 paper-based; 100 iBT). *Application deadline:* For fall admission, 12/15 priority date for domestic and international students. Applications are processed on a rolling basis. Application fee: $75. Electronic applications accepted. *Financial support:* In 2017–18, 22 students received support, including 12 research assistantships with full tuition reimbursements available (averaging $25,614 per year), 10 teaching assistantships with full tuition reimbursements available (averaging $25,614 per year); fellowships, scholarships/grants, health care benefits, and unspecified assistantships also available. Financial award application deadline: 1/31. *Faculty research:* Addiction, sleep and performance, body weight and energy balance, emotion and well being, learning and memory, reproduction, vision, movement. *Total annual research expenditures:* $3.5 million. *Unit head:* Dr. Steve Simasko, Chair, 509-335-6624, Fax: 509-335-4650, E-mail: simasko@vetmed.wsu.edu. *Application contact:* Becky Morton, Department Manager, 509-335-6621, Fax: 509-335-4650, E-mail: grad.neuro@vetmed.wsu.edu.
Website: http://ipn.vetmed.wsu.edu/neuroscience/graduate

Washington University in St. Louis, The Graduate School, Department of Philosophy, Program in Philosophy-Neuroscience-Psychology, St. Louis, MO 63130-4899. Offers PhD. *Degree requirements:* For doctorate, thesis/dissertation. *Entrance requirements:* For doctorate, GRE General Test, sample of written work. Additional exam requirements/recommendations for international students: Required—TOEFL. Electronic applications accepted. *Faculty research:* Philosophy of mind and language with a special emphasis on the philosophical dimensions of psychology, neuroscience, and linguistics.

Washington University in St. Louis, The Graduate School, Division of Biology and Biomedical Sciences, Program in Neurosciences, St. Louis, MO 63130-4899. Offers PhD. *Degree requirements:* For doctorate, thesis/dissertation. *Entrance requirements:* For doctorate, GRE General Test, GRE Subject Test. Additional exam requirements/recommendations for international students: Required—TOEFL. Electronic applications accepted. *Faculty research:* Neurobiology, neurology, functional imaging, behavior, cognition, computational neuroscience, electrophysiology, sensory systems, motor systems, neuroglia, neuronal development, learning, memory, language, synaptic plasticity, mind, consciousness, neurodegeneration, diseases of the nervous system, neuronal injury, clinical neuroscience, motor control, biological rhythms, connectivity mapping.

Wayne State University, College of Liberal Arts and Sciences, Department of Psychology, Detroit, MI 48202. Offers behavioral and cognitive neuroscience (PhD); clinical psychology (PhD); developmental science (PhD); industrial/organizational psychology (MA, PhD); social personality (PhD). Doctoral program admits for fall only. *Accreditation:* APA (one or more programs are accredited). *Faculty:* 38. *Students:* 94 full-time (63 women), 43 part-time (29 women); includes 23 minority (6 Black or African American, non-Hispanic/Latino; 3 Asian, non-Hispanic/Latino; 10 Hispanic/Latino; 4 Two or more races, non-Hispanic/Latino), 12 international. Average age 27. 478 applicants, 11% accepted, 39 enrolled. In 2017, 29 master's, 27 doctorates awarded. Terminal master's awarded for partial completion of doctoral program. *Degree requirements:* For master's, thesis (for some programs); for doctorate, thesis/dissertation, training assignments. *Entrance requirements:* For master's, GRE General Test, minimum undergraduate upper-division cumulative GPA of 3.0, courses in psychology and statistics; for doctorate, GRE General Test, bachelor's, master's, or other advanced degree; at least twelve credits in psychology with minimum GPA of 3.0; courses in laboratory psychology and statistical methods in psychology; at least three letters of recommendation; statement of purpose. Additional exam requirements/recommendations for international students: Required—TOEFL (minimum score 550 paper-based; 79 iBT), TWE (minimum score 5.5), Michigan English Language Assessment Battery (minimum score 85); Recommended—IELTS (minimum score 6.5). Application fee: $50. Electronic applications accepted. *Expenses:* Tuition, state resident: full-time $10,224; part-time $638.98 per credit hour. Tuition, nonresident: full-time $22,145; part-time $1384.04 per credit hour. Tuition and fees vary according to course load and program. *Financial support:* In 2017–18, 90 students received support, including 13 fellowships with tuition reimbursements available (averaging $11,212 per year), 8 research assistantships with tuition reimbursements available (averaging $18,534 per year), 50 teaching assistantships with tuition reimbursements available (averaging $18,534 per year); scholarships/grants, health care benefits, and unspecified assistantships also available. Financial award applicants required to submit FAFSA. *Faculty research:* Behavioral neuroscience, cognitive/neuroscience of development and aging research, children, adolescents, and family research, cognition research, emotion research, health psychology research, homelessness and poverty research, memory research, neuropsychology research, personality/cognition, relationships research, substance use and abuse research, workplace adaptation, well-being and evaluation research. *Unit head:* Boris Baltes, PhD, Chair/Professor, 313-577-2803, E-mail: b.baltes@wayne.edu. *Application contact:* Alia Allen, Academic Services Officer, 313-577-2823, E-mail: aallen@wayne.edu.
Website: http://clas.wayne.edu/psychology/

Wayne State University, School of Medicine, Office of Biomedical Graduate Programs, Detroit, MI 48202. Offers anatomy and cell biology (MS, PhD); basic medical sciences (MS); biochemistry and molecular biology (MS, PhD); cancer biology (MS, PhD); clinical and translational science (Graduate Certificate); family medicine and public health sciences (MPH, Graduate Certificate), including public health practice; genetic counseling (MS); immunology and microbiology (MS, PhD); medical physics (MS, PhD, Graduate Certificate); medical research (MS); molecular medicine and genomics (MS, PhD), including molecular genetics and genomics; pathology (PhD); pharmacology (MS, PhD); physiology (MS, PhD), including physiology, reproductive sciences (PhD); psychiatry and behavioral neurosciences (PhD), including translational neuroscience; MD/MPH; MD/PhD; MPH/MA; MSW/MPH. *Program availability:* Part-time, evening/weekend. *Students:* 268 full-time (152 women), 117 part-time (59 women); includes 108 minority (19 Black or African American, non-Hispanic/Latino; 1 American Indian or Alaska Native, non-Hispanic/Latino; 62 Asian, non-Hispanic/Latino; 9 Hispanic/Latino; 17 Two or more races, non-Hispanic/Latino), 48 international. Average age 26. 1,133 applicants, 21% accepted, 151 enrolled. In 2017, 70 master's, 25 doctorates, 10 other advanced degrees awarded. Terminal master's awarded for partial completion of doctoral program. *Degree requirements:* For master's, thesis (for some programs); for doctorate, thesis/dissertation. *Entrance requirements:* For master's, doctorate, and Graduate Certificate, GRE. Additional exam requirements/recommendations for international students: Required—TOEFL (minimum score 550 paper-based; 100 iBT), Michigan English Language Assessment Battery (minimum score 85); Recommended—IELTS (minimum score 6.5), TWE (minimum score 5.5). *Application deadline:* For fall admission, 2/1 for domestic and international students. Applications are processed on a rolling basis. Application fee: $50. Electronic applications accepted. *Expenses:* Contact institution. *Financial support:* In 2017–18, 177 students received support, including 64 fellowships with full tuition reimbursements available (averaging $24,388 per year), 79 research assistantships with full tuition reimbursements available (averaging $26,894 per year); scholarships/grants, traineeships, and health care benefits also available. *Faculty research:* Cancer biology, neurosciences, vision sciences, molecular biology, pathology, physiology, pharmacology, public health, medical physics. *Unit head:* Dr. Daniel A. Walz, Associate Dean for Biomedical Graduate Programs, 313-577-1455, Fax: 313-577-8796, E-mail: gradprogs@med.wayne.edu.
Website: https://www.med.wayne.edu/biomedical-graduate-programs/

Weill Cornell Medicine, Weill Cornell Graduate School of Medical Sciences, Neuroscience Program, New York, NY 10065. Offers MS, PhD. Terminal master's awarded for partial completion of doctoral program. *Degree requirements:* For master's, comprehensive exam; for doctorate, thesis/dissertation, final exam. *Entrance requirements:* For doctorate, GRE General Test, undergraduate training in biology, organic chemistry, physics, and mathematics. Additional exam requirements/recommendations for international students: Required—TOEFL. Electronic applications accepted. *Faculty research:* Neural disease, synaptic transmission, developmental neurobiology and regeneration, vision and computational and systems neuroscience, neuropharmacology.

Wilfrid Laurier University, Faculty of Graduate and Postdoctoral Studies, Faculty of Science, Department of Psychology, Waterloo, ON N2L 3C5, Canada. Offers behavioral neuroscience (M Sc, PhD); cognitive neuroscience (M Sc, PhD); community psychology (MA, PhD); social and developmental psychology (MA, PhD). *Program availability:* Part-time. *Degree requirements:* For master's, thesis; for doctorate, thesis/dissertation. *Entrance requirements:* For master's, GRE General Test, honors BA or the equivalent in psychology, minimum B average in undergraduate course work; for doctorate, GRE General Test, master's degree, minimum A- average. Additional exam requirements/recommendations for international students: Required—TOEFL (minimum score 89 iBT). Electronic applications accepted. *Faculty research:* Brain and cognition, community psychology, social and developmental psychology.

Wright State University, Graduate School, College of Science and Mathematics, Department of Neuroscience, Cell Biology, and Physiology, Dayton, OH 45435. Offers anatomy (MS); physiology and neuroscience (MS). *Degree requirements:* For master's, thesis optional. *Entrance requirements:* Additional exam requirements/recommendations for international students: Required—TOEFL. *Faculty research:* Reproductive cell biology, neurobiology of pain, neurohistochemistry.

Yale University, Graduate School of Arts and Sciences, Department of Psychology, New Haven, CT 06520. Offers behavioral neuroscience (PhD); clinical psychology (PhD); cognitive psychology (PhD); developmental psychology (PhD); social/personality psychology (PhD). *Accreditation:* APA. *Degree requirements:* For doctorate, thesis/dissertation. *Entrance requirements:* For doctorate, GRE General Test.

Yale University, Graduate School of Arts and Sciences, Interdepartmental Neuroscience Program, New Haven, CT 06520. Offers PhD. *Degree requirements:* For doctorate, thesis/dissertation. *Entrance requirements:* For doctorate, GRE General Test. *Expenses:* Contact institution.

Yale University, Yale School of Medicine and Graduate School of Arts and Sciences, Combined Program in Biological and Biomedical Sciences (BBS), Neuroscience Track, New Haven, CT 06520. Offers PhD, MD/PhD. *Degree requirements:* For doctorate, thesis/dissertation. *Entrance requirements:* For doctorate, GRE General Test. Additional exam requirements/recommendations for international students: Required—TOEFL. Electronic applications accepted.

UNIFORMED SERVICES UNIVERSITY OF THE HEALTH SCIENCES

F. Edward Hébert School of Medicine
Graduate Program in Neuroscience

Program of Study

The Uniformed Services University of the Health Sciences (USUHS) offers the Graduate Program in Neuroscience, a broadly based interdisciplinary program leading to the Ph.D. degree in neuroscience. Courses and research training are provided by the neuroscience faculty members, who hold primary appointments in the Departments of Anatomy, Physiology, and Genetics; Biochemistry; Medical and Clinical Psychology; Microbiology and Immunology; Neurology; Pathology; Pediatrics; Pharmacology; and Psychiatry at the University. The program permits considerable flexibility in the choice of courses and research areas; training programs are tailored to meet the individual requirements of each student. The program is designed for students with strong undergraduate training in the physical sciences, biology, or psychology who wish to pursue a professional career in neuroscience research. Integrated instruction in the development, structure, function, and pathology of the nervous system and its interaction with the environment is provided. Students in the program conduct their research under the direction of neuroscience faculty members in laboratories that are located in the medical school. During the first year of study, students begin formal course work. Each student is required to take laboratory training rotations in the research laboratories of program faculty members. By the end of the first year, students select a research area and a faculty thesis adviser. During the second year, students complete requirements for advancement to candidacy, including required course work and passage of the qualifying examination. After advancement to candidacy, each student develops an original research project and prepares and defends a written dissertation under the guidance of his or her faculty adviser and advisory committee.

Research Facilities

Each academic department at the University is provided with laboratories for the support of a variety of research projects. Neuroscience research laboratories available to students are suitable for research in most areas of neuroscience, including behavioral studies, electrophysiology, molecular and cellular neurobiology, neuroanatomy, neurochemistry, neuropathology, neuropharmacology, and neurophysiology. High-resolution electron microscopes, confocal microscopes, two photon microscopes, deconvolution wide-field fluorescence microscopes, a central resource facility providing custom synthesis of oligonucleotides and peptides and DNA sequencing, RNA sequencing, centralized animal facilities, computer support, a medical library, and a learning resources center are available within the University.

Financial Aid

USUHS provides an attractive package of financial support that is administered as a federal salary. This support is available on a competitive basis to all civilian graduate students. Awards are made on an annual basis and are renewable for up to three years. For the 2018 academic year, financial support for graduate students is $44,981. In addition to this base support, health insurance and transit benefits are provided if needed.

Cost of Study

Graduate students in the neuroscience program are not required to pay any tuition or fees. Civilian students incur no obligation to the United States government for service after completion of their graduate training program. Students are required to carry health insurance.

Living and Housing Costs

There is a reasonable supply of affordable rental housing in the area. The University does not have housing for graduate students. Students are responsible for making their own arrangements for accommodations. Costs in the Washington, D.C., area are comparable to those in other major metropolitan areas.

Student Group

The neuroscience graduate program is an active and growing graduate program; approximately 31 students are enrolled. The Uniformed Services University (USU) also has Ph.D. programs in departmentally based basic biomedical sciences, as well as interdisciplinary graduate programs in molecular and cell biology and in emerging infectious diseases. In addition to the graduate and medical programs in the medical school, the nursing school has graduate programs for nurse practitioners and nurse anesthetists.

Student Outcomes

Graduates hold faculty, research associate, postdoctoral, science policy, and other positions in universities, medical schools, government, and industrial research institutions. Over 60 Ph.D.'s have been awarded since 1998. Currently 3 USU neuroscience graduates hold faculty positions within the Neuroscience Graduate Program.

Location

Metropolitan Washington has a population of about 5 million residents in the District of Columbia and the surrounding areas of Maryland and Virginia. The region is a center of education and research and is home to five major universities, four medical schools, the National Library of Medicine and the National Institutes of Health (next to the USUHS campus), Walter Reed National Military Medical Center, the Armed Forces Institute of Pathology, the Library of Congress, the Smithsonian Institution, the National Bureau of Standards, and many other private and government research centers. Many cultural advantages of the area include the theater, a major symphony orchestra, major league sports, and world-famous museums. The Metro subway system has a station near campus and provides a convenient connection from the University to museums and cultural attractions of downtown Washington. The University is within an easy distance of three major airports, Baltimore Washington International, Reagan International, and Dulles International. Both Reagan and Dulles International airports are accessible from the campus via Metro subway. For outdoor activities, the Blue Ridge Mountains, the Chesapeake Bay, and the Atlantic coast beaches are all within a few hours of driving distance.

The University

The University was established by Congress in 1972 to provide a comprehensive education in medicine to those who demonstrate potential for careers as Medical Corps officers in the uniformed services. Graduate programs in the basic medical sciences are offered to both civilian and military students and are an essential part of the academic environment at the University. The University is located in proximity to major research facilities, including the National Institutes of Health (NIH), the National Library of Medicine, Walter Reed Army Medical Center at the National Naval Medical Center, the Armed Forces Institute of Pathology, the National Institute of Standards and Technology, and numerous biotechnology companies.

Uniformed Services University subscribes fully to the policy of equal educational opportunity and accepts students on a competitive basis without regard to race, color, sex, age, or creed.

Applying

Civilian applicants are accepted as full-time students only. Each applicant must have a bachelor's degree from an accredited academic institution. A strong background in science with courses in several of the following disciplines—biochemistry, biology, chemistry, mathematics, physics, physiology, and psychology—is desirable. Applicants must arrange for official transcripts of all prior college-level courses taken and their GRE scores (taken within the last two years) to be sent to the Office of Graduate Education. Students may elect to submit scores obtained in one or more GRE Subject Tests (from the subject areas listed above) in support of their application, but this is not required. Applicants must also arrange for letters of recommendation from 3 people who are familiar with their academic work to be sent to the University. For full consideration and evaluation for stipend support, completed applications should be received before **December 1** for matriculation in late August. Late applications are evaluated on a space-available basis. There is no application fee. Students may complete an application at https://registrar.usuhs.edu.

Correspondence and Information

For information about the neuroscience program:

Sharon L. Juliano, Ph.D.
Director, Graduate Program in Neuroscience
Uniformed Services University
4301 Jones Bridge Road
Bethesda, Maryland 20814-4799
United States
Phone: 301-295-3642
Fax: 301-295-1996
E-mail: sharon.juliano@usuhs.edu
Website: http://www.usuhs.edu/nes/

Tina Finley
Administrative Officer
Uniformed Services University
4301 Jones Bridge Road
Bethesda, Maryland 20814-4799
United States
Phone: 301-295-3642
E-mail: netina.finley@usuhs.edu

THE FACULTY AND THEIR RESEARCH

Denes V. Agoston, M.D., Ph.D.; Professor, Department of Anatomy, Physiology, and Genetics. The pathobiology of traumatic brain injury (TBI); clinical and experimental studies; blood and CSF based protein biomarkers of post-traumatic epilepsy and repeated mild TBI.

Juanita Anders, Ph.D.; Professor, Department of Anatomy, Physiology, and Genetics. Innovative therapies for neuropathic pain and regeneration of the injured peripheral nervous systems; light-cellular interaction and mechanistic basis of photobiomodulation.

Uniformed Services University of the Health Sciences

Regina Armstrong, Ph.D.; Professor, Department of Anatomy, Physiology, and Genetics, and Director of Translational Research, Center for Neuroscience and Regenerative Medicine. Cellular and molecular mechanisms of neural stem/progenitor cell development and regeneration in demyelinating diseases and brain injury models.

David Benedek, M.D.; Professor and Chair, Department of Psychiatry. Pathology of the traumatic stress response and mitigation strategies at the individual, community, and population levels.

Maria F. Braga, D.D.S., Ph.D.; Professor, Department of Anatomy, Physiology, and Genetics. Cellular and molecular mechanisms regulating neuronal excitability in the amygdala; pathophysiology of anxiety disorders and epilepsy.

Barrington G. Burnett, Ph.D.; Associate Professor, Department of Anatomy, Physiology, and Genetics. The ubiquitin-proteasome system in neuronal maintenance and neurodegeneration.

Howard Bryant, Ph.D.; Associate Professor, Department of Anatomy, Physiology, and Genetics. Electrophysiology of vascular smooth muscle.

Kimberly Byrnes, Ph.D.; Associate Professor, Department of Anatomy, Physiology, and Genetics. Microglial and macrophage-based chronic inflammation after traumatic brain and spinal cord injury; noninvasive imaging of post-injury metabolic and inflammatory events.

Kwang Choi, Ph.D.; Assistant Professor, Department of Psychiatry. Translational research on posttraumatic stress and substance use disorders using intravenous drug self-administration, Pavlovian fear conditioning, and PET brain imaging in rodents.

Thomas Côté, Ph.D.; Associate Professor, Department of Pharmacology. Mu opioid receptor interaction with GTP-binding proteins and RGS proteins.

Brian Cox, Ph.D.; Professor, Department of Pharmacology. Synaptic plasticity and its role in stress, brain injury, and responses to drug administration; biomarkers for brain injury.

Clifton Dalgard, Ph.D.; Associate Professor, Core Director, The American Genome Center, Ph.D. C.L.S., Uniformed Services University of the Health Sciences, 2005. Identification of a Small Molecule That Selectively Inhibits ERG-Positive Cancer Cell Growth. *Cancer Research* 78(13), 2018.

Bernard Dardzinski, Ph.D.; Associate Professor, Radiology; Director and Principal Investigator, Translational Imaging Facility (TIF); Center for Neuroscience and Regenerative Medicine; diagnostic medical imaging physicist. Developing non-invasive imaging biomarkers to diagnose disease and evaluate therapeutic efficacy.

Patricia A. Deuster, Ph.D., M.P.H.; Professor, Department of Military and Emergency Medicine. Mechanisms of neuroendocrine and immune activation with stress.

Dara L. Dickstein, Ph.D., Adjunct Assistant Professor, Department of Pathology, Center for Neuroscience and Regenerative Medicine, Synaptic plasticity and its role in neurodegeneration in traumatic brain injury and radiation exposure.

Martin Doughty, Ph.D., Associate Professor, Department of Anatomy, Physiology, and Genetics. Optimizing induced pluripotent stem cells (iPSCs) for cell replacement therapy to treat traumatic brain injury (TBI); identifying transcriptional programs that function in cerebellar neurogenesis and pattern formation.

Ying-Hong Feng, Associate Professor, M.D., Ph.D. Angiotensin receptor and signal transduction.

Zygmunt Galdzicki, Ph.D.; Professor, Department of Anatomy, Physiology, and Genetics. Molecular and electrophysiological approach to understand mental retardation in Down syndrome; neuroepigenetics and role of stress and brain trauma in neurodegenerative disorders.

Neil Grunberg, Ph.D.; Professor, Military and Emergency Medicine, Medical and Clinical Psychology, Neuroscience. Nicotine and tobacco; stress; TBI; PTSD; leadership.

Diego Iacono, M.D., Ph.D., Associate Professor Department of Neurology and Deputy Director BTR-CNRM: "CTE lesions in non-contact sports military brains."

Sharon Juliano, Ph.D.; Professor, Department of Anatomy, Physiology, and Genetics. Assessing levels of glial reactivity and inflammation in the neocortex of a gyrencephalic animal after traumatic brain injury. Evaluating changes in the expression of various forms of tau and phosphorylated tau as result of injury involving blast. Live imaging of neuronal migration.

Jason Lees, Ph.D.; Assistant Professor, Department of Medicine. Neuroimmunology; Inflammatory Demyelination."

Fabio Leonessa, M.D.; Research Assistant Professor, Department of Neurology. Pathobiology and biomarkers of blast-related neurotrauma.

He Li, M.D., Ph.D.; Associate Professor, Department of Psychiatry. Neurobiological basis of post-traumatic stress disorder; synaptic metaplasticity and neuronal signaling in traumatic stressed amygdala circuitry.

Geoffrey Ling, M.D., Ph.D.; Professor, Departments of Anesthesiology, Neurology, and Surgery. Novel therapeutics and diagnostic tools for traumatic brain injury and hemorrhagic shock; mechanisms of cellular injury and edema formation in traumatic brain injury.

Irwin Lucki, Ph.D.; Professor and Chair, Department of Pharmacology and Molecular Therapeutics. Behavioral models and neural mechanisms of rapidly acting antidepressant drugs (ketamine and kappa opioid receptor antagonists) developed for affective disturbances in treatment-resistant depression, post-traumatic stress disorder, substance abuse, and traumatic brain injury.

Ann M. Marini, Ph.D., M.D.; Professor, Department of Neurology. Molecular and cellular mechanisms of intrinsic survival pathways to protect against neurodegenerative disorders.

Joseph McCabe, Ph.D.; Professor and Vice Chair, Department of Anatomy, Physiology, and Genetics. Traumatic brain injury and modeling; neuroprotection.

David Mears, Ph.D.; Associate Professor, Department of Anatomy, Physiology, and Genetics. Electrophysiology and calcium signaling in neuroendocrine cells.

Chantal Moratz, Ph.D.; Assistant Professor, Department of Medicine. Mechanisms of inflammation regulation in systemic lupus erythematosus; neuroinflammation in mild traumatic brain injury.

Gregory Mueller, Ph.D.; Professor, Department of Anatomy, Physiology, and Genetics. Neuroimmunology; brain autoantibodies; brain injury biomarkers and the proteomics of brain injury.

Aryan Namboodiri, Ph.D.; Associate Professor, Department of Anatomy, Physiology, and Genetics. Neurobiology of N-acetylaspartate (NAA); pathogenesis and treatment of Canavan disease and intranasal brain delivery of neuroprotectants.

Fereshteh Nugent, Ph.D.; Associate Professor, Department of Pharmacology. Synaptic studies of reward-related behaviors, addiction, and depression.

Paul Pasquina, M.D.; Chairman, Department of Physical Medicine and Rehabilitation, and Director, Center for Rehabilitation Sciences Research. Clinical studies on advanced prosthetics; neurorehabilitation; traumatic brain injury, and pain management.

Daniel Perl, M.D.; Professor of Pathology, Director, Neuropathology Core, Center for Neuroscience and Regenerative Medicine and Director, USU/CNRM Brain Tissue Repository. Neuropathology of traumatic brain injury; brain banking, association of neurodegenerative phenomena to brain trauma.

Harvey B. Pollard, M.D., Ph.D.; Professor and Chair, Department of Anatomy, Physiology, and Genetics. Molecular biology of secretory processes.

Sylvie Poluch, Ph.D.; Research Assistant Professor, Department of Anatomy, Physiology, and Genetics. Development of the cerebral cortex.

Brian Schaefer, Ph.D.; Professor, Department of Microbiology and Immunology. Mechanisms of leukocyte activation, particularly regulation of cytoplasmic signals to NF-kappaB; development of therapeutic approaches for neurotropic viral infections; role of inflammation in traumatic brain injury.

Jeremy T. Smyth, Ph.D.; Assistant Professor, Department of Anatomy, Physiology, and Genetics. Physiology of the endoplasmic reticulum in developmental and neurodegenerative processes; intracellular calcium signaling; Drosophila developmental genetics.

Aviva Symes, Ph.D.; Professor, Department of Pharmacology. Neuroinflammation and neuroprotection after traumatic brain injury.

Robert J. Ursano, M.D.; Professor and Chairman, Department of Psychiatry, and Director, Center for the Study of Traumatic Stress. Posttraumatic stress disorder.

Gary H. Wynn, M.D.; Associate Professor, Department of Psychiatry. Neurobiology and clinical treatment of trauma-related disorders.

T. John Wu, Ph.D.; Professor, Department of Obstetrics and Gynecology. Molecular neuroendocrine regulation of reproduction and stress.

Lei Zhang, M.D.; Associate Professor, Department of Psychiatry. PTSD and biomarkers.

Yumin Zhang, M.D., Ph.D.; Associate Professor, Department of Anatomy, Physiology, and Genetics. Cellular and molecular mechanisms of oligodendroglial and neuronal toxicity.

Section 14
Nutrition

This section contains a directory of institutions offering graduate work in nutrition, followed by an in-depth entry submitted by an institution that chose to prepare a detailed program description. Additional information about programs listed in the directory but not augmented by an in-depth entry may be obtained by writing directly to the dean of a graduate school or chair of a department at the address given in the directory.

For programs offering related work, see also in this book *Allied Health, Biochemistry, Biological and Biomedical Sciences, Botany and Plant Biology, Microbiological Sciences, Pathology and Pathobiology, Pharmacology and Toxicology, Physiology, Public Health,* and *Veterinary Medicine and Sciences.* In the other guides in this series:

Graduate Programs in the Humanities, Arts & Social Sciences

See *Economics (Agricultural Economics and Agribusiness)* and *Family and Consumer Sciences*

Graduate Programs in the Physical Sciences, Mathematics, Agricultural Sciences, the Environment & Natural Resources

See *Agricultural and Food Sciences* and *Chemistry*

Graduate Programs in Engineering & Applied Sciences

See *Agricultural Engineering and Bioengineering* and *Biomedical Engineering and Biotechnology*

CONTENTS

Nutrition

Abilene Christian University, Graduate Programs, College of Education and Human Services, Department of Kinesiology and Nutrition, Abilene, TX 79699. Offers dietetic internship (Certificate); nutrition (MS). *Faculty:* 3 part-time/adjunct (all women). *Students:* 1 (woman) full-time, 20 part-time (all women); includes 1 minority (Hispanic/Latino). 24 applicants, 92% accepted, 21 enrolled. *Entrance requirements:* Additional exam requirements/recommendations for international students: Required—TOEFL (minimum score 80 iBT), IELTS (minimum score 6), PTE. *Application deadline:* For fall admission, 2/15 for domestic students. Application fee: $45. *Expenses:* $875 per hour. *Financial support:* Application deadline: 4/1; applicants required to submit FAFSA. *Unit head:* Dr. Sheila Jones, Program Director, 325-674-2089, Fax: 325-674-6788, E-mail: joness@acu.edu. *Application contact:* Graduate Admissions, 325-674-6911, Fax: 325-674-6717, E-mail: gradinfo@acu.edu.
Website: http://www.acu.edu/undergraduate/academics/education-and-human-services/kinesiology-and-nutrition.html

Adelphi University, College of Nursing and Public Health, Garden City, NY 11530. Offers adult health nurse (MS); health information technology (Advanced Certificate); nurse practitioner in adult health nursing (Certificate); nursing (PhD); nursing administration (MS, Certificate); nursing education (MS, Certificate); nutrition (MS); public health (MPH). *Accreditation:* AACN. *Program availability:* Part-time, evening/weekend. *Faculty:* 45 full-time (36 women), 234 part-time/adjunct (209 women). *Students:* 36 full-time (23 women), 395 part-time (337 women); includes 259 minority (123 Black or African American, non-Hispanic/Latino; 1 American Indian or Alaska Native, non-Hispanic/Latino; 88 Asian, non-Hispanic/Latino; 35 Hispanic/Latino; 12 Two or more races, non-Hispanic/Latino), 10 international. Average age 36. 388 applicants, 51% accepted, 122 enrolled. In 2017, 73 master's, 6 doctorates, 3 other advanced degrees awarded. *Degree requirements:* For master's, thesis or alternative. *Entrance requirements:* For master's, BSN, clinical experience, course in basic statistics, minimum GPA of 3.0, 2 letters of recommendation, resume or curriculum vitae; for doctorate, GRE, licensure as RN in New York, professional writing sample (scholarly writing), 3 letters of recommendation, resume or curriculum vitae; for other advanced degree, MSN. Additional exam requirements/recommendations for international students: Required—TOEFL (minimum score 550 paper-based; 80 iBT), IELTS (minimum score 6.5). *Application deadline:* For fall admission, 3/15 for domestic students, 4/1 for international students; for spring admission, 11/1 for international students. Application fee: $50. Electronic applications accepted. *Expenses:* Contact institution. *Financial support:* In 2017–18, 35 teaching assistantships with full and partial tuition reimbursements (averaging $5,178 per year) were awarded; fellowships, research assistantships, career-related internships or fieldwork, Federal Work-Study, scholarships/grants, traineeships, tuition waivers, unspecified assistantships, and tuition remission for employees also available. Support available to part-time students. Financial award application deadline: 2/15; financial award applicants required to submit FAFSA. *Faculty research:* Social practices in healthcare, bereavement, family grief, historiography, gerontology. *Unit head:* Dr. Elaine Smith, Interim Dean, 516-833-8181, E-mail: elsmith@adelphi.edu. *Application contact:* Kristen Capezza, Associate Vice President for Enrollment Management, 516-877-3021, Fax: 516-877-3039, E-mail: graduateadmissions@adelphi.edu.
Website: http://nursing.adelphi.edu/

Alabama Agricultural and Mechanical University, School of Graduate Studies, College of Agricultural, Life and Natural Sciences, Department of Family and Consumer Sciences, Huntsville, AL 35811. Offers apparel, merchandising and design (MS); family and consumer sciences (MS); human development and family studies (MS); nutrition and hospitality management (MS). *Program availability:* Part-time, evening/weekend. *Degree requirements:* For master's, comprehensive exam, thesis optional. *Entrance requirements:* For master's, GRE General Test. Additional exam requirements/recommendations for international students: Required—TOEFL (minimum score 500 paper-based; 61 iBT). Electronic applications accepted. *Faculty research:* Food biotechnology, nutrition, food microbiology, food engineering, food chemistry.

American College of Healthcare Sciences, Graduate Programs, Portland, OR 97239-3719. Offers anatomy and physiology (Graduate Certificate); aromatherapy (MS, Graduate Certificate); botanical safety (Graduate Certificate); complementary alternative medicine (MS, Graduate Certificate); health and wellness (MS); herbal medicine (MS, Graduate Certificate); holistic nutrition (MS, Graduate Certificate); wellness coaching (Graduate Certificate). *Program availability:* Part-time, evening/weekend, online learning. *Degree requirements:* For master's, capstone project. *Entrance requirements:* For master's, interview, letters of recommendation, essay.

American University, College of Arts and Sciences, Department of Health Studies, Program in Nutrition Education, Washington, DC 20016-8001. Offers MS, Certificate. *Program availability:* Part-time, online only, 100% online. *Students:* 1 (woman) full-time, 64 part-time (56 women); includes 2 minority (1 Black or African American, non-Hispanic/Latino; 1 Hispanic/Latino). Average age 35. 50 applicants, 90% accepted, 35 enrolled. In 2017, 37 master's, 2 other advanced degrees awarded. *Entrance requirements:* For master's, GRE; for Certificate, statement of purpose, transcripts, resume. Additional exam requirements/recommendations for international students: Required—TOEFL (minimum score 600 paper-based; 100 iBT), IELTS (minimum score 7). *Application deadline:* For fall admission, 2/1 priority date for domestic students; for spring admission, 11/1 priority date for domestic students. Application fee: $55. *Expenses:* Contact institution. *Financial support:* Applicants required to submit FAFSA. *Unit head:* Dr. Anastasia Snelling, Chair, Department of Health Studies, 202-885-6278, Fax: 202-885-1187, E-mail: stacey@american.edu. *Application contact:* Jonathan Harper, Assistant Director, Graduate Recruitment, 202-855-3622, E-mail: jharper@american.edu.
Website: http://www.american.edu/cas/nutrition/nutrition-education-ms.cfm

American University of Beirut, Graduate Programs, Faculty of Agricultural and Food Sciences, Beirut, Lebanon. Offers agricultural economics (MS); animal science (MS); ecosystem management (MSES); food safety (MS); food security (MS); food technology (MS); irrigation (MS); nutrition (MS); plant protection (MS); plant science (MS); poultry science (MS); public health nutrition (MS); rural community development (MS). *Program availability:* Part-time. *Faculty:* 16 full-time (4 women), 1 part-time/adjunct (0 women). *Students:* 76 full-time (58 women), 19 part-time (13 women); includes 6 minority (all Black or African American, non-Hispanic/Latino). Average age 25. 142 applicants, 72% accepted, 32 enrolled. In 2017, 20 master's awarded. *Degree requirements:* For master's, one foreign language, comprehensive exam, thesis (for some programs). *Entrance requirements:* Additional exam requirements/recommendations for international students: Required—TOEFL (minimum score 600 paper-based; 100 iBT), IELTS (minimum score 7.5). *Application deadline:* For fall admission, 2/10 for domestic and international students; for spring admission, 11/2 for domestic and international students. Application fee: $50. Electronic applications accepted. *Expenses: Tuition:* Full-time $17,244; part-time $958 per credit. *Required fees:* $740. Tuition and fees vary according to course load and program. *Financial support:* In 2017–18, 9 research assistantships with partial tuition reimbursements (averaging $1,800 per year), 47 teaching assistantships with full and partial tuition reimbursements (averaging $1,400 per year) were awarded; scholarships/grants, health care benefits, and unspecified assistantships also available. Financial award application deadline: 2/2. *Faculty research:* Refugee socio-economic vulnerability, nutrition in emergencies, forest and landscape restoration, broiler immunological response, vegetated infrastructure in deserts. *Total annual research expenditures:* $600,000. *Unit head:* Rabi Hassan Mohtar, Dean of Faculty of Agricultural and Food Sciences, 961-1-350000 Ext. 4400, Fax: 961-1-744460, E-mail: mohtar@aub.edu.lb. *Application contact:* Prof. Zaher Dawy, Graduate Council Chairperson, 961-1-374374 Ext. 4386, Fax: 961-1-374376, E-mail: graduate.council@aub.edu.lb.
Website: http://www.aub.edu.lb/fafs/Pages/default.aspx

American University of Beirut, Graduate Programs, Faculty of Health Sciences, 1107 2020, Lebanon. Offers environmental sciences (MS), including environmental health; epidemiology (MS, PhD); epidemiology and biostatistics (MPH); health care leadership (EMHCL); health management and policy (MPH), including health service administration; health promotion and community health (MPH); health research (MS); public health nutrition (MS). *Program availability:* Part-time. *Faculty:* 33 full-time (22 women), 5 part-time/adjunct (2 women). *Students:* 75 full-time (60 women), 78 part-time (67 women). Average age 27. 274 applicants, 56% accepted, 47 enrolled. In 2017, 63 master's awarded. *Degree requirements:* For master's, one foreign language, comprehensive exam (for some programs), thesis (for MS); for doctorate, one foreign language, comprehensive exam, thesis/dissertation. *Entrance requirements:* For master's, 2 letters of recommendations, personal statement, transcript; for doctorate, GRE, 3 letters of recommendations, personal statement, interview. Additional exam requirements/recommendations for international students: Required—TOEFL (minimum score 583 paper-based; 97 iBT), IELTS (minimum score 7). *Application deadline:* For fall admission, 4/4 for domestic and international students; for spring admission, 11/3 for domestic and international students. Application fee: $50. Electronic applications accepted. *Expenses:* Contact institution. *Financial support:* In 2017–18, 75 students received support. Scholarships/grants, health care benefits, and unspecified assistantships available. Financial award application deadline: 4/4. *Faculty research:* Reproductive and sexual health; occupational and environmental health; conflict and health; mental health; quality in health care delivery, tobacco control. *Total annual research expenditures:* $2 million. *Unit head:* Prof. Iman Adel Nuwayhid, Dean/Professor, 961-1-759683 Ext. 4600, Fax: 961-1-744470, E-mail: nuwayhid@aub.edu.lb. *Application contact:* Mitra Tauk, Administrative Coordinator, 961-1-350000 Ext. 4687, E-mail: mt12@aub.edu.lb.
Website: http://www.aub.edu.lb/fhs/fhs_home/Pages/index.aspx

Andrews University, School of Health Professions, Department of Nutrition, Berrien Springs, MI 49104. Offers nutrition (MS); nutrition and dietetics (Certificate); public health (MPH). *Program availability:* Part-time. *Faculty:* 1 (woman) full-time, 7 part-time/adjunct (2 women). *Students:* 1 (woman) full-time, 22 part-time (20 women); includes 13 minority (8 Black or African American, non-Hispanic/Latino; 1 Asian, non-Hispanic/Latino; 4 Hispanic/Latino), 5 international. Average age 35. 59 applicants, 78% accepted, 14 enrolled. In 2017, 10 master's, 14 other advanced degrees awarded. *Entrance requirements:* For master's, GRE. Additional exam requirements/recommendations for international students: Required—TOEFL (minimum score 550 paper-based). *Application deadline:* Applications are processed on a rolling basis. Application fee: $40. *Faculty research:* Exercise education. *Unit head:* Dr. Sherine Brown-Fraser, Chairperson, 269-471-3370. *Application contact:* Justina Clayburn, Supervisor of Graduate Admission, 800-253-2874, Fax: 269-471-6321, E-mail: graduate@andrews.edu.
Website: http://www.andrews.edu/shp/nutrition/

Appalachian State University, Cratis D. Williams Graduate School, Department of Nutrition and Health Care Management, Boone, NC 28608. Offers nutrition (MS). *Program availability:* Part-time. Electronic applications accepted. *Faculty research:* Food antioxidants and nutrition.

Arizona State University at the Tempe campus, College of Health Solutions, School of Nutrition and Health Promotion, Tempe, AZ 85287. Offers clinical exercise physiology (MS); exercise and wellness (MS); nutrition (MS), including dietetics, human nutrition; obesity prevention and management (MS); physical activity, nutrition and wellness (PhD).

Auburn University, Graduate School, College of Human Sciences, Department of Nutrition and Food Science, Auburn University, AL 36849. Offers MS, PhD, Graduate Certificate. *Program availability:* Part-time. *Faculty:* 15 full-time (6 women). *Students:* 28 full-time (25 women), 55 part-time (27 women). Average age 32. 81 applicants, 70% accepted, 43 enrolled. In 2017, 12 master's, 11 doctorates, 5 other advanced degrees awarded. *Degree requirements:* For master's, thesis (for some programs); for doctorate, thesis/dissertation. *Entrance requirements:* For master's and doctorate, GRE General Test. *Application deadline:* Applications are processed on a rolling basis. Application fee: $50 ($60 for international students). Electronic applications accepted. *Expenses:* Tuition, state resident: full-time $10,974; part-time $519 per credit hour. Tuition, nonresident: full-time $29,658; part-time $1557 per credit hour. *Required fees:* $816 per semester. Tuition and fees vary according to degree level and program. *Financial support:* Research assistantships, teaching assistantships, career-related internships or fieldwork, and Federal Work-Study available. Support available to part-time students. Financial award application deadline: 3/15; financial award applicants required to submit FAFSA. *Faculty research:* Food quality and safety, diet, food supply, physical activity in maintenance of health, prevention of selected chronic disease states. *Unit head:* Dr. Martin O'Neill, Head, 334-844-3266. *Application contact:* Dr. George Flowers, Dean of the Graduate School, 334-844-2125.
Website: http://www.humsci.auburn.edu/ndhm/grad.php

Ball State University, Graduate School, Teachers College, Department of Family, Consumer, and Technology Education, Muncie, IN 47306. Offers family and consumer science (MS), including apparel design (MA, MS), fashion merchandising (MA, MS), interior design (MA, MS), residential property management (MA, MS); family and consumer sciences (MA), including apparel design (MA, MS), fashion merchandising (MA, MS), interior design (MA, MS), residential property management (MA, MS); nutrition and dietetics (MA, MS). *Program availability:* Part-time, evening/weekend, 100% online. *Students:* 9 full-time (5 women), 54 part-time (20 women); includes 9 minority (5 Black or African American, non-Hispanic/Latino; 1 Asian, non-Hispanic/Latino; 3 Hispanic/Latino), 6 international. Average age 36. 63 applicants, 48% accepted, 26 enrolled. In 2017, 19 master's awarded. *Entrance requirements:* For

master's, letter of intent, resume, two letters of recommendation, portfolio (for interior design option). Additional exam requirements/recommendations for international students: Required—TOEFL (minimum score 550 paper-based; 79 iBT), IELTS (minimum score 6.5). *Application deadline:* For fall admission, 2/15 for domestic students; for spring admission, 9/25 for domestic students. Applications are processed on a rolling basis. Application fee: $60. Electronic applications accepted. *Financial support:* Research assistantships with partial tuition reimbursements and unspecified assistantships available. Financial award application deadline: 3/1; financial award applicants required to submit FAFSA. *Unit head:* Dr. Scott Hall, Chairperson, 765-285-5943, Fax: 765-285-2314, E-mail: sshall@bsu.edu.
Website: http://www.bsu.edu/fcs/

Bastyr University, School of Natural Health Arts and Sciences, Kenmore, WA 98028-4966. Offers counseling psychology (MA); maternal-child health systems (MA); midwifery (MS); nutrition (Certificate); nutrition and clinical health psychology (MS); nutrition and wellness (MS). *Accreditation:* AND. *Program availability:* Part-time. *Degree requirements:* For master's, thesis optional. *Entrance requirements:* For master's, 1-2 years' basic sciences course work (depending on program). Additional exam requirements/recommendations for international students: Required—TOEFL (minimum score 550 paper-based; 79 iBT). *Application deadline:* For fall admission, 3/15 priority date for domestic and international students. Applications are processed on a rolling basis. Application fee: $75. *Expenses: Tuition:* Part-time $714 per credit hour. *Required fees:* $75. *Financial support:* Career-related internships or fieldwork, Federal Work-Study, and scholarships/grants available. Support available to part-time students. Financial award application deadline: 4/15; financial award applicants required to submit FAFSA. *Faculty research:* Whole-food nutrition for type 2 diabetes; meditation in end-of-life care; stress management; Qi Gong, Tai Chi and yoga for older adults; Echinacea and immunology. *Unit head:* Dr. Lynelle Golden, Dean, 425-602-3110, Fax: 425-823-6222, E-mail: lgolden@bastyr.edu. *Application contact:* Admissions Office, 425-602-3330, Fax: 425-602-3090, E-mail: admissions@bastyr.edu.
Website: http://www.bastyr.edu/academics/schools-departments/school-natural-health-arts-sciences

Baylor University, Graduate School, Military Programs, Program in Nutrition, Waco, TX 76798. Offers MS. *Faculty:* 7 full-time (6 women), 6 part-time/adjunct (all women). *Students:* 19 full-time (16 women); includes 3 minority (1 Asian, non-Hispanic/Latino; 1 Hispanic/Latino; 1 Two or more races, non-Hispanic/Latino). Average age 26. 25 applicants, 48% accepted, 12 enrolled. In 2017, 8 master's awarded. *Degree requirements:* For master's, comprehensive exam, thesis. *Entrance requirements:* For master's, GRE. Additional exam requirements/recommendations for international students: Required—TOEFL, IELTS. *Application deadline:* Applications are processed on a rolling basis. Electronic applications accepted. *Faculty research:* Weight control, critical care nutrition, breast feeding, intuitive eating. *Unit head:* Stephanie Meyer, Graduate Program Director, 210-221-6274, Fax: 210-221-7363, E-mail: stephanie.a.meyer.mil@mail.mil. *Application contact:* Clint McKinley, Administrative Assistant, 210-295-6274, E-mail: clint.w.mckinley.mil@mail.mil.
Website: http://www.baylor.edu/graduate/nutrition/

Baylor University, Graduate School, Robbins College of Health and Human Sciences, Department of Family and Consumer Sciences, Waco, TX 76798. Offers nutrition sciences (MS). *Program availability:* Part-time. *Students:* 3 full-time (2 women), 1 (woman) part-time; includes 1 minority (Two or more races, non-Hispanic/Latino). In 2017, 3 master's awarded. *Unit head:* Dr. Rodney G. Bowden, Interim Dean, 254-710-6111, Fax: 254-710-3699, E-mail: rodney_bowden@baylor.edu. *Application contact:* Lori McNamara, Graduate Admissions Coordinator, 254-710-3588, Fax: 254-710-3870, E-mail: lori_mcnamara@baylor.edu.
Website: http://www.baylor.edu/fcs/

Baylor University, Graduate School, Robbins College of Health and Human Sciences, Department of Health, Human Performance and Recreation, Waco, TX 76798. Offers athletic training (MS); community health (MPH); exercise physiology (MS); kinesiology, exercise nutrition, and health promotion (PhD); sport pedagogy (MS). *Accreditation:* NCATE. *Program availability:* Part-time. *Faculty:* 24 full-time (11 women). *Students:* 86 full-time (52 women), 9 part-time (6 women); includes 24 minority (7 Black or African American, non-Hispanic/Latino; 3 Asian, non-Hispanic/Latino; 10 Hispanic/Latino; 1 Native Hawaiian or other Pacific Islander, non-Hispanic/Latino; 3 Two or more races, non-Hispanic/Latino), 8 international. 109 applicants, 59% accepted, 44 enrolled. In 2017, 30 master's, 3 doctorates awarded. *Degree requirements:* For master's, comprehensive exam, thesis optional; for doctorate, comprehensive exam, thesis/dissertation. *Entrance requirements:* For master's and doctorate, GRE General Test. Additional exam requirements/recommendations for international students: Required—TOEFL (minimum score 550 paper-based; 80 iBT). *Application deadline:* For fall admission, 2/1 priority date for domestic students, 2/1 for international students; for spring admission, 10/1 for domestic and international students. Applications are processed on a rolling basis. Application fee: $25. Electronic applications accepted. *Financial support:* In 2017–18, 60 students received support, including 1 research assistantship with full tuition reimbursement available (averaging $12,700 per year), 33 teaching assistantships with full tuition reimbursements available (averaging $7,650 per year); career-related internships or fieldwork, Federal Work-Study, institutionally sponsored loans, scholarships/grants, tuition waivers (full), and unspecified assistantships also available. Financial award application deadline: 2/1. *Faculty research:* Exercise testing, cardio-metabolic health, resistance exercise and training, nutritional intervention, population health, health promotion, global health epidemiology, coaching, natural resource management, stimulant misuse, diet, microbiome and colon cancer etiology. *Total annual research expenditures:* $250,118. *Unit head:* Dr. Jaeho Shim, Graduate Program Director, 254-710-4009, Fax: 254-710-3527, E-mail: joe_shim@baylor.edu. *Application contact:* Deepa Morris, Graduate Program Coordinator, 254-710-3526, Fax: 254-710-3527, E-mail: deepa_morris@baylor.edu.
Website: http://www.baylor.edu/HHPR/

Benedictine University, Graduate Programs, Program in Nutrition and Wellness, Lisle, IL 60532. Offers MS. *Entrance requirements:* Additional exam requirements/recommendations for international students: Required—TOEFL (minimum score 550 paper-based). Electronic applications accepted. *Faculty research:* Community and corporate wellness risk assessment, health behavior change, self-efficacy, evaluation of health program impact and effectiveness.

Benedictine University, Graduate Programs, Program in Public Health, Lisle, IL 60532. Offers administration of health care institutions (MPH); dietetics (MPH); disaster management (MPH); health education (MPH); health information systems (MPH); MBA/MPH; MPH/MS. *Accreditation:* CEPH. *Program availability:* Part-time, evening/weekend, online learning. *Entrance requirements:* For master's, MAT, GRE, or GMAT. Additional exam requirements/recommendations for international students: Required—TOEFL (minimum score 550 paper-based).

Boston University, College of Health and Rehabilitation Sciences: Sargent College, Department of Health Sciences, Program in Nutrition, Boston, MA 02215. Offers MS. *Faculty:* 10 full-time (9 women), 5 part-time/adjunct (3 women). *Students:* 56 full-time (47 women), 2 part-time (both women); includes 10 minority (1 Black or African American, non-Hispanic/Latino; 5 Asian, non-Hispanic/Latino; 3 Hispanic/Latino; 1 Two or more races, non-Hispanic/Latino), 6 international. Average age 24. 118 applicants, 33% accepted, 28 enrolled. In 2017, 19 master's awarded. *Entrance requirements:* For master's, GRE General Test, minimum GPA of 3.0. Additional exam requirements/recommendations for international students: Required—TOEFL (minimum score 550 paper-based; 84 iBT). *Application deadline:* For fall admission, 2/1 priority date for domestic students, 2/15 priority date for international students. Applications are processed on a rolling basis. Application fee: $95. Electronic applications accepted. *Financial support:* In 2017–18, 37 students received support, including 4 teaching assistantships (averaging $2,500 per year); career-related internships or fieldwork, Federal Work-Study, institutionally sponsored loans, and scholarships/grants also available. Financial award application deadline: 2/1; financial award applicants required to submit FAFSA. *Faculty research:* Metabolism, health promotion, obesity, epidemiology. *Total annual research expenditures:* $194,000. *Unit head:* Dr. Paula Quatromoni, Chair, 617-353-5797, Fax: 617-353-7567, E-mail: paulaq@bu.edu. *Application contact:* Sharon Sankey, Assistant Dean, Student Services, 617-353-2713, Fax: 617-353-7500, E-mail: ssankey@bu.edu.

Boston University, School of Medicine, Division of Graduate Medical Sciences, Program in Nutrition and Metabolism, Boston, MA 02215. Offers MS, PhD. *Degree requirements:* For master's, thesis; for doctorate, thesis/dissertation. *Application deadline:* For fall admission, 1/15 for domestic students; for spring admission, 10/15 for domestic students. *Unit head:* Dr. Lynn L. Moore, Director, 617-638-8008, E-mail: llmoore@bu.edu. *Application contact:* GMS Admissions Office, 617-638-5255, Fax: 617-638-5740, E-mail: askgms@bu.edu.
Website: http://www.bumc.bu.edu/gms/nutrition-metabolism/

Bradley University, The Graduate School, College of Education and Health Sciences, Department of Family and Consumer Sciences, Peoria, IL 61625-0002. Offers dietetic internship (MS).

Brigham Young University, Graduate Studies, College of Life Sciences, Department of Nutrition, Dietetics and Food Science, Provo, UT 84602. Offers food science (MS); nutrition (MS), including dietetics, nutritional science. *Faculty:* 15 full-time (6 women). *Students:* 16 full-time (10 women); includes 2 minority (1 Asian, non-Hispanic/Latino; 1 Hispanic/Latino), 1 international. Average age 28. 10 applicants, 50% accepted, 5 enrolled. In 2017, 7 master's awarded. *Degree requirements:* For master's, comprehensive exam, thesis. *Entrance requirements:* For master's, GRE General Test, MCAT, DAT, GMAT, LSAT. Additional exam requirements/recommendations for international students: Required—TOEFL (minimum score 580 paper-based; 85 iBT); Recommended—IELTS (minimum score 7). *Application deadline:* For fall admission, 2/1 priority date for domestic and international students; for winter admission, 6/30 priority date for domestic and international students; for spring admission, 3/1 priority date for domestic and international students; for summer admission, 3/1 priority date for domestic and international students. Application fee: $50. Electronic applications accepted. *Expenses: Tuition:* Full-time $6880; part-time $405 per credit hour. Tuition and fees vary according to course load, program and student's religious affiliation. *Financial support:* In 2017–18, 28 students received support, including 27 research assistantships with partial tuition reimbursements available (averaging $6,828 per year); teaching assistantships, institutionally sponsored loans, and scholarships/grants also available. Financial award application deadline: 4/1; financial award applicants required to submit FAFSA. *Faculty research:* Nutrition assessment, diabetes research, product development, cancer, food microbiology. *Total annual research expenditures:* $256,597. *Unit head:* Dr. Merrill J. Christensen, Chair, 801-422-5255, Fax: 801-422-0258, E-mail: merrill_christensen@byu.edu. *Application contact:* Judy Stoudt, Graduate Secretary, 801-422-4296, Fax: 801-422-0258, E-mail: judy.stoudt@byu.edu.
Website: http://ndfs.byu.edu/

Brooklyn College of the City University of New York, School of Natural and Behavioral Sciences, Department of Health and Nutrition Sciences, Program in Nutrition, Brooklyn, NY 11210-2889. Offers MS. *Program availability:* Part-time. *Degree requirements:* For master's, thesis or comprehensive exam. *Entrance requirements:* For master's, 18 credits in health-related areas, 2 letters of recommendation, essay. Additional exam requirements/recommendations for international students: Required—TOEFL. Electronic applications accepted. *Faculty research:* Medical ethics, AIDS, history of public health, diet restriction, palliative care, risk reduction/disease prevention, metabolism, diabetes.

★ **California Polytechnic State University, San Luis Obispo,** College of Agriculture, Food and Environmental Sciences, Department of Food Science and Nutrition, San Luis Obispo, CA 93407. Offers food science and nutrition (MS); nutrition (MS). *Students:* 6 full-time (5 women), 3 part-time (2 women); includes 4 minority (1 Asian, non-Hispanic/Latino; 3 Hispanic/Latino). Average age 28. 15 applicants, 27% accepted, 3 enrolled. In 2017, 1 master's awarded. *Degree requirements:* For master's, thesis. *Entrance requirements:* For master's, GRE. Additional exam requirements/recommendations for international students: Required—TOEFL (minimum score 80 iBT). *Application deadline:* For fall admission, 4/1 for domestic students. Application fee: $55. *Expenses:* Tuition, state resident: full-time $7176; part-time $4164 per year. *Required fees:* $3690; $3219 per year. $1073 per trimester. *Financial support:* Fellowships, teaching assistantships, scholarships/grants, tuition waivers, and unspecified assistantships available. Financial award application deadline: 3/2; financial award applicants required to submit FAFSA. *Unit head:* Dr. Johan Ubbink, Head, 805-756-2660, E-mail: jubbink@calpoly.edu. *Application contact:* Dr. Jim Prince, Associate Dean, Research and Graduate Programs, 805-756-5104, E-mail: jpprince@calpoly.edu.
Website: http://www.fsn.calpoly.edu

See Display on the next page and Close-Up on page 351.

California State University, Chico, Office of Graduate Studies, College of Natural Sciences, Department of Nutrition and Food Science, Chico, CA 95929-0722. Offers general nutritional science (MS); nutrition education (MS). *Program availability:* Part-time. *Degree requirements:* For master's, thesis, professional paper, or oral defense. *Entrance requirements:* For master's, GRE General Test, two letters of recommendation, statement of purpose, resume. Additional exam requirements/recommendations for international students: Required—TOEFL (minimum score 550 paper-based; 80 iBT), IELTS (minimum score 6.5), PTE (minimum score 59). Electronic applications accepted.

California State University, Long Beach, Graduate Studies, College of Health and Human Services, Department of Kinesiology, Long Beach, CA 90840. Offers adapted physical education (MA); coaching and student athlete development (MA); exercise physiology and nutrition (MS); exercise science (MS); individualized studies (MA); kinesiology (MA); pedagogical studies (MA); sport and exercise psychology (MS); sport management (MA); sports medicine and injury studies (MS). *Program availability:* Part-time. *Degree requirements:* For master's, oral and written comprehensive exams or thesis. *Entrance requirements:* For master's, GRE General Test, minimum GPA of 2.75 during previous 2 years of course work. Electronic applications accepted. *Faculty research:* Pulmonary functioning, feedback and practice structure, strength training, history and politics of sports, special population research issues.

California State University, Los Angeles, Graduate Studies, College of Health and Human Services, Department of Kinesiology and Nutritional Sciences, Los Angeles, CA 90032-8530. Offers nutritional science (MS); physical education and kinesiology (MA). *Accreditation:* AND. *Program availability:* Part-time, evening/weekend. *Degree requirements:* For master's, comprehensive exam, project or thesis. *Entrance requirements:* For master's, minimum GPA of 2.75. Additional exam requirements/recommendations for international students: Required—TOEFL (minimum score 500 paper-based).

California University of Pennsylvania, School of Graduate Studies and Research, College of Education and Human Services, Department of Exercise Science and Sport Studies, California, PA 15419-1394. Offers applied sport science (MS); exercise science (MS), including group fitness leadership, nutrition, performance enhancement and injury prevention, rehabilitation science; group fitness leadership (MS); nutrition (MS); wellness coaching (MS). *Program availability:* Part-time, evening/weekend, online learning. *Degree requirements:* For master's, comprehensive exam, thesis optional. *Entrance requirements:* For master's, minimum GPA of 3.0. Additional exam requirements/recommendations for international students: Required—TOEFL (minimum score 550 paper-based; 80 iBT). *Application deadline:* For winter admission, 12/1 priority date for domestic and international students. Applications are processed on a rolling basis. Application fee: $25. Electronic applications accepted. *Expenses:* Contact institution. *Financial support:* Applicants required to submit FAFSA. *Faculty research:* Reducing obesity in children, sport performance, creating unique biomechanical assessment techniques, web-based training for fitness professionals, Webcams. *Unit head:* Dr. William B. Biddington, Interim Dean, 724-938-4356, E-mail: biddington_w@calu.edu. *Application contact:* Suzanne C. Powers, Director of Graduate Admissions and Recruitment, 724-938-4029, Fax: 724-938-5712, E-mail: powers_s@cup.edu.

Canisius College, Graduate Division, School of Education and Human Services, Office of Professional Studies, Buffalo, NY 14208-1098. Offers applied nutrition (MS, Certificate); community and school health (MS); health and human performance (MS); health information technology (MS); respiratory care (MS). *Program availability:* Part-time, evening/weekend, 100% online, blended/hybrid learning. *Faculty:* 2 full-time (0 women), 8 part-time/adjunct (6 women). *Students:* 21 full-time (11 women), 40 part-time (34 women); includes 9 minority (7 Black or African American, non-Hispanic/Latino; 1 Hispanic/Latino; 1 Two or more races, non-Hispanic/Latino), 1 international. Average age 36. 18 applicants, 94% accepted, 17 enrolled. In 2017, 31 master's awarded. *Entrance requirements:* For master's, GRE (recommended), bachelor's degree transcript, two letters of recommendation, current licensure (for applied nutrition), minimum GPA of 2.7, current resume. Additional exam requirements/recommendations for international students: Required—TOEFL (minimum score 550 paper-based, 79 iBT), IELTS (minimum score 6.5), or CAEL (minimum score 70). *Application deadline:* Applications are processed on a rolling basis. Application fee: $0. Electronic applications accepted. *Expenses: Tuition:* Full-time $22,860; part-time $820 per credit. *Required fees:* $720; $25 per credit. $65 per semester. One-time fee: $425. *Financial support:* Career-related internships or fieldwork, Federal Work-Study, scholarships/grants, tuition waivers (partial), and unspecified assistantships available. Support available to part-time students. Financial award application deadline: 4/30; financial award applicants required to submit FAFSA. *Faculty research:* Nutrition, community and school health; community and health; health and human performance applied; nutrition and respiratory care. *Unit head:* Dennis W. Koch, Director, Office of Professional Studies, 716-888-8292, E-mail: koch5@canisius.edu.
Website: http://www.canisius.edu/graduate/

Case Western Reserve University, School of Medicine and School of Graduate Studies, Graduate Programs in Medicine, Department of Nutrition, Cleveland, OH 44106. Offers dietetics (MS); molecular nutrition (MS); nutrition (MS, PhD), including molecular nutrition (PhD); nutritional biochemistry and metabolism (MS); public health nutrition (MS). *Program availability:* Part-time. Terminal master's awarded for partial completion of doctoral program. *Degree requirements:* For master's, thesis (for some programs); for doctorate, thesis/dissertation. *Entrance requirements:* For master's, GRE General Test; for doctorate, GRE General Test, GRE Subject Test. Additional exam requirements/recommendations for international students: Required—TOEFL. *Expenses: Tuition:* Full-time $43,854; part-time $1827 per credit hour. *Required fees:* $50; $50 per credit hour. Tuition and fees vary according to course load and program. *Faculty research:* Fatty acid metabolism, application of gene therapy to nutritional problems, dietary intake methodology, nutrition and physical fitness, metabolism during infancy and pregnancy.

Cedar Crest College, Dietetic Internship Certificate Program, Allentown, PA 18104-6196. Offers Graduate Certificate. *Program availability:* Part-time, evening/weekend, blended/hybrid learning. *Faculty:* 3 full-time (all women), 3 part-time/adjunct (2 women). *Students:* 27 part-time (24 women). Average age 26. In 2017, 26 Graduate Certificates awarded. *Entrance requirements:* For degree, two semesters of medical nutrition therapy coursework completed no more than four years prior to application; one biochemistry course completed no more than five years prior to application. *Application deadline:* Applications are processed on a rolling basis. Electronic applications accepted. *Expenses:* Contact institution. *Unit head:* Marilou Wieder, Director, 610-606-4666 Ext. 3445, E-mail: mwieder@cedarcrest.edu. *Application contact:* Nancy Wunderly, Director of School of Adult and Graduate Education, 610-437-4471, E-mail: sage@cedarcrest.edu.
Website: http://sage.cedarcrest.edu/graduate/dietetic-internship/

Central Michigan University, Central Michigan University Global Campus, Program in Health Administration, Mount Pleasant, MI 48859. Offers health administration (DHA); international health (Certificate); nutrition and dietetics (MS). *Program availability:* Part-time, evening/weekend, online learning. Electronic applications accepted.

Central Michigan University, College of Graduate Studies, College of Education and Human Services, Department of Human Environmental Studies, Mount Pleasant, MI 48859. Offers apparel product development and merchandising technology (MS); gerontology (Graduate Certificate); human development and family studies (MA); nutrition and dietetics (MS). *Program availability:* Part-time, evening/weekend. *Degree requirements:* For master's, thesis or alternative. Electronic applications accepted. *Faculty research:* Human growth and development, family studies and human sexuality, human nutrition and dietetics, apparel and textile retailing, computer-aided design for apparel.

Central Washington University, School of Graduate Studies and Research, College of Education and Professional Studies, Department of Health Sciences, Ellensburg, WA 98926. Offers integrative human physiology (MS); nutrition (MS). *Program availability:* Part-time. *Entrance requirements:* For master's, GRE, minimum GPA of 3.0. Additional exam requirements/recommendations for international students: Required—TOEFL (minimum score 550 paper-based; 79 iBT). *Application deadline:* For fall admission, 2/1 priority date for domestic students; for winter admission, 10/1 for domestic students; for spring admission, 1/1 for domestic students. Applications are processed on a rolling basis. Application fee: $50. Electronic applications accepted. *Financial support:* Application deadline: 3/1; applicants required to submit FAFSA. *Unit head:* Dr. Ethan Bergman, Chair, 509-963-2366, E-mail: bergmane@cwu.edu. *Application contact:* Justine Eason, Admissions Program Coordinator, 509-963-3103, Fax: 509-963-1799, E-mail: masters@cwu.edu.
Website: http://www.cwu.edu/~nehs/

Chapman University, Schmid College of Science and Technology, Food Science Program, Orange, CA 92866. Offers MS, MS/MBA. *Program availability:* Part-time, evening/weekend. *Faculty:* 4 full-time (3 women), 9 part-time/adjunct (all women). *Students:* 16 full-time (7 women), 32 part-time (24 women); includes 19 minority (2 Black or African American, non-Hispanic/Latino; 10 Asian, non-Hispanic/Latino; 3 Hispanic/Latino; 4 Two or more races, non-Hispanic/Latino), 10 international. Average age 26. 41 applicants, 76% accepted, 26 enrolled. In 2017, 14 master's awarded. *Degree requirements:* For master's, thesis or alternative. *Entrance requirements:* For master's, GRE or GMAT. *Application deadline:* For fall admission, 5/1 for domestic students. Applications are processed on a rolling basis. Application fee: $60. Electronic applications accepted. *Expenses:* Contact institution. *Financial support:* Fellowships, research assistantships, teaching assistantships, Federal Work-Study, and scholarships/grants available. Financial award applicants required to submit FAFSA. *Unit head:* Dr. Anuradha Prakash, Program Director, 714-744-7895, E-mail: prakash@chapman.edu. *Application contact:* Sharnique Dow, Graduate Admission Counselor, 714-997-6770, E-mail: sdow@chapman.edu.
Website: https://www.chapman.edu/scst/graduate/ms-food-science/index.aspx

College of Saint Elizabeth, Department of Foods and Nutrition, Morristown, NJ 07960-6989. Offers dietetics verification (Certificate); nutrition (MS), including community nutrition and wellness, entrepreneurial nutrition practice; nutrition/dietetic internship (MS). *Program availability:* Part-time, blended/hybrid learning. *Faculty:* 4 full-time (all women), 2 part-time/adjunct (both women). *Students:* 23 full-time (21 women), 52 part-time (49 women); includes 14 minority (2 Asian, non-Hispanic/Latino; 10 Hispanic/Latino; 2 Two or more races, non-Hispanic/Latino), 1 international. Average age 26. 39 applicants, 100% accepted, 35 enrolled. In 2017, 31 master's awarded. *Degree requirements:* For master's, thesis. *Entrance requirements:* Additional exam requirements/recommendations for international students: Required—TOEFL (minimum score 550 paper-based; 79 iBT), IELTS (minimum score 6.5). *Application deadline:* For fall admission, 5/1 for international students. Applications are processed on a rolling basis. Application fee: $35. Electronic applications accepted. Application fee is waived when completed online. *Financial support:* Career-related internships or fieldwork, scholarships/grants, and unspecified assistantships available. Financial award applicants required to submit FAFSA. *Faculty research:* Medical nutrition intervention, public policy, obesity, hunger and food security, osteoporosis, nutrition and exercise. *Unit head:* Dr. Anne Buison Pellizzon, Program Chair, 973-290-4065, Fax: 973-290-4167, E-mail: apellizzon@cse.edu. *Application contact:* Lori J. Fragoso, Director of Graduate and Continuing Studies Admissions, 973-290-4413, Fax: 973-290-4710, E-mail: apply@cse.edu.
Website: http://www.cse.edu/academics/prof-studies/foods-and-nutrition/

Colorado State University, College of Health and Human Sciences, Department of Food Science and Human Nutrition, Fort Collins, CO 80523-1571. Offers dietetics (MS); food science and human nutrition (PhD); food science and nutrition (MS); nutrition and exercise science (MS). *Accreditation:* AND. *Program availability:* Part-time, 100% online, blended/hybrid learning. *Faculty:* 15 full-time (11 women), 2 part-time/adjunct (1 woman). *Students:* 51 full-time (42 women), 85 part-time (46 women); includes 8 minority (6 Hispanic/Latino; 2 Two or more races, non-Hispanic/Latino), 3 international. Average age 31. 114 applicants, 35% accepted, 22 enrolled. In 2017, 20 master's, 1 doctorate awarded. Terminal master's awarded for partial completion of doctoral program. *Degree requirements:* For master's, thesis; for doctorate, thesis/dissertation. *Entrance requirements:* For master's and doctorate, GRE (minimum 50th percentile), minimum GPA of 3.0; statement of purpose; resume; letters of recommendation; transcript. Additional exam requirements/recommendations for international students: Required—TOEFL (minimum score 550 paper-based; 80 iBT), IELTS (minimum score 6.5). *Application deadline:* For fall admission, 2/1 priority date for domestic and international students. Application fee: $60 ($70 for international students). Electronic applications accepted. *Expenses:* $580 per credit hour. *Financial support:* In 2017–18, 12 research assistantships (averaging $13,851 per year), 15 teaching assistantships (averaging $8,316 per year) were awarded; fellowships, scholarships/grants, and unspecified assistantships also available. Financial award application deadline: 2/1. *Faculty research:* Community-based interventions on public health outcomes; consumer food handling behavior; adult learning and assessment; food and culture issues; role of microbes in ecosystem functioning. *Total annual research expenditures:* $2.2 million. *Unit head:* Dr. Michael Pagliassotti, Department Head, 970-491-1390, E-mail: michael.pagliassotti@colostate.edu. *Application contact:* Paula Coleman, Administrative Assistant, 970-491-3819, Fax: 970-491-3875, E-mail: paula.coleman@colostate.edu.
Website: http://www.fshn.chhs.colostate.edu/

Colorado State University, College of Health and Human Sciences, Department of Health and Exercise Science, Fort Collins, CO 80523-1582. Offers exercise science and nutrition (MS); human bioenergetics (PhD). *Faculty:* 9 full-time (5 women), 1 (woman) part-time/adjunct. *Students:* 25 full-time (9 women), 9 part-time (2 women); includes 5 minority (3 Hispanic/Latino; 2 Two or more races, non-Hispanic/Latino), 3 international. Average age 28. 57 applicants, 23% accepted, 7 enrolled. In 2017, 8 master's, 1 doctorate awarded. Terminal master's awarded for partial completion of doctoral program. *Degree requirements:* For master's, thesis or alternative; for doctorate, comprehensive exam, thesis/dissertation. *Entrance requirements:* For master's, minimum GPA of 3.0; personal statement; identification of faculty mentor; for doctorate, minimum GPA of 3.0; personal statement; funding plan with PhD mentor for all 4 years; bachelor's or master's degree. Additional exam requirements/recommendations for international students: Recommended—TOEFL. *Application deadline:* For fall admission, 1/1 for domestic and international students; for spring admission, 5/1 for domestic and international students. Application fee: $60 ($70 for international students). Electronic applications accepted. *Expenses:* Tuition, state resident: full-time $9917. Tuition, nonresident: full-time $24,312. *Required fees:* $2284. Tuition and fees vary according to course load and program. *Financial support:* In 2017–18, 28 students received support, including 1 fellowship with full tuition reimbursement available (averaging $19,637 per year), 8 research assistantships with full tuition reimbursements available (averaging $17,906 per year), 14 teaching assistantships with full tuition reimbursements available (averaging $16,422 per year); scholarships/grants, health care benefits, and unspecified assistantships also available. *Faculty research:* Age-related disease and disability, cardiovascular physiology, rehabilitation, neurophysiology, human performance. *Total annual research expenditures:* $1.3 million. *Unit head:* Dr. Barry Braun, Professor and Department Head, 970-491-7875, Fax: 970-491-0445, E-mail: barry.braun@colostate.edu. *Application contact:* Dr. Matt Hickey, Professor, 970-491-5727, Fax: 970-491-0445, E-mail: matthew.hickey@colostate.edu.
Website: http://www.hes.chhs.colostate.edu/

Columbia University, College of Physicians and Surgeons, Institute of Human Nutrition, MS Program in Nutrition, New York, NY 10032. Offers MS, MPH/MS. *Program availability:* Part-time. *Degree requirements:* For master's, thesis. *Entrance requirements:* For master's, GRE General Test, MCAT. Additional exam requirements/recommendations for international students: Required—TOEFL; Recommended—IELTS. Electronic applications accepted. *Expenses: Tuition:* Full-time $44,864; part-time $1704 per credit. *Required fees:* $2370 per semester. One-time fee: $105.

Columbia University, College of Physicians and Surgeons, Institute of Human Nutrition and Graduate School of Arts and Sciences at the College of Physicians and Surgeons, PhD Program in Nutrition, New York, NY 10032. Offers PhD. *Degree requirements:* For doctorate, thesis/dissertation. *Entrance requirements:* For doctorate, GRE General Test. Additional exam requirements/recommendations for international students: Required—TOEFL. *Expenses: Tuition:* Full-time $44,864; part-time $1704 per credit. *Required fees:* $2370 per semester. One-time fee: $105. *Faculty research:* Growth and development, nutrition and metabolism.

Cornell University, Graduate School, Graduate Fields of Agriculture and Life Sciences, Field of Global Development, Ithaca, NY 14853. Offers development policy (MPS); international agriculture and development (MPS); international development (MPS); international nutrition (MPS); international planning (MPS); international population (MPS); science and technology policy (MPS). *Degree requirements:* For master's, project paper. *Entrance requirements:* For master's, GRE General Test (recommended), 2 years of development experience, 2 letters of recommendation. Additional exam requirements/recommendations for international students: Required—TOEFL (minimum score 550 paper-based; 77 iBT). Electronic applications accepted.

Cornell University, Graduate School, Graduate Fields of Agriculture and Life Sciences and Graduate Fields of Human Ecology, Field of Nutrition, Ithaca, NY 14853. Offers animal nutrition (MPS, PhD); community nutrition (MPS, PhD); human nutrition (MPS, PhD); international nutrition (MPS, PhD); molecular biochemistry (MPS, PhD). *Degree requirements:* For master's, thesis (MS), project papers (MPS); for doctorate, comprehensive exam, thesis/dissertation. *Entrance requirements:* For master's and doctorate, GRE General Test, previous course work in organic chemistry (with laboratory) and biochemistry; 2 letters of recommendation. Additional exam requirements/recommendations for international students: Required—TOEFL (minimum score 550 paper-based; 77 iBT). Electronic applications accepted. *Faculty research:* Nutritional biochemistry, experimental human and animal nutrition, international nutrition, community nutrition.

D'Youville College, Department of Dietetics, Buffalo, NY 14201-1084. Offers MS. Five-year program begins at freshman entry. *Degree requirements:* For master's, thesis. *Entrance requirements:* Additional exam requirements/recommendations for international students: Required—TOEFL (minimum score 500 paper-based). Electronic applications accepted. *Faculty research:* Nutrition education, clinical nutrition, herbal supplements, obesity.

East Carolina University, Graduate School, College of Allied Health Sciences, Department of Nutrition Science, Greenville, NC 27858-4353. Offers MS. *Program availability:* Part-time, online learning. *Students:* 13 full-time (10 women), 24 part-time (all women); includes 4 minority (2 Black or African American, non-Hispanic/Latino; 2 Hispanic/Latino). Average age 26. 24 applicants, 71% accepted, 16 enrolled. In 2017, 14 master's awarded. *Degree requirements:* For master's, comprehensive exam, thesis optional. *Entrance requirements:* For master's, GRE. Additional exam requirements/recommendations for international students: Recommended—TOEFL (minimum score 78 iBT), IELTS (minimum score 6.5). *Application deadline:* For fall admission, 3/1 for domestic students. Applications are processed on a rolling basis. Application fee: $75. Electronic applications accepted. *Expenses:* Tuition, state resident: full-time $4749; part-time $297 per credit hour. Tuition, nonresident: full-time $17,898; part-time $1119 per credit hour. *Required fees:* $2691; $224 per credit hour. Part-time tuition and fees vary according to course load and program. *Financial support:* Fellowships, teaching assistantships with partial tuition reimbursements, Federal Work-Study, institutionally sponsored loans, scholarships/grants, and unspecified assistantships available. Support available to part-time students. Financial award application deadline: 3/1; financial award applicants required to submit FAFSA. *Faculty research:* Lifecycle nutrition, nutrition and disease, nutrition for fish species, food service management. *Unit head:* Dr. Melani Duffrin, Interim Chair, 252-328-5698, E-mail: duffrinm@ecu.edu.
Website: http://www.ecu.edu/nutr/

Eastern Illinois University, Graduate School, College of Health and Human Services, Program in Nutrition and Dietetics, Charleston, IL 61920. Offers MS. *Program availability:* Part-time, evening/weekend. *Degree requirements:* For master's, comprehensive exam (for some programs), thesis (for some programs). *Entrance requirements:* For master's, GMAT or GRE. Additional exam requirements/recommendations for international students: Required—TOEFL (minimum score 500 paper-based; 61 iBT), IELTS (minimum score 6). *Application deadline:* For fall admission, 5/15 for domestic and international students; for spring admission, 10/15 for domestic and international students. Applications are processed on a rolling basis. Application fee: $30. Electronic applications accepted. *Financial support:* Teaching assistantships with full tuition reimbursements, career-related internships or fieldwork, Federal Work-Study, and unspecified assistantships available. Support available to part-time students. Financial award application deadline: 3/1; financial award applicants required to submit FAFSA. *Unit head:* Melanie T. Burns, Interim Chair/Graduate Coordinator, 217-581-6353, Fax: 217-581-6090, E-mail: mdburns@eiu.edu. *Application contact:* Melanie T. Burns, Interim Chair/Graduate Coordinator, 217-581-6353, Fax: 217-581-6090, E-mail: mdburns@eiu.edu.
Website: http://www.eiu.edu/dieteticsgrad/

Eastern Kentucky University, The Graduate School, College of Health Sciences, Department of Family and Consumer Sciences, Richmond, KY 40475-3102. Offers M Ed. Program offered in cooperation with the College of Education. *Program availability:* Part-time. *Entrance requirements:* For master's, GRE General Test, minimum GPA of 2.5.

Eastern Kentucky University, The Graduate School, College of Health Sciences, Program in Public Health, Richmond, KY 40475-3102. Offers community health education (MPH); environmental health science (MPH); industrial hygiene (MPH); public health nutrition (MPH). *Accreditation:* CEPH. *Degree requirements:* For master's, comprehensive exam, thesis optional, practicum, capstone course. *Entrance requirements:* For master's, GRE. *Faculty research:* Water quality, food safety, occupational health, air quality.

Eastern Michigan University, Graduate School, College of Health and Human Services, School of Health Sciences, Programs in Dietetics and Human Nutrition, Ypsilanti, MI 48197. Offers dietetics (MS); human nutrition (MS). *Program availability:* Part-time, evening/weekend, online learning. *Students:* 29 full-time (28 women), 37 part-time (34 women); includes 11 minority (4 Black or African American, non-Hispanic/Latino; 3 Asian, non-Hispanic/Latino; 2 Hispanic/Latino; 2 Two or more races, non-Hispanic/Latino), 1 international. Average age 33. 46 applicants, 54% accepted, 13 enrolled. In 2017, 31 master's awarded. *Entrance requirements:* Additional exam requirements/recommendations for international students: Required—TOEFL. *Application deadline:* Applications are processed on a rolling basis. Application fee: $45. *Financial support:* Fellowships, research assistantships with full tuition reimbursements, teaching assistantships with full tuition reimbursements, career-related internships or fieldwork, Federal Work-Study, institutionally sponsored loans, scholarships/grants, tuition waivers (partial), and unspecified assistantships available. Support available to part-time students. Financial award applicants required to submit FAFSA. *Application contact:* Dr. Alica Jo Rainville, Program Coordinator, 734-487-0430, Fax: 734-487-4095, E-mail: arainville@emich.edu.

Nutrition

East Tennessee State University, School of Graduate Studies, College of Clinical and Rehabilitative Health Sciences, Department of Allied Health Sciences, Elizabethton, TN 37643. Offers allied health (MSAH); clinical nutrition (MS). *Program availability:* Part-time, online learning. *Degree requirements:* For master's, comprehensive exam, thesis or advanced practice seminar (for MSAH); internship (for MS). *Entrance requirements:* For master's, GRE General Test, professional license in allied health discipline, minimum GPA of 2.75, and three professional letters of recommendation (for MSAH); bachelor's degree from an undergraduate didactic program in dietetics with minimum GPA of 3.0 in DPD coursework and three letters of recommendation (for MS). Additional exam requirements/recommendations for international students: Required—TOEFL (minimum score 550 paper-based; 79 iBT). *Application deadline:* For fall admission, 2/15 for domestic and international students; for spring admission, 11/1 for domestic students, 9/29 for international students. Application fee: $55 ($65 for international students). Electronic applications accepted. *Financial support:* Research assistantships with partial tuition reimbursements, teaching assistantships with partial tuition reimbursements, career-related internships or fieldwork, institutionally sponsored loans, scholarships/grants, and unspecified assistantships available. Financial award application deadline: 7/1; financial award applicants required to submit FAFSA. *Faculty research:* Recruitment and retention of allied health professionals, relationship between APACHEE II scores and the need for a tracheotomy, health care workers, patient care, occupational stress, radiofrequency lesioning, absorption of lipophilic compounds, Vitamin D status in college-age students, childhood and adolescence obesity, nutrition education/interventions. *Unit head:* Dr. Ester Verhovsek, Chair, 423-547-4900, Fax: 423-439-4921, E-mail: verhovse@etsu.edu. *Application contact:* Dr. Ester Verhovsek, Chair, 423-547-4900, Fax: 423-439-4921, E-mail: verhovse@etsu.edu.
Website: http://www.etsu.edu/crhs/alliedhealth/

Emory University, Laney Graduate School, Division of Biological and Biomedical Sciences, Program in Nutrition and Health Sciences, Atlanta, GA 30322-1100. Offers PhD. *Degree requirements:* For doctorate, comprehensive exam, thesis/dissertation. *Entrance requirements:* For doctorate, GRE General Test, minimum GPA of 3.0 in science course work (recommended). Additional exam requirements/recommendations for international students: Required—TOEFL. Electronic applications accepted. *Faculty research:* Biochemistry, molecular and cell biology, clinical nutrition, community and preventive health, nutritional epidemiology.

Emory University, Rollins School of Public Health, Hubert Department of Global Health, Atlanta, GA 30322-1100. Offers global health (MPH); public nutrition (MSPH). *Degree requirements:* For master's, thesis, practicum. *Entrance requirements:* For master's, GRE General Test. Additional exam requirements/recommendations for international students: Required—TOEFL (minimum score 550 paper-based; 80 iBT). Electronic applications accepted.

Florida International University, Robert Stempel College of Public Health and Social Work, Department of Dietetics and Nutrition, Miami, FL 33199. Offers MS, PhD. *Program availability:* Part-time. *Faculty:* 11 full-time (10 women), 8 part-time/adjunct (all women). *Students:* 82 full-time (70 women), 41 part-time (34 women); includes 79 minority (10 Black or African American, non-Hispanic/Latino; 7 Asian, non-Hispanic/Latino; 59 Hispanic/Latino; 3 Two or more races, non-Hispanic/Latino), 15 international. Average age 30. 74 applicants, 46% accepted, 25 enrolled. In 2017, 38 master's, 2 doctorates awarded. *Degree requirements:* For master's, thesis; for doctorate, comprehensive exam, thesis/dissertation. *Entrance requirements:* For master's, minimum GPA of 3.0; for doctorate, GRE General Test, minimum GPA of 3.0, resume, letters of recommendation, faculty sponsor. Additional exam requirements/recommendations for international students: Required—TOEFL (minimum score 550 paper-based; 80 iBT). *Application deadline:* For fall admission, 6/1 for domestic students, 4/1 for international students; for spring admission, 10/1 for domestic students, 9/1 for international students. Applications are processed on a rolling basis. Application fee: $30. Electronic applications accepted. *Expenses:* Tuition, state resident: full-time $8912; part-time $446 per credit hour. Tuition, nonresident: full-time $21,393; part-time $992 per credit hour. *Required fees:* $390; $195 per semester. *Financial support:* Career-related internships or fieldwork, Federal Work-Study, institutionally sponsored loans, and scholarships/grants available. Financial award application deadline: 3/1; financial award applicants required to submit FAFSA. *Faculty research:* Clinical nutrition, cultural food habits, pediatric nutrition, diabetes, dietetic education. *Unit head:* Dr. Fatma Ercanli-Huffman, Chair, 305-348-3788, Fax: 305-348-1996, E-mail: huffmanf@fiu.edu. *Application contact:* Nanett Rojas, Assistant Director, Graduate Admissions, 305-348-7464, Fax: 305-348-7441, E-mail: gradadm@fiu.edu.

Florida State University, The Graduate School, College of Human Sciences, Department of Nutrition, Food and Exercise Sciences, Tallahassee, FL 32306-1493. Offers exercise physiology (MS, PhD); nutrition and food science (MS, PhD), including clinical nutrition (MS), food science, human nutrition (PhD), nutrition education and health promotion (MS), nutrition science (MS); sports nutrition (MS); sports sciences (MS). *Program availability:* Part-time. *Faculty:* 21 full-time (8 women). *Students:* 86 full-time (56 women), 5 part-time (2 women); includes 13 minority (1 Black or African American, non-Hispanic/Latino; 1 Asian, non-Hispanic/Latino; 2 Hispanic/Latino; 9 Two or more races, non-Hispanic/Latino), 17 international. 116 applicants, 57% accepted, 29 enrolled. In 2017, 23 master's, 9 doctorates awarded. *Degree requirements:* For master's, thesis optional; for doctorate, thesis/dissertation, preliminary examination, minimum of 24 credit hours dissertation, dissertation defense. *Entrance requirements:* For master's and doctorate, GRE General Test, minimum upper-division GPA of 3.0. Additional exam requirements/recommendations for international students: Required—TOEFL (minimum score 550 paper-based; 80 iBT). *Application deadline:* For fall admission, 4/1 for domestic and international students; for spring admission, 10/1 for domestic and international students. Applications are processed on a rolling basis. Application fee: $30. Electronic applications accepted. *Expenses:* $480 per credit hour in-state; $1,111 per credit hour out-of-state. *Financial support:* In 2017–18, 53 students received support, including 22 research assistantships with full tuition reimbursements available (averaging $9,446 per year), 36 teaching assistantships with full tuition reimbursements available (averaging $14,725 per year); career-related internships or fieldwork, Federal Work-Study, institutionally sponsored loans, scholarships/grants, and unspecified assistantships also available. Financial award application deadline: 2/1; financial award applicants required to submit FAFSA. *Faculty research:* Body composition, functional food, chronic disease and aging response; food safety, food allergy, and safety/quality detection methods; sports nutrition, energy and human performance; strength training, functional performance, cardiovascular physiology, sarcopenia. *Total annual research expenditures:* $613,329. *Unit head:* Dr. Chester Ray, Department Chair, 850-644-1850, Fax: 850-645-5000, E-mail: caray@fsu.edu. *Application contact:* Mary-Sue McLemore, Academic Support Assistant, 850-644-1117, E-mail: mmclemore@fsu.edu.
Website: https://humansciences.fsu.edu/nutrition-food-exercise-sciences/students/graduate-programs/

Framingham State University, Graduate Studies, Programs in Food and Nutrition, Coordinated Program in Dietetics, Framingham, MA 01701-9101. Offers MS. *Unit head:* Suzanne Neubauer, Coordinator and Advisor, E-mail: sneubauer@framingham.edu. *Application contact:* Graduate Office, 508-626-4550, Fax: 508-626-4030, E-mail: dgce@frc.mass.edu.

Framingham State University, Graduate Studies, Programs in Food and Nutrition, Program in Nutrition Science and Informatics, Framingham, MA 01701-9101. Offers MS. *Program availability:* Part-time, evening/weekend. *Entrance requirements:* For master's, GRE General Test. *Unit head:* Dr. Sarah Pilkenton, Coordinator, E-mail: spilkenton@framingham.edu. *Application contact:* 508-626-4550, Fax: 508-626-4030, E-mail: dgce@frc.mass.edu.

Franciscan Missionaries of Our Lady University, School of Health Professions, Baton Rouge, LA 70808. Offers health administration (MHA); nutritional sciences (MS); physical therapy (DPT); physician assistant studies (MMS). *Unit head:* Dr. Susan K. Steele-Moses, Dean, 225-768-1676. *Application contact:* Dr. Susan K. Steele-Moses, Dean, 225-768-1676.
Website: https://www.franu.edu/academics/schools/school-of-health-professions

George Mason University, College of Health and Human Services, Department of Nutrition and Food Studies, Fairfax, VA 22030. Offers food security (Certificate); nutrition (MS). *Program availability:* Part-time. *Faculty:* 6 full-time (all women), 5 part-time/adjunct (3 women). *Students:* 28 full-time (24 women), 26 part-time (25 women); includes 18 minority (7 Black or African American, non-Hispanic/Latino; 4 Asian, non-Hispanic/Latino; 4 Hispanic/Latino; 3 Two or more races, non-Hispanic/Latino), 13 international. Average age 34. 29 applicants, 90% accepted, 16 enrolled. In 2017, 19 master's, 1 other advanced degree awarded. *Degree requirements:* For master's, comprehensive exam, thesis optional. *Entrance requirements:* For master's, resume, 2 letters of recommendation, expanded goal statement, college transcripts; for Certificate, college transcripts, goals statement, 2 recommendation letters, resume. Additional exam requirements/recommendations for international students: Required—TOEFL (minimum score 575 paper-based; 88 iBT), IELTS (minimum score 6.5), PTE (minimum score 59). *Application deadline:* For fall admission, 4/1 for domestic and international students; for spring admission, 11/1 for domestic and international students. Application fee: $75 ($80 for international students). Electronic applications accepted. *Expenses:* Tuition, state resident: full-time $11,228; part-time $459.50 per credit. Tuition, nonresident: full-time $30,932; part-time $1280.50 per credit. *Required fees:* $3252; $135.50 per credit. Part-time tuition and fees vary according to course load and program. *Financial support:* In 2017–18, 4 students received support, including 4 research assistantships with tuition reimbursements available (averaging $15,750 per year); career-related internships or fieldwork, Federal Work-Study, and health care benefits (for full-time research or teaching assistantship recipients) also available. Support available to part-time students. Financial award applicants required to submit FAFSA. *Total annual research expenditures:* $51,812. *Unit head:* Lisa Pawloski, Chair, 703-993-4628, E-mail: lpawlosk@gmu.edu. *Application contact:* Joe Wilson, Office Manager, 703-993-9709, Fax: 703-993-2193, E-mail: jwilso25@gmu.edu.
Website: https://chhs.gmu.edu/nfs/

Georgia Southern University, Jack N. Averitt College of Graduate Studies, College of Health and Human Sciences, School of Health and Kinesiology, Dietetic Internship Program, Statesboro, GA 30458. Offers Certificate. *Students:* 16 part-time (15 women); includes 4 minority (1 Black or African American, non-Hispanic/Latino; 2 Asian, non-Hispanic/Latino; 1 Two or more races, non-Hispanic/Latino). Average age 25. *Degree requirements:* For Certificate, 1,200 hours of supervised practice experiences. *Entrance requirements:* Additional exam requirements/recommendations for international students: Required—TOEFL (minimum score 550 paper-based; 80 iBT), IELTS (minimum score 6). *Application deadline:* For fall admission, 1/16 for domestic students. Application fee: $50. Electronic applications accepted. *Expenses:* Tuition, state resident: full-time $4986; part-time $3324 per year. Tuition, nonresident: full-time $21,982; part-time $15,352 per year. *Required fees:* $2092; $1802 per credit hour. $901 per semester. Tuition and fees vary according to course load, campus/location and program. *Financial support:* In 2017–18, 4 students received support. Application deadline: 4/20; applicants required to submit FAFSA. *Faculty research:* Community and school nutrition, energy balance, medical nutrition. *Unit head:* Dr. Karen Spears, Dietetic Internship Coordinator, 912-478-2123, E-mail: kspears@georgiasouthern.edu.
Website: http://chhs.georgiasouthern.edu/hk/graduate/dietetic-internship/

Georgia State University, Byrdine F. Lewis School of Nursing, Division of Nutrition, Atlanta, GA 30302-3083. Offers MS. *Program availability:* Part-time. *Faculty:* 9 full-time (6 women). *Students:* 35 full-time (all women), 8 part-time (4 women); includes 8 minority (1 Black or African American, non-Hispanic/Latino; 2 Asian, non-Hispanic/Latino; 4 Hispanic/Latino; 1 Two or more races, non-Hispanic/Latino), 1 international. Average age 28. 53 applicants, 60% accepted, 25 enrolled. In 2017, 22 master's awarded. *Degree requirements:* For master's, portfolio or thesis. *Entrance requirements:* For master's, GRE, prerequisite courses in inorganic chemistry (1 semester), organic chemistry (1 semester), and human anatomy and physiology (2 semesters); transcripts; resume; statement of goals; letters of recommendation. Additional exam requirements/recommendations for international students: Required—TOEFL (minimum score 550 paper-based; 80 iBT). *Application deadline:* For fall admission, 5/15 for domestic and international students; for spring admission, 10/1 for domestic and international students. Application fee: $50. Electronic applications accepted. *Expenses:* Tuition, state resident: full-time $7020. Tuition, nonresident: full-time $22,518. *Required fees:* $2128. Tuition and fees vary according to degree level and program. *Financial support:* In 2017–18, research assistantships with tuition reimbursements (averaging $1,647 per year), teaching assistantships with full tuition reimbursements (averaging $2,666 per year) were awarded. Financial award application deadline: 4/1. *Faculty research:* Energy balance and body composition, nutrition and HIV in Kenya, lipid peroxidation, energy requirements in obese children, diet and incidence of type I diabetes. *Unit head:* Dr. Anita Nucci, Department Head, 404-413-1234, Fax: 404-413-1228.
Website: http://nutrition.gsu.edu/

Grand Valley State University, College of Health Professions, Clinical Dietetics Program, Allendale, MI 49401-9403. Offers MS. *Program availability:* Part-time. *Students:* 39 full-time (35 women), 1 (woman) part-time; includes 6 minority (3 Asian, non-Hispanic/Latino; 1 Hispanic/Latino; 2 Two or more races, non-Hispanic/Latino). Average age 24. 41 applicants, 63% accepted, 24 enrolled. In 2017, 14 master's awarded. *Degree requirements:* For master's, project or thesis. *Entrance requirements:* For master's, minimum cumulative undergraduate GPA of 3.0, 2.7 in clinical or advanced nutrition, pharmacology, pathophysiology, and biochemistry courses; resume; personal statement; two professional or academic recommendations. Additional exam requirements/recommendations for international students: Required—TOEFL (minimum iBT score of 80), IELTS (6.5), or Michigan English Language Assessment Battery (77). *Application deadline:* For fall admission, 4/1 for domestic students. Applications are processed on a rolling basis. Application fee: $30. Electronic applications accepted. *Expenses:* $686 per credit hour. *Financial support:* Unspecified assistantships available. *Faculty research:* Health behavior and food insecurity. *Unit head:* Dr. Jody Vogelzang, Director, 616-331-5059, Fax: 616-331-5550, E-mail: vogelzjo@gvsu.edu. *Application contact:* Darlene Zwart, Student Services Coordinator/Recruiting Contact, 616-331-3958, Fax: 616-331-5999, E-mail: zwartda@gvsu.edu.
Website: http://www.gvsu.edu/grad/clinicaldiet/

Harvard University, Harvard T.H. Chan School of Public Health, Department of Nutrition, Boston, MA 02115-6096. Offers PhD. *Accreditation:* CEPH. *Faculty:* 25 full-time (10 women), 17 part-time/adjunct (6 women). *Students:* 15 full-time (9 women);

includes 3 minority (1 Asian, non-Hispanic/Latino; 2 Two or more races, non-Hispanic/Latino), 8 international. Average age 29. In 2017, 3 doctorates awarded. *Degree requirements:* For doctorate, thesis/dissertation, qualifying exam. *Entrance requirements:* For doctorate, GRE. Additional exam requirements/recommendations for international students: Recommended—TOEFL (minimum score 600 paper-based; 100 iBT), IELTS (minimum score 7). *Application deadline:* For fall admission, 12/1 for domestic and international students. Application fee: $120. Electronic applications accepted. *Financial support:* Fellowships, research assistantships, teaching assistantships, Federal Work-Study, scholarships/grants, traineeships, and unspecified assistantships available. Support available to part-time students. Financial award application deadline: 2/15; financial award applicants required to submit FAFSA. *Faculty research:* Dietary and genetic factors affecting heart diseases in humans; interactions among nutrition, immunity, and infection; role of diet and lifestyle in preventing macrovascular complications in diabetics. *Unit head:* Dr. Frank Hu, Chair. *Application contact:* Vincent W. James, Director of Admissions, 617-432-1031, Fax: 617-432-7080, E-mail: admissions@hsph.harvard.edu.
Website: http://www.hsph.harvard.edu/nutrition/

Harvard University, Harvard T.H. Chan School of Public Health, PhD Program in Population Health Sciences, Boston, MA 02115. Offers environmental health (PhD); epidemiology (PhD); global health and population (PhD); nutrition (PhD); social and behavioral sciences (PhD). *Students:* 80 full-time (56 women); includes 23 minority (5 Black or African American, non-Hispanic/Latino; 7 Asian, non-Hispanic/Latino; 6 Hispanic/Latino; 5 Two or more races, non-Hispanic/Latino), 26 international. Average age 29. 469 applicants, 11% accepted, 42 enrolled. *Entrance requirements:* Additional exam requirements/recommendations for international students: Recommended—TOEFL, IELTS. *Application deadline:* For fall admission, 12/1 for domestic and international students. Electronic applications accepted. *Financial support:* Application deadline: 2/15; applicants required to submit FAFSA. *Unit head:* Bruce Villineau, Assistant Director, E-mail: phdphs@hsph.harvard.edu. *Application contact:* Vincent W. James, Director of Admissions, 617-432-1031, Fax: 617-432-7080, E-mail: admissions@hsph.harvard.edu.

Howard University, Graduate School, Department of Nutritional Sciences, Washington, DC 20059-0002. Offers nutrition (MS, PhD). *Program availability:* Part-time, evening/weekend. *Degree requirements:* For master's, comprehensive exam, thesis; for doctorate, comprehensive exam, thesis/dissertation. *Entrance requirements:* For master's and doctorate, minimum GPA of 3.0, general chemistry, organic chemistry, biochemistry, nutrition. Additional exam requirements/recommendations for international students: Required—TOEFL. Electronic applications accepted. *Faculty research:* Dietary fiber, phytate, trace minerals, cardio-vascular diseases, overweight/obesity.

Hunter College of the City University of New York, Graduate School, School of Urban Public Health, Program in Nutrition, New York, NY 10065-5085. Offers MS. *Accreditation:* AND. *Program availability:* Part-time, evening/weekend. *Degree requirements:* For master's, comprehensive exam, thesis optional, internship. *Entrance requirements:* For master's, GRE General Test, previous course work in calculus and statistics. Additional exam requirements/recommendations for international students: Required—TOEFL.

Huntington University of Health Sciences, Program in Nutrition, Knoxville, TN 37918. Offers clinical nutrition (DHS); nutrition (MS); personalized option (DHS). *Program availability:* Part-time, evening/weekend, online learning. *Degree requirements:* For doctorate, comprehensive exam, thesis/dissertation. *Entrance requirements:* For master's, bachelor's degree, essay, resume/curriculum vitae; for doctorate, master's degree, essay, references, interview, resume/curriculum vitae. Additional exam requirements/recommendations for international students: Required—TOEFL (minimum score 550 paper-based; 80 iBT); Recommended—IELTS. Electronic applications accepted.

Immaculata University, College of Graduate Studies, Program in Nutrition Education, Immaculata, PA 19345. Offers nutrition education for the registered dietitian (MA); nutrition education with dietetic internship (MA); nutrition education with wellness promotion (MA). *Program availability:* Part-time, evening/weekend. *Degree requirements:* For master's, comprehensive exam, thesis optional. *Entrance requirements:* For master's, GRE or MAT, minimum GPA of 3.0. Additional exam requirements/recommendations for international students: Required—TOEFL. Electronic applications accepted. *Faculty research:* Sports nutrition, pediatric nutrition, changes in food consumption patterns in weight loss, nutritional counseling.

Indiana University Bloomington, School of Public Health, Department of Applied Health Science, Bloomington, IN 47405. Offers behavioral, social, and community health (MPH); family health (MPH); health behavior (PhD); nutrition science (MS); professional health education (MPH); public health administration (MPH); safety management (MS); school and college health education (MS). *Degree requirements:* For master's, thesis optional; for doctorate, comprehensive exam, thesis/dissertation. *Entrance requirements:* For master's, GRE (for MS in nutrition science), 3 recommendations; for doctorate, GRE, 3 recommendations. Additional exam requirements/recommendations for international students: Required—TOEFL (minimum score 550 paper-based; 80 iBT). Electronic applications accepted. *Faculty research:* Cancer education, HIV/AIDS and drug education, public health, parent-child interactions, safety education, obesity, public health policy, public health administration, school health, health education, human development, nutrition, human sexuality, chronic disease, early childhood health.

Indiana University of Pennsylvania, School of Graduate Studies and Research, College of Health and Human Services, Department of Food and Nutrition, Indiana, PA 15705. Offers MS. *Program availability:* Part-time, online learning. *Faculty:* 4 full-time (all women). *Students:* 7 full-time (6 women), 53 part-time (49 women); includes 4 minority (2 Black or African American, non-Hispanic/Latino; 1 Hispanic/Latino; 1 Two or more races, non-Hispanic/Latino), 1 international. Average age 27. 43 applicants, 84% accepted, 24 enrolled. In 2017, 17 master's awarded. *Degree requirements:* For master's, thesis optional. *Entrance requirements:* For master's, GRE General Test, 2 letters of recommendation. Additional exam requirements/recommendations for international students: Required—TOEFL (minimum score 540 paper-based). *Application deadline:* Applications are processed on a rolling basis. Application fee: $50. Electronic applications accepted. *Expenses:* Tuition, state resident: full-time $12,000; part-time $500 per credit. Tuition, nonresident: full-time $18,000; part-time $750 per credit. *Required fees:* $4073; $165.55 per credit. $64 per term. *Financial support:* In 2017–18, 5 research assistantships with tuition reimbursements (averaging $5,166 per year) were awarded; fellowships with partial tuition reimbursements and Federal Work-Study also available. Support available to part-time students. Financial award application deadline: 4/15; financial award applicants required to submit FAFSA. *Unit head:* Dr. Rita M. Johnson, Chairperson, 724-357-4440, E-mail: rjohnson@iup.edu. *Application contact:* Dr. Stephanie Taylor-Davis, Graduate Coordinator, 724-357-7733, E-mail: stdavis@iup.edu.

Indiana University–Purdue University Indianapolis, School of Health and Rehabilitation Sciences, Indianapolis, IN 46202. Offers health and rehabilitation sciences (PhD); health sciences (MS); nutrition and dietetics (MS); occupational therapy (OTD); physical therapy (DPT); physician assistant (MPAS). *Program availability:* Part-time, evening/weekend. *Degree requirements:* For master's, thesis (for some programs). *Entrance requirements:* For master's, GRE General Test, minimum GPA of 3.0 (for MS in health sciences, nutrition and dietetics), 3.2 (for MS in occupational therapy), 3.0 cumulative and prerequisite math/science (for MPAS); for doctorate, GRE, minimum cumulative and prerequisite math/science GPA of 3.2. Additional exam requirements/recommendations for international students: Required—TOEFL (minimum score 550 paper-based; 79 iBT), IELTS (minimum score 6.5), PTE (minimum score 54). Electronic applications accepted. *Expenses:* Contact institution. *Faculty research:* Function and mobility across the lifespan, pediatric nutrition, driving and mobility rehabilitation, neurorehabilitation and biomechanics, rehabilitation and integrative therapy.

Instituto Tecnologico de Santo Domingo, Graduate School, Area of Health Sciences, Santo Domingo, Dominican Republic. Offers bioethics (M Bioethics); clinical bioethics (Certificate); clinical nutrition (Certificate); comprehensive health and the adolescent (Certificate); comrehensive adloescent health (MS); health and social security (M Mgmt).

Iowa State University of Science and Technology, Program in Diet and Exercise, Ames, IA 50011. Offers MS. *Entrance requirements:* For master's, GRE, minimum GPA of 3.5, 3 letters of recommendation. Additional exam requirements/recommendations for international students: Required—TOEFL (minimum score 550 paper-based; 79 iBT), IELTS (minimum score 6.5). Electronic applications accepted.

Iowa State University of Science and Technology, Program in Nutritional Sciences, Ames, IA 50011. Offers MS, PhD. *Entrance requirements:* For master's and doctorate, GRE General Test. Additional exam requirements/recommendations for international students: Required—TOEFL (minimum score 550 paper-based; 79 iBT), IELTS (minimum score 6.5). Electronic applications accepted.

James Madison University, The Graduate School, College of Health and Behavioral Studies, Program in Health Sciences, Harrisonburg, VA 22801. Offers nutrition and physical activity (MS). *Program availability:* Part-time. *Students:* 3 full-time (all women), 1 part-time (0 women); includes 1 minority (Black or African American, non-Hispanic/Latino). Average age 30. In 2017, 4 master's awarded. Application fee: $55. Electronic applications accepted. *Expenses:* Tuition, state resident: full-time $10,512; part-time $438 per credit hour. Tuition, nonresident: full-time $28,358; part-time $1162 per credit hour. *Required fees:* $1128. *Financial support:* In 2017–18, 2 students received support. Federal Work-Study and 2 assistantships (averaging $7911) available. Financial award application deadline: 3/1; financial award applicants required to submit FAFSA. *Unit head:* Dr. Allen Lewis, Department Head, 540-568-6510, E-mail: amatohk@jmu.edu. *Application contact:* Lynette D. Michael, Director of Graduate Admissions and Student Records, 540-568-6131 Ext. 6395, Fax: 540-568-7860, E-mail: michaeld@jmu.edu.
Website: http://www.healthsci.jmu.edu/index.html

James Madison University, The Graduate School, College of Health and Behavioral Studies, Program in Kinesiology, Harrisonburg, VA 22801. Offers clinical exercise physiology (MS); exercise physiology (MS); kinesiology (MAT, MS); nutrition and exercise (MS); physical and health education (MAT); sport and recreation leadership (MS). *Program availability:* Part-time, evening/weekend. *Students:* 43 full-time (22 women), 3 part-time (2 women); includes 10 minority (4 Black or African American, non-Hispanic/Latino; 1 Asian, non-Hispanic/Latino; 4 Hispanic/Latino; 1 Two or more races, non-Hispanic/Latino). Average age 30. In 2017, 46 master's awarded. Application fee: $55. Electronic applications accepted. *Expenses:* Tuition, state resident: full-time $10,512; part-time $438 per credit hour. Tuition, nonresident: full-time $28,358; part-time $1162 per credit hour. *Required fees:* $1128. *Financial support:* In 2017–18, 32 students received support, including 13 teaching assistantships with full tuition reimbursements available (averaging $8,837 per year); Federal Work-Study and 19 assistantships (averaging $7911), 20 athletic assistantships (averaging $9284) also available. Financial award application deadline: 3/1; financial award applicants required to submit FAFSA. *Unit head:* Dr. Christopher J. Womack, Department Head, 540-568-6145, E-mail: womackcx@jmu.edu. *Application contact:* Lynette D. Michael, Director of Graduate Admissions, 540-568-6131 Ext. 6395, Fax: 540-568-7860, E-mail: michaeld@jmu.edu.
Website: http://www.jmu.edu/kinesiology/

Johns Hopkins University, Bloomberg School of Public Health, Department of International Health, Baltimore, MD 21205. Offers global disease epidemiology and control (MSPH, PhD); global health economics (MHS); health systems (MSPH, PhD); human nutrition (MSPH, PhD); social and behavioral interventions (MSPH, PhD). *Students:* 270 full-time (216 women); includes 80 minority (8 Black or African American, non-Hispanic/Latino; 1 American Indian or Alaska Native, non-Hispanic/Latino; 52 Asian, non-Hispanic/Latino; 8 Hispanic/Latino; 11 Two or more races, non-Hispanic/Latino), 70 international. Average age 28. 562 applicants, 40% accepted, 82 enrolled. *Degree requirements:* For master's, comprehensive exam, thesis (for some programs), 1-year full-time residency, 4-9 month internship; for doctorate, comprehensive exam, thesis/dissertation or alternative, 1.5 years' full-time residency, oral and written exams. *Entrance requirements:* For master's, GRE General Test or MCAT, 3 letters of recommendation, resume; for doctorate, GRE General Test or MCAT, 3 letters of recommendation, resume, transcripts. Additional exam requirements/recommendations for international students: Required—TOEFL (minimum score 600 paper-based; 100 iBT); Recommended—IELTS (minimum score 7). Electronic applications accepted. *Financial support:* Fellowships, Federal Work-Study, scholarships/grants, traineeships, and stipends available. *Faculty research:* Nutrition, infectious diseases, health systems, health economics, humanitarian emergencies. *Unit head:* Dr. David Peters, Chair, 410-955-3928, Fax: 410-955-7159, E-mail: dpeters@jhsph.edu. *Application contact:* Cristina G. Salazar, Academic Program Manager, 410-955-3734, Fax: 410-955-7159, E-mail: csalazar@jhsph.edu.
Website: http://www.jhsph.edu/dept/IH/

Kansas State University, Graduate School, College of Human Ecology, Department of Food, Nutrition, Dietetics and Health, Manhattan, KS 66506. Offers dietetics (MS); human nutrition (PhD); nutrition, dietetics and sensory sciences (MS); nutritional sciences (PhD); public health nutrition (PhD); public health physical activity (PhD); sensory analysis and consumer behavior (PhD). *Program availability:* Part-time. *Degree requirements:* For master's, thesis or alternative, residency; for doctorate, thesis/dissertation, residency. *Entrance requirements:* For master's, GRE General Test, minimum undergraduate GPA of 3.0; for doctorate, GRE General Test, minimum graduate GPA of 3.0. Additional exam requirements/recommendations for international students: Required—TOEFL (minimum score 550 paper-based; 79 iBT), IELTS (minimum score 6.5). Electronic applications accepted. *Faculty research:* Cancer and immunology, obesity, sensory analysis and consumer behavior, nutrient metabolism, clinical and community interventions.

Kent State University, College of Education, Health and Human Services, School of Health Sciences, Program in Nutrition, Kent, OH 44242-0001. Offers MS. *Degree requirements:* For master's, thesis optional. *Entrance requirements:* For master's, 3 letters of reference, goals statement, minimum GPA of 3.0. Additional exam requirements/recommendations for international students: Required—TOEFL (minimum score 550 paper-based; 80 iBT). *Expenses:* Tuition, state resident: full-time $11,310; part-time $515 per credit hour. Tuition, nonresident: full-time $20,396; part-time $928 per credit hour. *International tuition:* $18,544 full-time.

Nutrition

Lehman College of the City University of New York, School of Health Sciences, Human Services and Nursing, Department of Health Sciences, Program in Nutrition, Bronx, NY 10468-1589. Offers clinical nutrition (MS); community nutrition (MS); dietetic internship (MS). *Degree requirements:* For master's, thesis or alternative.

Liberty University, School of Health Sciences, Lynchburg, VA 24515. Offers anatomy and cell biology (PhD); biomedical sciences (MS); epidemiology (MPH); exercise science (MS), including clinical, community physical activity, human performance, nutrition; global health (MPH); health promotion (MPH); medical sciences (MA), including biopsychology, business management, health informatics, molecular medicine, public health; nutrition (MPH). *Program availability:* Part-time, online learning. *Students:* 542 full-time (394 women), 696 part-time (541 women); includes 402 minority (286 Black or African American, non-Hispanic/Latino; 10 American Indian or Alaska Native, non-Hispanic/Latino; 34 Asian, non-Hispanic/Latino; 46 Hispanic/Latino; 1 Native Hawaiian or other Pacific Islander, non-Hispanic/Latino; 25 Two or more races, non-Hispanic/Latino), 59 international. Average age 32. 1,592 applicants, 40% accepted, 297 enrolled. In 2017, 204 master's awarded. *Degree requirements:* For master's, thesis (for some programs); for doctorate, thesis/dissertation. *Entrance requirements:* For doctorate, MAT or GRE, minimum GPA of 3.25 in master's program, 2-3 recommendations, writing samples (for some programs), letter of intent, professional vitae. Additional exam requirements/recommendations for international students: Required—TOEFL (minimum score 600 paper-based; 100 iBT). Application fee: $50. *Financial support:* Applicants required to submit FAFSA. *Unit head:* Dr. Ralph Linstra, Dean. *Application contact:* Jay Bridge, Director of Admissions, 800-424-9595, Fax: 800-628-7977, E-mail: gradadmissions@liberty.edu.

Life University, College of Graduate and Undergraduate Studies, Marietta, GA 30060-2903. Offers athletic training (MAT); chiropractic sport science (MS); nutrition and sport science (MS), including chiropractic sport science; positive psychology (MS), including life coaching psychology; sport coaching (MS), including exercise sport science; sport injury management (MS), including nutrition and sport science; sports health science (MS), including sports injury management. *Program availability:* Part-time, 100% online, blended/hybrid learning. *Faculty:* 11 full-time (6 women), 12 part-time/adjunct (10 women). *Students:* 82 full-time (58 women), 131 part-time (86 women); includes 116 minority (85 Black or African American, non-Hispanic/Latino; 2 American Indian or Alaska Native, non-Hispanic/Latino; 3 Asian, non-Hispanic/Latino; 26 Hispanic/Latino), 25 international. Average age 30. In 2017, 53 master's awarded. *Degree requirements:* For master's, comprehensive exam (for some programs), thesis optional. *Entrance requirements:* For master's, GRE General Test, minimum GPA of 3.0, 3 letters of recommendation, curriculum vitae. Additional exam requirements/recommendations for international students: Required—TOEFL (minimum score 500 paper-based). *Application deadline:* For fall admission, 4/1 priority date for domestic and international students; for winter admission, 12/1 priority date for domestic and international students; for spring admission, 3/1 priority date for domestic and international students. Applications are processed on a rolling basis. Application fee: $50. Electronic applications accepted. *Expenses:* Contact institution. *Financial support:* Career-related internships or fieldwork, Federal Work-Study, and tuition waivers (full and partial) available. Support available to part-time students. Financial award application deadline: 9/1; financial award applicants required to submit FAFSA. *Faculty research:* Nutrient metabolism, organizational effectiveness, injury prevention, athlete development, recovery modalities and treatment, sport nutrition, functional neurology, peace and conflict studies. *Unit head:* Dr. Jana Holwick, Dean of Graduate and Undergraduate Studies, 678-331-4407, Fax: 770-426-2699, E-mail: jana.holwick@life.edu. *Application contact:* Robyn Stanley, Director of Enrollment, 770-426-2889, E-mail: robin.stanley@life.edu.
Website: http://www.life.edu/enrollment/admissions/graduate-admissions

Lipscomb University, Program in Exercise and Nutrition Science, Nashville, TN 37204-3951. Offers MS. *Program availability:* Part-time, evening/weekend. *Faculty:* 6 full-time (3 women). *Students:* 40 full-time (33 women), 20 part-time (15 women); includes 12 minority (4 Black or African American, non-Hispanic/Latino; 2 Asian, non-Hispanic/Latino; 5 Hispanic/Latino; 1 Two or more races, non-Hispanic/Latino), 1 international. Average age 25. 59 applicants, 44% accepted, 12 enrolled. In 2017, 14 master's awarded. *Degree requirements:* For master's, comprehensive exam (for some programs), thesis optional. *Entrance requirements:* For master's, GRE (minimum score of 800), minimum GPA of 2.75 on all undergraduate work; 2 letters of recommendation; resume. Additional exam requirements/recommendations for international students: Required—TOEFL (minimum score 570 paper-based; 80 iBT). *Application deadline:* For fall admission, 6/1 for domestic students; for spring admission, 12/1 for domestic students. Applications are processed on a rolling basis. Application fee: $50 ($75 for international students). Electronic applications accepted. *Expenses:* Contact institution. *Financial support:* Unspecified assistantships available. Financial award applicants required to submit FAFSA. *Unit head:* Dr. Karen Robichaud, Director, 615-966-5602, E-mail: karen.robichaud@lipscomb.edu. *Application contact:* Julie Lillicrap, Administrative Assistant, 615-966-5700, E-mail: julie.lillicrap@lipscomb.edu.
Website: http://www.lipscomb.edu/kinesiology/graduate-programs

Logan University, College of Health Sciences, Chesterfield, MO 63017. Offers health informatics (MS); health professionals education (DHPE); nutrition and human performance (MS); sports science and rehabilitation (MS). *Program availability:* Part-time, online only, 100% online. *Faculty:* 4 full-time (1 woman), 25 part-time/adjunct (13 women). *Students:* 84 full-time (63 women), 417 part-time (314 women); includes 75 minority (36 Black or African American, non-Hispanic/Latino; 3 American Indian or Alaska Native, non-Hispanic/Latino; 15 Asian, non-Hispanic/Latino; 17 Hispanic/Latino; 4 Two or more races, non-Hispanic/Latino), 1 international. Average age 36. 238 applicants, 72% accepted, 134 enrolled. In 2017, 61 master's awarded. *Entrance requirements:* For master's, minimum GPA of 2.5; 6 hours of biology and physical science; bachelor's degree and 9 hours of business health administration (for health informatics). Additional exam requirements/recommendations for international students: Required—TOEFL (minimum score 500 paper-based; 79 iBT); Recommended—IELTS (minimum score 6.5). *Application deadline:* Applications are processed on a rolling basis. Application fee: $50. Electronic applications accepted. *Expenses:* $450 per credit hour (for MS), $650 per credit hour (for DHPE), $80 fee per trimester. *Financial support:* In 2017–18, 4 students received support. Federal Work-Study available. Support available to part-time students. Financial award applicants required to submit FAFSA. *Faculty research:* Ankle injury prevention in high school athletes, low back pain in college football players, short arc banding and low back pain, the effects of enzymes on inflammatory blood markers, gait analysis in high school and college athletes. *Unit head:* Dr. Sherri Cole, Dean, College of Health Sciences, 636-227-2100 Ext. 2702, Fax: 636-207-2418, E-mail: sherri.cole@logan.edu. *Application contact:* Natacha Douglas, Executive Director of Admissions, 636-227-2100 Ext. 1718, Fax: 636-207-2425, E-mail: admissions@logan.edu.

Loma Linda University, School of Public Health, Programs in Nutrition, Loma Linda, CA 92350. Offers public health nutrition (MPH, Dr PH). *Degree requirements:* For doctorate, thesis/dissertation. *Entrance requirements:* For doctorate, GRE General Test. Additional exam requirements/recommendations for international students: Required—Michigan English Language Assessment Battery or TOEFL. *Expenses:* Contact institution. *Faculty research:* Sports nutrition in minorities, dietary determinance of chronic disease, protein adequacy in vegetarian diets, relationship of dietary intake to hormone level.

London Metropolitan University, Graduate Programs, London, United Kingdom. Offers applied psychology (M Sc); architecture (MA); biomedical science (M Sc); blood science (M Sc); cancer pharmacology (M Sc); computer networking and cyber security (M Sc); computing and information systems (M Sc); conference interpreting (MA); counter-terrorism studies (M Sc); creative, digital and professional writing (MA); crime, violence and prevention (M Sc); criminology (M Sc); curating contemporary art (MA); data analytics (M Sc); digital media (MA); early childhood studies (MA); education (MA, Ed D); financial services law, regulation and compliance (LL M); food science (M Sc); forensic psychology (M Sc); health and social care management and policy (M Sc); human nutrition (M Sc); human resource management (MA); human rights and international conflict (MA); information technology (M Sc); intelligence and security studies (M Sc); international oil, gas and energy law (LL M); international relations (MA); interpreting (MA); learning and teaching in higher education (MA); legal practice (LL M); media and entertainment law (LL M); organizational and consumer psychology (M Sc); psychological therapy (M Sc); psychology of mental health (M Sc); public health (M Sc); public policy and management (MPA); security studies (M Sc); social work (M Sc); spatial planning and urban design (MA); sports therapy (M Sc); supporting older children and young people with dyslexia (MA); teaching languages (MA), including Arabic, English; translation (MA); woman and child abuse (MA).

Long Island University–LIU Post, School of Health Professions and Nursing, Brookville, NY 11548-1300. Offers biomedical science (MS); cardiovascular perfusion (MS); clinical lab sciences (MS); clinical laboratory management (MS); dietetic internship (Advanced Certificate); family nurse practitioner (MS, Advanced Certificate); forensic social work (Advanced Certificate); gerontology (Advanced Certificate); health administration (MPA); non-profit management (Advanced Certificate); nursing education (MS); nutrition (MS); public administration (MPA); social work (MSW). *Program availability:* Part-time, blended/hybrid learning. *Faculty:* 23 full-time (17 women), 33 part-time/adjunct (19 women). *Students:* 228 full-time (174 women), 227 part-time (185 women); includes 172 minority (76 Black or African American, non-Hispanic/Latino; 1 American Indian or Alaska Native, non-Hispanic/Latino; 44 Asian, non-Hispanic/Latino; 48 Hispanic/Latino; 3 Two or more races, non-Hispanic/Latino), 60 international. Average age 31. 392 applicants, 67% accepted, 138 enrolled. In 2017, 180 master's, 26 other advanced degrees awarded. *Degree requirements:* For master's, comprehensive exam (for some programs), thesis (for some programs). *Entrance requirements:* Additional exam requirements/recommendations for international students: Required—TOEFL (minimum score 85 iBT) or IELTS (7.5). *Application deadline:* Applications are processed on a rolling basis. Application fee: $50. Electronic applications accepted. *Expenses: Tuition:* Full-time $21,618; part-time $1201 per credit. *Required fees:* $1840; $920 per term. Tuition and fees vary according to course load. *Financial support:* In 2017–18, 102 students received support. Research assistantships, teaching assistantships, career-related internships or fieldwork, Federal Work-Study, scholarships/grants, and unspecified assistantships available. Support available to part-time students. Financial award application deadline: 2/15; financial award applicants required to submit FAFSA. *Faculty research:* Antibiotic resistance, evidence-based practice, family care, interprofessional learning, simulation learning. *Unit head:* Dr. Stacy Gropack, Dean, 516-299-2485, Fax: 516-299-2527, E-mail: post-shpn@liu.edu. *Application contact:* Kathy Riley, Associate Director of Graduate Admissions, 516-299-2900, Fax: 516-299-2137, E-mail: post-enroll@liu.edu.
Website: http://liu.edu/post/health

Louisiana State University and Agricultural & Mechanical College, Graduate School, College of Agriculture, School of Nutrition and Food Sciences, Baton Rouge, LA 70803. Offers MS, PhD. *Faculty:* 12 full-time (6 women). *Students:* 46 full-time (25 women), 8 part-time (7 women); includes 14 minority (9 Black or African American, non-Hispanic/Latino; 2 Asian, non-Hispanic/Latino; 3 Hispanic/Latino), 32 international. Average age 30. 21 applicants, 24% accepted, 5 enrolled. In 2017, 8 master's, 5 doctorates awarded. *Financial support:* In 2017–18, 1 fellowship (averaging $36,781 per year), 41 research assistantships (averaging $19,858 per year) were awarded. *Total annual research expenditures:* $11,988.
Website: https://www.lsu.edu/departments/nfs/

Louisiana Tech University, Graduate School, College of Applied and Natural Sciences, Ruston, LA 71272. Offers biology (MS); dietetics (Graduate Certificate); health informatics (MHI); molecular science and nanotechnology (MS, PhD). *Program availability:* Part-time. *Faculty:* 56 full-time (31 women), 10 part-time/adjunct (4 women). *Students:* 75 full-time (49 women), 32 part-time (23 women); includes 32 minority (19 Black or African American, non-Hispanic/Latino; 4 Asian, non-Hispanic/Latino; 8 Hispanic/Latino; 1 Two or more races, non-Hispanic/Latino), 9 international. Average age 29. 46 applicants, 67% accepted, 10 enrolled. In 2017, 36 master's, 1 doctorate, 15 other advanced degrees awarded. *Degree requirements:* For master's, comprehensive exam (for some programs), thesis (for some programs); for doctorate, comprehensive exam, thesis/dissertation. *Entrance requirements:* For master's and doctorate, GRE General Test, transcript with bachelor's degree awarded; for Graduate Certificate, transcript with bachelor's degree awarded. Additional exam requirements/recommendations for international students: Required—TOEFL (minimum score 550 paper-based; 80 iBT), IELTS (minimum score 6.5). *Application deadline:* For fall admission, 8/1 priority date for domestic students, 6/1 for international students; for winter admission, 11/1 priority date for domestic students, 9/1 for international students; for spring admission, 2/1 priority date for domestic students, 12/1 for international students; for summer admission, 5/1 priority date for domestic students, 3/1 for international students. Applications are processed on a rolling basis. Application fee: $40. Electronic applications accepted. *Expenses:* Tuition, state resident: full-time $5146. Tuition, nonresident: full-time $10,147. *International tuition:* $10,267 full-time. *Required fees:* $2273. *Financial support:* In 2017–18, 19 students received support, including 19 research assistantships with partial tuition reimbursements available (averaging $8,817 per year); career-related internships or fieldwork, Federal Work-Study, scholarships/grants, and unspecified assistantships also available. Financial award application deadline: 2/1. *Faculty research:* Developmentally appropriate practices in early childhood education, maternal and child nutrition, nutrition and cardiovascular disease, and early intervention for infants and toddlers; research in cell and molecular biology; health promotion in emerging adults, insulin pump use, forensic nursing, qualitative research, empathy in nursing students, civility in nursing education, and STI education; gene expression data analysis and data mining, knowledge discovery for health related data. *Unit head:* Dr. Gary A. Kennedy, Dean, 318-257-4287, Fax: 318-257-5060, E-mail: kennedy@latech.edu.
Website: http://ans.latech.edu/

Loyola University Chicago, Graduate School, Marcella Niehoff School of Nursing, Maywood, IL 60141. Offers adult clinical nurse specialist (MSN, Certificate); adult nurse practitioner (Certificate); dietetics (MS); family nurse practitioner (Certificate); family, adult, and women's health nurse practitioner (MSN); health systems leadership (MSN); healthcare quality using education in safety and technology (DNP); infection prevention (MSN, DNP); nursing science (PhD); women's health clinical nurse specialist (Certificate). *Accreditation:* AACN. *Program availability:* Part-time, blended/hybrid learning. *Faculty:* 24 full-time (22 women), 21 part-time/adjunct (19 women). *Students:* 188 full-time (178 women), 222 part-time (208 women); includes 105 minority (23 Black or African American, non-Hispanic/Latino; 40 Asian, non-Hispanic/Latino; 30 Hispanic/Latino; 2 Native

Hawaiian or other Pacific Islander, non-Hispanic/Latino; 10 Two or more races, non-Hispanic/Latino), 4 international. Average age 36. 197 applicants, 55% accepted, 80 enrolled. In 2017, 94 master's, 17 doctorates, 26 other advanced degrees awarded. *Degree requirements:* For master's, comprehensive exam; for doctorate, thesis/dissertation, qualifying examination (for PhD); capstone project (for DNP). *Entrance requirements:* For master's, BSN, minimum nursing GPA of 3.0, Illinois RN license, 3 letters of recommendation, 1000 hours of experience in area of specialty prior to starting clinical rotations, personal statement; for doctorate, BSN or MSN, minimum GPA of 3.0, professional nursing license, 3 letters of recommendation, personal statement. Additional exam requirements/recommendations for international students: Required—TOEFL (minimum score 550 paper-based; 79 iBT), IELTS (minimum score 6.5). *Application deadline:* For fall admission, 6/1 priority date for domestic and international students; for spring admission, 11/15 priority date for domestic and international students; for summer admission, 3/15 priority date for domestic and international students. Applications are processed on a rolling basis. Application fee: $50. Electronic applications accepted. Application fee is waived when completed online. *Expenses:* Contact institution. *Financial support:* In 2017–18, 10 students received support, including 3 research assistantships with full tuition reimbursements available (averaging $18,000 per year), 1 teaching assistantship with full tuition reimbursement available (averaging $18,000 per year); scholarships/grants, unspecified assistantships, and nurse faculty loan program also available. Financial award application deadline: 5/1; financial award applicants required to submit FAFSA. *Faculty research:* Epigenetics and social determinants of health; women's health; vitamin D; health equity; interprofessional education; prevention and self-management of chronic disease; body mass in oncology patients. *Total annual research expenditures:* $1.4 million. *Unit head:* Dr. Vickie Keough, Dean, 708-216-5448, Fax: 708-216-9555, E-mail: vkeough@luc.edu. *Application contact:* Toni Topalova, Enrollment Advisor, 708-216-3751, Fax: 708-216-9555, E-mail: atopalova@luc.edu.
Website: http://www.luc.edu/nursing/

Marshall University, Academic Affairs Division, College of Health Professions, Department of Dietetics, Huntington, WV 25755. Offers MS, Certificate. *Students:* 12 full-time (10 women), 2 part-time (1 woman); includes 1 minority (Asian, non-Hispanic/Latino). Average age 28. In 2017, 13 master's awarded. *Unit head:* Dr. Kelli Williams, Chairperson, 304-696-4336, E-mail: williamsk@marshall.edu. *Application contact:* Information Contact, 304-746-1900, Fax: 304-746-1902, E-mail: services@marshall.edu.

Maryland University of Integrative Health, Programs in Nutrition, Laurel, MD 20723. Offers clinical nutrition (DCN), nutrition and integrative health (MS, Post Master's Certificate).

Marywood University, Academic Affairs, College of Health and Human Services, Department of Nutrition and Dietetics, Program in Dietetic Internship, Scranton, PA 18509-1598. Offers Certificate. *Program availability:* Online learning. Electronic applications accepted.

Marywood University, Academic Affairs, College of Health and Human Services, Department of Nutrition and Dietetics, Program in Nutrition, Scranton, PA 18509-1598. Offers MS. *Program availability:* Part-time. Electronic applications accepted.

Marywood University, Academic Affairs, College of Health and Human Services, Department of Nutrition and Dietetics, Program in Sports Nutrition and Exercise Science, Scranton, PA 18509-1598. Offers MS. *Program availability:* Part-time. Electronic applications accepted.

McGill University, Faculty of Graduate and Postdoctoral Studies, Faculty of Agricultural and Environmental Sciences, School of Dietetics and Human Nutrition, Montréal, QC H3A 2T5, Canada. Offers dietetics (M Sc A, Graduate Diploma); human nutrition (M Sc, M Sc A, PhD).

McMaster University, Faculty of Health Sciences and School of Graduate Studies, Program in Medical Sciences, Metabolism and Nutrition Area, Hamilton, ON L8S 4M2, Canada. Offers M Sc, PhD, MD/PhD. *Degree requirements:* For master's, thesis; for doctorate, comprehensive exam, thesis/dissertation. *Entrance requirements:* For master's, honors B Sc, B+ average in related field; for doctorate, M Sc, minimum B+ average, students with proven research experience and an A average may be admitted with a B Sc degree. Additional exam requirements/recommendations for international students: Required—TOEFL (minimum score 580 paper-based; 92 iBT).

McNeese State University, Doré School of Graduate Studies, Burton College of Education, Department of Health and Human Performance, Lake Charles, LA 70609. Offers exercise physiology (MS); health promotion (MS); nutrition and wellness (MS). *Accreditation:* NCATE. *Program availability:* Evening/weekend. *Entrance requirements:* For master's, GRE, undergraduate major or minor in health and human performance or related field of study. *Application deadline:* For fall admission, 5/15 priority date for domestic and international students; for spring admission, 10/15 priority date for domestic and international students. Applications are processed on a rolling basis. Application fee: $20 ($30 for international students). *Financial support:* Application deadline: 5/1. *Unit head:* Dr. Michael Soileau, Department Head, 337-475-5274, Fax: 337-475-5947, E-mail: msoileau@mcneese.edu. *Application contact:* Dr. Dustin M. Hebert, Director of Dore' School of Graduate Studies, 337-475-5396, Fax: 337-475-5397, E-mail: admissions@mcneese.edu.

Meredith College, School of Education, Health and Human Sciences, Nutrition, Health and Human Performance Department, Raleigh, NC 27607-5298. Offers dietetic internship (Postbaccalaureate Certificate); nutrition (MS). *Accreditation:* AND. *Students:* 60 full-time (53 women), 53 part-time (52 women); includes 15 minority (3 Black or African American, non-Hispanic/Latino; 5 Asian, non-Hispanic/Latino; 5 Hispanic/Latino; 2 Two or more races, non-Hispanic/Latino). Average age 26. 144 applicants, 56% accepted, 71 enrolled. In 2017, 18 master's, 27 other advanced degrees awarded. *Degree requirements:* For master's, thesis optional. *Entrance requirements:* For master's, GRE, recommendations, interview. Additional exam requirements/recommendations for international students: Required—TOEFL. *Application deadline:* For fall admission, 7/1 priority date for domestic and international students; for spring admission, 11/1 priority date for domestic and international students. Applications are processed on a rolling basis. Application fee: $50. Electronic applications accepted. *Expenses:* Contact institution. *Financial support:* Application deadline: 2/15; applicants required to submit FAFSA. *Unit head:* Dr. Judy Peel, Head, 919-760-8014, E-mail: peeljudy@meredith.edu. *Application contact:* Dr. William H. Landis, Director, 919-760-2355, Fax: 919-760-2819, E-mail: landisb@meredith.edu.

Michigan State University, The Graduate School, College of Agriculture and Natural Resources and College of Natural Science, Department of Food Science and Human Nutrition, East Lansing, MI 48824. Offers food science (MS, PhD); food science - environmental toxicology (PhD); human nutrition (MS, PhD); human nutrition-environmental toxicology (PhD). *Entrance requirements:* Additional exam requirements/recommendations for international students: Required—TOEFL (minimum score 550 paper-based), Michigan State University ELT (minimum score 85), Michigan English Language Assessment Battery (minimum score 83). Electronic applications accepted.

Mississippi State University, College of Agriculture and Life Sciences, Department of Food Science, Nutrition and Health Promotion, Mississippi State, MS 39762. Offers food science and technology (MS, PhD); health promotion (MS); nutrition (MS, PhD). *Program availability:* Blended/hybrid learning. *Faculty:* 17 full-time (6 women). *Students:* 57 full-time (41 women), 29 part-time (25 women); includes 20 minority (12 Black or African American, non-Hispanic/Latino; 3 Asian, non-Hispanic/Latino; 5 Hispanic/Latino), 21 international. Average age 30. 73 applicants, 32% accepted, 18 enrolled. In 2017, 21 master's, 9 doctorates awarded. *Degree requirements:* For master's, comprehensive exam, thesis; for doctorate, comprehensive exam, thesis/dissertation. *Entrance requirements:* For master's, GRE General Test, minimum GPA of 2.75; for doctorate, GRE General Test, minimum GPA of 2.75 undergraduate, 3.0 graduate. Additional exam requirements/recommendations for international students: Required—TOEFL (minimum score 550 paper-based; 79 iBT); Recommended—IELTS (minimum score 6.5). *Application deadline:* For fall admission, 7/1 for domestic students, 5/1 for international students; for spring admission, 11/1 for domestic students, 9/1 for international students. Applications are processed on a rolling basis. Application fee: $60 ($80 for international students). Electronic applications accepted. *Expenses:* Tuition, state resident: full-time $8318; part-time $462.12 per credit hour. Tuition, nonresident: full-time $22,358; part-time $1242.12 per credit hour. *Required fees:* $110; $12.24 per credit hour. $6.12 per semester. *Financial support:* Federal Work-Study, institutionally sponsored loans, scholarships/grants, and unspecified assistantships available. Financial award application deadline: 4/1; financial award applicants required to submit FAFSA. *Faculty research:* Food preservation, food chemistry, food safety, food processing, product development. *Unit head:* Dr. Marion Will Evans, Professor and Head, 662-325-5508, Fax: 662-325-8728, E-mail: mwe59@msstate.edu. *Application contact:* Marina Hunt, Admissions and Enrollment Assistant, 662-325-5188, E-mail: mhunt@grad.msstate.edu.
Website: http://www.fsnhp.msstate.edu

Missouri State University, Graduate College, College of Health and Human Services, Department of Biomedical Sciences, Springfield, MO 65897. Offers cell and molecular biology (MS); dietetic internship (Certificate); nurse anesthesia (DNAP). *Accreditation:* AANA/CANAEP (one or more programs are accredited). *Program availability:* Part-time. *Faculty:* 15 full-time (6 women), 17 part-time/adjunct (8 women). *Students:* 98 full-time (52 women), 55 part-time (32 women); includes 25 minority (12 Black or African American, non-Hispanic/Latino; 6 Asian, non-Hispanic/Latino; 5 Hispanic/Latino; 1 Native Hawaiian or other Pacific Islander, non-Hispanic/Latino; 1 Two or more races, non-Hispanic/Latino). Average age 28. 37 applicants, 70% accepted, 26 enrolled. In 2017, 10 master's, 42 doctorates awarded. *Degree requirements:* For master's, thesis or alternative, oral exam. *Entrance requirements:* For master's, GRE, minimum GPA of 3.0. Additional exam requirements/recommendations for international students: Required—TOEFL (minimum score 550 paper-based; 79 iBT), IELTS (minimum score 6). *Application deadline:* For fall admission, 7/20 for domestic students, 5/1 for international students; for spring admission, 12/20 for domestic students, 9/1 for international students. Application fee: $35 ($50 for international students). Electronic applications accepted. *Expenses:* Tuition, state resident: full-time $2915; part-time $2021 per credit hour. Tuition, nonresident: full-time $5354; part-time $3647 per credit hour. *International tuition:* $11,992 full-time. *Required fees:* $173; $173 per credit hour. Tuition and fees vary according to class time, course level, course load, degree level, campus/location and program. *Financial support:* In 2017–18, 11 teaching assistantships with full tuition reimbursements (averaging $8,772 per year) were awarded; Federal Work-Study, institutionally sponsored loans, scholarships/grants, and unspecified assistantships also available. Financial award application deadline: 3/31; financial award applicants required to submit FAFSA. *Unit head:* Dr. Colette Witkowski, Department Head, 417-836-6161, Fax: 417-836-5588, E-mail: biomedicalsciences@missouristate.edu. *Application contact:* Stephanie Praschan, Director, Graduate Enrollment Management, 417-836-5330, Fax: 417-836-6200, E-mail: stephaniepraschan@missouristate.edu.
Website: http://www.missouristate.edu/bms/

Montclair State University, The Graduate School, College of Education and Human Services, American Dietetics Certificate Program, Montclair, NJ 07043-1624. Offers Postbaccalaureate Certificate. *Program availability:* Part-time, evening/weekend. *Entrance requirements:* Additional exam requirements/recommendations for international students: Required—TOEFL (minimum score 65 iBT), IELTS. Electronic applications accepted.

Montclair State University, The Graduate School, College of Education and Human Services, Nutrition and Exercise Science Certificate Program, Montclair, NJ 07043-1624. Offers Certificate. Electronic applications accepted.

Montclair State University, The Graduate School, College of Education and Human Services, Program in Nutrition and Food Science, Montclair, NJ 07043-1624. Offers MS. *Program availability:* Part-time, evening/weekend. *Degree requirements:* For master's, comprehensive exam, thesis or alternative. *Entrance requirements:* For master's, GRE General Test, essay, 2 letters of recommendation. Additional exam requirements/recommendations for international students: Required—TOEFL (minimum score 83 iBT), IELTS (minimum score 6.5). Electronic applications accepted.

Mount Mary University, Graduate Programs, Program in Dietetics, Milwaukee, WI 53222-4597. Offers dietetics (MS); dietetics internship (MS). *Program availability:* Part-time, evening/weekend. *Degree requirements:* For master's, thesis or alternative. *Entrance requirements:* For master's, minimum GPA of 2.75, completion of ADA and DPD requirements. Additional exam requirements/recommendations for international students: Required—TOEFL (minimum score 550 paper-based; 80 iBT); Recommended—IELTS (minimum score 6.5). Electronic applications accepted. *Expenses:* Contact institution.

Mount Saint Vincent University, Graduate Programs, Department of Applied Human Nutrition, Halifax, NS B3M 2J6, Canada. Offers M Sc AHN, MAHN. *Program availability:* Part-time, evening/weekend. *Degree requirements:* For master's, thesis (for some programs). *Entrance requirements:* For master's, bachelor's degree in related field, minimum GPA of 3.0, professional experience. Electronic applications accepted.

Murray State University, School of Nursing and Health Professions, Department of Applied Health Sciences, Murray, KY 42071. Offers nutrition (MS); registered dietitian (Certificate). *Program availability:* Part-time, evening/weekend, 100% online. *Faculty:* 4 full-time (all women). *Students:* 10 full-time (9 women), 7 part-time (6 women). Average age 26. 1 applicant. In 2017, 4 master's awarded. *Entrance requirements:* For master's and Certificate, GRE or GMAT, minimum university GPA of 2.75. Additional exam requirements/recommendations for international students: Required—TOEFL (minimum score 527 paper-based; 71 iBT). *Application deadline:* Applications are processed on a rolling basis. Application fee: $40 ($50 for international students). Electronic applications accepted. *Expenses:* Tuition, state resident: full-time $9504. Tuition, nonresident: full-time $26,811. *International tuition:* $14,400 full-time. Tuition and fees vary according to course load, degree level and reciprocity agreements. *Financial support:* Federal Work-Study and unspecified assistantships available. Financial award applicants required to submit FAFSA. *Unit head:* Dr. Amelia Dodd, Chair, Department of Applied Health Sciences, 270-809-6463, Fax: 270-809-3413, E-mail: adodd@murraystate.edu. *Application contact:* Kaitlyn Burzynski, Interim Assistant Director for Graduate Admission and Records, 270-809-5732, Fax: 270-809-3780, E-mail: msu.graduateadmissions@murraystate.edu.
Website: http://www.murraystate.edu/academics/CollegesDepartments/nursing-and-health-professions/AHS/index.aspx

Nutrition

National University of Natural Medicine, School of Graduate Studies, Portland, OR 97201. Offers Ayurveda (MS); global health (MS); integrative medicine research (MS); integrative mental health (MS); nutrition (MS). *Faculty:* 7 full-time (5 women), 35 part-time/adjunct (25 women). *Students:* 184 (161 women). Average age 31. In 2017, 67 master's awarded. *Entrance requirements:* Additional exam requirements/recommendations for international students: Recommended—TOEFL, IELTS, TSE. *Application deadline:* For fall and winter admission, 5/1 for domestic and international students. Applications are processed on a rolling basis. Application fee: $75. Electronic applications accepted. *Expenses: Tuition:* Full-time $23,979. *Financial support:* Federal Work-Study and scholarships/grants available. Financial award application deadline: 2/15; financial award applicants required to submit FAFSA. *Faculty research:* Reliability of three constitutional questionnaires in Ayurveda diagnosis; mindfulness-based stress reduction for MS: feasibility, durability, and clinical outcomes; meditative neuroplasticity: the effect of qigong meditation on brain-derived neurotrophic factor and cortisol levels; food as medicine everyday research (FAMER): evaluating physiological changes associated with a shift toward a whole-foods diet. *Unit head:* Dr. Charles Kunert, Dean, 503-552-1742, Fax: 503-499-0027, E-mail: admission@nunm.edu. *Application contact:* Ryan Hollister, Associate Director of Admissions and Operations, 503-552-1665, Fax: 503-499-0027, E-mail: admissions@numn.edu.
Website: http://nunm.edu/academics/school-of-research-graduate-studies/

New York Chiropractic College, Program in Applied Clinical Nutrition, Seneca Falls, NY 13148-0800. Offers MS. *Program availability:* Part-time, evening/weekend. *Entrance requirements:* For master's, minimum GPA of 2.5, transcripts, writing sample. Additional exam requirements/recommendations for international students: Recommended—TOEFL. Electronic applications accepted.

New York Institute of Technology, School of Health Professions, Department of Interdisciplinary Health Sciences, Old Westbury, NY 11568-8000. Offers clinical nutrition (MS). *Program availability:* Part-time, evening/weekend, online only, 100% online. *Faculty:* 1 (woman) full-time, 6 part-time/adjunct (all women). *Students:* 4 full-time (all women), 20 part-time (18 women); includes 8 minority (1 Black or African American, non-Hispanic/Latino; 3 Asian, non-Hispanic/Latino; 4 Hispanic/Latino). Average age 32. 26 applicants, 69% accepted, 12 enrolled. In 2017, 6 master's awarded. *Degree requirements:* For master's, comprehensive exam, thesis optional. *Entrance requirements:* For master's, bachelor's degree or equivalent; minimum undergraduate GPA of 2.85 with satisfactory preparation in science courses. Additional exam requirements/recommendations for international students: Required—TOEFL (minimum score 79 iBT), IELTS (minimum score 6). *Application deadline:* Applications are processed on a rolling basis. Application fee: $50. Electronic applications accepted. *Expenses:* $1,285 per credit plus fees. *Financial support:* Career-related internships or fieldwork, Federal Work-Study, scholarships/grants, tuition waivers (full and partial), and unspecified assistantships available. Support available to part-time students. Financial award application deadline: 2/15; financial award applicants required to submit FAFSA. *Faculty research:* Diabetes prevention and treatment, college students' health behavior, online education in health sciences, health policy, wellness in underserved populations. *Unit head:* Dr. Mindy Haar, Chair, 516-686-3818, Fax: 516-686-3795, E-mail: mhaar@nyit.edu. *Application contact:* Alice Dolitsky, Director, Graduate Admissions, 516-686-7520, Fax: 516-686-1116, E-mail: nyitgrad@nyit.edu.
Website: http://www.nyit.edu/degrees/clinical_nutrition

New York University, College of Global Public Health, New York, NY 10012. Offers biological basis of public health (PhD); community and international health (MPH); global health leadership (MPH); health systems and health services research (PhD); population and community health (PhD); public health nutrition (MPH); social and behavioral sciences (MPH); socio-behavioral health (PhD). *Accreditation:* CEPH. *Program availability:* Part-time, online learning. *Faculty:* 26 full-time (20 women), 104 part-time/adjunct (53 women). *Students:* 161 full-time (136 women), 70 part-time (54 women); includes 74 minority (24 Black or African American, non-Hispanic/Latino; 1 American Indian or Alaska Native, non-Hispanic/Latino; 27 Asian, non-Hispanic/Latino; 11 Hispanic/Latino; 4 Native Hawaiian or other Pacific Islander, non-Hispanic/Latino; 7 Two or more races, non-Hispanic/Latino), 39 international. Average age 29. 802 applicants, 70% accepted, 97 enrolled. In 2017, 1 master's awarded. *Degree requirements:* For master's, thesis (for some programs); for doctorate, thesis/dissertation. *Entrance requirements:* For master's and doctorate, GRE. Additional exam requirements/recommendations for international students: Required—TOEFL. *Application deadline:* For fall admission, 2/1 for domestic and international students. Applications are processed on a rolling basis. Electronic applications accepted. *Expenses:* Contact institution. *Financial support:* Federal Work-Study and scholarships/grants available. *Unit head:* Dr. Cheryl G. Healton, Director, 212-992-6741. *Application contact:* New York University Information, 212-998-1212.
Website: http://publichealth.nyu.edu/

New York University, Steinhardt School of Culture, Education, and Human Development, Department of Nutrition, Food Studies, and Public Health, Programs in Nutrition and Dietetics, New York, NY 10012. Offers clinical nutrition (MS); nutrition and dietetics (MS, PhD), including food and nutrition (MS); rehabilitation sciences (PhD). *Program availability:* Part-time. *Students:* Average age 33. 221 applicants, 24% accepted, 34 enrolled. In 2017, 51 master's, 1 doctorate awarded. *Entrance requirements:* For doctorate, GRE General Test, interview. Additional exam requirements/recommendations for international students: Required—TOEFL (minimum score 100 iBT). *Application deadline:* For fall admission, 12/1 priority date for domestic students, 12/1 for international students; for spring admission, 10/1 for domestic and international students. Applications are processed on a rolling basis. Application fee: $75. Electronic applications accepted. *Expenses: Tuition:* Full-time $41,352; part-time $19,968 per year. *Required fees:* $2496; $1628 per unit. $814 per term. Tuition and fees vary according to course load and program. *Financial support:* Fellowships with full and partial tuition reimbursements, career-related internships or fieldwork, Federal Work-Study, institutionally sponsored loans, scholarships/grants, tuition waivers (partial), and unspecified assistantships available. Financial award application deadline: 2/1; financial award applicants required to submit FAFSA. *Faculty research:* Nutrition and race, childhood obesity and other eating disorders, nutritional epidemiology, nutrition policy, nutrition and health promotion. *Unit head:* Dr. Krishnendu Ray, Associate Professor of Food Studies/Department Chair, 212-998-5580, Fax: 212-995-4194, E-mail: krishnendu.ray@nyu.edu. *Application contact:* 212-998-5030, Fax: 212-995-4328, E-mail: steinhardt.gradadmissions@nyu.edu.
Website: http://steinhardt.nyu.edu/nutrition/dietetics

North Carolina Agricultural and Technical State University, School of Graduate Studies, School of Agriculture and Environmental Sciences, Department of Family and Consumer Sciences, Greensboro, NC 27411. Offers child development early education and family studies (MAT); family and consumer sciences (MAT); food and nutrition (MS). *Program availability:* Part-time, evening/weekend. *Degree requirements:* For master's, comprehensive exam, thesis or alternative, qualifying exam. *Entrance requirements:* For master's, GRE General Test, minimum GPA of 2.6.

North Carolina State University, Graduate School, College of Agriculture and Life Sciences and College of Veterinary Medicine, Program in Nutrition, Raleigh, NC 27695. Offers MN, MS, PhD. *Program availability:* Part-time. *Degree requirements:* For master's, thesis (for some programs); for doctorate, thesis/dissertation. *Entrance requirements:* For master's and doctorate, GRE General Test. Additional exam requirements/recommendations for international students: Required—TOEFL (minimum score 550 paper-based). Electronic applications accepted. *Faculty research:* Effects of food/feed ingredients and components on health and growth, community nutrition, waste management and reduction, experimental animal nutrition.

North Dakota State University, College of Graduate and Interdisciplinary Studies, College of Human Development and Education, Department of Health, Nutrition, and Exercise Sciences, Fargo, ND 58102. Offers advanced athletic training (MS); athletic training (MAT); dietetics (MS); exercise science and nutrition (PhD); health, nutrition and exercise science (MS). *Program availability:* Part-time, evening/weekend, online learning. *Entrance requirements:* For master's, minimum GPA of 3.0. Additional exam requirements/recommendations for international students: Required—TOEFL (minimum score 525 paper-based; 71 iBT). *Application deadline:* For fall admission, 3/1 priority date for domestic and international students. Applications are processed on a rolling basis. Application fee: $35. Electronic applications accepted. *Expenses:* Tuition, state resident: full-time $4323; part-time $360.21 per credit. Tuition, nonresident: full-time $6484; part-time $540.31 per credit. *Required fees:* $668; $55.70 per credit. Part-time tuition and fees vary according to degree level, program and reciprocity agreements. *Financial support:* Application deadline: 3/31. *Faculty research:* Biomechanics, sport specialization, recreation, nutrition, athletic training. *Unit head:* Dr. Yeong Rhee, Department Head, 701-231-7476, Fax: 701-231-8872, E-mail: yeong.rhee@ndsu.edu. *Application contact:* Nancy Moberg, Academic Assistant, 701-231-7474, Fax: 701-231-6524.
Website: http://www.ndsu.edu/hnes/

Northeastern University, College of Professional Studies, Boston, MA 02115-5096. Offers applied nutrition (MS); college athletics administration (MSL); commerce and economic development (MS); corporate and organizational communication (MS); criminal justice (MS); digital media (MPS); elearning and instructional design (M Ed); elementary education (MAT); geographic information technology (MPS); global studies and international relations (MS); higher education administration (M Ed); homeland security (MA); human services (MS); informatics (MPS); leadership (MS); learning analytics (M Ed); learning and instruction (M Ed); nonprofit management (MS); professional sports administration (MSL); project management (MS); regulatory affairs for drugs, biologics, and medical devices (MS); respiratory care leadership (MS); special education (M Ed); technical communication (MS). *Program availability:* Part-time, evening/weekend, 100% online, blended/hybrid learning. *Faculty:* 82 full-time (51 women), 853 part-time/adjunct (366 women). *Students:* 5,278 part-time (3,230 women). In 2017, 1,586 master's awarded. *Application deadline:* Applications are processed on a rolling basis. Application fee: $0. Electronic applications accepted. *Expenses:* Contact institution. *Financial support:* Applicants required to submit FAFSA. *Unit head:* Dr. Mary Loeffelholz, Dean of the College of Professional Studies. *Application contact:* E-mail: cpsadmissions@northeastern.edu.
Website: https://cps.northeastern.edu/

Northern Illinois University, Graduate School, College of Health and Human Sciences, School of Health Studies, De Kalb, IL 60115-2854. Offers nutrition and dietetics (MS); public health (MPH). *Students:* 15 full-time (11 women), 33 part-time (24 women); includes 13 minority (6 Black or African American, non-Hispanic/Latino; 6 Asian, non-Hispanic/Latino; 1 Hispanic/Latino), 4 international. Average age 33. 37 applicants, 49% accepted, 5 enrolled. *Unit head:* Jim Ciesla, Interim Chair, 815-753-1384. *Application contact:* Graduate School Office, 815-753-0395, E-mail: gradsch@niu.edu.
Website: http://chhs.niu.edu/health-studies/

Northwestern Health Sciences University, College of Health and Wellness, Bloomington, MN 55431-1599. Offers acupuncture (M Ac); applied clinical nutrition (MHS); Oriental medicine (MOM). *Accreditation:* ACAOM. *Entrance requirements:* For master's, 60 semester credits of course work with minimum GPA of 2.5. Additional exam requirements/recommendations for international students: Required—TOEFL (minimum score 540 paper-based; 76 iBT). Electronic applications accepted.

Nova Southeastern University, Dr. Kiran C. Patel College of Osteopathic Medicine, Fort Lauderdale, FL 33328. Offers biomedical informatics (MS, Graduate Certificate), including biomedical informatics (MS), clinical informatics (Graduate Certificate), public health informatics (Graduate Certificate); disaster and emergency management (MS); medical education (MS); nutrition (MS, Graduate Certificate), including functional nutrition and herbal therapy (Graduate Certificate); osteopathic medicine (DO); public health (MPH, Graduate Certificate), including health education (Graduate Certificate); social medicine (Graduate Certificate); DO/DMD. *Accreditation:* AOsA. *Faculty:* 98 full-time (58 women), 1,484 part-time/adjunct (401 women). *Students:* 1,032 full-time (479 women), 197 part-time (129 women); includes 656 minority (97 Black or African American, non-Hispanic/Latino; 308 Asian, non-Hispanic/Latino; 215 Hispanic/Latino; 1 Native Hawaiian or other Pacific Islander, non-Hispanic/Latino; 35 Two or more races, non-Hispanic/Latino), 67 international. Average age 26. 5,226 applicants, 9% accepted, 248 enrolled. In 2017, 110 master's, 239 doctorates, 7 other advanced degrees awarded. *Degree requirements:* For master's, comprehensive exam (for MPH); field/special projects; for doctorate, comprehensive exam, COMLEX Board Exams; for Graduate Certificate, thesis or alternative. *Entrance requirements:* For master's, GRE; for doctorate, MCAT, coursework in biology, chemistry, organic chemistry, physics (all with labs), biochemistry, and English. *Application deadline:* For fall admission, 1/15 for domestic students. Applications are processed on a rolling basis. Application fee: $50. Electronic applications accepted. *Expenses:* Contact institution. *Financial support:* In 2017–18, 83 students received support, including 24 fellowships with tuition reimbursements available; Federal Work-Study and scholarships/grants also available. Financial award application deadline: 6/1; financial award applicants required to submit FAFSA. *Faculty research:* Teaching strategies, simulated patient use, HIV/AIDS education, minority health issues, immune disorders. *Unit head:* Elaine M. Wallace, Dean, 954-262-1457, Fax: 954-262-2250, E-mail: ewallace@nova.edu. *Application contact:* HPD Admissions, 877-640-0218, E-mail: hpdinfo@nova.edu.
Website: https://www.osteopathic.nova.edu/

The Ohio State University, Graduate School, College of Education and Human Ecology, Department of Human Sciences, Columbus, OH 43210. Offers consumer sciences (MS, PhD); human development and family science (PhD); human nutrition (MS, PhD); kinesiology (MA, Ed D, PhD). *Program availability:* Part-time. *Faculty:* 55. *Students:* 127 full-time (71 women), 14 part-time (12 women). Average age 27. In 2017, 31 master's, 14 doctorates awarded. *Degree requirements:* For master's, thesis optional; for doctorate, thesis/dissertation. *Entrance requirements:* For master's and doctorate, GRE. Additional exam requirements/recommendations for international students: Required—TOEFL (minimum score 550 paper-based; 79 iBT), Michigan English Language Assessment Battery (minimum score 82); Recommended—IELTS (minimum score 7). *Application deadline:* For fall admission, 12/1 priority date for domestic and international students. Applications are processed on a rolling basis. Application fee: $60 ($70 for international students). Electronic applications accepted. *Financial support:* Fellowships with tuition reimbursements, research assistantships with tuition reimbursements, teaching assistantships with tuition reimbursements,

Federal Work-Study, and institutionally sponsored loans available. Support available to part-time students. *Unit head:* Dr. Brian Focht, Associate Chair and Professor, E-mail: focht.10@osu.edu. *Application contact:* Graduate and Professional Admissions, 614-292-9444, Fax: 614-292-3895, E-mail: gpadmissions@osu.edu.
Website: http://ehe.osu.edu/human-sciences/

The Ohio State University, Graduate School, College of Education and Human Ecology, Human Nutrition Program, Columbus, OH 43210. Offers PhD. Program offered jointly with College of Food, Agricultural, and Environmental Sciences, College of Medicine, and College of Veterinary Medicine. *Faculty:* 38. *Students:* 34 (21 women). Average age 28. In 2017, 5 doctorates awarded. *Degree requirements:* For doctorate, thesis/dissertation. *Entrance requirements:* For doctorate, GRE. Additional exam requirements/recommendations for international students: Required—TOEFL (minimum score 600 paper-based; 100 iBT); Recommended—IELTS (minimum score 8). *Application deadline:* For fall admission, 12/1 priority date for domestic and international students. Applications are processed on a rolling basis. Application fee: $60 ($70 for international students). Electronic applications accepted. *Financial support:* Applicants required to submit FAFSA. *Unit head:* Dr. Amanda Bird, Director, 614-292-9957, E-mail: osun@osu.edu. *Application contact:* Graduate and Professional Admissions, 614-292-9444, Fax: 614-292-3895, E-mail: gpadmissions@osu.edu.
Website: http://osun.osu.edu/

Ohio University, Graduate College, College of Health Sciences and Professions, School of Applied Health Sciences and Wellness, Program in Food and Nutrition, Athens, OH 45701-2979. Offers human and consumer sciences (MS).

Oklahoma State University, College of Human Sciences, Department of Nutritional Sciences, Stillwater, OK 74078. Offers MS, PhD. *Program availability:* Online learning. *Faculty:* 19 full-time (14 women), 4 part-time/adjunct (all women). *Students:* 22 full-time (21 women), 38 part-time (29 women); includes 10 minority (3 Black or African American, non-Hispanic/Latino; 2 American Indian or Alaska Native, non-Hispanic/Latino; 3 Asian, non-Hispanic/Latino; 2 Hispanic/Latino), 9 international. Average age 29. 31 applicants, 55% accepted, 16 enrolled. In 2017, 16 master's, 3 doctorates awarded. *Entrance requirements:* For master's and doctorate, GRE or GMAT. Additional exam requirements/recommendations for international students: Required—TOEFL (minimum score 550 paper-based; 79 iBT). *Application deadline:* For fall admission, 3/1 priority date for international students; for spring admission, 8/1 priority date for international students. Applications are processed on a rolling basis. Application fee: $40 ($75 for international students). Electronic applications accepted. *Expenses:* Tuition, state resident: full-time $4019; part-time $2679.60 per year. Tuition, nonresident: full-time $15,286; part-time $10,190.40 per year. *Required fees:* $2129; $1419 per unit. Tuition and fees vary according to program. *Financial support:* Research assistantships, teaching assistantships, career-related internships or fieldwork, Federal Work-Study, scholarships/grants, health care benefits, tuition waivers (partial), and unspecified assistantships available. Support available to part-time students. Financial award application deadline: 3/1; financial award applicants required to submit FAFSA. *Faculty research:* Nutritional sciences, micronutrients and chronic disease, phytochemicals, nutrition education, osteoporosis, food service administration. *Unit head:* Dr. Nancy M. Betts, Department Head, 405-744-5040, Fax: 405-744-1357, E-mail: nancy.betts@okstate.edu. *Application contact:* Dr. Gail Gates, Graduate Coordinator, 405-744-3845, Fax: 405-744-1357, E-mail: gail.gates@okstate.edu.
Website: http://humansciences.okstate.edu/nsci/

Oregon Health & Science University, School of Medicine, Graduate Programs in Medicine, Program in Clinical Nutrition, Portland, OR 97239-3098. Offers dietetics (Certificate); human nutrition (MS). *Program availability:* Part-time. *Faculty:* 1 (woman) full-time, 10 part-time/adjunct (all women). *Students:* 27 full-time (26 women), 1 (woman) part-time; includes 4 minority (3 Asian, non-Hispanic/Latino; 1 Hispanic/Latino), 1 international. Average age 27. 23 applicants, 43% accepted, 9 enrolled. In 2017, 8 master's awarded. *Degree requirements:* For master's, thesis optional. *Entrance requirements:* For master's, GRE General Test (minimum scores: 153 Verbal/148 Quantitative/4.5 Analytical), Registered Dietitian. *Application deadline:* For fall admission, 1/1 for domestic students. Application fee: $120. *Financial support:* Fellowships, career-related internships or fieldwork, and travel and conference funding awards available. Financial award application deadline: 3/1; financial award applicants required to submit FAFSA. *Faculty research:* Inborn errors of metabolism, weight loss/weight regulation, body composition/energy expenditure, nutritional epidemiology, medical nutrition therapy. *Unit head:* Dr. Diane Stadler, Program Director, E-mail: gphn@ohsu.edu. *Application contact:* Alexis Young, Administrative Coordinator, E-mail: gphn@ohsu.edu.

Oregon State University, College of Public Health and Human Sciences, Program in Nutrition, Corvallis, OR 97331. Offers MS, PhD. *Entrance requirements:* For master's and doctorate, GRE, minimum GPA of 3.0 in last 90 hours of course work. Additional exam requirements/recommendations for international students: Required—TOEFL (minimum score 80 iBT), IELTS (minimum score 6.5). *Application deadline:* For fall admission, 12/1 for domestic and international students. Applications are processed on a rolling basis. Electronic applications accepted. *Financial support:* Application deadline: 12/1. *Faculty research:* Human metabolic studies, trace minerals, food science, food management. *Application contact:* Debi Rothermund, Administrative Program Specialist, 541-737-3324, Fax: 541-737-6914, E-mail: debi.rothermund@oregonstate.edu.
Website: http://health.oregonstate.edu/degrees/graduate/nutrition

Penn State University Park, Graduate School, College of Health and Human Development, Department of Nutritional Sciences, University Park, PA 16802. Offers MS, PhD. *Unit head:* Dr. Ann C. Crouter, Dean, 814-865-1420, Fax: 814-865-3282. *Application contact:* Lori Hawn, Director, Graduate Student Services, 814-865-1795, Fax: 814-863-4627, E-mail: l-gswww@lists.psu.edu.
Website: http://nutrition.hhd.psu.edu/

Purdue University, Graduate School, College of Health and Human Sciences, Department of Nutrition Science, West Lafayette, IN 47907. Offers animal health (MS, PhD); biochemical and molecular nutrition (MS, PhD); growth and development (MS, PhD); human and clinical nutrition (MS, PhD); public health and education (MS, PhD). *Faculty:* 21 full-time (15 women), 1 part-time/adjunct (0 women). *Students:* 40 full-time (29 women), 9 part-time (7 women); includes 5 minority (3 Black or African American, non-Hispanic/Latino; 1 Asian, non-Hispanic/Latino; 1 Two or more races, non-Hispanic/Latino), 20 international. Average age 28. 66 applicants, 33% accepted, 13 enrolled. In 2017, 2 master's, 6 doctorates awarded. *Degree requirements:* For master's, thesis; for doctorate, thesis/dissertation. *Entrance requirements:* For master's and doctorate, GRE General Test (minimum scores in verbal and quantitative areas of 1000 or 300 on new scoring), minimum undergraduate GPA of 3.0 or equivalent. Additional exam requirements/recommendations for international students: Required—TOEFL (minimum score 600 paper-based; 77 iBT). *Application deadline:* For fall admission, 1/10 for domestic and international students. Applications are processed on a rolling basis. Application fee: $60 ($75 for international students). Electronic applications accepted. *Financial support:* Fellowships, research assistantships, and teaching assistantships available. Support available to part-time students. Financial award applicants required to submit FAFSA. *Faculty research:* Nutrient requirements, nutrient metabolism, nutrition and disease prevention. *Unit head:* Michele R. Forman, Head, 765-494-9921, E-mail: mforman@purdue.edu. *Application contact:* Jon A. Story, Graduate Contact for Admissions, 765-494-6843, E-mail: jastory@purdue.edu.
Website: http://www.cfs.purdue.edu/fn/

Queens College of the City University of New York, Mathematics and Natural Sciences Division, Department of Family, Nutrition and Exercise Sciences, Queens, NY 11367-1597. Offers exercise science specialist (MS); family and consumer science (K-12) (AC); family and consumer science/teaching curriculum (K-12) (MS Ed); nutrition and exercise science (MS); nutrition specialist (MS); physical education (K-12) (AC); physical education/teaching curriculum (pre K-12) (MS Ed). *Program availability:* Part-time, evening/weekend. *Faculty:* 13 full-time (11 women), 7 part-time/adjunct (4 women). *Students:* 15 full-time (7 women), 136 part-time (75 women); includes 67 minority (19 Black or African American, non-Hispanic/Latino; 1 American Indian or Alaska Native, non-Hispanic/Latino; 21 Asian, non-Hispanic/Latino; 25 Hispanic/Latino; 1 Two or more races, non-Hispanic/Latino), 3 international. Average age 30. 95 applicants, 76% accepted, 45 enrolled. In 2017, 34 master's, 12 other advanced degrees awarded. *Degree requirements:* For master's, research project. *Entrance requirements:* For master's, minimum GPA of 3.0. Additional exam requirements/recommendations for international students: Required—TOEFL (minimum paper-based score of 600) or IELTS (for program in nutrition). *Application deadline:* For fall admission, 4/1 for domestic students; for spring admission, 11/1 for domestic students. Applications are processed on a rolling basis. Application fee: $125. Electronic applications accepted. *Financial support:* Career-related internships or fieldwork and unspecified assistantships available. Financial award application deadline: 4/1; financial award applicants required to submit FAFSA. *Faculty research:* Health disparities; correlates of taste acuity, structuring and implementation of competition and competitive activities in physical education; exercise and metabolic risk in people living with HIV/AIDS; biomechanics, motor learning and motor control. *Unit head:* Dr. Ashima K. Kant, Chair, 718-997-4156 Ext. 4475, Fax: 718-997-4163, E-mail: ashima.kant@qc.cuny.edu. *Application contact:* Elizabeth D'Amico-Ramirez, Assistant Director of Graduate Admissions, 718-997-5203, E-mail: elizabeth.damicoramirez@qc.cuny.edu.

Rosalind Franklin University of Medicine and Science, College of Health Professions, Department of Nutrition, North Chicago, IL 60064-3095. Offers clinical nutrition (MS); health promotion and wellness (MS); nutrition education (MS). *Program availability:* Part-time, evening/weekend, online learning. *Degree requirements:* For master's, thesis optional, portfolio. *Entrance requirements:* For master's, minimum GPA of 2.75, registered dietitian (RD), professional certificate or license. Additional exam requirements/recommendations for international students: Required—TOEFL. *Expenses:* Contact institution. *Faculty research:* Nutrition education, distance learning, computer-based graduate education, childhood obesity, nutrition medical education.

Rush University, College of Health Sciences, Department of Clinical Nutrition, Chicago, IL 60612. Offers MS. *Program availability:* Part-time. *Degree requirements:* For master's, thesis. *Entrance requirements:* For master's, GRE General Test, minimum GPA of 3.0, course work in statistics, undergraduate didactic program approved by the American Dietetic Association. Additional exam requirements/recommendations for international students: Required—TOEFL. *Application deadline:* For winter admission, 2/15 for domestic and international students. Application fee: $40. Electronic applications accepted. *Financial support:* Career-related internships or fieldwork, Federal Work-Study, institutionally sponsored loans, scholarships/grants, and stipends available. Support available to part-time students. Financial award applicants required to submit FAFSA. *Faculty research:* Food service management, chronic disease prevention/treatment, obesity, Alzheimer's. *Unit head:* Dr. Kathryn S. Keim, Interim Chair, 312-942-5926, Fax: 312-942-5203.
Website: http://www.rushu.rush.edu/nutrition/

Rutgers University–Newark, School of Health Related Professions, Department of Nutritional Sciences, Dietetic Internship Program, Newark, NJ 07102. Offers Certificate. *Program availability:* Online learning. *Entrance requirements:* For degree, bachelor's degree in dietetics, nutrition, or related field; interview; minimum GPA of 2.9. Additional exam requirements/recommendations for international students: Required—TOEFL (minimum score 500 paper-based; 79 iBT). Electronic applications accepted.

Rutgers University–Newark, School of Health Related Professions, Department of Nutritional Sciences, Program in Clinical Nutrition, Newark, NJ 07102. Offers MS, DCN. *Program availability:* Part-time, evening/weekend, online learning. *Entrance requirements:* For master's, statement of career goals, minimum GPA of 3.2, proof of registered dietician status, interview, transcript of highest degree, bachelor's degree, 1 reference letter; for doctorate, minimum GPA of 3.4, transcript of highest degree, statement of career goals, interview, master's degree, 1 reference letter. Additional exam requirements/recommendations for international students: Required—TOEFL (minimum score 500 paper-based; 79 iBT). Electronic applications accepted.

Rutgers University–New Brunswick, Graduate School-New Brunswick, Program in Nutritional Sciences, Piscataway, NJ 08854-8097. Offers MS, PhD. *Program availability:* Part-time. Terminal master's awarded for partial completion of doctoral program. *Degree requirements:* For master's, thesis; for doctorate, thesis/dissertation, written qualifying exam. *Entrance requirements:* For master's and doctorate, GRE General Test, 3 letters of recommendation. Additional exam requirements/recommendations for international students: Required—TOEFL (minimum score 560 paper-based; 83 iBT). Electronic applications accepted. *Faculty research:* Nutrition and gene expression, nutrition and disease (obesity, diabetes, cancer, osteoporosis, alcohol), community nutrition and nutrition education, cellular lipid transport and metabolism.

Sacred Heart University, Graduate Programs, College of Health Professions, Department of Exercise Science, Fairfield, CT 06825. Offers exercise science and nutrition (MS). *Program availability:* Part-time, evening/weekend. *Faculty:* 8 full-time (2 women). *Students:* 31 full-time (14 women), 1 part-time (0 women); includes 5 minority (2 Black or African American, non-Hispanic/Latino; 1 American Indian or Alaska Native, non-Hispanic/Latino; 1 Asian, non-Hispanic/Latino; 1 Hispanic/Latino). Average age 24. 42 applicants, 79% accepted, 16 enrolled. In 2017, 9 master's awarded. *Degree requirements:* For master's, thesis. *Entrance requirements:* For master's, bachelor's degree in related major, minimum GPA of 3.0, anatomy and physiology (with labs), exercise physiology, nutrition, statistics or health/exercise-specific research methods course, kinesiology (preferred). Additional exam requirements/recommendations for international students: Required—TOEFL (minimum score 570 paper-based, 80 iBT), TWE, or IELTS (6.5). *Application deadline:* Applications are processed on a rolling basis. Application fee: $75. Electronic applications accepted. *Expenses:* Contact institution. *Financial support:* Unspecified assistantships available. Financial award applicants required to submit FAFSA. *Unit head:* Beau Greer, Director of Graduate Exercise Science and Nutrition, 203-396-8064, E-mail: greerb@sacredheart.edu. *Application contact:* Tara Chudy, Executive Director of Graduate Admissions, 203-365-4735, E-mail: chudyt@sacredheart.edu.
Website: http://www.sacredheart.edu/academics/collegeofhealthprofessions/academicprograms/exercisescience/masterofscienceinexercisesciencenutrition/

Sage Graduate School, School of Health Sciences, Program in Nutrition, Troy, NY 12180-4115. Offers applied nutrition (MS); dietetic internship (Certificate); nutrition

(Certificate). *Program availability:* Part-time, evening/weekend, 100% online. *Faculty:* 8 full-time (7 women), 4 part-time/adjunct (all women). *Students:* 63 full-time (60 women), 51 part-time (47 women); includes 13 minority (2 Black or African American, non-Hispanic/Latino; 1 American Indian or Alaska Native, non-Hispanic/Latino; 5 Asian, non-Hispanic/Latino; 2 Hispanic/Latino; 3 Two or more races, non-Hispanic/Latino), 2 international. Average age 28. 158 applicants, 43% accepted, 53 enrolled. In 2017, 22 master's, 28 other advanced degrees awarded. *Entrance requirements:* For master's, minimum GPA of 3.0, resume, 2 letters of recommendation, interview with director. Additional exam requirements/recommendations for international students: Required—TOEFL (minimum score 550 paper-based). *Application deadline:* Applications are processed on a rolling basis. Application fee: $30. Electronic applications accepted. Tuition and fees vary according to degree level and program. *Financial support:* Fellowships, research assistantships, scholarships/grants, and unspecified assistantships available. Financial award applicants required to submit FAFSA. *Unit head:* Dr. Theresa Hand, Dean, School of Health Sciences, 518-244-2264, Fax: 518-244-4571, E-mail: handt@sage.edu. *Application contact:* Rayane AbuSabha, Program Director, Nutrition, 518-935-3214, E-mail: abusar@sage.edu.

Saint Louis University, Graduate Programs, Doisy College of Health Sciences and Graduate Programs, Department of Nutrition and Dietetics, St. Louis, MO 63103. Offers medical dietetics (MS); nutrition and physical performance (MS). *Program availability:* Part-time. *Degree requirements:* For master's, comprehensive exam (for some programs). *Entrance requirements:* For master's, GRE General Test, letters of recommendation, resume, interview. Additional exam requirements/recommendations for international students: Required—TOEFL (minimum score 525 paper-based). Electronic applications accepted. *Faculty research:* Sustainable food systems, nutrition education, public health nutrition, culinary nutrition and physical performance.

Samford University, School of Public Health, Birmingham, AL 35229. Offers health informatics (MSHI); healthcare administration (MHA); nutrition (MS); public health (MPH); social work (MSW). *Program availability:* Part-time, 100% online. *Faculty:* 17 full-time (12 women), 4 part-time/adjunct (2 women). *Students:* 93 full-time (87 women), 5 part-time (all women); includes 20 minority (14 Black or African American, non-Hispanic/Latino; 2 Asian, non-Hispanic/Latino; 2 Hispanic/Latino; 2 Two or more races, non-Hispanic/Latino), 1 international. Average age 27. 90 applicants, 44% accepted, 32 enrolled. In 2017, 34 master's awarded. *Degree requirements:* For master's, capstone course. *Entrance requirements:* For master's, GRE, MAT, recommendations, resume, personal statement. Additional exam requirements/recommendations for international students: Required—TOEFL (minimum score 550 paper-based); Recommended—IELTS. *Application deadline:* For fall admission, 10/1 for domestic students; for spring admission, 5/1 for domestic students. Application fee: $75. Electronic applications accepted. *Expenses:* $813 per credit hour. *Financial support:* In 2017–18, 32 students received support. Scholarships/grants available. Financial award application deadline: 2/15; financial award applicants required to submit FAFSA. *Faculty research:* Chronic kidney disease, disasters and vulnerable populations, children's health, obesity, metabolism and diabetes, health policy and health care delivery. *Unit head:* Dr. Keith Elder, Dean, School of Public Health, 205-726-4655, E-mail: kelder@samford.edu. *Application contact:* Dr. Marian Carter, Assistant Dean of Enrollment Management and Student Services, 205-726-2611, E-mail: mwcarter@samford.edu.
Website: http://www.samford.edu/publichealth/

Sam Houston State University, College of Health Sciences, Department of Family and Consumer Sciences, Huntsville, TX 77341. Offers dietetics (MS); family and consumer sciences (MS). *Program availability:* Part-time, evening/weekend. *Degree requirements:* For master's, comprehensive exam, thesis optional, internship. *Entrance requirements:* For master's, GRE General Test, letters of recommendation, personal statement, writing sample. Additional exam requirements/recommendations for international students: Required—TOEFL (minimum score 550 paper-based; 79 iBT), IELTS (minimum score 6.5). Electronic applications accepted.

San Diego State University, Graduate and Research Affairs, College of Health and Human Services, School of Exercise and Nutritional Sciences, Program in Nutritional Sciences, San Diego, CA 92182. Offers MS, MS/MS. *Degree requirements:* For master's, thesis. *Entrance requirements:* For master's, GRE General Test, 2 letters of reference. Additional exam requirements/recommendations for international students: Required—TOEFL. Electronic applications accepted.

San Jose State University, Graduate Studies and Research, College of Health and Human Sciences, San Jose, CA 95192-0049. Offers criminology (MS), including global criminology, law and justice; justice studies (MS); kinesiology (MA), including athletic training, exercise physiology, interdisciplinary, sport studies, sports management; library and information science (MLIS); mass communications (MS); nursing (MS), including family nurse practitioner; nutritional science (MS); occupational therapy (MS); public health (MPH); social work (MSW); MD/M Div. *Program availability:* Part-time, 100% online, blended/hybrid learning. *Faculty:* 15 full-time (7 women), 6 part-time/adjunct (3 women). *Students:* 517 full-time (407 women), 405 part-time (302 women); includes 523 minority (39 Black or African American, non-Hispanic/Latino; 2 American Indian or Alaska Native, non-Hispanic/Latino; 141 Asian, non-Hispanic/Latino; 226 Hispanic/Latino; 2 Native Hawaiian or other Pacific Islander, non-Hispanic/Latino; 113 Two or more races, non-Hispanic/Latino), 14 international. Average age 32. 1,250 applicants, 45% accepted, 375 enrolled. In 2017, 808 master's awarded. *Degree requirements:* For master's, thesis (for some programs), graduate writing assessment. *Entrance requirements:* Additional exam requirements/recommendations for international students: Required—TOEFL (minimum score 550 paper-based; 80 iBT), IELTS (minimum score 6.5), PTE (minimum score 53). *Application deadline:* For fall admission, 2/1 for domestic and international students. Applications are processed on a rolling basis. Application fee: $55. Electronic applications accepted. *Expenses:* Tuition, state resident: full-time $7176. Tuition, nonresident: full-time $16,680. Tuition and fees vary according to course load and program. *Financial support:* Fellowships, research assistantships, teaching assistantships, career-related internships or fieldwork, Federal Work-Study, scholarships/grants, and tuition waivers (full and partial) available. Support available to part-time students. Financial award application deadline: 4/24; financial award applicants required to submit FAFSA. *Unit head:* Dr. Mary Schutten, Dean, College of Health and Human Sciences, 408-924-2900, Fax: 408-924-2901, E-mail: mary.schutten@sjsu.edu.
Website: http://www.sjsu.edu/casa/

Saybrook University, School of Mind-Body Medicine, San Francisco, CA 94612. Offers MS, PhD, Certificate. *Entrance requirements:* Additional exam requirements/recommendations for international students: Required—TOEFL (minimum score 580 paper-based; 93 iBT). Electronic applications accepted.

Simmons College, School of Nursing and Health Sciences, Boston, MA 02115. Offers didactic dietetics (Certificate); dietetic internship (Certificate); health professions education (PhD, CAGS); nursing (MS, MSN), including family nurse practitioner (MS); nursing practice (DNP); nutrition and health promotion (MS); physical therapy (DPT); sports nutrition (Certificate). *Accreditation:* AACN. *Program availability:* Part-time, 100% online, blended/hybrid learning. *Faculty:* 34 full-time (28 women), 44 part-time/adjunct (40 women). *Students:* 390 full-time (350 women), 1,286 part-time (1,169 women); includes 346 minority (131 Black or African American, non-Hispanic/Latino; 6 American Indian or Alaska Native, non-Hispanic/Latino; 75 Asian, non-Hispanic/Latino; 91 Hispanic/Latino; 3 Native Hawaiian or other Pacific Islander, non-Hispanic/Latino; 40 Two or more races, non-Hispanic/Latino), 9 international. Average age 34. 1,219 applicants, 74% accepted, 481 enrolled. In 2017, 423 master's, 39 doctorates, 55 other advanced degrees awarded. *Entrance requirements:* For doctorate, GRE. Additional exam requirements/recommendations for international students: Required—TOEFL (minimum score 570 paper-based; 88 iBT). *Application deadline:* For fall admission, 6/1 for international students. Application fee: $50. Electronic applications accepted. *Expenses:* $1,278 per credit, $116 activity fee per semester. *Financial support:* In 2017–18, 15 research assistantships with partial tuition reimbursements were awarded; scholarships/grants and unspecified assistantships also available. Financial award applicants required to submit FAFSA. *Unit head:* Dr. Judy Beal, Dean, 617-521-2139. *Application contact:* Brett DiMarzo, Director of Graduate Admission, 617-521-2651, Fax: 617-521-3137, E-mail: brett.dimarzo@simmons.edu.
Website: http://www.simmons.edu/snhs/

South Carolina State University, College of Graduate and Professional Studies, Department of Family and Consumer Sciences, Orangeburg, SC 29117-0001. Offers individual and family development (MS); nutritional sciences (MS). *Program availability:* Part-time, evening/weekend. *Faculty:* 4 full-time (3 women), 4 part-time/adjunct (all women). *Students:* 11 full-time (8 women), 6 part-time (4 women); all minorities (all Black or African American, non-Hispanic/Latino). Average age 35. 14 applicants, 93% accepted, 9 enrolled. In 2017, 2 master's awarded. *Degree requirements:* For master's, comprehensive exam, thesis optional, departmental qualifying exam. *Entrance requirements:* For master's, GRE, MAT, or NTE, minimum GPA of 2.7. *Application deadline:* For fall admission, 6/15 priority date for domestic students, 6/15 for international students; for spring admission, 11/1 for domestic and international students. Application fee: $25. Electronic applications accepted. *Expenses:* Tuition, state resident: full-time $9388; part-time $607 per credit hour. Tuition, nonresident: full-time $19,968; part-time $1194 per credit hour. *Required fees:* $766; $766 per credit hour. *Financial support:* Fellowships, Federal Work-Study, and scholarships/grants available. Financial award application deadline: 6/1. *Unit head:* Dr. William H. Whitaker, Chair, Department of Family and Consumer Sciences, 803-536-8958, Fax: 803-533-3268, E-mail: wwhitak3@scsu.edu. *Application contact:* Curtis Foskey, Coordinator of Graduate Admission, 803-536-8419, Fax: 803-536-8812, E-mail: cfoskey@scsu.edu.

South Dakota State University, Graduate School, College of Education and Human Sciences, Department of Health and Nutritional Sciences, Brookings, SD 57007. Offers athletic training (MS); dietetics (MS); nutrition and exercise sciences (MS, PhD); sport and recreation studies (MS). *Program availability:* Part-time. *Degree requirements:* For master's, comprehensive exam (for some programs), thesis (for some programs), oral exam. *Entrance requirements:* Additional exam requirements/recommendations for international students: Required—TOEFL (minimum score 525 paper-based). *Faculty research:* Food chemistry, bone density, functional food, nutrition education, nutrition biochemistry.

Southern Illinois University Carbondale, Graduate School, College of Agriculture, Department of Animal Science, Food and Nutrition, Program in Food and Nutrition, Carbondale, IL 62901-4701. Offers MS. *Degree requirements:* For master's, thesis or alternative. *Entrance requirements:* For master's, GRE, minimum GPA of 2.7. Additional exam requirements/recommendations for international students: Required—TOEFL (minimum score 550 paper-based; 80 iBT). Electronic applications accepted. *Faculty research:* Public health nutrition, nutrition physiology, soybean utilization, nutrition education.

State University of New York College at Oneonta, Graduate Programs, Department of Human Ecology, Oneonta, NY 13820-4015. Offers nutrition and dietetics (MS). *Program availability:* Online learning.

Stony Brook University, State University of New York, Stony Brook Medicine, School of Medicine and Graduate School, Graduate Programs in Medicine, Department of Family, Population and Preventive Medicine, Stony Brook, NY 11794. Offers nutrition (MS, Advanced Certificate). *Program availability:* Online learning. *Faculty:* 15 full-time (8 women), 7 part-time/adjunct (6 women). *Students:* 2 full-time (both women), 60 part-time (51 women); includes 14 minority (1 Black or African American, non-Hispanic/Latino; 1 American Indian or Alaska Native, non-Hispanic/Latino; 5 Asian, non-Hispanic/Latino; 7 Hispanic/Latino). Average age 29. 39 applicants, 69% accepted, 20 enrolled. In 2017, 24 master's, 2 other advanced degrees awarded. *Entrance requirements:* For master's, baccalaureate degree with minimum preferred GPA of 3.0; physiology (laboratory not required) and statistics; for Advanced Certificate, physiology (laboratory not required). Additional exam requirements/recommendations for international students: Required—TOEFL. *Application deadline:* For fall admission, 7/1 for domestic students; for spring admission, 11/1 for domestic students; for summer admission, 4/7 for domestic students. Application fee: $100. Electronic applications accepted. *Expenses:* Contact institution. *Faculty research:* Diabetes, eating disorders, heart diseases, nutrition or dietetics, obesity, anxiety, disorders, behavioral medicine, chronic illness, depression, family medicine. *Total annual research expenditures:* $3.4 million. *Unit head:* Dr. Iris A. Granek, Founding Chair, 631-444-3936, Fax: 631-444-1122, E-mail: emily.birgeles@stonybrookmedicine.edu. *Application contact:* Emily Birgeles, Assistant to the Chair, 631-638-3936, Fax: 631-444-1122, E-mail: emily.birgeles@stonybrookmedicine.edu.
Website: http://medicine.stonybrookmedicine.edu/gradnutrition

Syracuse University, David B. Falk College of Sport and Human Dynamics, Programs in Nutrition Science, Syracuse, NY 13244. Offers MA, MS, PhD. *Program availability:* Part-time. In 2017, 17 master's awarded. *Degree requirements:* For master's, comprehensive exam, thesis. *Entrance requirements:* For master's, GRE General Test, personal statement, resume, official transcripts, three letters of recommendation. Additional exam requirements/recommendations for international students: Required—TOEFL (minimum score 100 iBT). *Application deadline:* For fall admission, 2/15 priority date for domestic and international students; for spring admission, 11/1 priority date for domestic and international students. Application fee: $75. Electronic applications accepted. *Financial support:* Fellowships with full tuition reimbursements, research assistantships with tuition reimbursements, teaching assistantships with tuition reimbursements, career-related internships or fieldwork, and tuition waivers available. Financial award application deadline: 1/1; financial award applicants required to submit FAFSA. *Faculty research:* Vegetarianism, cultural food practices, consequences of global nutrition transition, food and agricultural policy. *Unit head:* Dr. Lynn Brann, Director of Graduate Programs in Nutrition, 315-443-2556, E-mail: lbrann@syr.edu. *Application contact:* Felicia Otero, Information Contact, 315-443-5555, E-mail: falk@syr.edu.
Website: https://falk.syr.edu/nutrition-science-dietetics/

Teachers College, Columbia University, Department of Health and Behavior Studies, New York, NY 10027-6696. Offers applied behavior analysis (MA, PhD); applied educational psychology: school psychology (Ed M, PhD); behavioral nutrition (PhD), including nutrition (Ed D, PhD); community health education (MS); community nutrition education (Ed M), including community nutrition education; education of deaf and hard of hearing (MA, PhD); health education (MA, Ed D); hearing impairment (Ed D); intellectual disability/autism (MA, Ed D, PhD); nursing education (Ed D, Advanced Certificate); nutrition and education (MS); nutrition and exercise physiology (MS);

nutrition and public health (MS); nutrition education (Ed D), including nutrition (Ed D, PhD); physical disabilities (Ed D); reading specialist (MA); severe or multiple disabilities (MA); special education (Ed M, MA, Ed D); teaching of sign language (MA). *Program availability:* Part-time, evening/weekend. *Students:* 245 full-time (226 women), 242 part-time (219 women); includes 167 minority (52 Black or African American, non-Hispanic/Latino; 2 American Indian or Alaska Native, non-Hispanic/Latino; 55 Asian, non-Hispanic/Latino; 48 Hispanic/Latino; 1 Native Hawaiian or other Pacific Islander, non-Hispanic/Latino, 9 Two or more races, non-Hispanic/Latino), 60 international. Average age 30. 480 applicants, 59% accepted, 157 enrolled. Terminal master's awarded for partial completion of doctoral program. *Unit head:* Prof. Dolores Perin, Chair, E-mail: dp111@tc.columbia.edu. *Application contact:* David Estrella, Director of Admission, 212-678-3305, E-mail: estrella@tc.columbia.edu.
Website: http://www.tc.columbia.edu/health-and-behavior-studies/

Texas A&M University, College of Agriculture and Life Sciences, Department of Nutrition and Food Science, College Station, TX 77843. Offers food science and technology (M Agr, MS); nutrition (MS, PhD). *Faculty:* 15. *Students:* 46 full-time (29 women), 13 part-time (9 women); includes 13 minority (5 Black or African American, non-Hispanic/Latino; 8 Hispanic/Latino), 27 international. Average age 30. 80 applicants, 19% accepted, 12 enrolled. In 2017, 11 master's, 9 doctorates awarded. *Degree requirements:* For master's, thesis; for doctorate, thesis/dissertation. *Entrance requirements:* For master's and doctorate, GRE General Test. Additional exam requirements/recommendations for international students: Required—TOEFL (minimum score 550 paper-based; 80 iBT), IELTS (minimum score 6), PTE (minimum score 53). *Application deadline:* For fall admission, 12/1 priority date for domestic students, 12/1 for international students; for spring admission, 6/1 for domestic and international students; for summer admission, 12/1 priority date for domestic students, 12/1 for international students. Applications are processed on a rolling basis. Application fee: $50 ($90 for international students). Electronic applications accepted. *Expenses:* Contact institution. *Financial support:* In 2017–18, 53 students received support, including 7 fellowships with tuition reimbursements available (averaging $31,660 per year), 25 research assistantships with tuition reimbursements available (averaging $8,381 per year), 20 teaching assistantships with tuition reimbursements available (averaging $7,578 per year); career-related internships or fieldwork, institutionally sponsored loans, scholarships/grants, traineeships, health care benefits, tuition waivers (full and partial), and unspecified assistantships also available. Support available to part-time students. Financial award application deadline: 3/15; financial award applicants required to submit FAFSA. *Faculty research:* Food safety, microbiology, product development. *Unit head:* Dr. Boon Chew, Department Head, 979-862-6655, E-mail: boon.chew@tamu.edu. *Application contact:* Graduate Admissions, 979-845-1044, E-mail: admissions@tamu.edu.
Website: http://nfs.tamu.edu

Texas State University, The Graduate College, College of Applied Arts, Program in Human Nutrition, San Marcos, TX 78666. Offers MS. *Program availability:* Part-time. *Faculty:* 6 full-time (all women), 2 part-time/adjunct (both women). *Students:* 26 full-time (21 women), 10 part-time (9 women); includes 15 minority (1 Asian, non-Hispanic/Latino; 12 Hispanic/Latino; 2 Two or more races, non-Hispanic/Latino), 1 international. Average age 27. 38 applicants, 58% accepted, 10 enrolled. In 2017, 10 master's awarded. *Degree requirements:* For master's, comprehensive exam, thesis (for some programs). *Entrance requirements:* For master's, baccalaureate degree from regionally-accredited institution with minimum GPA of 3.0 in last 60 hours of undergraduate work; 3 letters of reference; statement of goals and professional aspirations; curriculum vitae/resume; background course work in physiology, biochemistry, biology, nutrition, and chemistry. Additional exam requirements/recommendations for international students: Required—TOEFL (minimum score 550 paper-based; 78 iBT), IELTS (minimum score 6.5). *Application deadline:* For fall admission, 1/15 priority date for domestic and international students; for spring admission, 10/15 for domestic students, 10/1 for international students. Application fee: $40 ($90 for international students). Electronic applications accepted. *Expenses:* Tuition, state resident: full-time $7868; part-time $3934 per semester. Tuition, nonresident: full-time $17,828; part-time $8914 per semester. *Required fees:* $2092; $1435 per semester. Tuition and fees vary according to course load. *Financial support:* In 2017–18, 22 students received support, including 8 research assistantships (averaging $11,160 per year), 8 teaching assistantships (averaging $12,269 per year); scholarships/grants and unspecified assistantships also available. Financial award application deadline: 3/1; financial award applicants required to submit FAFSA. *Faculty research:* Egg protein supplementation for muscle mass and function in food; innovation approach to promoting healthy weight women;. *Total annual research expenditures:* $10,965. *Unit head:* Dr. Michelle Lane, Graduate Advisor, 512-245-4654, E-mail: ml48@txstate.edu. *Application contact:* Dr. Andrea Golato, Dean of the Graduate College, 512-245-2581, Fax: 512-245-8365, E-mail: gradcollege@txstate.edu.
Website: http://www.gradcollege.txstate.edu/programs/human-nutrition.html

Texas Tech University, Graduate School, College of Human Sciences, Department of Nutritional Sciences, Lubbock, TX 79409-1270. Offers nutrition and dietetics (MS); nutritional sciences (MS, PhD). *Program availability:* Part-time, 100% online. *Faculty:* 21 full-time (12 women), 4 part-time/adjunct (all women). *Students:* 64 full-time (49 women), 20 part-time (19 women); includes 13 minority (2 Asian, non-Hispanic/Latino; 11 Hispanic/Latino), 32 international. Average age 27. 57 applicants, 63% accepted, 29 enrolled. In 2017, 22 master's, 7 doctorates awarded. Terminal master's awarded for partial completion of doctoral program. *Degree requirements:* For master's, comprehensive exam (for some programs), thesis (for some programs); for doctorate, thesis/dissertation. *Entrance requirements:* For master's, GRE, minimum undergraduate cumulative GPA of 3.0; for doctorate, GRE, minimum undergraduate or graduate cumulative GPA of 3.0. Additional exam requirements/recommendations for international students: Required—TOEFL (minimum score 550 paper-based, 79 iBT) or IELTS (6.5). *Application deadline:* For fall admission, 6/1 priority date for domestic students, 1/15 priority date for international students; for spring admission, 9/1 priority date for domestic students, 6/15 priority date for international students. Applications are processed on a rolling basis. Application fee: $60. Electronic applications accepted. *Expenses:* Contact institution. *Financial support:* In 2017–18, 68 students received support, including 66 fellowships (averaging $4,226 per year), 25 research assistantships (averaging $15,519 per year), 18 teaching assistantships (averaging $12,795 per year); Federal Work-Study, scholarships/grants, and unspecified assistantships also available. Financial award application deadline: 1/15; financial award applicants required to submit FAFSA. *Faculty research:* Obesity and chronic diseases, clinical and cellular lipid metabolism, community nutrition education, domestic and international food security. *Total annual research expenditures:* $783,690. *Unit head:* Dr. Nikhil V. Dhurandhar, Professor and Chair, 806-742-5270, Fax: 806-742-2926, E-mail: nikhil.dhurandhar@ttu.edu. *Application contact:* Ashley Wenzel, Coordinator, 806-834-8271, Fax: 806-742-2926, E-mail: ashley.wenzel@ttu.edu.
Website: http://www.depts.ttu.edu/hs/ns/

Texas Woman's University, Graduate School, College of Health Sciences, Department of Nutrition and Food Sciences, Denton, TX 76204. Offers exercise and sports nutrition (MS); food science and flavor chemistry (MS); food systems administration (MS); nutrition (MS, PhD). *Program availability:* Part-time, evening/weekend. *Faculty:* 15 full-time (12 women), 1 (woman) part-time/adjunct. *Students:* 92 full-time (83 women), 109 part-time (100 women); includes 58 minority (10 Black or African American, non-Hispanic/Latino; 17 Asian, non-Hispanic/Latino; 24 Hispanic/Latino; 7 Two or more races, non-Hispanic/Latino), 10 international. Average age 29. 102 applicants, 84% accepted, 54 enrolled. In 2017, 71 master's, 1 doctorate awarded. *Degree requirements:* For master's, thesis or alternative, thesis (for food and flavor chemistry); thesis or coursework (for exercise and sports nutrition, nutrition); for doctorate, comprehensive exam, thesis/dissertation, qualifying exam, 50% of all required hours must be earned at TWU. *Entrance requirements:* For master's, GRE General Test (preferred minimum score 143 [350 old version] Verbal, 141 [450 old version] Quantitative), minimum GPA of 3.25, resume, personal statement of interest (food science and flavor chemistry only); for doctorate, GRE General Test (preferred minimum score 150 [450 old version] Verbal, 146 [550 old version] Quantitative), minimum GPA of 3.5 on last 60 undergraduate hours and graduate course work, 2 letters of reference, resume, statement of purpose. Additional exam requirements/recommendations for international students: Required—TOEFL (minimum score 550 paper-based; 79 iBT); Recommended—IELTS (minimum score 6.5), TSE (minimum score 53). *Application deadline:* For fall admission, 3/1 priority date for domestic and international students; for spring admission, 11/1 priority date for domestic students, 7/1 priority date for international students; for summer admission, 5/1 priority date for domestic students, 2/1 priority date for international students. Applications are processed on a rolling basis. Application fee: $50 ($75 for international students). Electronic applications accepted. *Expenses:* $7,520 per year full-time in-state; $16,829 per year full-time out-of-state. *Financial support:* In 2017–18, 66 students received support, including 5 research assistantships (averaging $19,791 per year), 4 teaching assistantships (averaging $19,586 per year); career-related internships or fieldwork, Federal Work-Study, institutionally sponsored loans, scholarships/grants, traineeships, health care benefits, and unspecified assistantships also available. Support available to part-time students. Financial award application deadline: 3/1; financial award applicants required to submit FAFSA. *Faculty research:* Bioactive food components and cancer, nutraceuticals and functional foods in diabetes, obesity and bone health, food safety, obesity prevention in children. *Total annual research expenditures:* $186,045. *Unit head:* Dr. K. Shane Broughton, Chair, 940-898-2636, Fax: 940-898-2634, E-mail: nutrfdsci@twu.edu. *Application contact:* Korie Hawkins, Associate Director of Admissions, Graduate Recruitment, 940-898-3188, Fax: 940-898-3081, E-mail: admissions@twu.edu.
Website: http://www.twu.edu/nutrition-food-sciences/

Tufts University, The Gerald J. and Dorothy R. Friedman School of Nutrition Science and Policy, Boston, MA 02111. Offers agriculture, food and environment (MS, PhD); biochemical and molecular nutrition (PhD); dietetic internship (MS); food policy and applied nutrition (MS, PhD); humanitarian assistance (MAHA); nutrition (MS, PhD); nutrition communication (MS); nutritional epidemiology (MS, PhD). *Program availability:* Part-time. *Degree requirements:* For doctorate, comprehensive exam, thesis/dissertation. *Entrance requirements:* For master's and doctorate, GRE General Test. Additional exam requirements/recommendations for international students: Required—TOEFL. Electronic applications accepted. *Expenses:* Contact institution. *Faculty research:* Nutritional biochemistry and metabolism, cell and molecular biochemistry, epidemiology, policy/planning, applied nutrition.

Tufts University, School of Medicine, Public Health and Professional Degree Programs, Boston, MA 02111. Offers biomedical sciences (MS); health communication (MS, Certificate); pain research, education and policy (MS, Certificate); physician assistant (MS); public health (MPH, Dr PH), including behavioral science (MPH), biostatistics (MPH), epidemiology (MPH), health communication (MPH), health services (MPH), management and policy (MPH), nutrition (MPH); DMD/MPH; DVM/MPH; JD/MPH; MD/MPH; MMS/MPH; MS/MBA; MS/MPH. *Accreditation:* CEPH (one or more programs are accredited). *Program availability:* Part-time, evening/weekend. *Faculty:* 62 full-time (25 women), 50 part-time/adjunct (25 women). *Students:* 449 full-time (280 women), 60 part-time (46 women); includes 188 minority (23 Black or African American, non-Hispanic/Latino; 112 Asian, non-Hispanic/Latino; 35 Hispanic/Latino; 18 Two or more races, non-Hispanic/Latino), 23 international. Average age 27. 1,750 applicants, 46% accepted, 252 enrolled. In 2017, 283 master's awarded. Terminal master's awarded for partial completion of doctoral program. *Degree requirements:* For master's, thesis (for some programs); for doctorate, thesis/dissertation. *Entrance requirements:* For master's, GRE General Test, MCAT, or GMAT; for doctorate, GRE General Test or MCAT. Additional exam requirements/recommendations for international students: Required—TOEFL (minimum score 100 iBT); Recommended—IELTS (minimum score 7). *Application deadline:* For fall admission, 1/15 priority date for domestic and international students; for spring admission, 10/25 priority date for domestic and international students. Applications are processed on a rolling basis. Application fee: $70. Electronic applications accepted. *Expenses:* Contact institution. *Financial support:* In 2017–18, 13 students received support, including 1 fellowship (averaging $3,000 per year), 50 research assistantships (averaging $1,000 per year), 65 teaching assistantships (averaging $2,000 per year); Federal Work-Study and scholarships/grants also available. Financial award application deadline: 2/23; financial award applicants required to submit FAFSA. *Faculty research:* Environmental and occupational health, nutrition, epidemiology, health communication, biostatics, obesity/chronic disease, health policy and health care delivery, global health, health inequality and social determinants of health. *Unit head:* Dr. Aviva Must, Dean, 617-636-0935, Fax: 617-636-0898, E-mail: aviva.must@tufts.edu. *Application contact:* Emily Keily, Director of Admissions, 617-636-0935, Fax: 617-636-0898, E-mail: med-phpd@tufts.edu.
Website: http://publichealth.tufts.edu

Tuskegee University, Graduate Programs, College of Agriculture, Environment and Nutrition Sciences, Department of Food and Nutritional Sciences, Tuskegee, AL 36088. Offers MS. *Degree requirements:* For master's, thesis. *Entrance requirements:* For master's, GRE General Test. Additional exam requirements/recommendations for international students: Required—TOEFL (minimum score 500 paper-based).

Université de Moncton, School of Food Science, Nutrition and Family Studies, Moncton, NB E1A 3E9, Canada. Offers foods/nutrition (M Sc). *Program availability:* Part-time. *Degree requirements:* For master's, one foreign language, thesis. *Entrance requirements:* For master's, previous course work in statistics. Electronic applications accepted. *Faculty research:* Clinic nutrition (anemia, elderly, osteoporosis), applied nutrition, metabolic activities of lactic bacteria, solubility of low density lipoproteins, bile acids.

Université de Montréal, Faculty of Medicine, Department of Nutrition, Montréal, QC H3C 3J7, Canada. Offers M Sc, PhD, DESS. Terminal master's awarded for partial completion of doctoral program. *Degree requirements:* For master's, thesis; for doctorate, thesis/dissertation, general exam. *Entrance requirements:* For master's, MD, B Sc in nutrition or equivalent, proficiency in French; for doctorate, M Sc in nutrition or equivalent, proficiency in French. Electronic applications accepted. *Faculty research:* Nutritional aspects of diabetes, obesity, anorexia nervosa, lipid metabolism, hepatic function.

Université Laval, Faculty of Agricultural and Food Sciences, Department of Food Sciences and Nutrition, Programs in Nutrition, Québec, QC G1K 7P4, Canada. Offers M Sc, PhD. Terminal master's awarded for partial completion of doctoral program. *Degree requirements:* For master's, thesis; for doctorate, comprehensive exam, thesis/dissertation. *Entrance requirements:* For master's and doctorate, knowledge of French and English. Electronic applications accepted.

Nutrition

University at Buffalo, the State University of New York, Graduate School, School of Public Health and Health Professions, Department of Exercise and Nutrition Sciences, Buffalo, NY 14260. Offers exercise science (MS, PhD); nutrition (MS, Advanced Certificate). *Program availability:* Part-time. *Faculty:* 18 full-time (8 women), 8 part-time/adjunct (4 women). *Students:* 74 full-time (62 women), 3 part-time (2 women); includes 5 minority (2 Black or African American, non-Hispanic/Latino; 3 Asian, non-Hispanic/Latino), 18 international. Average age 24. 109 applicants, 52% accepted, 50 enrolled. In 2017, 30 master's, 1 doctorate, 19 other advanced degrees awarded. *Entrance requirements:* For master's, doctorate, and Advanced Certificate, GRE General Test, minimum GPA of 3.0. Additional exam requirements/recommendations for international students: Required—TOEFL (minimum score 550 paper-based; 79 IBT), IELTS (minimum score 6.5). *Application deadline:* For fall admission, 4/1 for domestic students, 3/1 for international students; for spring admission, 8/15 for international students. Applications are processed on a rolling basis. Application fee: $50. Electronic applications accepted. *Financial support:* In 2017–18, 14 students received support, including 1 research assistantship with full tuition reimbursement available (averaging $15,000 per year), 11 teaching assistantships with tuition reimbursements available (averaging $6,980 per year); tuition waivers (full) and Fulbright scholarship also available. Financial award application deadline: 3/15; financial award applicants required to submit FAFSA. *Faculty research:* Cardiovascular disease-diet and exercise, respiratory control and muscle function, plasticity of connective and neural tissue, exercise nutrition, diet and cancer. *Total annual research expenditures:* $891,096. *Unit head:* Dr. David Hostler, Chair, 716-829-6756, Fax: 716-829-2428, E-mail: dhostler@buffalo.edu. *Application contact:* Dr. Jennifer Temple, Director of Graduate Studies, 716-829-5593, Fax: 716-829-2428, E-mail: jltemple@buffalo.edu.
Website: http://sphhp.buffalo.edu/exercise-and-nutrition-sciences.html

The University of Alabama, Graduate School, College of Human Environmental Sciences, Department of Human Nutrition and Hospitality Management, Tuscaloosa, AL 35487. Offers MSHES. *Program availability:* Part-time, online only, 100% online. *Faculty:* 16 full-time (13 women), 2 part-time/adjunct (1 woman). *Students:* 21 full-time (all women), 112 part-time (110 women); includes 10 minority (2 Asian, non-Hispanic/Latino; 4 Hispanic/Latino; 1 Native Hawaiian or other Pacific Islander, non-Hispanic/Latino; 3 Two or more races, non-Hispanic/Latino). Average age 29. 84 applicants, 68% accepted, 46 enrolled. In 2017, 52 master's awarded. *Degree requirements:* For master's, comprehensive exam, thesis optional. *Entrance requirements:* For master's, minimum GPA of 3.0. Additional exam requirements/recommendations for international students: Required—TOEFL, IELTS. *Application deadline:* For fall admission, 6/1 for domestic students; for spring admission, 11/1 for domestic students; for summer admission, 4/1 for domestic students. Applications are processed on a rolling basis. Application fee: $50 ($60 for international students). Electronic applications accepted. *Financial support:* In 2017–18, 11 students received support, including research assistantships (averaging $8,100 per year), teaching assistantships (averaging $8,100 per year); career-related internships or fieldwork also available. Financial award application deadline: 3/15. *Faculty research:* Maternal and child nutrition, childhood obesity, community nutrition interventions, geriatric nutrition, family eating patterns, food chemistry, phytochemicals, dietary antioxidants. *Total annual research expenditures:* $52,184. *Unit head:* Dr. Jeannine C. Lawrence, Chair/Associate Professor, 205-348-6252, Fax: 205-348-2982, E-mail: jlawrence@ches.ua.edu. *Application contact:* Patrick D. Fuller, Admissions Officer, 205-348-5923, Fax: 205-348-0400, E-mail: patrick.d.fuller@ua.edu.
Website: http://www.nhm.ches.ua.edu/

The University of Alabama at Birmingham, School of Health Professions, Program in Nutrition Sciences, Birmingham, AL 35294. Offers MS, PhD. Terminal master's awarded for partial completion of doctoral program. *Degree requirements:* For master's, thesis optional; for doctorate, thesis/dissertation. *Entrance requirements:* For master's, GRE or MAT, letters of recommendation; for doctorate, GRE. Additional exam requirements/recommendations for international students: Required—TOEFL. *Faculty research:* Energy metabolism, obesity, body composition, cancer prevention, bone metabolism, diabetes.

The University of Arizona, College of Agriculture and Life Sciences, Department of Nutritional Sciences, Tucson, AZ 85721. Offers MS, PhD. *Entrance requirements:* For master's, GRE, minimum GPA of 3.0, 2 letters of recommendation; for doctorate, GRE, minimum GPA of 3.0, 2 letters of recommendation, statement of purpose. Additional exam requirements/recommendations for international students: Required—TOEFL (minimum score 550 paper-based; 79 iBT). Electronic applications accepted. *Faculty research:* Bioactive compounds, nutrients and lifestyle: relationships to cancer; metabolic and behavior factors Influencing body composition; diabetes, obesity, musculoskeletal and cardiovascular diseases.

University of Arkansas for Medical Sciences, Graduate School, Little Rock, AR 72205. Offers biochemistry and molecular biology (MS, PhD); bioinformatics (MS, PhD); cellular physiology and molecular biophysics (MS, PhD); clinical nutrition (MS); interdisciplinary biomedical sciences (MS, PhD, Certificate); interdisciplinary toxicology (MS); microbiology and immunology (PhD); neurobiology and developmental sciences (PhD); pharmacology (PhD); MD/PhD. Bioinformatics programs hosted jointly with the University of Arkansas at Little Rock. *Program availability:* Part-time. Terminal master's awarded for partial completion of doctoral program. *Degree requirements:* For master's, comprehensive exam (for some programs), thesis (for some programs); for doctorate, thesis/dissertation. *Entrance requirements:* For master's and doctorate, GRE. Additional exam requirements/recommendations for international students: Required—TOEFL. Electronic applications accepted. *Expenses:* Contact institution.

University of Bridgeport, Nutrition Institute, Bridgeport, CT 06604. Offers human nutrition (MS). *Program availability:* Part-time, evening/weekend, online learning. *Degree requirements:* For master's, thesis, research project. *Entrance requirements:* For master's, previous course work in anatomy, biochemistry, organic chemistry, or physiology. Additional exam requirements/recommendations for international students: Recommended—TOEFL (minimum score 550 paper-based; 80 iBT), IELTS (minimum score 6.5). Electronic applications accepted. *Expenses:* Contact institution.

The University of British Columbia, Faculty of Land and Food Systems, Human Nutrition Program, Vancouver, BC V6T 1Z4, Canada. Offers M Sc, PhD. *Program availability:* Part-time. Terminal master's awarded for partial completion of doctoral program. *Degree requirements:* For master's, thesis; for doctorate, comprehensive exam, thesis/dissertation. *Entrance requirements:* Additional exam requirements/recommendations for international students: Required—TOEFL, IELTS. Electronic applications accepted. *Expenses:* Contact institution. *Faculty research:* Basic nutrition, clinical nutrition, community nutrition, women's health, pediatric nutrition.

University of California, Berkeley, Graduate Division, College of Natural Resources, Program in Metabolic Biology, Berkeley, CA 94720-1500. Offers MS, PhD. *Degree requirements:* For doctorate, thesis/dissertation, qualifying exam. *Entrance requirements:* For doctorate, GRE General Test, minimum GPA of 3.0, 3 letters of recommendation. Additional exam requirements/recommendations for international students: Required—TOEFL. Electronic applications accepted. *Faculty research:* Regulation of metabolism; nutritional genomics and nutrient-gene interactions; transport, metabolism and function of minerals; carcinogenesis and dietary anti-carcinogens.

University of California, Davis, Graduate Studies, Graduate Group in Nutritional Biology, Davis, CA 95616. Offers MS, PhD. *Degree requirements:* For master's, thesis; for doctorate, thesis/dissertation. *Entrance requirements:* For master's and doctorate, GRE General Test, minimum GPA of 3.0. Additional exam requirements/recommendations for international students: Required—TOEFL (minimum score 550 paper-based). Electronic applications accepted. *Faculty research:* Human/animal nutrition.

University of California, Davis, Graduate Studies, Program in Maternal and Child Nutrition, Davis, CA 95616. Offers MAS. *Degree requirements:* For master's, comprehensive exam. *Entrance requirements:* Additional exam requirements/recommendations for international students: Required—TOEFL (minimum score 550 paper-based).

University of Central Arkansas, Graduate School, College of Health and Behavioral Sciences, Department of Family and Consumer Sciences, Conway, AR 72035-0001. Offers family and consumer sciences (MS); nutrition (MS). *Program availability:* Part-time, evening/weekend, online learning. *Degree requirements:* For master's, comprehensive exam, thesis optional. *Entrance requirements:* For master's, GRE General Test, minimum GPA of 2.7. Additional exam requirements/recommendations for international students: Required—TOEFL (minimum score 550 paper-based). *Application deadline:* For fall admission, 3/1 priority date for domestic students; for spring admission, 10/1 for domestic students. Applications are processed on a rolling basis. Application fee: $25 ($40 for international students). Electronic applications accepted. *Expenses:* Contact institution. *Financial support:* Career-related internships or fieldwork, scholarships/grants, and unspecified assistantships available. Support available to part-time students. Financial award application deadline: 2/15. *Faculty research:* Neurology, developmental disabilities, diet consequences. *Unit head:* Dr. Mary Harlan, Chairperson, 501-450-5950, Fax: 501-450-5958, E-mail: maryh@uca.edu. *Application contact:* Sandy Burks, Administrative Specialist, 501-450-3124, Fax: 501-450-5678, E-mail: slburks@uca.edu.
Website: http://uca.edu/facs/

University of Central Oklahoma, The Jackson College of Graduate Studies, College of Education and Professional Studies, Department of Human Environmental Sciences, Edmond, OK 73034-5209. Offers family and child studies (MS), including family life education, infant/child specialist, marriage and family therapy; nutrition-food science (MS). *Program availability:* Part-time. *Faculty:* 5 full-time (4 women), 8 part-time/adjunct (6 women). *Students:* 46 full-time (38 women), 65 part-time (62 women); includes 48 minority (27 Black or African American, non-Hispanic/Latino; 3 American Indian or Alaska Native, non-Hispanic/Latino; 3 Asian, non-Hispanic/Latino; 7 Hispanic/Latino; 8 Two or more races, non-Hispanic/Latino), 13 international. Average age 29. 68 applicants, 93% accepted, 31 enrolled. In 2017, 37 master's awarded. *Degree requirements:* For master's, comprehensive exam (for some programs), thesis (for some programs). *Entrance requirements:* For master's, GRE, essay, physical, CPR and First Aid training. Additional exam requirements/recommendations for international students: Required—TOEFL (minimum score 550 paper-based; 79 iBT), IELTS (minimum score 6.5). *Application deadline:* For fall admission, 1/15 for domestic students, 7/15 for international students; for spring admission, 11/15 for international students. Applications are processed on a rolling basis. Application fee: $60. Electronic applications accepted. *Expenses:* Tuition, state resident: full-time $5375; part-time $268.75 per credit hour. Tuition, nonresident: full-time $13,295; part-time $664.75 per credit hour. *Required fees:* $626; $31.30 per credit hour. One-time fee: $50. Tuition and fees vary according to program. *Financial support:* In 2017–18, 11 students received support, including 8 research assistantships with partial tuition reimbursements available (averaging $4,436 per year); teaching assistantships, career-related internships or fieldwork, scholarships/grants, tuition waivers (partial), and unspecified assistantships also available. Financial award application deadline: 3/31; financial award applicants required to submit FAFSA. *Unit head:* Dr. Kaye Sears, Chair, 405-974-5551, Fax: 405-974-3850. *Application contact:* Carlie Wellington, Assistant Director, CEPS Graduate Enrollment, 405-974-5105, Fax: 405-974-3851, E-mail: gradcoll@uco.edu.
Website: http://sites.uco.edu/ceps/dept/Professional-Studies-Programs/hes/index.asp

University of Chicago, Division of the Biological Sciences, Committee on Molecular Metabolism and Nutrition, Chicago, IL 60637. Offers PhD. *Faculty:* 43 full-time. *Students:* 11 full-time (5 women). 18 applicants, 17% accepted, 2 enrolled. In 2017, 4 doctorates awarded. *Degree requirements:* For doctorate, thesis/dissertation, ethics class, 2 teaching assistantships, mock grant proposal. *Entrance requirements:* For doctorate, GRE General Test, transcripts, statement of purpose, 3 letters of recommendation. Additional exam requirements/recommendations for international students: Required—TOEFL (minimum score 600 paper-based; 104 iBT), IELTS (minimum score 7). *Application deadline:* For fall admission, 12/1 for domestic and international students. Application fee: $90. Electronic applications accepted. *Financial support:* In 2017–18, 11 students received support, including fellowships with full tuition reimbursements available (averaging $31,000 per year), research assistantships with full tuition reimbursements available (averaging $31,000 per year); institutionally sponsored loans, scholarships/grants, traineeships, and health care benefits also available. Financial award application deadline: 12/1. *Faculty research:* Regulation of lipoprotein metabolism, cellular vitamin metabolism, adipocyte differentiation, digestive diseases and nutrition, diabetes. *Unit head:* Matthew Brady, PhD, Chair, E-mail: biomed@bsd.uchicago.edu. *Application contact:* Lisa Abston-Leftridge, PhD, Administrator, E-mail: biomed@bsd.uchicago.edu.
Website: http://biomedsciences.uchicago.edu/page/molecular-metabolism-and-nutrition

University of Cincinnati, Graduate School, College of Allied Health Sciences, Department of Rehabilitation, Exercise, and Nutrition Sciences, Cincinnati, OH 45221. Offers nutritional sciences (MS). *Program availability:* Part-time. *Faculty:* 6 full-time (5 women). *Students:* 17 full-time (13 women), 16 part-time (14 women); includes 3 minority (2 Black or African American, non-Hispanic/Latino; 1 Hispanic/Latino), 4 international. Average age 25. 19 applicants, 84% accepted, 13 enrolled. In 2017, 8 master's awarded. *Degree requirements:* For master's, thesis. *Entrance requirements:* For master's, GRE General Test. Additional exam requirements/recommendations for international students: Required—TOEFL (minimum score 550 paper-based). *Application deadline:* For fall admission, 8/1 for domestic and international students; for spring admission, 11/1 for domestic and international students. Applications are processed on a rolling basis. Application fee: $40. Electronic applications accepted. *Expenses: Tuition, area resident:* Full-time $14,468. Tuition, state resident: full-time $14,968; part-time $754 per credit hour. Tuition, nonresident: full-time $24,210; part-time $1311 per credit hour. *International tuition:* $26,460 full-time. *Required fees:* $3958; $84 per credit hour. One-time fee: $85 full-time. Tuition and fees vary according to course load, degree level and program. *Financial support:* In 2017–18, 5 students received support, including 3 research assistantships with full tuition reimbursements available, 1 teaching assistantship with full tuition reimbursement available; scholarships/grants, tuition waivers (partial), and unspecified assistantships also available. Financial award application deadline: 4/1. *Faculty research:* Maternal and infant nutrition, pediatric hypertension and dyslipidemia, food insecurity, food literacy, diabetes self-management. *Total annual research expenditures:* $100,000. *Unit head:* Dr. Sarah C. Couch, Vice Chair, 513-558-7504, Fax: 513-558-7500, E-mail: sarah.couch@uc.edu. *Application contact:* Kim Maco, Program Coordinator, 513-558-7503, Fax: 513-558-7500, E-mail: macokr@ucmail.uc.edu.
Website: http://www.cahs.uc.edu/departments/rens/

University of Connecticut, Graduate School, College of Agriculture, Health and Natural Resources, Department of Nutritional Sciences, Storrs, CT 06269. Offers MS, PhD. Terminal master's awarded for partial completion of doctoral program. *Degree requirements:* For master's, comprehensive exam, thesis; for doctorate, thesis/dissertation. *Entrance requirements:* For master's and doctorate, GRE General Test. Additional exam requirements/recommendations for international students: Required—TOEFL (minimum score 550 paper-based). Electronic applications accepted.

University of Delaware, College of Health Sciences, Department of Behavioral Health and Nutrition, Newark, DE 19716. Offers health promotion (MS); human nutrition (MS). *Program availability:* Part-time. *Degree requirements:* For master's, thesis. *Entrance requirements:* For master's, GRE General Test, interview, minimum GPA of 3.0. Additional exam requirements/recommendations for international students: Required—TOEFL (minimum score 550 paper-based). Electronic applications accepted. *Faculty research:* Sport biomechanics, rehabilitation biomechanics, vascular dynamics.

University of Florida, Graduate School, College of Agricultural and Life Sciences, Department of Food Science and Human Nutrition, Gainesville, FL 32611. Offers food science (PhD), including toxicology; food science and human nutrition (MS), including nutritional sciences; nutritional sciences (MS, PhD), including clinical and translational science (PhD). *Degree requirements:* For master's, thesis optional; for doctorate, thesis/dissertation. *Entrance requirements:* For master's and doctorate, GRE General Test, minimum GPA of 3.0. Additional exam requirements/recommendations for international students: Required—TOEFL. Electronic applications accepted. *Faculty research:* Pesticide research, nutritional biochemistry and microbiology, food safety and toxicology assessment and dietetics, food chemistry.

University of Georgia, College of Family and Consumer Sciences, Department of Foods and Nutrition, Athens, GA 30602. Offers MS, PhD. *Degree requirements:* For master's, thesis (MS); for doctorate, thesis/dissertation. *Entrance requirements:* For master's, GRE General Test, minimum GPA of 3.0, course work in biochemistry and physiology; for doctorate, GRE General Test, master's degree, minimum GPA of 3.0. Electronic applications accepted.

University of Guelph, Graduate Studies, College of Biological Science, Department of Human Health and Nutritional Sciences, Guelph, ON N1G 2W1, Canada. Offers nutritional sciences (M Sc, PhD). *Program availability:* Part-time. *Degree requirements:* For master's, thesis (for some programs); for doctorate, comprehensive exam, thesis/dissertation. *Entrance requirements:* For master's, minimum B-average during previous 2 years of coursework; for doctorate, minimum A-average. Additional exam requirements/recommendations for international students: Required—TOEFL (minimum score 550 paper-based). Electronic applications accepted. *Faculty research:* Nutrition and biochemistry, exercise metabolism and physiology, toxicology, gene expression, biomechanics and ergonomics.

University of Guelph, Graduate Studies, College of Social and Applied Human Sciences, Department of Family Relations and Applied Nutrition, Guelph, ON N1G 2W1, Canada. Offers applied nutrition (MAN); family relations and human development (M Sc, PhD), including applied human nutrition, couple and family therapy (M Sc), family relations and human development. *Accreditation:* AAMFT/COAMFTE (one or more programs are accredited). *Program availability:* Part-time. *Degree requirements:* For master's, thesis (for some programs); for doctorate, comprehensive exam, thesis/dissertation. *Entrance requirements:* For master's, minimum B+ average; for doctorate, master's degree in family relations and human development or related field with a minimum B+ average or master's degree in applied human nutrition. Additional exam requirements/recommendations for international students: Required—TOEFL (minimum score 600 paper-based). Electronic applications accepted. *Faculty research:* Child and adolescent development, social gerontology, family roles and relations, couple and family therapy, applied human nutrition.

University of Hawaii at Manoa, Office of Graduate Education, College of Tropical Agriculture and Human Resources, Department of Human Nutrition, Food and Animal Sciences, Program in Nutrition, Honolulu, HI 96822. Offers PhD. *Program availability:* Part-time. *Degree requirements:* For doctorate, comprehensive exam, thesis/dissertation. *Entrance requirements:* For doctorate, GRE General Test. Additional exam requirements/recommendations for international students: Required—TOEFL (minimum score 580 paper-based; 92 iBT), IELTS (minimum score 5).

University of Hawaii at Manoa, Office of Graduate Education, College of Tropical Agriculture and Human Resources, Department of Human Nutrition, Food and Animal Sciences, Program in Nutritional Sciences, Honolulu, HI 96822. Offers MS, PhD. *Program availability:* Part-time. *Degree requirements:* For master's, thesis optional; for doctorate, comprehensive exam, thesis/dissertation. *Entrance requirements:* For master's and doctorate, GRE General Test. Additional exam requirements/recommendations for international students: Required—TOEFL (minimum score 580 paper-based; 92 iBT), IELTS (minimum score 5). *Faculty research:* Nutritional biochemistry, human nutrition, nutrition education, international nutrition, nutritional epidemiology.

University of Houston, College of Liberal Arts and Social Sciences, Department of Health and Human Performance, Houston, TX 77204. Offers exercise science (MS); human nutrition (MS); human space exploration sciences (MS); kinesiology (PhD); physical education (M Ed). *Accreditation:* NCATE (one or more programs are accredited). *Program availability:* Part-time, evening/weekend. *Degree requirements:* For master's, comprehensive exam (for some programs), thesis (for some programs); for doctorate, comprehensive exam, thesis/dissertation, qualifying exam, candidacy paper. *Entrance requirements:* For master's, GRE (minimum 35th percentile on each section), minimum cumulative GPA of 3.0; for doctorate, GRE (minimum 35th percentile on each section), minimum cumulative GPA of 3.3. Additional exam requirements/recommendations for international students: Required—TOEFL (minimum score 550 paper-based; 79 iBT). Electronic applications accepted. *Faculty research:* Biomechanics, exercise physiology, obesity, nutrition, space exploration science.

University of Illinois at Chicago, College of Applied Health Sciences, Program in Nutrition, Chicago, IL 60607-7128. Offers MS, PhD. *Degree requirements:* For master's, thesis; for doctorate, thesis/dissertation. *Entrance requirements:* For master's and doctorate, GRE General Test, minimum GPA of 2.75. Additional exam requirements/recommendations for international students: Required—TOEFL. Electronic applications accepted. *Expenses:* Contact institution. *Faculty research:* Nutrition for the elderly, inborn errors of metabolism, nutrition and cancer, lipid metabolism, dietary fat markers.

University of Illinois at Urbana–Champaign, Graduate College, College of Agricultural, Consumer and Environmental Sciences, Department of Food Science and Human Nutrition, Champaign, IL 61820. Offers food science (MS); food science and human nutrition (MS, PhD), including professional science (MS); human nutrition (MS). *Program availability:* Part-time, online learning.

University of Illinois at Urbana–Champaign, Graduate College, College of Agricultural, Consumer and Environmental Sciences, Division of Nutritional Sciences, Champaign, IL 61820. Offers MS, PhD, PhD/MPH.

The University of Kansas, University of Kansas Medical Center, School of Health Professions, Department of Dietetics and Nutrition, Kansas City, KS 66160. Offers dietetic internship (Graduate Certificate); dietetics and nutrition (MS); medical nutrition science (PhD). *Program availability:* Part-time. *Faculty:* 28. *Students:* 35 full-time (34 women), 34 part-time (33 women); includes 7 minority (1 Black or African American, non-Hispanic/Latino; 1 American Indian or Alaska Native, non-Hispanic/Latino; 2 Asian, non-Hispanic/Latino; 1 Hispanic/Latino; 2 Two or more races, non-Hispanic/Latino), 3 international. Average age 28. 66 applicants, 44% accepted, 27 enrolled. In 2017, 24 master's, 1 doctorate, 21 other advanced degrees awarded. *Degree requirements:* For master's, comprehensive exam, thesis, oral exam; for doctorate, comprehensive exam, thesis/dissertation, oral exam. *Entrance requirements:* For master's, GRE, prerequisite courses in nutrition, biochemistry, and physiology; for doctorate, GRE; for Graduate Certificate, GRE, minimum cumulative GPA of 3.0. Additional exam requirements/recommendations for international students: Required—TOEFL. *Application deadline:* For fall admission, 7/1 for domestic students, 6/1 for international students; for spring admission, 12/1 for domestic students, 11/1 for international students; for summer admission, 5/1 for domestic students, 4/1 for international students. Applications are processed on a rolling basis. Application fee: $60. Electronic applications accepted. *Expenses:* Contact institution. *Financial support:* Fellowships, research assistantships with partial tuition reimbursements, teaching assistantships with full tuition reimbursements, career-related internships or fieldwork, Federal Work-Study, institutionally sponsored loans, scholarships/grants, traineeships, tuition waivers, and unspecified assistantships available. Support available to part-time students. Financial award application deadline: 3/1; financial award applicants required to submit FAFSA. *Faculty research:* Obesity prevention and treatment, omega-3 fatty acids impact on infant development and immunity, vitamin D and bone metabolism in osteosarcoma cells, cancer prevention and recovery, maternal diet intake and weight gain impact on infant body composition and development. *Total annual research expenditures:* $807,651. *Unit head:* Dr. Debra Kay Sullivan, Chairperson, 913-588-5357, Fax: 913-588-8946, E-mail: dsulliva@kumc.edu. *Application contact:* Dr. Heather Gibbs, Graduate Director, 913-945-9138.
Website: http://www.kumc.edu/school-of-health-professions/dietetics-and-nutrition.html

University of Kentucky, Graduate School, College of Agriculture, Food and Environment, Program in Hospitality and Dietetics Administration, Lexington, KY 40506-0032. Offers MS. *Degree requirements:* For master's, comprehensive exam, thesis optional. *Entrance requirements:* For master's, GRE General Test, minimum undergraduate GPA of 2.75. Additional exam requirements/recommendations for international students: Required—TOEFL (minimum score 550 paper-based). Electronic applications accepted.

University of Kentucky, Graduate School, College of Health Sciences, Program in Nutritional Sciences, Lexington, KY 40506-0032. Offers MSNS, PhD. *Degree requirements:* For doctorate, comprehensive exam, thesis/dissertation. *Entrance requirements:* For master's, GRE General Test, minimum undergraduate GPA of 2.75; for doctorate, GRE General Test, minimum graduate GPA of 3.0. Additional exam requirements/recommendations for international students: Required—TOEFL (minimum score 550 paper-based). Electronic applications accepted. *Faculty research:* Nutrition and AIDS, nutrition and alcoholism, nutrition and cardiovascular disease, nutrition and cancer, nutrition and diabetes.

University of Manitoba, Faculty of Graduate Studies, Faculty of Agricultural and Food Sciences, Department of Food and Human Nutritional Sciences, Winnipeg, MB R3T 2N2, Canada. Offers food science (M Sc, PhD); human nutritional sciences (M Sc, PhD). *Degree requirements:* For master's, thesis.

University of Maryland, College Park, Academic Affairs, College of Agriculture and Natural Resources, Department of Nutrition and Food Science, Program in Nutrition, College Park, MD 20742. Offers MS, PhD. *Degree requirements:* For master's, thesis; for doctorate, comprehensive exam, thesis/dissertation, candidacy exam. *Entrance requirements:* For master's, GRE General Test, minimum GPA of 3.0, 3 letters of recommendation; for doctorate, GRE General Test, minimum GPA of 3.0. Additional exam requirements/recommendations for international students: Required—TOEFL. Electronic applications accepted. *Faculty research:* Nutrition education, carbohydrates and physical activity.

University of Massachusetts Amherst, Graduate School, School of Public Health and Health Sciences, Department of Nutrition, Amherst, MA 01003. Offers community nutrition (MS); nutrition (MPH); nutrition science (MS). *Program availability:* Part-time, evening/weekend, online learning. Terminal master's awarded for partial completion of doctoral program. *Degree requirements:* For master's, thesis or alternative. *Entrance requirements:* For master's, GRE General Test. Additional exam requirements/recommendations for international students: Required—TOEFL (minimum score 550 paper-based; 80 iBT), IELTS (minimum score 6.5). Electronic applications accepted.

University of Massachusetts Amherst, Graduate School, School of Public Health and Health Sciences, Department of Public Health, Amherst, MA 01003. Offers biostatistics (MPH, MS, PhD); community health education (MPH, MS, PhD); environmental health sciences (MPH, MS, PhD); epidemiology (MPH, MS, PhD); health policy and management (MPH, MS, PhD); nutrition (MPH, PhD); public health practice (MPH); MPH/MPPA. *Program availability:* Part-time, evening/weekend, online learning. Terminal master's awarded for partial completion of doctoral program. *Degree requirements:* For master's, thesis (for some programs); for doctorate, comprehensive exam, thesis/dissertation. *Entrance requirements:* For master's and doctorate, GRE General Test. Additional exam requirements/recommendations for international students: Required—TOEFL (minimum score 550 paper-based; 80 iBT), IELTS (minimum score 6.5). Electronic applications accepted.

University of Memphis, Graduate School, School of Health Studies, Memphis, TN 38152. Offers faith and health (Graduate Certificate); health studies (MS), including exercise, sport and movement sciences, health promotion, physical education teacher education; nutrition (MS), including clinical nutrition, environmental nutrition, nutrition science; sport nutrition and dietary supplementation (Graduate Certificate). *Program availability:* 100% online. *Faculty:* 19 full-time (10 women), 2 part-time/adjunct (both women). In 2017, 42 master's awarded. *Degree requirements:* For master's, comprehensive exam, thesis or alternative, culminating experience; for Graduate Certificate, practicum. *Entrance requirements:* For master's, GRE or PRAXIS II, letters of recommendation, statement of goals, minimum undergraduate GPA of 2.5; for Graduate Certificate, minimum undergraduate GPA of 2.5. Additional exam requirements/recommendations for international students: Required—TOEFL (minimum score 550 paper-based; 79 iBT). *Application deadline:* For fall admission, 4/15 priority date for domestic students; for spring admission, 10/15 priority date for domestic students; for summer admission, 4/15 priority date for domestic students. Application fee: $35 ($60 for international students). *Expenses:* Contact institution. *Financial support:* In 2017–18, 33 research assistantships (averaging $11,930 per year), 4 teaching assistantships (averaging $10,000 per year) were awarded; career-related internships or fieldwork, Federal Work-Study, scholarships/grants, and unspecified assistantships also available. Financial award application deadline: 2/1; financial award applicants required to submit FAFSA. *Unit head:* Dr. Richard J. Bloomer, Director, 901-678-4316, Fax: 901-678-3591, E-mail: rbloomer@memphis.edu. *Application contact:* Dr. Lawrence Weiss, Director of Graduate Programs, 901-678-5037, E-mail: lweiss@memphis.edu.
Website: http://www.memphis.edu/shs/

Nutrition

University of Miami, Graduate School, School of Education and Human Development, Department of Kinesiology and Sport Sciences, Program in Nutrition for Health and Human Performance, Coral Gables, FL 33124. Offers MS Ed. *Program availability:* Part-time, evening/weekend. *Degree requirements:* For master's, comprehensive exam, special project. *Entrance requirements:* For master's, GRE General Test. Additional exam requirements/recommendations for international students: Required—TOEFL (minimum score 550 paper-based; 80 iBT); Recommended—IELTS (minimum score 6.5). Electronic applications accepted.

University of Michigan, School of Public Health, Department of Nutritional Sciences, Ann Arbor, MI 48109. Offers dietetics (MPH); nutritional sciences (MPH, MS, PhD). *Accreditation:* AND. *Entrance requirements:* For master's, GRE, MCAT; for doctorate, GRE. Additional exam requirements/recommendations for international students: Required—TOEFL (minimum score 100 iBT). Electronic applications accepted. *Expenses:* Tuition, state resident: full-time $22,368; part-time $1201 per credit hour. Tuition, nonresident: full-time $45,156; part-time $2467 per credit hour. *Required fees:* $376 per term. Tuition and fees vary according to course load, degree level and program.

University of Minnesota, Twin Cities Campus, Graduate School, College of Food, Agricultural and Natural Resource Sciences, Program in Nutrition, St. Paul, MN 55108. Offers MS, PhD. *Program availability:* Part-time. *Faculty:* 15 full-time (8 women), 30 part-time/adjunct (20 women). *Students:* 44 full-time (39 women), 5 part-time (3 women); includes 5 minority (1 Black or African American, non-Hispanic/Latino; 1 American Indian or Alaska Native, non-Hispanic/Latino; 2 Hispanic/Latino; 1 Native Hawaiian or other Pacific Islander, non-Hispanic/Latino), 9 international. Average age 25. 47 applicants, 38% accepted, 16 enrolled. In 2017, 6 master's, 4 doctorates awarded. Terminal master's awarded for partial completion of doctoral program. *Degree requirements:* For master's, comprehensive exam, thesis; for doctorate, comprehensive exam, thesis/dissertation. *Entrance requirements:* For master's, GRE General Test, previous course work in general chemistry, organic chemistry, physiology, biology, biochemistry, and statistics; minimum GPA of 3.0 (preferred); for doctorate, GRE General Test, previous course work in general chemistry, organic chemistry, biology, physiology, biochemistry, and statistics; minimum GPA of 3.0 (preferred). Additional exam requirements/recommendations for international students: Required—TOEFL (minimum score 550 paper-based; 79 iBT), IELTS (minimum score 6.5). *Application deadline:* Applications are processed on a rolling basis. Application fee: $75 ($95 for international students). Electronic applications accepted. *Expenses:* $17,832 per year resident tuition and fees; $26,988 per year non-resident tuition and fees. *Financial support:* In 2017–18, fellowships with full tuition reimbursements (averaging $40,000 per year), research assistantships with tuition reimbursements (averaging $40,000 per year), teaching assistantships with tuition reimbursements (averaging $40,000 per year) were awarded; career-related internships or fieldwork, tuition waivers (full and partial), and unspecified assistantships also available. Support available to part-time students. *Faculty research:* Diet and chronic disease: from basic biological and molecular biology approaches to a public health/intervention/epidemiology perspective. *Total annual research expenditures:* $3 million. *Unit head:* Dr. Xiaoli Chen, Director of Graduate Studies, 612-626-1220, Fax: 612-625-5272, E-mail: xlchen@umn.edu. *Application contact:* Nancy L. Toedt, Program Coordinator, 612-624-6753, Fax: 612-625-5272, E-mail: ntoedt@umn.edu.
Website: http://fscn.cfans.umn.edu/graduate-programs/nutrition

University of Minnesota, Twin Cities Campus, School of Public Health, Major in Public Health Nutrition, Minneapolis, MN 55455-0213. Offers MPH. *Program availability:* Part-time. *Degree requirements:* For master's, fieldwork, project. *Entrance requirements:* For master's, GRE General Test. Additional exam requirements/recommendations for international students: Required—TOEFL. Electronic applications accepted. *Expenses:* Contact institution. *Faculty research:* Nutrition and pregnancy outcomes, nutrition and women's health, child growth and nutrition, child and adolescent nutrition and eating behaviors, obesity and eating disorder prevention.

University of Mississippi, Graduate School, School of Applied Sciences, University, MS 38677. Offers communicative disorders (MS); criminal justice (MCJ); exercise science (MS); food and nutrition services (MS); health and kinesiology (PhD); health promotion (MS); nutrition and hospitality management (PhD); park and recreation management (MA); social welfare (PhD); social work (MSW). *Faculty:* 66 full-time (38 women), 33 part-time/adjunct (14 women). *Students:* 182 full-time (139 women), 41 part-time (27 women); includes 49 minority (41 Black or African American, non-Hispanic/Latino; 1 American Indian or Alaska Native, non-Hispanic/Latino; 3 Asian, non-Hispanic/Latino; 3 Hispanic/Latino; 1 Two or more races, non-Hispanic/Latino), 13 international. Average age 26. *Entrance requirements:* For master's, GRE General Test, minimum GPA of 3.0. Additional exam requirements/recommendations for international students: Required—TOEFL. *Application deadline:* For fall admission, 4/1 for domestic students; for spring admission, 10/1 for domestic students. Applications are processed on a rolling basis. Application fee: $50. Electronic applications accepted. *Financial support:* Scholarships/grants available. Financial award application deadline: 3/1; financial award applicants required to submit FAFSA. *Unit head:* Dr. Teresa C. Carithers, Dean, 662-915-1081, Fax: 662-915-5717, E-mail: applsci@olemiss.edu.

University of Missouri, Office of Research and Graduate Studies, College of Human Environmental Sciences, Department of Nutrition and Exercise Physiology, Columbia, MO 65211. Offers exercise physiology (MS, PhD); nutritional sciences (MS, PhD). *Entrance requirements:* For master's and doctorate, GRE General Test, minimum GPA of 3.0. Additional exam requirements/recommendations for international students: Required—TOEFL. *Expenses:* Tuition, state resident: full-time $6480. Tuition, nonresident: full-time $17,744. *Required fees:* $1108. Tuition and fees vary according to course load, campus/location and program. *Financial support:* Fellowships, research assistantships, teaching assistantships, institutionally sponsored loans, scholarships/grants, health care benefits, and unspecified assistantships available. Support available to part-time students.
Website: http://ns.missouri.edu/

University of Nebraska–Lincoln, Graduate College, College of Agricultural Sciences and Natural Resources, Interdepartmental Area of Nutrition, Lincoln, NE 68588. Offers MS, PhD. *Degree requirements:* For master's, thesis optional; for doctorate, comprehensive exam, thesis/dissertation. *Entrance requirements:* For master's and doctorate, GRE General Test. Additional exam requirements/recommendations for international students: Required—TOEFL (minimum score 550 paper-based). Electronic applications accepted. *Faculty research:* Human nutrition and metabolism, animal nutrition and metabolism, biochemistry, community and clinical nutrition.

University of Nebraska–Lincoln, Graduate College, College of Education and Human Sciences, Department of Nutrition and Health Sciences, Lincoln, NE 68588. Offers community nutrition and health promotion (MS); nutrition (MS, PhD); nutrition and exercise (MS); nutrition and health sciences (MS, PhD). *Degree requirements:* For master's, thesis optional. *Entrance requirements:* For master's, GRE General Test. Additional exam requirements/recommendations for international students: Required—TOEFL (minimum score 550 paper-based). Electronic applications accepted. *Faculty research:* Foods/food service administration, community nutrition science, diet-health relationships.

University of Nebraska Medical Center, College of Allied Health Professions and College of Medicine, UNMC Dietetic Internship Program (Medical Nutrition Education Division), Omaha, NE 68198. Offers Certificate. *Entrance requirements:* Additional exam requirements/recommendations for international students: Required—TOEFL. *Expenses:* Tuition, state resident: full-time $8451; part-time $4225 per semester. Tuition, nonresident: full-time $24,219; part-time $11,295 per semester. *Required fees:* $589; $117 per term. *Faculty research:* Nutrition intervention outcomes.

University of Nevada, Las Vegas, Graduate College, School of Allied Health Sciences, Department of Kinesiology and Nutrition Sciences, Las Vegas, NV 89154-3034. Offers exercise physiology (MS); kinesiology (PhD); nutrition sciences (MS). *Program availability:* Part-time. *Faculty:* 10 full-time (5 women), 2 part-time/adjunct (1 woman). *Students:* 34 full-time (19 women), 11 part-time (4 women); includes 10 minority (2 Black or African American, non-Hispanic/Latino; 1 American Indian or Alaska Native, non-Hispanic/Latino; 2 Asian, non-Hispanic/Latino; 4 Hispanic/Latino; 1 Two or more races, non-Hispanic/Latino), 2 international. Average age 27. 54 applicants, 52% accepted, 17 enrolled. In 2017, 15 master's awarded. *Degree requirements:* For master's, thesis (for some programs), professional paper; for doctorate, comprehensive exam, thesis/dissertation. *Entrance requirements:* For master's, GRE General Test, bachelor's degree; statement of purpose; 2 letters of recommendation; for doctorate, GRE General Test (minimum 70th percentile on the Verbal section), master's degree/bachelor's degree with minimum GPA of 3.25; 3 letters of recommendation; statement of purpose; personal interview. Additional exam requirements/recommendations for international students: Required—TOEFL (minimum score 550 paper-based; 80 iBT), IELTS (minimum score 7). *Application deadline:* For fall admission, 6/15 for domestic and international students; for spring admission, 11/15 for domestic and international students. Application fee: $60 ($95 for international students). Electronic applications accepted. *Expenses:* $275 per credit, $850 per course, $7,969 per year resident, $22,157 per year non-resident, $7,094 non-resident fee (7 credits or more), $1,307 annual health insurance fee. *Financial support:* In 2017–18, 12 students received support, including 12 research assistantships with full and partial tuition reimbursements available (averaging $14,396 per year), 10 teaching assistantships with full and partial tuition reimbursements available (averaging $12,350 per year); institutionally sponsored loans, scholarships/grants, health care benefits, and unspecified assistantships also available. Financial award application deadline: 3/15; financial award applicants required to submit FAFSA. *Faculty research:* Biomechanics of gait, factors in motor skill acquisition and performance, nutritional supplements and performance, lipoprotein biochemistry, transcranial direct current stimulation. *Total annual research expenditures:* $49,804. *Unit head:* Dr. Brian Schilling, Chair/Professor, 702-895-1130, Fax: 702-895-1500, E-mail: brian.schilling@unlv.edu. *Application contact:* Dr. James Navalta, Graduate Coordinator, 702-895-2344, E-mail: james.navalta@unlv.edu.

University of Nevada, Reno, Graduate School, College of Agriculture, Biotechnology and Natural Resources, Department of Nutrition, Reno, NV 89557. Offers MS. *Degree requirements:* For master's, thesis optional. *Entrance requirements:* For master's, GRE, minimum GPA of 2.75. Additional exam requirements/recommendations for international students: Required—TOEFL (minimum score 500 paper-based; 61 iBT), IELTS (minimum score 6). Electronic applications accepted. *Faculty research:* Nutritional education, food technology, therapeutic human nutrition, human nutritional requirements, diet and disease.

University of New England, College of Graduate and Professional Studies, Portland, ME 04005-9526. Offers advanced educational leadership (CAGS); applied nutrition (MS); career and technical education (MS Ed); curriculum and instruction (MS Ed); education (CAGS, Post-Master's Certificate); educational leadership (MS Ed, Ed D); generalist (MS Ed); health informatics (MS, Graduate Certificate); inclusion education (MS Ed); literacy K-12 (MS Ed); medical education leadership (MMEL); public health (MPH); public health (Graduate Certificate); reading specialist (MS Ed); social work (MSW). *Program availability:* Part-time, evening/weekend, online only, 100% online. *Faculty:* 125 part-time/adjunct (94 women). *Students:* 1,403 full-time (1,128 women), 594 part-time (475 women); includes 474 minority (332 Black or African American, non-Hispanic/Latino; 13 American Indian or Alaska Native, non-Hispanic/Latino; 83 Asian, non-Hispanic/Latino; 27 Hispanic/Latino; 11 Native Hawaiian or other Pacific Islander, non-Hispanic/Latino; 8 Two or more races, non-Hispanic/Latino). Average age 35. 3,153 applicants, 41% accepted, 990 enrolled. In 2017, 307 master's, 59 doctorates, 124 other advanced degrees awarded. *Application deadline:* Applications are processed on a rolling basis. Electronic applications accepted. Tuition and fees vary according to degree level, program and student level. *Financial support:* Application deadline: 5/1; applicants required to submit FAFSA. *Unit head:* Dr. Martha Wilson, Associate Provost for Online Worldwide Learning/Dean of the College of Graduate and Professional Studies, 207-221-4985, E-mail: mwilson13@une.edu.
Website: http://online.une.edu

University of New Hampshire, Graduate School, College of Life Sciences and Agriculture, Department of Molecular, Cellular and Biomedical Sciences, Program in Animal and Nutritional Sciences, Durham, NH 03824. Offers agricultural sciences (MS, PhD); nutritional sciences (MS, PhD). *Program availability:* Part-time. *Students:* 6 full-time (5 women), 9 part-time (4 women), 4 international. Average age 28. 19 applicants, 42% accepted, 7 enrolled. In 2017, 1 master's, 3 doctorates awarded. *Entrance requirements:* For master's and doctorate, GRE. Additional exam requirements/recommendations for international students: Required—TOEFL (minimum score 550 paper-based; 80 iBT). *Application deadline:* For fall admission, 3/15 for domestic and international students; for spring admission, 12/1 for domestic students. Application fee: $65. Electronic applications accepted. *Financial support:* In 2017–18, 13 students received support, including 7 research assistantships, 6 teaching assistantships; fellowships, scholarships/grants, traineeships, and unspecified assistantships also available. Support available to part-time students. Financial award application deadline: 2/15. *Unit head:* Joanne Curran-Celentana, Chair, 603-862-2573. *Application contact:* Jen Surina, Administrative Assistant, 603-862-0822, E-mail: ansc.grad.program.info@unh.edu.

University of New Haven, Graduate School, College of Arts and Sciences, Program in Human Nutrition, West Haven, CT 06516. Offers human nutrition (MS); nutritional genomics (MS, Graduate Certificate). *Program availability:* Part-time, evening/weekend. *Faculty:* 3 full-time (all women), 1 (woman) part-time/adjunct. *Students:* 7 full-time (6 women), 13 part-time (9 women); includes 3 minority (1 Black or African American, non-Hispanic/Latino; 1 Asian, non-Hispanic/Latino; 1 Hispanic/Latino), 1 international. Average age 28. 31 applicants, 97% accepted, 14 enrolled. In 2017, 5 master's, 1 other advanced degree awarded. *Entrance requirements:* Additional exam requirements/recommendations for international students: Required—TOEFL (minimum score 80 iBT), IELTS, PTE. *Application deadline:* Applications are processed on a rolling basis. Application fee: $50. Electronic applications accepted. Application fee is waived when completed online. *Expenses: Tuition:* Full-time $16,020; part-time $890 per credit hour. *Required fees:* $220; $90 per term. *Financial support:* Research assistantships with partial tuition reimbursements, teaching assistantships with partial tuition reimbursements, career-related internships or fieldwork, Federal Work-Study, scholarships/grants, tuition waivers, and unspecified assistantships available. Support available to part-time students. Financial award applicants required to submit FAFSA. *Unit head:* Dr. Rosa A. Mo, Chair of Nutrition and Dietetics, 203-932-7040, E-mail: rmo@newhaven.edu. *Application contact:* Michelle Mason, Director of Graduate Enrollment, 203-932-7067, E-mail: mmason@newhaven.edu.

University of New Mexico, Graduate Studies, College of Education, Program in Nutrition, Albuquerque, NM 87131. Offers MS. *Program availability:* Part-time. *Faculty:* 5 full-time (3 women). *Students:* 12 full-time (9 women), 13 part-time (12 women); includes 12 minority (1 Asian, non-Hispanic/Latino; 10 Hispanic/Latino; 1 Two or more races, non-Hispanic/Latino). Average age 34. 15 applicants, 87% accepted, 12 enrolled. In 2017, 5 master's awarded. *Entrance requirements:* For master's, GRE. Additional exam requirements/recommendations for international students: Required—TOEFL. *Application deadline:* For fall admission, 2/1 priority date for domestic students, 2/1 for international students; for spring admission, 11/1 priority date for domestic students, 11/1 for international students. Application fee: $50. Electronic applications accepted. *Financial support:* Teaching assistantships and unspecified assistantships available. Financial award application deadline: 3/1; financial award applicants required to submit FAFSA. *Faculty research:* Nutritional needs of children, obesity prevention, phytochemicals, international nutrition. *Unit head:* Dr. Carole Conn, Graduate Coordinator, 505-277-8185, Fax: 505-277-8361, E-mail: cconn@unm.edu. *Application contact:* Cynthia Salas, Program Office, 505-277-4535, Fax: 505-277-8361, E-mail: casalas@unm.edu.
Website: http://coe.unm.edu/departments-programs/ifce/nutrition/

The University of North Carolina at Chapel Hill, Graduate School, Gillings School of Global Public Health, Department of Nutrition, Chapel Hill, NC 27599. Offers nutrition (MPH, PhD); nutrition/registered dietitian (MPH); nutritional biochemistry (MS). *Accreditation:* AND. *Faculty:* 43 full-time (29 women), 18 part-time/adjunct (15 women). *Students:* 114 full-time (103 women), 2 part-time (1 woman); includes 29 minority (5 Black or African American, non-Hispanic/Latino; 6 Asian, non-Hispanic/Latino; 11 Hispanic/Latino; 7 Two or more races, non-Hispanic/Latino), 13 international. Average age 28. 202 applicants, 27% accepted, 35 enrolled. In 2017, 27 master's, 12 doctorates awarded. *Degree requirements:* For master's, comprehensive exam, thesis, major paper, 10 weeks of advanced nutrition field work; for doctorate, comprehensive exam, thesis/dissertation. *Entrance requirements:* For master's, GRE General Test, MCAT, or DAT, three letters of recommendation (academic and/or professional; academic preferred); coursework in biochemistry, anatomy and physiology, organic chemistry, microbiology with lab, psychology, sociology or anthropology, and human nutrition; for doctorate, GRE General Test, MCAT, or DAT, three letters of recommendation (academic and/or professional; academic preferred); coursework in biochemistry, anatomy and physiology, organic chemistry, and human nutrition. Additional exam requirements/recommendations for international students: Required—TOEFL (minimum score 90 iBT), IELTS (minimum score 7). *Application deadline:* For fall admission, 1/9 for domestic and international students. Applications are processed on a rolling basis. Application fee: $85. Electronic applications accepted. *Financial support:* Fellowships with tuition reimbursements, research assistantships with tuition reimbursements, teaching assistantships with tuition reimbursements, career-related internships or fieldwork, Federal Work-Study, institutionally sponsored loans, scholarships/grants, traineeships, health care benefits, and unspecified assistantships available. Financial award application deadline: 12/10; financial award applicants required to submit FAFSA. *Faculty research:* Nutrition policy, management and leadership development, lipid and carbohydrate metabolism, dietary trends and determinants, transmembrane signal transduction and carcinogenesis, maternal and child nutrition. *Unit head:* Dr. Elizabeth Mayer-Davis, Chair, 919-966-7218, Fax: 919-966-7215, E-mail: mayerdav@email.unc.edu. *Application contact:* Jonathan Earnest, Student Services Manager, 919-966-7212, E-mail: earnestj@email.unc.edu.
Website: http://sph.unc.edu/nutr/unc-nutrition/

The University of North Carolina at Greensboro, Graduate School, School of Health and Human Sciences, Department of Nutrition, Greensboro, NC 27412-5001. Offers MS, PhD. *Degree requirements:* For master's, thesis; for doctorate, thesis/dissertation. *Entrance requirements:* For master's and doctorate, GRE General Test. Additional exam requirements/recommendations for international students: Required—TOEFL. Electronic applications accepted.

University of North Florida, Brooks College of Health, Department of Nutrition and Dietetics, Jacksonville, FL 32224. Offers MSH. *Program availability:* Part-time. *Entrance requirements:* For master's, GRE General Test, minimum GPA of 3.0 in last 60 hours. Additional exam requirements/recommendations for international students: Required—TOEFL (minimum score 500 paper-based; 61 iBT). Electronic applications accepted.

University of Oklahoma Health Sciences Center, Graduate College, College of Allied Health, Department of Nutritional Sciences, Oklahoma City, OK 73190. Offers MS. *Degree requirements:* For master's, comprehensive exam, thesis optional. *Entrance requirements:* For master's, GRE General Test, interview, 3 letters of reference. Additional exam requirements/recommendations for international students: Required—TOEFL (minimum score 550 paper-based).

University of Pittsburgh, School of Health and Rehabilitation Sciences, Department of Sports Medicine and Nutrition, Pittsburgh, PA 15260. Offers health and rehabilitation sciences (MS), including sports medicine, wellness and human performance; nutrition and dietetics (MS). *Program availability:* Online learning. *Faculty:* 15 full-time (8 women), 3 part-time/adjunct (all women). *Students:* 55 full-time (48 women), 8 part-time (7 women); includes 8 minority (1 Black or African American, non-Hispanic/Latino; 1 American Indian or Alaska Native, non-Hispanic/Latino; 2 Hispanic/Latino; 4 Two or more races, non-Hispanic/Latino), 4 international. Average age 26. 128 applicants, 65% accepted, 28 enrolled. In 2017, 29 master's awarded. *Degree requirements:* For master's, comprehensive exam (for some programs). *Entrance requirements:* Additional exam requirements/recommendations for international students: Required—TOEFL (minimum score 550 paper-based; 80 iBT), IELTS (minimum score 6.5). *Application deadline:* For fall admission, 3/15 for domestic and international students. Application fee: $50. Electronic applications accepted. *Financial support:* In 2017–18, 6 fellowships (averaging $15,060 per year), 7 research assistantships (averaging $27,400 per year) were awarded; career-related internships or fieldwork, Federal Work-Study, scholarships/grants, traineeships, and unspecified assistantships also available. *Faculty research:* Nutrition and fitness; movement science; injury prevention and human performance; molecular transducers of physical activity; characterization of psychological resilience and readiness. *Total annual research expenditures:* $2.4 million. *Unit head:* Dr. Kevin Conley, Chair/Associate Professor, 412-383-6737, Fax: 412-383-6636, E-mail: kconley@pitt.edu. *Application contact:* Jessica Maguire, Director of Admissions, 412-383-6557, Fax: 412-383-6535, E-mail: maguire@pitt.edu.
Website: http://www.shrs.pitt.edu/smn

University of Puerto Rico–Medical Sciences Campus, Graduate School of Public Health, Department of Human Development, Program in Nutrition, San Juan, PR 00936-5067. Offers MS. *Program availability:* Part-time. *Degree requirements:* For master's, thesis. *Entrance requirements:* For master's, GRE, previous course work in algebra, biochemistry, biology, chemistry, and social sciences.

University of Puerto Rico–Medical Sciences Campus, School of Health Professions, Program in Dietetics Internship, San Juan, PR 00936-5067. Offers Certificate. *Degree requirements:* For Certificate, one foreign language, clinical practice. *Entrance requirements:* For degree, minimum GPA of 2.5, interview, participation in the computer matching process by the American Dietetic Association.

University of Puerto Rico–Medical Sciences Campus, School of Medicine, Biomedical Sciences Graduate Program, Department of Biochemistry, San Juan, PR 00936-5067. Offers MS, PhD. *Degree requirements:* For master's, thesis; for doctorate, comprehensive exam, thesis/dissertation. *Entrance requirements:* For master's and doctorate, GRE General Test, GRE Subject Test, interview, minimum GPA of 3.0. Electronic applications accepted. *Faculty research:* Genetics, cell and molecular biology, cancer biology, protein structure/function, glycosilation of proteins.

University of Puerto Rico–Río Piedras, College of Education, Program in Family Ecology and Nutrition, San Juan, PR 00931-3300. Offers M Ed. *Program availability:* Part-time. *Degree requirements:* For master's, thesis. *Entrance requirements:* For master's, PAEG or GRE, minimum GPA of 3.0, letter of recommendation.

University of Rhode Island, Graduate School, College of Health Sciences, Department of Nutrition and Food Sciences, Kingston, RI 02881. Offers dietetic internship (MS); nutrition (MS); online dietetics (MS). *Program availability:* Part-time, 100% online. *Faculty:* 10 full-time (9 women), 1 (woman) part-time/adjunct. *Students:* 44 full-time (40 women), 40 part-time (38 women); includes 9 minority (2 Black or African American, non-Hispanic/Latino; 6 Asian, non-Hispanic/Latino; 1 Hispanic/Latino), 1 international. 76 applicants, 64% accepted, 42 enrolled. In 2017, 3 master's awarded. *Entrance requirements:* Additional exam requirements/recommendations for international students: Required—TOEFL. *Application deadline:* For fall admission, 2/15 for domestic students, 2/1 for international students. Application fee: $65. Electronic applications accepted. *Expenses:* Tuition, state resident: full-time $12,706; part-time $786 per credit. Tuition, nonresident: full-time $25,216; part-time $1401 per credit. *Required fees:* $1598; $45 per credit. One-time fee: $30 part-time. *Financial support:* In 2017–18, 2 research assistantships with tuition reimbursements (averaging $13,753 per year), 7 teaching assistantships (averaging $18,089 per year) were awarded. Financial award application deadline: 2/1; financial award applicants required to submit FAFSA. *Unit head:* Dr. Cathy English, Chair, 401-874-5689, Fax: 401-874-5974, E-mail: cathy@uri.edu. *Application contact:* Dr. Ingrid Lofgren, Graduate Coordinator, 401-874-5706, E-mail: ingridlofgren@uri.edu.
Website: http://web.uri.edu/nfs/

University of Saint Joseph, Department of Nutrition and Public Health, West Hartford, CT 06117-2700. Offers nutrition (MS); public health (MPH). *Program availability:* Part-time, evening/weekend, online learning. *Entrance requirements:* For master's, 2 letters of recommendation, letter of intent. *Application deadline:* Applications are processed on a rolling basis. Application fee: $50. Electronic applications accepted. Application fee is waived when completed online. *Financial support:* Career-related internships or fieldwork and unspecified assistantships available. Support available to part-time students. Financial award applicants required to submit FAFSA.
Website: https://www.usj.edu/academics/schools/sihs/nutrition-public-health/

University of Southern Mississippi, College of Health, Department of Nutrition and Food Systems, Hattiesburg, MS 39406-0001. Offers MS. *Program availability:* Part-time, online learning. *Students:* 2 full-time (both women). 13 applicants, 62% accepted, 2 enrolled. In 2017, 1 master's awarded. *Degree requirements:* For master's, comprehensive exam, thesis (for some programs). *Entrance requirements:* For master's, GRE General Test, minimum GPA of 2.75 on last 60 hours. Additional exam requirements/recommendations for international students: Required—TOEFL, IELTS. *Application deadline:* For fall admission, 3/1 for domestic and international students; for spring admission, 1/10 priority date for domestic and international students. Application fee: $60. Electronic applications accepted. *Expenses:* Tuition, state resident: full-time $3830. *Financial support:* Research assistantships with full tuition reimbursements, teaching assistantships with full tuition reimbursements, career-related internships or fieldwork, Federal Work-Study, institutionally sponsored loans, scholarships/grants, traineeships, health care benefits, and unspecified assistantships available. Financial award applicants required to submit FAFSA. *Unit head:* Dr. Elaine F. Molaison, Chair, 601-266-5377, Fax: 601-266-6343. *Application contact:* Erin Whittington, Academic Service Specialist, Fax: 601-266-6343.
Website: https://www.usm.edu/nutrition

University of South Florida, Innovative Education, Tampa, FL 33620-9951. Offers adult, career and higher education (Graduate Certificate), including college teaching, leadership in developing human resources, leadership in higher education; Africana studies (Graduate Certificate), including diasporas and health disparities, genocide and human rights; aging studies (Graduate Certificate), including gerontology; art research (Graduate Certificate), including museum studies; business foundations (Graduate Certificate); chemical and biomedical engineering (Graduate Certificate), including materials science and engineering, water, health and sustainability; child and family studies (Graduate Certificate), including positive behavior support; civil and industrial engineering (Graduate Certificate), including transportation systems analysis; community and family health (Graduate Certificate), including maternal and child health, social marketing and public health, violence and injury: prevention and intervention, women's health; criminology (Graduate Certificate), including criminal justice administration; data science for public administration (Graduate Certificate); digital humanities (Graduate Certificate); educational measurement and research (Graduate Certificate), including evaluation; English (Graduate Certificate), including comparative literary studies, creative writing, professional and technical communication; entrepreneurship (Graduate Certificate); environmental health (Graduate Certificate), including safety management; epidemiology and biostatistics (Graduate Certificate), including applied biostatistics, biostatistics, concepts and tools of epidemiology, epidemiology, epidemiology of infectious diseases; geography, environment and planning (Graduate Certificate), including community development, environmental policy and management, geographical information systems; geology (Graduate Certificate), including hydrogeology; global health (Graduate Certificate), including disaster management, global health and Latin American and Caribbean studies, global health practice, humanitarian assistance, infection control; government and international affairs (Graduate Certificate), including Cuban studies, globalization studies; health policy and management (Graduate Certificate), including health management and leadership, public health policy and programs; hearing specialist: early intervention (Graduate Certificate); industrial and management systems engineering (Graduate Certificate), including systems engineering, technology management; information studies (Graduate Certificate), including school library media specialist; information systems/decision sciences (Graduate Certificate), including analytics and business intelligence; instructional technology (Graduate Certificate), including distance education, Florida digital/virtual educator, instructional design, multimedia design, Web design; internal medicine, bioethics and medical humanities (Graduate Certificate), including biomedical ethics; Latin American and Caribbean studies (Graduate Certificate); leadership for coastal resiliency planning (Graduate Certificate); mass communications (Graduate Certificate), including multimedia journalism; mathematics and statistics (Graduate Certificate), including mathematics; medicine (Graduate Certificate), including aging and neuroscience, bioinformatics, biotechnology, brain fitness and memory management, clinical investigation, hand and upper limb rehabilitation, health informatics, health sciences, integrative weight management, intellectual property, medicine and gender, metabolic and nutritional medicine, metabolic cardiology, pharmacy sciences; national and competitive intelligence (Graduate Certificate); nursing (Graduate Certificate),

including simulation based academic fellowship in advanced pain management; psychological and social foundations (Graduate Certificate), including career counseling, college teaching, diversity in education, mental health counseling, school counseling; public affairs (Graduate Certificate), including nonprofit management, public management, research administration; public health (Graduate Certificate), including assessing chemical toxicity and public health risks, health equity, pharmacoepidemiology, public health generalist, toxicology, translational research in adolescent behavioral health; public health practices (Graduate Certificate), including planning for healthy communities; rehabilitation and mental health counseling (Graduate Certificate), including integrative mental health care, marriage and family therapy, rehabilitation technology; secondary education (Graduate Certificate), including ESOL, foreign language education: culture and content, foreign language education: professional; social work (Graduate Certificate), including geriatric social work/clinical gerontology; special education (Graduate Certificate), including autism spectrum disorder, disabilities education: severe/profound; world languages (Graduate Certificate), including teaching English as a second language (TESL) or foreign language. *Unit head:* Dr. Cynthia DeLuca, Associate Vice President and Assistant Vice Provost, 813-974-3077, Fax: 813-974-7061, E-mail: deluca@usf.edu. *Application contact:* Owen Hooper, Director, Summer and Alternative Calendar Programs, 813-974-6917, E-mail: hooper@usf.edu.
Website: http://www.usf.edu/innovative-education/

University of South Florida, Morsani College of Medicine and College of Graduate Studies, Graduate Programs in Medical Sciences, Tampa, FL 33620-9951. Offers advanced athletic training (MS); athletic training (MS); bioinformatics and computational biology (MSBCB); biotechnology (MSB); health informatics (MSHI); medical sciences (MSMS, PhD), including aging and neuroscience (MSMS), allergy, immunology and infectious disease (PhD), anatomy, biochemistry and molecular biology, clinical and translational research, health science (MSMS), interdisciplinary medical sciences (MSMS), medical microbiology and immunology (MSMS), metabolic and nutritional medicine (MSMS), microbiology and immunology (PhD), molecular medicine, molecular pharmacology and physiology (PhD), neuroscience (PhD), pathology and cell biology (PhD), women's health (MSMS). *Students:* 372 full-time (212 women), 216 part-time (142 women); includes 257 minority (78 Black or African American, non-Hispanic/Latino; 1 American Indian or Alaska Native, non-Hispanic/Latino; 79 Asian, non-Hispanic/Latino; 84 Hispanic/Latino; 15 Two or more races, non-Hispanic/Latino), 62 international. Average age 28. 1,048 applicants, 46% accepted, 309 enrolled. In 2017, 351 master's, 56 doctorates awarded. Terminal master's awarded for partial completion of doctoral program. *Degree requirements:* For master's, comprehensive exam, thesis; for doctorate, comprehensive exam, thesis/dissertation. *Entrance requirements:* For master's, GRE General Test or GMAT, bachelor's degree or equivalent from regionally-accredited university with minimum GPA of 3.0 in upper-division sciences coursework; prerequisites in general biology, general chemistry, general physics, organic chemistry, quantitative analysis, and integral and differential calculus; for doctorate, GRE General Test, bachelor's degree from regionally-accredited university with minimum GPA of 3.0 in upper-division sciences coursework; 3 letters of recommendation; personal interview; 1-2 page personal statement; prerequisites in biology, chemistry, physics, organic chemistry, quantitative analysis, and integral/differential calculus. Additional exam requirements/recommendations for international students: Required—TOEFL (minimum score 550 paper-based; 79 iBT) or IELTS (minimum score 6.5). *Application deadline:* For fall admission, 2/1 priority date for domestic students, 2/1 for international students. Application fee: $30. Electronic applications accepted. *Expenses:* Contact institution. *Financial support:* In 2017–18, 109 students received support. *Faculty research:* Anatomy, biochemistry, cancer biology, cardiovascular disease, cell biology, immunology, microbiology, molecular biology, neuroscience, pharmacology, physiology. *Total annual research expenditures:* $45.3 million. *Unit head:* Dr. Michael Barber, Professor/Associate Dean for Graduate and Postdoctoral Affairs, 813-974-9908, Fax: 813-974-4317, E-mail: mbarber@health.usf.edu. *Application contact:* Dr. Eric Bennett, Graduate Director, PhD Program in Medical Sciences, 813-974-1545, Fax: 813-974-4317, E-mail: esbennet@health.usf.edu.
Website: http://health.usf.edu/nocms/medicine/graduatestudies/

The University of Tampa, Program in Exercise and Nutrition Science, Tampa, FL 33606-1490. Offers MS. *Program availability:* Part-time, evening/weekend. *Faculty:* 3 full-time (1 woman), 1 (woman) part-time/adjunct. *Students:* 37 full-time (20 women), 7 part-time (6 women); includes 7 minority (4 Black or African American, non-Hispanic/Latino; 1 Asian, non-Hispanic/Latino; 2 Two or more races, non-Hispanic/Latino), 3 international. Average age 26. 207 applicants, 52% accepted, 33 enrolled. In 2017, 44 master's awarded. *Degree requirements:* For master's, comprehensive exam, practicum. *Entrance requirements:* For master's, GMAT or GRE, official transcripts from all colleges and/or universities previously attended, resume, personal statement, letters of recommendation, bachelor's degree in related field. Additional exam requirements/recommendations for international students: Required—TOEFL (minimum score 577 paper-based; 90 iBT), IELTS (minimum score 7.5). *Application deadline:* Applications are processed on a rolling basis. Application fee: $40. Electronic applications accepted. *Expenses:* Contact institution. *Financial support:* In 2017–18, 1 student received support. Career-related internships or fieldwork, scholarships/grants, and unspecified assistantships available. Financial award applicants required to submit FAFSA. *Unit head:* Dr. Ronda C. Sturgill, Associate Professor, Health Sciences and Human Performance, 813-257-3445, E-mail: rsturgill@ut.edu. *Application contact:* Chanelle Cox, Staff Assistant, Admissions for Graduate and Continuing Studies, 813-253-6249, E-mail: ccox@ut.edu.
Website: http://www.ut.edu/msexercisenutrition/

The University of Tennessee, Graduate School, College of Education, Health and Human Sciences, Department of Nutrition, Knoxville, TN 37996. Offers nutrition (MS), including nutrition science, public health nutrition; MS/MPH. *Program availability:* Part-time. *Degree requirements:* For master's, thesis or alternative. *Entrance requirements:* For master's, GRE General Test, minimum GPA of 2.7. Additional exam requirements/recommendations for international students: Required—TOEFL. Electronic applications accepted.

The University of Tennessee at Martin, Graduate Programs, College of Agriculture and Applied Sciences, Department of Family and Consumer Sciences, Martin, TN 38238. Offers dietetics (MSFCS); general family and consumer sciences (MSFCS). *Program availability:* Part-time, 100% online. *Faculty:* 9. *Students:* 10 full-time (7 women), 31 part-time (27 women); includes 11 minority (9 Black or African American, non-Hispanic/Latino; 1 Hispanic/Latino; 1 Two or more races, non-Hispanic/Latino). Average age 30. 50 applicants, 86% accepted, 20 enrolled. In 2017, 12 master's awarded. *Degree requirements:* For master's, comprehensive exam, thesis optional. *Entrance requirements:* For master's, GRE General Test, minimum GPA of 2.5. Additional exam requirements/recommendations for international students: Required—TOEFL (minimum score 525 paper-based; 71 iBT). *Application deadline:* For fall admission, 7/27 priority date for domestic and international students; for spring admission, 12/17 priority date for domestic and international students; for summer admission, 5/10 priority date for domestic and international students. Applications are processed on a rolling basis. Application fee: $30 ($130 for international students). Electronic applications accepted. *Expenses:* Tuition, state resident: full-time $8658; part-time $481 per credit hour. Tuition, nonresident: full-time $14,418; part-time $801 per credit hour. *International tuition:* $22,602 full-time. *Required fees:* $1404; $79 per credit hour. Part-time tuition and fees vary according to course load. *Financial support:* In 2017–18, 20 students received support, including 1 research assistantship with full tuition reimbursement available (averaging $7,540 per year), 7 teaching assistantships with full tuition reimbursements available (averaging $7,432 per year); scholarships/grants and tuition waivers (full and partial) also available. Financial award application deadline: 2/1; financial award applicants required to submit FAFSA. *Faculty research:* Children with developmental disabilities, regional food product development and marketing, parent education. *Unit head:* Dr. Lisa LeBleu, Coordinator, 731-881-7116, Fax: 731-881-7106, E-mail: llebleu@utm.edu. *Application contact:* Jolene L. Cunningham, Student Services Specialist, 731-881-7012, Fax: 731-881-7499, E-mail: jcunningham@utm.edu.
Website: http://www.utm.edu/departments/caas/fcs/index.php

The University of Texas at Austin, Graduate School, College of Natural Sciences, School of Human Ecology, Program in Nutritional Sciences, Austin, TX 78712-1111. Offers nutrition (MA); nutritional sciences (MS, PhD). *Program availability:* Online learning. *Degree requirements:* For master's, thesis; for doctorate, thesis/dissertation. *Entrance requirements:* For master's and doctorate, GRE General Test. Additional exam requirements/recommendations for international students: Required—TOEFL. Electronic applications accepted. *Faculty research:* Nutritional biochemistry, nutrient health assessment, obesity, nutrition education, molecular/cellular aspects of nutrient functions.

The University of Texas Rio Grande Valley, College of Health Affairs, Department of Health and Biomedical Sciences, Brownville, TX 78520. Offers clinical laboratory sciences (MSHS); health care administration (MSHS); nutrition (MSHS). *Faculty:* 2 full-time (both women), 10 part-time/adjunct (all women). *Students:* 129 part-time (94 women); includes 103 minority (8 Black or African American, non-Hispanic/Latino; 4 Asian, non-Hispanic/Latino; 90 Hispanic/Latino; 1 Two or more races, non-Hispanic/Latino), 6 international. 51 applicants, 96% accepted, 49 enrolled. *Application deadline:* For fall admission, 7/20 for domestic and international students; for spring admission, 12/2 for domestic students, 12/1 for international students. Application fee: $50 ($100 for international students). *Expenses:* Tuition, state resident: full-time $5550; part-time $417 per credit hour. Tuition, nonresident: full-time $13,020; part-time $832 per credit hour. *Required fees:* $1169. *Faculty research:* Health disparities, post-menopausal osteoporosis bone loss and bone density, alternative medicine and nutritional supplements, health informatics competencies, online learning and quality matters, health literacy. *Unit head:* Dr. Saraswathy Nair, Associate Professor and Chair, Health and Biomedical, 956-882-5108, Fax: 956-882-6835, E-mail: saraswathy.nair@utrgv.edu. *Application contact:* Kim Garcia, Lecturer III/Associate Chair, Health and Biomedical Sciences, 956-665-4781, E-mail: kim.garcia@utrgv.edu.
Website: http://www.utrgv.edu/hbs/

The University of Texas Southwestern Medical Center, Southwestern School of Health Professions, Clinical Nutrition Program, Dallas, TX 75390. Offers MCN.

University of the District of Columbia, College of Agriculture, Urban Sustainability and Environmental Sciences, Program in Nutrition and Dietetics, Washington, DC 20008-1175. Offers MS. *Degree requirements:* For master's, thesis. *Entrance requirements:* For master's, GRE, 3 letters of recommendation, personal interview.

University of the Incarnate Word, School of Mathematics, Science, and Engineering, San Antonio, TX 78209-6397. Offers applied statistics (MS); biology (MA, MS); mathematics (MA), including teaching; multidisciplinary sciences (MA); nutrition (MS). *Program availability:* Part-time, evening/weekend. *Faculty:* 9 full-time (4 women), 3 part-time/adjunct (1 woman). *Students:* 42 full-time (33 women), 6 part-time (5 women); includes 27 minority (2 Black or African American, non-Hispanic/Latino; 1 American Indian or Alaska Native, non-Hispanic/Latino; 1 Asian, non-Hispanic/Latino; 23 Hispanic/Latino), 6 international. In 2017, 13 master's awarded. *Degree requirements:* For master's, comprehensive exam (for some programs), thesis optional, capstone. *Entrance requirements:* For master's, GRE, recommendation letter. Additional exam requirements/recommendations for international students: Required—TOEFL (minimum score 560 paper-based; 83 iBT). *Application deadline:* Applications are processed on a rolling basis. Application fee: $20. Electronic applications accepted. *Expenses: Tuition:* Full-time $16,470; part-time $915 per credit hour. Tuition and fees vary according to degree level, program and student level. *Financial support:* In 2017–18, 1 research assistantship (averaging $5,000 per year) was awarded; Federal Work-Study, scholarships/grants, tuition waivers (partial), and unspecified assistantships also available. Financial award applicants required to submit FAFSA. *Faculty research:* Neural morphallaxis in lumbriculus variegatus, igneous and metamorphic petrology, applied cloud and precipitation physics, DNA-protein interactions, evolution of adenoviruses and picornaviruses. *Unit head:* Dr. Carlos A. Garcia, Dean, 210-829-2717, Fax: 210-829-3153, E-mail: cagarci9@uiwtx.edu. *Application contact:* Johnny Garcia, Graduate Admissions Counselor, 210-805-3554, Fax: 210-829-3921, E-mail: admis@uiwtx.edu.
Website: http://www.uiw.edu/smse/index.htm

The University of Toledo, College of Graduate Studies, College of Medicine and Life Sciences, Department of Public Health and Preventative Medicine, Toledo, OH 43606-3390. Offers biostatistics and epidemiology (Certificate); contemporary gerontological practice (Certificate); environmental and occupational health and safety (MPH); epidemiology (Certificate); global public health (Certificate); health promotion and education (MPH); industrial hygiene (MSOH); medical and health science teaching and learning (Certificate); occupational health (Certificate); public health administration (MPH); public health and emergency response (Certificate); public health epidemiology (MPH); public health nutrition (MPH); MD/MPH. *Program availability:* Part-time, evening/weekend. *Degree requirements:* For master's, thesis or alternative. *Entrance requirements:* For master's, GRE, minimum undergraduate GPA of 3.0, three letters of recommendation, statement of purpose, transcripts from all prior institutions attended, resume; for Certificate, minimum undergraduate GPA of 3.0, three letters of recommendation, statement of purpose, transcripts from all prior institutions attended, resume. Additional exam requirements/recommendations for international students: Required—TOEFL (minimum score 550 paper-based; 80 iBT), IELTS (minimum score 6.5). Electronic applications accepted.

University of Toronto, Faculty of Medicine, Department of Nutritional Sciences, Toronto, ON M5S 1A1, Canada. Offers M Sc, PhD. *Program availability:* Part-time. *Degree requirements:* For master's, thesis, oral thesis defense; for doctorate, comprehensive exam, thesis/dissertation, departmental examination, oral examination. *Entrance requirements:* For master's, minimum B average, background in nutrition or an area of biological or health sciences, 2 letters of reference; for doctorate, minimum B+ average in final 2 years, background in nutrition or an area of biological or health sciences, 2 letters of reference. Additional exam requirements/recommendations for international students: Required—TOEFL (minimum score 580 paper-based), TWE (minimum score 5), IELTS (minimum score 7), Michigan English Language Assessment Battery (minimum score 85), or COPE (minimum score 4). Electronic applications accepted.

University of Toronto, School of Graduate Studies, Department of Public Health Sciences, Toronto, ON M5S 1A1, Canada. Offers biostatistics (M Sc, PhD); community health (M Sc); community nutrition (MPH), including nutrition and dietetics; epidemiology (MPH, PhD); family and community medicine (MPH); occupational and environmental health (MPH); social and behavioral health science (PhD); social and behavioral health sciences (MPH), including health promotion. *Accreditation:* CAHME (one or more programs are accredited). *Program availability:* Part-time. *Degree requirements:* For master's, thesis (for some programs), practicum; for doctorate, comprehensive exam, thesis/dissertation, oral thesis defense. *Entrance requirements:* For master's, 2 letters of reference, relevant professional/research experience, minimum B average in final year; for doctorate, 2 letters of reference, relevant professional/research experience, minimum B+ average. Additional exam requirements/recommendations for international students: Required—TOEFL (minimum score 580 paper-based; 93 iBT), TWE (minimum score 5). Electronic applications accepted. *Expenses:* Contact institution.

University of Utah, Graduate School, College of Health, Division of Nutrition and Integrative Physiology, Salt Lake City, UT 84112. Offers nutrition and integrative physiology (MS, PhD), including integrative physiology, nutrition, nutrition and dietetics (MS). *Program availability:* 100% online. *Faculty:* 6 full-time (3 women), 11 part-time/adjunct (10 women). *Students:* 53 full-time (32 women), 5 part-time (all women); includes 6 minority (1 Asian, non-Hispanic/Latino; 4 Hispanic/Latino; 1 Two or more races, non-Hispanic/Latino), 5 international. Average age 28. 47 applicants, 36% accepted, 15 enrolled. In 2017, 20 master's awarded. Terminal master's awarded for partial completion of doctoral program. *Entrance requirements:* For master's, GRE General Test, minimum undergraduate GPA of 3.0; for doctorate, GRE General Test. Additional exam requirements/recommendations for international students: Required—TOEFL (minimum score 500 paper-based). *Application deadline:* For winter admission, 2/15 priority date for domestic and international students. Application fee: $55 ($65 for international students). Electronic applications accepted. *Expenses:* Contact institution. *Financial support:* In 2017–18, 41 students received support, including 15 research assistantships with full tuition reimbursements available (averaging $25,000 per year), 24 teaching assistantships with partial tuition reimbursements available (averaging $7,500 per year); career-related internships or fieldwork, scholarships/grants, health care benefits, and unspecified assistantships also available. Financial award application deadline: 2/15; financial award applicants required to submit FAFSA. *Faculty research:* Diabetes and metabolism, sport nutrition education, diabetes education, cardiovascular nutrition, pediatric nutrition. *Total annual research expenditures:* $120,000. *Unit head:* Dr. Scott Summers, Chair, 801-587-3024, Fax: 801-585-3874, E-mail: scott.a.summers@health.utah.edu. *Application contact:* Jean Zancanella, Academic Adviser, 801-581-5280, Fax: 801-585-3874, E-mail: jean.zancanella@health.utah.edu.
Website: http://www.health.utah.edu/fdnu/

University of Vermont, Graduate College, College of Agriculture and Life Sciences, Program in Dietetics, Burlington, VT 05405-0086. Offers dietetics (MS), including community health and nutrition. *Students:* 12 full-time (10 women). Average age 26. 18 applicants, 50% accepted, 6 enrolled. In 2017, 5 master's awarded. *Entrance requirements:* For master's, GRE General Test. Additional exam requirements/recommendations for international students: Required—TOEFL (minimum score 550 paper-based, 90 iBT) or IELTS (6.5). *Application deadline:* For fall admission, 2/15 for domestic students, 12/15 for international students. Application fee: $65. Electronic applications accepted. *Expenses:* Tuition, state resident: full-time $11,628; part-time $646 per credit. Tuition, nonresident: full-time $29,340; part-time $1630 per credit. *Required fees:* $1994; $10 per credit. Tuition and fees vary according to course load and program. *Unit head:* Amy Nickerson, Director, 802-656-0670, E-mail: uvmmsd@uvm.edu.
Website: https://www.uvm.edu/cals/nfs/ms_dietetics

University of Vermont, Graduate College, College of Agriculture and Life Sciences, Program in Nutrition and Food Sciences, Burlington, VT 05405-0086. Offers nutrition and food sciences (MS). *Accreditation:* AND. *Students:* 5 full-time (3 women). Average age 23. 13 applicants, 23% accepted, 2 enrolled. In 2017, 3 master's awarded. *Degree requirements:* For master's, thesis. *Entrance requirements:* For master's, GRE General Test. Additional exam requirements/recommendations for international students: Required—TOEFL (minimum score 550 paper-based, 90 iBT) or IELTS (6.5). *Application deadline:* For fall admission, 2/15 priority date for domestic and international students. Applications are processed on a rolling basis. Application fee: $65. Electronic applications accepted. *Expenses:* Tuition, state resident: full-time $11,628; part-time $646 per credit. Tuition, nonresident: full-time $29,340; part-time $1630 per credit. *Required fees:* $1994; $10 per credit. Tuition and fees vary according to course load and program. *Financial support:* In 2017–18, 2 research assistantships with full tuition reimbursements (averaging $27,000 per year), 3 teaching assistantships with full tuition reimbursements (averaging $23,500 per year) were awarded; health care benefits also available. Financial award application deadline: 2/15. *Unit head:* Dr. Stephen Pintauro, Coordinator, 802-656-0541, E-mail: stephen.pintauro@uvm.edu.
Website: https://www.uvm.edu/cals/nfs/ms_nutrition_and_food_sciences

University of Washington, Graduate School, School of Public Health, Nutritional Sciences Program, Seattle, WA 98195. Offers MPH, MS, PhD. *Program availability:* Part-time. *Students:* 16 full-time (15 women), 1 (woman) part-time; includes 6 minority (5 Asian, non-Hispanic/Latino; 1 Hispanic/Latino), 1 international. Average age 27. 136 applicants, 29% accepted, 17 enrolled. In 2017, 19 master's, 1 doctorate awarded. Terminal master's awarded for partial completion of doctoral program. Electronic applications accepted. *Financial support:* Fellowships, research assistantships, teaching assistantships, and scholarships/grants available. *Faculty research:* Dietary behavior, dietary supplements, obesity, clinical nutrition, addictive behaviors. *Unit head:* Dr. Adam Drewnowski, Director, 206-543-8016. *Application contact:* 206-543-1730, E-mail: nutr@uw.edu.
Website: http://depts.washington.edu/nutr/

University of Wisconsin–Madison, Graduate School, College of Agricultural and Life Sciences, Department of Nutritional Sciences, Madison, WI 53706. Offers MS, PhD. Terminal master's awarded for partial completion of doctoral program. *Degree requirements:* For master's, thesis or research report; for doctorate, comprehensive exam, thesis/dissertation. *Entrance requirements:* For master's and doctorate, GRE General Test. Additional exam requirements/recommendations for international students: Required—TOEFL (minimum score 550 paper-based; 80 iBT). Electronic applications accepted. *Faculty research:* Human and animal nutrition, nutrition epidemiology, nutrition education, biochemical and molecular nutrition.

University of Wisconsin–Milwaukee, Graduate School, College of Health Sciences, Department of Kinesiology, Milwaukee, WI 53201-0413. Offers athletic training (MS); kinesiology (MS, PhD), including exercise and nutrition in health and disease (MS), integrative human performance (MS), neuromechanics (MS); physical therapy (DPT). *Program availability:* Part-time. *Students:* 100 full-time (60 women), 16 part-time (9 women); includes 11 minority (1 Black or African American, non-Hispanic/Latino; 1 American Indian or Alaska Native, non-Hispanic/Latino; 9 Two or more races, non-Hispanic/Latino), 3 international. Average age 27. 36 applicants, 42% accepted, 5 enrolled. In 2017, 2 master's awarded. *Degree requirements:* For master's, comprehensive exam, thesis optional. *Entrance requirements:* For master's, GRE General Test. Additional exam requirements/recommendations for international students: Required—TOEFL (minimum score 550 paper-based; 79 iBT), IELTS (minimum score 6.5). *Application deadline:* For fall admission, 1/1 priority date for domestic students; for spring admission, 9/1 for domestic students. Applications are processed on a rolling basis. Application fee: $56 ($96 for international students). *Financial support:* Fellowships, research assistantships, teaching assistantships, career-related internships or fieldwork, unspecified assistantships, and project assistantships available. Support available to part-time students. Financial award application deadline: 4/15. *Unit head:* Dr. Kyle T. Ebersole, Department Chair, 414-229-6717, Fax: 414-229-3366, E-mail: ebersole@uwm.edu. *Application contact:* Stephen C. Cobb, Graduate Program Coordinator, 414-229-3369, Fax: 414-229-3366, E-mail: cobbsc@uwm.edu.
Website: http://uwm.edu/healthsciences/academics/kinesiology/

University of Wisconsin–Stevens Point, College of Professional Studies, School of Health Promotion and Human Development, Program in Nutritional Sciences, Stevens Point, WI 54481-3897. Offers MS. *Program availability:* Part-time. *Degree requirements:* For master's, thesis or alternative. *Entrance requirements:* For master's, minimum GPA of 2.75. *Application deadline:* For fall admission, 5/1 priority date for domestic students. Applications are processed on a rolling basis. *Expenses:* Tuition, state resident: part-time $562.55 per credit. Tuition, nonresident: part-time $1085.04 per credit. Part-time tuition and fees vary according to course load, program and reciprocity agreements. *Financial support:* Research assistantships, teaching assistantships, career-related internships or fieldwork, and Federal Work-Study available. Support available to part-time students. Financial award application deadline: 5/1; financial award applicants required to submit FAFSA. *Unit head:* Dr. Marty Loy, Head, 715-346-2830, Fax: 715-346-2720. *Application contact:* Dr. Jasia Steinmetz, Information Contact, 715-346-2830, Fax: 715-346-2720, E-mail: jsteinme@uwsp.edu.
Website: http://www.uwsp.edu/hphd/academics/

University of Wisconsin–Stout, Graduate School, College of Education, Health and Human Sciences, Program in Food and Nutritional Sciences, Menomonie, WI 54751. Offers MS. *Program availability:* Part-time. *Degree requirements:* For master's, thesis. *Entrance requirements:* For master's, minimum GPA of 3.0. Additional exam requirements/recommendations for international students: Required—TOEFL (minimum score 500 paper-based; 61 iBT). Electronic applications accepted. *Faculty research:* Disease states and nutrition, childhood obesity, nutraceuticals, food safety, nanotechnology.

University of Wyoming, College of Agriculture and Natural Resources, Department of Animal Sciences, Program in Food Science and Human Nutrition, Laramie, WY 82071. Offers MS. *Degree requirements:* For master's, thesis. *Entrance requirements:* For master's, GRE General Test, minimum GPA of 3.0. Additional exam requirements/recommendations for international students: Required—TOEFL (minimum score 525 paper-based). Electronic applications accepted. *Faculty research:* Protein and lipid metabolism, food microbiology, food safety, meat science.

Utah State University, School of Graduate Studies, College of Agriculture and Applied Sciences, Department of Nutrition, Dietetics, and Food Sciences, Logan, UT 84322. Offers dietetic administration (MDA); nutrition and food sciences (MS, PhD). *Program availability:* Online learning. *Degree requirements:* For master's, thesis; for doctorate, comprehensive exam, thesis/dissertation, teaching experience. *Entrance requirements:* For master's, GRE General Test, minimum GPA of 3.0, course work in chemistry, biochemistry, physics, math, bacteriology, physiology; for doctorate, GRE General Test, minimum GPA of 3.2, course work in chemistry, MS or manuscript in referred journal. Additional exam requirements/recommendations for international students: Required—TOEFL (minimum score 550 paper-based). Electronic applications accepted. *Faculty research:* Mineral balance, meat microbiology and nitrate interactions, milk ultrafiltration, lactic culture, milk coagulation.

Virginia Polytechnic Institute and State University, Graduate School, College of Agriculture and Life Sciences, Blacksburg, VA 24061. Offers agricultural and applied economics (MS, PhD); agricultural and life sciences (MS); agriculture, leadership, and community education (MS, PhD); animal and poultry science (MS, PhD); biochemistry (MS, PhD); crop and soil environmental sciences (MS, PhD); dairy science (MS, PhD); entomology (MS, PhD); food science and technology (MS, PhD); horticulture (PhD); human nutrition, foods and exercise (MS, PhD); plant pathology, physiology, and weed science (MS, PhD). *Faculty:* 241 full-time (73 women), 1 (woman) part-time/adjunct. *Students:* 379 full-time (221 women), 126 part-time (75 women); includes 64 minority (21 Black or African American, non-Hispanic/Latino; 15 Asian, non-Hispanic/Latino; 14 Hispanic/Latino; 14 Two or more races, non-Hispanic/Latino), 119 international. Average age 29. 357 applicants, 46% accepted, 118 enrolled. In 2017, 105 master's, 54 doctorates awarded. *Degree requirements:* For master's, comprehensive exam (for some programs), thesis (for some programs); for doctorate, comprehensive exam (for some programs), thesis/dissertation (for some programs). *Entrance requirements:* For master's and doctorate, GRE/GMAT. Additional exam requirements/recommendations for international students: Required—TOEFL (minimum score 80 iBT). *Application deadline:* For fall admission, 8/1 for domestic students, 4/1 for international students; for spring admission, 1/1 for domestic students, 9/1 for international students. Applications are processed on a rolling basis. Application fee: $75. Electronic applications accepted. *Expenses:* Tuition, state resident: full-time $15,072; part-time $718.50 per credit hour. Tuition, nonresident: full-time $28,810; part-time $1448.25 per credit hour. *Required fees:* $2741; $502 per semester. Tuition and fees vary according to course load, campus/location and program. *Financial support:* In 2017–18, 232 research assistantships with full tuition reimbursements (averaging $21,852 per year), 94 teaching assistantships with full tuition reimbursements (averaging $21,643 per year) were awarded. Financial award application deadline: 3/1; financial award applicants required to submit FAFSA. *Total annual research expenditures:* $44.3 million. *Unit head:* Dr. Alan L. Grant, Dean, 540-231-4152, Fax: 540-231-4163, E-mail: algrant@vt.edu. *Application contact:* Crystal Tawney, Administrative Assistant, 540-231-4152, Fax: 540-231-4163, E-mail: cdtawney@vt.edu.
Website: http://www.cals.vt.edu/

Washington State University, College of Pharmacy, Nutrition and Exercise Physiology Program, Pullman, WA 99164. Offers MS. Programs offered at the Spokane campus. *Degree requirements:* For master's, internship. *Entrance requirements:* For master's, BS in nutrition and exercise physiology, exercise science, human nutrition, or related degree; interview.

Wayne State University, College of Liberal Arts and Sciences, Department of Nutrition and Food Science, Detroit, MI 48202. Offers dietetics (Postbaccalaureate Certificate); food science (PhD); nutrition (PhD); nutrition and food science (MA, MS); MA/MPH. Postbaccalaureate certificate program admits only in fall with April 1 application deadline. *Faculty:* 8. *Students:* 28 full-time (23 women), 1 (woman) part-time; includes 1 minority (Asian, non-Hispanic/Latino), 15 international. Average age 32. 56 applicants, 23% accepted, 2 enrolled. In 2017, 18 master's, 3 doctorates awarded. *Degree requirements:* For master's, thesis (for some programs), essay (for MA); for doctorate, thesis/dissertation. *Entrance requirements:* For master's, GRE General Test (recommended), two letters of recommendation; minimum GPA of 3.0; undergraduate degree in science; for doctorate, GRE (recommended), MS in nutrition and/or food

science or in a cognate science with minimum GPA of 3.5; three letters of recommendation; personal statement; interview (live or Web-based). Additional exam requirements/recommendations for international students: Required—TOEFL (minimum score 550 paper-based; 79 iBT), TWE (minimum score 5.5), Michigan English Language Assessment Battery (minimum score 85); Recommended—IELTS (minimum score 6.5). *Application deadline:* For fall admission, 3/1 priority date for domestic and international students. Applications are processed on a rolling basis. Application fee: $50. Electronic applications accepted. *Expenses:* Tuition, state resident: full-time $10,224; part-time $638.98 per credit hour. Tuition, nonresident: full-time $22,145; part-time $1384.04 per credit hour. Tuition and fees vary according to course load and program. *Financial support:* In 2017–18, 17 students received support, including 1 fellowship with tuition reimbursement available (averaging $24,000 per year), 2 research assistantships with tuition reimbursements available (averaging $21,500 per year), 9 teaching assistantships with tuition reimbursements available (averaging $19,560 per year); scholarships/grants, health care benefits, and unspecified assistantships also available. Financial award applicants required to submit FAFSA. *Faculty research:* Metabolomics and the study of nutrition and disease; understanding the effect of nutrition intervention (i.e., caloric restriction, folate deficiency) on the molecular mechanisms of aging and cancer; obesity and diabetes; study of how different dietary constituents (e.g. fatty acids) interact with each other to modulate key parameters related to plasma lipoprotein metabolism. *Unit head:* Dr. Ahmad R. Heydari, Professor and Chair, 313-577-2500, E-mail: ahmad.heydari@wayne.edu. *Application contact:* Dr. Diane Cress, Associate Professor and Graduate Officer, E-mail: gradprogramnfs@wayne.edu.
Website: http://clas.wayne.edu/nfs/

West Chester University of Pennsylvania, College of Health Sciences, Department of Nutrition, West Chester, PA 19383. Offers community nutrition (MS). *Program availability:* Part-time, online only, 100% online. *Students:* 34 full-time (30 women), 33 part-time (32 women); includes 6 minority (4 Black or African American, non-Hispanic/Latino; 1 Hispanic/Latino; 1 Two or more races, non-Hispanic/Latino). Average age 28. 46 applicants, 91% accepted, 29 enrolled. In 2017, 17 master's awarded. *Degree requirements:* For master's, completion of nutrition capstone. *Entrance requirements:* For master's, college transcripts, two letters of recommendation, professional goals statement, minimum undergraduate GPA of 3.0, baccalaureate degree from regionally-accredited college or university, nutrition degree or other undergraduate degree that includes certain prerequisite courses with minimum B grade. Additional exam requirements/recommendations for international students: Required—TOEFL or IELTS. *Application deadline:* For fall admission, 5/15 for international students; for spring admission, 10/15 for international students. Applications are processed on a rolling basis. Application fee: $50. Electronic applications accepted. *Expenses:* Tuition, state resident: full-time $9000; part-time $500 per credit. Tuition, nonresident: full-time $13,500; part-time $750 per credit. *Required fees:* $2959; $149.79 per credit. *Financial support:* Scholarships/grants and unspecified assistantships available. Financial award application deadline: 2/15; financial award applicants required to submit FAFSA. *Faculty research:* Statistics, obesity, diabetes management and prevention, community and public health nutrition, life cycle nutrition, older adults, sports nutrition. *Unit head:* Dr. Christine Karpinski, Chair, 610-436-2125, E-mail: ckarpinski@wcupa.edu. *Application contact:* Dr. Mary Beth Gilboy, Graduate Coordinator, 610-738-0559, E-mail: mgilboy@wcupa.edu.
Website: http://www.wcupa.edu/healthsciences/nutritionanddietetics/

West Virginia University, Davis College of Agriculture, Forestry and Consumer Sciences, Morgantown, WV 26506. Offers agricultural and extension education (MS, PhD); agriculture and resource management (MS); agriculture, natural resources and design (M Agr); agronomy (MS); animal and food science (PhD); animal physiology (MS); applied and environmental microbiology (MS); design and merchandising (MS); entomology (MS); forest resource science (PhD); forestry (MSF); genetics and developmental biology (MS, PhD); horticulture (MS); human and community development (PhD); landscape architecture (MLA); natural resource economics (PhD); nutritional and food science (MS); plant and soil science (PhD); plant pathology (MS); recreation, parks and tourism resources (MS); reproductive physiology (MS, PhD); wildlife and fisheries resources (PhD). *Program availability:* Part-time. *Students:* 200 full-time (97 women), 53 part-time (32 women); includes 27 minority (6 Black or African American, non-Hispanic/Latino; 1 American Indian or Alaska Native, non-Hispanic/Latino; 4 Asian, non-Hispanic/Latino; 11 Hispanic/Latino; 5 Two or more races, non-Hispanic/Latino), 67 international. *Degree requirements:* For master's, thesis; for doctorate, thesis/dissertation. *Entrance requirements:* Additional exam requirements/recommendations for international students: Required—TOEFL (minimum score 550 paper-based). *Application deadline:* For fall admission, 6/1 priority date for domestic students, 6/1 for international students; for spring admission, 1/5 for domestic and international students. Applications are processed on a rolling basis. Application fee: $60. Electronic applications accepted. *Expenses:* Tuition, state resident: full-time $9450. Tuition, nonresident: full-time $24,390. *Financial support:* Fellowships, research assistantships, teaching assistantships, career-related internships or fieldwork, Federal Work-Study, institutionally sponsored loans, tuition waivers (full and partial), and unspecified assistantships available. Financial award application deadline: 2/1; financial award applicants required to submit FAFSA. *Faculty research:* Reproductive physiology, soil and water quality, human nutrition, aquaculture, wildlife management. *Unit head:* Dr. Dan J. Robison, Dean, 304-293-2395, Fax: 304-293-3740, E-mail: dan.robison@mail.wvu.edu. *Application contact:* Dr. Dennis K. Smith, Associate Dean, 304-293-2275, Fax: 304-293-3740, E-mail: denny.smith@mail.wvu.edu.
Website: https://www.davis.wvu.edu

Winthrop University, College of Arts and Sciences, Department of Human Nutrition, Rock Hill, SC 29733. Offers dietetics (Certificate); human nutrition (MS). *Program availability:* Part-time. *Students:* 32 full-time (27 women), 15 part-time (13 women); includes 12 minority (7 Black or African American, non-Hispanic/Latino; 1 Asian, non-Hispanic/Latino; 2 Hispanic/Latino; 2 Two or more races, non-Hispanic/Latino), 2 international. Average age 31. In 2017, 20 master's, 18 other advanced degrees awarded. *Degree requirements:* For master's, thesis. *Entrance requirements:* For master's, GRE General Test, PRAXIS, or MAT, interview, minimum GPA of 3.0. Additional exam requirements/recommendations for international students: Required—TOEFL (minimum score 550 paper-based; 79 iBT), IELTS (minimum score 6). *Application deadline:* For fall admission, 7/15 priority date for domestic students; for spring admission, 12/1 for domestic students. Applications are processed on a rolling basis. Application fee: $50. Electronic applications accepted. *Financial support:* Research assistantships with full tuition reimbursements, career-related internships or fieldwork, Federal Work-Study, scholarships/grants, and unspecified assistantships available. Support available to part-time students. Financial award application deadline: 2/1. *Unit head:* Dr. Wanda Koszewski, Chair, 803-323-4520, E-mail: humannutrition@winthrop.edu. *Application contact:* 800-411-7041, Fax: 803-323-2292, E-mail: gradschool@winthrop.edu.

CALIFORNIA POLYTECHNIC STATE UNIVERSITY

Master of Science in Nutrition Program

★ For more information, visit http://petersons.to/cpsunutrition

CAL POLY
Graduate Education

Program of Study

The Master of Science (M.S.) in Nutrition program at California Polytechnic State University prepares graduates for advancement in nutrition and other healthcare fields. It also prepares them for further education through allied health professions, dietetic internships, doctoral programs, and professional schools.

The program encompasses a wide-range of nutrition subjects from molecular nutrition to public health. Its interdisciplinary nature allows students to work closely with faculty from several departments and choose research topics from a wide-variety of areas including animal nutrition, business, human nutrition, kinesiology, public health, and social science.

The program is part of the Food Science and Nutrition Department, which provides comprehensive education in nutrition and food science. The department's research-driven and practice-oriented approach ensures that students become highly skilled and well-prepared nutrition and food science professionals.

The M.S. in Nutrition curriculum consists of 24 units of required courses including a thesis and 21 units of elective courses. Students can choose one of three emphasis areas: health and wellness, molecular nutrition, or public health nutrition. Upon graduation, students will have the ability to complete the following academic and professional activities:

- Apply basic principles of nutrition science to required coursework and research
- Explain, evaluate, and interpret fundamental scientific theories pertaining to thesis research
- Apply the scientific method to nutrition research by designing, conducting, and defending a thesis research project
- Use critical thinking skills to analyze published research literature and design and interpret a thesis research project
- Demonstrate strong oral and written communication skills
- Use creative and independent thinking skills to formulate, design, conduct, and interpret nutrition research
- Work productively in research teams and in other group settings
- Exhibit leadership skills, commitment to community values, and ethical conduct

According to the U.S. Department of Labor, employment of dietitians and nutritionists is projected to grow 16 percent from 2014 to 2024. This is much faster than the average for all occupations. A combination of factors is fueling this demand, such an aging baby-boomer population that will require dietetic services to help them stay healthy, an increasing number of dietitians and nutritionists needed to treat obesity and obesity-related conditions like diabetes and kidney disease, and the need for more nutritionists and dietitians employed by nursing homes as the population ages. Students in the M.S. in Nutrition program at California Polytechnic State University acquire the theoretical foundation and clinical experience to successfully address these needs. They graduate fully prepared to excel in a number of areas, such as clinical nutrition, community nutrition, the food industry, food service and management, postsecondary education, and public health.

Research Opportunities

California Polytechnic State University has a thesis-based program that gives students strong research experience under the direct leadership of their faculty supervisor. The interdisciplinary Graduate Group in Nutrition (GGN) allows students to work with faculty from several departments and to choose a research topic from a broad range of themes including human nutrition, animal nutrition, kinesiology, public health, business, or social sciences.

Applicants are strongly encouraged to contact individual faculty members to discuss research interests and availability for supervision of M.S. students. This is an important part of the admission process as it is the practice of the NGG to admit a student only when a faculty member (from any of the above departments) has agreed to serve as the student's major professor. Students will work closely with their faculty advisor to determine which elective courses beyond the core curriculum is most appropriate. Areas of emphasis may include molecular nutrition, public health nutrition, health and wellness, or others.

Financial Aid

Graduate students may qualify for federal loans, emergency loans, state grants, scholarships, and veteran's benefits. Students may also pursue loans from private lenders, employer tuition remission programs, and scholarships from private sources.

Cost of Study

For the 2017–18 academic year, tuition for the M.S. in Nutrition program was $3,622 per term for California residents. Nonresidents added $264 per enrolled unit. The most current information on tuition and fees is available at https://afd.calpoly.edu/fees/.

Living and Housing Costs

Graduate students can live in campus apartments complete with a full kitchen, private bathrooms, and the option of private or shared bedrooms. Costs for a University apartment per academic year range from $5,770 for an apartment with a double suite bedroom to $9,014 for an apartment with a private bedroom. There are also many opportunities for off-campus housing.

Location

California Polytechnic State University is located in San Luis Obispo, California. According to Colleges in California, its campus is one of the most beautiful in the state. The University is situated in an area known for its mild climate, natural beauty, and outdoor recreational options. Biking, hiking, and sailing are just some of the activities students can enjoy most of the year.

The University

California Polytechnic State University fosters scholarship, service, and teaching in a Learn-by-Doing environment. The application of theory to practice, active-learning methods, and field and laboratory work form the core of this academic approach. The University offers approximately 21,300 students nearly 190 bachelor's, master's, minor, and credential programs. This large offering enables students to create programs of study that reflect their academic and career interests.

California Polytechnic State University's commitment to providing high quality education earns it top honors. In its 2017 guidebook, U.S. News & World Report named it the best public, master's-level university in the west. This is the 24th consecutive year that the university has received this honor. The publisher also ranked it ninth among the best universities in the western region.

Faculty

Graduate faculty members in the Food Science and Nutrition Department are committed to helping their students succeed. They integrate theory, research, and practice to provide extensive knowledge and training in nutrition and food science.

Peggy Callaghan Papathakis, Ph.D., RD and Doris Derelian, Ph.D., J.D., RDN are two of the department's talented faculty members. Professor Papathakis is an expert on child/global and clinical/maternal nutrition. She conducts nutrition research concerning developing countries and provides students with global nutrition experiences. Professor Derelian has expertise in education, communications, counseling, world/cultural foods, and food law. Her research focuses on the development of food products for nutritional purposes and the effect of nutrition on academic performance as well as consumer awareness of health behaviors.

Applying

Most applicants with undergraduate degrees in nutrition, biology, or public health are eligible to apply for the M.S. program. Applicants with other undergraduate degrees are also eligible to apply but may require prerequisite course work. Students with undergraduate degrees other than nutrition must discuss their situation with potential thesis supervisors and the Nutrition Graduate Group to coordinate curriculum requirements and to develop an appropriate study plan. Applicants should make sure courses from other institutions are appropriate equivalents (use www.assist.org if using transfer courses from another CA public institution).

All applicants must submit a statement of purpose; 3 letters of reference; and GRE scores. For applicants with degrees from outside the U.S., all of the above applies. In addition, the applicant's international credentials must be evaluated by AACRAO, ACEI, WES or IERF; proficiency in English must be demonstrated by taking TOEFL (Test of English as a Foreign Language) within the last 2 years with an Internet score of 80 or greater or ELTS (International English Language Testing System) must be taken within 2 years with a score of 6.5 or greater. TOFEL or ELTS is required to issue an I20 visa.

Candidates are strongly encouraged to submit by mid-January. As a relatively small, non-cohort program, it is important that candidates connect with the graduate coordinator, discuss potential areas of research, include these considerations in their statement of interest, and submit applications early. Applications are accepted through the online system Cal State Apply. The filing periods are listed at https://admissions.calpoly.edu/applicants/graduate/deadlines.html and all applicants are responsible for using the University's established applicant checklist for meeting admission deadlines. More information is available at grad.calpoly.edu.

Correspondence and Information

California Polytechnic State University
Department of Food Science and Nutrition
1 Grand Avenue
San Luis Obispo, California 93407
Phone: 805-756-2660
E-mail: fsn@calpoly.edu
Website: www.fsn.calpoly.edu

Section 15
Parasitology

This section contains a directory of institutions offering graduate work in parasitology. Additional information about programs listed in the directory may be obtained by writing directly to the dean of a graduate school or chair of a department at the address given in the directory.

For programs offering related work, see also in this book *Allied Health, Biological and Biomedical Sciences, Microbiological Sciences,* and *Public Health.*

CONTENTS

Program Directory

Parasitology

Illinois State University, Graduate School, College of Arts and Sciences, School of Biological Sciences, Normal, IL 61790. Offers animal behavior (MS); bacteriology (MS); biochemistry (MS); biological sciences (MS); biology (PhD); biophysics (MS); biotechnology (MS); botany (MS, PhD); cell biology (MS); conservation biology (MS); developmental biology (MS); ecology (MS, PhD); entomology (MS); evolutionary biology (MS); genetics (MS, PhD); immunology (MS); microbiology (MS, PhD); molecular biology (MS); molecular genetics (MS); neurobiology (MS); neuroscience (MS); parasitology (MS); physiology (MS, PhD); plant biology (MS); plant molecular biology (MS); plant sciences (MS); structural biology (MS); zoology (MS, PhD). *Program availability:* Part-time. *Degree requirements:* For master's, thesis or alternative; for doctorate, variable foreign language requirement, thesis/dissertation, 2 terms of residency. *Entrance requirements:* For master's, GRE General Test, minimum GPA of 2.6 in last 60 hours of course work; for doctorate, GRE General Test. *Faculty research:* Redoc balance and drug development in schistosoma mansoni, control of the growth of listeria monocytogenes at low temperature, regulation of cell expansion and microtubule function by SPRI, CRUI: physiology and fitness consequences of different life history phenotypes.

Louisiana State University Health Sciences Center, School of Graduate Studies in New Orleans, Department of Microbiology, Immunology, and Parasitology, New Orleans, LA 70112-1393. Offers microbiology and immunology (PhD); MD/PhD. *Faculty:* 22 full-time (5 women). *Students:* 10 full-time (6 women). Average age 26. 15 applicants, 27% accepted, 4 enrolled. In 2017, 4 doctorates awarded. *Degree requirements:* For doctorate, comprehensive exam, thesis/dissertation, preliminary exam, qualifying exam. *Entrance requirements:* For doctorate, GRE General Test. Additional exam requirements/recommendations for international students: Recommended—TOEFL, IELTS. *Application deadline:* For fall admission, 4/1 for domestic and international students. Applications are processed on a rolling basis. Application fee: $30. *Expenses:* Tuition, state resident: full-time $11,835; part-time $518 per hour. Tuition, nonresident: full-time $24,108; part-time $1079 per hour. *Required fees:* $1254; $55 per hour. *Financial support:* Unspecified assistantships available. Financial award application deadline: 4/15. *Faculty research:* Microbial physiology, animal virology, vaccine development, AIDS drug studies, pathogenic mechanisms, molecular immunology. *Unit head:* Dr. Alistair Ramsay, Professor and Head, 504-568-4062, Fax: 504-568-2918, E-mail: aramsa@lsuhsc.edu. *Application contact:* Dr. Doug Johnston, Assistant Professor, E-mail: mipapp@lsuhsc.edu.
Website: http://www.medschool.lsuhsc.edu/microbiology/

McGill University, Faculty of Graduate and Postdoctoral Studies, Faculty of Agricultural and Environmental Sciences, Institute of Parasitology, Montréal, QC H3A 2T5, Canada. Offers biotechnology (M Sc A, Certificate); parasitology (M Sc, PhD).

Oregon State University, College of Science, Program in Microbiology, Corvallis, OR 97331. Offers environmental microbiology (MA, MS, PhD); food microbiology (MA, MS, PhD); genomics (MA, MS, PhD); immunology (MA, MS, PhD); microbial ecology (MA, MS, PhD); microbial evolution (MA, MS, PhD); parasitology (MA, MS, PhD); pathogenic microbiology (MA, MS, PhD); virology (MA). Terminal master's awarded for partial completion of doctoral program. *Entrance requirements:* For master's and doctorate, GRE. Additional exam requirements/recommendations for international students: Required—TOEFL (minimum score 600 paper-based; 100 iBT). *Application deadline:* For fall admission, 1/1 for domestic and international students. Application fee: $75 ($85 for international students). *Financial support:* Application deadline: 1/15. *Faculty research:* Genetics, physiology, biotechnology, pathogenic microbiology, plant virology. *Unit head:* Dr. Jerri Bartholomew, Professor and Department Head, 541-737-1834, E-mail: bartholj@science.oregonstate.edu. *Application contact:* Kim Halsey, Graduate Admissions Committee Chair, 541-737-1831, E-mail: kim.halsey@oregonstate.edu.
Website: http://microbiology.science.oregonstate.edu/

Tulane University, School of Public Health and Tropical Medicine, Department of Tropical Medicine, New Orleans, LA 70118-5669. Offers clinical tropical medicine and travelers health (Diploma); parasitology (PhD); public health (MSPH); public health and tropical medicine (MPHTM); MD/MPHTM. PhD offered through the Graduate School. *Degree requirements:* For master's, thesis; for doctorate, comprehensive exam, thesis/dissertation. *Entrance requirements:* For master's, GRE General Test, minimum B average in undergraduate course work; for doctorate, GRE General Test. Additional exam requirements/recommendations for international students: Required—TOEFL. *Expenses: Tuition:* Full-time $50,920; part-time $2829 per credit hour. *Required fees:* $2040; $44.50 per credit hour. $580 per term. Tuition and fees vary according to course load, degree level and program.

University of Notre Dame, Graduate School, College of Science, Department of Biological Sciences, Notre Dame, IN 46556. Offers aquatic ecology, evolution and environmental biology (MS, PhD); cellular and molecular biology (MS, PhD); genetics (MS, PhD); physiology (MS, PhD); vector biology and parasitology (MS, PhD). Terminal master's awarded for partial completion of doctoral program. *Degree requirements:* For master's, comprehensive exam, thesis; for doctorate, comprehensive exam, thesis/dissertation, candidacy exam. *Entrance requirements:* For master's and doctorate, GRE General Test. Additional exam requirements/recommendations for international students: Required—TOEFL (minimum score 600 paper-based; 80 iBT). Electronic applications accepted. *Faculty research:* Tropical disease, molecular genetics, neurobiology, evolutionary biology, aquatic biology.

University of Prince Edward Island, Atlantic Veterinary College, Graduate Program in Veterinary Medicine, Charlottetown, PE C1A 4P3, Canada. Offers anatomy (M Sc, PhD); bacteriology (M Sc, PhD); clinical pharmacology (M Sc, PhD); clinical sciences (M Sc, PhD); epidemiology (M Sc, PhD), including reproduction; fish health (M Sc, PhD); food animal nutrition (M Sc, PhD); immunology (M Sc, PhD); microanatomy (M Sc, PhD); parasitology (M Sc, PhD); pathology (M Sc, PhD); pharmacology (M Sc, PhD); physiology (M Sc, PhD); toxicology (M Sc, PhD); veterinary science (M Vet Sc); virology (M Sc, PhD). *Program availability:* Part-time. *Degree requirements:* For master's, thesis; for doctorate, thesis/dissertation. *Entrance requirements:* For master's, DVM, B Sc honors degree, or equivalent; for doctorate, M Sc. Additional exam requirements/recommendations for international students: Required—TOEFL (minimum score 550 paper-based; 80 iBT). *Expenses:* Contact institution. *Faculty research:* Animal health management, infectious diseases, fin fish and shellfish health, basic biomedical sciences, ecosystem health.

Section 16
Pathology and Pathobiology

This section contains a directory of institutions offering graduate work in pathology and pathobiology, followed by an in-depth entry submitted by an institution that chose to submit a detailed program description. Additional information about programs listed in the directory but not augmented by an in-depth entry may be obtained by writing directly to the dean of a graduate school or chair of a department at the address given in the directory.

For programs offering related work, see also in this book *Allied Health; Anatomy; Biochemistry; Biological and Biomedical Sciences; Cell, Molecular, and Structural Biology; Genetics, Developmental Biology, and Reproductive Biology; Microbiological Sciences; Pharmacology and Toxicology; Physiology, Public Health,* and *Veterinary Medicine and Sciences.*

CONTENTS

Program Directories

Molecular Pathogenesis

Dartmouth College, Graduate Program in Molecular and Cellular Biology, Department of Microbiology and Immunology, Program in Microbiology and Molecular Pathogenesis, Hanover, NH 03755. Offers PhD, MBA/PhD, MD/PhD. *Application deadline:* For fall admission, 12/8 for domestic students. Application fee: $75. Electronic applications accepted. *Financial support:* Fellowships and health care benefits available. *Unit head:* Dr. William R. Green, Chair, 603-650-8607, Fax: 603-650-6223. *Application contact:* Janet Cheney, Program Administrator, 608-650-1612, Fax: 608-650-6223.
Website: https://www.dartmouth.edu/~m2p2/

Emory University, Laney Graduate School, Division of Biological and Biomedical Sciences, Program in Immunology and Molecular Pathogenesis, Atlanta, GA 30322-1100. Offers PhD. *Degree requirements:* For doctorate, comprehensive exam, thesis/dissertation. *Entrance requirements:* For doctorate, GRE General Test, minimum GPA of 3.0 in science course work (recommended). Additional exam requirements/recommendations for international students: Required—TOEFL. Electronic applications accepted. *Faculty research:* Transplantation immunology, autoimmunity, microbial pathogenesis.

North Dakota State University, College of Graduate and Interdisciplinary Studies, College of Agriculture, Food Systems, and Natural Resources, Department of Microbiological Sciences, Fargo, ND 58102. Offers microbiology (MS); molecular pathogenesis (PhD). *Program availability:* Part-time. *Degree requirements:* For master's, thesis; for doctorate, thesis/dissertation, oral and written preliminary exams. *Entrance requirements:* For master's and doctorate, GRE. Additional exam requirements/recommendations for international students: Required—TOEFL (minimum score 525 paper-based; 71 iBT). *Application deadline:* For fall admission, 2/15 priority date for domestic students. Applications are processed on a rolling basis. Application fee: $35. *Expenses:* Tuition, state resident: full-time $4323; part-time $360.21 per credit. Tuition, nonresident: full-time $6484; part-time $540.31 per credit. *Required fees:* $668; $55.70 per credit. Part-time tuition and fees vary according to degree level, program and reciprocity agreements. *Financial support:* Application deadline: 4/15. *Faculty research:* Bacterial gene regulation, antibiotic resistance, molecular virology, mechanisms of bacterial pathogenesis, immunology of animals. *Unit head:* Peter Bergholz, Graduate Coordinator, 701-231-5946, E-mail: peter.bergholz@ndsu.edu. *Application contact:* Eugene Berry, Associate Professor, 701-231-7520, Fax: 701-231-7514, E-mail: eugene.berry@ndsu.edu.
Website: http://www.ndsu.edu/micro/

Washington University in St. Louis, The Graduate School, Division of Biology and Biomedical Sciences, Program in Molecular Microbiology and Microbial Pathogenesis, St. Louis, MO 63130-4899. Offers PhD. *Degree requirements:* For doctorate, thesis/dissertation. *Entrance requirements:* For doctorate, GRE General Test, GRE Subject Test. Additional exam requirements/recommendations for international students: Required—TOEFL. Electronic applications accepted. *Faculty research:* Host-pathogen interactions, cellular microbiology, molecular microbiology, microbial pathogenesis, pathogen discovery, emerging infectious diseases, microbial physiology and biochemistry, comparative genomics, gene expression and regulation, microbiome and host interactions, virology, bacteriology, mycology, parasitology.

Molecular Pathology

Rutgers University–Newark, Graduate School of Biomedical Sciences, Program in Molecular Pathology and Immunology, Newark, NJ 07107. Offers PhD. *Accreditation:* NAACLS. *Entrance requirements:* Additional exam requirements/recommendations for international students: Required—TOEFL. Electronic applications accepted.

Texas Tech University Health Sciences Center, School of Health Professions, Program in Molecular Pathology, Lubbock, TX 79430. Offers MS. *Faculty:* 12 full-time (8 women), 1 part-time/adjunct (0 women). *Students:* 32 full-time (15 women); includes 10 minority (3 Black or African American, non-Hispanic/Latino; 3 Asian, non-Hispanic/Latino; 4 Hispanic/Latino). Average age 24. 79 applicants, 49% accepted, 32 enrolled. In 2017, 32 master's awarded. *Entrance requirements:* Additional exam requirements/recommendations for international students: Required—TOEFL (minimum score 550 paper-based; 79 iBT). *Application deadline:* For spring admission, 2/1 priority date for domestic students. Applications are processed on a rolling basis. Application fee: $75. Electronic applications accepted. *Financial support:* Career-related internships or fieldwork, institutionally sponsored loans, and scholarships/grants available. Financial award application deadline: 9/1; financial award applicants required to submit FAFSA. *Unit head:* Dr. Ericka Hendrix, Program Director, 806-743-4473, Fax: 806-743-4470, E-mail: ericka.hendrix@ttuhsc.edu. *Application contact:* Lindsay Johnson, Associate Dean for Admissions and Student Affairs, 806-743-3220, Fax: 806-743-2994, E-mail: lindsay.johnson@ttuhsc.edu.
Website: http://www.ttuhsc.edu/health-professions/master-of-science-molecular-pathology/

University of Michigan, Rackham Graduate School, Program in Biomedical Sciences (PIBS), Program in Molecular and Cellular Pathology, Ann Arbor, MI 48109. Offers PhD. *Faculty:* 35 full-time (10 women). *Students:* 23 full-time (13 women); includes 7 minority (2 Black or African American, non-Hispanic/Latino; 2 Asian, non-Hispanic/Latino; 2 Hispanic/Latino; 1 Two or more races, non-Hispanic/Latino), 7 international. Average age 28. 57 applicants, 16% accepted, 5 enrolled. In 2017, 4 doctorates awarded. *Degree requirements:* For doctorate, comprehensive exam, thesis/dissertation, preliminary exam; oral defense of dissertation. *Entrance requirements:* For doctorate, GRE General Test, 3 letters of recommendation, research experience, personal statement. Additional exam requirements/recommendations for international students: Required—TOEFL (minimum score 84 iBT). *Application deadline:* For fall admission, 12/1 for domestic and international students. Application fee: $75 ($90 for international students). Electronic applications accepted. *Expenses:* Tuition, state resident: full-time $22,368; part-time $1201 per credit hour. Tuition, nonresident: full-time $45,156; part-time $2467 per credit hour. *Required fees:* $376 per term. Tuition and fees vary according to course load, degree level and program. *Financial support:* In 2017–18, 9 fellowships with full tuition reimbursements (averaging $30,600 per year), 14 research assistantships with full tuition reimbursements (averaging $30,600 per year) were awarded; scholarships/grants, traineeships, health care benefits, and unspecified assistantships also available. Financial award applicants required to submit FAFSA. *Faculty research:* Cancer biology, stem cell and developmental biology, immunopathology and inflammatory disease, epigenetics and gene regulation, cell death and regulation. *Total annual research expenditures:* $23.5 million. *Unit head:* Dr. Zaneta Nikolovska-Coleska, Associate Professor of Pathology/Director, 734-763-0846, Fax: 734-936-7361, E-mail: laszczem@med.umich.edu. *Application contact:* Jim Musgrave, Recruiting Coordinator, 734-615-1660, Fax: 734-647-7022, E-mail: jdmusg@umich.edu.
Website: http://www.pathology.med.umich.edu/

University of Pittsburgh, School of Medicine, Graduate Programs in Medicine, Cellular and Molecular Pathology Graduate Program, Pittsburgh, PA 15260. Offers PhD. *Accreditation:* NAACLS. *Faculty:* 78 full-time (22 women). *Students:* 25 full-time (15 women); includes 4 minority (1 Asian, non-Hispanic/Latino; 2 Hispanic/Latino; 1 Two or more races, non-Hispanic/Latino), 7 international. Average age 27. 350 applicants, 21% accepted, 16 enrolled. In 2017, 4 doctorates awarded. *Degree requirements:* For doctorate, comprehensive exam, thesis/dissertation. *Entrance requirements:* For doctorate, GRE General Test, minimum GPA of 3.2, 3 letters of recommendation, official transcripts, baccalaureate degree. Additional exam requirements/recommendations for international students: Required—TOEFL (minimum score 600 paper-based; 100 iBT), IELTS (minimum score 7). *Application deadline:* For fall admission, 12/1 priority date for domestic and international students. Application fee: $50. Electronic applications accepted. *Expenses:* $26,782 in-state, $42,006 out-of-state. *Financial support:* In 2017–18, 25 students received support, including 6 fellowships with full tuition reimbursements available (averaging $29,500 per year), 13 research assistantships with full tuition reimbursements available (averaging $29,500 per year); traineeships also available. *Faculty research:* Stem cells, fibrosis, inmate immunity, tissue regeneration. *Unit head:* Dr. Wendy Mars, Director, 412-648-9690, Fax: 412-648-1916, E-mail: wmars@pitt.edu. *Application contact:* Carol Williams, Admissions and Recruiting Manager, 412-648-9003, Fax: 412-648-1077, E-mail: gradstudies@medschool.pitt.edu.
Website: http://www.gradbiomed.pitt.edu

University of Wisconsin–Madison, School of Medicine and Public Health, Cellular and Molecular Pathology Graduate Program, Madison, WI 53706. Offers PhD. *Application contact:* Joanne Thornton, Graduate Program Coordinator, 608-262-2665, E-mail: jmthornt@wisc.edu.
Website: http://www.cmp.wisc.edu/

Pathobiology

Brown University, Graduate School, Division of Biology and Medicine, Department of Pathology and Laboratory Medicine, Providence, RI 02912. Offers Sc M, PhD, MD/PhD. Terminal master's awarded for partial completion of doctoral program. *Degree requirements:* For doctorate, thesis/dissertation, preliminary exam. *Entrance requirements:* For master's and doctorate, GRE General Test, GRE Subject Test. Additional exam requirements/recommendations for international students: Required—TOEFL. Electronic applications accepted. *Faculty research:* Environmental pathology, carcinogenesis, immunopathology, signal transduction, innate immunity.

Columbia University, College of Physicians and Surgeons, Department of Pathology, New York, NY 10032. Offers pathobiology (M Phil, MA, PhD); MD/PhD. Only candidates for the PhD are admitted. Terminal master's awarded for partial completion of doctoral program. *Degree requirements:* For doctorate, thesis/dissertation. *Entrance requirements:* For master's and doctorate, GRE General Test. Additional exam requirements/recommendations for international students: Required—TOEFL. *Expenses: Tuition:* Full-time $44,864; part-time $1704 per credit. *Required fees:* $2370 per semester. One-time fee: $105. *Faculty research:* Virology, molecular biology, cell biology, neurobiology, immunology.

Drexel University, College of Medicine, Biomedical Graduate Programs, Interdisciplinary Program in Molecular Pathobiology, Philadelphia, PA 19104-2875. Offers MS, PhD, MD/PhD. *Degree requirements:* For doctorate, comprehensive exam, thesis/dissertation, qualifying exams. *Entrance requirements:* For doctorate, GRE General Test, minimum GPA of 3.0. Additional exam requirements/recommendations for international students: Required—TOEFL. Electronic applications accepted. *Faculty research:* Cell and molecular immunology, tumor immunology, molecular genetics, immunopathology, immunology of aging.

Johns Hopkins University, School of Medicine, Graduate Programs in Medicine, Graduate Program in Pathobiology, Baltimore, MD 21218. Offers pathobiology (PhD). *Degree requirements:* For doctorate, thesis/dissertation, qualifying oral exam. *Entrance requirements:* For doctorate, GRE General Test, previous course work with laboratory in organic and inorganic chemistry, general biology, calculus; interview. Additional exam requirements/recommendations for international students: Required—TOEFL. Electronic applications accepted. *Faculty research:* Role of mutant proteins in Alzheimer's disease, nuclear protein function in breast and prostate cancer, medically important fungi, glycoproteins in HIV pathogenesis.

Kansas State University, Graduate School, College of Veterinary Medicine, Department of Diagnostic Medicine/Pathobiology, Manhattan, KS 66506. Offers biomedical science (MS); diagnostic medicine/pathobiology (PhD). Terminal master's awarded for partial completion of doctoral program. *Degree requirements:* For doctorate, thesis/dissertation. *Entrance requirements:* For master's and doctorate, interviews. Additional exam requirements/recommendations for international students: Required—TOEFL (minimum score 550 paper-based). Electronic applications accepted. *Faculty research:* Infectious disease of animals, food safety and security, epidemiology and public health, toxicology, pathology.

Medical University of South Carolina, College of Graduate Studies, Program in Molecular and Cellular Biology and Pathobiology, Charleston, SC 29425. Offers cancer biology (PhD); cardiovascular biology (PhD); cardiovascular imaging (PhD); cell regulation (PhD); craniofacial biology (PhD); genetics and development (PhD); marine biomedicine (PhD); DMD/PhD; MD/PhD. *Degree requirements:* For doctorate, thesis/dissertation, oral and written exams. *Entrance requirements:* For doctorate, GRE General Test, interview, minimum GPA of 3.0. Additional exam requirements/recommendations for international students: Required—TOEFL (minimum score 600 paper-based; 100 iBT). Electronic applications accepted.

Michigan State University, College of Veterinary Medicine and The Graduate School, Graduate Programs in Veterinary Medicine, Department of Pathobiology and Diagnostic Investigation, East Lansing, MI 48824. Offers pathology (MS, PhD); pathology–environmental toxicology (PhD). *Entrance requirements:* Additional exam requirements/recommendations for international students: Required—TOEFL. Electronic applications accepted.

Penn State University Park, Graduate School, College of Agricultural Sciences, Department of Veterinary and Biomedical Sciences, University Park, PA 16802. Offers pathobiology (MS, PhD). *Unit head:* Dr. Richard T. Roush, Dean, 814-865-2541, Fax: 814-865-3103. *Application contact:* Lori Stania, Director, Graduate Student Services, 814-865-1795, Fax: 814-863-4627, E-mail: l-gswww@lists.psu.edu.
Website: http://vbs.psu.edu/

Purdue University, School of Veterinary Medicine and Graduate School, Graduate Programs in Veterinary Medicine, Department of Comparative Pathobiology, West Lafayette, IN 47907-2027. Offers comparative epidemiology and public health (MS); comparative epidemiology and public heath (PhD); comparative microbiology and immunology (MS, PhD); comparative pathobiology (MS, PhD); interdisciplinary studies (PhD), including microbial pathogenesis, molecular signaling and cancer biology, molecular virology; lab animal medicine (MS), veterinary anatomic pathology (MS), veterinary clinical pathology (MS). Terminal master's awarded for partial completion of doctoral program. *Degree requirements:* For master's, thesis (for some programs); for doctorate, thesis/dissertation. *Entrance requirements:* For master's and doctorate, GRE General Test. Additional exam requirements/recommendations for international students: Required—TOEFL (minimum score 575 paper-based), IELTS (minimum score 6.5), TWE (minimum score 4). Electronic applications accepted.

The University of Alabama at Birmingham, Joint Health Sciences, Pathobiology and Molecular Medicine Theme, Birmingham, AL 35294. Offers PhD. *Faculty:* 370. *Students:* 37 full-time (24 women); includes 15 minority (6 Black or African American, non-Hispanic/Latino; 5 Asian, non-Hispanic/Latino; 4 Hispanic/Latino). Average age 28. 30 applicants, 27% accepted, 6 enrolled. In 2017, 9 doctorates awarded. *Degree requirements:* For doctorate, comprehensive exam, thesis/dissertation. *Entrance requirements:* For doctorate, personal statement, resume or curriculum vitae, letters of recommendation, research experience, interview. Additional exam requirements/recommendations for international students: Required—TOEFL (minimum score 80 iBT), IELTS (minimum score 6.5). *Application deadline:* For fall admission, 12/31 for domestic and international students. Applications are processed on a rolling basis. Electronic applications accepted. *Financial support:* In 2017–18, fellowships with full tuition reimbursements (averaging $29,000 per year), research assistantships with full tuition reimbursements (averaging $30,000 per year) were awarded; health care benefits also available. *Unit head:* Dr. Yabing Chen, Theme Director, 205-996-6293, E-mail: ybchen@uab.edu. *Application contact:* Alyssa Zasada, Admissions Manager for Graduate Biomedical Sciences, 205-934-3857, E-mail: grad-gbs@uab.edu.
Website: http://www.uab.edu/gbs/home/themes/pbmm

University of Cincinnati, Graduate School, College of Medicine, Graduate Programs in Biomedical Sciences, Program in Pathobiology and Molecular Medicine, Cincinnati, OH 45267-0529. Offers pathology (PhD), including anatomic pathology, laboratory medicine, pathobiology and molecular medicine. *Degree requirements:* For doctorate, thesis/dissertation, qualifying exam. *Entrance requirements:* For doctorate, GRE General Test. Additional exam requirements/recommendations for international students: Required—TOEFL. Electronic applications accepted. *Expenses: Tuition, area resident:* Full-time $14,468. Tuition, state resident: full-time $14,968; part-time $754 per credit hour. Tuition, nonresident: full-time $24,210; part-time $1311 per credit hour. *International tuition:* $26,460 full-time. *Required fees:* $3958; $84 per credit hour. One-time fee: $85 full-time. Tuition and fees vary according to course load, degree level and program. *Faculty research:* Cardiovascular and lipid disorders, digestive and kidney disease, endocrine and metabolic disorders, hematologic and oncogenic, immunology and infectious disease.

University of Connecticut, Graduate School, College of Agriculture, Health and Natural Resources, Department of Pathobiology and Veterinary Science, Storrs, CT 06269. Offers pathobiology (MS, PhD). Terminal master's awarded for partial completion of doctoral program. *Degree requirements:* For master's, comprehensive exam; for doctorate, thesis/dissertation. *Entrance requirements:* For master's and doctorate, GRE General Test, GRE Subject Test. Additional exam requirements/recommendations for international students: Required—TOEFL (minimum score 550 paper-based). Electronic applications accepted.

University of Illinois at Urbana–Champaign, College of Veterinary Medicine, Department of Pathobiology, Urbana, IL 61802. Offers MS, PhD, DVM/PhD. Terminal master's awarded for partial completion of doctoral program. *Degree requirements:* For doctorate, thesis/dissertation.

University of Missouri, College of Veterinary Medicine and Office of Research and Graduate Studies, Graduate Programs in Veterinary Medicine, Department of Veterinary Pathobiology, Columbia, MO 65211. Offers comparative medicine (MS); pathobiology (MS, PhD). *Entrance requirements:* For master's and doctorate, GRE General Test, minimum GPA of 3.0. *Expenses:* Tuition, state resident: full-time $6480. Tuition, nonresident: full-time $17,744. *Required fees:* $1108. Tuition and fees vary according to course load, campus/location and program. *Financial support:* Traineeships available. *Faculty research:* Bacteriology, cell biology, clinical pathology, comparative medicine, cytoskeletal regulation, gene expression and control, gene therapy, immunology, infectious disease, inflammatory diseases, microbiology, microscopy, molecular diagnostics, molecular genetics and genomic analysis.
Website: http://vpbio.missouri.edu/

University of Toronto, Faculty of Medicine, Department of Laboratory Medicine and Pathobiology, Toronto, ON M5S 1A1, Canada. Offers M Sc, PhD. *Degree requirements:* For master's, thesis; for doctorate, thesis/dissertation, oral defense of thesis. *Entrance requirements:* For master's, minimum B+ average in final 2 years, research experience, 2 letters of recommendation, resume, interview; for doctorate, minimum A- average, 2 letters of recommendation, research experience, resume, interview. Additional exam requirements/recommendations for international students: Required—TOEFL (minimum score 600 paper-based), TWE (minimum score 5, or IELTS (minimum score 7). Electronic applications accepted.

University of Washington, Graduate School, School of Public Health, Department of Global Health, Interdisciplinary Doctoral Program in Pathobiology, Seattle, WA 98195. Offers PhD. *Students:* 26 full-time (20 women); includes 7 minority (5 Asian, non-Hispanic/Latino; 2 Hispanic/Latino), 5 international. Average age 28. 71 applicants, 21% accepted, 7 enrolled. In 2017, 3 doctorates awarded. Terminal master's awarded for partial completion of doctoral program. Electronic applications accepted. *Financial support:* Fellowships, research assistantships, institutionally sponsored loans, scholarships/grants, traineeships, and health care benefits available. *Unit head:* 206-543-4338, E-mail: pabio@u.washington.edu. *Application contact:* 206-543-4338, E-mail: pabio@u.washington.edu.
Website: https://globalhealth.washington.edu/education-training/phd-pathobiology

University of Wyoming, College of Agriculture and Natural Resources, Department of Veterinary Sciences, Laramie, WY 82071. Offers pathobiology (MS). *Degree requirements:* For master's, thesis. *Entrance requirements:* For master's, GRE General Test, minimum GPA of 3.0. Additional exam requirements/recommendations for international students: Required—TOEFL. *Faculty research:* Infectious diseases, pathology, toxicology, immunology, microbiology.

Wake Forest University, School of Medicine and Graduate School of Arts and Sciences, Graduate Programs in Medicine, Program in Molecular and Cellular Pathobiology, Winston-Salem, NC 27109. Offers MS, PhD, MD/PhD. *Degree requirements:* For master's, thesis; for doctorate, thesis/dissertation. *Entrance requirements:* For master's and doctorate, GRE General Test. Additional exam requirements/recommendations for international students: Required—TOEFL. Electronic applications accepted. *Faculty research:* Atherosclerosis, lipoproteins, arterial wall metabolism.

Pathology

Albert Einstein College of Medicine, Graduate Programs in the Biomedical Sciences, Department of Pathology, Bronx, NY 10461. Offers PhD, MD/PhD. *Degree requirements:* For doctorate, thesis/dissertation. *Entrance requirements:* For doctorate, GRE General Test. Additional exam requirements/recommendations for international students: Required—TOEFL. *Application deadline:* For fall admission, 1/15 for domestic students. Application fee: $0. *Financial support:* Fellowships available. *Faculty research:* Clinical and disease-related research at tissue, cellular, and subcellular levels; biochemistry and morphology of enzyme and lysosome disorders. *Unit head:* Dr. Michael Prystowsky, Chairman, 718-430-2827. *Application contact:* Sheila Cleeton, Executive Director and Registrar, Einstein Graduate Division, 718-430-2128, Fax: 718-430-8655, E-mail: sheila.cleeton@einstein.yu.edu.
Website: http://www.einstein.yu.edu/departments/pathology/

Boston University, School of Medicine, Division of Graduate Medical Sciences, Department of Pathology and Laboratory Medicine, Boston, MA 02118. Offers MS, PhD, MD/PhD. *Program availability:* Part-time. *Degree requirements:* For doctorate, thesis/dissertation. *Entrance requirements:* Additional exam requirements/recommendations for international students: Required—TOEFL. *Application deadline:* For fall admission, 1/15 for domestic students; for spring admission, 10/15 for domestic students. *Financial support:* Scholarships/grants and traineeships available. Financial award applicants required to submit FAFSA. *Unit head:* Dr. Daniel G. Remick, Chairman, 617-414-7043, E-mail: remickd@bu.edu. *Application contact:* GMS Admissions Office, 617-638-5255, E-mail: askgms@bu.edu.
Website: http://www.bumc.bu.edu/busm-pathology/

Case Western Reserve University, School of Medicine and School of Graduate Studies, Graduate Programs in Medicine, Programs in Molecular and Cellular Basis of Disease/Pathology, Cleveland, OH 44106. Offers molecular and cellular basis of disease (PhD); pathology (MS); MD/PhD. Terminal master's awarded for partial completion of doctoral program. *Degree requirements:* For master's, thesis; for doctorate, thesis/dissertation. *Entrance requirements:* For master's and doctorate, GRE General Test, GRE Subject Test. Additional exam requirements/recommendations for international students: Required—TOEFL (minimum score 550 paper-based). Electronic applications accepted. *Expenses: Tuition:* Full-time $43,854; part-time $1827 per credit hour. *Required fees:* $50; $50 per credit hour. Tuition and fees vary according to course load and program. *Faculty research:* Neurobiology, molecular biology, cancer biology, biomaterials, biocompatibility.

Colorado State University, College of Veterinary Medicine and Biomedical Sciences, Department of Microbiology, Immunology and Pathology, Fort Collins, CO 80523-1682. Offers microbiology, immunology and pathology (MS, PhD); pathology (PhD). *Faculty:* 76 full-time (35 women), 11 part-time/adjunct (7 women). *Students:* 73 full-time (52 women), 36 part-time (29 women); includes 18 minority (2 Black or African American, non-Hispanic/Latino; 1 American Indian or Alaska Native, non-Hispanic/Latino; 7 Asian, non-Hispanic/Latino; 6 Hispanic/Latino; 2 Two or more races, non-Hispanic/Latino), 7 international. Average age 29. 200 applicants, 32% accepted, 54 enrolled. In 2017, 43 master's, 12 doctorates awarded. Terminal master's awarded for partial completion of doctoral program. *Degree requirements:* For master's, comprehensive exam (for some programs), thesis (for some programs); for doctorate, comprehensive exam, thesis/dissertation. *Entrance requirements:* For master's and doctorate, GRE General Test or MCAT, minimum GPA of 3.0; written statement; transcripts; resume/curriculum vitae; three recommendations. Additional exam requirements/recommendations for international students: Required—TOEFL (minimum score 550 paper-based; 80 iBT), IELTS (minimum score 6.5). *Application deadline:* For fall admission, 4/1 for domestic

and international students; for spring admission, 12/15 for domestic and international students. Application fee: $60 ($70 for international students). Electronic applications accepted. *Expenses:* $120 per credit hour. *Financial support:* In 2017–18, 20 research assistantships with full and partial tuition reimbursements (averaging $24,368 per year), 6 teaching assistantships with full and partial tuition reimbursements (averaging $17,883 per year) were awarded; fellowships with full and partial tuition reimbursements and health care benefits also available. Financial award application deadline: 12/15. *Faculty research:* Bacteriology, immunology, prion biology, vector biology, virology. *Total annual research expenditures:* $20.9 million. *Unit head:* Dr. Mark Zabel, Associate Department Head for Graduate Education, 970-491-1455, E-mail: mark.zabel@colostate.edu. *Application contact:* Heidi Runge, Academic Support Coordinator for Graduate Studies, 970-491-1630, Fax: 970-491-1815, E-mail: heidi.runge@colostate.edu.
Website: http://csu-cvmbs.colostate.edu/academics/mip/graduate/Pages/microbiology-immunology-professional-masters.aspx

Columbia University, College of Physicians and Surgeons, Department of Pathology, New York, NY 10032. Offers pathobiology (M Phil, MA, PhD); MD/PhD. Only candidates for the PhD are admitted. Terminal master's awarded for partial completion of doctoral program. *Degree requirements:* For doctorate, thesis/dissertation. *Entrance requirements:* For master's and doctorate, GRE General Test. Additional exam requirements/recommendations for international students: Required—TOEFL. *Expenses: Tuition:* Full-time $44,864; part-time $1704 per credit. *Required fees:* $2370 per semester. One-time fee: $105. *Faculty research:* Virology, molecular biology, cell biology, neurobiology, immunology.

Dalhousie University, Faculty of Graduate Studies and Faculty of Medicine, Graduate Programs in Medicine, Department of Pathology, Halifax, NS B3H 4R2, Canada. Offers M Sc, PhD. *Degree requirements:* For master's, oral defense of thesis. *Entrance requirements:* Additional exam requirements/recommendations for international students: Required—1 of 5 approved tests: TOEFL, IELTS, CANTEST, CAEL, Michigan English Language Assessment Battery. Electronic applications accepted. *Faculty research:* Tumor immunology, molecular oncology, clinical chemistry, hematology, molecular genetics/oncology.

Duke University, Graduate School, Department of Pathology, Durham, NC 27710. Offers PhD. *Accreditation:* NAACLS. *Degree requirements:* For doctorate, thesis/dissertation. *Entrance requirements:* For doctorate, GRE General Test, GRE Subject Test (recommended). Additional exam requirements/recommendations for international students: Required—TOEFL (minimum score 577 paper-based; 90 iBT) or IELTS (minimum score 7). Electronic applications accepted.

Duke University, School of Medicine, Pathologists' Assistant Program, Durham, NC 27710. Offers MHS. *Accreditation:* NAACLS. *Faculty:* 1 (woman) full-time, 56 part-time/adjunct (30 women). *Students:* 16 full-time (10 women); includes 2 minority (both Asian, non-Hispanic/Latino). Average age 26. 66 applicants, 12% accepted, 8 enrolled. In 2017, 8 master's awarded. *Degree requirements:* For master's, comprehensive exam. *Entrance requirements:* For master's, GRE. Additional exam requirements/recommendations for international students: Required—TOEFL. *Application deadline:* For fall admission, 1/15 for domestic students. Application fee: $55. Electronic applications accepted. Application fee is waived when completed online. *Financial support:* Application deadline: 5/1; applicants required to submit FAFSA. *Unit head:* Dr. Rex C. Bentley, Program Director, 919-684-6423, Fax: 919-681-7634, E-mail: bentl003@mc.duke.edu. *Application contact:* Pamela Vollmer, Associate Director, 919-684-2159, Fax: 919-684-8693, E-mail: pamela.vollmer@duke.edu.
Website: http://pathology.duke.edu/academic-programs/pathologists-assistant-program

Harvard University, Graduate School of Arts and Sciences, Division of Medical Sciences, Boston, MA 02115. Offers biological chemistry and molecular pharmacology (PhD); cell biology (PhD); genetics (PhD); microbiology and molecular genetics (PhD); pathology (PhD), including experimental pathology. *Degree requirements:* For doctorate, thesis/dissertation. *Entrance requirements:* For doctorate, GRE General Test, GRE Subject Test. Additional exam requirements/recommendations for international students: Required—TOEFL.

Indiana University–Purdue University Indianapolis, Indiana University School of Medicine, Department of Pathology and Laboratory Medicine, Indianapolis, IN 46202. Offers MS, PhD, MD/PhD. *Degree requirements:* For master's, thesis; for doctorate, thesis/dissertation. *Entrance requirements:* For master's and doctorate, GRE General Test. Additional exam requirements/recommendations for international students: Required—TOEFL. *Faculty research:* Intestinal microecology and anaerobes, molecular pathogenesis of infectious diseases, AIDS, pneumocystis, sports medicine toxicology, neuropathology of aging.

Iowa State University of Science and Technology, Department of Veterinary Pathology, Ames, IA 50011. Offers MS, PhD. *Entrance requirements:* For master's and doctorate, GRE General Test. Additional exam requirements/recommendations for international students: Recommended—TOEFL (minimum score 550 paper-based; 79 iBT), IELTS (minimum score 6.5). Electronic applications accepted.

Johns Hopkins University, School of Medicine, Graduate Programs in Medicine, Graduate Program in Pathobiology, Baltimore, MD 21218. Offers pathobiology (PhD). *Degree requirements:* For doctorate, thesis/dissertation, qualifying oral exam. *Entrance requirements:* For doctorate, GRE General Test, previous course work with laboratory in organic and inorganic chemistry, general biology, calculus; interview. Additional exam requirements/recommendations for international students: Required—TOEFL. Electronic applications accepted. *Faculty research:* Role of mutant proteins in Alzheimer's disease, nuclear protein function in breast and prostate cancer, medically important fungi, glycoproteins in HIV pathogenesis.

Loma Linda University, School of Medicine, Programs in Pathology and Human Anatomy, Loma Linda, CA 92350. Offers human anatomy (PhD); pathology (PhD). *Accreditation:* NAACLS. *Program availability:* Part-time. Terminal master's awarded for partial completion of doctoral program. *Degree requirements:* For doctorate, 2 foreign languages, thesis/dissertation. *Entrance requirements:* For doctorate, GRE General Test. Additional exam requirements/recommendations for international students: Required—TOEFL (minimum score 550 paper-based). *Faculty research:* Neuroendocrine system, histochemistry and image analysis, effect of age and diabetes on PNS, electron microscopy, histology.

McGill University, Faculty of Graduate and Postdoctoral Studies, Faculty of Medicine, Department of Pathology, Montréal, QC H3A 2T5, Canada. Offers M Sc, PhD.

Medical University of South Carolina, College of Graduate Studies, Department of Pathology and Laboratory Medicine, Charleston, SC 29425. Offers MS, PhD, DMD/PhD, MD/PhD. *Accreditation:* NAACLS. Terminal master's awarded for partial completion of doctoral program. *Degree requirements:* For master's, thesis; for doctorate, thesis/dissertation, oral and written exams. *Entrance requirements:* For master's, GRE General Test; for doctorate, GRE General Test, interview, minimum GPA of 3.0. Additional exam requirements/recommendations for international students: Required—TOEFL (minimum score 600 paper-based; 100 iBT). Electronic applications accepted. *Faculty research:* Neurobiology of hearing loss; inner ear ion homeostasis; cancer biology, genetics and stem cell biology; cellular defense mechanisms.

Michigan State University, College of Veterinary Medicine and The Graduate School, Graduate Programs in Veterinary Medicine, Department of Pathobiology and Diagnostic Investigation, East Lansing, MI 48824. Offers pathology (MS, PhD); pathology–environmental toxicology (PhD). *Entrance requirements:* Additional exam requirements/recommendations for international students: Required—TOEFL. Electronic applications accepted.

New York Medical College, Graduate School of Basic Medical Sciences, Valhalla, NY 10595. Offers biochemistry and molecular biology (MS, PhD); cell biology (MS, PhD); microbiology and immunology (MS, PhD); pathology (MS, PhD); pharmacology (MS, PhD); physiology (MS, PhD); MD/PhD. *Program availability:* Part-time, evening/weekend. *Faculty:* 70 full-time (17 women), 25 part-time/adjunct (9 women). *Students:* 116 full-time (63 women), 25 part-time (11 women); includes 65 minority (17 Black or African American, non-Hispanic/Latino; 1 American Indian or Alaska Native, non-Hispanic/Latino; 23 Asian, non-Hispanic/Latino; 21 Hispanic/Latino; 3 Two or more races, non-Hispanic/Latino), 27 international. Average age 27. 273 applicants, 56% accepted, 59 enrolled. In 2017, 32 master's, 3 doctorates awarded. *Degree requirements:* For master's, thesis; for doctorate, comprehensive exam, thesis/dissertation. *Entrance requirements:* For master's, GRE General Test, MCAT, or DAT; for doctorate, GRE General Test. Additional exam requirements/recommendations for international students: Required—TOEFL. *Application deadline:* For fall admission, 7/1 priority date for domestic students, 5/1 priority date for international students; for spring admission, 12/1 priority date for domestic students, 9/15 priority date for international students. Applications are processed on a rolling basis. Application fee: $75 ($100 for international students). Electronic applications accepted. *Expenses:* $1,125 per credit, $655 fees. *Financial support:* Fellowships, research assistantships, Federal Work-Study, institutionally sponsored loans, scholarships/grants, tuition waivers, and health benefits (for PhD candidates only) available. Support available to part-time students. Financial award application deadline: 4/30; financial award applicants required to submit FAFSA. *Faculty research:* Cardiovascular science, infectious diseases, neuroscience, cancer, cell signaling. *Unit head:* Dr. Francis L. Belloni, Dean, 914-594-4110, Fax: 914-594-4944, E-mail: francis_belloni@nymc.edu. *Application contact:* Valerie Romeo-Messana, Director of Admissions, 914-594-4110, Fax: 914-594-4944, E-mail: v_romeomessana@nymc.edu.
Website: https://www.nymc.edu/graduate-school-of-basic-medical-sciences-gsbms/gsbms-academics/

North Carolina State University, College of Veterinary Medicine, Program in Comparative Biomedical Sciences, Raleigh, NC 27695. Offers cell biology (MS, PhD); infectious disease (MS, PhD); pathology (MS, PhD); pharmacology (MS, PhD); population medicine (MS, PhD). *Program availability:* Part-time. *Degree requirements:* For master's, thesis; for doctorate, thesis/dissertation. *Entrance requirements:* For master's and doctorate, GRE General Test. Additional exam requirements/recommendations for international students: Required—TOEFL (minimum score 550 paper-based). Electronic applications accepted. *Expenses:* Contact institution. *Faculty research:* Infectious diseases, cell biology, pharmacology and toxicology, genomics, pathology and population medicine.

North Dakota State University, College of Graduate and Interdisciplinary Studies, College of Agriculture, Food Systems, and Natural Resources, Department of Microbiological Sciences, Fargo, ND 58102. Offers microbiology (MS); molecular pathogenesis (PhD). *Program availability:* Part-time. *Degree requirements:* For master's, thesis; for doctorate, thesis/dissertation, oral and written preliminary exams. *Entrance requirements:* For master's and doctorate, GRE. Additional exam requirements/recommendations for international students: Required—TOEFL (minimum score 525 paper-based; 71 iBT). *Application deadline:* For fall admission, 2/15 priority date for domestic students. Applications are processed on a rolling basis. Application fee: $35. *Expenses:* Tuition, state resident: full-time $4323; part-time $360.21 per credit. Tuition, nonresident: full-time $6484; part-time $540.31 per credit. *Required fees:* $668; $55.70 per credit. Part-time tuition and fees vary according to degree level, program and reciprocity agreements. *Financial support:* Application deadline: 4/15. *Faculty research:* Bacterial gene regulation, antibiotic resistance, molecular virology, mechanisms of bacterial pathogenesis, immunology of animals. *Unit head:* Peter Bergholz, Graduate Coordinator, 701-231-5946, E-mail: peter.bergholz@ndsu.edu. *Application contact:* Eugene Berry, Associate Professor, 701-231-7520, Fax: 701-231-7514, E-mail: eugene.berry@ndsu.edu.
Website: http://www.ndsu.edu/micro/

Purdue University, School of Veterinary Medicine and Graduate School, Graduate Programs in Veterinary Medicine, Department of Comparative Pathobiology, West Lafayette, IN 47907-2027. Offers comparative epidemiology and public health (MS); comparative epidemiology and public heath (PhD); comparative microbiology and immunology (MS, PhD); comparative pathobiology (MS, PhD); interdisciplinary studies (PhD), including microbial pathogenesis, molecular signaling and cancer biology, molecular virology; lab animal medicine (MS); veterinary anatomic pathology (MS); veterinary clinical pathology (MS). Terminal master's awarded for partial completion of doctoral program. *Degree requirements:* For master's, thesis (for some programs); for doctorate, thesis/dissertation. *Entrance requirements:* For master's and doctorate, GRE General Test. Additional exam requirements/recommendations for international students: Required—TOEFL (minimum score 575 paper-based), IELTS (minimum score 6.5), TWE (minimum score 4). Electronic applications accepted.

Queen's University at Kingston, School of Graduate Studies, Faculty of Health Sciences, Department of Pathology and Molecular Medicine, Kingston, ON K7L 3N6, Canada. Offers M Sc, PhD. *Program availability:* Part-time. *Degree requirements:* For master's, thesis; for doctorate, comprehensive exam, thesis/dissertation. *Entrance requirements:* Additional exam requirements/recommendations for international students: Required—TOEFL. *Faculty research:* Immunopathology, cancer biology, immunology and metastases, cell differentiation, blood coagulation.

Quinnipiac University, School of Health Sciences, Program for Pathologists' Assistant, Hamden, CT 06518-1940. Offers MHS. *Accreditation:* NAACLS. *Faculty:* 3 full-time (0 women), 1 part-time/adjunct (0 women). *Students:* 46 full-time (33 women); includes 15 minority (2 Black or African American, non-Hispanic/Latino; 7 Asian, non-Hispanic/Latino; 4 Hispanic/Latino; 2 Two or more races, non-Hispanic/Latino). 123 applicants, 22% accepted, 24 enrolled. In 2017, 23 master's awarded. *Degree requirements:* For master's, residency. *Entrance requirements:* For master's, interview, coursework in biological and health sciences, minimum GPA of 3.0. *Application deadline:* For summer admission, 9/1 for domestic students. Applications are processed on a rolling basis. Application fee: $45. Electronic applications accepted. *Financial support:* Scholarships/grants and unspecified assistantships available. Financial award application deadline: 5/1; financial award applicants required to submit FAFSA. *Faculty research:* ACL injury mechanism and running injuries and performance; transcriptional activators upstream stimulatory factor (USF); identification of novel antimicrobials; vaccines, formites and opportunistic pathogens; molecular biology of the Lyme Disease agent, Borrelia burgdorferi; molecular and microscopic techniques in host-pathogen interactions; non-invasive vascular biology, external pneumatic compression, sports performance. *Unit head:* Robert Cottrell, Program Director, 203-582-8672, E-mail: paadmissions@qu.edu. *Application contact:* Office of Graduate Admissions, 800-462-1944, Fax: 203-582-3443, E-mail: paadmissions@qu.edu.
Website: http://www.qu.edu/gradpathologists

Rosalind Franklin University of Medicine and Science, College of Health Professions, Pathologists' Assistant Department, North Chicago, IL 60064-3095. Offers MS. *Accreditation:* NAACLS. *Entrance requirements:* For master's, bachelor's degree from an accredited college or university, minimum cumulative GPA of 3.0. Additional exam requirements/recommendations for international students: Required—TOEFL. *Faculty research:* Adaptation of ACGME/ADASP pathology resident training competencies to pathologists' assistant clinical education, utilization of structural portfolios in pathologists' assistant clinical education.

Rutgers University–Newark, Graduate School of Biomedical Sciences, Program in Molecular Pathology and Immunology, Newark, NJ 07107. Offers PhD. *Accreditation:* NAACLS. *Entrance requirements:* Additional exam requirements/recommendations for international students: Required—TOEFL. Electronic applications accepted.

Saint Louis University, Graduate Programs, School of Medicine, Graduate Programs in Biomedical Sciences and Graduate Programs, Department of Pathology, St. Louis, MO 63103. Offers PhD. *Accreditation:* NAACLS. *Degree requirements:* For doctorate, comprehensive exam, thesis/dissertation, oral and written preliminary exams, oral defense of dissertation. *Entrance requirements:* For doctorate, GRE General Test (GRE Subject Test optional), letters of recommendation, resume, interview. Additional exam requirements/recommendations for international students: Required—TOEFL (minimum score 525 paper-based). Electronic applications accepted. *Faculty research:* Cancer research, hepatitis C virology, cell imaging, liver disease.

Stony Brook University, State University of New York, Graduate School, College of Arts and Sciences, Department of Biochemistry and Cell Biology, Molecular and Cellular Biology Program, Stony Brook, NY 11794. Offers biochemistry and molecular biology (PhD); biological sciences (MA); immunology and pathology (PhD); molecular and cellular biology (PhD). *Students:* 63 full-time (35 women); includes 12 minority (3 Black or African American, non-Hispanic/Latino; 6 Asian, non-Hispanic/Latino; 3 Hispanic/Latino), 35 international. Average age 28. 131 applicants, 25% accepted, 11 enrolled. In 2017, 12 doctorates awarded. *Degree requirements:* For doctorate, comprehensive exam, thesis/dissertation, teaching experience. *Entrance requirements:* For doctorate, GRE General Test, GRE Subject Test. Additional exam requirements/recommendations for international students: Required—TOEFL. *Application deadline:* For fall admission, 1/15 for domestic students; for spring admission, 10/1 for domestic students. Application fee: $100. Electronic applications accepted. *Expenses:* Contact institution. *Financial support:* In 2017–18, 4 fellowships, 29 research assistantships, 12 teaching assistantships were awarded; Federal Work-Study also available. *Unit head:* Prof. Aaron Neiman, Chair, 631-632-8550, Fax: 631-632-8575, E-mail: aaron.neiman@stonybrook.edu. *Application contact:* Amy Saas, Graduate Program Administrator, 631-632-8613, Fax: 631-632-9730, E-mail: mcbgraduateprogram@stonybrook.edu.
Website: https://www.stonybrook.edu/mcb/

Tufts University, Cummings School of Veterinary Medicine, North Grafton, MA 01536. Offers animals and public policy (MS); biomedical sciences (PhD), including digestive diseases, infectious diseases, neuroscience and reproductive biology, pathology; conservation medicine (MS); veterinary medicine (DVM); DVM/MPH; DVM/MS. *Accreditation:* AVMA (one or more programs are accredited). *Degree requirements:* For master's, thesis (for some programs); for doctorate, comprehensive exam, thesis/dissertation (for some programs). *Entrance requirements:* For master's and doctorate, GRE General Test. Additional exam requirements/recommendations for international students: Required—TOEFL or IELTS. Electronic applications accepted. *Expenses:* Contact institution. *Faculty research:* Oncology, veterinary ethics, international veterinary medicine, veterinary genomics, pathogenesis of Clostridium difficile, wildlife fertility control.

Université de Montréal, Faculty of Medicine, Department of Pathology and Cellular Biology, Montréal, QC H3C 3J7, Canada. Offers M Sc, PhD. Terminal master's awarded for partial completion of doctoral program. *Degree requirements:* For master's, thesis; for doctorate, thesis/dissertation, general exam. *Entrance requirements:* For master's and doctorate, proficiency in French, knowledge of English. Electronic applications accepted. *Faculty research:* Immunopathology, cardiovascular pathology, oncogenetics, cellular neurocytology, muscular dystrophy.

Université Laval, Faculty of Medicine, Post-Professional Programs in Medical Studies, Québec, QC G1K 7P4, Canada. Offers anatomy–pathology (DESS); anesthesiology (DESS); cardiology (DESS); care of older people (Diploma); clinical research (DESS); community health (DESS); dermatology (DESS); diagnostic radiology (DESS); emergency medicine (Diploma); family medicine (DESS); general surgery (DESS); geriatrics (DESS); hematology (DESS); internal medicine (DESS); maternal and fetal medicine (Diploma); medical biochemistry (DESS); medical microbiology and infectious diseases (DESS); medical oncology (DESS); nephrology (DESS); neurology (DESS); neurosurgery (DESS); obstetrics and gynecology (DESS); ophthalmology (DESS); orthopedic surgery (DESS); oto-rhino-laryngology (DESS); palliative medicine (Diploma); pediatrics (DESS); plastic surgery (DESS); psychiatry (DESS); pulmonary medicine (DESS); radiology–oncology (DESS); thoracic surgery (DESS); urology (DESS). *Degree requirements:* For other advanced degree, comprehensive exam. *Entrance requirements:* For degree, knowledge of French. Electronic applications accepted.

University at Buffalo, the State University of New York, Graduate School, Graduate Programs in Cancer Research and Biomedical Sciences at Roswell Park Cancer Institute, Department of Cancer Pathology and Prevention at Roswell Park Cancer Institute, Buffalo, NY 14263-0001. Offers PhD. *Faculty:* 27 full-time (13 women). *Students:* 13 full-time (5 women); includes 1 minority (Black or African American, non-Hispanic/Latino), 5 international. 36 applicants, 11% accepted, 2 enrolled. In 2017, 4 doctorates awarded. *Degree requirements:* For doctorate, comprehensive exam, thesis/dissertation, oral defense of dissertation. *Entrance requirements:* For doctorate, GRE General Test. Additional exam requirements/recommendations for international students: Required—TOEFL (minimum score 79 iBT). *Application deadline:* For fall admission, 1/5 priority date for domestic and international students. Application fee: $75. Electronic applications accepted. *Financial support:* In 2017–18, 19 students received support, including 19 research assistantships with full tuition reimbursements available (averaging $27,000 per year); scholarships/grants, health care benefits, and unspecified assistantships also available. Financial award application deadline: 1/5. *Faculty research:* Molecular pathology of cancer, chemoprevention of cancer, genomic instability, molecular diagnosis and prognosis of cancer, molecular epidemiology. *Unit head:* Dr. Kirsten Moysich, Chairman, 716-845-8004, Fax: 716-845-1126, E-mail: kirsten.moysich@roswellpark.org. *Application contact:* Dr. Norman J. Karin, Associate Dean, 716-845-2339, Fax: 716-845-8178, E-mail: norman.karin@roswellpark.edu.
Website: http://www.roswellpark.edu/education/phd-programs/cancer-pathology-and-prevention

University at Buffalo, the State University of New York, Graduate School, Jacobs School of Medicine and Biomedical Sciences, Graduate Programs in Medicine and Biomedical Sciences, Department of Pathology and Anatomical Sciences, Buffalo, NY 14203. Offers anatomical sciences (MA, PhD); computational cell biology, anatomy, and pathology (PhD); pathology (MA, PhD). *Program availability:* Part-time. *Faculty:* 17 full-time (4 women). *Students:* 14 full-time (3 women); includes 2 minority (1 American Indian or Alaska Native, non-Hispanic/Latino; 1 Asian, non-Hispanic/Latino), 1 international. Average age 29. 26 applicants, 27% accepted, 6 enrolled. In 2017, 2 master's, 2 doctorates awarded. *Degree requirements:* For master's, thesis; for doctorate, comprehensive exam, thesis/dissertation. *Entrance requirements:* For master's, GRE, MCAT or DAT, 2 letters of recommendation; for doctorate, GRE, MCAT, or DAT, 3 letters of recommendation. Additional exam requirements/recommendations for international students: Required—TOEFL (minimum score 600 paper-based; 100 iBT). *Application deadline:* For fall admission, 5/1 priority date for domestic students, 3/1 priority date for international students. Applications are processed on a rolling basis. Application fee: $85. Electronic applications accepted. *Expenses:* Contact institution. *Financial support:* In 2017–18, 7 students received support, including 1 research assistantship with full tuition reimbursement available (averaging $24,900 per year), 1 teaching assistantship with full tuition reimbursement available (averaging $24,900 per year); Federal Work-Study, health care benefits, and unspecified assistantships also available. Financial award application deadline: 2/1; financial award applicants required to submit FAFSA. *Faculty research:* Immunopathology-immunobiology, experimental hypertension, neuromuscular disease, molecular pathology, cell motility and cytoskeleton. *Total annual research expenditures:* $138,370. *Unit head:* Dr. John E. Tomaszewski, Department Chair, 716-829-2846, Fax: 716-829-2911, E-mail: johntoma@buffalo.edu. *Application contact:* Lannette M. Garcia, Graduate Program Coordinator, 716-829-5204, Fax: 716-829-2911, E-mail: ubpathad@buffalo.edu.
Website: http://medicine.buffalo.edu/departments/pathology.html

University of Alberta, Faculty of Medicine and Dentistry and Faculty of Graduate Studies and Research, Graduate Programs in Medicine, Department of Laboratory Medicine and Pathology, Edmonton, AB T6G 2E1, Canada. Offers medical sciences (M Sc, PhD). *Program availability:* Part-time. Terminal master's awarded for partial completion of doctoral program. *Degree requirements:* For master's, thesis; for doctorate, thesis/dissertation, candidacy exam. *Entrance requirements:* For master's and doctorate, 3 letters of recommendation, minimum GPA of 3.0. Additional exam requirements/recommendations for international students: Required—TOEFL. *Faculty research:* Transplantation, renal pathology, molecular mechanisms of diseases, cryobiology, immunodiagnostics, informatics/cyber medicine, neuroimmunology, microbiology.

The University of British Columbia, Faculty of Medicine, Department of Pathology and Laboratory Medicine, Vancouver, BC V6T 2B5, Canada. Offers pathology (M Sc, PhD). *Degree requirements:* For master's, thesis; for doctorate, comprehensive exam, thesis/dissertation, internal oral defense. *Entrance requirements:* For master's, GRE, upper-level course work in biochemistry and physiology; for doctorate, GRE. Additional exam requirements/recommendations for international students: Required—TOEFL, IELTS. Electronic applications accepted. *Expenses:* Contact institution. *Faculty research:* Molecular biology of disease processes, cancer, hematopathology, atherosclerosis, pulmonary and cardiovascular pathophysiology.

University of Calgary, Cumming School of Medicine and Faculty of Graduate Studies, Medical Science Graduate Program, Calgary, AB T2N 1N4, Canada. Offers cancer biology (M Sc, PhD); critical care medicine (M Sc, PhD); joint injury and arthritis (M Sc, PhD); molecular and medical genetics (M Sc, PhD); mountain medicine and high altitude physiology (M Sc, PhD); pathologists' assistant (M Sc, PhD). *Degree requirements:* For master's, thesis; for doctorate, thesis/dissertation, candidacy exam. *Entrance requirements:* For master's, minimum undergraduate GPA of 3.2; for doctorate, minimum graduate GPA of 3.2. Additional exam requirements/recommendations for international students: Required—TOEFL (minimum score 600 paper-based). Electronic applications accepted. *Faculty research:* Cancer biology, immunology, joint injury and arthritis, medical education, population genomics.

University of California, Davis, Graduate Studies, Graduate Group in Comparative Pathology, Davis, CA 95616. Offers MS, PhD. *Accreditation:* NAACLS. Terminal master's awarded for partial completion of doctoral program. *Degree requirements:* For master's, comprehensive exam (for some programs), thesis (for some programs); for doctorate, thesis/dissertation. *Entrance requirements:* For master's and doctorate, GRE General Test. Additional exam requirements/recommendations for international students: Required—TOEFL (minimum score 550 paper-based). Electronic applications accepted. *Faculty research:* Immunopathology, toxicological and environmental pathology, reproductive pathology, pathology of infectious diseases.

University of California, Irvine, School of Medicine, Department of Pathology and Laboratory Medicine, Irvine, CA 92697. Offers experimental pathology (PhD). *Accreditation:* NAACLS. *Students:* 3 full-time (2 women); includes 1 minority (Hispanic/Latino), 1 international. Average age 33. In 2017, 1 doctorate awarded. Application fee: $105 ($125 for international students). *Unit head:* Dr. Edwin S. Monuki, Chair, 949-824-9604, Fax: 949-824-2160, E-mail: emonuki@uci.edu. *Application contact:* Stefani Ching, Graduate Student Coordinator, 949-824-5367, E-mail: shching@uci.edu.
Website: http://www.pathology.uci.edu/

University of California, Los Angeles, David Geffen School of Medicine and Graduate Division, Graduate Programs in Medicine, Program in Cellular and Molecular Pathology, Los Angeles, CA 90095. Offers MS, PhD. Terminal master's awarded for partial completion of doctoral program. *Degree requirements:* For master's, thesis; for doctorate, thesis/dissertation, written and oral qualifying examinations; 2 quarters of teaching experience. *Entrance requirements:* For doctorate, GRE General Test, bachelor's degree; minimum undergraduate GPA of 3.0 (or its equivalent if letter grade system not used). Additional exam requirements/recommendations for international students: Required—TOEFL. Electronic applications accepted.

University of California, Los Angeles, David Geffen School of Medicine and Graduate Division, Graduate Programs in Medicine, Program in Experimental Pathology, Los Angeles, CA 90095. Offers MS, PhD. *Degree requirements:* For doctorate, thesis/dissertation, oral and written qualifying exams. *Entrance requirements:* For master's, GRE General Test; for doctorate, GRE General Test, previous course work in physical chemistry and physics.

University of California, Los Angeles, Graduate Division, College of Letters and Science and David Geffen School of Medicine, UCLA ACCESS to Programs in the Molecular, Cellular and Integrative Life Sciences, Los Angeles, CA 90095. Offers biochemistry and molecular biology (PhD); biological chemistry (PhD); cellular and molecular pathology (PhD); human genetics (PhD); microbiology, immunology, and molecular genetics (PhD); molecular biology (PhD); molecular toxicology (PhD); molecular, cellular and integrative physiology (PhD); neurobiology (PhD); oral biology (PhD); physiology (PhD). *Degree requirements:* For doctorate, thesis/dissertation, oral and written qualifying exams. *Entrance requirements:* For doctorate, GRE General Test, bachelor's degree; minimum undergraduate GPA of 3.0 (or its equivalent if letter grade system not used). Additional exam requirements/recommendations for international students: Required—TOEFL. Electronic applications accepted.

University of Cincinnati, Graduate School, College of Medicine, Graduate Programs in Biomedical Sciences, Program in Pathobiology and Molecular Medicine, Cincinnati, OH 45267-0529. Offers pathology (PhD), including anatomic pathology, laboratory medicine, pathobiology and molecular medicine. *Degree requirements:* For doctorate, thesis/dissertation, qualifying exam. *Entrance requirements:* For doctorate, GRE

General Test. Additional exam requirements/recommendations for international students: Required—TOEFL. Electronic applications accepted. *Expenses: Tuition, area resident:* Full-time $14,468. Tuition, state resident: full-time $14,968; part-time $754 per credit hour. Tuition, nonresident: full-time $24,210; part-time $1311 per credit hour. *International tuition:* $26,460 full-time. *Required fees:* $3958; $84 per credit hour. One-time fee: $85 full-time. Tuition and fees vary according to course load, degree level and program. *Faculty research:* Cardiovascular and lipid disorders, digestive and kidney disease, endocrine and metabolic disorders, hematologic and oncogenic, immunology and infectious disease.

University of Georgia, College of Veterinary Medicine, Department of Veterinary Pathology, Athens, GA 30602. Offers MS, PhD. *Degree requirements:* For master's, thesis; for doctorate, one foreign language, thesis/dissertation. *Entrance requirements:* For master's and doctorate, GRE General Test. Electronic applications accepted.

University of Guelph, Ontario Veterinary College and Graduate Studies, Graduate Programs in Veterinary Sciences, Department of Pathobiology, Guelph, ON N1G 2W1, Canada. Offers anatomic pathology (DV Sc, Diploma); clinical pathology (Diploma); comparative pathology (M Sc, PhD); immunology (M Sc, PhD); laboratory animal science (DV Sc); pathology (M Sc, PhD, Diploma); veterinary infectious diseases (M Sc, PhD); zoo animal/wildlife medicine (DV Sc). *Degree requirements:* For master's, thesis; for doctorate, thesis/dissertation. *Entrance requirements:* For master's, DVM with B average or an honours degree in biological sciences; for doctorate, DVM or MSC degree, minimum B+ average. Additional exam requirements/recommendations for international students: Required—TOEFL (minimum score 550 paper-based). *Faculty research:* Pathogenesis; diseases of animals, wildlife, fish, and laboratory animals; parasitology; immunology; veterinary infectious diseases; laboratory animal science.

The University of Iowa, Roy J. and Lucille A. Carver College of Medicine and Graduate College, Graduate Programs in Medicine, Department of Pathology, Iowa City, IA 52242-1316. Offers MS. *Degree requirements:* For master's, thesis. *Entrance requirements:* For master's, GRE, minimum GPA of 3.0. Additional exam requirements/recommendations for international students: Required—TOEFL. Electronic applications accepted. *Faculty research:* Oncology, microbiology, vascular biology, immunology, neuroscience, virology, signaling and cell death.

The University of Kansas, University of Kansas Medical Center, School of Medicine, Department of Pathology and Laboratory Medicine, Kansas City, KS 66160. Offers MS, PhD, MD/PhD. *Accreditation:* NAACLS. *Faculty:* 24. *Students:* 11 full-time (5 women), 1 (woman) part-time; includes 1 minority (Asian, non-Hispanic/Latino), 7 international. Average age 30. 15 applicants, 20% accepted, 1 enrolled. In 2017, 1 master's, 6 doctorates awarded. Terminal master's awarded for partial completion of doctoral program. *Degree requirements:* For master's, thesis; for doctorate, one foreign language, comprehensive exam, thesis/dissertation. *Entrance requirements:* For master's, GRE, curriculum vitae, official transcripts for all undergraduate coursework, 3 reference letters; for doctorate, GRE, curriculum vitae, statement of research and career interests, official transcripts for all undergraduate and graduate coursework, 3 reference letters. Additional exam requirements/recommendations for international students: Required—TOEFL (preferred) or IELTS. *Application deadline:* For fall admission, 1/15 priority date for domestic and international students. Applications are processed on a rolling basis. Application fee: $60. Electronic applications accepted. *Financial support:* In 2017–18, 1 fellowship with full tuition reimbursement (averaging $31,000 per year), 10 research assistantships with full tuition reimbursements (averaging $24,000 per year), 2 teaching assistantships with full tuition reimbursements (averaging $24,000 per year) were awarded; Federal Work-Study, scholarships/grants, traineeships, and unspecified assistantships also available. Financial award application deadline: 3/1; financial award applicants required to submit FAFSA. *Faculty research:* Cancer biology, developmental biology and cell differentiation, stem cell biology, microbial and viral pathogenesis. *Total annual research expenditures:* $5.5 million. *Unit head:* Dr. Soumen Paul, Director, Pathology Graduate Program, 913-588-7236, Fax: 913-588-5242, E-mail: spaul2@kumc.edu.
Website: http://www.kumc.edu/school-of-medicine/pathology.html

University of Manitoba, Max Rady College of Medicine and Faculty of Graduate Studies, Graduate Programs in Medicine, Department of Pathology, Winnipeg, MB R3E 3P5, Canada. Offers M Sc. *Degree requirements:* For master's, thesis. *Entrance requirements:* For master's, B Sc honours degree. Additional exam requirements/recommendations for international students: Required—TOEFL (minimum score 550 paper-based; 80 iBT), IELTS (minimum score 6.5). *Faculty research:* Experimental hydrocephalus; brain development; stroke; developmental neurobiology; myelination in Rett Syndrome; glial migration during cortical development; growth factors and breast cancer; transgenic models of breast cancer; molecular genetics and cancer diagnosis; graft-vs-host disease; biology of natural killer cells; transplantation immunology.

University of Maryland, Baltimore, School of Medicine, Department of Pathology, Baltimore, MD 21201. Offers pathologists' assistant (MS). *Accreditation:* NAACLS. *Students:* 20 full-time (17 women); includes 8 minority (1 Black or African American, non-Hispanic/Latino; 2 Asian, non-Hispanic/Latino; 3 Hispanic/Latino; 2 Two or more races, non-Hispanic/Latino), 1 international. Average age 27. 94 applicants, 33% accepted, 10 enrolled. In 2017, 10 master's awarded. *Entrance requirements:* For master's, GRE General Test. Additional exam requirements/recommendations for international students: Required—TOEFL (minimum score 600 paper-based; 100 iBT); Recommended—IELTS (minimum score 8). *Application deadline:* For fall admission, 2/1 for domestic and international students. Application fee: $75. Electronic applications accepted. *Expenses:* Contact institution. *Financial support:* Application deadline: 3/1; applicants required to submit FAFSA. *Unit head:* Dr. Rudy Castellani, Program Director, 410-328-5555, Fax: 410-706-8414, E-mail: rcastellani@som.umaryland.edu. *Application contact:* Carlen Miller, Associate Program Director, 410-328-5555, Fax: 410-706-8414, E-mail: cmiller@som.umaryland.edu.
Website: http://medschool.umaryland.edu/pathology/pa/default.asp

University of Michigan, Rackham Graduate School, Program in Biomedical Sciences (PIBS), Program in Molecular and Cellular Pathology, Ann Arbor, MI 48109. Offers PhD. *Faculty:* 35 full-time (10 women). *Students:* 23 full-time (13 women); includes 7 minority (2 Black or African American, non-Hispanic/Latino; 2 Asian, non-Hispanic/Latino; 2 Hispanic/Latino; 1 Two or more races, non-Hispanic/Latino), 7 international. Average age 28. 57 applicants, 16% accepted, 5 enrolled. In 2017, 4 doctorates awarded. *Degree requirements:* For doctorate, comprehensive exam, thesis/dissertation, preliminary exam; oral defense of dissertation. *Entrance requirements:* For doctorate, GRE General Test, 3 letters of recommendation, research experience, personal statement. Additional exam requirements/recommendations for international students: Required—TOEFL (minimum score 84 iBT). *Application deadline:* For fall admission, 12/1 for domestic and international students. Application fee: $75 ($90 for international students). Electronic applications accepted. *Expenses:* Tuition, state resident: full-time $22,368; part-time $1201 per credit hour. Tuition, nonresident: full-time $45,156; part-time $2467 per credit hour. *Required fees:* $376 per term. Tuition and fees vary according to course load, degree level and program. *Financial support:* In 2017–18, 9 fellowships with full tuition reimbursements (averaging $30,600 per year), 14 research assistantships with full tuition reimbursements (averaging $30,600 per year) were awarded; scholarships/grants, traineeships, health care benefits, and unspecified assistantships also available. Financial award applicants required to submit FAFSA. *Faculty research:* Cancer biology, stem cell and developmental biology, immunopathology and inflammatory disease, epigenetics and gene regulation, cell death and regulation. *Total annual research expenditures:* $23.5 million. *Unit head:* Dr. Zaneta Nikolovska-Coleska, Associate Professor of Pathology/Director, 734-763-0846, Fax: 734-936-7361, E-mail: laszczem@med.umich.edu. *Application contact:* Jim Musgrave, Recruiting Coordinator, 734-615-1660, Fax: 734-647-7022, E-mail: jdmusg@umich.edu.
Website: http://www.pathology.med.umich.edu/

University of Mississippi Medical Center, School of Graduate Studies in the Health Sciences, Department of Pathology, Jackson, MS 39216-4505. Offers PhD, MD/PhD. *Accreditation:* NAACLS. *Degree requirements:* For doctorate, thesis/dissertation, first authored publication in peer-reviewed journal. *Entrance requirements:* For doctorate, GRE General Test, GRE Subject Test, minimum GPA of 3.0. Additional exam requirements/recommendations for international students: Required—TOEFL. *Faculty research:* Toll-like receptor expression and function in metastatic breast cancer patients, innate immunity, circulating tumor cells, natural killer cells, pro-inflammatory T cell transcriptional profile during progression of HIV-1 infection, renal allografts hinges on microvascular endothelium response, immunoregulatory gene expression affecting regulatory cells.

University of Missouri, School of Medicine and Office of Research and Graduate Studies, Graduate Programs in Medicine, Department of Pathology and Anatomical Sciences, Columbia, MO 65211. Offers MS, PhD. *Entrance requirements:* For master's, GRE (minimum Verbal and Analytical score of 1250), letters of recommendation, minimum GPA of 3.5. Additional exam requirements/recommendations for international students: Required—TOEFL. Electronic applications accepted. *Expenses:* Tuition, state resident: full-time $6480. Tuition, nonresident: full-time $17,744. *Required fees:* $1108. Tuition and fees vary according to course load, campus/location and program. *Unit head:* Dr. Lester Layfield, Chair. *Application contact:* Dr. Lester Layfield, Chair.
Website: http://pathology-anatomy.missouri.edu/

University of Nebraska Medical Center, Interdisciplinary Graduate Program in Biomedical Sciences, Immunology, Pathology and Infectious Disease Graduate Program, Omaha, NE 68198-5900. Offers MS, PhD. *Program availability:* Part-time. *Faculty:* 84 full-time (26 women). *Students:* 41 full-time (27 women), 4 part-time (3 women); includes 5 minority (1 Black or African American, non-Hispanic/Latino; 1 American Indian or Alaska Native, non-Hispanic/Latino; 3 Asian, non-Hispanic/Latino), 21 international. Average age 28. 21 applicants, 38% accepted, 7 enrolled. In 2017, 4 master's, 2 doctorates awarded. Terminal master's awarded for partial completion of doctoral program. *Degree requirements:* For master's, comprehensive exam, thesis; for doctorate, comprehensive exam, thesis/dissertation. *Entrance requirements:* For master's, previous course work in biology, chemistry, mathematics, and physics; for doctorate, GRE General Test, previous course work in biology, chemistry, mathematics, and physics. Additional exam requirements/recommendations for international students: Required—TOEFL (minimum score 550 paper-based; 90 iBT), IELTS (minimum score 6.5). *Application deadline:* For fall admission, 4/1 for domestic and international students; for spring admission, 10/1 for domestic and international students; for summer admission, 3/1 for domestic students, 1/1 for international students. Applications are processed on a rolling basis. Application fee: $60. Electronic applications accepted. *Expenses:* Tuition, state resident: full-time $8451; part-time $4225 per semester. Tuition, nonresident: full-time $24,219; part-time $11,295 per semester. *Required fees:* $589; $117 per term. *Financial support:* In 2017–18, 5 students received support, including 2 fellowships with full tuition reimbursements available (averaging $24,000 per year), 3 research assistantships with full tuition reimbursements available (averaging $24,000 per year); scholarships/grants, health care benefits, and unspecified assistantships also available. Financial award application deadline: 3/1; financial award applicants required to submit FAFSA. *Faculty research:* Infectious diseases, cancer biology, immunobiology, molecular virology, molecular genetics. *Unit head:* Dr. Rakesh K. Singh, Chair, Graduate Committee, 402-559-9949, Fax: 402-559-5900, E-mail: rsingh@unmc.edu. *Application contact:* Tuire Cechin, Graduate Program Coordinator, 402-559-4042, Fax: 402-559-5900, E-mail: tcechin@unmc.edu.
Website: http://www.unmc.edu/pathology/

University of New Mexico, Graduate Studies, Health Sciences Center, Program in Biomedical Sciences, Albuquerque, NM 87131-5196. Offers biochemistry and molecular biology (MS, PhD); cell biology and physiology (MS, PhD); molecular genetics and microbiology (MS, PhD); neuroscience (MS, PhD); pathology (MS, PhD); toxicology (MS, PhD). *Program availability:* Part-time. *Students:* Average age 29. 61 applicants, 16% accepted, 10 enrolled. In 2017, 11 master's, 14 doctorates awarded. Terminal master's awarded for partial completion of doctoral program. *Degree requirements:* For master's, thesis; for doctorate, comprehensive exam, thesis/dissertation, qualifying exam at the end of year 1/core curriculum. *Entrance requirements:* For master's and doctorate, GRE General Test, minimum undergraduate GPA of 3.0. Additional exam requirements/recommendations for international students: Required—TOEFL. *Application deadline:* For fall admission, 3/1 priority date for domestic and international students. Applications are processed on a rolling basis. Application fee: $50. Electronic applications accepted. *Financial support:* Fellowships, research assistantships with full tuition reimbursements, teaching assistantships, career-related internships or fieldwork, Federal Work-Study, institutionally sponsored loans, scholarships/grants, traineeships, health care benefits, and unspecified assistantships available. Financial award application deadline: 1/1; financial award applicants required to submit FAFSA. *Faculty research:* Infectious disease/immunity, cancer biology, cardiovascular and metabolic diseases, brain and behavioral illness, environmental health. *Unit head:* Dr. Helen J. Hathaway, Program Director, 505-272-1887, Fax: 505-272-2412, E-mail: hhathaway@salud.unm.edu. *Application contact:* Mary Fenton, Admissions Coordinator, 505-272-1887, Fax: 505-272-2412, E-mail: mfenton@salud.unm.edu.

The University of North Carolina at Chapel Hill, School of Medicine and Graduate School, Graduate Programs in Medicine, Department of Pathology and Laboratory Medicine, Chapel Hill, NC 27599-7525. Offers experimental pathology (PhD). *Accreditation:* NAACLS. *Degree requirements:* For doctorate, comprehensive exam, thesis/dissertation, oral exam, proposal defense. *Entrance requirements:* For doctorate, GRE General Test. Additional exam requirements/recommendations for international students: Required—TOEFL (minimum score 550 paper-based). Electronic applications accepted. *Faculty research:* Carcinogenesis, mutagenesis and cancer biology; molecular biology, genetics and animal models of human disease; cardiovascular biology, hemostasis, and thrombosis; immunology and infectious disease; progenitor cell research.

University of Oklahoma Health Sciences Center, College of Medicine and Graduate College, Graduate Programs in Medicine, Department of Pathology, Oklahoma City, OK 73190. Offers PhD. *Degree requirements:* For doctorate, thesis/dissertation. *Entrance requirements:* For doctorate, GRE General Test, 3 letters of recommendation. Additional exam requirements/recommendations for international students: Required—TOEFL. *Faculty research:* Molecular pathology, tissue response in disease, anatomic pathology, immunopathology, histocytochemistry.

University of Pittsburgh, School of Medicine, Graduate Programs in Medicine, Cellular and Molecular Pathology Graduate Program, Pittsburgh, PA 15260. Offers PhD. *Accreditation:* NAACLS. *Faculty:* 78 full-time (22 women). *Students:* 25 full-time (15 women); includes 4 minority (1 Asian, non-Hispanic/Latino; 2 Hispanic/Latino; 1 Two or more races, non-Hispanic/Latino), 7 international. Average age 27. 350 applicants, 21% accepted, 16 enrolled. In 2017, 4 doctorates awarded. *Degree requirements:* For doctorate, comprehensive exam, thesis/dissertation. *Entrance requirements:* For doctorate, GRE General Test, minimum GPA of 3.2, 3 letters of recommendation, official transcripts, baccalaureate degree. Additional exam requirements/recommendations for international students: Required—TOEFL (minimum score 600 paper-based; 100 iBT), IELTS (minimum score 7). *Application deadline:* For fall admission, 12/1 priority date for domestic and international students. Application fee: $50. Electronic applications accepted. *Expenses:* $26,782 in-state, $42,006 out-of-state. *Financial support:* In 2017–18, 25 students received support, including 6 fellowships with full tuition reimbursements available (averaging $29,500 per year), 13 research assistantships with full tuition reimbursements available (averaging $29,500 per year); traineeships also available. *Faculty research:* Stem cells, fibrosis, inmate immunity, tissue regeneration. *Unit head:* Dr. Wendy Mars, Director, 412-648-9690, Fax: 412-648-1916, E-mail: wmars@pitt.edu. *Application contact:* Carol Williams, Admissions and Recruiting Manager, 412-648-9003, Fax: 412-648-1077, E-mail: gradstudies@medschool.pitt.edu.
Website: http://www.gradbiomed.pitt.edu

University of Prince Edward Island, Atlantic Veterinary College, Graduate Program in Veterinary Medicine, Charlottetown, PE C1A 4P3, Canada. Offers anatomy (M Sc, PhD); bacteriology (M Sc, PhD); clinical pharmacology (M Sc, PhD); clinical sciences (M Sc, PhD); epidemiology (M Sc, PhD), including reproduction; fish health (M Sc, PhD); food animal nutrition (M Sc, PhD); immunology (M Sc, PhD); microanatomy (M Sc, PhD); parasitology (M Sc, PhD); pathology (M Sc, PhD); pharmacology (M Sc, PhD); physiology (M Sc, PhD); toxicology (M Sc, PhD); veterinary science (M Vet Sc); virology (M Sc, PhD). *Program availability:* Part-time. *Degree requirements:* For master's, thesis; for doctorate, thesis/dissertation. *Entrance requirements:* For master's, DVM, B Sc honors degree, or equivalent; for doctorate, M Sc. Additional exam requirements/recommendations for international students: Required—TOEFL (minimum score 550 paper-based; 80 iBT). *Expenses:* Contact institution. *Faculty research:* Animal health management, infectious diseases, fin fish and shellfish health, basic biomedical sciences, ecosystem health.

University of Rochester, School of Medicine and Dentistry, Graduate Programs in Medicine and Dentistry, Department of Pathology and Laboratory Medicine, Rochester, NY 14627. Offers pathology (PhD). *Degree requirements:* For doctorate, variable foreign language requirement, thesis/dissertation, qualifying exam. *Entrance requirements:* For doctorate, GRE General Test, GRE Subject Test.

University of Saskatchewan, College of Medicine, Department of Pathology, Saskatoon, SK S7N 5A2, Canada. Offers M Sc, PhD. *Degree requirements:* For master's, thesis; for doctorate, thesis/dissertation. *Entrance requirements:* Additional exam requirements/recommendations for international students: Required—TOEFL.

University of Saskatchewan, Western College of Veterinary Medicine and College of Graduate Studies and Research, Graduate Programs in Veterinary Medicine, Department of Veterinary Pathology, Saskatoon, SK S7N 5A2, Canada. Offers M Sc, M Vet Sc, PhD. *Degree requirements:* For master's, thesis; for doctorate, comprehensive exam (for some programs), thesis/dissertation. *Entrance requirements:* Additional exam requirements/recommendations for international students: Required—TOEFL or IELTS (minimum score 6.5). Electronic applications accepted. *Faculty research:* Thyroid, oncology, immunology/infectious diseases, vaccinology.

University of Southern California, Keck School of Medicine and Graduate School, Graduate Programs in Medicine, Department of Pathology, Los Angeles, CA 90033. Offers experimental and molecular pathology (MS). *Faculty:* 32 full-time (6 women). *Students:* 13 full-time (5 women); includes 5 minority (2 Asian, non-Hispanic/Latino; 3 Hispanic/Latino), 2 international. Average age 27. 5 applicants, 40% accepted, 2 enrolled. In 2017, 2 master's awarded. *Degree requirements:* For master's, experiment-based thesis or theory-based scholarly review. *Entrance requirements:* For master's, GRE General Test, minimum GPA of 3.0. Additional exam requirements/recommendations for international students: Required—TOEFL (minimum score 600 paper-based; 100 iBT); Recommended—IELTS (minimum score 6.5). *Application deadline:* For fall admission, 6/15 priority date for domestic and international students; for spring admission, 12/1 for domestic and international students. Applications are processed on a rolling basis. Application fee: $90. Electronic applications accepted. *Financial support:* Federal Work-Study and scholarships/grants available. *Faculty research:* Cellular and molecular biology of cancer; chemical carcinogenesis; virology; stem cell and developmental pathology; liver and pulmonary diseases; circulatory, endocrine, and neurodegenerative diseases. *Total annual research expenditures:* $6.9 million. *Unit head:* Dr. Michael E. Selsted, Chair, 323-442-1180, Fax: 323-442-3049, E-mail: selsted@usc.edu. *Application contact:* Lisa A. Doumak, Student Services Assistant, 323-442-1168, Fax: 323-442-3049, E-mail: doumak@med.usc.edu.
Website: http://keck.usc.edu/pathology/training-education/

University of South Florida, Morsani College of Medicine and College of Graduate Studies, Graduate Programs in Medical Sciences, Tampa, FL 33620-9951. Offers advanced athletic training (MS); athletic training (MS); bioinformatics and computational biology (MSBCB); biotechnology (MSB); health informatics (MSHI); medical sciences (MSMS, PhD), including aging and neuroscience (MSMS), allergy, immunology and infectious disease (PhD), anatomy, biochemistry and molecular biology, clinical and translational research, health science (MSMS), interdisciplinary medical sciences (MSMS), medical microbiology and immunology (MSMS), metabolic and nutritional medicine (MSMS), microbiology and immunology (PhD), molecular medicine, molecular pharmacology and physiology (PhD), neuroscience (PhD), pathology and cell biology (PhD), women's health (MSMS). *Students:* 372 full-time (212 women), 216 part-time (142 women); includes 257 minority (78 Black or African American, non-Hispanic/Latino; 1 American Indian or Alaska Native, non-Hispanic/Latino; 79 Asian, non-Hispanic/Latino; 84 Hispanic/Latino; 15 Two or more races, non-Hispanic/Latino), 62 international. Average age 28. 1,048 applicants, 46% accepted, 309 enrolled. In 2017, 351 master's, 56 doctorates awarded. Terminal master's awarded for partial completion of doctoral program. *Degree requirements:* For master's, comprehensive exam, thesis; for doctorate, comprehensive exam, thesis/dissertation. *Entrance requirements:* For master's, GRE General Test or GMAT, bachelor's degree or equivalent from regionally-accredited university with minimum GPA of 3.0 in upper-division sciences coursework; prerequisites in general biology, general chemistry, general physics, organic chemistry, quantitative analysis, and integral and differential calculus; for doctorate, GRE General Test, bachelor's degree from regionally-accredited university with minimum GPA of 3.0 in upper-division sciences coursework; 3 letters of recommendation; personal interview; 1-2 page personal statement; prerequisites in biology, chemistry, physics, organic chemistry, quantitative analysis, and integral/differential calculus. Additional exam requirements/recommendations for international students: Required—TOEFL (minimum score 550 paper-based; 79 iBT) or IELTS (minimum score 6.5). *Application deadline:* For fall admission, 2/1 priority date for domestic students, 2/1 for international students. Application fee: $30. Electronic applications accepted. *Expenses:* Contact institution. *Financial support:* In 2017–18, 109 students received support. *Faculty research:* Anatomy, biochemistry, cancer biology, cardiovascular disease, cell biology, immunology, microbiology, molecular biology, neuroscience, pharmacology, physiology. *Total annual research expenditures:* $45.3 million. *Unit head:* Dr. Michael Barber, Professor/Associate Dean for Graduate and Postdoctoral Affairs, 813-974-9908, Fax: 813-974-4317, E-mail: mbarber@health.usf.edu. *Application contact:* Dr. Eric Bennett, Graduate Director, PhD Program in Medical Sciences, 813-974-1545, Fax: 813-974-4317, E-mail: esbennet@health.usf.edu.
Website: http://health.usf.edu/nocms/medicine/graduatestudies/

The University of Tennessee Health Science Center, College of Health Professions, Memphis, TN 38163-0002. Offers audiology (MS, Au D); clinical laboratory science (MSCLS); cytopathology practice (MCP); health informatics and information management (MHIIM); occupational therapy (MOT); physical therapy (DPT, ScDPT); physician assistant (MMS); speech-language pathology (MS). *Accreditation:* AOTA; APTA. *Program availability:* Part-time, evening/weekend, online learning. Terminal master's awarded for partial completion of doctoral program. *Degree requirements:* For master's, comprehensive exam, thesis; for doctorate, comprehensive exam, residency. *Entrance requirements:* For master's, GRE (MOT, MSCLS), minimum GPA of 3.0, 3 letters of reference, national accreditation (MSCLS), GRE if GPA is less than 3.0 (MCP); for doctorate, GRE. Additional exam requirements/recommendations for international students: Required—TOEFL (minimum score 550 paper-based; 80 iBT). Electronic applications accepted. *Expenses:* Contact institution. *Faculty research:* Gait deviation, muscular dystrophy and strength, hemophilia and exercise, pediatric neurology, self-efficacy.

The University of Texas Medical Branch, Graduate School of Biomedical Sciences, Program in Experimental Pathology, Galveston, TX 77555. Offers PhD. *Accreditation:* NAACLS. *Degree requirements:* For doctorate, thesis/dissertation. *Entrance requirements:* For doctorate, GRE General Test. Additional exam requirements/recommendations for international students: Required—TOEFL (minimum score 550 paper-based). Electronic applications accepted.

The University of Toledo, College of Graduate Studies, College of Medicine and Life Sciences, Department of Pathology, Toledo, OH 43606-3390. Offers pathology (Certificate); pathology assistant (MSBS). *Accreditation:* NAACLS. *Entrance requirements:* For degree, second-year medical student in good academic standing with recommendation by UT Medical School. Electronic applications accepted.

University of Utah, School of Medicine and Graduate School, Graduate Programs in Medicine, Department of Pathology, Salt Lake City, UT 84112-1107. Offers experimental pathology (PhD); laboratory medicine and biomedical science (MS). PhD offered after acceptance into the combined Program in Molecular Biology. *Degree requirements:* For doctorate, comprehensive exam, thesis/dissertation. *Entrance requirements:* For doctorate, GRE, minimum GPA of 3.0. *Faculty research:* Immunology, cell biology, signal transduction, gene regulation, receptor biology.

University of Vermont, The Robert Larner, MD College of Medicine and Graduate College, Graduate Programs in Medicine, Department of Pathology and Laboratory Medicine, Burlington, VT 05405. Offers MS. *Accreditation:* NAACLS. *Students:* 2 (both women). Average age 33. 3 applicants, 67% accepted, 2 enrolled. Terminal master's awarded for partial completion of doctoral program. *Entrance requirements:* For master's, GRE General Test or MCAT. Additional exam requirements/recommendations for international students: Required—TOEFL (minimum score 550 paper-based, 90 iBT) or IELTS (6.5). *Application deadline:* For fall admission, 3/15 for domestic and international students. Application fee: $65. Electronic applications accepted. *Expenses:* Tuition, state resident: full-time $11,628; part-time $646 per credit. Tuition, nonresident: full-time $29,340; part-time $1630 per credit. *Required fees:* $1994; $10 per credit. Tuition and fees vary according to course load and program. *Financial support:* Fellowships, research assistantships, and traineeships available. Financial award application deadline: 3/1. *Faculty research:* Molecular epidemiology, redox biology, histology. *Unit head:* Dr. Debra Leonard, Chair, 802-656-0359. *Application contact:* Dr. Vikas Leonard, Assistant Professor, 802-656-9625, E-mail: vikas.anathy@med.uvm.edu.
Website: http://www.med.uvm.edu/pathology/education_old/graduate-students

University of Virginia, School of Medicine, Department of Pathology, Charlottesville, VA 22903. Offers PhD. *Students:* 26 full-time (14 women); includes 5 minority (4 Black or African American, non-Hispanic/Latino; 1 Hispanic/Latino), 2 international. Average age 28. In 2017, 4 doctorates awarded. *Degree requirements:* For doctorate, thesis/dissertation, oral defense of thesis. *Entrance requirements:* For doctorate, GRE General Test; GRE Subject Test (recommended), 2 letters of recommendation. Additional exam requirements/recommendations for international students: Required—TOEFL. *Application deadline:* For fall admission, 1/15 for domestic and international students. *Financial support:* Application deadline: 1/15. *Unit head:* Christopher A. Moskaluk, Chair, Fax: 434-924-9312, E-mail: cam5p@virginia.edu.
Website: http://www.medicine.virginia.edu/clinical/departments/pathology/Education/mcbd

University of Washington, Graduate School, School of Medicine, Graduate Programs in Medicine, Department of Pathology, Seattle, WA 98195. Offers experimental and molecular pathology (PhD). *Degree requirements:* For doctorate, thesis/dissertation. *Entrance requirements:* For doctorate, GRE General Test. *Faculty research:* Viral oncogenesis, aging, mutagenesis and repair, extracellular matrix biology, vascular biology.

The University of Western Ontario, Faculty of Graduate Studies, Biosciences Division, Department of Pathology, London, ON N6A 5B8, Canada. Offers M Sc, PhD. *Degree requirements:* For master's, thesis; for doctorate, comprehensive exam, thesis/dissertation. *Entrance requirements:* For master's and doctorate, minimum B+ average, honors degree. Additional exam requirements/recommendations for international students: Required—TOEFL. *Faculty research:* Heavy metal toxicology, transplant pathology, immunopathology, immunological cancers, neurochemistry, aging and dementia, cancer pathology.

University of Wisconsin–Madison, School of Medicine and Public Health, Cellular and Molecular Pathology Graduate Program, Madison, WI 53706. Offers PhD. *Application contact:* Joanne Thornton, Graduate Program Coordinator, 608-262-2665, E-mail: jmthornt@wisc.edu.
Website: http://www.cmp.wisc.edu/

Vanderbilt University, School of Medicine, Department of Molecular Pathology and Immunology, Nashville, TN 37240-1001. Offers PhD, MD/PhD. *Faculty:* 32 full-time (10 women). *Students:* 14 full-time (8 women); includes 3 minority (1 American Indian or Alaska Native, non-Hispanic/Latino; 1 Hispanic/Latino; 1 Two or more races, non-Hispanic/Latino), 2 international. Average age 29. In 2017, 2 doctorates awarded. *Degree requirements:* For doctorate, thesis/dissertation, qualifying and final exams. *Entrance requirements:* For doctorate, GRE General Test. Additional exam requirements/recommendations for international students: Required—TOEFL (minimum score 570 paper-based; 88 iBT). *Application deadline:* For fall admission, 1/15 for domestic and international students. Application fee: $0. Electronic applications accepted. *Financial support:* Fellowships with full tuition reimbursements, research

assistantships with full tuition reimbursements, Federal Work-Study, institutionally sponsored loans, traineeships, health care benefits, and tuition waivers (partial) available. Financial award application deadline: 1/15; financial award applicants required to submit CSS PROFILE or FAFSA. *Faculty research:* Vascular biology and biochemistry, tumor pathology, the immune response, inflammation and repair, the biology of the extracellular matrix in response to disease processes, the pathogenesis of infectious agents, the regulation of gene expression in disease. *Unit head:* Lorie Franklin, Administrative Assistant/Assistant Director of Graduate Studies, 615-343-8324, Fax: 615-322-0576, E-mail: lorie.franklin@vanderbilt.edu. *Application contact:* Walter B. Bieschke, Program Coordinator for Graduate Admissions, 615-342-0236, E-mail: vandygrad@vanderbilt.edu.
Website: https://medschool.vanderbilt.edu/igp/molecular-pathology-immunology

Wayne State University, School of Medicine, Office of Biomedical Graduate Programs, Detroit, MI 48202. Offers anatomy and cell biology (MS, PhD); basic medical sciences (MS); biochemistry and molecular biology (MS, PhD); cancer biology (MS, PhD); clinical and translational science (Graduate Certificate); family medicine and public health sciences (MPH, Graduate Certificate), including public health practice; genetic counseling (MS); immunology and microbiology (MS, PhD); medical physics (MS, PhD, Graduate Certificate); medical research (MS); molecular medicine and genomics (MS, PhD), including molecular genetics and genomics; pathology (PhD); pharmacology (MS, PhD); physiology (MS, PhD), including physiology, reproductive sciences (PhD); psychiatry and behavioral neurosciences (PhD), including translational neuroscience; MD/MPH; MD/PhD; MPH/MA; MSW/MPH. *Program availability:* Part-time, evening/weekend. *Students:* 268 full-time (152 women), 117 part-time (59 women); includes 108 minority (19 Black or African American, non-Hispanic/Latino; 1 American Indian or Alaska Native, non-Hispanic/Latino; 62 Asian, non-Hispanic/Latino; 9 Hispanic/Latino; 17 Two or more races, non-Hispanic/Latino), 48 international. Average age 26. 1,133 applicants, 21% accepted, 151 enrolled. In 2017, 70 master's, 25 doctorates, 10 other advanced degrees awarded. Terminal master's awarded for partial completion of doctoral program. *Degree requirements:* For master's, thesis (for some programs); for doctorate, thesis/dissertation. *Entrance requirements:* For master's, doctorate, and Graduate Certificate, GRE. Additional exam requirements/recommendations for international students: Required—TOEFL (minimum score 550 paper-based; 100 iBT), Michigan English Language Assessment Battery (minimum score 85); Recommended—IELTS (minimum score 6.5), TWE (minimum score 5.5). *Application deadline:* For fall admission, 2/1 for domestic and international students. Applications are processed on a rolling basis. Application fee: $50. Electronic applications accepted. *Expenses:* Contact institution. *Financial support:* In 2017–18, 177 students received support, including 64 fellowships with full tuition reimbursements available (averaging $24,388 per year), 79 research assistantships with full tuition reimbursements available (averaging $26,894 per year); scholarships/grants, traineeships, and health care benefits also available. *Faculty research:* Cancer biology, neurosciences, vision sciences, molecular biology, pathology, physiology, pharmacology, public health, medical physics. *Unit head:* Dr. Daniel A. Walz, Associate Dean for Biomedical Graduate Programs, 313-577-1455, Fax: 313-577-8796, E-mail: gradprogs@med.wayne.edu.
Website: https://www.med.wayne.edu/biomedical-graduate-programs/

West Virginia University, School of Medicine, Morgantown, WV 26506-9600. Offers biochemistry and molecular biology (PhD); biomedical science (MS); cancer cell biology (PhD); cellular and integrative physiology (PhD); exercise physiology (MS, PhD); health sciences (MS); immunology (PhD); medicine (MD); occupational therapy (MOT); pathologists assistant (MHS); physical therapy (DPT). *Program availability:* Part-time, evening/weekend. *Students:* 781 full-time (440 women), 25 part-time (13 women); includes 140 minority (15 Black or African American, non-Hispanic/Latino; 1 American Indian or Alaska Native, non-Hispanic/Latino; 68 Asian, non-Hispanic/Latino; 37 Hispanic/Latino; 1 Native Hawaiian or other Pacific Islander, non-Hispanic/Latino; 18 Two or more races, non-Hispanic/Latino), 19 international. *Entrance requirements:* Additional exam requirements/recommendations for international students: Required—TOEFL. *Application deadline:* Applications are processed on a rolling basis. Application fee: $60. Electronic applications accepted. *Expenses:* Contact institution. *Financial support:* Fellowships, research assistantships, teaching assistantships, career-related internships or fieldwork, Federal Work-Study, institutionally sponsored loans, health care benefits, tuition waivers (full and partial), and administrative assistantships available. Financial award applicants required to submit FAFSA. *Unit head:* Dr. Clay Marsh, Executive Dean, 304-293-6607, Fax: 304-293-6627, E-mail: clay.marsh@hsc.wvu.edu. *Application contact:* Lisa M. Salati, Assistant Vice President, Graduate Education, 304-293-7759, Fax: 304-293-3080, E-mail: lsalati@hsc.wvu.edu.
Website: https://medicine.hsc.wvu.edu

Yale University, Graduate School of Arts and Sciences, Department of Experimental Pathology, New Haven, CT 06520. Offers MS, PhD. *Degree requirements:* For doctorate, thesis/dissertation, qualifying exam. *Entrance requirements:* For doctorate, GRE General Test.

Section 17
Pharmacology and Toxicology

This section contains a directory of institutions offering graduate work in pharmacology and toxicology. Additional information about programs listed in the directory but not augmented by an in-depth entry may be obtained by writing directly to the dean of a graduate school or chair of a department at the address given in the directory.

For programs offering related work, see also in this book *Biochemistry; Biological and Biomedical Sciences; Cell, Molecular, and Structural Biology; Ecology, Environmental Biology, and Evolutionary Biology; Genetics, Developmental Biology, and Reproductive Biology; Neuroscience and Neurobiology; Nutrition; Pathology and Pathobiology; Pharmacy and Pharmaceutical Sciences; Physiology; Public Health;* and *Veterinary Medicine and Sciences.* In the other guides in this series:

Graduate Programs in the Humanities, Arts & Social Sciences
See *Psychology and Counseling*

Graduate Programs in the Physical Sciences, Mathematics, Agricultural Sciences, the Environment & Natural Resources
See *Chemistry* and *Environmental Sciences and Management*

Graduate Programs in Engineering & Applied Sciences
See *Chemical Engineering* and *Civil and Environmental Engineering*

CONTENTS

Program Directories

Featured School: Display and Close-Up

See:

Molecular Pharmacology

Albert Einstein College of Medicine, Graduate Programs in the Biomedical Sciences, Department of Molecular Pharmacology, Bronx, NY 10461. Offers PhD, MD/PhD. *Degree requirements:* For doctorate, thesis/dissertation. *Entrance requirements:* For doctorate, GRE General Test. Additional exam requirements/recommendations for international students: Required—TOEFL. *Application deadline:* For fall admission, 1/15 for domestic students. Application fee: $0. *Financial support:* Fellowships available. *Faculty research:* Effects of drugs on macromolecules, enzyme systems, cell morphology and function. *Unit head:* Dr. Jonathan M. Backer, Chair, 718-430-2153. *Application contact:* Sheila Cleeton, Executive Director and Registrar, Einstein Graduate Division, 718-430-2128, E-mail: sheila.cleeton@einstein.yu.edu.
Website: http://www.einstein.yu.edu/departments/molecular-pharmacology/

Brown University, Graduate School, Division of Biology and Medicine, Department of Molecular Pharmacology, Physiology and Biotechnology, Providence, RI 02912. Offers biomedical engineering (Sc M, PhD); biotechnology (PhD); molecular pharmacology and physiology (PhD); MD/PhD. *Degree requirements:* For doctorate, thesis/dissertation, preliminary exam. *Entrance requirements:* For master's and doctorate, GRE General Test, GRE Subject Test. Additional exam requirements/recommendations for international students: Required—TOEFL. Electronic applications accepted. *Faculty research:* Structural biology, antiplatelet drugs, nicotinic receptor structure/function.

Harvard University, Graduate School of Arts and Sciences, Division of Medical Sciences, Boston, MA 02115. Offers biological chemistry and molecular pharmacology (PhD); cell biology (PhD); genetics (PhD); microbiology and molecular genetics (PhD); pathology (PhD), including experimental pathology. *Degree requirements:* For doctorate, thesis/dissertation. *Entrance requirements:* For doctorate, GRE General Test, GRE Subject Test. Additional exam requirements/recommendations for international students: Required—TOEFL.

Loyola University Chicago, Graduate School, Integrated Program in Biomedical Sciences, Maywood, IL 60141. Offers biochemistry and molecular biology (MS, PhD); cell and molecular physiology (MS, PhD); infectious disease and immunology (MS); integrative cell biology (MS, PhD); microbiology and immunology (MS, PhD); molecular pharmacology and therapeutics (MS, PhD); neuroscience (MS, PhD). *Faculty:* 84 full-time (32 women). *Students:* 126 full-time (65 women), 1 (woman) part-time; includes 36 minority (5 Black or African American, non-Hispanic/Latino; 14 Asian, non-Hispanic/Latino; 14 Hispanic/Latino; 3 Two or more races, non-Hispanic/Latino), 13 international. Average age 26. 748 applicants, 34% accepted, 124 enrolled. In 2017, 41 master's, 18 doctorates awarded. *Degree requirements:* For master's, thesis; for doctorate, comprehensive exam, thesis/dissertation. *Entrance requirements:* For doctorate, GRE. Additional exam requirements/recommendations for international students: Required—TOEFL (minimum score 94 iBT), IELTS (minimum score 7.5). *Application deadline:* For fall admission, 2/7 for domestic students. Applications are processed on a rolling basis. Electronic applications accepted. *Expenses:* Contact institution. *Financial support:* In 2017–18, 20 students received support. Schmitt Fellowships and yearly tuition scholarships (averaging $25,032) available. Financial award application deadline: 6/15; financial award applicants required to submit FAFSA. *Unit head:* Dr. Leanne L. Cribbs, Associate Dean, Graduate Education, 708-327-2817, Fax: 708-216-8216, E-mail: lcribbs@luc.edu. *Application contact:* Margarita Quesada, Graduate Program Secretary, 708-216-3532, Fax: 708-216-8216, E-mail: mquesad@luc.edu.
Website: http://ssom.luc.edu/graduate_school/degree-programs/ipbsphd/

Mayo Clinic Graduate School of Biomedical Sciences, Program in Molecular Pharmacology and Experimental Therapeutics, Rochester, MN 55905. Offers MS, PhD. *Faculty:* 19 full-time (1 woman). *Students:* 38 full-time (24 women); includes 13 minority (2 Black or African American, non-Hispanic/Latino; 1 American Indian or Alaska Native, non-Hispanic/Latino; 8 Asian, non-Hispanic/Latino; 2 Hispanic/Latino). 30 applicants, 23% accepted, 6 enrolled. Terminal master's awarded for partial completion of doctoral program. *Degree requirements:* For master's, thesis; for doctorate, comprehensive exam, thesis/dissertation, oral defense of dissertation, qualifying oral and written exam. *Entrance requirements:* For doctorate, GRE, 1 year of chemistry, biology, calculus, and physics. Additional exam requirements/recommendations for international students: Required—TOEFL. *Application deadline:* For fall admission, 12/1 for domestic and international students. Application fee: $50. Electronic applications accepted. *Financial support:* Fellowships with full tuition reimbursements available. *Faculty research:* Patch clamping, G-proteins, pharmacogenetics, receptor-induced transcriptional events, cholinesterase biology. *Unit head:* Dr. Richard Weinshilboum, Director, 507-284-4308, E-mail: weinshilboum.richard@mayo.edu. *Application contact:* Sarah E Giese, Admissions Coordinator, 507-538-1160, E-mail: phd.training@mayo.edu.
Website: http://www.mayo.edu.mgs/

Medical University of South Carolina, College of Graduate Studies, Program in Cell and Molecular Pharmacology and Experimental Therapeutics, Charleston, SC 29425. Offers MS, PhD, DMD/PhD, MD/PhD. Terminal master's awarded for partial completion of doctoral program. *Degree requirements:* For master's, thesis; for doctorate, comprehensive exam, thesis/dissertation, oral and written exams. *Entrance requirements:* For master's, GRE General Test; for doctorate, GRE General Test, interview, minimum GPA of 3.0. Additional exam requirements/recommendations for international students: Required—TOEFL (minimum score 600 paper-based; 100 iBT). Electronic applications accepted. *Faculty research:* Cancer drug discovery and development, growth factor receptor signaling, regulation of G-protein signaling, redox signal transduction, proteomics and mass spectrometry.

New York University, School of Medicine and Graduate School of Arts and Science, Sackler Institute of Graduate Biomedical Sciences, New York, NY 10016. Offers biomedical imaging and technology (PhD); biostatistics (PhD); cellular and molecular biology (PhD); developmental genetics (PhD); epidemiology (PhD); genome integrity (PhD); immunology and inflammation (PhD); microbiology (PhD); molecular biophysics (PhD); molecular oncology and tumor immunology (PhD); molecular pharmacology (PhD); neuroscience and physiology (PhD), including immunology, molecular oncology; stem cell biology (PhD); systems and computational biomedicine (PhD); MD/PhD. *Faculty:* 207 full-time (51 women). *Students:* 236 full-time (138 women), 1 part-time (0 women); includes 68 minority (13 Black or African American, non-Hispanic/Latino; 26 Asian, non-Hispanic/Latino; 28 Hispanic/Latino; 1 Native Hawaiian or other Pacific Islander, non-Hispanic/Latino), 79 international. Average age 27. 761 applicants, 18% accepted, 59 enrolled. In 2017, 35 doctorates awarded. *Degree requirements:* For doctorate, comprehensive exam, thesis/dissertation, qualifying exam; thesis defense. *Entrance requirements:* For doctorate, GRE. Additional exam requirements/recommendations for international students: Required—TOEFL, IELTS. *Application deadline:* For fall admission, 12/1 for domestic and international students. Applications are processed on a rolling basis. Application fee: $100. Electronic applications accepted. Application fee is waived when completed online. *Expenses:* Contact institution. *Financial support:* Health care benefits, tuition waivers (full), and unspecified assistantships available. *Faculty research:* Biomedical sciences. *Unit head:* Dr. Naoko Tanese, Associate Dean for Biomedical Sciences/Director, Sackler Institute, 212-263-8945, E-mail: naoko.tanese@nyumc.org. *Application contact:* Jessica Dong, Program Manager, 212-263-5648, E-mail: sackler-info@nyumc.org.
Website: https://med.nyu.edu/research/sackler-institute-graduate-biomedical-sciences/

Purdue University, College of Pharmacy and Graduate School, Graduate Programs in Pharmacy and Pharmacal Sciences, Department of Medicinal Chemistry and Molecular Pharmacology, West Lafayette, IN 47907. Offers biophysical and computational chemistry (PhD); cancer research (PhD); immunology and infectious disease (PhD); medicinal biochemistry and molecular biology (PhD); medicinal chemistry and chemical biology (PhD); molecular pharmacology (PhD); neuropharmacology, neurodegeneration, and neurotoxicity (PhD); systems biology and functional genomics (PhD). *Faculty:* 26 full-time (5 women). *Students:* 52 full-time (22 women), 3 part-time (all women); includes 4 minority (1 Black or African American, non-Hispanic/Latino; 2 Asian, non-Hispanic/Latino; 1 Hispanic/Latino), 29 international. Average age 26. 151 applicants, 19% accepted, 13 enrolled. In 2017, 18 doctorates awarded. *Degree requirements:* For doctorate, thesis/dissertation. *Entrance requirements:* For doctorate, GRE General Test; GRE Subject Test in biology, biochemistry, and chemistry (recommended), minimum undergraduate GPA of 3.0. Additional exam requirements/recommendations for international students: Required—TOEFL (minimum score 550 paper-based; 77 iBT); Recommended—TWE. *Application deadline:* For fall admission, 2/1 for domestic and international students. Applications are processed on a rolling basis. Application fee: $60 ($75 for international students). Electronic applications accepted. *Financial support:* Fellowships, research assistantships, teaching assistantships, and traineeships available. Support available to part-time students. Financial award applicants required to submit FAFSA. *Faculty research:* Drug design and development, cancer research, drug synthesis and analysis, chemical pharmacology, environmental toxicology. *Unit head:* Zhong-Yin Zhang, Head, 765-494-1403, E-mail: zhang-yn@purdue.edu. *Application contact:* Delayne Graham, Graduate Contact, 765-494-1362, E-mail: dkgraham@purdue.edu.

Rosalind Franklin University of Medicine and Science, School of Graduate and Postdoctoral Studies - Interdisciplinary Graduate Program in Biomedical Sciences, Department of Cellular and Molecular Pharmacology, North Chicago, IL 60064-3095. Offers MS, PhD, MD/PhD. Terminal master's awarded for partial completion of doctoral program. *Degree requirements:* For master's, comprehensive exam, thesis; for doctorate, comprehensive exam, thesis/dissertation. *Entrance requirements:* For master's and doctorate, GRE General Test. Additional exam requirements/recommendations for international students: Required—TOEFL, TWE. Electronic applications accepted. *Faculty research:* Control of gene expression in higher organisms, molecular mechanism of action of growth factors and hormones, hormonal regulation in brain neuropsychopharmacology.

Rutgers University–New Brunswick, Graduate School of Biomedical Sciences, Program in Cellular and Molecular Pharmacology, Piscataway, NJ 08854-5635. Offers MS, PhD, MD/PhD. *Degree requirements:* For master's, thesis, qualifying exam; for doctorate, thesis/dissertation, qualifying exam. *Entrance requirements:* Additional exam requirements/recommendations for international students: Required—TOEFL. Electronic applications accepted.

Thomas Jefferson University, Jefferson College of Biomedical Sciences, PhD Program in Biochemistry and Molecular Pharmacology, Philadelphia, PA 19107. Offers PhD. *Faculty:* 57 full-time (12 women). *Students:* 20 full-time (11 women); includes 2 minority (1 Black or African American, non-Hispanic/Latino; 1 Asian, non-Hispanic/Latino), 3 international. In 2017, 7 doctorates awarded. *Degree requirements:* For doctorate, comprehensive exam, thesis/dissertation. *Entrance requirements:* For doctorate, GRE General Test or MCAT, minimum GPA of 3.2. Additional exam requirements/recommendations for international students: Required—TOEFL, IELTS (minimum score 7). *Application deadline:* For fall admission, 12/1 priority date for domestic and international students. Applications are processed on a rolling basis. Application fee: $60. Electronic applications accepted. *Financial support:* In 2017–18, 20 students received support, including 20 fellowships with full tuition reimbursements available (averaging $62,653 per year); Federal Work-Study, institutionally sponsored loans, scholarships/grants, traineeships, health care benefits, and stipends also available. Financial award application deadline: 5/1; financial award applicants required to submit FAFSA. *Faculty research:* Signal transduction and molecular genetics, translational biochemistry, human mitochondrial genetics, molecular biology of protein-RNA interaction, mammalian mitochondrial biogenesis and function. *Unit head:* Dr. Michael J. Root, MD, Program Director, 215-503-4564, Fax: 215-923-2117, E-mail: michael.root@jefferson.edu. *Application contact:* Marc E. Stearns, Senior Associate Director of Admissions, 215-503-0155, Fax: 215-503-3433, E-mail: jgsbs-info@jefferson.edu.
Website: http://www.jefferson.edu/university/biomedical-sciences/degrees-programs/phd-programs/biochemistry-pharmacology.html

University at Buffalo, the State University of New York, Graduate School, Graduate Programs in Cancer Research and Biomedical Sciences at Roswell Park Cancer Institute, Department of Molecular Pharmacology and Cancer Therapeutics at Roswell Park Cancer Institute, Buffalo, NY 14260. Offers PhD. *Faculty:* 22 full-time (7 women). *Students:* 14 full-time (10 women); includes 4 minority (1 Black or African American, non-Hispanic/Latino; 1 Asian, non-Hispanic/Latino; 1 Native Hawaiian or other Pacific Islander, non-Hispanic/Latino; 1 Two or more races, non-Hispanic/Latino), 4 international. 32 applicants, 19% accepted, 3 enrolled. In 2017, 5 doctorates awarded. *Degree requirements:* For doctorate, comprehensive exam, thesis/dissertation, oral defense of dissertation. *Entrance requirements:* For doctorate, GRE General Test. Additional exam requirements/recommendations for international students: Required—TOEFL (minimum score 79 iBT). *Application deadline:* For fall admission, 1/5 priority date for domestic and international students. Application fee: $75. Electronic applications accepted. *Financial support:* In 2017–18, 16 students received support, including 16 research assistantships with full tuition reimbursements available (averaging $27,000 per year); scholarships/grants, health care benefits, and unspecified assistantships also available. Financial award application deadline: 1/5. *Faculty research:* Cell cycle regulation, apoptosis, signal transduction, k+s signaling pathway, drug development. *Unit head:* Dr. Pamela Hershberger, Director of Graduate Studies, 716-845-1697, Fax: 716-845-8857, E-mail: pamela.hershberger@roswellpark.org. *Application contact:* Dr. Norman J. Karin, Associate Dean, 716-845-2339, Fax: 716-845-8178, E-mail: norman.karin@roswellpark.edu.
Website: http://www.roswellpark.edu/education/phd-programs/molecular-pharmacology-cancer-therapeutics

University of Massachusetts Medical School, Graduate School of Biomedical Sciences, Worcester, MA 01655-0115. Offers biomedical sciences (PhD), including biochemistry and molecular pharmacology, bioinformatics and computational biology, cancer biology, immunology and microbiology, interdisciplinary, neuroscience, translational science; biomedical sciences (millennium program) (PhD); clinical and population health research (PhD); clinical investigation (MS). *Faculty:* 1,316 full-time (526 women), 357 part-time/adjunct (229 women). *Students:* 347 full-time (180 women); includes 61 minority (10 Black or African American, non-Hispanic/Latino; 1 American Indian or Alaska Native, non-Hispanic/Latino; 35 Asian, non-Hispanic/Latino; 15 Hispanic/Latino), 130 international. Average age 29. 608 applicants, 28% accepted, 54 enrolled. In 2017, 6 master's, 51 doctorates awarded. Terminal master's awarded for partial completion of doctoral program. *Degree requirements:* For master's, comprehensive exam, thesis; for doctorate, comprehensive exam, thesis/dissertation. *Entrance requirements:* For master's, MD, PhD, DVM, or PharmD; for doctorate, GRE General Test, bachelor's degree. Additional exam requirements/recommendations for international students: Required—TOEFL (minimum score 90 iBT) or IELTS (minimum score 7.0). *Application deadline:* For fall admission, 12/15 for domestic and international students. Applications are processed on a rolling basis. Application fee: $80. Electronic applications accepted. Application fee is waived when completed online. *Expenses:* $14,883 in-state tuition and mandatory fees; $31,406 out-of-state. *Financial support:* In 2017–18, 15 fellowships with partial tuition reimbursements (averaging $29,000 per year), 296 research assistantships with full tuition reimbursements (averaging $31,212 per year) were awarded; institutionally sponsored loans and scholarships/grants also available. Financial award application deadline: 5/15. *Faculty research:* RNA biology, molecular/cell/developmental/metabolic biology, bioinformatics and computational biology, clinical/translational research, infectious disease and immunology. *Total annual research expenditures:* $279 million. *Unit head:* Dr. Mary Ellen Lane, Dean, 508-856-4018, E-mail: maryellen.lane@umassmed.edu. *Application contact:* Dr. Kendall Knight, Assistant Vice Provost for Admissions, 508-856-5628, Fax: 508-856-3659, E-mail: kendall.knight@umassmed.edu.
Website: http://www.umassmed.edu/gsbs/

University of Nevada, Reno, Graduate School, Interdisciplinary Program in Cellular and Molecular Pharmacology and Physiology, Reno, NV 89557. Offers PhD. *Degree requirements:* For doctorate, one foreign language, thesis/dissertation. *Entrance requirements:* For doctorate, GRE General Test or MCAT, minimum GPA of 3.0. Additional exam requirements/recommendations for international students: Required—TOEFL (minimum score 500 paper-based; 61 iBT), IELTS (minimum score 6). Electronic applications accepted. *Faculty research:* Neuropharmacology, toxicology, cardiovascular pharmacology, neuromuscular pharmacology.

University of Pittsburgh, School of Medicine, Graduate Programs in Medicine, Molecular Pharmacology Graduate Program, Pittsburgh, PA 15260. Offers PhD. *Faculty:* 65 full-time (11 women). *Students:* 29 full-time (13 women); includes 5 minority (1 Black or African American, non-Hispanic/Latino; 3 Asian, non-Hispanic/Latino; 1 Hispanic/Latino), 6 international. Average age 27. 350 applicants, 21% accepted, 16 enrolled. In 2017, 3 doctorates awarded. *Degree requirements:* For doctorate, comprehensive exam, thesis/dissertation. *Entrance requirements:* For doctorate, GRE General Test, minimum GPA of 3.2, 3 letters of recommendation, official transcripts, baccalaureate degree. Additional exam requirements/recommendations for international students: Required—TOEFL (minimum score 600 paper-based; 100 iBT), IELTS (minimum score 7). *Application deadline:* For fall admission, 12/1 priority date for domestic and international students. Application fee: $50. Electronic applications accepted. *Financial support:* In 2017–18, 29 students received support, including 8 fellowships with full tuition reimbursements available (averaging $29,500 per year), 15 research assistantships with full tuition reimbursements available (averaging $29,500 per year); teaching assistantships, traineeships, and tuition waivers also available. *Faculty research:* Drug discovery, signal transduction, cancer pharmacology, neuropharmacology, cell and organ system pharmacology. *Unit head:* Dr. Patrick Pagano, Director, 412-383-6505, Fax: 412-648-1077, E-mail: pagano@pitt.edu. *Application contact:* Carol Williams, Admissions and Recruiting Manager, 412-648-8957, Fax: 412-648-1077, E-mail: gradstudies@medschool.pitt.edu.
Website: http://www.gradbiomed.pitt.edu/

University of Southern California, Graduate School, School of Pharmacy, Graduate Programs in Molecular Pharmacology and Toxicology, Los Angeles, CA 90033. Offers pharmacology and pharmaceutical sciences (MS, PhD). Terminal master's awarded for partial completion of doctoral program. *Degree requirements:* For master's, comprehensive exam, thesis, 24 units of formal course work, excluding research and seminar courses; for doctorate, comprehensive exam, thesis/dissertation, 24 units of formal course work, excluding research and seminar courses. *Entrance requirements:* For master's and doctorate, GRE. Additional exam requirements/recommendations for international students: Required—TOEFL (minimum score 603 paper-based; 100 iBT). Electronic applications accepted. *Expenses:* Contact institution. *Faculty research:* Degenerative diseases, toxicology of drugs.

University of South Florida, Morsani College of Medicine and College of Graduate Studies, Graduate Programs in Medical Sciences, Tampa, FL 33620-9951. Offers advanced athletic training (MS); athletic training (MS); bioinformatics and computational biology (MSBCB); biotechnology (MSB); health informatics (MSHI); medical sciences (MSMS, PhD), including aging and neuroscience (MSMS), allergy, immunology and infectious disease (PhD), anatomy, biochemistry and molecular biology, clinical and translational research, health science (MSMS), interdisciplinary medical sciences (MSMS), medical microbiology and immunology (MSMS), metabolic and nutritional medicine (MSMS), microbiology and immunology (PhD), molecular medicine, molecular pharmacology and physiology (PhD), neuroscience (PhD), pathology and cell biology (PhD), women's health (MSMS). *Students:* 372 full-time (212 women), 216 part-time (142 women); includes 257 minority (78 Black or African American, non-Hispanic/Latino; 1 American Indian or Alaska Native, non-Hispanic/Latino; 79 Asian, non-Hispanic/Latino; 84 Hispanic/Latino; 15 Two or more races, non-Hispanic/Latino), 62 international. Average age 28. 1,048 applicants, 46% accepted, 309 enrolled. In 2017, 351 master's, 56 doctorates awarded. Terminal master's awarded for partial completion of doctoral program. *Degree requirements:* For master's, comprehensive exam, thesis; for doctorate, comprehensive exam, thesis/dissertation. *Entrance requirements:* For master's, GRE General Test or GMAT, bachelor's degree or equivalent from regionally-accredited university with minimum GPA of 3.0 in upper-division sciences coursework; prerequisites in general biology, general chemistry, general physics, organic chemistry, quantitative analysis, and integral and differential calculus; for doctorate, GRE General Test, bachelor's degree from regionally-accredited university with minimum GPA of 3.0 in upper-division sciences coursework; 3 letters of recommendation; personal interview; 1-2 page personal statement; prerequisites in biology, chemistry, physics, organic chemistry, quantitative analysis, and integral/differential calculus. Additional exam requirements/recommendations for international students: Required—TOEFL (minimum score 550 paper-based; 79 iBT) or IELTS (minimum score 6.5). *Application deadline:* For fall admission, 2/1 priority date for domestic students, 2/1 for international students. Application fee: $30. Electronic applications accepted. *Expenses:* Contact institution. *Financial support:* In 2017–18, 109 students received support. *Faculty research:* Anatomy, biochemistry, cancer biology, cardiovascular disease, cell biology, immunology, microbiology, molecular biology, neuroscience, pharmacology, physiology. *Total annual research expenditures:* $45.3 million. *Unit head:* Dr. Michael Barber, Professor/Associate Dean for Graduate and Postdoctoral Affairs, 813-974-9908, Fax: 813-974-4317, E-mail: mbarber@health.usf.edu. *Application contact:* Dr. Eric Bennett, Graduate Director, PhD Program in Medical Sciences, 813-974-1545, Fax: 813-974-4317, E-mail: esbennet@health.usf.edu.
Website: http://health.usf.edu/nocms/medicine/graduatestudies/

Molecular Toxicology

Massachusetts Institute of Technology, School of Science, Department of Biology, Cambridge, MA 02139. Offers biochemistry (PhD); biological oceanography (PhD); biology (PhD); biophysical chemistry and molecular structure (PhD); cell biology (PhD); computational and systems biology (PhD); developmental biology (PhD); genetics (PhD); immunology (PhD); microbiology (PhD); molecular biology (PhD); neurobiology (PhD). *Degree requirements:* For doctorate, comprehensive exam, thesis/dissertation, teaching assistantship during two semesters. *Entrance requirements:* For doctorate, GRE General Test. Additional exam requirements/recommendations for international students: Required—TOEFL, IELTS. Electronic applications accepted. *Faculty research:* Cellular, developmental and molecular (plant and animal) biology; biochemistry, bioengineering, biophysics and structural biology; classical and molecular genetics, stem cell and epigenetics; immunology and microbiology; cancer biology, molecular medicine, neurobiology and human disease; computational and systems biology.

New York University, Graduate School of Arts and Science, Department of Environmental Medicine, New York, NY 10012-1019. Offers environmental health sciences (MS, PhD), including biostatistics (PhD), environmental hygiene (MS), epidemiology (PhD), ergonomics and biomechanics (PhD), exposure assessment and health effects (PhD), molecular toxicology/carcinogenesis (PhD), toxicology. *Program availability:* Part-time. *Students:* Average age 30. 79 applicants, 44% accepted, 20 enrolled. In 2017, 8 master's, 6 doctorates awarded. Terminal master's awarded for partial completion of doctoral program. *Degree requirements:* For master's, thesis or alternative; for doctorate, one foreign language, thesis/dissertation, oral and written exams. *Entrance requirements:* For master's and doctorate, GRE General Test, minimum GPA of 3.0; bachelor's degree in biological, physical, or engineering science. Additional exam requirements/recommendations for international students: Required—TOEFL. *Application deadline:* For fall admission, 12/18 for domestic and international students. Application fee: $100. *Expenses: Tuition:* Full-time $41,352; part-time $19,968 per year. *Required fees:* $2496; $1628 per unit. $814 per term. Tuition and fees vary according to course load and program. *Financial support:* Fellowships, teaching assistantships, career-related internships or fieldwork, Federal Work-Study, institutionally sponsored loans, and health care benefits available. Financial award application deadline: 12/18; financial award applicants required to submit FAFSA. *Unit head:* Dr. Max Costa, Chair, 845-731-3661, Fax: 845-351-4510, E-mail: ehs@env.med.nyu.edu. *Application contact:* Dr. Jerome J. Solomon, Director of Graduate Studies, 845-731-3661, Fax: 845-351-4510, E-mail: ehs@env.med.nyu.edu.
Website: http://environmental-medicine.med.nyu.edu/

See Close-Up on page 843.

North Carolina State University, Graduate School, College of Agriculture and Life Sciences and College of Veterinary Medicine, Department of Environmental and Molecular Toxicology, Raleigh, NC 27695. Offers M Tox, MS, PhD. Terminal master's awarded for partial completion of doctoral program. *Degree requirements:* For master's, thesis (for some programs); for doctorate, thesis/dissertation. *Entrance requirements:* For master's and doctorate, GRE General Test, minimum GPA of 3.0. Electronic applications accepted. *Faculty research:* Chemical fate, carcinogenesis, developmental and endocrine toxicity, xenobiotic metabolism, signal transduction.

Oregon State University, College of Agricultural Sciences, Program in Toxicology, Corvallis, OR 97331. Offers environmental chemistry and ecotoxicology (MS, PhD); mechanistic toxicology (MS, PhD); molecular and cellular toxicology (MS, PhD); neurotoxicology (MS, PhD). *Degree requirements:* For master's, thesis; for doctorate, thesis/dissertation. *Entrance requirements:* For master's and doctorate, GRE, bachelor's degree in chemistry or biological sciences, minimum GPA of 3.0 in last 90 hours of course work. Additional exam requirements/recommendations for international students: Required—TOEFL (minimum score 80 iBT), IELTS (minimum score 6.5). *Application deadline:* For fall admission, 12/31 for domestic and international students. Application fee: $75 ($85 for international students). *Financial support:* Application deadline: 12/31. *Application contact:* Mary Mucia, Advisor, 541-737-9079, E-mail: mary.mucia@oregonstate.edu.
Website: http://emt.oregonstate.edu/prospectivegrads

Penn State Hershey Medical Center, College of Medicine, Graduate School Programs in the Biomedical Sciences, Huck Institutes of the Life Sciences, Intercollege Graduate Program in Molecular Cellular and Integrative Biosciences, Hershey, PA 17000. Offers cell and developmental biology (PhD); molecular medicine (PhD); molecular toxicology (PhD); neurobiology (PhD). *Students:* 3 full-time (2 women); includes 2 minority (both Asian, non-Hispanic/Latino). 2 applicants, 100% accepted, 2 enrolled. In 2017, 1 doctorate awarded. *Degree requirements:* For doctorate, comprehensive exam, thesis/dissertation, oral exam. *Entrance requirements:* For doctorate, GRE, minimum GPA of 3.0. Additional exam requirements/recommendations for international students: Required—TOEFL (minimum score 500 paper-based). *Application deadline:* For fall admission, 1/31 priority date for domestic students, 2/1 priority date for international students. Applications are processed on a rolling basis. Application fee: $65. Electronic applications accepted. *Financial support:* In 2017–18, research assistantships with full tuition reimbursements (averaging $26,196 per year) were awarded; fellowships with full tuition reimbursements, career-related internships or fieldwork, Federal Work-Study, scholarships/grants, health care benefits, and unspecified assistantships also available. Financial award applicants required to submit FAFSA. *Faculty research:* Vascular biology, molecular toxicology, chemical biology,

immune system, pathophysiological basis of human disease. *Unit head:* Dr. Peter Hudson, Director, 814-865-6057, E-mail: pjh18@psu.edu. *Application contact:* Kathy Shuey, Administrative Assistant, 717-531-8982, Fax: 717-531-0786, E-mail: grad-hmc@psu.edu.
Website: http://www.huck.psu.edu/education/molecular-cellular-and-integrative-biosciences

University of California, Berkeley, Graduate Division, College of Natural Resources, Group in Molecular Toxicology, Berkeley, CA 94720-1500. Offers PhD. *Entrance requirements:* For doctorate, GRE General Test, 3 letters of recommendation.

University of California, Los Angeles, Graduate Division, School of Public Health, Department of Environmental Health Sciences, Interdepartmental Program in Molecular Toxicology, Los Angeles, CA 90095. Offers PhD. *Degree requirements:* For doctorate, thesis/dissertation, oral and written qualifying exams. *Entrance requirements:* For doctorate, GRE General Test. Electronic applications accepted.

University of Cincinnati, Graduate School, College of Medicine, Graduate Programs in Biomedical Sciences, Department of Environmental Health, Programs in Environmental Genetics and Molecular Toxicology, Cincinnati, OH 45221. Offers MS, PhD. *Degree requirements:* For doctorate, thesis/dissertation. *Entrance requirements:* For master's, GRE, minimum GPA of 3.0, 3 letters of recommendation. Additional exam requirements/recommendations for international students: Required—TOEFL (minimum score 520 paper-based). *Expenses: Tuition, area resident:* Full-time $14,468. Tuition, state resident: full-time $14,968; part-time $754 per credit hour. Tuition, nonresident: full-time $24,210; part-time $1311 per credit hour. *International tuition:* $26,460 full-time. *Required fees:* $3958; $84 per credit hour. One-time fee: $85 full-time. Tuition and fees vary according to course load, degree level and program.

Pharmacology

Albany College of Pharmacy and Health Sciences, School of Pharmacy and Pharmaceutical Sciences, Albany, NY 12208. Offers health outcomes research (MS); pharmaceutical sciences (MS), including pharmaceutics, pharmacology; pharmacy (Pharm D). *Accreditation:* ACPE. *Degree requirements:* For master's, thesis; for doctorate, practice experience. *Entrance requirements:* For master's, GRE, minimum GPA of 3.0; for doctorate, PCAT, minimum GPA of 2.5. Additional exam requirements/recommendations for international students: Required—TOEFL (minimum score 84 iBT). Electronic applications accepted. *Faculty research:* Therapeutic use of drugs, pharmacokinetics, drug delivery and design.

Albany Medical College, Center for Neuropharmacology and Neuroscience, Albany, NY 12208-3479. Offers MS, PhD. Terminal master's awarded for partial completion of doctoral program. *Degree requirements:* For master's, thesis; for doctorate, comprehensive exam, thesis/dissertation. *Entrance requirements:* For master's, GRE General Test, all transcripts, letters of recommendation; for doctorate, GRE General Test, letters of recommendation. Additional exam requirements/recommendations for international students: Required—TOEFL. *Faculty research:* Molecular and cellular neuroscience, neuronal development, addiction.

Alliant International University–San Francisco, California School of Professional Psychology, Program in Psychopharmacology, San Francisco, CA 94133. Offers Post-Doctoral MS. *Program availability:* Part-time, online learning. *Entrance requirements:* For master's, doctorate in clinical psychology. Additional exam requirements/recommendations for international students: Required—TOEFL (minimum score 550 paper-based; 80 iBT), TWE (minimum score 5). Electronic applications accepted.

American University of Beirut, Graduate Programs, Faculty of Medicine, Beirut, Lebanon. Offers biochemistry (MS); biomedical engineering (MS); biomedical sciences (PhD); health research (MS); human morphology (MS); medicine (MD); microbiology and immunology (MS); neuroscience (MS); orthodontics (clinical) (MS); pharmacology and therapeutics (MS); physiology (MS). *Program availability:* Part-time. *Faculty:* 335 full-time (117 women), 54 part-time/adjunct (5 women). *Students:* 513 full-time (274 women). Average age 23. 527 applicants, 47% accepted, 169 enrolled. In 2017, 18 master's, 98 doctorates awarded. *Degree requirements:* For master's, one foreign language, comprehensive exam, thesis (for some programs); for doctorate, one foreign language, comprehensive exam, thesis/dissertation. *Entrance requirements:* For doctorate, MCAT (for MD); GRE (for PhD). Additional exam requirements/recommendations for international students: Required—TOEFL (minimum score 600 paper-based; 100 iBT), IELTS (minimum score 7.5). *Application deadline:* Applications are processed on a rolling basis. Application fee: $75. Electronic applications accepted. *Expenses:* Contact institution. *Financial support:* In 2017–18, 302 students received support. Fellowships, research assistantships, teaching assistantships, institutionally sponsored loans, scholarships/grants, tuition waivers, and unspecified assistantships available. *Unit head:* Dr. Mohamed Sayegh, Dean, 961-1-135000 Ext. 4700, Fax: 961-1-744489, E-mail: msayegh@aub.edu.lb. *Application contact:* Dr. Salim Kanaan, Director, Admission's Office, 961-1-350000 Ext. 2594, Fax: 961-1-750775, E-mail: sk00@aub.edu.lb.

Argosy University, Hawai`i, Hawai'i School of Professional Psychology, Program in Psychopharmacology, Honolulu, HI 96813. Offers MS, Certificate.

Augusta University, Program in Pharmacology, Augusta, GA 30912. Offers PhD. *Degree requirements:* For doctorate, comprehensive exam, thesis/dissertation. *Entrance requirements:* For doctorate, GRE General Test. Additional exam requirements/recommendations for international students: Required—TOEFL (minimum score 550 paper-based; 79 iBT). Electronic applications accepted. *Faculty research:* Protein signaling, neural development, cardiovascular pharmacology, endothelial cell function, neuropharmacology.

Baylor College of Medicine, Graduate School of Biomedical Sciences, Department of Pharmacology, Houston, TX 77030-3498. Offers PhD, MD/PhD. *Degree requirements:* For doctorate, thesis/dissertation, public defense. *Entrance requirements:* For doctorate, GRE General Test, GRE Subject Test (strongly recommended), minimum GPA of 3.0. Additional exam requirements/recommendations for international students: Required—TOEFL. Electronic applications accepted. *Faculty research:* Drug discovery, antibiotics, antitumor, computational drug design, signal transduction complex.

Boston University, School of Medicine, Division of Graduate Medical Sciences, Department of Pharmacology and Experimental Therapeutics, Boston, MA 02118. Offers PhD, MD/PhD. Terminal master's awarded for partial completion of doctoral program. *Degree requirements:* For doctorate, thesis/dissertation. *Application deadline:* For fall admission, 1/15 for domestic students; for spring admission, 10/15 for domestic students. *Unit head:* Dr. David H. Farb, Chairman, 617-638-4300, Fax: 617-638-4329, E-mail: dfarb@bu.edu. *Application contact:* GMS Admissions Office, 617-638-5255, E-mail: askgms@bu.edu.
Website: http://www.bumc.bu.edu/busm-pm/

Boston University, School of Medicine, Division of Graduate Medical Sciences, Program in Clinical Research, Boston, MA 02215. Offers MA. *Degree requirements:* For master's, thesis. *Application deadline:* For spring admission, 10/15 for domestic students. *Unit head:* Dr. Janice Weinberg, Director, 617-638-5470, E-mail: janicew@bu.edu. *Application contact:* Stacey Hess Pino, Assistant Director, 617-638-5211, Fax: 617-638-5740, E-mail: sahess@bu.edu.
Website: http://www.bumc.bu.edu/gms/maci/

Case Western Reserve University, School of Medicine and School of Graduate Studies, Graduate Programs in Medicine, Department of Pharmacology, Cleveland, OH 44106. Offers PhD, MD/PhD. Terminal master's awarded for partial completion of doctoral program. *Degree requirements:* For doctorate, comprehensive exam, thesis/dissertation. *Entrance requirements:* For doctorate, GRE General Test or MCAT. Additional exam requirements/recommendations for international students: Required—TOEFL (minimum score 577 paper-based; 90 iBT). Electronic applications accepted. *Expenses: Tuition:* Full-time $43,854; part-time $1827 per credit hour. *Required fees:* $50; $50 per credit hour. Tuition and fees vary according to course load and program. *Faculty research:* Neuroendocrine pharmacology, translational therapeutics, cancer therapeutics, molecular pharmacology and cell regulation, membrane and structural biology and pharmacology.

The Chicago School of Professional Psychology: Online, Program in Clinical Psychopharmacology, Chicago, IL 60654. Offers MS. *Program availability:* Online learning.

Columbia University, College of Physicians and Surgeons, Department of Pharmacology, New York, NY 10032. Offers pharmacology (M Phil, MA, PhD); pharmacology-toxicology (M Phil, MA, PhD); MD/PhD. Only candidates for the PhD are admitted. Terminal master's awarded for partial completion of doctoral program. *Degree requirements:* For doctorate, thesis/dissertation. *Entrance requirements:* For master's and doctorate, GRE General Test. Additional exam requirements/recommendations for international students: Required—TOEFL. *Expenses: Tuition:* Full-time $44,864; part-time $1704 per credit. *Required fees:* $2370 per semester. One-time fee: $105. *Faculty research:* Cardiovascular pharmacology, receptor pharmacology, neuropharmacology, membrane biophysics, eicosanoids.

Creighton University, School of Medicine and Graduate School, Graduate Programs in Medicine, Department of Pharmacology, Omaha, NE 68178-0001. Offers pharmaceutical sciences (MS); pharmacology (MS, PhD); Pharm D/MS. Terminal master's awarded for partial completion of doctoral program. *Degree requirements:* For master's, comprehensive exam, thesis; for doctorate, comprehensive exam, thesis/dissertation, oral and written preliminary exams. *Entrance requirements:* For master's and doctorate, GRE General Test, minimum GPA of 3.0, undergraduate degree in sciences. Additional exam requirements/recommendations for international students: Required—TOEFL. Electronic applications accepted. Part-time tuition and fees vary according to course load, degree level, campus/location and program. *Faculty research:* Pharmacology secretion, cardiovascular-renal pharmacology, adrenergic receptors, signal transduction, genetic regulation of receptors.

Dalhousie University, Faculty of Graduate Studies and Faculty of Medicine, Graduate Programs in Medicine, Department of Pharmacology, Halifax, NS B3H 4R2, Canada. Offers M Sc, PhD. *Degree requirements:* For master's, thesis; for doctorate, comprehensive exam, thesis/dissertation. *Entrance requirements:* Additional exam requirements/recommendations for international students: Required—1 of 5 approved tests: TOEFL, IELTS, CANTEST, CAEL, Michigan English Language Assessment Battery. Electronic applications accepted. *Faculty research:* Electrophysiology and neurochemistry; endocrinology, immunology and cancer research; molecular biology; cardiovascular and autonomic; drug biotransformation and metabolism; ocular pharmacology.

Drexel University, College of Medicine, Biomedical Graduate Programs, Pharmacology and Physiology Program, Philadelphia, PA 19104-2875. Offers MS, PhD, MD/PhD. *Program availability:* Part-time. Terminal master's awarded for partial completion of doctoral program. *Degree requirements:* For master's, comprehensive exam; for doctorate, thesis/dissertation, qualifying exam. *Entrance requirements:* For master's, GRE General Test, minimum GPA of 2.75; for doctorate, GRE General Test, minimum GPA of 3.0. Additional exam requirements/recommendations for international students: Required—TOEFL. Electronic applications accepted. *Faculty research:* Cardiovascular pharmacology, drugs of abuse, neurotransmitter mechanisms.

Duke University, Graduate School, Department of Pharmacology and Cancer Biology, Durham, NC 27710. Offers pharmacology (PhD). *Faculty:* 42 full-time. *Students:* 44 full-time (22 women); includes 20 minority (3 Black or African American, non-Hispanic/Latino; 1 American Indian or Alaska Native, non-Hispanic/Latino; 14 Asian, non-Hispanic/Latino; 2 Hispanic/Latino). Average age 23. 67 applicants, 22% accepted, 8 enrolled. In 2017, 7 doctorates awarded. *Degree requirements:* For doctorate, thesis/dissertation. *Entrance requirements:* For doctorate, GRE General Test, minimum GPA of 3.0. Additional exam requirements/recommendations for international students: Required—TOEFL or IELTS. *Application deadline:* For fall admission, 12/1 priority date for domestic and international students. Application fee: $85. Electronic applications accepted. *Financial support:* In 2017–18, 10 fellowships with tuition reimbursements (averaging $30,550 per year), 13 research assistantships with tuition reimbursements (averaging $30,550 per year) were awarded; scholarships/grants, traineeships, health care benefits, and unspecified assistantships also available. Financial award application deadline: 12/1. *Faculty research:* Developmental pharmacology, neuropharmacology, molecular pharmacology, toxicology, cell growth and metabolism. *Unit head:* Dr. David MacAlpine, Director of Graduate Studies, 919-681-6077, E-mail: david.macalpine@duke.edu. *Application contact:* Jamie Baize-Smith, Assistant Director of Graduate Studies, 919-613-8600, E-mail: baize@duke.edu.
Website: http://pharmacology.mc.duke.edu/

Duquesne University, School of Pharmacy, Graduate School of Pharmaceutical Sciences, Program in Pharmacology, Pittsburgh, PA 15282-0001. Offers MS, PhD. *Faculty:* 6 full-time (4 women). *Students:* 11 full-time (6 women), 8 international. Average age 26. 12 applicants, 25% accepted, 1 enrolled. In 2017, 1 master's, 1 doctorate awarded. *Degree requirements:* For master's, thesis; for doctorate,

comprehensive exam, thesis/dissertation. *Entrance requirements:* For master's and doctorate, GRE General Test. Additional exam requirements/recommendations for international students: Required—TOEFL (minimum score 100 iBT). *Application deadline:* For fall admission, 12/1 priority date for domestic and international students; for spring admission, 10/1 priority date for domestic and international students. Applications are processed on a rolling basis. Electronic applications accepted. *Expenses:* $1,542 per credit. *Financial support:* In 2017–18, 12 students received support, including 1 research assistantship with full tuition reimbursement available, 11 teaching assistantships with full tuition reimbursements available. *Unit head:* Dr. Christopher K. Surratt, Head, 412-396-5007. *Application contact:* Information Contact, 412-396-1172, E-mail: gsps-adm@duq.edu.
Website: http://www.duq.edu/academics/schools/pharmacy/graduate-school-of-pharmaceutical-sciences

East Carolina University, Brody School of Medicine, Department of Pharmacology and Toxicology, Greenville, NC 27858-4353. Offers PhD. *Students:* 16 full-time (8 women); includes 1 minority (Hispanic/Latino), 2 international. Average age 29. *Entrance requirements:* For doctorate, GRE General Test, GRE Subject Test. *Expenses:* Tuition, state resident: full-time $4749; part-time $297 per credit hour. Tuition, nonresident: full-time $17,898; part-time $1119 per credit hour. *Required fees:* $2691; $224 per credit hour. Part-time tuition and fees vary according to course load and program. *Financial support:* Fellowships with full tuition reimbursements available. Financial award application deadline: 6/1. *Faculty research:* GNS/behavioral pharmacology, cardiovascular pharmacology, cell signaling and second messenger, effects of calcium channel blockers. *Unit head:* Dr. David A. Taylor, Chairman, 252-744-2734, Fax: 252-744-3203, E-mail: taylorda@ecu.edu. *Application contact:* Contact Center, 252-744-1020.
Website: http://www.ecu.edu/cs-dhs/pharmacology/

East Tennessee State University, Quillen College of Medicine, Department of Biomedical Sciences, Johnson City, TN 37614. Offers anatomy (PhD); biochemistry (PhD); microbiology (PhD); pharmaceutical sciences (PhD); pharmacology (PhD); physiology (PhD); quantitative biosciences (PhD). In 2017, 5 doctorates awarded. *Degree requirements:* For doctorate, comprehensive exam, thesis/dissertation, comprehensive qualifying exam; one-year residency. *Entrance requirements:* For doctorate, GRE General Test, GRE Subject Test, 3 letters of recommendation, minimum of 60 credit hours beyond the baccalaureate degree. Additional exam requirements/recommendations for international students: Required—TOEFL (minimum score 550 paper-based; 79 iBT). *Application deadline:* For fall admission, 6/1 priority date for domestic students, 4/29 for international students; for spring admission, 11/1 for domestic students, 9/29 for international students; for summer admission, 3/15 for domestic students, 2/1 for international students. Applications are processed on a rolling basis. Application fee: $55 ($65 for international students). Electronic applications accepted. *Expenses:* Contact institution. *Financial support:* Research assistantships with full tuition reimbursements, career-related internships or fieldwork, institutionally sponsored loans, scholarships/grants, and unspecified assistantships available. Financial award application deadline: 7/1; financial award applicants required to submit FAFSA. *Faculty research:* Cardiovascular, infectious disease, neurosciences, cancer, immunology. *Unit head:* Theo Hagg, Chair, 423-439-6294, Fax: 423-439-2140, E-mail: haggt1@etsu.edu. *Application contact:* Theo Hagg, Chair, 423-439-6294, Fax: 423-439-2140, E-mail: haggt1@etsu.edu.
Website: http://www.etsu.edu/com/dbms/

Emory University, Laney Graduate School, Division of Biological and Biomedical Sciences, Program in Molecular and Systems Pharmacology, Atlanta, GA 30322-1100. Offers PhD. *Degree requirements:* For doctorate, comprehensive exam, thesis/dissertation. *Entrance requirements:* For doctorate, GRE General Test, minimum GPA of 3.0 in science course work (recommended). Additional exam requirements/recommendations for international students: Required—TOEFL. Electronic applications accepted. *Faculty research:* Transmembrane signaling, neuropharmacology, neurophysiology and neurodegeneration, metabolism and molecular toxicology, cell and developmental biology.

Fairleigh Dickinson University, Florham Campus, Silberman College of Business, Program in Pharmaceutical Studies, Madison, NJ 07940-1099. Offers MBA, Certificate. *Expenses:* *Tuition:* Full-time $22,410; part-time $1245 per credit. *Required fees:* $888; $414 per unit. Tuition and fees vary according to course load, degree level and program.

Florida Agricultural and Mechanical University, Division of Graduate Studies, Research, and Continuing Education, College of Pharmacy and Pharmaceutical Sciences, Graduate Programs in Pharmaceutical Sciences, Tallahassee, FL 32307-3200. Offers environmental toxicology (PhD); health outcomes research and pharmacoeconomics (PhD); medicinal chemistry (MS, PhD); pharmaceutics (MS, PhD); pharmacology/toxicology (MS, PhD); pharmacy administration (MS). *Accreditation:* CEPH. *Degree requirements:* For master's, comprehensive exam, thesis, publishable paper; for doctorate, comprehensive exam, thesis/dissertation, publishable paper. *Entrance requirements:* For master's and doctorate, GRE General Test, minimum GPA of 3.0 in last 60 hours. Additional exam requirements/recommendations for international students: Required—TOEFL. *Faculty research:* Anticancer agents, anti-inflammatory drugs, chronopharmacology, neuroendocrinology, microbiology.

Georgetown University, Graduate School of Arts and Sciences, Department of Pharmacology and Physiology, Washington, DC 20057. Offers pharmacology (MS, PhD); physiology (MS); MD/PhD. *Degree requirements:* For doctorate, comprehensive exam, thesis/dissertation. *Entrance requirements:* For doctorate, GRE General Test, previous course work in biology and chemistry. Additional exam requirements/recommendations for international students: Required—TOEFL. *Faculty research:* Neuropharmacology, techniques in biochemistry and tissue culture.

Howard University, College of Medicine, Department of Pharmacology, Washington, DC 20059-0002. Offers MS, PhD, MD/PhD. *Program availability:* Part-time. *Degree requirements:* For master's, comprehensive exam, thesis; for doctorate, one foreign language, comprehensive exam, thesis/dissertation, qualifying exam. *Entrance requirements:* For master's, GRE General Test, minimum GPA of 3.2, BS in chemistry, biology, pharmacy, psychology or related field; for doctorate, GRE General Test, minimum graduate GPA of 3.2. Additional exam requirements/recommendations for international students: Recommended—TOEFL. *Faculty research:* Biochemical pharmacology, molecular pharmacology, neuropharmacology, drug metabolism, cancer research.

Husson University, School of Pharmacy, Bangor, ME 04401-2999. Offers pharmacology (MS); pharmacy (Pharm D). *Accreditation:* ACPE. *Faculty:* 24 full-time (7 women), 1 part-time/adjunct (0 women). *Students:* 189 full-time (109 women); includes 55 minority (26 Black or African American, non-Hispanic/Latino; 2 American Indian or Alaska Native, non-Hispanic/Latino; 20 Asian, non-Hispanic/Latino; 6 Hispanic/Latino; 1 Two or more races, non-Hispanic/Latino), 7 international. Average age 26. 158 applicants, 48% accepted, 46 enrolled. In 2017, 56 doctorates awarded. *Entrance requirements:* For doctorate, PCAT, PharmCAS application. Additional exam requirements/recommendations for international students: Required—TOEFL (minimum score 550 paper-based; 80 iBT), IELTS (minimum score 6.5). *Application deadline:* For fall admission, 3/1 for domestic students. Application fee: $50 ($0 for international students). Electronic applications accepted. *Expenses:* $968 per credit; $580 in fees per year. *Financial support:* In 2017–18, 112 students received support. Federal Work-Study, scholarships/grants, and unspecified assistantships available. Financial award application deadline: 3/1; financial award applicants required to submit FAFSA. *Faculty research:* Development of nanoparticles for noninvasive delivery of therapeutic agents; clinical implications in anti-infective resistance; using stochastic modeling to determine appropriate antibiotic selection, infectious diseases surveillance and epidemiology; impaired healing in individuals with diabetes; assessment of pharmaceutical needs in rural settings in the midst of the changing health care environment. *Total annual research expenditures:* $25,460. *Unit head:* Dr. Rodney A. Larson, Dean, 207-941-7122, E-mail: larsonr@husson.edu. *Application contact:* Kristen Card, Director of Graduate Admissions, 207-404-5660, E-mail: cardk@husson.edu.
Website: http://www.husson.edu/pharmacy

Idaho State University, Office of Graduate Studies, College of Pharmacy, Department of Biomedical and Pharmaceutical Sciences, Pocatello, ID 83209-8334. Offers biopharmaceutical analysis (PhD); drug delivery (PhD); medicinal chemistry (PhD); pharmaceutical sciences (MS); pharmacology (PhD). *Program availability:* Part-time. *Degree requirements:* For master's, one foreign language, comprehensive exam, thesis, thesis research, classes in speech and technical writing; for doctorate, comprehensive exam, thesis/dissertation, written and oral exams, classes in speech and technical writing. *Entrance requirements:* For master's, GRE General Test, minimum GPA of 3.0, 3 letters of recommendation; for doctorate, GRE General Test, BS in pharmacy or related field, minimum GPA of 3.0, 3 letters of recommendation. Additional exam requirements/recommendations for international students: Required—TOEFL (minimum score 550 paper-based; 80 iBT). Electronic applications accepted. *Expenses:* Contact institution. *Faculty research:* Metabolic toxicity of heavy metals, neuroendocrine pharmacology, cardiovascular pharmacology, cancer biology, immunopharmacology.

Indiana University–Purdue University Indianapolis, Indiana University School of Medicine, Department of Pharmacology and Toxicology, Indianapolis, IN 46202. Offers pharmacology (MS, PhD); toxicology (MS, PhD); MD/PhD. *Degree requirements:* For master's, thesis; for doctorate, thesis/dissertation. *Entrance requirements:* For master's, GRE General Test, GRE Subject Test, minimum GPA of 3.2 in core science courses; for doctorate, GRE General Test, GRE Subject Test. Additional exam requirements/recommendations for international students: Required—TOEFL, IELTS, GRE or MCAT. Electronic applications accepted. *Expenses:* Contact institution. *Faculty research:* Neuropharmacology, cardiovascular biopharmacology, chemotherapy, oncogenesis.

Johns Hopkins University, School of Medicine, Graduate Programs in Medicine, Department of Pharmacology and Molecular Sciences, Baltimore, MD 21205. Offers PhD. *Degree requirements:* For doctorate, comprehensive exam, thesis/dissertation, departmental seminar. *Entrance requirements:* For doctorate, GRE General Test. Additional exam requirements/recommendations for international students: Required—TOEFL. Electronic applications accepted.

Kent State University, College of Arts and Sciences, School of Biomedical Sciences, Kent, OH 44242-0001. Offers biological anthropology (PhD); biomedical mathematics (MS, PhD); cellular and molecular biology (MS, PhD), including cellular biology and structures, molecular biology and genetics; neurosciences (MS, PhD); pharmacology (MS, PhD); physiology (MS, PhD). *Faculty:* 22 full-time (9 women), 3 part-time/adjunct (1 woman). *Students:* 75 full-time (46 women); includes 8 minority (1 Black or African American, non-Hispanic/Latino; 3 Asian, non-Hispanic/Latino; 2 Hispanic/Latino; 2 Two or more races, non-Hispanic/Latino), 25 international. Average age 28. 70 applicants, 23% accepted, 13 enrolled. In 2017, 23 master's, 5 doctorates awarded. Terminal master's awarded for partial completion of doctoral program. *Degree requirements:* For master's, thesis; for doctorate, comprehensive exam, thesis/dissertation. *Entrance requirements:* For master's, GRE, bachelor's degree, transcripts, minimum GPA of 3.0, goal statement, three letters of recommendation, academic preparation adequate to perform graduate work in the desired field; for doctorate, GRE, master's degree, minimum GPA of 3.0, transcripts, goal statement, three letters of recommendation. Additional exam requirements/recommendations for international students: Required—TOEFL (minimum score 600 paper-based, 100 iBT), Michigan English Language Assessment Battery (minimum score 85), IELTS (minimum score 7.0) or PTE (minimum score 68). *Application deadline:* For fall admission, 1/1 for domestic and international students. Applications are processed on a rolling basis. Application fee: $45 ($70 for international students). Electronic applications accepted. *Expenses:* Tuition, state resident: full-time $11,310; part-time $515 per credit hour. Tuition, nonresident: full-time $20,396; part-time $928 per credit hour. *International tuition:* $18,544 full-time. *Financial support:* Research assistantships with full tuition reimbursements, teaching assistantships, and unspecified assistantships available. Financial award application deadline: 1/1. *Unit head:* Dr. Ernest J. Freeman, Director, School of Biomedical Sciences, 330-672-2363, E-mail: efreema2@kent.edu.
Website: http://www.kent.edu/biomedical/

Loma Linda University, School of Medicine, Programs in Physiology and Pharmacology, Loma Linda, CA 92350. Offers pharmacology (PhD); physiology (PhD). *Program availability:* Part-time. *Degree requirements:* For doctorate, 2 foreign languages, thesis/dissertation. *Entrance requirements:* For doctorate, GRE General Test. *Faculty research:* Drug metabolism, biochemical pharmacology, structure and function of cell membranes, neuropharmacology.

London Metropolitan University, Graduate Programs, London, United Kingdom. Offers applied psychology (M Sc); architecture (MA); biomedical science (M Sc); blood science (M Sc); cancer pharmacology (M Sc); computer networking and cyber security (M Sc); computing and information systems (M Sc); conference interpreting (MA); counter-terrorism studies (M Sc); creative, digital and professional writing (MA); crime, violence and prevention (M Sc); criminology (M Sc); curating contemporary art (MA); data analytics (M Sc); digital media (MA); early childhood studies (MA); education (MA, Ed D); financial services law, regulation and compliance (LL M); food science (M Sc); forensic psychology (M Sc); health and social care management and policy (M Sc); human nutrition (M Sc); human resource management (MA); human rights and international conflict (MA); information technology (M Sc); intelligence and security studies (M Sc); international oil, gas and energy law (LL M); international relations (MA); interpreting (MA); learning and teaching in higher education (MA); legal practice (LL M); media and entertainment law (LL M); organizational and consumer psychology (M Sc); psychological therapy (M Sc); psychology of mental health (M Sc); public health (M Sc); public policy and management (MPA); security studies (M Sc); social work (M Sc); spatial planning and urban design (MA); sports therapy (M Sc); supporting older children and young people with dyslexia (MA); teaching languages (MA), including Arabic, English; translation (MA); woman and child abuse (MA).

Long Island University–LIU Brooklyn, Arnold and Marie Schwartz College of Pharmacy and Health Sciences, Brooklyn, NY 11201-8423. Offers drug regulatory affairs (MS); pharmaceutics (MS, PhD), including cosmetic science (MS), industrial pharmacy (MS); pharmacology and toxicology (MS); pharmacy (Pharm D). *Accreditation:* ACPE. *Program availability:* Part-time. *Faculty:* 51 full-time (29 women), 33 part-time/adjunct (14 women). *Students:* 497 full-time (296 women), 77 part-time (42 women); includes 228 minority (26 Black or African American, non-Hispanic/Latino; 143

Asian, non-Hispanic/Latino; 31 Hispanic/Latino; 28 Two or more races, non-Hispanic/Latino), 137 international. Average age 25. 241 applicants, 62% accepted, 38 enrolled. In 2017, 57 master's, 183 doctorates awarded. Terminal master's awarded for partial completion of doctoral program. *Degree requirements:* For master's, comprehensive exam, thesis; for doctorate, comprehensive exam, thesis/dissertation. *Entrance requirements:* For master's and doctorate, GRE. Additional exam requirements/recommendations for international students: Required—TOEFL (minimum score 550 paper-based, 79 iBT) or IELTS. *Application deadline:* Applications are processed on a rolling basis. Application fee: $50. Electronic applications accepted. *Expenses:* Contact institution. *Financial support:* In 2017–18, 200 students received support. Research assistantships, teaching assistantships, career-related internships or fieldwork, Federal Work-Study, scholarships/grants, tuition waivers (full and partial), and unspecified assistantships available. Support available to part-time students. Financial award application deadline: 2/15; financial award applicants required to submit FAFSA. *Faculty research:* Preformulation, formulation and drug delivery; pharmacokinetics; pharmacology research; drug regulatory affairs; pharmaceutical analysis. *Total annual research expenditures:* $100,000. *Unit head:* Dr. John M. Pezzuto, Dean, 718-488-1004, Fax: 718-488-0628, E-mail: john.pezzuto@liu.edu. *Application contact:* Michael Young, Senior Assistant Director of Admissions, 718-488-1000, E-mail: michael.young@liu.edu.
Website: http://liu.edu/Pharmacy

Louisiana State University Health Sciences Center, School of Graduate Studies in New Orleans, Department of Pharmacology and Experimental Therapeutics, New Orleans, LA 70112-2223. Offers PhD, MD/PhD. *Faculty:* 21 full-time (4 women). *Students:* 14 full-time (5 women); includes 3 minority (2 Black or African American, non-Hispanic/Latino; 1 Asian, non-Hispanic/Latino), 3 international. Average age 25. 6 applicants, 33% accepted, 2 enrolled. In 2017, 6 doctorates awarded. *Degree requirements:* For doctorate, comprehensive exam, thesis/dissertation. *Entrance requirements:* For doctorate, GRE General Test. Additional exam requirements/recommendations for international students: Recommended—TOEFL, IELTS. *Application deadline:* For fall admission, 4/1 for domestic and international students. Applications are processed on a rolling basis. Application fee: $30. *Expenses:* Tuition, state resident: full-time $11,835; part-time $518 per hour. Tuition, nonresident: full-time $24,108; part-time $1079 per hour. *Required fees:* $1254; $55 per hour. *Financial support:* Unspecified assistantships available. Financial award application deadline: 4/15. *Faculty research:* Neuropharmacology, gastrointestinal pharmacology, drug metabolism, behavioral pharmacology, cardiovascular pharmacology. *Unit head:* Dr. Kurt Varner, Professor/Head, 504-568-4740, Fax: 504-568-2361, E-mail: kvarne@lsuhsc.edu. *Application contact:* Dr. Andrew Catling, Graduate Coordinator and Professor, 504-568-2222, E-mail: acatli@lsuhsc.edu.
Website: http://www.medschool.lsumc.edu/pharmacology/

Louisiana State University Health Sciences Center at Shreveport, Department of Pharmacology, Toxicology and Neuroscience, Shreveport, LA 71130-3932. Offers pharmacology (PhD); MD/PhD. Terminal master's awarded for partial completion of doctoral program. *Degree requirements:* For master's, thesis; for doctorate, thesis/dissertation. *Entrance requirements:* For master's, GRE General Test; for doctorate, GRE General Test, minimum GPA of 3.0. Additional exam requirements/recommendations for international students: Required—TOEFL (minimum score 550 paper-based). *Faculty research:* Behavioral, cardiovascular, clinical, and gastrointestinal pharmacology; neuropharmacology; psychopharmacology; drug abuse; pharmacokinetics; neuroendocrinology, psychoneuroimmunology, and stress; toxicology.

McGill University, Faculty of Graduate and Postdoctoral Studies, Faculty of Medicine, Department of Pharmacology and Therapeutics, Montréal, QC H3A 2T5, Canada. Offers M Sc, PhD.

McMaster University, Faculty of Health Sciences and School of Graduate Studies, Program in Medical Sciences, Physiology/Pharmacology Area, Hamilton, ON L8S 4M2, Canada. Offers M Sc, PhD, MD/PhD. *Degree requirements:* For master's, thesis; for doctorate, comprehensive exam, thesis/dissertation. *Entrance requirements:* For master's, honors B Sc, B+ average in related field; for doctorate, M Sc, minimum B+ average, students with proven research experience and an A average may be admitted with a B Sc degree. Additional exam requirements/recommendations for international students: Required—TOEFL (minimum score 580 paper-based; 92 iBT).

MCPHS University, Graduate Studies, Program in Pharmacology, Boston, MA 02115-5896. Offers MS, PhD. *Accreditation:* ACPE (one or more programs are accredited). Terminal master's awarded for partial completion of doctoral program. *Degree requirements:* For master's, oral defense of thesis; for doctorate, one foreign language, oral defense of dissertation, qualifying exam. *Entrance requirements:* For master's and doctorate, GRE General Test, minimum QPA of 3.0. Additional exam requirements/recommendations for international students: Required—TOEFL (minimum score 550 paper-based; 79 iBT). *Faculty research:* Neuropharmacology, cardiovascular pharmacology, nutritional pharmacology, pulmonary physiology, drug metabolism.

Medical College of Wisconsin, Graduate School, Department of Pharmacology and Toxicology, Milwaukee, WI 53226-0509. Offers PhD, MD/PhD. *Degree requirements:* For doctorate, comprehensive exam, thesis/dissertation, oral and written qualifying exams. *Entrance requirements:* For doctorate, GRE, official transcripts, three letters of recommendation. Additional exam requirements/recommendations for international students: Required—TOEFL. *Application deadline:* For fall admission, 12/15 priority date for domestic and international students. Applications are processed on a rolling basis. Application fee: $50. Electronic applications accepted. *Financial support:* Fellowships, research assistantships, career-related internships or fieldwork, institutionally sponsored loans, and scholarships/grants available. Financial award application deadline: 2/15; financial award applicants required to submit FAFSA. *Faculty research:* Cardiovascular physiology and pharmacology, drugs of abuse, environmental and aquatic toxicology, central nervous system and biochemical pharmacology, signal transduction. *Unit head:* Dr. William D. Campbell, Chair, 414-955-8267, Fax: 414-955-6555, E-mail: gradschool@mcw.edu. *Application contact:* Recruitment Office, 414-955-4402, Fax: 414-955-6555, E-mail: gradschoolrecruit@mcw.edu.
Website: https://www.mcw.edu/Pharmacology.htm

Meharry Medical College, School of Graduate Studies, Program in Biomedical Sciences, Pharmacology Emphasis, Nashville, TN 37208-9989. Offers PhD, MD/PhD. *Degree requirements:* For doctorate, comprehensive exam, thesis/dissertation. *Entrance requirements:* For doctorate, GRE.

Michigan State University, College of Human Medicine and The Graduate School, Graduate Programs in Human Medicine, East Lansing, MI 48824. Offers biochemistry and molecular biology (MS, PhD); epidemiology (MS, PhD); microbiology (MS); microbiology and molecular genetics (PhD); pharmacology and toxicology (MS, PhD); physiology (MS, PhD); public health (MPH). *Entrance requirements:* Additional exam requirements/recommendations for international students: Required—TOEFL.

Michigan State University, College of Osteopathic Medicine and The Graduate School, Graduate Studies in Osteopathic Medicine and Graduate Programs in Human Medicine and Graduate Programs in Veterinary Medicine, Department of Pharmacology and Toxicology, East Lansing, MI 48824. Offers integrative pharmacology (MS); pharmacology and toxicology (MS, PhD); pharmacology and toxicology-environmental toxicology (PhD). *Entrance requirements:* Additional exam requirements/recommendations for international students: Required—TOEFL (minimum score 600 paper-based). Electronic applications accepted.

Michigan State University, College of Veterinary Medicine and The Graduate School, Graduate Programs in Veterinary Medicine, East Lansing, MI 48824. Offers comparative medicine and integrative biology (MS, PhD), including comparative medicine and integrative biology, comparative medicine and integrative biology–environmental toxicology (PhD); food safety and toxicology (MS), including food safety; integrative toxicology (PhD), including animal science–environmental toxicology, biochemistry and molecular biology–environmental toxicology, chemistry–environmental toxicology, crop and soil sciences–environmental toxicology, environmental engineering–environmental toxicology, environmental geosciences–environmental toxicology, fisheries and wildlife–environmental toxicology, food science–environmental toxicology, forestry–environmental toxicology, genetics–environmental toxicology, human nutrition–environmental toxicology, microbiology–environmental toxicology, pharmacology and toxicology–environmental toxicology, zoology–environmental toxicology; large animal clinical sciences (MS, PhD); microbiology and molecular genetics (MS, PhD), including industrial microbiology, microbiology, microbiology and molecular genetics, microbiology–environmental toxicology (PhD); pathobiology and diagnostic investigation (MS, PhD), including pathology, pathology–environmental toxicology (PhD); pharmacology and toxicology (MS, PhD); pharmacology and toxicology–environmental toxicology (PhD); physiology (MS, PhD); small animal clinical sciences (MS). Electronic applications accepted. *Faculty research:* Molecular genetics, food safety/toxicology, comparative orthopedics, airway disease, population medicine.

Montclair State University, The Graduate School, College of Science and Mathematics, Program in Pharmaceutical Biochemistry, Montclair, NJ 07043-1624. Offers MS. *Program availability:* Part-time, evening/weekend. *Entrance requirements:* For master's, GRE General Test, 24 undergraduate credits in chemistry, 2 letters of recommendation, essay. Electronic applications accepted. *Faculty research:* Enzyme kinetics, enzyme expression, pharmaceutical biochemistry, medicinal chemistry, biophysical chemistry.

New Jersey Institute of Technology, Newark College of Engineering, Newark, NJ 07102. Offers biomedical engineering (MS, PhD); chemical engineering (MS, PhD); computer engineering (MS, PhD); electrical engineering (MS, PhD); engineering management (MS); environmental engineering (PhD); healthcare systems management (MS); industrial engineering (MS, PhD); Internet engineering (MS); manufacturing engineering (MS); mechanical engineering (MS, PhD); occupational safety and health engineering (MS); pharmaceutical bioprocessing (MS); pharmaceutical engineering (MS); pharmaceutical systems management (MS); power and energy systems (MS); telecommunications (MS); transportation (MS, PhD). *Program availability:* Part-time, evening/weekend. *Students:* Average age 27. 2,959 applicants, 51% accepted, 442 enrolled. In 2017, 595 master's, 29 doctorates awarded. Terminal master's awarded for partial completion of doctoral program. *Entrance requirements:* For master's, GRE General Test; for doctorate, GRE General Test, minimum graduate GPA of 3.5. Additional exam requirements/recommendations for international students: Required—TOEFL (minimum score 550 paper-based; 79 iBT). *Application deadline:* For fall admission, 6/1 priority date for domestic students, 5/1 priority date for international students; for spring admission, 11/15 priority date for domestic and international students. Applications are processed on a rolling basis. Application fee: $75. Electronic applications accepted. *Expenses:* Contact institution. *Financial support:* In 2017–18, 172 students received support, including 24 fellowships (averaging $7,124 per year), 112 research assistantships (averaging $19,407 per year), 101 teaching assistantships (averaging $24,173 per year); scholarships/grants also available. Financial award application deadline: 1/15. *Faculty research:* Nonlinear signal processing, intelligent medical image analysis, calibration issues in coherent localization, computer-aided design, neural network for tool wear measurement. *Total annual research expenditures:* $11.1 million. *Unit head:* Dr. Moshe Kam, Dean, 973-596-5534, E-mail: moshe.kam@njit.edu. *Application contact:* Stephen Eck, Director of Admissions, 973-596-3300, Fax: 973-596-3461, E-mail: admissions@njit.edu.
Website: http://engineering.njit.edu/

New York Medical College, Graduate School of Basic Medical Sciences, Valhalla, NY 10595. Offers biochemistry and molecular biology (MS, PhD); cell biology (MS, PhD); microbiology and immunology (MS, PhD); pathology (MS, PhD); pharmacology (MS, PhD); physiology (MS, PhD); MD/PhD. *Program availability:* Part-time, evening/weekend. *Faculty:* 70 full-time (17 women), 25 part-time/adjunct (9 women). *Students:* 116 full-time (63 women), 25 part-time (11 women); includes 65 minority (17 Black or African American, non-Hispanic/Latino; 1 American Indian or Alaska Native, non-Hispanic/Latino; 23 Asian, non-Hispanic/Latino; 21 Hispanic/Latino; 3 Two or more races, non-Hispanic/Latino), 27 international. Average age 27. 273 applicants, 56% accepted, 59 enrolled. In 2017, 32 master's, 3 doctorates awarded. *Degree requirements:* For master's, thesis; for doctorate, comprehensive exam, thesis/dissertation. *Entrance requirements:* For master's, GRE General Test, MCAT, or DAT; for doctorate, GRE General Test. Additional exam requirements/recommendations for international students: Required—TOEFL. *Application deadline:* For fall admission, 7/1 priority date for domestic students, 5/1 priority date for international students; for spring admission, 12/1 priority date for domestic students, 9/15 priority date for international students. Applications are processed on a rolling basis. Application fee: $75 ($100 for international students). Electronic applications accepted. *Expenses:* $1,125 per credit, $655 fees. *Financial support:* Fellowships, research assistantships, Federal Work-Study, institutionally sponsored loans, scholarships/grants, tuition waivers, and health benefits (for PhD candidates only) available. Support available to part-time students. Financial award application deadline: 4/30; financial award applicants required to submit FAFSA. *Faculty research:* Cardiovascular science, infectious diseases, neuroscience, cancer, cell signaling. *Unit head:* Dr. Francis L. Belloni, Dean, 914-594-4110, Fax: 914-594-4944, E-mail: francis_belloni@nymc.edu. *Application contact:* Valerie Romeo-Messana, Director of Admissions, 914-594-4110, Fax: 914-594-4944, E-mail: v_romeomessana@nymc.edu.
Website: https://www.nymc.edu/graduate-school-of-basic-medical-sciences-gsbms/gsbms-academics/

North Carolina State University, College of Veterinary Medicine, Program in Comparative Biomedical Sciences, Raleigh, NC 27695. Offers cell biology (MS, PhD); infectious disease (MS, PhD); pathology (MS, PhD); pharmacology (MS, PhD); population medicine (MS, PhD). *Program availability:* Part-time. *Degree requirements:* For master's, thesis; for doctorate, thesis/dissertation. *Entrance requirements:* For master's and doctorate, GRE General Test. Additional exam requirements/recommendations for international students: Required—TOEFL (minimum score 550 paper-based). Electronic applications accepted. *Expenses:* Contact institution. *Faculty research:* Infectious diseases, cell biology, pharmacology and toxicology, genomics, pathology and population medicine.

Northeastern University, Bouvé College of Health Sciences, Boston, MA 02115-5096. Offers applied behavior analysis (MS); audiology (Au D); counseling psychology (MS, PhD, CAGS); exercise science (MS); nursing (MS, PhD, CAGS), including

administration (MS), adult-gerontology acute care nurse practitioner (MS, CAGS), adult-gerontology primary care nurse practitioner (MS, CAGS), anesthesia (MS), family nurse practitioner (MS, CAGS), neonatal nurse practitioner (MS, CAGS), pediatric nurse practitioner (MS, CAGS), psychiatric mental health nurse practitioner (MS, CAGS); nursing practice (DNP); pharmaceutical sciences (MS, PhD), including interdisciplinary concentration, pharmaceutics and drug delivery systems; pharmacology (MS); pharmacy (Pharm D); school psychology (PhD); speech-language pathology (MS); urban health (MPH); MS/MBA. *Accreditation:* ACPE (one or more programs are accredited). *Program availability:* Part-time, evening/weekend, online learning. *Faculty:* 192 full-time. *Students:* 1,685. In 2017, 352 master's, 312 doctorates, 25 other advanced degrees awarded. *Degree requirements:* For doctorate, thesis/dissertation (for some programs); for CAGS, comprehensive exam. Application fee: $75. Electronic applications accepted. *Expenses:* Contact institution. *Financial support:* Fellowships, research assistantships, teaching assistantships, career-related internships or fieldwork, scholarships/grants, health care benefits, tuition waivers, and unspecified assistantships available. Support available to part-time students. Financial award applicants required to submit FAFSA. *Unit head:* Susan L. Parish, Dean, Bouve College of Health Sciences, 617-373-3321, Fax: 617-373-3030, E-mail: s.parish@northeastern.edu. *Application contact:* 617-373-2708, Fax: 617-373-4701, E-mail: bouvegrad@northeastern.edu.
Website: https://www.northeastern.edu/bouve/

The Ohio State University, College of Pharmacy, Columbus, OH 43210. Offers MS, PhD, Pharm D, Pharm D/MBA, Pharm D/MPH, Pharm D/PhD. *Accreditation:* ACPE (one or more programs are accredited). *Faculty:* 53. *Students:* 608 (331 women); includes 175 minority (42 Black or African American, non-Hispanic/Latino; 97 Asian, non-Hispanic/Latino; 22 Hispanic/Latino; 14 Two or more races, non-Hispanic/Latino), 61 international. Average age 25. In 2017, 15 master's, 127 doctorates awarded. Terminal master's awarded for partial completion of doctoral program. *Degree requirements:* For doctorate, comprehensive exam (for some programs), thesis/dissertation (for some programs). *Entrance requirements:* For master's, GRE General Test, minimum GPA of 3.0; for doctorate, GRE General Test; PCAT (for PharmD), minimum GPA of 3.0. Additional exam requirements/recommendations for international students: Required—TOEFL minimum score 600 paper-based, 100 iBT (for MS and PhD); TOEFL minimum score 577 paper-based; 90 iBT, Michigan English Language Assessment Battery minimum score 84, IELTS minimum score 7.5 (for PharmD). *Application deadline:* For fall admission, 12/15 for domestic and international students. Application fee: $60 ($70 for international students). Electronic applications accepted. *Expenses:* Contact institution. *Financial support:* Fellowships with full tuition reimbursements, research assistantships with full tuition reimbursements, teaching assistantships with full tuition reimbursements, career-related internships or fieldwork, Federal Work-Study, institutionally sponsored loans, scholarships/grants, and traineeships available. *Unit head:* Dr. Henry J. Mann, Dean and Professor, 614-292-5711, Fax: 614-292-2588, E-mail: mann.414@osu.edu. *Application contact:* E-mail: admissions@pharmacy.ohio-state.edu.
Website: http://www.pharmacy.osu.edu

Oregon Health & Science University, School of Medicine, Graduate Programs in Medicine, Program in Molecular and Cellular Biosciences, Department of Physiology and Pharmacology, Portland, OR 97239-3098. Offers PhD. *Faculty:* 15 full-time (5 women), 20 part-time/adjunct (7 women). *Students:* 15 full-time (10 women); includes 6 minority (4 Asian, non-Hispanic/Latino; 2 Hispanic/Latino). Average age 27. In 2017, 2 doctorates awarded. *Degree requirements:* For doctorate, comprehensive exam, thesis/dissertation. *Entrance requirements:* For doctorate, GRE General Test (minimum scores: 153 Verbal/148 Quantitative/4.5 Analytical) or MCAT (for some programs). *Application deadline:* For fall admission, 12/1 for domestic and international students. Application fee: $70. Electronic applications accepted. *Financial support:* Health care benefits, tuition waivers (full), and full-tuition and stipends available. Financial award application deadline: 3/1; financial award applicants required to submit FAFSA. *Faculty research:* Ion conduction and gating in K+ channels, autonomic neuron plasticity, neurotransmitter/receptor expression, fetal/neonatal pharmacology, molecular pharmacology. *Unit head:* Dr. Robert Duvoisin, Program Director, E-mail: somgrad@ohsu.edu. *Application contact:* Brandi Colbert, Program Coordinator, E-mail: somgrad@ohsu.edu.

Purdue University, College of Pharmacy and Graduate School, Graduate Programs in Pharmacy and Pharmacal Sciences, Department of Medicinal Chemistry and Molecular Pharmacology, West Lafayette, IN 47907. Offers biophysical and computational chemistry (PhD); cancer research (PhD); immunology and infectious disease (PhD); medicinal biochemistry and molecular biology (PhD); medicinal chemistry and chemical biology (PhD); molecular pharmacology (PhD); neuropharmacology, neurodegeneration, and neurotoxicity (PhD); systems biology and functional genomics (PhD). *Faculty:* 26 full-time (5 women). *Students:* 52 full-time (22 women), 3 part-time (all women); includes 4 minority (1 Black or African American, non-Hispanic/Latino; 2 Asian, non-Hispanic/Latino; 1 Hispanic/Latino), 29 international. Average age 26. 151 applicants, 19% accepted, 13 enrolled. In 2017, 18 doctorates awarded. *Degree requirements:* For doctorate, thesis/dissertation. *Entrance requirements:* For doctorate, GRE General Test; GRE Subject Test in biology, biochemistry, and chemistry (recommended), minimum undergraduate GPA of 3.0. Additional exam requirements/recommendations for international students: Required—TOEFL (minimum score 550 paper-based; 77 iBT); Recommended—TWE. *Application deadline:* For fall admission, 2/1 for domestic and international students. Applications are processed on a rolling basis. Application fee: $60 ($75 for international students). Electronic applications accepted. *Financial support:* Fellowships, research assistantships, teaching assistantships, and traineeships available. Support available to part-time students. Financial award applicants required to submit FAFSA. *Faculty research:* Drug design and development, cancer research, drug synthesis and analysis, chemical pharmacology, environmental toxicology. *Unit head:* Zhong-Yin Zhang, Head, 765-494-1403, E-mail: zhang-yn@purdue.edu. *Application contact:* Delayne Graham, Graduate Contact, 765-494-1362, E-mail: dkgraham@purdue.edu.

Purdue University, School of Veterinary Medicine and Graduate School, Graduate Programs in Veterinary Medicine, Department of Basic Medical Sciences, West Lafayette, IN 47907. Offers anatomy (MS, PhD); pharmacology (MS, PhD); physiology (MS, PhD). *Program availability:* Part-time. Terminal master's awarded for partial completion of doctoral program. *Degree requirements:* For master's, thesis; for doctorate, thesis/dissertation. *Entrance requirements:* For master's and doctorate, GRE General Test. Additional exam requirements/recommendations for international students: Required—TOEFL. Electronic applications accepted. *Faculty research:* Development and regeneration, tissue injury and shock, biomedical engineering, ovarian function, bone and cartilage biology, cell and molecular biology.

Queen's University at Kingston, School of Graduate Studies, Faculty of Health Sciences, Department of Pharmacology and Toxicology, Kingston, ON K7L 3N6, Canada. Offers M Sc, PhD. *Degree requirements:* For master's, thesis; for doctorate, comprehensive exam, thesis/dissertation. *Entrance requirements:* For master's, minimum 2nd class standing, honors bachelor of science degree (life sciences, health sciences, or equivalent); for doctorate, masters of science degree or outstanding performance in honors bachelor of science program. Additional exam requirements/recommendations for international students: Required—TOEFL (minimum score 600 paper-based). Electronic applications accepted. *Faculty research:* Biochemical toxicology, cardiovascular pharmacology and neuropharmacology.

Rush University, Graduate College, Division of Pharmacology, Chicago, IL 60612-3832. Offers clinical research (MS); pharmacology (MS, PhD); MD/PhD. Terminal master's awarded for partial completion of doctoral program. *Degree requirements:* For master's, thesis; for doctorate, thesis/dissertation. *Entrance requirements:* For master's and doctorate, GRE General Test, interview. Additional exam requirements/recommendations for international students: Required—TOEFL (minimum score 550 paper-based). *Faculty research:* Dopamine neurobiology and Parkinson's disease; cardiac electrophysiology and clinical pharmacology; neutrophil motility, apoptosis, and adhesion; angiogenesis; pulmonary vascular physiology.

Rutgers University–Newark, Graduate School of Biomedical Sciences, Department of Pharmacology and Physiology, Newark, NJ 07107. Offers PhD. *Degree requirements:* For doctorate, thesis/dissertation, qualifying exam. *Entrance requirements:* For doctorate, GRE General Test. Additional exam requirements/recommendations for international students: Required—TOEFL. Electronic applications accepted.

Saint Louis University, Graduate Programs, School of Medicine, Graduate Programs in Biomedical Sciences and Graduate Programs, Department of Pharmacological and Physiological Science, St. Louis, MO 63103. Offers PhD. *Degree requirements:* For doctorate, comprehensive exam, thesis/dissertation, departmental qualifying exams. *Entrance requirements:* For doctorate, GRE General Test (GRE Subject Test optional), letters of recommendation, resume, interview. Additional exam requirements/recommendations for international students: Required—TOEFL (minimum score 525 paper-based). Electronic applications accepted. *Faculty research:* Molecular endocrinology, neuropharmacology, cardiovascular science, drug abuse, neurotransmitter and hormonal signaling mechanisms.

Southern Illinois University Carbondale, Graduate School, Graduate Programs in Medicine, Program in Pharmacology, Springfield, IL 62794-9629. Offers MS, PhD. *Degree requirements:* For master's, thesis; for doctorate, thesis/dissertation. *Entrance requirements:* For master's, GRE, minimum GPA of 3.0; for doctorate, GRE, minimum GPA of 3.25. Additional exam requirements/recommendations for international students: Required—TOEFL. *Faculty research:* Autonomic nervous system pharmacology, biochemical pharmacology, neuropharmacology, toxicology, cardiovascular pharmacology.

State University of New York Upstate Medical University, College of Graduate Studies, Program in Pharmacology, Syracuse, NY 13210. Offers PhD, MD/PhD. Terminal master's awarded for partial completion of doctoral program. *Degree requirements:* For doctorate, comprehensive exam, thesis/dissertation. *Entrance requirements:* For doctorate, GRE General Test, telephone interview. Additional exam requirements/recommendations for international students: Required—TOEFL. Electronic applications accepted. *Faculty research:* Cancer, disorders of the nervous system, infectious diseases, diabetes/metabolic disorders/cardiovascular diseases.

Stony Brook University, State University of New York, Stony Brook Medicine, School of Medicine and Graduate School, Graduate Programs in Medicine, Department of Pharmacological Sciences, Graduate Program in Molecular and Cellular Pharmacology, Stony Brook, NY 11794. Offers MS, PhD. *Faculty:* 19 full-time (5 women). *Students:* 54 full-time (30 women); includes 19 minority (5 Black or African American, non-Hispanic/Latino; 6 Asian, non-Hispanic/Latino; 7 Hispanic/Latino; 1 Two or more races, non-Hispanic/Latino), 9 international. Average age 26. 47 applicants, 32% accepted, 6 enrolled. In 2017, 5 doctorates awarded. *Degree requirements:* For doctorate, thesis/dissertation, departmental qualifying exam. *Entrance requirements:* For doctorate, GRE General Test. Additional exam requirements/recommendations for international students: Required—TOEFL. *Application deadline:* For fall admission, 1/15 priority date for domestic students; for spring admission, 10/1 for domestic students. Applications are processed on a rolling basis. Application fee: $100. Electronic applications accepted. *Expenses:* Contact institution. *Financial support:* In 2017–18, 18 fellowships, 17 research assistantships were awarded; teaching assistantships and Federal Work-Study also available. Financial award application deadline: 3/15; financial award applicants required to submit FAFSA. *Faculty research:* Bioimaging, pharmacology, DNA repair, DNA replication, cancer or carcinogenesis. *Total annual research expenditures:* $5.4 million. *Unit head:* Dr. Michael A. Frohman, Chair, 631-444-3050, Fax: 631-444-9749, E-mail: michael.frohman@stonybrook.edu. *Application contact:* Odalis Hernandez, Coordinator, 631-444-3057, Fax: 631-444-9749, E-mail: odalis.hernandez@stonybrook.edu.
Website: http://www.pharm.stonybrook.edu/about-graduate-program

Thomas Jefferson University, Jefferson College of Biomedical Sciences, MS Program in Pharmacology, Philadelphia, PA 19107. Offers MS. *Program availability:* Part-time, evening/weekend. *Faculty:* 43 full-time (16 women), 28 part-time/adjunct (9 women). *Students:* 32 part-time (18 women); includes 6 minority (1 Black or African American, non-Hispanic/Latino; 2 Asian, non-Hispanic/Latino; 3 Hispanic/Latino), 2 international. 15 applicants, 73% accepted, 5 enrolled. In 2017, 6 master's awarded. *Degree requirements:* For master's, thesis, clerkship. *Entrance requirements:* For master's, GRE General Test or MCAT, minimum GPA of 3.0. Additional exam requirements/recommendations for international students: Required—TOEFL, IELTS (minimum score 7). *Application deadline:* For fall admission, 8/1 priority date for domestic students, 3/1 priority date for international students; for winter admission, 12/1 priority date for domestic students, 6/1 priority date for international students; for spring admission, 4/1 priority date for domestic students. Applications are processed on a rolling basis. Application fee: $50. Electronic applications accepted. *Financial support:* Federal Work-Study and institutionally sponsored loans available. Support available to part-time students. Financial award application deadline: 5/1; financial award applicants required to submit FAFSA. *Faculty research:* Pharmacology, drug development, planning and management, biostatistics. *Unit head:* Dr. Carol L. Beck, Associate Dean/Program Director, 215-503-6539, Fax: 215-503-3433, E-mail: carol.beck@jefferson.edu. *Application contact:* Marc E. Stearns, Senior Associate Director of Admissions, 215-503-0155, Fax: 215-503-3433, E-mail: jgsbs-info@jefferson.edu.
Website: http://www.jefferson.edu/university/biomedical-sciences/degrees-programs/master-programs/pharmacology.html

Tulane University, School of Medicine and School of Liberal Arts, Graduate Programs in Biomedical Sciences, Department of Pharmacology, New Orleans, LA 70118-5669. Offers MS. MS and PhD offered through the Graduate School. *Degree requirements:* For master's, one foreign language, thesis. *Entrance requirements:* For master's, GRE General Test, minimum B average in undergraduate course work. Additional exam requirements/recommendations for international students: Required—TOEFL. Electronic applications accepted. *Expenses: Tuition:* Full-time $50,920; part-time $2829 per credit hour. *Required fees:* $2040; $44.50 per credit hour. $580 per term. Tuition and fees vary according to course load, degree level and program.

Universidad Central del Caribe, School of Medicine, Program in Biomedical Sciences, Bayamón, PR 00960-6032. Offers anatomy and cell biology (MA, MS); biochemistry (MS); biomedical sciences (MA); cellular and molecular biology (PhD); microbiology and immunology (MA, MS); pharmacology (MS); physiology (MS).

Pharmacology

Université de Montréal, Faculty of Medicine, Department of Pharmacology, Montréal, QC H3C 3J7, Canada. Offers M Sc, PhD. Terminal master's awarded for partial completion of doctoral program. *Degree requirements:* For master's, thesis; for doctorate, thesis/dissertation, general exam. *Entrance requirements:* For master's, proficiency in French, knowledge of English; for doctorate, master's degree, proficiency in French. Electronic applications accepted. *Faculty research:* Molecular, clinical, and cardiovascular pharmacology; pharmacokinetics; mechanisms of drug interactions and toxicity; neuropharmacology and receptology.

Université de Sherbrooke, Faculty of Medicine and Health Sciences, Graduate Programs in Medicine, Department of Pharmacology, Sherbrooke, QC J1H 5N4, Canada. Offers M Sc, PhD. Terminal master's awarded for partial completion of doctoral program. *Degree requirements:* For master's, thesis; for doctorate, thesis/dissertation. Electronic applications accepted. *Faculty research:* Pharmacology of peptide hormones, pharmacology of lipid mediators, protein-protein interactions, medicinal pharmacology.

University at Buffalo, the State University of New York, Graduate School, Jacobs School of Medicine and Biomedical Sciences, Graduate Programs in Medicine and Biomedical Sciences, Department of Pharmacology and Toxicology, Buffalo, NY 14203. Offers pharmacology (MS, PhD); MD/PhD. *Faculty:* 20 full-time (3 women), 1 part-time/adjunct (0 women). *Students:* 29 full-time (15 women); includes 9 minority (5 Black or African American, non-Hispanic/Latino; 1 American Indian or Alaska Native, non-Hispanic/Latino; 2 Asian, non-Hispanic/Latino; 1 Hispanic/Latino), 10 international. Average age 26. 47 applicants, 47% accepted, 12 enrolled. In 2017, 1 master's, 2 doctorates awarded. Terminal master's awarded for partial completion of doctoral program. *Degree requirements:* For master's, thesis; for doctorate, thesis/dissertation. *Entrance requirements:* For master's and doctorate, GRE General Test, 3 letters of recommendation. Additional exam requirements/recommendations for international students: Required—TOEFL (minimum score 79 iBT). *Application deadline:* For fall admission, 2/14 priority date for domestic and international students. Applications are processed on a rolling basis. Application fee: $85. Electronic applications accepted. *Financial support:* In 2017–18, 3 students received support, including 15 research assistantships with full tuition reimbursements available (averaging $27,000 per year); fellowships, teaching assistantships, Federal Work-Study, scholarships/grants, health care benefits, and unspecified assistantships also available. Financial award application deadline: 2/14; financial award applicants required to submit FAFSA. *Faculty research:* Neuropharmacology, toxicology, signal transduction, molecular pharmacology, behavioral pharmacology. *Total annual research expenditures:* $3.7 million. *Unit head:* Dr. David Dietz, Associate Professor/Chair, 716-829-2071, Fax: 716-829-2801, E-mail: ddietz@buffalo.edu. *Application contact:* Linda M. LeRoy, Admissions Assistant, 716-829-2800, Fax: 716-829-2801, E-mail: pmygrad@buffalo.edu.
Website: http://medicine.buffalo.edu/pharmtox

University of Alberta, Faculty of Graduate Studies and Research, Department of Pharmacology, Edmonton, AB T6G 2E1, Canada. Offers M Sc, PhD. Terminal master's awarded for partial completion of doctoral program. *Degree requirements:* For master's, thesis; for doctorate, thesis/dissertation. *Entrance requirements:* For master's, B Sc, minimum GPA of 3.3; for doctorate, M Sc in pharmacology or closely related field, honors B Sc in pharmacology. *Faculty research:* Cardiovascular pharmacology, neuropharmacology, cancer pharmacology, molecular pharmacology, toxicology.

The University of Arizona, College of Pharmacy, Department of Pharmacology and Toxicology, Graduate Program in Medical Pharmacology, Tucson, AZ 85721. Offers medical pharmacology (PhD); perfusion science (MS). *Degree requirements:* For master's, thesis; for doctorate, comprehensive exam, thesis/dissertation. *Entrance requirements:* For master's, GRE General Test, 3 letters of recommendation; for doctorate, GRE General Test, personal statement, 3 letters of recommendation. Additional exam requirements/recommendations for international students: Required—TOEFL (minimum score 550 paper-based; 79 iBT). Electronic applications accepted. *Faculty research:* Immunopharmacology, pharmacogenetics, pharmacogenomics, clinical pharmacology, ocularpharmacology and neuropharmacology.

University of Arkansas for Medical Sciences, Graduate School, Little Rock, AR 72205. Offers biochemistry and molecular biology (MS, PhD); bioinformatics (MS, PhD); cellular physiology and molecular biophysics (MS, PhD); clinical nutrition (MS); interdisciplinary biomedical sciences (MS, PhD, Certificate); interdisciplinary toxicology (MS); microbiology and immunology (PhD); neurobiology and developmental sciences (PhD); pharmacology (PhD); MD/PhD. Bioinformatics programs hosted jointly with the University of Arkansas at Little Rock. *Program availability:* Part-time. Terminal master's awarded for partial completion of doctoral program. *Degree requirements:* For master's, comprehensive exam (for some programs), thesis (for some programs); for doctorate, thesis/dissertation. *Entrance requirements:* For master's and doctorate, GRE. Additional exam requirements/recommendations for international students: Required—TOEFL. Electronic applications accepted. *Expenses:* Contact institution.

The University of British Columbia, Faculty of Medicine, Department of Anesthesiology, Pharmacology and Therapeutics, Vancouver, BC V6T 1Z3, Canada. Offers pharmacology (M Sc, PhD). Terminal master's awarded for partial completion of doctoral program. *Degree requirements:* For master's, thesis; for doctorate, comprehensive exam, thesis/dissertation. *Entrance requirements:* For master's, MD or appropriate bachelor's degree; for doctorate, MD or M Sc. Additional exam requirements/recommendations for international students: Required—TOEFL. Electronic applications accepted. *Expenses:* Contact institution. *Faculty research:* Cellular, biochemical, autonomic, and cardiovascular pharmacology; neuropharmacology and pulmonary pharmacology.

University of California, Davis, Graduate Studies, Graduate Group in Pharmacology and Toxicology, Davis, CA 95616. Offers MS, PhD. Terminal master's awarded for partial completion of doctoral program. *Degree requirements:* For master's, comprehensive exam or thesis; for doctorate, thesis/dissertation, qualifying exam. *Entrance requirements:* For master's and doctorate, GRE General Test, minimum GPA of 3.0, course work in biochemistry and/or physiology. Additional exam requirements/recommendations for international students: Required—TOEFL (minimum score 550 paper-based). Electronic applications accepted. *Faculty research:* Respiratory, neurochemical, molecular, genetic, and ecological toxicology.

University of California, Los Angeles, David Geffen School of Medicine and Graduate Division, Graduate Programs in Medicine, Department of Molecular and Medical Pharmacology, Los Angeles, CA 90095. Offers MS, PhD. *Degree requirements:* For master's, thesis; for doctorate, thesis/dissertation, written and oral qualifying exams; 2 quarters of teaching experience. *Entrance requirements:* For doctorate, GRE General Test, bachelor's degree; minimum undergraduate GPA of 3.0 (or its equivalent if letter grade system not used). Additional exam requirements/recommendations for international students: Required—TOEFL. Electronic applications accepted.

University of California, San Francisco, School of Pharmacy and Graduate Division, Pharmaceutical Sciences and Pharmacogenomics Program, San Francisco, CA 94158-0775. Offers PhD. *Degree requirements:* For doctorate, comprehensive exam, thesis/dissertation. *Entrance requirements:* For doctorate, GRE General Test, bachelor's degree, 3 letters of recommendation, personal statement. Additional exam requirements/recommendations for international students: Required—TOEFL. Electronic applications accepted. *Faculty research:* Drug development sciences, molecular pharmacology, therapeutic bioengineering, pharmacogenomics and functional genomics, quantitative and systems pharmacology, computational genomics.

University of Cincinnati, Graduate School, College of Medicine, Graduate Programs in Biomedical Sciences, Department of Pharmacology and Cell Biophysics, Cincinnati, OH 45221. Offers cell biophysics (PhD); pharmacology (PhD). *Degree requirements:* For doctorate, thesis/dissertation, qualifying exam. *Entrance requirements:* For doctorate, GRE General Test. Additional exam requirements/recommendations for international students: Required—TOEFL. Electronic applications accepted. *Expenses: Tuition, area resident:* Full-time $14,468. Tuition, state resident: full-time $14,968; part-time $754 per credit hour. Tuition, nonresident: full-time $24,210; part-time $1311 per credit hour. *International tuition:* $26,460 full-time. *Required fees:* $3958; $84 per credit hour. One-time fee: $85 full-time. Tuition and fees vary according to course load, degree level and program. *Faculty research:* Lipoprotein research, enzyme regulation, electrophysiology, gene actuation.

University of Colorado Denver, School of Medicine, Program in Pharmacology, Aurora, CO 80206. Offers bioinformatics (PhD); biomolecular structure (PhD). *Students:* 26 full-time (12 women); includes 7 minority (2 Asian, non-Hispanic/Latino; 4 Hispanic/Latino; 1 Two or more races, non-Hispanic/Latino), 2 international. Average age 27. 28 applicants, 14% accepted, 4 enrolled. In 2017, 3 doctorates awarded. *Degree requirements:* For doctorate, comprehensive exam, thesis/dissertation, major seminar, 3 research rotations in the first year, 30 hours each of course work and thesis. *Entrance requirements:* For doctorate, GRE General Test, three letters of recommendation, personal statement. Additional exam requirements/recommendations for international students: Required—TOEFL (minimum score 550 paper-based; 80 iBT). *Application deadline:* For fall admission, 12/15 for domestic students, 11/15 for international students. Application fee: $50 ($75 for international students). Electronic applications accepted. *Financial support:* Fellowships, research assistantships, teaching assistantships, institutionally sponsored loans, scholarships/grants, traineeships, health care benefits, tuition waivers (full), and unspecified assistantships available. *Faculty research:* Cancer biology, drugs of abuse, neuroscience, signal transduction, structural biology. *Unit head:* Dr. Andrew Thorburn, Interim Chair, 303-724-3290, Fax: 303-724-3663, E-mail: andrew.thorburn@ucdenver.edu. *Application contact:* Elizabeth Bowen, Graduate Program Coordinator, 303-724-3565, E-mail: elizabeth.bowen@ucdenver.edu.
Website: http://www.ucdenver.edu/academics/colleges/medicalschool/departments/Pharmacology/Pages/Pharmacology.aspx

University of Connecticut, Graduate School, School of Pharmacy, Department of Pharmaceutical Sciences, Graduate Program in Pharmacology and Toxicology, Storrs, CT 06269. Offers pharmacology (MS, PhD); toxicology (MS, PhD). Terminal master's awarded for partial completion of doctoral program. *Degree requirements:* For master's, comprehensive exam, thesis; for doctorate, thesis/dissertation. *Entrance requirements:* For master's and doctorate, GRE General Test. Additional exam requirements/recommendations for international students: Required—TOEFL (minimum score 550 paper-based). Electronic applications accepted.

University of Florida, College of Medicine and Graduate School, Interdisciplinary Program in Biomedical Sciences, Concentration in Physiology and Pharmacology, Gainesville, FL 32611. Offers PhD. *Degree requirements:* For doctorate, thesis/dissertation. *Entrance requirements:* For doctorate, GRE General Test, minimum GPA of 3.0, biochemistry before enrollment. Electronic applications accepted.

University of Florida, Graduate School, College of Pharmacy, Graduate Programs in Pharmacy, Department of Pharmacodynamics, Gainesville, FL 32611. Offers MSP, PhD, Pharm D/PhD. *Degree requirements:* For doctorate, comprehensive exam, thesis/dissertation. *Entrance requirements:* For master's and doctorate, GRE General Test, minimum GPA of 3.0. Additional exam requirements/recommendations for international students: Required—TOEFL (minimum score 550 paper-based; 80 iBT), IELTS (minimum score 6). Electronic applications accepted. *Faculty research:* Neurological mechanisms involved in addiction, stress, and body fluid homeostasis; cellular and molecular neurobiology of epilepsy, age-related cognitive decline, and Parkinson's Disease; hypertension and cardiac hypertrophy; stress hormone effects on fetal and neonatal development.

University of Georgia, College of Veterinary Medicine, Department of Physiology and Pharmacology, Athens, GA 30602. Offers pharmacology (MS, PhD). *Degree requirements:* For master's, thesis; for doctorate, one foreign language, thesis/dissertation. *Entrance requirements:* For master's and doctorate, GRE General Test. Electronic applications accepted.

University of Guelph, Ontario Veterinary College and Graduate Studies, Graduate Programs in Veterinary Sciences, Department of Biomedical Sciences, Guelph, ON N1G 2W1, Canada. Offers morphology (M Sc, DV Sc, PhD); neuroscience (M Sc, DV Sc, PhD); pharmacology (M Sc, DV Sc, PhD); physiology (M Sc, DV Sc, PhD); toxicology (M Sc, DV Sc, PhD). *Program availability:* Part-time. *Degree requirements:* For master's, thesis; for doctorate, comprehensive exam, thesis/dissertation. *Entrance requirements:* For master's, honors B Sc, minimum 75% average in last 20 courses; for doctorate, M Sc with thesis from accredited institution. Additional exam requirements/recommendations for international students: Required—TOEFL (minimum score 550 paper-based; 89 iBT). Electronic applications accepted. *Faculty research:* Cellular morphology; endocrine, vascular and reproductive physiology; clinical pharmacology; veterinary toxicology; developmental biology, neuroscience.

University of Hawaii at Hilo, Program in Clinical Psychopharmacology, Hilo, HI 96720-4091. Offers MS. *Entrance requirements:* Additional exam requirements/recommendations for international students: Required—TOEFL, IELTS. Electronic applications accepted.

University of Houston, College of Pharmacy, Houston, TX 77204. Offers pharmaceutics (MSPHR, PhD); pharmacology (MSPHR, PhD); pharmacy (Pharm D); pharmacy administration (MSPHR, PhD). *Accreditation:* ACPE. *Program availability:* Part-time. Terminal master's awarded for partial completion of doctoral program. *Entrance requirements:* For doctorate, PCAT (for Pharm D). Additional exam requirements/recommendations for international students: Required—TOEFL. Electronic applications accepted. *Faculty research:* Drug screening and design, cardiovascular pharmacology, infectious disease, asthma research, herbal medicine.

University of Illinois at Chicago, College of Medicine and Graduate College, Graduate Programs in Medicine, Department of Pharmacology, Chicago, IL 60612. Offers PhD, MD/PhD. *Degree requirements:* For doctorate, thesis/dissertation. *Entrance requirements:* For doctorate, GRE General Test. Additional exam requirements/recommendations for international students: Required—TOEFL. *Faculty research:* Cardiovascular and lung biology, cell signaling, molecular pharmacology of G-proteins, immunopharmacology, molecular and cellular basis of inflammation, neuroscience.

The University of Iowa, Roy J. and Lucille A. Carver College of Medicine and Graduate College, Graduate Programs in Medicine, Department of Pharmacology, Iowa City, IA 52242-1316. Offers MS, PhD. Terminal master's awarded for partial completion of doctoral program. *Degree requirements:* For master's, thesis. *Entrance requirements:*

For master's, GRE General Test. Additional exam requirements/recommendations for international students: Required—TOEFL (minimum score 600 paper-based). Electronic applications accepted. *Faculty research:* Cancer and cell cycle, hormones and growth factors, nervous system function and dysfunction, receptors and signal transduction, stroke and hypertension.

The University of Kansas, Graduate Studies, School of Pharmacy, Department of Pharmacology and Toxicology, Lawrence, KS 66045. Offers MS, PhD. *Students:* 32 full-time (24 women), 1 part-time (0 women); includes 4 minority (1 American Indian or Alaska Native, non-Hispanic/Latino; 1 Asian, non-Hispanic/Latino; 2 Hispanic/Latino), 14 international. Average age 28. 64 applicants, 17% accepted, 10 enrolled. In 2017, 7 master's, 4 doctorates awarded. Terminal master's awarded for partial completion of doctoral program. *Entrance requirements:* For master's and doctorate, GRE General Test, bachelor's degree in related field, 3 letters of recommendation, resume or curriculum vitae, official transcripts, 1-2 page personal statement. *Application deadline:* For fall admission, 1/15 priority date for domestic and international students. Application fee: $65 ($85 for international students). Electronic applications accepted. *Financial support:* Fellowships, research assistantships, and teaching assistantships available. Financial award application deadline: 2/1. *Faculty research:* Molecular neurobiology, gene regulation, neurotransmitter receptors, drug metabolism. *Unit head:* Nancy Muma, Chair, 785-864-4002, E-mail: nmuma@ku.edu. *Application contact:* Sarah Hoadley, Graduate Admissions Contact, 785-864-4002, E-mail: sarahhoadley@ku.edu.
Website: http://pharmtox.ku.edu/

The University of Kansas, University of Kansas Medical Center, School of Medicine, Department of Pharmacology, Toxicology and Therapeutics, Kansas City, KS 66160. Offers pharmacology (PhD); toxicology (PhD); MD/PhD. *Faculty:* 17. *Students:* 19 full-time (10 women); includes 3 minority (2 Black or African American, non-Hispanic/Latino; 1 Two or more races, non-Hispanic/Latino), 12 international. Average age 30. 1 applicant, 100% accepted, 1 enrolled. In 2017, 4 doctorates awarded. Terminal master's awarded for partial completion of doctoral program. *Degree requirements:* For doctorate, one foreign language, comprehensive exam, thesis/dissertation. *Entrance requirements:* For doctorate, GRE General Test. Additional exam requirements/recommendations for international students: Required—TOEFL. *Application deadline:* For fall admission, 12/1 priority date for domestic and international students. Applications are processed on a rolling basis. Application fee: $60. Electronic applications accepted. Application fee is waived when completed online. *Financial support:* Fellowships with full tuition reimbursements, research assistantships with full tuition reimbursements, teaching assistantships with full tuition reimbursements, Federal Work-Study, scholarships/grants, traineeships, and unspecified assistantships available. Support available to part-time students. Financial award application deadline: 3/1; financial award applicants required to submit FAFSA. *Faculty research:* Liver nuclear receptors, hepatobiliary transporters, pharmacogenomics, neuropharmacology of pain and depression, hepatotoxicity. *Total annual research expenditures:* $4.2 million. *Unit head:* Dr. Hartmut Jaeschke, Professor and Chair, 913-588-7500, Fax: 913-588-7501, E-mail: hjaeschke@kumc.edu. *Application contact:* Dr. Bruno Hagenbuch, Chair, Departmental Graduate Committee, 913-588-7500, Fax: 913-588-7501, E-mail: bhagenbuch@kumc.edu.
Website: http://www.kumc.edu/school-of-medicine/pharmacology-toxicology-and-therapeutics.html

University of Kentucky, Graduate School, Graduate School Programs from the College of Medicine, Program in Molecular and Biomedical Pharmacology, Lexington, KY 40506-0032. Offers PhD, MD/PhD. *Degree requirements:* For doctorate, comprehensive exam, thesis/dissertation. *Entrance requirements:* For doctorate, GRE General Test, minimum undergraduate GPA of 2.75, graduate 3.0. Additional exam requirements/recommendations for international students: Required—TOEFL (minimum score 550 paper-based). Electronic applications accepted.

University of Louisville, School of Medicine, Department of Pharmacology and Toxicology, Louisville, KY 40292-0001. Offers MS, PhD, MD/PhD. *Program availability:* Part-time. *Faculty:* 20 full-time (5 women). *Students:* 34 full-time (18 women), 16 part-time (10 women); includes 10 minority (3 Black or African American, non-Hispanic/Latino; 2 Asian, non-Hispanic/Latino; 5 Two or more races, non-Hispanic/Latino), 14 international. Average age 29. 21 applicants, 43% accepted, 9 enrolled. In 2017, 3 master's, 5 doctorates awarded. Terminal master's awarded for partial completion of doctoral program. *Degree requirements:* For master's, thesis; for doctorate, comprehensive exam, thesis/dissertation. *Entrance requirements:* For master's and doctorate, GRE General Test (minimum score of 1000 verbal and quantitative), minimum GPA of 3.0. Additional exam requirements/recommendations for international students: Required—TOEFL; Recommended—IELTS. *Application deadline:* For fall admission, 12/1 priority date for domestic and international students. Application fee: $65. *Expenses:* Tuition, state resident: full-time $12,246; part-time $681 per credit hour. Tuition, nonresident: full-time $25,486; part-time $1417 per credit hour. *Required fees:* $196. Tuition and fees vary according to course load, program and reciprocity agreements. *Financial support:* In 2017–18, 5 fellowships with full tuition reimbursements (averaging $25,000 per year) were awarded. Financial award application deadline: 12/1. *Faculty research:* Carcinogenesis, cardiometabolic disease, metal toxicology, drug development, diabetes. *Total annual research expenditures:* $4.1 million. *Unit head:* Dr. David W. Hein, Chair, 502-852-5141, Fax: 502-852-7868, E-mail: dhein@louisville.edu. *Application contact:* Heddy R. Rubin, Information Contact, 502-852-5741, Fax: 502-852-7868, E-mail: hrrubi01@gwise.louisville.edu.
Website: http://louisville.edu/medicine/departments/pharmacology

The University of Manchester, School of Biological Sciences, Manchester, United Kingdom. Offers adaptive organismal biology (M Phil, PhD); animal biology (M Phil, PhD); biochemistry (M Phil, PhD); bioinformatics (M Phil, PhD); biomolecular sciences (M Phil, PhD); biotechnology (M Phil, PhD); cell biology (M Phil, PhD); cell matrix research (M Phil, PhD); channels and transporters (M Phil, PhD); developmental biology (M Phil, PhD); environmental biology (M Phil, PhD); evolutionary biology (M Phil, PhD); gene expression (M Phil, PhD); genetics (M Phil, PhD); history of science, technology and medicine (M Phil, PhD); immunology (M Phil, PhD); integrative neurobiology and behavior (M Phil, PhD); membrane trafficking (M Phil, PhD); microbiology (M Phil, PhD); molecular and cellular neuroscience (M Phil, PhD); molecular biology (M Phil, PhD); molecular cancer studies (M Phil, PhD); neuroscience (M Phil, PhD); ophthalmology (M Phil, PhD); optometry (M Phil, PhD); organelle function (M Phil, PhD); pharmacology (M Phil, PhD); physiology (M Phil, PhD); plant sciences (M Phil, PhD); stem cell research (M Phil, PhD); structural biology (M Phil, PhD); systems neuroscience (M Phil, PhD); toxicology (M Phil, PhD).

University of Manitoba, Max Rady College of Medicine and Faculty of Graduate Studies, Graduate Programs in Medicine, Department of Pharmacology and Therapeutics, Winnipeg, MB R3T 2N2, Canada. Offers M Sc, PhD. *Program availability:* Part-time. Terminal master's awarded for partial completion of doctoral program. *Degree requirements:* For master's, thesis; for doctorate, thesis/dissertation. *Entrance requirements:* For master's and doctorate, GRE. Additional exam requirements/recommendations for international students: Required—TOEFL. *Faculty research:* Clinical pharmacology; neuropharmacology; cardiac, hepatic, and renal pharmacology.

University of Maryland, Baltimore, Graduate School, Graduate Program in Life Sciences, Program in Molecular Medicine, Baltimore, MD 21201. Offers cancer biology (PhD); cell and molecular physiology (PhD); human genetics and genomic medicine (PhD); molecular toxicology and pharmacology (PhD); MD/PhD. *Students:* 62 full-time (35 women), 2 part-time (0 women); includes 21 minority (7 Black or African American, non-Hispanic/Latino; 8 Asian, non-Hispanic/Latino; 4 Hispanic/Latino; 2 Two or more races, non-Hispanic/Latino), 4 international. Average age 27. 89 applicants, 30% accepted, 3 enrolled. In 2017, 13 doctorates awarded. *Degree requirements:* For doctorate, comprehensive exam, thesis/dissertation. *Entrance requirements:* For doctorate, GRE, minimum GPA of 3.0, curriculum vitae, essay, 3 letters of recommendation. Additional exam requirements/recommendations for international students: Required—TOEFL (minimum score 80 iBT); Recommended—IELTS (minimum score 7). *Application deadline:* For fall admission, 12/1 priority date for domestic students, 1/15 for international students. Application fee: $75. Electronic applications accepted. *Expenses:* Tuition, state resident: full-time $13,990; part-time $661 per credit. Tuition, nonresident: full-time $30,484; part-time $1310 per credit. *Required fees:* $1894; $94 per credit. $415 per semester. Part-time tuition and fees vary according to course load, degree level and program. *Financial support:* In 2017–18, research assistantships with partial tuition reimbursements (averaging $26,000 per year) were awarded; fellowships and health care benefits also available. Financial award application deadline: 3/1; financial award applicants required to submit FAFSA. *Unit head:* Dr. Toni Antalis, Director, 410-706-8222, E-mail: tantalis@som.umaryland.edu. *Application contact:* Marcina Garner, Program Coordinator, 410-706-6044, Fax: 410-706-6040, E-mail: mgarner@som.umaryland.edu.
Website: http://molecularmedicine.umaryland.edu

University of Maryland, Baltimore, Graduate School, Graduate Programs in Pharmacy, Program in Pharmacometrics, Baltimore, MD 21201. Offers MS. *Expenses:* Tuition, state resident: full-time $13,990; part-time $661 per credit. Tuition, nonresident: full-time $30,484; part-time $1310 per credit. *Required fees:* $1894; $94 per credit. $415 per semester. Part-time tuition and fees vary according to course load, degree level and program.

University of Miami, Graduate School, Miller School of Medicine, Graduate Programs in Medicine, Department of Molecular and Cellular Pharmacology, Coral Gables, FL 33124. Offers PhD, MD/PhD. *Degree requirements:* For doctorate, thesis/dissertation, dissertation defense, laboratory rotations, qualifying exam. *Entrance requirements:* For doctorate, GRE General Test. Additional exam requirements/recommendations for international students: Required—TOEFL (minimum score 550 paper-based). *Faculty research:* Membrane and cardiovascular pharmacology, muscle contraction, hormone action signal transduction, nuclear transport.

University of Michigan, Rackham Graduate School, Program in Biomedical Sciences (PIBS), Department of Pharmacology, Ann Arbor, MI 48109-5632. Offers MS, PhD. Final fall application deadline for MS is April 15. *Faculty:* 17 full-time (6 women). *Students:* 26 full-time (15 women), 1 (woman) part-time; includes 6 minority (2 Black or African American, non-Hispanic/Latino; 1 Asian, non-Hispanic/Latino; 2 Hispanic/Latino; 1 Two or more races, non-Hispanic/Latino), 6 international. Average age 27. 117 applicants, 29% accepted, 17 enrolled. In 2017, 8 master's, 6 doctorates awarded. Terminal master's awarded for partial completion of doctoral program. *Degree requirements:* For master's, thesis, oral presentation; for doctorate, thesis/dissertation, oral and written preliminary exam, oral defense of written dissertation. *Entrance requirements:* For master's and doctorate, 3 letters of recommendation, research experience, all undergraduate transcripts. Additional exam requirements/recommendations for international students: Required—TOEFL (minimum score 560 paper-based; 84 iBT). *Application deadline:* For fall admission, 12/1 for domestic and international students. Applications are processed on a rolling basis. Application fee: $75 ($90 for international students). Electronic applications accepted. *Expenses:* $22,414 full-time in-state, $45,240 out-of-state. *Financial support:* In 2017–18, 23 students received support, including 16 fellowships with full tuition reimbursements available (averaging $30,600 per year), 7 research assistantships with full tuition reimbursements available (averaging $30,600 per year); scholarships/grants, traineeships, health care benefits, and unspecified assistantships also available. Financial award application deadline: 12/1. *Faculty research:* Signal transduction, addiction research, cancer pharmacology, drug metabolism and pharmacogenetics. *Total annual research expenditures:* $5.1 million. *Unit head:* Dr. Lori L. Isom, Professor/Chair of Pharmacology, 734-764-8166, Fax: 734-763-4450, E-mail: lisom@umich.edu. *Application contact:* Jim Musgrave, Director of Graduate Admissions and Recruitment, 734-615-1581, Fax: 734-647-7022, E-mail: jdmusg@umich.edu.
Website: https://medicine.umich.edu/pharmacology

University of Minnesota, Duluth, Medical School, Program in Pharmacology, Duluth, MN 55812-2496. Offers MS, PhD. MS, PhD offered jointly with University of Minnesota, Twin Cities Campus. Terminal master's awarded for partial completion of doctoral program. *Degree requirements:* For master's, thesis, final oral exam; for doctorate, thesis/dissertation, final oral exam, oral and written preliminary exams. *Entrance requirements:* For master's and doctorate, GRE General Test. Additional exam requirements/recommendations for international students: Required—TOEFL. *Faculty research:* Drug addiction, alcohol and hypertension, neurotransmission, allergic airway disease, auditory neuroscience.

University of Minnesota, Twin Cities Campus, College of Pharmacy and Graduate School, Graduate Programs in Pharmacy, Graduate Program in Experimental and Clinical Pharmacology, Minneapolis, MN 55455-0213. Offers MS, PhD. *Degree requirements:* For doctorate, thesis/dissertation.

University of Minnesota, Twin Cities Campus, Medical School, Department of Pharmacology, Minneapolis, MN 55455. Offers MS, PhD. Terminal master's awarded for partial completion of doctoral program. *Degree requirements:* For master's, thesis (for some programs); for doctorate, thesis/dissertation. *Entrance requirements:* For master's and doctorate, GRE General Test. Additional exam requirements/recommendations for international students: Required—TOEFL (minimum score 603 paper-based; 100 iBT). Electronic applications accepted. *Faculty research:* Molecular pharmacology, cancer chemotherapy, neuropharmacology, biochemical pharmacology, behavioral pharmacology.

University of Mississippi, Graduate School, School of Pharmacy, University, MS 38677. Offers environmental toxicology (MS, PhD); industrial pharmacy (MS); medicinal chemistry (MS, PhD); pharmaceutics (MS, PhD); pharmacognosy (MS, PhD); pharmacology (MS, PhD); pharmacy (Pharm D); pharmacy administration (MS, PhD). *Accreditation:* ACPE (one or more programs are accredited). *Program availability:* Part-time. *Faculty:* 71 full-time (32 women), 17 part-time/adjunct (6 women). *Students:* 417 full-time (256 women), 16 part-time (7 women); includes 71 minority (24 Black or African American, non-Hispanic/Latino; 1 American Indian or Alaska Native, non-Hispanic/Latino; 36 Asian, non-Hispanic/Latino; 4 Hispanic/Latino; 6 Two or more races, non-Hispanic/Latino), 88 international. Average age 25. In 2017, 22 master's, 49 doctorates awarded. Terminal master's awarded for partial completion of doctoral program. *Degree requirements:* For master's, thesis; for doctorate, thesis/dissertation (for some programs). *Entrance requirements:* For master's, GRE General Test, minimum GPA of 3.0; for doctorate, GRE General Test (for PhD). Additional exam requirements/recommendations for international students: Required—TOEFL. *Application deadline:* For fall admission, 2/1 priority date for domestic students; for spring admission, 10/1 priority date for domestic students. Applications are processed on a rolling basis.

Application fee: $50. Electronic applications accepted. *Financial support:* Fellowships, research assistantships, teaching assistantships, career-related internships or fieldwork, Federal Work-Study, institutionally sponsored loans, scholarships/grants, tuition waivers (full), and unspecified assistantships available. Financial award application deadline: 3/1; financial award applicants required to submit FAFSA. *Unit head:* Dr. David D. Allen, II, Dean, 662-915-7265, Fax: 662-915-5118, E-mail: sopdean@olemiss.edu.
Website: http://www.pharmacy.olemiss.edu/

University of Mississippi Medical Center, School of Graduate Studies in the Health Sciences, Department of Pharmacology and Toxicology, Jackson, MS 39216-4505. Offers PhD. *Degree requirements:* For doctorate, comprehensive exam, thesis/dissertation, first authored publication. *Entrance requirements:* For doctorate, GRE General Test, minimum GPA of 3.0. Additional exam requirements/recommendations for international students: Required—TOEFL (minimum score 550 paper-based, 79 iBT), IELTS or PTE. Electronic applications accepted. *Faculty research:* Renal and cardiovascular pharmacology, genetic basis of cardio-renal diseases, diabetes, obesity, metabolic diseases, cancer chemotherapy.

University of Missouri, School of Medicine and Office of Research and Graduate Studies, Graduate Programs in Medicine, Department of Medical Pharmacology and Physiology, Columbia, MO 65211. Offers MS, PhD. *Degree requirements:* For master's, thesis; for doctorate, thesis/dissertation. *Entrance requirements:* For master's and doctorate, GRE General Test, minimum GPA of 3.0. Additional exam requirements/recommendations for international students: Required—TOEFL (minimum score 500 paper-based; 61 iBT). Application fee: $75 ($90 for international students). *Expenses:* Tuition, state resident: full-time $6480. Tuition, nonresident: full-time $17,744. *Required fees:* $1108. Tuition and fees vary according to course load, campus/location and program. *Financial support:* Fellowships, research assistantships, teaching assistantships, institutionally sponsored loans, scholarships/grants, health care benefits, and unspecified assistantships available. Support available to part-time students.
Website: http://mpp.missouri.edu/

University of Nebraska Medical Center, Interdisciplinary Graduate Program in Biomedical Sciences, Department of Pharmacology and Experimental Neuroscience, Omaha, NE 68198-5800. Offers PhD. *Faculty:* 26 full-time (8 women), 2 part-time/adjunct (0 women). *Students:* 31 full-time (10 women); includes 1 minority (Black or African American, non-Hispanic/Latino), 11 international. Average age 28. 12 applicants, 42% accepted, 5 enrolled. In 2017, 6 doctorates awarded. Terminal master's awarded for partial completion of doctoral program. *Degree requirements:* For doctorate, comprehensive exam, thesis/dissertation. *Entrance requirements:* For doctorate, GRE General Test. Additional exam requirements/recommendations for international students: Required—TOEFL (minimum score 90 iBT). *Application deadline:* For fall admission, 6/1 for domestic students, 4/1 for international students. Applications are processed on a rolling basis. Application fee: $45. Electronic applications accepted. *Expenses:* Tuition, state resident: full-time $8451; part-time $4225 per semester. Tuition, nonresident: full-time $24,219; part-time $11,295 per semester. *Required fees:* $589; $117 per term. *Financial support:* In 2017–18, 6 students received support, including 6 fellowships with full tuition reimbursements available (averaging $23,400 per year); research assistantships, scholarships/grants, health care benefits, and unspecified assistantships also available. Financial award application deadline: 2/15. *Faculty research:* Neuropharmacology, molecular pharmacology, toxicology, molecular biology, neuroscience. *Unit head:* Dr. Keshore Bidasee, Chair, Graduate Studies, 402-559-9018, Fax: 402-559-7495, E-mail: kbidasee@unmc.edu. *Application contact:* Reed Felderman, Office Administrator, 402-559-4044, Fax: 402-559-7495, E-mail: reed.felderman@unmc.edu.
Website: http://www.unmc.edu/pharmacology/

The University of North Carolina at Chapel Hill, School of Medicine and Graduate School, Graduate Programs in Medicine, Department of Pharmacology, Chapel Hill, NC 27599-7365. Offers PhD. *Degree requirements:* For doctorate, comprehensive exam, thesis/dissertation. *Entrance requirements:* For doctorate, GRE General Test, minimum GPA of 3.0. Additional exam requirements/recommendations for international students: Required—TOEFL. Electronic applications accepted. *Faculty research:* Signal transduction, cell adhesion, receptors, ion channels.

University of North Texas Health Science Center at Fort Worth, Graduate School of Biomedical Sciences, Fort Worth, TX 76107-2699. Offers biochemistry and cancer biology (MS, PhD); biotechnology (MS); cell biology, immunology and microbiology (MS, PhD); clinical research management (MS); forensic genetics (MS); genetics (MS, PhD); integrative physiology (MS, PhD); medical sciences (MS); pharmaceutical sciences and pharmacotherapy (MS, PhD); pharmacology and neuroscience (MS, PhD); structural anatomy and rehabilitation sciences (MS, PhD); DO/MS; DO/PhD. Terminal master's awarded for partial completion of doctoral program. *Degree requirements:* For master's, thesis; for doctorate, thesis/dissertation. *Entrance requirements:* For master's and doctorate, GRE General Test. Additional exam requirements/recommendations for international students: Required—TOEFL. *Expenses:* Contact institution. *Faculty research:* Alzheimer's disease, aging, eye diseases, cancer, cardiovascular disease.

University of Pennsylvania, Perelman School of Medicine, Biomedical Graduate Studies, Graduate Group in Pharmacology, Philadelphia, PA 19104. Offers PhD, MD/PhD, VMD/PhD. *Faculty:* 117. *Students:* 69 full-time (40 women); includes 32 minority (9 Black or African American, non-Hispanic/Latino; 14 Asian, non-Hispanic/Latino; 8 Hispanic/Latino; 1 Two or more races, non-Hispanic/Latino), 4 international. 80 applicants, 34% accepted, 17 enrolled. In 2017, 14 doctorates awarded. *Degree requirements:* For doctorate, thesis/dissertation. *Entrance requirements:* For doctorate, GRE General Test, previous course work in physical or natural science. Additional exam requirements/recommendations for international students: Required—TOEFL. *Application deadline:* For fall admission, 12/1 priority date for domestic and international students. Applications are processed on a rolling basis. Application fee: $80. Electronic applications accepted. *Financial support:* In 2017–18, 60 students received support. Fellowships, research assistantships, teaching assistantships, and tuition waivers available. *Faculty research:* Properties and regulation of receptors for biogenic amines, molecular aspects of transduction, mechanisms of biosynthesis, biological mechanisms of depression, developmental events in the nervous system. *Unit head:* Dr. Julie Blendy, Chair, 215-898-0730. *Application contact:* Sarah Squire, Coordinator, 215-898-1790.
Website: http://www.med.upenn.edu/ggps

University of Prince Edward Island, Atlantic Veterinary College, Graduate Program in Veterinary Medicine, Charlottetown, PE C1A 4P3, Canada. Offers anatomy (M Sc, PhD); bacteriology (M Sc, PhD); clinical pharmacology (M Sc, PhD); clinical sciences (M Sc, PhD); epidemiology (M Sc, PhD), including reproduction; fish health (M Sc, PhD); food animal nutrition (M Sc, PhD); immunology (M Sc, PhD); microanatomy (M Sc, PhD); parasitology (M Sc, PhD); pathology (M Sc, PhD); pharmacology (M Sc, PhD); physiology (M Sc, PhD); toxicology (M Sc, PhD); veterinary science (M Vet Sc); virology (M Sc, PhD). *Program availability:* Part-time. *Degree requirements:* For master's, thesis; for doctorate, thesis/dissertation. *Entrance requirements:* For master's, DVM, B Sc honors degree, or equivalent; for doctorate, M Sc. Additional exam requirements/recommendations for international students: Required—TOEFL (minimum score 550 paper-based; 80 iBT). *Expenses:* Contact institution. *Faculty research:* Animal health management, infectious diseases, fin fish and shellfish health, basic biomedical sciences, ecosystem health.

University of Puerto Rico–Medical Sciences Campus, School of Medicine, Biomedical Sciences Graduate Program, Department of Pharmacology and Toxicology, San Juan, PR 00936-5067. Offers MS, PhD. *Degree requirements:* For master's, one foreign language, thesis; for doctorate, one foreign language, comprehensive exam, thesis/dissertation. *Entrance requirements:* For master's and doctorate, GRE General Test, GRE Subject Test, interview, minimum GPA of 3.0, 3 letters of recommendation. Electronic applications accepted. *Faculty research:* Cardiovascular, central nervous system, and endocrine pharmacology; anti-cancer drugs; sodium pump; mitochondrial DNA repair; Huntington's disease.

University of Rhode Island, Graduate School, College of Pharmacy, Department of Biomedical and Pharmaceutical Sciences, Kingston, RI 02881. Offers health outcomes (MS, PhD); medicinal chemistry and pharmacognosy (MS, PhD); pharmaceutics and pharmacokinetics (MS, PhD); pharmacology and toxicology (MS, PhD). *Program availability:* Part-time. *Faculty:* 23 full-time (11 women). *Students:* 36 full-time (14 women), 9 part-time (4 women); includes 4 minority (1 Black or African American, non-Hispanic/Latino; 1 American Indian or Alaska Native, non-Hispanic/Latino; 2 Asian, non-Hispanic/Latino), 22 international. 138 applicants, 18% accepted, 14 enrolled. In 2017, 3 master's, 6 doctorates awarded. *Entrance requirements:* Additional exam requirements/recommendations for international students: Required—TOEFL. *Application deadline:* For fall admission, 7/15 for domestic students, 2/1 for international students. Application fee: $65. Electronic applications accepted. *Expenses:* Tuition, state resident: full-time $12,706; part-time $786 per credit. Tuition, nonresident: full-time $25,216; part-time $1401 per credit. *Required fees:* $1598; $45 per credit. One-time fee: $30 part-time. *Financial support:* In 2017–18, 10 research assistantships with tuition reimbursements (averaging $13,958 per year), 10 teaching assistantships with tuition reimbursements (averaging $11,291 per year) were awarded. Financial award application deadline: 2/1; financial award applicants required to submit FAFSA. *Unit head:* Dr. David Rowley, Chair, 401-874-9228, E-mail: drowley@uri.edu.
Website: http://www.uri.edu/pharmacy/departments/bps/index.shtml

University of Rochester, School of Medicine and Dentistry, Graduate Programs in Medicine and Dentistry, Department of Pharmacology and Physiology, Programs in Pharmacology, Rochester, NY 14627. Offers MS, PhD. Terminal master's awarded for partial completion of doctoral program. *Degree requirements:* For master's, thesis; for doctorate, thesis/dissertation, qualifying exam. *Entrance requirements:* For master's and doctorate, GRE General Test.

University of Saskatchewan, College of Medicine, Department of Pharmacology, Saskatoon, SK S7N 5A2, Canada. Offers M Sc, PhD. *Degree requirements:* For master's, thesis; for doctorate, thesis/dissertation. *Entrance requirements:* Additional exam requirements/recommendations for international students: Required—TOEFL. *Faculty research:* Neuropharmacology, mechanisms of action of anticancer drugs, clinical pharmacology, cardiovascular pharmacology, toxicology: alcohol-related changes in fetal brain development.

University of South Dakota, Graduate School, Sanford School of Medicine and Graduate School, Biomedical Sciences Graduate Program, Physiology and Pharmacology Group, Vermillion, SD 57069. Offers MS, PhD. In 2017, 1 master's, 3 doctorates awarded. Terminal master's awarded for partial completion of doctoral program. *Degree requirements:* For master's, thesis; for doctorate, comprehensive exam, thesis/dissertation. *Entrance requirements:* For master's and doctorate, GRE General Test, minimum GPA of 3.0. Additional exam requirements/recommendations for international students: Required—TOEFL (minimum score 550 paper-based; 80 iBT), IELTS (minimum score 6). *Application deadline:* For fall admission, 4/15 priority date for domestic students, 3/15 for international students. Applications are processed on a rolling basis. Application fee: $35. Electronic applications accepted. *Expenses:* Contact institution. *Financial support:* In 2017–18, 12 students received support. Fellowships with partial tuition reimbursements available, research assistantships with partial tuition reimbursements available, scholarships/grants, and unspecified assistantships available. Financial award application deadline: 4/15; financial award applicants required to submit FAFSA. *Faculty research:* Pulmonary physiology and pharmacology, drug abuse, reproduction, signal transduction, cardiovascular physiology and pharmacology. *Unit head:* 605-658-6322, Fax: 605-677-6381, E-mail: biomed@usd.edu. *Application contact:* Graduate School, 605-658-6140, Fax: 605-677-6118.
Website: http://www.usd.edu/medicine/basic-biomedical-sciences

The University of Tennessee Health Science Center, College of Graduate Health Sciences, Memphis, TN 38163. Offers biomedical engineering (MS, PhD); biomedical sciences (PhD); dental sciences (MDS); epidemiology (MS); health outcomes and policy research (PhD); laboratory research and management (MS); nursing science (PhD); pharmaceutical sciences (PhD); pharmacology (MS); speech and hearing science (PhD); DDS/PhD; DNP/PhD; MD/PhD; Pharm D/PhD. MS and PhD programs in biomedical engineering offered jointly with University of Memphis. *Faculty:* 528 full-time (176 women). *Students:* 258 full-time (130 women); includes 87 minority (14 Black or African American, non-Hispanic/Latino; 68 Asian, non-Hispanic/Latino; 5 Hispanic/Latino). Average age 28. 673 applicants, 17% accepted, 102 enrolled. In 2017, 23 master's, 30 doctorates awarded. Terminal master's awarded for partial completion of doctoral program. *Degree requirements:* For master's, comprehensive exam, thesis; for doctorate, thesis/dissertation, oral and written preliminary and comprehensive exams. *Entrance requirements:* For master's and doctorate, GRE General Test, minimum GPA of 3.0. Additional exam requirements/recommendations for international students: Recommended—TOEFL (minimum score 79 iBT), IELTS (minimum score 6.5). *Application deadline:* For winter admission, 1/1 for domestic and international students; for spring admission, 3/1 for domestic and international students. Applications are processed on a rolling basis. Application fee: $0. Electronic applications accepted. *Expenses:* Contact institution. *Financial support:* In 2017–18, 150 students received support, including 150 research assistantships (averaging $25,000 per year); fellowships, institutionally sponsored loans, scholarships/grants, health care benefits, and tuition waivers (full and partial) also available. Support available to part-time students. *Faculty research:* Cell biology, epidemiology, biomedical engineering, speech and hearing science, health policy, pharmaceutical sciences, dental sciences, nursing science, pharmacology. *Unit head:* Dr. Donald B. Thomason, Dean, 901-448-5538, E-mail: dthomaso@uthsc.edu. *Application contact:* Dr. Isaac O. Donkor, Associate Dean for Student Affairs, 901-448-5538, E-mail: idonkor@uthsc.edu.
Website: http://grad.uthsc.edu/

The University of Texas at Austin, Graduate School, College of Pharmacy, Graduate Programs in Pharmacy, Austin, TX 78712-1111. Offers health outcomes and pharmacy practice (PhD); health outcomes and pharmacy practice (MS); medicinal chemistry (PhD); pharmaceutics (PhD); pharmacology and toxicology (PhD); pharmacotherapy (MS, PhD); translational science (PhD). PhD in translational science offered jointly with The University of Texas Health Science Center at San Antonio and The University of Texas at San Antonio. *Degree requirements:* For master's, thesis; for doctorate, thesis/dissertation. *Entrance requirements:* For master's and doctorate, GRE General Test. Electronic applications accepted. *Faculty research:* Synthetic medical chemistry, synthetic molecular biology, bio-organic chemistry, pharmacoeconomics, pharmacy practice.

The University of Texas Health Science Center at Houston, MD Anderson UTHealth Graduate School, Houston, TX 77225-0036. Offers biochemistry and cell biology (PhD); biomedical sciences (MS); cancer biology (PhD); genetic counseling (MS); genetics and epigenetics (PhD); immunology (PhD); medical physics (MS, PhD); microbiology and infectious diseases (PhD); neuroscience (PhD); quantitative sciences (PhD); therapeutics and pharmacology (PhD); MD/PhD. Terminal master's awarded for partial completion of doctoral program. *Degree requirements:* For master's, thesis; for doctorate, thesis/dissertation. *Entrance requirements:* For master's and doctorate, GRE General Test. Additional exam requirements/recommendations for international students: Required—TOEFL. Electronic applications accepted. *Faculty research:* Biomedical sciences.

The University of Texas Health Science Center at San Antonio, Graduate School of Biomedical Sciences, Department of Pharmacology, San Antonio, TX 78229-3900. Offers neuroscience (PhD). *Degree requirements:* For doctorate, comprehensive exam, thesis/dissertation.

The University of Texas Medical Branch, Graduate School of Biomedical Sciences, Program in Pharmacology and Toxicology, Galveston, TX 77555. Offers pharmacology (MS); pharmacology and toxicology (PhD). *Degree requirements:* For master's, thesis or alternative; for doctorate, thesis/dissertation. *Entrance requirements:* For master's and doctorate, GRE General Test. Additional exam requirements/recommendations for international students: Required—TOEFL (minimum score 550 paper-based).

University of the Sciences, Program in Chemistry, Biochemistry and Pharmacognosy, Philadelphia, PA 19104-4495. Offers biochemistry (MS, PhD); chemistry (MS, PhD); pharmacognosy (MS, PhD). *Program availability:* Part-time. *Degree requirements:* For master's, thesis, qualifying exams; for doctorate, comprehensive exam, thesis/dissertation, qualifying exams. *Entrance requirements:* For master's and doctorate, GRE General Test, GRE Subject Test. Additional exam requirements/recommendations for international students: Required—TOEFL, TWE. *Expenses:* Contact institution.

University of the Sciences, Program in Pharmacology and Toxicology, Philadelphia, PA 19104-4495. Offers pharmacology (MS, PhD); toxicology (MS, PhD). Terminal master's awarded for partial completion of doctoral program. *Degree requirements:* For master's, thesis; for doctorate, comprehensive exam, thesis/dissertation. *Entrance requirements:* For master's and doctorate, GRE General Test. Additional exam requirements/recommendations for international students: Required—TOEFL, TWE. *Expenses:* Contact institution.

The University of Toledo, College of Graduate Studies, College of Pharmacy and Pharmaceutical Sciences, Program in Experimental Therapeutics, Toledo, OH 43606-3390. Offers PhD. *Entrance requirements:* For doctorate, GRE, bachelor's degree in chemistry, biology, pharmaceutical sciences, pharmacy or a related discipline. Additional exam requirements/recommendations for international students: Required—TOEFL.

The University of Toledo, College of Graduate Studies, College of Pharmacy and Pharmaceutical Sciences, Program in Pharmaceutical Sciences, Toledo, OH 43606-3390. Offers administrative pharmacy (MSPS); industrial pharmacy (MSPS); pharmacology toxicology (MSPS). *Degree requirements:* For master's, thesis. *Entrance requirements:* For master's, GRE General Test. Additional exam requirements/recommendations for international students: Required—TOEFL (minimum score 550 paper-based; 80 iBT). Electronic applications accepted.

University of Toronto, Faculty of Medicine, Department of Pharmacology and Toxicology, Toronto, ON M5S 1A1, Canada. Offers pharmacology (M Sc, PhD). *Program availability:* Part-time. *Degree requirements:* For master's, thesis; for doctorate, thesis/dissertation. *Entrance requirements:* For master's, B Sc or equivalent; background in pharmacology, biochemistry, and physiology; minimum B+ earned in at least 4 senior level classes; for doctorate, minimum B+ average. Additional exam requirements/recommendations for international students: Required—TOEFL (minimum score 580 paper-based; 93 iBT), TWE (minimum score 5). Electronic applications accepted.

University of Utah, Graduate School, College of Pharmacy, Department of Pharmacology and Toxicology, Salt Lake City, UT 84112. Offers PhD. *Faculty:* 10 full-time (3 women), 7 part-time/adjunct (1 woman). *Students:* 3 full-time (2 women), 1 (woman) part-time. In 2017, 3 doctorates awarded. Terminal master's awarded for partial completion of doctoral program. *Entrance requirements:* For doctorate, GRE General Test, BS in biology, chemistry, or neuroscience. Application fee: $0. Electronic applications accepted. *Expenses:* Contact institution. *Financial support:* In 2017–18, 9 students received support, including 9 research assistantships with full tuition reimbursements available (averaging $25,000 per year); health care benefits and tuition waivers (full) also available. Financial award application deadline: 1/15. *Faculty research:* Neuropharmacology of anti-seizure drugs and drugs of abuse, drug metabolism, signal transduction pathways and oncogenic processes, drug analyses in biological samples, natural products drug discovery. *Unit head:* Dr. Karen Wilcox, Department Chair, 801-581-6287, Fax: 801-585-5111, E-mail: karen.wilcox@hsc.utah.edu. *Application contact:* Linda Wright, Program Assistant, 801-581-6281, Fax: 801-585-5111, E-mail: linda.wright@utah.edu.
Website: http://www.pharmacy.utah.edu/pharmtox/

University of Vermont, The Robert Larner, MD College of Medicine and Graduate College, Graduate Programs in Medicine, Department of Pharmacology, Burlington, VT 05405-0068. Offers MS, PhD. *Students:* 13 (4 women). Average age 23. 23 applicants, 83% accepted, 4 enrolled. In 2017, 7 master's awarded. *Degree requirements:* For master's, thesis optional; for doctorate, thesis/dissertation. *Entrance requirements:* For doctorate, GRE General Test. Additional exam requirements/recommendations for international students: Required—TOEFL (minimum score 550 paper-based, 90 iBT) or IELTS (6.5). *Application deadline:* For fall admission, 3/15 priority date for domestic and international students. Applications are processed on a rolling basis. Application fee: $65. Electronic applications accepted. *Expenses:* Tuition, state resident: full-time $11,628; part-time $646 per credit. Tuition, nonresident: full-time $29,340; part-time $1630 per credit. *Required fees:* $1994; $10 per credit. Tuition and fees vary according to course load and program. *Financial support:* Fellowships, research assistantships, and teaching assistantships available. Financial award application deadline: 3/1. *Faculty research:* Cardiovascular drugs, anticancer drugs. *Unit head:* Dr. Anthony Morielli, Director, 802-656-2500, E-mail: anthony.morielli@uvm.edu.
Website: http://www.med.uvm.edu/pharmacology/graduate

University of Virginia, School of Medicine, Department of Pharmacology, Charlottesville, VA 22903. Offers PhD, MD/PhD. *Faculty:* 26 full-time (7 women), 2 part-time/adjunct (0 women). *Students:* 12 full-time (4 women), 1 part-time (0 women); includes 2 minority (1 Asian, non-Hispanic/Latino; 1 Hispanic/Latino). Average age 26. In 2017, 3 doctorates awarded. *Degree requirements:* For doctorate, thesis/dissertation. *Entrance requirements:* For doctorate, GRE General Test, GRE Subject Test (recommended), 2 letters of recommendation. Additional exam requirements/recommendations for international students: Required—TOEFL. *Application deadline:* For fall admission, 1/15 for domestic and international students. Applications are processed on a rolling basis. Application fee: $60. Electronic applications accepted. *Financial support:* Fellowships, research assistantships, and teaching assistantships available. Financial award applicants required to submit FAFSA. *Unit head:* Dr. Douglas A. Bayliss, Chairman, 434-924-1919, Fax: 434-982-3878, E-mail: dab3y@virginia.edu. *Application contact:* Biomedical Sciences Graduate Program, E-mail: bims@virginia.edu.
Website: http://www.healthsystem.virginia.edu/internet/pharmacology/

University of Washington, Graduate School, School of Medicine, Graduate Programs in Medicine, Department of Pharmacology, Seattle, WA 98195. Offers PhD. *Degree requirements:* For doctorate, thesis/dissertation. *Entrance requirements:* For doctorate, GRE General Test, minimum GPA of 3.0. *Faculty research:* Neuroscience, cell physiology, molecular biology, regulation of metabolism, signal transduction.

University of Wisconsin–Madison, School of Medicine and Public Health, Molecular and Cellular Pharmacology Graduate Training Program, Madison, WI 53705. Offers PhD. *Students:* 28. *Degree requirements:* For doctorate, comprehensive exam, thesis/dissertation. *Entrance requirements:* Additional exam requirements/recommendations for international students: Required—TOEFL (minimum score 580 paper-based; 92 iBT). *Application deadline:* For fall admission, 12/1 priority date for domestic and international students. Application fee: $75 ($81 for international students). Electronic applications accepted. *Financial support:* Fellowships, research assistantships, teaching assistantships, scholarships/grants, traineeships, health care benefits, and unspecified assistantships available. *Faculty research:* Protein kinases, signaling pathways, neurotransmitters, molecular recognition, receptors and transporters. *Unit head:* Dr. Anjon Audhya, Director, 608-262-3761, E-mail: audhya@wisc.edu. *Application contact:* Kristin Cooper, Program Coordinator, E-mail: kgcooper@wisc.edu.
Website: http://molpharm.wisc.edu/

Vanderbilt University, School of Medicine, Department of Pharmacology, Nashville, TN 37240-1001. Offers PhD, MD/PhD. *Faculty:* 24 full-time (9 women). *Students:* 45 full-time (23 women); includes 15 minority (3 Black or African American, non-Hispanic/Latino; 5 Asian, non-Hispanic/Latino; 3 Hispanic/Latino; 4 Two or more races, non-Hispanic/Latino), 4 international. Average age 26. In 2017, 8 doctorates awarded. *Degree requirements:* For doctorate, comprehensive exam, thesis/dissertation, preliminary, qualifying, and final exams. *Entrance requirements:* For doctorate, GRE General Test, GRE Subject Test (recommended). Additional exam requirements/recommendations for international students: Required—TOEFL (minimum score 570 paper-based; 88 iBT). *Application deadline:* For fall admission, 1/15 for domestic and international students. Application fee: $0. Electronic applications accepted. *Financial support:* Fellowships with full tuition reimbursements, research assistantships with full tuition reimbursements, Federal Work-Study, institutionally sponsored loans, scholarships/grants, traineeships, health care benefits, and tuition waivers (partial) available. Financial award application deadline: 1/15; financial award applicants required to submit CSS PROFILE or FAFSA. *Faculty research:* Molecular pharmacology, neuropharmacology, drug disposition and toxicology, genetic mechanics, cell regulation. *Unit head:* Dr. David Sweatt, Chair, 615-322-2207, Fax: 615-936-3910, E-mail: david.sweatt@vanderbilt.edu. *Application contact:* Christine Konradi, Director of Graduate Studies, 615-322-2207, E-mail: christine.konradi@vanderbilt.edu.
Website: http://medschool.vanderbilt.edu/pharmacology/

Virginia Commonwealth University, Medical College of Virginia-Professional Programs, School of Medicine, Graduate Programs in Medicine, Department of Pharmacology and Toxicology, Richmond, VA 23284-9005. Offers neuroscience (PhD); pharmacology (Certificate); pharmacology and toxicology (MS, PhD); MD/PhD. Terminal master's awarded for partial completion of doctoral program. *Degree requirements:* For master's, thesis; for doctorate, thesis/dissertation, comprehensive oral and written exams. *Entrance requirements:* For master's and doctorate, GRE or MCAT. Additional exam requirements/recommendations for international students: Required—TOEFL (minimum score 600 paper-based; 100 iBT). Electronic applications accepted. *Faculty research:* Drug abuse, drug metabolism, pharmacodynamics, peptide synthesis, receptor mechanisms.

Wake Forest University, School of Medicine and Graduate School of Arts and Sciences, Graduate Programs in Medicine, Program in Physiology and Pharmacology, Winston-Salem, NC 27109. Offers pharmacology (PhD); physiology (PhD); MD/PhD. *Degree requirements:* For doctorate, thesis/dissertation. *Entrance requirements:* For doctorate, GRE General Test. Additional exam requirements/recommendations for international students: Required—TOEFL. Electronic applications accepted. *Faculty research:* Aging, substance abuse, cardiovascular control, endocrine systems, toxicology.

Wayne State University, Eugene Applebaum College of Pharmacy and Health Sciences, Department of Pharmaceutical Sciences, Detroit, MI 48202. Offers medicinal chemistry (MS, PhD); pharmaceutics (MS, PhD), including medicinal chemistry (PhD); pharmacology and toxicology (MS, PhD). *Faculty:* 20. *Students:* 23 full-time (17 women), 1 (woman) part-time, 19 international. Average age 29. 119 applicants, 9% accepted, 7 enrolled. In 2017, 7 master's, 3 doctorates awarded. *Degree requirements:* For master's, thesis; for doctorate, thesis/dissertation. *Entrance requirements:* For master's, GRE General Test, bachelor's degree; adequate background in biology, physics, calculus, and chemistry; three letters of recommendation; personal statement; for doctorate, GRE General Test, bachelor's or master's degree in one of the behavioral, biological, pharmaceutical or physical sciences; three letters of recommendation. Additional exam requirements/recommendations for international students: Required—TOEFL (minimum score 550 paper-based; 79 iBT), Michigan English Language Assessment Battery (minimum score 85); Recommended—IELTS (minimum score 6.5), TWE (minimum score 5.5). *Application deadline:* For fall admission, 12/1 priority date for domestic and international students. Applications are processed on a rolling basis. Application fee: $50. Electronic applications accepted. *Expenses:* Contact institution. *Financial support:* In 2017–18, 16 students received support, including 2 fellowships with tuition reimbursements available (averaging $26,000 per year), 11 research assistantships with full tuition reimbursements available (averaging $25,182 per year); scholarships/grants, health care benefits, and unspecified assistantships also available. Financial award applicants required to submit FAFSA. *Faculty research:* Design of new anthracyclines, genetic and epigenetic effects of extracellular inducers, cellular injury and cell death, drug metabolism and nutrition, anti-infective agents, carcinogenesis, diabetes research, Thera gnostic nanomedicines, neurotoxicity, drug discovery, insulin resistance. *Unit head:* Dr. George Corcoran, Chair and Professor, 313-577-1737, E-mail: corcoran@wayne.edu. *Application contact:* 313-577-5415, Fax: 313-577-2033, E-mail: pscgrad@wayne.edu.
Website: http://cphs.wayne.edu/sciences/index.php

Wayne State University, School of Medicine, Office of Biomedical Graduate Programs, Detroit, MI 48202. Offers anatomy and cell biology (MS, PhD); basic medical sciences (MS); biochemistry and molecular biology (MS, PhD); cancer biology (MS, PhD); clinical and translational science (Graduate Certificate); family medicine and public health sciences (MPH, Graduate Certificate), including public health practice; genetic counseling (MS); immunology and microbiology (MS, PhD); medical physics (MS, PhD, Graduate Certificate); medical research (MS); molecular medicine and genomics (MS, PhD), including molecular genetics and genomics; pathology (PhD); pharmacology (MS, PhD); physiology (MS, PhD), including physiology, reproductive sciences (PhD); psychiatry and behavioral neurosciences (PhD), including translational neuroscience;

MD/MPH; MD/PhD; MPH/MA; MSW/MPH. *Program availability:* Part-time, evening/ weekend. *Students:* 268 full-time (152 women), 117 part-time (59 women); includes 108 minority (19 Black or African American, non-Hispanic/Latino; 1 American Indian or Alaska Native, non-Hispanic/Latino; 62 Asian, non-Hispanic/Latino; 9 Hispanic/Latino; 17 Two or more races, non-Hispanic/Latino), 48 international. Average age 26. 1,133 applicants, 21% accepted, 151 enrolled. In 2017, 70 master's, 25 doctorates, 10 other advanced degrees awarded. Terminal master's awarded for partial completion of doctoral program. *Degree requirements:* For master's, thesis (for some programs); for doctorate, thesis/dissertation. *Entrance requirements:* For master's, doctorate, and Graduate Certificate, GRE. Additional exam requirements/recommendations for international students: Required—TOEFL (minimum score 550 paper-based; 100 iBT), Michigan English Language Assessment Battery (minimum score 85); Recommended—IELTS (minimum score 6.5), TWE (minimum score 5.5). *Application deadline:* For fall admission, 2/1 for domestic and international students. Applications are processed on a rolling basis. Application fee: $50. Electronic applications accepted. *Expenses:* Contact institution. *Financial support:* In 2017–18, 177 students received support, including 64 fellowships with full tuition reimbursements available (averaging $24,388 per year), 79 research assistantships with full tuition reimbursements available (averaging $26,894 per year); scholarships/grants, traineeships, and health care benefits also available. *Faculty research:* Cancer biology, neurosciences, vision sciences, molecular biology, pathology, physiology, pharmacology, public health, medical physics. *Unit head:* Dr. Daniel A. Walz, Associate Dean for Biomedical Graduate Programs, 313-577-1455, Fax: 313-577-8796, E-mail: gradprogs@med.wayne.edu.
Website: https://www.med.wayne.edu/biomedical-graduate-programs/

Weill Cornell Medicine, Weill Cornell Graduate School of Medical Sciences, Pharmacology Program, New York, NY 10065. Offers MS, PhD. Terminal master's awarded for partial completion of doctoral program. *Degree requirements:* For master's, comprehensive exam; for doctorate, thesis/dissertation, final exam. *Entrance requirements:* For doctorate, GRE General Test, previous course work in natural and/or health sciences. Additional exam requirements/recommendations for international students: Required—TOEFL. *Faculty research:* Understanding how drugs and chemicals modify biological systems; using and developing new drugs to treat diseases, such as cancer, diabetes, atherosclerosis, epilepsy, anxiety disorders, Alzheimer's disease, and autism.

Wright State University, Boonshoft School of Medicine, Program in Pharmacology and Toxicology, Dayton, OH 45435. Offers MS. *Degree requirements:* For master's, thesis optional.

Yale University, Yale School of Medicine and Graduate School of Arts and Sciences, Combined Program in Biological and Biomedical Sciences (BBS), Department of Pharmacology, New Haven, CT 06520. Offers PhD. *Degree requirements:* For doctorate, thesis/dissertation. *Entrance requirements:* For doctorate, GRE General Test. Additional exam requirements/recommendations for international students: Required—TOEFL. *Expenses:* Contact institution.

Yale University, Yale School of Medicine and Graduate School of Arts and Sciences, Combined Program in Biological and Biomedical Sciences (BBS), Pharmacological Sciences and Molecular Medicine Track, New Haven, CT 06520. Offers PhD, MD/PhD. *Degree requirements:* For doctorate, thesis/dissertation. *Entrance requirements:* For doctorate, GRE General Test. Additional exam requirements/recommendations for international students: Required—TOEFL. Electronic applications accepted.

Toxicology

Clemson University, Graduate School, College of Science, Department of Biological Sciences, Clemson, SC 29634. Offers biological sciences (MS, PhD); biological sciences for science educators (MBS); environmental toxicology (MS, PhD); microbiology (MS, PhD). *Program availability:* Part-time, 100% online. *Faculty:* 46 full-time (15 women), 9 part-time/adjunct (4 women). *Students:* 136 full-time (86 women), 546 part-time (386 women); includes 76 minority (26 Black or African American, non-Hispanic/Latino; 2 American Indian or Alaska Native, non-Hispanic/Latino; 10 Asian, non-Hispanic/Latino; 20 Hispanic/Latino; 18 Two or more races, non-Hispanic/Latino), 34 international. Average age 35. 245 applicants, 75% accepted, 143 enrolled. In 2017, 182 master's, 12 doctorates awarded. *Degree requirements:* For master's, comprehensive exam (for some programs), thesis (for some programs); for doctorate, comprehensive exam, thesis/dissertation. *Entrance requirements:* For master's and doctorate, GRE General Test, unofficial transcripts, letters of recommendation. Additional exam requirements/recommendations for international students: Required—TOEFL (minimum score 100 iBT), IELTS (minimum score 7.5), PTE (minimum score 72). *Application deadline:* For fall admission, 1/5 for domestic and international students. Application fee: $80 ($90 for international students). Electronic applications accepted. *Expenses:* $5,174 per semester full-time resident, $9,714 per semester full-time non-resident, $511 per credit hour part-time resident, $1,017 per credit hour part-time non-resident; $741 per credit hour online; other fees may apply per session. *Financial support:* In 2017–18, 47 students received support, including 2 fellowships with partial tuition reimbursements available (averaging $17,000 per year), 8 research assistantships with partial tuition reimbursements available (averaging $23,063 per year), 37 teaching assistantships with partial tuition reimbursements available (averaging $21,662 per year). Financial award application deadline: 1/5. *Faculty research:* Microbiology, cell and developmental biology, evolutionary biology, ecology, molecular biology. *Total annual research expenditures:* $1.5 million. *Unit head:* Dr. Robert Cohen, Department Chair, 864-656-1112, Fax: 864-656-0435, E-mail: rscohen@clemson.edu. *Application contact:* Jay Lyn Martin, Student Services Program Coordinator, 864-656-3587, Fax: 864-656-0435, E-mail: jaylyn@clemson.edu.
Website: http://www.clemson.edu/science/departments/biosci/

Columbia University, College of Physicians and Surgeons, Department of Pharmacology, New York, NY 10032. Offers pharmacology (M Phil, MA, PhD); pharmacology-toxicology (M Phil, MA, PhD); MD/PhD. Only candidates for the PhD are admitted. Terminal master's awarded for partial completion of doctoral program. *Degree requirements:* For doctorate, thesis/dissertation. *Entrance requirements:* For master's and doctorate, GRE General Test. Additional exam requirements/recommendations for international students: Required—TOEFL. *Expenses: Tuition:* Full-time $44,864; part-time $1704 per credit. *Required fees:* $2370 per semester. One-time fee: $105. *Faculty research:* Cardiovascular pharmacology, receptor pharmacology, neuropharmacology, membrane biophysics, eicosanoids.

Columbia University, Columbia University Mailman School of Public Health, Department of Environmental Health Sciences, New York, NY 10032. Offers environmental health sciences (MPH, Dr PH, PhD); radiological sciences (MS); toxicology (MS). PhD offered in cooperation with the Graduate School of Arts and Sciences. *Accreditation:* CEPH (one or more programs are accredited). *Program availability:* Part-time. *Students:* 54 full-time (43 women), 25 part-time (16 women); includes 28 minority (3 Black or African American, non-Hispanic/Latino; 15 Asian, non-Hispanic/Latino; 8 Hispanic/Latino; 2 Two or more races, non-Hispanic/Latino), 10 international. Average age 28. 173 applicants, 55% accepted, 38 enrolled. In 2017, 30 master's, 7 doctorates awarded. *Degree requirements:* For master's, thesis optional; for doctorate, thesis/dissertation. *Entrance requirements:* For master's, GRE General Test, 1 year of course work in biology, general chemistry, organic chemistry, and mathematics; for doctorate, GRE General Test, MPH or equivalent (for Dr PH). Additional exam requirements/recommendations for international students: Required—TOEFL (minimum score 600 paper-based; 100 iBT). *Application deadline:* For fall admission, 12/1 priority date for domestic and international students. Applications are processed on a rolling basis. Application fee: $120. Electronic applications accepted. *Expenses: Tuition:* Full-time $44,864; part-time $1704 per credit. *Required fees:* $2370 per semester. One-time fee: $105. *Financial support:* Research assistantships, teaching assistantships, career-related internships or fieldwork, and Federal Work-Study available. Support available to part-time students. Financial award application deadline: 2/1; financial award applicants required to submit FAFSA. *Faculty research:* Laboratory science, field research, and community-based efforts to understand the impact of environmental exposures on human health, including areas of molecular epidemiology, environmental toxicology, environmental health policy, global health, air pollution, children's health, climate and health, epigenetics, radiological sciences, and health physics. *Unit head:* Dr. Andrea Baccarelli, Chair, 212-305-3466, Fax: 212-305-4012. *Application contact:* Clare Norton, Associate Dean for Enrollment Management, 212-305-8698, Fax: 212-342-1861, E-mail: ph-admit@columbia.edu.
Website: https://www.mailman.columbia.edu/become-student/departments/environmental-health-sciences

Cornell University, Graduate School, Graduate Fields of Agriculture and Life Sciences, Field of Environmental Toxicology, Ithaca, NY 14853. Offers cellular and molecular toxicology (MS, PhD); ecotoxicology and environmental chemistry (MS, PhD); nutritional and food toxicology (MS, PhD); risk assessment, management and public policy (MS, PhD). *Degree requirements:* For master's, thesis; for doctorate, comprehensive exam, thesis/dissertation. *Entrance requirements:* For master's and doctorate, GRE General Test, GRE Subject Test (biology or chemistry recommended), 2 letters of recommendation. Additional exam requirements/recommendations for international students: Required—TOEFL (minimum score 600 paper-based; 77 iBT). Electronic applications accepted. *Faculty research:* Cellular and molecular toxicology, cancer toxicology, bioremediation, ecotoxicology, nutritional and food toxicology, reproductive toxicology.

Duke University, Graduate School, Integrated Toxicology and Environmental Health Program, Durham, NC 27708. Offers Certificate. *Entrance requirements:* Additional exam requirements/recommendations for international students: Required—TOEFL (minimum score 577 paper-based; 90 iBT) or IELTS (minimum score 7). Electronic applications accepted.

Florida Agricultural and Mechanical University, Division of Graduate Studies, Research, and Continuing Education, College of Pharmacy and Pharmaceutical Sciences, Graduate Programs in Pharmaceutical Sciences, Tallahassee, FL 32307-3200. Offers environmental toxicology (PhD); health outcomes research and pharmacoeconomics (PhD); medicinal chemistry (MS, PhD); pharmaceutics (MS, PhD); pharmacology/toxicology (MS, PhD); pharmacy administration (MS). *Accreditation:* CEPH. *Degree requirements:* For master's, comprehensive exam, thesis, publishable paper; for doctorate, comprehensive exam, thesis/dissertation, publishable paper. *Entrance requirements:* For master's and doctorate, GRE General Test, minimum GPA of 3.0 in last 60 hours. Additional exam requirements/recommendations for international students: Required—TOEFL. *Faculty research:* Anticancer agents, anti-inflammatory drugs, chronopharmacology, neuroendocrinology, microbiology.

The George Washington University, Columbian College of Arts and Sciences, Department of Forensic Sciences, Washington, DC 20052. Offers crime scene investigation (MFS); forensic chemistry (MFS); forensic molecular biology (MFS); forensic toxicology (MFS); high-technology crime investigation (MS); security management (MFS). MFS programs in high-technology crime investigation and in security management offered in Arlington, VA. *Program availability:* Part-time, evening/weekend. *Faculty:* 10 full-time (1 woman), 12 part-time/adjunct (3 women). *Students:* 65 full-time (54 women), 23 part-time (15 women); includes 41 minority (14 Black or African American, non-Hispanic/Latino; 12 Asian, non-Hispanic/Latino; 13 Hispanic/Latino; 1 Native Hawaiian or other Pacific Islander, non-Hispanic/Latino; 1 Two or more races, non-Hispanic/Latino), 5 international. Average age 25. 192 applicants, 67% accepted, 44 enrolled. In 2017, 43 master's, 1 other advanced degree awarded. *Degree requirements:* For master's, comprehensive exam. *Entrance requirements:* For master's, GRE General Test, minimum GPA of 3.0. Additional exam requirements/recommendations for international students: Required—TOEFL (minimum score 550 paper-based; 80 iBT). *Application deadline:* For fall admission, 1/16 priority date for international students; for spring admission, 10/1 priority date for domestic students, 9/1 priority date for international students. Applications are processed on a rolling basis. Application fee: $75. Electronic applications accepted. *Expenses: Tuition:* Full-time $28,800; part-time $1655 per credit hour. *Required fees:* $45; $2.75 per credit hour. *Financial support:* In 2017–18, 19 students received support. Fellowships with partial tuition reimbursements available, Federal Work-Study, and tuition waivers available. *Unit head:* Dr. Walter F. Rowe, Chair, 202-242-5757, E-mail: wfrowe@gwu.edu. *Application contact:* 202-242-5758, Fax: 202-994-6213, E-mail: forsc@gwu.edu.
Website: http://forensicsciences.columbian.gwu.edu/

Indiana University Bloomington, School of Public and Environmental Affairs, Environmental Science Programs, Bloomington, IN 47405. Offers applied ecology (MSES); energy (MSES); environmental chemistry, toxicology, and risk assessment (MSES); environmental science (PhD); hazardous materials management (Certificate); specialized environmental science (MSES); water resources (MSES); JD/MSES; MSES/MA; MSES/MPA; MSES/MS. *Program availability:* Part-time. Terminal master's awarded for partial completion of doctoral program. *Degree requirements:* For master's, capstone or thesis; internship; for doctorate, comprehensive exam, thesis/dissertation. *Entrance requirements:* For master's, GRE General Test or GMAT, official transcripts, 3 letters of recommendation, resume, personal statement; for doctorate, GRE General Test or

LSAT, official transcripts, 3 letters of recommendation, resume or curriculum vitae, statement of purpose. Additional exam requirements/recommendations for international students: Required—TOEFL (minimum score 600 paper-based; 96 iBT); Recommended—IELTS (minimum score 7). Electronic applications accepted. *Faculty research:* Applied ecology, bio-geochemistry, toxicology, wetlands ecology, environmental microbiology, forest ecology, environmental chemistry.

Indiana University–Purdue University Indianapolis, Indiana University School of Medicine, Department of Pharmacology and Toxicology, Indianapolis, IN 46202. Offers pharmacology (MS, PhD); toxicology (MS, PhD), MD/PhD. *Degree requirements:* For master's, thesis; for doctorate, thesis/dissertation. *Entrance requirements:* For master's, GRE General Test, GRE Subject Test, minimum GPA of 3.2 in core science courses; for doctorate, GRE General Test, GRE Subject Test. Additional exam requirements/recommendations for international students: Required—TOEFL, IELTS, GRE or MCAT. Electronic applications accepted. *Expenses:* Contact institution. *Faculty research:* Neuropharmacology, cardiovascular biopharmacology, chemotherapy, oncogenesis.

Iowa State University of Science and Technology, Program in Toxicology, Ames, IA 50011. Offers MS, PhD. *Entrance requirements:* For master's and doctorate, GRE General Test. Additional exam requirements/recommendations for international students: Required—TOEFL (minimum score 550 paper-based; 79 iBT), IELTS (minimum score 6.5). Electronic applications accepted.

Long Island University–LIU Brooklyn, Arnold and Marie Schwartz College of Pharmacy and Health Sciences, Brooklyn, NY 11201-8423. Offers drug regulatory affairs (MS); pharmaceutics (MS, PhD), including cosmetic science (MS), industrial pharmacy (MS); pharmacology and toxicology (MS); pharmacy (Pharm D). *Accreditation:* ACPE. *Program availability:* Part-time. *Faculty:* 51 full-time (29 women), 33 part-time/adjunct (14 women). *Students:* 497 full-time (296 women), 77 part-time (42 women); includes 228 minority (26 Black or African American, non-Hispanic/Latino; 143 Asian, non-Hispanic/Latino; 31 Hispanic/Latino; 28 Two or more races, non-Hispanic/Latino), 137 international. Average age 25. 241 applicants, 62% accepted, 38 enrolled. In 2017, 57 master's, 183 doctorates awarded. Terminal master's awarded for partial completion of doctoral program. *Degree requirements:* For master's, comprehensive exam, thesis; for doctorate, comprehensive exam, thesis/dissertation. *Entrance requirements:* For master's and doctorate, GRE. Additional exam requirements/recommendations for international students: Required—TOEFL (minimum score 550 paper-based, 79 iBT) or IELTS. *Application deadline:* Applications are processed on a rolling basis. Application fee: $50. Electronic applications accepted. *Expenses:* Contact institution. *Financial support:* In 2017–18, 200 students received support. Research assistantships, teaching assistantships, career-related internships or fieldwork, Federal Work-Study, scholarships/grants, tuition waivers (full and partial), and unspecified assistantships available. Support available to part-time students. Financial award application deadline: 2/15; financial award applicants required to submit FAFSA. *Faculty research:* Preformulation, formulation and drug delivery; pharmacokinetics; pharmacology research; drug regulatory affairs; pharmaceutical analysis. *Total annual research expenditures:* $100,000. *Unit head:* Dr. John M. Pezzuto, Dean, 718-488-1004, Fax: 718-488-0628, E-mail: john.pezzuto@liu.edu. *Application contact:* Michael Young, Senior Assistant Director of Admissions, 718-488-1000, E-mail: michael.young@liu.edu.
Website: http://liu.edu/Pharmacy

Louisiana State University and Agricultural & Mechanical College, Graduate School, School of the Coast and Environment, Department of Environmental Sciences, Baton Rouge, LA 70803. Offers environmental planning and management (MS); environmental science (PhD); environmental toxicology (MS). *Faculty:* 12 full-time (5 women), 1 part-time/adjunct (0 women). *Students:* 25 full-time (11 women), 12 part-time (2 women); includes 2 minority (1 Black or African American, non-Hispanic/Latino; 1 Hispanic/Latino), 10 international. Average age 31. 14 applicants, 50% accepted, 4 enrolled. In 2017, 10 master's, 2 doctorates awarded. *Financial support:* In 2017–18, 12 research assistantships (averaging $19,100 per year), 6 teaching assistantships (averaging $16,776 per year) were awarded. *Total annual research expenditures:* $1.9 million.

Massachusetts Institute of Technology, School of Engineering, Department of Biological Engineering, Cambridge, MA 02139. Offers applied biosciences (PhD, Sc D); bioengineering (PhD, Sc D); biological engineering (PhD, Sc D); biomedical engineering (M Eng); toxicology (SM); SM/MBA. Terminal master's awarded for partial completion of doctoral program. *Degree requirements:* For master's, thesis; for doctorate, comprehensive exam, thesis/dissertation. *Entrance requirements:* For master's and doctorate, GRE General Test. Additional exam requirements/recommendations for international students: Required—IELTS. Electronic applications accepted. *Faculty research:* Biomaterials; biophysics; cell and tissue engineering; computational modeling of biological and physiological systems; discovery and delivery of molecular therapeutics; new tools for genomics; functional genomics; proteomics and glycomics; macromolecular biochemistry and biophysics; molecular, cell and tissue biomechanics; synthetic biology; systems biology.

Medical College of Wisconsin, Graduate School, Department of Pharmacology and Toxicology, Milwaukee, WI 53226-0509. Offers PhD, MD/PhD. *Degree requirements:* For doctorate, comprehensive exam, thesis/dissertation, oral and written qualifying exams. *Entrance requirements:* For doctorate, GRE, official transcripts, three letters of recommendation. Additional exam requirements/recommendations for international students: Required—TOEFL. *Application deadline:* For fall admission, 12/15 priority date for domestic and international students. Applications are processed on a rolling basis. Application fee: $50. Electronic applications accepted. *Financial support:* Fellowships, research assistantships, career-related internships or fieldwork, institutionally sponsored loans, and scholarships/grants available. Financial award application deadline: 2/15; financial award applicants required to submit FAFSA. *Faculty research:* Cardiovascular physiology and pharmacology, drugs of abuse, environmental and aquatic toxicology, central nervous system and biochemical pharmacology, signal transduction. *Unit head:* Dr. William D. Campbell, Chair, 414-955-8267, Fax: 414-955-6555, E-mail: gradschool@mcw.edu. *Application contact:* Recruitment Office, 414-955-4402, Fax: 414-955-6555, E-mail: gradschoolrecruit@mcw.edu.
Website: https://www.mcw.edu/Pharmacology.htm

Medical University of South Carolina, College of Graduate Studies, Department of Pharmaceutical and Biomedical Sciences, Charleston, SC 29425. Offers cell injury and repair (PhD); drug discovery (PhD); medicinal chemistry (PhD); toxicology (PhD); DMD/PhD; MD/PhD; Pharm D/PhD. *Degree requirements:* For doctorate, thesis/dissertation, oral and written exams, teaching and research seminar. *Entrance requirements:* For doctorate, GRE General Test, interview, minimum GPA of 3.0. Additional exam requirements/recommendations for international students: Required—TOEFL (minimum score 600 paper-based; 100 iBT). Electronic applications accepted. *Faculty research:* Drug discovery, toxicology, metabolomics, cell stress and injury.

Michigan State University, College of Human Medicine and The Graduate School, Graduate Programs in Human Medicine, East Lansing, MI 48824. Offers biochemistry and molecular biology (MS, PhD); epidemiology (MS, PhD); microbiology (MS); microbiology and molecular genetics (PhD); pharmacology and toxicology (MS, PhD); physiology (MS, PhD); public health (MPH). *Entrance requirements:* Additional exam requirements/recommendations for international students: Required—TOEFL.

Michigan State University, College of Osteopathic Medicine and The Graduate School, Graduate Studies in Osteopathic Medicine and Graduate Programs in Human Medicine and Graduate Programs in Veterinary Medicine, Department of Pharmacology and Toxicology, East Lansing, MI 48824. Offers integrative pharmacology (MS); pharmacology and toxicology (MS, PhD); pharmacology and toxicology-environmental toxicology (PhD). *Entrance requirements:* Additional exam requirements/recommendations for international students: Required—TOEFL (minimum score 600 paper-based). Electronic applications accepted.

Michigan State University, College of Veterinary Medicine and The Graduate School, Graduate Programs in Veterinary Medicine, Center for Integrative Toxicology, East Lansing, MI 48824. Offers animal science–environmental toxicology (PhD); biochemistry and molecular biology–environmental toxicology (PhD); chemistry–environmental toxicology (PhD); crop and soil sciences–environmental toxicology (PhD); environmental engineering–environmental toxicology (PhD); environmental geosciences–environmental toxicology (PhD); fisheries and wildlife–environmental toxicology (PhD); food science–environmental toxicology (PhD); forestry–environmental toxicology (PhD); genetics–environmental toxicology (PhD); human nutrition–environmental toxicology (PhD); microbiology–environmental toxicology (PhD); pharmacology and toxicology–environmental toxicology (PhD); zoology–environmental toxicology (PhD). *Entrance requirements:* Additional exam requirements/recommendations for international students: Required—TOEFL (minimum score 550 paper-based), Michigan State University ELT (minimum score 85), Michigan English Language Assessment Battery (minimum score 83). Electronic applications accepted. *Faculty research:* Environmental risk assessment, toxicogenomics, phytoremediation, storage and disposal of hazardous waste, environmental regulation.

Michigan State University, College of Veterinary Medicine and The Graduate School, Graduate Programs in Veterinary Medicine and College of Natural Science, Department of Microbiology and Molecular Genetics, East Lansing, MI 48824. Offers industrial microbiology (MS, PhD); microbiology (MS, PhD); microbiology and molecular genetics (MS, PhD); microbiology–environmental toxicology (PhD). *Entrance requirements:* For master's, GRE General Test. Additional exam requirements/recommendations for international students: Required—TOEFL (minimum score 550 paper-based), Michigan State University ELT (minimum score 85), Michigan English Language Assessment Battery (minimum score 83). Electronic applications accepted.

Michigan State University, The Graduate School, College of Agriculture and Natural Resources, Department of Animal Science, East Lansing, MI 48824. Offers animal science (MS, PhD); animal science-environmental toxicology (PhD). *Entrance requirements:* Additional exam requirements/recommendations for international students: Required—TOEFL (minimum score 550 paper-based), Michigan State University ELT (minimum score 85), Michigan English Language Assessment Battery (minimum score 83). Electronic applications accepted.

Michigan State University, The Graduate School, College of Agriculture and Natural Resources, Department of Crop and Soil Sciences, East Lansing, MI 48824. Offers crop and soil sciences (MS, PhD); crop and soil sciences-environmental toxicology (PhD); plant breeding and genetics-crop and soil sciences (MS); plant breeding, genetics and biotechnology-crop and soil sciences (PhD). *Entrance requirements:* Additional exam requirements/recommendations for international students: Required—TOEFL (minimum score 550 paper-based), Michigan State University ELT (minimum score 85), Michigan Michigan English Language Assessment Battery (minimum score 83). Electronic applications accepted.

Michigan State University, The Graduate School, College of Agriculture and Natural Resources and College of Natural Science, Department of Food Science and Human Nutrition, East Lansing, MI 48824. Offers food science (MS, PhD); food science - environmental toxicology (PhD); human nutrition (MS, PhD); human nutrition-environmental toxicology (PhD). *Entrance requirements:* Additional exam requirements/recommendations for international students: Required—TOEFL (minimum score 550 paper-based), Michigan State University ELT (minimum score 85), Michigan English Language Assessment Battery (minimum score 83). Electronic applications accepted.

Michigan State University, The Graduate School, College of Engineering, Department of Civil and Environmental Engineering, East Lansing, MI 48824. Offers civil engineering (MS, PhD); environmental engineering (MS, PhD); environmental engineering-environmental toxicology (PhD). *Program availability:* Part-time. *Entrance requirements:* Additional exam requirements/recommendations for international students: Required—TOEFL. Electronic applications accepted.

Michigan State University, The Graduate School, College of Natural Science and Graduate Programs in Human Medicine and Graduate Studies in Osteopathic Medicine, Department of Biochemistry and Molecular Biology, East Lansing, MI 48824. Offers biochemistry and molecular biology (MS, PhD); biochemistry and molecular biology/environmental toxicology (PhD). *Entrance requirements:* Additional exam requirements/recommendations for international students: Required—TOEFL. Electronic applications accepted.

Michigan State University, The Graduate School, College of Natural Science, Department of Chemistry, East Lansing, MI 48824. Offers chemical physics (PhD); chemistry (MS, PhD); chemistry-environmental toxicology (PhD); computational chemistry (MS). *Entrance requirements:* Additional exam requirements/recommendations for international students: Required—TOEFL. Electronic applications accepted. *Faculty research:* Analytical chemistry, inorganic and organic chemistry, nuclear chemistry, physical chemistry, theoretical and computational chemistry.

Michigan State University, The Graduate School, College of Natural Science, Department of Geological Sciences, East Lansing, MI 48824. Offers environmental geosciences (MS, PhD); environmental geosciences-environmental toxicology (PhD); geological sciences (MS, PhD). *Degree requirements:* For master's, thesis (for those without prior thesis work); for doctorate, thesis/dissertation. *Entrance requirements:* For master's, GRE General Test, minimum GPA of 3.0, course work in geoscience, 3 letters of recommendation; for doctorate, GRE General Test, 3 letters of recommendation. Additional exam requirements/recommendations for international students: Required—TOEFL (minimum score 550 paper-based), Michigan State University ELT (minimum score 85), Michigan English Language Assessment Battery (minimum score 83). Electronic applications accepted. *Faculty research:* Water in the environment, global and biological change, crystal dynamics.

Michigan State University, The Graduate School, College of Natural Science, Program in Genetics, East Lansing, MI 48824. Offers genetics (MS, PhD); genetics–environmental toxicology (PhD). *Entrance requirements:* Additional exam requirements/recommendations for international students: Required—TOEFL. Electronic applications accepted.

New York University, Graduate School of Arts and Science, Department of Environmental Medicine, New York, NY 10012-1019. Offers environmental health sciences (MS, PhD), including biostatistics (PhD), environmental hygiene (MS), epidemiology (PhD), ergonomics and biomechanics (PhD), exposure assessment and health effects (PhD), molecular toxicology/carcinogenesis (PhD), toxicology. *Program availability:* Part-time. *Students:* Average age 30. 79 applicants, 44% accepted, 20

enrolled. In 2017, 8 master's, 6 doctorates awarded. Terminal master's awarded for partial completion of doctoral program. *Degree requirements:* For master's, thesis or alternative; for doctorate, one foreign language, thesis/dissertation, oral and written exams. *Entrance requirements:* For master's and doctorate, GRE General Test, minimum GPA of 3.0; bachelor's degree in biological, physical, or engineering science. Additional exam requirements/recommendations for international students: Required—TOEFL. *Application deadline:* For fall admission, 12/18 for domestic and international students. Application fee: $100. *Expenses: Tuition:* Full-time $41,352; part-time $19,968 per year. *Required fees:* $2496; $1628 per unit. $814 per term. Tuition and fees vary according to course load and program. *Financial support:* Fellowships, teaching assistantships, career-related internships or fieldwork, Federal Work-Study, institutionally sponsored loans, and health care benefits available. Financial award application deadline: 12/18; financial award applicants required to submit FAFSA. *Unit head:* Dr. Max Costa, Chair, 845-731-3661, Fax: 845-351-4510, E-mail: ehs@env.med.nyu.edu. *Application contact:* Dr. Jerome J. Solomon, Director of Graduate Studies, 845-731-3661, Fax: 845-351-4510, E-mail: ehs@env.med.nyu.edu.
Website: http://environmental-medicine.med.nyu.edu/

See Close-Up on page 843.

North Carolina State University, Graduate School, College of Agriculture and Life Sciences and College of Veterinary Medicine, Department of Environmental and Molecular Toxicology, Raleigh, NC 27695. Offers M Tox, MS, PhD. Terminal master's awarded for partial completion of doctoral program. *Degree requirements:* For master's, thesis (for some programs); for doctorate, thesis/dissertation. *Entrance requirements:* For master's and doctorate, GRE General Test, minimum GPA of 3.0. Electronic applications accepted. *Faculty research:* Chemical fate, carcinogenesis, developmental and endocrine toxicity, xenobiotic metabolism, signal transduction.

Oklahoma State University Center for Health Sciences, Graduate Program in Forensic Sciences, Tulsa, OK 74107-1898. Offers forensic sciences (MS), including arson and explosives investigation, forensic biology/DNA, forensic document examination, forensic pathology/death scene investigations, forensic psychology, forensic science administration, forensic toxicology/trace evidence. *Program availability:* Part-time, evening/weekend, 100% online, blended/hybrid learning. *Degree requirements:* For master's, comprehensive exam, thesis (for some programs), thesis or creative component. *Entrance requirements:* For master's, GRE (for thesis tracks); GRE or MAT (for options in arson and explosives investigation, forensic science administration, and forensic document examination), professional experience (for options in arson and explosives investigation, forensic science administration and forensic document examination). Additional exam requirements/recommendations for international students: Required—TOEFL (minimum score 100 iBT) or IELTS (minimum score 7.0). Electronic applications accepted. *Faculty research:* Studies on the variability in chromosomal DNA; development/enhancement of accessory methods useful for forensic DNA typing; forensic chemistry in the areas of controlled substances, explosives, and technology; research on explosives and IEDs (non-chemistry); therapeutic jurisprudence, issues involving inmates and their families, institutional stress suicide.

Oregon State University, College of Agricultural Sciences, Program in Fisheries Science, Corvallis, OR 97331. Offers aquaculture (MS); conservation biology (MS, PhD); fish genetics (MS, PhD); ichthyology (MS, PhD); limnology (MS, PhD); parasites and diseases (MS, PhD); physiology and ecology of marine and freshwater fishes (MS, PhD); stream ecology (MS, PhD); toxicology (MS, PhD); water pollution biology (MS, PhD). *Program availability:* Part-time. *Entrance requirements:* For master's and doctorate, GRE, minimum GPA of 3.0 in last 90 hours. Additional exam requirements/recommendations for international students: Required—TOEFL (minimum score 80 iBT), IELTS (minimum score 6.5). *Application deadline:* For fall admission, 5/1 for domestic students, 4/1 for international students. Application fee: $75 ($85 for international students). *Faculty research:* Fisheries ecology, fish toxicology, stream ecology, quantitative analyses of marine and freshwater fish populations. *Unit head:* Dr. Selina Heppell, Department Head/Professor of Fisheries, 541-737-9039, Fax: 541-737-3590, E-mail: selina.heppell@oregonstate.edu. *Application contact:* Dr. Selina Heppell, Department Head/Professor of Fisheries, 541-737-9039, Fax: 541-737-3590, E-mail: selina.heppell@oregonstate.edu.
Website: http://fw.oregonstate.edu/content/graduate

Oregon State University, College of Agricultural Sciences, Program in Toxicology, Corvallis, OR 97331. Offers environmental chemistry and ecotoxicology (MS, PhD); mechanistic toxicology (MS, PhD); molecular and cellular toxicology (MS, PhD); neurotoxicology (MS, PhD). *Degree requirements:* For master's, thesis; for doctorate, thesis/dissertation. *Entrance requirements:* For master's and doctorate, GRE, bachelor's degree in chemistry or biological sciences, minimum GPA of 3.0 in last 90 hours of course work. Additional exam requirements/recommendations for international students: Required—TOEFL (minimum score 80 iBT), IELTS (minimum score 6.5). *Application deadline:* For fall admission, 12/31 for domestic and international students. Application fee: $75 ($85 for international students). *Financial support:* Application deadline: 12/31. *Application contact:* Mary Mucia, Advisor, 541-737-9079, E-mail: mary.mucia@oregonstate.edu.
Website: http://emt.oregonstate.edu/prospectivegrads

Purdue University, Graduate School, College of Health and Human Sciences, School of Health Sciences, West Lafayette, IN 47907. Offers health physics (MS, PhD); medical physics (MS, PhD); occupational and environmental health science (MS, PhD), including aerosol deposition and lung disease, ergonomics, exposure and risk assessment, indoor air quality and bioaerosols (PhD), liver/lung toxicology; radiation biology (PhD); toxicology (PhD); MS/PhD. *Program availability:* Part-time. *Faculty:* 12 full-time (4 women), 1 part-time/adjunct (0 women). *Students:* 37 full-time (16 women), 5 part-time (1 woman); includes 6 minority (2 Black or African American, non-Hispanic/Latino; 2 Asian, non-Hispanic/Latino; 1 Hispanic/Latino; 1 Two or more races, non-Hispanic/Latino), 9 international. Average age 28. 57 applicants, 65% accepted, 15 enrolled. In 2017, 10 master's, 4 doctorates awarded. *Degree requirements:* For master's, thesis optional; for doctorate, one foreign language, thesis/dissertation. *Entrance requirements:* For master's and doctorate, GRE General Test, minimum undergraduate GPA of 3.0 or equivalent. Additional exam requirements/recommendations for international students: Required—TOEFL (minimum score 550 paper-based; 77 iBT); Recommended—TWE. *Application deadline:* For fall admission, 5/15 for domestic and international students; for spring admission, 10/15 for domestic and international students. Applications are processed on a rolling basis. Application fee: $60 ($75 for international students). Electronic applications accepted. *Financial support:* In 2017–18, fellowships with tuition reimbursements (averaging $14,400 per year), research assistantships with tuition reimbursements (averaging $12,000 per year), teaching assistantships with tuition reimbursements (averaging $12,000 per year) were awarded; career-related internships or fieldwork and traineeships also available. Support available to part-time students. Financial award applicants required to submit FAFSA. *Faculty research:* Environmental toxicology, industrial hygiene, radiation dosimetry. *Unit head:* Jason T. Harris, Interim Head of the Graduate Program, 765-496-1271, E-mail: jtharris@purdue.edu. *Application contact:* Karen E. Walker, Graduate Contact, 765-494-1419, E-mail: kwalker@purdue.edu.
Website: https://www.purdue.edu/hhs/hsci/

Queen's University at Kingston, School of Graduate Studies, Faculty of Health Sciences, Department of Pharmacology and Toxicology, Kingston, ON K7L 3N6, Canada. Offers M Sc, PhD. *Degree requirements:* For master's, thesis; for doctorate, comprehensive exam, thesis/dissertation. *Entrance requirements:* For master's, minimum 2nd class standing, honors bachelor of science degree (life sciences, health sciences, or equivalent); for doctorate, masters of science degree or outstanding performance in honors bachelor of science program. Additional exam requirements/recommendations for international students: Required—TOEFL (minimum score 600 paper-based). Electronic applications accepted. *Faculty research:* Biochemical toxicology, cardiovascular pharmacology and neuropharmacology.

Rutgers University–New Brunswick, Graduate School-New Brunswick, Department of Environmental Sciences, Piscataway, NJ 08854-8097. Offers air pollution and resources (MS, PhD); aquatic biology (MS, PhD); aquatic chemistry (MS, PhD); atmospheric science (MS, PhD); chemistry and physics of aerosol and hydrosol systems (MS, PhD); environmental chemistry (MS, PhD); environmental microbiology (MS, PhD); environmental toxicology (PhD); exposure assessment (PhD); fate and effects of pollutants (MS, PhD); pollution prevention and control (MS, PhD); water and wastewater treatment (MS, PhD); water resources (MS, PhD). Terminal master's awarded for partial completion of doctoral program. *Degree requirements:* For master's, comprehensive exam, thesis or alternative, oral final exam; for doctorate, comprehensive exam, thesis/dissertation, thesis defense, qualifying exam. *Entrance requirements:* For master's and doctorate, GRE General Test. Additional exam requirements/recommendations for international students: Required—TOEFL. Electronic applications accepted. *Faculty research:* Biological waste treatment; contaminant fate and transport; air, soil and water quality.

Rutgers University–New Brunswick, Graduate School-New Brunswick, Joint Program in Toxicology, Piscataway, NJ 08854-8097. Offers environmental toxicology (MS, PhD); industrial-occupational toxicology (MS, PhD); nutritional toxicology (MS, PhD); pharmaceutical toxicology (MS, PhD). MS, PhD offered jointly with University of Medicine and Dentistry of New Jersey. *Degree requirements:* For master's, thesis; for doctorate, comprehensive exam, thesis/dissertation, qualifying exams (written and oral). *Entrance requirements:* For master's and doctorate, GRE General Test. Additional exam requirements/recommendations for international students: Required—TOEFL. Electronic applications accepted. *Faculty research:* Neurotoxicants, immunotoxicology, carcinogenesis and chemoprevention, molecular toxicology, xenobiotic metabolism.

Rutgers University–New Brunswick, Graduate School of Biomedical Sciences, Piscataway, NJ 08854-5635. Offers biochemistry and molecular biology (MS, PhD); biomedical engineering (MS, PhD); biomedical science (MS); cellular and molecular pharmacology (MS, PhD); clinical and translational science (MS); environmental sciences/exposure assessment (PhD); molecular genetics, microbiology and immunology (MS, PhD); neuroscience (MS, PhD); physiology and integrative biology (MS, PhD); toxicology (PhD); MD/PhD. Terminal master's awarded for partial completion of doctoral program. *Degree requirements:* For master's, thesis (for some programs), ethics training; for doctorate, comprehensive exam, thesis/dissertation, ethics training. *Entrance requirements:* For master's, GRE General Test, MCAT, DAT; for doctorate, GRE General Test. Additional exam requirements/recommendations for international students: Required—TOEFL. Electronic applications accepted.

St. John's University, College of Pharmacy and Health Sciences, Graduate Programs in Pharmaceutical Sciences, Program in Toxicology, Queens, NY 11439. Offers MS. *Program availability:* Part-time. *Students:* 8 full-time (4 women), 5 part-time (3 women); includes 9 minority (5 Asian, non-Hispanic/Latino; 1 Hispanic/Latino; 3 Two or more races, non-Hispanic/Latino), 1 international. Average age 24. 19 applicants, 63% accepted, 5 enrolled. In 2017, 4 master's awarded. Terminal master's awarded for partial completion of doctoral program. *Degree requirements:* For master's, comprehensive exam (for some programs), thesis (for some programs). *Entrance requirements:* For master's, GRE General Test, letters of recommendation, transcripts, resume, personal statement. Additional exam requirements/recommendations for international students: Required—TOEFL (minimum score 100 iBT), IELTS (minimum score 7). *Application deadline:* For fall admission, 3/1 for domestic students; for spring admission, 11/1 for domestic students. Applications are processed on a rolling basis. Application fee: $70. Electronic applications accepted. *Expenses:* $2,110 per credit tuition, $170 per semester fees; tuition may vary by program. *Financial support:* Fellowships, teaching assistantships, career-related internships or fieldwork, scholarships/grants, and unspecified assistantships available. Support available to part-time students. Financial award application deadline: 2/1; financial award applicants required to submit FAFSA. *Faculty research:* Neurotoxicology, renal toxicology, toxicology of metals, hepatic toxicology, pulmonary toxicology. *Unit head:* Dr. Vijaya L. Korlipara, Chair, 718-990-5369, Fax: 718-990-1877, E-mail: korlipav@stjohns.edu. *Application contact:* Robert Medrano, Director of Graduate Admission, 718-990-1601, Fax: 718-990-5686, E-mail: gradhelp@stjohns.edu.
Website: http://www.stjohns.edu//academics/schools-and-colleges/college-pharmacy-and-health-sciences/programs-and-majors/toxicology-master-science

San Diego State University, Graduate and Research Affairs, College of Health and Human Services, Graduate School of Public Health, San Diego, CA 92182. Offers environmental health (MPH); epidemiology (MPH, PhD), including biostatistics (MPH); global emergency preparedness and response (MS); global health (PhD); health behavior (PhD); health promotion (MPH); health services administration (MPH); toxicology (MS); MPH/MA; MSW/MPH. *Accreditation:* CAHME (one or more programs are accredited). *Program availability:* Part-time. *Degree requirements:* For master's, comprehensive exam (for some programs), thesis (for some programs); for doctorate, thesis/dissertation. *Entrance requirements:* For master's, GMAT (MPH in health services administration), GRE General Test; for doctorate, GRE General Test. Additional exam requirements/recommendations for international students: Required—TOEFL. *Faculty research:* Evaluation of tobacco, AIDS prevalence and prevention, mammography, infant death project, Alzheimer's in elderly Chinese.

Simon Fraser University, Office of Graduate Studies and Postdoctoral Fellows, Faculty of Science, Department of Biological Sciences, Burnaby, BC V5A 1S6, Canada. Offers bioinformatics (Graduate Diploma); biological sciences (M Sc, PhD); environmental toxicology (MET); pest management (MPM). *Degree requirements:* For master's, thesis; for doctorate, thesis/dissertation, candidacy exam; for Graduate Diploma, practicum. *Entrance requirements:* For master's, minimum GPA of 3.0 (on scale of 4.33) or 3.33 based on last 60 credits of undergraduate courses; for doctorate, minimum GPA of 3.5 (on scale of 4.33); for Graduate Diploma, minimum GPA of 2.5 (on scale of 4.33) or 2.67 based on last 60 credits of undergraduate courses. Additional exam requirements/recommendations for international students: Recommended—TOEFL (minimum score 580 paper-based; 93 iBT), IELTS (minimum score 7), TWE (minimum score 5). Electronic applications accepted. *Faculty research:* Cell biology, wildlife ecology, environmental and evolutionary physiology, environmental toxicology, pest management.

Texas Southern University, School of Science and Technology, Program in Environmental Toxicology, Houston, TX 77004-4584. Offers MS, PhD. *Program availability:* Part-time. *Degree requirements:* For master's, thesis; for doctorate, thesis/dissertation. *Entrance requirements:* For master's, minimum GPA of 2.75; for doctorate, GRE, minimum GPA of 2.75. Electronic applications accepted. *Expenses:* Contact institution. *Faculty research:* Air quality, water quality, soil remediation, computer modeling.

Texas Tech University, Graduate School, College of Arts and Sciences, Department of Environmental Toxicology, Lubbock, TX 79409. Offers MS, PhD, JD/MS, MBA/MS. *Program availability:* Part-time. *Faculty:* 17 full-time (5 women). *Students:* 38 full-time (22 women), 3 part-time (2 women); includes 7 minority (3 Black or African American, non-Hispanic/Latino; 2 Hispanic/Latino; 2 Two or more races, non-Hispanic/Latino), 11 international. Average age 30. 20 applicants, 70% accepted, 7 enrolled. In 2017, 4 master's, 8 doctorates awarded. Terminal master's awarded for partial completion of doctoral program. *Degree requirements:* For master's, thesis; for doctorate, comprehensive exam, thesis/dissertation. *Entrance requirements:* For master's and doctorate, GRE. Additional exam requirements/recommendations for international students: Required—TOEFL (minimum score 550 paper-based; 79 iBT); Recommended—IELTS (minimum score 6.5), TSE (minimum score 60). *Application deadline:* For fall admission, 6/1 priority date for domestic students, 1/15 priority date for international students; for spring admission, 9/1 priority date for domestic students, 6/15 priority date for international students. Applications are processed on a rolling basis. Application fee: $60. Electronic applications accepted. *Expenses:* Contact institution. *Financial support:* In 2017–18, 44 students received support, including 42 fellowships (averaging $2,282 per year), 42 research assistantships (averaging $14,540 per year); teaching assistantships, Federal Work-Study, institutionally sponsored loans, scholarships/grants, health care benefits, and unspecified assistantships also available. Financial award application deadline: 5/15; financial award applicants required to submit FAFSA. *Faculty research:* Wildlife toxicology; human health epidemiology and toxicology; endangered species toxicology; reproductive, molecular, and developmental toxicology; environmental and forensic chemistry. *Total annual research expenditures:* $1.2 million. *Unit head:* Dr. Steven M. Presley, Chair and Professor, 806-885-0236, Fax: 806-885-2132, E-mail: steve.presley@ttu.edu. *Application contact:* Dr. Kamaleshwar Singh, Graduate Officer, 806-834-8407, Fax: 806-885-2132, E-mail: kamaleshwar.singh@ttu.edu.
Website: http://www.tiehh.ttu.edu/

Thomas Jefferson University, Jefferson College of Biomedical Sciences, MS Program in Forensic Toxicology, Philadelphia, PA 19107. Offers MS. *Program availability:* Part-time, evening/weekend. *Faculty:* 43 full-time (16 women), 28 part-time/adjunct (9 women). *Students:* 7 part-time (4 women). 10 applicants, 70% accepted, 3 enrolled. *Degree requirements:* For master's, thesis, clerkship. *Entrance requirements:* For master's, GRE General Test or MCAT, minimum GPA of 3.0. Additional exam requirements/recommendations for international students: Required—TOEFL, IELTS (minimum score 7). *Application deadline:* For fall admission, 8/1 priority date for domestic students, 3/1 priority date for international students. Applications are processed on a rolling basis. Application fee: $50. Electronic applications accepted. *Financial support:* Federal Work-Study and institutionally sponsored loans available. Support available to part-time students. Financial award application deadline: 5/1; financial award applicants required to submit FAFSA. *Unit head:* Barry Logan, PhD, Program Director, E-mail: barry.logan@jefferson.edu. *Application contact:* Marc E. Stearns, Senior Associate Director of Admissions, 215-503-0155, Fax: 215-503-3433, E-mail: jgsbs-info@jefferson.edu.
Website: http://www.jefferson.edu/university/biomedical-sciences/degrees-programs/master-programs/forensic-toxicology.html

Université de Montréal, Faculty of Medicine, Program in Toxicology and Risk Analysis, Montréal, QC H3C 3J7, Canada. Offers DESS. Electronic applications accepted.

University at Albany, State University of New York, School of Public Health, Department of Environmental Health Sciences, Albany, NY 12222-0001. Offers environmental and occupational health (MS, PhD); environmental chemistry (MS, PhD); toxicology (MS, PhD). *Accreditation:* CEPH. *Faculty:* 15 full-time (8 women), 2 part-time/adjunct (1 woman). *Students:* 7 full-time (5 women), 8 part-time (all women); includes 4 minority (3 Black or African American, non-Hispanic/Latino; 1 Asian, non-Hispanic/Latino), 5 international. 16 applicants, 75% accepted, 3 enrolled. In 2017, 2 doctorates awarded. *Degree requirements:* For master's, thesis; for doctorate, comprehensive exam, thesis/dissertation. *Entrance requirements:* For master's and doctorate, GRE General Test, GRE Subject Test, 3 letters of reference. Additional exam requirements/recommendations for international students: Required—TOEFL (minimum score 600 paper-based). *Application deadline:* For fall admission, 1/15 for domestic and international students; for winter admission, 4/1 for domestic and international students; for spring admission, 10/1 for domestic students, 11/1 for international students. Applications are processed on a rolling basis. Application fee: $75. Electronic applications accepted. *Expenses:* Tuition, state resident: full-time $10,870; part-time $453 per credit hour. Tuition, nonresident: full-time $22,210; part-time $925 per credit hour. *Required fees:* $84.68 per credit hour. $508.06 per semester. Part-time tuition and fees vary according to course load and program. *Financial support:* Fellowships, research assistantships with full tuition reimbursements, teaching assistantships with full tuition reimbursements, scholarships/grants, health care benefits, tuition waivers (partial), and unspecified assistantships available. Financial award application deadline: 1/15. *Faculty research:* Xenobiotic metabolism, neurotoxicity of halogenated hydrocarbons, pharmacy/toxic genomics, environmental analytical chemistry. *Unit head:* Dr. David Lawrence, Chair, 518-474-7161, E-mail: dalawrence@albany.edu.
Website: http://www.albany.edu/sph/eht/index.html

University at Buffalo, the State University of New York, Graduate School, Jacobs School of Medicine and Biomedical Sciences, Graduate Programs in Medicine and Biomedical Sciences, Department of Pharmacology and Toxicology, Buffalo, NY 14203. Offers pharmacology (MS, PhD); MD/PhD. *Faculty:* 20 full-time (3 women), 1 part-time/adjunct (0 women). *Students:* 29 full-time (15 women); includes 9 minority (5 Black or African American, non-Hispanic/Latino; 1 American Indian or Alaska Native, non-Hispanic/Latino; 2 Asian, non-Hispanic/Latino; 1 Hispanic/Latino), 10 international. Average age 26. 47 applicants, 47% accepted, 12 enrolled. In 2017, 1 master's, 2 doctorates awarded. Terminal master's awarded for partial completion of doctoral program. *Degree requirements:* For master's, thesis; for doctorate, thesis/dissertation. *Entrance requirements:* For master's and doctorate, GRE General Test, 3 letters of recommendation. Additional exam requirements/recommendations for international students: Required—TOEFL (minimum score 79 iBT). *Application deadline:* For fall admission, 2/14 priority date for domestic and international students. Applications are processed on a rolling basis. Application fee: $85. Electronic applications accepted. *Financial support:* In 2017–18, 3 students received support, including 15 research assistantships with full tuition reimbursements available (averaging $27,000 per year); fellowships, teaching assistantships, Federal Work-Study, scholarships/grants, health care benefits, and unspecified assistantships also available. Financial award application deadline: 2/14; financial award applicants required to submit FAFSA. *Faculty research:* Neuropharmacology, toxicology, signal transduction, molecular pharmacology, behavioral pharmacology. *Total annual research expenditures:* $3.7 million. *Unit head:* Dr. David Dietz, Associate Professor/Chair, 716-829-2071, Fax: 716-829-2801, E-mail: ddietz@buffalo.edu. *Application contact:* Linda M. LeRoy, Admissions Assistant, 716-829-2800, Fax: 716-829-2801, E-mail: pmygrad@buffalo.edu.
Website: http://medicine.buffalo.edu/pharmtox

The University of Alabama at Birmingham, School of Public Health, Program in Public Health, Birmingham, AL 35294. Offers applied epidemiology and pharmacoepidemiology (MSPH); biostatistics (MPH); clinical and translational science (MSPH); environmental health (MPH); environmental health and toxicology (MSPH); epidemiology (MPH); general theory and practice (MPH); health behavior (MPH); health care organization (MPH); health policy quantitative policy analysis (MPH); industrial hygiene (MPH, MSPH); maternal and child health policy (Dr PH); maternal and child health policy and leadership (MPH); occupational health and safety (MPH); outcomes research (MSPH, Dr PH); public health (PhD); public health management (Dr PH); public health preparedness management (MPH). *Program availability:* Part-time, online learning. *Degree requirements:* For doctorate, comprehensive exam, thesis/dissertation. *Entrance requirements:* For master's and doctorate, GRE. Additional exam requirements/recommendations for international students: Recommended—TOEFL (minimum score 550 paper-based; 79 iBT), IELTS (minimum score 6.5). Electronic applications accepted.

University of Arkansas for Medical Sciences, Graduate School, Little Rock, AR 72205. Offers biochemistry and molecular biology (MS, PhD); bioinformatics (MS, PhD); cellular physiology and molecular biophysics (MS, PhD); clinical nutrition (MS); interdisciplinary biomedical sciences (MS, PhD, Certificate); interdisciplinary toxicology (MS); microbiology and immunology (PhD); neurobiology and developmental sciences (PhD); pharmacology (PhD); MD/PhD. Bioinformatics programs hosted jointly with the University of Arkansas at Little Rock. *Program availability:* Part-time. Terminal master's awarded for partial completion of doctoral program. *Degree requirements:* For master's, comprehensive exam (for some programs), thesis (for some programs); for doctorate, thesis/dissertation. *Entrance requirements:* For master's and doctorate, GRE. Additional exam requirements/recommendations for international students: Required—TOEFL. Electronic applications accepted. *Expenses:* Contact institution.

University of California, Davis, Graduate Studies, Graduate Group in Pharmacology and Toxicology, Davis, CA 95616. Offers MS, PhD. Terminal master's awarded for partial completion of doctoral program. *Degree requirements:* For master's, comprehensive exam or thesis; for doctorate, thesis/dissertation, qualifying exam. *Entrance requirements:* For master's and doctorate, GRE General Test, minimum GPA of 3.0, course work in biochemistry and/or physiology. Additional exam requirements/recommendations for international students: Required—TOEFL (minimum score 550 paper-based). Electronic applications accepted. *Faculty research:* Respiratory, neurochemical, molecular, genetic, and ecological toxicology.

University of California, Irvine, School of Medicine, Program in Environmental Health Sciences, Irvine, CA 92697. Offers environmental health sciences (MS); environmental toxicology (PhD); exposure sciences and risk assessment (PhD). *Students:* 16 full-time (11 women); includes 6 minority (3 Asian, non-Hispanic/Latino; 2 Hispanic/Latino; 1 Two or more races, non-Hispanic/Latino), 2 international. Average age 30. 19 applicants, 32% accepted, 4 enrolled. In 2017, 2 master's, 1 doctorate awarded. Terminal master's awarded for partial completion of doctoral program. *Degree requirements:* For master's, comprehensive exam; for doctorate, comprehensive exam, thesis/dissertation. *Entrance requirements:* For master's and doctorate, GRE General Test, GRE Subject Test, minimum GPA of 3.0. Additional exam requirements/recommendations for international students: Required—TOEFL (minimum score 550 paper-based). *Application deadline:* For fall admission, 1/15 for domestic students. Applications are processed on a rolling basis. Application fee: $105 ($125 for international students). Electronic applications accepted. *Financial support:* Fellowships, research assistantships with full tuition reimbursements, teaching assistantships, institutionally sponsored loans, traineeships, health care benefits, and unspecified assistantships available. Financial award application deadline: 12/15; financial award applicants required to submit FAFSA. *Faculty research:* Inhalation/pulmonary toxicology, environmental carcinogenesis, biochemical neurotoxicology, toxic kinetics, chemical pathology. *Unit head:* Dr. Ulrike Luderer, Director, 949-824-8848, E-mail: uluderer@uci.edu. *Application contact:* Armando Villalpando, Student Affairs Officer, 949-824-8848, E-mail: avillal@uci.edu.
Website: http://www.medicine.uci.edu/occupational/graduate.asp

University of California, Los Angeles, Graduate Division, College of Letters and Science and David Geffen School of Medicine, UCLA ACCESS to Programs in the Molecular, Cellular and Integrative Life Sciences, Los Angeles, CA 90095. Offers biochemistry and molecular biology (PhD); biological chemistry (PhD); cellular and molecular pathology (PhD); human genetics (PhD); microbiology, immunology, and molecular genetics (PhD); molecular biology (PhD); molecular toxicology (PhD); molecular, cellular and integrative physiology (PhD); neurobiology (PhD); oral biology (PhD); physiology (PhD). *Degree requirements:* For doctorate, thesis/dissertation, oral and written qualifying exams. *Entrance requirements:* For doctorate, GRE General Test, bachelor's degree; minimum undergraduate GPA of 3.0 (or its equivalent if letter grade system not used). Additional exam requirements/recommendations for international students: Required—TOEFL. Electronic applications accepted.

University of California, Riverside, Graduate Division, Program in Environmental Toxicology, Riverside, CA 92521. Offers MS, PhD. *Faculty:* 43 full-time (19 women). Terminal master's awarded for partial completion of doctoral program. *Degree requirements:* For master's, thesis; for doctorate, comprehensive exam, thesis/dissertation, preliminary written exam, oral qualifying exam. *Entrance requirements:* For master's and doctorate, GRE General Test, minimum GPA of 3.25. Additional exam requirements/recommendations for international students: Required—TOEFL (minimum score 550 paper-based, 80 iBT) or IELTS. *Application deadline:* For fall admission, 1/5 priority date for domestic students, 1/5 for international students; for winter admission, 11/15 for domestic students, 7/1 for international students; for spring admission, 3/1 for domestic students, 10/1 for international students. Application fee: $80 ($100 for international students). Electronic applications accepted. *Expenses:* Tuition, state resident: full-time $5746. Tuition, nonresident: full-time $10,780. Tuition and fees vary according to campus/location and program. *Financial support:* Fellowships with full tuition reimbursements, research assistantships with full tuition reimbursements, teaching assistantships with full tuition reimbursements, career-related internships or fieldwork, institutionally sponsored loans, scholarships/grants, traineeships, health care benefits, and unspecified assistantships available. Financial award application deadline: 1/5; financial award applicants required to submit FAFSA. *Faculty research:* Cellular/molecular toxicology, atmospheric chemistry, bioremediation, carcinogenesis, mechanism of toxicity. *Unit head:* Dr. Yinsheng Wang, Program Director, E-mail: yinsheng.wang@ucr.edu. *Application contact:* Antonio Knox, E-mail: etox@ucr.edu.
Website: http://www.etox.ucr.edu/

University of California, Santa Cruz, Division of Graduate Studies, Division of Physical and Biological Sciences, Environmental Toxicology Department, Santa Cruz, CA 95064. Offers MS, PhD. Terminal master's awarded for partial completion of doctoral program. *Degree requirements:* For master's, comprehensive exam, thesis; for doctorate, thesis/dissertation, qualifying exams. *Entrance requirements:* For master's and doctorate, GRE. Additional exam requirements/recommendations for international students: Required—TOEFL (minimum score 550 paper-based; 83 iBT); Recommended—IELTS (minimum score 8). Electronic applications accepted. *Faculty research:* Molecular mechanisms of reactive DNA methylation toxicity, anthropogenic perturbations of biogeochemical cycles, anaerobic microbiology and biotransformation of pollutants and toxic metals, organismal responses and therapeutic treatment of toxins, microbiology, molecular genetics, genomics.

Toxicology

University of Colorado Denver, Skaggs School of Pharmacy and Pharmaceutical Sciences, Program in Toxicology, Aurora, CO 80045. Offers PhD. *Entrance requirements:* For doctorate, GRE, minimum undergraduate GPA of 3.0; prior coursework in general chemistry, organic chemistry, calculus, biology, and physics. Additional exam requirements/recommendations for international students: Required—TOEFL. Application fee: $0. *Financial support:* Applicants required to submit FAFSA. *Faculty research:* Regulation of apoptotic cell death; cancer chemoprevention; innate immunity and hepatotoxicity; role of chronic inflammation in cancer; Parkinson's disease, epilepsy and oxidative stress.
Website: http://www.ucdenver.edu/academics/colleges/pharmacy/AcademicPrograms/PhDPrograms/PhDToxicology/Pages/PhDToxicology.aspx

University of Connecticut, Graduate School, School of Pharmacy, Department of Pharmaceutical Sciences, Graduate Program in Pharmacology and Toxicology, Storrs, CT 06269. Offers pharmacology (MS, PhD); toxicology (MS, PhD). Terminal master's awarded for partial completion of doctoral program. *Degree requirements:* For master's, comprehensive exam, thesis; for doctorate, thesis/dissertation. *Entrance requirements:* For master's and doctorate, GRE General Test. Additional exam requirements/recommendations for international students: Required—TOEFL (minimum score 550 paper-based). Electronic applications accepted.

University of Florida, College of Veterinary Medicine, Graduate Program in Veterinary Medical Sciences, Gainesville, FL 32611. Offers forensic toxicology (Certificate); veterinary medical sciences (MS, PhD), including forensic toxicology (MS). *Program availability:* Online learning. Terminal master's awarded for partial completion of doctoral program. *Degree requirements:* For master's, thesis; for doctorate, thesis/dissertation. *Entrance requirements:* For master's and doctorate, GRE General Test, minimum GPA of 3.0. Additional exam requirements/recommendations for international students: Required—TOEFL (minimum score 550 paper-based). Electronic applications accepted. *Expenses:* Contact institution.

University of Florida, Graduate School, College of Pharmacy, Programs in Forensic Science, Gainesville, FL 32611. Offers clinical toxicology (Certificate); drug chemistry (Certificate); environmental forensics (Certificate); forensic death investigation (Certificate); forensic DNA and serology (MSP, Certificate); forensic drug chemistry (MSP); forensic science (MSP); forensic toxicology (Certificate). *Program availability:* Part-time, evening/weekend, online learning. *Degree requirements:* For master's, comprehensive exam. *Entrance requirements:* For master's, GRE General Test, minimum GPA of 3.0. Additional exam requirements/recommendations for international students: Required—TOEFL (minimum score 550 paper-based; 80 iBT), IELTS (minimum score 6).

University of Guelph, Graduate Studies, Ontario Agricultural College, Department of Environmental Biology, Guelph, ON N1G 2W1, Canada. Offers entomology (M Sc, PhD); environmental microbiology and biotechnology (M Sc, PhD); environmental toxicology (M Sc, PhD); plant and forest systems (M Sc, PhD); plant pathology (M Sc, PhD). *Program availability:* Part-time. *Degree requirements:* For master's, thesis; for doctorate, comprehensive exam, thesis/dissertation. *Entrance requirements:* For master's, minimum 75% average during previous 2 years of course work; for doctorate, minimum 75% average. Additional exam requirements/recommendations for international students: Required—TOEFL or IELTS. Electronic applications accepted. *Faculty research:* Entomology, environmental microbiology and biotechnology, environmental toxicology, forest ecology, plant pathology.

University of Guelph, Ontario Veterinary College and Graduate Studies, Graduate Programs in Veterinary Sciences, Department of Biomedical Sciences, Guelph, ON N1G 2W1, Canada. Offers morphology (M Sc, DV Sc, PhD); neuroscience (M Sc, DV Sc, PhD); pharmacology (M Sc, DV Sc, PhD); physiology (M Sc, DV Sc, PhD); toxicology (M Sc, DV Sc, PhD). *Program availability:* Part-time. *Degree requirements:* For master's, thesis; for doctorate, comprehensive exam, thesis/dissertation. *Entrance requirements:* For master's, honors B Sc, minimum 75% average in last 20 courses; for doctorate, M Sc with thesis from accredited institution. Additional exam requirements/recommendations for international students: Required—TOEFL (minimum score 550 paper-based; 89 iBT). Electronic applications accepted. *Faculty research:* Cellular morphology; endocrine, vascular and reproductive physiology; clinical pharmacology; veterinary toxicology; developmental biology, neuroscience.

University of Guelph, Ontario Veterinary College, Interdepartmental Program in Toxicology, Guelph, ON N1G 2W1, Canada. Offers M Sc, PhD. *Program availability:* Part-time. *Degree requirements:* For master's, thesis (for some programs); for doctorate, comprehensive exam, thesis/dissertation. *Entrance requirements:* For master's, B Sc; for doctorate, M Sc. Additional exam requirements/recommendations for international students: Required—TOEFL (minimum score 550 paper-based; 89 iBT).

University of Illinois at Chicago, College of Pharmacy and Graduate College, Graduate Programs in Pharmacy, Chicago, IL 60607-7128. Offers comparative effectiveness research (MS); forensic science (MS); forensic toxicology (MS); medicinal chemistry (MS, PhD); pharmacognosy (MS, PhD); pharmacy (PhD). Terminal master's awarded for partial completion of doctoral program. *Degree requirements:* For master's, variable foreign language requirement, thesis; for doctorate, variable foreign language requirement, thesis/dissertation. *Entrance requirements:* For master's and doctorate, GRE General Test. Additional exam requirements/recommendations for international students: Required—TOEFL. Electronic applications accepted. *Faculty research:* Biopharmaceutical science, forensic science, forensic toxicology, medicinal chemistry, pharmacognosy.

The University of Iowa, Graduate College, Program in Human Toxicology, Iowa City, IA 52242-1316. Offers MS, PhD. *Degree requirements:* For master's, thesis; for doctorate, comprehensive exam, thesis/dissertation. *Entrance requirements:* For master's and doctorate, GRE General Test, minimum GPA of 3.0. Additional exam requirements/recommendations for international students: Required—TOEFL (minimum score 600 paper-based; 100 iBT). Electronic applications accepted.

The University of Kansas, Graduate Studies, School of Pharmacy, Department of Pharmacology and Toxicology, Lawrence, KS 66045. Offers MS, PhD. *Students:* 32 full-time (24 women), 1 part-time (0 women); includes 4 minority (1 American Indian or Alaska Native, non-Hispanic/Latino; 1 Asian, non-Hispanic/Latino; 2 Hispanic/Latino), 14 international. Average age 28. 64 applicants, 17% accepted, 10 enrolled. In 2017, 7 master's, 4 doctorates awarded. Terminal master's awarded for partial completion of doctoral program. *Entrance requirements:* For master's and doctorate, GRE General Test, bachelor's degree in related field, 3 letters of recommendation, resume or curriculum vitae, official transcripts, 1-2 page personal statement. *Application deadline:* For fall admission, 1/15 priority date for domestic and international students. Application fee: $65 ($85 for international students). Electronic applications accepted. *Financial support:* Fellowships, research assistantships, and teaching assistantships available. Financial award application deadline: 2/1. *Faculty research:* Molecular neurobiology, gene regulation, neurotransmitter receptors, drug metabolism. *Unit head:* Nancy Muma, Chair, 785-864-4002, E-mail: nmuma@ku.edu. *Application contact:* Sarah Hoadley, Graduate Admissions Contact, 785-864-4002, E-mail: sarahhoadley@ku.edu.
Website: http://pharmtox.ku.edu/

The University of Kansas, University of Kansas Medical Center, School of Medicine, Department of Pharmacology, Toxicology and Therapeutics, Kansas City, KS 66160. Offers pharmacology (PhD); toxicology (PhD); MD/PhD. *Faculty:* 17. *Students:* 19 full-time (10 women); includes 3 minority (2 Black or African American, non-Hispanic/Latino; 1 Two or more races, non-Hispanic/Latino), 12 international. Average age 30. 1 applicant, 100% accepted, 1 enrolled. In 2017, 4 doctorates awarded. Terminal master's awarded for partial completion of doctoral program. *Degree requirements:* For doctorate, one foreign language, comprehensive exam, thesis/dissertation. *Entrance requirements:* For doctorate, GRE General Test. Additional exam requirements/recommendations for international students: Required—TOEFL. *Application deadline:* For fall admission, 12/1 priority date for domestic and international students. Applications are processed on a rolling basis. Application fee: $60. Electronic applications accepted. Application fee is waived when completed online. *Financial support:* Fellowships with full tuition reimbursements, research assistantships with full tuition reimbursements, teaching assistantships with full tuition reimbursements, Federal Work-Study, scholarships/grants, traineeships, and unspecified assistantships available. Support available to part-time students. Financial award application deadline: 3/1; financial award applicants required to submit FAFSA. *Faculty research:* Liver nuclear receptors, hepatobiliary transporters, pharmacogenomics, neuropharmacology of pain and depression, hepatotoxicity. *Total annual research expenditures:* $4.2 million. *Unit head:* Dr. Hartmut Jaeschke, Professor and Chair, 913-588-7500, Fax: 913-588-7501, E-mail: hjaeschke@kumc.edu. *Application contact:* Dr. Bruno Hagenbuch, Chair, Departmental Graduate Committee, 913-588-7500, Fax: 913-588-7501, E-mail: bhagenbuch@kumc.edu.
Website: http://www.kumc.edu/school-of-medicine/pharmacology-toxicology-and-therapeutics.html

University of Kentucky, Graduate School, Graduate School Programs from the College of Medicine, Program in Toxicology, Lexington, KY 40506-0032. Offers MS, PhD. Terminal master's awarded for partial completion of doctoral program. *Degree requirements:* For master's, comprehensive exam, thesis optional; for doctorate, comprehensive exam, thesis/dissertation. *Entrance requirements:* For master's, GRE General Test, minimum undergraduate GPA of 2.75; for doctorate, GRE General Test, minimum graduate GPA of 3.0. Additional exam requirements/recommendations for international students: Required—TOEFL (minimum score 550 paper-based). Electronic applications accepted. *Faculty research:* Chemical carcinogenesis, immunotoxicology, neurotoxicology, metabolism and disposition, gene regulation.

University of Louisiana at Monroe, Graduate School, College of Health and Pharmaceutical Sciences, School of Pharmacy, Monroe, LA 71209-0001. Offers pharmacy (PhD); toxicology (PhD). *Accreditation:* ACPE. *Faculty:* 22 full-time (10 women). *Students:* 390 full-time (236 women), 5 part-time (2 women); includes 96 minority (41 Black or African American, non-Hispanic/Latino; 1 American Indian or Alaska Native, non-Hispanic/Latino; 39 Asian, non-Hispanic/Latino; 5 Hispanic/Latino; 10 Two or more races, non-Hispanic/Latino), 30 international. Average age 24. 48 applicants, 96% accepted, 45 enrolled. In 2017, 108 doctorates awarded. *Degree requirements:* For doctorate, comprehensive exam, thesis/dissertation. *Entrance requirements:* For doctorate, GRE General Test, minimum undergraduate GPA of 2.5. Additional exam requirements/recommendations for international students: Required—TOEFL (minimum score 500 paper-based; 61 iBT). *Application deadline:* For fall admission, 3/1 for domestic and international students; for winter admission, 12/14 for domestic students; for spring admission, 9/1 for domestic and international students. Applications are processed on a rolling basis. Application fee: $20 ($30 for international students). Electronic applications accepted. *Expenses:* $11,792 per semester tuition and fees. *Financial support:* In 2017–18, 63 students received support. Research assistantships, Federal Work-Study, and unspecified assistantships available. Financial award application deadline: 4/1; financial award applicants required to submit FAFSA. *Unit head:* Dr. Glenn Anderson, Dean, 318-342-1600, E-mail: ganderson@ulm.edu. *Application contact:* Dr. Paul W. Sylvester, Director, Research and Graduate Studies, 318-342-1958, Fax: 318-342-1606, E-mail: sylvester@ulm.edu.
Website: http://www.ulm.edu/pharmacy/

University of Louisville, School of Medicine, Department of Pharmacology and Toxicology, Louisville, KY 40292-0001. Offers MS, PhD, MD/PhD. *Program availability:* Part-time. *Faculty:* 20 full-time (5 women). *Students:* 34 full-time (18 women), 16 part-time (10 women); includes 10 minority (3 Black or African American, non-Hispanic/Latino; 2 Asian, non-Hispanic/Latino; 5 Two or more races, non-Hispanic/Latino), 14 international. Average age 29. 21 applicants, 43% accepted, 9 enrolled. In 2017, 3 master's, 5 doctorates awarded. Terminal master's awarded for partial completion of doctoral program. *Degree requirements:* For master's, thesis; for doctorate, comprehensive exam, thesis/dissertation. *Entrance requirements:* For master's and doctorate, GRE General Test (minimum score of 1000 verbal and quantitative), minimum GPA of 3.0. Additional exam requirements/recommendations for international students: Required—TOEFL; Recommended—IELTS. *Application deadline:* For fall admission, 12/1 priority date for domestic and international students. Application fee: $65. *Expenses:* Tuition, state resident: full-time $12,246; part-time $681 per credit hour. Tuition, nonresident: full-time $25,486; part-time $1417 per credit hour. *Required fees:* $196. Tuition and fees vary according to course load, program and reciprocity agreements. *Financial support:* In 2017–18, 5 fellowships with full tuition reimbursements (averaging $25,000 per year) were awarded. Financial award application deadline: 12/1. *Faculty research:* Carcinogenesis, cardiometabolic disease, metal toxicology, drug development, diabetes. *Total annual research expenditures:* $4.1 million. *Unit head:* Dr. David W. Hein, Chair, 502-852-5141, Fax: 502-852-7868, E-mail: dhein@louisville.edu. *Application contact:* Heddy R. Rubin, Information Contact, 502-852-5741, Fax: 502-852-7868, E-mail: hrrubi01@gwise.louisville.edu.
Website: http://louisville.edu/medicine/departments/pharmacology

The University of Manchester, School of Biological Sciences, Manchester, United Kingdom. Offers adaptive organismal biology (M Phil, PhD); animal biology (M Phil, PhD); biochemistry (M Phil, PhD); bioinformatics (M Phil, PhD); biomolecular sciences (M Phil, PhD); biotechnology (M Phil, PhD); cell biology (M Phil, PhD); cell matrix research (M Phil, PhD); channels and transporters (M Phil, PhD); developmental biology (M Phil, PhD); environmental biology (M Phil, PhD); evolutionary biology (M Phil, PhD); gene expression (M Phil, PhD); genetics (M Phil, PhD); history of science, technology and medicine (M Phil, PhD); immunology (M Phil, PhD); integrative neurobiology and behavior (M Phil, PhD); membrane trafficking (M Phil, PhD); microbiology (M Phil, PhD); molecular and cellular neuroscience (M Phil, PhD); molecular biology (M Phil, PhD); molecular cancer studies (M Phil, PhD); neuroscience (M Phil, PhD); ophthalmology (M Phil, PhD); optometry (M Phil, PhD); organelle function (M Phil, PhD); pharmacology (M Phil, PhD); physiology (M Phil, PhD); plant sciences (M Phil, PhD); stem cell research (M Phil, PhD); structural biology (M Phil, PhD); systems neuroscience (M Phil, PhD); toxicology (M Phil, PhD).

University of Maryland, Baltimore, Graduate School, Graduate Program in Life Sciences, Program in Toxicology, Baltimore, MD 21201. Offers MS, PhD, MD/MS, MD/PhD. *Program availability:* Part-time. *Students:* 13 full-time (10 women), 6 part-time (4 women); includes 3 minority (1 Asian, non-Hispanic/Latino; 1 Hispanic/Latino; 1 Two or more races, non-Hispanic/Latino), 4 international. Average age 28. 29 applicants, 21% accepted, 1 enrolled. In 2017, 3 master's, 6 doctorates awarded. *Degree requirements:*

For master's, thesis (for some programs). *Entrance requirements:* For master's, GRE General Test, GRE Subject Test, minimum GPA of 3.0, curriculum vitae, essay, 3 letters of recommendation. Additional exam requirements/recommendations for international students: Required—TOEFL (minimum score 80 iBT); Recommended—IELTS (minimum score 7). *Application deadline:* For fall admission, 3/15 for domestic students, 1/15 for international students. Application fee: $75. Electronic applications accepted. *Expenses:* Tuition, state resident: full-time $13,990; part-time $661 per credit. Tuition, nonresident: full-time $30,484; part-time $1310 per credit. *Required fees:* $1894; $94 per credit. $415 per semester. Part-time tuition and fees vary according to course load, degree level and program. *Financial support:* In 2017–18, research assistantships with partial tuition reimbursements (averaging $26,000 per year) were awarded; fellowships, Federal Work-Study, and health care benefits also available. Financial award application deadline: 3/1; financial award applicants required to submit FAFSA. *Unit head:* Dr. William Randall, Director, 410-706-7530, E-mail: wrandall@umaryland.edu. *Application contact:* Linda Horne, Program Coordinator, 410-706-5422, E-mail: lhorne@som.umaryland.edu.
Website: http://lifesciences.umaryland.edu/Toxicology/

University of Maryland, Baltimore, School of Medicine, Department of Epidemiology and Public Health, Baltimore, MD 21201. Offers biostatistics (MS); clinical research (MS); epidemiology and preventive medicine (MPH, MS, PhD); gerontology (PhD); human genetics and genomic medicine (MS, PhD); molecular epidemiology (MS, PhD); toxicology (MS, PhD); JD/MS; MD/PhD; MS/PhD. *Accreditation:* CEPH. *Program availability:* Part-time. *Students:* 88 full-time (72 women), 53 part-time (38 women); includes 51 minority (21 Black or African American, non-Hispanic/Latino; 20 Asian, non-Hispanic/Latino; 7 Hispanic/Latino; 3 Two or more races, non-Hispanic/Latino), 29 international. Average age 30. In 2017, 24 master's, 14 doctorates awarded. *Degree requirements:* For doctorate, comprehensive exam, thesis/dissertation. *Entrance requirements:* For master's and doctorate, GRE General Test. Additional exam requirements/recommendations for international students: Required—TOEFL (minimum score 550 paper-based; 80 iBT); Recommended—IELTS (minimum score 7). *Application deadline:* For fall admission, 1/15 for domestic and international students. Application fee: $75. Electronic applications accepted. *Expenses:* Contact institution. *Financial support:* In 2017–18, research assistantships with partial tuition reimbursements (averaging $26,000 per year) were awarded; fellowships, Federal Work-Study, scholarships/grants, and unspecified assistantships also available. Financial award application deadline: 3/1; financial award applicants required to submit FAFSA. *Unit head:* Dr. Laura Hungerford, Program Director, 410-706-8492, Fax: 410-706-4225. *Application contact:* Jessica Kelley, Program Coordinator, 410-706-8492, Fax: 410-706-4225, E-mail: jkelley@som.umaryland.edu.
Website: http://lifesciences.umaryland.edu/epidemiology/

University of Maryland Eastern Shore, Graduate Programs, Department of Natural Sciences, Program in Toxicology, Princess Anne, MD 21853. Offers MS, PhD. *Expenses:* Tuition, state resident: part-time $325 per credit hour. Tuition, nonresident: part-time $604 per credit hour. *Required fees:* $85 per credit hour. Part-time tuition and fees vary according to campus/location, program and reciprocity agreements. *Financial support:* Teaching assistantships available. *Unit head:* Dr. Ali Ishaque, Coordinator, 410-651-6050, E-mail: abishaque@umes.edu. *Application contact:* Benita Sims-Tucker, Associate Vice President for Academic Affairs, 410-651-6508, E-mail: bsimstucker@umes.edu.

University of Michigan, School of Public Health, Department of Environmental Health Sciences, Ann Arbor, MI 48109. Offers environmental health policy and promotion (MPH); environmental health sciences (MS, PhD); environmental quality, sustainability and health (MPH); industrial hygiene (MPH, MS); occupational and environmental epidemiology (MPH); toxicology (MPH, MS, PhD). *Accreditation:* CEPH (one or more programs are accredited). Terminal master's awarded for partial completion of doctoral program. *Degree requirements:* For master's, thesis (for some programs); for doctorate, thesis/dissertation, preliminary exam, oral defense of dissertation. *Entrance requirements:* For master's and doctorate, GRE General Test and/or MCAT. Additional exam requirements/recommendations for international students: Required—TOEFL (minimum score 100 iBT). Electronic applications accepted. *Expenses:* Tuition, state resident: full-time $22,368; part-time $1201 per credit hour. Tuition, nonresident: full-time $45,156; part-time $2467 per credit hour. *Required fees:* $376 per term. Tuition and fees vary according to course load, degree level and program. *Faculty research:* Toxicology, occupational hygiene, environmental exposure sciences, environmental epidemiology.

University of Minnesota, Duluth, Graduate School, Program in Toxicology, Duluth, MN 55812-2496. Offers MS, PhD. MS, PhD offered jointly with University of Minnesota, Twin Cities Campus. Terminal master's awarded for partial completion of doctoral program. *Degree requirements:* For master's, thesis; for doctorate, comprehensive exam, thesis/dissertation, written and oral preliminary and final exams. *Entrance requirements:* For master's and doctorate, GRE General Test, BS in basic science; full year each of biology, chemistry, and physics; mathematics coursework through calculus. Additional exam requirements/recommendations for international students: Required—TOEFL (minimum score 550 paper-based; 79 iBT). Electronic applications accepted. *Faculty research:* Structure activity correlations, neurotoxicity, aquatic toxicology, biochemical mechanisms, immunotoxicology.

University of Minnesota, Duluth, Medical School, Department of Biochemistry, Molecular Biology and Biophysics, Duluth, MN 55812-2496. Offers biochemistry, molecular biology and biophysics (MS); biology and biophysics (PhD); social, administrative, and clinical pharmacy (MS, PhD); toxicology (MS, PhD). Terminal master's awarded for partial completion of doctoral program. *Degree requirements:* For master's, comprehensive exam, thesis; for doctorate, comprehensive exam, thesis/dissertation. *Entrance requirements:* For master's and doctorate, GRE General Test. Additional exam requirements/recommendations for international students: Required—TOEFL. Electronic applications accepted. *Faculty research:* Intestinal cancer biology; hepatotoxins and mitochondriopathies; toxicology; cell cycle regulation in stem cells; neurobiology of brain development, trace metal function and blood-brain barrier; hibernation biology.

University of Minnesota, Twin Cities Campus, School of Public Health, Division of Environmental Health Sciences, Area in Environmental Toxicology, Minneapolis, MN 55455-0213. Offers MPH, MS, PhD. *Degree requirements:* For doctorate, thesis/dissertation. *Entrance requirements:* For master's and doctorate, GRE General Test. Electronic applications accepted.

University of Mississippi, Graduate School, School of Pharmacy, University, MS 38677. Offers environmental toxicology (MS, PhD); industrial pharmacy (MS); medicinal chemistry (MS, PhD); pharmaceutics (MS, PhD); pharmacognosy (MS, PhD); pharmacology (MS, PhD); pharmacy (Pharm D); pharmacy administration (MS, PhD). *Accreditation:* ACPE (one or more programs are accredited). *Program availability:* Part-time. *Faculty:* 71 full-time (32 women), 17 part-time/adjunct (6 women). *Students:* 417 full-time (256 women), 16 part-time (7 women); includes 71 minority (24 Black or African American, non-Hispanic/Latino; 1 American Indian or Alaska Native, non-Hispanic/Latino; 36 Asian, non-Hispanic/Latino; 4 Hispanic/Latino; 6 Two or more races, non-Hispanic/Latino), 88 international. Average age 25. In 2017, 22 master's, 49 doctorates awarded. Terminal master's awarded for partial completion of doctoral program. *Degree requirements:* For master's, thesis; for doctorate, thesis/dissertation (for some programs). *Entrance requirements:* For master's, GRE General Test, minimum GPA of 3.0; for doctorate, GRE General Test (for PhD). Additional exam requirements/recommendations for international students: Required—TOEFL. *Application deadline:* For fall admission, 2/1 priority date for domestic students; for spring admission, 10/1 priority date for domestic students. Applications are processed on a rolling basis. Application fee: $50. Electronic applications accepted. *Financial support:* Fellowships, research assistantships, teaching assistantships, career-related internships or fieldwork, Federal Work-Study, institutionally sponsored loans, scholarships/grants, tuition waivers (full), and unspecified assistantships available. Financial award application deadline: 3/1; financial award applicants required to submit FAFSA. *Unit head:* Dr. David D. Allen, II, Dean, 662-915-7265, Fax: 662-915-5118, E-mail: sopdean@olemiss.edu.
Website: http://www.pharmacy.olemiss.edu/

University of Mississippi Medical Center, School of Graduate Studies in the Health Sciences, Department of Pharmacology and Toxicology, Jackson, MS 39216-4505. Offers PhD. *Degree requirements:* For doctorate, comprehensive exam, thesis/dissertation, first authored publication. *Entrance requirements:* For doctorate, GRE General Test, minimum GPA of 3.0. Additional exam requirements/recommendations for international students: Required—TOEFL (minimum score 550 paper-based, 79 iBT), IELTS or PTE. Electronic applications accepted. *Faculty research:* Renal and cardiovascular pharmacology, genetic basis of cardio-renal diseases, diabetes, obesity, metabolic diseases, cancer chemotherapy.

University of Montana, Graduate School, College of Health Professions and Biomedical Sciences, Skaggs School of Pharmacy, Department of Biomedical and Pharmaceutical Sciences, Missoula, MT 59812. Offers biomedical sciences (PhD); medicinal chemistry (MS, PhD); molecular and cellular toxicology (MS, PhD); neuroscience (PhD); pharmaceutical sciences (MS). *Accreditation:* ACPE. *Degree requirements:* For master's, oral defense of thesis; for doctorate, research dissertation defense. *Entrance requirements:* For master's and doctorate, GRE General Test. Additional exam requirements/recommendations for international students: Required—TOEFL (minimum score 540 paper-based). Electronic applications accepted. *Faculty research:* Cardiovascular pharmacology, medicinal chemistry, neurosciences, environmental toxicology, pharmacogenetics, cancer.

University of Nebraska–Lincoln, Graduate College, Interdepartmental Area of Environmental Health, Occupational Health and Toxicology, Lincoln, NE 68588. Offers MS, PhD. MS, PhD offered jointly with University of Nebraska Medical Center. *Entrance requirements:* Additional exam requirements/recommendations for international students: Required—TOEFL (minimum score 550 paper-based). Electronic applications accepted.

University of Nebraska Medical Center, Environmental Health, Occupational Health and Toxicology Graduate Program, Omaha, NE 68198-4388. Offers PhD. *Degree requirements:* For doctorate, comprehensive exam, thesis/dissertation. *Entrance requirements:* For doctorate, GRE General Test, BS in chemistry, biology, biochemistry or related area. Additional exam requirements/recommendations for international students: Required—TOEFL (minimum score 550 paper-based; 80 iBT). Electronic applications accepted. *Expenses:* Tuition, state resident: full-time $8451; part-time $4225 per semester. Tuition, nonresident: full-time $24,219; part-time $11,295 per semester. *Required fees:* $589; $117 per term. *Faculty research:* Mechanisms of carcinogenesis, alcohol and metal toxicity, DNA damage, human molecular genetics, agrochemicals in soil and water.

University of New Mexico, Graduate Studies, Health Sciences Center, Program in Biomedical Sciences, Albuquerque, NM 87131-5196. Offers biochemistry and molecular biology (MS, PhD); cell biology and physiology (MS, PhD); molecular genetics and microbiology (MS, PhD); neuroscience (MS, PhD); pathology (MS, PhD); toxicology (MS, PhD). *Program availability:* Part-time. *Students:* Average age 29. 61 applicants, 16% accepted, 10 enrolled. In 2017, 11 master's, 14 doctorates awarded. Terminal master's awarded for partial completion of doctoral program. *Degree requirements:* For master's, thesis; for doctorate, comprehensive exam, thesis/dissertation, qualifying exam at the end of year 1/core curriculum. *Entrance requirements:* For master's and doctorate, GRE General Test, minimum undergraduate GPA of 3.0. Additional exam requirements/recommendations for international students: Required—TOEFL. *Application deadline:* For fall admission, 3/1 priority date for domestic and international students. Applications are processed on a rolling basis. Application fee: $50. Electronic applications accepted. *Financial support:* Fellowships, research assistantships with full tuition reimbursements, teaching assistantships, career-related internships or fieldwork, Federal Work-Study, institutionally sponsored loans, scholarships/grants, traineeships, health care benefits, and unspecified assistantships available. Financial award application deadline: 1/1; financial award applicants required to submit FAFSA. *Faculty research:* Infectious disease/immunity, cancer biology, cardiovascular and metabolic diseases, brain and behavioral illness, environmental health. *Unit head:* Dr. Helen J. Hathaway, Program Director, 505-272-1887, Fax: 505-272-2412, E-mail: hhathaway@salud.unm.edu. *Application contact:* Mary Fenton, Admissions Coordinator, 505-272-1887, Fax: 505-272-2412, E-mail: mfenton@salud.unm.edu.

The University of North Carolina at Chapel Hill, School of Medicine, Curriculum in Toxicology, Chapel Hill, NC 27599. Offers MS, PhD. Terminal master's awarded for partial completion of doctoral program. *Degree requirements:* For master's, comprehensive exam, thesis; for doctorate, comprehensive exam, thesis/dissertation. *Entrance requirements:* For doctorate, GRE General Test. Electronic applications accepted. *Faculty research:* Molecular and cellular toxicology, carcinogenesis, neurotoxicology, pulmonary toxicology, developmental toxicology.

University of Prince Edward Island, Atlantic Veterinary College, Graduate Program in Veterinary Medicine, Charlottetown, PE C1A 4P3, Canada. Offers anatomy (M Sc, PhD); bacteriology (M Sc, PhD); clinical pharmacology (M Sc, PhD); clinical sciences (M Sc, PhD); epidemiology (M Sc, PhD), including reproduction; fish health (M Sc, PhD); food animal nutrition (M Sc, PhD); immunology (M Sc, PhD); microanatomy (M Sc, PhD); parasitology (M Sc, PhD); pathology (M Sc, PhD); pharmacology (M Sc, PhD); physiology (M Sc, PhD); toxicology (M Sc, PhD); veterinary science (M Vet Sc); virology (M Sc, PhD). *Program availability:* Part-time. *Degree requirements:* For master's, thesis; for doctorate, thesis/dissertation. *Entrance requirements:* For master's, DVM, B Sc honors degree, or equivalent; for doctorate, M Sc. Additional exam requirements/recommendations for international students: Required—TOEFL (minimum score 550 paper-based; 80 iBT). *Expenses:* Contact institution. *Faculty research:* Animal health management, infectious diseases, fin fish and shellfish health, basic biomedical sciences, ecosystem health.

University of Puerto Rico–Medical Sciences Campus, School of Medicine, Biomedical Sciences Graduate Program, Department of Pharmacology and Toxicology, San Juan, PR 00936-5067. Offers MS, PhD. *Degree requirements:* For master's, one foreign language, thesis; for doctorate, one foreign language, comprehensive exam, thesis/dissertation. *Entrance requirements:* For master's and doctorate, GRE General Test, GRE Subject Test, interview, minimum GPA of 3.0, 3 letters of recommendation. Electronic applications accepted. *Faculty research:* Cardiovascular, central nervous system, and endocrine pharmacology; anti-cancer drugs; sodium pump; mitochondrial DNA repair; Huntington's disease.

Toxicology

University of Rhode Island, Graduate School, College of Pharmacy, Department of Biomedical and Pharmaceutical Sciences, Kingston, RI 02881. Offers health outcomes (MS, PhD); medicinal chemistry and pharmacognosy (MS, PhD); pharmaceutics and pharmacokinetics (MS, PhD); pharmacology and toxicology (MS, PhD). *Program availability:* Part-time. *Faculty:* 23 full-time (11 women). *Students:* 36 full-time (14 women), 9 part-time (4 women); includes 4 minority (1 Black or African American, non-Hispanic/Latino; 1 American Indian or Alaska Native, non-Hispanic/Latino; 2 Asian, non-Hispanic/Latino), 22 international. 138 applicants, 18% accepted, 14 enrolled. In 2017, 3 master's, 6 doctorates awarded. *Entrance requirements:* Additional exam requirements/recommendations for international students: Required—TOEFL. *Application deadline:* For fall admission, 7/15 for domestic students, 2/1 for international students. Application fee: $65. Electronic applications accepted. *Expenses:* Tuition, state resident: full-time $12,706; part-time $786 per credit. Tuition, nonresident: full-time $25,216; part-time $1401 per credit. *Required fees:* $1598; $45 per credit. One-time fee: $30 part-time. *Financial support:* In 2017–18, 10 research assistantships with tuition reimbursements (averaging $13,958 per year), 10 teaching assistantships with tuition reimbursements (averaging $11,291 per year) were awarded. Financial award application deadline: 2/1; financial award applicants required to submit FAFSA. *Unit head:* Dr. David Rowley, Chair, 401-874-9228, E-mail: drowley@uri.edu.
Website: http://www.uri.edu/pharmacy/departments/bps/index.shtml

University of Rochester, School of Medicine and Dentistry, Graduate Programs in Medicine and Dentistry, Department of Environmental Medicine, Programs in Toxicology, Rochester, NY 14627. Offers PhD. *Degree requirements:* For doctorate, thesis/dissertation, qualifying exam. *Entrance requirements:* For doctorate, GRE General Test.

University of Saskatchewan, College of Graduate Studies and Research, Toxicology Centre, Saskatoon, SK S7N 5A2, Canada. Offers M Sc, PhD, Diploma. *Degree requirements:* For master's, thesis; for doctorate, thesis/dissertation. *Entrance requirements:* Additional exam requirements/recommendations for international students: Required—TOEFL.

University of South Alabama, Graduate School, Program in Environmental Toxicology, Mobile, AL 36688. Offers basic medical sciences (MS); biology (MS); chemistry (MS); environmental toxicology (MS); exposure route and chemical transport (MS). *Faculty:* 3 full-time (0 women), 1 (woman) part-time/adjunct. *Students:* 9 full-time (2 women), 2 part-time (both women); includes 1 minority (Black or African American, non-Hispanic/Latino). Average age 26. 7 applicants, 29% accepted, 2 enrolled. In 2017, 3 master's awarded. *Degree requirements:* For master's, comprehensive exam, research project or thesis. *Entrance requirements:* For master's, GRE, BA/BS in related discipline, minimum undergraduate GPA of 3.0. Additional exam requirements/recommendations for international students: Required—TOEFL (minimum score 525 paper-based; 71 iBT). *Application deadline:* For fall admission, 7/15 for domestic students, 6/15 for international students; for spring admission, 12/1 for domestic students, 11/1 for international students. Application fee: $35. Electronic applications accepted. *Expenses:* Tuition, state resident: full-time $10,104; part-time $421 per semester hour. Tuition, nonresident: full-time $20,208; part-time $842 per semester hour. *Financial support:* Fellowships, research assistantships, teaching assistantships, career-related internships or fieldwork, Federal Work-Study, institutionally sponsored loans, scholarships/grants, and unspecified assistantships available. Support available to part-time students. Financial award application deadline: 3/31; financial award applicants required to submit FAFSA. *Unit head:* Dr. Harold Pardue, Dean of the Graduate School, 251-460-6310, E-mail: hpardue@southalabama.edu. *Application contact:* Dr. David Forbes, Chair, Chemistry, 251-460-6181, E-mail: dforbes@southalabama.edu.
Website: http://www.southalabama.edu/graduatemajors/etox/index.html

University of Southern California, Graduate School, School of Pharmacy, Graduate Programs in Molecular Pharmacology and Toxicology, Los Angeles, CA 90033. Offers pharmacology and pharmaceutical sciences (MS, PhD). Terminal master's awarded for partial completion of doctoral program. *Degree requirements:* For master's, comprehensive exam, thesis, 24 units of formal course work, excluding research and seminar courses; for doctorate, comprehensive exam, thesis/dissertation, 24 units of formal course work, excluding research and seminar courses. *Entrance requirements:* For master's and doctorate, GRE. Additional exam requirements/recommendations for international students: Required—TOEFL (minimum score 603 paper-based; 100 iBT). Electronic applications accepted. *Expenses:* Contact institution. *Faculty research:* Degenerative diseases, toxicology of drugs.

University of South Florida, Innovative Education, Tampa, FL 33620-9951. Offers adult, career and higher education (Graduate Certificate), including college teaching, leadership in developing human resources, leadership in higher education; Africana studies (Graduate Certificate), including diasporas and health disparities, genocide and human rights; aging studies (Graduate Certificate), including gerontology; art research (Graduate Certificate), including museum studies; business foundations (Graduate Certificate); chemical and biomedical engineering (Graduate Certificate), including materials science and engineering, water, health and sustainability; child and family studies (Graduate Certificate), including positive behavior support; civil and industrial engineering (Graduate Certificate), including transportation systems analysis; community and family health (Graduate Certificate), including maternal and child health, social marketing and public health, violence and injury: prevention and intervention, women's health; criminology (Graduate Certificate), including criminal justice administration; data science for public administration (Graduate Certificate); digital humanities (Graduate Certificate); educational measurement and research (Graduate Certificate), including evaluation; English (Graduate Certificate), including comparative literary studies, creative writing, professional and technical communication; entrepreneurship (Graduate Certificate); environmental health (Graduate Certificate), including safety management; epidemiology and biostatistics (Graduate Certificate), including applied biostatistics, biostatistics, concepts and tools of epidemiology, epidemiology, epidemiology of infectious diseases; geography, environment and planning (Graduate Certificate), including community development, environmental policy and management, geographical information systems; geology (Graduate Certificate), including hydrogeology; global health (Graduate Certificate), including disaster management, global health and Latin American and Caribbean studies, global health practice, humanitarian assistance, infection control; government and international affairs (Graduate Certificate), including Cuban studies, globalization studies; health policy and management (Graduate Certificate), including health management and leadership, public health policy and programs; hearing specialist: early intervention (Graduate Certificate); industrial and management systems engineering (Graduate Certificate), including systems engineering, technology management; information studies (Graduate Certificate), including school library media specialist; information systems/decision sciences (Graduate Certificate), including analytics and business intelligence; instructional technology (Graduate Certificate), including distance education, Florida digital/virtual educator, instructional design, multimedia design, Web design; internal medicine, bioethics and medical humanities (Graduate Certificate), including biomedical ethics; Latin American and Caribbean studies (Graduate Certificate); leadership for coastal resiliency planning (Graduate Certificate); mass communications (Graduate Certificate), including multimedia journalism; mathematics and statistics (Graduate Certificate), including mathematics; medicine (Graduate Certificate), including aging and neuroscience, bioinformatics, biotechnology, brain fitness and memory management, clinical investigation, hand and upper limb rehabilitation, health informatics, health sciences, integrative weight management, intellectual property, medicine and gender, metabolic and nutritional medicine, metabolic cardiology, pharmacy sciences; national and competitive intelligence (Graduate Certificate); nursing (Graduate Certificate), including simulation based academic fellowship in advanced pain management; psychological and social foundations (Graduate Certificate), including career counseling, college teaching, diversity in education, mental health counseling, school counseling; public affairs (Graduate Certificate), including nonprofit management, public management, research administration; public health (Graduate Certificate), including assessing chemical toxicity and public health risks, health equity, pharmacoepidemiology, public health generalist, toxicology, translational research in adolescent behavioral health; public health practices (Graduate Certificate), including planning for healthy communities; rehabilitation and mental health counseling (Graduate Certificate), including integrative mental health care, marriage and family therapy, rehabilitation technology; secondary education (Graduate Certificate), including ESOL, foreign language education: culture and content, foreign language education: professional; social work (Graduate Certificate), including geriatric social work/clinical gerontology; special education (Graduate Certificate), including autism spectrum disorder, disabilities education: severe/profound; world languages (Graduate Certificate), including teaching English as a second language (TESL) or foreign language. *Unit head:* Dr. Cynthia DeLuca, Associate Vice President and Assistant Vice Provost, 813-974-3077, Fax: 813-974-7061, E-mail: deluca@usf.edu. *Application contact:* Owen Hooper, Director, Summer and Alternative Calendar Programs, 813-974-6917, E-mail: hooper@usf.edu.
Website: http://www.usf.edu/innovative-education/

The University of Texas at Austin, Graduate School, College of Pharmacy, Graduate Programs in Pharmacy, Austin, TX 78712-1111. Offers health outcomes and pharmacy practice (PhD); health outcomes and pharmacy practice (MS); medicinal chemistry (PhD); pharmaceutics (PhD); pharmacology and toxicology (PhD); pharmacotherapy (MS, PhD); translational science (PhD). PhD in translational science offered jointly with The University of Texas Health Science Center at San Antonio and The University of Texas at San Antonio. *Degree requirements:* For master's, thesis; for doctorate, thesis/dissertation. *Entrance requirements:* For master's and doctorate, GRE General Test. Electronic applications accepted. *Faculty research:* Synthetic medical chemistry, synthetic molecular biology, bio-organic chemistry, pharmacoeconomics, pharmacy practice.

The University of Texas Health Science Center at San Antonio, Graduate School of Biomedical Sciences, Program in Toxicology, San Antonio, TX 78229-3900. Offers MS.

The University of Texas Medical Branch, Graduate School of Biomedical Sciences, Program in Pharmacology and Toxicology, Galveston, TX 77555. Offers pharmacology (MS); pharmacology and toxicology (PhD). *Degree requirements:* For master's, thesis or alternative; for doctorate, thesis/dissertation. *Entrance requirements:* For master's and doctorate, GRE General Test. Additional exam requirements/recommendations for international students: Required—TOEFL (minimum score 550 paper-based).

University of the Sciences, Program in Pharmacology and Toxicology, Philadelphia, PA 19104-4495. Offers pharmacology (MS, PhD); toxicology (MS, PhD). Terminal master's awarded for partial completion of doctoral program. *Degree requirements:* For master's, thesis; for doctorate, comprehensive exam, thesis/dissertation. *Entrance requirements:* For master's and doctorate, GRE General Test. Additional exam requirements/recommendations for international students: Required—TOEFL, TWE. *Expenses:* Contact institution.

University of Utah, Graduate School, College of Pharmacy, Department of Pharmacology and Toxicology, Salt Lake City, UT 84112. Offers PhD. *Faculty:* 10 full-time (3 women), 7 part-time/adjunct (1 woman). *Students:* 3 full-time (2 women), 1 (woman) part-time. In 2017, 3 doctorates awarded. Terminal master's awarded for partial completion of doctoral program. *Entrance requirements:* For doctorate, GRE General Test, BS in biology, chemistry, or neuroscience. Application fee: $0. Electronic applications accepted. *Expenses:* Contact institution. *Financial support:* In 2017–18, 9 students received support, including 9 research assistantships with full tuition reimbursements available (averaging $25,000 per year); health care benefits and tuition waivers (full) also available. Financial award application deadline: 1/15. *Faculty research:* Neuropharmacology of anti-seizure drugs and drugs of abuse, drug metabolism, signal transduction pathways and oncogenic processes, drug analyses in biological samples, natural products drug discovery. *Unit head:* Dr. Karen Wilcox, Department Chair, 801-581-6287, Fax: 801-585-5111, E-mail: karen.wilcox@hsc.utah.edu. *Application contact:* Linda Wright, Program Assistant, 801-581-6281, Fax: 801-585-5111, E-mail: linda.wright@utah.edu.
Website: http://www.pharmacy.utah.edu/pharmtox/

University of Washington, Graduate School, School of Public Health, Department of Environmental and Occupational Health Sciences, Seattle, WA 98195. Offers applied toxicology (MS); environmental and occupational health (MPH); environmental and occupational hygiene (PhD); environmental health (MS); environmental toxicology (MS, PhD); occupational and environmental exposure sciences (MS); occupational and environmental medicine (MPH). *Accreditation:* CEPH. *Program availability:* Part-time. *Faculty:* 38 full-time (14 women), 17 part-time/adjunct (8 women). *Students:* 68 full-time (51 women), 9 part-time (3 women); includes 21 minority (2 Black or African American, non-Hispanic/Latino; 1 American Indian or Alaska Native, non-Hispanic/Latino; 11 Asian, non-Hispanic/Latino; 6 Hispanic/Latino; 1 Native Hawaiian or other Pacific Islander, non-Hispanic/Latino), 9 international. Average age 31. 121 applicants, 50% accepted, 33 enrolled. In 2017, 20 master's, 10 doctorates awarded. Terminal master's awarded for partial completion of doctoral program. *Entrance requirements:* For master's and doctorate, GRE General Test. Additional exam requirements/recommendations for international students: Required—TOEFL. Electronic applications accepted. *Expenses:* Contact institution. *Financial support:* Fellowships, research assistantships, teaching assistantships, career-related internships or fieldwork, institutionally sponsored loans, scholarships/grants, traineeships, health care benefits, and unspecified assistantships available. *Faculty research:* Developmental and behavioral toxicology, biochemical toxicology, exposure assessment, hazardous waste, industrial chemistry. *Unit head:* Dr. Michael Yost, Chair, 206-543-3199, Fax: 206-543-9616. *Application contact:* Trina Sterry, Manager of Student and Academic Services, 206-543-3199, E-mail: ehgrad@uw.edu.
Website: http://deohs.washington.edu/

University of Wisconsin–Madison, School of Medicine and Public Health, Molecular and Environmental Toxicology Graduate Program, Madison, WI 53706. Offers MS, PhD. *Application contact:* Mark Marohl, Graduate Program Coordinator, 608-263-4580, E-mail: mdmarohl@wisc.edu.
Website: http://www.med.wisc.edu/metc/

Utah State University, School of Graduate Studies, College of Agriculture and Applied Sciences, Program in Toxicology, Logan, UT 84322. Offers MS, PhD. Terminal master's awarded for partial completion of doctoral program. *Degree requirements:* For master's, thesis; for doctorate, thesis/dissertation. *Entrance requirements:* For master's and doctorate, GRE General Test, minimum GPA of 3.0. Additional exam requirements/ recommendations for international students: Required—TOEFL. *Faculty research:* Free-radical mechanisms, toxicity of iron, carcinogenesis of natural compounds, molecular mechanisms of retinoid toxicity, aflatoxins.

Virginia Commonwealth University, Graduate School, College of Humanities and Sciences, Department of Forensic Science, Richmond, VA 23284-9005. Offers forensic biology (MS); forensic chemistry/drugs and toxicology (MS); forensic chemistry/trace evidence (MS); forensic physical analysis (MS). *Program availability:* Part-time. *Entrance requirements:* For master's, GRE General Test, bachelor's degree in a natural science discipline, including forensic science, or a degree with equivalent work. Additional exam requirements/recommendations for international students: Required—TOEFL (minimum score 600 paper-based; 100 iBT) or IELTS (minimum score 6.5). Electronic applications accepted.

Virginia Commonwealth University, Medical College of Virginia-Professional Programs, School of Medicine, Graduate Programs in Medicine, Department of Pharmacology and Toxicology, Richmond, VA 23284-9005. Offers neuroscience (PhD); pharmacology (Certificate); pharmacology and toxicology (MS, PhD); MD/PhD. Terminal master's awarded for partial completion of doctoral program. *Degree requirements:* For master's, thesis; for doctorate, thesis/dissertation, comprehensive oral and written exams. *Entrance requirements:* For master's and doctorate, GRE or MCAT. Additional exam requirements/recommendations for international students: Required—TOEFL (minimum score 600 paper-based; 100 iBT). Electronic applications accepted. *Faculty research:* Drug abuse, drug metabolism, pharmacodynamics, peptide synthesis, receptor mechanisms.

Wayne State University, Eugene Applebaum College of Pharmacy and Health Sciences, Department of Pharmaceutical Sciences, Detroit, MI 48202. Offers medicinal chemistry (MS, PhD); pharmaceutics (MS, PhD), including medicinal chemistry (PhD); pharmacology and toxicology (MS, PhD). *Faculty:* 20. *Students:* 23 full-time (17 women), 1 (woman) part-time, 19 international. Average age 29. 119 applicants, 9% accepted, 7 enrolled. In 2017, 7 master's, 3 doctorates awarded. *Degree requirements:* For master's, thesis; for doctorate, thesis/dissertation. *Entrance requirements:* For master's, GRE General Test, bachelor's degree; adequate background in biology, physics, calculus, and chemistry; three letters of recommendation; personal statement; for doctorate, GRE General Test, bachelor's or master's degree in one of the behavioral, biological, pharmaceutical or physical sciences; three letters of recommendation. Additional exam requirements/recommendations for international students: Required—TOEFL (minimum score 550 paper-based; 79 iBT), Michigan English Language Assessment Battery (minimum score 85); Recommended—IELTS (minimum score 6.5), TWE (minimum score 5.5). *Application deadline:* For fall admission, 12/1 priority date for domestic and international students. Applications are processed on a rolling basis. Application fee: $50. Electronic applications accepted. *Expenses:* Contact institution. *Financial support:* In 2017–18, 16 students received support, including 2 fellowships with tuition reimbursements available (averaging $26,000 per year), 11 research assistantships with full tuition reimbursements available (averaging $25,182 per year); scholarships/grants, health care benefits, and unspecified assistantships also available. Financial award applicants required to submit FAFSA. *Faculty research:* Design of new anthracyclines, genetic and epigenetic effects of extracellular Inducers, cellular injury and cell death, drug metabolism and nutrition, anti-infective agents, carcinogenesis, diabetes research, Thera gnostic nanomedicines, neurotoxicity, drug discovery, insulin resistance. *Unit head:* Dr. George Corcoran, Chair and Professor, 313-577-1737, E-mail: corcoran@wayne.edu. *Application contact:* 313-577-5415, Fax: 313-577-2033, E-mail: pscgrad@wayne.edu.
Website: http://cphs.wayne.edu/sciences/index.php

Wright State University, Boonshoft School of Medicine, Program in Pharmacology and Toxicology, Dayton, OH 45435. Offers MS. *Degree requirements:* For master's, thesis optional.

Section 18
Physiology

This section contains a directory of institutions offering graduate work in physiology, followed by an in-depth entry submitted by an institution that chose to prepare a detailed program description. Additional information about programs listed in the directory but not augmented by an in-depth entry may be obtained by writing directly to the dean of a graduate school or chair of a department at the address given in the directory.

For programs offering related work, see also all other sections in this book. In the other guides in this series:

Graduate Programs in the Physical Sciences, Mathematics, Agricultural Sciences, the Environment & Natural Resources

See *Agricultural and Food Sciences, Chemistry,* and *Marine Sciences and Oceanography*

Graduate Programs in Engineering & Applied Sciences

See *Agricultural Engineering and Bioengineering, Biomedical Engineering and Biotechnology, Electrical and Computer Engineering,* and *Mechanical Engineering and Mechanics*

CONTENTS

Program Directories

Cardiovascular Sciences

Albany Medical College, Center for Cardiovascular Sciences, Albany, NY 12208-3479. Offers MS, PhD. *Program availability:* Part-time. Terminal master's awarded for partial completion of doctoral program. *Degree requirements:* For master's, thesis; for doctorate, comprehensive exam, thesis/dissertation, candidacy exam, written preliminary exam, 1 published paper-peer review. *Entrance requirements:* For master's, GRE General Test, letters of recommendation; for doctorate, GRE General Test, all transcripts, letters of recommendation. Additional exam requirements/recommendations for international students: Required—TOEFL. *Faculty research:* Vascular smooth muscle, endothelial cell biology, molecular and genetic bases underlying cardiac disease, reactive oxygen and nitrogen species biology, fatty acid trafficking and fatty acid mediated transcription control.

Augusta University, Program in Vascular Biology, Augusta, GA 30912. Offers PhD. *Degree requirements:* For doctorate, comprehensive exam, thesis/dissertation. *Entrance requirements:* For doctorate, GRE General Test. Additional exam requirements/recommendations for international students: Required—TOEFL.

Baylor College of Medicine, Graduate School of Biomedical Sciences, Department of Molecular Physiology and Biophysics, Houston, TX 77030-3498. Offers cardiovascular sciences (PhD); molecular physiology and biophysics (PhD); MD/PhD. *Degree requirements:* For doctorate, thesis/dissertation, public defense. *Entrance requirements:* For doctorate, GRE General Test, GRE Subject Test (strongly recommended), minimum GPA of 3.0. Additional exam requirements/recommendations for international students: Required—TOEFL. Electronic applications accepted. *Faculty research:* Cardiovascular disease; skeletal muscle disease (myasthenia gravis, muscular dystrophy, malignant hyperthermia, central core disease); cancer; Alzheimer's disease; developmental diseases of the nervous system, eye and heart; diabetes; motor neuron disease (amyotrophic lateral sclerosis and spinal muscular atrophy); asthma; autoimmune diseases.

Johns Hopkins University, Bloomberg School of Public Health, Department of Epidemiology, Baltimore, MD 21205. Offers cancer epidemiology (MHS, Sc M, PhD, Sc D); cardiovascular disease and clinical epidemiology (MHS, Sc M, PhD, Sc D); clinical trials (PhD, Sc D); clinical trials and evidence synthesis (MHS, Sc M, PhD, Sc D); environmental epidemiology (MHS, Sc M, PhD, Sc D); epidemiology of aging (MHS, Sc M, PhD, Sc D); general epidemiology and methodology (MHS, Sc M); genetic epidemiology (MHS, Sc M, PhD, Sc D); infectious disease epidemiology (MHS, Sc M, PhD, Sc D). *Students:* 160 full-time (111 women), 14 part-time (9 women); includes 44 minority (9 Black or African American, non-Hispanic/Latino; 1 American Indian or Alaska Native, non-Hispanic/Latino; 20 Asian, non-Hispanic/Latino; 9 Hispanic/Latino; 1 Native Hawaiian or other Pacific Islander, non-Hispanic/Latino; 4 Two or more races, non-Hispanic/Latino), 64 international. Average age 29. 408 applicants, 29% accepted, 61 enrolled. In 2017, 36 master's, 16 doctorates awarded. *Degree requirements:* For master's, comprehensive exam, thesis, 1-year full-time residency; for doctorate, comprehensive exam, thesis/dissertation, 2 years' full-time residency, oral and written exams, student teaching. *Entrance requirements:* For master's, GRE General Test or MCAT, 3 letters of recommendation, curriculum vitae; for doctorate, GRE General Test, minimum 1 year of work experience, 3 letters of recommendation, curriculum vitae, academic records from all schools. Additional exam requirements/recommendations for international students: Required—TOEFL (minimum score 100 iBT), IELTS (minimum score 7.5). *Application deadline:* Applications are processed on a rolling basis. Application fee: $135. Electronic applications accepted. *Financial support:* Fellowships, Federal Work-Study, institutionally sponsored loans, scholarships/grants, traineeships, and stipends available. Support available to part-time students. Financial award application deadline: 3/15. *Faculty research:* Cancer and congenital malformations, nutritional epidemiology, AIDS, tuberculosis, cardiovascular disease, risk assessment. *Unit head:* Dr. David D. Celentano, Chair, 410-955-3286, Fax: 410-955-0863. *Application contact:* Frances S. Burman, Academic Program Manager, 410-955-3926, Fax: 410-955-0863, E-mail: fburman@jhsph.edu.
Website: http://www.jhsph.edu/dept/epi/index.html

Marquette University, Graduate School, Program in Transfusion Medicine, Milwaukee, WI 53201-1881. Offers MSTM. Program is held in collaboration with BloodCenter of Wisconsin. *Program availability:* Part-time. *Entrance requirements:* For master's, official transcripts from all current and previous colleges, three letters of recommendation. Additional exam requirements/recommendations for international students: Required—TOEFL.

McMaster University, Faculty of Health Sciences and School of Graduate Studies, Program in Medical Sciences, Blood and Vascular Area, Hamilton, ON L8S 4M2, Canada. Offers M Sc, PhD, MD/PhD. *Degree requirements:* For master's, thesis; for doctorate, comprehensive exam, thesis/dissertation. *Entrance requirements:* For master's, honors B Sc, B+ average in related field; for doctorate, M Sc, minimum B+ average, students with proven research experience and an A average may be admitted with a B Sc degree. Additional exam requirements/recommendations for international students: Required—TOEFL (minimum score 580 paper-based; 92 iBT).

Medical University of South Carolina, College of Graduate Studies, Program in Molecular and Cellular Biology and Pathobiology, Charleston, SC 29425. Offers cancer biology (PhD); cardiovascular biology (PhD); cardiovascular imaging (PhD); cell regulation (PhD); craniofacial biology (PhD); genetics and development (PhD); marine biomedicine (PhD); DMD/PhD; MD/PhD. *Degree requirements:* For doctorate, thesis/dissertation, oral and written exams. *Entrance requirements:* For doctorate, GRE General Test, interview, minimum GPA of 3.0. Additional exam requirements/recommendations for international students: Required—TOEFL (minimum score 600 paper-based; 100 iBT). Electronic applications accepted.

Memorial University of Newfoundland, Faculty of Medicine and School of Graduate Studies, Graduate Programs in Medicine, Division of Biomedical Sciences, St. John's, NL A1C 5S7, Canada. Offers cancer (M Sc, PhD); cardiovascular (M Sc, PhD); immunology (M Sc, PhD); neuroscience (M Sc, PhD). *Program availability:* Part-time. *Degree requirements:* For master's, thesis; for doctorate, comprehensive exam, thesis/dissertation, oral defense of thesis. *Entrance requirements:* For master's, MD or B Sc; for doctorate, MD or M Sc. Additional exam requirements/recommendations for international students: Required—TOEFL. *Faculty research:* Neuroscience, immunology, cardiovascular, and cancer.

Midwestern University, Glendale Campus, College of Health Sciences, Arizona Campus, Program in Cardiovascular Science, Glendale, AZ 85308. Offers MCVS. Application fee: $50. *Expenses:* Contact institution.

Milwaukee School of Engineering, MS Program in Perfusion, Milwaukee, WI 53202-3109. Offers MS. *Students:* 14 full-time (7 women). Average age 27. 69 applicants, 13% accepted, 7 enrolled. In 2017, 5 master's awarded. *Degree requirements:* For master's, comprehensive exam, thesis. *Entrance requirements:* For master's, GRE General Test (percentiles must average 50% or better), baccalaureate degree with minimum undergraduate GPA of 2.8; at least one undergraduate course in each of the following areas: physiology (or anatomy and physiology), chemistry, mathematics and physics; 3 letters of recommendation; personal interview; observation of 2 perfusion clinical cases. Additional exam requirements/recommendations for international students: Required—TOEFL (minimum score 90 iBT), IELTS (minimum score 7). *Application deadline:* Applications are processed on a rolling basis. Application fee: $0. Electronic applications accepted. *Expenses: Tuition:* Part-time $814 per credit hour. *Required fees:* $12.50 per credit hour. *Financial support:* Career-related internships or fieldwork, institutionally sponsored loans, and scholarships/grants available. Financial award application deadline: 3/15; financial award applicants required to submit FAFSA. *Faculty research:* Heart medicine. *Unit head:* Dr. Ronald Gerrits, Program Director, 414-277-7561, Fax: 414-277-7494, E-mail: gerrits@msoe.edu. *Application contact:* Brian Rutz, Graduate Admission Counselor, 414-277-7200, E-mail: rutz@msoe.edu.
Website: https://www.msoe.edu/academics/graduate-degrees/health/perfusion/

Queen's University at Kingston, School of Graduate Studies, Faculty of Health Sciences, Department of Anatomy and Cell Biology, Kingston, ON K7L 3N6, Canada. Offers biology of reproduction (M Sc, PhD); cancer (M Sc, PhD); cardiovascular pathophysiology (M Sc, PhD); cell and molecular biology (M Sc, PhD); drug metabolism (M Sc, PhD); endocrinology (M Sc, PhD); motor control (M Sc, PhD); neural regeneration (M Sc, PhD); neurophysiology (M Sc, PhD). *Program availability:* Part-time. *Degree requirements:* For master's, thesis; for doctorate, one foreign language, comprehensive exam, thesis/dissertation. *Entrance requirements:* Additional exam requirements/recommendations for international students: Required—TOEFL. Electronic applications accepted. *Faculty research:* Human kinetics, neuroscience, reproductive biology, cardiovascular.

Quinnipiac University, School of Health Sciences, Program in Cardiovascular Perfusion, Hamden, CT 06518-1940. Offers MHS. *Faculty:* 1 full-time (0 women), 3 part-time/adjunct (0 women). *Students:* 8 full-time (2 women), 7 part-time (5 women); includes 2 minority (1 Black or African American, non-Hispanic/Latino; 1 Two or more races, non-Hispanic/Latino). 49 applicants, 27% accepted, 8 enrolled. In 2017, 6 master's awarded. *Entrance requirements:* For master's, bachelor's degree in science or health-related discipline from an accredited American or Canadian college or university; 2 years of health care work experience; interview. *Application deadline:* For fall admission, 2/1 for domestic students. Applications are processed on a rolling basis. Application fee: $45. Electronic applications accepted. *Financial support:* Federal Work-Study, scholarships/grants, and unspecified assistantships available. Financial award application deadline: 6/1; financial award applicants required to submit FAFSA. *Faculty research:* Methods of preventing systemic inflammatory response syndrome (SIRS) during extracorporeal circulation of blood, investigations into the role of P-selectin in causing monocyte-platelet interaction, effect of simulated cardiopulmonary bypass on platelets and other formed elements in the blood. *Unit head:* Dr. Michael Smith, Director, 203-582-3427, E-mail: graduate@qu.edu. *Application contact:* Office of Graduate Admissions, 800-462-1944, Fax: 208-582-3443, E-mail: graduate@qu.edu.
Website: http://www.qu.edu/gradperfusion

Université Laval, Faculty of Medicine, Post-Professional Programs in Medical Studies, Québec, QC G1K 7P4, Canada. Offers anatomy–pathology (DESS); anesthesiology (DESS); cardiology (DESS); care of older people (Diploma); clinical research (DESS); community health (DESS); dermatology (DESS); diagnostic radiology (DESS); emergency medicine (Diploma); family medicine (DESS); general surgery (DESS); geriatrics (DESS); hematology (DESS); internal medicine (DESS); maternal and fetal medicine (Diploma); medical biochemistry (DESS); medical microbiology and infectious diseases (DESS); medical oncology (DESS); nephrology (DESS); neurology (DESS); neurosurgery (DESS); obstetrics and gynecology (DESS); ophthalmology (DESS); orthopedic surgery (DESS); oto-rhino-laryngology (DESS); palliative medicine (Diploma); pediatrics (DESS); plastic surgery (DESS); psychiatry (DESS); pulmonary medicine (DESS); radiology–oncology (DESS); thoracic surgery (DESS); urology (DESS). *Degree requirements:* For other advanced degree, comprehensive exam. *Entrance requirements:* For degree, knowledge of French. Electronic applications accepted.

University of Calgary, Cumming School of Medicine and Faculty of Graduate Studies, Program in Cardiovascular and Respiratory Sciences, Calgary, AB T2N 1N4, Canada. Offers M Sc, PhD. *Degree requirements:* For master's, thesis; for doctorate, thesis/dissertation, candidacy exam. *Entrance requirements:* For master's and doctorate, minimum GPA of 3.2. Additional exam requirements/recommendations for international students: Required—TOEFL (minimum score 600 paper-based). Electronic applications accepted. *Faculty research:* Cardiac mechanics, physiology and pharmacology; lung mechanics, physiology and pathophysiology; smooth muscle biochemistry; physiology and pharmacology.

University of Guelph, Ontario Veterinary College and Graduate Studies, Graduate Programs in Veterinary Sciences, Department of Clinical Studies, Guelph, ON N1G 2W1, Canada. Offers anesthesiology (M Sc, DV Sc); cardiology (DV Sc, Diploma); clinical studies (Diploma); dermatology (M Sc); diagnostic imaging (M Sc, DV Sc); emergency/critical care (M Sc, DV Sc, Diploma); medicine (M Sc, DV Sc); neurology (M Sc, DV Sc); ophthalmology (M Sc, DV Sc); surgery (M Sc, DV Sc). *Degree requirements:* For master's, thesis; for doctorate, comprehensive exam, thesis/dissertation. *Entrance requirements:* Additional exam requirements/recommendations for international students: Required—TOEFL (minimum score 550 paper-based), IELTS (minimum score 6.5). Electronic applications accepted. *Faculty research:* Orthopedics, respirology, oncology, exercise physiology, cardiology.

University of Mary, School of Health Sciences, Program in Respiratory Therapy, Bismarck, ND 58504-9652. Offers MS. *Entrance requirements:* For master's, minimum GPA of 3.0, 3 letters of reference, interview. Additional exam requirements/recommendations for international students: Required—TOEFL (minimum score 500 paper-based; 71 iBT). Electronic applications accepted.

University of South Dakota, Graduate School, Sanford School of Medicine and Graduate School, Biomedical Sciences Graduate Program, Cardiovascular Research Program, Vermillion, SD 57069. Offers MS, PhD. In 2017, 1 master's, 1 doctorate awarded. Terminal master's awarded for partial completion of doctoral program. *Degree requirements:* For master's, thesis; for doctorate, comprehensive exam, thesis/dissertation. *Entrance requirements:* For master's and doctorate, GRE General Test, minimum GPA of 3.0. Additional exam requirements/recommendations for international students: Required—TOEFL (minimum score 550 paper-based; 80 iBT), IELTS (minimum score 6). *Application deadline:* For fall admission, 4/15 priority date for domestic students, 3/15 for international students. Applications are processed on a rolling basis. Application fee: $35. Electronic applications accepted. *Expenses:* Contact institution. *Financial support:* In 2017–18, 4 students received support, including 4 fellowships with partial tuition reimbursements available (averaging $20,772 per year), research assistantships with partial tuition reimbursements available (averaging $10,386 per year); teaching assistantships and unspecified assistantships also available. Financial award application deadline: 4/15; financial award applicants required to submit FAFSA. *Faculty research:* Cardiovascular disease. *Total annual research expenditures:* $1.4 million. *Unit head:* 605-658-6322, Fax: 605-677-6381, E-mail: biomed@usd.edu.

University of South Florida, Innovative Education, Tampa, FL 33620-9951. Offers adult, career and higher education (Graduate Certificate), including college teaching, leadership in developing human resources, leadership in higher education; Africana studies (Graduate Certificate), including diasporas and health disparities, genocide and human rights; aging studies (Graduate Certificate), including gerontology; art research (Graduate Certificate), including museum studies; business foundations (Graduate Certificate); chemical and biomedical engineering (Graduate Certificate), including materials science and engineering, water, health and sustainability; child and family studies (Graduate Certificate), including positive behavior support; civil and industrial engineering (Graduate Certificate), including transportation systems analysis; community and family health (Graduate Certificate), including maternal and child health, social marketing and public health, violence and injury: prevention and intervention, women's health; criminology (Graduate Certificate), including criminal justice administration; data science for public administration (Graduate Certificate); digital humanities (Graduate Certificate); educational measurement and research (Graduate Certificate), including evaluation; English (Graduate Certificate), including comparative literary studies, creative writing, professional and technical communication; entrepreneurship (Graduate Certificate); environmental health (Graduate Certificate), including safety management; epidemiology and biostatistics (Graduate Certificate), including applied biostatistics, biostatistics, concepts and tools of epidemiology, epidemiology, epidemiology of infectious diseases; geography, environment and planning (Graduate Certificate), including community development, environmental policy and management, geographical information systems; geology (Graduate Certificate), including hydrogeology; global health (Graduate Certificate), including disaster management, global health and Latin American and Caribbean studies, global health practice, humanitarian assistance, infection control; government and international affairs (Graduate Certificate), including Cuban studies, globalization studies; health policy and management (Graduate Certificate), including health management and leadership, public health policy and programs; hearing specialist: early intervention (Graduate Certificate); industrial and management systems engineering (Graduate Certificate), including systems engineering, technology management; information studies (Graduate Certificate), including school library media specialist; information systems/decision sciences (Graduate Certificate), including analytics and business intelligence; instructional technology (Graduate Certificate), including distance education, Florida digital/virtual educator, instructional design, multimedia design, Web design; internal medicine, bioethics and medical humanities (Graduate Certificate), including biomedical ethics; Latin American and Caribbean studies (Graduate Certificate); leadership for coastal resiliency planning (Graduate Certificate); mass communications (Graduate Certificate), including multimedia journalism; mathematics and statistics (Graduate Certificate), including mathematics; medicine (Graduate Certificate), including aging and neuroscience, bioinformatics, biotechnology, brain fitness and memory management, clinical investigation, hand and upper limb rehabilitation, health informatics, health sciences, integrative weight management, intellectual property, medicine and gender, metabolic and nutritional medicine, metabolic cardiology, pharmacy sciences; national and competitive intelligence (Graduate Certificate); nursing (Graduate Certificate), including simulation based academic fellowship in advanced pain management; psychological and social foundations (Graduate Certificate), including career counseling, college teaching, diversity in education, mental health counseling, school counseling; public affairs (Graduate Certificate), including nonprofit management, public management, research administration; public health (Graduate Certificate), including assessing chemical toxicity and public health risks, health equity, pharmacoepidemiology, public health generalist, toxicology, translational research in adolescent behavioral health; public health practices (Graduate Certificate), including planning for healthy communities; rehabilitation and mental health counseling (Graduate Certificate), including integrative mental health care, marriage and family therapy, rehabilitation technology; secondary education (Graduate Certificate), including ESOL, foreign language education: culture and content, foreign language education: professional; social work (Graduate Certificate), including geriatric social work/clinical gerontology; special education (Graduate Certificate), including autism spectrum disorder, disabilities education: severe/profound; world languages (Graduate Certificate), including teaching English as a second language (TESL) or foreign language. *Unit head:* Dr. Cynthia DeLuca, Associate Vice President and Assistant Vice Provost, 813-974-3077, Fax: 813-974-7061, E-mail: deluca@usf.edu. *Application contact:* Owen Hooper, Director, Summer and Alternative Calendar Programs, 813-974-6917, E-mail: hooper@usf.edu.
Website: http://www.usf.edu/innovative-education/

The University of Toledo, College of Graduate Studies, College of Medicine and Life Sciences, Department of Physiology and Pharmacology, Toledo, OH 43606-3390. Offers cardiovascular and metabolic diseases (MSBS, PhD); MD/MSBS; MD/PhD. Terminal master's awarded for partial completion of doctoral program. *Degree requirements:* For master's, thesis, qualifying exam; for doctorate, thesis/dissertation, qualifying exam. *Entrance requirements:* For master's and doctorate, GRE, minimum undergraduate GPA of 3.0, three letters of recommendation, statement of purpose, transcripts from all prior institutions attended, resume. Additional exam requirements/recommendations for international students: Required—TOEFL (minimum score 550 paper-based; 80 iBT). Electronic applications accepted.

Molecular Physiology

Baylor College of Medicine, Graduate School of Biomedical Sciences, Department of Molecular Physiology and Biophysics, Houston, TX 77030-3498. Offers cardiovascular sciences (PhD); molecular physiology and biophysics (PhD); MD/PhD. *Degree requirements:* For doctorate, thesis/dissertation, public defense. *Entrance requirements:* For doctorate, GRE General Test, GRE Subject Test (strongly recommended), minimum GPA of 3.0. Additional exam requirements/recommendations for international students: Required—TOEFL. Electronic applications accepted. *Faculty research:* Cardiovascular disease; skeletal muscle disease (myasthenia gravis, muscular dystrophy, malignant hyperthermia, central core disease); cancer; Alzheimer's disease; developmental diseases of the nervous system, eye and heart; diabetes; motor neuron disease (amyotrophic lateral sclerosis and spinal muscular atrophy); asthma; autoimmune diseases.

Loyola University Chicago, Graduate School, Integrated Program in Biomedical Sciences, Maywood, IL 60141. Offers biochemistry and molecular biology (MS, PhD); cell and molecular physiology (MS, PhD); infectious disease and immunology (MS); integrative cell biology (MS, PhD); microbiology and immunology (MS, PhD); molecular pharmacology and therapeutics (MS, PhD); neuroscience (MS, PhD). *Faculty:* 84 full-time (32 women). *Students:* 126 full-time (65 women), 1 (woman) part-time; includes 36 minority (5 Black or African American, non-Hispanic/Latino; 14 Asian, non-Hispanic/Latino; 14 Hispanic/Latino; 3 Two or more races, non-Hispanic/Latino), 13 international. Average age 26. 748 applicants, 34% accepted, 124 enrolled. In 2017, 41 master's, 18 doctorates awarded. *Degree requirements:* For master's, thesis; for doctorate, comprehensive exam, thesis/dissertation. *Entrance requirements:* For doctorate, GRE. Additional exam requirements/recommendations for international students: Required—TOEFL (minimum score 94 iBT), IELTS (minimum score 7.5). *Application deadline:* For fall admission, 2/7 for domestic students. Applications are processed on a rolling basis. Electronic applications accepted. *Expenses:* Contact institution. *Financial support:* In 2017–18, 20 students received support. Schmitt Fellowships and yearly tuition scholarships (averaging $25,032) available. Financial award application deadline: 6/15; financial award applicants required to submit FAFSA. *Unit head:* Dr. Leanne L. Cribbs, Associate Dean, Graduate Education, 708-327-2817, Fax: 708-216-8216, E-mail: lcribbs@luc.edu. *Application contact:* Margarita Quesada, Graduate Program Secretary, 708-216-3532, Fax: 708-216-8216, E-mail: mquesad@luc.edu.
Website: http://ssom.luc.edu/graduate_school/degree-programs/ipbsphd/

Rutgers University–New Brunswick, Graduate School-New Brunswick, Program in Endocrinology and Animal Biosciences, Piscataway, NJ 08854-8097. Offers MS, PhD. Terminal master's awarded for partial completion of doctoral program. *Degree requirements:* For master's, thesis; for doctorate, comprehensive exam, thesis/dissertation. *Entrance requirements:* For master's and doctorate, GRE General Test. Additional exam requirements/recommendations for international students: Required—TOEFL. Electronic applications accepted. *Faculty research:* Comparative and behavioral endocrinology, epigenetic regulation of the endocrine system, exercise physiology and immunology, fetal and neonatal developmental programming, mammary gland biology and breast cancer, neuroendocrinology and alcohol studies, reproductive and developmental toxicology.

Stony Brook University, State University of New York, Stony Brook Medicine, School of Medicine and Graduate School, Graduate Programs in Medicine, Department of Physiology and Biophysics, Stony Brook, NY 11794. Offers PhD. *Faculty:* 12 full-time (4 women), 1 part-time/adjunct (0 women). *Students:* 31 full-time (6 women); includes 14 minority (3 Black or African American, non-Hispanic/Latino; 4 Asian, non-Hispanic/Latino; 7 Hispanic/Latino), 1 international. Average age 23. 5 applicants. In 2017, 2 doctorates awarded. *Degree requirements:* For doctorate, comprehensive exam, thesis/dissertation. *Entrance requirements:* For doctorate, GRE General Test, GRE Subject Test, BS in related field, minimum GPA of 3.0, recommendation. Additional exam requirements/recommendations for international students: Required—TOEFL (minimum score 550 paper-based). *Application deadline:* For fall admission, 1/15 for domestic students; for spring admission, 10/1 for domestic students. Application fee: $100. *Expenses:* Contact institution. *Financial support:* In 2017–18, 1 research assistantship was awarded; fellowships, teaching assistantships, and Federal Work-Study also available. Financial award application deadline: 3/15. *Faculty research:* Biophysics, human physiology, ion channels, physiology, signal transduction. *Total annual research expenditures:* $3.8 million. *Unit head:* Dr. Todd Miller, Chair, 631-444-3533, Fax: 631-444-3432, E-mail: todd.miller@stonybrook.edu. *Application contact:* Odalis Hernandez, Coordinator, 631-444-3057, Fax: 631-444-9749, E-mail: odalis.hernandez@stonybrook.edu.
Website: https://medicine.stonybrookmedicine.edu/pnb

University of California, Los Angeles, Graduate Division, College of Letters and Science, Program in Molecular, Cellular and Integrative Physiology, Los Angeles, CA 90095. Offers PhD. *Degree requirements:* For doctorate, thesis/dissertation, oral and written qualifying exams. *Entrance requirements:* For doctorate, GRE General Test; GRE Subject Test (biology or applicant's undergraduate major), bachelor's degree; minimum undergraduate GPA of 3.0 (or its equivalent if letter grade system not used); interview. Additional exam requirements/recommendations for international students: Required—TOEFL. Electronic applications accepted.

University of Illinois at Urbana–Champaign, Graduate College, College of Liberal Arts and Sciences, School of Molecular and Cellular Biology, Department of Molecular and Integrative Physiology, Champaign, IL 61820. Offers MS, PhD.

The University of North Carolina at Chapel Hill, School of Medicine and Graduate School, Graduate Programs in Medicine, Department of Cell and Molecular Physiology, Chapel Hill, NC 27599. Offers PhD. Terminal master's awarded for partial completion of doctoral program. *Degree requirements:* For doctorate, comprehensive exam, thesis/dissertation, ethics training. *Entrance requirements:* For doctorate, GRE General Test. Electronic applications accepted. *Faculty research:* Signal transduction; growth factors; cardiovascular diseases; neurobiology; hormones, receptors, ion channels.

University of Pittsburgh, School of Medicine, Graduate Programs in Medicine, Cell Biology and Molecular Physiology Graduate Program, Pittsburgh, PA 15260. Offers PhD. *Faculty:* 46 full-time (11 women). *Students:* 6 full-time (5 women). Average age 26. 350 applicants, 21% accepted, 16 enrolled. In 2017, 2 doctorates awarded. *Degree requirements:* For doctorate, comprehensive exam, thesis/dissertation. *Entrance requirements:* For doctorate, GRE General Test, minimum GPA of 3.2, 3 letters of recommendation, official transcripts, baccalaureate degree. Additional exam requirements/recommendations for international students: Required—TOEFL (minimum score 600 paper-based; 100 iBT), IELTS (minimum score 7). *Application deadline:* For fall admission, 12/1 priority date for domestic and international students. Application fee: $50. Electronic applications accepted. *Expenses:* $26,782 in-state, $42,006 out-of-state. *Financial support:* In 2017–18, 6 students received support, including 1 research assistantship with full tuition reimbursement available (averaging $29,500 per year), 4 teaching assistantships with full tuition reimbursements available (averaging $29,500 per year); traineeships also available. *Faculty research:* Genetic disorders of ion channels, regulation of gene expression development, membrane traffic of proteins and lipids, reproductive biology, signal transduction in diabetes and metabolism. *Unit head:* Dr. Michael Butterworth, Program Director, 412-383-8591, E-mail: michael7@pitt.edu. *Application contact:* Carol Williams, Admissions and Recruiting Manager, 412-648-9003, Fax: 412-648-1077, E-mail: gradstudies@medschool.pitt.edu.
Website: http://www.gradbiomed.pitt.edu

Molecular Physiology

University of Virginia, School of Medicine, Department of Molecular Physiology and Biological Physics, Charlottesville, VA 22903. Offers biological and physical sciences (MS); physiology (PhD); MD/PhD. *Faculty:* 26 full-time (6 women), 1 part-time/adjunct (0 women). *Students:* 3 full-time (1 woman); includes 1 minority (Hispanic/Latino). Average age 28. In 2017, 17 master's, 1 doctorate awarded. *Entrance requirements:* For doctorate, GRE General Test, GRE Subject Test. Additional exam requirements/recommendations for international students: Required—TOEFL. *Application deadline:* For fall admission, 2/15 for domestic and international students. Applications are processed on a rolling basis. Application fee: $60. Electronic applications accepted. *Financial support:* Fellowships, research assistantships, and teaching assistantships available. Financial award applicants required to submit FAFSA. *Unit head:* Dr. Mark Yeager, Chair, 434-924-5108, Fax: 434-982-1616, E-mail: my3r@virginia.edu. *Application contact:* Director of Graduate Studies, E-mail: physiograd@virginia.edu.
Website: http://www.healthsystem.virginia.edu/internet/physio/

Vanderbilt University, School of Medicine, Department of Molecular Physiology and Biophysics, Nashville, TN 37240-1001. Offers MS, PhD, MD/PhD. *Faculty:* 26 full-time (3 women). *Students:* 27 full-time (15 women); includes 7 minority (2 Black or African American, non-Hispanic/Latino; 2 Asian, non-Hispanic/Latino; 3 Hispanic/Latino). Average age 27. In 2017, 9 doctorates awarded. *Degree requirements:* For doctorate, comprehensive exam, thesis/dissertation, preliminary, qualifying, and final exams. *Entrance requirements:* For doctorate, GRE General Test, GRE Subject Test (recommended). Additional exam requirements/recommendations for international students: Required—TOEFL (minimum score 570 paper-based; 88 iBT). *Application deadline:* For fall admission, 1/15 for domestic and international students. Application fee: $0. Electronic applications accepted. *Financial support:* Fellowships with full tuition reimbursements, research assistantships with full tuition reimbursements, Federal Work-Study, institutionally sponsored loans, scholarships/grants, traineeships, health care benefits, and tuition waivers (partial) available. Financial award application deadline: 1/15; financial award applicants required to submit CSS PROFILE or FAFSA. *Faculty research:* Biophysics, cell signaling and gene regulation, human genetics, diabetes and obesity, neuroscience. *Unit head:* Dr. Roger Cone, Acting Chair, 615-322-7000, Fax: 615-343-0490, E-mail: roger.cone@vanderbilt.edu. *Application contact:* Richard O'Brien, Director of Graduate Studies, 615-322-7000, E-mail: richard.obrien@vanderbilt.edu.
Website: http://www.mc.vanderbilt.edu/root/vumc.php?site-MPB

Yale University, Graduate School of Arts and Sciences, Department of Cellular and Molecular Physiology, New Haven, CT 06520. Offers PhD. *Degree requirements:* For doctorate, thesis/dissertation. *Entrance requirements:* For doctorate, GRE General Test, GRE Subject Test.

Physiology

Albert Einstein College of Medicine, Graduate Programs in the Biomedical Sciences, Department of Physiology and Biophysics, Bronx, NY 10461. Offers PhD, MD/PhD. *Degree requirements:* For doctorate, thesis/dissertation. *Entrance requirements:* For doctorate, GRE General Test. Additional exam requirements/recommendations for international students: Required—TOEFL. *Application deadline:* For fall admission, 1/15 for domestic students. Application fee: $0. *Financial support:* Fellowships available. *Faculty research:* Biophysical and biochemical basis of body function at the subcellular, cellular, organ, and whole-body level. *Unit head:* Dr. Denis M. Rousseau, Chairperson, 718-430-3592. *Application contact:* Sheila Cleeton, Executive Director and Registrar, Einstein Graduate Division, 718-430-2128, Fax: 718-430-8655, E-mail: sheila.cleeton@einstein.yu.edu.
Website: http://www.einstein.yu.edu/departments/physiology-biophysics/

American College of Healthcare Sciences, Graduate Programs, Portland, OR 97239-3719. Offers anatomy and physiology (Graduate Certificate); aromatherapy (MS, Graduate Certificate); botanical safety (Graduate Certificate); complementary alternative medicine (MS, Graduate Certificate); health and wellness (MS); herbal medicine (MS, Graduate Certificate); holistic nutrition (MS, Graduate Certificate); wellness coaching (Graduate Certificate). *Program availability:* Part-time, evening/weekend, online learning. *Degree requirements:* For master's, capstone project. *Entrance requirements:* For master's, interview, letters of recommendation, essay.

American University of Beirut, Graduate Programs, Faculty of Medicine, Beirut, Lebanon. Offers biochemistry (MS); biomedical engineering (MS); biomedical sciences (PhD); health research (MS); human morphology (MS); medicine (MD); microbiology and immunology (MS); neuroscience (MS); orthodontics (clinical) (MS); pharmacology and therapeutics (MS); physiology (MS). *Program availability:* Part-time. *Faculty:* 335 full-time (117 women), 54 part-time/adjunct (5 women). *Students:* 513 full-time (274 women). Average age 23. 527 applicants, 47% accepted, 169 enrolled. In 2017, 18 master's, 98 doctorates awarded. *Degree requirements:* For master's, one foreign language, comprehensive exam, thesis (for some programs); for doctorate, one foreign language, comprehensive exam, thesis/dissertation. *Entrance requirements:* For doctorate, MCAT (for MD); GRE (for PhD). Additional exam requirements/recommendations for international students: Required—TOEFL (minimum score 600 paper-based; 100 iBT), IELTS (minimum score 7.5). *Application deadline:* Applications are processed on a rolling basis. Application fee: $75. Electronic applications accepted. *Expenses:* Contact institution. *Financial support:* In 2017–18, 302 students received support. Fellowships, research assistantships, teaching assistantships, institutionally sponsored loans, scholarships/grants, tuition waivers, and unspecified assistantships available. *Unit head:* Dr. Mohamed Sayegh, Dean, 961-1-135000 Ext. 4700, Fax: 961-1-744489, E-mail: msayegh@aub.edu.lb. *Application contact:* Dr. Salim Kanaan, Director, Admission's Office, 961-1-350000 Ext. 2594, Fax: 961-1-750775, E-mail: sk00@aub.edu.lb.

Augusta University, Program in Physiology, Augusta, GA 30912. Offers PhD. *Degree requirements:* For doctorate, comprehensive exam, thesis/dissertation. *Entrance requirements:* For doctorate, GRE General Test. Additional exam requirements/recommendations for international students: Required—TOEFL. Electronic applications accepted. *Faculty research:* Cardiovascular and renal physiology, behavioral neuroscience and genetics, neurophysiology, adrenal steroid endocrinology and genetics, inflammatory mediators and cardiovascular disease, hypertension, diabetes and stroke.

Ball State University, Graduate School, College of Sciences and Humanities, Department of Biology, Program in Physiology, Muncie, IN 47306. Offers MA, MS. *Program availability:* Part-time. *Students:* 17 full-time (8 women), 5 part-time (3 women); includes 2 minority (1 Black or African American, non-Hispanic/Latino; 1 Hispanic/Latino), 3 international. Average age 25. 20 applicants, 75% accepted, 13 enrolled. In 2017, 7 master's awarded. *Entrance requirements:* For master's, minimum baccalaureate GPA of 2.75 or 3.0 in latter half of baccalaureate, three letters of recommendation, resume or curriculum vitae. Additional exam requirements/recommendations for international students: Required—TOEFL (minimum score 550 paper-based; 79 iBT), IELTS (minimum score 6.5). *Application deadline:* Applications are processed on a rolling basis. Application fee: $60. Electronic applications accepted. *Financial support:* In 2017–18, 9 students received support. Teaching assistantships with partial tuition reimbursements available available. Financial award application deadline: 3/1; financial award applicants required to submit FAFSA. *Unit head:* Dr. Kemuel Badger, Chairperson, 765-285-8820, Fax: 765-285-8804, E-mail: kbadger@bsu.edu. *Application contact:* Dr. Marianna Zamalauski-Tucker, Assistant Professor/Graduate Advisor, 765-285-8630, Fax: 765-285-8804, E-mail: mzamlaus@bsu.edu.
Website: http://www.bsu.edu/biology

Baylor University, Graduate School, Robbins College of Health and Human Sciences, Department of Health, Human Performance and Recreation, Waco, TX 76798. Offers athletic training (MS); community health (MPH); exercise physiology (MS); kinesiology, exercise nutrition, and health promotion (PhD); sport pedagogy (MS). *Accreditation:* NCATE. *Program availability:* Part-time. *Faculty:* 24 full-time (11 women). *Students:* 86 full-time (52 women), 9 part-time (6 women); includes 24 minority (7 Black or African American, non-Hispanic/Latino; 3 Asian, non-Hispanic/Latino; 10 Hispanic/Latino; 1 Native Hawaiian or other Pacific Islander, non-Hispanic/Latino; 3 Two or more races, non-Hispanic/Latino), 8 international. 109 applicants, 59% accepted, 44 enrolled. In 2017, 30 master's, 3 doctorates awarded. *Degree requirements:* For master's, comprehensive exam, thesis optional; for doctorate, comprehensive exam, thesis/dissertation. *Entrance requirements:* For master's and doctorate, GRE General Test. Additional exam requirements/recommendations for international students: Required—TOEFL (minimum score 550 paper-based; 80 iBT). *Application deadline:* For fall admission, 2/1 priority date for domestic students, 2/1 for international students; for spring admission, 10/1 for domestic and international students. Applications are processed on a rolling basis. Application fee: $25. Electronic applications accepted. *Financial support:* In 2017–18, 60 students received support, including 1 research assistantship with full tuition reimbursement available (averaging $12,700 per year), 33 teaching assistantships with full tuition reimbursements available (averaging $7,650 per year); career-related internships or fieldwork, Federal Work-Study, institutionally sponsored loans, scholarships/grants, tuition waivers (full), and unspecified assistantships also available. Financial award application deadline: 2/1. *Faculty research:* Exercise testing, cardio-metabolic health, resistance exercise and training, nutritional intervention, population health, health promotion, global health epidemiology, coaching, natural resource management, stimulant misuse, diet, microbiome and colon cancer etiology. *Total annual research expenditures:* $250,118. *Unit head:* Dr. Jaeho Shim, Graduate Program Director, 254-710-4009, Fax: 254-710-3527, E-mail: joe_shim@baylor.edu. *Application contact:* Deepa Morris, Graduate Program Coordinator, 254-710-3526, Fax: 254-710-3527, E-mail: deepa_morris@baylor.edu.
Website: http://www.baylor.edu/HHPR/

Boston University, College of Health and Rehabilitation Sciences: Sargent College, Department of Health Sciences, Programs in Human Physiology, Boston, MA 02215. Offers MS, PhD. *Faculty:* 10 full-time (9 women), 5 part-time/adjunct (2 women). *Students:* 8 full-time (5 women), 7 part-time (5 women); includes 2 minority (1 Asian, non-Hispanic/Latino; 1 Hispanic/Latino), 4 international. Average age 24. 49 applicants, 51% accepted, 11 enrolled. In 2017, 10 master's, 3 doctorates awarded. Terminal master's awarded for partial completion of doctoral program. *Degree requirements:* For master's, thesis or alternative; for doctorate, comprehensive exam, thesis/dissertation. *Entrance requirements:* For master's, GRE General Test, minimum GPA of 3.0; for doctorate, GRE General Test. Additional exam requirements/recommendations for international students: Required—TOEFL (minimum score 550 paper-based; 84 iBT). *Application deadline:* For fall admission, 1/15 priority date for domestic and international students. Applications are processed on a rolling basis. Application fee: $95. Electronic applications accepted. *Financial support:* In 2017–18, 9 students received support, including 2 research assistantships with full tuition reimbursements available (averaging $22,000 per year); career-related internships or fieldwork, Federal Work-Study, institutionally sponsored loans, and scholarships/grants also available. Support available to part-time students. Financial award application deadline: 1/15; financial award applicants required to submit FAFSA. *Faculty research:* Skeletal muscle, neural systems, smooth muscle, muscular dystrophy. *Total annual research expenditures:* $3.3 million. *Unit head:* Dr. Paula Quatromoni, Chair, 617-353-5797, Fax: 617-353-7567, E-mail: paulaq@bu.edu. *Application contact:* Sharon Sankey, Assistant Dean, Student Services, 617-353-2713, Fax: 617-353-7500, E-mail: ssankey@bu.edu.

Boston University, School of Medicine, Division of Graduate Medical Sciences, Department of Physiology and Biophysics, Boston, MA 02118. Offers MA, PhD, MD/PhD. *Program availability:* Part-time. Terminal master's awarded for partial completion of doctoral program. *Degree requirements:* For master's, thesis; for doctorate, thesis/dissertation. *Application deadline:* For fall admission, 1/15 for domestic students; for spring admission, 10/15 for domestic students. *Faculty research:* X-ray scattering, NMR spectroscopy, protein crystallography, structural electron. *Unit head:* Dr. David Atkinson, Chairman, 617-638-4015, Fax: 617-638-4041, E-mail: atkinson@bu.edu. *Application contact:* GMS Admissions Office, 617-638-5255, E-mail: askgms@bu.edu.
Website: http://www.bumc.bu.edu/phys-biophys/

Brigham Young University, Graduate Studies, College of Life Sciences, Department of Physiology and Developmental Biology, Provo, UT 84602. Offers neuroscience (MS, PhD); physiology and developmental biology (MS, PhD). *Program availability:* Part-time. *Faculty:* 19 full-time (1 woman), 4 part-time/adjunct (3 women). *Students:* 33 full-time (16 women); includes 6 minority (5 Asian, non-Hispanic/Latino; 1 Hispanic/Latino). Average age 30. 14 applicants, 43% accepted, 3 enrolled. In 2017, 6 master's, 4 doctorates awarded. Terminal master's awarded for partial completion of doctoral program. *Degree requirements:* For master's, thesis, oral exam; for doctorate, comprehensive exam, thesis/dissertation. *Entrance requirements:* For master's, GRE General Test, MCAT, or DAT, minimum GPA of 3.0 during previous 2 years; for doctorate, GRE General Test, minimum GPA of 3.0 overall. Additional exam requirements/recommendations for international students: Required—TOEFL (minimum score 580 paper-based; 85 iBT); Recommended—IELTS. *Application deadline:* For fall admission, 2/1 priority date for domestic and international students; for winter admission, 9/10 priority date for domestic students, 9/10 for international students; for spring

admission, 2/1 for domestic and international students; for summer admission, 2/1 for domestic and international students. Application fee: $50. Electronic applications accepted. *Expenses:* $6,880 full-time first year for members of the Church of Jesus Christ of Latter-day Saints; $13,760 for those who are not members of the Church; $405 per credit for additional years. *Financial support:* In 2017–18, 33 students received support, including 1 fellowship with partial tuition reimbursement available (averaging $15,000 per year), 16 research assistantships with full tuition reimbursements available (averaging $15,500 per year), 18 teaching assistantships with partial tuition reimbursements available (averaging $14,900 per year); career-related internships or fieldwork, institutionally sponsored loans, scholarships/grants, tuition waivers (full and partial), unspecified assistantships, and tuition awards also available. Financial award application deadline: 2/1. *Faculty research:* Sex differentiation of the brain, exercise physiology, developmental biology, membrane biophysics, neuroscience, heart differentiation/birth defects. *Total annual research expenditures:* $435,024. *Unit head:* Dr. Dixon J. Woodbury, Chair, 801-422-7562, Fax: 801-422-0004, E-mail: dixon_woodbury@byu.edu. *Application contact:* Connie L. Provost, Graduate Program Manager, 801-422-3706, Fax: 801-422-0004, E-mail: connie_provost@byu.edu.
Website: http://pdbio.byu.edu

Brown University, Graduate School, Division of Biology and Medicine, Department of Molecular Pharmacology, Physiology and Biotechnology, Providence, RI 02912. Offers biomedical engineering (Sc M, PhD); biotechnology (PhD); molecular pharmacology and physiology (PhD); MD/PhD. *Degree requirements:* For doctorate, thesis/dissertation, preliminary exam. *Entrance requirements:* For master's and doctorate, GRE General Test, GRE Subject Test. Additional exam requirements/recommendations for international students: Required—TOEFL. Electronic applications accepted. *Faculty research:* Structural biology, antiplatelet drugs, nicotinic receptor structure/function.

Case Western Reserve University, School of Medicine and School of Graduate Studies, Graduate Programs in Medicine, Department of Physiology and Biophysics, Cleveland, OH 44106. Offers medical physiology (MS); physiology and biophysics (PhD); MD/PhD. Terminal master's awarded for partial completion of doctoral program. *Degree requirements:* For master's, thesis; for doctorate, thesis/dissertation. *Entrance requirements:* For master's, GRE General Test, minimum GPA of 3.28; for doctorate, GRE General Test, minimum GPA of 3.6. Additional exam requirements/recommendations for international students: Required—TOEFL. Electronic applications accepted. *Expenses: Tuition:* Full-time $43,854; part-time $1827 per credit hour. *Required fees:* $50; $50 per credit hour. Tuition and fees vary according to course load and program. *Faculty research:* Cardiovascular physiology, calcium metabolism, epithelial cell biology.

Central Washington University, School of Graduate Studies and Research, College of Education and Professional Studies, Department of Health Sciences, Ellensburg, WA 98926. Offers integrative human physiology (MS); nutrition (MS). *Program availability:* Part-time. *Entrance requirements:* For master's, GRE, minimum GPA of 3.0. Additional exam requirements/recommendations for international students: Required—TOEFL (minimum score 550 paper-based; 79 iBT). *Application deadline:* For fall admission, 2/1 priority date for domestic students; for winter admission, 10/1 for domestic students; for spring admission, 1/1 for domestic students. Applications are processed on a rolling basis. Application fee: $50. Electronic applications accepted. *Financial support:* Application deadline: 3/1; applicants required to submit FAFSA. *Unit head:* Dr. Ethan Bergman, Chair, 509-963-2366, E-mail: bergmane@cwu.edu. *Application contact:* Justine Eason, Admissions Program Coordinator, 509-963-3103, Fax: 509-963-1799, E-mail: masters@cwu.edu.
Website: http://www.cwu.edu/~nehs/

Columbia University, College of Physicians and Surgeons, Department of Physiology and Cellular Biophysics, New York, NY 10032. Offers M Phil, MA, PhD, MD/PhD. Only candidates for the PhD are admitted. Terminal master's awarded for partial completion of doctoral program. *Degree requirements:* For doctorate, thesis/dissertation. *Entrance requirements:* For master's and doctorate, GRE General Test. Additional exam requirements/recommendations for international students: Required—TOEFL. *Expenses: Tuition:* Full-time $44,864; part-time $1704 per credit. *Required fees:* $2370 per semester. One-time fee: $105. *Faculty research:* Membrane physiology, cellular biology, cardiovascular physiology, neurophysiology.

Cornell University, Graduate School, Graduate Fields of Agriculture and Life Sciences, Field of Horticulture, Ithaca, NY 14853. Offers breeding of horticultural crops (MPS); horticultural crop management systems (MPS); human-plant interactions (MPS, PhD); physiology and ecology of horticultural crops (MPS, MS, PhD). *Degree requirements:* For master's, thesis (MS); for doctorate, comprehensive exam, thesis/dissertation. *Entrance requirements:* For master's and doctorate, GRE General Test, 3 letters of recommendation. Additional exam requirements/recommendations for international students: Required—TOEFL (minimum score 550 paper-based; 77 iBT). Electronic applications accepted. *Faculty research:* Plant selection/plant materials, greenhouse management, greenhouse crop production, urban landscape management, turfgrass management.

Dalhousie University, Faculty of Agriculture, Halifax, NS B3H 4R2, Canada. Offers agriculture (M Sc), including air quality, animal behavior, animal molecular genetics, animal nutrition, animal technology, aquaculture, botany, crop management, crop physiology, ecology, environmental microbiology, food science, horticulture, nutrient management, pest management, physiology, plant biotechnology, plant pathology, soil chemistry, soil fertility, waste management and composting, water quality. *Program availability:* Part-time. *Degree requirements:* For master's, thesis, ATC Exam Teaching Assistantship. *Entrance requirements:* For master's, honors B Sc, minimum GPA of 3.0. Additional exam requirements/recommendations for international students: Required—TOEFL (minimum score 580 paper-based; 92 iBT), IELTS, Michigan English Language Assessment Battery, CanTEST, CAEL. *Faculty research:* Bio-product development, organic agriculture, nutrient management, air and water quality, agricultural biotechnology.

Dalhousie University, Faculty of Medicine, Department of Physiology and Biophysics, Halifax, NS B3H 1X5, Canada. Offers M Sc, PhD, M Sc/PhD. *Degree requirements:* For master's, thesis; for doctorate, thesis/dissertation. *Entrance requirements:* For master's and doctorate, GRE Subject Test (for international students). Additional exam requirements/recommendations for international students: Required—1 of 5 approved tests: TOEFL, IELTS, CANTEST, CAEL, Michigan English Language Assessment Battery. Electronic applications accepted. *Faculty research:* Computer modeling, reproductive and endocrine physiology, cardiovascular physiology, neurophysiology, membrane biophysics.

Eastern Michigan University, Graduate School, College of Health and Human Services, School of Health Promotion and Human Performance, Programs in Exercise Physiology, Ypsilanti, MI 48197. Offers exercise physiology (MS); sports medicine-biomechanics (MS); sports medicine-corporate adult fitness (MS); sports medicine-exercise physiology (MS). *Program availability:* Part-time, evening/weekend. *Students:* 9 full-time (3 women), 13 part-time (5 women); includes 5 minority (2 Black or African American, non-Hispanic/Latino; 1 Asian, non-Hispanic/Latino; 1 Hispanic/Latino; 1 Two or more races, non-Hispanic/Latino), 1 international. Average age 29. 43 applicants, 56% accepted, 7 enrolled. In 2017, 13 master's awarded. *Degree requirements:* For master's, comprehensive exam, thesis or 450-hour internship. *Entrance requirements:* Additional exam requirements/recommendations for international students: Required—TOEFL. *Application deadline:* For fall admission, 8/1 for domestic students, 5/1 for international students; for winter admission, 12/1 for domestic students, 10/1 for international students; for spring admission, 3/15 for domestic students, 3/1 for international students. Application fee: $45. *Application contact:* Dr. Becca Moore, Program Coordinator, 734-487-2824, Fax: 734-487-2024, E-mail: rmoore41@emich.edu.

East Tennessee State University, Quillen College of Medicine, Department of Biomedical Sciences, Johnson City, TN 37614. Offers anatomy (PhD); biochemistry (PhD); microbiology (PhD); pharmaceutical sciences (PhD); pharmacology (PhD); physiology (PhD); quantitative biosciences (PhD). In 2017, 5 doctorates awarded. *Degree requirements:* For doctorate, comprehensive exam, thesis/dissertation, comprehensive qualifying exam; one-year residency. *Entrance requirements:* For doctorate, GRE General Test, GRE Subject Test, 3 letters of recommendation, minimum of 60 credit hours beyond the baccalaureate degree. Additional exam requirements/recommendations for international students: Required—TOEFL (minimum score 550 paper-based; 79 iBT). *Application deadline:* For fall admission, 6/1 priority date for domestic students, 4/29 for international students; for spring admission, 11/1 for domestic students, 9/29 for international students; for summer admission, 3/15 for domestic students, 2/1 for international students. Applications are processed on a rolling basis. Application fee: $55 ($65 for international students). Electronic applications accepted. *Expenses:* Contact institution. *Financial support:* Research assistantships with full tuition reimbursements, career-related internships or fieldwork, institutionally sponsored loans, scholarships/grants, and unspecified assistantships available. Financial award application deadline: 7/1; financial award applicants required to submit FAFSA. *Faculty research:* Cardiovascular, infectious disease, neurosciences, cancer, immunology. *Unit head:* Theo Hagg, Chair, 423-439-6294, Fax: 423-439-2140, E-mail: haggt1@etsu.edu. *Application contact:* Theo Hagg, Chair, 423-439-6294, Fax: 423-439-2140, E-mail: haggt1@etsu.edu.
Website: http://www.etsu.edu/com/dbms/

Georgetown University, Graduate School of Arts and Sciences, Department of Pharmacology and Physiology, Washington, DC 20057. Offers pharmacology (MS, PhD); physiology (MS); MD/PhD. *Degree requirements:* For doctorate, comprehensive exam, thesis/dissertation. *Entrance requirements:* For doctorate, GRE General Test, previous course work in biology and chemistry. Additional exam requirements/recommendations for international students: Required—TOEFL. *Faculty research:* Neuropharmacology, techniques in biochemistry and tissue culture.

Georgia Institute of Technology, Graduate Studies, College of Sciences, School of Biological Sciences, Program in Applied Physiology, Atlanta, GA 30332-0001. Offers PhD. *Degree requirements:* For doctorate, comprehensive exam, thesis/dissertation. *Entrance requirements:* For doctorate, GRE. Additional exam requirements/recommendations for international students: Required—TOEFL (minimum score 550 paper-based; 79 iBT). Electronic applications accepted.

Georgia Institute of Technology, Graduate Studies, College of Sciences, School of Biological Sciences, Program in Prosthetics and Orthotics, Atlanta, GA 30332-0001. Offers MS. Terminal master's awarded for partial completion of doctoral program. *Degree requirements:* For master's, capstone research project plus minimum 500 contact hours of clinical practicum in medicine, prosthetics and orthotics, and pedorthics combined. *Entrance requirements:* For master's, GRE. Additional exam requirements/recommendations for international students: Required—TOEFL (minimum score 550 paper-based; 79 iBT). Electronic applications accepted. *Expenses:* Contact institution.

Georgia State University, College of Arts and Sciences, Department of Biology, Program in Cellular and Molecular Biology and Physiology, Atlanta, GA 30302-3083. Offers bioinformatics (MS); cellular and molecular biology and physiology (MS, PhD). *Program availability:* Part-time. Terminal master's awarded for partial completion of doctoral program. *Entrance requirements:* For master's and doctorate, GRE. *Application deadline:* Applications are processed on a rolling basis. Application fee: $50. Electronic applications accepted. *Expenses:* Tuition, state resident: full-time $7020. Tuition, nonresident: full-time $22,518. *Required fees:* $2128. Tuition and fees vary according to degree level and program. *Financial support:* Fellowships and research assistantships available. Financial award application deadline: 12/3. *Faculty research:* Membrane transport, viral infection, molecular immunology, protein modeling, gene regulation. *Unit head:* Dr. Charles Derby, Director of Graduate Studies, 404-413-5393, Fax: 404-413-5446, E-mail: cderby@gsu.edu.
Website: http://biology.gsu.edu/

Gonzaga University, School of Nursing and Human Physiology, Spokane, WA 99258. Offers MSN, DNP, DNP-A. *Accreditation:* AACN; AANA/CANAEP. *Program availability:* Part-time, evening/weekend, 100% online, immersion weekends. *Faculty:* 10 full-time (all women), 57 part-time/adjunct (48 women). *Students:* 34 full-time (22 women), 673 part-time (566 women); includes 106 minority (18 Black or African American, non-Hispanic/Latino; 4 American Indian or Alaska Native, non-Hispanic/Latino; 29 Asian, non-Hispanic/Latino; 28 Hispanic/Latino; 1 Native Hawaiian or other Pacific Islander, non-Hispanic/Latino; 26 Two or more races, non-Hispanic/Latino), 3 international. Average age 38. 454 applicants, 38% accepted, 130 enrolled. In 2017, 180 master's, 4 doctorates awarded. *Entrance requirements:* For master's, MAT or GRE within the last 5 years if GPA is lower than 3.0, official transcripts, two letters of recommendation, statement of purpose, current resume/curriculum vitae, current registered nurse license. Additional exam requirements/recommendations for international students: Required—TOEFL (minimum score 88 iBT) or IELTS (minimum score 6.5). *Application deadline:* For spring admission, 9/1 for domestic students; for summer admission, 3/28 for domestic students. Applications are processed on a rolling basis. Application fee: $50. Electronic applications accepted. *Expenses:* $955 per credit. *Financial support:* In 2017–18, 28 students received support. Scholarships/grants, traineeships, and unspecified assistantships available. Support available to part-time students. Financial award applicants required to submit FAFSA. *Unit head:* Dr. Lin Murphy, Interim Dean, 509-313-3569, E-mail: murpheyl1@gonzaga.edu. *Application contact:* Shannon Zaranski, Assistant to the Dean, 509-313-3569, E-mail: zaranski@gonzaga.edu.
Website: https://www.gonzaga.edu/school-of-nursing-human-physiology

Howard University, Graduate School, Department of Physiology and Biophysics, Washington, DC 20059-0002. Offers biophysics (PhD); physiology (PhD). *Degree requirements:* For doctorate, comprehensive exam, thesis/dissertation. *Entrance requirements:* For doctorate, GRE General Test, minimum B average in field. *Faculty research:* Cardiovascular physiology, pulmonary physiology, renal physiology, neurophysiology, endocrinology.

Illinois State University, Graduate School, College of Arts and Sciences, School of Biological Sciences, Normal, IL 61790. Offers animal behavior (MS); bacteriology (MS); biochemistry (MS); biological sciences (MS); biology (PhD); biophysics (MS); biotechnology (MS); botany (MS, PhD); cell biology (MS); conservation biology (MS); developmental biology (MS); ecology (MS, PhD); entomology (MS); evolutionary biology (MS); genetics (MS, PhD); immunology (MS); microbiology (MS, PhD); molecular biology (MS); molecular genetics (MS); neurobiology (MS); neuroscience (MS); parasitology (MS); physiology (MS, PhD); plant biology (MS); plant molecular biology (MS); plant sciences (MS); structural biology (MS); zoology (MS, PhD). *Program availability:* Part-time. *Degree requirements:* For master's, thesis or alternative; for doctorate, variable foreign language requirement, thesis/dissertation, 2 terms of residency. *Entrance requirements:* For master's, GRE General Test, minimum GPA of 2.6 in last 60 hours of course work; for doctorate, GRE General Test. *Faculty research:* Redoc balance and drug development in schistosoma mansoni, control of the growth of listeria monocytogenes at low temperature, regulation of cell expansion and microtubule function by SPRI, CRUI: physiology and fitness consequences of different life history phenotypes.

Indiana State University, College of Graduate and Professional Studies, College of Arts and Sciences, Department of Biology, Terre Haute, IN 47809. Offers cellular and molecular biology (PhD); ecology, systematics and evolution (PhD); life sciences (MS); physiology (PhD); science education (MS). *Degree requirements:* For master's, thesis optional; for doctorate, comprehensive exam, thesis/dissertation. *Entrance requirements:* For master's and doctorate, GRE General Test. Electronic applications accepted.

James Madison University, The Graduate School, College of Health and Behavioral Studies, Program in Kinesiology, Harrisonburg, VA 22801. Offers clinical exercise physiology (MS); exercise physiology (MS); kinesiology (MAT, MS); nutrition and exercise (MS); physical and health education (MAT); sport and recreation leadership (MS). *Program availability:* Part-time, evening/weekend. *Students:* 43 full-time (22 women), 3 part-time (2 women); includes 10 minority (4 Black or African American, non-Hispanic/Latino; 1 Asian, non-Hispanic/Latino; 4 Hispanic/Latino; 1 Two or more races, non-Hispanic/Latino). Average age 30. In 2017, 46 master's awarded. Application fee: $55. Electronic applications accepted. *Expenses:* Tuition, state resident: full-time $10,512; part-time $438 per credit hour. Tuition, nonresident: full-time $28,358; part-time $1162 per credit hour. *Required fees:* $1128. *Financial support:* In 2017–18, 32 students received support, including 13 teaching assistantships with full tuition reimbursements available (averaging $8,837 per year); Federal Work-Study and 19 assistantships (averaging $7911), 20 athletic assistantships (averaging $9284) also available. Financial award application deadline: 3/1; financial award applicants required to submit FAFSA. *Unit head:* Dr. Christopher J. Womack, Department Head, 540-568-6145, E-mail: womackcx@jmu.edu. *Application contact:* Lynette D. Michael, Director of Graduate Admissions, 540-568-6131 Ext. 6395, Fax: 540-568-7860, E-mail: michaeld@jmu.edu.
Website: http://www.jmu.edu/kinesiology/

Johns Hopkins University, School of Medicine, Graduate Programs in Medicine, Department of Physiology, Baltimore, MD 21205. Offers cellular and molecular physiology (PhD); physiology (PhD). *Degree requirements:* For doctorate, thesis/dissertation, oral and qualifying exams. *Entrance requirements:* For doctorate, GRE General Test, previous course work in biology, calculus, chemistry, and physics. Additional exam requirements/recommendations for international students: Required—TOEFL. Electronic applications accepted. *Expenses:* Contact institution. *Faculty research:* Membrane biochemistry and biophysics; signal transduction; developmental genetics and physiology; physiology and biochemistry; transporters, carriers, and ion channels.

Kansas State University, Graduate School, College of Agriculture, Department of Animal Sciences and Industry, Manhattan, KS 66506. Offers genetics (MS, PhD); meat science (MS, PhD); monogastric nutrition (MS, PhD); physiology (MS, PhD); ruminant nutrition (MS, PhD). *Degree requirements:* For master's, comprehensive exam, thesis, oral exam; for doctorate, comprehensive exam, thesis/dissertation, preliminary exams. *Entrance requirements:* Additional exam requirements/recommendations for international students: Required—TOEFL (minimum score 550 paper-based; 79 iBT). Electronic applications accepted. *Faculty research:* Animal nutrition, animal physiology, meat science, animal genetics.

Kansas State University, Graduate School, College of Veterinary Medicine, Department of Anatomy and Physiology, Manhattan, KS 66506. Offers physiology (PhD). Terminal master's awarded for partial completion of doctoral program. *Entrance requirements:* For doctorate, GRE. Additional exam requirements/recommendations for international students: Required—TOEFL. Electronic applications accepted. *Faculty research:* Cardiovascular and pulmonary, immunophysiology, neuroscience, pharmacology, epithelial.

Kent State University, College of Arts and Sciences, Department of Biological Sciences, Kent, OH 44242-0001. Offers biological sciences (MA, MS, PhD), including botany (MS, PhD), cell biology (MS, PhD), ecology (MS, PhD), physiology (MS, PhD). *Program availability:* Part-time. *Faculty:* 28 full-time (10 women), 3 part-time/adjunct (2 women). *Students:* 55 full-time (37 women), 10 part-time (6 women); includes 6 minority (3 Black or African American, non-Hispanic/Latino; 1 Asian, non-Hispanic/Latino; 2 Two or more races, non-Hispanic/Latino), 12 international. Average age 28. 27 applicants, 56% accepted, 11 enrolled. In 2017, 4 master's, 6 doctorates awarded. Terminal master's awarded for partial completion of doctoral program. *Degree requirements:* For master's, thesis (for some programs), departmental seminar presentation about research (for MS); for doctorate, thesis/dissertation, departmental seminar presentation about research, admitted to doctoral candidacy following written and oral candidacy. *Entrance requirements:* For master's, GRE, minimum GPA of 3.0, official transcripts, goal statement, three letters of recommendation, list of up to five potential faculty advisors, undergraduate coursework roughly equivalent to a biology minor; for doctorate, GRE, official transcripts, goal statement, three letters of recommendation, list of up to five potential faculty advisors, baccalaureate degree with strong background in biology and related subjects such as chemistry and mathematics. Additional exam requirements/recommendations for international students: Required—TOEFL (minimum score 587 paper-based, 94 iBT), Michigan English Language Assessment Battery (minimum score 82), IELTS (7.0), or PTE (65). *Application deadline:* For fall admission, 12/15 for domestic students, 12/5 for international students. Applications are processed on a rolling basis. Application fee: $45 ($70 for international students). Electronic applications accepted. *Expenses:* Tuition, state resident: full-time $11,310; part-time $515 per credit hour. Tuition, nonresident: full-time $20,396; part-time $928 per credit hour. *International tuition:* $18,544 full-time. *Financial support:* Research assistantships with full tuition reimbursements, teaching assistantships with full tuition reimbursements, Federal Work-Study, scholarships/grants, and unspecified assistantships available. Financial award application deadline: 12/15. *Unit head:* Dr. James L. Blank, Dean, 330-672-2650, E-mail: jblank@kent.edu. *Application contact:* Dr. Heather K. Caldwell, Associate Professor and Graduate Coordinator, 330-672-3636, E-mail: hcaldwel@kent.edu.
Website: http://www.kent.edu/biology

Kent State University, College of Arts and Sciences, School of Biomedical Sciences, Kent, OH 44242-0001. Offers biological anthropology (PhD); biomedical mathematics (MS, PhD); cellular and molecular biology (MS, PhD), including cellular biology and structures, molecular biology and genetics; neurosciences (MS, PhD); pharmacology (MS, PhD); physiology (MS, PhD). *Faculty:* 22 full-time (9 women), 3 part-time/adjunct (1 woman). *Students:* 75 full-time (46 women); includes 8 minority (1 Black or African American, non-Hispanic/Latino; 3 Asian, non-Hispanic/Latino; 2 Hispanic/Latino; 2 Two or more races, non-Hispanic/Latino), 25 international. Average age 28. 70 applicants, 23% accepted, 13 enrolled. In 2017, 23 master's, 5 doctorates awarded. Terminal master's awarded for partial completion of doctoral program. *Degree requirements:* For master's, thesis; for doctorate, comprehensive exam, thesis/dissertation. *Entrance requirements:* For master's, GRE, bachelor's degree, transcripts, minimum GPA of 3.0, goal statement, three letters of recommendation, academic preparation adequate to perform graduate work in the desired field; for doctorate, GRE, master's degree, minimum GPA of 3.0, transcripts, goal statement, three letters of recommendation. Additional exam requirements/recommendations for international students: Required—TOEFL (minimum score 600 paper-based, 100 iBT), Michigan English Language Assessment Battery (minimum score 85), IELTS (minimum score 7.0) or PTE (minimum score 68). *Application deadline:* For fall admission, 1/1 for domestic and international students. Applications are processed on a rolling basis. Application fee: $45 ($70 for international students). Electronic applications accepted. *Expenses:* Tuition, state resident: full-time $11,310; part-time $515 per credit hour. Tuition, nonresident: full-time $20,396; part-time $928 per credit hour. *International tuition:* $18,544 full-time. *Financial support:* Research assistantships with full tuition reimbursements, teaching assistantships, and unspecified assistantships available. Financial award application deadline: 1/1. *Unit head:* Dr. Ernest J. Freeman, Director, School of Biomedical Sciences, 330-672-2363, E-mail: efreema2@kent.edu.
Website: http://www.kent.edu/biomedical/

Loma Linda University, School of Medicine, Programs in Physiology and Pharmacology, Loma Linda, CA 92350. Offers pharmacology (PhD); physiology (PhD). *Program availability:* Part-time. *Degree requirements:* For doctorate, 2 foreign languages, thesis/dissertation. *Entrance requirements:* For doctorate, GRE General Test. *Faculty research:* Drug metabolism, biochemical pharmacology, structure and function of cell membranes, neuropharmacology.

Louisiana State University Health Sciences Center, School of Graduate Studies in New Orleans, Department of Physiology, New Orleans, LA 70112-2223. Offers PhD, MD/PhD. *Faculty:* 9 full-time (3 women). *Students:* 7 full-time (4 women); includes 2 minority (both Asian, non-Hispanic/Latino). Average age 26. 2 applicants. In 2017, 4 doctorates awarded. *Degree requirements:* For doctorate, comprehensive exam, thesis/dissertation. *Entrance requirements:* For doctorate, GRE General Test. Additional exam requirements/recommendations for international students: Recommended—TOEFL, IELTS. *Application deadline:* For fall admission, 4/1 for domestic and international students. Applications are processed on a rolling basis. Application fee: $30. *Expenses:* Tuition, state resident: full-time $11,835; part-time $518 per hour. Tuition, nonresident: full-time $24,108; part-time $1079 per hour. *Required fees:* $1254; $55 per hour. *Financial support:* Unspecified assistantships available. *Faculty research:* Host defense, lipoprotein metabolism, regulation of cardiopulmonary function, alcohol and drug abuse, cell to cell communication, cytokinesis, physiologic functions of nitric oxide. *Unit head:* Dr. Patricia Molina, Professor and Interim Head, 504-568-6171, Fax: 504-568-6158, E-mail: pmolin@lsuhsc.edu. *Application contact:* Dr. Scott Edwards, Graduate Coordinator and Professor, 504-568-2669, E-mail: sedwa5@lsuhsc.edu.
Website: http://www.medschool.lsuhsc.edu/physiology/

Louisiana State University Health Sciences Center at Shreveport, Department of Molecular and Cellular Physiology, Shreveport, LA 71130-3932. Offers physiology (MS, PhD); MD/PhD. *Degree requirements:* For master's, thesis; for doctorate, thesis/dissertation. *Entrance requirements:* For master's and doctorate, GRE General Test. Additional exam requirements/recommendations for international students: Required—TOEFL (minimum score 550 paper-based). *Expenses:* Contact institution. *Faculty research:* Cardiovascular, gastrointestinal, renal, and neutrophil function; cellular detoxification systems; hypoxia and mitochondria function.

Loyola University Chicago, Graduate School, Integrated Program in Biomedical Sciences, Maywood, IL 60141. Offers biochemistry and molecular biology (MS, PhD); cell and molecular physiology (MS, PhD); infectious disease and immunology (MS); integrative cell biology (MS, PhD); microbiology and immunology (MS, PhD); molecular pharmacology and therapeutics (MS, PhD); neuroscience (MS, PhD). *Faculty:* 84 full-time (32 women). *Students:* 126 full-time (65 women), 1 (woman) part-time; includes 36 minority (5 Black or African American, non-Hispanic/Latino; 14 Asian, non-Hispanic/Latino; 14 Hispanic/Latino; 3 Two or more races, non-Hispanic/Latino), 13 international. Average age 26. 748 applicants, 34% accepted, 124 enrolled. In 2017, 41 master's, 18 doctorates awarded. *Degree requirements:* For master's, thesis; for doctorate, comprehensive exam, thesis/dissertation. *Entrance requirements:* For doctorate, GRE. Additional exam requirements/recommendations for international students: Required—TOEFL (minimum score 94 iBT), IELTS (minimum score 7.5). *Application deadline:* For fall admission, 2/7 for domestic students. Applications are processed on a rolling basis. Electronic applications accepted. *Expenses:* Contact institution. *Financial support:* In 2017–18, 20 students received support. Schmitt Fellowships and yearly tuition scholarships (averaging $25,032) available. Financial award application deadline: 6/15; financial award applicants required to submit FAFSA. *Unit head:* Dr. Leanne L. Cribbs, Associate Dean, Graduate Education, 708-327-2817, Fax: 708-216-8216, E-mail: lcribbs@luc.edu. *Application contact:* Margarita Quesada, Graduate Program Secretary, 708-216-3532, Fax: 708-216-8216, E-mail: mquesad@luc.edu.
Website: http://ssom.luc.edu/graduate_school/degree-programs/ipbsphd/

Maharishi University of Management, Graduate Studies, Program in Physiology, Fairfield, IA 52557. Offers PhD. *Degree requirements:* For doctorate, thesis/dissertation. *Faculty research:* The effects of Maharishi AyurVeda and the Transcendental Meditation program on health and physiology.

Marquette University, Graduate School, College of Arts and Sciences, Department of Biology, Milwaukee, WI 53201-1881. Offers cell biology (MS, PhD); developmental biology (MS, PhD); ecology (MS, PhD); epithelial physiology (MS, PhD); genetics (MS, PhD); microbiology (MS, PhD); molecular biology (MS, PhD); muscle and exercise physiology (MS, PhD); neuroscience (PhD). Terminal master's awarded for partial completion of doctoral program. *Degree requirements:* For master's, comprehensive exam, thesis, 1 year of teaching experience or equivalent; for doctorate, thesis/dissertation, 1 year of teaching experience or equivalent, qualifying exam. *Entrance requirements:* For master's and doctorate, GRE General Test, GRE Subject Test, official transcripts from all current and previous colleges/universities except Marquette, statement of professional goals and aspirations, three letters of recommendation. Additional exam requirements/recommendations for international students: Required—TOEFL (minimum score 530 paper-based). Electronic applications accepted. *Faculty research:* Neurobiology, neuroendocrinology, epithelial physiology, neuropeptide interactions, synaptic transmission.

Mayo Clinic Graduate School of Biomedical Sciences, Program in Biomedical Engineering and Physiology, Rochester, MN 55905. Offers MS, PhD. *Faculty:* 77 full-time (10 women). *Students:* 28 full-time (11 women); includes 3 minority (1 American Indian or Alaska Native, non-Hispanic/Latino; 2 Asian, non-Hispanic/Latino). 38 applicants, 32% accepted, 6 enrolled. Terminal master's awarded for partial completion of doctoral program. *Degree requirements:* For master's, thesis; for doctorate, comprehensive exam, thesis/dissertation, oral defense of dissertation, qualifying oral and written exam. *Entrance requirements:* For doctorate, GRE, 1 year of chemistry,

biology, calculus, and physics; courses in quantitative science and engineering, e.g., signal processing, computer science, instrumentation (encouraged). Additional exam requirements/recommendations for international students: Required—TOEFL. *Application deadline:* For fall admission, 12/1 for domestic and international students. Application fee: $50. Electronic applications accepted. *Financial support:* Fellowships with full tuition reimbursements available. *Faculty research:* Biomechanics, biomedical imaging, molecular biophysics, physiology, likelihood-based metabolic modeling, tissue engineering and tendon surgery in the hand, role of neurotrophic signaling in restoration of respiratory function after cervical spinal cord injury. *Unit head:* Dr. Carlos B. Mantilla, Director, 507-255-8544, E-mail: mantilla.carlos@mayo.edu. *Application contact:* Sarah E. Giese, Admissions Coordinator, 507-538-1160, E-mail: phd.training@mayo.edu.
Website: http://www.mayo.edu/mgs/

McGill University, Faculty of Graduate and Postdoctoral Studies, Faculty of Medicine, Department of Physiology, Montréal, QC H3A 2T5, Canada. Offers M Sc, PhD.

McMaster University, Faculty of Health Sciences and School of Graduate Studies, Program in Medical Sciences, Physiology/Pharmacology Area, Hamilton, ON L8S 4M2, Canada. Offers M Sc, PhD, MD/PhD. *Degree requirements:* For master's, thesis; for doctorate, comprehensive exam, thesis/dissertation. *Entrance requirements:* For master's, honors B Sc, B+ average in related field; for doctorate, M Sc, minimum B+ average, students with proven research experience and an A average may be admitted with a B Sc degree. Additional exam requirements/recommendations for international students: Required—TOEFL (minimum score 580 paper-based; 92 iBT).

Medical College of Wisconsin, Graduate School, Department of Physiology, Milwaukee, WI 53226-0509. Offers PhD, MD/PhD. *Degree requirements:* For doctorate, comprehensive exam, thesis/dissertation. *Entrance requirements:* For doctorate, GRE, official transcripts, three letters of recommendation. Additional exam requirements/recommendations for international students: Required—TOEFL. *Application deadline:* For fall admission, 1/15 for domestic and international students. Applications are processed on a rolling basis. Application fee: $50. *Financial support:* Fellowships with full tuition reimbursements, research assistantships with full tuition reimbursements, institutionally sponsored loans, and scholarships/grants available. Support available to part-time students. Financial award application deadline: 2/15. *Faculty research:* Cardiovascular, respiratory, renal, and exercise physiology; mathematical modeling; molecular and cellular biology. *Unit head:* Dr. Allen W. Cowley, Jr., Chair, 414-955-8277, Fax: 414-955-6555, E-mail: cowley@mcw.edu. *Application contact:* Recruitment Office, 414-955-4402, Fax: 414-955-6555, E-mail: gradschoolrecruit@mcw.edu.
Website: https://www.mcw.edu/Physiology/Education.htm

Michigan State University, College of Human Medicine and The Graduate School, Graduate Programs in Human Medicine, East Lansing, MI 48824. Offers biochemistry and molecular biology (MS, PhD); epidemiology (MS, PhD); microbiology (MS); microbiology and molecular genetics (PhD); pharmacology and toxicology (MS, PhD); physiology (MS, PhD); public health (MPH). *Entrance requirements:* Additional exam requirements/recommendations for international students: Required—TOEFL.

Michigan State University, College of Osteopathic Medicine and The Graduate School, Graduate Studies in Osteopathic Medicine, East Lansing, MI 48824. Offers biochemistry and molecular biology (MS, PhD); microbiology (MS); microbiology and molecular genetics (PhD); pharmacology and toxicology (MS, PhD), including integrative pharmacology (MS), pharmacology and toxicology, pharmacology and toxicology-environmental toxicology (PhD); physiology (MS, PhD).

Michigan State University, College of Veterinary Medicine and The Graduate School, Graduate Programs in Veterinary Medicine, East Lansing, MI 48824. Offers comparative medicine and integrative biology (MS, PhD), including comparative medicine and integrative biology, comparative medicine and integrative biology–environmental toxicology (PhD); food safety and toxicology (MS), including food safety, integrative toxicology (PhD), including animal science–environmental toxicology, biochemistry and molecular biology–environmental toxicology, chemistry–environmental toxicology, crop and soil sciences–environmental toxicology, environmental engineering–environmental toxicology, environmental geosciences–environmental toxicology, fisheries and wildlife–environmental toxicology, food science–environmental toxicology, forestry–environmental toxicology, genetics–environmental toxicology, human nutrition–environmental toxicology, microbiology–environmental toxicology, pharmacology and toxicology–environmental toxicology, zoology–environmental toxicology; large animal clinical sciences (MS, PhD); microbiology and molecular genetics (MS, PhD), including industrial microbiology, microbiology, microbiology and molecular genetics, microbiology–environmental toxicology (PhD); pathobiology and diagnostic investigation (MS, PhD), including pathology, pathology–environmental toxicology (PhD); pharmacology and toxicology (MS, PhD); pharmacology and toxicology–environmental toxicology (PhD); physiology (MS, PhD); small animal clinical sciences (MS). Electronic applications accepted. *Faculty research:* Molecular genetics, food safety/toxicology, comparative orthopedics, airway disease, population medicine.

Michigan State University, The Graduate School, College of Natural Science and Graduate Programs in Human Medicine and Graduate Studies in Osteopathic Medicine, Department of Physiology, East Lansing, MI 48824. Offers MS, PhD. *Entrance requirements:* Additional exam requirements/recommendations for international students: Required—TOEFL (minimum score 600 paper-based). Electronic applications accepted.

Montclair State University, The Graduate School, College of Science and Mathematics, Program in Biology, Montclair, NJ 07043-1624. Offers biological science/education (MS); biology (MS); ecology and evolution (MS); physiology (MS).

New York Medical College, Graduate School of Basic Medical Sciences, Valhalla, NY 10595. Offers biochemistry and molecular biology (MS, PhD); cell biology (MS, PhD); microbiology and immunology (MS, PhD); pathology (MS, PhD); pharmacology (MS, PhD); physiology (MS, PhD); MD/PhD. *Program availability:* Part-time, evening/weekend. *Faculty:* 70 full-time (17 women), 25 part-time/adjunct (9 women). *Students:* 116 full-time (63 women), 25 part-time (11 women); includes 65 minority (17 Black or African American, non-Hispanic/Latino; 1 American Indian or Alaska Native, non-Hispanic/Latino; 23 Asian, non-Hispanic/Latino; 21 Hispanic/Latino; 3 Two or more races, non-Hispanic/Latino), 27 international. Average age 27. 273 applicants, 56% accepted, 59 enrolled. In 2017, 32 master's, 3 doctorates awarded. *Degree requirements:* For master's, thesis; for doctorate, comprehensive exam, thesis/dissertation. *Entrance requirements:* For master's, GRE General Test, MCAT, or DAT; for doctorate, GRE General Test. Additional exam requirements/recommendations for international students: Required—TOEFL. *Application deadline:* For fall admission, 7/1 priority date for domestic students, 5/1 priority date for international students; for spring admission, 12/1 priority date for domestic students, 9/15 priority date for international students. Applications are processed on a rolling basis. Application fee: $75 ($100 for international students). Electronic applications accepted. *Expenses:* $1,125 per credit, $655 fees. *Financial support:* Fellowships, research assistantships, Federal Work-Study, institutionally sponsored loans, scholarships/grants, tuition waivers, and health benefits (for PhD candidates only) available. Support available to part-time students. Financial award application deadline: 4/30; financial award applicants required to submit FAFSA. *Faculty research:* Cardiovascular science, infectious diseases, neuroscience, cancer, cell signaling. *Unit head:* Dr. Francis L. Belloni, Dean, 914-594-4110, Fax: 914-594-4944, E-mail: francis_belloni@nymc.edu. *Application contact:* Valerie Romeo-Messana, Director of Admissions, 914-594-4110, Fax: 914-594-4944, E-mail: v_romeomessana@nymc.edu.
Website: https://www.nymc.edu/graduate-school-of-basic-medical-sciences-gsbms/gsbms-academics/

New York University, School of Medicine and Graduate School of Arts and Science, Sackler Institute of Graduate Biomedical Sciences, New York, NY 10016. Offers biomedical imaging and technology (PhD); biostatistics (PhD); cellular and molecular biology (PhD); developmental genetics (PhD); epidemiology (PhD); genome integrity (PhD); immunology and inflammation (PhD); microbiology (PhD); molecular biophysics (PhD); molecular oncology and tumor immunology (PhD); molecular pharmacology (PhD); neuroscience and physiology (PhD), including immunology, molecular oncology; stem cell biology (PhD); systems and computational biomedicine (PhD); MD/PhD. *Faculty:* 207 full-time (51 women). *Students:* 236 full-time (138 women), 1 part-time (0 women); includes 68 minority (13 Black or African American, non-Hispanic/Latino; 26 Asian, non-Hispanic/Latino; 28 Hispanic/Latino; 1 Native Hawaiian or other Pacific Islander, non-Hispanic/Latino), 79 international. Average age 27. 761 applicants, 18% accepted, 59 enrolled. In 2017, 35 doctorates awarded. *Degree requirements:* For doctorate, comprehensive exam, thesis/dissertation, qualifying exam; thesis defense. *Entrance requirements:* For doctorate, GRE. Additional exam requirements/recommendations for international students: Required—TOEFL, IELTS. *Application deadline:* For fall admission, 12/1 for domestic and international students. Applications are processed on a rolling basis. Application fee: $100. Electronic applications accepted. Application fee is waived when completed online. *Expenses:* Contact institution. *Financial support:* Health care benefits, tuition waivers (full), and unspecified assistantships available. *Faculty research:* Biomedical sciences. *Unit head:* Dr. Naoko Tanese, Associate Dean for Biomedical Sciences/Director, Sackler Institute, 212-263-8945, E-mail: naoko.tanese@nyumc.org. *Application contact:* Jessica Dong, Program Manager, 212-263-5648, E-mail: sackler-info@nyumc.org.
Website: https://med.nyu.edu/research/sackler-institute-graduate-biomedical-sciences/

North Carolina State University, Graduate School, College of Agriculture and Life Sciences and College of Veterinary Medicine, Program in Physiology, Raleigh, NC 27695. Offers MP, MS, PhD. *Degree requirements:* For master's, thesis (for some programs); for doctorate, thesis/dissertation. *Entrance requirements:* For master's and doctorate, GRE General Test. Electronic applications accepted. *Faculty research:* Neurophysiology, gastrointestinal physiology, reproductive physiology, environmental/stress physiology, cardiovascular physiology.

Northwestern University, The Graduate School, Judd A. and Marjorie Weinberg College of Arts and Sciences, Department of Neurobiology, Evanston, IL 60208. Offers neurobiology and physiology (MS). Admissions and degrees offered through The Graduate School. *Program availability:* Part-time. *Degree requirements:* For master's, thesis. *Entrance requirements:* For master's, GRE General Test and MCAT (strongly recommended). Additional exam requirements/recommendations for international students: Required—TOEFL. Electronic applications accepted. *Expenses:* Contact institution. *Faculty research:* Sensory neurobiology and neuroendocrinology, reproductive biology, vision physiology and psychophysics, cell and developmental biology.

Ohio University, Graduate College, College of Arts and Sciences, Department of Biological Sciences, Athens, OH 45701-2979. Offers biological sciences (MS, PhD); cell biology and physiology (MS, PhD); ecology and evolutionary biology (MS, PhD); exercise physiology and muscle biology (MS, PhD); microbiology (MS, PhD); neuroscience (MS, PhD). Terminal master's awarded for partial completion of doctoral program. *Degree requirements:* For master's, comprehensive exam, thesis, 1 quarter of teaching experience; for doctorate, comprehensive exam, thesis/dissertation, 2 quarters of teaching experience. *Entrance requirements:* For master's, GRE General Test, names of three faculty members whose research interests most closely match the applicant's interest; for doctorate, GRE General Test, essay concerning prior training, research interest and career goals, plus names of three faculty members whose research interests most closely match the applicant's interest. Additional exam requirements/recommendations for international students: Required—TOEFL (minimum score 620 paper-based; 105 iBT) or IELTS (minimum score 7.5). Electronic applications accepted. *Faculty research:* Ecology and evolutionary biology, exercise physiology and muscle biology, neurobiology, cell biology, physiology.

Oregon Health & Science University, School of Medicine, Graduate Programs in Medicine, Program in Molecular and Cellular Biosciences, Department of Physiology and Pharmacology, Portland, OR 97239-3098. Offers PhD. *Faculty:* 15 full-time (5 women), 20 part-time/adjunct (7 women). *Students:* 15 full-time (10 women); includes 6 minority (4 Asian, non-Hispanic/Latino; 2 Hispanic/Latino). Average age 27. In 2017, 2 doctorates awarded. *Degree requirements:* For doctorate, comprehensive exam, thesis/dissertation. *Entrance requirements:* For doctorate, GRE General Test (minimum scores: 153 Verbal/148 Quantitative/4.5 Analytical) or MCAT (for some programs). *Application deadline:* For fall admission, 12/1 for domestic and international students. Application fee: $70. Electronic applications accepted. *Financial support:* Health care benefits, tuition waivers (full), and full-tuition and stipends available. Financial award application deadline: 3/1; financial award applicants required to submit FAFSA. *Faculty research:* Ion conduction and gating in K+ channels, autonomic neuron plasticity, neurotransmitter/receptor expression, fetal/neonatal pharmacology, molecular pharmacology. *Unit head:* Dr. Robert Duvoisin, Program Director, E-mail: somgrad@ohsu.edu. *Application contact:* Brandi Colbert, Program Coordinator, E-mail: somgrad@ohsu.edu.

Oregon State University, College of Agricultural Sciences, Program in Fisheries Science, Corvallis, OR 97331. Offers aquaculture (MS); conservation biology (MS, PhD); fish genetics (MS, PhD); ichthyology (MS, PhD); limnology (MS, PhD); parasites and diseases (MS, PhD); physiology and ecology of marine and freshwater fishes (MS, PhD); stream ecology (MS, PhD); toxicology (MS, PhD); water pollution biology (MS, PhD). *Program availability:* Part-time. *Entrance requirements:* For master's and doctorate, GRE, minimum GPA of 3.0 in last 90 hours. Additional exam requirements/recommendations for international students: Required—TOEFL (minimum score 80 iBT), IELTS (minimum score 6.5). *Application deadline:* For fall admission, 5/1 for domestic students, 4/1 for international students. Application fee: $75 ($85 for international students). *Faculty research:* Fisheries ecology, fish toxicology, stream ecology, quantitative analyses of marine and freshwater fish populations. *Unit head:* Dr. Selina Heppell, Department Head/Professor of Fisheries, 541-737-9039, Fax: 541-737-3590, E-mail: selina.heppell@oregonstate.edu. *Application contact:* Dr. Selina Heppell, Department Head/Professor of Fisheries, 541-737-9039, Fax: 541-737-3590, E-mail: selina.heppell@oregonstate.edu.
Website: http://fw.oregonstate.edu/content/graduate

Penn State University Park, Graduate School, Intercollege Graduate Programs, Integrative and Biomedical Physiology Program, University Park, PA 16802. Offers integrative and biomedical physiology (MS, PhD). *Unit head:* Dr. Regina Vasilatos-Younken, Dean, 814-531-8567, Fax: 814-865-4627. *Application contact:* Lori Hawn, Director, Graduate Student Services, 814-865-1795, Fax: 814-863-4627, E-mail: l-gswww@lists.psu.edu.
Website: https://www.huck.psu.edu/content/graduate-programs/physiology

Physiology

Purdue University, School of Veterinary Medicine and Graduate School, Graduate Programs in Veterinary Medicine, Department of Basic Medical Sciences, West Lafayette, IN 47907. Offers anatomy (MS, PhD); pharmacology (MS, PhD); physiology (MS, PhD). *Program availability:* Part-time. Terminal master's awarded for partial completion of doctoral program. *Degree requirements:* For master's, thesis; for doctorate, thesis/dissertation. *Entrance requirements:* For master's and doctorate, GRE General Test. Additional exam requirements/recommendations for international students: Required—TOEFL. Electronic applications accepted. *Faculty research:* Development and regeneration, tissue injury and shock, biomedical engineering, ovarian function, bone and cartilage biology, cell and molecular biology.

Queen's University at Kingston, School of Graduate Studies, Faculty of Health Sciences, Department of Physiology, Kingston, ON K7L 3N6, Canada. Offers M Sc, PhD. *Degree requirements:* For master's, thesis; for doctorate, comprehensive exam, thesis/dissertation. *Entrance requirements:* For master's, minimum upper B average. Additional exam requirements/recommendations for international students: Required—TOEFL. *Faculty research:* Cardiovascular and respiratory physiology, exercise, gastrointestinal physiology, neuroscience.

Rocky Mountain University of Health Professions, Doctor of Science Program in Clinical Electrophysiology, Provo, UT 84606. Offers D Sc. *Program availability:* Online learning. *Degree requirements:* For doctorate, thesis/dissertation. *Entrance requirements:* For doctorate, clinical entry-level master's or doctorate degree; professional licensure as a chiropractor, nurse practitioner, occupational therapist, physical therapist, physician or physician assistant; minimum of 100 hours experience in electroneuromyography.

Rosalind Franklin University of Medicine and Science, School of Graduate and Postdoctoral Studies - Interdisciplinary Graduate Program in Biomedical Sciences, Department of Physiology and Biophysics, North Chicago, IL 60064-3095. Offers MS, PhD, MD/PhD. Terminal master's awarded for partial completion of doctoral program. *Degree requirements:* For master's, comprehensive exam, thesis; for doctorate, comprehensive exam, thesis/dissertation. *Entrance requirements:* For master's and doctorate, GRE General Test. Additional exam requirements/recommendations for international students: Required—TOEFL, TWE. *Faculty research:* Membrane transport, mechanisms of cellular regulation, brain metabolism, peptide metabolism.

Rush University, Graduate College, Department of Molecular Biophysics and Physiology, Chicago, IL 60612-3832. Offers physiology (PhD); MD/PhD. *Degree requirements:* For doctorate, thesis/dissertation. *Entrance requirements:* For doctorate, GRE General Test. Additional exam requirements/recommendations for international students: Required—TOEFL. *Faculty research:* Physiological exocytosis, raft formation and growth, voltage-gated proton channels, molecular biophysics and physiology.

Rutgers University–Newark, Graduate School of Biomedical Sciences, Department of Pharmacology and Physiology, Newark, NJ 07107. Offers PhD. *Degree requirements:* For doctorate, thesis/dissertation, qualifying exam. *Entrance requirements:* For doctorate, GRE General Test. Additional exam requirements/recommendations for international students: Required—TOEFL. Electronic applications accepted.

Rutgers University–New Brunswick, Graduate School-New Brunswick, Program in Endocrinology and Animal Biosciences, Piscataway, NJ 08854-8097. Offers MS, PhD. Terminal master's awarded for partial completion of doctoral program. *Degree requirements:* For master's, thesis; for doctorate, comprehensive exam, thesis/dissertation. *Entrance requirements:* For master's and doctorate, GRE General Test. Additional exam requirements/recommendations for international students: Required—TOEFL. Electronic applications accepted. *Faculty research:* Comparative and behavioral endocrinology, epigenetic regulation of the endocrine system, exercise physiology and immunology, fetal and neonatal developmental programming, mammary gland biology and breast cancer, neuroendocrinology and alcohol studies, reproductive and developmental toxicology.

Rutgers University–New Brunswick, Graduate School of Biomedical Sciences, Program in Physiology and Integrative Biology, Piscataway, NJ 08854-5635. Offers MS, PhD, MD/PhD. *Entrance requirements:* Additional exam requirements/recommendations for international students: Required—TOEFL. Electronic applications accepted.

Saint Louis University, Graduate Programs, School of Medicine, Graduate Programs in Biomedical Sciences and Graduate Programs, Department of Pharmacological and Physiological Science, St. Louis, MO 63103. Offers PhD. *Degree requirements:* For doctorate, comprehensive exam, thesis/dissertation, departmental qualifying exams. *Entrance requirements:* For doctorate, GRE General Test (GRE Subject Test optional), letters of recommendation, resume, interview. Additional exam requirements/recommendations for international students: Required—TOEFL (minimum score 525 paper-based). Electronic applications accepted. *Faculty research:* Molecular endocrinology, neuropharmacology, cardiovascular science, drug abuse, neurotransmitter and hormonal signaling mechanisms.

Salisbury University, Program in Applied Health Physiology, Salisbury, MD 21801-6837. Offers MS. *Program availability:* Part-time. *Faculty:* 5 full-time (0 women). *Students:* 27 full-time (11 women), 3 part-time (1 woman); includes 7 minority (4 Black or African American, non-Hispanic/Latino; 2 Asian, non-Hispanic/Latino; 1 Two or more races, non-Hispanic/Latino). Average age 24. 23 applicants, 74% accepted, 11 enrolled. In 2017, 20 master's awarded. *Entrance requirements:* For master's, GRE, two letters of recommendation; official transcripts from all colleges and universities attended; personal statement; minimum GPA of 3.0. Additional exam requirements/recommendations for international students: Required—TOEFL (minimum score 550 paper-based; 79 iBT), IELTS (minimum score 6.5). *Application deadline:* For fall admission, 8/1 for domestic and international students; for spring admission, 12/1 for domestic and international students. Application fee: $65. Electronic applications accepted. *Expenses:* $392 per credit hour resident; $703 per credit hour non-resident; $92 per credit hour fees. *Financial support:* In 2017–18, 10 students received support, including 15 teaching assistantships with full tuition reimbursements available (averaging $8,099 per year); career-related internships or fieldwork and scholarships/grants also available. Support available to part-time students. Financial award application deadline: 3/1; financial award applicants required to submit FAFSA. *Faculty research:* Peripheral arterial disease; pulmonary rehabilitation; professional perspectives of credentialing strata. *Unit head:* Dr. Carlton Insley, Graduate Program Director, Applied Health Physiology, 410-677-0145, E-mail: rcinsley@salisbury.edu. *Application contact:* Dr. Thomas Pellinger, Faculty, Applied Health Physiology, 410-677-0144, E-mail: tkpellinger@salisbury.edu.
Website: http://www.salisbury.edu/gsr/gradstudies/MSAHPHpage.html

San Francisco State University, Division of Graduate Studies, College of Science and Engineering, Department of Biology, Program in Physiology and Behavioral Biology, San Francisco, CA 94132-1722. Offers MS. *Application deadline:* Applications are processed on a rolling basis. *Unit head:* Dr. Megumi Fuse, Coordinator, 415-405-0728, Fax: 415-338-2295, E-mail: fuse@sfsu.edu.
Website: http://biology.sfsu.edu/graduate/physiology_and_behavior

San Jose State University, Graduate Studies and Research, College of Science, San Jose, CA 95192-0099. Offers bioinformatics (MS); biological sciences (MA, MS), including ecology and evolution (MS), molecular biology and microbiology (MS), physiology (MS); biotechnology (MBT); chemistry (MA, MS); computer science (MS); geology (MS); marine science (MS); mathematics (MA, MS), including mathematics education (MA); medical products development management (MS); meteorology (MS); physics (MS), including computational physics, modern optics, physics; statistics (MS). MS in marine science offered through Moss Landing Marine Labs. *Program availability:* Part-time. *Faculty:* 78 full-time (27 women), 25 part-time/adjunct (13 women). *Students:* 154 full-time (76 women), 212 part-time (102 women); includes 135 minority (4 Black or African American, non-Hispanic/Latino; 78 Asian, non-Hispanic/Latino; 27 Hispanic/Latino; 1 Native Hawaiian or other Pacific Islander, non-Hispanic/Latino; 25 Two or more races, non-Hispanic/Latino), 135 international. Average age 28. 1,156 applicants, 26% accepted, 179 enrolled. In 2017, 196 master's awarded. *Degree requirements:* For master's, comprehensive exam (for some programs), thesis (for some programs), directed reading, colloquium, project, writing project, statistical consulting. *Entrance requirements:* Additional exam requirements/recommendations for international students: Required—TOEFL (minimum score 550 paper-based; 80 iBT), IELTS (minimum score 6.5), TWE, PTE (minimum score 53). *Application deadline:* For fall admission, 2/1 for domestic and international students. Applications are processed on a rolling basis. Application fee: $55. Electronic applications accepted. *Expenses:* Tuition, state resident: full-time $7176. Tuition, nonresident: full-time $16,680. Tuition and fees vary according to course load and program. *Financial support:* Fellowships, research assistantships, career-related internships or fieldwork, Federal Work-Study, scholarships/grants, traineeships, tuition waivers (full and partial), and unspecified assistantships available. Support available to part-time students. Financial award application deadline: 4/28; financial award applicants required to submit FAFSA. *Unit head:* Dr. Michael Kaufman, Dean, 408-924-4800, Fax: 408-924-4815, E-mail: michael.kaufman@sjsu.edu.
Website: http://www.sjsu.edu/science/

Southern Illinois University Carbondale, Graduate School, Graduate Programs in Medicine, Program in Molecular, Cellular and Systemic Physiology, Carbondale, IL 62901-4701. Offers MS, PhD. *Degree requirements:* For doctorate, thesis/dissertation. *Entrance requirements:* For master's and doctorate, GRE.

Southern Methodist University, Simmons School of Education and Human Development, Department of Allied Physiology and Wellness, Dallas, TX 75275. Offers applied physiology (PhD); health promotion management (MS); sport management (MS). Program offered jointly with Cox School of Business. *Entrance requirements:* For master's, GMAT, resume, essays, transcripts from all colleges and universities attended, two references. Additional exam requirements/recommendations for international students: Required—TOEFL or PTE. *Unit head:* Dr. Lynn Romejko Jacobs, Department Chair, 214-768-1811, E-mail: lromejko@smu.edu. *Application contact:* Michael Lysko, Program Director, 214-768-7834, E-mail: mlysko@smu.edu.
Website: http://smu.edu/education/APW/

Stanford University, School of Medicine, Graduate Programs in Medicine, Department of Molecular and Cellular Physiology, Stanford, CA 94305-2004. Offers PhD. *Degree requirements:* For doctorate, thesis/dissertation, qualifying exams. *Entrance requirements:* For doctorate, GRE General Test, GRE Subject Test. Additional exam requirements/recommendations for international students: Required—TOEFL. Electronic applications accepted. *Expenses: Tuition:* Full-time $48,987; part-time $10,620 per quarter. One-time fee: $400. Tuition and fees vary according to program. *Faculty research:* Signal transduction, ion channels, intracellular calcium, synaptic transmission.

State University of New York Upstate Medical University, College of Graduate Studies, Program in Physiology, Syracuse, NY 13210. Offers MS, PhD, MD/PhD. Terminal master's awarded for partial completion of doctoral program. *Degree requirements:* For master's, thesis; for doctorate, comprehensive exam, thesis/dissertation. *Entrance requirements:* For master's, GRE General Test, interview; for doctorate, GRE General Test, telephone interview. Additional exam requirements/recommendations for international students: Required—TOEFL. Electronic applications accepted.

Stony Brook University, State University of New York, Stony Brook Medicine, School of Medicine and Graduate School, Graduate Programs in Medicine, Department of Physiology and Biophysics, Stony Brook, NY 11794. Offers PhD. *Faculty:* 12 full-time (4 women), 1 part-time/adjunct (0 women). *Students:* 31 full-time (6 women); includes 14 minority (3 Black or African American, non-Hispanic/Latino; 4 Asian, non-Hispanic/Latino; 7 Hispanic/Latino), 1 international. Average age 23. 5 applicants. In 2017, 2 doctorates awarded. *Degree requirements:* For doctorate, comprehensive exam, thesis/dissertation. *Entrance requirements:* For doctorate, GRE General Test, GRE Subject Test, BS in related field, minimum GPA of 3.0, recommendation. Additional exam requirements/recommendations for international students: Required—TOEFL (minimum score 550 paper-based). *Application deadline:* For fall admission, 1/15 for domestic students; for spring admission, 10/1 for domestic students. Application fee: $100. *Expenses:* Contact institution. *Financial support:* In 2017–18, 1 research assistantship was awarded; fellowships, teaching assistantships, and Federal Work-Study also available. Financial award application deadline: 3/15. *Faculty research:* Biophysics, human physiology, ion channels, physiology, signal transduction. *Total annual research expenditures:* $3.8 million. *Unit head:* Dr. Todd Miller, Chair, 631-444-3533, Fax: 631-444-3432, E-mail: todd.miller@stonybrook.edu. *Application contact:* Odalis Hernandez, Coordinator, 631-444-3057, Fax: 631-444-9749, E-mail: odalis.hernandez@stonybrook.edu.
Website: https://medicine.stonybrookmedicine.edu/pnb

Teachers College, Columbia University, Department of Biobehavioral Sciences, New York, NY 10027-6696. Offers applied exercise physiology (Ed M, MA, Ed D); communication sciences and disorders (MS, Ed D, PhD); kinesiology (PhD); motor learning and control (Ed M, MA); motor learning/movement science (Ed D); neuroscience and education (MS); physical education (MA, Ed D). *Accreditation:* ASHA. *Program availability:* Part-time, evening/weekend. *Students:* 180 full-time (160 women), 176 part-time (141 women); includes 149 minority (17 Black or African American, non-Hispanic/Latino; 40 Asian, non-Hispanic/Latino; 83 Hispanic/Latino; 9 Two or more races, non-Hispanic/Latino), 30 international. Average age 29. 738 applicants, 41% accepted, 164 enrolled. *Financial support:* Fellowships, teaching assistantships, career-related internships or fieldwork, Federal Work-Study, institutionally sponsored loans, traineeships, and tuition waivers (full and partial) available. Support available to part-time students. *Unit head:* Prof. Carol Garber, Chair, 212-678-3891, E-mail: garber@tc.columbia.edu. *Application contact:* David Estrella, Director of Admissions, 212-678-3305, E-mail: estrella@tc.columbia.edu.
Website: http://www.tc.columbia.edu/biobehavioral-sciences/

Tulane University, School of Medicine and School of Liberal Arts, Graduate Programs in Biomedical Sciences, Department of Physiology, New Orleans, LA 70118-5669. Offers MS. MS and PhD offered through the Graduate School. *Degree requirements:* For master's, one foreign language, thesis. *Entrance requirements:* For master's, GRE General Test, minimum B average in undergraduate course work. Additional exam requirements/recommendations for international students: Required—TOEFL. Electronic applications accepted. *Expenses: Tuition:* Full-time $50,920; part-time $2829 per credit hour. *Required fees:* $2040; $44.50 per credit hour. $580 per term. Tuition and fees vary according to course load, degree level and program. *Faculty research:* Renal microcirculation, neurophysiology, NA+ transport, renin/angio tensin system, cell and molecular endocrinology.

Universidad Central del Caribe, School of Medicine, Program in Biomedical Sciences, Bayamón, PR 00960-6032. Offers anatomy and cell biology (MA, MS); biochemistry (MS); biomedical sciences (MA); cellular and molecular biology (PhD); microbiology and immunology (MA, MS); pharmacology (MS); physiology (MS).

Université de Montréal, Faculty of Medicine, Department of Physiology, Montréal, QC H3C 3J7, Canada. Offers neurological sciences (M Sc, PhD); physiology (M Sc, PhD). Terminal master's awarded for partial completion of doctoral program. *Degree requirements:* For master's, thesis; for doctorate, thesis/dissertation, general exam. *Entrance requirements:* For master's and doctorate, proficiency in French, knowledge of English. Electronic applications accepted. *Faculty research:* Cardiovascular, neuropeptides, membrane transport and biophysics, signaling pathways.

Université de Sherbrooke, Faculty of Medicine and Health Sciences, Graduate Programs in Medicine, Department of Physiology and Biophysics, Sherbrooke, QC J1H 5N4, Canada. Offers M Sc, PhD. Terminal master's awarded for partial completion of doctoral program. *Degree requirements:* For master's, thesis; for doctorate, thesis/dissertation. Electronic applications accepted. *Faculty research:* Ion channels, neurological basis of pain, insulin resistance, obesity.

Université Laval, Faculty of Medicine, Graduate Programs in Medicine, Programs in Physiology-Endocrinology, Québec, QC G1K 7P4, Canada. Offers M Sc, PhD. Terminal master's awarded for partial completion of doctoral program. *Degree requirements:* For master's, thesis; for doctorate, comprehensive exam, thesis/dissertation. Electronic applications accepted.

University at Buffalo, the State University of New York, Graduate School, Jacobs School of Medicine and Biomedical Sciences, Graduate Programs in Medicine and Biomedical Sciences, Department of Physiology and Biophysics, Buffalo, NY 14203. Offers biophysics (MS, PhD); physiology (MA, PhD). *Faculty:* 17 full-time (4 women). *Students:* 6 full-time (1 woman); includes 4 minority (1 Black or African American, non-Hispanic/Latino; 3 Asian, non-Hispanic/Latino). Average age 27. 13 applicants, 23% accepted, 2 enrolled. In 2017, 2 master's, 3 doctorates awarded. Terminal master's awarded for partial completion of doctoral program. *Degree requirements:* For master's, comprehensive exam, thesis or alternative, oral exam, project; for doctorate, comprehensive exam, thesis/dissertation, oral and written qualifying exam or 2 research proposals. *Entrance requirements:* For master's, GRE General Test, unofficial transcripts, 3 letters of recommendation, personal statement, curriculum vitae; for doctorate, GRE General Test or MCAT, unofficial transcripts, 3 letters of recommendation, personal statement, curriculum vitae. Additional exam requirements/recommendations for international students: Required—TOEFL (minimum score 550 paper-based; 79 iBT). *Application deadline:* Applications are processed on a rolling basis. Application fee: $85. Electronic applications accepted. *Expenses:* Contact institution. *Financial support:* In 2017–18, 1 research assistantship with full tuition reimbursement (averaging $27,000 per year) was awarded; health care benefits also available. Financial award applicants required to submit FAFSA. *Faculty research:* Neurosciences, ion channels, cardiac physiology, renal/epithelial transport, cardiopulmonary exercise. *Total annual research expenditures:* $2.7 million. *Unit head:* Dr. Perry M. Hogan, Chair, 716-829-2738, Fax: 716-829-2344, E-mail: phogan@buffalo.edu. *Application contact:* Kara M. Rickicki, Graduate Programs Coordinator, 716-829-2417, Fax: 716-829-2344, E-mail: rickicki@buffalo.edu.
Website: https://medicine.buffalo.edu/departments/physiology.html

University of Alberta, Faculty of Graduate Studies and Research, Department of Biological Sciences, Edmonton, AB T6G 2E1, Canada. Offers environmental biology and ecology (M Sc, PhD); microbiology and biotechnology (M Sc, PhD); molecular biology and genetics (M Sc, PhD); physiology and cell biology (M Sc, PhD); plant biology (M Sc, PhD); systematics and evolution (M Sc, PhD). Terminal master's awarded for partial completion of doctoral program. *Degree requirements:* For master's, thesis; for doctorate, thesis/dissertation. *Entrance requirements:* Additional exam requirements/recommendations for international students: Required—TOEFL.

University of Alberta, Faculty of Medicine and Dentistry and Faculty of Graduate Studies and Research, Graduate Programs in Medicine, Department of Physiology, Edmonton, AB T6G 2E1, Canada. Offers M Sc, PhD. Terminal master's awarded for partial completion of doctoral program. *Degree requirements:* For master's, thesis; for doctorate, thesis/dissertation. *Entrance requirements:* For master's and doctorate, minimum GPA of 3.0. Additional exam requirements/recommendations for international students: Required—TOEFL (minimum score 580 paper-based). Electronic applications accepted. *Faculty research:* Membrane transport, cell biology, perinatal endocrinology, neurophysiology, cardiovascular.

The University of Arizona, Graduate Interdisciplinary Programs, Graduate Interdisciplinary Program in Physiological Sciences, Tucson, AZ 85721. Offers MS, PhD. *Degree requirements:* For doctorate, thesis/dissertation. *Entrance requirements:* For master's, GRE General Test, 3 letters of recommendation, statement of purpose; for doctorate, GRE General Test, 3 letters of recommendation. Additional exam requirements/recommendations for international students: Required—TOEFL (minimum score 600 paper-based). Electronic applications accepted. *Faculty research:* Cellular transport and signaling, receptor and messenger modulation, neural interaction and biomechanics, fluid network regulation, environmental adaptation.

University of Arkansas for Medical Sciences, Graduate School, Little Rock, AR 72205. Offers biochemistry and molecular biology (MS, PhD); bioinformatics (MS, PhD); cellular physiology and molecular biophysics (MS, PhD); clinical nutrition (MS); interdisciplinary biomedical sciences (MS, PhD, Certificate); interdisciplinary toxicology (MS); microbiology and immunology (PhD); neurobiology and developmental sciences (PhD); pharmacology (PhD); MD/PhD. Bioinformatics programs hosted jointly with the University of Arkansas at Little Rock. *Program availability:* Part-time. Terminal master's awarded for partial completion of doctoral program. *Degree requirements:* For master's, comprehensive exam (for some programs), thesis (for some programs); for doctorate, thesis/dissertation. *Entrance requirements:* For master's and doctorate, GRE. Additional exam requirements/recommendations for international students: Required—TOEFL. Electronic applications accepted. *Expenses:* Contact institution.

University of Calgary, Cumming School of Medicine and Faculty of Graduate Studies, Medical Science Graduate Program, Calgary, AB T2N 1N4, Canada. Offers cancer biology (M Sc, PhD); critical care medicine (M Sc, PhD); joint injury and arthritis (M Sc, PhD); molecular and medical genetics (M Sc, PhD); mountain medicine and high altitude physiology (M Sc, PhD); pathologists' assistant (M Sc, PhD). *Degree requirements:* For master's, thesis; for doctorate, thesis/dissertation, candidacy exam. *Entrance requirements:* For master's, minimum undergraduate GPA of 3.2; for doctorate, minimum graduate GPA of 3.2. Additional exam requirements/recommendations for international students: Required—TOEFL (minimum score 600 paper-based). Electronic applications accepted. *Faculty research:* Cancer biology, immunology, joint injury and arthritis, medical education, population genomics.

University of Calgary, Cumming School of Medicine and Faculty of Graduate Studies, Program in Gastrointestinal Sciences, Calgary, AB T2N 1N4, Canada. Offers M Sc, PhD. *Degree requirements:* For master's, thesis; for doctorate, thesis/dissertation, candidacy exam. *Entrance requirements:* For master's and doctorate, minimum GPA of 3.2 during previous 2 years. Additional exam requirements/recommendations for international students: Required—TOEFL. Electronic applications accepted. *Faculty research:* Physiology, biochemistry, molecular biology, pharmacology, immunology.

University of California, Berkeley, Graduate Division, College of Letters and Science, Group in Endocrinology, Berkeley, CA 94720-1500. Offers MA, PhD. *Degree requirements:* For doctorate, thesis/dissertation, oral qualifying exam. *Entrance requirements:* For master's, GRE General Test or the equivalent (MCAT), minimum GPA of 3.0, 3 letters of recommendation; for doctorate, GRE General Test or the equivalent (MCAT), minimum GPA of 3.4, 3 letters of recommendation. Additional exam requirements/recommendations for international students: Required—TOEFL. Electronic applications accepted.

University of California, Davis, Graduate Studies, Molecular, Cellular and Integrative Physiology Graduate Group, Davis, CA 95616. Offers MS, PhD. *Degree requirements:* For master's, comprehensive exam (for some programs), thesis (for some programs); for doctorate, thesis/dissertation. *Entrance requirements:* For master's and doctorate, GRE General Test. Additional exam requirements/recommendations for international students: Required—TOEFL (minimum score 550 paper-based). Electronic applications accepted. *Faculty research:* Systemic physiology, cellular physiology, neurophysiology, cardiovascular physiology, endocrinology.

University of California, Irvine, School of Medicine and Francisco J. Ayala School of Biological Sciences, Department of Physiology and Biophysics, Irvine, CA 92697. Offers biological sciences (PhD); MD/PhD. *Students:* 14 full-time (6 women), 1 part-time (0 women); includes 7 minority (1 American Indian or Alaska Native, non-Hispanic/Latino; 4 Asian, non-Hispanic/Latino; 2 Hispanic/Latino), 4 international. Average age 29. In 2017, 3 doctorates awarded. *Entrance requirements:* For doctorate, GRE General Test, GRE Subject Test, minimum GPA of 3.0. Additional exam requirements/recommendations for international students: Required—TOEFL (minimum score 550 paper-based). *Application deadline:* For fall admission, 1/15 priority date for domestic students, 1/15 for international students. Application fee: $105 ($125 for international students). Electronic applications accepted. *Financial support:* Fellowships, research assistantships with full tuition reimbursements, teaching assistantships, institutionally sponsored loans, traineeships, health care benefits, and unspecified assistantships available. Financial award application deadline: 3/1; financial award applicants required to submit FAFSA. *Faculty research:* Membrane physiology, exercise physiology, regulation of hormone biosynthesis and action, endocrinology, ion channels and signal transduction. *Unit head:* Prof. Michael Cahalan, Chair, 949-824-7776, Fax: 949-824-3143, E-mail: mcahalan@uci.edu. *Application contact:* Janita Parpana, Chief Administrative Officer, 949-824-6833, Fax: 949-824-8540, E-mail: jparpana@uci.edu.
Website: http://www.physiology.uci.edu/

University of California, Los Angeles, David Geffen School of Medicine and Graduate Division, Graduate Programs in Medicine, Department of Physiology, Los Angeles, CA 90095. Offers PhD. *Degree requirements:* For doctorate, thesis/dissertation, oral and written qualifying exams. *Entrance requirements:* For doctorate, GRE General Test, GRE Subject Test. *Faculty research:* Membrane physiology, cell physiology, muscle physiology, neurophysiology, cardiopulmonary physiology.

University of California, Los Angeles, Graduate Division, College of Letters and Science, Department of Integrative Biology and Physiology, Los Angeles, CA 90095. Offers physiological science (MS). *Degree requirements:* For master's, thesis. *Entrance requirements:* For master's, GRE General Test or MCAT, bachelor's degree; minimum undergraduate GPA of 3.0 (or its equivalent if letter grade system not used). Additional exam requirements/recommendations for international students: Required—TOEFL. Electronic applications accepted.

University of California, Los Angeles, Graduate Division, College of Letters and Science and David Geffen School of Medicine, UCLA ACCESS to Programs in the Molecular, Cellular and Integrative Life Sciences, Los Angeles, CA 90095. Offers biochemistry and molecular biology (PhD); biological chemistry (PhD); cellular and molecular pathology (PhD); human genetics (PhD); microbiology, immunology, and molecular genetics (PhD); molecular biology (PhD); molecular toxicology (PhD); molecular, cellular and integrative physiology (PhD); neurobiology (PhD); oral biology (PhD); physiology (PhD). *Degree requirements:* For doctorate, thesis/dissertation, oral and written qualifying exams. *Entrance requirements:* For doctorate, GRE General Test, bachelor's degree; minimum undergraduate GPA of 3.0 (or its equivalent if letter grade system not used). Additional exam requirements/recommendations for international students: Required—TOEFL. Electronic applications accepted.

University of Central Florida, College of Community Innovation and Education, Department of Learning Sciences and Educational Research, Program in Sport and Exercise Science, Orlando, FL 32816. Offers applied exercise physiology (MS). *Program availability:* Part-time, evening/weekend. *Students:* 51 full-time (23 women), 16 part-time (7 women); includes 18 minority (4 Black or African American, non-Hispanic/Latino; 1 American Indian or Alaska Native, non-Hispanic/Latino; 2 Asian, non-Hispanic/Latino; 10 Hispanic/Latino; 1 Two or more races, non-Hispanic/Latino), 5 international. Average age 26. 95 applicants, 66% accepted, 39 enrolled. In 2017, 41 master's awarded. *Degree requirements:* For master's, thesis or alternative. *Entrance requirements:* For master's, GRE General Test, letters of recommendation, resume. Additional exam requirements/recommendations for international students: Required—TOEFL. *Application deadline:* For fall admission, 7/15 for domestic students; for spring admission, 12/1 for domestic students; for summer admission, 4/15 for domestic students. Application fee: $30. Electronic applications accepted. *Expenses:* Tuition, state resident: part-time $288.16 per credit hour. Tuition, nonresident: part-time $1073.31 per credit hour. Tuition and fees vary according to program. *Financial support:* In 2017–18, 6 students received support, including 6 research assistantships with partial tuition reimbursements available (averaging $7,380 per year), 2 teaching assistantships with partial tuition reimbursements available (averaging $8,406 per year); fellowships, career-related internships or fieldwork, Federal Work-Study, institutionally sponsored loans, tuition waivers (partial), and unspecified assistantships also available. Financial award application deadline: 3/1; financial award applicants required to submit FAFSA. *Unit head:* Dr. David Fukuda, Program Coordinator, 407-823-0442, E-mail: david.fukuda@ucf.edu. *Application contact:* Associate Director, Graduate Admissions, 407-823-2766, Fax: 407-823-6442, E-mail: gradadmissions@ucf.edu.
Website: http://education.ucf.edu/sportexscience/

University of Colorado Boulder, Graduate School, College of Arts and Sciences, Department of Integrative Physiology, Boulder, CO 80309. Offers MS, PhD. *Faculty:* 23 full-time (7 women). *Students:* 62 full-time (29 women); includes 10 minority (1 Black or African American, non-Hispanic/Latino; 3 Asian, non-Hispanic/Latino; 5 Hispanic/Latino; 1 Two or more races, non-Hispanic/Latino), 3 international. Average age 27. 78 applicants, 19% accepted, 14 enrolled. In 2017, 15 master's, 8 doctorates awarded. Terminal master's awarded for partial completion of doctoral program. *Degree requirements:* For master's, comprehensive exam, thesis or alternative; for doctorate,

thesis/dissertation. *Entrance requirements:* For master's, GRE General Test, minimum undergraduate GPA of 2.75. *Application deadline:* For fall admission, 1/10 for domestic students; for spring admission, 12/1 for domestic students. Applications are processed on a rolling basis. Application fee: $60 ($80 for international students). Electronic applications accepted. Application fee is waived when completed online. *Financial support:* In 2017–18, 183 students received support, including 52 fellowships (averaging $5,252 per year), 22 research assistantships with full and partial tuition reimbursements available (averaging $23,500 per year), 44 teaching assistantships with full and partial tuition reimbursements available (averaging $35,806 per year); institutionally sponsored loans, scholarships/grants, health care benefits, and unspecified assistantships also available. Financial award application deadline: 2/15; financial award applicants required to submit FAFSA. *Faculty research:* Aging/gerontology; nervous system; neurophysiology; neuroscience; physiological controls and systems. *Total annual research expenditures:* $8.2 million. *Application contact:* E-mail: iphygrad@colorado.edu.
Website: http://www.colorado.edu/intphys/

University of Connecticut, Graduate School, College of Liberal Arts and Sciences, Department of Physiology and Neurobiology, Storrs, CT 06269. Offers comparative physiology (MS, PhD). Terminal master's awarded for partial completion of doctoral program. *Degree requirements:* For master's, comprehensive exam; for doctorate, thesis/dissertation. *Entrance requirements:* For master's and doctorate, GRE General Test, GRE Subject Test. Additional exam requirements/recommendations for international students: Required—TOEFL (minimum score 550 paper-based). Electronic applications accepted.

University of Delaware, College of Arts and Sciences, Department of Biological Sciences, Newark, DE 19716. Offers biotechnology (MS); cancer biology (MS, PhD); cell and extracellular matrix biology (MS, PhD); cell and systems physiology (MS, PhD); developmental biology (MS, PhD); ecology and evolution (MS, PhD); microbiology (MS, PhD); molecular biology and genetics (MS, PhD). Terminal master's awarded for partial completion of doctoral program. *Degree requirements:* For master's, thesis, preliminary exam; for doctorate, comprehensive exam, thesis/dissertation, preliminary exam. *Entrance requirements:* For master's and doctorate, GRE General Test. Additional exam requirements/recommendations for international students: Required—TOEFL (minimum score 600 paper-based); Recommended—TWE. Electronic applications accepted. *Faculty research:* Microorganisms, bone, cancer metastasis, developmental biology, cell biology, DNA.

University of Delaware, College of Health Sciences, Department of Kinesiology and Applied Physiology, Newark, DE 19716. Offers MS, PhD.

University of Florida, College of Medicine and Graduate School, Interdisciplinary Program in Biomedical Sciences, Concentration in Physiology and Pharmacology, Gainesville, FL 32611. Offers PhD. *Degree requirements:* For doctorate, thesis/dissertation. *Entrance requirements:* For doctorate, GRE General Test, minimum GPA of 3.0, biochemistry before enrollment. Electronic applications accepted.

University of Florida, Graduate School, College of Health and Human Performance, Department of Applied Physiology and Kinesiology, Gainesville, FL 32611. Offers applied physiology and kinesiology (MS); athletic training/sports medicine (MS); biobehavioral science (MS); clinical exercise physiology (MS); exercise physiology (MS); health and human performance (PhD), including applied physiology and kinesiology, biobehavioral science, exercise physiology; human performance (MS). *Degree requirements:* For master's, comprehensive exam, thesis (for some programs); for doctorate, comprehensive exam, thesis/dissertation. *Entrance requirements:* For master's and doctorate, GRE General Test, minimum GPA of 3.0. Additional exam requirements/recommendations for international students: Required—TOEFL (minimum score 550 paper-based; 80 iBT), IELTS (minimum score 6). Electronic applications accepted. *Faculty research:* Cardiovascular disease; basic mechanisms that underlie exercise-induced changes in the body at the organ, tissue, cellular and molecular level; development of rehabilitation techniques for regaining motor control after stroke or as a consequence of Parkinson's disease; maintaining optimal health and delaying age-related declines in physiological function; psychomotor mechanisms impacting health and performance across the life span.

University of Georgia, College of Veterinary Medicine, Department of Physiology and Pharmacology, Athens, GA 30602. Offers pharmacology (MS, PhD). *Degree requirements:* For master's, thesis; for doctorate, one foreign language, thesis/dissertation. *Entrance requirements:* For master's and doctorate, GRE General Test. Electronic applications accepted.

University of Guelph, Ontario Veterinary College and Graduate Studies, Graduate Programs in Veterinary Sciences, Department of Biomedical Sciences, Guelph, ON N1G 2W1, Canada. Offers morphology (M Sc, DV Sc, PhD); neuroscience (M Sc, DV Sc, PhD); pharmacology (M Sc, DV Sc, PhD); physiology (M Sc, DV Sc, PhD); toxicology (M Sc, DV Sc, PhD). *Program availability:* Part-time. *Degree requirements:* For master's, thesis; for doctorate, comprehensive exam, thesis/dissertation. *Entrance requirements:* For master's, honors B Sc, minimum 75% average in last 20 courses; for doctorate, M Sc with thesis from accredited institution. Additional exam requirements/recommendations for international students: Required—TOEFL (minimum score 550 paper-based; 89 iBT). Electronic applications accepted. *Faculty research:* Cellular morphology; endocrine, vascular and reproductive physiology; clinical pharmacology; veterinary toxicology; developmental biology, neuroscience.

University of Hawaii at Manoa, John A. Burns School of Medicine, Program in Developmental and Reproductive Biology, Honolulu, HI 96813. Offers MS, PhD. *Program availability:* Part-time. *Degree requirements:* For doctorate, thesis/dissertation. *Entrance requirements:* For doctorate, GRE General Test, GRE Subject Test. Additional exam requirements/recommendations for international students: Recommended—TOEFL (minimum score 560 paper-based), IELTS (minimum score 5). *Faculty research:* Biology of gametes and fertilization, reproductive endocrinology.

University of Illinois at Chicago, College of Medicine and Graduate College, Graduate Programs in Medicine, Department of Physiology and Biophysics, Chicago, IL 60607-7128. Offers MS, PhD. Terminal master's awarded for partial completion of doctoral program. *Degree requirements:* For master's, thesis; for doctorate, thesis/dissertation. *Entrance requirements:* For master's and doctorate, GRE General Test. Additional exam requirements/recommendations for international students: Required—TOEFL. Electronic applications accepted. *Faculty research:* Neuroscience, endocrinology and reproduction, cell physiology, exercise physiology, NMR, cardiovascular physiology and metabolism, cytoskeleton and vascular biology, gastrointestinal and epithelial cell biology, reproductive and endocrine sciences.

University of Illinois at Urbana–Champaign, Graduate College, College of Liberal Arts and Sciences, School of Molecular and Cellular Biology, Department of Molecular and Integrative Physiology, Champaign, IL 61820. Offers MS, PhD.

The University of Iowa, Roy J. and Lucille A. Carver College of Medicine and Graduate College, Graduate Programs in Medicine, Department of Molecular Physiology and Biophysics, Iowa City, IA 52242. Offers MS, PhD. *Degree requirements:* For master's, comprehensive exam; for doctorate, comprehensive exam, thesis/dissertation. *Entrance requirements:* For master's, GRE General Test; for doctorate, GRE. Additional exam requirements/recommendations for international students: Required—TOEFL. Electronic applications accepted. *Faculty research:* Cellular and molecular endocrinology, membrane structure and function, cardiac cell electrophysiology, regulation of gene expression, neurophysiology.

The University of Kansas, University of Kansas Medical Center, School of Medicine, Department of Molecular and Integrative Physiology, Kansas City, KS 66160. Offers PhD, MD/PhD. *Faculty:* 33. *Students:* 16 full-time (10 women); includes 1 minority (Hispanic/Latino), 7 international. Average age 29. In 2017, 10 doctorates awarded. Terminal master's awarded for partial completion of doctoral program. *Degree requirements:* For doctorate, comprehensive exam, thesis/dissertation. *Entrance requirements:* For doctorate, GRE. Additional exam requirements/recommendations for international students: Required—TOEFL. *Application deadline:* For fall admission, 12/1 priority date for domestic and international students. Applications are processed on a rolling basis. Application fee: $60. Electronic applications accepted. *Expenses:* $412.89 per credit hour in-state, $418.77 per semester campus fees (not including summer). *Financial support:* In 2017–18, 2 fellowships with full tuition reimbursements (averaging $30,000 per year), 8 research assistantships with partial tuition reimbursements (averaging $24,000 per year), 2 teaching assistantships with full tuition reimbursements (averaging $24,000 per year) were awarded; scholarships/grants and unspecified assistantships also available. Financial award application deadline: 3/1; financial award applicants required to submit FAFSA. *Faculty research:* Male reproductive physiology and contraception, ovarian development and regulation by pituitary and hypothalamus, neural control of movement and stroke recovery, cardio-pulmonary physiology and hypoxia, plasticity of the autonomic nervous system, renal physiology, exercise physiology, diabetes, cancer biology. *Total annual research expenditures:* $2.8 million. *Unit head:* Dr. Victor G. Blanco, Chair, 913-588-7400, Fax: 913-588-7430, E-mail: gblanco@kumc.edu. *Application contact:* Dr. Michael W. Wolfe, Director of Graduate Studies, 913-588-7418, Fax: 913-588-7430, E-mail: mwolfe2@kumc.edu.
Website: http://www.kumc.edu/school-of-medicine/molecular-and-integrative-physiology.html

University of Kentucky, Graduate School, Graduate School Programs from the College of Medicine, Program in Physiology, Lexington, KY 40506-0032. Offers PhD. *Degree requirements:* For doctorate, comprehensive exam, thesis/dissertation. *Entrance requirements:* For doctorate, GRE General Test, minimum undergraduate GPA of 2.75, graduate 3.0. Additional exam requirements/recommendations for international students: Required—TOEFL (minimum score 550 paper-based). Electronic applications accepted.

University of Louisville, School of Medicine, Department of Physiology, Louisville, KY 40292-0001. Offers MS, PhD, MD/PhD. *Faculty:* 17 full-time (3 women), 4 part-time/adjunct (0 women). *Students:* 45 full-time (26 women), 3 part-time (2 women); includes 17 minority (9 Black or African American, non-Hispanic/Latino; 7 Asian, non-Hispanic/Latino; 1 Two or more races, non-Hispanic/Latino), 5 international. Average age 27. 52 applicants, 65% accepted, 33 enrolled. In 2017, 2 master's, 2 doctorates awarded. *Degree requirements:* For doctorate, comprehensive exam, thesis/dissertation. *Entrance requirements:* For master's and doctorate, GRE General Test (minimum score of 1000 verbal and quantitative), minimum GPA of 3.0. Additional exam requirements/recommendations for international students: Required—TOEFL (minimum score 550 paper-based). *Application deadline:* For winter admission, 2/15 for international students; for spring admission, 2/15 for domestic students; for summer admission, 7/15 for domestic students, 7/1 for international students. Applications are processed on a rolling basis. Application fee: $65. Electronic applications accepted. *Expenses:* Tuition, state resident: full-time $12,246; part-time $681 per credit hour. Tuition, nonresident: full-time $25,486; part-time $1417 per credit hour. *Required fees:* $196. Tuition and fees vary according to course load, program and reciprocity agreements. *Financial support:* In 2017–18, 4 fellowships with full tuition reimbursements (averaging $23,500 per year) were awarded; health care benefits also available. Financial award application deadline: 4/15. *Faculty research:* Cardiac regeneration, vascular remodeling, cerebral microcirculation, renal vasculature. *Total annual research expenditures:* $3 million. *Unit head:* Dr. Irving G. Joshua, Chair, 502-852-5371, Fax: 502-852-6239, E-mail: igjosh01@louisville.edu. *Application contact:* Dr. William Wead, Director of Admissions, 502-852-7571, Fax: 502-852-6849, E-mail: wbwead01@gwise.louisville.edu.
Website: http://louisville.edu/medicine/departments/physiology

The University of Manchester, School of Biological Sciences, Manchester, United Kingdom. Offers adaptive organismal biology (M Phil, PhD); animal biology (M Phil, PhD); biochemistry (M Phil, PhD); bioinformatics (M Phil, PhD); biomolecular sciences (M Phil, PhD); biotechnology (M Phil, PhD); cell biology (M Phil, PhD); cell matrix research (M Phil, PhD); channels and transporters (M Phil, PhD); developmental biology (M Phil, PhD); environmental biology (M Phil, PhD); evolutionary biology (M Phil, PhD); gene expression (M Phil, PhD); genetics (M Phil, PhD); history of science, technology and medicine (M Phil, PhD); immunology (M Phil, PhD); integrative neurobiology and behavior (M Phil, PhD); membrane trafficking (M Phil, PhD); microbiology (M Phil, PhD); molecular and cellular neuroscience (M Phil, PhD); molecular biology (M Phil, PhD); molecular cancer studies (M Phil, PhD); neuroscience (M Phil, PhD); ophthalmology (M Phil, PhD); optometry (M Phil, PhD); organelle function (M Phil, PhD); pharmacology (M Phil, PhD); physiology (M Phil, PhD); plant sciences (M Phil, PhD); stem cell research (M Phil, PhD); structural biology (M Phil, PhD); systems neuroscience (M Phil, PhD); toxicology (M Phil, PhD).

University of Manitoba, Max Rady College of Medicine and Faculty of Graduate Studies, Graduate Programs in Medicine, Department of Physiology and Pathophysiology, Winnipeg, MB R3T 2N2, Canada. Offers M Sc, PhD, MD/PhD. Terminal master's awarded for partial completion of doctoral program. *Degree requirements:* For master's, one foreign language, thesis; for doctorate, one foreign language, thesis/dissertation. *Entrance requirements:* For master's, minimum GPA of 3.5; for doctorate, minimum GPA of 3.5, M Sc. *Faculty research:* Cardiovascular research, gene technology, cell biology, neuroscience, respiration.

University of Massachusetts Amherst, Graduate School, Interdisciplinary Programs, Program in Plant Biology, Amherst, MA 01003. Offers biochemistry and metabolism (MS, PhD); cell biology and physiology (MS, PhD); environmental, ecological and integrative biology (MS, PhD); genetics and evolution (MS, PhD). *Degree requirements:* For master's, thesis; for doctorate, 2 foreign languages, comprehensive exam, thesis/dissertation. *Entrance requirements:* For master's and doctorate, GRE General Test. Additional exam requirements/recommendations for international students: Required—TOEFL (minimum score 550 paper-based; 80 iBT), IELTS (minimum score 6.5). Electronic applications accepted.

University of Miami, Graduate School, Miller School of Medicine, Graduate Programs in Medicine, Department of Physiology and Biophysics, Coral Gables, FL 33124. Offers PhD, MD/PhD. *Degree requirements:* For doctorate, thesis/dissertation, qualifying exam. *Entrance requirements:* For doctorate, GRE General Test, minimum GPA of 3.0 in sciences. Additional exam requirements/recommendations for international students: Required—TOEFL. *Faculty research:* Cell and membrane physiology, cell-to-cell communication, molecular neurobiology, neuroimmunology, neural development.

University of Michigan, Rackham Graduate School, Program in Biomedical Sciences (PIBS), Department of Molecular and Integrative Physiology, Ann Arbor, MI 48109-5622. Offers MS, PhD. *Faculty:* 48 full-time (16 women), 12 part-time/adjunct (5 women). *Students:* 78 full-time (36 women); includes 20 minority (2 Black or African American, non-Hispanic/Latino; 1 American Indian or Alaska Native, non-Hispanic/Latino; 12 Asian, non-Hispanic/Latino; 5 Hispanic/Latino). Average age 25. 194 applicants, 33% accepted, 43 enrolled. In 2017, 31 master's, 5 doctorates awarded. *Degree requirements:* For master's, thesis (for some programs), capstone project (for some programs); for doctorate, thesis/dissertation, oral defense of dissertation, preliminary exam. *Entrance requirements:* For master's, GRE, MCAT, DAT or PCAT, minimum science and overall GPA of 3.0; for doctorate, GRE General Test, 3 letters of recommendation, research experience. Additional exam requirements/recommendations for international students: Required—TOEFL (minimum score 84 iBT) or Michigan English Language Assessment Battery. *Application deadline:* For fall admission, 12/1 for domestic and international students. Application fee: $75 ($90 for international students). Electronic applications accepted. *Expenses:* Tuition, state resident: full-time $22,368; part-time $1201 per credit hour. Tuition, nonresident: full-time $45,156; part-time $2467 per credit hour. *Required fees:* $376 per term. Tuition and fees vary according to course load, degree level and program. *Financial support:* In 2017–18, 33 students received support, including 33 fellowships with full tuition reimbursements available (averaging $30,600 per year); scholarships/grants, health care benefits, tuition waivers (full), and unspecified assistantships also available. Financial award application deadline: 12/1. *Faculty research:* Ion transport, cardiovascular physiology, gene expression, hormone action, gastrointestinal physiology, endocrinology, muscle, signal transduction. *Unit head:* Dr. Santiago Schnell, Interim Chair, 734-764-4376, Fax: 734-936-8813, E-mail: schnells@umich.edu. *Application contact:* Michelle DiMondo, Director of Student Life, 734-647-5773, Fax: 734-647-7022, E-mail: mdimondo@umich.edu.
Website: http://medicine.umich.edu/dept/molecular-integrative-physiology

University of Minnesota, Duluth, Medical School, Graduate Program in Physiology, Duluth, MN 55812-2496. Offers MS, PhD. MS, PhD offered jointly with University of Minnesota, Twin Cities Campus. Terminal master's awarded for partial completion of doctoral program. *Degree requirements:* For master's, thesis; for doctorate, thesis/dissertation. *Entrance requirements:* For master's, GRE or MCAT; for doctorate, GRE or MCAT, 1 year of course work in each calculus, physics, and biology; 2 years of course work in chemistry; minimum GPA of 3.0 in science. Additional exam requirements/recommendations for international students: Required—TOEFL. *Faculty research:* Neural control of posture and locomotion, transport and metabolic phenomena in biological systems, control of organ blood flow, intracellular means of communication.

University of Minnesota, Twin Cities Campus, Graduate School, Department of Integrative Biology and Physiology, Minneapolis, MN 55455-0213. Offers PhD. *Program availability:* Part-time. *Degree requirements:* For doctorate, comprehensive exam, thesis/dissertation. *Entrance requirements:* For doctorate, GRE General Test. Electronic applications accepted. *Faculty research:* Cardiovascular physiology.

University of Mississippi Medical Center, School of Graduate Studies in the Health Sciences, Department of Physiology and Biophysics, Jackson, MS 39216-4505. Offers PhD, MD/PhD. *Degree requirements:* For doctorate, thesis/dissertation, first authored publication. *Entrance requirements:* For doctorate, GRE General Test, minimum GPA of 3.0. *Faculty research:* Cardiovascular, renal, endocrine, and cellular neurophysiology; molecular physiology.

University of Missouri, School of Medicine and Office of Research and Graduate Studies, Graduate Programs in Medicine, Department of Medical Pharmacology and Physiology, Columbia, MO 65211. Offers MS, PhD. *Degree requirements:* For master's, thesis; for doctorate, thesis/dissertation. *Entrance requirements:* For master's and doctorate, GRE General Test, minimum GPA of 3.0. Additional exam requirements/recommendations for international students: Required—TOEFL (minimum score 500 paper-based; 61 iBT). Application fee: $75 ($90 for international students). *Expenses:* Tuition, state resident: full-time $6480. Tuition, nonresident: full-time $17,744. *Required fees:* $1108. Tuition and fees vary according to course load, campus/location and program. *Financial support:* Fellowships, research assistantships, teaching assistantships, institutionally sponsored loans, scholarships/grants, health care benefits, and unspecified assistantships available. Support available to part-time students.
Website: http://mpp.missouri.edu/

University of Nebraska Medical Center, Interdisciplinary Graduate Program in Biomedical Sciences, Integrative Physiology and Molecular Medicine Doctoral Program, Omaha, NE 68198-5850. Offers PhD. *Program availability:* Part-time. *Faculty:* 12 full-time (2 women). *Students:* 2 full-time (both women), both international. Average age 29. 3 applicants, 33% accepted, 1 enrolled. *Degree requirements:* For doctorate, comprehensive exam, thesis/dissertation, at least one first-author research publication. *Entrance requirements:* For doctorate, GRE General Test or MCAT, course work in biology, chemistry, mathematics, and physics; minimum GPA of 3.25. Additional exam requirements/recommendations for international students: Required—TOEFL (minimum score 600 paper-based; 95 iBT), IELTS (minimum score 7). *Application deadline:* For fall admission, 6/1 for domestic students, 4/1 for international students. Applications are processed on a rolling basis. Electronic applications accepted. *Expenses:* Tuition, state resident: full-time $8451; part-time $4225 per semester. Tuition, nonresident: full-time $24,219; part-time $11,295 per semester. *Required fees:* $589; $117 per term. *Financial support:* In 2017–18, 2 research assistantships with full tuition reimbursements (averaging $26,500 per year) were awarded; fellowships, scholarships/grants, health care benefits, and unspecified assistantships also available. Support available to part-time students. Financial award application deadline: 2/1; financial award applicants required to submit FAFSA. *Faculty research:* Cardiovascular, neuroscience, renal physiology and pathophysiology, cardiopulmonary and renal consequences of heart failure, free radical biology, reproductive endocrinology, inflammation. *Total annual research expenditures:* $4.1 million. *Unit head:* Dr. Pamela K. Carmines, Vice Chair for Graduate Education, Department of Cellular and Integrative Physiology, 402-559-9343, Fax: 402-559-4438, E-mail: pcarmines@unmc.edu. *Application contact:* Kim Kavan, Office Associate, 402-559-4426, E-mail: kimberly.kavan@unmc.edu.
Website: https://www.unmc.edu/physiology/education/ipmmprogram/index.html

University of Nevada, Reno, Graduate School, Interdisciplinary Program in Cellular and Molecular Pharmacology and Physiology, Reno, NV 89557. Offers PhD. *Degree requirements:* For doctorate, one foreign language, thesis/dissertation. *Entrance requirements:* For doctorate, GRE General Test or MCAT, minimum GPA of 3.0. Additional exam requirements/recommendations for international students: Required—TOEFL (minimum score 500 paper-based; 61 iBT), IELTS (minimum score 6). Electronic applications accepted. *Faculty research:* Neuropharmacology, toxicology, cardiovascular pharmacology, neuromuscular pharmacology.

University of New Mexico, Graduate Studies, Health Sciences Center, Program in Biomedical Sciences, Albuquerque, NM 87131-5196. Offers biochemistry and molecular biology (MS, PhD); cell biology and physiology (MS, PhD); molecular genetics and microbiology (MS, PhD); neuroscience (MS, PhD); pathology (MS, PhD); toxicology (MS, PhD). *Program availability:* Part-time. *Students:* Average age 29. 61 applicants, 16% accepted, 10 enrolled. In 2017, 11 master's, 14 doctorates awarded. Terminal master's awarded for partial completion of doctoral program. *Degree requirements:* For master's, thesis; for doctorate, comprehensive exam, thesis/dissertation, qualifying exam at the end of year 1/core curriculum. *Entrance requirements:* For master's and doctorate, GRE General Test, minimum undergraduate GPA of 3.0. Additional exam requirements/recommendations for international students: Required—TOEFL. *Application deadline:* For fall admission, 3/1 priority date for domestic and international students. Applications are processed on a rolling basis. Application fee: $50. Electronic applications accepted. *Financial support:* Fellowships, research assistantships with full tuition reimbursements, teaching assistantships, career-related internships or fieldwork, Federal Work-Study, institutionally sponsored loans, scholarships/grants, traineeships, health care benefits, and unspecified assistantships available. Financial award application deadline: 1/1; financial award applicants required to submit FAFSA. *Faculty research:* Infectious disease/immunity, cancer biology, cardiovascular and metabolic diseases, brain and behavioral illness, environmental health. *Unit head:* Dr. Helen J. Hathaway, Program Director, 505-272-1887, Fax: 505-272-2412, E-mail: hhathaway@salud.unm.edu. *Application contact:* Mary Fenton, Admissions Coordinator, 505-272-1887, Fax: 505-272-2412, E-mail: mfenton@salud.unm.edu.

University of North Texas Health Science Center at Fort Worth, Graduate School of Biomedical Sciences, Fort Worth, TX 76107-2699. Offers biochemistry and cancer biology (MS, PhD); biotechnology (MS); cell biology, immunology and microbiology (MS, PhD); clinical research management (MS); forensic genetics (MS); genetics (MS, PhD); integrative physiology (MS, PhD); medical sciences (MS); pharmaceutical sciences and pharmacotherapy (MS, PhD); pharmacology and neuroscience (MS, PhD); structural anatomy and rehabilitation sciences (MS, PhD); DO/MS; DO/PhD. Terminal master's awarded for partial completion of doctoral program. *Degree requirements:* For master's, thesis; for doctorate, thesis/dissertation. *Entrance requirements:* For master's and doctorate, GRE General Test. Additional exam requirements/recommendations for international students: Required—TOEFL. *Expenses:* Contact institution. *Faculty research:* Alzheimer's disease, aging, eye diseases, cancer, cardiovascular disease.

University of Notre Dame, Graduate School, College of Science, Department of Biological Sciences, Notre Dame, IN 46556. Offers aquatic ecology, evolution and environmental biology (MS, PhD); cellular and molecular biology (MS, PhD); genetics (MS, PhD); physiology (MS, PhD); vector biology and parasitology (MS, PhD). Terminal master's awarded for partial completion of doctoral program. *Degree requirements:* For master's, comprehensive exam, thesis; for doctorate, comprehensive exam, thesis/dissertation, candidacy exam. *Entrance requirements:* For master's and doctorate, GRE General Test. Additional exam requirements/recommendations for international students: Required—TOEFL (minimum score 600 paper-based; 80 iBT). Electronic applications accepted. *Faculty research:* Tropical disease, molecular genetics, neurobiology, evolutionary biology, aquatic biology.

University of Oklahoma Health Sciences Center, College of Medicine and Graduate College, Graduate Programs in Medicine, Department of Physiology, Oklahoma City, OK 73190. Offers MS, PhD. *Program availability:* Part-time. Terminal master's awarded for partial completion of doctoral program. *Degree requirements:* For master's, thesis (for some programs); for doctorate, thesis/dissertation. *Entrance requirements:* For master's, GRE General Test, statement of career goals, 3 letters of recommendation; for doctorate, GRE General Test, 3 letters of recommendation. Additional exam requirements/recommendations for international students: Required—TOEFL. *Faculty research:* Cardiopulmonary physiology, neurophysiology, exercise physiology, cell and molecular physiology.

University of Oregon, Graduate School, College of Arts and Sciences, Department of Human Physiology, Eugene, OR 97403. Offers MS, PhD. *Degree requirements:* For master's, thesis optional; for doctorate, one foreign language, thesis/dissertation. *Entrance requirements:* For master's, GRE General Test, minimum GPA of 2.75 in undergraduate course work; for doctorate, GRE General Test. *Faculty research:* Balance control, muscle fatigue, lower extremity function, knee control.

University of Pennsylvania, Perelman School of Medicine, Biomedical Graduate Studies, Graduate Group in Cell and Molecular Biology, Philadelphia, PA 19104. Offers cancer biology (PhD); cell biology, physiology, and metabolism (PhD); developmental stem cell regenerative biology (PhD); gene therapy and vaccines (PhD); genetics and gene regulation (PhD); microbiology, virology, and parasitology (PhD); MD/PhD; VMD/PhD. *Faculty:* 363. *Students:* 343 full-time (197 women); includes 114 minority (7 Black or African American, non-Hispanic/Latino; 51 Asian, non-Hispanic/Latino; 41 Hispanic/Latino; 15 Two or more races, non-Hispanic/Latino), 50 international. 588 applicants, 22% accepted, 61 enrolled. In 2017, 61 doctorates awarded. *Degree requirements:* For doctorate, thesis/dissertation. *Entrance requirements:* For doctorate, GRE General Test. Additional exam requirements/recommendations for international students: Required—TOEFL. *Application deadline:* For fall admission, 12/1 priority date for domestic and international students. Applications are processed on a rolling basis. Application fee: $80. Electronic applications accepted. *Financial support:* In 2017–18, 339 students received support. Fellowships, research assistantships, teaching assistantships, and tuition waivers available. *Unit head:* Dr. Daniel Kessler, Graduate Group Chair, 215-898-1478. *Application contact:* Meagan Schofer, Coordinator, 215-898-1478.
Website: http://www.med.upenn.edu/camb/

University of Prince Edward Island, Atlantic Veterinary College, Graduate Program in Veterinary Medicine, Charlottetown, PE C1A 4P3, Canada. Offers anatomy (M Sc, PhD); bacteriology (M Sc, PhD); clinical pharmacology (M Sc, PhD); clinical sciences (M Sc, PhD); epidemiology (M Sc, PhD), including reproduction; fish health (M Sc, PhD); food animal nutrition (M Sc, PhD); immunology (M Sc, PhD); microanatomy (M Sc, PhD); parasitology (M Sc, PhD); pathology (M Sc, PhD); pharmacology (M Sc, PhD); physiology (M Sc, PhD); toxicology (M Sc, PhD); veterinary science (M Vet Sc); virology (M Sc, PhD). *Program availability:* Part-time. *Degree requirements:* For master's, thesis; for doctorate, thesis/dissertation. *Entrance requirements:* For master's, DVM, B Sc honors degree, or equivalent; for doctorate, M Sc. Additional exam requirements/recommendations for international students: Required—TOEFL (minimum score 550 paper-based; 80 iBT). *Expenses:* Contact institution. *Faculty research:* Animal health management, infectious diseases, fin fish and shellfish health, basic biomedical sciences, ecosystem health.

University of Puerto Rico–Medical Sciences Campus, School of Medicine, Biomedical Sciences Graduate Program, Department of Physiology, San Juan, PR 00936-5067. Offers MS, PhD. Terminal master's awarded for partial completion of doctoral program. *Degree requirements:* For master's, one foreign language, thesis; for doctorate, one foreign language, comprehensive exam, thesis/dissertation. *Entrance requirements:* For master's and doctorate, GRE General Test, GRE Subject Test, interview; course work in biology, chemistry and physics; minimum GPA of 3.0; 3 letters of recommendation. Electronic applications accepted. *Faculty research:* Respiration, neuroendocrinology, cellular and molecular physiology, cardiovascular, exercise physiology and neurobiology.

University of Rochester, School of Medicine and Dentistry, Graduate Programs in Medicine and Dentistry, Department of Pharmacology and Physiology, Programs in Physiology, Rochester, NY 14627. Offers MS, PhD. Terminal master's awarded for partial completion of doctoral program. *Degree requirements:* For master's, thesis; for doctorate, thesis/dissertation, qualifying exam. *Entrance requirements:* For master's and doctorate, GRE General Test.

Physiology

University of Saskatchewan, College of Medicine, Department of Physiology, Saskatoon, SK S7N 5A2, Canada. Offers M Sc, PhD. *Degree requirements:* For master's, thesis; for doctorate, thesis/dissertation. *Entrance requirements:* Additional exam requirements/recommendations for international students: Required—TOEFL.

University of Saskatchewan, Western College of Veterinary Medicine and College of Graduate Studies and Research, Graduate Programs in Veterinary Medicine, Department of Veterinary Biomedical Sciences, Saskatoon, SK S7N 5A2, Canada. Offers veterinary anatomy (M Sc); veterinary biomedical sciences (M Vet Sc); veterinary physiological sciences (M Sc, PhD). *Degree requirements:* For master's, thesis; for doctorate, comprehensive exam (for some programs), thesis/dissertation. *Entrance requirements:* Additional exam requirements/recommendations for international students: Required—TOEFL (minimum score 80 iBT); Recommended—IELTS (minimum score 6.5). Electronic applications accepted. *Faculty research:* Toxicology, animal reproduction, pharmacology, chloride channels, pulmonary pathobiology.

University of South Dakota, Graduate School, Sanford School of Medicine and Graduate School, Biomedical Sciences Graduate Program, Physiology and Pharmacology Group, Vermillion, SD 57069. Offers MS, PhD. In 2017, 1 master's, 3 doctorates awarded. Terminal master's awarded for partial completion of doctoral program. *Degree requirements:* For master's, thesis; for doctorate, comprehensive exam, thesis/dissertation. *Entrance requirements:* For master's and doctorate, GRE General Test, minimum GPA of 3.0. Additional exam requirements/recommendations for international students: Required—TOEFL (minimum score 550 paper-based; 80 iBT), IELTS (minimum score 6). *Application deadline:* For fall admission, 4/15 priority date for domestic students, 3/15 for international students. Applications are processed on a rolling basis. Application fee: $35. Electronic applications accepted. *Expenses:* Contact institution. *Financial support:* In 2017–18, 12 students received support. Fellowships with partial tuition reimbursements available, research assistantships with partial tuition reimbursements available, scholarships/grants, and unspecified assistantships available. Financial award application deadline: 4/15; financial award applicants required to submit FAFSA. *Faculty research:* Pulmonary physiology and pharmacology, drug abuse, reproduction, signal transduction, cardiovascular physiology and pharmacology. *Unit head:* 605-658-6322, Fax: 605-677-6381, E-mail: biomed@usd.edu. *Application contact:* Graduate School, 605-658-6140, Fax: 605-677-6118.
Website: http://www.usd.edu/medicine/basic-biomedical-sciences

University of Southern California, Keck School of Medicine and Graduate School, Graduate Programs in Medicine, Department of Physiology and Biophysics, Los Angeles, CA 90089. Offers MS. *Program availability:* Part-time. *Faculty:* 13 full-time (2 women). *Students:* 3 full-time (all women), 1 part-time (0 women); includes 2 minority (1 Asian, non-Hispanic/Latino; 1 Hispanic/Latino). Average age 23. 7 applicants, 43% accepted, 2 enrolled. In 2017, 2 master's awarded. *Degree requirements:* For master's, thesis optional. *Entrance requirements:* For master's, GRE General Test, minimum GPA of 3.0. Additional exam requirements/recommendations for international students: Required—TOEFL (minimum score 600 paper-based; 100 iBT). *Application deadline:* For fall admission, 12/1 priority date for domestic and international students. Applications are processed on a rolling basis. Application fee: $85. Electronic applications accepted. *Expenses:* Contact institution. *Financial support:* Application deadline: 4/15; applicants required to submit FAFSA. *Faculty research:* Endocrinology and metabolism, neurophysiology, mathematical modeling, cell transport, autoimmunity and cancer immunotherapy. *Unit head:* Dr. Berislav Zlokavic, Chair, 323-442-2566, Fax: 323-442-2230, E-mail: zlokovic@usc.edu. *Application contact:* Monica Pan, Student Services Advisor, 323-442-0230, Fax: 323-442-1610, E-mail: monicap@med.usc.edu.

University of South Florida, College of Arts and Sciences, Department of Integrative Biology, Tampa, FL 33620-9951. Offers biology (MS), including ecology and evolution (MS, PhD), environmental and ecological microbiology (MS, PhD), physiology and morphology (MS, PhD); integrative biology (PhD), including ecology and evolution (MS, PhD), environmental and ecological microbiology (MS, PhD), physiology and morphology (MS, PhD). *Program availability:* Part-time. *Faculty:* 14 full-time (5 women). *Students:* 21 full-time (11 women), 1 (woman) part-time; includes 1 minority (Asian, non-Hispanic/Latino), 2 international. Average age 30. 35 applicants, 17% accepted, 5 enrolled. In 2017, 7 master's, 5 doctorates awarded. *Degree requirements:* For master's, comprehensive exam, thesis (for some programs); for doctorate, comprehensive exam, thesis/dissertation. *Entrance requirements:* For master's and doctorate, GRE General Test, minimum GPA of 3.0 in last 60 hours of BS. *Application deadline:* For fall admission, 11/30 priority date for domestic and international students; for spring admission, 7/1 priority date for domestic and international students. Application fee: $30. Electronic applications accepted. *Financial support:* In 2017–18, 7 students received support. Research assistantships, teaching assistantships, and unspecified assistantships available. Financial award application deadline: 6/30; financial award applicants required to submit FAFSA. *Faculty research:* Marine ecology, ecosystem responses to urbanization, biomechanical and physiological mechanisms of animal movement, population biology and conservation, microbial ecology and public health microbiology, natural diversity of parasites and herbivores; ecosystems, vertebrates, disturbance ecology, functional and ecological morphology of feeding in fishes, rare amphibians and reptiles, genomics in ecological experiments, ecotoxicology, global carbon cycle, plant-animal interactions. *Total annual research expenditures:* $1.9 million. *Unit head:* Dr. Valerie Harwood, Professor and Chair, 813-974-1524, Fax: 813-974-3263, E-mail: vharwood@usf.edu. *Application contact:* Dr. Stephen Deban, Associate Professor and Graduate Program Director, 813-974-2242, E-mail: sdeban@usf.edu.
Website: http://biology.usf.edu/ib/grad/

University of South Florida, Morsani College of Medicine and College of Graduate Studies, Graduate Programs in Medical Sciences, Tampa, FL 33620-9951. Offers advanced athletic training (MS); athletic training (MS); bioinformatics and computational biology (MSBCB); biotechnology (MSB); health informatics (MSHI); medical sciences (MSMS, PhD), including aging and neuroscience (MSMS), allergy, immunology and infectious disease (PhD), anatomy, biochemistry and molecular biology, clinical and translational research, health science (MSMS), interdisciplinary medical sciences (MSMS), medical microbiology and immunology (MSMS), metabolic and nutritional medicine (MSMS), microbiology and immunology (PhD), molecular medicine, molecular pharmacology and physiology (PhD), neuroscience (PhD), pathology and cell biology (PhD), women's health (MSMS). *Students:* 372 full-time (212 women), 216 part-time (142 women); includes 257 minority (78 Black or African American, non-Hispanic/Latino; 1 American Indian or Alaska Native, non-Hispanic/Latino; 79 Asian, non-Hispanic/Latino; 84 Hispanic/Latino; 15 Two or more races, non-Hispanic/Latino), 62 international. Average age 28. 1,048 applicants, 46% accepted, 309 enrolled. In 2017, 351 master's, 56 doctorates awarded. Terminal master's awarded for partial completion of doctoral program. *Degree requirements:* For master's, comprehensive exam, thesis; for doctorate, comprehensive exam, thesis/dissertation. *Entrance requirements:* For master's, GRE General Test or GMAT, bachelor's degree or equivalent from regionally-accredited university with minimum GPA of 3.0 in upper-division sciences coursework; prerequisites in general biology, general chemistry, general physics, organic chemistry, quantitative analysis, and integral and differential calculus; for doctorate, GRE General Test, bachelor's degree from regionally-accredited university with minimum GPA of 3.0 in upper-division sciences coursework; 3 letters of recommendation; personal interview; 1-2 page personal statement; prerequisites in biology, chemistry, physics, organic chemistry, quantitative analysis, and integral/differential calculus. Additional exam requirements/recommendations for international students: Required—TOEFL (minimum score 550 paper-based; 79 iBT) or IELTS (minimum score 6.5). *Application deadline:* For fall admission, 2/1 priority date for domestic students, 2/1 for international students. Application fee: $30. Electronic applications accepted. *Expenses:* Contact institution. *Financial support:* In 2017–18, 109 students received support. *Faculty research:* Anatomy, biochemistry, cancer biology, cardiovascular disease, cell biology, immunology, microbiology, molecular biology, neuroscience, pharmacology, physiology. *Total annual research expenditures:* $45.3 million. *Unit head:* Dr. Michael Barber, Professor/Associate Dean for Graduate and Postdoctoral Affairs, 813-974-9908, Fax: 813-974-4317, E-mail: mbarber@health.usf.edu. *Application contact:* Dr. Eric Bennett, Graduate Director, PhD Program in Medical Sciences, 813-974-1545, Fax: 813-974-4317, E-mail: esbennet@health.usf.edu.
Website: http://health.usf.edu/nocms/medicine/graduatestudies/

The University of Tennessee, Graduate School, College of Agricultural Sciences and Natural Resources, Department of Animal Science, Knoxville, TN 37996. Offers animal anatomy (PhD); breeding (MS, PhD); management (MS, PhD); nutrition (MS, PhD); physiology (MS, PhD). *Program availability:* Part-time. *Degree requirements:* For master's, thesis; for doctorate, thesis/dissertation. *Entrance requirements:* For master's and doctorate, GRE General Test, minimum GPA of 2.7. Additional exam requirements/recommendations for international students: Required—TOEFL. Electronic applications accepted.

The University of Texas Medical Branch, Graduate School of Biomedical Sciences, Program in Human Pathophysiology and Translational Medicine, Galveston, TX 77555. Offers MS, PhD. *Degree requirements:* For master's, thesis or alternative; for doctorate, thesis/dissertation. *Entrance requirements:* For master's and doctorate, GRE General Test. Additional exam requirements/recommendations for international students: Required—TOEFL (minimum score 550 paper-based). Electronic applications accepted.

University of Toronto, Faculty of Medicine, Department of Physiology, Toronto, ON M5S 1A1, Canada. Offers M Sc, PhD, MD/PhD. *Degree requirements:* For master's, thesis; for doctorate, thesis/dissertation. *Entrance requirements:* For master's and doctorate, minimum B+ average in final year, 2 letters of reference. Additional exam requirements/recommendations for international students: Required—TOEFL (minimum score 600 paper-based), Michigan English Language Assessment Battery (minimum score 95), IELTS (minimum score 8), or COPE (minimum score 5). Electronic applications accepted.

University of Utah, Graduate School, College of Health, Division of Nutrition and Integrative Physiology, Salt Lake City, UT 84112. Offers nutrition and integrative physiology (MS, PhD), including integrative physiology, nutrition, nutrition and dietetics (MS). *Program availability:* 100% online. *Faculty:* 6 full-time (3 women), 11 part-time/adjunct (10 women). *Students:* 53 full-time (32 women), 5 part-time (all women); includes 6 minority (1 Asian, non-Hispanic/Latino; 4 Hispanic/Latino; 1 Two or more races, non-Hispanic/Latino), 5 international. Average age 28. 47 applicants, 36% accepted, 15 enrolled. In 2017, 20 master's awarded. Terminal master's awarded for partial completion of doctoral program. *Entrance requirements:* For master's, GRE General Test, minimum undergraduate GPA of 3.0; for doctorate, GRE General Test. Additional exam requirements/recommendations for international students: Required—TOEFL (minimum score 500 paper-based). *Application deadline:* For winter admission, 2/15 priority date for domestic and international students. Application fee: $55 ($65 for international students). Electronic applications accepted. *Expenses:* Contact institution. *Financial support:* In 2017–18, 41 students received support, including 15 research assistantships with full tuition reimbursements available (averaging $25,000 per year), 24 teaching assistantships with partial tuition reimbursements available (averaging $7,500 per year); career-related internships or fieldwork, scholarships/grants, health care benefits, and unspecified assistantships also available. Financial award application deadline: 2/15; financial award applicants required to submit FAFSA. *Faculty research:* Diabetes and metabolism, sport nutrition education, diabetes education, cardiovascular nutrition, pediatric nutrition. *Total annual research expenditures:* $120,000. *Unit head:* Dr. Scott Summers, Chair, 801-587-3024, Fax: 801-585-3874, E-mail: scott.a.summers@health.utah.edu. *Application contact:* Jean Zancanella, Academic Adviser, 801-581-5280, Fax: 801-585-3874, E-mail: jean.zancanella@health.utah.edu.
Website: http://www.health.utah.edu/fdnu/

University of Utah, School of Medicine and Graduate School, Graduate Programs in Medicine, Department of Physiology, Salt Lake City, UT 84112-1107. Offers PhD. *Degree requirements:* For doctorate, thesis/dissertation, comprehensive qualifying exam, preliminary exam. *Entrance requirements:* For doctorate, GRE General Test, GRE Subject Test, minimum GPA of 3.0. Additional exam requirements/recommendations for international students: Required—TOEFL (minimum score 650 paper-based; 100 iBT); Recommended—TWE (minimum score 6). Electronic applications accepted. *Faculty research:* Cell neurobiology, chemosensory systems, cardiovascular and kidney physiology, endocrinology.

University of Virginia, School of Medicine, Department of Molecular Physiology and Biological Physics, Program in Physiology, Charlottesville, VA 22903. Offers PhD, MD/PhD. *Students:* 3 full-time (1 woman); includes 1 minority (Hispanic/Latino). Average age 28. In 2017, 1 doctorate awarded. *Entrance requirements:* For doctorate, GRE General Test, 2 letters of recommendation. Additional exam requirements/recommendations for international students: Required—TOEFL. *Application deadline:* For fall admission, 1/15 for domestic and international students. Applications are processed on a rolling basis. Application fee: $60. Electronic applications accepted. *Financial support:* Fellowships, research assistantships, and teaching assistantships available. Financial award applicants required to submit FAFSA. *Unit head:* Dr. Mark Yeager, Chair, 434-924-5108, Fax: 434-982-1616, E-mail: my3r@virginia.edu. *Application contact:* E-mail: physiograd@virginia.edu.
Website: http://www.healthsystem.virginia.edu/internet/physio/

University of Washington, Graduate School, School of Medicine, Graduate Programs in Medicine, Department of Physiology and Biophysics, Seattle, WA 98195. Offers PhD. *Degree requirements:* For doctorate, thesis/dissertation. *Entrance requirements:* For doctorate, GRE General Test. Additional exam requirements/recommendations for international students: Required—TOEFL (minimum score 580 paper-based; 70 iBT). *Faculty research:* Membrane and cell biophysics, neuroendocrinology, cardiovascular and respiratory physiology, systems neurophysiology and behavior, molecular physiology.

The University of Western Ontario, Faculty of Graduate Studies, Biosciences Division, Department of Physiology and Pharmacology, London, ON N6A 5B8, Canada. Offers M Sc, PhD. *Degree requirements:* For master's, thesis, seminar course; for doctorate, comprehensive exam, thesis/dissertation. *Entrance requirements:* For master's, minimum B average, honors degree; for doctorate, minimum B average, honors degree, M Sc. *Faculty research:* Reproductive and endocrine physiology, neurophysiology, cardiovascular and renal physiology, cell physiology, gastrointestinal and metabolic physiology.

University of Wisconsin–La Crosse, College of Science and Health, Department of Biology, La Crosse, WI 54601-3742. Offers aquatic sciences (MS); biology (MS); cellular and molecular biology (MS); clinical microbiology (MS); microbiology (MS); nurse anesthesia (MS); physiology (MS). *Accreditation:* AANA/CANAEP. *Program availability:* Part-time. *Students:* 11 full-time (2 women), 29 part-time (14 women); includes 1 minority (Two or more races, non-Hispanic/Latino). Average age 30. 67 applicants, 28% accepted, 18 enrolled. In 2017, 24 master's awarded. *Degree requirements:* For master's, comprehensive exam, thesis. *Entrance requirements:* For master's, GRE General Test, minimum GPA of 2.85. Additional exam requirements/recommendations for international students: Required—TOEFL (minimum score 550 paper-based; 79 iBT). *Application deadline:* For fall admission, 2/1 priority date for domestic and international students; for spring admission, 1/4 priority date for domestic and international students. Applications are processed on a rolling basis. Electronic applications accepted. *Financial support:* Research assistantships with partial tuition reimbursements, Federal Work-Study, scholarships/grants, health care benefits, and tuition waivers (partial) available. Support available to part-time students. Financial award application deadline: 3/15; financial award applicants required to submit FAFSA. *Unit head:* Dr. Mark Sandheinrich, Department Chair, 608-785-8261, E-mail: msandheinrich@uwlax.edu. *Application contact:* Brandon Schaller, Senior Graduate Student Status Examiner, 608-785-8941, E-mail: admissions@uwlax.edu.
Website: http://uwlax.edu/biology/

University of Wisconsin–Madison, School of Medicine and Public Health, Endocrinology-Reproductive Physiology Program, Madison, WI 53706. Offers MS, PhD. *Application contact:* Grace Jensen, Student Services Coordinator, 608-265-5838, E-mail: gjensen2@wisc.edu.
Website: http://www.erp.wisc.edu/

University of Wisconsin–Madison, School of Medicine and Public Health, Physiology Graduate Training Program, Madison, WI 53706. Offers PhD.
Website: http://www.pgtp.wisc.edu/

University of Wyoming, College of Arts and Sciences, Department of Zoology and Physiology, Laramie, WY 82071. Offers MS, PhD. *Program availability:* Part-time. *Degree requirements:* For master's, comprehensive exam (for some programs), thesis; for doctorate, comprehensive exam (for some programs), thesis/dissertation. *Entrance requirements:* For master's and doctorate, GRE General Test, minimum GPA of 3.0. Additional exam requirements/recommendations for international students: Required—TOEFL. Electronic applications accepted. *Faculty research:* Cell biology, ecology/wildlife, organismal physiology, zoology.

Virginia Commonwealth University, Medical College of Virginia-Professional Programs, School of Medicine, Graduate Programs in Medicine, Department of Physiology and Biophysics, Richmond, VA 23284-9005. Offers molecular biology and genetics (MS); physical therapy (PhD); physiology (MS, PhD); MD/PhD. Terminal master's awarded for partial completion of doctoral program. *Degree requirements:* For master's, thesis; for doctorate, thesis/dissertation, comprehensive oral and written exams. *Entrance requirements:* For master's, GRE General Test, MCAT, or DAT; for doctorate, GRE, MCAT or DAT. Additional exam requirements/recommendations for international students: Required—TOEFL (minimum score 600 paper-based; 100 iBT). Electronic applications accepted.

Wake Forest University, School of Medicine and Graduate School of Arts and Sciences, Graduate Programs in Medicine, Program in Physiology and Pharmacology, Winston-Salem, NC 27109. Offers pharmacology (PhD); physiology (PhD); MD/PhD. *Degree requirements:* For doctorate, thesis/dissertation. *Entrance requirements:* For doctorate, GRE General Test. Additional exam requirements/recommendations for international students: Required—TOEFL. Electronic applications accepted. *Faculty research:* Aging, substance abuse, cardiovascular control, endocrine systems, toxicology.

Wayne State University, School of Medicine, Office of Biomedical Graduate Programs, Detroit, MI 48202. Offers anatomy and cell biology (MS, PhD); basic medical sciences (MS); biochemistry and molecular biology (MS, PhD); cancer biology (MS, PhD); clinical and translational science (Graduate Certificate); family medicine and public health sciences (MPH, Graduate Certificate), including public health practice; genetic counseling (MS); immunology and microbiology (MS, PhD); medical physics (MS, PhD, Graduate Certificate); medical research (MS); molecular medicine and genomics (MS, PhD), including molecular genetics and genomics; pathology (PhD); pharmacology (MS, PhD); physiology (MS, PhD), including physiology, reproductive sciences (PhD); psychiatry and behavioral neurosciences (PhD), including translational neuroscience; MD/MPH; MD/PhD; MPH/MA; MSW/MPH. *Program availability:* Part-time, evening/weekend. *Students:* 268 full-time (152 women), 117 part-time (59 women); includes 108 minority (19 Black or African American, non-Hispanic/Latino; 1 American Indian or Alaska Native, non-Hispanic/Latino; 62 Asian, non-Hispanic/Latino; 9 Hispanic/Latino; 17 Two or more races, non-Hispanic/Latino), 48 international. Average age 26. 1,133 applicants, 21% accepted, 151 enrolled. In 2017, 70 master's, 25 doctorates, 10 other advanced degrees awarded. Terminal master's awarded for partial completion of doctoral program. *Degree requirements:* For master's, thesis (for some programs); for doctorate, thesis/dissertation. *Entrance requirements:* For master's, doctorate, and Graduate Certificate, GRE. Additional exam requirements/recommendations for international students: Required—TOEFL (minimum score 550 paper-based; 100 iBT), Michigan English Language Assessment Battery (minimum score 85); Recommended—IELTS (minimum score 6.5), TWE (minimum score 5.5). *Application deadline:* For fall admission, 2/1 for domestic and international students. Applications are processed on a rolling basis. Application fee: $50. Electronic applications accepted. *Expenses:* Contact institution. *Financial support:* In 2017–18, 177 students received support, including 64 fellowships with full tuition reimbursements available (averaging $24,388 per year), 79 research assistantships with full tuition reimbursements available (averaging $26,894 per year); scholarships/grants, traineeships, and health care benefits also available. *Faculty research:* Cancer biology, neurosciences, vision sciences, molecular biology, pathology, physiology, pharmacology, public health, medical physics. *Unit head:* Dr. Daniel A. Walz, Associate Dean for Biomedical Graduate Programs, 313-577-1455, Fax: 313-577-8796, E-mail: gradprogs@med.wayne.edu.
Website: https://www.med.wayne.edu/biomedical-graduate-programs/

Weill Cornell Medicine, Weill Cornell Graduate School of Medical Sciences, Physiology, Biophysics and Systems Biology Program, New York, NY 10065. Offers MS, PhD. Terminal master's awarded for partial completion of doctoral program. *Degree requirements:* For master's, comprehensive exam; for doctorate, thesis/dissertation, final exam. *Entrance requirements:* For doctorate, GRE General Test, introductory courses in biology, inorganic and organic chemistry, physics, and mathematics. Additional exam requirements/recommendations for international students: Required—TOEFL. *Faculty research:* Receptor-mediated regulation of cell function, molecular properties of channels or receptors, bioinformatics, mathematical modeling.

Western Michigan University, Graduate College, College of Education and Human Development, Department of Health, Physical Education and Recreation, Kalamazoo, MI 49008. Offers athletic training (MS), including exercise physiology; sport management (MA), including pedagogy, special physical education.

Wright State University, Graduate School, College of Science and Mathematics, Department of Neuroscience, Cell Biology, and Physiology, Dayton, OH 45435. Offers anatomy (MS); physiology and neuroscience (MS). *Degree requirements:* For master's, thesis optional. *Entrance requirements:* Additional exam requirements/recommendations for international students: Required—TOEFL. *Faculty research:* Reproductive cell biology, neurobiology of pain, neurohistochemistry.

Yale University, Yale School of Medicine and Graduate School of Arts and Sciences, Combined Program in Biological and Biomedical Sciences (BBS), Physiology and Integrative Medical Biology Track, New Haven, CT 06520. Offers PhD, MD/PhD. *Entrance requirements:* Additional exam requirements/recommendations for international students: Required—TOEFL.

Youngstown State University, Graduate School, College of Science, Technology, Engineering and Mathematics, Department of Biological Sciences, Youngstown, OH 44555-0001. Offers environmental biology (MS); molecular biology, microbiology, and genetic (MS); physiology and anatomy (MS). *Program availability:* Part-time. *Degree requirements:* For master's, comprehensive exam, thesis, oral review. *Entrance requirements:* For master's, GRE General Test, minimum GPA of 2.7. Additional exam requirements/recommendations for international students: Required—TOEFL. *Faculty research:* Cell biology, neurophysiology, molecular biology, neurobiology, gene regulation.

Section 19
Zoology

This section contains a directory of institutions offering graduate work in zoology. Additional information about programs listed in the directory may be obtained by writing directly to the dean of a graduate school or chair of a department at the address given in the directory.

For programs offering related work, see also in this book *Anatomy; Biochemistry; Biological and Biomedical Sciences; Cell, Molecular, and Structural Biology; Ecology, Environmental Biology, and Evolutionary Biology; Entomology; Genetics, Developmental Biology, and Reproductive Biology; Microbiological Sciences; Neuroscience and Neurobiology; Neurobiology; Physiology;* and *Veterinary Medicine and Sciences.* In the other guides in this series:

Graduate Programs in the Physical Sciences, Mathematics, Agricultural Sciences, the Environment & Natural Resources

See *Agricultural and Food Sciences, Environmental Sciences and Management,* and *Marine Sciences and Oceanography*

Graduate Programs in Engineering & Applied Sciences

See *Agricultural Engineering and Bioengineering* and *Ocean Engineering*

CONTENTS

Program Directories

Animal Behavior

Arizona State University at the Tempe campus, College of Liberal Arts and Sciences, School of Life Sciences, Tempe, AZ 85287-4601. Offers animal behavior (PhD); applied ethics (biomedical and health ethics) (MA); biology (MS, PhD), including biology, biology and society, complex adaptive systems science (PhD), plant biology and conservation (MS); environmental life sciences (PhD); evolutionary biology (PhD); history and philosophy of science (PhD); human and social dimensions of science and technology (PhD); microbiology (PhD); molecular and cellular biology (PhD); neuroscience (PhD). Terminal master's awarded for partial completion of doctoral program. *Degree requirements:* For master's, thesis (for some programs), interactive Program of Study (iPOS) submitted before completing 50 percent of required credit hours; for doctorate, variable foreign language requirement, comprehensive exam, thesis/dissertation, interactive Program of Study (iPOS) submitted before completing 50 percent of required credit hours. *Entrance requirements:* For master's and doctorate, GRE, minimum GPA of 3.0 or equivalent in last 2 years of work leading to bachelor's degree. Additional exam requirements/recommendations for international students: Required—TOEFL (minimum score 600 paper-based; 100 iBT). Electronic applications accepted.

Bucknell University, Graduate Studies, College of Arts and Sciences, Department of Animal Behavior, Lewisburg, PA 17837. Offers MS. *Degree requirements:* For master's, thesis. *Entrance requirements:* For master's, GRE General Test, GRE Subject Test, minimum GPA of 3.0. Additional exam requirements/recommendations for international students: Required—TOEFL (minimum score 600 paper-based).

Cornell University, Graduate School, Graduate Fields of Agriculture and Life Sciences, Field of Neurobiology and Behavior, Ithaca, NY 14853. Offers behavioral biology (PhD), including behavioral ecology, chemical ecology, ethology, neuroethology, sociobiology; neurobiology (PhD), including cellular and molecular neurobiology, neuroanatomy, neurochemistry, neuropharmacology, neurophysiology, sensory physiology. *Degree requirements:* For doctorate, comprehensive exam, thesis/dissertation, 1 year of teaching experience, seminar presentation. *Entrance requirements:* For doctorate, GRE General Test, GRE Subject Test (biology), 3 letters of recommendation. Additional exam requirements/recommendations for international students: Required—TOEFL (minimum score 550 paper-based; 77 iBT). Electronic applications accepted. *Faculty research:* Cellular neurobiology and neuropharmacology, integrative neurobiology, social behavior, chemical ecology, neuroethology.

Emory University, Laney Graduate School, Department of Psychology, Atlanta, GA 30322-1100. Offers clinical psychology (PhD); cognition and development (PhD); neuroscience and animal behavior (PhD). *Accreditation:* APA. *Degree requirements:* For doctorate, comprehensive exam, thesis/dissertation. *Entrance requirements:* For doctorate, GRE General Test, minimum GPA of 3.25. Additional exam requirements/recommendations for international students: Required—TOEFL. Electronic applications accepted. *Faculty research:* Neuroscience and animal behavior; adult and child psychopathology, cognition development assessment.

Hunter College of the City University of New York, Graduate School, School of Arts and Sciences, Department of Psychology, New York, NY 10065-5085. Offers animal behavior and conservation (MA, Certificate); general psychology (MA). *Program availability:* Part-time, evening/weekend. *Degree requirements:* For master's, comprehensive exam, thesis. *Entrance requirements:* For master's, GRE General Test, minimum 12 credits of course work in psychology, including statistics and experimental psychology; 2 letters of recommendation. Additional exam requirements/recommendations for international students: Required—TOEFL. *Faculty research:* Personality, cognitive and linguistic development, hormonal and neural control of behavior, gender and culture, social cognition of health and attitudes.

Illinois State University, Graduate School, College of Arts and Sciences, School of Biological Sciences, Normal, IL 61790. Offers animal behavior (MS); bacteriology (MS); biochemistry (MS); biological sciences (MS); biology (PhD); biophysics (MS); biotechnology (MS); botany (MS, PhD); cell biology (MS); conservation biology (MS); developmental biology (MS); ecology (MS, PhD); entomology (MS); evolutionary biology (MS); genetics (MS, PhD); immunology (MS); microbiology (MS, PhD); molecular biology (MS); molecular genetics (MS); neurobiology (MS); neuroscience (MS); parasitology (MS); physiology (MS, PhD); plant biology (MS); plant molecular biology (MS); plant sciences (MS); structural biology (MS); zoology (MS, PhD). *Program availability:* Part-time. *Degree requirements:* For master's, thesis or alternative; for doctorate, variable foreign language requirement, thesis/dissertation, 2 terms of residency. *Entrance requirements:* For master's, GRE General Test, minimum GPA of 2.6 in last 60 hours of course work; for doctorate, GRE General Test. *Faculty research:* Redoc balance and drug development in schistosoma mansoni, control of the growth of listeria monocytogenes at low temperature, regulation of cell expansion and microtubule function by SPRI, CRUI: physiology and fitness consequences of different life history phenotypes.

University of California, Davis, Graduate Studies, Graduate Group in Animal Behavior, Davis, CA 95616. Offers PhD. *Degree requirements:* For doctorate, thesis/dissertation. *Entrance requirements:* For doctorate, GRE General Test. Additional exam requirements/recommendations for international students: Required—TOEFL (minimum score 550 paper-based), IELTS (minimum score 7). Electronic applications accepted. *Faculty research:* Wildlife behavior, conservation biology, companion animal behavior, behavioral endocrinology, animal communication.

University of Massachusetts Amherst, Graduate School, Interdisciplinary Programs, Program in Neuroscience and Behavior, Amherst, MA 01003. Offers animal behavior and learning (PhD); molecular and cellular neuroscience (PhD); neural and behavioral development (PhD); neuroendocrinology (PhD); neuroscience and behavior (MS); sensorimotor, cognitive, and computational neuroscience (PhD). Terminal master's awarded for partial completion of doctoral program. *Degree requirements:* For master's, thesis or alternative; for doctorate, comprehensive exam, thesis/dissertation. *Entrance requirements:* For master's, GRE General Test; for doctorate, GRE General Test; GRE Subject Test in psychology, biology, or mathematics (recommended). Additional exam requirements/recommendations for international students: Required—TOEFL (minimum score 550 paper-based; 80 iBT), IELTS (minimum score 6.5). Electronic applications accepted.

University of Minnesota, Twin Cities Campus, Graduate School, College of Biological Sciences, Department of Ecology, Evolution, and Behavior, St. Paul, MN 55418. Offers MS, PhD. Terminal master's awarded for partial completion of doctoral program. *Degree requirements:* For master's, comprehensive exam, thesis or projects; for doctorate, comprehensive exam, thesis/dissertation. *Entrance requirements:* For master's and doctorate, GRE General Test, minimum GPA of 3.0. Additional exam requirements/recommendations for international students: Required—TOEFL (minimum score 550 paper-based; 79 iBT), Michigan English Language Assessment Battery. Electronic applications accepted. *Faculty research:* Behavioral ecology, community ecology, community genetics, ecosystem and global change, evolution and systematics.

University of Montana, Graduate School, College of Humanities and Sciences, Department of Psychology, Missoula, MT 59812. Offers clinical psychology (PhD); experimental psychology (PhD), including animal behavior psychology, developmental psychology; school psychology (MA, PhD, Ed S). *Accreditation:* APA (one or more programs are accredited). Terminal master's awarded for partial completion of doctoral program. *Degree requirements:* For master's, thesis; for doctorate, thesis/dissertation. *Entrance requirements:* For master's, doctorate, and Ed S, GRE General Test. Additional exam requirements/recommendations for international students: Required—TOEFL.

The University of Tennessee, Graduate School, College of Arts and Sciences, Department of Ecology and Evolutionary Biology, Knoxville, TN 37996. Offers behavior (MS, PhD); ecology (MS, PhD); evolutionary biology (MS, PhD). *Program availability:* Part-time. *Degree requirements:* For master's, thesis; for doctorate, thesis/dissertation. *Entrance requirements:* For master's and doctorate, GRE General Test, minimum GPA of 2.7. Additional exam requirements/recommendations for international students: Required—TOEFL. Electronic applications accepted.

The University of Texas at Austin, Graduate School, College of Natural Sciences, School of Biological Sciences, Program in Ecology, Evolution and Behavior, Austin, TX 78712-1111. Offers PhD. *Entrance requirements:* For doctorate, GRE General Test. Additional exam requirements/recommendations for international students: Required—TOEFL. Electronic applications accepted.

University of Washington, Graduate School, College of Arts and Sciences, Department of Psychology, Seattle, WA 98195. Offers animal behavior (PhD); applied child and adolescent psychology: prevention and treatment (MA); behavioral neuroscience (PhD); clinical psychology (PhD); cognition and perception (PhD); developmental psychology (PhD); quantitative psychology (PhD); social psychology and personality (PhD). *Accreditation:* APA (one or more programs are accredited). *Degree requirements:* For doctorate, thesis/dissertation. *Entrance requirements:* For doctorate, GRE General Test, minimum GPA of 3.0. Electronic applications accepted. *Faculty research:* Addictive behaviors, artificial intelligence, child psychopathology, mechanisms and development of vision, physiology of ingestive behaviors.

Zoology

Auburn University, Graduate School, College of Sciences and Mathematics, Department of Biological Sciences, Auburn University, AL 36849. Offers botany (MS); zoology (MS). *Faculty:* 37 full-time (16 women), 1 (woman) part-time/adjunct. *Students:* 42 full-time (19 women), 65 part-time (43 women); includes 15 minority (8 Black or African American, non-Hispanic/Latino; 1 Asian, non-Hispanic/Latino; 2 Hispanic/Latino; 4 Two or more races, non-Hispanic/Latino), 15 international. Average age 27. 83 applicants, 41% accepted, 23 enrolled. In 2017, 22 master's, 7 doctorates awarded. *Entrance requirements:* For master's and doctorate, GRE General Test. Additional exam requirements/recommendations for international students: Required—TOEFL. Application fee: $50 ($60 for international students). Electronic applications accepted. *Expenses:* Tuition, state resident: full-time $10,974; part-time $519 per credit hour. Tuition, nonresident: full-time $29,658; part-time $1557 per credit hour. *Required fees:* $816 per semester. Tuition and fees vary according to degree level and program. *Financial support:* Research assistantships and teaching assistantships available. Financial award applicants required to submit FAFSA. *Unit head:* Dr. Jason E. Bond, Chair, 334-844-3906, Fax: 334-844-1645. *Application contact:* Dr. George Flowers, Dean of the Graduate School, 334-844-2125.

Canisius College, Graduate Division, College of Arts and Sciences, Department of Animal Behavior, Ecology and Conservation, Buffalo, NY 14208-1098. Offers anthrozoology (MS). Applicants accepted in fall only. *Program availability:* Part-time, evening/weekend, blended/hybrid learning. *Faculty:* 5 full-time (3 women), 3 part-time/adjunct (all women). *Students:* 23 full-time (all women), 32 part-time (26 women); includes 3 minority (1 Black or African American, non-Hispanic/Latino; 1 Hispanic/Latino; 1 Two or more races, non-Hispanic/Latino), 1 international. Average age 35. 78 applicants, 36% accepted, 20 enrolled. In 2017, 15 master's awarded. *Entrance requirements:* For master's, GRE (recommended), official transcript of all college work, bachelor's degree, minimum GPA of 3.0, three essays. Additional exam requirements/recommendations for international students: Required—TOEFL (minimum score 550 paper-based, 80 iBT), IELTS (minimum score 6.5), or CAEL (minimum score 70). *Application deadline:* For fall admission, 3/1 for domestic and international students. Applications are processed on a rolling basis. Application fee: $0. Electronic applications accepted. *Expenses: Tuition:* Full-time $22,860; part-time $820 per credit. *Required fees:* $720; $25 per credit. $65 per semester. One-time fee: $425. *Financial support:* Career-related internships or fieldwork, Federal Work-Study, scholarships/grants, tuition waivers (partial), and unspecified assistantships available. Support available to part-time students. Financial award application deadline: 4/30; financial award applicants required to submit FAFSA. *Faculty research:* Human animal relations; advocacy of animal welfare and conservation. *Unit head:* Dr. Sue Margulis, Program Director, 716-888-2773, E-mail: margulis@canisius.edu.
Website: http://www.canisius.edu/abec/

Colorado State University, College of Natural Sciences, Programs in Natural Sciences Education, Fort Collins, CO 80523. Offers material science and engineering (PhD);

natural science education (MNSE); zoo, aquarium, and animal shelter management (MS). *Program availability:* 100% online. *Faculty:* 1 (woman) full-time. *Students:* 28 full-time (21 women), 53 part-time (34 women); includes 13 minority (3 Black or African American, non-Hispanic/Latino; 1 Asian, non-Hispanic/Latino; 7 Hispanic/Latino; 2 Two or more races, non-Hispanic/Latino), 3 international. Average age 29. 35 applicants, 91% accepted, 29 enrolled. In 2017, 18 master's awarded. *Degree requirements:* For master's, comprehensive exam (for some programs), thesis (for some programs); for doctorate, comprehensive exam (for some programs), thesis/dissertation. *Entrance requirements:* Additional exam requirements/recommendations for international students: Required—TOEFL (minimum score 550 paper-based). Application fee: $60 ($70 for international students). Electronic applications accepted. *Expenses:* $609 per credit hour (for online MNSE); $2,000 per semester (for MPSN); $125 per credit hour (for materials science and engineering program). *Unit head:* Dr. Janice Nerger, Dean, 970-491-1300, Fax: 970-491-6639, E-mail: janice.nerger@colostate.edu. *Application contact:* Dr. Simon Tavener, Associate Dean for Academics, 970-491-1300, Fax: 970-491-6639, E-mail: cns@colostate.edu.
Website: https://www.online.colostate.edu/degrees/natural-sciences-education/

Emporia State University, Department of Biological Sciences, Emporia, KS 66801-5415. Offers botany (MS); environmental biology (MS); forensic science (MS); general biology (MS); microbial and cellular biology (MS); zoology (MS). *Program availability:* Part-time. *Faculty:* 13 full-time (3 women), 1 part-time/adjunct (0 women). *Students:* 20 full-time (11 women), 15 part-time (3 women); includes 3 minority (2 Hispanic/Latino; 1 Two or more races, non-Hispanic/Latino), 17 international. 17 applicants, 59% accepted, 8 enrolled. In 2017, 21 master's awarded. *Degree requirements:* For master's, comprehensive exam or thesis. *Entrance requirements:* For master's, GRE, appropriate undergraduate degree, interview, letters of reference. Additional exam requirements/recommendations for international students: Required—TOEFL (minimum score 520 paper-based; 68 iBT). *Application deadline:* For fall admission, 8/15 priority date for domestic students. Applications are processed on a rolling basis. Application fee: $30 ($75 for international students). Electronic applications accepted. *Expenses:* Tuition, state resident: full-time $6084; part-time $253.50 per credit hour. Tuition, nonresident: full-time $18,924; part-time $788.50 per credit hour. *Required fees:* $1943; $80.95 per credit hour. Tuition and fees vary according to campus/location. *Financial support:* In 2017–18, 7 research assistantships with full tuition reimbursements (averaging $9,747 per year), 15 teaching assistantships with full tuition reimbursements (averaging $7,499 per year) were awarded; career-related internships or fieldwork, Federal Work-Study, institutionally sponsored loans, health care benefits, and unspecified assistantships also available. Financial award application deadline: 3/15; financial award applicants required to submit FAFSA. *Faculty research:* Fisheries, range, and wildlife management; aquatic, plant, grassland, vertebrate, and invertebrate ecology; mammalian and plant systematics, taxonomy, and evolution; immunology, virology, and molecular biology. *Unit head:* Dr. Tim Burnett, Interim Chair, 620-341-5910, Fax: 620-341-5608, E-mail: tburnett@emporia.edu.
Website: http://www.emporia.edu/info/degrees-courses/grad/biology

Illinois State University, Graduate School, College of Arts and Sciences, School of Biological Sciences, Normal, IL 61790. Offers animal behavior (MS); bacteriology (MS); biochemistry (MS); biological sciences (MS); biology (PhD); biophysics (MS); biotechnology (MS); botany (MS, PhD); cell biology (MS); conservation biology (MS); developmental biology (MS); ecology (MS, PhD); entomology (MS); evolutionary biology (MS); genetics (MS, PhD); immunology (MS); microbiology (MS, PhD); molecular biology (MS); molecular genetics (MS); neurobiology (MS); neuroscience (MS); parasitology (MS); physiology (MS, PhD); plant biology (MS); plant molecular biology (MS); plant sciences (MS); structural biology (MS); zoology (MS, PhD). *Program availability:* Part-time. *Degree requirements:* For master's, thesis or alternative; for doctorate, variable foreign language requirement, thesis/dissertation, 2 terms of residency. *Entrance requirements:* For master's, GRE General Test, minimum GPA of 2.6 in last 60 hours of course work; for doctorate, GRE General Test. *Faculty research:* Redoc balance and drug development in schistosoma mansoni, control of the growth of listeria monocytogenes at low temperature, regulation of cell expansion and microtubule function by SPRI, CRUI: physiology and fitness consequences of different life history phenotypes.

Indiana University Bloomington, University Graduate School, College of Arts and Sciences, Department of Biology, Bloomington, IN 47405. Offers biology teaching (MAT); biotechnology (MA); evolution, ecology, and behavior (MA, PhD); genetics (PhD); microbiology (MA, PhD); molecular, cellular, and developmental biology (PhD); plant sciences (MA, PhD); zoology (MA, PhD). Terminal master's awarded for partial completion of doctoral program. *Degree requirements:* For master's, thesis, oral defense; for doctorate, thesis/dissertation, oral defense. *Entrance requirements:* For master's and doctorate, GRE General Test. Additional exam requirements/recommendations for international students: Required—TOEFL (minimum score 100 iBT). Electronic applications accepted. *Faculty research:* Evolution, ecology and behavior; microbiology; molecular biology and genetics; plant biology.

Michigan State University, The Graduate School, College of Natural Science, Department of Zoology, East Lansing, MI 48824. Offers zoo and aquarium management (MS); zoology (MS, PhD); zoology-environmental toxicology (PhD). *Entrance requirements:* Additional exam requirements/recommendations for international students: Required—TOEFL. Electronic applications accepted.

North Carolina State University, Graduate School, College of Agriculture and Life Sciences, Department of Zoology, Raleigh, NC 27695. Offers MS, MZS, PhD. Terminal master's awarded for partial completion of doctoral program. *Degree requirements:* For master's, thesis (for some programs), oral exam; for doctorate, thesis/dissertation, oral and written exams. *Entrance requirements:* For master's and doctorate, GRE General Test, minimum GPA of 3.0. Additional exam requirements/recommendations for international students: Required—TOEFL. Electronic applications accepted. *Faculty research:* Acquatic and terrestrial ecology, herpetology, behavioral biology, neurobiology, avian ecology.

North Dakota State University, College of Graduate and Interdisciplinary Studies, College of Science and Mathematics, Department of Biological Sciences, Fargo, ND 58102. Offers biology (MS); botany (MS, PhD); zoology (MS, PhD). *Entrance requirements:* For master's and doctorate, GRE General Test. Additional exam requirements/recommendations for international students: Required—TOEFL. *Application deadline:* For fall admission, 1/15 for domestic students. Applications are processed on a rolling basis. Application fee: $35. Electronic applications accepted. *Expenses:* Tuition, state resident: full-time $4323; part-time $360.21 per credit. Tuition, nonresident: full-time $6484; part-time $540.31 per credit. *Required fees:* $668; $55.70 per credit. Part-time tuition and fees vary according to degree level, program and reciprocity agreements. *Financial support:* Application deadline: 4/15; applicants required to submit FAFSA. *Faculty research:* Comparative endocrinology, physiology, behavioral ecology, plant cell biology, aquatic biology. *Unit head:* Dr. Katie Reindl, Graduate Coordinator, 701-231-7087, E-mail: katie.reindl@ndsu.edu. *Application contact:* Elizabeth Worth, Marketing, Recruitment, and Public Relations Coordinator, 701-231-8476, Fax: 701-231-6524, E-mail: elizabeth.worth@ndsu.edu.
Website: http://www.ndsu.edu/biology/

Southern Illinois University Carbondale, Graduate School, College of Science, Department of Zoology, Carbondale, IL 62901-4701. Offers MS, PhD. *Degree requirements:* For master's, thesis; for doctorate, thesis/dissertation. *Entrance requirements:* For master's, GRE, minimum GPA of 2.7; for doctorate, GRE, minimum GPA of 3.25. Additional exam requirements/recommendations for international students: Required—TOEFL. *Faculty research:* Ecology, fisheries and wildlife, systematics, behavior, vertebrate and invertebrate biology.

Texas Tech University, Graduate School, College of Arts and Sciences, Department of Biological Sciences, Lubbock, TX 79409-3131. Offers biology (MS, PhD); environmental sustainability and natural resource management (PSM); microbiology (MS); zoology (MS, PhD). *Program availability:* Part-time, blended/hybrid learning. *Faculty:* 44 full-time (16 women). *Students:* 103 full-time (56 women), 13 part-time (5 women); includes 12 minority (2 Black or African American, non-Hispanic/Latino; 2 Asian, non-Hispanic/Latino; 6 Hispanic/Latino; 2 Two or more races, non-Hispanic/Latino), 51 international. Average age 29. 77 applicants, 36% accepted, 17 enrolled. In 2017, 13 master's, 10 doctorates awarded. *Degree requirements:* For master's, comprehensive exam, thesis or alternative; for doctorate, comprehensive exam, thesis/dissertation. *Entrance requirements:* For master's and doctorate, GRE General Test. Additional exam requirements/recommendations for international students: Required—TOEFL (minimum score 550 paper-based; 79 iBT). *Application deadline:* For fall admission, 6/1 priority date for domestic students, 1/15 priority date for international students; for spring admission, 9/1 priority date for domestic students, 6/15 priority date for international students. Applications are processed on a rolling basis. Application fee: $60. Electronic applications accepted. *Expenses:* Contact institution. *Financial support:* In 2017–18, 110 students received support, including 85 fellowships (averaging $1,960 per year), 28 research assistantships (averaging $8,365 per year), 93 teaching assistantships (averaging $15,744 per year); Federal Work-Study and health care benefits also available. Financial award application deadline: 2/15; financial award applicants required to submit FAFSA. *Faculty research:* Biodiversity, genomics and evolution; climate change in arid ecosystems, plant biology and biotechnology; animal communication and behavior; microbiomes, zoonosis and emerging diseases. *Total annual research expenditures:* $1.7 million. *Unit head:* Dr. Ron Chesser, Chair, 806-834-0121, Fax: 806-742-2963, E-mail: ron.chesser@ttu.edu. *Application contact:* Dr. Lou Densmore, Graduate Adviser, 806-834-6479, Fax: 806-742-2963, E-mail: lou.densmore@ttu.edu.
Website: http://www.depts.ttu.edu/biology/

Uniformed Services University of the Health Sciences, F. Edward Hebert School of Medicine, Graduate Programs in the Biomedical Sciences and Public Health, Bethesda, MD 20814. Offers emerging infectious diseases (PhD); medical and clinical psychology (PhD), including clinical psychology, medical psychology; medicine (MS, PhD), including health professions education; molecular and cell biology (MS, PhD); neuroscience (PhD); preventive medicine and biometrics (MPH, MS, MSPH, MTMH, PhD), including environmental health sciences (PhD), healthcare administration and policy (MS), medical zoology (PhD), public health (MPH, MSPH), tropical medicine and hygiene (MTMH). *Students:* Average age 25. 598 applicants, 17% accepted, 77 enrolled. In 2017, 19 master's, 50 doctorates awarded. Terminal master's awarded for partial completion of doctoral program. *Degree requirements:* For master's, comprehensive exam, thesis or alternative; for doctorate, comprehensive exam, thesis/dissertation, qualifying exam. *Entrance requirements:* For master's, GRE General Test; for doctorate, GRE General Test, minimum GPA of 3.0. *Application deadline:* For fall admission, 12/1 priority date for domestic students. Application fee: $0. Electronic applications accepted. *Expenses:* There are no tuition charges or fees for graduate students at USU. *Financial support:* In 2017–18, 50 fellowships (averaging $43,000 per year) were awarded; research assistantships, career-related internships or fieldwork, scholarships/grants, and health care benefits also available. *Unit head:* Dr. Gregory Mueller, Associate Dean, 301-295-3507, E-mail: gregory.mueller@usuhs.edu. *Application contact:* Tina Finley, Administrative Officer, 301-295-3642, Fax: 301-295-6772, E-mail: netina.finley@usuhs.edu.
Website: http://www.usuhs.mil/graded

Uniformed Services University of the Health Sciences, F. Edward Hebert School of Medicine, Graduate Programs in the Biomedical Sciences and Public Health, Department of Preventive Medicine and Biometrics, Program in Medical Zoology, Bethesda, MD 20814-4799. Offers PhD. *Degree requirements:* For doctorate, comprehensive exam, thesis/dissertation, qualifying exam. *Entrance requirements:* For doctorate, GRE General Test, GRE Subject Test, minimum GPA of 3.0, U.S. citizenship. Additional exam requirements/recommendations for international students: Required—TOEFL. *Faculty research:* Epidemiology, biostatistics, tropical public health, parasitology, vector biology.

The University of British Columbia, Faculty of Science, Department of Zoology, Vancouver, BC V6T 1Z4, Canada. Offers M Sc, PhD. *Degree requirements:* For master's, thesis, final defense; for doctorate, comprehensive exam, thesis/dissertation, final defense. *Entrance requirements:* For master's and doctorate, faculty support. Additional exam requirements/recommendations for international students: Required—TOEFL. Electronic applications accepted. *Expenses:* Contact institution. *Faculty research:* Cell and developmental biology; community, environmental, and population biology; comparative physiology and biochemistry; fisheries; ecology and evolutionary biology.

University of California, Davis, Graduate Studies, Graduate Group in Avian Sciences, Davis, CA 95616. Offers MS. *Degree requirements:* For master's, comprehensive exam (for some programs), thesis (for some programs). *Entrance requirements:* For master's, GRE General Test, minimum GPA of 3.0. Additional exam requirements/recommendations for international students: Required—TOEFL (minimum score 550 paper-based). Electronic applications accepted. *Faculty research:* Reproduction, nutrition, toxicology, food products, ecology of avian species.

University of Chicago, Division of the Biological Sciences, Department of Organismal Biology and Anatomy, Chicago, IL 60637. Offers integrative biology (PhD). *Faculty:* 20. *Students:* 20 full-time (13 women). 28 applicants, 21% accepted, 4 enrolled. In 2017, 6 doctorates awarded. *Degree requirements:* For doctorate, thesis/dissertation, ethics class, 2 teaching assistantships, preliminary examinations. *Entrance requirements:* For doctorate, GRE General Test, transcripts, statement of purpose, 3 letters of recommendation. Additional exam requirements/recommendations for international students: Required—TOEFL (minimum score 600 paper-based; 104 iBT), IELTS (minimum score 7). *Application deadline:* For fall admission, 12/1 for domestic and international students. Application fee: $90. Electronic applications accepted. *Financial support:* In 2017–18, 12 students received support, including fellowships with full tuition reimbursements available (averaging $31,000 per year), research assistantships with full tuition reimbursements available (averaging $31,000 per year); institutionally sponsored loans, scholarships/grants, traineeships, and health care benefits also available. Financial award application deadline: 12/1. *Faculty research:* Evolution and development, behavioral neurobiology, comparative biomechanics, vertebrate paleontology, integrative neuromechanics. *Unit head:* Dr. Robert Ho, Chair, E-mail: rkh@uchicago.edu. *Application contact:* Audrey Aronowsky, Graduate Research, Education, and Outreach Manager, 773-702-3891, E-mail: aronowsky@uchicago.edu.
Website: http://pondside.uchicago.edu/oba/

Zoology

University of Florida, Graduate School, College of Liberal Arts and Sciences, Department of Biology, Gainesville, FL 32611. Offers botany (MS, MST, PhD), including botany, tropical conservation and development, wetland sciences; zoology (MS, MST, PhD), including animal molecular and cellular biology (PhD), tropical conservation and development, wetland sciences, zoology. *Degree requirements:* For master's, comprehensive exam (for some programs), thesis; for doctorate, comprehensive exam, thesis/dissertation. *Entrance requirements:* For master's and doctorate, GRE General Test, minimum GPA of 3.0. Additional exam requirements/recommendations for international students: Required—TOEFL (minimum score 550 paper-based; 80 iBT), IELTS (minimum score 6). Electronic applications accepted. *Faculty research:* Ecology of natural populations, plant and animal genome evolution, biodiversity, plant biology, behavior.

University of Guelph, Graduate Studies, College of Biological Science, Department of Integrative Biology, Botany and Zoology, Guelph, ON N1G 2W1, Canada. Offers botany (M Sc, PhD); zoology (M Sc, PhD). *Program availability:* Part-time. *Degree requirements:* For master's, thesis, research proposal; for doctorate, thesis/dissertation, research proposal, qualifying exam. *Entrance requirements:* For master's, minimum B average during previous 2 years of course work. Additional exam requirements/recommendations for international students: Required—TOEFL (minimum score 550 paper-based), IELTS (minimum score 6.5). Electronic applications accepted. *Faculty research:* Aquatic science, environmental physiology, parasitology, wildlife biology, management.

University of Hawaii at Manoa, Office of Graduate Education, College of Natural Sciences, Department of Biology, Honolulu, HI 96822. Offers zoology (MS, PhD). *Program availability:* Part-time. *Degree requirements:* For master's, one foreign language, thesis optional; for doctorate, one foreign language, comprehensive exam, thesis/dissertation, seminar. *Entrance requirements:* For master's and doctorate, GRE General Test, GRE Subject Test. Additional exam requirements/recommendations for international students: Required—TOEFL (minimum score 600 paper-based; 100 iBT), IELTS (minimum score 7). *Faculty research:* Molecular evolution, reproductive biology, animal behavior, conservation biology, avian biology.

University of Illinois at Urbana–Champaign, Graduate College, College of Liberal Arts and Sciences, School of Integrative Biology, Department of Animal Biology, Champaign, IL 61820. Offers animal biology (ecology, ethology and evolution) (MS, PhD).

University of Maine, Graduate School, College of Natural Sciences, Forestry, and Agriculture, School of Biology and Ecology, Orono, ME 04469. Offers biological sciences (PhD); botany and plant pathology (MS); entomology (MS); zoology (MS, PhD). *Program availability:* Part-time. *Faculty:* 30 full-time (16 women), 2 part-time/adjunct (1 woman). *Students:* 61 full-time (40 women), 22 part-time (11 women); includes 7 minority (1 American Indian or Alaska Native, non-Hispanic/Latino; 3 Asian, non-Hispanic/Latino; 3 Hispanic/Latino), 14 international. Average age 30. 69 applicants, 87% accepted, 28 enrolled. In 2017, 7 master's, 9 doctorates awarded. Terminal master's awarded for partial completion of doctoral program. *Degree requirements:* For master's, thesis (for some programs); for doctorate, comprehensive exam, thesis/dissertation. *Entrance requirements:* For master's and doctorate, GRE General Test. Additional exam requirements/recommendations for international students: Required—TOEFL (minimum score 80 iBT), IELTS (minimum score 6.5). *Application deadline:* For fall admission, 2/1 priority date for domestic students. Applications are processed on a rolling basis. Application fee: $65. Electronic applications accepted. *Expenses:* Tuition, state resident: full-time $7722; part-time $429 per credit hour. Tuition, nonresident: full-time $25,146; part-time $1397 per credit hour. *Required fees:* $1162; $581 per credit hour. *Financial support:* In 2017–18, 92 students received support, including 2 fellowships with full tuition reimbursements available (averaging $25,000 per year), 47 research assistantships with full tuition reimbursements available (averaging $19,800 per year), 32 teaching assistantships with full tuition reimbursements available (averaging $15,200 per year); career-related internships or fieldwork, Federal Work-Study, institutionally sponsored loans, tuition waivers (full and partial), and unspecified assistantships also available. Financial award application deadline: 3/1. *Faculty research:* Ecology and evolution (aquatic, terrestrial, paleo); development and genetics; biomedical research; ecophysiology and stress; invasion ecology and pest management. *Total annual research expenditures:* $3.1 million. *Unit head:* Dr. Andrei Aloykhin, Director, 207-581-2977, Fax: 207-581-2537. *Application contact:* Scott G. Delcourt, Assistant Vice President for Graduate Studies and Senior Associate Dean, 207-581-3291, Fax: 207-581-3232, E-mail: graduate@maine.edu.
Website: http://sbe.umaine.edu/

University of Manitoba, Faculty of Graduate Studies, Faculty of Science, Department of Biological Sciences, Winnipeg, MB R3T 2N2, Canada. Offers botany (M Sc, PhD); ecology (M Sc, PhD); zoology (M Sc, PhD).

University of Montana, Graduate School, College of Humanities and Sciences, Division of Biological Sciences, Program in Organismal Biology and Ecology, Missoula, MT 59812. Offers MS, PhD. Terminal master's awarded for partial completion of doctoral program. *Degree requirements:* For master's, one foreign language, thesis; for doctorate, 2 foreign languages, thesis/dissertation. *Entrance requirements:* For master's and doctorate, GRE General Test. *Faculty research:* Conservation biology, ecology and behavior, evolutionary genetics, avian biology.

University of North Dakota, Graduate School, College of Arts and Sciences, Department of Biology, Grand Forks, ND 58202. Offers biology (MS); fisheries/wildlife (PhD); genetics (PhD); zoology (PhD). Terminal master's awarded for partial completion of doctoral program. *Degree requirements:* For master's, thesis, final exam; for doctorate, comprehensive exam, thesis/dissertation, final exam. *Entrance requirements:* For master's, GRE General Test, GRE Subject Test, minimum GPA of 3.0; for doctorate, GRE General Test, GRE Subject Test, minimum GPA of 3.5. Additional exam requirements/recommendations for international students: Required—TOEFL (minimum score 550 paper-based; 79 iBT), IELTS (minimum score 6.5). Electronic applications accepted. *Faculty research:* Population biology, wildlife ecology, RNA processing, hormonal control of behavior.

University of Wisconsin–Madison, Graduate School, College of Letters and Science, Department of Zoology, Madison, WI 53706-1380. Offers MA, MS, PhD. *Program availability:* Part-time. *Degree requirements:* For master's, thesis; for doctorate, one foreign language, thesis/dissertation. *Entrance requirements:* For master's and doctorate, GRE General Test. Additional exam requirements/recommendations for international students: Required—TOEFL. Electronic applications accepted. *Faculty research:* Developmental biology, ecology, neurobiology, aquatic ecology, animal behavior.

University of Wisconsin–Oshkosh, Graduate Studies, College of Letters and Science, Department of Biology and Microbiology, Oshkosh, WI 54901. Offers biology (MS), including botany, microbiology, zoology. *Degree requirements:* For master's, comprehensive exam, thesis. *Entrance requirements:* For master's, GRE General Test, minimum GPA of 3.0, BS in biology. Additional exam requirements/recommendations for international students: Required—TOEFL (minimum score 550 paper-based; 79 iBT). Electronic applications accepted.

University of Wyoming, College of Arts and Sciences, Department of Zoology and Physiology, Laramie, WY 82071. Offers MS, PhD. *Program availability:* Part-time. *Degree requirements:* For master's, comprehensive exam (for some programs), thesis; for doctorate, comprehensive exam (for some programs), thesis/dissertation. *Entrance requirements:* For master's and doctorate, GRE General Test, minimum GPA of 3.0. Additional exam requirements/recommendations for international students: Required—TOEFL. Electronic applications accepted. *Faculty research:* Cell biology, ecology/wildlife, organismal physiology, zoology.

Western Illinois University, School of Graduate Studies, College of Arts and Sciences, Department of Biological Sciences, Macomb, IL 61455-1390. Offers biology (MS); environmental GIS (Certificate); zoo and aquarium studies (Certificate). *Program availability:* Part-time. *Students:* 43 full-time (24 women), 24 part-time (14 women); includes 5 minority (1 Black or African American, non-Hispanic/Latino; 2 Hispanic/Latino; 2 Two or more races, non-Hispanic/Latino), 21 international. Average age 28. 20 applicants, 90% accepted, 12 enrolled. In 2017, 22 master's awarded. *Degree requirements:* For master's, thesis or alternative. *Entrance requirements:* Additional exam requirements/recommendations for international students: Required—TOEFL (minimum score 550 paper-based; 80 iBT); Recommended—IELTS. *Application deadline:* Applications are processed on a rolling basis. Application fee: $30. Electronic applications accepted. *Financial support:* In 2017–18, 13 research assistantships with full tuition reimbursements (averaging $7,544 per year), 19 teaching assistantships with full tuition reimbursements (averaging $8,688 per year) were awarded; unspecified assistantships also available. Financial award applicants required to submit FAFSA. *Unit head:* Dr. Richard Musser, Chairperson, 309-298-1546. *Application contact:* Dr. Nancy Parsons, Associate Provost and Director of Graduate Studies, 309-298-1806, Fax: 309-298-2345, E-mail: grad-office@wiu.edu.
Website: http://wiu.edu/biology

West Liberty University, College of Sciences, West Liberty, WV 26074. Offers biology (MA, MS); biomedical science (MA); physician assistant studies (MS); zoo science (MA, MS). Tuition and fees vary according to course load and program. *Unit head:* Dr. Karen Kettler, Interim Dean, E-mail: kkettler@westliberty.edu. *Application contact:* Sara Sweeney, Director, Office of Graduate Studies, 304-336-8545, E-mail: sara.sweeney@westliberty.edu.
Website: http://westliberty.edu/college-of-sciences/

ACADEMIC AND PROFESSIONAL PROGRAMS IN HEALTH-RELATED PROFESSIONS

Section 20
Allied Health

This section contains a directory of institutions offering graduate work in allied health, followed by an in-depth entry submitted by an institution that chose to prepare a detailed program description. Additional information about programs listed in the directory but not augmented by an in-depth entry may be obtained by writing directly to the dean of a graduate school or chair of a department at the address given in the directory.

For programs offering related work, see also in this book *Anatomy, Biophysics, Dentistry and Dental Sciences, Health Services, Microbiological Sciences, Pathology and Pathobiology, Physiology,* and *Public Health.* In the other guides in this series:

Graduate Programs in the Humanities, Arts & Social Sciences

See *Art and Art History (Art Therapy), Family and Consumer Sciences (Gerontology), Performing Arts (Therapies),* and *Psychology and Counseling'*

Graduate Programs in the Physical Sciences, Mathematics, Agricultural Sciences, the Environment & Natural Resources

See *Physics (Acoustics)*

Graduate Programs in Engineering & Applied Sciences

See *Agricultural Engineering and Bioengineering (Bioengineering), Biomedical Engineering and Biotechnology,* and *Energy and Power Engineering (Nuclear Engineering)*

Graduate Programs in Business, Education, Information Studies, Law & Social Work

See *Administration, Instruction, and Theory (Educational Psychology); Special Focus (Education of the Multiply Handicapped); Social Work;* and *Subject Areas (Counselor Education)*

CONTENTS

Program Directories

Featured School: Display and Close-Up

Allied Health—General

Alabama State University, College of Health Sciences, Montgomery, AL 36101-0271. Offers MRC, MS, DPT. *Faculty:* 19 full-time (16 women), 19 part-time/adjunct (10 women). *Students:* 168 full-time (117 women), 5 part-time (2 women); includes 71 minority (56 Black or African American, non-Hispanic/Latino; 10 Asian, non-Hispanic/Latino; 3 Hispanic/Latino; 2 Two or more races, non-Hispanic/Latino), 4 international. Average age 22. 172 applicants, 35% accepted, 58 enrolled. In 2017, 21 master's, 21 doctorates awarded. *Degree requirements:* For master's, comprehensive exam; for doctorate, thesis/dissertation or alternative. *Entrance requirements:* For doctorate, GRE (recommended minimum scores: Verbal 145, Quantitative 140), baccalaureate degree from accredited educational institution with minimum cumulative GPA of 3.0. Additional exam requirements/recommendations for international students: Required—TOEFL (minimum score 500 paper-based). *Application deadline:* For fall admission, 4/15 for domestic and international students; for spring admission, 11/15 for domestic and international students; for summer admission, 3/15 for domestic and international students. Applications are processed on a rolling basis. Application fee: $25. Electronic applications accepted. *Expenses:* Tuition, state resident: part-time $412 per credit hour. Tuition, nonresident: part-time $824 per credit hour. *Required fees:* $685 per semester. *Financial support:* In 2017–18, 3 students received support. Research assistantships and unspecified assistantships available. Financial award application deadline: 6/30; financial award applicants required to submit FAFSA. *Unit head:* Dr. Cheryl E. Easley, Dean, College of Health Sciences, 334-229-5053, E-mail: bdawson@alasu.edu. *Application contact:* Dr. William Person, Dean of Graduate Studies, 334-229-4274, Fax: 334-229-4928, E-mail: wperson@alasu.edu.
Website: http://www.alasu.edu/academics/colleges—departments/health-sciences/index.aspx

American College of Healthcare Sciences, Graduate Programs, Portland, OR 97239-3719. Offers anatomy and physiology (Graduate Certificate); aromatherapy (MS, Graduate Certificate); botanical safety (Graduate Certificate); complementary alternative medicine (MS, Graduate Certificate); health and wellness (MS); herbal medicine (MS, Graduate Certificate); holistic nutrition (MS, Graduate Certificate); wellness coaching (Graduate Certificate). *Program availability:* Part-time, evening/weekend, online learning. *Degree requirements:* For master's, capstone project. *Entrance requirements:* For master's, interview, letters of recommendation, essay.

Andrews University, School of Health Professions, Department of Medical Laboratory Sciences, Berrien Springs, MI 49104. Offers MSMLS. *Accreditation:* APTA. *Faculty:* 2 full-time (1 woman). *Students:* 1 (woman) full-time; minority (Asian, non-Hispanic/Latino). Average age 23. 6 applicants, 33% accepted. In 2017, 2 master's awarded. *Entrance requirements:* For master's, GRE. Additional exam requirements/recommendations for international students: Required—TOEFL (minimum score 550 paper-based). *Application deadline:* Applications are processed on a rolling basis. Application fee: $40. *Unit head:* Karen Reiner, Chair, 269-471-3336. *Application contact:* Justina Clayburn, Supervisor of Graduate Admission, 800-253-2874, Fax: 269-471-6321, E-mail: graduate@andrews.edu.
Website: http://www.andrews.edu/shp/mls/

Athabasca University, Faculty of Health Disciplines, Athabasca, AB T9S 3A3, Canada. Offers advanced nursing practice (MN, Advanced Diploma); generalist (MN); health studies (MHS). *Program availability:* Part-time, online learning. *Degree requirements:* For master's, comprehensive exam (for some programs). *Entrance requirements:* For master's, bachelor's degree in health-related field and 2 years of professional health service experience (MHS); bachelor's degree in nursing and 2 years' nursing experience (MN); minimum GPA of 3.0 in final 30 credits; for Advanced Diploma, RN license, 2 years of health care experience. Electronic applications accepted. *Expenses:* Contact institution.

A.T. Still University, Arizona School of Health Sciences, Mesa, AZ 85206. Offers advanced occupational therapy (MS); advanced physician assistant studies (MS); athletic training (MS, DAT); audiology (Au D); clinical decision making in athletic training (Graduate Certificate); occupational therapy (MS, OTD); orthopedic rehabilitation (Graduate Certificate); physical therapy (DPT); physician assistant studies (MS); transitional audiology (Au D); transitional physical therapy (DPT). *Accreditation:* AOTA (one or more programs are accredited); ASHA. *Program availability:* Part-time, 100% online. *Faculty:* 59 full-time (39 women), 221 part-time/adjunct (155 women). *Students:* 608 full-time (405 women), 431 part-time (310 women); includes 247 minority (54 Black or African American, non-Hispanic/Latino; 13 American Indian or Alaska Native, non-Hispanic/Latino; 151 Asian, non-Hispanic/Latino; 2 Hispanic/Latino; 1 Native Hawaiian or other Pacific Islander, non-Hispanic/Latino; 26 Two or more races, non-Hispanic/Latino), 1 international. Average age 33. 4,882 applicants, 9% accepted, 278 enrolled. In 2017, 132 master's, 270 doctorates awarded. *Degree requirements:* For master's, thesis (for some programs); for doctorate, thesis/dissertation (for some programs). *Entrance requirements:* For master's, GRE General Test; for doctorate, GRE, Physical Therapist Evaluation Tool (for DPT), current state licensure. Additional exam requirements/recommendations for international students: Required—TOEFL (minimum score 80 iBT). *Application deadline:* For fall admission, 7/7 for domestic and international students; for winter admission, 10/3 for domestic and international students; for spring admission, 1/16 for domestic and international students; for summer admission, 4/17 for domestic and international students. Applications are processed on a rolling basis. Application fee: $70. Electronic applications accepted. Application fee is waived when completed online. *Financial support:* In 2017–18, 161 students received support. Federal Work-Study and scholarships/grants available. Financial award application deadline: 6/1; financial award applicants required to submit FAFSA. *Faculty research:* Pediatric sport-related concussion, adolescent athlete health-related quality of life; geriatric and pediatric well-being, pain management for participation, practice-based research network, BMI and dental caries. *Total annual research expenditures:* $63,003. *Unit head:* Dr. Randy Danielsen, Dean, 480-219-6009, Fax: 480-219-6110, E-mail: rdanielsen@atsu.edu. *Application contact:* Donna Sparks, Director, Admissions Processing, 660-626-2117, Fax: 660-626-2969, E-mail: admissions@atsu.edu.
Website: http://www.atsu.edu/ashs

Augusta University, College of Allied Health Sciences, Program in Applied Health Sciences, Augusta, GA 30912. Offers diagnostic sciences (PhD); health care outcomes (PhD); rehabilitation science (PhD). *Program availability:* Part-time, online learning. *Entrance requirements:* For doctorate, GRE General Test, bachelor's degree, official transcripts, minimum undergraduate GPA of 3.0, three letters of recommendation. Additional exam requirements/recommendations for international students: Required—TOEFL (minimum score 550 paper-based; 79 iBT). Electronic applications accepted. *Faculty research:* Patient- and family-centered care, public health informatics, vascular health promotion through physical activity, improving air quality for school children, movement therapies for Parkinson's Disease.

Baylor University, Graduate School, Military Programs, Waco, TX 76798. Offers MHA, MS, D Sc, D Sc PA, DPT, DScPT, MHA/MBA. *Accreditation:* APTA (one or more programs are accredited). *Faculty:* 44 full-time (4 women), 21 part-time/adjunct (5 women). *Students:* 199 full-time (82 women); includes 29 minority (6 Black or African American, non-Hispanic/Latino; 1 American Indian or Alaska Native, non-Hispanic/Latino; 7 Asian, non-Hispanic/Latino; 7 Hispanic/Latino; 8 Two or more races, non-Hispanic/Latino). In 2017, 63 master's, 49 doctorates awarded. *Entrance requirements:* For master's and doctorate, GRE General Test. *Application deadline:* Applications are processed on a rolling basis. *Expenses:* Contact institution. *Unit head:* Skip Gill, Dean, 210-221-7100, Fax: 210-221-6457, E-mail: norman.w.gill2.mil@mail.mil. *Application contact:* Lori McNamara, Admissions Coordinator, 254-710-3588, Fax: 254-710-3870.

Belmont University, College of Health Sciences, Nashville, TN 37212. Offers nursing (MSN, DNP); occupational therapy (MSOT, OTD); physical therapy (DPT). *Program availability:* Part-time, blended/hybrid learning. *Faculty:* 29 full-time (25 women), 16 part-time/adjunct (11 women). *Students:* 394 full-time (330 women), 9 part-time (8 women); includes 34 minority (9 Black or African American, non-Hispanic/Latino; 12 Asian, non-Hispanic/Latino; 7 Hispanic/Latino; 6 Two or more races, non-Hispanic/Latino). Average age 26. In 2017, 52 master's, 79 doctorates awarded. *Degree requirements:* For master's, comprehensive exam, thesis; for doctorate, comprehensive exam. *Entrance requirements:* For master's, GRE, BSN, minimum GPA of 3.0. Additional exam requirements/recommendations for international students: Required—TOEFL (minimum score 550 paper-based). *Application deadline:* Applications are processed on a rolling basis. Application fee: $50. Electronic applications accepted. *Expenses:* Contact institution. *Financial support:* Teaching assistantships with full tuition reimbursements, career-related internships or fieldwork, scholarships/grants, and traineeships available. Financial award application deadline: 3/1; financial award applicants required to submit FAFSA. *Unit head:* Dr. Cathy Taylor, Dean, 615-460-6916, Fax: 615-460-6750. *Application contact:* Bill Nichols, Director of Enrollment Services, 615-460-6107, E-mail: bill.nichols@belmont.edu.
Website: http://www.belmont.edu/healthsciences/

Bennington College, Graduate Programs, Post Baccalaureate Premedical Program, Bennington, VT 05201. Offers allied and health sciences (Certificate). Electronic applications accepted. *Expenses:* Contact institution. *Faculty research:* Cellular functions of Hsp90, foundations of quantum mechanics, history and philosophy of physics, cytosolic quality control, forest ecology, plate tectonics of rift systems, amphibian evolutionary physiology, photochemistry of gold complexes.

Boston University, College of Health and Rehabilitation Sciences: Sargent College, Boston, MA 02215. Offers MS, DPT, OTD, PhD. *Accreditation:* APTA (one or more programs are accredited). *Program availability:* Blended/hybrid learning. *Faculty:* 54 full-time (42 women), 44 part-time/adjunct (28 women). *Students:* 459 full-time (380 women), 74 part-time (65 women); includes 91 minority (5 Black or African American, non-Hispanic/Latino; 47 Asian, non-Hispanic/Latino; 26 Hispanic/Latino; 13 Two or more races, non-Hispanic/Latino), 39 international. Average age 26. 1,687 applicants, 24% accepted, 146 enrolled. In 2017, 118 master's, 85 doctorates awarded. Terminal master's awarded for partial completion of doctoral program. *Degree requirements:* For master's, comprehensive exam, thesis optional; for doctorate, comprehensive exam (for some programs), thesis/dissertation. *Entrance requirements:* For master's and doctorate, GRE General Test. Additional exam requirements/recommendations for international students: Required—TOEFL (minimum score 550 paper-based; 84 iBT). *Application deadline:* For fall admission, 1/1 priority date for domestic and international students. Applications are processed on a rolling basis. Application fee: $95. Electronic applications accepted. *Financial support:* In 2017–18, 300 students received support, including 30 research assistantships with full tuition reimbursements available (averaging $22,000 per year), 18 teaching assistantships (averaging $2,500 per year); career-related internships or fieldwork, Federal Work-Study, institutionally sponsored loans, scholarships/grants, and health care benefits also available. Support available to part-time students. Financial award application deadline: 1/1; financial award applicants required to submit FAFSA. *Faculty research:* Outcome measurement, gerontology, neuroanatomy, aphasia, autism, Parkinson's Disease, psychiatric rehabilitation, obesity prevention, speech production and imaging. *Total annual research expenditures:* $13.1 million. *Unit head:* Dr. Christopher Moore, Dean, 617-353-2705, Fax: 617-353-7500, E-mail: mooreca@bu.edu. *Application contact:* Sharon Sankey, Assistant Dean, Student Services, 617-353-2713, Fax: 617-353-7500, E-mail: ssankey@bu.edu.
Website: http://www.bu.edu/sargent/

Brock University, Faculty of Graduate Studies, Faculty of Applied Health Sciences, St. Catharines, ON L2S 3A1, Canada. Offers M Sc, MA, PhD. *Degree requirements:* For master's, thesis. *Entrance requirements:* For master's, honors degree, BA and/or B Sc. Additional exam requirements/recommendations for international students: Required—TOEFL (minimum score 550 paper-based; 80 iBT), IELTS (minimum score 6.5), TWE (minimum score 4). Electronic applications accepted. *Faculty research:* Health and physical activity, aging and health, health advocacy, exercise psychology, community development.

Canisius College, Graduate Division, School of Education and Human Services, Office of Professional Studies, Buffalo, NY 14208-1098. Offers applied nutrition (MS, Certificate); community and school health (MS); health and human performance (MS); health information technology (MS); respiratory care (MS). *Program availability:* Part-time, evening/weekend, 100% online, blended/hybrid learning. *Faculty:* 2 full-time (0 women), 8 part-time/adjunct (6 women). *Students:* 21 full-time (11 women), 40 part-time (34 women); includes 9 minority (7 Black or African American, non-Hispanic/Latino; 1 Hispanic/Latino; 1 Two or more races, non-Hispanic/Latino), 1 international. Average age 36. 18 applicants, 94% accepted, 17 enrolled. In 2017, 31 master's awarded. *Entrance requirements:* For master's, GRE (recommended), bachelor's degree transcript, two letters of recommendation, current licensure (for applied nutrition), minimum GPA of 2.7, current resume. Additional exam requirements/recommendations for international students: Required—TOEFL (minimum score 550 paper-based, 79 iBT), IELTS (minimum score 6.5), or CAEL (minimum score 70). *Application deadline:* Applications are processed on a rolling basis. Application fee: $0. Electronic applications accepted. *Expenses: Tuition:* Full-time $22,860; part-time $820 per credit. *Required fees:* $720; $25 per credit. $65 per semester. One-time fee: $425. *Financial support:* Career-related internships or fieldwork, Federal Work-Study, scholarships/grants, tuition waivers (partial), and unspecified assistantships available. Support available to part-time students. Financial award application deadline: 4/30; financial award applicants required to submit FAFSA. *Faculty research:* Nutrition, community and school health; community and health; health and human performance applied; nutrition and respiratory care. *Unit head:* Dennis W. Koch, Director, Office of Professional Studies, 716-888-8292, E-mail: koch5@canisius.edu.
Website: http://www.canisius.edu/graduate/

Cleveland State University, College of Graduate Studies, College of Sciences and Health Professions, School of Health Sciences, Program in Health Sciences, Cleveland, OH 44115. Offers health sciences (MS); physician assistant science (MS). *Program availability:* Part-time, evening/weekend, online learning. *Faculty:* 7 full-time (6 women), 6 part-time/adjunct (all women). *Students:* 67 full-time (48 women), 26 part-time (20 women); includes 24 minority (7 Black or African American, non-Hispanic/Latino; 6 Asian, non-Hispanic/Latino; 9 Hispanic/Latino; 2 Two or more races, non-Hispanic/Latino), 1 international. Average age 31. 85 applicants, 73% accepted, 48 enrolled. In 2017, 52 master's awarded. *Entrance requirements:* For master's, GRE (minimum scores of 50th percentile in all areas; analytical writing 3.5), bachelor's degree from accredited institution, minimum prerequisite course GPA of 3.0, all courses completed with minimum grade of C. Additional exam requirements/recommendations for international students: Required—TOEFL (minimum score 550 paper-based; 78 iBT). Application fee: $40. Electronic applications accepted. *Financial support:* Research assistantships with partial tuition reimbursements, career-related internships or fieldwork, Federal Work-Study, institutionally sponsored loans, scholarships/grants, traineeships, tuition waivers (partial), and unspecified assistantships available. Support available to part-time students. Financial award applicants required to submit FAFSA. *Faculty research:* Assisted technologies, biomechanics, clinical administration, cultural health, gerontology. *Unit head:* Dr. Stephen Slane, Chairperson and Professor Emeritus, 216-687-2379, E-mail: s.slane@csuohio.edu. *Application contact:* Karen Armstrong, Administrative Assistant, 216-687-3567, Fax: 216-687-9316, E-mail: healthsci@csuohio.edu.
Website: http://www.csuohio.edu/sciences/dept/healthsciences/graduate/index.html

Concordia University, St. Paul, College of Health and Science, St. Paul, MN 55104-5494. Offers exercise science (MS); orthotics and prosthetics (MS); physical therapy (DPT); sports management (MA). *Program availability:* Part-time, evening/weekend, 100% online, blended/hybrid learning. *Faculty:* 14 full-time (8 women), 22 part-time/adjunct (8 women). *Students:* 260 full-time (127 women), 20 part-time (6 women); includes 48 minority (24 Black or African American, non-Hispanic/Latino; 5 Asian, non-Hispanic/Latino; 11 Hispanic/Latino; 1 Native Hawaiian or other Pacific Islander, non-Hispanic/Latino; 7 Two or more races, non-Hispanic/Latino), 4 international. Average age 28. 218 applicants, 43% accepted, 84 enrolled. In 2017, 57 master's, 26 doctorates awarded. *Degree requirements:* For master's, comprehensive exam (for some programs), thesis (for some programs); for doctorate, at least one 8-12 week clinical rotation outside the St. Paul area. *Entrance requirements:* For master's, official transcripts from regionally-accredited institution stating the conferral of a bachelor's degree with minimum cumulative GPA of 3.0; personal statement; resume; for doctorate, GRE, official transcript from regionally-accredited institution showing bachelor's degree and minimum coursework GPA of 3.0; 100 physical therapy observation hours; two letters of professional recommendation. Additional exam requirements/recommendations for international students: Recommended—TOEFL (minimum score 547 paper-based; 78 iBT), IELTS (minimum score 6), TSE (minimum score 52). *Application deadline:* For fall admission, 4/1 for domestic students. Applications are processed on a rolling basis. Application fee: $0. Electronic applications accepted. *Expenses:* $475 per credit (for MA and MS); $810 per credit (for DPT). *Financial support:* In 2017–18, 60 students received support. Scholarships/grants and unspecified assistantships available. Financial award applicants required to submit FAFSA. *Faculty research:* Developmental screening in early childhood, cardiovascular responses to aerobic exercise. *Unit head:* Dr. Katie Fischer, Dean, 651-641-8735, E-mail: fischer@csp.edu. *Application contact:* Amber Faletti, Director of Enrollment Management, 651-641-8838, Fax: 651-603-6320, E-mail: faletti@csp.edu.

Creighton University, School of Pharmacy and Health Professions, Omaha, NE 68178-0001. Offers MS, DPT, OTD, Pharm D, Pharm D/MS. *Accreditation:* ACPE (one or more programs are accredited). *Program availability:* Online learning. *Entrance requirements:* For doctorate, PCAT (for Pharm D); GRE (for DPT). Electronic applications accepted. *Expenses:* Contact institution. *Faculty research:* Patient safety in health services research, health information technology and health services research, interdisciplinary educational research in the health professions, outcomes research in the health professions, cross-cultural care in the health professions.

Dominican College, Division of Allied Health, Orangeburg, NY 10962-1210. Offers MS, DPT. *Program availability:* Part-time, evening/weekend, online learning. *Faculty:* 10 full-time (4 women), 26 part-time/adjunct (18 women). *Students:* 152 full-time (108 women), 191 part-time (116 women); includes 146 minority (11 Black or African American, non-Hispanic/Latino; 1 American Indian or Alaska Native, non-Hispanic/Latino; 97 Asian, non-Hispanic/Latino; 26 Hispanic/Latino; 3 Native Hawaiian or other Pacific Islander, non-Hispanic/Latino; 8 Two or more races, non-Hispanic/Latino), 36 international. Average age 37. In 2017, 54 master's, 112 doctorates awarded. *Entrance requirements:* Additional exam requirements/recommendations for international students: Required—TOEFL (minimum score 550 paper-based; 90 iBT). *Application deadline:* Applications are processed on a rolling basis. Application fee: $50. Electronic applications accepted. *Expenses: Tuition:* Part-time $900 per credit. One-time fee: $200. Tuition and fees vary according to degree level and program. *Financial support:* Applicants required to submit FAFSA. *Unit head:* Margaret Boyd, Coordinator of Academic Study and Fieldwork, 845-848-6033, Fax: 845-398-4893, E-mail: margaret.boyd@dc.edu. *Application contact:* Christina Lifshey, Assistant Director of Graduate Admissions, 845-848-7900, Fax: 845-365-3150, E-mail: admissions@dc.edu.

Drexel University, College of Nursing and Health Professions, Philadelphia, PA 19104-2875. Offers MA, MFT, MHS, MS, MSN, DPT, Dr NP, PPDPT, PhD, Certificate, PMC. *Accreditation:* ACEN. *Program availability:* Part-time, evening/weekend. Terminal master's awarded for partial completion of doctoral program. *Degree requirements:* For master's, comprehensive exam, thesis (for some programs); for doctorate, thesis/dissertation, qualifying exam. *Entrance requirements:* For doctorate, GRE General Test. Electronic applications accepted.

Duquesne University, John G. Rangos, Sr. School of Health Sciences, Pittsburgh, PA 15282-0001. Offers health management systems (MHMS); occupational therapy (MS, OTD); physical therapy (DPT); physician assistant studies (MPAS); rehabilitation science (MS, PhD); speech-language pathology (MS). *Accreditation:* AOTA (one or more programs are accredited); APTA (one or more programs are accredited); ASHA. *Program availability:* Part-time, minimal on-campus study. *Faculty:* 51 full-time (38 women), 33 part-time/adjunct (17 women). *Students:* 247 full-time (199 women), 11 part-time (7 women); includes 15 minority (2 Black or African American, non-Hispanic/Latino; 7 Asian, non-Hispanic/Latino; 3 Hispanic/Latino; 3 Two or more races, non-Hispanic/Latino), 42 international. Average age 23. 283 applicants, 31% accepted, 54 enrolled. In 2017, 134 master's, 39 doctorates awarded. *Degree requirements:* For doctorate, comprehensive exam (for some programs), thesis/dissertation (for some programs). *Entrance requirements:* For master's, GRE General Test (speech-language pathology), 3 letters of recommendation; minimum GPA of 2.75 (health management systems), 3.0 (speech-language pathology); for doctorate, GRE General Test (for physical therapy and rehabilitation science), 3 letters of recommendation, minimum GPA of 3.0, personal interview. Additional exam requirements/recommendations for international students: Required—TOEFL (minimum score 550 paper-based; 90 iBT); Recommended—IELTS. *Application deadline:* For fall admission, 2/1 for domestic and international students; for spring admission, 7/1 for domestic and international students. Applications are processed on a rolling basis. Application fee: $0. Electronic applications accepted. *Expenses:* $1,351 per credit ($1,259 for health management systems). *Financial support:* Federal Work-Study available. Financial award applicants required to submit FAFSA. *Faculty research:* Neuronal processing, electrical stimulation on peripheral neuropathy, central nervous system (CNS) stimulatory and inhibitory signals, behavioral genetic methodologies to development disorders of speech, neurogenic communication disorders. *Total annual research expenditures:* $24,578. *Unit head:* Dr. Fevzi Akinci, Dean, 412-396-5303, Fax: 412-396-5554, E-mail: akincif@duq.edu. *Application contact:* Christopher R. Hilf, Director of Enrollment Management, 412-396-5653, Fax: 412-396-5554, E-mail: hilfc@duq.edu.
Website: http://www.duq.edu/academics/schools/health-sciences

Duquesne University, Post-Baccalaureate Pre-Medical and Health Professions Program, Pittsburgh, PA 15282-0001. Offers Postbaccalaureate Certificate. *Faculty:* 1 (woman) full-time. *Students:* 6 full-time (4 women); includes 3 minority (2 Black or African American, non-Hispanic/Latino; 1 Hispanic/Latino). Average age 23. 40 applicants, 38% accepted, 3 enrolled. In 2017, 6 Postbaccalaureate Certificates awarded. *Entrance requirements:* For degree, undergraduate degree from accredited college or university; minimum cumulative undergraduate GPA of 3.0, 2.75 for all relevant math/science courses taken; official transcripts with no final grades of D or F. *Application deadline:* For fall admission, 5/15 for domestic students. Applications are processed on a rolling basis. Application fee: $0. Electronic applications accepted. *Expenses:* $1,259 per credit. *Financial support:* Applicants required to submit FAFSA. *Unit head:* Dr. Paula Sammarone-Turocy, Director, 412-396-6335, Fax: 412-396-5587, E-mail: turocyp@duq.edu. *Application contact:* Todd Eicker, Director of Graduate Admission, 412-396-6219, E-mail: eickert@duq.edu.

East Carolina University, Graduate School, College of Allied Health Sciences, Greenville, NC 27834. Offers MS, MSOT, Au D, DPT, PhD, Certificate. *Program availability:* Part-time, evening/weekend, online learning. *Students:* 472 full-time (400 women), 194 part-time (165 women); includes 116 minority (65 Black or African American, non-Hispanic/Latino; 2 American Indian or Alaska Native, non-Hispanic/Latino; 19 Asian, non-Hispanic/Latino; 20 Hispanic/Latino; 10 Two or more races, non-Hispanic/Latino), 2 international. Average age 29. 1,173 applicants, 27% accepted, 203 enrolled. In 2017, 144 master's, 39 doctorates, 65 other advanced degrees awarded. *Degree requirements:* For master's, comprehensive exam (for some programs), thesis (for some programs); for doctorate, comprehensive exam (for some programs), thesis/dissertation (for some programs). *Entrance requirements:* For master's and doctorate, GRE, MAT or GMAT. Additional exam requirements/recommendations for international students: Recommended—TOEFL, IELTS. *Application deadline:* For fall admission, 2/1 for domestic and international students; for spring admission, 9/1 for domestic students, 10/1 for international students. Applications are processed on a rolling basis. Application fee: $75. Electronic applications accepted. *Expenses:* Tuition, state resident: full-time $4749; part-time $297 per credit hour. Tuition, nonresident: full-time $17,898; part-time $1119 per credit hour. *Required fees:* $2691; $224 per credit hour. Part-time tuition and fees vary according to course load and program. *Financial support:* Research assistantships with partial tuition reimbursements, teaching assistantships with partial tuition reimbursements, career-related internships or fieldwork, Federal Work-Study, scholarships/grants, and unspecified assistantships available. Support available to part-time students. Financial award application deadline: 3/1; financial award applicants required to submit FAFSA. *Faculty research:* Hearing, stuttering, therapeutic activities, ACL injury. *Unit head:* Dr. Greg Hassler, Interim Dean, 252-744-6010, E-mail: hasslerg@ecu.edu.
Website: http://www.ecu.edu/cs-dhs/ah/

Eastern Kentucky University, The Graduate School, College of Health Sciences, Richmond, KY 40475-3102. Offers MPH, MS, MSN. *Program availability:* Part-time. *Entrance requirements:* For master's, GRE General Test, minimum GPA of 2.75.

East Tennessee State University, School of Graduate Studies, College of Clinical and Rehabilitative Health Sciences, Department of Allied Health Sciences, Elizabethton, TN 37643. Offers allied health (MSAH); clinical nutrition (MS). *Program availability:* Part-time, online learning. *Degree requirements:* For master's, comprehensive exam, thesis or advanced practice seminar (for MSAH); internship (for MS). *Entrance requirements:* For master's, GRE General Test, professional license in allied health discipline, minimum GPA of 2.75, and three professional letters of recommendation (for MSAH); bachelor's degree from an undergraduate didactic program in dietetics with minimum GPA of 3.0 in DPD coursework and three letters of recommendation (for MS). Additional exam requirements/recommendations for international students: Required—TOEFL (minimum score 550 paper-based; 79 iBT). *Application deadline:* For fall admission, 2/15 for domestic and international students; for spring admission, 11/1 for domestic students, 9/29 for international students. Application fee: $55 ($65 for international students). Electronic applications accepted. *Financial support:* Research assistantships with partial tuition reimbursements, teaching assistantships with partial tuition reimbursements, career-related internships or fieldwork, institutionally sponsored loans, scholarships/grants, and unspecified assistantships available. Financial award application deadline: 7/1; financial award applicants required to submit FAFSA. *Faculty research:* Recruitment and retention of allied health professionals, relationship between APACHEE II scores and the need for a tracheotomy, health care workers, patient care, occupational stress, radiofrequency lesioning, absorption of lipophilic compounds, Vitamin D status in college-age students, childhood and adolescence obesity, nutrition education/interventions. *Unit head:* Dr. Ester Verhovsek, Chair, 423-547-4900, Fax: 423-439-4921, E-mail: verhovse@etsu.edu. *Application contact:* Dr. Ester Verhovsek, Chair, 423-547-4900, Fax: 423-439-4921, E-mail: verhovse@etsu.edu.
Website: http://www.etsu.edu/crhs/alliedhealth/

Emory University, School of Medicine, Programs in Allied Health Professions, Atlanta, GA 30322-1100. Offers anesthesiology assistant (MM Sc); genetic counseling (MM Sc), including human genetics and genetic counseling; physical therapy (DPT); physician assistant (MM Sc). *Entrance requirements:* For master's, GRE or MCAT; for doctorate, GRE. Electronic applications accepted. *Expenses:* Contact institution.

Ferris State University, College of Health Professions, Big Rapids, MI 49307. Offers MHA, MPH, MSN. *Program availability:* Part-time, evening/weekend, 100% online. *Faculty:* 16 full-time (13 women), 2 part-time/adjunct (both women). *Students:* 28 full-time (25 women), 129 part-time (116 women); includes 22 minority (4 Black or African American, non-Hispanic/Latino; 6 American Indian or Alaska Native, non-Hispanic/Latino; 3 Asian, non-Hispanic/Latino; 3 Hispanic/Latino; 1 Native Hawaiian or other Pacific Islander, non-Hispanic/Latino; 5 Two or more races, non-Hispanic/Latino). Average age 34. 64 applicants, 91% accepted, 54 enrolled. In 2017, 25 master's awarded. *Degree requirements:* For master's, practicum, practicum project. *Entrance requirements:* Additional exam requirements/recommendations for international students: Required—TOEFL (minimum score 500 paper-based; 61 iBT). *Application deadline:* For fall admission, 4/15 priority date for domestic students; for spring admission, 10/15 for domestic students. Applications are processed on a rolling basis. Application fee: $0. Electronic applications accepted. *Financial support:* In 2017–18, 3 students received support. Career-related internships or fieldwork and scholarships/grants available. Financial award application deadline: 4/15; financial award applicants

required to submit FAFSA. *Unit head:* Dr. Matthew Adeyanju, Dean, 231-591-2342, E-mail: matthewadeyanju@ferris.edu. *Application contact:* Dr. Kristen Salomonson, Dean of Enrollment Services and Director of Admissions and Records, 231-591-3963, Fax: 231-591-3179, E-mail: kristensalomonson@ferris.edu.
Website: http://www.ferris.edu/htmls/colleges/alliedhe/

Florida Agricultural and Mechanical University, Division of Graduate Studies, Research, and Continuing Education, School of Allied Health Sciences, Tallahassee, FL 32307-3200. Offers health administration (MS); occupational therapy (MOT); physical therapy (DPT). *Degree requirements:* For master's, thesis (for some programs). *Entrance requirements:* For master's, GRE General Test or GMAT, minimum GPA of 3.0. Additional exam requirements/recommendations for international students: Required—TOEFL (minimum score 550 paper-based).

Florida Gulf Coast University, Elaine Nicpon Marieb College of Health and Human Services, Fort Myers, FL 33965-6565. Offers MA, MPAS, MS, MSN, MSW, DNP, DPT. *Accreditation:* AOTA. *Program availability:* Part-time, evening/weekend, online learning. *Faculty:* 71 full-time (49 women), 49 part-time/adjunct (32 women). *Students:* 187 full-time (147 women), 133 part-time (98 women); includes 114 minority (33 Black or African American, non-Hispanic/Latino; 12 Asian, non-Hispanic/Latino; 61 Hispanic/Latino; 8 Two or more races, non-Hispanic/Latino), 3 international. Average age 29. 473 applicants, 51% accepted, 186 enrolled. In 2017, 111 master's, 32 doctorates awarded. *Degree requirements:* For master's, thesis or alternative. *Entrance requirements:* For master's, GRE General Test or MAT, minimum GPA of 3.0. Additional exam requirements/recommendations for international students: Required—TOEFL (minimum score 550 paper-based). *Application deadline:* For fall admission, 2/15 priority date for domestic students; for spring admission, 12/1 for domestic students. Applications are processed on a rolling basis. Application fee: $30. Electronic applications accepted. *Expenses:* Tuition, state resident: part-time $290 per credit hour. Tuition, nonresident: part-time $1173 per credit hour. *Required fees:* $127 per credit hour. Tuition and fees vary according to course load. *Financial support:* In 2017–18, 62 students received support. Career-related internships or fieldwork, Federal Work-Study, and institutionally sponsored loans available. Financial award application deadline: 6/30; financial award applicants required to submit FAFSA. *Faculty research:* Health care policy, health administration, community-based services. *Total annual research expenditures:* $140,292. *Unit head:* Dr. Joan Glacken, Interim Dean, 239-590-7498, E-mail: jglacken@fgcu.edu. *Application contact:* Susan Baurer, Administrative Assistant, 239-590-7451, E-mail: sbaurer@fgcu.edu.
Website: https://www2.fgcu.edu/mariebcollege/

Georgia Southern University, Jack N. Averitt College of Graduate Studies, College of Health and Human Sciences, Statesboro, GA 30460. Offers MS, MSN, DNP, Certificate. *Program availability:* Part-time, evening/weekend, 100% online, blended/hybrid learning. *Faculty:* 78 full-time (54 women), 6 part-time/adjunct (5 women). *Students:* 110 full-time (68 women), 154 part-time (102 women); includes 77 minority (52 Black or African American, non-Hispanic/Latino; 7 Asian, non-Hispanic/Latino; 13 Hispanic/Latino; 5 Two or more races, non-Hispanic/Latino), 5 international. Average age 31. 287 applicants, 45% accepted, 98 enrolled. In 2017, 88 master's, 7 other advanced degrees awarded. *Degree requirements:* For master's, comprehensive exam (for some programs), thesis (for some programs), exams; for doctorate, comprehensive exam, practicum. *Entrance requirements:* For master's, GRE General Test, MAT or GMAT; for doctorate, GRE or MAT. Additional exam requirements/recommendations for international students: Required—TOEFL (minimum score 550 paper-based; 80 iBT), IELTS (minimum score 6). *Application deadline:* For fall admission, 3/1 priority date for domestic students, 3/1 for international students; for spring admission, 10/1 priority date for domestic students, 10/1 for international students. Applications are processed on a rolling basis. Application fee: $50. Electronic applications accepted. *Expenses:* Tuition, state resident: full-time $4986; part-time $3324 per year. Tuition, nonresident: full-time $21,982; part-time $15,352 per year. *Required fees:* $2092; $1802 per credit hour. $901 per semester. Tuition and fees vary according to course load, campus/location and program. *Financial support:* In 2017–18, 134 students received support, including 24 fellowships with full tuition reimbursements available (averaging $7,750 per year), 9 research assistantships with full tuition reimbursements available (averaging $7,750 per year), 33 teaching assistantships with full tuition reimbursements available (averaging $7,750 per year); career-related internships or fieldwork, Federal Work-Study, scholarships/grants, traineeships, and unspecified assistantships also available. Support available to part-time students. Financial award application deadline: 4/15; financial award applicants required to submit FAFSA. *Faculty research:* Kinesiology, sport performance, coaching, nursing, nutrition. *Total annual research expenditures:* $99,590. *Unit head:* Dr. Barry Joyner, Dean, 912-478-5322, Fax: 912-478-5349, E-mail: joyner@georgiasouthern.edu.
Website: http://chhs.georgiasouthern.edu/

Georgia State University, Byrdine F. Lewis School of Nursing, Division of Respiratory Therapy, Atlanta, GA 30302-3083. Offers MS. *Faculty:* 3 full-time (2 women). *Students:* 39 full-time (28 women), 6 part-time (5 women); includes 15 minority (10 Black or African American, non-Hispanic/Latino; 4 Asian, non-Hispanic/Latino; 1 Hispanic/Latino), 14 international. Average age 30. 34 applicants, 85% accepted, 16 enrolled. In 2017, 20 master's awarded. *Degree requirements:* For master's, thesis. *Entrance requirements:* For master's, GRE, transcripts, resume, statement of goals, letters of recommendation. Additional exam requirements/recommendations for international students: Required—TOEFL (minimum score 550 paper-based; 80 iBT). *Application deadline:* For fall admission, 5/1 for domestic and international students; for spring admission, 9/15 for domestic and international students. Application fee: $50. Electronic applications accepted. *Expenses:* Tuition, state resident: full-time $7020. Tuition, nonresident: full-time $22,518. *Required fees:* $2128. Tuition and fees vary according to degree level and program. *Financial support:* In 2017–18, research assistantships with full tuition reimbursements (averaging $2,000 per year), teaching assistantships with full tuition reimbursements (averaging $2,000 per year) were awarded; scholarships/grants and unspecified assistantships also available. Financial award application deadline: 6/1; financial award applicants required to submit FAFSA. *Faculty research:* Aerosol delivery methods, aerosol devices, smoking cessation, continuing and professional respiratory therapy education, chronic lung disease management. *Unit head:* Dr. Douglas Gardenhire, Department Head, 404-413-1270, Fax: 404-413-1230, E-mail: dgardenhire@gsu.edu.
Website: http://respiratorytherapy.gsu.edu/

Grand Valley State University, College of Health Professions, Allendale, MI 49401-9403. Offers MPAS, MPH, MS, DPT. *Faculty:* 59 full-time (45 women), 13 part-time/adjunct (all women). *Students:* 644 full-time (503 women), 48 part-time (34 women); includes 63 minority (13 Black or African American, non-Hispanic/Latino; 1 American Indian or Alaska Native, non-Hispanic/Latino; 14 Asian, non-Hispanic/Latino; 20 Hispanic/Latino; 15 Two or more races, non-Hispanic/Latino), 7 international. Average age 25. 1,181 applicants, 29% accepted, 273 enrolled. In 2017, 207 master's, 58 doctorates awarded. *Entrance requirements:* For master's, volunteer work, interview, minimum GPA of 3.0, writing sample; for doctorate, GRE, 50 hours of volunteer work, interview, minimum GPA of 3.0 in last 60 hours and in prerequisites, writing sample. Additional exam requirements/recommendations for international students: Required—TOEFL (minimum score 610 paper-based). *Application deadline:* For winter admission, 1/15 priority date for domestic and international students. Applications are processed on a rolling basis. Electronic applications accepted. Tuition and fees vary according to degree level and program. *Financial support:* In 2017–18, 104 students received support, including 75 fellowships, 37 research assistantships with full and partial tuition reimbursements available (averaging $8,000 per year); career-related internships or fieldwork, Federal Work-Study, institutionally sponsored loans, and scholarships/grants also available. Financial award application deadline: 2/15. *Faculty research:* Skeletal muscle structure, blood platelets, thrombospondin activity, FES exercise for quadriplegics, balance. *Unit head:* Dr. Roy Olsson, Dean, 616-331-3356, Fax: 616-331-3350, E-mail: olssonr@gvsu.edu. *Application contact:* Darlene Zwart, Student Services Coordinator, 616-331-3958, E-mail: zwartda@gvsu.edu.
Website: http://www.gvsu.edu/shp/

Hampton University, School of Science, Program in Medical Science, Hampton, VA 23668. Offers MS. *Students:* 59 full-time (43 women); includes 57 minority (56 Black or African American, non-Hispanic/Latino; 1 Hispanic/Latino). Average age 25. 112 applicants, 30% accepted, 10 enrolled. In 2017, 21 master's awarded. *Degree requirements:* For master's, comprehensive exam. *Entrance requirements:* For master's, MCAT or DAT. Additional exam requirements/recommendations for international students: Required—TOEFL (minimum score 525 paper-based) or IELTS (6.5). *Application deadline:* For fall admission, 6/1 priority date for domestic students, 4/1 priority date for international students; for summer admission, 6/1 for domestic students. Applications are processed on a rolling basis. Application fee: $35. Electronic applications accepted. *Expenses: Tuition:* Full-time $22,630; part-time $575 per semester hour. *Required fees:* $70. Tuition and fees vary according to program. *Financial support:* In 2017–18, 4 students received support. Unspecified assistantships available. Financial award application deadline: 6/30; financial award applicants required to submit FAFSA. *Faculty research:* Cancer, health disparities, protein kinases, neurodegeneration, nanoparticles, cellular differentiation, experimental physical chemistry, laser spectroscopy, RNA biology, bioinformatics, genomics. *Unit head:* Michael Darnell Druitt, Medical Science Coordinator, 757-727-5795, E-mail: michael.druitt@hamptonu.edu.
Website: http://science.hamptonu.edu/prehealth/mprograms.cfm

Harding University, College of Allied Health, Searcy, AR 72149-0001. Offers MS, DPT. *Faculty:* 27 full-time (16 women), 4 part-time/adjunct (2 women). *Students:* 245 full-time (170 women), 78 part-time (2 women); includes 30 minority (8 Black or African American, non-Hispanic/Latino; 3 American Indian or Alaska Native, non-Hispanic/Latino; 9 Asian, non-Hispanic/Latino; 9 Hispanic/Latino; 1 Two or more races, non-Hispanic/Latino). Average age 26. 1,084 applicants, 16% accepted, 90 enrolled. In 2017, 53 master's, 28 doctorates awarded. *Entrance requirements:* Additional exam requirements/recommendations for international students: Required—TOEFL. Tuition and fees vary according to course load, degree level, campus/location and program. *Financial support:* In 2017–18, 6 students received support. *Application contact:* Dr. Julie Hixson-Wallace, Vice Provost, 501-279-5205, Fax: 501-279-5192, E-mail: jahixson@harding.edu.
Website: http://www.harding.edu/academics/colleges-departments/allied-health

Howard University, College of Nursing and Allied Health Sciences, Division of Allied Health Sciences, Washington, DC 20059-0002. Offers occupational therapy (MSOT); physical therapy (DPT); physician assistant (MPA). *Accreditation:* AOTA.

Idaho State University, Office of Graduate Studies, School of Health Professions, Pocatello, ID 83209-8090. Offers M Coun, MHE, MPH, MS, PhD, Ed S. *Accreditation:* APTA (one or more programs are accredited). *Program availability:* Part-time. *Degree requirements:* For master's, comprehensive exam, thesis (for some programs), 8-week externship; for doctorate, comprehensive exam, thesis/dissertation, clinical rotation (for some programs); for Ed S, comprehensive exam, thesis, case study, oral exam. *Entrance requirements:* For master's, GRE General Test or MAT, minimum GPA of 3.0, 3 letters of recommendation; for doctorate, GRE General Test or MAT, minimum GPA of 3.0, counseling license, professional research, interview, work experience, 3 letters of recommendation; for Ed S, GRE General Test or MAT, master's degree in similar field of study, 3 letters of recommendation, 2 years of work experience. Additional exam requirements/recommendations for international students: Required—TOEFL (minimum score 600 paper-based; 80 iBT). Electronic applications accepted. *Expenses:* Contact institution. *Faculty research:* Mental health, information technology, dental health, nursing.

Ithaca College, School of Health Sciences and Human Performance, Ithaca, NY 14850. Offers MS, DPT. *Program availability:* Part-time. *Faculty:* 59 full-time (40 women), 3 part-time/adjunct (all women). *Students:* 311 full-time (238 women), 15 part-time (8 women); includes 48 minority (9 Black or African American, non-Hispanic/Latino; 15 Asian, non-Hispanic/Latino; 11 Hispanic/Latino; 13 Two or more races, non-Hispanic/Latino), 3 international. Average age 23. 371 applicants, 50% accepted, 184 enrolled. In 2017, 99 master's, 78 doctorates awarded. *Degree requirements:* For master's, thesis (for some programs); for doctorate, thesis/dissertation optional. *Entrance requirements:* Additional exam requirements/recommendations for international students: Required—TOEFL (minimum score 550 paper-based; 80 iBT). *Application deadline:* Applications are processed on a rolling basis. Application fee: $40. Electronic applications accepted. *Expenses:* Contact institution. *Financial support:* In 2017–18, 214 students received support, including 69 research assistantships (averaging $12,462 per year); career-related internships or fieldwork, Federal Work-Study, scholarships/grants, and unspecified assistantships also available. Support available to part-time students. Financial award applicants required to submit FAFSA. *Unit head:* Dr. John Sigg, Interim Dean, 607-274-3237, Fax: 607-274-1263, E-mail: sigg@ithaca.edu. *Application contact:* Nicole Eversley Bradwell, Director, Office of Admission, 607-274-3124, Fax: 607-274-1263, E-mail: admission@ithaca.edu.
Website: http://www.ithaca.edu/hshp

Jacksonville University, Brooks Rehabilitation College of Healthcare Sciences, School of Applied Health Sciences, Jacksonville, FL 32211. Offers clinical mental health counseling (MS), including clinical mental health counseling; health informatics (MS); kinesiological sciences (MS); occupational therapy (OTD); speech-language pathology (MS); sport management (MS). *Program availability:* Part-time, 100% online, blended/hybrid learning. *Faculty:* 18 full-time (10 women), 19 part-time/adjunct (9 women). *Students:* 150 full-time (118 women), 100 part-time (69 women); includes 108 minority (62 Black or African American, non-Hispanic/Latino; 2 American Indian or Alaska Native, non-Hispanic/Latino; 11 Asian, non-Hispanic/Latino; 29 Hispanic/Latino; 4 Two or more races, non-Hispanic/Latino), 3 international. Average age 31. 145 applicants, 91% accepted, 93 enrolled. In 2017, 43 master's awarded. *Degree requirements:* For doctorate, observation of occupational therapy practice; minimum of 40 hours total among three different settings (hospital, school system, home health, clinic, etc.). *Entrance requirements:* For master's, GRE (for speech language pathology and kinesiological sciences), baccalaureate degree from accredited college or university with minimum GPA of 3.0; official transcripts; essay on professional goals (minimum 1000 words); resume (education, work experience); 3 letters of recommendation; interview; for doctorate, GRE, baccalaureate degree from accredited college or university with minimum GPA of 3.0; official transcripts; observation of occupational therapy practice with minimum of 40 hours total among three settings (hospital, school system, home

health, clinic, etc.); interview. Additional exam requirements/recommendations for international students: Required—TOEFL (minimum score 650 paper-based; 114 iBT), IELTS (minimum score 8). *Application deadline:* For fall admission, 2/1 for domestic and international students. Applications are processed on a rolling basis. Application fee: $50. Electronic applications accepted. *Expenses:* $795 per credit hour (health informatics); $780 per credit hour (kinesiology); $680 per credit hour (mental health); $895 per credit hour (speech and language pathology); $630 per credit hour (sport management). *Financial support:* Federal Work-Study, institutionally sponsored loans, scholarships/grants, and health care benefits available. Support available to part-time students. Financial award application deadline: 3/15; financial award applicants required to submit FAFSA. *Faculty research:* PTSD, biomechanics, aphasia, autism, pediatric bilingual-multicultural speech disorders. *Unit head:* Dr. Heather Hausenblas, Associate Dean, School of Applied Health Sciences, 904-256-7975, E-mail: hhausen@ju.edu. *Application contact:* Ashlea Rieser, Assistant Director of Enrollment and Advising, 904-256-8934, E-mail: arieser0@ju.edu.
Website: https://www.ju.edu/appliedhealth/index.php

Loma Linda University, School of Allied Health Professions, Loma Linda, CA 92350. Offers MOT, MPA, MS, DPT, OTD, PhD, SLPD. *Accreditation:* AOTA; APTA. *Entrance requirements:* For master's, minimum GPA of 2.0; for doctorate, minimum GPA of 2.0, associate degree in physical therapy. Additional exam requirements/recommendations for international students: Required—TOEFL (minimum score 550 paper-based). Electronic applications accepted.

Long Island University–LIU Post, School of Health Professions and Nursing, Brookville, NY 11548-1300. Offers biomedical science (MS); cardiovascular perfusion (MS); clinical lab sciences (MS); clinical laboratory management (MS); dietetic internship (Advanced Certificate); family nurse practitioner (MS, Advanced Certificate); forensic social work (Advanced Certificate); gerontology (Advanced Certificate); health administration (MPA); non-profit management (Advanced Certificate); nursing education (MS); nutrition (MS); public administration (MPA); social work (MSW). *Program availability:* Part-time, blended/hybrid learning. *Faculty:* 23 full-time (17 women), 33 part-time/adjunct (19 women). *Students:* 228 full-time (174 women), 227 part-time (185 women); includes 172 minority (76 Black or African American, non-Hispanic/Latino; 1 American Indian or Alaska Native, non-Hispanic/Latino; 44 Asian, non-Hispanic/Latino; 48 Hispanic/Latino; 3 Two or more races, non-Hispanic/Latino), 60 international. Average age 31. 392 applicants, 67% accepted, 138 enrolled. In 2017, 180 master's, 26 other advanced degrees awarded. *Degree requirements:* For master's, comprehensive exam (for some programs), thesis (for some programs). *Entrance requirements:* Additional exam requirements/recommendations for international students: Required—TOEFL (minimum score 85 iBT) or IELTS (7.5). *Application deadline:* Applications are processed on a rolling basis. Application fee: $50. Electronic applications accepted. *Expenses: Tuition:* Full-time $21,618; part-time $1201 per credit. *Required fees:* $1840; $920 per term. Tuition and fees vary according to course load. *Financial support:* In 2017–18, 102 students received support. Research assistantships, teaching assistantships, career-related internships or fieldwork, Federal Work-Study, scholarships/grants, and unspecified assistantships available. Support available to part-time students. Financial award application deadline: 2/15; financial award applicants required to submit FAFSA. *Faculty research:* Antibiotic resistance, evidence-based practice, family care, interprofessional learning, simulation learning. *Unit head:* Dr. Stacy Gropack, Dean, 516-299-2485, Fax: 516-299-2527, E-mail: post-shpn@liu.edu. *Application contact:* Kathy Riley, Associate Director of Graduate Admissions, 516-299-2900, Fax: 516-299-2137, E-mail: post-enroll@liu.edu.
Website: http://liu.edu/post/health

Marymount University, Malek School of Health Professions, Arlington, VA 22207-4299. Offers MS, MSN, DNP, DPT, Certificate. *Program availability:* Part-time, evening/weekend. *Faculty:* 18 full-time (16 women), 21 part-time/adjunct (17 women). *Students:* 146 full-time (105 women), 50 part-time (46 women); includes 65 minority (26 Black or African American, non-Hispanic/Latino; 14 Asian, non-Hispanic/Latino; 17 Hispanic/Latino; 8 Two or more races, non-Hispanic/Latino), 7 international. Average age 30. 322 applicants, 53% accepted, 63 enrolled. In 2017, 25 master's, 38 doctorates, 3 other advanced degrees awarded. *Degree requirements:* For master's, comprehensive exam (for some programs), internship/clinical practicum; for doctorate, comprehensive exam (for some programs), thesis/dissertation, research presentation/residency. *Entrance requirements:* For master's, GRE, MAT, 2 letters of recommendation, interview, resume, personal statement; for doctorate, GRE, 2 letters of recommendation, interview, resume, 40 hours of clinical work experience whether volunteer or observation, essay, minimum GPA of 3.0 from previous university coursework; for Certificate, interview, master's degree in nursing with minimum of GPA of 3.3, current RN licensure. Additional exam requirements/recommendations for international students: Required—TOEFL (minimum score 600 paper-based; 96 iBT), IELTS (minimum score 6.5). *Application deadline:* For fall admission, 3/1 priority date for domestic and international students; for spring admission, 11/1 priority date for domestic and international students. Applications are processed on a rolling basis. Application fee: $40. Electronic applications accepted. *Expenses: Tuition:* Full-time $17,550; part-time $975 per credit hour. *Required fees:* $198; $11 per credit hour. One-time fee: $250. Tuition and fees vary according to program. *Financial support:* In 2017–18, 22 students received support, including 11 teaching assistantships with full and partial tuition reimbursements available (averaging $13,199 per year); research assistantships with full and partial tuition reimbursements available, career-related internships or fieldwork, Federal Work-Study, scholarships/grants, and unspecified assistantships also available. Support available to part-time students. Financial award application deadline: 3/1; financial award applicants required to submit FAFSA. *Unit head:* Dr. Jeanne Matthews, Dean, 703-284-1580, Fax: 703-284-3819, E-mail: jeanne.matthews@marymount.edu. *Application contact:* Francesca Reed, Director, Graduate Admissions, 703-284-5901, Fax: 703-527-3815, E-mail: grad.admissions@marymount.edu.
Website: http://www.marymount.edu/Academics/Malek-School-of-Health-Professions

Maryville University of Saint Louis, Myrtle E. and Earl E. Walker College of Health Professions, St. Louis, MO 63141-7299. Offers MARC, MMT, MOT, MS, MSN, DNP, DPT, Post-MSN Certificate. *Accreditation:* CORE. *Program availability:* Part-time, 100% online, blended/hybrid learning. *Faculty:* 52 full-time (43 women), 152 part-time/adjunct (132 women). *Students:* 269 full-time (229 women), 3,090 part-time (2,719 women); includes 795 minority (385 Black or African American, non-Hispanic/Latino; 51 American Indian or Alaska Native, non-Hispanic/Latino; 136 Asian, non-Hispanic/Latino; 158 Hispanic/Latino; 65 Two or more races, non-Hispanic/Latino), 23 international. Average age 35. In 2017, 895 master's, 80 doctorates awarded. *Entrance requirements:* Additional exam requirements/recommendations for international students: Required—TOEFL (minimum score 550 paper-based). *Application deadline:* Applications are processed on a rolling basis. Electronic applications accepted. *Expenses: Tuition:* Part-time $675 per credit hour. One-time fee: $350 part-time. Tuition and fees vary according to program. *Financial support:* Career-related internships or fieldwork, Federal Work-Study, and campus employment available. Financial award application deadline: 4/1; financial award applicants required to submit FAFSA. *Unit head:* Dr. Charles Gulas, Dean, 314-529-9625, Fax: 314-529-9495, E-mail: hlthprofessions@maryville.edu. *Application contact:* Jeannie DeLuca, Director of Admissions and Advising, 314-529-9355, Fax: 314-529-9927, E-mail: jdeluca@maryville.edu.
Website: http://www.maryville.edu/hp/

Medical University of South Carolina, College of Health Professions, Charleston, SC 29425. Offers MHA, MS, MSNA, MSOT, DHA, DPT, PhD. *Accreditation:* CAHME (one or more programs are accredited). *Program availability:* Part-time. *Degree requirements:* For doctorate, comprehensive exam, thesis/dissertation. *Entrance requirements:* For master's, GRE. Additional exam requirements/recommendations for international students: Required—TOEFL (minimum score 600 paper-based). Electronic applications accepted. *Expenses:* Contact institution. *Faculty research:* Spinal cord injury, geriatrics, rehabilitation sciences, behavioral medicine.

Mercy College, School of Health and Natural Sciences, Dobbs Ferry, NY 10522-1189. Offers communication disorders (MS); nursing (MS), including nursing administration, nursing education; occupational therapy (MS); physical therapy (DPT); physician assistant studies (MS). *Program availability:* Part-time, evening/weekend, blended/hybrid learning. *Students:* 379 full-time (290 women), 205 part-time (182 women); includes 273 minority (85 Black or African American, non-Hispanic/Latino; 76 Asian, non-Hispanic/Latino; 100 Hispanic/Latino; 3 Native Hawaiian or other Pacific Islander, non-Hispanic/Latino; 9 Two or more races, non-Hispanic/Latino), 1 international. Average age 33. 1,117 applicants, 20% accepted, 151 enrolled. In 2017, 184 master's, 25 doctorates awarded. *Degree requirements:* For master's, comprehensive exam (for some programs), thesis (for some programs). *Entrance requirements:* For master's and doctorate, essay, interview, resume, letters of recommendation, undergraduate transcripts. Additional exam requirements/recommendations for international students: Required—TOEFL (minimum score 600 paper-based; 79 iBT), IELTS (minimum score 8). *Application deadline:* For fall admission, 8/1 for international students. Applications are processed on a rolling basis. Application fee: $40. Electronic applications accepted. *Expenses:* Contact institution. *Financial support:* Career-related internships or fieldwork, Federal Work-Study, scholarships/grants, and unspecified assistantships available. Support available to part-time students. Financial award applicants required to submit FAFSA. *Unit head:* Dr. Joan Toglia, Dean, School of Health and Natural Sciences, 914-674-7837, E-mail: jtoglia@mercy.edu. *Application contact:* Allison Gurdineer, Senior Director of Admissions, 877-637-2946, Fax: 914-674-7382, E-mail: admissions@mercy.edu.
Website: https://www.mercy.edu/health-and-natural-sciences/

Midwestern University, Glendale Campus, College of Health Sciences, Arizona Campus, Glendale, AZ 85308. Offers MA, MBS, MCVS, MMS, MOT, MS, DPM, DPT, Psy D. *Program availability:* Part-time. *Application deadline:* For fall admission, 6/4 for domestic students. Applications are processed on a rolling basis. Application fee: $50. *Expenses:* Contact institution. *Financial support:* Federal Work-Study available.

Minnesota State University Mankato, College of Graduate Studies and Research, College of Allied Health and Nursing, Mankato, MN 56001. Offers MA, MS, MSN, DNP, Postbaccalaureate Certificate. *Program availability:* Part-time. *Degree requirements:* For master's, comprehensive exam; for Postbaccalaureate Certificate, thesis. *Entrance requirements:* For master's, GRE (for some programs), minimum GPA of 3.0 during previous 2 years; for Postbaccalaureate Certificate, GRE General Test, minimum GPA of 3.0. Electronic applications accepted.

Misericordia University, College of Health Sciences and Education, Dallas, PA 18612-1098. Offers MS, MSN, MSOT, MSSLP, DNP, DPT, OTD. *Program availability:* Part-time, evening/weekend. *Entrance requirements:* For doctorate, interview, references. Additional exam requirements/recommendations for international students: Required—TOEFL. Electronic applications accepted.

Moravian College, Graduate and Continuing Studies, Business and Management Programs, Bethlehem, PA 18018-6650. Offers accounting (MBA); business analytics (MBA); business management (MBA); health administration (MHA); healthcare management (MBA); HR leadership (MSHRM); human resource management (MBA); learning and performance management (MSHRM); supply chain management (MBA). *Program availability:* Part-time, evening/weekend. *Faculty:* 5 full-time (2 women), 9 part-time/adjunct (3 women). *Students:* 13 full-time (10 women), 80 part-time (45 women); includes 13 minority (6 Black or African American, non-Hispanic/Latino; 6 Hispanic/Latino; 1 Two or more races, non-Hispanic/Latino). Average age 31. 55 applicants, 91% accepted, 31 enrolled. In 2017, 29 master's awarded. *Entrance requirements:* For master's, current resume, official transcripts, 2 letters of recommendation. Additional exam requirements/recommendations for international students: Required—TOEFL (minimum score 550 paper-based), IELTS (minimum score 6.5). *Application deadline:* For fall admission, 8/1 priority date for domestic and international students; for spring admission, 1/1 priority date for domestic and international students; for summer admission, 5/1 priority date for domestic and international students. Applications are processed on a rolling basis. Electronic applications accepted. *Expenses: Tuition:* Full-time $15,714; part-time $2619 per course. *Required fees:* $45 per semester. Tuition and fees vary according to program. *Financial support:* In 2017–18, 3 students received support, including 2 research assistantships with full tuition reimbursements available. Financial award applicants required to submit FAFSA. *Faculty research:* Leadership, change management, human resources. *Unit head:* Dr. Liz Kleintop, Associate Chair of Graduate Business, 610-861-1400, Fax: 610-861-1466, E-mail: graduate@moravian.edu. *Application contact:* Sean Rossi, Student Experience Mentor, 610-861-1400, Fax: 610-861-1466, E-mail: graduate@moravian.edu.
Website: https://www.moravian.edu/graduate

New Jersey City University, College of Professional Studies, Department of Health Sciences, Jersey City, NJ 07305-1597. Offers community health education (MS); health administration (MS); school health education (MS). *Program availability:* Part-time, evening/weekend. *Degree requirements:* For master's, thesis or alternative, internship. *Entrance requirements:* Additional exam requirements/recommendations for international students: Required—TOEFL (minimum score 79 iBT).

Northeastern University, Bouvé College of Health Sciences, Boston, MA 02115-5096. Offers applied behavior analysis (MS); audiology (Au D); counseling psychology (MS, PhD, CAGS); exercise science (MS); nursing (MS, PhD, CAGS), including administration (MS), adult-gerontology acute care nurse practitioner (MS, CAGS), adult-gerontology primary care nurse practitioner (MS, CAGS), anesthesia (MS), family nurse practitioner (MS, CAGS), neonatal nurse practitioner (MS, CAGS), pediatric nurse practitioner (MS, CAGS), psychiatric mental health nurse practitioner (MS, CAGS); nursing practice (DNP); pharmaceutical sciences (MS, PhD), including interdisciplinary concentration, pharmaceutics and drug delivery systems; pharmacology (MS); pharmacy (Pharm D); school psychology (PhD); speech-language pathology (MS); urban health (MPH); MS/MBA. *Accreditation:* ACPE (one or more programs are accredited). *Program availability:* Part-time, evening/weekend, online learning. *Faculty:* 192 full-time. *Students:* 1,685. In 2017, 352 master's, 312 doctorates, 25 other advanced degrees awarded. *Degree requirements:* For doctorate, thesis/dissertation (for some programs); for CAGS, comprehensive exam. Application fee: $75. Electronic applications accepted. *Expenses:* Contact institution. *Financial support:* Fellowships, research assistantships, teaching assistantships, career-related internships or fieldwork, scholarships/grants, health care benefits, tuition waivers, and unspecified assistantships available. Support available to part-time students. Financial award applicants required to submit FAFSA. *Unit head:* Susan L. Parish, Dean, Bouve College of Health Sciences, 617-373-3321, Fax: 617-373-3030, E-mail: s.parish@northeastern.edu. *Application contact:* 617-373-2708, Fax: 617-373-4701, E-mail: bouvegrad@northeastern.edu.
Website: https://www.northeastern.edu/bouve/

Allied Health—General

Northern Arizona University, College of Health and Human Services, Flagstaff, AZ 86011. Offers MPAS, MS, DNP, DPT, OTD, Certificate. *Accreditation:* APTA (one or more programs are accredited). *Program availability:* Part-time, 100% online, blended/hybrid learning. *Faculty:* 137 full-time (112 women), 88 part-time/adjunct (65 women). *Students:* 601 full-time (434 women), 268 part-time (240 women); includes 239 minority (17 Black or African American, non-Hispanic/Latino; 19 American Indian or Alaska Native, non-Hispanic/Latino; 33 Asian, non-Hispanic/Latino; 131 Hispanic/Latino; 1 Native Hawaiian or other Pacific Islander, non-Hispanic/Latino; 38 Two or more races, non-Hispanic/Latino), 2 international. Average age 29. 2,297 applicants, 14% accepted, 316 enrolled. In 2017, 158 master's, 109 doctorates, 4 other advanced degrees awarded. *Degree requirements:* For master's, variable foreign language requirement, comprehensive exam (for some programs), thesis (for some programs); for doctorate, variable foreign language requirement, comprehensive exam (for some programs), thesis/dissertation (for some programs); for Certificate, comprehensive exam (for some programs). *Entrance requirements:* Additional exam requirements/recommendations for international students: Required—TOEFL (minimum score 80 iBT), IELTS (minimum score 6.5). *Application deadline:* For fall admission, 3/1 for domestic and international students; for spring admission, 10/1 for domestic and international students. Application fee: $65. Electronic applications accepted. *Expenses:* Tuition, state resident: full-time $9240; part-time $458 per credit hour. Tuition, nonresident: full-time $21,588; part-time $1199 per credit hour. *Required fees:* $1021; $14 per credit hour. $646 per semester. Tuition and fees vary according to course load, campus/location and program. *Financial support:* In 2017–18, 10 students received support, including 3 research assistantships with partial tuition reimbursements available (averaging $5,000 per year); institutionally sponsored loans, health care benefits, tuition waivers (full and partial), and unspecified assistantships also available. Financial award application deadline: 2/1; financial award applicants required to submit FAFSA. *Unit head:* Dr. Lynda Ransdell, Dean, 928-523-4331, Fax: 928-523-4315, E-mail: lynda.ransdell@nau.edu. *Application contact:* Tina Sutton, Coordinator, Graduate College, 928-523-4348, Fax: 928-523-8950, E-mail: graduate@nau.edu.
Website: https://nau.edu/chhs/

Northern Kentucky University, Office of Graduate Programs, School of Nursing and Health Professions, Program in Health Science, Highland Heights, KY 41099. Offers MS. *Program availability:* Online learning. *Degree requirements:* For master's, capstone, internship. *Entrance requirements:* For master's, official transcripts, minimum GPA of 3.0 on last 40 hours of undergraduate work, letter of intent, resume, undergraduate course in statistical methods with minimum C grade, interview. Additional exam requirements/recommendations for international students: Required—TOEFL (minimum score 79 iBT); Recommended—IELTS (minimum score 6.5).

Nova Southeastern University, Dr. Pallavi Patel College of Health Care Sciences, Fort Lauderdale, FL 33314-7796. Offers anesthesiologist assistant (MSA); audiology (Au D); health science (MH Sc, DHSc, PhD); occupational therapy (MOT, Dr OT, PhD); physical therapy (DPT, TDPT); physician assistant (MMS); speech-language pathology (MS). *Accreditation:* AOTA. *Faculty:* 54 full-time (31 women), 15 part-time/adjunct (7 women). *Students:* 501 full-time (407 women); includes 131 minority (18 Black or African American, non-Hispanic/Latino; 2 American Indian or Alaska Native, non-Hispanic/Latino; 45 Asian, non-Hispanic/Latino; 65 Hispanic/Latino; 1 Two or more races, non-Hispanic/Latino). Average age 24. 7,600 applicants, 7% accepted, 452 enrolled. In 2017, 616 master's, 225 doctorates awarded. *Degree requirements:* For doctorate, comprehensive exam, thesis/dissertation (for some programs), 12-month full-time clinical externship experience. *Entrance requirements:* For master's, GRE General Test; for doctorate, GRE General Test, personal interview, essay in application, on-site essay. *Application deadline:* For spring admission, 2/15 for domestic and international students; for summer admission, 12/1 for domestic and international students. Applications are processed on a rolling basis. Application fee: $50. Electronic applications accepted. *Expenses:* Contact institution. *Financial support:* Federal Work-Study, institutionally sponsored loans, and scholarships/grants available. Financial award application deadline: 4/15; financial award applicants required to submit FAFSA. *Faculty research:* Efferent suppression and auditory processing delay, subjective visual vertical in vestibular assessment, competency-based clinical evaluation, hearing instrument performance for frequency lowering, hearing instrument performance for noise suppression, anxiety and dizziness in college students, audiology assistants. *Unit head:* Dr. Stanley Wilson, Dean, 954-262-1203, E-mail: swilson@nova.edu. *Application contact:* Joey Jankie, Admissions Counselor, 954-262-7249, E-mail: joey@nova.edu.
Website: http://healthsciences.nova.edu/

Oakland University, Graduate Study and Lifelong Learning, School of Health Sciences, Rochester, MI 48309-4401. Offers MS, DPT, Dr Sc PT, TDPT, Graduate Certificate. *Accreditation:* APTA (one or more programs are accredited). *Entrance requirements:* For master's, minimum GPA of 3.0; for doctorate, GRE General Test. Additional exam requirements/recommendations for international students: Required—TOEFL (minimum score 550 paper-based). Electronic applications accepted. *Expenses:* Contact institution.

The Ohio State University, College of Medicine, School of Health and Rehabilitation Sciences, Program in Allied Health, Columbus, OH 43210. Offers MS. *Students:* 43 full-time (37 women), 14 part-time (8 women). Average age 26. In 2017, 24 master's awarded. *Entrance requirements:* For master's, GRE. Additional exam requirements/recommendations for international students: Required—TOEFL (minimum score 550 paper-based; 79 iBT), Michigan English Language Assessment Battery (minimum score 82); Recommended—IELTS (minimum score 7). *Application deadline:* For fall admission, 11/1 priority date for domestic students, 10/1 priority date for international students; for spring admission, 12/12 for domestic students, 11/10 for international students; for summer admission, 4/10 for domestic students, 3/13 for international students. Applications are processed on a rolling basis. Application fee: $60 ($70 for international students). Electronic applications accepted. *Unit head:* Dr. Deborah S. Larsen, Associate Dean and Director, 614-292-5645, E-mail: larsen.64@osu.edu. *Application contact:* Graduate and Professional Admissions, 614-292-9444, Fax: 614-292-3895, E-mail: gpadmissions@osu.edu.
Website: https://hrs.osu.edu/academics/graduate-programs/ms-in-allied-health

Old Dominion University, College of Health Sciences, Norfolk, VA 23529. Offers MS, MSAT, MSN, DNP, DPT, PhD. *Program availability:* Part-time, evening/weekend, 100% online, blended/hybrid learning. *Faculty:* 64 full-time (42 women), 2 part-time/adjunct (0 women). *Students:* 332 full-time (242 women), 112 part-time (98 women); includes 108 minority (55 Black or African American, non-Hispanic/Latino; 1 American Indian or Alaska Native, non-Hispanic/Latino; 17 Asian, non-Hispanic/Latino; 18 Hispanic/Latino; 17 Two or more races, non-Hispanic/Latino), 12 international. Average age 32. 1,047 applicants, 25% accepted, 202 enrolled. In 2017, 91 master's, 79 doctorates awarded. *Degree requirements:* For master's, comprehensive exam; for doctorate, comprehensive exam, thesis/dissertation. *Entrance requirements:* For master's and doctorate, GRE or MAT. Additional exam requirements/recommendations for international students: Required—TOEFL (minimum score 550 paper-based; 79 iBT). *Application deadline:* Applications are processed on a rolling basis. Application fee: $50. Electronic applications accepted. *Expenses:* Tuition, state resident: full-time $8928; part-time $496 per credit. Tuition, nonresident: full-time $22,482; part-time $1249 per credit. *Required fees:* $66 per semester. *Financial support:* In 2017–18, 40 students received support, including 7 fellowships with full tuition reimbursements available (averaging $15,000 per year), 12 research assistantships with partial tuition reimbursements available (averaging $15,000 per year), 9 teaching assistantships with partial tuition reimbursements available (averaging $13,000 per year); career-related internships or fieldwork, institutionally sponsored loans, scholarships/grants, health care benefits, tuition waivers (full and partial), and unspecified assistantships also available. Support available to part-time students. Financial award application deadline: 2/15; financial award applicants required to submit FAFSA. *Faculty research:* Health promotion and wellness, health care ethics, health policy, health services, cultural competency, environmental health, global health, falls prevention, breast cancer detection. *Total annual research expenditures:* $2.7 million. *Unit head:* Dr. Bonnie Van Lunen, Dean, 757-683-3516, Fax: 757-683-5674, E-mail: bvanlune@odu.edu. *Application contact:* William Heffelfinger, Director of Graduate Admissions, 757-683-5554, Fax: 757-683-3255, E-mail: gradadmit@odu.edu.
Website: http://hs.odu.edu/

Oregon State University, Interdisciplinary/Institutional Programs, Program in Comparative Health Sciences, Corvallis, OR 97331. Offers biomedical sciences (MS, PhD). *Entrance requirements:* For master's and doctorate, GRE. Additional exam requirements/recommendations for international students: Required—TOEFL (minimum score 80 iBT), IELTS (minimum score 6.5). *Application deadline:* For fall admission, 12/10 for domestic and international students. Application fee: $75 ($85 for international students). *Unit head:* Lynette Hawthorne, Administrative Assistant, E-mail: lynette.hawthorne@oregonstate.edu. *Application contact:* Carolyn Cowan, Assistant to the Department Head, 541-737-6921, E-mail: carolyn.cowan@oregonstate.edu.

Purdue University, Graduate School, College of Health and Human Sciences, School of Health Sciences, West Lafayette, IN 47907. Offers health physics (MS, PhD); medical physics (MS, PhD); occupational and environmental health science (MS, PhD), including aerosol deposition and lung disease, ergonomics, exposure and risk assessment, indoor air quality and bioaerosols (PhD), liver/lung toxicology; radiation biology (PhD); toxicology (PhD); MS/PhD. *Program availability:* Part-time. *Faculty:* 12 full-time (4 women), 1 part-time/adjunct (0 women). *Students:* 37 full-time (16 women), 5 part-time (1 woman); includes 6 minority (2 Black or African American, non-Hispanic/Latino; 2 Asian, non-Hispanic/Latino; 1 Hispanic/Latino; 1 Two or more races, non-Hispanic/Latino), 9 international. Average age 28. 57 applicants, 65% accepted, 15 enrolled. In 2017, 10 master's, 4 doctorates awarded. *Degree requirements:* For master's, thesis optional; for doctorate, one foreign language, thesis/dissertation. *Entrance requirements:* For master's and doctorate, GRE General Test, minimum undergraduate GPA of 3.0 or equivalent. Additional exam requirements/recommendations for international students: Required—TOEFL (minimum score 550 paper-based; 77 iBT); Recommended—TWE. *Application deadline:* For fall admission, 5/15 for domestic and international students; for spring admission, 10/15 for domestic and international students. Applications are processed on a rolling basis. Application fee: $60 ($75 for international students). Electronic applications accepted. *Financial support:* In 2017–18, fellowships with tuition reimbursements (averaging $14,400 per year), research assistantships with tuition reimbursements (averaging $12,000 per year), teaching assistantships with tuition reimbursements (averaging $12,000 per year) were awarded; career-related internships or fieldwork and traineeships also available. Support available to part-time students. Financial award applicants required to submit FAFSA. *Faculty research:* Environmental toxicology, industrial hygiene, radiation dosimetry. *Unit head:* Jason T. Harris, Interim Head of the Graduate Program, 765-496-1271, E-mail: jtharris@purdue.edu. *Application contact:* Karen E. Walker, Graduate Contact, 765-494-1419, E-mail: kwalker@purdue.edu.
Website: https://www.purdue.edu/hhs/hsci/

Quinnipiac University, School of Health Sciences, Hamden, CT 06518-1940. Offers MHS, MSW. *Accreditation:* AOTA. *Faculty:* 58 full-time (41 women), 89 part-time/adjunct (48 women). *Students:* 529 full-time (385 women), 206 part-time (170 women); includes 138 minority (36 Black or African American, non-Hispanic/Latino; 39 Asian, non-Hispanic/Latino; 54 Hispanic/Latino; 9 Two or more races, non-Hispanic/Latino), 23 international. 1,453 applicants, 18% accepted, 152 enrolled. In 2017, 303 master's awarded. *Entrance requirements:* Additional exam requirements/recommendations for international students: Required—TOEFL (minimum score 575 paper-based; 90 iBT), IELTS (minimum score 6.5). *Application deadline:* Applications are processed on a rolling basis. Application fee: $45. Electronic applications accepted. *Financial support:* Federal Work-Study, scholarships/grants, and unspecified assistantships available. Financial award applicants required to submit FAFSA. *Application contact:* Office of Graduate Admissions, 800-462-1944, Fax: 203-582-3443, E-mail: graduate@qu.edu.
Website: http://www.qu.edu/gradprograms

Regis University, Rueckert-Hartman College for Health Professions, Denver, CO 80221-1099. Offers advanced practice nurse (DNP); counseling (MA); counseling children and adolescents (Post-Graduate Certificate); counseling military families (Post-Graduate Certificate); depth psychotherapy (Post-Graduate Certificate); fellowship in orthopedic manual physical therapy (Certificate); health care business management (Certificate); health care quality and patient safety (Certificate); health industry leadership (MBA); health services administration (MS); marriage and family therapy (MA, Post-Graduate Certificate); neonatal nurse practitioner (MSN); nursing education (MSN); nursing leadership (MSN); occupational therapy (OTD); pharmacy (Pharm D); physical therapy (DPT). *Program availability:* Part-time, evening/weekend, 100% online, blended/hybrid learning. *Degree requirements:* For master's, thesis (for some programs), internship. *Entrance requirements:* For master's, official transcript reflecting baccalaureate degree awarded from regionally-accredited college or university. Additional exam requirements/recommendations for international students: Required—TOEFL (minimum score 550 paper-based; 82 iBT). Electronic applications accepted. *Expenses:* Contact institution. *Faculty research:* Normal and pathological balance and gait research, normal/pathological upper limb motor control/biomechanics, exercise energy/metabolism research, optical treatment protocols for therapeutic modalities.

Rosalind Franklin University of Medicine and Science, College of Health Professions, North Chicago, IL 60064-3095. Offers MS, D Sc, DNAP, DPT, PhD, TDPT, Certificate. *Program availability:* Part-time, online learning. Terminal master's awarded for partial completion of doctoral program.

Rutgers University–Newark, School of Health Related Professions, Newark, NJ 07102. Offers MS, DCN, DPT, PhD, Certificate, DMD/MS, MD/MS. *Accreditation:* APTA (one or more programs are accredited); NAACLS. *Program availability:* Part-time. *Degree requirements:* For master's, thesis (for some programs). *Entrance requirements:* Additional exam requirements/recommendations for international students: Required—TOEFL. Electronic applications accepted. *Expenses:* Contact institution. *Faculty research:* Clinical outcomes.

Saint Louis University, Graduate Programs, Doisy College of Health Sciences, St. Louis, MO 63103. Offers MAT, MMS, MOT, MS, DPT, PhD, Certificate. *Program availability:* Part-time. *Degree requirements:* For master's, comprehensive exam. *Entrance requirements:* Additional exam requirements/recommendations for international students: Required—TOEFL (minimum score 525 paper-based).

Sam Houston State University, College of Health Sciences, Department of Health Services and Promotion, Huntsville, TX 77341. Offers health (MA). *Accreditation:* NCATE. *Program availability:* Part-time. *Degree requirements:* For master's, comprehensive exam, thesis optional, internship. *Entrance requirements:* For master's, GRE General Test, MAT, letters of recommendation, statement of interest/intent. Additional exam requirements/recommendations for international students: Required—TOEFL (minimum score 550 paper-based; 79 iBT), IELTS (minimum score 6.5). Electronic applications accepted.

Seton Hall University, School of Health and Medical Sciences, Program in Health Sciences, South Orange, NJ 07079-2697. Offers PhD. *Program availability:* Part-time, evening/weekend. *Degree requirements:* For doctorate, comprehensive exam (for some programs), thesis/dissertation, candidacy exam, practicum, research projects. *Entrance requirements:* For doctorate, GRE (preferred), interview, minimum GPA of 3.0, letters of recommendation. Additional exam requirements/recommendations for international students: Required—TOEFL. Electronic applications accepted. *Faculty research:* Movement science, motor learning, dual tasks, clinical decision making, online education, teaching strategies.

Shenandoah University, School of Health Professions, Winchester, VA 22601. Offers athletic training (MSAT); non-traditional physical therapy (MS); occupational training (MS); performing arts medicine (Certificate); physician assistant studies (MS); public health (MPH, Certificate); transitional physical therapy (DPT). *Program availability:* Part-time, all online except for two on-site weekend sessions (for DPT). *Faculty:* 35 full-time (27 women), 18 part-time/adjunct (13 women). *Students:* 446 full-time (355 women), 134 part-time (112 women); includes 78 minority (14 Black or African American, non-Hispanic/Latino; 28 Asian, non-Hispanic/Latino; 25 Hispanic/Latino; 11 Two or more races, non-Hispanic/Latino), 22 international. Average age 28. 839 applicants, 31% accepted, 166 enrolled. In 2017, 100 master's, 75 doctorates, 4 other advanced degrees awarded. *Degree requirements:* For master's and Certificate, thesis; for doctorate, comprehensive exam. *Entrance requirements:* For master's, GRE; for doctorate, GRE, minimum cumulative and prerequisite GPA of 2.8. Additional exam requirements/recommendations for international students: Required—TOEFL (minimum score 558 paper-based; 83 iBT). *Application deadline:* For fall admission, 10/1 for domestic and international students; for summer admission, 4/1 for domestic and international students. Application fee: $30. Electronic applications accepted. *Expenses:* Contact institution. *Financial support:* In 2017–18, 53 students received support. Scholarships/grants and unspecified assistantships available. Financial award applicants required to submit FAFSA. *Faculty research:* 3D motion analysis of running mechanics; quality improvement in clinical practice; functional movement screen to predict injury in professional athletes and dancers; sensory integration for children with autism; chronic ankle instability. *Total annual research expenditures:* $15,000. *Unit head:* Dr. Karen Elizabeth Abraham, Dean of School of Health Professions, 540-545.6209, Fax: 540-665.5530, E-mail: kabraham@su.edu. *Application contact:* Jon Brannon, Graduate Admissions Specialist, Office of Admissions, 540-545-7394, Fax: 540-665-4627, E-mail: jbannan09@su.edu.
Website: http://www.health.su.edu

South Carolina State University, College of Graduate and Professional Studies, Department of Health Sciences, Orangeburg, SC 29117-0001. Offers speech pathology and audiology (MA). *Accreditation:* ASHA. *Program availability:* Part-time, evening/weekend. *Faculty:* 6 full-time (5 women), 4 part-time/adjunct (all women). *Students:* 74 full-time (68 women), 7 part-time (6 women); includes 53 minority (all Black or African American, non-Hispanic/Latino). Average age 27. 84 applicants, 51% accepted, 40 enrolled. In 2017, 38 master's awarded. *Degree requirements:* For master's, thesis optional, departmental qualifying exam. *Entrance requirements:* For master's, GRE or NTE, minimum GPA of 3.0. *Application deadline:* For fall admission, 6/15 for domestic and international students; for spring admission, 11/1 for domestic and international students. Application fee: $25. Electronic applications accepted. *Expenses:* Tuition, state resident: full-time $9388; part-time $607 per credit hour. Tuition, nonresident: full-time $19,968; part-time $1194 per credit hour. *Required fees:* $766; $766 per credit hour. *Financial support:* Fellowships, career-related internships or fieldwork, Federal Work-Study, and scholarships/grants available. Financial award application deadline: 6/1. *Unit head:* Dr. Cecelia Jeffries, Chair, Department of Health Sciences, 803-536-8074, Fax: 803-536-8593, E-mail: cjeffrie@scsu.edu. *Application contact:* Curtis Foskey, Coordinator of Graduate Admission, 803-536-8419, Fax: 803-536-8812, E-mail: cfoskey@scsu.edu.

Southwestern Oklahoma State University, College of Professional and Graduate Studies, School of Behavioral Sciences and Education, Specialization in Health Sciences and Microbiology, Weatherford, OK 73096-3098. Offers M Ed.

Temple University, College of Public Health, Philadelphia, PA 19122. Offers MA, MOT, MPH, MS, MSAT, MSW, DAT, DNP, DOT, DPT, PhD, TDPT. *Accreditation:* APTA (one or more programs are accredited). *Program availability:* Part-time, evening/weekend, online learning. *Faculty:* 109 full-time (78 women), 18 part-time/adjunct (13 women). *Students:* 687 full-time (556 women), 387 part-time (296 women); includes 343 minority (173 Black or African American, non-Hispanic/Latino; 1 American Indian or Alaska Native, non-Hispanic/Latino; 56 Asian, non-Hispanic/Latino; 74 Hispanic/Latino; 39 Two or more races, non-Hispanic/Latino), 31 international. 1,222 applicants, 50% accepted, 232 enrolled. In 2017, 333 master's, 117 doctorates awarded. *Entrance requirements:* Additional exam requirements/recommendations for international students: Required—TOEFL (minimum score 550 paper-based; 79 iBT). Application fee: $60. *Expenses:* Contact institution. *Financial support:* Fellowships, research assistantships, teaching assistantships, career-related internships or fieldwork, Federal Work-Study, institutionally sponsored loans, traineeships, and tuition waivers (partial) available. Support available to part-time students. Financial award application deadline: 1/15. *Total annual research expenditures:* $10.1 million. *Unit head:* Dr. Laura Siminoff, Dean, 215-707-8624, Fax: 215-707-7819, E-mail: laura.siminoff@temple.edu.
Website: http://cph.temple.edu/

Tennessee State University, The School of Graduate Studies and Research, College of Health Sciences, Nashville, TN 37209-1561. Offers MA Ed, MOT, MPH, MS, MSN, DPT, Certificate. *Accreditation:* ASHA (one or more programs are accredited). *Program availability:* Part-time, evening/weekend. *Entrance requirements:* For master's, GRE General Test, MAT, minimum GPA of 3.5. Electronic applications accepted.

Texas Christian University, Harris College of Nursing and Health Sciences, Fort Worth, TX 76129. Offers MS, MSN, MSW, DNP, DNP-A, Certificate. *Program availability:* Part-time, 100% online, blended/hybrid learning. *Faculty:* 62 full-time (48 women), 9 part-time/adjunct (5 women). *Students:* 341 full-time (245 women), 20 part-time (19 women); includes 75 minority (17 Black or African American, non-Hispanic/Latino; 15 Asian, non-Hispanic/Latino; 32 Hispanic/Latino; 1 Native Hawaiian or other Pacific Islander, non-Hispanic/Latino; 10 Two or more races, non-Hispanic/Latino), 7 international. Average age 31. 582 applicants, 35% accepted, 166 enrolled. In 2017, 101 master's, 89 doctorates, 4 other advanced degrees awarded. *Degree requirements:* For master's and Certificate, comprehensive exam (for some programs), thesis (for some programs); for doctorate, comprehensive exam (for some programs), thesis/dissertation (for some programs). *Entrance requirements:* For master's, GRE (for some programs), resume, two transcripts from each institution attended, bachelor's degree in related field, recommendation letters; certification or license (for some programs); for doctorate, GRE (for some programs), resume, two transcripts from each institution attended, bachelor's degree in related field, recommendation letters; certification or license (for some programs); master's degree (for some programs); for Certificate, resume, two transcripts from each institution attended, bachelor's degree in related field, recommendation letters; certification or license (for some programs); master's degree (for some programs). Additional exam requirements/recommendations for international students: Required—TOEFL (minimum score 550 paper-based, 80 iBT) or IELTS (6.5). Application fee: $60. Electronic applications accepted. *Expenses:* $1,630 per semester hour, fees vary per program. *Financial support:* Application deadline: 5/1; applicants required to submit FAFSA. *Faculty research:* Children and movement, oncology education and research, translational research, collaborative practice, sports science. *Unit head:* Dr. Suzy Lockwood, Interim Dean, 817-257-6749, E-mail: s.lockwood@tcu.edu. *Application contact:* Debbie Rhea, Associate Dean, 817-257-5263, E-mail: d.rhea@tcu.edu.
Website: http://www.harriscollege.tcu.edu/

Texas State University, The Graduate College, College of Health Professions, San Marcos, TX 78666. Offers MA, MHA, MHIIM, MSCD, MSN, DPT. *Program availability:* Part-time, evening/weekend, blended/hybrid learning. *Faculty:* 63 full-time (43 women), 25 part-time/adjunct (14 women). *Students:* 348 full-time (270 women), 31 part-time (20 women); includes 162 minority (27 Black or African American, non-Hispanic/Latino; 2 American Indian or Alaska Native, non-Hispanic/Latino; 18 Asian, non-Hispanic/Latino; 102 Hispanic/Latino; 13 Two or more races, non-Hispanic/Latino), 19 international. Average age 28. 694 applicants, 32% accepted, 120 enrolled. In 2017, 109 master's awarded. *Degree requirements:* For master's, comprehensive exam. *Entrance requirements:* For master's, GRE General Test (for some programs), baccalaureate degree from regionally-accredited institution; for doctorate, GRE (preferred minimum score of 295 with no less than 150 on the verbal and 145 on the quantitative), baccalaureate degree from regionally-accredited institution in physical therapy with minimum GPA of 3.0 on last 60 hours of undergraduate work. Additional exam requirements/recommendations for international students: Required—TOEFL (minimum score 550 paper-based; 78 iBT), IELTS (minimum score 6.5). *Application deadline:* For fall admission, 1/15 priority date for domestic and international students; for spring admission, 10/1 for domestic and international students. Applications are processed on a rolling basis. Application fee: $40 ($90 for international students). Electronic applications accepted. *Expenses:* Tuition, state resident: full-time $7868; part-time $3934 per semester. Tuition, nonresident: full-time $17,828; part-time $8914 per semester. *Required fees:* $2092; $1435 per semester. Tuition and fees vary according to course load. *Financial support:* In 2017–18, 249 students received support, including 3 research assistantships (averaging $5,752 per year), 34 teaching assistantships (averaging $9,794 per year); fellowships, career-related internships or fieldwork, Federal Work-Study, institutionally sponsored loans, scholarships/grants, unspecified assistantships, and stipends also available. Support available to part-time students. Financial award application deadline: 3/1; financial award applicants required to submit FAFSA. *Faculty research:* Overpowering osteoarthritis, exploring trunk stability and balance, employee well being, sarcoidosis research, nursing and allied health, post-concussion patient response. *Total annual research expenditures:* $30,219. *Unit head:* Dr. Ruth Welborn, Dean, 512-245-3300, Fax: 512-245-3791, E-mail: mw01@txstate.edu. *Application contact:* Dr. Andrea Golato, Dean of Graduate School, 512-245-2581, Fax: 512-245-8365, E-mail: gradcollege@txstate.edu.
Website: http://www.health.txstate.edu/

Texas Woman's University, Graduate School, College of Health Sciences, Denton, TX 76204. Offers MA, MOT, MS, DPT, OTD, PhD. *Program availability:* Part-time, evening/weekend, 100% online, blended/hybrid learning. *Faculty:* 99 full-time (76 women), 27 part-time/adjunct (21 women). *Students:* 1,167 full-time (1,015 women), 476 part-time (393 women); includes 615 minority (166 Black or African American, non-Hispanic/Latino; 4 American Indian or Alaska Native, non-Hispanic/Latino; 156 Asian, non-Hispanic/Latino; 248 Hispanic/Latino; 41 Two or more races, non-Hispanic/Latino), 45 international. Average age 29. 1,393 applicants, 37% accepted, 409 enrolled. In 2017, 395 master's, 154 doctorates awarded. Terminal master's awarded for partial completion of doctoral program. *Degree requirements:* For master's, comprehensive exam (for some programs), thesis (for some programs); for doctorate, comprehensive exam, thesis/dissertation, qualifying exam. *Entrance requirements:* For master's and doctorate, minimum GPA of 3.0. Additional exam requirements/recommendations for international students: Required—TOEFL (minimum score 550 paper-based; 79 iBT); Recommended—IELTS (minimum score 6.5), TSE (minimum score 53). *Application deadline:* For fall admission, 7/1 priority date for domestic students, 3/1 priority date for international students; for spring admission, 12/1 priority date for domestic students, 7/1 priority date for international students. Applications are processed on a rolling basis. Application fee: $50 ($75 for international students). Electronic applications accepted. *Expenses:* Contact institution. *Financial support:* In 2017–18, 619 students received support, including 59 research assistantships (averaging $11,499 per year), 15 teaching assistantships (averaging $11,499 per year); career-related internships or fieldwork, Federal Work-Study, institutionally sponsored loans, scholarships/grants, traineeships, health care benefits, and unspecified assistantships also available. Support available to part-time students. Financial award application deadline: 3/1; financial award applicants required to submit FAFSA. *Total annual research expenditures:* $506,307. *Unit head:* Dr. Christopher T. Ray, Dean, 940-898-2852, Fax: 940-898-2853. *Application contact:* Korie Hawkins, Associate Director of Admissions, Graduate Recruitment, 940-898-3188, Fax: 940-898-3081, E-mail: admissions@twu.edu.
Website: http://www.twu.edu/college-health-sciences/

Towson University, College of Health Professions, Program in Health Science, Towson, MD 21252-0001. Offers MS. *Program availability:* Part-time, evening/weekend. *Students:* 23 full-time (21 women), 52 part-time (40 women); includes 48 minority (40 Black or African American, non-Hispanic/Latino; 3 Asian, non-Hispanic/Latino; 4 Hispanic/Latino; 1 Two or more races, non-Hispanic/Latino), 2 international. *Degree requirements:* For master's, thesis optional. *Entrance requirements:* For master's, undergraduate degree in a health science field or substantial upper-division course work in those fields, or experience in those same areas; minimum B grade in previous statistics course; minimum GPA of 3.0. *Application deadline:* For fall admission, 1/17 for domestic students, 5/15 for international students; for spring admission, 10/15 for domestic students, 12/1 for international students. Applications are processed on a rolling basis. Application fee: $45. Electronic applications accepted. *Expenses:* Tuition, state resident: full-time $7960; part-time $398 per unit. Tuition, nonresident: full-time $16,480; part-time $824 per unit. *Required fees:* $2600; $130 per year. $390 per term. *Financial support:* Application deadline: 4/1. *Unit head:* Dr. Niya Werts, Graduate Program Director, 410-704-2378, E-mail: nwerts@towson.edu. *Application contact:* Coverley Beidleman, Assistant Director of Graduate Admissions, 410-704-5630, Fax: 410-704-3030, E-mail: cbeidleman@towson.edu.
Website: https://www.towson.edu/chp/departments/healthsci/gradhealthsci/

University at Buffalo, the State University of New York, Graduate School, School of Public Health and Health Professions, Buffalo, NY 14260. Offers MA, MPH, MS, DPT, PhD, Advanced Certificate, Certificate. *Program availability:* Part-time. *Faculty:* 73 full-time (42 women), 28 part-time/adjunct (14 women). *Students:* 475 full-time (343

women), 45 part-time (25 women); includes 74 minority (13 Black or African American, non-Hispanic/Latino; 1 American Indian or Alaska Native, non-Hispanic/Latino; 59 Asian, non-Hispanic/Latino; 1 Hispanic/Latino), 80 international. Average age 25. 597 applicants, 48% accepted, 229 enrolled. In 2017, 151 master's, 53 doctorates, 21 other advanced degrees awarded. Terminal master's awarded for partial completion of doctoral program. *Degree requirements:* For master's, comprehensive exam (for some programs), thesis (for some programs); for doctorate, comprehensive exam, thesis/dissertation. *Entrance requirements:* For master's and doctorate, GRE General Test. Additional exam requirements/recommendations for international students: Required—TOEFL (minimum score 79 iBT). *Application deadline:* For fall admission, 2/1 priority date for domestic and international students. Application fee: $50. Electronic applications accepted. *Financial support:* In 2017–18, 47 students received support, including 8 fellowships with full tuition reimbursements available (averaging $2,500 per year), 15 research assistantships with full tuition reimbursements available (averaging $15,000 per year), 16 teaching assistantships with full tuition reimbursements available (averaging $8,500 per year); career-related internships or fieldwork, Federal Work-Study, institutionally sponsored loans, scholarships/grants, tuition waivers (full and partial), and unspecified assistantships also available. Financial award application deadline: 3/15; financial award applicants required to submit FAFSA. *Faculty research:* Public health, epidemiology, rehabilitation, assistive technology, exercise and nutrition science. *Total annual research expenditures:* $7.3 million. *Unit head:* Dr. Lynn Kozlowski, Dean, 716-829-6951, Fax: 716-829-6040, E-mail: lk22@buffalo.edu.
Website: http://sphhp.buffalo.edu/

The University of Alabama at Birmingham, School of Health Professions, Birmingham, AL 35294. Offers MS, MSHA, MSHI, MSPAS, D Sc, DPT, PhD, Certificate. *Accreditation:* AANA/CANAEP (one or more programs are accredited); APTA (one or more programs are accredited); CAHME (one or more programs are accredited). *Program availability:* Part-time, online learning. *Degree requirements:* For doctorate, thesis/dissertation. Electronic applications accepted. *Expenses:* Contact institution.

University of Detroit Mercy, College of Health Professions, Detroit, MI 48221. Offers clinical nurse leader (MSN); family nurse practitioner (MSN); health services administration (MHSA); health systems management (MSN); nurse anesthesia (MS); nursing (DNP); nursing education (MSN, Certificate); nursing leadership and financial management (Certificate); outcomes performance management (Certificate); physician assistant (MS). *Entrance requirements:* For master's, GRE General Test, minimum GPA of 3.0. *Faculty research:* Research design, respiratory physiology, AIDS prevention, adolescent health, community, low income health education.

University of Florida, Graduate School, College of Public Health and Health Professions, Gainesville, FL 32611. Offers MA, MHA, MHS, MHS, MOT, MPH, MS, Au D, DPT, PhD, Certificate, DPT/MPH, DVM/MPH, JD/MPH, MBA/MHA, MD/MPH, PhD/MPH, Pharm D/MPH. *Accreditation:* CAHME (one or more programs are accredited). *Program availability:* Part-time. Terminal master's awarded for partial completion of doctoral program. *Degree requirements:* For master's, thesis (for some programs); for doctorate, comprehensive exam, thesis/dissertation. *Entrance requirements:* For master's and doctorate, GRE General Test, minimum GPA of 3.0. Additional exam requirements/recommendations for international students: Required—TOEFL (minimum score 550 paper-based; 80 iBT), IELTS (minimum score 6). Electronic applications accepted.

University of Illinois at Chicago, College of Applied Health Sciences, Chicago, IL 60607-7128. Offers MS, DPT, OTD, PhD, CAS, Certificate. *Accreditation:* AOTA. *Program availability:* Part-time. *Degree requirements:* For doctorate, thesis/dissertation. *Entrance requirements:* For master's, GRE General Test, minimum GPA of 2.75. Additional exam requirements/recommendations for international students: Required—TOEFL. Electronic applications accepted. *Expenses:* Contact institution. *Faculty research:* The impact of cultural competence training on service providers, interventions to improve the functional skills and independent living capacity of those with long term disabilities and conditions; fall prevention in the elderly and veterans with ambulatory prosthetics; helping people with chronic conditions manage their disease and prevent secondary conditions.

The University of Kansas, University of Kansas Medical Center, School of Health Professions, Kansas City, KS 66160. Offers MOT, MS, Au D, DNAP, DPT, OTD, PhD, SLPD, Graduate Certificate. *Faculty:* 110. *Students:* 451 full-time (325 women), 75 part-time (67 women); includes 60 minority (11 Black or African American, non-Hispanic/Latino; 4 American Indian or Alaska Native, non-Hispanic/Latino; 9 Asian, non-Hispanic/Latino; 19 Hispanic/Latino; 1 Native Hawaiian or other Pacific Islander, non-Hispanic/Latino; 16 Two or more races, non-Hispanic/Latino), 22 international. Average age 27. In 2017, 60 master's, 100 doctorates, 21 other advanced degrees awarded. *Total annual research expenditures:* $1.4 million. *Unit head:* Dr. Abiodun Akinwuntan, Dean, 913-588-5235, Fax: 913-588-5254, E-mail: aakinwuntan@kumc.edu.
Website: http://www.kumc.edu/school-of-health-professions.html

University of Kentucky, Graduate School, College of Health Sciences, Lexington, KY 40506-0032. Offers MHA, MS, MSCD, MSHP, MSNS, MSPAS, MSPT, MSRMP, DS, PhD. *Program availability:* Part-time. *Degree requirements:* For master's, comprehensive exam, thesis (for some programs). *Entrance requirements:* For master's, GRE General Test, minimum undergraduate GPA of 2.75; for doctorate, GRE General Test, minimum undergraduate GPA of 3.0. Additional exam requirements/recommendations for international students: Required—TOEFL (minimum score 550 paper-based). Electronic applications accepted.

University of Maryland, Baltimore, Graduate School, Program in Health Science, Baltimore, MD 21201. Offers MS. *Students:* 91 part-time (68 women); includes 39 minority (10 Black or African American, non-Hispanic/Latino; 18 Asian, non-Hispanic/Latino; 8 Hispanic/Latino; 3 Two or more races, non-Hispanic/Latino), 9 international. Average age 30. 19 applicants, 21% accepted. In 2017, 53 master's awarded. *Degree requirements:* For master's, comprehensive exam, thesis optional. *Entrance requirements:* For master's, GRE, minimum GPA of 3.0, curriculum vitae, essay, three letters of recommendation. Additional exam requirements/recommendations for international students: Required—TOEFL (minimum score 80 iBT); Recommended—IELTS (minimum score 7). *Application deadline:* For fall admission, 7/15 for domestic students, 1/15 for international students; for spring admission, 12/15 for domestic students. Application fee: $75. Electronic applications accepted. *Expenses:* Tuition, state resident: full-time $13,990; part-time $661 per credit. Tuition, nonresident: full-time $30,484; part-time $1310 per credit. *Required fees:* $1894; $94 per credit. $415 per semester. Part-time tuition and fees vary according to course load, degree level and program. *Unit head:* Dr. Bruce E. Jarrell, Chief Academic and Research Officer/Dean of the Graduate School, 410-706-2304, Fax: 410-706-0500, E-mail: bjarrell@som.umaryland.edu. *Application contact:* Keith T. Brooks, Assistant Dean, 410-706-7131, Fax: 410-706-3473, E-mail: kbrooks@umaryland.edu.

University of Massachusetts Lowell, College of Health Sciences, Lowell, MA 01854. Offers MS, DNP, DPT, PhD. *Accreditation:* APTA (one or more programs are accredited). *Program availability:* Part-time. *Degree requirements:* For master's, thesis optional; for doctorate, thesis/dissertation. *Entrance requirements:* For master's and doctorate, GRE General Test.

University of Memphis, Graduate School, School of Health Studies, Memphis, TN 38152. Offers faith and health (Graduate Certificate); health studies (MS), including exercise, sport and movement sciences, health promotion, physical education teacher education; nutrition (MS), including clinical nutrition, environmental nutrition, nutrition science; sport nutrition and dietary supplementation (Graduate Certificate). *Program availability:* 100% online. *Faculty:* 19 full-time (10 women), 2 part-time/adjunct (both women). In 2017, 42 master's awarded. *Degree requirements:* For master's, comprehensive exam, thesis or alternative, culminating experience; for Graduate Certificate, practicum. *Entrance requirements:* For master's, GRE or PRAXIS II, letters of recommendation, statement of goals, minimum undergraduate GPA of 2.5; for Graduate Certificate, minimum undergraduate GPA of 2.5. Additional exam requirements/recommendations for international students: Required—TOEFL (minimum score 550 paper-based; 79 iBT). *Application deadline:* For fall admission, 4/15 priority date for domestic students; for spring admission, 10/15 priority date for domestic students; for summer admission, 4/15 priority date for domestic students. Application fee: $35 ($60 for international students). *Expenses:* Contact institution. *Financial support:* In 2017–18, 33 research assistantships (averaging $11,930 per year), 4 teaching assistantships (averaging $10,000 per year) were awarded; career-related internships or fieldwork, Federal Work-Study, scholarships/grants, and unspecified assistantships also available. Financial award application deadline: 2/1; financial award applicants required to submit FAFSA. *Unit head:* Dr. Richard J. Bloomer, Director, 901-678-4316, Fax: 901-678-3591, E-mail: rbloomer@memphis.edu. *Application contact:* Dr. Lawrence Weiss, Director of Graduate Programs, 901-678-5037, E-mail: lweiss@memphis.edu.
Website: http://www.memphis.edu/shs/

University of Mississippi Medical Center, School of Health Related Professions, Jackson, MS 39216-4505. Offers MOT, MPT. *Accreditation:* AOTA; NAACLS. *Program availability:* Part-time.

University of Nebraska Medical Center, College of Allied Health Professions, Omaha, NE 68198-4000. Offers MPAS, MPS, DPT, Certificate. *Accreditation:* APTA (one or more programs are accredited). *Entrance requirements:* For master's and doctorate, GRE. Additional exam requirements/recommendations for international students: Required—TOEFL. *Expenses:* Tuition, state resident: full-time $8451; part-time $4225 per semester. Tuition, nonresident: full-time $24,219; part-time $11,295 per semester. *Required fees:* $589; $117 per term.

University of Nevada, Las Vegas, Graduate College, School of Allied Health Sciences, Las Vegas, NV 89154-3018. Offers MS, DMP, DPT, PhD, Advanced Certificate. *Program availability:* Part-time. *Faculty:* 19 full-time (7 women), 13 part-time/adjunct (8 women). *Students:* 173 full-time (75 women), 24 part-time (10 women); includes 57 minority (4 Black or African American, non-Hispanic/Latino; 1 American Indian or Alaska Native, non-Hispanic/Latino; 22 Asian, non-Hispanic/Latino; 19 Hispanic/Latino; 11 Two or more races, non-Hispanic/Latino), 8 international. Average age 28. 82 applicants, 54% accepted, 28 enrolled. In 2017, 19 master's, 33 doctorates awarded. *Degree requirements:* For master's, thesis (for some programs); for doctorate, comprehensive exam (for some programs), thesis/dissertation. *Entrance requirements:* For master's and doctorate, GRE General Test, letter of recommendation; statement of purpose. Additional exam requirements/recommendations for international students: Required—TOEFL (minimum score 550 paper-based; 80 iBT), IELTS (minimum score 7). Application fee: $60 ($95 for international students). Electronic applications accepted. *Expenses:* $275 per credit, $850 per course, $7,969 per year resident, $22,157 per year non-resident, $7,094 non-resident fee (7 credits or more), $1,307 annual health insurance fee. *Financial support:* In 2017–18, 49 students received support, including 1 fellowship with full and partial tuition reimbursement available (averaging $20,000 per year), 27 research assistantships with full and partial tuition reimbursements available (averaging $17,009 per year), 22 teaching assistantships with full and partial tuition reimbursements available (averaging $14,239 per year); institutionally sponsored loans, scholarships/grants, health care benefits, and unspecified assistantships also available. Financial award application deadline: 3/15; financial award applicants required to submit FAFSA. *Faculty research:* Clinical trials for the treatment of Parkinson's Disease; radiation exposure and cancer; diabetes management; obesity; prosthesis. *Total annual research expenditures:* $3.9 million. *Unit head:* Dr. Ronald T. Brown, Dean, 702-895-3693, Fax: 702-895-1356, E-mail: ronald.brown@unlv.edu.
Website: https://www.unlv.edu/ahs

University of New Mexico, Graduate Studies, Health Sciences Center, Albuquerque, NM 87131-2039. Offers MOT, MPH, MPT, MS, MSN, DNP, DPT, MD, PhD, Pharm D, Certificate, MSN/MA. *Students:* Average age 30. 218 applicants, 47% accepted, 94 enrolled. *Unit head:* Dr. R. Philip Eaton, Interim Vice President, 505-272-5849. *Application contact:* Deborah Kieltyka, Associate Director, Admissions, 505-277-3140, Fax: 505-277-6686, E-mail: deborahk@unm.edu.

The University of North Carolina at Chapel Hill, School of Medicine and Graduate School, Graduate Programs in Medicine, Department of Allied Health Sciences, Chapel Hill, NC 27599. Offers clinical rehabilitation and mental health counseling (MS); human movement science (PhD); occupational science and occupational therapy (MS, PhD), including occupational science (PhD), occupational therapy (MS); physical therapy (DPT); speech and hearing sciences (MS, Au D, PhD), including audiology (Au D), speech and hearing sciences (PhD), speech-language pathology (MS). *Accreditation:* APTA (one or more programs are accredited). *Program availability:* Online learning. *Entrance requirements:* For master's, GRE General Test; for doctorate, GRE General Test, minimum GPA of 3.0. Additional exam requirements/recommendations for international students: Required—TOEFL (minimum score 550 paper-based), TWE. Electronic applications accepted.

University of Northern Iowa, Graduate College, College of Education, Ed D Program in Education, Cedar Falls, IA 50614. Offers allied health, recreation, and community services (Ed D); curriculum and instruction (Ed D); educational leadership (Ed D). *Program availability:* Part-time, evening/weekend. *Degree requirements:* For doctorate, thesis/dissertation. *Entrance requirements:* For doctorate, GRE, minimum GPA of 3.0, master's degree. Additional exam requirements/recommendations for international students: Required—TOEFL (minimum score 500 paper-based; 61 iBT).

University of Northern Iowa, Graduate College, College of Education, School of Kinesiology, Allied Health and Human Services, Cedar Falls, IA 50614. Offers athletic training (MS); health education (MA), including community health education, health promotion/fitness management, school health education; leisure, youth and human services (MA); physical education (MA), including kinesiology, teaching/coaching. *Program availability:* Part-time, evening/weekend. *Degree requirements:* For master's, comprehensive exam, thesis or alternative. *Entrance requirements:* For master's, minimum GPA of 3.0. Additional exam requirements/recommendations for international students: Required—TOEFL (minimum score 500 paper-based; 61 iBT).

University of North Florida, Brooks College of Health, Jacksonville, FL 32224. Offers MHA, MPH, MS, MSH, MSN, DNP, DPT, Certificate. *Program availability:* Part-time, evening/weekend. *Entrance requirements:* For master's, GRE General Test, minimum GPA of 3.0 in last 60 hours. Additional exam requirements/recommendations for international students: Required—TOEFL (minimum score 500 paper-based; 61 iBT).

Electronic applications accepted. *Expenses:* Contact institution. *Faculty research:* Adolescent substance abuse, detection of bacterial agents, spirituality and health, non-vitamin and non-mineral supplements, analyzing ticks and their ability to transfer diseases to humans.

University of Oklahoma Health Sciences Center, Graduate College, College of Allied Health, Oklahoma City, OK 73190. Offers MOT, MPT, MS, Au D, PhD, Certificate. *Accreditation:* AOTA; APTA. *Program availability:* Part-time. Terminal master's awarded for partial completion of doctoral program. *Degree requirements:* For master's, comprehensive exam, thesis optional; for doctorate, one foreign language, comprehensive exam, thesis/dissertation. *Entrance requirements:* For master's and doctorate, GRE General Test, 3 letters of recommendation. Additional exam requirements/recommendations for international students: Required—TOEFL.

University of Phoenix–Las Vegas Campus, College of Human Services, Las Vegas, NV 89135. Offers marriage, family, and child therapy (MSC); mental health counseling (MSC); school counseling (MSC). *Program availability:* Online learning. *Entrance requirements:* For master's, minimum undergraduate GPA of 2.5, 3 years of work experience. Additional exam requirements/recommendations for international students: Required—TOEFL (minimum score 550 paper-based; 79 iBT). Electronic applications accepted.

University of Puerto Rico–Medical Sciences Campus, School of Health Professions, San Juan, PR 00936-5067. Offers MS, Au D, Certificate. *Degree requirements:* For master's, one foreign language, thesis (for some programs). *Entrance requirements:* For master's, GRE or EXADEP, interview; for doctorate, EXADEP; for Certificate, Allied Health Professions Admissions Test, minimum GPA of 2.5, interview. Electronic applications accepted. *Faculty research:* Infantile autism, aphasia, language problems, toxicology, immunohematology, medical record documentation and quality.

University of South Alabama, Pat Capps Covey College of Allied Health Professions, Mobile, AL 36688. Offers MHS, MS, Au D, DPT, PhD. *Faculty:* 31 full-time (26 women), 5 part-time/adjunct (4 women). *Students:* 365 full-time (287 women), 1 (woman) part-time; includes 14 minority (4 Black or African American, non-Hispanic/Latino; 1 American Indian or Alaska Native, non-Hispanic/Latino; 1 Asian, non-Hispanic/Latino; 2 Hispanic/Latino; 1 Native Hawaiian or other Pacific Islander, non-Hispanic/Latino; 5 Two or more races, non-Hispanic/Latino), 2 international. Average age 25. 902 applicants, 27% accepted, 96 enrolled. In 2017, 89 master's, 51 doctorates awarded. *Degree requirements:* For master's, thesis optional, externship; for doctorate, thesis/dissertation, clinical internship. *Entrance requirements:* For master's, GRE General Test; for doctorate, GRE, minimum GPA of 3.0. Additional exam requirements/recommendations for international students: Required—TOEFL (minimum score 600 paper-based; 100 iBT). *Application deadline:* For fall admission, 7/15 priority date for domestic students, 6/15 priority date for international students; for spring admission, 12/1 priority date for domestic students, 11/1 priority date for international students. Applications are processed on a rolling basis. Application fee: $35. Electronic applications accepted. *Expenses:* Contact institution. *Financial support:* Fellowships, research assistantships, teaching assistantships, career-related internships or fieldwork, Federal Work-Study, institutionally sponsored loans, scholarships/grants, and unspecified assistantships available. Support available to part-time students. Financial award application deadline: 3/31; financial award applicants required to submit FAFSA. *Unit head:* Dr. Gregory Frazer, Dean, College of Allied Health, 251-445-9250, Fax: 251-445-9259, E-mail: gfrazer@southalabama.edu. *Application contact:* Dr. Susan Gordon-Hickey, Associate Dean, College of Allied Health, 251-445-9250, Fax: 251-445-9259, E-mail: gordonhickey@southalabama.edu.
Website: http://www.southalabama.edu/colleges/alliedhealth/index.html

University of South Dakota, Graduate School, School of Health Sciences, Vermillion, SD 57069. Offers MA, MPH, MS, MSW, DPT, OTD, PhD, Graduate Certificate. *Program availability:* Part-time. *Entrance requirements:* For master's, GRE General Test, GRE Subject Test. Application fee: $35. *Financial support:* Research assistantships, teaching assistantships, career-related internships or fieldwork, Federal Work-Study, scholarships/grants, traineeships, and unspecified assistantships available. Financial award applicants required to submit FAFSA. *Faculty research:* Occupational therapy, physical therapy, vision, pediatrics, geriatrics. *Application contact:* Graduate School, 605-658-6140, Fax: 605-677-6118, E-mail: grad@usd.edu.
Website: http://www.usd.edu/health-sciences

The University of Tennessee Health Science Center, College of Graduate Health Sciences, Memphis, TN 38163. Offers biomedical engineering (MS, PhD); biomedical sciences (PhD); dental sciences (MDS); epidemiology (MS); health outcomes and policy research (PhD); laboratory research and management (MS); nursing science (PhD); pharmaceutical sciences (PhD); pharmacology (MS); speech and hearing science (PhD); DDS/PhD; DNP/PhD; MD/PhD; Pharm D/PhD. MS and PhD programs in biomedical engineering offered jointly with University of Memphis. *Faculty:* 528 full-time (176 women). *Students:* 258 full-time (130 women); includes 87 minority (14 Black or African American, non-Hispanic/Latino; 68 Asian, non-Hispanic/Latino; 5 Hispanic/Latino). Average age 28. 673 applicants, 17% accepted, 102 enrolled. In 2017, 23 master's, 30 doctorates awarded. Terminal master's awarded for partial completion of doctoral program. *Degree requirements:* For master's, comprehensive exam, thesis; for doctorate, thesis/dissertation, oral and written preliminary and comprehensive exams. *Entrance requirements:* For master's and doctorate, GRE General Test, minimum GPA of 3.0. Additional exam requirements/recommendations for international students: Recommended—TOEFL (minimum score 79 iBT), IELTS (minimum score 6.5). *Application deadline:* For winter admission, 1/1 for domestic and international students; for spring admission, 3/1 for domestic and international students. Applications are processed on a rolling basis. Application fee: $0. Electronic applications accepted. *Expenses:* Contact institution. *Financial support:* In 2017–18, 150 students received support, including 150 research assistantships (averaging $25,000 per year); fellowships, institutionally sponsored loans, scholarships/grants, health care benefits, and tuition waivers (full and partial) also available. Support available to part-time students. *Faculty research:* Cell biology, epidemiology, biomedical engineering, speech and hearing science, health policy, pharmaceutical sciences, dental sciences, nursing science, pharmacology. *Unit head:* Dr. Donald B. Thomason, Dean, 901-448-5538, E-mail: dthomaso@uthsc.edu. *Application contact:* Dr. Isaac O. Donkor, Associate Dean for Student Affairs, 901-448-5538, E-mail: idonkor@uthsc.edu.
Website: http://grad.uthsc.edu/

The University of Tennessee Health Science Center, College of Health Professions, Memphis, TN 38163-0002. Offers audiology (MS, Au D); clinical laboratory science (MSCLS); cytopathology practice (MCP); health informatics and information management (MHIIM); occupational therapy (MOT); physical therapy (DPT, ScDPT); physician assistant (MMS); speech-language pathology (MS). *Accreditation:* AOTA; APTA. *Program availability:* Part-time, evening/weekend, online learning. Terminal master's awarded for partial completion of doctoral program. *Degree requirements:* For master's, comprehensive exam, thesis; for doctorate, comprehensive exam, residency. *Entrance requirements:* For master's, GRE (MOT, MSCLS), minimum GPA of 3.0, 3 letters of reference, national accreditation (MSCLS), GRE if GPA is less than 3.0 (MCP); for doctorate, GRE. Additional exam requirements/recommendations for international students: Required—TOEFL (minimum score 550 paper-based; 80 iBT). Electronic applications accepted. *Expenses:* Contact institution. *Faculty research:* Gait deviation, muscular dystrophy and strength, hemophilia and exercise, pediatric neurology, self-efficacy.

The University of Texas at El Paso, Graduate School, College of Health Sciences, Program in Interdisciplinary Health Sciences, El Paso, TX 79968-0001. Offers PhD. *Degree requirements:* For doctorate, thesis/dissertation. *Entrance requirements:* For doctorate, GRE, three letters of reference, relevant personal/professional experience, evidence of a master's degree (MS or MA) or other terminal degree, official transcripts. Additional exam requirements/recommendations for international students: Required—TOEFL (minimum score 550 paper-based); Recommended—IELTS. *Application deadline:* For fall admission, 1/30 for domestic and international students; for spring admission, 11/1 for domestic students, 9/3 for international students. Applications are processed on a rolling basis. Application fee: $45 ($80 for international students). Electronic applications accepted. *Financial support:* Fellowships with partial tuition reimbursements, research assistantships with partial tuition reimbursements, teaching assistantships with partial tuition reimbursements, institutionally sponsored loans, scholarships/grants, health care benefits, tuition waivers (partial), and unspecified assistantships available. Support available to part-time students. Financial award application deadline: 3/15; financial award applicants required to submit FAFSA. *Unit head:* Dr. Christina Sobin, Director, 915-747-7256, Fax: 915-747-7274, E-mail: casobin@utep.edu. *Application contact:* Dr. Benjamin Flores, Dean of the Graduate School, 915-747-5491, Fax: 915-747-5788, E-mail: bflores@utep.edu.

The University of Texas Medical Branch, School of Health Professions, Galveston, TX 77555. Offers MOT, MPAS, MPT, DPT. *Degree requirements:* For master's, thesis or alternative; for doctorate, thesis/dissertation or alternative. *Entrance requirements:* For master's, GRE, experience in field, minimum GPA of 3.0; for doctorate, GRE, documentation of 40 hours experience. Additional exam requirements/recommendations for international students: Required—TOEFL (minimum score 550 paper-based). Electronic applications accepted.

University of Vermont, Graduate College, College of Nursing and Health Sciences, Burlington, VT 05405-0068. Offers MS, DNP, DPT, PhD, Post-Graduate Certificate. *Students:* 560 applicants, 48% accepted, 95 enrolled. In 2017, 29 master's, 38 doctorates awarded. *Degree requirements:* For master's, thesis. *Entrance requirements:* For master's and doctorate, GRE General Test. Additional exam requirements/recommendations for international students: Required—TOEFL (minimum score 550 paper-based, 90 iBT) or IELTS (6.5). *Application deadline:* Applications are processed on a rolling basis. Application fee: $65. Electronic applications accepted. *Expenses:* Tuition, state resident: full-time $11,628; part-time $646 per credit. Tuition, nonresident: full-time $29,340; part-time $1630 per credit. *Required fees:* $1994; $10 per credit. Tuition and fees vary according to course load and program. *Financial support:* Fellowships, research assistantships, teaching assistantships, and Federal Work-Study available. Financial award application deadline: 3/1. *Unit head:* Dr. Patricia A. Prelock, Dean, 802-656-2216, E-mail: patricia.prelock@med.uvm.edu. *Application contact:* Kristen Cella, Admissions Specialist, 802-656-3858, E-mail: cnhsgrad@uvm.edu.
Website: https://www.uvm.edu/cnhs

University of Wisconsin–Milwaukee, Graduate School, College of Health Sciences, Milwaukee, WI 53211. Offers MHA, MS, DPT, PhD, Graduate Certificate. *Program availability:* Part-time. *Students:* 303 full-time (231 women), 44 part-time (28 women); includes 38 minority (6 Black or African American, non-Hispanic/Latino; 1 American Indian or Alaska Native, non-Hispanic/Latino; 12 Asian, non-Hispanic/Latino; 1 Hispanic/Latino; 18 Two or more races, non-Hispanic/Latino), 25 international. Average age 28. 292 applicants, 42% accepted, 88 enrolled. In 2017, 32 master's, 1 doctorate, 1 other advanced degree awarded. *Degree requirements:* For master's, thesis; for doctorate, comprehensive exam, thesis/dissertation. *Entrance requirements:* For doctorate, GRE General Test, master's degree. Additional exam requirements/recommendations for international students: Required—TOEFL (minimum score 600 paper-based), IELTS (minimum score 6.5). *Application deadline:* For fall admission, 1/1 priority date for domestic students; for spring admission, 9/1 for domestic students. Applications are processed on a rolling basis. Application fee: $56 ($96 for international students). *Expenses:* Contact institution. *Financial support:* Research assistantships, teaching assistantships, career-related internships or fieldwork, Federal Work-Study, and unspecified assistantships available. Support available to part-time students. Financial award application deadline: 3/30. *Unit head:* Ron A. Cisler, PhD, Dean, 414-229-5663, E-mail: rac@uwm.edu. *Application contact:* Office of Student Affairs, 414-229-2758, Fax: 414-229-3373, E-mail: chs-info@uwm.edu.
Website: http://uwm.edu/healthsciences/

Virginia Commonwealth University, Graduate School, School of Allied Health Professions, Doctoral Program in Health Related Sciences, Richmond, VA 23284-9005. Offers clinical laboratory sciences (PhD); gerontology (PhD); health administration (PhD); nurse anesthesia (PhD); occupational therapy (PhD); physical therapy (PhD); radiation sciences (PhD); rehabilitation leadership (PhD). *Entrance requirements:* For doctorate, GRE General Test or MAT, minimum GPA of 3.3 in master's degree. Additional exam requirements/recommendations for international students: Required—TOEFL (minimum score 600 paper-based; 100 iBT); Recommended—IELTS (minimum score 6.5). Electronic applications accepted.

Western University of Health Sciences, College of Allied Health Professions, Pomona, CA 91766-1854. Offers MS, DPT. *Accreditation:* APTA (one or more programs are accredited). *Faculty:* 29 full-time (22 women), 1 part-time/adjunct (0 women). *Students:* 361 full-time (233 women), 37 part-time (20 women); includes 229 minority (27 Black or African American, non-Hispanic/Latino; 1 American Indian or Alaska Native, non-Hispanic/Latino; 72 Asian, non-Hispanic/Latino; 91 Hispanic/Latino; 2 Native Hawaiian or other Pacific Islander, non-Hispanic/Latino; 36 Two or more races, non-Hispanic/Latino), 3 international. Average age 28. 2,755 applicants, 8% accepted, 144 enrolled. In 2017, 96 master's, 73 doctorates awarded. *Degree requirements:* For master's, thesis; for doctorate, comprehensive exam (for some programs). *Entrance requirements:* For master's, GRE, minimum GPA of 2.5, letters of recommendation; for doctorate, GRE, minimum GPA of 2.8, letters of recommendation, bachelor's degree. Additional exam requirements/recommendations for international students: Required—TOEFL. *Application deadline:* For fall admission, 11/1 for domestic and international students. Applications are processed on a rolling basis. Application fee: $60. Electronic applications accepted. *Expenses:* Contact institution. *Financial support:* Scholarships/grants available. Financial award application deadline: 3/2; financial award applicants required to submit FAFSA. *Total annual research expenditures:* $90,133. *Unit head:* Dr. Stephanie Bowlin, Dean, 909-469-5390, Fax: 909-469-5438, E-mail: sbowlin@westernu.edu. *Application contact:* Karen Hutton-Lopez, Director of Admissions, 909-469-5650, Fax: 909-469-5570, E-mail: admissions@westernu.edu.
Website: http://www.westernu.edu/allied-health/

Wichita State University, Graduate School, College of Health Professions, Wichita, KS 67260. Offers MA, MPA, MSN, Au D, DNP, DPT, PhD. *Accreditation:* APTA (one or more programs are accredited). *Program availability:* Part-time. *Unit head:* Dr. Sandra C. Bibb, Dean, 316-978-3600, Fax: 316-978-3025, E-mail: sandra.bibb@wichita.edu. *Application contact:* Jordan Oleson, Admissions Coordinator, 316-978-3095, Fax: 316-978-3253, E-mail: jordan.oleson@wichita.edu.
Website: http://www.wichita.edu/chp

Anesthesiologist Assistant Studies

Case Western Reserve University, School of Medicine and School of Graduate Studies, Graduate Programs in Medicine, Anesthesiologist Assistant Program, Cleveland, OH 44106. Offers MS. *Degree requirements:* For master's, thesis. *Entrance requirements:* For master's, MCAT. Additional exam requirements/recommendations for international students: Required—TOEFL. Electronic applications accepted. *Expenses:* Contact institution. *Faculty research:* Metabolism of bio-amines, cerebral metabolism, cardiovascular hemodynamics, genetics.

Emory University, School of Medicine, Programs in Allied Health Professions, Anesthesiology Assistant Program, Atlanta, GA 30322. Offers MM Sc. *Entrance requirements:* For master's, GRE General Test, MCAT. Additional exam requirements/recommendations for international students: Required—TOEFL (minimum score 600 paper-based; 94 iBT). Electronic applications accepted. *Expenses:* Contact institution.

Nova Southeastern University, Dr. Pallavi Patel College of Health Care Sciences, Fort Lauderdale, FL 33314-7796. Offers anesthesiologist assistant (MSA); audiology (Au D); health science (MH Sc, DHSc, PhD); occupational therapy (MOT, Dr OT, PhD); physical therapy (DPT, TDPT); physician assistant (MMS); speech-language pathology (MS). *Accreditation:* AOTA. *Faculty:* 54 full-time (31 women), 15 part-time/adjunct (7 women). *Students:* 501 full-time (407 women); includes 131 minority (18 Black or African American, non-Hispanic/Latino; 2 American Indian or Alaska Native, non-Hispanic/Latino; 45 Asian, non-Hispanic/Latino; 65 Hispanic/Latino; 1 Two or more races, non-Hispanic/Latino). Average age 24. 7,600 applicants, 7% accepted, 452 enrolled. In 2017, 616 master's, 225 doctorates awarded. *Degree requirements:* For doctorate, comprehensive exam, thesis/dissertation (for some programs), 12-month full-time clinical externship experience. *Entrance requirements:* For master's, GRE General Test; for doctorate, GRE General Test, personal interview, essay in application, on-site essay. *Application deadline:* For spring admission, 2/15 for domestic and international students; for summer admission, 12/1 for domestic and international students. Applications are processed on a rolling basis. Application fee: $50. Electronic applications accepted. *Expenses:* Contact institution. *Financial support:* Federal Work-Study, institutionally sponsored loans, and scholarships/grants available. Financial award application deadline: 4/15; financial award applicants required to submit FAFSA. *Faculty research:* Efferent suppression and auditory processing delay, subjective visual vertical in vestibular assessment, competency-based clinical evaluation, hearing instrument performance for frequency lowering, hearing instrument performance for noise suppression, anxiety and dizziness in college students, audiology assistants. *Unit head:* Dr. Stanley Wilson, Dean, 954-262-1203, E-mail: swilson@nova.edu. *Application contact:* Joey Jankie, Admissions Counselor, 954-262-7249, E-mail: joey@nova.edu. Website: http://healthsciences.nova.edu/

Quinnipiac University, Frank H. Netter MD School of Medicine, Program for Anesthesiologist Assistant, Hamden, CT 06518-1940. Offers MMS. *Degree requirements:* For master's, comprehensive exam. *Entrance requirements:* For master's, GRE or MCAT, bachelor's degree; official transcripts of all undergraduate and graduate course work; three letters of recommendation; essay; interview; criminal background check. Additional exam requirements/recommendations for international students: Required—TOEFL. Electronic applications accepted. *Expenses:* Contact institution.

South University, Graduate Programs, College of Health Professions, Program in Anesthesiologist Assistant, Savannah, GA 31406. Offers MM Sc.

Université Laval, Faculty of Medicine, Post-Professional Programs in Medical Studies, Québec, QC G1K 7P4, Canada. Offers anatomy–pathology (DESS); anesthesiology (DESS); cardiology (DESS); care of older people (Diploma); clinical research (DESS); community health (DESS); dermatology (DESS); diagnostic radiology (DESS); emergency medicine (Diploma); family medicine (DESS); general surgery (DESS); geriatrics (DESS); hematology (DESS); internal medicine (DESS); maternal and fetal medicine (Diploma); medical biochemistry (DESS); medical microbiology and infectious diseases (DESS); medical oncology (DESS); nephrology (DESS); neurology (DESS); neurosurgery (DESS); obstetrics and gynecology (DESS); ophthalmology (DESS); orthopedic surgery (DESS); oto-rhino-laryngology (DESS); palliative medicine (Diploma); pediatrics (DESS); plastic surgery (DESS); psychiatry (DESS); pulmonary medicine (DESS); radiology–oncology (DESS); thoracic surgery (DESS); urology (DESS). *Degree requirements:* For other advanced degree, comprehensive exam. *Entrance requirements:* For degree, knowledge of French. Electronic applications accepted.

University of Colorado Denver, School of Medicine, Program in Anesthesiology, Aurora, CO 80045. Offers MS. *Students:* 16 applicants, 88% accepted, 14 enrolled. In 2017, 6 master's awarded. *Entrance requirements:* For master's, GRE or MCAT, three letters of recommendation; curriculum vitae or resume; statement of purpose. Additional exam requirements/recommendations for international students: Required—TOEFL. *Unit head:* Dr. Vesna Jevtovic-Todorovic, Professor and Chair, 720-848-6709, E-mail: vesna.jevtovic-todorovic@ucdenver.edu. *Application contact:* Carlos Rodriguez, Program Coordinator, 303-724-1764, E-mail: carlos.r.rodriguez@ucdenver.edu. Website: http://www.ucdenver.edu/academics/colleges/medicalschool/departments/Anesthesiology/Pages/Anesthesiology.aspx

University of Guelph, Ontario Veterinary College and Graduate Studies, Graduate Programs in Veterinary Sciences, Department of Clinical Studies, Guelph, ON N1G 2W1, Canada. Offers anesthesiology (M Sc, DV Sc); cardiology (DV Sc, Diploma); clinical studies (Diploma); dermatology (M Sc); diagnostic imaging (M Sc, DV Sc); emergency/critical care (M Sc, DV Sc, Diploma); medicine (M Sc, DV Sc); neurology (M Sc, DV Sc); ophthalmology (M Sc, DV Sc); surgery (M Sc, DV Sc). *Degree requirements:* For master's, thesis; for doctorate, comprehensive exam, thesis/dissertation. *Entrance requirements:* Additional exam requirements/recommendations for international students: Required—TOEFL (minimum score 550 paper-based), IELTS (minimum score 6.5). Electronic applications accepted. *Faculty research:* Orthopedics, respirology, oncology, exercise physiology, cardiology.

Clinical Laboratory Sciences/Medical Technology

Albany College of Pharmacy and Health Sciences, School of Arts and Sciences, Albany, NY 12208. Offers clinical laboratory sciences (MS); cytotechnology and molecular cytology (MS); health outcomes research (MS); molecular biosciences (MS). *Degree requirements:* For master's, thesis. *Entrance requirements:* For master's, GRE, minimum GPA of 3.0. Additional exam requirements/recommendations for international students: Required—TOEFL (minimum score 84 iBT). Electronic applications accepted.

Austin Peay State University, College of Graduate Studies, College of Science, Technology, Engineering and Mathematics, Department of Biology, Clarksville, TN 37044. Offers clinical laboratory science (MS). *Program availability:* Part-time. *Faculty:* 12 full-time (5 women). *Students:* 1 full-time (0 women), 27 part-time (15 women); includes 3 minority (2 Hispanic/Latino; 1 Two or more races, non-Hispanic/Latino), 1 international. Average age 27. 24 applicants, 71% accepted, 13 enrolled. In 2017, 16 master's awarded. *Degree requirements:* For master's, comprehensive exam, thesis optional. *Entrance requirements:* For master's, GRE General Test, 3 letters of recommendation, minimum undergraduate GPA of 2.75. Additional exam requirements/recommendations for international students: Required—TOEFL (minimum score 500 paper-based). *Application deadline:* For fall admission, 8/8 priority date for domestic students. Applications are processed on a rolling basis. Application fee: $45 ($50 for international students). Electronic applications accepted. *Expenses:* Tuition, state resident: full-time $7686; part-time $427 per credit hour. Tuition, nonresident: full-time $20,268; part-time $1126 per credit hour. *Required fees:* $1529; $76.45 per credit hour. *Financial support:* Research assistantships with full tuition reimbursements, career-related internships or fieldwork, Federal Work-Study, institutionally sponsored loans, scholarships/grants, and unspecified assistantships available. Support available to part-time students. Financial award application deadline: 4/1; financial award applicants required to submit FAFSA. *Faculty research:* Molecular basis of microbial pathogenesis, avian ecology, aquatic toxicology, endocrinology, aquatic biology. *Unit head:* Dr. Don Dailey, Chair, 931-221-7781, Fax: 931-221-6323, E-mail: daileyd@apsu.edu. *Application contact:* Megan Mitchell, Coordinator of Graduate Admissions, 800-859-4723, Fax: 931-221-7641, E-mail: gradadmissions@apsu.edu. Website: http://www.apsu.edu/biology/

Baylor College of Medicine, Graduate School of Biomedical Sciences, Program in Clinical Scientist Training, Houston, TX 77030-3498. Offers MS, PhD. Terminal master's awarded for partial completion of doctoral program. *Degree requirements:* For master's, thesis; for doctorate, thesis/dissertation, public defense. Electronic applications accepted. *Faculty research:* Cardiology, pulmonary, HIV, rheumatology, cancer.

The Catholic University of America, School of Arts and Sciences, Department of Biology, Washington, DC 20064. Offers biotechnology (MS); cell and microbial biology (MS, PhD), including cell biology; clinical laboratory science (MS, PhD); MSLS/MS. MSLS/MS offered jointly with Department of Library and Information Science. *Program availability:* Part-time. *Faculty:* 10 full-time (4 women), 7 part-time/adjunct (1 woman). *Students:* 24 full-time (18 women), 43 part-time (20 women); includes 7 minority (2 Black or African American, non-Hispanic/Latino; 3 Asian, non-Hispanic/Latino; 2 Two or more races, non-Hispanic/Latino), 48 international. Average age 31. 56 applicants, 61% accepted, 18 enrolled. In 2017, 7 master's, 1 doctorate awarded. Terminal master's awarded for partial completion of doctoral program. *Degree requirements:* For master's and doctorate, comprehensive exam. *Entrance requirements:* For master's and doctorate, GRE General Test, GRE Subject Test, statement of purpose, official copies of academic transcripts, three letters of recommendation. Additional exam requirements/recommendations for international students: Required—TOEFL (minimum score 550 paper-based; 80 iBT). *Application deadline:* For fall admission, 7/15 priority date for domestic students, 7/1 for international students; for spring admission, 11/15 priority date for domestic students, 11/1 for international students. Applications are processed on a rolling basis. Application fee: $55. Electronic applications accepted. *Expenses:* Contact institution. *Financial support:* Fellowships, research assistantships, teaching assistantships, Federal Work-Study, scholarships/grants, tuition waivers (full and partial), and unspecified assistantships available. Financial award application deadline: 2/1; financial award applicants required to submit FAFSA. *Faculty research:* Virus structure and assembly, hepatic and epithelial cell biology, drug resistance and genome stabilization in yeast, biophysics of ion-conductive nanostructures, eukaryotic gene regulation, cancer and vaccine research. *Total annual research expenditures:* $1.7 million. *Unit head:* Dr. Venigalla Rao, Chair, 202-319-5271, Fax: 202-319-5721, E-mail: rao@cua.edu. *Application contact:* Dr. Steven Brown, Director of Graduate Admissions, 202-319-5057, Fax: 202-319-6533, E-mail: cua-admissions@cua.edu. Website: http://biology.cua.edu/

The College of William and Mary, Faculty of Arts and Sciences, Department of Applied Science, Williamsburg, VA 23185. Offers accelerator science (PhD); applied mathematics (PhD); applied mechanics (PhD); applied robotics (PhD); applied science (MS); atmospheric and environmental science (PhD); computational neuroscience (PhD); interface, thin film and surface science (PhD); lasers and optics (PhD); magnetic resonance (PhD); materials science and engineering (PhD); mathematical and computational biology (PhD); medical imaging (PhD); nanotechnology (PhD); neuroscience (PhD); non-destructive evaluation (PhD); polymer chemistry (PhD); remote sensing (PhD). *Program availability:* Part-time. *Faculty:* 11 full-time (3 women). *Students:* 30 full-time (11 women), 3 part-time (0 women); includes 6 minority (2 Black or African American, non-Hispanic/Latino; 1 Asian, non-Hispanic/Latino; 2 Hispanic/Latino; 1 Two or more races, non-Hispanic/Latino), 13 international. Average age 27. 34 applicants, 47% accepted, 10 enrolled. In 2017, 5 doctorates awarded. Terminal master's awarded for partial completion of doctoral program. *Degree requirements:* For master's, comprehensive exam, thesis; for doctorate, comprehensive exam, thesis/dissertation, 4 core courses. *Entrance requirements:* For master's and doctorate, GRE General Test, GRE Subject Test. Additional exam requirements/recommendations for international students: Required—TOEFL, IELTS. *Application deadline:* For fall admission, 2/1 priority date for domestic students, 2/1 for international students; for spring admission, 10/5 priority date for domestic students, 10/5 for international students. Applications are processed on a rolling basis. Application fee: $50. Electronic applications accepted. *Expenses:* Contact institution. *Financial support:* In 2017–18, 8 students received support, including 27 research assistantships (averaging $26,000 per year), 1 teaching assistantship (averaging $9,500 per year); fellowships, scholarships/grants, health care

benefits, tuition waivers (full), and unspecified assistantships also available. Financial award application deadline: 4/15; financial award applicants required to submit FAFSA. *Faculty research:* Computational biology, non-destructive evaluation, neurophysiology, laser spectroscopy, nanotechnology. *Total annual research expenditures:* $536,220. *Unit head:* Dr. Christopher Del Negro, Chair, 757-221-7808, Fax: 757-221-2050, E-mail: cadeln@wm.edu. *Application contact:* Lianne Rios Ashburne, Graduate Program Coordinator, 757-221-2563, Fax: 757-221-2050, E-mail: lrashburne@wm.edu.
Website: http://www.wm.edu/as/appliedscience

Dominican University of California, School of Health and Natural Sciences, Program in Clinical Laboratory Sciences, San Rafael, CA 94901-2298. Offers MS. *Program availability:* Part-time, evening/weekend. *Faculty:* 4 full-time (2 women), 5 part-time/adjunct (2 women). *Students:* 1 full-time (0 women), 20 part-time (11 women); includes 15 minority (1 Black or African American, non-Hispanic/Latino; 12 Asian, non-Hispanic/Latino; 2 Hispanic/Latino), 1 international. Average age 41. 10 applicants, 100% accepted, 7 enrolled. In 2017, 8 master's awarded. *Degree requirements:* For master's, thesis. *Entrance requirements:* For master's, GRE, minimum GPA of 3.0. Additional exam requirements/recommendations for international students: Required—TOEFL (minimum score 550 paper-based; 80 iBT), IELTS (minimum score 6.5). *Application deadline:* For fall admission, 5/15 priority date for domestic and international students. Applications are processed on a rolling basis. Application fee: $0. Electronic applications accepted. *Expenses:* $1,100 per unit. *Financial support:* Application deadline: 3/2; applicants required to submit FAFSA. *Unit head:* Dr. Mary Sevigny, Program Director, 415-482-3544, E-mail: mary.sevigny@dominican.edu. *Application contact:* Michael Lavigna, Assistant Director of Graduate Admissions, 415-485-3253, Fax: 415-485-3214, E-mail: gradmissions@dominican.edu.
Website: https://www.dominican.edu/academics/hns2/sciencemath/graduate/ms-in-clinical-laboratory-sciences

Duke University, School of Medicine, Clinical Leadership Program, Durham, NC 27701. Offers MHS. *Faculty:* 15 part-time/adjunct (7 women). *Students:* 2 applicants. *Degree requirements:* For master's, project. *Entrance requirements:* For master's, GRE. Additional exam requirements/recommendations for international students: Required—TOEFL. *Application deadline:* For fall admission, 7/20 for domestic students; for spring admission, 12/1 priority date for domestic students; for summer admission, 4/1 for domestic students. Applications are processed on a rolling basis. Application fee: $100. *Financial support:* Application deadline: 5/1; applicants required to submit FAFSA. *Unit head:* Dr. Anh N. Tran, Vice Chief of Education, 919-681-6079, Fax: 919-681-6899, E-mail: anh.tran@duke.edu. *Application contact:* Jan Willis, Training Coordinator for Educational Programs, 919-681-7007, Fax: 919-681-0676, E-mail: jan.willis@duke.edu.
Website: http://clinical-leadership.mc.duke.edu

Fairleigh Dickinson University, Metropolitan Campus, University College: Arts, Sciences, and Professional Studies, Henry P. Becton School of Nursing and Allied Health, Program in Medical Technology, Teaneck, NJ 07666-1914. Offers MS. *Expenses: Tuition:* Full-time $22,410; part-time $1245 per credit. *Required fees:* $888; $414 per unit. Tuition and fees vary according to course load, degree level and program.

Inter American University of Puerto Rico, Metropolitan Campus, Graduate Programs, Program in Medical Technology, San Juan, PR 00919-1293. Offers administration of clinical laboratories (MS); molecular microbiology (MS). *Accreditation:* NAACLS. *Program availability:* Part-time. *Degree requirements:* For master's, comprehensive exam. *Entrance requirements:* For master's, BS in medical technology, minimum GPA of 2.5. Electronic applications accepted.

Lipscomb University, Program in Biomolecular Science, Nashville, TN 37204-3951. Offers human disease (MS); laboratory research (MS). *Program availability:* Part-time, evening/weekend. *Faculty:* 6 full-time (4 women). *Students:* 31 full-time (15 women); includes 10 minority (6 Black or African American, non-Hispanic/Latino; 2 Asian, non-Hispanic/Latino; 2 Hispanic/Latino). Average age 26. 67 applicants, 51% accepted, 11 enrolled. In 2017, 23 master's awarded. *Degree requirements:* For master's, capstone project. *Entrance requirements:* For master's, GRE (minimum score of 300/1000 on prior scoring system), MCAT (minimum score of 24), DAT (minimum score of 17), BS in related field, transcripts, minimum undergraduate GPA of 3.0, 2 letters of recommendation, resume. Additional exam requirements/recommendations for international students: Required—TOEFL (minimum score 570 paper-based). *Application deadline:* For fall admission, 8/1 for domestic students; for winter admission, 12/14 for domestic students; for spring admission, 5/14 for domestic students. Applications are processed on a rolling basis. Application fee: $50 ($75 for international students). Electronic applications accepted. *Expenses:* Contact institution. *Financial support:* Unspecified assistantships available. Financial award applicants required to submit FAFSA. *Unit head:* Dr. Kent Gallaher, Director, 615-966-5721, E-mail: kent.gallaher@lipscomb.edu. *Application contact:* Tina Fulford, Administrative Assistant, 615-966-5330, E-mail: tina.fulford@lipscomb.edu.
Website: http://www.lipscomb.edu/biology/Graduate-Program

Mayo Clinic Graduate School of Biomedical Sciences, Program in Clinical and Translational Science, Rochester, MN 55905. Offers clinical and translational science (MS); laboratory-based translational science (PhD); patient-based translational science (PhD); population-based translational science (PhD). *Faculty:* 69 full-time (16 women). *Students:* 28 full-time (20 women); includes 15 minority (4 Black or African American, non-Hispanic/Latino; 6 Asian, non-Hispanic/Latino; 4 Hispanic/Latino; 1 Native Hawaiian or other Pacific Islander, non-Hispanic/Latino). 14 applicants, 36% accepted, 4 enrolled. Terminal master's awarded for partial completion of doctoral program. *Degree requirements:* For master's, thesis; for doctorate, comprehensive exam, thesis/dissertation. *Application deadline:* For fall admission, 12/1 for domestic and international students. Application fee: $50. Electronic applications accepted. *Financial support:* Fellowships with full tuition reimbursements available. *Faculty research:* Population-/patient-/laboratory-based translational science; cellular mechanisms underlying the host systemic inflammatory response; obesity and diabetes prevention; sex-specific mechanisms of blood pressure regulation in women. *Unit head:* Anthony J. Windebank, MD, Director, 507-293-7602, E-mail: windebank.anthony@mayo.edu. *Application contact:* Sarah E. Giese, PhD Admissions Coordinator, 507-538-1160, E-mail: phd.training@mayo.edu.
Website: http://www.mayo.edu/mgs

Medical College of Wisconsin, Graduate School, Program in Clinical and Translational Science, Milwaukee, WI 53226-0509. Offers MS. Program offered in collaboration with the Clinical and Translational Science Institute (CTSI) of Southeast Wisconsin. *Entrance requirements:* For master's, GRE, official transcripts, three letters of recommendation. Additional exam requirements/recommendations for international students: Required—TOEFL (minimum score 600 paper-based; 100 iBT). *Application deadline:* For fall admission, 7/1 for domestic and international students; for spring admission, 11/1 for domestic and international students; for summer admission, 4/1 for domestic and international students. Application fee: $50. *Unit head:* Leonard Egede, MD, Director, 414-955-8218, Fax: 414-955-6555, E-mail: legede@mcw.edu. *Application contact:* Recruitment Office, 414-955-4402, Fax: 414-955-6555, E-mail: gradschoolrecruit@mcw.edu.
Website: http://ctsi.mcw.edu/

Michigan State University, The Graduate School, College of Natural Science, Biomedical Laboratory Diagnostics Program, East Lansing, MI 48824. Offers biomedical laboratory operations (MS); clinical laboratory sciences (MS). *Entrance requirements:* Additional exam requirements/recommendations for international students: Required—TOEFL. Electronic applications accepted.

Milwaukee School of Engineering, MS Program in Perfusion, Milwaukee, WI 53202-3109. Offers MS. *Students:* 14 full-time (7 women). Average age 27. 69 applicants, 13% accepted, 7 enrolled. In 2017, 5 master's awarded. *Degree requirements:* For master's, comprehensive exam, thesis. *Entrance requirements:* For master's, GRE General Test (percentiles must average 50% or better), baccalaureate degree with minimum undergraduate GPA of 2.8; at least one undergraduate course in each of the following areas: physiology (or anatomy and physiology), chemistry, mathematics and physics; 3 letters of recommendation; personal interview; observation of 2 perfusion clinical cases. Additional exam requirements/recommendations for international students: Required—TOEFL (minimum score 90 iBT), IELTS (minimum score 7). *Application deadline:* Applications are processed on a rolling basis. Application fee: $0. Electronic applications accepted. *Expenses: Tuition:* Part-time $814 per credit hour. *Required fees:* $12.50 per credit hour. *Financial support:* Career-related internships or fieldwork, institutionally sponsored loans, and scholarships/grants available. Financial award application deadline: 3/15; financial award applicants required to submit FAFSA. *Faculty research:* Heart medicine. *Unit head:* Dr. Ronald Gerrits, Program Director, 414-277-7561, Fax: 414-277-7494, E-mail: gerrits@msoe.edu. *Application contact:* Brian Rutz, Graduate Admission Counselor, 414-277-7200, E-mail: rutz@msoe.edu.
Website: https://www.msoe.edu/academics/graduate-degrees/health/perfusion/

Northern Michigan University, Office of Graduate Education and Research, College of Health Sciences and Professional Studies, School of Clinical Sciences, Marquette, MI 49855-5301. Offers clinical molecular genetics (MS). *Program availability:* Part-time. *Degree requirements:* For master's, thesis or project to be presented as a seminar at the conclusion of the program. *Entrance requirements:* For master's, minimum undergraduate GPA of 3.0; bachelor's degree in clinical laboratory science or biology; laboratory experience; statement of intent that includes lab skills and experiences along with reason for pursuing this degree; 3 letters of recommendation (instructors or professional references). Additional exam requirements/recommendations for international students: Required—TOEFL (minimum score 550 paper-based; 79 iBT), IELTS (minimum score 6.5). *Application deadline:* For fall admission, 7/1 for domestic students. Applications are processed on a rolling basis. Application fee: $50. Electronic applications accepted. *Expenses:* Tuition, state resident: full-time $9417; part-time $542 per credit hour. Tuition, nonresident: full-time $12,873; part-time $758 per credit hour. Tuition and fees vary according to course load, degree level and program. *Financial support:* Federal Work-Study, scholarships/grants, and unspecified assistantships available. Support available to part-time students. Financial award application deadline: 3/1; financial award applicants required to submit FAFSA. *Unit head:* Paul Mann, Associate Dean/Director, 906-227-2338, E-mail: pmann@nmu.edu. *Application contact:* Paul Mann, Associate Dean/Director, 906-227-2338, E-mail: pmann@nmu.edu.
Website: http://www.nmu.edu/clinicalsciences/

Northwestern University, School of Professional Studies, Program in Regulatory Compliance, Evanston, IL 60208. Offers clinical research (MS); healthcare compliance (MS); quality systems (MS). Offered in partnership with Northwestern Univesity's Clinical and Translational Sciences Institute. *Program availability:* Part-time, evening/weekend.
Website: https://sps.northwestern.edu/masters/regulatory-compliance/index.php

Pontifical Catholic University of Puerto Rico, College of Sciences, School of Medical Technology, Ponce, PR 00717-0777. Offers Certificate. *Entrance requirements:* For degree, letters of recommendation, interview, minimum GPA of 2.75.

Rush University, College of Health Sciences, Department of Medical Laboratory Science, Chicago, IL 60612-3832. Offers clinical laboratory management (MS); medical laboratory science (MS). *Accreditation:* NAACLS. *Degree requirements:* For master's, comprehensive exam, project. *Entrance requirements:* For master's, 16 semester hours of chemistry, 12 semester hours of biology, 3 semester hours of mathematics, interview. Additional exam requirements/recommendations for international students: Required—TOEFL. *Application deadline:* For fall admission, 8/1 for domestic and international students; for winter admission, 12/1 for domestic and international students; for spring admission, 3/1 for domestic and international students. Applications are processed on a rolling basis. Application fee: $40. Electronic applications accepted. *Financial support:* Federal Work-Study, institutionally sponsored loans, and scholarships/grants available. Support available to part-time students. Financial award application deadline: 4/15; financial award applicants required to submit FAFSA. *Faculty research:* Hematopoietic disorders, molecular techniques, biochemistry, microbial susceptibility, immunology. *Unit head:* Dr. Maribeth Flaws, Acting Chair, 312-942-2115, E-mail: maribeth_l_flaws@rush.edu. *Application contact:* 312-942-7120, E-mail: chs_admissions@rush.edu.
Website: http://www.rushu.rush.edu/mls

Rutgers University–Newark, School of Health Related Professions, Department of Clinical Laboratory Sciences, Newark, NJ 07102. Offers MS. *Program availability:* Part-time, online learning. *Degree requirements:* For master's, project. *Entrance requirements:* For master's, two recommendations, personal statement, current resume or curriculum vita, minimum GPA of 2.75. Additional exam requirements/recommendations for international students: Required—TOEFL.

Rutgers University–New Brunswick, Graduate School of Biomedical Sciences, Program in Clinical and Translational Science, Piscataway, NJ 08854-8097. Offers MS. *Program availability:* Part-time. *Degree requirements:* For master's, thesis.

State University of New York Upstate Medical University, Program in Medical Technology, Syracuse, NY 13210. Offers MS. *Accreditation:* NAACLS. *Degree requirements:* For master's, thesis. *Entrance requirements:* For master's, GRE General Test, GRE Subject Test, 2 years of medical technology experience.

Tarleton State University, College of Graduate Studies, College of Health Sciences and Human Services, Department of Medical Laboratory Sciences and Public Health, Fort Worth, TX 76104. Offers medical laboratory sciences (MS). *Program availability:* Part-time, evening/weekend. *Faculty:* 5 full-time (4 women), 2 part-time/adjunct (both women). *Students:* 7 full-time (3 women), 5 part-time (all women); includes 6 minority (2 Black or African American, non-Hispanic/Latino; 1 American Indian or Alaska Native, non-Hispanic/Latino; 3 Asian, non-Hispanic/Latino), 2 international. Average age 30. 14 applicants, 79% accepted, 10 enrolled. In 2017, 1 master's awarded. *Degree requirements:* For master's, comprehensive exam, thesis optional. *Entrance requirements:* For master's, GRE, minimum GPA of 3.0. Additional exam requirements/recommendations for international students: Required—TOEFL (minimum score 550 paper-based; 80 iBT), IELTS (minimum score 6). *Application deadline:* For fall admission, 8/15 for domestic students; for spring admission, 1/7 for domestic students. Applications are processed on a rolling basis. Application fee: $45 ($145 for international students). Electronic applications accepted. *Expenses:* Contact institution. *Financial support:* Career-related internships or fieldwork, Federal Work-Study, and scholarships/grants available. Support available to part-time students. Financial award application deadline: 5/1; financial award applicants required to submit FAFSA. *Unit head:* Sally Lewis, Head, 817-926-1101, E-mail: slewis@tarleton.edu. *Application contact:* Information Contact, 254-968-9104, Fax: 254-968-9670, E-mail: gradoffice@tarleton.edu.
Website: http://www.tarleton.edu/degrees/masters/ms-medical-laboratory-science/

Clinical Laboratory Sciences/Medical Technology

Thomas Jefferson University, Jefferson College of Health Professions, Department of Medical Laboratory Sciences and Biotechnology, Philadelphia, PA 19107. Offers biotechnology (MS); cytotechnology (MS); medical laboratory science (MS). *Program availability:* Part-time. *Degree requirements:* For master's, comprehensive exam. *Entrance requirements:* Additional exam requirements/recommendations for international students: Required—TOEFL (minimum score 87 iBT), IELTS (minimum score 6.5). Electronic applications accepted. *Expenses:* Contact institution. *Faculty research:* Women's health; transportation of islet cells to remedy diabetes/insulin deficiency; bone regeneration; the use of stem cells to remedy cardiac injuries.

Tufts University, Sackler School of Graduate Biomedical Sciences, Clinical and Translational Science Program, Medford, MA 02155. Offers MS, PhD, Certificate. *Degree requirements:* For master's, thesis; for doctorate, comprehensive exam, thesis/dissertation. *Entrance requirements:* For master's and doctorate, strong clinical research background; resume; personal statement; 3 letters of recommendation. Electronic applications accepted. *Expenses:* Contact institution. *Faculty research:* Clinical study design, mathematical modeling, meta analysis, epidemiologic research, coronary heart disease.

Universidad de las Américas Puebla, Division of Graduate Studies, School of Sciences, Program in Clinical Analysis (Biomedicine), Puebla, Mexico. Offers MS. *Program availability:* Part-time, evening/weekend. *Degree requirements:* For master's, one foreign language, thesis. *Faculty research:* Clinical techniques, clinical research.

Université de Sherbrooke, Faculty of Medicine and Health Sciences, Graduate Programs in Medicine, Program in Clinical Sciences, Sherbrooke, QC J1H 5N4, Canada. Offers M Sc, PhD. *Program availability:* Part-time. Terminal master's awarded for partial completion of doctoral program. *Degree requirements:* For master's, thesis; for doctorate, thesis/dissertation. Electronic applications accepted. *Faculty research:* Population health, health services, ethics, clinical research.

University at Buffalo, the State University of New York, Graduate School, Jacobs School of Medicine and Biomedical Sciences, Graduate Programs in Medicine and Biomedical Sciences, Department of Biotechnical and Clinical Laboratory Sciences, Buffalo, NY 14214. Offers biotechnology (MS). *Accreditation:* NAACLS. *Program availability:* Part-time. *Faculty:* 6 full-time (2 women). *Students:* 10 full-time (6 women), 1 (woman) part-time, 6 international. Average age 24. 68 applicants, 13% accepted, 3 enrolled. In 2017, 4 master's awarded. *Degree requirements:* For master's, thesis. *Entrance requirements:* For master's, GRE General Test, minimum GPA of 3.0 or equivalent. Additional exam requirements/recommendations for international students: Required—TOEFL (minimum score 79 iBT), IELTS. *Application deadline:* For fall admission, 3/1 priority date for domestic students, 2/1 priority date for international students. Applications are processed on a rolling basis. Application fee: $85. Electronic applications accepted. *Financial support:* In 2017–18, 6 students received support, including 1 research assistantship with tuition reimbursement available (averaging $15,000 per year), 5 teaching assistantships with full tuition reimbursements available (averaging $10,000 per year). Financial award application deadline: 3/1. *Faculty research:* Immunology, cancer biology, toxicology, analytical clinical chemistry, hematology, chemistry, microbial genomics. *Total annual research expenditures:* $1.2 million. *Unit head:* Dr. Paul J. Kostyniak, Chair, 716-829-5188, Fax: 716-829-3601, E-mail: pjkost@buffalo.edu. *Application contact:* Dr. Stephen T. Koury, Director of Graduate Studies, 716-829-5188, Fax: 716-829-3601, E-mail: stvkoury@buffalo.edu.
Website: http://www.smbs.buffalo.edu/cls/biotech-ms.html

The University of Alabama at Birmingham, School of Health Professions, Program in Clinical Laboratory Science, Birmingham, AL 35294. Offers MS. *Accreditation:* NAACLS. *Degree requirements:* For master's, thesis optional. *Entrance requirements:* For master's, GRE General Test, interview, related undergraduate major, minimum undergraduate GPA of 3.0 computed from all undergraduate credits or from the last 60 semester hours of undergraduate course credit. Additional exam requirements/recommendations for international students: Required—TOEFL (minimum score 550 paper-based; 80 iBT), TWE. Electronic applications accepted. *Faculty research:* Computer-enhanced instruction, antiphospholipid antibodies, alternate site testing, technology assessment.

The University of Alabama at Birmingham, School of Public Health, Program in Public Health, Birmingham, AL 35294. Offers applied epidemiology and pharmacoepidemiology (MSPH); biostatistics (MPH); clinical and translational science (MSPH); environmental health (MPH); environmental health and toxicology (MSPH); epidemiology (MPH); general theory and practice (MPH); health behavior (MPH); health care organization (MPH); health policy quantitative policy analysis (MPH); industrial hygiene (MPH, MSPH); maternal and child health policy (Dr PH); maternal and child health policy and leadership (MPH); occupational health and safety (MPH); outcomes research (MSPH, Dr PH); public health (PhD); public health management (Dr PH); public health preparedness management (MPH). *Program availability:* Part-time, online learning. *Degree requirements:* For doctorate, comprehensive exam, thesis/dissertation. *Entrance requirements:* For master's and doctorate, GRE. Additional exam requirements/recommendations for international students: Recommended—TOEFL (minimum score 550 paper-based; 79 iBT), IELTS (minimum score 6.5). Electronic applications accepted.

University of Alberta, Faculty of Medicine and Dentistry and Faculty of Graduate Studies and Research, Graduate Programs in Medicine, Department of Laboratory Medicine and Pathology, Edmonton, AB T6G 2E1, Canada. Offers medical sciences (M Sc, PhD). *Program availability:* Part-time. Terminal master's awarded for partial completion of doctoral program. *Degree requirements:* For master's, thesis; for doctorate, thesis/dissertation, candidacy exam. *Entrance requirements:* For master's and doctorate, 3 letters of recommendation, minimum GPA of 3.0. Additional exam requirements/recommendations for international students: Required—TOEFL. *Faculty research:* Transplantation, renal pathology, molecular mechanisms of diseases, cryobiology, immunodiagnostics, informatics/cyber medicine, neuroimmunology, microbiology.

University of California, San Diego, Graduate Division, Department of Electrical and Computer Engineering, La Jolla, CA 92093. Offers applied ocean science (MS, PhD); applied physics (MS, PhD); communication theory and systems (MS, PhD); computer engineering (MS, PhD); electronic circuits and systems (MS, PhD); intelligent systems, robotics and control (MS, PhD); medical devices and systems (MS, PhD); nanoscale devices and systems (MS, PhD); photonics (MS, PhD); signal and image processing (MS, PhD). Program offered jointly with San Diego State University. *Students:* 697 full-time (135 women), 75 part-time (11 women). 2,651 applicants, 32% accepted, 283 enrolled. In 2017, 180 master's, 33 doctorates awarded. Terminal master's awarded for partial completion of doctoral program. *Degree requirements:* For master's, comprehensive exam (for some programs), thesis (for some programs); for doctorate, comprehensive exam, thesis/dissertation. *Entrance requirements:* For master's and doctorate, GRE General Test, minimum GPA of 3.0, resume or curriculum vitae (recommended). Additional exam requirements/recommendations for international students: Required—TOEFL (minimum score 550 paper-based; 80 iBT), IELTS (minimum score 7), PTE (minimum score 65). *Application deadline:* For fall admission, 12/15 for domestic students. Application fee: $105 ($125 for international students). Electronic applications accepted. *Financial support:* Fellowships, research assistantships, teaching assistantships, scholarships/grants, traineeships, and unspecified assistantships available. Financial award applicants required to submit FAFSA. *Faculty research:* Applied ocean science; applied physics; communication theory and systems; computer engineering; electronic circuits and systems; intelligent systems, robotics and control; medical devices and systems; nanoscale devices and systems; photonics; signal and image processing. *Unit head:* Truong Nguyen, Chair, 858-822-5554, E-mail: nguyent@ece.ucsd.edu. *Application contact:* Sean Jones, Graduate Admissions Coordinator, 858-534-3213, E-mail: ecegradapps@ece.ucsd.edu.
Website: http://ece.ucsd.edu/

University of California, San Diego, Graduate Division, Program in Medical Device Engineering, La Jolla, CA 92093. Offers MAS. *Program availability:* Part-time. *Students:* 27 part-time (7 women). 20 applicants, 90% accepted, 16 enrolled. In 2017, 19 master's awarded. *Degree requirements:* For master's, capstone project. *Entrance requirements:* For master's, 3 letters of recommendation; statement of purpose; bachelor's degree in engineering, science, or mathematics; minimum undergraduate GPA of 3.0 in final two years of study; two years of relevant work experience; curriculum vitae/resume. Additional exam requirements/recommendations for international students: Required—TOEFL (minimum score 550 paper-based; 80 iBT), IELTS (minimum score 7). *Application deadline:* For fall admission, 5/1 priority date for domestic students. Applications are processed on a rolling basis. Application fee: $105 ($125 for international students). Electronic applications accepted. *Expenses:* Contact institution. *Financial support:* Applicants required to submit FAFSA. *Faculty research:* Mechanics and transport, anatomy and physiology, biomaterials, business processes, regulatory affairs, life science technologies. *Unit head:* Juan C. Lasheras, Director, 858-534-5437, E-mail: jlasheras@ucsd.edu. *Application contact:* Sally Binney, Program Coordinator, 858-246-1463, E-mail: mde-mas@ucsd.edu.
Website: http://maseng.ucsd.edu/mde/

University of Colorado Denver, School of Medicine, Clinical Science Graduate Program, Aurora, CO 80045. Offers clinical investigation (PhD); clinical sciences (MS); health information technology (PhD); health services research (PhD). *Students:* 46 full-time (31 women), 26 part-time (15 women); includes 7 minority (2 Black or African American, non-Hispanic/Latino; 4 Asian, non-Hispanic/Latino; 1 Hispanic/Latino). Average age 37. 18 applicants, 67% accepted, 11 enrolled. In 2017, 21 master's, 1 doctorate awarded. *Degree requirements:* For master's, thesis, minimum of 30 credit hours, defense/final exam of thesis or publishable paper; for doctorate, comprehensive exam, thesis/dissertation, at least 30 credit hours of thesis work. *Entrance requirements:* For master's, GRE General Test or MCAT (waived if candidate has earned MS/MA or PhD from accredited U.S. school), minimum undergraduate GPA of 3.0, 3-4 letters of recommendation; for doctorate, GRE General Test or MCAT (waived if candidate has earned MS/MA or PhD from accredited U.S. school), health care graduate, professional degree, or graduate degree related to health sciences; minimum GPA of 3.0; 3-4 letters of recommendation. Additional exam requirements/recommendations for international students: Required—TOEFL (minimum score 550 paper-based; 80 iBT). *Application deadline:* For fall admission, 2/1 for domestic students, 1/15 priority date for international students; for spring admission, 10/1 for domestic students. Application fee: $50 ($75 for international students). Electronic applications accepted. *Unit head:* Dr. Lisa Cicutto, Program Director, 303-398-1539, E-mail: cicuttol@njhealth.org. *Application contact:* Galit Mankin, Program Administrator, 720-848-6249, Fax: 303-848-7381, E-mail: galit.mankin@ucdenver.edu.
Website: http://www.ucdenver.edu/research/CCTSI/education-training/clsc/Pages/default.aspx

University of Florida, Graduate School, College of Nursing, Gainesville, FL 32611. Offers clinical and translational science (PhD); clinical nursing (DNP); nursing (MSN); nursing sciences (PhD). *Accreditation:* AACN; ACNM/ACME (one or more programs are accredited). *Program availability:* Part-time. *Degree requirements:* For master's, thesis optional; for doctorate, thesis/dissertation. *Entrance requirements:* For master's and doctorate, GRE General Test, minimum GPA of 3.0. Additional exam requirements/recommendations for international students: Required—TOEFL (minimum score 550 paper-based; 80 iBT), IELTS (minimum score 6). Electronic applications accepted. *Faculty research:* Aging and health: cancer survivorship, interventions to promote healthy aging, and symptom management; women's health, fetal and infant development; biobehavioral interventions: interrelationships among the biological, behavioral, psychological, social and spiritual factors that influence wellness and disease; health policy: influence of local and national policy on physical and psychological health.

University of Florida, Graduate School, College of Pharmacy, Graduate Programs in Pharmacy, Department of Pharmaceutics, Gainesville, FL 32611. Offers clinical and translational sciences (PhD); pharmaceutical sciences (MSP, PhD); pharmacy (MSP, PhD). *Degree requirements:* For doctorate, comprehensive exam, thesis/dissertation. *Entrance requirements:* For master's and doctorate, GRE General Test, minimum GPA of 3.0. Additional exam requirements/recommendations for international students: Required—TOEFL (minimum score 550 paper-based; 80 iBT), IELTS (minimum score 6). Electronic applications accepted. *Faculty research:* Basic, applied, and clinical investigations in pharmacokinetics/biopharmaceutics; pharmaceutical analysis, pharmaceutical biotechnology and drug delivery; herbal medicine.

University of Florida, Graduate School, College of Public Health and Health Professions, Department of Clinical and Health Psychology, Gainesville, FL 32611. Offers clinical and translational science (PhD); psychology (MS). *Accreditation:* APA (one or more programs are accredited). *Degree requirements:* For doctorate, comprehensive exam, thesis/dissertation, pre-doctoral internship. *Entrance requirements:* For master's and doctorate, GRE General Test, minimum GPA of 3.0. Additional exam requirements/recommendations for international students: Required—TOEFL (minimum score 550 paper-based; 80 iBT), IELTS (minimum score 6). Electronic applications accepted. *Faculty research:* Clinical child and pediatric psychology, medical psychology, neuropsychology, health promotion and aging.

University of Florida, Graduate School, College of Public Health and Health Professions, Department of Epidemiology, Gainesville, FL 32611. Offers clinical and translational science (PhD); epidemiology (MS, PhD). *Degree requirements:* For master's, thesis; for doctorate, thesis/dissertation. *Entrance requirements:* For master's and doctorate, GRE (minimum score verbal/quantitative combined 300), minimum GPA of 3.0. Additional exam requirements/recommendations for international students: Required—TOEFL (minimum score 550 paper-based; 80 iBT), IELTS (minimum score 6). *Faculty research:* Substance abuse, psychiatric epidemiology, cancer epidemiology, infectious disease epidemiology, bioinformatics.

University of Florida, Graduate School, Herbert Wertheim College of Engineering, Department of Materials Science and Engineering, Gainesville, FL 32611. Offers material science and engineering (MS), including clinical and translational science; materials science and engineering (ME, PhD); nuclear engineering (ME, PhD), including imaging science and technology (PhD), nuclear engineering sciences (ME, MS, PhD); nuclear engineering (MS), including nuclear engineering sciences (ME, MS, PhD); JD/MS. *Program availability:* Part-time, online learning. Terminal master's awarded for partial completion of doctoral program. *Degree requirements:* For master's, comprehensive exam, thesis; for doctorate, comprehensive exam, thesis/dissertation. *Entrance requirements:* For master's and doctorate, minimum GPA of 3.0. Additional exam requirements/recommendations for international students: Required—TOEFL (minimum score 550 paper-based; 80 iBT), IELTS (minimum score 6). Electronic applications accepted. *Faculty research:* Polymeric system, biomaterials and biomimetics; inorganic and organic electronic materials; functional ceramic materials for energy systems and microelectronic applications; advanced metallic systems for aerospace, transportation and biological applications; nuclear materials.

University of Maryland, Baltimore, Graduate School, Department of Medical and Research Technology, Baltimore, MD 21201. Offers MS. *Accreditation:* NAACLS. *Program availability:* Part-time. *Students:* 4 full-time (all women), 3 part-time (all women); includes 3 minority (2 Black or African American, non-Hispanic/Latino; 1 Two or more races, non-Hispanic/Latino), 3 international. Average age 29. 4 applicants, 50% accepted. In 2017, 3 master's awarded. *Degree requirements:* For master's, thesis or management project. *Entrance requirements:* For master's, GRE General Test, minimum GPA of 3.0, curriculum vitae, essay, 3 letters of recommendation. Additional exam requirements/recommendations for international students: Required—TOEFL (minimum score 80 iBT) or IELTS (minimum score 7). *Application deadline:* For fall admission, 5/1 priority date for domestic students, 1/15 for international students; for spring admission, 11/30 priority date for domestic students. Application fee: $75. Electronic applications accepted. *Expenses:* Tuition, state resident: full-time $13,990; part-time $661 per credit. Tuition, nonresident: full-time $30,484; part-time $1310 per credit. *Required fees:* $1894; $94 per credit. $415 per semester. Part-time tuition and fees vary according to course load, degree level and program. *Financial support:* Fellowships and research assistantships available. Financial award application deadline: 3/1; financial award applicants required to submit FAFSA. *Faculty research:* Clinical microbiology, immunology, immunohematology, hematology, clinical chemistry, molecular biology. *Unit head:* Dr. Sanford Stass, Chair, 410-328-1237. *Application contact:* Dr. Ivana Vucenik, Graduate Program Director, 410-706-1832, E-mail: ivucenik@som.umaryland.edu.

University of Massachusetts Lowell, College of Health Sciences, Department of Clinical Laboratory and Nutritional Sciences, Lowell, MA 01854. Offers clinical laboratory sciences (MS). *Accreditation:* NAACLS. *Program availability:* Part-time, online learning. *Degree requirements:* For master's, thesis optional. *Entrance requirements:* For master's, GRE General Test, minimum GPA of 3.0, letters of recommendation. *Faculty research:* Cardiovascular disease, lipoprotein metabolism, micronutrient evaluation, alcohol metabolism, mycobacterial drug resistance.

University of Minnesota, Twin Cities Campus, College of Science and Engineering, Technological Leadership Institute, Program in Medical Device Innovation, Minneapolis, MN 55455-0213. Offers MS. *Entrance requirements:* Additional exam requirements/recommendations for international students: Required—TOEFL. Electronic applications accepted. *Faculty research:* Dynamics of medical device innovation, including technology innovation, project and business management, intellectual property, regulatory affairs, and public policy.

University of Nebraska Medical Center, College of Allied Health Professions, Program in Clinical Perfusion Education, Omaha, NE 68198-4144. Offers distance education perfusion education (MPS); perfusion science (MPS). *Accreditation:* NAACLS. *Program availability:* Online learning. *Degree requirements:* For master's, comprehensive exam, thesis. *Entrance requirements:* For master's, GRE. Electronic applications accepted. *Expenses:* Tuition, state resident: full-time $8451; part-time $4225 per semester. Tuition, nonresident: full-time $24,219; part-time $11,295 per semester. *Required fees:* $589; $117 per term. *Faculty research:* Platelet gel, hemoconcentrators.

University of Nebraska Medical Center, College of Allied Health Professions, Program in Cytotechnology, Omaha, NE 68198. Offers Certificate. *Accreditation:* NAACLS. *Program availability:* Online learning. Electronic applications accepted. *Expenses:* Tuition, state resident: full-time $8451; part-time $4225 per semester. Tuition, nonresident: full-time $24,219; part-time $11,295 per semester. *Required fees:* $589; $117 per term. *Faculty research:* HPV vaccine.

University of New Mexico, Graduate Studies, Health Sciences Center, Master's in Clinical Laboratory Science Program, Albuquerque, NM 87131. Offers education (MS); laboratory management (MS); research and development (MS). *Program availability:* Part-time. *Faculty:* 10 full-time (4 women). *Students:* 2 full-time (1 woman), 4 part-time (2 women), 1 international. Average age 34. 3 applicants. *Entrance requirements:* For master's, ASCP Board of Certification Exam. Additional exam requirements/recommendations for international students: Required—TOEFL. *Application deadline:* For fall admission, 7/15 priority date for domestic students, 6/15 priority date for international students. Application fee: $50. Electronic applications accepted. *Financial support:* Career-related internships or fieldwork available. Financial award application deadline: 7/15; financial award applicants required to submit FAFSA. *Faculty research:* Prostate cancer, educational techniques, online training, molecular diagnostics, laboratory medicine, laboratory management, laboratory test assessment. *Unit head:* Dr. Paul B. Roth, Dean, 505-272-8273, Fax: 505-272-6857. *Application contact:* Dr. Roberto Gomez, Associate Dean of Students, 505-272-3414, Fax: 505-272-6857, E-mail: rgomez@unm.edu.
Website: http://pathology.unm.edu/medical-laboratory-sciences/program/graduate-m.s.-degree-program.html

University of New Mexico, Graduate Studies, Health Sciences Center, Program in Clinical and Translational Science, Albuquerque, NM 87131-2039. Offers Certificate. *Students:* Average age 33. In 2017, 6 Certificates awarded. *Unit head:* Dr. Helen J. Hathaway, Program Director, 505-272-1469, E-mail: hhathaway@salud.unm.edu. *Application contact:* Angel Cooke-Jackson, Coordinator, 505-272-1887, Fax: 505-272-8738, E-mail: acooke-jackson@salud.unm.edu.

University of North Dakota, Graduate School and Graduate School, Graduate Programs in Medicine, Department of Clinical Translation Science, Grand Forks, ND 58202. Offers MS, PhD. *Accreditation:* NAACLS. *Program availability:* Online learning. *Degree requirements:* For master's, comprehensive exam, thesis or alternative. *Entrance requirements:* For master's, minimum GPA of 3.0. Additional exam requirements/recommendations for international students: Required—TOEFL (minimum score 550 paper-based; 79 iBT), IELTS (minimum score 5.5). Electronic applications accepted.

University of Pennsylvania, Perelman School of Medicine, Master of Regulatory Affairs Program, Philadelphia, PA 19104. Offers MRA. *Unit head:* Dr. Emma Meagher, MD, Director, Regulatory Education Programs, 215-662-2174, E-mail: itmated@mail.med.upenn.edu. *Application contact:* Dr. Anna Greene, Program Coordinator, 215-662-4619, E-mail: acgreene@upenn.edu.
Website: http://www.itmat.upenn.edu/mra.html

University of Pennsylvania, Perelman School of Medicine, Master's in Translational Research Program, Philadelphia, PA 19104. Offers MTR. *Unit head:* Dr. Emma Meagher, MD, Director, Translational Research Programs, 215-662-2174, E-mail: itmated@mail.med.upenn.edu. *Application contact:* Rachel Bastian, Administrative Director, 215-614-1835, E-mail: itmated@mail.med.upenn.edu.
Website: http://www.itmat.upenn.edu/

University of Pittsburgh, School of Medicine, Graduate Programs in Medicine, Clinical and Translational Science Graduate Program, Pittsburgh, PA 15260. Offers PhD. *Program availability:* Part-time, blended/hybrid learning. *Faculty:* 31 full-time (16 women). *Students:* 3 full-time (1 woman), 8 part-time (5 women); includes 1 minority (Black or African American, non-Hispanic/Latino), 1 international. Average age 39. 4 applicants, 75% accepted, 3 enrolled. In 2017, 1 doctorate awarded. *Degree requirements:* For doctorate, comprehensive exam, thesis/dissertation, 8 hours of responsible conduct in research training. *Entrance requirements:* For doctorate, MCAT or GRE, transcripts, curriculum vitae, 2 letters of recommendation. Additional exam requirements/recommendations for international students: Required—TOEFL (minimum score 600 paper-based; 100 iBT), IELTS (minimum score 7). *Application deadline:* For summer admission, 1/31 priority date for domestic and international students. Application fee: $0. Electronic applications accepted. *Expenses:* $26,782 in-state, $42,006 out-of-state. *Financial support:* In 2017–18, 3 students received support. Fellowships with full tuition reimbursements available, research assistantships, scholarships/grants, traineeships, tuition waivers, and employee benefits available. *Faculty research:* Design and analysis of observational studies and clinical trials; evaluating the effectiveness of mind-body and complementary interventions for chronic pain and high blood pressure; cost effectiveness of common medical interventions. *Unit head:* Dr. Wishwa Kapoor, Director, 412-586-9632, Fax: 412-586-9672, E-mail: icre@pitt.edu. *Application contact:* Juliana Tambellini, Program Administrator, 412-586-9632, Fax: 412-586-9672, E-mail: icre@pitt.edu.
Website: http://www.icre.pitt.edu/phd

University of Puerto Rico–Medical Sciences Campus, School of Health Professions, Program in Clinical Laboratory Science, San Juan, PR 00936-5067. Offers MS. *Accreditation:* NAACLS. *Program availability:* Part-time, evening/weekend. *Degree requirements:* For master's, one foreign language, thesis or alternative. *Entrance requirements:* For master's, EXADEP or GRE General Test, minimum GPA of 2.75, bachelor's degree in medical technology, 1 year lab experience, interview. *Faculty research:* Toxicology, virology, biochemistry, immunohematology, nervous system regeneration.

University of Puerto Rico–Medical Sciences Campus, School of Health Professions, Program in Cytotechnology, San Juan, PR 00936-5067. Offers Certificate. *Degree requirements:* For Certificate, one foreign language, research project. *Entrance requirements:* For degree, minimum GPA of 2.5, interview.

University of Puerto Rico–Medical Sciences Campus, School of Health Professions, Program in Medical Technology, San Juan, PR 00936-5067. Offers Certificate. *Program availability:* Part-time. *Degree requirements:* For Certificate, one foreign language, clinical practice. *Entrance requirements:* For degree, bachelor's degree in science, minimum GPA of 2.5.

University of Rhode Island, Graduate School, College of the Environment and Life Sciences, Department of Cell and Molecular Biology, Kingston, RI 02881. Offers biochemistry (MS, PhD); clinical laboratory sciences (MS), including biotechnology, clinical laboratory science, cytopathology; microbiology (MS, PhD); molecular genetics (MS, PhD). *Program availability:* Part-time. *Faculty:* 14 full-time (6 women). *Students:* 17 full-time (9 women), 19 part-time (15 women); includes 9 minority (2 Black or African American, non-Hispanic/Latino; 4 Asian, non-Hispanic/Latino; 2 Hispanic/Latino; 1 Two or more races, non-Hispanic/Latino), 10 international. 26 applicants, 62% accepted, 6 enrolled. In 2017, 17 master's awarded. *Entrance requirements:* Additional exam requirements/recommendations for international students: Required—TOEFL. *Application deadline:* For fall admission, 1/15 for domestic and international students. Application fee: $65. Electronic applications accepted. *Expenses:* Tuition, state resident: full-time $12,706; part-time $786 per credit. Tuition, nonresident: full-time $25,216; part-time $1401 per credit. *Required fees:* $1598; $45 per credit. One-time fee: $30 part-time. *Financial support:* In 2017–18, 4 teaching assistantships with tuition reimbursements (averaging $12,698 per year) were awarded; traineeships also available. Financial award application deadline: 1/15; financial award applicants required to submit FAFSA. *Unit head:* Dr. Gongqing Sun, Chair and Professor, 401-874-5937, Fax: 401-874-2202, E-mail: gsun@mail.uri.edu. *Application contact:* Bethany Jenkins, Professor, 401-874-7551, E-mail: bjenkins@uri.edu.
Website: https://web.uri.edu/cmb/

University of Southern Mississippi, College of Health, Department of Medical Laboratory Science, Hattiesburg, MS 39406-0001. Offers MLS. *Accreditation:* NAACLS. *Program availability:* Part-time, online learning. *Students:* 2 full-time (both women). 3 applicants, 100% accepted, 2 enrolled. In 2017, 4 master's awarded. *Degree requirements:* For master's, comprehensive exam, thesis (for some programs). *Entrance requirements:* For master's, GRE General Test, minimum GPA of 2.75. Additional exam requirements/recommendations for international students: Required—TOEFL, IELTS. *Application deadline:* For fall admission, 3/1 priority date for domestic students, 3/1 for international students; for spring admission, 1/10 priority date for domestic and international students. Application fee: $60. Electronic applications accepted. *Expenses:* Tuition, state resident: full-time $3830. *Financial support:* Research assistantships, teaching assistantships with full tuition reimbursements, career-related internships or fieldwork, Federal Work-Study, institutionally sponsored loans, scholarships/grants, health care benefits, and unspecified assistantships available. Financial award application deadline: 3/15; financial award applicants required to submit FAFSA. *Faculty research:* Clinical chemistry, clinical microbiology, hematology, clinical management and education, immunohematology. *Unit head:* Dr. Mary Lux, Chair, 601-266-4908. *Application contact:* Shonna Breland, Manager of Graduate Admissions, 601-266-6563, Fax: 601-266-5138.
Website: https://www.usm.edu/medical-laboratory-science

The University of Tennessee Health Science Center, College of Graduate Health Sciences, Memphis, TN 38163. Offers biomedical engineering (MS, PhD); biomedical sciences (PhD); dental sciences (MDS); epidemiology (MS); health outcomes and policy research (PhD); laboratory research and management (MS); nursing science (PhD); pharmaceutical sciences (PhD); pharmacology (MS); speech and hearing science (PhD); DDS/PhD; DNP/PhD; MD/PhD; Pharm D/PhD. MS and PhD programs in biomedical engineering offered jointly with University of Memphis. *Faculty:* 528 full-time (176 women). *Students:* 258 full-time (130 women); includes 87 minority (14 Black or African American, non-Hispanic/Latino; 68 Asian, non-Hispanic/Latino; 5 Hispanic/Latino). Average age 28. 673 applicants, 17% accepted, 102 enrolled. In 2017, 23 master's, 30 doctorates awarded. Terminal master's awarded for partial completion of doctoral program. *Degree requirements:* For master's, comprehensive exam, thesis; for doctorate, thesis/dissertation, oral and written preliminary and comprehensive exams. *Entrance requirements:* For master's and doctorate, GRE General Test, minimum GPA of 3.0. Additional exam requirements/recommendations for international students: Recommended—TOEFL (minimum score 79 iBT), IELTS (minimum score 6.5). *Application deadline:* For winter admission, 1/1 for domestic and international students; for spring admission, 3/1 for domestic and international students. Applications are processed on a rolling basis. Application fee: $0. Electronic applications accepted. *Expenses:* Contact institution. *Financial support:* In 2017–18, 150 students received support, including 150 research assistantships (averaging $25,000 per year); fellowships, institutionally sponsored loans, scholarships/grants, health care benefits,

and tuition waivers (full and partial) also available. Support available to part-time students. *Faculty research:* Cell biology, epidemiology, biomedical engineering, speech and hearing science, health policy, pharmaceutical sciences, dental sciences, nursing science, pharmacology. *Unit head:* Dr. Donald B. Thomason, Dean, 901-448-5538, E-mail: dthomaso@uthsc.edu. *Application contact:* Dr. Isaac O. Donkor, Associate Dean for Student Affairs, 901-448-5538, E-mail: idonkor@uthsc.edu.
Website: http://grad.uthsc.edu/

The University of Tennessee Health Science Center, College of Health Professions, Memphis, TN 38163-0002. Offers audiology (MS, Au D); clinical laboratory science (MSCLS); cytopathology practice (MCP); health informatics and information management (MHIIM); occupational therapy (MOT); physical therapy (DPT, ScDPT); physician assistant (MMS); speech-language pathology (MS). *Accreditation:* AOTA; APTA. *Program availability:* Part-time, evening/weekend, online learning. Terminal master's awarded for partial completion of doctoral program. *Degree requirements:* For master's, comprehensive exam, thesis; for doctorate, comprehensive exam, residency. *Entrance requirements:* For master's, GRE (MOT, MSCLS), minimum GPA of 3.0, 3 letters of reference, national accreditation (MSCLS), GRE if GPA is less than 3.0 (MCP); for doctorate, GRE. Additional exam requirements/recommendations for international students: Required—TOEFL (minimum score 550 paper-based; 80 iBT). Electronic applications accepted. *Expenses:* Contact institution. *Faculty research:* Gait deviation, muscular dystrophy and strength, hemophilia and exercise, pediatric neurology, self-efficacy.

The University of Texas at Austin, Graduate School, College of Pharmacy, Graduate Programs in Pharmacy, Austin, TX 78712-1111. Offers health outcomes and pharmacy practice (PhD); health outcomes and pharmacy practice (MS); medicinal chemistry (PhD); pharmaceutics (PhD); pharmacology and toxicology (PhD); pharmacotherapy (MS, PhD); translational science (PhD). PhD in translational science offered jointly with The University of Texas Health Science Center at San Antonio and The University of Texas at San Antonio. *Degree requirements:* For master's, thesis; for doctorate, thesis/dissertation. *Entrance requirements:* For master's and doctorate, GRE General Test. Electronic applications accepted. *Faculty research:* Synthetic medical chemistry, synthetic molecular biology, bio-organic chemistry, pharmacoeconomics, pharmacy practice.

The University of Texas Health Science Center at San Antonio, Graduate School of Biomedical Sciences, Translational Science Program, San Antonio, TX 78229-3900. Offers PhD. *Program availability:* Part-time. *Degree requirements:* For doctorate, comprehensive exam, thesis/dissertation.

The University of Texas Medical Branch, Graduate School of Biomedical Sciences, Program in Clinical Science, Galveston, TX 77555. Offers MS, PhD.

The University of Texas Rio Grande Valley, College of Health Affairs, Department of Health and Biomedical Sciences, Brownville, TX 78520. Offers clinical laboratory sciences (MSHS); health care administration (MSHS); nutrition (MSHS). *Faculty:* 2 full-time (both women), 10 part-time/adjunct (all women). *Students:* 129 part-time (94 women); includes 103 minority (8 Black or African American, non-Hispanic/Latino; 4 Asian, non-Hispanic/Latino; 90 Hispanic/Latino; 1 Two or more races, non-Hispanic/Latino), 6 international. 51 applicants, 96% accepted, 49 enrolled. *Application deadline:* For fall admission, 7/20 for domestic and international students; for spring admission, 12/2 for domestic students, 12/1 for international students. Application fee: $50 ($100 for international students). *Expenses:* Tuition, state resident: full-time $5550; part-time $417 per credit hour. Tuition, nonresident: full-time $13,020; part-time $832 per credit hour. *Required fees:* $1169. *Faculty research:* Health disparities, post-menopausal osteoporosis bone loss and bone density, alternative medicine and nutritional supplements, health informatics competencies, online learning and quality matters, health literacy. *Unit head:* Dr. Saraswathy Nair, Associate Professor and Chair, Health and Biomedical, 956-882-5108, Fax: 956-882-6835, E-mail: saraswathy.nair@utrgv.edu. *Application contact:* Kim Garcia, Lecturer III/Associate Chair, Health and Biomedical Sciences, 956-665-4781, E-mail: kim.garcia@utrgv.edu.
Website: http://www.utrgv.edu/hbs/

University of Utah, School of Medicine and Graduate School, Graduate Programs in Medicine, Department of Pathology, Program in Laboratory Medicine and Biomedical Science, Salt Lake City, UT 84112-1107. Offers MS. *Program availability:* Part-time. *Degree requirements:* For master's, comprehensive exam, thesis, thesis research. *Entrance requirements:* For master's, minimum GPA of 3.0 during last 2 years of undergraduate course work, BS in medical laboratory science or related field. Additional exam requirements/recommendations for international students: Required—TOEFL (minimum score 550 paper-based). *Faculty research:* Clinical chemistry, hematology, diagnostic microbiology, immunohematology, cell biology, immunology.

University of Vermont, Graduate College, College of Nursing and Health Sciences, Program in Medical Laboratory Science, Burlington, VT 05405. Offers MS. *Students:* 11 (8 women). 12 applicants, 92% accepted, 8 enrolled. *Entrance requirements:* For master's, GRE General Test. Additional exam requirements/recommendations for international students: Required—TOEFL (minimum iBT score of 90) or IELTS (6.5). *Application deadline:* For fall admission, 4/15 for domestic and international students. Application fee: $65. Electronic applications accepted. *Expenses:* Tuition, state resident: full-time $11,628; part-time $646 per credit. Tuition, nonresident: full-time $29,340; part-time $1630 per credit. *Required fees:* $1994; $10 per credit. Tuition and fees vary according to course load and program. *Financial support:* Scholarships/grants available. *Application contact:* Kristen Cella, Admissions Specialist, 802-656-3858, E-mail: cnhsgrad@uvm.edu.
Website: https://www.uvm.edu/cnhs/mlrs/medical_laboratory_science_ms

University of Vermont, The Robert Larner, MD College of Medicine and Graduate College, Graduate Programs in Medicine, Program in Clinical and Translational Science, Burlington, VT 05405. Offers MS, PhD, Certificate. *Students:* 9 (5 women). 6 applicants, 17% accepted, 1 enrolled. In 2017, 2 doctorates awarded. Terminal master's awarded for partial completion of doctoral program. *Degree requirements:* For master's, thesis; for doctorate, thesis/dissertation. *Entrance requirements:* For master's and doctorate, GRE (recommended). Additional exam requirements/recommendations for international students: Required—TOEFL (minimum score 550 paper-based; 90 iBT), IELTS (minimum score 6.5). *Application deadline:* For fall admission, 3/1 for domestic and international students; for spring admission, 10/1 for domestic and international students. Application fee: $65. Electronic applications accepted. *Expenses:* Tuition, state resident: full-time $11,628; part-time $646 per credit. Tuition, nonresident: full-time $29,340; part-time $1630 per credit. *Required fees:* $1994; $10 per credit. Tuition and fees vary according to course load and program. *Financial support:* Teaching assistantships available. *Faculty research:* Mood disorders, survivors of torture, geomedical science, electronic information resources and patient outcomes. *Unit head:* Dr. Alan Rubin, Director, 802-656-8228, E-mail: alan.rubin@uvm.edu.
Website: http://med.uvm.edu/medicine/gimr/ctseducation/overview

University of Washington, Graduate School, School of Medicine, Graduate Programs in Medicine, Department of Laboratory Medicine, Seattle, WA 98195. Offers MS. *Accreditation:* NAACLS. *Program availability:* Part-time. *Degree requirements:* For master's, thesis. *Entrance requirements:* For master's, GRE General Test, medical technology certification or specialist in an area of laboratory medicine.

Virginia Commonwealth University, Graduate School, School of Allied Health Professions, Department of Clinical Laboratory Sciences, Richmond, VA 23284-9005. Offers MS. *Accreditation:* NAACLS. *Degree requirements:* For master's, one foreign language, thesis. *Entrance requirements:* For master's, GRE General Test, major in clinical laboratory sciences, biology, or chemistry; minimum GPA of 2.7. Additional exam requirements/recommendations for international students: Required—TOEFL (minimum score 600 paper-based; 100 iBT); Recommended—IELTS (minimum score 6.5). Electronic applications accepted. *Faculty research:* Educational outcomes assessment, virtual instrumentation development, cost-effective treatment of bacteremia using third generation cephalosporins.

Virginia Commonwealth University, Graduate School, School of Allied Health Professions, Doctoral Program in Health Related Sciences, Richmond, VA 23284-9005. Offers clinical laboratory sciences (PhD); gerontology (PhD); health administration (PhD); nurse anesthesia (PhD); occupational therapy (PhD); physical therapy (PhD); radiation sciences (PhD); rehabilitation leadership (PhD). *Entrance requirements:* For doctorate, GRE General Test or MAT, minimum GPA of 3.3 in master's degree. Additional exam requirements/recommendations for international students: Required—TOEFL (minimum score 600 paper-based; 100 iBT); Recommended—IELTS (minimum score 6.5). Electronic applications accepted.

Clinical Research

Albert Einstein College of Medicine, Graduate Programs in the Biomedical Sciences, Clinical Investigation Program, Bronx, NY 10461. Offers PhD. *Unit head:* Dr. Paul Marantz, Associate Dean for Clinical Research Education, 718-430-4187, Fax: 718-430-4035. *Application contact:* Salvatore Calabro, Director of Graduate Admissions, 718-430-2345, Fax: 718-430-8655, E-mail: phd@einstein.yu.edu.
Website: http://www.einstein.yu.edu/centers/ictr/ret/phd-in-clinical-investigation/

American University of Beirut, Graduate Programs, Faculty of Medicine, Beirut, Lebanon. Offers biochemistry (MS); biomedical engineering (MS); biomedical sciences (PhD); health research (MS); human morphology (MS); medicine (MD); microbiology and immunology (MS); neuroscience (MS); orthodontics (clinical) (MS); pharmacology and therapeutics (MS); physiology (MS). *Program availability:* Part-time. *Faculty:* 335 full-time (117 women), 54 part-time/adjunct (5 women). *Students:* 513 full-time (274 women). Average age 23. 527 applicants, 47% accepted, 169 enrolled. In 2017, 18 master's, 98 doctorates awarded. *Degree requirements:* For master's, one foreign language, comprehensive exam, thesis (for some programs); for doctorate, one foreign language, comprehensive exam, thesis/dissertation. *Entrance requirements:* For doctorate, MCAT (for MD); GRE (for PhD). Additional exam requirements/recommendations for international students: Required—TOEFL (minimum score 600 paper-based; 100 iBT), IELTS (minimum score 7.5). *Application deadline:* Applications are processed on a rolling basis. Application fee: $75. Electronic applications accepted. *Expenses:* Contact institution. *Financial support:* In 2017–18, 302 students received support. Fellowships, research assistantships, teaching assistantships, institutionally sponsored loans, scholarships/grants, tuition waivers, and unspecified assistantships available. *Unit head:* Dr. Mohamed Sayegh, Dean, 961-1-135000 Ext. 4700, Fax: 961-1-744489, E-mail: msayegh@aub.edu.lb. *Application contact:* Dr. Salim Kanaan, Director, Admission's Office, 961-1-350000 Ext. 2594, Fax: 961-1-750775, E-mail: sk00@aub.edu.lb.

American University of Health Sciences, School of Clinical Research, Signal Hill, CA 90755. Offers MSCR.

Augusta University, College of Allied Health Sciences, Program in Clinical Laboratory Sciences, Augusta, GA 30912. Offers MHS.

Boston University, School of Medicine, Division of Graduate Medical Sciences, Program in Clinical Research, Boston, MA 02215. Offers MA. *Degree requirements:* For master's, thesis. *Application deadline:* For spring admission, 10/15 for domestic students. *Unit head:* Dr. Janice Weinberg, Director, 617-638-5470, E-mail: janicew@bu.edu. *Application contact:* Stacey Hess Pino, Assistant Director, 617-638-5211, Fax: 617-638-5740, E-mail: sahess@bu.edu.
Website: http://www.bumc.bu.edu/gms/maci/

Case Western Reserve University, School of Medicine, Clinical Research Scholars Program, Cleveland, OH 44106. Offers MS, PhD. *Expenses: Tuition:* Full-time $43,854; part-time $1827 per credit hour. *Required fees:* $50; $50 per credit hour. Tuition and fees vary according to course load and program.

Clemson University, Graduate School, College of Behavioral, Social and Health Sciences, Department of Public Health Sciences, Clemson, SC 29634. Offers applied health research and evaluation (MS, PhD); biomedical data science and informatics (PhD); clinical and translational research (Certificate). *Program availability:* Part-time, 100% online. *Faculty:* 22 full-time (13 women). *Students:* 13 full-time (9 women), 25 part-time (17 women); includes 3 minority (1 Black or African American, non-Hispanic/Latino; 1 Asian, non-Hispanic/Latino; 1 Hispanic/Latino), 4 international. Average age 36. 25 applicants, 68% accepted, 11 enrolled. In 2017, 1 master's, 10 other advanced degrees awarded. *Degree requirements:* For doctorate, comprehensive exam, thesis/dissertation. *Entrance requirements:* For master's and Certificate, GRE General Test, curriculum vitae, statement of career goals, letters of recommendation, unofficial transcripts; for doctorate, GRE General Test, MS/MA thesis or publications, curriculum vitae, statement of career goals, letters of recommendation, unofficial transcripts. Additional exam requirements/recommendations for international students: Required—TOEFL (minimum score 80 iBT), IELTS (minimum score 6.5), PTE (minimum score 54). *Application deadline:* For fall admission, 4/15 for international students; for spring admission, 10/15 for international students. Applications are processed on a rolling basis. Application fee: $80 ($90 for international students). Electronic applications accepted. *Expenses:* $6,564 per semester full-time resident, $12,538 per semester full-time non-resident, $743 per credit hour part-time resident, $1,486 per credit hour part-

time non-resident, $1,203 per credit hour online, other fees may apply per session. *Financial support:* In 2017–18, 7 students received support, including 2 research assistantships with partial tuition reimbursements available (averaging $16,596 per year), 5 teaching assistantships with partial tuition reimbursements available (averaging $14,400 per year); career-related internships or fieldwork also available. *Faculty research:* Health promotion and behavior, epidemiology and outcomes research, public health informatics, health policy and health services research, global health, evaluation. *Total annual research expenditures:* $1.2 million. *Unit head:* Dr. Ronald Gimbel, Department Chair, 864-656-1969, E-mail: rgimbel@clemson.edu. *Application contact:* Dr. Joel Williams, Graduate Program Coordinator, 864-656-1017, E-mail: joel2@clemson.edu.
Website: http://www.clemson.edu/cbshs/departments/public-health/index.html

Clemson University, Graduate School, College of Behavioral, Social and Health Sciences, School of Nursing, Clemson, SC 29634. Offers clinical and translational research (PhD); global health (Certificate), including low resource countries; healthcare genetics (PhD); nursing (MS, DNP), including adult/gerontology nurse practitioner (MS), family nurse practitioner (MS). *Accreditation:* AACN. *Program availability:* Part-time, 100% online, blended/hybrid learning. *Faculty:* 37 full-time (35 women). *Students:* 130 full-time (118 women), 195 part-time (170 women); includes 50 minority (23 Black or African American, non-Hispanic/Latino; 5 Asian, non-Hispanic/Latino; 16 Hispanic/Latino; 6 Two or more races, non-Hispanic/Latino), 14 international. Average age 34. 71 applicants, 66% accepted, 33 enrolled. In 2017, 88 master's, 2 doctorates, 10 other advanced degrees awarded. *Degree requirements:* For master's, comprehensive exam, thesis or alternative; for doctorate, comprehensive exam, thesis/dissertation. *Entrance requirements:* For master's, GRE General Test, South Carolina RN license, unofficial transcripts, resume, letters of recommendation; for doctorate, GRE General Test, unofficial transcripts, MS/MA thesis or publications, curriculum vitae, statement of career goals, letters of recommendation. Additional exam requirements/recommendations for international students: Required—TOEFL (minimum score 80 iBT), IELTS (minimum score 6.5), PTE (minimum score 54). *Application deadline:* For fall admission, 3/1 priority date for domestic and international students; for spring admission, 10/1 priority date for domestic and international students. Application fee: $80 ($90 for international students). Electronic applications accepted. *Expenses:* Contact institution. *Financial support:* In 2017–18, 41 students received support, including 46 teaching assistantships with partial tuition reimbursements available (averaging $4,919 per year); career-related internships or fieldwork and unspecified assistantships also available. Financial award application deadline: 3/1. *Faculty research:* Breast cancer, healthcare, genetics, international healthcare, educational innovation and technology. *Total annual research expenditures:* $371,674. *Unit head:* Dr. Kathleen Valentine, Director and Associate College Dean, 864-656-4758, E-mail: klvalen@clemson.edu. *Application contact:* Dr. Stephanie Davis, Graduate Studies Coordinator, 864-656-2588, E-mail: stephad@clemson.edu.
Website: http://www.clemson.edu/cbshs/departments/nursing/

Duke University, School of Medicine, Clinical Research Program, Durham, NC 27708. Offers MHS. *Program availability:* Part-time. *Faculty:* 17 part-time/adjunct (4 women). *Students:* 123 part-time (71 women); includes 50 minority (6 Black or African American, non-Hispanic/Latino; 1 American Indian or Alaska Native, non-Hispanic/Latino; 36 Asian, non-Hispanic/Latino; 7 Hispanic/Latino). 58 applicants, 97% accepted, 56 enrolled. In 2017, 17 master's awarded. *Degree requirements:* For master's, research project. *Entrance requirements:* For master's, GRE. Additional exam requirements/recommendations for international students: Required—TOEFL, IELTS. *Application deadline:* For fall admission, 5/15 for domestic students. *Financial support:* Fellowships, research assistantships, teaching assistantships, and scholarships/grants available. Financial award application deadline: 5/1; financial award applicants required to submit FAFSA. *Unit head:* Dr. Steven C. Grambow, Director, 919-684-1292, Fax: 919-681-4569, E-mail: steven.grambow@duke.edu. *Application contact:* Gail Ladd, Program Coordinator, 919-681-4560, Fax: 919-681-4569, E-mail: gail.ladd@duke.edu.
Website: http://crtp.mc.duke.edu/

Eastern Michigan University, Graduate School, College of Health and Human Services, School of Health Sciences, Programs in Clinical Research Administration, Ypsilanti, MI 48197. Offers MS, Graduate Certificate. *Program availability:* Part-time, evening/weekend, online learning. *Students:* 4 full-time (all women), 16 part-time (12 women); includes 2 minority (1 Black or African American, non-Hispanic/Latino; 1 Asian, non-Hispanic/Latino), 7 international. Average age 34. 26 applicants, 85% accepted, 9 enrolled. In 2017, 10 master's, 1 other advanced degree awarded. *Entrance requirements:* Additional exam requirements/recommendations for international students: Required—TOEFL. *Application deadline:* Applications are processed on a rolling basis. Application fee: $45. *Financial support:* Fellowships, research assistantships with full tuition reimbursements, teaching assistantships with full tuition reimbursements, career-related internships or fieldwork, Federal Work-Study, institutionally sponsored loans, scholarships/grants, tuition waivers (partial), and unspecified assistantships available. Support available to part-time students. Financial award applicants required to submit FAFSA. *Application contact:* Dr. Jean Rowan, Program Director, 734-487-1238, Fax: 734-487-4095, E-mail: jrowan3@emich.edu.

Emory University, Laney Graduate School, Program in Clinical Research, Atlanta, GA 30322-1100. Offers MS. *Degree requirements:* For master's, thesis. *Entrance requirements:* Additional exam requirements/recommendations for international students: Recommended—TOEFL. Electronic applications accepted.

Fordham University, Graduate School of Arts and Sciences, Department of Psychology, Program in Clinical Research Methods, New York, NY 10458. Offers MS. *Program availability:* Part-time. *Students:* 19 full-time (15 women), 1 (woman) part-time; includes 4 minority (1 Asian, non-Hispanic/Latino; 3 Hispanic/Latino), 2 international. 278 applicants, 5% accepted, 8 enrolled. In 2017, 1 master's awarded. *Degree requirements:* For master's, thesis, practicum. *Entrance requirements:* Additional exam requirements/recommendations for international students: Required—TOEFL. Application fee: $70. *Application contact:* Bernadette Valentino-Morrison, Director of Graduate Admissions, 718-817-4419, Fax: 718-817-3566, E-mail: valentinomor@fordham.edu.

Icahn School of Medicine at Mount Sinai, Graduate School of Biomedical Sciences, New York, NY 10029-6504. Offers biomedical sciences (MS, PhD); clinical research education (MS, PhD); community medicine (MPH); genetic counseling (MS); neurosciences (PhD); MD/PhD. Terminal master's awarded for partial completion of doctoral program. *Degree requirements:* For master's, thesis; for doctorate, comprehensive exam, thesis/dissertation. *Entrance requirements:* For master's, GRE General Test; for doctorate, GRE General Test, GRE Subject Test, 3 years of college pre-med course work. Additional exam requirements/recommendations for international students: Required—TOEFL. Electronic applications accepted. *Faculty research:* Cancer, genetics and genomics, immunology, neuroscience, developmental and stem cell biology, translational research.

Johns Hopkins University, Bloomberg School of Public Health, Graduate Training Program in Clinical Investigation, Baltimore, MD 21287. Offers MHS, PhD. *Degree requirements:* For master's, comprehensive exam, thesis; for doctorate, comprehensive exam, thesis/dissertation. *Entrance requirements:* For master's, GRE or MCAT; United States Medical Licensing Exam, 2 letters of recommendation, curriculum vitae, transcripts, statement of purpose; for doctorate, GRE or MCAT; United States Medical Licensing Exam, 2 letters of recommendation, curriculum vitae. Additional exam requirements/recommendations for international students: Required—TOEFL (minimum score 600 paper-based). Electronic applications accepted. *Faculty research:* Ethical issues, biomedical writing, grant writing, epidemiology, biostatistics.

Loyola University Chicago, Graduate School, Program in Clinical Research Methods, Chicago, IL 60660. Offers MS. *Program availability:* Part-time-only. *Faculty:* 5 full-time (2 women). *Students:* 5 part-time (2 women); includes 3 minority (1 Black or African American, non-Hispanic/Latino; 1 Asian, non-Hispanic/Latino; 1 Hispanic/Latino). Average age 31. 6 applicants, 33% accepted, 1 enrolled. In 2017, 8 master's awarded. *Degree requirements:* For master's, research project. *Entrance requirements:* For master's, MCAT; GRE. Additional exam requirements/recommendations for international students: Recommended—TOEFL (minimum score 550 paper-based; 79 iBT). *Application deadline:* For fall admission, 5/15 for domestic students, 5/1 for international students; for spring admission, 11/15 for domestic students, 11/1 for international students. Applications are processed on a rolling basis. Electronic applications accepted. *Expenses:* $1,069 per credit hour tuition, $527 per semester mandatory fees. *Financial support:* Applicants required to submit FAFSA. *Faculty research:* Genetics of hypertension and obesity, vitamin D metabolism, kidney diseases. *Unit head:* Dr. David Shoham, MPH Program Director, 708-327-9006, Fax: 708-327-9009, E-mail: dshoham@luc.edu. *Application contact:* Ilze Berzina-Galbreath, Administrative Coordinator, 708-327-9224, E-mail: iberzin@luc.edu.

Medical College of Wisconsin, Graduate School, Medical Scientist Training Program, Milwaukee, WI 53226-0509. Offers MD/PhD. *Entrance requirements:* Additional exam requirements/recommendations for international students: Required—TOEFL. *Application deadline:* For fall admission, 12/1 for domestic and international students. Application fee: $50. *Unit head:* Dr. Joseph T. Barbieri, Director, 414-456-8412, E-mail: jtb01@mcw.edu. *Application contact:* Dr. Joseph T. Barbieri, Director, 414-456-8412, E-mail: jtb01@mcw.edu.
Website: https://www.mcw.edu/Medical-Scientist-Training-Program-MSTP.htm

Medical University of South Carolina, College of Graduate Studies, South Carolina Clinical and Translational Research Institute, Charleston, SC 29425-5010. Offers MS. *Program availability:* Online learning. *Degree requirements:* For master's, thesis, oral dissertation of grant proposal. *Entrance requirements:* For master's, essay, letter of support. Additional exam requirements/recommendations for international students: Required—TOEFL (minimum score 600 paper-based; 100 iBT). Electronic applications accepted. *Faculty research:* Cardiovascular epidemiology/hypertension, cystic fibrosis, comparative effectivenessstudies, community-engaged research.

Memorial University of Newfoundland, Faculty of Medicine and School of Graduate Studies, Graduate Programs in Medicine, Division of Applied Health Services Research, St. John's, NL A1C 5S7, Canada. Offers M Sc.

Morehouse School of Medicine, Master of Science in Clinical Research Program, Atlanta, GA 30310-1495. Offers MS. *Program availability:* Part-time. *Degree requirements:* For master's, thesis. Electronic applications accepted.

National University of Natural Medicine, School of Graduate Studies, Portland, OR 97201. Offers Ayurveda (MS); global health (MS); integrative medicine research (MS); integrative mental health (MS); nutrition (MS). *Faculty:* 7 full-time (5 women), 35 part-time/adjunct (25 women). *Students:* 184 (161 women). Average age 31. In 2017, 67 master's awarded. *Entrance requirements:* Additional exam requirements/recommendations for international students: Recommended—TOEFL, IELTS, TSE. *Application deadline:* For fall and winter admission, 5/1 for domestic and international students. Applications are processed on a rolling basis. Application fee: $75. Electronic applications accepted. *Expenses: Tuition:* Full-time $23,979. *Financial support:* Federal Work-Study and scholarships/grants available. Financial award application deadline: 2/15; financial award applicants required to submit FAFSA. *Faculty research:* Reliability of three constitutional questionnaires in Ayurveda diagnosis; mindfulness-based stress reduction for MS: feasibility, durability, and clinical outcomes; meditative neuroplasticity: the effect of qigong meditation on brain-derived neurotrophic factor and cortisol levels; food as medicine everyday research (FAMER): evaluating physiological changes associated with a shift toward a whole-foods diet. *Unit head:* Dr. Charles Kunert, Dean, 503-552-1742, Fax: 503-499-0027, E-mail: admission@nunm.edu. *Application contact:* Ryan Hollister, Associate Director of Admissions and Operations, 503-552-1665, Fax: 503-499-0027, E-mail: admissions@numn.edu.
Website: http://nunm.edu/academics/school-of-research-graduate-studies/

New York University, College of Dentistry, Program in Clinical Research, New York, NY 10010. Offers MS. *Program availability:* Part-time. *Faculty:* 6 full-time (1 woman), 3 part-time/adjunct (1 woman). *Students:* 22 full-time (14 women); includes 12 minority (2 Black or African American, non-Hispanic/Latino; 6 Asian, non-Hispanic/Latino; 4 Hispanic/Latino). Average age 33. 30 applicants, 50% accepted, 12 enrolled. In 2017, 14 master's awarded. *Entrance requirements:* For master's, GRE or GRE or another standardized test (such as DAT, CDAT, National Dental Board Part I and National Dental Board Part II), academic transcripts, personal statement, resume or curriculum vitae, three letters of recommendation. Additional exam requirements/recommendations for international students: Required—TOEFL (minimum score 600 paper-based; 100 iBT). *Application deadline:* For fall admission, 7/1 for domestic and international students. Applications are processed on a rolling basis. Application fee: $100. Electronic applications accepted. *Expenses:* $1,664 per credit, $2,834 fees. *Financial support:* Application deadline: 4/1; applicants required to submit FAFSA. *Faculty research:* Clinical research methodology, epidemiology and biostatistics, ethical and regulatory principles, and evidence-based healthcare. *Unit head:* Dr. Ryan Ruff, Director, 212-998-9663, E-mail: ryan.ruff@nyu.edu. *Application contact:* Julianna Cools, Program Coordinator, 212-998-9934, E-mail: jc1290@nyu.edu.
Website: https://dental.nyu.edu/academicprograms/masters-degree-programs/clinical-research.html

Northwestern University, Feinberg School of Medicine, Program in Clinical Investigation, Evanston, IL 60208. Offers MSCI. *Program availability:* Part-time, evening/weekend. *Entrance requirements:* For master's, GRE or MCAT, doctoral degree in healthcare-related field. Additional exam requirements/recommendations for international students: Required—TOEFL. Electronic applications accepted. *Faculty research:* Clinical research.

Northwestern University, The Graduate School, Program in Clinical Investigation, Evanston, IL 60208. Offers MSCI, Certificate. *Program availability:* Part-time, evening/weekend.

Northwestern University, School of Professional Studies, Program in Regulatory Compliance, Evanston, IL 60208. Offers clinical research (MS); healthcare compliance (MS); quality systems (MS). Offered in partnership with Northwestern University's Clinical and Translational Sciences Institute. *Program availability:* Part-time, evening/weekend.
Website: https://sps.northwestern.edu/masters/regulatory-compliance/index.php

Oregon Health & Science University, School of Medicine, Graduate Programs in Medicine, Human Investigations Program, Portland, OR 97239-3098. Offers clinical

research (MCR, Certificate). MCR program only open to those currently enrolled in the certificate program. *Program availability:* Part-time-only. *Faculty:* 17 part-time/adjunct (10 women). *Students:* 9 full-time (5 women), 84 part-time (59 women); includes 25 minority (1 American Indian or Alaska Native, non-Hispanic/Latino; 16 Asian, non-Hispanic/Latino; 6 Hispanic/Latino; 2 Two or more races, non-Hispanic/Latino), 7 international. Average age 37. 62 applicants, 97% accepted, 58 enrolled. In 2017, 12 master's, 19 Certificates awarded. *Entrance requirements:* For master's and Certificate, MD, MD/PhD, DO, DDS, DMD, DC, Pharm D, OD, ND or PhD with clinical responsibilities or patient-oriented research; faculty or staff member, clinical or post-doctoral fellows and graduate students at OHSU, Kaiser Permanente, Portland VA Medical Center or other health care facilities in Oregon or the Northwest. *Application deadline:* For fall admission, 7/15 for domestic students; for winter admission, 12/15 for domestic students; for spring admission, 3/15 for domestic students. Applications are processed on a rolling basis. Electronic applications accepted. *Financial support:* Application deadline: 3/1; applicants required to submit FAFSA. *Faculty research:* Clinical and translational research. *Unit head:* Dr. Cynthia Morris, Director, E-mail: hip@ohsu.edu. *Application contact:* Karen McCracken, Education Program Coordinator, E-mail: hip@ohsu.edu.
Website: http://www.ohsu.edu/hip

Palmer College of Chiropractic, Division of Graduate Studies, Davenport, IA 52803-5287. Offers clinical research (MS). *Program availability:* Part-time. *Degree requirements:* For master's, 2 mentored practicum projects. *Entrance requirements:* For master's, GRE General Test, minimum GPA of 2.5, bachelor's and doctoral-level health professions degrees. Additional exam requirements/recommendations for international students: Required—TOEFL. Electronic applications accepted. *Expenses:* Contact institution. *Faculty research:* Chiropractic clinical research.

Stanford University, School of Medicine, Graduate Programs in Medicine, Department of Health Research and Policy, Program in Epidemiology and Clinical Research, Stanford, CA 94305-2004. Offers MS, PhD. *Degree requirements:* For master's, thesis; for doctorate, thesis/dissertation, qualifying examinations. *Entrance requirements:* For doctorate, GRE General Test or MCAT. Additional exam requirements/recommendations for international students: Required—TOEFL. Electronic applications accepted. *Expenses: Tuition:* Full-time $48,987; part-time $10,620 per quarter. One-time fee: $400. Tuition and fees vary according to program.

Thomas Jefferson University, Jefferson College of Biomedical Sciences, Certificate Program in Clinical Research and Trials: Implementation, Philadelphia, PA 19107. Offers Certificate. *Program availability:* Part-time. *Faculty:* 43 full-time (16 women), 28 part-time/adjunct (9 women). *Students:* 3 part-time (all women); includes 1 minority (Asian, non-Hispanic/Latino). 6 applicants, 83% accepted, 3 enrolled. *Entrance requirements:* For degree, GRE General Test (recommended), scientific/medical background. Additional exam requirements/recommendations for international students: Required—TOEFL, IELTS (minimum score 7). *Application deadline:* For fall admission, 8/1 priority date for domestic students, 3/1 priority date for international students; for winter admission, 12/1 priority date for domestic students, 6/1 priority date for international students; for spring admission, 4/1 priority date for domestic students. Applications are processed on a rolling basis. Application fee: $50. *Financial support:* Federal Work-Study and institutionally sponsored loans available. Support available to part-time students. Financial award application deadline: 5/1; financial award applicants required to submit FAFSA. *Unit head:* Suzanne Adams, Program Director, 215-955-8848, Fax: 215-503-7420, E-mail: suzanne.adams@jefferson.edu. *Application contact:* Marc E. Stearns, Senior Associate Director of Admissions, 215-503-0155, Fax: 215-503-3433, E-mail: jgsbs-info@jefferson.edu.
Website: http://www.jefferson.edu/university/biomedical-sciences/degrees-programs/graduate-certificate.html

Thomas Jefferson University, Jefferson College of Biomedical Sciences, Certificate Program in Clinical Research: Operations, Philadelphia, PA 19107. Offers Certificate. *Faculty:* 43 full-time (16 women), 28 part-time/adjunct (9 women). *Students:* 3 part-time (2 women). 6 applicants, 83% accepted, 3 enrolled. *Entrance requirements:* For degree, BA. Additional exam requirements/recommendations for international students: Required—TOEFL, IELTS (minimum score 7). *Application deadline:* For fall admission, 8/1 priority date for domestic students, 3/1 for international students; for winter admission, 12/1 priority date for domestic students, 6/1 for international students; for spring admission, 4/1 priority date for domestic students. Applications are processed on a rolling basis. Application fee: $50. *Financial support:* Federal Work-Study and institutionally sponsored loans available. Support available to part-time students. Financial award application deadline: 5/1; financial award applicants required to submit FAFSA. *Unit head:* Suzanne Adams, Program Director, 215-955-8848, Fax: 215-503-3433, E-mail: suzanne.adams@jefferson.edu. *Application contact:* Marc E. Stearns, Senior Associate Director of Admissions, 215-503-0155, Fax: 215-503-3433, E-mail: jgsbs-info@jefferson.edu.

Thomas Jefferson University, Jefferson College of Biomedical Sciences, Certificate Program in Human Clinical Investigation: Theory, Philadelphia, PA 19107. Offers Certificate. *Program availability:* Part-time. *Faculty:* 43 full-time (16 women), 28 part-time/adjunct (9 women). *Students:* 2 part-time (1 woman). 2 applicants, 100% accepted, 2 enrolled. *Entrance requirements:* For degree, GRE General Test (recommended), scientific/medical background. Additional exam requirements/recommendations for international students: Required—TOEFL, IELTS (minimum score 7). *Application deadline:* For fall admission, 8/1 priority date for domestic students, 3/1 for international students; for winter admission, 12/1 priority date for domestic students, 6/1 for international students; for spring admission, 4/1 priority date for domestic students. Applications are processed on a rolling basis. Application fee: $50. *Financial support:* Federal Work-Study and institutionally sponsored loans available. Support available to part-time students. Financial award application deadline: 5/1; financial award applicants required to submit FAFSA. *Unit head:* Dr. Carol L. Beck, Associate Dean/Program Director, 215-503-6539, E-mail: carol.beck@jefferson.edu. *Application contact:* Marc E. Stearns, Senior Associate Director of Admissions, 215-503-0155, Fax: 215-503-3433, E-mail: jgsbs-info@jefferson.edu.

Thomas Jefferson University, Jefferson College of Biomedical Sciences, MS Program in Clinical Research, Philadelphia, PA 19107. Offers MS. *Program availability:* Part-time, evening/weekend. *Faculty:* 43 full-time (16 women), 28 part-time/adjunct (9 women). *Students:* 6 part-time (5 women), 1 international. 5 applicants, 100% accepted, 2 enrolled. *Degree requirements:* For master's, thesis, clerkship. *Entrance requirements:* For master's, GRE General Test or MCAT, minimum GPA of 3.0. Additional exam requirements/recommendations for international students: Required—TOEFL, IELTS (minimum score 7). *Application deadline:* For fall admission, 8/1 priority date for domestic students, 3/1 priority date for international students; for winter admission, 12/1 priority date for domestic students, 6/1 priority date for international students; for spring admission, 4/1 priority date for domestic students. Applications are processed on a rolling basis. Application fee: $50. Electronic applications accepted. *Financial support:* Federal Work-Study and institutionally sponsored loans available. Support available to part-time students. Financial award application deadline: 5/1; financial award applicants required to submit FAFSA. *Unit head:* Suzanne Adams, Program Director, 215-503-8848, Fax: 215-503-7420, E-mail: suzanne.adams@jefferson.edu. *Application contact:* Marc E. Stearns, Senior Associate Director of Admissions, 215-503-0155, Fax: 215-503-3433, E-mail: jgsbs-info@jefferson.edu.
Website: http://www.jefferson.edu/university/biomedical-sciences/degrees-programs/master-programs/clinical-research-MS.html

Trident University International, College of Health Sciences, Program in Health Sciences, Cypress, CA 90630. Offers clinical research administration (MS, Certificate); emergency and disaster management (MS, Certificate); environmental health science (Certificate); health care administration (PhD); health care management (MS), including health informatics; health education (MS, Certificate); health informatics (Certificate); health sciences (PhD); international health (MS); international health: educator or researcher option (PhD); international health: practitioner option (PhD); law and expert witness studies (MS, Certificate); public health (MS); quality assurance (Certificate). *Program availability:* Part-time, evening/weekend, online learning. *Degree requirements:* For doctorate, comprehensive exam, thesis/dissertation, defense of dissertation. *Entrance requirements:* For master's, minimum GPA of 2.5 (students with GPA 3.0 or greater may transfer up to 30% of graduate level credits); for doctorate, minimum GPA of 3.4, curriculum vitae, course work in research methods or statistics. Additional exam requirements/recommendations for international students: Required—TOEFL. Electronic applications accepted.

University of California, Berkeley, UC Berkeley Extension, Certificate Programs in Sciences, Biotechnology and Mathematics, Berkeley, CA 94720-1500. Offers clinical research conduct and management (Certificate). *Program availability:* Online learning.

University of California, Davis, Graduate Studies, Graduate Group in Clinical Research, Davis, CA 95616. Offers MAS. *Degree requirements:* For master's, comprehensive exam. *Entrance requirements:* Additional exam requirements/recommendations for international students: Required—TOEFL (minimum score 550 paper-based).

University of California, Los Angeles, David Geffen School of Medicine and Graduate Division, Graduate Programs in Medicine, Department of Biomathematics, Program in Clinical Research, Los Angeles, CA 90095. Offers MS. *Degree requirements:* For master's, thesis. *Entrance requirements:* For master's, GRE General Test, bachelor's degree; minimum undergraduate GPA of 3.0 (or its equivalent if letter grade system not used). Additional exam requirements/recommendations for international students: Required—TOEFL. Electronic applications accepted.

University of California, San Diego, School of Medicine, Program in Clinical Research, La Jolla, CA 92093. Offers MAS. *Program availability:* Part-time, evening/weekend. *Students:* 13 full-time (4 women), 44 part-time (20 women). 69 applicants, 77% accepted, 41 enrolled. In 2017, 31 master's awarded. *Degree requirements:* For master's, independent study project. *Entrance requirements:* For master's, minimum GPA of 3.0, advanced degree (recommended); professional work experience in clinical research, medical practice, or related field (recommended); resume or curriculum vitae, statement of purpose, three letters of recommendation. Additional exam requirements/recommendations for international students: Required—TOEFL (minimum score 550 paper-based; 80 iBT), IELTS (minimum score 7). *Application deadline:* For winter admission, 9/27 for domestic students; for summer admission, 3/20 for domestic students. Application fee: $105 ($125 for international students). Electronic applications accepted. *Expenses:* Contact institution. *Financial support:* Scholarships/grants available. Financial award applicants required to submit FAFSA. *Faculty research:* Epidemiology, biostatistics, quantitative analysis, health services. *Unit head:* Ravindra Mehta, Chair, 619-543-7310, E-mail: rmehta@ucsd.edu. *Application contact:* Tam Nguyen, Graduate Coordinator, 858-534-9164, E-mail: clre@ucsd.edu.
Website: http://clre.ucsd.edu/

University of Colorado Denver, School of Medicine, Clinical Science Graduate Program, Aurora, CO 80045. Offers clinical investigation (PhD); clinical sciences (MS); health information technology (PhD); health services research (PhD). *Students:* 46 full-time (31 women), 26 part-time (15 women); includes 7 minority (2 Black or African American, non-Hispanic/Latino; 4 Asian, non-Hispanic/Latino; 1 Hispanic/Latino). Average age 37. 18 applicants, 67% accepted, 11 enrolled. In 2017, 21 master's, 1 doctorate awarded. *Degree requirements:* For master's, thesis, minimum of 30 credit hours, defense/final exam of thesis or publishable paper; for doctorate, comprehensive exam, thesis/dissertation, at least 30 credit hours of thesis work. *Entrance requirements:* For master's, GRE General Test or MCAT (waived if candidate has earned MS/MA or PhD from accredited U.S. school), minimum undergraduate GPA of 3.0, 3-4 letters of recommendation; for doctorate, GRE General Test or MCAT (waived if candidate has earned MS/MA or PhD from accredited U.S. school), health care graduate, professional degree, or graduate degree related to health sciences; minimum GPA of 3.0; 3-4 letters of recommendation. Additional exam requirements/recommendations for international students: Required—TOEFL (minimum score 550 paper-based; 80 iBT). *Application deadline:* For fall admission, 2/1 for domestic students, 1/15 priority date for international students; for spring admission, 10/1 for domestic students. Application fee: $50 ($75 for international students). Electronic applications accepted. *Unit head:* Dr. Lisa Cicutto, Program Director, 303-398-1539, E-mail: cicuttol@njhealth.org. *Application contact:* Galit Mankin, Program Administrator, 720-848-6249, Fax: 303-848-7381, E-mail: galit.mankin@ucdenver.edu.
Website: http://www.ucdenver.edu/research/CCTSI/education-training/clsc/Pages/default.aspx

University of Connecticut Health Center, Graduate School, Program in Clinical and Translational Research, Farmington, CT 06030. Offers MS. *Program availability:* Part-time. *Entrance requirements:* For master's, GRE. Additional exam requirements/recommendations for international students: Required—TOEFL (minimum score 600 paper-based).

University of Florida, College of Medicine, Program in Clinical Investigation, Gainesville, FL 32611. Offers clinical investigation (MS); epidemiology (MS); public health (MPH). *Program availability:* Part-time. *Entrance requirements:* For master's, GRE, MD, PhD, DMD/DDS or Pharm D.

University of Florida, Graduate School, Herbert Wertheim College of Engineering, J. Crayton Pruitt Family Department of Biomedical Engineering, Gainesville, FL 32611. Offers biomedical engineering (ME, MS, PhD, Certificate); clinical and translational science (PhD); medical physics (MS, PhD); MD/PhD. Terminal master's awarded for partial completion of doctoral program. *Degree requirements:* For master's, comprehensive exam (for some programs), thesis (for some programs); for doctorate, comprehensive exam (for some programs), thesis/dissertation (for some programs). *Entrance requirements:* Additional exam requirements/recommendations for international students: Required—TOEFL (minimum score 550 paper-based; 80 iBT), IELTS (minimum score 6). Electronic applications accepted. *Faculty research:* Neural engineering, imaging and medical physics, biomaterials and regenerative medicine, biomedical informatics and modeling.

The University of Iowa, Graduate College, College of Public Health, Department of Epidemiology, Iowa City, IA 52242-1316. Offers clinical investigation (MS); epidemiology (MPH, MS, PhD). *Degree requirements:* For master's, thesis optional, exam; for doctorate, comprehensive exam, thesis/dissertation. *Entrance requirements:* For master's and doctorate, GRE General Test, minimum GPA of 3.0. Additional exam requirements/recommendations for international students: Required—TOEFL (minimum score 600 paper-based; 100 iBT). Electronic applications accepted.

The University of Kansas, University of Kansas Medical Center, School of Medicine, Department of Preventive Medicine and Public Health, Kansas City, KS 66160. Offers clinical research (MS); epidemiology (MPH); public health management (MPH); social and behavioral health (MPH); MD/MPH; PhD/MPH. *Accreditation:* CEPH. *Program availability:* Part-time. *Faculty:* 71. *Students:* 39 full-time (30 women), 40 part-time (28 women); includes 21 minority (10 Black or African American, non-Hispanic/Latino; 1 American Indian or Alaska Native, non-Hispanic/Latino; 4 Asian, non-Hispanic/Latino; 3 Hispanic/Latino; 3 Two or more races, non-Hispanic/Latino), 7 international. Average age 30. 66 applicants, 68% accepted, 32 enrolled. In 2017, 33 master's awarded. *Degree requirements:* For master's, thesis, capstone practicum defense. *Entrance requirements:* For master's, GRE, MCAT, LSAT, GMAT or other equivalent graduate professional exam. Additional exam requirements/recommendations for international students: Required—TOEFL. *Application deadline:* For fall admission, 3/1 for domestic and international students. Applications are processed on a rolling basis. Application fee: $60. Electronic applications accepted. *Financial support:* In 2017–18, 9 research assistantships (averaging $15,000 per year) were awarded; career-related internships or fieldwork, Federal Work-Study, scholarships/grants, and unspecified assistantships also available. Support available to part-time students. Financial award application deadline: 3/1; financial award applicants required to submit FAFSA. *Faculty research:* Cancer screening and prevention, smoking cessation, obesity and physical activity, health services/outcomes research, health disparities. *Total annual research expenditures:* $8.4 million. *Unit head:* Dr. Edward F. Ellerbeck, Chairman, 913-588-2774, Fax: 913-588-2780, E-mail: eellerbe@kumc.edu. *Application contact:* Tanya Honderick, MPH Director, 913-588-2720, Fax: 913-588-8505, E-mail: thonderick@kumc.edu.
Website: http://www.kumc.edu/school-of-medicine/preventive-medicine-and-public-health.html

University of Kentucky, Graduate School, College of Public Health, Program in Clinical Research Design, Lexington, KY 40506-0032. Offers MS.

University of Maryland, Baltimore, Graduate School, Clinical Research Certificate Program, Baltimore, MD 21201. Offers Postbaccalaureate Certificate. *Students:* 1 full-time (0 women), 5 part-time (1 woman); includes 5 minority (1 Black or African American, non-Hispanic/Latino; 3 Asian, non-Hispanic/Latino; 1 Hispanic/Latino), 1 international. Average age 42. 12 applicants, 58% accepted, 5 enrolled. In 2017, 3 Postbaccalaureate Certificates awarded. *Entrance requirements:* For degree, GRE General Test, minimum GPA of 3.0, curriculum vitae, essay. Additional exam requirements/recommendations for international students: Required—TOEFL (minimum score 80 iBT); Recommended—IELTS (minimum score 7). *Application deadline:* For fall admission, 3/1 for domestic and international students. Application fee: $75. Electronic applications accepted. *Expenses:* Tuition, state resident: full-time $13,990; part-time $661 per credit. Tuition, nonresident: full-time $30,484; part-time $1310 per credit. *Required fees:* $1894; $94 per credit. $415 per semester. Part-time tuition and fees vary according to course load, degree level and program. *Financial support:* Fellowships and Federal Work-Study available. Financial award application deadline: 3/1; financial award applicants required to submit FAFSA. *Unit head:* Dr. Jay Magaziner, Departmental Chair, 410-706-3553, Fax: 410-706-4433, E-mail: jmagazin@epi.umaryland.edu. *Application contact:* Dr. Kristen Stafford, Program Director, 410-706-8492, E-mail: kstafford@ihv.umaryland.edu.
Website: http://medschool.umaryland.edu/K30/certificate_clinical.asp

University of Maryland, Baltimore, Graduate School, Graduate Program in Life Sciences, Baltimore, MD 21201. Offers biochemistry and molecular biology (MS, PhD), including biochemistry; cellular and molecular biomedical science (MS); clinical research (Postbaccalaureate Certificate); epidemiology (PhD); gerontology (PhD); molecular medicine (PhD), including cancer biology, cell and molecular physiology, human genetics and genomic medicine, molecular toxicology and pharmacology; molecular microbiology and immunology (PhD); neuroscience (PhD); physical rehabilitation science (PhD); toxicology (MS, PhD); MD/MS; MD/PhD. *Students:* 251 full-time (153 women), 53 part-time (37 women); includes 88 minority (29 Black or African American, non-Hispanic/Latino; 34 Asian, non-Hispanic/Latino; 16 Hispanic/Latino; 9 Two or more races, non-Hispanic/Latino), 47 international. Average age 29. 579 applicants, 23% accepted, 46 enrolled. In 2017, 22 master's, 52 doctorates awarded. *Degree requirements:* For master's, comprehensive exam (for some programs), thesis (for some programs); for doctorate, comprehensive exam, thesis/dissertation. *Entrance requirements:* For master's and doctorate, GRE. Additional exam requirements/recommendations for international students: Required—TOEFL (minimum score 80 iBT); Recommended—IELTS (minimum score 7). *Application deadline:* For fall admission, 12/15 for domestic students, 1/15 for international students. Application fee: $75. Electronic applications accepted. *Expenses:* Tuition, state resident: full-time $13,990; part-time $661 per credit. Tuition, nonresident: full-time $30,484; part-time $1310 per credit. *Required fees:* $1894; $94 per credit. $415 per semester. Part-time tuition and fees vary according to course load, degree level and program. *Financial support:* In 2017–18, research assistantships with partial tuition reimbursements (averaging $26,000 per year) were awarded; fellowships, scholarships/grants, health care benefits, and unspecified assistantships also available. Financial award application deadline: 3/1; financial award applicants required to submit FAFSA. *Faculty research:* Cancer, reproduction, cardiovascular, immunology. *Unit head:* Dr. Dudley Strickland, Assistant Dean for Graduate Studies, 410-706-8010. *Application contact:* Keith T. Brooks, Assistant Dean, 410-706-7131, Fax: 410-706-3473, E-mail: kbrooks@umaryland.edu.
Website: http://lifesciences.umaryland.edu

University of Maryland, Baltimore, School of Medicine, Department of Epidemiology and Public Health, Baltimore, MD 21201. Offers biostatistics (MS); clinical research (MS); epidemiology and preventive medicine (MPH, MS, PhD); gerontology (PhD); human genetics and genomic medicine (MS, PhD); molecular epidemiology (MS, PhD); toxicology (MS, PhD); JD/MS; MD/PhD; MS/PhD. *Accreditation:* CEPH. *Program availability:* Part-time. *Students:* 88 full-time (72 women), 53 part-time (38 women); includes 51 minority (21 Black or African American, non-Hispanic/Latino; 20 Asian, non-Hispanic/Latino; 7 Hispanic/Latino; 3 Two or more races, non-Hispanic/Latino), 29 international. Average age 30. In 2017, 24 master's, 14 doctorates awarded. *Degree requirements:* For doctorate, comprehensive exam, thesis/dissertation. *Entrance requirements:* For master's and doctorate, GRE General Test. Additional exam requirements/recommendations for international students: Required—TOEFL (minimum score 550 paper-based; 80 iBT); Recommended—IELTS (minimum score 7). *Application deadline:* For fall admission, 1/15 for domestic and international students. Application fee: $75. Electronic applications accepted. *Expenses:* Contact institution. *Financial support:* In 2017–18, research assistantships with partial tuition reimbursements (averaging $26,000 per year) were awarded; fellowships, Federal Work-Study, scholarships/grants, and unspecified assistantships also available. Financial award application deadline: 3/1; financial award applicants required to submit FAFSA. *Unit head:* Dr. Laura Hungerford, Program Director, 410-706-8492, Fax: 410-706-4225. *Application contact:* Jessica Kelley, Program Coordinator, 410-706-8492, Fax: 410-706-4225, E-mail: jkelley@som.umaryland.edu.
Website: http://lifesciences.umaryland.edu/epidemiology/

University of Massachusetts Medical School, Graduate School of Biomedical Sciences, Worcester, MA 01655-0115. Offers biomedical sciences (PhD), including biochemistry and molecular pharmacology, bioinformatics and computational biology, cancer biology, immunology and microbiology, interdisciplinary, neuroscience, translational science; biomedical sciences (millennium program) (PhD); clinical and population health research (PhD); clinical investigation (MS). *Faculty:* 1,316 full-time (526 women), 357 part-time/adjunct (229 women). *Students:* 347 full-time (180 women); includes 61 minority (10 Black or African American, non-Hispanic/Latino; 1 American Indian or Alaska Native, non-Hispanic/Latino; 35 Asian, non-Hispanic/Latino; 15 Hispanic/Latino), 130 international. Average age 29. 608 applicants, 28% accepted, 54 enrolled. In 2017, 6 master's, 51 doctorates awarded. Terminal master's awarded for partial completion of doctoral program. *Degree requirements:* For master's, comprehensive exam, thesis; for doctorate, comprehensive exam, thesis/dissertation. *Entrance requirements:* For master's, MD, PhD, DVM, or PharmD; for doctorate, GRE General Test, bachelor's degree. Additional exam requirements/recommendations for international students: Required—TOEFL (minimum score 90 iBT) or IELTS (minimum score 7.0). *Application deadline:* For fall admission, 12/15 for domestic and international students. Applications are processed on a rolling basis. Application fee: $80. Electronic applications accepted. Application fee is waived when completed online. *Expenses:* $14,883 in-state tuition and mandatory fees; $31,486 out-of-state. *Financial support:* In 2017–18, 15 fellowships with partial tuition reimbursements (averaging $29,000 per year), 296 research assistantships with full tuition reimbursements (averaging $31,212 per year) were awarded; institutionally sponsored loans and scholarships/grants also available. Financial award application deadline: 5/15. *Faculty research:* RNA biology, molecular/cell/developmental/metabolic biology, bioinformatics and computational biology, clinical/translational research, infectious disease and immunology. *Total annual research expenditures:* $279 million. *Unit head:* Dr. Mary Ellen Lane, Dean, 508-856-4018, E-mail: maryellen.lane@umassmed.edu. *Application contact:* Dr. Kendall Knight, Assistant Vice Provost for Admissions, 508-856-5628, Fax: 508-856-3659, E-mail: kendall.knight@umassmed.edu.
Website: http://www.umassmed.edu/gsbs/

University of Michigan, School of Public Health, Program in Clinical Research Design and Statistical Analysis, Ann Arbor, MI 48109. Offers MS. Offered through the Rackham Graduate School; program admits applicants in odd-numbered calendar years only. *Program availability:* Evening/weekend. *Degree requirements:* For master's, comprehensive exam. *Entrance requirements:* For master's, GRE General Test or MCAT. Additional exam requirements/recommendations for international students: Recommended—TOEFL (minimum score 560 paper-based; 100 iBT). Electronic applications accepted. *Expenses:* Contact institution. *Faculty research:* Survival analysis, missing data, Bayesian inference, health economics, quality of life.

University of Minnesota, Twin Cities Campus, School of Public Health, Major in Clinical Research, Minneapolis, MN 55455-0213. Offers MS. *Program availability:* Part-time. *Degree requirements:* For master's, thesis. *Entrance requirements:* For master's, advanced health professional degree. Additional exam requirements/recommendations for international students: Required—TOEFL. Electronic applications accepted. *Faculty research:* Osteoporosis prevention; heart disease prevention; role of inflammatory dental disease in the genesis of atherosclerosis; interventional research into AIDS and cancer.

The University of North Carolina at Chapel Hill, Graduate School, Gillings School of Global Public Health, Department of Epidemiology, Chapel Hill, NC 27599. Offers clinical research (MSCR); epidemiology (MPH, PhD); veterinary epidemiology (MPH); Pharm D/MPH. *Faculty:* 56 full-time (36 women), 93 part-time/adjunct (52 women). *Students:* 180 full-time (137 women), 11 part-time (6 women); includes 59 minority (13 Black or African American, non-Hispanic/Latino; 1 American Indian or Alaska Native, non-Hispanic/Latino; 21 Asian, non-Hispanic/Latino; 11 Hispanic/Latino; 13 Two or more races, non-Hispanic/Latino), 21 international. Average age 31. 259 applicants, 31% accepted, 43 enrolled. In 2017, 12 master's, 36 doctorates awarded. Terminal master's awarded for partial completion of doctoral program. *Degree requirements:* For master's, comprehensive exam, major paper; for doctorate, comprehensive exam, thesis/dissertation. *Entrance requirements:* For master's, GRE General Test or MCAT, doctoral degree (completed or in-progress); for doctorate, GRE General Test, strong quantitative and biological preparation, 3 letters of recommendation (academic and/or professional). Additional exam requirements/recommendations for international students: Required—TOEFL (minimum score 90 iBT), IELTS (minimum score 7). *Application deadline:* For fall admission, 1/10 for domestic and international students. Applications are processed on a rolling basis. Application fee: $85. Electronic applications accepted. *Financial support:* Fellowships with tuition reimbursements, research assistantships with tuition reimbursements, teaching assistantships with tuition reimbursements, career-related internships or fieldwork, Federal Work-Study, institutionally sponsored loans, scholarships/grants, traineeships, and health care benefits available. Support available to part-time students. Financial award application deadline: 12/10; financial award applicants required to submit FAFSA. *Faculty research:* Chronic disease: cancer, cardiovascular, nutritional; environmental/occupational injury; infectious diseases; reproductive diseases; healthcare. *Unit head:* Dr. Andrew Olshan, Chair, 919-966-7424, Fax: 919-966-2089, E-mail: andy_olshan@unc.edu. *Application contact:* Jennifer Joyce Moore, Student Services Specialist, 919-966-7458, Fax: 919-966-2089, E-mail: jenjoyce@email.unc.edu.
Website: https://sph.unc.edu/epid/epidemiology-landing/

The University of North Carolina Wilmington, School of Nursing, Wilmington, NC 28403-3297. Offers clinical research and product development (MS); family nurse practitioner (Post-Master's Certificate); nurse educator (Post-Master's Certificate); nursing (MSN); nursing practice (DNP). *Accreditation:* AACN; ACEN. *Program availability:* Part-time, 100% online. *Faculty:* 44 full-time (38 women). *Students:* 160 full-time (148 women), 237 part-time (213 women); includes 79 minority (55 Black or African American, non-Hispanic/Latino; 3 American Indian or Alaska Native, non-Hispanic/Latino; 6 Asian, non-Hispanic/Latino; 9 Hispanic/Latino; 6 Two or more races, non-Hispanic/Latino). Average age 36. 287 applicants, 71% accepted, 167 enrolled. In 2017, 40 master's awarded. *Degree requirements:* For master's, thesis or alternative, research project, presentation; for doctorate, clinical scholarly project, 1000 clinical hours. *Entrance requirements:* For master's, GRE General Test, 3 recommendations, statement of interest, resume, writing sample, RN experience, RN license (for MSN), bachelor's degree in related field; for doctorate, 3 recommendations, Advanced Practice Registered Nurse with current unrestricted RN license in state in which practice will occur, minimum GPA of 3.0, essay, resume or curriculum vitae, interview, criminal background check and 12-panel drug screening. Additional exam requirements/recommendations for international students: Required—TOEFL (minimum score 550 paper-based; 79 iBT), IELTS (minimum score 6.5). *Application deadline:* For fall admission, 3/1 for domestic students. Applications are processed on a rolling basis. Application fee: $75. Electronic applications accepted. *Expenses:* $318.15 per credit hour in-state, $965.60 per credit hour out-of-state (for DNP). *Financial support:* Application deadline: 1/1; applicants required to submit FAFSA. *Unit head:* Dr. Laurie Badzek, Director, 910-962-7410, Fax: 910-962-3723, E-mail: badzekl@uncw.edu. *Application contact:* Dr. Micah Scott, MSN Graduate Coordinator, 910-962-7534, E-mail: scottmi@uncw.edu.
Website: https://www.uncw.edu/son/academicprograms.html

Clinical Research

University of Pittsburgh, School of Medicine, Graduate Programs in Medicine, Clinical Research Graduate Programs, Pittsburgh, PA 15260. Offers MS, Certificate. *Program availability:* Part-time, blended/hybrid learning. *Faculty:* 51 full-time (32 women). *Students:* 1 (woman) full-time, 57 part-time (34 women); includes 17 minority (5 Black or African American, non-Hispanic/Latino; 9 Asian, non-Hispanic/Latino; 2 Hispanic/Latino; 1 Two or more races, non-Hispanic/Latino), 7 international. Average age 32. 33 applicants, 94% accepted, 27 enrolled. In 2017, 28 master's, 17 other advanced degrees awarded. *Degree requirements:* For master's, thesis, 8 hours of responsible conduct in research training. *Entrance requirements:* For master's, MCAT or GRE, official transcripts, 2 letters of recommendation, curriculum vitae. Additional exam requirements/recommendations for international students: Required—TOEFL (minimum score 600 paper-based; 100 iBT), IELTS (minimum score 7). *Application deadline:* For summer admission, 2/28 priority date for domestic and international students. Application fee: $0. Electronic applications accepted. *Expenses:* $26,782 in-state, $42,006 out-of-state. *Financial support:* In 2017–18, 25 students received support, including 5 fellowships with full tuition reimbursements available (averaging $24,500 per year); traineeships also available. *Faculty research:* Design and analysis of observational studies and clinical trials; evaluating the effectiveness of mind-body and complementary interventions for chronic pain and high blood pressure; cost effectiveness of common medical interventions. *Unit head:* Dr. Wishwa Kapoor, Program Director, 412-586-9632, Fax: 412-586-9672, E-mail: icre@pitt.edu. *Application contact:* Juliana Tambellini, Program Coordinator, 412-586-9632, Fax: 412-586-9672, E-mail: icre@pitt.edu.
Website: http://www.icre.pitt.edu/degrees

University of Puerto Rico–Medical Sciences Campus, School of Health Professions, Program in Clinical Research, San Juan, PR 00936-5067. Offers MS, Graduate Certificate.

University of Rochester, School of Medicine and Dentistry, Graduate Programs in Medicine and Dentistry, Department of Community and Preventive Medicine, Programs in Public Health and Clinical Investigation, Rochester, NY 14627. Offers clinical investigation (MS); public health (MPH); MBA/MPH; MD/MPH; MPH/MS; MPH/PhD. *Entrance requirements:* For master's, GRE General Test.

University of Rochester, School of Medicine and Dentistry, Graduate Programs in Medicine and Dentistry, Interdepartmental Program in Clinical Translational Research, Rochester, NY 14627. Offers MS.

University of Southern California, Graduate School, School of Pharmacy, Regulatory Science Programs, Los Angeles, CA 90089. Offers clinical research design and management (Graduate Certificate); food safety (Graduate Certificate); patient and product safety (Graduate Certificate); preclinical drug development (Graduate Certificate); regulatory and clinical affairs (Graduate Certificate); regulatory science (MS, DRSc). *Program availability:* Part-time, evening/weekend, online learning. Terminal master's awarded for partial completion of doctoral program. *Degree requirements:* For master's, thesis optional; for doctorate, comprehensive exam, thesis/dissertation. *Entrance requirements:* For master's, GRE. Additional exam requirements/recommendations for international students: Required—TOEFL (minimum score 603 paper-based; 100 iBT). Electronic applications accepted.

University of South Florida, Innovative Education, Tampa, FL 33620-9951. Offers adult, career and higher education (Graduate Certificate), including college teaching, leadership in developing human resources, leadership in higher education; Africana studies (Graduate Certificate), including diasporas and health disparities, genocide and human rights; aging studies (Graduate Certificate), including gerontology; art research (Graduate Certificate), including museum studies; business foundations (Graduate Certificate); chemical and biomedical engineering (Graduate Certificate), including materials science and engineering, water, health and sustainability; child and family studies (Graduate Certificate), including positive behavior support; civil and industrial engineering (Graduate Certificate), including transportation systems analysis; community and family health (Graduate Certificate), including maternal and child health, social marketing and public health, violence and injury: prevention and intervention, women's health; criminology (Graduate Certificate), including criminal justice administration; data science for public administration (Graduate Certificate); digital humanities (Graduate Certificate); educational measurement and research (Graduate Certificate), including evaluation; English (Graduate Certificate), including comparative literary studies, creative writing, professional and technical communication; entrepreneurship (Graduate Certificate); environmental health (Graduate Certificate), including safety management; epidemiology and biostatistics (Graduate Certificate), including applied biostatistics, biostatistics, concepts and tools of epidemiology, epidemiology, epidemiology of infectious diseases; geography, environment and planning (Graduate Certificate), including community development, environmental policy and management, geographical information systems; geology (Graduate Certificate), including hydrogeology; global health (Graduate Certificate), including disaster management, global health and Latin American and Caribbean studies, global health practice, humanitarian assistance, infection control; government and international affairs (Graduate Certificate), including Cuban studies, globalization studies; health policy and management (Graduate Certificate), including health management and leadership, public health policy and programs; hearing specialist: early intervention (Graduate Certificate); industrial and management systems engineering (Graduate Certificate), including systems engineering, technology management; information studies (Graduate Certificate), including school library media specialist; information systems/decision sciences (Graduate Certificate), including analytics and business intelligence; instructional technology (Graduate Certificate), including distance education, Florida digital/virtual educator, instructional design, multimedia design, Web design; internal medicine, bioethics and medical humanities (Graduate Certificate), including biomedical ethics; Latin American and Caribbean studies (Graduate Certificate); leadership for coastal resiliency planning (Graduate Certificate); mass communications (Graduate Certificate), including multimedia journalism; mathematics and statistics (Graduate Certificate), including mathematics; medicine (Graduate Certificate), including aging and neuroscience, bioinformatics, biotechnology, brain fitness and memory management, clinical investigation, hand and upper limb rehabilitation, health informatics, health sciences, integrative weight management, intellectual property, medicine and gender, metabolic and nutritional medicine, metabolic cardiology, pharmacy sciences; national and competitive intelligence (Graduate Certificate); nursing (Graduate Certificate), including simulation based academic fellowship in advanced pain management; psychological and social foundations (Graduate Certificate), including career counseling, college teaching, diversity in education, mental health counseling, school counseling; public affairs (Graduate Certificate), including nonprofit management, public management, research administration; public health (Graduate Certificate), including assessing chemical toxicity and public health risks, health equity, pharmacoepidemiology, public health generalist, toxicology, translational research in adolescent behavioral health; public health practices (Graduate Certificate), including planning for healthy communities; rehabilitation and mental health counseling (Graduate Certificate), including integrative mental health care, marriage and family therapy, rehabilitation technology; secondary education (Graduate Certificate), including ESOL, foreign language education: culture and content, foreign language education: professional; social work (Graduate Certificate), including geriatric social work/clinical gerontology; special education (Graduate Certificate), including autism spectrum disorder, disabilities education: severe/profound; world languages (Graduate Certificate), including teaching English as a second language (TESL) or foreign language. *Unit head:* Dr. Cynthia DeLuca, Associate Vice President and Assistant Vice Provost, 813-974-3077, Fax: 813-974-7061, E-mail: deluca@usf.edu. *Application contact:* Owen Hooper, Director, Summer and Alternative Calendar Programs, 813-974-6917, E-mail: hooper@usf.edu.
Website: http://www.usf.edu/innovative-education/

University of South Florida, Morsani College of Medicine and College of Graduate Studies, Graduate Programs in Medical Sciences, Tampa, FL 33620-9951. Offers advanced athletic training (MS); athletic training (MS); bioinformatics and computational biology (MSBCB); biotechnology (MSB); health informatics (MSHI); medical sciences (MSMS, PhD), including aging and neuroscience (MSMS), allergy, immunology and infectious disease (PhD), anatomy, biochemistry and molecular biology, clinical and translational research, health science (MSMS), interdisciplinary medical sciences (MSMS), medical microbiology and immunology (MSMS), metabolic and nutritional medicine (MSMS), microbiology and immunology (PhD), molecular medicine, molecular pharmacology and physiology (PhD), neuroscience (PhD), pathology and cell biology (PhD), women's health (MSMS). *Students:* 372 full-time (212 women), 216 part-time (142 women); includes 257 minority (78 Black or African American, non-Hispanic/Latino; 1 American Indian or Alaska Native, non-Hispanic/Latino; 79 Asian, non-Hispanic/Latino; 84 Hispanic/Latino; 15 Two or more races, non-Hispanic/Latino), 62 international. Average age 28. 1,048 applicants, 46% accepted, 309 enrolled. In 2017, 351 master's, 56 doctorates awarded. Terminal master's awarded for partial completion of doctoral program. *Degree requirements:* For master's, comprehensive exam, thesis; for doctorate, comprehensive exam, thesis/dissertation. *Entrance requirements:* For master's, GRE General Test or GMAT, bachelor's degree or equivalent from regionally-accredited university with minimum GPA of 3.0 in upper-division sciences coursework; prerequisites in general biology, general chemistry, general physics, organic chemistry, quantitative analysis, and integral and differential calculus; for doctorate, GRE General Test, bachelor's degree from regionally-accredited university with minimum GPA of 3.0 in upper-division sciences coursework; 3 letters of recommendation; personal interview; 1-2 page personal statement; prerequisites in biology, chemistry, physics, organic chemistry, quantitative analysis, and integral/differential calculus. Additional exam requirements/recommendations for international students: Required—TOEFL (minimum score 550 paper-based; 79 iBT) or IELTS (minimum score 6.5). *Application deadline:* For fall admission, 2/1 priority date for domestic students, 2/1 for international students. Application fee: $30. Electronic applications accepted. *Expenses:* Contact institution. *Financial support:* In 2017–18, 109 students received support. *Faculty research:* Anatomy, biochemistry, cancer biology, cardiovascular disease, cell biology, immunology, microbiology, molecular biology, neuroscience, pharmacology, physiology. *Total annual research expenditures:* $45.3 million. *Unit head:* Dr. Michael Barber, Professor/Associate Dean for Graduate and Postdoctoral Affairs, 813-974-9908, Fax: 813-974-4317, E-mail: mbarber@health.usf.edu. *Application contact:* Dr. Eric Bennett, Graduate Director, PhD Program in Medical Sciences, 813-974-1545, Fax: 813-974-4317, E-mail: esbennet@health.usf.edu.
Website: http://health.usf.edu/nocms/medicine/graduatestudies/

The University of Texas Health Science Center at San Antonio, Graduate School of Biomedical Sciences, Master of Science in Clinical Investigation Program, San Antonio, TX 78229-3900. Offers MS. *Program availability:* Part-time. *Degree requirements:* For master's, comprehensive exam.

University of Virginia, School of Medicine, Department of Public Health Sciences, Program in Clinical Research, Charlottesville, VA 22903. Offers clinical investigation and patient-oriented research (MS); informatics in medicine (MS). *Program availability:* Part-time. *Students:* 5 full-time (4 women), 9 part-time (5 women); includes 6 minority (4 Asian, non-Hispanic/Latino; 2 Two or more races, non-Hispanic/Latino). Average age 34. 21 applicants, 76% accepted, 14 enrolled. In 2017, 7 master's awarded. *Degree requirements:* For master's, thesis (for some programs). *Entrance requirements:* For master's, 2 letters of recommendation. Additional exam requirements/recommendations for international students: Required—TOEFL (minimum score 600 paper-based; 90 iBT). *Application deadline:* For fall admission, 3/1 priority date for domestic and international students. Application fee: $60. Electronic applications accepted. *Financial support:* Career-related internships or fieldwork available. Financial award applicants required to submit FAFSA. *Unit head:* Dr. Jean Eby, Program Director, 434-924-8430, Fax: 434-924-8437, E-mail: jmg5b@virginia.edu. *Application contact:* Tracey C. Brookman, Academic Programs Administrator, 434-924-8430, Fax: 434-924-8437, E-mail: phsdegrees@virginia.edu.
Website: http://research.med.virginia.edu/clinicalresearch/

University of Washington, Graduate School, School of Public Health, Department of Epidemiology, Seattle, WA 98195. Offers clinical research methods (MS); epidemiology (PhD); general epidemiology (MPH, MS); global health (MPH); maternal and child health (MPH); MPH/MPA. *Accreditation:* CEPH (one or more programs are accredited). *Faculty:* 51 full-time (30 women), 40 part-time/adjunct (20 women). *Students:* 145 full-time (104 women), 30 part-time (23 women); includes 54 minority (6 Black or African American, non-Hispanic/Latino; 2 American Indian or Alaska Native, non-Hispanic/Latino; 32 Asian, non-Hispanic/Latino; 13 Hispanic/Latino; 1 Native Hawaiian or other Pacific Islander, non-Hispanic/Latino), 17 international. Average age 31. 395 applicants, 43% accepted, 58 enrolled. In 2017, 40 master's, 9 doctorates awarded. *Entrance requirements:* For master's, GRE (except for those MD/DO from U.S. institutions); for doctorate, GRE. Additional exam requirements/recommendations for international students: Required—TOEFL. Electronic applications accepted. *Financial support:* Fellowships, research assistantships, teaching assistantships, career-related internships or fieldwork, scholarships/grants, traineeships, health care benefits, and tuition waivers (full and partial) available. Support available to part-time students. Financial award applicants required to submit FAFSA. *Faculty research:* Chronic disease, health disparities and social determinants of health, aging and neuroepidemiology, maternal and child health, molecular and genetic epidemiology. *Unit head:* E-mail: epiadmin@uw.edu. *Application contact:* John Paulson, Assistant Director of Student Academic Services, 206-685-1762, E-mail: epi@uw.edu.
Website: https://epi.washington.edu/

University of Wisconsin–Madison, School of Medicine and Public Health, Program in Clinical Investigation, Madison, WI 53706-1380. Offers MS, PhD. *Application contact:* Sally Wedde, Student Services, 608-262-3768, E-mail: sally.wedde@wisc.edu.
Website: https://ictr.wisc.edu/graduate-program-in-clinical-investigation/

Walden University, Graduate Programs, School of Health Sciences, Minneapolis, MN 55401. Offers clinical research administration (MS, Graduate Certificate); health education and promotion (MS, PhD), including behavioral health (PhD), disease surveillance (PhD), emergency preparedness (MS), general (MHA, MS), global health (PhD), health policy (PhD), health policy and advocacy (MS), population health (PhD); health informatics (MS); health services (PhD), including community health, healthcare administration, leadership, public health policy, self-designed; healthcare administration (MHA, DHA), including general (MHA, MS); leadership and organizational development (MHA); public health (MPH, Dr PH, PhD, Graduate Certificate), including community health education (PhD), epidemiology (PhD); systems policy (MHA). *Program availability:* Part-time, evening/weekend, online only, 100% online. *Degree requirements:* For doctorate, thesis/dissertation, residency. *Entrance requirements:* For master's, bachelor's degree or higher; minimum GPA of 2.5; official transcripts; goal statement (for some programs); access to computer and Internet; for doctorate, master's degree or higher; three years of related professional or academic experience (preferred); minimum GPA of 3.0; goal statement and current resume (for select programs); official transcripts; access to computer and Internet; for Graduate Certificate, relevant work experience; access to computer and Internet. Additional exam requirements/recommendations for international students: Required—TOEFL (minimum score 550 paper-based, 79 iBT), IELTS (minimum score 6.5), Michigan English Language Assessment Battery (minimum score 82), or PTE (minimum score 53). Electronic applications accepted.

Washington University in St. Louis, School of Medicine, Program in Clinical Investigation, St. Louis, MO 63130-4899. Offers clinical investigation (MS), including bioethics, entrepreneurship, genetics/genomics, translational medicine. *Program availability:* Part-time, evening/weekend. *Degree requirements:* For master's, thesis. *Entrance requirements:* For master's, doctoral-level degree or in process of obtaining doctoral-level degree. Electronic applications accepted. *Faculty research:* Anesthesiology, infectious diseases, neurology, obstetrics and gynecology, orthopedic surgery.

Communication Disorders

Abilene Christian University, Graduate Programs, College of Education and Human Services, Department of Communication Sciences and Disorders, Abilene, TX 79699. Offers MS. *Accreditation:* ASHA. *Faculty:* 10 part-time/adjunct (9 women). *Students:* 83 full-time (81 women); includes 13 minority (3 Black or African American, non-Hispanic/Latino; 1 American Indian or Alaska Native, non-Hispanic/Latino; 4 Asian, non-Hispanic/Latino; 5 Hispanic/Latino). 311 applicants, 35% accepted, 51 enrolled. In 2017, 25 master's awarded. *Degree requirements:* For master's, one foreign language, comprehensive exam. *Entrance requirements:* For master's, GRE General Test. Additional exam requirements/recommendations for international students: Required—TOEFL (minimum score 80 iBT), IELTS (minimum score 6), PTE. *Application deadline:* For fall admission, 2/1 priority date for domestic students. Applications are processed on a rolling basis. Application fee: $50. Electronic applications accepted. *Expenses:* $1,105 per hour. *Financial support:* In 2017–18, 60 students received support. Research assistantships and scholarships/grants available. Financial award application deadline: 4/1; financial award applicants required to submit FAFSA. *Unit head:* Dr. Lynette Austin, Co-Chair, 325-674-2074, Fax: 325-674-2552, E-mail: dla08a@acu.edu. *Application contact:* Graduate Admission, 325-674-6911, Fax: 325-674-6717, E-mail: gradinfo@acu.edu.
Website: http://www.acu.edu/graduate/academics/speech-language-pathology.html

Adelphi University, Ruth S. Ammon School of Education, Program in Communication Sciences and Disorders, Garden City, NY 11530-0701. Offers audiology (MS, DA); speech-language pathology (MS, DA). *Accreditation:* ASHA. *Program availability:* Part-time. *Students:* 206 full-time (197 women), 21 part-time (20 women); includes 77 minority (10 Black or African American, non-Hispanic/Latino; 16 Asian, non-Hispanic/Latino; 48 Hispanic/Latino; 3 Two or more races, non-Hispanic/Latino). Average age 25. 711 applicants, 45% accepted, 103 enrolled. In 2017, 95 master's, 7 doctorates awarded. *Degree requirements:* For master's, comprehensive exam, clinical practice; for doctorate, one foreign language, comprehensive exam, thesis/dissertation. *Entrance requirements:* For master's, GRE General Test, writing exam, 3 letters of recommendation, interview, resume, 19 credits of prerequisite course work or communications disorders training; for doctorate, GRE General Test, 3 letters of recommendation, interview. Additional exam requirements/recommendations for international students: Required—TOEFL (minimum score 550 paper-based; 80 iBT), IELTS (minimum score 6.5). *Application deadline:* For fall admission, 3/1 priority date for domestic students, 3/1 for international students; for spring admission, 10/1 priority date for domestic students, 10/1 for international students. Applications are processed on a rolling basis. Application fee: $50. Electronic applications accepted. *Expenses:* Contact institution. *Financial support:* Research assistantships, teaching assistantships, career-related internships or fieldwork, institutionally sponsored loans, scholarships/grants, traineeships, and unspecified assistantships available. Support available to part-time students. Financial award application deadline: 2/15; financial award applicants required to submit FAFSA. *Faculty research:* Pediatric audiology, child speech perception with hearing loss, auditory deprivation, fluency, cultural diversity. *Unit head:* Dr. Robert Goldfarb, Chairperson, 516-877-4785, E-mail: goldfarb2@adelphi.edu. *Application contact:* E-mail: graduateadmissions@adelphi.edu.

Alabama Agricultural and Mechanical University, School of Graduate Studies, College of Education, Humanities, and Behavioral Sciences, Department of Health Sciences, Human Performance, and Communicative Disorders, Huntsville, AL 35811. Offers kinesiology (MS); physical education (MS); speech-language pathology (MS). *Program availability:* Part-time, evening/weekend. *Degree requirements:* For master's, comprehensive exam. *Entrance requirements:* For master's, GRE General Test. Additional exam requirements/recommendations for international students: Required—TOEFL (minimum score 500 paper-based; 61 iBT). Electronic applications accepted. *Faculty research:* Cardiorespiratory assessment.

Andrews University, School of Health Professions, Department of Speech-Language Pathology and Audiology, Berrien Springs, MI 49104. Offers speech-language pathology (MS). *Faculty:* 5 full-time (all women). *Students:* 35 full-time (32 women); includes 17 minority (6 Black or African American, non-Hispanic/Latino; 4 Asian, non-Hispanic/Latino; 6 Hispanic/Latino; 1 Two or more races, non-Hispanic/Latino), 3 international. Average age 24. 66 applicants, 38% accepted, 19 enrolled. In 2017, 12 master's awarded. *Unit head:* Heather Ferguson, Chair, 269-471-6369, E-mail: hferguson@andrews.edu. *Application contact:* Justina Clayburn, Supervisor of Graduate Admission, 800-253-2874, Fax: 269-471-3228, E-mail: graduate@andrews.edu.
Website: http://www.andrews.edu/shp/speech/

Appalachian State University, Cratis D. Williams Graduate School, Department of Communication Sciences and Disorders, Boone, NC 28608. Offers speech-language pathology (MS). *Accreditation:* ASHA. *Program availability:* Part-time. *Degree requirements:* For master's, comprehensive exam, thesis optional. *Entrance requirements:* For master's, GRE General Test, 3 letters of recommendation. Additional exam requirements/recommendations for international students: Required—TOEFL (minimum score 570 paper-based), IELTS (minimum score 6.5). Electronic applications accepted. *Faculty research:* Clinical service delivery, voice disorders, language disorders, fluency disorders, neurogenic disorders.

Arizona State University at the Tempe campus, College of Health Solutions, Department of Speech and Hearing Science, Tempe, AZ 85287-0102. Offers audiology (Au D); communication disorders (MS); speech and hearing science (PhD). *Accreditation:* ASHA (one or more programs are accredited). *Degree requirements:* For master's, comprehensive exam (for some programs), thesis optional, interactive Program of Study (iPOS) submitted before completing 50 percent of required credit hours; for doctorate, comprehensive exam, thesis/dissertation (for some programs), academic/practicum components (Au D); interactive Program of Study (iPOS) submitted before completing 50 percent of required credit hours. *Entrance requirements:* For master's and doctorate, GRE, minimum GPA of 3.0 or equivalent in last 2 years of work leading to bachelor's degree. Additional exam requirements/recommendations for international students: Required—TOEFL, IELTS, or PTE. *Expenses:* Contact institution.

Arkansas State University, Graduate School, College of Nursing and Health Professions, Department of Communication Disorders, State University, AR 72467. Offers communication disorders (MCD); dyslexia therapy (Graduate Certificate). *Accreditation:* ASHA. *Program availability:* Part-time. *Degree requirements:* For master's, comprehensive exam, thesis or alternative. *Entrance requirements:* For master's, GRE General Test, appropriate bachelor's degree, letters of recommendation, official transcripts, immunization records. Additional exam requirements/recommendations for international students: Required—TOEFL (minimum score 550 paper-based; 79 iBT), IELTS (minimum score 6), PTE (minimum score 56). Electronic applications accepted. *Expenses:* Contact institution.

A.T. Still University, Arizona School of Health Sciences, Mesa, AZ 85206. Offers advanced occupational therapy (MS); advanced physician assistant studies (MS); athletic training (MS, DAT); audiology (Au D); clinical decision making in athletic training (Graduate Certificate); occupational therapy (MS, OTD); orthopedic rehabilitation (Graduate Certificate); physical therapy (DPT); physician assistant studies (MS); transitional audiology (Au D); transitional physical therapy (DPT). *Accreditation:* AOTA (one or more programs are accredited); ASHA. *Program availability:* Part-time, 100% online. *Faculty:* 59 full-time (39 women), 221 part-time/adjunct (155 women). *Students:* 608 full-time (405 women), 431 part-time (310 women); includes 247 minority (54 Black or African American, non-Hispanic/Latino; 13 American Indian or Alaska Native, non-Hispanic/Latino; 151 Asian, non-Hispanic/Latino; 2 Hispanic/Latino; 1 Native Hawaiian or other Pacific Islander, non-Hispanic/Latino; 26 Two or more races, non-Hispanic/Latino), 1 international. Average age 33. 4,882 applicants, 9% accepted, 278 enrolled. In 2017, 132 master's, 270 doctorates awarded. *Degree requirements:* For master's, thesis (for some programs); for doctorate, thesis/dissertation (for some programs). *Entrance requirements:* For master's, GRE General Test; for doctorate, GRE, Physical Therapist Evaluation Tool (for DPT), current state licensure. Additional exam requirements/recommendations for international students: Required—TOEFL (minimum score 80 iBT). *Application deadline:* For fall admission, 7/7 for domestic and international students; for winter admission, 10/3 for domestic and international students; for spring admission, 1/16 for domestic and international students; for summer admission, 4/17 for domestic and international students. Applications are processed on a rolling basis. Application fee: $70. Electronic applications accepted. Application fee is waived when completed online. *Financial support:* In 2017–18, 161 students received support. Federal Work-Study and scholarships/grants available. Financial award application deadline: 6/1; financial award applicants required to submit FAFSA. *Faculty research:* Pediatric sport-related concussion, adolescent athlete health-related quality of life; geriatric and pediatric well-being, pain management for participation, practice-based research network, BMI and dental caries. *Total annual research expenditures:* $63,003. *Unit head:* Dr. Randy Danielsen, Dean, 480-219-6009, Fax: 480-219-6110, E-mail: rdanielsen@atsu.edu. *Application contact:* Donna Sparks, Director, Admissions Processing, 660-626-2117, Fax: 660-626-2969, E-mail: admissions@atsu.edu.
Website: http://www.atsu.edu/ashs

Auburn University, Graduate School, College of Liberal Arts, Department of Communication Disorders, Auburn University, AL 36849. Offers audiology (MCD, Au D). *Accreditation:* ASHA (one or more programs are accredited). *Program availability:* Part-time. *Faculty:* 19 full-time (15 women). *Students:* 78 full-time (74 women), 9 part-time (all women); includes 6 minority (2 Black or African American, non-Hispanic/Latino; 1 American Indian or Alaska Native, non-Hispanic/Latino; 1 Asian, non-Hispanic/Latino; 2 Hispanic/Latino), 1 international. Average age 23. 294 applicants, 13% accepted, 35 enrolled. In 2017, 25 master's, 7 doctorates awarded. *Degree requirements:* For master's, comprehensive exam (MCD), thesis (MS). *Entrance requirements:* For master's, GRE General Test. *Application deadline:* Applications are processed on a rolling basis. Application fee: $50 ($60 for international students). Electronic applications accepted. *Expenses:* Tuition, state resident: full-time $10,974; part-time $519 per credit hour. Tuition, nonresident: full-time $29,658; part-time $1557 per credit hour. *Required fees:* $816 per semester. Tuition and fees vary according to degree level and program. *Financial support:* Research assistantships, teaching assistantships, and Federal Work-Study available. Support available to part-time students. Financial award application deadline: 3/15; financial award applicants required to submit FAFSA. *Unit head:* Dr. Nancy Haak, Chair, 334-844-9600. *Application contact:* Dr. George Flowers, Dean of the Graduate School, 334-844-2125.
Website: http://www.cla.auburn.edu/communicationdisorders/

Baldwin Wallace University, Graduate Programs, Speech-Language Pathology Program, Berea, OH 44017-2088. Offers MS. *Faculty:* 9 full-time (all women), 5 part-time/adjunct (all women). *Students:* 42 full-time (40 women); includes 7 minority (2 Black or African American, non-Hispanic/Latino; 1 Asian, non-Hispanic/Latino; 3 Hispanic/Latino; 1 Two or more races, non-Hispanic/Latino), 1 international. Average age 23. 146 applicants, 34% accepted, 22 enrolled. In 2017, 15 master's awarded. *Entrance requirements:* For master's, GRE, 3 letters of recommendation, bachelor's degree, 25 clinical observation hours in speech and/or language therapy or evaluation, CSDCAS online application. Additional exam requirements/recommendations for international students: Required—TOEFL. *Application deadline:* For fall admission, 1/15 for domestic students. Applications are processed on a rolling basis. Electronic applications accepted. *Expenses:* Contact institution. *Financial support:* Applicants required to submit FAFSA. *Faculty research:* Scholarship of teaching and learning, clinical training, traumatic brain injury and concussions, feeding and swallowing disorders across the life span, voice disorders. *Unit head:* Stephen D. Stahl, Provost, Academic Affairs, 440-826-2251, Fax: 440-826-2329, E-mail: sstahl@bw.edu. *Application contact:* Winnie W. Gerhardt, Director of Transfer, Adult and Graduate Admission, 440-826-2222, Fax: 440-826-3830, E-mail: slp@bw.edu.
Website: http://www.bw.edu/graduate/speech-language-pathology/

Ball State University, Graduate School, College of Health, Department of Speech Pathology and Audiology, Muncie, IN 47306. Offers audiology (Au D); speech-language

pathology (MA). *Accreditation:* ASHA. *Faculty:* 21 full-time (17 women). *Students:* 101 full-time (96 women), 28 part-time (27 women); includes 8 minority (2 Black or African American, non-Hispanic/Latino; 2 Asian, non-Hispanic/Latino; 3 Hispanic/Latino; 1 Two or more races, non-Hispanic/Latino). Average age 23. 209 applicants, 21% accepted, 35 enrolled. In 2017, 49 master's, 7 doctorates awarded. *Degree requirements:* For doctorate, comprehensive exam. *Entrance requirements:* For master's, GRE General Test (minimum preferred combined score of 900 on verbal and quantitative sections), minimum baccalaureate GPA of 3.0, three letters of reference, transcripts of all previous course work; for doctorate, GRE General Test, statement of purpose, on-campus interview. Additional exam requirements/recommendations for international students: Required—TOEFL (minimum score 550 paper-based; 79 iBT), IELTS (minimum score 6.5). *Application deadline:* For fall admission, 2/1 for domestic students; for spring admission, 10/31 for domestic students; for summer admission, 2/1 for domestic students. Applications are processed on a rolling basis. Application fee: $60. Electronic applications accepted. *Financial support:* In 2017 18, 16 students received support, including 15 teaching assistantships with partial tuition reimbursements available (averaging $7,803 per year); research assistantships with partial tuition reimbursements available and unspecified assistantships also available. Support available to part-time students. Financial award application deadline: 3/1; financial award applicants required to submit FAFSA. *Faculty research:* Adult neurological disorders, stuttering, tinnitus masking, brain stem responses. *Unit head:* Dr. Mary Jo Germani, Chairperson, 765-285-8162, Fax: 765-285-5623, E-mail: mgermani@bsu.edu.
Website: http://www.bsu.edu/spaa

Barry University, School of Education, Program in Education for Teachers of Students with Hearing Impairments, Miami Shores, FL 33161-6695. Offers MS.

Baylor University, Graduate School, Robbins College of Health and Human Sciences, Department of Communication Sciences and Disorders, Waco, TX 76798. Offers MS. *Accreditation:* ASHA. *Students:* 68 full-time (all women); includes 13 minority (1 Asian, non-Hispanic/Latino; 5 Hispanic/Latino; 7 Two or more races, non-Hispanic/Latino), 1 international. Average age 24. 177 applicants, 23% accepted, 9 enrolled. In 2017, 33 master's awarded. *Entrance requirements:* For master's, GRE General Test. Additional exam requirements/recommendations for international students: Required—TOEFL. Electronic applications accepted. *Expenses:* Contact institution. *Financial support:* In 2017–18, 25 students received support. Fellowships, research assistantships, teaching assistantships, Federal Work-Study, institutionally sponsored loans, and tuition waivers (partial) available. Financial award application deadline: 5/1. *Faculty research:* Nasality, language impairment, stuttering, Spanish speech perception, language literacy. *Unit head:* Dr. David Garrett, Program Director, 254-710-2567, Fax: 254-710-2590. *Application contact:* Kathryn Fadal Williams, Manager, 254-710-2571, Fax: 254-710-2590, E-mail: kathryn_williams@baylor.edu.
Website: http://www.baylor.edu/csd/

Biola University, School of Arts and Sciences, La Mirada, CA 90639-0001. Offers Christian apologetics (MA, Certificate); science and religion (MA); speech language pathology (MA). *Program availability:* Part-time, evening/weekend, online learning. *Faculty:* 20. *Students:* 24 full-time (7 women), 251 part-time (49 women); includes 80 minority (21 Black or African American, non-Hispanic/Latino; 1 American Indian or Alaska Native, non-Hispanic/Latino; 31 Asian, non-Hispanic/Latino; 19 Hispanic/Latino; 8 Two or more races, non-Hispanic/Latino), 15 international. 168 applicants, 70% accepted, 77 enrolled. In 2017, 64 master's awarded. *Entrance requirements:* For master's, minimum GPA of 3.0, bachelor's degree from accredited college or university (in science-related field for science and religion program). Additional exam requirements/recommendations for international students: Required—TOEFL (minimum score 600 paper-based; 100 iBT). *Application deadline:* For fall admission, 7/1 for domestic students, 6/1 for international students; for spring admission, 12/1 for domestic students. Applications are processed on a rolling basis. Application fee: $65. Electronic applications accepted. *Financial support:* Scholarships/grants and unspecified assistantships available. Support available to part-time students. Financial award applicants required to submit FAFSA. *Faculty research:* Apologetics, science and religion, intelligent design. *Application contact:* Graduate Admissions Office, 562-903-4752, E-mail: graduate.admissions@biola.edu.
Website: http://www.biola.edu/academics/sas/

Bloomsburg University of Pennsylvania, School of Graduate Studies, College of Education, Department of Exceptionality Programs, Program in Education of the Deaf/Hard of Hearing, Bloomsburg, PA 17815-1301. Offers MS. *Degree requirements:* For master's, thesis, minimum QPA of 3.0, practicum. *Entrance requirements:* For master's, PRAXIS, GRE, minimum QPA of 3.0, letter of intent, 3 letters of recommendation, interview. Additional exam requirements/recommendations for international students: Required—TOEFL (minimum score 550 paper-based), IELTS. Electronic applications accepted. *Expenses:* Tuition, state resident: full-time $10,000; part-time $500 per credit hour. Tuition, nonresident: full-time $15,000; part-time $750 per credit hour. *Required fees:* $2484; $110.75 per credit hour. $75 per term. Tuition and fees vary according to program.

Bloomsburg University of Pennsylvania, School of Graduate Studies, College of Science and Technology, Department of Audiology and Speech Pathology, Program in Audiology, Bloomsburg, PA 17815-1301. Offers Au D. *Accreditation:* ASHA. *Degree requirements:* For doctorate, comprehensive exam, thesis/dissertation, minimum QPA of 3.0, practicum. *Entrance requirements:* For doctorate, GRE, 3 letters of recommendation, interview, personal statement, minimum QPA of 3.0. Additional exam requirements/recommendations for international students: Required—TOEFL, IELTS. Electronic applications accepted. *Expenses:* Contact institution.

Bloomsburg University of Pennsylvania, School of Graduate Studies, College of Science and Technology, Department of Audiology and Speech Pathology, Program in Speech Pathology, Bloomsburg, PA 17815-1301. Offers speech-language pathology (MS). *Accreditation:* ASHA. *Degree requirements:* For master's, thesis optional, minimum QPA of 3.0, clinical experience. *Entrance requirements:* For master's, GRE, minimum QPA of 3.0, 3 letters of recommendation, personal statement. Additional exam requirements/recommendations for international students: Required—TOEFL (minimum score 550 paper-based), IELTS. Electronic applications accepted. *Expenses:* Contact institution.

Boston University, College of Health and Rehabilitation Sciences: Sargent College, Department of Speech, Language and Hearing Sciences, Boston, MA 02215. Offers speech, language and hearing sciences (PhD); speech-language pathology (MS). *Accreditation:* ASHA. *Faculty:* 18 full-time (14 women), 12 part-time/adjunct (5 women). *Students:* 90 full-time (84 women), 3 part-time (all women); includes 14 minority (10 Asian, non-Hispanic/Latino; 3 Hispanic/Latino; 1 Two or more races, non-Hispanic/Latino), 7 international. Average age 24. 500 applicants, 32% accepted, 35 enrolled. In 2017, 28 master's, 2 doctorates awarded. Terminal master's awarded for partial completion of doctoral program. *Degree requirements:* For master's, comprehensive exam, thesis optional; for doctorate, comprehensive exam, thesis/dissertation. *Entrance requirements:* For master's and doctorate, GRE General Test. Additional exam requirements/recommendations for international students: Required—TOEFL (minimum score 550 paper-based; 94 iBT). *Application deadline:* For fall admission, 1/1 priority date for domestic and international students. Applications are processed on a rolling basis. Application fee: $125. Electronic applications accepted. *Financial support:* In 2017–18, 58 students received support, including 12 research assistantships with full tuition reimbursements available (averaging $22,000 per year), 6 teaching assistantships (averaging $3,000 per year); career-related internships or fieldwork, Federal Work-Study, institutionally sponsored loans, scholarships/grants, and tuition waivers (full and partial) also available. Financial award application deadline: 1/1; financial award applicants required to submit FAFSA. *Faculty research:* Child language, fluency, autism, speech science, perception of complex sounds. *Total annual research expenditures:* $6.2 million. *Unit head:* Dr. Melanie Matthies, Chair, 617-353-3188, E-mail: slhs@bu.edu. *Application contact:* Sharon Sankey, Assistant Dean, Student Services, 617-353-2713, Fax: 617-353-7500, E-mail: ssankey@bu.edu.
Website: http://www.bu.edu/sargent/

Bowling Green State University, Graduate College, College of Health and Human Services, Department of Communication Sciences and Disorders, Bowling Green, OH 43403. Offers communication disorders (PhD); speech-language pathology (MS). *Accreditation:* ASHA (one or more programs are accredited). *Degree requirements:* For master's, thesis or alternative; for doctorate, comprehensive exam, thesis/dissertation, foreign language or research tool. *Entrance requirements:* For master's, GRE General Test, minimum GPA of 3.0; for doctorate, GRE General Test, minimum GPA of 3.2. Additional exam requirements/recommendations for international students: Required—TOEFL. Electronic applications accepted. *Faculty research:* Rehabilitation and mental disorders, forensic rehabilitation, rehabilitation and substance abuse, private rehabilitation and disability management, adjustment to disability.

Bridgewater State University, College of Graduate Studies, College of Education and Allied Studies, Department of Communication Science and Disorders, Bridgewater, MA 02325. Offers speech/language pathology (MS).

Brigham Young University, Graduate Studies, David O. McKay School of Education, Department of Communication Disorders, Provo, UT 84602. Offers speech language pathology (MS). *Accreditation:* ASHA. *Faculty:* 9 full-time (3 women). *Students:* 17 full-time (all women), 20 part-time (18 women); includes 2 minority (1 American Indian or Alaska Native, non-Hispanic/Latino; 1 Hispanic/Latino). Average age 26. 98 applicants, 29% accepted, 17 enrolled. In 2017, 18 master's awarded. *Degree requirements:* For master's, comprehensive exam, thesis, exit interview, PRAXIS. *Entrance requirements:* For master's, GRE General Test, 3 letters of recommendation, statement of intent. Additional exam requirements/recommendations for international students: Required—TOEFL (minimum score 580 paper-based; 85 iBT), IELTS (minimum score 7). *Application deadline:* For fall admission, 2/1 for domestic and international students. Application fee: $50. Electronic applications accepted. *Expenses:* Contact institution. *Financial support:* In 2017–18, 37 students received support, including 20 research assistantships (averaging $1,701 per year), 18 teaching assistantships (averaging $2,786 per year); scholarships/grants also available. *Faculty research:* Foreign language speech argiometry materials; language sample analysis; language measurement; speech motor control physiology; aerodynamic and kinetic analysis of speech production. *Unit head:* Dr. Martin Fujiki, Chair, 801-422-5994, Fax: 801-422-0197, E-mail: martin_fujiki@byu.edu. *Application contact:* Sandy Alger, Department Secretary, 801-422-5117, Fax: 801-422-0197, E-mail: sandy_alger@byu.edu.
Website: http://education.byu.edu/comd/

Brooklyn College of the City University of New York, School of Humanities and Social Sciences, Department of Speech Communication Arts and Sciences, Brooklyn, NY 11210-2889. Offers audiology (Au D); speech (MA), including public communication; speech-language pathology (MS). Au D offered jointly with Hunter College of the City University of New York. *Accreditation:* ASHA (one or more programs are accredited). *Program availability:* Part-time. Terminal master's awarded for partial completion of doctoral program. *Degree requirements:* For master's, comprehensive exam, NTE. *Entrance requirements:* For master's, GRE, minimum GPA of 3.0, interview, essay. Additional exam requirements/recommendations for international students: Required—TOEFL (minimum score 500 paper-based; 61 iBT). Electronic applications accepted. *Faculty research:* Language and learning disorders, aphasia, auditory disorders, public and business communication, voice and fluency disorders.

Buffalo State College, State University of New York, The Graduate School, Faculty of Applied Science and Education, Department of Speech-Language Pathology, Buffalo, NY 14222-1095. Offers MS Ed. *Accreditation:* ASHA. *Program availability:* Part-time, evening/weekend. *Degree requirements:* For master's, thesis or alternative, project. *Entrance requirements:* For master's, minimum GPA of 3.0 in last 60 hours, 22 hours in communication disorders. Additional exam requirements/recommendations for international students: Required—TOEFL (minimum score 550 paper-based).

California Baptist University, Program in Speech Language Pathology, Riverside, CA 92504-3206. Offers MS. *Program availability:* Part-time. *Faculty:* 6 full-time (5 women), 5 part-time/adjunct (3 women). *Students:* 48 full-time (44 women); includes 25 minority (2 Black or African American, non-Hispanic/Latino; 5 Asian, non-Hispanic/Latino; 16 Hispanic/Latino; 2 Two or more races, non-Hispanic/Latino). Average age 25. 148 applicants, 29% accepted, 24 enrolled. *Degree requirements:* For master's, comprehensive exam, capstone, PRAXIS, clinical practicum. *Entrance requirements:* For master's, minimum undergraduate GPA of 3.0, bachelor's transcripts, three letters of recommendation, essay, resume, interview. Additional exam requirements/recommendations for international students: Required—TOEFL (minimum score 80 iBT). *Application deadline:* For fall admission, 12/1 priority date for domestic students, 11/1 priority date for international students; for spring admission, 8/1 priority date for domestic students, 7/1 priority date for international students. Applications are processed on a rolling basis. Application fee: $45. Electronic applications accepted. *Expenses:* Contact institution. *Financial support:* In 2017–18, 1 student received support. Federal Work-Study and scholarships/grants available. Financial award applicants required to submit CSS PROFILE or FAFSA. *Faculty research:* Neurogenic communication disorders, autism, early intervention, phonological acquisition, traumatic brain injury. *Unit head:* Dr. Candace Vickers, Director, 951-552-8129, E-mail: cvickers@calbaptist.edu. *Application contact:* Stephanie Fluitt, Graduate Admissions Counselor, 951-343-4696, Fax: 877-228-8877, E-mail: sfluitt@calbaptist.edu.

California State University, Chico, Office of Graduate Studies, College of Communication and Education, Department of Communication Arts and Sciences, Program in Communication Sciences and Disorders, Chico, CA 95929-0722. Offers MA. *Accreditation:* ASHA. *Degree requirements:* For master's, thesis or comprehensive exam. *Entrance requirements:* For master's, GRE General Test, 3 letters of recommendation, statement of purpose, resume. Additional exam requirements/recommendations for international students: Required—TOEFL (minimum score 550 paper-based; 80 iBT), IELTS (minimum score 6.5), PTE (minimum score 59). Electronic applications accepted.

California State University, East Bay, Office of Graduate Studies, College of Letters, Arts, and Social Sciences, Department of Communicative Sciences and Disorders, Hayward, CA 94542-3000. Offers speech-language pathology (MS). *Accreditation:* ASHA. *Program availability:* Part-time. *Faculty:* 4 full-time (3 women), 4 part-time/adjunct (all women). *Students:* 92 full-time (84 women), 20 part-time (17 women); includes 50 minority (3 Black or African American, non-Hispanic/Latino; 1 American

Indian or Alaska Native, non-Hispanic/Latino; 24 Asian, non-Hispanic/Latino; 18 Hispanic/Latino; 4 Two or more races, non-Hispanic/Latino), 4 international. Average age 30. 302 applicants, 10% accepted, 26 enrolled. In 2017, 27 master's awarded. *Degree requirements:* For master's, comprehensive exam, internship or thesis. *Entrance requirements:* For master's, minimum GPA of 3.0 in last 2 years of course work; baccalaureate degree in speech pathology and audiology; minimum of 60 hours' supervised clinical practice. Additional exam requirements/recommendations for international students: Required—TOEFL (minimum score 550 paper-based). *Application deadline:* For fall admission, 6/1 for domestic and international students. Application fee: $55. Electronic applications accepted. *Financial support:* Fellowships, teaching assistantships, career-related internships or fieldwork, Federal Work-Study, institutionally sponsored loans, and scholarships/grants available. Support available to part-time students. Financial award application deadline: 3/2. *Faculty research:* Aphasia, autism, dementia, diversity, voice. *Unit head:* Dr. Shubha Kashinath, Interim Chair, 510-885-3090, E-mail: shubha.kashinath@csueastbay.edu. *Application contact:* Dr. Elena Dukhovny, Graduate Coordinator, 510-885-2631, Fax: 510-885-2186, E-mail: elena.dukhovny@csueastbay.edu.
Website: http://www20.csueastbay.edu/class/departments/commsci/index.html

California State University, Fresno, Division of Research and Graduate Studies, College of Health and Human Services, Department of Communicative Sciences and Deaf Studies, Fresno, CA 93740-8027. Offers communicative disorders (MA), including deaf education, speech/language pathology. *Accreditation:* ASHA. *Program availability:* Part-time. *Degree requirements:* For master's, thesis or alternative. *Entrance requirements:* For master's, GRE General Test, minimum GPA of 3.0. Additional exam requirements/recommendations for international students: Required—TOEFL. Electronic applications accepted. *Faculty research:* Disabilities education, technology, writing skills at multiple levels, stuttering treatment.

California State University, Fullerton, Graduate Studies, College of Communications, Department of Communication Sciences and Disorders, Fullerton, CA 92831-3599. Offers communicative disorders (MA). *Accreditation:* ASHA. *Faculty:* 8 full-time (5 women), 3 part-time/adjunct (2 women). *Students:* 60 full-time (56 women), 14 part-time (all women); includes 46 minority (4 Black or African American, non-Hispanic/Latino; 16 Asian, non-Hispanic/Latino; 19 Hispanic/Latino; 7 Two or more races, non-Hispanic/Latino), 4 international. Average age 28. 377 applicants, 5% accepted, 18 enrolled. *Unit head:* HyeKyeung Seung, Chair, 657-278-7602, E-mail: hseung@fullerton.edu. *Application contact:* Admissions/Applications, 657-278-2371.
Website: http://communications.fullerton.edu/comd/

California State University, Long Beach, Graduate Studies, College of Health and Human Services, Department of Speech-Language Pathology, Long Beach, CA 90840. Offers MA. *Accreditation:* ASHA. *Program availability:* Part-time. *Degree requirements:* For master's, comprehensive exam or thesis. *Entrance requirements:* For master's, GRE, minimum GPA of 3.0 in last 60 units. Electronic applications accepted.

California State University, Los Angeles, Graduate Studies, College of Health and Human Services, Department of Communication Disorders, Los Angeles, CA 90032-8530. Offers speech and hearing (MA); speech-language pathology (MA). *Accreditation:* ASHA. *Program availability:* Part-time, evening/weekend. *Degree requirements:* For master's, comprehensive exam. *Entrance requirements:* For master's, undergraduate major in communication disorders or related area, minimum GPA of 2.75 in last 90 units. Additional exam requirements/recommendations for international students: Required—TOEFL (minimum score 500 paper-based). *Faculty research:* Language disabilities, minority child language learning.

California State University, Northridge, Graduate Studies, College of Health and Human Development, Department of Communication Disorders and Sciences, Northridge, CA 91330. Offers audiology (MS); speech language pathology (MS). *Accreditation:* ASHA. *Students:* 118 full-time (104 women), 30 part-time (29 women); includes 71 minority (2 Black or African American, non-Hispanic/Latino; 15 Asian, non-Hispanic/Latino; 43 Hispanic/Latino; 1 Native Hawaiian or other Pacific Islander, non-Hispanic/Latino; 10 Two or more races, non-Hispanic/Latino), 5 international. Average age 27. 250 applicants, 16% accepted, 39 enrolled. In 2017, 107 master's awarded. *Degree requirements:* For master's, PRAXIS. *Entrance requirements:* For master's, GRE or minimum GPA of 3.5. Additional exam requirements/recommendations for international students: Required—TOEFL. *Application deadline:* For fall admission, 11/30 for domestic students. Application fee: $55. *Financial support:* Application deadline: 3/1. *Faculty research:* Infant stimulation, early intervention program. *Unit head:* Dr. Patricia Seymour, Chair, 818-677-2852.
Website: http://www.csun.edu/hhd/cd/

California State University, Sacramento, College of Health and Human Services, Department of Communication Sciences and Disorders, Sacramento, CA 95819. Offers communication sciences and disorders (MS). *Accreditation:* ASHA. *Program availability:* Part-time. *Students:* 68 full-time (64 women), 14 part-time (13 women); includes 19 minority (1 Black or African American, non-Hispanic/Latino; 11 Asian, non-Hispanic/Latino; 7 Hispanic/Latino). Average age 28. 149 applicants, 21% accepted, 31 enrolled. In 2017, 62 master's awarded. *Degree requirements:* For master's, thesis, project, or comprehensive exam; writing proficiency exam. *Entrance requirements:* For master's, GRE General Test; CBEST, appropriate bachelor's degree, minimum GPA of 3.0 in last 2 years of course work. Additional exam requirements/recommendations for international students: Required—TOEFL (minimum score 550 paper-based; 80 iBT); Recommended—IELTS, TSE. *Application deadline:* For fall admission, 2/15 for domestic students, 3/1 for international students; for spring admission, 9/30 for international students. Applications are processed on a rolling basis. Application fee: $55. Electronic applications accepted. *Expenses:* Contact institution. *Financial support:* Career-related internships or fieldwork, Federal Work-Study, and scholarships/grants available. Support available to part-time students. Financial award application deadline: 3/1; financial award applicants required to submit FAFSA. *Unit head:* Dr. Robert Pieretti, Chair, 916-278-6759, E-mail: rpieretti@csus.edu. *Application contact:* Jose Martinez, Graduate Admissions Supervisor, 916-278-7871, E-mail: martinj@skymail.csus.edu.
Website: http://www.csus.edu/hhs/csad/

California State University, San Marcos, College of Education, Health and Human Services, Department of Speech-Language Pathology, San Marcos, CA 92096-0001. Offers MS. *Accreditation:* ASHA. *Application deadline:* For fall admission, 1/1 priority date for domestic students. *Expenses:* Contact institution. *Unit head:* Dr. Lori Heisler, Department Chair, 760-750-8596, E-mail: lheisler@csusm.edu.
Website: http://www.csusm.edu/slp/

California University of Pennsylvania, School of Graduate Studies and Research, College of Education and Human Services, Department of Communication Disorders, California, PA 15419-1394. Offers MS. *Accreditation:* ASHA. *Program availability:* Part-time, evening/weekend. *Degree requirements:* For master's, comprehensive exam, thesis optional. *Entrance requirements:* For master's, GRE General Test, minimum GPA of 3.0, references. Additional exam requirements/recommendations for international students: Required—TOEFL (minimum score 550 paper-based; 80 iBT). *Application deadline:* For fall admission, 2/15 priority date for domestic and international students. Applications are processed on a rolling basis. Application fee: $25. Electronic applications accepted. *Financial support:* Applicants required to submit FAFSA. *Faculty research:* Normative voice database, communication disorders and health. *Unit head:* Dr. Ralph Belsterling, Program Coordinator, 724-938-4175, E-mail: belsterling@calu.edu. *Application contact:* Suzanne C. Powers, Director of Graduate Admissions and Recruitment, 724-938-4029, Fax: 724-938-5712, E-mail: powers_s@cup.edu.
Website: http://www.calu.edu/academics/colleges/education/communication-disorders/

Canisius College, Graduate Division, School of Education and Human Services, Department of Graduate Education and Leadership, Buffalo, NY 14208-1098. Offers business and marketing education (MS Ed); college student personnel (MS Ed); deaf education (MS Ed); deaf/adolescent education, grades 7-12 (MS Ed); deaf/childhood education, grades 1-6 (MS Ed); differentiated instruction (MS Ed); education administration (MS); educational administration (MS Ed); educational technologies (Certificate); gifted education extension (Certificate); literacy (MS Ed); reading (Certificate); school building leadership (MS Ed, Certificate); school district leadership (Certificate); teacher leader (Certificate); TESOL (MS Ed). *Accreditation:* NCATE. *Program availability:* Part-time, evening/weekend, 100% online, blended/hybrid learning. *Faculty:* 5 full-time (all women), 21 part-time/adjunct (16 women). *Students:* 85 full-time (67 women), 189 part-time (151 women); includes 31 minority (18 Black or African American, non-Hispanic/Latino; 3 American Indian or Alaska Native, non-Hispanic/Latino; 3 Asian, non-Hispanic/Latino; 4 Hispanic/Latino; 3 Two or more races, non-Hispanic/Latino), 1 international. Average age 31. 83 applicants, 96% accepted, 74 enrolled. In 2017, 94 master's, 47 other advanced degrees awarded. *Entrance requirements:* For master's, GRE (if cumulative GPA less than 2.7), transcripts, two letters of recommendation. Additional exam requirements/recommendations for international students: Required—TOEFL (minimum score 550 paper-based, 79 iBT), IELTS (minimum score 6.5), or CAEL (minimum score 70). *Application deadline:* Applications are processed on a rolling basis. Application fee: $0. Electronic applications accepted. *Expenses: Tuition:* Full-time $22,860; part-time $820 per credit. *Required fees:* $720; $25 per credit. $65 per semester. One-time fee: $425. *Financial support:* Career-related internships or fieldwork, Federal Work-Study, scholarships/grants, tuition waivers (partial), and unspecified assistantships available. Support available to part-time students. Financial award application deadline: 4/30; financial award applicants required to submit FAFSA. *Faculty research:* Asperger's disease, autism, private higher education, reading strategies. *Unit head:* Dr. Anne Marie Tryjankowski, Chair/Associate Professor of Graduate Education and Leadership, 716-888-3715, Fax: 716-888-3142, E-mail: tryjanka@canisius.edu.

Carlos Albizu University, Graduate Programs, San Juan, PR 00901. Offers clinical psychology (MS, PhD, Psy D); general psychology (PhD); industrial/organizational psychology (MS, PhD); speech and language pathology (MS). *Accreditation:* APA (one or more programs are accredited). *Program availability:* Part-time, evening/weekend. Terminal master's awarded for partial completion of doctoral program. *Degree requirements:* For master's, one foreign language, comprehensive exam, thesis; for doctorate, one foreign language, comprehensive exam, thesis/dissertation, written qualifying exams. *Entrance requirements:* For master's, GRE General Test or EXADEP, interview; minimum GPA of 2.8 (industrial/organizational psychology); for doctorate, GRE General Test or EXADEP, interview; minimum GPA of 3.0 (PhD in industrial/organizational psychology and clinical psychology), 3.25 (Psy D). *Faculty research:* Psychotherapeutic techniques for Hispanics, psychology of the aged, school dropouts, stress, violence.

Carlos Albizu University, Miami Campus, Graduate Programs, Miami, FL 33172-2209. Offers clinical psychology (PhD, Psy D); entrepreneurship (MBA); exceptional student education (MS); human services (PhD); industrial/organizational psychology (MS); marriage and family therapy (MS); mental health counseling (MS); nonprofit management (MBA); organizational management (MBA); psychology (MS); speech and language pathology (MS); teaching English for speakers of other languages (MS). *Accreditation:* APA. *Program availability:* Part-time, evening/weekend, 100% online, blended/hybrid learning. *Faculty:* 32 full-time (24 women), 27 part-time/adjunct (15 women). *Students:* 411 full-time (345 women), 248 part-time (215 women); includes 562 minority (53 Black or African American, non-Hispanic/Latino; 4 Asian, non-Hispanic/Latino; 498 Hispanic/Latino; 7 Two or more races, non-Hispanic/Latino), 23 international. Average age 34. 391 applicants, 42% accepted, 154 enrolled. In 2017, 96 master's, 54 doctorates awarded. Terminal master's awarded for partial completion of doctoral program. *Degree requirements:* For master's, comprehensive exam (for some programs), integrative project (for MBA); research project (for exceptional student education, teaching English as a second language); for doctorate, comprehensive examinations, internship, project/dissertation. *Entrance requirements:* For master's, GRE/EXADEP, bachelor's degree from accredited institution, minimum GPA of 3.0, 3 letters of recommendation, interview, resume, statement of purpose, official transcripts; for doctorate, GRE (for Psy D), 3 letters of recommendation, resume, interview, statement of purpose, official transcripts; bachelor's degree and minimum GPA of 3.25 (for Psy D); master's degree and minimum GPA of 3.0 (for PhD). Additional exam requirements/recommendations for international students: Required—Michigan Test of English Language Proficiency. *Application deadline:* For fall admission, 4/1 priority date for domestic students, 5/1 priority date for international students; for spring admission, 11/1 priority date for domestic students, 9/1 priority date for international students. Applications are processed on a rolling basis. Application fee: $50. Electronic applications accepted. Application fee is waived when completed online. *Expenses:* Contact institution. *Financial support:* In 2017–18, 145 students received support. Federal Work-Study, scholarships/grants, unspecified assistantships, and tuition discounts available. Financial award application deadline: 6/1; financial award applicants required to submit FAFSA. *Faculty research:* Psychotherapy, forensic psychology, neuropsychology, special education, speech-language pathology, criminal justice. *Unit head:* Dr. Etiony Aldarondo, Provost, 305-593-1223 Ext. 3138, Fax: 305-592-7930, E-mail: ealdarondo@albizu.edu. *Application contact:* Sonia Feliciano, Institutional Director of Student Recruitment, 305-593-1223 Ext. 3108, Fax: 305-477-8983, E-mail: sfeliciano@albizu.edu.

Case Western Reserve University, School of Graduate Studies, Psychological Sciences Department, Program in Communication Sciences, Cleveland, OH 44106. Offers speech-language pathology (MA, PhD). *Accreditation:* ASHA (one or more programs are accredited). *Program availability:* Part-time. *Faculty:* 4 full-time (all women), 10 part-time/adjunct (8 women). *Students:* 15 full-time (14 women), 7 part-time (all women). Average age 29. 132 applicants, 9% accepted, 10 enrolled. In 2017, 9 master's awarded. Terminal master's awarded for partial completion of doctoral program. *Degree requirements:* For master's, comprehensive exam, thesis optional; for doctorate, thesis/dissertation. *Entrance requirements:* For master's and doctorate, GRE General Test, statement of objectives; curriculum vitae; 3 letters of recommendation; interview. Additional exam requirements/recommendations for international students: Required—TOEFL (minimum score 577 paper-based; 90 iBT); Recommended—IELTS (minimum score 7). *Application deadline:* For fall admission, 1/15 for domestic students. Application fee: $50. Electronic applications accepted. *Expenses: Tuition:* Full-time $43,854; part-time $1827 per credit hour. *Required fees:* $50; $50 per credit hour. Tuition and fees vary according to course load and program. *Financial support:* Research assistantships, tuition waivers (partial), and unspecified assistantships available. Financial award application deadline: 1/15; financial award applicants required

to submit FAFSA. *Faculty research:* Traumatic brain injury, phonological disorders, child language disorders, communication problems in the aged and Alzheimer's patients, cleft palate, voice disorders. *Unit head:* Dr. Heath Demaree, Professor and Chair, 216-368-6468, E-mail: psychsciences@case.edu. *Application contact:* Kori Kosek, Department Administrator, 216-368-6469, Fax: 216-368-6078, E-mail: psychsciences@case.edu.
Website: http://psychsciences.case.edu/graduate/

Central Michigan University, College of Graduate Studies, The Herbert H. and Grace A. Dow College of Health Professions, Department of Communication Sciences and Disorders, Doctor of Audiology Program, Mount Pleasant, MI 48859. Offers Au D. *Accreditation:* ASHA. *Degree requirements:* For doctorate, comprehensive exam, thesis/dissertation or alternative. *Entrance requirements:* For doctorate, GRE, interview. Electronic applications accepted. *Faculty research:* Auditory electrophysiology, auditory process disorders, neuroanatomy, pediatric audiology, rehabilitative audiology.

Central Michigan University, College of Graduate Studies, The Herbert H. and Grace A. Dow College of Health Professions, Department of Communication Sciences and Disorders, Program in Speech-Language Pathology, Mount Pleasant, MI 48859. Offers MA. *Accreditation:* ASHA. *Degree requirements:* For master's, thesis or alternative. Electronic applications accepted. *Expenses:* Contact institution. *Faculty research:* Traumatic brain injury, neuro-linguistics, multidisciplinary and transdisciplinary therapy, speech audiometry, phonological disorders.

Chapman University, Crean College of Health and Behavioral Sciences, Department of Communication Sciences and Disorders, Orange, CA 92866. Offers MS. *Program availability:* Evening/weekend. *Faculty:* 5 full-time (all women), 4 part-time/adjunct (all women). *Students:* 83 full-time (74 women); includes 32 minority (10 Asian, non-Hispanic/Latino; 18 Hispanic/Latino; 4 Two or more races, non-Hispanic/Latino). Average age 26. 291 applicants, 24% accepted, 42 enrolled. In 2017, 31 master's awarded. *Degree requirements:* For master's, comprehensive exam, thesis, 400 hours of supervised practicum. *Entrance requirements:* For master's, GRE. *Application deadline:* For fall admission, 1/15 for domestic students. Application fee: $60. Electronic applications accepted. *Expenses:* Contact institution. *Financial support:* Fellowships, scholarships/grants, and unspecified assistantships available. Financial award applicants required to submit FAFSA. *Unit head:* Dr. Mary Kennedy, Director, 714-744-2132, E-mail: markenne@chapman.edu. *Application contact:* Sharnique Dow, Graduate Admission Counselor, 714-997-6770, E-mail: sdow@chapman.edu.

Clarion University of Pennsylvania, College of Health and Human Services, MS Program in Speech Language Pathology, Clarion, PA 16214. Offers MS. *Accreditation:* ASHA. *Program availability:* Part-time. *Faculty:* 8 full-time (7 women), 6 part-time/adjunct (5 women). *Students:* 99 full-time (92 women), 20 part-time (18 women); includes 10 minority (3 Hispanic/Latino; 7 Two or more races, non-Hispanic/Latino). Average age 23. 179 applicants, 46% accepted, 46 enrolled. In 2017, 57 master's awarded. *Degree requirements:* For master's, comprehensive exam, thesis or alternative. *Entrance requirements:* For master's, GRE, minimum QPA of 3.0, interview. Additional exam requirements/recommendations for international students: Required—TOEFL (minimum score 573 paper-based; 89 iBT). *Application deadline:* For fall admission, 1/31 priority date for domestic students, 9/1 priority date for international students. Applications are processed on a rolling basis. Application fee: $40. Electronic applications accepted. *Expenses:* $747.80 per credit. *Financial support:* Career-related internships or fieldwork, scholarships/grants, and unspecified assistantships available. Support available to part-time students. Financial award application deadline: 3/1; financial award applicants required to submit FAFSA. *Unit head:* Dr. Janis Jarecki-Liu, 814-393-2581, Fax: 814-393-2206, E-mail: jjareckiliu@clarion.edu. *Application contact:* Dana Bearer, Associate Director, Transfer, Adult, and Graduate Programs, 814-393-2337, Fax: 814-393-2722, E-mail: gradstudies@clarion.edu.

Cleveland State University, College of Graduate Studies, College of Sciences and Health Professions, School of Health Sciences, Program in Speech Pathology and Audiology, Cleveland, OH 44115. Offers MA. *Accreditation:* ASHA. *Faculty:* 7 full-time (6 women), 5 part-time/adjunct (all women). *Students:* 68 full-time (64 women); includes 5 minority (1 Black or African American, non-Hispanic/Latino; 1 American Indian or Alaska Native, non-Hispanic/Latino; 1 Asian, non-Hispanic/Latino; 1 Hispanic/Latino; 1 Two or more races, non-Hispanic/Latino). Average age 23. In 2017, 32 master's awarded. *Entrance requirements:* For master's, GRE. Additional exam requirements/recommendations for international students: Required—TOEFL (minimum score 550 paper-based; 78 iBT). Application fee: $40. Electronic applications accepted. *Financial support:* In 2017–18, 9 students received support, including 13 research assistantships (averaging $6,960 per year); teaching assistantships with partial tuition reimbursements available, career-related internships or fieldwork, Federal Work-Study, and unspecified assistantships also available. Financial award application deadline: 2/1; financial award applicants required to submit FAFSA. *Faculty research:* Child language and literacy development, cultural diversity, variant dialects, voice disorders, neurogenic communication disorders. *Unit head:* Dr. Monica Gordon Pershey, Program Director, 216-687-4534, Fax: 216-687-6993, E-mail: m.pershey@csuohio.edu. *Application contact:* Donna Helwig, Administrative Coordinator to the Chairperson, 216-687-3807, Fax: 216-687-6993, E-mail: d.helwig@csuohio.edu.
Website: http://www.csuohio.edu/sciences/dept/healthsciences/graduate/SPH/index.html

The College of Saint Rose, Graduate Studies, Thelma P. Lally School of Education, Program in Communication Sciences and Disorders, Albany, NY 12203-1419. Offers MS Ed. *Accreditation:* ASHA. *Students:* 104 full-time (102 women), 6 part-time (all women); includes 7 minority (6 Hispanic/Latino; 1 Two or more races, non-Hispanic/Latino), 5 international. Average age 24. 208 applicants, 50% accepted, 47 enrolled. In 2017, 51 master's awarded. *Degree requirements:* For master's, comprehensive exam (for some programs), thesis (for some programs), comprehensive exam or thesis. *Entrance requirements:* For master's, minimum undergraduate GPA of 3.0, on-campus interview, 32 undergraduate credits (if undergraduate degree is not in communication disorders). Additional exam requirements/recommendations for international students: Required—TOEFL (minimum score 550 paper-based; 80 iBT), IELTS (minimum score 6), PTE (minimum score 56). *Application deadline:* For fall admission, 1/15 for domestic and international students; for spring admission, 9/15 for domestic and international students; for summer admission, 1/15 for domestic and international students. Application fee: $125. Electronic applications accepted. *Expenses: Tuition:* Full-time $7191; part-time $799 per credit hour. *Required fees:* $924; $462 per credit hour. Tuition and fees vary according to course load. *Financial support:* Career-related internships or fieldwork, scholarships/grants, tuition waivers, and unspecified assistantships available. Support available to part-time students. Financial award application deadline: 4/15. *Unit head:* Dr. Jim Feeney, Chair, 518-454-5255, E-mail: feenyj@strose.edu. *Application contact:* Cris Murray, Assistant Vice President for Graduate Recruitment and Enrollment, 518-485-3390, E-mail: grad@strose.edu.
Website: https://www.strose.edu/communication-sciences-disorders-ms/

Dalhousie University, Faculty of Health Professions, School of Human Communication Disorders, Halifax, NS B3H 1R2, Canada. Offers audiology (M Sc); speech-language pathology (M Sc). *Degree requirements:* For master's, thesis or alternative. *Entrance requirements:* Additional exam requirements/recommendations for international students: Required—TOEFL, IELTS, CANTEST, CAEL, or Michigan English Language Assessment Battery. Electronic applications accepted. *Expenses:* Contact institution. *Faculty research:* Audiology, hearing aids, speech and voice disorders, language development and disorders, treatment efficacy.

Duquesne University, John G. Rangos, Sr. School of Health Sciences, Pittsburgh, PA 15282-0001. Offers health management systems (MHMS); occupational therapy (MS, OTD); physical therapy (DPT); physician assistant studies (MPAS); rehabilitation science (MS, PhD); speech-language pathology (MS). *Accreditation:* AOTA (one or more programs are accredited); APTA (one or more programs are accredited); ASHA. *Program availability:* Part-time, minimal on-campus study. *Faculty:* 51 full-time (38 women), 33 part-time/adjunct (17 women). *Students:* 247 full-time (199 women), 11 part-time (7 women); includes 15 minority (2 Black or African American, non-Hispanic/Latino; 7 Asian, non-Hispanic/Latino; 3 Hispanic/Latino; 3 Two or more races, non-Hispanic/Latino), 42 international. Average age 23. 283 applicants, 31% accepted, 54 enrolled. In 2017, 134 master's, 39 doctorates awarded. *Degree requirements:* For doctorate, comprehensive exam (for some programs), thesis/dissertation (for some programs). *Entrance requirements:* For master's, GRE General Test (speech-language pathology), 3 letters of recommendation; minimum GPA of 2.75 (health management systems), 3.0 (speech-language pathology); for doctorate, GRE General Test (for physical therapy and rehabilitation science), 3 letters of recommendation, minimum GPA of 3.0, personal interview. Additional exam requirements/recommendations for international students: Required—TOEFL (minimum score 550 paper-based; 90 iBT); Recommended—IELTS. *Application deadline:* For fall admission, 2/1 for domestic and international students; for spring admission, 7/1 for domestic and international students. Applications are processed on a rolling basis. Application fee: $0. Electronic applications accepted. *Expenses:* $1,351 per credit ($1,259 for health management systems). *Financial support:* Federal Work-Study available. Financial award applicants required to submit FAFSA. *Faculty research:* Neuronal processing, electrical stimulation on peripheral neuropathy, central nervous system (CNS) stimulatory and inhibitory signals, behavioral genetic methodologies to development disorders of speech, neurogenic communication disorders. *Total annual research expenditures:* $24,578. *Unit head:* Dr. Fevzi Akinci, Dean, 412-396-5303, Fax: 412-396-5554, E-mail: akincif@duq.edu. *Application contact:* Christopher R. Hilf, Director of Enrollment Management, 412-396-5653, Fax: 412-396-5554, E-mail: hilfc@duq.edu.
Website: http://www.duq.edu/academics/schools/health-sciences

East Carolina University, Graduate School, College of Allied Health Sciences, Department of Communication Sciences and Disorders, Greenville, NC 27858-4353. Offers MS, Au D, PhD. *Accreditation:* ASHA (one or more programs are accredited). *Program availability:* Part-time, evening/weekend, online learning. *Students:* 120 full-time (117 women), 22 part-time (21 women); includes 11 minority (2 Black or African American, non-Hispanic/Latino; 3 Asian, non-Hispanic/Latino; 6 Hispanic/Latino), 2 international. Average age 28. 339 applicants, 37% accepted, 53 enrolled. In 2017, 43 master's, 5 doctorates awarded. *Degree requirements:* For master's, comprehensive exam, thesis or alternative, clinical clock hours; for doctorate, comprehensive exam, thesis/dissertation. *Entrance requirements:* For master's and doctorate, GRE General Test. Additional exam requirements/recommendations for international students: Recommended—TOEFL (minimum score 78 iBT), IELTS (minimum score 6.5). *Application deadline:* For fall admission, 1/15 for domestic students. Applications are processed on a rolling basis. Application fee: $75. Electronic applications accepted. *Expenses:* Tuition, state resident: full-time $4749; part-time $297 per credit hour. Tuition, nonresident: full-time $17,898; part-time $1119 per credit hour. *Required fees:* $2691; $224 per credit hour. Part-time tuition and fees vary according to course load and program. *Financial support:* Research assistantships with partial tuition reimbursements, teaching assistantships with partial tuition reimbursements, and unspecified assistantships available. Financial award application deadline: 3/1; financial award applicants required to submit FAFSA. *Faculty research:* Hearing, language disorders, stuttering, reading disorder. *Unit head:* Dr. Kathleen Cox, Interim Chair, 252-744-6095, E-mail: coxka@ecu.edu.
Website: http://www.ecu.edu/cs-dhs/csd/index.cfm

Eastern Illinois University, Graduate School, College of Health and Human Services, Department of Communication Disorders and Sciences, Charleston, IL 61920. Offers MS. *Accreditation:* ASHA. *Program availability:* Part-time, evening/weekend, online learning. *Degree requirements:* For master's, comprehensive exam (for some programs), thesis (for some programs). *Entrance requirements:* For master's, GMAT or GRE. Additional exam requirements/recommendations for international students: Required—TOEFL (minimum score 500 paper-based; 61 iBT), IELTS (minimum score 6). *Application deadline:* For fall admission, 5/15 for domestic and international students; for spring admission, 10/15 for domestic and international students. Applications are processed on a rolling basis. Application fee: $30. Electronic applications accepted. *Financial support:* Teaching assistantships with full tuition reimbursements, career-related internships or fieldwork, Federal Work-Study, and unspecified assistantships available. Support available to part-time students. Financial award application deadline: 3/1; financial award applicants required to submit FAFSA. *Unit head:* Angela Anthony, Chair, 217-581-2712, Fax: 217-581-7105, E-mail: abanthony@eiu.edu. *Application contact:* Rebecca Throneburg, Graduate Coordinator, 217-581-7447, Fax: 217-581-7105, E-mail: rmthroneburg@eiu.edu.
Website: http://www.eiu.edu/commdisgrad/

Eastern Kentucky University, The Graduate School, College of Education, Department of Special Education, Program in Communication Disorders, Richmond, KY 40475-3102. Offers MA Ed. *Accreditation:* ASHA. *Degree requirements:* For master's, comprehensive exam, thesis optional, 375 clinical clock hours. *Entrance requirements:* For master's, GRE General Test, minimum GPA of 3.0. *Faculty research:* Distance learning, fluency, phonemic awareness, technology, autism.

Eastern Michigan University, Graduate School, College of Education, Department of Special Education, Program in Speech-Language Pathology, Ypsilanti, MI 48197. Offers MA. *Accreditation:* ASHA. *Program availability:* Part-time, evening/weekend, online learning. *Students:* 75 full-time (74 women), 26 part-time (all women); includes 8 minority (5 Asian, non-Hispanic/Latino; 1 Hispanic/Latino; 2 Two or more races, non-Hispanic/Latino), 4 international. Average age 27. 226 applicants, 20% accepted, 21 enrolled. In 2017, 39 master's awarded. *Entrance requirements:* For master's, GRE General Test. Additional exam requirements/recommendations for international students: Required—TOEFL. *Application deadline:* Applications are processed on a rolling basis. Application fee: $45. *Financial support:* Fellowships, research assistantships with full tuition reimbursements, teaching assistantships with full tuition reimbursements, career-related internships or fieldwork, Federal Work-Study, institutionally sponsored loans, scholarships/grants, tuition waivers (partial), and unspecified assistantships available. Support available to part-time students. Financial award applicants required to submit FAFSA. *Application contact:* Dr. Sarah Ginsberg, Program Director, 734-487-3300, Fax: 734-487-2473, E-mail: sginsberg@emich.edu.
Website: http://www.emich.edu/coe/slp/

Eastern New Mexico University, Graduate School, College of Liberal Arts and Sciences, Department of Health and Human Services, Portales, NM 88130. Offers communicative disorders (MS); nursing (MSN). *Accreditation:* ASHA. *Program availability:* Part-time, online learning. *Degree requirements:* For master's, thesis

optional, oral and written comprehensive exam, oral presentation of professional portfolio. *Entrance requirements:* For master's, GRE, three letters of recommendation, resume, two essays. Additional exam requirements/recommendations for international students: Required—TOEFL (minimum score 550 paper-based; 79 iBT), IELTS (minimum score 6). *Application deadline:* For fall admission, 3/1 priority date for domestic and international students. Applications are processed on a rolling basis. Application fee: $10. Electronic applications accepted. *Financial support:* Applicants required to submit FAFSA. *Unit head:* Dr. Suzanne Swift, Chair/Interim Graduate Coordinator, 575-562-2724, Fax: 575-562-2380, E-mail: suzanne.swift@enmu.edu. *Application contact:* Wendy Turner, Department Secretary, 575-562-2156, Fax: 575-562-2380, E-mail: wendy.turner@enmu.edu.
Website: http://liberal-arts.enmu.edu/health/cdis/graduate-cdis.shtml

Eastern Washington University, Graduate Studies, College of Health Science and Public Health, Department of Communication Sciences and Disorders, Cheney, WA 99004-2431. Offers MS. *Accreditation:* ASHA. *Faculty:* 9 part-time/adjunct (all women). *Students:* 48 full-time (47 women). Average age 26. 235 applicants, 10% accepted, 23 enrolled. In 2017, 25 master's awarded. *Degree requirements:* For master's, comprehensive exam, thesis or alternative. *Entrance requirements:* For master's, GRE General Test, minimum GPA of 3.0. Additional exam requirements/recommendations for international students: Required—TOEFL (minimum score 580 paper-based; 92 iBT), IELTS (minimum score 7), PTE (minimum score 63). *Application deadline:* For fall admission, 3/1 for domestic students. Applications are processed on a rolling basis. Application fee: $75. Electronic applications accepted. *Expenses:* Tuition, state resident: full-time $11,191; part-time $373.06 per credit. Tuition, nonresident: full-time $25,995; part-time $866.52 per credit. *Financial support:* Teaching assistantships with partial tuition reimbursements, career-related internships or fieldwork, Federal Work-Study, institutionally sponsored loans, scholarships/grants, health care benefits, tuition waivers (partial), and unspecified assistantships available. Support available to part-time students. Financial award application deadline: 2/1; financial award applicants required to submit FAFSA. *Application contact:* Dr. Roberta Jackson, Advisor, 509-359-6622, Fax: 509-359-6802.
Website: http://www.ewu.edu/CSHE/Programs/Communication-Disorders/ComD-Degrees/MSCD.xml

East Stroudsburg University of Pennsylvania, Graduate and Extended Studies, College of Health Sciences, Department of Communication Sciences and Disorders, East Stroudsburg, PA 18301-2999. Offers MS. *Accreditation:* ASHA. *Program availability:* Part-time, evening/weekend, online learning. *Faculty:* 5 full-time (all women), 3 part-time/adjunct (all women). *Students:* 61 full-time (58 women); includes 4 minority (1 Asian, non-Hispanic/Latino; 1 Hispanic/Latino; 2 Two or more races, non-Hispanic/Latino). Average age 24. 182 applicants, 26% accepted, 31 enrolled. In 2017, 12 master's awarded. *Degree requirements:* For master's, comprehensive exam, portfolio. *Entrance requirements:* For master's, GRE General Test, minimum undergraduate QPA of 3.0 overall and in major, 3 letters of recommendation. Additional exam requirements/recommendations for international students: Recommended—TOEFL (minimum score 560 paper-based; 83 iBT), IELTS. *Application deadline:* For fall admission, 2/1 priority date for domestic and international students; for spring admission, 11/30 for domestic and international students. Applications are processed on a rolling basis. Application fee: $50. Electronic applications accepted. *Expenses:* Tuition, state resident: full-time $4500; part-time $3000 per credit. Tuition, nonresident: full-time $6750; part-time $4500 per credit. *Required fees:* $2642; $1756 per credit. $878 per semester. Tuition and fees vary according to course load, campus/location and program. *Financial support:* Research assistantships with tuition reimbursements, Federal Work-Study, and unspecified assistantships available. Support available to part-time students. Financial award application deadline: 3/1; financial award applicants required to submit FAFSA. *Faculty research:* Computer-assisted classroom instruction. *Unit head:* Dr. LuAnn Batson-Magnuson, Graduate Coordinator, 570-422-3311, Fax: 570-422-3850, E-mail: lmagnuson@esu.edu. *Application contact:* Kevin Quintero, Associate Director, Graduate and Extended Studies, 570-422-3890, Fax: 570-422-2711, E-mail: kquintero@esu.edu.

East Tennessee State University, School of Graduate Studies, College of Clinical and Rehabilitative Health Sciences, Department of Audiology and Speech-Language Pathology, Johnson City, TN 37614-1710. Offers audiology (Au D); speech-language pathology (MS). *Accreditation:* ASHA (one or more programs are accredited). *Degree requirements:* For master's, comprehensive exam, case study or thesis; for doctorate, comprehensive exam, externship, research project. *Entrance requirements:* For master's, GRE General Test, minimum GPA of 3.0; 3 letters of recommendation; resume; 3 credits each in biological science, physical science, and statistics; 6 credits in the behavioral and/or social sciences; 15 credits in basic human communication processes; 25 clinical observation credits; for doctorate, GRE General Test, minimum GPA of 3.25, three letters of recommendation, 6 credit hours each in college-level mathematics (of which at least 3 must statistics) and in the behavioral and/or social sciences, interview. Additional exam requirements/recommendations for international students: Required—TOEFL (minimum score 550 paper-based; 79 iBT). *Application deadline:* For fall admission, 2/1 for domestic and international students. Application fee: $55 ($65 for international students). Electronic applications accepted. *Financial support:* Research assistantships with tuition reimbursements, teaching assistantships with full tuition reimbursements, career-related internships or fieldwork, institutionally sponsored loans, scholarships/grants, and unspecified assistantships available. Financial award application deadline: 7/1; financial award applicants required to submit FAFSA. *Faculty research:* Vestibular assessment and management, tinnitus management, speech perception, hearing amplification, early speech and language intervention for children with cleft palate, assessment and management of speech sound disorders, pediatric language intervention, voice disorders and vocal fatigue. *Unit head:* Dr. Brenda Louw, Chair, 423-439-4315, Fax: 423-439-4607, E-mail: louwb1@etsu.edu. *Application contact:* Dr. Brenda Louw, Chair, 423-439-4315, Fax: 423-439-4607, E-mail: louwb1@etsu.edu.
Website: http://www.etsu.edu/crhs/aslp/

Edinboro University of Pennsylvania, Department of Speech, Language and Hearing, Edinboro, PA 16444. Offers speech language pathology (MA). *Accreditation:* ASHA. *Program availability:* Part-time, evening/weekend. *Degree requirements:* For master's, thesis or alternative, competency exam. *Entrance requirements:* For master's, GRE or MAT, minimum QPA of 2.5. Electronic applications accepted.

Elmhurst College, Graduate Programs, Program in Communication Sciences and Disorders, Elmhurst, IL 60126-3296. Offers MS. *Faculty:* 9 full-time (8 women), 1 (woman) part-time/adjunct. *Students:* 45 full-time (44 women), 1 (woman) part-time; includes 7 minority (all Hispanic/Latino). Average age 25. 306 applicants, 31% accepted, 22 enrolled. In 2017, 21 master's awarded. *Degree requirements:* For master's, clinical practicum. *Entrance requirements:* For master's, GRE General Test, 3 recommendations, resume, statement of purpose. Additional exam requirements/recommendations for international students: Required—TOEFL (minimum score 550 paper-based; 79 iBT). *Application deadline:* Applications are processed on a rolling basis. Application fee: $0. Electronic applications accepted. *Expenses:* Contact institution. *Financial support:* In 2017–18, 39 students received support. Fellowships and scholarships/grants available. Financial award application deadline: 1/15; financial award applicants required to submit FAFSA. *Unit head:* Brenda Gorman, Director, 630-617-6122, E-mail: brenda.gorman@elmhurst.edu. *Application contact:* Timothy J. Panfil, Director of Enrollment Management, 630-617-3300 Ext. 3256, Fax: 630-617-6471, E-mail: panfilt@elmhurst.edu.
Website: http://www.elmhurst.edu/masters_communication_sciences_disorders

Emerson College, Graduate Studies, Boston, MA 02116-4624. Offers civic media (MA), including art and practice; communication disorders (MS); creative writing (MFA); digital marketing (MA), including data analytics; film and media art (MFA); journalism (MA); popular fiction writing and publishing (MFA); public relations (MA); publishing and writing (MA); strategic communication for marketing (MA); theatre education (MA); writing for film and television (MFA). *Program availability:* Part-time, evening/weekend. *Faculty:* 202 full-time (86 women), 252 part-time/adjunct (125 women). *Students:* 571 full-time (423 women), 82 part-time (60 women); includes 102 minority (24 Black or African American, non-Hispanic/Latino; 19 Asian, non-Hispanic/Latino; 38 Hispanic/Latino; 1 Native Hawaiian or other Pacific Islander, non-Hispanic/Latino; 20 Two or more races, non-Hispanic/Latino), 170 international. Average age 27. 1,578 applicants, 57% accepted, 297 enrolled. In 2017, 271 master's awarded. *Entrance requirements:* For master's, GRE or GMAT (for certain programs). Additional exam requirements/recommendations for international students: Required—TOEFL (minimum score 550 paper-based; 80 iBT), IELTS (minimum score 6.5). *Application deadline:* Applications are processed on a rolling basis. Application fee: $60 ($75 for international students). Electronic applications accepted. *Expenses: Tuition:* Full-time $20,016; part-time $1251 per credit. *Required fees:* $624; $232 per credit. $116 per semester. *Financial support:* In 2017–18, 382 students received support, including 382 fellowships with partial tuition reimbursements available (averaging $7,551 per year); research assistantships with partial tuition reimbursements available, Federal Work-Study, scholarships/grants, and unspecified assistantships also available. Financial award application deadline: 3/1; financial award applicants required to submit FAFSA. *Application contact:* Leanda Ferland, Director of Graduate Admission, 617-824-8610, Fax: 617-824-8614, E-mail: gradadmission@emerson.edu.
Website: http://www.emerson.edu/academics/graduate-degrees

Florida Atlantic University, College of Education, Department of Communication Sciences and Disorders, Boca Raton, FL 33431-0991. Offers speech-language pathology (MS). *Accreditation:* ASHA. *Faculty:* 3 full-time (1 woman). *Students:* 44 full-time (43 women), 4 part-time (2 women); includes 10 minority (1 Black or African American, non-Hispanic/Latino; 2 Asian, non-Hispanic/Latino; 7 Hispanic/Latino). Average age 25. 354 applicants, 16% accepted, 20 enrolled. In 2017, 24 master's awarded. *Degree requirements:* For master's, thesis optional. *Entrance requirements:* For master's, GRE General Test, minimum undergraduate GPA of 3.0 in last 60 hours of course work or graduate 3.5. Additional exam requirements/recommendations for international students: Required—TOEFL (minimum score 500 paper-based; 61 iBT), IELTS (minimum score 6). *Application deadline:* For fall admission, 2/1 for domestic and international students. Application fee: $30. *Expenses:* Tuition, state resident: full-time $7400; part-time $369.82 per credit. Tuition, nonresident: full-time $20,496; part-time $1042.81 per credit. *Financial support:* Career-related internships or fieldwork available. *Faculty research:* Fluency disorders, auditory processing, child language, adult language and cognition, multicultural speech and language issues. *Unit head:* Dr. Deena Louise Wener, Chair, 561-297-2258, Fax: 561-297-2268, E-mail: wener@fau.edu. *Application contact:* Dr. Eliah Watlington, Associate Dean, 561-296-8520, Fax: 261-297-2991, E-mail: ewatling@fau.edu.
Website: http://www.coe.fau.edu/academicdepartments/csd/

Florida International University, Nicole Wertheim College of Nursing and Health Sciences, Department of Communication Sciences and Disorders, Miami, FL 33199. Offers speech-language pathology (MS). *Accreditation:* ASHA. *Program availability:* Part-time, evening/weekend. *Faculty:* 4 full-time (3 women), 5 part-time/adjunct (4 women). *Students:* 88 full-time (84 women), 2 part-time (both women); includes 80 minority (3 Black or African American, non-Hispanic/Latino; 77 Hispanic/Latino), 2 international. Average age 25. 206 applicants, 30% accepted, 45 enrolled. In 2017, 43 master's awarded. *Degree requirements:* For master's, thesis optional. *Entrance requirements:* For master's, minimum undergraduate GPA of 3.0 in upper-level coursework; letter of intent; 2 letters of recommendation. Additional exam requirements/recommendations for international students: Required—TOEFL (minimum score 550 paper-based; 80 iBT). *Application deadline:* For fall admission, 2/1 for domestic and international students. Application fee: $30. Electronic applications accepted. *Expenses:* Tuition, state resident: full-time $8912; part-time $446 per credit hour. Tuition, nonresident: full-time $21,393; part-time $992 per credit hour. *Required fees:* $390; $195 per semester. *Financial support:* Institutionally sponsored loans, scholarships/grants, and unspecified assistantships available. Financial award application deadline: 3/1; financial award applicants required to submit FAFSA. *Unit head:* Dr. Monica Hough, Chair, 305-348-2710, E-mail: monica.hough@fiu.edu. *Application contact:* Nanett Rojas, Manager, Admissions Operations, 305-348-7464, Fax: 305-348-7441, E-mail: gradadm@fiu.edu.
Website: http://cnhs.fiu.edu/

Florida State University, The Graduate School, College of Communication and Information, School of Communication Science and Disorders, Tallahassee, FL 32306-1200. Offers MS, PhD. *Accreditation:* ASHA (one or more programs are accredited). *Program availability:* Part-time, blended/hybrid learning. *Faculty:* 5 full-time (1 woman), 4 part-time/adjunct (3 women). *Students:* 77 full-time (73 women), 133 part-time (130 women); includes 58 minority (8 Black or African American, non-Hispanic/Latino; 5 Asian, non-Hispanic/Latino; 29 Hispanic/Latino; 16 Two or more races, non-Hispanic/Latino). 357 applicants, 30% accepted, 66 enrolled. In 2017, 62 master's awarded. *Degree requirements:* For master's, comprehensive exam, thesis optional; for doctorate, thesis/dissertation. *Entrance requirements:* For master's, GRE General Test, minimum GPA of 3.0; for doctorate, GRE General Test, minimum GPA of 3.0 (undergraduate), 3.5 (graduate). Additional exam requirements/recommendations for international students: Required—TOEFL (minimum score 550 paper-based; 80 iBT). *Application deadline:* For fall admission, 1/15 for domestic and international students. Application fee: $30. Electronic applications accepted. *Financial support:* In 2017–18, 80 students received support, including 3 fellowships with full tuition reimbursements available (averaging $21,000 per year), 27 research assistantships with partial tuition reimbursements available (averaging $8,842 per year), 20 teaching assistantships with partial tuition reimbursements available (averaging $9,364 per year); career-related internships or fieldwork, Federal Work-Study, institutionally sponsored loans, scholarships/grants, tuition waivers (full and partial), and unspecified assistantships also available. Financial award application deadline: 1/1; financial award applicants required to submit FAFSA. *Faculty research:* Autism, neurogenic disorders, early intervention, child language disorders, literacy development and disorders, augmentative communication, dialectal influences on language development, speech development. *Unit head:* Dr. Hugh W. Catts, Director, 850-644-6566, Fax: 850-645-8994, E-mail: hugh.catts@cci.fsu.edu. *Application contact:* Jennifer Boss Kekelis, Assistant Director, Academic and Student Services, 850-644-2253, Fax: 850-644-8994, E-mail: jennifer.kekelis@cci.fsu.edu.
Website: http://commdisorders.cci.fsu.edu/Academic-Programs-Admissions/Doctoral-Program-Admissions/?_ga-1.91886682.1375024079.1443718977

Communication Disorders

Fontbonne University, Graduate Programs, St. Louis, MO 63105-3098. Offers accounting (MBA, MS); art (MA); art (K-12) (MAT); business (MBA); computer science (MS); deaf education (MA); early intervention in deaf education (MA); education (MA), including autism spectrum disorders, curriculum and instruction, diverse learners, early childhood education, reading, special education; elementary education (MAT); family and consumer sciences (MA), including multidisciplinary health communication studies; fine arts (MFA); instructional design and technology (MS); management and leadership (MM); middle school education (MAT); secondary education (MAT); special education (MAT); speech-language pathology (MS); supply chain management (MS); theatre (MA). *Program availability:* Part-time, evening/weekend, online learning. *Degree requirements:* For master's, comprehensive exam (for some programs), thesis (for some programs). *Entrance requirements:* Additional exam requirements/recommendations for international students: Required—TOEFL (minimum score 500 paper-based; 65 iBT). Electronic applications accepted.

Fort Hays State University, Graduate School, College of Health and Life Sciences, Department of Communication Sciences and Disorders, Hays, KS 67601-4099. Offers speech-language pathology (MS). *Accreditation:* ASHA. *Program availability:* Part-time. *Degree requirements:* For master's, comprehensive exam, thesis optional. *Entrance requirements:* For master's, GRE General Test. Additional exam requirements/recommendations for international students: Required—TOEFL (minimum score 550 paper-based). Electronic applications accepted. *Faculty research:* Aural rehabilitation, phonological and articulation skills, middle ear diseases, output capability of stereo cassette units, language development.

Gallaudet University, The Graduate School, Washington, DC 20002-3625. Offers American Sign Language/English bilingual early childhood deaf education: birth to 5 (Certificate); audiology (Au D); clinical psychology (PhD); deaf and hard of hearing infants, toddlers, and their families (Certificate); deaf education (MA, Ed S); deaf history (Certificate); deaf studies (Certificate); educating deaf students with disabilities (Certificate); education: teacher preparation (MA), including deaf education, early childhood education and deaf education, elementary education and deaf education, secondary education and deaf education; educational neuroscience (PhD); hearing, speech and language sciences (MS, PhD); international development (MA); interpretation (MA, PhD), including combined interpreting practice and research (MA), interpreting research (MA); linguistics (MA, PhD); mental health counseling (MA); peer mentoring (Certificate); public administration (MPA); school counseling (MA); school psychology (Psy S); sign language teaching (MA); social work (MSW); speech-language pathology (MS). *Program availability:* Part-time. Terminal master's awarded for partial completion of doctoral program. *Degree requirements:* For master's, comprehensive exam (for some programs), thesis optional; for doctorate, comprehensive exam, thesis/dissertation. *Entrance requirements:* For master's and doctorate, GRE General Test or MAT, letters of recommendation, interviews, goals statement, American Sign Language proficiency interview, written English competency. Additional exam requirements/recommendations for international students: Required—TOEFL. Electronic applications accepted. *Faculty research:* Signing math dictionaries, telecommunications access, cancer genetics, linguistics, visual language and visual learning, integrated quantum materials, deaf legal discourse, advance recruitment and retention in geosciences.

The George Washington University, Columbian College of Arts and Sciences, Department of Speech and Hearing Sciences, Washington, DC 20052. Offers speech-language pathology (MA). *Accreditation:* ASHA. *Faculty:* 13 full-time (8 women), 4 part-time/adjunct (1 woman). *Students:* 74 full-time (70 women), 37 part-time (33 women); includes 33 minority (9 Black or African American, non-Hispanic/Latino; 9 Asian, non-Hispanic/Latino; 12 Hispanic/Latino; 3 Two or more races, non-Hispanic/Latino). Average age 25. 413 applicants, 40% accepted, 62 enrolled. In 2017, 33 master's awarded. *Degree requirements:* For master's, comprehensive exam, thesis or alternative. *Entrance requirements:* For master's, GRE General Test, interview, minimum GPA of 3.0. Additional exam requirements/recommendations for international students: Required—TOEFL (minimum score 550 paper-based; 80 iBT). *Application deadline:* For fall admission, 2/1 priority date for domestic students, 1/15 priority date for international students. Applications are processed on a rolling basis. Application fee: $75. Electronic applications accepted. *Expenses: Tuition:* Full-time $28,800; part-time $1655 per credit hour. *Required fees:* $45; $2.75 per credit hour. *Financial support:* In 2017–18, 16 students received support. Fellowships with tuition reimbursements available, teaching assistantships with tuition reimbursements available, career-related internships or fieldwork, Federal Work-Study, and tuition waivers available. Financial award application deadline: 1/15. *Unit head:* James Mahshie, Chair, 202-994-7362, E-mail: jmahshie@gwu.edu. *Application contact:* Information Contact, 202-994-7362, Fax: 202-994-2589, E-mail: gwusphr@gwu.edu.
Website: http://speechhearing.columbian.gwu.edu/

Georgia Southern University–Armstrong Campus, College of Graduate Studies, Program in Communication Sciences and Disorders, Savannah, GA 31419-1997. Offers MS. *Accreditation:* ASHA. *Faculty:* 4 full-time (all women), 1 (woman) part-time/adjunct. *Students:* 40 full-time (all women); includes 3 minority (2 Black or African American, non-Hispanic/Latino; 1 Hispanic/Latino). Average age 25. In 2017, 19 master's awarded. *Degree requirements:* For master's, comprehensive exam, 400 client contact hours, PRAXIS II, minimum B average. *Entrance requirements:* For master's, GRE, minimum GPA of 3.0, recommendations, letter of interest. Additional exam requirements/recommendations for international students: Required—TOEFL (minimum score 523 paper-based; 70 iBT). *Application deadline:* For fall admission, 1/15 for domestic and international students. Applications are processed on a rolling basis. Application fee: $30. Electronic applications accepted. *Expenses:* Tuition, state resident: part-time $211 per credit hour. Tuition, nonresident: part-time $782 per credit hour. *Required fees:* $737 per semester. Tuition and fees vary according to course load, degree level, campus/location and program. *Financial support:* In 2017–18, 1 research assistantship with full tuition reimbursement (averaging $5,000 per year) was awarded; teaching assistantships, Federal Work-Study, scholarships/grants, and unspecified assistantships also available. Support available to part-time students. Financial award application deadline: 3/15; financial award applicants required to submit FAFSA. *Faculty research:* School age children, literacy, linguistic variation, social pragmatic issues, adult language impairment, service-learning, and clinical growth in CSD programs. *Unit head:* Maya Clark, Program Coordinator, 912-344-2969, Fax: 912-344-3439, E-mail: maya.clark@armstrong.edu. *Application contact:* McKenzie Peterman, Graduate Admissions Specialist, 912-478-5678, Fax: 912-478-0740, E-mail: mpeterman@georgiasouthern.edu.
Website: https://www.armstrong.edu/academic-departments/rs-communication-sciences-ms

Georgia State University, College of Education and Human Development, Department of Educational Psychology, Special Education, and Communication Disorders, Program in Communication Disorders, Atlanta, GA 30302-3083. Offers M Ed. *Accreditation:* ASHA; NCATE. *Entrance requirements:* For master's, GRE, minimum undergraduate GPA of 3.0. Additional exam requirements/recommendations for international students: Required—TOEFL (minimum score 550 paper-based; 79 iBT), IELTS (minimum score 6.5). Application fee: $50. Electronic applications accepted. *Expenses:* Tuition, state resident: full-time $7020. Tuition, nonresident: full-time $22,518. *Required fees:* $2128. Tuition and fees vary according to degree level and program. *Faculty research:* Dialect, aphasia, motor speech disorders, child language development, high risk populations. *Unit head:* Dr. Jacqueline Sue Laures-Gore, Program Coordinator, 404-413-8299, E-mail: jlaures@gsu.edu. *Application contact:* Sandy Vaughn, Senior Administrative Coordinator, 404-413-8318, Fax: 404-413-8043, E-mail: svaughn@gsu.edu.
Website: http://esc.education.gsu.edu/academics-and-admissions/communication-sciences-and-disorders/

Georgia State University, College of Education and Human Development, Department of Educational Psychology, Special Education, and Communication Disorders, Program in Education of Students with Exceptionalities, Atlanta, GA 30302-3083. Offers autism spectrum disorders (PhD); behavior disorders (PhD); communication disorders (PhD); early childhood special education (PhD); learning disabilities (PhD); mental retardation (PhD); orthopedic impairments (PhD); sensory impairments (PhD). *Accreditation:* NCATE. *Program availability:* Part-time, evening/weekend. Application fee: $50. Electronic applications accepted. *Expenses:* Tuition, state resident: full-time $7020. Tuition, nonresident: full-time $22,518. *Required fees:* $2128. Tuition and fees vary according to degree level and program. *Financial support:* Fellowships, research assistantships, scholarships/grants, health care benefits, and unspecified assistantships available. *Faculty research:* Academic and behavioral supports for students with emotional/behavior disorders; academic interventions for learning disabilities; cultural, socioeconomic, and linguistic diversity; language and literacy development, disorders, and instruction. *Unit head:* Dr. Kristine Jolivette, Associate Professor, 404-413-8040, Fax: 404-413-8043, E-mail: kjolivette@gsu.edu. *Application contact:* Sandy Vaughn, Senior Administrative Coordinator, 404-413-8318, Fax: 404-413-8043, E-mail: svaughn@gsu.edu.
Website: http://esc.education.gsu.edu/academics-and-admissions/special-education/education-of-students-with-exceptionalities-ph-d/

Georgia State University, College of Education and Human Development, Department of Educational Psychology, Special Education, and Communication Disorders, Program in Multiple and Severe Disabilities, Atlanta, GA 30302-3083. Offers early childhood special education (M Ed); special education adapted curriculum (intellectual disabilities) (M Ed); special education deaf education (M Ed); special education general and adapted curriculum (autism spectrum disorders) (M Ed); special education physical and health disabilities (orthopedic impairments) (M Ed). *Accreditation:* NCATE. *Program availability:* Part-time. *Entrance requirements:* For master's, GRE. Application fee: $50. Electronic applications accepted. *Expenses:* Tuition, state resident: full-time $7020. Tuition, nonresident: full-time $22,518. *Required fees:* $2128. Tuition and fees vary according to degree level and program. *Financial support:* Fellowships, research assistantships, teaching assistantships, scholarships/grants, health care benefits, and unspecified assistantships available. *Faculty research:* Literacy, language, behavioral supports. *Unit head:* Dr. Kathryn Wolff Heller, Professor, 404-413-8040, E-mail: kheller@gsu.edu. *Application contact:* Sandy Vaughn, Senior Administrative Coordinator, 404-413-8318, Fax: 404-413-8043, E-mail: svaughn@gsu.edu.

Governors State University, College of Health and Human Services, Program in Communication Disorders, University Park, IL 60484. Offers MHS. *Accreditation:* ASHA. *Program availability:* Part-time. *Faculty:* 5 full-time (4 women), 15 part-time/adjunct (all women). *Students:* 62 full-time (57 women), 44 part-time (all women); includes 27 minority (8 Black or African American, non-Hispanic/Latino; 3 Asian, non-Hispanic/Latino; 14 Hispanic/Latino; 2 Two or more races, non-Hispanic/Latino). Average age 28. 53 applicants, 100% accepted, 42 enrolled. In 2017, 38 master's awarded. *Application deadline:* For fall admission, 4/1 for domestic students. Applications are processed on a rolling basis. Application fee: $50. Electronic applications accepted. *Expenses:* Tuition, state resident: full-time $8472; part-time $353 per credit hour. Tuition, nonresident: full-time $16,944; part-time $706 per credit hour. *Required fees:* $1824; $76 per credit hour. $38 per term. Tuition and fees vary according to course load, degree level and program. *Financial support:* Application deadline: 5/1; applicants required to submit FAFSA. *Unit head:* Jessica Bonner, Interim Chair, Department of Communication Disorders, 708-534-5000 Ext. 4591, E-mail: jbonner@govst.edu.

The Graduate Center, City University of New York, Graduate Studies, Program in Audiology, New York, NY 10016-4039. Offers Au D. *Accreditation:* ASHA. *Students:* 41 full-time (all women); includes 10 minority (2 Black or African American, non-Hispanic/Latino; 3 Asian, non-Hispanic/Latino; 3 Hispanic/Latino; 2 Two or more races, non-Hispanic/Latino), 2 international. Average age 28. 101 applicants, 17% accepted, 9 enrolled. In 2017, 15 doctorates awarded. *Entrance requirements:* For doctorate, GRE General Test. Additional exam requirements/recommendations for international students: Required—TOEFL. *Application deadline:* For fall admission, 2/1 for domestic students. Application fee: $125. Electronic applications accepted. *Financial support:* In 2017–18, 14 students received support. Application deadline: 4/15. *Unit head:* John Preece, Executive Officer, 212-817-7980, E-mail: jpreece@gc.cuny.edu. *Application contact:* Les Gribben, Director of Admissions, 212-817-7470, Fax: 212-817-1624, E-mail: lgribben@gc.cuny.edu.
Website: http://web.gc.cuny.edu/ClinicalDoctoral/audio/

The Graduate Center, City University of New York, Graduate Studies, Program in Speech and Hearing Sciences, New York, NY 10016-4039. Offers PhD. *Accreditation:* ASHA. *Faculty:* 19 full-time (3 women). *Students:* 44 full-time (36 women); includes 9 minority (2 Black or African American, non-Hispanic/Latino; 4 Asian, non-Hispanic/Latino; 3 Hispanic/Latino), 15 international. Average age 37. 17 applicants, 59% accepted, 6 enrolled. In 2017, 8 doctorates awarded. *Degree requirements:* For doctorate, one foreign language, thesis/dissertation. *Entrance requirements:* For doctorate, GRE General Test. Additional exam requirements/recommendations for international students: Required—TOEFL. *Application deadline:* For fall admission, 1/1 priority date for domestic students; for spring admission, 10/15 for domestic students. Application fee: $125. Electronic applications accepted. *Financial support:* In 2017–18, 29 students received support, including 35 fellowships, 1 teaching assistantship; research assistantships, career-related internships or fieldwork, Federal Work-Study, institutionally sponsored loans, and tuition waivers (full and partial) also available. Financial award application deadline: 2/1; financial award applicants required to submit FAFSA. *Unit head:* Klara Marton, Executive Officer, 212-817-8802, Fax: 212-817-1537, E-mail: kmarton@gc.cuny.edu. *Application contact:* Les Gribben, Director of Admissions, 212-817-7470, Fax: 212-817-1624, E-mail: lgribben@gc.cuny.edu.

Grand Valley State University, College of Health Professions, Speech-Language Pathology Program, Allendale, MI 49401-9403. Offers MS. *Program availability:* Part-time. *Faculty:* 8 full-time (7 women), 2 part-time/adjunct (both women). *Students:* 76 full-time (64 women), 1 (woman) part-time; includes 6 minority (1 Black or African American, non-Hispanic/Latino; 4 Hispanic/Latino; 1 Two or more races, non-Hispanic/Latino). Average age 25. 197 applicants, 19% accepted, 29 enrolled. In 2017, 42 master's awarded. *Degree requirements:* For master's, thesis optional, internship. *Entrance requirements:* For master's, GRE, minimum GPA of 3.0, professional vita or resume, 3 letters of reference, interview. Additional exam requirements/recommendations for international students: Required—TOEFL (minimum iBT score of 80), IELTS (6.5), or Michigan English Language Assessment Battery (77). *Application deadline:* For fall admission, 1/15 for domestic and international students. Applications are processed on a rolling basis. Application fee: $30. Electronic applications accepted. *Expenses:* $686 per credit hour. *Financial support:* In 2017–18, 5 students received support, including 5 fellowships; unspecified assistantships also available. *Unit head:* Dr. Dan Halling, Department Chair, 616-331-5604, Fax: 616-331-5556, E-mail: halling@gvsu.edu. *Application contact:* Dr. Courtney Karasinski, Graduate Program Director, 616-331-5670, Fax: 616-331-5544, E-mail: karasinc@gvsu.edu.

Hampton University, School of Science, Department of Communicative Sciences and Disorders, Hampton, VA 23668. Offers speech-language pathology (MA). *Accreditation:* ASHA. *Program availability:* Part-time, online learning. *Students:* 55 full-time (all women), 15 part-time (13 women); includes 45 minority (38 Black or African American, non-Hispanic/Latino; 2 American Indian or Alaska Native, non-Hispanic/Latino; 2 Asian, non-Hispanic/Latino; 3 Hispanic/Latino), 1 international. Average age 26. 90 applicants, 23% accepted, 11 enrolled. In 2017, 21 master's awarded. *Degree requirements:* For master's, comprehensive exam. *Entrance requirements:* For master's, GRE General Test. Additional exam requirements/recommendations for international students: Required—TOEFL (minimum score 525 paper-based) or IELTS (6.5). *Application deadline:* For fall admission, 6/1 priority date for domestic students, 4/1 priority date for international students; for spring admission, 11/1 for domestic and international students. Applications are processed on a rolling basis. Application fee: $35. Electronic applications accepted. *Expenses: Tuition:* Full-time $22,630; part-time $575 per semester hour. *Required fees:* $70. Tuition and fees vary according to program. *Financial support:* Fellowships, research assistantships, teaching assistantships, career-related internships or fieldwork, Federal Work-Study, institutionally sponsored loans, and scholarships/grants available. Support available to part-time students. Financial award application deadline: 6/30; financial award applicants required to submit FAFSA. *Faculty research:* Language development, the scholarship of teaching and learning, post-stroke care, multicultural issues, family intervention. *Unit head:* Dr. Dorian Lee-Wilkerson, Chairperson, Department of Communicative Sciences and Disorders, 757-727-5435, Fax: 757-727-5765, E-mail: dorian.wilkerson@hamptonu.edu. *Application contact:* Dr. Tamara Freeman-Nichols, Graduate Coordinator, Department of Communicative Sciences and Disorders, 757-727-5435, Fax: 757-727-5765, E-mail: tamara.freeman@hamptonu.edu.
Website: http://science.hamptonu.edu/csad/

Harding University, College of Allied Health, Program in Communication Sciences and Disorders, Searcy, AR 72149-0001. Offers MS. *Accreditation:* ASHA. *Faculty:* 11 full-time (9 women), 2 part-time/adjunct (1 woman). *Students:* 40 full-time (all women), 1 (woman) part-time; includes 3 minority (2 Black or African American, non-Hispanic/Latino; 1 Hispanic/Latino). Average age 24. 92 applicants, 22% accepted, 18 enrolled. In 2017, 18 master's awarded. *Application deadline:* For fall admission, 3/1 for domestic and international students. Application fee: $40. Tuition and fees vary according to course load, degree level, campus/location and program. *Financial support:* In 2017–18, 6 students received support. Application deadline: 3/1; applicants required to submit FAFSA. *Unit head:* Dr. Dan Tullos, Professor and Chair, 501-279-4633, Fax: 501-279-4325, E-mail: tullos@harding.edu. *Application contact:* Martha Vendetti, Administrative Assistant, 501-279-4335, Fax: 501-279-5192, E-mail: mvendett@harding.edu.
Website: http://www.harding.edu/academics/colleges-departments/allied-health/communication-sciences-disorders/graduate-program

Hofstra University, School of Education, Programs in Teacher Education, Hempstead, NY 11549. Offers bilingual education (MA); bilingual extension (Advanced Certificate), including education/speech language pathology, intensive teacher institute; business education (MS Ed); curriculum studies (MS Ed); early childhood and childhood education (MS Ed); early childhood education (MA, MS Ed); educational technology (Advanced Certificate); elementary education (MA, MS Ed), including science, technology, engineering, and mathematics (STEM) (MA); English education (MS Ed); family and consumer science (MS Ed); fine arts and music education (Advanced Certificate); fine arts education (MS Ed); foreign language and TESOL (MS Ed); foreign language education (MA, MS Ed), including Arabic (MS Ed), biology, chemistry, Chinese (MS Ed), earth science, French, German, Italian (MS Ed), Mandarin (MS Ed), physics, Russian, Spanish; foundations of education (Advanced Certificate), including grades 5-6, grades 7-9; languages other than English and teaching English as a second language (MA); learning and teaching (Ed D), including applied linguistics, art education, arts and humanities, early childhood education, English education, human development, math education, math, science, and technology, multicultural education, physical education, science education, social studies education, special education; mathematics education (MA, MS Ed); music education (MA, MS Ed); science education (MA), including biology (MA, MS Ed), chemistry (MA, MS Ed), earth science (MA, MS Ed), physics (MA, MS Ed); secondary education (Advanced Certificate); social studies education (MA, MS Ed); teaching languages other than English and TESOL (MS Ed); technology for learning (MA); TESOL (MS Ed, Advanced Certificate); TESOL with specialization in STEM (MA); work based learning extension (Advanced Certificate). *Program availability:* Part-time, evening/weekend, blended/hybrid learning. *Students:* 119 full-time (83 women), 124 part-time (90 women); includes 54 minority (15 Black or African American, non-Hispanic/Latino; 9 Asian, non-Hispanic/Latino; 29 Hispanic/Latino; 1 Native Hawaiian or other Pacific Islander, non-Hispanic/Latino), 12 international. Average age 29. 205 applicants, 88% accepted, 93 enrolled. In 2017, 103 master's, 4 doctorates, 32 other advanced degrees awarded. *Degree requirements:* For master's, comprehensive exam, thesis (for some programs), exit project, student teaching, fieldwork, electronic portfolio, curriculum project, minimum GPA of 3.0; for doctorate, thesis/dissertation; for Advanced Certificate, 3 foreign languages, comprehensive exam (for some programs), thesis project. *Entrance requirements:* For master's, GRE, 2 letters of recommendation, portfolio, teacher certification (MA), interview, essay; for doctorate, GMAT, GRE, LSAT, or MAT; for Advanced Certificate, 2 letters of recommendation, essay, interview and/or portfolio, teaching certificate. Additional exam requirements/recommendations for international students: Required—TOEFL (minimum score 550 paper-based; 80 iBT). *Application deadline:* Applications are processed on a rolling basis. Application fee: $75. Electronic applications accepted. *Expenses: Tuition:* Full-time $1292. *Required fees:* $970. Tuition and fees vary according to program. *Financial support:* In 2017–18, 112 students received support, including 56 fellowships with full and partial tuition reimbursements available (averaging $4,998 per year), 2 research assistantships with full and partial tuition reimbursements available (averaging $8,753 per year); career-related internships or fieldwork, Federal Work-Study, institutionally sponsored loans, scholarships/grants, traineeships, tuition waivers (full and partial), and unspecified assistantships also available. Support available to part-time students. Financial award applicants required to submit FAFSA. *Faculty research:* Educational interventions that foster critical-thinking skills; teachers' attitudes about professional development; threats to teacher quality. *Unit head:* Dr. Eustace Thompson, Chairperson, 516-463-5749, Fax: 516-463-6275, E-mail: eustace.g.thompson@hofstra.edu. *Application contact:* Sunil Samuel, Assistant Vice President of Admissions, 516-463-4723, Fax: 516-463-4664, E-mail: graduateadmission@hofstra.edu.
Website: http://www.hofstra.edu/education/

Hofstra University, School of Health Professions and Human Services, Programs in Health, Hempstead, NY 11549. Offers foundations of public health (Advanced Certificate); health administration (MHA); health informatics (MS); occupational therapy (MS); public health (MPH); security and privacy in health information systems (Advanced Certificate); sports science (MS), including exercise physiology, strength and conditioning; teacher of students with speech-language disabilities (Advanced Certificate). *Program availability:* Part-time, evening/weekend. *Students:* 257 full-time (176 women), 128 part-time (95 women); includes 197 minority (76 Black or African American, non-Hispanic/Latino; 2 American Indian or Alaska Native, non-Hispanic/Latino; 70 Asian, non-Hispanic/Latino; 42 Hispanic/Latino; 6 Native Hawaiian or other Pacific Islander, non-Hispanic/Latino; 1 Two or more races, non-Hispanic/Latino), 25 international. Average age 28. 620 applicants, 50% accepted, 151 enrolled. In 2017, 87 master's awarded. *Degree requirements:* For master's, internship, minimum GPA of 3.0. *Entrance requirements:* For master's, interview, 2 letters of recommendation, essay, resume. Additional exam requirements/recommendations for international students: Required—TOEFL (minimum score 550 paper-based; 80 iBT). *Application deadline:* Applications are processed on a rolling basis. Application fee: $75. Electronic applications accepted. *Expenses: Tuition:* Full-time $1292. *Required fees:* $970. Tuition and fees vary according to program. *Financial support:* In 2017–18, 148 students received support, including 88 fellowships with full and partial tuition reimbursements available (averaging $3,026 per year), 4 research assistantships with full and partial tuition reimbursements available (averaging $5,619 per year); career-related internships or fieldwork, Federal Work-Study, institutionally sponsored loans, scholarships/grants, traineeships, tuition waivers (full and partial), and unspecified assistantships also available. Support available to part-time students. Financial award applicants required to submit FAFSA. *Faculty research:* Hand and upper extremity rehabilitation; orthotic fabrication; palliative care; neurorehabilitation; public health and health inequities, particularly in the American suburbs and minority communities; obesity; physical activity; social justice in physical education pedagogy. *Unit head:* Dr. Corinne Kyriacou, Chairperson, 516-463-4553, E-mail: corinne.m.kyriacou@hofstra.edu. *Application contact:* Sunil Samuel, Assistant Vice President of Admissions, 516-463-4723, Fax: 516-463-4664, E-mail: graduateadmission@hofstra.edu.
Website: http://www.hofstra.edu/academics/colleges/healthscienceshumanservices/

Hofstra University, School of Health Professions and Human Services, Programs in Speech Language Pathology and Audiology, Hempstead, NY 11549. Offers audiology (Au D); speech-language pathology (MA). *Accreditation:* ASHA (one or more programs are accredited). *Students:* 105 full-time (104 women), 6 part-time (all women); includes 17 minority (1 Black or African American, non-Hispanic/Latino; 3 Asian, non-Hispanic/Latino; 12 Hispanic/Latino; 1 Native Hawaiian or other Pacific Islander, non-Hispanic/Latino). Average age 24. 410 applicants, 43% accepted, 46 enrolled. In 2017, 50 master's, 5 doctorates awarded. *Degree requirements:* For master's, comprehensive exam, thesis optional; for doctorate, comprehensive exam, thesis/dissertation. *Entrance requirements:* For master's, GRE, 3 letters of recommendation, essay; for doctorate, GRE or master's degree, 3 letters of recommendation, essay. Additional exam requirements/recommendations for international students: Required—TOEFL (minimum score 550 paper-based; 80 iBT). *Application deadline:* For fall admission, 1/15 for domestic and international students. Application fee: $75. Electronic applications accepted. *Expenses: Tuition:* Full-time $1292. *Required fees:* $970. Tuition and fees vary according to program. *Financial support:* In 2017–18, 39 students received support, including 34 fellowships with full and partial tuition reimbursements available (averaging $4,767 per year), 3 research assistantships with full and partial tuition reimbursements available (averaging $8,316 per year); career-related internships or fieldwork, Federal Work-Study, institutionally sponsored loans, scholarships/grants, traineeships, tuition waivers (full and partial), and unspecified assistantships also available. Support available to part-time students. Financial award applicants required to submit FAFSA. *Faculty research:* Tinnitus, hyperacusis, amplification, and hearing conservation; stuttering; diagnostic, geriatric, and rehabilitation audiology; language/literacy development and disorders; language development of children adopted internationally. *Unit head:* Dr. Jenny Roberts, Chairperson, 516-463-5514, E-mail: jennifer.a.roberts@hofstra.edu. *Application contact:* Sunil Samuel, Assistant Vice President of Admissions, 516-463-4723, Fax: 516-463-4664, E-mail: graduateadmission@hofstra.edu.
Website: http://www.hofstra.edu/academics/colleges/healthscienceshumanservices/

Howard University, Cathy Hughes School of Communications, Department of Communication Sciences and Disorders, Washington, DC 20059-0002. Offers communication sciences (PhD); speech pathology (MS). Offered through the Graduate School of Arts and Sciences. *Accreditation:* ASHA (one or more programs are accredited). *Program availability:* Part-time. *Degree requirements:* For master's, comprehensive exam, thesis or alternative; for doctorate, one foreign language, comprehensive exam, thesis/dissertation. *Entrance requirements:* For master's, GRE General Test, minimum GPA of 3.2; for doctorate, GRE General Test, minimum GPA of 3.5. Additional exam requirements/recommendations for international students: Required—TOEFL. Electronic applications accepted. *Faculty research:* Multiculturalism, augmentative communication, adult neurological disorders, child language disorders.

Hunter College of the City University of New York, Graduate School, School of Health Professions, Department of Speech-Language Pathology and Audiology, New York, NY 10065-5085. Offers speech-language pathology (MS). *Accreditation:* ASHA. *Program availability:* Part-time. *Degree requirements:* For master's, comprehensive exam (for some programs), NTE, research project. *Entrance requirements:* For master's, GRE, letters of reference. Additional exam requirements/recommendations for international students: Required—TOEFL. *Faculty research:* Aging and communication disorders, fluency, speech science, diagnostic audiology, amplification.

Idaho State University, Office of Graduate Studies, School of Rehabilitation and Communication Sciences, Department of Communication Sciences and Disorders, Pocatello, ID 83209-8116. Offers audiology (Au D); speech language pathology (MS). *Accreditation:* ASHA (one or more programs are accredited). *Program availability:* Part-time. *Degree requirements:* For master's, thesis optional, written and oral comprehensive exams; for doctorate, comprehensive exam, thesis/dissertation optional, externship, 1 year full time clinical practicum, 3rd year spent in Boise. *Entrance requirements:* For master's, GRE General Test, minimum GPA of 3.0, 3 letters of recommendation; for doctorate, GRE General Test (at least 2 scores minimum 40th percentile), minimum GPA of 3.0, 3 letters of recommendation, bachelor's degree. Additional exam requirements/recommendations for international students: Required—TOEFL (minimum score 600 paper-based; 80 iBT). Electronic applications accepted. *Faculty research:* Neurogenic disorders, central auditory processing disorders, vestibular disorders, cochlear implants, language disorders, professional burnout, swallowing disorders.

Illinois State University, Graduate School, College of Arts and Sciences, Department of Communication Sciences and Disorders, Normal, IL 61790. Offers MA, MS. *Accreditation:* ASHA. *Degree requirements:* For master's, thesis or alternative, 1 term of residency, 2 practica. *Entrance requirements:* For master's, GRE General Test, minimum GPA of 3.0 in last 60 hours.

Indiana State University, College of Graduate and Professional Studies, Bayh College of Education, Department of Communication Disorders and Counseling, School, and Educational Psychology, Terre Haute, IN 47809. Offers clinical mental health counseling (MS); communication disorders (MS); school counseling (M Ed); school psychology (PhD, Ed S); MA/MS. *Accreditation:* ACA; ASHA; NCATE. *Program availability:* Part-time, evening/weekend. *Degree requirements:* For master's, thesis optional; for doctorate, thesis/dissertation, research tools proficiency tests. *Entrance requirements:* For master's, GRE General Test or MAT, minimum undergraduate GPA of 2.75; for doctorate, GRE General Test, master's degree, minimum undergraduate GPA of 3.5. Electronic applications accepted. *Faculty research:* Vocational development supervision.

Indiana University Bloomington, University Graduate School, College of Arts and Sciences, Department of Speech and Hearing Sciences, Clinical Program in Audiology, Bloomington, IN 47405-7000. Offers Au D. *Accreditation:* ASHA.

Indiana University Bloomington, University Graduate School, College of Arts and Sciences, Department of Speech and Hearing Sciences, Program in Speech and Hearing Sciences, Bloomington, IN 47405-7000. Offers auditory sciences (Au D, PhD); language sciences (PhD); speech and voice sciences (PhD); speech-language pathology (MA). *Accreditation:* ASHA.

Indiana University of Pennsylvania, School of Graduate Studies and Research, College of Education and Communications, Department of Communication Disorders, Special Education, and Disability Services, Program in Speech-Language Pathology, Indiana, PA 15705. Offers MS. *Accreditation:* ASHA. *Program availability:* Part-time. *Faculty:* 10 full-time (8 women), 3 part-time/adjunct (2 women). *Students:* 42 full-time (40 women), 2 part-time (both women). Average age 23. 93 applicants, 25% accepted, 22 enrolled. In 2017, 23 master's awarded. *Degree requirements:* For master's, comprehensive exam, thesis optional. *Entrance requirements:* For master's, GRE, 2 letters of recommendation, minimum undergraduate GPA of 3.0. Additional exam requirements/recommendations for international students: Required—TOEFL. *Application deadline:* For fall admission, 2/15 priority date for domestic students. Application fee: $50. Electronic applications accepted. *Expenses:* Contact institution. *Financial support:* In 2017–18, 12 research assistantships with tuition reimbursements (averaging $2,607 per year) were awarded; fellowships with partial tuition reimbursements, career-related internships or fieldwork, Federal Work-Study, scholarships/grants, and unspecified assistantships also available. Support available to part-time students. Financial award application deadline: 4/15; financial award applicants required to submit FAFSA. *Unit head:* Dr. Lisa Hammett Price, Professor/ Program Director, 724-357-5687, E-mail: lisa.price@iup.edu.
Website: http://www.iup.edu/grad/speechlanguage/default.aspx

Iona College, School of Arts and Science, Department of Speech Communication Studies, New Rochelle, NY 10801-1890. Offers communication sciences and disorders (MA). *Faculty:* 6 full-time (all women). *Students:* 47 full-time (45 women); includes 13 minority (1 Black or African American, non-Hispanic/Latino; 2 Asian, non-Hispanic/ Latino; 8 Hispanic/Latino; 2 Native Hawaiian or other Pacific Islander, non-Hispanic/ Latino). Average age 24. 160 applicants, 60% accepted, 23 enrolled. In 2017, 22 master's awarded. *Degree requirements:* For master's, comprehensive exam. *Entrance requirements:* For master's, GRE, 3 letters of recommendation, personal statement, interview. Additional exam requirements/recommendations for international students: Required—TOEFL (minimum score 550 paper-based; 80 iBT). *Application deadline:* For fall admission, 2/1 priority date for domestic students, 2/1 for international students. Application fee: $50. *Expenses:* Contact institution. *Financial support:* In 2017–18, 12 students received support. Application deadline: 4/15; applicants required to submit FAFSA. *Faculty research:* Child language development, adult language disorders, social language disorders, neuropathology. *Unit head:* Diane Ferrero-Paluzzi, PhD, Department Chair, Speech Communications Studies, 914-633-2112, Fax: 914-633-2023, E-mail: dferrero-paluzzi@iona.edu. *Application contact:* Katelyn Brunck, Graduate Admissions, 914-633-2420, Fax: 914-633-2277, E-mail: kbrunck@iona.edu.

Ithaca College, School of Health Sciences and Human Performance, Program in Speech-Language Pathology and Audiology, Ithaca, NY 14850. Offers speech-language pathology (MS); speech-language pathology with teacher certification (MS). *Accreditation:* ASHA. *Program availability:* Part-time. *Faculty:* 12 full-time (10 women). *Students:* 39 full-time (38 women); includes 6 minority (1 Black or African American, non-Hispanic/Latino; 1 Asian, non-Hispanic/Latino; 1 Hispanic/Latino; 3 Two or more races, non-Hispanic/Latino). Average age 23. 165 applicants, 47% accepted, 17 enrolled. In 2017, 25 master's awarded. *Degree requirements:* For master's, comprehensive exam, thesis optional, clinical experience. *Entrance requirements:* For master's, GRE General Test. Additional exam requirements/recommendations for international students: Required—TOEFL (minimum score 550 paper-based; 80 iBT). *Application deadline:* For fall admission, 2/1 for domestic and international students. Applications are processed on a rolling basis. Application fee: $40. Electronic applications accepted. *Expenses:* Contact institution. *Financial support:* In 2017–18, 23 students received support, including 23 research assistantships (averaging $12,085 per year); career-related internships or fieldwork, Federal Work-Study, scholarships/grants, and unspecified assistantships also available. Support available to part-time students. Financial award application deadline: 2/1; financial award applicants required to submit FAFSA. *Unit head:* Dr. Mary Pitti, Chair, 607-274-1765, E-mail: mpitti@ithaca.edu. *Application contact:* Nicole Eversley Bradwell, Director, Office of Admission, 607-274-3124, Fax: 607-274-1263, E-mail: admission@ithaca.edu.
Website: http://www.ithaca.edu/gradprograms/slpa

Jackson State University, Graduate School, School of Public Health, Department of Communicative Disorders, Jackson, MS 39217. Offers MS. *Accreditation:* ASHA. *Degree requirements:* For master's, comprehensive exam. *Entrance requirements:* For master's, GRE General Test. Additional exam requirements/recommendations for international students: Required—TOEFL (minimum score 520 paper-based; 67 iBT).

Jacksonville University, Brooks Rehabilitation College of Healthcare Sciences, School of Applied Health Sciences, Program in Speech-Language Pathology, Jacksonville, FL 32211. Offers MS. *Program availability:* Part-time. *Faculty:* 6 full-time (5 women), 10 part-time/adjunct (6 women). *Students:* 68 full-time (64 women); includes 20 minority (7 Black or African American, non-Hispanic/Latino; 4 Asian, non-Hispanic/Latino; 9 Hispanic/Latino). Average age 25. 51 applicants, 100% accepted, 34 enrolled. In 2017, 33 master's awarded. *Entrance requirements:* For master's, GRE (quantitative, verbal and writing components), baccalaureate degree from accredited college or university with minimum GPA of 3.0; official transcripts; essay on personal professional goals (minimum 1000 words); resume (education, work experience); 3 letters of recommendation; interview. Additional exam requirements/recommendations for international students: Required—TOEFL (minimum score 650 paper-based; 114 iBT), IELTS (minimum score 8). *Application deadline:* For fall admission, 2/1 for domestic and international students. Applications are processed on a rolling basis. Application fee: $50. Electronic applications accepted. *Expenses:* $895 per credit hour. *Financial support:* Federal Work-Study, institutionally sponsored loans, scholarships/grants, and health care benefits available. Support available to part-time students. Financial award application deadline: 3/15; financial award applicants required to submit FAFSA. *Faculty research:* PTSD, biomechanics, aphasia, autism, pediatric bilingual-multicultural speech disorders. *Unit head:* Dr. Judith M. Wingate, Department Chair and Associate Professor of Communication Sciences and Disorders, E-mail: jwingat2@ju.edu. *Application contact:* Ashlea Rieser, Assistant Director of Enrollment and Advising, 904-256-8934, E-mail: arieser0@ju.edu.
Website: https://www.ju.edu/communicationsciences/programs/ms-speech-language-pathology.php

James Madison University, The Graduate School, College of Health and Behavioral Studies, Program in Audiology, Harrisonburg, VA 22801. Offers Au D. *Accreditation:* ASHA. *Program availability:* Part-time. *Students:* 23 full-time (19 women); includes 3 minority (1 Black or African American, non-Hispanic/Latino; 1 Hispanic/Latino; 1 Two or more races, non-Hispanic/Latino). Average age 30. In 2017, 6 doctorates awarded. Application fee: $55. Electronic applications accepted. *Expenses:* Tuition, state resident: full-time $10,512; part-time $438 per credit hour. Tuition, nonresident: full-time $28,358; part-time $1162 per credit hour. *Required fees:* $1128. *Financial support:* In 2017–18, 18 students received support, including 1 teaching assistantship (averaging $7,000 per year); fellowships, Federal Work-Study, and 6 assistantships (averaging $7911), 12 doctoral assistantships (stipend varies) also available. Financial award application deadline: 3/1; financial award applicants required to submit FAFSA. *Unit head:* Dr. Cynthia R. O'Donoghue, Department Head, 540-568-6440, E-mail: odonogcr@jmu.edu. *Application contact:* Lynette D. Michael, Director of Graduate Admissions, 540-568-6131 Ext. 6395, Fax: 540-568-7860, E-mail: michaeld@jmu.edu.
Website: http://www.csd.jmu.edu/aud/

James Madison University, The Graduate School, College of Health and Behavioral Studies, Program in Communication Sciences and Disorders, Harrisonburg, VA 22807. Offers PhD. *Program availability:* Part-time. *Students:* 5 full-time (all women), 2 part-time (both women), 2 international. Average age 30. In 2017, 1 doctorate awarded. *Application deadline:* For fall admission, 7/1 priority date for domestic students. Applications are processed on a rolling basis. Application fee: $55. *Expenses:* Tuition, state resident: full-time $10,512; part-time $438 per credit hour. Tuition, nonresident: full-time $28,358; part-time $1162 per credit hour. *Required fees:* $1128. *Financial support:* In 2017–18, 5 students received support. Teaching assistantships, Federal Work-Study, unspecified assistantships, and 5 doctoral assistantships (stipend varies) available. Financial award application deadline: 3/1; financial award applicants required to submit FAFSA. *Unit head:* Dr. Sharon E. Lovell, Dean, 540-568-2705, Fax: 540-568-2747, E-mail: lovellse@jmu.edu. *Application contact:* Lynette D. Michael, Director of Graduate Admissions, 540-568-6131 Ext. 6395, Fax: 540-568-7860, E-mail: michaeld@jmu.edu.

James Madison University, The Graduate School, College of Health and Behavioral Studies, Program in Speech-Language Pathology, Harrisonburg, VA 22801. Offers MS. *Accreditation:* ASHA. *Program availability:* Part-time. *Students:* 57 full-time (55 women), 38 part-time (all women); includes 11 minority (1 Black or African American, non-Hispanic/Latino; 5 Asian, non-Hispanic/Latino; 4 Hispanic/Latino; 1 Two or more races, non-Hispanic/Latino). Average age 30. In 2017, 44 master's awarded. Application fee: $55. Electronic applications accepted. *Expenses:* Tuition, state resident: full-time $10,512; part-time $438 per credit hour. Tuition, nonresident: full-time $28,358; part-time $1162 per credit hour. *Required fees:* $1128. *Financial support:* In 2017–18, 20 students received support. Fellowships, Federal Work-Study, and 20 assistantships (averaging $7911) available. Financial award application deadline: 3/1; financial award applicants required to submit FAFSA. *Unit head:* Dr. Cynthia R. O'Donoghue, Department Head, 540-568-6440, E-mail: odonogcr@jmu.edu. *Application contact:* Lynette D. Michael, Director of Graduate Admissions, 540-568-6131 Ext. 6395, Fax: 540-568-7860, E-mail: michaeld@jmu.edu.
Website: http://www.csd.jmu.edu/MS-SLP/

Kansas State University, Graduate School, College of Human Ecology, School of Family Studies and Human Services, Manhattan, KS 66506-1403. Offers applied family sciences (MS); communication sciences and disorders (MS); conflict resolution (Graduate Certificate); couple and family therapy (MS); early childhood education (MS); family and community service (MS); life-span human development (MS); personal financial planning (MS, PhD, Graduate Certificate); youth development (MS, Graduate Certificate). *Accreditation:* AAMFT/COAMFTE; ASHA. *Program availability:* Part-time, online learning. *Degree requirements:* For master's, comprehensive exam (for some programs), thesis optional. *Entrance requirements:* For master's, GRE, minimum GPA of 3.0 in last 2 years (60 semester hours) of undergraduate study; for doctorate, GRE. Additional exam requirements/recommendations for international students: Required—TOEFL (minimum score 600 paper-based). Electronic applications accepted. *Faculty research:* Health and security of military families, training in and evaluation of professional human services (marriage and couple therapy, family life education, treatment of speech and swallowing disorders, financial therapy), disorders of communication and swallowing, family and relationship development and health, financial decision-making.

Kean University, Nathan Weiss Graduate College, Doctorate Program in Speech-Language Pathology, Union, NJ 07083. Offers SLPD. *Faculty:* 12 full-time (9 women). *Students:* 11 part-time (all women); includes 6 minority (3 Black or African American, non-Hispanic/Latino; 2 Asian, non-Hispanic/Latino; 1 Hispanic/Latino). Average age 40. 25 applicants, 44% accepted, 11 enrolled. *Entrance requirements:* For doctorate, master's degree in speech-language pathology or its equivalent from accredited institution of higher education; minimum master's GPA of 3.2; curriculum vitae; three letters of recommendation; statement of goals and research career interests; personal interview. Additional exam requirements/recommendations for international students: Required—TOEFL (minimum score 550 paper-based; 79 iBT), IELTS (minimum score 6.5). *Application deadline:* For fall admission, 4/15 for domestic students. Application fee: $75. Electronic applications accepted. *Expenses:* Contact institution. *Financial support:* Scholarships/grants and unspecified assistantships available. Financial award applicants required to submit FAFSA. *Unit head:* Dr. Mahchid Namazi, Coordinator, 908-737-5804, E-mail: mnamazi@kean.edu. *Application contact:* Helen Ramirez, Associate Director, Graduate Admissions, 908-737-7100, E-mail: gradadmissions@kean.edu.
Website: https://www.kean.edu/academics/programs/speech-language-pathology-doctorate-slpd

Kean University, Nathan Weiss Graduate College, Program in Speech-Language Pathology, Union, NJ 07083. Offers MA. *Accreditation:* ASHA. *Program availability:* Part-time. *Faculty:* 12 full-time (9 women). *Students:* 94 full-time (88 women), 9 part-time (8 women); includes 29 minority (3 Black or African American, non-Hispanic/Latino; 6 Asian, non-Hispanic/Latino; 18 Hispanic/Latino; 2 Two or more races, non-Hispanic/ Latino), 1 international. Average age 25. 257 applicants, 24% accepted, 42 enrolled. In 2017, 45 master's awarded. *Degree requirements:* For master's, comprehensive exam, thesis, six credits of research, minimum of 400 supervised clinical hours, PRAXIS. *Entrance requirements:* For master's, GRE General Test, minimum cumulative GPA of 3.2, official transcripts from all institutions attended, personal statement, three letters of recommendation, professional resume/curriculum vitae. Additional exam requirements/ recommendations for international students: Required—TOEFL (minimum score 550 paper-based; 79 iBT), IELTS (minimum score 6.5). *Application deadline:* For fall admission, 2/15 for domestic and international students; for summer admission, 1/15 for domestic and international students. Application fee: $75. Electronic applications accepted. *Expenses:* Contact institution. *Financial support:* Scholarships/grants and unspecified assistantships available. Financial award applicants required to submit FAFSA. *Unit head:* Dr. JoAnne Cascia, Program Coordinator, 908-737-5822, E-mail: gradcoordinatorcdd@kean.edu. *Application contact:* Helen Ramirez, Associate Director, Graduate Admissions, 908-737-7137, E-mail: grad-adm@kean.edu.
Website: http://grad.kean.edu/slp

Kent State University, College of Education, Health and Human Services, School of Health Sciences, Program in Audiology, Kent, OH 44242-0001. Offers Au D, PhD. *Entrance requirements:* For doctorate, GRE, 3 letters of reference, goals statement. Additional exam requirements/recommendations for international students: Required—TOEFL (minimum score 550 paper-based; 80 iBT). *Expenses:* Tuition, state resident: full-time $11,310; part-time $515 per credit hour. Tuition, nonresident: full-time $20,396; part-time $928 per credit hour. *International tuition:* $18,544 full-time.

Kent State University, College of Education, Health and Human Services, School of Health Sciences, Program in Speech Language Pathology, Kent, OH 44242-0001. Offers MA, PhD. *Accreditation:* ASHA. *Degree requirements:* For doctorate, comprehensive exam, thesis/dissertation. *Entrance requirements:* For master's and doctorate, GRE, 3 letters of reference, goals statement. Additional exam requirements/recommendations for international students: Required—TOEFL (minimum score 550 paper-based; 80 iBT). *Expenses:* Tuition, state resident: full-time $11,310; part-time $515 per credit hour. Tuition, nonresident: full-time $20,396; part-time $928 per credit hour. *International tuition:* $18,544 full-time.

Kent State University, College of Education, Health and Human Services, School of Lifespan Development and Educational Sciences, Program in Special Education, Kent, OH 44242-0001. Offers deaf education (M Ed); early childhood education (M Ed); educational interpreter K-12 (M Ed); general special education (M Ed); mild/moderate intervention (M Ed); special education (PhD, Ed S); transition to work (M Ed). *Accreditation:* NCATE. *Degree requirements:* For doctorate, comprehensive exam, thesis/dissertation. *Entrance requirements:* For master's, minimum undergraduate GPA of 2.75, moral character form, 2 letters of reference, goals statement; for doctorate and Ed S, GRE General Test, goals statement, 2 letters of reference, interview, resume. Additional exam requirements/recommendations for international students: Required—TOEFL (minimum score 550 paper-based; 80 iBT). Electronic applications accepted. *Expenses:* Tuition, state resident: full-time $11,310; part-time $515 per credit hour. Tuition, nonresident: full-time $20,396; part-time $928 per credit hour. *International tuition:* $18,544 full-time. *Faculty research:* Social/emotional needs of gifted, inclusion transition services, early intervention/ecobehavioral assessments, applied behavioral analysis.

Lamar University, College of Graduate Studies, College of Fine Arts and Communication, Department of Speech and Hearing Science, Beaumont, TX 77701. Offers audiology (Au D); speech language pathology (MS). *Accreditation:* ASHA. *Faculty:* 13 full-time (7 women), 2 part-time/adjunct (1 woman). *Students:* 88 full-time (80 women), 14 part-time (13 women); includes 38 minority (10 Black or African American, non-Hispanic/Latino; 5 Asian, non-Hispanic/Latino; 21 Hispanic/Latino; 2 Two or more races, non-Hispanic/Latino), 1 international. Average age 25. 63 applicants, 83% accepted, 42 enrolled. In 2017, 27 master's, 7 doctorates awarded. *Degree requirements:* For master's, thesis optional; for doctorate, thesis/dissertation. *Entrance requirements:* For master's, GRE General Test, performance IQ score of 115 (for deaf students), minimum GPA of 2.5; for doctorate, GRE General Test, performance IQ score of 115 (for deaf students). Additional exam requirements/recommendations for international students: Required—TOEFL (minimum score 550 paper-based; 79 iBT), IELTS (minimum score 6.5). *Application deadline:* For fall admission, 8/10 for domestic students, 7/1 for international students; for spring admission, 1/5 for domestic students, 12/1 for international students. Applications are processed on a rolling basis. Application fee: $25 ($50 for international students). Electronic applications accepted. *Expenses:* Contact institution. *Financial support:* Fellowships with tuition reimbursements, teaching assistantships, and institutionally sponsored loans available. Support available to part-time students. Financial award application deadline: 4/1; financial award applicants required to submit FAFSA. *Unit head:* Dr. Monica Harn, Chair, 409-880-8338. *Application contact:* Deidre Mayer, Interim Director, Admissions and Academic Services, 409-880-8888, Fax: 409-880-7419, E-mail: gradmissions@lamar.edu.
Website: http://fineartscomm.lamar.edu/speech-and-hearing-sciences

La Salle University, School of Nursing and Health Sciences, Program in Speech-Language Pathology, Philadelphia, PA 19141-1199. Offers MS. *Accreditation:* ASHA. *Faculty:* 5 full-time (3 women), 5 part-time/adjunct (all women). *Students:* 59 full-time (58 women); includes 5 minority (2 Asian, non-Hispanic/Latino; 2 Hispanic/Latino; 1 Two or more races, non-Hispanic/Latino). Average age 23. 338 applicants, 28% accepted, 23 enrolled. In 2017, 33 master's awarded. *Degree requirements:* For master's, comprehensive exam, capstone project, which includes a written manuscript suitable for publication in a scholarly journal. *Entrance requirements:* For master's, GRE, personal essay; 3 letters of recommendation; CSDCAS centralized application. Additional exam requirements/recommendations for international students: Required—TOEFL. *Application deadline:* For fall admission, 2/1 for domestic and international students. Application fee: $100. *Expenses:* Contact institution. *Financial support:* In 2017–18, 10 students received support. Federal Work-Study and scholarships/grants available. Financial award application deadline: 8/31; financial award applicants required to submit FAFSA. *Unit head:* Dr. Barbara Amster, Director, 215-951-1986, Fax: 215-951-5171, E-mail: slh@lasalle.edu. *Application contact:* Elizabeth Heenan, Director, Graduate and Adult Enrollment, 215-951-1100, Fax: 215-951-1462, E-mail: heenan@lasalle.edu.
Website: http://www.lasalle.edu/master-speech-language-pathology/

Lebanon Valley College, Program in Speech-Language Pathology, Annville, PA 17003. Offers MSLP. *Faculty:* 2 full-time (both women). *Students:* 47 applicants, 81% accepted, 23 enrolled. *Expenses:* Contact institution. *Financial support:* Federal Work-Study and scholarships/grants available. Financial award applicants required to submit FAFSA. *Unit head:* Dr. Michelle Scesa, Chair/Assistant Professor of Speech Language Pathology, 717-867-6710, E-mail: scesa@lvc.edu. *Application contact:* EJ Smith, Associate Director of Admissions and Recruitment, 717-867-6183, E-mail: ejsmith@lvc.edu.
Website: http://www.lvc.edu/academics/graduate-studies/speech-language-pathology/

Lehman College of the City University of New York, School of Health Sciences, Human Services and Nursing, Department of Speech–Language–Hearing Sciences, Bronx, NY 10468-1589. Offers speech-language pathology (MA). *Accreditation:* ASHA. *Program availability:* Part-time, evening/weekend. *Degree requirements:* For master's, thesis or alternative.

Lewis & Clark College, Graduate School of Education and Counseling, Department of Teacher Education, Program in Special Education, Portland, OR 97219-7899. Offers M Ed. *Accreditation:* NCATE. *Program availability:* Part-time, evening/weekend. *Entrance requirements:* For master's, minimum GPA of 2.75. Additional exam requirements/recommendations for international students: Required—TOEFL (minimum score 575 paper-based). Electronic applications accepted.

Lindenwood University, Graduate Programs, School of Education, St. Charles, MO 63301-1695. Offers behavioral analysis (MA); education (MA), including autism spectrum disorders, character education, early intervention in autism and sensory impairment, gifted, technology; educational administration (MA, Ed D, Ed S); English to speakers of other languages (MA); instructional leadership (Ed D, Ed S); library media (MA); professional counseling (MA); school administration (MA, Ed S); school counseling (MA); teaching (MA). *Program availability:* Part-time, evening/weekend, 100% online, blended/hybrid learning. *Faculty:* 47 full-time (31 women), 213 part-time/adjunct (135 women). *Students:* 434 full-time (319 women), 1,292 part-time (989 women); includes 387 minority (313 Black or African American, non-Hispanic/Latino; 9 American Indian or Alaska Native, non-Hispanic/Latino; 13 Asian, non-Hispanic/Latino; 37 Hispanic/Latino; 1 Native Hawaiian or other Pacific Islander, non-Hispanic/Latino; 14 Two or more races, non-Hispanic/Latino), 20 international. Average age 36. 828 applicants, 61% accepted, 378 enrolled. In 2017, 431 master's, 63 doctorates, 94 other advanced degrees awarded. *Degree requirements:* For master's, thesis (for some programs), minimum GPA of 3.0; for doctorate, thesis/dissertation, minimum GPA of 3.0; for Ed S, comprehensive exam, project, minimum GPA of 3.0. *Entrance requirements:* For master's, interview, minimum undergraduate cumulative GPA of 3.0, writing sample, letter of recommendation; for doctorate, GRE, minimum graduate GPA of 3.4, resume, interview, writing sample, 4 letters of recommendation; for Ed S, master's degree in education, relevant work experience. Additional exam requirements/recommendations for international students: Required—TOEFL (minimum score 550 paper-based; 80 iBT); Recommended—IELTS (minimum score 6.5). *Application deadline:* For fall admission, 8/27 priority date for domestic and international students; for spring admission, 1/14 priority date for domestic and international students; for summer admission, 6/4 priority date for domestic and international students. Applications are processed on a rolling basis. Application fee: $30 ($100 for international students). Electronic applications accepted. *Expenses: Tuition:* Full-time $16,300; part-time $460 per credit. *Required fees:* $660; $330 per credit. Tuition and fees vary according to degree level and program. *Financial support:* In 2017–18, 1,615 students received support. Career-related internships or fieldwork, Federal Work-Study, institutionally sponsored loans, scholarships/grants, tuition waivers (partial), and unspecified assistantships available. Financial award application deadline: 6/30; financial award applicants required to submit FAFSA. *Unit head:* Dr. Anthony Scheffler, Dean, School of Education, 636-949-4618, Fax: 636-949-4197, E-mail: ascheffler@lindenwood.edu. *Application contact:* Kara Schilli, Director, Evening and Graduate Admissions, 636-949-4349, Fax: 636-949-4109, E-mail: adultadmissions@lindenwood.edu.
Website: http://www.lindenwood.edu/academics/academic-schools/school-of-education/

Loma Linda University, School of Allied Health Professions, Department of Communication Sciences and Disorders, Loma Linda, CA 92350. Offers speech-language pathology (MS, SLPD). *Accreditation:* ASHA (one or more programs are accredited). *Program availability:* Part-time. *Degree requirements:* For master's, thesis or alternative. *Entrance requirements:* For master's, GRE General Test. Additional exam requirements/recommendations for international students: Required—TOEFL (minimum score 550 paper-based). Electronic applications accepted.

Long Island University–LIU Brooklyn, School of Health Professions, Brooklyn, NY 11201-8423. Offers athletic training and sport sciences (MS); community health (MS Ed); exercise science (MS); forensic social work (Advanced Certificate); occupational therapy (MS); physical therapy (DPT); physician assistant (MS); public health (MPH); social work (MSW); speech-language pathology (MS). *Faculty:* 33 full-time (23 women), 82 part-time/adjunct (55 women). *Students:* 690 full-time (508 women), 86 part-time (74 women); includes 259 minority (120 Black or African American, non-Hispanic/Latino; 1 American Indian or Alaska Native, non-Hispanic/Latino; 52 Asian, non-Hispanic/Latino; 76 Hispanic/Latino; 10 Two or more races, non-Hispanic/Latino), 65 international. Average age 27. 1,241 applicants, 45% accepted, 255 enrolled. In 2017, 249 master's, 42 doctorates, 8 other advanced degrees awarded. *Degree requirements:* For master's, comprehensive exam (for some programs), thesis (for some programs); for doctorate, comprehensive exam (for some programs). *Entrance requirements:* For master's and doctorate, GRE. Additional exam requirements/recommendations for international students: Required—TOEFL (minimum score 550 paper-based; 79 iBT). *Application deadline:* Applications are processed on a rolling basis. Application fee: $50. Electronic applications accepted. *Expenses: Tuition:* Full-time $21,618; part-time $1201 per credit. *Required fees:* $1840; $920 per term. Tuition and fees vary according to course load. *Financial support:* In 2017–18, 187 students received support. Research assistantships, teaching assistantships, career-related internships or fieldwork, Federal Work-Study, scholarships/grants, and unspecified assistantships available. Support available to part-time students. Financial award application deadline: 2/15; financial award applicants required to submit FAFSA. *Faculty research:* Pediatric physical therapy, complementary and alternative medicine, global health and human rights, sport leadership and entrepreneurship, feminist sport psychology. *Unit head:* Dr. Barry S. Eckert, Dean, 718-780-6578, Fax: 718-780-4561, E-mail: barry.eckert@liu.edu. *Application contact:* Dr. Dominick Fortugno, Associate Dean, 718-488-1496, Fax: 718-780-4561, E-mail: dominick.fortugno@liu.edu.
Website: http://liu.edu/brooklyn/academics/school-of-health-professions

Long Island University–LIU Post, College of Education, Information and Technology, Brookville, NY 11548-1300. Offers adolescence education (MS); adolescence education 7-12 (MS); archives and records management (AC); art education (MS); childhood education (MS); childhood education/literacy B-6 (MS); childhood education/special education (MS); clinical mental health counseling (MS, AC); early childhood education (MS); early childhood education/childhood education (MS); educational leadership (AC); educational technology (MS); information studies (PhD); interdisciplinary educational studies (Ed D); middle childhood education (MS); music education (MS); public library administration (AC); school counselor (MS); special education (MS Ed); speech-language pathology (MA); students with disabilities, 7-12 generalist (AC); TESOL (MA). *Accreditation:* TEAC. *Program availability:* Part-time, 100% online, blended/hybrid learning. *Faculty:* 40 full-time (26 women), 73 part-time/adjunct (38 women). *Students:* 472 full-time (400 women), 696 part-time (543 women); includes 254 minority (93 Black or African American, non-Hispanic/Latino; 46 Asian, non-Hispanic/Latino; 105 Hispanic/Latino; 10 Two or more races, non-Hispanic/Latino), 33 international. Average age 33. 917 applicants, 82% accepted, 357 enrolled. In 2017, 408 master's, 31 other advanced degrees awarded. Terminal master's awarded for partial completion of doctoral program. *Degree requirements:* For master's, variable foreign language requirement, comprehensive exam (for some programs), thesis optional; for doctorate, comprehensive exam, thesis/dissertation. *Entrance requirements:* For master's and AC, GRE (for some programs). Additional exam requirements/recommendations for international students: Required—TOEFL (minimum score 550 paper-based, 75 iBT), IELTS, or PTE. *Application deadline:* Applications are processed on a rolling basis. Application fee: $50. Electronic applications accepted. *Expenses: Tuition:* Full-time $21,618; part-time $1201 per credit. *Required fees:* $1840; $920 per term. Tuition and fees vary according to course load. *Financial support:* In 2017–18, 376 students received support. Career-related internships or fieldwork, Federal Work-Study, institutionally sponsored loans, scholarships/grants, tuition waivers (partial), and unspecified assistantships available. Support available to part-time students. Financial award application deadline: 2/15; financial award applicants required to submit FAFSA. *Faculty research:* Sleep; use of technology to develop executive function by students with disabilities; early childhood literacy development through play; social justice through education; using a structured protocol to discuss Bad News. *Unit head:* Dr. Albert Inserra, Dean, 516-299-2210, E-mail: albert.inserra@liu.edu. *Application contact:* Rita Langdon, Graduate Admissions, 516-299-2900, Fax: 516-299-2137, E-mail: post-enroll@liu.edu.
Website: http://liu.edu/CWPost/Academics/College-of-Education-Information-and-Technology

Communication Disorders

Longwood University, College of Graduate and Professional Studies, College of Education and Human Services, Department of Social Work and Communication Sciences and Disorders, Farmville, VA 23909. Offers communication sciences and disorders (MS). *Accreditation:* ASHA. *Degree requirements:* For master's, comprehensive exam, thesis optional. *Entrance requirements:* For master's, GRE, bachelor's degree from regionally-accredited institution, minimum GPA of 3.0, CSDCAS application. Additional exam requirements/recommendations for international students: Required—TOEFL (minimum score 570 paper-based), IELTS (minimum score 6.5). Electronic applications accepted. *Expenses:* Contact institution.

Louisiana State University and Agricultural & Mechanical College, Graduate School, College of Humanities and Social Sciences, Department of Communication Sciences and Disorders, Baton Rouge, LA 70803. Offers MA, PhD. *Accreditation:* ASHA (one or more programs are accredited). *Faculty:* 13 full-time (11 women), 2 part-time/adjunct (both women). *Students:* 71 full-time (66 women), 1 (woman) part-time; includes 15 minority (8 Black or African American, non-Hispanic/Latino; 3 Asian, non-Hispanic/Latino; 4 Hispanic/Latino), 3 international. Average age 25. 139 applicants, 24% accepted, 30 enrolled. In 2017, 22 master's, 1 doctorate awarded. *Financial support:* In 2017–18, 1 fellowship (averaging $22,595 per year), 3 research assistantships (averaging $13,889 per year), 29 teaching assistantships (averaging $17,397 per year) were awarded. *Total annual research expenditures:* $99,726.

Louisiana State University Health Sciences Center, School of Allied Health Professions, Department of Communication Disorders, New Orleans, LA 70112. Offers audiology (Au D); speech pathology (MCD). *Accreditation:* ASHA (one or more programs are accredited). *Faculty:* 9 full-time (6 women), 7 part-time/adjunct (6 women). *Students:* 91 full-time (90 women); includes 11 minority (4 Black or African American, non-Hispanic/Latino; 1 Asian, non-Hispanic/Latino; 1 Hispanic/Latino; 5 Two or more races, non-Hispanic/Latino). Average age 24. 219 applicants, 14% accepted, 31 enrolled. In 2017, 28 master's, 12 doctorates awarded. *Degree requirements:* For master's, comprehensive exam or thesis. *Entrance requirements:* For master's, GRE General Test (minimum score of 296), 3 letters of recommendation, minimum GPA of 3.0; for doctorate, GRE General Test (minimum score of 294), 3 letters of recommendation, minimum GPA of 3.0. Additional exam requirements/recommendations for international students: Required—TOEFL (minimum score 550 paper-based; 79 iBT). *Application deadline:* For fall admission, 2/15 for domestic students; for summer admission, 1/15 for domestic students. Application fee: $125. Electronic applications accepted. *Expenses:* Contact institution. *Financial support:* Application deadline: 4/15; applicants required to submit FAFSA. *Faculty research:* Hearing aids, clinical audiology, swallowing respiration, language acquisition, speech science. *Unit head:* Dr. Annette E. Hurley-Larmeu, Interim Head, 504-568-4337, Fax: 504-568-4352, E-mail: ahurle@lsuhsc.edu. *Application contact:* Yudialys Delgado Cazanas, Student Affairs Director, 504-568-4253, Fax: 504-568-3185, E-mail: ydelga@lsuhsc.edu.
Website: http://alliedhealth.lsuhsc.edu/cd/default.aspx

Louisiana Tech University, Graduate School, College of Liberal Arts, Ruston, LA 71272. Offers architecture (M Arch); art (MFA), including graphic design, photography, studio; audiology (Au D); communication (MA), including speech communication, theatre; English (MA), including literature, technical writing; history (MA); speech pathology (MA); technical writing and communication (Graduate Certificate). *Program availability:* Part-time. *Faculty:* 63 full-time (25 women), 5 part-time/adjunct (3 women). *Students:* 114 full-time (29 women), 31 part-time (19 women); includes 12 minority (4 Black or African American, non-Hispanic/Latino; 1 Asian, non-Hispanic/Latino; 3 Hispanic/Latino; 4 Two or more races, non-Hispanic/Latino), 5 international. Average age 30. 146 applicants, 59% accepted, 37 enrolled. In 2017, 49 master's, 3 doctorates awarded. *Degree requirements:* For master's, thesis (for some programs); for doctorate, thesis/dissertation. *Entrance requirements:* For master's, GRE General Test; for doctorate, GRE General Test, bachelor's degree, minimum GPA of 3.0 or 3.2 on last 60 hours attempted. Additional exam requirements/recommendations for international students: Required—TOEFL (minimum score 550 paper-based; 80 iBT), IELTS (minimum score 6.5). *Application deadline:* For fall admission, 8/1 priority date for domestic students, 6/1 for international students; for winter admission, 11/1 priority date for domestic students, 9/1 for international students; for spring admission, 2/1 priority date for domestic students, 12/1 for international students; for summer admission, 5/1 priority date for domestic students, 3/1 for international students. Application fee: $40 ($50 for international students). Electronic applications accepted. *Expenses:* Tuition, state resident: full-time $5146. Tuition, nonresident: full-time $10,147. *International tuition:* $10,267 full-time. *Required fees:* $2273. *Financial support:* In 2017–18, 63 students received support, including 46 research assistantships (averaging $5,229 per year), 7 teaching assistantships (averaging $5,543 per year); fellowships, career-related internships or fieldwork, Federal Work-Study, institutionally sponsored loans, tuition waivers (partial), and unspecified assistantships also available. Financial award application deadline: 2/1. *Faculty research:* Contributing to the expansion of historical and social scientific knowledge and understanding through original research and publication; diverse language, ethnic, cultural, and socioeconomic backgrounds with disorders of speech, language, swallowing, hearing, and cognitive aspects of communication; prevention of communication, swallowing, and hearing disorders. *Unit head:* Dr. Donald P. Kaczvinsky, Dean, 318-257-4805, Fax: 318-257-3935, E-mail: dkaczv@latech.edu. *Application contact:* Mary Green, Administrative Assistant, 318-257-2924, Fax: 318-257-4487, E-mail: meg@latech.edu.
Website: http://liberalarts.latech.edu/

Loyola University Maryland, Graduate Programs, Loyola College of Arts and Sciences, Department of Speech-Language-Hearing Sciences, Baltimore, MD 21210-2699. Offers speech-language pathology (MS). *Accreditation:* ASHA. *Faculty:* 64 full-time (37 women), 31 part-time/adjunct (20 women). *Students:* 99 full-time (98 women); includes 12 minority (1 Black or African American, non-Hispanic/Latino; 2 Asian, non-Hispanic/Latino; 5 Hispanic/Latino; 1 Native Hawaiian or other Pacific Islander, non-Hispanic/Latino; 3 Two or more races, non-Hispanic/Latino). Average age 24. In 2017, 52 master's awarded. *Entrance requirements:* Additional exam requirements/recommendations for international students: Required—TOEFL (minimum score 550 paper-based), IELTS (minimum score 7). *Application deadline:* For fall admission, 2/1 for domestic and international students. Applications are processed on a rolling basis. Application fee: $60. Electronic applications accepted. *Expenses:* Contact institution. *Financial support:* Scholarships/grants, tuition waivers, and unspecified assistantships available. Financial award application deadline: 4/15; financial award applicants required to submit FAFSA. *Unit head:* Dr. Lisa Schoenbrodt, Chair, 410-617-2506, E-mail: lschoenbrodt@loyola.edu. *Application contact:* Office of Graduate Admissions, 410-617-5020, E-mail: graduate@loyola.edu.
Website: http://www.loyola.edu/speech/

Marquette University, Graduate School, College of Health Sciences, Department of Speech Pathology and Audiology, Milwaukee, WI 53201-1881. Offers bilingual English/Spanish (Certificate); speech-language pathology (MS). *Accreditation:* ASHA (one or more programs are accredited). *Program availability:* Part-time. *Degree requirements:* For master's, comprehensive exam, thesis (for some programs). *Entrance requirements:* For master's, GRE General Test, official transcripts from all current and previous colleges/universities except Marquette, three letters of recommendation, personal statement. Additional exam requirements/recommendations for international students: Required—TOEFL (minimum score 530 paper-based). Electronic applications accepted. *Faculty research:* Language processing in the brain, vocal aging, early language development, birth-to-three intervention, computer applications.

Marshall University, Academic Affairs Division, College of Health Professions, Department of Communication Disorders, Huntington, WV 25755. Offers MS. *Accreditation:* ASHA. *Students:* 60 full-time (59 women), 5 part-time (all women); includes 1 minority (Hispanic/Latino). Average age 25. In 2017, 25 master's awarded. *Entrance requirements:* For master's, GRE General Test. Application fee: $40. *Financial support:* Fellowships available. *Unit head:* Karen McNealy, Chairperson, 304-696-3634, E-mail: mcnealy@marshall.edu. *Application contact:* Information Contact, 304-746-1900, Fax: 304-746-1902, E-mail: services@marshall.edu.

Maryville University of Saint Louis, Myrtle E. and Earl E. Walker College of Health Professions, Program in Speech-Language Pathology, St. Louis, MO 63141-7299. Offers MS. *Faculty:* 5 full-time (all women), 1 (woman) part-time/adjunct. *Students:* 40 full-time (all women); includes 1 minority (Hispanic/Latino), 1 international. Average age 24. *Entrance requirements:* For master's, minimum cumulative GPA of 3.0. Additional exam requirements/recommendations for international students: Required—TOEFL (minimum score 603 paper-based; 79 iBT). *Application deadline:* For fall admission, 2/1 for domestic students. Applications are processed on a rolling basis. Electronic applications accepted. *Expenses:* $797 per credit hour, $1,200 per semester full-time. *Financial support:* Application deadline: 4/1; applicants required to submit FAFSA. *Unit head:* Dr. Charles Gulas, Dean, 314-529-9625, Fax: 314-529-9495, E-mail: hlthprofessions@maryville.edu. *Application contact:* Jeannie DeLuca, Director, Admissions and Advising, 314-529-9355, Fax: 314-529-9927, E-mail: jdeluca@maryville.edu.
Website: http://www.maryville.edu/hp/speech-language-pathology/

Marywood University, Academic Affairs, Reap College of Education and Human Development, Department of Communication Sciences and Disorders, Scranton, PA 18509-1598. Offers speech-language pathology (MS). *Accreditation:* ASHA. *Program availability:* Part-time. Electronic applications accepted.

Massachusetts Institute of Technology, School of Engineering, Harvard-MIT Health Sciences and Technology Program, Cambridge, MA 02139. Offers health sciences and technology (SM, PhD, Sc D), including bioastronautics (PhD, Sc D), bioinformatics and integrative genomics (PhD, Sc D), medical engineering and medical physics (PhD, Sc D), speech and hearing bioscience and technology (PhD, Sc D). Terminal master's awarded for partial completion of doctoral program. *Degree requirements:* For doctorate, comprehensive exam, thesis/dissertation. *Entrance requirements:* For doctorate, GRE General Test. Additional exam requirements/recommendations for international students: Required—TOEFL, IELTS. Electronic applications accepted. *Faculty research:* Biomedical imaging, drug delivery, medical devices, medical diagnostics, regenerative biomedical technologies.

McGill University, Faculty of Graduate and Postdoctoral Studies, Faculty of Medicine, School of Communication Sciences and Disorders, Montréal, QC H3A 2T5, Canada. Offers communication science and disorders (M Sc); communication sciences and disorders (PhD); speech-language pathology (M Sc A). *Accreditation:* ASHA.

Mercy College, School of Health and Natural Sciences, Program in Communication Disorders, Dobbs Ferry, NY 10522-1189. Offers MS. *Accreditation:* ASHA. *Program availability:* Part-time, evening/weekend. *Students:* 82 full-time (all women), 17 part-time (15 women); includes 35 minority (4 Black or African American, non-Hispanic/Latino; 5 Asian, non-Hispanic/Latino; 24 Hispanic/Latino; 2 Two or more races, non-Hispanic/Latino). Average age 33. 366 applicants, 17% accepted, 47 enrolled. In 2017, 45 master's awarded. *Entrance requirements:* For master's, essay, interview, resume, 2 letters of recommendation, undergraduate transcripts. Additional exam requirements/recommendations for international students: Required—TOEFL (minimum score 600 paper-based; 100 iBT), IELTS (minimum score 8). *Application deadline:* Applications are processed on a rolling basis. Application fee: $62. Electronic applications accepted. *Expenses:* Contact institution. *Financial support:* Career-related internships or fieldwork, Federal Work-Study, scholarships/grants, and unspecified assistantships available. Support available to part-time students. Financial award applicants required to submit FAFSA. *Faculty research:* Phonology, articulation, hearing deficits, fluency, attention. *Unit head:* Dr. Joan Toglia, Dean, School of Health and Natural Sciences, 914-674-7837, E-mail: jtoglia@mercy.edu. *Application contact:* Allison Gurdineer, Senior Director of Admissions, 877-637-2946, Fax: 914-674-7382, E-mail: admissions@mercy.edu.
Website: https://www.mercy.edu/degrees-programs/ms-communication-disorders

MGH Institute of Health Professions, School of Health and Rehabilitation Sciences, Department of Communication Sciences and Disorders, Boston, MA 02129. Offers reading (Certificate); speech-language pathology (MS). *Accreditation:* ASHA (one or more programs are accredited). *Program availability:* Part-time. *Degree requirements:* For master's, thesis or alternative, research proposal. *Entrance requirements:* For master's, GRE General Test, bachelor's degree from regionally-accredited college or university. Additional exam requirements/recommendations for international students: Required—TOEFL (minimum score 550 paper-based; 80 iBT). Electronic applications accepted. *Faculty research:* Children's language disorders, reading, speech disorders, voice disorders, augmentative communication, autism.

Miami University, College of Arts and Science, Department of Speech Pathology and Audiology, Oxford, OH 45056. Offers MA, MS. *Accreditation:* ASHA. *Students:* 52 full-time (49 women); includes 6 minority (3 Black or African American, non-Hispanic/Latino; 2 Asian, non-Hispanic/Latino; 1 Two or more races, non-Hispanic/Latino). Average age 23. In 2017, 26 master's awarded. *Expenses:* Tuition, state resident: full-time $13,812; part-time $575 per credit hour. Tuition, nonresident: full-time $30,860; part-time $1286 per credit hour. *Unit head:* Dr. Susan Baker Brehm, Chair, 513-529-2500, E-mail: bakerse1@miamioh.edu. *Application contact:* Dr. Donna Scarborough, Director of Graduate Studies, 513-529-2506, E-mail: scarbod@miamioh.edu.
Website: http://www.miamioh.edu/spa/

Michigan State University, The Graduate School, College of Communication Arts and Sciences, Department of Communicative Sciences and Disorders, East Lansing, MI 48824. Offers MA, PhD. *Accreditation:* ASHA (one or more programs are accredited). *Entrance requirements:* Additional exam requirements/recommendations for international students: Required—TOEFL. Electronic applications accepted.

Midwestern University, Glendale Campus, College of Health Sciences, Arizona Campus, Program in Speech-Language Pathology, Glendale, AZ 85308. Offers MS. *Entrance requirements:* For master's, bachelor's degree, minimum cumulative GPA of 3.0.

Minnesota State University Mankato, College of Graduate Studies and Research, College of Allied Health and Nursing, Program in Communication Disorders, Mankato, MN 56001. Offers MS. *Accreditation:* ASHA. *Program availability:* Part-time. *Degree requirements:* For master's, thesis or alternative, internship. *Entrance requirements:* For master's, GRE General Test, minimum GPA of 3.0 during previous 2 years, references, writing sample. Additional exam requirements/recommendations for international students: Required—TOEFL.

Minnesota State University Moorhead, Graduate Studies, College of Education and Human Services, Moorhead, MN 56563. Offers counseling and student affairs (MS); curriculum and instruction (MS); educational leadership (MS, Ed D, Ed S); special education (MS); speech-language pathology (MS). *Accreditation:* NCATE. *Program availability:* Part-time, 100% online, blended/hybrid learning. *Faculty:* 22. *Students:* 117 full-time (101 women), 337 part-time (253 women). Average age 32. 248 applicants, 49% accepted. In 2017, 149 master's, 16 other advanced degrees awarded. *Degree requirements:* For master's, comprehensive exam (for some programs), thesis, final oral defense; for doctorate, comprehensive exam (for some programs), thesis/dissertation, final oral defense. *Entrance requirements:* For master's, GRE, essay, letter of intent, letters of reference, teaching license, teaching verification, minimum cumulative GPA of 3.0; for doctorate, official transcripts; letter of intent; resume or curriculum vitae; master's degree; personal essay. Additional exam requirements/recommendations for international students: Required—TOEFL (minimum score 550 paper-based); Recommended—IELTS (minimum score 6.5). *Application deadline:* Applications are processed on a rolling basis. Application fee: $20. Electronic applications accepted. *Expenses:* Tuition, state resident: full-time $9000; part-time $374 per credit. Tuition, nonresident: full-time $18,000; part-time $748 per credit. *Required fees:* $1055; $43.96 per credit. Tuition and fees vary according to degree level, program and reciprocity agreements. *Financial support:* Federal Work-Study and unspecified assistantships available. Financial award application deadline: 10/1; financial award applicants required to submit FAFSA. *Unit head:* Dr. Ok-Hee Lee, Dean, 218-477-2095, E-mail: okheelee@mnstate.edu. *Application contact:* Karla Wenger, Office Manager, 218-477-2344, Fax: 218-477-2482, E-mail: wengerk@mnstate.edu.
Website: http://www.mnstate.edu/cehs/

Minot State University, Graduate School, Department of Communication Disorders, Minot, ND 58707-0002. Offers speech-language pathology (MS). *Accreditation:* ASHA. *Degree requirements:* For master's, comprehensive exam (for some programs), thesis (for some programs). *Entrance requirements:* For master's, GRE General Test, minimum GPA of 3.25. Additional exam requirements/recommendations for international students: Required—TOEFL (minimum score 79 iBT), IELTS (minimum score 6). *Faculty research:* Auditory evoked potentials, pathologies of auditory system, newborn hearing screening, cleft palate research, intervention, the diagnostic process, early language, the pedagogy of clinical teaching, phonology, geriatric communication problems, dysphagia, brain functioning after injury.

Minot State University, Graduate School, Program in Special Education, Minot, ND 58707-0002. Offers deaf/hard of hearing education (MS); specific learning disabilities (MS). *Accreditation:* NCATE. *Degree requirements:* For master's, comprehensive exam (for some programs), thesis (for some programs). *Entrance requirements:* For master's, minimum GPA of 2.75, bachelor's degree in education or related field, teacher licensure (for some concentrations). Additional exam requirements/recommendations for international students: Required—TOEFL (minimum score 79 iBT), IELTS (minimum score 6).

Misericordia University, College of Health Sciences and Education, Program in Speech-Language Pathology, Dallas, PA 18612-1098. Offers MSSLP. *Accreditation:* ASHA. *Entrance requirements:* For master's, GRE, minimum undergraduate GPA of 3.5. Additional exam requirements/recommendations for international students: Required—TOEFL.

Mississippi University for Women, Graduate School, College of Nursing and Health Sciences, Columbus, MS 39701-9998. Offers nursing (MSN, DNP, PMC); public health education (MPH); speech-language pathology (MS). *Accreditation:* AACN; ASHA. *Program availability:* Part-time. *Degree requirements:* For master's, comprehensive exam, thesis. *Entrance requirements:* For master's, GRE General Test, bachelor's degree in nursing, previous course work in statistics, proficiency in English.

Missouri State University, Graduate College, College of Health and Human Services, Department of Communication Sciences and Disorders, Springfield, MO 65897. Offers communication sciences and disorders (Au D); speech language pathology (MS). *Accreditation:* ASHA (one or more programs are accredited). *Faculty:* 18 full-time (15 women), 13 part-time/adjunct (4 women). *Students:* 101 full-time (92 women), 2 part-time (both women); includes 8 minority (1 Black or African American, non-Hispanic/Latino; 3 Hispanic/Latino; 1 Native Hawaiian or other Pacific Islander, non-Hispanic/Latino; 3 Two or more races, non-Hispanic/Latino), 3 international. Average age 22. 23 applicants, 43% accepted, 10 enrolled. In 2017, 33 master's, 10 doctorates awarded. *Degree requirements:* For master's, comprehensive exam, thesis or alternative; for doctorate, comprehensive exam, thesis/dissertation or alternative, clinical externship. *Entrance requirements:* For master's and doctorate, GRE, minimum GPA of 3.0. Additional exam requirements/recommendations for international students: Required—TOEFL (minimum score 550 paper-based; 79 iBT), IELTS (minimum score 6). *Application deadline:* For fall admission, 2/1 for domestic and international students. Application fee: $35 ($50 for international students). Electronic applications accepted. *Expenses:* Tuition, state resident: full-time $2915; part-time $2021 per credit hour. Tuition, nonresident: full-time $5354; part-time $3647 per credit hour. *International tuition:* $11,992 full-time. *Required fees:* $173; $173 per credit hour. Tuition and fees vary according to class time, course level, course load, degree level, campus/location and program. *Financial support:* In 2017–18, 1 research assistantship with full tuition reimbursement (averaging $8,772 per year) was awarded; career-related internships or fieldwork, Federal Work-Study, scholarships/grants, and unspecified assistantships also available. Support available to part-time students. Financial award application deadline: 3/31; financial award applicants required to submit FAFSA. *Faculty research:* Dysphagia, phonological intervention, elderly adult aural rehabilitation, vestibular disorders. *Unit head:* Dr. Letitia White, Department Head, 417-836-5368, Fax: 417-836-4242, E-mail: csd@missouristate.edu. *Application contact:* Stephanie Praschan, Director, Graduate Enrollment Management, 417-836-5330, Fax: 417-836-6200, E-mail: stephaniepraschan@missouristate.edu.
Website: http://www.missouristate.edu/CSD/

Molloy College, Program in Speech Language Pathology, Rockville Centre, NY 11571-5002. Offers MS. *Accreditation:* ASHA. *Program availability:* Part-time, evening/weekend. *Faculty:* 7 full-time (6 women), 3 part-time/adjunct (all women). *Students:* 81 full-time (80 women); includes 16 minority (1 Black or African American, non-Hispanic/Latino; 1 American Indian or Alaska Native, non-Hispanic/Latino; 2 Asian, non-Hispanic/Latino; 12 Hispanic/Latino). Average age 29. 270 applicants, 45% accepted, 44 enrolled. In 2017, 43 master's awarded. *Entrance requirements:* Additional exam requirements/recommendations for international students: Required—TOEFL (minimum score 550 paper-based; 79 iBT). *Application deadline:* For fall admission, 2/1 for domestic and international students. Application fee: $60. Electronic applications accepted. *Expenses: Tuition:* Full-time $19,980; part-time $1110 per credit. *Required fees:* $1040. Tuition and fees vary according to course load and degree level. *Financial support:* Application deadline: 3/1; applicants required to submit FAFSA. *Faculty research:* Biofeedback speech interventions such as EPG and ultrasound; peer mentoring; electrophysiology; language interventions for school age children; jaw kinematics in speech and non-speech tasks. *Unit head:* Susan Alimonti, Associate Dean, 516-323-3517, E-mail: salimonti@molloy.edu. *Application contact:* Jaclyn Machowicz, Assistant Director for Admissions, 516-323-4010, E-mail: jmachowicz@molloy.edu.

Monmouth University, Graduate Studies, School of Education, West Long Branch, NJ 07764-1898. Offers applied behavior analysis (Certificate); autism (Certificate); director of school counseling services (Post-Master's Certificate); early childhood (M Ed); educational leadership (Ed D); elementary education (MAT), including elementary level, secondary level; English as a second language (M Ed); learning disabilities teacher-consultant (Post-Master's Certificate); literacy (MS Ed); school counseling (MS Ed); special education (MS Ed), including autism, learning disabilities teacher-consultant, teacher of students with disabilities, teaching in inclusive settings; speech-language pathology (MS Ed); student affairs and college counseling (MS Ed); supervisor (Post-Master's Certificate); teaching English to speakers of other languages (Certificate). *Accreditation:* NCATE. *Program availability:* Part-time, evening/weekend, 100% online, blended/hybrid learning. *Faculty:* 23 full-time (19 women), 33 part-time/adjunct (25 women). *Students:* 175 full-time (163 women), 168 part-time (142 women); includes 54 minority (10 Black or African American, non-Hispanic/Latino; 4 Asian, non-Hispanic/Latino; 32 Hispanic/Latino; 8 Two or more races, non-Hispanic/Latino). Average age 27. In 2017, 160 master's, 3 other advanced degrees awarded. *Entrance requirements:* For master's, GRE taken within last 5 years (for MS Ed in speech-language pathology); SAT (minimum combined score of 1660 in 3 sections), ACT (23), GRE (minimum score of 4.0 on analytical writing section and minimum combined score of 310 on quantitative and verbal sections), or passing scores on 3 parts of Core Academic Skills Educators, minimum GPA of 3.0 in major; 2 letters of recommendation (for some programs); resume, personal statement or essay (depending on program). Additional exam requirements/recommendations for international students: Required—TOEFL (minimum score 550 paper-based; 79 iBT), IELTS (minimum score 6), Michigan English Language Assessment Battery (minimum score 77) or Certificate of Advanced English (minimum score 160). *Application deadline:* For fall admission, 7/15 priority date for domestic students, 7/1 for international students; for spring admission, 12/1 priority date for domestic students, 11/1 for international students; for summer admission, 5/1 for domestic students. Applications are processed on a rolling basis. Application fee: $50. Electronic applications accepted. *Expenses: Tuition:* Full-time $21,366; part-time $7122 per credit. *Required fees:* $700; $175 per term. *Financial support:* In 2017–18, 125 students received support. Institutionally sponsored loans, scholarships/grants, and unspecified assistantships available. Support available to part-time students. Financial award applicants required to submit FAFSA. *Faculty research:* Multicultural literacy, science and mathematics teaching strategies, teacher as reflective practitioner, children with disabilities. *Unit head:* Dr. John E. Henning, Dean, 732-263-5513, Fax: 732-263-5277. *Application contact:* Laurie Kuhn, Associate Director of Graduate Admission, 732-571-3452, Fax: 732-263-5123, E-mail: gradadm@monmouth.edu.
Website: http://www.monmouth.edu/academics/schools/education/default.asp

Montclair State University, The Graduate School, College of Humanities and Social Sciences, Doctoral Program in Audiology, Montclair, NJ 07043-1624. Offers Sc D. *Accreditation:* ASHA. *Program availability:* Part-time, evening/weekend. *Degree requirements:* For doctorate, comprehensive exam (for some programs), thesis/dissertation (for some programs). *Entrance requirements:* For doctorate, GRE General Test, essay, 2 letters of recommendation. Additional exam requirements/recommendations for international students: Required—TOEFL (minimum score 83 iBT), IELTS (minimum score 6.5). Electronic applications accepted. *Faculty research:* Child language development and disorders, word finding in discourse of aphasic and non-aphasics, phonological assessment and remediation, behavioral and electrophysiological measures of aging and spatial hearing, behavioral and electrophysiological measures of bilingual speech perception.

Montclair State University, The Graduate School, College of Humanities and Social Sciences, Program in Communication Sciences and Disorders, Montclair, NJ 07043-1624. Offers MA. *Accreditation:* ASHA. *Program availability:* Part-time, evening/weekend. *Degree requirements:* For master's, comprehensive exam, thesis (for some programs). *Entrance requirements:* For master's, GRE General Test, 2 letters of recommendation, essay. Additional exam requirements/recommendations for international students: Required—TOEFL (minimum score 83 iBT), IELTS (minimum score 6.5). Electronic applications accepted. *Faculty research:* Child language development and disorders, word finding in discourse of aphasic and non-aphasics, phonological assessment and remediation, behavioral and electrophysiological measures of aging and spatial hearing, behavioral and electrophysiological measures of bilingual speech perception.

Murray State University, College of Education and Human Services, Center for Communication Disorders, Murray, KY 42071. Offers interdisciplinary brain injury studies (Certificate); speech-language pathology (MS). *Accreditation:* ASHA (one or more programs are accredited). *Program availability:* Part-time. *Faculty:* 4 full-time (all women). *Students:* 63 full-time (62 women); includes 2 minority (1 Asian, non-Hispanic/Latino; 1 Two or more races, non-Hispanic/Latino). Average age 23. 84 applicants, 43% accepted, 16 enrolled. In 2017, 14 master's awarded. *Entrance requirements:* For master's and Certificate, GRE or GMAT, minimum university GPA of 2.75. Additional exam requirements/recommendations for international students: Required—TOEFL (minimum score 527 paper-based; 71 iBT). *Application deadline:* Applications are processed on a rolling basis. Application fee: $40 ($50 for international students). Electronic applications accepted. *Expenses:* Tuition, state resident: full-time $9504. Tuition, nonresident: full-time $26,811. *International tuition:* $14,400 full-time. Tuition and fees vary according to course load, degree level and reciprocity agreements. *Financial support:* Federal Work-Study and unspecified assistantships available. Financial award applicants required to submit FAFSA. *Unit head:* Dr. Robert Lyons, Interim Academic Director and Graduate Coordinator, 270-809-3807, Fax: 809-809-3889, E-mail: rlyons@murraystate.edu. *Application contact:* Kaitlyn Burzynski, Interim Assistant Director for Graduate Admission and Records, 270-809-5732, Fax: 270-809-3780, E-mail: msu.graduateadmissions@murraystate.edu.
Website: http://www.murraystate.edu/academics/CollegesDepartments/CollegeOfEducationandHumanServices/coehsacademicunits/centerforcommunicationdisorders/index.a

Nazareth College of Rochester, Graduate Studies, Department of Speech-Language Pathology, Communication Sciences and Disorders Program, Rochester, NY 14618. Offers MS. *Accreditation:* ASHA. *Program availability:* Part-time. *Entrance requirements:* For master's, GRE General Test, minimum GPA of 3.0. Additional exam requirements/recommendations for international students: Required—TOEFL or IELTS.

New Mexico State University, College of Education, Department of Communication Disorders, Las Cruces, NM 88003. Offers communication disorders (MA); curriculum and instruction (Ed S), including special education (MA, Ed S), special education/deaf-hard of hearing (MA, Ed S); education (MA), including autism spectrum disorders (MA, Ed D, PhD), special education (MA, Ed S), special education/deaf-hard of hearing (MA, Ed S), speech-language pathology; special education (Ed D, PhD), including autism spectrum disorders (MA, Ed D, PhD), bilingual/multicultural special education. *Accreditation:* ASHA (one or more programs are accredited); NCATE. *Program availability:* Part-time, evening/weekend, online learning. *Faculty:* 13 full-time (10 women), 4 part-time/adjunct (3 women). *Students:* 45 full-time (41 women), 56 part-time (45 women); includes 64 minority (1 Black or African American, non-Hispanic/Latino; 2 American Indian or Alaska Native, non-Hispanic/Latino; 4 Asian, non-Hispanic/Latino;

56 Hispanic/Latino; 1 Two or more races, non-Hispanic/Latino), 6 international. Average age 33. 164 applicants, 36% accepted, 32 enrolled. In 2017, 41 master's, 3 doctorates, 7 other advanced degrees awarded. *Degree requirements:* For master's, comprehensive exam, thesis optional; for doctorate, comprehensive exam, thesis/dissertation. *Entrance requirements:* For master's, GRE General Test or MAT. Additional exam requirements/recommendations for international students: Required—TOEFL (minimum score 550 paper-based; 79 iBT), IELTS (minimum score 6.5). *Application deadline:* For fall admission, 2/1 priority date for domestic students. Applications are processed on a rolling basis. Application fee: $40 ($50 for international students). Electronic applications accepted. *Expenses:* Tuition, state resident: full-time $4390. Tuition, nonresident: full-time $15,309. *Required fees:* $853. *Financial support:* In 2017–18, 33 students received support, including 1 fellowship (averaging $4,390 per year), 1 research assistantship (averaging $8,482 per year), 14 teaching assistantships (averaging $10,386 per year); career-related internships or fieldwork, Federal Work-Study, scholarships/grants, traineeships, health care benefits, and unspecified assistantships also available. Support available to part-time students. Financial award application deadline: 3/1. *Faculty research:* Multicultural special education, multicultural communication disorders, mild disability, multicultural assessment, deaf education, early childhood, bilingual special education. *Total annual research expenditures:* $182,251. *Unit head:* Dr. Victoria White, Interim Department Head, 575-646-5973, Fax: 575-646-7712, E-mail: vwhite@nmsu.edu.
Website: https://cd.nmsu.edu/

New York Medical College, School of Health Sciences and Practice, Valhalla, NY 10595. Offers behavioral sciences and health promotion (MPH); biostatistics (MS); children with special health care (Graduate Certificate); emergency preparedness (Graduate Certificate); environmental health science (MPH); epidemiology (MPH, MS); global health (Graduate Certificate); health education (Graduate Certificate); health policy and management (MPH, Dr PH); industrial hygiene (Graduate Certificate); pediatric dysphagia (Post-Graduate Certificate); physical therapy (DPT); public health (Graduate Certificate); speech-language pathology (MS). *Accreditation:* CEPH. *Program availability:* Part-time, evening/weekend, 100% online, blended/hybrid learning. *Faculty:* 48 full-time (33 women), 235 part-time/adjunct (141 women). *Students:* 221 full-time (153 women), 270 part-time (194 women); includes 202 minority (83 Black or African American, non-Hispanic/Latino; 2 American Indian or Alaska Native, non-Hispanic/Latino; 64 Asian, non-Hispanic/Latino; 47 Hispanic/Latino; 1 Native Hawaiian or other Pacific Islander, non-Hispanic/Latino; 5 Two or more races, non-Hispanic/Latino), 19 international. Average age 29. 1,118 applicants, 38% accepted, 169 enrolled. In 2017, 110 master's, 41 doctorates awarded. *Degree requirements:* For master's, comprehensive exam (for some programs), thesis (for some programs); for doctorate, thesis/dissertation. *Entrance requirements:* For master's, GRE (for MS in speech-language pathology); for doctorate, GRE. Additional exam requirements/recommendations for international students: Required—TOEFL, IELTS. *Application deadline:* For fall admission, 8/1 for domestic students, 4/15 for international students; for spring admission, 12/1 for domestic students; for summer admission, 5/1 for domestic students, 4/15 for international students. Application fee: $125. Electronic applications accepted. *Expenses:* $1,125 per credit, $245 fees. *Financial support:* In 2017–18, 10,000 students received support. Scholarships/grants and unspecified assistantships available. Financial award application deadline: 4/30; financial award applicants required to submit FAFSA. *Unit head:* Ben Watson, PhD, Vice Dean, 914-594-4531, E-mail: ben_watson@nymc.edu. *Application contact:* Irene Bundziak, Assistant to Director of Admissions, 914-594-4905, E-mail: irene_bundziak@nymc.edu.
Website: http://www.nymc.edu/school-of-health-sciences-and-practice-shsp/

New York University, Steinhardt School of Culture, Education, and Human Development, Department of Communication Sciences and Disorders, New York, NY 10003-6860. Offers MS, PhD. *Accreditation:* ASHA. *Program availability:* Part-time. *Students:* Average age 33. 422 applicants, 39% accepted, 59 enrolled. In 2017, 60 master's, 2 doctorates awarded. *Entrance requirements:* For master's, GRE General Test; for doctorate, GRE General Test, interview. Additional exam requirements/recommendations for international students: Required—TOEFL (minimum score 100 iBT). *Application deadline:* For fall admission, 12/1 priority date for domestic and international students. Applications are processed on a rolling basis. Application fee: $75. Electronic applications accepted. *Expenses: Tuition:* Full-time $41,352; part-time $19,968 per year. *Required fees:* $2496; $1628 per unit. $814 per term. Tuition and fees vary according to course load and program. *Financial support:* Fellowships with full and partial tuition reimbursements, research assistantships with full and partial tuition reimbursements, career-related internships or fieldwork, Federal Work-Study, institutionally sponsored loans, scholarships/grants, tuition waivers (partial), and unspecified assistantships available. Support available to part-time students. Financial award application deadline: 2/1; financial award applicants required to submit FAFSA. *Faculty research:* Evidence-based practice, phonological acquisition, dysphagia, child language acquisition and disorders, neuromotor disorders. *Unit head:* Prof. Adam Buchwald, Director, 212-998-5260, E-mail: buchwald@nyu.edu. *Application contact:* 212-998-5030, Fax: 212-995-4328, E-mail: steinhardt.gradadmissions@nyu.edu.
Website: http://steinhardt.nyu.edu/csd

North Carolina Central University, School of Education, Program in Communication Disorders, Durham, NC 27707-3129. Offers MS. *Accreditation:* ASHA. *Program availability:* Part-time, evening/weekend. *Degree requirements:* For master's, comprehensive exam, thesis or alternative. *Entrance requirements:* For master's, GRE, minimum GPA of 3.0 in major, 2.5 overall. Additional exam requirements/recommendations for international students: Required—TOEFL. *Application deadline:* For fall admission, 8/1 for domestic students. Application fee: $30. *Expenses:* Tuition, state resident: full-time $2770; part-time $692.50 per credit hour. Tuition, nonresident: full-time $9247; part-time $2311.75 per credit hour. *Financial support:* Application deadline: 5/1; applicants required to submit FAFSA. *Unit head:* Sheila J. Bridges-Bond, Program Coordinator, 919-530-7299, E-mail: bridges@nccu.edu. *Application contact:* Sheila J. Bridges-Bond, Program Coordinator, 919-530-7299, E-mail: bridges@nccu.edu.

Northeastern State University, College of Science and Health Professions, Department of Health Professions, Program in Speech-Language Pathology, Tahlequah, OK 74464-2399. Offers MS. *Accreditation:* ASHA. *Program availability:* Part-time, evening/weekend. *Faculty:* 5 full-time (4 women), 1 (woman) part-time/adjunct. *Students:* 73 full-time (72 women); includes 27 minority (2 Black or African American, non-Hispanic/Latino; 8 American Indian or Alaska Native, non-Hispanic/Latino; 4 Hispanic/Latino; 13 Two or more races, non-Hispanic/Latino). Average age 26. In 2017, 36 master's awarded. *Degree requirements:* For master's, thesis, capstone experience. *Entrance requirements:* For master's, GRE, minimum GPA of 2.75. Additional exam requirements/recommendations for international students: Required—TOEFL. *Application deadline:* For fall admission, 6/1 priority date for domestic students. Applications are processed on a rolling basis. Application fee: $25. Electronic applications accepted. *Expenses:* Tuition, state resident: part-time $222 per credit hour. Tuition, nonresident: part-time $501.75 per credit hour. *Required fees:* $37.40 per credit hour. Tuition and fees vary according to degree level. *Financial support:* Teaching assistantships, career-related internships or fieldwork, and Federal Work-Study available. Financial award application deadline: 3/1. *Unit head:* Dr. Julie Beard, Program Chair, 918-444-3780, E-mail: beard03@nsuok.edu. *Application contact:* Josh McCollum, Graduate Coordinator, 918-444-2093, E-mail: mccolluj@nsuok.edu.
Website: https://academics.nsuok.edu/healthprofessions/DegreePrograms/Speech-LangPath.aspx

Northeastern University, Bouvé College of Health Sciences, Boston, MA 02115-5096. Offers applied behavior analysis (MS); audiology (Au D); counseling psychology (MS, PhD, CAGS); exercise science (MS); nursing (MS, PhD, CAGS), including administration (MS), adult-gerontology acute care nurse practitioner (MS, CAGS), adult-gerontology primary care nurse practitioner (MS, CAGS), anesthesia (MS), family nurse practitioner (MS, CAGS), neonatal nurse practitioner (MS, CAGS), pediatric nurse practitioner (MS, CAGS), psychiatric mental health nurse practitioner (MS, CAGS); nursing practice (DNP); pharmaceutical sciences (MS, PhD), including interdisciplinary concentration, pharmaceutics and drug delivery systems; pharmacology (MS); pharmacy (Pharm D); school psychology (PhD); speech-language pathology (MS); urban health (MPH); MS/MBA. *Accreditation:* ACPE (one or more programs are accredited). *Program availability:* Part-time, evening/weekend, online learning. *Faculty:* 192 full-time. *Students:* 1,685. In 2017, 352 master's, 312 doctorates, 25 other advanced degrees awarded. *Degree requirements:* For doctorate, thesis/dissertation (for some programs); for CAGS, comprehensive exam. Application fee: $75. Electronic applications accepted. *Expenses:* Contact institution. *Financial support:* Fellowships, research assistantships, teaching assistantships, career-related internships or fieldwork, scholarships/grants, health care benefits, tuition waivers, and unspecified assistantships available. Support available to part-time students. Financial award applicants required to submit FAFSA. *Unit head:* Susan L. Parish, Dean, Bouve College of Health Sciences, 617-373-3321, Fax: 617-373-3030, E-mail: s.parish@northeastern.edu. *Application contact:* 617-373-2708, Fax: 617-373-4701, E-mail: bouvegrad@northeastern.edu.
Website: https://www.northeastern.edu/bouve/

Northern Arizona University, College of Health and Human Services, Department of Communication Sciences and Disorders, Flagstaff, AZ 86011. Offers clinical speech-language pathology (MS). *Accreditation:* ASHA. *Program availability:* Part-time. *Faculty:* 15 full-time (11 women), 2 part-time/adjunct (both women). *Students:* 74 full-time (67 women), 90 part-time (88 women); includes 48 minority (4 Black or African American, non-Hispanic/Latino; 5 American Indian or Alaska Native, non-Hispanic/Latino; 9 Asian, non-Hispanic/Latino; 25 Hispanic/Latino; 5 Two or more races, non-Hispanic/Latino), 2 international. Average age 27. 321 applicants, 12% accepted, 40 enrolled. In 2017, 46 master's awarded. *Degree requirements:* For master's, variable foreign language requirement, comprehensive exam (for some programs), thesis (for some programs). *Entrance requirements:* For master's, GRE General Test. Additional exam requirements/recommendations for international students: Required—TOEFL (minimum score 100 iBT), IELTS (minimum score 6.5). *Application deadline:* For fall admission, 1/15 for domestic and international students; for spring admission, 10/1 for domestic and international students. Application fee: $65. Electronic applications accepted. *Expenses:* Tuition, state resident: full-time $9240; part-time $458 per credit hour. Tuition, nonresident: full-time $21,588; part-time $1199 per credit hour. *Required fees:* $1021; $14 per credit hour. $646 per semester. Tuition and fees vary according to course load, campus/location and program. *Financial support:* In 2017–18, 10 students received support, including 3 research assistantships with partial tuition reimbursements available (averaging $5,000 per year); institutionally sponsored loans, health care benefits, tuition waivers (partial), and unspecified assistantships also available. Financial award application deadline: 2/1; financial award applicants required to submit FAFSA. *Unit head:* Dr. Elise Lindstedt, Chair, 928-523-2969, Fax: 928-523-0034, E-mail: elise.lindstedt@nau.edu. *Application contact:* Joan Brakefield, Senior Program Coordinator, 928-523-7444, Fax: 928-523-0034, E-mail: speech@nau.edu.
Website: https://nau.edu/CHHS/CSD/

Northern Illinois University, Graduate School, College of Health and Human Sciences, School of Allied Health and Communicative Disorders, Program in Communicative Disorders, De Kalb, IL 60115-2854. Offers audiology (Au D); speech-language pathology (MA). *Accreditation:* ASHA (one or more programs are accredited); CORE. *Faculty:* 9 full-time (6 women), 2 part-time/adjunct (1 woman). *Students:* 82 full-time (76 women), 2 part-time (1 woman); includes 16 minority (2 Black or African American, non-Hispanic/Latino; 5 Asian, non-Hispanic/Latino; 8 Hispanic/Latino; 1 Two or more races, non-Hispanic/Latino), 1 international. Average age 26. 155 applicants, 30% accepted, 9 enrolled. In 2017, 19 master's, 8 doctorates awarded. *Degree requirements:* For master's, comprehensive exam, thesis optional, practicum; for doctorate, practicum, research project. *Entrance requirements:* For master's, GRE General Test, minimum undergraduate GPA of 3.0; for doctorate, GRE General Test, minimum undergraduate GPA of 3.2. Additional exam requirements/recommendations for international students: Required—TOEFL (minimum score 550 paper-based). *Application deadline:* For fall admission, 2/1 priority date for domestic students, 5/1 for international students; for spring admission, 9/1 priority date for domestic students, 10/1 for international students. Applications are processed on a rolling basis. Application fee: $40. Electronic applications accepted. *Financial support:* Fellowships with full tuition reimbursements, research assistantships with full tuition reimbursements, teaching assistantships with full tuition reimbursements, career-related internships or fieldwork, Federal Work-Study, scholarships/grants, tuition waivers (full), and unspecified assistantships available. Support available to part-time students. Financial award applicants required to submit FAFSA. *Faculty research:* Impact of disability employment, deaf education, American Sign Language, autism, bilingualism. *Unit head:* Dr. Sherrill Morris, Chair, 815-753-1484, Fax: 815-753-9123, E-mail: ahcd@niu.edu. *Application contact:* Graduate School Office, 815-753-0395, E-mail: gradsch@niu.edu.
Website: http://www.chhs.niu.edu/slp/graduate/index.shtml

Northwestern University, The Graduate School, School of Communication, The Roxelyn and Richard Pepper Department of Communication Sciences and Disorders, Evanston, IL 60208. Offers audiology (Au D); communication sciences and disorders (PhD); speech, language, and learning (MS). Admissions and degrees offered through The Graduate School. *Accreditation:* ASHA (one or more programs are accredited). Terminal master's awarded for partial completion of doctoral program. *Degree requirements:* For master's, seminar paper; for doctorate, thesis/dissertation, pre-dissertation research project, qualifying exam. *Entrance requirements:* For master's and doctorate, GRE General Test, letters of recommendation. Additional exam requirements/recommendations for international students: Required—TOEFL. *Faculty research:* Swallow behavior, verb structure in aphasia, language decline in dementia, cognitive processing in children, word-finding defects in children.

Nova Southeastern University, Dr. Pallavi Patel College of Health Care Sciences, Fort Lauderdale, FL 33314-7796. Offers anesthesiologist assistant (MSA); audiology (Au D); health science (MH Sc, DHSc, PhD); occupational therapy (MOT, Dr OT, PhD); physical therapy (DPT, TDPT); physician assistant (MMS); speech-language pathology (MS). *Accreditation:* AOTA. *Faculty:* 54 full-time (31 women), 15 part-time/adjunct (7 women). *Students:* 501 full-time (407 women); includes 131 minority (18 Black or African American, non-Hispanic/Latino; 2 American Indian or Alaska Native, non-Hispanic/Latino; 45 Asian, non-Hispanic/Latino; 65 Hispanic/Latino; 1 Two or more races, non-Hispanic/Latino). Average age 24. 7,600 applicants, 7% accepted, 452 enrolled. In 2017, 616 master's, 225 doctorates awarded. *Degree requirements:* For doctorate,

comprehensive exam, thesis/dissertation (for some programs), 12-month full-time clinical externship experience. *Entrance requirements:* For master's, GRE General Test; for doctorate, GRE General Test, personal interview, essay in application, on-site essay. *Application deadline:* For spring admission, 2/15 for domestic and international students; for summer admission, 12/1 for domestic and international students. Applications are processed on a rolling basis. Application fee: $50. Electronic applications accepted. *Expenses:* Contact institution. *Financial support:* Federal Work-Study, institutionally sponsored loans, and scholarships/grants available. Financial award application deadline: 4/15; financial award applicants required to submit FAFSA. *Faculty research:* Efferent suppression and auditory processing delay, subjective visual vertical in vestibular assessment, competency-based clinical evaluation, hearing instrument performance for frequency lowering, hearing instrument performance for noise suppression, anxiety and dizziness in college students, audiology assistants. *Unit head:* Dr. Stanley Wilson, Dean, 954-262-1203, E-mail: swilson@nova.edu. *Application contact:* Joey Jankie, Admissions Counselor, 954-262-7249, E-mail: joey@nova.edu.
Website: http://healthsciences.nova.edu/

The Ohio State University, Graduate School, College of Arts and Sciences, Division of Social and Behavioral Sciences, Department of Speech and Hearing Science, Columbus, OH 43210. Offers audiology (Au D); hearing science (PhD); speech-language pathology (MA); speech-language science (PhD). *Accreditation:* ASHA (one or more programs are accredited). *Faculty:* 22. *Students:* 113 full-time (105 women), 5 part-time (all women). Average age 25. In 2017, 28 master's, 17 doctorates awarded. *Entrance requirements:* For master's and doctorate, GRE General Test. Additional exam requirements/recommendations for international students: Required—TOEFL (minimum score 600 paper-based; 100 iBT); Recommended—IELTS (minimum score 9). *Application deadline:* For fall admission, 12/1 for domestic students, 11/30 for international students. Applications are processed on a rolling basis. Electronic applications accepted. *Financial support:* Fellowships, research assistantships, teaching assistantships, Federal Work-Study, and institutionally sponsored loans available. Support available to part-time students. *Unit head:* Dr. Robert A. Fox, Chair, 614-292-1628, E-mail: fox.2@osu.edu. *Application contact:* Graduate and Professional Admissions, 614-292-9444, E-mail: gpadmissions@osu.edu.
Website: http://sphs.osu.edu/

Ohio University, Graduate College, College of Health Sciences and Professions, School of Rehabilitation and Communication Sciences, Division of Communication Sciences and Disorders, Athens, OH 45701-2979. Offers clinical audiology (Au D); hearing science (PhD); speech language pathology (MA); speech language science (PhD). *Accreditation:* ASHA.

Oklahoma State University, College of Arts and Sciences, Department of Communication Sciences and Disorders, Stillwater, OK 74078. Offers MS. *Accreditation:* ASHA. *Faculty:* 13 full-time (8 women), 6 part-time/adjunct (all women). *Students:* 39 full-time (all women); includes 6 minority (1 American Indian or Alaska Native, non-Hispanic/Latino; 1 Asian, non-Hispanic/Latino; 3 Hispanic/Latino; 1 Two or more races, non-Hispanic/Latino). Average age 23. 108 applicants, 21% accepted, 13 enrolled. In 2017, 22 master's awarded. *Entrance requirements:* For master's, GRE, minimum GPA of 3.0 in undergraduate major. Additional exam requirements/ recommendations for international students: Required—TOEFL (minimum score 550 paper-based; 79 iBT). *Application deadline:* For fall admission, 3/1 priority date for international students; for spring admission, 8/1 priority date for international students. Applications are processed on a rolling basis. Application fee: $40 ($75 for international students). Electronic applications accepted. *Expenses:* Tuition, state resident: full-time $4019; part-time $2679.60 per year. Tuition, nonresident: full-time $15,286; part-time $10,190.40 per year. *Required fees:* $2129; $1419 per unit. Tuition and fees vary according to program. *Financial support:* Research assistantships, teaching assistantships, career-related internships or fieldwork, Federal Work-Study, scholarships/grants, health care benefits, tuition waivers (partial), and unspecified assistantships available. Support available to part-time students. Financial award application deadline: 3/1; financial award applicants required to submit FAFSA. *Faculty research:* Speech communications. *Unit head:* Dr. Maureen Sullivan, Interim Department Head, 405-744-8938, E-mail: maureen.sullivan@okstate.edu. *Application contact:* Abby Grantham, Graduate Advisor, 405-744-8922, E-mail: abby.l.grantham@okstate.edu.
Website: http://cdis.okstate.edu/

Old Dominion University, Darden College of Education, Program in Speech-Language Pathology, Norfolk, VA 23529. Offers MS. *Accreditation:* ASHA. *Faculty:* 9 full-time (all women), 6 part-time/adjunct (5 women). *Students:* 56 full-time (55 women), 1 (woman) part-time; includes 14 minority (2 Black or African American, non-Hispanic/Latino; 3 Asian, non-Hispanic/Latino; 3 Hispanic/Latino; 6 Two or more races, non-Hispanic/ Latino). Average age 25. 252 applicants, 31% accepted, 27 enrolled. In 2017, 26 master's awarded. *Degree requirements:* For master's, comprehensive exam, written exams, case studies paper, practica. *Entrance requirements:* For master's, GRE General Test, minimum GPA of 3.0 in major, 2.8 overall. Additional exam requirements/ recommendations for international students: Required—TOEFL, IELTS. *Application deadline:* For fall admission, 2/1 for domestic and international students. Application fee: $50. Electronic applications accepted. *Expenses:* $496 per credit; additional healthcare and activity fees apply. *Financial support:* In 2017–18, 18 students received support, including 6 fellowships (averaging $6,000 per year), 8 research assistantships (averaging $4,500 per year); scholarships/grants and unspecified assistantships also available. Financial award application deadline: 2/1. *Faculty research:* Childhood language disorders, phonological disorders, stuttering, aphasia, apraxia of speech, augmentative communication, auditory attention, Executive functions. *Total annual research expenditures:* $370,000. *Unit head:* Dr. Anastasia M. Raymer, Graduate Program Director, 757-683-4117, Fax: 757-683-5593, E-mail: sraymer@odu.edu. *Application contact:* William Heffelfinger, Director of Graduate Admissions, 757-683-5554, Fax: 757-683-3255, E-mail: gradadmit@odu.edu.
Website: http://www.odu.edu/cdse

Our Lady of the Lake University, College of Professional Studies, Program in Communication and Learning Disorders, San Antonio, TX 78207-4689. Offers MA. *Accreditation:* ASHA. *Program availability:* Part-time. *Faculty:* 5 full-time (4 women), 1 (woman) part-time/adjunct. *Students:* 45 full-time (44 women), 1 (woman) part-time; includes 24 minority (1 Asian, non-Hispanic/Latino; 23 Hispanic/Latino), 1 international. Average age 26. 135 applicants, 17% accepted, 16 enrolled. In 2017, 25 master's awarded. *Degree requirements:* For master's, comprehensive exam, comprehensive clinical practicum. *Entrance requirements:* For master's, GRE General Test, official transcripts. Additional exam requirements/recommendations for international students: Required—TOEFL. *Application deadline:* For fall admission, 2/1 for domestic and international students. Application fee: $40 ($50 for international students). Electronic applications accepted. Application fee is waived when completed online. *Expenses:* *Tuition:* Full-time $10,668; part-time $5334 per year. *Required fees:* $816; $816 per year. $408 per semester. *Financial support:* In 2017–18, 8 students received support, including 3 research assistantships, 5 teaching assistantships; Federal Work-Study, scholarships/grants, unspecified assistantships, and tuition discounts also available. Support available to part-time students. Financial award application deadline: 5/1; financial award applicants required to submit FAFSA. *Unit head:* Dr. Eva Nwokah, Communication Disorders Department Chair, 210-431-2608, E-mail: eenwokah@ollusa.edu. *Application contact:* Office of Graduate Admissions, 210-431-3995, Fax: 210-431-3945, E-mail: gradadm@lake.ollusa.edu.
Website: http://www.ollusa.edu/s/1190/hybrid/default-hybrid-ollu.aspx?sid-1190&gid-1&pgid-7874

Pacific University, College of Education, Forest Grove, OR 97116-1797. Offers early childhood education (MAT), education (MAE); elementary education (MAT); ESOL (MAT); high school education (MAT); middle school education (MAT); special education (MAT); speech-language pathology (MS); STEM education (MAT); talented and gifted (M Ed); visual function in learning (M Ed). *Accreditation:* ASHA; NCATE. *Program availability:* Part-time, evening/weekend. *Degree requirements:* For master's, research project. *Entrance requirements:* For master's, California Basic Educational Skills Test, PRAXIS II, minimum undergraduate GPA of 2.75, 3.0 graduate. Additional exam requirements/recommendations for international students: Required—TOEFL. Electronic applications accepted. *Expenses:* Contact institution. *Faculty research:* Defining a culturally competent classroom, technology in the K-12 classroom, Socratic seminars, social studies education.

Pacific University, School of Audiology, Forest Grove, OR 97116-1797. Offers Au D. *Accreditation:* ASHA.

Penn State University Park, Graduate School, College of Health and Human Development, Department of Communication Sciences and Disorders, University Park, PA 16802. Offers MS, PhD, Certificate. *Accreditation:* ASHA (one or more programs are accredited). *Unit head:* Dr. Ann C. Crouter, Dean, 814-865-1420, Fax: 814-865-3282. *Application contact:* Lori Hawn, Director, Graduate Student Services, 814-865-1795, Fax: 814-863-4627, E-mail: l-gswww@lists.psu.edu.
Website: http://csd.hhd.psu.edu/

Portland State University, Graduate Studies, College of Liberal Arts and Sciences, Department of Speech and Hearing Sciences, Portland, OR 97207-0751. Offers speech-language pathology (MA, MS). *Accreditation:* ASHA (one or more programs are accredited). *Faculty:* 14 full-time (11 women), 6 part-time/adjunct (all women). *Students:* 76 full-time (71 women), 9 part-time (all women); includes 18 minority (6 Asian, non-Hispanic/Latino; 11 Hispanic/Latino; 1 Two or more races, non-Hispanic/Latino), 4 international. Average age 29. 13 applicants, 8% accepted, 1 enrolled. In 2017, 44 master's awarded. *Degree requirements:* For master's, variable foreign language requirement, thesis or alternative, oral exam, clinic. *Entrance requirements:* For master's, GRE General Test, minimum GPA of 3.0 in upper-division course work or 2.75 overall, BA/BS in speech and hearing sciences. Additional exam requirements/recommendations for international students: Required—TOEFL (minimum score 550 paper-based; 80 iBT), IELTS (minimum score 6.5). *Application deadline:* For fall admission, 2/1 for domestic and international students. Application fee: $65. *Expenses:* Tuition, state resident: full-time $14,436; part-time $401 per credit. Tuition, nonresident: full-time $21,780; part-time $605 per credit. *Required fees:* $1380; $22 per credit. $119 per quarter. One-time fee: $325. Tuition and fees vary according to program. *Financial support:* In 2017–18, 3 teaching assistantships with full and partial tuition reimbursements (averaging $6,390 per year) were awarded; research assistantships, career-related internships or fieldwork, Federal Work-Study, and institutionally sponsored loans also available. Support available to part-time students. Financial award application deadline: 3/1; financial award applicants required to submit FAFSA. *Faculty research:* Adolescents with clefts, spectral analysis of stuttering, communication in late talkers, speech intelligibility, brainstem response in fitting hearing aids. *Total annual research expenditures:* $169,308. *Unit head:* Christina Gildersleeve-Neumann, PhD, Chair, 503-725-3230, Fax: 503-725-5385, E-mail: cegn@pdx.edu. *Application contact:* Dr. Sarah Key-DeLyria, Graduate Program Coordinator, 503-725-3698, E-mail: keydel@pdx.edu.
Website: http://www.pdx.edu/sphr/

Purdue University, Graduate School, College of Health and Human Sciences, Department of Speech, Language, and Hearing Sciences, West Lafayette, IN 47907. Offers audiology clinic (MS, Au D, PhD); linguistics (MS, PhD); speech and hearing science (MS, PhD); speech-language pathology (MS, PhD). *Accreditation:* ASHA. *Faculty:* 32 full-time (21 women), 9 part-time/adjunct (8 women). *Students:* 106 full-time (98 women), 7 part-time (6 women); includes 10 minority (1 Black or African American, non-Hispanic/Latino; 4 Asian, non-Hispanic/Latino; 1 Hispanic/Latino; 4 Two or more races, non-Hispanic/Latino), 7 international. Average age 25. 301 applicants, 35% accepted, 48 enrolled. In 2017, 31 master's, 5 doctorates awarded. *Degree requirements:* For master's, comprehensive exam (for some programs), thesis optional; for doctorate, comprehensive exam, thesis/dissertation. *Entrance requirements:* For master's and doctorate, GRE General Test, minimum undergraduate GPA of 3.0 or equivalent. Additional exam requirements/recommendations for international students: Required—TOEFL (minimum score 77 iBT). *Application deadline:* For fall admission, 1/1 priority date for domestic and international students; for spring admission, 8/1 priority date for domestic and international students. Applications are processed on a rolling basis. Application fee: $60 ($75 for international students). Electronic applications accepted. *Financial support:* Fellowships with full tuition reimbursements, research assistantships with full tuition reimbursements, teaching assistantships with full tuition reimbursements, career-related internships or fieldwork, and scholarships/grants available. Support available to part-time students. Financial award application deadline: 2/1; financial award applicants required to submit FAFSA. *Faculty research:* Psychoacoustics, speech perception, speech physiology, stuttering, child language. *Unit head:* Dr. Keith R. Kluender, Head, 765-494-3788, E-mail: kkluender@purdue.edu. *Application contact:* Vickie L. Parker-Black, Graduate Contact, 765-494-3786, E-mail: vpblack@purdue.edu.
Website: http://www.purdue.edu/hhs/slhs/

Queens College of the City University of New York, Arts and Humanities Division, Department of Linguistics and Communication Disorders, Queens, NY 11367-1597. Offers applied linguistics (MA); speech-language pathology (MA); TESOL (MS Ed, Post-Master's Certificate); TESOL and bilingual education (Post-Master's Certificate). *Accreditation:* ASHA. *Program availability:* Part-time. *Faculty:* 22 full-time (16 women), 19 part-time/adjunct (13 women). *Students:* 37 full-time (34 women), 123 part-time (112 women); includes 62 minority (10 Black or African American, non-Hispanic/Latino; 17 Asian, non-Hispanic/Latino; 32 Hispanic/Latino; 3 Two or more races, non-Hispanic/ Latino), 3 international. Average age 27. 390 applicants, 25% accepted, 81 enrolled. In 2017, 59 master's, 24 other advanced degrees awarded. *Degree requirements:* For master's, 400 hours of supervised clinical teaching (for MA in speech-language pathology); 50-100 hours of student teaching (for MS Ed). *Entrance requirements:* For master's, minimum GPA of 3.0. Additional exam requirements/recommendations for international students: Required—TOEFL, IELTS. *Application deadline:* For fall admission, 4/1 for domestic students; for winter admission, 1/1 for domestic students. Applications are processed on a rolling basis. Application fee: $125. Electronic applications accepted. *Expenses:* Contact institution. *Financial support:* Career-related internships or fieldwork available. Financial award application deadline: 4/1; financial award applicants required to submit FAFSA. *Unit head:* Arlene Kraat, Chair, 718-997-2940, E-mail: arlene.kraat@qc.cuny.edu. *Application contact:* Elizabeth D'Amico-Ramirez, Assistant Director of Graduate Admissions, 718-997-5203, E-mail: elizabeth.damicoramirez@qc.cuny.edu.

Communication Disorders

Radford University, College of Graduate Studies and Research, Program in Communication Sciences and Disorders, Radford, VA 24142. Offers MA, MS. *Accreditation:* ASHA (one or more programs are accredited). *Program availability:* Part-time. *Faculty:* 7 full-time (all women), 7 part-time/adjunct (all women). *Students:* 54 full-time (50 women); includes 4 minority (1 Black or African American, non-Hispanic/Latino; 2 Hispanic/Latino; 1 Two or more races, non-Hispanic/Latino). Average age 24. 171 applicants, 61% accepted, 24 enrolled. In 2017, 26 master's awarded. *Degree requirements:* For master's, comprehensive exam, thesis (for some programs). *Entrance requirements:* For master's, GRE, minimum GPA of 3.0; completed CSDCAS application with 3 letters of reference; personal essay; resume. Additional exam requirements/recommendations for international students: Required—TOEFL (minimum score 550 paper-based; 79 iBT), IELTS (minimum score 6.5). *Application deadline:* For fall admission, 2/1 priority date for domestic students, 12/1 for international students; for spring admission, 7/1 for international students. Applications are processed on a rolling basis. Application fee: $50. Electronic applications accepted. *Expenses:* Tuition, state resident: full-time $8336; part-time $347 per credit hour. Tuition, nonresident: full-time $16,862; part-time $702 per credit hour. *Required fees:* $3220; $135 per credit hour. Tuition and fees vary according to course load and program. *Financial support:* In 2017–18, 10 students received support, including 3 teaching assistantships (averaging $7,000 per year); career-related internships or fieldwork, scholarships/grants, and unspecified assistantships also available. Support available to part-time students. Financial award application deadline: 3/1; financial award applicants required to submit FAFSA. *Unit head:* Dr. Lauren Flora, Coordinator, 540-831-7639, E-mail: lflora2@radford.edu.
Website: http://www.radford.edu/content/wchs/home/cosd/academic-programs/master-cosd.html

Rockhurst University, College of Health and Human Services, Program in Communication Sciences and Disorders, Kansas City, MO 64110-2561. Offers MS. *Accreditation:* ASHA. *Program availability:* Part-time. *Faculty:* 6 full-time (all women), 1 (woman) part-time/adjunct. *Students:* 45 full-time (all women), 27 part-time (all women); includes 1 minority (Asian, non-Hispanic/Latino). Average age 23. 298 applicants, 53% accepted, 36 enrolled. In 2017, 32 master's awarded. *Entrance requirements:* For master's, GRE General Test, interview, minimum GPA of 3.0, letters of recommendation. Additional exam requirements/recommendations for international students: Required—TOEFL (minimum score 550 paper-based; 79 iBT). *Application deadline:* Applications are processed on a rolling basis. Electronic applications accepted. *Expenses:* $855 per credit hour tuition; $790 per year fees, additional fees may apply. *Financial support:* Applicants required to submit FAFSA. *Faculty research:* Bioacoustics, physiology, applied speech science, pediatric nutrition/dysphagia, communication/cognition. *Unit head:* Kathy Ermgodts, Chair, 816-501-4505, E-mail: kathy.ermgodts@rockhurst.edu. *Application contact:* Kevin Roy, Graduate Admissions Coordinator, 816-501-4097, E-mail: kevin.roy@rockhurst.edu.
Website: https://www.rockhurst.edu/communication-sciences-disorders

Rocky Mountain University of Health Professions, Program in Speech-Language Pathology, Provo, UT 84606. Offers Clin Sc D.

Rush University, College of Health Sciences, Department of Communication Disorders and Sciences, Chicago, IL 60612-3832. Offers audiology (Au D); speech-language pathology (MS). *Accreditation:* ASHA (one or more programs are accredited). *Degree requirements:* For master's, comprehensive exam, thesis optional; for doctorate, comprehensive exam, investigative project. *Entrance requirements:* For master's and doctorate, GRE General Test, minimum GPA of 3.0. Additional exam requirements/recommendations for international students: Required—TOEFL. *Application deadline:* For fall admission, 1/1 for domestic students. Applications are processed on a rolling basis. Application fee: $40. Electronic applications accepted. *Expenses:* Contact institution. *Financial support:* Research assistantships with partial tuition reimbursements, career-related internships or fieldwork, Federal Work-Study, institutionally sponsored loans, scholarships/grants, traineeships, tuition waivers (partial), and stipends available. Support available to part-time students. Financial award application deadline: 4/1; financial award applicants required to submit FAFSA. *Faculty research:* Electrostimulation of subthalamic nucleus, sensory feedback in speech modulation, sentence complexity in children's writing, velopharyngeal function, adult neurology. *Unit head:* Dr. Gail Kempster, Chairperson, E-mail: gail_b_kempster@rush.edu. *Application contact:* 312-942-7120, E-mail: chs_admissions@rush.edu.

Sacred Heart University, Graduate Programs, College of Health Professions, Department of Speech-Language Pathology, Fairfield, CT 06825. Offers MS. *Faculty:* 7 full-time (all women), 10 part-time/adjunct (9 women). *Students:* 76 full-time (74 women); includes 12 minority (2 Black or African American, non-Hispanic/Latino; 1 American Indian or Alaska Native, non-Hispanic/Latino; 3 Asian, non-Hispanic/Latino; 6 Hispanic/Latino), 1 international. Average age 25. 207 applicants, 46% accepted, 41 enrolled. In 2017, 27 master's awarded. *Degree requirements:* For master's, capstone. *Entrance requirements:* For master's, GRE, bachelor's degree with minimum GPA of 3.0. Additional exam requirements/recommendations for international students: Required—TOEFL (minimum score 570 paper-based, 80 iBT), TWE, or IELTS (6.5). *Application deadline:* For fall admission, 1/15 for domestic students. Applications are processed on a rolling basis. Application fee: $75. Electronic applications accepted. *Expenses:* Contact institution. *Financial support:* Unspecified assistantships available. Financial award applicants required to submit FAFSA. *Unit head:* Rhea Paul, Chair/Professor of Speech Language Pathology, 203-416-3947, E-mail: paulr4@sacredheart.edu. *Application contact:* Tara Chudy, Executive Director of Graduate Admissions, 203-365-4735, E-mail: chudyt@sacredheart.edu.
Website: http://www.sacredheart.edu/academics/collegeofhealthprofessions/academicprograms/speech-languagepathology/

St. Ambrose University, College of Health and Human Services, Program in Speech-Language Pathology, Davenport, IA 52803-2898. Offers MSLP. *Accreditation:* ASHA. *Program availability:* Part-time, evening/weekend. *Entrance requirements:* Additional exam requirements/recommendations for international students: Required—TOEFL. Electronic applications accepted.

St. Cloud State University, School of Graduate Studies, School of Health and Human Services, Department of Communication Sciences and Disorders, St. Cloud, MN 56301-4498. Offers MS. *Accreditation:* ASHA. *Degree requirements:* For master's, comprehensive exam (for some programs), thesis or alternative. *Entrance requirements:* For master's, GRE General Test, minimum GPA of 2.75. Additional exam requirements/recommendations for international students: Required—Michigan English Language Assessment Battery; Recommended—TOEFL (minimum score 550 paper-based), IELTS (minimum score 6.5). *Application deadline:* For fall admission, 2/1 for domestic and international students. Application fee: $35. Electronic applications accepted. *Expenses:* Tuition, state resident: full-time $8220; part-time $398.75 per credit. Tuition, nonresident: full-time $11,948; part-time $605.79 per credit. Tuition and fees vary according to degree level, campus/location, program and reciprocity agreements. *Financial support:* Federal Work-Study, scholarships/grants, and unspecified assistantships available. Financial award application deadline: 3/1.
Website: http://www.stcloudstate.edu/csd/

St. John's University, St. John's College of Liberal Arts and Sciences, Department of Communication Sciences and Disorders, Queens, NY 11439. Offers audiology (Au D); speech language pathology (MA). *Accreditation:* ASHA. *Program availability:* Evening/weekend. *Faculty:* 11 full-time (8 women), 11 part-time/adjunct (1 woman). *Students:* 113 full-time (109 women), 57 part-time (55 women); includes 39 minority (4 Black or African American, non-Hispanic/Latino; 14 Asian, non-Hispanic/Latino; 14 Hispanic/Latino; 2 Native Hawaiian or other Pacific Islander, non-Hispanic/Latino; 5 Two or more races, non-Hispanic/Latino), 1 international. Average age 24. 461 applicants, 34% accepted, 54 enrolled. In 2017, 57 master's, 4 doctorates awarded. *Degree requirements:* For master's, comprehensive exam, thesis, practicum, residency; for doctorate, practicum. *Entrance requirements:* For master's, GRE, letters of recommendation, transcripts, resume, personal statement, 21 prerequisite credits in speech language pathology; for doctorate, GRE, letters of recommendation, transcripts, resume, personal statement. Additional exam requirements/recommendations for international students: Required—TOEFL (minimum score 80 iBT), IELTS (minimum score 6.5). *Application deadline:* For fall admission, 2/1 for domestic students. Application fee: $70. Electronic applications accepted. *Expenses:* $23,130 per year. *Financial support:* Fellowships, research assistantships, teaching assistantships, scholarships/grants, tuition waivers, and unspecified assistantships available. Support available to part-time students. Financial award application deadline: 2/1; financial award applicants required to submit FAFSA. *Faculty research:* Bilingualism and adult and child language disorders, neural processing of speech, dysphagia, speech motor control, electrophysiological measurement of hearing. *Unit head:* Dr. Nancy Colodny, Chair, 718-990-2052, E-mail: colodnyn@stjohns.edu. *Application contact:* Robert Medrano, Director of Graduate Admission, 718-990-1601, Fax: 718-990-5686, E-mail: gradhelp@stjohns.edu.
Website: https://www.stjohns.edu/academics/schools-and-colleges/st-johns-college-liberal-arts-and-sciences/communication-sciences-and-disorders

Saint Joseph's University, College of Arts and Sciences, Graduate Programs in Education, Philadelphia, PA 19131-1395. Offers curriculum supervisor (Certificate); educational leadership (MS, Ed D); elementary education (MS, Certificate); elementary/middle school education (Certificate); organizational development and leadership (MS); principal (Certificate); professional education (MS); reading specialist (MS, Certificate); reading supervisor (Certificate); secondary education (MS, Certificate); special education (MS); special education 7-12 (Certificate); special education PK-8 (Certificate); superintendent's letter of eligibility (Certificate); supervisor of special education (Certificate); teacher of the deaf and hard of hearing (Certificate). *Program availability:* Part-time, evening/weekend, blended/hybrid learning. *Faculty:* 18 full-time (16 women), 63 part-time/adjunct (44 women). *Students:* 79 full-time (60 women), 793 part-time (604 women); includes 179 minority (125 Black or African American, non-Hispanic/Latino; 5 American Indian or Alaska Native, non-Hispanic/Latino; 15 Asian, non-Hispanic/Latino; 27 Hispanic/Latino; 1 Native Hawaiian or other Pacific Islander, non-Hispanic/Latino; 6 Two or more races, non-Hispanic/Latino), 12 international. Average age 34. 375 applicants, 75% accepted, 189 enrolled. In 2017, 340 master's, 13 doctorates, 3 other advanced degrees awarded. *Degree requirements:* For master's, thesis or alternative; for doctorate, comprehensive exam, thesis/dissertation. *Entrance requirements:* For master's, 2 letters of recommendation, minimum GPA of 3.0, official transcripts, personal statement; for doctorate, GRE, master's degree from accredited institution, minimum graduate GPA of 3.5, computer competence, interview with program director. Additional exam requirements/recommendations for international students: Required—TOEFL (minimum score 550 paper-based; 80 iBT), IELTS (minimum score 6.5), PTE (minimum score 60). *Application deadline:* For fall admission, 7/15 for international students; for spring admission, 11/1 for international students. Applications are processed on a rolling basis. Application fee: $35. Electronic applications accepted. *Expenses:* Contact institution. *Financial support:* Scholarships/grants and unspecified assistantships available. Financial award application deadline: 5/1; financial award applicants required to submit FAFSA. *Faculty research:* Factors predicting early mathematics skills for low income children, early child care and development, preschool quality, parent communication and home-school collaboration issues, education of terminally ill children, preparing literacy teachers for urban schools. *Unit head:* Dr. John Vacca, Associate Dean, Education, 610-660-3131, E-mail: gradcas@sju.edu. *Application contact:* Graduate Admissions, College of Arts and Sciences, 610-660-3131, E-mail: gradcas@sju.edu.
Website: https://sites.sju.edu/education/graduate-programs/

Saint Louis University, Graduate Programs, Doisy College of Health Sciences, Department of Communication Sciences and Disorders, St. Louis, MO 63103. Offers MA. *Accreditation:* ASHA. *Degree requirements:* For master's, thesis optional, comprehensive oral and written exams. *Entrance requirements:* For master's, GRE General Test, letters of recommendation, resume. Additional exam requirements/recommendations for international students: Required—TOEFL (minimum score 525 paper-based). Electronic applications accepted. *Faculty research:* Communication disorders in culturally and linguistically diverse populations, disability study-specific to World Health Organization classifications, early intervention in communication disorders and literacy skills, communication difficulties in internationally adopted children, voice and swallowing disorders secondary to cancer treatments.

Saint Mary's College, Graduate Programs, Master of Science Program in Speech Language Pathology, Notre Dame, IN 46556. Offers MS. *Faculty:* 6 full-time (all women), 7 part-time/adjunct (6 women). *Students:* 56 full-time (all women); includes 5 minority (1 Black or African American, non-Hispanic/Latino; 2 Asian, non-Hispanic/Latino; 2 Hispanic/Latino). Average age 24. 217 applicants, 39% accepted, 30 enrolled. In 2017, 20 master's awarded. *Degree requirements:* For master's, comprehensive exam (for some programs), thesis optional, 400 hours of a supervised clinical practicum. *Entrance requirements:* For master's, GRE, bachelor's degree in communication sciences and disorders or related field, official transcripts, current resume or curriculum vitae, 3 letters of recommendation, personal statement, video interview. Additional exam requirements/recommendations for international students: Recommended—TOEFL (minimum score 80 iBT), IELTS (minimum score 6.5). *Application deadline:* For fall admission, 1/15 for domestic and international students. Application fee: $125. Electronic applications accepted. *Expenses:* $10,901 per semester. *Financial support:* In 2017–18, 4 students received support, including 2 fellowships (averaging $11,000 per year). Financial award application deadline: 3/1; financial award applicants required to submit FAFSA. *Faculty research:* Autism, children's develop of speech perception, auditory middle latency response in individuals with tinnitus, speech analysis app development to identify neurodegenerative disease processes. *Unit head:* Susan Latham, Program Director, Master of Science in Speech Language Pathology, 574-284-4686, E-mail: slatham@saintmarys.edu. *Application contact:* Melissa Fruscione, Graduate Admission, 574-284-5098, E-mail: graduateadmission@saintmarys.edu.
Website: http://grad.saintmarys.edu/academic-programs/ms-speech-pathology

Saint Xavier University, Graduate Studies, College of Arts and Sciences, Department of Communication Sciences and Disorders, Chicago, IL 60655-3105. Offers speech-language pathology (MS). *Accreditation:* ASHA. *Entrance requirements:* For master's, GRE General Test, minimum GPA of 3.0, undergraduate course work in speech. *Expenses:* Contact institution.

Salus University, College of Education and Rehabilitation, Elkins Park, PA 19027-1598. Offers education of children and youth with visual and multiple impairments (M Ed, Certificate); low vision rehabilitation (MS, Certificate); occupational therapy (MS); orientation and mobility therapy (MS, Certificate); speech-language pathology (MS); vision rehabilitation therapy (MS, Certificate); OD/MS. *Accreditation:* AOTA. *Program availability:* Part-time, online learning. *Entrance requirements:* For master's, GRE or MAT, letters of reference (3), interviews (2). Additional exam requirements/recommendations for international students: Required—TOEFL, TWE. *Expenses:* Contact institution. *Faculty research:* Knowledge utilization, technology transfer.

Salus University, Osborne College of Audiology, Elkins Park, PA 19027-1598. Offers Au D. *Accreditation:* ASHA. *Entrance requirements:* Additional exam requirements/recommendations for international students: Required—TOEFL. Electronic applications accepted.

Samford University, School of Health Professions, Birmingham, AL 35229. Offers athletic training (MAT); physical therapy (DPT); respiratory care (MS); speech language pathology (MS). *Faculty:* 20 full-time (12 women), 1 part-time/adjunct (0 women). *Students:* 140 full-time (105 women), 2 part-time (both women); includes 14 minority (3 Black or African American, non-Hispanic/Latino; 1 Asian, non-Hispanic/Latino; 4 Hispanic/Latino; 6 Two or more races, non-Hispanic/Latino). Average age 24. 191 applicants, 60% accepted, 5 enrolled. In 2017, 17 master's awarded. *Degree requirements:* For master's and doctorate, capstone course. *Entrance requirements:* For master's and doctorate, GRE, recommendations, resume, on-campus interview, personal statement, shadowing hours. Additional exam requirements/recommendations for international students: Required—TOEFL (minimum score 550 paper-based). *Application deadline:* For fall admission, 10/1 for domestic students; for spring admission, 5/1 for domestic students. Application fee: $120. Electronic applications accepted. *Expenses:* $813 per credit hour. *Financial support:* In 2017–18, 36 students received support. Scholarships/grants available. Financial award application deadline: 2/15; financial award applicants required to submit FAFSA. *Faculty research:* Physical disabilities related to Parkinson's disease, neurogenic communication disorders, skeletal muscle physiology, spinal cord injuries, medical ventilation and tobacco treatment and prevention. *Unit head:* Dr. Alan Jung, Dean of the School of Health Professions, 205-726-2716, E-mail: apjung@samford.edu. *Application contact:* Dr. Marian Carter, Assistant Dean of Enrollment Management and Student Services, 205-726-2611, E-mail: mwcarter@samford.edu.
Website: http://www.samford.edu/healthprofessions

San Diego State University, Graduate and Research Affairs, College of Health and Human Services, School of Speech, Language, and Hearing Sciences, San Diego, CA 92182. Offers audiology (Au D); communicative disorders (MA); language and communicative disorders (PhD). PhD offered jointly with University of California, San Diego. *Program availability:* Part-time. *Degree requirements:* For master's, comprehensive exam (for some programs), thesis (for some programs); for doctorate, thesis/dissertation. *Entrance requirements:* For master's and doctorate, GRE General Test. Additional exam requirements/recommendations for international students: Required—TOEFL. Electronic applications accepted. *Faculty research:* Brain/behavior relationships in language development, grammatical processing and language disorders, interdisciplinary training of bilingual speech pathologists.

San Francisco State University, Division of Graduate Studies, College of Education, Department of Speech, Language and Hearing Sciences, San Francisco, CA 94132-1722. Offers speech-language pathology (MS). *Accreditation:* ASHA. *Unit head:* Dr. Laura Epstein, Chair, 415-338-1058, Fax: 415-338-0916, E-mail: lepstein@sfsu.edu.
Website: http://slhs.sfsu.edu/

San Jose State University, Graduate Studies and Research, Connie L. Lurie College of Education, San Jose, CA 95192-0071. Offers child and adolescent development (MA); education (MA), including counseling and student personnel, curriculum and instruction, speech pathology; educational leadership (MA, Ed D), including administration and supervision (MA), educational leadership (MA); elementary education (MA), including curriculum and instruction. *Accreditation:* NCATE. *Program availability:* Part-time, evening/weekend. *Faculty:* 29 full-time (22 women), 47 part-time/adjunct (40 women). *Students:* 414 full-time (339 women), 115 part-time (93 women); includes 341 minority (14 Black or African American, non-Hispanic/Latino; 87 Asian, non-Hispanic/Latino; 176 Hispanic/Latino; 64 Two or more races, non-Hispanic/Latino), 9 international. Average age 30. 654 applicants, 34% accepted, 161 enrolled. In 2017, 286 master's, 7 doctorates awarded. Terminal master's awarded for partial completion of doctoral program. *Degree requirements:* For master's, project or theses, graduate writing assessment; for doctorate, thesis/dissertation. *Entrance requirements:* For master's, GRE General Test (for some programs). Additional exam requirements/recommendations for international students: Required—TOEFL (minimum score 550 paper-based; 80 iBT), IELTS (minimum score 6.5), PTE (minimum score 53). *Application deadline:* For fall admission, 2/1 for domestic and international students. Applications are processed on a rolling basis. Application fee: $55. Electronic applications accepted. *Expenses:* Tuition, state resident: full-time $7176. Tuition, nonresident: full-time $16,680. Tuition and fees vary according to course load and program. *Financial support:* In 2017–18, 4 research assistantships with partial tuition reimbursements (averaging $2,500 per year) were awarded; fellowships, career-related internships or fieldwork, Federal Work-Study, scholarships/grants, traineeships, and tuition waivers (full and partial) also available. Support available to part-time students. Financial award application deadline: 4/28; financial award applicants required to submit FAFSA. *Faculty research:* Equity and social justice in public education, interdisciplinary practices, teacher training, and effective pedagogy, clinical efficacy, typical and atypical development in children. *Unit head:* Dr. Paul Cascella, Interim Dean, 408-924-3600, Fax: 408-924-3713, E-mail: paul.cascella@sjsu.edu.
Website: http://www.sjsu.edu/education/

Seton Hall University, School of Health and Medical Sciences, Program in Speech-Language Pathology, South Orange, NJ 07079-2697. Offers MS. *Accreditation:* ASHA. *Entrance requirements:* For master's, GRE, bachelor's degree, clinical experience; minimum GPA of 3.0, undergraduate preprofessional coursework in communication sciences and disorders. Additional exam requirements/recommendations for international students: Recommended—TOEFL. Electronic applications accepted. *Faculty research:* Child language disorders, motor speech control, voice disorders, dysphagia, early intervention/teaming.

South Carolina State University, College of Graduate and Professional Studies, Department of Health Sciences, Orangeburg, SC 29117-0001. Offers speech pathology and audiology (MA). *Accreditation:* ASHA. *Program availability:* Part-time, evening/weekend. *Faculty:* 6 full-time (5 women), 4 part-time/adjunct (all women). *Students:* 74 full-time (68 women), 7 part-time (6 women); includes 53 minority (all Black or African American, non-Hispanic/Latino). Average age 27. 84 applicants, 51% accepted, 40 enrolled. In 2017, 38 master's awarded. *Degree requirements:* For master's, thesis optional, departmental qualifying exam. *Entrance requirements:* For master's, GRE or NTE, minimum GPA of 3.0. *Application deadline:* For fall admission, 6/15 for domestic and international students; for spring admission, 11/1 for domestic and international students. Application fee: $25. Electronic applications accepted. *Expenses:* Tuition, state resident: full-time $9388; part-time $607 per credit hour. Tuition, nonresident: full-time $19,968; part-time $1194 per credit hour. *Required fees:* $766; $766 per credit hour. *Financial support:* Fellowships, career-related internships or fieldwork, Federal Work-Study, and scholarships/grants available. Financial award application deadline: 6/1. *Unit head:* Dr. Cecelia Jeffries, Chair, Department of Health Sciences, 803-536-8074, Fax: 803-536-8593, E-mail: cjeffrie@scsu.edu. *Application contact:* Curtis Foskey, Coordinator of Graduate Admission, 803-536-8419, Fax: 803-536-8812, E-mail: cfoskey@scsu.edu.

Southeastern Louisiana University, College of Nursing and Health Sciences, Department of Health and Human Sciences, Hammond, LA 70402. Offers communication sciences and disorders (MS); counseling (MS). *Accreditation:* ACA; ASHA; NCATE. *Program availability:* Part-time. *Faculty:* 15 full-time (14 women), 2 part-time/adjunct (both women). *Students:* 193 full-time (96 women), 41 part-time (38 women); includes 40 minority (13 Black or African American, non-Hispanic/Latino; 1 Asian, non-Hispanic/Latino; 13 Hispanic/Latino; 1 Native Hawaiian or other Pacific Islander, non-Hispanic/Latino; 12 Two or more races, non-Hispanic/Latino). Average age 28. 28 applicants, 57% accepted, 11 enrolled. In 2017, 53 master's awarded. *Degree requirements:* For master's, comprehensive exam, thesis optional, 25 clock hours of clinical observation (for communication sciences and disorders). *Entrance requirements:* For master's, GRE (minimum combined score of 279), minimum GPA of 2.8. Additional exam requirements/recommendations for international students: Required—TOEFL (minimum score 500 paper-based; 61 iBT). *Application deadline:* For fall admission, 3/1 priority date for domestic students, 6/1 priority date for international students; for spring admission, 10/1 priority date for domestic and international students. Applications are processed on a rolling basis. Application fee: $20 ($30 for international students). Electronic applications accepted. *Expenses:* Tuition, state resident: full-time $6684. Tuition, nonresident: full-time $19,162. *Required fees:* $2088. *Financial support:* In 2017–18, 65 students received support. Career-related internships or fieldwork, Federal Work-Study, institutionally sponsored loans, scholarships/grants, and unspecified assistantships available. Support available to part-time students. Financial award application deadline: 5/1; financial award applicants required to submit FAFSA. *Faculty research:* School counseling, play therapy, family counseling, grief counseling, transformational teaching. *Unit head:* Dr. Jacqueline Guendouzi, Department Head, 985-549-2309, Fax: 985-549-3758, E-mail: jguendouzi@southeastern.edu. *Application contact:* Amanda Harper, Graduate Admissions Analyst, 985-549-5620, Fax: 985-549-5632, E-mail: admissions@southeastern.edu.
Website: http://www.southeastern.edu/acad_research/depts/hhs/index.html

Southeast Missouri State University, School of Graduate Studies, Department of Communication Disorders, Cape Girardeau, MO 63701-4799. Offers MA. *Accreditation:* ASHA. *Faculty:* 8 full-time (all women). *Students:* 30 full-time (all women); includes 1 minority (Black or African American, non-Hispanic/Latino). Average age 23. 113 applicants, 15% accepted, 16 enrolled. In 2017, 14 master's awarded. *Degree requirements:* For master's, comprehensive exam, research project or thesis. *Entrance requirements:* For master's, GRE General Test. Additional exam requirements/recommendations for international students: Required—TOEFL (minimum score 550 paper-based; 79 iBT), IELTS (minimum score 6), PTE (minimum score 53). *Application deadline:* For fall admission, 2/1 for domestic and international students. Applications are processed on a rolling basis. Application fee: $30 ($40 for international students). Electronic applications accepted. *Expenses:* $270.35 per credit hour in-state tuition, $33.40 per credit hour fees. *Financial support:* In 2017–18, 9 students received support. Teaching assistantships with full tuition reimbursements available, career-related internships or fieldwork, Federal Work-Study, scholarships/grants, traineeships, tuition waivers (full), and unspecified assistantships available. Financial award application deadline: 6/30; financial award applicants required to submit FAFSA. *Faculty research:* Dysphagia, fluency disorders, voice disorders, language disorders, speech disorders, autism spectrum disorders, quality of life, AAC. *Unit head:* Dr. Marcia Brown Haims, Department of Communication Disorders Chair, 573-651-2488, Fax: 573-651-2827, E-mail: mjbrown@semo.edu.
Website: http://www.semo.edu/commdisorders/

Southern Connecticut State University, School of Graduate Studies, School of Health and Human Services, Department of Communication Disorders, New Haven, CT 06515-1355. Offers speech pathology (MS). *Accreditation:* ASHA. *Program availability:* Part-time. *Degree requirements:* For master's, thesis or alternative, clinical experience. *Entrance requirements:* For master's, GRE, interview, minimum QPA of 3.0. Electronic applications accepted.

Southern Illinois University Carbondale, Graduate School, College of Education and Human Services, Department of Communication Disorders and Sciences, Carbondale, IL 62901-4701. Offers MS. *Accreditation:* ASHA. *Degree requirements:* For master's, thesis. *Entrance requirements:* For master's, GRE, minimum GPA of 3.0. Additional exam requirements/recommendations for international students: Required—TOEFL (minimum score 550 paper-based; 80 iBT). Electronic applications accepted. *Faculty research:* Neurolinguistics, language processing, child language, fluency, phonology.

Southern Illinois University Edwardsville, Graduate School, School of Education, Health, and Human Behavior, Department of Special Education and Communication Disorders, Program in Speech-Language Pathology, Edwardsville, IL 62026. Offers MS. *Accreditation:* ASHA. *Program availability:* Part-time, evening/weekend. *Degree requirements:* For master's, thesis (for some programs), final exam. *Entrance requirements:* For master's, GRE, minimum GPA of 3.0. Additional exam requirements/recommendations for international students: Required—TOEFL (minimum score 550 paper-based; 79 iBT), IELTS (minimum score 6.5). Electronic applications accepted.

Southern University and Agricultural and Mechanical College, College of Nursing and Allied Health, Department of Speech-Language Pathology, Baton Rouge, LA 70813. Offers MS. *Accreditation:* ASHA.

State University of New York at Fredonia, College of Liberal Arts and Sciences, Fredonia, NY 14063-1136. Offers biology (MS); English (MA); English education 7-12 (MA); interdisciplinary studies (MA, MS); math education (MS Ed); professional writing (CAS); speech pathology (MS); MA/MS. *Program availability:* Part-time, evening/weekend. *Students:* 73 full-time (62 women), 9 part-time (6 women); includes 7 minority (1 Black or African American, non-Hispanic/Latino; 1 Asian, non-Hispanic/Latino; 2 Hispanic/Latino; 1 Native Hawaiian or other Pacific Islander, non-Hispanic/Latino; 2 Two or more races, non-Hispanic/Latino). Average age 24. 200 applicants, 25% accepted, 43 enrolled. In 2017, 41 master's, 1 other advanced degree awarded. *Degree requirements:* For master's, comprehensive exam (for some programs), thesis (for some programs). *Entrance requirements:* For master's, GRE. Additional exam requirements/recommendations for international students: Required—TOEFL (minimum score 79 iBT), IELTS (minimum score 6.5). *Application deadline:* Applications are processed on a rolling basis. Application fee: $75. Electronic applications accepted. *Expenses:* Tuition, state resident: full-time $8154. Tuition, nonresident: full-time $16,650. *Required fees:* $1209. *Financial support:* In 2017–18, 5 students received support, including 14 teaching assistantships with full and partial tuition reimbursements available (averaging $5,957 per year); tuition waivers (full and partial) and unspecified assistantships also available. *Faculty research:* Immunology/microbiology, applied human physiology, ecology and evolution, invertebrate biology, molecular biology, biochemistry, physiology, animal behavior, science education, vertebrate physiology, cell biology, plant biology,

developmental biology, aquatic ecology, bilingual language acquisition, bilingual language acquisition and disorders, augmentative and alternate communication with ALS, World War I, Zweig, environmental literature, editing, adolescent literature, pedagogy. *Unit head:* Dr. Andy Karafa, Dean, 716-673-3173, Fax: 716-673-3338, E-mail: andy.karafa@gmail.com. *Application contact:* Wendy S. Dunst, Interim Graduate Recruitment and Admissions Associate, 716-673-3808, Fax: 716-673-3712, E-mail: wendy.dunst@fredonia.edu.
Website: http://www.fredonia.edu/clas/

State University of New York at New Paltz, Graduate and Extended Learning School, School of Liberal Arts and Sciences, Department of Communication Disorders, New Paltz, NY 12561. Offers communication disorders (MS), including speech-language disabilities, speech-language pathology. *Accreditation:* ASHA. *Program availability:* Part-time, evening/weekend. *Faculty:* 8 full-time (all women), 5 part-time/adjunct (all women). *Students:* 54 full-time (47 women); includes 3 minority (1 Hispanic/Latino; 2 Two or more races, non-Hispanic/Latino). 149 applicants, 23% accepted, 6 enrolled. In 2017, 9 master's awarded. *Degree requirements:* For master's, comprehensive exam, thesis. *Entrance requirements:* For master's, GRE General Test or MAT, minimum GPA of 3.0. Additional exam requirements/recommendations for international students: Required—TOEFL (minimum score 550 paper-based; 80 iBT), IELTS (minimum score 6.5). *Application deadline:* For fall admission, 3/1 for domestic and international students. Application fee: $50. Electronic applications accepted. *Financial support:* In 2017–18, 4 teaching assistantships with partial tuition reimbursements (averaging $5,000 per year) were awarded. Financial award application deadline: 8/1. *Unit head:* Dr. Wendy Bower, Program Coordinator, 845-257-3452, E-mail: commdisgrad@newpaltz.edu.
Website: http://www.newpaltz.edu/commdis/

State University of New York at Plattsburgh, School of Education, Health, and Human Services, Department of Communication Sciences and Disorders, Plattsburgh, NY 12901-2681. Offers speech-language pathology (MA). *Accreditation:* ASHA. *Program availability:* Part-time. *Entrance requirements:* For master's, GRE General Test, minimum GPA of 3.0. Additional exam requirements/recommendations for international students: Required—TOEFL. *Faculty research:* Autotoxins and noise effects on hearing, language impairment in Alzheimer's disease, attitudes on stuttering, diagnostic audiology.

State University of New York College at Cortland, Graduate Studies, School of Professional Studies, Department of Communication Disorders and Sciences, Cortland, NY 13045. Offers communication sciences and disorders (MS).

Stephen F. Austin State University, Graduate School, College of Education, Department of Human Services, Nacogdoches, TX 75962. Offers counseling (MA); school psychology (MA); special education (M Ed); speech-language pathology (MS). *Accreditation:* ACA (one or more programs are accredited); ASHA (one or more programs are accredited); CORE; NCATE. *Degree requirements:* For master's, comprehensive exam, thesis (for some programs). *Entrance requirements:* For master's, GRE General Test, minimum GPA of 2.8. Additional exam requirements/recommendations for international students: Required—TOEFL.

Stockton University, Office of Graduate Studies, Program in Communication Disorders, Galloway, NJ 08205-9441. Offers MS. *Accreditation:* ASHA. *Faculty:* 4 full-time (3 women), 5 part-time/adjunct (all women). *Students:* 58 full-time (56 women), 1 (woman) part-time; includes 9 minority (1 Black or African American, non-Hispanic/Latino; 3 Asian, non-Hispanic/Latino; 4 Hispanic/Latino; 1 Two or more races, non-Hispanic/Latino). Average age 23. 258 applicants, 23% accepted, 27 enrolled. In 2017, 31 master's awarded. *Degree requirements:* For master's, comprehensive exam (for some programs), thesis optional. *Entrance requirements:* For master's, GRE, 3 letters of recommendation, official transcripts from all colleges/universities attended, minimum undergraduate cumulative GPA of 3.2. *Application deadline:* For fall admission, 2/1 for domestic students. Electronic applications accepted. *Expenses:* Contact institution. *Financial support:* Fellowships, research assistantships with partial tuition reimbursements, career-related internships or fieldwork, Federal Work-Study, scholarships/grants, and unspecified assistantships available. Support available to part-time students. Financial award application deadline: 3/1. *Unit head:* Dr. Stacy Cassel, Program Director, 609-626-3640, E-mail: graduatestudies@stockton.edu. *Application contact:* Tara Williams, Assistant Director of Enrollment Management, 609-626-3640, Fax: 609-626-6050, E-mail: gradschool@stockton.edu.

Syracuse University, College of Arts and Sciences, MS Program in Speech-Language Pathology, Syracuse, NY 13244. Offers MS. *Accreditation:* ASHA. *Degree requirements:* For master's, comprehensive exam, thesis or alternative. *Entrance requirements:* For master's, GRE, three letters of recommendation, personal statement, resume, transcripts. Additional exam requirements/recommendations for international students: Required—TOEFL (minimum score 100 iBT). *Application deadline:* For fall admission, 1/1 priority date for domestic and international students. Application fee: $75. Electronic applications accepted. *Financial support:* Scholarships/grants, tuition waivers, and unspecified assistantships available. Financial award application deadline: 1/1. *Faculty research:* Auditory electrophysiology, hearing science, pediatric auditory, speech production, aphasia and psycholinguistics. *Unit head:* Dr. Karen Doherty, Professor and Chair, Communications Sciences and Disorders, 315-443-5662, E-mail: kadohert@syr.edu. *Application contact:* Jennifer Steigerwald, Information Contact, 315-443-9615, E-mail: jssteige@syr.edu.
Website: http://csd.syr.edu/graduate/overview.html

Syracuse University, College of Arts and Sciences, Programs in Audiology, Syracuse, NY 13244. Offers Au D, PhD. *Accreditation:* ASHA. *Program availability:* Part-time. *Degree requirements:* For doctorate, thesis/dissertation, internship. *Entrance requirements:* For doctorate, GRE General Test, undergraduate and graduate transcripts, three letters of recommendation, resume, personal statement. Additional exam requirements/recommendations for international students: Required—TOEFL (minimum score 620 paper-based; 105 iBT). *Application deadline:* For fall admission, 1/1 for domestic and international students. Application fee: $75. Electronic applications accepted. *Financial support:* Scholarships/grants and unspecified assistantships available. Financial award application deadline: 1/1. *Faculty research:* Auditory electrophysiology, hearing science, pediatric auditory, speech production, aphasia and psycholinguistics. *Unit head:* Dr. Karen Doherty, Department Chair, 315-443-9637, E-mail: csd@syr.edu. *Application contact:* Jennifer Steigerwald, Information Contact, 315-443-9615, E-mail: csdcasinfo@csdcas.org.
Website: http://csd.syr.edu/graduate/overview.html

Teachers College, Columbia University, Department of Biobehavioral Sciences, New York, NY 10027-6696. Offers applied exercise physiology (Ed M, MA, Ed D); communication sciences and disorders (MS, Ed D, PhD); kinesiology (PhD); motor learning and control (Ed M, MA); motor learning/movement science (Ed D); neuroscience and education (MS); physical education (MA, Ed D). *Accreditation:* ASHA. *Program availability:* Part-time, evening/weekend. *Students:* 180 full-time (160 women), 176 part-time (141 women); includes 149 minority (17 Black or African American, non-Hispanic/Latino; 40 Asian, non-Hispanic/Latino; 83 Hispanic/Latino; 9 Two or more races, non-Hispanic/Latino), 30 international. Average age 29. 738 applicants, 41% accepted, 164 enrolled. *Financial support:* Fellowships, teaching assistantships, career-related internships or fieldwork, Federal Work-Study, institutionally sponsored loans, traineeships, and tuition waivers (full and partial) available. Support available to part-time students. *Unit head:* Prof. Carol Garber, Chair, 212-678-3891, E-mail: garber@tc.columbia.edu. *Application contact:* David Estrella, Director of Admissions, 212-678-3305, E-mail: estrella@tc.columbia.edu.
Website: http://www.tc.columbia.edu/biobehavioral-sciences/

Teachers College, Columbia University, Department of Health and Behavior Studies, New York, NY 10027-6696. Offers applied behavior analysis (MA, PhD); applied educational psychology: school psychology (Ed M, PhD); behavioral nutrition (PhD), including nutrition (Ed D, PhD); community health education (MS); community nutrition education (Ed M), including community nutrition education; education of deaf and hard of hearing (MA, PhD); health education (MA, Ed D); hearing impairment (Ed D); intellectual disability/autism (MA, Ed D, PhD); nursing education (Ed D, Advanced Certificate); nutrition and education (MS); nutrition and exercise physiology (MS); nutrition and public health (MS); nutrition education (Ed D), including nutrition (Ed D, PhD); physical disabilities (Ed D); reading specialist (MA); severe or multiple disabilities (MA); special education (Ed M, MA, Ed D); teaching of sign language (MA). *Program availability:* Part-time, evening/weekend. *Students:* 245 full-time (226 women), 242 part-time (219 women); includes 167 minority (52 Black or African American, non-Hispanic/Latino; 2 American Indian or Alaska Native, non-Hispanic/Latino; 55 Asian, non-Hispanic/Latino; 48 Hispanic/Latino; 1 Native Hawaiian or other Pacific Islander, non-Hispanic/Latino; 9 Two or more races, non-Hispanic/Latino), 60 international. Average age 30. 480 applicants, 59% accepted, 157 enrolled. Terminal master's awarded for partial completion of doctoral program. *Unit head:* Prof. Dolores Perin, Chair, E-mail: dp111@tc.columbia.edu. *Application contact:* David Estrella, Director of Admission, 212-678-3305, E-mail: estrella@tc.columbia.edu.
Website: http://www.tc.columbia.edu/health-and-behavior-studies/

Temple University, College of Public Health, Department of Communication Sciences and Disorders, Philadelphia, PA 19122. Offers communication sciences and disorders (PhD); speech-language-hearing (MA). *Accreditation:* ASHA. *Faculty:* 17 full-time (13 women), 3 part-time/adjunct (all women). *Students:* 63 full-time (57 women), 1 (woman) part-time; includes 10 minority (3 Black or African American, non-Hispanic/Latino; 4 Asian, non-Hispanic/Latino; 2 Hispanic/Latino; 1 Two or more races, non-Hispanic/Latino), 1 international. 391 applicants, 25% accepted, 29 enrolled. In 2017, 28 master's, 3 doctorates awarded. *Degree requirements:* For master's, comprehensive exam; for doctorate, comprehensive exam, thesis/dissertation. *Entrance requirements:* For master's, GRE General Test, minimum GPA of 3.0, 2 letters of reference, statement of goals; for doctorate, GRE General Test, minimum GPA of 3.0, 3 letters of reference, statement of goals, writing sample, resume. Additional exam requirements/recommendations for international students: Required—TOEFL (minimum score 550 paper-based; 79 iBT). *Application deadline:* For fall admission, 1/1 for domestic and international students; for spring admission, 11/1 for domestic students, 10/1 for international students. Application fee: $60. Electronic applications accepted. *Expenses:* Contact institution. *Financial support:* Federal Work-Study, institutionally sponsored loans, and unspecified assistantships available. Financial award application deadline: 1/15. *Faculty research:* Bilingualism; biliteracy; adult neurogenic language disorders, including aphasia; dementia; school readiness. *Unit head:* Gayle DeDe, Interim Chair, 215-204-7543, E-mail: gayle.dede@temple.edu. *Application contact:* Dawn Dandridge, Academic Coordinator, 215-204-9005, E-mail: ddandrid@temple.edu.
Website: https://cph.temple.edu/commsci/home

Tennessee State University, The School of Graduate Studies and Research, College of Health Sciences, Department of Speech Pathology and Audiology, Nashville, TN 37209-1561. Offers speech and hearing science (MS). *Accreditation:* ASHA. *Program availability:* Part-time, online learning. *Degree requirements:* For master's, comprehensive exam, thesis optional. *Entrance requirements:* For master's, GRE General Test or MAT, minimum GPA of 3.5. Additional exam requirements/recommendations for international students: Required—TOEFL. *Faculty research:* Assessment and management of dysphagia, early intervention language disorders, multicultural diversity.

Texas A&M University–Kingsville, College of Graduate Studies, College of Arts and Sciences, Program in Communication Sciences and Disorders, Kingsville, TX 78363. Offers MS. *Accreditation:* ASHA. *Entrance requirements:* Additional exam requirements/recommendations for international students: Required—TOEFL (minimum score 550 paper-based; 79 iBT); Recommended—IELTS. Electronic applications accepted.

Texas Christian University, Harris College of Nursing and Health Sciences, Davies School of Communication Sciences and Disorders, Fort Worth, TX 76129. Offers speech-language pathology (MS). *Accreditation:* ASHA. *Faculty:* 11 full-time (9 women). *Students:* 40 full-time (38 women); includes 9 minority (1 Asian, non-Hispanic/Latino; 8 Hispanic/Latino), 2 international. Average age 23. 220 applicants, 9% accepted, 20 enrolled. In 2017, 20 master's awarded. *Degree requirements:* For master's, comprehensive exam, thesis optional. *Entrance requirements:* For master's, GRE General Test. Additional exam requirements/recommendations for international students: Required—TOEFL. *Application deadline:* For fall admission, 1/15 for domestic and international students. Application fee: $60. Electronic applications accepted. *Financial support:* In 2017–18, 40 students received support, including 40 research assistantships (averaging $35,000 per year); tuition waivers (partial) and unspecified assistantships also available. Financial award application deadline: 1/15; financial award applicants required to submit FAFSA. *Faculty research:* Voice disorders, hearing loss, cochlear implants, aphasia, child language. *Total annual research expenditures:* $75,000. *Unit head:* Dr. Christopher Watts, Director, 817-257-7620, E-mail: c.watts@tcu.edu. *Application contact:* Janet Schwartz, Administrative Assistant, 817-257-7620, E-mail: janet.schwartz@tcu.edu.
Website: http://csd.tcu.edu

Texas State University, The Graduate College, College of Health Professions, Program in Communication Disorders, San Marcos, TX 78666. Offers MA, MSCD. *Accreditation:* ASHA (one or more programs are accredited). *Faculty:* 13 full-time (11 women). *Students:* 65 full-time (62 women); includes 35 minority (2 Black or African American, non-Hispanic/Latino; 1 American Indian or Alaska Native, non-Hispanic/Latino; 2 Asian, non-Hispanic/Latino; 27 Hispanic/Latino; 3 Two or more races, non-Hispanic/Latino), 1 international. Average age 25. 425 applicants, 20% accepted, 34 enrolled. In 2017, 31 master's awarded. *Degree requirements:* For master's, comprehensive exam, thesis (for some programs), clinical practicum. *Entrance requirements:* For master's, baccalaureate degree in communication disorders from regionally-accredited institution with minimum GPA of 3.0 in communication disorders courses and in last 60 hours of course work; 3 forms of recommendation; resume; statement of purpose and interests. Additional exam requirements/recommendations for international students: Required—TOEFL (minimum score 550 paper-based; 78 iBT), IELTS (minimum score 6.5). *Application deadline:* For fall admission, 1/15 for domestic and international students. Applications are processed on a rolling basis. Application fee: $40 ($90 for international students). Electronic applications accepted. *Expenses:* Tuition, state resident: full-time $7868; part-time $3934 per semester. Tuition,

nonresident: full-time $17,828; part-time $8914 per semester. *Required fees:* $2092; $1435 per semester. Tuition and fees vary according to course load. *Financial support:* In 2017–18, 52 students received support, including 2 research assistantships (averaging $5,927 per year), 5 teaching assistantships (averaging $6,076 per year); fellowships, career-related internships or fieldwork, Federal Work-Study, institutionally sponsored loans, scholarships/grants, and unspecified assistantships also available. Support available to part-time students. Financial award application deadline: 3/1; financial award applicants required to submit FAFSA. *Unit head:* Dr. Valarie Fleming, Graduate Advisor, 512-245-2330, Fax: 512-245-2029, E-mail: vf13@txstate.edu. *Application contact:* Dr. Andrea Golato, Dean of Graduate School, 512-245-2581, Fax: 512-245-8365, E-mail: gradcollege@txstate.edu.
Website: http://www.health.txstate.edu/CDIS/

Texas Tech University Health Sciences Center, School of Health Professions, Program in Audiology, Lubbock, TX 79430. Offers Au D. *Faculty:* 8 full-time (6 women). *Students:* 37 full-time (35 women), 6 part-time (all women); includes 12 minority (1 Asian, non-Hispanic/Latino; 11 Hispanic/Latino). Average age 27. 88 applicants, 34% accepted, 11 enrolled. In 2017, 11 doctorates awarded. *Entrance requirements:* For doctorate, GRE, official transcripts, bachelor's degree, minimum cumulative GPA of 3.0. Additional exam requirements/recommendations for international students: Required—TOEFL (minimum score 550 paper-based; 79 iBT). *Application deadline:* For fall admission, 11/1 for domestic students; for winter admission, 2/1 for domestic students. Applications are processed on a rolling basis. Application fee: $75. Electronic applications accepted. *Financial support:* Application deadline: 9/1; applicants required to submit FAFSA. *Unit head:* Dr. Candace Hicks, Program Director, 806-743-5660, Fax: 806-743-5670, E-mail: candace.hicks@ttuhsc.edu. *Application contact:* Lindsay Johnson, Associate Dean for Admissions and Student Affairs, 806-743-3220, Fax: 806-743-2994, E-mail: lindsay.johnson@ttuhsc.edu.
Website: http://www.ttuhsc.edu/health-professions/doctor-of-audiology/

Texas Tech University Health Sciences Center, School of Health Professions, Program in Speech-Language Pathology, Lubbock, TX 79430. Offers MS. *Accreditation:* ASHA. *Faculty:* 13 full-time (11 women), 5 part-time/adjunct (all women). *Students:* 66 full-time (all women), 13 part-time (all women); includes 8 minority (1 Black or African American, non-Hispanic/Latino; 1 Asian, non-Hispanic/Latino; 6 Hispanic/Latino). Average age 23. 297 applicants, 31% accepted, 42 enrolled. In 2017, 38 master's awarded. *Degree requirements:* For master's, comprehensive exam, thesis optional. *Entrance requirements:* For master's, GRE. Additional exam requirements/recommendations for international students: Required—TOEFL (minimum score 550 paper-based; 79 iBT), IELTS. *Application deadline:* For winter admission, 1/15 for domestic students. Applications are processed on a rolling basis. Application fee: $75. Electronic applications accepted. *Financial support:* Research assistantships, teaching assistantships, career-related internships or fieldwork, institutionally sponsored loans, scholarships/grants, and unspecified assistantships available. Financial award application deadline: 9/1; financial award applicants required to submit FAFSA. *Unit head:* Sherry Sancibrian, Program Director, 806-743-5660, Fax: 806-743-5670, E-mail: sherry.sancibrian@ttuhsc.edu. *Application contact:* Lindsay Johnson, Associate Dean for Admissions and Student Affairs, 806-743-3220, Fax: 806-742-2994, E-mail: lindsay.johnson@ttuhsc.edu.
Website: http://www.ttuhsc.edu/health-professions/master-of-science-speech-language-pathology/

Texas Woman's University, Graduate School, College of Health Sciences, Department of Communication Sciences and Disorders, Denton, TX 76204. Offers education of the deaf (MS); speech-language pathology (MS). *Accreditation:* ASHA. *Program availability:* Part-time, 100% online, blended/hybrid learning. *Faculty:* 19 full-time (17 women), 4 part-time/adjunct (all women). *Students:* 199 full-time (193 women), 23 part-time (21 women); includes 103 minority (10 Black or African American, non-Hispanic/Latino; 11 Asian, non-Hispanic/Latino; 81 Hispanic/Latino; 1 Two or more races, non-Hispanic/Latino). Average age 30. 250 applicants, 13% accepted, 25 enrolled. In 2017, 164 master's awarded. *Degree requirements:* For master's, comprehensive exam, thesis (for some programs), internship, practicum. *Entrance requirements:* For master's, GRE General Test, 2 letters of reference (3 for speech/language pathology), personal essay, minimum GPA of 3.0 in last 60 hours of undergraduate work and all graduate course work. Additional exam requirements/recommendations for international students: Required—TOEFL (minimum score 550 paper-based; 79 iBT); Recommended—IELTS (minimum score 6.5), TSE (minimum score 53). *Application deadline:* For fall admission, 3/1 priority date for domestic and international students; for summer admission, 4/15 for domestic students, 2/1 priority date for international students. Applications are processed on a rolling basis. Application fee: $50 ($75 for international students). Electronic applications accepted. *Expenses:* $7,880 per year full-time in-state; $17,180 per year full-time out-of-state. *Financial support:* In 2017–18, 85 students received support. Research assistantships, career-related internships or fieldwork, Federal Work-Study, institutionally sponsored loans, scholarships/grants, traineeships, health care benefits, and unspecified assistantships available. Support available to part-time students. Financial award application deadline: 3/1; financial award applicants required to submit FAFSA. *Faculty research:* Adult neurocognition, literacy skills and inclusion for children who are deaf/hard of hearing, dysphagia, improving language literacy development of bilingual populations, treatment of language cognitive and motor disorders using non-invasive electrical brain stimulation. *Total annual research expenditures:* $25,000. *Unit head:* Dr. Erika Armstrong, Chair, 940-898-2025, Fax: 940-898-2070, E-mail: coms@twu.edu. *Application contact:* Korie Hawkins, Associate Director of Admissions, Graduate Recruitment, 940-898-3188, Fax: 940-898-3081, E-mail: admissions@twu.edu.
Website: http://www.twu.edu/communication-sciences/

Touro College, School of Health Sciences, Bay Shore, NY 11706. Offers industrial-organizational psychology (MS); mental health counseling (MS); occupational therapy (MS); physical therapy (DPT); physician assistant (MS); speech-language pathology (MS). *Faculty:* 81 full-time (55 women), 77 part-time/adjunct (46 women). *Students:* 628 full-time (470 women), 113 part-time (73 women); includes 143 minority (31 Black or African American, non-Hispanic/Latino; 1 American Indian or Alaska Native, non-Hispanic/Latino; 61 Asian, non-Hispanic/Latino; 42 Hispanic/Latino; 1 Native Hawaiian or other Pacific Islander, non-Hispanic/Latino; 7 Two or more races, non-Hispanic/Latino), 00 international. Average age 28. *Expenses:* Contact institution. *Financial support:* Fellowships available. *Unit head:* Dr. Louis Primavera, Dean, School of Health Sciences, 516-673-3200, E-mail: louis.primavera@touro.edu. *Application contact:* Brian J. Diele, Director of Student Administrative Services, 631-665-1600 Ext. 6311, E-mail: brian.diele@touro.edu.

Towson University, College of Health Professions, Program in Audiology, Towson, MD 21252-0001. Offers Au D. *Accreditation:* ASHA. *Students:* 45 full-time (43 women); includes 3 minority (all Black or African American, non-Hispanic/Latino), 1 international. *Entrance requirements:* For doctorate, GRE, 3 letters of recommendation, minimum GPA of 3.0, interview, essay. Additional exam requirements/recommendations for international students: Required—TOEFL (minimum score 600 paper-based). *Application deadline:* For fall admission, 1/17 for domestic students, 5/15 for international students; for spring admission, 10/15 for domestic students, 12/1 for international students. Applications are processed on a rolling basis. Application fee: $45. Electronic applications accepted. *Expenses:* Tuition, state resident: full-time $7960; part-time $398 per unit. Tuition, nonresident: full-time $16,480; part-time $824 per unit. *Required fees:* $2600; $130 per year. $390 per term. *Financial support:* Application deadline: 4/1. *Unit head:* Dr. Jennifer Smart, Graduate Program Director, 410-704-5903, E-mail: audiology@towson.edu. *Application contact:* Coverley Beidleman, Assistant Director of Graduate Admissions, 410-704-5630, Fax: 410-704-3030, E-mail: cbeidleman@towson.edu.
Website: http://www.towson.edu/chp/departments/asld/grad/audiology/

Towson University, College of Health Professions, Program in Speech-Language Pathology, Towson, MD 21252-0001. Offers MS. *Accreditation:* ASHA. *Students:* 94 full-time (93 women); includes 7 minority (3 Black or African American, non-Hispanic/Latino; 3 Hispanic/Latino; 1 Two or more races, non-Hispanic/Latino). *Degree requirements:* For master's, thesis (for some programs). *Entrance requirements:* For master's, GRE, bachelor's degree in speech-language pathology and audiology; CLEP or advanced placement (AP) examination credits in biological sciences, physical sciences, social/behavioral sciences and statistics; minimum GPA of 3.0 in major; 3 letters of recommendation; essay. Additional exam requirements/recommendations for international students: Required—TOEFL (minimum score 600 paper-based). *Application deadline:* For fall admission, 1/17 for domestic students, 5/15 for international students; for spring admission, 10/15 for domestic students, 12/1 for international students. Applications are processed on a rolling basis. Application fee: $45. Electronic applications accepted. *Expenses:* Tuition, state resident: full-time $7960; part-time $398 per unit. Tuition, nonresident: full-time $16,480; part-time $824 per unit. *Required fees:* $2600; $130 per year. $390 per term. *Financial support:* Application deadline: 4/1. *Unit head:* Dr. Karen Fallon, Graduate Program Director, 410-704-2437, E-mail: slpgradprogram@towson.edu. *Application contact:* Coverley Beidleman, Assistant Director of Graduate Admissions, 410-704-5630, Fax: 410-704-3030, E-mail: cbeidleman@towson.edu.
Website: http://www.towson.edu/chp/departments/asld/grad/speech/

Truman State University, Graduate School, School of Health Sciences and Education, Program in Communication Disorders, Kirksville, MO 63501-4221. Offers MA. *Accreditation:* ASHA. *Degree requirements:* For master's, comprehensive exam, thesis optional. *Entrance requirements:* For master's, GRE General Test, minimum GPA of 3.0. Additional exam requirements/recommendations for international students: Required—TOEFL (minimum score 550 paper-based). Electronic applications accepted.

Universidad del Turabo, Graduate Programs, School of Health Sciences, Program in Speech and Language Pathology, Gurabo, PR 00778-3030. Offers MS. *Entrance requirements:* For master's, EXADEP, GRE OR GMAT, interview, essay, official transcript, recommendation letters. Electronic applications accepted.

Université de Montréal, Faculty of Medicine, School of Speech Therapy and Audiology, Montréal, QC H3C 3J7, Canada. Offers audiology (PMS); speech therapy (PMS, DESS). *Degree requirements:* For master's, thesis. *Entrance requirements:* For master's, B Sc in speech-language pathology and audiology, proficiency in French. Electronic applications accepted. *Faculty research:* Aphasia in adults, dysarthria, speech and hearing-impaired children, noise-induced hearing impairment, computerized audiometry.

Université Laval, Faculty of Medicine, Graduate Programs in Medicine, Program in Speech Therapy, Québec, QC G1K 7P4, Canada. Offers M Sc. *Entrance requirements:* For master's, knowledge of French, interview. Electronic applications accepted.

University at Buffalo, the State University of New York, Graduate School, College of Arts and Sciences, Department of Communicative Disorders and Sciences, Buffalo, NY 14214. Offers audiology (Au D); communicative disorders and sciences (MA, PhD). *Accreditation:* ASHA (one or more programs are accredited). *Faculty:* 19 full-time (11 women), 3 part-time/adjunct (all women). *Students:* 110 full-time (101 women); includes 16 minority (1 Black or African American, non-Hispanic/Latino; 12 Asian, non-Hispanic/Latino; 3 Hispanic/Latino). Average age 24. 249 applicants, 36% accepted, 39 enrolled. In 2017, 36 master's, 2 doctorates awarded. *Degree requirements:* For master's, thesis or alternative, exam; for doctorate, thesis/dissertation, exams. *Entrance requirements:* For master's and doctorate, GRE General Test, minimum GPA of 3.0. Additional exam requirements/recommendations for international students: Required—TOEFL (minimum score 550 paper-based; 79 iBT). *Application deadline:* For fall admission, 1/1 priority date for domestic and international students. Application fee: $75. Electronic applications accepted. *Expenses:* Contact institution. *Financial support:* In 2017–18, 21 students received support, including 4 research assistantships with partial tuition reimbursements available (averaging $7,000 per year), 20 teaching assistantships with partial tuition reimbursements available (averaging $7,600 per year); fellowships with partial tuition reimbursements available, career-related internships or fieldwork, Federal Work-Study, institutionally sponsored loans, scholarships/grants, health care benefits, tuition waivers (full and partial), and unspecified assistantships also available. Financial award applicants required to submit FAFSA. *Faculty research:* Hearing and speech science, child and adult language disorders, augmentative communication, cochlear implants, tinnitus. *Total annual research expenditures:* $454,000. *Unit head:* Dr. Jeffery Higginbotham, Chairperson, 716-829-5542, Fax: 716-829-3979, E-mail: cdsjeff@buffalo.edu. *Application contact:* Virginia L. Majewski, Graduate Coordinator, 716-829-5570, Fax: 716-829-3979, E-mail: vmajewsk@buffalo.edu.
Website: http://cdswebserver.med.buffalo.edu/drupal/

The University of Akron, Graduate School, College of Health Professions, School of Speech-Language Pathology and Audiology, Program in Audiology, Akron, OH 44325. Offers Au D. *Accreditation:* ASHA. *Students:* 41 full-time (39 women); includes 5 minority (2 Asian, non-Hispanic/Latino; 1 Hispanic/Latino; 2 Two or more races, non-Hispanic/Latino), 1 international. Average age 23. 82 applicants, 23% accepted, 11 enrolled. In 2017, 20 doctorates awarded. *Degree requirements:* For doctorate, 2,000 clock hours of clinical experience, academic and clinical competency-based exams. *Entrance requirements:* For doctorate, GRE, minimum GPA of 3.0, letters of recommendation, statement of purpose, interview. Additional exam requirements/recommendations for international students: Required—TOEFL (minimum score 79 iBT), IELTS (minimum score 6.5). *Application deadline:* For fall admission, 1/15 for domestic and international students. Application fee: $45 ($70 for international students). Electronic applications accepted. *Total annual research expenditures:* $500,935. *Unit head:* Dr. James Steiger, School Director, 330-972-8190, E-mail: steiger@uakron.edu.
Website: https://www.uakron.edu/sslpa/dap/

The University of Akron, Graduate School, College of Health Professions, School of Speech-Language Pathology and Audiology, Program in Speech-Language Pathology, Akron, OH 44325. Offers MA. *Accreditation:* ASHA. *Students:* 75 full-time (73 women), 31 part-time (30 women); includes 7 minority (2 Black or African American, non-Hispanic/Latino; 1 Asian, non-Hispanic/Latino; 2 Hispanic/Latino; 2 Two or more races, non-Hispanic/Latino). Average age 26. 228 applicants, 28% accepted, 35 enrolled. In 2017, 55 master's awarded. *Entrance requirements:* For master's, GRE, baccalaureate degree in speech-language pathology, minimum GPA of 3.0, three letters of recommendation, statement of purpose, resume, interview. Additional exam

requirements/recommendations for international students: Required—TOEFL (minimum score 79 iBT), IELTS (minimum score 6.5). *Application deadline:* For fall admission, 1/1 for domestic and international students. Application fee: $45 ($70 for international students). Electronic applications accepted. *Unit head:* Dr. James Steiger, School Director, 330-972-8190, E-mail: steiger@uakron.edu. *Application contact:* Dr. Charles Carlin, Graduate Coordinator, 330-972-6556, E-mail: carlin@uakron.edu.
Website: http://www.uakron.edu/sslpa/

The University of Alabama, Graduate School, College of Arts and Sciences, Department of Communicative Disorders, Tuscaloosa, AL 35487. Offers speech language pathology (MS). *Accreditation:* ASHA. *Faculty:* 9 full-time (8 women). *Students:* 61 full-time (60 women); includes 7 minority (2 Black or African American, non-Hispanic/Latino; 1 Asian, non-Hispanic/Latino; 3 Hispanic/Latino; 1 Two or more races, non-Hispanic/Latino). Average age 24. 211 applicants, 30% accepted, 36 enrolled. In 2017, 25 master's awarded. *Degree requirements:* For master's, comprehensive exam, thesis optional. *Entrance requirements:* For master's, GRE or MAT, minimum GPA of 3.0. Additional exam requirements/recommendations for international students: Required—TOEFL. *Application deadline:* For fall and spring admission, 1/15 for domestic and international students. Application fee: $50 ($60 for international students). Electronic applications accepted. *Financial support:* In 2017–18, 12 students received support, including 3 fellowships with tuition reimbursements available (averaging $6,000 per year), 20 teaching assistantships with partial tuition reimbursements available (averaging $6,660 per year); career-related internships or fieldwork, Federal Work-Study, scholarships/grants, traineeships, health care benefits, and unspecified assistantships also available. Financial award application deadline: 1/15. *Faculty research:* Aphasia, cochlear implants, autism, voice, balance, multicultural, fluency, dysphagia, rural health. *Total annual research expenditures:* $248,805. *Unit head:* Dr. Angela B. Barber, Associate Professor and Chair, 205-348-2010, Fax: 205-348-1845, E-mail: abarber@ua.edu. *Application contact:* Lacey Watts, Office Associate, 205-348-7131, Fax: 205-348-1845, E-mail: lwatts@ua.edu.
Website: http://cd.ua.edu/

University of Alberta, Faculty of Graduate Studies and Research, Department of Speech Pathology and Audiology, Edmonton, AB T6G 2E1, Canada. Offers speech pathology and audiology (PhD); speech-language pathology (M Sc). *Degree requirements:* For master's, thesis (for some programs), clinical practicum (MSLP). *Entrance requirements:* For master's, GRE, minimum GPA of 6.5 on a 9.0 scale. Additional exam requirements/recommendations for international students: Required—TOEFL. *Faculty research:* Clinical education, hearing conservation, motor speech disorders, child language, voice resonance.

The University of Arizona, College of Science, Department of Speech, Language, and Hearing Sciences, Tucson, AZ 85721. Offers MS, PhD, Certificate. *Accreditation:* ASHA (one or more programs are accredited). *Degree requirements:* For master's, thesis optional; for doctorate, thesis/dissertation. *Entrance requirements:* For master's, GRE General Test, 3 letters of recommendation; for doctorate, GRE General Test, 3 letters of recommendation, personal statement, writing sample. Additional exam requirements/recommendations for international students: Required—TOEFL (minimum score 550 paper-based; 79 iBT). Electronic applications accepted. *Faculty research:* Alzheimer's disease, speech motor control, auditory-evoked potentials, analyzing pathological speech.

University of Arkansas, Graduate School, College of Education and Health Professions, Department of Rehabilitation, Human Resources and Communication Disorders, Program in Communication Disorders, Fayetteville, AR 72701. Offers MS. *Accreditation:* ASHA. *Program availability:* Part-time. In 2017, 37 master's awarded. *Degree requirements:* For master's, thesis optional, 8-week externship. *Entrance requirements:* For master's, GRE General Test. *Application deadline:* For fall admission, 8/1 for domestic students, 4/1 for international students; for spring admission, 12/1 for domestic students, 10/1 for international students; for summer admission, 4/15 for domestic students, 3/1 for international students. Applications are processed on a rolling basis. Application fee: $60. Electronic applications accepted. *Expenses:* Tuition, state resident: full-time $3782. Tuition, nonresident: full-time $10,238. *Financial support:* In 2017–18, 5 research assistantships were awarded; fellowships, teaching assistantships, career-related internships or fieldwork, and Federal Work-Study also available. Support available to part-time students. Financial award application deadline: 4/1; financial award applicants required to submit FAFSA. *Unit head:* Dr. Kimberly Frazier, Program Coordinator, 479-575-4916, E-mail: kimfraz@uark.edu. *Application contact:* Dr. Kimberly Baker Frazier, Graduate Coordinator, 479-575-4916, E-mail: kimfraz@uark.edu.
Website: http://cdis.uark.edu

University of Arkansas for Medical Sciences, College of Health Professions, Little Rock, AR 72205-7199. Offers audiology (Au D); communication sciences and disorders (MS, PhD); genetic counseling (MS); nuclear medicine advanced associate (MIS); physician assistant studies (MPAS); radiologist assistant (MIS). PhD offered through consortium with University of Arkansas at Little Rock and University of Central Arkansas. *Program availability:* Part-time, online learning. *Degree requirements:* For master's, thesis (for some programs); for doctorate, comprehensive exam (for some programs), thesis/dissertation (for some programs). *Entrance requirements:* For master's, GRE. Additional exam requirements/recommendations for international students: Required—TOEFL (minimum score 550 paper-based; 79 iBT). Electronic applications accepted. *Expenses:* Contact institution. *Faculty research:* Auditory-based intervention, soy diet, nutrition and cancer.

The University of British Columbia, Faculty of Medicine, School of Audiology and Speech Sciences, Vancouver, BC V6T 1Z3, Canada. Offers M Sc, PhD. *Accreditation:* ASHA. *Degree requirements:* For master's, thesis or alternative, externship; for doctorate, comprehensive exam, thesis/dissertation. *Entrance requirements:* For master's, 4-year undergraduate degree; for doctorate, master's degree, research proposal. Additional exam requirements/recommendations for international students: Required—TOEFL, IELTS. Electronic applications accepted. *Expenses:* Contact institution. *Faculty research:* Language development, experimental phonetics, linguistic physiology, amplification, auditory physiology.

University of California, San Diego, Graduate Division, Interdisciplinary Program in Language and Communicative Disorders, La Jolla, CA 92093. Offers PhD. Program offered jointly with San Diego State University. *Students:* 13 part-time (9 women). In 2017, 2 doctorates awarded. *Degree requirements:* For doctorate, one foreign language, comprehensive exam, thesis/dissertation, teaching assistantship. *Entrance requirements:* For doctorate, GRE General Test, minimum GPA of 3.25. Additional exam requirements/recommendations for international students: Required—TOEFL (minimum score 550 paper-based; 80 iBT), IELTS (minimum score 7). *Application deadline:* For fall admission, 5/5 for domestic students. Electronic applications accepted. *Financial support:* Teaching assistantships available. Financial award applicants required to submit FAFSA. *Faculty research:* Language acquisition and development, sign languages, bilingualism, neural bases of language use and loss, language development in disorders. *Unit head:* Seana Coulson, Program Director, 858-534-7486, E-mail: scoulson@ucsd.edu. *Application contact:* Janet Shin, Graduate Coordinator, 858-822-2698, E-mail: jshin@ucsd.edu.
Website: http://slhs.sdsu.edu/programs/phd/

University of California, San Diego, School of Medicine, Program in Audiology, La Jolla, CA 92093. Offers Au D. Program offered jointly with San Diego State University. *Students:* 11 full-time (6 women). In 2017, 8 doctorates awarded. *Degree requirements:* For doctorate, comprehensive exam, thesis/dissertation, 2,950 clinic hours; externship. *Entrance requirements:* For doctorate, GRE General Test, minimum GPA of 3.0; at least one course in each of the following areas: statistics, biological science, physical science, and American Sign Language; additional courses in behavioral/social sciences and biological or physical sciences. Additional exam requirements/recommendations for international students: Required—TOEFL (minimum score 550 paper-based; 80 iBT), IELTS (minimum score 7). Electronic applications accepted. *Expenses:* Contact institution. *Financial support:* Fellowships, research assistantships, scholarships/grants, and unspecified assistantships available. Financial award applicants required to submit FAFSA. *Faculty research:* Peripheral auditory physiology, auditory evoked potentials, psychoacoustics, epidemiology of age-related hearing loss, aural rehabilitation. *Unit head:* Erika Zettner, Chair, 858-657-8057, E-mail: ezettner@ucsd.edu.
Website: http://slhs.sdsu.edu/programs/aud/

University of Central Arkansas, Graduate School, College of Health and Behavioral Sciences, Department of Communication Sciences and Disorders, Conway, AR 72035-0001. Offers communication sciences and disorders (PhD); speech-language pathology (MS). *Accreditation:* ASHA (one or more programs are accredited). *Degree requirements:* For master's, comprehensive exam, thesis optional, portfolio, internship. *Entrance requirements:* For master's, GRE General Test, NTE, minimum GPA of 2.7. Additional exam requirements/recommendations for international students: Required—TOEFL (minimum score 550 paper-based). *Application deadline:* For fall admission, 3/1 priority date for domestic students; for spring admission, 10/1 for domestic students. Applications are processed on a rolling basis. Application fee: $25 ($50 for international students). Electronic applications accepted. *Expenses:* Contact institution. *Financial support:* Research assistantships with full and partial tuition reimbursements, teaching assistantships, career-related internships or fieldwork, Federal Work-Study, scholarships/grants, traineeships, and unspecified assistantships available. Financial award application deadline: 2/15; financial award applicants required to submit FAFSA.
Website: http://www.uca.edu/divisions/academic/slp/

University of Central Florida, College of Community Innovation and Education, Education Doctoral Programs, Orlando, FL 32816. Offers curriculum and instruction (Ed D); education (PhD), including communication sciences and disorders, counselor education, early childhood education, elementary education, exceptional education, exercise physiology, higher education, instructional design and technology, mathematics education, methodology, measurement and analysis, reading education, science education, social science education, TESOL; educational leadership (Ed D). *Students:* 122 full-time (86 women), 129 part-time (88 women); includes 64 minority (24 Black or African American, non-Hispanic/Latino; 1 American Indian or Alaska Native, non-Hispanic/Latino; 9 Asian, non-Hispanic/Latino; 24 Hispanic/Latino; 6 Two or more races, non-Hispanic/Latino), 26 international. Average age 38. 195 applicants, 47% accepted, 72 enrolled. In 2017, 89 doctorates awarded. *Entrance requirements:* For doctorate, GRE, letters of recommendation, goal statement, resume, writing sample. Application fee: $30. Electronic applications accepted. *Expenses:* Tuition, state resident: part-time $288.16 per credit hour. Tuition, nonresident: part-time $1073.31 per credit hour. Tuition and fees vary according to program. *Financial support:* In 2017–18, 77 students received support, including 28 fellowships with partial tuition reimbursements available (averaging $5,733 per year), 29 research assistantships with partial tuition reimbursements available (averaging $10,230 per year), 54 teaching assistantships with partial tuition reimbursements available (averaging $11,614 per year); health care benefits also available. Financial award application deadline: 3/1; financial award applicants required to submit FAFSA. *Unit head:* Dr. Edward Robinson, Director of Doctoral Programs, 407-823-6106, E-mail: edward.robinson@ucf.edu. *Application contact:* Associate Director, Graduate Admissions, 407-823-2766, Fax: 407-823-6442, E-mail: gradadmissions@ucf.edu.
Website: https://edcollege.ucf.edu/academic-programs/graduate/

University of Central Florida, College of Health Professions and Sciences, School of Communication Sciences and Disorders, Orlando, FL 32816. Offers communication sciences and disorders (MA); medical speech-language pathology (Certificate). *Accreditation:* ASHA (one or more programs are accredited). *Program availability:* Part-time, evening/weekend. *Students:* 204 full-time (192 women), 6 part-time (5 women); includes 62 minority (7 Black or African American, non-Hispanic/Latino; 1 American Indian or Alaska Native, non-Hispanic/Latino; 8 Asian, non-Hispanic/Latino; 41 Hispanic/Latino; 5 Two or more races, non-Hispanic/Latino), 1 international. Average age 26. 332 applicants, 36% accepted, 31 enrolled. In 2017, 94 master's awarded. *Degree requirements:* For master's, comprehensive exam, thesis or alternative. *Entrance requirements:* For master's, GRE General Test, minimum GPA of 3.0 in last 60 hours, letters of recommendation, resume, personal statement. Additional exam requirements/recommendations for international students: Required—TOEFL. *Application deadline:* For fall admission, 2/1 for domestic students; for spring admission, 10/1 for domestic students. Application fee: $30. Electronic applications accepted. *Expenses:* Tuition, state resident: part-time $288.16 per credit hour. Tuition, nonresident: part-time $1073.31 per credit hour. Tuition and fees vary according to program. *Financial support:* In 2017–18, 15 students received support, including 6 fellowships with partial tuition reimbursements available (averaging $3,833 per year), 4 research assistantships with partial tuition reimbursements available (averaging $6,020 per year), 7 teaching assistantships with partial tuition reimbursements available (averaging $7,138 per year); career-related internships or fieldwork, Federal Work-Study, institutionally sponsored loans, and unspecified assistantships also available. Financial award application deadline: 3/1; financial award applicants required to submit FAFSA. *Unit head:* Dr. Linda Rosa-Lugo, Program Coordinator, 407-823-4798, E-mail: csdgraduate@ucf.edu. *Application contact:* Associate Director, Graduate Admissions, 407-823-2766, Fax: 407-823-6442, E-mail: gradadmissions@ucf.edu.
Website: https://healthprofessions.ucf.edu/csd/

University of Central Missouri, The Graduate School, Warrensburg, MO 64093. Offers accountancy (MA); accounting (MBA); applied mathematics (MS); aviation safety (MA); biology (MS); business administration (MBA); career and technical education leadership (MS); college student personnel administration (MS); communication (MA); computer science (MS); counseling (MS); criminal justice (MS); educational leadership (Ed D); educational technology (MS); elementary and early childhood education (MSE); English (MA); environmental studies (MA); finance (MBA); history (MA); human services/educational technology (Ed S); human services/learning resources (Ed S); human services/professional counseling (Ed S); industrial hygiene (MS); industrial management (MS); information systems (MBA); information technology (MS); kinesiology (MS); library science and information services (MS); literacy education (MSE); marketing (MBA); mathematics (MS); music (MA); occupational safety management (MS); psychology (MS); rural family nursing (MS); school administration (MSE); social gerontology (MS); sociology (MA); special education (MSE); speech language pathology (MS); superintendency (Ed S); teaching (MAT); teaching English as a second language (MA); technology (MS); technology management (PhD); theatre (MA). *Program availability:* Part-time, 100% online, blended/hybrid learning. *Faculty:* 337 full-time (145 women), 41 part-time/adjunct (28 women). *Students:* 785 full-time (398 women), 1,633 part-time

(1,063 women); includes 231 minority (102 Black or African American, non-Hispanic/Latino; 4 American Indian or Alaska Native, non-Hispanic/Latino; 16 Asian, non-Hispanic/Latino; 52 Hispanic/Latino; 57 Two or more races, non-Hispanic/Latino), 692 international. Average age 30. In 2017, 2,605 master's, 122 other advanced degrees awarded. *Degree requirements:* For master's and Ed S, comprehensive exam (for some programs), thesis (for some programs). *Entrance requirements:* Additional exam requirements/recommendations for international students: Required—TOEFL (minimum score 550 paper-based; 79 iBT). *Application deadline:* For fall admission, 6/1 priority date for domestic and international students; for spring admission, 10/1 priority date for domestic and international students; for summer admission, 4/1 priority date for domestic and international students. Applications are processed on a rolling basis. Application fee: $30 ($75 for international students). Electronic applications accepted. *Expenses:* Tuition, state resident: full-time $8771; part-time $292.35 per credit hour. Tuition, nonresident: full-time $17,541; part-time $584.70 per credit hour. *Required fees:* $372; $24.78 per credit hour. *Financial support:* In 2017–18, 99 students received support. Research assistantships, teaching assistantships, career-related internships or fieldwork, Federal Work-Study, scholarships/grants, and administrative and laboratory assistantships available. Support available to part-time students. Financial award application deadline: 3/1; financial award applicants required to submit FAFSA. *Unit head:* Shellie Hewitt, Director of Graduate and International Student Services, 660-543-4621, Fax: 660-543-4778, E-mail: hewitt@ucmo.edu. *Application contact:* 660-543-4621, E-mail: admit_intl@ucmo.edu.
Website: http://www.ucmo.edu/graduate/

University of Central Oklahoma, The Jackson College of Graduate Studies, College of Education and Professional Studies, Donna Nigh Department of Advanced Professional and Special Services, Edmond, OK 73034-5209. Offers educational leadership (M Ed); library media education (M Ed); reading (M Ed); school counseling (M Ed); special education (M Ed), including mild/moderate disabilities, severe-profound/multiple disabilities; speech-language pathology (MS). *Accreditation:* ASHA. *Program availability:* Part-time. *Faculty:* 17 full-time (12 women), 8 part-time/adjunct (4 women). *Students:* 73 full-time (65 women), 286 part-time (239 women); includes 91 minority (41 Black or African American, non-Hispanic/Latino; 8 American Indian or Alaska Native, non-Hispanic/Latino; 5 Asian, non-Hispanic/Latino; 20 Hispanic/Latino; 17 Two or more races, non-Hispanic/Latino), 3 international. Average age 35. 146 applicants, 83% accepted, 91 enrolled. In 2017, 128 master's awarded. *Degree requirements:* For master's, comprehensive exam (for some programs), thesis (for some programs). *Entrance requirements:* Additional exam requirements/recommendations for international students: Required—TOEFL (minimum score 550 paper-based; 79 iBT), IELTS (minimum score 6.5). *Application deadline:* For fall admission, 7/15 for international students; for spring admission, 11/15 for international students; for summer admission, 1/31 for domestic students. Applications are processed on a rolling basis. Application fee: $60. Electronic applications accepted. *Expenses:* Tuition, state resident: full-time $5375; part-time $268.75 per credit hour. Tuition, nonresident: full-time $13,295; part-time $664.75 per credit hour. *Required fees:* $626; $31.30 per credit hour. One-time fee: $50. Tuition and fees vary according to program. *Financial support:* In 2017–18, 74 students received support, including 1 research assistantship with partial tuition reimbursement available (averaging $2,958 per year), 1 teaching assistantship with partial tuition reimbursement available (averaging $5,915 per year); career-related internships or fieldwork, scholarships/grants, tuition waivers (partial), and unspecified assistantships also available. Financial award application deadline: 3/31; financial award applicants required to submit FAFSA. *Unit head:* Dr. Cheryl Evans, Chair, 405-974-5437, Fax: 405-974-3857. *Application contact:* Carlie Wellington, Assistant Director, CEPS Graduate Enrollment, 405-974-5105, Fax: 405-974-3851, E-mail: gradcoll@uco.edu.
Website: http://sites.uco.edu/ceps/dept/Education-Programs/apss/index.asp

University of Cincinnati, Graduate School, College of Allied Health Sciences, Department of Communication Sciences and Disorders, Cincinnati, OH 45221. Offers MA, Au D, PhD. *Accreditation:* ASHA (one or more programs are accredited). *Degree requirements:* For master's, thesis optional; for doctorate, comprehensive exam, thesis/dissertation. *Entrance requirements:* For master's and doctorate, GRE General Test, minimum GPA of 3.0. Additional exam requirements/recommendations for international students: Required—TOEFL (minimum score 600 paper-based). Electronic applications accepted. *Expenses: Tuition, area resident:* Full-time $14,468. Tuition, state resident: full-time $14,968; part-time $754 per credit hour. Tuition, nonresident: full-time $24,210; part-time $1311 per credit hour. *International tuition:* $26,460 full-time. *Required fees:* $3958; $84 per credit hour. One-time fee: $85 full-time. Tuition and fees vary according to course load, degree level and program. *Faculty research:* Neurogenic speech and language disorders, speech science, linguistics, swallowing disorders, speech-language pathology.

University of Colorado Boulder, Graduate School, College of Arts and Sciences, Department of Speech, Language and Hearing Sciences, Boulder, CO 80309. Offers MA, Au D, PhD. *Accreditation:* ASHA (one or more programs are accredited). *Faculty:* 10 full-time (all women). *Students:* 101 full-time (92 women), 9 part-time (8 women); includes 24 minority (1 Black or African American, non-Hispanic/Latino; 5 Asian, non-Hispanic/Latino; 9 Hispanic/Latino; 9 Two or more races, non-Hispanic/Latino), 1 international. Average age 27. 610 applicants, 20% accepted, 42 enrolled. In 2017, 36 master's, 12 doctorates awarded. Terminal master's awarded for partial completion of doctoral program. *Degree requirements:* For master's, comprehensive exam, thesis or alternative; for doctorate, one foreign language, thesis/dissertation. *Entrance requirements:* For master's, GRE General Test, minimum undergraduate GPA of 3.25; for doctorate, GRE General Test. *Application deadline:* For fall admission, 1/10 for domestic students, 12/1 for international students; for spring admission, 9/15 for domestic students, 10/1 for international students. Applications are processed on a rolling basis. Application fee: $60 ($80 for international students). Electronic applications accepted. Application fee is waived when completed online. *Financial support:* In 2017–18, 77 students received support, including 49 fellowships (averaging $4,274 per year), 10 teaching assistantships with full and partial tuition reimbursements available (averaging $20,427 per year); research assistantships, institutionally sponsored loans, scholarships/grants, health care benefits, and unspecified assistantships also available. Financial award application deadline: 2/15; financial award applicants required to submit FAFSA. *Faculty research:* Audiology; speech communicative disorders; cognitive development/processes; hearing; hearing communicative disorders. *Total annual research expenditures:* $850,726. *Application contact:* E-mail: slhsgrad@colorado.edu.
Website: http://slhs.colorado.edu

University of Connecticut, Graduate School, College of Liberal Arts and Sciences, Department of Communication Sciences, Program in Speech-Language Pathology, Storrs, CT 06269. Offers MA, Au D, PhD. *Accreditation:* ASHA. Terminal master's awarded for partial completion of doctoral program. *Degree requirements:* For master's, comprehensive exam, thesis optional; for doctorate, thesis/dissertation. *Entrance requirements:* For master's and doctorate, GRE General Test. Additional exam requirements/recommendations for international students: Required—TOEFL (minimum score 550 paper-based). Electronic applications accepted.

University of Delaware, College of Health Sciences, Department of Communication Sciences and Disorders, Newark, DE 19716. Offers speech-language pathology (MA). *Entrance requirements:* For master's, GRE General Test, letters of recommendation, personal essay.

University of Florida, Graduate School, College of Public Health and Health Professions, Department of Speech, Language and Hearing Sciences, Gainesville, FL 32611. Offers audiology (Au D); communication sciences and disorders (MA, PhD). *Accreditation:* ASHA (one or more programs are accredited). *Degree requirements:* For master's, thesis optional; for doctorate, comprehensive exam, thesis/dissertation. *Entrance requirements:* For master's and doctorate, GRE General Test, minimum GPA of 3.0. Additional exam requirements/recommendations for international students: Required—TOEFL (minimum score 550 paper-based; 80 iBT), IELTS (minimum score 6). Electronic applications accepted. *Faculty research:* Phonetic science, cochlear implant, dyslexia, auditory development, voice.

University of Georgia, College of Education, Department of Communication Sciences and Special Education, Athens, GA 30602. Offers communication science and disorders (M Ed, MA, PhD, Ed S); special education (Ed D). *Accreditation:* ASHA (one or more programs are accredited). Terminal master's awarded for partial completion of doctoral program. *Degree requirements:* For master's, comprehensive exam (for some programs), thesis (for some programs); for doctorate, thesis/dissertation. *Entrance requirements:* For master's, doctorate, and Ed S, GRE General Test. Additional exam requirements/recommendations for international students: Required—TOEFL. Electronic applications accepted.

University of Hawaii at Manoa, John A. Burns School of Medicine, Department of Communication Sciences and Disorders, Honolulu, HI 96822. Offers MS. *Accreditation:* ASHA. *Program availability:* Part-time. *Degree requirements:* For master's, thesis optional. *Entrance requirements:* For master's, GRE General Test, minimum GPA of 3.0. Additional exam requirements/recommendations for international students: Required—TOEFL (minimum score 580 paper-based; 92 iBT), IELTS (minimum score 5). *Faculty research:* Emerging language (child phonology and special populations), central auditory function, developmental phonology, processing in the aging.

University of Houston, College of Liberal Arts and Social Sciences, Department of Communication Sciences and Disorders, Houston, TX 77204. Offers MA. *Accreditation:* ASHA. *Program availability:* Part-time. *Degree requirements:* For master's, comprehensive exam, thesis optional. *Entrance requirements:* For master's, GRE General Test, minimum GPA of 3.0 in last 60 hours. Additional exam requirements/recommendations for international students: Required—TOEFL (minimum score 550 paper-based; 79 iBT). *Faculty research:* Stuttering, voice disorders, language disorders, phonological processing, cognition.

University of Illinois at Urbana–Champaign, Graduate College, College of Applied Health Sciences, Department of Speech and Hearing Science, Champaign, IL 61820. Offers audiology (Au D); speech and hearing science (MA, PhD). *Accreditation:* ASHA (one or more programs are accredited).

The University of Iowa, Graduate College, College of Liberal Arts and Sciences, Department of Communication Sciences and Disorders, Iowa City, IA 52242-1316. Offers MA, Au D, PhD, Au D/PhD. *Accreditation:* ASHA. *Degree requirements:* For master's, thesis optional, exam; for doctorate, comprehensive exam (for some programs), thesis/dissertation (for some programs). *Entrance requirements:* For master's and doctorate, GRE General Test, minimum GPA of 3.0. Additional exam requirements/recommendations for international students: Required—TOEFL (minimum score 550 paper-based; 81 iBT). Electronic applications accepted.

The University of Kansas, Graduate Studies, College of Liberal Arts and Sciences, Intercampus Program in Communicative Disorders: Speech-Language Pathology, Lawrence, KS 66045. Offers audiology (PhD); speech-language pathology (MA, PhD). *Accreditation:* ASHA. *Program availability:* Part-time. *Students:* 80 full-time (74 women), 5 part-time (all women); includes 17 minority (5 Black or African American, non-Hispanic/Latino; 1 American Indian or Alaska Native, non-Hispanic/Latino; 1 Asian, non-Hispanic/Latino; 2 Hispanic/Latino; 8 Two or more races, non-Hispanic/Latino), 5 international. Average age 26. 189 applicants, 38% accepted, 30 enrolled. In 2017, 27 master's, 8 doctorates awarded. Terminal master's awarded for partial completion of doctoral program. *Entrance requirements:* For master's, GRE General Test, minimum GPA of 3.0, bachelor's degree, one- to two-page resume, three letters of recommendation, official transcript, 500-word essay on one of three topics provided; for doctorate, GRE General Test, minimum GPA of 3.0, bachelor's degree, one- to two-page resume, three letters of recommendation, official transcript. Additional exam requirements/recommendations for international students: Required—TOEFL. *Application deadline:* For fall admission, 12/10 priority date for domestic students, 10/10 priority date for international students. Application fee: $65 ($85 for international students). Electronic applications accepted. *Financial support:* Research assistantships, teaching assistantships, career-related internships or fieldwork, Federal Work-Study, institutionally sponsored loans, scholarships/grants, traineeships, and unspecified assistantships available. Support available to part-time students. Financial award application deadline: 12/10; financial award applicants required to submit FAFSA. *Faculty research:* Reading disorders, language acquisition, auditory electrophysiology, genetics of language, phonological development. *Unit head:* Holly L. Storkel, Chair, 785-864-0497, E-mail: hstorkel@ku.edu. *Application contact:* Graduate Admissions Coordinator, 913-588-5935, Fax: 913-588-5923, E-mail: ipcd@ku.edu.
Website: http://splh.ku.edu/ipcd/

The University of Kansas, University of Kansas Medical Center, School of Health Professions, Intercampus Program in Communicative Disorders: Audiology and Speech-Language Pathology, Lawrence, KS 66045. Offers audiology (Au D); speech-language pathology (SLPD). *Accreditation:* ASHA. *Faculty:* 21. *Students:* 25 full-time (22 women), 14 part-time (12 women); includes 8 minority (3 Black or African American, non-Hispanic/Latino; 1 American Indian or Alaska Native, non-Hispanic/Latino; 1 Hispanic/Latino; 3 Two or more races, non-Hispanic/Latino), 1 international. Average age 28. 38 applicants, 74% accepted, 13 enrolled. In 2017, 11 doctorates awarded. *Degree requirements:* For doctorate, comprehensive exam, oral comprehensive exam (for AuD); capstone oral exam (for SLPD). *Entrance requirements:* For doctorate, GRE (for Au D), bachelor's degree and/or prerequisites in communication sciences and disorders (for Au D); master's degree in speech-language pathology (for SLPD). Additional exam requirements/recommendations for international students: Required—TOEFL or IELTS. *Application deadline:* For fall admission, 1/15 for domestic and international students. Application fee: $60. Electronic applications accepted. *Financial support:* Research assistantships with partial tuition reimbursements, teaching assistantships with partial tuition reimbursements, institutionally sponsored loans, scholarships/grants, traineeships, health care benefits, and unspecified assistantships available. Financial award application deadline: 3/1; financial award applicants required to submit FAFSA. *Unit head:* Dr. John A. Ferraro, Professor/Chair/Program Co-Director, 913-588-5937, Fax: 913-588-5923, E-mail: jferraro@kumc.edu. *Application contact:* Angela Carrasco, Admissions Coordinator, 913-588-5935, Fax: 913-588-5923, E-mail: ipcd@ku.edu.
Website: http://ipcd.ku.edu

Communication Disorders

University of Kentucky, Graduate School, College of Health Sciences, Program in Communication Disorders, Lexington, KY 40506-0032. Offers MS. *Accreditation:* ASHA. *Degree requirements:* For master's, comprehensive exam. *Entrance requirements:* For master's, GRE General Test, minimum undergraduate GPA of 2.75. Additional exam requirements/recommendations for international students: Required—TOEFL (minimum score 550 paper-based). Electronic applications accepted. *Faculty research:* Swallowing disorders, infant speech development, child language intervention, augmentative communication.

University of Louisiana at Lafayette, College of Liberal Arts, Department of Communicative Disorders, Lafayette, LA 70504. Offers applied language and speech sciences (PhD); speech pathology and audiology (MS). *Accreditation:* ASHA (one or more programs are accredited). *Entrance requirements:* For master's, GRE General Test, minimum GPA of 2.75. Additional exam requirements/recommendations for international students: Required—TOEFL (minimum score 550 paper-based). *Application deadline:* For fall admission, 5/15 for domestic and international students; for spring admission, 10/1 for domestic and international students. Application fee: $25 ($30 for international students). *Financial support:* Application deadline: 5/1. *Unit head:* Dr. Nancye C. Roussel, Head of Department, 337-482-6727, E-mail: ncroussel@louisiana.edu. *Application contact:* Dr. John Tetnowski, Coordinator, 337-482-6869, Fax: 337-482-6195, E-mail: tetnowski@louisiana.edu.

University of Louisiana at Monroe, Graduate School, College of Health and Pharmaceutical Sciences, Department of Speech-Language Pathology, Monroe, LA 71209-0001. Offers MS. *Accreditation:* ASHA. *Faculty:* 7 full-time (6 women). *Students:* 42 full-time (all women), 6 part-time (all women); includes 7 minority (3 Black or African American, non-Hispanic/Latino; 2 Hispanic/Latino; 2 Two or more races, non-Hispanic/Latino). Average age 24. 113 applicants, 15% accepted, 15 enrolled. In 2017, 23 master's awarded. *Degree requirements:* For master's, thesis. *Entrance requirements:* For master's, GRE, minimum GPA of 2.5. Additional exam requirements/recommendations for international students: Required—TOEFL (minimum score 500 paper-based; 61 iBT). *Application deadline:* For fall admission, 8/24 priority date for domestic students, 7/1 for international students; for winter admission, 12/14 priority date for domestic students; for spring admission, 1/19 for domestic students, 11/1 for international students. Applications are processed on a rolling basis. Application fee: $20 ($30 for international students). Electronic applications accepted. *Expenses:* Tuition, state resident: full-time $6489; part-time $479 per hour. Tuition, nonresident: full-time $12,100; part-time $479 per hour. *Required fees:* $8860; $802 per hour. $3273 per semester. *Financial support:* In 2017–18, 29 students received support. Research assistantships, career-related internships or fieldwork, Federal Work-Study, and unspecified assistantships available. Financial award application deadline: 4/1; financial award applicants required to submit FAFSA. *Faculty research:* Child language, stuttering, multicultural issues, ethics.
Website: http://www.ulm.edu/slp/

University of Louisville, School of Medicine, Department of Otolaryngology Head and Neck Surgery and Communicative Disorders, Louisville, KY 40292-0001. Offers audiology (Au D); speech-language pathology (MS). *Accreditation:* ASHA. *Faculty:* 92 full-time (18 women), 3 part-time/adjunct (0 women). *Students:* 93 full-time (84 women), 1 (woman) part-time; includes 5 minority (2 Black or African American, non-Hispanic/Latino; 2 Hispanic/Latino; 1 Two or more races, non-Hispanic/Latino), 1 international. Average age 25. 183 applicants, 33% accepted, 32 enrolled. In 2017, 26 master's, 12 doctorates awarded. *Entrance requirements:* For doctorate, GRE. Additional exam requirements/recommendations for international students: Required—TOEFL (minimum score 79 iBT); Recommended—IELTS. *Application deadline:* For fall admission, 1/1 for domestic students; for winter admission, 1/1 for international students. Application fee: $65. *Expenses:* Tuition, state resident: full-time $12,246; part-time $681 per credit hour. Tuition, nonresident: full-time $25,486; part-time $1417 per credit hour. *Required fees:* $196. Tuition and fees vary according to course load, program and reciprocity agreements. *Financial support:* Career-related internships or fieldwork and stipends available. *Faculty research:* Adult auditory rehabilitation, cochlear implant outcomes, auditory neuroscience, scholarship related to teaching and service delivery, sound localization and spatial hearing. *Total annual research expenditures:* $2.7 million. *Unit head:* Dr. Jeffrey M. Bumpous, Professor of Otolaryngology/Chairman, 502-561-7268, Fax: 502-561-7280, E-mail: jmbump01@louisville.edu. *Application contact:* Angela Smith, Program Coordinator, 502-852-5277, E-mail: angela.smith@louisville.edu.
Website: http://louisville.edu/medicine/departments/otolaryngology

University of Maine, Graduate School, College of Natural Sciences, Forestry, and Agriculture, Department of Communication Sciences and Disorders, Orono, ME 04469. Offers MA. *Accreditation:* ASHA. *Faculty:* 7 full-time (6 women), 4 part-time/adjunct (2 women). *Students:* 32 full-time (all women); includes 1 minority (American Indian or Alaska Native, non-Hispanic/Latino), 5 international. Average age 24. 93 applicants, 45% accepted, 15 enrolled. In 2017, 15 master's awarded. *Degree requirements:* For master's, comprehensive exam. *Entrance requirements:* For master's, GRE General Test. Additional exam requirements/recommendations for international students: Required—TOEFL (minimum score 80 iBT). *Application deadline:* For fall admission, 1/15 priority date for domestic students, 1/15 for international students. Applications are processed on a rolling basis. Application fee: $65. Electronic applications accepted. *Expenses:* Tuition, state resident: full-time $7722; part-time $429 per credit hour. Tuition, nonresident: full-time $25,146; part-time $1397 per credit hour. *Required fees:* $1162; $581 per credit hour. *Financial support:* In 2017–18, 8 students received support, including 4 research assistantships (averaging $7,500 per year), 1 teaching assistantship with partial tuition reimbursement available (averaging $15,200 per year); career-related internships or fieldwork, Federal Work-Study, institutionally sponsored loans, scholarships/grants, and tuition waivers (full and partial) also available. Support available to part-time students. Financial award application deadline: 3/1. *Faculty research:* Telepractice speech therapy with aphasia clients, linguistic processing in adults with brain injury, communication dynamics of AAC users and their partners, clinical observation in CSD, needs and concerns of parents raising children with communication disorders, stuttering and language. *Total annual research expenditures:* $5,000. *Unit head:* Dr. Nancy Hall, Chair, 207-581-2006, Fax: 207-581-1953. *Application contact:* Scott G. Delcourt, Assistant Vice President for Graduate Studies and Senior Associate Dean, 207-581-3291, Fax: 207-581-3232, E-mail: graduate@maine.edu.
Website: http://umaine.edu/comscidis/

The University of Manchester, School of Psychological Sciences, Manchester, United Kingdom. Offers audiology (M Phil, PhD); clinical psychology (M Phil, PhD, Psy D); psychology (M Phil, PhD).

University of Maryland, College Park, Academic Affairs, College of Behavioral and Social Sciences, Department of Hearing and Speech Sciences, College Park, MD 20742. Offers audiology (MA, PhD); hearing and speech sciences (Au D); language pathology (MA, PhD); neuroscience (PhD); speech (MA, PhD). *Accreditation:* ASHA (one or more programs are accredited). *Degree requirements:* For master's, thesis optional; for doctorate, thesis/dissertation, written and oral exams. *Entrance requirements:* For master's, GRE General Test, minimum GPA of 3.5, 3 letters of recommendation; for doctorate, GRE General Test, minimum GPA of 3.5. Additional exam requirements/recommendations for international students: Required—TOEFL. Electronic applications accepted. *Faculty research:* Speech perception, language acquisition, bilingualism, hearing loss.

University of Massachusetts Amherst, Graduate School, School of Public Health and Health Sciences, Department of Communication Disorders, Amherst, MA 01003. Offers audiology (Au D, PhD); clinical audiology (PhD); speech-language pathology (MA, PhD). *Accreditation:* ASHA (one or more programs are accredited). *Program availability:* Part-time. Terminal master's awarded for partial completion of doctoral program. *Degree requirements:* For master's, thesis optional; for doctorate, comprehensive exam, thesis/dissertation. *Entrance requirements:* For master's and doctorate, GRE General Test. Additional exam requirements/recommendations for international students: Required—TOEFL (minimum score 550 paper-based; 80 iBT), IELTS (minimum score 6.5). Electronic applications accepted.

University of Memphis, Graduate School, School of Communication Sciences and Disorders, Memphis, TN 38152. Offers audiology (Au D); communication sciences and disorders (PhD), including hearing sciences and disorders; speech-language pathology (MA). *Accreditation:* ASHA. *Program availability:* Part-time. *Students:* Average age 28. 442 applicants, 26% accepted, 40 enrolled. In 2017, 16 master's, 10 doctorates awarded. Terminal master's awarded for partial completion of doctoral program. *Degree requirements:* For master's, comprehensive exam, thesis or alternative, clinical practicum; for doctorate, comprehensive exam, thesis/dissertation (for some programs), qualifying exam, research project, externship. *Entrance requirements:* For master's, GRE General Test, minimum GPA of 3.0, three letters of recommendation, personal statement, ASHA certification; for doctorate, GRE General Test, minimum GPA of 3.0, three letters of recommendation, personal statement, curriculum vitae, interview. Additional exam requirements/recommendations for international students: Required—TOEFL (minimum score 550 paper-based; 79 iBT). *Application deadline:* For fall admission, 2/1 priority date for domestic students. Applications are processed on a rolling basis. Application fee: $35 ($60 for international students). Electronic applications accepted. *Expenses:* Contact institution. *Financial support:* In 2017–18, 25 research assistantships with full tuition reimbursements (averaging $8,560 per year) were awarded; Federal Work-Study, scholarships/grants, and unspecified assistantships also available. Financial award application deadline: 2/1; financial award applicants required to submit FAFSA. *Faculty research:* Hearing aid characteristic selection, language acquisition, speech disorders, characteristics of the aging voice, hearing science. *Total annual research expenditures:* $1.5 million. *Unit head:* Dr. Linda Jarmulowicz, Interim Dean, 901-678-5800, Fax: 901-525-1282, E-mail: ljrmlwcz@memphis.edu. *Application contact:* Dr. Lisa Mendel, Interim Associate Dean, 901-678-5800, E-mail: lmendel@memphis.edu.
Website: http://www.memphis.edu/csd

University of Minnesota, Duluth, Graduate School, College of Education and Human Service Professions, Department of Communication Sciences and Disorders, Duluth, MN 55812-2496. Offers MA. *Accreditation:* ASHA. *Program availability:* Part-time. *Degree requirements:* For master's, research project, oral exam. *Entrance requirements:* For master's, minimum GPA of 3.0, undergraduate degree in communication sciences and disorders. Additional exam requirements/recommendations for international students: Required—TOEFL (minimum score 550 paper-based). *Faculty research:* Clinical supervision, augmentative communication, speech understanding, fluency, developmental apraxia of speech.

University of Minnesota, Twin Cities Campus, Graduate School, College of Liberal Arts, Department of Speech-Language-Hearing Sciences, Minneapolis, MN 55455. Offers audiology (Au D); speech-language pathology (MA); speech-language-hearing sciences (PhD). Terminal master's awarded for partial completion of doctoral program. *Degree requirements:* For master's, thesis, 375 client contact hours; for doctorate, comprehensive exam, thesis/dissertation. *Entrance requirements:* For master's and doctorate, GRE General Test, minimum GPA of 3.0. Additional exam requirements/recommendations for international students: Required—TOEFL. Electronic applications accepted. *Faculty research:* Normal and disordered child phonology, specific language impairment, bilingual and multicultural aspects of language, TBI, AAC.

University of Mississippi, Graduate School, School of Applied Sciences, University, MS 38677. Offers communicative disorders (MS); criminal justice (MCJ); exercise science (MS); food and nutrition services (MS); health and kinesiology (PhD); health promotion (MS); nutrition and hospitality management (PhD); park and recreation management (MA); social welfare (PhD); social work (MSW). *Faculty:* 66 full-time (38 women), 33 part-time/adjunct (14 women). *Students:* 182 full-time (139 women), 41 part-time (27 women); includes 49 minority (41 Black or African American, non-Hispanic/Latino; 1 American Indian or Alaska Native, non-Hispanic/Latino; 3 Asian, non-Hispanic/Latino; 3 Hispanic/Latino; 1 Two or more races, non-Hispanic/Latino), 13 international. Average age 26. *Entrance requirements:* For master's, GRE General Test, minimum GPA of 3.0. Additional exam requirements/recommendations for international students: Required—TOEFL. *Application deadline:* For fall admission, 4/1 for domestic students; for spring admission, 10/1 for domestic students. Applications are processed on a rolling basis. Application fee: $50. Electronic applications accepted. *Financial support:* Scholarships/grants available. Financial award application deadline: 3/1; financial award applicants required to submit FAFSA. *Unit head:* Dr. Teresa C. Carithers, Dean, 662-915-1081, Fax: 662-915-5717, E-mail: applsci@olemiss.edu.

University of Missouri, School of Health Professions, Program in Communication Science and Disorders, Columbia, MO 65211. Offers MHS, PhD, MHS/Phd. *Accreditation:* ASHA (one or more programs are accredited). *Entrance requirements:* For master's, GRE General Test, minimum GPA of 3.0. Additional exam requirements/recommendations for international students: Required—TOEFL. *Application deadline:* Applications are processed on a rolling basis. Electronic applications accepted. *Expenses:* Tuition, state resident: full-time $6480. Tuition, nonresident: full-time $17,744. *Required fees:* $1108. Tuition and fees vary according to course load, campus/location and program. *Financial support:* Research assistantships, teaching assistantships, and institutionally sponsored loans available.
Website: http://shp.missouri.edu/csd/

University of Montana, Graduate School, Phyllis J. Washington College of Education and Human Sciences, Department of Communicative Sciences and Disorders, Missoula, MT 59812. Offers speech-language pathology (MS, Postbaccalaureate Certificate). *Accreditation:* ASHA.

University of Montevallo, College of Arts and Sciences, Department of Communication Science and Disorders, Montevallo, AL 35115. Offers MS. *Accreditation:* ASHA. *Students:* 50 full-time (all women); includes 3 minority (2 Black or African American, non-Hispanic/Latino; 1 Hispanic/Latino). *Degree requirements:* For master's, comprehensive exam. *Entrance requirements:* For master's, GRE General Test, MAT. Additional exam requirements/recommendations for international students: Required—TOEFL (minimum score 550 paper-based). *Application deadline:* For fall admission, 7/15 for domestic students; for spring admission, 11/15 for domestic students. Application fee: $30. *Expenses:* Tuition, state resident: full-time $9888. Tuition, nonresident: full-time $21,144. *Required fees:* $1920. *Financial support:* Federal Work-Study, scholarships/grants, and unspecified assistantships available. *Unit head:* Dr. Claire Edwards, Chair, 205-665-6724, E-mail: edwardsc@montevallo.edu. *Application contact:* Christine Soria, Graduate Admissions Assistant, 205-665-6510, E-mail: csoria@montevallo.edu.
Website: http://www.montevallo.edu/csd/

University of Nebraska at Kearney, College of Education, Department of Communication Disorders, Kearney, NE 68849-0001. Offers speech/language pathology (MS Ed). *Accreditation:* ASHA. *Program availability:* Part-time. *Degree requirements:* For master's, comprehensive exam, thesis optional. *Entrance requirements:* For master's, GRE General Test, personal statement, letters of recommendation, phase 2 video response. Additional exam requirements/recommendations for international students: Recommended—TOEFL (minimum score 550 paper-based; 79 iBT), IELTS (minimum score 6.5). Electronic applications accepted. *Faculty research:* Neurogenic, communication disorders in adults, phonological development and disorders, orofacial anomalies, audio logic rehabilitation of the elderly.

University of Nebraska at Omaha, Graduate Studies, College of Education, Department of Special Education and Communication Disorders, Omaha, NE 68182. Offers special education (MS); speech-language pathology (MS). *Accreditation:* ASHA; NCATE. *Program availability:* Part-time, evening/weekend. *Degree requirements:* For master's, comprehensive exam, thesis (for some programs). *Entrance requirements:* For master's, minimum GPA of 3.0, statement of purpose, 2 letters of recommendation, copy of teaching certificate. Additional exam requirements/recommendations for international students: Required—TOEFL, IELTS, PTE. Electronic applications accepted.

University of Nebraska–Lincoln, Graduate College, College of Education and Human Sciences, Department of Special Education and Communication Disorders, Program in Speech-Language Pathology and Audiology, Lincoln, NE 68588. Offers audiology and hearing science (Au D); speech-language pathology and audiology (MS). *Accreditation:* ASHA. *Degree requirements:* For master's, thesis optional. *Entrance requirements:* For master's, GRE. Additional exam requirements/recommendations for international students: Required—TOEFL (minimum score 500 paper-based). Electronic applications accepted.

University of Nevada, Reno, Graduate School, Division of Health Sciences, Department of Speech Pathology and Audiology, Reno, NV 89557. Offers speech pathology (PhD); speech pathology and audiology (MS). *Accreditation:* ASHA (one or more programs are accredited). Terminal master's awarded for partial completion of doctoral program. *Degree requirements:* For master's, thesis optional; for doctorate, thesis/dissertation. *Entrance requirements:* For master's, GRE General Test, minimum GPA of 2.75; for doctorate, GRE General Test, minimum GPA of 3.0. Additional exam requirements/recommendations for international students: Required—TOEFL (minimum score 500 paper-based; 61 iBT), IELTS (minimum score 6). Electronic applications accepted. *Faculty research:* Language impairment in children, voice disorders, stuttering.

University of New Hampshire, Graduate School, College of Health and Human Services, Department of Communication Sciences and Disorders, Durham, NH 03824. Offers adult neurogenic communication (MS); communication sciences and disorders (MS); early childhood intervention (MS); language and literacy disorders (MS). *Accreditation:* ASHA. *Program availability:* Part-time. *Students:* 40 full-time (39 women), 2 part-time (both women); includes 3 minority (2 Asian, non-Hispanic/Latino; 1 Hispanic/Latino), 1 international. Average age 26. 138 applicants, 36% accepted, 20 enrolled. In 2017, 33 master's awarded. *Entrance requirements:* For master's, GRE General Test. Additional exam requirements/recommendations for international students: Required—TOEFL (minimum score 550 paper-based; 80 iBT). *Application deadline:* For fall admission, 1/15 priority date for domestic students, 1/15 for international students. Application fee: $65. Electronic applications accepted. *Financial support:* In 2017–18, 15 students received support, including 12 teaching assistantships; fellowships, research assistantships, career-related internships or fieldwork, Federal Work-Study, scholarships/grants, and tuition waivers (full and partial) also available. Support available to part-time students. Financial award application deadline: 2/15. *Unit head:* Stephen Calculator, Chair, 603-862-3836. *Application contact:* Jane Dodge, Administrative Assistant III, 603-862-0965, E-mail: communication.disorders@unh.edu. Website: http://chhs.unh.edu/csd

University of New Mexico, Graduate Studies, College of Arts and Sciences, Program in Speech-Language Pathology, Albuquerque, NM 87131. Offers MS. *Accreditation:* ASHA. *Students:* Average age 30. 150 applicants, 24% accepted, 27 enrolled. In 2017, 17 master's awarded. *Degree requirements:* For master's, comprehensive exam, thesis optional. *Entrance requirements:* For master's, GRE General Test, minimum GPA of 3.4 in speech and hearing sciences coursework. Additional exam requirements/recommendations for international students: Required—TOEFL (minimum score 550 paper-based; 80 iBT). *Application deadline:* For fall admission, 2/1 for domestic students, 1/1 for international students. Application fee: $50. Electronic applications accepted. *Financial support:* Research assistantships with partial tuition reimbursements, career-related internships or fieldwork, Federal Work-Study, scholarships/grants, health care benefits, and unspecified assistantships available. Financial award application deadline: 2/1; financial award applicants required to submit FAFSA. *Faculty research:* Augmentative and alternative communication (AAC), behavioral genetic studies of language, child language assessment, bilingual language acquisition, bilingual phonology, speech perception, swallowing disorders, transition from oral language to literacy. *Total annual research expenditures:* $172,031. *Unit head:* Dr. Barbara Rodriguez, Chair, 505-277-9728, Fax: 505-277-0968, E-mail: brodrig@unm.edu. *Application contact:* Tracy Wenzl, Department Administrator, 505-277-4453, Fax: 505-277-0968, E-mail: twenzl@unm.edu.
Website: http://shs.unm.edu/programs/master-of-science/index.html

The University of North Carolina at Chapel Hill, School of Medicine and Graduate School, Graduate Programs in Medicine, Department of Allied Health Sciences, Division of Speech and Hearing Sciences, Chapel Hill, NC 27599. Offers audiology (Au D); speech and hearing sciences (PhD); speech-language pathology (MS). *Accreditation:* ASHA (one or more programs are accredited). *Program availability:* Online learning. *Degree requirements:* For master's, comprehensive exam, thesis optional; for doctorate, comprehensive exam, thesis/dissertation. *Entrance requirements:* For master's, GRE General Test, minimum GPA of 3.0; for doctorate, GRE, minimum GPA of 3.0. Additional exam requirements/recommendations for international students: Required—TOEFL (minimum score 550 paper-based). Electronic applications accepted. *Faculty research:* Child language and literacy, family participation in early intervention, child and adult hearing loss and treatment, vocal characteristics of African American speakers and aging populations, adult apraxia of speech.

The University of North Carolina at Greensboro, Graduate School, School of Health and Human Sciences, Department of Communication Sciences and Disorders, Greensboro, NC 27412-5001. Offers speech language pathology (PhD); speech pathology and audiology (MA). *Accreditation:* ASHA. *Degree requirements:* For master's, thesis or alternative. *Entrance requirements:* For master's, GRE General Test. Additional exam requirements/recommendations for international students: Required—TOEFL. Electronic applications accepted.

University of North Dakota, Graduate School, College of Arts and Sciences, Department of Communication Sciences and Disorders, Grand Forks, ND 58202. Offers speech-language pathology (MS). *Accreditation:* ASHA. *Program availability:* Part-time. *Degree requirements:* For master's, comprehensive exam, thesis or alternative. *Entrance requirements:* For master's, GRE General Test, minimum GPA of 3.0. Additional exam requirements/recommendations for international students: Required—TOEFL (minimum score 550 paper-based; 79 iBT), IELTS (minimum score 6.5). Electronic applications accepted. *Faculty research:* Mass communications, journalism, community law, international communications, cultural studies.

University of Northern Colorado, Graduate School, College of Natural and Health Sciences, School of Human Sciences, Program in Audiology and Speech-Language Sciences, Greeley, CO 80639. Offers audiology (Au D); speech-language pathology (MA). *Accreditation:* ASHA (one or more programs are accredited). *Program availability:* Part-time, evening/weekend, online learning. *Degree requirements:* For master's, comprehensive exam, thesis or alternative; for doctorate, comprehensive exam, thesis/dissertation. *Entrance requirements:* For master's and doctorate, GRE General Test. Electronic applications accepted.

University of Northern Iowa, Graduate College, College of Humanities, Arts and Sciences, Department of Communication Sciences and Disorders, Cedar Falls, IA 50614. Offers speech-language pathology (MA). *Accreditation:* ASHA. *Program availability:* Part-time, evening/weekend. *Degree requirements:* For master's, comprehensive exam, thesis or alternative. *Entrance requirements:* For master's, GRE, minimum GPA of 3.0. Additional exam requirements/recommendations for international students: Required—TOEFL (minimum score 500 paper-based; 61 iBT).

University of North Florida, College of Education and Human Services, Department of Exceptional, Deaf, and Interpreter Education, Jacksonville, FL 32224. Offers American Sign Language (MS); American Sign Language/English interpreting (M Ed); applied behavior analysis (M Ed); autism (M Ed); deaf education (M Ed); disability services (M Ed); exceptional student education (M Ed). *Accreditation:* NCATE. *Program availability:* Part-time, evening/weekend. *Entrance requirements:* For master's, GRE General Test, minimum GPA of 3.0 in last 60 hours, interview, 3 letters of recommendation. Additional exam requirements/recommendations for international students: Required—TOEFL (minimum score 500 paper-based). Electronic applications accepted. *Faculty research:* Transportation, energy, communications, healthcare, nano-science and engineering, unmanned aircraft systems, biomedical applications.

University of North Texas, Robert B. Toulouse School of Graduate Studies, Denton, TX 76203-5459. Offers accounting (MS); applied anthropology (MA, MS); applied behavior analysis (Certificate); applied geography (MA); applied technology and performance improvement (M Ed, MS); art education (MA); art history (MA); art museum education (Certificate); arts leadership (Certificate); audiology (Au D); behavior analysis (MS); behavioral science (PhD); biochemistry and molecular biology (MS); biology (MA, MS); biomedical engineering (MS); business analysis (MS); chemistry (MS); clinical health psychology (PhD); communication studies (MA, MS); computer engineering (MS); computer science (MS); counseling (M Ed, MS), including clinical mental health counseling (MS), college and university counseling, elementary school counseling, secondary school counseling; creative writing (MA); criminal justice (MS); curriculum and instruction (M Ed); decision sciences (MBA); design (MA, MFA), including fashion design (MFA), innovation studies, interior design (MFA); early childhood studies (MS); economics (MS); educational leadership (M Ed, Ed D); educational psychology (MS, PhD), including family studies (MS), gifted and talented (MS), human development (MS), learning and cognition (MS), research, measurement and evaluation (MS); electrical engineering (MS); emergency management (MPA); engineering technology (MS); English (MA); English as a second language (MA); environmental science (MS); finance (MBA, MS); financial management (MPA); French (MA); health services management (MBA); higher education (M Ed, Ed D); history (MA, MS); hospitality management (MS); human resources management (MPA); information science (MS); information systems (PhD); information technologies (MBA); interdisciplinary studies (MA, MS); international studies (MA); international sustainable tourism (MS); jazz studies (MM); journalism (MA, MJ, Graduate Certificate), including interactive and virtual digital communication (Graduate Certificate), narrative journalism (Graduate Certificate), public relations (Graduate Certificate); kinesiology (MS); linguistics (MA); local government management (MPA); logistics (PhD); logistics and supply chain management (MBA); long-term care, senior housing, and aging services (MA); management (PhD); marketing (MBA); mathematics (MA, MS); mechanical and energy engineering (MS, PhD); music (MA), including ethnomusicology, music theory, musicology, performance; music composition (PhD); music education (MM Ed, PhD); nonprofit management (MPA); operations and supply chain management (MBA); performance (MM, DMA); philosophy (MA); political science (MA); professional and technical communication (MA); radio, television and film (MA, MFA); rehabilitation counseling (Certificate); sociology (MA); Spanish (MA); special education (M Ed); speech-language pathology (MA); strategic management (MBA); studio art (MFA); teaching (M Ed); MBA/MS. *Program availability:* Part-time, evening/weekend, online learning. Terminal master's awarded for partial completion of doctoral program. *Degree requirements:* For master's, variable foreign language requirement, comprehensive exam (for some programs), thesis (for some programs); for doctorate, variable foreign language requirement, comprehensive exam (for some programs), thesis/dissertation; for other advanced degree, variable foreign language requirement, comprehensive exam (for some programs). *Entrance requirements:* For master's and doctorate, GRE, GMAT. Additional exam requirements/recommendations for international students: Required—TOEFL (minimum score 550 paper-based; 79 iBT). Electronic applications accepted.

University of Oklahoma Health Sciences Center, Graduate College, College of Allied Health, Department of Communication Sciences and Disorders, Oklahoma City, OK 73190. Offers audiology (MS, Au D, PhD); communication sciences and disorders (Certificate), including reading, speech-language pathology; education of the deaf (MS); speech-language pathology (MS, PhD). *Accreditation:* ASHA (one or more programs are accredited). *Program availability:* Part-time. Terminal master's awarded for partial completion of doctoral program. *Degree requirements:* For master's, comprehensive exam, thesis optional; for doctorate, one foreign language, comprehensive exam, thesis/dissertation. *Entrance requirements:* For master's and doctorate, GRE General Test, 3 letters of recommendation. Additional exam requirements/recommendations for international students: Required—TOEFL (minimum score 550 paper-based). *Faculty research:* Event-related potentials, cleft palate, fluency disorders, language disorders, hearing and speech science.

University of Oregon, Graduate School, College of Education, Eugene, OR 97403. Offers communication disorders and sciences (MA, MS, PhD); counseling psychology (PhD); couples and family therapy (MS); critical and sociocultural studies in education (PhD); curriculum and teacher education (MA, MS); educational leadership (MS, D Ed, PhD); prevention science (M Ed, MS, PhD); school psychology (MS, PhD); special education (M Ed, MA, MS, PhD). *Program availability:* Part-time. Terminal master's awarded for partial completion of doctoral program. *Degree requirements:* For master's, exam, paper, or project; for doctorate, comprehensive exam, thesis/dissertation. *Entrance requirements:* Additional exam requirements/recommendations for international students: Required—TOEFL. *Faculty research:* Basic and applied research in teaching, learning and habilitation in all settings, schooling effectiveness.

University of Ottawa, Faculty of Graduate and Postdoctoral Studies, Faculty of Health Sciences, School of Rehabilitation Sciences, Ottawa, ON K1N 6N5, Canada. Offers audiology (M Sc); orthophony (M Sc). *Program availability:* Part-time, evening/weekend. *Entrance requirements:* For master's, honors degree or equivalent, minimum B average. Electronic applications accepted.

Communication Disorders

University of Pittsburgh, School of Health and Rehabilitation Sciences, Department of Communication Science and Disorders, Pittsburgh, PA 15260. Offers audiology (MA, MS, Au D); communication science and disorders (PhD); medical speech language pathology (CScD); speech language pathology (MA, MS). *Accreditation:* ASHA (one or more programs are accredited). *Faculty:* 12 full-time (9 women), 8 part-time/adjunct (6 women). *Students:* 137 full-time (128 women), 16 part-time (15 women); includes 12 minority (1 Black or African American, non-Hispanic/Latino; 5 Asian, non-Hispanic/Latino; 4 Hispanic/Latino; 1 Native Hawaiian or other Pacific Islander, non-Hispanic/Latino; 1 Two or more races, non-Hispanic/Latino), 7 international. Average age 26. 468 applicants, 44% accepted, 82 enrolled. In 2017, 66 master's, 15 doctorates awarded. *Degree requirements:* For master's, comprehensive exam, thesis (for some programs); for doctorate, comprehensive exam, thesis/dissertation (for some programs). *Entrance requirements:* For master's and doctorate, GRE General Test. Additional exam requirements/recommendations for international students: Required—TOEFL (minimum score 600 paper-based; 100 iBT), IELTS (minimum score 7). *Application deadline:* For fall admission, 1/15 for domestic and international students; for summer admission, 12/1 for domestic and international students. Applications are processed on a rolling basis. Electronic applications accepted. *Financial support:* In 2017–18, 5 fellowships with full tuition reimbursements (averaging $15,060 per year), 7 research assistantships with full tuition reimbursements (averaging $22,590 per year), 3 teaching assistantships with full tuition reimbursements (averaging $27,675 per year) were awarded; career-related internships or fieldwork, Federal Work-Study, scholarships/grants, traineeships, tuition waivers, and unspecified assistantships also available. *Faculty research:* Cognition and learning; sensation and perception; structure and movement; service delivery and outcomes. *Total annual research expenditures:* $2.1 million. *Unit head:* Dr. Cheryl Messick, Interim Chair/Director of Clinical Education/Professor, 412-383-6547, E-mail: cmessick@pitt.edu. *Application contact:* Jessica Maguire, Director of Admissions, 412-383-6557, Fax: 412-383-6535, E-mail: maguire@pitt.edu.
Website: http://www.shrs.pitt.edu/csd

University of Puerto Rico–Medical Sciences Campus, School of Health Professions, Program in Audiology, San Juan, PR 00936-5067. Offers Au D. *Accreditation:* ASHA. *Faculty research:* Hearing, auditory brainstem responses, otoacoustic emissions.

University of Puerto Rico–Medical Sciences Campus, School of Health Professions, Program in Speech-Language Pathology, San Juan, PR 00936-5067. Offers MS. *Accreditation:* ASHA. *Degree requirements:* For master's, one foreign language, comprehensive exam, thesis or alternative. *Entrance requirements:* For master's, EXADEP, interview; previous course work in linguistics, statistics, human development, and basic concepts in speech-language pathology; minimum GPA of 2.5. *Faculty research:* Aphasia, autism, language, aphasia, assistive technology.

University of Redlands, College of Arts and Sciences, Department of Communicative Disorders, Redlands, CA 92373-0999. Offers MS. *Accreditation:* ASHA. *Degree requirements:* For master's, final exam. *Entrance requirements:* For master's, GMAT or GRE, minimum GPA of 3.0, 3 letters of recommendation. Additional exam requirements/recommendations for international students: Required—TOEFL (minimum score 550 paper-based). Electronic applications accepted. *Expenses:* Contact institution. *Faculty research:* Neuropathy.

University of Rhode Island, Graduate School, College of Health Sciences, Department of Communicative Disorders, Kingston, RI 02881. Offers speech-language pathology (MS). *Accreditation:* ASHA. *Program availability:* Part-time. *Faculty:* 10 full-time (8 women). *Students:* 38 full-time (36 women), 1 part-time (0 women); includes 2 minority (1 Asian, non-Hispanic/Latino; 1 Two or more races, non-Hispanic/Latino). 131 applicants, 27% accepted, 13 enrolled. In 2017, 22 master's awarded. *Entrance requirements:* Additional exam requirements/recommendations for international students: Required—TOEFL. *Application deadline:* For fall admission, 2/15 for domestic and international students; for spring admission, 10/15 for domestic and international students. Application fee: $65. Electronic applications accepted. *Expenses:* Tuition, state resident: full-time $12,706; part-time $786 per credit. Tuition, nonresident: full-time $25,216; part-time $1401 per credit. *Required fees:* $1598; $45 per credit. One-time fee: $30 part-time. *Financial support:* In 2017–18, 4 teaching assistantships with tuition reimbursements (averaging $8,862 per year) were awarded. Financial award application deadline: 2/1; financial award applicants required to submit FAFSA. *Unit head:* Dr. Dana Kovarsky, Chair, 401-874-2735, E-mail: dana@uri.edu. *Application contact:* Dr. Ann Weiss, Graduate Program Coordinator, 401-874-9071, E-mail: alw@uri.edu.
Website: http://www.uri.edu/hss/cmd/

University of South Alabama, Pat Capps Covey College of Allied Health Professions, Department of Speech Pathology and Audiology, Mobile, AL 36688. Offers audiology (Au D); communication sciences and disorders (PhD); speech-language pathology (MS). *Accreditation:* ASHA. *Faculty:* 12 full-time (11 women), 2 part-time/adjunct (both women). *Students:* 90 full-time (86 women), 1 (woman) part-time; includes 6 minority (1 Black or African American, non-Hispanic/Latino; 1 American Indian or Alaska Native, non-Hispanic/Latino; 1 Asian, non-Hispanic/Latino; 3 Two or more races, non-Hispanic/Latino), 2 international. Average age 24. 244 applicants, 46% accepted, 35 enrolled. In 2017, 21 master's, 11 doctorates awarded. *Degree requirements:* For master's, thesis optional, externship; for doctorate, thesis/dissertation, clinical externship; minimum of 11 full-time semesters of academic study. *Entrance requirements:* For master's, GRE, bachelor's degree in communication sciences and disorders, three faculty references from undergraduate program; for doctorate, GRE, minimum GPA of 3.5. Additional exam requirements/recommendations for international students: Required—TOEFL (minimum score 600 paper-based; 100 iBT). *Application deadline:* For fall admission, 1/15 for domestic students. Application fee: $35. Electronic applications accepted. *Expenses:* Contact institution. *Financial support:* Fellowships, research assistantships, teaching assistantships, career-related internships or fieldwork, Federal Work-Study, institutionally sponsored loans, scholarships/grants, and unspecified assistantships available. Support available to part-time students. Financial award application deadline: 3/31; financial award applicants required to submit FAFSA. *Faculty research:* Adult speech and language, background noise, child language, developmental stuttering, evoked potentials and multicultural issues, vestibular research. *Unit head:* Dr. Elizabeth Adams, Department Chair, 251-445-9596, Fax: 251-445-9376, E-mail: eadams@southalabama.edu. *Application contact:* Dr. Susan Gordon-Hickey, Associate Dean, Allied Health, 251-445-9250, Fax: 251-445-9259, E-mail: gordonhickey@southalabama.edu.
Website: http://www.southalabama.edu/colleges/alliedhealth/speechandhearing/

University of South Carolina, The Graduate School, Arnold School of Public Health, Department of Communication Sciences and Disorders, Columbia, SC 29208. Offers MCD, MSP, PhD. *Accreditation:* ASHA (one or more programs are accredited). *Program availability:* Online learning. *Degree requirements:* For master's, thesis optional; for doctorate, comprehensive exam, thesis/dissertation. *Entrance requirements:* For master's, GRE General Test, minimum GPA of 3.0; for doctorate, GRE General Test. Electronic applications accepted. *Faculty research:* Noise-induced hearing loss, recurrent laryngeal nerve regeneration, cleft palate, child language-phonology, epidemiology of craniofacial anomalies.

University of South Dakota, Graduate School, College of Arts and Sciences, Department of Communication Sciences and Disorders, Vermillion, SD 57069. Offers audiology (Au D); speech-language pathology (MA). *Accreditation:* ASHA (one or more programs are accredited). *Program availability:* Part-time. *Degree requirements:* For master's, comprehensive exam; for doctorate, comprehensive exam, thesis/dissertation. *Entrance requirements:* For master's, GRE General Test, minimum GPA of 3.0. Additional exam requirements/recommendations for international students: Required—TOEFL (minimum score 550 paper-based; 79 iBT). *Application deadline:* For fall admission, 1/15 for domestic students. Application fee: $35. Electronic applications accepted. *Financial support:* Research assistantships with partial tuition reimbursements, teaching assistantships with partial tuition reimbursements, career-related internships or fieldwork, Federal Work-Study, scholarships/grants, and unspecified assistantships available. Support available to part-time students. Financial award application deadline: 5/1; financial award applicants required to submit FAFSA. *Faculty research:* Craniofacial anomalies, central auditory processing, phonological disorders. *Application contact:* Graduate School, 605-658-6140, Fax: 605-677-6118, E-mail: grad@usd.edu.
Website: http://www.usd.edu/arts-and-sciences/communication-sciences-and-disorders

University of Southern Mississippi, College of Health, Department of Speech and Hearing Sciences, Hattiesburg, MS 39406-0001. Offers MA, MS, Au D. *Accreditation:* ASHA (one or more programs are accredited). *Students:* 29 full-time (25 women). 166 applicants, 39% accepted, 26 enrolled. In 2017, 4 master's, 5 doctorates awarded. *Degree requirements:* For master's, comprehensive exam, thesis or alternative; for doctorate, comprehensive exam, thesis/dissertation. *Entrance requirements:* For master's, GRE General Test, minimum GPA of 3.0 in field of study, 2.75 in last 60 hours; for doctorate, GRE General Test, minimum GPA of 3.5. Additional exam requirements/recommendations for international students: Required—TOEFL, IELTS. *Application deadline:* For fall admission, 3/1 for domestic and international students; for spring admission, 1/10 priority date for domestic and international students. Application fee: $60. Electronic applications accepted. *Expenses:* Tuition, state resident: full-time $3830. *Financial support:* Research assistantships with full and partial tuition reimbursements, teaching assistantships with full and partial tuition reimbursements, career-related internships or fieldwork, Federal Work-Study, institutionally sponsored loans, scholarships/grants, health care benefits, and unspecified assistantships available. Financial award application deadline: 3/15; financial award applicants required to submit FAFSA. *Faculty research:* Voice disorders, auditory-evoked responses, acoustic analysis of speech, child language, parent-child interaction. *Unit head:* Dr. Edward Goshorn, Chair, 601-266-5217.
Website: https://www.usm.edu/speech-hearing-sciences

University of South Florida, College of Behavioral and Community Sciences, Department of Communication Sciences and Disorders, Tampa, FL 33620. Offers audiology (Au D); communication sciences and disorders (PhD), including hearing sciences and audiology, neurocommunicative science, speech-language sciences; speech-language pathology (MS). *Accreditation:* ASHA (one or more programs are accredited). *Program availability:* Part-time, evening/weekend, online learning. *Faculty:* 30 full-time (24 women). *Students:* 183 full-time (172 women), 60 part-time (57 women); includes 43 minority (4 Black or African American, non-Hispanic/Latino; 6 Asian, non-Hispanic/Latino; 31 Hispanic/Latino; 2 Two or more races, non-Hispanic/Latino), 7 international. Average age 26. 584 applicants, 17% accepted, 89 enrolled. In 2017, 63 master's, 13 doctorates awarded. *Degree requirements:* For master's, comprehensive exam, thesis (for some programs); for doctorate, comprehensive exam, thesis/dissertation. *Entrance requirements:* For master's, GRE General Test (for MS in speech language pathology and audiology), demonstrated competency in communication skills, 3 letters of recommendation, and letter of intent; minimum GPA of 3.2 in upper-division undergraduate course work and resume (for speech language pathology); minimum GPA of 3.0 for last 60 hours of bachelor's degree (for audiology); for doctorate, GRE General Test, minimum GPA of 3.5 during bachelor's, master's, and/or graduate study (for PhD), 3.0 during last 60 hours of bachelor's degree (for Au D); three letters of recommendation; letter of intent. Additional exam requirements/recommendations for international students: Required—TOEFL (minimum score 550 paper-based; 79 iBT) or IELTS (minimum score 6.5). *Application deadline:* For fall admission, 12/1 for domestic and international students; for spring admission, 10/15 for domestic students, 9/15 for international students. Application fee: $30. Electronic applications accepted. *Financial support:* In 2017–18, 65 students received support, including 1 research assistantship with tuition reimbursement available (averaging $10,920 per year), 15 teaching assistantships with tuition reimbursements available (averaging $10,881 per year); career-related internships or fieldwork, traineeships, health care benefits, and unspecified assistantships also available. Financial award application deadline: 2/1; financial award applicants required to submit FAFSA. *Faculty research:* Auditory perception and intervention; language and literacy; neurophysiology of hearing, speech, and language; adult neurogenics; bilingualism and language variation; language processing and intervention; speech and voice production; speech perception; translational science. *Total annual research expenditures:* $1.9 million. *Unit head:* Dr. Jennifer Lister, Interim Chair/Professor, 813-974-9712, Fax: 813-974-0822, E-mail: jlister@usf.edu. *Application contact:* Dr. Joseph Walton, PhD Program Director/Associate Professor, 813-974-4080, Fax: 813-974-0822, E-mail: jwalton1@usf.edu.
Website: http://csd.cbcs.usf.edu/

University of South Florida, Innovative Education, Tampa, FL 33620-9951. Offers adult, career and higher education (Graduate Certificate), including college teaching, leadership in developing human resources, leadership in higher education; Africana studies (Graduate Certificate), including diasporas and health disparities, genocide and human rights; aging studies (Graduate Certificate), including gerontology; art research (Graduate Certificate), including museum studies; business foundations (Graduate Certificate); chemical and biomedical engineering (Graduate Certificate), including materials science and engineering, water, health and sustainability; child and family studies (Graduate Certificate), including positive behavior support; civil and industrial engineering (Graduate Certificate), including transportation systems analysis; community and family health (Graduate Certificate), including maternal and child health, social marketing and public health, violence and injury: prevention and intervention, women's health; criminology (Graduate Certificate), including criminal justice administration; data science for public administration (Graduate Certificate); digital humanities (Graduate Certificate); educational measurement and research (Graduate Certificate), including evaluation; English (Graduate Certificate), including comparative literary studies, creative writing, professional and technical communication; entrepreneurship (Graduate Certificate); environmental health (Graduate Certificate), including safety management; epidemiology and biostatistics (Graduate Certificate), including applied biostatistics, biostatistics, concepts and tools of epidemiology, epidemiology, epidemiology of infectious diseases; geography, environment and planning (Graduate Certificate), including community development, environmental policy and management, geographical information systems; geology (Graduate Certificate), including hydrogeology; global health (Graduate Certificate), including disaster management, global health and Latin American and Caribbean studies, global health practice, humanitarian assistance, infection control; government and international affairs (Graduate Certificate), including Cuban studies, globalization studies; health policy and management (Graduate Certificate), including health management and leadership, public health policy and programs; hearing specialist: early intervention (Graduate

Certificate); industrial and management systems engineering (Graduate Certificate), including systems engineering, technology management; information studies (Graduate Certificate), including school library media specialist; information systems/decision sciences (Graduate Certificate), including analytics and business intelligence; instructional technology (Graduate Certificate), including distance education, Florida digital/virtual educator, instructional design, multimedia design, Web design; internal medicine, bioethics and medical humanities (Graduate Certificate), including biomedical ethics; Latin American and Caribbean studies (Graduate Certificate); leadership for coastal resiliency planning (Graduate Certificate); mass communications (Graduate Certificate), including multimedia journalism; mathematics and statistics (Graduate Certificate), including mathematics; medicine (Graduate Certificate), including aging and neuroscience, bioinformatics, biotechnology, brain fitness and memory management, clinical investigation, hand and upper limb rehabilitation, health informatics, health sciences, integrative weight management, intellectual property, medicine and gender, metabolic and nutritional medicine, metabolic cardiology, pharmacy sciences; national and competitive intelligence (Graduate Certificate); nursing (Graduate Certificate), including simulation based academic fellowship in advanced pain management; psychological and social foundations (Graduate Certificate), including career counseling, college teaching, diversity in education, mental health counseling, school counseling; public affairs (Graduate Certificate), including nonprofit management, public management, research administration; public health (Graduate Certificate), including assessing chemical toxicity and public health risks, health equity, pharmacoepidemiology, public health generalist, toxicology, translational research in adolescent behavioral health; public health practices (Graduate Certificate), including planning for healthy communities; rehabilitation and mental health counseling (Graduate Certificate), including integrative mental health care, marriage and family therapy, rehabilitation technology; secondary education (Graduate Certificate), including ESOL, foreign language education: culture and content, foreign language education: professional; social work (Graduate Certificate), including geriatric social work/clinical gerontology; special education (Graduate Certificate), including autism spectrum disorder, disabilities education: severe/profound; world languages (Graduate Certificate), including teaching English as a second language (TESL) or foreign language. *Unit head:* Dr. Cynthia DeLuca, Associate Vice President and Assistant Vice Provost, 813-974-3077, Fax: 813-974-7061, E-mail: deluca@usf.edu. *Application contact:* Owen Hooper, Director, Summer and Alternative Calendar Programs, 813-974-6917, E-mail: hooper@usf.edu.
Website: http://www.usf.edu/innovative-education/

The University of Tennessee, Graduate School, College of Arts and Sciences, Department of Audiology and Speech Pathology, Program in Audiology, Knoxville, TN 37996. Offers MA. *Accreditation:* ASHA. *Degree requirements:* For master's, thesis or alternative. *Entrance requirements:* For master's, GRE General Test, minimum GPA of 2.7. Additional exam requirements/recommendations for international students: Required—TOEFL. Electronic applications accepted.

The University of Tennessee, Graduate School, College of Arts and Sciences, Department of Audiology and Speech Pathology, Program in Speech and Hearing Science, Knoxville, TN 37996. Offers audiology (PhD); hearing science (PhD); speech and language pathology (PhD); speech and language science (PhD). *Degree requirements:* For doctorate, thesis/dissertation. *Entrance requirements:* For doctorate, GRE General Test, minimum GPA of 2.7. Additional exam requirements/recommendations for international students: Required—TOEFL. Electronic applications accepted.

The University of Tennessee, Graduate School, College of Arts and Sciences, Department of Audiology and Speech Pathology, Program in Speech Pathology, Knoxville, TN 37996. Offers MA. *Accreditation:* ASHA. *Degree requirements:* For master's, thesis or alternative. *Entrance requirements:* For master's, GRE General Test, minimum GPA of 2.7. Additional exam requirements/recommendations for international students: Required—TOEFL. Electronic applications accepted.

The University of Tennessee, Graduate School, College of Education, Health and Human Sciences, Program in Education, Knoxville, TN 37996. Offers art education (MS); counseling education (PhD); cultural studies in education (PhD); curriculum (MS, Ed S); curriculum, educational research and evaluation (Ed D, PhD); early childhood education (PhD); early childhood special education (MS); education of deaf and hard of hearing (MS); educational administration and policy studies (Ed D, PhD); educational administration and supervision (Ed S); educational psychology (Ed D, PhD); elementary education (MS, Ed S); elementary teaching (MS); English education (MS, Ed S); exercise science (PhD); foreign language/ESL education (MS, Ed S); instructional technology (MS, Ed D, PhD, Ed S); literacy, language and ESL education (PhD); literacy, language education, and ESL education (Ed D); mathematics education (MS, Ed S); modified and comprehensive special education (MS); reading education (MS, Ed S); school counseling (Ed S); school psychology (PhD, Ed S); science education (MS, Ed S); secondary teaching (MS); social foundations (MS); social science education (MS, Ed S); socio-cultural foundations of sports and education (PhD); special education (Ed S); teacher education (Ed D, PhD). *Accreditation:* NCATE. *Program availability:* Part-time, evening/weekend. *Degree requirements:* For master's and Ed S, thesis optional; for doctorate, variable foreign language requirement, thesis/dissertation. *Entrance requirements:* For master's, minimum GPA of 2.7; for doctorate and Ed S, GRE General Test, minimum GPA of 2.7. Additional exam requirements/recommendations for international students: Required—TOEFL. Electronic applications accepted.

The University of Tennessee Health Science Center, College of Graduate Health Sciences, Memphis, TN 38163. Offers biomedical engineering (MS, PhD); biomedical sciences (PhD); dental sciences (MDS); epidemiology (MS); health outcomes and policy research (PhD); laboratory research and management (MS); nursing science (PhD); pharmaceutical sciences (PhD); pharmacology (MS); speech and hearing science (PhD); DDS/PhD; DNP/PhD; MD/PhD; Pharm D/PhD. MS and PhD programs in biomedical engineering offered jointly with University of Memphis. *Faculty:* 528 full-time (176 women). *Students:* 258 full-time (130 women); includes 87 minority (14 Black or African American, non-Hispanic/Latino; 68 Asian, non-Hispanic/Latino; 5 Hispanic/Latino). Average age 28. 673 applicants, 17% accepted, 102 enrolled. In 2017, 23 master's, 30 doctorates awarded. Terminal master's awarded for partial completion of doctoral program. *Degree requirements:* For master's, comprehensive exam, thesis; for doctorate, thesis/dissertation, oral and written preliminary and comprehensive exams. *Entrance requirements:* For master's and doctorate, GRE General Test, minimum GPA of 3.0. Additional exam requirements/recommendations for international students: Recommended—TOEFL (minimum score 79 iBT), IELTS (minimum score 6.5). *Application deadline:* For winter admission, 1/1 for domestic and international students; for spring admission, 3/1 for domestic and international students. Applications are processed on a rolling basis. Application fee: $0. Electronic applications accepted. *Expenses:* Contact institution. *Financial support:* In 2017–18, 150 students received support, including 150 research assistantships (averaging $25,000 per year); fellowships, institutionally sponsored loans, scholarships/grants, health care benefits, and tuition waivers (full and partial) also available. Support available to part-time students. *Faculty research:* Cell biology, epidemiology, biomedical engineering, speech and hearing science, health policy, pharmaceutical sciences, dental sciences, nursing science, pharmacology. *Unit head:* Dr. Donald B. Thomason, Dean, 901-448-5538, E-mail: dthomaso@uthsc.edu. *Application contact:* Dr. Isaac O. Donkor, Associate Dean for Student Affairs, 901-448-5538, E-mail: idonkor@uthsc.edu.
Website: http://grad.uthsc.edu/

The University of Tennessee Health Science Center, College of Health Professions, Memphis, TN 38163-0002. Offers audiology (MS, Au D); clinical laboratory science (MSCLS); cytopathology practice (MCP); health informatics and information management (MHIIM); occupational therapy (MOT); physical therapy (DPT, ScDPT); physician assistant (MMS); speech-language pathology (MS). *Accreditation:* AOTA; APTA. *Program availability:* Part-time, evening/weekend, online learning. Terminal master's awarded for partial completion of doctoral program. *Degree requirements:* For master's, comprehensive exam, thesis; for doctorate, comprehensive exam, residency. *Entrance requirements:* For master's, GRE (MOT, MSCLS), minimum GPA of 3.0, 3 letters of reference, national accreditation (MSCLS), GRE if GPA is less than 3.0 (MCP); for doctorate, GRE. Additional exam requirements/recommendations for international students: Required—TOEFL (minimum score 550 paper-based; 80 iBT). Electronic applications accepted. *Expenses:* Contact institution. *Faculty research:* Gait deviation, muscular dystrophy and strength, hemophilia and exercise, pediatric neurology, self efficacy.

The University of Texas at Austin, Graduate School, College of Communication, Department of Communication Sciences and Disorders, Austin, TX 78712-1111. Offers audiology (Au D); communication sciences and disorders (PhD); speech language pathology (MA). *Accreditation:* ASHA (one or more programs are accredited). *Entrance requirements:* For master's and doctorate, GRE General Test.

The University of Texas at Dallas, School of Behavioral and Brain Sciences, Program in Communication Sciences and Disorders, Richardson, TX 75080. Offers audiology (Au D); communication disorders (MS); communication sciences and disorders (PhD). *Program availability:* Part-time, evening/weekend. *Faculty:* 16 full-time (10 women), 11 part-time/adjunct (10 women). *Students:* 276 full-time (262 women), 14 part-time (12 women); includes 71 minority (3 Black or African American, non-Hispanic/Latino; 1 American Indian or Alaska Native, non-Hispanic/Latino; 19 Asian, non-Hispanic/Latino; 30 Hispanic/Latino; 18 Two or more races, non-Hispanic/Latino), 14 international. Average age 25. 715 applicants, 15% accepted, 70 enrolled. In 2017, 116 master's, 14 doctorates awarded. *Degree requirements:* For doctorate, thesis/dissertation. *Entrance requirements:* For master's and doctorate, GRE General Test, minimum GPA of 3.0 in upper-level course work in field. Additional exam requirements/recommendations for international students: Required—TOEFL (minimum score 550 paper-based). *Application deadline:* For fall admission, 7/15 for domestic students, 5/1 priority date for international students; for spring admission, 11/15 for domestic students, 9/1 priority date for international students. Applications are processed on a rolling basis. Application fee: $50 ($100 for international students). Electronic applications accepted. *Expenses:* Tuition, state resident: full-time $12,916; part-time $718 per credit hour. Tuition, nonresident: full-time $25,252; part-time $1403 per credit hour. *Financial support:* In 2017–18, 221 students received support, including 1 fellowship (averaging $1,500 per year), 10 research assistantships with partial tuition reimbursements available (averaging $24,181 per year), 21 teaching assistantships with partial tuition reimbursements available (averaging $18,335 per year); Federal Work-Study, institutionally sponsored loans, scholarships/grants, and unspecified assistantships also available. Support available to part-time students. Financial award application deadline: 4/30; financial award applicants required to submit FAFSA. *Faculty research:* Developmental neurolinguistics, brain plasticity and biofeedback treatment, autism spectrum disorders, speech production, neurogenic speech and language disorders. *Unit head:* Dr. Robert D. Stillman, Area Head, 214-905-3106, Fax: 972-883-3022, E-mail: stillman@utdallas.edu.
Website: http://www.utdallas.edu/bbs/degrees/csd-degrees/

The University of Texas at El Paso, Graduate School, College of Health Sciences, Program in Speech-Language Pathology, El Paso, TX 79968-0001. Offers MS. *Accreditation:* ASHA. *Degree requirements:* For master's, comprehensive exam, thesis optional. *Entrance requirements:* For master's, GRE, minimum GPA of 3.0, resume, letters of recommendation, writing sample, interview. Additional exam requirements/recommendations for international students: Required—TOEFL; Recommended—IELTS. *Application deadline:* For fall admission, 8/1 for domestic students, 3/1 for international students; for spring admission, 11/1 for domestic students, 9/3 for international students. Applications are processed on a rolling basis. Application fee: $45 ($80 for international students). Electronic applications accepted. *Financial support:* Fellowships with partial tuition reimbursements, research assistantships with partial tuition reimbursements, teaching assistantships with partial tuition reimbursements, institutionally sponsored loans, scholarships/grants, health care benefits, tuition waivers (partial), and unspecified assistantships available. Support available to part-time students. Financial award application deadline: 3/15; financial award applicants required to submit FAFSA. *Faculty research:* Bilingual language disorders, clinical supervision, hearing loss, traumatic brain injury, aphasia, policy, augmentative communication.

The University of Texas Health Science Center at San Antonio, Joe R. and Teresa Lozano Long School of Medicine, San Antonio, TX 78229-3900. Offers deaf education and hearing (MS); medicine (MD); MPH/MD. *Accreditation:* LCME/AMA. *Degree requirements:* For master's, comprehensive exam, practicum assignments. *Entrance requirements:* For master's, minimum GPA of 3.0, interview, 3 professional letters of recommendation; for doctorate, MCAT. Electronic applications accepted. *Expenses:* Contact institution. *Faculty research:* Geriatrics, diabetes, cancer, AIDS, obesity.

The University of Texas Health Science Center at San Antonio, School of Health Professions, San Antonio, TX 78229-3900. Offers occupational therapy (MOT); physical therapy (DPT); physician assistant studies (MS); speech language pathology (MS). *Accreditation:* AOTA; APTA; ARC-PA; ASHA. *Degree requirements:* For master's, comprehensive exam, thesis (for some programs); for doctorate, comprehensive exam.

The University of Texas Rio Grande Valley, College of Health Affairs, Department of Communication Sciences and Disorders, Edinburg, TX 78539. Offers MS. *Accreditation:* ASHA. *Faculty:* 9 full-time (7 women), 1 (woman) part-time/adjunct. *Students:* 45 full-time (42 women); includes 43 minority (1 Black or African American, non-Hispanic/Latino; 2 Asian, non-Hispanic/Latino; 40 Hispanic/Latino). Average age 24. 85 applicants, 29% accepted, 24 enrolled. In 2017, 21 master's awarded. *Degree requirements:* For master's, comprehensive exam, thesis optional, PRAXIS in speech-language pathology. *Entrance requirements:* For master's, GRE General Test (taken within prior two years), minimum GPA of 3.0, three letters of recommendation or reference check lists, resume, 500-word essay on goals in pursuing graduate degree. Additional exam requirements/recommendations for international students: Required—TOEFL (minimum score 550 paper-based). *Application deadline:* For fall admission, 2/3 for domestic and international students. Application fee: $50. Electronic applications accepted. *Expenses:* Contact institution. *Financial support:* In 2017–18, 29 students received support, including 3 research assistantships (averaging $5,000 per year); teaching assistantships, career-related internships or fieldwork, Federal Work-Study, institutionally sponsored loans, and scholarships/grants also available. Financial award application deadline: 9/1; financial award applicants required to submit FAFSA. *Faculty*

research: Augmentative and alternative communication; autism; bilingual/bicultural language development/disorders; elementary-age language disorders; voice disorders. *Total annual research expenditures:* $53,000. *Unit head:* Dr. Donald R. Fuller, Department Chair, 956-665-2387, Fax: 956-665-5238, E-mail: donald.fuller@utrgv.edu. *Application contact:* Dr. Teri Mata-Pistokache, Graduate Program Coordinator, 956-665-3582, E-mail: theresa.matapistokache@utrgv.edu.
Website: http://www.utrgv.edu/communication-disorders/

University of the District of Columbia, College of Arts and Sciences, Program in Speech-Language Pathology, Washington, DC 20008-1175. Offers MS. *Accreditation:* ASHA. *Program availability:* Part-time. *Degree requirements:* For master's, comprehensive exam, thesis optional. *Entrance requirements:* For master's, GRE General Test, writing proficiency exam. *Faculty research:* Child language, dialect variation, English as a second language.

University of the Pacific, Thomas J. Long School of Pharmacy and Health Sciences, Department of Audiology, San Francisco, CA 94103. Offers Au D. *Faculty:* 15 full-time (8 women), 26 part-time/adjunct (24 women). *Students:* 62 full-time (53 women); includes 28 minority (2 Black or African American, non-Hispanic/Latino; 11 Asian, non-Hispanic/Latino; 11 Hispanic/Latino; 4 Two or more races, non-Hispanic/Latino), 2 international. Average age 26. *Unit head:* Dr. Philip Oppenheimer, Dean, 209-946-2561. *Application contact:* 209-946-2211.
Website: http://www.pacific.edu/Academics/Schools-and-Colleges/Thomas-J-Long-School-of-Pharmacy-and-Health-Sciences/Faculty-and-Departments/Audiology.html

University of the Pacific, Thomas J. Long School of Pharmacy and Health Sciences, Department of Speech-Language Pathology, Stockton, CA 95211-0197. Offers MS. *Accreditation:* ASHA. *Students:* 60 full-time (56 women); includes 22 minority (2 Black or African American, non-Hispanic/Latino; 10 Asian, non-Hispanic/Latino; 6 Hispanic/Latino; 4 Two or more races, non-Hispanic/Latino). Average age 24. 159 applicants, 40% accepted, 30 enrolled. In 2017, 28 master's awarded. *Entrance requirements:* For master's, GRE General Test. Additional exam requirements/recommendations for international students: Required—TOEFL. *Application deadline:* For fall admission, 2/1 for domestic students. Application fee: $75. *Financial support:* Institutionally sponsored loans available. Support available to part-time students. Financial award application deadline: 2/1; financial award applicants required to submit FAFSA. *Unit head:* Dr. Robert Hanyak, Chairman, 209-946-3233, Fax: 209-946-2647, E-mail: rhanyak@pacific.edu. *Application contact:* Ron Espejo, Recruitment Specialist, 209-946-3957, Fax: 209-946-3147, E-mail: respejo@pacific.edu.

The University of Toledo, College of Graduate Studies, College of Health and Human Services, School of Intervention and Wellness, Toledo, OH 43606-3390. Offers counselor education (MA, PhD); school psychology (Ed S); speech-language pathology (MA). *Accreditation:* ACA (one or more programs are accredited); NCATE. *Degree requirements:* For master's, seminar paper. *Entrance requirements:* For master's, GRE General Test, interview, minimum GPA of 3.0. Electronic applications accepted. *Faculty research:* Training and supervision, ethics and standards, therapist development, multicultural issues, substance abuse screening.

University of Toronto, Faculty of Medicine, Department of Speech-Language Pathology, Toronto, ON M5S 1A1, Canada. Offers M Sc, MH Sc, PhD. *Program availability:* Part-time. *Degree requirements:* For master's, thesis (for some programs), clinical internship (MH Sc), oral thesis defense (M Sc); for doctorate, comprehensive exam, thesis/dissertation, oral thesis defense. *Entrance requirements:* For master's, minimum B+ average in last 2 years (MH Sc), B average in final year (M Sc); volunteer/work experience in a clinical setting (MH Sc); for doctorate, previous research experience or thesis, resume, 3 writing samples, 3 letters of recommendation. Electronic applications accepted.

The University of Tulsa, Graduate School, Oxley College of Health Sciences, Department of Communication Sciences and Disorders, Tulsa, OK 74104-3189. Offers MS. *Accreditation:* ASHA. *Program availability:* Part-time. *Faculty:* 7 full-time (all women). *Students:* 35 full-time (33 women), 2 part-time (both women); includes 11 minority (2 Black or African American, non-Hispanic/Latino; 4 American Indian or Alaska Native, non-Hispanic/Latino; 1 Asian, non-Hispanic/Latino; 1 Hispanic/Latino; 1 Native Hawaiian or other Pacific Islander, non-Hispanic/Latino; 2 Two or more races, non-Hispanic/Latino), 1 international. Average age 24. 117 applicants, 29% accepted, 16 enrolled. In 2017, 18 master's awarded. *Degree requirements:* For master's, thesis optional. *Entrance requirements:* For master's, GRE General Test. Additional exam requirements/recommendations for international students: Required—TOEFL (minimum score 577 paper-based; 90 iBT), IELTS (minimum score 6.5). *Application deadline:* For fall admission, 2/1 priority date for domestic students. Application fee: $55. Electronic applications accepted. *Expenses: Tuition:* Full-time $22,230. *Required fees:* $2000. Tuition and fees vary according to course load and program. *Financial support:* In 2017–18, 27 students received support, including 4 fellowships with full tuition reimbursements available (averaging $9,895 per year), 29 teaching assistantships with full tuition reimbursements available (averaging $8,381 per year); career-related internships or fieldwork, Federal Work-Study, scholarships/grants, traineeships, health care benefits, tuition waivers (full and partial), and unspecified assistantships also available. Support available to part-time students. Financial award application deadline: 2/1; financial award applicants required to submit FAFSA. *Faculty research:* Disorders of fluency, delayed language and literacy, aphasia, voice, speech articulation, swallowing, cognition. *Unit head:* Dr. Paula Cadogan, Chair, 918-631-2897, Fax: 918-631-3668, E-mail: paula-cadogan@utulsa.edu.

University of Utah, Graduate School, College of Education, Department of Special Education, Salt Lake City, UT 84112. Offers board certified behavior analyst (M Ed, MS, PhD); deaf and hard of hearing (M Ed); deaf/blind (M Ed, MS); early childhood deaf and hard of hearing (MS); early childhood special education (M Ed, MS, PhD); early childhood vision impairments (M Ed); mild/moderate disabilities (M Ed, MS, PhD); severe disabilities (M Ed, MS, PhD); visual impairment (M Ed, MS). *Program availability:* Part-time, evening/weekend, 100% online, blended/hybrid learning. *Faculty:* 9 full-time (6 women), 8 part-time/adjunct (7 women). *Students:* 45 full-time (41 women), 26 part-time (24 women); includes 6 minority (4 Asian, non-Hispanic/Latino; 2 Hispanic/Latino). Average age 31. 30 applicants, 97% accepted, 28 enrolled. In 2017, 29 master's awarded. Terminal master's awarded for partial completion of doctoral program. *Degree requirements:* For master's, comprehensive exam, thesis (for some programs), qualifying exam; for doctorate, thesis/dissertation, qualifying exam. *Entrance requirements:* For master's, GRE, minimum GPA of 3.0; for doctorate, GRE General Test, minimum GPA of 3.5. Additional exam requirements/recommendations for international students: Required—TOEFL (minimum score 600 paper-based; 100 iBT); Recommended—IELTS (minimum score 7). *Application deadline:* For fall admission, 3/1 for domestic and international students; for spring admission, 11/1 for domestic and international students; for summer admission, 5/16 for domestic and international students. Application fee: $55 ($65 for international students). Electronic applications accepted. *Financial support:* In 2017–18, 22 students received support, including 33 fellowships with partial tuition reimbursements available (averaging $4,350 per year), 3 teaching assistantships with tuition reimbursements available (averaging $10,000 per year); career-related internships or fieldwork and health care benefits also available. Support available to part-time students. Financial award application deadline: 3/1; financial award applicants required to submit FAFSA. *Faculty research:* Inclusive education, positive behavior support, reading, instruction and intervention strategies. *Total annual research expenditures:* $139,750. *Unit head:* Dr. Robert E. O'Neill, Chair, 801-581-8121, Fax: 801-585-6476, E-mail: rob.oneill@utah.edu. *Application contact:* Patty Davis, Academic Advisor, 801-581-4764, Fax: 801-585-6476, E-mail: patty.davis@utah.edu.
Website: http://special-ed.utah.edu/

University of Utah, Graduate School, College of Health, Department of Communication Sciences and Disorders, Salt Lake City, UT 84112. Offers audiology (Au D, PhD); speech-language pathology (MA, MS, PhD). *Accreditation:* ASHA (one or more programs are accredited). *Faculty:* 8 full-time (4 women), 14 part-time/adjunct (12 women). *Students:* 125 full-time (106 women), 4 part-time (3 women); includes 20 minority (2 Black or African American, non-Hispanic/Latino; 3 Asian, non-Hispanic/Latino; 11 Hispanic/Latino; 4 Two or more races, non-Hispanic/Latino), 2 international. Average age 26. 258 applicants, 46% accepted, 53 enrolled. In 2017, 75 master's, 22 doctorates awarded. Terminal master's awarded for partial completion of doctoral program. *Entrance requirements:* For master's and doctorate, GRE General Test, minimum GPA of 3.0. Additional exam requirements/recommendations for international students: Required—TOEFL (minimum score 600 paper-based; 100 iBT). *Application deadline:* For fall admission, 1/15 for domestic and international students. Application fee: $55 ($65 for international students). Electronic applications accepted. *Expenses:* Contact institution. *Financial support:* In 2017–18, 31 students received support, including 13 research assistantships with partial tuition reimbursements available (averaging $9,680 per year); teaching assistantships, career-related internships or fieldwork, Federal Work-Study, scholarships/grants, tuition waivers (full and partial), and unspecified assistantships also available. Financial award application deadline: 3/15; financial award applicants required to submit FAFSA. *Faculty research:* Motor speech disorders, fluency disorders, language disorders, voice disorders, speech perception, audiology disorders. *Total annual research expenditures:* $441,812. *Unit head:* Dr. Michael Blomgren, Department Chair, 801-581-6725, Fax: 801-581-7955, E-mail: michael.blomgren@hsc.utah.edu. *Application contact:* Dr. Kathy Chapman, Director of Graduate Studies, 801-581-6725, Fax: 801-581-7955, E-mail: kathy.chapman@hsc.utah.edu.
Website: http://www.health.utah.edu/csd

University of Vermont, Graduate College, College of Nursing and Health Sciences, Department of Communication Sciences and Disorders, Burlington, VT 05405. Offers MS. *Accreditation:* ASHA. *Students:* 31 full-time (27 women); includes 4 minority (1 Asian, non-Hispanic/Latino; 3 Hispanic/Latino), 2 international. 135 applicants, 50% accepted, 18 enrolled. In 2017, 10 master's awarded. *Entrance requirements:* For master's, GRE General Test. Additional exam requirements/recommendations for international students: Required—TOEFL (minimum iBT score of 90) or IELTS (6.5). *Application deadline:* For fall admission, 1/15 for domestic and international students. Application fee: $65. Electronic applications accepted. *Expenses:* Tuition, state resident: full-time $11,628; part-time $646 per credit. Tuition, nonresident: full-time $29,340; part-time $1630 per credit. *Required fees:* $1994; $10 per credit. Tuition and fees vary according to course load and program. *Financial support:* In 2017–18, 5 students received support. Fellowships and scholarships/grants available. Financial award application deadline: 3/1. *Unit head:* Dr. Michael S. Cannizzaro, Chair, 802-656-9725, E-mail: michael.cannizzaro@med.uvm.edu. *Application contact:* Kristen Cella, Admissions Specialist, 802-656-3858, E-mail: cnhsgrad@uvm.edu.
Website: http://www.uvm.edu/cnhs/csd

University of Virginia, Curry School of Education, Department of Human Services, Program in Speech Communication Disorders, Charlottesville, VA 22903. Offers M Ed, PhD. *Accreditation:* ASHA (one or more programs are accredited). *Students:* 86 full-time (83 women); includes 12 minority (3 Black or African American, non-Hispanic/Latino; 1 Asian, non-Hispanic/Latino; 5 Hispanic/Latino; 3 Two or more races, non-Hispanic/Latino), 2 international. Average age 24. 230 applicants, 32% accepted, 33 enrolled. In 2017, 23 master's awarded. *Entrance requirements:* For master's, GRE General Test, 2 letters of recommendation. Additional exam requirements/recommendations for international students: Required—TOEFL (minimum score 600 paper-based; 90 iBT), IELTS (minimum score 7). *Application deadline:* Applications are processed on a rolling basis. Application fee: $60. Electronic applications accepted. *Financial support:* Applicants required to submit FAFSA. *Unit head:* Randall R. Robey, Director, 434-924-6351, E-mail: robey@virginia.edu. *Application contact:* E-mail: curry-admissions@virginia.edu.

University of Washington, Graduate School, College of Arts and Sciences, Department of Speech and Hearing Sciences, Seattle, WA 98195. Offers audiology (Au D); speech and hearing sciences (PhD); speech-language pathology (MS). *Accreditation:* ASHA (one or more programs are accredited). *Degree requirements:* For master's, comprehensive exam, thesis or alternative; for doctorate, thesis/dissertation. *Entrance requirements:* For master's and doctorate, GRE, minimum GPA of 3.0. Additional exam requirements/recommendations for international students: Required—TOEFL. Electronic applications accepted. *Faculty research:* Treatment of communication disorders across the life span, speech physiology, auditory perception, behavioral and physiologic audiology.

The University of Western Ontario, Faculty of Graduate Studies, Health Sciences Division, School of Communication Sciences and Disorders, London, ON N6A 5B8, Canada. Offers audiology (M Cl Sc, M Sc); speech-language pathology (M Cl Sc, M Sc). *Degree requirements:* For master's, thesis (for some programs), supervised clinical practicum. *Entrance requirements:* For master's, 14 hours volunteer experience in field of study, minimum B average during last 2 years, previous course work in developmental psychology and statistics, 4 year honors degree. Additional exam requirements/recommendations for international students: Required—TOEFL (minimum score 620 paper-based). *Faculty research:* Child language, voice, neurogenics; auditory function, stuttering.

University of West Georgia, College of Education, Carrollton, GA 30118. Offers business education (M Ed); early childhood education (M Ed, Ed S); educational leadership (M Ed, Ed S); media (M Ed, Ed S); professional counseling (M Ed, Ed S); professional counseling and supervision (Ed D); reading instruction (M Ed); school improvement (Ed D); secondary education (M Ed); special education (M Ed, Ed S), including teaching (M Ed); speech language pathology (M Ed); teaching (MAT). *Accreditation:* NCATE. *Program availability:* Part-time, evening/weekend, 100% online, blended/hybrid learning. *Faculty:* 45 full-time (28 women). *Students:* 344 full-time (286 women), 1,243 part-time (1,039 women); includes 538 minority (456 Black or African American, non-Hispanic/Latino; 19 Asian, non-Hispanic/Latino; 46 Hispanic/Latino; 1 Native Hawaiian or other Pacific Islander, non-Hispanic/Latino; 16 Two or more races, non-Hispanic/Latino), 7 international. Average age 36. 685 applicants, 78% accepted, 429 enrolled. In 2017, 299 master's, 30 doctorates, 218 other advanced degrees awarded. *Entrance requirements:* Additional exam requirements/recommendations for international students: Required—TOEFL (minimum score 523 paper-based; 69 iBT); Recommended—IELTS (minimum score 6.5). *Application deadline:* For fall admission, 7/21 for domestic students, 6/1 for international students; for spring admission, 11/30 for domestic students, 10/15 for international students; for summer admission, 4/15 for

domestic students, 3/30 for international students. Applications are processed on a rolling basis. Application fee: $40. Electronic applications accepted. Tuition and fees vary according to degree level and program. *Financial support:* Fellowships, research assistantships, teaching assistantships, career-related internships or fieldwork, Federal Work-Study, institutionally sponsored loans, scholarships/grants, and unspecified assistantships available. Support available to part-time students. Financial award application deadline: 4/1; financial award applicants required to submit FAFSA. *Unit head:* Dr. Diane Hoff, Dean, College of Education, 678-839-6570, Fax: 678-839-6098, E-mail: dhoff@westga.edu. *Application contact:* Dr. Toby Ziglar, Assistant Dean of the Graduate School, 678-839-1394, Fax: 678-839-1395, E-mail: graduate@westga.edu.
Website: http://www.westga.edu/education/

University of Wisconsin–Eau Claire, College of Education and Human Sciences, Program in Communication Sciences and Disorders, Eau Claire, WI 54702-4004. Offers MS. *Accreditation:* ASHA. *Program availability:* Part-time. *Degree requirements:* For master's, comprehensive exam, thesis optional, written or oral exam with thesis, externship. *Entrance requirements:* For master's, GRE, Wisconsin residency; minimum GPA of 3.0 in communication disorders, 2.75 overall. Additional exam requirements/recommendations for international students: Required—TOEFL (minimum score 79 iBT).

University of Wisconsin–Madison, Graduate School, College of Letters and Science, Department of Communication Sciences and Disorders, Madison, WI 53706-1380. Offers audiology (Au D); normal aspects of speech, language and hearing (MS, PhD); speech-language pathology (MS, PhD); MS/PhD. *Accreditation:* ASHA (one or more programs are accredited). *Degree requirements:* For doctorate, thesis/dissertation. *Entrance requirements:* For master's and doctorate, GRE. Electronic applications accepted. *Faculty research:* Language disorders in children and adults, disorders of speech production, intelligibility, fluency, hearing impairment, deafness.

University of Wisconsin–Milwaukee, Graduate School, College of Health Sciences, Department of Communication Sciences and Disorders, Milwaukee, WI 53211. Offers MS. *Accreditation:* ASHA. *Program availability:* Part-time. *Students:* 52 full-time (51 women), 1 part-time (0 women); includes 1 minority (Two or more races, non-Hispanic/Latino), 1 international. Average age 25. 59 applicants, 44% accepted, 26 enrolled. In 2017, 1 master's awarded. *Degree requirements:* For master's, comprehensive exam, thesis optional. *Entrance requirements:* For master's, GRE General Test, minimum GPA of 3.0. Additional exam requirements/recommendations for international students: Required—TOEFL (minimum score 550 paper-based; 79 iBT), IELTS (minimum score 6.5). *Application deadline:* For fall admission, 1/1 priority date for domestic students, for spring admission, 9/1 for domestic students. Applications are processed on a rolling basis. Application fee: $56 ($96 for international students). *Financial support:* In 2017–18, 1 teaching assistantship was awarded; fellowships, research assistantships, career-related internships or fieldwork, unspecified assistantships, and project assistantships also available. Support available to part-time students. Financial award application deadline: 4/15. *Unit head:* Carol H. Seery, PhD, Department Chair, 414-229-4291, Fax: 414-229-2620, E-mail: cseery@uwm.edu. *Application contact:* Marylou Gelfer, PhD, Graduate Program Coordinator, 414-229-6465, Fax: 414-229-2620, E-mail: gelfer@uwm.edu.
Website: http://uwm.edu/healthsciences/academics/communication-sciences-disorders/

University of Wisconsin–River Falls, Outreach and Graduate Studies, College of Education and Professional Studies, Department of Communication Sciences and Disorders, River Falls, WI 54022. Offers communicative disorders (MS); secondary education-communicative disorders (MSE). *Accreditation:* ASHA (one or more programs are accredited). *Program availability:* Part-time. *Degree requirements:* For master's, comprehensive exam. *Entrance requirements:* For master's, minimum GPA of 2.75, 3 letters of reference. Additional exam requirements/recommendations for international students: Required—TOEFL (minimum score 500 paper-based; 65 iBT), IELTS (minimum score 5.5). *Faculty research:* Voice, language, audiology.

University of Wisconsin–Stevens Point, College of Professional Studies, School of Communication Sciences and Disorders, Stevens Point, WI 54481-3897. Offers audiology (Au D); speech and language pathology (MS). *Accreditation:* ASHA (one or more programs are accredited). *Degree requirements:* For master's, thesis optional, clinical semester and capstone project; for doctorate, capstone project, full-time clinical externship. *Entrance requirements:* For master's, completion of specific course contents and practicum experiences at the undergraduate level. *Application deadline:* For fall admission, 1/10 for domestic students. Application fee: $45. *Expenses:* Tuition, state resident: part-time $562.55 per credit. Tuition, nonresident: part-time $1085.04 per credit. Part-time tuition and fees vary according to course load, program and reciprocity agreements. *Financial support:* Research assistantships, teaching assistantships, Federal Work-Study, and unspecified assistantships available. Financial award application deadline: 5/1; financial award applicants required to submit FAFSA. *Unit head:* Dr. Gary Cumley, Chair, 715-346-4699, Fax: 715-346-2157, E-mail: gcumley@uwsp.edu. *Application contact:* Leslie Plonsker, Information Contact, 715-346-4835, Fax: 715-346-2157, E-mail: lplonske@uwsp.edu.
Website: http://www.uwsp.edu/csd/

University of Wisconsin–Whitewater, School of Graduate Studies, College of Education and Professional Studies, Program in Communication Sciences and Disorders, Whitewater, WI 53190-1790. Offers MS. *Accreditation:* ASHA. *Program availability:* Part-time, evening/weekend, online learning. *Degree requirements:* For master's, comprehensive exam. *Entrance requirements:* For master's, 2 letters of recommendation. Additional exam requirements/recommendations for international students: Required—TOEFL (minimum score 550 paper-based; 80 iBT), IELTS (minimum score 6). Electronic applications accepted. *Faculty research:* Occupational hearing conservation.

University of Wyoming, College of Health Sciences, Division of Communication Disorders, Laramie, WY 82071. Offers speech-language pathology (MS). *Accreditation:* ASHA. *Program availability:* Part-time, online learning. *Entrance requirements:* For master's, GRE General Test, minimum GPA of 3.0. Additional exam requirements/recommendations for international students: Required—TOEFL. Electronic applications accepted. *Faculty research:* Child language, visual reinforcement audiometry, voice, auditory brain response, TBI.

Utah State University, School of Graduate Studies, Emma Eccles Jones College of Education and Human Services, Department of Communicative Disorders and Deaf Education, Logan, UT 84322. Offers audiology (Au D, Ed S); communication disorders and deaf education (M Ed); communicative disorders and deaf education (MA, MS). *Accreditation:* ASHA (one or more programs are accredited). *Program availability:* Evening/weekend, online learning. *Degree requirements:* For master's, thesis optional; for Ed S, thesis or alternative. *Entrance requirements:* For master's, GRE General Test, minimum GPA of 3.0, 3 recommendations; for doctorate, GRE General Test, interview, minimum GPA of 3.25. Additional exam requirements/recommendations for international students: Required—TOEFL. *Expenses:* Contact institution. *Faculty research:* Parent-infant intervention with hearing-impaired infants, voice disorders, language development and disorders, oto-accoustic emissions, deaf or hard-of-hearing infants.

Valdosta State University, Department of Communication Sciences and Disorders, Valdosta, GA 31698. Offers communication disorders (M Ed); communication sciences and disorders (SLPD); special education (MAT, Ed S). *Accreditation:* ASHA. *Degree requirements:* For master's, comprehensive exam. *Entrance requirements:* For master's, GRE or MAT. Additional exam requirements/recommendations for international students: Required—TOEFL. *Application deadline:* For fall admission, 3/1 for domestic and international students; for spring admission, 7/1 for domestic and international students. Application fee: $45. Electronic applications accepted. *Financial support:* Research assistantships, Federal Work-Study, scholarships/grants, and unspecified assistantships available. *Unit head:* Dr. Corine Myers-Jennings, Head, 229-219-1327, Fax: 229-219-1335, E-mail: cmjennin@valdosta.edu. *Application contact:* Tonya R. Crawford, Administrative Secretary, 229-219-1327, Fax: 229-245-3853, E-mail: tocrawford@valdosta.edu.
Website: https://www.valdosta.edu/colleges/education/communication-sciences-and-disorders/

Vanderbilt University, School of Medicine, Department of Hearing and Speech Sciences, Nashville, TN 37240-1001. Offers audiology (Au D, PhD); education of the deaf (MDE); speech-language pathology (MS, PhD). *Accreditation:* ASHA. *Faculty:* 21 full-time (7 women). *Students:* 31 full-time (21 women); includes 2 minority (1 Hispanic/Latino; 1 Two or more races, non-Hispanic/Latino), 4 international. Average age 28. 21 applicants, 33% accepted, 4 enrolled. In 2017, 7 doctorates awarded. *Degree requirements:* For master's, thesis optional; for doctorate, thesis/dissertation, final and qualifying exams. *Entrance requirements:* For master's and doctorate, GRE General Test. Additional exam requirements/recommendations for international students: Required—TOEFL. *Application deadline:* For fall admission, 1/15 for domestic and international students. Application fee: $0. Electronic applications accepted. *Financial support:* Fellowships with full tuition reimbursements, research assistantships with full tuition reimbursements, career-related internships or fieldwork, institutionally sponsored loans, traineeships, and tuition waivers (full and partial) available. Financial award application deadline: 1/15; financial award applicants required to submit FAFSA. *Faculty research:* Child language. *Total annual research expenditures:* $3.6 million. *Unit head:* Dr. Anne Marie Tharpe, Chair, 615-936-5103, Fax: 615-936-5014, E-mail: anne.m.tharpe@vanderbilt.edu. *Application contact:* Todd Ricketts, Director of Graduate Studies, 615-936-5103, Fax: 615-936-6914, E-mail: todd.a.ricketts@vanderbilt.edu.
Website: https://ww2.mc.vanderbilt.edu/ghss/

Washington State University, Elson S. Floyd College of Medicine, Program in Speech and Hearing Sciences, Spokane, WA 99210. Offers MS. Program offered at the Spokane campus. *Accreditation:* ASHA. *Degree requirements:* For master's, comprehensive exam, thesis (for some programs). *Entrance requirements:* For master's, GRE, minimum GPA of 3.0, 3 letters of recommendation. Additional exam requirements/recommendations for international students: Required—TOEFL (minimum score 550 paper-based). Electronic applications accepted. *Faculty research:* Autism spectrum disorder, childhood apraxia of speech, cleft palate and craniofacial disorders, motor speech disorders in patients with neurodegenerative disease and galactosemia, early language and literacy in multicultural populations.

Washington University in St. Louis, School of Medicine, Program in Audiology and Communication Sciences, St. Louis, MO 63110. Offers audiology (Au D); deaf education (MS); speech and hearing sciences (PhD). *Accreditation:* ASHA (one or more programs are accredited). *Faculty:* 22 full-time (12 women), 18 part-time/adjunct (12 women). *Students:* 67 full-time (61 women). Average age 24. 129 applicants, 34% accepted, 20 enrolled. In 2017, 8 master's, 14 doctorates awarded. *Degree requirements:* For master's, comprehensive exam, thesis, independent study project, oral exam; for doctorate, comprehensive exam, thesis/dissertation, capstone project. *Entrance requirements:* For master's and doctorate, GRE General Test, minimum B average in previous college/university coursework (recommended). Additional exam requirements/recommendations for international students: Required—TOEFL (minimum score 100 iBT). *Application deadline:* For fall admission, 2/15 for domestic and international students. Application fee: $25. Electronic applications accepted. *Expenses:* $38,000 per academic year (all-inclusive). *Financial support:* In 2017–18, 67 students received support, including 67 fellowships with full and partial tuition reimbursements available (averaging $17,879 per year), 6 teaching assistantships with partial tuition reimbursements available (averaging $1,500 per year); Federal Work-Study, scholarships/grants, traineeships, health care benefits, tuition waivers (partial), and unspecified assistantships also available. Financial award application deadline: 2/15; financial award applicants required to submit FAFSA. *Faculty research:* Audiology, deaf education, speech and hearing sciences, sensory neuroscience. *Unit head:* Dr. William W. Clark, Program Director, 314-747-0104, Fax: 314-747-0105. *Application contact:* Beth Elliott, Director, Finance and Student/Academic Affairs, 314-747-0104, Fax: 314-747-0105, E-mail: elliottb@wustl.edu.
Website: http://pacs.wustl.edu/

Wayne State University, College of Liberal Arts and Sciences, Department of Communication Sciences and Disorders, Detroit, MI 48202. Offers audiology (Au D); communication disorders and science (PhD); speech-language pathology (MA). *Accreditation:* ASHA (one or more programs are accredited). *Faculty:* 7. *Students:* 116 full-time (113 women), 2 part-time (1 woman); includes 9 minority (2 Black or African American, non-Hispanic/Latino; 3 Asian, non-Hispanic/Latino; 2 Hispanic/Latino; 2 Two or more races, non-Hispanic/Latino), 14 international. Average age 25. 309 applicants, 17% accepted, 48 enrolled. In 2017, 42 master's, 10 doctorates awarded. *Degree requirements:* For master's, comprehensive exam (for some programs), thesis (for some programs); for doctorate, thesis/dissertation (for some programs), written and oral comprehensive examinations. *Entrance requirements:* For master's, GRE, minimum GPA of 3.0, three letters of recommendation, written statement of intent, official transcripts, CSDCAS Centralized Application Service; for doctorate, GRE, minimum GPA of 3.0, three letters of recommendation, written statement of intent, official transcripts, CSDCAS Centralized Application Service (for audiology applicants). Additional exam requirements/recommendations for international students: Required—TOEFL (minimum score 620 paper-based; 105 iBT), TWE (minimum score 5.5), Michigan English Language Assessment Battery (minimum score 85); Recommended—IELTS. *Application deadline:* For fall admission, 1/15 for domestic and international students. Application fee: $50. Electronic applications accepted. *Expenses:* Tuition, state resident: full-time $10,224; part-time $638.98 per credit hour. Tuition, nonresident: full-time $22,145; part-time $1384.04 per credit hour. Tuition and fees vary according to course load and program. *Financial support:* In 2017–18, 42 students received support, including 1 fellowship with tuition reimbursement available (averaging $19,000 per year), 1 research assistantship with tuition reimbursement available (averaging $17,606 per year); scholarships/grants and unspecified assistantships also available. Financial award applicants required to submit FAFSA. *Faculty research:* Aphasia, stuttering/fluency, speech and auditory genetics, neuroscience, tinnitus. *Unit head:* Dr. Margaret Greenwald, Chair, 313-577-0608, E-mail: mgreenwald@wayne.edu. *Application contact:* Dr. Derek Daniels, Associate Professor/Director of Graduate Studies, 313-577-3339, E-mail: dedaniels@wayne.edu.
Website: http://clas.wayne.edu/csd/

Communication Disorders

Webster University, School of Education, Department of Communication Arts, Reading and Early Childhood, St. Louis, MO 63119-3194. Offers communication arts (MAT); reading (MA). *Entrance requirements:* For master's, minimum GPA of 2.5. Additional exam requirements/recommendations for international students: Required—TOEFL.

West Chester University of Pennsylvania, College of Health Sciences, Department of Communication Sciences and Disorders, West Chester, PA 19383. Offers speech-language pathology (MA). *Accreditation:* ASHA. *Program availability:* Part-time. *Students:* 52 full-time (51 women), 4 part-time (3 women); includes 2 minority (1 Asian, non-Hispanic/Latino; 1 Hispanic/Latino). Average age 25. 335 applicants, 40% accepted, 27 enrolled. In 2017, 26 master's awarded. *Degree requirements:* For master's, comprehensive exam, thesis optional, 62 semester credit hours. *Entrance requirements:* For master's, GRE, two letters of recommendation; personal statement of academic and professional goals; logs of 25-clinical observation, practicum hours, and structured vita. Additional exam requirements/recommendations for international students: Required—TOEFL or IELTS. *Application deadline:* For fall admission, 5/15 for international students; for spring admission, 10/15 for international students. Applications are processed on a rolling basis. Application fee: $50. Electronic applications accepted. *Expenses:* $550 per credit in-state, $825 per credit out-of-state. *Financial support:* Scholarships/grants and unspecified assistantships available. Financial award application deadline: 2/15; financial award applicants required to submit FAFSA. *Faculty research:* Identification/interaction with students with communicative disorders, voice therapy, autism, bilingual assessment and intervention, critical thinking, literacy development, fluency, interprofessional collaboration, scholarship of teaching, audiological assessment. *Unit head:* Dr. Cheryl Gunter, Chair, 610-436-2115, Fax: 610-436-3388, E-mail: cgunter@wcupa.edu. *Application contact:* Dr. Mareile Koenig, Graduate Coordinator, 610-436-3218, Fax: 610-436-3388, E-mail: mkoenig@wcupa.edu.
Website: http://www.wcupa.edu/healthsciences/commdisorder/

Western Carolina University, Graduate School, College of Health and Human Sciences, Department of Communication Sciences and Disorders, Cullowhee, NC 28723. Offers MS. *Accreditation:* ASHA. *Program availability:* Part-time. *Degree requirements:* For master's, comprehensive exam, thesis or alternative. *Entrance requirements:* For master's, GRE, appropriate undergraduate degree with minimum GPA of 3.0, 3 letters of recommendation. Additional exam requirements/recommendations for international students: Required—TOEFL (minimum score 550 paper-based; 79 iBT). *Expenses:* Tuition, state resident: full-time $4436. Tuition, nonresident: full-time $14,842. *Required fees:* $2926. *Faculty research:* Early assessment and intervention in language, stuttering, school-family partnerships, voice and organic disorders, accent reduction.

Western Illinois University, School of Graduate Studies, College of Fine Arts and Communication, Department of Communication Sciences and Disorders, Macomb, IL 61455-1390. Offers MS. *Accreditation:* ASHA. *Program availability:* Part-time. *Students:* 42 full-time (all women); includes 1 minority (Hispanic/Latino), 3 international. Average age 24. 158 applicants, 54% accepted, 21 enrolled. In 2017, 20 master's awarded. *Degree requirements:* For master's, comprehensive exam, thesis or alternative. *Entrance requirements:* For master's, GRE, minimum GPA of 3.0. Additional exam requirements/recommendations for international students: Required—TOEFL (minimum score 550 paper-based; 80 iBT). *Application deadline:* For fall admission, 2/1 priority date for domestic students. Applications are processed on a rolling basis. Application fee: $30. Electronic applications accepted. *Financial support:* Research assistantships with full tuition reimbursements and unspecified assistantships available. Financial award applicants required to submit FAFSA. *Unit head:* Dr. Pete Jorgensen, Chairperson, 309-298-1858. *Application contact:* Dr. Nancy Parsons, Associate Provost and Director of Graduate Studies, 309-298-1806, Fax: 309-298-2345, E-mail: grad-office@wiu.edu.
Website: http://wiu.edu/csd

Western Kentucky University, Graduate Studies, College of Health and Human Services, Department of Communication Disorders, Bowling Green, KY 42101. Offers MS. *Accreditation:* ASHA. *Program availability:* Part-time, evening/weekend, online learning. *Degree requirements:* For master's, comprehensive exam, written exam. *Entrance requirements:* For master's, GRE General Test, 3 letters of recommendation. Additional exam requirements/recommendations for international students: Required—TOEFL (minimum score 555 paper-based; 79 iBT).

Western Michigan University, Graduate College, College of Health and Human Services, Department of Speech, Language and Hearing Sciences, Kalamazoo, MI 49008. Offers audiology (Au D); speech pathology and audiology (MA). *Accreditation:* ASHA. *Degree requirements:* For master's, thesis optional.

Western Washington University, Graduate School, College of Humanities and Social Sciences, Department of Communication Sciences and Disorders, Bellingham, WA 98225-5996. Offers MA. *Accreditation:* ASHA. *Program availability:* Part-time. *Degree requirements:* For master's, comprehensive exam, thesis optional. *Entrance requirements:* For master's, GRE General Test, minimum GPA of 3.0 in last 60 semester hours or last 90 quarter hours. Additional exam requirements/recommendations for international students: Required—TOEFL (minimum score 567 paper-based). Electronic applications accepted. *Faculty research:* Autism, stroke and stroke perception, aural rehabilitation and cochlear implants, auditory processing, speech in individuals with Parkinson's disease.

West Texas A&M University, College of Nursing and Health Sciences, Department of Communication Disorders, Canyon, TX 79015. Offers MS. *Accreditation:* ASHA. *Program availability:* Part-time. *Degree requirements:* For master's, comprehensive exam, thesis optional. *Entrance requirements:* For master's, GRE General Test, minimum B average in all clinical courses, liability insurance, immunizations. Additional exam requirements/recommendations for international students: Required—TOEFL. Electronic applications accepted.

West Virginia University, College of Education and Human Services, Morgantown, WV 26506. Offers audiology (Au D); autism spectrum disorder (MA); clinical rehabilitation and mental health counseling (MS); communication science and disorders (PhD); counseling (MA); counseling psychology (PhD); curriculum and instruction (Ed D); early childhood education (MA); early intervention (MA); education (PhD); educational leadership (MA, Ed D); educational leadership/public school administration (MA); educational psychology (MA, Ed D); elementary education (MA); gifted education (MA); higher education administration (MA, Ed D); higher education curriculum and teaching (MA); institutional design and technology (MA); instructional design and technology (Ed D); literacy education (MA); secondary education (MA); secondary education/English (MA); special education (Ed D); speech pathology (MS). *Accreditation:* NCATE. *Program availability:* Part-time, evening/weekend, online learning. *Students:* 423 full-time (347 women), 367 part-time (316 women); includes 57 minority (14 Black or African American, non-Hispanic/Latino; 7 Asian, non-Hispanic/Latino; 20 Hispanic/Latino; 16 Two or more races, non-Hispanic/Latino), 13 international. *Degree requirements:* For master's, content exams; for doctorate, comprehensive exam, thesis/dissertation. *Entrance requirements:* Additional exam requirements/recommendations for international students: Required—TOEFL (minimum score 500 paper-based; 61 iBT). *Application deadline:* For fall admission, 8/1 for domestic students; for spring admission, 1/1 for domestic students; for summer admission, 5/1 for domestic students. Application fee: $60. Electronic applications accepted. *Expenses:* Tuition, state resident: full-time $9450. Tuition, nonresident: full-time $24,390. *Financial support:* Fellowships, research assistantships, teaching assistantships, career-related internships or fieldwork, Federal Work-Study, institutionally sponsored loans, health care benefits, tuition waivers (full and partial), and administrative assistantships available. Financial award applicants required to submit FAFSA. *Faculty research:* Internet training and integration for teachers, rural education, teacher preparation, organization of schools, evaluation of personnel. *Unit head:* Dr. Gypsy Denzine, Dean, 304-293-5703, Fax: 304-293-7565, E-mail: gypsy.denzine@mail.wvu.edu. *Application contact:* Dr. M. Cecil Smith, Associate Dean for Research and Graduate Education, 304-293-2174, Fax: 304-293-3802, E-mail: mcecil.smith@mail.wvu.edu.
Website: http://cehs.wvu.edu/

Wichita State University, Graduate School, College of Health Professions, Department of Communication Sciences and Disorders, Wichita, KS 67260. Offers MA, Au D, PhD. *Accreditation:* ASHA (one or more programs are accredited). *Financial support:* Teaching assistantships available. *Unit head:* Dr. Julie Scherz, Chairperson, 316-978-3240, Fax: 316-978-3302, E-mail: julie.scherz@wichita.edu. *Application contact:* Jordan Oleson, Admissions Coordinator, 316-978-3095, Fax: 316-978-3253, E-mail: jordan.oleson@wichita.edu.
Website: http://www.wichita.edu/csd

William Paterson University of New Jersey, College of Science and Health, Wayne, NJ 07470-8420. Offers adult gerontology nurse practitioner (Certificate); biology (MS); biotechnology (MS); communication disorders (MS); exercise and sport studies (MS); materials chemistry (MS); nurse practitioner (Certificate); nursing (MSN); nursing education (Certificate); nursing practice (DNP); school nurse (Certificate). *Program availability:* Part-time. *Faculty:* 29 full-time (15 women), 25 part-time/adjunct (24 women). *Students:* 66 full-time (56 women), 197 part-time (163 women); includes 104 minority (15 Black or African American, non-Hispanic/Latino; 45 Asian, non-Hispanic/Latino; 38 Hispanic/Latino; 6 Two or more races, non-Hispanic/Latino), 3 international. Average age 33. 387 applicants, 34% accepted, 77 enrolled. In 2017, 87 master's, 5 doctorates awarded. *Degree requirements:* For master's, comprehensive exam (for some programs), thesis (for some programs), non-thesis internship/practicum (for some programs). *Entrance requirements:* For master's, GRE/MAT, minimum GPA of 3.0; 2-3 letters of recommendation; personal statement; work experience (for some programs); for doctorate, GRE/MAT, minimum GPA of 3.3; work experience; 3 letters of recommendation; interview; master's degree in nursing. Additional exam requirements/recommendations for international students: Required—TOEFL (minimum score 550 paper-based; 79 iBT), IELTS (minimum score 6). *Application deadline:* For fall admission, 6/1 for domestic students, 3/1 for international students; for spring admission, 11/1 for domestic students, 10/1 for international students. Applications are processed on a rolling basis. Application fee: $50. Electronic applications accepted. *Expenses:* Tuition, state resident: full-time $13,920; part-time $6264 per year. Tuition, nonresident: full-time $21,700; part-time $9765 per year. *Required fees:* $80; $36 per year. Tuition and fees vary according to course load, degree level and program. *Financial support:* In 2017–18, 9,800 students received support. Career-related internships or fieldwork, Federal Work-Study, scholarships/grants, and unspecified assistantships available. Support available to part-time students. Financial award application deadline: 3/15; financial award applicants required to submit FAFSA. *Faculty research:* Behaviors of American long-eared bats, postpartum fatigue, methodologies for coating carbon nano-tubes, paleoclimatology, and pre-linguistic gestures in children with language disorders. *Total annual research expenditures:* $291,600. *Unit head:* Dr. Venkat Sharma, Dean, 973-720-2194, Fax: 973-720-3414, E-mail: sharmav@wpunj.edu. *Application contact:* Christina Aiello, Assistant Director, Graduate Admissions, 973-720-2506, Fax: 973-720-2035, E-mail: aielloc@wpunj.edu.
Website: http://www.wpunj.edu/cosh

Worcester State University, Graduate School, Program in Speech-Language Pathology, Worcester, MA 01602-2597. Offers MS. *Accreditation:* ASHA. *Program availability:* Part-time, evening/weekend. *Faculty:* 8 full-time, 4 part-time/adjunct. *Students:* 46 full-time (44 women), 40 part-time (38 women); includes 4 minority (1 Black or African American, non-Hispanic/Latino; 1 Asian, non-Hispanic/Latino; 1 Hispanic/Latino; 1 Two or more races, non-Hispanic/Latino). Average age 26. 213 applicants, 42% accepted, 29 enrolled. In 2017, 27 master's awarded. *Degree requirements:* For master's, comprehensive exam, thesis, practicum; national licensing exam; clinical observation and participation in diagnostic/therapeutic work. *Entrance requirements:* For master's, GRE General Test or MAT. Additional exam requirements/recommendations for international students: Required—TOEFL (minimum score 550 paper-based; 79 iBT). *Application deadline:* For fall admission, 2/1 priority date for domestic and international students. Applications are processed on a rolling basis. Application fee: $50. Electronic applications accepted. *Expenses:* Contact institution. *Financial support:* Career-related internships or fieldwork, scholarships/grants, and unspecified assistantships available. Financial award application deadline: 3/1; financial award applicants required to submit FAFSA. *Unit head:* Dr. Kenneth Melnick, Program Coordinator, 508-929-8836, E-mail: kmelnick@worcester.edu. *Application contact:* Sara Grady, Associate Dean, Graduate Studies and Professional Development, 508-929-8130, E-mail: sara.grady@worcester.edu.

Yeshiva University, The Katz School, Program in Speech-Language Pathology, New York, NY 10033-3201. Offers MS.

Dental Hygiene

Eastern Washington University, Graduate Studies, College of Health Science and Public Health, Department of Dental Hygiene, Cheney, WA 99004-2431. Offers MS. *Faculty:* 8. *Students:* 11 full-time (all women), 9 part-time (8 women); includes 1 minority (Asian, non-Hispanic/Latino). Average age 39. 8 applicants, 75% accepted, 4 enrolled. In 2017, 3 master's awarded. *Degree requirements:* For master's, comprehensive exam, thesis. *Entrance requirements:* For master's, Dental Hygiene National Board examination, current dental hygiene license in the U.S. or Canada. Additional exam requirements/recommendations for international students: Required—TOEFL (minimum score 580 paper-based; 92 iBT), IELTS (minimum score 7), PTE (minimum score 63). *Application deadline:* For fall admission, 7/1 for domestic students; for spring admission, 12/1 for domestic students. Applications are processed on a rolling basis. Application fee: $75. Electronic applications accepted. *Expenses:* Tuition, state resident: full-time $11,191; part-time $373.06 per credit. Tuition, nonresident: full-time $25,995; part-time $866.52 per credit. *Financial support:* Teaching assistantships with partial tuition reimbursements available. Financial award application deadline: 2/1; financial award applicants required to submit FAFSA. *Unit head:* Kasey Clark, 509-828-1317, E-mail: kclark56@ewu.edu.
Website: http://www.ewu.edu/cshe/programs/dental-hygiene.xml

Idaho State University, Office of Graduate Studies, Office of Medical and Oral Health, Department of Dental Hygiene, Pocatello, ID 83209-8048. Offers MS. *Program availability:* Part-time. *Degree requirements:* For master's, comprehensive exam, thesis, thesis defense, practicum experience, oral exam. *Entrance requirements:* For master's, GRE, MAT, baccalaureate degree in dental hygiene, minimum GPA of 3.0 in upper-division and dental hygiene coursework, current dental hygiene licensure in good standing. Additional exam requirements/recommendations for international students: Required—TOEFL (minimum score 600 paper-based; 80 iBT). Electronic applications accepted.

Missouri Southern State University, Program in Dental Hygiene, Joplin, MO 64801-1595. Offers MS. Program offered jointly with University of Missouri–Kansas City. *Program availability:* Part-time. *Degree requirements:* For master's, project. *Entrance requirements:* For master's, copy of current dental hygiene license. Electronic applications accepted.

The Ohio State University, College of Dentistry, Columbus, OH 43210. Offers dental anesthesiology (MS); dental hygiene (MDH); dentistry (DDS); endodontics (MS); oral and maxillofacial pathology (MS); oral and maxillofacial surgery (MS); oral biology (PhD); orthodontics (MS); pediatric dentistry (MS); periodontology (MS); prosthodontics (MS); DDS/PhD. *Accreditation:* ADA (one or more programs are accredited). *Faculty:* 86. *Students:* 506 full-time (213 women), 11 part-time (8 women). Average age 26. In 2017, 34 master's, 109 doctorates awarded. Terminal master's awarded for partial completion of doctoral program. *Degree requirements:* For master's, thesis; for doctorate, thesis/dissertation (for some programs). *Entrance requirements:* For master's, GRE General Test (for all applicants with cumulative GPA below 3.0); for doctorate, DAT (for DDS); GRE General Test, GRE Subject Test in biology recommended (for PhD). Additional exam requirements/recommendations for international students: Required—TOEFL (minimum score 550 paper-based; 79 iBT), IELTS (minimum score 7), Michigan English Language Assessment Battery (minimum score 82). *Application deadline:* For fall admission, 10/1 for domestic and international students; for summer admission, 4/11 for domestic students, 3/10 for international students. Applications are processed on a rolling basis. Electronic applications accepted. *Expenses:* Contact institution. *Financial support:* Fellowships with tuition reimbursements, research assistantships with tuition reimbursements, teaching assistantships with tuition reimbursements, Federal Work-Study, institutionally sponsored loans, and health care benefits available. Financial award application deadline: 2/15. *Faculty research:* Neurobiology, inflammation and immunity, materials science, bone biology. *Unit head:* Dr. Patrick M. Lloyd, Dean, 614-292-9755, E-mail: lloyd.256@osu.edu. *Application contact:* Graduate and Professional Admissions, 614-292-9444, Fax: 614-292-3895, E-mail: gpadmissions@osu.edu.
Website: http://www.dentistry.osu.edu/

Old Dominion University, College of Health Sciences, School of Dental Hygiene, Norfolk, VA 23529. Offers dental hygiene (MS), including community/public health, education, generalist, global health, marketing, modeling and simulation, research. *Program availability:* Part-time, evening/weekend, blended/hybrid learning. *Faculty:* 10 full-time (9 women). *Students:* 3 full-time (1 woman), 22 part-time (21 women); includes 5 minority (3 Black or African American, non-Hispanic/Latino; 1 Asian, non-Hispanic/Latino; 1 Hispanic/Latino), 3 international. Average age 38. 12 applicants, 25% accepted, 2 enrolled. In 2017, 8 master's awarded. *Degree requirements:* For master's, comprehensive exam, thesis optional, writing proficiency exam, responsible conduct of research training. *Entrance requirements:* For master's, Dental Hygiene National Board Examination or copy of license to practice dental hygiene, BS or certificate in dental hygiene or related area, minimum GPA of 2.8 (3.0 in major), 4 letters of recommendation. Additional exam requirements/recommendations for international students: Required—TOEFL (minimum score 550 paper-based, 79 iBT) or IELTS (minimum score 6.5). *Application deadline:* For fall admission, 7/1 for domestic students, 4/15 for international students; for spring admission, 12/1 for domestic students, 10/1 for international students; for summer admission, 3/1 for domestic students, 2/1 for international students. Applications are processed on a rolling basis. Application fee: $50. Electronic applications accepted. *Expenses:* Contact institution. *Financial support:* In 2017–18, 4 students received support, including 4 teaching assistantships with partial tuition reimbursements available (averaging $13,000 per year); scholarships/grants and health care benefits also available. Support available to part-time students. Financial award application deadline: 2/15; financial award applicants required to submit CSS PROFILE or FAFSA. *Faculty research:* Clinical dental hygiene, dental hygiene client health behaviors, dental hygiene education interventions, oral product testing, cold plasma. *Total annual research expenditures:* $43,581. *Unit head:* Dr. Denise M. Claiborne, Assistant Professor/Graduate Program Director, 757-683-5949, Fax: 757-683-5239, E-mail: dclaibor@odu.edu. *Application contact:* William Heffelfinger, Director of Graduate Admissions, 757-683-5554, Fax: 757-683-3255, E-mail: gradadmit@odu.edu.
Website: http://www.odu.edu/academics/programs/masters/dental-hygiene

Texas A&M University, College of Dentistry, Dallas, TX 75266-0677. Offers advanced education in general dentistry (Certificate); biomedical sciences (MS); dental hygiene (MS); dental public health (Certificate); endodontics (Certificate); maxillofacial surgery (Certificate); oral and maxillofacial pathology (Certificate); oral and maxillofacial radiology (Certificate); oral and maxillofacial surgery (Certificate); oral biology (MS, PhD); orthodontics (Certificate); pediatric dentistry (Certificate); periodontics (Certificate); prosthodontics (Certificate). *Accreditation:* ADA; SACS/CC. *Faculty:* 44. *Enrollment:* 499 full-time matriculated graduate/professional students (251 women), 37 part-time matriculated graduate/professional students (12 women). *Students:* 499 full-time (251 women), 37 part-time (12 women); includes 275 minority (54 Black or African American, non-Hispanic/Latino; 2 American Indian or Alaska Native, non-Hispanic/Latino; 100 Asian, non-Hispanic/Latino; 109 Hispanic/Latino; 10 Two or more races, non-Hispanic/Latino), 30 international. Average age 27. In 2017, 18 master's, 2 doctorates, 101 other advanced degrees awarded. *Entrance requirements:* Additional exam requirements/recommendations for international students: Required—TOEFL (minimum score 550 paper-based; 79 iBT). Application fee: $35. Electronic applications accepted. *Expenses:* Contact institution. *Financial support:* In 2017–18, 235 students received support, including 32 research assistantships with tuition reimbursements available (averaging $8,712 per year), 43 teaching assistantships with tuition reimbursements available (averaging $14,231 per year); career-related internships or fieldwork, institutionally sponsored loans, scholarships/grants, traineeships, health care benefits, tuition waivers (full and partial), and unspecified assistantships also available. Support available to part-time students. Financial award applicants required to submit FAFSA. *Unit head:* Dr. Lawrence E. Wolinsky, Dean, 214-828-8300, E-mail: wolinsky@tamhsc.edu. *Application contact:* Ernestine S. Lacy, Associate Dean for Student Affairs and Student Diversity, 214-828-8374, Fax: 214-874-4572, E-mail: eslacy@tamhsc.edu.
Website: http://www.dentistry.tamhsc.edu/

Texas Woman's University, Graduate School, College of Health Sciences, Department of Health Studies, Denton, TX 76204. Offers health studies (MS, PhD), including dental hygiene (MS). *Program availability:* Part-time, evening/weekend. *Faculty:* 8 full-time (7 women), 5 part-time/adjunct (2 women). *Students:* 35 full-time (32 women), 93 part-time (82 women); includes 68 minority (37 Black or African American, non-Hispanic/Latino; 1 American Indian or Alaska Native, non-Hispanic/Latino; 6 Asian, non-Hispanic/Latino; 20 Hispanic/Latino; 4 Two or more races, non-Hispanic/Latino), 1 international. Average age 34. 49 applicants, 57% accepted, 22 enrolled. In 2017, 8 master's, 3 doctorates awarded. *Degree requirements:* For master's, comprehensive exam, thesis, non-thesis options, or work-site health (for dental hygiene); for doctorate, comprehensive exam, thesis/dissertation, qualifying exam. *Entrance requirements:* For master's, minimum undergraduate GPA of 3.0 in last 60 credit hours of bachelor's degree, [illegible] curriculum vitae, 2 letters of recommendation, personal statement letter; for doctorate, GRE General Test (preferred minimum scores 152 [480 old version] Verbal, 140 [400 old version] Quantitative), minimum GPA of 3.5 on all master's course work, 2 letters of recommendation, curriculum vitae, essay, writing sample. Additional exam requirements/recommendations for international students: Required—TOEFL (minimum score 575 paper-based; 79 iBT); Recommended—IELTS (minimum score 6.5), TSE (minimum score 53). *Application deadline:* For fall admission, 3/1 priority date for domestic and international students; for spring admission, 11/1 priority date for domestic students, 7/1 priority date for international students. Applications are processed on a rolling basis. Application fee: $50 ($75 for international students). Electronic applications accepted. *Expenses:* $8,240 per year full-time in-state, $17,540 per year full-time out-of-state. *Financial support:* In 2017–18, 29 students received support, including 2 research assistantships (averaging $11,926 per year), 3 teaching assistantships (averaging $11,926 per year); career-related internships or fieldwork, Federal Work-Study, institutionally sponsored loans, scholarships/grants, traineeships, health care benefits, and unspecified assistantships also available. Support available to part-time students. Financial award application deadline: 3/1; financial award applicants required to submit FAFSA. *Faculty research:* Teen pregnancy prevention, eating disorder and obesity prevention, body image issues, adolescent and women's health, chronic disease prevention. *Total annual research expenditures:* $158,000. *Unit head:* Dr. George King, Chair, 940-898-2860, Fax: 940-898-2859, E-mail: healthstudiesinfo@twu.edu. *Application contact:* Korie Hawkins, Associate Director of Admissions, Graduate Recruitment, 940-898-3188, Fax: 940-898-3081, E-mail: admissions@twu.edu.
Website: http://www.twu.edu/health-studies/

Université de Montréal, Faculty of Dental Medicine, Program in Stomatology Residency, Montréal, QC H3C 3J7, Canada. Offers Certificate.

University of Alberta, Faculty of Medicine and Dentistry, Department of Dentistry, Program in Dental Hygiene, Edmonton, AB T6G 2E1, Canada. Offers Diploma. Electronic applications accepted.

University of Bridgeport, Fones School of Dental Hygiene, Bridgeport, CT 06604. Offers MS. *Program availability:* Part-time, evening/weekend, online learning. *Degree requirements:* For master's, thesis. *Entrance requirements:* For master's, Dental Hygiene National Board Examination. Additional exam requirements/recommendations for international students: Recommended—TOEFL (minimum score 550 paper-based; 80 iBT), IELTS (minimum score 6.5). *Expenses:* Contact institution.

University of Michigan, School of Dentistry and Rackham Graduate School, Graduate Programs in Dentistry, Dental Hygiene Program, Ann Arbor, MI 48109-1078. Offers MS. *Program availability:* Part-time. *Students:* 11 full-time (all women); includes 5 minority (1 Black or African American, non-Hispanic/Latino; 2 Asian, non-Hispanic/Latino; 2 Hispanic/Latino). 8 applicants, 100% accepted, 6 enrolled. In 2017, 2 master's awarded. *Degree requirements:* For master's, thesis. *Entrance requirements:* For master's, bachelor's degree in dental hygiene. Additional exam requirements/recommendations for international students: Required—TOEFL (minimum score 84 iBT). *Application deadline:* Applications are processed on a rolling basis. Application fee: $75 ($90 for international students). Electronic applications accepted. *Expenses:* Contact institution. *Financial support:* In 2017–18, 1 student received support, including 1 fellowship with full tuition reimbursement available. *Unit head:* Dr. Danielle Furgeson, Director, 734-763-3392, E-mail: furgeson@umich.edu. *Application contact:* Patricia Katcher, Associate Admissions Director, 734-763-3316, Fax: 734-764-1922, E-mail: graddentinquiry@umich.edu.
Website: http://www.dent.umich.edu/dentalhygiene/education/MShome

University of Missouri–Kansas City, School of Dentistry, Kansas City, MO 64110-2499. Offers advanced education in dentistry (Graduate Dental Certificate); dental hygiene education (MS); endodontics (Graduate Dental Certificate); oral and maxillofacial surgery (Graduate Dental Certificate); oral biology (MS, PhD); orthodontics and dentofacial orthopedics (Graduate Dental Certificate); periodontics (Graduate Dental Certificate). PhD (interdisciplinary) offered through the School of Graduate Studies. *Accreditation:* ADA (one or more programs are accredited). *Degree requirements:* For master's, thesis; for doctorate, thesis/dissertation (for some programs). *Entrance requirements:* For master's, DAT, letters of evaluation, personal interview; for doctorate, DAT (for DDS); for Graduate Dental Certificate, DDS. Additional exam requirements/recommendations for international students: Required—TOEFL (minimum score 550 paper-based; 80 iBT). *Expenses:* Contact institution. *Faculty research:* Biomaterials, dental use of lasers, effectiveness of periodontal treatments, temporomandibular joint dysfunction.

Dental Hygiene

University of New Mexico, Graduate Studies, Health Sciences Center, Program in Dental Hygiene, Albuquerque, NM 87131-2039. Offers MS. *Program availability:* Part-time, evening/weekend, online learning. *Students:* 9 full-time (all women), 16 part-time (all women); includes 15 minority (1 Black or African American, non-Hispanic/Latino; 2 American Indian or Alaska Native, non-Hispanic/Latino; 1 Asian, non-Hispanic/Latino; 10 Hispanic/Latino; 1 Two or more races, non-Hispanic/Latino). Average age 35. 14 applicants, 86% accepted, 10 enrolled. In 2017, 3 master's awarded. *Application deadline:* For fall admission, 4/15 for domestic and international students; for winter admission, 1/31 priority date for domestic and international students. Application fee: $50. *Total annual research expenditures:* $1.3 million. *Unit head:* Prof. Christine N. Nathe, Director, 505-272-8147, Fax: 505-272-5584, E-mail: cnathe@unm.edu. *Application contact:* Prof. Demetra D. Logothetis, Graduate Program Director, 505-272-6687, Fax: 505-272-5584, E-mail: dlogothetis@salud.unm.edu.

The University of North Carolina at Chapel Hill, School of Dentistry and Graduate School, Graduate Programs in Dentistry, Chapel Hill, NC 27599. Offers dental hygiene (MS); endodontics (MS); epidemiology (PhD); operative dentistry (MS); oral and maxillofacial pathology (MS); oral and maxillofacial radiology (MS); oral biology (PhD); orthodontics (MS); pediatric dentistry (MS); periodontology (MS); prosthodontics (MS). *Degree requirements:* For master's, thesis; for doctorate, thesis/dissertation. *Entrance requirements:* For master's, GRE General Test (for orthodontics and oral biology only); National Dental Board Part I (Part II if available), dental degree (for all except dental hygiene); for doctorate, GRE General Test. Additional exam requirements/recommendations for international students: Required—TOEFL (minimum score 550 paper-based; 79 iBT). Electronic applications accepted. *Expenses:* Contact institution. *Faculty research:* Clinical research, inflammation, immunology, neuroscience, molecular biology.

West Virginia University, School of Dentistry, Morgantown, WV 26506-9400. Offers dental hygiene (MS); dentistry (DDS); endodontics (MS); orthodontics (MS); periodontics (MS); prosthodontics (MS). *Accreditation:* ADA (one or more programs are accredited). *Students:* 223 full-time (109 women), 1 part-time (0 women); includes 22 minority (1 Black or African American, non-Hispanic/Latino; 16 Asian, non-Hispanic/Latino; 3 Hispanic/Latino; 2 Two or more races, non-Hispanic/Latino), 12 international. *Degree requirements:* For master's, thesis; for doctorate, comprehensive exam. *Entrance requirements:* For doctorate, DAT, letters of recommendation, interview, minimum of 50 semester credit hours. Additional exam requirements/recommendations for international students: Required—TOEFL (minimum score 500 paper-based). *Application deadline:* For fall admission, 11/1 for domestic and international students. Applications are processed on a rolling basis. Application fee: $60. Electronic applications accepted. *Expenses:* Contact institution. *Financial support:* Research assistantships, teaching assistantships, Federal Work-Study, institutionally sponsored loans, scholarships/grants, health care benefits, and tuition waivers (partial) available. Financial award application deadline: 3/1; financial award applicants required to submit FAFSA. *Faculty research:* Growth and development, cephalography, endodontic interpretation and therapy, basic biological and clinical sciences, genetics and oral health. *Unit head:* Dr. Tom Borgia, Dean, 304-293-2521, E-mail: aborgia@hsc.wvu.edu. *Application contact:* Dr. Sheila Price, Associate Dean for Admissions, Recruitment, and Access, 304-293-1980, E-mail: sprice@hsc.wvu.edu.
Website: http://www.dentistry.hsc.wvu.edu

Emergency Medical Services

Baylor University, Graduate School, Military Programs, Program in Emergency Medicine, Waco, TX 76798. Offers D Sc PA. *Faculty:* 49 full-time (7 women), 19 part-time/adjunct (3 women). *Students:* 30 full-time (11 women); includes 9 minority (2 Black or African American, non-Hispanic/Latino; 2 Asian, non-Hispanic/Latino; 4 Hispanic/Latino; 1 Two or more races, non-Hispanic/Latino). In 2017, 13 doctorates awarded. *Degree requirements:* For doctorate, comprehensive exam. *Entrance requirements:* For doctorate, GRE. Additional exam requirements/recommendations for international students: Required—TOEFL, IELTS. *Unit head:* Brian Burk, Graduate Program Director, 210-221-7483, E-mail: brian.e.burk.mil@mail.mil. *Application contact:* Dr. Sue Love, 210-916-4542, Fax: 254-710-3870, E-mail: sue.love@us.army.mil.

Creighton University, Graduate School, Program in Emergency Medical Services, Omaha, NE 68178-0001. Offers MS. Program offered jointly with School of Pharmacy and Health Professions. *Program availability:* Part-time, online only, 100% online, blended/hybrid learning. *Faculty:* 6 full-time (1 woman). *Students:* 2 full-time (both women), 8 part-time (3 women). Average age 34. 6 applicants, 50% accepted, 3 enrolled. In 2017, 4 master's awarded. *Entrance requirements:* Additional exam requirements/recommendations for international students: Required—TOEFL (minimum score 90 iBT). *Application deadline:* For fall admission, 8/1 for domestic students, 6/1 for international students; for spring admission, 11/15 for domestic students, 10/1 for international students; for summer admission, 3/1 for domestic students, 2/1 for international students. Applications are processed on a rolling basis. Application fee: $50. Electronic applications accepted. Part-time tuition and fees vary according to course load, degree level, campus/location and program. *Financial support:* Scholarships/grants available. *Unit head:* Dr. Michael Miller, Director, 402-280-1189, E-mail: mikemiller@creighton.edu. *Application contact:* Lindsay Johnson, Director of Graduate and Adult Recruitment, 402-280-2703, Fax: 402-280-2423, E-mail: gradschool@creighton.edu.
Website: http://ems.creighton.edu/

Drexel University, College of Nursing and Health Professions, Emergency and Public Safety Services Program, Philadelphia, PA 19104-2875. Offers MS. *Program availability:* Part-time, evening/weekend. *Degree requirements:* For master's, comprehensive exam. *Entrance requirements:* For master's, GRE General Test, minimum GPA of 2.75.

San Diego State University, Graduate and Research Affairs, College of Health and Human Services, Graduate School of Public Health, San Diego, CA 92182. Offers environmental health (MPH); epidemiology (MPH, PhD), including biostatistics (MPH); global emergency preparedness and response (MS); global health (PhD); health behavior (PhD); health promotion (MPH); health services administration (MPH); toxicology (MS); MPH/MA; MSW/MPH. *Accreditation:* CAHME (one or more programs are accredited). *Program availability:* Part-time. *Degree requirements:* For master's, comprehensive exam (for some programs), thesis (for some programs); for doctorate, thesis/dissertation. *Entrance requirements:* For master's, GMAT (MPH in health services administration), GRE General Test; for doctorate, GRE General Test. Additional exam requirements/recommendations for international students: Required—TOEFL. *Faculty research:* Evaluation of tobacco, AIDS prevalence and prevention, mammography, infant death project, Alzheimer's in elderly Chinese.

Université Laval, Faculty of Medicine, Post-Professional Programs in Medical Studies, Québec, QC G1K 7P4, Canada. Offers anatomy–pathology (DESS); anesthesiology (DESS); cardiology (DESS); care of older people (Diploma); clinical research (DESS); community health (DESS); dermatology (DESS); diagnostic radiology (DESS); emergency medicine (Diploma); family medicine (DESS); general surgery (DESS); geriatrics (DESS); hematology (DESS); internal medicine (DESS); maternal and fetal medicine (Diploma); medical biochemistry (DESS); medical microbiology and infectious diseases (DESS); medical oncology (DESS); nephrology (DESS); neurology (DESS); neurosurgery (DESS); obstetrics and gynecology (DESS); ophthalmology (DESS); orthopedic surgery (DESS); oto-rhino-laryngology (DESS); palliative medicine (Diploma); pediatrics (DESS); plastic surgery (DESS); psychiatry (DESS); pulmonary medicine (DESS); radiology–oncology (DESS); thoracic surgery (DESS); urology (DESS). *Degree requirements:* For other advanced degree, comprehensive exam. *Entrance requirements:* For degree, knowledge of French. Electronic applications accepted.

University of Guelph, Ontario Veterinary College and Graduate Studies, Graduate Programs in Veterinary Sciences, Department of Clinical Studies, Guelph, ON N1G 2W1, Canada. Offers anesthesiology (M Sc, DV Sc); cardiology (DV Sc, Diploma); clinical studies (Diploma); dermatology (M Sc); diagnostic imaging (M Sc, DV Sc); emergency/critical care (M Sc, DV Sc, Diploma); medicine (M Sc, DV Sc); neurology (M Sc, DV Sc); ophthalmology (M Sc, DV Sc); surgery (M Sc, DV Sc). *Degree requirements:* For master's, thesis; for doctorate, comprehensive exam, thesis/dissertation. *Entrance requirements:* Additional exam requirements/recommendations for international students: Required—TOEFL (minimum score 550 paper-based), IELTS (minimum score 6.5). Electronic applications accepted. *Faculty research:* Orthopedics, respirology, oncology, exercise physiology, cardiology.

Occupational Therapy

Abilene Christian University, Graduate Programs, College of Education and Human Services, Department of Occupational Therapy, Abilene, TX 79699. Offers MS. *Accreditation:* AOTA. *Faculty:* 3 full-time (all women), 4 part-time/adjunct (3 women). *Students:* 55 full-time (49 women); includes 5 minority (1 Black or African American, non-Hispanic/Latino; 1 Asian, non-Hispanic/Latino; 3 Hispanic/Latino). 190 applicants, 34% accepted, 30 enrolled. In 2017, 22 master's awarded. *Entrance requirements:* Additional exam requirements/recommendations for international students: Required—TOEFL (minimum score 80 iBT), IELTS (minimum score 6), PTE. *Application deadline:* For fall admission, 2/1 for domestic students. Application fee: $50. *Expenses:* $910 per hour. *Financial support:* In 2017–18, 7 students received support. Institutionally sponsored loans, scholarships/grants, and unspecified assistantships available. Support available to part-time students. Financial award application deadline: 4/1; financial award applicants required to submit FAFSA. *Unit head:* Dr. Hope Martin, Program Director, 325-674-2474, Fax: 325-674-6568, E-mail: msot@acu.edu. *Application contact:* Graduate Admissions, 325-674-6911, Fax: 325-674-6717, E-mail: gradinfo@acu.edu.
Website: http://www.acu.edu/graduate/academics/occupational-therapy.html

Adventist University of Health Sciences, Program in Occupational Therapy, Orlando, FL 32803. Offers MOT.

Alabama State University, College of Health Sciences, Department of Occupational Therapy, Montgomery, AL 36101-0271. Offers MS. *Accreditation:* AOTA. *Faculty:* 6 full-time (all women). *Students:* 23 full-time (19 women). Average age 22. 24 applicants, 100% accepted, 23 enrolled. *Degree requirements:* For master's, comprehensive exam. *Entrance requirements:* For master's, interview. Additional exam requirements/recommendations for international students: Required—TOEFL. *Application deadline:* For fall admission, 4/15 for domestic and international students; for spring admission, 11/15 for domestic and international students; for summer admission, 3/15 for domestic and international students. Application fee: $25. Electronic applications accepted. *Expenses:* Tuition, state resident: part-time $412 per credit hour. Tuition, nonresident: part-time $824 per credit hour. *Required fees:* $685 per semester. *Financial support:* Application deadline: 6/30; applicants required to submit FAFSA. *Unit head:* Dr. Susan Denham, Chair, 334-229-5056, Fax: 334-229-5882, E-mail: sdenham@alasu.edu. *Application contact:* Dr. William Person, Dean of Graduate Studies, 334-229-4274, Fax: 334-229-4928, E-mail: wperson@alasu.edu.
Website: http://www.alasu.edu/academics/colleges—departments/health-sciences/occupational-therapy/index.aspx

Allen College, Graduate Programs, Waterloo, IA 50703. Offers adult-gerontology acute care nurse practitioner (MSN); community/public health nursing (MSN); education (MSN); family nurse practitioner (MSN); health sciences (Ed D); leadership in health care delivery (MSN); leadership in health care informatics (MSN); nursing (DNP); occupational therapy (MS); psychiatric mental health nurse practitioner (MSN). MSN in leadership in healthcare informatics offered in partnership with University of Minnesota. *Accreditation:* AACN; ACEN. *Program availability:* Part-time, 100% online, blended/hybrid learning. *Faculty:* 24 full-time (all women), 8 part-time/adjunct (7 women). *Students:* 106 full-time (91 women), 187 part-time (164 women); includes 22 minority

(12 Black or African American, non-Hispanic/Latino; 1 American Indian or Alaska Native, non-Hispanic/Latino; 2 Asian, non-Hispanic/Latino; 3 Hispanic/Latino; 4 Two or more races, non-Hispanic/Latino), 2 international. Average age 33. 352 applicants, 56% accepted, 131 enrolled. In 2017, 73 master's, 2 doctorates awarded. *Entrance requirements:* For master's, minimum GPA of 3.0 in the last 60 hours of undergraduate coursework; for doctorate, minimum GPA of 3.25 in graduate coursework. *Application deadline:* For fall admission, 2/1 priority date for domestic students; for spring admission, 9/1 priority date for domestic students. Applications are processed on a rolling basis. Application fee: $50. Electronic applications accepted. *Expenses:* $17,860 per year. *Financial support:* In 2017–18, 97 students received support. Federal Work-Study, institutionally sponsored loans, scholarships/grants, and traineeships available. Support available to part-time students. Financial award application deadline: 8/1; financial award applicants required to submit FAFSA. *Faculty research:* Poverty. *Unit head:* Dr. Nancy Kramer, Vice Chancellor for Academic Affairs, 319-226-2040, Fax: 319-226-2070, E-mail: nancy.kramer@allencollege.edu. *Application contact:* Molly Quinn, Director of Admissions, 319-226-2001, Fax: 319-226-2010, E-mail: molly.quinn@allencollege.edu.
Website: http://www.allencollege.edu/

Alvernia University, School of Graduate Studies, Program in Occupational Therapy, Reading, PA 19607-1799. Offers MSOT. *Accreditation:* AOTA. *Program availability:* Part-time, evening/weekend. *Degree requirements:* For master's, thesis optional. Electronic applications accepted.

American International College, School of Health Sciences, Springfield, MA 01109-3189. Offers exercise science (MS); family nurse practitioner (MSN, Post-Master's Certificate); nursing administrator (MSN); nursing educator (MSN); occupational therapy (MSOT, OTD); physical therapy (DPT). *Program availability:* Part-time, 100% online. *Faculty:* 14 full-time (13 women), 10 part-time/adjunct (all women). *Students:* 286 full-time (220 women), 11 part-time (9 women); includes 75 minority (30 Black or African American, non-Hispanic/Latino; 21 Asian, non-Hispanic/Latino; 19 Hispanic/Latino; 5 Two or more races, non-Hispanic/Latino), 2 international. Average age 27. 652 applicants, 49% accepted, 109 enrolled. In 2017, 48 master's, 28 doctorates, 2 other advanced degrees awarded. *Degree requirements:* For master's, practicum; for doctorate, thesis/dissertation, practicum. *Entrance requirements:* For master's, 3 letters of recommendation, personal goal statement; minimum GPA of 3.2, interview, BS or BA, and 2 clinical PT observations (for DPT); minimum GPA of 3.0, MSOT, OT licensen, and 2 clinical OT observations (for OTD); for doctorate, personal goal statement, 2 letters of recommendation; minimum GPA of 3.0, BS or BA, 2 clinical OT observations (for MSOT); RN license and minimum GPA of 3.0 (for MSN). Additional exam requirements/recommendations for international students: Required—TOEFL (minimum score 577 paper-based; 91 iBT). *Application deadline:* For fall admission, 12/1 priority date for domestic and international students; for spring admission, 11/15 priority date for domestic and international students. Application fee: $50. Electronic applications accepted. *Expenses:* Contact institution. *Faculty research:* Teaching simulation, ergonomics, orthopedics, use of social media in health care. *Unit head:* Dr. Cesarina Thompson, Dean, 413-205-3056, Fax: 413-654-1430, E-mail: cesarina.thompson@aic.edu. *Application contact:* Kerry Barnes, Director of Graduate Admissions, 413-205-3703, Fax: 413-205-3051, E-mail: kerry.barnes@aic.edu.
Website: http://www.aic.edu/academics/hs

Arkansas State University, Graduate School, College of Nursing and Health Professions, Program in Occupational Therapy, State University, AR 72467. Offers DOT. *Degree requirements:* For doctorate, comprehensive exam, thesis/dissertation. *Entrance requirements:* For doctorate, GRE or MAT, bachelor's degree; transcripts; minimum GPA of 3.0 on prerequisites, 2.5 overall; 3 letters of recommendation; CPR Certification; TB Test; immunizations; health insurance; professional liability insurance; resume; personal statement. Additional exam requirements/recommendations for international students: Required—TOEFL (minimum score 550 paper-based; 79 iBT), IELTS (minimum score 6), PTE (minimum score 56). Electronic applications accepted. *Expenses:* Contact institution.

A.T. Still University, Arizona School of Health Sciences, Mesa, AZ 85206. Offers advanced occupational therapy (MS); advanced physician assistant studies (MS); athletic training (MS, DAT); audiology (Au D); clinical decision making in athletic training (Graduate Certificate); occupational therapy (MS, OTD); orthopedic rehabilitation (Graduate Certificate); physical therapy (DPT); physician assistant studies (MS); transitional audiology (Au D); transitional physical therapy (DPT). *Accreditation:* AOTA (one or more programs are accredited); ASHA. *Program availability:* Part-time, 100% online. *Faculty:* 59 full-time (39 women), 221 part-time/adjunct (155 women). *Students:* 608 full-time (405 women), 431 part-time (310 women); includes 247 minority (54 Black or African American, non-Hispanic/Latino; 13 American Indian or Alaska Native, non-Hispanic/Latino; 151 Asian, non-Hispanic/Latino; 2 Hispanic/Latino; 1 Native Hawaiian or other Pacific Islander, non-Hispanic/Latino; 26 Two or more races, non-Hispanic/Latino), 1 international. Average age 33. 4,882 applicants, 9% accepted, 278 enrolled. In 2017, 132 master's, 270 doctorates awarded. *Degree requirements:* For master's, thesis (for some programs); for doctorate, thesis/dissertation (for some programs). *Entrance requirements:* For master's, GRE General Test; for doctorate, GRE, Physical Therapist Evaluation Tool (for DPT), current state licensure. Additional exam requirements/recommendations for international students: Required—TOEFL (minimum score 80 iBT). *Application deadline:* For fall admission, 7/7 for domestic and international students; for winter admission, 10/3 for domestic and international students; for spring admission, 1/16 for domestic and international students; for summer admission, 4/17 for domestic and international students. Applications are processed on a rolling basis. Application fee: $70. Electronic applications accepted. Application fee is waived when completed online. *Financial support:* In 2017–18, 161 students received support. Federal Work-Study and scholarships/grants available. Financial award application deadline: 6/1; financial award applicants required to submit FAFSA. *Faculty research:* Pediatric sport-related concussion, adolescent athlete health-related quality of life; geriatric and pediatric well-being, pain management for participation, practice-based research network, BMI and dental caries. *Total annual research expenditures:* $63,003. *Unit head:* Dr. Randy Danielsen, Dean, 480-219-6009, Fax: 480-219-6110, E-mail: rdanielsen@atsu.edu. *Application contact:* Donna Sparks, Director, Admissions Processing, 660-626-2117, Fax: 660-626-2969, E-mail: admissions@atsu.edu.
Website: http://www.atsu.edu/ashs

Augusta University, College of Allied Health Sciences, Occupational Therapy Program, Augusta, GA 30912. Offers MHS. *Accreditation:* AOTA. *Program availability:* Part-time. *Degree requirements:* For master's, thesis. *Entrance requirements:* For master's, GRE General Test. Additional exam requirements/recommendations for international students: Required—TOEFL (minimum score 550 paper-based; 79 iBT). Electronic applications accepted.

Barry University, College of Health Sciences, Program in Occupational Therapy, Miami Shores, FL 33161-6695. Offers MS. *Accreditation:* AOTA. Electronic applications accepted.

Bay Path University, Program in Occupational Therapy, Longmeadow, MA 01106-2292. Offers MOT, OTD. *Accreditation:* AOTA. *Program availability:* Part-time. *Students:* 280 full-time (256 women), 36 part-time (33 women); includes 56 minority (20 Black or African American, non-Hispanic/Latino; 2 American Indian or Alaska Native, non-Hispanic/Latino; 13 Asian, non-Hispanic/Latino; 14 Hispanic/Latino; 7 Two or more races, non-Hispanic/Latino), 1 international. Average age 28. In 2017, 81 master's, 36 doctorates awarded. *Degree requirements:* For master's, 78 credits and 24 weeks of full-time level II fieldwork following completion of all academic courses; for doctorate, 36 credits (12 courses). *Entrance requirements:* For master's, bachelor's degree with minimum GPA of 3.0; two courses in anatomy and physiology, and one course each in developmental psychology, statistics, and sociology or culture (for occupational therapy); for doctorate, master's or baccalaureate degree in occupational therapy; minimum of one year of full-time clinical experience. *Application deadline:* Applications are processed on a rolling basis. Application fee: $45. Electronic applications accepted. Application fee is waived when completed online. *Expenses:* $935 per credit (for MS); $975 per credit (for OTD). *Financial support:* Unspecified assistantships available. Financial award applicants required to submit FAFSA. *Unit head:* Dr. Beverly St. Pierre, Program Director, E-mail: bstpierre@baypath.edu. *Application contact:* Diane Ranaldi, Dean of Graduate Admissions, 413-565-1332, Fax: 413-565-1250, E-mail: dranaldi@baypath.edu.
Website: http://graduate.baypath.edu/Graduate-Programs/Programs-On-Campus/MS-Programs/Master-of-Occupational-Therapy

Belmont University, College of Health Sciences, Nashville, TN 37212. Offers nursing (MSN, DNP); occupational therapy (MSOT, OTD); physical therapy (DPT). *Program availability:* Part-time, blended/hybrid learning. *Faculty:* 29 full-time (25 women), 16 part-time/adjunct (11 women). *Students:* 394 full-time (330 women), 9 part-time (8 women); includes 34 minority (9 Black or African American, non-Hispanic/Latino; 12 Asian, non-Hispanic/Latino; 7 Hispanic/Latino; 6 Two or more races, non-Hispanic/Latino). Average age 26. In 2017, 52 master's, 79 doctorates awarded. *Degree requirements:* For master's, comprehensive exam, thesis; for doctorate, comprehensive exam. *Entrance requirements:* For master's, GRE, BSN, minimum GPA of 3.0. Additional exam requirements/recommendations for international students: Required—TOEFL (minimum score 550 paper-based). *Application deadline:* Applications are processed on a rolling basis. Application fee: $50. Electronic applications accepted. *Expenses:* Contact institution. *Financial support:* Teaching assistantships with full tuition reimbursements, career-related internships or fieldwork, scholarships/grants, and traineeships available. Financial award application deadline: 3/1; financial award applicants required to submit FAFSA. *Unit head:* Dr. Cathy Taylor, Dean, 615-460-6916, Fax: 615-460-6750. *Application contact:* Bill Nichols, Director of Enrollment Services, 615-460-6107, E-mail: bill.nichols@belmont.edu.
Website: http://www.belmont.edu/healthsciences/

Boston University, College of Health and Rehabilitation Sciences: Sargent College, Department of Occupational Therapy, Boston, MA 02215. Offers occupational therapy (OTD); rehabilitation sciences (PhD). *Accreditation:* AOTA (one or more programs are accredited). *Program availability:* Blended/hybrid learning. *Faculty:* 15 full-time (12 women), 7 part-time/adjunct (all women). *Students:* 118 full-time (106 women), 58 part-time (53 women); includes 38 minority (3 Black or African American, non-Hispanic/Latino; 17 Asian, non-Hispanic/Latino; 13 Hispanic/Latino; 5 Two or more races, non-Hispanic/Latino), 13 international. Average age 28. 269 applicants, 27% accepted, 45 enrolled. In 2017, 14 doctorates awarded. *Degree requirements:* For doctorate, scholarly project (for OTD); comprehensive exam and thesis (for PhD). *Entrance requirements:* For doctorate, GRE General Test. Additional exam requirements/recommendations for international students: Required—TOEFL (minimum score 550 paper-based; 84 iBT), TWE (minimum score 5). *Application deadline:* For fall admission, 12/15 priority date for domestic students, 1/15 priority date for international students. Applications are processed on a rolling basis. Application fee: $140. Electronic applications accepted. *Financial support:* In 2017–18, 60 students received support, including 12 teaching assistantships (averaging $2,500 per year); career-related internships or fieldwork, Federal Work-Study, institutionally sponsored loans, and scholarships/grants also available. Financial award application deadline: 12/15; financial award applicants required to submit FAFSA. *Faculty research:* Sensory integration, outcomes measurement, impact of Parkinson's disease, families of people with autism. *Total annual research expenditures:* $1.9 million. *Unit head:* Dr. Ellen Cohn, Program Director, 617-358-1063, Fax: 617-353-2926, E-mail: ecohn@bu.edu. *Application contact:* Sharon Sankey, Assistant Dean, Student Services, 617-353-2713, Fax: 617-353-7500, E-mail: ssankey@bu.edu.
Website: http://www.bu.edu/sargent/

Brenau University, Sydney O. Smith Graduate School, College of Health Sciences, Gainesville, GA 30501. Offers family nurse practitioner (MSN); nurse educator (MSN); nursing management (MSN); occupational therapy (MS); psychology (MS). *Accreditation:* AOTA. *Program availability:* Part-time, evening/weekend. *Degree requirements:* For master's, comprehensive exam (for some programs), thesis (for some programs), clinical practicum hours. *Entrance requirements:* For master's, GRE General Test or MAT (for some programs), interview, writing sample, references (for some programs). Additional exam requirements/recommendations for international students: Required—TOEFL (minimum score 500 paper-based; 61 iBT); Recommended—IELTS (minimum score 5). Electronic applications accepted. *Expenses:* Contact institution.

Cabarrus College of Health Sciences, Program in Occupational Therapy, Concord, NC 28025. Offers MOT. *Accreditation:* AOTA.

California State University, Dominguez Hills, College of Health, Human Services and Nursing, Program in Occupational Therapy, Carson, CA 90747-0001. Offers MS. *Accreditation:* AOTA. *Degree requirements:* For master's, comprehensive exam. *Entrance requirements:* For master's, GRE. Additional exam requirements/recommendations for international students: Required—TOEFL, TWE. Electronic applications accepted. *Faculty research:* Child school functioning, assessment, lifespan occupational development, low vision occupational therapy intervention.

Carroll University, Program in Occupational Therapy, Waukesha, WI 53186-5593. Offers MOT.

Chatham University, Program in Occupational Therapy, Pittsburgh, PA 15232-2826. Offers MOT, OTD. *Accreditation:* AOTA. *Faculty:* 7 full-time (all women), 11 part-time/adjunct (all women). *Students:* 100 full-time (91 women), 30 part-time (28 women); includes 11 minority (7 Black or African American, non-Hispanic/Latino; 2 Hispanic/Latino; 2 Two or more races, non-Hispanic/Latino). Average age 31. 501 applicants, 23% accepted, 65 enrolled. In 2017, 40 master's, 35 doctorates awarded. *Entrance requirements:* For master's, recommendation letter, community service, volunteer service. Additional exam requirements/recommendations for international students: Required—TOEFL (minimum score 600 paper-based; 100 iBT), IELTS (minimum score 7), TWE. *Application deadline:* For fall admission, 12/5 priority date for domestic and international students. Applications are processed on a rolling basis. Application fee: $45. Electronic applications accepted. Application fee is waived when completed online. *Expenses:* Contact institution. *Financial support:* Applicants required to submit FAFSA. *Unit head:* Dr. Joyce Salls, Director, 412-365-1177, E-mail: salls@chatham.edu. *Application contact:* Ashlee Bartko, Senior Assistant Director of Graduate Admission, 412-365-1115, Fax: 412-365-1609, E-mail: gradadmissions@chatham.edu.
Website: http://www.chatham.edu/ot

Occupational Therapy

Chicago State University, School of Graduate and Professional Studies, College of Health Sciences, Department of Occupational Therapy, Chicago, IL 60628. Offers MOT. *Accreditation:* AOTA. *Program availability:* Part-time. *Entrance requirements:* For master's, bachelor's degree from accredited college or university with minimum GPA of 3.0 in final 60 semester credit hours; two recommendations; human service experience; essay; interview. *Application deadline:* For fall admission, 2/1 priority date for domestic students. *Unit head:* Elizabeth Wittbrodt, Program Coordinator, 773-995-2530, E-mail: ewittbro@csu.edu. *Application contact:* Daphne G. Townsend, Admissions and Records Officer II, 773-995-2404, Fax: 773-995-3671, E-mail: g-studies1@csu.edu.
Website: http://www.csu.edu/OccupationalTherapy/

Clarkson University, Division of Health Sciences, Department of Occupational Therapy, Potsdam, NY 13699. Offers MS. *Faculty:* 14 full-time (9 women), 7 part-time/adjunct (6 women). *Students:* 51 full-time (45 women), 1 (woman) part-time; includes 13 minority (2 Black or African American, non-Hispanic/Latino; 9 Asian, non-Hispanic/Latino; 2 Hispanic/Latino). 383 applicants, 4% accepted, 16 enrolled. *Entrance requirements:* For master's, minimum undergraduate GPA of 3.0; OTCAS application. *Application deadline:* For spring admission, 4/18 for domestic and international students. Applications are processed on a rolling basis. Application fee: $190. Electronic applications accepted. *Expenses:* Contact institution. *Financial support:* Scholarships/grants available. *Unit head:* Dr. Victoria Priganc, Chair of Occupational Therapy, 315-268-4412, E-mail: vpriganc@clarkson.edu. *Application contact:* Jennifer Zoanetti, Graduate Admissions Coordinator, 315-268-4476, E-mail: jzoanett@clarkson.edu.
Website: https://www.clarkson.edu/academics/graduate

Cleveland State University, College of Graduate Studies, College of Sciences and Health Professions, School of Health Sciences, Program in Occupational Therapy, Cleveland, OH 44115. Offers MOT. *Accreditation:* AOTA. *Faculty:* 7 full-time (5 women), 2 part-time/adjunct (both women). *Students:* 118 full-time (106 women), 19 part-time (17 women); includes 11 minority (4 Black or African American, non-Hispanic/Latino; 5 Hispanic/Latino; 2 Two or more races, non-Hispanic/Latino). Average age 26. 163 applicants, 30% accepted, 45 enrolled. In 2017, 40 master's awarded. *Entrance requirements:* For master's, GRE (if overall GPA less than 3.0). Additional exam requirements/recommendations for international students: Recommended—TOEFL (minimum score 550 paper-based; 78 iBT), IELTS (minimum score 6). Application fee: $55. Electronic applications accepted. *Financial support:* In 2017–18, 9 students received support. Teaching assistantships and unspecified assistantships available. Financial award application deadline: 3/15; financial award applicants required to submit FAFSA. *Faculty research:* Pediatrics, psychology, daily living, exercise physiology, neuromuscular disorders. *Total annual research expenditures:* $620,000. *Unit head:* Dr. Glenn D. Goodman, Director, 216-687-2493, Fax: 216-687-9316, E-mail: g.goodman@csuohio.edu. *Application contact:* Karen Armstrong, Administrative Assistant, 216-687-3567, Fax: 216-687-9316, E-mail: k.bradley@csuohio.edu.
Website: http://www.csuohio.edu/sciences/dept/healthsciences/graduate/MOT/index.html

College of Saint Mary, Program in Occupational Therapy, Omaha, NE 68106. Offers MOT. *Accreditation:* AOTA.

The College of St. Scholastica, Graduate Studies, Department of Occupational Therapy, Duluth, MN 55811-4199. Offers MA. *Accreditation:* AOTA. *Program availability:* Part-time. *Degree requirements:* For master's, thesis. *Entrance requirements:* Additional exam requirements/recommendations for international students: Required—TOEFL (minimum score 550 paper-based; 79 iBT). Electronic applications accepted. *Faculty research:* Gerontology, occupational therapy administration, neurorehabilitation, occupational therapy in nontraditional settings, clinical fieldwork issues.

Colorado State University, College of Health and Human Sciences, Department of Occupational Therapy, Fort Collins, CO 80523-1573. Offers MOT, MS, PhD. *Accreditation:* AOTA. *Faculty:* 11 full-time (8 women), 4 part-time/adjunct (all women). *Students:* 112 full-time (103 women), 13 part-time (10 women); includes 11 minority (2 Asian, non-Hispanic/Latino; 6 Hispanic/Latino; 3 Two or more races, non-Hispanic/Latino), 2 international. Average age 27. 633 applicants, 13% accepted, 51 enrolled. In 2017, 52 master's awarded. Terminal master's awarded for partial completion of doctoral program. *Degree requirements:* For master's, thesis (for some programs); for doctorate, comprehensive exam, thesis/dissertation. *Entrance requirements:* For master's and doctorate, GRE General Test, OTCAS; departmental application. Additional exam requirements/recommendations for international students: Required—TOEFL. *Application deadline:* For fall admission, 1/5 priority date for domestic and international students. Application fee: $60 ($70 for international students). Electronic applications accepted. *Expenses:* $2,000 per semester. *Financial support:* In 2017–18, 5 fellowships with full and partial tuition reimbursements (averaging $7,390 per year), 6 research assistantships with full and partial tuition reimbursements (averaging $24,652 per year), 1 teaching assistantship with full and partial tuition reimbursement (averaging $7,390 per year) were awarded; scholarships/grants and unspecified assistantships also available. *Faculty research:* Children's play; development of neurophysiological mechanisms that underlie cognitive and motor behaviors in children with and without disorders; TBI screening tool development; neuro-rehabilitation. *Total annual research expenditures:* $558,864. *Unit head:* Dr. Anita Bundy, Department Head, 970-491-3105, Fax: 970-491-6290, E-mail: anita.bundy@colostate.edu. *Application contact:* Linda McDowell, Graduate Programs Coordinator, 970-491-6243, Fax: 970-491-6290, E-mail: linda.mcdowell@colostate.edu.
Website: http://www.ot.chhs.colostate.edu/

Columbia University, College of Physicians and Surgeons, Programs in Occupational Therapy, New York, NY 10032. Offers movement science (Ed D), including occupational therapy; occupational therapy (MS); occupational therapy and cognition (OTD); MPH/MS. EdD offered in tandem with Teachers College, Columbia University. *Accreditation:* AOTA. *Degree requirements:* For master's, project, 6 months of fieldwork, thesis (for post-professional students); for doctorate, comprehensive exam, thesis/dissertation. *Entrance requirements:* For master's, undergraduate course work in anatomy, physiology, statistics, psychology, social sciences, humanities, and English composition; for doctorate, master's degree in occupational therapy (for OTD). Additional exam requirements/recommendations for international students: Required—TOEFL (minimum score 100 iBT) or IELTS (minimum score 8). Electronic applications accepted. *Expenses:* Contact institution. *Faculty research:* Community mental health, motor learning, cognition, literacy, LGBTQ.

Concordia University Wisconsin, Graduate Programs, School of Health Professions, Program in Occupational Therapy, Mequon, WI 53097-2402. Offers MOT. *Accreditation:* AOTA. *Degree requirements:* For master's, comprehensive exam, thesis or alternative. *Entrance requirements:* Additional exam requirements/recommendations for international students: Required—TOEFL.

Creighton University, School of Pharmacy and Health Professions, Program in Occupational Therapy, Omaha, NE 68178-0001. Offers OTD. *Accreditation:* AOTA. *Program availability:* Online learning. *Entrance requirements:* Additional exam requirements/recommendations for international students: Required—TOEFL. Electronic applications accepted. Part-time tuition and fees vary according to course load, degree level, campus/location and program. *Faculty research:* Patient safety in health services research, health information technology and health services research, health care services in minority and underserved populations, occupational therapy in school-based programs, educational technology use in the classroom.

Dalhousie University, Faculty of Health Professions, School of Occupational Therapy, Halifax, NS B3H3J5, Canada. Offers occupational therapy (entry to profession) (M Sc); occupational therapy (post-professional) (M Sc). *Program availability:* Part-time, evening/weekend, online learning. *Degree requirements:* For master's, thesis. *Entrance requirements:* Additional exam requirements/recommendations for international students: Required—TOEFL, IELTS, CANTEST, CAEL, or Michigan English Language Assessment Battery. Electronic applications accepted. *Faculty research:* Gender, health systems, design, geriatrics power and empowerment.

Dominican College, Division of Allied Health, Department of Occupational Therapy, Orangeburg, NY 10962-1210. Offers MS. *Accreditation:* AOTA. *Program availability:* Part-time, evening/weekend. *Faculty:* 5 full-time (3 women), 9 part-time/adjunct (all women). *Students:* 81 full-time (71 women), 20 part-time (17 women); includes 32 minority (6 Black or African American, non-Hispanic/Latino; 8 Asian, non-Hispanic/Latino; 13 Hispanic/Latino; 2 Native Hawaiian or other Pacific Islander, non-Hispanic/Latino; 3 Two or more races, non-Hispanic/Latino), 1 international. In 2017, 54 master's awarded. *Degree requirements:* For master's, 2 clinical affiliations. *Entrance requirements:* For master's, minimum GPA of 3.0, writing sample, 3 letters of recommendation. Additional exam requirements/recommendations for international students: Required—TOEFL (minimum score 550 paper-based; 90 iBT). *Application deadline:* Applications are processed on a rolling basis. Application fee: $50. Electronic applications accepted. *Expenses: Tuition:* Part-time $900 per credit. One-time fee: $200. Tuition and fees vary according to degree level and program. *Financial support:* Application deadline: 2/1; applicants required to submit FAFSA. *Unit head:* Jan Garbarini, Program Director, 845-848-6034, Fax: 845-398-4893, E-mail: jan.garbarini@dc.edu. *Application contact:* Christina Lifshey, Assistant Director of Graduate Admissions, 845-848-7900, Fax: 845-365-3150, E-mail: admissions@dc.edu.
Website: http://www.dc.edu/

Dominican University of California, School of Health and Natural Sciences, Program in Occupational Therapy, San Rafael, CA 94901-2298. Offers MS. *Accreditation:* AOTA. *Faculty:* 8 full-time (all women), 7 part-time/adjunct (all women). *Students:* 102 full-time (93 women), 5 part-time (all women); includes 60 minority (2 Black or African American, non-Hispanic/Latino; 40 Asian, non-Hispanic/Latino; 12 Hispanic/Latino; 1 Native Hawaiian or other Pacific Islander, non-Hispanic/Latino; 5 Two or more races, non-Hispanic/Latino), 1 international. Average age 27. 62 applicants, 100% accepted, 50 enrolled. In 2017, 51 master's awarded. *Degree requirements:* For master's, thesis. *Entrance requirements:* For master's, GRE, minimum GPA of 3.0, minimum of 60 hours of volunteer experience. Additional exam requirements/recommendations for international students: Required—TOEFL (minimum score 550 paper-based; 80 iBT), IELTS (minimum score 6.5). *Application deadline:* For fall admission, 2/1 priority date for domestic students. Application fee: $0. Electronic applications accepted. *Expenses:* $1,100 per unit. *Financial support:* In 2017–18, 6 students received support. Scholarships/grants available. Financial award application deadline: 3/2; financial award applicants required to submit FAFSA. *Unit head:* Dr. Ruth Ramsey, Department Chair and Program Director, 415-257-1393, E-mail: rramsey@dominican.edu. *Application contact:* Michael Lavigna, Assistant Director of Graduate Admissions, 415-485-3253, Fax: 415-485-3214, E-mail: gradmissions@dominican.edu.
Website: https://www.dominican.edu/academics/hns2/ot/graduate-program

Drake University, College of Pharmacy and Health Sciences, Des Moines, IA 50311-4516. Offers athletic training (MAT); occupational therapy (OTD); pharmacy (Pharm D); Pharm D/JD; Pharm D/MBA; Pharm D/MPA. *Accreditation:* ACPE. *Degree requirements:* For doctorate, rotations. *Entrance requirements:* For doctorate, PCAT, interview. Additional exam requirements/recommendations for international students: Required—TOEFL. *Application deadline:* For fall admission, 2/1 priority date for domestic students. Application fee: $135. Electronic applications accepted. *Expenses:* Contact institution. *Financial support:* Teaching assistantships, career-related internships or fieldwork, Federal Work-Study, institutionally sponsored loans, and scholarships/grants available. Support available to part-time students. Financial award application deadline: 3/1; financial award applicants required to submit FAFSA. *Faculty research:* Cost-benefit and cost-analysis of pharmaceutical products and services, patient satisfaction, community health planning and development, nutrition, ambulatory care. *Unit head:* Dr. Renae Chesnut, Dean, 515-271-3018, Fax: 515-271-4171, E-mail: renae.chesnut@drake.edu.
Website: http://www.drake.edu/cphs/

Duquesne University, John G. Rangos, Sr. School of Health Sciences, Pittsburgh, PA 15282-0001. Offers health management systems (MHMS); occupational therapy (MS, OTD); physical therapy (DPT); physician assistant studies (MPAS); rehabilitation science (MS, PhD); speech-language pathology (MS). *Accreditation:* AOTA (one or more programs are accredited); APTA (one or more programs are accredited); ASHA. *Program availability:* Part-time, minimal on-campus study. *Faculty:* 51 full-time (38 women), 33 part-time/adjunct (17 women). *Students:* 247 full-time (199 women), 11 part-time (7 women); includes 15 minority (2 Black or African American, non-Hispanic/Latino; 7 Asian, non-Hispanic/Latino; 3 Hispanic/Latino; 3 Two or more races, non-Hispanic/Latino), 42 international. Average age 23. 283 applicants, 31% accepted, 54 enrolled. In 2017, 134 master's, 39 doctorates awarded. *Degree requirements:* For doctorate, comprehensive exam (for some programs), thesis/dissertation (for some programs). *Entrance requirements:* For master's, GRE General Test (speech-language pathology), 3 letters of recommendation; minimum GPA of 2.75 (health management systems), 3.0 (speech-language pathology); for doctorate, GRE General Test (for physical therapy and rehabilitation science), 3 letters of recommendation, minimum GPA of 3.0, personal interview. Additional exam requirements/recommendations for international students: Required—TOEFL (minimum score 550 paper-based; 90 iBT); Recommended—IELTS. *Application deadline:* For fall admission, 2/1 for domestic and international students; for spring admission, 7/1 for domestic and international students. Applications are processed on a rolling basis. Application fee: $0. Electronic applications accepted. *Expenses:* $1,351 per credit ($1,259 for health management systems). *Financial support:* Federal Work-Study available. Financial award applicants required to submit FAFSA. *Faculty research:* Neuronal processing, electrical stimulation on peripheral neuropathy, central nervous system (CNS) stimulatory and inhibitory signals, behavioral genetic methodologies to development disorders of speech, neurogenic communication disorders. *Total annual research expenditures:* $24,578. *Unit head:* Dr. Fevzi Akinci, Dean, 412-396-5303, Fax: 412-396-5554, E-mail: akincif@duq.edu. *Application contact:* Christopher R. Hilf, Director of Enrollment Management, 412-396-5653, Fax: 412-396-5554, E-mail: hilfc@duq.edu.
Website: http://www.duq.edu/academics/schools/health-sciences

D'Youville College, Occupational Therapy Department, Buffalo, NY 14201-1084. Offers MS. *Accreditation:* AOTA. *Degree requirements:* For master's, research project or thesis. *Entrance requirements:* For master's, minimum undergraduate GPA of 3.0. Additional exam requirements/recommendations for international students: Required—TOEFL (minimum score 500 paper-based). Electronic applications accepted. *Faculty research:* Learning styles, range of motion in the elderly, hospice care, culture, health, differences in education and performance of Afro-American children, autistic spectrum disorder and social stories, autistic disorders and listening programs.

East Carolina University, Graduate School, College of Allied Health Sciences, Department of Addictions and Rehabilitation Studies, Greenville, NC 27858-4353. Offers clinical counseling (MS); military and trauma counseling (Certificate); rehabilitation and career counseling (MS); rehabilitation counseling (Certificate); rehabilitation counseling and administration (PhD); substance abuse counseling (Certificate); vocational evaluation (Certificate). *Accreditation:* CORE. *Program availability:* Part-time, evening/weekend. *Students:* 82 full-time (64 women), 55 part-time (43 women); includes 39 minority (28 Black or African American, non-Hispanic/Latino; 1 American Indian or Alaska Native, non-Hispanic/Latino; 2 Asian, non-Hispanic/Latino; 5 Hispanic/Latino; 3 Two or more races, non-Hispanic/Latino). Average age 33. 51 applicants, 73% accepted, 31 enrolled. In 2017, 19 master's, 5 doctorates, 34 other advanced degrees awarded. *Degree requirements:* For master's, comprehensive exam, thesis or alternative, internship; for doctorate, thesis/dissertation, internship. *Entrance requirements:* For master's and doctorate, GRE General Test or MAT. Additional exam requirements/recommendations for international students: Recommended—TOEFL (minimum score 78 iBT), IELTS (minimum score 6.5). *Application deadline:* For fall admission, 3/1 priority date for domestic students; for spring admission, 10/1 priority date for domestic students. Applications are processed on a rolling basis. Application fee: $75. Electronic applications accepted. *Expenses:* Tuition, state resident: full-time $4749; part-time $297 per credit hour. Tuition, nonresident: full-time $17,898; part-time $1119 per credit hour. *Required fees:* $2691; $224 per credit hour. Part-time tuition and fees vary according to course load and program. *Financial support:* Research assistantships with partial tuition reimbursements, teaching assistantships with partial tuition reimbursements, Federal Work-Study, scholarships/grants, and unspecified assistantships available. Support available to part-time students. Financial award application deadline: 3/1; financial award applicants required to submit FAFSA. *Unit head:* Dr. Paul Toriello, Chair, 252-744-6292, E-mail: toriellop@ecu.edu.
Website: http://www.ecu.edu/rehb/

East Carolina University, Graduate School, College of Allied Health Sciences, Department of Occupational Therapy, Greenville, NC 27858-4353. Offers MSOT. *Accreditation:* AOTA. *Students:* 52 full-time (51 women), 20 part-time (19 women); includes 3 minority (1 Black or African American, non-Hispanic/Latino; 1 Asian, non-Hispanic/Latino; 1 Two or more races, non-Hispanic/Latino). Average age 24. 108 applicants, 37% accepted, 24 enrolled. In 2017, 26 master's awarded. *Degree requirements:* For master's, comprehensive exam, thesis or research project. *Entrance requirements:* For master's, GRE General Test. Additional exam requirements/recommendations for international students: Required—TOEFL. *Application deadline:* For fall admission, 11/1 for domestic students. Applications are processed on a rolling basis. Application fee: $75. Electronic applications accepted. *Expenses:* Tuition, state resident: full-time $4749; part-time $297 per credit hour. Tuition, nonresident: full-time $17,898; part-time $1119 per credit hour. *Required fees:* $2691; $224 per credit hour. Part-time tuition and fees vary according to course load and program. *Financial support:* Research assistantships, career-related internships or fieldwork, and Federal Work-Study available. Financial award application deadline: 3/1; financial award applicants required to submit FAFSA. *Faculty research:* Quality of life, assistive technology, environmental contributions, modifications of occupation to health, therapeutic activities. *Unit head:* Dr. Leonard Trujillo, Chair, 252-744-6195, E-mail: trujillol@ecu.edu.
Website: http://www.ecu.edu/ot/

Eastern Kentucky University, The Graduate School, College of Health Sciences, Department of Occupational Therapy, Richmond, KY 40475-3102. Offers MS. *Accreditation:* AOTA. *Program availability:* Part-time. *Degree requirements:* For master's, thesis optional. *Entrance requirements:* For master's, GRE General Test, minimum GPA of 3.0. *Faculty research:* Rehabilitation, pediatrics, leadership issues.

Eastern Michigan University, Graduate School, College of Health and Human Services, School of Health Sciences, Programs in Occupational Therapy, Ypsilanti, MI 48197. Offers MOT, MS. *Accreditation:* AOTA. *Program availability:* Part-time, evening/weekend, online learning. *Students:* 60 full-time (51 women), 1 (woman) part-time; includes 5 minority (2 Asian, non-Hispanic/Latino; 1 Hispanic/Latino; 2 Two or more races, non-Hispanic/Latino), 1 international. Average age 26. 5 applicants, 60% accepted, 3 enrolled. In 2017, 39 master's awarded. *Entrance requirements:* Additional exam requirements/recommendations for international students: Required—TOEFL. *Application deadline:* Applications are processed on a rolling basis. Application fee: $45. *Financial support:* Fellowships, research assistantships with full tuition reimbursements, teaching assistantships with full tuition reimbursements, career-related internships or fieldwork, Federal Work-Study, institutionally sponsored loans, scholarships/grants, tuition waivers (partial), and unspecified assistantships available. Support available to part-time students. Financial award applicants required to submit FAFSA. *Application contact:* Sharon Holt, Advisor, 734-487-0430, Fax: 734-487-4095, E-mail: ot_intent_advising@emich.edu.

Eastern Washington University, Graduate Studies, College of Health Science and Public Health, Department of Occupational Therapy, Cheney, WA 99004-2431. Offers MOT. *Accreditation:* AOTA. *Faculty:* 7. *Students:* 91 full-time (76 women), 3 part-time (2 women); includes 4 minority (1 American Indian or Alaska Native, non-Hispanic/Latino; 3 Hispanic/Latino), 1 international. Average age 29. 2 applicants, 50% accepted, 1 enrolled. In 2017, 30 master's awarded. *Degree requirements:* For master's, comprehensive exam. *Entrance requirements:* For master's, GRE. Additional exam requirements/recommendations for international students: Required—TOEFL (minimum score 580 paper-based; 92 iBT), IELTS (minimum score 7), PTE (minimum score 63). *Application deadline:* For summer admission, 12/15 for domestic students. Applications are processed on a rolling basis. Application fee: $75. Electronic applications accepted. *Expenses:* Tuition, state resident: full-time $11,191; part-time $373.06 per credit. Tuition, nonresident: full-time $25,995; part-time $866.52 per credit. *Financial support:* Career-related internships or fieldwork, Federal Work-Study, institutionally sponsored loans, scholarships/grants, tuition waivers (partial), and unspecified assistantships available. Support available to part-time students. Financial award application deadline: 2/1; financial award applicants required to submit FAFSA. *Unit head:* Dr. Roberta Snover, 509-368-1347, E-mail: rsnover@ewu.edu.
Website: http://www.ewu.edu/cshe/programs/occupational-therapy.xml

Elizabethtown College, Department of Occupational Therapy, Elizabethtown, PA 17022-2298. Offers MS. *Accreditation:* AOTA.

Elmhurst College, Graduate Programs, Program in Occupational Therapy, Elmhurst, IL 60126-3296. Offers MOT. *Faculty:* 4 full-time (all women), 1 (woman) part-time/adjunct. *Students:* 39 full-time (34 women); includes 6 minority (1 Asian, non-Hispanic/Latino; 5 Hispanic/Latino). Average age 23. 318 applicants, 15% accepted, 21 enrolled. *Entrance requirements:* For master's, GRE, minimum cumulative GPA of 3.2, 3 recommendations, resume, statement of purpose. Additional exam requirements/recommendations for international students: Required—TOEFL (minimum score 550 paper-based; 79 iBT). *Application deadline:* Applications are processed on a rolling basis. Application fee: $0. Electronic applications accepted. *Expenses:* Contact institution. *Financial support:* In 2017–18, 32 students received support. Scholarships/grants available. Support available to part-time students. Financial award application deadline: 3/1; financial award applicants required to submit FAFSA. *Unit head:* Dr. Elizabeth Wanka, Program Director, 630-617-5854, E-mail: elizabeth.wanka@elmhurst.edu. *Application contact:* Timothy J. Panfil, Director of Enrollment Management, 630-617-3300 Ext. 3256, Fax: 630-617-6471, E-mail: panfilt@elmhurst.edu.
Website: http://www.elmhurst.edu/admission/graduate/master_of_occupational_therapy

Emory & Henry College, Graduate Programs, Emory, VA 24327. Offers American history (MA Ed); education professional studies (M Ed); occupational therapy (MOT); organizational leadership (MCOL); physical therapy (DPT); physician assistant studies (MPAS); reading specialist (MA Ed). *Program availability:* Part-time. *Faculty:* 7 full-time (3 women). *Students:* 194 full-time (128 women), 4 part-time (2 women); includes 6 minority (2 Black or African American, non-Hispanic/Latino; 1 American Indian or Alaska Native, non-Hispanic/Latino; 1 Asian, non-Hispanic/Latino; 2 Hispanic/Latino). Average age 25. 525 applicants, 21% accepted, 74 enrolled. In 2017, 24 master's awarded. *Degree requirements:* For master's, thesis optional; for doctorate, thesis/dissertation optional. *Entrance requirements:* For master's, GRE or PRAXIS I, official transcripts from all colleges previously attended, three professional recommendations, essay. Additional exam requirements/recommendations for international students: Recommended—TOEFL, IELTS (minimum score 6). *Application deadline:* Applications are processed on a rolling basis. Electronic applications accepted. *Expenses:* Contact institution. *Financial support:* Application deadline: 10/15; applicants required to submit FAFSA. *Unit head:* Dr. Michael Puglisi, Associate Dean for Academic Affairs, 276-944-6662, E-mail: mpuglisi@ehc.edu. *Application contact:* Mary Bolt, Director of Transfer and Graduate Admission, 276-944-6135, E-mail: mbolt@ehc.edu.

Florida Agricultural and Mechanical University, Division of Graduate Studies, Research, and Continuing Education, School of Allied Health Sciences, Division of Occupational Therapy, Tallahassee, FL 32307-3200. Offers MOT. *Accreditation:* AOTA.

Florida Gulf Coast University, Elaine Nicpon Marieb College of Health and Human Services, Program in Occupational Therapy, Fort Myers, FL 33965-6565. Offers MS. *Accreditation:* AOTA. *Faculty:* 71 full-time (49 women), 49 part-time/adjunct (32 women). *Students:* 64 full-time (54 women); includes 14 minority (2 Black or African American, non-Hispanic/Latino; 1 Asian, non-Hispanic/Latino; 11 Hispanic/Latino). Average age 25. 208 applicants, 20% accepted, 32 enrolled. In 2017, 34 master's awarded. *Entrance requirements:* For master's, GRE General Test, MAT, minimum GPA of 3.0. Additional exam requirements/recommendations for international students: Required—TOEFL (minimum score 550 paper-based). *Application deadline:* For fall admission, 1/15 priority date for domestic students. Applications are processed on a rolling basis. Application fee: $30. Electronic applications accepted. *Expenses:* Tuition, state resident: part-time $290 per credit hour. Tuition, nonresident: part-time $1173 per credit hour. *Required fees:* $127 per credit hour. Tuition and fees vary according to course load. *Financial support:* In 2017–18, 29 students received support. Application deadline: 6/30; applicants required to submit FAFSA. *Unit head:* Dr. Lynn Jaffe, Program Director, 239-590-4315, E-mail: ljaffe@fgcu.edu. *Application contact:* Wanda Smith, Office Manager, 239-590-7550, E-mail: wsmith@fgcu.edu.

Florida International University, Nicole Wertheim College of Nursing and Health Sciences, Department of Occupational Therapy, Miami, FL 33199. Offers MSOT. *Accreditation:* AOTA. *Program availability:* Part-time. *Faculty:* 4 full-time (3 women), 9 part-time/adjunct (7 women). *Students:* 147 full-time (132 women), 8 part-time (5 women); includes 124 minority (14 Black or African American, non-Hispanic/Latino; 5 Asian, non-Hispanic/Latino; 101 Hispanic/Latino; 4 Two or more races, non-Hispanic/Latino), 1 international. Average age 26. 190 applicants, 32% accepted, 52 enrolled. In 2017, 48 master's awarded. *Degree requirements:* For master's, thesis or alternative. *Entrance requirements:* For master's, minimum undergraduate GPA of 3.0 in upper-level course work, letter of intent, 3 letters of recommendation, resume. Additional exam requirements/recommendations for international students: Required—TOEFL (minimum score 550 paper-based; 80 iBT). *Application deadline:* For fall admission, 2/15 for domestic and international students. Applications are processed on a rolling basis. Application fee: $30. Electronic applications accepted. *Expenses:* Contact institution. *Financial support:* Career-related internships or fieldwork, Federal Work-Study, institutionally sponsored loans, scholarships/grants, and unspecified assistantships available. Financial award application deadline: 3/1; financial award applicants required to submit FAFSA. *Faculty research:* Senior transportation and driving, foster care, adolescent transitions, independent living skills development, family and patient-centered care, aging, quality of life, social justice, cognition. *Unit head:* Dr. Lynn Richard, Interim Chair, 305-348-2921, E-mail: lyrichar@fiu.edu. *Application contact:* Nanett Rojas, Manager, Admissions Operations, 305-348-7464, Fax: 305-348-7441, E-mail: gradadm@fiu.edu.
Website: http://cnhs.fiu.edu/index.html

Gannon University, School of Graduate Studies, Morosky College of Health Professions and Sciences, School of Health Professions, Program in Occupational Therapy, Erie, PA 16541-0001. Offers MS, OTD. *Accreditation:* AOTA. *Degree requirements:* For master's, thesis, field work; for doctorate, thesis/dissertation. *Entrance requirements:* For master's, bachelor's degree, Student Self-Report Transcript Evaluation, minimum GPA of 3.0, 40 hours of volunteer experience; for doctorate, bachelor's degree from accredited college or university with minimum GPA of 3.0, transcript, minimum of 40 hours of volunteer experience in an OT setting, Student Self-Report Transcript Evaluation. Additional exam requirements/recommendations for international students: Required—TOEFL (minimum score 79 iBT). Electronic applications accepted. Application fee is waived when completed online. *Expenses:* Contact institution.

Governors State University, College of Health and Human Services, Program in Occupational Therapy, University Park, IL 60484. Offers MOT. *Accreditation:* AOTA. *Program availability:* Part-time. *Faculty:* 6 full-time (all women), 7 part-time/adjunct (all women). *Students:* 89 full-time (78 women), 3 part-time (all women); includes 26 minority (9 Black or African American, non-Hispanic/Latino; 1 Asian, non-Hispanic/Latino; 15 Hispanic/Latino; 1 Two or more races, non-Hispanic/Latino). Average age 28. In 2017, 29 master's awarded. *Application deadline:* For fall admission, 4/1 for domestic students. Applications are processed on a rolling basis. Application fee: $50. Electronic applications accepted. *Expenses:* Contact institution. *Financial support:* Application deadline: 5/1; applicants required to submit FAFSA. *Unit head:* Cynthia Carr, Interim Chair, Department of Occupational Therapy, 708-534-5000 Ext. 7292, E-mail: ccarr@govst.edu.

Grand Valley State University, College of Health Professions, Occupational Therapy Program, Allendale, MI 49401-9403. Offers MS. *Accreditation:* AOTA. *Program availability:* Part-time, evening/weekend. *Faculty:* 9 full-time (8 women), 6 part-time/adjunct (all women). *Students:* 120 full-time (108 women), 18 part-time (14 women); includes 17 minority (3 Black or African American, non-Hispanic/Latino; 4 Asian, non-Hispanic/Latino; 6 Hispanic/Latino; 4 Two or more races, non-Hispanic/Latino). Average age 26. 159 applicants, 40% accepted, 58 enrolled. In 2017, 50 master's awarded. *Degree requirements:* For master's, thesis or alternative, fieldwork, project. *Entrance requirements:* For master's, minimum GPA of 3.0 in prerequisite courses and last 60 hours of work, 2 letters of recommendation, interview, volunteer work (minimum of 50 hours), writing sample, completion of Achievement Summary Form. Additional exam requirements/recommendations for international students: Required—TOEFL (minimum iBT score of 80), IELTS (6.5), or Michigan English Language Assessment Battery (77).

Application deadline: For fall admission, 1/15 for domestic and international students. Applications are processed on a rolling basis. Application fee: $30. Electronic applications accepted. *Expenses:* $686 per credit hour. *Financial support:* In 2017–18, 21 students received support, including 19 fellowships; research assistantships and unspecified assistantships also available. Financial award application deadline: 2/15. *Faculty research:* Teaching/learning methods, continuing professional education, clinical reasoning, geriatrics, performing artists. *Unit head:* Dr. Scott Truskowski, Department Chair, 616-331-3128, Fax: 616-331-5654, E-mail: truskows@gvsu.edu. *Application contact:* Darlene Zwart, Student Services Coordinator, 616-331-3958, Fax: 616-331-5643, E-mail: zwartda@gvsu.edu.
Website: http://www.gvsu.edu/ot/

Hofstra University, School of Health Professions and Human Services, Programs in Health, Hempstead, NY 11549. Offers foundations of public health (Advanced Certificate); health administration (MHA); health informatics (MS); occupational therapy (MS); public health (MPH); security and privacy in health information systems (Advanced Certificate); sports science (MS), including exercise physiology, strength and conditioning; teacher of students with speech-language disabilities (Advanced Certificate). *Program availability:* Part-time, evening/weekend. *Students:* 257 full-time (176 women), 128 part-time (95 women); includes 197 minority (76 Black or African American, non-Hispanic/Latino; 2 American Indian or Alaska Native, non-Hispanic/Latino; 70 Asian, non-Hispanic/Latino; 42 Hispanic/Latino; 6 Native Hawaiian or other Pacific Islander, non-Hispanic/Latino; 1 Two or more races, non-Hispanic/Latino), 25 international. Average age 28. 620 applicants, 50% accepted, 151 enrolled. In 2017, 87 master's awarded. *Degree requirements:* For master's, internship, minimum GPA of 3.0. *Entrance requirements:* For master's, interview, 2 letters of recommendation, essay, resume. Additional exam requirements/recommendations for international students: Required—TOEFL (minimum score 550 paper-based; 80 iBT). *Application deadline:* Applications are processed on a rolling basis. Application fee: $75. Electronic applications accepted. *Expenses: Tuition:* Full-time $1292. *Required fees:* $970. Tuition and fees vary according to program. *Financial support:* In 2017–18, 148 students received support, including 88 fellowships with full and partial tuition reimbursements available (averaging $3,026 per year), 4 research assistantships with full and partial tuition reimbursements available (averaging $5,619 per year); career-related internships or fieldwork, Federal Work-Study, institutionally sponsored loans, scholarships/grants, traineeships, tuition waivers (full and partial), and unspecified assistantships also available. Support available to part-time students. Financial award applicants required to submit FAFSA. *Faculty research:* Hand and upper extremity rehabilitation; orthotic fabrication; palliative care; neurorehabilitation; public health and health inequities, particularly in the American suburbs and minority communities; obesity; physical activity; social justice in physical education pedagogy. *Unit head:* Dr. Corinne Kyriacou, Chairperson, 516-463-4553, E-mail: corinne.m.kyriacou@hofstra.edu. *Application contact:* Sunil Samuel, Assistant Vice President of Admissions, 516-463-4723, Fax: 516-463-4664, E-mail: graduateadmission@hofstra.edu.
Website: http://www.hofstra.edu/academics/colleges/healthscienceshumanservices/

Howard University, College of Nursing and Allied Health Sciences, Division of Allied Health Sciences, Washington, DC 20059-0002. Offers occupational therapy (MSOT); physical therapy (DPT); physician assistant (MPA). *Accreditation:* AOTA.

Huntington University, Graduate School, Huntington, IN 46750-1299. Offers adolescent and young adult education (M Ed); business administration (MBA); counseling (MA), including licensed mental health counselor; early adolescent education (M Ed); elementary education (M Ed); global youth ministry (MA); occupational therapy (OTD); organizational leadership (MA); pastoral leadership (MA); TESOL education (M Ed). *Program availability:* Part-time, online learning. *Faculty:* 17 full-time (10 women), 14 part-time/adjunct (4 women). *Students:* 221 full-time (163 women), 22 part-time (13 women). *Degree requirements:* For master's, comprehensive exam (for some programs), thesis (for some programs). *Entrance requirements:* For master's, GRE (for counseling and education students only); for doctorate, GRE (for occupational therapy students). Additional exam requirements/recommendations for international students: Required—TOEFL (minimum score 85 iBT), IELTS (minimum score 6.5). *Application deadline:* For fall admission, 7/1 for domestic students, 5/1 for international students; for winter admission, 10/1 for domestic students, 9/1 for international students; for spring admission, 11/30 for domestic students, 10/30 for international students. Applications are processed on a rolling basis. Application fee: $30. Electronic applications accepted. *Expenses:* Contact institution. *Financial support:* Scholarships/grants and unspecified assistantships available. Support available to part-time students. Financial award application deadline: 8/1; financial award applicants required to submit FAFSA. *Faculty research:* Leadership, educational technology trends, evangelism, youth ministry, mental health. *Unit head:* Michael Wanous, Vice President for Academic Affairs, 260-359-4008, Fax: 260-359-4126, E-mail: mwanous@huntington.edu. *Application contact:* Evan Bennett, Assistant Director of Graduate Admissions, 260-359-4111, Fax: 260-359-4126, E-mail: graduate@huntington.edu.
Website: http://www.huntington.edu/graduate

Idaho State University, Office of Graduate Studies, School of Rehabilitation and Communication Sciences, Department of Physical and Occupational Therapy, Program in Occupational Therapy, Pocatello, ID 83209-8045. Offers MOT. *Accreditation:* AOTA. *Degree requirements:* For master's, comprehensive exam, thesis, oral and written exam. *Entrance requirements:* For master's, GRE General Test, minimum GPA of 3.0, 80 hours in 2 practice settings of occupational therapy. Additional exam requirements/recommendations for international students: Required—TOEFL (minimum score 600 paper-based). Electronic applications accepted. *Expenses:* Contact institution. *Faculty research:* Human movement, health care.

Indiana State University, College of Graduate and Professional Studies, College of Health and Human Services, Department of Applied Medicine and Rehabilitation, Terre Haute, IN 47809. Offers athletic training (MS, DAT); occupational therapy (MS); physical therapy (DPT); physician assistant (MS). *Degree requirements:* For master's, thesis or alternative. *Entrance requirements:* For master's, GRE General Test. Electronic applications accepted.

Indiana University–Purdue University Indianapolis, School of Health and Rehabilitation Sciences, Indianapolis, IN 46202. Offers health and rehabilitation sciences (PhD); health sciences (MS); nutrition and dietetics (MS); occupational therapy (OTD); physical therapy (DPT); physician assistant (MPAS). *Program availability:* Part-time, evening/weekend. *Degree requirements:* For master's, thesis (for some programs). *Entrance requirements:* For master's, GRE General Test, minimum GPA of 3.0 (for MS in health sciences, nutrition and dietetics), 3.2 (for MS in occupational therapy), 3.0 cumulative and prerequisite math/science (for MPAS); for doctorate, GRE, minimum cumulative and prerequisite math/science GPA of 3.2. Additional exam requirements/recommendations for international students: Required—TOEFL (minimum score 550 paper-based; 79 iBT), IELTS (minimum score 6.5), PTE (minimum score 54). Electronic applications accepted. *Expenses:* Contact institution. *Faculty research:* Function and mobility across the lifespan, pediatric nutrition, driving and mobility rehabilitation, neurorehabilitation and biomechanics, rehabilitation and integrative therapy.

Ithaca College, School of Health Sciences and Human Performance, Program in Occupational Therapy, Ithaca, NY 14850. Offers MS. *Accreditation:* AOTA. *Program availability:* Part-time. *Faculty:* 14 full-time (all women). *Students:* 65 full-time (62 women), 1 (woman) part-time; includes 6 minority (4 Asian, non-Hispanic/Latino; 1 Hispanic/Latino; 1 Two or more races, non-Hispanic/Latino). Average age 23. 75 applicants, 41% accepted, 26 enrolled. In 2017, 50 master's awarded. *Degree requirements:* For master's, thesis optional, clinical electives/fieldwork. *Entrance requirements:* Additional exam requirements/recommendations for international students: Required—TOEFL (minimum score 550 paper-based; 80 iBT). *Application deadline:* For fall admission, 3/1 for domestic and international students. Applications are processed on a rolling basis. Application fee: $40. Electronic applications accepted. *Expenses:* Contact institution. *Financial support:* In 2017–18, 41 students received support, including 14 research assistantships (averaging $11,965 per year); career-related internships or fieldwork, Federal Work-Study, scholarships/grants, and unspecified assistantships also available. Support available to part-time students. Financial award application deadline: 2/1; financial award applicants required to submit FAFSA. *Unit head:* Dr. Melinda Cozzolino, Chair, 607-274-3618, Fax: 607-274-1263, E-mail: mcozzoli@ithaca.edu. *Application contact:* Nicole Eversley Bradwell, Director, Office of Admission, 607-274-3124, Fax: 607-274-1263, E-mail: admission@ithaca.edu.
Website: http://www.ithaca.edu/gradprograms/ot

Jacksonville University, Brooks Rehabilitation College of Healthcare Sciences, School of Applied Health Sciences, Program in Occupational Therapy, Jacksonville, FL 32211. Offers OTD. *Degree requirements:* For doctorate, observation of occupational therapy practice; minimum of 40 hours total among three different settings (hospital, school system, home health, clinic, etc.). *Entrance requirements:* For doctorate, GRE, baccalaureate degree from accredited college or university with minimum GPA of 3.0; official transcripts; observation of occupational therapy practice with minimum of 40 hours total among three different settings (hospital, school system, home health, clinic, etc.); interview. Additional exam requirements/recommendations for international students: Required—TOEFL (minimum score 650 paper-based; 114 iBT), IELTS (minimum score 8). *Application deadline:* For spring admission, 10/30 for domestic and international students. Applications are processed on a rolling basis. Application fee: $50. Electronic applications accepted. *Expenses:* $950 per credit hour. *Financial support:* Application deadline: 3/15; applicants required to submit FAFSA. *Unit head:* Dr. Heather Hausenblas, Associate Dean, School of Applied Health Sciences, 904-256-7975, E-mail: hhausen@ju.edu. *Application contact:* Ashlea Rieser, Assistant Director, Enrollment and Advising, 904-256-8934, E-mail: arieser0@ju.edu.
Website: https://www.ju.edu/occupationaltherapy/

James Madison University, The Graduate School, College of Health and Behavioral Studies, Program in Occupational Therapy, Harrisonburg, VA 22801. Offers MOT. *Accreditation:* AOTA. *Program availability:* Part-time. *Students:* 65 full-time (55 women); includes 10 minority (3 Black or African American, non-Hispanic/Latino; 2 Asian, non-Hispanic/Latino; 1 Hispanic/Latino; 4 Two or more races, non-Hispanic/Latino). Average age 30. In 2017, 21 master's awarded. Application fee: $55. Electronic applications accepted. *Expenses:* Tuition, state resident: full-time $10,512; part-time $438 per credit hour. Tuition, nonresident: full-time $28,358; part-time $1162 per credit hour. *Required fees:* $1128. *Financial support:* In 2017–18, 2 students received support. Fellowships available. Financial award application deadline: 3/1; financial award applicants required to submit FAFSA. *Unit head:* Dr. Allen Lewis, Academic Unit Head, 540-568-6510. *Application contact:* Lynette D. Michael, Director of Graduate Admissions and Student Records, 540-568-6131 Ext. 6395, Fax: 540-568-7860, E-mail: michaeld@jmu.edu.
Website: http://www.healthsci.jmu.edu/occupationaltherapy

Jefferson College of Health Sciences, Program in Occupational Therapy, Roanoke, VA 24013. Offers MS. *Accreditation:* AOTA. *Program availability:* Part-time. *Entrance requirements:* For master's, GRE. Additional exam requirements/recommendations for international students: Required—TOEFL (minimum score 550 paper-based; 80 iBT). Electronic applications accepted.

Johnson & Wales University, Graduate Studies, Occupational Therapy Doctorate Program, Providence, RI 02903-3703. Offers OTD. *Entrance requirements:* For doctorate, GRE, bachelor's degree with minimum cumulative GPA of 3.0, 3 letters of recommendation, background check. *Expenses: Tuition:* Full-time $12,636; part-time $702 per credit hour. *Unit head:* Dr. Ann Burkhardt, Director, 401-598-5106, E-mail: ann.burkhardt@jwu.edu. *Application contact:* Graduate School Admissions, 401-598-1015, Fax: 401-598-1286, E-mail: pvdgrad@admissions.jwu.edu.
Website: https://www.jwu.edu/academics/programs-by-campus/providence-programs/occupational-therapy-otd.html

Kean University, Nathan Weiss Graduate College, Program in Occupational Therapy, Union, NJ 07083. Offers MS. *Accreditation:* AOTA. *Program availability:* Part-time. *Faculty:* 4 full-time (all women). *Students:* 67 full-time (62 women), 40 part-time (36 women); includes 28 minority (2 Black or African American, non-Hispanic/Latino; 7 Asian, non-Hispanic/Latino; 17 Hispanic/Latino; 2 Two or more races, non-Hispanic/Latino). Average age 25. 236 applicants, 19% accepted, 35 enrolled. In 2017, 34 master's awarded. *Degree requirements:* For master's, 6 months of field work, final project. *Entrance requirements:* For master's, minimum GPA of 3.0, minimum grade of B in each prerequisite course, official transcripts from all institutions attended, three letters of recommendation (one letter must be from an occupational therapist), documented observation of occupational therapy services in two or more practice settings for a minimum of 40 hours, resume, personal statement. Additional exam requirements/recommendations for international students: Required—TOEFL (minimum score 550 paper-based; 79 iBT), IELTS (minimum score 6.5). *Application deadline:* For fall admission, 2/2 for domestic and international students. Applications are processed on a rolling basis. Application fee: $75. Electronic applications accepted. *Expenses:* Contact institution. *Financial support:* Scholarships/grants and unspecified assistantships available. Financial award applicants required to submit FAFSA. *Unit head:* Dr. Mariann Moran, Program Coordinator, 908-737-5850, Fax: 908-737-5855, E-mail: ot@kean.edu. *Application contact:* Brittany Gerstenhaber, Admissions Counselor, 908-737-7100, E-mail: gradadmissions@kean.edu.
Website: http://grad.kean.edu/ot

Keiser University, MS in Occupational Therapy Program, Fort Lauderdale, FL 33309. Offers MS. *Unit head:* Dr. Tamara Pinchevsky-Font, Program Chair.

Keuka College, Program in Occupational Therapy, Keuka Park, NY 14478. Offers MS. *Accreditation:* AOTA. *Degree requirements:* For master's, thesis, clinical internships. *Entrance requirements:* For master's, BS in occupational science from Keuka College. Additional exam requirements/recommendations for international students: Required—TOEFL (minimum score 550 paper-based). Electronic applications accepted. *Expenses:* Contact institution. *Faculty research:* Continuing education needs of occupational therapists in community-based settings; the meaning of driving at different ages; interprofessional learning from international field work experiences.

Le Moyne College, Department of Occupational Therapy, Syracuse, NY 13214. Offers MS. *Faculty:* 3 full-time (all women), 6 part-time/adjunct (4 women). *Students:* 81 full-time (72 women); includes 9 minority (1 Black or African American, non-Hispanic/Latino; 6 Asian, non-Hispanic/Latino; 1 Hispanic/Latino; 1 Native Hawaiian or other Pacific Islander, non-Hispanic/Latino), 1 international. Average age 25. 99 applicants, 85% accepted, 43 enrolled. In 2017, 29 master's awarded. *Degree requirements:* For master's, scholarly

project. *Entrance requirements:* For master's, MAT, bachelor's degree with minimum GPA of 3.0; three references from academic advisors, licensed occupational therapists, and/or work managers; background check. Additional exam requirements/recommendations for international students: Required—TOEFL (minimum score 550 paper-based, 79 iBT) or IELTS (6.5). *Application deadline:* For fall admission, 3/30 for domestic and international students. Applications are processed on a rolling basis. Application fee: $125. Electronic applications accepted. *Expenses:* $13,820 per semester. *Financial support:* Career-related internships or fieldwork, scholarships/grants, and health care benefits available. Financial award applicants required to submit FAFSA. *Unit head:* Dr. Deborah Marr, Interim Chair, 315-445-5432, E-mail: occupationaltherapy@lemoyne.edu. *Application contact:* Kristen P. Richards, Senior Director of Enrollment Management, 315-445-5444, Fax: 315-445-6092, E-mail: trapaskp@lemoyne.edu.
Website: http://www.lemoyne.edu/apply/graduate-and-professional-admission/occupational-therapy

Lenoir-Rhyne University, Graduate Programs, School of Occupational Therapy, Hickory, NC 28601. Offers MS. *Accreditation:* AOTA. *Entrance requirements:* For master's, GRE, official transcripts, three letters of recommendation, essay, criminal background check. *Expenses:* Contact institution.

Loma Linda University, School of Allied Health Professions, Department of Occupational Therapy, Loma Linda, CA 92350. Offers MOT, OTD. *Accreditation:* AOTA.

Long Island University–LIU Brooklyn, School of Health Professions, Brooklyn, NY 11201-8423. Offers athletic training and sport sciences (MS); community health (MS Ed); exercise science (MS); forensic social work (Advanced Certificate); occupational therapy (MS); physical therapy (DPT); physician assistant (MS); public health (MPH); social work (MSW); speech-language pathology (MS). *Faculty:* 33 full-time (23 women), 82 part-time/adjunct (55 women). *Students:* 690 full-time (508 women), 86 part-time (74 women); includes 259 minority (120 Black or African American, non-Hispanic/Latino; 1 American Indian or Alaska Native, non-Hispanic/Latino; 52 Asian, non-Hispanic/Latino; 76 Hispanic/Latino; 10 Two or more races, non-Hispanic/Latino), 65 international. Average age 27. 1,241 applicants, 45% accepted, 255 enrolled. In 2017, 249 master's, 42 doctorates, 8 other advanced degrees awarded. *Degree requirements:* For master's, comprehensive exam (for some programs), thesis (for some programs); for doctorate, comprehensive exam (for some programs). *Entrance requirements:* For master's and doctorate, GRE. Additional exam requirements/recommendations for international students: Required—TOEFL (minimum score 550 paper-based; 79 iBT). *Application deadline:* Applications are processed on a rolling basis. Application fee: $50. Electronic applications accepted. *Expenses:* Tuition: Full-time $21,618; part-time $1201 per credit. *Required fees:* $1840; $920 per term. Tuition and fees vary according to course load. *Financial support:* In 2017–18, 187 students received support. Research assistantships, teaching assistantships, career-related internships or fieldwork, Federal Work-Study, scholarships/grants, and unspecified assistantships available. Support available to part-time students. Financial award application deadline: 2/15; financial award applicants required to submit FAFSA. *Faculty research:* Pediatric physical therapy, complementary and alternative medicine, global health and human rights, sport leadership and entrepreneurship, feminist sport psychology. *Unit head:* Dr. Barry S. Eckert, Dean, 718-780-6578, Fax: 718-780-4561, E-mail: barry.eckert@liu.edu. *Application contact:* Dr. Dominick Fortugno, Associate Dean, 718-488-1496, Fax: 718-780-4561, E-mail: dominick.fortugno@liu.edu.
Website: http://liu.edu/brooklyn/academics/school-of-health-professions

Louisiana State University Health Sciences Center, School of Allied Health Professions, Department of Occupational Therapy, New Orleans, LA 70112. Offers MOT. *Accreditation:* AOTA. *Faculty:* 4 full-time (3 women), 1 (woman) part-time/adjunct. *Students:* 69 full-time (62 women); includes 9 minority (2 Black or African American, non-Hispanic/Latino; 1 Asian, non-Hispanic/Latino; 2 Hispanic/Latino; 1 Native Hawaiian or other Pacific Islander, non-Hispanic/Latino; 3 Two or more races, non-Hispanic/Latino). Average age 25. 209 applicants, 17% accepted, 35 enrolled. In 2017, 32 master's awarded. *Entrance requirements:* For master's, GRE (minimum scores: 150 verbal, 141 quantitative, and 3.5 analytical), bachelor's degree; 40 hours of observation in occupational therapy; minimum cumulative GPA of 2.8, cumulative prerequisite 3.0. Additional exam requirements/recommendations for international students: Required—TOEFL (minimum score 550 paper-based; 79 iBT). *Application deadline:* For spring admission, 6/16 priority date for domestic students. Application fee: $140. Electronic applications accepted. *Expenses:* Contact institution. *Financial support:* Application deadline: 4/15; applicants required to submit FAFSA. *Faculty research:* Rehabilitation for clients with neurological diagnoses (especially stroke), teaching and learning strategies in OT education, interprofessional education, occupation-based interventions, early intervention in occupational therapy. *Unit head:* Dr. Kelly L. Alig, Department Head, 504-568-4303, Fax: 504-568-4306, E-mail: kalig@lsuhsc.edu. *Application contact:* Yudialys Delgado Cazanas, Student Affairs Director, 504-568-4253, Fax: 504-568-3185, E-mail: ydelga@lsuhsc.edu.
Website: http://alliedhealth.lsuhsc.edu/ot/default.aspx

Mary Baldwin University, Graduate Studies, Program in Occupational Therapy, Staunton, VA 24401-3610. Offers OTD. *Accreditation:* AOTA.

Maryville University of Saint Louis, Myrtle E. and Earl E. Walker College of Health Professions, Occupational Therapy Program, St. Louis, MO 63141-7299. Offers MOT. *Accreditation:* AOTA. *Faculty:* 5 full-time (4 women), 6 part-time/adjunct (5 women). *Students:* 75 full-time (70 women), 26 part-time (25 women); includes 4 minority (3 Hispanic/Latino; 1 Two or more races, non-Hispanic/Latino). Average age 24. In 2017, 33 master's awarded. *Entrance requirements:* For master's, GRE or MAT, minimum cumulative GPA of 3.0, resume, interview, writing sample. Additional exam requirements/recommendations for international students: Required—TOEFL (minimum score 563 paper-based). *Application deadline:* Applications are processed on a rolling basis. Electronic applications accepted. *Expenses:* $797 per credit hour, $450 per semester part-time fee, $1,200 per semester full-time. *Financial support:* Career-related internships or fieldwork, Federal Work-Study, and campus employment available. Financial award application deadline: 4/1; financial award applicants required to submit FAFSA. *Unit head:* Robert Cunningham, Director, 314-529-9682, Fax: 314-529-9191, E-mail: rcunningham@maryville.edu. *Application contact:* Jeannie DeLuca, Director of Admissions and Advising, 314-529-9355, Fax: 314-529-9927, E-mail: jdeluca@maryville.edu.
Website: http://www.maryville.edu/hp/occupational-therapy/

McMaster University, Faculty of Health Sciences, Professional Program in Occupational Therapy, Hamilton, ON L8S 4M2, Canada. Offers M Sc. *Degree requirements:* For master's, fieldwork and independent research project. *Entrance requirements:* For master's, minimum B average over last 60 undergraduate units. Additional exam requirements/recommendations for international students: Required—TOEFL (minimum score 600 paper-based).

Medical University of South Carolina, College of Health Professions, Program in Occupational Therapy, Charleston, SC 29425. Offers MSOT. *Accreditation:* AOTA. *Degree requirements:* For master's, thesis or alternative, research project. *Entrance requirements:* For master's, GRE General Test, interview, minimum GPA of 3.0, references. Additional exam requirements/recommendations for international students: Required—TOEFL (minimum score 600 paper-based). Electronic applications accepted. *Faculty research:* Therapeutic interventions for children with cerebral palsy; function, well being, quality of life for adults with chronic conditions and health disparities; driving interventions for adults with head and neck cancer; oral health for adults with tetraplegia; interprofessional education.

Mercy College, School of Health and Natural Sciences, Program in Occupational Therapy, Dobbs Ferry, NY 10522-1189. Offers MS. *Accreditation:* AOTA. *Program availability:* Evening/weekend. *Students:* 22 full-time (19 women), 6 part-time (5 women). Average age 33. 218 applicants, 20% accepted, 37 enrolled. In 2017, 35 master's awarded. *Degree requirements:* For master's, comprehensive exam (for some programs), thesis, fieldwork. *Entrance requirements:* For master's, essay, 3 letters of recommendation, interview, resume, undergraduate transcripts with minimum GPA of 3.0. Additional exam requirements/recommendations for international students: Required—TOEFL (minimum score 600 paper-based; 100 iBT), IELTS (minimum score 8). *Application deadline:* Applications are processed on a rolling basis. Application fee: $62. Electronic applications accepted. *Expenses:* Contact institution. *Financial support:* Career-related internships or fieldwork, Federal Work-Study, scholarships/grants, and unspecified assistantships available. Support available to part-time students. Financial award applicants required to submit FAFSA. *Unit head:* Dr. Joan Toglia, Dean, School of Health and Natural Sciences, 914-674-7837, E-mail: jtoglia@mercy.edu. *Application contact:* Allison Gurdineer, Senior Director of Admissions, 877-637-2946, Fax: 914-674-7382, E-mail: admissions@mercy.edu.
Website: https://www.mercy.edu/degrees-programs/ms-occupational-therapy

MGH Institute of Health Professions, School of Health and Rehabilitation Sciences, Department of Occupational Therapy, Boston, MA 02129. Offers OTD. *Accreditation:* AOTA. *Entrance requirements:* For doctorate, GRE, bachelor's degree from regionally-accredited U.S. college or university with minimum undergraduate GPA of 3.0; official transcripts; personal statement; recommendation letters. Additional exam requirements/recommendations for international students: Required—TOEFL (minimum score 80 iBT). Electronic applications accepted.

Midwestern University, Downers Grove Campus, College of Health Sciences, Illinois Campus, Program in Occupational Therapy, Downers Grove, IL 60515-1235. Offers MOT. *Accreditation:* AOTA. *Entrance requirements:* For master's, GRE General Test. *Application deadline:* Applications are processed on a rolling basis. Application fee: $50. *Expenses:* Contact institution. *Financial support:* Federal Work-Study and scholarships/grants available. Financial award applicants required to submit FAFSA.

Midwestern University, Glendale Campus, College of Health Sciences, Arizona Campus, Program in Occupational Therapy, Glendale, AZ 85308. Offers MOT. *Accreditation:* AOTA. *Entrance requirements:* For master's, GRE. *Application deadline:* Applications are processed on a rolling basis. Application fee: $50. *Expenses:* Contact institution.

Milligan College, Program in Occupational Therapy, Milligan College, TN 37682. Offers MSOT. *Accreditation:* AOTA. *Degree requirements:* For master's, thesis or alternative. *Entrance requirements:* For master's, GRE. Additional exam requirements/recommendations for international students: Required—TOEFL (minimum score 550 paper-based; 80 iBT). Electronic applications accepted. *Expenses:* Contact institution. *Faculty research:* Handwriting, creativity, leadership in health care and rehabilitation, prevention and rehabilitation of work-related musculoskeletal disorders, parent-child interaction therapy, community-based occupational therapy programs.

Misericordia University, College of Health Sciences and Education, Program in Occupational Therapy, Dallas, PA 18612-1098. Offers MSOT, OTD. *Accreditation:* AOTA. *Entrance requirements:* For master's, minimum undergraduate GPA of 2.8, 2 letters of reference; for doctorate, minimum graduate GPA of 3.0, interview, 3 letters of reference. Additional exam requirements/recommendations for international students: Required—TOEFL. Electronic applications accepted.

Missouri State University, Graduate College, College of Health and Human Services, Department of Sports Medicine and Athletic Training, Springfield, MO 65897. Offers athletic training (MS); occupational therapy (MOT). *Program availability:* Part-time. *Faculty:* 7 full-time (4 women), 5 part-time/adjunct (3 women). *Students:* 21 full-time (11 women), 4 part-time (2 women); includes 1 minority (Two or more races, non-Hispanic/Latino). Average age 23. 28 applicants, 43% accepted, 11 enrolled. In 2017, 12 master's awarded. *Degree requirements:* For master's, comprehensive exam, thesis or alternative. *Entrance requirements:* For master's, GRE, current Professional Rescuer and AED certification, BOC certification, licensure as an athletic trainer, minimum undergraduate GPA of 3.0 (for MS); OTCAS application (for MOT). Additional exam requirements/recommendations for international students: Required—TOEFL (minimum score 550 paper-based; 79 iBT), IELTS (minimum score 6). *Application deadline:* For fall admission, 1/15 for domestic and international students. Application fee: $35 ($50 for international students). Electronic applications accepted. *Expenses:* Tuition, state resident: full-time $2915; part-time $2021 per credit hour. Tuition, nonresident: full-time $5354; part-time $3647 per credit hour. *International tuition:* $11,992 full-time. *Required fees:* $173; $173 per credit hour. Tuition and fees vary according to class time, course level, course load, degree level, campus/location and program. *Financial support:* In 2017–18, 5 teaching assistantships with partial tuition reimbursements (averaging $8,772 per year) were awarded; Federal Work-Study, institutionally sponsored loans, and unspecified assistantships also available. Financial award application deadline: 3/31; financial award applicants required to submit FAFSA. *Unit head:* Dr. Tona Hetzler, Head, 417-836-8924, Fax: 417-836-8554, E-mail: tonahetzler@missouristate.edu. *Application contact:* Stephanie Praschan, Director, Graduate Enrollment Management, 417-836-5330, Fax: 417-836-6200, E-mail: stephaniepraschan@missouristate.edu.
Website: http://sportsmed.missouristate.edu/

Mount Mary University, Graduate Programs, Program in Occupational Therapy, Milwaukee, WI 53222-4597. Offers MS, OTD. *Accreditation:* AOTA. *Program availability:* Part-time, evening/weekend, 100% online, blended/hybrid learning. *Degree requirements:* For master's, comprehensive exam, thesis or alternative, professional development portfolio. *Entrance requirements:* For master's, minimum GPA of 3.0, occupational therapy license, 1 year of work experience. Additional exam requirements/recommendations for international students: Required—TOEFL (minimum score 550 paper-based; 80 iBT); Recommended—IELTS (minimum score 6.5). Electronic applications accepted. *Expenses:* Contact institution. *Faculty research:* Clinical reasoning, occupational science, sensory integration.

New England Institute of Technology, Program in Occupational Therapy, East Greenwich, RI 02818. Offers MS. *Accreditation:* AOTA. *Program availability:* Part-time-only, evening/weekend, 100% online, blended/hybrid learning. *Degree requirements:* For master's, fieldwork. *Entrance requirements:* For master's, minimum GPA of 2.5, associate degree and certification as an Occupational Therapy Assistant. Additional exam requirements/recommendations for international students: Required—TOEFL. *Application deadline:* Applications are processed on a rolling basis. Application fee: $25. Electronic applications accepted. *Expenses:* $725 per credit, $14 per quarter lab fees. *Unit head:* Douglas H. Sherman, Senior Vice President and Provost, 401-739-5000 Ext. 3481, Fax: 401-886-0859, E-mail: dsherman@neit.edu. *Application contact:* Michael Caruso, Director of Admissions, 800-736-7744 Ext. 3411, Fax: 401-886-0868, E-mail: mcaruso@neit.edu.
Website: http://www.neit.edu/Programs/Masters-Degree-Programs/Occupational-Therapy

Occupational Therapy

New York Institute of Technology, School of Health Professions, Department of Occupational Therapy, Old Westbury, NY 11568-8000. Offers MS. *Accreditation:* AOTA. *Faculty:* 8 full-time (6 women), 4 part-time/adjunct (all women). *Students:* 91 full-time (81 women), 19 part-time (15 women); includes 24 minority (3 Black or African American, non-Hispanic/Latino; 14 Asian, non-Hispanic/Latino; 5 Hispanic/Latino; 2 Two or more races, non-Hispanic/Latino). Average age 24. 140 applicants, 41% accepted, 42 enrolled. In 2017, 37 master's awarded. *Entrance requirements:* For master's, bachelor's degree; minimum undergraduate GPA of 3.0; academic record with coursework in humanities, social sciences, and life sciences; competence in written and spoken English; 100 hours of volunteer work under the supervision of licensed occupational therapist; 3 professional letters of recommendation; essay. Additional exam requirements/recommendations for international students: Required—TOEFL (minimum score 79 iBT), IELTS (minimum score 6). *Application deadline:* For fall admission, 10/31 for domestic and international students. Applications are processed on a rolling basis. Application fee: $50. Electronic applications accepted. *Expenses:* $1,285 per credit plus fees. *Financial support:* Federal Work-Study, scholarships/grants, tuition waivers (full and partial), and unspecified assistantships available. Support available to part-time students. Financial award application deadline: 2/15; financial award applicants required to submit FAFSA. *Faculty research:* Pediatric interventions; virtual reality; concussions and brain injury in college athletes; health and well-being in the LGBTQ community; community health; assessment and technology use in substance abuse. *Unit head:* Dr. Razan Hamed, Chair, 516-686-3863, E-mail: rhamed@nyit.edu. *Application contact:* Alice Dolitsky, Director, Graduate Admissions, 516-686-7520, Fax: 516-686-1116, E-mail: nyitgrad@nyit.edu.
Website: http://www.nyit.edu/degrees/occupational_therapy

New York University, Steinhardt School of Culture, Education, and Human Development, Department of Occupational Therapy, New York, NY 10012. Offers advanced occupational therapy (MA); occupational therapy (MS, DPS); research in occupational therapy (PhD). *Accreditation:* AOTA (one or more programs are accredited). *Program availability:* Part-time. *Students:* Average age 33. 598 applicants, 21% accepted, 63 enrolled. In 2017, 68 master's, 3 doctorates awarded. *Degree requirements:* For master's, thesis (for some programs), terminal project; fieldwork; for doctorate, thesis/dissertation, terminal project. *Entrance requirements:* For doctorate, GRE General Test, interview. Additional exam requirements/recommendations for international students: Required—TOEFL (minimum score 100 iBT). *Application deadline:* For fall admission, 12/1 priority date for domestic and international students. Applications are processed on a rolling basis. Application fee: $75. Electronic applications accepted. *Expenses: Tuition:* Full-time $41,352; part-time $19,968 per year. *Required fees:* $2496; $1628 per unit. $814 per term. Tuition and fees vary according to course load and program. *Financial support:* Fellowships with full and partial tuition reimbursements, teaching assistantships with full and partial tuition reimbursements, career-related internships or fieldwork, Federal Work-Study, institutionally sponsored loans, scholarships/grants, traineeships, tuition waivers (partial), and unspecified assistantships available. Support available to part-time students. Financial award application deadline: 2/1; financial award applicants required to submit FAFSA. *Faculty research:* Pediatrics, assistive rehabilitation technology, adaptive computer technology for children with disabilities, cognitive bases of adult disablement, upper limb rehabilitation. *Unit head:* Prof. Kristie Patten Koenig, Chairperson, 212-998-5852, Fax: 212-995-4044, E-mail: kpk3@nyu.edu. *Application contact:* 212-998-5030, Fax: 212-995-4328, E-mail: steinhardt.gradadmissions@nyu.edu.
Website: http://steinhardt.nyu.edu/ot

Northeastern State University, College of Science and Health Professions, Department of Health Professions, Program in Occupational Therapy, Tahlequah, OK 74464-2399. Offers MS. *Faculty:* 4 full-time (3 women). *Students:* 39 full-time (34 women), 1 part-time (0 women); includes 11 minority (7 American Indian or Alaska Native, non-Hispanic/Latino; 2 Hispanic/Latino; 2 Two or more races, non-Hispanic/Latino). Average age 27. In 2017, 10 master's awarded. *Application deadline:* For fall admission, 7/1 priority date for domestic and international students. Applications are processed on a rolling basis. Electronic applications accepted. *Expenses:* Tuition, state resident: part-time $222 per credit hour. Tuition, nonresident: part-time $501.75 per credit hour. *Required fees:* $37.40 per credit hour. Tuition and fees vary according to degree level. *Unit head:* Dr. Judith A. Melvin, Program Director, 918-444-5232, E-mail: melvin02@nsuok.edu. *Application contact:* Josh McCollum, Graduate Coordinator, 918-444-2093, E-mail: mccolluj@nsuok.edu.
Website: http://academics.nsuok.edu/healthprofessions/DegreePrograms/Graduate/OccupatTherapy.aspx

Northern Arizona University, College of Health and Human Services, Department of Occupational Therapy, Phoenix, AZ 85004. Offers OTD. *Accreditation:* AOTA. *Program availability:* Blended/hybrid learning. *Faculty:* 9 full-time (8 women), 3 part-time/adjunct (2 women). *Students:* 108 full-time (90 women); includes 23 minority (2 Black or African American, non-Hispanic/Latino; 4 Asian, non-Hispanic/Latino; 11 Hispanic/Latino; 6 Two or more races, non-Hispanic/Latino). Average age 27. 98 applicants, 54% accepted, 53 enrolled. In 2017, 24 doctorates awarded. *Degree requirements:* For doctorate, variable foreign language requirement, comprehensive exam (for some programs), thesis/dissertation (for some programs). *Entrance requirements:* For doctorate, minimum of 80 volunteer and observation hours. Additional exam requirements/recommendations for international students: Required—TOEFL (minimum score 80 iBT), IELTS (minimum score 6.5). *Application deadline:* For fall admission, 1/9 for domestic and international students; for spring admission, 10/1 for domestic and international students. Application fee: $65. Electronic applications accepted. *Expenses:* Tuition, state resident: full-time $9240; part-time $458 per credit hour. Tuition, nonresident: full-time $21,588; part-time $1199 per credit hour. *Required fees:* $1021; $14 per credit hour. $646 per semester. Tuition and fees vary according to course load, campus/location and program. *Financial support:* Institutionally sponsored loans available. Financial award application deadline: 2/1; financial award applicants required to submit FAFSA. *Unit head:* Dr. Oaklee Rogers, Interim Chair, 602-827-2583, Fax: 602-827-2425, E-mail: oaklee.rogers@nau.edu. *Application contact:* Tina Sutton, Coordinator, Graduate College, 928-523-4348, Fax: 928-523-8950, E-mail: graduate@nau.edu.
Website: https://nau.edu/CHHS/Occupational-Therapy/

Nova Southeastern University, Dr. Pallavi Patel College of Health Care Sciences, Fort Lauderdale, FL 33314-7796. Offers anesthesiologist assistant (MSA); audiology (Au D); health science (MH Sc, DHSc, PhD); occupational therapy (MOT, Dr OT, PhD); physical therapy (DPT, TDPT); physician assistant (MMS); speech-language pathology (MS). *Accreditation:* AOTA. *Faculty:* 54 full-time (31 women), 15 part-time/adjunct (7 women). *Students:* 501 full-time (407 women); includes 131 minority (18 Black or African American, non-Hispanic/Latino; 2 American Indian or Alaska Native, non-Hispanic/Latino; 45 Asian, non-Hispanic/Latino; 65 Hispanic/Latino; 1 Two or more races, non-Hispanic/Latino). Average age 24. 7,600 applicants, 7% accepted, 452 enrolled. In 2017, 616 master's, 225 doctorates awarded. *Degree requirements:* For doctorate, comprehensive exam, thesis/dissertation (for some programs), 12-month full-time clinical externship experience. *Entrance requirements:* For master's, GRE General Test; for doctorate, GRE General Test, personal interview, essay in application, on-site essay. *Application deadline:* For spring admission, 2/15 for domestic and international students; for summer admission, 12/1 for domestic and international students. Applications are processed on a rolling basis. Application fee: $50. Electronic applications accepted. *Expenses:* Contact institution. *Financial support:* Federal Work-Study, institutionally sponsored loans, and scholarships/grants available. Financial award application deadline: 4/15; financial award applicants required to submit FAFSA. *Faculty research:* Efferent suppression and auditory processing delay, subjective visual vertical in vestibular assessment, competency-based clinical evaluation, hearing instrument performance for frequency lowering, hearing instrument performance for noise suppression, anxiety and dizziness in college students, audiology assistants. *Unit head:* Dr. Stanley Wilson, Dean, 954-262-1203, E-mail: swilson@nova.edu. *Application contact:* Joey Jankie, Admissions Counselor, 954-262-7249, E-mail: joey@nova.edu.
Website: http://healthsciences.nova.edu/

The Ohio State University, College of Medicine, School of Health and Rehabilitation Sciences, Program in Occupational Therapy, Columbus, OH 43210. Offers MOT, MOT/PhD. *Accreditation:* AOTA. *Faculty:* 11. *Students:* 108 full-time (100 women); includes 8 minority (all Asian, non-Hispanic/Latino). Average age 23. In 2017, 44 master's awarded. *Degree requirements:* For master's, fieldwork. *Entrance requirements:* For master's, GRE General Test. Additional exam requirements/recommendations for international students: Required—TOEFL (minimum score 550 paper-based; 79 iBT), Michigan English Language Assessment Battery (minimum score 82); Recommended—IELTS (minimum score 7). *Application deadline:* For summer admission, 11/1 for domestic and international students. Applications are processed on a rolling basis. Application fee: $60 ($70 for international students). Electronic applications accepted. *Unit head:* Dr. Deborah S. Larsen, Associate Dean and Director, 614-292-5645, Fax: 614-292-0210, E-mail: larsen.64@osu.edu. *Application contact:* Graduate and Professional Admissions, 614-292-9444, Fax: 614-292-3895, E-mail: gpadmissions@osu.edu.
Website: http://medicine.osu.edu/hrs/ot

Pacific University, School of Occupational Therapy, Forest Grove, OR 97116-1797. Offers OTD. *Accreditation:* AOTA. Electronic applications accepted. *Expenses:* Contact institution. *Faculty research:* Cultural competency development, disability policy, scholarship of teaching and learning, driver rehabilitation and older adult visual perception, neurorehabilitation and motor learning.

Queen's University at Kingston, School of Graduate Studies, Faculty of Health Sciences, School of Rehabilitation Therapy, Kingston, ON K7L 3N6, Canada. Offers occupational therapy (M Sc OT); physical therapy (M Sc PT); rehabilitation science (M Sc, PhD). *Program availability:* Part-time. *Degree requirements:* For master's, thesis; for doctorate, comprehensive exam, thesis/dissertation. *Entrance requirements:* Additional exam requirements/recommendations for international students: Required—TOEFL. *Faculty research:* Disability, community, motor performance, rehabilitation, treatment efficiency.

Radford University, College of Graduate Studies and Research, Program in Occupational Therapy, Radford, VA 24142. Offers MOT. *Accreditation:* AOTA. *Program availability:* Part-time, evening/weekend. *Faculty:* 6 full-time (5 women), 2 part-time/adjunct (both women). *Students:* 64 full-time (58 women); includes 11 minority (4 Black or African American, non-Hispanic/Latino; 1 Asian, non-Hispanic/Latino; 4 Hispanic/Latino; 2 Two or more races, non-Hispanic/Latino). Average age 24. 69 applicants, 41% accepted, 23 enrolled. In 2017, 22 master's awarded. *Degree requirements:* For master's, comprehensive exam. *Entrance requirements:* For master's, GRE, minimum GPA of 3.25, minimum B grade in prerequisite courses, 2 letters of recommendation, professional resume, 40 hours of observation, official transcripts, completion of a college or community course to learn a new occupation. Additional exam requirements/recommendations for international students: Required—TOEFL (minimum score 550 paper-based; 79 iBT), IELTS (minimum score 6.5). *Application deadline:* For fall admission, 5/15 priority date for domestic students, 12/1 for international students; for spring admission, 7/1 for international students. Applications are processed on a rolling basis. Application fee: $50. Electronic applications accepted. *Expenses:* Contact institution. *Financial support:* In 2017–18, 3 students received support. Career-related internships or fieldwork, scholarships/grants, and unspecified assistantships available. Support available to part-time students. Financial award application deadline: 3/1; financial award applicants required to submit FAFSA. *Unit head:* Dr. Douglas Mitchell, Chair, 540-831-2693, Fax: 540-831-6802, E-mail: ot@radford.edu.
Website: http://www.radford.edu/content/wchs/home/occupational-therapy.html

Regis College, Nursing and Health Sciences School, Weston, MA 02493. Offers applied behavior analysis (MS); counseling psychology (MA); health administration (MS); nurse practitioner (Certificate); nursing (MS, DNP); nursing education (Certificate); occupational therapy (MS). *Accreditation:* ACEN. *Program availability:* Part-time, evening/weekend, 100% online, blended/hybrid learning. *Degree requirements:* For doctorate, thesis/dissertation. *Entrance requirements:* For master's, GRE General Test or MAT, minimum GPA of 3.0, official transcripts, recommendations, personal statement, resume/curriculum vitae, interview; for doctorate, MAT or GRE if GPA from master's lower than 3.5. Additional exam requirements/recommendations for international students: Required—TOEFL (minimum score 560 paper-based; 79 iBT); Recommended—IELTS (minimum score 6.5). *Application deadline:* Applications are processed on a rolling basis. Application fee: $75. Electronic applications accepted. *Financial support:* Federal Work-Study, scholarships/grants, traineeships, and unspecified assistantships available. Support available to part-time students. Financial award applicants required to submit FAFSA. *Faculty research:* Global public health, health policy, education, aging, job satisfaction, psychiatric nursing, critical thinking. *Application contact:* Hillary Lyons, Graduate Admission Counselor, 781-768-7746, E-mail: hillary.lyons@regiscollege.edu.

Regis University, Rueckert-Hartman College for Health Professions, Denver, CO 80221-1099. Offers advanced practice nurse (DNP); counseling (MA); counseling children and adolescents (Post-Graduate Certificate); counseling military families (Post-Graduate Certificate); depth psychotherapy (Post-Graduate Certificate); fellowship in orthopedic manual physical therapy (Certificate); health care business management (Certificate); health care quality and patient safety (Certificate); health industry leadership (MBA); health services administration (MS); marriage and family therapy (MA, Post-Graduate Certificate); neonatal nurse practitioner (MSN); nursing education (MSN); nursing leadership (MSN); occupational therapy (OTD); pharmacy (Pharm D); physical therapy (DPT). *Program availability:* Part-time, evening/weekend, 100% online, blended/hybrid learning. *Degree requirements:* For master's, thesis (for some programs), internship. *Entrance requirements:* For master's, official transcript reflecting baccalaureate degree awarded from regionally-accredited college or university. Additional exam requirements/recommendations for international students: Required—TOEFL (minimum score 550 paper-based; 82 iBT). Electronic applications accepted. *Expenses:* Contact institution. *Faculty research:* Normal and pathological balance and gait research, normal/pathological upper limb motor control/biomechanics, exercise energy/metabolism research, optical treatment protocols for therapeutic modalities.

Rochester Institute of Technology, Graduate Enrollment Services, National Technical Institute for the Deaf, Research and Teacher Education Department, Rochester, NY 14623. Offers secondary education for the deaf and hard of hearing (MS). *Accreditation:* TEAC. *Students:* 18 full-time (13 women), 1 (woman) part-time; includes 5 minority (1 Black or African American, non-Hispanic/Latino; 2 Hispanic/Latino; 2 Two or more races,

non-Hispanic/Latino), 4 international. Average age 28. 24 applicants, 33% accepted, 5 enrolled. In 2017, 11 master's awarded. *Entrance requirements:* For master's, minimum GPA of 3.0. Additional exam requirements/recommendations for international students: Required—PTE (minimum score 58). *Application deadline:* For fall admission, 2/15 priority date for domestic and international students. Applications are processed on a rolling basis. Application fee: $65. Electronic applications accepted. *Expenses:* $1,815 per credit hour. *Financial support:* Fellowships with full tuition reimbursements, research assistantships with partial tuition reimbursements, teaching assistantships with partial tuition reimbursements, career-related internships or fieldwork, scholarships/grants, and unspecified assistantships available. Support available to part-time students. Financial award applicants required to submit FAFSA. *Faculty research:* Effective use of technology and online learning in teaching deaf students; strategies for inclusive instruction/deaf students with other disabilities; effective literacy instruction strategies for DHH readers; single case experimental design methods; STEM language, literacy and learning; deaf studies; international deaf education; stereotype threat effects on mathematical performance. *Unit head:* Dr. Gerald C. Bateman, Director, 585-475-6480, Fax: 585-475-2525, E-mail: gcbnmp@rit.edu. *Application contact:* Diane Ellison, Senior Associate Vice President, Graduate Enrollment Services, 585-475-2229, Fax: 585-475-7164, E-mail: gradinfo@rit.edu.
Website: http://www.ntid.rit.edu/msse/

Rockhurst University, College of Health and Human Services, Program in Occupational Therapy, Kansas City, MO 64110-2561. Offers MOT. *Accreditation:* AOTA. *Program availability:* Part-time. *Faculty:* 7 full-time (all women), 2 part-time/adjunct (both women). *Students:* 93 full-time (88 women), 1 (woman) part-time; includes 6 minority (2 Black or African American, non-Hispanic/Latino; 1 Asian, non-Hispanic/Latino; 1 Hispanic/Latino; 2 Two or more races, non-Hispanic/Latino). Average age 23. 396 applicants, 27% accepted, 56 enrolled. In 2017, 60 master's awarded. *Entrance requirements:* For master's, minimum GPA of 3.0. Additional exam requirements/recommendations for international students: Required—TOEFL (minimum score 550 paper-based; 79 iBT). *Application deadline:* Applications are processed on a rolling basis. Electronic applications accepted. *Expenses:* $855 per credit hour tuition; $790 per year fees, additional fees may apply. *Financial support:* Applicants required to submit FAFSA. *Faculty research:* Problem-based learning, cognitive rehabilitation behavioral state in infants and children, adult neurological defects and prosthetics. *Unit head:* Dr. Mylene Schriner, Interim Chair, 816-501-4635, Fax: 816-501-4643, E-mail: mylene.schriner@rockhurst.edu. *Application contact:* Beth Harris, Graduate Admissions Coordinator and Recruiter, 816-501-4059, E-mail: beth.harris@rockhurst.edu.
Website: https://www.rockhurst.edu/ot

Rocky Mountain University of Health Professions, Program in Occupational Therapy, Provo, UT 84606. Offers OTD. *Program availability:* Online learning. *Entrance requirements:* For doctorate, bachelor's or master's degree from accredited institution with minimum cumulative GPA of 3.0; current U.S. occupational therapy license; resume/curriculum vitae; two letters of recommendation; official transcripts. Electronic applications accepted.

Rush University, College of Health Sciences, Department of Occupational Therapy, Chicago, IL 60612-3832. Offers OTD. *Accreditation:* AOTA. *Program availability:* Part-time. *Application deadline:* For fall admission, 12/1 for domestic students. Applications are processed on a rolling basis. Application fee: $40. Electronic applications accepted. *Financial support:* Career-related internships or fieldwork, Federal Work-Study, institutionally sponsored loans, and scholarships/grants available. Support available to part-time students. Financial award application deadline: 3/15; financial award applicants required to submit FAFSA. *Faculty research:* Intervention and practice strategies in the stroke population and the impact of evidenced based interventions. *Unit head:* Dr. Linda M. Olson, Chairperson, 312-942-8721, E-mail: linda_m_olson@rush.edu. *Application contact:* 312-942-7120, E-mail: chs_admissions@rush.edu.
Website: http://www.rushu.rush.edu/occuth/

Sacred Heart University, Graduate Programs, College of Health Professions, Department of Occupational Therapy, Fairfield, CT 06825. Offers MSOT. *Accreditation:* AOTA. *Faculty:* 7 full-time (all women), 9 part-time/adjunct (all women). *Students:* 38 full-time (27 women), 61 part-time (39 women); includes 10 minority (1 Black or African American, non-Hispanic/Latino; 2 Asian, non-Hispanic/Latino; 4 Hispanic/Latino; 3 Two or more races, non-Hispanic/Latino). Average age 32. 542 applicants, 13% accepted, 49 enrolled. In 2017, 46 master's awarded. *Degree requirements:* For master's, capstone. *Entrance requirements:* For master's, GRE, minimum overall and prerequisites GPA of 3.2 (science 3.0) with no prerequisite course below a C; statistics and human anatomy and physiology completed in the past 10 years. Additional exam requirements/recommendations for international students: Required—TOEFL (minimum score 570 paper-based, 80 iBT), TWE, or IELTS (6.5). *Application deadline:* For fall admission, 12/15 for domestic students. Applications are processed on a rolling basis. Application fee: $75. Electronic applications accepted. *Expenses:* Contact institution. *Financial support:* Career-related internships or fieldwork, institutionally sponsored loans, and unspecified assistantships available. Financial award applicants required to submit FAFSA. *Unit head:* Dr. Jody Bortone, Associate Dean of College of Health Professions/Chair, Occupational Therapy and Health Professions/Clinical Associate Professor, 203-396-8023, Fax: 203-365-7508, E-mail: bortonej@sacredheart.edu. *Application contact:* Tara Chudy, Executive Director of Graduate Admissions, 203-365-4735, E-mail: chudyt@sacredheart.edu.
Website: http://www.sacredheart.edu/academics/collegeofhealthprofessions/academicprograms/occupationaltherapy/

Sage Graduate School, School of Health Sciences, Program in Occupational Therapy, Troy, NY 12180-4115. Offers MS. *Accreditation:* AOTA. *Faculty:* 9 full-time (all women), 3 part-time/adjunct (all women). *Students:* 70 full-time (68 women), 39 part-time (36 women); includes 7 minority (4 Asian, non-Hispanic/Latino; 2 Hispanic/Latino; 1 Two or more races, non-Hispanic/Latino). Average age 24. 197 applicants, 19% accepted, 28 enrolled. In 2017, 38 master's awarded. *Entrance requirements:* For master's, baccalaureate degree, minimum undergraduate GPA of 3.0, completion of 20 hours of clinical observation. Additional exam requirements/recommendations for international students: Required—TOEFL (minimum score 550 paper-based). *Application deadline:* For fall admission, 2/1 for domestic students. Applications are processed on a rolling basis. Application fee: $30. Electronic applications accepted. *Expenses:* Contact institution. *Financial support:* Fellowships, research assistantships, scholarships/grants, and unspecified assistantships available. Financial award applicants required to submit FAFSA. *Unit head:* Dr. Theresa Hand, Dean of Health Sciences/Program Director, 518-244-2264, Fax: 518-244-4524, E-mail: handt@sage.edu. *Application contact:* Wendy D. Diefendorf, Director of Graduate and Adult Admission, 518-244-2443, Fax: 518-244-6880, E-mail: diefew@sage.edu.

Saginaw Valley State University, College of Health and Human Services, Program in Occupational Therapy, University Center, MI 48710. Offers MSOT. *Accreditation:* AOTA. *Program availability:* Part-time, evening/weekend. *Students:* 119 full-time (105 women), 59 part-time (51 women); includes 11 minority (1 Asian, non-Hispanic/Latino; 5 Hispanic/Latino; 5 Two or more races, non-Hispanic/Latino), 1 international. Average age 24. In 2017, 61 master's awarded. *Entrance requirements:* For master's, minimum GPA of 3.0. Additional exam requirements/recommendations for international students: Required—TOEFL (minimum score 525 paper-based; 71 iBT). *Application deadline:* For spring admission, 1/23 for domestic and international students. Applications are processed on a rolling basis. Application fee: $30 ($90 for international students). Electronic applications accepted. *Expenses:* Tuition, state resident: full-time $10,156; part-time $564.20 per credit hour. Tuition, nonresident: full-time $19,336; part-time $1074.20 per credit hour. *Required fees:* $263; $14.60 per credit hour. Tuition and fees vary according to degree level and program. *Financial support:* Federal Work-Study and scholarships/grants available. Support available to part-time students. *Unit head:* Don Earley, Professor of Occupational Therapy, 989-964-4689, E-mail: dwe@svsu.edu. *Application contact:* Jenna Briggs, Director, Graduate and International Admissions, 989-964-6096, Fax: 989-964-2788, E-mail: gradadm@svsu.edu.

St. Ambrose University, College of Health and Human Services, Program in Occupational Therapy, Davenport, IA 52803-2898. Offers OTD. *Accreditation:* AOTA. *Entrance requirements:* Additional exam requirements/recommendations for international students: Required—TOEFL. Electronic applications accepted.

St. Catherine University, Graduate Programs, Program in Occupational Therapy, St. Paul, MN 55105. Offers MA, OTD. *Accreditation:* AOTA. *Program availability:* Part-time, evening/weekend. *Degree requirements:* For master's, thesis. *Entrance requirements:* For master's, GRE, minimum GPA of 3.0. Additional exam requirements/recommendations for international students: Required—Michigan English Language Assessment Battery or TOEFL. *Application deadline:* For fall admission, 2/1 priority date for domestic students. Applications are processed on a rolling basis. Application fee: $35. *Expenses:* Contact institution. *Financial support:* Career-related internships or fieldwork and institutionally sponsored loans available. Support available to part-time students. Financial award application deadline: 4/1; financial award applicants required to submit FAFSA. *Unit head:* Dr. Kathleen Matuska, Department Chair, 651-690-6627, Fax: 651-690-8804. *Application contact:* Kristin Chalberg, Associate Director of Non-Traditional Admissions, 651-690-6868, Fax: 651-690-6064.

Saint Francis University, Department of Occupational Therapy, Loretto, PA 15940-0600. Offers MOT. *Accreditation:* AOTA. *Faculty:* 6 full-time (5 women). *Students:* 42 full-time (39 women), 1 (woman) part-time; includes 3 minority (1 Black or African American, non-Hispanic/Latino; 2 Asian, non-Hispanic/Latino). Average age 23. 5 applicants, 100% accepted, 2 enrolled. In 2017, 35 master's awarded. *Degree requirements:* For master's, one foreign language, thesis. Application fee: $30. Electronic applications accepted. *Expenses:* Contact institution. *Faculty research:* Retention, technology, work injury, distance learning. *Unit head:* Dr. Edward Mihelcic, Department Chair, 814-472-2760, E-mail: emihelcic@francis.edu. *Application contact:* Amy Hudkins, Instructor, 814-472-2792, E-mail: ahudkins@francis.edu.
Website: http://www.francis.edu/ot

Saint Louis University, Graduate Programs, Doisy College of Health Sciences, Department of Occupational Science and Occupational Therapy, St. Louis, MO 63103. Offers MOT. *Accreditation:* AOTA. *Degree requirements:* For master's, project. *Entrance requirements:* For master's, minimum GPA of 2.8. Additional exam requirements/recommendations for international students: Required—TOEFL (minimum score 525 paper-based; 55 iBT). Electronic applications accepted. *Faculty research:* Autism spectrum and Asperger's disease, early intervention with children of homeless families, disability awareness program development of developing countries, environmental adaptations and universal design for persons who are disabled and/or aging, physical activity models for persons with dementia.

Salem State University, School of Graduate Studies, Program in Occupational Therapy, Salem, MA 01970-5353. Offers MS. *Accreditation:* AOTA. *Program availability:* Part-time, evening/weekend. *Entrance requirements:* For master's, GRE or MAT. Additional exam requirements/recommendations for international students: Required—TOEFL (minimum score 550 paper-based; 80 iBT), IELTS (minimum score 5.5).

Salus University, College of Education and Rehabilitation, Elkins Park, PA 19027-1598. Offers education of children and youth with visual and multiple impairments (M Ed, Certificate); low vision rehabilitation (MS, Certificate); occupational therapy (MS); orientation and mobility therapy (MS, Certificate); speech-language pathology (MS); vision rehabilitation therapy (MS, Certificate); OD/MS. *Accreditation:* AOTA. *Program availability:* Part-time, online learning. *Entrance requirements:* For master's, GRE or MAT, letters of reference (3), interviews (2). Additional exam requirements/recommendations for international students: Required—TOEFL, TWE. *Expenses:* Contact institution. *Faculty research:* Knowledge utilization, technology transfer.

Samuel Merritt University, Department of Occupational Therapy, Oakland, CA 94609-3108. Offers OTD. *Accreditation:* AOTA. *Faculty:* 12 full-time (11 women), 10 part-time/adjunct (8 women). *Students:* 85 full-time (71 women), 39 part-time (34 women); includes 70 minority (6 Black or African American, non-Hispanic/Latino; 1 American Indian or Alaska Native, non-Hispanic/Latino; 28 Asian, non-Hispanic/Latino; 29 Hispanic/Latino; 6 Two or more races, non-Hispanic/Latino). 246 applicants, 25% accepted, 42 enrolled. *Degree requirements:* For doctorate, project. *Entrance requirements:* For doctorate, minimum GPA of 3.0 in science and overall; 40-70 hours of volunteer or professional occupational therapy experience; interview. Additional exam requirements/recommendations for international students: Required—TOEFL (minimum score 100 iBT). *Application deadline:* For fall admission, 10/1 priority date for domestic students. Application fee: $140. Electronic applications accepted. *Expenses:* $41,458 annual tuition (for first-year doctoral students). *Financial support:* Career-related internships or fieldwork, Federal Work-Study, and scholarships/grants available. Support available to part-time students. Financial award applicants required to submit FAFSA. *Faculty research:* Neurological rehabilitation, attention, social responsiveness, computer assisted remediation. *Unit head:* Kate Hayner, Chair, 510-869-4780, E-mail: khayner@samuelmerritt.edu. *Application contact:* Timothy Cranford, Dean of Admission, 510-869-1550, Fax: 510-869-6525, E-mail: admission@samuelmerritt.edu.
Website: http://www.samuelmerritt.edu/occupational_therapy

San Jose State University, Graduate Studies and Research, College of Health and Human Sciences, San Jose, CA 95192-0049. Offers criminology (MS), including global criminology, law and justice; justice studies (MS); kinesiology (MA), including athletic training, exercise physiology, interdisciplinary, sport studies, sports management; library and information science (MLIS); mass communications (MS); nursing (MS), including family nurse practitioner; nutritional science (MS); occupational therapy (MS); public health (MPH); social work (MSW); MD/M Div. *Program availability:* Part-time, 100% online, blended/hybrid learning. *Faculty:* 15 full-time (7 women), 6 part-time/adjunct (3 women). *Students:* 517 full-time (407 women), 405 part-time (302 women); includes 523 minority (39 Black or African American, non-Hispanic/Latino; 2 American Indian or Alaska Native, non-Hispanic/Latino; 141 Asian, non-Hispanic/Latino; 226 Hispanic/Latino; 2 Native Hawaiian or other Pacific Islander, non-Hispanic/Latino; 113 Two or more races, non-Hispanic/Latino), 14 international. Average age 32. 1,250 applicants, 45% accepted, 375 enrolled. In 2017, 808 master's awarded. *Degree requirements:* For master's, thesis (for some programs), graduate writing assessment. *Entrance requirements:* Additional exam requirements/recommendations for international students: Required—TOEFL (minimum score 550 paper-based; 80 iBT), IELTS (minimum score 6.5), PTE (minimum score 53). *Application deadline:* For fall admission, 2/1 for domestic and international students. Applications are processed on a rolling

basis. Application fee: $55. Electronic applications accepted. *Expenses:* Tuition, state resident: full-time $7176. Tuition, nonresident: full-time $16,680. Tuition and fees vary according to course load and program. *Financial support:* Fellowships, research assistantships, teaching assistantships, career-related internships or fieldwork, Federal Work-Study, scholarships/grants, and tuition waivers (full and partial) available. Support available to part-time students. Financial award application deadline: 4/24; financial award applicants required to submit FAFSA. *Unit head:* Dr. Mary Schutten, Dean, College of Health and Human Sciences, 408-924-2900, Fax: 408-924-2901, E-mail: mary.schutten@sjsu.edu.
Website: http://www.sjsu.edu/casa/

Seton Hall University, School of Health and Medical Sciences, Program in Occupational Therapy, South Orange, NJ 07079-2697. Offers MS. *Accreditation:* AOTA. *Entrance requirements:* For master's, health care experience, minimum GPA of 3.0, 50 hours of occupational therapy volunteer work, pre-requisite courses. Additional exam requirements/recommendations for international students: Required—TOEFL. Electronic applications accepted. *Faculty research:* Occupational genesis, occupational technology, pediatric OT, community practice, families of children with special needs; family routines; complementary medicine and wellness.

Shawnee State University, Program in Occupational Therapy, Portsmouth, OH 45662. Offers MOT. *Accreditation:* AOTA.

Sonoma State University, School of Science and Technology, Department of Kinesiology, Rohnert Park, CA 94928. Offers exercise science/pre-physical therapy (MA); interdisciplinary (MA); interdisciplinary pre-occupational therapy (MA); lifetime physical activity (MA), including coach education, fitness and wellness. *Program availability:* Part-time. *Degree requirements:* For master's, thesis, oral exam. *Entrance requirements:* For master's, minimum GPA of 2.8. Additional exam requirements/recommendations for international students: Required—TOEFL (minimum score 500 paper-based). *Application deadline:* For fall admission, 11/30 for domestic students; for spring admission, 9/1 for domestic students. Applications are processed on a rolling basis. Application fee: $55. *Financial support:* Career-related internships or fieldwork available. Financial award application deadline: 3/2; financial award applicants required to submit FAFSA. *Unit head:* Dr. Steven Winter, Chair, 707-664-2188, E-mail: steven.winter@sonoma.edu. *Application contact:* Dr. Bulent Sokmen, Graduate Coordinator, 707-664-2789, E-mail: sokmen@sonoma.edu.
Website: http://www.sonoma.edu/kinesiology/

South University, Program in Occupational Therapy, Royal Palm Beach, FL 33411. Offers OTD.

Spalding University, Graduate Studies, Kosair College of Health and Natural Sciences, Auerbach School of Occupational Therapy, Louisville, KY 40203-2188. Offers MS. *Accreditation:* AOTA. *Entrance requirements:* For master's, interview, letters of recommendation, transcripts, 20 observation hours, MSOT mission alignment policy. Additional exam requirements/recommendations for international students: Required—TOEFL (minimum score 535 paper-based). *Faculty research:* High-risk youth, community-dwelling older adults, assistive technology, mother-infant relationships, community accessibility.

Springfield College, Graduate Programs, Program in Occupational Therapy, Springfield, MA 01109-3797. Offers MS. *Accreditation:* AOTA. *Program availability:* Part-time. *Faculty:* 6 full-time (all women), 8 part-time/adjunct (7 women). *Students:* 702 applicants, 8% accepted, 24 enrolled. *Degree requirements:* For master's, comprehensive exam, research project; 6 months of full-time fieldwork. *Entrance requirements:* For master's, prerequisite courses in anatomy and physiology, other physical science, introduction to psychology, introduction to sociology, abnormal psychology, developmental psychology, English composition, additional English course, and statistics; minimum undergraduate GPA of 3.0; prior experience in/exposure to occupational therapy services. Additional exam requirements/recommendations for international students: Required—TOEFL (minimum score 90 iBT); Recommended—IELTS (minimum score 7). *Application deadline:* For fall admission, 1/15 for domestic and international students; for winter admission, 11/1 for domestic and international students; for spring admission, 11/1 for domestic and international students. Applications are processed on a rolling basis. Application fee: $50. Electronic applications accepted. *Financial support:* Fellowships with partial tuition reimbursements, teaching assistantships with partial tuition reimbursements, career-related internships or fieldwork, Federal Work-Study, institutionally sponsored loans, scholarships/grants, and unspecified assistantships available. Financial award application deadline: 3/1; financial award applicants required to submit FAFSA. *Faculty research:* Gerontology and dementia, service learning in higher education, students with learning disabilities, domestic violence, pediatric assessment. *Unit head:* Dr. Katherine M. Post, Department Chair and Professor, 413-748-3785, Fax: 413-748-3371, E-mail: kpost@springfield.edu. *Application contact:* Anne Griffin, Director of Graduate Admissions, 413-748-3225, Fax: 413-748-3694, E-mail: agriffin2@springfield.edu.
Website: http://springfield.edu/ot

Stanbridge University, Program in Occupational Therapy, Irvine, CA 92612. Offers MS.

State University of New York Downstate Medical Center, School of Graduate Studies, Program in Occupational Therapy, Brooklyn, NY 11203-2098. Offers MS. *Accreditation:* AOTA.

Stockton University, Office of Graduate Studies, Program in Occupational Therapy, Galloway, NJ 08205-9441. Offers MSOT. *Accreditation:* AOTA. *Faculty:* 5 full-time (all women), 1 (woman) part-time/adjunct. *Students:* 60 full-time (50 women), 30 part-time (28 women); includes 19 minority (2 Black or African American, non-Hispanic/Latino; 8 Asian, non-Hispanic/Latino; 7 Hispanic/Latino; 2 Two or more races, non-Hispanic/Latino). Average age 25. 345 applicants, 12% accepted, 30 enrolled. In 2017, 25 master's awarded. *Entrance requirements:* For master's, minimum GPA of 3.0; 60 hours of work, volunteer or community service. Additional exam requirements/recommendations for international students: Required—TOEFL. *Application deadline:* For fall admission, 11/17 for domestic and international students. Application fee: $50. Electronic applications accepted. *Expenses:* Contact institution. *Financial support:* Fellowships, research assistantships, career-related internships or fieldwork, institutionally sponsored loans, scholarships/grants, and unspecified assistantships available. Support available to part-time students. Financial award application deadline: 3/1; financial award applicants required to submit FAFSA. *Faculty research:* Home health-based occupational therapy for women with HIV/AIDS. *Unit head:* Dr. Kim Furphy, Program Director, 609-626-3640, E-mail: msot@stockton.edu. *Application contact:* Tara Williams, Assistant Director of Graduate Enrollment Management, 609-626-3640, Fax: 609-626-6050, E-mail: gradschool@stockton.edu.

Stony Brook University, State University of New York, Stony Brook Medicine, School of Health Technology and Management, Stony Brook, NY 11794. Offers applied health informatics (MS); disability studies (Certificate); health administration (MHA); health and rehabilitation sciences (PhD); health care management (Advanced Certificate); health care policy and management (MS); occupational therapy (MS); physical therapy (DPT); physician assistant (MS). *Accreditation:* APTA. *Faculty:* 62 full-time (42 women), 59 part-time/adjunct (36 women). *Students:* 565 full-time (382 women), 67 part-time (53 women); includes 179 minority (29 Black or African American, non-Hispanic/Latino; 83 Asian, non-Hispanic/Latino; 59 Hispanic/Latino; 2 Native Hawaiian or other Pacific Islander, non-Hispanic/Latino; 6 Two or more races, non-Hispanic/Latino), 14 international. Average age 27. 2,516 applicants, 16% accepted, 266 enrolled. In 2017, 162 master's, 84 doctorates, 39 other advanced degrees awarded. *Degree requirements:* For master's, thesis; for doctorate, thesis/dissertation. *Entrance requirements:* For master's, GRE General Test, minimum GPA of 3.0, work experience in field, references; for doctorate, GRE, three references, essay. Additional exam requirements/recommendations for international students: Required—TOEFL (minimum score 550 paper-based). *Application deadline:* For fall admission, 1/15 for domestic students; for spring admission, 10/1 for domestic students. Application fee: $100. *Expenses:* Contact institution. *Financial support:* Fellowships, research assistantships, teaching assistantships, career-related internships or fieldwork, Federal Work-Study, and institutionally sponsored loans available. Financial award application deadline: 3/15. *Faculty research:* Developmental disabilities, disability studies, health promotion, multiple sclerosis, quality of life program, internal medicine, lung disease, palliative care, respiratory diseases, neuromuscular disorders, orthopedics, physical medicine and rehabilitation, physical therapy, prostheses or implants, advance directives, advocacy alienation, allied health education, allied health occupations, adolescents, adoption, child or adolescent mental health, multiple sclerosis, youth policy. *Total annual research expenditures:* $1.2 million. *Unit head:* Dr. Carlos Vidal, Dean, 631-444-1009, Fax: 631-444-7621, E-mail: carlos.vidal@stonybrook.edu. *Application contact:* Frances Shaw, 631-444-3240, Fax: 631-444-7621, E-mail: frances.shaw@stonybrook.edu.
Website: http://healthtechnology.stonybrookmedicine.edu/

Temple University, College of Public Health, Department of Rehabilitation Sciences, Philadelphia, PA 19122. Offers occupational therapy (MOT, DOT); therapeutic recreation (MS), including recreation therapy. *Accreditation:* AOTA. *Program availability:* Part-time. *Faculty:* 17 full-time (16 women), 3 part-time/adjunct (2 women). *Students:* 117 full-time (108 women), 24 part-time (22 women); includes 24 minority (5 Black or African American, non-Hispanic/Latino; 6 Asian, non-Hispanic/Latino; 7 Hispanic/Latino; 6 Two or more races, non-Hispanic/Latino). 12 applicants, 100% accepted, 10 enrolled. In 2017, 49 master's, 7 doctorates awarded. *Degree requirements:* For doctorate, comprehensive exam (for some programs), thesis/dissertation (for some programs). *Entrance requirements:* For master's and doctorate, GRE General Test, minimum GPA of 3.0. Additional exam requirements/recommendations for international students: Required—TOEFL (minimum score 550 paper-based; 79 iBT). *Application deadline:* For fall admission, 2/1 for domestic students, 1/1 for international students; for spring admission, 11/1 for domestic students, 10/1 for international students. Applications are processed on a rolling basis. Application fee: $60. Electronic applications accepted. *Expenses:* Contact institution. *Financial support:* Career-related internships or fieldwork and Federal Work-Study available. *Faculty research:* Participation, community inclusion, disability issues, leisure/recreation, occupation, quality of life, adaptive equipment and technology. *Unit head:* Dr. Mark Salzer, Chair, 215-204-7879, E-mail: mark.salzer@temple.edu.
Website: http://cph.temple.edu/rs/home

Tennessee State University, The School of Graduate Studies and Research, College of Health Sciences, Department of Occupational Therapy, Nashville, TN 37209-1561. Offers MOT. *Accreditation:* AOTA. *Entrance requirements:* For master's, GRE taken within the last 5 years, undergraduate degree with minimum GPA of 3.0; 30 hours of observation, volunteer, or work with an occupational therapist; 3 professional and/or academic references.

Texas Tech University Health Sciences Center, School of Health Professions, Program in Occupational Therapy, Lubbock, TX 79430. Offers MOT. *Accreditation:* AOTA. *Faculty:* 7 full-time (6 women), 1 (woman) part-time/adjunct. *Students:* 96 full-time (85 women), 1 (woman) part-time; includes 24 minority (5 Black or African American, non-Hispanic/Latino; 1 Asian, non-Hispanic/Latino; 16 Hispanic/Latino; 1 Native Hawaiian or other Pacific Islander, non-Hispanic/Latino; 1 Two or more races, non-Hispanic/Latino). Average age 25. 474 applicants, 19% accepted, 51 enrolled. In 2017, 49 master's awarded. *Entrance requirements:* Additional exam requirements/recommendations for international students: Required—TOEFL (minimum score 550 paper-based; 79 iBT), IELTS. *Application deadline:* For summer admission, 11/15 priority date for domestic students. Applications are processed on a rolling basis. Application fee: $75. Electronic applications accepted. *Financial support:* Career-related internships or fieldwork, institutionally sponsored loans, and scholarships/grants available. Financial award application deadline: 9/1; financial award applicants required to submit FAFSA. *Unit head:* Dr. Sandra Whisner, Program Director, 806-743-3240, Fax: 806-743-2189, E-mail: sandra.whisner@ttuhsc.edu. *Application contact:* Lindsay Johnson, Associate Dean for Admissions and Student Affairs, 806-743-3220, Fax: 806-743-2994, E-mail: lindsay.johnson@ttuhsc.edu.
Website: http://www.ttuhsc.edu/health-professions/master-occupational-therapy/

Texas Woman's University, Graduate School, College of Health Sciences, School of Occupational Therapy, Denton, TX 76204. Offers MOT, OTD, PhD. *Accreditation:* AOTA (one or more programs are accredited). *Program availability:* Part-time, evening/weekend. *Faculty:* 21 full-time (18 women), 8 part-time/adjunct (7 women). *Students:* 403 full-time (374 women), 63 part-time (58 women); includes 173 minority (29 Black or African American, non-Hispanic/Latino; 1 American Indian or Alaska Native, non-Hispanic/Latino; 50 Asian, non-Hispanic/Latino; 82 Hispanic/Latino; 11 Two or more races, non-Hispanic/Latino), 2 international. Average age 29. 500 applicants, 50% accepted, 155 enrolled. In 2017, 116 master's, 15 doctorates awarded. *Degree requirements:* For master's, comprehensive exam, thesis or alternative, capstone course, internship; for doctorate, comprehensive exam, thesis/dissertation, capstone; completion of program within 6 years of initial registration (for OTD), 10 years (for PhD); qualification exam. *Entrance requirements:* For master's, GRE General Test (within 5 years of completion date), minimum GPA of 3.0 on prerequisites, interview, 20 hours of observation with one supervising OTR, 2 faculty references; for doctorate, GRE General Test (within last 5 years), essay, interview, 3 letters of reference, certification and master's degree in occupational therapy or related field, minimum GPA of 3.2 in previous graduate work, occupational therapy license (OTD only), initial certification as an OT by NBCOT (PhD only). Additional exam requirements/recommendations for international students: Required—TOEFL (minimum score 550 paper-based; 89 iBT); Recommended—IELTS (minimum score 6.5), TSE (minimum score 53). *Application deadline:* For fall admission, 10/15 for domestic and international students. Applications are processed on a rolling basis. Application fee: $50 ($75 for international students). Electronic applications accepted. *Expenses:* $7,610 per year full-time in-state; $16,910 per year full-time out-of-state. *Financial support:* In 2017–18, 216 students received support, including 13 research assistantships (averaging $8,697 per year); career-related internships or fieldwork, Federal Work-Study, institutionally sponsored loans, scholarships/grants, traineeships, health care benefits, and unspecified assistantships also available. Support available to part-time students. Financial award application deadline: 3/1; financial award applicants required to submit FAFSA. *Faculty research:* Quality of life/wellness, mental health promotion, hand rehabilitation, psychosocial dysfunction, adaptation/chronic disability. *Total annual research expenditures:* $75,071. *Unit head:* Dr. Cynthia Evetts, Director, 940-898-2801, Fax: 940-898-2806, E-mail: ot@twu.edu. *Application contact:* Korie Hawkins, Associate Director of Admissions, Graduate Recruitment, 940-898-3188, Fax: 940-898-3081, E-mail: admissions@twu.edu.
Website: http://www.twu.edu/occupational-therapy/

Thomas Jefferson University, College of Science, Health and the Liberal Arts, Program in Occupational Therapy, Philadelphia, PA 19107. Offers MS. *Accreditation:* AOTA. *Program availability:* Evening/weekend. *Degree requirements:* For master's, portfolio. *Entrance requirements:* For master's, GRE or MAT. Additional exam requirements/recommendations for international students: Required—TOEFL (minimum score 550 paper-based; 79 iBT). Electronic applications accepted.

Thomas Jefferson University, Jefferson College of Health Professions, Department of Occupational Therapy, Philadelphia, PA 19107. Offers MS, OTD. *Accreditation:* AOTA. *Program availability:* Part-time. *Degree requirements:* For master's, capstone project; for doctorate, capstone project plus fellowship and project oral defense. *Entrance requirements:* For master's and doctorate, GRE or MAT. Additional exam requirements/recommendations for international students: Required—TOEFL (minimum score 87 iBT). Electronic applications accepted.

Touro College, School of Health Sciences, Bay Shore, NY 11706. Offers industrial-organizational psychology (MS); mental health counseling (MS); occupational therapy (MS); physical therapy (DPT); physician assistant (MS); speech-language pathology (MS). *Faculty:* 81 full-time (55 women), 77 part-time/adjunct (46 women). *Students:* 628 full-time (470 women), 113 part-time (73 women); includes 143 minority (31 Black or African American, non-Hispanic/Latino; 1 American Indian or Alaska Native, non-Hispanic/Latino; 61 Asian, non-Hispanic/Latino; 42 Hispanic/Latino; 1 Native Hawaiian or other Pacific Islander, non-Hispanic/Latino; 7 Two or more races, non-Hispanic/Latino), 63 international. Average age 28. *Expenses:* Contact institution. *Financial support:* Fellowships available. *Unit head:* Dr. Louis Primavera, Dean, School of Health Sciences, 516-673-3200, E-mail: louis.primavera@touro.edu. *Application contact:* Brian J. Diele, Director of Student Administrative Services, 631-665-1600 Ext. 6311, E-mail: brian.diele@touro.edu.

Towson University, College of Health Professions, Program in Occupational Therapy, Towson, MD 21252-0001. Offers MS. *Accreditation:* AOTA. *Students:* 118 full-time (109 women); includes 12 minority (6 Black or African American, non-Hispanic/Latino; 5 Asian, non-Hispanic/Latino; 1 Hispanic/Latino), 1 international. *Degree requirements:* For master's, thesis optional. *Entrance requirements:* For master's, bachelor's degree with minimum GPA of 3.25, master's degree, or doctorate; 3 letters of recommendation; human service/OT observation hours; personal statement. *Application deadline:* For fall admission, 1/17 for domestic students, 5/15 for international students; for spring admission, 10/15 for domestic students, 12/1 for international students. Applications are processed on a rolling basis. Application fee: $45. Electronic applications accepted. *Expenses:* Tuition, state resident: full-time $7960; part-time $398 per unit. Tuition, nonresident: full-time $16,480; part-time $824 per unit. *Required fees:* $2600; $130 per year. $390 per term. *Financial support:* Application deadline: 4/1. *Unit head:* Dr. Sonia Lawson, Graduate Program Director, 410-704-2762, E-mail: slawson@towson.edu. *Application contact:* Coverley Beidleman, Assistant Director of Graduate Admissions, 410-704-5630, Fax: 410-704-3030, E-mail: cbeidleman@towson.edu.
Website: http://www.towson.edu/chp/departments/occutherapy/programs/gradoccutherapy/

Tufts University, Graduate School of Arts and Sciences, Department of Occupational Therapy, Medford, MA 02155. Offers MS, OTD. *Accreditation:* AOTA. *Students:* 133 full-time (122 women), 4 part-time (2 women); includes 36 minority (6 Black or African American, non-Hispanic/Latino; 13 Asian, non-Hispanic/Latino; 8 Hispanic/Latino; 9 Two or more races, non-Hispanic/Latino), 11 international. Average age 27. 277 applicants, 29% accepted, 38 enrolled. In 2017, 37 master's, 3 doctorates awarded. *Degree requirements:* For master's, thesis optional; for doctorate, leadership project. *Entrance requirements:* For master's and doctorate, GRE General Test. Additional exam requirements/recommendations for international students: Required—TOEFL (minimum score 550 paper-based; 80 iBT), IELTS (minimum score 6.5). *Application deadline:* For fall admission, 1/15 for domestic and international students; for spring admission, 10/15 for domestic students. Applications are processed on a rolling basis. Application fee: $85. Electronic applications accepted. *Expenses:* Contact institution. *Financial support:* Teaching assistantships, Federal Work-Study, scholarships/grants, and tuition waivers (full and partial) available. Support available to part-time students. Financial award application deadline: 1/15. *Unit head:* Dr. Gary Bedell, Graduate Program Director, 617-627-2854. *Application contact:* Jill Rocca, Admissions Coordinator, 617-627-5720, E-mail: bsot@tufts.edu.
Website: http://ase.tufts.edu/bsot/

Tufts University, Graduate School of Arts and Sciences, Graduate Certificate Programs, Advanced Professional Study in Occupational Therapy Program, Medford, MA 02155. Offers Certificate. *Program availability:* Part-time, evening/weekend. Electronic applications accepted. *Expenses:* Contact institution.

Tuskegee University, Graduate Programs, College of Veterinary Medicine, Nursing and Allied Health, School of Nursing and Allied Health, Tuskegee, AL 36088. Offers occupational therapy (MS). *Accreditation:* AOTA.

Université de Montréal, Faculty of Medicine, Programs in Ergonomics, Montréal, QC H3C 3J7, Canada. Offers occupational therapy (DESS). Program offered jointly with École Polytechnique de Montréal.

University at Buffalo, the State University of New York, Graduate School, School of Public Health and Health Professions, Department of Rehabilitation Science, Program in Occupational Therapy, Buffalo, NY 14260. Offers MS. *Accreditation:* AOTA. *Faculty:* 6 full-time (all women), 3 part-time/adjunct (all women). *Students:* 141 full-time (130 women); includes 29 minority (3 Black or African American, non-Hispanic/Latino; 25 Asian, non-Hispanic/Latino; 1 Hispanic/Latino), 1 international. Average age 23. 80 applicants, 99% accepted, 78 enrolled. In 2017, 61 master's awarded. *Entrance requirements:* Additional exam requirements/recommendations for international students: Required—TOEFL (minimum score 79 iBT). *Application deadline:* For fall admission, 2/1 priority date for domestic students, 4/1 for international students; for spring admission, 11/1 priority date for domestic students, 9/1 for international students. Application fee: $50. Electronic applications accepted. *Financial support:* In 2017–18, 5 teaching assistantships with tuition reimbursements (averaging $2,750 per year) were awarded; unspecified assistantships also available. Financial award application deadline: 2/1; financial award applicants required to submit FAFSA. *Faculty research:* Sensory integration, assistive technology, aging and technology, transition for students with emotional/behavioral problems. *Unit head:* Dr. Susan Nochajski, Graduate Program Director, 716-829-6942, Fax: 716-829-3217, E-mail: phhpadv@buffalo.edu. *Application contact:* MaryAnn Venezia, Program Coordinator, 716-829-6942, Fax: 716-829-3217, E-mail: venezia3@buffalo.edu.
Website: http://sphhp.buffalo.edu/rehabilitation-science/education/occupational-therapy-bsms.html

The University of Alabama at Birmingham, School of Health Professions, Program in Occupational Therapy, Birmingham, AL 35294. Offers low vision rehabilitation (Certificate); occupational therapy (MS). *Accreditation:* AOTA. *Program availability:* Part-time, online learning. *Entrance requirements:* Additional exam requirements/recommendations for international students: Recommended—TOEFL, IELTS.

University of Alberta, Faculty of Graduate Studies and Research, Department of Occupational Therapy, Edmonton, AB T6G 2E1, Canada. Offers M Sc, PhD. *Program availability:* Part-time. *Degree requirements:* For master's, thesis. *Entrance requirements:* For master's, bachelor's degree in occupational therapy, minimum GPA of 6.9 on a 9.0 scale. Additional exam requirements/recommendations for international students: Required—TOEFL. Electronic applications accepted. *Faculty research:* Work evaluation, pediatrics, geriatrics, program evaluation, community-based rehabilitation.

The University of British Columbia, Faculty of Medicine, Department of Occupational Science and Occupational Therapy, Vancouver, BC V6T 2B5, Canada. Offers occupational therapy (MOT). *Entrance requirements:* Additional exam requirements/recommendations for international students: Required—TOEFL, IELTS. Electronic applications accepted. *Expenses:* Contact institution.

University of Central Arkansas, Graduate School, College of Health and Behavioral Sciences, Department of Occupational Therapy, Conway, AR 72035-0001. Offers MS. *Accreditation:* AOTA. *Degree requirements:* For master's, thesis optional, internship. *Entrance requirements:* For master's, GRE General Test, minimum GPA of 2.7. Additional exam requirements/recommendations for international students: Required—TOEFL (minimum score 550 paper-based; 80 iBT). *Application deadline:* For fall admission, 3/1 priority date for domestic students; for spring admission, 10/1 for domestic students. Applications are processed on a rolling basis. Application fee: $25 ($50 for international students). Electronic applications accepted. *Expenses:* Contact institution. *Financial support:* Research assistantships, Federal Work-Study, scholarships/grants, and unspecified assistantships available. Financial award application deadline: 2/15; financial award applicants required to submit FAFSA.
Website: http://uca.edu/ot/

The University of Findlay, Office of Graduate Admissions, Findlay, OH 45840. Offers applied security and analytics (MSAS); athletic training (MAT); business (MBA), including certified management accountant, certified public accountant, health care management, hospitality management; education (MA Ed, Ed D), including children's literature (MA Ed), curriculum and teaching (MA Ed), education (MA Ed), educational administration (MA Ed), human resource development (MA Ed), mathematics (MA Ed), reading (MA Ed), science education (MA Ed), superintendent (Ed D), teaching (Ed D), technology (MA Ed); environmental, safety, and health management (MSEM); health informatics (MS); occupational therapy (MOT); pharmacy (Pharm D); physical therapy (DPT); physician assistant (MPA); rhetoric and writing (MA); teaching English to speakers of other languages (TESOL) and applied linguistics (MA). *Program availability:* Part-time, evening/weekend, 100% online, blended/hybrid learning. *Students:* 688 full-time (430 women), 553 part-time (308 women), 170 international. Average age 28. In 2017, 366 master's, 137 doctorates awarded. *Degree requirements:* For master's, comprehensive exam (for some programs), thesis (for some programs), cumulative project, capstone project; for doctorate, thesis/dissertation (for some programs). *Entrance requirements:* For master's, GRE/GMAT, bachelor's degree from accredited institution, minimum undergraduate GPA of 2.5 in last 64 hours of course work; for doctorate, GRE, MAT, minimum cumulative GPA of 3.0. Additional exam requirements/recommendations for international students: Required—TOEFL (minimum score 79 iBT), IELTS (minimum score 7), PTE (minimum score 61). *Application deadline:* Applications are processed on a rolling basis. Electronic applications accepted. *Financial support:* In 2017–18, 10 research assistantships with partial tuition reimbursements (averaging $7,200 per year), 35 teaching assistantships with partial tuition reimbursements (averaging $7,200 per year) were awarded; Federal Work-Study, institutionally sponsored loans, and unspecified assistantships also available. Financial award applicants required to submit FAFSA. *Unit head:* Christopher M. Harris, Director of Admissions, 419-434-4347, E-mail: harrisc1@findlay.edu. *Application contact:* Madeline Fauser Brennan, Graduate Admissions Counselor, 419-434-4636, Fax: 419-434-4898, E-mail: fauserbrennan@findlay.edu.
Website: http://www.findlay.edu/admissions/graduate/Pages/default.aspx

University of Florida, Graduate School, College of Public Health and Health Professions, Department of Occupational Therapy, Gainesville, FL 32611. Offers MHS, MOT. *Accreditation:* AOTA. *Degree requirements:* For master's, clinical rotations. *Entrance requirements:* For master's, GRE General Test, minimum GPA of 3.0. Additional exam requirements/recommendations for international students: Required—TOEFL (minimum score 550 paper-based; 80 iBT), IELTS (minimum score 6). Electronic applications accepted. *Faculty research:* Rehabilitation intervention outcomes assessment, safe driving and community participation, assessment of driving skills and impact on participation, stroke and upper extremity rehabilitation, effective rehabilitation outcomes, community participation in families and children with muscular dystrophy, assessment of the impact of MD on community participation, assistive technology, AT effectiveness and availability.

University of Illinois at Chicago, College of Applied Health Sciences, Department of Occupational Therapy, Chicago, IL 60607-7128. Offers MS, OTD. *Accreditation:* AOTA. *Program availability:* Part-time. *Degree requirements:* For master's, thesis. *Entrance requirements:* For master's, GRE General Test, minimum GPA of 2.75, previous course work in statistics. Additional exam requirements/recommendations for international students: Required—TOEFL. Electronic applications accepted. *Expenses:* Contact institution. *Faculty research:* Sensory integration, perception, play, treatment efficacy, instrument development.

University of Indianapolis, Graduate Programs, College of Health Sciences, School of Occupational Therapy, Indianapolis, IN 46227-3697. Offers MOT, DHS, OTD. *Accreditation:* AOTA. *Program availability:* Part-time, evening/weekend. *Degree requirements:* For master's, thesis. *Entrance requirements:* For master's, minimum GPA of 3.0, interview; for doctorate, minimum GPA of 3.3, BA/BS or MA/MS from occupational therapy program, current state license, currently in practice as occupational therapist or have 1000 hours of practice in last 5 years. Additional exam requirements/recommendations for international students: Required—TOEFL (minimum score 550 paper-based; 92 iBT), TWE (minimum score 5). *Expenses:* Contact institution.

The University of Kansas, University of Kansas Medical Center, School of Health Professions, Department of Occupational Therapy Education, Kansas City, KS 66160. Offers occupational therapy (MOT, OTD); therapeutic science (PhD). *Accreditation:* AOTA. *Program availability:* Part-time. *Faculty:* 15. *Students:* 127 full-time (113 women), 25 part-time (22 women); includes 18 minority (1 Black or African American, non-Hispanic/Latino; 1 American Indian or Alaska Native, non-Hispanic/Latino; 4 Asian, non-Hispanic/Latino; 7 Hispanic/Latino; 5 Two or more races, non-Hispanic/Latino), 5 international. Average age 27. 218 applicants, 22% accepted, 48 enrolled. In 2017, 36 master's, 3 doctorates awarded. *Degree requirements:* For doctorate, comprehensive exam, thesis/dissertation, oral defense. *Entrance requirements:* For master's, 40 hours of paid work or volunteer experience working directly with people with special needs, 3 letters of recommendation, personal statement, program statement of interest, bachelor's degree with 40 hours of prerequisite work, minimum GPA of 3.0; for doctorate, 24 hours of master's-level research. Additional exam requirements/recommendations for international students: Required—TOEFL; Recommended—IELTS. *Application deadline:* For fall admission, 12/1 for domestic students, 4/1 for international students. Application fee: $60. Electronic applications accepted. *Financial support:* In 2017–18, 2 teaching assistantships with full and partial tuition reimbursements were awarded; research assistantships with partial tuition reimbursements, scholarships/grants, traineeships, and unspecified assistantships also

available. Financial award application deadline: 3/1; financial award applicants required to submit FAFSA. *Faculty research:* Impact of sensory processing in everyday life; improving balance, motor skills, and independence with community nonprofit organizations serving people with special needs; improving self-confidence and self-sufficiency with poverty-based services in community; working with autism population in a community-wide aquatics program; improving quality of life of people living with cancer and chronic illness. *Total annual research expenditures:* $12,331. *Unit head:* Dr. Winifred W. Dunn, Professor/Chair, 913-588-7195, Fax: 913-588-4568, E-mail: wdunn@kumc.edu. *Application contact:* Wendy Hildenbrand, Admissions Representative, 913-588-7174, Fax: 913-588-4568, E-mail: whildenb@kumc.edu.
Website: http://www.kumc.edu/school-of-health-professions/occupational-therapy-education.html

University of Louisiana at Monroe, Graduate School, College of Health and Pharmaceutical Sciences, Department of Occupational Therapy, Monroe, LA 71209-0001. Offers MOT. *Accreditation:* AOTA. *Faculty:* 4 full-time (all women), 1 (woman) part-time/adjunct. *Students:* 60 full-time (46 women), 29 part-time (23 women); includes 26 minority (6 Black or African American, non-Hispanic/Latino; 1 American Indian or Alaska Native, non-Hispanic/Latino; 1 Asian, non-Hispanic/Latino; 9 Hispanic/Latino; 9 Two or more races, non-Hispanic/Latino). Average age 32. 59 applicants, 51% accepted, 29 enrolled. In 2017, 25 master's awarded. Application fee: $50. *Expenses:* Tuition, state resident: full-time $6489; part-time $479 per hour. Tuition, nonresident: full-time $12,100; part-time $479 per hour. *Required fees:* $8860; $802 per hour. $3273 per semester. *Financial support:* In 2017–18, 38 students received support. *Unit head:* Dr. Patti Calk, Program Director, 318-342-5581, E-mail: calk@ulm.edu.
Website: http://www.ulm.edu/ot/

University of Manitoba, Faculty of Graduate Studies, College of Rehabilitation Sciences, Winnipeg, MB R3T 2N2, Canada. Offers applied health sciences (PhD); occupational therapy (MOT); physical therapy (MPT); rehabilitation sciences (M Sc).

University of Mary, School of Health Sciences, Program in Occupational Therapy, Bismarck, ND 58504-9652. Offers MSOT. *Accreditation:* AOTA. *Program availability:* Part-time, online learning. *Degree requirements:* For master's, thesis or alternative, seminar. *Entrance requirements:* For master's, minimum cumulative GPA of 3.0, 48 hours of volunteer experience, 3 letters of reference. Additional exam requirements/recommendations for international students: Required—TOEFL (minimum score 550 paper-based). Electronic applications accepted. *Expenses:* Contact institution. *Faculty research:* Safe homes for well elderly, occupation and spirituality, professional development in the spiritual domain, case method instruction, ergonomics, assistive technology.

University of Minnesota Rochester, Graduate Programs, Rochester, MN 55904. Offers bioinformatics and computational biology (MS, PhD); business administration (MBA); occupational therapy (MOT).

University of Mississippi Medical Center, School of Health Related Professions, Department of Occupational Therapy, Jackson, MS 39216-4505. Offers MOT. *Accreditation:* AOTA.

University of Missouri, School of Health Professions, Program in Occupational Therapy, Columbia, MO 65211. Offers MOT. *Accreditation:* AOTA. *Entrance requirements:* Additional exam requirements/recommendations for international students: Required—TOEFL. *Application deadline:* Applications are processed on a rolling basis. Electronic applications accepted. *Expenses:* Tuition, state resident: full-time $6480. Tuition, nonresident: full-time $17,744. *Required fees:* $1108. Tuition and fees vary according to course load, campus/location and program.
Website: http://shp.missouri.edu/ot/degrees.php

University of New England, Westbrook College of Health Professions, Biddeford, ME 04005-9526. Offers nurse anesthesia (MSNA); occupational therapy (MS); physical therapy (DPT); physician assistant (MS); social work (MSW). *Program availability:* Part-time. *Faculty:* 43 full-time (30 women), 26 part-time/adjunct (19 women). *Students:* 527 full-time (401 women), 5 part-time (4 women); includes 50 minority (11 Black or African American, non-Hispanic/Latino; 1 American Indian or Alaska Native, non-Hispanic/Latino; 24 Asian, non-Hispanic/Latino; 5 Hispanic/Latino; 1 Native Hawaiian or other Pacific Islander, non-Hispanic/Latino; 8 Two or more races, non-Hispanic/Latino), 1 international. Average age 27. 2,499 applicants, 18% accepted, 226 enrolled. In 2017, 440 master's, 71 doctorates awarded. *Application deadline:* Applications are processed on a rolling basis. Electronic applications accepted. Tuition and fees vary according to degree level, program and student level. *Financial support:* Application deadline: 5/1; applicants required to submit FAFSA. *Unit head:* Dr. Elizabeth Francis- Connolly, Dean, Westbrook College of Health Professions, 207-221-4523, E-mail: efrancisconnolly@une.edu. *Application contact:* Scott Steinberg, Dean of University Admission, 207-221-4225, Fax: 207-523-1925, E-mail: ssteinberg@une.edu.
Website: http://www.une.edu/wchp/index.cfm

University of New Hampshire, Graduate School, College of Health and Human Services, Department of Occupational Therapy, Durham, NH 03824. Offers assistive technology (Postbaccalaureate Certificate); occupational therapy (MS). *Accreditation:* AOTA. *Program availability:* Part-time. *Students:* 136 full-time (122 women), 7 part-time (all women); includes 5 minority (1 Black or African American, non-Hispanic/Latino; 2 Asian, non-Hispanic/Latino; 2 Hispanic/Latino), 2 international. Average age 24. 114 applicants, 67% accepted, 67 enrolled. In 2017, 62 master's, 7 other advanced degrees awarded. *Entrance requirements:* For master's, OT Course Prerequisite Verification Form. Additional exam requirements/recommendations for international students: Required—TOEFL (minimum score 550 paper-based; 80 iBT). *Application deadline:* For fall admission, 1/15 for domestic and international students. Application fee: $65. Electronic applications accepted. *Financial support:* In 2017–18, 4 students received support. Fellowships, research assistantships, teaching assistantships, career-related internships or fieldwork, Federal Work-Study, and scholarships/grants available. Support available to part-time students. Financial award application deadline: 2/15. *Unit head:* Lou Ann Griswold, Chair, 603-862-3416. *Application contact:* Deb Smith, Administrative Assistant, 603-862-3221, E-mail: deb.smith@unh.edu.
Website: http://www.chhs.unh.edu/ot

University of New Mexico, Graduate Studies, Health Sciences Center, Program in Occupational Therapy, Albuquerque, NM 87131-5196. Offers MOT. *Accreditation:* AOTA. *Program availability:* Part-time. *Faculty:* 7 full-time (all women), 1 (woman) part-time/adjunct. *Students:* 88 full-time (73 women), 5 part-time (4 women); includes 38 minority (2 Black or African American, non-Hispanic/Latino; 3 American Indian or Alaska Native, non-Hispanic/Latino; 4 Asian, non-Hispanic/Latino; 27 Hispanic/Latino; 2 Two or more races, non-Hispanic/Latino). Average age 32. 66 applicants, 39% accepted, 26 enrolled. In 2017, 23 master's awarded. *Degree requirements:* For master's, thesis, clinical fieldwork. *Entrance requirements:* For master's, interview, writing sample, volunteer experience. *Application deadline:* For fall admission, 12/1 priority date for domestic students. Applications are processed on a rolling basis. Application fee: $50. Electronic applications accepted. *Financial support:* Research assistantships, Federal Work-Study, institutionally sponsored loans, scholarships/grants, traineeships, and unspecified assistantships available. Financial award application deadline: 3/1; financial award applicants required to submit FAFSA. *Faculty research:* Sensory processing, scleroderma treatment, use of therapy dogs, educational scholarship. *Total annual research expenditures:* $290,062. *Unit head:* Dr. Betsy VanLeit, Director, 505-272-1753, Fax: 505-272-3583, E-mail: bvanleit@salud.unm.edu. *Application contact:* Janet Werner, Coordinator, 505-272-1753, Fax: 505-272-3583, E-mail: werner@salud.unm.edu.
Website: http://hsc.unm.edu/som/ot/

The University of North Carolina at Chapel Hill, School of Medicine and Graduate School, Graduate Programs in Medicine, Department of Allied Health Sciences, Division of Occupational Science and Occupational Therapy, Chapel Hill, NC 27599. Offers occupational science (PhD); occupational therapy (MS). *Accreditation:* AOTA. *Degree requirements:* For master's, comprehensive exam, thesis optional, collaborative research project; for doctorate, thesis/dissertation. *Entrance requirements:* For master's, GRE General Test; for doctorate, GRE, master's degree in occupational therapy, relevant social behavioral sciences or health field. Additional exam requirements/recommendations for international students: Required—TOEFL (minimum score 550 paper-based). Electronic applications accepted. *Faculty research:* Parents and infants in co-occupations, psychosocial dysfunction, predictors of autism, factors influencing the occupation of primates, factors influencing occupations of people with dementia, occupational development of young children.

University of North Dakota, Graduate School and Graduate School, Graduate Programs in Medicine, Department of Occupational Therapy, Grand Forks, ND 58202. Offers MOT. *Accreditation:* AOTA. *Program availability:* Part-time. *Entrance requirements:* For master's, letter of reference; volunteer or work experience, preferably from health-related field; interview; minimum GPA of 2.7. Additional exam requirements/recommendations for international students: Required—TOEFL (minimum score 550 paper-based; 79 iBT), IELTS (minimum score 6.5). Electronic applications accepted.

University of Oklahoma Health Sciences Center, Graduate College, College of Allied Health, Department of Occupational Therapy, Oklahoma City, OK 73190. Offers MOT. *Accreditation:* AOTA.

University of Pittsburgh, School of Health and Rehabilitation Sciences, Department of Occupational Therapy, Pittsburgh, PA 15260. Offers MS, CScD, OTD. *Accreditation:* AOTA. *Program availability:* Online learning. *Faculty:* 15 full-time (14 women). *Students:* 103 full-time (98 women), 3 part-time (2 women); includes 12 minority (2 Black or African American, non-Hispanic/Latino; 5 Asian, non-Hispanic/Latino; 4 Hispanic/Latino; 1 Two or more races, non-Hispanic/Latino). Average age 25. 170 applicants, 59% accepted, 52 enrolled. In 2017, 53 master's awarded. *Degree requirements:* For master's and doctorate, comprehensive exam (for some programs). *Entrance requirements:* For master's and doctorate, GRE General Test. Additional exam requirements/recommendations for international students: Required—TOEFL (minimum score 550 paper-based; 80 iBT), IELTS (minimum score 6.5). *Application deadline:* For summer admission, 2/1 for domestic and international students. Application fee: $140. Electronic applications accepted. *Financial support:* In 2017–18, 2 fellowships with full tuition reimbursements (averaging $28,770 per year), 5 research assistantships (averaging $22,590 per year) were awarded; career-related internships or fieldwork, Federal Work-Study, scholarships/grants, traineeships, and unspecified assistantships also available. *Faculty research:* Biobehavioral rehabilitation; illness, injury and disability prevention; vocational and life skills training; cognition and everyday activities with and without impairment; palliative care. *Total annual research expenditures:* $772,055. *Unit head:* Dr. Elizabeth Skidmore, Chair/Associate Professor, 412-383-6617, Fax: 412-383-6613, E-mail: skidmore@pitt.edu. *Application contact:* Jessica Maguire, Director of Admissions, 412-383-6557, Fax: 412-383-6535, E-mail: maguire@pitt.edu.
Website: http://www.shrs.pitt.edu/ot

University of Puerto Rico–Medical Sciences Campus, School of Health Professions, Program in Occupational Therapy, San Juan, PR 00936-5067. Offers MS. *Accreditation:* AOTA.

University of Puget Sound, School of Occupational Therapy, Tacoma, WA 98416. Offers MSOT, Dr OT. *Accreditation:* AOTA. *Degree requirements:* For master's, thesis, publishable paper or program development project. *Entrance requirements:* For master's, GRE General Test, minimum baccalaureate GPA of 3.0, three letters of recommendation. Additional exam requirements/recommendations for international students: Required—TOEFL (minimum score 550 paper-based; 90 iBT). Electronic applications accepted. *Expenses:* Contact institution.

University of St. Augustine for Health Sciences, Graduate Programs, Doctor of Occupational Therapy Program, San Marcos, CA 92069. Offers OTD. Program offered in Austin TX and San Marcos CA.

University of St. Augustine for Health Sciences, Graduate Programs, Master of Occupational Therapy Program, San Marcos, CA 92069. Offers MOT. *Accreditation:* AOTA. *Entrance requirements:* For master's, GRE General Test. Application fee is waived when completed online.

University of St. Augustine for Health Sciences, Graduate Programs, Post Professional Programs, San Marcos, CA 92069. Offers health science (DH Sc); health sciences education (Ed D); occupational therapy (TOTD); physical therapy (TDPT). *Program availability:* Part-time, online learning. *Entrance requirements:* For doctorate, GRE General Test, master's degree in related field. Additional exam requirements/recommendations for international students: Required—TOEFL.

The University of Scranton, Panuska College of Professional Studies, Program in Occupational Therapy, Scranton, PA 18510. Offers MS. *Accreditation:* AOTA. *Degree requirements:* For master's, comprehensive exam (for some programs), thesis (for some programs), capstone experience. *Entrance requirements:* For master's, minimum GPA of 3.0, three letters of reference. Additional exam requirements/recommendations for international students: Required—TOEFL (minimum score 500 paper-based; 80 iBT), IELTS (minimum score 6.5). Electronic applications accepted. *Faculty research:* Low vision; developmental visual perception; home safety for elderly; history of occupational therapy; telehealth.

University of South Alabama, Pat Capps Covey College of Allied Health Professions, Department of Occupational Therapy, Mobile, AL 36688. Offers MS. *Accreditation:* AOTA. *Faculty:* 6 full-time (all women), 1 (woman) part-time/adjunct. *Students:* 86 full-time (80 women); includes 2 minority (1 Native Hawaiian or other Pacific Islander, non-Hispanic/Latino; 1 Two or more races, non-Hispanic/Latino). Average age 24. 199 applicants, 32% accepted, 27 enrolled. In 2017, 29 master's awarded. *Degree requirements:* For master's, clinical externship. *Entrance requirements:* For master's, GRE, minimum GPA of 3.0; bachelor's degree or 96 semester hours of prerequisites and electives; minimum of 25 documented OT observation hours. Additional exam requirements/recommendations for international students: Required—TOEFL (minimum score 600 paper-based; 100 iBT), TWE (minimum score 5.5). *Application deadline:* For fall admission, 12/1 for domestic and international students. Application fee: $75. Electronic applications accepted. *Expenses:* Contact institution. *Financial support:* Fellowships, research assistantships, teaching assistantships, career-related internships or fieldwork, Federal Work-Study, institutionally sponsored loans, scholarships/grants, and unspecified assistantships available. Support available to part-time students. Financial award application deadline: 3/31; financial award applicants

required to submit FAFSA. *Unit head:* Dr. Donna M. Wooster, Chair, 251-445-9222, Fax: 251-445-9211, E-mail: otdept@southalabama.edu. *Application contact:* Dr. Susan Gordon-Hickey, Associate Dean, Allied Health, 251-445-9250, Fax: 251-460-9259, E-mail: gordonhickey@southalabama.edu.
Website: http://www.southalabama.edu/colleges/alliedhealth/ot/

University of South Dakota, Graduate School, School of Health Sciences, Department of Occupational Therapy, Vermillion, SD 57069. Offers occupational therapy (OTD); post-professional clinical occupational therapy (OTD). *Accreditation:* AOTA. *Program availability:* Part-time. *Degree requirements:* For master's, thesis optional, 6 months of supervised fieldwork. *Entrance requirements:* For master's, courses in human anatomy, human physiology, general psychology, abnormal psychology, lifespan development, and statistics. Additional exam requirements/recommendations for international students: Required—TOEFL (minimum score 550 paper-based). *Application deadline:* For fall admission, 10/1 priority date for domestic and international students. Applications are processed on a rolling basis. Application fee: $35. *Expenses:* Contact institution. *Financial support:* Research assistantships with partial tuition reimbursements, teaching assistantships with partial tuition reimbursements, scholarships/grants, and traineeships available. Financial award application deadline: 3/1; financial award applicants required to submit FAFSA. *Faculty research:* Low vision in youth and adults, agricultural/rural health, childhood obesity, adolescent mental health, elder health and well being. *Application contact:* Graduate School, 605-658-6140, Fax: 605-677-6118, E-mail: grad@usd.edu.
Website: http://www.usd.edu/ot

University of Southern California, Graduate School, Herman Ostrow School of Dentistry, Chan Division of Occupational Science and Occupational Therapy, Graduate Program in Occupational Science, Los Angeles, CA 90089. Offers PhD. *Accreditation:* AOTA. *Degree requirements:* For doctorate, thesis/dissertation, qualifying exam. *Entrance requirements:* For doctorate, GRE (minimum combined score of 1100), minimum GPA of 3.0. Additional exam requirements/recommendations for international students: Required—TOEFL (minimum score 600 paper-based; 100 iBT). Electronic applications accepted. *Faculty research:* Health and well-being; health disparities and cultural influences on health and recovery; family life; community re-integration and social participation; engagement, activity and neuroscience; rehabilitation science and ethics; society and social justice; autism and sensory integration; interventions; health disparities in autism diagnosis.

University of Southern California, Graduate School, Herman Ostrow School of Dentistry, Chan Division of Occupational Science and Occupational Therapy, Graduate Programs in Occupational Therapy, Los Angeles, CA 90089. Offers MA, OTD. *Accreditation:* AOTA. *Program availability:* Part-time. *Degree requirements:* For master's, comprehensive exam (for some programs), thesis or alternative; for doctorate, residency, portfolio. *Entrance requirements:* For master's and doctorate, GRE (minimum score 1000), minimum cumulative GPA of 3.0. Additional exam requirements/recommendations for international students: Required—TOEFL (minimum score 600 paper-based; 100 iBT). Electronic applications accepted. *Faculty research:* Health and well-being; health disparities and cultural influences on health and recovery; family life; community re-integration and social participation; engagement, activity and neuroscience; rehabilitation science and ethics; society and social justice; autism and sensory integration; interventions; health disparities in autism diagnosis.

University of Southern Indiana, Graduate Studies, College of Nursing and Health Professions, Program in Occupational Therapy, Evansville, IN 47712-3590. Offers MSOT. *Accreditation:* AOTA. *Program availability:* Part-time. *Faculty:* 1 full-time (0 women). *Students:* 59 full-time (49 women), 2 part-time (both women); includes 2 minority (1 Black or African American, non-Hispanic/Latino; 1 Two or more races, non-Hispanic/Latino). Average age 24. In 2017, 30 master's awarded. *Entrance requirements:* For master's, minimum GPA of 3.0, two letters of recommendation (one professional letter from previous employer or practicing OT; one academic letter from professor or advisor from undergraduate degree). Additional exam requirements/recommendations for international students: Required—TOEFL (minimum score 550 paper-based; 79 iBT), IELTS (minimum score 6). *Application deadline:* For fall admission, 2/15 for domestic and international students. Applications are processed on a rolling basis. Application fee: $40. Electronic applications accepted. *Expenses:* Contact institution. *Financial support:* In 2017–18, 6 students received support. Federal Work-Study, scholarships/grants, tuition waivers (full and partial), and unspecified assistantships available. Financial award application deadline: 3/1; financial award applicants required to submit FAFSA. *Unit head:* Dr. Mary Kay Arvin, Program Chair, 812-465-1103, E-mail: mkarvin@usi.edu. *Application contact:* Dr. Mayola Rowser, Director, Graduate Studies, 812-465-7015, Fax: 812-464-1956, E-mail: mrowser@usi.edu.
Website: http://www.usi.edu/health/occupational-therapy

University of Southern Maine, Lewiston-Auburn College, Program in Occupational Therapy, Lewiston, ME 04240. Offers MOT. *Accreditation:* AOTA. *Degree requirements:* For master's, fieldwork, original research. *Entrance requirements:* For master's, minimum GPA of 3.0, writing sample, interview, reference letters, job shadow observation. Electronic applications accepted. *Faculty research:* Multicultural curricula, cultural competence, parents responses to fussy infants, chronic pain, early childhood eating disorders.

The University of Tennessee at Chattanooga, Department of Occupational Therapy, Chattanooga, TN 37403-2598. Offers OTD. *Faculty:* 4 full-time (all women), 1 (woman) part-time/adjunct. *Students:* 64 full-time (62 women), 1 (woman) part-time; includes 7 minority (2 Hispanic/Latino; 5 Two or more races, non-Hispanic/Latino). Average age 24. 32 applicants, 88% accepted, 24 enrolled. In 2017, 13 doctorates awarded. *Degree requirements:* For doctorate, thesis/dissertation, internship. *Entrance requirements:* For doctorate, GRE General Test, OTCAS application. Additional exam requirements/recommendations for international students: Required—TOEFL (minimum score 550 paper-based; 79 iBT), IELTS (minimum score 6). *Application deadline:* For fall admission, 6/15 priority date for domestic students, 7/1 for international students; for spring admission, 11/1 priority date for domestic students, 11/1 for international students. Applications are processed on a rolling basis. Application fee: $35 ($40 for international students). Electronic applications accepted. *Expenses:* Contact institution. *Financial support:* Fellowships, research assistantships, career-related internships or fieldwork, scholarships/grants, and unspecified assistantships available. Support available to part-time students. Financial award application deadline: 7/1; financial award applicants required to submit FAFSA. *Unit head:* Susan McDonald, Department Head, 423-425-5759, E-mail: susan-mcdonald@utc.edu. *Application contact:* Dr. Joanne Romagni, Dean of the Graduate School, 423-425-4478, Fax: 423-425-5223, E-mail: joanne-romagni@utc.edu.
Website: http://www.utc.edu/occupational-therapy/

The University of Tennessee Health Science Center, College of Health Professions, Memphis, TN 38163-0002. Offers audiology (MS, Au D); clinical laboratory science (MSCLS); cytopathology practice (MCP); health informatics and information management (MHIIM); occupational therapy (MOT); physical therapy (DPT, ScDPT); physician assistant (MMS); speech-language pathology (MS). *Accreditation:* AOTA; APTA. *Program availability:* Part-time, evening/weekend, online learning. Terminal master's awarded for partial completion of doctoral program. *Degree requirements:* For master's, comprehensive exam, thesis; for doctorate, comprehensive exam, residency. *Entrance requirements:* For master's, GRE (MOT, MSCLS), minimum GPA of 3.0, 3 letters of reference, national accreditation (MSCLS), GRE if GPA is less than 3.0 (MCP); for doctorate, GRE. Additional exam requirements/recommendations for international students: Required—TOEFL (minimum score 550 paper-based; 80 iBT). Electronic applications accepted. *Expenses:* Contact institution. *Faculty research:* Gait deviation, muscular dystrophy and strength, hemophilia and exercise, pediatric neurology, self-efficacy.

The University of Texas at El Paso, Graduate School, College of Health Sciences, Master of Occupational Therapy Program, El Paso, TX 79968-0001. Offers MOT. *Accreditation:* AOTA. *Degree requirements:* For master's, thesis optional. *Entrance requirements:* For master's, GRE, minimum cumulative and prerequisite GPA of 3.0, bachelor's degree, 40 clock hours of supervised observations with an OT. Additional exam requirements/recommendations for international students: Required—TOEFL; Recommended—IELTS. *Application deadline:* For fall admission, 10/15 for domestic and international students; for spring admission, 11/1 for domestic students, 9/3 for international students. Application fee: $45 ($80 for international students). *Financial support:* Fellowships with partial tuition reimbursements, research assistantships with partial tuition reimbursements, teaching assistantships with partial tuition reimbursements, institutionally sponsored loans, scholarships/grants, health care benefits, tuition waivers (partial), and unspecified assistantships available. Support available to part-time students. Financial award application deadline: 3/15; financial award applicants required to submit FAFSA. *Faculty research:* Falls prevention, coping of mothers with children with disabilities.
Website: https://www.utep.edu/chs/ot/

The University of Texas Health Science Center at San Antonio, School of Health Professions, San Antonio, TX 78229-3900. Offers occupational therapy (MOT); physical therapy (DPT); physician assistant studies (MS); speech language pathology (MS). *Accreditation:* AOTA; APTA; ARC-PA; ASHA. *Degree requirements:* For master's, comprehensive exam, thesis (for some programs); for doctorate, comprehensive exam.

The University of Texas Medical Branch, School of Health Professions, Department of Occupational Therapy, Galveston, TX 77555. Offers MOT. *Accreditation:* AOTA. *Entrance requirements:* For master's, MAT, 20 volunteer hours, telephone interview, 2 references.

The University of Texas Rio Grande Valley, College of Health Affairs, Department of Occupational Therapy, Edinburg, TX 78539. Offers MS. *Accreditation:* AOTA. *Program availability:* Evening/weekend. *Faculty:* 6 full-time (1 woman), 1 (woman) part-time/adjunct. *Students:* 61 full-time (50 women); includes 55 minority (1 Black or African American, non-Hispanic/Latino; 5 Asian, non-Hispanic/Latino; 49 Hispanic/Latino). Average age 24. 66 applicants, 48% accepted, 31 enrolled. In 2017, 21 master's awarded. *Degree requirements:* For master's, National Board of Certified Occupational Therapist (NBCOT) Practice Exam. *Entrance requirements:* For master's, Health Occupations Aptitude Examination. *Application deadline:* For fall admission, 5/31 for domestic students; for winter admission, 11/1 priority date for domestic students. Application fee: $35. *Expenses:* Tuition, state resident: full-time $5550; part-time $417 per credit hour. Tuition, nonresident: full-time $13,020; part-time $832 per credit hour. *Required fees:* $1169. *Financial support:* In 2017–18, 3 research assistantships were awarded; fellowships, Federal Work-Study, institutionally sponsored loans, scholarships/grants, traineeships, and unspecified assistantships also available. *Faculty research:* Recruiting African Americans into Hispanic serving institution graduate health programs; pedagogy for diversity students; efficiency of pediatric OT evaluations; driving skills among individuals with disabilities; physical activities vs. academic performance. *Total annual research expenditures:* $106,000. *Unit head:* Dr. Shirley A. Wells, Chair, 956-665-2475, E-mail: shirley.wells@utrgv.edu. *Application contact:* Stephanie Ozuna, Graduate Student Recruiter, 956-665-3558, E-mail: stephanie.ozuna@utrgv.edu.
Website: http://www.utrgv.edu/ot

University of the Sciences, Program in Occupational Therapy, Philadelphia, PA 19104-4495. Offers MOT, Dr OT. *Accreditation:* AOTA. *Program availability:* Online learning. *Degree requirements:* For doctorate, capstone project. *Entrance requirements:* For doctorate, master's degree, two years of occupational therapy practice experience, 500-word essay. Electronic applications accepted.

The University of Toledo, College of Graduate Studies, College of Health and Human Services, School of Exercise and Rehabilitation Sciences, Toledo, OH 43606-3390. Offers athletic training (MSES); exercise physiology (MSES); exercise science (PhD); occupational therapy (OTD); physical therapy (DPT); recreation and leisure studies (MA), including recreation administration, recreation therapy. *Degree requirements:* For master's, comprehensive exam, thesis; for doctorate, thesis/dissertation or alternative. *Entrance requirements:* For master's, GRE, minimum cumulative GPA of 2.7 for all previous academic work, letters of recommendation; for doctorate, GRE, minimum cumulative GPA of 3.0 for all previous academic work, letters of recommendation; OTCAS or PTCAS application and UT supplemental application (for OTD and DPT). Additional exam requirements/recommendations for international students: Required—TOEFL (minimum score 550 paper-based; 80 iBT). Electronic applications accepted.

University of Toronto, Faculty of Medicine, Department of Occupational Science and Occupational Therapy, Toronto, ON M5S 1A1, Canada. Offers occupational therapy (M Sc OT). *Entrance requirements:* For master's, bachelor's degree with high academic standing from recognized university with minimum B average in final year, personal statement. Additional exam requirements/recommendations for international students: Required—TOEFL (minimum score 600 paper-based; 100 iBT), TWE (minimum score 5). Electronic applications accepted.

University of Utah, Graduate School, College of Health, Department of Occupational and Recreational Therapies, Salt Lake City, UT 84108. Offers MOT, OTD. *Accreditation:* AOTA. *Program availability:* Part-time, evening/weekend, 100% online. *Faculty:* 5 full-time (all women), 9 part-time/adjunct (7 women). *Students:* 100 full-time (82 women), 19 part-time (16 women); includes 18 minority (1 Black or African American, non-Hispanic/Latino; 4 Asian, non-Hispanic/Latino; 8 Hispanic/Latino; 5 Two or more races, non-Hispanic/Latino), 1 international. Average age 28. 200 applicants, 23% accepted, 34 enrolled. In 2017, 34 master's, 5 doctorates awarded. *Entrance requirements:* For master's, GRE General Test. Additional exam requirements/recommendations for international students: Required—TOEFL (minimum score 575 paper-based). *Application deadline:* For fall admission, 11/20 for domestic and international students. Application fee: $125. Electronic applications accepted. *Expenses:* Contact institution. *Financial support:* In 2017–18, 10 students received support. Career-related internships or fieldwork, Federal Work-Study, institutionally sponsored loans, scholarships/grants, and unspecified assistantships available. Financial award application deadline: 2/15; financial award applicants required to submit FAFSA. *Faculty research:* Community-based practice, occupational science, refugees, resilience, executive function, traumatic brain injury, pediatrics. *Total annual research expenditures:* $13,409. *Unit head:* Dr. Lorie Richards, Chairperson, 801-585-1069, Fax: 801-585-1001, E-mail: lorie.richards@hsc.utah.edu. *Application contact:* Kelly C. Brown, Academic Advisor, 801-585-0555, Fax: 801-585-1001, E-mail: kelly.brown@hsc.utah.edu.
Website: http://health.utah.edu/occupational-recreational-therapies/

Occupational Therapy

University of Washington, Graduate School, School of Medicine, Graduate Programs in Medicine, Department of Rehabilitation Medicine, Seattle, WA 98195-6490. Offers occupational therapy (MOT); physical therapy (DPT); prosthetics and orthotics (MPO); rehabilitation science (PhD). *Accreditation:* AOTA. *Degree requirements:* For doctorate, comprehensive exam (for some programs), thesis/dissertation (for some programs). *Entrance requirements:* For master's and doctorate, GRE. Additional exam requirements/recommendations for international students: Required—TOEFL. *Faculty research:* Biomechanics, balance, brain injury, spinal cord injury, pain, degenerative diseases.

The University of Western Ontario, Faculty of Graduate Studies, Health Sciences Division, School of Occupational Therapy, London, ON N6A 5B8, Canada. Offers M Sc. *Program availability:* Part-time. *Degree requirements:* For master's, thesis. *Entrance requirements:* For master's, Canadian BA in occupational therapy or equivalent, minimum B+ average in last 2 years of 4 year degree. Additional exam requirements/recommendations for international students: Required—TOEFL (minimum score 570 paper-based). *Faculty research:* Human occupation, clumsy children, biomechanics, learning disabilities, ergonomics.

University of Wisconsin–La Crosse, College of Science and Health, Department of Health Professions, Program in Occupational Therapy, La Crosse, WI 54601-3742. Offers MS. *Accreditation:* AOTA. *Students:* 46 full-time (43 women), 28 part-time (24 women); includes 4 minority (3 Asian, non-Hispanic/Latino; 1 Hispanic/Latino). Average age 25. 155 applicants, 28% accepted, 24 enrolled. In 2017, 23 master's awarded. *Degree requirements:* For master's, 6-month clinical internship. *Entrance requirements:* For master's, minimum GPA of 3.0, 20 job shadowing hours. Additional exam requirements/recommendations for international students: Required—TOEFL (minimum score 550 paper-based; 79 iBT). *Application deadline:* For fall admission, 1/4 for domestic students. Application fee: $50. Electronic applications accepted. *Expenses:* Contact institution. *Financial support:* Federal Work-Study, scholarships/grants, and health care benefits available. Support available to part-time students. Financial award application deadline: 3/15; financial award applicants required to submit FAFSA. *Unit head:* Dr. Peggy Denton, Director, 608-785-8470, E-mail: pdenton@uwlax.edu. *Application contact:* Brandon Schaller, Senior Graduate Student Status Examiner, 608-785-8941, E-mail: admissions@uwlax.edu.
Website: http://www.uwlax.edu/ot/

University of Wisconsin–Madison, Graduate School, School of Education, Department of Kinesiology, Occupational Therapy Program, Madison, WI 53706-1380. Offers MS, PhD. *Accreditation:* AOTA. *Degree requirements:* For doctorate, thesis/dissertation.

University of Wisconsin–Milwaukee, Graduate School, College of Health Sciences, Department of Occupational Science and Technology, Milwaukee, WI 53201-0413. Offers assistive technology and design (MS); disability and occupation (MS); ergonomics (MS); therapeutic recreation (MS). *Accreditation:* AOTA. *Students:* 86 full-time (74 women), 1 (woman) part-time; includes 6 minority (3 Asian, non-Hispanic/Latino; 1 Hispanic/Latino; 2 Two or more races, non-Hispanic/Latino), 1 international. Average age 27. 115 applicants, 30% accepted, 32 enrolled. In 2017, 22 master's awarded. *Degree requirements:* For master's, thesis or alternative. *Entrance requirements:* Additional exam requirements/recommendations for international students: Required—TOEFL (minimum score 550 paper-based; 79 iBT), IELTS (minimum score 6.5). *Application deadline:* For fall admission, 1/1 priority date for domestic students; for spring admission, 9/1 for domestic students. Applications are processed on a rolling basis. Application fee: $56 ($75 for international students). *Financial support:* Fellowships, research assistantships, teaching assistantships, and unspecified assistantships available. Support available to part-time students. Financial award application deadline: 4/15. *Unit head:* Jay Kapellusch, PhD, Department Chair, 414-229-5292, Fax: 414-229-2619, E-mail: kap@uwm.edu. *Application contact:* Bhagwant S. Sindhu, PhD, Graduate Program Coordinator, 414-229-1180, Fax: 414-229-5100, E-mail: sindhu@uwm.edu.
Website: http://uwm.edu/healthsciences/academics/occupational-science-technology/

Utica College, Program in Occupational Therapy, Utica, NY 13502-4892. Offers MS. *Accreditation:* AOTA. *Program availability:* Part-time, evening/weekend. *Faculty:* 7 full-time (all women). *Students:* 90 full-time (82 women), 1 (woman) part-time; includes 10 minority (3 Black or African American, non-Hispanic/Latino; 2 Asian, non-Hispanic/Latino; 3 Hispanic/Latino; 2 Two or more races, non-Hispanic/Latino). Average age 26. 62 applicants, 98% accepted, 58 enrolled. In 2017, 59 master's awarded. *Degree requirements:* For master's, thesis. *Entrance requirements:* For master's, physical health exam, CPR certification, 60 hours of volunteer experience, minimum GPA of 3.0. Additional exam requirements/recommendations for international students: Required—TOEFL (minimum score 525 paper-based). *Application deadline:* Applications are processed on a rolling basis. Application fee: $50. Electronic applications accepted. *Expenses:* Contact institution. *Financial support:* Career-related internships or fieldwork, scholarships/grants, tuition waivers (partial), and unspecified assistantships available. Support available to part-time students. Financial award application deadline: 3/15; financial award applicants required to submit FAFSA. *Unit head:* Cora Bruns, Director, 315-792-3125, E-mail: cbruns@utica.edu. *Application contact:* John D. Rowe, Director of Graduate Admissions, 315-792-3824, Fax: 315-792-3003, E-mail: jrowe@utica.edu.

Virginia Commonwealth University, Graduate School, School of Allied Health Professions, Department of Occupational Therapy, Richmond, VA 23284-9005. Offers MSOT, OTD. *Accreditation:* AOTA (one or more programs are accredited). *Degree requirements:* For master's, fieldwork. *Entrance requirements:* For master's, GRE General Test. Additional exam requirements/recommendations for international students: Required—TOEFL (minimum score 600 paper-based; 100 iBT); Recommended—IELTS (minimum score 6.5). Electronic applications accepted. *Faculty research:* Children with complex care needs, instrument development, carpal tunnel syndrome, development of oral-motor feeding programs, school system practice.

Virginia Commonwealth University, Graduate School, School of Allied Health Professions, Doctoral Program in Health Related Sciences, Richmond, VA 23284-9005. Offers clinical laboratory sciences (PhD); gerontology (PhD); health administration (PhD); nurse anesthesia (PhD); occupational therapy (PhD); physical therapy (PhD); radiation sciences (PhD); rehabilitation leadership (PhD). *Entrance requirements:* For doctorate, GRE General Test or MAT, minimum GPA of 3.3 in master's degree. Additional exam requirements/recommendations for international students: Required—TOEFL (minimum score 600 paper-based; 100 iBT); Recommended—IELTS (minimum score 6.5). Electronic applications accepted.

Washington University in St. Louis, School of Medicine, Program in Occupational Therapy, Saint Louis, MO 63108. Offers MSOT, OTD. *Accreditation:* AOTA. Terminal master's awarded for partial completion of doctoral program. *Degree requirements:* For master's, fieldwork experiences; for doctorate, fieldwork and apprenticeship experiences. *Entrance requirements:* For master's and doctorate, GRE General Test, bachelor's degree in another field or enrollment in an affiliated institution. Additional exam requirements/recommendations for international students: Required—TOEFL, TWE (minimum score 5). Electronic applications accepted. *Faculty research:* Brain injury, ergonomics, work performance, care giving, quality of life, rehabilitation.

Wayne State University, Eugene Applebaum College of Pharmacy and Health Sciences, Department of Health Care Sciences, Program in Occupational Therapy, Detroit, MI 48202. Offers MOT. Students begin the program as undergraduates. *Accreditation:* AOTA. *Faculty:* 10. *Students:* 28 full-time (26 women); includes 7 minority (3 Black or African American, non-Hispanic/Latino; 2 Asian, non-Hispanic/Latino; 2 Two or more races, non-Hispanic/Latino), 1 international. Average age 25. In 2017, 35 master's awarded. *Degree requirements:* For master's, fieldwork. *Entrance requirements:* For master's, minimum cumulative GPA of 3.0 and in science prerequisite coursework; personal resume; 20 contact hours under supervision of an OTR; interview; background check; OTCAS application. Additional exam requirements/recommendations for international students: Required—TOEFL (minimum score 550 paper-based; 79 iBT), Michigan English Language Assessment Battery (minimum score 85); Recommended—IELTS (minimum score 6.5), TWE (minimum score 5.5). *Application deadline:* For fall admission, 12/1 for domestic and international students. Electronic applications accepted. *Expenses:* Contact institution. *Financial support:* Scholarships/grants available. Financial award applicants required to submit FAFSA. *Faculty research:* Technology for neurorehabilitation, body shape and movement analysis, grasp and manipulation, methods of measurement of quality-of-life outcomes of the entire family of a person with chronic illnesses or disabilities, evaluating the efficacy of different types of family support interventions for persons of low socio-economic status, program evaluation for persons with disabilities across the lifespan. *Unit head:* Dr. Doreen Head, Program Director, 313-577-5884, E-mail: doreen.head@wayne.edu. *Application contact:* 617-612-2860, Fax: 313-577-1432, E-mail: cphsinfo@wayne.edu.
Website: http://cphs.wayne.edu/occupational-therapy/

West Coast University, Graduate Programs, North Hollywood, CA 91606. Offers advanced generalist (MSN); family nurse practitioner (MSN); health administration (MHA); occupational therapy (MS); pharmacy (Pharm D); physical therapy (DPT).

Western Michigan University, Graduate College, College of Health and Human Services, Department of Occupational Therapy, Kalamazoo, MI 49008. Offers MS. *Accreditation:* AOTA.

Western New England University, College of Pharmacy and Health Sciences, Doctor of Occupational Therapy Program, Springfield, MA 01119. Offers OTD. *Faculty:* 8 full-time (all women). *Students:* 29 full-time (25 women); includes 12 minority (4 Black or African American, non-Hispanic/Latino; 7 Asian, non-Hispanic/Latino; 1 Hispanic/Latino). Average age 24. 49 applicants, 80% accepted, 29 enrolled. *Degree requirements:* For doctorate, thesis/dissertation. *Entrance requirements:* For doctorate, baccalaureate degree from accredited institution, documented volunteer/observation hours, two recommendations, personal statement. Additional exam requirements/recommendations for international students: Required—TOEFL (minimum score 80 iBT). *Application deadline:* For fall admission, 4/1 priority date for domestic students. Applications are processed on a rolling basis. Application fee: $140. Electronic applications accepted. *Expenses:* $36,636 tuition, $2,775 fees. *Financial support:* Unspecified assistantships available. Financial award application deadline: 4/15; financial award applicants required to submit FAFSA. *Unit head:* Dr. Cathy Dow-Royer, Chair and Director of Occupational Therapy, 413-782-1423, E-mail: cathy.dow-royer@wne.edu. *Application contact:* Matthew Fox, Director of Admissions for Graduate Students and Adult Learners, 413-782-1410, Fax: 413-782-1777, E-mail: study@wne.edu.
Website: http://www1.wne.edu/pharmacy-and-health-sciences/academics/otd/

Western New Mexico University, Graduate Division, Program in Occupational Therapy, Silver City, NM 88062-0680. Offers MOT. *Program availability:* Part-time.

West Virginia University, School of Medicine, Morgantown, WV 26506-9600. Offers biochemistry and molecular biology (PhD); biomedical science (MS); cancer cell biology (PhD); cellular and integrative physiology (PhD); exercise physiology (MS, PhD); health sciences (MS); immunology (PhD); medicine (MD); occupational therapy (MOT); pathologists assistant (MHS); physical therapy (DPT). *Program availability:* Part-time, evening/weekend. *Students:* 781 full-time (440 women), 25 part-time (13 women); includes 140 minority (15 Black or African American, non-Hispanic/Latino; 1 American Indian or Alaska Native, non-Hispanic/Latino; 68 Asian, non-Hispanic/Latino; 37 Hispanic/Latino; 1 Native Hawaiian or other Pacific Islander, non-Hispanic/Latino; 18 Two or more races, non-Hispanic/Latino), 19 international. *Entrance requirements:* Additional exam requirements/recommendations for international students: Required—TOEFL. *Application deadline:* Applications are processed on a rolling basis. Application fee: $60. Electronic applications accepted. *Expenses:* Contact institution. *Financial support:* Fellowships, research assistantships, teaching assistantships, career-related internships or fieldwork, Federal Work-Study, institutionally sponsored loans, health care benefits, tuition waivers (full and partial), and administrative assistantships available. Financial award applicants required to submit FAFSA. *Unit head:* Dr. Clay Marsh, Executive Dean, 304-293-6607, Fax: 304-293-6627, E-mail: clay.marsh@hsc.wvu.edu. *Application contact:* Lisa M. Salati, Assistant Vice President, Graduate Education, 304-293-7759, Fax: 304-293-3080, E-mail: lsalati@hsc.wvu.edu.
Website: https://medicine.hsc.wvu.edu

Winston-Salem State University, Department of Occupational Therapy, Winston-Salem, NC 27110-0003. Offers MS. *Accreditation:* AOTA. *Entrance requirements:* For master's, GRE, 3 letters of recommendation (one from a licensed occupational therapist where volunteer or work experiences were performed; the other two from former professors or persons acquainted with academic potential); writing sample. Additional exam requirements/recommendations for international students: Required—TOEFL. Electronic applications accepted. *Faculty research:* Assistive technology, environmental adaptations, comprehensive performance evaluations.

Worcester State University, Graduate School, Program in Occupational Therapy, Worcester, MA 01602-2597. Offers MOT. *Accreditation:* AOTA. *Faculty:* 8 full-time. *Students:* 42 full-time (35 women), 18 part-time (all women); includes 1 minority (Two or more races, non-Hispanic/Latino). Average age 25. 80 applicants, 38% accepted, 26 enrolled. In 2017, 25 master's awarded. *Degree requirements:* For master's, comprehensive exam (for some programs), thesis, fieldwork. *Entrance requirements:* For master's, GRE General Test or MAT, minimum undergraduate GPA of 3.0. Additional exam requirements/recommendations for international students: Required—TOEFL (minimum score 550 paper-based; 79 iBT). *Application deadline:* For fall admission, 3/1 priority date for domestic and international students. Applications are processed on a rolling basis. Application fee: $50. Electronic applications accepted. *Expenses:* Contact institution. *Financial support:* Career-related internships or fieldwork, scholarships/grants, and unspecified assistantships available. Financial award application deadline: 3/1; financial award applicants required to submit FAFSA. *Unit head:* Dr. Cheryl Lucas, Coordinator, 508-929-8795, E-mail: clucas2@worcester.edu. *Application contact:* Sara Grady, Associate Dean, Graduate Studies and Professional Development, 508-929-8130, E-mail: sara.grady@worcester.edu.

Xavier University, College of Social Sciences, Health and Education, Department of Occupational Therapy, Cincinnati, OH 45207. Offers MOT. *Accreditation:* AOTA. *Degree requirements:* For master's, one foreign language, group research project. *Entrance requirements:* For master's, GRE (minimum of 33% average across all GRE sections - verbal, quantitative, analytical writing), minimum GPA of 3.0, completion of 40 volunteer hours, completion of all prerequisite courses with no more than 2 grades of C or lower; official transcript; personal statement; interview. Additional exam requirements/recommendations for international students: Required—TOEFL (minimum score 550 paper-based; 70 iBT) or IELTS. Electronic applications accepted. Application fee is waived when completed online. *Expenses:* Contact institution. *Faculty research:* Occupation, ethics, pediatric, occupational therapy interventions, pediatric occupational therapy assessment.

Perfusion

Milwaukee School of Engineering, MS Program in Perfusion, Milwaukee, WI 53202-3109. Offers MS. *Students:* 14 full-time (7 women). Average age 27. 69 applicants, 13% accepted, 7 enrolled. In 2017, 5 master's awarded. *Degree requirements:* For master's, comprehensive exam, thesis. *Entrance requirements:* For master's, GRE General Test (percentiles must average 50% or better), baccalaureate degree with minimum undergraduate GPA of 2.8; at least one undergraduate course in each of the following areas: physiology (or anatomy and physiology), chemistry, mathematics and physics; 3 letters of recommendation; personal interview; observation of 2 perfusion clinical cases. Additional exam requirements/recommendations for international students: Required—TOEFL (minimum score 90 iBT), IELTS (minimum score 7). *Application deadline:* Applications are processed on a rolling basis. Application fee: $0. Electronic applications accepted. *Expenses: Tuition:* Part-time $814 per credit hour. *Required fees:* $12.50 per credit hour. *Financial support:* Career-related internships or fieldwork, institutionally sponsored loans, and scholarships/grants available. Financial award application deadline: 3/15; financial award applicants required to submit FAFSA. *Faculty research:* Heart medicine. *Unit head:* Dr. Ronald Gerrits, Program Director, 414-277-7561, Fax: 414-277-7494, E-mail: gerrits@msoe.edu. *Application contact:* Brian Rutz, Graduate Admission Counselor, 414-277-7200, E-mail: rutz@msoe.edu.
Website: https://www.msoe.edu/academics/graduate-degrees/health/perfusion/

Quinnipiac University, School of Health Sciences, Program in Cardiovascular Perfusion, Hamden, CT 06518-1940. Offers MHS. *Faculty:* 1 full-time (0 women), 3 part-time/adjunct (0 women). *Students:* 8 full-time (2 women), 7 part-time (5 women); includes 2 minority (1 Black or African American, non-Hispanic/Latino; 1 Two or more races, non-Hispanic/Latino). 49 applicants, 27% accepted, 8 enrolled. In 2017, 6 master's awarded. *Entrance requirements:* For master's, bachelor's degree in science or health-related discipline from an accredited American or Canadian college or university; 2 years of health care work experience; interview. *Application deadline:* For fall admission, 2/1 for domestic students. Applications are processed on a rolling basis. Application fee: $45. Electronic applications accepted. *Financial support:* Federal Work-Study, scholarships/grants, and unspecified assistantships available. Financial award application deadline: 6/1; financial award applicants required to submit FAFSA. *Faculty research:* Methods of preventing systemic inflammatory response syndrome (SIRS) during extracorporeal circulation of blood, investigations into the role of P-selectin in causing monocyte-platelet interaction, effect of simulated cardiopulmonary bypass on platelets and other formed elements in the blood. *Unit head:* Dr. Michael Smith, Director, 203-582-3427, E-mail: graduate@qu.edu. *Application contact:* Office of Graduate Admissions, 800-462-1944, Fax: 208-582-3443, E-mail: graduate@qu.edu.
Website: http://www.qu.edu/gradperfusion

Rush University, College of Health Sciences, Program in Perfusion Technology, Chicago, IL 60612-3832. Offers MS. *Unit head:* Mindy Blackwell, Director, 312-942-7120, E-mail: charlotte_m_blackwell@rush.edu. *Application contact:* E-mail: chs_admissions@rush.edu.

The University of Arizona, College of Pharmacy, Department of Pharmacology and Toxicology, Graduate Program in Medical Pharmacology, Tucson, AZ 85721. Offers medical pharmacology (PhD); perfusion science (MS). *Degree requirements:* For master's, thesis; for doctorate, comprehensive exam, thesis/dissertation. *Entrance requirements:* For master's, GRE General Test, 3 letters of recommendation; for doctorate, GRE General Test, personal statement, 3 letters of recommendation. Additional exam requirements/recommendations for international students: Required—TOEFL (minimum score 550 paper-based; 79 iBT). Electronic applications accepted. *Faculty research:* Immunopharmacology, pharmacogenetics, pharmacogenomics, clinical pharmacology, ocularpharmacology and neuropharmacology.

University of Nebraska Medical Center, College of Allied Health Professions, Program in Clinical Perfusion Education, Omaha, NE 68198-4144. Offers distance education perfusion education (MPS); perfusion science (MPS). *Accreditation:* NAACLS. *Program availability:* Online learning. *Degree requirements:* For master's, comprehensive exam, thesis. *Entrance requirements:* For master's, GRE. Electronic applications accepted. *Expenses:* Tuition, state resident: full-time $8451; part-time $4225 per semester. Tuition, nonresident: full-time $24,219; part-time $11,295 per semester. *Required fees:* $589; $117 per term. *Faculty research:* Platelet gel, hemoconcentrators.

Physical Therapy

Adventist University of Health Sciences, Program in Physical Therapy, Orlando, FL 32803. Offers DPT. *Entrance requirements:* For doctorate, minimum GPA of 3.0.

Alabama State University, College of Health Sciences, Department of Physical Therapy, Montgomery, AL 36101-0271. Offers DPT. *Accreditation:* APTA. *Faculty:* 7 full-time (6 women), 3 part-time/adjunct (0 women). *Students:* 70 full-time (41 women), 2 part-time (0 women); includes 28 minority (19 Black or African American, non-Hispanic/Latino; 5 Asian, non-Hispanic/Latino; 2 Hispanic/Latino; 2 Two or more races, non-Hispanic/Latino), 3 international. Average age 22. 139 applicants, 18% accepted, 24 enrolled. In 2017, 21 doctorates awarded. Terminal master's awarded for partial completion of doctoral program. *Degree requirements:* For doctorate, thesis/dissertation or alternative. *Entrance requirements:* Additional exam requirements/recommendations for international students: Required—TOEFL (minimum score 500 paper-based). *Application deadline:* For fall admission, 4/15 for domestic and international students; for spring admission, 11/15 for domestic and international students; for summer admission, 3/15 for domestic and international students. Applications are processed on a rolling basis. Application fee: $25. Electronic applications accepted. *Expenses:* Tuition, state resident: part-time $412 per credit hour. Tuition, nonresident: part-time $824 per credit hour. *Required fees:* $685 per semester. *Financial support:* Application deadline: 6/30; applicants required to submit FAFSA. *Unit head:* Dr. Susan Denham, Interim Chair, 334-229-4709, Fax: 334-229-4945, E-mail: asupt@alasu.edu. *Application contact:* Dr. William Person, Dean of Graduate Studies, 334-229-4274, Fax: 334-229-4928, E-mail: wperson@alasu.edu.
Website: http://www.alasu.edu/academics/colleges—departments/health-sciences/physical-therapy/index.aspx

American International College, School of Health Sciences, Springfield, MA 01109-3189. Offers exercise science (MS); family nurse practitioner (MSN, Post-Master's Certificate); nursing administrator (MSN); nursing educator (MSN); occupational therapy (MSOT, OTD); physical therapy (DPT). *Program availability:* Part-time, 100% online. *Faculty:* 14 full-time (13 women), 10 part-time/adjunct (all women). *Students:* 286 full-time (220 women), 11 part-time (9 women); includes 75 minority (30 Black or African American, non-Hispanic/Latino; 21 Asian, non-Hispanic/Latino; 19 Hispanic/Latino; 5 Two or more races, non-Hispanic/Latino), 2 international. Average age 27. 652 applicants, 49% accepted, 109 enrolled. In 2017, 48 master's, 28 doctorates, 2 other advanced degrees awarded. *Degree requirements:* For master's, practicum; for doctorate, thesis/dissertation, practicum. *Entrance requirements:* For master's, 3 letters of recommendation, personal goal statement; minimum GPA of 3.2, interview, BS or BA, and 2 clinical PT observations (for DPT); minimum GPA of 3.0, MSOT, OT licensen, and 2 clinical OT observations (for OTD); for doctorate, personal goal statement, 2 letters of recommendation; minimum GPA of 3.0, BS or BA, 2 clinical OT observations (for MSOT); RN license and minimum GPA of 3.0 (for MSN). Additional exam requirements/recommendations for international students: Required—TOEFL (minimum score 577 paper-based; 91 iBT). *Application deadline:* For fall admission, 12/1 priority date for domestic and international students; for spring admission, 11/15 priority date for domestic and international students. Application fee: $50. Electronic applications accepted. *Expenses:* Contact institution. *Faculty research:* Teaching simulation, ergonomics, orthopedics, use of social media in health care. *Unit head:* Dr. Cesarina Thompson, Dean, 413-205-3056, Fax: 413-654-1430, E-mail: cesarina.thompson@aic.edu. *Application contact:* Kerry Barnes, Director of Graduate Admissions, 413-205-3703, Fax: 413-205-3051, E-mail: kerry.barnes@aic.edu.
Website: http://www.aic.edu/academics/hs

Andrews University, School of Health Professions, Department of Physical Therapy, Postprofessional Physical Therapy Program, Berrien Springs, MI 49104. Offers orthopedic manual therapy (Dr Sc PT); physical therapy (TDPT). *Accreditation:* APTA. *Students:* 12 full-time (6 women), 47 part-time (18 women); includes 13 minority (1 Black or African American, non-Hispanic/Latino; 6 Asian, non-Hispanic/Latino; 6 Hispanic/Latino), 22 international. Average age 39. In 2017, 14 doctorates awarded. *Application deadline:* For fall admission, 12/1 priority date for domestic students. Applications are processed on a rolling basis. Application fee: $40. *Expenses:* Contact institution. *Financial support:* Federal Work-Study, institutionally sponsored loans, and scholarships/grants available. Financial award application deadline: 9/1; financial award applicants required to submit FAFSA. *Faculty research:* Home health patient profile, clinical education, breeding success of marine birds, trends in home health care for physical therapy, patient motivation in acute rehabilitation. *Unit head:* Kathy Berglund, Director of Professional Programs, 269-471-6076, Fax: 269-471-2866, E-mail: berglund@andrews.edu. *Application contact:* Jillian Panigot, Director of Admissions, 800-827-2878, Fax: 269-471-2867, E-mail: pt-info@andrews.edu.
Website: http://www.andrews.edu/PHTH/

Angelo State University, College of Graduate Studies and Research, Archer College of Health and Human Services, Department of Physical Therapy, San Angelo, TX 76909. Offers DPT. *Accreditation:* APTA. *Students:* 78 full-time (42 women); includes 12 minority (1 Black or African American, non-Hispanic/Latino; 4 Asian, non-Hispanic/Latino; 7 Hispanic/Latino). Average age 25. *Degree requirements:* For doctorate, 3 clinical placements. *Entrance requirements:* For doctorate, GRE General Test, interview, minimum undergraduate GPA of 3.0 in all prerequisite courses, essay, letters of recommendation, self-report transcript, volunteer hours. Additional exam requirements/recommendations for international students: Required—TOEFL or IELTS. *Application deadline:* For fall admission, 2/1 for domestic students, 3/10 for international students. Application fee: $40 ($50 for international students). Electronic applications accepted. *Expenses:* Tuition, state resident: full-time $3856. Tuition, nonresident: full-time $11,324. *Required fees:* $2650. *Financial support:* Scholarships/grants available. Financial award application deadline: 3/1; financial award applicants required to submit FAFSA. *Faculty research:* Women and lipoproteins, international distance education, quadriceps femoris and the vastus medialis obliquus (VMO), ergonomics, children and obesity. *Unit head:* Dr. Shelly D. Weise, Chair, 325-486-6474, Fax: 325-942-2548, E-mail: shelly.weise@angelo.edu.
Website: http://www.angelo.edu/dept/physical_therapy/

Arcadia University, College of Health Sciences, Department of Physical Therapy, Glenside, PA 19038-3295. Offers DPT, DPT/MPH. *Accreditation:* APTA. *Expenses:* Contact institution.

Arkansas State University, Graduate School, College of Nursing and Health Professions, Department of Physical Therapy, State University, AR 72467. Offers DPT. *Accreditation:* APTA. *Program availability:* Part-time. *Degree requirements:* For doctorate, comprehensive exam, thesis/dissertation. *Entrance requirements:* For doctorate, GRE, Allied Health Professions Admissions Test, appropriate bachelor's or master's degree, letters of reference, resume, official transcript, volunteer experience, criminal background check, immunization records, writing sample, PTCAS Application. Additional exam requirements/recommendations for international students: Required—TOEFL (minimum score 550 paper-based; 79 iBT), IELTS (minimum score 6), PTE (minimum score 56). Electronic applications accepted. *Expenses:* Contact institution.

A.T. Still University, Arizona School of Health Sciences, Mesa, AZ 85206. Offers advanced occupational therapy (MS); advanced physician assistant studies (MS); athletic training (MS, DAT); audiology (Au D); clinical decision making in athletic training (Graduate Certificate); occupational therapy (MS, OTD); orthopedic rehabilitation (Graduate Certificate); physical therapy (DPT); physician assistant studies (MS); transitional audiology (Au D); transitional physical therapy (DPT). *Accreditation:* AOTA (one or more programs are accredited); ASHA. *Program availability:* Part-time, 100% online. *Faculty:* 59 full-time (39 women), 221 part-time/adjunct (155 women). *Students:* 608 full-time (405 women), 431 part-time (310 women); includes 247 minority (54 Black or African American, non-Hispanic/Latino; 13 American Indian or Alaska Native, non-Hispanic/Latino; 151 Asian, non-Hispanic/Latino; 2 Hispanic/Latino; 1 Native Hawaiian or other Pacific Islander, non-Hispanic/Latino; 26 Two or more races, non-Hispanic/Latino), 1 international. Average age 33. 4,882 applicants, 9% accepted, 278 enrolled. In 2017, 132 master's, 270 doctorates awarded. *Degree requirements:* For master's, thesis (for some programs); for doctorate, thesis/dissertation (for some programs). *Entrance requirements:* For master's, GRE General Test; for doctorate, GRE, Physical Therapist Evaluation Tool (for DPT), current state licensure. Additional exam requirements/recommendations for international students: Required—TOEFL (minimum score 80 iBT). *Application deadline:* For fall admission, 7/7 for domestic and international students; for winter admission, 10/3 for domestic and international students; for spring admission, 1/16 for domestic and international students; for summer admission, 4/17 for domestic and international students. Applications are processed on a rolling basis. Application fee: $70. Electronic applications accepted. Application fee is waived when completed online. *Financial support:* In 2017–18, 161 students received support. Federal Work-Study and scholarships/grants available. Financial award application deadline: 6/1; financial award applicants required to submit FAFSA. *Faculty research:* Pediatric sport-related concussion, adolescent athlete health-related quality of life; geriatric and pediatric well-being, pain management for participation, practice-based research network, BMI and dental caries. *Total annual research expenditures:* $63,003. *Unit head:* Dr. Randy Danielsen, Dean, 480-219-6009, Fax: 480-219-6110, E-mail: rdanielsen@atsu.edu. *Application contact:* Donna Sparks, Director, Admissions Processing, 660-626-2117, Fax: 660-626-2969, E-mail: admissions@atsu.edu.
Website: http://www.atsu.edu/ashs

Augusta University, College of Allied Health Sciences, Physical Therapy Program, Augusta, GA 30912. Offers DPT. *Accreditation:* APTA. *Program availability:* Part-time, online learning. *Degree requirements:* For doctorate, acute experience, rehabilitation experience. *Entrance requirements:* For doctorate, GRE, at least 100 hours of observational, volunteer or other work experiences in physical therapy settings. Additional exam requirements/recommendations for international students: Required—TOEFL (minimum score 550 paper-based; 79 iBT). Electronic applications accepted.

Azusa Pacific University, School of Behavioral and Applied Sciences, Department of Physical Therapy, Azusa, CA 91702-7000. Offers DPT. *Accreditation:* APTA. *Degree requirements:* For doctorate, thesis/dissertation. *Entrance requirements:* For doctorate, GRE General Test. Additional exam requirements/recommendations for international students: Required—TOEFL (minimum score 600 paper-based). Electronic applications accepted. *Expenses:* Contact institution. *Faculty research:* Antioxidants and endothelial function, EEG and pain, metabolic function in obesity.

Baylor University, Graduate School, Military Programs, Program in Orthopedics, Waco, TX 76798. Offers D Sc. *Students:* 13 full-time (2 women); includes 2 minority (1 American Indian or Alaska Native, non-Hispanic/Latino; 1 Hispanic/Latino). In 2017, 12 doctorates awarded. *Degree requirements:* For doctorate, comprehensive exam. *Entrance requirements:* Additional exam requirements/recommendations for international students: Required—TOEFL, IELTS. *Unit head:* Brian Burk, Graduate Program Director, 210-916-7142, E-mail: brian.e.burk.mil@mail.mil. *Application contact:* Lori McNamara, Admissions Coordinator, 254-710-3588, Fax: 254-710-3870.

Baylor University, Graduate School, Military Programs, Program in Physical Therapy, Waco, TX 76798. Offers DPT, DScPT. Program offered jointly with the U.S. Army. *Accreditation:* APTA. *Students:* 52 full-time (25 women); includes 1 minority (Two or more races, non-Hispanic/Latino). In 2017, 24 doctorates awarded. *Degree requirements:* For doctorate, comprehensive exam. *Entrance requirements:* Additional exam requirements/recommendations for international students: Required—TOEFL, IELTS. *Application deadline:* For fall admission, 2/1 for domestic students. Applications are processed on a rolling basis. Application fee: $0. *Faculty research:* Effect of electrical stimulation on normal and immobilized muscle, effects of inversion traction. *Unit head:* Ted Croy, Graduate Program Director, 210-221-6897, Fax: 210-221-7585, E-mail: theodore.w.croy2.mil@mail.mil.

Bellarmine University, College of Health Professions, School of Movement and Rehabilitation Sciences, Louisville, KY 40205. Offers athletic training (MSAT); physical therapy (DPT). *Program availability:* Part-time. *Faculty:* 22 full-time (15 women), 27 part-time/adjunct (17 women). *Students:* 212 full-time (136 women), 2 part-time (both women); includes 18 minority (2 Black or African American, non-Hispanic/Latino; 4 Asian, non-Hispanic/Latino; 2 Hispanic/Latino; 10 Two or more races, non-Hispanic/Latino), 1 international. Average age 25. In 2017, 62 doctorates awarded. *Degree requirements:* For master's and doctorate, comprehensive exam. *Entrance requirements:* For master's, minimum undergraduate GPA of 2.75 or GRE, 3.0 in prerequisite courses; grade of C or better in all prerequisites; for doctorate, GRE, minimum undergraduate GPA of 2.75, 3.0 in prerequisite courses; grade of C or better in all prerequisites; documented work/volunteer hours in PT setting; physical ability to perform tasks required of a physical therapist. Additional exam requirements/recommendations for international students: Required—TOEFL (minimum iBT score of 83, 26 on speaking test), IELTS (minimum score 7, speaking band score of 8). *Application deadline:* Applications are processed on a rolling basis. Application fee: $40. Electronic applications accepted. Tuition and fees vary according to program. *Financial support:* Applicants required to submit FAFSA. *Unit head:* Dr. Tony Brosky, Dean, 502-272-8375, E-mail: jbrosky@bellarmine.edu. *Application contact:* Dr. Sara Pettingill, Dean of Graduate Admission, 502-272-8401, Fax: 502-272-8002, E-mail: spettingill@bellarmine.edu.
Website: https://www.bellarmine.edu/movement/

Belmont University, College of Health Sciences, Nashville, TN 37212. Offers nursing (MSN, DNP); occupational therapy (MSOT, OTD); physical therapy (DPT). *Program availability:* Part-time, blended/hybrid learning. *Faculty:* 29 full-time (25 women), 16 part-time/adjunct (11 women). *Students:* 394 full-time (330 women), 9 part-time (8 women); includes 34 minority (9 Black or African American, non-Hispanic/Latino; 12 Asian, non-Hispanic/Latino; 7 Hispanic/Latino; 6 Two or more races, non-Hispanic/Latino). Average age 26. In 2017, 52 master's, 79 doctorates awarded. *Degree requirements:* For master's, comprehensive exam, thesis; for doctorate, comprehensive exam. *Entrance requirements:* For master's, GRE, BSN, minimum GPA of 3.0. Additional exam requirements/recommendations for international students: Required—TOEFL (minimum score 550 paper-based). *Application deadline:* Applications are processed on a rolling basis. Application fee: $50. Electronic applications accepted. *Expenses:* Contact institution. *Financial support:* Teaching assistantships with full tuition reimbursements, career-related internships or fieldwork, scholarships/grants, and traineeships available. Financial award application deadline: 3/1; financial award applicants required to submit FAFSA. *Unit head:* Dr. Cathy Taylor, Dean, 615-460-6916, Fax: 615-460-6750. *Application contact:* Bill Nichols, Director of Enrollment Services, 615-460-6107, E-mail: bill.nichols@belmont.edu.
Website: http://www.belmont.edu/healthsciences/

Boston University, College of Health and Rehabilitation Sciences: Sargent College, Department of Physical Therapy and Athletic Training, Boston, MA 02215. Offers athletic training (MS); physical therapy (DPT); rehabilitation sciences (PhD). *Accreditation:* APTA (one or more programs are accredited). *Faculty:* 13 full-time (10 women), 26 part-time/adjunct (12 women). *Students:* 187 full-time (138 women), 4 part-time (2 women); includes 27 minority (1 Black or African American, non-Hispanic/Latino; 14 Asian, non-Hispanic/Latino; 6 Hispanic/Latino; 6 Two or more races, non-Hispanic/Latino), 9 international. Average age 25. 812 applicants, 16% accepted, 41 enrolled. In 2017, 66 doctorates awarded. *Degree requirements:* For doctorate, comprehensive exam and thesis (for PhD). *Entrance requirements:* For master's, GRE General Test, bachelor's degree; for doctorate, GRE General Test, bachelor's degree (for DPT), master's degree (for PhD). Additional exam requirements/recommendations for international students: Required—TOEFL (minimum score 550 paper-based; 84 iBT). *Application deadline:* For fall admission, 12/15 priority date for domestic and international students. Applications are processed on a rolling basis. Application fee: $145. Electronic applications accepted. *Financial support:* In 2017–18, 120 students received support, including 16 research assistantships with full tuition reimbursements available (averaging $22,000 per year), 6 teaching assistantships (averaging $2,500 per year); fellowships, career-related internships or fieldwork, Federal Work-Study, institutionally sponsored loans, scholarships/grants, and tuition waivers (full and partial) also available. Financial award application deadline: 12/15; financial award applicants required to submit FAFSA. *Faculty research:* Gait, balance, motor control, dynamic systems analysis, spinal cord injury. *Total annual research expenditures:* $1.5 million. *Unit head:* Dr. LaDora Thompson, Department Chair, 617-353-2724, E-mail: pt@bu.edu. *Application contact:* Sharon Sankey, Assistant Dean, Student Services, 617-353-2713, Fax: 617-353-7500, E-mail: ssankey@bu.edu.

Bradley University, The Graduate School, College of Education and Health Sciences, Department of Physical Therapy and Health Science, Peoria, IL 61625-0002. Offers physical therapy (DPT). *Accreditation:* APTA. *Entrance requirements:* For doctorate, GRE, 2 letters of recommendation. Additional exam requirements/recommendations for international students: Required—TOEFL (minimum score 600 paper-based; 100 iBT), IELTS (minimum score 6.5). Electronic applications accepted. *Expenses:* Contact institution.

California State University, Fresno, Division of Research and Graduate Studies, College of Health and Human Services, Department of Physical Therapy, Fresno, CA 93740-8027. Offers DPT. *Accreditation:* APTA. *Entrance requirements:* Additional exam requirements/recommendations for international students: Required—TOEFL. Electronic applications accepted. *Faculty research:* Dance, occupational health, ethics.

California State University, Long Beach, Graduate Studies, College of Health and Human Services, Department of Physical Therapy, Long Beach, CA 90840. Offers DPT. *Accreditation:* APTA. *Entrance requirements:* Additional exam requirements/recommendations for international students: Required—TOEFL. Electronic applications accepted.

California State University, Northridge, Graduate Studies, College of Health and Human Development, Department of Physical Therapy, Northridge, CA 91330. Offers MPT. *Accreditation:* APTA. *Students:* 90 full-time (53 women); includes 33 minority (23 Asian, non-Hispanic/Latino; 10 Hispanic/Latino), 1 international. Average age 27. *Entrance requirements:* For master's, GRE General Test or minimum GPA of 3.0. Additional exam requirements/recommendations for international students: Required—TOEFL. *Application deadline:* For fall admission, 11/30 for domestic students. Application fee: $55. *Financial support:* Application deadline: 3/1. *Unit head:* Dr. Janna Beling, Chair, 818-677-2203. *Application contact:* E-mail: pt@csun.edu.
Website: http://www.csun.edu/hhd/pt/

California State University, Sacramento, College of Health and Human Services, Department of Physical Therapy, Sacramento, CA 95819. Offers DPT. *Students:* 94 full-time (48 women), 2 part-time (both women); includes 24 minority (16 Asian, non-Hispanic/Latino; 7 Hispanic/Latino; 1 Native Hawaiian or other Pacific Islander, non-Hispanic/Latino). Average age 28. 106 applicants, 31% accepted, 33 enrolled. In 2017, 29 doctorates awarded. *Degree requirements:* For doctorate, project. *Entrance requirements:* For doctorate, GRE. Additional exam requirements/recommendations for international students: Required—TOEFL (minimum score 550 paper-based; 80 iBT); Recommended—IELTS, TSE. *Application deadline:* For fall admission, 2/15 for domestic and international students. Applications are processed on a rolling basis. Application fee: $55. Electronic applications accepted. *Expenses:* Contact institution. *Financial support:* Teaching assistantships, Federal Work-Study, and scholarships/grants available. Support available to part-time students. Financial award application deadline: 3/1; financial award applicants required to submit FAFSA. *Unit head:* Dr. Bryan Coleman-Salgado, Director, 916-278-4871, E-mail: mmckeough@csus.edu. *Application contact:* Jose Martinez, Graduate Admissions Supervisor, 916-278-7871, E-mail: martinj@skymail.csus.edu.
Website: http://www.csus.edu/hhs/pt/

Campbell University, Graduate and Professional Programs, College of Pharmacy and Health Sciences, Buies Creek, NC 27506. Offers clinical research (MS); pharmaceutical sciences (MS); pharmacy (Pharm D); physician assistant (MPAP); public health (MS). *Accreditation:* ACPE. *Program availability:* Part-time, evening/weekend. *Entrance requirements:* For master's, MCAT, PCAT, GRE, bachelor's degree in health sciences or related field; for doctorate, PCAT. Additional exam requirements/recommendations for international students: Required—TOEFL (minimum score 550 paper-based; 79 iBT). Electronic applications accepted. *Expenses:* Contact institution. *Faculty research:* Immunology, medicinal chemistry, pharmaceutics, applied pharmacology.

Carroll University, Program in Physical Therapy, Waukesha, WI 53186-5593. Offers DPT. *Accreditation:* APTA. *Entrance requirements:* Additional exam requirements/recommendations for international students: Required—TOEFL. *Expenses:* Contact institution. *Faculty research:* Physical therapy education, geriatrics, neural control of movement, wellness and prevention in apparently healthy individuals with disease and disability.

Central Michigan University, College of Graduate Studies, The Herbert H. and Grace A. Dow College of Health Professions, School of Rehabilitation and Medical Sciences, Mount Pleasant, MI 48859. Offers physical therapy (DPT); physician assistant (MS). *Accreditation:* APTA; ARC-PA. *Degree requirements:* For master's, thesis or alternative; for doctorate, thesis/dissertation or alternative. *Entrance requirements:* For master's and doctorate, GRE. Electronic applications accepted.

Chapman University, Crean College of Health and Behavioral Sciences, Department of Physical Therapy, Orange, CA 92866. Offers DPT, TDPT. *Accreditation:* APTA. *Faculty:* 18 full-time (14 women), 12 part-time/adjunct (9 women). *Students:* 127 full-time (56 women), 142 part-time (76 women); includes 147 minority (3 Black or African American, non-Hispanic/Latino; 103 Asian, non-Hispanic/Latino; 21 Hispanic/Latino; 20 Two or more races, non-Hispanic/Latino), 4 international. Average age 28. 1,312 applicants, 9% accepted, 55 enrolled. In 2017, 57 doctorates awarded. *Degree requirements:* For doctorate, 1440 hours of clinical experience. *Entrance requirements:* For doctorate, GRE, 40 hours of physical therapy observation (or paid work). *Application deadline:* For fall admission, 12/15 for domestic students; for summer admission, 10/16 for domestic students. Electronic applications accepted. *Expenses:* Contact institution. *Financial support:* Fellowships, Federal Work-Study, and scholarships/grants available. Financial award applicants required to submit FAFSA. *Unit head:* Dr. Emmanuel John, Chair, 714-744-7906, E-mail: john@chapman.edu. *Application contact:* Anuja Nanjappa, 714-744-7620, E-mail: cudptadmissions@chapman.edu.

Chatham University, Program in Physical Therapy, Pittsburgh, PA 15232-2826. Offers DPT, TDPT. *Accreditation:* APTA. *Faculty:* 8 full-time (5 women), 3 part-time/adjunct (2 women). *Students:* 114 full-time (76 women), 1 part-time (0 women); includes 8 minority (1 Black or African American, non-Hispanic/Latino; 4 Asian, non-Hispanic/Latino; 3 Hispanic/Latino). Average age 25. 415 applicants, 21% accepted, 40 enrolled. In 2017, 41 doctorates awarded. *Entrance requirements:* For doctorate, GRE, community service, interview, minimum GPA of 3.0, writing sample, volunteer/work experience, 3 references. Additional exam requirements/recommendations for international students: Required—TOEFL (minimum score 600 paper-based; 100 iBT), IELTS (minimum score 7), TWE. *Application deadline:* For fall admission, 12/1 priority date for domestic and international students. Application fee: $45. Electronic applications accepted. Application fee is waived when completed online. *Expenses: Tuition:* Full-time $16,740; part-time $930 per credit. *Required fees:* $486; $27 per credit. $243 per semester. *Financial support:* Career-related internships or fieldwork available. Financial award applicants required to submit FAFSA. *Faculty research:* Stroke rehabilitation, osteoporosis and fall prevention, physical therapy for children with disabilities, evidence-based practice and decision-making, low back pain in children and adolescents. *Unit head:* Dr. Patricia Downey, Director, 412-365-1199, Fax: 412-365-1505, E-mail: downey@chatham.edu. *Application contact:* Ashlee Bartko, Senior Assistant Director of Graduate Admission, 412-365-2988, Fax: 412-365-1609, E-mail: gradadmissions@chatham.edu.
Website: http://www.chatham.edu/departments/healthmgmt/graduate/pt

Clarke University, Physical Therapy Program, Dubuque, IA 52001-3198. Offers DPT. *Accreditation:* APTA. *Faculty:* 8 full-time (5 women), 6 part-time/adjunct (3 women). *Students:* 72 full-time (46 women); includes 2 minority (1 Hispanic/Latino; 1 Two or more races, non-Hispanic/Latino). Average age 24. 221 applicants, 20% accepted, 20 enrolled. In 2017, 27 doctorates awarded. *Entrance requirements:* For doctorate, GRE, minimum GPA of 3.0; total of 30 hours observing in three of the following areas: pediatrics, geriatrics, in-patient, acute/subacute care, neurological rehabilitation, orthopedics, or sports medicine; essay; three recommendations. Additional exam requirements/recommendations for international students: Required—TOEFL (minimum score 550 paper-based; 80 iBT), IELTS (minimum score 6.5). *Application deadline:* For fall admission, 11/2 for domestic students. Application fee: $0. Electronic applications accepted. *Expenses:* Contact institution. *Financial support:* Applicants required to submit FAFSA. *Faculty research:* Qualitative research, occupational health, discontinuous anaerobic studies, low back dysfunction. *Unit head:* Dr. Bill O'Dell, Chair, 563-588-6618, E-mail: bill.odell@clarke.edu. *Application contact:* Kimberly Roush, Director of Admission, Graduate and Adult Programs, 563-588-6539, Fax: 563-552-7994, E-mail: graduate@clarke.edu.
Website: https://www.clarke.edu/admission-aid/#graduate

Clarkson University, Division of Health Sciences, Department of Physical Therapy, Potsdam, NY 13699. Offers DPT. *Accreditation:* APTA. *Faculty:* 14 full-time (9 women), 7 part-time/adjunct (6 women). *Students:* 63 full-time (46 women), 1 (woman) part-time; includes 4 minority (1 Black or African American, non-Hispanic/Latino; 1 Asian, non-Hispanic/Latino; 2 Hispanic/Latino), 1 international. 206 applicants, 36% accepted, 18 enrolled. In 2017, 24 doctorates awarded. *Entrance requirements:* For doctorate, minimum undergraduate GPA of 3.2; PTCAS application. *Application deadline:* For fall admission, 3/1 for domestic and international students. Applications are processed on a rolling basis. Application fee: $140. Electronic applications accepted. *Expenses:* Contact institution. *Financial support:* Scholarships/grants available. *Unit head:* Dr. George Fulk, Chair of Physical Therapy, 315-268-3786, E-mail: gfulk@clarkson.edu. *Application contact:* Anne Gilbert, Graduate Admissions Contact, 315-268-3786, E-mail: agilbert@clarkson.edu.
Website: https://www.clarkson.edu/academics/graduate

Cleveland State University, College of Graduate Studies, College of Sciences and Health Professions, School of Health Sciences, Program in Physical Therapy, Cleveland, OH 44115. Offers DPT. *Accreditation:* APTA. *Faculty:* 7 full-time (6 women), 7 part-time/adjunct (5 women). *Students:* 112 full-time (71 women); includes 7 minority (1 Black or African American, non-Hispanic/Latino; 1 Asian, non-Hispanic/Latino; 3 Hispanic/Latino; 2 Two or more races, non-Hispanic/Latino). Average age 25. In 2017, 35 doctorates awarded. *Entrance requirements:* For doctorate, GRE (minimum scores: 450 verbal; 550 quantitative; 4.0 analytical writing), minimum overall GPA of 3.0. Additional exam requirements/recommendations for international students: Required—TOEFL (minimum score 550 paper-based; 78 iBT). Application fee: $40. Electronic applications accepted. Application fee is waived when completed online. *Expenses:* Contact institution. *Financial support:* Research assistantships, career-related internships or fieldwork, and unspecified assistantships available. Financial award application deadline: 1/1; financial award applicants required to submit FAFSA. *Faculty research:* Electronic gaming to increase balance, clinical education in physical therapy, use of ankle foot orthotics, function of patients on dialysis, student impressions on working with the elderly. *Unit head:* Dr. Karen Ann O'Loughlin, Associate Professor of Physical Therapy/Program Director, 216-687-3581, Fax: 216-687-9316, E-mail: s.m.giuffre@csuohio.edu. *Application contact:* Lisa Pistone, Administrative Secretary, 216-687-3566, Fax: 216-687-9316, E-mail: l.pistone@csuohio.edu.

The College of St. Scholastica, Graduate Studies, Department of Physical Therapy, Duluth, MN 55811-4199. Offers DPT. *Accreditation:* APTA. *Entrance requirements:* For doctorate, GRE. Additional exam requirements/recommendations for international students: Required—TOEFL (minimum score 550 paper-based; 79 iBT). Electronic applications accepted. *Faculty research:* Postural control, reliability and validity of spinal assessment tools, biomechanics of golf swing and low back pain, gait assessment and treatment, ethical issues.

College of Staten Island of the City University of New York, Graduate Programs, School of Health Sciences, Program in Physical Therapy, Staten Island, NY 10314-6600. Offers DPT. *Accreditation:* APTA. *Faculty:* 10 full-time, 14 part-time/adjunct. *Students:* 59. 189 applicants, 11% accepted, 20 enrolled. In 2017, 17 doctorates awarded. *Degree requirements:* For doctorate, comprehensive exam, 105 credits, examinations, four clinical affiliations, publishable research project. *Entrance requirements:* For doctorate, GRE, bachelor's degree from accredited college with minimum GPA of 3.0; 2 semesters of anatomy and physiology; 2 semesters of physics and chemistry; 1 semester each of pre-calculus/algebra/trigonometry, statistics, and English composition. Additional exam requirements/recommendations for international students: Required—TOEFL (minimum score 550 paper-based; 79 iBT), IELTS (minimum score 6.5). *Application deadline:* For fall admission, 11/2 for domestic and international students. Application fee: $125. Electronic applications accepted. *Expenses:* Contact institution. *Faculty research:* Spinal cord injury treatment, treatment of spasticity as a result of neurological disorders, transcranial stimulation, osteoarthritis, carpal tunnel treatment, balance and coordination evaluation and treatment. *Unit head:* Michael Chiacchiero, 718-982-2987, E-mail: michael.chiacchiero@csi.cuny.edu. *Application contact:* Sasha Spence, Associate Director for Graduate Admissions, 718-982-2019, Fax: 718-982-2500, E-mail: sasha.spence@csi.cuny.edu.
Website: https://www.csi.cuny.edu/sites/default/files/pdf/admissions/grad/pdf/DPT%20Fact%20Sheet.pdf

Columbia University, College of Physicians and Surgeons, Program in Physical Therapy, New York, NY 10032. Offers DPT. *Accreditation:* APTA. *Degree requirements:* For doctorate, fieldwork, capstone project. *Entrance requirements:* For doctorate, GRE General Test, undergraduate course work in biology, chemistry, physics, psychology, statistics and humanities. Additional exam requirements/recommendations for international students: Required—TOEFL. Electronic applications accepted. *Expenses:* Contact institution. *Faculty research:* Motor control, motion analysis, back assessment, recovery of function following neurological injury, women's health, disability awareness, pediatrics, orthopedics.

Concordia University, St. Paul, College of Health and Science, St. Paul, MN 55104-5494. Offers exercise science (MS); orthotics and prosthetics (MS); physical therapy (DPT); sports management (MA). *Program availability:* Part-time, evening/weekend, 100% online, blended/hybrid learning. *Faculty:* 14 full-time (8 women), 22 part-time/adjunct (8 women). *Students:* 260 full-time (127 women), 20 part-time (6 women); includes 48 minority (24 Black or African American, non-Hispanic/Latino; 5 Asian, non-Hispanic/Latino; 11 Hispanic/Latino; 1 Native Hawaiian or other Pacific Islander, non-Hispanic/Latino; 7 Two or more races, non-Hispanic/Latino), 4 international. Average age 28. 218 applicants, 43% accepted, 84 enrolled. In 2017, 57 master's, 26 doctorates awarded. *Degree requirements:* For master's, comprehensive exam (for some programs), thesis (for some programs); for doctorate, at least one 8-12 week clinical rotation outside the St. Paul area. *Entrance requirements:* For master's, official transcripts from regionally-accredited institution stating the conferral of a bachelor's degree with minimum cumulative GPA of 3.0; personal statement; resume; for doctorate, GRE, official transcript from regionally-accredited institution showing bachelor's degree and minimum coursework GPA of 3.0; 100 physical therapy observation hours; two letters of professional recommendation. Additional exam requirements/recommendations for international students: Recommended—TOEFL (minimum score 547 paper-based; 78 iBT), IELTS (minimum score 6), TSE (minimum score 52). *Application deadline:* For fall admission, 4/1 for domestic students. Applications are processed on a rolling basis. Application fee: $0. Electronic applications accepted. *Expenses:* $475 per credit (for MA and MS); $810 per credit (for DPT). *Financial support:* In 2017–18, 60 students received support. Scholarships/grants and unspecified assistantships available. Financial award applicants required to submit FAFSA. *Faculty research:* Developmental screening in early childhood, cardiovascular responses to aerobic exercise. *Unit head:* Dr. Katie Fischer, Dean, 651-641-8735, E-mail: fischer@csp.edu. *Application contact:* Amber Faletti, Director of Enrollment Management, 651-641-8838, Fax: 651-603-6320, E-mail: faletti@csp.edu.

Concordia University Wisconsin, Graduate Programs, School of Health Professions, Program in Physical Therapy, Mequon, WI 53097-2402. Offers DPT. *Accreditation:* APTA. *Entrance requirements:* Additional exam requirements/recommendations for international students: Required—TOEFL. *Expenses:* Contact institution.

Creighton University, School of Pharmacy and Health Professions, Program in Physical Therapy, Omaha, NE 68178-0001. Offers DPT. *Accreditation:* APTA. *Entrance requirements:* For doctorate, GRE. Additional exam requirements/recommendations for international students: Required—TOEFL. Electronic applications accepted. Part-time tuition and fees vary according to course load, degree level, campus/location and program. *Faculty research:* Patient safety in health services research, health information technology and health services research, Parkinson's rigidity and rehabilitation sciences, prion disease transmission, outcomes research in the rehabilitation sciences.

Daemen College, Department of Physical Therapy, Amherst, NY 14226-3592. Offers orthopedic manual physical therapy (Advanced Certificate); physical therapy-direct entry (DPT); transitional (DPT). *Accreditation:* APTA. *Program availability:* Part-time. *Degree requirements:* For doctorate, minimum C grade in all coursework; for Advanced Certificate, minimum GPA of 3.0; degree completion in maximum of 3 years. *Entrance requirements:* For doctorate, baccalaureate degree with minimum GPA of 2.8 in science coursework; letter of intent; resume; 2 letters of reference; 120 hours of PT exposure; transcripts; for Advanced Certificate, BS/BA; license to practice physical therapy; current registration; 2 recommendations; letter of intent; 2 years of physical therapy experience. Additional exam requirements/recommendations for international students: Required—TOEFL (minimum score 500 paper-based; 63 iBT), IELTS (minimum score 5.5). Electronic applications accepted. *Faculty research:* Athletic injuries, myofacial pain syndrome, electrical stimulation and tissue healing, lumbar spine dysfunction, temporomandibular joint syndrome.

Dalhousie University, Faculty of Health Professions, School of Physiotherapy, Halifax, NS B3H 3J5, Canada. Offers physiotherapy (entry to profession) (M Sc); physiotherapy (rehabilitation research) (M Sc). *Entrance requirements:* Additional exam requirements/recommendations for international students: Required—TOEFL, IELTS, CANTEST, CAEL, or Michigan English Language Assessment Battery. Electronic applications accepted.

Des Moines University, College of Health Sciences, Program in Physical Therapy, Des Moines, IA 50312-4104. Offers DPT. *Accreditation:* APTA. *Entrance requirements:* For doctorate, GRE. Additional exam requirements/recommendations for international students: Required—TOEFL. Electronic applications accepted. *Expenses:* Contact institution.

Dominican College, Division of Allied Health, Department of Physical Therapy, Orangeburg, NY 10962-1210. Offers MS, DPT. *Accreditation:* APTA. *Program availability:* Part-time, evening/weekend. *Faculty:* 5 full-time (1 woman), 27 part-time/adjunct (20 women). *Students:* 71 full-time (37 women), 171 part-time (99 women); includes 114 minority (5 Black or African American, non-Hispanic/Latino; 1 American Indian or Alaska Native, non-Hispanic/Latino; 89 Asian, non-Hispanic/Latino; 13 Hispanic/Latino; 1 Native Hawaiian or other Pacific Islander, non-Hispanic/Latino; 5 Two or more races, non-Hispanic/Latino), 35 international. In 2017, 131 doctorates awarded. *Degree requirements:* For master's, 3 clinical affiliations, 100 hours of voluntary or work experience in setting where licensed physical therapist is employed. *Entrance requirements:* For master's, minimum GPA of 3.0. Additional exam requirements/recommendations for international students: Required—TOEFL (minimum score 550 paper-based; 90 iBT). *Application deadline:* Applications are processed on a rolling basis. Application fee: $50. Electronic applications accepted. *Expenses: Tuition:* Part-time $900 per credit. One-time fee: $200. Tuition and fees vary according to degree level and program. *Financial support:* Application deadline: 2/3; applicants required to submit FAFSA. *Unit head:* Dr. Emil Euaparadorn, Program Director, 845-848-6048, Fax: 845-398-4893, E-mail: emil.euaparadorn@dc.edu. *Application contact:* Heather Bergling, Assistant Director of Graduate Admissions, 845-848-7900, Fax: 845-365-3150, E-mail: admissions@dc.edu.

Drexel University, College of Nursing and Health Professions, Department of Physical Therapy and Rehabilitation Sciences, Philadelphia, PA 19102. Offers clinical biomechanics and orthopedics (PhD); hand and upper quarter rehabilitation (Certificate); hand therapy (MHS, PPDPT); orthopedics (MHS, PPDPT); pediatric rehabilitation (Certificate); pediatrics (MHS, PPDPT, PhD); physical therapy (DPT). *Accreditation:* APTA. *Program availability:* Part-time. Terminal master's awarded for partial completion of doctoral program. *Degree requirements:* For master's, comprehensive exam; for doctorate, thesis/dissertation, qualifying exam. *Entrance requirements:* For master's and doctorate, GRE General Test. Additional exam requirements/recommendations for international students: Required—TOEFL. Electronic applications accepted. *Faculty research:* Cerebral palsy, chronic low back pain, shoulder dysfunction, early intervention/community programs.

Duke University, School of Medicine, Physical Therapy Division, Durham, NC 27708. Offers DPT. *Accreditation:* APTA. *Faculty:* 17 full-time (8 women). *Students:* 226 full-time (152 women); includes 53 minority (12 Black or African American, non-Hispanic/Latino; 1 American Indian or Alaska Native, non-Hispanic/Latino; 23 Asian, non-Hispanic/Latino; 13 Hispanic/Latino; 4 Native Hawaiian or other Pacific Islander, non-Hispanic/Latino). 924 applicants, 15% accepted, 80 enrolled. In 2017, 73 doctorates awarded. *Degree requirements:* For doctorate, comprehensive exam, scholarly project. *Entrance requirements:* For doctorate, GRE, previous course work in anatomy, physiology, biological sciences, chemistry, physics, psychology, and statistics. Additional exam requirements/recommendations for international students: Recommended—TOEFL, IELTS. *Application deadline:* For fall admission, 11/1 priority date for domestic and international students. Applications are processed on a rolling basis. Application fee: $50. Electronic applications accepted. *Financial support:* In 2017–18, 22 students received support. Application deadline: 5/1; applicants required to submit FAFSA. *Faculty research:* Geriatrics, visual plasticity, educational outcomes, orthopedics, neurology. *Unit head:* Dr. Chad Cook, Program Director, 919-684-8905, Fax: 919-684-1846, E-mail: chad.cook@duke.edu. *Application contact:* Mya Shackleford, Admissions Coordinator, 919-668-5206, Fax: 919-684-1846, E-mail: mya.shackleford@duke.edu.
Website: http://dpt.duhs.duke.edu

Duquesne University, John G. Rangos, Sr. School of Health Sciences, Pittsburgh, PA 15282-0001. Offers health management systems (MHMS); occupational therapy (MS, OTD); physical therapy (DPT); physician assistant studies (MPAS); rehabilitation science (MS, PhD); speech-language pathology (MS). *Accreditation:* AOTA (one or more programs are accredited); APTA (one or more programs are accredited); ASHA. *Program availability:* Part-time, minimal on-campus study. *Faculty:* 51 full-time (38 women), 33 part-time/adjunct (17 women). *Students:* 247 full-time (199 women), 11 part-time (7 women); includes 15 minority (2 Black or African American, non-Hispanic/Latino; 7 Asian, non-Hispanic/Latino; 3 Hispanic/Latino; 3 Two or more races, non-Hispanic/Latino), 42 international. Average age 23. 283 applicants, 31% accepted, 54 enrolled. In 2017, 134 master's, 39 doctorates awarded. *Degree requirements:* For doctorate, comprehensive exam (for some programs), thesis/dissertation (for some programs). *Entrance requirements:* For master's, GRE General Test (speech-language pathology), 3 letters of recommendation; minimum GPA of 2.75 (health management systems), 3.0 (speech-language pathology); for doctorate, GRE General Test (for physical therapy and rehabilitation science), 3 letters of recommendation, minimum GPA of 3.0, personal interview. Additional exam requirements/recommendations for international students: Required—TOEFL (minimum score 550 paper-based; 90 iBT); Recommended—IELTS. *Application deadline:* For fall admission, 2/1 for domestic and international students; for spring admission, 7/1 for domestic and international students. Applications are processed on a rolling basis. Application fee: $0. Electronic applications accepted. *Expenses:* $1,351 per credit ($1,259 for health management systems). *Financial support:* Federal Work-Study available. Financial award applicants required to submit FAFSA. *Faculty research:* Neuronal processing, electrical stimulation on peripheral neuropathy, central nervous system (CNS) stimulatory and inhibitory signals, behavioral genetic methodologies to development disorders of speech, neurogenic communication disorders. *Total annual research expenditures:* $24,578. *Unit head:* Dr. Fevzi Akinci, Dean, 412-396-5303, Fax: 412-396-5554, E-mail: akincif@duq.edu. *Application contact:* Christopher R. Hilf, Director of Enrollment Management, 412-396-5653, Fax: 412-396-5554, E-mail: hilfc@duq.edu.
Website: http://www.duq.edu/academics/schools/health-sciences

D'Youville College, Department of Physical Therapy, Buffalo, NY 14201-1084. Offers advanced orthopedic physical therapy (Certificate); manual physical therapy (Certificate); physical therapy (DPT). *Accreditation:* APTA. *Program availability:* Part-time, online learning. *Degree requirements:* For doctorate, comprehensive exam, project or thesis. *Entrance requirements:* For doctorate, bachelor's degree, minimum GPA of 3.0. Additional exam requirements/recommendations for international students: Required—TOEFL (minimum score 500 paper-based). Electronic applications accepted. *Faculty research:* Therapeutic effects of Tai Chi, orthopedics, health promotion in type 2 diabetes, athletic performance in youth and college sports, behavioral determinants in childhood obesity.

East Carolina University, Graduate School, College of Allied Health Sciences, Department of Physical Therapy, Greenville, NC 27858-4353. Offers DPT. *Accreditation:* APTA. *Students:* 85 full-time (61 women); includes 10 minority (2 Black or African American, non-Hispanic/Latino; 3 Asian, non-Hispanic/Latino; 2 Hispanic/Latino; 3 Two or more races, non-Hispanic/Latino). Average age 24. 305 applicants, 12% accepted, 33 enrolled. In 2017, 29 doctorates awarded. *Entrance requirements:* Additional exam requirements/recommendations for international students: Recommended—TOEFL (minimum score 78 iBT), IELTS (minimum score 6.5). *Application deadline:* For fall admission, 10/2 for domestic students. Applications are processed on a rolling basis. Application fee: $75. Electronic applications accepted. *Expenses:* Tuition, state resident: full-time $4749; part-time $297 per credit hour. Tuition, nonresident: full-time $17,898; part-time $1119 per credit hour. *Required fees:* $2691; $224 per credit hour. Part-time tuition and fees vary according to course load and program. *Financial support:* Application deadline: 3/1. *Faculty research:* Diabetes and obesity, diabetic foot, ACL injury. *Unit head:* Dr. Walter L. Jenkins, Chair, 252-744-6234, E-mail: jenkinsw@ecu.edu.
Website: http://www.ecu.edu/pt/

Eastern Washington University, Graduate Studies, College of Health Science and Public Health, Department of Physical Therapy, Cheney, WA 99004-2431. Offers DPT. *Accreditation:* APTA. *Faculty:* 10. *Students:* 113 full-time (74 women). Average age 26. 512 applicants, 7% accepted, 38 enrolled. In 2017, 38 doctorates awarded. *Degree requirements:* For doctorate, comprehensive exam, thesis/dissertation or final project. *Entrance requirements:* For doctorate, GRE General Test (minimum score of 4.0 on writing section), minimum GPA of 3.0, 75 hours of experience, 3 letters of recommendation. Additional exam requirements/recommendations for international students: Required—TOEFL (minimum score 580 paper-based; 92 iBT), IELTS (minimum score 7), TWE, PTE (minimum score 63). *Application deadline:* For fall admission, 7/1 for domestic students. Application fee: $75. Electronic applications accepted. *Expenses:* Tuition, state resident: full-time $11,191; part-time $373.06 per credit. Tuition, nonresident: full-time $25,995; part-time $866.52 per credit. *Financial support:* In 2017–18, 1 teaching assistantship was awarded; career-related internships or fieldwork, Federal Work-Study, institutionally sponsored loans, scholarships/grants, health care benefits, tuition waivers (partial), and unspecified assistantships also available. Support available to part-time students. Financial award application deadline: 2/1; financial award applicants required to submit FAFSA. *Unit head:* Jenna McDonald, 509-828-1354.

East Tennessee State University, School of Graduate Studies, College of Clinical and Rehabilitative Health Sciences, Department of Physical Therapy, Johnson City, TN 37614. Offers DPT. *Accreditation:* APTA. *Degree requirements:* For doctorate, comprehensive exam, internship. *Entrance requirements:* For doctorate, GRE General Test, minimum prerequisite GPA of 3.0, three letters of recommendation with at least one from a licensed PT, interview with the physical therapy Admissions Committee. Additional exam requirements/recommendations for international students: Required—TOEFL (minimum score 550 paper-based; 79 iBT). *Application deadline:* For spring admission, 3/1 priority date for domestic and international students. Application fee: $55 ($65 for international students). Electronic applications accepted. *Financial support:* Research assistantships with tuition reimbursements, career-related internships or fieldwork, institutionally sponsored loans, scholarships/grants, and unspecified assistantships available. Financial award application deadline: 7/1; financial award applicants required to submit FAFSA. *Faculty research:* Health and wellness across the lifespan; relationships between scapular kinematics, pain, and function; cognitive training and dual-task ability in older adult; vestibular rehabilitation and dizziness in geriatric patients; assessment tools for patients with TMJ dysfunction; proprioceptive training and gait variability in older adults. *Unit head:* Dr. Patricia King, Chair, 423-439-8794, Fax: 423-439-8077, E-mail: kingpm@etsu.edu. *Application contact:* Dr. Patricia King, Chair, 423-439-8794, Fax: 423-439-8077, E-mail: kingpm@etsu.edu.
Website: http://www.etsu.edu/crhs/physther/default.php

Elon University, Program in Physical Therapy, Elon, NC 27244-2010. Offers DPT. *Accreditation:* APTA. *Faculty:* 14 full-time (9 women), 16 part-time/adjunct (13 women). *Students:* 139 full-time (99 women); includes 17 minority (5 Black or African American, non-Hispanic/Latino; 2 Asian, non-Hispanic/Latino; 2 Hispanic/Latino; 8 Two or more races, non-Hispanic/Latino), 2 international. Average age 26. 916 applicants, 10% accepted, 47 enrolled. In 2017, 48 doctorates awarded. *Entrance requirements:* For doctorate, GRE General Test. Additional exam requirements/recommendations for international students: Required—TOEFL (minimum score 550 paper-based; 79 iBT). *Application deadline:* For fall admission, 11/1 for domestic students. Applications are processed on a rolling basis. Application fee: $50. Electronic applications accepted. *Financial support:* Federal Work-Study and scholarships/grants available. Financial award application deadline: 10/1; financial award applicants required to submit FAFSA. *Faculty research:* Exercise readiness in female survivors of domestic violence, animal-assisted therapy, locomotor training for multiple sclerosis patients, effect of infant positioning on the attainment of gross motor skills, physical activity levels for methadone maintenance treatment patients. *Unit head:* Dr. Becky Neiduski, Dean of the School of Health Sciences, 336-278-6350, E-mail: bneiduski@elon.edu. *Application contact:* Art Fadde, Director of Graduate Admissions, 800-334-8448 Ext. 3, Fax: 336-278-7699, E-mail: afadde@elon.edu.
Website: http://www.elon.edu/dpt/

Emory & Henry College, Graduate Programs, Emory, VA 24327. Offers American history (MA Ed); education professional studies (M Ed); occupational therapy (MOT); organizational leadership (MCOL); physical therapy (DPT); physician assistant studies (MPAS); reading specialist (MA Ed). *Program availability:* Part-time. *Faculty:* 7 full-time (3 women). *Students:* 194 full-time (128 women), 4 part-time (2 women); includes 6 minority (2 Black or African American, non-Hispanic/Latino; 1 American Indian or Alaska Native, non-Hispanic/Latino; 1 Asian, non-Hispanic/Latino; 2 Hispanic/Latino). Average age 25. 525 applicants, 21% accepted, 74 enrolled. In 2017, 24 master's awarded. *Degree requirements:* For master's, thesis optional; for doctorate, thesis/dissertation optional. *Entrance requirements:* For master's, GRE or PRAXIS I, official transcripts from all colleges previously attended, three professional recommendations, essay. Additional exam requirements/recommendations for international students: Recommended—TOEFL, IELTS (minimum score 6). *Application deadline:* Applications are processed on a rolling basis. Electronic applications accepted. *Expenses:* Contact institution. *Financial support:* Application deadline: 10/15; applicants required to submit FAFSA. *Unit head:* Dr. Michael Puglisi, Associate Dean for Academic Affairs, 276-944-6662, E-mail: mpuglisi@ehc.edu. *Application contact:* Mary Bolt, Director of Transfer and Graduate Admission, 276-944-6135, E-mail: mbolt@ehc.edu.

Emory University, School of Medicine, Programs in Allied Health Professions, Doctor of Physical Therapy Program, Atlanta, GA 30322. Offers DPT. *Accreditation:* APTA. *Entrance requirements:* For doctorate, GRE General Test. Additional exam requirements/recommendations for international students: Recommended—TOEFL. Electronic applications accepted. *Expenses:* Contact institution. *Faculty research:* Sensorimotor plasticity, biomechanics of walking, qualitative distinctions of moral practice, constraint induced therapy following stroke.

Florida Agricultural and Mechanical University, Division of Graduate Studies, Research, and Continuing Education, School of Allied Health Sciences, Division of Physical Therapy, Tallahassee, FL 32307-3200. Offers DPT. *Accreditation:* APTA. *Entrance requirements:* Additional exam requirements/recommendations for international students: Required—TOEFL.

Florida Gulf Coast University, Elaine Nicpon Marieb College of Health and Human Services, Program in Physical Therapy, Fort Myers, FL 33965-6565. Offers DPT. *Accreditation:* APTA. *Program availability:* Part-time, online learning. *Faculty:* 71 full-time (49 women), 49 part-time/adjunct (32 women). *Students:* 88 full-time (44 women), 7 part-time (6 women); includes 17 minority (3 Black or African American, non-Hispanic/Latino; 1 Asian, non-Hispanic/Latino; 11 Hispanic/Latino; 2 Two or more races, non-Hispanic/Latino), 2 international. Average age 26. 45 applicants, 78% accepted, 29 enrolled. In 2017, 32 doctorates awarded. *Entrance requirements:* Additional exam requirements/recommendations for international students: Required—TOEFL (minimum score 550 paper-based). *Application deadline:* For fall admission, 11/15 priority date for domestic students. Applications are processed on a rolling basis. Application fee: $30. Electronic applications accepted. *Expenses:* Tuition, state resident: part-time $290 per credit hour. Tuition, nonresident: part-time $1173 per credit hour. *Required fees:* $127 per credit hour. Tuition and fees vary according to course load. *Financial support:* In 2017–18, 61 students received support. Career-related internships or fieldwork, Federal Work-Study, and institutionally sponsored loans available. Financial award application deadline: 6/30; financial award applicants required to submit FAFSA. *Faculty research:* Physical therapy practice and education. *Unit head:* Dr. Eric Shamus, Chair/Program Director, 239-590-1418, E-mail: eshamus@fgcu.edu. *Application contact:* MeLinda Coffey, Administrative Assistant, 239-590-7530, Fax: 239-590-7474, E-mail: mcoffey@fgcu.edu.

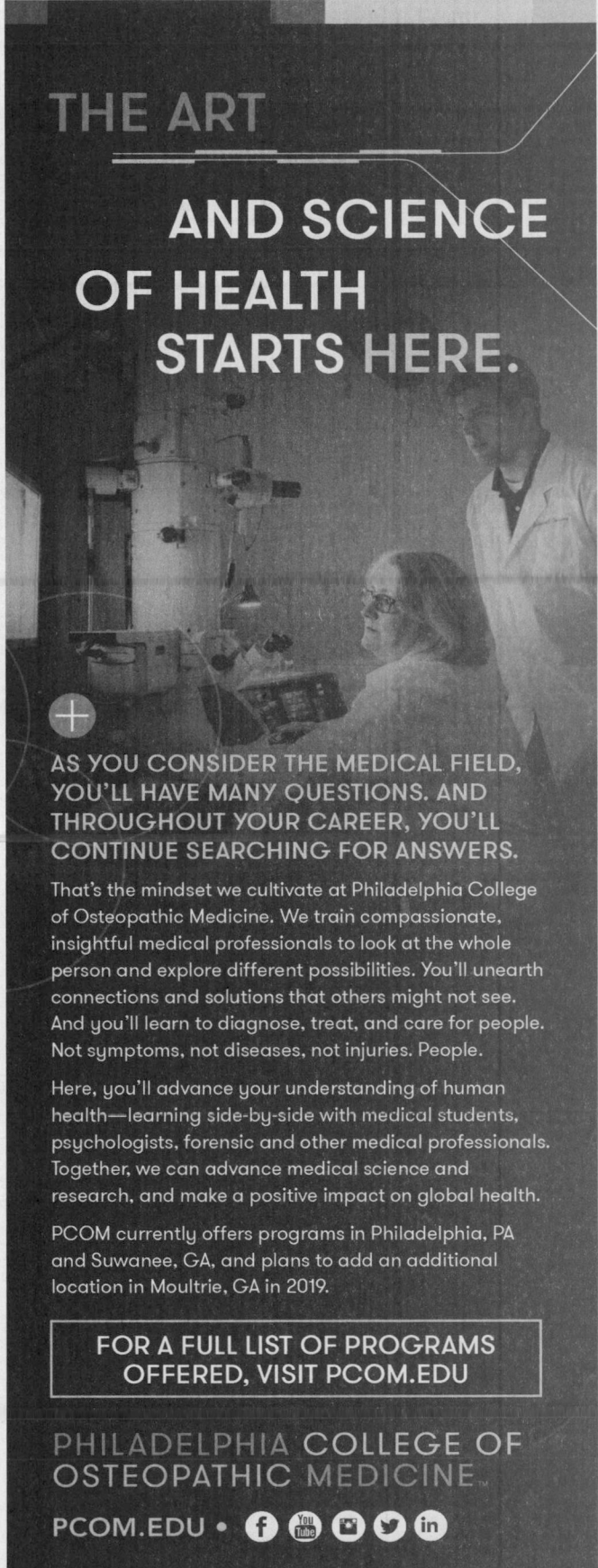

Florida International University, Nicole Wertheim College of Nursing and Health Sciences, Department of Physical Therapy, Miami, FL 33199. Offers DPT. *Accreditation:* APTA. *Program availability:* Part-time. *Faculty:* 7 full-time (4 women), 12 part-time/adjunct (6 women). *Students:* 174 full-time (112 women), 2 part-time (1 woman); includes 111 minority (14 Black or African American, non-Hispanic/Latino; 16 Asian, non-Hispanic/Latino; 78 Hispanic/Latino; 3 Two or more races, non-Hispanic/Latino), 1 international. Average age 26. 739 applicants, 11% accepted, 61 enrolled. In 2017, 53 doctorates awarded. *Degree requirements:* For doctorate, comprehensive exam. *Entrance requirements:* For doctorate, minimum undergraduate GPA of 3.0 in upper-level coursework; letter of intent; resume; at least 40 hours of observation within physical therapy clinic or facility. Additional exam requirements/recommendations for international students: Required—TOEFL (minimum score 550 paper-based; 80 iBT). *Application deadline:* For fall admission, 1/15 for domestic and international students. Application fee: $30. Electronic applications accepted. *Expenses:* Tuition, state resident: full-time $8912; part-time $446 per credit hour. Tuition, nonresident: full-time $21,393; part-time $992 per credit hour. *Required fees:* $390; $195 per semester. *Financial support:* Institutionally sponsored loans, scholarships/grants, and unspecified assistantships available. Financial award application deadline: 3/1; financial award applicants required to submit FAFSA. *Faculty research:* Isokinetic test results and gait abnormalities after knee arthroscopy. *Unit head:* Dr. Mark Rossi, Interim Chair, 305-348-3478, Fax: 305-348-1979, E-mail: mark.rossi@fiu.edu. *Application contact:* Nanett Rojas, Manager, Admissions Operations, 305-348-7464, Fax: 305-348-7441, E-mail: gradadm@fiu.edu.
Website: http://cnhs.fiu.edu/index.html

Franciscan Missionaries of Our Lady University, School of Health Professions, Baton Rouge, LA 70808. Offers health administration (MHA); nutritional sciences (MS); physical therapy (DPT); physician assistant studies (MMS). *Unit head:* Dr. Susan K. Steele-Moses, Dean, 225-768-1676. *Application contact:* Dr. Susan K. Steele-Moses, Dean, 225-768-1676.
Website: https://www.franu.edu/academics/schools/school-of-health-professions

Franklin Pierce University, Graduate and Professional Studies, Rindge, NH 03461-0060. Offers curriculum and instruction (M Ed); elementary education (MS Ed); emerging network technologies (Graduate Certificate); energy and sustainability studies (MBA, Graduate Certificate); health administration (MBA, Graduate Certificate); human resource management (MBA, Graduate Certificate); information technology (MBA); leadership (MBA); nursing education (MS); nursing leadership (MS); physical therapy (DPT); physician assistant studies (MPAS); special education (M Ed); sports management (MBA). *Accreditation:* APTA. *Program availability:* Part-time, 100% online, blended/hybrid learning. *Degree requirements:* For master's, concentrated original research projects; student teaching; fieldwork and/or internship; leadership project; PRAXIS I and II (for M Ed); for doctorate, concentrated original research projects, clinical fieldwork and/or internship, leadership project. *Entrance requirements:* For master's, minimum GPA of 2.5, 3 letters of recommendation; competencies in accounting, economics, statistics, and computer skills through life experience or undergraduate coursework (for MBA); certification/e-portfolio, minimum C grade in all education courses (for M Ed); license to practice as RN (for MS); for doctorate, GRE, 80 hours of observation/work in PT settings; completion of anatomy, chemistry, physics, and statistics; minimum GPA of 3.0. Additional exam requirements/recommendations for international students: Required—TOEFL (minimum score 550 paper-based; 61 iBT). Electronic applications accepted. *Faculty research:* Evidence-based practice in sports physical therapy, human resource management in economic crisis, leadership in nursing, innovation in sports facility management, differentiated learning and understanding by design.

Gannon University, School of Graduate Studies, Morosky College of Health Professions and Sciences, School of Health Professions, Program in Physical Therapy, Erie, PA 16541-0001. Offers DPT. *Accreditation:* APTA. *Degree requirements:* For doctorate, thesis/dissertation or alternative, research project, practicum. *Entrance requirements:* For doctorate, baccalaureate degree from accredited college or university with minimum GPA of 3.0, interview. Additional exam requirements/recommendations for international students: Required—TOEFL (minimum score 79 iBT). Electronic applications accepted. *Expenses:* Contact institution.

George Fox University, Program in Physical Therapy, Newberg, OR 97132-2697. Offers DPT. *Accreditation:* APTA. *Entrance requirements:* For doctorate, bachelor's degree from regionally-accredited university or college, minimum GPA of 3.0. Additional exam requirements/recommendations for international students: Required—TOEFL, IELTS. Electronic applications accepted.

The George Washington University, School of Medicine and Health Sciences, Health Sciences Programs, Program in Physical Therapy, Washington, DC 20052. Offers DPT. *Accreditation:* APTA. *Students:* 133 full-time (99 women); includes 31 minority (15 Asian, non-Hispanic/Latino; 8 Hispanic/Latino; 2 Native Hawaiian or other Pacific Islander, non-Hispanic/Latino; 6 Two or more races, non-Hispanic/Latino), 1 international. Average age 26. 729 applicants, 18% accepted, 47 enrolled. In 2017, 41 doctorates awarded. *Entrance requirements:* Additional exam requirements/recommendations for international students: Required—TOEFL (minimum score 550 paper-based). *Application deadline:* For spring admission, 7/31 priority date for domestic students. Applications are processed on a rolling basis. Application fee: $75. *Expenses: Tuition:* Full-time $28,800; part-time $1655 per credit hour. *Required fees:* $45; $2.75 per credit hour. *Unit head:* Dr. Joyce Maring, Director, 202-994-0053, E-mail: maringj@gwu.edu. *Application contact:* Marsha White, Program Administrator, 202-994-5105, E-mail: hsp@gwu.edu.

Georgia Campus–Philadelphia College of Osteopathic Medicine, Doctor of Physical Therapy Program, Suwanee, GA 30024. Offers DPT.

See Display on this page and Close-Up on page 493.

Georgia Southern University–Armstrong Campus, College of Graduate Studies, Program in Physical Therapy, Savannah, GA 31419-1997. Offers DPT. *Accreditation:* APTA. *Faculty:* 10 full-time (6 women). *Students:* 107 full-time (66 women); includes 7 minority (4 Black or African American, non-Hispanic/Latino; 3 Hispanic/Latino). Average age 25. In 2017, 32 doctorates awarded. *Degree requirements:* For doctorate, thesis/dissertation, licensure exam. *Entrance requirements:* For doctorate, GRE General Test, course work in general biology, chemistry, physical anatomy, physiology, and statistics; letters of recommendation; bachelor's degree; minimum GPA of 3.0; observation hours (recommended); PTCAS application. Additional exam requirements/recommendations for international students: Required—TOEFL (minimum score 600 paper-based; 70 iBT). *Application deadline:* For fall admission, 10/15 priority date for domestic students; for summer admission, 8/15 priority date for domestic students. Applications are processed on a rolling basis. Application fee: $30. Electronic applications accepted. *Expenses:* Contact institution. *Financial support:* In 2017–18, research assistantships with full tuition reimbursements (averaging $5,000 per year) were awarded; career-related internships or fieldwork, scholarships/grants, and unspecified assistantships also available. Financial award application deadline: 3/5; financial award applicants required to submit FAFSA. *Faculty research:* Therapeutic exercise, effectiveness of therapeutic

interventions, injury prevention and prediction, effective teaching and learning in health professions. *Unit head:* Dr. James Karnes, Program Director, 912-344-2580, Fax: 912-344-3439, E-mail: james.karnes@armstrong.edu. *Application contact:* McKenzie Peterman, Graduate Admissions Specialist, 912-478-5678, Fax: 912-478-0740, E-mail: mpeterman@georgiasouthern.edu.
Website: https://www.armstrong.edu/academic-departments/rs-doctor-of-physical-therapy

Georgia State University, Byrdine F. Lewis School of Nursing, Division of Physical Therapy, Atlanta, GA 30302-3083. Offers DPT. *Accreditation:* APTA. *Faculty:* 10 full-time (5 women). *Students:* 120 full-time (70 women); includes 23 minority (7 Black or African American, non-Hispanic/Latino; 5 Asian, non-Hispanic/Latino; 6 Hispanic/Latino; 5 Two or more races, non-Hispanic/Latino). Average age 25. In 2017, 36 doctorates awarded. *Degree requirements:* For doctorate, comprehensive exam, thesis/dissertation or alternative, clinical education. *Entrance requirements:* For doctorate, GRE, transcripts, documentation of Physical Therapy Experience Form, statement of goals. Additional exam requirements/recommendations for international students: Required—TOEFL (minimum score 550 paper-based; 80 iBT). *Application deadline:* For fall admission, 11/15 for domestic and international students. Application fee: $50. Electronic applications accepted. *Expenses:* Contact institution. *Financial support:* In 2017–18, research assistantships with full tuition reimbursements (averaging $2,000 per year), teaching assistantships with full tuition reimbursements (averaging $2,000 per year) were awarded; scholarships/grants, tuition waivers (partial), and unspecified assistantships also available. Financial award application deadline: 4/1; financial award applicants required to submit FAFSA. *Faculty research:* Tissue regeneration, wheelchair propulsion, neurophysiology, function in cerebral palsy, musculoskeletal anatomy and function. *Unit head:* Dr. Andrew Butler, Department Head, 404-413-1415, Fax: 404-413-1230, E-mail: andrewbutler@gsu.edu.
Website: http://physicaltherapy.gsu.edu/

Governors State University, College of Health and Human Services, Program in Physical Therapy, University Park, IL 60484. Offers DPT. *Accreditation:* APTA. *Program availability:* Part-time. *Faculty:* 6 full-time (4 women), 15 part-time/adjunct (8 women). *Students:* 96 full-time (47 women), 7 part-time (6 women); includes 47 minority (4 Black or African American, non-Hispanic/Latino; 3 Asian, non-Hispanic/Latino; 40 Hispanic/Latino). Average age 27. 1 applicant. In 2017, 39 doctorates awarded. *Application deadline:* For fall admission, 4/1 for domestic students. Applications are processed on a rolling basis. Application fee: $75. Electronic applications accepted. *Expenses:* Contact institution. *Financial support:* Application deadline: 5/1; applicants required to submit FAFSA. *Unit head:* Rebecca Wojcik, Chair, Department of Physical Therapy, 708-534-5000 Ext. 2231, E-mail: rwojcik@govst.edu.

Grand Valley State University, College of Health Professions, Physical Therapy Program, Allendale, MI 49401-9403. Offers DPT. *Accreditation:* APTA. *Faculty:* 15 full-time (10 women), 5 part-time/adjunct (all women). *Students:* 178 full-time (124 women); includes 6 minority (1 Black or African American, non-Hispanic/Latino; 1 Hispanic/Latino; 4 Two or more races, non-Hispanic/Latino). Average age 24. 299 applicants, 24% accepted, 58 enrolled. In 2017, 58 doctorates awarded. *Degree requirements:* For doctorate, thesis/dissertation optional. *Entrance requirements:* For doctorate, GRE, PTCAS Application, minimum GPA of 3.0 in most recent 60 hours and in prerequisites, official transcripts from all colleges/universities attended, 50 hours of volunteer work, writing sample, 2 recommendations. Additional exam requirements/recommendations for international students: Required—TOEFL (minimum iBT score of 80), IELTS (6.5), or Michigan English Language Assessment Battery (77). *Application deadline:* For fall admission, 10/15 priority date for domestic and international students. Applications are processed on a rolling basis. Application fee: $30. Electronic applications accepted. *Expenses:* $792 per credit hour. *Financial support:* In 2017–18, 47 students received support, including 25 fellowships, 28 research assistantships with partial tuition reimbursements available (averaging $2,000 per year); career-related internships or fieldwork, Federal Work-Study, institutionally sponsored loans, and unspecified assistantships also available. Financial award application deadline: 2/15. *Faculty research:* Balance deficits, motion analysis, nutritional knowledge of female athletes, trust in athletic performance, spinal functions dysfunction. *Unit head:* Dr. Daniel Vaughn, Director, 616-331-2678, Fax: 616-331-3350, E-mail: vaughnd@gvsu.edu. *Application contact:* Darlene Zwart, Student Services Coordinator, 616-331-3958, Fax: 616-331-5643, E-mail: zwartda@gvsu.edu.
Website: http://www.gvsu.edu/pt/

Hampton University, School of Science, Department of Physical Therapy, Hampton, VA 23668. Offers DPT. *Accreditation:* APTA. *Students:* 81 full-time (52 women); includes 56 minority (44 Black or African American, non-Hispanic/Latino; 1 American Indian or Alaska Native, non-Hispanic/Latino; 5 Asian, non-Hispanic/Latino; 6 Hispanic/Latino). Average age 25. 572 applicants, 5% accepted, 24 enrolled. In 2017, 20 doctorates awarded. *Degree requirements:* For doctorate, thesis/dissertation. *Entrance requirements:* For doctorate, GRE General Test, bachelor's degree, minimum cumulative and prerequisite GPA of 3.0. *Application deadline:* For fall admission, 1/15 priority date for domestic and international students; for winter admission, 1/15 for domestic students; for spring admission, 11/1 for domestic students. Application fee: $35. Electronic applications accepted. *Expenses:* Contact institution. *Financial support:* In 2017–18, 50 students received support. Scholarships/grants available. Financial award application deadline: 2/15; financial award applicants required to submit FAFSA. *Faculty research:* Physical therapy, cardiovascular disease, neuromuscular diseases and conditions, health disparities, cancer. *Unit head:* Dr. Senobia D. Crawford, Chair, 757-727-5260, E-mail: senobia.crawford@hamptonu.edu. *Application contact:* Dr. Stephen Chris Owens, Admissions Coordinator, 757-727-5847, E-mail: stephen.owens@hamptonu.edu.
Website: http://science.hamptonu.edu/pt/

Harding University, College of Allied Health, Program in Physical Therapy, Searcy, AR 72149-0001. Offers DPT. *Accreditation:* APTA. *Faculty:* 9 full-time (3 women). *Students:* 100 full-time (54 women), 2 part-time (1 woman); includes 8 minority (4 Black or African American, non-Hispanic/Latino; 1 American Indian or Alaska Native, non-Hispanic/Latino; 3 Hispanic/Latino). Average age 26. 309 applicants, 27% accepted, 38 enrolled. In 2017, 28 doctorates awarded. *Entrance requirements:* For doctorate, GRE. Additional exam requirements/recommendations for international students: Required—TOEFL (minimum score 550 paper-based). Application fee: $50. *Expenses:* Contact institution. *Unit head:* Dr. Michael McGalliard, Chair and Associate Professor, 501-279-5990, E-mail: mmcgalliard@harding.edu. *Application contact:* 501-279-5990, E-mail: pt@harding.edu.
Website: http://www.harding.edu/pt/

Hardin-Simmons University, Graduate School, Holland School of Sciences and Mathematics, Department of Physical Therapy, Abilene, TX 79698. Offers DPT. *Accreditation:* APTA. *Faculty:* 8 full-time (3 women), 1 part-time/adjunct (0 women). *Students:* 81 full-time (54 women); includes 15 minority (4 Black or African American, non-Hispanic/Latino; 1 Asian, non-Hispanic/Latino; 10 Hispanic/Latino). Average age 23. 326 applicants, 10% accepted, 28 enrolled. In 2017, 28 doctorates awarded. *Degree requirements:* For doctorate, comprehensive exam, thesis/dissertation or alternative. *Entrance requirements:* For doctorate, GRE, letters of recommendation, interview, transcripts from all colleges attended. Additional exam requirements/recommendations for international students: Required—TOEFL (minimum score 550 paper-based; 75 iBT). *Application deadline:* For fall admission, 11/1 priority date for domestic and international students. Application fee: $100 for international students. Electronic applications accepted. *Expenses:* $9,270 per semester tuition; $600 fees per fall/spring semester, $200 summer. *Financial support:* In 2017–18, 80 students received support. Scholarships/grants available. Financial award application deadline: 6/1; financial award applicants required to submit FAFSA. *Faculty research:* Upper limb tension (treatment effects); health promotion for seniors/disabled populations, sports injuries and recovery, sensory integration, postural stability, breathing techniques in tennis players. *Unit head:* Dr. Janelle K. O'Connell, Department Head/Professor, 325-670-5860, Fax: 325-670-5868, E-mail: ptoffice@hsutx.edu.
Website: http://www.hsutx.edu/academics/holland/graduate/physicaltherapy

High Point University, Norcross Graduate School, High Point, NC 27268. Offers athletic training (MSAT); business administration (MBA); educational leadership (M Ed, Ed D); elementary education (M Ed, MAT); pharmacy (Pharm D); physical therapy (DPT); physician assistant studies (MPAS); secondary mathematics (M Ed, MAT); special education (M Ed); strategic communication (MA). *Accreditation:* NCATE. *Program availability:* Part-time, evening/weekend. *Degree requirements:* For master's, comprehensive exam (for some programs), thesis (for some programs). *Entrance requirements:* For master's, GMAT (MBA), GRE, MAT, minimum GPA of 3.0. Additional exam requirements/recommendations for international students: Required—TOEFL (minimum score 550 paper-based). Electronic applications accepted.

Howard University, College of Nursing and Allied Health Sciences, Division of Allied Health Sciences, Washington, DC 20059-0002. Offers occupational therapy (MSOT); physical therapy (DPT); physician assistant (MPA). *Accreditation:* AOTA.

Hunter College of the City University of New York, Graduate School, School of Health Professions, Program in Physical Therapy, New York, NY 10065-5085. Offers DPT. *Accreditation:* APTA. *Entrance requirements:* For doctorate, 2 semesters of course work in biology, physics, chemistry, and psychology; 1 semester of mathematics, statistics, and English composition; CPR certification; minimum GPA of 3.0; documented clinical experience of at least 75 hours under the supervision of a licensed physical therapist, with a minimum of 50 hours in a hospital-based setting. Additional exam requirements/recommendations for international students: Required—TOEFL (minimum score 550 paper-based). Electronic applications accepted. *Faculty research:* Kinematic analysis, Parkinson's disease, gait dysfunction, electrotherapy, brain neurotransmitters.

Husson University, Doctorate in Physical Therapy Program, Bangor, ME 04401-2999. Offers DPT. *Accreditation:* APTA. *Faculty:* 10 full-time (5 women), 2 part-time/adjunct (both women). *Students:* 87 full-time (51 women), 1 (woman) part-time; includes 2 minority (1 Asian, non-Hispanic/Latino; 1 Two or more races, non-Hispanic/Latino), 2 international. Average age 25. 236 applicants, 17% accepted, 15 enrolled. In 2017, 32 doctorates awarded. *Degree requirements:* For doctorate, group research project. *Entrance requirements:* For doctorate, GRE, essay, minimum GPA of 3.0. Additional exam requirements/recommendations for international students: Required—TOEFL (minimum score 550 paper-based; 75 iBT). *Application deadline:* For fall admission, 4/15 for domestic and international students. Application fee: $50. Electronic applications accepted. *Expenses:* $24,747 per year. *Financial support:* In 2017–18, 20 students received support. Federal Work-Study, scholarships/grants, and unspecified assistantships available. Financial award application deadline: 4/15; financial award applicants required to submit FAFSA. *Faculty research:* Educational and leadership processes within physical therapy programs; use of motor control and learning principles in treating clinical populations; approaches from dynamic systems to understand how social, cognitive, and physical development impact motor behavior and physical activity in children with and without disabilities; nervous system plasticity and spinal cord physiology. *Unit head:* Dr. Karen Huhn, Director, 207-941-7620, E-mail: huhnk@husson.edu. *Application contact:* Cecile Ferguson, Administrative Assistant, 207-941-7101, E-mail: fergusonc@husson.edu.
Website: http://www.husson.edu/college-of-health-and-education/school-of-physical-therapy/

Idaho State University, Office of Graduate Studies, School of Rehabilitation and Communication Sciences, Department of Physical and Occupational Therapy, Program in Physical Therapy, Pocatello, ID 83209-8045. Offers DPT. *Accreditation:* APTA. *Degree requirements:* For doctorate, comprehensive exam, thesis/dissertation, oral and written exam. *Entrance requirements:* For doctorate, GRE General Test, minimum GPA of 3.0, 80 hours in 2 practice settings of physical therapy. Additional exam requirements/recommendations for international students: Required—TOEFL (minimum score 600 paper-based). Electronic applications accepted. *Expenses:* Contact institution. *Faculty research:* Cardiovascular/pulmonary balance, neural plasticity, orthopedics, geriatrics, hypertension.

Indiana State University, College of Graduate and Professional Studies, College of Health and Human Services, Department of Applied Medicine and Rehabilitation, Terre Haute, IN 47809. Offers athletic training (MS, DAT); occupational therapy (MS); physical therapy (DPT); physician assistant (MS). *Degree requirements:* For master's, thesis or alternative. *Entrance requirements:* For master's, GRE General Test. Electronic applications accepted.

Indiana University–Purdue University Indianapolis, School of Health and Rehabilitation Sciences, Indianapolis, IN 46202. Offers health and rehabilitation sciences (PhD); health sciences (MS); nutrition and dietetics (MS); occupational therapy (OTD); physical therapy (DPT); physician assistant (MPAS). *Program availability:* Part-time, evening/weekend. *Degree requirements:* For master's, thesis (for some programs). *Entrance requirements:* For master's, GRE General Test, minimum GPA of 3.0 (for MS in health sciences, nutrition and dietetics), 3.2 (for MS in occupational therapy), 3.0 cumulative and prerequisite math/science (for MPAS); for doctorate, GRE, minimum cumulative and prerequisite math/science GPA of 3.2. Additional exam requirements/recommendations for international students: Required—TOEFL (minimum score 550 paper-based; 79 iBT), IELTS (minimum score 6.5), PTE (minimum score 54). Electronic applications accepted. *Expenses:* Contact institution. *Faculty research:* Function and mobility across the lifespan, pediatric nutrition, driving and mobility rehabilitation, neurorehabilitation and biomechanics, rehabilitation and integrative therapy.

Ithaca College, School of Health Sciences and Human Performance, Program in Physical Therapy, Ithaca, NY 14850. Offers DPT. *Accreditation:* APTA. *Faculty:* 19 full-time (11 women), 3 part-time/adjunct (all women). *Students:* 174 full-time (121 women); includes 29 minority (3 Black or African American, non-Hispanic/Latino; 10 Asian, non-Hispanic/Latino; 7 Hispanic/Latino; 9 Two or more races, non-Hispanic/Latino). Average age 22. In 2017, 78 doctorates awarded. *Degree requirements:* For doctorate, thesis/dissertation optional, clinical experience. *Expenses:* Contact institution. *Financial support:* In 2017–18, 117 students received support. Career-related internships or fieldwork, Federal Work-Study, scholarships/grants, and unspecified assistantships available. Support available to part-time students. Financial award application deadline: 3/1; financial award applicants required to submit FAFSA. *Unit head:* Dr. Stephen Lahr, Chair, 607-274-3743, E-mail: lahr@ithaca.edu. *Application contact:* Nicole Eversley Bradwell, Director, Office of Admission, 607-274-3124, Fax: 607-274-1263, E-mail: admission@ithaca.edu.
Website: http://www.ithaca.edu/hshp/depts/pt

Kean University, Nathan Weiss Graduate College, Doctorate Program in Physical Therapy, Union, NJ 07083. Offers DPT. *Faculty:* 6 full-time (4 women). *Students:* 44 full-time (25 women); includes 11 minority (2 Black or African American, non-Hispanic/Latino; 1 Asian, non-Hispanic/Latino; 4 Hispanic/Latino; 4 Two or more races, non-Hispanic/Latino). Average age 24. 496 applicants, 11% accepted, 21 enrolled. *Entrance requirements:* For doctorate, GRE, minimum cumulative GPA of 3.0, satisfactory completion of all course prerequisites with minimum C grade, letters of recommendation, PT Experience form. Additional exam requirements/recommendations for international students: Required—TOEFL (minimum score 550 paper-based; 79 iBT), IELTS (minimum score 6.5). *Application deadline:* For summer admission, 10/1 priority date for domestic and international students. Application fee: $75. Electronic applications accepted. *Expenses:* Contact institution. *Financial support:* Scholarships/grants and unspecified assistantships available. Financial award applicants required to submit FAFSA. *Unit head:* Dr. Shannon N. Clifford, Executive Director, 908-737-6179, E-mail: cliffosh@kean.edu. *Application contact:* Pedro Lopes, Admissions Counselor, 908-737-7100, E-mail: gradadmissions@kean.edu.
Website: http://grad.kean.edu/dpt

Langston University, School of Physical Therapy, Langston, OK 73050. Offers DPT. *Accreditation:* APTA.

Lebanon Valley College, Program in Physical Therapy, Annville, PA 17003-1400. Offers DPT. *Accreditation:* APTA. *Faculty:* 9 full-time (4 women), 32 part-time/adjunct (13 women). *Students:* 70 full-time (47 women); includes 3 minority (1 Black or African American, non-Hispanic/Latino; 1 Asian, non-Hispanic/Latino; 1 Native Hawaiian or other Pacific Islander, non-Hispanic/Latino). Average age 23. 252 applicants, 51% accepted, 66 enrolled. In 2017, 38 doctorates awarded. *Degree requirements:* For doctorate, minimum GPA of 3.0. *Entrance requirements:* For doctorate, GRE, documented clinical hours; minimum overall undergraduate GPA of 3.0, 2.8 science. Additional exam requirements/recommendations for international students: Required—TOEFL (minimum score 80 iBT). *Application deadline:* For fall admission, 2/1 for domestic and international students. Applications are processed on a rolling basis. Application fee: $50. Electronic applications accepted. *Expenses:* $43,320 per academic year; $884 per credit hour (for summer). *Financial support:* In 2017–18, 100 students received support. Federal Work-Study and scholarships/grants available. Financial award application deadline: 3/1; financial award applicants required to submit FAFSA. *Faculty research:* Injury prevention programs, concussions in sports, community based exercise programs for children with autism, effects of manual therapy, benefits of interprofessional educational experiences, walking programs for the elderly and cardiopulmonary effects. *Unit head:* Dr. Katie Oriel, Co-Chair/Professor of Physical Therapy, 717-867-6852, E-mail: oriel@lvc.edu. *Application contact:* EJ Smith, Assistant Director of Admission, 717-867-6183, E-mail: ejsmith@lvc.edu.
Website: http://www.lvc.edu/academics/programs-of-study/physical-therapy

Loma Linda University, School of Allied Health Professions, Department of Physical Therapy, Loma Linda, CA 92350. Offers physical therapy (DPT, PhD); rehabilitation (MS). *Accreditation:* APTA. *Entrance requirements:* Additional exam requirements/recommendations for international students: Required—TOEFL (minimum score 550 paper-based). Electronic applications accepted.

Long Island University–LIU Brooklyn, School of Health Professions, Brooklyn, NY 11201-8423. Offers athletic training and sport sciences (MS); community health (MS Ed); exercise science (MS); forensic social work (Advanced Certificate); occupational therapy (MS); physical therapy (DPT); physician assistant (MS); public health (MPH); social work (MSW); speech-language pathology (MS). *Faculty:* 33 full-time (23 women), 82 part-time/adjunct (55 women). *Students:* 690 full-time (508 women), 86 part-time (74 women); includes 259 minority (120 Black or African American, non-Hispanic/Latino; 1 American Indian or Alaska Native, non-Hispanic/Latino; 52 Asian, non-Hispanic/Latino; 76 Hispanic/Latino; 10 Two or more races, non-Hispanic/Latino), 65 international. Average age 27. 1,241 applicants, 45% accepted, 255 enrolled. In 2017, 249 master's, 42 doctorates, 8 other advanced degrees awarded. *Degree requirements:* For master's, comprehensive exam (for some programs), thesis (for some programs); for doctorate, comprehensive exam (for some programs). *Entrance requirements:* For master's and doctorate, GRE. Additional exam requirements/recommendations for international students: Required—TOEFL (minimum score 550 paper-based; 79 iBT). *Application deadline:* Applications are processed on a rolling basis. Application fee: $50. Electronic applications accepted. *Expenses: Tuition:* Full-time $21,618; part-time $1201 per credit. *Required fees:* $1840; $920 per term. Tuition and fees vary according to course load. *Financial support:* In 2017–18, 187 students received support. Research assistantships, teaching assistantships, career-related internships or fieldwork, Federal Work-Study, scholarships/grants, and unspecified assistantships available. Support available to part-time students. Financial award application deadline: 2/15; financial award applicants required to submit FAFSA. *Faculty research:* Pediatric physical therapy, complementary and alternative medicine, global health and human rights, sport leadership and entrepreneurship, feminist sport psychology. *Unit head:* Dr. Barry S. Eckert, Dean, 718-780-6578, Fax: 718-780-4561, E-mail: barry.eckert@liu.edu. *Application contact:* Dr. Dominick Fortugno, Associate Dean, 718-488-1496, Fax: 718-780-4561, E-mail: dominick.fortugno@liu.edu.
Website: http://liu.edu/brooklyn/academics/school-of-health-professions

Louisiana State University Health Sciences Center, School of Allied Health Professions, Department of Physical Therapy, New Orleans, LA 70112-2223. Offers DPT. *Accreditation:* APTA. *Faculty:* 6 full-time (5 women), 1 (woman) part-time/adjunct. *Students:* 105 full-time (64 women); includes 4 minority (1 Black or African American, non-Hispanic/Latino; 3 Asian, non-Hispanic/Latino). Average age 26. 284 applicants, 12% accepted, 35 enrolled. In 2017, 39 doctorates awarded. *Degree requirements:* For doctorate, thesis/dissertation optional. *Entrance requirements:* For doctorate, GRE General Test (minimum combined score: 296), 60 hours of experience in physical therapy, minimum GPA of 3.0 in math and science, bachelor's degree. *Application deadline:* For fall admission, 10/1 for domestic students; for summer admission, 10/1 for domestic students. Application fee: $140. Electronic applications accepted. *Expenses:* Tuition, state resident: full-time $11,835; part-time $518 per hour. Tuition, nonresident: full-time $24,108; part-time $1079 per hour. *Required fees:* $1254; $55 per hour. *Financial support:* Application deadline: 4/15; applicants required to submit FAFSA. *Faculty research:* Wound healing, spinal cord injury, pain management, geriatrics, muscle physiology, muscle damage, motor control, balance. *Total annual research expenditures:* $101,546. *Unit head:* Dr. Jane M. Eason, Head, 504-568-4288, Fax: 504-568-6552, E-mail: jeason@lsuhsc.edu. *Application contact:* Yudialys Delgado Cazanas, Student Affairs Director, 504-568-4253, Fax: 504-568-3185, E-mail: ydelga@lsuhsc.edu.
Website: http://alliedhealth.lsuhsc.edu/pt/

Marist College, Graduate Programs, School of Science, Poughkeepsie, NY 12601-1387. Offers physical therapy (DPT).

Marquette University, Graduate School, College of Health Sciences, Department of Physical Therapy, Milwaukee, WI 53201-1881. Offers DPT. *Accreditation:* APTA. *Degree requirements:* For doctorate, clinical rotations. *Entrance requirements:* For doctorate, GRE General Test. Additional exam requirements/recommendations for international students: Required—TOEFL. Electronic applications accepted. *Expenses:* Contact institution. *Faculty research:* Urban health issues, mechanisms and management of pain, kinesiologic principles, brain and spinal cord control of human locomotion, mechanisms of motor impairment.

Marshall University, Academic Affairs Division, College of Health Professions, School of Physical Therapy, Huntington, WV 25755. Offers DPT. *Accreditation:* APTA. *Students:* 113 part-time (49 women); includes 3 minority (all Asian, non-Hispanic/Latino). Average age 25. In 2017, 38 doctorates awarded. *Application deadline:* Applications are processed on a rolling basis. *Unit head:* Dr. Penny G. Kroll, Program Director, 800-642-3463, E-mail: kroll@marshall.edu. *Application contact:* Information Contact, 304-746-1900, Fax: 304-746-1902, E-mail: services@marshall.edu.

Marymount University, Malek School of Health Professions, Program in Physical Therapy, Arlington, VA 22207-4299. Offers DPT. *Accreditation:* APTA. *Faculty:* 7 full-time (6 women), 19 part-time/adjunct (15 women). *Students:* 116 full-time (81 women), 2 part-time (1 woman); includes 33 minority (7 Black or African American, non-Hispanic/Latino; 6 Asian, non-Hispanic/Latino; 13 Hispanic/Latino; 7 Two or more races, non-Hispanic/Latino), 2 international. Average age 27. 273 applicants, 50% accepted, 40 enrolled. In 2017, 37 doctorates awarded. *Degree requirements:* For doctorate, comprehensive exam, thesis/dissertation, research presentation. *Entrance requirements:* For doctorate, GRE, 2 letters of recommendation, interview, resume, 40 hours of clinical work experience whether volunteer or observation, essay, minimum GPA of 3.0 from previous university coursework including many standard prerequisites. Additional exam requirements/recommendations for international students: Required—TOEFL (minimum score 600 paper-based; 96 iBT), IELTS (minimum score 6.5). *Application deadline:* For fall admission, 10/15 priority date for domestic and international students. Application fee: $180. Electronic applications accepted. *Expenses:* $37,500 per year. *Financial support:* In 2017–18, 13 students received support, including 7 teaching assistantships with partial tuition reimbursements available (averaging $14,891 per year); research assistantships with partial tuition reimbursements available, career-related internships or fieldwork, Federal Work-Study, scholarships/grants, and unspecified assistantships also available. Financial award application deadline: 3/1; financial award applicants required to submit FAFSA. *Unit head:* Dr. Jennifer Donovan, Chair, Physical Therapy, 703-284-5988, Fax: 703-284-5981, E-mail: jennifer.donovan@marymount.edu. *Application contact:* Francesca Reed, Director, Graduate Admissions, 703-284-5901, Fax: 703-527-3815, E-mail: grad.admissions@marymount.edu.
Website: http://www.marymount.edu/Academics/Malek-School-of-Health-Professions/Graduate-Programs/Physical-Therapy-(D-P-T-)

Maryville University of Saint Louis, Myrtle E. and Earl E. Walker College of Health Professions, Physical Therapy Program, St. Louis, MO 63141-7299. Offers DPT. *Accreditation:* APTA. *Faculty:* 16 full-time (10 women), 3 part-time/adjunct (2 women). *Students:* 81 full-time (54 women), 38 part-time (28 women); includes 6 minority (1 Black or African American, non-Hispanic/Latino; 1 Asian, non-Hispanic/Latino; 4 Hispanic/Latino). Average age 23. In 2017, 38 doctorates awarded. *Degree requirements:* For doctorate, clinical rotations. *Entrance requirements:* For doctorate, minimum cumulative GPA of 3.25 or ACT composite of 24, 2 letters of recommendation, interview, documentation of observation hours. Additional exam requirements/recommendations for international students: Required—TOEFL (minimum score 573 paper-based). *Application deadline:* Applications are processed on a rolling basis. Electronic applications accepted. *Expenses:* $897 per credit hour, $450 per semester part-time fee, $1,200 per semester full-time. *Financial support:* Career-related internships or fieldwork, Federal Work-Study, and campus employment available. Financial award application deadline: 4/1; financial award applicants required to submit FAFSA. *Faculty research:* Memory and exercise. *Unit head:* Dr. Michelle Unterberg, Director, 314-529-9590, Fax: 314-529-9946, E-mail: munterberg@maryville.edu. *Application contact:* Jeannie DeLuca, Director of Admissions and Advising, 314-529-9355, Fax: 314-529-9927, E-mail: jdeluca@maryville.edu.
Website: http://www.maryville.edu/hp/physical-therapy/

Mayo Clinic School of Health Sciences, Program in Physical Therapy, Rochester, MN 55905. Offers DPT. *Accreditation:* APTA. *Degree requirements:* For doctorate, comprehensive exam. *Entrance requirements:* For doctorate, GRE, official transcripts, three letters of recommendation. Additional exam requirements/recommendations for international students: Required—TOEFL. *Application deadline:* For fall admission, 10/16 for domestic and international students. Applications are processed on a rolling basis. Electronic applications accepted. *Expenses:* Contact institution. *Financial support:* Scholarships/grants available. Financial award applicants required to submit FAFSA. *Faculty research:* Biomechanics, gait analysis, growth factor-mediated plasticity in muscle, musculoskeletal clinical tests and measures, Parkinson's disease, coordination testing. *Unit head:* Dr. John Hollman, Director, 507-284-2054, Fax: 507-284-0656, E-mail: hollman.john@mayo.edu. *Application contact:* Carol Cooper, Administrative Assistant, 507-284-2054, Fax: 507-284-0656, E-mail: cooper.carol@mayo.edu.
Website: http://www.mayo.edu/mayo-clinic-school-of-health-sciences/careers/physical-therapy/physical-therapy-doctoral-program-minnesota

McMaster University, Faculty of Health Sciences, Professional Program in Physiotherapy, Hamilton, ON L8S 4M2, Canada. Offers M Sc. *Degree requirements:* For master's, clinical placements, independent research project. *Entrance requirements:* For master's, minimum B average over last 60 undergraduate units. Additional exam requirements/recommendations for international students: Required—TOEFL (minimum score 600 paper-based).

MCPHS University, School of Physical Therapy, Boston, MA 02115-5896. Offers DPT.

Medical University of South Carolina, College of Health Professions, Program in Physical Therapy, Charleston, SC 29425. Offers DPT. *Accreditation:* APTA. *Program availability:* Online learning. *Entrance requirements:* For doctorate, GRE, references, minimum GPA of 3.0, volunteer hours. Additional exam requirements/recommendations for international students: Required—TOEFL (minimum score 600 paper-based). Electronic applications accepted. *Faculty research:* Low back pain, spinal cord injury.

Mercer University, Graduate Studies, Cecil B. Day Campus, College of Health Professions, Atlanta, GA 30341. Offers athletic training (MAT); clinical medical psychology (Psy D); physical therapy (DPT); physician assistant studies (MM Sc); public health (MPH); DPT/MBA; DPT/MPH; MM Sc/MPH; Pharm D/MPH. *Faculty:* 23 full-time (14 women), 10 part-time/adjunct (7 women). *Students:* 345 full-time (261 women), 67 part-time (55 women); includes 167 minority (116 Black or African American, non-Hispanic/Latino; 28 Asian, non-Hispanic/Latino; 21 Hispanic/Latino; 2 Two or more races, non-Hispanic/Latino), 2 international. Average age 26. In 2017, 83 master's, 37 doctorates awarded. *Expenses:* Contact institution. *Financial support:* Federal Work-Study, traineeships, and unspecified assistantships available. *Faculty research:* Scholarship of teaching and learning, health disparities, clinical outcomes, health promotion. *Unit head:* Dr. Lisa Lundquist, Dean/Clinical Professor, 678-547-6308, E-mail: lundquist_lm@mercer.edu. *Application contact:* Laura Ellison, Director of Admissions and Student Affairs, 678-547-6391, E-mail: ellison_la@mercer.edu.
Website: http://chp.mercer.edu/

Physical Therapy

Mercy College, School of Health and Natural Sciences, Program in Physical Therapy, Dobbs Ferry, NY 10522-1189. Offers DPT. *Accreditation:* APTA. *Program availability:* Evening/weekend. *Students:* 100 full-time (49 women), 16 part-time (8 women); includes 51 minority (6 Black or African American, non-Hispanic/Latino; 23 Asian, non-Hispanic/Latino; 18 Hispanic/Latino; 4 Two or more races, non-Hispanic/Latino). Average age 33. 453 applicants, 14% accepted, 29 enrolled. In 2017, 25 doctorates awarded. *Entrance requirements:* For doctorate, interview, two letters of recommendations, official college transcripts with minimum GPA of 3.0, two-page typewritten essay on reasons for pursuing career in physical therapy, volunteer/work experience forms demonstrating at least 80 hours of volunteer work or work-related experience. Additional exam requirements/recommendations for international students: Required—TOEFL (minimum score 600 paper-based; 100 iBT), IELTS (minimum score 8). *Application deadline:* Applications are processed on a rolling basis. Application fee: $62. Electronic applications accepted. *Expenses:* Contact institution. *Financial support:* Career-related internships or fieldwork, Federal Work-Study, scholarships/grants, and unspecified assistantships available. Support available to part-time students. Financial award applicants required to submit FAFSA. *Unit head:* Dr. Joan Toglia, Dean, School of Health and Natural Sciences, 914-674-7837, E-mail: jtoglia@mercy.edu. *Application contact:* Allison Gurdineer, Senior Director of Admissions, 877-637-2946, Fax: 914-674-7382, E-mail: admissions@mercy.edu.
Website: https://www.mercy.edu/degrees-programs/doctorate-physical-therapy

MGH Institute of Health Professions, School of Health and Rehabilitation Sciences, Doctor of Physical Therapy Program, Boston, MA 02129. Offers DPT. *Accreditation:* APTA. *Degree requirements:* For doctorate, thesis/dissertation or alternative, research project. *Entrance requirements:* For doctorate, GRE General Test, interview, minimum of 10 physical therapy observation hours, bachelor's degree from regionally-accredited college or university. Additional exam requirements/recommendations for international students: Required—TOEFL (minimum score 550 paper-based; 80 iBT). Electronic applications accepted. *Faculty research:* Disability in the elderly; gait, balance, and posture; cardiac rehabilitation: relationship of impairment to disability.

MGH Institute of Health Professions, School of Health and Rehabilitation Sciences, MS Program in Physical Therapy, Boston, MA 02129. Offers MS, Certificate. *Program availability:* Part-time, evening/weekend. *Degree requirements:* For master's, thesis, clinical preceptorship. *Entrance requirements:* For master's, GRE General Test, graduation from an approved program in physical therapy. Additional exam requirements/recommendations for international students: Required—TOEFL (minimum score 550 paper-based; 80 iBT). Electronic applications accepted. *Faculty research:* Disability in the elderly; gait, balance and posture; cardiac rehabilitation; relationship of impairment to disability; effect of muscle strengthening in the elderly.

Midwestern University, Downers Grove Campus, College of Health Sciences, Illinois Campus, Program in Physical Therapy, Downers Grove, IL 60515-1235. Offers DPT. *Accreditation:* APTA. *Entrance requirements:* For doctorate, GRE General Test. *Application deadline:* Applications are processed on a rolling basis. Application fee: $50. *Expenses:* Contact institution. *Financial support:* Federal Work-Study available.
Website: http://www.midwestern.edu/

Midwestern University, Glendale Campus, College of Health Sciences, Arizona Campus, Program in Physical Therapy, Glendale, AZ 85308. Offers DPT. *Accreditation:* APTA. *Entrance requirements:* For doctorate, GRE General Test, bachelor's degree, minimum cumulative GPA of 2.75. *Application deadline:* For fall admission, 12/15 for domestic students. Applications are processed on a rolling basis.

Misericordia University, College of Health Sciences and Education, Program in Physical Therapy, Dallas, PA 18612-1098. Offers DPT. *Accreditation:* APTA. *Entrance requirements:* For doctorate, GRE General Test, minimum undergraduate GPA of 3.0, volunteer experience. Additional exam requirements/recommendations for international students: Required—TOEFL. Electronic applications accepted. *Faculty research:* Wound care, computer-assisted instruction, instruction in applied physiology, isokinetics, prosthetics.

Missouri State University, Graduate College, College of Health and Human Services, Department of Physical Therapy, Springfield, MO 65897. Offers DPT. *Accreditation:* APTA. *Faculty:* 7 full-time (4 women), 13 part-time/adjunct (4 women). *Students:* 115 full-time (67 women); includes 12 minority (1 Black or African American, non-Hispanic/Latino; 2 American Indian or Alaska Native, non-Hispanic/Latino; 2 Asian, non-Hispanic/Latino; 3 Hispanic/Latino; 4 Two or more races, non-Hispanic/Latino). Average age 24. 69 applicants, 64% accepted, 38 enrolled. In 2017, 40 doctorates awarded. *Degree requirements:* For doctorate, comprehensive exam, thesis/dissertation or alternative. *Entrance requirements:* For doctorate, GRE, minimum GPA of 3.0, PTCAS. Additional exam requirements/recommendations for international students: Required—TOEFL (minimum score 550 paper-based; 79 iBT), IELTS (minimum score 6). *Application deadline:* For fall admission, 12/15 for domestic and international students. Application fee: $35 ($50 for international students). Electronic applications accepted. *Expenses:* Tuition, state resident: full-time $2915; part-time $2021 per credit hour. Tuition, nonresident: full-time $5354; part-time $3647 per credit hour. *International tuition:* $11,992 full-time. *Required fees:* $173; $173 per credit hour. Tuition and fees vary according to class time, course level, course load, degree level, campus/location and program. *Financial support:* Federal Work-Study, institutionally sponsored loans, and unspecified assistantships available. Financial award application deadline: 3/31; financial award applicants required to submit FAFSA. *Faculty research:* Complex regional pain syndrome (CRPS), posture and the temporomandibular joint, clinical orthopedics, aging of the motor system. *Unit head:* Dr. Jeanne Cook, Department Head, 417-836-6179, Fax: 417-836-6229, E-mail: physicaltherapy@missouristate.edu. *Application contact:* Stephanie Praschan, Director, Graduate Enrollment Management, 417-836-5330, Fax: 417-836-6200, E-mail: stephaniepraschan@missouristate.edu.
Website: http://www.missouristate.edu/physicaltherapy/

Mount St. Joseph University, Physical Therapy Program, Cincinnati, OH 45233-1670. Offers DPT. *Accreditation:* APTA. *Faculty:* 6 full-time (4 women), 12 part-time/adjunct (8 women). *Students:* 83 full-time (53 women), 37 part-time (20 women); includes 1 minority (Black or African American, non-Hispanic/Latino). Average age 24. In 2017, 32 doctorates awarded. *Degree requirements:* For doctorate, clinical internship; integrative project. *Entrance requirements:* For doctorate, GRE, minimum GPA of 3.0; prerequisite coursework in sciences, humanities, social sciences, and statistics; 80 observation hours; at least 80 hours of clinical observation in 2 different physical therapy settings; PTCAS application. Additional exam requirements/recommendations for international students: Required—TOEFL (minimum score 560 paper-based; 83 iBT). *Application deadline:* For fall admission, 11/1 for domestic students. Application fee: $50. Electronic applications accepted. *Expenses:* Contact institution. *Financial support:* Applicants required to submit FAFSA. *Faculty research:* Utilizing technology in learning, neurobiology, assessment of student learning, critical thinking, effectiveness of distance education methods. *Unit head:* Dr. Rosanne Thomas, Chair, 513-244-4519, Fax: 513-451-2547, E-mail: rosanne.thomas@msj.edu. *Application contact:* Mary Brigham, Assistant Director of Graduate Recruitment, 513-244-4233, Fax: 513-244-4629, E-mail: mary.brigham@msj.edu.
Website: http://www.msj.edu/academics/graduate-programs/doctor-of-physical-therapy1/

Mount Saint Mary's University, Graduate Division, Los Angeles, CA 90049. Offers business administration (MBA); counseling psychology (MS); creative writing (MFA); education (MS, Certificate); film and television (MFA); health policy and management (MS); humanities (MA); nursing (MSN, Certificate); physical therapy (DPT); religious studies (MA). *Program availability:* Part-time, evening/weekend. *Faculty:* 50 full-time (35 women), 116 part-time/adjunct (81 women). *Students:* 670 full-time (518 women), 147 part-time (116 women); includes 414 minority (73 Black or African American, non-Hispanic/Latino; 4 American Indian or Alaska Native, non-Hispanic/Latino; 60 Asian, non-Hispanic/Latino; 259 Hispanic/Latino; 7 Native Hawaiian or other Pacific Islander, non-Hispanic/Latino; 11 Two or more races, non-Hispanic/Latino), 4 international. Average age 32. 1,398 applicants, 21% accepted, 242 enrolled. In 2017, 170 master's, 28 doctorates, 35 other advanced degrees awarded. *Entrance requirements:* Additional exam requirements/recommendations for international students: Required—TOEFL. *Application deadline:* For fall admission, 6/30 priority date for domestic and international students; for spring admission, 10/30 priority date for domestic and international students; for summer admission, 3/30 priority date for domestic and international students. Applications are processed on a rolling basis. Application fee: $50. Electronic applications accepted. *Expenses: Tuition:* Part-time $905 per unit. One-time fee: $155 part-time. Tuition and fees vary according to degree level and program. *Financial support:* Career-related internships or fieldwork, Federal Work-Study, institutionally sponsored loans, and tuition waivers (full and partial) available. Support available to part-time students. Financial award application deadline: 3/15; financial award applicants required to submit FAFSA. *Unit head:* Albert Ramos, Director of Graduate Admissions, 213-477-2800, E-mail: gradprograms@msmu.edu. *Application contact:* Shawn Peters, Graduate Admission Counselor, 213-477-2676, E-mail: gradprograms@msmu.edu.
Website: http://www.msmu.edu/graduate-programs/

Nazareth College of Rochester, Graduate Studies, Department of Physical Therapy, Rochester, NY 14618. Offers DPT. *Entrance requirements:* For doctorate, minimum GPA of 3.0 in prerequisite coursework and overall. Additional exam requirements/recommendations for international students: Required—TOEFL (minimum score 550 paper-based, 79 iBT) or IELTS (6.5). *Expenses:* Contact institution.

Neumann University, Program in Physical Therapy, Aston, PA 19014-1298. Offers DPT. *Accreditation:* APTA. *Program availability:* Evening/weekend. *Faculty:* 6 full-time (5 women), 3 part-time/adjunct (2 women). *Students:* 82 full-time (45 women); includes 18 minority (6 Black or African American, non-Hispanic/Latino; 1 American Indian or Alaska Native, non-Hispanic/Latino; 4 Asian, non-Hispanic/Latino; 5 Hispanic/Latino; 2 Two or more races, non-Hispanic/Latino). Average age 26. 169 applicants, 28% accepted, 32 enrolled. In 2017, 25 doctorates awarded. *Degree requirements:* For doctorate, comprehensive exam. *Entrance requirements:* For doctorate, GRE, official transcripts from all institutions attended, resume, letter of intent, documentation of at least 200 observation hours, 3 letters of recommendation. Additional exam requirements/recommendations for international students: Required—TOEFL (minimum score 89 iBT). *Application deadline:* For summer admission, 5/14 for domestic students. Applications are processed on a rolling basis. Application fee: $0. Electronic applications accepted. *Expenses:* $950 per credit hour. *Financial support:* Scholarships/grants and health care benefits available. Support available to part-time students. Financial award application deadline: 3/15; financial award applicants required to submit FAFSA. *Unit head:* Dr. Robert E Post, Program Director, Physical Therapy, 610-558-5233, Fax: 610-459-1370, E-mail: postr@neumann.edu. *Application contact:* Dr. Erika K. Davis, Director of Adult and Graduate Admissions, 800-9-NEUMANN Ext. 5208, Fax: 610-361-2548, E-mail: gradadultadmiss@neumann.edu.

New York Institute of Technology, School of Health Professions, Department of Physical Therapy, Old Westbury, NY 11568-8000. Offers DPT. *Accreditation:* APTA. *Faculty:* 10 full-time (5 women), 8 part-time/adjunct (5 women). *Students:* 122 full-time (63 women), 2 part-time (0 women); includes 47 minority (7 Black or African American, non-Hispanic/Latino; 19 Asian, non-Hispanic/Latino; 17 Hispanic/Latino; 4 Two or more races, non-Hispanic/Latino), 1 international. Average age 25. 673 applicants, 10% accepted, 40 enrolled. In 2017, 32 doctorates awarded. *Entrance requirements:* For doctorate, bachelor's or master's degree; minimum undergraduate GPA of 3.0; previous coursework in humanities, social sciences, and natural sciences; competency in English writing; essay; 100 hours of volunteer or paid work under direct supervision of a physical therapist; 2 professional letters of recommendation. Additional exam requirements/recommendations for international students: Required—TOEFL (minimum score 79 iBT), IELTS (minimum score 6). *Application deadline:* For summer admission, 10/16 for domestic and international students. Applications are processed on a rolling basis. Application fee: $50. Electronic applications accepted. *Expenses:* $1,285 per credit plus fees. *Financial support:* Federal Work-Study, scholarships/grants, tuition waivers (full and partial), and unspecified assistantships available. Support available to part-time students. Financial award application deadline: 2/15; financial award applicants required to submit FAFSA. *Faculty research:* Parkinson's disease; response to different exercise protocols; virtual reality in rehabilitation; running mechanics; dual task training. *Unit head:* Dr. Karen Friel, Department Chair, 516-686-7651, Fax: 516-686-7699, E-mail: kfriel@nyit.edu. *Application contact:* Alice Dolitsky, Director, Graduate Admissions, 516-686-7520, Fax: 516-686-1116, E-mail: nyitgrad@nyit.edu.
Website: http://www.nyit.edu/degrees/physical_therapy

New York Medical College, School of Health Sciences and Practice, Valhalla, NY 10595. Offers behavioral sciences and health promotion (MPH); biostatistics (MS); children with special health care (Graduate Certificate); emergency preparedness (Graduate Certificate); environmental health science (MPH); epidemiology (MPH, MS); global health (Graduate Certificate); health education (Graduate Certificate); health policy and management (MPH, Dr PH); industrial hygiene (Graduate Certificate); pediatric dysphagia (Post-Graduate Certificate); physical therapy (DPT); public health (Graduate Certificate); speech-language pathology (MS). *Accreditation:* CEPH. *Program availability:* Part-time, evening/weekend, 100% online, blended/hybrid learning. *Faculty:* 48 full-time (33 women), 235 part-time/adjunct (141 women). *Students:* 221 full-time (153 women), 270 part-time (194 women); includes 202 minority (83 Black or African American, non-Hispanic/Latino; 2 American Indian or Alaska Native, non-Hispanic/Latino; 64 Asian, non-Hispanic/Latino; 47 Hispanic/Latino; 1 Native Hawaiian or other Pacific Islander, non-Hispanic/Latino; 5 Two or more races, non-Hispanic/Latino), 19 international. Average age 29. 1,118 applicants, 38% accepted, 169 enrolled. In 2017, 110 master's, 41 doctorates awarded. *Degree requirements:* For master's, comprehensive exam (for some programs), thesis (for some programs); for doctorate, thesis/dissertation. *Entrance requirements:* For master's, GRE (for MS in speech-language pathology); for doctorate, GRE. Additional exam requirements/recommendations for international students: Required—TOEFL, IELTS. *Application deadline:* For fall admission, 8/1 for domestic students, 4/15 for international students; for spring admission, 12/1 for domestic students; for summer admission, 5/1 for domestic students, 4/15 for international students. Application fee: $125. Electronic applications accepted. *Expenses:* $1,125 per credit, $245 fees. *Financial support:* In 2017–18, 10,000 students received support. Scholarships/grants and unspecified assistantships available. Financial award application deadline: 4/30; financial award applicants required to submit FAFSA. *Unit head:* Ben Watson, PhD, Vice Dean, 914-594-4531, E-mail: ben_watson@nymc.edu. *Application contact:* Irene Bundziak, Assistant to Director of Admissions, 914-594-4905, E-mail: irene_bundziak@nymc.edu.
Website: http://www.nymc.edu/school-of-health-sciences-and-practice-shsp/

New York University, Steinhardt School of Culture, Education, and Human Development, Department of Physical Therapy, New York, NY 10010-5615. Offers orthopedic physical therapy (Advanced Certificate); physical therapy (MA, DPT, PhD), including pathokinesiology (MA). *Accreditation:* APTA (one or more programs are accredited). *Program availability:* Part-time. *Students:* Average age 29. 479 applicants, 23% accepted, 51 enrolled. In 2017, 5 master's, 36 doctorates, 6 other advanced degrees awarded. *Entrance requirements:* For master's, physical therapy certificate; for doctorate, GRE General Test, interview, physical therapy certificate. Additional exam requirements/recommendations for international students: Required—TOEFL (minimum score 100 iBT). *Application deadline:* For fall admission, 12/1 priority date for domestic and international students; for spring admission, 10/1 for domestic and international students. Applications are processed on a rolling basis. Application fee: $75. Electronic applications accepted. *Expenses: Tuition:* Full-time $41,352; part-time $19,968 per year. *Required fees:* $2496; $1628 per unit. $814 per term. Tuition and fees vary according to course load and program. *Financial support:* Fellowships with full and partial tuition reimbursements, research assistantships with full and partial tuition reimbursements, career-related internships or fieldwork, Federal Work-Study, scholarships/grants, tuition waivers (partial), and unspecified assistantships available. Support available to part-time students. Financial award application deadline: 2/1; financial award applicants required to submit FAFSA. *Faculty research:* Motor learning and control, neuromuscular disorders, biomechanics and ergonomics, movement analysis, pathomechanics. *Unit head:* Prof. Mitchell Batavia, Chairperson, 212-998-9400, Fax: 212-995-4190, E-mail: mitchell.batavia@nyu.edu. *Application contact:* 212-998-5030, Fax: 212-995-4328, E-mail: steinhardt.gradadmissions@nyu.edu.
Website: http://steinhardt.nyu.edu/pt

Northern Arizona University, College of Health and Human Services, Department of Physical Therapy, Flagstaff, AZ 86011. Offers DPT. *Accreditation:* APTA. *Program availability:* Blended/hybrid learning. *Faculty:* 22 full-time (14 women), 13 part-time/adjunct (8 women). *Students:* 307 full-time (197 women), 2 part-time (1 woman); includes 67 minority (2 Black or African American, non-Hispanic/Latino; 3 American Indian or Alaska Native, non-Hispanic/Latino; 8 Asian, non-Hispanic/Latino; 39 Hispanic/Latino; 15 Two or more races, non-Hispanic/Latino). Average age 25. 1,128 applicants, 11% accepted, 118 enrolled. In 2017, 80 doctorates awarded. *Degree requirements:* For doctorate, variable foreign language requirement, comprehensive exam (for some programs), thesis/dissertation (for some programs), fieldwork experience/internship, individualized research. *Entrance requirements:* For doctorate, GRE General Test. Additional exam requirements/recommendations for international students: Required—TOEFL (minimum score 100 iBT), IELTS (minimum score 6.5). *Application deadline:* For fall admission, 3/1 for domestic and international students; for spring admission, 10/1 for domestic and international students. Applications are processed on a rolling basis. Application fee: $65. Electronic applications accepted. *Expenses:* Contact institution. *Financial support:* Health care benefits and tuition waivers (full and partial) available. Financial award application deadline: 2/1; financial award applicants required to submit FAFSA. *Unit head:* Dr. Patricia S. Pohl, Chair, 602-827-2427, E-mail: patricia.pohl@nau.edu. *Application contact:* Tina Sutton, Coordinator, Graduate College, 928-523-4348, Fax: 928-523-8950, E-mail: graduate@nau.edu.
Website: https://nau.edu/chhs/physical-therapy/

Northern Illinois University, Graduate School, College of Health and Human Sciences, School of Allied Health and Communicative Disorders, Program in Physical Therapy, De Kalb, IL 60115-2854. Offers DPT. *Accreditation:* APTA; CEPH. *Program availability:* Part-time. *Students:* 104 full-time (50 women); includes 16 minority (1 Black or African American, non-Hispanic/Latino; 3 Asian, non-Hispanic/Latino; 7 Hispanic/Latino; 5 Two or more races, non-Hispanic/Latino). Average age 26. 137 applicants, 34% accepted, 34 enrolled. In 2017, 32 doctorates awarded. *Entrance requirements:* Additional exam requirements/recommendations for international students: Required—TOEFL (minimum score 550 paper-based). *Application deadline:* For fall admission, 6/1 for domestic students, 5/1 for international students; for spring admission, 11/1 for domestic students, 10/1 for international students. Applications are processed on a rolling basis. Application fee: $40. Electronic applications accepted. *Financial support:* Fellowships with full tuition reimbursements, research assistantships with full tuition reimbursements, teaching assistantships with full tuition reimbursements, career-related internships or fieldwork, Federal Work-Study, scholarships/grants, tuition waivers (full), and unspecified assistantships available. Support available to part-time students. Financial award applicants required to submit FAFSA. *Faculty research:* Stroke rehabilitation, radon exposure prevention, environmental causes of cancer, body image in young girls. *Unit head:* Dr. Russell Carter, Program Director, 815-753-1486, Fax: 815-753-6169, E-mail: ahcd@niu.edu. *Application contact:* Graduate School Office, 815-753-0395, E-mail: gradsch@niu.edu.
Website: http://www.chhs.niu.edu/physical_therapy/

Northwestern University, Feinberg School of Medicine, Department of Physical Therapy and Human Movement Sciences, Chicago, IL 60611-2814. Offers neuroscience (PhD), including movement and rehabilitation science; physical therapy (DPT); DPT/MPH; DPT/PhD. *Accreditation:* APTA. *Degree requirements:* For doctorate, research project. *Entrance requirements:* For doctorate, GRE General Test (for DPT), baccalaureate degree with minimum GPA of 3.0 in required course work (DPT). Additional exam requirements/recommendations for international students: Required—TOEFL (minimum score 100 iBT). *Application deadline:* For fall admission, 10/1 for domestic and international students. Applications are processed on a rolling basis. Electronic applications accepted. *Expenses:* Contact institution. *Financial support:* Institutionally sponsored loans and scholarships/grants available. Financial award application deadline: 3/1; financial award applicants required to submit FAFSA. *Unit head:* Dr. Julius P. A. Dewald, Professor and Chair, 312-908-8160, Fax: 312-908-0741. *Application contact:* Dr. Jane Sullivan, Professor/Assistant Chair for Recruitment and Admissions, 312-908-8160, Fax: 312-908-0741, E-mail: dpt-admissions@northwestern.edu.
Website: http://www.feinberg.northwestern.edu/sites/pthms/

Nova Southeastern University, Dr. Pallavi Patel College of Health Care Sciences, Fort Lauderdale, FL 33314-7796. Offers anesthesiologist assistant (MSA); audiology (Au D); health science (MH Sc, DHSc, PhD); occupational therapy (MOT, Dr OT, PhD); physical therapy (DPT, TDPT); physician assistant (MMS); speech-language pathology (MS). *Accreditation:* AOTA. *Faculty:* 54 full-time (31 women), 15 part-time/adjunct (7 women). *Students:* 501 full-time (407 women); includes 131 minority (18 Black or African American, non-Hispanic/Latino; 2 American Indian or Alaska Native, non-Hispanic/Latino; 45 Asian, non-Hispanic/Latino; 65 Hispanic/Latino; 1 Two or more races, non-Hispanic/Latino). Average age 24. 7,600 applicants, 7% accepted, 452 enrolled. In 2017, 616 master's, 225 doctorates awarded. *Degree requirements:* For doctorate, comprehensive exam, thesis/dissertation (for some programs), 12-month full-time clinical externship experience. *Entrance requirements:* For master's, GRE General Test; for doctorate, GRE General Test, personal interview, essay in application, on-site essay. *Application deadline:* For spring admission, 2/15 for domestic and international students; for summer admission, 12/1 for domestic and international students. Applications are processed on a rolling basis. Application fee: $50. Electronic applications accepted. *Expenses:* Contact institution. *Financial support:* Federal Work-Study, institutionally sponsored loans, and scholarships/grants available. Financial award application deadline: 4/15; financial award applicants required to submit FAFSA. *Faculty research:* Efferent suppression and auditory processing delay, subjective visual vertical in vestibular assessment, competency-based clinical evaluation, hearing instrument performance for frequency lowering, hearing instrument performance for noise suppression, anxiety and dizziness in college students, audiology assistants. *Unit head:* Dr. Stanley Wilson, Dean, 954-262-1203, E-mail: swilson@nova.edu. *Application contact:* Joey Jankie, Admissions Counselor, 954-262-7249, E-mail: joey@nova.edu.
Website: http://healthsciences.nova.edu/

Oakland University, Graduate Study and Lifelong Learning, School of Health Sciences, Program in Physical Therapy, Rochester, MI 48309-4401. Offers clinical exercise science (Dr Sc PT); complementary medicine and wellness (Dr Sc PT); corporate worksite wellness (Dr Sc PT); exercise science (Dr Sc PT); neurological rehabilitation (Dr Sc PT, TDPT); orthopedic manual physical therapy (Dr Sc PT, TDPT, Graduate Certificate); orthopedic physical therapy (Graduate Certificate); orthopedics (Dr Sc PT, TDPT); pediatric rehabilitation (Dr Sc PT, TDPT); physical therapy (DPT); teaching and learning for rehabilitation professionals (Dr Sc PT, TDPT). *Accreditation:* APTA. *Entrance requirements:* For doctorate, GRE General Test. Additional exam requirements/recommendations for international students: Required—TOEFL (minimum score 550 paper-based). *Expenses:* Contact institution.

The Ohio State University, College of Medicine, School of Health and Rehabilitation Sciences, Program in Physical Therapy, Columbus, OH 43210. Offers DPT. *Accreditation:* APTA. *Faculty:* 13. *Students:* 144 full-time (100 women); includes 5 minority (all Hispanic/Latino). Average age 24. In 2017, 46 doctorates awarded. *Degree requirements:* For doctorate, thesis/dissertation. *Entrance requirements:* For doctorate, GRE General Test. Additional exam requirements/recommendations for international students: Required—TOEFL (minimum score 550 paper-based; 79 iBT), Michigan English Language Assessment Battery (minimum score 82); Recommended—IELTS (minimum score 7). *Application deadline:* For summer admission, 10/3 for domestic and international students. Applications are processed on a rolling basis. Application fee: $60 ($70 for international students). Electronic applications accepted. *Financial support:* Fellowships with tuition reimbursements available. *Unit head:* Dr. Deborah S. Larsen, Associate Dean and Director, 614-292-5645, Fax: 614-292-0210, E-mail: larsen.64@osu.edu. *Application contact:* Graduate and Professional Admissions, 614-292-9444, Fax: 614-292-3895, E-mail: gpadmissions@osu.edu.
Website: http://medicine.osu.edu/hrs/pt

Ohio University, Graduate College, College of Health Sciences and Professions, School of Rehabilitation and Communication Sciences, Division of Physical Therapy, Athens, OH 45701-2979. Offers DPT. Applications accepted for summer term only. *Accreditation:* APTA. *Entrance requirements:* For doctorate, GRE. Additional exam requirements/recommendations for international students: Required—TOEFL (minimum score 550 paper-based; 80 iBT) or IELTS (minimum score 6.5). Electronic applications accepted. *Faculty research:* Motor control, muscle architecture, postural control, morphometrics, sensory integration.

Old Dominion University, College of Health Sciences, School of Physical Therapy and Athletic Training, Doctor of Physical Therapy Program, Norfolk, VA 23529. Offers DPT. *Faculty:* 8 full-time (6 women), 10 part-time/adjunct (6 women). *Students:* 122 full-time (66 women); includes 15 minority (6 Black or African American, non-Hispanic/Latino; 7 Asian, non-Hispanic/Latino; 2 Hispanic/Latino). Average age 26. 542 applicants, 16% accepted, 44 enrolled. In 2017, 42 doctorates awarded. *Degree requirements:* For doctorate, 5 full-time two-month long supervised clinical experiences; oral and written comprehensive exams. *Entrance requirements:* For doctorate, GRE, bachelor's degree; completion of prerequisite courses in biology, anatomy and physiology, chemistry, physics, and psychology; 3 letters of recommendation (1 from a physical therapist); 80 hours of volunteer experience in two separate physical therapy settings (hospital, private practice, rehab center, home health agency). Additional exam requirements/recommendations for international students: Required—TOEFL (minimum score 550 paper-based). *Application deadline:* For fall admission, 11/1 for domestic and international students. Application fee: $50. Electronic applications accepted. *Expenses:* Contact institution. *Financial support:* In 2017–18, 4 students received support, including 2 teaching assistantships with partial tuition reimbursements available (averaging $5,000 per year); scholarships/grants also available. Financial award applicants required to submit FAFSA. *Faculty research:* Falls risk assessment; gait and balance; motor learning/ motor control in rehabilitation; inter-professional education for health professional students; concussion prevention and treatment. *Total annual research expenditures:* $200,000. *Unit head:* Dr. Martha Walker, Program Director, 757-683-4519, E-mail: mlwalker@odu.edu. *Application contact:* William Heffelfinger, Director of Graduate Admissions, 757-683-5554, Fax: 757-683-3255, E-mail: gradadmit@odu.edu.
Website: http://www.odu.edu/ptat/dpt

Pacific University, School of Physical Therapy, Forest Grove, OR 97116-1797. Offers athletic training (MSAT); physical therapy (DPT). *Accreditation:* APTA. *Degree requirements:* For doctorate, evidence-based capstone project thesis. *Entrance requirements:* For doctorate, 100 hours of volunteer/observational hours, minimum cumulative GPA of 3.0, prerequisite courses with a C grade or better, minimum GPA of 2.5 in science/statistics. Additional exam requirements/recommendations for international students: Required—TOEFL (minimum score 600 paper-based). Electronic applications accepted. *Expenses:* Contact institution. *Faculty research:* Balance disorders, geriatrics, orthopedic treatment outcomes, obesity, women's health.

Queen's University at Kingston, School of Graduate Studies, Faculty of Health Sciences, School of Rehabilitation Therapy, Kingston, ON K7L 3N6, Canada. Offers occupational therapy (M Sc OT); physical therapy (M Sc PT); rehabilitation science (M Sc, PhD). *Program availability:* Part-time. *Degree requirements:* For master's, thesis; for doctorate, comprehensive exam, thesis/dissertation. *Entrance requirements:* Additional exam requirements/recommendations for international students: Required—TOEFL. *Faculty research:* Disability, community, motor performance, rehabilitation, treatment efficiency.

Radford University, College of Graduate Studies and Research, Program in Physical Therapy, Roanoke, VA 24013. Offers DPT. *Accreditation:* APTA. *Faculty:* 7 full-time (2 women), 4 part-time/adjunct (3 women). *Students:* 85 full-time (63 women); includes 5 minority (2 Asian, non-Hispanic/Latino; 1 Hispanic/Latino; 2 Two or more races, non-Hispanic/Latino), 1 international. Average age 24. 348 applicants, 24% accepted, 29 enrolled. In 2017, 18 doctorates awarded. *Degree requirements:* For doctorate, comprehensive exam, capstone research project suitable for publication. *Entrance requirements:* For doctorate, GRE, PTCAS application with 3 letters of reference, personal essay, resume, 40 hours of clinical experience, minimum overall GPA of 3.25, 3.0 in math and science prerequisites. Additional exam requirements/recommendations for international students: Required—TOEFL (minimum score 575 paper-based; 88 iBT). *Application deadline:* For fall admission, 2/15 priority date for domestic students. Applications are processed on a rolling basis. Application fee: $50. Electronic applications accepted. *Expenses:* Contact institution. *Financial support:* In 2017–18, 10 students received support, including 2 research assistantships (averaging $5,000 per year); career-related internships or fieldwork, scholarships/grants, and unspecified assistantships also available. Support available to part-time students. Financial award application deadline: 3/1; financial award applicants required to submit FAFSA. *Unit head:* Dr. Brent Harper, Program Director, 540-224-6657, Fax: 540-224-6660, E-mail: dpt@radford.edu.
Website: http://www.radford.edu/content/wchs/home/pt.html

Regis University, Rueckert-Hartman College for Health Professions, Denver, CO 80221-1099. Offers advanced practice nurse (DNP); counseling (MA); counseling children and adolescents (Post-Graduate Certificate); counseling military families (Post-Graduate Certificate); depth psychotherapy (Post-Graduate Certificate); fellowship in orthopedic manual physical therapy (Certificate); health care business management (Certificate); health care quality and patient safety (Certificate); health industry leadership (MBA); health services administration (MS); marriage and family therapy (MA, Post-Graduate Certificate); neonatal nurse practitioner (MSN); nursing education (MSN); nursing leadership (MSN); occupational therapy (OTD); pharmacy (Pharm D); physical therapy (DPT). *Program availability:* Part-time, evening/weekend, 100% online, blended/hybrid learning. *Degree requirements:* For master's, thesis (for some programs), internship. *Entrance requirements:* For master's, official transcript reflecting baccalaureate degree awarded from regionally-accredited college or university. Additional exam requirements/recommendations for international students: Required—TOEFL (minimum score 550 paper-based; 82 iBT). Electronic applications accepted. *Expenses:* Contact institution. *Faculty research:* Normal and pathological balance and gait research, normal/pathological upper limb motor control/biomechanics, exercise energy/metabolism research, optical treatment protocols for therapeutic modalities.

Rockhurst University, College of Health and Human Services, Program in Physical Therapy, Kansas City, MO 64110-2561. Offers DPT. *Accreditation:* APTA. *Faculty:* 13 full-time (11 women), 4 part-time/adjunct (3 women). *Students:* 140 full-time (94 women), 1 (woman) part-time; includes 14 minority (1 American Indian or Alaska Native, non-Hispanic/Latino; 1 Asian, non-Hispanic/Latino; 2 Hispanic/Latino; 4 Native Hawaiian or other Pacific Islander, non-Hispanic/Latino; 6 Two or more races, non-Hispanic/Latino), 1 international. Average age 24. 203 applicants, 44% accepted, 46 enrolled. In 2017, 46 doctorates awarded. *Entrance requirements:* For doctorate, 3 letters of recommendation, interview, minimum GPA of 3.0, physical therapy experience. Additional exam requirements/recommendations for international students: Required—TOEFL (minimum score 550 paper-based; 79 iBT). *Application deadline:* Applications are processed on a rolling basis. Application fee: $0. Electronic applications accepted. *Expenses:* $855 per credit hour tuition; $790 per year fees, additional fees may apply. *Financial support:* Applicants required to submit FAFSA. *Faculty research:* Clinical decision-making, geriatrics, balance in persons with neurological disorders, physical rehabilitation following total joint replacement, clinical education. *Unit head:* Dr. Jean Hiebert, Chair, 816-501-4059, Fax: 816-501-4169, E-mail: jean.hiebert@rockhurst.edu. *Application contact:* Beth Harris, Graduate Admissions Coordinator and Recruiter, 816-501-4059, E-mail: beth.harris@rockhurst.edu.
Website: https://www.rockhurst.edu/physical-therapy

Rocky Mountain University of Health Professions, Programs in Physical Therapy, Provo, UT 84606. Offers DPT, TDPT. *Accreditation:* APTA. *Entrance requirements:* For doctorate, GRE, bachelor's degree; two courses each of general chemistry and general physics with lab (for science majors); one course each in biology, human anatomy (with lab), and physiology (with lab); three semester hours of statistics; six semester hours in the behavioral sciences (life span development preferred); minimum cumulative GPA of 3.0.

Rosalind Franklin University of Medicine and Science, College of Health Professions, Department of Physical Therapy, North Chicago, IL 60064-3095. Offers MS, DPT, TDPT. *Accreditation:* APTA. *Program availability:* Online learning. *Degree requirements:* For master's, thesis. *Entrance requirements:* For master's, physical therapy license. Additional exam requirements/recommendations for international students: Required—TOEFL. *Faculty research:* Clinical research, development/analysis of tests, measures, education.

Rush University, College of Health Sciences, Department of Respiratory Care, Chicago, IL 60612-3832. Offers MS. *Unit head:* David L. Vines, Chairperson, 312-563-2353. *Application contact:* 312-942-7120, E-mail: chs_admissions@rush.edu.

Rutgers University–Camden, Graduate School of Arts and Sciences, Program in Physical Therapy, Stratford, NJ 08084. Offers DPT. Program offered jointly with University of Medicine and Dentistry of New Jersey. *Accreditation:* APTA. *Entrance requirements:* For doctorate, GRE, physical therapy experience, 3 letters of recommendation, statement of personal, professional and academic goals, resume. Additional exam requirements/recommendations for international students: Required—TOEFL, IELTS. Electronic applications accepted. *Faculty research:* Clinical education, migrant workers, biomechanical constraints on motor control, high intensity strength training and the elderly, posture and ergonomics.

Rutgers University–Newark, School of Health Related Professions, Department of Rehabilitation and Movement Sciences, Program in Physical Therapy–Newark, Newark, NJ 07102. Offers DPT. *Entrance requirements:* For doctorate, GRE, chemistry, physics, calculus, psychology, statistics, interview, 3 reference letters. Additional exam requirements/recommendations for international students: Required—TOEFL (minimum score 500 paper-based; 79 iBT). Electronic applications accepted.

Rutgers University–Newark, School of Health Related Professions, Department of Rehabilitation and Movement Sciences, Program in Physical Therapy–Stratford, Newark, NJ 07102. Offers DPT. *Entrance requirements:* For doctorate, GRE, BS, 3 reference letters, interview. Additional exam requirements/recommendations for international students: Required—TOEFL (minimum score 500 paper-based; 79 iBT). Electronic applications accepted.

Sacred Heart University, Graduate Programs, College of Health Professions, Department of Physical Therapy, Fairfield, CT 06825. Offers DPT. *Accreditation:* APTA. *Faculty:* 10 full-time (6 women), 19 part-time/adjunct (15 women). *Students:* 148 full-time (108 women); includes 15 minority (1 Black or African American, non-Hispanic/Latino; 1 American Indian or Alaska Native, non-Hispanic/Latino; 4 Asian, non-Hispanic/Latino; 7 Hispanic/Latino; 2 Two or more races, non-Hispanic/Latino), 1 international. Average age 24. 447 applicants, 19% accepted, 75 enrolled. In 2017, 62 doctorates awarded. *Degree requirements:* For doctorate, capstone. *Entrance requirements:* For doctorate, GRE (recommended), minimum overall and prerequisites GPA of 3.2. Additional exam requirements/recommendations for international students: Required—TOEFL (minimum score 570 paper-based, 80 iBT), TWE, or IELTS (6.5). *Application deadline:* For fall admission, 12/15 for domestic and international students. Applications are processed on a rolling basis. Application fee: $75. *Expenses:* Contact institution. *Financial support:* Unspecified assistantships available. Financial award applicants required to submit FAFSA. *Unit head:* Dr. Chris Petrosino, Professor/Chair, Physical Therapy and Human Movement, 203-371-7976, E-mail: petrosinoc@sacredheart.edu. *Application contact:* Tara Chudy, Executive Director of Graduate Admissions, 203-365-4735, E-mail: chudyt@sacredheart.edu.
Website: http://www.sacredheart.edu/academics/collegeofhealthprofessions/academicprograms/physicaltherapy/

Sage Graduate School, School of Health Sciences, Program in Physical Therapy, Troy, NY 12180-4115. Offers DPT. *Accreditation:* APTA. *Faculty:* 10 full-time (7 women), 4 part-time/adjunct (3 women). *Students:* 97 full-time (64 women), 2 part-time (1 woman); includes 15 minority (4 Black or African American, non-Hispanic/Latino; 4 Asian, non-Hispanic/Latino; 6 Hispanic/Latino; 1 Two or more races, non-Hispanic/Latino). Average age 25. 219 applicants, 14% accepted, 29 enrolled. In 2017, 37 doctorates awarded. *Entrance requirements:* For doctorate, baccalaureate degree; current resume; 2 letters of recommendation; minimum GPA of 3.0 overall and in science prerequisites; completion of 40 hours of physical therapy observation. Additional exam requirements/recommendations for international students: Required—TOEFL (minimum score 550 paper-based). *Application deadline:* Applications are processed on a rolling basis. Application fee: $30. Electronic applications accepted. *Expenses:* Contact institution. *Financial support:* Scholarships/grants and unspecified assistantships available. Financial award application deadline: 3/1; financial award applicants required to submit FAFSA. *Unit head:* Dr. Theresa Hand, Dean, School of Health Sciences, 518-244-2265, Fax: 518-244-4571, E-mail: handt@sage.edu. *Application contact:* Dr. James Brennan, Chair and Assistant Professor, 518-244-2058, Fax: 518-244-4524, E-mail: brennj@sage.edu.

St. Ambrose University, College of Health and Human Services, Program in Physical Therapy, Davenport, IA 52803-2898. Offers DPT. *Accreditation:* APTA. *Degree requirements:* For doctorate, board exams. *Entrance requirements:* For doctorate, GRE, interview. Additional exam requirements/recommendations for international students: Required—TOEFL. *Faculty research:* Human motor control, orthopedic physical therapy, cardiopulmonary physical therapy, kinesiology/biomechanics.

St. Catherine University, Graduate Programs, Program in Physical Therapy, St. Paul, MN 55105. Offers DPT. Offered on the Minneapolis campus only. *Accreditation:* APTA. *Degree requirements:* For doctorate, research project. *Entrance requirements:* For doctorate, GRE, minimum GPA of 3.0; coursework in biology/zoology, anatomy, physiology, chemistry, physics, psychology, statistics, mathematics and medical terminology. Additional exam requirements/recommendations for international students: Required—Michigan English Language Assessment Battery or TOEFL (minimum score 600 paper-based; 100 iBT). *Application deadline:* For fall admission, 1/20 priority date for domestic students. Application fee: $35. *Expenses:* Contact institution. *Financial support:* Institutionally sponsored loans available. Financial award application deadline: 4/1; financial award applicants required to submit FAFSA. *Unit head:* Cort Cieminski, Director, 651-690-7884, Fax: 651-690-7876. *Application contact:* Kristin Chalberg, Associate Director of Non-Traditional Admissions, 651-690-6868, Fax: 651-690-6064.
Website: https://www.stkate.edu/academics/graduate-degrees/academic-programs/dpt

Saint Francis University, Department of Physical Therapy, Loretto, PA 15940-0600. Offers DPT. *Accreditation:* APTA. *Faculty:* 9 full-time (5 women), 2 part-time/adjunct (0 women). *Students:* 67 full-time (37 women), 4 part-time (3 women); includes 3 minority (2 Black or African American, non-Hispanic/Latino; 1 Asian, non-Hispanic/Latino), 1 international. Average age 24. 339 applicants, 30% accepted, 40 enrolled. In 2017, 33 doctorates awarded. *Entrance requirements:* Additional exam requirements/recommendations for international students: Required—TOEFL. *Application deadline:* For winter admission, 1/15 for domestic and international students. Application fee: $30. Electronic applications accepted. *Expenses:* Contact institution. *Financial support:* Teaching assistantships with partial tuition reimbursements and unspecified assistantships available. Financial award applicants required to submit FAFSA. *Faculty research:* Childhood asthma, athletic performance, energy expenditure, sports injuries, balance and falls, concussion management, physical therapy administration, orthopedic assignment. *Unit head:* Dr. Ivan J. Mulligan, Chair/Associate Professor, 814-472-3123, Fax: 814-472-3140, E-mail: imulligan@francis.edu. *Application contact:* Dr. Peter Raymond Skoner, Associate Provost, 814-472-3085, Fax: 814-472-3365, E-mail: pskoner@francis.edu.

Saint Louis University, Graduate Programs, Doisy College of Health Sciences, Department of Physical Therapy, St. Louis, MO 63103. Offers athletic training (MAT); physical therapy (DPT). *Accreditation:* APTA. *Program availability:* Part-time. *Entrance requirements:* Additional exam requirements/recommendations for international students: Required—TOEFL (minimum score 525 paper-based; 55 iBT). Electronic applications accepted. *Faculty research:* Patellofemoral pain and associated risk factors; prevalence of disordered eating in physical therapy students; effects of selected interventions for children with cerebral palsy on gait and posture: hippotherapy, ankle strengthening, supported treadmill training, spirituality in physical therapy/patient care, risk factors for exercise-related leg pain in running athletes.

Samford University, School of Health Professions, Birmingham, AL 35229. Offers athletic training (MAT); physical therapy (DPT); respiratory care (MS); speech language pathology (MS). *Faculty:* 20 full-time (12 women), 1 part-time/adjunct (0 women). *Students:* 140 full-time (105 women), 2 part-time (both women); includes 14 minority (3 Black or African American, non-Hispanic/Latino; 1 Asian, non-Hispanic/Latino; 4 Hispanic/Latino; 6 Two or more races, non-Hispanic/Latino). Average age 24. 191 applicants, 60% accepted, 5 enrolled. In 2017, 17 master's awarded. *Degree requirements:* For master's and doctorate, capstone course. *Entrance requirements:* For master's and doctorate, GRE, recommendations, resume, on-campus interview, personal statement, shadowing hours. Additional exam requirements/recommendations for international students: Required—TOEFL (minimum score 550 paper-based). *Application deadline:* For fall admission, 10/1 for domestic students; for spring admission, 5/1 for domestic students. Application fee: $120. Electronic applications accepted. *Expenses:* $813 per credit hour. *Financial support:* In 2017–18, 36 students received support. Scholarships/grants available. Financial award application deadline: 2/15; financial award applicants required to submit FAFSA. *Faculty research:* Physical disabilities related to Parkinson's disease, neurogenic communication disorders, skeletal muscle physiology, spinal cord injuries, medical ventilation and tobacco treatment and prevention. *Unit head:* Dr. Alan Jung, Dean of the School of Health Professions, 205-726-2716, E-mail: apjung@samford.edu. *Application contact:* Dr. Marian Carter, Assistant Dean of Enrollment Management and Student Services, 205-726-2611, E-mail: mwcarter@samford.edu.
Website: http://www.samford.edu/healthprofessions

Samuel Merritt University, Department of Physical Therapy, Oakland, CA 94609-3108. Offers DPT. *Accreditation:* APTA. *Faculty:* 12 full-time (10 women), 23 part-time/adjunct (10 women). *Students:* 114 full-time (73 women), 3 part-time (2 women); includes 69 minority (2 Black or African American, non-Hispanic/Latino; 34 Asian, non-Hispanic/Latino; 23 Hispanic/Latino; 2 Native Hawaiian or other Pacific Islander, non-Hispanic/Latino; 8 Two or more races, non-Hispanic/Latino). 486 applicants, 18% accepted, 40 enrolled. In 2017, 32 doctorates awarded. *Entrance requirements:* For doctorate, GRE General Test, minimum GPA of 3.0 in science and overall; related work experience; interview. Additional exam requirements/recommendations for international students: Required—TOEFL (minimum score 100 iBT). *Application deadline:* For fall admission, 10/1 priority date for domestic students. Application fee: $140. Electronic applications accepted. *Expenses:* $50,943 per year (for first two years); $18,481 (for third year). *Financial support:* Career-related internships or fieldwork, Federal Work-Study, and scholarships/grants available. Financial award applicants required to submit FAFSA. *Faculty research:* Human movement, motor control, falls prevention in the elderly. *Unit head:* Dr. Nicole Christensen, Co-Chair, 510-869-6567, Fax: 510-869-6282, E-mail: nchristensen@samuelmerritt.edu. *Application contact:* Timothy Cranford, Dean of Admissions, 510-869-1550, Fax: 510-869-6525, E-mail: admission@samuelmerritt.edu.
Website: http://www.samuelmerritt.edu/physical_therapy

San Diego State University, Graduate and Research Affairs, College of Health and Human Services, School of Exercise and Nutritional Sciences, Program in Physical Therapy, San Diego, CA 92182. Offers DPT. *Accreditation:* APTA.

San Francisco State University, Division of Graduate Studies, College of Health and Social Sciences, Program in Physical Therapy, San Francisco, CA 94132-1722. Offers DPT. Programs offered jointly with University of California, San Francisco. *Accreditation:* APTA. *Financial support:* Career-related internships or fieldwork and institutionally sponsored loans available. *Unit head:* Dr. Linda Wanek, Director, 415-338-2001, Fax: 415-338-0907, E-mail: lwanek@sfsu.edu. *Application contact:* Jill Lienau, Academic Office Coordinator, 415-338-2001, Fax: 415-338-0907, E-mail: jlienau@sfsu.edu.
Website: http://www.pt.sfsu.edu/

Seton Hall University, School of Health and Medical Sciences, Program in Physical Therapy, South Orange, NJ 07079-2697. Offers professional physical therapy (DPT). *Accreditation:* APTA. *Degree requirements:* For doctorate, research project. *Entrance requirements:* Additional exam requirements/recommendations for international students: Required—TOEFL. Electronic applications accepted. *Faculty research:* Electrical stimulation, motor learning, backpacks, gait and balance, orthopedic injury, women's health, pediatric obesity.

Shenandoah University, School of Health Professions, Winchester, VA 22601. Offers athletic training (MSAT); non-traditional physical therapy (MS); occupational training (MS); performing arts medicine (Certificate); physician assistant studies (MS); public health (MPH, Certificate); transitional physical therapy (DPT). *Program availability:* Part-time, all online except for two on-site weekend sessions (for DPT). *Faculty:* 35 full-time (27 women), 18 part-time/adjunct (13 women). *Students:* 446 full-time (355 women), 134 part-time (112 women); includes 78 minority (14 Black or African American, non-Hispanic/Latino; 28 Asian, non-Hispanic/Latino; 25 Hispanic/Latino; 11 Two or more races, non-Hispanic/Latino), 22 international. Average age 28. 839 applicants, 31% accepted, 166 enrolled. In 2017, 100 master's, 75 doctorates, 4 other advanced degrees awarded. *Degree requirements:* For master's and Certificate, thesis; for doctorate, comprehensive exam. *Entrance requirements:* For master's, GRE; for doctorate, GRE, minimum cumulative and prerequisite GPA of 2.8. Additional exam requirements/recommendations for international students: Required—TOEFL (minimum score 558 paper-based; 83 iBT). *Application deadline:* For fall admission, 10/1 for domestic and international students; for summer admission, 4/1 for domestic and international students. Application fee: $30. Electronic applications accepted. *Expenses:* Contact institution. *Financial support:* In 2017–18, 53 students received support. Scholarships/grants and unspecified assistantships available. Financial award applicants required to submit FAFSA. *Faculty research:* 3D motion analysis of running mechanics; quality improvement in clinical practice; functional movement screen to predict injury in professional athletes and dancers; sensory integration for children with autism; chronic ankle instability. *Total annual research expenditures:* $15,000. *Unit head:* Dr. Karen Elizabeth Abraham, Dean of School of Health Professions, 540-545.6209, Fax: 540-665.5530, E-mail: kabraham@su.edu. *Application contact:* Jon Brannon, Graduate Admissions Specialist, Office of Admissions, 540-545-7394, Fax: 540-665-4627, E-mail: jbannan09@su.edu.
Website: http://www.health.su.edu

Simmons College, School of Nursing and Health Sciences, Boston, MA 02115. Offers didactic dietetics (Certificate); dietetic internship (Certificate); health professions education (PhD, CAGS); nursing (MS, MSN), including family nurse practitioner (MS); nursing practice (DNP); nutrition and health promotion (MS); physical therapy (DPT); sports nutrition (Certificate). *Accreditation:* AACN. *Program availability:* Part-time, 100% online, blended/hybrid learning. *Faculty:* 34 full-time (28 women), 44 part-time/adjunct (40 women). *Students:* 390 full-time (350 women), 1,286 part-time (1,169 women); includes 346 minority (131 Black or African American, non-Hispanic/Latino; 6 American Indian or Alaska Native, non-Hispanic/Latino; 75 Asian, non-Hispanic/Latino; 91 Hispanic/Latino; 3 Native Hawaiian or other Pacific Islander, non-Hispanic/Latino; 40 Two or more races, non-Hispanic/Latino), 9 international. Average age 34. 1,219 applicants, 74% accepted, 481 enrolled. In 2017, 423 master's, 39 doctorates, 55 other advanced degrees awarded. *Entrance requirements:* For doctorate, GRE. Additional exam requirements/recommendations for international students: Required—TOEFL (minimum score 570 paper-based; 88 iBT). *Application deadline:* For fall admission, 6/1 for international students. Application fee: $50. Electronic applications accepted. *Expenses:* $1,278 per credit, $116 activity fee per semester. *Financial support:* In 2017–18, 15 research assistantships with partial tuition reimbursements were awarded; scholarships/grants and unspecified assistantships also available. Financial award applicants required to submit FAFSA. *Unit head:* Dr. Judy Beal, Dean, 617-521-2139. *Application contact:* Brett DiMarzo, Director of Graduate Admission, 617-521-2651, Fax: 617-521-3137, E-mail: brett.dimarzo@simmons.edu.
Website: http://www.simmons.edu/snhs/

Slippery Rock University of Pennsylvania, Graduate Studies (Recruitment), College of Health, Environment, and Science, School of Physical Therapy, Slippery Rock, PA 16057-1383. Offers DPT. *Accreditation:* APTA. *Degree requirements:* For doctorate, clinical residency. *Entrance requirements:* For doctorate, GRE General Test, minimum GPA of 3.0, three letters of recommendation, essay, 100 hours of PT experience with licensed physical therapist, CPR certification. Additional exam requirements/recommendations for international students: Required—TOEFL (minimum score 550 paper-based; 80 iBT). Electronic applications accepted. *Expenses:* Contact institution.

Sonoma State University, School of Science and Technology, Department of Kinesiology, Rohnert Park, CA 94928. Offers exercise science/pre-physical therapy (MA); interdisciplinary (MA); interdisciplinary pre-occupational therapy (MA); lifetime physical activity (MA), including coach education, fitness and wellness. *Program availability:* Part-time. *Degree requirements:* For master's, thesis, oral exam. *Entrance requirements:* For master's, minimum GPA of 2.8. Additional exam requirements/recommendations for international students: Required—TOEFL (minimum score 500 paper-based). *Application deadline:* For fall admission, 11/30 for domestic students; for spring admission, 9/1 for domestic students. Applications are processed on a rolling basis. Application fee: $55. *Financial support:* Career-related internships or fieldwork available. Financial award application deadline: 3/2; financial award applicants required to submit FAFSA. *Unit head:* Dr. Steven Winter, Chair, 707-664-2188, E-mail: steven.winter@sonoma.edu. *Application contact:* Dr. Bulent Sokmen, Graduate Coordinator, 707-664-2789, E-mail: sokmen@sonoma.edu.
Website: http://www.sonoma.edu/kinesiology/

Southwest Baptist University, Program in Physical Therapy, Bolivar, MO 65613-2597. Offers DPT. *Accreditation:* APTA. *Degree requirements:* For doctorate, comprehensive exam, 3-4 clinical education experiences. *Entrance requirements:* Additional exam requirements/recommendations for international students: Required—TOEFL (minimum score 550 paper-based). *Expenses:* Contact institution. *Faculty research:* Balance and falls prevention, distance and web based learning, foot and ankle intervention, pediatrics, musculoskeletal management.

Springfield College, Graduate Programs, Program in Physical Therapy, Springfield, MA 01109. Offers DPT. *Accreditation:* APTA. *Program availability:* Part-time. *Faculty:* 10 full-time, 18 part-time/adjunct. In 2017, 34 doctorates awarded. *Degree requirements:* For doctorate, comprehensive exam, thesis/dissertation, research project. *Entrance requirements:* For doctorate, GRE General Test. Additional exam requirements/recommendations for international students: Required—TOEFL (minimum score 550 paper-based); Recommended—IELTS (minimum score 7). *Application deadline:* For fall admission, 12/1 for domestic and international students. Applications are processed on a rolling basis. Application fee: $50. Electronic applications accepted. *Financial support:* Fellowships with partial tuition reimbursements, teaching assistantships with partial tuition reimbursements, career-related internships or fieldwork, Federal Work-Study, institutionally sponsored loans, scholarships/grants, and unspecified assistantships available. Financial award application deadline: 3/1; financial award applicants required to submit FAFSA. *Unit head:* Dr. Julia Chevan, Chair, 413-748-3569, Fax: 413-748-3371, E-mail: jchevan@springfieldcollege.edu. *Application contact:* Anne Griffin, Director of Graduate Admissions, 413-748-3225, Fax: 413-748-3694, E-mail: agriffin2@springfield.edu.
Website: https://springfield.edu/programs/physical-therapy-doctoral-degree

State University of New York Upstate Medical University, Department of Physical Therapy, Syracuse, NY 13210. Offers DPT. *Accreditation:* APTA. *Program availability:* Part-time, evening/weekend, online learning. Electronic applications accepted.

Stockton University, Office of Graduate Studies, Program in Physical Therapy, Galloway, NJ 08205-9441. Offers DPT. *Accreditation:* APTA. *Faculty:* 8 full-time (6 women), 1 (woman) part-time/adjunct. *Students:* 91 full-time (57 women), 1 (woman) part-time; includes 19 minority (2 Black or African American, non-Hispanic/Latino; 8 Asian, non-Hispanic/Latino; 5 Hispanic/Latino; 4 Two or more races, non-Hispanic/Latino). Average age 24. 351 applicants, 19% accepted, 37 enrolled. In 2017, 39 doctorates awarded. *Entrance requirements:* For doctorate, GRE. Additional exam requirements/recommendations for international students: Required—TOEFL. *Application deadline:* For fall admission, 10/15 priority date for domestic students, 10/15 for international students. Application fee: $50. Electronic applications accepted. *Expenses:* Contact institution. *Financial support:* Fellowships, research assistantships, career-related internships or fieldwork, Federal Work-Study, scholarships/grants, and unspecified assistantships available. Support available to part-time students. Financial award application deadline: 3/1; financial award applicants required to submit FAFSA. *Faculty research:* Spinal flexibility in the well elderly, use of traditional Chinese medicine concepts in physical therapy, computerized vs. traditional study in human gross anatomy. *Unit head:* Dr. Bess Kathrins, Program Director, 609-626-3640, E-mail: gradschool@stockton.edu. *Application contact:* Tara Williams, Assistant Director of Graduate Enrollment Management, 609-626-3640, Fax: 609-626-6050, E-mail: gradschool@stockton.edu.

Stony Brook University, State University of New York, Stony Brook Medicine, School of Health Technology and Management, Stony Brook, NY 11794. Offers applied health informatics (MS); disability studies (Certificate); health administration (MHA); health and rehabilitation sciences (PhD); health care management (Advanced Certificate); health care policy and management (MS); occupational therapy (MS); physical therapy (DPT); physician assistant (MS). *Accreditation:* APTA. *Faculty:* 62 full-time (42 women), 59 part-time/adjunct (36 women). *Students:* 565 full-time (382 women), 67 part-time (53 women); includes 179 minority (29 Black or African American, non-Hispanic/Latino; 83 Asian, non-Hispanic/Latino; 59 Hispanic/Latino; 2 Native Hawaiian or other Pacific Islander, non-Hispanic/Latino; 6 Two or more races, non-Hispanic/Latino), 14 international. Average age 27. 2,516 applicants, 16% accepted, 266 enrolled. In 2017, 162 master's, 84 doctorates, 39 other advanced degrees awarded. *Degree requirements:* For master's, thesis; for doctorate, thesis/dissertation. *Entrance requirements:* For master's, GRE General Test, minimum GPA of 3.0, work experience in field, references; for doctorate, GRE, three references, essay. Additional exam requirements/recommendations for international students: Required—TOEFL (minimum score 550 paper-based). *Application deadline:* For fall admission, 1/15 for domestic students; for spring admission, 10/1 for domestic students. Application fee: $100. *Expenses:* Contact institution. *Financial support:* Fellowships, research assistantships, teaching assistantships, career-related internships or fieldwork, Federal Work-Study, and institutionally sponsored loans available. Financial award application deadline: 3/15. *Faculty research:* Developmental disabilities, disability studies, health promotion, multiple sclerosis, quality of life program, internal medicine, lung disease, palliative care, respiratory diseases, neuromuscular disorders, orthopedics, physical medicine and rehabilitation, physical therapy, prostheses or implants, advance directives, advocacy alienation, allied health education, allied health occupations, adolescents, adoption, child or adolescent mental health, multiple sclerosis, youth policy. *Total annual research expenditures:* $1.2 million. *Unit head:* Dr. Carlos Vidal, Dean, 631-444-1009, Fax: 631-444-7621, E-mail: carlos.vidal@stonybrook.edu. *Application contact:* Frances Shaw, 631-444-3240, Fax: 631-444-7621, E-mail: frances.shaw@stonybrook.edu.
Website: http://healthtechnology.stonybrookmedicine.edu/

Temple University, College of Public Health, Department of Physical Therapy, Philadelphia, PA 19122. Offers DPT, TDPT. *Accreditation:* APTA (one or more programs are accredited). *Program availability:* Part-time, online learning. *Faculty:* 9 full-time (5 women), 2 part-time/adjunct (1 woman). *Students:* 159 full-time (110 women), 7 part-time (4 women); includes 29 minority (3 Black or African American, non-Hispanic/Latino; 14 Asian, non-Hispanic/Latino; 6 Hispanic/Latino; 6 Two or more races, non-Hispanic/Latino), 1 international. In 2017, 83 doctorates awarded. *Degree requirements:* For doctorate, comprehensive exam, thesis/dissertation. *Entrance requirements:* For doctorate, GRE General Test, essay, interview, clinical experience. Additional exam requirements/recommendations for international students: Required—TOEFL (minimum score 550 paper-based; 79 iBT). *Application deadline:* For fall admission, 3/1 for domestic students, 2/1 for international students; for spring admission, 11/1 for domestic students, 10/1 for international students; for summer admission, 3/1 for domestic students, 2/1 for international students. Applications are processed on a rolling basis. Application fee: $60. Electronic applications accepted. *Expenses:* Contact institution. *Financial support:* Teaching assistantships with tuition reimbursements, career-related internships or fieldwork, Federal Work-Study, scholarships/grants, and unspecified assistantships available. Financial award application deadline: 1/1; financial award applicants required to submit FAFSA. *Faculty research:* Balance dysfunction, biomechanics, development, qualitative research, developmental neuroscience, health services. *Unit head:* Dr. Emily A. Keshner, Chair, 215-707-4815, Fax: 215-707-7500, E-mail: deptpt@temple.edu. *Application contact:* Scott Burns, Director of Program Administration/Director of Admissions/Director of the Transition DPT, 215-707-4815, E-mail: dptadmissions@temple.edu.
Website: https://cph.temple.edu/department-physical-therapy

Tennessee State University, The School of Graduate Studies and Research, College of Health Sciences, Department of Physical Therapy, Nashville, TN 37209-1561. Offers DPT. *Accreditation:* APTA. *Program availability:* Part-time, online learning. *Entrance requirements:* For doctorate, GRE, baccalaureate degree, 2 letters of recommendation, interview, essay. Electronic applications accepted. *Faculty research:* Evidence-based research clinical research case studies/reports qualitative research education assessment total knee anthroplasty; ergonomics; childhood obesity.

Texas State University, The Graduate College, College of Health Professions, Doctor of Physical Therapy Program, San Marcos, TX 78666. Offers DPT. *Accreditation:* APTA.

Faculty: 15 full-time (13 women), 5 part-time/adjunct (1 woman). *Students:* 125 full-time (77 women); includes 42 minority (6 Black or African American, non-Hispanic/Latino; 1 American Indian or Alaska Native, non-Hispanic/Latino; 1 Asian, non-Hispanic/Latino; 29 Hispanic/Latino; 5 Two or more races, non-Hispanic/Latino), 2 international. Average age 26. 622 applicants, 11% accepted, 42 enrolled. *Degree requirements:* For doctorate, comprehensive exam. *Entrance requirements:* For doctorate, GRE General Test (preferred minimum score of 295 with no less than 150 verbal and 145 quantitative), baccalaureate degree from regionally-accredited institution with minimum GPA of 3.0 on last 60 hours of undergraduate work and in all science courses; completion of volunteer, observation or employment hours in a variety of physical therapy settings. Additional exam requirements/recommendations for international students: Required—TOEFL (minimum score 550 paper-based; 78 iBT). *Application deadline:* For summer admission, 8/29 priority date for domestic and international students. Applications are processed on a rolling basis. Application fee: $65 ($115 for international students). Electronic applications accepted. *Expenses:* Tuition, state resident: full-time $7868; part-time $3934 per semester. Tuition, nonresident: full-time $17,828; part-time $8914 per semester. *Required fees:* $2092; $1435 per semester. Tuition and fees vary according to course load. *Financial support:* In 2017–18, 105 students received support, including 1 research assistantship (averaging $5,400 per year), 13 teaching assistantships (averaging $8,249 per year); career-related internships or fieldwork, Federal Work-Study, institutionally sponsored loans, scholarships/grants, and unspecified assistantships also available. Support available to part-time students. Financial award application deadline: 3/1; financial award applicants required to submit FAFSA. *Faculty research:* Overpowering osteoarthritis, exploring trunk stability and balance, post-concussion patient response. *Total annual research expenditures:* $14,291. *Unit head:* Dr. Barbara Sanders, Graduate Advisor, 512-245-8351, Fax: 512-245-8736, E-mail: bs04@txstate.edu. *Application contact:* Dr. Andrea Golato, Dean of Graduate School, 512-245-2581, Fax: 512-245-8365, E-mail: gradcollege@txstate.edu.
Website: http://www.health.txstate.edu/pt/

Texas Tech University Health Sciences Center, School of Health Professions, Program in Physical Therapy, Lubbock, TX 79430. Offers DPT, Sc D, TDPT. *Accreditation:* APTA. *Program availability:* Blended/hybrid learning. *Faculty:* 19 full-time (6 women), 4 part-time/adjunct (3 women). *Students:* 205 full-time (131 women), 153 part-time (83 women); includes 94 minority (9 Black or African American, non-Hispanic/Latino; 1 American Indian or Alaska Native, non-Hispanic/Latino; 25 Asian, non-Hispanic/Latino; 54 Hispanic/Latino; 1 Native Hawaiian or other Pacific Islander, non-Hispanic/Latino; 4 Two or more races, non-Hispanic/Latino). Average age 32. 792 applicants, 26% accepted, 116 enrolled. In 2017, 102 doctorates awarded. *Entrance requirements:* For doctorate, GRE. Additional exam requirements/recommendations for international students: Required—TOEFL (minimum score 550 paper-based; 79 iBT), IELTS. *Application deadline:* For summer admission, 10/1 priority date for domestic students. Applications are processed on a rolling basis. Application fee: $75. Electronic applications accepted. *Financial support:* Career-related internships or fieldwork, Federal Work-Study, institutionally sponsored loans, and scholarships/grants available. Financial award application deadline: 9/1; financial award applicants required to submit FAFSA. *Unit head:* Dr. Steven Sawyer, Department Chair, 806-743-3226, Fax: 806-743-2189, E-mail: steven.sawyer@ttuhsc.edu. *Application contact:* Lindsay Johnson, Associate Dean for Admissions and Student Affairs, 806-743-3220, Fax: 806-743-2994, E-mail: lindsay.johnson@ttuhsc.edu.
Website: http://www.ttuhsc.edu/health-professions/doctor-of-physical-therapy/

Texas Woman's University, Graduate School, College of Health Sciences, School of Physical Therapy, Houston, TX 77030. Offers DPT, PhD. *Accreditation:* APTA (one or more programs are accredited). *Program availability:* Part-time. *Faculty:* 25 full-time (19 women), 7 part-time/adjunct (5 women). *Students:* 297 full-time (216 women), 61 part-time (41 women); includes 110 minority (13 Black or African American, non-Hispanic/Latino; 27 Asian, non-Hispanic/Latino; 62 Hispanic/Latino; 8 Two or more races, non-Hispanic/Latino), 13 international. Average age 30. 423 applicants, 32% accepted, 112 enrolled. In 2017, 126 doctorates awarded. *Degree requirements:* For doctorate, comprehensive exam, thesis/dissertation, professional project, internship, residency (for PhD), qualification exam. *Entrance requirements:* For doctorate, GRE General Test (DPT only), interview, resume, essay; license to practice physical therapy (preferred) or eligibility for licensure and 2 letters of recommendation (PhD); 3 letters of recommendation on department form (DPT); minimum GPA of 3.0, CPR and AED certificates, 80 observation hours. Additional exam requirements/recommendations for international students: Required—TOEFL (minimum score 550 paper-based; 79 iBT); Recommended—IELTS (minimum score 6.5), TSE (minimum score 53). *Application deadline:* For fall admission, 10/15 for domestic and international students. Applications are processed on a rolling basis. Application fee: $50 ($75 for international students). Electronic applications accepted. *Expenses:* $7,520 per year full-time in-state; $16,829 per year full-time out-of-state. *Financial support:* In 2017–18, 187 students received support, including 3 research assistantships (averaging $3,095 per year); career-related internships or fieldwork, Federal Work-Study, institutionally sponsored loans, scholarships/grants, traineeships, health care benefits, and unspecified assistantships also available. Support available to part-time students. Financial award application deadline: 3/1; financial award applicants required to submit FAFSA. *Faculty research:* Gait training and outcomes, physical activity to promote health in youth and adults, exercise training for individuals with amputation, spine related injuries and rehabilitation. *Total annual research expenditures:* $62,191. *Unit head:* Dr. Ann Medley, Director, 713-794-2070, Fax: 713-794-2071, E-mail: pt@twu.edu. *Application contact:* Korie Hawkins, Associate Director of Admissions, Graduate Recruitment, 940-898-3188, Fax: 940-898-3081, E-mail: admissions@twu.edu.
Website: http://www.twu.edu/physical-therapy/

Thomas Jefferson University, Jefferson College of Health Professions, Department of Physical Therapy, Philadelphia, PA 19107. Offers DPT. *Accreditation:* APTA. *Degree requirements:* For doctorate, capstone project. *Entrance requirements:* Additional exam requirements/recommendations for international students: Required—TOEFL (minimum score 87 iBT). Electronic applications accepted. *Expenses:* Contact institution. *Faculty research:* Motion analysis/biomedical and EMG analysis of individuals with musculoskeletal and neuromuscular impairment; scholarship of teaching and learning; clinical reasoning; PT effectiveness and outcomes research in specific patient populations: cystic fibrosis, spina bifida, stroke; global health.

Touro College, School of Health Sciences, Bay Shore, NY 11706. Offers industrial-organizational psychology (MS); mental health counseling (MS); occupational therapy (MS); physical therapy (DPT); physician assistant (MS); speech-language pathology (MS). *Faculty:* 81 full-time (55 women), 77 part-time/adjunct (46 women). *Students:* 628 full-time (470 women), 113 part-time (73 women); includes 143 minority (31 Black or African American, non-Hispanic/Latino; 1 American Indian or Alaska Native, non-Hispanic/Latino; 61 Asian, non-Hispanic/Latino; 42 Hispanic/Latino; 1 Native Hawaiian or other Pacific Islander, non-Hispanic/Latino; 7 Two or more races, non-Hispanic/Latino), 63 international. Average age 28. *Expenses:* Contact institution. *Financial support:* Fellowships available. *Unit head:* Dr. Louis Primavera, Dean, School of Health Sciences, 516-673-3200, E-mail: louis.primavera@touro.edu. *Application contact:* Brian J. Diele, Director of Student Administrative Services, 631-665-1600 Ext. 6311, E-mail: brian.diele@touro.edu.

Trine University, Program in Physical Therapy, Angola, IN 46703-1764. Offers DPT. *Accreditation:* APTA. *Faculty:* 9. *Students:* 97 full-time (60 women). *Degree requirements:* For doctorate, internship. *Application deadline:* Applications are processed on a rolling basis. *Expenses: Tuition:* Part-time $515 per credit hour. Tuition and fees vary according to degree level and program. *Unit head:* Dr. Thomas Ruediger, Director, 260-203-2901, E-mail: ruedigert@trine.edu. *Application contact:* Dr. Thomas Ruediger, Director, 260-203-2901, E-mail: ruedigert@trine.edu.

University at Buffalo, the State University of New York, Graduate School, School of Public Health and Health Professions, Department of Rehabilitation Science, Program in Physical Therapy, Buffalo, NY 14260. Offers DPT. *Accreditation:* APTA. *Faculty:* 9 full-time (5 women), 5 part-time/adjunct (2 women). *Students:* 130 full-time (68 women), 1 part-time (0 women); includes 19 minority (2 Black or African American, non-Hispanic/Latino; 17 Asian, non-Hispanic/Latino), 3 international. Average age 23. 99 applicants, 45% accepted, 44 enrolled. In 2017, 43 doctorates awarded. *Entrance requirements:* For doctorate, GRE. Additional exam requirements/recommendations for international students: Required—TOEFL (minimum score 79 iBT). *Application deadline:* For fall admission, 11/1 for domestic and international students. Application fee: $50. Electronic applications accepted. *Financial support:* Application deadline: 2/1; applicants required to submit FAFSA. *Faculty research:* Functional limitations and rehabilitation for individuals with osteoporosis, multiple sclerosis, juvenile arthritis and aging; neuroscience concepts as they relate to rehabilitation in stroke and cerebral palsy; neural mechanisms associated with development, aging and neuromuscular disorders; sleep apnea and episodic hypoxia as it relates to muscles in the upper airway and cardiovascular system, neurobiological changes in ventilator control. *Unit head:* Dr. Kirkwood Personious, Program Director, 716-829-6742, Fax: 716-829-3217, E-mail: phhpadv@buffalo.edu. *Application contact:* MaryAnn Venezia, Program Coordinator, 716-829-6742, Fax: 716-829-3217, E-mail: venezia3@buffalo.edu.
Website: http://sphhp.buffalo.edu/rehabilitation-science/education/doctor-of-physical-therapy-dpt.html

The University of Alabama at Birmingham, School of Health Professions, Program in Physical Therapy, Birmingham, AL 35294. Offers DPT. *Accreditation:* APTA. *Entrance requirements:* For doctorate, GRE, interview; letters of recommendation; minimum GPA of 3.0 overall, in prerequisite courses, and last 60 hours; 40 hours of PT observation. Electronic applications accepted. *Faculty research:* Geriatrics, exercise physiology, aquatic therapy, industrial rehabilitation, outcome measurement.

University of Alberta, Faculty of Graduate Studies and Research, Department of Physical Therapy, Edmonton, AB T6G 2E1, Canada. Offers M Sc, PhD. *Program availability:* Part-time. *Degree requirements:* For master's, thesis. *Entrance requirements:* For master's, bachelor's degree in physical therapy, minimum GPA of 6.5 on a 9.0 scale. Additional exam requirements/recommendations for international students: Required—TOEFL. Electronic applications accepted. *Faculty research:* Spinal disorders, musculoskeletal disorders, ergonomics, sports therapy, motor development, cardiac rehabilitation/therapeutic exercise.

The University of British Columbia, Faculty of Medicine, Department of Physical Therapy, Vancouver, BC V6T 1Z1, Canada. Offers MPT.

University of California, San Francisco, Graduate Division, Program in Physical Therapy, San Francisco, CA 94143. Offers DPT, DPTSc. Programs offered jointly with San Francisco State University. *Accreditation:* APTA. *Entrance requirements:* For doctorate, GRE General Test, letters of recommendation.

University of Central Arkansas, Graduate School, College of Health and Behavioral Sciences, Department of Physical Therapy, Conway, AR 72035-0001. Offers DPT, PhD. *Accreditation:* APTA. *Degree requirements:* For doctorate, comprehensive exam, thesis/dissertation. *Entrance requirements:* Additional exam requirements/recommendations for international students: Required—TOEFL (minimum score 550 paper-based; 80 iBT). *Application deadline:* For fall admission, 3/1 priority date for domestic students; for spring admission, 10/1 for domestic students. Applications are processed on a rolling basis. Application fee: $25 ($50 for international students). Electronic applications accepted. *Expenses:* Contact institution. *Financial support:* Research assistantships with partial tuition reimbursements, Federal Work-Study, scholarships/grants, and unspecified assistantships available. Financial award application deadline: 2/15; financial award applicants required to submit FAFSA.
Website: http://uca.edu/pt/

University of Central Florida, College of Health Professions and Sciences, Program in Physical Therapy, Orlando, FL 32816. Offers physical therapy (DPT). *Accreditation:* APTA. *Faculty:* 22 full-time (11 women), 17 part-time/adjunct (11 women). *Students:* 108 full-time (59 women), 1 part-time (0 women); includes 41 minority (5 Black or African American, non-Hispanic/Latino; 6 Asian, non-Hispanic/Latino; 26 Hispanic/Latino; 4 Two or more races, non-Hispanic/Latino), 1 international. Average age 26. In 2017, 33 doctorates awarded. *Application deadline:* For summer admission, 11/1 for domestic students. Application fee: $30. Electronic applications accepted. *Expenses:* Contact institution. *Financial support:* In 2017–18, 5 students received support, including 2 fellowships with partial tuition reimbursements available (averaging $4,000 per year), 3 research assistantships with partial tuition reimbursements available (averaging $10,902 per year); career-related internships or fieldwork, institutionally sponsored loans, scholarships/grants, tuition waivers (partial), and unspecified assistantships also available. Financial award application deadline: 3/1; financial award applicants required to submit FAFSA. *Unit head:* Dr. Patrick Pabian, Program Director, 407-823-3457, E-mail: patrick.pabian@ucf.edu. *Application contact:* Associate Director, Graduate Admissions, 407-823-2766, Fax: 407-823-6442, E-mail: gradadmissions@ucf.edu.
Website: https://www.cohpa.ucf.edu/hp/physical-therapy-program/

University of Cincinnati, Graduate School, College of Allied Health Sciences, Department of Rehabilitation Sciences, Cincinnati, OH 45221. Offers physical therapy (DPT). *Accreditation:* APTA. *Entrance requirements:* For doctorate, GRE General Test, bachelor's degree with minimum GPA of 3.0, 50 hours volunteer/work in physical therapy setting. Additional exam requirements/recommendations for international students: Required—TOEFL. Electronic applications accepted. *Expenses: Tuition, area resident:* Full-time $14,468. Tuition, state resident: full-time $14,968; part-time $754 per credit hour. Tuition, nonresident: full-time $24,210; part-time $1311 per credit hour. *International tuition:* $26,460 full-time. *Required fees:* $3958; $84 per credit hour. One-time fee: $85 full-time. Tuition and fees vary according to course load, degree level and program. *Faculty research:* Biomechanics, sports-related injuries, motor learning, stroke rehabilitation.

University of Colorado Denver, School of Medicine, Program in Physical Therapy, Aurora, CO 80045. Offers DPT. *Accreditation:* APTA. *Program availability:* Part-time. *Students:* 205 full-time (157 women); includes 30 minority (3 Black or African American, non-Hispanic/Latino; 6 Asian, non-Hispanic/Latino; 10 Hispanic/Latino; 11 Two or more races, non-Hispanic/Latino), 1 international. Average age 26. 956 applicants, 7% accepted, 68 enrolled. In 2017, 65 doctorates awarded. *Degree requirements:* For doctorate, thesis/dissertation or alternative, 116 credit hours, 44 weeks of clinical experiences, capstone project at end of year 3. *Entrance requirements:* For doctorate, GRE, minimum GPA of 3.0; prerequisite coursework in anatomy, physiology, chemistry, physics, psychology, English composition or writing, college-level math, statistics, and

upper-level science; 45 hours of observation. Additional exam requirements/recommendations for international students: Required—TOEFL (minimum score 550 paper-based). *Application deadline:* For fall admission, 10/1 for domestic students, 8/8 priority date for international students. Application fee: $120. Electronic applications accepted. *Faculty research:* Interventions for early and mid-stages of Parkinson's disease, physical therapy for individuals with recurrent lower back pain. *Unit head:* Margaret Schenkman, Program Director, 303-724-9375, E-mail: margaret.schenkman@ucdenver.edu. *Application contact:* Lauren Wahlquist, Administrative Assistant, 303-724-2878, E-mail: pt.admissions@ucdenver.edu.
Website: http://www.ucdenver.edu/academics/colleges/medicalschool/education/degree_programs/pt/Pages/PT.aspx

University of Connecticut, Graduate School, College of Agriculture, Health and Natural Resources, Department of Kinesiology, Program in Physical Therapy, Storrs, CT 06269. Offers DPT. *Accreditation:* APTA. *Entrance requirements:* Additional exam requirements/recommendations for international students: Required—TOEFL (minimum score 550 paper-based). Electronic applications accepted.

University of Dayton, Department of Physical Therapy, Dayton, OH 45469. Offers DPT. *Accreditation:* APTA. *Faculty:* 10 full-time (4 women), 19 part-time/adjunct (15 women). *Students:* 109 full-time (71 women); includes 6 minority (1 Black or African American, non-Hispanic/Latino; 1 Asian, non-Hispanic/Latino; 1 Hispanic/Latino; 3 Two or more races, non-Hispanic/Latino), 1 international. Average age 24. 70 applicants, 87% accepted, 44 enrolled. In 2017, 37 doctorates awarded. *Degree requirements:* For doctorate, comprehensive exam, 4 clinical rotations; research project presented at a professional conference. *Entrance requirements:* For doctorate, GRE, bachelor's degree from accredited college or university; minimum cumulative GPA of 3.0 across all schools attended; minimum of 64 semester credits and four or more prerequisite science courses with labs; minimum grade of C+ in all prerequisite courses. Additional exam requirements/recommendations for international students: Required—TOEFL (minimum score 550 paper-based; 89 iBT). *Application deadline:* For fall admission, 10/1 priority date for domestic and international students. Application fee: $50 for international students. Electronic applications accepted. *Expenses:* Contact institution. *Financial support:* In 2017–18, 7 research assistantships with partial tuition reimbursements (averaging $13,920 per year) were awarded; institutionally sponsored loans and unspecified assistantships also available. Support available to part-time students. Financial award application deadline: 3/1; financial award applicants required to submit FAFSA. *Faculty research:* Biomechanics related to knee pathologies; rehabilitation oncology and upper extremity function; functional tests and clinical measures and injury in professional athletes; scapular performance with elbow, wrist and hand pathologies. *Unit head:* Dr. Philip A. Anloague, Chair/Associate Professor, 937-229-5600, Fax: 937-229-5601, E-mail: panalogue1@udayton.edu. *Application contact:* Trista Cathcart, Admissions Coordinator, 937-229-5611, Fax: 937-229-5601, E-mail: tcathcart1@udayton.edu.
Website: https://www.udayton.edu/education/departments_and_programs/dpt/index.php

University of Delaware, College of Health Sciences, Department of Physical Therapy, Newark, DE 19716. Offers DPT. *Accreditation:* APTA. *Entrance requirements:* For doctorate, GRE, 100 hours clinical experience, 3 letters of recommendation. Additional exam requirements/recommendations for international students: Required—TOEFL (minimum score 550 paper-based). Electronic applications accepted. *Faculty research:* Movement sciences, applied physiology, physical rehabilitation.

University of Evansville, College of Education and Health Sciences, Department of Physical Therapy, Evansville, IN 47722. Offers DPT. *Accreditation:* APTA. *Entrance requirements:* Additional exam requirements/recommendations for international students: Required—TOEFL (minimum score 88 iBT), IELTS (minimum score 6.5).

The University of Findlay, Office of Graduate Admissions, Findlay, OH 45840. Offers applied security and analytics (MSAS); athletic training (MAT); business (MBA), including certified management accountant, certified public accountant, health care management, hospitality management; education (MA Ed, Ed D), including children's literature (MA Ed), curriculum and teaching (MA Ed), education (MA Ed), educational administration (MA Ed), human resource development (MA Ed), mathematics (MA Ed), reading (MA Ed), science education (MA Ed), superintendent (Ed D), teaching (Ed D), technology (MA Ed); environmental, safety, and health management (MSEM); health informatics (MS); occupational therapy (MOT); pharmacy (Pharm D); physical therapy (DPT); physician assistant (MPA); rhetoric and writing (MA); teaching English to speakers of other languages (TESOL) and applied linguistics (MA). *Program availability:* Part-time, evening/weekend, 100% online, blended/hybrid learning. *Students:* 688 full-time (430 women), 553 part-time (308 women), 170 international. Average age 28. In 2017, 366 master's, 137 doctorates awarded. *Degree requirements:* For master's, comprehensive exam (for some programs), thesis (for some programs), cumulative project, capstone project; for doctorate, thesis/dissertation (for some programs). *Entrance requirements:* For master's, GRE/GMAT, bachelor's degree from accredited institution, minimum undergraduate GPA of 2.5 in last 64 hours of course work; for doctorate, GRE, MAT, minimum cumulative GPA of 3.0. Additional exam requirements/recommendations for international students: Required—TOEFL (minimum score 79 iBT), IELTS (minimum score 7), PTE (minimum score 61). *Application deadline:* Applications are processed on a rolling basis. Electronic applications accepted. *Financial support:* In 2017–18, 10 research assistantships with partial tuition reimbursements (averaging $7,200 per year), 35 teaching assistantships with partial tuition reimbursements (averaging $7,200 per year) were awarded; Federal Work-Study, institutionally sponsored loans, and unspecified assistantships also available. Financial award applicants required to submit FAFSA. *Unit head:* Christopher M. Harris, Director of Admissions, 419-434-4347, E-mail: harrisc1@findlay.edu. *Application contact:* Madeline Fauser Brennan, Graduate Admissions Counselor, 419-434-4636, Fax: 419-434-4898, E-mail: fauserbrennan@findlay.edu.
Website: http://www.findlay.edu/admissions/graduate/Pages/default.aspx

University of Florida, Graduate School, College of Public Health and Health Professions, Department of Physical Therapy, Gainesville, FL 32611. Offers DPT, DPT/MPH. *Accreditation:* APTA (one or more programs are accredited). *Entrance requirements:* For doctorate, GRE General Test, minimum GPA of 3.0. Additional exam requirements/recommendations for international students: Required—TOEFL (minimum score 515 paper-based; 80 iBT), IELTS (minimum score 6). Electronic applications accepted. *Faculty research:* Exercise physiology, motor control, rehabilitation, geriatrics.

University of Hartford, College of Education, Nursing, and Health Professions, Program in Physical Therapy, West Hartford, CT 06117-1599. Offers MSPT, DPT. *Accreditation:* APTA. *Entrance requirements:* For master's, GRE, 3 letters of recommendation. Additional exam requirements/recommendations for international students: Required—TOEFL (minimum score 550 paper-based).

University of Illinois at Chicago, College of Applied Health Sciences, Department of Physical Therapy, Chicago, IL 60607-7128. Offers MS, DPT. *Accreditation:* APTA. *Degree requirements:* For master's, thesis. *Entrance requirements:* For master's, GRE General Test, minimum GPA of 2.75. Additional exam requirements/recommendations for international students: Required—TOEFL. Electronic applications accepted. *Faculty research:* Diagnosing delayed development in high-risk infants, falling mechanics and prevention, posture and movement control in the elderly, healthy lifestyle behaviors of people with disabilities, motor dysfunction following spinal cord injury and stroke.

University of Indianapolis, Graduate Programs, College of Health Sciences, Krannert School of Physical Therapy, Indianapolis, IN 46227-3697. Offers MHS, DHS, DPT. *Accreditation:* APTA (one or more programs are accredited). *Program availability:* Part-time, evening/weekend. *Entrance requirements:* For doctorate, GRE General Test (for DPT), minimum GPA of 3.0 (for DPT), 3 letters of recommendation. Additional exam requirements/recommendations for international students: Required—TOEFL (minimum score 100 iBT), TWE (minimum score 5). Electronic applications accepted. *Expenses:* Contact institution. *Faculty research:* Patella positioning, reaction time, allocation of physical therapy resources.

The University of Iowa, Roy J. and Lucille A. Carver College of Medicine and Graduate College, Graduate Programs in Medicine, Department of Physical Therapy and Rehabilitation Science, Iowa City, IA 52242. Offers physical rehabilitation science (MA, PhD); physical therapy (DPT). *Accreditation:* APTA (one or more programs are accredited). Terminal master's awarded for partial completion of doctoral program. *Degree requirements:* For master's, thesis (for some programs); for doctorate, comprehensive exam (for some programs), thesis/dissertation (for some programs). *Entrance requirements:* For master's and doctorate, GRE. Additional exam requirements/recommendations for international students: Required—TOEFL. Electronic applications accepted. *Expenses:* Contact institution. *Faculty research:* Neuroplasticity and motor control, pain mechanisms, biomechanics and sports medicine, neuromuscular physiology, cardiovascular physiology.

University of Jamestown, Program in Physical Therapy, Jamestown, ND 58405. Offers DPT. *Accreditation:* APTA. *Entrance requirements:* For doctorate, bachelor's degree.

The University of Kansas, University of Kansas Medical Center, School of Health Professions, Department of Physical Therapy and Rehabilitation Science, Kansas City, KS 66160. Offers physical therapy (DPT); rehabilitation science (PhD). *Accreditation:* APTA. *Faculty:* 26. *Students:* 191 full-time (117 women), 1 part-time (0 women); includes 17 minority (3 Black or African American, non-Hispanic/Latino; 1 Asian, non-Hispanic/Latino; 8 Hispanic/Latino; 1 Native Hawaiian or other Pacific Islander, non-Hispanic/Latino; 4 Two or more races, non-Hispanic/Latino), 12 international. Average age 25. 398 applicants, 19% accepted, 62 enrolled. In 2017, 60 doctorates awarded. *Degree requirements:* For doctorate, comprehensive exam, research project with paper. *Entrance requirements:* For doctorate, GRE General Test, minimum GPA of 3.0. Additional exam requirements/recommendations for international students: Required—TOEFL. *Application deadline:* For fall admission, 11/1 for domestic students. Application fee: $75. Electronic applications accepted. *Expenses:* Contact institution. *Financial support:* Research assistantships with tuition reimbursements, teaching assistantships with tuition reimbursements, career-related internships or fieldwork, Federal Work-Study, institutionally sponsored loans, scholarships/grants, traineeships, and unspecified assistantships available. Financial award application deadline: 3/1; financial award applicants required to submit FAFSA. *Faculty research:* Stroke rehabilitation and the effects on balance and coordination; deep brain stimulation and Parkinson's disease; peripheral neuropathies, pain and the effects of exercise; islet transplants for Type 1 diabetes; cardiac disease associated with diabetes. *Total annual research expenditures:* $333,916. *Unit head:* Dr. Patricia Kluding, Chair, 913-588-6799, Fax: 913-588-6910, E-mail: pkluding@kumc.edu. *Application contact:* Robert Bagley, Senior Coordinator, 913-588-6799, Fax: 913-588-6910, E-mail: rbagley@kumc.edu.
Website: http://www.kumc.edu/school-of-health-professions/physical-therapy-and-rehabilitation-science.html

University of Kentucky, Graduate School, College of Health Sciences, Program in Physical Therapy, Lexington, KY 40506-0032. Offers DPT. *Accreditation:* APTA. *Degree requirements:* For doctorate, comprehensive exam, thesis/dissertation optional. *Entrance requirements:* For doctorate, GRE General Test, minimum undergraduate GPA of 2.75, U.S. physical therapist license. Additional exam requirements/recommendations for international students: Required—TOEFL (minimum score 550 paper-based). Electronic applications accepted. *Faculty research:* Orthopedics, biomechanics, electrophysiological stimulation, neural plasticity, brain damage and mechanism.

University of Lynchburg, Graduate Studies, Doctor of Physical Therapy Program, Lynchburg, VA 24501-3199. Offers physical therapy (DPT). *Accreditation:* APTA. *Faculty:* 13 full-time (7 women). *Students:* 147 full-time (89 women); includes 2 minority (1 Black or African American, non-Hispanic/Latino; 1 Asian, non-Hispanic/Latino), 1 international. Average age 25. 677 applicants, 13% accepted, 45 enrolled. In 2017, 45 doctorates awarded. *Degree requirements:* For doctorate, comprehensive exam, clinical internships; comprehensive review. *Entrance requirements:* For doctorate, GRE, baccalaureate degree from institution accredited by a CHEA-recognized regional accrediting organization; official transcripts; minimum GPA of 3.0 overall and for prerequisite science coursework; personal essay as described on PTCAS; 80 hours' experience under supervision of licensed physical therapist; 2 letters of recommendation. Additional exam requirements/recommendations for international students: Required—TOEFL. *Application deadline:* For spring admission, 2/1 priority date for domestic and international students. Applications are processed on a rolling basis. Application fee: $135. Electronic applications accepted. *Expenses:* $15,400 per semester (fall and spring) plus $5,600 (summer); $100 fees. *Financial support:* Scholarships/grants, tuition waivers (partial), and unspecified assistantships available. Financial award application deadline: 7/31; financial award applicants required to submit FAFSA. *Unit head:* Dr. A. Russell Smith, Jr., Associate Professor/Director of DPT Program, 434-544-8880, E-mail: smith.ar@lynchburg.edu. *Application contact:* Carrington Pritchard, Admissions Coordinator, 434-544-8885, Fax: 434-544-8887, E-mail: pritchard@lynchburg.edu.
Website: http://www.lynchburg.edu/graduate/doctor-of-physical-therapy/

University of Manitoba, Faculty of Graduate Studies, College of Rehabilitation Sciences, Winnipeg, MB R3T 2N2, Canada. Offers applied health sciences (PhD); occupational therapy (MOT); physical therapy (MPT); rehabilitation sciences (M Sc).

University of Mary, School of Health Sciences, Program in Physical Therapy, Bismarck, ND 58504-9652. Offers DPT. *Accreditation:* APTA. *Degree requirements:* For doctorate, comprehensive exam, professional paper. *Entrance requirements:* For doctorate, GRE, minimum GPA of 2.75, 3.0 in core requirements; 40 hours of paid/volunteer experience; 2 letters of recommendation. Additional exam requirements/recommendations for international students: Required—TOEFL (minimum score 500 paper-based; 71 iBT). Electronic applications accepted. *Expenses:* Contact institution.

University of Mary Hardin-Baylor, Graduate Studies in Physical Therapy, Belton, TX 76513. Offers DPT. *Faculty:* 10 full-time (7 women), 10 part-time/adjunct (5 women). *Students:* 112 full-time (71 women); includes 29 minority (6 Black or African American, non-Hispanic/Latino; 7 Asian, non-Hispanic/Latino; 15 Hispanic/Latino; 1 Two or more races, non-Hispanic/Latino). Average age 26. 120 applicants, 45% accepted, 40 enrolled. *Degree requirements:* For doctorate, comprehensive exam, professional portfolio. *Entrance requirements:* For doctorate, minimum GPA of 3.2 in last 60 hours of

bachelor's or relevant master's degree, 3.0 in prerequisites; therapy and other healthcare-related experience; resume; letters of recommendation. Additional exam requirements/recommendations for international students: Required—TOEFL (minimum score 60 iBT), IELTS (minimum score 4.5). *Application deadline:* For fall admission, 6/1 for domestic students, 4/30 priority date for international students; for spring admission, 11/1 for domestic students, 9/30 priority date for international students. Applications are processed on a rolling basis. Application fee: $35 ($135 for international students). Electronic applications accepted. *Expenses:* $920 per credit hour. *Financial support:* In 2017–18, 110 students received support. Federal Work-Study, unspecified assistantships, and scholarships for some active duty military personnel available. Financial award applicants required to submit FAFSA. *Faculty research:* Dry needling; balance and balance training; burnout and stress in DPT students; blood flow restriction training; motor control and injury prediction in athletes. *Unit head:* Dr. Barbara Gresham, Director, Doctor of Physical Therapy Program/Associate Professor, 254-295-4921, E-mail: bgresham@umhb.edu. *Application contact:* Sharon Aguilera, Assistant Director, Graduate Admissions, 254-295-4835, E-mail: saguilera@umhb.edu.
Website: https://go.umhb.edu/graduate/physical-therapy/home

University of Maryland, Baltimore, School of Medicine, Department of Physical Therapy and Rehabilitation Science, Baltimore, MD 21201. Offers physical rehabilitation science (PhD); physical therapy and rehabilitation science (DPT). *Accreditation:* APTA. *Students:* 183 full-time (124 women), 2 part-time (1 woman); includes 26 minority (5 Black or African American, non-Hispanic/Latino; 1 American Indian or Alaska Native, non-Hispanic/Latino; 9 Asian, non-Hispanic/Latino; 8 Hispanic/Latino; 3 Two or more races, non-Hispanic/Latino), 2 international. Average age 25. 187 applicants, 91% accepted, 65 enrolled. In 2017, 56 doctorates awarded. *Entrance requirements:* For doctorate, GRE General Test, BS, science coursework. Additional exam requirements/recommendations for international students: Required—TOEFL (minimum score 80 iBT). Electronic applications accepted. *Expenses:* Contact institution. *Financial support:* Career-related internships or fieldwork, Federal Work-Study, scholarships/grants, traineeships, health care benefits, and unspecified assistantships available. Financial award application deadline: 3/1; financial award applicants required to submit FAFSA. *Unit head:* Dr. Mark W. Rogers, Chair, 410-706-0841, Fax: 410-706-4903, E-mail: mrogers@som.umaryland.edu. *Application contact:* Aynsley Hamel, Program Coordinator, 410-706-0566, Fax: 410-706-6387, E-mail: ptadmissions@som.umaryland.edu.
Website: http://pt.umaryland.edu/pros.asp

University of Maryland Eastern Shore, Graduate Programs, Department of Physical Therapy, Princess Anne, MD 21853. Offers DPT. *Accreditation:* APTA. *Degree requirements:* For doctorate, thesis/dissertation, clinical practicum, research project. *Entrance requirements:* For doctorate, minimum GPA of 3.0, course work in science and mathematics, interview, knowledge of the physical therapy field. Additional exam requirements/recommendations for international students: Required—TOEFL (minimum score 80 iBT). *Application deadline:* For fall admission, 1/1 for domestic and international students. Application fee: $30. Electronic applications accepted. *Expenses:* Tuition, state resident: part-time $325 per credit hour. Tuition, nonresident: part-time $604 per credit hour. *Required fees:* $85 per credit hour. Part-time tuition and fees vary according to campus/location, program and reciprocity agreements. *Financial support:* Research assistantships, teaching assistantships, career-related internships or fieldwork, scholarships/grants, and unspecified assistantships available. Financial award application deadline: 3/1; financial award applicants required to submit FAFSA. *Faculty research:* Allied health projects. *Unit head:* Dr. Raymond Blakely, Chair, 410-651-6310, Fax: 410-651-6259, E-mail: rblakely@umes.edu. *Application contact:* Benita Sims-Tucker, Associate Vice President for Academic Affairs, 410-651-6508, E-mail: bsimstucker@umes.edu.

University of Massachusetts Lowell, College of Health Sciences, Department of Physical Therapy, Lowell, MA 01854. Offers DPT. *Accreditation:* APTA. *Entrance requirements:* For doctorate, GRE General Test, minimum GPA of 3.0, 3 letters of recommendation. Additional exam requirements/recommendations for international students: Required—TOEFL (minimum score 560 paper-based). *Faculty research:* Orthopedics, pediatrics, electrophysiology, cardiopulmonary, neurology.

University of Miami, Graduate School, Miller School of Medicine, Graduate Programs in Medicine, Department of Physical Therapy, Coral Gables, FL 33124. Offers DPT, PhD. *Accreditation:* APTA (one or more programs are accredited). *Degree requirements:* For doctorate, comprehensive exam, thesis/dissertation. *Entrance requirements:* For doctorate, GRE General Test. Additional exam requirements/recommendations for international students: Required—TOEFL. Electronic applications accepted. *Expenses:* Contact institution. *Faculty research:* Central pattern generators in SCI balance and vestibular function in children, amputee rehabilitation.

University of Michigan–Flint, School of Health Professions and Studies, Program in Physical Therapy, Flint, MI 48502-1950. Offers adult neurology (PhD); neurology (Certificate); orthopedics (PhD, Certificate); pediatrics (PhD, Certificate); physical therapy (DPT). *Accreditation:* APTA. *Program availability:* Part-time, evening/weekend, 100% online. *Faculty:* 16 full-time (12 women), 17 part-time/adjunct (10 women). *Students:* 176 full-time (104 women), 44 part-time (27 women); includes 34 minority (2 Black or African American, non-Hispanic/Latino; 1 American Indian or Alaska Native, non-Hispanic/Latino; 23 Asian, non-Hispanic/Latino; 2 Hispanic/Latino; 6 Two or more races, non-Hispanic/Latino), 16 international. Average age 27. 346 applicants, 38% accepted, 67 enrolled. In 2017, 88 doctorates, 4 other advanced degrees awarded. *Degree requirements:* For doctorate, thesis/dissertation or alternative. *Entrance requirements:* For doctorate, GRE (minimum Verbal score between 340-480; Quantitative 370-710), bachelor's or master's physical therapy degree from regionally-accredited institution, current physical therapy license in the United States or Canada, minimum overall GPA of 3.0 in the physical therapy degree, current CPR certification (depending on program); for Certificate, DPT from accredited institution; current physical therapy license in the United States or Canada; minimum overall GPA of 3.0 in the physical therapy degree; current CPR certification. Additional exam requirements/recommendations for international students: Required—TOEFL (minimum score 84 iBT), IELTS (minimum score 6.5). *Application deadline:* For fall admission, 5/1 for domestic students, 2/1 for international students; for winter admission, 7/31 for domestic students, 4/1 for international students; for spring admission, 3/1 for domestic students, 12/1 for international students. Application fee: $55. Electronic applications accepted. *Expenses:* Contact institution. *Financial support:* Federal Work-Study and unspecified assistantships available. Support available to part-time students. Financial award application deadline: 3/1; financial award applicants required to submit FAFSA. *Faculty research:* Cumulative trauma disorders, oncology rehabilitation, neurological rehabilitation, musculoskeletal rehabilitation, cardiopulmonary rehabilitation. *Unit head:* Dr. Amy Yorke, Department Admissions Chair, 810-762-3373, E-mail: amyorke@umflint.edu. *Application contact:* Frank Fanzone, Senior Administrative Assistant, 810-762-3373, Fax: 810-766-6668, E-mail: ffanzone@umflint.edu.
Website: https://www.umflint.edu/pt

University of Minnesota, Twin Cities Campus, Medical School, Minneapolis, MN 55455-0213. Offers MA, MS, DPT, MD, PhD, JD/MD, MD/MBA, MD/MHI, MD/MPH, MD/MS, MD/PhD. *Accreditation:* LCME/AMA. *Program availability:* Part-time, evening/weekend. *Expenses:* Contact institution.

University of Mississippi Medical Center, School of Health Related Professions, Department of Physical Therapy, Jackson, MS 39216-4505. Offers MPT. *Accreditation:* APTA. *Faculty research:* Pain, acupressure, seating, patient satisfaction, physical therapy educational issues.

University of Missouri, School of Health Professions, Program in Physical Therapy, Columbia, MO 65211. Offers DPT. *Accreditation:* APTA. *Entrance requirements:* Additional exam requirements/recommendations for international students: Required—TOEFL. *Application deadline:* Applications are processed on a rolling basis. Electronic applications accepted. *Expenses:* Tuition, state resident: full-time $6480. Tuition, nonresident: full-time $17,744. *Required fees:* $1108. Tuition and fees vary according to course load, campus/location and program. *Financial support:* Research assistantships, teaching assistantships, and institutionally sponsored loans available.
Website: http://shp.missouri.edu/pt/index.php

University of Montana, Graduate School, College of Health Professions and Biomedical Sciences, School of Physical Therapy and Rehabilitation Science, Missoula, MT 59812. Offers physical therapy (DPT). *Accreditation:* APTA. *Degree requirements:* For doctorate, professional paper. *Entrance requirements:* For doctorate, GRE General Test. Additional exam requirements/recommendations for international students: Required—TOEFL. Electronic applications accepted. *Expenses:* Contact institution. *Faculty research:* Muscle stiffness, fitness with a disability, psychosocial aspects of disability, clinical learning, motion analysis.

University of Mount Union, Program in Physical Therapy, Alliance, OH 44601-3993. Offers DPT. *Faculty:* 7 full-time (4 women), 4 part-time/adjunct (1 woman). *Students:* 58 full-time (33 women); includes 6 minority (2 Black or African American, non-Hispanic/Latino; 2 Asian, non-Hispanic/Latino; 1 Hispanic/Latino; 1 Two or more races, non-Hispanic/Latino). Average age 24. 190 applicants, 22% accepted, 30 enrolled. *Entrance requirements:* Additional exam requirements/recommendations for international students: Required—TOEFL (minimum score 89 iBT). *Application deadline:* For fall admission, 10/2 for domestic and international students. Electronic applications accepted. *Expenses:* $34,380. *Financial support:* Applicants required to submit FAFSA. *Unit head:* Dr. Robert Frampton, Director, 330-823-4786, E-mail: framptrm@mountunion.edu. *Application contact:* Brandon Crites, Admission Representative, 330-823-2587, E-mail: critesbr@mountunion.edu.
Website: http://www.mountunion.edu/dpt

University of Nebraska Medical Center, College of Allied Health Professions, Division of Physical Therapy Education, Omaha, NE 68198. Offers DPT. *Accreditation:* APTA. *Expenses:* Tuition, state resident: full-time $8451; part-time $4225 per semester. Tuition, nonresident: full-time $24,219; part-time $11,295 per semester. *Required fees:* $589; $117 per term.

University of Nevada, Las Vegas, Graduate College, School of Allied Health Sciences, Department of Physical Therapy, Las Vegas, NV 89154-3029. Offers DPT. *Accreditation:* APTA. *Faculty:* 6 full-time (2 women), 10 part-time/adjunct (7 women). *Students:* 116 full-time (50 women); includes 39 minority (18 Asian, non-Hispanic/Latino; 13 Hispanic/Latino; 8 Two or more races, non-Hispanic/Latino). Average age 27. In 2017, 33 doctorates awarded. *Degree requirements:* For doctorate, comprehensive exam (for some programs), thesis/dissertation, final research report/professional paper/case report. *Entrance requirements:* For doctorate, GRE General Test, PTCAS application; hours of observation; 3 letters of recommendation; statement of purpose; personal interview; bachelor's degree. Additional exam requirements/recommendations for international students: Required—TOEFL (minimum score 550 paper-based; 80 iBT), IELTS (minimum score 7). *Application deadline:* For summer admission, 11/1 for domestic and international students. Application fee: $60 ($95 for international students). Electronic applications accepted. *Expenses:* $275 per credit, $850 per course, $7,969 per year resident, $22,157 per year non-resident, $7,094 non-resident fee (7 credits or more), $1,307 annual health insurance fee. *Financial support:* In 2017–18, 6 students received support, including 5 research assistantships with full and partial tuition reimbursements available (averaging $20,000 per year), 1 teaching assistantship with full and partial tuition reimbursement available (averaging $20,000 per year); institutionally sponsored loans, scholarships/grants, health care benefits, and unspecified assistantships also available. Financial award application deadline: 3/15; financial award applicants required to submit FAFSA. *Faculty research:* Pathobiomechanics of prosthetics, knee osteoarthritis, patellofemoral pain, balance assessment and impairment, Parkinson's disease, Alzheimer's disease, falls and fall avoidance behavior, cerebral vascular accident, wound care and acute care delivery services, transcranial magnetic stimulation, transcranial direct current stimulation. *Total annual research expenditures:* $14,057. *Unit head:* Dr. Merrill Landers, Chair/Associate Professor, 702-895-1377, Fax: 702-895-4883, E-mail: merrill.landers@unlv.edu. *Application contact:* Dr. Keoni Kins, Graduate Coordinator, 702-895-3072, Fax: 702-895-4883, E-mail: keoni.kins@unlv.edu.
Website: http://pt.unlv.edu/

University of New England, Westbrook College of Health Professions, Biddeford, ME 04005-9526. Offers nurse anesthesia (MSNA); occupational therapy (MS); physical therapy (DPT); physician assistant (MS); social work (MSW). *Program availability:* Part-time. *Faculty:* 43 full-time (30 women), 26 part-time/adjunct (19 women). *Students:* 527 full-time (401 women), 5 part-time (4 women); includes 50 minority (11 Black or African American, non-Hispanic/Latino; 1 American Indian or Alaska Native, non-Hispanic/Latino; 24 Asian, non-Hispanic/Latino; 5 Hispanic/Latino; 1 Native Hawaiian or other Pacific Islander, non-Hispanic/Latino; 8 Two or more races, non-Hispanic/Latino), 1 international. Average age 27. 2,499 applicants, 18% accepted, 226 enrolled. In 2017, 440 master's, 71 doctorates awarded. *Application deadline:* Applications are processed on a rolling basis. Electronic applications accepted. Tuition and fees vary according to degree level, program and student level. *Financial support:* Application deadline: 5/1; applicants required to submit FAFSA. *Unit head:* Dr. Elizabeth Francis- Connolly, Dean, Westbrook College of Health Professions, 207-221-4523, E-mail: efrancisconnolly@une.edu. *Application contact:* Scott Steinberg, Dean of University Admission, 207-221-4225, Fax: 207-523-1925, E-mail: ssteinberg@une.edu.
Website: http://www.une.edu/wchp/index.cfm

University of New Mexico, Graduate Studies, Health Sciences Center, Division of Physical Therapy, Albuquerque, NM 87131. Offers DPT. *Accreditation:* APTA. *Faculty:* 8 full-time (6 women). *Students:* 85 full-time (45 women); includes 42 minority (1 Black or African American, non-Hispanic/Latino; 5 American Indian or Alaska Native, non-Hispanic/Latino; 1 Asian, non-Hispanic/Latino; 32 Hispanic/Latino; 3 Two or more races, non-Hispanic/Latino), 1 international. Average age 29. 31 applicants, 100% accepted, 30 enrolled. In 2017, 26 doctorates awarded. *Degree requirements:* For doctorate, comprehensive exam, thesis/dissertation or alternative. *Entrance requirements:* For doctorate, GRE General Test, GRE Writing Assessment Test, interview, minimum GPA of 3.0. *Application deadline:* For fall admission, 12/15 priority date for domestic students. Applications are processed on a rolling basis. Application fee: $50. *Financial support:* Fellowships, Federal Work-Study, institutionally sponsored loans, and scholarships/grants available. Financial award application deadline: 3/1; financial award applicants required to submit FAFSA. *Faculty research:* Gait analysis, motion analysis, balance, articular cartilage, quality of life. *Total annual research expenditures:* $7,428. *Unit head:* Dr. Susan A. Queen, Director, 505-272-5756, Fax: 505-272-8079, E-mail: squeen@salud.unm.edu. *Application contact:* Rosalia Loya Vejar, Administrative Assistant, 505-272-6956, Fax: 505-272-8079, E-mail: rloyavejar@salud.unm.edu.

The University of North Carolina at Chapel Hill, School of Medicine and Graduate School, Graduate Programs in Medicine, Department of Allied Health Sciences, Program in Physical Therapy, Chapel Hill, NC 27599. Offers DPT. *Accreditation:* APTA. *Program availability:* Part-time, evening/weekend, online learning. *Degree requirements:* For doctorate, thesis/dissertation or alternative. *Entrance requirements:* For doctorate, physical therapy license. Additional exam requirements/recommendations for international students: Required—TOEFL (minimum score 550 paper-based). Electronic applications accepted. *Faculty research:* Traumatic brain injury, quality of life after heart and/or lung transplant, cultural diversity, life care planning, rehabilitation education and supervision.

University of North Dakota, Graduate School and Graduate School, Graduate Programs in Medicine, Department of Physical Therapy, Grand Forks, ND 58202. Offers DPT. *Accreditation:* APTA. *Entrance requirements:* For doctorate, minimum GPA of 3.0, pre-physical therapy program. Additional exam requirements/recommendations for international students: Required—TOEFL (minimum score 550 paper-based; 79 iBT), IELTS (minimum score 6.5).

University of North Florida, Brooks College of Health, Department of Clinical and Applied Movement Sciences, Jacksonville, FL 32224. Offers MSH, DPT. *Accreditation:* APTA. *Program availability:* Part-time, evening/weekend. *Entrance requirements:* For master's, GRE General Test, minimum GPA of 3.0 in last 60 hours, volunteer/observation experience. Additional exam requirements/recommendations for international students: Required—TOEFL (minimum score 500 paper-based). Electronic applications accepted. *Faculty research:* Clinical outcomes related to orthopedic physical therapy interventions, instructional multimedia in physical therapy education, effect of functional electrical stimulation orthostatic hypotension in acute complete spinal cord injury individuals.

University of North Georgia, Department of Physical Therapy, Dahlonega, GA 30597. Offers DPT. *Accreditation:* APTA. *Faculty:* 8 full-time (4 women). *Students:* 87 full-time (62 women); includes 7 minority (2 Black or African American, non-Hispanic/Latino; 3 Hispanic/Latino; 2 Two or more races, non-Hispanic/Latino). Average age 25. In 2017, 30 doctorates awarded. *Degree requirements:* For doctorate, research project. *Entrance requirements:* For doctorate, GRE (minimum combined score of 297 on verbal and quantitative sections), interview, recommendations, physical therapy observations hours, minimum GPA of 2.8. Additional exam requirements/recommendations for international students: Required—TOEFL (minimum score 550 paper-based; 79 iBT), IELTS (minimum score 6.5). *Application deadline:* For summer admission, 10/3 for domestic students. Applications are processed on a rolling basis. Application fee: $50. Electronic applications accepted. *Expenses:* Contact institution. *Financial support:* Unspecified assistantships available. Financial award application deadline: 5/1; financial award applicants required to submit CSS PROFILE or FAFSA. *Faculty research:* Ergonomics, spinal mobility measurements, electrophysiology, orthopedic physical therapy. *Unit head:* Dr. Mary Ellen Oesterle, Department Head, 706-867-4589, E-mail: maryellen.oesterle@ung.edu. *Application contact:* Melinda Maxwell, Director of Graduate Admissions, 706-864-1543, E-mail: melinda.maxwell@ung.edu.
Website: http://ung.edu/physical-therapy/

University of North Texas Health Science Center at Fort Worth, School of Health Professions, Fort Worth, TX 76107-2699. Offers physical therapy (DPT); physician assistant studies (MPAS). *Accreditation:* ARC-PA. *Degree requirements:* For master's, thesis or alternative, research paper. *Entrance requirements:* For master's, minimum GPA of 2.85. *Faculty research:* Impact of mid-level providers on medical treatment, curriculum development, pain in geriatric patients, biopsychosocial risk factors.

University of Oklahoma Health Sciences Center, Graduate College, College of Allied Health, Department of Physical Therapy, Oklahoma City, OK 73190. Offers MPT. *Accreditation:* APTA.

University of Pittsburgh, School of Health and Rehabilitation Sciences, Department of Physical Therapy, Pittsburgh, PA 15260. Offers MS, DPT, DPT/PhD. *Accreditation:* APTA. *Faculty:* 31 full-time (17 women), 4 part-time/adjunct (2 women). *Students:* 196 full-time (132 women), 2 part-time (both women); includes 20 minority (2 Black or African American, non-Hispanic/Latino; 1 American Indian or Alaska Native, non-Hispanic/Latino; 12 Asian, non-Hispanic/Latino; 4 Hispanic/Latino; 1 Two or more races, non-Hispanic/Latino), 24 international. Average age 24. 753 applicants, 27% accepted, 84 enrolled. In 2017, 41 master's, 60 doctorates awarded. *Degree requirements:* For doctorate, comprehensive exam. *Entrance requirements:* For doctorate, GRE General Test. Additional exam requirements/recommendations for international students: Required—TOEFL (minimum score 550 paper-based; 80 iBT), IELTS (minimum score 6.5). *Application deadline:* For fall admission, 4/15 for domestic and international students; for summer admission, 11/15 for domestic and international students. Application fee: $140. Electronic applications accepted. *Financial support:* In 2017–18, 1 research assistantship (averaging $24,590 per year), 1 teaching assistantship (averaging $27,675 per year) were awarded; career-related internships or fieldwork, Federal Work-Study, scholarships/grants, traineeships, and unspecified assistantships also available. *Faculty research:* Pain management; development, aging, and transitions across the lifespan; health systems safety for patients and providers; chronic low back pain; osteoarthritis. *Total annual research expenditures:* $5 million. *Unit head:* Dr. James Irrgang, Chair/Professor, 412-383-9865, Fax: 412-648-5970, E-mail: jirrgang@pitt.edu. *Application contact:* Jessica Maguire, Director of Admissions, 412-383-6557, Fax: 412-383-6535, E-mail: maguire@pitt.edu.
Website: http://www.shrs.pitt.edu/pt

University of Puerto Rico–Medical Sciences Campus, School of Health Professions, Program in Physical Therapy, San Juan, PR 00936-5067. Offers MS. *Accreditation:* APTA. *Program availability:* Part-time, evening/weekend. *Degree requirements:* For master's, one foreign language, thesis. *Entrance requirements:* For master's, EXADEP, minimum GPA of 2.8, interview, first aid training and CPR certification.

University of Puget Sound, School of Physical Therapy, Tacoma, WA 98416. Offers DPT. *Accreditation:* APTA. *Degree requirements:* For doctorate, comprehensive exam, thesis/dissertation or alternative, successful completion of 36 weeks of full-time internships and a research project. *Entrance requirements:* For doctorate, GRE General Test, minimum baccalaureate GPA of 3.0, observation hours (at least 100 recommended), four letters of recommendation. Additional exam requirements/recommendations for international students: Required—TOEFL. Electronic applications accepted. *Expenses:* Contact institution. *Faculty research:* Manual therapy, pain studies, injury prevention, movement assessment in children, global health.

University of Rhode Island, Graduate School, College of Health Sciences, Physical Therapy Department, Kingston, RI 02881. Offers DPT. *Accreditation:* APTA. *Program availability:* Part-time. *Faculty:* 9 full-time (5 women). *Students:* 57 full-time (33 women), 28 part-time (19 women); includes 7 minority (1 Black or African American, non-Hispanic/Latino; 4 Asian, non-Hispanic/Latino; 2 Hispanic/Latino), 1 international. 33 applicants, 3% accepted. In 2017, 34 doctorates awarded. *Entrance requirements:* Additional exam requirements/recommendations for international students: Required—TOEFL. *Application deadline:* For fall admission, 10/15 for domestic and international students. Application fee: $65. Electronic applications accepted. *Expenses:* Tuition, state resident: full-time $12,706; part-time $786 per credit. Tuition, nonresident: full-time $25,216; part-time $1401 per credit. *Required fees:* $1598; $45 per credit. One-time fee: $30 part-time. *Financial support:* In 2017–18, 4 teaching assistantships with tuition reimbursements (averaging $4,985 per year) were awarded. Financial award application deadline: 10/15; financial award applicants required to submit FAFSA. *Unit head:* Dr. Jeff Konin, Chair, 401-574-5627, E-mail: jkonin@mail.uri.edu.
Website: http://www.uri.edu/hss/pt/

University of St. Augustine for Health Sciences, Graduate Programs, Doctor of Physical Therapy Program, San Marcos, CA 92069. Offers DPT. *Accreditation:* APTA. *Entrance requirements:* Additional exam requirements/recommendations for international students: Required—TOEFL. Application fee is waived when completed online.

University of St. Augustine for Health Sciences, Graduate Programs, Post Professional Programs, San Marcos, CA 92069. Offers health science (DH Sc); health sciences education (Ed D); occupational therapy (TOTD); physical therapy (TDPT). *Program availability:* Part-time, online learning. *Entrance requirements:* For doctorate, GRE General Test, master's degree in related field. Additional exam requirements/recommendations for international students: Required—TOEFL.

University of Saint Mary, Graduate Programs, Program in Physical Therapy, Leavenworth, KS 66048-5082. Offers DPT. *Accreditation:* APTA. Electronic applications accepted. *Expenses:* Contact institution.

The University of Scranton, Panuska College of Professional Studies, Department of Physical Therapy, Scranton, PA 18510. Offers DPT. *Accreditation:* APTA. *Program availability:* Part-time. *Degree requirements:* For doctorate, capstone experience. *Entrance requirements:* For doctorate, minimum undergraduate GPA of 3.0, minimum 60 hours of observation. Additional exam requirements/recommendations for international students: Required—TOEFL (minimum score 500 paper-based; 80 iBT), IELTS (minimum score 6.5). Electronic applications accepted.

University of South Alabama, Pat Capps Covey College of Allied Health Professions, Department of Physical Therapy, Mobile, AL 36688. Offers DPT. *Accreditation:* APTA. *Faculty:* 8 full-time (5 women). *Students:* 111 full-time (74 women); includes 1 minority (Hispanic/Latino). Average age 24. 481 applicants, 14% accepted, 34 enrolled. In 2017, 40 doctorates awarded. *Entrance requirements:* For doctorate, GRE, minimum GPA of 3.0. Additional exam requirements/recommendations for international students: Required—TOEFL (minimum score 600 paper-based; 100 iBT), TWE (minimum score 4.5). *Application deadline:* For fall admission, 12/1 for domestic students, 10/1 for international students. Application fee: $75. Electronic applications accepted. *Expenses:* Contact institution. *Financial support:* Fellowships, research assistantships, teaching assistantships, career-related internships or fieldwork, Federal Work-Study, institutionally sponsored loans, scholarships/grants, and unspecified assistantships available. Support available to part-time students. Financial award application deadline: 3/31; financial award applicants required to submit FAFSA. *Unit head:* Dr. Barry Dale, Chair, 251-445-9330, Fax: 251-445-9238, E-mail: ptdept@southalabama.edu. *Application contact:* Dr. Susan Gordon-Hickey, Associate Dean, Allied Health, 251-445-9250, Fax: 251-445-9259, E-mail: gordonhickey@southalabama.edu.
Website: http://www.southalabama.edu/alliedhealth/pt/

University of South Dakota, Graduate School, School of Health Sciences, Department of Physical Therapy, Vermillion, SD 57069. Offers DPT. *Accreditation:* APTA. *Entrance requirements:* For doctorate, GRE General Test. Additional exam requirements/recommendations for international students: Required—TOEFL (minimum score 550 paper-based; 79 iBT), IELTS (minimum score 6). *Application deadline:* For spring admission, 9/15 priority date for domestic students. Applications are processed on a rolling basis. Application fee: $35. *Expenses:* Contact institution. *Financial support:* Scholarships/grants available. *Faculty research:* Physical therapy, knee rehabilitation, pediatric intervention, wound care, motion analysis. *Application contact:* Graduate School, 605-658-6140, Fax: 605-677-6118, E-mail: grad@usd.edu.
Website: http://www.usd.edu/pt

University of Southern California, Graduate School, Herman Ostrow School of Dentistry, Division of Biokinesiology and Physical Therapy, Los Angeles, CA 90089. Offers biokinesiology (MS, PhD); physical therapy (DPT). *Accreditation:* APTA (one or more programs are accredited). *Degree requirements:* For master's, comprehensive exam; for doctorate, thesis/dissertation. *Entrance requirements:* For master's and doctorate, GRE (minimum combined score 1200, verbal 600, quantitative 600). Additional exam requirements/recommendations for international students: Required—TOEFL. Electronic applications accepted. *Expenses:* Contact institution. *Faculty research:* Exercise and aging biomechanics, musculoskeletal biomechanics, exercise and hormones related to muscle wasting, computational neurorehabilitation, motor behavior and neurorehabilitation, motor development, infant motor performance.

University of South Florida, Morsani College of Medicine, School of Physical Therapy, Tampa, FL 33620-9951. Offers physical therapy (DPT); rehabilitation sciences (PhD), including chronic disease, neuromusculoskeletal disability, veteran's health/reintegration. *Accreditation:* APTA. *Faculty:* 11 full-time (6 women). *Students:* 139 full-time (94 women); includes 28 minority (6 Black or African American, non-Hispanic/Latino; 1 American Indian or Alaska Native, non-Hispanic/Latino; 9 Asian, non-Hispanic/Latino; 11 Hispanic/Latino; 1 Two or more races, non-Hispanic/Latino). Average age 24. 1,433 applicants, 5% accepted, 50 enrolled. In 2017, 80 doctorates awarded. *Degree requirements:* For doctorate, comprehensive exam, thesis/dissertation. *Entrance requirements:* For doctorate, GRE General Test, bachelor's degree from regionally-accredited university with minimum GPA of 3.0 in all upper-division coursework; interview; at least 20 hours of documented volunteer or work experience in hospital outpatient/inpatient physical therapy settings; written personal statement of values and purpose for attending. Additional exam requirements/recommendations for international students: Required—TOEFL (minimum score 600 paper-based; 79 iBT). *Application deadline:* For fall admission, 6/1 for domestic students, 1/1 for international students; for spring admission, 10/15 for domestic students, 9/15 for international students. Application fee: $30. Electronic applications accepted. *Financial support:* In 2017–18, 83 students received support. Teaching assistantships available. *Faculty research:* Veteran's reintegration and resilience, prosthetics and orthotics (microprocessor prosthetic knee), neuromusculoskeletal disorders (occupational ergonomics, fall risk and prevention, exercise adherence and compliance, and orthotic and prosthetic wear and use), human movement and function. *Total annual research expenditures:* $908,954. *Unit head:* Dr. William S. Quillen, Director, 813-974-9863, Fax: 813-974-8915, E-mail: wquillen@health.usf.edu. *Application contact:* Dr. Gina Maria Musolino, Associate Professor and Coordinator for Clinical Education, 813-974-2254, Fax: 813-974-8915, E-mail: gmusolin@health.usf.edu.
Website: http://health.usf.edu/medicine/dpt/index.htm

The University of Tennessee at Chattanooga, Program in Physical Therapy, Chattanooga, TN 37403. Offers DPT. *Accreditation:* APTA. *Faculty:* 10 full-time (7 women), 3 part-time/adjunct (2 women). *Students:* 107 full-time (70 women); includes 17 minority (1 Black or African American, non-Hispanic/Latino; 1 Asian, non-Hispanic/Latino; 1 Hispanic/Latino; 14 Two or more races, non-Hispanic/Latino). Average age 24. 45 applicants, 84% accepted, 36 enrolled. In 2017, 33 doctorates awarded. *Degree requirements:* For doctorate, qualifying exams, internship. *Entrance requirements:* For

doctorate, GRE, minimum GPA of 3.2 in science and overall, criminal background check, two letters of reference (one of which must be from a licensed physical therapist). Additional exam requirements/recommendations for international students: Required—TOEFL (minimum score 550 paper-based; 79 iBT); Recommended—IELTS (minimum score 6). *Application deadline:* For fall admission, 6/15 priority date for domestic students, 7/1 for international students; for spring admission, 11/1 priority date for domestic students, 11/1 for international students. Applications are processed on a rolling basis. Application fee: $35 ($40 for international students). Electronic applications accepted. *Expenses:* Contact institution. *Financial support:* Research assistantships, teaching assistantships, career-related internships or fieldwork, scholarships/grants, and unspecified assistantships available. Support available to part-time students. Financial award application deadline: 7/1; financial award applicants required to submit FAFSA. *Faculty research:* Diabetes and wound management, disabilities, animal physical therapy and rehabilitation, orthopedics. *Unit head:* Dr. Debbie Ingram, Interim Department Head, 423-425-4767, Fax: 423-425-2380, E-mail: debbie-ingram@utc.edu. *Application contact:* Dr. Joanne Romagni, Dean of the Graduate School, 423-425-4478, Fax: 423-425-5223, E-mail: joanne-romagni@utc.edu.
Website: http://www.utc.edu/physical-therapy/

The University of Tennessee Health Science Center, College of Health Professions, Memphis, TN 38163-0002. Offers audiology (MS, Au D); clinical laboratory science (MSCLS); cytopathology practice (MCP); health informatics and information management (MHIIM); occupational therapy (MOT); physical therapy (DPT, ScDPT); physician assistant (MMS); speech-language pathology (MS). *Accreditation:* AOTA; APTA. *Program availability:* Part-time, evening/weekend, online learning. Terminal master's awarded for partial completion of doctoral program. *Degree requirements:* For master's, comprehensive exam, thesis; for doctorate, comprehensive exam, residency. *Entrance requirements:* For master's, GRE (MOT, MSCLS), minimum GPA of 3.0, 3 letters of reference, national accreditation (MSCLS), GRE if GPA is less than 3.0 (MCP); for doctorate, GRE. Additional exam requirements/recommendations for international students: Required—TOEFL (minimum score 550 paper-based; 80 iBT). Electronic applications accepted. *Expenses:* Contact institution. *Faculty research:* Gait deviation, muscular dystrophy and strength, hemophilia and exercise, pediatric neurology, self-efficacy.

The University of Texas at El Paso, Graduate School, College of Health Sciences, Program in Physical Therapy, El Paso, TX 79968-0001. Offers DPT. *Accreditation:* APTA. *Entrance requirements:* For doctorate, GRE General Test. Additional exam requirements/recommendations for international students: Required—TOEFL. *Application deadline:* For fall admission, 11/15 for domestic students, 10/15 for international students; for spring admission, 1/10 for domestic and international students. Application fee: $45 ($80 for international students). Electronic applications accepted. *Financial support:* Research assistantships, teaching assistantships, institutionally sponsored loans, and scholarships/grants available. Financial award application deadline: 3/15; financial award applicants required to submit FAFSA.
Website: http://chs.utep.edu/pt/

The University of Texas Health Science Center at San Antonio, School of Health Professions, San Antonio, TX 78229-3900. Offers occupational therapy (MOT); physical therapy (DPT); physician assistant studies (MS); speech language pathology (MS). *Accreditation:* AOTA; APTA; ARC-PA; ASHA. *Degree requirements:* For master's, comprehensive exam, thesis (for some programs); for doctorate, comprehensive exam.

The University of Texas Medical Branch, School of Health Professions, Department of Physical Therapy, Galveston, TX 77555. Offers MPT, DPT. *Accreditation:* APTA. *Degree requirements:* For master's, thesis or alternative. *Entrance requirements:* For master's and doctorate, GRE, documentation of 40 hours' experience. Electronic applications accepted.

The University of Texas Southwestern Medical Center, Southwestern School of Health Professions, Physical Therapy Program, Dallas, TX 75390. Offers DPT. *Accreditation:* APTA. *Entrance requirements:* For doctorate, GRE, minimum GPA of 3.0. Additional exam requirements/recommendations for international students: Required—TOEFL (minimum score 600 paper-based). Electronic applications accepted.

University of the Incarnate Word, School of Physical Therapy, San Antonio, TX 78209-6397. Offers DPT. *Accreditation:* APTA. *Faculty:* 16 full-time (9 women), 12 part-time/adjunct (10 women). *Students:* 107 full-time (68 women), 73 part-time (35 women); includes 96 minority (10 Black or African American, non-Hispanic/Latino; 32 Asian, non-Hispanic/Latino; 51 Hispanic/Latino; 3 Two or more races, non-Hispanic/Latino), 4 international. In 2017, 65 doctorates awarded. *Degree requirements:* For doctorate, comprehensive exam. *Entrance requirements:* For doctorate, GRE, minimum of 100 verified observation hours in at least two different physical therapy settings which focus on different physical therapy specialties; three letters of reference (at least one letter from licensed Physical Therapist). Additional exam requirements/recommendations for international students: Required—TOEFL (minimum score 560 paper-based). *Application deadline:* For fall admission, 10/1 priority date for domestic students. Application fee: $50. *Expenses:* $900 per credit hour. *Financial support:* Scholarships/grants and unspecified assistantships available. Financial award applicants required to submit FAFSA. *Unit head:* Dr. Caroline Goulet, Dean, 210-283-6924, E-mail: goulet@uiwtx.edu. *Application contact:* Christina Immel, Director of Enrollment, 210-283-6918, E-mail: cimmel@uiwtx.edu.
Website: http://www.uiw.edu/physicaltherapy/

University of the Pacific, Thomas J. Long School of Pharmacy and Health Sciences, Department of Physical Therapy, Stockton, CA 95211-0197. Offers MS, DPT. *Accreditation:* APTA. *Faculty:* 8 full-time (4 women), 12 part-time/adjunct (8 women). *Students:* 71 full-time (53 women); includes 29 minority (20 Asian, non-Hispanic/Latino; 9 Hispanic/Latino), 1 international. Average age 25. 562 applicants, 12% accepted, 35 enrolled. In 2017, 38 doctorates awarded. *Entrance requirements:* For master's, GRE General Test, minimum GPA of 3.0. Additional exam requirements/recommendations for international students: Required—TOEFL. *Application deadline:* For fall admission, 1/4 for domestic students. Application fee: $75. *Financial support:* Federal Work-Study available. Financial award application deadline: 3/1; financial award applicants required to submit FAFSA. *Unit head:* Dr. Cathy Peterson, Chair, 209-946-2397, Fax: 209-946-2410, E-mail: cpeterson@pacific.edu. *Application contact:* Ron Espejo, Recruitment Specialist, 209-946-3957, Fax: 209-946-3147, E-mail: respejo@pacific.edu.

University of the Sciences, Doctor of Physical Therapy Program, Philadelphia, PA 19104-4495. Offers DPT. *Accreditation:* APTA. *Program availability:* Part-time, evening/weekend, online learning. *Entrance requirements:* For doctorate, interview. *Expenses:* Contact institution.

The University of Toledo, College of Graduate Studies, College of Health and Human Services, School of Exercise and Rehabilitation Sciences, Toledo, OH 43606-3390. Offers athletic training (MSES); exercise physiology (MSES); exercise science (PhD); occupational therapy (OTD); physical therapy (DPT); recreation and leisure studies (MA), including recreation administration, recreation therapy. *Degree requirements:* For master's, comprehensive exam, thesis; for doctorate, thesis/dissertation or alternative. *Entrance requirements:* For master's, GRE, minimum cumulative GPA of 2.7 for all previous academic work, letters of recommendation; for doctorate, GRE, minimum cumulative GPA of 3.0 for all previous academic work, letters of recommendation; OTCAS or PTCAS application and UT supplemental application (for OTD and DPT). Additional exam requirements/recommendations for international students: Required—TOEFL (minimum score 550 paper-based; 80 iBT). Electronic applications accepted.

The University of Toledo, College of Graduate Studies, College of Medicine and Life Sciences, Department of Orthopedic Surgery, Toledo, OH 43606-3390. Offers MSBS. *Accreditation:* APTA. *Degree requirements:* For master's, thesis or alternative. *Entrance requirements:* For master's, GRE, minimum undergraduate GPA of 3.0, three letters of recommendation, statement of purpose, transcripts from all prior institutions attended, resume. Additional exam requirements/recommendations for international students: Required—TOEFL (minimum score 550 paper-based; 80 iBT). Electronic applications accepted.

University of Toronto, Faculty of Medicine, Department of Physical Therapy, Toronto, ON M5S 1A1, Canada. Offers M Sc PT. *Accreditation:* APTA. *Entrance requirements:* For master's, minimum B average in final year, 2 references. Additional exam requirements/recommendations for international students: Required—TOEFL (minimum score 600 paper-based; 100 iBT), TWE (minimum score 5). Electronic applications accepted.

University of Utah, Graduate School, College of Health, Department of Physical Therapy and Athletic Training, Salt Lake City, UT 84112-1290. Offers physical therapy (DPT); rehabilitation science (PhD). *Accreditation:* APTA. *Faculty:* 7 full-time (1 woman), 12 part-time/adjunct (9 women). *Students:* 180 full-time (98 women), 4 part-time (3 women); includes 26 minority (3 Black or African American, non-Hispanic/Latino; 4 Asian, non-Hispanic/Latino; 13 Hispanic/Latino; 6 Two or more races, non-Hispanic/Latino), 2 international. Average age 25. 437 applicants, 11% accepted, 48 enrolled. In 2017, 49 doctorates awarded. *Entrance requirements:* For doctorate, GRE, minimum GPA of 3.0, volunteer work, bachelor's degree. Additional exam requirements/recommendations for international students: Required—TOEFL (minimum score 90 iBT); Recommended—IELTS (minimum score 7). *Application deadline:* For fall admission, 10/3 priority date for domestic students, 10/3 for international students. Application fee: $55 ($65 for international students). Electronic applications accepted. *Expenses:* Contact institution. *Financial support:* In 2017–18, 29 students received support. Research assistantships with full tuition reimbursements available, teaching assistantships with full tuition reimbursements available, Federal Work-Study, scholarships/grants, tuition waivers (full), and unspecified assistantships available. Financial award application deadline: 10/1; financial award applicants required to submit FAFSA. *Faculty research:* Rehabilitation and Parkinson's disease, motor control and musculoskeletal dysfunction, burns/wound care, rehabilitation and multiple sclerosis, cancer. *Total annual research expenditures:* $600,129. *Unit head:* Dr. R. Scott Ward, Chair, 801-581-4895, E-mail: scott.ward@hsc.utah.edu. *Application contact:* Dee-Dee Darby-Duffin, Academic Advisor, 801-585-9510, E-mail: d.darby-duffin@hsc.utah.edu.
Website: http://www.health.utah.edu/pt

University of Vermont, Graduate College, College of Nursing and Health Sciences, Program in Physical Therapy, Burlington, VT 05405. Offers DPT. *Accreditation:* APTA. *Students:* 110 full-time (74 women); includes 7 minority (1 Black or African American, non-Hispanic/Latino; 3 Asian, non-Hispanic/Latino; 2 Hispanic/Latino; 1 Two or more races, non-Hispanic/Latino). 314 applicants, 43% accepted, 42 enrolled. In 2017, 36 doctorates awarded. *Entrance requirements:* For doctorate, GRE General Test. Additional exam requirements/recommendations for international students: Required—TOEFL (minimum score 550 paper-based; 90 iBT). *Application deadline:* For summer admission, 11/1 for domestic and international students. Application fee: $65. Electronic applications accepted. *Expenses:* Contact institution. *Financial support:* In 2017–18, 16 students received support. Federal Work-Study and scholarships/grants available. Financial award application deadline: 3/1. *Unit head:* Dr. Barbara Ann Tschoepe, 802-656-8647. *Application contact:* Kristen Cella, Admissions Specialist, 802-656-3858, E-mail: cnhsgrad@uvm.edu.
Website: https://www.uvm.edu/cnhs/rms/physical_therapy

University of Washington, Graduate School, School of Medicine, Graduate Programs in Medicine, Department of Rehabilitation Medicine, Seattle, WA 98195-6490. Offers occupational therapy (MOT); physical therapy (DPT); prosthetics and orthotics (MPO); rehabilitation science (PhD). *Accreditation:* AOTA. *Degree requirements:* For doctorate, comprehensive exam (for some programs), thesis/dissertation (for some programs). *Entrance requirements:* For master's and doctorate, GRE. Additional exam requirements/recommendations for international students: Required—TOEFL. *Faculty research:* Biomechanics, balance, brain injury, spinal cord injury, pain, degenerative diseases.

The University of Western Ontario, Faculty of Graduate Studies, Biosciences Division, School of Physical Therapy, London, ON N6A 5B8, Canada. Offers manipulative therapy (CAS); physical therapy (MPT); wound healing (CAS). *Program availability:* Part-time. *Degree requirements:* For master's, thesis. *Entrance requirements:* For master's, B Sc in physical therapy. Additional exam requirements/recommendations for international students: Required—TOEFL. *Faculty research:* Muscle strength, wound healing, motor control, respiratory physiology, exercise physiology.

University of Wisconsin–La Crosse, College of Science and Health, Department of Health Professions, Program in Physical Therapy, La Crosse, WI 54601-3742. Offers DPT. *Accreditation:* APTA. *Students:* 86 full-time (54 women), 43 part-time (32 women); includes 4 minority (1 Asian, non-Hispanic/Latino; 3 Two or more races, non-Hispanic/Latino). Average age 24. 560 applicants, 9% accepted, 45 enrolled. In 2017, 41 doctorates awarded. *Entrance requirements:* Additional exam requirements/recommendations for international students: Required—TOEFL (minimum score 550 paper-based; 79 iBT). Application fee: $50. Electronic applications accepted. *Expenses:* Contact institution. *Financial support:* Federal Work-Study, scholarships/grants, and health care benefits available. Support available to part-time students. Financial award application deadline: 11/1; financial award applicants required to submit FAFSA. *Unit head:* Dr. Michele Thorman, Director, 608-785-8466, E-mail: thorman.mich@uwlax.edu. *Application contact:* Brandon Schaller, Senior Graduate Student Status Examiner, 608-785-8941, E-mail: admissions@uwlax.edu.
Website: http://www.uwlax.edu/pt/

University of Wisconsin–Madison, School of Medicine and Public Health, Doctor of Physical Therapy Program, Madison, WI 53706. Offers DPT. *Accreditation:* APTA. *Faculty:* 12 full-time (9 women), 7 part-time/adjunct (6 women). *Students:* 118 full-time (59 women); includes 16 minority (1 Black or African American, non-Hispanic/Latino; 1 American Indian or Alaska Native, non-Hispanic/Latino; 3 Asian, non-Hispanic/Latino; 4 Hispanic/Latino; 7 Two or more races, non-Hispanic/Latino). Average age 24. 589 applicants, 11% accepted, 40 enrolled. In 2017, 40 doctorates awarded. *Entrance requirements:* For doctorate, GRE. Additional exam requirements/recommendations for international students: Required—TOEFL (minimum score 580 paper-based; 92 iBT). *Application deadline:* For fall admission, 11/1 for domestic and international students. Application fee: $50. Electronic applications accepted. *Expenses:* Contact institution. *Faculty research:* Running injuries, Tai Chi and physical therapy, female athlete, human factors in engineering, children's muscular disorders. *Unit head:* Lisa Steinkamp, Program Director, 608-263-9427, E-mail: steinkamp@pt.wisc.edu. *Application contact:* Reenie Euhardy, Program Advisor, 608-265-4815, Fax: 608-262-7809, E-mail: euhardy@pt.wisc.edu.
Website: http://www.med.wisc.edu/pt

University of Wisconsin–Milwaukee, Graduate School, College of Health Sciences, Department of Kinesiology, Milwaukee, WI 53201-0413. Offers athletic training (MS); kinesiology (MS, PhD), including exercise and nutrition in health and disease (MS), integrative human performance (MS), neuromechanics (MS); physical therapy (DPT). *Program availability:* Part-time. *Students:* 100 full-time (60 women), 16 part-time (9 women); includes 11 minority (1 Black or African American, non-Hispanic/Latino; 1 American Indian or Alaska Native, non-Hispanic/Latino; 9 Two or more races, non-Hispanic/Latino), 3 international. Average age 27. 36 applicants, 42% accepted, 5 enrolled. In 2017, 2 master's awarded. *Degree requirements:* For master's, comprehensive exam, thesis optional. *Entrance requirements:* For master's, GRE General Test. Additional exam requirements/recommendations for international students: Required—TOEFL (minimum score 550 paper-based; 79 iBT), IELTS (minimum score 6.5). *Application deadline:* For fall admission, 1/1 priority date for domestic students; for spring admission, 9/1 for domestic students. Applications are processed on a rolling basis. Application fee: $56 ($96 for international students). *Financial support:* Fellowships, research assistantships, teaching assistantships, career-related internships or fieldwork, unspecified assistantships, and project assistantships available. Support available to part-time students. Financial award application deadline: 4/15. *Unit head:* Dr. Kyle T. Ebersole, Department Chair, 414-229-6717, Fax: 414-229-3366, E-mail: ebersole@uwm.edu. *Application contact:* Stephen C. Cobb, Graduate Program Coordinator, 414-229-3369, Fax: 414-229-3366, E-mail: cobbsc@uwm.edu.
Website: http://uwm.edu/healthsciences/academics/kinesiology/

Utica College, Department of Physical Therapy, Utica, NY 13502-4892. Offers DPT, TDPT. *Accreditation:* APTA. *Program availability:* Part-time, evening/weekend, online learning. *Faculty:* 10 full-time (4 women). *Students:* 86 full-time (46 women), 386 part-time (253 women); includes 246 minority (17 Black or African American, non-Hispanic/Latino; 220 Asian, non-Hispanic/Latino; 8 Hispanic/Latino; 1 Native Hawaiian or other Pacific Islander, non-Hispanic/Latino), 4 international. Average age 34. 240 applicants, 98% accepted, 232 enrolled. In 2017, 299 doctorates awarded. *Degree requirements:* For doctorate, comprehensive exam, thesis/dissertation (for some programs). *Entrance requirements:* For doctorate, GRE, MCAT, DAT or OPT, BS, minimum GPA of 3.0. Additional exam requirements/recommendations for international students: Required—TOEFL (minimum score 525 paper-based). *Application deadline:* Applications are processed on a rolling basis. Application fee: $50. Electronic applications accepted. *Expenses:* Contact institution. *Financial support:* Career-related internships or fieldwork, scholarships/grants, tuition waivers (partial), and unspecified assistantships available. Support available to part-time students. Financial award application deadline: 3/15; financial award applicants required to submit FAFSA. *Faculty research:* Forensic paleopathology, biomechanical analysis of movement, neuronal plasticity, somatosensory mechanotransduction. *Unit head:* Dr. Ashraf Elazzazi, Director, 315-792-3313, E-mail: aelazza@utica.edu. *Application contact:* John D. Rowe, Director of Graduate Admissions, 315-792-3824, Fax: 315-792-3003, E-mail: jrowe@utica.edu.

Virginia Commonwealth University, Graduate School, School of Allied Health Professions, Department of Physical Therapy, Richmond, VA 23284-9005. Offers DPT. *Accreditation:* APTA. *Degree requirements:* For doctorate, thesis/dissertation. *Entrance requirements:* For doctorate, GRE General Test, Physical Therapist Centralized Application Service (PTCAS). Additional exam requirements/recommendations for international students: Required—TOEFL (minimum score 600 paper-based; 100 iBT). Electronic applications accepted. *Faculty research:* Eye movement, bilabyrinthectomy on ferret muscle fiber typing, neck disability index, cost-effective care, training effect on muscle.

Virginia Commonwealth University, Medical College of Virginia-Professional Programs, School of Medicine, Graduate Programs in Medicine, Department of Physiology and Biophysics, Richmond, VA 23284-9005. Offers molecular biology and genetics (MS); physical therapy (PhD); physiology (MS, PhD); MD/PhD. Terminal master's awarded for partial completion of doctoral program. *Degree requirements:* For master's, thesis; for doctorate, thesis/dissertation, comprehensive oral and written exams. *Entrance requirements:* For master's, GRE General Test, MCAT, or DAT; for doctorate, GRE, MCAT or DAT. Additional exam requirements/recommendations for international students: Required—TOEFL (minimum score 600 paper-based; 100 iBT). Electronic applications accepted.

Walsh University, Graduate Programs, Program in Physical Therapy, North Canton, OH 44720-3396. Offers DPT. *Accreditation:* APTA. *Degree requirements:* For doctorate, comprehensive exam, research project, 3 clinical placements. *Entrance requirements:* For doctorate, GRE General Test (minimum scores: verbal 150, quantitative 150, or combined score of 291), previous coursework in anatomy, human physiology, exercise physiology, chemistry, statistics, psychology, biology, and physics; minimum GPA of 3.0. Additional exam requirements/recommendations for international students: Required—TOEFL (minimum score 500 paper-based; 61 iBT). Electronic applications accepted. Application fee is waived when completed online. *Expenses:* Contact institution. *Faculty research:* Physical therapy, education, clinical decision making, outcomes.

Washington University in St. Louis, School of Medicine, Program in Physical Therapy, Saint Louis, MO 63108. Offers DPT. *Accreditation:* APTA. *Degree requirements:* For doctorate, thesis/dissertation (for some programs). *Entrance requirements:* For doctorate, GRE. Additional exam requirements/recommendations for international students: Required—TOEFL (minimum score 600 paper-based; 100 iBT), TWE (minimum score 5). Electronic applications accepted. *Expenses:* Contact institution. *Faculty research:* Movement and movement dysfunction.

Wayne State University, Eugene Applebaum College of Pharmacy and Health Sciences, Department of Health Care Sciences, Program in Physical Therapy, Detroit, MI 48202. Offers DPT. *Accreditation:* APTA. *Program availability:* Part-time, blended/hybrid learning. *Faculty:* 12. *Students:* 140 full-time (86 women), 6 part-time (4 women); includes 17 minority (5 Black or African American, non-Hispanic/Latino; 5 Asian, non-Hispanic/Latino; 4 Hispanic/Latino; 3 Two or more races, non-Hispanic/Latino), 3 international. Average age 26. 211 applicants, 33% accepted, 36 enrolled. In 2017, 00 doctorates awarded. *Degree requirements:* For doctorate, clinical internship. *Entrance requirements:* For doctorate, GRE, interview; 90 undergraduate credit hours; minimum GPA of 3.0 overall and in all prerequisite courses with no less than a C grade in prerequisite courses; PTCAS application; essay. Additional exam requirements/recommendations for international students: Required—TOEFL (minimum score 550 paper-based; 79 iBT), Michigan English Language Assessment Battery (minimum score 85); Recommended—IELTS (minimum score 6.5), TWE (minimum score 5.5). *Application deadline:* For fall admission, 10/15 for domestic and international students. Application fee: $50. Electronic applications accepted. *Expenses:* Contact institution. *Financial support:* In 2017–18, 60 students received support. Scholarships/grants available. Financial award applicants required to submit FAFSA. *Faculty research:* Muscle dysfunction, response to immobility and exercise. *Unit head:* Dr. Kristina Reid, Interim Director, 313-577-1432, E-mail: cphsinfo@wayne.edu. *Application contact:* E-mail: cphsinfo@wayne.edu.
Website: http://cphs.wayne.edu/physical-therapy/

West Coast University, Graduate Programs, North Hollywood, CA 91606. Offers advanced generalist (MSN); family nurse practitioner (MSN); health administration (MHA); occupational therapy (MS); pharmacy (Pharm D); physical therapy (DPT).

Western Carolina University, Graduate School, College of Health and Human Sciences, Department of Physical Therapy, Cullowhee, NC 28723. Offers DPT. *Accreditation:* APTA. *Entrance requirements:* Additional exam requirements/recommendations for international students: Required—TOEFL (minimum score 550 paper-based; 79 iBT). *Expenses:* Tuition, state resident: full-time $4436. Tuition, nonresident: full-time $14,842. *Required fees:* $2926. *Faculty research:* Bone density, disability in older adults, neuroanatomy, intervention of musculoskeletal conditions.

Western Kentucky University, Graduate Studies, College of Health and Human Services, Department of Allied Health, Bowling Green, KY 42101. Offers physical therapy (DPT).

Western University of Health Sciences, College of Allied Health Professions, Program in Physical Therapy, Pomona, CA 91766-1854. Offers DPT. *Accreditation:* APTA. *Faculty:* 15 full-time (11 women). *Students:* 155 full-time (96 women), 24 part-time (11 women); includes 107 minority (11 Black or African American, non-Hispanic/Latino; 44 Asian, non-Hispanic/Latino; 35 Hispanic/Latino; 1 Native Hawaiian or other Pacific Islander, non-Hispanic/Latino; 16 Two or more races, non-Hispanic/Latino). Average age 28. 1,021 applicants, 9% accepted, 47 enrolled. In 2017, 73 doctorates awarded. *Degree requirements:* For doctorate, comprehensive exam (for some programs). *Entrance requirements:* For doctorate, GRE, bachelor's degree, letters of recommendation, volunteer or paid work experience, access to a computer meeting minimum technical standards, health screening and immunization, background check, minimum GPA of 3.0. *Application deadline:* For fall admission, 11/1 for domestic and international students. Applications are processed on a rolling basis. Application fee: $60. Electronic applications accepted. *Expenses:* $41,430 first-year tuition and fees. *Financial support:* In 2017–18, 9 students received support. Scholarships/grants available. Financial award application deadline: 3/2; financial award applicants required to submit FAFSA. *Unit head:* Dr. Dayle Armstrong, Chair, 909-469-5322, Fax: 909-469-5692, E-mail: darmstrong@westernu.edu. *Application contact:* Karen Hutton-Lopez, Director of Admissions, 909-469-5335, Fax: 909-469-5570, E-mail: admissions@westernu.edu.
Website: http://www.westernu.edu/allied-health/allied-health-dpt/

West Virginia University, School of Medicine, Morgantown, WV 26506-9600. Offers biochemistry and molecular biology (PhD); biomedical science (MS); cancer cell biology (PhD); cellular and integrative physiology (PhD); exercise physiology (MS, PhD); health sciences (MS); immunology (PhD); medicine (MD); occupational therapy (MOT); pathologists assistant (MHS); physical therapy (DPT). *Program availability:* Part-time, evening/weekend. *Students:* 781 full-time (440 women), 25 part-time (13 women); includes 140 minority (15 Black or African American, non-Hispanic/Latino; 1 American Indian or Alaska Native, non-Hispanic/Latino; 68 Asian, non-Hispanic/Latino; 37 Hispanic/Latino; 1 Native Hawaiian or other Pacific Islander, non-Hispanic/Latino; 18 Two or more races, non-Hispanic/Latino), 19 international. *Entrance requirements:* Additional exam requirements/recommendations for international students: Required—TOEFL. *Application deadline:* Applications are processed on a rolling basis. Application fee: $60. Electronic applications accepted. *Expenses:* Contact institution. *Financial support:* Fellowships, research assistantships, teaching assistantships, career-related internships or fieldwork, Federal Work-Study, institutionally sponsored loans, health care benefits, tuition waivers (full and partial), and administrative assistantships available. Financial award applicants required to submit FAFSA. *Unit head:* Dr. Clay Marsh, Executive Dean, 304-293-6607, Fax: 304-293-6627, E-mail: clay.marsh@hsc.wvu.edu. *Application contact:* Lisa M. Salati, Assistant Vice President, Graduate Education, 304-293-7759, Fax: 304-293-3080, E-mail: lsalati@hsc.wvu.edu.
Website: https://medicine.hsc.wvu.edu

Wheeling Jesuit University, Department of Physical Therapy, Wheeling, WV 26003-6295. Offers DPT. *Accreditation:* APTA. *Degree requirements:* For doctorate, comprehensive exam, thesis/dissertation. *Entrance requirements:* For doctorate, GRE, minimum GPA of 3.0. Additional exam requirements/recommendations for international students: Required—TOEFL (minimum score 650 paper-based). Electronic applications accepted. Application fee is waived when completed online. *Expenses:* Contact institution. *Faculty research:* Service-learning, clinical prediction rules, ergonomics, public health, pediatrics.

Wichita State University, Graduate School, College of Health Professions, Department of Physical Therapy, Wichita, KS 67260. Offers DPT. *Accreditation:* APTA. *Unit head:* Dr. Robert C. Manske, Chair, 316-978-3604, Fax: 316-978-3025, E-mail: robert.manske@wichita.edu. *Application contact:* Jordan Oleson, Admissions Coordinator, 316-978-3095, Fax: 316-978-3253, E-mail: jordan.oleson@wichita.edu.
Website: http://www.wichita.edu/pt

Widener University, School of Human Service Professions, Institute for Physical Therapy Education, Chester, PA 19013-5792. Offers MS, DPT. *Accreditation:* APTA. *Faculty:* 8 full-time (5 women), 1 (woman) part-time/adjunct. *Students:* 118 full-time (66 women), 2 part-time (both women); includes 10 minority (4 Black or African American, non-Hispanic/Latino; 2 American Indian or Alaska Native, non-Hispanic/Latino; 3 Hispanic/Latino; 1 Two or more races, non-Hispanic/Latino). Average age 24. 524 applicants, 11% accepted, 30 enrolled. In 2017, 53 doctorates awarded. *Degree requirements:* For master's, thesis. *Entrance requirements:* For master's, GRE. *Application deadline:* For fall admission, 1/30 for domestic students. Applications are processed on a rolling basis. Application fee: $40. *Expenses:* Contact institution. *Financial support:* Teaching assistantships, Federal Work-Study, institutionally sponsored loans, and scholarships/grants available. Financial award application deadline: 5/1; financial award applicants required to submit FAFSA. *Faculty research:* Social support, aquatics, children and adults with movement dysfunction, physical therapy modalities. *Unit head:* Dr. Robin Dole, Associate Dean and Director, 610-499-1159, Fax: 610-499-1231, E-mail: rldole@widener.edu. *Application contact:* 610-499-4124, E-mail: gradprograms@widener.edu.

Wingate University, Department of Physical Therapy, Wingate, NC 28174. Offers DPT.

Winston-Salem State University, Department of Physical Therapy, Winston-Salem, NC 27110-0003. Offers DPT. *Accreditation:* APTA. Electronic applications accepted. *Faculty research:* Tissue healing; neuroimaging with functional recovery; visual, proprioceptive and vestibular sensor inputs roles.

Youngstown State University, Graduate School, Bitonte College of Health and Human Services, Department of Physical Therapy, Youngstown, OH 44555-0001. Offers DPT. *Accreditation:* APTA. *Entrance requirements:* Additional exam requirements/recommendations for international students: Required—TOEFL.

Physician Assistant Studies

Adventist University of Health Sciences, Program in Physician Assistant Studies, Orlando, FL 32803. Offers MS. *Entrance requirements:* For master's, minimum GPA of 3.0.

Albany Medical College, Center for Physician Assistant Studies, Albany, NY 12208-3479. Offers MS. *Accreditation:* ARC-PA. *Degree requirements:* For master's, comprehensive exam, clinical portfolio. *Entrance requirements:* For master's, GRE. Additional exam requirements/recommendations for international students: Required—TOEFL. Electronic applications accepted. *Expenses:* Contact institution. *Faculty research:* Genetics, education, informatics.

Alderson Broaddus University, Program in Physician Assistant Studies, Philippi, WV 26416. Offers MPAS. *Degree requirements:* For master's, comprehensive exam, thesis. *Entrance requirements:* For master's, minimum 60 semester hours plus specific science. Electronic applications accepted.

Arcadia University, College of Health Sciences, Department of Medical Science, Glenside, PA 19038-3295. Offers physician assistant (MMS); MMS/MPH. *Entrance requirements:* For master's, GRE General Test or MCAT. Additional exam requirements/recommendations for international students: Required—TOEFL. *Expenses:* Contact institution.

A.T. Still University, Arizona School of Health Sciences, Mesa, AZ 85206. Offers advanced occupational therapy (MS); advanced physician assistant studies (MS); athletic training (MS, DAT); audiology (Au D); clinical decision making in athletic training (Graduate Certificate); occupational therapy (MS, OTD); orthopedic rehabilitation (Graduate Certificate); physical therapy (DPT); physician assistant studies (MS); transitional audiology (Au D); transitional physical therapy (DPT). *Accreditation:* AOTA (one or more programs are accredited); ASHA. *Program availability:* Part-time, 100% online. *Faculty:* 59 full-time (39 women), 221 part-time/adjunct (155 women). *Students:* 608 full-time (405 women), 431 part-time (310 women); includes 247 minority (54 Black or African American, non-Hispanic/Latino; 13 American Indian or Alaska Native, non-Hispanic/Latino; 151 Asian, non-Hispanic/Latino; 2 Hispanic/Latino; 1 Native Hawaiian or other Pacific Islander, non-Hispanic/Latino; 26 Two or more races, non-Hispanic/Latino), 1 international. Average age 33. 4,882 applicants, 9% accepted, 278 enrolled. In 2017, 132 master's, 270 doctorates awarded. *Degree requirements:* For master's, thesis (for some programs); for doctorate, thesis/dissertation (for some programs). *Entrance requirements:* For master's, GRE General Test; for doctorate, GRE, Physical Therapist Evaluation Tool (for DPT), current state licensure. Additional exam requirements/recommendations for international students: Required—TOEFL (minimum score 80 iBT). *Application deadline:* For fall admission, 7/7 for domestic and international students; for winter admission, 10/3 for domestic and international students; for spring admission, 1/16 for domestic and international students; for summer admission, 4/17 for domestic and international students. Applications are processed on a rolling basis. Application fee: $70. Electronic applications accepted. Application fee is waived when completed online. *Financial support:* In 2017–18, 161 students received support. Federal Work-Study and scholarships/grants available. Financial award application deadline: 6/1; financial award applicants required to submit FAFSA. *Faculty research:* Pediatric sport-related concussion, adolescent athlete health-related quality of life; geriatric and pediatric well-being, pain management for participation, practice-based research network, BMI and dental caries. *Total annual research expenditures:* $63,003. *Unit head:* Dr. Randy Danielsen, Dean, 480-219-6009, Fax: 480-219-6110, E-mail: rdanielsen@atsu.edu. *Application contact:* Donna Sparks, Director, Admissions Processing, 660-626-2117, Fax: 660-626-2969, E-mail: admissions@atsu.edu.
Website: http://www.atsu.edu/ashs

Augsburg University, Program in Physician Assistant Studies, Minneapolis, MN 55454-1351. Offers MS. *Accreditation:* ARC-PA.

Augusta University, College of Allied Health Sciences, Physician Assistant Program, Augusta, GA 30912. Offers MPA. *Accreditation:* ARC-PA. *Program availability:* Part-time. *Degree requirements:* For master's, thesis or alternative. *Entrance requirements:* For master's, GRE General Test, minimum of 100 hours of hands-on health care experience. Additional exam requirements/recommendations for international students: Required—TOEFL (minimum score 600 paper-based; 100 iBT), TWE. Electronic applications accepted.

Baldwin Wallace University, Graduate Programs, Physician Assistant Program, Berea, OH 44017-2088. Offers MMS. *Faculty:* 5 full-time (3 women), 2 part-time/adjunct (0 women). *Students:* 56 full-time (41 women); includes 3 minority (1 Asian, non-Hispanic/Latino; 2 Two or more races, non-Hispanic/Latino). Average age 25. 544 applicants, 8% accepted, 29 enrolled. In 2017, 31 master's awarded. *Degree requirements:* For master's, comprehensive exam, thesis or alternative, capstone project. *Entrance requirements:* For master's, GRE, 3 letters of recommendation, personal statement, 40 hours of shadowing. Additional exam requirements/recommendations for international students: Required—TOEFL (minimum score 550 paper-based; 100 iBT). *Application deadline:* For fall admission, 11/1 for domestic and international students. Applications are processed on a rolling basis. Electronic applications accepted. *Expenses:* Contact institution. *Financial support:* Applicants required to submit FAFSA. *Unit head:* Jared R. Pennington, Director/Chair, 440-826-2221, E-mail: jpenning@bw.edu. *Application contact:* Michele Siverd, Program Support Specialist, 440-826-8585, E-mail: msiverd@bw.edu.
Website: http://www.bw.edu/graduate/physician-assistant/

Barry University, Physician Assistant Program, Miami Shores, FL 33161-6695. Offers MCMS. *Accreditation:* ARC-PA. *Entrance requirements:* For master's, GRE General Test. Electronic applications accepted.

Baylor College of Medicine, School of Allied Health Sciences, Physician Assistant Program, Houston, TX 77030-3498. Offers MS. *Accreditation:* ARC-PA. *Degree requirements:* For master's, comprehensive exam, thesis. *Entrance requirements:* For master's, GRE General Test, bachelor's degree; minimum GPA of 3.0; prerequisite courses in general chemistry, organic chemistry, microbiology, general psychology, human anatomy, human physiology, statistics, and expository writing. Additional exam requirements/recommendations for international students: Required—TOEFL. Electronic applications accepted. *Expenses:* Contact institution. *Faculty research:* Cultural competency attainment, health behavioral counseling skills mastery, readiness for inter-professional learning, probability error in differential diagnosis, shared decision-making.

Bay Path University, Program in Physician Assistant Studies, Longmeadow, MA 01106-2292. Offers MS. *Students:* 61 full-time (39 women); includes 13 minority (4 Black or African American, non-Hispanic/Latino; 1 American Indian or Alaska Native, non-Hispanic/Latino; 5 Asian, non-Hispanic/Latino; 2 Hispanic/Latino; 1 Two or more races, non-Hispanic/Latino). Average age 30. In 2017, 23 master's awarded. *Degree requirements:* For master's, 116 credits with minimum cumulative GPA of 3.0 and no grade below a B. *Entrance requirements:* For master's, minimum of 500 hours of patient contact hours; minimum of 24 hours of documented PA shadowing; all prerequisite courses completed with minimum C grade and cumulative GPA of 3.0. *Application deadline:* Applications are processed on a rolling basis. Application fee: $60. Electronic applications accepted. Application fee is waived when completed online. *Expenses:* $15,800 per year. *Financial support:* Unspecified assistantships available. Financial award applicants required to submit FAFSA. *Unit head:* Theresa Riethle, Director, 413-565-1206, E-mail: triethle@baypath.edu. *Application contact:* Diane Ranaldi, Dean of Graduate Admissions, 413-565-1332, Fax: 413-565-1250, E-mail: dranaldi@baypath.edu.
Website: http://graduate.baypath.edu/Graduate-Programs/Programs-On-Campus/MS-Programs/Physician-Assistant-Studies

Bethel University, Graduate Programs, McKenzie, TN 38201. Offers administration and supervision (MA Ed); business administration (MBA); conflict resolution (MA); physician assistant studies (MS). *Program availability:* Part-time, evening/weekend. *Degree requirements:* For master's, thesis (for some programs). *Entrance requirements:* For master's, GRE General Test or MAT, minimum undergraduate GPA of 2.5.

Bethel University, Graduate School, St. Paul, MN 55112-6999. Offers business administration (MBA); classroom management (Certificate); counseling (MA); K-12 education (MA); leadership (Ed D); leadership foundations (Certificate); nurse educator (MS, Certificate); nurse-midwifery (MS); physician assistant (MS); special education (MA); strategic leadership (MA); teaching (MA); teaching and learning (Certificate). *Program availability:* Part-time, evening/weekend, 100% online, blended/hybrid learning. *Faculty:* 22 full-time (16 women), 70 part-time/adjunct (44 women). *Students:* 611 full-time (431 women), 393 part-time (249 women); includes 176 minority (82 Black or African American, non-Hispanic/Latino; 4 American Indian or Alaska Native, non-Hispanic/Latino; 31 Asian, non-Hispanic/Latino; 39 Hispanic/Latino; 2 Native Hawaiian or other Pacific Islander, non-Hispanic/Latino; 18 Two or more races, non-Hispanic/Latino), 9 international. Average age 36. 668 applicants, 42% accepted, 223 enrolled. In 2017, 287 master's, 30 doctorates, 172 other advanced degrees awarded. *Degree requirements:* For master's, comprehensive exam (for some programs), thesis (for some programs); for doctorate, comprehensive exam, thesis/dissertation. *Entrance requirements:* Additional exam requirements/recommendations for international students: Required—TOEFL (minimum score 550 paper-based, 80 iBT) or IELTS. *Application deadline:* Applications are processed on a rolling basis. Application fee: $0. Electronic applications accepted. *Expenses:* Contact institution. *Financial support:* Teaching assistantships, career-related internships or fieldwork, and scholarships/grants available. Support available to part-time students. Financial award applicants required to submit FAFSA. *Unit head:* Dr. Randy Bergen, Associate Provost, 651-635-8000, Fax: 651-635-8004, E-mail: r-bergen@bethel.edu. *Application contact:* Director of Admissions, 651-635-8000, Fax: 651-635-8004, E-mail: gs@bethel.edu.
Website: https://www.bethel.edu/graduate/

Boston University, School of Medicine, Division of Graduate Medical Sciences, Physician Assistant Program, Boston, MA 02215. Offers MS. *Entrance requirements:* For master's, GRE, three letters of recommendation. Additional exam requirements/recommendations for international students: Required—TOEFL (minimum score 550 paper-based; 80 iBT). *Application deadline:* For spring admission, 10/1 for domestic students. Electronic applications accepted. *Unit head:* Mary Warner, Director, 617-638-5744, E-mail: paoffice@bu.edu. *Application contact:* GMS Admissions Office, 617-638-5255, E-mail: askgms@bu.edu.
Website: http://www.bu.edu/paprogram/

Bryant University, School of Health Sciences, Smithfield, RI 02917. Offers physician assistant studies (MPAS). *Faculty:* 8 full-time (6 women), 3 part-time/adjunct (2 women). *Students:* 43 full-time (32 women), 37 part-time (25 women); includes 9 minority (2 American Indian or Alaska Native, non-Hispanic/Latino; 2 Asian, non-Hispanic/Latino; 2 Hispanic/Latino; 3 Two or more races, non-Hispanic/Latino). Average age 28. 811 applicants, 7% accepted, 43 enrolled. In 2017, 30 master's awarded. *Degree requirements:* For master's, comprehensive exam. *Entrance requirements:* For master's, GRE (taken within past five years), baccalaureate degree, minimum overall undergraduate GPA of 3.0, three professional references, 2000 hours of direct patient care experience. Additional exam requirements/recommendations for international students: Required—TOEFL (minimum score 100 iBT). *Application deadline:* For winter admission, 10/1 for domestic and international students. Applications are processed on a rolling basis. Application fee: $80. Electronic applications accepted. *Expenses:* $683 per credit hour. *Financial support:* Fund for a Healthy Rhode Island awards available. Financial award application deadline: 10/1; financial award applicants required to submit FAFSA. *Unit head:* Jay Amrien, Program Director, 401-232-6556, E-mail: jamrien@bryant.edu. *Application contact:* Kayla Cetrone, Director, Physician Assistant Admissions, 401-232-6404, E-mail: pa_program@bryant.edu.
Website: http://gradschool.bryant.edu/health-sciences.htm

Butler University, College of Pharmacy and Health Sciences, Indianapolis, IN 46208-3485. Offers pharmaceutical science (MS); pharmacy (Pharm D), including medical Spanish, research; physician assistant studies (MS). *Accreditation:* ACPE (one or more programs are accredited). *Faculty:* 62 full-time (42 women). *Students:* 390 full-time (302 women), 10 part-time (6 women); includes 35 minority (3 Black or African American, non-Hispanic/Latino; 21 Asian, non-Hispanic/Latino; 7 Hispanic/Latino; 4 Two or more races, non-Hispanic/Latino), 3 international. Average age 24. 581 applicants, 25% accepted, 131 enrolled. In 2017, 75 master's, 116 doctorates awarded. *Degree requirements:* For master's, comprehensive exam, research paper or thesis. *Entrance requirements:* For master's, GRE General Test, CASPA application, official transcripts, baccalaureate degree from accredited institution (for physician assistant studies). Additional exam requirements/recommendations for international students: Required—TOEFL (minimum score 550 paper-based; 79 iBT), IELTS (minimum score 6). *Application deadline:* For fall admission, 4/1 for domestic and international students. Application fee: $0. Electronic applications accepted. *Expenses:* Contact institution. *Financial support:* In 2017–18, 8 students received support. Scholarships/grants, tuition waivers (full and partial), and unspecified assistantships available. Financial award application deadline: 7/15; financial award applicants required to submit FAFSA. *Faculty research:* Cancer research; targeted drug delivery and pharmacokinetics; neuropharmacology; gene regulation; next generation sequencing. *Unit head:* Dr. Robert Soltis, Dean, 317-940-8056, E-mail: rsoltis@butler.edu. *Application contact:* Diane Dubord, Graduate Student Services Specialist, 317-940-8107, E-mail: ddubord@butler.edu.
Website: https://www.butler.edu/pharmacy-pa/about

California Baptist University, Program in Physician Assistant Studies, Riverside, CA 92504-3206. Offers MS. *Program availability:* Part-time. *Faculty:* 5 full-time (3 women). *Students:* 60 full-time (44 women); includes 33 minority (1 Black or African American, non-Hispanic/Latino; 15 Asian, non-Hispanic/Latino; 12 Hispanic/Latino; 1 Native Hawaiian or other Pacific Islander, non-Hispanic/Latino; 4 Two or more races, non-Hispanic/Latino). Average age 26. 1,134 applicants, 4% accepted, 30 enrolled. *Entrance requirements:* For master's, minimum undergraduate GPA of 3.0, bachelor's transcripts, three letters of recommendation, essay, interview. Additional exam requirements/recommendations for international students: Required—TOEFL (minimum score 80 iBT). *Application deadline:* For fall admission, 12/1 priority date for domestic students, 11/1 priority date for international students; for spring admission, 8/1 priority date for domestic students, 7/1 priority date for international students. Applications are processed on a rolling basis. Application fee: $45. Electronic applications accepted. *Expenses:* Contact institution. *Financial support:* In 2017–18, 2 students received support. Federal Work-Study and scholarships/grants available. Financial award applicants required to submit CSS PROFILE or FAFSA. *Faculty research:* Curriculum and instruction design, missions and under-served populations, the anti-vaccine movement, emergency medicine, occupational medicine. *Unit head:* Dr. Allan M. Bedashi, Director, 951-552-8838, E-mail: abedashi@calbaptist.edu. *Application contact:* Stephanie Fluitt, Graduate Admissions Counselor, 951-343-4696, Fax: 877-228-8877, E-mail: sfluitt@calbaptist.edu.

Campbell University, Graduate and Professional Programs, College of Pharmacy and Health Sciences, Buies Creek, NC 27506. Offers clinical research (MS); pharmaceutical sciences (MS); pharmacy (Pharm D); physician assistant (MPAP); public health (MS). *Accreditation:* ACPE. *Program availability:* Part-time, evening/weekend. *Entrance requirements:* For master's, MCAT, PCAT, GRE, bachelor's degree in health sciences or related field; for doctorate, PCAT. Additional exam requirements/recommendations for international students: Required—TOEFL (minimum score 550 paper-based; 79 iBT). Electronic applications accepted. *Expenses:* Contact institution. *Faculty research:* Immunology, medicinal chemistry, pharmaceutics, applied pharmacology.

Carroll University, Program in Physician Assistant Studies, Waukesha, WI 53186-5593. Offers MS. *Entrance requirements:* For master's, GRE, three letters of reference, personal essay, patient care experience, transcripts. Additional exam requirements/recommendations for international students: Required—TOEFL.

Case Western Reserve University, School of Medicine, Physician Assistant Program, Cleveland, OH 44106. Offers MS. *Degree requirements:* For master's, thesis. *Entrance requirements:* For master's, GRE, statement of objectives, letters of recommendation (minimum of 3). Additional exam requirements/recommendations for international students: Required—TOEFL (minimum score 577 paper-based; 90 iBT); Recommended—IELTS (minimum score 7). Electronic applications accepted. *Expenses: Tuition:* Full-time $43,854; part-time $1827 per credit hour. *Required fees:* $50; $50 per credit hour. Tuition and fees vary according to course load and program.

Central Michigan University, College of Graduate Studies, The Herbert H. and Grace A. Dow College of Health Professions, School of Rehabilitation and Medical Sciences, Mount Pleasant, MI 48859. Offers physical therapy (DPT); physician assistant (MS). *Accreditation:* APTA; ARC-PA. *Degree requirements:* For master's, thesis or alternative; for doctorate, thesis/dissertation or alternative. *Entrance requirements:* For master's and doctorate, GRE. Electronic applications accepted.

Chapman University, Crean College of Health and Behavioral Sciences, Physician Assistant Studies Program, Orange, CA 92866. Offers MMS. *Faculty:* 4 full-time (1 woman). *Students:* 24 full-time (18 women); includes 9 minority (4 Asian, non-Hispanic/Latino; 4 Hispanic/Latino; 1 Two or more races, non-Hispanic/Latino). Average age 25. *Application deadline:* For spring admission, 10/1 for domestic students. Electronic applications accepted. *Expenses:* Contact institution. *Financial support:* Applicants required to submit FAFSA. *Unit head:* Dr. Michael Burney, Director, 714-744-5420, E-mail: paprogram@chapman.edu. *Application contact:* Laurel Hasper, 714-744-2190, E-mail: hasper@chapman.edu.

Chatham University, Program in Physician Assistant Studies, Pittsburgh, PA 15232-2826. Offers MPAS. *Accreditation:* ARC-PA. *Faculty:* 8 full-time (all women), 16 part-time/adjunct (15 women). *Students:* 135 full-time (112 women); includes 14 minority (1 Black or African American, non-Hispanic/Latino; 3 Asian, non-Hispanic/Latino; 6 Hispanic/Latino; 4 Two or more races, non-Hispanic/Latino). Average age 25. 723 applicants, 15% accepted, 73 enrolled. In 2017, 67 master's awarded. *Degree requirements:* For master's, thesis, clinical experience, research project. *Entrance requirements:* For master's, community service, minimum GPA of 3.0, health science work or shadowing, volunteer work experience, PA shadowing form, 3 references. Additional exam requirements/recommendations for international students: Required—TOEFL (minimum score 600 paper-based; 100 iBT), IELTS (minimum score 7), TWE. *Application deadline:* For fall admission, 10/1 priority date for domestic and international students. Application fee: $45. Electronic applications accepted. Application fee is waived when completed online. *Expenses:* Contact institution. *Financial support:* Career-related internships or fieldwork available. Financial award applicants required to submit FAFSA. *Faculty research:* Complementary and alternative medicine, education methods, physician assistant practice. *Unit head:* Carl Garrubba, Director, 412-365-1425, Fax: 412-365-1213, E-mail: cgarrubba@chatham.edu. *Application contact:* Maureen Stokan, Assistant Director of Graduate Admission, 412-365-2988, Fax: 412-365-1609, E-mail: gradadmissions@chatham.edu.
Website: http://www.chatham.edu/departments/healthmgmt/graduate/pa

Christian Brothers University, School of Sciences, Memphis, TN 38104-5581. Offers physician assistant studies (MS).

Clarkson University, Division of Health Sciences, Department of Physician Assistant Studies, Potsdam, NY 13699. Offers MS. *Faculty:* 6 full-time (4 women), 10 part-time/adjunct (6 women). *Students:* 53 full-time (35 women); includes 10 minority (6 Asian, non-Hispanic/Latino; 2 Hispanic/Latino; 2 Two or more races, non-Hispanic/Latino). 1,766 applicants, 2% accepted, 29 enrolled. In 2017, 19 master's awarded. *Entrance requirements:* For master's, minimum undergraduate GPA of 3.0; CASPA application. *Application deadline:* For fall admission, 3/1 for domestic and international students. Applications are processed on a rolling basis. Application fee: $227. Electronic applications accepted. *Expenses:* Contact institution. *Financial support:* Scholarships/grants available. *Unit head:* Joan Caruso, Interim Chair of Physician Assistant Studies, 315-268-7942, E-mail: jcaruso@clarkson.edu. *Application contact:* Amy Thompson, Graduate Admissions Coordinator, 315-268-7942, E-mail: athompso@clarkson.edu.
Website: https://www.clarkson.edu/academics/graduate

Cleveland State University, College of Graduate Studies, College of Sciences and Health Professions, School of Health Sciences, Program in Health Sciences, Cleveland, OH 44115. Offers health sciences (MS); physician assistant science (MS). *Program availability:* Part-time, evening/weekend, online learning. *Faculty:* 7 full-time (6 women), 6 part-time/adjunct (all women). *Students:* 67 full-time (48 women), 26 part-time (20 women); includes 24 minority (7 Black or African American, non-Hispanic/Latino; 6 Asian, non-Hispanic/Latino; 9 Hispanic/Latino; 2 Two or more races, non-Hispanic/Latino), 1 international. Average age 31. 85 applicants, 73% accepted, 48 enrolled. In 2017, 52 master's awarded. *Entrance requirements:* For master's, GRE (minimum scores of 50th percentile in all areas; analytical writing 3.5), bachelor's degree from accredited institution, minimum prerequisite course GPA of 3.0, all courses completed with minimum grade of C. Additional exam requirements/recommendations for international students: Required—TOEFL (minimum score 550 paper-based; 78 iBT). Application fee: $40. Electronic applications accepted. *Financial support:* Research assistantships with partial tuition reimbursements, career-related internships or fieldwork, Federal Work-Study, institutionally sponsored loans, scholarships/grants, traineeships, tuition waivers (partial), and unspecified assistantships available. Support available to part-time students. Financial award applicants required to submit FAFSA. *Faculty research:* Assisted technologies, biomechanics, clinical administration, cultural health, gerontology. *Unit head:* Dr. Stephen Slane, Chairperson and Professor Emeritus, 216-687-2379, E-mail: s.slane@csuohio.edu. *Application contact:* Karen Armstrong, Administrative Assistant, 216-687-3567, Fax: 216-687-9316, E-mail: healthsci@csuohio.edu.
Website: http://www.csuohio.edu/sciences/dept/healthsciences/graduate/index.html

Daemen College, Physician Assistant Department, Amherst, NY 14226-3592. Offers MS. *Accreditation:* ARC-PA. *Degree requirements:* For master's, 30 credits (40 weeks) in clinical clerk-ships; 2 research courses; 3 final year seminars. *Entrance requirements:* For master's, minimum GPA of 3.0 overall and in math and science prerequisites; 120 hours of direct patient contact; admission to professional phase. Additional exam requirements/recommendations for international students: Required—TOEFL (minimum score 500 paper-based; 63 iBT), IELTS (minimum score 5.5). Electronic applications accepted.

Des Moines University, College of Health Sciences, Physician Assistant Program, Des Moines, IA 50312-4104. Offers MS. *Accreditation:* ARC-PA. *Degree requirements:* For master's, research project. *Entrance requirements:* For master's, GRE, interview, minimum GPA of 2.8, related work experience. Additional exam requirements/recommendations for international students: Recommended—TOEFL. Electronic applications accepted. *Expenses:* Contact institution.

Drexel University, College of Nursing and Health Professions, Physician Assistant Department, Philadelphia, PA 19104-2875. Offers MHS. *Accreditation:* ARC-PA. Electronic applications accepted.

Duke University, School of Medicine, Physician Assistant Program, Durham, NC 27701. Offers MHS. *Accreditation:* ARC-PA. *Faculty:* 17 full-time (15 women), 2 part-time/adjunct (1 woman). *Students:* 183 full-time (131 women); includes 63 minority (7 Black or African American, non-Hispanic/Latino; 42 Asian, non-Hispanic/Latino; 14 Hispanic/Latino). 1,628 applicants, 6% accepted, 90 enrolled. In 2017, 89 master's awarded. *Entrance requirements:* For master's, GRE, bachelor's degree from regionally-accredited college; 8 core courses: anatomy, physiology, microbiology, biology (choice of 2), chemistry including labs (choice of 2), and statistics. Additional exam requirements/recommendations for international students: Recommended—TOEFL. *Application deadline:* For fall admission, 11/1 for domestic students. Application fee: $50. Electronic applications accepted. *Financial support:* In 2017–18, 47 students received support. Fellowships, research assistantships, teaching assistantships, institutionally sponsored loans, and scholarships/grants available. Financial award application deadline: 5/1; financial award applicants required to submit FAFSA. *Unit head:* Patricia Dieter, Professor in Community and Family Medicine, 919-681-3259, Fax: 919-681-9666, E-mail: patricia.dieter@duke.edu. *Application contact:* Wendy Z. Elwell, Admissions Coordinator, 919-668-4710, Fax: 919-681-9666, E-mail: wendy.elwell@duke.edu.
Website: http://pa.mc.duke.edu/

Duquesne University, John G. Rangos, Sr. School of Health Sciences, Pittsburgh, PA 15282-0001. Offers health management systems (MHMS); occupational therapy (MS, OTD); physical therapy (DPT); physician assistant studies (MPAS); rehabilitation science (MS, PhD); speech-language pathology (MS). *Accreditation:* AOTA (one or more programs are accredited); APTA (one or more programs are accredited); ASHA. *Program availability:* Part-time, minimal on-campus study. *Faculty:* 51 full-time (38 women), 33 part-time/adjunct (17 women). *Students:* 247 full-time (199 women), 11 part-time (7 women); includes 15 minority (2 Black or African American, non-Hispanic/Latino; 7 Asian, non-Hispanic/Latino; 3 Hispanic/Latino; 3 Two or more races, non-Hispanic/Latino), 42 international. Average age 23. 283 applicants, 31% accepted, 54 enrolled. In 2017, 134 master's, 39 doctorates awarded. *Degree requirements:* For doctorate, comprehensive exam (for some programs), thesis/dissertation (for some programs). *Entrance requirements:* For master's, GRE General Test (speech-language pathology), 3 letters of recommendation; minimum GPA of 2.75 (health management systems), 3.0 (speech-language pathology); for doctorate, GRE General Test (for physical therapy and rehabilitation science), 3 letters of recommendation, minimum GPA of 3.0, personal interview. Additional exam requirements/recommendations for international students: Required—TOEFL (minimum score 550 paper-based; 90 iBT); Recommended—IELTS. *Application deadline:* For fall admission, 2/1 for domestic and international students; for spring admission, 7/1 for domestic and international students. Applications are processed on a rolling basis. Application fee: $0. Electronic applications accepted. *Expenses:* $1,351 per credit ($1,259 for health management systems). *Financial support:* Federal Work-Study available. Financial award applicants required to submit FAFSA. *Faculty research:* Neuronal processing, electrical stimulation on peripheral neuropathy, central nervous system (CNS) stimulatory and inhibitory signals, behavioral genetic methodologies to development disorders of speech, neurogenic communication disorders. *Total annual research expenditures:* $24,578. *Unit head:* Dr. Fevzi Akinci, Dean, 412-396-5303, Fax: 412-396-5554, E-mail: akincif@duq.edu. *Application contact:* Christopher R. Hilf, Director of Enrollment Management, 412-396-5653, Fax: 412-396-5554, E-mail: hilfc@duq.edu.
Website: http://www.duq.edu/academics/schools/health-sciences

D'Youville College, Physician Assistant Department, Buffalo, NY 14201-1084. Offers MS. *Accreditation:* ARC-PA. *Entrance requirements:* For master's, BS, patient contact, 3 letters of recommendation. Additional exam requirements/recommendations for international students: Required—TOEFL (minimum score 500 paper-based). Electronic applications accepted.

East Carolina University, Graduate School, College of Allied Health Sciences, Department of Physician Assistant Studies, Greenville, NC 27858-4353. Offers MS. *Accreditation:* ARC-PA. *Students:* 106 full-time (83 women), 1 (woman) part-time; includes 10 minority (2 Black or African American, non-Hispanic/Latino; 4 Asian, non-Hispanic/Latino; 3 Hispanic/Latino; 1 Two or more races, non-Hispanic/Latino). Average age 26. 333 applicants, 15% accepted, 36 enrolled. In 2017, 34 master's awarded. *Entrance requirements:* For master's, GRE. *Application deadline:* For fall admission, 9/1 for domestic students. Applications are processed on a rolling basis. Application fee: $75. Electronic applications accepted. *Expenses:* Tuition, state resident: full-time $4749; part-time $297 per credit hour. Tuition, nonresident: full-time $17,898; part-time $1119 per credit hour. *Required fees:* $2691; $224 per credit hour. Part-time tuition and fees vary according to course load and program. *Unit head:* Dr. Alan Gindoff, Chair, 252-744-6271, E-mail: gindoffa@ecu.edu.
Website: http://www.ecu.edu/pa/

Eastern Michigan University, Graduate School, College of Health and Human Services, School of Health Promotion and Human Performance, Program in Physician Assistant Studies, Ypsilanti, MI 48197. Offers MS. *Program availability:* Part-time, evening/weekend. *Students:* 55 full-time (43 women); includes 7 minority (2 Black or African American, non-Hispanic/Latino; 1 Asian, non-Hispanic/Latino; 3 Hispanic/Latino; 1 Two or more races, non-Hispanic/Latino), 1 international. Average age 28. 9 applicants. In 2017, 30 master's awarded. *Entrance requirements:* Additional exam requirements/recommendations for international students: Required—TOEFL. Application fee: $45. *Financial support:* Research assistantships with full tuition reimbursements, teaching assistantships with full tuition reimbursements, career-related internships or fieldwork, Federal Work-Study, institutionally sponsored loans, scholarships/grants, tuition waivers (full and partial), and unspecified assistantships available. Support available to part-time students. *Application contact:* Karin Olson, Program Director, 734-487-2843, Fax: 734-483-1834, E-mail: kolson14@emich.edu.

Eastern Virginia Medical School, Master of Physician Assistant Program, Norfolk, VA 23501-1980. Offers MPA. *Accreditation:* ARC-PA. *Entrance requirements:* Additional exam requirements/recommendations for international students: Required—TOEFL. Electronic applications accepted. *Expenses:* Contact institution.

Elon University, Program in Physician Assistant Studies, Elon, NC 27244-2010. Offers MS. *Faculty:* 8 full-time (7 women), 2 part-time/adjunct (1 woman). *Students:* 76 full-time (60 women); includes 9 minority (2 Black or African American, non-Hispanic/Latino; 5 Asian, non-Hispanic/Latino; 1 Hispanic/Latino; 1 Two or more races, non-Hispanic/Latino). Average age 27. 1,286 applicants, 4% accepted, 38 enrolled. In 2017, 38 master's awarded. *Entrance requirements:* Additional exam requirements/recommendations for international students: Required—TOEFL. *Application deadline:* For spring admission, 11/1 for domestic students. Applications are processed on a rolling basis. Application fee: $50. Electronic applications accepted. *Financial support:* Federal Work-Study and scholarships/grants available. Financial award application deadline: 10/1; financial award applicants required to submit FAFSA. *Unit head:* Dr. Becky Neiduski, Dean of the School of Health Sciences, 336-278-6350, E-mail: bneiduski@elon.edu. *Application contact:* Art Fadde, Director of Graduate Admissions, 800-334-8448 Ext. 3, Fax: 336-278-7699, E-mail: afadde@elon.edu.
Website: https://www.elon.edu/pa/

Emory & Henry College, Graduate Programs, Emory, VA 24327. Offers American history (MA Ed); education professional studies (M Ed); occupational therapy (MOT); organizational leadership (MCOL); physical therapy (DPT); physician assistant studies (MPAS); reading specialist (MA Ed). *Program availability:* Part-time. *Faculty:* 7 full-time (3 women). *Students:* 194 full-time (128 women), 4 part-time (2 women); includes 6 minority (2 Black or African American, non-Hispanic/Latino; 1 American Indian or Alaska Native, non-Hispanic/Latino; 1 Asian, non-Hispanic/Latino; 2 Hispanic/Latino). Average age 25. 525 applicants, 21% accepted, 74 enrolled. In 2017, 24 master's awarded. *Degree requirements:* For master's, thesis optional; for doctorate, thesis/dissertation optional. *Entrance requirements:* For master's, GRE or PRAXIS I, official transcripts from all colleges previously attended, three professional recommendations, essay. Additional exam requirements/recommendations for international students: Recommended—TOEFL, IELTS (minimum score 6). *Application deadline:* Applications are processed on a rolling basis. Electronic applications accepted. *Expenses:* Contact institution. *Financial support:* Application deadline: 10/15; applicants required to submit FAFSA. *Unit head:* Dr. Michael Puglisi, Associate Dean for Academic Affairs, 276-944-6662, E-mail: mpuglisi@ehc.edu. *Application contact:* Mary Bolt, Director of Transfer and Graduate Admission, 276-944-6135, E-mail: mbolt@ehc.edu.

Emory University, School of Medicine, Programs in Allied Health Professions, Physician Assistant Program, Atlanta, GA 30322. Offers MM Sc. *Accreditation:* ARC-PA. *Entrance requirements:* For master's, GRE General Test. Additional exam requirements/recommendations for international students: Required—TOEFL (minimum score 69 iBT). Electronic applications accepted. *Expenses:* Contact institution. *Faculty research:* Cultural competency in medical education, farm worker health, technology in medicine, physician assistants in primary care, interprofessional education.

Florida Gulf Coast University, Elaine Nicpon Marieb College of Health and Human Services, Program in Physician Assistant Studies, Fort Myers, FL 33965-6565. Offers MPAS. *Faculty:* 71 full-time (49 women), 49 part-time/adjunct (32 women). *Students:* 20 full-time (16 women); includes 8 minority (1 Asian, non-Hispanic/Latino; 5 Hispanic/Latino; 2 Two or more races, non-Hispanic/Latino). Average age 26. 23 applicants, 91% accepted, 20 enrolled. *Entrance requirements:* Additional exam requirements/recommendations for international students: Required—TOEFL (minimum score 550 paper-based). *Application deadline:* For fall admission, 1/15 priority date for domestic students. Applications are processed on a rolling basis. Application fee: $30. Electronic applications accepted. *Expenses:* Tuition, state resident: part-time $290 per credit hour. Tuition, nonresident: part-time $1173 per credit hour. *Required fees:* $127 per credit hour. Tuition and fees vary according to course load. *Financial support:* In 2017–18, 8 students received support. Application deadline: 6/30; applicants required to submit FAFSA. *Unit head:* Robert Hawkes, Director, 239-745-4417, E-mail: rhawkes@fgcu.edu. *Application contact:* Susan Baurer, Administrative Assistant, 239-590-7451; E-mail: sbaurer@fgcu.edu.

Florida International University, Herbert Wertheim College of Medicine, Miami, FL 33199. Offers biomedical sciences (PhD); medicine (MD); physician assistant studies (MPAS). *Accreditation:* LCME/AMA. *Faculty:* 84 full-time (45 women), 83 part-time/adjunct (28 women). *Students:* 638 full-time (364 women); includes 418 minority (42 Black or African American, non-Hispanic/Latino; 124 Asian, non-Hispanic/Latino; 228 Hispanic/Latino; 24 Two or more races, non-Hispanic/Latino), 13 international. Average age 26. 5,410 applicants, 7% accepted, 170 enrolled. In 2017, 115 doctorates awarded. *Entrance requirements:* For doctorate, MCAT (minimum score of 25), minimum overall GPA of 3.0; 3 letters of recommendation, 2 from basic science faculty (biology, chemistry, physics, math) and 1 from any other faculty member. *Application deadline:* For fall admission, 12/15 for domestic students. Application fee: $160. Electronic applications accepted. *Expenses:* Contact institution. *Financial support:* Institutionally sponsored loans and scholarships/grants available. Financial award application deadline: 3/1; financial award applicants required to submit FAFSA. *Unit head:* Dr. John Rock, Dean, 305-348-0570, E-mail: med.admissions@fiu.edu. *Application contact:* Cristina M. Arabatzis, Assistant Director of Admissions, 305-348-0639, Fax: 305-348-0650, E-mail: carabatz@fiu.edu.
Website: http://medicine.fiu.edu/

Franciscan Missionaries of Our Lady University, School of Health Professions, Baton Rouge, LA 70808. Offers health administration (MHA); nutritional sciences (MS); physical therapy (DPT); physician assistant studies (MMS). *Unit head:* Dr. Susan K. Steele-Moses, Dean, 225-768-1676. *Application contact:* Dr. Susan K. Steele-Moses, Dean, 225-768-1676.
Website: https://www.franu.edu/academics/schools/school-of-health-professions

Francis Marion University, Graduate Programs, Physician Assistant Program, Florence, SC 29502-0547. Offers MPAS. *Entrance requirements:* For master's, GRE, bachelor's degree with minimum GPA of 3.0, official transcripts, 3 letters of recommendation, 250 hours of clinical work, criminal background check, personal statement, proof of immunizations. Electronic applications accepted.

Franklin Pierce University, Graduate and Professional Studies, Rindge, NH 03461-0060. Offers curriculum and instruction (M Ed); elementary education (MS Ed); emerging network technologies (Graduate Certificate); energy and sustainability studies (MBA, Graduate Certificate); health administration (MBA, Graduate Certificate); human resource management (MBA, Graduate Certificate); information technology (MBA); leadership (MBA); nursing education (MS); nursing leadership (MS); physical therapy (DPT); physician assistant studies (MPAS); special education (M Ed); sports management (MBA). *Accreditation:* APTA. *Program availability:* Part-time, 100% online, blended/hybrid learning. *Degree requirements:* For master's, concentrated original research projects; student teaching; fieldwork and/or internship; leadership project; PRAXIS I and II (for M Ed); for doctorate, concentrated original research projects, clinical fieldwork and/or internship, leadership project. *Entrance requirements:* For master's, minimum GPA of 2.5, 3 letters of recommendation; competencies in accounting, economics, statistics, and computer skills through life experience or undergraduate coursework (for MBA); certification/e-portfolio, minimum C grade in all education courses (for M Ed); license to practice as RN (for MS); for doctorate, GRE, 80 hours of observation/work in PT settings; completion of anatomy, chemistry, physics, and statistics; minimum GPA of 3.0. Additional exam requirements/recommendations for international students: Required—TOEFL (minimum score 550 paper-based; 61 iBT). Electronic applications accepted. *Faculty research:* Evidence-based practice in sports physical therapy, human resource management in economic crisis, leadership in nursing, innovation in sports facility management, differentiated learning and understanding by design.

Gannon University, School of Graduate Studies, Morosky College of Health Professions and Sciences, School of Health Professions, Program in Physician Assistant Science, Erie, PA 16541-0001. Offers MPAS. *Accreditation:* ARC-PA. *Degree requirements:* For master's, thesis or alternative, research project, practicum. *Entrance requirements:* For master's, baccalaureate degree with minimum GPA of 3.0, 3 letters of recommendation, interview, transcript, 30 hours of documented volunteer/paid medical experience or shadowing a physician assistant. Additional exam requirements/recommendations for international students: Required—TOEFL (minimum score 600 paper-based). Electronic applications accepted. Application fee is waived when completed online. *Expenses:* Contact institution.

Gardner-Webb University, Graduate School, Program in Physician Assistant Studies, Boiling Springs, NC 28017. Offers MPAS. *Faculty:* 5 full-time (4 women). *Students:* 59 full-time (45 women); includes 7 minority (3 Asian, non-Hispanic/Latino; 1 Hispanic/Latino; 3 Two or more races, non-Hispanic/Latino). Average age 25. *Expenses:* Contact institution. *Unit head:* Dr. Franki Burch, Dean, 704-406-4723, E-mail: gradschool@gardner-webb.edu. *Application contact:* Melissa Hamrick, Secretary, 704-406-2369, Fax: 704-406-2370, E-mail: mhamrick8@gardner-webb.edu.
Website: http://www.gardner-webb.edu/academic-programs-and-resources/colleges-and-schools/health-sciences/schools-and-departments/physician-assistant-studies/%

The George Washington University, School of Medicine and Health Sciences, Health Sciences Programs, Physician Assistant Program, Washington, DC 20052. Offers MSHS. *Accreditation:* ARC-PA. *Students:* 138 full-time (107 women), 1 (woman) part-time; includes 37 minority (3 Black or African American, non-Hispanic/Latino; 1 American Indian or Alaska Native, non-Hispanic/Latino; 15 Asian, non-Hispanic/Latino; 14 Hispanic/Latino; 1 Native Hawaiian or other Pacific Islander, non-Hispanic/Latino; 3 Two or more races, non-Hispanic/Latino). Average age 29. 1,332 applicants, 10% accepted, 61 enrolled. In 2017, 60 master's awarded. *Entrance requirements:* For master's, GRE General Test, BA/BS with clinical experience. *Application deadline:* For fall admission, 10/15 for domestic students. Applications are processed on a rolling basis. Application fee: $75. Electronic applications accepted. *Expenses: Tuition:* Full-time $28,800; part-time $1655 per credit hour. *Required fees:* $45; $2.75 per credit hour. *Unit head:* Dr. Karen Wright, Program Director, 202-994-9279, E-mail: kawright@gwu.edu. *Application contact:* Erin C. McKan Thomas, Assistant Director of Admissions and Enrollment Services, 202-994-6395, E-mail: emckan@gwu.edu.

Grand Valley State University, College of Health Professions, Physician Assistant Studies Program, Allendale, MI 49401-9403. Offers MPAS. *Accreditation:* ARC-PA. *Faculty:* 11 full-time (8 women). *Students:* 136 full-time (96 women); includes 8 minority (1 Asian, non-Hispanic/Latino; 3 Hispanic/Latino; 4 Two or more races, non-Hispanic/Latino). Average age 25. 374 applicants, 14% accepted, 43 enrolled. In 2017, 44 master's awarded. *Degree requirements:* For master's, thesis optional, clinical rotations, project. *Entrance requirements:* For master's, United States Medical Licensing Exam, minimum GPA of 3.0 overall, in last 60 hours, and on prerequisite courses; 2 recommendations; interview; minimum of 500 hours in volunteer, work, or observational experience in health care environment. Additional exam requirements/recommendations for international students: Required—TOEFL (minimum iBT score of 80), IELTS (6.5), or Michigan English Language Assessment Battery (77). *Application deadline:* For fall admission, 9/15 priority date for domestic and international students. Application fee: $30. Electronic applications accepted. *Expenses:* $686 per credit hour. *Financial support:* In 2017–18, 17 students received support, including 17 fellowships, 2 research assistantships with full and partial tuition reimbursements available (averaging $8,000 per year); institutionally sponsored loans also available. Financial award application deadline: 2/15. *Faculty research:* Women's health, pain management, PA practice issues, hematology/hemostasis, patient education. *Unit head:* Andrew Booth, Director, 616-331-5991, Fax: 616-331-5654, E-mail: bootha@gvsu.edu. *Application contact:* Darlene Zwart, Student Services Coordinator, 616-331-3958, Fax: 616-331-5643, E-mail: zwartda@gvsu.edu.
Website: http://www.gvsu.edu/pas/

Harding University, College of Allied Health, Program in Physician Assistant, Searcy, AR 72149-0001. Offers MS. *Faculty:* 7 full-time (4 women), 2 part-time/adjunct (1 woman). *Students:* 106 full-time (76 women); includes 17 minority (2 Black or African American, non-Hispanic/Latino; 2 American Indian or Alaska Native, non-Hispanic/Latino; 7 Asian, non-Hispanic/Latino; 5 Hispanic/Latino; 1 Two or more races, non-Hispanic/Latino). Average age 27. 776 applicants, 6% accepted, 36 enrolled. In 2017, 35 master's awarded. *Entrance requirements:* For master's, GRE. Additional exam requirements/recommendations for international students: Required—TOEFL. *Application deadline:* For fall admission, 11/1 for domestic and international students. Application fee: $25. *Expenses:* Contact institution. *Unit head:* Dr. Mike Murphy, Professor/Program Director, 501-279-5642, E-mail: mmurphy1@harding.edu. *Application contact:* Marci Murphy, Admissions Director, 501-279-5642, Fax: 501-279-4811, E-mail: paprogram@harding.edu.
Website: http://www.harding.edu/paprogram/

Hardin-Simmons University, Graduate School, Holland School of Sciences and Mathematics, Abilene, TX 79698-0001. Offers environmental management (MS); mathematics (MS); physical therapy (DPT); physician assistant studies (MPAS). *Program availability:* Part-time. *Faculty:* 29 full-time (15 women), 6 part-time/adjunct (4 women). *Students:* 115 full-time (77 women), 8 part-time (6 women); includes 25 minority (6 Black or African American, non-Hispanic/Latino; 2 Asian, non-Hispanic/Latino; 17 Hispanic/Latino), 1 international. Average age 25. 1,156 applicants, 7% accepted, 62 enrolled. In 2017, 10 master's, 29 doctorates awarded. *Degree requirements:* For master's, comprehensive exam, thesis or alternative, internship; for doctorate, comprehensive

exam, thesis/dissertation or alternative. *Entrance requirements:* For master's, minimum undergraduate GPA of 3.0 in major, 2.7 overall; 2 semesters of course work each in biology, chemistry and geology; interview; writing sample; occupational experience; for doctorate, letters of recommendation, interview, writing sample. Additional exam requirements/recommendations for international students: Required—TOEFL (minimum score 550 paper-based; 79 iBT). *Application deadline:* For fall admission, 8/15 priority date for domestic students, 4/1 for international students; for spring admission, 1/5 priority date for domestic students, 9/1 for international students. Applications are processed on a rolling basis. Application fee: $50 ($150 for international students). Electronic applications accepted. *Expenses: Tuition:* Full-time $13,500; part-time $750 per semester hour. *Required fees:* $220 per term. One-time fee: $50. Tuition and fees vary according to course load, campus/location and program. *Financial support:* In 2017–18, 108 students received support. Fellowships, career-related internships or fieldwork, and scholarships/grants available. Support available to part-time students. Financial award application deadline: 6/30; financial award applicants required to submit FAFSA. *Unit head:* Dr. Christopher McNair, Dean, 325-670-1401, Fax: 325-670-1385, E-mail: cmcnair@hsutx.edu. *Application contact:* Dr. Nancy Kucinski, Dean of Graduate Studies, 325-670-1298, Fax: 325-670-1564, E-mail: gradoff@hsutx.edu.
Website: http://www.hsutx.edu/academics/holland

High Point University, Norcross Graduate School, High Point, NC 27268. Offers athletic training (MSAT); business administration (MBA); educational leadership (M Ed, Ed D); elementary education (M Ed, MAT); pharmacy (Pharm D); physical therapy (DPT); physician assistant studies (MPAS); secondary mathematics (M Ed, MAT); special education (M Ed); strategic communication (MA). *Accreditation:* NCATE. *Program availability:* Part-time, evening/weekend. *Degree requirements:* For master's, comprehensive exam (for some programs), thesis (for some programs). *Entrance requirements:* For master's, GMAT (MBA), GRE, MAT, minimum GPA of 3.0. Additional exam requirements/recommendations for international students: Required—TOEFL (minimum score 550 paper-based). Electronic applications accepted.

Hofstra University, Hofstra Northwell School of Graduate Nursing and Physician Assistant Studies, Program in Physician Assistant, Hempstead, NY 11549. Offers physician assistant studies (MS). *Students:* 123 full-time (93 women), 4 part-time (3 women); includes 17 minority (1 American Indian or Alaska Native, non-Hispanic/Latino; 7 Asian, non-Hispanic/Latino; 6 Hispanic/Latino; 1 Native Hawaiian or other Pacific Islander, non-Hispanic/Latino; 2 Two or more races, non-Hispanic/Latino), 2 international. Average age 25. 1,616 applicants, 3% accepted, 43 enrolled. In 2017, 48 master's awarded. *Degree requirements:* For master's, comprehensive exam, minimum GPA of 3.0. *Entrance requirements:* For master's, bachelor's degree in biology or equivalent, 2 letters of recommendation, essay, minimum GPA of 3.0. Additional exam requirements/recommendations for international students: Required—TOEFL (minimum score 550 paper-based; 80 iBT). *Application deadline:* For fall admission, 11/1 for domestic students. Application fee: $0. Electronic applications accepted. *Expenses: Tuition:* Full-time $1292. *Required fees:* $970. Tuition and fees vary according to program. *Financial support:* In 2017–18, 15 students received support, including 15 fellowships with full and partial tuition reimbursements available (averaging $4,925 per year); research assistantships with full and partial tuition reimbursements available, career-related internships or fieldwork, Federal Work-Study, institutionally sponsored loans, scholarships/grants, traineeships, tuition waivers (full and partial), and unspecified assistantships also available. Support available to part-time students. Financial award applicants required to submit FAFSA. *Faculty research:* Autism and PA education; addressing mental health issues in PA education; pregnancy, childbirth, and postpartum mental health; novel modalities in teaching evidence-based medicine; optimal team practice for PA's. *Unit head:* Carina Loscalzo, Chairperson, 516-463-4412, Fax: 516-463-5177, E-mail: carina.loscalzo@hofstra.edu. *Application contact:* Sunil Samuel, Assistant Vice President of Admissions, 516-463-4723, Fax: 516-463-4664, E-mail: graduateadmission@hofstra.edu.
Website: http://www.hofstra.edu/academics/colleges/healthscienceshumanservices/

Howard University, College of Nursing and Allied Health Sciences, Division of Allied Health Sciences, Washington, DC 20059-0002. Offers occupational therapy (MSOT); physical therapy (DPT); physician assistant (MPA). *Accreditation:* AOTA.

Idaho State University, Office of Graduate Studies, Office of Medical and Oral Health, Department of Physician Assistant Studies, Pocatello, ID 83209-8253. Offers MPAS. *Accreditation:* ARC-PA. *Degree requirements:* For master's, comprehensive exam, thesis (for some programs), portfolio, clinical year, oral case presentation. *Entrance requirements:* For master's, GRE General Test, minimum GPA of 3.0, letters of reference. Additional exam requirements/recommendations for international students: Required—TOEFL (minimum score 500 paper-based). Electronic applications accepted. *Expenses:* Contact institution.

Indiana State University, College of Graduate and Professional Studies, College of Health and Human Services, Department of Applied Medicine and Rehabilitation, Terre Haute, IN 47809. Offers athletic training (MS, DAT); occupational therapy (MS); physical therapy (DPT); physician assistant (MS). *Degree requirements:* For master's, thesis or alternative. *Entrance requirements:* For master's, GRE General Test. Electronic applications accepted.

James Madison University, The Graduate School, College of Health and Behavioral Studies, Program in Physician Assistant Studies, Harrisonburg, VA 22801. Offers MPAS. *Accreditation:* ARC-PA. *Program availability:* Part-time. *Students:* 61 full-time (48 women), 28 part-time (26 women); includes 11 minority (2 Black or African American, non-Hispanic/Latino; 5 Asian, non-Hispanic/Latino; 1 Hispanic/Latino; 3 Two or more races, non-Hispanic/Latino). Average age 30. In 2017, 31 master's awarded. Application fee: $55. Electronic applications accepted. *Expenses:* Tuition, state resident: full-time $10,512; part-time $438 per credit hour. Tuition, nonresident: full-time $28,358; part-time $1162 per credit hour. *Required fees:* $1128. *Financial support:* Fellowships available. Financial award application deadline: 3/1; financial award applicants required to submit FAFSA. *Unit head:* Dr. Allen Lewis, Department Head, 540-568-6510, E-mail: lewis6an@jmu.edu. *Application contact:* Lynette D. Michael, Director of Graduate Admissions and Student Records, 540-568-6131 Ext. 6395, Fax: 540-568-7860, E-mail: michaeld@jmu.edu.
Website: http://www.healthsci.jmu.edu/PA/index.html

Jefferson College of Health Sciences, Program in Physician Assistant, Roanoke, VA 24013. Offers MS. *Accreditation:* ARC-PA. *Degree requirements:* For master's, rotations. *Entrance requirements:* For master's, GRE. Additional exam requirements/recommendations for international students: Required—TOEFL (minimum score 550 paper-based; 80 iBT). Electronic applications accepted. *Faculty research:* Community health, chronic disease management, geriatrics, rheumatology, medically underserved populations.

Johnson & Wales University, Graduate Studies, Master of Science Program in Physician Assistant Studies, Providence, RI 02903-3703. Offers MS. *Expenses: Tuition:* Full-time $12,636; part-time $702 per credit hour. *Unit head:* Dr. George S. Bottomley, Director, 410-598-4558. *Application contact:* Katie Spolidoro, Admissions Counselor, 401-598-2381, E-mail: pastudies@admissions.jwu.edu.
Website: https://www.jwu.edu/academics/colleges/college-of-health-and-wellness/physician-assistant-studies/index.html

Keiser University, MS in Physician Assistant Program, Fort Lauderdale, FL 33309. Offers MS. *Unit head:* Christine Kessler, Program Director, 888-753-4737.
Website: http://www.keiseruniversity.edu/graduateschool/PA/

Kettering College, Program in Physician Assistant Studies, Kettering, OH 45429-1299. Offers MPAS.

King's College, Program in Physician Assistant Studies, Wilkes-Barre, PA 18711-0801. Offers MSPAS. *Accreditation:* ARC-PA. *Degree requirements:* For master's, thesis. *Entrance requirements:* For master's, bachelor's degree; minimum cumulative GPA of 3.2 overall and in science; 500 clinical hours of health care experience; 2 letters of reference; personal statement. Additional exam requirements/recommendations for international students: Required—TOEFL (minimum score 610 paper-based; 108 iBT). Electronic applications accepted. *Expenses:* Contact institution.

Le Moyne College, Department of Physician Assistant Studies, Syracuse, NY 13214. Offers MS. *Accreditation:* ARC-PA. *Faculty:* 6 full-time (4 women), 14 part-time/adjunct (10 women). *Students:* 131 full-time (100 women), 3 part-time (all women); includes 14 minority (5 Black or African American, non-Hispanic/Latino; 5 Asian, non-Hispanic/Latino; 2 Hispanic/Latino; 2 Two or more races, non-Hispanic/Latino), 1 international. Average age 26. 1,292 applicants, 7% accepted, 73 enrolled. In 2017, 74 master's awarded. *Degree requirements:* For master's, project. *Entrance requirements:* For master's, bachelor's degree with minimum GPA of 3.0, patient contact, interview, 3 letters of recommendation. Additional exam requirements/recommendations for international students: Required—TOEFL (minimum score 550 paper-based; 79 iBT); Recommended—IELTS (minimum score 6.5). *Application deadline:* For fall admission, 10/1 priority date for domestic and international students. Application fee: $177. Electronic applications accepted. *Expenses:* $13,310 per semester. *Financial support:* In 2017–18, 20 students received support. Career-related internships or fieldwork, scholarships/grants, and health care benefits available. Financial award applicants required to submit FAFSA. *Faculty research:* Cultural competence, educational outcomes, preventive medicine, health literacy. *Unit head:* Mary E. Springston, Clinical Assistant Professor/Director of Department of Physician Assistant Studies, 315-445-4163, Fax: 315-445-4602, E-mail: springme@lemoyne.edu. *Application contact:* Kristen P. Richards, Senior Director of Enrollment Management, 315-445-5444, Fax: 315-445-6092, E-mail: trapaskp@lemoyne.edu.
Website: http://www.lemoyne.edu/pa

Lenoir-Rhyne University, Graduate Programs, School of Physician Assistant Studies, Hickory, NC 28601. Offers MS. *Expenses:* Contact institution.

Lock Haven University of Pennsylvania, College of Natural, Behavioral and Health Sciences, Lock Haven, PA 17745-2390. Offers actuarial science (PSM); athletic training (MS); health promotion/education (MHS); healthcare management (MHS); physician assistant (MHS). Program also offered at the Clearfield, Coudersport, and Harrisburg campuses. *Accreditation:* ARC-PA. *Entrance requirements:* For master's, minimum undergraduate GPA of 3.0. Additional exam requirements/recommendations for international students: Required—TOEFL. Electronic applications accepted.

Loma Linda University, School of Allied Health Professions, Department of Physician Assistant Sciences, Loma Linda, CA 92350. Offers MPA. *Accreditation:* ARC-PA. *Entrance requirements:* For master's, minimum GPA of 3.0. Additional exam requirements/recommendations for international students: Required—TOEFL (minimum score 550 paper-based).

Long Island University–LIU Brooklyn, School of Health Professions, Brooklyn, NY 11201-8423. Offers athletic training and sport sciences (MS); community health (MS Ed); exercise science (MS); forensic social work (Advanced Certificate); occupational therapy (MS); physical therapy (DPT); physician assistant (MS); public health (MPH); social work (MSW); speech-language pathology (MS). *Faculty:* 33 full-time (23 women), 82 part-time/adjunct (55 women). *Students:* 690 full-time (508 women), 86 part-time (74 women); includes 259 minority (120 Black or African American, non-Hispanic/Latino; 1 American Indian or Alaska Native, non-Hispanic/Latino; 52 Asian, non-Hispanic/Latino; 76 Hispanic/Latino; 10 Two or more races, non-Hispanic/Latino), 65 international. Average age 27. 1,241 applicants, 45% accepted, 255 enrolled. In 2017, 249 master's, 42 doctorates, 8 other advanced degrees awarded. *Degree requirements:* For master's, comprehensive exam (for some programs), thesis (for some programs); for doctorate, comprehensive exam (for some programs). *Entrance requirements:* For master's and doctorate, GRE. Additional exam requirements/recommendations for international students: Required—TOEFL (minimum score 550 paper-based; 79 iBT). *Application deadline:* Applications are processed on a rolling basis. Application fee: $50. Electronic applications accepted. *Expenses: Tuition:* Full-time $21,618; part-time $1201 per credit. *Required fees:* $1840; $920 per term. Tuition and fees vary according to course load. *Financial support:* In 2017–18, 187 students received support. Research assistantships, teaching assistantships, career-related internships or fieldwork, Federal Work-Study, scholarships/grants, and unspecified assistantships available. Support available to part-time students. Financial award application deadline: 2/15; financial award applicants required to submit FAFSA. *Faculty research:* Pediatric physical therapy, complementary and alternative medicine, global health and human rights, sport leadership and entrepreneurship, feminist sport psychology. *Unit head:* Dr. Barry S. Eckert, Dean, 718-780-6578, Fax: 718-780-4561, E-mail: barry.eckert@liu.edu. *Application contact:* Dr. Dominick Fortugno, Associate Dean, 718-488-1496, Fax: 718-780-4561, E-mail: dominick.fortugno@liu.edu.
Website: http://liu.edu/brooklyn/academics/school-of-health-professions

Louisiana State University Health Sciences Center, School of Allied Health Professions, Program in Physician Assistant Studies, New Orleans, LA 70112. Offers MPAS. *Faculty:* 4 full-time (all women). *Students:* 59 full-time (45 women); includes 6 minority (1 Black or African American, non-Hispanic/Latino; 4 Asian, non-Hispanic/Latino; 1 Two or more races, non-Hispanic/Latino). Average age 25. 308 applicants, 10% accepted, 30 enrolled. In 2017, 29 master's awarded. *Entrance requirements:* For master's, GRE (minimum score 153 verbal, 144 quantitative, and 3.5 analytical), minimum cumulative and overall science GPA of 3.0, 80 hours of documented healthcare experience. Additional exam requirements/recommendations for international students: Required—TOEFL (minimum score 550 paper-based; 79 iBT). *Application deadline:* For fall admission, 8/1 for domestic students. Application fee: $175. Electronic applications accepted. *Expenses:* Contact institution. *Financial support:* Application deadline: 4/15; applicants required to submit FAFSA. *Faculty research:* PA workforce issues, evaluation of clinical competence, curriculum development. *Unit head:* Dr. Debra S. Munsell, Director, 504-556-3420, Fax: 504-556-3421, E-mail: dmunse@lsuhsc.edu. *Application contact:* Yudialys Delgado Cazanas, Student Affairs Director, 504-568-4253, Fax: 504-568-3185, E-mail: ydelga@lsuhsc.edu.
Website: http://alliedhealth.lsuhsc.edu/pa/

Marietta College, Program in Physician Assistant Studies, Marietta, OH 45750-4000. Offers MS. *Accreditation:* ARC-PA. *Faculty:* 5 full-time (2 women), 2 part-time/adjunct (0 women). *Students:* 72 full-time (56 women); includes 11 minority (1 Black or African American, non-Hispanic/Latino; 4 Asian, non-Hispanic/Latino; 3 Hispanic/Latino; 3 Two or more races, non-Hispanic/Latino). Average age 25. 963 applicants, 5% accepted, 36 enrolled. In 2017, 36 master's awarded. *Degree requirements:* For master's, capstone project. *Entrance requirements:* For master's, MCAT and/or GRE, official transcripts.

Physician Assistant Studies

Additional exam requirements/recommendations for international students: Recommended—TOEFL (minimum score 100 iBT). *Application deadline:* For fall admission, 11/1 for domestic students. Application fee: $100. Electronic applications accepted. *Expenses:* Contact institution. *Financial support:* Scholarships/grants available. *Faculty research:* Meniscal tears, radiology, oncology, clinical medicine, hospitalist care. *Unit head:* Miranda Collins, Director, 740-376-4953, E-mail: miranda.collins@marietta.edu. *Application contact:* Lori Hart, Administrative Coordinator, 740-376-4458, E-mail: lori.hart@marietta.edu.
Website: http://www.marietta.edu/pa-program

Marquette University, Graduate School, College of Health Sciences, Department of Physician Assistant Studies, Milwaukee, WI 53201-1881. Offers MPAS. *Accreditation:* ARC-PA. *Degree requirements:* For master's, clinical clerkship experience, capstone project. *Entrance requirements:* For master's, GRE General Test, three letters of recommendation, minimum GPA of 3.0, official transcripts from all current and previous institutions except Marquette. Additional exam requirements/recommendations for international students: Required—TOEFL (minimum score 530 paper-based). Electronic applications accepted. *Expenses:* Contact institution.

Marywood University, Academic Affairs, College of Health and Human Services, Department of Physician Assistant Studies, Scranton, PA 18509-1598. Offers MS. *Accreditation:* ARC-PA. Electronic applications accepted. *Expenses:* Contact institution.

MCPHS University, Graduate Studies, Programs in Physician Assistant Studies, Accelerated Program in Physician Assistant Studies (Manchester/Worcester), Boston, MA 02115-5896. Offers MPAS. *Accreditation:* ARC-PA. *Entrance requirements:* Additional exam requirements/recommendations for international students: Required—TOEFL (minimum score 550 paper-based; 79 iBT). Electronic applications accepted.

MCPHS University, Graduate Studies, Programs in Physician Assistant Studies, Program in Physician Assistant Studies (Boston), Boston, MA 02115-5896. Offers MPAS. *Entrance requirements:* Additional exam requirements/recommendations for international students: Required—TOEFL (minimum score 550 paper-based; 79 iBT).

Medical University of South Carolina, College of Health Professions, Physician Assistant Studies Program, Charleston, SC 29425. Offers MS. *Accreditation:* ARC-PA. *Degree requirements:* For master's, clinical clerkship, research project. *Entrance requirements:* For master's, GRE General Test, interview, minimum GPA of 3.0, 3 references. Additional exam requirements/recommendations for international students: Required—TOEFL (minimum score 600 paper-based). Electronic applications accepted. *Faculty research:* Oral health, pediatric emergency medicine, simulation technology in education, health manpower needs, cultural competency.

Mercer University, Graduate Studies, Cecil B. Day Campus, College of Health Professions, Atlanta, GA 30341. Offers athletic training (MAT); clinical medical psychology (Psy D); physical therapy (DPT); physician assistant studies (MM Sc); public health (MPH); DPT/MBA; DPT/MPH; MM Sc/MPH; Pharm D/MPH. *Faculty:* 23 full-time (14 women), 10 part-time/adjunct (7 women). *Students:* 345 full-time (261 women), 67 part-time (55 women); includes 167 minority (116 Black or African American, non-Hispanic/Latino; 28 Asian, non-Hispanic/Latino; 21 Hispanic/Latino; 2 Two or more races, non-Hispanic/Latino), 2 international. Average age 26. In 2017, 83 master's, 37 doctorates awarded. *Expenses:* Contact institution. *Financial support:* Federal Work-Study, traineeships, and unspecified assistantships available. *Faculty research:* Scholarship of teaching and learning, health disparities, clinical outcomes, health promotion. *Unit head:* Dr. Lisa Lundquist, Dean/Clinical Professor, 678-547-6308, E-mail: lundquist_lm@mercer.edu. *Application contact:* Laura Ellison, Director of Admissions and Student Affairs, 678-547-6391, E-mail: ellison_la@mercer.edu.
Website: http://chp.mercer.edu/

Mercy College, School of Health and Natural Sciences, Program in Physician Assistant Studies, Dobbs Ferry, NY 10522-1189. Offers MS. *Accreditation:* ARC-PA. *Program availability:* Evening/weekend. *Students:* 121 full-time (91 women), 8 part-time (4 women); includes 51 minority (10 Black or African American, non-Hispanic/Latino; 22 Asian, non-Hispanic/Latino; 18 Hispanic/Latino; 1 Two or more races, non-Hispanic/Latino), 1 international. Average age 33. 50 applicants, 20% accepted. In 2017, 62 master's awarded. *Entrance requirements:* For master's, essay, interview, two letters of reference, undergraduate transcripts with minimum GPA of 3.0. Additional exam requirements/recommendations for international students: Required—TOEFL (minimum score 600 paper-based; 100 iBT), IELTS (minimum score 8). *Application deadline:* Applications are processed on a rolling basis. Application fee: $62. Electronic applications accepted. *Expenses:* Contact institution. *Financial support:* Career-related internships or fieldwork, Federal Work-Study, scholarships/grants, and unspecified assistantships available. Support available to part-time students. Financial award applicants required to submit FAFSA. *Unit head:* Dr. Joan Toglia, Dean, School of Health and Natural Sciences, 914-674-7837, E-mail: jtoglia@mercy.edu. *Application contact:* Allison Gurdineer, Senior Director of Admissions, 877-637-2946, Fax: 914-674-7382, E-mail: admissions@mercy.edu.
Website: https://www.mercy.edu/degrees-programs/ms-physician-assistant

Mercyhurst University, Graduate Studies, Program in Physician Assistant Studies, Erie, PA 16546. Offers MS.

Methodist University, School of Graduate Studies, Program in Physician Assistant Studies, Fayetteville, NC 28311-1498. Offers MMS. *Accreditation:* ARC-PA. *Degree requirements:* For master's, comprehensive exam. *Entrance requirements:* For master's, GRE, bachelor's degree from four-year, regionally-accredited college or university; minimum of 500 hours' clinical experience with direct patient contact; minimum GPA of 3.0 on all college level work attempted, 3.2 on medical core prerequisites (recommended). Additional exam requirements/recommendations for international students: Required—TOEFL (minimum score 500 paper-based; 60 iBT).

MGH Institute of Health Professions, School of Health and Rehabilitation Sciences, Program in Physician Assistant Studies, Boston, MA 02129. Offers MPAS.

Midwestern University, Downers Grove Campus, College of Health Sciences, Illinois Campus, Program in Physician Assistant Studies, Downers Grove, IL 60515-1235. Offers MMS. *Accreditation:* ARC-PA. *Entrance requirements:* For master's, GRE General Test. *Application deadline:* Applications are processed on a rolling basis. Application fee: $50. *Expenses:* Contact institution. *Financial support:* Federal Work-Study available.
Website: http://www.midwestern.edu/

Midwestern University, Glendale Campus, College of Health Sciences, Arizona Campus, Program in Physician Assistant Studies, Glendale, AZ 85308. Offers MMS. *Accreditation:* ARC-PA. *Entrance requirements:* For master's, GRE. *Application deadline:* Applications are processed on a rolling basis. Application fee: $50. *Expenses:* Contact institution. *Financial support:* Applicants required to submit FAFSA.

Milligan College, Area of Physician Assistant Studies, Milligan College, TN 37682. Offers MSPAS. *Degree requirements:* For master's, thesis or alternative. *Entrance requirements:* For master's, GRE, CASPA application, baccalaureate degree with minimum cumulative GPA of 3.0 overall and for prerequisite science courses, health care experience with minimum of 300 documented hours of direct patient care or observation experience, three references, background check, CPR certification. Additional exam requirements/recommendations for international students: Required—TOEFL (minimum score 550 paper-based, 79 iBT) or IELTS (6.5). *Application deadline:* For spring admission, 9/1 for domestic students. Electronic applications accepted. *Expenses:* $730 per hour tuition; $325 per semester tech/activity fees. *Financial support:* Scholarships/grants available. Financial award application deadline: 12/1; financial award applicants required to submit FAFSA. *Faculty research:* Development, maintenance and evaluation of clinical sites; curriculum development; PA program admissions process; student remediation; first-time test taker PANCE data. *Unit head:* Andrew Hull, Area Chair and Director, 423-461-1558, Fax: 423-461-1518, E-mail: awhull@milligan.edu. *Application contact:* Rebekah Bess, Program Secretary, 423-461-1557, Fax: 423-461-1518, E-mail: rbess@milligan.edu.
Website: http://www.milligan.edu/pa/

Missouri State University, Graduate College, College of Health and Human Services, Department of Physician Assistant Studies, Springfield, MO 65897. Offers MS. *Accreditation:* ARC-PA. *Faculty:* 6 full-time (4 women), 50 part-time/adjunct (11 women). *Students:* 63 full-time (45 women); includes 6 minority (5 Asian, non-Hispanic/Latino; 1 Hispanic/Latino). Average age 24. In 2017, 32 master's awarded. *Degree requirements:* For master's, comprehensive exam, thesis or alternative. *Entrance requirements:* For master's, GRE General Test, minimum GPA of 3.0; CASPA. Additional exam requirements/recommendations for international students: Required—TOEFL (minimum score 550 paper-based; 79 iBT), IELTS (minimum score 6). *Application deadline:* For spring admission, 8/1 for domestic and international students. Application fee: $35 ($50 for international students). Electronic applications accepted. *Expenses:* Tuition, state resident: full-time $2915; part-time $2021 per credit hour. Tuition, nonresident: full-time $5354; part-time $3647 per credit hour. *International tuition:* $11,992 full-time. *Required fees:* $173; $173 per credit hour. Tuition and fees vary according to class time, course level, course load, degree level, campus/location and program. *Financial support:* Application deadline: 3/31; applicants required to submit FAFSA. *Unit head:* Dr. Steven Dodge, Department Head, 417-836-6151, Fax: 417-836-6406, E-mail: physicianasststudies@missouristate.edu. *Application contact:* Stephanie Praschan, Director, Graduate Enrollment Management, 417-836-5330, Fax: 417-836-6200, E-mail: stephaniepraschan@missouristate.edu.
Website: http://www.missouristate.edu/pas/

Monmouth University, Graduate Studies, Marjorie K. Unterberg School of Nursing and Health Studies, West Long Branch, NJ 07764-1898. Offers adult-gerontological primary care nurse practitioner (MSN, Post-Master's Certificate); family nurse practitioner (MSN, Post-Master's Certificate); forensic nursing (MSN, Certificate); nursing (MSN); nursing administration (MSN); nursing education (MSN, Post-Master's Certificate); nursing practice (DNP); physician assistant (MS); psychiatric and mental health nurse practitioner (MSN, Post-Master's Certificate); school nursing (MSN, Certificate). *Accreditation:* AACN. *Program availability:* Part-time, evening/weekend, 100% online, blended/hybrid learning. *Faculty:* 12 full-time (all women), 20 part-time/adjunct (12 women). *Students:* 90 full-time (66 women), 329 part-time (302 women); includes 129 minority (51 Black or African American, non-Hispanic/Latino; 43 Asian, non-Hispanic/Latino; 31 Hispanic/Latino; 1 Native Hawaiian or other Pacific Islander, non-Hispanic/Latino; 3 Two or more races, non-Hispanic/Latino), 1 international. Average age 36. In 2017, 85 master's, 4 other advanced degrees awarded. *Degree requirements:* For master's, practicum (for some tracks); for doctorate, practicum, capstone course. *Entrance requirements:* For master's, GRE General Test (waived for MSN applicants with minimum B grade in each of the first four courses and for MS applicants with master's degree), BSN with minimum GPA of 2.75, current RN license, proof of liability and malpractice policy, personal statement, two letters of recommendation, college course work in health assessment, resume; CASPA application (for MS); for doctorate, accredited master's nursing program degree with minimum GPA of 3.2, active RN license, national certification as nurse practitioner or nurse administrator, working knowledge of statistics, statement of goals and vision for change, 2 letters of recommendation (professional or academic), resume, interview. Additional exam requirements/recommendations for international students: Required—TOEFL (minimum score 550 paper-based; 79 iBT), IELTS (minimum score 6) or Michigan English Language Assessment Battery (minimum score 77). *Application deadline:* For fall admission, 7/15 priority date for domestic students, 6/1 for international students; for spring admission, 12/1 priority date for domestic students, 11/1 for international students; for summer admission, 5/1 for domestic students. Applications are processed on a rolling basis. Application fee: $50. Electronic applications accepted. *Expenses:* Contact institution. *Financial support:* In 2017–18, 197 students received support. Institutionally sponsored loans, scholarships/grants, and unspecified assistantships available. Support available to part-time students. Financial award applicants required to submit FAFSA. *Faculty research:* School nursing, health policy, and smoking cessation in teens; Multiple Sclerosis; adherence and self-efficacy; aging issues and geriatric care. *Unit head:* Dr. Janet Mahoney, Dean, 732-571-3443, Fax: 732-263-5131, E-mail: jmahoney@monmouth.edu. *Application contact:* Lucia Fedele, Graduate Admission Counselor, 732-571-3452, Fax: 732-263-5123, E-mail: gradadm@monmouth.edu.
Website: https://www.monmouth.edu/graduate/nursing-programs-of-study/

New York Institute of Technology, School of Health Professions, Department of Physician Assistant Studies, Old Westbury, NY 11568-8000. Offers MS. *Accreditation:* ARC-PA. *Faculty:* 7 full-time (5 women), 16 part-time/adjunct (11 women). *Students:* 150 full-time (118 women), 3 part-time (all women); includes 49 minority (5 Black or African American, non-Hispanic/Latino; 23 Asian, non-Hispanic/Latino; 18 Hispanic/Latino; 3 Two or more races, non-Hispanic/Latino). Average age 25. 1,791 applicants, 6% accepted, 55 enrolled. In 2017, 46 master's awarded. *Entrance requirements:* For master's, bachelor's degree (preferably in science or health-related field); minimum undergraduate GPA of 3.0; academic record that includes a strong emphasis on science and math; minimum grade of B- in prerequisite courses; minimum of 100 hours of verifiable patient care experience in the U.S. healthcare system. Additional exam requirements/recommendations for international students: Required—TOEFL (minimum score 79 iBT), IELTS (minimum score 6). *Application deadline:* For fall admission, 10/1 for domestic and international students. Applications are processed on a rolling basis. Application fee: $50. Electronic applications accepted. *Expenses:* $1,285 per credit plus fees. *Financial support:* Federal Work-Study, scholarships/grants, tuition waivers (full and partial), and unspecified assistantships available. Support available to part-time students. Financial award application deadline: 2/15; financial award applicants required to submit FAFSA. *Faculty research:* Healthcare workforce issues, point-of-care ultrasound, cultural competency, palliative care, diet and disease prevention. *Unit head:* Dr. Zehra Ahmed, Department Chair, 516-686-3871, E-mail: zahmed01@nyit.edu. *Application contact:* Alice Dolitsky, Director, Graduate Admissions, 516-686-7520, Fax: 516-686-1116, E-mail: nyitgrad@nyit.edu.
Website: http://www.nyit.edu/degrees/physician_assistant_studies

Northern Arizona University, College of Health and Human Services, Department of Physician Assistant Studies, Phoenix, AZ 85004. Offers MPAS. *Faculty:* 6 full-time (4 women), 13 part-time/adjunct (11 women). *Students:* 100 full-time (70 women), 1 part-time (0 women); includes 44 minority (4 Black or African American, non-Hispanic/Latino; 2 American Indian or Alaska Native, non-Hispanic/Latino; 4 Asian, non-Hispanic/Latino; 24 Hispanic/Latino; 10 Two or more races, non-Hispanic/Latino). Average age 28. 684 applicants, 8% accepted, 53 enrolled. In 2017, 46 master's awarded. *Degree*

requirements: For master's, variable foreign language requirement, comprehensive exam (for some programs), thesis (for some programs), fieldwork experience/internship. *Entrance requirements:* For master's, GRE General Test, minimum overall and science course GPA of 3.0; minimum of 40 credits of science courses; minimum of 500 hours of direct patient care experience, paid or volunteer; in-person interview. Additional exam requirements/recommendations for international students: Required—TOEFL (minimum score 80 iBT), IELTS (minimum score 6.5). *Application deadline:* For fall admission, 9/1 for domestic and international students. Application fee: $65. Electronic applications accepted. *Expenses:* Tuition, state resident: full-time $9240; part-time $458 per credit hour. Tuition, nonresident: full-time $21,588; part-time $1199 per credit hour. *Required fees:* $1021; $14 per credit hour. $646 per semester. Tuition and fees vary according to course load, campus/location and program. *Financial support:* Institutionally sponsored loans available. Financial award application deadline: 2/1; financial award applicants required to submit FAFSA. *Unit head:* Elias Villarreal, Jr., Chair, 602-827-2828, E-mail: paprog@nau.edu. *Application contact:* Tina Sutton, Coordinator, Graduate College, 928-523-4348, Fax: 928-523-8950, E-mail: graduate@nau.edu.
Website: https://nau.edu/CHHS/PA/

Nova Southeastern University, Dr. Pallavi Patel College of Health Care Sciences, Fort Lauderdale, FL 33314-7796. Offers anesthesiologist assistant (MSA); audiology (Au D); health science (MH Sc, DHSc, PhD); occupational therapy (MOT, Dr OT, PhD); physical therapy (DPT, TDPT); physician assistant (MMS); speech-language pathology (MS). *Accreditation:* AOTA. *Faculty:* 54 full-time (31 women), 15 part-time/adjunct (7 women). *Students:* 501 full-time (407 women); includes 131 minority (18 Black or African American, non-Hispanic/Latino; 2 American Indian or Alaska Native, non-Hispanic/Latino; 45 Asian, non-Hispanic/Latino; 65 Hispanic/Latino; 1 Two or more races, non-Hispanic/Latino). Average age 24. 7,600 applicants, 7% accepted, 452 enrolled. In 2017, 616 master's, 225 doctorates awarded. *Degree requirements:* For doctorate, comprehensive exam, thesis/dissertation (for some programs), 12-month full-time clinical externship experience. *Entrance requirements:* For master's, GRE General Test; for doctorate, GRE General Test, personal interview, essay in application, on-site essay. *Application deadline:* For spring admission, 2/15 for domestic and international students; for summer admission, 12/1 for domestic and international students. Applications are processed on a rolling basis. Application fee: $50. Electronic applications accepted. *Expenses:* Contact institution. *Financial support:* Federal Work-Study, institutionally sponsored loans, and scholarships/grants available. Financial award application deadline: 4/15; financial award applicants required to submit FAFSA. *Faculty research:* Efferent suppression and auditory processing delay, subjective visual vertical in vestibular assessment, competency-based clinical evaluation, hearing instrument performance for frequency lowering, hearing instrument performance for noise suppression, anxiety and dizziness in college students, audiology assistants. *Unit head:* Dr. Stanley Wilson, Dean, 954-262-1203, E-mail: swilson@nova.edu. *Application contact:* Joey Jankie, Admissions Counselor, 954-262-7249, E-mail: joey@nova.edu.
Website: http://healthsciences.nova.edu/

Ohio Dominican University, Division of Physician Assistant Studies, Columbus, OH 43219-2099. Offers physician assistant studies (MS). *Faculty:* 7 full-time (4 women), 2 part-time/adjunct (0 women). *Students:* 101 full-time (73 women), 48 part-time (31 women); includes 11 minority (1 Black or African American, non-Hispanic/Latino; 1 American Indian or Alaska Native, non-Hispanic/Latino; 4 Asian, non-Hispanic/Latino; 3 Hispanic/Latino; 2 Two or more races, non-Hispanic/Latino). Average age 25. 504 applicants, 15% accepted, 49 enrolled. In 2017, 48 master's awarded. *Entrance requirements:* For master's, GRE and/or MCAT, bachelor's degree from accredited college or university with minimum GPA of 3.0 overall and in science; minimum of 250 hours of documented patient-care experience. Additional exam requirements/ recommendations for international students: Required—TOEFL (minimum score 550 paper-based), IELTS (minimum score 6.5). *Application deadline:* For fall admission, 10/1 for domestic and international students. Applications are processed on a rolling basis. Electronic applications accepted. *Expenses:* Contact institution. *Financial support:* Applicants required to submit FAFSA. *Unit head:* Prof. Shonna Riedlinger, Program Director, 614-251-8988, E-mail: riedlins@ohiodominican.edu. *Application contact:* John W. Naughton, Associate Vice President for Enrollment Management, 614-251-4721, Fax: 614-251-6654, E-mail: grad@ohiodominican.edu.
Website: http://www.ohiodominican.edu/academics/graduate/mspas

Oregon Health & Science University, School of Medicine, Graduate Programs in Medicine, Division of Physician Assistant Education, Portland, OR 97239-3098. Offers physician assistant studies (MPAS). *Accreditation:* ARC-PA. *Faculty:* 6 full-time (5 women), 10 part-time/adjunct (7 women). *Students:* 82 full-time (56 women); includes 27 minority (6 Black or African American, non-Hispanic/Latino; 1 American Indian or Alaska Native, non-Hispanic/Latino; 6 Asian, non-Hispanic/Latino; 7 Hispanic/Latino; 7 Two or more races, non-Hispanic/Latino), 2 international. Average age 30. 1,592 applicants, 3% accepted, 42 enrolled. In 2017, 41 master's awarded. *Entrance requirements:* For master's, GRE, bachelor's degree, 2000 hours of health care experience. *Application deadline:* For fall admission, 10/1 for domestic students. Electronic applications accepted. *Expenses:* Contact institution. *Financial support:* Application deadline: 3/1; applicants required to submit FAFSA. *Unit head:* J. Glenn Forister, Program Director/ Division Head, E-mail: papgrm@ohsu.edu. *Application contact:* Colleen Schierholtz, Director of Admissions, 503-494-1408, E-mail: paprgm@ohsu.edu.
Website: http://www.ohsu.edu/xd/education/schools/school-of-medicine/academic-programs/physician-assistant/index.cfm

Pace University, College of Health Professions, Department of Physician Assistant Studies, New York, NY 10038. Offers MS. *Accreditation:* ARC-PA. *Faculty:* 10 full-time (all women). *Students:* 149 full-time (121 women), 191 part-time (155 women); includes 92 minority (6 Black or African American, non-Hispanic/Latino; 1 American Indian or Alaska Native, non-Hispanic/Latino; 50 Asian, non-Hispanic/Latino; 27 Hispanic/Latino; 8 Two or more races, non-Hispanic/Latino). Average age 28. 1,469 applicants, 10% accepted, 77 enrolled. In 2017, 364 master's awarded. *Degree requirements:* For master's, summative evaluations including 2 objective structured clinical evaluations and comprehensive written clinical exam; final paper; final project including clinical review article suitable for publication in JAAPA. *Entrance requirements:* For master's, baccalaureate degree from accredited institution, minimum science and cumulative GPA of 3.0, minimum 200 hours of direct patient care, 3 references from professionals (1 must be a health care professional), completion of all prerequisite courses at time of CASPA e-submission, no more than 1 grade that is less than a B- in a prerequisite course. Additional exam requirements/recommendations for international students: Required—TOEFL (minimum score 100 iBT), IELTS (minimum score 7.5) or PTE (minimum score 61). *Application deadline:* For spring admission, 9/1 for domestic and international students. Applications are processed on a rolling basis. Application fee: $70. Electronic applications accepted. *Financial support:* Institutionally sponsored loans and scholarships/grants available. Financial award application deadline: 2/15; financial award applicants required to submit FAFSA. *Unit head:* Susan Cappelmann, Program Director, 212-618-6052, E-mail: paprogram_admissions@pace.edu. *Application contact:* Susan Ford-Goldschein, Director of Graduate Admissions, 212-346-1531, Fax: 212-346-1585, E-mail: graduateadmission@pace.edu.
Website: http://www.pace.edu/physician-assistant/

Pace University, College of Health Professions, Physician Assistant Program - Pleasantville, New York, NY 10038. Offers MS. *Students:* 30 full-time (23 women); includes 16 minority (2 Black or African American, non-Hispanic/Latino; 6 Asian, non-Hispanic/Latino; 8 Hispanic/Latino). Average age 25. 85 applicants, 41% accepted, 30 enrolled. *Degree requirements:* For master's, comprehensive exam. *Entrance requirements:* For master's, baccalaureate degree from accredited institution, minimum GPA of 3.0, minimum 500 hours of patient care experience, personal statement, resume, three references (one must be health professional), no more than one grade less than a B-. Additional exam requirements/recommendations for international students: Required—TOEFL (minimum score 102 iBT); Recommended—IELTS (minimum score 7.5), TSE (minimum score 73). *Application deadline:* For fall admission, 1/1 for domestic students. Applications are processed on a rolling basis. Application fee: $70. *Financial support:* Application deadline: 8/1; applicants required to submit FAFSA. *Unit head:* Steven Sweitzer, Director, 914-773-3005, Fax: 914-989-8652, E-mail: ssweitzer@pace.edu. *Application contact:* Susan Ford-Goldschein, Dean of Graduate Admissions, 212-346-1531, Fax: 212-346-1585, E-mail: graduateadmission@pace.edu.
Website: http://www.pace.edu/college-health-professions/graduate-degree-programs/physician-assistant-program-pleasantville

Pacific University, School of Physician Assistant Studies, Forest Grove, OR 97116-1797. Offers MS. *Accreditation:* ARC-PA. *Degree requirements:* For master's, comprehensive exam, thesis, clinical project. *Entrance requirements:* For master's, minimum of 1000 hours of direct clinical patient care, prerequisite coursework in science with minimum C average. Additional exam requirements/recommendations for international students: Required—TOEFL (minimum score 600 paper-based). *Expenses:* Contact institution. *Faculty research:* Public health, evidenced based medicine.

Philadelphia College of Osteopathic Medicine, Graduate and Professional Programs, Physician Assistant Studies Program, Philadelphia, PA 19131-1694. Offers health sciences (MS). *Accreditation:* ARC-PA. *Faculty:* 9 full-time (6 women), 34 part-time/ adjunct (11 women). *Students:* 108 full-time (91 women); includes 31 minority (4 Black or African American, non-Hispanic/Latino; 4 Asian, non-Hispanic/Latino; 6 Hispanic/ Latino; 17 Two or more races, non-Hispanic/Latino). Average age 25. 2,011 applicants, 4% accepted, 55 enrolled. In 2017, 51 master's awarded. *Degree requirements:* For master's, thesis. *Entrance requirements:* For master's, minimum GPA of 3.0; 200 hours of patient contact. Additional exam requirements/recommendations for international students: Required—TOEFL (minimum score 79 iBT). *Application deadline:* For fall admission, 12/1 for domestic students. Applications are processed on a rolling basis. Application fee: $75. Electronic applications accepted. *Expenses:* Contact institution. *Financial support:* In 2017–18, 80 students received support. Federal Work-Study, institutionally sponsored loans, and scholarships/grants available. Financial award application deadline: 3/15; financial award applicants required to submit FAFSA. *Unit head:* Laura Levy, Program Director, 215-871-6772, E-mail: lauramo@pcom.edu. *Application contact:* Kevin A. Zajac, Assistant Director of Admissions, 215-871-6700, E-mail: kevinzaj@pcom.edu.
Website: http://www.pcom.edu

Quinnipiac University, School of Health Sciences, Program for Physician Assistant, Hamden, CT 06518-1940. Offers MHS. *Accreditation:* ARC-PA. *Faculty:* 8 full-time (7 women), 25 part-time/adjunct (11 women). *Students:* 106 full-time (73 women), 1 (woman) part-time; includes 21 minority (1 Black or African American, non-Hispanic/ Latino; 10 Asian, non-Hispanic/Latino; 9 Hispanic/Latino; 1 Two or more races, non-Hispanic/Latino), 1 international. 1,086 applicants, 7% accepted, 54 enrolled. In 2017, 61 master's awarded. *Degree requirements:* For master's, comprehensive exam. *Entrance requirements:* For master's, minimum GPA of 3.2; course work in biological, physical, and behavioral sciences; interviews; 2500 hours of direct patient care experience. *Application deadline:* For summer admission, 9/1 for domestic students. Electronic applications accepted. *Financial support:* Scholarships/grants and unspecified assistantships available. Financial award application deadline: 5/1; financial award applicants required to submit FAFSA. *Application contact:* Office of Graduate Admissions, 800-462-1944, Fax: 203-582-3443, E-mail: paadmissions@qu.edu.
Website: http://www.qu.edu/gradphysicianasst

Rocky Mountain College, Program in Physician Assistant Studies, Billings, MT 59102-1796. Offers MPAS. *Accreditation:* ARC-PA. *Faculty:* 4 full-time (3 women), 3 part-time/ adjunct (1 woman). *Students:* 72 full-time (41 women); includes 5 minority (3 Asian, non-Hispanic/Latino; 1 Hispanic/Latino; 1 Two or more races, non-Hispanic/Latino). Average age 27. In 2017, 36 master's awarded. *Entrance requirements:* For master's, GRE (minimum combined verbal and quantitative score of 291), 1500 hours of direct, hands-on patient care. Additional exam requirements/recommendations for international students: Required—TOEFL (minimum score 570 paper-based; 88 iBT), IELTS (minimum score 6.5). *Application deadline:* Applications are processed on a rolling basis. Application fee: $45. Electronic applications accepted. *Expenses:* Contact institution. *Financial support:* Applicants required to submit FAFSA. *Unit head:* Heather Heggem, Program Director, 406-657-1190, E-mail: heather.heggem@rocky.edu. *Application contact:* Calley Thompson, PA Admissions Counselor, 406-657-1198, E-mail: calley.thompson@rocky.edu.
Website: http://rocky.edu/academics/academic-programs/graduate-programs/mpas/index.php

Rocky Mountain University of Health Professions, Program in Physician Assistant Studies, Provo, UT 84606. Offers MPAS.

Rocky Vista University, Program in Physician Assistant Studies, Parker, CO 80134. Offers MPAS.

Rosalind Franklin University of Medicine and Science, College of Health Professions, Physician Assistant Department, North Chicago, IL 60064-3095. Offers MS. *Accreditation:* ARC-PA. *Degree requirements:* For master's, thesis. *Entrance requirements:* For master's, GRE, writing sample. Additional exam requirements/ recommendations for international students: Required—TOEFL. Electronic applications accepted. *Faculty research:* Ortho-spine, diabetes education, cultural competency, interprofessional medical education.

Rush University, College of Health Sciences, Physician Assistant Studies Program, Chicago, IL 60612-3832. Offers MS. *Entrance requirements:* For master's, GRE General Test. Additional exam requirements/recommendations for international students: Required—TOEFL (minimum score 570 paper-based; 88 iBT). *Application deadline:* For summer admission, 12/1 for domestic students. Electronic applications accepted. *Unit head:* Regina Chen, Director, 312-563-3234, E-mail: pa_admissions@rush.edu. *Application contact:* 312-942-7120, E-mail: chs_admissions@rush.edu.

Rutgers University–Newark, School of Health Related Professions, Department of Primary Care, Physician Assistant Program, Newark, NJ 07102. Offers MS. *Accreditation:* ARC-PA. *Degree requirements:* For master's, internship. *Entrance requirements:* For master's, GRE, interview, minimum GPA of 3.0, BS, 3 reference letters. Additional exam requirements/recommendations for international students: Required—TOEFL. Electronic applications accepted.

Sacred Heart University, Graduate Programs, College of Health Professions, Department of Physician Assistant Studies, Fairfield, CT 06825. Offers MPAS. *Faculty:*

5 full-time (1 woman), 2 part-time/adjunct (1 woman). *Students:* 60 full-time (46 women); includes 22 minority (3 Black or African American, non-Hispanic/Latino; 13 Asian, non-Hispanic/Latino; 5 Hispanic/Latino; 1 Two or more races, non-Hispanic/Latino). Average age 27. 640 applicants, 9% accepted, 34 enrolled. Application fee: $75. *Expenses:* Contact institution. *Unit head:* Dr. Teresa Thetford, Chair, 203-989-9237, E-mail: thetfordt@sacredheart.edu. *Application contact:* Tara Chudy, Executive Director of Graduate Admissions, 203-365-4735, Fax: 203-365-4732, E-mail: chudyt@sacredheart.edu.

St. Ambrose University, College of Health and Human Services, Program in Physician Assistant Studies, Davenport, IA 52803-2898. Offers MPAS.

St. Catherine University, Graduate Programs, Program in Physician Assistant Studies, St. Paul, MN 55105. Offers MPAS. *Entrance requirements:* For master's, GRE, personal essay. *Application deadline:* For fall admission, 9/1 for domestic students. Application fee: $35. *Expenses:* Contact institution. *Financial support:* Applicants required to submit FAFSA. *Unit head:* Heather Bidinger, Director, 651-690-7880, E-mail: hkbidinger@stkate.edu.
Website: https://www.stkate.edu/academics/graduate-degrees/academic-programs/mpas

Saint Francis University, Department of Physician Assistant Sciences, Loretto, PA 15940-0600. Offers MPAS. *Accreditation:* ARC-PA. *Faculty:* 9 full-time (7 women), 3 part-time/adjunct (2 women). *Students:* 47 full-time (38 women), 3 part-time (2 women); includes 1 minority (Asian, non-Hispanic/Latino). Average age 22. In 2017, 52 master's awarded. *Degree requirements:* For master's, capstone, summative evaluation. *Entrance requirements:* For master's, interview. Additional exam requirements/recommendations for international students: Required—TOEFL (minimum score 550 paper-based; 70 iBT). *Application deadline:* For fall admission, 10/1 for domestic and international students. Applications are processed on a rolling basis. Application fee: $175. Electronic applications accepted. *Expenses:* Contact institution. *Financial support:* Applicants required to submit FAFSA. *Unit head:* Marie Link, 814-472-3128, E-mail: mlink@francis.edu.
Website: http://francis.edu/physician-assistant-science/

Saint Louis University, Graduate Programs, Doisy College of Health Sciences, Department of Physician Assistant Education, St. Louis, MO 63103. Offers MMS. *Accreditation:* ARC-PA. *Entrance requirements:* Additional exam requirements/recommendations for international students: Required—TOEFL (minimum score 86 iBT). Electronic applications accepted.

Salus University, College of Health Sciences, Elkins Park, PA 19027-1598. Offers physician assistant (MMS); public health (MPH). *Accreditation:* ARC-PA. *Entrance requirements:* For master's, GRE (recommended). Additional exam requirements/recommendations for international students: Required—TOEFL. Electronic applications accepted.

Samuel Merritt University, Department of Physician Assistant Studies, Oakland, CA 94609-3108. Offers MPA. *Accreditation:* ARC-PA. *Faculty:* 10 full-time (5 women), 18 part-time/adjunct (9 women). *Students:* 89 full-time (62 women), 47 part-time (38 women); includes 80 minority (9 Black or African American, non-Hispanic/Latino; 34 Asian, non-Hispanic/Latino; 31 Hispanic/Latino; 1 Native Hawaiian or other Pacific Islander, non-Hispanic/Latino; 5 Two or more races, non-Hispanic/Latino). 2,174 applicants, 2% accepted, 44 enrolled. In 2017, 40 master's awarded. *Entrance requirements:* For master's, health care experience, minimum GPA of 3.0, previous course work in statistics. Additional exam requirements/recommendations for international students: Required—TOEFL (minimum score 100 iBT). *Application deadline:* For fall admission, 10/1 priority date for domestic students. Application fee: $175. Electronic applications accepted. *Expenses:* $50,943 annual tuition for first year. *Financial support:* Federal Work-Study, institutionally sponsored loans, and scholarships/grants available. Financial award applicants required to submit FAFSA. *Application contact:* Timothy Cranford, Dean of Admission, 510-869-1550, Fax: 510-869-6525, E-mail: admission@samuelmerritt.edu.
Website: http://www.samuelmerritt.edu/

Seton Hall University, School of Health and Medical Sciences, Physician Assistant Program, South Orange, NJ 07079-2697. Offers MS. *Accreditation:* ARC-PA. *Entrance requirements:* For master's, GRE, health care experience, interview, minimum GPA of 3.0. Additional exam requirements/recommendations for international students: Required—TOEFL. Electronic applications accepted.

Seton Hill University, Master of Science Program in Physician Assistant, Greensburg, PA 15601. Offers MS. *Accreditation:* ARC-PA. *Entrance requirements:* For master's, minimum GPA of 3.2, transcripts, 3 letters of recommendation, personal statement. Additional exam requirements/recommendations for international students: Required—TOEFL (minimum score 650 paper-based; 114 iBT), IELTS (minimum score 7). *Application deadline:* Applications are processed on a rolling basis. Electronic applications accepted. *Expenses: Tuition:* Part-time $734 per credit. Tuition and fees vary according to class time, course level, course load and program. *Financial support:* Application deadline: 8/15; applicants required to submit FAFSA.
Website: http://www.setonhill.edu/academics/gradaute_programs/physician_assistant

Shenandoah University, School of Health Professions, Winchester, VA 22601. Offers athletic training (MSAT); non-traditional physical therapy (MS); occupational training (MS); performing arts medicine (Certificate); physician assistant studies (MS); public health (MPH, Certificate); transitional physical therapy (DPT). *Program availability:* Part-time, all online except for two on-site weekend sessions (for DPT). *Faculty:* 35 full-time (27 women), 18 part-time/adjunct (13 women). *Students:* 446 full-time (355 women), 134 part-time (112 women); includes 78 minority (14 Black or African American, non-Hispanic/Latino; 28 Asian, non-Hispanic/Latino; 25 Hispanic/Latino; 11 Two or more races, non-Hispanic/Latino), 22 international. Average age 28. 839 applicants, 31% accepted, 166 enrolled. In 2017, 100 master's, 75 doctorates, 4 other advanced degrees awarded. *Degree requirements:* For master's and Certificate, thesis; for doctorate, comprehensive exam. *Entrance requirements:* For master's, GRE; for doctorate, GRE, minimum cumulative and prerequisite GPA of 2.8. Additional exam requirements/recommendations for international students: Required—TOEFL (minimum score 558 paper-based; 83 iBT). *Application deadline:* For fall admission, 10/1 for domestic and international students; for summer admission, 4/1 for domestic and international students. Application fee: $30. Electronic applications accepted. *Expenses:* Contact institution. *Financial support:* In 2017–18, 53 students received support. Scholarships/grants and unspecified assistantships available. Financial award applicants required to submit FAFSA. *Faculty research:* 3D motion analysis of running mechanics; quality improvement in clinical practice; functional movement screen to predict injury in professional athletes and dancers; sensory integration for children with autism; chronic ankle instability. *Total annual research expenditures:* $15,000. *Unit head:* Dr. Karen Elizabeth Abraham, Dean of School of Health Professions, 540-545.6209, Fax: 540-665.5530, E-mail: kabraham@su.edu. *Application contact:* Jon Brannon, Graduate Admissions Specialist, Office of Admissions, 540-545-7394, Fax: 540-665-4627, E-mail: jbannan09@su.edu.
Website: http://www.health.su.edu

Slippery Rock University of Pennsylvania, Graduate Studies (Recruitment), College of Health, Environment, and Science, Department of Physician Assistant Studies, Slippery Rock, PA 16057-1383. Offers MS. *Degree requirements:* For master's, clinical rotations. *Entrance requirements:* Additional exam requirements/recommendations for international students: Required—TOEFL (minimum score 550 paper-based; 80 iBT). Electronic applications accepted. *Expenses:* Contact institution.

South College, Program in Physician Assistant Studies, Knoxville, TN 37917. Offers MHS. *Accreditation:* ARC-PA.

Southern Illinois University Carbondale, Graduate School, Graduate Programs in Medicine, Program in Physician Assistant Studies, Carbondale, IL 62901-4701. Offers MSPA. *Accreditation:* ARC-PA. *Entrance requirements:* For master's, GRE, MAT, or MCAT. Additional exam requirements/recommendations for international students: Required—TOEFL.

South University, Graduate Programs, College of Health Professions, Program in Physician Assistant Studies, Savannah, GA 31406. Offers MS. *Accreditation:* ARC-PA.

South University, Program in Physician Assistant Studies, Tampa, FL 33614. Offers MS.

Springfield College, Graduate Programs, Program in Physician Assistant, Springfield, MA 01109-3797. Offers MS. *Accreditation:* ARC-PA. *Program availability:* Part-time. *Faculty:* 6 full-time, 5 part-time/adjunct. *Students:* 70 full-time. Average age 21. In 2017, 37 master's awarded. *Degree requirements:* For master's, comprehensive exam. *Entrance requirements:* Additional exam requirements/recommendations for international students: Required—TOEFL (minimum score 550 paper-based); Recommended—IELTS (minimum score 7). *Application deadline:* For spring admission, 6/1 for domestic and international students. Applications are processed on a rolling basis. Application fee: $50. Electronic applications accepted. *Financial support:* Fellowships with partial tuition reimbursements, teaching assistantships with partial tuition reimbursements, career-related internships or fieldwork, Federal Work-Study, institutionally sponsored loans, scholarships/grants, and unspecified assistantships available. Financial award application deadline: 3/1; financial award applicants required to submit FAFSA. *Unit head:* Charles Milch, Director, 413-748-3554, Fax: 413-748-3595, E-mail: cmilch@springfieldcollege.edu. *Application contact:* Anne Griffin, Director of Graduate Admissions, 413-748-3524, Fax: 413-748-3694, E-mail: agriffin2@springfield.edu.
Website: http://springfield.edu/gradpa

Stephens College, Division of Graduate and Continuing Studies, Columbia, MO 65215-0002. Offers counseling (M Ed), including addictions counseling, clinical mental health counseling, school counseling; health information administration (Postbaccalaureate Certificate); physician assistant studies (MPAS); TV and screenwriting (MFA). *Program availability:* Part-time, evening/weekend, online learning. *Entrance requirements:* For master's, minimum GPA of 3.0 in last 60 hours. Additional exam requirements/recommendations for international students: Required—TOEFL (minimum score 79 iBT). Electronic applications accepted. *Faculty research:* Educational psychology, outcomes assessment.

Stony Brook University, State University of New York, Stony Brook Medicine, School of Health Technology and Management, Stony Brook, NY 11794. Offers applied health informatics (MS); disability studies (Certificate); health administration (MHA); health and rehabilitation sciences (PhD); health care management (Advanced Certificate); health care policy and management (MS); occupational therapy (MS); physical therapy (DPT); physician assistant (MS). *Accreditation:* APTA. *Faculty:* 62 full-time (42 women), 59 part-time/adjunct (36 women). *Students:* 565 full-time (382 women), 67 part-time (53 women); includes 179 minority (29 Black or African American, non-Hispanic/Latino; 83 Asian, non-Hispanic/Latino; 59 Hispanic/Latino; 2 Native Hawaiian or other Pacific Islander, non-Hispanic/Latino; 6 Two or more races, non-Hispanic/Latino), 14 international. Average age 27. 2,516 applicants, 16% accepted, 266 enrolled. In 2017, 162 master's, 84 doctorates, 39 other advanced degrees awarded. *Degree requirements:* For master's, thesis; for doctorate, thesis/dissertation. *Entrance requirements:* For master's, GRE General Test, minimum GPA of 3.0, work experience in field, references; for doctorate, GRE, three references, essay. Additional exam requirements/recommendations for international students: Required—TOEFL (minimum score 550 paper-based). *Application deadline:* For fall admission, 1/15 for domestic students; for spring admission, 10/1 for domestic students. Application fee: $100. *Expenses:* Contact institution. *Financial support:* Fellowships, research assistantships, teaching assistantships, career-related internships or fieldwork, Federal Work-Study, and institutionally sponsored loans available. Financial award application deadline: 3/15. *Faculty research:* Developmental disabilities, disability studies, health promotion, multiple sclerosis, quality of life program, internal medicine, lung disease, palliative care, respiratory diseases, neuromuscular disorders, orthopedics, physical medicine and rehabilitation, physical therapy, prostheses or implants, advance directives, advocacy alienation, allied health education, allied health occupations, adolescents, adoption, child or adolescent mental health, multiple sclerosis, youth policy. *Total annual research expenditures:* $1.2 million. *Unit head:* Dr. Carlos Vidal, Dean, 631-444-1009, Fax: 631-444-7621, E-mail: carlos.vidal@stonybrook.edu. *Application contact:* Frances Shaw, 631-444-3240, Fax: 631-444-7621, E-mail: frances.shaw@stonybrook.edu.
Website: http://healthtechnology.stonybrookmedicine.edu/

Texas Tech University Health Sciences Center, School of Health Professions, Program in Physician Assistant Studies, Midland, TX 79705. Offers MPAS. *Accreditation:* ARC-PA. *Faculty:* 6 full-time (3 women), 2 part-time/adjunct (1 woman). *Students:* 111 full-time (86 women); includes 60 minority (10 Black or African American, non-Hispanic/Latino; 1 American Indian or Alaska Native, non-Hispanic/Latino; 18 Asian, non-Hispanic/Latino; 31 Hispanic/Latino). Average age 27. 1,628 applicants, 7% accepted, 58 enrolled. In 2017, 57 master's awarded. *Entrance requirements:* For master's, GRE. *Application deadline:* For summer admission, 10/1 priority date for domestic students. Applications are processed on a rolling basis. Application fee: $75. Electronic applications accepted. *Financial support:* Career-related internships or fieldwork, institutionally sponsored loans, and scholarships/grants available. Financial award application deadline: 9/1; financial award applicants required to submit FAFSA. *Unit head:* Christina Robohm, Program Director, 432-620-1120, Fax: 432-620-8605, E-mail: christina.robohm@ttuhsc.edu. *Application contact:* Lindsay Johnson, Associate Dean for Admissions and Student Affairs, 806-743-3220, Fax: 806-743-2994, E-mail: lindsay.johnson@ttuhsc.edu.
Website: http://www.ttuhsc.edu/health-professions/master-physician-assistant-studies/

Thomas Jefferson University, College of Science, Health and the Liberal Arts, Program in Physician Assistant Studies, Philadelphia, PA 19107. Offers MS. *Accreditation:* ARC-PA. *Entrance requirements:* For master's, MCAT, GRE, or MAT. Additional exam requirements/recommendations for international students: Required—TOEFL (minimum score 550 paper-based; 79 iBT), IELTS (minimum score 6.5).

Thomas Jefferson University, Jefferson College of Health Professions, Department of Physician Assistant Studies, Philadelphia, PA 19107. Offers MS. *Degree requirements:* For master's, comprehensive exam, thesis. *Entrance requirements:* Additional exam requirements/recommendations for international students: Required—TOEFL (minimum score 87 iBT). Electronic applications accepted.

Touro College, School of Health Sciences, Bay Shore, NY 11706. Offers industrial-organizational psychology (MS); mental health counseling (MS); occupational therapy (MS); physical therapy (DPT); physician assistant (MS); speech-language pathology (MS). *Faculty:* 81 full-time (55 women), 77 part-time/adjunct (46 women). *Students:* 628 full-time (470 women), 113 part-time (73 women); includes 143 minority (31 Black or African American, non-Hispanic/Latino; 1 American Indian or Alaska Native, non-Hispanic/Latino; 61 Asian, non-Hispanic/Latino; 42 Hispanic/Latino; 1 Native Hawaiian or other Pacific Islander, non-Hispanic/Latino; 7 Two or more races, non-Hispanic/Latino), 63 international. Average age 28. *Expenses:* Contact institution. *Financial support:* Fellowships available. *Unit head:* Dr. Louis Primavera, Dean, School of Health Sciences, 516-673-3200, E-mail: louis.primavera@touro.edu. *Application contact:* Brian J. Diele, Director of Student Administrative Services, 631-665-1600 Ext. 6311, E-mail: brian.diele@touro.edu.

Towson University, College of Health Professions, Program in Physician Assistant Studies, Towson, MD 21252-0001. Offers MS. *Accreditation:* ARC-PA. *Students:* 79 full-time (51 women); includes 31 minority (8 Black or African American, non-Hispanic/Latino; 14 Asian, non-Hispanic/Latino; 6 Hispanic/Latino; 3 Two or more races, non-Hispanic/Latino), 2 international. *Entrance requirements:* For master's, bachelor's degree with minimum GPA of 3.0, completion of prerequisite math and science courses, minimum of 800 hours of patient contact experience or medical/health-related experience. Additional exam requirements/recommendations for international students: Required—TOEFL (minimum score 550 paper-based; 80 iBT). *Application deadline:* For fall admission, 1/17 for domestic students, 5/15 for international students; for spring admission, 10/15 for domestic students, 12/1 for international students. Applications are processed on a rolling basis. Application fee: $45. Electronic applications accepted. *Expenses:* Contact institution. *Financial support:* Application deadline: 4/1. *Unit head:* Mark McKinnon, Graduate Program Director, 410-704-2016, E-mail: paprogram@towson.edu. *Application contact:* Coverley Beidleman, Assistant Director of Graduate Admissions, 410-704-5630, Fax: 410-704-3030, E-mail: cbeidleman@towson.edu.
Website: https://www.towson.edu/chp/departments/interprofessional/grad/physassistant/

Trevecca Nazarene University, Graduate Physician Assistant Program, Nashville, TN 37210-2877. Offers MS. *Accreditation:* ARC-PA. *Faculty:* 5 full-time (all women), 4 part-time/adjunct (3 women). *Students:* 93 full-time (70 women), 1 part-time (0 women); includes 8 minority (1 Black or African American, non-Hispanic/Latino; 5 Asian, non-Hispanic/Latino; 2 Hispanic/Latino). Average age 25. In 2017, 45 master's awarded. *Degree requirements:* For master's, comprehensive exam, 9 clinical skills rotations, professional assessment, OSCE exam. *Entrance requirements:* For master's, GRE (minimum score: 300 combined verbal and quantitative), minimum cumulative and science GPA of 3.25; 3 letters of recommendation (one by physician assistant); minimum of 250 hours of direct patient care and 10 hours of shadowing; prerequisites in human anatomy and physiology with lab, general chemistry with lab, microbiology with lab, general psychology, developmental psychology, and medical terminology. Additional exam requirements/recommendations for international students: Required—TOEFL (minimum score 550 paper-based; 80 iBT). *Application deadline:* For fall admission, 10/1 for domestic students. *Expenses:* $13,185 per semester. *Financial support:* Applicants required to submit FAFSA. *Unit head:* Bret Reeves, Director, 615-248-1225, E-mail: admissions_pa@trevecca.edu. *Application contact:* 615-248-1225, E-mail: admissions_pa@trevecca.edu.
Website: http://www.trevecca.edu/pa

Trine University, Program in Physician Assistant Studies, Angola, IN 46703-1764. Offers MPAS. *Expenses:* $13,150 per semester. *Unit head:* Dr. Emilio de Jesus Vazquez, Interim Director, 260-702-3597, E-mail: vazqueze@trine.edu. *Application contact:* Kristina Brewer, Admissions Coordinator, 260-665-4161, E-mail: brewerk@trine.edu.
Website: https://www.trine.edu/academics/majors-degrees/graduate/master-physician-assistant-studies/

Tufts University, School of Medicine, Public Health and Professional Degree Programs, Boston, MA 02111. Offers biomedical sciences (MS); health communication (MS, Certificate); pain research, education and policy (MS, Certificate); physician assistant (MS); public health (MPH, Dr PH), including behavioral science (MPH), biostatistics (MPH), epidemiology (MPH), health communication (MPH), health services (MPH), management and policy (MPH), nutrition (MPH); DMD/MPH; DVM/MPH; JD/MPH; MD/MPH; MMS/MPH; MS/MBA; MS/MPH. *Accreditation:* CEPH (one or more programs are accredited). *Program availability:* Part-time, evening/weekend. *Faculty:* 62 full-time (25 women), 50 part-time/adjunct (25 women). *Students:* 449 full-time (280 women), 60 part-time (46 women); includes 188 minority (23 Black or African American, non-Hispanic/Latino; 112 Asian, non-Hispanic/Latino; 35 Hispanic/Latino; 18 Two or more races, non-Hispanic/Latino), 23 international. Average age 27. 1,750 applicants, 46% accepted, 252 enrolled. In 2017, 283 master's awarded. Terminal master's awarded for partial completion of doctoral program. *Degree requirements:* For master's, thesis (for some programs); for doctorate, thesis/dissertation. *Entrance requirements:* For master's, GRE General Test, MCAT, or GMAT; for doctorate, GRE General Test or MCAT. Additional exam requirements/recommendations for international students: Required—TOEFL (minimum score 100 iBT); Recommended—IELTS (minimum score 7). *Application deadline:* For fall admission, 1/15 priority date for domestic and international students; for spring admission, 10/25 priority date for domestic and international students. Applications are processed on a rolling basis. Application fee: $70. Electronic applications accepted. *Expenses:* Contact institution. *Financial support:* In 2017–18, 13 students received support, including 1 fellowship (averaging $3,000 per year), 50 research assistantships (averaging $1,000 per year), 65 teaching assistantships (averaging $2,000 per year); Federal Work-Study and scholarships/grants also available. Financial award application deadline: 2/23; financial award applicants required to submit FAFSA. *Faculty research:* Environmental and occupational health, nutrition, epidemiology, health communication, biostatics, obesity/chronic disease, health policy and health care delivery, global health, health inequality and social determinants of health. *Unit head:* Dr. Aviva Must, Dean, 617-636-0935, Fax: 617-636-0898, E-mail: aviva.must@tufts.edu. *Application contact:* Emily Keily, Director of Admissions, 617-636-0935, Fax: 617-636-0898, E-mail: med-phpd@tufts.edu.
Website: http://publichealth.tufts.edu

Union College, Physician Assistant Program, Lincoln, NE 68506-4300. Offers MPAS. *Accreditation:* ARC-PA. *Faculty:* 5 full-time (3 women), 8 part-time/adjunct (2 women). *Students:* 87 full-time (65 women); includes 12 minority (2 Black or African American, non-Hispanic/Latino; 2 Asian, non-Hispanic/Latino; 8 Hispanic/Latino). Average age 28. *Entrance requirements:* Additional exam requirements/recommendations for international students: Required—TOEFL (minimum score 600 paper-based; 100 iBT). *Application deadline:* For fall admission, 11/1 for domestic and international students. Applications are processed on a rolling basis. Electronic applications accepted. *Expenses:* $1,060 per credit hour. *Financial support:* Applicants required to submit FAFSA. *Faculty research:* Servant leadership, cultural competency. *Unit head:* Megan Heidtbrink, Director, 402-486-2527, Fax: 402-486-2559. *Application contact:* Jan Lemon, Admissions Coordinator/Office Manager, 402-486-2527, Fax: 402-486-2559, E-mail: jan.lemon@ucollege.edu.
Website: http://www.ucollege.edu/pa

The University of Alabama at Birmingham, School of Health Professions, Program in Physician Assistant Studies, Birmingham, AL 35294. Offers MSPAS. *Accreditation:* ARC-PA. *Entrance requirements:* For master's, GRE or MCAT, minimum GPA of 3.0. Additional exam requirements/recommendations for international students: Required—TOEFL. Electronic applications accepted. *Faculty research:* Primary care and public health, infectious disease/HIV, oral health.

University of Arkansas for Medical Sciences, College of Health Professions, Little Rock, AR 72205-7199. Offers audiology (Au D); communication sciences and disorders (MS, PhD); genetic counseling (MS); nuclear medicine advanced associate (MIS); physician assistant studies (MPAS); radiologist assistant (MIS). PhD offered through consortium with University of Arkansas at Little Rock and University of Central Arkansas. *Program availability:* Part-time, online learning. *Degree requirements:* For master's, thesis (for some programs); for doctorate, comprehensive exam (for some programs), thesis/dissertation (for some programs). *Entrance requirements:* For master's, GRE. Additional exam requirements/recommendations for international students: Required—TOEFL (minimum score 550 paper-based; 79 iBT). Electronic applications accepted. *Expenses:* Contact institution. *Faculty research:* Auditory-based intervention, soy diet, nutrition and cancer.

University of Bridgeport, Physician Assistant Institute, Bridgeport, CT 06604. Offers MS. *Degree requirements:* For master's, thesis. *Entrance requirements:* Additional exam requirements/recommendations for international students: Recommended—TOEFL (minimum score 550 paper-based; 80 iBT), IELTS (minimum score 6.5).

University of Charleston, Physician Assistant Program, Charleston, WV 25304-1099. Offers MPAS. Electronic applications accepted.

University of Colorado Denver, School of Medicine, Physician Assistant Program, Aurora, CO 80045. Offers child health associate (MPAS), including global health, leadership, education, advocacy, development, and scholarship, pediatric critical and acute care, rural health, urban/underserved populations. *Accreditation:* ARC-PA. *Students:* 130 full-time (108 women); includes 21 minority (4 Black or African American, non-Hispanic/Latino; 4 Asian, non-Hispanic/Latino; 8 Hispanic/Latino; 5 Two or more races, non-Hispanic/Latino). Average age 27. 57 applicants, 96% accepted, 44 enrolled. *Degree requirements:* For master's, comprehensive exam. *Entrance requirements:* For master's, GRE General Test, minimum GPA of 2.8; 3 letters of recommendation; prerequisite courses in chemistry, biology, general genetics, psychology and statistics; interview. Additional exam requirements/recommendations for international students: Required—TOEFL (minimum score 550 paper-based; 80 iBT). *Application deadline:* For fall admission, 9/1 for domestic students, 9/15 for international students. Application fee: $170. Electronic applications accepted. *Faculty research:* Clinical genetics and genetic counseling, evidence-based medicine, pediatric allergy and asthma, childhood diabetes, standardized patient assessment. *Unit head:* Jonathan Bowser, Program Director, 303-724-1349, E-mail: jonathan.bowser@ucdenver.edu. *Application contact:* Kay Denler, Academic Services Program Manager, 303-724-7963, E-mail: kay.denler@ucdenver.edu.
Website: http://www.ucdenver.edu/academics/colleges/medicalschool/education/degree_programs/PAProgram/Pages/Home.aspx

University of Dayton, Department of Physician Assistant Education, Dayton, OH 45469. Offers physician assistant practice (MPAP). *Faculty:* 6 full-time (all women), 2 part-time/adjunct (both women). *Students:* 111 full-time (83 women), 1 (woman) part-time; includes 12 minority (4 Black or African American, non-Hispanic/Latino; 4 Asian, non-Hispanic/Latino; 3 Hispanic/Latino; 1 Two or more races, non-Hispanic/Latino). Average age 26. 48 applicants. In 2017, 30 master's awarded. *Degree requirements:* For master's, comprehensive exam. *Entrance requirements:* For master's, minimum GPA of 3.0, 250 hours' health care experience, interview, written and oral communication skills, 20 hours' community service, 20 hours' prior shadowing experience. Additional exam requirements/recommendations for international students: Required—TOEFL (minimum score 550 paper-based; 85 iBT). *Application deadline:* For fall admission, 11/1 for domestic and international students. Application fee: $0 ($50 for international students). Electronic applications accepted. *Expenses:* Contact institution. *Financial support:* In 2017–18, 9 research assistantships with partial tuition reimbursements (averaging $9,640 per year) were awarded; teaching assistantships, career-related internships or fieldwork, institutionally sponsored loans, and unspecified assistantships also available. Financial award application deadline: 3/1; financial award applicants required to submit FAFSA. *Faculty research:* Efficacy and safety of anticoagulation therapy; treatment and care of burn and skin wounds; enhanced skills for physician assistant faculty; behavioral-based interviewing for PA admission. *Unit head:* Lindsey Hammett, Director/Chair, 937-229-4847, E-mail: lhammett1@udayton.edu. *Application contact:* Amy Kidwell, Admissions Coordinator/Senior Administrative Secretary, 937-229-2900, E-mail: akidwell1@udayton.edu.
Website: https://www.udayton.edu/education/departments_and_programs/pa/index.php

University of Detroit Mercy, College of Health Professions, Detroit, MI 48221. Offers clinical nurse leader (MSN); family nurse practitioner (MSN); health services administration (MHSA); health systems management (MSN); nurse anesthesia (MS); nursing (DNP); nursing education (MSN, Certificate); nursing leadership and financial management (Certificate); outcomes performance management (Certificate); physician assistant (MS). *Entrance requirements:* For master's, GRE General Test, minimum GPA of 3.0. *Faculty research:* Research design, respiratory physiology, AIDS prevention, adolescent health, community, low income health education.

The University of Findlay, Office of Graduate Admissions, Findlay, OH 45840. Offers applied security and analytics (MSAS); athletic training (MAT); business (MBA), including certified management accountant, certified public accountant, health care management, hospitality management; education (MA Ed, Ed D), including children's literature (MA Ed), curriculum and teaching (MA Ed), education (MA Ed), educational administration (MA Ed), human resource development (MA Ed), mathematics (MA Ed), reading (MA Ed), science education (MA Ed), superintendent (Ed D), teaching (Ed D), technology (MA Ed); environmental, safety, and health management (MSEM); health informatics (MS); occupational therapy (MOT); pharmacy (Pharm D); physical therapy (DPT); physician assistant (MPA); rhetoric and writing (MA); teaching English to speakers of other languages (TESOL) and applied linguistics (MA). *Program availability:* Part-time, evening/weekend, 100% online, blended/hybrid learning. *Students:* 688 full-time (430 women), 553 part-time (308 women), 170 international. Average age 28. In 2017, 366 master's, 137 doctorates awarded. *Degree requirements:* For master's, comprehensive exam (for some programs), thesis (for some programs), cumulative project, capstone project; for doctorate, thesis/dissertation (for some programs). *Entrance requirements:* For master's, GRE/GMAT, bachelor's degree from accredited institution, minimum undergraduate GPA of 2.5 in last 64 hours of course work; for doctorate, GRE, MAT, minimum cumulative GPA of 3.0. Additional exam requirements/recommendations for international students: Required—TOEFL (minimum score 79 iBT), IELTS (minimum score 7), PTE (minimum score 61). *Application deadline:* Applications are processed on a rolling basis. Electronic applications accepted. *Financial support:* In 2017–18, 10 research assistantships with partial tuition reimbursements (averaging $7,200 per year), 35 teaching assistantships with partial tuition reimbursements (averaging $7,200 per year) were awarded; Federal Work-Study, institutionally sponsored loans, and unspecified assistantships also available. Financial

award applicants required to submit FAFSA. *Unit head:* Christopher M. Harris, Director of Admissions, 419-434-4347, E-mail: harrisc1@findlay.edu. *Application contact:* Madeline Fauser Brennan, Graduate Admissions Counselor, 419-434-4636, Fax: 419-434-4898, E-mail: fauserbrennan@findlay.edu.
Website: http://www.findlay.edu/admissions/graduate/Pages/default.aspx

University of Florida, College of Medicine, Program in Physician Assistant, Gainesville, FL 32611. Offers MPAS. *Accreditation:* ARC-PA. *Entrance requirements:* For master's, GRE General Test, interview. Electronic applications accepted.

The University of Iowa, Roy J. and Lucille A. Carver College of Medicine and Graduate College, Graduate Programs in Medicine, Department of Physician Assistant Studies and Services, Iowa City, IA 52242-1110. Offers MPAS. *Accreditation:* ARC-PA. *Degree requirements:* For master's, comprehensive exam, comprehensive clinical exam, clinical presentation. *Entrance requirements:* For master's, GRE General Test or MCAT, minimum of 1,000 hours of health care and/or research experience. Additional exam requirements/recommendations for international students: Required—TOEFL (minimum score 93 iBT). Electronic applications accepted. *Expenses:* Contact institution.

University of Kentucky, Graduate School, College of Health Sciences, Program in Physician Assistant Studies, Lexington, KY 40506-0032. Offers MSPAS. *Accreditation:* ARC-PA. *Degree requirements:* For master's, comprehensive exam. *Entrance requirements:* For master's, GRE General Test, minimum undergraduate GPA of 2.75. Additional exam requirements/recommendations for international students: Required—TOEFL (minimum score 550 paper-based). Electronic applications accepted.

University of Lynchburg, Graduate Studies, MA Program in Physician Assistant Medicine, Lynchburg, VA 24501-3199. Offers MA. *Faculty:* 9 full-time (4 women), 1 part-time/adjunct (0 women). *Students:* 60 full-time (48 women), 1 part-time (0 women); includes 12 minority (3 Black or African American, non-Hispanic/Latino; 3 Asian, non-Hispanic/Latino; 3 Hispanic/Latino; 3 Two or more races, non-Hispanic/Latino), 1 international. Average age 26. 628 applicants, 5% accepted, 28 enrolled. *Entrance requirements:* Additional exam requirements/recommendations for international students: Required—TOEFL (minimum score 550 paper-based; 80 iBT). *Application deadline:* For spring admission, 1/15 for domestic students; for summer admission, 1/15 for domestic students. Applications are processed on a rolling basis. Application fee: $50. Electronic applications accepted. Application fee is waived when completed online. *Expenses:* $11,670 per semester. *Financial support:* Institutionally sponsored loans, scholarships/grants, traineeships, unspecified assistantships, and tobacco fund awards available. *Faculty research:* Anatomy lab featuring flat screen monitors and 21 cadaver stations; low student-faculty ratio; advanced clinical procedures emphasis; modular organ based format; extensive clinical rotation exposure; custom-designed facilities in the newly renovated graduate health science building featuring state-of-the-art equipment and technology. *Unit head:* Dr. Jeremy Welsh, Director, 434-544-8876. *Application contact:* E-mail: pa@lynchburg.edu.
Website: https://www.lynchburg.edu/graduate/physician-assistant-medicine/

University of Mount Union, Program in Physician Assistant Studies, Alliance, OH 44601-3993. Offers MS. *Faculty:* 5 full-time (3 women), 3 part-time/adjunct (2 women). *Students:* 76 full-time (56 women); includes 4 minority (2 Asian, non-Hispanic/Latino; 2 Two or more races, non-Hispanic/Latino). Average age 24. 273 applicants, 18% accepted, 40 enrolled. In 2017, 28 master's awarded. *Entrance requirements:* For master's, GRE, 40 hours of PA shadowing, interview, 3 letters of recommendation. Additional exam requirements/recommendations for international students: Required—TOEFL (minimum score 590 paper-based; 100 iBT). *Application deadline:* For summer admission, 10/1 for domestic and international students. Electronic applications accepted. *Expenses:* $31,335. *Financial support:* Applicants required to submit FAFSA. *Faculty research:* Motivational interviewing, board exam predictors, medical professionalism. *Unit head:* Betsy Ekey, Director, 330-829-8954, E-mail: ekeybd@mountunion.edu. *Application contact:* Laurie Scarpitti, Admission Representative, 330-823-2419, E-mail: scarpill@mountunion.edu.
Website: http://www.mountunion.edu/physician-assistant-program

University of Nebraska Medical Center, College of Allied Health Professions, Division of Physician Assistant Education, Omaha, NE 68198-4300. Offers MPAS. *Accreditation:* ARC-PA. *Degree requirements:* For master's, comprehensive exam, research paper. *Entrance requirements:* For master's, GRE General Test, 16 undergraduate hours of course work in both biology and chemistry, 3 in math, 6 in English, 9 in psychology; minimum GPA of 3.0. Additional exam requirements/recommendations for international students: Required—TOEFL (minimum score 600 paper-based; 100 iBT). Electronic applications accepted. *Expenses:* Tuition, state resident: full-time $8451; part-time $4225 per semester. Tuition, nonresident: full-time $24,219; part-time $11,295 per semester. *Required fees:* $589; $117 per term. *Faculty research:* Substance abuse, mental health, women's health, geriatrics.

University of New England, Westbrook College of Health Professions, Biddeford, ME 04005-9526. Offers nurse anesthesia (MSNA); occupational therapy (MS); physical therapy (DPT); physician assistant (MS); social work (MSW). *Program availability:* Part-time. *Faculty:* 43 full-time (30 women), 26 part-time/adjunct (19 women). *Students:* 527 full-time (401 women), 5 part-time (4 women); includes 50 minority (11 Black or African American, non-Hispanic/Latino; 1 American Indian or Alaska Native, non-Hispanic/Latino; 24 Asian, non-Hispanic/Latino; 5 Hispanic/Latino; 1 Native Hawaiian or other Pacific Islander, non-Hispanic/Latino; 8 Two or more races, non-Hispanic/Latino), 1 international. Average age 27. 2,499 applicants, 18% accepted, 226 enrolled. In 2017, 440 master's, 71 doctorates awarded. *Application deadline:* Applications are processed on a rolling basis. Electronic applications accepted. Tuition and fees vary according to degree level, program and student level. *Financial support:* Application deadline: 5/1; applicants required to submit FAFSA. *Unit head:* Dr. Elizabeth Francis- Connolly, Dean, Westbrook College of Health Professions, 207-221-4523, E-mail: efrancisconnolly@une.edu. *Application contact:* Scott Steinberg, Dean of University Admission, 207-221-4225, Fax: 207-523-1925, E-mail: ssteinberg@une.edu.
Website: http://www.une.edu/wchp/index.cfm

University of New Mexico, Graduate Studies, Health Sciences Center, Program in Physician Assistant Studies, Albuquerque, NM 87131. Offers MS. *Accreditation:* ARC-PA. *Faculty:* 5 full-time (all women). *Students:* 34 full-time (24 women); includes 18 minority (1 Black or African American, non-Hispanic/Latino; 1 American Indian or Alaska Native, non-Hispanic/Latino; 15 Hispanic/Latino; 1 Two or more races, non-Hispanic/Latino). Average age 30. In 2017, 15 master's awarded. *Entrance requirements:* For master's, GRE. Additional exam requirements/recommendations for international students: Recommended—TOEFL. *Application deadline:* For fall admission, 8/1 for domestic and international students; for winter admission, 8/1 for domestic and international students; for spring admission, 8/8 for domestic students, 8/1 for international students. Applications are processed on a rolling basis. Application fee: $50. Electronic applications accepted. *Financial support:* Application deadline: 6/30; applicants required to submit FAFSA. *Unit head:* Dr. Nikki Katalanos, Program Director, 505-272-9864, E-mail: paprogram@salud.unm.edu. *Application contact:* Marlys Harrison, Program Manager, 505-272-9864, E-mail: mharrison@salud.unm.edu.
Website: http://fcm.unm.edu/education/physician-assistant-program/index.html

University of North Dakota, Graduate School and Graduate School, Graduate Programs in Medicine, Physician Assistant Program, Grand Forks, ND 58202. Offers MPAS. *Accreditation:* ARC-PA. *Entrance requirements:* For master's, current RN licensure, minimum of 4 years of clinical experience, current ACLS certification, interview, letters of recommendation. Additional exam requirements/recommendations for international students: Required—TOEFL (minimum score 550 paper-based; 79 iBT), IELTS (minimum score 6.5).

University of North Texas Health Science Center at Fort Worth, School of Health Professions, Fort Worth, TX 76107-2699. Offers physical therapy (DPT); physician assistant studies (MPAS). *Accreditation:* ARC-PA. *Degree requirements:* For master's, thesis or alternative, research paper. *Entrance requirements:* For master's, minimum GPA of 2.85. *Faculty research:* Impact of mid-level providers on medical treatment, curriculum development, pain in geriatric patients, biopsychosocial risk factors.

University of Oklahoma Health Sciences Center, College of Medicine, Program in Physician Associate, Oklahoma City, OK 73190. Offers MHS.

University of Pittsburgh, School of Health and Rehabilitation Sciences, Department of Rehabilitation Science and Technology, Pittsburgh, PA 15260. Offers clinical rehabilitation and mental health counseling (MS); physician assistant studies (MS); prosthetics and orthotics (DPT); rehabilitation technology (MS). *Program availability:* Online learning. *Faculty:* 27 full-time (14 women), 7 part-time/adjunct (3 women). *Students:* 177 full-time (118 women), 9 part-time (8 women); includes 26 minority (6 Black or African American, non-Hispanic/Latino; 5 Asian, non-Hispanic/Latino; 9 Hispanic/Latino; 6 Two or more races, non-Hispanic/Latino), 12 international. Average age 25. 611 applicants, 25% accepted, 101 enrolled. In 2017, 72 master's awarded. *Degree requirements:* For master's, comprehensive exam (for some programs). *Entrance requirements:* For master's, GRE General Test, hands-on patient care experience, CPR certification. Additional exam requirements/recommendations for international students: Required—TOEFL (minimum score 550 paper-based; 80 iBT), IELTS (minimum score 6.5). *Application deadline:* For fall admission, 12/31 for domestic and international students; for spring admission, 11/1 for domestic students, 9/1 for international students. Application fee: $177. Electronic applications accepted. *Financial support:* In 2017–18, 14 research assistantships (averaging $23,650 per year) were awarded; career-related internships or fieldwork, Federal Work-Study, scholarships/grants, traineeships, and unspecified assistantships also available. *Faculty research:* Assistive and rehabilitation technology development; prevention and management of chronic conditions; universal design and accessibility; environmental optimization; rehabilitation outcomes measurement. *Total annual research expenditures:* $9.2 million. *Unit head:* Dr. Rory Cooper, Associate Dean for Inclusion/Chair/Professor, 412-822-3700, E-mail: rcooper@pitt.edu. *Application contact:* Jessica Maguire, Director of Admissions, 412-383-6557, Fax: 412-383-6535, E-mail: maguire@pitt.edu.
Website: http://www.shrs.pitt.edu/rst

University of St. Francis, College of Arts and Sciences, Joliet, IL 60435-6169. Offers forensic social work (Post-Master's Certificate); physician assistant practice (MS); social work (MSW). *Program availability:* Part-time. *Faculty:* 7 full-time (5 women), 5 part-time/adjunct (4 women). *Students:* 107 full-time (82 women), 24 part-time (22 women); includes 40 minority (13 Black or African American, non-Hispanic/Latino; 3 Asian, non-Hispanic/Latino; 20 Hispanic/Latino; 2 Native Hawaiian or other Pacific Islander, non-Hispanic/Latino; 2 Two or more races, non-Hispanic/Latino), 6 international. Average age 28. 69 applicants, 48% accepted, 26 enrolled. In 2017, 64 master's awarded. *Entrance requirements:* For master's, GRE (for MS). Additional exam requirements/recommendations for international students: Required—TOEFL (minimum score 550 paper-based; 79 iBT), IELTS (minimum score 6). *Application deadline:* Applications are processed on a rolling basis. Application fee: $30. Electronic applications accepted. Application fee is waived when completed online. *Expenses:* $748 per credit. *Financial support:* In 2017–18, 10 students received support. Scholarships/grants and unspecified assistantships available. Support available to part-time students. Financial award applicants required to submit FAFSA. *Unit head:* Dr. Robert Kase, Dean, 815-740-3367, Fax: 815-740-6366. *Application contact:* Sandra Sloka, Director of Admissions for Graduate and Degree Completion Programs, 800-735-7500, Fax: 815-740-3431, E-mail: ssloka@stfrancis.edu.
Website: http://www.stfrancis.edu/academics/cas

University of Saint Francis, Graduate School, Department of Physician Assistant Studies, Fort Wayne, IN 46808-3994. Offers MS. *Accreditation:* ARC-PA. *Faculty:* 4 full-time (2 women), 2 part-time/adjunct (both women). *Students:* 48 full-time (37 women), 1 part-time (0 women); includes 4 minority (1 Asian, non-Hispanic/Latino; 2 Hispanic/Latino; 1 Two or more races, non-Hispanic/Latino), 1 international. Average age 27. In 2017, 25 master's awarded. *Degree requirements:* For master's, comprehensive exam. *Entrance requirements:* For master's, GRE, 12 credit hours of chemistry, 15 credit hours of biology, and 6 credit hours of psychology; direct patient care experience. Additional exam requirements/recommendations for international students: Required—TOEFL (minimum score 550 paper-based) or IELTS (minimum score 6.5). *Application deadline:* For summer admission, 12/1 for domestic and international students. Application fee: $177. Electronic applications accepted. *Expenses:* Contact institution. *Financial support:* Scholarships/grants available. Financial award application deadline: 4/15; financial award applicants required to submit FAFSA. *Unit head:* Christopher Carlin, Program Director, Physician Assistant Studies, 260-399-7700 Ext. 8560, E-mail: cscarlin@sf.edu. *Application contact:* Kyle Richardson, Associate Director of Enrollment Services for Adult Learning, 260-399-7700 Ext. 6310, E-mail: krichardson@sf.edu.
Website: https://pa.sf.edu/

University of South Alabama, Pat Capps Covey College of Allied Health Professions, Department of Physician Assistant Studies, Mobile, AL 36688. Offers MHS. *Accreditation:* ARC-PA. *Faculty:* 5 full-time (4 women), 2 part-time/adjunct (1 woman). *Students:* 78 full-time (47 women); includes 5 minority (3 Black or African American, non-Hispanic/Latino; 1 Hispanic/Latino; 1 Two or more races, non-Hispanic/Latino). Average age 29. In 2017, 39 master's awarded. *Degree requirements:* For master's, comprehensive exam, thesis optional, externship; 121 hours consisting of 73 credit hours of didactic course work and 48 hours of clinical work. *Entrance requirements:* For master's, GRE General Test, minimum GPA of 3.0; 500 hours in direct patient contact experience. Additional exam requirements/recommendations for international students: Required—TOEFL (minimum score 600 paper-based; 100 iBT). *Application deadline:* For fall admission, 9/1 for domestic students, 8/1 for international students. Application fee: $110. Electronic applications accepted. *Expenses:* Contact institution. *Financial support:* Fellowships, research assistantships, teaching assistantships, career-related internships or fieldwork, Federal Work-Study, institutionally sponsored loans, scholarships/grants, and unspecified assistantships available. Support available to part-time students. Financial award application deadline: 3/31; financial award applicants required to submit FAFSA. *Unit head:* Stephanie McGilvray, Department Chair and Program Director, 251-445-9334, Fax: 251-445-9336, E-mail: pastudies@southalabama.edu. *Application contact:* Dr. Nancy Dunn, Admissions Coordinator, 251-445-9334, Fax: 251-445-9336, E-mail: ndunn@southalabama.edu.
Website: http://www.southalabama.edu/colleges/alliedhealth/pa/

University of South Dakota, Graduate School, School of Health Sciences, Department of Physician Assistant Studies, Vermillion, SD 57069. Offers MS. *Accreditation:* ARC-

PA. *Entrance requirements:* Additional exam requirements/recommendations for international students: Required—TOEFL (minimum score 550 paper-based). *Application deadline:* For spring admission, 9/1 for domestic and international students. Application fee: $150. Electronic applications accepted. *Expenses:* Contact institution. *Financial support:* Scholarships/grants available. Financial award application deadline: 3/15; financial award applicants required to submit FAFSA. *Faculty research:* Neuroscience, teaching techniques in physician assistant education. *Application contact:* Graduate School, 605-658-6140, Fax: 605-677-6118, E-mail: grad@usd.edu.
Website: http://www.usd.edu/pa

University of Southern California, Keck School of Medicine and Graduate School, Graduate Programs in Medicine, Primary Care Physician Assistant Program, Alhambra, CA 91803. Offers MPAP. *Accreditation:* ARC-PA. *Faculty:* 12 full-time (8 women), 7 part-time/adjunct (4 women). *Students:* 176 full-time (134 women); includes 116 minority (10 Black or African American, non-Hispanic/Latino; 44 Asian, non-Hispanic/Latino; 56 Hispanic/Latino; 6 Two or more races, non-Hispanic/Latino). Average age 27. 864 applicants, 8% accepted, 60 enrolled. In 2017, 58 master's awarded. *Degree requirements:* For master's, comprehensive exam, clinical training. *Entrance requirements:* For master's, GRE or MCAT, bachelor's degree; minimum cumulative GPA of 3.0, cumulative science 2.75. Additional exam requirements/recommendations for international students: Required—TOEFL (minimum score 90 iBT). *Application deadline:* For fall admission, 11/1 for domestic and international students. Applications are processed on a rolling basis. Application fee: $50. Electronic applications accepted. *Expenses:* Contact institution. *Financial support:* In 2017–18, 26 students received support. Institutionally sponsored loans and scholarships/grants available. Financial award application deadline: 5/4; financial award applicants required to submit FAFSA. *Faculty research:* Technology in education, interprofessional education; clinical case topics and medical review; clinical education and best practices; faculty development, street medicine. *Total annual research expenditures:* $450,000. *Unit head:* Dr. Kevin C. Lohenry, Program Director, 626-457-4262, Fax: 626-457-4245, E-mail: lohenry@med.usc.edu. *Application contact:* Sara Diosdado-Ortiz, Admissions Counselor II, 626-457-4240, Fax: 626-457-4245, E-mail: uscpa@usc.edu.
Website: http://www.usc.edu/pa

The University of Tennessee Health Science Center, College of Health Professions, Memphis, TN 38163-0002. Offers audiology (MS, Au D); clinical laboratory science (MSCLS); cytopathology practice (MCP); health informatics and information management (MHIIM); occupational therapy (MOT); physical therapy (DPT, ScDPT); physician assistant (MMS); speech language pathology (MS). *Accreditation:* AOTA; APTA. *Program availability:* Part-time, evening/weekend, online learning. Terminal master's awarded for partial completion of doctoral program. *Degree requirements:* For master's, comprehensive exam, thesis; for doctorate, comprehensive exam, residency. *Entrance requirements:* For master's, GRE (MOT, MSCLS), minimum GPA of 3.0, 3 letters of reference, national accreditation (MSCLS), GRE if GPA is less than 3.0 (MCP); for doctorate, GRE. Additional exam requirements/recommendations for international students: Required—TOEFL (minimum score 550 paper-based; 80 iBT). Electronic applications accepted. *Expenses:* Contact institution. *Faculty research:* Gait deviation, muscular dystrophy and strength, hemophilia and exercise, pediatric neurology, self-efficacy.

The University of Texas Health Science Center at San Antonio, School of Health Professions, San Antonio, TX 78229-3900. Offers occupational therapy (MOT); physical therapy (DPT); physician assistant studies (MS); speech language pathology (MS). *Accreditation:* AOTA; APTA; ARC-PA; ASHA. *Degree requirements:* For master's, comprehensive exam, thesis (for some programs); for doctorate, comprehensive exam.

The University of Texas Medical Branch, School of Health Professions, Department of Physician Assistant Studies, Galveston, TX 77555. Offers MPAS. *Accreditation:* ARC-PA. *Entrance requirements:* For master's, GRE, interview. Electronic applications accepted.

The University of Texas Rio Grande Valley, College of Health Affairs, Department of Physician Assistant Studies, Edinburg, TX 78539. Offers primary care (MPAS). *Faculty:* 20 full-time (12 women). *Students:* 158 full-time (105 women); includes 133 minority (5 Black or African American, non-Hispanic/Latino; 27 Asian, non-Hispanic/Latino; 99 Hispanic/Latino; 2 Two or more races, non-Hispanic/Latino). Average age 27. 1,200 applicants, 6% accepted, 65 enrolled. In 2017, 49 master's awarded. *Degree requirements:* For master's, comprehensive exam, thesis or alternative, capstone research paper. *Entrance requirements:* For master's, GRE. Additional exam requirements/recommendations for international students: Required—TOEFL. *Application deadline:* For fall admission, 9/1 for domestic and international students. Application fee: $50. Application fee is waived when completed online. *Expenses:* Contact institution. *Financial support:* In 2017–18, 155 students received support, including 6 research assistantships (averaging $10,000 per year); scholarships/grants also available. Financial award application deadline: 8/15; financial award applicants required to submit FAFSA. *Faculty research:* Holistic admission and academic performance; the GRE as a predictor of academic performance in professional programs; barriers to healthcare in Hispanic underserved areas; experience as a scribe as related to academic performance in PA school. *Unit head:* Frank Ambriz, Chair and Clinical Associate Professor, 956-665-2298, Fax: 956-665-2438, E-mail: frank.ambriz@utrgv.edu. *Application contact:* Stephanie Ozuna, Graduate Student Recruiter, 956-665-3558, E-mail: stephanie.ozuna@utrgv.edu.
Website: http://www.utrgv.edu/pa/

The University of Texas Southwestern Medical Center, Southwestern School of Health Professions, Physician Assistant Studies Program, Dallas, TX 75390. Offers MPAS. *Accreditation:* ARC-PA. *Entrance requirements:* For master's, GRE, minimum GPA of 3.0. Electronic applications accepted.

University of the Cumberlands, Program in Physician Assistant Studies, Williamsburg, KY 40769-1372. Offers MPAS. *Accreditation:* ARC-PA. *Entrance requirements:* Additional exam requirements/recommendations for international students: Required—TOEFL. Electronic applications accepted.

The University of Toledo, College of Graduate Studies, College of Medicine and Life Sciences, Department of Physician Assistant Studies, Toledo, OH 43606-3390. Offers MSBS. *Accreditation:* ARC-PA. *Degree requirements:* For master's, thesis or alternative, scholarly project. *Entrance requirements:* For master's, GRE, interview, minimum undergraduate GPA of 3.0, writing sample, transcripts. Additional exam requirements/recommendations for international students: Required—TOEFL (minimum score 550 paper-based; 80 iBT). Electronic applications accepted. *Expenses:* Contact institution.

University of Utah, School of Medicine and Graduate School, Graduate Programs in Medicine, Department of Family and Preventive Medicine, Utah Physician Assistant Program, Salt Lake City, UT 84112-1107. Offers MPAS. *Accreditation:* ARC-PA. *Degree requirements:* For master's, comprehensive exam, thesis or alternative. *Entrance requirements:* Additional exam requirements/recommendations for international students: Required—TOEFL (minimum score 550 paper-based). Electronic applications accepted. *Expenses:* Contact institution. *Faculty research:* Physical assistant education, evidence-based medicine, technology and education, international medicine education.

University of Wisconsin–La Crosse, College of Science and Health, Department of Health Professions, Program in Physician Assistant Studies, La Crosse, WI 54601-3742. Offers MS. *Accreditation:* ARC-PA. *Students:* 37 full-time (30 women); includes 1 minority (Asian, non-Hispanic/Latino). Average age 24. 373 applicants, 8% accepted, 19 enrolled. In 2017, 18 master's awarded. *Degree requirements:* For master's, comprehensive exam. *Entrance requirements:* For master's, GRE. Additional exam requirements/recommendations for international students: Required—TOEFL (minimum score 104 iBT). *Application deadline:* For fall admission, 8/1 for domestic and international students. Application fee: $50. Electronic applications accepted. *Expenses:* Contact institution. *Financial support:* Federal Work-Study and scholarships/grants available. Support available to part-time students. *Unit head:* Sandra Sieck, MD, Director, 608-785-6621, E-mail: ssieck@uwlax.edu. *Application contact:* Brandon Schaller, Senior Graduate Student Status Examiner, 608-785-8941, E-mail: admissions@uwlax.edu.
Website: http://www.uwlax.edu/pastudies/

University of Wisconsin–Madison, School of Medicine and Public Health, Physician Assistant Program, Madison, WI 53706. Offers MPA. *Application contact:* 608-263-5620, E-mail: paprogram@mailplus.wisc.edu.
Website: https://www.med.wisc.edu/education/physician-assistant-pa-program/

Valparaiso University, Graduate School and Continuing Education, College of Nursing and Health Professions, Valparaiso, IN 46383. Offers nursing (DNP); nursing education (MSN, Certificate); physician assistant (MSPA); public health (MPH); MSN/MHA. *Accreditation:* AACN. *Program availability:* Part-time, evening/weekend, online learning. *Entrance requirements:* For master's, minimum GPA of 3.0, undergraduate major in nursing, Indiana registered nursing license, undergraduate courses in research and statistics. Additional exam requirements/recommendations for international students: Required—TOEFL (minimum score 550 paper-based; 80 iBT), IELTS (minimum score 6). Electronic applications accepted. *Expenses:* Contact institution.

Wayne State University, Eugene Applebaum College of Pharmacy and Health Sciences, Department of Health Care Sciences, Program in Physician Assistant Studies, Detroit, MI 48202. Offers MS. *Accreditation:* ARC-PA. *Faculty:* 10. *Students:* 100 full-time (76 women); includes 11 minority (6 Asian, non-Hispanic/Latino; 1 Hispanic/Latino; 4 Two or more races, non-Hispanic/Latino). Average age 26. 381 applicants, 13% accepted, 49 enrolled. In 2017, 51 master's awarded. *Degree requirements:* For master's, clinical rotation. *Entrance requirements:* For master's, GRE General Test, course work in science, 500 hours of work experience in patient care in a health-service environment, three letters of recommendation, personal statement, interview, bachelor's degree from accredited institution with minimum GPA of 3.0 overall and in prerequisites, CASPA application. Additional exam requirements/recommendations for international students: Required—TOEFL (minimum score 600 paper-based; 100 iBT), TWE, Michigan English Language Assessment Battery (minimum score 85); Recommended—IELTS. *Application deadline:* For spring admission, 9/1 for domestic and international students. Application fee: $50. Electronic applications accepted. *Expenses:* Contact institution. *Financial support:* In 2017–18, 12 students received support. Scholarships/grants available. Financial award applicants required to submit FAFSA. *Faculty research:* Professionalism in physician assistant programs, interprofessional education, including advancements in neurological surgery, vestibular dysfunction, special needs populations. *Unit head:* John G. McGinnity, Program Director/Professor, 313-577-3707, E-mail: jmcginnity@wayne.edu. *Application contact:* E-mail: paadmit@wayne.edu.
Website: http://cphs.wayne.edu/physician-assistant/

Weill Cornell Medicine, Weill Cornell Graduate School of Medical Sciences, Physician Assistant Program, New York, NY 10022. Offers health sciences (MS), including surgery. *Accreditation:* ARC-PA. *Degree requirements:* For master's, thesis. *Entrance requirements:* For master's, GRE. Additional exam requirements/recommendations for international students: Required—TOEFL. Electronic applications accepted.

Western Michigan University, Graduate College, College of Health and Human Services, Department of Physician Assistant, Kalamazoo, MI 49008. Offers MSM. *Accreditation:* ARC-PA. *Program availability:* Part-time.

Western University of Health Sciences, College of Allied Health Professions, Program in Physician Assistant Studies, Pomona, CA 91766-1854. Offers MS. *Accreditation:* ARC-PA. *Faculty:* 11 full-time (8 women), 1 part-time/adjunct (0 women). *Students:* 192 full-time (124 women); includes 106 minority (12 Black or African American, non-Hispanic/Latino; 1 American Indian or Alaska Native, non-Hispanic/Latino; 25 Asian, non-Hispanic/Latino; 51 Hispanic/Latino; 1 Native Hawaiian or other Pacific Islander, non-Hispanic/Latino; 16 Two or more races, non-Hispanic/Latino). Average age 28. 1,720 applicants, 8% accepted, 95 enrolled. In 2017, 96 master's awarded. *Degree requirements:* For master's, comprehensive exam. *Entrance requirements:* For master's, bachelor's degree, minimum GPA of 3.0, letters of recommendation, interview, demonstrated history of ongoing community service and involvement, health screenings and immunizations, background check. Additional exam requirements/recommendations for international students: Recommended—TOEFL. *Application deadline:* For fall admission, 11/1 for domestic and international students. Application fee: $50. Electronic applications accepted. *Expenses:* $42,615 first-year tuition and fees. *Financial support:* In 2017–18, 97 students received support. Scholarships/grants available. Financial award application deadline: 3/2; financial award applicants required to submit FAFSA. *Unit head:* Roy Guizado, Chair, 909-469-5445, Fax: 909-469-5407, E-mail: roygpac@westernu.edu. *Application contact:* Karen Hutton-Lopez, Director of Admissions, 909-469-5335, Fax: 909-469-5570, E-mail: admissions@westernu.edu.
Website: http://www.westernu.edu/allied-health/allied-health-mspas/

Westfield State University, College of Graduate and Continuing Education, Department of Health Sciences, Westfield, MA 01086. Offers physician assistant studies (MS). *Faculty:* 5 full-time (4 women). *Students:* 24 full-time (18 women); includes 4 minority (2 Black or African American, non-Hispanic/Latino; 2 Hispanic/Latino). Average age 28. *Degree requirements:* For master's, comprehensive exam, thesis. *Entrance requirements:* For master's, CASPA application, minimum of 500 hours of patient contact, completion of prerequisite courses within previous ten years. Additional exam requirements/recommendations for international students: Required—TOEFL (minimum score 550 paper-based; 90 iBT). *Application deadline:* For fall admission, 8/1 for domestic students. Applications are processed on a rolling basis. Application fee: $50. *Expenses:* Contact institution. *Financial support:* Applicants required to submit FAFSA. *Unit head:* Dr. Jennifer Hixon, Chair, 413-572-8149, E-mail: jhixon@westfield.ma.edu. *Application contact:* Shelly Henrichon, Coordinator of College of Graduate and Continuing Education Admissions, 413-572-8022, Fax: 413-572-5227, E-mail: mhenrichon@westfield.ma.edu.

West Liberty University, College of Sciences, West Liberty, WV 26074. Offers biology (MA, MS); biomedical science (MA); physician assistant studies (MS); zoo science (MA, MS). Tuition and fees vary according to course load and program. *Unit head:* Dr. Karen Kettler, Interim Dean, E-mail: kkettler@westliberty.edu. *Application contact:* Sara Sweeney, Director, Office of Graduate Studies, 304-336-8545, E-mail: sara.sweeney@westliberty.edu.
Website: http://westliberty.edu/college-of-sciences/

Wichita State University, Graduate School, College of Health Professions, Department of Physician Assistant, Wichita, KS 67260. Offers MPA. *Accreditation:* ARC-PA. *Unit head:* Dr. Kimberly Darden, Interim Department Chair, 316-978-3011, Fax: 316-978-3669, E-mail: kim.darden@wichita.edu. *Application contact:* Jordan Oleson, Admissions Coordinator, 316-978-3095, Fax: 316-978-3253, E-mail: jordan.oleson@wichita.edu.
Website: http://www.wichita.edu/pa

Wingate University, Harris Department of Physician Assistant Studies, Wingate, NC 28174. Offers MPAS.

Yale University, Yale School of Medicine, Physician Associate Program, New Haven, CT 06510. Offers MM Sc, MM Sc/MPH. *Accreditation:* ARC-PA. *Program availability:* Online learning. *Degree requirements:* For master's, thesis. *Entrance requirements:* For master's, GRE General Test, course work in science. Additional exam requirements/recommendations for international students: Required—TOEFL. Electronic applications accepted. *Expenses:* Contact institution. *Faculty research:* Correlation of GRE scores and program performance, relationship of PA programs and pharmaceutical companies, career patterns in physician assistants, PA utilization and satisfaction with care, factors influencing PAs in their decision to pursue postgraduate residencies.

York College of the City University of New York, School of Health Sciences and Professional Programs, Jamaica, NY 11451. Offers physician assistant (MSPAS). *Entrance requirements:* For master's, GRE, bachelor's degree with minimum cumulative GPA of 3.0; 1 year each of general biology, general chemistry, human anatomy and physiology, and behavioral sciences; 1 semester each of biochemistry, microbiology (preferably clinical microbiology), and statistics; 500 hours of documented healthcare experience (volunteer or paid); personal interview.

Rehabilitation Sciences

Alabama State University, College of Health Sciences, Department of Prosthetics and Orthotics, Montgomery, AL 36101-0271. Offers MS. *Faculty:* 2 full-time (both women), 1 (woman) part-time/adjunct. *Students:* 8 full-time (5 women); includes 1 minority (Black or African American, non-Hispanic/Latino). Average age 22. 8 applicants, 100% accepted. In 2017, 8 master's awarded. *Degree requirements:* For master's, thesis. *Entrance requirements:* For master's, OPCAS application, interviews. Additional exam requirements/recommendations for international students: Required—TOEFL (minimum score 500 paper-based). *Application deadline:* For fall admission, 4/15 for domestic and international students; for spring admission, 11/15 for domestic and international students; for summer admission, 3/15 for domestic and international students. Application fee: $25. Electronic applications accepted. *Expenses:* Tuition, state resident: part-time $412 per credit hour. Tuition, nonresident: part-time $824 per credit hour. *Required fees:* $685 per semester. *Financial support:* Application deadline: 6/30; applicants required to submit FAFSA. *Unit head:* Kimberly K. Hill, Interim Program Director, 334-229-5888, E-mail: asupando@alasu.edu. *Application contact:* Dr. William Person, Dean of Graduate Studies, 334-229-4274, Fax: 334-229-4928, E-mail: wperson@alasu.edu.
Website: http://www.alasu.edu/academics/colleges—departments/health-sciences/prosthetics-orthotics/index.aspx

Augusta University, College of Allied Health Sciences, Program in Applied Health Sciences, Augusta, GA 30912. Offers diagnostic sciences (PhD); health care outcomes (PhD); rehabilitation science (PhD). *Program availability:* Part-time, online learning. *Entrance requirements:* For doctorate, GRE General Test, bachelor's degree, official transcripts, minimum undergraduate GPA of 3.0, three letters of recommendation. Additional exam requirements/recommendations for international students: Required—TOEFL (minimum score 550 paper-based; 79 iBT). Electronic applications accepted. *Faculty research:* Patient- and family-centered care, public health informatics, vascular health promotion through physical activity, improving air quality for school children, movement therapies for Parkinson's Disease.

Boston University, College of Health and Rehabilitation Sciences: Sargent College, Department of Occupational Therapy, Boston, MA 02215. Offers occupational therapy (OTD); rehabilitation sciences (PhD). *Accreditation:* AOTA (one or more programs are accredited). *Program availability:* Blended/hybrid learning. *Faculty:* 15 full-time (12 women), 7 part-time/adjunct (all women). *Students:* 118 full-time (106 women), 58 part-time (53 women); includes 38 minority (3 Black or African American, non-Hispanic/Latino; 17 Asian, non-Hispanic/Latino; 13 Hispanic/Latino; 5 Two or more races, non-Hispanic/Latino), 13 international. Average age 28. 269 applicants, 27% accepted, 45 enrolled. In 2017, 14 doctorates awarded. *Degree requirements:* For doctorate, scholarly project (for OTD); comprehensive exam and thesis (for PhD). *Entrance requirements:* For doctorate, GRE General Test. Additional exam requirements/recommendations for international students: Required—TOEFL (minimum score 550 paper-based; 84 iBT), TWE (minimum score 5). *Application deadline:* For fall admission, 12/15 priority date for domestic students, 1/15 priority date for international students. Applications are processed on a rolling basis. Application fee: $140. Electronic applications accepted. *Financial support:* In 2017–18, 60 students received support, including 12 teaching assistantships (averaging $2,500 per year); career-related internships or fieldwork, Federal Work-Study, institutionally sponsored loans, and scholarships/grants also available. Financial award application deadline: 12/15; financial award applicants required to submit FAFSA. *Faculty research:* Sensory integration, outcomes measurement, impact of Parkinson's disease, families of people with autism. *Total annual research expenditures:* $1.9 million. *Unit head:* Dr. Ellen Cohn, Program Director, 617-358-1063, Fax: 617-353-2926, E-mail: ecohn@bu.edu. *Application contact:* Sharon Sankey, Assistant Dean, Student Services, 617-353-2713, Fax: 617-353-7500, E-mail: ssankey@bu.edu.
Website: http://www.bu.edu/sargent/

Boston University, College of Health and Rehabilitation Sciences: Sargent College, Department of Physical Therapy and Athletic Training, Boston, MA 02215. Offers athletic training (MS); physical therapy (DPT); rehabilitation sciences (PhD). *Accreditation:* APTA (one or more programs are accredited). *Faculty:* 13 full-time (10 women), 26 part-time/adjunct (12 women). *Students:* 187 full-time (138 women), 4 part-time (2 women); includes 27 minority (1 Black or African American, non-Hispanic/Latino; 14 Asian, non-Hispanic/Latino; 6 Hispanic/Latino; 6 Two or more races, non-Hispanic/Latino), 9 international. Average age 25. 812 applicants, 16% accepted, 41 enrolled. In 2017, 66 doctorates awarded. *Degree requirements:* For doctorate, comprehensive exam and thesis (for PhD). *Entrance requirements:* For master's, GRE General Test, bachelor's degree; for doctorate, GRE General Test, bachelor's degree (for DPT), master's degree (for PhD). Additional exam requirements/recommendations for international students: Required—TOEFL (minimum score 550 paper-based; 84 iBT). *Application deadline:* For fall admission, 12/15 priority date for domestic and international students. Applications are processed on a rolling basis. Application fee: $145. Electronic applications accepted. *Financial support:* In 2017–18, 120 students received support, including 16 research assistantships with full tuition reimbursements available (averaging $22,000 per year), 6 teaching assistantships (averaging $2,500 per year); fellowships, career-related internships or fieldwork, Federal Work-Study, institutionally sponsored loans, scholarships/grants, and tuition waivers (full and partial) also available. Financial award application deadline: 12/15; financial award applicants required to submit FAFSA. *Faculty research:* Gait, balance, motor control, dynamic systems analysis, spinal cord injury. *Total annual research expenditures:* $1.5 million. *Unit head:* Dr. LaDora Thompson, Department Chair, 617-353-2724, E-mail: pt@bu.edu. *Application contact:* Sharon Sankey, Assistant Dean, Student Services, 617-353-2713, Fax: 617-353-7500, E-mail: ssankey@bu.edu.

Central Michigan University, College of Graduate Studies, The Herbert H. and Grace A. Dow College of Health Professions, School of Rehabilitation and Medical Sciences, Mount Pleasant, MI 48859. Offers physical therapy (DPT); physician assistant (MS). *Accreditation:* APTA; ARC-PA. *Degree requirements:* For master's, thesis or alternative; for doctorate, thesis/dissertation or alternative. *Entrance requirements:* For master's and doctorate, GRE. Electronic applications accepted.

Clarion University of Pennsylvania, College of Health and Human Services, Master's in Clinical Mental Health Counseling Program, Clarion, PA 16214. Offers MS. *Program availability:* Part-time, evening/weekend, online only, 100% online, blended/hybrid learning. *Faculty:* 2 full-time (1 woman), 1 part-time/adjunct (0 women). *Students:* 4 full-time (all women), 46 part-time (35 women); includes 3 minority (all Black or African American, non-Hispanic/Latino). Average age 32. 47 applicants, 74% accepted, 23 enrolled. In 2017, 1 master's awarded. *Entrance requirements:* For master's, GRE General Test, MAT, or minimum QPA of 3.0, goals letter. Additional exam requirements/recommendations for international students: Required—TOEFL (minimum score 550 paper-based, 80 iBT) or IELTS (7). *Application deadline:* For fall admission, 8/15 priority date for domestic students, 7/15 priority date for international students. Applications are processed on a rolling basis. Application fee: $40. Electronic applications accepted. *Expenses:* $655.05 per credit. *Financial support:* Career-related internships or fieldwork available. Support available to part-time students. Financial award application deadline: 3/1; financial award applicants required to submit FAFSA. *Unit head:* Dr. Ray Feroz, Chair, 814-393-2325, Fax: 814-393-1951. *Application contact:* Dana Bearer, Associate Director for Transfer, Adult and Graduate Admissions, 814-393-2337, Fax: 814-393-2772, E-mail: gradstudies@clarion.edu.

Concordia University Wisconsin, Graduate Programs, School of Health Professions, Program in Rehabilitation Science, Mequon, WI 53097-2402. Offers MSRS.

Duquesne University, John G. Rangos, Sr. School of Health Sciences, Pittsburgh, PA 15282-0001. Offers health management systems (MHMS); occupational therapy (MS, OTD); physical therapy (DPT); physician assistant studies (MPAS); rehabilitation science (MS, PhD); speech-language pathology (MS). *Accreditation:* AOTA (one or more programs are accredited); APTA (one or more programs are accredited); ASHA. *Program availability:* Part-time, minimal on-campus study. *Faculty:* 51 full-time (38 women), 33 part-time/adjunct (17 women). *Students:* 247 full-time (199 women), 11 part-time (7 women); includes 15 minority (2 Black or African American, non-Hispanic/Latino; 7 Asian, non-Hispanic/Latino; 3 Hispanic/Latino; 3 Two or more races, non-Hispanic/Latino), 42 international. Average age 23. 283 applicants, 31% accepted, 54 enrolled. In 2017, 134 master's, 39 doctorates awarded. *Degree requirements:* For doctorate, comprehensive exam (for some programs), thesis/dissertation (for some programs). *Entrance requirements:* For master's, GRE General Test (speech-language pathology), 3 letters of recommendation; minimum GPA of 2.75 (health management systems), 3.0 (speech-language pathology); for doctorate, GRE General Test (for physical therapy and rehabilitation science), 3 letters of recommendation, minimum GPA of 3.0, personal interview. Additional exam requirements/recommendations for international students: Required—TOEFL (minimum score 550 paper-based; 90 iBT); Recommended—IELTS. *Application deadline:* For fall admission, 2/1 for domestic and international students; for spring admission, 7/1 for domestic and international students. Applications are processed on a rolling basis. Application fee: $0. Electronic applications accepted. *Expenses:* $1,351 per credit ($1,259 for health management systems). *Financial support:* Federal Work-Study available. Financial award applicants required to submit FAFSA. *Faculty research:* Neuronal processing, electrical stimulation on peripheral neuropathy, central nervous system (CNS) stimulatory and inhibitory signals, behavioral genetic methodologies to development disorders of speech, neurogenic communication disorders. *Total annual research expenditures:* $24,578. *Unit head:* Dr. Fevzi Akinci, Dean, 412-396-5303, Fax: 412-396-5554, E-mail: akincif@duq.edu. *Application contact:* Christopher R. Hilf, Director of Enrollment Management, 412-396-5653, Fax: 412-396-5554, E-mail: hilfc@duq.edu.
Website: http://www.duq.edu/academics/schools/health-sciences

East Carolina University, Graduate School, College of Allied Health Sciences, Department of Addictions and Rehabilitation Studies, Greenville, NC 27858-4353. Offers clinical counseling (MS); military and trauma counseling (Certificate); rehabilitation and career counseling (MS); rehabilitation counseling (Certificate); rehabilitation counseling and administration (PhD); substance abuse counseling (Certificate); vocational evaluation (Certificate). *Accreditation:* CORE. *Program availability:* Part-time, evening/weekend. *Students:* 82 full-time (64 women), 55 part-time (43 women); includes 39 minority (28 Black or African American, non-Hispanic/Latino; 1 American Indian or Alaska Native, non-Hispanic/Latino; 2 Asian, non-Hispanic/Latino; 5 Hispanic/Latino; 3 Two or more races, non-Hispanic/Latino). Average age 33. 51 applicants, 73% accepted, 31 enrolled. In 2017, 19 master's, 5 doctorates, 34 other advanced degrees awarded. *Degree requirements:* For master's, comprehensive exam, thesis or alternative, internship; for doctorate, thesis/dissertation, internship. *Entrance requirements:* For master's and doctorate, GRE General Test or MAT. Additional exam requirements/recommendations for international students: Recommended—TOEFL (minimum score 78 iBT), IELTS (minimum score 6.5). *Application deadline:* For fall admission, 3/1 priority date for domestic students; for spring admission, 10/1 priority date for domestic students. Applications are processed on a rolling basis. Application fee: $75. Electronic applications accepted. *Expenses:* Tuition, state resident: full-time $4749; part-time $297 per credit hour. Tuition, nonresident: full-time $17,898; part-time $1119 per credit hour. *Required fees:* $2691; $224 per credit hour. Part-time tuition and fees vary according to course load and program. *Financial support:* Research assistantships with partial tuition reimbursements, teaching assistantships with partial tuition reimbursements, Federal Work-Study, scholarships/grants, and unspecified

assistantships available. Support available to part-time students. Financial award application deadline: 3/1; financial award applicants required to submit FAFSA. *Unit head:* Dr. Paul Toriello, Chair, 252-744-6292, E-mail: toriellop@ecu.edu.
Website: http://www.ecu.edu/rehb/

East Stroudsburg University of Pennsylvania, Graduate and Extended Studies, College of Education, Department of Special Education and Rehabilitation, East Stroudsburg, PA 18301-2999. Offers special education (M Ed). *Program availability:* Part-time, evening/weekend, online learning. *Faculty:* 4 full-time (3 women), 1 (woman) part-time/adjunct. *Students:* 11 full-time (8 women), 49 part-time (46 women); includes 4 minority (2 Black or African American, non-Hispanic/Latino; 1 American Indian or Alaska Native, non-Hispanic/Latino; 1 Hispanic/Latino). Average age 31. 32 applicants, 78% accepted, 19 enrolled. In 2017, 15 master's awarded. *Degree requirements:* For master's, comprehensive exam. *Entrance requirements:* For master's, PRAXIS/teacher certification, letter of recommendation, Pennsylvania Department of Education requirements. Additional exam requirements/recommendations for international students: Recommended—TOEFL (minimum score 560 paper-based; 83 iBT), IELTS. *Application deadline:* For fall admission, 7/31 priority date for domestic students, 6/30 priority date for international students; for spring admission, 11/30 for domestic students, 10/31 for international students. Applications are processed on a rolling basis. Application fee: $50. Electronic applications accepted. *Expenses:* Tuition, state resident: full-time $4500; part-time $3000 per credit. Tuition, nonresident: full-time $6750; part-time $4500 per credit. *Required fees:* $2642; $1756 per credit. $878 per semester. Tuition and fees vary according to course load, campus/location and program. *Financial support:* Research assistantships with tuition reimbursements, career-related internships or fieldwork, Federal Work-Study, and unspecified assistantships available. Support available to part-time students. Financial award application deadline: 3/1; financial award applicants required to submit FAFSA. *Unit head:* Dr. Gina Scala, Chair, 570-422-3781, Fax: 570-422-3198, E-mail: gscala@esu.edu. *Application contact:* Kevin Quintero, Associate Director, Graduate and Extended Studies, 570-422-3890, Fax: 570-422-2711, E-mail: kquintero@esu.edu.

George Mason University, College of Health and Human Services, Department of Rehabilitation Science, Fairfax, VA 22030. Offers PhD, Certificate. *Program availability:* Part-time. *Faculty:* 6 full-time (1 woman), 2 part-time/adjunct (0 women). *Students:* 13 full-time (7 women), 8 part-time (6 women); includes 2 minority (both Asian, non-Hispanic/Latino), 7 international. Average age 32. 14 applicants, 64% accepted, 3 enrolled. In 2017, 2 doctorates, 1 other advanced degree awarded. *Degree requirements:* For doctorate, comprehensive exam, thesis/dissertation; for Certificate, 15 credits, minimum GPA of 3.0. *Entrance requirements:* For doctorate, GRE, college transcripts, expanded goals statement, 2 letters of recommendation, resume, professional and volunteer experience in related fields; for Certificate, college transcripts, expanded goals statement. 2 letters of recommendation, resume, bachelor's degree in a discipline related to health sciences from regionally-accredited institution, minimum GPA of 3.0, professional and volunteer experience in related fields. Additional exam requirements/recommendations for international students: Required—TOEFL (minimum score 570 paper-based; 88 iBT), IELTS (minimum score 6.5), PTE (minimum score 59). *Application deadline:* For fall admission, 2/1 for domestic and international students. Application fee: $75 ($80 for international students). Electronic applications accepted. *Expenses:* Contact institution. *Financial support:* In 2017–18, 8 students received support, including 7 research assistantships (averaging $23,000 per year), 1 teaching assistantship; career-related internships or fieldwork, Federal Work-Study, scholarships/grants, unspecified assistantships, and health care benefits (for full-time research or teaching assistantship recipients) also available. Support available to part-time students. Financial award applicants required to submit FAFSA. *Faculty research:* Exercise and cognition; oxygen uptake kinetics, nonlinear analysis of movement complexity in gait and balance, central circulatory and microvascular mechanisms of performance fatigability, microvascular dysfunction and muscle fatigue in sleep disorders, multimodal exercise interventions for movement disorders. *Total annual research expenditures:* $219,104. *Unit head:* Andrew Guccione, Chair, 703-993-4650, E-mail: aguccion@gmu.edu. *Application contact:* Joshua Bowen, Program Coordinator, 703-993-1950, E-mail: jbowen6@gmu.edu.
Website: http://chhs.gmu.edu/rehabscience/

Indiana University–Purdue University Indianapolis, School of Health and Rehabilitation Sciences, Indianapolis, IN 46202. Offers health and rehabilitation sciences (PhD); health sciences (MS); nutrition and dietetics (MS); occupational therapy (OTD); physical therapy (DPT); physician assistant (MPAS). *Program availability:* Part-time, evening/weekend. *Degree requirements:* For master's, thesis (for some programs). *Entrance requirements:* For master's, GRE General Test, minimum GPA of 3.0 (for MS in health sciences, nutrition and dietetics), 3.2 (for MS in occupational therapy), 3.0 cumulative and prerequisite math/science (for MPAS); for doctorate, GRE, minimum cumulative and prerequisite math/science GPA of 3.2. Additional exam requirements/recommendations for international students: Required—TOEFL (minimum score 550 paper-based; 79 iBT), IELTS (minimum score 6.5), PTE (minimum score 54). Electronic applications accepted. *Expenses:* Contact institution. *Faculty research:* Function and mobility across the lifespan, pediatric nutrition, driving and mobility rehabilitation, neurorehabilitation and biomechanics, rehabilitation and integrative therapy.

Jackson State University, Graduate School, College of Education and Human Development, Department of Counseling, Rehabilitation and Psychometric Services, Jackson, MS 39217. Offers clinical mental health (MS); rehabilitation counseling (MS); school counseling (MS Ed). *Accreditation:* ACA; CORE (one or more programs are accredited); NCATE. *Program availability:* Part-time, evening/weekend, 100% online, blended/hybrid learning. *Degree requirements:* For master's, comprehensive exam, thesis. *Entrance requirements:* For master's, GRE General Test. Additional exam requirements/recommendations for international students: Required—TOEFL (minimum score 520 paper-based; 67 iBT). Electronic applications accepted. *Expenses:* Contact institution.

Lasell College, Graduate and Professional Studies in Rehabilitation Science, Newton, MA 02466-2709. Offers MS. *Program availability:* Part-time, evening/weekend, online only, 100% online. *Faculty:* 4 full-time (2 women), 1 (woman) part-time/adjunct. *Students:* 14 full-time (12 women), 7 part-time (6 women); includes 3 minority (2 Black or African American, non-Hispanic/Latino; 1 Two or more races, non-Hispanic/Latino). Average age 26. 21 applicants, 43% accepted, 8 enrolled. *Degree requirements:* For master's, minimum GPA of 3.0. *Entrance requirements:* For master's, one-page personal statement, 2 letters of recommendation, resume, bachelor's degree transcript, BA/BS in health-related field from accredited institution, minimum GPA of 2.75, 8 credits in anatomy and physiology, 3-4 credits in kinesiology, 3 credits in statistics. Additional exam requirements/recommendations for international students: Required—TOEFL (minimum score 550 paper-based, 79 iBT) or IELTS (minimum score 6). *Application deadline:* For fall admission, 8/31 priority date for domestic students, 6/30 priority date for international students; for spring admission, 12/31 priority date for domestic students, 10/31 priority date for international students. Applications are processed on a rolling basis. Electronic applications accepted. *Expenses:* $600 per credit. *Financial support:* Federal Work-Study, scholarships/grants, and tuition discounts available. Support available to part-time students. Financial award application deadline: 8/31; financial award applicants required to submit FAFSA. *Unit head:* Eric Turner, Dean of Graduate and Professional Studies, 617-243-2071, Fax: 617-243-2450, E-mail: gradinfo@lasell.edu. *Application contact:* Adrienne Franciosi, Director of Graduate Enrollment, 617-243-2214, Fax: 617-243-2450, E-mail: gradinfo@lasell.edu.
Website: http://www.lasell.edu/academics/graduate-and-professional-studies/programs-of-study/master-of-science-in-rehabilitation-science.html

Logan University, College of Health Sciences, Chesterfield, MO 63017. Offers health informatics (MS); health professionals education (DHPE); nutrition and human performance (MS); sports science and rehabilitation (MS). *Program availability:* Part-time, online only, 100% online. *Faculty:* 4 full-time (1 woman), 25 part-time/adjunct (13 women). *Students:* 84 full-time (63 women), 417 part-time (314 women); includes 75 minority (36 Black or African American, non-Hispanic/Latino; 3 American Indian or Alaska Native, non-Hispanic/Latino; 15 Asian, non-Hispanic/Latino; 17 Hispanic/Latino; 4 Two or more races, non-Hispanic/Latino), 1 international. Average age 36. 238 applicants, 72% accepted, 134 enrolled. In 2017, 61 master's awarded. *Entrance requirements:* For master's, minimum GPA of 2.5; 6 hours of biology and physical science; bachelor's degree and 9 hours of business health administration (for health informatics). Additional exam requirements/recommendations for international students: Required—TOEFL (minimum score 500 paper-based; 79 iBT); Recommended—IELTS (minimum score 6.5). *Application deadline:* Applications are processed on a rolling basis. Application fee: $50. Electronic applications accepted. *Expenses:* $450 per credit hour (for MS), $650 per credit hour (for DHPE), $80 fee per trimester. *Financial support:* In 2017–18, 4 students received support. Federal Work-Study available. Support available to part-time students. Financial award applicants required to submit FAFSA. *Faculty research:* Ankle injury prevention in high school athletes, low back pain in college football players, short arc banding and low back pain, the effects of enzymes on inflammatory blood markers, gait analysis in high school and college athletes. *Unit head:* Dr. Sherri Cole, Dean, College of Health Sciences, 636-227-2100 Ext. 2702, Fax: 636-207-2418, E-mail: sherri.cole@logan.edu. *Application contact:* Natacha Douglas, Executive Director of Admissions, 636-227-2100 Ext. 1718, Fax: 636-207-2425, E-mail: admissions@logan.edu.

Loma Linda University, School of Allied Health Professions, Department of Physical Therapy, Loma Linda, CA 92350. Offers physical therapy (DPT, PhD); rehabilitation (MS). *Accreditation:* APTA. *Entrance requirements:* Additional exam requirements/recommendations for international students: Required—TOEFL (minimum score 550 paper-based). Electronic applications accepted.

Marquette University, Graduate School, College of Health Sciences, Clinical and Translational Rehabilitation Science Program, Milwaukee, WI 53201-1881. Offers MS, PhD. *Entrance requirements:* For master's and doctorate, GRE, official transcripts, curriculum vitae, personal statement, three letters of recommendation, interview. Additional exam requirements/recommendations for international students: Required—TOEFL (minimum score 90 iBT).

McGill University, Faculty of Graduate and Postdoctoral Studies, Faculty of Medicine, School of Physical and Occupational Therapy, Montréal, QC H3A 2T5, Canada. Offers assessing driving capability (PGC); rehabilitation science (M Sc, PhD).

McMaster University, Faculty of Health Sciences and School of Graduate Studies, Program in Rehabilitation Science (course-based), Hamilton, ON L8S 4M2, Canada. Offers M Sc. *Program availability:* Part-time. *Degree requirements:* For master's, online courses and scholarly paper. *Entrance requirements:* For master's, minimum B+ average in final year of a 4-year undergraduate health professional program or other relevant program. Additional exam requirements/recommendations for international students: Required—TOEFL (minimum score 600 paper-based).

McMaster University, Faculty of Health Sciences and School of Graduate Studies, Program in Rehabilitation Science (Thesis Option), Hamilton, ON L8S 4M2, Canada. Offers M Sc, PhD. *Program availability:* Part-time. *Degree requirements:* For master's, thesis. *Entrance requirements:* For master's, minimum B+ average in final year of a 4-year undergraduate health professional program or other relevant program. Additional exam requirements/recommendations for international students: Required—TOEFL (minimum score 600 paper-based).

Medical University of South Carolina, College of Health Professions, PhD Program in Health and Rehabilitation Science, Charleston, SC 29425. Offers PhD. *Degree requirements:* For doctorate, comprehensive exam, thesis/dissertation. *Entrance requirements:* Additional exam requirements/recommendations for international students: Required—TOEFL (minimum score 600 paper-based). Electronic applications accepted. *Faculty research:* Spinal cord injury, geriatrics, health economics, health psychology, behavioral medicine.

New York University, Steinhardt School of Culture, Education, and Human Development, Department of Nutrition, Food Studies, and Public Health, Programs in Nutrition and Dietetics, New York, NY 10012. Offers clinical nutrition (MS); nutrition and dietetics (MS, PhD), including food and nutrition (MS); rehabilitation sciences (PhD). *Program availability:* Part-time. *Students:* Average age 33. 221 applicants, 24% accepted, 34 enrolled. In 2017, 51 master's, 1 doctorate awarded. *Entrance requirements:* For doctorate, GRE General Test, interview. Additional exam requirements/recommendations for international students: Required—TOEFL (minimum score 100 iBT). *Application deadline:* For fall admission, 12/1 priority date for domestic students, 12/1 for international students; for spring admission, 10/1 for domestic and international students. Applications are processed on a rolling basis. Application fee: $75. Electronic applications accepted. *Expenses: Tuition:* Full-time $41,352; part-time $19,968 per year. *Required fees:* $2496; $1628 per unit. $814 per term. Tuition and fees vary according to course load and program. *Financial support:* Fellowships with full and partial tuition reimbursements, career-related internships or fieldwork, Federal Work-Study, institutionally sponsored loans, scholarships/grants, tuition waivers (partial), and unspecified assistantships available. Financial award application deadline: 2/1; financial award applicants required to submit FAFSA. *Faculty research:* Nutrition and race, childhood obesity and other eating disorders, nutritional epidemiology, nutrition policy, nutrition and health promotion. *Unit head:* Dr. Krishnendu Ray, Associate Professor of Food Studies/Department Chair, 212-998-5580, Fax: 212-995-4194, E-mail: krishnendu.ray@nyu.edu. *Application contact:* 212-998-5030, Fax: 212-995-4328, E-mail: steinhardt.gradadmissions@nyu.edu.
Website: http://steinhardt.nyu.edu/nutrition/dietetics

Northwestern University, Feinberg School of Medicine, Department of Physical Therapy and Human Movement Sciences, Chicago, IL 60611-2814. Offers neuroscience (PhD), including movement and rehabilitation science; physical therapy (DPT); DPT/MPH; DPT/PhD. *Accreditation:* APTA. *Degree requirements:* For doctorate, research project. *Entrance requirements:* For doctorate, GRE General Test (for DPT), baccalaureate degree with minimum GPA of 3.0 in required course work (DPT). Additional exam requirements/recommendations for international students: Required—TOEFL (minimum score 100 iBT). *Application deadline:* For fall admission, 10/1 for domestic and international students. Applications are processed on a rolling basis. Electronic applications accepted. *Expenses:* Contact institution. *Financial support:* Institutionally sponsored loans and scholarships/grants available. Financial award application deadline: 3/1; financial award applicants required to submit FAFSA. *Unit*

head: Dr. Julius P. A. Dewald, Professor and Chair, 312-908-8160, Fax: 312-908-0741. *Application contact:* Dr. Jane Sullivan, Professor/Assistant Chair for Recruitment and Admissions, 312-908-8160, Fax: 312-908-0741, E-mail: dpt-admissions@northwestern.edu.
Website: http://www.feinberg.northwestern.edu/sites/pthms/

The Ohio State University, College of Medicine, School of Health and Rehabilitation Sciences, Program in Health and Rehabilitation Sciences, Columbus, OH 43210. Offers PhD. *Students:* 18 (15 women). Average age 30. In 2017, 4 doctorates awarded. *Degree requirements:* For doctorate, thesis/dissertation. *Entrance requirements:* For doctorate, GRE. Additional exam requirements/recommendations for international students: Required—TOEFL (minimum score 550 paper-based; 79 iBT), Michigan English Language Assessment Battery (minimum score 82); Recommended—IELTS (minimum score 7). *Application deadline:* For fall admission, 11/1 priority date for domestic students, 10/1 priority date for international students; for spring admission, 12/12 for domestic students, 11/10 for international students; for summer admission, 4/10 for domestic students, 3/13 for international students. Applications are processed on a rolling basis. Application fee: $60 ($70 for international students). Electronic applications accepted. *Financial support:* Fellowships with tuition reimbursements, research assistantships with tuition reimbursements, and teaching assistantships with tuition reimbursements available. *Unit head:* Dr. Deborah S. Larsen, Associate Dean and Director, 614-292-5645, Fax: 614-292-0210, E-mail: larsen.64@osu.edu. *Application contact:* Graduate and Professional Admissions, 614-292-9444, Fax: 614-292-3895, E-mail: gpadmissions@osu.edu.
Website: http://medicine.osu.edu/hrs/phd

Old Dominion University, College of Health Sciences, School of Physical Therapy and Athletic Training, Doctor of Kinesiology and Rehabilitation Program, Norfolk, VA 23529. Offers PhD. *Faculty:* 3 full-time (1 woman), 7 part-time/adjunct (3 women). *Students:* 9 full-time (6 women), 2 part-time (both women); includes 2 minority (1 Hispanic/Latino; 1 Two or more races, non-Hispanic/Latino). Average age 30. 11 applicants, 82% accepted, 9 enrolled. *Degree requirements:* For doctorate, comprehensive exam, thesis/dissertation. *Entrance requirements:* For doctorate, master's degree or higher in an associated area of basic science, such as kinesiology, exercise science, or biomechanics, or in a health profession such as athletic training, nursing, occupational therapy, physical therapy, or speech/language pathology. Additional exam requirements/recommendations for international students: Recommended—TOEFL (minimum score 550 paper-based; 79 iBT), IELTS (minimum score 6.5). *Application deadline:* For fall admission, 2/1 for domestic and international students. Application fee: $50. Electronic applications accepted. *Expenses:* $496 per credit. *Financial support:* In 2017–18, 5 students received support, including 5 research assistantships with full tuition reimbursements available (averaging $15,000 per year); unspecified assistantships also available. *Faculty research:* Balance and falls, gait, perceptual information in action and virtual reality, sensorimotor compromise following joint injury, evidence-based practice and patient-centered care. *Unit head:* Daniel Russell, Director, 757-683-6016, E-mail: dmrussel@odu.edu. *Application contact:* William Heffelfinger, Director of Graduate Admissions, 757-683-5554, Fax: 757-683-3255, E-mail: gradadmit@odu.edu.
Website: http://www.odu.edu/ptat/phd-kinesiology-rehabilitation

Queen's University at Kingston, School of Graduate Studies, Faculty of Health Sciences, School of Rehabilitation Therapy, Kingston, ON K7L 3N6, Canada. Offers occupational therapy (M Sc OT); physical therapy (M Sc PT); rehabilitation science (M Sc, PhD). *Program availability:* Part-time. *Degree requirements:* For master's, thesis; for doctorate, comprehensive exam, thesis/dissertation. *Entrance requirements:* Additional exam requirements/recommendations for international students: Required—TOEFL. *Faculty research:* Disability, community, motor performance, rehabilitation, treatment efficiency.

Salus University, College of Education and Rehabilitation, Elkins Park, PA 19027-1598. Offers education of children and youth with visual and multiple impairments (M Ed, Certificate); low vision rehabilitation (MS, Certificate); occupational therapy (MS); orientation and mobility therapy (MS, Certificate); speech-language pathology (MS); vision rehabilitation therapy (MS, Certificate); OD/MS. *Accreditation:* AOTA. *Program availability:* Part-time, online learning. *Entrance requirements:* For master's, GRE or MAT, letters of reference (3), interviews (2). Additional exam requirements/recommendations for international students: Required—TOEFL, TWE. *Expenses:* Contact institution. *Faculty research:* Knowledge utilization, technology transfer.

Stony Brook University, State University of New York, Stony Brook Medicine, School of Health Technology and Management, Stony Brook, NY 11794. Offers applied health informatics (MS); disability studies (Certificate); health administration (MHA); health and rehabilitation sciences (PhD); health care management (Advanced Certificate); health care policy and management (MS); occupational therapy (MS); physical therapy (DPT); physician assistant (MS). *Accreditation:* APTA. *Faculty:* 62 full-time (42 women), 59 part-time/adjunct (36 women). *Students:* 565 full-time (382 women), 67 part-time (53 women); includes 179 minority (29 Black or African American, non-Hispanic/Latino; 83 Asian, non-Hispanic/Latino; 59 Hispanic/Latino; 2 Native Hawaiian or other Pacific Islander, non-Hispanic/Latino; 6 Two or more races, non-Hispanic/Latino), 14 international. Average age 27. 2,516 applicants, 16% accepted, 266 enrolled. In 2017, 162 master's, 84 doctorates, 39 other advanced degrees awarded. *Degree requirements:* For master's, thesis; for doctorate, thesis/dissertation. *Entrance requirements:* For master's, GRE General Test, minimum GPA of 3.0, work experience in field, references; for doctorate, GRE, three references, essay. Additional exam requirements/recommendations for international students: Required—TOEFL (minimum score 550 paper-based). *Application deadline:* For fall admission, 1/15 for domestic students; for spring admission, 10/1 for domestic students. Application fee: $100. *Expenses:* Contact institution. *Financial support:* Fellowships, research assistantships, teaching assistantships, career-related internships or fieldwork, Federal Work-Study, and institutionally sponsored loans available. Financial award application deadline: 3/15. *Faculty research:* Developmental disabilities, disability studies, health promotion, multiple sclerosis, quality of life program, internal medicine, lung disease, palliative care, respiratory diseases, neuromuscular disorders, orthopedics, physical medicine and rehabilitation, physical therapy, prostheses or implants, advance directives, advocacy alienation, allied health education, allied health occupations, adolescents, adoption, child or adolescent mental health, multiple sclerosis, youth policy. *Total annual research expenditures:* $1.2 million. *Unit head:* Dr. Carlos Vidal, Dean, 631-444-1009, Fax: 631-444-7621, E-mail: carlos.vidal@stonybrook.edu. *Application contact:* Frances Shaw, 631-444-3240, Fax: 631-444-7621, E-mail: frances.shaw@stonybrook.edu.
Website: http://healthtechnology.stonybrookmedicine.edu/

Temple University, College of Public Health, Department of Rehabilitation Sciences, Philadelphia, PA 19122. Offers occupational therapy (MOT, DOT); therapeutic recreation (MS), including recreation therapy. *Accreditation:* AOTA. *Program availability:* Part-time. *Faculty:* 17 full-time (16 women), 3 part-time/adjunct (2 women). *Students:* 117 full-time (108 women), 24 part-time (22 women); includes 24 minority (5 Black or African American, non-Hispanic/Latino; 6 Asian, non-Hispanic/Latino; 7 Hispanic/Latino; 6 Two or more races, non-Hispanic/Latino). 12 applicants, 100% accepted, 10 enrolled. In 2017, 49 master's, 7 doctorates awarded. *Degree requirements:* For doctorate, comprehensive exam (for some programs), thesis/dissertation (for some programs). *Entrance requirements:* For master's and doctorate, GRE General Test, minimum GPA of 3.0. Additional exam requirements/recommendations for international students: Required—TOEFL (minimum score 550 paper-based; 79 iBT). *Application deadline:* For fall admission, 2/1 for domestic students, 1/1 for international students; for spring admission, 11/1 for domestic students, 10/1 for international students. Applications are processed on a rolling basis. Application fee: $60. Electronic applications accepted. *Expenses:* Contact institution. *Financial support:* Career-related internships or fieldwork and Federal Work-Study available. *Faculty research:* Participation, community inclusion, disability issues, leisure/recreation, occupation, quality of life, adaptive equipment and technology. *Unit head:* Dr. Mark Salzer, Chair, 215-204-7879, E-mail: mark.salzer@temple.edu.
Website: http://cph.temple.edu/rs/home

Texas Tech University Health Sciences Center, School of Health Professions, Program in Rehabilitation Science, Lubbock, TX 79430. Offers PhD. *Program availability:* Part-time. *Faculty:* 22 full-time (9 women), 8 part-time/adjunct (3 women). *Students:* 9 full-time (7 women), 12 part-time (5 women); includes 9 minority (2 Black or African American, non-Hispanic/Latino; 5 Asian, non-Hispanic/Latino; 2 Hispanic/Latino). Average age 35. 30 applicants, 30% accepted, 5 enrolled. In 2017, 1 doctorate awarded. *Entrance requirements:* For doctorate, GRE. Additional exam requirements/recommendations for international students: Required—TOEFL (minimum score 550 paper-based; 79 iBT), IELTS. *Application deadline:* For fall admission, 3/15 for domestic students; for spring admission, 10/15 for domestic students; for summer admission, 2/1 for domestic students. Applications are processed on a rolling basis. Application fee: $75. Electronic applications accepted. *Financial support:* Research assistantships, teaching assistantships, institutionally sponsored loans, and scholarships/grants available. Financial award application deadline: 9/1; financial award applicants required to submit FAFSA. *Unit head:* Dr. Roger James, Program Director, 806-743-3226, Fax: 806-743-2189, E-mail: roger.james@ttuhsc.edu. *Application contact:* Lindsay Johnson, Associate Dean for Admissions and Student Affairs, 806-743-3220, Fax: 806-743-2994, E-mail: lindsay.johnson@ttuhsc.edu.
Website: http://www.ttuhsc.edu/health-professions/phd-rehabilitation-science/default.aspx

Université de Montréal, Faculty of Medicine, Program in Mobility and Posture, Montréal, QC H3C 3J7, Canada. Offers DESS.

University at Buffalo, the State University of New York, Graduate School, School of Public Health and Health Professions, Department of Rehabilitation Science, Program in Assistive and Rehabilitation Technology, Buffalo, NY 14260. Offers Certificate. *Program availability:* Part-time. *Faculty:* 2 full-time (1 woman). In 2017, 1 Certificate awarded. *Entrance requirements:* For degree, bachelor's degree. Additional exam requirements/recommendations for international students: Required—TOEFL (minimum score 550 paper-based; 79 iBT). *Application deadline:* For fall admission, 6/1 priority date for domestic students; for spring admission, 11/1 priority date for international students. Applications are processed on a rolling basis. Application fee: $50. Electronic applications accepted. *Faculty research:* Assistive technology outcomes. *Total annual research expenditures:* $1.1 million. *Unit head:* Dr. Robert Burkard, Chair, 716-829-6720, Fax: 716-829-2317, E-mail: phhpadv@buffalo.edu. *Application contact:* Dr. James A. Lenker, Program Director, 716-829-6726, Fax: 716-829-3217, E-mail: lenker@buffalo.edu.
Website: http://sphhp.buffalo.edu/rehabilitation-science/education/adv-grad-cert-assistive-and-rehabilitation-technology.html

The University of Alabama at Birmingham, School of Health Professions, Program in Rehabilitation Science, Birmingham, AL 35294. Offers PhD. Program offered jointly by Departments of Occupational Therapy and Physical Therapy. *Program availability:* Part-time. *Faculty:* 20 full-time (8 women). *Students:* 23 full-time (16 women), 1 part-time (0 women); includes 4 minority (2 Asian, non-Hispanic/Latino; 1 Hispanic/Latino; 1 Two or more races, non-Hispanic/Latino), 11 international. Average age 29. 28 applicants, 36% accepted, 9 enrolled. In 2017, 2 doctorates awarded. *Degree requirements:* For doctorate, comprehensive exam, thesis/dissertation. *Entrance requirements:* For doctorate, GRE, references, minimum GPA of 3.0, interview. Additional exam requirements/recommendations for international students: Required—TOEFL (minimum score 500 paper-based; 80 iBT); Recommended—IELTS (minimum score 5). *Application deadline:* For fall admission, 1/31 priority date for domestic and international students. Applications are processed on a rolling basis. Application fee: $50 ($60 for international students). Electronic applications accepted. *Financial support:* In 2017–18, 15 students received support, including 3 fellowships with full tuition reimbursements available (averaging $29,000 per year), 12 research assistantships with full tuition reimbursements available (averaging $29,000 per year); scholarships/grants, traineeships, and health care benefits also available. Financial award application deadline: 2/1. *Faculty research:* Motor control physiology, occupation science, disability health behavior, exercise physiology, physical rehabilitation. *Total annual research expenditures:* $30,000. *Unit head:* Dr. David A. Brown, Graduate Program Director/Professor, 205-975-2788, E-mail: dbrownpt@uab.edu. *Application contact:* Holly Hebard, Director of Graduate School Operations, 205-934-8227, Fax: 205-934-8413, E-mail: gradschool@uab.edu.
Website: http://www.uab.edu/shp/pt/rsphd

University of Alberta, Faculty of Graduate Studies and Research, Faculty of Rehabilitation Medicine, Edmonton, AB T6G 2E1, Canada. Offers PhD. *Degree requirements:* For doctorate, thesis/dissertation. *Entrance requirements:* For doctorate, GRE, minimum GPA of 7.0 on a 9.0 scale. Additional exam requirements/recommendations for international students: Required—TOEFL. Electronic applications accepted. *Faculty research:* Musculoskeletal disorders, neuromotor control, exercise physiology, motor speech disorders, assistive technologies, cardiac rehabilitation/therapeutic exercise.

The University of British Columbia, Faculty of Medicine, School of Rehabilitation Sciences, Vancouver, BC V6T 1Z3, Canada. Offers M Sc, MRSc, PhD. *Degree requirements:* For master's, thesis; for doctorate, comprehensive exam, thesis/dissertation. *Entrance requirements:* For master's, minimum B+ average; for doctorate, minimum B+ average, master's degree. Additional exam requirements/recommendations for international students: Required—TOEFL. Electronic applications accepted. *Expenses:* Contact institution. *Faculty research:* Disability, rehabilitation and society, exercise science and rehabilitation, neurorehabilitation and motor control.

University of Colorado Denver, School of Medicine, Program in Rehabilitation Science, Aurora, CO 80045. Offers PhD. In 2017, 1 doctorate awarded. *Degree requirements:* For doctorate, comprehensive exam, 60 credit hours (30 of core coursework and 30 of thesis). *Entrance requirements:* For doctorate, GRE, bachelor's degree with minimum GPA of 3.0, research experience (preferred), three letters of recommendation, interview. Application fee: $0. *Financial support:* Fellowships, research assistantships, teaching assistantships, career-related internships or fieldwork, Federal Work-Study, institutionally sponsored loans, scholarships/grants, traineeships, and unspecified assistantships available. *Unit head:* Margaret Schenkman, Director of Physical Therapy Program, 303-724-9375, E-mail: margaret.schenkman@ucdenver.edu. *Application contact:* Vonelle Kelly, Program Administrator, 303-724-3102, E-mail: vonelle.kelly@ucdenver.edu.
Website: http://www.ucdenver.edu/academics/colleges/medicalschool/education/degree_programs/pt/EducationPrograms/PhD/Pages/Overview.aspx

University of Florida, Graduate School, College of Public Health and Health Professions, Program in Rehabilitation Science, Gainesville, FL 32611. Offers PhD, PhD/MPH. *Degree requirements:* For doctorate, comprehensive exam, thesis/dissertation. *Entrance requirements:* For doctorate, GRE (minimum scores: 150 Verbal, 145 Quantitative), minimum GPA of 3.0. Additional exam requirements/recommendations for international students: Required—TOEFL (minimum score 550 paper-based; 80 iBT), IELTS (minimum score 6). Electronic applications accepted. *Faculty research:* Neuroplasticity and neurorehabilitation, musculoskeletal pain, cardiopulmonary and respiratory, rehabilitation, muscle degeneration, regeneration and pathology, clinical and patient outcome measures.

University of Illinois at Urbana–Champaign, Graduate College, College of Applied Health Sciences, Department of Kinesiology and Community Health, Champaign, IL 61820. Offers community health (MS, MSPH, PhD); kinesiology (MS, PhD); public health (MPH); rehabilitation (MS); PhD/MPH.

The University of Iowa, Roy J. and Lucille A. Carver College of Medicine and Graduate College, Graduate Programs in Medicine, Department of Physical Therapy and Rehabilitation Science, Iowa City, IA 52242. Offers physical rehabilitation science (MA, PhD); physical therapy (DPT). *Accreditation:* APTA (one or more programs are accredited). Terminal master's awarded for partial completion of doctoral program. *Degree requirements:* For master's, thesis (for some programs); for doctorate, comprehensive exam (for some programs), thesis/dissertation (for some programs). *Entrance requirements:* For master's and doctorate, GRE. Additional exam requirements/recommendations for international students: Required—TOEFL. Electronic applications accepted. *Expenses:* Contact institution. *Faculty research:* Neuroplasticity and motor control, pain mechanisms, biomechanics and sports medicine, neuromuscular physiology, cardiovascular physiology.

The University of Kansas, University of Kansas Medical Center, School of Health Professions, Department of Occupational Therapy Education, Kansas City, KS 66160. Offers occupational therapy (MOT, OTD); therapeutic science (PhD). *Accreditation:* AOTA. *Program availability:* Part-time. *Faculty:* 15. *Students:* 127 full-time (113 women), 25 part-time (22 women); includes 18 minority (1 Black or African American, non-Hispanic/Latino; 1 American Indian or Alaska Native, non-Hispanic/Latino; 4 Asian, non-Hispanic/Latino; 7 Hispanic/Latino; 5 Two or more races, non-Hispanic/Latino), 5 international. Average age 27. 218 applicants, 22% accepted, 48 enrolled. In 2017, 36 master's, 3 doctorates awarded. *Degree requirements:* For doctorate, comprehensive exam, thesis/dissertation, oral defense. *Entrance requirements:* For master's, 40 hours of paid work or volunteer experience working directly with people with special needs, 3 letters of recommendation, personal statement, program statement of interest, bachelor's degree with 40 hours of prerequisite work, minimum GPA of 3.0; for doctorate, 24 hours of master's-level research. Additional exam requirements/recommendations for international students: Required—TOEFL; Recommended—IELTS. *Application deadline:* For fall admission, 12/1 for domestic students, 4/1 for international students. Application fee: $60. Electronic applications accepted. *Financial support:* In 2017–18, 2 teaching assistantships with full and partial tuition reimbursements were awarded; research assistantships with partial tuition reimbursements, scholarships/grants, traineeships, and unspecified assistantships also available. Financial award application deadline: 3/1; financial award applicants required to submit FAFSA. *Faculty research:* Impact of sensory processing in everyday life; improving balance, motor skills, and independence with community nonprofit organizations serving people with special needs; improving self-confidence and self-sufficiency with poverty-based services in community; working with autism population in a community-wide aquatics program; improving quality of life of people living with cancer and chronic illness. *Total annual research expenditures:* $12,331. *Unit head:* Dr. Winifred W. Dunn, Professor/Chair, 913-588-7195, Fax: 913-588-4568, E-mail: wdunn@kumc.edu. *Application contact:* Wendy Hildenbrand, Admissions Representative, 913-588-7174, Fax: 913-588-4568, E-mail: whildenb@kumc.edu.
Website: http://www.kumc.edu/school-of-health-professions/occupational-therapy-education.html

The University of Kansas, University of Kansas Medical Center, School of Health Professions, Department of Physical Therapy and Rehabilitation Science, Kansas City, KS 66160. Offers physical therapy (DPT); rehabilitation science (PhD). *Accreditation:* APTA. *Faculty:* 26. *Students:* 191 full-time (117 women), 1 part-time (0 women); includes 17 minority (3 Black or African American, non-Hispanic/Latino; 1 Asian, non-Hispanic/Latino; 8 Hispanic/Latino; 1 Native Hawaiian or other Pacific Islander, non-Hispanic/Latino; 4 Two or more races, non-Hispanic/Latino), 12 international. Average age 25. 398 applicants, 19% accepted, 62 enrolled. In 2017, 60 doctorates awarded. *Degree requirements:* For doctorate, comprehensive exam, research project with paper. *Entrance requirements:* For doctorate, GRE General Test, minimum GPA of 3.0. Additional exam requirements/recommendations for international students: Required—TOEFL. *Application deadline:* For fall admission, 11/1 for domestic students. Application fee: $75. Electronic applications accepted. *Expenses:* Contact institution. *Financial support:* Research assistantships with tuition reimbursements, teaching assistantships with tuition reimbursements, career-related internships or fieldwork, Federal Work-Study, institutionally sponsored loans, scholarships/grants, traineeships, and unspecified assistantships available. Financial award application deadline: 3/1; financial award applicants required to submit FAFSA. *Faculty research:* Stroke rehabilitation and the effects on balance and coordination; deep brain stimulation and Parkinson's disease; peripheral neuropathies, pain and the effects of exercise; islet transplants for Type 1 diabetes; cardiac disease associated with diabetes. *Total annual research expenditures:* $333,916. *Unit head:* Dr. Patricia Kluding, Chair, 913-588-6799, Fax: 913-588-6910, E-mail: pkluding@kumc.edu. *Application contact:* Robert Bagley, Senior Coordinator, 913-588-6799, Fax: 913-588-6910, E-mail: rbagley@kumc.edu.
Website: http://www.kumc.edu/school-of-health-professions/physical-therapy-and-rehabilitation-science.html

University of Kentucky, Graduate School, College of Health Sciences, Program in Rehabilitation Sciences, Lexington, KY 40506-0032. Offers PhD. *Degree requirements:* For doctorate, comprehensive exam, thesis/dissertation. *Entrance requirements:* For doctorate, GRE General Test, minimum undergraduate GPA of 2.75. Additional exam requirements/recommendations for international students: Required—TOEFL (minimum score 550 paper-based). Electronic applications accepted.

University of Manitoba, Faculty of Graduate Studies, College of Rehabilitation Sciences, Winnipeg, MB R3T 2N2, Canada. Offers applied health sciences (PhD); occupational therapy (MOT); physical therapy (MPT); rehabilitation sciences (M Sc).

University of Maryland, Baltimore, Graduate School, Graduate Program in Life Sciences, Program in Physical Rehabilitation Science, Baltimore, MD 21201. Offers PhD, MD/PhD. *Students:* 3 full-time (2 women), 4 part-time (3 women); includes 2 minority (1 Black or African American, non-Hispanic/Latino; 1 Hispanic/Latino), 2 international. Average age 31. 3 applicants, 33% accepted. *Degree requirements:* For doctorate, comprehensive exam, thesis/dissertation. *Entrance requirements:* For doctorate, GRE, minimum GPA of 3.0, curriculum vitae, essay, 3 letters of recommendation. Additional exam requirements/recommendations for international students: Required—TOEFL (minimum score 80 iBT); Recommended—IELTS (minimum score 7). *Application deadline:* For fall admission, 3/15 for domestic students, 1/15 for international students. Application fee: $75. Electronic applications accepted. *Expenses:* Tuition, state resident: full-time $13,990; part-time $661 per credit. Tuition, nonresident: full-time $30,484; part-time $1310 per credit. *Required fees:* $1894; $94 per credit. $415 per semester. Part-time tuition and fees vary according to course load, degree level and program. *Financial support:* In 2017–18, research assistantships with partial tuition reimbursements (averaging $26,000 per year) were awarded; health care benefits and unspecified assistantships also available. Financial award application deadline: 3/1; financial award applicants required to submit FAFSA. *Faculty research:* Applied physiology, biomechanics, epidemiology of disability, neuromotor control. *Unit head:* Dr. Larry Forester, Program Director, 410-706-5212, Fax: 410-706-4903, E-mail: lforrester@som.umaryland.edu. *Application contact:* Janice Abarro, Senior Research Analyst, 410-706-0856, E-mail: jabarro@som.umaryland.edu.
Website: http://lifesciences.umaryland.edu/rehabscience/

University of Maryland, Baltimore, School of Medicine, Department of Physical Therapy and Rehabilitation Science, Baltimore, MD 21201. Offers physical rehabilitation science (PhD); physical therapy and rehabilitation science (DPT). *Accreditation:* APTA. *Students:* 183 full-time (124 women), 2 part-time (1 woman); includes 26 minority (5 Black or African American, non-Hispanic/Latino; 1 American Indian or Alaska Native, non-Hispanic/Latino; 9 Asian, non-Hispanic/Latino; 8 Hispanic/Latino; 3 Two or more races, non-Hispanic/Latino), 2 international. Average age 25. 187 applicants, 91% accepted, 65 enrolled. In 2017, 56 doctorates awarded. *Entrance requirements:* For doctorate, GRE General Test, BS, science coursework. Additional exam requirements/recommendations for international students: Required—TOEFL (minimum score 80 iBT). Electronic applications accepted. *Expenses:* Contact institution. *Financial support:* Career-related internships or fieldwork, Federal Work-Study, scholarships/grants, traineeships, health care benefits, and unspecified assistantships available. Financial award application deadline: 3/1; financial award applicants required to submit FAFSA. *Unit head:* Dr. Mark W. Rogers, Chair, 410-706-0841, Fax: 410-706-4903, E-mail: mrogers@som.umaryland.edu. *Application contact:* Aynsley Hamel, Program Coordinator, 410-706-0566, Fax: 410-706-6387, E-mail: ptadmissions@som.umaryland.edu.
Website: http://pt.umaryland.edu/pros.asp

University of Maryland Eastern Shore, Graduate Programs, Department of Rehabilitation Services, Princess Anne, MD 21853. Offers rehabilitation counseling (MS). *Accreditation:* CORE. *Program availability:* Part-time, evening/weekend. *Degree requirements:* For master's, internship. *Entrance requirements:* For master's, interview. Additional exam requirements/recommendations for international students: Required—TOEFL (minimum score 80 iBT). *Application deadline:* For fall admission, 5/1 priority date for domestic and international students. Application fee: $30. Electronic applications accepted. *Expenses:* Tuition, state resident: part-time $325 per credit hour. Tuition, nonresident: part-time $604 per credit hour. *Required fees:* $85 per credit hour. Part-time tuition and fees vary according to campus/location, program and reciprocity agreements. *Financial support:* Research assistantships, scholarships/grants, and unspecified assistantships available. Financial award application deadline: 3/1. *Faculty research:* Long-term rehabilitation training. *Unit head:* Dr. Leslie Santos, 410-651-6262, E-mail: lsantos@umes.edu. *Application contact:* Dr. Leslie Santos, 410-651-6262, E-mail: lsantos@umes.edu.

University of Northern Colorado, Graduate School, College of Natural and Health Sciences, School of Human Sciences, Program in Rehabilitation Counseling and Sciences, Greeley, CO 80639. Offers rehabilitation counseling (MA); rehabilitation sciences (PhD). *Accreditation:* CORE (one or more programs are accredited). *Program availability:* Part-time. *Degree requirements:* For master's, comprehensive exam, thesis or alternative; for doctorate, comprehensive exam, thesis/dissertation. *Entrance requirements:* For master's, GRE General Test or MAT, 2 letters of recommendation; for doctorate, GRE General Test, 2 letters of recommendation. Electronic applications accepted.

University of North Texas Health Science Center at Fort Worth, Graduate School of Biomedical Sciences, Fort Worth, TX 76107-2699. Offers biochemistry and cancer biology (MS, PhD); biotechnology (MS); cell biology, immunology and microbiology (MS, PhD); clinical research management (MS); forensic genetics (MS); genetics (MS, PhD); integrative physiology (MS, PhD); medical sciences (MS); pharmaceutical sciences and pharmacotherapy (MS, PhD); pharmacology and neuroscience (MS, PhD); structural anatomy and rehabilitation sciences (MS, PhD); DO/MS; DO/PhD. Terminal master's awarded for partial completion of doctoral program. *Degree requirements:* For master's, thesis; for doctorate, thesis/dissertation. *Entrance requirements:* For master's and doctorate, GRE General Test. Additional exam requirements/recommendations for international students: Required—TOEFL. *Expenses:* Contact institution. *Faculty research:* Alzheimer's disease, aging, eye diseases, cancer, cardiovascular disease.

University of Oklahoma Health Sciences Center, Graduate College, College of Allied Health, Department of Rehabilitation Sciences, Oklahoma City, OK 73190. Offers MS. *Degree requirements:* For master's, comprehensive exam, thesis optional. *Entrance requirements:* For master's, GRE General Test, 2 years of clinical experience, 3 letters of reference. Additional exam requirements/recommendations for international students: Required—TOEFL (minimum score 550 paper-based).

University of Ottawa, Faculty of Graduate and Postdoctoral Studies, Faculty of Health Sciences, School of Rehabilitation Sciences, Ottawa, ON K1N 6N5, Canada. Offers audiology (M Sc); orthophony (M Sc). *Program availability:* Part-time, evening/weekend. *Entrance requirements:* For master's, honors degree or equivalent, minimum B average. Electronic applications accepted.

University of Pittsburgh, School of Health and Rehabilitation Sciences, Department of Rehabilitation Science and Technology, Pittsburgh, PA 15260. Offers clinical rehabilitation and mental health counseling (MS); physician assistant studies (MS); prosthetics and orthotics (DPT); rehabilitation technology (MS). *Program availability:* Online learning. *Faculty:* 27 full-time (14 women), 7 part-time/adjunct (3 women). *Students:* 177 full-time (118 women), 9 part-time (8 women); includes 26 minority (6 Black or African American, non-Hispanic/Latino; 5 Asian, non-Hispanic/Latino; 9 Hispanic/Latino; 6 Two or more races, non-Hispanic/Latino), 12 international. Average age 25. 611 applicants, 25% accepted, 101 enrolled. In 2017, 72 master's awarded. *Degree requirements:* For master's, comprehensive exam (for some programs). *Entrance requirements:* For master's, GRE General Test, hands-on patient care experience, CPR certification. Additional exam requirements/recommendations for international students: Required—TOEFL (minimum score 550 paper-based; 80 iBT), IELTS (minimum score 6.5). *Application deadline:* For fall admission, 12/31 for domestic and international students; for spring admission, 11/1 for domestic students, 9/1 for international students. Application fee: $177. Electronic applications accepted. *Financial support:* In 2017–18, 14 research assistantships (averaging $23,650 per year) were awarded; career-related internships or fieldwork, Federal Work-Study, scholarships/grants, traineeships, and unspecified assistantships also available. *Faculty research:* Assistive and rehabilitation technology development; prevention and management of chronic conditions; universal design and accessibility; environmental optimization; rehabilitation outcomes measurement. *Total annual research expenditures:* $9.2 million. *Unit head:* Dr. Rory Cooper, Associate Dean for Inclusion/Chair/Professor, 412-822-3700, E-mail: rcooper@pitt.edu. *Application contact:* Jessica Maguire, Director of Admissions, 412-383-6557, Fax: 412-383-6535, E-mail: maguire@pitt.edu.
Website: http://www.shrs.pitt.edu/rst

Rehabilitation Sciences

University of Pittsburgh, School of Health and Rehabilitation Sciences, Department of Sports Medicine and Nutrition, Pittsburgh, PA 15260. Offers health and rehabilitation sciences (MS), including sports medicine, wellness and human performance; nutrition and dietetics (MS). *Program availability:* Online learning. *Faculty:* 15 full-time (8 women), 3 part-time/adjunct (all women). *Students:* 55 full-time (48 women), 8 part-time (7 women); includes 8 minority (1 Black or African American, non-Hispanic/Latino; 1 American Indian or Alaska Native, non-Hispanic/Latino; 2 Hispanic/Latino; 4 Two or more races, non-Hispanic/Latino), 4 international. Average age 26. 128 applicants, 65% accepted, 28 enrolled. In 2017, 29 master's awarded. *Degree requirements:* For master's, comprehensive exam (for some programs). *Entrance requirements:* Additional exam requirements/recommendations for international students: Required—TOEFL (minimum score 550 paper-based; 80 iBT), IELTS (minimum score 6.5). *Application deadline:* For fall admission, 3/15 for domestic and international students. Application fee: $50. Electronic applications accepted. *Financial support:* In 2017–18, 6 fellowships (averaging $15,060 per year), 7 research assistantships (averaging $27,400 per year) were awarded; career-related internships or fieldwork, Federal Work-Study, scholarships/grants, traineeships, and unspecified assistantships also available. *Faculty research:* Nutrition and fitness; movement science; injury prevention and human performance; molecular transducers of physical activity; characterization of psychological resilience and readiness. *Total annual research expenditures:* $2.4 million. *Unit head:* Dr. Kevin Conley, Chair/Associate Professor, 412-383-6737, Fax: 412-383-6636, E-mail: kconley@pitt.edu. *Application contact:* Jessica Maguire, Director of Admissions, 412-383-6557, Fax: 412-383-6535, E-mail: maguire@pitt.edu.
Website: http://www.shrs.pitt.edu/smn

University of Pittsburgh, School of Health and Rehabilitation Sciences, PhD Program in Rehabilitation Science, Pittsburgh, PA 15260. Offers PhD. *Program availability:* Part-time. *Students:* 41 full-time (18 women), 4 part-time (2 women); includes 7 minority (3 Black or African American, non-Hispanic/Latino; 1 Asian, non-Hispanic/Latino; 1 Hispanic/Latino; 2 Two or more races, non-Hispanic/Latino), 12 international. Average age 32. 18 applicants, 56% accepted, 7 enrolled. In 2017, 22 doctorates awarded. *Degree requirements:* For doctorate, thesis/dissertation. *Entrance requirements:* For doctorate, GRE General Test. Additional exam requirements/recommendations for international students: Required—TOEFL (minimum score 600 paper-based; 100 iBT), IELTS (minimum score 7). *Application deadline:* Applications are processed on a rolling basis. Application fee: $50. Electronic applications accepted. *Financial support:* Career-related internships or fieldwork, Federal Work-Study, scholarships/grants, traineeships, and unspecified assistantships available. *Faculty research:* Human performance optimization, psychological aspects of rehabilitation, clinical observational and randomized trials and clinical outcomes research, health service research, biomechanical analyses of human movement in health and diseased states, assistive technologies, rehabilitation technical product development, health and wellness, rehabilitation counseling. *Unit head:* Dr. G. Kelley Fitzgerald, Associate Dean of Graduate Studies/Professor, 412-383-6643, Fax: 412-383-6535, E-mail: kfitzger@pitt.edu. *Application contact:* Jessica Maguire, Director of Admissions, 412-383-6557, Fax: 412-383-6535, E-mail: maguire@pitt.edu.
Website: http://www.shrs.pitt.edu/phdrs/

University of South Carolina, School of Medicine and The Graduate School, Graduate Programs in Medicine, Program in Rehabilitation Counseling, Columbia, SC 29208. Offers psychiatric rehabilitation (Certificate); rehabilitation counseling (MRC). *Accreditation:* CORE. *Program availability:* Part-time, evening/weekend. *Degree requirements:* For master's, comprehensive exam, internship, practicum. *Entrance requirements:* For master's and Certificate, GRE General Test or GMAT. Electronic applications accepted. *Expenses:* Contact institution. *Faculty research:* Quality of life, alcohol dependency, technology for disabled, psychiatric rehabilitation, women with disabilities.

University of South Florida, Morsani College of Medicine, School of Physical Therapy, Tampa, FL 33620-9951. Offers physical therapy (DPT); rehabilitation sciences (PhD), including chronic disease, neuromusculoskeletal disability, veteran's health/reintegration. *Accreditation:* APTA. *Faculty:* 11 full-time (6 women). *Students:* 139 full-time (94 women); includes 28 minority (6 Black or African American, non-Hispanic/Latino; 1 American Indian or Alaska Native, non-Hispanic/Latino; 9 Asian, non-Hispanic/Latino; 11 Hispanic/Latino; 1 Two or more races, non-Hispanic/Latino). Average age 24. 1,433 applicants, 5% accepted, 50 enrolled. In 2017, 80 doctorates awarded. *Degree requirements:* For doctorate, comprehensive exam, thesis/dissertation. *Entrance requirements:* For doctorate, GRE General Test, bachelor's degree from regionally-accredited university with minimum GPA of 3.0 in all upper-division coursework; interview; at least 20 hours of documented volunteer or work experience in hospital outpatient/inpatient physical therapy settings; written personal statement of values and purpose for attending. Additional exam requirements/recommendations for international students: Required—TOEFL (minimum score 600 paper-based; 79 iBT). *Application deadline:* For fall admission, 6/1 for domestic students, 1/1 for international students; for spring admission, 10/15 for domestic students, 9/15 for international students. Application fee: $30. Electronic applications accepted. *Financial support:* In 2017–18, 83 students received support. Teaching assistantships available. *Faculty research:* Veteran's reintegration and resilience, prosthetics and orthotics (microprocessor prosthetic knee), neuromusculoskeletal disorders (occupational ergonomics, fall risk and prevention, exercise adherence and compliance, and orthotic and prosthetic wear and use), human movement and function. *Total annual research expenditures:* $908,954. *Unit head:* Dr. William S. Quillen, Director, 813-974-9863, Fax: 813-974-8915, E-mail: wquillen@health.usf.edu. *Application contact:* Dr. Gina Maria Musolino, Associate Professor and Coordinator for Clinical Education, 813-974-2254, Fax: 813-974-8915, E-mail: gmusolin@health.usf.edu.
Website: http://health.usf.edu/medicine/dpt/index.htm

The University of Texas Medical Branch, Graduate School of Biomedical Sciences, Program in Rehabilitation Sciences, Galveston, TX 77555. Offers PhD. *Accreditation:* CEPH. *Degree requirements:* For doctorate, thesis/dissertation. *Entrance requirements:* For doctorate, GRE General Test. Additional exam requirements/recommendations for international students: Required—TOEFL (minimum score 550 paper-based). Electronic applications accepted.

University of Toronto, Faculty of Medicine, Department of Rehabilitation Science, Toronto, ON M5S 1A1, Canada. Offers M Sc, PhD. *Degree requirements:* For master's, thesis. *Entrance requirements:* For master's, B Sc or equivalent; specialization in occupational therapy, physical therapy, or a related field; minimum B+ average in final 2 years. Additional exam requirements/recommendations for international students: Required—TOEFL (minimum score 580 paper-based; 93 iBT), TWE (minimum score 5). Electronic applications accepted.

The University of Tulsa, Graduate School, Oxley College of Health Sciences, Department of Kinesiology and Rehabilitative Sciences, Tulsa, OK 74104-3189. Offers MAT. Summer enrollment only. *Faculty:* 10 full-time (4 women), 7 part-time/adjunct (2 women). *Students:* 5 full-time (2 women), 2 part-time (1 woman), 4 international. Average age 24. 1 applicant, 100% accepted, 1 enrolled. *Entrance requirements:* For master's, GRE General Test. Additional exam requirements/recommendations for international students: Required—TOEFL (minimum score 577 paper-based; 90 iBT), IELTS (minimum score 6.5). Application fee: $55. *Expenses:* $800 per credit hour tuition. *Financial support:* Applicants required to submit FAFSA. *Unit head:* Robin Ploeger, Interim Dean, 918-631-3170, E-mail: robin-ploeger@utulsa.edu. *Application contact:* Dr. Rachel Hildebrand, Program Advisor, 918-631-3204, Fax: 918-631-2156, E-mail: rachel-hildebrand@utulsa.edu.
Website: https://healthsciences.utulsa.edu/departments-schools/athletic-training/graduate-program/

University of Utah, Graduate School, College of Health, Department of Physical Therapy and Athletic Training, Salt Lake City, UT 84112-1290. Offers physical therapy (DPT); rehabilitation science (PhD). *Accreditation:* APTA. *Faculty:* 7 full-time (1 woman), 12 part-time/adjunct (9 women). *Students:* 180 full-time (98 women), 4 part-time (3 women); includes 26 minority (3 Black or African American, non-Hispanic/Latino; 4 Asian, non-Hispanic/Latino; 13 Hispanic/Latino; 6 Two or more races, non-Hispanic/Latino), 2 international. Average age 25. 437 applicants, 11% accepted, 48 enrolled. In 2017, 49 doctorates awarded. *Entrance requirements:* For doctorate, GRE, minimum GPA of 3.0, volunteer work, bachelor's degree. Additional exam requirements/recommendations for international students: Required—TOEFL (minimum score 90 iBT); Recommended—IELTS (minimum score 7). *Application deadline:* For fall admission, 10/3 priority date for domestic students, 10/3 for international students. Application fee: $55 ($65 for international students). Electronic applications accepted. *Expenses:* Contact institution. *Financial support:* In 2017–18, 29 students received support. Research assistantships with full tuition reimbursements available, teaching assistantships with full tuition reimbursements available, Federal Work-Study, scholarships/grants, tuition waivers (full), and unspecified assistantships available. Financial award application deadline: 10/1; financial award applicants required to submit FAFSA. *Faculty research:* Rehabilitation and Parkinson's disease, motor control and musculoskeletal dysfunction, burns/wound care, rehabilitation and multiple sclerosis, cancer. *Total annual research expenditures:* $600,129. *Unit head:* Dr. R. Scott Ward, Chair, 801-581-4895, E-mail: scott.ward@hsc.utah.edu. *Application contact:* Dee-Dee Darby-Duffin, Academic Advisor, 801-585-9510, E-mail: d.darby-duffin@hsc.utah.edu.
Website: http://www.health.utah.edu/pt

University of Vermont, Graduate College, College of Nursing and Health Sciences, Program in Human Functioning and Rehabilitation Science, Burlington, VT 05405. Offers PhD. *Students:* 3 (2 women). 3 applicants, 100% accepted, 3 enrolled. *Entrance requirements:* For doctorate, GRE General Test. Additional exam requirements/recommendations for international students: Required—TOEFL (minimum iBT score of 90) or IELTS (6.5). *Application deadline:* For fall admission, 2/15 for domestic and international students. Application fee: $65. Electronic applications accepted. *Expenses:* Tuition, state resident: full-time $11,628; part-time $646 per credit. Tuition, nonresident: full-time $29,340; part-time $1630 per credit. *Required fees:* $1994; $10 per credit. Tuition and fees vary according to course load and program. *Financial support:* In 2017–18, 3 students received support, including 5 research assistantships with full tuition reimbursements available (averaging $26,500 per year); fellowships, teaching assistantships, and health care benefits also available. Financial award application deadline: 3/1. *Application contact:* Shelley Velleman, Coordinator, 802-656-3858, E-mail: cnhsgrad@uvm.edu.
Website: https://www.uvm.edu/cnhs/doctor_philosophy_human_functioning_and_rehabilitation_science

University of Washington, Graduate School, School of Medicine, Graduate Programs in Medicine, Department of Rehabilitation Medicine, Seattle, WA 98195-6490. Offers occupational therapy (MOT); physical therapy (DPT); prosthetics and orthotics (MPO); rehabilitation science (PhD). *Accreditation:* AOTA. *Degree requirements:* For doctorate, comprehensive exam (for some programs), thesis/dissertation (for some programs). *Entrance requirements:* For master's and doctorate, GRE. Additional exam requirements/recommendations for international students: Required—TOEFL. *Faculty research:* Biomechanics, balance, brain injury, spinal cord injury, pain, degenerative diseases.

University of Wisconsin–La Crosse, College of Science and Health, Department of Exercise and Sport Science, Program in Clinical Exercise Physiology, La Crosse, WI 54601-3742. Offers MS. *Students:* 15 full-time (8 women), 2 part-time (both women), 2 international. Average age 24. 28 applicants, 54% accepted, 15 enrolled. In 2017, 15 master's awarded. *Degree requirements:* For master's, thesis optional. *Entrance requirements:* Additional exam requirements/recommendations for international students: Required—TOEFL (minimum score 550 paper-based; 79 iBT). *Application deadline:* For fall admission, 2/1 priority date for domestic and international students. Electronic applications accepted. *Financial support:* Federal Work-Study, scholarships/grants, health care benefits, and tuition waivers (partial) available. Support available to part-time students. Financial award application deadline: 3/15; financial award applicants required to submit FAFSA. *Unit head:* Dr. John Porcari, Director, 608-785-8684, Fax: 608-785-8686, E-mail: porcari.john@uwlax.edu. *Application contact:* Brandon Schaller, Senior Graduate Student Status Examiner, 608-785-8941, E-mail: admissions@uwlax.edu.
Website: http://www.uwlax.edu/sah/ess/cep/

University of Wisconsin–Milwaukee, Graduate School, College of Health Sciences, Program in Health Sciences, Milwaukee, WI 53201-0413. Offers health sciences (PhD), including diagnostic and biomedical sciences, disability and rehabilitation, health administration and policy, human movement sciences, population health. *Students:* 17 full-time (10 women), 7 part-time (4 women); includes 6 minority (1 Black or African American, non-Hispanic/Latino; 3 Asian, non-Hispanic/Latino; 2 Two or more races, non-Hispanic/Latino), 11 international. Average age 33. 7 applicants, 43% accepted, 3 enrolled. In 2017, 1 doctorate awarded. *Degree requirements:* For doctorate, comprehensive exam, thesis/dissertation. *Entrance requirements:* For doctorate, GRE. Additional exam requirements/recommendations for international students: Required—TOEFL (minimum score 600 paper-based), IELTS (minimum score 6.5). Application fee: $56 ($96 for international students). *Financial support:* Fellowships, research assistantships, teaching assistantships, and project assistantships available. *Application contact:* Susan Cashin, PhD, Assistant Dean, 414-229-3303, E-mail: scashin@uwm.edu.
Website: http://uwm.edu/healthsciences/academics/phd-health-sciences/

Virginia Commonwealth University, Graduate School, College of Humanities and Sciences, Department of Kinesiology and Health Sciences, Program in Rehabilitation and Movement Science, Richmond, VA 23284-9005. Offers PhD. *Entrance requirements:* Additional exam requirements/recommendations for international students: Required—TOEFL (minimum score 600 paper-based; 100 iBT). Electronic applications accepted.

Washington University in St. Louis, School of Medicine, Program in Rehabilitation and Participation Science, St. Louis, MO 63130-4899. Offers PhD.

Western Michigan University, Graduate College, College of Health and Human Services, Department of Blindness and Low Vision Studies, Kalamazoo, MI 49008. Offers orientation and mobility (MA); orientation and mobility of children (MA); vision rehabilitation therapy (MA). *Accreditation:* CORE.

PHILADELPHIA COLLEGE OF OSTEOPATHIC MEDICINE

Doctoral of Physical Therapy Program

PCOM

Program of Study

The Physical Therapy program at Philadelphia College of Osteopathic Medicine (PCOM) is a three-year (12 terms, four terms each year) program that leads to a Doctor of Physical Therapy (D.P.T.) degree. The 140-credit-hour curriculum is built around five content areas: basic/foundational sciences, clinicisal/physical therapy sciences, evidence-based practice, professional engagement, and clinical experience. The three years of learning includes 36 weeks of full-time clinical experience (integrated and terminal).

The program, offered at PCOM's Georgia campus, is designed to prepare individuals who demonstrate excellence in the practice of physical therapy, emphasize a "whole person" approach to patient management, commitment to the advancement of knowledge and intellectual growth, and engage in the well-being of the community.

PCOM's physical therapy program focuses on the clinical perspective and takes a wellness orientation approach. Students receive experiential training all three years, with multiple opportunities to practice and serve the community in real-world settings. PCOM has a 12,000-square-foot dedicated facility with clinical learning and assessment laboratories designed for education and research. Physical therapy students have access to a clinical learning and assessment laboratory (Simulation Center); they practice skills using standardized patients and they learn applied anatomy in a cadaver lab.

Effective May 2, 2018, the Doctor of Physical Therapy Program at Philadelphia College of Osteopathic Medicine in Suwanee, Georgia has been granted Candidate for Accreditation status by the Commission on Accreditation in Physical Therapy Education (1111 North Fairfax Street, Alexandria, Virginia 22314; phone: 703-706-3245; e-mail: accreditation@apta.org). The program/institution can be contacted directly at 770-682-2306 or e-mail phillippa@pcom.edu.

Candidate for Accreditation is a pre-accreditation status of affiliation with the Commission on Accreditation in Physical Therapy Education that indicates that the program is progressing toward accreditation and may matriculate students in professional courses. Candidate for Accreditation is not an accreditation status nor does it assure eventual accreditation.

Research Facilities

PCOM's libraries feature both a well-developed collection of medical journals and texts and new capabilities for access to online medical references and Internet searching in a facility that provides individual student stations, Internet terminals, advanced audiovisual resources, and a large student computer lab.

Financial Aid

The Financial Aid Office at PCOM offers financial assistance to students through the Federal Direct Loan program, institutional grants, and various alternative private loan programs.

Cost of Study

In 2018–19, the tuition and fees for the first year of the PCOM Physical Therapy program is $29,075.

Living and Housing Costs

Students live off campus within the Suwanee, Georgia metropolitan and suburban areas; there is no on-campus housing. Room and board costs vary by each student's individual preferences.

Student Group

Admission to the Physical Therapy program is competitive and selective. The Faculty Committee on Admissions looks for academically and socially well-rounded individuals who are committed to caring for patients. The class of 2021 is comprised of 39 students (24 women and 15 men) ranging in age from 21 to 51. Thirty-five percent of the class reports their ethnicity to be Asian and Black/African American. Thirty-four incoming students were residents of Georgia. The average GPA of the entering class was 3.4.

Location

Philadelphia College of Osteopathic Medicine is one of the largest of thirty-four osteopathic colleges in the United States, with campuses located in Philadelphia, Pennsylvania; Suwanee, Georgia; and Moultrie, Georgia. The Physical Therapy Studies program is offered at the Suwanee, Georgia campus. PCOM's facilities include large lecture halls, small classrooms; labs for teaching, clinical skills, robotic and human actor simulation, and research; a state-of-the-art library; and scenic landscaping, all in a suburban setting.

The College

PCOM, chartered in 1899, enrolls approximately 2,800 students in its various programs across three campuses, and is committed to educating community-responsive, primary care–oriented physicians and physical therapists to practice medicine in the twenty-first century. Supported by the latest in medical and educational technology, PCOM emphasizes treating the whole person, not merely the symptoms. Students have a committed, professional, humanistic faculty who are leaders in the osteopathic and physical therapy national health-care community.

Applying

Selection for the Physical Therapy program is very competitive. Applicants must complete a baccalaureate degree at a regionally accredited college or university: Prior to matriculation, an applicant must have successfully completed the following courses:

- General/introductory biology: two-course sequence for science majors (8 semester-hours credit), must include labs; or two-course sequence in anatomy and physiology (8 semester-hours credit), must include labs
- Anatomy, physiology, or biology course (4 semester-hour credits) must include labs
- General/introductory physics: two-course sequence for science majors (8 semester-hours credit), must include labs (sequence should include content related to mechanics, electricity, magnetism, and light)
- General/introductory chemistry: two-course sequence for science majors (8 semester-hours credit), must include labs
- Statistics or biostatistics: one course (3 semester-credit hours)
- Psychology: one course (3 semester-credit hours)
- Sociology/anthropology: one course (3 semester-credit hours)

If all prerequisite courses identified above and all coursework required for the baccalaureate degree have not been completed, a document specifying when these requirements will be met must be supplied. The document should provide specific information as to when the courses will be completed. Note that the requirements for the baccalaureate and all prerequisite courses must be completed prior to matriculation. At least six of the ten required prerequisite courses must be completed before an application will be considered.

Philadelphia College of Osteopathic Medicine

A complete list of application requirements and deadline information is available online at https://www.pcom.edu/admissions/apply/physical-therapy.html.

Correspondence and Information

Georgia Campus—Philadelphia College of Osteopathic Medicine

Office of Admissions

625 Old Peachtree Road

Suwanee, Georgia 30024

Phone: 866-282-4544 (toll-free)

678-225-7500 (local)

Fax: 678-225-7509

E-mail: GAAdmissions@pcom.edu

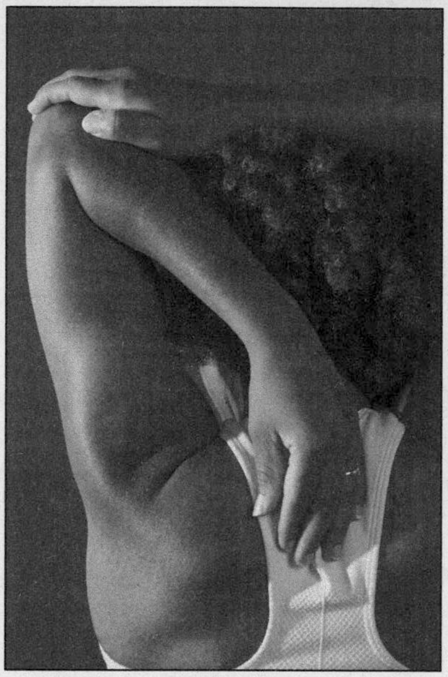

THE FACULTY AND THEIR RESEARCH

Full-Time Faculty

Phillip B. Palmer, PT, Ph.D., University of North Texas. Professor; Chair, Department of Physical Therapy Studies.

Philip A. Fabrizio, PT, D.P.T., M.S., CIDN, Marymount University. Associate Professor of Physical Therapy, Department of Physical Therapy Studies.

Robert Friberg, Ph.D., PT, CFMT, University of Iowa. Professor, Director of Faculty and Student Development, Department of Physical Therapy Studies.

Carol A. Milller, PT, Ph.D., GCS, Walden University. Professor, Director of Curriculum and Instruction, De-partment of Physical Therapy Studies.

Jennifer Wiley, PT, D.P.T., Medical College of Georgia. Associate Professor, Associate Director for Clinical Education, Department of Physical Therapy Studies.

Adjunct Faculty

Stefanie D. Palma, PT, D.P.T., M.Ed., NCS, CBIS, University of Central Arkansas.

Joseph M. Powers, M.D., FAAP, CAQ Sports Medicine, Medical College of Georgia.

Karlyn J. Schiltgen, PT, D.P.T., OCS, CCS, Mount St. Mary's College.

Section 21
Health Sciences

This section contains a directory of institutions offering graduate work in health sciences. Additional information about programs listed in the directory may be obtained by writing directly to the dean of a graduate school or chair of a department at the address given in the directory.

For programs offering related work, see also in this book *Biological and Biomedical Sciences, Biophysics (Radiation Biology), Dentistry and Dental Sciences, Health Services, Medicine, Nursing,* and *Public Health.* In the other guides in this series:

Graduate Programs in the Physical Sciences, Mathematics, Agricultural Sciences, the Environment & Natural Resources

See *Physics*

Graduate Programs in Engineering & Applied Sciences

See *Agricultural Engineering and Bioengineering (Bioengineering), Biomedical Engineering and Biotechnology,* and *Energy and Power Engineering (Nuclear Engineering)*

CONTENTS

Program Directories

Health Physics/Radiological Health

East Carolina University, Graduate School, Thomas Harriot College of Arts and Sciences, Department of Physics, Greenville, NC 27858-4353. Offers applied physics (MS); biomedical physics (PhD); health physics (MS); medical physics (MS). *Program availability:* Part-time. *Students:* 39 full-time (10 women), 8 part-time (2 women); includes 11 minority (4 Black or African American, non-Hispanic/Latino; 4 Asian, non-Hispanic/Latino; 2 Hispanic/Latino; 1 Two or more races, non-Hispanic/Latino), 5 international. Average age 29. 37 applicants, 70% accepted, 16 enrolled. In 2017, 4 master's, 1 doctorate awarded. *Degree requirements:* For master's, comprehensive exam; for doctorate, comprehensive exam, thesis/dissertation. *Entrance requirements:* For master's and doctorate, GRE General Test. Additional exam requirements/recommendations for international students: Recommended—TOEFL (minimum score 78 iBT), IELTS (minimum score 6.5). *Application deadline:* For fall admission, 3/1 priority date for domestic and international students. Applications are processed on a rolling basis. Application fee: $75. Electronic applications accepted. *Expenses:* Tuition, state resident: full-time $4749; part-time $297 per credit hour. Tuition, nonresident: full-time $17,898; part-time $1119 per credit hour. *Required fees:* $2691; $224 per credit hour. Part-time tuition and fees vary according to course load and program. *Financial support:* Research assistantships with partial tuition reimbursements, teaching assistantships with partial tuition reimbursements, and Federal Work-Study available. Support available to part-time students. Financial award application deadline: 3/1. *Faculty research:* Health and medical physics, biological and biomedical physics, radiological physics, acoustics and bioacoustics, theoretical and computational physics. *Unit head:* Dr. Jefferson Shinpaugh, Chair, 252-328-1852, E-mail: shinpaughj@ecu.edu. *Application contact:* Dean of Graduate School, 252-328-6012, Fax: 252-328-6071, E-mail: gradschool@ecu.edu.
Website: http://www.ecu.edu/cs-cas/physics/

Georgetown University, Graduate School of Arts and Sciences, Department of Health Physics and Radiation Protection, Washington, DC 20057. Offers health physics (MS); nuclear nonproliferation (MS). *Degree requirements:* For master's, thesis. *Entrance requirements:* Additional exam requirements/recommendations for international students: Required—TOEFL.

Georgia Institute of Technology, Graduate Studies, College of Engineering, George W. Woodruff School of Mechanical Engineering, Nuclear and Radiological Engineering and Medical Physics Programs, Atlanta, GA 30332-0001. Offers medical physics (MS, MSMP); nuclear and radiological engineering (PhD); nuclear engineering (MSNE). *Program availability:* Part-time, online learning. Terminal master's awarded for partial completion of doctoral program. *Degree requirements:* For master's, thesis optional; for doctorate, comprehensive exam, thesis/dissertation. *Entrance requirements:* For master's and doctorate, GRE General Test, minimum GPA of 3.0. Additional exam requirements/recommendations for international students: Required—TOEFL (minimum score 580 paper-based; 94 iBT). Electronic applications accepted. *Faculty research:* Reactor physics, nuclear materials, plasma physics, radiation detection, radiological assessment.

Idaho State University, Office of Graduate Studies, College of Science and Engineering, Department of Physics, Pocatello, ID 83209-8106. Offers applied physics (PhD); health physics (MS); physics (MNS). *Program availability:* Part-time. *Degree requirements:* For master's, comprehensive exam, thesis (for some programs), oral exam (for some programs); for doctorate, comprehensive exam, thesis/dissertation (for some programs), oral exam, written qualifying exam in physics or health physics after 1st year. *Entrance requirements:* For master's, GRE General Test, 3 letters of recommendation, BS or BA in physics, teaching certificate (MNS); for doctorate, GRE General Test (minimum 50th percentile), 3 letters of recommendation, statement of career goals. Additional exam requirements/recommendations for international students: Required—TOEFL (minimum score 550 paper-based; 80 iBT). Electronic applications accepted. *Faculty research:* Ion beam applications, low-energy nuclear physics, relativity and cosmology, observational astronomy.

Illinois Institute of Technology, Graduate College, College of Science, Department of Physics, Chicago, IL 60616. Offers applied physics (MS); health physics (MAS); physics (MS, PhD). *Program availability:* Part-time, evening/weekend, online learning. Terminal master's awarded for partial completion of doctoral program. *Degree requirements:* For master's, comprehensive exam (for some programs), thesis (for some programs); for doctorate, comprehensive exam, thesis/dissertation. *Entrance requirements:* For master's, GRE General Test (minimum score 295 Quantitative and Verbal, 2.5 Analytical Writing), minimum undergraduate GPA of 3.0; for doctorate, GRE General Test (minimum score 310 Quantitative and Verbal, 3.0 Analytical Writing); GRE Subject Test in physics (strongly recommended), minimum undergraduate GPA of 3.0. Additional exam requirements/recommendations for international students: Required—TOEFL (minimum score 550 paper-based; 80 iBT). Electronic applications accepted. *Faculty research:* Elementary particle physics, condensed matter, superconductivity, experimental and computational biophysics.

McMaster University, School of Graduate Studies, Faculty of Science, Department of Medical Physics and Applied Radiation Sciences, Hamilton, ON L8S 4M2, Canada. Offers health and radiation physics (M Sc); medical physics (M Sc, PhD). *Program availability:* Part-time. *Degree requirements:* For master's, thesis or alternative. *Entrance requirements:* For master's, minimum B+ average. Additional exam requirements/recommendations for international students: Required—TOEFL (minimum score 550 paper-based). *Faculty research:* Imaging, toxicology, dosimetry, body composition, medical lasers.

Midwestern State University, Billie Doris McAda Graduate School, Robert D. and Carol Gunn College of Health Sciences and Human Services, Program in Radiologic Sciences, Wichita Falls, TX 76308. Offers MS. *Program availability:* Part-time, evening/weekend, online learning. *Degree requirements:* For master's, comprehensive exam, thesis optional. *Entrance requirements:* For master's, GRE General Test, MAT or GMAT, credentials in one of the medical imaging modalities or radiation therapy; 1 year of experience; 3 letters of recommendation from past and/or present educators and employers. Additional exam requirements/recommendations for international students: Required—TOEFL (minimum score 550 paper-based). Electronic applications accepted. *Faculty research:* Bone densitometry, radiologic dose trends, teaching of radiologic science, radiographic positioning landmarks.

Northwestern State University of Louisiana, Graduate Studies and Research, College of Nursing and School of Allied Health, Department of Radiologic Sciences, Natchitoches, LA 71497. Offers MS. *Degree requirements:* For master's, comprehensive exam, thesis (for some programs). *Entrance requirements:* Additional exam requirements/recommendations for international students: Required—TOEFL. Electronic applications accepted.

Oregon State University, College of Engineering, Program in Radiation Health Physics, Corvallis, OR 97331. Offers application of nuclear techniques (MHP, MS, PhD). *Program availability:* Part-time, blended/hybrid learning. *Entrance requirements:* For master's and doctorate, GRE. Additional exam requirements/recommendations for international students: Required—TOEFL (minimum score 80 iBT), IELTS (minimum score 6.5). *Application deadline:* For fall admission, 2/1 priority date for domestic and international students. Application fee: $75 ($85 for international students). *Expenses:* Contact institution. *Financial support:* Application deadline: 2/1. *Faculty research:* Radioactive material transport, research reactor health physics, radiation instrumentation, radiation shielding, environmental monitoring. *Unit head:* Dr. Kathryn A. Higley, Department Head/Professor, 541-737-2343, E-mail: kathryn.higley@oregonstate.edu. *Application contact:* Radiation Health Physics Advisor, 541-737-2343, E-mail: nuc_engr@ne.oregonstate.edu.
Website: http://ne.oregonstate.edu/health-physics-program

Purdue University, Graduate School, College of Health and Human Sciences, School of Health Sciences, West Lafayette, IN 47907. Offers health physics (MS, PhD); medical physics (MS, PhD); occupational and environmental health science (MS, PhD), including aerosol deposition and lung disease, ergonomics, exposure and risk assessment, indoor air quality and bioaerosols (PhD), liver/lung toxicology; radiation biology (PhD); toxicology (PhD); MS/PhD. *Program availability:* Part-time. *Faculty:* 12 full-time (4 women), 1 part-time/adjunct (0 women). *Students:* 37 full-time (16 women), 5 part-time (1 woman); includes 6 minority (2 Black or African American, non-Hispanic/Latino; 2 Asian, non-Hispanic/Latino; 1 Hispanic/Latino; 1 Two or more races, non-Hispanic/Latino), 9 international. Average age 28. 57 applicants, 65% accepted, 15 enrolled. In 2017, 10 master's, 4 doctorates awarded. *Degree requirements:* For master's, thesis optional; for doctorate, one foreign language, thesis/dissertation. *Entrance requirements:* For master's and doctorate, GRE General Test, minimum undergraduate GPA of 3.0 or equivalent. Additional exam requirements/recommendations for international students: Required—TOEFL (minimum score 550 paper-based; 77 iBT); Recommended—TWE. *Application deadline:* For fall admission, 5/15 for domestic and international students; for spring admission, 10/15 for domestic and international students. Applications are processed on a rolling basis. Application fee: $60 ($75 for international students). Electronic applications accepted. *Financial support:* In 2017–18, fellowships with tuition reimbursements (averaging $14,400 per year), research assistantships with tuition reimbursements (averaging $12,000 per year), teaching assistantships with tuition reimbursements (averaging $12,000 per year) were awarded; career-related internships or fieldwork and traineeships also available. Support available to part-time students. Financial award applicants required to submit FAFSA. *Faculty research:* Environmental toxicology, industrial hygiene, radiation dosimetry. *Unit head:* Jason T. Harris, Interim Head of the Graduate Program, 765-496-1271, E-mail: jtharris@purdue.edu. *Application contact:* Karen E. Walker, Graduate Contact, 765-494-1419, E-mail: kwalker@purdue.edu.
Website: https://www.purdue.edu/hhs/hsci/

Quinnipiac University, School of Health Sciences, Program for Radiologist Assistant, Hamden, CT 06518-1940. Offers MHS. *Faculty:* 2 full-time (1 woman), 2 part-time/adjunct (1 woman). *Students:* 5 full-time (3 women), 3 part-time (2 women); includes 2 minority (1 Asian, non-Hispanic/Latino; 1 Hispanic/Latino). 6 applicants, 100% accepted, 6 enrolled. In 2017, 2 master's awarded. *Entrance requirements:* For master's, proof of certification from American Registry of Radiologic Technologists; 2000 hours of direct patient care; CPR certification. Additional exam requirements/recommendations for international students: Required—TOEFL (minimum score 575 paper-based; 90 iBT), IELTS (minimum score 6.5). *Application deadline:* For summer admission, 4/30 priority date for domestic students, 4/30 for international students. Applications are processed on a rolling basis. Application fee: $45. Electronic applications accepted. *Financial support:* Federal Work-Study, scholarships/grants, and unspecified assistantships available. Financial award application deadline: 5/1; financial award applicants required to submit FAFSA. *Faculty research:* Curriculum development, assessment of student learning, radiation safety. *Unit head:* John Candler, Director, 203-582-6205, E-mail: john.candler@qu.edu. *Application contact:* Office of Graduate Admissions, 800-462-1944, Fax: 203-582-3443, E-mail: graduate@qu.edu.
Website: http://www.qu.edu/gradradiologistasst

Rutgers University–Newark, School of Health Related Professions, Department of Medical Imaging Sciences, Newark, NJ 07102. Offers radiologist assistant (MS). *Program availability:* Part-time, evening/weekend. *Entrance requirements:* For master's, BS with minimum GPA of 3.0, RT license, coursework in intro to pathopsychology, interview, all transcripts, personal statement, BCLS certification. Additional exam requirements/recommendations for international students: Required—TOEFL (minimum score 500 paper-based; 79 iBT). Electronic applications accepted.

San Diego State University, Graduate and Research Affairs, College of Sciences, Department of Physics, Program in Radiological Physics, San Diego, CA 92182. Offers MS. *Program availability:* Part-time. *Degree requirements:* For master's, thesis optional, oral or written exam. *Entrance requirements:* For master's, GRE General Test, GRE Subject Test (physics), 2 letters of recommendation. Additional exam requirements/recommendations for international students: Required—TOEFL. Electronic applications accepted. *Faculty research:* Computational radiological physics, medical physics.

Thomas Jefferson University, Jefferson College of Health Professions, Department of Radiologic Sciences, Philadelphia, PA 19107. Offers radiologic and imaging sciences (MS). *Program availability:* Part-time. *Degree requirements:* For master's, capstone project. *Entrance requirements:* For master's, bachelor's degree. Additional exam requirements/recommendations for international students: Required—TOEFL (minimum score 87 iBT), IELTS (minimum score 6.5). Electronic applications accepted. *Faculty research:* MRI safety; reducing patient anxiety in radiation oncology; use of standardized patient; simulation for competency; interprofessional education in radiology.

Université Laval, Faculty of Medicine, Post-Professional Programs in Medical Studies, Québec, QC G1K 7P4, Canada. Offers anatomy–pathology (DESS); anesthesiology (DESS); cardiology (DESS); care of older people (Diploma); clinical research (DESS); community health (DESS); dermatology (DESS); diagnostic radiology (DESS); emergency medicine (Diploma); family medicine (DESS); general surgery (DESS); geriatrics (DESS); hematology (DESS); internal medicine (DESS); maternal and fetal medicine (Diploma); medical biochemistry (DESS); medical microbiology and infectious diseases (DESS); medical oncology (DESS); nephrology (DESS); neurology (DESS); neurosurgery (DESS); obstetrics and gynecology (DESS); ophthalmology (DESS); orthopedic surgery (DESS); oto-rhino-laryngology (DESS); palliative medicine (Diploma); pediatrics (DESS); plastic surgery (DESS); psychiatry (DESS); pulmonary medicine (DESS); radiology–oncology (DESS); thoracic surgery (DESS); urology (DESS). *Degree requirements:* For other advanced degree, comprehensive exam. *Entrance requirements:* For degree, knowledge of French. Electronic applications accepted.

University of Alberta, Faculty of Medicine and Dentistry and Faculty of Graduate Studies and Research, Graduate Programs in Medicine, Department of Radiology and Diagnostic Imaging, Edmonton, AB T6G 2E1, Canada. Offers medical sciences (PhD); radiology and diagnostic imaging (M Sc). Terminal master's awarded for partial completion of doctoral program. *Degree requirements:* For master's, thesis; for doctorate, thesis/dissertation. *Entrance requirements:* For master's, minimum GPA of 6.5 on a 9.0 scale; for doctorate, M Sc. *Faculty research:* Spectroscopic attenuation correction, nuclear medicine technology, monoclonal antibody labeling, bone mineral analysis using ultrasound.

University of Arkansas for Medical Sciences, College of Health Professions, Little Rock, AR 72205-7199. Offers audiology (Au D); communication sciences and disorders (MS, PhD); genetic counseling (MS); nuclear medicine advanced associate (MIS); physician assistant studies (MPAS); radiologist assistant (MIS). PhD offered through consortium with University of Arkansas at Little Rock and University of Central Arkansas. *Program availability:* Part-time, online learning. *Degree requirements:* For master's, thesis (for some programs); for doctorate, comprehensive exam (for some programs), thesis/dissertation (for some programs). *Entrance requirements:* For master's, GRE. Additional exam requirements/recommendations for international students: Required—TOEFL (minimum score 550 paper-based; 79 iBT). Electronic applications accepted. *Expenses:* Contact institution. *Faculty research:* Auditory-based intervention, soy diet, nutrition and cancer.

University of Cincinnati, Graduate School, College of Medicine, Graduate Programs in Biomedical Sciences, Department of Radiology, Cincinnati, OH 45267. Offers medical physics (MS). *Program availability:* Part-time. *Degree requirements:* For master's, comprehensive exam, project. *Entrance requirements:* For master's, GRE General Test. Additional exam requirements/recommendations for international students: Required—TOEFL (minimum score 575 paper-based). Electronic applications accepted. *Expenses: Tuition, area resident:* Full-time $14,468. Tuition, state resident: full-time $14,968; part-time $754 per credit hour. Tuition, nonresident: full-time $24,210; part-time $1311 per credit hour. *International tuition:* $26,460 full-time. *Required fees:* $3958; $84 per credit hour. One-time fee: $85 full-time. Tuition and fees vary according to course load, degree level and program. *Faculty research:* Radiation oncology, radiologic imaging, dosimetry, radiation biology, radiation therapy.

University of Kentucky, Graduate School, Graduate School Programs from the College of Medicine, Program in Radiation Sciences, Lexington, KY 40506-0032. Offers MSRMP. *Program availability:* Part-time. *Degree requirements:* For master's, comprehensive exam, thesis. *Entrance requirements:* For master's, GRE General Test, minimum undergraduate GPA of 2.75. Additional exam requirements/recommendations for international students: Required—TOEFL (minimum score 550 paper-based). Electronic applications accepted. *Faculty research:* Dosimetry, manpower studies, diagnostic imaging physics, shielding.

University of Massachusetts Lowell, College of Sciences, Department of Physics, Program in Radiological Sciences and Protection, Lowell, MA 01854. Offers MS, PSM. *Degree requirements:* For master's, one foreign language, thesis. *Entrance requirements:* For master's, GRE General Test, 3 letters of reference. Additional exam requirements/recommendations for international students: Required—TOEFL. Electronic applications accepted.

University of Michigan, College of Engineering, Department of Nuclear Engineering and Radiological Sciences, Ann Arbor, MI 48109. Offers nuclear engineering (Nuc E); nuclear engineering and radiological sciences (MSE, PhD); nuclear science (MS, PhD). *Students:* 133 full-time (22 women), 1 part-time (0 women). 169 applicants, 37% accepted, 39 enrolled. In 2017, 29 master's, 19 doctorates awarded. Terminal master's awarded for partial completion of doctoral program. *Degree requirements:* For master's, thesis optional; for doctorate, thesis/dissertation, oral defense of dissertation, preliminary exams. *Entrance requirements:* For master's and doctorate, GRE General Test. Additional exam requirements/recommendations for international students: Required—TOEFL. *Application deadline:* Applications are processed on a rolling basis. Electronic applications accepted. *Expenses:* Tuition, state resident: full-time $22,368; part-time $1201 per credit hour. Tuition, nonresident: full-time $45,156; part-time $2467 per credit hour. *Required fees:* $376 per term. Tuition and fees vary according to course load, degree level and program. *Financial support:* Fellowships, research assistantships, teaching assistantships, career-related internships or fieldwork, institutionally sponsored loans, scholarships/grants, traineeships, health care benefits, and unspecified assistantships available. Financial award applicants required to submit FAFSA. *Faculty research:* Radiation safety, environmental sciences, medical physics, fission systems and radiation transport, materials, plasmas and fusion, radiation measurements and imaging. *Total annual research expenditures:* $21.4 million. *Unit head:* Dr. Ronald Gilgenbach, Department Chair, 734-763-1261, Fax: 734-763-4540, E-mail: rongilg@umich.edu. *Application contact:* Garnette Roberts, Graduate Program Coordinator, 734-615-8810, Fax: 734-763-4540, E-mail: ners-grad-admissions@umich.edu.
Website: https://ners.engin.umich.edu/

University of Missouri, School of Health Professions, Department of Clinical and Diagnostic Sciences, Columbia, MO 65211. Offers diagnostic medical ultrasound (MHS). *Entrance requirements:* Additional exam requirements/recommendations for international students: Required—TOEFL. *Application deadline:* Applications are processed on a rolling basis. Electronic applications accepted. *Expenses:* Tuition, state resident: full-time $6480. Tuition, nonresident: full-time $17,744. *Required fees:* $1108. Tuition and fees vary according to course load, campus/location and program.
Website: http://shp.missouri.edu/cds/index.php

University of Nevada, Las Vegas, Graduate College, School of Allied Health Sciences, Department of Health Physics and Diagnostic Sciences, Las Vegas, NV 89154-3037. Offers health physics (MS); interdisciplinary health sciences (PhD); medical physics (DMP, Advanced Certificate). *Accreditation:* ABET. *Program availability:* Part-time. *Faculty:* 3 full-time (0 women), 1 part-time/adjunct (0 women). *Students:* 23 full-time (6 women), 13 part-time (6 women); includes 8 minority (2 Black or African American, non-Hispanic/Latino; 2 Asian, non-Hispanic/Latino; 2 Hispanic/Latino; 2 Two or more races, non-Hispanic/Latino), 6 international. Average age 32. 28 applicants, 57% accepted, 11 enrolled. In 2017, 4 master's awarded. *Degree requirements:* For master's, thesis, professional paper, oral exam; for doctorate, comprehensive exam (for some programs), thesis/dissertation. *Entrance requirements:* For master's and doctorate, GRE General Test, bachelor's degree with minimum GPA 3.0; 3 letters of recommendation; statement of purpose; for Advanced Certificate, GRE General Test, minimum overall GPA of 3.0 in graduate work. Additional exam requirements/recommendations for international students: Required—TOEFL (minimum score 550 paper-based; 80 iBT), IELTS (minimum score 7). *Application deadline:* For fall admission, 6/15 for domestic students, 5/1 for international students; for spring admission, 11/15 for domestic students, 10/1 for international students. Application fee: $60 ($95 for international students). Electronic applications accepted. *Expenses:* $275 per credit, $850 per course, $7,969 per year resident, $22,157 per year non-resident, $7,094 non-resident fee (7 credits or more), $1,307 annual health insurance fee. *Financial support:* In 2017–18, 21 students received support, including 1 fellowship with full and partial tuition reimbursement available (averaging $20,000 per year), 10 research assistantships with full and partial tuition reimbursements available (averaging $18,650 per year), 11 teaching assistantships with full and partial tuition reimbursements available (averaging $15,432 per year); institutionally sponsored loans, scholarships/grants, health care benefits, and unspecified assistantships also available. Financial award application deadline: 3/15; financial award applicants required to submit FAFSA. *Faculty research:* Biomechanics of human movement, exercise immunology, micro dosimetry and cancer initiation processes, medical imaging and diagnostics, white blood cell response to skeletal muscle injury. *Total annual research expenditures:* $117,557. *Unit head:* Dr. Steen Madsen, Chair/Associate Professor, 702-895-1805, Fax: 702-895-4819, E-mail: steen.madsen@unlv.edu.
Website: http://healthphysics.unlv.edu/

University of Oklahoma Health Sciences Center, College of Medicine and Graduate College, Graduate Programs in Medicine, Department of Radiological Sciences, Oklahoma City, OK 73190. Offers medical radiation physics (MS, PhD), including diagnostic radiology, nuclear medicine, radiation therapy, ultrasound. *Program availability:* Part-time. Terminal master's awarded for partial completion of doctoral program. *Degree requirements:* For master's, thesis; for doctorate, thesis/dissertation. *Entrance requirements:* For master's, GRE General Test; for doctorate, GRE General Test, 3 letters of recommendation. Additional exam requirements/recommendations for international students: Required—TOEFL. *Faculty research:* Monte Carlo applications in radiation therapy, observer-performed studies in diagnostic radiology, error analysis in gated cardiac nuclear medicine studies, nuclear medicine absorbed fraction determinations.

University of Toronto, Faculty of Medicine, Institute of Medical Science, Toronto, ON M5S 1A1, Canada. Offers bioethics (MH Sc); biomedical communications (M Sc BMC); medical radiation science (MH Sc); medical science (PhD). *Degree requirements:* For master's, thesis; for doctorate, thesis/dissertation, thesis defense. *Entrance requirements:* For master's, minimum GPA of 3.7 in 3 of 4 years (M Sc), interview; for doctorate, M Sc or equivalent, defended thesis, minimum A- average, interview. Additional exam requirements/recommendations for international students: Required—TOEFL (minimum score 600 paper-based; 93 iBT), TWE (minimum score 5). Electronic applications accepted.

Vanderbilt University, Department of Physics and Astronomy, Nashville, TN 37240-1001. Offers astronomy (MS); health physics (MA); physics (MAT, MS, PhD). *Faculty:* 25 full-time (4 women). *Students:* 42 full-time (8 women), 1 part-time (0 women); includes 5 minority (1 Black or African American, non-Hispanic/Latino; 1 Asian, non-Hispanic/Latino; 2 Hispanic/Latino; 1 Two or more races, non-Hispanic/Latino), 13 international. Average age 27. 89 applicants, 26% accepted, 9 enrolled. In 2017, 3 master's, 16 doctorates awarded. *Degree requirements:* For master's, thesis; for doctorate, comprehensive exam, thesis/dissertation, final and qualifying exams. *Entrance requirements:* For master's, GRE General Test; for doctorate, GRE General Test, GRE Subject Test. Additional exam requirements/recommendations for international students: Required—TOEFL (minimum score 570 paper-based; 88 iBT). *Application deadline:* For fall admission, 1/1 for domestic and international students. Electronic applications accepted. *Financial support:* Fellowships, research assistantships with full tuition reimbursements, teaching assistantships with full tuition reimbursements, career-related internships or fieldwork, Federal Work-Study, and institutionally sponsored loans available. Financial award application deadline: 1/15; financial award applicants required to submit CSS PROFILE or FAFSA. *Faculty research:* Experimental and theoretical physics, free electron laser, living-state physics, heavy-ion physics, nuclear structure. *Unit head:* Dr. Robert Sherrer, Chair, 615-322-2828, E-mail: robert.scherrer@vanderbilt.edu. *Application contact:* Julia Velkovska, Director of Graduate Studies, 615-322-2828, E-mail: julia.velkovska@vanderbilt.edu.
Website: http://www.vanderbilt.edu/physics/

Virginia Commonwealth University, Graduate School, School of Allied Health Professions, Doctoral Program in Health Related Sciences, Richmond, VA 23284-9005. Offers clinical laboratory sciences (PhD); gerontology (PhD); health administration (PhD); nurse anesthesia (PhD); occupational therapy (PhD); physical therapy (PhD); radiation sciences (PhD); rehabilitation leadership (PhD). *Entrance requirements:* For doctorate, GRE General Test or MAT, minimum GPA of 3.3 in master's degree. Additional exam requirements/recommendations for international students: Required—TOEFL (minimum score 600 paper-based; 100 iBT); Recommended—IELTS (minimum score 6.5). Electronic applications accepted.

Weber State University, Dumke College of Health Professions, Department of Radiologic Sciences, Ogden, UT 84408-1001. Offers MSRS. *Faculty:* 5 full-time (2 women). *Students:* 18 full-time (12 women), 3 part-time (1 woman); includes 4 minority (1 Black or African American, non-Hispanic/Latino; 2 Asian, non-Hispanic/Latino; 1 Hispanic/Latino). Average age 41. In 2017, 18 master's awarded. *Degree requirements:* For master's, thesis. *Entrance requirements:* Additional exam requirements/recommendations for international students: Required—TOEFL (minimum score 550 paper-based). *Application deadline:* For fall admission, 5/1 priority date for domestic and international students. Application fee: $60 ($90 for international students). Electronic applications accepted. *Expenses:* Tuition, state resident: full-time $7283. Tuition, nonresident: full-time $17,166. *Required fees:* $898. Tuition and fees vary according to program. *Financial support:* In 2017–18, 15 students received support. Scholarships/grants available. Financial award application deadline: 4/1; financial award applicants required to submit FAFSA. *Unit head:* Dr. Robert Walker, Program Director, 801-626-7156, Fax: 801-626-7683, E-mail: rwalker2@weber.edu. *Application contact:* Lonnie Lujan, Graduate Enrollment Director, 801-626-6088, Fax: 801-626-7966, E-mail: lonnielujan@weber.edu.
Website: http://www.weber.edu/msrs

Medical Imaging

Boston University, School of Medicine, Division of Graduate Medical Sciences, Program in Bioimaging, Boston, MA 02215. Offers MS. *Degree requirements:* For master's, thesis. *Financial support:* Applicants required to submit FAFSA. *Unit head:* Dr. Mark Moss, Chair, 617-638-4200, E-mail: markmoss@bu.edu. *Application contact:* GMS Admissions Office, 617-638-5255, E-mail: askgms@bu.edu.
Website: http://www.bumc.bu.edu/mbi/

Cedars-Sinai Medical Center, Graduate Programs, Los Angeles, CA 90048. Offers biomedical and translational sciences (PhD); magnetic resonance in medicine (MS). *Faculty:* 60 full-time (15 women). *Students:* 40 full-time (26 women); includes 12 minority (2 Black or African American, non-Hispanic/Latino; 4 Asian, non-Hispanic/Latino; 4 Hispanic/Latino; 2 Native Hawaiian or other Pacific Islander, non-Hispanic/Latino). Average age 29. 55 applicants, 15% accepted, 8 enrolled. *Degree requirements:* For doctorate, comprehensive exam, thesis/dissertation. *Entrance requirements:* For doctorate, GRE, 3 letters of recommendation. Additional exam requirements/recommendations for international students: Required—TOEFL (minimum score 550 paper-based; 80 iBT), IELTS (minimum score 6.5). *Application deadline:* For fall admission, 1/31 for domestic students. Application fee: $35. Electronic applications accepted. *Financial support:* Health care benefits and annual stipends (averaging $36,000) available. *Faculty research:* Regenerative medicine, immunology and host-pathogen interactions, cancer biology, genomics, tissue fibrosis and repair, neurosciences, metabolism, heart biology. *Total annual research expenditures:* $36 million. *Application contact:* Emma Yates Casler, Program Coordinator, 310-423-8294, E-mail: yatese@cshs.org.
Website: https://www.cedars-sinai.edu/Education/Graduate-Research-Education/

Illinois Institute of Technology, Graduate College, Armour College of Engineering, Department of Electrical and Computer Engineering, Chicago, IL 60616. Offers biomedical imaging and signals (MAS); computer engineering (MS, PhD); electrical engineering (MS, PhD); electricity markets (MAS); network engineering (MAS); power engineering (MAS); telecommunications and software engineering (MAS); VLSI and microelectronics (MAS); MS/MS. *Program availability:* Part-time, evening/weekend, online learning. Terminal master's awarded for partial completion of doctoral program. *Degree requirements:* For master's, comprehensive exam (for some programs), thesis (for some programs); for doctorate, comprehensive exam, thesis/dissertation. *Entrance requirements:* For master's and doctorate, GRE General Test (minimum score 1100 Quantitative and Verbal, 3.5 Analytical Writing), minimum undergraduate GPA of 3.0. Additional exam requirements/recommendations for international students: Required—TOEFL (minimum score 550 paper-based; 80 iBT); Recommended—IELTS (minimum score 5.5). Electronic applications accepted. *Faculty research:* Communication systems, wireless networks, computer systems, computer networks, wireless security, cloud computing and micro-electronics; electromagnetics and electronics; power and control systems; signal and image processing.

Medical University of South Carolina, College of Graduate Studies, Program in Molecular and Cellular Biology and Pathobiology, Charleston, SC 29425. Offers cancer biology (PhD); cardiovascular biology (PhD); cardiovascular imaging (PhD); cell regulation (PhD); craniofacial biology (PhD); genetics and development (PhD); marine biomedicine (PhD); DMD/PhD; MD/PhD. *Degree requirements:* For doctorate, thesis/dissertation, oral and written exams. *Entrance requirements:* For doctorate, GRE General Test, interview, minimum GPA of 3.0. Additional exam requirements/recommendations for international students: Required—TOEFL (minimum score 600 paper-based; 100 iBT). Electronic applications accepted.

National University of Health Sciences, Graduate Programs, Lombard, IL 60148-4583. Offers acupuncture (MSAC); chiropractic (DC); diagnostic imaging (MS); naturopathic medicine (ND); Oriental medicine (MSOM).

New York University, School of Medicine and Graduate School of Arts and Science, Sackler Institute of Graduate Biomedical Sciences, New York, NY 10016. Offers biomedical imaging and technology (PhD); biostatistics (PhD); cellular and molecular biology (PhD); developmental genetics (PhD); epidemiology (PhD); genome integrity (PhD); immunology and inflammation (PhD); microbiology (PhD); molecular biophysics (PhD); molecular oncology and tumor immunology (PhD); molecular pharmacology (PhD); neuroscience and physiology (PhD), including immunology, molecular oncology; stem cell biology (PhD); systems and computational biomedicine (PhD); MD/PhD. *Faculty:* 207 full-time (51 women). *Students:* 236 full-time (138 women), 1 part-time (0 women); includes 68 minority (13 Black or African American, non-Hispanic/Latino; 26 Asian, non-Hispanic/Latino; 28 Hispanic/Latino; 1 Native Hawaiian or other Pacific Islander, non-Hispanic/Latino), 79 international. Average age 27. 761 applicants, 18% accepted, 59 enrolled. In 2017, 35 doctorates awarded. *Degree requirements:* For doctorate, comprehensive exam, thesis/dissertation, qualifying exam; thesis defense. *Entrance requirements:* For doctorate, GRE. Additional exam requirements/recommendations for international students: Required—TOEFL, IELTS. *Application deadline:* For fall admission, 12/1 for domestic and international students. Applications are processed on a rolling basis. Application fee: $100. Electronic applications accepted. Application fee is waived when completed online. *Expenses:* Contact institution. *Financial support:* Health care benefits, tuition waivers (full), and unspecified assistantships available. *Faculty research:* Biomedical sciences. *Unit head:* Dr. Naoko Tanese, Associate Dean for Biomedical Sciences/Director, Sackler Institute, 212-263-8945, E-mail: naoko.tanese@nyumc.org. *Application contact:* Jessica Dong, Program Manager, 212-263-5648, E-mail: sackler-info@nyumc.org.
Website: https://med.nyu.edu/research/sackler-institute-graduate-biomedical-sciences/

Oregon State University, College of Engineering, Program in Bioengineering, Corvallis, OR 97331. Offers biomaterials (M Eng, MS, PhD); biomedical devices and instrumentation (M Eng, MS, PhD); human performance engineering (M Eng, MS, PhD); medical imaging (M Eng, MS, PhD); systems and computational biology (M Eng, MS, PhD). Electronic applications accepted. *Expenses:* Contact institution. *Faculty research:* Biomaterials, biomedical devices and instrumentation, human performance engineering, medical imaging, systems and computational biology. *Unit head:* Anita Hughes, Graduate Program Coordinator, E-mail: anita.hughes@oregonstate.edu.

Rutgers University–Newark, School of Health Related Professions, Department of Medical Imaging Sciences, Newark, NJ 07102. Offers radiologist assistant (MS). *Program availability:* Part-time, evening/weekend. *Entrance requirements:* For master's, BS with minimum GPA of 3.0, RT license, coursework in intro to pathopsychology, interview, all transcripts, personal statement, BCLS certification. Additional exam requirements/recommendations for international students: Required—TOEFL (minimum score 500 paper-based; 79 iBT). Electronic applications accepted.

University of California, San Francisco, Graduate Division, Biomedical Imaging Program, San Francisco, CA 94143. Offers MS. *Program availability:* Part-time. *Faculty:* 14 full-time (7 women). *Students:* 18 full-time (8 women), 1 part-time (0 women). In 2017, 19 master's awarded. *Degree requirements:* For master's, comprehensive exam or thesis. *Entrance requirements:* For master's, MCAT or GRE General Test. Additional exam requirements/recommendations for international students: Required—TOEFL (minimum score 550 paper-based, 80 iBT) or IELTS (minimum score 7.0). *Application deadline:* For fall admission, 2/28 for domestic and international students. Application fee: $105 ($125 for international students). Electronic applications accepted. *Expenses:* Contact institution. *Financial support:* Applicants required to submit FAFSA. *Faculty research:* Cancer imaging, musculoskeletal imaging, neurological imaging, abdominal and pelvic imaging, cardiovascular imaging, MR pulse sequences, image processing and analysis, nuclear and optical imaging, magnetic resonance imaging. *Unit head:* Rukayah Abdolcader, Program Administrator, 415-514-8246, E-mail: msbi@ucsf.edu.
Website: http://radiology.ucsf.edu/education/graduate-programs/msbi-program

University of Cincinnati, Graduate School, College of Engineering and Applied Science, Department of Biomedical, Chemical and Environmental Engineering, Cincinnati, OH 45221. Offers biomechanics (PhD); chemical engineering (MS, PhD); environmental engineering (MS, PhD); environmental sciences (MS, PhD); medical imaging (PhD); tissue engineering (PhD). *Program availability:* Part-time. *Degree requirements:* For master's, thesis or alternative; for doctorate, one foreign language, thesis/dissertation. *Entrance requirements:* For master's and doctorate, GRE General Test. Additional exam requirements/recommendations for international students: Required—TOEFL (minimum score 600 paper-based). *Expenses: Tuition, area resident:* Full-time $14,468. Tuition, state resident: full-time $14,968; part-time $754 per credit hour. Tuition, nonresident: full-time $24,210; part-time $1311 per credit hour. *International tuition:* $26,460 full-time. *Required fees:* $3958; $84 per credit hour. One-time fee: $85 full-time. Tuition and fees vary according to course load, degree level and program.

University of Guelph, Ontario Veterinary College and Graduate Studies, Graduate Programs in Veterinary Sciences, Department of Clinical Studies, Guelph, ON N1G 2W1, Canada. Offers anesthesiology (M Sc, DV Sc); cardiology (DV Sc, Diploma); clinical studies (Diploma); dermatology (M Sc); diagnostic imaging (M Sc, DV Sc); emergency/critical care (M Sc, DV Sc, Diploma); medicine (M Sc, DV Sc); neurology (M Sc, DV Sc); ophthalmology (M Sc, DV Sc); surgery (M Sc, DV Sc). *Degree requirements:* For master's, thesis; for doctorate, comprehensive exam, thesis/dissertation. *Entrance requirements:* Additional exam requirements/recommendations for international students: Required—TOEFL (minimum score 550 paper-based), IELTS (minimum score 6.5). Electronic applications accepted. *Faculty research:* Orthopedics, respirology, oncology, exercise physiology, cardiology.

University of Southern California, Graduate School, Viterbi School of Engineering, Department of Biomedical Engineering, Los Angeles, CA 90089. Offers biomedical engineering (PhD); medical device and diagnostic engineering (MS); medical imaging and imaging informatics (MS). *Program availability:* Online learning. Terminal master's awarded for partial completion of doctoral program. *Degree requirements:* For master's, thesis optional; for doctorate, thesis/dissertation. *Entrance requirements:* For master's and doctorate, GRE General Test. Additional exam requirements/recommendations for international students: Recommended—TOEFL. Electronic applications accepted. *Faculty research:* Medical ultrasound, BioMEMS, neural prosthetics, computational bioengineering, bioengineering of vision, medical devices.

University of Wisconsin–Milwaukee, Graduate School, College of Engineering and Applied Science, Biomedical and Health Informatics Program, Milwaukee, WI 53201-0413. Offers health information systems (PhD); health services management and policy (PhD); knowledge based systems (PhD); medical imaging and instrumentation (PhD); public health informatics (PhD). *Students:* 8 full-time (3 women), 14 part-time (6 women); includes 3 minority (2 Black or African American, non-Hispanic/Latino; 1 Asian, non-Hispanic/Latino), 9 international. Average age 37. 18 applicants, 56% accepted, 4 enrolled. *Degree requirements:* For doctorate, comprehensive exam, thesis/dissertation. *Entrance requirements:* For doctorate, GRE, GMAT or MCAT. Additional exam requirements/recommendations for international students: Required—TOEFL (minimum score 600 paper-based; 79 iBT), IELTS (minimum score 6.5). Application fee: $56 ($96 for international students). Electronic applications accepted. *Financial support:* Fellowships, research assistantships, teaching assistantships, and project assistantships available. *Unit head:* Devendra Misra, PhD, Chair, 414-229-3327, E-mail: misra@uwm.edu. *Application contact:* Betty Warras, Engineering and Computer Science Graduate Programs, 414-229-6169, E-mail: ceas-graduate@uwm.edu.
Website: http://uwm.edu/engineering/academics-2/departments/biomedical-engineering/

Wayne State University, College of Engineering, Department of Biomedical Engineering, Detroit, MI 48202. Offers biomedical engineering (MS, PhD), including biomedical imaging (PhD); injury biomechanics (Graduate Certificate). *Faculty:* 17. *Students:* 79 full-time (40 women), 32 part-time (15 women); includes 16 minority (4 Black or African American, non-Hispanic/Latino; 8 Asian, non-Hispanic/Latino; 2 Hispanic/Latino; 2 Two or more races, non-Hispanic/Latino), 41 international. Average age 27. 152 applicants, 40% accepted, 30 enrolled. In 2017, 38 master's, 6 doctorates awarded. Terminal master's awarded for partial completion of doctoral program. *Degree requirements:* For master's, thesis optional; for doctorate, thesis/dissertation. *Entrance requirements:* For master's, GRE (recommended), bachelor's degree, minimum undergraduate GPA of 3.0, one-page statement of purpose, completion of prerequisite coursework in calculus and engineering physics; for doctorate, GRE, bachelor's degree in biomedical engineering with minimum undergraduate GPA of 3.5, or master's degree in biomedical engineering with minimum GPA of 3.3; personal statement; three letters of recommendation; for Graduate Certificate, minimum undergraduate GPA of 3.0, bachelor's degree in engineering or in a mathematics-based science program. Additional exam requirements/recommendations for international students: Required—TOEFL (minimum score 550 paper-based; 79 iBT), TWE; Recommended—IELTS (minimum score 6.5). *Application deadline:* For fall admission, 6/1 priority date for domestic students, 5/1 priority date for international students; for winter admission, 10/1 priority date for domestic students, 9/1 priority date for international students; for spring admission, 2/1 priority date for domestic students, 1/1 priority date for international students. Applications are processed on a rolling basis. Application fee: $50. Electronic applications accepted. *Expenses:* Contact institution. *Financial support:* In 2017–18, 41 students received support, including 4 fellowships with tuition reimbursements available (averaging $16,000 per year), 4 research assistantships with tuition reimbursements available (averaging $18,795 per year), 8 teaching assistantships with tuition reimbursements available (averaging $19,560 per year); Federal Work-Study, scholarships/grants, health care benefits, and unspecified assistantships also available. Support available to part-time students. Financial award applicants required to submit FAFSA. *Faculty research:* Injury and orthopedic biomechanics, neurophysiology of pain, smart sensors, biomaterials and imaging. *Unit head:* Dr. John Cavanaugh, Interim Department Chair, 313-577-3916, E-mail: jmc@wayne.edu. *Application contact:* Ellen Cope, Graduate Program Coordinator, 313-577-0409, Fax: 313-577-8333, E-mail: escope@wayne.edu.
Website: http://engineering.wayne.edu/bme/

Medical Physics

The College of William and Mary, Faculty of Arts and Sciences, Department of Applied Science, Williamsburg, VA 23185. Offers accelerator science (PhD); applied mathematics (PhD); applied mechanics (PhD); applied robotics (PhD); applied science (MS); atmospheric and environmental science (PhD); computational neuroscience (PhD); interface, thin film and surface science (PhD); lasers and optics (PhD); magnetic resonance (PhD); materials science and engineering (PhD); mathematical and computational biology (PhD); medical imaging (PhD); nanotechnology (PhD); neuroscience (PhD); non-destructive evaluation (PhD); polymer chemistry (PhD); remote sensing (PhD). *Program availability:* Part-time. *Faculty:* 11 full-time (3 women). *Students:* 30 full-time (11 women), 3 part-time (0 women); includes 6 minority (2 Black or African American, non-Hispanic/Latino; 1 Asian, non-Hispanic/Latino; 2 Hispanic/Latino; 1 Two or more races, non-Hispanic/Latino), 13 international. Average age 27. 34 applicants, 47% accepted, 10 enrolled. In 2017, 5 doctorates awarded. Terminal master's awarded for partial completion of doctoral program. *Degree requirements:* For master's, comprehensive exam, thesis; for doctorate, comprehensive exam, thesis/dissertation, 4 core courses. *Entrance requirements:* For master's and doctorate, GRE General Test, GRE Subject Test. Additional exam requirements/recommendations for international students: Required—TOEFL, IELTS. *Application deadline:* For fall admission, 2/1 priority date for domestic students, 2/1 for international students; for spring admission, 10/5 priority date for domestic students, 10/5 for international students. Applications are processed on a rolling basis. Application fee: $50. Electronic applications accepted. *Expenses:* Contact institution. *Financial support:* In 2017–18, 8 students received support, including 27 research assistantships (averaging $26,000 per year), 1 teaching assistantship (averaging $9,500 per year); fellowships, scholarships/grants, health care benefits, tuition waivers (full), and unspecified assistantships also available. Financial award application deadline: 4/15; financial award applicants required to submit FAFSA. *Faculty research:* Computational biology, non-destructive evaluation, neurophysiology, laser spectroscopy, nanotechnology. *Total annual research expenditures:* $536,220. *Unit head:* Dr. Christopher Del Negro, Chair, 757-221-7808, Fax: 757-221-2050, E-mail: cadeln@wm.edu. *Application contact:* Lianne Rios Ashburne, Graduate Program Coordinator, 757-221-2563, Fax: 757-221-2050, E-mail: lrashburne@wm.edu.
Website: http://www.wm.edu/as/appliedscience

Columbia University, Fu Foundation School of Engineering and Applied Science, Department of Applied Physics and Applied Mathematics, New York, NY 10027. Offers applied mathematics (MS, Eng Sc D, PhD); applied physics (MS, Eng Sc D, PhD); materials science and engineering (MS, Eng Sc D, PhD); medical physics (MS). *Program availability:* Part-time, online learning. Terminal master's awarded for partial completion of doctoral program. *Degree requirements:* For master's, comprehensive exam; for doctorate, thesis/dissertation, qualifying exam. *Entrance requirements:* For master's, GRE General Test, GRE Subject Test (strongly recommended); for doctorate, GRE General Test, GRE Subject Test (applied physics). Additional exam requirements/recommendations for international students: Required—TOEFL, IELTS, PTE. Electronic applications accepted. *Expenses: Tuition:* Full-time $44,864; part-time $1704 per credit. *Required fees:* $2370 per semester. One-time fee: $105. *Faculty research:* Plasma physics and fusion energy; optical and laser physics; atmospheric, oceanic and earth physics; applied mathematics; solid state science and processing of materials, their properties, and their structure; medical physics.

Creighton University, Graduate School, College of Arts and Sciences, Program in Physics, Omaha, NE 68178-0001. Offers medical physics (MS); physics (MS). *Program availability:* Part-time. *Faculty:* 11 full-time (2 women), 2 part-time/adjunct (0 women). *Students:* 10 full-time (1 woman), 2 part-time (0 women), 4 international. Average age 28. 21 applicants, 62% accepted, 9 enrolled. *Degree requirements:* For master's, comprehensive exam, thesis (for some programs). *Entrance requirements:* For master's, GRE General Test, 3 letters of recommendation. Additional exam requirements/recommendations for international students: Required—TOEFL (minimum score 90 iBT). *Application deadline:* For fall admission, 3/1 for domestic and international students. Applications are processed on a rolling basis. Application fee: $50. Electronic applications accepted. Part-time tuition and fees vary according to course load, degree level, campus/location and program. *Financial support:* In 2017–18, 8 students received support, including 8 teaching assistantships with full tuition reimbursements available (averaging $11,865 per year). Financial award applicants required to submit FAFSA. *Unit head:* Dr. Michael Nichols, Chair, 402-280-2159, E-mail: mnichols@creighton.edu. *Application contact:* Lindsay Johnson, Director of Graduate and Adult Recruitment, 402-280-2703, Fax: 402-280-2423, E-mail: gradschool@creighton.edu.

Duke University, Graduate School, Medical Physics Graduate Program, Durham, NC 27705. Offers MS, PhD. *Entrance requirements:* For master's and doctorate, GRE General Test. Additional exam requirements/recommendations for international students: Required—TOEFL (minimum score 577 paper-based; 90 iBT) or IELTS (minimum score 7). Electronic applications accepted.

East Carolina University, Graduate School, Thomas Harriot College of Arts and Sciences, Department of Physics, Greenville, NC 27858-4353. Offers applied physics (MS); biomedical physics (PhD); health physics (MS); medical physics (MS). *Program availability:* Part-time. *Students:* 39 full-time (10 women), 8 part-time (2 women); includes 11 minority (4 Black or African American, non-Hispanic/Latino; 4 Asian, non-Hispanic/Latino; 2 Hispanic/Latino; 1 Two or more races, non-Hispanic/Latino), 5 international. Average age 29. 37 applicants, 70% accepted, 16 enrolled. In 2017, 4 master's, 1 doctorate awarded. *Degree requirements:* For master's, comprehensive exam; for doctorate, comprehensive exam, thesis/dissertation. *Entrance requirements:* For master's and doctorate, GRE General Test. Additional exam requirements/recommendations for international students: Recommended—TOEFL (minimum score 78 iBT), IELTS (minimum score 6.5). *Application deadline:* For fall admission, 3/1 priority date for domestic and international students. Applications are processed on a rolling basis. Application fee: $75. Electronic applications accepted. *Expenses:* Tuition, state resident: full-time $4749; part-time $297 per credit hour. Tuition, nonresident: full-time $17,898; part-time $1119 per credit hour. *Required fees:* $2691; $224 per credit hour. Part-time tuition and fees vary according to course load and program. *Financial support:* Research assistantships with partial tuition reimbursements, teaching assistantships with partial tuition reimbursements, and Federal Work-Study available. Support available to part-time students. Financial award application deadline: 3/1. *Faculty research:* Health and medical physics, biological and biomedical physics, radiological physics, acoustics and bioacoustics, theoretical and computational physics. *Unit head:* Dr. Jefferson Shinpaugh, Chair, 252-328-1852, E-mail: shinpaughj@ecu.edu. *Application contact:* Dean of Graduate School, 252-328-6012, Fax: 252-328-6071, E-mail: gradschool@ecu.edu.
Website: http://www.ecu.edu/cs-cas/physics/

Hampton University, School of Science, Department of Physics, Hampton, VA 23668. Offers medical physics (MS, PhD); nuclear physics (MS, PhD); optical physics (MS, PhD). *Students:* 13 full-time (3 women), 5 part-time (1 woman); includes 8 minority (6 Black or African American, non-Hispanic/Latino; 2 Asian, non-Hispanic/Latino), 7 international. Average age 30. 14 applicants, 29% accepted, 1 enrolled. In 2017, 1 doctorate awarded. *Degree requirements:* For master's, thesis optional; for doctorate, thesis/dissertation, oral defense, qualifying exam. *Entrance requirements:* For master's, GRE General Test; for doctorate, GRE General Test, minimum GPA of 3.0 or master's degree in physics or related field. Additional exam requirements/recommendations for international students: Required—TOEFL (minimum score 525 paper-based) or IELTS (6.5). *Application deadline:* For fall admission, 6/1 priority date for domestic students, 4/1 priority date for international students; for spring admission, 11/1 priority date for domestic students, 9/1 priority date for international students; for summer admission, 4/1 priority date for domestic students, 2/1 priority date for international students. Applications are processed on a rolling basis. Application fee: $35. Electronic applications accepted. *Expenses: Tuition:* Full-time $22,630; part-time $575 per semester hour. *Required fees:* $70. Tuition and fees vary according to program. *Financial support:* In 2017–18, 17 research assistantships were awarded; fellowships, teaching assistantships, career-related internships or fieldwork, Federal Work-Study, institutionally sponsored loans, and scholarships/grants also available. Support available to part-time students. Financial award application deadline: 6/30; financial award applicants required to submit FAFSA. *Faculty research:* Laser optics, remote sensing. *Unit head:* Dr. Paul Gueye, Chairperson, 757-727-5277.
Website: http://science.hamptonu.edu/physics/

Harvard University, Graduate School of Arts and Sciences, Department of Physics, Cambridge, MA 02138. Offers experimental physics (PhD); medical engineering/medical physics (PhD), including applied physics, engineering sciences, physics; theoretical physics (PhD). *Degree requirements:* For doctorate, thesis/dissertation, final exams, laboratory experience. *Entrance requirements:* For doctorate, GRE General Test, GRE Subject Test. Additional exam requirements/recommendations for international students: Required—TOEFL. *Faculty research:* Particle physics, condensed matter physics, atomic physics.

Hofstra University, College of Liberal Arts and Sciences, Program in Medical Physics, Hempstead, NY 11549. Offers MS. *Program availability:* Part-time, evening/weekend. *Students:* 7 full-time (1 woman); includes 4 minority (2 Asian, non-Hispanic/Latino; 2 Hispanic/Latino). Average age 25. 28 applicants, 64% accepted, 2 enrolled. In 2017, 4 master's awarded. *Degree requirements:* For master's, comprehensive exam, minimum GPA of 3.0. *Entrance requirements:* For master's, bachelor's degree in science, minimum GPA of 3.0, 2 letters of recommendation. Additional exam requirements/recommendations for international students: Required—TOEFL (minimum score 550 paper-based; 80 iBT). *Application deadline:* Applications are processed on a rolling basis. Application fee: $75. Electronic applications accepted. *Expenses: Tuition:* Full-time $1292. *Required fees:* $970. Tuition and fees vary according to program. *Financial support:* In 2017–18, 7 students received support, including 6 fellowships with full and partial tuition reimbursements available (averaging $5,814 per year); research assistantships with full and partial tuition reimbursements available, career-related internships or fieldwork, Federal Work-Study, institutionally sponsored loans, scholarships/grants, traineeships, tuition waivers (full and partial), and unspecified assistantships also available. Support available to part-time students. Financial award applicants required to submit FAFSA. *Faculty research:* General medical physics; radiation therapy physics; diagnostic radiological physics; nuclear medicine; radiation protection and safety. *Unit head:* Dr. Gregory Levine, Chairperson, 516-463-5583, E-mail: gregory.c.levine@hofstra.edu. *Application contact:* Sunil Samuel, Assistant Vice President of Admissions, 516-463-4723, Fax: 516-463-4664, E-mail: graduateadmission@hofstra.edu.
Website: http://www.hofstra.edu/hclas

Indiana University Bloomington, University Graduate School, College of Arts and Sciences, Department of Physics, Bloomington, IN 47405. Offers medical physics (MS); physics (MAT, MS, PhD). *Program availability:* Part-time, online learning. Terminal master's awarded for partial completion of doctoral program. *Degree requirements:* For master's, comprehensive exam (for some programs), thesis (for some programs), qualifying exam; for doctorate, comprehensive exam, thesis/dissertation, qualifying exam. *Entrance requirements:* For master's and doctorate, GRE General Test, GRE Subject Test (physics), minimum GPA of 3.0. Additional exam requirements/recommendations for international students: Required—TOEFL (minimum score 550 paper-based; 80 iBT) or IELTS (minimum score 6.5). Electronic applications accepted. *Expenses:* Contact institution. *Faculty research:* Accelerator physics, astrophysics and cosmology, biophysics (biocomplexity, neural networks, visual systems, chemical signaling), condensed matter physics (neutron scattering, complex fluids, quantum computing), particle physics (collider physics, hybrid mesons, lattice gauge, symmetries, collider phenomenology), neutrino physics, nuclear physics (proton and neutron physics, neutrinos, symmetries, nuclear astrophysics, hadron structure).

Louisiana State University and Agricultural & Mechanical College, Graduate School, College of Science, Department of Physics and Astronomy, Baton Rouge, LA 70803. Offers astronomy (PhD); astrophysics (PhD); medical physics (MS); physics (MS, PhD). *Faculty:* 47 full-time (8 women), 1 part-time/adjunct (0 women). *Students:* 101 full-time (29 women), 5 part-time (1 woman); includes 6 minority (1 Black or African American, non-Hispanic/Latino; 2 Asian, non-Hispanic/Latino; 2 Hispanic/Latino; 1 Two or more races, non-Hispanic/Latino), 38 international. Average age 27. 185 applicants, 11% accepted, 21 enrolled. In 2017, 9 master's, 14 doctorates awarded. *Financial support:* In 2017–18, 6 fellowships (averaging $36,213 per year), 59 research assistantships (averaging $24,339 per year), 37 teaching assistantships (averaging $22,235 per year) were awarded. *Total annual research expenditures:* $8.4 million.

Massachusetts Institute of Technology, School of Engineering, Harvard-MIT Health Sciences and Technology Program, Cambridge, MA 02139. Offers health sciences and technology (SM, PhD, Sc D), including bioastronautics (PhD, Sc D), bioinformatics and integrative genomics (PhD, Sc D), medical engineering and medical physics (PhD, Sc D), speech and hearing bioscience and technology (PhD, Sc D). Terminal master's awarded for partial completion of doctoral program. *Degree requirements:* For doctorate, comprehensive exam, thesis/dissertation. *Entrance requirements:* For doctorate, GRE General Test. Additional exam requirements/recommendations for international students: Required—TOEFL, IELTS. Electronic applications accepted. *Faculty research:* Biomedical imaging, drug delivery, medical devices, medical diagnostics, regenerative biomedical technologies.

McGill University, Faculty of Graduate and Postdoctoral Studies, Faculty of Medicine, Medical Physics Unit, Montréal, QC H3A 2T5, Canada. Offers M Sc, PhD. *Entrance requirements:* Additional exam requirements/recommendations for international students: Required—TOEFL.

Medical Physics

McMaster University, School of Graduate Studies, Faculty of Science, Department of Medical Physics and Applied Radiation Sciences, Hamilton, ON L8S 4M2, Canada. Offers health and radiation physics (M Sc); medical physics (M Sc, PhD). *Program availability:* Part-time. *Degree requirements:* For master's, thesis or alternative. *Entrance requirements:* For master's, minimum B+ average. Additional exam requirements/recommendations for international students: Required—TOEFL (minimum score 550 paper-based). *Faculty research:* Imaging, toxicology, dosimetry, body composition, medical lasers.

Oakland University, Graduate Study and Lifelong Learning, College of Arts and Sciences, Department of Physics, Rochester, MI 48309-4401. Offers medical physics (PhD); physics (MS). *Degree requirements:* For doctorate, thesis/dissertation. *Entrance requirements:* For master's, minimum GPA of 3.0; for doctorate, GRE Subject Test, GRE General Test, minimum GPA of 3.0. Additional exam requirements/recommendations for international students: Required—TOEFL (minimum score 550 paper-based). Electronic applications accepted. *Expenses:* Contact institution.

Oregon State University, College of Engineering, Program in Medical Physics, Corvallis, OR 97331. Offers medical health physics (MMP, MS); therapeutic radiologic physics (PhD). *Entrance requirements:* For master's and doctorate, GRE. Additional exam requirements/recommendations for international students: Required—TOEFL (minimum score 80 iBT), IELTS (minimum score 6.5). *Application deadline:* For fall admission, 12/15 for domestic students. Application fee: $75 ($85 for international students). *Expenses:* Contact institution. *Financial support:* Application deadline: 2/1. *Unit head:* Grant Rommel, Administrative Assistant, 503-494-7461, E-mail: rommel@ohsu.edu. *Application contact:* Medical Physics Advisor, 541-737-2343, E-mail: nuc_engr@ne.oregonstate.edu.
Website: http://ne.oregonstate.edu/content/medical-physics-program

Purdue University, Graduate School, College of Health and Human Sciences, School of Health Sciences, West Lafayette, IN 47907. Offers health physics (MS, PhD); medical physics (MS, PhD); occupational and environmental health science (MS, PhD), including aerosol deposition and lung disease, ergonomics, exposure and risk assessment, indoor air quality and bioaerosols (PhD), liver/lung toxicology; radiation biology (PhD); toxicology (PhD); MS/PhD. *Program availability:* Part-time. *Faculty:* 12 full-time (4 women), 1 part-time/adjunct (0 women). *Students:* 37 full-time (16 women), 5 part-time (1 woman); includes 6 minority (2 Black or African American, non-Hispanic/Latino; 2 Asian, non-Hispanic/Latino; 1 Hispanic/Latino; 1 Two or more races, non-Hispanic/Latino), 9 international. Average age 28. 57 applicants, 65% accepted, 15 enrolled. In 2017, 10 master's, 4 doctorates awarded. *Degree requirements:* For master's, thesis optional; for doctorate, one foreign language, thesis/dissertation. *Entrance requirements:* For master's and doctorate, GRE General Test, minimum undergraduate GPA of 3.0 or equivalent. Additional exam requirements/recommendations for international students: Required—TOEFL (minimum score 550 paper-based; 77 iBT); Recommended—TWE. *Application deadline:* For fall admission, 5/15 for domestic and international students; for spring admission, 10/15 for domestic and international students. Applications are processed on a rolling basis. Application fee: $60 ($75 for international students). Electronic applications accepted. *Financial support:* In 2017–18, fellowships with tuition reimbursements (averaging $14,400 per year), research assistantships with tuition reimbursements (averaging $12,000 per year), teaching assistantships with tuition reimbursements (averaging $12,000 per year) were awarded; career-related internships or fieldwork and traineeships also available. Support available to part-time students. Financial award applicants required to submit FAFSA. *Faculty research:* Environmental toxicology, industrial hygiene, radiation dosimetry. *Unit head:* Jason T. Harris, Interim Head of the Graduate Program, 765-496-1271, E-mail: jtharris@purdue.edu. *Application contact:* Karen E. Walker, Graduate Contact, 765-494-1419, E-mail: kwalker@purdue.edu.
Website: https://www.purdue.edu/hhs/hsci/

Rush University, Graduate College, Division of Medical Physics, Chicago, IL 60612-3832. Offers MS, PhD. Terminal master's awarded for partial completion of doctoral program. *Degree requirements:* For master's, thesis, qualifying exam; for doctorate, thesis/dissertation, preliminary and qualifying exams. *Entrance requirements:* For master's, GRE General Test, BS in physics or physical science; for doctorate, GRE General Test, GRE Subject Test. Additional exam requirements/recommendations for international students: Required—TOEFL. Electronic applications accepted. *Faculty research:* Radiation therapy treatment planning, dosimetry, diagnostic radiology and nuclear imaging.

Southern Illinois University Carbondale, Graduate School, College of Applied Science, Program in Medical Dosimetry, Carbondale, IL 62901-4701. Offers MS. *Entrance requirements:* Additional exam requirements/recommendations for international students: Required—TOEFL. Electronic applications accepted.

Stony Brook University, State University of New York, Graduate School, College of Engineering and Applied Sciences, Department of Biomedical Engineering, Program in Medical Physics, Stony Brook, NY 11794. Offers MS, PhD. *Entrance requirements:* For doctorate, GRE. Additional exam requirements/recommendations for international students: Required—TOEFL (minimum score 90 iBT). *Application deadline:* For fall admission, 1/1 for domestic students. Application fee: $100. *Expenses:* Tuition, state resident: full-time $10,870; part-time $453 per credit. Tuition, nonresident: full-time $22,210; part-time $925 per credit. *Financial support:* Fellowships available. *Unit head:* Dr. Terry Button, Director, 631-444-3841, Fax: 631-444-7538, E-mail: terry.button@stonybrook.edu. *Application contact:* Jessica Anne Kuhn, Assistant to Chair/Graduate Program Coordinator, 631-632-8371, Fax: 631-632-8577, E-mail: jessica.kuhn@stonybrook.edu.
Website: http://bme.sunysb.edu/grad/medicalphysics.html

University at Buffalo, the State University of New York, Graduate School, Jacobs School of Medicine and Biomedical Sciences, Graduate Programs in Medicine and Biomedical Sciences, Program in Medical Physics, Williamsville, NY 14221. Offers MS, PhD. *Faculty:* 14 full-time (1 woman). *Students:* 22 full-time (5 women); includes 12 minority (1 Black or African American, non-Hispanic/Latino; 11 Asian, non-Hispanic/Latino). Average age 29. 47 applicants, 23% accepted, 5 enrolled. In 2017, 6 master's, 5 doctorates awarded. *Degree requirements:* For master's, thesis or project; for doctorate, thesis/dissertation. *Entrance requirements:* For master's and doctorate, GRE. Additional exam requirements/recommendations for international students: Required—TOEFL (minimum score 550 paper-based; 79 iBT). *Application deadline:* Applications are processed on a rolling basis. Application fee: $85. Electronic applications accepted. *Expenses:* Contact institution. *Financial support:* Research assistantships and traineeships available. *Faculty research:* Radiation dose distribution tracking for patients and staff, development of improved dynamic x-ray image guidance systems for interventional procedures, development and testing of improved endovascular interventional devices, external beam therapy dose planning and optimization, 3D printing phantoms for CT and angiographic procedures. *Total annual research expenditures:* $200,000. *Unit head:* Dr. Stephen Rudin, Director, 716-829-5408, E-mail: srudin@buffalo.edu. *Application contact:* Kara M. Rickicki, Graduate Programs Coordinator, 716-829-2417, Fax: 716-829-2344, E-mail: rickicki@buffalo.edu.
Website: http://medicine.buffalo.edu/education/medical-physics.html

University of Alberta, Faculty of Graduate Studies and Research, Department of Physics, Edmonton, AB T6G 2E1, Canada. Offers astrophysics (M Sc, PhD); condensed matter (M Sc, PhD); geophysics (M Sc, PhD); medical physics (M Sc, PhD); subatomic physics (M Sc, PhD). *Degree requirements:* For master's, thesis; for doctorate, thesis/dissertation. *Entrance requirements:* For master's and doctorate, minimum GPA of 7.0 on a 9.0 scale. Additional exam requirements/recommendations for international students: Required—TOEFL. *Faculty research:* Cosmology, astroparticle physics, high-intermediate energy, magnetism, superconductivity.

The University of Arizona, College of Science, Department of Physics, Medical Physics Program, Tucson, AZ 85721. Offers PSM. *Program availability:* Part-time. *Degree requirements:* For master's, thesis or alternative, internship, colloquium, business courses. *Entrance requirements:* Additional exam requirements/recommendations for international students: Required—TOEFL (minimum score 550 paper-based; 79 iBT). Electronic applications accepted. *Faculty research:* Nanotechnology, optics, medical imaging, high energy physics, biophysics.

University of California, Los Angeles, David Geffen School of Medicine and Graduate Division, Graduate Programs in Medicine, Program in Biomedical Physics, Los Angeles, CA 90095. Offers MS, PhD. Terminal master's awarded for partial completion of doctoral program. *Degree requirements:* For master's, comprehensive exam or thesis; for doctorate, thesis/dissertation, oral and written qualifying exams. *Entrance requirements:* For master's and doctorate, GRE General Test. Additional exam requirements/recommendations for international students: Required—TOEFL. Electronic applications accepted.

University of Chicago, Division of the Biological Sciences, Committee on Medical Physics, Chicago, IL 60637-1513. Offers PhD. *Students:* 20 full-time (6 women). 59 applicants, 14% accepted, 4 enrolled. In 2017, 2 doctorates awarded. *Degree requirements:* For doctorate, comprehensive exam, thesis/dissertation, ethics class, 2 teaching assistantships. *Entrance requirements:* For doctorate, GRE General Test, transcripts, statement of purpose, 3 letters of recommendation. Additional exam requirements/recommendations for international students: Required—TOEFL (minimum score 600 paper-based; 104 iBT), IELTS (minimum score 7). *Application deadline:* For fall admission, 12/1 for domestic and international students. Application fee: $90. Electronic applications accepted. *Financial support:* In 2017–18, 20 students received support, including fellowships with full tuition reimbursements available (averaging $31,000 per year), research assistantships with full tuition reimbursements available (averaging $31,000 per year); institutionally sponsored loans, scholarships/grants, traineeships, and health care benefits also available. Financial award application deadline: 12/1. *Faculty research:* Imaging techniques and technologies, diagnostic radiography, electron paramagnetic resonance imagine, computer-aided diagnostics and quantitative image analysis, multi-modality image correlation. *Unit head:* Dr. Samuel Armato, III, Chair, 773-834-7769, E-mail: bsdadmissions@uchicago.edu. *Application contact:* Ruth Magana, Program Administrator, 773-834-7769, E-mail: rmagana@radiology.bsd.uchicago.edu.
Website: http://medicalphysics.uchicago.edu/

University of Cincinnati, Graduate School, College of Medicine, Graduate Programs in Biomedical Sciences, Department of Radiology, Cincinnati, OH 45267. Offers medical physics (MS). *Program availability:* Part-time. *Degree requirements:* For master's, comprehensive exam, project. *Entrance requirements:* For master's, GRE General Test. Additional exam requirements/recommendations for international students: Required—TOEFL (minimum score 575 paper-based). Electronic applications accepted. *Expenses: Tuition, area resident:* Full-time $14,468. Tuition, state resident: full-time $14,968; part-time $754 per credit hour. Tuition, nonresident: full-time $24,210; part-time $1311 per credit hour. *International tuition:* $26,460 full-time. *Required fees:* $3958; $84 per credit hour. One-time fee: $85 full-time. Tuition and fees vary according to course load, degree level and program. *Faculty research:* Radiation oncology, radiologic imaging, dosimetry, radiation biology, radiation therapy.

University of Florida, Graduate School, Herbert Wertheim College of Engineering, J. Crayton Pruitt Family Department of Biomedical Engineering, Gainesville, FL 32611. Offers biomedical engineering (ME, MS, PhD, Certificate); clinical and translational science (PhD); medical physics (MS, PhD); MD/PhD. Terminal master's awarded for partial completion of doctoral program. *Degree requirements:* For master's, comprehensive exam (for some programs), thesis (for some programs); for doctorate, comprehensive exam (for some programs), thesis/dissertation (for some programs). *Entrance requirements:* Additional exam requirements/recommendations for international students: Required—TOEFL (minimum score 550 paper-based; 80 iBT), IELTS (minimum score 6). Electronic applications accepted. *Faculty research:* Neural engineering, imaging and medical physics, biomaterials and regenerative medicine, biomedical informatics and modeling.

University of Kentucky, Graduate School, Graduate School Programs from the College of Medicine, Program in Radiation Sciences, Lexington, KY 40506-0032. Offers MSRMP. *Program availability:* Part-time. *Degree requirements:* For master's, comprehensive exam, thesis. *Entrance requirements:* For master's, GRE General Test, minimum undergraduate GPA of 2.75. Additional exam requirements/recommendations for international students: Required—TOEFL (minimum score 550 paper-based). Electronic applications accepted. *Faculty research:* Dosimetry, manpower studies, diagnostic imaging physics, shielding.

University of Minnesota, Twin Cities Campus, Graduate School, Program in Biophysical Sciences and Medical Physics, Minneapolis, MN 55455-0213. Offers MS, PhD. *Program availability:* Part-time. *Degree requirements:* For master's, thesis optional, research paper, oral exam; for doctorate, thesis/dissertation, oral/written preliminary exam, oral final exam. *Faculty research:* Theoretical biophysics, radiological physics, cellular and molecular biophysics.

University of Oklahoma Health Sciences Center, College of Medicine and Graduate College, Graduate Programs in Medicine, Department of Radiological Sciences, Oklahoma City, OK 73190. Offers medical radiation physics (MS, PhD), including diagnostic radiology, nuclear medicine, radiation therapy, ultrasound. *Program availability:* Part-time. Terminal master's awarded for partial completion of doctoral program. *Degree requirements:* For master's, thesis; for doctorate, thesis/dissertation. *Entrance requirements:* For master's, GRE General Test; for doctorate, GRE General Test, 3 letters of recommendation. Additional exam requirements/recommendations for international students: Required—TOEFL. *Faculty research:* Monte Carlo applications in radiation therapy, observer-performed studies in diagnostic radiology, error analysis in gated cardiac nuclear medicine studies, nuclear medicine absorbed fraction determinations.

University of Pennsylvania, School of Arts and Sciences, College of Liberal and Professional Studies, Philadelphia, PA 19104. Offers applied geosciences (MSAG); applied positive psychology (MAP); chemical sciences (MCS); environmental studies (MES); individualized study (MLA); liberal arts (M Phil); medical physics (MMP); organization dynamics (M Phil). *Students:* 191 full-time (112 women), 311 part-time (178 women); includes 99 minority (34 Black or African American, non-Hispanic/Latino; 2 American Indian or Alaska Native, non-Hispanic/Latino; 28 Asian, non-Hispanic/Latino; 24 Hispanic/Latino; 11 Two or more races, non-Hispanic/Latino), 83 international.

Average age 34. 633 applicants, 52% accepted, 249 enrolled. In 2017, 141 master's awarded. *Unit head:* Nora Lewis, Vice Dean, Professional and Liberal Education, 215-898-7326, E-mail: nlewis@sas.upenn.edu.
Website: http://www.sas.upenn.edu/lps/graduate

University of Pennsylvania, School of Arts and Sciences, Graduate Group in Physics and Astronomy, Philadelphia, PA 19104. Offers medical physics (MS); physics (PhD). *Program availability:* Part-time. *Faculty:* 44 full-time (8 women), 11 part-time/adjunct (0 women). *Students:* 100 full-time (29 women), 1 part-time (0 women); includes 18 minority (1 Black or African American, non-Hispanic/Latino; 8 Asian, non-Hispanic/Latino; 6 Hispanic/Latino; 3 Two or more races, non-Hispanic/Latino), 25 international. Average age 26. 460 applicants, 13% accepted, 13 enrolled. In 2017, 19 master's, 14 doctorates awarded. *Financial support:* Application deadline: 12/1.
Website: http://www.physics.upenn.edu/graduate/

University of Rhode Island, Graduate School, College of Arts and Sciences, Department of Physics, Kingston, RI 02881. Offers medical physics (MS); physics (MS, PhD). *Program availability:* Part-time, evening/weekend. *Faculty:* 17 full-time (1 woman). *Students:* 18 full-time (5 women); includes 2 minority (1 Black or African American, non-Hispanic/Latino; 1 Asian, non-Hispanic/Latino), 7 international. 49 applicants, 14% accepted, 2 enrolled. In 2017, 1 master's, 2 doctorates awarded. *Entrance requirements:* For master's and doctorate, GRE General Test; GRE Subject Test in physics (recommended), 2 letters of recommendation. Additional exam requirements/recommendations for international students: Required—TOEFL. *Application deadline:* For fall admission, 3/1 for domestic students, 2/1 for international students; for spring admission, 7/15 for international students. Application fee: $65. Electronic applications accepted. *Expenses:* Tuition, state resident: full-time $12,706; part-time $786 per credit. Tuition, nonresident: full-time $25,216; part-time $1401 per credit. *Required fees:* $1598; $45 per credit. One-time fee: $30 part-time. *Financial support:* In 2017–18, 17 teaching assistantships with tuition reimbursements (averaging $17,165 per year) were awarded. Financial award application deadline: 3/1; financial award applicants required to submit FAFSA. *Unit head:* Dr. Oleg Andreev, Chair, 401-874-2060, Fax: 401-874-2380, E-mail: andreev@mail.uri.edu. *Application contact:* Dr. Leonard M. Kahn, Director of Graduate Studies, 401-874-2503, Fax: 401-874-2380, E-mail: lkahn@uri.edu.
Website: http://www.phys.uri.edu/index.html

University of South Florida, College of Arts and Sciences, Department of Physics, Tampa, FL 33620-9951. Offers applied physics (PhD), including medical physics; physics (MS), including applied physics, atomic and molecular physics, laser physics, materials physics, optical physics, semiconductor physics, solid state physics. *Program availability:* Part-time. *Faculty:* 22 full-time (2 women), 2 part-time/adjunct (1 woman). *Students:* 64 full-time (17 women), 9 part-time (2 women); includes 13 minority (1 Black or African American, non-Hispanic/Latino; 1 Asian, non-Hispanic/Latino; 11 Hispanic/Latino), 31 international. Average age 30. 110 applicants, 24% accepted, 14 enrolled. In 2017, 10 master's, 13 doctorates awarded. *Degree requirements:* For master's, comprehensive exam, thesis optional; for doctorate, comprehensive exam, thesis/dissertation. *Entrance requirements:* For master's and doctorate, GRE General Test; GRE Subject Test in physics (recommended), minimum GPA of 3.0, three letters of recommendation, statement of purpose. Additional exam requirements/recommendations for international students: Required—TOEFL (minimum score 550 paper-based; 79 iBT) or IELTS (minimum score 6.5). *Application deadline:* For fall admission, 2/1 priority date for domestic students, 2/1 for international students; for spring admission, 9/1 for domestic and international students. Applications are processed on a rolling basis. Application fee: $30. Electronic applications accepted. *Financial support:* In 2017–18, 9 students received support, including 27 research assistantships with tuition reimbursements available (averaging $15,272 per year), 43 teaching assistantships with tuition reimbursements available (averaging $16,267 per year); unspecified assistantships also available. *Faculty research:* Molecular organization of collagen, lipid rafts in biological membranes, formation of Alzheimer plaques, the role of cellular ion pumps in wound healing, carbon nanotubes as biological detectors, optical imaging of neuronal activity, three-dimensional imaging of intact tissues, motility of cancer cells, optical detection of pathogens in water. *Total annual research expenditures:* $2.7 million. *Unit head:* Dr. David Rabson, Professor and Chairperson, 813-974-1207, E-mail: davidra@ewald.cas.usf.edu. *Application contact:* Dr. Xiaomei Jiang, Associate Professor and Director of Graduate Admissions, 813-974-7765, E-mail: xjiang@usf.edu.
Website: http://physics.usf.edu/

The University of Texas Health Science Center at Houston, MD Anderson UTHealth Graduate School, Houston, TX 77225-0036. Offers biochemistry and cell biology (PhD); biomedical sciences (MS); cancer biology (PhD); genetic counseling (MS); genetics and epigenetics (PhD); immunology (PhD); medical physics (MS, PhD); microbiology and infectious diseases (PhD); neuroscience (PhD); quantitative sciences (PhD); therapeutics and pharmacology (PhD); MD/PhD. Terminal master's awarded for partial completion of doctoral program. *Degree requirements:* For master's, thesis; for doctorate, thesis/dissertation. *Entrance requirements:* For master's and doctorate, GRE General Test. Additional exam requirements/recommendations for international students: Required—TOEFL. Electronic applications accepted. *Faculty research:* Biomedical sciences.

The University of Texas Health Science Center at San Antonio, Graduate School of Biomedical Sciences, Radiological Sciences Graduate Program, San Antonio, TX 78229-3900. Offers PhD. *Degree requirements:* For doctorate, comprehensive exam, thesis/dissertation.

The University of Toledo, College of Graduate Studies, College of Medicine and Life Sciences, Program in Medical Physics, Toledo, OH 43606-3390. Offers MSBS. *Degree requirements:* For master's, thesis. *Entrance requirements:* For master's, GRE, minimum undergraduate GPA of 3.0, three letters of recommendation, statement of purpose, transcripts from all prior institutions attended, resume. Additional exam requirements/recommendations for international students: Required—TOEFL (minimum score 550 paper-based; 80 iBT). Electronic applications accepted.

The University of Toledo, College of Graduate Studies, College of Natural Sciences and Mathematics, Department of Physics and Astronomy, Toledo, OH 43606-3390. Offers photovoltaics (PSM); physics (MS, PhD), including astrophysics (PhD), materials science, medical physics (PhD); MS/PhD. *Degree requirements:* For master's, thesis; for doctorate, thesis/dissertation, departmental qualifying exam. *Entrance requirements:* For master's and doctorate, GRE General Test, GRE Subject Test, minimum cumulative point-hour ratio of 2.7 for all previous academic work, three letters of recommendation, statement of purpose, transcripts from all prior institutions attended. Additional exam requirements/recommendations for international students: Required—TOEFL (minimum score 550 paper-based; 80 iBT). Electronic applications accepted. *Faculty research:* Atomic physics, solid-state physics, materials science, astrophysics.

University of Utah, Graduate School, College of Science, Department of Physics and Astronomy, Salt Lake City, UT 84112. Offers chemical physics (PhD); medical physics (MS, PhD); physics (MA, MS, PhD); physics teaching (PhD). *Program availability:* Part-time. *Faculty:* 34 full-time (5 women), 16 part-time/adjunct (1 woman). *Students:* 71 full-time (22 women), 29 part-time (12 women); includes 5 minority (1 Asian, non-Hispanic/Latino; 3 Hispanic/Latino; 1 Two or more races, non-Hispanic/Latino), 58 international. Average age 25. 137 applicants, 31% accepted, 19 enrolled. In 2017, 14 master's, 12 doctorates awarded. Terminal master's awarded for partial completion of doctoral program. *Entrance requirements:* For master's and doctorate, GRE Subject Test, minimum GPA of 3.0. Additional exam requirements/recommendations for international students: Required—TOEFL (minimum score 550 paper-based; 85 iBT). *Application deadline:* Applications are processed on a rolling basis. Application fee: $55 ($65 for international students). Electronic applications accepted. *Expenses:* Contact institution. *Financial support:* In 2017–18, 76 students received support, including 23 research assistantships with full tuition reimbursements available (averaging $23,500 per year), 52 teaching assistantships with full tuition reimbursements available (averaging $20,641 per year); unspecified assistantships also available. Financial award application deadline: 2/15; financial award applicants required to submit FAFSA. *Faculty research:* High-energy, cosmic-ray, medical physics, condensed matter, relativity applied physics, biophysics, astronomy and astrophysics. *Total annual research expenditures:* $5.6 million. *Unit head:* Dr. Benjamin Bromley, Chair, 801-581-3538, Fax: 801-581-4801, E-mail: bromley@physics.utah.edu. *Application contact:* Krista Perkins, Academic Coordinator, 801-581-6861, Fax: 801-581-4801, E-mail: krista@physics.utah.edu.
Website: http://www.physics.utah.edu/

University of Victoria, Faculty of Graduate Studies, Faculty of Science, Department of Physics and Astronomy, Victoria, BC V8W 2Y2, Canada. Offers astronomy and astrophysics (M Sc, PhD); condensed matter physics (M Sc, PhD); experimental particle physics (M Sc, PhD); medical physics (M Sc, PhD); ocean physics (M Sc, PhD); theoretical physics (M Sc, PhD). *Degree requirements:* For master's, thesis; for doctorate, comprehensive exam, thesis/dissertation, candidacy exam. *Entrance requirements:* For master's and doctorate, GRE. Additional exam requirements/recommendations for international students: Required—TOEFL (minimum score 575 paper-based), IELTS (minimum score 7). Electronic applications accepted. *Faculty research:* Old stellar populations; observational cosmology and large scale structure; cp violation; atlas.

University of Wisconsin–Madison, School of Medicine and Public Health, Medical Physics Graduate Program, Madison, WI 53705-2275. Offers medical physics (MS, PhD). *Program availability:* Part-time. *Faculty:* 46 full-time (6 women). *Students:* 82 full-time (24 women); includes 22 minority (2 Black or African American, non-Hispanic/Latino; 1 American Indian or Alaska Native, non-Hispanic/Latino; 7 Asian, non-Hispanic/Latino; 8 Hispanic/Latino; 1 Native Hawaiian or other Pacific Islander, non-Hispanic/Latino; 3 Two or more races, non-Hispanic/Latino), 17 international. Average age 27. 70 applicants, 14% accepted, 10 enrolled. In 2017, 3 master's, 13 doctorates awarded. Terminal master's awarded for partial completion of doctoral program. *Degree requirements:* For master's, comprehensive exam; for doctorate, comprehensive exam, thesis/dissertation. *Entrance requirements:* For master's and doctorate, GRE General Test, minimum GPA of 3.0. Additional exam requirements/recommendations for international students: Required—TOEFL (minimum score 550 paper-based; 80 iBT), IELTS (minimum score 6.5). *Application deadline:* For fall admission, 12/1 priority date for domestic students, 11/15 for international students. Application fee: $56 ($64 for international students). Electronic applications accepted. *Financial support:* In 2017–18, 77 students received support, including 4 fellowships with full tuition reimbursements available (averaging $24,289 per year), 63 research assistantships with full tuition reimbursements available (averaging $24,289 per year), 2 teaching assistantships with full tuition reimbursements available (averaging $17,131 per year); career-related internships or fieldwork, scholarships/grants, traineeships, health care benefits, and unspecified assistantships also available. Financial award application deadline: 11/15. *Faculty research:* Biomagnetism, anatomic and functional imaging, medical image processing, radiation therapy physics, radiation metrology, molecular imaging, novel radionuclide production. *Total annual research expenditures:* $4.5 million. *Unit head:* Dr. Edward F. Jackson, Chair, 608-262-2171, Fax: 608-262-2413, E-mail: efjackson@wisc.edu. *Application contact:* Carol A. Aspinwall, Graduate Coordinator, 608-265-6504, Fax: 608-262-2413, E-mail: caaspinwall@wisc.edu.
Website: http://www.medphysics.wisc.edu/

Virginia Commonwealth University, Graduate School, College of Humanities and Sciences, Department of Physics, Programs in Medical Physics, Richmond, VA 23284-9005. Offers MS, PhD. *Entrance requirements:* For master's and doctorate, GRE General Test. Additional exam requirements/recommendations for international students: Required—TOEFL (minimum score 600 paper-based; 100 iBT); Recommended—IELTS (minimum score 6.5). Electronic applications accepted. *Faculty research:* Functional imaging using PET and NMR, computed tomography (CT) image artifact removal and deformation, intensity-modulated radiation therapy, radiation therapy dose calculations, 4D radiation therapy, brachytherapy dose calculations.

Wayne State University, School of Medicine, Office of Biomedical Graduate Programs, Detroit, MI 48202. Offers anatomy and cell biology (MS, PhD); basic medical sciences (MS); biochemistry and molecular biology (MS, PhD); cancer biology (MS, PhD); clinical and translational science (Graduate Certificate); family medicine and public health sciences (MPH, Graduate Certificate), including public health practice; genetic counseling (MS); immunology and microbiology (MS, PhD); medical physics (MS, PhD, Graduate Certificate); medical research (MS); molecular medicine and genomics (MS, PhD), including molecular genetics and genomics; pathology (PhD); pharmacology (MS, PhD); physiology (MS, PhD), including physiology, reproductive sciences (PhD); psychiatry and behavioral neurosciences (PhD), including translational neuroscience; MD/MPH; MD/PhD; MPH/MA; MSW/MPH. *Program availability:* Part-time, evening/weekend. *Students:* 268 full-time (152 women), 117 part-time (59 women); includes 108 minority (19 Black or African American, non-Hispanic/Latino; 1 American Indian or Alaska Native, non-Hispanic/Latino; 62 Asian, non-Hispanic/Latino; 9 Hispanic/Latino; 17 Two or more races, non-Hispanic/Latino), 48 international. Average age 26. 1,133 applicants, 21% accepted, 151 enrolled. In 2017, 70 master's, 25 doctorates, 10 other advanced degrees awarded. Terminal master's awarded for partial completion of doctoral program. *Degree requirements:* For master's, thesis (for some programs); for doctorate, thesis/dissertation. *Entrance requirements:* For master's, doctorate, and Graduate Certificate, GRE. Additional exam requirements/recommendations for international students: Required—TOEFL (minimum score 550 paper-based; 100 iBT), Michigan English Language Assessment Battery (minimum score 85); Recommended—IELTS (minimum score 6.5), TWE (minimum score 5.5). *Application deadline:* For fall admission, 2/1 for domestic and international students. Applications are processed on a rolling basis. Application fee: $50. Electronic applications accepted. *Expenses:* Contact institution. *Financial support:* In 2017–18, 177 students received support, including 64 fellowships with full tuition reimbursements available (averaging $24,388 per year), 79 research assistantships with full tuition reimbursements available (averaging $26,894 per year); scholarships/grants, traineeships, and health care benefits also available. *Faculty research:* Cancer biology, neurosciences, vision sciences, molecular biology, pathology, physiology, pharmacology, public health, medical physics. *Unit head:* Dr. Daniel A. Walz, Associate Dean for Biomedical Graduate Programs, 313-577-1455, Fax: 313-577-8796, E-mail: gradprogs@med.wayne.edu.
Website: https://www.med.wayne.edu/biomedical-graduate-programs/

Section 22
Health Services

This section contains a directory of institutions offering graduate work in health services. Additional information about programs listed in the directory may be obtained by writing directly to the dean of a graduate school or chair of a department at the address given in the directory.

For programs offering related work, see also in this book *Allied Health, Nursing,* and *Public Health.* In another book in this series:

Graduate Programs in Business, Education, Information Studies, Law & Social Work

See *Business Administration and Management*

CONTENTS

Program Directories

Featured School: Display and Close-Up

Health Services Management and Hospital Administration

Abilene Christian University, College of Graduate and Professional Studies, Program in Business Administration, Addison, TX 75001. Offers business analytics (MBA); corporate finance (MBA); general management (MBA); healthcare administration (MBA); human resource management (MBA); international business (MBA); management: business analytics (MS); management: healthcare administration (MS); management: international business (MS); management: marketing (MS); management: operations and supply chain management (MS); marketing (MBA); nonprofit leadership (MBA); operations and supply chain management (MBA). *Program availability:* Part-time, online only, 100% online. *Faculty:* 2 full-time (0 women), 6 part-time/adjunct (2 women). *Students:* 109 full-time (47 women), 51 part-time (22 women); includes 42 minority (33 Black or African American, non-Hispanic/Latino; 1 American Indian or Alaska Native, non-Hispanic/Latino; 2 Asian, non-Hispanic/Latino; 6 Hispanic/Latino). 125 applicants, 65% accepted, 58 enrolled. *Entrance requirements:* Additional exam requirements/recommendations for international students: Required—TOEFL (minimum score 80 iBT), IELTS (minimum score 6). *Application deadline:* For fall admission, 8/14 priority date for domestic students; for winter admission, 10/1 priority date for domestic students; for spring admission, 12/15 priority date for domestic students; for summer admission, 4/15 priority date for domestic students. Applications are processed on a rolling basis. Application fee: $50. Electronic applications accepted. *Expenses:* $700 per hour. *Financial support:* In 2017–18, 2 students received support. Application deadline: 4/1; applicants required to submit FAFSA. *Faculty research:* Organizational structure, financial management, cost accounting, unit analysis management. *Unit head:* Phil Vardiman, Program Director, 325-674-2153, E-mail: pxv02b@acu.edu. *Application contact:* Graduate Advisor, 817-219-7300, E-mail: gradonline@acu.edu.
Website: http://www.acu.edu/online/academics/mba-business-administration.html

Adelphi University, Robert B. Willumstad School of Business, MBA Program, Garden City, NY 11530-0701. Offers accounting (MBA); finance (MBA); health services administration (MBA); human resource management (MBA); management (MBA); management information systems (MBA); marketing (MBA); sport management (MBA). *Accreditation:* AACSB. *Program availability:* Part-time, evening/weekend. *Students:* 257 full-time (110 women), 78 part-time (38 women); includes 56 minority (18 Black or African American, non-Hispanic/Latino; 16 Asian, non-Hispanic/Latino; 19 Hispanic/Latino; 3 Two or more races, non-Hispanic/Latino), 181 international. Average age 28. 435 applicants, 61% accepted, 205 enrolled. In 2017, 130 master's awarded. *Degree requirements:* For master's, capstone course. *Entrance requirements:* For master's, GMAT, 2 letters of recommendation. Additional exam requirements/recommendations for international students: Required—TOEFL (minimum score 550 paper-based; 80 iBT), IELTS (minimum score 6.5). *Application deadline:* For fall admission, 4/1 for international students; for spring admission, 11/1 for international students. Applications are processed on a rolling basis. Application fee: $50. Electronic applications accepted. *Expenses:* Contact institution. *Financial support:* Research assistantships with partial tuition reimbursements, career-related internships or fieldwork, Federal Work-Study, institutionally sponsored loans, scholarships/grants, tuition waivers (partial), and unspecified assistantships available. Financial award application deadline: 3/1; financial award applicants required to submit FAFSA. *Faculty research:* Supply chain management, distribution channels, productivity benchmark analysis, data envelopment analysis, financial portfolio analysis. *Unit head:* Dr. Rakesh Gupta, Associate Dean, 516-877-4629. *Application contact:* E-mail: graduateadmissions@adelphi.edu.
Website: http://business.adelphi.edu/degree-programs/graduate-degree-programs/m-b-a/

Adventist University of Health Sciences, Program in Healthcare Administration, Orlando, FL 32803. Offers MHA. *Entrance requirements:* For master's, minimum GPA of 3.0.

Alaska Pacific University, Graduate Programs, Business Administration Department, Program in Business Administration, Anchorage, AK 99508-4672. Offers business administration (MBA); health services administration (MBA). *Program availability:* Part-time, evening/weekend. *Degree requirements:* For master's, capstone course. *Entrance requirements:* For master's, GMAT or GRE General Test, minimum GPA of 3.0.

Albany State University, College of Arts and Humanities, Albany, GA 31705-2717. Offers criminal justice (MS); English education (M Ed); public administration (MPA), including community and economic development, criminal justice administration, health administration and policy, human resources management, public management, public policy, water resources management and policy; social work (MSW). *Accreditation:* NASPAA. *Program availability:* Part-time. *Degree requirements:* For master's, comprehensive exam, professional portfolio (for MPA), internship, capstone report. *Entrance requirements:* For master's, GRE, MAT, minimum GPA of 3.0, official transcript, pre-medical record/certificate of immunization, letters of reference. Electronic applications accepted. *Faculty research:* HIV prevention for minority students.

Albany State University, College of Business, Albany, GA 31705-2717. Offers accounting (MBA); general business administration (MBA); healthcare (MBA); public administration (MBA); supply chain and logistics (MBA). *Accreditation:* ACBSP. *Program availability:* Part-time, evening/weekend. *Degree requirements:* For master's, comprehensive exam, internship, 3 hours of physical education. *Entrance requirements:* For master's, GMAT (minimum score of 450)/GRE (minimum score of 800) for those without earned master's degree or higher, minimum undergraduate GPA of 2.5, 2 letters of reference, official transcript, pre-entrance medical record and certificate of immunization. Electronic applications accepted. *Faculty research:* Diversity issues, ancestry, understanding finance through use of technology.

Albertus Magnus College, Master of Business Administration Program, New Haven, CT 06511-1189. Offers accounting (MBA); general management (MBA); health care management (MBA); human resource management (MBA); leadership (MBA); project management (MBA). Program also offered in East Hartford, CT. *Program availability:* Part-time, evening/weekend, 100% online, blended/hybrid learning. *Degree requirements:* For master's, thesis, capstone project, business plan, minimum cumulative GPA of 3.0, completion of all requirements within seven years of matriculation. *Entrance requirements:* For master's, 3 years of management or related experience, minimum GPA of 2.5, 2 letters of recommendation, official transcripts. Additional exam requirements/recommendations for international students: Recommended—TOEFL (minimum score 550 paper-based; 80 iBT). *Application deadline:* Applications are processed on a rolling basis. Application fee: $50. Electronic applications accepted. *Expenses:* Contact institution. *Financial support:* Federal Work-Study and unspecified assistantships available. Support available to part-time students. Financial award applicants required to submit FAFSA. *Faculty research:* Finance, project management, accounting, business administration, generalist. *Unit head:* Dr. Wayne Gineo, Director, 203-672-6670, E-mail: wgineo@albertus.edu. *Application contact:* Anthony Reich, Director of Admission, Division of Professional and Graduate Studies, 203-773-5302, E-mail: arreich@albertus.edu.
Website: http://www.albertus.edu/business-administration/ms/

American InterContinental University Online, Program in Business Administration, Schaumburg, IL 60173. Offers accounting and finance (MBA); finance (MBA); healthcare management (MBA); human resource management (MBA); international business (MBA); management (MBA); marketing (MBA); operations management (MBA); organizational psychology and development (MBA); project management (MBA). *Accreditation:* ACBSP. *Program availability:* Evening/weekend, online learning. *Entrance requirements:* Additional exam requirements/recommendations for international students: Required—TOEFL (minimum score 550 paper-based). Electronic applications accepted.

American Sentinel University, Graduate Programs, Aurora, CO 80014. Offers business administration (MBA); business intelligence (MS); computer science (MSCS); health information management (MS); healthcare (MBA); information systems (MSIS); nursing (MSN). *Program availability:* Part-time, evening/weekend, online learning. *Entrance requirements:* Additional exam requirements/recommendations for international students: Required—TOEFL (minimum score 600 paper-based). Electronic applications accepted.

American University, School of Professional and Extended Studies, Washington, DC 20016-8030. Offers agile project management (MS); healthcare management (MS, Graduate Certificate); human resource analytics and management (MS, Graduate Certificate); instructional design and learning analytics (MS); measurement and evaluation (MS); project monitoring and evaluation (Graduate Certificate); sports analytics and management (MS, Graduate Certificate). *Program availability:* Part-time, evening/weekend, 100% online. *Faculty:* 27 full-time (13 women), 21 part-time/adjunct (10 women). *Students:* 17 full-time (8 women), 59 part-time (34 women); includes 9 minority (5 Black or African American, non-Hispanic/Latino; 2 Asian, non-Hispanic/Latino; 1 Hispanic/Latino; 1 Two or more races, non-Hispanic/Latino), 5 international. Average age 31. 55 applicants, 89% accepted, 38 enrolled. In 2017, 8 other advanced degrees awarded. *Entrance requirements:* For master's, official transcript(s), resume. Additional exam requirements/recommendations for international students: Required—TOEFL (minimum score 600 paper-based; 100 iBT). *Application deadline:* Applications are processed on a rolling basis. Application fee: $55. Electronic applications accepted. *Expenses:* Contact institution. *Financial support:* Applicants required to submit FAFSA. *Unit head:* Carola Weil, Dean, 202-885-5990, Fax: 202-895-4960, E-mail: weil@american.edu. *Application contact:* Emily Aronoff, Assistant Director for Recruitment and Admission, 202-895-4953, E-mail: aronoff@american.edu.
Website: http://www.american.edu/spexs/

American University of Beirut, Graduate Programs, Faculty of Health Sciences, 1107 2020, Lebanon. Offers environmental sciences (MS), including environmental health; epidemiology (MS, PhD); epidemiology and biostatistics (MPH); health care leadership (EMHCL); health management and policy (MPH), including health service administration; health promotion and community health (MPH); health research (MS); public health nutrition (MS). *Program availability:* Part-time. *Faculty:* 33 full-time (22 women), 5 part-time/adjunct (2 women). *Students:* 75 full-time (60 women), 78 part-time (67 women). Average age 27. 274 applicants, 56% accepted, 47 enrolled. In 2017, 63 master's awarded. *Degree requirements:* For master's, one foreign language, comprehensive exam (for some programs), thesis (for MS); for doctorate, one foreign language, comprehensive exam, thesis/dissertation. *Entrance requirements:* For master's, 2 letters of recommendations, personal statement, transcript; for doctorate, GRE, 3 letters of recommendations, personal statement, interview. Additional exam requirements/recommendations for international students: Required—TOEFL (minimum score 583 paper-based; 97 iBT), IELTS (minimum score 7). *Application deadline:* For fall admission, 4/4 for domestic and international students; for spring admission, 11/3 for domestic and international students. Application fee: $50. Electronic applications accepted. *Expenses:* Contact institution. *Financial support:* In 2017–18, 75 students received support. Scholarships/grants, health care benefits, and unspecified assistantships available. Financial award application deadline: 4/4. *Faculty research:* Reproductive and sexual health; occupational and environmental health; conflict and health; mental health; quality in health care delivery, tobacco control. *Total annual research expenditures:* $2 million. *Unit head:* Prof. Iman Adel Nuwayhid, Dean/Professor, 961-1-759683 Ext. 4600, Fax: 961-1-744470, E-mail: nuwayhid@aub.edu.lb. *Application contact:* Mitra Tauk, Administrative Coordinator, 961-1-350000 Ext. 4687, E-mail: mt12@aub.edu.lb.
Website: http://www.aub.edu.lb/fhs/fhs_home/Pages/index.aspx

Anderson University, College of Business, Anderson, SC 29621-4035. Offers business administration (MBA); healthcare leadership (MBA); human resources (MBA); marketing (MBA); organizational leadership (MOL); supply chain management (MBA). *Accreditation:* ACBSP. *Expenses:* Contact institution. *Financial support:* Tuition waivers available. Financial award application deadline: 3/1; financial award applicants required to submit FAFSA. *Unit head:* Steve Nail, Dean, 864-MBA-6000. *Application contact:* Mallory Knight, Graduate Admission Counselor, 864-231-2182, Fax: 864-231-2115, E-mail: malloryknight@andersonuniversity.edu.
Website: http://www.andersonuniversity.edu/business

Antioch University Midwest, MBA Program in Healthcare Leadership, Yellow Springs, OH 45387-1609. Offers MBA. *Program availability:* Part-time, evening/weekend, online learning. *Degree requirements:* For master's, capstone (thesis or practicum). *Entrance requirements:* For master's, resume, interview, essay. *Application deadline:* For fall admission, 9/1 for domestic students; for winter admission, 12/1 for domestic students; for spring admission, 3/10 for domestic students. Applications are processed on a rolling basis. Application fee: $50. Electronic applications accepted. *Expenses:* Contact institution. *Financial support:* Federal Work-Study available. Financial award applicants required to submit FAFSA. *Unit head:* Randolph Oliver, Chair, Graduate Management Programs, 937-769-1841, Fax: 937-769-1807, E-mail: roliver@antioch.edu. *Application contact:* Sarah Klemm, Enrollment Advisor, 937-769-1814, Fax: 937-769-1804, E-mail: sklemm@antioch.edu.
Website: https://www.antioch.edu/midwest/degrees-programs/business-management-leadership/mba-concentration-healthcare-leadership/

Aquinas Institute of Theology, Graduate and Professional Programs, St. Louis, MO 63108. Offers biblical studies (Certificate); church music (MM); health care mission (MAHCM); ministry (M Div); pastoral care (Certificate); pastoral ministry (MAPM); pastoral studies (MAPS); preaching (D Min); spiritual direction (Certificate); theology (M Div, MA); Thomistic studies (Certificate); M Div/MA; MA/PhD; MAPS/MSW. *Accreditation:* ATS (one or more programs are accredited). *Program availability:* Part-time, evening/weekend, online learning. *Degree requirements:* For master's, variable foreign language requirement, comprehensive exam (for some programs), thesis (for some programs); for doctorate, thesis/dissertation. *Entrance requirements:* For master's and Certificate, MAT; for doctorate, 3 years of ministerial experience, 6 hours of graduate course work in homiletics, M Div or the equivalent, minimum GPA of 3.0. Additional exam requirements/recommendations for international students: Required—TOEFL. *Expenses:* Contact institution. *Faculty research:* Theology of preaching, hermeneutics, lay ecclesial ministry, pastoral and practical theology.

Argosy University, Atlanta, College of Business, Atlanta, GA 30328. Offers accounting (DBA); corporate compliance (MBA); customized professional concentration (MBA, DBA); finance (MBA); healthcare administration (MBA); information systems (DBA); information systems management (MBA); international business (MBA, DBA); management (MBA, MSM, DBA); marketing (MBA, DBA). *Accreditation:* ACBSP.

Argosy University, Chicago, College of Business, Chicago, IL 60601. Offers accounting (DBA); customized professional concentration (MBA, DBA); finance (MBA); fraud examination (MBA); global business sustainability (DBA); healthcare administration (MBA); information systems (DBA); information systems management (MBA); international business (MBA, DBA); management (MBA, MSM, DBA); marketing (MBA, DBA); organizational leadership (Ed D); public administration (MBA); sustainable management (MBA). *Accreditation:* ACBSP. *Program availability:* Online learning.

Argosy University, Hawai`i, College of Business, Honolulu, HI 96813. Offers accounting (DBA); corporate compliance (MBA); customized professional concentration (MBA, DBA); finance (MBA, Certificate); fraud examination (MBA); global business sustainability (DBA); healthcare administration (MBA, Certificate); information systems (DBA); information systems management (MBA, Certificate); international business (MBA, DBA, Certificate); management (MBA, MSM, DBA); marketing (MBA, DBA, Certificate); organizational leadership (Ed D); public administration (MBA); sustainable management (MBA).

Argosy University, Los Angeles, College of Business, Los Angeles, CA 90045. Offers accounting (DBA); corporate compliance (MBA); customized professional concentration (MBA, DBA); finance (MBA); fraud examination (MBA); global business sustainability (DBA); healthcare administration (MBA); information systems (DBA); information systems management (MBA); international business (MBA, DBA); management (MBA, MSM, DBA); marketing (MBA, DBA); organizational leadership (Ed D); public administration (MBA); sustainable management (MBA).

Argosy University, Northern Virginia, College of Business, Arlington, VA 22209. Offers accounting (DBA); customized professional concentration (MBA, DBA); finance (MBA); fraud examination (MBA); global business sustainability (DBA); healthcare administration (MBA); information systems (DBA); information systems management (MBA); international business (MBA, DBA, Certificate); management (MBA, MSM, DBA); marketing (MBA, DBA, Certificate); organizational leadership (Ed D); public administration (MBA); sustainable management (MBA).

Argosy University, Orange County, College of Business, Orange, CA 92868. Offers accounting (DBA, Adv C); corporate compliance (MBA); customized professional concentration (MBA, DBA); finance (MBA, Certificate); fraud examination (MBA); global business sustainability (DBA); healthcare administration (MBA, Certificate); information systems (DBA, Adv C, Certificate); information systems management (MBA); international business (MBA, DBA, Adv C, Certificate); management (MBA, MSM, DBA, Adv C); marketing (MBA, DBA, Adv C, Certificate); organizational leadership (Ed D); public administration (MBA, Certificate); sustainable management (MBA).

Argosy University, Phoenix, College of Business, Phoenix, AZ 85021. Offers accounting (DBA); corporate compliance (MBA); customized professional concentration (MBA, DBA); finance (MBA); fraud examination (MBA); global business sustainability (DBA); healthcare administration (MBA); information systems (DBA); information systems management (MBA); international business (MBA, DBA); management (MBA, DBA); marketing (MBA, DBA); public administration (MBA); sustainable management (MBA).

Argosy University, Seattle, College of Business, Seattle, WA 98121. Offers accounting (DBA); corporate compliance (MBA); customized professional concentration (MBA, DBA); finance (MBA); fraud examination (MBA); global business sustainability (DBA); healthcare administration (MBA); information systems (DBA); information systems management (MBA); international business (MBA, DBA); management (MBA, MSM, DBA); marketing (MBA, DBA); organizational leadership (Ed D); public administration (MBA); sustainable management (MBA).

Argosy University, Tampa, College of Business, Tampa, FL 33607. Offers accounting (DBA); corporate compliance (MBA); customized professional concentration (MBA, DBA); finance (MBA); fraud examination (MBA); global business sustainability (DBA); healthcare administration (MBA); information systems (DBA); information systems management (MBA); international business (MBA, DBA); management (MBA, MSM, DBA); marketing (MBA, DBA); organizational leadership (Ed D); public administration (MBA); sustainable management (MBA).

Argosy University, Twin Cities, College of Business, Eagan, MN 55121. Offers accounting (DBA); customized professional concentration (MBA, DBA); finance (MBA); fraud examination (MBA); global business sustainability (DBA); healthcare administration (MBA); information systems (DBA); information systems management (MBA); international business (MBA, DBA); management (MBA, MSM, DBA); marketing (MBA, DBA); organizational leadership (Ed D); public administration (MBA); sustainable management (MBA).

Argosy University, Twin Cities, College of Health Sciences, Eagan, MN 55121. Offers health services management (MS); public health (MPH).

Arizona State University at the Tempe campus, W. P. Carey School of Business, Program in Business Administration, Tempe, AZ 85287-4906. Offers entrepreneurship (MBA); finance (MBA); health sector management (MBA); international business (MBA); leadership (MBA); marketing (MBA); organizational behavior (PhD); strategic management (PhD); supply chain management (MBA, PhD); JD/MBA; MBA/M Acc; MBA/M Arch. *Accreditation:* AACSB. *Program availability:* Part-time, evening/weekend, online learning. Terminal master's awarded for partial completion of doctoral program. *Degree requirements:* For master's, thesis or alternative, internship, interactive Program of Study (iPOS) submitted before completing 50 percent of required credit hours; for doctorate, comprehensive exam, thesis/dissertation, interactive Program of Study (iPOS) submitted before completing 50 percent of required credit hours. *Entrance requirements:* For master's, GMAT, minimum GPA of 3.0 in last 2 years of work leading to bachelor's degree, 2 letters of recommendation, professional resume, official transcripts, 3 essays; for doctorate, GMAT or GRE, minimum GPA of 3.0 in last 2 years of work leading to bachelor's degree, 3 letters of recommendation, resume, personal statement/essay. Additional exam requirements/recommendations for international students: Required—TOEFL (minimum score 550 paper-based; 80 iBT), IELTS (minimum score 6.5). Electronic applications accepted. *Expenses:* Contact institution.

Arkansas State University, Graduate School, College of Nursing and Health Professions, School of Nursing, State University, AR 72467. Offers aging studies (Graduate Certificate); health care management (Graduate Certificate); health sciences (MS); health sciences education (Graduate Certificate); nurse anesthesia (MSN); nursing (MSN); nursing practice (DNP). *Accreditation:* AANA/CANAEP (one or more programs are accredited); ACEN. *Program availability:* Part-time. *Degree requirements:* For master's and Graduate Certificate, comprehensive exam, thesis or alternative; for doctorate, comprehensive exam, thesis/dissertation. *Entrance requirements:* For master's, GRE General Test or MAT, appropriate bachelor's degree, current Arkansas nursing license, CPR certification, physical examination, professional liability insurance, critical care experience, ACLS Certification, PALS Certification, interview, immunization records, personal goal statement, health assessment; for doctorate, GRE or MAT, NCLEX-RN Exam, appropriate master's degree, current Arkansas nursing license, CPR certification, physical examination, professional liability insurance, critical care experience, ACLS Certification, PALS Certification, interview, immunization records, personal goal statement, health assessment, TB skin test, background check; for Graduate Certificate, GRE or MAT, appropriate bachelor's degree, official transcripts, immunization records, proof of employment in healthcare, TB Skin Test, TB Mask Fit Test, CPR Certification. Additional exam requirements/recommendations for international students: Required—TOEFL (minimum score 550 paper-based; 79 iBT), IELTS (minimum score 6), PTE (minimum score 56). Electronic applications accepted. *Expenses:* Contact institution.

Ashland University, Dauch College of Business and Economics, Ashland, OH 44805-3702. Offers accounting (MBA); business analytics (MBA); entrepreneurship (MBA); financial management (MBA); global management (MBA); health care management and leadership (MBA); human resource management (MBA); human resources (MBA); management information systems (MBA); project management (MBA); sport management (MBA); supply chain management (MBA). *Accreditation:* ACBSP. *Program availability:* Part-time, evening/weekend, 100% online, blended/hybrid learning. *Faculty:* 20 full-time (8 women), 13 part-time/adjunct (2 women). *Students:* 458 full-time (210 women), 144 part-time (52 women); includes 88 minority (63 Black or African American, non-Hispanic/Latino; 1 American Indian or Alaska Native, non-Hispanic/Latino; 10 Asian, non-Hispanic/Latino; 11 Hispanic/Latino), 302 international. Average age 31. 216 applicants, 74% accepted, 115 enrolled. In 2017, 184 master's awarded. Terminal master's awarded for partial completion of doctoral program. *Degree requirements:* For master's, thesis optional, capstone course. *Entrance requirements:* For master's, 2 years of full-time work experience. Additional exam requirements/recommendations for international students: Required—TOEFL (minimum score 550 paper-based; 78 iBT). *Application deadline:* For fall admission, 8/1 priority date for domestic students; for spring admission, 12/1 priority date for domestic students. Applications are processed on a rolling basis. Application fee: $30. Electronic applications accepted. *Expenses:* $815 per credit hour, $15 technology fee for online sections. *Financial support:* Scholarships/grants, tuition waivers (partial), and unspecified assistantships available. Financial award application deadline: 4/15; financial award applicants required to submit FAFSA. *Faculty research:* Relationship marketing strategy, executive compensation and company performance, online marketplaces in electronic commerce, diversity training in campus recreation departments, entrepreneurship in developing and emerging economies. *Unit head:* Dr. Elad Granot, Dean, 419-289-5932, E-mail: egranot@ashland.edu. *Application contact:* Stephen W. Krispinsky, Executive Director of MBA Program, 419-289-5236, Fax: 419-289-5910, E-mail: skrispin@ashland.edu.
Website: http://www.mba.ashland.edu

Ashworth College, Graduate Programs, Norcross, GA 30092. Offers business administration (MBA); criminal justice (MS); health care administration (MBA, MS); human resource management (MBA, MS); international business (MBA); management (MS); marketing (MBA, MS).

Assumption College, Health Advocacy Program, Worcester, MA 01609-1296. Offers MA, Professional Certificate. *Program availability:* Part-time, evening/weekend, online only, 100% online. *Faculty:* 1 (woman) full-time, 5 part-time/adjunct (3 women). *Students:* 15 part-time (all women). Average age 50. 8 applicants, 88% accepted, 7 enrolled. In 2017, 2 other advanced degrees awarded. *Degree requirements:* For master's, research course, practicum, capstone. *Entrance requirements:* For master's and Professional Certificate, bachelor's degree, three letters of recommendation, official transcripts, personal statement, current resume. Additional exam requirements/recommendations for international students: Required—TOEFL (minimum score 540 paper-based; 76 iBT), IELTS (minimum score 6). *Application deadline:* For fall admission, 7/1 for domestic and international students; for spring admission, 12/1 for domestic and international students. Application fee: $30. Electronic applications accepted. *Expenses: Tuition:* Full-time $11,952; part-time $664 per credit. *Required fees:* $70 per term. *Financial support:* In 2017–18, 1 student received support. Tuition waivers (full and partial) and institutional discounts available. Financial award applicants required to submit FAFSA. *Unit head:* Lea Christo, Director, 508-767-7503, Fax: 508-798-2872, E-mail: l.christo@assumption.edu. *Application contact:* Karen Stoyanoff, Director of Recruitment for Graduate Enrollment, 508-767-7442, Fax: 508-799-4412, E-mail: graduate@assumption.edu.
Website: http://graduate.assumption.edu/health-advocacy/graduate-programs-health-advocacy

Assumption College, Healthcare Management Program, Worcester, MA 01609-1296. Offers MBA, CAGS, CGS. *Program availability:* Part-time, evening/weekend, online only, 100% online, blended/hybrid learning. *Degree requirements:* For master's, capstone. *Entrance requirements:* For master's, bachelor's degree, three letters of recommendation, official transcripts, personal statement, current resume; for other advanced degree, three letters of recommendation, official transcripts, personal statement, current resume; bachelor's degree in closely-related field (for CGS); MBA or equivalent degree in closely-related field (for CAGS). Additional exam requirements/recommendations for international students: Required—TOEFL (minimum score 540 paper-based; 76 iBT), IELTS (minimum score 6). *Application deadline:* For fall admission, 8/10 priority date for domestic and international students; for spring admission, 1/4 priority date for domestic and international students; for summer admission, 5/10 priority date for domestic and international students. Application fee: $30. Electronic applications accepted. *Expenses: Tuition:* Full-time $11,952; part-time $664 per credit. *Required fees:* $70 per term. *Financial support:* Tuition waivers (full and partial), unspecified assistantships, and institutional discounts available. Financial award applicants required to submit FAFSA. *Unit head:* Dr. Robin Frkal, Co-Director, 508-767-7622, E-mail: ra.frkal@assumption.edu. *Application contact:* Karen Stoyanoff, Director of Recruitment for Graduate Enrollment, 508-767-7442, Fax: 508-799-4412, E-mail: graduate@assumption.edu.
Website: http://graduate.assumption.edu/mba/mba-healthcare-management

Health Services Management and Hospital Administration

Atlantis University, School of Health Care, Miami, FL 33132. Offers healthcare management (MS).

A.T. Still University, College of Graduate Health Studies, Kirksville, MO 63501. Offers dental public health (MPH); exercise and sport psychology (Certificate); fundamentals of education (Certificate); geriatric exercise science (Certificate); global health (Certificate); health administration (MHA, DHA); health professions (Ed D); health sciences (DH Sc); kinesiology (MS); leadership and organizational behavior (Certificate); public health (MPH); sports conditioning (Certificate). *Program availability:* Part-time, evening/weekend, online only, 100% online, blended/hybrid learning. *Faculty:* 28 full-time (18 women), 83 part-time/adjunct (43 women). *Students:* 537 full-time (334 women), 516 part-time (316 women); includes 397 minority (171 Black or African American, non-Hispanic/Latino; 14 American Indian or Alaska Native, non-Hispanic/Latino; 84 Asian, non-Hispanic/Latino; 106 Hispanic/Latino; 1 Native Hawaiian or other Pacific Islander, non-Hispanic/Latino; 21 Two or more races, non-Hispanic/Latino), 43 international. Average age 36. 392 applicants, 84% accepted, 270 enrolled. In 2017, 138 master's, 102 doctorates, 116 other advanced degrees awarded. *Degree requirements:* For master's, thesis, integrated terminal project, practicum; for doctorate, thesis/dissertation. *Entrance requirements:* For master's, minimum GPA of 2.5, bachelor's degree or equivalent, essay, resume, English proficiency; for doctorate, minimum GPA of 2.5, master's or terminal degree, essay, past experience in relevant field, resume, English proficiency. Additional exam requirements/recommendations for international students: Required—TOEFL (minimum score 550 paper-based; 80 iBT). *Application deadline:* For fall admission, 6/26 for domestic students, 5/20 for international students; for winter admission, 9/11 for domestic students, 9/12 for international students; for spring admission, 12/11 for domestic students, 12/12 for international students; for summer admission, 3/5 for domestic students, 3/6 for international students. Applications are processed on a rolling basis. Application fee: $70. Electronic applications accepted. *Financial support:* In 2017–18, 18 students received support. Scholarships/grants available. Financial award applicants required to submit FAFSA. *Faculty research:* Public health: influence of availability of comprehensive wellness resources online, student wellness, oral health care needs assessment of community, oral health knowledge and behaviors of Medicaid-eligible pregnant women and mothers of young children in relations to early childhood caries and tooth decay, alcohol use and alcohol related problems among college students. *Unit head:* Dr. Donald Altman, Dean, 480-219-6008, Fax: 660-626-2826, E-mail: daltman@atsu.edu. *Application contact:* Amie Waldemer, Associate Director, Online Admissions, 480-219-6146, E-mail: awaldemer@atsu.edu.
Website: http://www.atsu.edu/college-of-graduate-health-studies

Avila University, School of Business, Kansas City, MO 64145-1698. Offers accounting (MBA); finance (MBA); health care administration (MBA); international business (MBA); management (MBA); management information systems (MBA); marketing (MBA). *Program availability:* Part-time, evening/weekend. *Faculty:* 6 full-time (2 women), 6 part-time/adjunct (2 women). *Students:* 49 full-time (19 women), 29 part-time (14 women); includes 16 minority (12 Black or African American, non-Hispanic/Latino; 1 Asian, non-Hispanic/Latino; 3 Hispanic/Latino), 19 international. Average age 32. 51 applicants, 47% accepted, 20 enrolled. In 2017, 31 master's awarded. *Degree requirements:* For master's, comprehensive exam, capstone course. *Entrance requirements:* For master's, GMAT (minimum score 420), minimum GPA of 3.0, interview. Additional exam requirements/recommendations for international students: Required—TOEFL (minimum score 550 paper-based). *Application deadline:* For fall admission, 7/30 priority date for domestic and international students; for winter admission, 11/30 priority date for domestic and international students; for spring admission, 2/28 priority date for domestic and international students; for summer admission, 6/1 priority date for domestic and international students. Applications are processed on a rolling basis. Application fee: $0. Electronic applications accepted. *Expenses:* Contact institution. *Financial support:* In 2017–18, 18 students received support. Career-related internships or fieldwork and scholarships/grants available. Support available to part-time students. Financial award applicants required to submit FAFSA. *Faculty research:* Leadership characteristics, financial hedging, group dynamics. *Unit head:* Dr. Wendy L. Acker, Interim Dean, 816-501-3720, Fax: 816-501-2463, E-mail: wendy.acker@avila.edu. *Application contact:* Brandon Black, MBA Admission Advisor, 816-501-3601, Fax: 816-501-2463, E-mail: brandon.black@avila.edu.
Website: https://www.avila.edu/mrk/mba

Baker College Center for Graduate Studies–Online, Graduate Programs, Flint, MI 48507. Offers accounting (MBA); business administration (DBA); finance (MBA); general business (MBA); health care management (MBA); human resources management (MBA); information management (MBA); leadership studies (MBA); management information systems (MSIS); marketing (MBA). *Program availability:* Part-time, evening/weekend, online learning. *Degree requirements:* For master's, portfolio. *Entrance requirements:* For master's, 3 years of work experience, minimum undergraduate GPA of 2.5, writing sample, 3 letters of recommendation; for doctorate, MBA or acceptable related master's degree from accredited association, 5 years work experience, minimum graduate GPA of 3.25, writing sample, 3 professional references. Additional exam requirements/recommendations for international students: Required—TOEFL (minimum score 550 paper-based). Electronic applications accepted.

Baldwin Wallace University, Graduate Programs, School of Business, Program in Health Care, Berea, OH 44017-2088. Offers MBA. *Program availability:* Part-time, evening/weekend. *Students:* 39 full-time (19 women), 5 part-time (3 women); includes 11 minority (4 Black or African American, non-Hispanic/Latino; 2 Asian, non-Hispanic/Latino; 5 Hispanic/Latino). Average age 38. 29 applicants, 55% accepted, 10 enrolled. In 2017, 14 master's awarded. *Degree requirements:* For master's, minimum overall GPA of 3.0. *Entrance requirements:* For master's, GMAT or minimum GPA or 3.0, interview, work experience, bachelor's degree in any field. Additional exam requirements/recommendations for international students: Required—TOEFL (minimum score 550 paper-based; 79 iBT). *Application deadline:* For fall admission, 7/25 priority date for domestic students, 4/30 priority date for international students; for spring admission, 12/10 priority date for domestic students, 9/30 priority date for international students. Applications are processed on a rolling basis. Application fee: $25. Electronic applications accepted. Application fee is waived when completed online. *Expenses:* $948 per credit hour. *Financial support:* Applicants required to submit FAFSA. *Unit head:* Tom Campanella, Director, 440-826-3818, Fax: 440-826-3868, E-mail: tcampane@bw.edu. *Application contact:* Laura Spencer, Graduate Application Specialist, 440-826-2191, Fax: 440-826-3868, E-mail: lspencer@bw.edu.
Website: http://www.bw.edu/graduate/business/health-care-mba/

Barry University, Andreas School of Business, Graduate Certificate Programs, Miami Shores, FL 33161-6695. Offers finance (Certificate); health services administration (Certificate); international business (Certificate); management (Certificate); management information systems (Certificate); marketing (Certificate).

Barry University, College of Health Sciences, Graduate Certificate Programs, Miami Shores, FL 33161-6695. Offers health care leadership (Certificate); health care planning and informatics (Certificate); histotechnology (Certificate); long term care management (Certificate); medical group practice management (Certificate); quality improvement and outcomes management (Certificate).

Barry University, College of Health Sciences, Program in Health Services Administration, Miami Shores, FL 33161-6695. Offers MS. *Program availability:* Part-time, evening/weekend. *Degree requirements:* For master's, comprehensive exam. *Entrance requirements:* For master's, GMAT or GRE General Test, 2 years of experience in the health field, minimum GPA of 3.0, 1 semester of course work in computer applications or the equivalent (business). Electronic applications accepted.

Baruch College of the City University of New York, Austin W. Marxe School of Public and International Affairs, Program in Public Administration, New York, NY 10010-5585. Offers general public administration (MPA); health care policy (MPA); nonprofit administration (MPA); policy analysis and evaluation (MPA); public management (MPA); urban development and sustainability (MPA); MS/MPA. *Accreditation:* NASPAA. *Program availability:* Part-time, evening/weekend. *Degree requirements:* For master's, thesis, capstone. *Entrance requirements:* For master's, GRE General Test. Additional exam requirements/recommendations for international students: Required—TOEFL. Electronic applications accepted. *Expenses:* Contact institution. *Faculty research:* Urbanization, population and poverty in the developing world, housing and community development, labor unions and housing, government-nongovernment relations, immigration policy, social network analysis, cross-sectoral governance, comparative healthcare systems, program evaluation, social welfare policy, health outcomes, educational policy and leadership, transnationalism, infant health, welfare reform, racial/ethnic disparities in health, urban politics, homelessness, race and ethnic relations.

Baruch College of the City University of New York, Zicklin School of Business, Zicklin Executive Programs, Baruch/Mt. Sinai Program in Health Care Administration, New York, NY 10010-5585. Offers MBA. *Accreditation:* CAHME. *Program availability:* Part-time, evening/weekend. *Entrance requirements:* For master's, GMAT, personal interview, work experience in health care. Additional exam requirements/recommendations for international students: Required—TOEFL. Electronic applications accepted. *Expenses:* Contact institution. *Faculty research:* Economics of reproductive health, multivariate point estimation.

Baylor University, Graduate School, Military Programs, Program in Health Care Administration, Waco, TX 76798. Offers MHA, MHA/MBA. Program offered jointly with the U.S. Army. *Accreditation:* CAHME. *Faculty:* 19 full-time (5 women), 18 part-time/adjunct (2 women). *Students:* 85 full-time (28 women); includes 14 minority (4 Black or African American, non-Hispanic/Latino; 4 Asian, non-Hispanic/Latino; 1 Hispanic/Latino; 5 Two or more races, non-Hispanic/Latino). In 2017, 55 master's awarded. *Degree requirements:* For master's, comprehensive exam. *Entrance requirements:* For master's, GRE General Test. Additional exam requirements/recommendations for international students: Required—TOEFL, IELTS. *Application deadline:* For fall admission, 6/15 for domestic students. Applications are processed on a rolling basis. *Faculty research:* Data quality, public health policy, organizational behavior, AIDS. *Unit head:* Alan Jones, Graduate Program Director, 210-295-8715, E-mail: alan.a.jones.mil@mail.mil. *Application contact:* Rene Pryor, Program Administrator, 210-221-6443, Fax: 210-221-6010, E-mail: rene.l.pryor.civ@mail.mil.
Website: http://www.cs.amedd.army.mil/baylorhca/

Belhaven University, School of Business, Jackson, MS 39202-1789. Offers business administration (MBA); health administration (MBA, MHA); human resources (MBA, MSL); leadership (MBA); public administration (MPA); sports administration (MBA, MSA). *Program availability:* Part-time, evening/weekend, 100% online. *Faculty:* 11 full-time (4 women), 93 part-time/adjunct (39 women). *Students:* 20 full-time (12 women), 1,441 part-time (1,061 women); includes 1,168 minority (1,100 Black or African American, non-Hispanic/Latino; 22 American Indian or Alaska Native, non-Hispanic/Latino; 2 Asian, non-Hispanic/Latino; 23 Hispanic/Latino; 1 Native Hawaiian or other Pacific Islander, non-Hispanic/Latino; 20 Two or more races, non-Hispanic/Latino), 21 international. Average age 35. 501 applicants, 74% accepted, 261 enrolled. In 2017, 326 master's awarded. *Degree requirements:* For master's, comprehensive exam (for some programs), thesis or alternative. *Entrance requirements:* For master's, minimum GPA of 2.8 (for MBA and MHA), 2.5 (for MSL, MPA and MSA). *Application deadline:* Applications are processed on a rolling basis. Application fee: $25. Electronic applications accepted. *Expenses:* Contact institution. *Financial support:* Applicants required to submit FAFSA. *Unit head:* Dr. Ralph Mason, Dean, 601-968-8949, Fax: 601-968-8951, E-mail: cmason@belhaven.edu. *Application contact:* Dr. Audrey Kelleher, Vice President of Adult and Graduate Marketing and Development, 407-804-1424, Fax: 407-620-5210, E-mail: akelleher@belhaven.edu.
Website: http://www.belhaven.edu/campuses/index.htm

Bellevue University, Graduate School, College of Arts and Sciences, Bellevue, NE 68005-3098. Offers clinical counseling (MS); healthcare administration (MHA); human services (MA); international security and intelligence studies (MS); managerial communication (MA). *Program availability:* Online learning.

Belmont University, Jack C. Massey Graduate School of Business, Nashville, TN 37212. Offers accounting (M Acc); business (AMBA, PMBA); healthcare (MBA). *Accreditation:* AACSB. *Program availability:* Part-time, evening/weekend. *Faculty:* 29 full-time (9 women), 7 part-time/adjunct (3 women). *Students:* 163 full-time (72 women), 42 part-time (19 women); includes 36 minority (13 Black or African American, non-Hispanic/Latino; 9 Asian, non-Hispanic/Latino; 5 Hispanic/Latino; 9 Two or more races, non-Hispanic/Latino), 10 international. Average age 30. 135 applicants, 96% accepted, 102 enrolled. In 2017, 110 master's awarded. *Entrance requirements:* For master's, GMAT, 2 years of work experience (MBA). Additional exam requirements/recommendations for international students: Required—TOEFL (minimum score 550 paper-based). *Application deadline:* For fall admission, 7/1 for domestic and international students; for spring admission, 11/1 for domestic and international students. Applications are processed on a rolling basis. Application fee: $50. Electronic applications accepted. *Expenses:* Contact institution. *Financial support:* In 2017–18, 86 students received support. Scholarships/grants, tuition waivers (partial), and unspecified assistantships available. Financial award application deadline: 7/1; financial award applicants required to submit FAFSA. *Faculty research:* Music business, strategy, ethics, finance, accounting systems. *Unit head:* Dr. Patrick Raines, Dean, 615-460-6480, Fax: 615-460-6455, E-mail: pat.raines@belmont.edu. *Application contact:* 615-460-6480, E-mail: masseyadmissions@belmont.edu.

Benedictine University, Graduate Programs, Program in Business Administration, Lisle, IL 60532. Offers accounting (MBA); entrepreneurship and managing innovation (MBA); financial management (MBA); health administration (MBA); human resource management (MBA); information systems security (MBA); international business (MBA); management consulting (MBA); management information systems (MBA); marketing management (MBA); operations management and logistics (MBA); organizational leadership (MBA). *Program availability:* Part-time, evening/weekend, online learning. *Entrance requirements:* For master's, GMAT. Additional exam requirements/recommendations for international students: Required—TOEFL (minimum score 550 paper-based). Electronic applications accepted. *Faculty research:* Strategic leadership in professional organizations, sociology of professions, organizational change, social identity theory, applications to change management.

Benedictine University, Graduate Programs, Program in Public Health, Lisle, IL 60532. Offers administration of health care institutions (MPH); dietetics (MPH); disaster management (MPH); health education (MPH); health information systems (MPH); MBA/MPH; MPH/MS. *Accreditation:* CEPH. *Program availability:* Part-time, evening/weekend, online learning. *Entrance requirements:* For master's, MAT, GRE, or GMAT. Additional exam requirements/recommendations for international students: Required—TOEFL (minimum score 550 paper-based).

Binghamton University, State University of New York, Graduate School, School of Management, Program in Business Administration, Binghamton, NY 13902-6000. Offers business administration (MBA); corporate executive (MBA); executive business administration (MBA); health care professional executive (MBA); professional business administration (MBA). Executive and Professional MBA programs offered in Manhattan. *Accreditation:* AACSB. *Program availability:* Part-time. *Students:* 120 full-time (37 women), 6 part-time (5 women); includes 23 minority (2 Black or African American, non-Hispanic/Latino; 11 Asian, non-Hispanic/Latino; 6 Hispanic/Latino; 4 Two or more races, non-Hispanic/Latino), 25 international. Average age 24. 209 applicants, 72% accepted, 99 enrolled. In 2017, 101 master's awarded. *Entrance requirements:* For master's, GMAT. Additional exam requirements/recommendations for international students: Required—TOEFL (minimum score 96 iBT). *Application deadline:* Applications are processed on a rolling basis. Application fee: $75. Electronic applications accepted. *Expenses:* Contact institution. *Financial support:* In 2017–18, 12 students received support, including 10 teaching assistantships with full tuition reimbursements available (averaging $17,000 per year); career-related internships or fieldwork, Federal Work-Study, institutionally sponsored loans, scholarships/grants, health care benefits, tuition waivers (full and partial), and unspecified assistantships also available. Financial award applicants required to submit FAFSA. *Unit head:* Dr. Upinder Dhillon, Dean, 607-777-2314, E-mail: dhillon@binghamton.edu. *Application contact:* Ben Balkaya, Assistant Dean and Director, 607-777-2151, Fax: 607-777-2501, E-mail: balkaya@binghamton.edu.

Binghamton University, State University of New York, Graduate School, Thomas J. Watson School of Engineering and Applied Science, Department of Systems Science and Industrial Engineering, Binghamton, NY 13902-6000. Offers executive health systems (MS); industrial and systems engineering (M Eng); systems science and industrial engineering (MS, PhD). MS in executive health systems also offered in Manhattan. *Program availability:* Part-time, evening/weekend, online learning. *Faculty:* 23 full-time (4 women). *Students:* 208 full-time (68 women), 164 part-time (47 women); includes 57 minority (21 Black or African American, non-Hispanic/Latino; 20 Asian, non-Hispanic/Latino; 13 Hispanic/Latino; 3 Two or more races, non-Hispanic/Latino), 252 international. Average age 29. 483 applicants, 87% accepted, 123 enrolled. In 2017, 131 master's, 11 doctorates awarded. *Degree requirements:* For master's, thesis; for doctorate, thesis/dissertation. *Entrance requirements:* For master's and doctorate, GRE General Test. Additional exam requirements/recommendations for international students: Required—TOEFL (minimum score 550 paper-based; 80 iBT). *Application deadline:* For fall admission, 4/1 priority date for domestic and international students; for spring admission, 11/15 priority date for domestic and international students. Applications are processed on a rolling basis. Application fee: $75. Electronic applications accepted. *Expenses:* Contact institution. *Financial support:* In 2017–18, 101 students received support, including 1 fellowship with full tuition reimbursement available (averaging $10,000 per year), 45 research assistantships with full tuition reimbursements available (averaging $16,500 per year), 13 teaching assistantships with full tuition reimbursements available (averaging $16,500 per year); career-related internships or fieldwork, Federal Work-Study, institutionally sponsored loans, scholarships/grants, health care benefits, tuition waivers (full and partial), and unspecified assistantships also available. Financial award application deadline: 2/1; financial award applicants required to submit FAFSA. *Faculty research:* Problem restructuring, protein modeling. *Unit head:* Ellen Tilden, Coordinator of Graduate Studies, 607-777-2873, E-mail: etilden@binghamton.edu. *Application contact:* Ben Balkaya, Assistant Dean and Director, 607-777-2151, Fax: 607-777-2501, E-mail: balkaya@binghamton.edu.
Website: http://www.ssie.binghamton.edu

Bluffton University, Programs in Business, Bluffton, OH 45817. Offers accounting and financial management (MBA); health care management (MBA); leadership (MAOM, MBA); production and operations management (MBA); sustainability management (MBA). *Program availability:* Evening/weekend, blended/hybrid learning, videoconference. *Faculty:* 5 full-time (2 women), 8 part-time/adjunct (2 women). *Students:* 48 full-time (31 women); includes 11 minority (5 Black or African American, non-Hispanic/Latino; 1 Asian, non-Hispanic/Latino; 3 Hispanic/Latino; 2 Two or more races, non-Hispanic/Latino), 1 international. Average age 33. 44 applicants, 70% accepted, 26 enrolled. In 2017, 41 master's awarded. *Degree requirements:* For master's, integrated research project (for some programs). *Entrance requirements:* For master's, current resume, official transcript, bachelor's degree, minimum GPA of 3.0, personal essay. Additional exam requirements/recommendations for international students: Recommended—TOEFL (minimum score 550 paper-based). *Application deadline:* For fall admission, 7/31 priority date for domestic and international students. Applications are processed on a rolling basis. Application fee: $0. Electronic applications accepted. *Expenses:* $550 per credit hour, $150 per semester technology fee, $25 per semester payment plan fee. *Financial support:* Unspecified assistantships and faculty/staff grants available. Financial award applicants required to submit FAFSA. *Unit head:* Dr. Melissa Green, Director of Graduate Programs in Business, 419-358-3447, E-mail: greenm@bluffton.edu. *Application contact:* Carrie Mast, Administrative Assistant, Graduate Programs in Business, 419-358-3065, E-mail: mastc@bluffton.edu.
Website: http://www.bluffton.edu/grad/

Boston University, School of Medicine, Division of Graduate Medical Sciences, Program in Healthcare Emergency Management, Boston, MA 02215. Offers MS. *Financial support:* Applicants required to submit FAFSA. *Unit head:* Dr. Kevin Thomas, Director, 617-414-2316, Fax: 617-414-2332, E-mail: kipthoma@bu.edu. *Application contact:* GMS Admissions Office, 617-638-5255, E-mail: askgms@bu.edu.
Website: http://www.bumc.bu.edu/bmcm/

Boston University, School of Medicine, Division of Graduate Medical Sciences, Program in Medical Sciences, Boston, MA 02215. Offers MS, MS/MPH. *Program availability:* Part-time. *Degree requirements:* For master's, thesis. *Entrance requirements:* For master's, MCAT or GRE. *Application deadline:* Applications are processed on a rolling basis. Application fee: $75. Electronic applications accepted. *Financial support:* Federal Work-Study available. Financial award applicants required to submit FAFSA. *Unit head:* Dr. Gwynneth D. Offner, Director, 617-638-8221, E-mail: goffner@bu.edu. *Application contact:* GMS Admissions Office, 617-638-5255, E-mail: askgms@bu.edu.
Website: http://www.bumc.bu.edu/gms/mams/

Boston University, School of Public Health, Health Law, Policy and Management Department, Boston, MA 02215. Offers health law, policy and management (MPH); health services and systems research (MS); health services research (PhD). *Accreditation:* CAHME. *Program availability:* Part-time, evening/weekend. *Degree requirements:* For master's, comprehensive exam (for some programs), thesis (for some programs); for doctorate, comprehensive exam, thesis/dissertation. *Entrance requirements:* For master's, GRE, MCAT, GMAT; for doctorate, GRE. Additional exam requirements/recommendations for international students: Required—TOEFL (minimum score 600 paper-based; 100 iBT), IELTS (minimum score 7). Electronic applications accepted. *Faculty research:* Health policy, health law and ethics, human rights, healthcare management.

Bradley University, The Graduate School, College of Education and Health Sciences, Department of Nursing, Peoria, IL 61625-0002. Offers family nurse practitioner (MSN, DNP, Certificate); leadership (DNP); nursing administration (MSN); nursing education (MSN, Certificate). *Accreditation:* AACN; ACEN. *Program availability:* Part-time, evening/weekend. *Degree requirements:* For master's, comprehensive exam, thesis optional. *Entrance requirements:* For master's, GRE General Test or MAT, interview, Illinois RN license, advanced cardiac life support certification, pediatric advanced life support certification, 3 letters of recommendation. Additional exam requirements/recommendations for international students: Required—TOEFL (minimum score 550 paper-based; 79 iBT), IELTS (minimum score 6.5). Electronic applications accepted.

Brandeis University, The Heller School for Social Policy and Management, Program in Nonprofit Management, Waltham, MA 02454-9110. Offers child, youth, and family management (MBA); health care management (MBA); social impact management (MBA); social policy and management (MBA); sustainable development (MBA); MBA/MA; MBA/MD. MBA/MD program offered in conjunction with Tufts University School of Medicine. *Accreditation:* AACSB. *Program availability:* Part-time. *Degree requirements:* For master's, team consulting project. *Entrance requirements:* For master's, GMAT (preferred) or GRE, 2 letters of recommendation, problem statement analysis, 3-5 years of professional experience. Additional exam requirements/recommendations for international students: Required—TOEFL (minimum score 600 paper-based; 100 iBT). Electronic applications accepted. *Expenses:* Contact institution. *Faculty research:* Health care; children and families; elder and disabled services; social impact management; organizations in the non-profit, for-profit, or public sector.

Brandman University, School of Business and Professional Studies, Irvine, CA 92618. Offers accounting (MBA); business administration (MBA); business intelligence and data analytics (MBA); e-business strategic management (MBA); entrepreneurship (MBA); finance (MBA); health administration (MBA); human resources (MBA, MS); international business (MBA); marketing (MBA); organizational leadership (MA, MBA, MPA); public administration (MPA). *Expenses: Tuition:* Part-time $640 per credit hour. Tuition and fees vary according to degree level and program. *Unit head:* Dr. Glenn Worthington, Dean, 253-861-1024, E-mail: gworthin@brandman.edu. *Application contact:* Dr. Glenn Worthington, Dean, 253-861-1024, E-mail: gworthin@brandman.edu.
Website: https://www.brandman.edu/academic-programs/business-and-professional-studies

Brenau University, Sydney O. Smith Graduate School, College of Business and Mass Communication, Gainesville, GA 30501. Offers accounting (MBA); business administration (MBA); healthcare management (MBA); organizational leadership (MS); project management (MBA). *Accreditation:* ACBSP. *Program availability:* Part-time, evening/weekend, online learning. *Degree requirements:* For master's, comprehensive exam (for some programs). *Entrance requirements:* For master's, resume, minimum undergraduate GPA of 2.5. Additional exam requirements/recommendations for international students: Required—TOEFL (minimum score 500 paper-based; 61 iBT); Recommended—IELTS (minimum score 5). Electronic applications accepted. *Expenses:* Contact institution.

Brigham Young University, Graduate Studies, BYU Marriott School of Business, Master of Public Administration Program, Provo, UT 84602. Offers healthcare (MPA); local government (MPA); nonprofit management (MPA); state and federal government (MPA); JD/MPA. *Accreditation:* NASPAA. *Faculty:* 134 full-time (15 women), 65 part-time/adjunct (16 women). *Students:* 105 full-time (50 women); includes 10 minority (3 Black or African American, non-Hispanic/Latino; 3 Asian, non-Hispanic/Latino; 3 Hispanic/Latino; 1 Native Hawaiian or other Pacific Islander, non-Hispanic/Latino), 14 international. Average age 27. 95 applicants, 73% accepted, 50 enrolled. In 2017, 41 master's awarded. *Entrance requirements:* For master's, GMAT or GRE, commitment to BYU Honor Code. Additional exam requirements/recommendations for international students: Required—TOEFL (minimum score 580 paper-based; 85 iBT). *Application deadline:* For fall admission, 1/15 for domestic and international students. Application fee: $50. Electronic applications accepted. *Expenses:* Contact institution. *Financial support:* Research assistantships, teaching assistantships, career-related internships or fieldwork, institutionally sponsored loans, and scholarships/grants available. Financial award application deadline: 4/15; financial award applicants required to submit FAFSA. *Faculty research:* Taxes, budgeting, nonprofit, ethics, decision modeling, work balance, organizational behavior. *Unit head:* Dr. Lori Wadsworth, Director, 801-422-5956, E-mail: mpa@byu.edu. *Application contact:* Catherine Cooper, Associate Director, 801-422-9173, E-mail: mpa@byu.edu.
Website: https://marriottschool.byu.edu/mpa/

Broadview University–West Jordan, Graduate Programs, West Jordan, UT 84088. Offers business administration (MBA); health care management (MSM); information technology (MSM); managerial leadership (MSM).

Brooklyn College of the City University of New York, School of Natural and Behavioral Sciences, Department of Health and Nutrition Sciences, Program in Public Health, Brooklyn, NY 11210-2889. Offers general public health (MPH); health care policy and administration (MPH). *Degree requirements:* For master's, thesis or alternative, 46 credits. *Entrance requirements:* For master's, GRE, 2 letters of recommendation, essay, interview. Electronic applications accepted.

Bryan College, MBA Program, Dayton, TN 37321. Offers business administration (MBA); healthcare administration (MBA); human resources (MBA); marketing (MBA); ministry (MBA); sports management (MBA). *Program availability:* Online only, 100% online. *Entrance requirements:* For master's, resume, 2 letters of recommendation. Additional exam requirements/recommendations for international students: Required—TOEFL. *Application deadline:* For fall admission, 7/1 for domestic and international students; for winter admission, 11/15 for domestic and international students; for spring admission, 12/1 for domestic and international students; for summer admission, 5/1 for domestic and international students. Applications are processed on a rolling basis. Application fee: $50. Electronic applications accepted. *Expenses:* Contact institution. *Financial support:* Scholarships/grants available. Financial award applicants required to submit FAFSA. *Unit head:* Dr. Adina Scruggs, Dean of Adult and Graduate Studies, 423-634-2057, E-mail: adina.scruggs@bryan.edu. *Application contact:* Mandi K Sullivan, Director of Academic Programs, 423-634-9880, E-mail: mandi.sullivan@bryan.edu.
Website: http://www.bryan.edu/academics/adult-education/graduate/online-mba/

California Baptist University, Program in Business Administration, Riverside, CA 92504-3206. Offers accounting (MBA); construction management (MBA); healthcare management (MBA); management (MBA). *Accreditation:* ACBSP. *Program availability:* Part-time, evening/weekend, 100% online, blended/hybrid learning. *Faculty:* 19 full-time (7 women), 18 part-time/adjunct (6 women). *Students:* 123 full-time (64 women), 101 part-time (55 women); includes 108 minority (22 Black or African American, non-Hispanic/Latino; 15 Asian, non-Hispanic/Latino; 62 Hispanic/Latino; 1 Native Hawaiian or other Pacific Islander, non-Hispanic/Latino; 8 Two or more races, non-Hispanic/Latino), 29 international. Average age 30. 285 applicants, 62% accepted, 142 enrolled.

In 2017, 147 master's awarded. *Degree requirements:* For master's, interdisciplinary capstone project. *Entrance requirements:* For master's, GMAT, minimum GPA of 2.5; two recommendations; comprehensive essay; resume; interview. Additional exam requirements/recommendations for international students: Required—TOEFL (minimum score 80 iBT). *Application deadline:* For fall admission, 8/1 priority date for domestic students, 7/1 for international students; for spring admission, 12/1 priority date for domestic students, 11/1 for international students. Applications are processed on a rolling basis. Application fee: $45. Electronic applications accepted. *Expenses:* Contact institution. *Financial support:* In 2017–18, 38 students received support. Federal Work-Study and scholarships/grants available. Financial award applicants required to submit CSS PROFILE or FAFSA. *Faculty research:* Behavioral economics, economic indicators, marketing ethics, international business, microfinance. *Unit head:* Dr. Andrea Scott, Dean, School of Business, 951-343-4701, Fax: 951-343-4361, E-mail: ascott@calbaptist.edu. *Application contact:* Deanna Meyer, Graduate Admissions Counselor, 951-343-4463, E-mail: dmeyer@calbaptist.edu.
Website: http://www.calbaptist.edu/mba/about/

California Baptist University, Program in Public Health, Riverside, CA 92504-3206. Offers health education and promotion (MPH); health policy and administration (MPH). *Program availability:* Part-time, evening/weekend. *Faculty:* 9 full-time (5 women), 4 part-time/adjunct (2 women). *Students:* 56 full-time (47 women), 37 part-time (30 women); includes 72 minority (18 Black or African American, non-Hispanic/Latino; 8 Asian, non-Hispanic/Latino; 38 Hispanic/Latino; 8 Two or more races, non-Hispanic/Latino), 4 international. Average age 28. 83 applicants, 64% accepted, 39 enrolled. In 2017, 4 master's awarded. *Degree requirements:* For master's, capstone project; practicum. *Entrance requirements:* For master's, minimum undergraduate GPA of 2.75, two recommendations, 500-word essay, resume. Additional exam requirements/recommendations for international students: Required—TOEFL (minimum score 80 iBT). *Application deadline:* For fall admission, 8/1 priority date for domestic students, 7/1 for international students; for spring admission, 12/1 priority date for domestic students, 11/1 for international students. Applications are processed on a rolling basis. Application fee: $45. Electronic applications accepted. *Expenses:* Contact institution. *Financial support:* In 2017–18, 22 students received support. Federal Work-Study and scholarships/grants available. Financial award applicants required to submit CSS PROFILE or FAFSA. *Faculty research:* Epidemiology, statistical education, exercise and immunity, obesity and chronic disease. *Unit head:* Dr. David Pearson, Dean, College of Health Science, 951-343-4298, E-mail: dpearson@calbaptist.edu. *Application contact:* Tamakia King, Graduate Admissions Counselor, 951-552-8138, E-mail: tking@calbaptist.edu.
Website: http://www.calbaptist.edu/explore-cbu/schools-colleges/college-allied-health/health-sciences/master-public-health/

California Coast University, School of Administration and Management, Santa Ana, CA 92701. Offers business marketing (MBA); health care management (MBA); human resource management (MBA); management (MBA, MS). *Program availability:* Online learning. Electronic applications accepted.

California Intercontinental University, School of Healthcare, Irvine, CA 92614. Offers healthcare management and leadership (MBA, DBA).

California State University, Bakersfield, Division of Graduate Studies, School of Business and Public Administration, Program in Health Care Administration, Bakersfield, CA 93311. Offers MS. *Faculty:* 1 (woman) full-time, 3 part-time/adjunct (2 women). *Students:* 16 full-time (11 women), 24 part-time (18 women); includes 29 minority (4 Black or African American, non-Hispanic/Latino; 11 Asian, non-Hispanic/Latino; 12 Hispanic/Latino; 2 Two or more races, non-Hispanic/Latino), 4 international. Average age 31. 39 applicants, 62% accepted, 21 enrolled. *Entrance requirements:* For master's, official transcripts, two letters of recommendation, personal statement. Additional exam requirements/recommendations for international students: Required—TOEFL (minimum score 550 paper-based; 79 iBT), IELTS (minimum score 7). *Application deadline:* Applications are processed on a rolling basis. Application fee: $55. Electronic applications accepted. *Expenses:* Tuition, state resident: full-time $7176; part-time $4164 per year. *Financial support:* In 2017–18, fellowships (averaging $1,850 per year) were awarded; Federal Work-Study, scholarships/grants, and tuition waivers (full and partial) also available. Financial award application deadline: 3/2; financial award applicants required to submit FAFSA. *Unit head:* Dr. BJ Moore, Coordinator, 661-654-3026, E-mail: bjmoore@csub.edu. *Application contact:* Debbie Blowers, Assistant Director of Admissions and Evaluations, 661-664-3381, E-mail: dblowers@csub.edu.
Website: https://bpa.csub.edu/departments/Master-of-Science-in-Health-Care-Administration.html

California State University, Chico, Office of Graduate Studies, College of Behavioral and Social Sciences, Department of Political Science and Criminal Justice, Program in Public Administration, Chico, CA 95929-0722. Offers health administration (MPA); local government management (MPA). *Accreditation:* NASPAA. *Program availability:* Part-time. *Degree requirements:* For master's, thesis or culminating practicum. *Entrance requirements:* For master's, 2 letters of recommendation. Additional exam requirements/recommendations for international students: Required—TOEFL (minimum score 550 paper-based; 80 iBT), IELTS (minimum score 6.5), PTE. Electronic applications accepted.

California State University, East Bay, Office of Graduate Studies, College of Letters, Arts, and Social Sciences, Department of Public Affairs and Administration, Program in Health Care Administration, Hayward, CA 94542-3000. Offers management and change in health care (MS). *Program availability:* Part-time, evening/weekend, online learning. *Students:* 4 full-time (3 women), 155 part-time (129 women); includes 117 minority (16 Black or African American, non-Hispanic/Latino; 64 Asian, non-Hispanic/Latino; 25 Hispanic/Latino; 2 Native Hawaiian or other Pacific Islander, non-Hispanic/Latino; 10 Two or more races, non-Hispanic/Latino), 17 international. Average age 30. 249 applicants, 44% accepted, 57 enrolled. In 2017, 153 master's awarded. *Degree requirements:* For master's, thesis or alternative, final project. *Entrance requirements:* For master's, minimum undergraduate cumulative GPA of 2.5, statement of purpose, two letters of academic and/or professional recommendation, professional resume/curriculum vitae, all undergraduate/graduate transcripts. Additional exam requirements/recommendations for international students: Required—TOEFL (minimum score 550 paper-based). *Application deadline:* For fall admission, 6/1 for domestic and international students. Application fee: $55. Electronic applications accepted. *Financial support:* Career-related internships or fieldwork, Federal Work-Study, institutionally sponsored loans, and scholarships/grants available. Support available to part-time students. Financial award application deadline: 3/2; financial award applicants required to submit FAFSA. *Unit head:* Dr. Toni Fogarty, Chair/Graduate Advisor, 510-885-2268, E-mail: toni.fogarty@csueastbay.edu. *Application contact:* Prof. Michael Moon, Public Administration Graduate Advisor, 510-885-2545, Fax: 510-885-3726, E-mail: michael.moon@csueastbay.edu.

California State University, East Bay, Office of Graduate Studies, College of Letters, Arts, and Social Sciences, Department of Public Affairs and Administration, Program in Public Administration, Hayward, CA 94542-3000. Offers health care administration (MPA); public management and policy analysis (MPA). *Program availability:* Part-time, evening/weekend. *Students:* 3 full-time (2 women), 125 part-time (79 women); includes 92 minority (30 Black or African American, non-Hispanic/Latino; 2 American Indian or Alaska Native, non-Hispanic/Latino; 19 Asian, non-Hispanic/Latino; 30 Hispanic/Latino; 3 Native Hawaiian or other Pacific Islander, non-Hispanic/Latino; 8 Two or more races, non-Hispanic/Latino), 9 international. Average age 33. 88 applicants, 74% accepted, 38 enrolled. In 2017, 87 master's awarded. *Degree requirements:* For master's, comprehensive exam (for some programs), comprehensive exam or thesis. *Entrance requirements:* For master's, minimum GPA of 2.5; statement of purpose; 2 letters of recommendation; professional resume/curriculum vitae. Additional exam requirements/recommendations for international students: Required—TOEFL (minimum score 550 paper-based; 79 iBT). *Application deadline:* For fall admission, 6/1 for domestic and international students. Application fee: $55. Electronic applications accepted. *Financial support:* Fellowships, teaching assistantships, career-related internships or fieldwork, Federal Work-Study, institutionally sponsored loans, and scholarships/grants available. Support available to part-time students. Financial award application deadline: 3/2; financial award applicants required to submit FAFSA. *Unit head:* Dr. Toni Fogarty, Chair, 510-885-2268, E-mail: toni.fogarty@csueastbay.edu. *Application contact:* Prof. Michael Moon, Public Administration Graduate Advisor, 510-885-2545, Fax: 510-885-3726, E-mail: michael.moon@csueastbay.edu.

California State University, Fresno, Division of Research and Graduate Studies, College of Health and Human Services, Department of Public Health, Fresno, CA 93740-8027. Offers health policy and management (MPH); health promotion (MPH). *Accreditation:* CEPH. *Program availability:* Part-time, evening/weekend. *Degree requirements:* For master's, thesis or alternative. *Entrance requirements:* For master's, GRE General Test, minimum GPA of 2.5. Additional exam requirements/recommendations for international students: Required—TOEFL. Electronic applications accepted. *Faculty research:* Foster parent training, geriatrics, tobacco control.

California State University, Long Beach, Graduate Studies, College of Health and Human Services, Program in Health Care Administration, Long Beach, CA 90840. Offers MS. *Accreditation:* CAHME. *Program availability:* Part-time. *Degree requirements:* For master's, comprehensive exam or thesis. *Entrance requirements:* For master's, minimum GPA of 3.0. Electronic applications accepted. *Faculty research:* Long-term care, Immigration Reform Act and health care, physician reimbursement.

California State University, Los Angeles, Graduate Studies, College of Business and Economics, Department of Management, Los Angeles, CA 90032-8530. Offers health care management (MS); management (MBA). *Accreditation:* AACSB. *Program availability:* Part-time, evening/weekend. *Entrance requirements:* For master's, GMAT, minimum GPA of 2.5 during previous 2 years of course work. Additional exam requirements/recommendations for international students: Required—TOEFL (minimum score 550 paper-based). Electronic applications accepted.

California State University, Northridge, Graduate Studies, College of Health and Human Development, Department of Health Sciences, Northridge, CA 91330. Offers health administration (MS); public health (MPH), including applied epidemiology, community health education. *Accreditation:* CEPH. *Students:* 128 full-time (96 women), 53 part-time (45 women); includes 96 minority (10 Black or African American, non-Hispanic/Latino; 21 Asian, non-Hispanic/Latino; 53 Hispanic/Latino; 1 Native Hawaiian or other Pacific Islander, non-Hispanic/Latino; 11 Two or more races, non-Hispanic/Latino), 6 international. Average age 30. 323 applicants, 38% accepted, 68 enrolled. In 2017, 70 master's awarded. *Entrance requirements:* For master's, GRE General Test or minimum GPA of 3.0. Additional exam requirements/recommendations for international students: Required—TOEFL. *Application deadline:* For fall admission, 11/30 for domestic students. Application fee: $55. *Financial support:* Teaching assistantships available. Financial award application deadline: 3/1. *Faculty research:* Labor market needs assessment, health education products, dental hygiene, independent practice prototype. *Unit head:* Louis Rubino, Chair, 818-677-3101.
Website: http://www.csun.edu/hhd/hsci/

California State University, Northridge, Graduate Studies, Tseng College, Program in Health Administration, Northridge, CA 91330. Offers MPA. Offered in collaboration with the College of Health and Human Development. *Program availability:* Online learning. *Degree requirements:* For master's, comprehensive exam. *Entrance requirements:* For master's, bachelor's degree from accredited college or university, minimum cumulative GPA of 2.5, at least two years of work experience. Additional exam requirements/recommendations for international students: Required—TOEFL (minimum score of 563 paper-based, 85 iBT) or IELTS (minimum score of 7). *Application deadline:* For fall admission, 6/1 for domestic students. Electronic applications accepted. *Unit head:* Louis Rubino, Director, 818-677-3332.
Website: http://tsengcollege.csun.edu/programs/MPA/online-healthadmin

California State University, San Bernardino, Graduate Studies, College of Natural Sciences, Program in Health Services Administration, San Bernardino, CA 92407. Offers MS. *Faculty:* 1 (woman) full-time, 4 part-time/adjunct (3 women). *Students:* 19 full-time (17 women), 13 part-time (9 women); includes 16 minority (3 Black or African American, non-Hispanic/Latino; 4 Asian, non-Hispanic/Latino; 8 Hispanic/Latino; 1 Native Hawaiian or other Pacific Islander, non-Hispanic/Latino), 4 international. Average age 27. 35 applicants, 57% accepted, 14 enrolled. In 2017, 5 master's awarded. *Degree requirements:* For master's, thesis or alternative. *Entrance requirements:* Additional exam requirements/recommendations for international students: Required—TOEFL. *Application deadline:* For fall admission, 5/5 for domestic students. Application fee: $55. *Unit head:* Dr. Paulchris Okpala, Assistant Professor, 909-537-5341, E-mail: pokpala@csusb.edu. *Application contact:* Dr. Dorota Huizinga, Dean of Graduate Studies, 909-537-3064, E-mail: dorota.huizinga@csusb.edu.

California University of Pennsylvania, School of Graduate Studies and Research, Eberly College of Science and Technology, Program in Business Administration, California, PA 15419-1394. Offers business analytics (MBA); entrepreneurship (MBA); healthcare management (MBA). *Program availability:* Part-time, evening/weekend. *Degree requirements:* For master's, comprehensive exam. *Entrance requirements:* For master's, minimum GPA of 3.0, official transcripts. Additional exam requirements/recommendations for international students: Required—TOEFL (minimum score 550 paper-based). *Application deadline:* For fall admission, 8/1 priority date for domestic and international students; for winter admission, 12/1 priority date for domestic and international students; for spring admission, 5/1 priority date for domestic and international students. Applications are processed on a rolling basis. Application fee: $25. Electronic applications accepted. *Financial support:* Applicants required to submit FAFSA. *Faculty research:* Economics, applied economics, consumer behavior, technology and business, impact of technology. *Unit head:* Dr. Arshad Chawdhry, Graduate Coordinator, 724-938-5990, Fax: 724-938-5908, E-mail: chawdhry@cup.edu. *Application contact:* Suzanne C. Powers, Director of Graduate Admissions and Recruitment, 724-938-4029, Fax: 724-938-5712, E-mail: powers_s@cup.edu.

Cambridge College, School of Management, Boston, MA 02129. Offers business administration (MBA); business negotiation and conflict resolution (M Mgt); general business (M Mgt); health care (MBA); health care management (M Mgt); small business development (M Mgt); technology management (M Mgt). *Program availability:* Part-time, evening/weekend. *Degree requirements:* For master's, thesis, seminars. *Entrance requirements:* For master's, resume, 2 professional references. Additional exam

requirements/recommendations for international students: Required—TOEFL (minimum score 550 paper-based; 79 iBT), Michigan English Language Assessment Battery (minimum score 85); Recommended—IELTS (minimum score 6). *Application deadline:* Applications are processed on a rolling basis. Application fee: $30. Electronic applications accepted. *Expenses:* Contact institution. *Financial support:* Career-related internships or fieldwork, Federal Work-Study, and scholarships/grants available. Financial award applicants required to submit FAFSA. *Faculty research:* Negotiation, mediation and conflict resolution; leadership; management of diverse organizations; case studies and simulation methodologies for management education, digital as a second language: social networking for digital immigrants, non-profit and public management. *Unit head:* Dr. Mary Ann Joseph, Dean, 617-873-0227, E-mail: maryann.joseph@cambridgecollege.edu. *Application contact:* Robyn Shahid-Bellot, Interim Director of Admissions, 800-877-4723, Fax: 617-349-3561, E-mail: robyn.shahid-bellot@cambridgecollege.edu.
Website: https://www.cambridgecollege.edu/school/school-management

Capella University, School of Business and Technology, Master's Programs in Business, Minneapolis, MN 55402. Offers accounting (MBA); business analysis (MS); business intelligence (MBA); entrepreneurship (MBA); finance (MBA); general business administration (MBA); general human resource management (MS); general leadership (MS); health care management (MBA); human resource management (MBA); marketing (MBA); project management (MBA, MS). *Accreditation:* ACBSP.

Capella University, School of Public Service Leadership, Doctoral Programs in Healthcare, Minneapolis, MN 55402. Offers criminal justice (PhD); emergency management (PhD); epidemiology (Dr PH); general health administration (DHA); general public administration (DPA); health advocacy and leadership (Dr PH); health care administration (PhD); health care leadership (DHA); health policy advocacy (DHA); multidisciplinary human services (PhD); nonprofit management and leadership (PhD); public safety leadership (PhD); social and community services (PhD).

Capella University, School of Public Service Leadership, Master's Programs in Healthcare, Minneapolis, MN 55402. Offers criminal justice (MS); emergency management (MS); general public health (MPH); gerontology (MS); health administration (MHA); health care operations (MHA); health management policy (MPH); health policy (MHA); homeland security (MS); multidisciplinary human services (MS); public administration (MPA); public safety leadership (MS); social and community services (MS); social behavioral sciences (MPH); MS/MPA.

Cardinal Stritch University, College of Business and Management, Milwaukee, WI 53217-3985. Offers cyber security (MBA); healthcare management (MBA); justice administration (MBA); marketing (MBA). *Accreditation:* ACBSP. *Program availability:* Part-time, evening/weekend, 100% online, blended/hybrid learning. *Students:* 133 full-time (72 women), 98 part-time (54 women); includes 88 minority (64 Black or African American, non-Hispanic/Latino; 1 American Indian or Alaska Native, non-Hispanic/Latino; 12 Asian, non-Hispanic/Latino; 10 Hispanic/Latino; 1 Two or more races, non-Hispanic/Latino), 8 international. Average age 36. 144 applicants, 100% accepted, 57 enrolled. In 2017, 118 master's awarded. *Degree requirements:* For master's, thesis. *Entrance requirements:* For master's, 3 years of management or related experience, minimum GPA of 2.5. Additional exam requirements/recommendations for international students: Required—TOEFL (minimum score 79 iBT), IELTS (minimum score 6.5). *Application deadline:* Applications are processed on a rolling basis. Application fee: $0. Electronic applications accepted. *Expenses:* $665 per credit. *Financial support:* Career-related internships or fieldwork, Federal Work-Study, and scholarships/grants available. Financial award applicants required to submit FAFSA. *Unit head:* Janette Braverman, Dean, 414-410-4004, E-mail: jmbraverman1@stritch.edu. *Application contact:* Graduate Admissions, 414-410-4042, E-mail: admissions@stritch.edu.
Website: http://www.stritch.edu/cbm

Carlow University, College of Leadership and Social Change, MBA Program, Pittsburgh, PA 15213-3165. Offers fraud and forensics (MBA); healthcare management (MBA); human resource management (MBA); leadership and management (MBA); project management (MBA). *Program availability:* Part-time, evening/weekend, 100% online, blended/hybrid learning. *Students:* 81 full-time (62 women), 28 part-time (18 women); includes 32 minority (26 Black or African American, non-Hispanic/Latino; 2 Asian, non-Hispanic/Latino; 1 Hispanic/Latino; 3 Two or more races, non-Hispanic/Latino). Average age 32. 46 applicants, 98% accepted, 32 enrolled. In 2017, 57 master's awarded. *Entrance requirements:* For master's, minimum undergraduate GPA of 3.0 (preferred); personal essay; resume; official transcripts; two professional recommendations. Additional exam requirements/recommendations for international students: Required—TOEFL (minimum score 550 paper-based). *Application deadline:* Applications are processed on a rolling basis. Electronic applications accepted. *Expenses: Tuition:* Full-time $12,103; part-time $825 per credit hour. Tuition and fees vary according to program. *Financial support:* Application deadline: 4/1; applicants required to submit FAFSA. *Unit head:* Dr. Howard Stern, Chair, MBA Program, 412-578-8828, E-mail: hastern@carlow.edu. *Application contact:* 412-578-6059, Fax: 412-578-6321, E-mail: gradstudies@carlow.edu.
Website: http://www.carlow.edu/Business_Administration.aspx

Carnegie Mellon University, Heinz College, School of Public Policy and Management, Master of Science Program in Health Care Policy and Management, Pittsburgh, PA 15213-3891. Offers MSHCPM. *Program availability:* Part-time, evening/weekend. *Degree requirements:* For master's, internship. *Entrance requirements:* For master's, GRE or GMAT, college-level course in advanced algebra/pre-calculus; college-level courses in economics and statistics (recommended). Additional exam requirements/recommendations for international students: Required—TOEFL or IELTS. Electronic applications accepted.

Carnegie Mellon University, Heinz College, School of Public Policy and Management, Programs in Medical Management, Pittsburgh, PA 15213-3891. Offers MMM.

Case Western Reserve University, Weatherhead School of Management, Program in Healthcare, Cleveland, OH 44106. Offers MSM. *Program availability:* Evening/weekend. *Entrance requirements:* For master's, GMAT/GRE, master's degree or higher in a medical to management-related field, or bachelor's degree plus 5 years of experience working in the healthcare industry, essay, current resume, letters of recommendation. Electronic applications accepted. *Expenses: Tuition:* Full-time $43,854; part-time $1827 per credit hour. *Required fees:* $50; $50 per credit hour. Tuition and fees vary according to course load and program.

The Catholic University of America, Metropolitan School of Professional Studies, Washington, DC 20064. Offers emergency service administration (MS); health administration (MHA); social service administration (MS). *Program availability:* Part-time, evening/weekend, 100% online. *Faculty:* 20 part-time/adjunct (6 women). *Students:* 14 full-time (8 women), 36 part-time (20 women); includes 26 minority (16 Black or African American, non-Hispanic/Latino; 1 Asian, non-Hispanic/Latino; 4 Hispanic/Latino; 5 Two or more races, non-Hispanic/Latino), 3 international. Average age 36. 45 applicants, 80% accepted, 21 enrolled. In 2017, 100 master's awarded. *Degree requirements:* For master's, minimum GPA of 3.0, capstone course. *Entrance requirements:* For master's, statement of purpose, official copies of academic transcripts, three letters of recommendation, resume. Additional exam requirements/recommendations for international students: Required—TOEFL (minimum score 550 paper-based; 80 iBT). *Application deadline:* For fall admission, 7/15 priority date for domestic students, 7/1 for international students; for spring admission, 11/15 priority date for domestic students, 11/1 for international students. Applications are processed on a rolling basis. Application fee: $55. Electronic applications accepted. *Expenses:* Contact institution. *Financial support:* Scholarships/grants available. Financial award application deadline: 3/15; financial award applicants required to submit FAFSA. *Unit head:* Dr. Vince Kiernan, Dean, 202-319-5256, Fax: 202-319-6260, E-mail: kiernan@cua.edu. *Application contact:* Dr. Steven Brown, Director of Graduate Admissions, 202-319-5057, Fax: 202-319-6533, E-mail: cua-admissions@cua.edu.
Website: https://metro.catholic.edu/

Cedarville University, Graduate Programs, Cedarville, OH 45314. Offers business administration (MBA); family nurse practitioner (MSN); global ministry (M Div); global public health nursing (MSN); healthcare administration (MBA); ministry (M Min); nurse educator (MSN); operations management (MBA); pharmacy (Pharm D). *Program availability:* Part-time, evening/weekend, 100% online, blended/hybrid learning. *Faculty:* 23 full-time (9 women), 48 part-time/adjunct (21 women). *Students:* 202 full-time (123 women), 146 part-time (96 women); includes 63 minority (39 Black or African American, non-Hispanic/Latino; 3 American Indian or Alaska Native, non-Hispanic/Latino; 15 Asian, non-Hispanic/Latino; 2 Hispanic/Latino; 1 Native Hawaiian or other Pacific Islander, non-Hispanic/Latino; 3 Two or more races, non-Hispanic/Latino), 3 international. Average age 24. 345 applicants, 37% accepted, 91 enrolled. In 2017, 53 master's, 47 doctorates awarded. *Degree requirements:* For master's, portfolio; for doctorate, comprehensive exam. *Entrance requirements:* For master's, GRE, 2 professional recommendations; for doctorate, PCAT, professional recommendation from a practicing pharmacist or current employer/supervisor, resume, essay, interview. Additional exam requirements/recommendations for international students: Required—TOEFL (minimum score 550 paper-based; 80 iBT). *Application deadline:* For fall admission, 5/1 priority date for domestic and international students; for spring admission, 11/1 priority date for domestic and international students. Applications are processed on a rolling basis. Application fee: $0. Electronic applications accepted. *Expenses: Tuition:* Full-time $12,594; part-time $566 per credit. One-time fee: $100 full-time. Tuition and fees vary according to degree level and program. *Financial support:* Scholarships/grants and unspecified assistantships available. Support available to part-time students. Financial award application deadline: 1/30; financial award applicants required to submit FAFSA. *Faculty research:* Establishing competencies of clinical reasoning for nursing students in Taiwan, social determinants of health in pediatric primary care, meeting needs of palliative care populations, natural product utility in cancer, monoclonal antibodies directed at angiogenesis regulation. *Total annual research expenditures:* $3,800. *Unit head:* Dr. Janice Supplee, Dean of Graduate Studies, 937-766-7700, E-mail: suppleej@cedarville.edu. *Application contact:* Jim Amstutz, Director of Graduate Admissions, 937-766-7878, Fax: 937-766-7575, E-mail: amstutzj@cedarville.edu.
Website: https://www.cedarville.edu/Admissions/Graduate/Graduate-Programs.aspx

Central Michigan University, Central Michigan University Global Campus, Program in Administration, Mount Pleasant, MI 48859. Offers acquisitions administration (MSA, Certificate); engineering management administration (MSA, Certificate); general administration (MSA, Certificate); health services administration (MSA, Certificate); human resources administration (MSA, Certificate); information resource management (MSA); information resource management administration (Certificate); international administration (MSA, Certificate); leadership (MSA, Certificate); philanthropy and fundraising administration (MSA, Certificate); public administration (MSA, Certificate); recreation and park administration (MSA); research administration (MSA, Certificate). *Program availability:* Part-time, evening/weekend, online learning. *Entrance requirements:* For master's, minimum GPA of 2.7 in major. Electronic applications accepted.

Central Michigan University, Central Michigan University Global Campus, Program in Health Administration, Mount Pleasant, MI 48859. Offers health administration (DHA); international health (Certificate); nutrition and dietetics (MS). *Program availability:* Part-time, evening/weekend, online learning. Electronic applications accepted.

Central Michigan University, College of Graduate Studies, The Herbert H. and Grace A. Dow College of Health Professions, School of Health Sciences, Mount Pleasant, MI 48859. Offers exercise science (MA); health administration (DHA). *Program availability:* Part-time, evening/weekend, online learning. *Degree requirements:* For doctorate, comprehensive exam, thesis/dissertation. *Entrance requirements:* For doctorate, accredited master's or doctoral degree, 5 years of related work experience. Electronic applications accepted. *Faculty research:* Exercise science.

Central Michigan University, College of Graduate Studies, Interdisciplinary Administration Programs, Mount Pleasant, MI 48859. Offers acquisitions administration (MSA, Graduate Certificate); general administration (MSA, Graduate Certificate); health services administration (MSA, Graduate Certificate); human resource administration (Graduate Certificate); human resources administration (MSA); information resource management (MSA, Graduate Certificate); international administration (MSA, Graduate Certificate); leadership (MSA, Graduate Certificate); public administration (MSA, Graduate Certificate); research administration (Graduate Certificate); sport administration (MSA). *Accreditation:* AACSB. *Program availability:* Part-time, evening/weekend, online learning. *Degree requirements:* For master's, thesis or alternative. *Entrance requirements:* For master's, bachelor's degree with minimum GPA of 2.7. Electronic applications accepted. *Faculty research:* Interdisciplinary studies in acquisitions administration, health services administration, sport administration, recreation and park administration, and international administration.

Champlain College, Graduate Studies, Burlington, VT 05402-0670. Offers business (MBA); digital forensic science (MS); early childhood education (M Ed); emergent media (MFA, MS); executive leadership (MS); health care administration (MS); information security operations (MS); law (MS); mediation and applied conflict studies (MS). MS in emergent media program held in Shanghai. *Program availability:* Part-time, online learning. *Degree requirements:* For master's, capstone project. *Entrance requirements:* Additional exam requirements/recommendations for international students: Required—TOEFL (minimum score 550 paper-based; 80 iBT). Electronic applications accepted.

The Chicago School of Professional Psychology: Online, Program in Health Services Administration, Chicago, IL 60654. Offers MHSA. *Program availability:* Online learning.

Clarion University of Pennsylvania, College of Business Administration and Information Sciences, Master of Business Administration Program, Clarion, PA 16214. Offers accounting (MBA); finance (MBA); health care administration (MBA); innovation and entrepreneurship (MBA); non-profit business (MBA). *Accreditation:* AACSB. *Program availability:* Part-time, evening/weekend, 100% online. *Faculty:* 4 full-time (1 woman), 3 part-time/adjunct (0 women). *Students:* 19 full-time (7 women), 66 part-time (34 women); includes 10 minority (6 Black or African American, non-Hispanic/Latino; 1 Asian, non-Hispanic/Latino; 3 Hispanic/Latino), 2 international. Average age 31. 86 applicants, 63% accepted, 21 enrolled. In 2017, 33 master's awarded. *Degree requirements:* For master's, portfolio. *Entrance requirements:* For master's, GMAT,

minimum QPA of 2.75. Additional exam requirements/recommendations for international students: Required—TOEFL (minimum score 550 paper-based, 80 iBT) or IELTS (7). *Application deadline:* For fall admission, 8/1 priority date for domestic students, 4/15 priority date for international students; for spring admission, 12/1 priority date for domestic students, 9/15 priority date for international students. Applications are processed on a rolling basis. Application fee: $40. Electronic applications accepted. *Expenses:* $655.05 per credit. *Financial support:* Unspecified assistantships available. Support available to part-time students. Financial award application deadline: 3/1; financial award applicants required to submit FAFSA. *Unit head:* Juanice Vega, Assistant to the Dean, 814-393-2600, Fax: 814-393-1910, E-mail: mba@clarion.edu. *Application contact:* Dana Bearer, Assistant Director, Graduate Programs, 814-393-2337, Fax: 814-393-2722, E-mail: gradstudies@clarion.edu.
Website: http://www.clarion.edu/admissions/graduate/index.html

Clarkson University, David D. Reh School of Business, Master's Programs in Healthcare Management and Leadership, Schenectady, NY 12308. Offers clinical leadership in healthcare management (MS); healthcare data analytics (MS); healthcare management (MBA, Advanced Certificate). *Program availability:* Part-time, evening/weekend, blended/hybrid learning. *Faculty:* 20 full-time (5 women), 13 part-time/adjunct (3 women). *Students:* 43 full-time (23 women), 35 part-time (21 women); includes 12 minority (4 Black or African American, non-Hispanic/Latino; 6 Asian, non-Hispanic/Latino; 2 Hispanic/Latino), 5 international. 64 applicants, 55% accepted, 28 enrolled. In 2017, 41 master's, 3 other advanced degrees awarded. *Entrance requirements:* For master's, GRE or GMAT. Additional exam requirements/recommendations for international students: Required—TOEFL (minimum score 550 paper-based, 80 iBT) or IELTS (6.5). *Application deadline:* Applications are processed on a rolling basis. Application fee: $50. Electronic applications accepted. *Expenses: Tuition:* Full-time $24,210; part-time $1345 per credit hour. Tuition and fees vary according to campus/location and program. *Financial support:* Scholarships/grants available. *Unit head:* Dr. John Huppertz, Director of Healthcare Management, 518-631-9892, E-mail: jhuppert@clarkson.edu. *Application contact:* Dan Capogna, Director of Graduate Admissions, 518-631-9910, E-mail: graduate@clarkson.edu.
Website: https://www.clarkson.edu/academics/graduate

Cleary University, Online Program in Business Administration, Howell, MI 48843. Offers analytics, technology, and innovation (MBA, Graduate Certificate); financial planning (Graduate Certificate); global leadership (MBA, Graduate Certificate); health care leadership (MBA, Graduate Certificate). *Program availability:* Part-time, evening/weekend, online learning. *Degree requirements:* For master's, thesis. *Entrance requirements:* For master's, bachelor's degree; minimum GPA of 2.5; professional resume indicating minimum of 2 years of management or related experience; undergraduate degree from accredited college or university with at least 18 quarter hours (or 12 semester hours) of accounting study (for MBA in accounting). Additional exam requirements/recommendations for international students: Required—TOEFL (minimum score 550 paper-based; 79 iBT), Michigan English Language Assessment Battery (minimum score 75). Electronic applications accepted.

Cleveland State University, College of Graduate Studies, Monte Ahuja College of Business, Department of Management, Cleveland, OH 44115. Offers health care administration (MBA); labor relations and human resources (MLRHR). *Program availability:* Part-time, evening/weekend. *Faculty:* 6 full-time (3 women), 8 part-time/adjunct (1 woman). *Students:* 101 full-time (45 women), 41 part-time (22 women); includes 19 minority (9 Black or African American, non-Hispanic/Latino; 6 Asian, non-Hispanic/Latino; 3 Hispanic/Latino; 1 Two or more races, non-Hispanic/Latino), 81 international. Average age 27. In 2017, 12 master's awarded. *Entrance requirements:* For master's, GMAT or GRE, minimum GPA of 3.0. Additional exam requirements/recommendations for international students: Required—TOEFL (minimum score 550 paper-based; 78 iBT). *Application deadline:* For fall admission, 7/15 for domestic students; for spring admission, 12/15 for domestic students. Applications are processed on a rolling basis. Application fee: $40. Electronic applications accepted. *Financial support:* In 2017–18, 3 students received support. Career-related internships or fieldwork, scholarships/grants, and unspecified assistantships available. Financial award application deadline: 5/1; financial award applicants required to submit FAFSA. *Faculty research:* Employee selection, individual differences, leadership, emotions, interviews. *Unit head:* Dr. Kenneth J. Dunegan, Chairperson, 216-687-4747, Fax: 216-687-4708, E-mail: t.degroot@csuohio.edu. *Application contact:* Lisa Marie Sample, Administrative Assistant, 216-687-4726, Fax: 216-687-6888, E-mail: l.m.sample@csuohio.edu.
Website: https://www.csuohio.edu/business/management/management

The College at Brockport, State University of New York, School of Business and Management, Department of Public Administration, Brockport, NY 14420-2997. Offers arts administration (AGC); nonprofit management (AGC); public administration (MPA), including health care management, nonprofit management, poverty studies, public management, public safety. *Accreditation:* NASPAA. *Program availability:* Part-time, evening/weekend. *Faculty:* 5 full-time (3 women), 5 part-time/adjunct (1 woman). *Students:* 54 full-time (38 women), 95 part-time (57 women); includes 38 minority (19 Black or African American, non-Hispanic/Latino; 3 Asian, non-Hispanic/Latino; 11 Hispanic/Latino; 5 Two or more races, non-Hispanic/Latino), 4 international. 53 applicants, 91% accepted, 31 enrolled. In 2017, 59 master's, 6 other advanced degrees awarded. *Degree requirements:* For master's, thesis or alternative. *Entrance requirements:* For master's, GRE or minimum GPA of 3.0, letters of recommendation, statement of objectives, current resume. Additional exam requirements/recommendations for international students: Required—TOEFL (minimum score 550 paper-based; 79 iBT), IELTS (minimum score 6.5). *Application deadline:* For fall admission, 8/15 priority date for domestic and international students; for spring admission, 1/15 priority date for domestic and international students; for summer admission, 4/15 priority date for domestic and international students. Application fee: $50. Electronic applications accepted. *Expenses:* Tuition, state resident: full-time $10,870; part-time $453 per credit hour. Tuition, nonresident: full-time $22,210. *Required fees:* $988; $246 per semester. *Financial support:* In 2017–18, 1 fellowship with full tuition reimbursement (averaging $7,500 per year), 1 teaching assistantship with full tuition reimbursement (averaging $6,000 per year) were awarded; Federal Work-Study, scholarships/grants, and unspecified assistantships also available. Support available to part-time students. Financial award application deadline: 3/15; financial award applicants required to submit FAFSA. *Faculty research:* E-government, performance management, nonprofits and policy implementation, Medicaid and disabilities. *Unit head:* Dr. Celia Watt, Graduate Director, 585-395-5538, Fax: 585-395-2172, E-mail: cwatt@brockport.edu. *Application contact:* Danielle A. Welch, Graduate Admissions Counselor, 585-395-2525, Fax: 585-395-2515.
Website: https://www.brockport.edu/academics/public_administration/graduate/masters.html

College of Saint Elizabeth, Health Administration Program, Morristown, NJ 07960-6989. Offers MS. *Program availability:* Part-time. *Faculty:* 2 full-time (both women), 3 part-time/adjunct (0 women). *Students:* 1 (woman) full-time, 21 part-time (16 women); includes 9 minority (5 Black or African American, non-Hispanic/Latino; 3 Asian, non-Hispanic/Latino; 1 Hispanic/Latino). Average age 42. 11 applicants, 100% accepted, 4 enrolled. In 2017, 5 master's awarded. *Degree requirements:* For master's, thesis. *Entrance requirements:* For master's, minimum cumulative undergraduate GPA of 3.0, personal statement, resume, two letters of professional recommendation. Additional exam requirements/recommendations for international students: Required—TOEFL (minimum score 550 paper-based; 79 iBT), IELTS (minimum score 6.5). *Application deadline:* For fall admission, 5/1 for international students. Applications are processed on a rolling basis. Application fee: $35. Electronic applications accepted. Application fee is waived when completed online. *Financial support:* Career-related internships or fieldwork, scholarships/grants, tuition waivers (partial), and unspecified assistantships available. Financial award applicants required to submit FAFSA. *Unit head:* Dr. Regina Riccioni, Program Chair and Director, Health Care Administration, 973-290-4271, Fax: 973-290-4167, E-mail: rriccioni@cse.edu. *Application contact:* Lori J. Fragoso, Director of Graduate and Continuing Studies Admissions, 973-290-4413, Fax: 973-290-4710, E-mail: apply@cse.edu.
Website: http://www.cse.edu/academics/prof-studies/health-administration/

College of Staten Island of the City University of New York, Graduate Programs, School of Business, Program in Healthcare Management, Staten Island, NY 10314-6600. Offers MS. *Program availability:* Evening/weekend. *Degree requirements:* For master's, comprehensive exam, 33 credit hours. *Entrance requirements:* For master's, baccalaureate degree, 1-2 page letter explaining interest in pursuing graduate program in healthcare management, brief 1-2 page resume, two letters of recommendation, transcripts. Additional exam requirements/recommendations for international students: Required—TOEFL (minimum score 79 iBT), IELTS (minimum score 6.5). *Application deadline:* For fall admission, 6/30 priority date for domestic students, 4/25 for international students; for spring admission, 11/25 priority date for domestic students, 11/25 for international students. Applications are processed on a rolling basis. Application fee: $125. Electronic applications accepted. *Expenses:* Tuition, state resident: full-time $10,450; part-time $440 per credit. Tuition, nonresident: full-time $19,320; part-time $440 per credit. *Required fees:* $181.10 per semester. Tuition and fees vary according to program. *Unit head:* Prof. Gordon DiPaolo, Department Chair, 718-982-2936, E-mail: gordon.dipalo@csi.cuny.edu. *Application contact:* Sasha Spence, Associate Director for Graduate Admissions, 718-982-2019, Fax: 718-982-2500, E-mail: sasha.spence@csi.cuny.edu.
Website: https://www.csi.cuny.edu/sites/default/files/pdf/admissions/grad/pdf/Healthcare_Management_Fact_Sheet.pdf

Colorado State University–Global Campus, Graduate Programs, Greenwood Village, CO 80111. Offers criminal justice and law enforcement administration (MS); education leadership (MS); finance (MS); healthcare administration and management (MS); human resource management (MHRM); information technology management (MITM); international management (MS); management (MS); organizational leadership (MS); professional accounting (MPA); project management (MS); teaching and learning (MS). *Accreditation:* ACBSP. *Program availability:* Online learning.

Columbia Southern University, MBA Program, Orange Beach, AL 36561. Offers finance (MBA); health care management (MBA); human resource management (MBA); marketing (MBA); project management (MBA); public administration (MBA). *Program availability:* Part-time, evening/weekend, online learning. *Entrance requirements:* For master's, bachelor's degree from accredited/approved institution. Additional exam requirements/recommendations for international students: Required—TOEFL. Electronic applications accepted.

Columbia University, Columbia University Mailman School of Public Health, Department of Health Policy and Management, New York, NY 10032. Offers Exec MHA, Exec MPH, MHA, MPH. *Accreditation:* CAHME. *Program availability:* Part-time, evening/weekend. *Students:* 221 full-time (163 women), 153 part-time (107 women); includes 160 minority (24 Black or African American, non-Hispanic/Latino; 1 American Indian or Alaska Native, non-Hispanic/Latino; 91 Asian, non-Hispanic/Latino; 33 Hispanic/Latino; 11 Two or more races, non-Hispanic/Latino), 52 international. Average age 29. 757 applicants, 60% accepted, 191 enrolled. In 2017, 183 master's awarded. *Degree requirements:* For master's, thesis optional. *Entrance requirements:* For master's, GRE General Test. Additional exam requirements/recommendations for international students: Required—TOEFL (minimum score 600 paper-based; 100 iBT). *Application deadline:* For fall admission, 12/1 priority date for domestic and international students. Application fee: $120. Electronic applications accepted. *Expenses: Tuition:* Full-time $44,864; part-time $1704 per credit. *Required fees:* $2370 per semester. One-time fee: $105. *Financial support:* Research assistantships, teaching assistantships, career-related internships or fieldwork, and Federal Work-Study available. Support available to part-time students. Financial award application deadline: 2/1; financial award applicants required to submit FAFSA. *Faculty research:* Health care reform, health care disparities, state and national and cross-national health policy, health care quality, organization structure and performance. *Unit head:* Dr. Michael Sparer, Chairperson, 212-305-3924. *Application contact:* Clare Norton, Associate Dean for Enrollment Management, 212-305-8698, Fax: 212-342-1861, E-mail: ph-admit@columbia.edu.
Website: https://www.mailman.columbia.edu/become-student/departments/health-policy-and-management

Columbus State University, Graduate Studies, College of Letters and Sciences, Department of Political Science and Public Administration, Columbus, GA 31907-5645. Offers public administration (MPA), including criminal justice, environmental policy, government administration, health services administration, political campaigning, urban policy. *Program availability:* Part-time, evening/weekend, 100% online, blended/hybrid learning. *Faculty:* 15 full-time (6 women), 14 part-time/adjunct (0 women). *Students:* 34 full-time (21 women), 44 part-time (24 women); includes 40 minority (32 Black or African American, non-Hispanic/Latino; 2 Asian, non-Hispanic/Latino; 3 Hispanic/Latino; 1 Native Hawaiian or other Pacific Islander, non-Hispanic/Latino; 2 Two or more races, non-Hispanic/Latino), 3 international. Average age 33. 68 applicants, 43% accepted, 21 enrolled. In 2017, 38 master's awarded. *Degree requirements:* For master's, comprehensive exam. *Entrance requirements:* For master's, GRE General Test, minimum GPA of 2.75, three letters of recommendation. Additional exam requirements/recommendations for international students: Required—TOEFL (minimum score 550 paper-based; 79 iBT). *Application deadline:* For fall admission, 6/30 for domestic students, 5/1 for international students; for spring admission, 11/1 for domestic and international students; for summer admission, 3/1 for domestic and international students. Applications are processed on a rolling basis. Application fee: $50. Electronic applications accepted. *Expenses:* Tuition, state resident: full-time $3708; part-time $2472 per year. Tuition, nonresident: full-time $14,418; part-time $9612 per year. *International tuition:* $19,218 full-time. *Required fees:* $1605. Tuition and fees vary according to program. *Financial support:* In 2017–18, 4 students received support, including 6 research assistantships with partial tuition reimbursements available (averaging $3,000 per year); career-related internships or fieldwork, Federal Work-Study, institutionally sponsored loans, scholarships/grants, tuition waivers (partial), and unspecified assistantships also available. Support available to part-time students. Financial award application deadline: 5/1; financial award applicants required to submit FAFSA. *Unit head:* Dr. Frederick Gordon, Director, 706-565-7875, E-mail: gordon_frederick@colstate.edu. *Application contact:* Catrina Smith-Edmond, Assistant Director for Graduate and Global Admission, 706-507-8824, Fax: 706-568-5091, E-mail: smithedmond_catrina@columbusstate.edu.
Website: http://politicalscience.columbusstate.edu/

Concordia University Irvine, School of Professional Studies, Irvine, CA 92612-3299. Offers healthcare administration (MHA); international studies (MAIS), including Africa, China; nursing (MSN).

Concordia University, St. Paul, College of Business and Technology, St. Paul, MN 55104-5494. Offers business administration (MBA), including cyber-security leadership; health care management (MBA); human resource management (MA); information technology (MBA); leadership and management (MA); strategic communication management (MA). *Accreditation:* ACBSP. *Program availability:* Part-time, evening/weekend, 100% online, blended/hybrid learning. *Faculty:* 12 full-time (5 women), 33 part-time/adjunct (16 women). *Students:* 475 full-time (293 women), 35 part-time (17 women); includes 122 minority (57 Black or African American, non-Hispanic/Latino; 1 American Indian or Alaska Native, non-Hispanic/Latino; 34 Asian, non-Hispanic/Latino; 12 Hispanic/Latino; 1 Native Hawaiian or other Pacific Islander, non-Hispanic/Latino; 17 Two or more races, non-Hispanic/Latino), 47 international. Average age 33. 203 applicants, 70% accepted, 136 enrolled. In 2017, 172 master's awarded. *Degree requirements:* For master's, thesis (for some programs). *Entrance requirements:* For master's, official transcripts from regionally-accredited institution stating the conferral of a bachelor's degree with minimum cumulative GPA of 3.0; personal statement; professional resume. Additional exam requirements/recommendations for international students: Recommended—TOEFL (minimum score 547 paper-based; 78 iBT), IELTS (minimum score 6). *Application deadline:* For fall admission, 8/1 for domestic and international students; for spring admission, 12/1 for domestic and international students; for summer admission, 5/1 for domestic and international students. Applications are processed on a rolling basis. Application fee: $0. Electronic applications accepted. *Expenses:* $625 per credit (for MBA); $475 per credit (for MA). *Financial support:* In 2017–18, 292 students received support. Scholarships/grants and unspecified assistantships available. Financial award applicants required to submit FAFSA. *Faculty research:* Alternative dispute resolution, franchising, entrepreneurship, applied business ethics, strategic leadership development. *Unit head:* Dr. Kevin Hall, Dean, 651-603-6165, Fax: 651-641-8807, E-mail: khall@csp.edu. *Application contact:* Amber Faletti, Director of Enrollment Management, 651-641-8838, Fax: 651-603-6320, E-mail: faletti@csp.edu.

Concordia University Wisconsin, Graduate Programs, School of Business Administration, MBA Program, Mequon, WI 53097-2402. Offers finance (MBA); health care administration (MBA); human resource management (MBA); international business (MBA); international business-bilingual English/Chinese (MBA); management (MBA); management information systems (MBA); managerial communications (MBA); marketing (MBA); public administration (MBA); risk management (MBA). *Program availability:* Online learning. *Degree requirements:* For master's, comprehensive exam, thesis or alternative. *Entrance requirements:* Additional exam requirements/recommendations for international students: Required—TOEFL. *Expenses:* Contact institution.

Copenhagen Business School, Graduate Programs, Copenhagen, Denmark. Offers business administration (Exec MBA, MBA, PhD); business administration and information systems (M Sc); business, language and culture (M Sc); economics and business administration (M Sc); health management (MHM); international business and politics (M Sc); public administration (MPA); shipping and logistics (Exec MBA); technology, market and organization (MBA).

Cornell University, Graduate School, Graduate Fields of Human Ecology, Field of Policy Analysis and Management, Ithaca, NY 14853. Offers consumer policy (PhD); family and social welfare policy (PhD); health administration (MHA); health management and policy (PhD); public policy (PhD). *Degree requirements:* For master's, thesis; for doctorate, thesis/dissertation. *Entrance requirements:* For master's, GRE General Test or GMAT, 2 letters of recommendation; for doctorate, GRE General Test, 2 letters of recommendation. Additional exam requirements/recommendations for international students: Required—TOEFL (minimum score 550 paper-based; 77 iBT). Electronic applications accepted. *Faculty research:* Health policy, family policy, social welfare policy, program evaluation, consumer policy.

Creighton University, Graduate School, Department of Interdisciplinary Studies, Master of Healthcare Management Program, Omaha, NE 68178-0001. Offers MHM. *Program availability:* Part-time. *Faculty:* 2 full-time (1 woman). *Students:* 5 full-time (4 women), 1 part-time (0 women); includes 1 minority (Asian, non-Hispanic/Latino). Average age 39. 9 applicants, 78% accepted, 6 enrolled. *Degree requirements:* For master's, practicum. *Entrance requirements:* For master's, resume; statement of purpose. Additional exam requirements/recommendations for international students: Required—TOEFL (minimum score 90 iBT), IELTS (minimum score 6.5). *Application deadline:* For fall admission, 7/1 for domestic and international students; for spring admission, 12/1 for domestic and international students. Application fee: $50. Electronic applications accepted. *Expenses:* $980 per credit hour. *Financial support:* Scholarships/grants available. Financial award applicants required to submit FAFSA. *Unit head:* Dr. Tanya Benedict, Director, 402-280-2646, E-mail: tjm19083@creighton.edu. *Application contact:* Lindsay Johnson, Director of Graduate and Adult Recruitment, 402-280-2703, Fax: 402-280-2423, E-mail: gradschool@creighton.edu.
Website: https://gradschool.creighton.edu/program/healthcare-management-mhm

Daemen College, Program in Executive Leadership and Change, Amherst, NY 14226-3592. Offers business (MS); health professions (MS); not-for-profit organizations (MS). *Program availability:* Part-time, evening/weekend. *Degree requirements:* For master's, thesis, cohort learning sequence (2 years for weekend cohort; 3 years for weeknight cohort). *Entrance requirements:* For master's, 2 letters of recommendation, interview, goal statement, official transcripts, resume. Additional exam requirements/recommendations for international students: Required—TOEFL (minimum score 500 paper-based; 63 iBT), IELTS (minimum score 5.5). Electronic applications accepted.

Dalhousie University, Faculty of Health Professions, School of Health Administration, Halifax, NS B3H 1R2, Canada. Offers MAHSR, MHA, MPH, PhD, LL B/MHA, MBA/MHA, MHA/MN. *Accreditation:* CAHME. *Program availability:* Part-time, online learning. *Entrance requirements:* For master's, GMAT. Additional exam requirements/recommendations for international students: Required—TOEFL, IELTS, CANTEST, CAEL, or Michigan English Language Assessment Battery. Electronic applications accepted. *Expenses:* Contact institution. *Faculty research:* Hospital, nursing, long-term, public, and community health administration; government administration in health areas.

Dallas Baptist University, College of Business, Management Program, Dallas, TX 75211-9299. Offers conflict resolution management (MA); general management (MA, MS); health care management (MA); human resource management (MA); organizational communication (MA); performance management (MA); professional sales and management optimization (MA). *Program availability:* Part-time, evening/weekend, online learning. *Application deadline:* Applications are processed on a rolling basis. Application fee: $25. Electronic applications accepted. Application fee is waived when completed online. *Expenses: Tuition:* Full-time $16,308; part-time $906 per credit hour. *Required fees:* $900; $450 per semester. Tuition and fees vary according to course load and degree level. *Unit head:* Dr. Sandra Reid, Chair, Graduate School of Business, 214-333-6860, E-mail: sandra@dbu.edu. *Application contact:* Richard Nassar, Director, 214-333-6801, E-mail: richardn@dbu.edu.
Website: http://www.dbu.edu/gsb/ma-in-management

Dallas Baptist University, College of Business, Master of Business Administration Program, Dallas, TX 75211-9299. Offers accounting (MBA); business communication (MBA); conflict resolution management (MBA); entrepreneurship (MBA); finance (MBA); health care management (MBA); international business (MBA); leading the non-profit organization (MBA); management (MBA); management information systems (MBA); marketing (MBA); project management (MBA); technology and engineering management (MBA). *Accreditation:* ACBSP. *Program availability:* Part-time, evening/weekend, 100% online, blended/hybrid learning. *Application deadline:* Applications are processed on a rolling basis. Application fee: $25. Electronic applications accepted. Application fee is waived when completed online. *Expenses: Tuition:* Full-time $16,308; part-time $906 per credit hour. *Required fees:* $900; $450 per semester. Tuition and fees vary according to course load and degree level. *Unit head:* Dr. Sandra Reid, Chair of Graduate Business Programs, 214-333-5280, E-mail: sandra@dbu.edu. *Application contact:* Bobby Soto, Director of Admissions, 214-333-5242, E-mail: graduate@dbu.edu.
Website: http://www.dbu.edu/gsb/mba

Dartmouth College, The Dartmouth Institute, Program in Health Policy and Clinical Practice, Hanover, NH 03755. Offers evaluative clinical sciences (MS, PhD). *Program availability:* Part-time. *Students:* 13 full-time (6 women), 10 part-time (5 women), 1 international. Average age 30. 24 applicants, 17% accepted. In 2017, 8 master's, 1 doctorate awarded. *Degree requirements:* For master's, research project or practicum; for doctorate, thesis/dissertation. *Entrance requirements:* For master's and doctorate, GRE or MCAT, 3 letters of recommendation. Additional exam requirements/recommendations for international students: Required—TOEFL. *Application deadline:* For fall admission, 1/15 for domestic students. Applications are processed on a rolling basis. Application fee: $135. *Financial support:* Fellowships with tuition reimbursements, research assistantships, teaching assistantships with tuition reimbursements, institutionally sponsored loans, and scholarships/grants available. Financial award application deadline: 6/1; financial award applicants required to submit FAFSA. *Faculty research:* Prevention and treatment of cardiovascular diseases, health care cost containment, variation of delivery of care, health care improvement, decision evaluation. *Unit head:* Dr. Elliot S. Fisher, Director, 603-653-0802. *Application contact:* Marc Aquila, Senior Director of Recruitment and Admissions, 603-650-1539.
Website: http://tdi.dartmouth.edu/

Davenport University, Sneden Graduate School, Grand Rapids, MI 49512. Offers accounting (MBA); business administration (EMBA); finance (MBA); health care management (MBA); human resources (MBA); information assurance (MS); public health (MPH); strategic management (MBA). *Program availability:* Evening/weekend. *Entrance requirements:* For master's, GMAT, minimum undergraduate GPA of 2.75. Additional exam requirements/recommendations for international students: Required—TOEFL. Electronic applications accepted. *Faculty research:* Leadership, management, marketing, organizational culture.

Delta State University, Graduate Programs, Robert E. Smith School of Nursing, Cleveland, MS 38733. Offers family nurse practitioner (MSN); nurse administrator (MSN); nurse educator (MSN). *Accreditation:* AACN. *Program availability:* Part-time. *Degree requirements:* For master's, thesis optional. *Entrance requirements:* For master's, GRE General Test. Electronic applications accepted.

DeSales University, Division of Business, Center Valley, PA 18034-9568. Offers accounting (MBA); computer information systems (MBA); finance (MBA); health care systems management (MBA); human resources management (MBA); management (MBA); marketing (MBA); project management (MBA); self-design (MBA); supply chain management (MBA); DNP/MBA; MSN/MBA. *Accreditation:* ACBSP. *Program availability:* Part-time, evening/weekend, 100% online, blended/hybrid learning. *Faculty:* 9 full-time (3 women), 32 part-time/adjunct (8 women). *Students:* 78 full-time (44 women), 323 part-time (164 women); includes 71 minority (22 Black or African American, non-Hispanic/Latino; 17 Asian, non-Hispanic/Latino; 24 Hispanic/Latino; 8 Two or more races, non-Hispanic/Latino), 1 international. Average age 34. 213 applicants, 40% accepted, 64 enrolled. In 2017, 123 master's awarded. *Entrance requirements:* For master's, GMAT (waived if undergraduate GPA is 3.0 or better), minimum GPA of 3.0 in undergraduate work, literacy in basic software, background or interest in the field of study, personal statement, 2 years of work experience. Additional exam requirements/recommendations for international students: Required—TOEFL. *Application deadline:* Applications are processed on a rolling basis. Application fee: $50. Electronic applications accepted. *Expenses:* Contact institution. *Financial support:* Applicants required to submit FAFSA. *Faculty research:* Quality improvement, executive development, productivity, cross-cultural managerial differences, leadership. *Unit head:* Dr. David M. Gilfoil, Director, MBA Program, 610-282-1100 Ext. 1828, Fax: 610-282-2869, E-mail: david.gilfoil@desales.edu. *Application contact:* Julia Ferraro, Director of Graduate Admissions, 610-282-1100 Ext. 1768, E-mail: gradadmissions@desales.edu.

Des Moines University, College of Health Sciences, Program in Healthcare Administration, Des Moines, IA 50312-4104. Offers MHA. *Accreditation:* CAHME. *Program availability:* Part-time, evening/weekend. *Entrance requirements:* For master's, minimum GPA of 3.0. Additional exam requirements/recommendations for international students: Required—TOEFL (minimum score 600 paper-based). Electronic applications accepted. *Expenses:* Contact institution. *Faculty research:* Quality improvement, rural sociology, women's health, health promotion, patient education.

Dominican College, MBA Program, Orangeburg, NY 10962-1210. Offers accounting (MBA); healthcare management (MBA); management (MBA). *Program availability:* Part-time, evening/weekend. *Faculty:* 1 full-time (0 women). *Students:* 1 (woman) full-time, 21 part-time (15 women); includes 11 minority (6 Black or African American, non-Hispanic/Latino; 1 Asian, non-Hispanic/Latino; 3 Hispanic/Latino; 1 Two or more races, non-Hispanic/Latino), 1 international. In 2017, 14 master's awarded. *Entrance requirements:* For master's, GMAT, 2 letters of recommendation. Additional exam requirements/recommendations for international students: Required—TOEFL (minimum score 550 paper-based; 90 iBT). *Application deadline:* Applications are processed on a rolling basis. Application fee: $50. Electronic applications accepted. *Expenses:* Contact institution. *Financial support:* Application deadline: 2/1; applicants required to submit FAFSA. *Unit head:* Ken Mias, MBA Director, 845-848-4102, E-mail: ken.mias@dc.edu. *Application contact:* Christina Lifshey, Assistant Director of Graduate Admissions, 845-848-7908, Fax: 845-365-3150, E-mail: admissions@dc.edu.

Drew University, Caspersen School of Graduate Studies, Madison, NJ 07940-1493. Offers conflict resolution and leadership (Certificate), including community leadership, moderation, peace building; education (M Ed); finance (MA); history and culture (MA, PhD), including American history, book history, British history, European history, Holocaust and genocide (M Litt, MA, D Litt, PhD), intellectual history, Irish history, print culture, public history; K-12 education (MAT), including art, biology, chemistry, elementary education, English, French, Italian, math, secondary education, special education, teacher of students with disabilities; liberal studies (M Litt, D Litt), including history, Holocaust and genocide (M Litt, MA, D Litt, PhD), Irish/Irish-American studies, literature (M Litt, MMH, D Litt, DMH, CMH), religion, spirituality, teaching in the two-year college, writing; medical humanities (MMH, DMH, CMH), including arts, health, healthcare, literature (M Litt, MMH, D Litt, DMH, CMH), scientific research; poetry (MFA). *Program availability:* Part-time, evening/weekend. *Faculty:* 4 full-time (2 women),

29 part-time/adjunct (15 women). *Students:* 77 full-time (42 women), 175 part-time (114 women); includes 39 minority (12 Black or African American, non-Hispanic/Latino; 6 Asian, non-Hispanic/Latino; 16 Hispanic/Latino; 5 Two or more races, non-Hispanic/Latino), 11 international. Average age 41. 126 applicants, 75% accepted, 52 enrolled. In 2017, 38 master's, 23 doctorates, 35 other advanced degrees awarded. Terminal master's awarded for partial completion of doctoral program. *Degree requirements:* For master's and other advanced degree, thesis (for some programs); for doctorate, one foreign language, comprehensive exam (for some programs), thesis/dissertation. *Entrance requirements:* For master's, PRAXIS Core and Subject Area tests (for MAT), GRE/GMAT (for M Fin), resume, transcripts, writing sample, personal statement, letters of recommendation; for doctorate, GRE (PhD in history and culture), resume, transcripts, writing sample, personal statement, letters of recommendation; for other advanced degree, resume, transcripts, personal statement. Additional exam requirements/recommendations for international students: Required—TOEFL (minimum score 587 paper-based; 80 iBT), IELTS (minimum score 6), TWE (minimum score 4). *Application deadline:* For fall admission, 8/1 for domestic students, 6/1 for international students; for spring admission, 12/1 for domestic students, 10/1 for international students. Applications are processed on a rolling basis. Application fee: $35. Electronic applications accepted. *Financial support:* Fellowships, research assistantships, teaching assistantships, career-related internships or fieldwork, Federal Work-Study, scholarships/grants, and unspecified assistantships available. Support available to part-time students. Financial award applicants required to submit FAFSA. *Faculty research:* Irish history and culture, conflict resolution and leadership. *Application contact:* Leanne Horinko, Director of Caspersen Admissions, 973-408-3280, E-mail: gradm@drew.edu.
Website: http://www.drew.edu/caspersen

Duke University, The Fuqua School of Business, The Duke MBA-Daytime Program, Durham, NC 27708-0586. Offers academic excellence in finance (Certificate); business administration (MBA); decision sciences (MBA); energy and environment (MBA); energy finance (MBA); entrepreneurship and innovation (MBA); finance (MBA); financial analysis (MBA); health sector management (Certificate); leadership and ethics (MBA); management (MBA); management science and technology management (Certificate); marketing (MBA); operations management (MBA); social entrepreneurship (MBA); strategy (MBA). *Faculty:* 96 full-time (19 women), 48 part-time/adjunct (15 women). *Students:* 876 full-time (297 women); includes 180 minority (39 Black or African American, non-Hispanic/Latino; 2 American Indian or Alaska Native, non-Hispanic/Latino; 83 Asian, non-Hispanic/Latino; 50 Hispanic/Latino; 6 Two or more races, non-Hispanic/Latino), 321 international. Average age 29. In 2017, 445 master's awarded. *Entrance requirements:* For master's, GMAT or GRE, transcripts, essays, resume, recommendation letters, interview. *Application deadline:* For fall admission, 9/12 for domestic and international students; for winter admission, 10/10 for domestic and international students; for spring admission, 1/3 for domestic and international students; for summer admission, 3/20 for domestic and international students. Application fee: $225. Electronic applications accepted. *Expenses:* $69,342 first-year tuition and fees. *Financial support:* In 2017–18, 423 students received support. Scholarships/grants available. Financial award applicants required to submit FAFSA. *Unit head:* Steve Misuraca, Assistant Dean, Daytime MBA Program. *Application contact:* Shari Hubert, Associate Dean, Office of Admissions, 919-660-7705, Fax: 919-681-8026, E-mail: admissions-info@fuqua.duke.edu.
Website: https://www.fuqua.duke.edu/programs/daytime-mba

Duke University, The Fuqua School of Business, The Duke MBA-Global Executive Program, Durham, NC 27708-0586. Offers business administration (MBA); energy and environment (MBA); entrepreneurship and innovation (MBA); finance (MBA); health sector management (Certificate); marketing (MBA); strategy (MBA). *Faculty:* 96 full-time (19 women), 48 part-time/adjunct (15 women). *Students:* 94 full-time (26 women); includes 34 minority (8 Black or African American, non-Hispanic/Latino; 21 Asian, non-Hispanic/Latino; 4 Hispanic/Latino; 1 Two or more races, non-Hispanic/Latino), 25 international. Average age 39. In 2017, 27 master's awarded. *Entrance requirements:* For master's, Executive Assessment, GMAT, or GRE, transcripts, essays, resume, recommendation letters, letter of company support, interview. *Application deadline:* For fall admission, 10/12 priority date for domestic and international students; for winter admission, 12/7 priority date for domestic and international students; for spring admission, 3/20 priority date for domestic and international students; for summer admission, 5/31 for domestic and international students. Applications are processed on a rolling basis. Application fee: $225. Electronic applications accepted. *Expenses:* Contact institution. *Financial support:* In 2017–18, 31 students received support. Scholarships/grants available. Financial award applicants required to submit FAFSA. *Unit head:* Karen Courtney, Associate Dean, Executive Programs. *Application contact:* Shari Hubert, Associate Dean, Office of Admissions, 919-660-7705, Fax: 919-681-8026, E-mail: admissions-info@fuqua.duke.edu.
Website: https://www.fuqua.duke.edu/programs/global-executive-mba

Duke University, The Fuqua School of Business, The Duke MBA-Weekend Executive Program, Durham, NC 27708-0586. Offers business administration (MBA); energy and environment (MBA); entrepreneurship and innovation (MBA); finance (MBA); health sector management (Certificate); marketing (MBA); strategy (MBA). *Faculty:* 96 full-time (19 women), 48 part-time/adjunct (15 women). *Students:* 219 full-time (59 women); includes 80 minority (13 Black or African American, non-Hispanic/Latino; 3 American Indian or Alaska Native, non-Hispanic/Latino; 45 Asian, non-Hispanic/Latino; 13 Hispanic/Latino; 6 Two or more races, non-Hispanic/Latino), 32 international. Average age 35. In 2017, 92 master's awarded. *Entrance requirements:* For master's, Executive Assessment, GMAT or GRE, transcripts, essays, resume, recommendation letters, letter of company support, interview. *Application deadline:* For fall admission, 10/12 priority date for domestic and international students; for winter admission, 12/7 priority date for domestic and international students; for spring admission, 2/7 priority date for domestic and international students; for summer admission, 3/20 for domestic and international students. Applications are processed on a rolling basis. Application fee: $225. Electronic applications accepted. *Expenses:* Contact institution. *Financial support:* In 2017–18, 44 students received support. Scholarships/grants available. Financial award applicants required to submit FAFSA. *Unit head:* Karen Courtney, Associate Dean, Executive Programs. *Application contact:* Shari Hubert, Associate Dean, Office of Admissions, 919-660-7705, Fax: 919-681-8026, E-mail: admissions-info@fuqua.duke.edu.
Website: https://www.fuqua.duke.edu/programs/weekend-executive-mba

Duquesne University, John G. Rangos, Sr. School of Health Sciences, Pittsburgh, PA 15282-0001. Offers health management systems (MHMS); occupational therapy (MS, OTD); physical therapy (DPT); physician assistant studies (MPAS); rehabilitation science (MS, PhD); speech-language pathology (MS). *Accreditation:* AOTA (one or more programs are accredited); APTA (one or more programs are accredited); ASHA. *Program availability:* Part-time, minimal on-campus study. *Faculty:* 51 full-time (38 women), 33 part-time/adjunct (17 women). *Students:* 247 full-time (199 women), 11 part-time (7 women); includes 15 minority (2 Black or African American, non-Hispanic/Latino; 7 Asian, non-Hispanic/Latino; 3 Hispanic/Latino; 3 Two or more races, non-Hispanic/Latino), 42 international. Average age 23. 283 applicants, 31% accepted, 54 enrolled. In 2017, 134 master's, 39 doctorates awarded. *Degree requirements:* For doctorate, comprehensive exam (for some programs), thesis/dissertation (for some programs). *Entrance requirements:* For master's, GRE General Test (speech-language pathology), 3 letters of recommendation; minimum GPA of 2.75 (health management systems), 3.0 (speech-language pathology); for doctorate, GRE General Test (for physical therapy and rehabilitation science), 3 letters of recommendation, minimum GPA of 3.0, personal interview. Additional exam requirements/recommendations for international students: Required—TOEFL (minimum score 550 paper-based; 90 iBT); Recommended—IELTS. *Application deadline:* For fall admission, 2/1 for domestic and international students; for spring admission, 7/1 for domestic and international students. Applications are processed on a rolling basis. Application fee: $0. Electronic applications accepted. *Expenses:* $1,351 per credit ($1,259 for health management systems). *Financial support:* Federal Work-Study available. Financial award applicants required to submit FAFSA. *Faculty research:* Neuronal processing, electrical stimulation on peripheral neuropathy, central nervous system (CNS) stimulatory and inhibitory signals, behavioral genetic methodologies to development disorders of speech, neurogenic communication disorders. *Total annual research expenditures:* $24,578. *Unit head:* Dr. Fevzi Akinci, Dean, 412-396-5303, Fax: 412-396-5554, E-mail: akincif@duq.edu. *Application contact:* Christopher R. Hilf, Director of Enrollment Management, 412-396-5653, Fax: 412-396-5554, E-mail: hilfc@duq.edu.
Website: http://www.duq.edu/academics/schools/health-sciences

D'Youville College, Department of Health Services Administration, Buffalo, NY 14201-1084. Offers clinical research associate (Certificate); health administration (Ed D); health services administration (MS, Certificate); long term care administration (Certificate). *Program availability:* Part-time, evening/weekend. *Degree requirements:* For master's, project or thesis. *Entrance requirements:* For master's, minimum GPA of 3.0 in major. Additional exam requirements/recommendations for international students: Required—TOEFL (minimum score 500 paper-based). Electronic applications accepted. *Faculty research:* Outcomes research in rehabilitation medicine, cost/benefit analysis of prospective payment systems.

East Carolina University, Graduate School, College of Allied Health Sciences, Department of Health Services and Information Management, Greenville, NC 27858-4353. Offers health care administration (Certificate); health care management (Certificate); health informatics (Certificate); health informatics and information management (MS); health information management (Certificate). *Program availability:* Part-time, evening/weekend, online learning. *Students:* 14 full-time (all women), 72 part-time (57 women); includes 39 minority (28 Black or African American, non-Hispanic/Latino; 5 Asian, non-Hispanic/Latino; 2 Hispanic/Latino; 2 Native Hawaiian or other Pacific Islander, non-Hispanic/Latino; 2 Two or more races, non-Hispanic/Latino). Average age 36. 13 applicants, 85% accepted, 10 enrolled. In 2017, 8 master's, 31 other advanced degrees awarded. *Degree requirements:* For master's, comprehensive exam, thesis optional. *Entrance requirements:* For master's, GRE General Test or GMAT. Additional exam requirements/recommendations for international students: Recommended—TOEFL, IELTS. *Application deadline:* For fall admission, 5/1 priority date for domestic students; for spring admission, 10/15 priority date for domestic students. Applications are processed on a rolling basis. Application fee: $75. Electronic applications accepted. *Expenses:* Tuition, state resident: full-time $4749; part-time $297 per credit hour. Tuition, nonresident: full-time $17,898; part-time $1119 per credit hour. *Required fees:* $2691; $224 per credit hour. Part-time tuition and fees vary according to course load and program. *Unit head:* Dr. Xiaoming Zeng, Chair, 252-744-6176, E-mail: zengx@ecu.edu.
Website: http://www.ecu.edu/cs-dhs/hsim/

Eastern Kentucky University, The Graduate School, College of Arts and Sciences, Department of Government, Program in General Public Administration, Richmond, KY 40475-3102. Offers community development (MPA); community health administration (MPA); general public administration (MPA). *Accreditation:* NASPAA. *Program availability:* Part-time, evening/weekend. *Entrance requirements:* For master's, GRE General Test, minimum GPA of 2.5.

Eastern Mennonite University, Program in Business Administration, Harrisonburg, VA 22802-2462. Offers general management (MBA); health services administration (MBA); non-profit leadership (MBA). *Program availability:* Part-time, evening/weekend. *Degree requirements:* For master's, final capstone course. *Entrance requirements:* For master's, GMAT, minimum GPA of 2.5, 2 years of work experience, 2 letters of reference. Additional exam requirements/recommendations for international students: Required—TOEFL (minimum score 500 paper-based). *Application deadline:* For fall admission, 3/1 priority date for domestic and international students. Applications are processed on a rolling basis. Application fee: $25. Electronic applications accepted. *Expenses:* Contact institution. *Financial support:* Application deadline: 6/30; applicants required to submit FAFSA. *Faculty research:* Information security, Anabaptist/Mennonite experiences and perspectives, limits of multi-cultural education, international development performance criteria. *Unit head:* Dr. James M. Leaman, Department Chair, 540-432-4152, Fax: 540-432-4071, E-mail: james.leaman@emu.edu. *Application contact:* Patricia S. Eckard, Administrative Coordinator, 540-432-4150, Fax: 540-432-4071, E-mail: eckardp@emu.edu.
Website: http://www.emu.edu/mba/

Eastern Michigan University, Graduate School, College of Arts and Sciences, Department of Political Science, Programs in Public Administration, Ypsilanti, MI 48197. Offers general public management (Graduate Certificate); local government management (Graduate Certificate); management of public healthcare services (Graduate Certificate); nonprofit management (Graduate Certificate); public administration (MPA); public budget management (Graduate Certificate); public land planning and development management (Graduate Certificate); public personnel management (Graduate Certificate); public policy analysis (Graduate Certificate). *Accreditation:* NASPAA. *Students:* 11 full-time (6 women), 41 part-time (19 women); includes 18 minority (13 Black or African American, non-Hispanic/Latino; 1 Hispanic/Latino; 4 Two or more races, non-Hispanic/Latino). Average age 34. 42 applicants, 79% accepted, 14 enrolled. In 2017, 23 master's, 4 other advanced degrees awarded. Application fee: $45. *Application contact:* Dr. Jeffrey L. Bernstein, Program Advisor, 734-487-6970, Fax: 734-487-3340, E-mail: jeffrey.bernstein@emich.edu.
Website: http://www.emich.edu/polisci/

Eastern Michigan University, Graduate School, College of Health and Human Services, Interdisciplinary Program in Health and Human Services, Ypsilanti, MI 48197. Offers Graduate Certificate. *Program availability:* Part-time, evening/weekend. In 2017, 2 Graduate Certificates awarded. *Entrance requirements:* Additional exam requirements/recommendations for international students: Required—TOEFL. Application fee: $45. *Unit head:* Dr. Marcia Bombyk, Program Coordinator, 734-487-0393, Fax: 734-487-8536, E-mail: mbombyk@emich.edu. *Application contact:* Graduate Admissions, 734-487-2400, Fax: 734-487-6559, E-mail: graduate.admissions@emich.edu.

Eastern Michigan University, Graduate School, College of Health and Human Services, School of Health Sciences, Programs in Health Administration, Ypsilanti, MI 48197. Offers MHA, MS, Graduate Certificate. *Students:* 5 full-time (3 women), 31 part-time (26 women); includes 11 minority (4 Black or African American, non-Hispanic/Latino; 5 Asian, non-Hispanic/Latino; 2 Hispanic/Latino), 1 international. Average age 46. 39 applicants, 59% accepted, 9 enrolled. In 2017, 19 master's, 4 other advanced degrees awarded. Application fee: $45. *Application contact:* Dr. Colleen Croxall, Program Director, 734-487-4096, Fax: 734-487-4095, E-mail: ccroxall@emich.edu.

Eastern University, Graduate Programs in Business and Leadership, St. Davids, PA 19087-3696. Offers health administration (MBA); health services management (MS); management (MBA); organizational leadership (MA); social impact (MBA). *Program availability:* Part-time, evening/weekend, online learning. *Students:* 55 full-time (34 women), 195 part-time (126 women); includes 123 minority (93 Black or African American, non-Hispanic/Latino; 1 American Indian or Alaska Native, non-Hispanic/Latino; 12 Asian, non-Hispanic/Latino; 12 Hispanic/Latino; 5 Two or more races, non-Hispanic/Latino), 23 international. Average age 34. In 2017, 123 master's awarded. *Application deadline:* Applications are processed on a rolling basis. Application fee: $35. Electronic applications accepted. Application fee is waived when completed online. *Expenses:* Contact institution. *Financial support:* Applicants required to submit FAFSA. *Unit head:* Michael Dziedziak, Executive Director of Enrollment, 800-452-0996, E-mail: gpsadmissions@eastern.edu.
Website: https://www.eastern.edu/academics/programs/graduate-business

East Tennessee State University, School of Graduate Studies, College of Business and Technology, Department of Management and Marketing, Johnson City, TN 37614. Offers business administration (MBA, Postbaccalaureate Certificate); digital marketing (MS); entrepreneurial leadership (Postbaccalaureate Certificate); health care management (Postbaccalaureate Certificate). *Program availability:* Part-time, evening/weekend. *Degree requirements:* For master's, comprehensive exam, capstone. *Entrance requirements:* For master's, GMAT, minimum GPA of 2.5 (for MBA), 3.0 (for MS); current resume; three letters of recommendation; for Postbaccalaureate Certificate, minimum GPA of 2.5, undergraduate degree. Additional exam requirements/recommendations for international students: Required—TOEFL (minimum score 550 paper-based; 79 iBT). *Application deadline:* For fall admission, 6/1 for domestic students, 4/29 for international students; for spring admission, 11/1 for domestic students, 9/29 for international students. Application fee: $55 ($65 for international students). Electronic applications accepted. *Financial support:* Research assistantships with full tuition reimbursements, teaching assistantships with full tuition reimbursements, career-related internships or fieldwork, institutionally sponsored loans, scholarships/grants, and unspecified assistantships available. Financial award application deadline: 7/1; financial award applicants required to submit FAFSA. *Faculty research:* Sustainability, healthcare effectiveness, consumer behavior, merchandising trends, organizational management issues. *Unit head:* Charles Gorman, Chair, 423-439-4433, Fax: 423-439-5661, E-mail: gormanc@etsu.edu. *Application contact:* Charles Gorman, Chair, 423-439-4433, Fax: 423-439-5661, E-mail: gormanc@etsu.edu.
Website: http://www.etsu.edu/chat/mgmtmkt/

East Tennessee State University, School of Graduate Studies, College of Public Health, Program in Public Health, Johnson City, TN 37614. Offers biostatistics (MPH, Postbaccalaureate Certificate); community health (MPH, DPH); environmental health (MPH); epidemiology (MPH, DPH, Postbaccalaureate Certificate); gerontology (Postbaccalaureate Certificate); global health (Postbaccalaureate Certificate); health care management (Postbaccalaureate Certificate); health management and policy (DPH); public health (Postbaccalaureate Certificate); public health services administration (MPH); rural health (Postbaccalaureate Certificate). *Accreditation:* CEPH. *Program availability:* Part-time, online learning. *Degree requirements:* For master's, comprehensive exam, field experience; for doctorate, thesis/dissertation, practicum. *Entrance requirements:* For master's, GRE General Test, minimum GPA of 2.75, SOPHAS application, three letters of recommendation; for doctorate, GRE General Test, SOPHAS application, three letters of recommendation; for Postbaccalaureate Certificate, minimum GPA of 2.5, three letters of recommendation, resume. Additional exam requirements/recommendations for international students: Required—TOEFL (minimum score 550 paper-based; 79 iBT), IELTS (minimum score 6.5). *Application deadline:* For fall admission, 3/1 for domestic and international students. Application fee: $35 ($45 for international students). Electronic applications accepted. *Financial support:* Research assistantships with tuition reimbursements, teaching assistantships with full tuition reimbursements, career-related internships or fieldwork, institutionally sponsored loans, scholarships/grants, and unspecified assistantships available. Financial award application deadline: 7/1; financial award applicants required to submit FAFSA. *Unit head:* Dr. Randy Wykoff, Dean, 423-439-4243, Fax: 423-439-5238, E-mail: wykoff@etsu.edu. *Application contact:* Dr. Randy Wykoff, Dean, 423-439-4243, Fax: 423-439-5238, E-mail: wykoff@etsu.edu.
Website: http://www.etsu.edu/cph/

Elmhurst College, Graduate Programs, Program in Health Care Management and Administration, Elmhurst, IL 60126-3296. Offers MHCA. *Program availability:* Part-time, evening/weekend, online learning. *Faculty:* 2 full-time (1 woman), 1 part-time/adjunct (0 women). *Students:* 2 part-time (both women). Average age 26. *Entrance requirements:* For master's, undergraduate degree, undergraduate or graduate statistics course, at least two years of professional or military experience. Additional exam requirements/recommendations for international students: Required—TOEFL (minimum score 550 paper-based; 79 iBT). *Application deadline:* Applications are processed on a rolling basis. Application fee: $0. Electronic applications accepted. *Expenses:* Contact institution. *Financial support:* In 2017–18, 2 students received support. Scholarships/grants available. Support available to part-time students. Financial award application deadline: 3/1; financial award applicants required to submit FAFSA. *Unit head:* Richard Pabst, Director, E-mail: richard.pabst@elmhurst.edu. *Application contact:* Timothy J. Panfil, Director of Enrollment Management, 630-617-3300 Ext. 3256, Fax: 630-617-6471, E-mail: panfilt@elmhurst.edu.

Elms College, Division of Business, Chicopee, MA 01013-2839. Offers accounting (MBA); accounting and finance (MS); financial planning (MBA, Certificate); healthcare leadership (MBA); lean entrepreneurship (MBA); management (MBA). *Program availability:* Part-time, evening/weekend. *Faculty:* 5 full-time (all women), 7 part-time/adjunct (4 women). *Students:* 51 part-time (30 women); includes 9 minority (4 Black or African American, non-Hispanic/Latino; 2 Asian, non-Hispanic/Latino; 3 Hispanic/Latino), 2 international. Average age 33. 14 applicants, 93% accepted, 10 enrolled. In 2017, 28 master's awarded. *Entrance requirements:* For master's, minimum GPA of 3.0. *Application deadline:* Applications are processed on a rolling basis. Application fee: $30. Electronic applications accepted. *Expenses: Tuition:* Full-time $13,860; part-time $770 per credit hour. *Required fees:* $200. Tuition and fees vary according to degree level and program. *Unit head:* Dr. David Kimball, Chair, Division of Business, 413-265-2300, E-mail: kimballd@elms.edu. *Application contact:* MBA Program Coordinator, 413-265-2592, E-mail: mba@elms.edu.

Emory University, Rollins School of Public Health, Department of Health Policy and Management, Atlanta, GA 30322-1100. Offers health policy (MPH); health policy research (MSPH); health services management (MPH); health services research and health policy (PhD). *Program availability:* Part-time. *Degree requirements:* For master's, thesis (for some programs), practicum, capstone course. *Entrance requirements:* For master's, GRE General Test. Additional exam requirements/recommendations for international students: Required—TOEFL (minimum score 550 paper-based; 80 iBT). Electronic applications accepted. *Faculty research:* U.S. health policy and financing, healthcare organization and financing.

Excelsior College, School of Business and Technology, Albany, NY 12203-5159. Offers business administration (MBA); cybersecurity - information assurance (MS); cybersecurity - medical data security (MS); cybersecurity - policy administration (MS); cybersecurity management (MBA, Graduate Certificate); general business management (MS); health care management (MBA); human performance technology (MBA); human resource management (MS); human resources management (MBA); leadership (MBA, MS); mediation and arbitration (MBA, MS); social media management (MBA); technology management (MBA). *Program availability:* Part-time, evening/weekend, online learning. *Faculty:* 30 part-time/adjunct (12 women). *Students:* 1,204 part-time (333 women); includes 560 minority (310 Black or African American, non-Hispanic/Latino; 7 American Indian or Alaska Native, non-Hispanic/Latino; 42 Asian, non-Hispanic/Latino; 140 Hispanic/Latino; 10 Native Hawaiian or other Pacific Islander, non-Hispanic/Latino; 51 Two or more races, non-Hispanic/Latino). Average age 40. In 2017, 294 master's awarded. *Application deadline:* Applications are processed on a rolling basis. Application fee: $50. Electronic applications accepted. *Expenses: Tuition:* Part-time $645 per credit. *Required fees:* $265 per credit. *Financial support:* Scholarships/grants available. *Unit head:* Dr. Lifang Shih, Dean, 888-647-2388. *Application contact:* Admissions, 888-647-2388 Ext. 133, Fax: 518-464-8777, E-mail: admissions@excelsior.edu.

Fairleigh Dickinson University, Florham Campus, Silberman College of Business, Executive MBA Programs, Executive MBA Program for Health Care and Life Sciences Professionals, Madison, NJ 07940-1099. Offers EMBA. *Expenses: Tuition:* Full-time $22,410; part-time $1245 per credit. *Required fees:* $888; $414 per unit. Tuition and fees vary according to course load, degree level and program.

Fairleigh Dickinson University, Metropolitan Campus, Silberman College of Business, Program in Healthcare and Life Sciences, Teaneck, NJ 07666-1914. Offers EMBA. *Expenses: Tuition:* Full-time $22,410; part-time $1245 per credit. *Required fees:* $888; $414 per unit. Tuition and fees vary according to course load, degree level and program.

Felician University, Program in Health Care Administration, Lodi, NJ 07644-2117. Offers MSHA. *Program availability:* Part-time, evening/weekend. *Faculty:* 1 full-time (0 women), 6 part-time/adjunct (2 women). *Students:* 9 full-time (8 women), 36 part-time (29 women); includes 30 minority (14 Black or African American, non-Hispanic/Latino; 5 Asian, non-Hispanic/Latino; 11 Hispanic/Latino), 2 international. Average age 33. 28 applicants, 93% accepted, 16 enrolled. In 2017, 6 master's awarded. Terminal master's awarded for partial completion of doctoral program. *Degree requirements:* For master's, thesis, scholarly project. *Entrance requirements:* For master's, GRE, resume, personal statement, graduation from accredited baccalaureate program. Additional exam requirements/recommendations for international students: Required—TOEFL (minimum score 550 paper-based; 79 iBT), IELTS (minimum score 6.5), PTE (minimum score 56). *Application deadline:* Applications are processed on a rolling basis. Application fee: $40. Electronic applications accepted. Application fee is waived when completed online. *Expenses:* Contact institution. *Financial support:* Federal Work-Study and scholarships/grants available. Financial award applicants required to submit FAFSA. *Faculty research:* Healthcare communications. *Unit head:* Dr. David M. Turi, Associate Dean/Associate Professor, School of Business, 201-559-3327, E-mail: turid@felician.edu. *Application contact:* Michael Szarek, Assistant Vice-President of Graduate Admissions, 201-355-1450, E-mail: szarekm@felician.edu.

Ferris State University, College of Health Professions, Program in Healthcare Administration, Big Rapids, MI 49307. Offers MHA. *Program availability:* Part-time, evening/weekend, online learning. *Faculty:* 4 full-time (3 women). *Students:* 20 full-time (all women), 11 part-time (8 women); includes 5 minority (1 Black or African American, non-Hispanic/Latino; 1 American Indian or Alaska Native, non-Hispanic/Latino; 1 Asian, non-Hispanic/Latino; 2 Two or more races, non-Hispanic/Latino). Average age 30. 25 applicants, 88% accepted, 20 enrolled. *Degree requirements:* For master's, 160-hour capstone project, program portfolio. *Entrance requirements:* Additional exam requirements/recommendations for international students: Required—TOEFL (minimum score 550 paper-based). *Application deadline:* For fall admission, 7/18 for domestic students; for spring admission, 12/8 for domestic students. Electronic applications accepted. *Financial support:* Application deadline: 4/15; applicants required to submit FAFSA. *Faculty research:* Rural healthcare; social media and healthcare delivery; health literacy. *Unit head:* Dr. Gail Bullard, Program Coordinator, 231-591-2279, E-mail: gailbullard@ferris.edu.
Website: https://ferris.edu/HTMLS/colleges/alliedhe/csrchca/MHA/homepage.htm

Florida Atlantic University, College of Business, Department of Management, Boca Raton, FL 33431-0991. Offers business administration (MBA); entrepreneurship (MBA); health administration (MBA); international business (MBA); sport management (MBA). *Faculty:* 4 full-time (1 woman). *Students:* 122 full-time (86 women), 81 part-time (67 women); includes 117 minority (61 Black or African American, non-Hispanic/Latino; 12 Asian, non-Hispanic/Latino; 44 Hispanic/Latino), 3 international. Average age 35. 124 applicants, 73% accepted, 75 enrolled. In 2017, 70 master's awarded. *Entrance requirements:* For master's, GMAT or GRE General Test, minimum GPA of 3.0 in last 60 hours of course work. Additional exam requirements/recommendations for international students: Required—TOEFL (minimum score 600 paper-based; 61 iBT), IELTS (minimum score 6). *Application deadline:* For fall admission, 7/25 for domestic students, 2/15 for international students; for spring admission, 12/10 for domestic students, 7/15 for international students. Applications are processed on a rolling basis. Application fee: $30. Electronic applications accepted. *Expenses:* Tuition, state resident: full-time $7400; part-time $369.82 per credit. Tuition, nonresident: full-time $20,496; part-time $1042.81 per credit. *Financial support:* Research assistantships with full tuition reimbursements, career-related internships or fieldwork, tuition waivers (partial), and unspecified assistantships available. *Faculty research:* Sports administration, healthcare, policy, finance, real estate, senior living. *Unit head:* Dr. Roland Kidwell, Chair, 561-297-5634, E-mail: kidwellr@fau.edu.
Website: http://business.fau.edu/departments/management/index.aspx

Florida Institute of Technology, Nathan M. Bisk College of Business, Program in Healthcare Management, Melbourne, FL 32901-6975. Offers MBA. *Program availability:* Part-time, evening/weekend. *Students:* Average age 30. 36 applicants, 53% accepted, 2 enrolled. In 2017, 46 master's awarded. *Entrance requirements:* For master's, GMAT, GRE General Test (recommended). Additional exam requirements/recommendations for international students: Required—TOEFL (minimum score 550 paper-based; 79 iBT). *Application deadline:* For fall admission, 4/1 for international students; for spring admission, 9/30 for international students. Applications are processed on a rolling basis. Electronic applications accepted. *Expenses: Tuition:* Part-time $1241 per credit hour. Part-time tuition and fees vary according to campus/location. *Financial support:* Career-related internships or fieldwork and tuition remissions available. Support available to part-time students. Financial award application deadline: 3/1; financial award applicants required to submit FAFSA. *Unit head:* Dr. S. Ann Becker, Dean, 321-674-7327, E-mail: abecker@fit.edu. *Application contact:* Cheryl A. Brown, Associate Director of Graduate Admissions, 321-674-7581, Fax: 321-723-9468, E-mail: cbrown@fit.edu.
Website: http://www.fit.edu/programs/8334/mba-healthcare-management#.VUI2Jk10ypo

Florida International University, Nicole Wertheim College of Nursing and Health Sciences, Department of Health Services Administration, Miami, FL 33199. Offers MHSA. *Program availability:* Part-time. *Faculty:* 9 full-time (5 women), 23 part-time/

adjunct (10 women). *Students:* 81 full-time (68 women), 1 (woman) part-time; includes 76 minority (23 Black or African American, non-Hispanic/Latino; 5 Asian, non-Hispanic/Latino; 43 Hispanic/Latino; 1 Native Hawaiian or other Pacific Islander, non-Hispanic/Latino; 4 Two or more races, non-Hispanic/Latino), 3 international. Average age 26. 94 applicants, 60% accepted, 42 enrolled. *Entrance requirements:* For master's, GRE General Test, minimum GPA of 3.0. Additional exam requirements/recommendations for international students: Required—TOEFL. *Application deadline:* For fall admission, 4/1 priority date for domestic students; for spring admission, 10/1 for domestic students. Applications are processed on a rolling basis. Application fee: $25. *Expenses:* Tuition, state resident: full-time $8912; part-time $446 per credit hour. Tuition, nonresident: full-time $21,393; part-time $992 per credit hour. *Required fees:* $390; $195 per semester. *Financial support:* In 2017–18, 1 fellowship, 1 research assistantship, 1 teaching assistantship were awarded; career-related internships or fieldwork, Federal Work-Study, and institutionally sponsored loans also available. *Faculty research:* International nutrition, parental nutrition, lactoferrin. *Unit head:* Prof. Salvatore Barbera, Interim Director, 305-348-7722, Fax: 305-348-6303, E-mail: sbarbera@fiu.edu. *Application contact:* Nanett Rojas, Manager, Admissions Operations, 305-348-7464, Fax: 305-348-7441, E-mail: gradadm@fiu.edu.
Website: http://cnhs.fiu.edu/hsa/

Florida International University, Robert Stempel College of Public Health and Social Work, Programs in Public Health, Miami, FL 33199. Offers biostatistics (MPH); environmental and occupational health (MPH, PhD); epidemiology (MPH, PhD); health policy and management (MPH); health promotion and disease prevention (MPH, PhD). PhD program has fall admissions only; MPH offered jointly with University of Miami. *Program availability:* Part-time, evening/weekend, online learning. *Faculty:* 34 full-time (18 women), 2 part-time/adjunct (both women). *Students:* 132 full-time (88 women), 63 part-time (49 women); includes 133 minority (50 Black or African American, non-Hispanic/Latino; 17 Asian, non-Hispanic/Latino; 60 Hispanic/Latino; 6 Two or more races, non-Hispanic/Latino), 30 international. Average age 29. 249 applicants, 54% accepted, 65 enrolled. In 2017, 37 master's, 14 doctorates awarded. *Degree requirements:* For master's, thesis optional; for doctorate, comprehensive exam, thesis/dissertation. *Entrance requirements:* For master's, minimum GPA of 3.0, letters of recommendation; for doctorate, GRE, resume, minimum GPA of 3.0, letters of recommendation, letter of intent. Additional exam requirements/recommendations for international students: Required—TOEFL (minimum score 550 paper-based; 80 iBT). *Application deadline:* For fall admission, 6/1 for domestic students, 4/1 for international students; for spring admission, 10/1 for domestic students, 9/1 for international students. Applications are processed on a rolling basis. Application fee: $30. Electronic applications accepted. *Expenses:* Contact institution. *Financial support:* Institutionally sponsored loans, scholarships/grants, and tuition waivers (full) available. Financial award application deadline: 3/1; financial award applicants required to submit FAFSA. *Faculty research:* Drugs/AIDS intervention among migrant workers, provision of services for active/recovering drug users with HIV. *Unit head:* Dr. Benjamin C. Amick, III, Chair, 305-348-7527, E-mail: benjamin.amickiii@fiu.edu. *Application contact:* Nanett Rojas, Assistant Director, Graduate Admissions, 305-348-7464, Fax: 305-348-7441, E-mail: gradadm@fiu.edu.

Florida National University, Program in Business Administration, Hialeah, FL 33012. Offers accounting (MBA); finance (MBA); general management (MBA); health services administration (MBA); marketing (MBA); public management and leadership (MBA). *Program availability:* Part-time, blended/hybrid learning. *Degree requirements:* For master's, capstone. *Entrance requirements:* For master's, writing assessment, bachelor's degree from accredited institution; official undergraduate transcripts; minimum undergraduate GPA of 2.5, GMAT (minimum score of 400), or GRE (minimum score of 900); two letters of recommendation; resume. Additional exam requirements/recommendations for international students: Required—TOEFL (minimum score 500 paper-based; 62 iBT), IELTS (minimum score 5.5). *Application deadline:* Applications are processed on a rolling basis. Electronic applications accepted. *Expenses:* Contact institution. *Financial support:* Federal Work-Study, institutionally sponsored loans, scholarships/grants, and tuition waivers available. Financial award applicants required to submit FAFSA. *Unit head:* Dr. Ernesto Gonzalez, Business and Economics Department Head, 305-821-3333 Ext. 1070, Fax: 305-362-0595, E-mail: egonzalez@fnu.edu.
Website: https://www.fnu.edu/prospective-students/our-programs/select-a-program/master-of-business-administration/business-administration-mba-masters/

Florida National University, Program in Health Services Administration, Hialeah, FL 33012. Offers MHSA. *Program availability:* Part-time, evening/weekend, 100% online, blended/hybrid learning. *Degree requirements:* For master's, capstone project. *Entrance requirements:* For master's, writing assessment, bachelor's degree from an accredited institution; official undergraduate transcripts; minimum undergraduate GPA of 2.5, GMAT (minimum score of 400), or GRE (minimum score of 900). Additional exam requirements/recommendations for international students: Required—TOEFL, IELTS. *Application deadline:* Applications are processed on a rolling basis. Electronic applications accepted. *Expenses: Tuition:* Full-time $15,600. *Required fees:* $650. *Financial support:* Scholarships/grants available. Financial award applicants required to submit FAFSA. *Unit head:* Dr. Loreto Almonte, Allied Health Division Head, 305-821-3333 Ext. 1074, Fax: 305-362-0595, E-mail: lalmonte@fnu.edu.
Website: http://www.fnu.edu/health-services-administration-hsa-master/

Fordham University, Gabelli School of Business, New York, NY 10023. Offers accounting (MBA, MS); applied statistics and decision-making (MS); business economics (DPS); capital markets (DPS); communications and media management (MBA); electronic business (MBA); entrepreneurship (MBA); finance (MBA, PhD); global finance (MS); global sustainability (MBA); health administration (MS); healthcare management (MBA); information systems (MBA, MS); investor relations (MS); management (EMBA, MBA, MS, PhD); marketing (MBA); marketing intelligence (MS); media management (MS); nonprofit leadership (MS); quantitative finance (MS); strategy and decision-making (DPS); taxation (MS); JD/MBA; MS/MBA. *Accreditation:* AACSB. *Program availability:* Part-time, evening/weekend. *Faculty:* 130 full-time (46 women), 42 part-time/adjunct (5 women). *Students:* 1,051 full-time (570 women), 563 part-time (313 women); includes 190 minority (48 Black or African American, non-Hispanic/Latino; 72 Asian, non-Hispanic/Latino; 69 Hispanic/Latino; 1 Native Hawaiian or other Pacific Islander, non-Hispanic/Latino), 1,106 international. Average age 27. 4,577 applicants, 58% accepted, 794 enrolled. In 2017, 937 master's awarded. Terminal master's awarded for partial completion of doctoral program. *Degree requirements:* For master's, internships (for some degrees); for doctorate, comprehensive exam (for some programs), thesis/dissertation. *Entrance requirements:* For master's, GMAT/GRE, 2 letters of recommendation, resume, 2 essays, transcripts, interview. Additional exam requirements/recommendations for international students: Required—TOEFL (minimum score 100 iBT), IELTS (minimum score 7). *Application deadline:* For fall admission, 11/15 priority date for domestic and international students; for winter admission, 1/19 priority date for domestic students, 1/1 priority date for international students; for spring admission, 4/15 for domestic students, 3/1 for international students; for summer admission, 6/1 for domestic students. Application fee: $130. Electronic applications accepted. *Expenses:* $1,495 per credit. *Financial support:* Career-related internships or fieldwork, institutionally sponsored loans, scholarships/grants, and unspecified assistantships available. Support available to part-time students. Financial award application deadline: 6/30; financial award applicants required to submit FAFSA. *Unit head:* Dr. Donna Rapaccioli, Dean, 212-636-6165, Fax: 212-307-1779, E-mail: rapaccioli@fordham.edu. *Application contact:* Lawrence Murray, Senior Assistant Dean of Graduate Admissions and Advising, 212-636-6200, Fax: 212-636-7076, E-mail: admissionsgb@fordham.edu.
Website: http://www.fordham.edu/gabelli

Framingham State University, Graduate Studies, Program in Healthcare Administration, Framingham, MA 01701-9101. Offers MHA. *Program availability:* Part-time, evening/weekend. *Unit head:* Dr. Paulette Melanson, Program Coordinator, E-mail: pmelanson@framingham.edu. *Application contact:* 508-626-4550, Fax: 508-626-4030, E-mail: dgce@frc.mass.edu.

Franciscan Missionaries of Our Lady University, School of Health Professions, Baton Rouge, LA 70808. Offers health administration (MHA); nutritional sciences (MS); physical therapy (DPT); physician assistant studies (MMS). *Unit head:* Dr. Susan K. Steele-Moses, Dean, 225-768-1676. *Application contact:* Dr. Susan K. Steele-Moses, Dean, 225-768-1676.
Website: https://www.franu.edu/academics/schools/school-of-health-professions

Francis Marion University, Graduate Programs, School of Business, Florence, SC 29502-0547. Offers business (MBA); health executive management (MBA). *Accreditation:* AACSB. *Program availability:* Part-time, evening/weekend. *Degree requirements:* For master's, comprehensive exam. *Entrance requirements:* For master's, GMAT or GRE, official transcripts, two letters of recommendation. Additional exam requirements/recommendations for international students: Required—TOEFL (minimum score 550 paper-based; 79 iBT). *Faculty research:* Ethics, directions of MBA, international business, regional economics, environmental issues.

Franklin Pierce University, Graduate and Professional Studies, Rindge, NH 03461-0060. Offers curriculum and instruction (M Ed); elementary education (MS Ed); emerging network technologies (Graduate Certificate); energy and sustainability studies (MBA, Graduate Certificate); health administration (MBA, Graduate Certificate); human resource management (MBA, Graduate Certificate); information technology (MBA); leadership (MBA); nursing education (MS); nursing leadership (MS); physical therapy (DPT); physician assistant studies (MPAS); special education (M Ed); sports management (MBA). *Accreditation:* APTA. *Program availability:* Part-time, 100% online, blended/hybrid learning. *Degree requirements:* For master's, concentrated original research projects; student teaching; fieldwork and/or internship; leadership project; PRAXIS I and II (for M Ed); for doctorate, concentrated original research projects, clinical fieldwork and/or internship, leadership project. *Entrance requirements:* For master's, minimum GPA of 2.5, 3 letters of recommendation; competencies in accounting, economics, statistics, and computer skills through life experience or undergraduate coursework (for MBA); certification/e-portfolio, minimum C grade in all education courses (for M Ed); license to practice as RN (for MS); for doctorate, GRE, 80 hours of observation/work in PT settings; completion of anatomy, chemistry, physics, and statistics; minimum GPA of 3.0. Additional exam requirements/recommendations for international students: Required—TOEFL (minimum score 550 paper-based; 61 iBT). Electronic applications accepted. *Faculty research:* Evidence-based practice in sports physical therapy, human resource management in economic crisis, leadership in nursing, innovation in sports facility management, differentiated learning and understanding by design.

Friends University, Graduate School, Wichita, KS 67213. Offers family therapy (MSFT); global business administration (MBA), including accounting, business law, change management, health care leadership, management information systems, supply chain management and logistics; health care leadership (MHCL); management information systems (MMIS); professional business administration (MBA), including accounting, business law, change management, health care leadership, management information systems, supply chain management and logistics. *Program availability:* Part-time, evening/weekend, online learning. *Degree requirements:* For master's, research project. *Entrance requirements:* For master's, bachelor's degree from accredited institution, official transcripts, interview with program director, letter(s) of recommendation. Additional exam requirements/recommendations for international students: Required—TOEFL (minimum score 560 paper-based). Electronic applications accepted.

George Mason University, College of Health and Human Services, Department of Health Administration and Policy, Fairfax, VA 22030. Offers health and medical policy (MS); health informatics (MS); health informatics and data analytics (Certificate); health services research (PhD); health systems management (MHA); quality improvement and outcomes management in health care systems (Certificate). *Accreditation:* CAHME. *Program availability:* Part-time, evening/weekend, 100% online. *Faculty:* 16 full-time (7 women), 29 part-time/adjunct (12 women). *Students:* 68 full-time (52 women), 97 part-time (73 women); includes 64 minority (22 Black or African American, non-Hispanic/Latino; 31 Asian, non-Hispanic/Latino; 10 Hispanic/Latino; 1 Two or more races, non-Hispanic/Latino), 37 international. Average age 32. 124 applicants, 73% accepted, 41 enrolled. In 2017, 63 master's, 18 other advanced degrees awarded. *Degree requirements:* For master's, comprehensive exam, internship; for doctorate, thesis/dissertation. *Entrance requirements:* For master's, GRE recommended if undergraduate GPA is below 3.0 (for MS in health and medical policy), 2 official transcripts; expanded goals statement; 3 letters of recommendation; resume; 1 year of work experience (for MHA in health systems management); minimum GPA of 3.25 preferred (for MS in health informatics); for doctorate, GRE, professional and volunteer experience, evidence of ability to write and conduct research at the doctoral level, master's degree or equivalent; for Certificate, 2 official transcripts; expanded goals statement; 3 letters of recommendation; resume. Additional exam requirements/recommendations for international students: Required—TOEFL (minimum score 575 paper-based; 88 iBT), IELTS (minimum score 6.5), PTE (minimum score 59). *Application deadline:* For fall admission, 4/1 for domestic and international students; for spring admission, 11/1 for domestic and international students. Application fee: $75 ($80 for international students). Electronic applications accepted. *Expenses:* $978 per credit (MHA); $900 per credit (MHI). *Financial support:* In 2017–18, 22 students received support, including 18 research assistantships with tuition reimbursements available (averaging $18,018 per year), 5 teaching assistantships (averaging $4,804 per year); career-related internships or fieldwork, Federal Work-Study, scholarships/grants, unspecified assistantships, and health care benefits (for full-time research or teaching assistantship recipients) also available. Support available to part-time students. Financial award application deadline: 3/1; financial award applicants required to submit FAFSA. *Faculty research:* Universal health care, publications, relationships between malpractice pressure and rates of Cesarean section and VBAC, seniors and Wii gaming, relationships between changes in physician's incomes and practice settings and their care to Medicaid and charity patients. *Total annual research expenditures:* $396,087. *Unit head:* Dr. P.J. Maddox, Chair, 703-993-1982, Fax: 703-993-1953, E-mail: pmaddox@gmu.edu. *Application contact:* Tracy Shevlin, Department Manager, 703-993-1929, Fax: 703-993-1953, E-mail: tshevlin@gmu.edu.
Website: http://chhs.gmu.edu/hap/index

George Mason University, College of Health and Human Services, School of Nursing, Fairfax, VA 22030. Offers adult gerontology (DNP); adult/gerontological nurse

practitioner (MSN); family nurse practitioner (MSN, DNP); nurse educator (MSN); nursing (PhD); nursing administration (MSN, DNP); nursing education (Certificate); psychiatric mental health (DNP). *Accreditation:* AACN. *Program availability:* Part-time, evening/weekend, blended/hybrid learning. *Faculty:* 28 full-time (27 women), 51 part-time/adjunct (47 women). *Students:* 51 full-time (40 women), 182 part-time (162 women); includes 110 minority (59 Black or African American, non-Hispanic/Latino; 1 American Indian or Alaska Native, non-Hispanic/Latino; 36 Asian, non-Hispanic/Latino; 10 Hispanic/Latino; 4 Two or more races, non-Hispanic/Latino), 8 international. Average age 37. 159 applicants, 70% accepted, 73 enrolled. In 2017, 33 master's, 24 doctorates, 1 other advanced degree awarded. *Degree requirements:* For master's, comprehensive exam (for some programs), thesis in clinical classes; for doctorate, comprehensive exam (for some programs), thesis/dissertation (for some programs). *Entrance requirements:* For master's, 2 official transcripts; expanded goals statement; resume; BSN from accredited institution; minimum GPA of 3.0 in last 60 credits of undergraduate work; 2 letters of recommendation; completion of undergraduate statistics and graduate-level bivariate statistics; certification in professional CPR; for doctorate, GRE, 2 official transcripts; expanded goals statement; resume; 2 recommendation letters; nursing license; at least 1 year of work experience as an RN; interview; writing sample; evidence of graduate-level course in applied statistics; master's degree in nursing with minimum GPA of 3.5; for Certificate, 2 official transcripts; expanded goals statement; resume; master's degree from accredited institution or currently enrolled with minimum GPA of 3.0. Additional exam requirements/recommendations for international students: Required—TOEFL (minimum score 570 paper-based; 88 iBT), IELTS (minimum score 6.5), PTE (minimum score 59). *Application deadline:* For fall admission, 2/1 for domestic and international students. Application fee: $75 ($80 for international students). Electronic applications accepted. *Expenses:* Contact institution. *Financial support:* In 2017–18, 7 students received support, including 5 research assistantships with tuition reimbursements available (averaging $20,500 per year), 2 teaching assistantships; career-related internships or fieldwork, Federal Work-Study, scholarships/grants, unspecified assistantships, and health care benefits (for full-time research or teaching assistantship recipients) also available. Financial award application deadline: 3/1; financial award applicants required to submit FAFSA. *Faculty research:* Health care, nursing science. *Total annual research expenditures:* $1.6 million. *Unit head:* Carol Urban, Director, 703-993-2991, Fax: 703-993-1949, E-mail: curban@gmu.edu. *Application contact:* Susan Eckis, Office Manager, 703-993-1938, Fax: 703-993-1949, E-mail: seckis@gmu.edu.
Website: http://chhs.gmu.edu/nursing

The George Washington University, College of Professional Studies, Program in Healthcare Corporate Compliance, Washington, DC 20052. Offers Graduate Certificate. Program offered jointly with Milken Institute School of Public Health and the law firm of Feldesman Tucker Leifer Fidel LLP. *Program availability:* Online learning. *Students:* 21 part-time (17 women); includes 5 minority (3 Black or African American, non-Hispanic/Latino; 1 Asian, non-Hispanic/Latino; 1 Hispanic/Latino). Average age 46. 32 applicants, 88% accepted, 20 enrolled. In 2017, 19 Graduate Certificates awarded. *Application deadline:* For fall admission, 8/31 for domestic students. *Expenses: Tuition:* Full-time $28,800; part-time $1655 per credit hour. *Required fees:* $45; $2.75 per credit hour. *Unit head:* Phyllis C. Borzi, Director, 202-530-2312, E-mail: borziph@gwu.edu. *Application contact:* Kristin Williams, Assistant Vice President for Graduate and Special Enrollment Management, 202-994-0467, Fax: 202-994-0371, E-mail: ksw@gwu.edu.
Website: http://cps.gwu.edu/hcc.html

The George Washington University, Milken Institute School of Public Health, Department of Health Policy and Management, Washington, DC 20052. Offers EMHA, MHA, MPH, MS, Graduate Certificate. *Accreditation:* CAHME. *Students:* 124 full-time (90 women), 361 part-time (240 women); includes 232 minority (97 Black or African American, non-Hispanic/Latino; 90 Asian, non-Hispanic/Latino; 31 Hispanic/Latino; 1 Native Hawaiian or other Pacific Islander, non-Hispanic/Latino; 13 Two or more races, non-Hispanic/Latino), 9 international. Average age 33. 675 applicants, 67% accepted, 168 enrolled. In 2017, 136 master's, 2 other advanced degrees awarded. *Entrance requirements:* For master's, GMAT, GRE General Test, or MCAT. Additional exam requirements/recommendations for international students: Required—TOEFL. *Application deadline:* For fall admission, 4/15 priority date for domestic students, 4/15 for international students; for spring admission, 11/1 for domestic and international students. Applications are processed on a rolling basis. Application fee: $75. *Expenses: Tuition:* Full-time $28,800; part-time $1655 per credit hour. *Required fees:* $45; $2.75 per credit hour. *Financial support:* In 2017–18, 10 students received support. Tuition waivers available. Financial award application deadline: 2/15. *Unit head:* Prof. Thomas LaVeist, Chair, 202-994-8354, E-mail: toml@gwu.edu. *Application contact:* Jane Smith, Director of Admissions, 202-994-0248, Fax: 202-994-1860, E-mail: sphhsinfo@gwumc.edu.

The George Washington University, School of Medicine and Health Sciences, Health Sciences Programs, Washington, DC 20052. Offers clinical practice management (MSHS); clinical research administration (MSHS); emergency services management (MSHS); end-of-life care (MSHS); immunohematology (MSHS); immunohematology and biotechnology (MSHS); physical therapy (DPT); physician assistant (MSHS). *Program availability:* Online learning. *Faculty:* 31 full-time (23 women), 4 part-time/adjunct (2 women). *Students:* 304 full-time (233 women), 321 part-time (248 women); includes 212 minority (70 Black or African American, non-Hispanic/Latino; 1 American Indian or Alaska Native, non-Hispanic/Latino; 64 Asian, non-Hispanic/Latino; 59 Hispanic/Latino; 3 Native Hawaiian or other Pacific Islander, non-Hispanic/Latino; 15 Two or more races, non-Hispanic/Latino), 18 international. Average age 33. 2,366 applicants, 19% accepted, 246 enrolled. In 2017, 159 master's, 49 doctorates, 2 other advanced degrees awarded. *Entrance requirements:* Additional exam requirements/recommendations for international students: Required—TOEFL (minimum score 550 paper-based). *Application deadline:* Applications are processed on a rolling basis. Application fee: $75. *Expenses:* Contact institution. *Unit head:* Jean E. Johnson, Senior Associate Dean, 202-994-3725, E-mail: jejohns@gwu.edu. *Application contact:* Joke Ogundiran, Director of Admission, 202-994-1668, Fax: 202-994-0870, E-mail: jokeogun@gwu.edu.

Georgia Institute of Technology, Graduate Studies, College of Engineering, H. Milton Stewart School of Industrial and Systems Engineering, Program in Health Systems, Atlanta, GA 30332-0001. Offers MS. *Program availability:* Part-time. *Entrance requirements:* For master's, GRE General Test. Additional exam requirements/recommendations for international students: Required—TOEFL (minimum score 550 paper-based; 79 iBT). Electronic applications accepted. *Faculty research:* Emergency medical services, health development planning, health services evaluations.

Georgia Southern University, Jack N. Averitt College of Graduate Studies, Jiann-Ping Hsu College of Public Health, Program in Healthcare Administration, Statesboro, GA 30460. Offers MHA. *Program availability:* Part-time. *Faculty:* 28 full-time (14 women). *Students:* 49 full-time (37 women), 1 (woman) part-time; includes 25 minority (20 Black or African American, non-Hispanic/Latino; 2 Asian, non-Hispanic/Latino; 2 Hispanic/Latino; 1 Two or more races, non-Hispanic/Latino), 1 international. Average age 24. 47 applicants, 72% accepted, 25 enrolled. In 2017, 14 master's awarded. *Degree requirements:* For master's, thesis optional, internship. *Entrance requirements:* For master's, GRE, GMAT, personal statement, minimum cumulative undergraduate GPA of 2.75, resume, 3 letters of recommendation. Additional exam requirements/recommendations for international students: Required—TOEFL (minimum score 537 paper-based; 75 iBT), IELTS (minimum score 6). *Application deadline:* For fall admission, 6/1 for domestic students, 5/1 for international students. Applications are processed on a rolling basis. Application fee: $135. Electronic applications accepted. *Expenses:* $3,918 in-state, $13,859 out-of-state. *Financial support:* In 2017–18, 26 students received support, including 1 research assistantship with full tuition reimbursement available (averaging $12,350 per year), 6 teaching assistantships with full tuition reimbursements available (averaging $12,350 per year); Federal Work-Study, scholarships/grants, tuition waivers (full), and unspecified assistantships also available. Financial award application deadline: 4/15; financial award applicants required to submit FAFSA. *Faculty research:* Health disparity elimination, cost effectiveness analysis, epidemiology of rural public health, health care system assessment, rural health care, health policy and healthcare financing. *Total annual research expenditures:* $415,747. *Unit head:* Dr. Robert Greg Evans, Dean, 912-478-2674, Fax: 912-478-5811, E-mail: rgevans@georgiasouthern.edu. *Application contact:* Shamia Garrett, Coordinator, Office of Student Services, 912-478-2674, Fax: 912-478-5811, E-mail: jphcoph-gradadvisor@georgiasouthern.edu.

Georgia Southern University, Jack N. Averitt College of Graduate Studies, Jiann-Ping Hsu College of Public Health, Program in Public Health, Statesboro, GA 30460. Offers biostatistics (MPH, Dr PH); community health behavior and education (Dr PH); community health education (MPH); environmental health sciences (MPH); epidemiology (MPH); health policy and management (MPH, Dr PH). *Program availability:* Part-time. *Faculty:* 11 full-time (5 women). *Students:* 146 full-time (90 women), 70 part-time (57 women); includes 112 minority (95 Black or African American, non-Hispanic/Latino; 9 Asian, non-Hispanic/Latino; 5 Hispanic/Latino; 3 Two or more races, non-Hispanic/Latino), 47 international. Average age 32. 190 applicants, 78% accepted, 89 enrolled. In 2017, 34 master's, 13 doctorates awarded. *Degree requirements:* For master's, thesis optional, practicum; for doctorate, comprehensive exam, thesis/dissertation, preceptorship. *Entrance requirements:* For master's, GRE General Test, minimum GPA of 2.75, 3 letters of recommendation, statement of purpose, resume or curriculum vitae; for doctorate, GRE, GMAT, MCAT, LSAT, minimum GPA of 3.0, 3 letters of recommendation, statement of purpose, resume or curriculum vitae. Additional exam requirements/recommendations for international students: Required—TOEFL (minimum score 537 paper-based; 75 iBT), IELTS (minimum score 6). *Application deadline:* For fall admission, 6/1 for domestic students, 5/1 for international students. Applications are processed on a rolling basis. Application fee: $135. Electronic applications accepted. *Expenses:* $3,949 in-state, $13,929 out-of-state (for MPH); $4,014 in-state, $14,159 out-of-state (for Dr PH). *Financial support:* In 2017–18, 106 students received support, including 1 research assistantship with full tuition reimbursement available (averaging $12,350 per year), 6 teaching assistantships with full tuition reimbursements available (averaging $12,350 per year); scholarships/grants, tuition waivers (full), and unspecified assistantships also available. Financial award application deadline: 4/15; financial award applicants required to submit FAFSA. *Faculty research:* Rural public health best practices, health disparity elimination, community initiatives to enhance public health, cost effectiveness analysis, epidemiology of rural public health, environmental health issues, health care system assessment, rural health care, health policy and healthcare financing, survival analysis, nonparametric statistics and resampling methods, micro-arrays and genomics, data imputation techniques and clinical trial methodology. *Total annual research expenditures:* $415,747. *Unit head:* Dr. Robert Greg Evans, Dean, 912-478-2674, E-mail: rgevans@georgiasouthern.edu. *Application contact:* Shamia Garrett, Coordinator, Office of Student Services, 912-478-2674, Fax: 912-478-5811, E-mail: jphcoph-gradadvisor@georgiasouthern.edu.
Website: http://jphcoph.georgiasouthern.edu/

Georgia Southern University–Armstrong Campus, College of Graduate Studies, Program in Health Services Administration, Savannah, GA 31419-1997. Offers MHSA. *Accreditation:* CAHME; CEPH. *Program availability:* Part-time, evening/weekend. *Faculty:* 5 full-time (3 women). *Students:* 20 full-time (12 women), 7 part-time (6 women); includes 14 minority (7 Black or African American, non-Hispanic/Latino; 3 Asian, non-Hispanic/Latino; 1 Hispanic/Latino; 1 Native Hawaiian or other Pacific Islander, non-Hispanic/Latino; 2 Two or more races, non-Hispanic/Latino), 4 international. Average age 28. 27 applicants, 96% accepted, 14 enrolled. In 2017, 14 master's awarded. *Degree requirements:* For master's, comprehensive exam, thesis optional, capstone project and internship, administration practicum, or research practicum. *Entrance requirements:* For master's, GMAT or GRE General Test, MAT, minimum GPA of 2.8, letter of intent, letters of recommendation. Additional exam requirements/recommendations for international students: Required—TOEFL (minimum score 523 paper-based; 70 iBT). *Application deadline:* For fall admission, 6/1 priority date for domestic students, 5/1 priority date for international students; for spring admission, 11/15 priority date for domestic students, 9/15 priority date for international students; for summer admission, 4/15 for domestic students, 9/15 for international students. Applications are processed on a rolling basis. Application fee: $30. Electronic applications accepted. *Expenses:* Contact institution. *Financial support:* In 2017–18, research assistantships with full tuition reimbursements (averaging $5,000 per year) were awarded; career-related internships or fieldwork, Federal Work-Study, scholarships/grants, tuition waivers (full), and unspecified assistantships also available. Support available to part-time students. Financial award applicants required to submit FAFSA. *Faculty research:* Health administration, community health, health education. *Unit head:* Dr. Robert LeFavi, Department Head, 912-344-3208, Fax: 912-344-3490, E-mail: robert.lefavi@armstrong.edu. *Application contact:* McKenzie Peterman, Graduate Admissions Specialist, 912-478-5678, Fax: 912-478-0740, E-mail: mpeterman@georgiasouthern.edu.
Website: https://www.armstrong.edu/degree-programs/health-services-administration-mhsa

Georgia State University, Andrew Young School of Policy Studies, Department of Public Management and Policy, Atlanta, GA 30303. Offers criminal justice (MPA); disaster management (Certificate); disaster policy (MPA); environmental policy (PhD); health policy (PhD); management and finance (MPA); nonprofit management (MPA, Certificate); nonprofit policy (MPA); planning and economic development (MPP, Certificate); policy analysis and evaluation (MPA), including planning and economic development; public and nonprofit management (PhD); public finance and budgeting (PhD), including science and technology policy, urban and regional economic development; public finance policy (MPA), including social policy; public health (MPA). *Accreditation:* NASPAA (one or more programs are accredited). *Program availability:* Part-time. *Faculty:* 17 full-time (9 women). *Students:* 125 full-time (75 women), 78 part-time (51 women); includes 90 minority (67 Black or African American, non-Hispanic/Latino; 5 Asian, non-Hispanic/Latino; 9 Hispanic/Latino; 9 Two or more races, non-Hispanic/Latino), 34 international. Average age 30. 275 applicants, 62% accepted, 88 enrolled. In 2017, 71 master's, 5 doctorates, 12 other advanced degrees awarded. Terminal master's awarded for partial completion of doctoral program. *Degree requirements:* For master's, thesis optional; for doctorate, comprehensive exam, thesis/dissertation. *Entrance requirements:* For master's and doctorate, GRE. Additional exam requirements/recommendations for international students: Required—TOEFL (minimum

score 603 paper-based; 100 iBT) or IELTS (minimum score 7). *Application deadline:* For fall admission, 1/15 for domestic and international students. Application fee: $50. Electronic applications accepted. *Expenses:* Tuition, state resident: full-time $7020. Tuition, nonresident: full-time $22,518. *Required fees:* $2128. Tuition and fees vary according to degree level and program. *Financial support:* In 2017–18, fellowships (averaging $8,194 per year), research assistantships (averaging $8,068 per year), teaching assistantships (averaging $3,600 per year) were awarded; institutionally sponsored loans, scholarships/grants, health care benefits, and unspecified assistantships also available. Financial award application deadline: 2/1. *Faculty research:* Public budgeting and finance, public management, nonprofit management, performance measurement and management, urban development. *Unit head:* Dr. Carolyn Bourdeaux, Chair and Professor, 404-413-0013, Fax: 404-413-0104, E-mail: cbourdeaux@gsu.edu.
Website: http://aysps.gsu.edu/pmap/

Georgia State University, J. Mack Robinson College of Business, Institute of Health Administration, Atlanta, GA 30302-3083. Offers health administration (MBA, MSHA); health informatics (MBA, MSCIS); MBA/MHA; PMBA/MHA. *Accreditation:* CAHME. *Program availability:* Part-time, evening/weekend. *Faculty:* 8 full-time (2 women). *Students:* 40 full-time (20 women), 14 part-time (6 women); includes 22 minority (8 Black or African American, non-Hispanic/Latino; 8 Asian, non-Hispanic/Latino; 3 Hispanic/Latino; 3 Two or more races, non-Hispanic/Latino), 1 international. Average age 28. 52 applicants, 25% accepted, 7 enrolled. In 2017, 64 master's awarded. *Entrance requirements:* For master's, GRE or GMAT, transcripts from all institutions attended, resume, essays. Additional exam requirements/recommendations for international students: Required—TOEFL (minimum score 610 paper-based; 101 iBT), IELTS (minimum score 7). *Application deadline:* For fall admission, 5/1 priority date for domestic students, 2/1 priority date for international students; for spring admission, 9/15 priority date for domestic students, 4/1 priority date for international students. Applications are processed on a rolling basis. Application fee: $50. Electronic applications accepted. *Expenses:* Tuition, state resident: full-time $7020. Tuition, nonresident: full-time $22,518. *Required fees:* $2128. Tuition and fees vary according to degree level and program. *Financial support:* Research assistantships, teaching assistantships, scholarships/grants, tuition waivers, and unspecified assistantships available. *Faculty research:* Health information technology, health insurance exchanges, health policy and economic impact, healthcare quality, healthcare transformation. *Unit head:* Dr. Andrew T. Sumner, Chair in Health Administration/Director of the Institute of Health, 404-413-7630, Fax: 404-413-7631. *Application contact:* Toby McChesney, Assistant Dean for Graduate Recruiting and Student Services, 404-413-7167, Fax: 404-413-7162, E-mail: rcbgradadmissions@gsu.edu.
Website: http://www.hagsu.org/

Goldey-Beacom College, Graduate Program, Wilmington, DE 19808-1999. Offers business administration (MBA); finance (MS); financial management (MBA); health care management (MBA); human resource management (MBA); information technology (MBA); international business management (MBA); major finance (MBA); major taxation (MBA); management (MM); marketing management (MBA); taxation (MBA, MS). *Accreditation:* ACBSP. *Program availability:* Part-time, evening/weekend. *Entrance requirements:* For master's, GMAT, MAT, GRE, minimum GPA of 3.0. Additional exam requirements/recommendations for international students: Required—TOEFL (minimum score 65 iBT); Recommended—IELTS (minimum score 6). Electronic applications accepted.

Governors State University, College of Health and Human Services, Program in Health Administration, University Park, IL 60484. Offers MHA. *Accreditation:* CAHME. *Program availability:* Part-time. *Faculty:* 5 full-time (4 women), 14 part-time/adjunct (5 women). *Students:* 30 full-time (22 women), 33 part-time (30 women); includes 37 minority (27 Black or African American, non-Hispanic/Latino; 8 Asian, non-Hispanic/Latino; 2 Hispanic/Latino), 7 international. Average age 32. 26 applicants, 77% accepted, 12 enrolled. In 2017, 6 master's awarded. *Application deadline:* For fall admission, 4/1 for domestic students. Applications are processed on a rolling basis. Application fee: $50. Electronic applications accepted. *Expenses:* Tuition, state resident: full-time $8472; part-time $353 per credit hour. Tuition, nonresident: full-time $16,944; part-time $706 per credit hour. *Required fees:* $1824; $76 per credit hour. $38 per term. Tuition and fees vary according to course load, degree level and program. *Financial support:* Application deadline: 5/1; applicants required to submit FAFSA. *Unit head:* Rupert Evans, Chair, Department of Health Administration, 708-534-5000 Ext. 2131, E-mail: revans@govst.edu.

Grambling State University, School of Graduate Studies and Research, College of Arts and Sciences, Department of Political Science and Public Administration, Grambling, LA 71270. Offers health services administration (MPA); human resource management (MPA); public management (MPA); state and local government (MPA). *Accreditation:* NASPAA. *Program availability:* Part-time. *Degree requirements:* For master's, comprehensive exam (for some programs), thesis optional. *Entrance requirements:* For master's, GRE, minimum GPA of 2.75 on last degree. Additional exam requirements/recommendations for international students: Required—TOEFL (minimum score 500 paper-based; 62 iBT). Electronic applications accepted.

Grand Canyon University, Colangelo College of Business, Phoenix, AZ 85017-1097. Offers accounting (MBA, MS); business analytics (MS); disaster preparedness and executive fire service leadership (MS); finance (MBA); general management (MBA); health systems management (MBA); information technology management (MS); leadership (MBA, MS); marketing (MBA); organizational leadership and entrepreneurship (MS); project management (MBA); sports business (MBA); strategic human resource management (MBA). *Accreditation:* ACBSP. *Program availability:* Part-time, evening/weekend, online learning. *Entrance requirements:* For master's, equivalent of two years' full-time professional work experience. Additional exam requirements/recommendations for international students: Required—TOEFL (minimum score 575 paper-based; 90 iBT), IELTS (minimum score 7). Electronic applications accepted.

Grand Canyon University, College of Doctoral Studies, Phoenix, AZ 85017-1097. Offers data analytics (DBA); general psychology (PhD), including cognition and instruction, industrial and organizational psychology, integrating technology, learning, and psychology, performance psychology; management (DBA); marketing (DBA); organizational leadership (Ed D), including behavioral health, Christian ministry, health care administration, organizational development. *Degree requirements:* For doctorate, comprehensive exam, thesis/dissertation. *Entrance requirements:* For doctorate, minimum GPA of 3.4 on earned advanced degree from regionally-accredited institution; transcripts; goals statement.

Grand Canyon University, College of Nursing and Health Care Professions, Phoenix, AZ 85017-1097. Offers acute care nurse practitioner (MSN, PMC); family nurse practitioner (MSN, PMC); health care administration (MS); health care informatics (MS, MSN); leadership in health care systems (MSN); nursing (DNP); nursing education (MSN, PMC); public health (MPH, MSN); MBA/MSN. *Accreditation:* AACN. *Program availability:* Part-time, evening/weekend, online learning. *Degree requirements:* For master's and PMC, comprehensive exam (for some programs). *Entrance requirements:* For master's, minimum cumulative and science course undergraduate GPA of 3.0. Additional exam requirements/recommendations for international students: Required—TOEFL (minimum score 575 paper-based; 90 iBT), IELTS (minimum score 7).

Grand Valley State University, College of Community and Public Service, School of Public, Nonprofit and Health Administration, Program in Health Administration, Allendale, MI 49401-9403. Offers MHA. *Program availability:* Part-time, evening/weekend. *Students:* 34 full-time (25 women), 33 part-time (24 women); includes 13 minority (2 Black or African American, non-Hispanic/Latino; 7 Asian, non-Hispanic/Latino; 1 Hispanic/Latino; 3 Two or more races, non-Hispanic/Latino), 7 international. Average age 28. 42 applicants, 74% accepted, 12 enrolled. In 2017, 24 master's awarded. *Degree requirements:* For master's, internship (for pre- and early-career students), capstone (for mid-career). *Entrance requirements:* For master's, minimum undergraduate GPA of 3.0, three letters of reference, 250-750 word essay on career and educational objectives, current resume. Additional exam requirements/recommendations for international students: Required—TOEFL (minimum iBT score of 80), IELTS (6.5), or Michigan English Language Assessment Battery (77). *Application deadline:* For fall admission, 5/1 priority date for domestic students; for winter admission, 11/1 priority date for domestic students. Applications are processed on a rolling basis. Application fee: $30. Electronic applications accepted. *Expenses:* $627 per credit hour. *Financial support:* In 2017–18, 11 students received support, including 4 fellowships, 1 research assistantship with full and partial tuition reimbursement available (averaging $4,000 per year). Financial award application deadline: 5/1. *Faculty research:* Long-term care and aging, Medicare and Medicaid finance and administration, health economics. *Unit head:* Dr. Richard Jelier, Director, 616-331-6575, Fax: 616-331-7120, E-mail: jelierr@gvsu.edu. *Application contact:* Dr. Greg Cline, Graduate Program Director, 616-331-6437, Fax: 616-331-7120, E-mail: clinegr@gvsu.edu.
Website: http://www.gvsu.edu/spna

Grantham University, College of Nursing and Allied Health, Lenexa, KS 66219. Offers case management (MSN); health systems management (MS); healthcare administration (MHA); nursing education (MSN); nursing informatics (MSN); nursing management and organizational leadership (MSN). *Program availability:* Part-time, evening/weekend, online only, 100% online. *Faculty:* 2 full-time, 34 part-time/adjunct. *Students:* 198 full-time (144 women), 113 part-time (83 women); includes 170 minority (118 Black or African American, non-Hispanic/Latino; 3 American Indian or Alaska Native, non-Hispanic/Latino; 27 Asian, non-Hispanic/Latino; 11 Hispanic/Latino; 2 Native Hawaiian or other Pacific Islander, non-Hispanic/Latino; 9 Two or more races, non-Hispanic/Latino). Average age 41. 95 applicants, 89% accepted, 72 enrolled. In 2017, 123 master's awarded. *Entrance requirements:* For master's, BSN from state-approved nursing program with minimum cumulative GPA of 2.5 from institution accredited by agency recognized by U.S. DOE or foreign equivalent; unencumbered and current RN license. Additional exam requirements/recommendations for international students: Required—TOEFL (minimum score 530 paper-based; 71 iBT), IELTS (minimum score 6.5), PTE (minimum score 50). *Application deadline:* Applications are processed on a rolling basis. Application fee: $0. Electronic applications accepted. *Expenses:* $325 per credit hour. *Financial support:* Scholarships/grants available. Financial award applicants required to submit FAFSA. *Faculty research:* Compassion in caring improving incivility in the ICU setting, get well network technology in enhancing patient education, opioid use and abuse in postpartum women. *Unit head:* Dr. Cheryl Rules, Dean of the College of Nursing and Allied Health, 913-309-4783, Fax: 844-897-6490, E-mail: crules@grantham.edu. *Application contact:* Jared Parlette, Vice President of Student Enrollment, 800-955-2527 Ext. 803, Fax: 866-914-4557, E-mail: admissions@grantham.edu.
Website: http://www.grantham.edu/nursing-and-allied-health/

Gwynedd Mercy University, School of Graduate and Professional Studies, Gwynedd Valley, PA 19437-0901. Offers health care administration (MBA); management (MSM); strategic management and leadership (MBA). *Program availability:* Part-time, evening/weekend. *Faculty:* 5 full-time (all women), 22 part-time/adjunct (8 women). *Students:* 63 full-time (37 women); includes 20 minority (16 Black or African American, non-Hispanic/Latino; 2 Asian, non-Hispanic/Latino; 2 Hispanic/Latino). Average age 39. In 2017, 56 master's awarded. *Degree requirements:* For master's, thesis. *Entrance requirements:* For master's, minimum GPA of 3.0. *Application deadline:* Applications are processed on a rolling basis. *Expenses:* $640 per credit, $17 per credit part-time fee, $165 graduation fee. *Financial support:* Career-related internships or fieldwork, Federal Work-Study, tuition waivers (full and partial), and unspecified assistantships available. Financial award application deadline: 8/31; financial award applicants required to submit FAFSA. *Unit head:* Dr. Mary Sortino, Dean, 215-646-7300, E-mail: sortino.m@gmercyu.edu. *Application contact:* Information Contact, 800-342-5462, Fax: 215-641-5556.

Harvard University, Graduate School of Arts and Sciences, Committee on Higher Degrees in Health Policy, Cambridge, MA 02138. Offers PhD. *Degree requirements:* For doctorate, thesis/dissertation. *Entrance requirements:* For doctorate, GMAT, GRE General Test, or MCAT. Additional exam requirements/recommendations for international students: Required—TOEFL.

Harvard University, Harvard Business School, Doctoral Programs in Management, Boston, MA 02163. Offers accounting and management (DBA); business economics (PhD); health policy management (PhD); management (DBA); marketing (DBA); organizational behavior (PhD); science, technology and management (PhD); strategy (DBA); technology and operations management (DBA). *Degree requirements:* For doctorate, comprehensive exam (for some programs), thesis/dissertation. *Entrance requirements:* For doctorate, GRE General Test or GMAT. Additional exam requirements/recommendations for international students: Required—TOEFL.

Harvard University, Harvard T.H. Chan School of Public Health, Department of Health Policy and Management, Boston, MA 02115-6096. Offers MHCM, SM, PhD. *Program availability:* Part-time. *Faculty:* 47 full-time (16 women), 23 part-time/adjunct (8 women). *Students:* 63 full-time (47 women), 57 part-time (9 women); includes 42 minority (2 Black or African American, non-Hispanic/Latino; 29 Asian, non-Hispanic/Latino; 9 Hispanic/Latino; 2 Two or more races, non-Hispanic/Latino), 22 international. Average age 29. 232 applicants, 20% accepted, 12 enrolled. In 2017, 19 master's, 11 doctorates awarded. *Degree requirements:* For doctorate, thesis/dissertation, qualifying exam. *Entrance requirements:* For master's, GRE, GMAT, MCAT; for doctorate, GRE. Additional exam requirements/recommendations for international students: Recommended—TOEFL (minimum score 600 paper-based; 100 iBT), IELTS (minimum score 7). *Application deadline:* For fall admission, 12/1 for domestic and international students. Application fee: $120. Electronic applications accepted. *Financial support:* Fellowships, research assistantships, teaching assistantships, Federal Work-Study, scholarships/grants, traineeships, and unspecified assistantships available. Support available to part-time students. Financial award application deadline: 2/15; financial award applicants required to submit FAFSA. *Unit head:* Dr. Arnold Epstein, Chair, 617-432-3415, Fax: 617-432-4494. *Application contact:* Vincent W. James, Director of Admissions, 617-432-1031, Fax: 617-432-7080, E-mail: admissions@hsph.harvard.edu.
Website: http://www.hsph.harvard.edu/departments/health-policy-and-management/

Herzing University Online, Program in Business Administration, Menomonee Falls, WI 53051. Offers accounting (MBA); business administration (MBA); business management (MBA); healthcare management (MBA); human resources (MBA); marketing (MBA); project management (MBA); technology management (MBA). *Program availability:* Online learning.

Hilbert College, Program in Public Administration, Hamburg, NY 14075-1597. Offers health administration (MPA); public administration (MPA). *Program availability:* Evening/

weekend. *Faculty:* 1 full-time (0 women), 12 part-time/adjunct (6 women). *Students:* 27 full-time (22 women), 1 part-time (0 women); includes 8 minority (3 Black or African American, non-Hispanic/Latino; 1 American Indian or Alaska Native, non-Hispanic/Latino; 1 Hispanic/Latino; 3 Two or more races, non-Hispanic/Latino), 1 international. Average age 30. In 2017, 14 master's awarded. *Degree requirements:* For master's, final capstone project. *Entrance requirements:* For master's, essay, official transcripts from all prior colleges, two letters of recommendation, current resume, relevant work experience, baccalaureate degree from accredited college or university with minimum cumulative GPA of 3.0, personal interview. Additional exam requirements/recommendations for international students: Recommended—TOEFL. *Application deadline:* Applications are processed on a rolling basis. Application fee: $25. Electronic applications accepted. Application fee is waived when completed online. *Expenses:* $800 per credit hour; $20 technology fee per course; $20 one-time orientation fee; $50 one-time graduation fee. *Financial support:* Scholarships/grants and tuition waivers (partial) available. Financial award application deadline: 7/1; financial award applicants required to submit FAFSA. *Unit head:* Kathryn Eskew, Director of Adult and Graduate Studies, 716-649-7900 Ext. 305, Fax: 716-649-0702, E-mail: keskew@hilbert.edu. *Application contact:* Kim Chiarmonte, Director for Adult and Graduate Recruitment, 716-926-8948, Fax: 716-649-0702, E-mail: kchiarmonte@hilbert.edu.
Website: http://www.hilbert.edu/grad/mpa

Hodges University, Graduate Programs, Naples, FL 34119. Offers accounting (M Acc); business administration (MBA); clinical mental health counseling (MS); health services administration (MS); information systems management (MIS); legal studies (MS); management (MSM). *Program availability:* Part-time, evening/weekend, 100% online, blended/hybrid learning. *Degree requirements:* For master's, comprehensive exam (for some programs), thesis (for some programs). *Entrance requirements:* For master's, essay. Additional exam requirements/recommendations for international students: Recommended—TOEFL. Electronic applications accepted.

Hofstra University, Frank G. Zarb School of Business, Programs in Management and General Business, Hempstead, NY 11549. Offers business administration (MBA), including health services management, management, sports and entertainment management, strategic business management, strategic healthcare management; general management (Advanced Certificate); human resource management (MS, Advanced Certificate). *Program availability:* Part-time, evening/weekend, blended/hybrid learning. *Students:* 131 full-time (58 women), 145 part-time (65 women); includes 102 minority (23 Black or African American, non-Hispanic/Latino; 39 Asian, non-Hispanic/Latino; 37 Hispanic/Latino; 3 Two or more races, non-Hispanic/Latino), 25 international. Average age 33. 327 applicants, 72% accepted, 104 enrolled. In 2017, 116 master's awarded. *Degree requirements:* For master's, thesis optional, capstone course (for MBA), thesis (for MS), minimum GPA of 3.0. *Entrance requirements:* For master's, GMAT/GRE, 2 letters of recommendation, resume, essay. Additional exam requirements/recommendations for international students: Required—TOEFL (minimum score 550 paper-based; 80 iBT); Recommended—IELTS (minimum score 6). *Application deadline:* Applications are processed on a rolling basis. Application fee: $75. Electronic applications accepted. *Expenses:* $1,322 per credit. *Financial support:* In 2017–18, 78 students received support, including 75 fellowships with full and partial tuition reimbursements available (averaging $4,785 per year); research assistantships with full and partial tuition reimbursements available, career-related internships or fieldwork, Federal Work-Study, institutionally sponsored loans, scholarships/grants, tuition waivers (full and partial), and unspecified assistantships also available. Support available to part-time students. Financial award applicants required to submit FAFSA. *Faculty research:* Organizational change; sustainability; entrepreneurial spawning; family business; global supply chain strategies. *Unit head:* Dr. Kaushik Sengupta, Chairperson, 516-463-7825, Fax: 516-463-4834, E-mail: kaushik.sengupta@hofstra.edu. *Application contact:* Sunil Samuel, Assistant Vice President of Admissions, 516-463-4723, Fax: 516-463-4664, E-mail: graduateadmission@hofstra.edu.
Website: http://www.hofstra.edu/business/

Hofstra University, School of Health Professions and Human Services, Programs in Health, Hempstead, NY 11549. Offers foundations of public health (Advanced Certificate); health administration (MHA); health informatics (MS); occupational therapy (MS); public health (MPH); security and privacy in health information systems (Advanced Certificate); sports science (MS), including exercise physiology, strength and conditioning; teacher of students with speech-language disabilities (Advanced Certificate). *Program availability:* Part-time, evening/weekend. *Students:* 257 full-time (176 women), 128 part-time (95 women); includes 197 minority (76 Black or African American, non-Hispanic/Latino; 2 American Indian or Alaska Native, non-Hispanic/Latino; 70 Asian, non-Hispanic/Latino; 42 Hispanic/Latino; 6 Native Hawaiian or other Pacific Islander, non-Hispanic/Latino; 1 Two or more races, non-Hispanic/Latino), 25 international. Average age 28. 620 applicants, 50% accepted, 151 enrolled. In 2017, 87 master's awarded. *Degree requirements:* For master's, internship, minimum GPA of 3.0. *Entrance requirements:* For master's, interview, 2 letters of recommendation, essay, resume. Additional exam requirements/recommendations for international students: Required—TOEFL (minimum score 550 paper-based; 80 iBT). *Application deadline:* Applications are processed on a rolling basis. Application fee: $75. Electronic applications accepted. *Expenses: Tuition:* Full-time $1292. *Required fees:* $970. Tuition and fees vary according to program. *Financial support:* In 2017–18, 148 students received support, including 88 fellowships with full and partial tuition reimbursements available (averaging $3,026 per year), 4 research assistantships with full and partial tuition reimbursements available (averaging $5,619 per year); career-related internships or fieldwork, Federal Work-Study, institutionally sponsored loans, scholarships/grants, traineeships, tuition waivers (full and partial), and unspecified assistantships also available. Support available to part-time students. Financial award applicants required to submit FAFSA. *Faculty research:* Hand and upper extremity rehabilitation; orthotic fabrication; palliative care; neurorehabilitation; public health and health inequities, particularly in the American suburbs and minority communities; obesity; physical activity; social justice in physical education pedagogy. *Unit head:* Dr. Corinne Kyriacou, Chairperson, 516-463-4553, E-mail: corinne.m.kyriacou@hofstra.edu. *Application contact:* Sunil Samuel, Assistant Vice President of Admissions, 516-463-4723, Fax: 516-463-4664, E-mail: graduateadmission@hofstra.edu.
Website: http://www.hofstra.edu/academics/colleges/healthscienceshumanservices/

Holy Family University, Graduate and Professional Programs, School of Business Administration, Philadelphia, PA 19114. Offers accountancy (MS); finance (MBA); health care administration (MBA); human resource management (MBA); information systems management (MBA). *Accreditation:* ACBSP. *Program availability:* Part-time, evening/weekend. *Degree requirements:* For master's, comprehensive exam, thesis optional. *Entrance requirements:* For master's, minimum GPA of 3.0, interview, essay/personal statement, current resume, official transcript of all college or university work. Additional exam requirements/recommendations for international students: Required—TOEFL (minimum score 550 paper-based; 79 iBT), IELTS (minimum score 6), PTE (minimum score 54). Electronic applications accepted. *Expenses: Tuition:* Full-time $13,518; part-time $9012 per credit hour. Tuition and fees vary according to degree level and program.

Husson University, Master of Business Administration Program, Bangor, ME 04401-2999. Offers athletic administration (MBA); biotechnology and innovation (MBA); general business administration (MBA); healthcare management (MBA); hospitality and tourism management (MBA); organizational management (MBA); risk management (MBA). *Program availability:* Part-time, evening/weekend, 100% online, blended/hybrid learning. *Faculty:* 11 full-time (5 women), 19 part-time/adjunct (4 women). *Students:* 83 full-time (44 women), 287 part-time (176 women); includes 25 minority (7 Black or African American, non-Hispanic/Latino; 11 Asian, non-Hispanic/Latino; 4 Hispanic/Latino; 3 Two or more races, non-Hispanic/Latino), 16 international. Average age 35. 158 applicants, 77% accepted, 49 enrolled. In 2017, 120 master's awarded. *Degree requirements:* For master's, comprehensive exam (for some programs), thesis optional. *Entrance requirements:* For master's, minimum GPA of 3.0, letter of recommendation. Additional exam requirements/recommendations for international students: Required—TOEFL (minimum score 550 paper-based; 80 iBT), IELTS (minimum score 6.5). *Application deadline:* Applications are processed on a rolling basis. Application fee: $50. Electronic applications accepted. *Expenses:* $464 per credit. *Financial support:* In 2017–18, 13 students received support. Career-related internships or fieldwork, Federal Work-Study, scholarships/grants, and unspecified assistantships available. Financial award application deadline: 4/15; financial award applicants required to submit FAFSA. *Unit head:* Prof. Stephanie Shayne, Director, Graduate and Online Programs, 207-404-5632, Fax: 207-992-4987, E-mail: shaynes@husson.edu. *Application contact:* Kristen Card, Director of Graduate Admissions, 207-404-5660, Fax: 207-941-7935, E-mail: cardk@husson.edu.
Website: http://www.husson.edu/college-of-business/school-of-business-and-management/master-of-business-administration-mba/

IGlobal University, Graduate Programs, Vienna, VA 22182. Offers accounting (MBA); data management and analytics (MSIT); entrepreneurship (MBA); finance (MBA); global business management (MBA); health care management (MBA); hospitality and tourism management (MBA); human resources management (MBA); information technology (MBA); information technology systems and management (MSIT); leadership and management (MBA); project management (MBA); public service and administration (MBA); software design and management (MSIT).

Independence University, Program in Business Administration in Health Care, Salt Lake City, UT 84107. Offers health care administration (MBA). *Program availability:* Part-time, evening/weekend, online learning. *Degree requirements:* For master's, fieldwork/internship.

Independence University, Program in Health Care Administration, Salt Lake City, UT 84107. Offers MSHCA. *Program availability:* Part-time, evening/weekend, online learning. *Degree requirements:* For master's, fieldwork, internship. *Entrance requirements:* For master's, previous course work in psychology.

Independence University, Program in Health Services, Salt Lake City, UT 84107. Offers community health (MSHS); wellness promotion (MSHS). *Program availability:* Part-time, evening/weekend, online learning. *Degree requirements:* For master's, fieldwork, internship, final project (wellness promotion). *Entrance requirements:* For master's, previous course work in psychology.

Indiana Tech, Program in Business Administration, Fort Wayne, IN 46803-1297. Offers accounting (MBA); health care management (MBA); human resources (MBA); management (MBA); marketing (MBA). *Program availability:* Part-time, evening/weekend, online learning. *Entrance requirements:* For master's, GMAT, bachelor's degree from regionally-accredited university; minimum undergraduate GPA of 2.5; 2 years of significant work experience; 3 letters of recommendation. Electronic applications accepted.

Indiana University Bloomington, School of Public Health, Department of Applied Health Science, Bloomington, IN 47405. Offers behavioral, social, and community health (MPH); family health (MPH); health behavior (PhD); nutrition science (MS); professional health education (MPH); public health administration (MPH); safety management (MS); school and college health education (MS). *Degree requirements:* For master's, thesis optional; for doctorate, comprehensive exam, thesis/dissertation. *Entrance requirements:* For master's, GRE (for MS in nutrition science), 3 recommendations; for doctorate, GRE, 3 recommendations. Additional exam requirements/recommendations for international students: Required—TOEFL (minimum score 550 paper-based; 80 iBT). Electronic applications accepted. *Faculty research:* Cancer education, HIV/AIDS and drug education, public health, parent-child interactions, safety education, obesity, public health policy, public health administration, school health, health education, human development, nutrition, human sexuality, chronic disease, early childhood health.

Indiana University Kokomo, Department of Public Administration and Health Management, Kokomo, IN 46904. Offers health management (MPM, Graduate Certificate); public management (Graduate Certificate); public management and policy (MPM). *Program availability:* Part-time, evening/weekend. *Entrance requirements:* For master's, GRE/GMAT for GPAs lower than 3.0, letters of recommendation. Additional exam requirements/recommendations for international students: Required—TOEFL (minimum score 550 paper-based; 73 iBT). Electronic applications accepted. *Expenses:* Contact institution.

Indiana University Northwest, School of Public and Environmental Affairs, Gary, IN 46408. Offers criminal justice (MPA); environmental affairs (Graduate Certificate); health services (MPA); nonprofit management (Certificate); public management (MPA, Graduate Certificate). *Accreditation:* NASPAA (one or more programs are accredited). *Program availability:* Part-time. *Entrance requirements:* For master's, GRE General Test (minimum combined verbal and quantitative score of 280), GMAT, or LSAT, letters of recommendation. Electronic applications accepted. *Faculty research:* Employment in income security policies, evidence in criminal justice, equal employment law, social welfare policy and welfare reform, public finance in developing countries.

Indiana University of Pennsylvania, School of Graduate Studies and Research, College of Health and Human Services, Department of Employment and Labor Relations, Program in Health Services Administration, Indiana, PA 15705. Offers MS. Program offered at Northpointe Campus near Pittsburgh, PA. *Program availability:* Part-time, evening/weekend, online learning. *Faculty:* 4 full-time (1 woman), 1 part-time/adjunct (0 women). *Students:* 14 full-time (9 women), 16 part-time (15 women); includes 8 minority (4 Black or African American, non-Hispanic/Latino; 1 American Indian or Alaska Native, non-Hispanic/Latino; 2 Asian, non-Hispanic/Latino; 1 Two or more races, non-Hispanic/Latino), 1 international. Average age 31. 37 applicants, 76% accepted, 16 enrolled. In 2017, 15 master's awarded. *Degree requirements:* For master's, thesis optional. *Application deadline:* Applications are processed on a rolling basis. Application fee: $50. Electronic applications accepted. *Expenses:* Tuition, state resident: full-time $12,000; part-time $500 per credit. Tuition, nonresident: full-time $18,000; part-time $750 per credit. *Required fees:* $4073; $165.55 per credit. $64 per term. *Financial support:* In 2017–18, 7 research assistantships with tuition reimbursements (averaging $1,686 per year) were awarded; career-related internships or fieldwork, Federal Work-Study, scholarships/grants, and unspecified assistantships also available. Financial award application deadline: 4/15; financial award applicants required to submit FAFSA. *Unit head:* Dr. Scott Decker, Graduate Coordinator, 724-357-4470, E-mail: s.e.decker@iup.edu.
Website: http://www.iup.edu/elr/grad/health-services-administration-ms/default.aspx

Health Services Management and Hospital Administration

Indiana University of Pennsylvania, School of Graduate Studies and Research, College of Health and Human Services, Department of Nursing and Allied Health Professions, Indiana, PA 15705. Offers health service administration (MS); nursing (MS, PhD); nursing administration (MS); nursing education (MS). *Program availability:* Part-time, evening/weekend. *Faculty:* 12 full-time (11 women), 1 (woman) part-time/adjunct. *Students:* 18 full-time (all women), 86 part-time (76 women); includes 3 minority (1 Asian, non-Hispanic/Latino; 2 Hispanic/Latino), 24 international. Average age 38. 49 applicants, 82% accepted, 15 enrolled. In 2017, 32 master's, 4 doctorates awarded. *Degree requirements:* For master's, thesis optional; for doctorate, comprehensive exam, thesis/dissertation. *Entrance requirements:* For master's, 2 letters of recommendation; for doctorate, GRE, 2 letters of recommendation, current nursing license, current curriculum vitae. Additional exam requirements/recommendations for international students: Required—TOEFL (minimum score 540 paper-based). *Application deadline:* Applications are processed on a rolling basis. Application fee: $50. Electronic applications accepted. *Expenses:* Tuition, state resident: full-time $12,000; part-time $500 per credit. Tuition, nonresident: full-time $18,000; part-time $750 per credit. *Required fees:* $4073; $165.55 per credit. $64 per term. *Financial support:* In 2017–18, 8 research assistantships with tuition reimbursements (averaging $2,505 per year), 1 teaching assistantship with partial tuition reimbursement (averaging $23,305 per year) were awarded; fellowships with partial tuition reimbursements, career-related internships or fieldwork, Federal Work-Study, scholarships/grants, and unspecified assistantships also available. Support available to part-time students. Financial award application deadline: 4/15; financial award applicants required to submit FAFSA. *Unit head:* Dr. Theresa Gropelli, Chairperson, 724-357-2279, E-mail: theresa.gropelli@iup.edu. *Application contact:* Paula Stossel, Assistant Dean of Administration, 724-357-4511, E-mail: pstoss@iup.edu.
Website: http://www.iup.edu/rn-alliedhealth

Indiana University–Purdue University Indianapolis, Kelley School of Business, Business of Medicine MBA Program, Indianapolis, IN 46202-5151. Offers MBA. *Program availability:* Part-time, evening/weekend, blended/hybrid learning. *Entrance requirements:* For master's, GMAT, previous course work in accounting and statistics; MD or DO with three years' experience post-residency. Electronic applications accepted. *Faculty research:* Accounting information systems, auditing, game theory e-commerce, industrial organization, online pricing, organizational change, leadership education and development, managerial skill assessment, exchange rate behavior, financial market impact of Federal Reserve policies, global financial markets, international economics and finance, consumer buying behavior, interventions to increase healthy behavior, marketing of medical products and services, marketing research.

Indiana University–Purdue University Indianapolis, Richard M. Fairbanks School of Public Health, Indianapolis, IN 46202. Offers biostatistics (MS, PhD); environmental health (MPH); epidemiology (MPH, PhD); global health leadership (Dr PH); health administration (MHA); health policy (Graduate Certificate); health policy and management (MPH, PhD); health systems management (Graduate Certificate); product stewardship (MS); public health (Graduate Certificate); social and behavioral sciences (MPH). *Expenses:* Contact institution.

Indiana University–Purdue University Indianapolis, School of Nursing, PhD Program in Nursing Science, Indianapolis, IN 46202. Offers clinical nursing science (PhD); health systems (PhD). *Program availability:* Part-time, blended/hybrid learning. *Degree requirements:* For doctorate, comprehensive exam, thesis/dissertation. *Entrance requirements:* For doctorate, GRE General Test, BSN or MSN from ACEN- or CCNE-accredited program; minimum baccalaureate cumulative GPA of 3.0 or master's degree 3.5. Additional exam requirements/recommendations for international students: Required—TOEFL (minimum score 550 paper-based; 79 iBT). Electronic applications accepted. *Expenses:* Contact institution. *Faculty research:* Quality of life, symptom management, cancer prevention and control, heart failure, pediatric oncology.

Indiana University South Bend, College of Liberal Arts and Sciences, South Bend, IN 46615. Offers advanced computer programming (Graduate Certificate); applied informatics (Graduate Certificate); applied mathematics and computer science (MS); behavior modification (Graduate Certificate); computer applications (Graduate Certificate); computer programming (Graduate Certificate); correctional management and supervision (Graduate Certificate); English (MA); health systems management (Graduate Certificate); international studies (Graduate Certificate); liberal studies (MLS); nonprofit management (Graduate Certificate); paralegal studies (Graduate Certificate); professional writing (Graduate Certificate); public affairs (MPA); public management (Graduate Certificate); social and cultural diversity (Graduate Certificate); strategic sustainability leadership (Graduate Certificate); technology for administration (Graduate Certificate). *Program availability:* Part-time, evening/weekend. *Degree requirements:* For master's, variable foreign language requirement, thesis (for some programs). *Entrance requirements:* For master's, minimum GPA of 3.0. Additional exam requirements/recommendations for international students: Required—TOEFL (minimum score 550 paper-based; 80 iBT). *Expenses:* Contact institution. *Faculty research:* Artificial intelligence, bioinformatics, English language and literature, creative writing, computer networks.

Indiana Wesleyan University, College of Adult and Professional Studies, Graduate Studies in Business, Marion, IN 46953. Offers accounting (MBA, Graduate Certificate); applied management (MBA); business administration (MBA); health care (MBA, Graduate Certificate); human resources (MBA, Graduate Certificate); management (MS); organizational leadership (MA). *Program availability:* Part-time, evening/weekend, online learning. *Degree requirements:* For master's, applied business or management project. *Entrance requirements:* For master's, minimum GPA of 2.5, 2 years of related work experience. Additional exam requirements/recommendations for international students: Required—TOEFL (minimum score 550 paper-based). Electronic applications accepted.

Institute of Public Administration, Programs in Public Administration, Dublin, Ireland. Offers healthcare management (MA); local government management (MA); public management (MA, Diploma).

Iona College, School of Business, Department of Management, Business Administration and Health Care Management, New Rochelle, NY 10801-1890. Offers business administration (MBA); health care analytics (AC); health care management (MBA, AC); human resource management (MBA, PMC); long term care services management (AC); management (MBA, PMC). *Program availability:* Part-time, evening/weekend. *Faculty:* 11 full-time (0 women), 6 part-time/adjunct (3 women). *Students:* 27 full-time (17 women), 62 part-time (41 women); includes 29 minority (14 Black or African American, non-Hispanic/Latino; 1 Asian, non-Hispanic/Latino; 13 Hispanic/Latino; 1 Native Hawaiian or other Pacific Islander, non-Hispanic/Latino), 4 international. Average age 29. 31 applicants, 94% accepted, 17 enrolled. In 2017, 40 master's, 30 other advanced degrees awarded. *Entrance requirements:* For master's, GMAT, 2 letters of recommendation, minimum GPA of 3.0; for other advanced degree, GMAT, minimum GPA of 3.0. Additional exam requirements/recommendations for international students: Required—TOEFL (minimum score 550 paper-based; 80 iBT), IELTS (minimum score 6.5). *Application deadline:* For fall admission, 8/15 priority date for domestic students, 8/1 priority date for international students; for winter admission, 11/15 priority date for domestic students, 11/1 priority date for international students; for spring admission, 2/15 priority date for domestic students, 2/1 priority date for international students; for summer admission, 5/15 priority date for domestic students, 5/1 priority date for international students. Applications are processed on a rolling basis. Application fee: $50. Electronic applications accepted. *Expenses:* Contact institution. *Financial support:* In 2017–18, 20 students received support. Scholarships/grants, tuition waivers (partial), and unspecified assistantships available. Support available to part-time students. Financial award application deadline: 4/15; financial award applicants required to submit FAFSA. *Faculty research:* Information systems, strategic management, corporate values and ethics. *Unit head:* George DeFeis, Chair, 914-633-2631, E-mail: gdefeis@iona.edu. *Application contact:* Katelyn Brunck, Director of MBA Admissions, 914-633-2451, Fax: 914-633-2277, E-mail: kbrunck@iona.edu.
Website: http://www.iona.edu/Academics/Hagan-School-of-Business/Departments/Management-Business-Administration-Health-Car/Graduate-Programs.aspx

Johns Hopkins University, Bloomberg School of Public Health, Department of Health Policy and Management, Baltimore, MD 21205-1996. Offers bioethics and policy (PhD); health administration (MHA); health and public policy (PhD); health economics (MHS); health economics and policy (PhD); health finance and management (MHS); health policy (MSPH); health policy and management (Dr PH); health services research and policy (PhD); public policy (MPP). *Accreditation:* CAHME (one or more programs are accredited). *Program availability:* Part-time. *Students:* 190 full-time (123 women), 135 part-time (73 women); includes 90 minority (10 Black or African American, non-Hispanic/Latino; 53 Asian, non-Hispanic/Latino; 17 Hispanic/Latino; 1 Native Hawaiian or other Pacific Islander, non-Hispanic/Latino; 9 Two or more races, non-Hispanic/Latino), 107 international. Average age 31. 729 applicants, 31% accepted, 96 enrolled. In 2017, 80 master's, 26 doctorates awarded. *Degree requirements:* For master's, thesis (for some programs), internship (for some programs); for doctorate, comprehensive exam, thesis/dissertation, 1-year full-time residency (for some programs), oral and written exams. *Entrance requirements:* For master's, GRE General Test or GMAT, 3 letters of recommendation, curriculum vitae/resume; for doctorate, GRE General Test or GMAT, 3 letters of recommendation, curriculum vitae, transcripts. Additional exam requirements/recommendations for international students: Required—TOEFL (minimum score 100 iBT), IELTS (minimum score 7). *Application deadline:* Applications are processed on a rolling basis. Application fee: $135. Electronic applications accepted. *Financial support:* Fellowships, research assistantships, teaching assistantships, career-related internships or fieldwork, Federal Work-Study, scholarships/grants, traineeships, and stipends available. Support available to part-time students. *Faculty research:* Quality of care and health outcomes, health care finance and technology, health disparities and vulnerable populations, injury prevention, health policy and health care policy. *Unit head:* Dr. Colleen Barry, Chairman. *Application contact:* Mary Sewell, Coordinator, 410-955-2489, Fax: 410-614-9152, E-mail: msewell@jhsph.edu.

Johns Hopkins University, Bloomberg School of Public Health, Department of International Health, Baltimore, MD 21205. Offers global disease epidemiology and control (MSPH, PhD); global health economics (MHS); health systems (MSPH, PhD); human nutrition (MSPH, PhD); social and behavioral interventions (MSPH, PhD). *Students:* 270 full-time (216 women); includes 80 minority (8 Black or African American, non-Hispanic/Latino; 1 American Indian or Alaska Native, non-Hispanic/Latino; 52 Asian, non-Hispanic/Latino; 8 Hispanic/Latino; 11 Two or more races, non-Hispanic/Latino), 70 international. Average age 28. 562 applicants, 40% accepted, 82 enrolled. *Degree requirements:* For master's, comprehensive exam, thesis (for some programs), 1-year full-time residency, 4-9 month internship; for doctorate, comprehensive exam, thesis/dissertation or alternative, 1.5 years' full-time residency, oral and written exams. *Entrance requirements:* For master's, GRE General Test or MCAT, 3 letters of recommendation, resume; for doctorate, GRE General Test or MCAT, 3 letters of recommendation, resume, transcripts. Additional exam requirements/recommendations for international students: Required—TOEFL (minimum score 600 paper-based; 100 iBT); Recommended—IELTS (minimum score 7). Electronic applications accepted. *Financial support:* Fellowships, Federal Work-Study, scholarships/grants, traineeships, and stipends available. *Faculty research:* Nutrition, infectious diseases, health systems, health economics, humanitarian emergencies. *Unit head:* Dr. David Peters, Chair, 410-955-3928, Fax: 410-955-7159, E-mail: dpeters@jhsph.edu. *Application contact:* Cristina G. Salazar, Academic Program Manager, 410-955-3734, Fax: 410-955-7159, E-mail: csalazar@jhsph.edu.
Website: http://www.jhsph.edu/dept/IH/

Johns Hopkins University, Carey Business School, MS in Health Care Management Program, Baltimore, MD 21218. Offers health care management (MS). *Program availability:* Part-time, evening/weekend, blended/hybrid learning, on-site residency requirement. *Faculty:* 93 full-time (33 women), 45 part-time/adjunct (11 women). *Students:* 26 full-time (13 women), 66 part-time (40 women); includes 32 minority (9 Black or African American, non-Hispanic/Latino; 16 Asian, non-Hispanic/Latino; 4 Hispanic/Latino; 1 Native Hawaiian or other Pacific Islander, non-Hispanic/Latino; 2 Two or more races, non-Hispanic/Latino), 16 international. Average age 30. 87 applicants, 72% accepted, 41 enrolled. In 2017, 26 master's awarded. *Degree requirements:* For master's, 36 credits. *Entrance requirements:* For master's, GMAT or GRE. Additional exam requirements/recommendations for international students: Required—TOEFL, IELTS. *Application deadline:* For fall admission, 5/1 for domestic and international students. Applications are processed on a rolling basis. Application fee: $100. Electronic applications accepted. *Expenses:* $66,500 (full-time); $1,330 per credit (part-time). *Financial support:* In 2017–18, 20 students received support. Scholarships/grants available. Support available to part-time students. Financial award application deadline: 4/15; financial award applicants required to submit FAFSA. *Faculty research:* Health economics, leading health care organizations, organization theory, strategy, technology entrepreneurship. *Unit head:* Dr. Kevin Frick, Vice Dean of Education, 410-234-9272, E-mail: kfrick@jhu.edu. *Application contact:* Office of Admissions, 410-234-9220, Fax: 443-529-1554, E-mail: carey.admissions@jhu.edu.
Website: http://carey.jhu.edu/academics/master-of-science/ms-in-healthcare-management/

Kean University, College of Business and Public Management, Program in Public Administration, Union, NJ 07083. Offers health services administration (MPA); non-profit management (MPA); public administration (MPA). *Accreditation:* NASPAA. *Program availability:* Part-time. *Faculty:* 14 full-time (4 women). *Students:* 55 full-time (40 women), 47 part-time (35 women); includes 86 minority (51 Black or African American, non-Hispanic/Latino; 10 Asian, non-Hispanic/Latino; 22 Hispanic/Latino; 3 Two or more races, non-Hispanic/Latino), 3 international. Average age 31. 62 applicants, 94% accepted, 33 enrolled. In 2017, 57 master's awarded. *Degree requirements:* For master's, thesis, internship, research seminar. *Entrance requirements:* For master's, minimum cumulative GPA of 3.0, official transcripts from all institutions attended, two letters of recommendation, personal statement, writing sample, professional resume/curriculum vitae. Additional exam requirements/recommendations for international students: Required—TOEFL (minimum score 550 paper-based; 79 iBT), IELTS (minimum score 6.5). *Application deadline:* For fall admission, 6/30 for domestic and international students; for spring admission, 12/1 for domestic and international students. Applications are processed on a rolling basis. Application fee: $75. Electronic applications accepted. *Expenses:* Tuition, state resident: full-time $13,419; part-time

$653 per credit. Tuition, nonresident: full-time $18,188; part-time $801 per credit. *Required fees:* $3382; $154 per credit. Tuition and fees vary according to course level, course load, degree level and program. *Financial support:* Scholarships/grants and unspecified assistantships available. Financial award applicants required to submit FAFSA. *Unit head:* Dr. Patricia Moore, Program Coordinator, 908-737-4314, E-mail: pmoore@kean.edu. *Application contact:* Pedro Lopes, Admissions Counselor, 908-737-7100, E-mail: gradadmissions@kean.edu.
Website: http://grad.kean.edu/masters-programs/public-administration

Keiser University, Master of Business Administration Program, Fort Lauderdale, FL 33309. Offers accounting (MBA); health services administration (MBA); international business (MBA); management (MBA); marketing (MBA); technology management (MBA). All concentrations except technology management also offered in Mandarin. *Program availability:* Part-time, online learning. *Unit head:* Yan Luo-Beitler, Department Chair.
Website: http://www.keiseruniversity.edu/graduateschool/mba.php#accounting

Kennesaw State University, Coles College of Business, Program in Health Management and Informatics, Kennesaw, GA 30144. Offers MS. Application fee: $60. *Unit head:* Dr. Sweta Sneha, Director, 770-853-0661, E-mail: ssneha@kennesaw.edu. *Application contact:* Timothy Isles, Admissions Counselor, 470-578-4470, Fax: 470-578-9172, E-mail: ksugrad@kennesaw.edu.
Website: http://coles.kennesaw.edu/mshmi/

Kent State University, College of Public Health, Kent, OH 44242-0001. Offers public health (MPH, PhD), including biostatistics (MPH), environmental health sciences (MPH), epidemiology, health policy and management, prevention science (PhD), social and behavioral sciences (MPH). *Accreditation:* CEPH. *Program availability:* Part-time, online learning. *Faculty:* 23 full-time (14 women), 12 part-time/adjunct (3 women). *Students:* 123 full-time (87 women), 152 part-time (120 women); includes 57 minority (37 Black or African American, non-Hispanic/Latino; 1 American Indian or Alaska Native, non-Hispanic/Latino; 8 Asian, non-Hispanic/Latino; 6 Hispanic/Latino; 5 Two or more races, non-Hispanic/Latino), 40 international. Average age 31. 176 applicants, 76% accepted, 81 enrolled. In 2017, 79 master's, 5 doctorates awarded. *Degree requirements:* For master's, comprehensive exam, 300 hours' placement at public health agency, final portfolio and presentation; for doctorate, comprehensive exam, thesis/dissertation. *Entrance requirements:* For master's, GRE, minimum GPA of 3.0, transcripts, goal statement, 3 letters of recommendation; for doctorate, GRE, minimum GPA of 3.0, personal statement, resume, interview, 3 letters of recommendation. Additional exam requirements/recommendations for international students: Required—TOEFL (minimum score 550 paper-based; 79 iBT), IELTS (minimum score 6.5), PTE (minimum score 58), Michigan English Language Assessment Battery. *Application deadline:* For fall admission, 6/15 for domestic and international students; for spring admission, 10/15 for domestic and international students; for summer admission, 3/15 for domestic and international students. Applications are processed on a rolling basis. Application fee: $45 ($70 for international students). Electronic applications accepted. *Expenses:* Tuition, state resident: full-time $11,310; part-time $515 per credit hour. Tuition, nonresident: full-time $20,396; part-time $928 per credit hour. *International tuition:* $18,544 full-time. *Financial support:* Unspecified assistantships available. *Unit head:* Dr. Sonia Alemagno, Dean and Professor of Health Policy and Management, 330-672-6500, E-mail: salemagn@kent.edu. *Application contact:* Dr. Mark A. James, Professor/Chair/Graduate Advisor, 330-672-6506, E-mail: mjames22@kent.edu.
Website: http://www.kent.edu/publichealth/

King's College, William G. McGowan School of Business, Wilkes-Barre, PA 18711-0801. Offers health care administration (MS). *Accreditation:* AACSB. *Program availability:* Part-time. *Entrance requirements:* Additional exam requirements/recommendations for international students: Required—TOEFL (minimum score 600 paper-based).

King University, School of Business and Economics, Bristol, TN 37620-2699. Offers accounting (MBA); finance (MBA); healthcare management (MBA); human resources management (MBA); leadership (MBA); management (MBA); marketing (MBA); project management (MBA). *Program availability:* Part-time, evening/weekend, online learning. *Degree requirements:* For master's, comprehensive exam, thesis optional. *Entrance requirements:* For master's, GMAT, 2 years of work experience. Additional exam requirements/recommendations for international students: Required—TOEFL (minimum score 550 paper-based). Electronic applications accepted. *Faculty research:* International monetary policy.

Lake Erie College, School of Business, Painesville, OH 44077-3389. Offers general management (MBA); health care administration (MBA); information technology management (MBA). *Program availability:* Part-time, evening/weekend. *Entrance requirements:* For master's, GMAT or minimum GPA of 3.0, resume, personal statement. Additional exam requirements/recommendations for international students: Required—TOEFL (minimum score 550 paper-based; 79 iBT), IELTS (minimum score 6), STEP Eiken 1st and pre-1st grade level (for Japanese students). Electronic applications accepted. Application fee is waived when completed online. *Expenses:* Contact institution.

Lake Forest Graduate School of Management, The Leadership MBA Program, Lake Forest, IL 60045. Offers finance (MBA); global business (MBA); healthcare management (MBA); management (MBA); marketing (MBA); organizational behavior (MBA). *Program availability:* Part-time, evening/weekend. *Entrance requirements:* For master's, 4 years of work experience in field, interview, 2 letters of recommendation. Electronic applications accepted.

Lakeland University, Graduate Studies Division, Program in Business Administration, Plymouth, WI 53073. Offers accounting (MBA); finance (MBA); healthcare management (MBA); project management (MBA). *Entrance requirements:* For master's, GMAT. *Expenses:* Contact institution.

Lamar University, College of Graduate Studies, College of Business, Beaumont, TX 77701. Offers accounting (MBA); experiential business and entrepreneurship (MBA); healthcare administration (MBA); MSA/MBA. *Accreditation:* AACSB. *Program availability:* Part-time, evening/weekend. *Faculty:* 50 full-time (14 women), 6 part-time/adjunct (2 women). *Students:* 20 full-time (11 women), 228 part-time (118 women); includes 98 minority (58 Black or African American, non-Hispanic/Latino; 10 Asian, non-Hispanic/Latino; 26 Hispanic/Latino; 4 Two or more races, non-Hispanic/Latino), 32 international. Average age 32. 205 applicants, 92% accepted, 78 enrolled. In 2017, 69 master's awarded. *Degree requirements:* For master's, comprehensive exam (for some programs), thesis optional. *Entrance requirements:* For master's, GMAT. Additional exam requirements/recommendations for international students: Required—TOEFL (minimum score 550 paper-based; 79 iBT), IELTS (minimum score 6.5). *Application deadline:* For fall admission, 8/10 for domestic students, 7/1 for international students; for spring admission, 1/5 for domestic students, 12/1 for international students. Applications are processed on a rolling basis. Application fee: $25 ($50 for international students). Electronic applications accepted. *Expenses:* Contact institution. *Financial support:* Fellowships with tuition reimbursements, research assistantships with partial tuition reimbursements, career-related internships or fieldwork, Federal Work-Study, institutionally sponsored loans, scholarships/grants, and tuition waivers (partial) available. Support available to part-time students. Financial award application deadline: 4/1; financial award applicants required to submit FAFSA. *Faculty research:* Marketing, finance, quantitative methods, management information systems, legal, environmental. *Unit head:* Dr. Enrique R. Venta, Dean, 409-880-8603, Fax: 409-880-8088, E-mail: henry.venta@lamar.edu. *Application contact:* Deidre Mayer, Interim Director, Admissions and Academic Services, 409-880-8888, Fax: 409-880-7419, E-mail: gradmissions@lamar.edu.
Website: http://business.lamar.edu

Lasell College, Graduate and Professional Studies in Management, Newton, MA 02466-2709. Offers business administration (MBA); elder care management (MSM); hospitality and event management (MSM); human resources management (MSM, Graduate Certificate); management (MSM, Graduate Certificate); marketing (MS, Graduate Certificate); project management (MSM, Graduate Certificate). *Accreditation:* ACBSP. *Program availability:* Part-time, evening/weekend, 100% online, blended/hybrid learning. *Faculty:* 1 full-time (0 women), 15 part-time/adjunct (11 women). *Students:* 41 full-time (25 women), 102 part-time (70 women); includes 34 minority (19 Black or African American, non-Hispanic/Latino; 5 Asian, non-Hispanic/Latino; 8 Hispanic/Latino; 2 Two or more races, non-Hispanic/Latino), 29 international. Average age 32. 128 applicants, 46% accepted, 38 enrolled. In 2017, 66 master's, 3 other advanced degrees awarded. *Degree requirements:* For master's, minimum GPA of 3.0; internship or research paper (for MSM). *Entrance requirements:* For master's, one-page personal statement, 2 letters of recommendation, resume, bachelor's degree transcript; proof of microeconomics and statistics (for MBA); for Graduate Certificate, bachelor's degree transcript, 2 letters of recommendation, 1-page personal statement, resume. Additional exam requirements/recommendations for international students: Required—TOEFL (minimum score 550 paper-based, 79 iBT) or IELTS (minimum score 6). *Application deadline:* For fall admission, 8/31 priority date for domestic students, 6/30 priority date for international students; for spring admission, 12/31 priority date for domestic students, 10/31 priority date for international students. Applications are processed on a rolling basis. Electronic applications accepted. *Expenses:* $600 per credit. *Financial support:* Federal Work-Study, scholarships/grants, and tuition discounts available. Support available to part-time students. Financial award application deadline: 8/31; financial award applicants required to submit FAFSA. *Unit head:* Eric Turner, Vice President of Graduate and Professional Studies, 617-243-2071, Fax: 617-243-2450, E-mail: gradinfo@lasell.edu. *Application contact:* Adrienne Franciosi, Director of Graduate Enrollment, 617-243-2214, Fax: 617-243-2450, E-mail: gradinfo@lasell.edu.
Website: http://www.lasell.edu/academics/graduate-and-professional-studies/programs-of-study/master-of-science-in-management.html

Lawrence Technological University, College of Management, Southfield, MI 48075-1058. Offers business administration (MBA, DBA), including business analytics (MBA, MS), cybersecurity (MBA, MS), finance (MBA), information systems (MBA), information technology (MBA), marketing (MBA), project management (MBA, MS); cybersecurity (Graduate Certificate); health IT management (Graduate Certificate); information assurance mangement (Graduate Certificate); information systems (MS), including enterprise resource planning, enterprise security management, project management (MBA, MS); information technology (MS, DM), including business analytics (MBA, MS), cybersecurity (MBA, MS), information assurance (MS), project management (MBA, MS); management (PhD); nonprofit management and leadership (Graduate Certificate); operations management (MS), including manufacturing operations, service operations; project management (Graduate Certificate). *Accreditation:* ACBSP. *Program availability:* Part-time, evening/weekend, 100% online. *Faculty:* 13 full-time (6 women), 7 part-time/adjunct (1 woman). *Students:* 8 full-time (3 women), 280 part-time (102 women); includes 70 minority (34 Black or African American, non-Hispanic/Latino; 2 American Indian or Alaska Native, non-Hispanic/Latino; 18 Asian, non-Hispanic/Latino; 11 Hispanic/Latino; 5 Two or more races, non-Hispanic/Latino), 73 international. Average age 34. 143 applicants, 50% accepted, 68 enrolled. In 2017, 114 master's, 7 doctorates, 10 other advanced degrees awarded. Terminal master's awarded for partial completion of doctoral program. *Degree requirements:* For master's, thesis (for some programs); for doctorate, comprehensive exam, thesis/dissertation. *Entrance requirements:* Additional exam requirements/recommendations for international students: Required—TOEFL (minimum score 550 paper-based; 79 iBT), IELTS (minimum score 6.5). *Application deadline:* For fall admission, 5/27 for international students; for spring admission, 10/8 for international students; for summer admission, 2/14 for international students. Applications are processed on a rolling basis. Application fee: $50. Electronic applications accepted. *Expenses: Tuition:* Full-time $15,274; part-time $1091 per credit. One-time fee: $150. *Financial support:* In 2017–18, 35 students received support, including 8 research assistantships with partial tuition reimbursements available (averaging $3,360 per year); career-related internships or fieldwork, unspecified assistantships, and corporate tuition incentives also available. Financial award application deadline: 4/1; financial award applicants required to submit FAFSA. *Faculty research:* Cybersecurity; risk management; IT governance; security controls and countermeasures; threat modeling cyber resilience; autonomous cars; natural language processing; text mining; machine learning; reflective leadership; emerging leadership theories and practice; motivational studies; teaching effectiveness strategies; teamwork; organization development; strategic planning; strengths-based and positive organizational scholarship; global leadership; globalization; corporate governance. *Unit head:* Dr. Bahman Mirshab, Dean, 248-204-3050, E-mail: mgtdean@ltu.edu. *Application contact:* Jane Rohrback, Director of Admissions, 248-204-3160, Fax: 248-204-2228, E-mail: admissions@ltu.edu.
Website: http://www.ltu.edu/management/index.asp

Lebanon Valley College, Program in Business Administration, Annville, PA 17003-1400. Offers business administration (MBA); healthcare management (MBA); human resources (MBA); leadership and ethics (MBA); project management (MBA). *Program availability:* Part-time, evening/weekend. *Faculty:* 7 full-time (1 woman), 8 part-time/adjunct (1 woman). *Students:* 11 full-time (5 women), 66 part-time (28 women); includes 11 minority (3 Black or African American, non-Hispanic/Latino; 4 Asian, non-Hispanic/Latino; 4 Hispanic/Latino), 3 international. Average age 34. 21 applicants, 81% accepted, 16 enrolled. In 2017, 32 master's awarded. *Degree requirements:* For master's, capstone course. *Entrance requirements:* For master's, GMAT, 3 years of work experience, resume, professional statement (application form, resume, personal statement, transcripts). Additional exam requirements/recommendations for international students: Required—TOEFL (minimum score 80 iBT), IELTS (minimum score 6.5) or STEP Eiken (grade 1). *Application deadline:* Applications are processed on a rolling basis. Application fee: $0. Electronic applications accepted. *Expenses:* $660 per credit hour. *Financial support:* Career-related internships or fieldwork and scholarships/grants available. Financial award application deadline: 3/1; financial award applicants required to submit FAFSA. *Faculty research:* Leadership, motivation, BI, information systems strategies, emerging market development, the role of informational business education, economic growth. *Unit head:* Dr. David Setley, Associate Professor/Chair of Business Administration/Director of the MBA Program, 717-867-6104, Fax: 717-867-6018, E-mail: setley@lvc.edu. *Application contact:* Christine M. Martin, Enrollment and Operations Specialist, 717-867-6486, Fax: 717-867-6013, E-mail: cmartin@lvc.edu.
Website: http://www.lvc.edu/mba

Health Services Management and Hospital Administration

Lehigh University, P.C. Rossin College of Engineering and Applied Science, Department of Industrial and Systems Engineering, Program in Healthcare Systems Engineering, Bethlehem, PA 18015. Offers M Eng, Certificate. *Program availability:* Part-time, blended/hybrid learning. *Faculty:* 3 part-time/adjunct (0 women). *Students:* 17 full-time (9 women), 26 part-time (14 women); includes 9 minority (1 Black or African American, non-Hispanic/Latino; 6 Asian, non-Hispanic/Latino; 1 Hispanic/Latino; 1 Two or more races, non-Hispanic/Latino), 7 international. Average age 28. 19 applicants, 68% accepted, 8 enrolled. In 2017, 18 master's awarded. *Degree requirements:* For master's, comprehensive exam, thesis or alternative, 30 credits. *Entrance requirements:* For master's, GRE (minimum scores in the 75th percentile). Additional exam requirements/recommendations for international students: Required—TOEFL (minimum score 79 iBT). Application fee: $75. *Expenses:* $1,460 per credit. *Financial support:* Application deadline: 1/15. *Faculty research:* Project management; engineering economics; statistics and stochastic processes; operations research; simulation, optimization, and IT. *Unit head:* Prof. Ana Iulia Alexandrescu, Professor of Practice, 610-758-3865, Fax: 610-758-6766, E-mail: aia210@lehigh.edu. *Application contact:* Linda Wismer, Coordinator, 610-758-5867, Fax: 610-758-6766, E-mail: liw511@lehigh.edu.
Website: http://hse.lehigh.edu/

Lenoir-Rhyne University, Graduate Programs, Charles M. Snipes School of Business, Hickory, NC 28601. Offers accounting (MBA); business analytics and information technology (MBA); entrepreneurship (MBA); global business (MBA); healthcare administration (MBA); innovation and change management (MBA); leadership development (MBA). *Accreditation:* ACBSP. *Program availability:* Part-time, evening/weekend, online learning. *Degree requirements:* For master's, capstone course. *Entrance requirements:* For master's, GMAT, GRE, MAT, minimum undergraduate GPA of 2.7, graduate 3.0. Additional exam requirements/recommendations for international students: Required—TOEFL (minimum score 600 paper-based). Electronic applications accepted. *Expenses:* Contact institution.

LeTourneau University, Graduate Programs, Longview, TX 75607-7001. Offers business (MBA); counseling (MA), including licensed professional counselor, marriage and family therapy, school counseling; curriculum and instruction (M Ed); educational administration (M Ed); engineering (ME, MS); engineering management (MEM); health care administration (MS); marriage and family therapy (MA); psychology (MA); strategic leadership (MSL); teacher leadership (M Ed); teaching and learning (M Ed). *Program availability:* Part-time, 100% online, blended/hybrid learning. *Students:* 55 full-time (35 women), 337 part-time (266 women); includes 218 minority (140 Black or African American, non-Hispanic/Latino; 2 American Indian or Alaska Native, non-Hispanic/Latino; 5 Asian, non-Hispanic/Latino; 32 Hispanic/Latino; 39 Two or more races, non-Hispanic/Latino), 3 international. Average age 37. *Entrance requirements:* Additional exam requirements/recommendations for international students: Required—TOEFL. *Application deadline:* For fall admission, 8/22 for domestic students, 8/29 for international students; for winter admission, 10/10 for domestic students; for spring admission, 1/2 for domestic students, 1/10 for international students; for summer admission, 5/1 for domestic and international students. Applications are processed on a rolling basis. Electronic applications accepted. *Expenses:* Contact institution. *Financial support:* Research assistantships, institutionally sponsored loans, and unspecified assistantships available. Financial award applicants required to submit FAFSA.
Website: http://www.letu.edu

Lewis University, College of Business, Program in Business Administration, Romeoville, IL 60446. Offers accounting (MBA); custom elective option (MBA); e-business (MBA); finance (MBA); healthcare management (MBA); human resources management (MBA); international business (MBA); management information systems (MBA); marketing (MBA); project management (MBA); technology and operations management (MBA). *Program availability:* Part-time, evening/weekend. *Students:* 130 full-time (77 women), 187 part-time (107 women); includes 83 minority (27 Black or African American, non-Hispanic/Latino; 3 American Indian or Alaska Native, non-Hispanic/Latino; 7 Asian, non-Hispanic/Latino; 40 Hispanic/Latino; 6 Two or more races, non-Hispanic/Latino), 31 international. Average age 31. In 2017, 99 master's awarded. *Degree requirements:* For master's, comprehensive exam. *Entrance requirements:* For master's, interview, bachelor's degree, resume, two recommendations. Additional exam requirements/recommendations for international students: Required—TOEFL (minimum score 550 paper-based), IELTS. *Application deadline:* For fall admission, 8/15 priority date for domestic students, 5/1 priority date for international students; for spring admission, 11/15 priority date for international students. Applications are processed on a rolling basis. Application fee: $40. Electronic applications accepted. Tuition and fees vary according to program. *Financial support:* Career-related internships or fieldwork, Federal Work-Study, scholarships/grants, and unspecified assistantships available. Financial award application deadline: 5/1; financial award applicants required to submit FAFSA. *Unit head:* Dr. Maureen Culleeney, Academic Program Director, 815-838-0500 Ext. 5631, E-mail: culleema@lewisu.edu. *Application contact:* Michele Ryan, Director of Admission, 815-838-0500 Ext. 5384, E-mail: ryanml@lewisu.edu.

Lindenwood University, Graduate Programs, School of Accelerated Degree Programs, St. Charles, MO 63301-1695. Offers administration (MSA), including management, marketing, project management; business administration (MBA); communications (MA), including digital and multimedia, media management, promotions, training and development; criminal justice and administration (MS); healthcare administration (MS); human resource management (MS); information technology (Certificate); managing information security (MS); managing information technology (MS); managing virtualization and cloud computing (MS); writing (MFA). *Program availability:* Part-time, evening/weekend, 100% online. *Faculty:* 12 full-time (5 women), 90 part-time/adjunct (37 women). *Students:* 597 full-time (383 women), 202 part-time (138 women); includes 248 minority (206 Black or African American, non-Hispanic/Latino; 3 American Indian or Alaska Native, non-Hispanic/Latino; 6 Asian, non-Hispanic/Latino; 21 Hispanic/Latino; 1 Native Hawaiian or other Pacific Islander, non-Hispanic/Latino; 11 Two or more races, non-Hispanic/Latino), 69 international. Average age 36. 526 applicants, 46% accepted, 204 enrolled. In 2017, 537 master's awarded. *Degree requirements:* For master's, thesis (for some programs), minimum cumulative GPA of 3.0; for Certificate, minimum cumulative GPA of 3.0. *Entrance requirements:* For master's, resume, personal statement, official undergraduate transcript, minimum undergraduate cumulative GPA of 3.0. Additional exam requirements/recommendations for international students: Required—TOEFL (minimum score 550 paper-based; 80 iBT); Recommended—IELTS (minimum score 6.5). *Application deadline:* For fall admission, 9/24 priority date for domestic and international students; for winter admission, 1/7 priority date for domestic and international students; for spring admission, 4/8 priority date for domestic and international students; for summer admission, 7/8 priority date for domestic and international students. Applications are processed on a rolling basis. Application fee: $30 ($100 for international students). Electronic applications accepted. *Expenses: Tuition:* Full-time $16,300; part-time $460 per credit. *Required fees:* $660; $330 per credit. Tuition and fees vary according to degree level and program. *Financial support:* In 2017–18, 738 students received support. Career-related internships or fieldwork, institutionally sponsored loans, scholarships/grants, tuition waivers (partial), and unspecified assistantships available. Financial award application deadline: 6/30; financial award applicants required to submit FAFSA. *Unit head:* Dr. Gina Ganahl, Dean, Accelerated Degree Programs, 636-949-4501, Fax: 636-949-4505, E-mail: gganahl@lindenwood.edu. *Application contact:* Kara Schilli, Director, Evening and Graduate Admissions, 636-949-4349, Fax: 636-949-4109, E-mail: adultadmissions@lindenwood.edu.
Website: http://www.lindenwood.edu/academics/academic-schools/school-of-accelerated-degree-programs/

Lindenwood University–Belleville, Graduate Programs, Belleville, IL 62226. Offers business administration (MBA); communications (MA), including digital and multimedia, media management, promotions, training and development; counseling (MA); criminal justice administration (MS); education (MA); healthcare administration (MS); human resource management (MS); school administration (MA); teaching (MAT).

Lipscomb University, College of Business, Nashville, TN 37204-3951. Offers accounting and finance (MBA); audit/accounting (M Acc); business (Certificate); business administration (MM); healthcare management (MBA); leadership (MBA); tax (M Acc); MBA/MS; Pharm D/MM. *Accreditation:* ACBSP. *Program availability:* Part-time, evening/weekend. *Faculty:* 14 full-time (2 women), 8 part-time/adjunct (1 woman). *Students:* 157 full-time (68 women), 9 part-time (6 women); includes 26 minority (9 Black or African American, non-Hispanic/Latino; 7 Asian, non-Hispanic/Latino; 8 Hispanic/Latino; 2 Two or more races, non-Hispanic/Latino), 9 international. Average age 30. 249 applicants, 49% accepted, 52 enrolled. In 2017, 130 master's awarded. *Entrance requirements:* For master's, GMAT, transcripts, interview, 2 references, resume. Additional exam requirements/recommendations for international students: Required—TOEFL (minimum score 570 paper-based). *Application deadline:* For fall admission, 6/15 for domestic students, 2/1 for international students; for winter admission, 6/1 for international students; for spring admission, 11/15 for domestic students. Applications are processed on a rolling basis. Application fee: $50 ($75 for international students). Electronic applications accepted. *Expenses:* Contact institution. *Financial support:* Career-related internships or fieldwork, scholarships/grants, tuition waivers (partial), and unspecified assistantships available. Support available to part-time students. Financial award application deadline: 7/1; financial award applicants required to submit FAFSA. *Faculty research:* Impact of spirituality on organization commitment, women in corporate leadership, psychological empowerment, training. *Unit head:* Allison Duke, Associate Dean of Graduate Business Programs, 615-966-5732, Fax: 615-966-1818, E-mail: allison.duke@lipscomb.edu. *Application contact:* Karen Risley, Manager, Graduate Business Recruiting, 615-966-5145, E-mail: karen.risley@lipscomb.edu.
Website: http://www.lipscomb.edu/business/Graduate-Programs

Lock Haven University of Pennsylvania, College of Natural, Behavioral and Health Sciences, Lock Haven, PA 17745-2390. Offers actuarial science (PSM); athletic training (MS); health promotion/education (MHS); healthcare management (MHS); physician assistant (MHS). Program also offered at the Clearfield, Coudersport, and Harrisburg campuses. *Accreditation:* ARC-PA. *Entrance requirements:* For master's, minimum undergraduate GPA of 3.0. Additional exam requirements/recommendations for international students: Required—TOEFL. Electronic applications accepted.

Loma Linda University, School of Public Health, Program in Healthcare Administration, Loma Linda, CA 92350. Offers MBA. *Entrance requirements:* Additional exam requirements/recommendations for international students: Required—Michigan Test of English Language Proficiency or TOEFL.

London Metropolitan University, Graduate Programs, London, United Kingdom. Offers applied psychology (M Sc); architecture (MA); biomedical science (M Sc); blood science (M Sc); cancer pharmacology (M Sc); computer networking and cyber security (M Sc); computing and information systems (M Sc); conference interpreting (MA); counter-terrorism studies (M Sc); creative, digital and professional writing (MA); crime, violence and prevention (M Sc); criminology (M Sc); curating contemporary art (MA); data analytics (M Sc); digital media (MA); early childhood studies (MA); education (MA, Ed D); financial services law, regulation and compliance (LL M); food science (M Sc); forensic psychology (M Sc); health and social care management and policy (M Sc); human nutrition (M Sc); human resource management (MA); human rights and international conflict (MA); information technology (M Sc); intelligence and security studies (M Sc); international oil, gas and energy law (LL M); international relations (MA); interpreting (MA); learning and teaching in higher education (MA); legal practice (LL M); media and entertainment law (LL M); organizational and consumer psychology (M Sc); psychological therapy (M Sc); psychology of mental health (M Sc); public health (M Sc); public policy and management (MPA); security studies (M Sc); social work (M Sc); spatial planning and urban design (MA); sports therapy (M Sc); supporting older children and young people with dyslexia (MA); teaching languages (MA), including Arabic, English; translation (MA); woman and child abuse (MA).

Long Island University–Brentwood Campus, Graduate Programs, Brentwood, NY 11717. Offers childhood education (MS), including grades 1-6; childhood education/literacy B-6 (MS); childhood education/special education (grades 1-6) (MS); clinical mental health counseling (MS, Advanced Certificate); criminal justice (MS); early childhood education (MS); educational leadership (MS Ed); family nurse practitioner (MS, Advanced Certificate); health administration (MPA); library and information science (MS); literacy (B-6) (MS Ed); school counselor (MS, Advanced Certificate); social work (MSW); special education (MS Ed); students with disabilities generalist (grades 7-12) (Advanced Certificate). *Program availability:* Part-time. *Faculty:* 14 full-time (9 women), 22 part-time/adjunct (11 women). *Students:* 111 full-time (89 women), 47 part-time (34 women); includes 35 minority (8 Black or African American, non-Hispanic/Latino; 1 American Indian or Alaska Native, non-Hispanic/Latino; 3 Asian, non-Hispanic/Latino; 22 Hispanic/Latino; 1 Two or more races, non-Hispanic/Latino), 1 international. Average age 30. 110 applicants, 82% accepted, 63 enrolled. In 2017, 58 master's, 5 other advanced degrees awarded. *Entrance requirements:* For master's and Advanced Certificate, GRE. Additional exam requirements/recommendations for international students: Required—TOEFL or IELTS. *Application deadline:* Applications are processed on a rolling basis. Application fee: $50. Electronic applications accepted. *Expenses: Tuition:* Full-time $21,168; part-time $1201 per credit. *Required fees:* $1840; $920 per term. Tuition and fees vary according to course load. *Financial support:* In 2017–18, 121 students received support. Scholarships/grants available. Support available to part-time students. Financial award application deadline: 2/15; financial award applicants required to submit FAFSA. *Unit head:* Dr. Abby Van Vlerah, Dean and Chief Operating Officer, 631-299-3831, E-mail: abagail.vanvlerah@liu.edu. *Application contact:* Scott Aug, Associate Director of Enrollment Management, 631-287-8506, E-mail: scott.aug@liu.edu.
Website: http://liu.edu/brentwood

Long Island University–Hudson, Graduate School, Purchase, NY 10577. Offers autism (Advanced Certificate); bilingual education (Advanced Certificate); childhood education (MS Ed); crisis management (Advanced Certificate); early childhood education (MS Ed); educational leadership (MS Ed); health administration (MPA); literacy (MS Ed); marriage and family therapy (MS); mental health counseling (MS, Advanced Certificate), including credentialed alcoholism and substance abuse counselor (MS); middle childhood and adolescence education (MS Ed); pharmaceutics (MS), including cosmetic science, industrial pharmacy; public administration (MPA); school counseling (MS Ed, Advanced Certificate); school psychology (MS Ed); special education (MS Ed); TESOL (MS Ed); TESOL (all grades) (Advanced Certificate). *Program availability:* Part-time, evening/weekend. *Faculty:* 8 full-time (6 women), 41 part-time/adjunct (24 women). *Students:* 69 full-time (54 women), 249 part-time (200 women); includes 102 minority (29 Black or African American, non-Hispanic/Latino; 1 American Indian or Alaska Native, non-Hispanic/Latino; 9 Asian, non-Hispanic/Latino; 62 Hispanic/Latino; 1 Native Hawaiian or other Pacific Islander, non-Hispanic/Latino). Average age 33. 153 applicants, 96% accepted, 103 enrolled. In 2017, 138 master's, 36 other advanced degrees awarded. *Entrance requirements:* Additional exam requirements/recommendations for international students: Required—TOEFL. *Application deadline:* Applications are processed on a rolling basis. Application fee: $50. Electronic applications accepted. *Expenses:* Contact institution. *Financial support:* In 2017–18, 32 students received support. Scholarships/grants available. Support available to part-time students. Financial award application deadline: 2/15; financial award applicants required to submit FAFSA. *Unit head:* Dr. Sylvia Blake, Dean and Chief Operating Officer, 914-831-2700, E-mail: westchester@liu.edu.

Long Island University–LIU Brooklyn, School of Business, Public Administration and Information Sciences, Brooklyn, NY 11201-8423. Offers accounting (MBA); accounting (MS); business administration (MBA); computer science (MS); gerontology (Advanced Certificate); health administration (MPA); human resources management (MS); not-for-profit management (Advanced Certificate); public administration (MPA); taxation (MS). *Program availability:* Part-time, evening/weekend. *Faculty:* 18 full-time (7 women), 28 part-time/adjunct (8 women). *Students:* 226 full-time (140 women), 232 part-time (150 women); includes 272 minority (192 Black or African American, non-Hispanic/Latino; 2 American Indian or Alaska Native, non-Hispanic/Latino; 35 Asian, non-Hispanic/Latino; 40 Hispanic/Latino; 3 Two or more races, non-Hispanic/Latino), 88 international. Average age 32. 495 applicants, 64% accepted, 149 enrolled. In 2017, 189 master's, 13 other advanced degrees awarded. *Entrance requirements:* Additional exam requirements/recommendations for international students: Required—TOEFL (minimum score 550 paper-based; 75 iBT). *Application deadline:* Applications are processed on a rolling basis. Application fee: $50. Electronic applications accepted. *Expenses: Tuition:* Full-time $21,618; part-time $1201 per credit. *Required fees:* $1840; $920 per term. Tuition and fees vary according to course load. *Financial support:* In 2017–18, 78 students received support. Career-related internships or fieldwork, Federal Work-Study, scholarships/grants, and unspecified assistantships available. Support available to part-time students. Financial award application deadline: 2/15; financial award applicants required to submit FAFSA. *Faculty research:* Tax policy; public sector budgeting and gender inequities; technology and innovation; game theory; knowledge management. *Unit head:* Dr. Edward Rogoff, Dean, 718-488-1159, E-mail: edward.rogoff@liu.edu. *Application contact:* Luis Santiago, Dean of Enrollment, 718-488-1011, Fax: 718-780-6110, E-mail: bkln-admissions@liu.edu.
Website: http://liu.edu/Brooklyn/Academics/School-of-Business-Public-Administration-and-Information-Sciences

Long Island University–LIU Post, School of Health Professions and Nursing, Brookville, NY 11548-1300. Offers biomedical science (MS); cardiovascular perfusion (MS); clinical lab sciences (MS); clinical laboratory management (MS); dietetic internship (Advanced Certificate); family nurse practitioner (MS, Advanced Certificate); forensic social work (Advanced Certificate); gerontology (Advanced Certificate); health administration (MPA); non-profit management (Advanced Certificate); nursing education (MS); nutrition (MS); public administration (MPA); social work (MSW). *Program availability:* Part-time, blended/hybrid learning. *Faculty:* 23 full-time (17 women), 33 part-time/adjunct (19 women). *Students:* 228 full-time (174 women), 227 part-time (185 women); includes 172 minority (76 Black or African American, non-Hispanic/Latino; 1 American Indian or Alaska Native, non-Hispanic/Latino; 44 Asian, non-Hispanic/Latino; 48 Hispanic/Latino; 3 Two or more races, non-Hispanic/Latino), 60 international. Average age 31. 392 applicants, 67% accepted, 138 enrolled. In 2017, 180 master's, 26 other advanced degrees awarded. *Degree requirements:* For master's, comprehensive exam (for some programs), thesis (for some programs). *Entrance requirements:* Additional exam requirements/recommendations for international students: Required—TOEFL (minimum score 85 iBT) or IELTS (7.5). *Application deadline:* Applications are processed on a rolling basis. Application fee: $50. Electronic applications accepted. *Expenses: Tuition:* Full-time $21,618; part-time $1201 per credit. *Required fees:* $1840; $920 per term. Tuition and fees vary according to course load. *Financial support:* In 2017–18, 102 students received support. Research assistantships, teaching assistantships, career-related internships or fieldwork, Federal Work-Study, scholarships/grants, and unspecified assistantships available. Support available to part-time students. Financial award application deadline: 2/15; financial award applicants required to submit FAFSA. *Faculty research:* Antibiotic resistance, evidence-based practice, family care, interprofessional learning, simulation learning. *Unit head:* Dr. Stacy Gropack, Dean, 516-299-2485, Fax: 516-299-2527, E-mail: post-shpn@liu.edu. *Application contact:* Kathy Riley, Associate Director of Graduate Admissions, 516-299-2900, Fax: 516-299-2137, E-mail: post-enroll@liu.edu.
Website: http://liu.edu/post/health

Louisiana State University Health Sciences Center, School of Public Health, New Orleans, LA 70112. Offers behavioral and community health sciences (MPH); biostatistics (MPH, MS, PhD); community health sciences (PhD); environmental and occupational health sciences (MPH); epidemiology (MPH, PhD); health policy and systems management (MPH). *Accreditation:* CEPH. *Program availability:* Part-time. *Faculty:* 51 full-time (23 women), 41 part-time/adjunct (12 women). *Students:* 98 full-time (77 women), 24 part-time (18 women); includes 55 minority (26 Black or African American, non-Hispanic/Latino; 1 American Indian or Alaska Native, non-Hispanic/Latino; 13 Asian, non-Hispanic/Latino; 13 Hispanic/Latino; 2 Two or more races, non-Hispanic/Latino), 16 international. Average age 24. 208 applicants, 67% accepted, 54 enrolled. *Degree requirements:* For doctorate, thesis/dissertation. *Entrance requirements:* For master's, GRE General Test. Additional exam requirements/recommendations for international students: Recommended—TOEFL (minimum score 550 paper-based; 79 iBT), IELTS. *Application deadline:* Applications are processed on a rolling basis. Application fee: $30. Electronic applications accepted. *Expenses:* Tuition, state resident: full-time $11,835; part-time $518 per hour. Tuition, nonresident: full-time $24,108; part-time $1079 per hour. *Required fees:* $1254; $55 per hour. *Unit head:* Dr. Dean Smith, Dean, 504-568-5700, E-mail: dgsmith@lsuhsc.edu. *Application contact:* Isabel Billiot, Director of Admissions and Student Affairs, 504-568-5773, E-mail: ibilli@lsuhsc.edu.
Website: http://publichealth.lsuhsc.edu/

Louisiana State University in Shreveport, College of Business, Education, and Human Development, Program in Health Administration, Shreveport, LA 71115-2399. Offers MHA. *Program availability:* Part-time, evening/weekend, online learning. *Students:* 170 full-time (134 women), 342 part-time (231 women); includes 193 minority (144 Black or African American, non-Hispanic/Latino; 13 Asian, non-Hispanic/Latino; 23 Hispanic/Latino; 1 Native Hawaiian or other Pacific Islander, non-Hispanic/Latino; 12 Two or more races, non-Hispanic/Latino), 12 international. Average age 34. 258 applicants, 98% accepted, 84 enrolled. In 2017, 139 master's awarded. *Entrance requirements:* For master's, GRE or GMAT, minimum GPA of 3.0, recommendations. Additional exam requirements/recommendations for international students: Required—TOEFL (minimum score 550 paper-based; 61 iBT). *Application deadline:* For fall admission, 6/30 for domestic and international students; for spring admission, 11/30 for domestic and international students; for summer admission, 4/30 for domestic and international students. Applications are processed on a rolling basis. Application fee: $20 ($30 for international students). Electronic applications accepted. *Expenses:* Tuition, state resident: full-time $3098; part-time $344 per credit hour. Tuition, nonresident: full-time $9923; part-time $1103 per credit hour. *Required fees:* $384 per semester. Tuition and fees vary according to program. *Financial support:* In 2017–18, 3 students received support. *Faculty research:* Healthcare marketing, law and ethics, leadership. *Unit head:* Dr. John Fortenberry, Program Director, 318-212-0240, E-mail: john.fortenberry@lsus.edu. *Application contact:* Mary Catherine Harvison, Director of Admissions, 318-797-2400, Fax: 318-797-5286, E-mail: mary.harvison@lsus.edu.

Loyola University Chicago, Quinlan School of Business, MBA Programs, Chicago, IL 60611. Offers accounting (MBA); business ethics (MBA); derivative markets (MBA); economics (MBA); entrepreneurship (MBA); finance (MBA); healthcare management (MBA); human resources management (MBA); information systems management (MBA); international business (MBA); management (MBA); marketing (MBA); risk management (MBA); supply chain management (MBA). *Program availability:* Part-time, evening/weekend. *Faculty:* 84 full-time (28 women), 12 part-time/adjunct (3 women). *Students:* 253 full-time (118 women), 76 part-time (35 women); includes 83 minority (21 Black or African American, non-Hispanic/Latino; 1 American Indian or Alaska Native, non-Hispanic/Latino; 33 Asian, non-Hispanic/Latino; 24 Hispanic/Latino; 4 Two or more races, non-Hispanic/Latino), 37 international. Average age 30. 334 applicants, 52% accepted, 80 enrolled. In 2017, 220 master's awarded. *Entrance requirements:* For master's, GMAT or GRE, official transcripts, two letters of recommendation, statement of purpose, resume. Additional exam requirements/recommendations for international students: Required—TOEFL (minimum score 90 iBT) or IELTS (minimum score 6.5). *Application deadline:* For fall admission, 7/15 for domestic and international students; for winter admission, 10/1 for domestic and international students; for spring admission, 1/15 for domestic and international students; for summer admission, 4/1 for domestic and international students. Applications are processed on a rolling basis. Application fee: $50. Electronic applications accepted. Application fee is waived when completed online. *Expenses:* $4,488 per course. *Financial support:* In 2017–18, 11 students received support. Research assistantships, career-related internships or fieldwork, Federal Work-Study, scholarships/grants, and health care benefits available. *Faculty research:* Social enterprise and responsibility, emerging markets, supply chain management, risk management. *Unit head:* Katherine Acles, Assistant Dean for Graduate Programs, 312-915-6124, Fax: 312-915-7207, E-mail: kacles@luc.edu.

Madonna University, Program in Health Services, Livonia, MI 48150-1173. Offers MSHS. *Program availability:* Part-time. *Degree requirements:* For master's, thesis or alternative. *Entrance requirements:* For master's, GRE General Test or minimum GPA of 3.25. Additional exam requirements/recommendations for international students: Required—TOEFL, TWE. Electronic applications accepted.

Marshall University, Academic Affairs Division, College of Business, Program in Health Care Administration, Huntington, WV 25755. Offers MS. *Program availability:* Part-time, evening/weekend. *Students:* 25 full-time (17 women), 24 part-time (19 women); includes 9 minority (4 Black or African American, non-Hispanic/Latino; 3 Asian, non-Hispanic/Latino; 1 Native Hawaiian or other Pacific Islander, non-Hispanic/Latino; 1 Two or more races, non-Hispanic/Latino). Average age 30. In 2017, 45 master's awarded. *Entrance requirements:* For master's, GMAT or GRE General Test. *Application deadline:* Applications are processed on a rolling basis. Application fee: $40. *Financial support:* Career-related internships or fieldwork and tuition waivers (full) available. Support available to part-time students. Financial award applicants required to submit FAFSA. *Unit head:* Dr. Margie McInerney, Associate Dean, 304-696-2575, E-mail: mcinerney@marshall.edu. *Application contact:* Wesley Spradlin, Academic Advisor, 304-746-8964, Fax: 304-746-1902, E-mail: spradlin2@marshall.edu.

Marymount University, School of Business Administration, Program in Health Care Management, Arlington, VA 22207-4299. Offers MS, MS/MBA, MS/MS. *Accreditation:* CAHME. *Program availability:* Part-time, evening/weekend. *Faculty:* 3 full-time (2 women), 2 part-time/adjunct (1 woman). *Students:* 14 full-time (8 women), 13 part-time (9 women); includes 14 minority (7 Black or African American, non-Hispanic/Latino; 3 Asian, non-Hispanic/Latino; 3 Hispanic/Latino; 1 Two or more races, non-Hispanic/Latino), 3 international. Average age 33. 18 applicants, 100% accepted, 8 enrolled. In 2017, 9 master's awarded. *Degree requirements:* For master's, thesis or alternative. *Entrance requirements:* For master's, GMAT or GRE General Test, resume, interview, personal statement. Additional exam requirements/recommendations for international students: Required—TOEFL (minimum score 600 paper-based; 96 iBT), IELTS (minimum score 6.5). *Application deadline:* For fall admission, 7/16 priority date for domestic and international students; for spring admission, 11/16 priority date for domestic and international students; for summer admission, 4/16 for domestic and international students. Applications are processed on a rolling basis. Application fee: $40. Electronic applications accepted. *Expenses:* $990 per credit. *Financial support:* In 2017–18, 2 students received support, including 1 research assistantship with full and partial tuition reimbursement available (averaging $5,940 per year), 1 teaching assistantship with full and partial tuition reimbursement available (averaging $17,550 per year); career-related internships or fieldwork, Federal Work-Study, scholarships/grants, and unspecified assistantships also available. Support available to part-time students. Financial award application deadline: 3/1; financial award applicants required to submit FAFSA. *Unit head:* Dr. Uma Kelekar, Director, Healthcare Management, 703-284-4984, Fax: 703-527-3830, E-mail: uma.kelekar@marymount.edu. *Application contact:* Francesca Reed, Director, Graduate Admissions, 703-284-5901, Fax: 703-527-3815, E-mail: grad.admissions@marymount.edu.
Website: http://www.marymount.edu/Academics/School-of-Business-Administration/Graduate-Programs/Health-Care-Management-(M-S-)

Maryville University of Saint Louis, The John E. Simon School of Business, St. Louis, MO 63141-7299. Offers accounting (MBA, MS, Certificate); business studies (Certificate); cybersecurity (MBA, MS, Certificate); financial services (MBA, Certificate); healthcare practice management (MBA, Certificate); human resource management (MBA, Certificate); information technology (MBA, Certificate); management (MBA, Certificate); management and leadership (MA); marketing (MBA, Certificate); project management (MBA, Certificate); sport business management (MBA); supply chain management (Certificate); supply chain management/logistics (MBA). *Accreditation:* ACBSP. *Program availability:* Part-time, 100% online, blended/hybrid learning. *Faculty:* 5 full-time (3 women), 31 part-time/adjunct (10 women). *Students:* 222 full-time (90 women), 400 part-time (222 women); includes 185 minority (104 Black or African American, non-Hispanic/Latino; 5 American Indian or Alaska Native, non-Hispanic/Latino; 30 Asian, non-Hispanic/Latino; 37 Hispanic/Latino; 9 Two or more races, non-Hispanic/Latino), 26 international. Average age 33. In 2017, 106 master's awarded. *Degree requirements:* For master's, capstone course (for MBA). *Entrance requirements:* Additional exam requirements/recommendations for international students: Required—TOEFL (minimum score 563 paper-based; 85 iBT). *Application deadline:* Applications are processed on a rolling basis. Electronic applications accepted. *Expenses:* Contact institution. *Financial support:* Career-related internships or fieldwork, Federal Work-Study, tuition waivers (partial), and campus employment available. Financial award application deadline: 4/1; financial award applicants required to submit FAFSA. *Unit head:* Pam Horwitz, Interim Dean, 314-529-9680, Fax: 314-529-9975. *Application contact:* Dustin Loeffler, Director for Graduate Studies in Business, 314-529-9571, Fax: 314-529-9975, E-mail: dloeffler@maryville.edu.
Website: http://www.maryville.edu/bu/business-administration-masters/

Health Services Management and Hospital Administration

Marywood University, Academic Affairs, College of Health and Human Services, School of Social Work, Program in Health Services Administration, Scranton, PA 18509-1598. Offers MHSA. *Program availability:* Part-time. Electronic applications accepted.

McGill University, Faculty of Graduate and Postdoctoral Studies, Faculty of Medicine, Department of Epidemiology and Biostatistics, Montréal, QC H3A 2T5, Canada. Offers community health (M Sc); environmental health (M Sc); epidemiology and biostatistics (M Sc, PhD, Diploma); health care evaluation (M Sc); medical statistics (M Sc).

MCPHS University, Graduate Studies, Program in Drug Regulatory Affairs and Health Policy, Boston, MA 02115-5896. Offers MS. *Program availability:* Part-time, evening/weekend. *Degree requirements:* For master's, thesis, oral defense of thesis. *Entrance requirements:* For master's, GRE General Test, minimum GPA of 3.0. Additional exam requirements/recommendations for international students: Required—TOEFL (minimum score 550 paper-based; 79 iBT). Electronic applications accepted. *Faculty research:* Epidemiology, drug policy, drug regulation, ethics.

Medical University of South Carolina, College of Health Professions, Doctoral Program in Health Administration, Charleston, SC 29425. Offers DHA. *Degree requirements:* For doctorate, comprehensive exam, thesis/dissertation. *Entrance requirements:* For doctorate, experience in health care, interview, master's degree in relevant field, resume, 3 references. Additional exam requirements/recommendations for international students: Required—TOEFL (minimum score 600 paper-based). *Faculty research:* HIV outcomes, health outcomes and statistics, inter-professional education.

Medical University of South Carolina, College of Health Professions, Program in Health Administration-Executive, Charleston, SC 29425. Offers MHA. *Accreditation:* CAHME. *Program availability:* Part-time, online learning. *Degree requirements:* For master's, 20 hours of community service. *Entrance requirements:* For master's, GRE General Test or GMAT, minimum GPA of 3.0. Additional exam requirements/recommendations for international students: Required—TOEFL (minimum score 600 paper-based). Electronic applications accepted. *Faculty research:* Electronic health records; telemedicine; fraud prediction and prevention; decision modeling; continuous quality improvement; empathy, caring, patient-centered health care and health outcomes; heath policy.

Medical University of South Carolina, College of Health Professions, Program in Health Administration-Global, Charleston, SC 29425. Offers MHA. *Entrance requirements:* Additional exam requirements/recommendations for international students: Required—TOEFL.

Medical University of South Carolina, College of Health Professions, Program in Health Administration-Residential, Charleston, SC 29425. Offers MHA. *Accreditation:* CAHME. *Program availability:* Part-time, online learning. *Degree requirements:* For master's, 20 hours of community service, internship or field project. *Entrance requirements:* For master's, GRE General Test, GMAT, minimum GPA of 3.0, 3 references, interview. Additional exam requirements/recommendations for international students: Required—TOEFL (minimum score 550 paper-based). *Faculty research:* Electronic health records; telemedicine; fraud prediction and prevention; decision modeling; continuous quality improvement; empathy, caring, patient-centered health care; health policy; health outcomes.

Meharry Medical College, School of Graduate Studies, Division of Public Health Practice, Nashville, TN 37208-9989. Offers occupational medicine (MSPH); public health administration (MSPH). *Accreditation:* CEPH. *Program availability:* Part-time, evening/weekend. *Degree requirements:* For master's, thesis, externship. *Entrance requirements:* For master's, GRE General Test, GMAT. *Expenses:* Contact institution.

Mercy College, School of Social and Behavioral Sciences, Program in Health Services Management, Dobbs Ferry, NY 10522-1189. Offers MPA, MS. *Program availability:* Part-time, evening/weekend, blended/hybrid learning. *Students:* 32 full-time (28 women), 27 part-time (24 women); includes 44 minority (18 Black or African American, non-Hispanic/Latino; 1 American Indian or Alaska Native, non-Hispanic/Latino; 2 Asian, non-Hispanic/Latino; 23 Hispanic/Latino). Average age 34. 41 applicants, 49% accepted, 14 enrolled. In 2017, 24 master's awarded. *Entrance requirements:* For master's, interview, resume, undergraduate transcript. Additional exam requirements/recommendations for international students: Required—TOEFL (minimum score 600 paper-based; 100 iBT), IELTS (minimum score 8). *Application deadline:* For fall admission, 8/1 for international students. Applications are processed on a rolling basis. Application fee: $40. Electronic applications accepted. *Expenses: Tuition:* Full-time $15,426; part-time $857 per credit hour. *Required fees:* $630; $158 per term. Tuition and fees vary according to course load, degree level and program. *Financial support:* Career-related internships or fieldwork, Federal Work-Study, scholarships/grants, and unspecified assistantships available. Support available to part-time students. Financial award applicants required to submit FAFSA. *Unit head:* Dr. Karol Dean, Dean, School of Social and Behavioral Sciences, 914-674-7517, E-mail: kdean@mercy.edu. *Application contact:* Allison Gurdineer, Senior Director of Admissions, 877-637-2946, Fax: 914-674-7382, E-mail: admissions@mercy.edu.
Website: https://www.mercy.edu/social-and-behavioral-sciences/social-sciences

Mercy College of Ohio, Program in Health Administration, Toledo, OH 43604. Offers MHA. *Program availability:* Part-time-only, online only. *Entrance requirements:* For master's, bachelor's degree or higher from regionally-accredited higher education institution, minimum overall GPA of 3.0 on undergraduate and graduate course work. Application fee: $50. Electronic applications accepted. *Expenses: Tuition:* Part-time $600 per credit hour. *Required fees:* $450 per semester. One-time fee: $250 part-time. *Financial support:* Applicants required to submit FAFSA. *Unit head:* Dr. Kimberly Watson, Director of Graduate Studies, 419-251-1852, E-mail: kim.watson@mercycollege.edu.
Website: https://www.mercycollege.edu/program/health-administration-master

Midwestern State University, Billie Doris McAda Graduate School, Robert D. and Carol Gunn College of Health Sciences and Human Services, Department of Criminal Justice and Health Services Administration, Wichita Falls, TX 76308. Offers criminal justice (MA); health information management (MHA); health services administration (Graduate Certificate); medical practice management (MHA); public and community sector health care management (MHA); rural and urban hospital management (MHA). *Program availability:* Part-time, evening/weekend. *Degree requirements:* For master's, comprehensive exam, thesis. *Entrance requirements:* For master's, GRE. Additional exam requirements/recommendations for international students: Required—TOEFL (minimum score 550 paper-based). Electronic applications accepted. *Faculty research:* Universal service policy, telehealth, bullying, healthcare financial management, public health ethics.

Milligan College, Area of Business Administration, Milligan College, TN 37682. Offers health sector management (MBA, Graduate Certificate); leadership (MBA, Graduate Certificate); operations management (MBA, Graduate Certificate). *Program availability:* 100% online, blended/hybrid learning. *Faculty:* 4 full-time (1 woman), 3 part-time/adjunct (2 women). *Students:* 30 full-time (16 women), 1 international. Average age 38. 30 applicants, 83% accepted, 24 enrolled. In 2017, 27 master's awarded. *Degree requirements:* For master's, thesis or alternative. *Entrance requirements:* For master's, GMAT if undergraduate GPA less than 3.0, undergraduate degree and supporting transcripts, relevant full-time work experience, essay/personal statement, professional recommendations. Additional exam requirements/recommendations for international students: Required—TOEFL (minimum score 550 paper-based, 79 iBT) or IELTS (6.5). *Application deadline:* For fall admission, 8/1 for domestic students, 6/1 for international students; for spring admission, 1/15 for domestic students, 12/1 for international students. Applications are processed on a rolling basis. Application fee: $30. Electronic applications accepted. *Expenses:* Contact institution. *Financial support:* Scholarships/grants available. Financial award application deadline: 12/1; financial award applicants required to submit FAFSA. *Faculty research:* International microfinance; economic development in Appalachia; job satisfaction; business ethics; internal migration. *Unit head:* Dr. David Campbell, Area Chair of Business, 423-461-8674, Fax: 423-461-8677, E-mail: dacampbell@milligan.edu. *Application contact:* Rebecca Banton, Graduate Admissions Recruiter, Business Area, 423-461-8662, Fax: 423-461-8789, E-mail: rbbanton@milligan.edu.
Website: http://www.milligan.edu/GPS

Milwaukee School of Engineering, MS Program in Nursing - Leadership and Management, Milwaukee, WI 53202-3109. Offers MSN. *Program availability:* Part-time, evening/weekend, 100% online, blended/hybrid learning. *Students:* 5 full-time (all women), 1 (woman) part-time; includes 2 minority (1 Asian, non-Hispanic/Latino; 1 Hispanic/Latino). Average age 31. 5 applicants, 60% accepted, 3 enrolled. In 2017, 3 master's awarded. *Entrance requirements:* For master's, GRE General Test or GMAT if undergraduate GPA less than 3.0, 2 letters of recommendation; BSN from accredited institution; current unrestricted licensure as a Registered Nurse. Additional exam requirements/recommendations for international students: Required—TOEFL (minimum score 90 iBT), IELTS (minimum score 7). *Application deadline:* Applications are processed on a rolling basis. Application fee: $0. Electronic applications accepted. *Expenses: Tuition:* Part-time $814 per credit hour. *Required fees:* $12.50 per credit hour. *Financial support:* In 2017–18, 2 students received support. Scholarships/grants available. Financial award application deadline: 3/15; financial award applicants required to submit FAFSA. *Unit head:* Dr. Debra Jenks, Program Director, 414-277-4516, E-mail: jenks@msoe.edu. *Application contact:* Brian Rutz, Graduate Admission Counselor, 414-277-7200, E-mail: rutz@msoe.edu.
Website: https://www.msoe.edu/academics/graduate-degrees/health/nursing/

Minnesota State University Moorhead, Graduate Studies, College of Science, Health and the Environment, Moorhead, MN 56563. Offers healthcare administration (MHA); nursing (MS); school psychology (MS, Psy S). *Program availability:* Part-time. *Faculty:* 24. *Students:* 34 full-time (25 women), 104 part-time (84 women). Average age 32. 42 applicants, 74% accepted. In 2017, 34 master's, 11 other advanced degrees awarded. *Degree requirements:* For master's, comprehensive exam (for some programs), thesis, final oral defense. *Entrance requirements:* For master's, GRE (for school psychology program), minimum GPA of 3.0, essay, letters of reference. Additional exam requirements/recommendations for international students: Required—TOEFL (minimum score 550 paper-based). *Application deadline:* Applications are processed on a rolling basis. Application fee: $20. Electronic applications accepted. *Expenses:* Tuition, state resident: full-time $9000; part-time $374 per credit. Tuition, nonresident: full-time $18,000; part-time $748 per credit. *Required fees:* $1055; $43.96 per credit. Tuition and fees vary according to degree level, program and reciprocity agreements. *Financial support:* Federal Work-Study and unspecified assistantships available. Financial award application deadline: 10/1; financial award applicants required to submit FAFSA. *Unit head:* Dr. Jeffrey Bodwin, Dean, 218-477-5892, E-mail: jeffrey.bodwin@mnstate.edu. *Application contact:* Karla Wenger, Graduate Studies Office Manager, 218-477-2344, Fax: 218-477-2482, E-mail: wengerk@mnstate.edu.
Website: http://www.mnstate.edu/cshe/

Misericordia University, College of Business, Master of Business Administration Program, Dallas, PA 18612-1098. Offers accounting (MBA); healthcare management (MBA); human resource management (MBA); management (MBA); sport management (MBA). *Program availability:* Part-time, evening/weekend, online learning. *Entrance requirements:* For master's, GMAT, MAT, GRE (50th percentile or higher), or minimum undergraduate GPA of 3.0, interview. Additional exam requirements/recommendations for international students: Required—TOEFL. Electronic applications accepted. Application fee is waived when completed online. *Expenses:* Contact institution.

Misericordia University, College of Business, Program in Organizational Management, Dallas, PA 18612-1098. Offers healthcare management (MS); human resource management (MS); management (MS). *Program availability:* Part-time, evening/weekend, online learning. *Entrance requirements:* For master's, GRE General Test, MAT (35th percentile or higher), or minimum undergraduate GPA of 3.0. Additional exam requirements/recommendations for international students: Required—TOEFL. Electronic applications accepted. Application fee is waived when completed online. *Expenses:* Contact institution.

Mississippi College, Graduate School, Program in Health Services Administration, Clinton, MS 39058. Offers MHSA. *Program availability:* Part-time. *Degree requirements:* For master's, comprehensive exam. *Entrance requirements:* For master's, GRE General Test, minimum GPA of 2.5. Additional exam requirements/recommendations for international students: Recommended—TOEFL, IELTS. Electronic applications accepted.

Missouri State University, Graduate College, College of Business, Department of Management and Information Technology, Springfield, MO 65897. Offers health administration (MHA). *Program availability:* Part-time, evening/weekend. *Faculty:* 12 full-time (4 women). *Students:* 27 full-time (19 women), 98 part-time (39 women); includes 26 minority (13 Black or African American, non-Hispanic/Latino; 7 Asian, non-Hispanic/Latino; 6 Hispanic/Latino), 12 international. Average age 27. 49 applicants, 41% accepted, 20 enrolled. In 2017, 70 master's awarded. *Degree requirements:* For master's, thesis optional. *Entrance requirements:* For master's, GMAT or GRE, minimum GPA of 2.75. Additional exam requirements/recommendations for international students: Required—TOEFL (minimum score 550 paper-based; 79 iBT), IELTS (minimum score 6). *Application deadline:* For fall admission, 7/20 priority date for domestic students, 5/1 for international students; for spring admission, 12/20 priority date for domestic students, 9/1 for international students; for summer admission, 5/20 priority date for domestic students. Applications are processed on a rolling basis. Application fee: $35 ($50 for international students). Electronic applications accepted. *Expenses:* Tuition, state resident: full-time $2915; part-time $2021 per credit hour. Tuition, nonresident: full-time $5354; part-time $3647 per credit hour. *International tuition:* $11,992 full-time. *Required fees:* $173; $173 per credit hour. Tuition and fees vary according to class time, course level, course load, degree level, campus/location and program. *Financial support:* Career-related internships or fieldwork, institutionally sponsored loans, scholarships/grants, tuition waivers (partial), and unspecified assistantships available. Support available to part-time students. Financial award application deadline: 3/31; financial award applicants required to submit FAFSA. *Faculty research:* Medical tourism, performance management, entrepreneurship. *Unit head:* Dr. Josh Davis, Department Head, 417-836-4131, E-mail: management@missouristate.edu. *Application contact:* Stephanie Praschan, Director, Graduate Enrollment Management, 417-836-5330, E-mail: stephaniepraschan@missouristate.edu.
Website: http://mgt.missouristate.edu/

Molloy College, The Barbara H. Hagan School of Nursing, Rockville Centre, NY 11571-5002. Offers adult - gerontology nurse practitioner (MS); adult-gerontology clinical nurse specialist (DNP); adult-gerontology nurse practitioner (DNP); clinical nurse specialist: adult - gerontology (MS); family nurse practitioner (MS, DNP); family psychiatric/mental health nurse practitioner (MS, DNP); nursing (PhD, Advanced Certificate); nursing administration with informatics (MS); nursing education (MS); pediatric nurse practitioner (MS, DNP). *Accreditation:* AACN. *Program availability:* Part-time, evening/weekend. *Faculty:* 28 full-time (all women), 7 part-time/adjunct (6 women). *Students:* 19 full-time (14 women), 574 part-time (527 women); includes 336 minority (179 Black or African American, non-Hispanic/Latino; 2 American Indian or Alaska Native, non-Hispanic/Latino; 107 Asian, non-Hispanic/Latino; 42 Hispanic/Latino; 1 Native Hawaiian or other Pacific Islander, non-Hispanic/Latino; 5 Two or more races, non-Hispanic/Latino), 4 international. Average age 44. 292 applicants, 65% accepted, 147 enrolled. In 2017, 135 master's, 9 doctorates, 5 other advanced degrees awarded. *Degree requirements:* For master's, thesis optional. *Entrance requirements:* For master's, 3 letters of reference, BS in nursing, minimum undergraduate GPA of 3.0; for Advanced Certificate, 3 letters of reference, master's degree in nursing. Additional exam requirements/recommendations for international students: Required—TOEFL (minimum score 550 paper-based; 79 iBT). *Application deadline:* For fall admission, 9/2 priority date for domestic students; for spring admission, 1/20 priority date for domestic students. Applications are processed on a rolling basis. Application fee: $60. Electronic applications accepted. *Expenses: Tuition:* Full-time $19,980; part-time $1110 per credit. *Required fees:* $1040. Tuition and fees vary according to course load and degree level. *Financial support:* Research assistantships with partial tuition reimbursements, teaching assistantships with partial tuition reimbursements, institutionally sponsored loans, scholarships/grants, and unspecified assistantships available. Support available to part-time students. Financial award application deadline: 3/1; financial award applicants required to submit FAFSA. *Faculty research:* Workplace violence involving nurses and psychiatric patients; moral distress in nursing; primary care of veterans; the role of service immersion programs in graduate nursing education; academic integrity. *Unit head:* Dr. Marcia R. Gardner, Dean, The Barbara H. Hagan School of Nursing, 516-323-3651, E-mail: mgardner@molloy.edu. *Application contact:* Jaclyn Machowicz, Assistant Director for Admissions, 516-323-4010, E-mail: jmachowicz@molloy.edu.

Molloy College, Graduate Business Program, Rockville Centre, NY 11571-5002. Offers accounting (MBA); finance (MBA, Post-Master's Certificate, Postbaccalaureate Certificate); healthcare (MBA, Post-Master's Certificate, Postbaccalaureate Certificate); management (MBA); marketing (MBA, Post-Master's Certificate, Postbaccalaureate Certificate); personal financial planning (MBA). *Program availability:* Part-time, evening/weekend. *Faculty:* 8 full-time (3 women), 7 part-time/adjunct (2 women). *Students:* 53 full-time (29 women), 175 part-time (89 women); includes 88 minority (38 Black or African American, non-Hispanic/Latino; 18 Asian, non-Hispanic/Latino; 30 Hispanic/Latino; 2 Two or more races, non-Hispanic/Latino), 3 international. Average age 39. 128 applicants, 68% accepted, 81 enrolled. In 2017, 125 master's awarded. *Entrance requirements:* Additional exam requirements/recommendations for international students: Required—TOEFL (minimum score 550 paper-based; 79 iBT). *Application deadline:* Applications are processed on a rolling basis. Application fee: $60. Electronic applications accepted. *Expenses: Tuition:* Full-time $19,980; part-time $1110 per credit. *Required fees:* $1040. Tuition and fees vary according to course load and degree level. *Financial support:* Application deadline: 3/1; applicants required to submit FAFSA. *Faculty research:* Graduate education - pedagogy and the capstone experience; Freedom of Speech in the workplace; employer liability for sexual harassment in the workplace; educational economics and industrial organization; corporate governance and distressed debt analysis; social network analysis; market segmentation. *Unit head:* Dr. Maureen Mackenzie, Dean, Division of Business/Director of Graduate Programs, 516-323-3080, E-mail: mmackenzie@molloy.edu. *Application contact:* Jaclyn Machowicz, Assistant Director for Admissions, 516-323-4010, E-mail: jmachowicz@molloy.edu.
Website: http://www.molloy.edu/academics/graduate-programs/graduate-business

Monroe College, King Graduate School, Bronx, NY 10468. Offers accounting (MS); business administration (MBA), including entrepreneurship, finance, general business administration, healthcare management, human resources, information technology, marketing; computer science (MS); criminal justice (MS); hospitality management (MS); public health (MPH), including biostatistics and epidemiology, community health, health administration and leadership. *Program availability:* Online learning. Application fee: $50.
Website: https://www.monroecollege.edu/Degrees/King-Graduate-School/

Montana State University Billings, College of Allied Health Professions, Program in Health Administration, Billings, MT 59101. Offers MHA. *Program availability:* Part-time, evening/weekend, 100% online, blended/hybrid learning. *Degree requirements:* For master's, thesis or professional paper and/or field experience. *Entrance requirements:* For master's, GRE General Test or GMAT, minimum undergraduate GPA of 3.0, graduate 3.25; 3 years' clinical or administrative experience in health care delivery or 5 years' experience in business or industry management. Additional exam requirements/recommendations for international students: Required—TOEFL (minimum score 79 iBT), IELTS (minimum score 6.5). *Application deadline:* For fall admission, 4/20 for domestic students. Applications are processed on a rolling basis. Application fee: $40. Electronic applications accepted. *Expenses:* Tuition, state resident: full-time $11,740; part-time $7880 per year. Tuition, nonresident: full-time $32,200; part-time $24,140 per year. *Financial support:* Career-related internships or fieldwork, Federal Work-Study, institutionally sponsored loans, scholarships/grants, tuition waivers (partial), and unspecified assistantships available. Support available to part-time students. Financial award application deadline: 5/1; financial award applicants required to submit FAFSA. *Unit head:* Dr. Catherine Grott, Interim Director, 406-896-5832. *Application contact:* Dr. Catherine Grott, Interim Director, 406-896-5832.

Moravian College, Graduate and Continuing Studies, Business and Management Programs, Bethlehem, PA 18018-6650. Offers accounting (MBA); business analytics (MBA); business management (MBA); health administration (MHA); healthcare management (MBA); HR leadership (MSHRM); human resource management (MBA); learning and performance management (MSHRM); supply chain management (MBA). *Program availability:* Part-time, evening/weekend. *Faculty:* 5 full-time (2 women), 9 part-time/adjunct (3 women). *Students:* 13 full-time (10 women), 80 part-time (45 women); includes 13 minority (6 Black or African American, non-Hispanic/Latino; 6 Hispanic/Latino; 1 Two or more races, non-Hispanic/Latino). Average age 31. 55 applicants, 91% accepted, 31 enrolled. In 2017, 29 master's awarded. *Entrance requirements:* For master's, current resume, official transcripts, 2 letters of recommendation. Additional exam requirements/recommendations for international students: Required—TOEFL (minimum score 550 paper-based), IELTS (minimum score 6.5). *Application deadline:* For fall admission, 8/1 priority date for domestic and international students; for spring admission, 1/1 priority date for domestic and international students; for summer admission, 5/1 priority date for domestic and international students. Applications are processed on a rolling basis. Electronic applications accepted. *Expenses: Tuition:* Full-time $15,714; part-time $2619 per course. *Required fees:* $45 per semester. Tuition and fees vary according to program. *Financial support:* In 2017–18, 3 students received support, including 2 research assistantships with full tuition reimbursements available. Financial award applicants required to submit FAFSA. *Faculty research:* Leadership, change management, human resources. *Unit head:* Dr. Liz Kleintop, Associate Chair of Graduate Business, 610-861-1400, Fax: 610-861-1466, E-mail: graduate@moravian.edu. *Application contact:* Sean Rossi, Student Experience Mentor, 610-861-1400, Fax: 610-861-1466, E-mail: graduate@moravian.edu.
Website: https://www.moravian.edu/graduate

Mount Aloysius College, Program in Business Administration, Cresson, PA 16630. Offers accounting (MBA); health and human services administration (MBA); non-profit management (MBA); project management (MBA). *Program availability:* Part-time, evening/weekend. *Entrance requirements:* Additional exam requirements/recommendations for international students: Required—IELTS (minimum score 5.5); Recommended—TOEFL. *Application deadline:* For fall admission, 8/1 for domestic students; for spring admission, 12/1 for domestic students. Applications are processed on a rolling basis. Application fee: $30. Electronic applications accepted. Application fee is waived when completed online. *Expenses: Tuition:* Full-time $14,000; part-time $790 per credit hour. *Financial support:* Unspecified assistantships available. Financial award applicants required to submit FAFSA. *Application contact:* Matthew P. Bodenschatz, Director of Graduate and Continuing Education Admissions, 814-886-6556, Fax: 814-886-6441, E-mail: mbodenschatz@mtaloy.edu.
Website: http://www.mtaloy.edu

Mount St. Joseph University, Doctor of Nursing Practice Program, Cincinnati, OH 45233-1670. Offers health systems leadership (DNP). *Accreditation:* AACN. *Program availability:* Part-time-only. *Faculty:* 9 full-time (all women), 15 part-time/adjunct (all women). *Students:* 53 part-time (50 women); includes 4 minority (all Black or African American, non-Hispanic/Latino). Average age 48. In 2017, 1 doctorate awarded. *Degree requirements:* For doctorate, capstone, minimum cumulative GPA of 3.0, completion of program within 5 years of enrollment, minimum of 75% of credits earned at Mount St. Joseph University, 1000 practicum hours between prior master's degree and DNP programs, minimum of 400 practicum hours in the DNP program. *Entrance requirements:* For doctorate, essay; MSN from regionally-accredited university; minimum graduate GPA of 3.0; professional resume; two professional references; interview; 2 years of clinical nursing experience; active RN license; minimum C grade in an undergraduate statistics course; official documentation of practicum hours post-BSN. Additional exam requirements/recommendations for international students: Required—TOEFL (minimum score 560 paper-based; 83 iBT). *Application deadline:* Applications are processed on a rolling basis. Application fee: $50. Electronic applications accepted. *Expenses:* $655 per credit hour. *Financial support:* Applicants required to submit FAFSA. *Unit head:* Dr. Nancy Hinzman, Assistant Dean of Nursing, 513-244-4325, Fax: 513-451-2547, E-mail: nancy.hinzman@msj.edu. *Application contact:* Autumn Richards, Admission Counselor for Graduate Studies, 513-244-4228, Fax: 513-244-4629, E-mail: autumn.richards@msj.edu.
Website: http://www.msj.edu/academics/graduate-programs/doctor-of-nursing-practice/

Mount Saint Mary College, School of Business, Newburgh, NY 12550-3494. Offers business (MBA); financial planning (MBA); health care management (MBA). *Program availability:* Part-time, evening/weekend. *Faculty:* 4 full-time (1 woman), 8 part-time/adjunct (4 women). *Students:* 48 full-time (21 women), 30 part-time (21 women); includes 20 minority (6 Black or African American, non-Hispanic/Latino; 1 Asian, non-Hispanic/Latino; 12 Hispanic/Latino; 1 Two or more races, non-Hispanic/Latino). Average age 32. 17 applicants, 65% accepted, 6 enrolled. In 2017, 41 master's awarded. *Degree requirements:* For master's, thesis or alternative. *Entrance requirements:* For master's, GMAT or minimum undergraduate GPA of 2.7. Additional exam requirements/recommendations for international students: Required—TOEFL (minimum score 80 iBT). *Application deadline:* Applications are processed on a rolling basis. Application fee: $45. Electronic applications accepted. Application fee is waived when completed online. *Expenses: Tuition:* Full-time $14,454; part-time $803 per credit. *Required fees:* $172; $86 per semester. *Financial support:* In 2017–18, 18 students received support. Unspecified assistantships available. Financial award application deadline: 4/15; financial award applicants required to submit FAFSA. *Faculty research:* Financial reform, entrepreneurship and small business development, global business relations, technology's impact on business decision-making, college-assisted business education. *Unit head:* Dr. Moira Tolan, Graduate Coordinator, 845-569-3121, Fax: 845-562-6762, E-mail: moira.tolan@msmc.edu. *Application contact:* Lisa Alvarez, Director of Admissions for Graduate Programs and Adult Degree Completion, 845-569-3166, Fax: 845-569-3450, E-mail: lisa.gallina@msmc.edu.
Website: http://www.msmc.edu/Academics/Graduate_Programs/master_of_business_administration.be

Mount Saint Mary's University, Graduate Division, Los Angeles, CA 90049. Offers business administration (MBA); counseling psychology (MS); creative writing (MFA); education (MS, Certificate); film and television (MFA); health policy and management (MS); humanities (MA); nursing (MSN, Certificate); physical therapy (DPT); religious studies (MA). *Program availability:* Part-time, evening/weekend. *Faculty:* 50 full-time (35 women), 116 part-time/adjunct (81 women). *Students:* 670 full-time (518 women), 147 part-time (116 women); includes 414 minority (73 Black or African American, non-Hispanic/Latino; 4 American Indian or Alaska Native, non-Hispanic/Latino; 60 Asian, non-Hispanic/Latino; 259 Hispanic/Latino; 7 Native Hawaiian or other Pacific Islander, non-Hispanic/Latino; 11 Two or more races, non-Hispanic/Latino), 4 international. Average age 32. 1,398 applicants, 21% accepted, 242 enrolled. In 2017, 170 master's, 28 doctorates, 35 other advanced degrees awarded. *Entrance requirements:* Additional exam requirements/recommendations for international students: Required—TOEFL. *Application deadline:* For fall admission, 6/30 priority date for domestic and international students; for spring admission, 10/30 priority date for domestic and international students; for summer admission, 3/30 priority date for domestic and international students. Applications are processed on a rolling basis. Application fee: $50. Electronic applications accepted. *Expenses: Tuition:* Part-time $905 per unit. One-time fee: $155 part-time. Tuition and fees vary according to degree level and program. *Financial support:* Career-related internships or fieldwork, Federal Work-Study, institutionally sponsored loans, and tuition waivers (full and partial) available. Support available to part-time students. Financial award application deadline: 3/15; financial award applicants required to submit FAFSA. *Unit head:* Albert Ramos, Director of Graduate Admissions, 213-477-2800, E-mail: gradprograms@msmu.edu. *Application contact:* Shawn Peters, Graduate Admission Counselor, 213-477-2676, E-mail: gradprograms@msmu.edu.
Website: http://www.msmu.edu/graduate-programs/

Mount St. Mary's University, Program in Health Administration, Emmitsburg, MD 21727-7799. Offers MHA. *Program availability:* Part-time, evening/weekend. *Degree requirements:* For master's, health care field practicum. *Entrance requirements:* For master's, undergraduate degree, minimum cumulative undergraduate GPA of 2.75. Additional exam requirements/recommendations for international students: Required—TOEFL (minimum score 550 paper-based; 83 iBT). Electronic applications accepted. *Expenses:* Contact institution.

National American University, Roueche Graduate Center, Austin, TX 78731. Offers accounting (MBA); aviation management (MBA, MM); care coordination (MSN); community college leadership (Ed D); criminal justice (MM); e-marketing (MBA, MM);

health care administration (MBA, MM); higher education (MM); human resources management (MBA, MM); information technology management (MBA, MM); international business (MBA); leadership (EMBA); management (MBA); nursing administration (MSN); nursing education (MSN); nursing informatics (MSN); operations and configuration management (MBA, MM); project and process management (MBA, MM). Master's programs offered online through the Harold D. Buckingham Graduate School. *Program availability:* Part-time, evening/weekend, online learning. *Entrance requirements:* For master's, minimum undergraduate GPA of 2.75. Additional exam requirements/recommendations for international students: Required—TOEFL, TWE. Electronic applications accepted. *Faculty research:* Tourism, finance, marketing.

National University, School of Health and Human Services, La Jolla, CA 92037-1011. Offers clinical affairs (MS); clinical regulatory affairs (MS); complementary and integrative healthcare (MS); family nurse practitioner (MSN); health and life science analytics (MS); health informatics (MS, Certificate); healthcare administration (MHA); nurse anesthesia (MSNA); nursing administration (MSN); nursing informatics (MSN); psychiatric-mental health nurse practitioner (MSN); public health (MPH), including health promotion, healthcare administration, mental health. *Program availability:* Part-time, evening/weekend, 100% online, blended/hybrid learning. *Degree requirements:* For master's, thesis (for some programs). *Entrance requirements:* For master's, interview, minimum GPA of 2.5. Additional exam requirements/recommendations for international students: Required—TOEFL (minimum score 550 paper-based; 79 iBT), IELTS (minimum score 6). *Application deadline:* Applications are processed on a rolling basis. Application fee: $60 ($65 for international students). Electronic applications accepted. *Expenses: Tuition:* Part-time $430 per quarter hour. *Financial support:* Career-related internships or fieldwork, institutionally sponsored loans, scholarships/grants, and tuition waivers (partial) available. Support available to part-time students. Financial award application deadline: 6/30; financial award applicants required to submit FAFSA. *Faculty research:* Nursing education, obesity prevention, workforce diversity. *Unit head:* Dr. Gloria J. McNeal, Dean, 858-309-3473, E-mail: shhs@nu.edu. *Application contact:* Brandon Jouganatos, Vice President for Enrollment Services, 800-628-8648, E-mail: advisor@nu.edu.
Website: http://www.nu.edu/OurPrograms/SchoolOfHealthAndHumanServices.html

Nebraska Methodist College, Program in Healthcare Operations Management, Omaha, NE 68114. Offers MS. *Program availability:* Part-time, evening/weekend, online learning. *Degree requirements:* For master's, thesis or alternative, capstone. *Entrance requirements:* Additional exam requirements/recommendations for international students: Required—TOEFL (minimum score 550 paper-based; 80 iBT).

New Charter University, College of Business, Salt Lake City, UT 84101. Offers finance (MBA); health care management (MBA); management (MBA). *Program availability:* Part-time, evening/weekend, online learning. *Entrance requirements:* For master's, course work in calculus, statistics, macroeconomics. Additional exam requirements/recommendations for international students: Required—TOEFL (minimum score 550 paper-based). Electronic applications accepted.

New England College, Program in Management, Henniker, NH 03242-3293. Offers accounting (MSA); healthcare administration (MS); international relations (MA); marketing management (MS); nonprofit leadership (MS); project management (MS); strategic leadership (MS). *Program availability:* Part-time, evening/weekend. *Degree requirements:* For master's, independent research project. Electronic applications accepted.

New Jersey City University, College of Professional Studies, Department of Health Sciences, Jersey City, NJ 07305-1597. Offers community health education (MS); health administration (MS); school health education (MS). *Program availability:* Part-time, evening/weekend. *Degree requirements:* For master's, thesis or alternative, internship. *Entrance requirements:* Additional exam requirements/recommendations for international students: Required—TOEFL (minimum score 79 iBT).

New Jersey Institute of Technology, Newark College of Engineering, Newark, NJ 07102. Offers biomedical engineering (MS, PhD); chemical engineering (MS, PhD); computer engineering (MS, PhD); electrical engineering (MS, PhD); engineering management (MS); environmental engineering (PhD); healthcare systems management (MS); industrial engineering (MS, PhD); Internet engineering (MS); manufacturing engineering (MS); mechanical engineering (MS, PhD); occupational safety and health engineering (MS); pharmaceutical bioprocessing (MS); pharmaceutical engineering (MS); pharmaceutical systems management (MS); power and energy systems (MS); telecommunications (MS); transportation (MS, PhD). *Program availability:* Part-time, evening/weekend. *Students:* Average age 27. 2,959 applicants, 51% accepted, 442 enrolled. In 2017, 595 master's, 29 doctorates awarded. Terminal master's awarded for partial completion of doctoral program. *Entrance requirements:* For master's, GRE General Test; for doctorate, GRE General Test, minimum graduate GPA of 3.5. Additional exam requirements/recommendations for international students: Required—TOEFL (minimum score 550 paper-based; 79 iBT). *Application deadline:* For fall admission, 6/1 priority date for domestic students, 5/1 priority date for international students; for spring admission, 11/15 priority date for domestic and international students. Applications are processed on a rolling basis. Application fee: $75. Electronic applications accepted. *Expenses:* Contact institution. *Financial support:* In 2017–18, 172 students received support, including 24 fellowships (averaging $7,124 per year), 112 research assistantships (averaging $19,407 per year), 101 teaching assistantships (averaging $24,173 per year); scholarships/grants also available. Financial award application deadline: 1/15. *Faculty research:* Nonlinear signal processing, intelligent medical image analysis, calibration issues in coherent localization, computer-aided design, neural network for tool wear measurement. *Total annual research expenditures:* $11.1 million. *Unit head:* Dr. Moshe Kam, Dean, 973-596-5534, E-mail: moshe.kam@njit.edu. *Application contact:* Stephen Eck, Director of Admissions, 973-596-3300, Fax: 973-596-3461, E-mail: admissions@njit.edu.
Website: http://engineering.njit.edu/

New York Medical College, School of Health Sciences and Practice, Valhalla, NY 10595. Offers behavioral sciences and health promotion (MPH); biostatistics (MS); children with special health care (Graduate Certificate); emergency preparedness (Graduate Certificate); environmental health science (MPH); epidemiology (MPH, MS); global health (Graduate Certificate); health education (Graduate Certificate); health policy and management (MPH, Dr PH); industrial hygiene (Graduate Certificate); pediatric dysphagia (Post-Graduate Certificate); physical therapy (DPT); public health (Graduate Certificate); speech-language pathology (MS). *Accreditation:* CEPH. *Program availability:* Part-time, evening/weekend, 100% online, blended/hybrid learning. *Faculty:* 48 full-time (33 women), 235 part-time/adjunct (141 women). *Students:* 221 full-time (153 women), 270 part-time (194 women); includes 202 minority (83 Black or African American, non-Hispanic/Latino; 2 American Indian or Alaska Native, non-Hispanic/Latino; 64 Asian, non-Hispanic/Latino; 47 Hispanic/Latino; 1 Native Hawaiian or other Pacific Islander, non-Hispanic/Latino; 5 Two or more races, non-Hispanic/Latino), 19 international. Average age 29. 1,118 applicants, 38% accepted, 169 enrolled. In 2017, 110 master's, 41 doctorates awarded. *Degree requirements:* For master's, comprehensive exam (for some programs), thesis (for some programs); for doctorate, thesis/dissertation. *Entrance requirements:* For master's, GRE (for MS in speech-language pathology); for doctorate, GRE. Additional exam requirements/recommendations for international students: Required—TOEFL, IELTS. *Application deadline:* For fall admission, 8/1 for domestic students, 4/15 for international students; for spring admission, 12/1 for domestic students; for summer admission, 5/1 for domestic students, 4/15 for international students. Application fee: $125. Electronic applications accepted. *Expenses:* $1,125 per credit, $245 fees. *Financial support:* In 2017–18, 10,000 students received support. Scholarships/grants and unspecified assistantships available. Financial award application deadline: 4/30; financial award applicants required to submit FAFSA. *Unit head:* Ben Watson, PhD, Vice Dean, 914-594-4531, E-mail: ben_watson@nymc.edu. *Application contact:* Irene Bundziak, Assistant to Director of Admissions, 914-594-4905, E-mail: irene_bundziak@nymc.edu.
Website: http://www.nymc.edu/school-of-health-sciences-and-practice-shsp/

New York University, College of Global Public Health, New York, NY 10012. Offers biological basis of public health (PhD); community and international health (MPH); global health leadership (MPH); health systems and health services research (PhD); population and community health (PhD); public health nutrition (MPH); social and behavioral sciences (MPH); socio-behavioral health (PhD). *Accreditation:* CEPH. *Program availability:* Part-time, online learning. *Faculty:* 26 full-time (20 women), 104 part-time/adjunct (53 women). *Students:* 161 full-time (136 women), 70 part-time (54 women); includes 74 minority (24 Black or African American, non-Hispanic/Latino; 1 American Indian or Alaska Native, non-Hispanic/Latino; 27 Asian, non-Hispanic/Latino; 11 Hispanic/Latino; 4 Native Hawaiian or other Pacific Islander, non-Hispanic/Latino; 7 Two or more races, non-Hispanic/Latino), 39 international. Average age 29. 802 applicants, 70% accepted, 97 enrolled. In 2017, 1 master's awarded. *Degree requirements:* For master's, thesis (for some programs); for doctorate, thesis/dissertation. *Entrance requirements:* For master's and doctorate, GRE. Additional exam requirements/recommendations for international students: Required—TOEFL. *Application deadline:* For fall admission, 2/1 for domestic and international students. Applications are processed on a rolling basis. Electronic applications accepted. *Expenses:* Contact institution. *Financial support:* Federal Work-Study and scholarships/grants available. *Unit head:* Dr. Cheryl G. Healton, Director, 212-992-6741. *Application contact:* New York University Information, 212-998-1212.
Website: http://publichealth.nyu.edu/

New York University, Wagner Graduate School of Public Service, Program in Health Policy and Management, New York, NY 10012. Offers health finance (MPA); health policy analysis (MPA); health services management (MPA); international health (MPA); MBA/MPA; MD/MPA; MPA/MPH. *Accreditation:* CAHME (one or more programs are accredited). *Program availability:* Part-time. *Students:* Average age 28. 186 applicants, 62% accepted, 56 enrolled. In 2017, 67 master's awarded. *Degree requirements:* For master's, thesis or alternative, capstone end event. *Entrance requirements:* Additional exam requirements/recommendations for international students: Required—TOEFL (minimum score 100 iBT), IELTS (minimum score 7.5), TWE. *Application deadline:* For fall admission, 1/5 for domestic and international students; for spring admission, 10/1 for domestic and international students. Application fee: $85. Electronic applications accepted. *Expenses:* Contact institution. *Financial support:* In 2017–18, 30 students received support, including 14 fellowships with partial tuition reimbursements available (averaging $18,307 per year), 1 research assistantship with full tuition reimbursement available (averaging $56,524 per year); career-related internships or fieldwork, Federal Work-Study, scholarships/grants, health care benefits, and unspecified assistantships also available. Support available to part-time students. Financial award application deadline: 1/5; financial award applicants required to submit FAFSA. *Unit head:* Prof. John Billings, Director, 212-998-7455, Fax: 212-995-4162. *Application contact:* Sandra Oliveira, Admissions Officer, 212-998-7414, Fax: 212-995-4611, E-mail: wagner.admissions@nyu.edu.
Website: http://wagner.nyu.edu/health

Niagara University, Graduate Division of Business Administration, Niagara University, NY 14109. Offers accounting (MBA); business administration (MBA); finance (MBA, MS); financial planning (MBA); healthcare administration (MBA, MHA); human resources (MBA); international business (MBA); marketing (MBA); professional accountancy (MBA); strategic management (MBA); supply chain management (MBA). *Accreditation:* AACSB. *Program availability:* Part-time, evening/weekend. *Faculty:* 17 full-time, 11 part-time/adjunct. *Students:* 173 full-time (92 women), 77 part-time (39 women); includes 38 minority (8 Black or African American, non-Hispanic/Latino; 3 American Indian or Alaska Native, non-Hispanic/Latino; 8 Asian, non-Hispanic/Latino; 8 Hispanic/Latino; 11 Two or more races, non-Hispanic/Latino), 46 international. Average age 27. In 2017, 139 master's awarded. *Entrance requirements:* For master's, GMAT. Additional exam requirements/recommendations for international students: Required—TOEFL (minimum score 550 paper-based; 79 iBT), IELTS (minimum score 6). *Application deadline:* For fall admission, 8/1 for domestic students; for spring admission, 11/1 for domestic students. Applications are processed on a rolling basis. Electronic applications accepted. *Expenses:* Contact institution. *Financial support:* Fellowships, research assistantships, career-related internships or fieldwork, and Federal Work-Study available. Support available to part-time students. Financial award application deadline: 4/15; financial award applicants required to submit FAFSA. *Faculty research:* Capital flows, Federal Reserve policy, human resource management, public policy, issues in marketing, auctions, economics of information, risk and capital markets, management strategy, consumer behavior, Internet and social media marketing. *Unit head:* Dr. Paul Richardson, MBA Director/Chair of the Marketing Department, 716-286-8169, Fax: 716-286-8206, E-mail: psr@niagara.edu. *Application contact:* Evan Pierce, Associate Director for Graduate Recruitment, 716-286-8769, Fax: 716-286-8170, E-mail: epierce@niagara.edu.
Website: http://mba.niagara.edu

Northeast Ohio Medical University, College of Graduate Studies, Rootstown, OH 44272-0095. Offers bioethics (Certificate); health-system pharmacy administration (MS); integrated pharmaceutical medicine (MS, PhD); medical ethics and humanities (MS); public health (MPH). MPH offered as part of consortium with The University of Akron, Youngstown State University, Ohio University, and Cleveland State University. *Program availability:* Part-time, evening/weekend. *Faculty:* 23 part-time/adjunct (14 women). *Students:* 22 full-time (13 women), 21 part-time (13 women); includes 10 minority (1 Black or African American, non-Hispanic/Latino; 8 Asian, non-Hispanic/Latino; 1 Two or more races, non-Hispanic/Latino). In 2017, 3 master's, 1 doctorate awarded. *Degree requirements:* For master's, thesis (for MS in medical ethics and humanities, integrated pharmaceutical medicine); for doctorate, thesis/dissertation. *Application deadline:* For fall admission, 5/1 priority date for domestic students; for winter admission, 1/5 priority date for domestic students. Applications are processed on a rolling basis. Application fee: $95. Electronic applications accepted. *Expenses:* Contact institution. *Financial support:* Institutionally sponsored loans and tuition waivers available. Financial award application deadline: 3/15; financial award applicants required to submit FAFSA. *Unit head:* Dr. Steven Schmidt, Dean, 330-325-6290. *Application contact:* Heidi Terry, Executive Director, Enrollment Services, 330-325-6479, E-mail: hterry@neomed.edu.
Website: https://www.neomed.edu/graduatestudies/

Northwestern University, Feinberg School of Medicine and Interdepartmental Programs, Driskill Graduate Program in Life Sciences, Chicago, IL 60611. Offers biostatistics (PhD); epidemiology (PhD); health and biomedical informatics (PhD); health services and outcomes research (PhD); healthcare quality and patient safety (PhD); translational outcomes in science (PhD). *Degree requirements:* For doctorate, comprehensive exam, thesis/dissertation, written and oral qualifying exams. *Entrance requirements:* For doctorate, GRE General Test. Additional exam requirements/recommendations for international students: Required—TOEFL (minimum score 600 paper-based). Electronic applications accepted.

Northwestern University, The Graduate School, Kellogg School of Management, Management Programs, Evanston, IL 60208. Offers accounting information and management (MBA, PhD); analytical finance (MBA); business administration (MBA); decision sciences (MBA); entrepreneurship and innovation (MBA); finance (MBA, PhD); health enterprise management (MBA); human resources management (MBA); international business (MBA); management and organizations (MBA, PhD); management and organizations and sociology (PhD); management and strategy (MBA); management studies (MS); managerial analytics (MBA); managerial economics (MBA); managerial economics and strategy (PhD); marketing (MBA, PhD); marketing management (MBA); media management (MBA); operations management (MBA, PhD); real estate (MBA); social enterprise at Kellogg (MBA); JD/MBA. *Program availability:* Part-time, evening/weekend. Terminal master's awarded for partial completion of doctoral program. *Degree requirements:* For doctorate, thesis/dissertation, 2 years of coursework, qualifying (field) exam and candidacy, summer research papers and presentations to faculty, proposal defense, final exam/defense. *Entrance requirements:* For master's, GMAT, GRE, interview, 2 letters of recommendation, college transcripts, resume, essays, Kellogg honor code; for doctorate, GMAT, GRE, statement of purpose, transcripts, 2 letters of recommendation, resume, interview. Additional exam requirements/recommendations for international students: Required—TOEFL, IELTS. Electronic applications accepted. *Expenses:* Contact institution. *Faculty research:* Business cycles and international finance, health policy, networks, non-market strategy, consumer psychology.

Northwestern University, School of Professional Studies, Program in Public Policy and Administration, Evanston, IL 60208. Offers global policy (MA); health services policy (MA); public administration (MA); public policy (MA). *Program availability:* Part-time, evening/weekend, online learning.
Website: https://sps.northwestern.edu/masters/public-policy/index.php

Ohio Christian University, Graduate Programs, Circleville, OH 43113. Offers accounting (MBA); business administration (MBA); digital marketing (MBA); finance (MBA), healthcare management (MBA); human resources (MBA); management (MM); organizational leadership (MBA); pastoral care and counseling (MAM); practical theology (MAM).

Ohio Dominican University, Division of Business, Program in Healthcare Administration, Columbus, OH 43219-2099. Offers MS. *Program availability:* Part-time, evening/weekend. *Faculty:* 1 full-time (0 women), 2 part-time/adjunct (1 woman). *Students:* 6 full-time (4 women), 11 part-time (7 women); includes 9 minority (all Black or African American, non-Hispanic/Latino), 4 international. Average age 33. 17 applicants, 35% accepted, 6 enrolled. In 2017, 5 master's awarded. *Entrance requirements:* For master's, minimum GPA of 3.0 in undergraduate degree from regionally-accredited institution, or 2.7 in the last 60 semester hours of bachelor's degree and at least two years of professional experience. Additional exam requirements/recommendations for international students: Required—TOEFL (minimum score 550 paper-based), IELTS (minimum score 6.5). *Application deadline:* For fall admission, 8/15 for domestic students, 6/10 for international students; for spring admission, 1/4 for domestic students, 11/2 for international students; for summer admission, 5/30 for domestic students. Applications are processed on a rolling basis. Application fee: $25. Electronic applications accepted. *Expenses:* $600 per credit hour, $175 per semester technology fee, $50 per semester activity fee. *Financial support:* Applicants required to submit FAFSA. *Unit head:* Dr. Kenneth C. Fah, Chair of Business Division, 614-251-4566, E-mail: fahk@ohiodominican.edu. *Application contact:* John W Naughton, Associate Vice President for Enrollment Management, 614-251-4721, Fax: 614-251-6654, E-mail: grad@ohiodominican.edu.
Website: http://www.ohiodominican.edu/academics/graduate/msha

The Ohio State University, College of Public Health, Columbus, OH 43210. Offers MHA, MPH, MS, PhD, DVM/MPH, JD/MHA, MHA/MBA, MHA/MD, MHA/MPA, MHA/MS, MPH/MBA, MPH/MD, MPH/MSW. *Accreditation:* CAHME. *Program availability:* Part-time. *Faculty:* 57. *Students:* 241 full-time (177 women), 77 part-time (57 women); includes 75 minority (25 Black or African American, non-Hispanic/Latino; 25 Asian, non-Hispanic/Latino; 15 Hispanic/Latino; 10 Two or more races, non-Hispanic/Latino), 18 international. Average age 27. In 2017, 123 master's, 7 doctorates awarded. Terminal master's awarded for partial completion of doctoral program. *Degree requirements:* For master's, thesis optional, practicum; for doctorate, thesis/dissertation. *Entrance requirements:* For master's and doctorate, GRE. Additional exam requirements/recommendations for international students: Required—TOEFL (minimum score 550 paper-based; 79 iBT); Recommended—IELTS (minimum score 7). *Application deadline:* For fall admission, 12/1 priority date for domestic students, 11/1 priority date for international students. Applications are processed on a rolling basis. Application fee: $60 ($70 for international students). Electronic applications accepted. *Financial support:* Fellowships with tuition reimbursements and research assistantships with tuition reimbursements available. *Unit head:* Dr. William J. Martin, II, Dean and Professor, 614-292-8350, E-mail: martin.3047@osu.edu. *Application contact:* 614-292-8350, Fax: 614-247-1846, E-mail: cph@cph.osu.edu.
Website: http://cph.osu.edu/

Ohio University, Graduate College, College of Health Sciences and Professions, Department of Social and Public Health, Athens, OH 45701-2979. Offers early child development and family life (MS); family studies (MS); health administration (MHA); public health (MPH); social work (MSW). *Program availability:* Part-time, evening/weekend, online learning. *Degree requirements:* For master's, capstone (MPH). *Entrance requirements:* For master's, GMAT, GRE General Test, previous course work in accounting, management, and statistics; previous public health background (MHA, MPH). Additional exam requirements/recommendations for international students: Required—TOEFL (minimum score 550 paper-based; 80 iBT) or IELTS (minimum score 6.5). Electronic applications accepted. *Expenses:* Contact institution. *Faculty research:* Health care management, health policy, managed care, health behavior, disease prevention.

Oklahoma Christian University, Graduate School of Business, Oklahoma City, OK 73136-1100. Offers accounting (M Acc, MBA); financial services (MBA); general business (MBA); health services management (MBA); human resources (MBA); international business (MBA); leadership and organizational development (MBA); marketing (MBA); nonprofit management (MBA); project management (MBA). *Accreditation:* ACBSP. *Program availability:* Part-time, 100% online. *Entrance requirements:* For master's, bachelor's degree. Additional exam requirements/recommendations for international students: Required—TOEFL (minimum score 550 paper-based). Electronic applications accepted. *Expenses:* Contact institution.

Oklahoma State University Center for Health Sciences, Program in Health Care Administration, Tulsa, OK 74107-1898. Offers MS. *Program availability:* Part-time, evening/weekend, 100% online. *Degree requirements:* For master's, thesis or alternative. *Entrance requirements:* For master's, official transcripts with minimum GPA of 3.0. Additional exam requirements/recommendations for international students: Required—TOEFL. *Faculty research:* Healthcare economics, emotional intelligence, leadership, organizational development.

Oregon Health & Science University, School of Medicine, Graduate Programs in Medicine, Division of Management, Portland, OR 97239-3098. Offers healthcare management (MBA, MS, Certificate). *Program availability:* Part-time. *Faculty:* 4 full-time (1 woman), 21 part-time/adjunct (5 women). *Students:* 182 part-time (96 women); includes 49 minority (5 Black or African American, non-Hispanic/Latino; 2 American Indian or Alaska Native, non-Hispanic/Latino; 25 Asian, non-Hispanic/Latino; 7 Hispanic/Latino; 10 Two or more races, non-Hispanic/Latino), 6 international. Average age 39. 83 applicants, 87% accepted, 68 enrolled. In 2017, 22 master's awarded. *Degree requirements:* For master's, thesis optional. *Entrance requirements:* For master's, GRE General Test (minimum scores: 153 Verbal/148 Quantitative/4.5 Analytical) or GMAT. *Application deadline:* For fall admission, 7/15 for domestic and international students; for winter admission, 10/15 for domestic and international students; for spring admission, 1/15 for domestic and international students. Applications are processed on a rolling basis. Application fee: $70. Electronic applications accepted. *Financial support:* Health care benefits available. Financial award application deadline: 3/1; financial award applicants required to submit FAFSA. *Faculty research:* Enhancing quality and reducing cost for healthcare by improving patient activation, identifying factors in hospital readmissions using system dynamics modeling, human and organizational dimensions of creating healthy communities. *Unit head:* Steve Kinder, Division Head, E-mail: hcmanagement@ohsu.edu. *Application contact:* Jessica Walter, Program Coordinator, E-mail: hcmanagement@ohsu.edu.

Oregon State University, College of Public Health and Human Sciences, Program in Public Health, Corvallis, OR 97331. Offers biostatistics (MPH); environmental and occupational health (MPH, PhD); epidemiology (MPH, PhD); global health (MPH, PhD). Terminal master's awarded for partial completion of doctoral program. *Entrance requirements:* For master's and doctorate, GRE, minimum GPA of 3.0 in last 90 hours. Additional exam requirements/recommendations for international students: Required—TOEFL (minimum score 80 iBT), IELTS (minimum score 6.5). *Application deadline:* For fall admission, 12/1 priority date for domestic and international students. Applications are processed on a rolling basis. Electronic applications accepted. *Expenses:* Contact institution. *Financial support:* Application deadline: 12/1. *Unit head:* Amanda Armington, MPH Program Manager, 541-737-3825, E-mail: amanda.armington@oregonstate.edu.

Our Lady of the Lake University, School of Business and Leadership, Program in Healthcare Management, San Antonio, TX 78207-4689. Offers MBA. *Program availability:* Part-time, evening/weekend, 100% online, blended/hybrid learning. *Faculty:* 1 full-time (0 women), 5 part-time/adjunct (0 women). *Students:* 61 full-time (45 women), 8 part-time (all women); includes 47 minority (9 Black or African American, non-Hispanic/Latino; 38 Hispanic/Latino). Average age 36. 24 applicants, 71% accepted, 12 enrolled. In 2017, 19 master's awarded. *Entrance requirements:* For master's, official transcripts showing 6 hours of coursework in economics and 3 hours of coursework in each of the following ares: statistics, management, business law, and finance; resume including detailed work history describing managerial or professional work experience. Additional exam requirements/recommendations for international students: Required—TOEFL. *Application deadline:* For fall admission, 6/15 for domestic and international students; for spring admission, 11/15 for domestic and international students; for summer admission, 4/15 for domestic and international students. Applications are processed on a rolling basis. Application fee: $40 ($50 for international students). Electronic applications accepted. Application fee is waived when completed online. *Expenses: Tuition:* Full-time $10,668; part-time $5334 per year. *Required fees:* $816; $816 per year. $408 per semester. *Financial support:* In 2017–18, 8 students received support. Federal Work-Study, scholarships/grants, unspecified assistantships, and tuition discounts available. Support available to part-time students. Financial award application deadline: 5/1; financial award applicants required to submit FAFSA. *Unit head:* Dr. Ronald Crowe, E-mail: rcrowe@ollusa.edu. *Application contact:* Office of Graduate Admissions, 210-431-3995, Fax: 210-431-3945, E-mail: gradadm@ollusa.edu.
Website: http://www.ollusa.edu/s/1190/hybrid/default-hybrid-ollu.aspx?sid-1190&gid-1&pgid-7873

Pace University, Dyson College of Arts and Sciences, Department of Public Administration, New York, NY 10038. Offers government management (MPA); health care administration (MPA); not-for-profit management (MPA); JD/MPA. *Program availability:* Part-time, evening/weekend. *Faculty:* 6 full-time (4 women), 4 part-time/adjunct (1 woman). *Students:* 34 full-time (18 women), 66 part-time (45 women); includes 59 minority (38 Black or African American, non-Hispanic/Latino; 9 Asian, non-Hispanic/Latino; 11 Hispanic/Latino; 1 Two or more races, non-Hispanic/Latino), 8 international. Average age 31. In 2017, 53 master's awarded. *Degree requirements:* For master's, comprehensive exam, thesis (for some programs), capstone project. *Entrance requirements:* For master's, 2 letters of recommendation, resume, personal statement, official transcripts, essay. Additional exam requirements/recommendations for international students: Required—TOEFL (minimum score 88 iBT), IELTS (minimum score 7) or PTE (minimum score 60). *Application deadline:* For fall admission, 8/1 priority date for domestic students, 6/1 for international students; for spring admission, 12/1 priority date for domestic students, 10/1 for international students. Applications are processed on a rolling basis. Application fee: $70. Electronic applications accepted. *Financial support:* Research assistantships, career-related internships or fieldwork, Federal Work-Study, and tuition waivers (partial) available. Support available to part-time students. Financial award application deadline: 2/15; financial award applicants required to submit FAFSA. *Unit head:* Dr. Hillary Knepper, Chairperson, 914-773-3140, E-mail: hknepper@pace.edu. *Application contact:* Susan Ford-Goldschein, Director of Admissions, 914-422-4283, Fax: 212-346-1585, E-mail: graduateadmission@pace.edu.
Website: http://www.pace.edu/dyson/academic-departments-and-programs/public-admin

Pacific University, Healthcare Administration Program, Forest Grove, OR 97116-1797. Offers MHA.

Park University, School of Graduate and Professional Studies, Kansas City, MO 54105. Offers adult education (M Ed); business and government leadership (Graduate Certificate); business, government, and global society (MPA); communication and leadership (MA); creative and life writing (Graduate Certificate); disaster and emergency management (MPA, Graduate Certificate); educational leadership (M Ed); finance (MBA, Graduate Certificate); general business (MBA); global business (Graduate Certificate); healthcare administration (MHA); healthcare services management and leadership (Graduate Certificate); international business (MBA); language and literacy (M Ed), including English for speakers of other languages, special reading teacher/literacy coach; leadership of international healthcare organizations (Graduate Certificate); management information systems (MBA, Graduate Certificate); music performance (ADP, Graduate Certificate), including cello (MM, ADP), piano (MM, ADP), viola (MM, ADP), violin (MM, ADP); nonprofit and community services management (MPA); nonprofit leadership (Graduate Certificate); performance (MM), including cello

(MM, ADP), piano (MM, ADP), viola (MM, ADP), violin (MM, ADP); public management (MPA); social work (MSW); teacher leadership (M Ed), including curriculum and assessment, instructional leader. *Program availability:* Part-time, evening/weekend, online learning. *Degree requirements:* For master's, comprehensive exam (for some programs), thesis (for some programs), internship (for some programs); exam (for some programs). *Entrance requirements:* For master's, GRE or GMAT (for some programs), teacher certification (for some M Ed programs), letters of recommendation, essay, resume (for some programs). Additional exam requirements/recommendations for international students: Required—TOEFL (minimum score 550 paper-based; 79 iBT), IELTS (minimum score 6). Electronic applications accepted.

Penn State Great Valley, Graduate Studies, Management Division, Malvern, PA 19355-1488. Offers business administration (MBA); cyber security (Certificate); data analytics (MPS, MS, Certificate); distributed energy and grid modernization (Certificate); finance (M Fin); health sector management (Certificate); human resource management (Certificate); information science (MSIS); leadership development (MLD); new ventures and entrepreneurship (Certificate); sustainable management practices (Certificate). *Accreditation:* AACSB. *Unit head:* Dr. James A. Nemes, Chancellor, 610-648-3202, Fax: 610-725-5296. *Application contact:* JoAnn Kelly, Director of Admissions, 610-648-3315, Fax: 610-725-5296, E-mail: jek2@psu.edu.
Website: http://greatvalley.psu.edu/academics/masters-degrees/engineering-management

Penn State Harrisburg, Graduate School, School of Public Affairs, Middletown, PA 17057. Offers criminal justice (MA); health administration (MHA); health administration: long term care (Certificate); homeland security (MPS, Certificate); public administration (MPA, PhD); public administration: non-profit administration (Certificate); public budgeting and financial management (Certificate); public sector human resource management (Certificate). *Accreditation:* NASPAA. *Unit head:* Dr. Mukund S. Kulkarni, Chancellor, 717-948-6105, Fax: 717-948-6452. *Application contact:* Robert W. Coffman, Jr., Director of Enrollment Management, Recruitment and Admissions, 717-948-6250, Fax: 717-948-6325, E-mail: hbgadmit@psu.edu.
Website: https://harrisburg.psu.edu/public-affairs

Penn State University Park, Graduate School, College of Health and Human Development, Department of Health Policy and Administration, University Park, PA 16802. Offers MHA, MS, PhD. *Accreditation:* CAHME. *Unit head:* Dr. Ann C. Crouter, Dean, 814-865-1420, Fax: 814-865-3282. *Application contact:* Lori Hawn, Director, Graduate Student Services, 814-865-1795, Fax: 814-863-4627, E-mail: l-gswww@lists.psu.edu.
Website: http://hhd.psu.edu/hpa

Pennsylvania College of Health Sciences, Graduate Programs, Lancaster, PA 17601. Offers administration (MSN); education (MSHS, MSN); healthcare administration (MHA). *Degree requirements:* For master's, internship (for MHA, MSN in administration); practicum (for MSHS, MSN in education).

Pfeiffer University, Program in Health Administration, Misenheimer, NC 28109-0960. Offers MHA, MBA/MHA.

Philadelphia College of Osteopathic Medicine, Graduate and Professional Programs, Department of Psychology, Philadelphia, PA 19131-1694. Offers applied behavior analysis (Certificate); clinical health psychology (Post-Doctoral Certificate); clinical neuropsychology (Post-Doctoral Certificate); clinical psychology (Psy D); educational psychology (PhD); mental health counseling (MS); organizational development and leadership (MS); psychology (Certificate); public health management and administration (MS); school psychology (MS, Psy D, Ed S). *Accreditation:* APA. *Faculty:* 19 full-time (11 women), 122 part-time/adjunct (58 women). *Students:* 487 (335 women); includes 138 minority (89 Black or African American, non-Hispanic/Latino; 4 American Indian or Alaska Native, non-Hispanic/Latino; 11 Asian, non-Hispanic/Latino; 12 Hispanic/Latino; 22 Two or more races, non-Hispanic/Latino). 298 applicants, 44% accepted, 100 enrolled. In 2017, 50 master's, 43 doctorates, 10 other advanced degrees awarded. Terminal master's awarded for partial completion of doctoral program. *Degree requirements:* For master's, comprehensive exam (for some programs), thesis (for some programs); for doctorate, comprehensive exam, thesis/dissertation. *Entrance requirements:* For master's, GRE or MAT, minimum GPA of 3.0; bachelor's degree from regionally-accredited college or university; for doctorate, PRAXIS II (for Psy D in school psychology), minimum undergraduate GPA of 3.0; for other advanced degree, GRE (for Ed S). Additional exam requirements/recommendations for international students: Required—TOEFL (minimum score 79 iBT). *Application deadline:* Applications are processed on a rolling basis. Application fee: $50. Electronic applications accepted. *Financial support:* In 2017–18, 28 teaching assistantships were awarded; Federal Work-Study, institutionally sponsored loans, and scholarships/grants also available. Financial award application deadline: 3/15; financial award applicants required to submit FAFSA. *Faculty research:* Adult and childhood anxiety and ADHD; coping with chronic illness; primary care psychology/integrated health care; applied behavior analysis; psychological, educational, and neuropsychological assessment. *Total annual research expenditures:* $533,489. *Unit head:* Dr. Robert DiTomasso, Chairman, 215-871-6442, Fax: 215-871-6458, E-mail: robertd@pcom.edu. *Application contact:* Johnathan Cox, Associate Director of Admissions, 215-871-6700, Fax: 215-871-6719, E-mail: johnathancox@pcom.edu.

Point Loma Nazarene University, Fermanian School of Business, San Diego, CA 92106-2899. Offers general business (MBA); healthcare management (MBA); innovation and entrepreneurship (MBA); organizational leadership (MBA); project management (MBA). *Accreditation:* ACBSP. *Program availability:* Part-time, evening/weekend. *Faculty:* 7 full-time (0 women), 5 part-time/adjunct (3 women). *Students:* 27 full-time (8 women), 94 part-time (45 women); includes 52 minority (6 Black or African American, non-Hispanic/Latino; 1 American Indian or Alaska Native, non-Hispanic/Latino; 7 Asian, non-Hispanic/Latino; 33 Hispanic/Latino; 5 Two or more races, non-Hispanic/Latino), 11 international. Average age 31. 74 applicants, 99% accepted, 56 enrolled. In 2017, 45 master's awarded. *Entrance requirements:* For master's, GMAT, letters of recommendation, essay, interview. Additional exam requirements/recommendations for international students: Required—TOEFL. *Application deadline:* For fall admission, 7/26 priority date for domestic students; for spring admission, 11/29 priority date for domestic students; for summer admission, 4/2 priority date for domestic students. Applications are processed on a rolling basis. Application fee: $50. Electronic applications accepted. *Expenses:* Contact institution. *Financial support:* Applicants required to submit FAFSA. *Unit head:* Jamie McIlwaine, Associate Dean, Graduate Business, 619-849-2721, E-mail: jmcilwai@pointloma.edu. *Application contact:* Joanie Joy, Senior Director of Enrollment Management, 619-329-6785, E-mail: gradinfo@pointloma.edu.
Website: https://www.pointloma.edu/schools-departments-colleges/fermanian-school-business

Point Park University, Rowland School of Business, Program in Management, Pittsburgh, PA 15222-1984. Offers health care administration and management (MS); leadership (MA). *Program availability:* 100% online.

Portland State University, Graduate Studies, College of Urban and Public Affairs, Hatfield School of Government, Division of Public Administration, Portland, OR 97207-0751. Offers collaborative governance (Certificate); energy policy and management (Certificate); global management and leadership (MPA); health administration (MPA); human resource management (MPA); local government (MPA); natural resource policy and administration (MPA); nonprofit and public management (Certificate); nonprofit management (MPA); public administration (EMPA); public affairs and policy (PhD); sustainable food systems (Certificate). *Accreditation:* NASPAA (one or more programs are accredited). *Program availability:* Part-time, evening/weekend. *Faculty:* 15 full-time (6 women), 6 part-time/adjunct (4 women). *Students:* 84 full-time (54 women), 109 part-time (75 women); includes 40 minority (8 Black or African American, non-Hispanic/Latino; 5 American Indian or Alaska Native, non-Hispanic/Latino; 8 Asian, non-Hispanic/Latino; 12 Hispanic/Latino; 1 Native Hawaiian or other Pacific Islander, non-Hispanic/Latino; 6 Two or more races, non-Hispanic/Latino), 14 international. Average age 35. 118 applicants, 84% accepted, 56 enrolled. In 2017, 60 master's, 1 doctorate awarded. *Degree requirements:* For master's, integrative field experience (MPA), practicum (MPH); for doctorate, comprehensive exam, thesis/dissertation. *Entrance requirements:* For master's, GRE (minimum scores: verbal 150, quantitative 149, and analytic writing 4.5), minimum GPA of 3.0, 3 recommendation letters, resume, 500-word statement of intent; for doctorate, GRE, 3 recommendation letters, resume, 500-word personal essay. Additional exam requirements/recommendations for international students: Required—TOEFL (minimum score 550 paper-based; 80 iBT), IELTS (minimum score 7). *Application deadline:* For fall admission, 4/1 for domestic students, 3/1 for international students; for winter admission, 9/1 for domestic students, 8/1 for international students; for spring admission, 11/1 for domestic and international students. Application fee: $65. *Expenses:* Tuition, state resident: full-time $14,436; part-time $401 per credit. Tuition, nonresident: full-time $21,780; part-time $605 per credit. *Required fees:* $1380; $22 per credit. $119 per quarter. One-time fee: $325. Tuition and fees vary according to program. *Financial support:* In 2017–18, 39 students received support, including 5 research assistantships with full and partial tuition reimbursements available (averaging $8,341 per year), 4 teaching assistantships (averaging $5,292 per year); career-related internships or fieldwork, Federal Work-Study, scholarships/grants, and unspecified assistantships also available. Support available to part-time students. Financial award application deadline: 3/1; financial award applicants required to submit FAFSA. *Faculty research:* Public budgeting, program evaluation, nonprofit management, natural resources policy and administration. *Total annual research expenditures:* $679,077. *Unit head:* Dr. Masami Nishishiba, Chair, 503-725-5151, E-mail: nishism@pdx.edu. *Application contact:* Megan Heljeson, Office Coordinator, 503-725-3921, Fax: 503-725-8250, E-mail: publicad@pdx.edu.
Website: https://www.pdx.edu/hatfieldschool/public-administration

Portland State University, Graduate Studies, OHSU-PSU School of Public Health, Health Management and Policy Program, Portland, OR 97207-0751. Offers health management and policy (MPH); health systems and policy (PhD). *Program availability:* Part-time, evening/weekend. *Students:* 7 full-time (6 women), 17 part-time (13 women); includes 4 minority (1 Black or African American, non-Hispanic/Latino; 1 American Indian or Alaska Native, non-Hispanic/Latino; 2 Two or more races, non-Hispanic/Latino). Average age 35. In 2017, 20 master's, 1 doctorate awarded. *Degree requirements:* For master's, comprehensive exam (for some programs), thesis (for some programs), internship (MPA), practicum (MPH); for doctorate, comprehensive exam, thesis/dissertation. *Entrance requirements:* For master's, GRE (for MPH program), minimum GPA of 3.0 in upper-division course work or 2.75 overall, resume, 3 recommendation letters; for doctorate, GRE, transcripts, personal statement, resume, writing sample, 3 recommendation letters. Additional exam requirements/recommendations for international students: Required—TOEFL (minimum score 550 paper-based; 80 iBT). *Application deadline:* For fall admission, 2/1 for domestic and international students. Applications are processed on a rolling basis. Application fee: $65. *Expenses:* Tuition, state resident: full-time $14,436; part-time $401 per credit. Tuition, nonresident: full-time $21,780; part-time $605 per credit. *Required fees:* $1380; $22 per credit. $119 per quarter. One-time fee: $325. Tuition and fees vary according to program. *Financial support:* In 2017–18, 6 research assistantships with full and partial tuition reimbursements (averaging $6,738 per year), 2 teaching assistantships with full and partial tuition reimbursements (averaging $9,585 per year) were awarded; career-related internships or fieldwork, Federal Work-Study, institutionally sponsored loans, scholarships/grants, and unspecified assistantships also available. Support available to part-time students. Financial award application deadline: 3/1; financial award applicants required to submit FAFSA. *Unit head:* Dr. David Bangsberg, Founding Dean, 503-282-7537, E-mail: bangsber@ohsu.edu. *Application contact:* Dr. Jill Rissi, Associate Dean for Academic Affairs, 502-725-8217, E-mail: jrissi@pdx.edu.
Website: https://ohsu-psu-sph.org/

Post University, Program in Business Administration, Waterbury, CT 06723-2540. Offers accounting (MSA); business administration (MBA); corporate finance (MBA); corporate innovation (MBA); healthcare systems leadership (MBA); leadership (MBA); marketing (MBA); project management (MBA, MS). *Accreditation:* ACBSP. *Program availability:* Online learning. *Entrance requirements:* For master's, resume. *Expenses: Tuition:* Part-time $730 per credit hour. Part-time tuition and fees vary according to degree level and program. *Application contact:* Veronica Montalvo, Vice President, Online Education Enrollment Management and Admissions, 203-596-6164, E-mail: vmontalvo@post.edu.

Purdue University Global, School of Business, Davenport, IA 52807. Offers business administration (MBA); change leadership (MS); entrepreneurship (MBA); finance (MBA); health care management (MBA, MS); human resource (MBA); international business (MBA); management (MS); marketing (MBA); project management (MBA, MS); supply chain management and logistics (MBA, MS). *Accreditation:* ACBSP. *Program availability:* Part-time, evening/weekend, online learning. *Entrance requirements:* Additional exam requirements/recommendations for international students: Required—TOEFL (minimum score 550 paper-based; 80 iBT). Electronic applications accepted.

Purdue University Global, School of Legal Studies, Davenport, IA 52807. Offers health care delivery (MS); pathway to paralegal (Postbaccalaureate Certificate); state and local government (MS). *Program availability:* Part-time, evening/weekend, online learning. *Entrance requirements:* Additional exam requirements/recommendations for international students: Required—TOEFL (minimum score 550 paper-based; 80 iBT).

Queen's University at Kingston, School of Graduate Studies, Faculty of Health Sciences, Department of Community Health and Epidemiology, Kingston, ON K7L 3N6, Canada. Offers epidemiology (PhD); epidemiology and population health (M Sc); health services (M Sc); policy research and clinical epidemiology (M Sc); public health (MPH). *Program availability:* Part-time. *Degree requirements:* For master's, thesis. *Entrance requirements:* For master's, GRE General Test (strongly recommended). Additional exam requirements/recommendations for international students: Required—TOEFL (minimum score 600 paper-based). *Faculty research:* Cancer epidemiology, clinical trials, biostatistics health services research, health policy.

Quinnipiac University, School of Business, Program in Business Administration, Hamden, CT 06518-1940. Offers finance (MBA); health care management (MBA); supply chain management (MBA); JD/MBA. *Accreditation:* AACSB. *Program availability:* Part-time, evening/weekend, 100% online, blended/hybrid learning. *Faculty:* 32 full-time (11 women), 8 part-time/adjunct (3 women). *Students:* 201 full-time (95 women), 215

part-time (95 women); includes 48 minority (9 Black or African American, non-Hispanic/Latino; 12 Asian, non-Hispanic/Latino; 20 Hispanic/Latino; 7 Two or more races, non-Hispanic/Latino), 19 international. 307 applicants, 79% accepted, 223 enrolled. In 2017, 264 master's awarded. *Entrance requirements:* For master's, GMAT or GRE, minimum GPA of 3.0. Additional exam requirements/recommendations for international students: Required—TOEFL (minimum score 575 paper-based; 90 iBT), IELTS (minimum score 6.5). *Application deadline:* For fall admission, 7/30 priority date for domestic students, 4/30 priority date for international students; for spring admission, 12/15 priority date for domestic students, 9/30 priority date for international students. Applications are processed on a rolling basis. Application fee: $45. Electronic applications accepted. *Expenses:* Contact institution. *Financial support:* Career-related internships or fieldwork, Federal Work-Study, scholarships/grants, and unspecified assistantships available. Financial award application deadline: 6/1; financial award applicants required to submit FAFSA. *Faculty research:* Financial markets and investments, international business, supply chain management, health care management, corporate governance. *Unit head:* Lisa Braiewa, Director of the MBA Program, 800-462-1944, Fax: 203-582-3443, E-mail: graduate@qu.edu. *Application contact:* Office of Graduate Admissions, 800-462-1944, Fax: 203-582-3443, E-mail: graduate@qu.edu.
Website: http://www.qu.edu/mba

Regent University, Graduate School, School of Business and Leadership, Virginia Beach, VA 23464-9800. Offers business administration (MBA), including accounting, economics, entrepreneurship, finance and investing, general management, healthcare management (MA, MBA), human resource management (MA, MBA), innovation management, leadership, marketing, not-for-profit management (MA, MBA); business analytics (MS); business and design management (MA); church leadership (MA); leadership (Certificate); organizational leadership (MA, PhD), including ecclesial leadership (DSL, PhD), entrepreneurial leadership (PhD), healthcare management (MA, MBA), human resource development (PhD), human resource management (MA, MBA), individualized studies (DSL, PhD), interdisciplinary studies (MA), leadership coaching and mentoring (MA), not-for-profit management (MA, MBA), organizational development consulting (MA), servant leadership (MA, DSL); strategic leadership (DSL), including ecclesial leadership (DSL, PhD), global consulting, healthcare leadership, individualized studies (DSL, PhD), leadership coaching, servant leadership (MA, DSL), strategic foresight. *Program availability:* Part-time, evening/weekend, 100% online, blended/hybrid learning. *Faculty:* 9 full-time (2 women), 38 part-time/adjunct (11 women). *Students:* 129 full-time (80 women), 1,152 part-time (598 women); includes 685 minority (546 Black or African American, non-Hispanic/Latino; 10 American Indian or Alaska Native, non-Hispanic/Latino; 29 Asian, non-Hispanic/Latino; 65 Hispanic/Latino; 6 Native Hawaiian or other Pacific Islander, non-Hispanic/Latino; 29 Two or more races, non-Hispanic/Latino), 62 international. Average age 41. 1,721 applicants, 48% accepted, 624 enrolled. In 2017, 125 master's, 69 doctorates awarded. *Degree requirements:* For master's, thesis or alternative, 3-credit hour culminating experience; for doctorate, thesis/dissertation. *Entrance requirements:* For master's, college transcripts, resume, essay; for doctorate, college transcripts, resume, essay, writing sample; for Certificate, writing sample, resume, transcripts. Additional exam requirements/recommendations for international students: Required—TOEFL (minimum score 577 paper-based). *Application deadline:* For fall admission, 5/1 priority date for domestic students; for spring admission, 10/1 priority date for domestic students. Applications are processed on a rolling basis. Application fee: $50. Electronic applications accepted. *Expenses:* $650 per credit (MA, MS, MBA); $995 per credit (PhD); $300 per semester technology fee. *Financial support:* In 2017–18, 829 students received support. Career-related internships or fieldwork, scholarships/grants, and unspecified assistantships available. Support available to part-time students. *Faculty research:* Servant leadership, global business, team effectiveness, technology utilization, leadership development. *Unit head:* Dr. Doris Gomez, Dean, 757-352-4686, Fax: 757-352-4634, E-mail: dorigom@regent.edu. *Application contact:* Heidi Cece, Assistant Vice President of Enrollment Management, 800-373-5504, Fax: 757-352-4381, E-mail: admissions@regent.edu.
Website: https://www.regent.edu/school-of-business-and-leadership/

Regis College, Nursing and Health Sciences School, Weston, MA 02493. Offers applied behavior analysis (MS); counseling psychology (MA); health administration (MS); nurse practitioner (Certificate); nursing (MS, DNP); nursing education (Certificate); occupational therapy (MS). *Accreditation:* ACEN. *Program availability:* Part-time, evening/weekend, 100% online, blended/hybrid learning. *Degree requirements:* For doctorate, thesis/dissertation. *Entrance requirements:* For master's, GRE General Test or MAT, minimum GPA of 3.0, official transcripts, recommendations, personal statement, resume/curriculum vitae, interview; for doctorate, MAT or GRE if GPA from master's lower than 3.5. Additional exam requirements/recommendations for international students: Required—TOEFL (minimum score 560 paper-based; 79 iBT); Recommended—IELTS (minimum score 6.5). *Application deadline:* Applications are processed on a rolling basis. Application fee: $75. Electronic applications accepted. *Financial support:* Federal Work-Study, scholarships/grants, traineeships, and unspecified assistantships available. Support available to part-time students. Financial award applicants required to submit FAFSA. *Faculty research:* Global public health, health policy, education, aging, job satisfaction, psychiatric nursing, critical thinking. *Application contact:* Hillary Lyons, Graduate Admission Counselor, 781-768-7746, E-mail: hillary.lyons@regiscollege.edu.

Regis University, College of Business and Economics, Denver, CO 80221-1099. Offers accounting (MS); executive leadership (Certificate); finance (MS); finance and accounting (MBA); health industry leadership (MBA); human resource management and leadership (MSOL); management (MBA); marketing (MBA); nonprofit leadership (Post-Graduate Certificate); nonprofit management (MNM); nonprofit organizational capacity building (Certificate); operations management (MBA); organizational leadership and management (MSOL); project leadership and management (MS, MSOL); strategic business management (Certificate); strategic human resource integration (Certificate); strategic management (MBA). Programs offered at Colorado Springs Campus, Northwest Denver Campus, Southeast Denver Campus, Fort Collins Campus, Broomfield Campus, Henderson (Nevada) Campus, and Summerlin (Nevada) Campus. *Program availability:* Part-time, evening/weekend, 100% online, blended/hybrid learning. *Degree requirements:* For master's, thesis (for some programs), capstone or final research project. *Entrance requirements:* For master's, official transcript reflecting baccalaureate degree awarded from regionally-accredited college or university, interview, 2 years of full-time related work experience, resume, letters of recommendation. Additional exam requirements/recommendations for international students: Required—TOEFL (minimum score 550 paper-based; 82 iBT). Electronic applications accepted. *Expenses:* Contact institution. *Faculty research:* Impact of information technology on small business regulation of accounting, international project financing, mineral development, delivery of healthcare to rural indigenous communities.

Regis University, Rueckert-Hartman College for Health Professions, Denver, CO 80221-1099. Offers advanced practice nurse (DNP); counseling (MA); counseling children and adolescents (Post-Graduate Certificate); counseling military families (Post-Graduate Certificate); depth psychotherapy (Post-Graduate Certificate); fellowship in orthopedic manual physical therapy (Certificate); health care business management (Certificate); health care quality and patient safety (Certificate); health industry leadership (MBA); health services administration (MS); marriage and family therapy (MA, Post-Graduate Certificate); neonatal nurse practitioner (MSN); nursing education (MSN); nursing leadership (MSN); occupational therapy (OTD); pharmacy (Pharm D); physical therapy (DPT). *Program availability:* Part-time, evening/weekend, 100% online, blended/hybrid learning. *Degree requirements:* For master's, thesis (for some programs), internship. *Entrance requirements:* For master's, official transcript reflecting baccalaureate degree awarded from regionally-accredited college or university. Additional exam requirements/recommendations for international students: Required—TOEFL (minimum score 550 paper-based; 82 iBT). Electronic applications accepted. *Expenses:* Contact institution. *Faculty research:* Normal and pathological balance and gait research, normal/pathological upper limb motor control/biomechanics, exercise energy/metabolism research, optical treatment protocols for therapeutic modalities.

Rhode Island College, School of Graduate Studies, School of Business, Program in Health Care Administration, Providence, RI 02908-1991. Offers MS. *Students:* 6 full-time (4 women), 5 part-time (4 women); includes 5 minority (4 Black or African American, non-Hispanic/Latino; 1 Hispanic/Latino). Average age 25. *Entrance requirements:* For master's, GMAT or GRE, bachelor's degree in health care administration or related field; official transcripts; one professional and one academic reference; completion of courses in elementary statistics, principles of economics and introductory accounting. Application fee: $50. *Expenses:* Tuition, state resident: full-time $9768; part-time $407 per credit. Tuition, nonresident: full-time $19,008; part-time $792 per credit. *Required fees:* $696; $29 per credit. One-time fee: $200 full-time; $100 part-time. Tuition and fees vary according to course load. *Financial support:* In 2017–18, 2 research assistantships with full tuition reimbursements (averaging $3,000 per year), 2 teaching assistantships with full tuition reimbursements (averaging $3,000 per year) were awarded. Financial award application deadline: 5/15; financial award applicants required to submit FAFSA. *Unit head:* Dr. Marianne Raimondo, Program Director, 401-456-8096, E-mail: mraimondo@ric.edu. *Application contact:* Graduate Studies, 401-456-8700.
Website: http://www.ric.edu/som/Master-of-Science-in-Health-Care-Administration.php

Rice University, Graduate Programs, Wiess School–Professional Science Master's Programs, Professional Master's Program in Bioscience Research and Health Policy, Houston, TX 77251-1892. Offers MS.

Robert Morris University Illinois, Morris Graduate School of Management, Chicago, IL 60605. Offers accounting (MBA); accounting/finance (MBA); business analytics (MIS); health care administration (MM); higher education administration (MM); human performance (MS); human resource management (MBA); information security (MIS); information systems management (MIS); law enforcement administration (MM); management (MBA); management/finance (MBA); management/human resource management (MBA); sports administration (MM). *Program availability:* Part-time, evening/weekend. *Faculty:* 2 full-time (0 women), 26 part-time/adjunct (8 women). *Students:* 186 full-time (108 women), 114 part-time (57 women); includes 167 minority (88 Black or African American, non-Hispanic/Latino; 15 Asian, non-Hispanic/Latino; 62 Hispanic/Latino; 1 Native Hawaiian or other Pacific Islander, non-Hispanic/Latino; 1 Two or more races, non-Hispanic/Latino), 18 international. Average age 32. 157 applicants, 78% accepted, 72 enrolled. In 2017, 191 master's awarded. *Entrance requirements:* For master's, official transcripts and letters of recommendation (for some programs); written personal statement. Additional exam requirements/recommendations for international students: Required—TOEFL (minimum score 550 paper-based). *Application deadline:* Applications are processed on a rolling basis. Application fee: $20 ($100 for international students). Electronic applications accepted. *Expenses: Tuition:* Full-time $17,100; part-time $2850 per course. *Financial support:* In 2017–18, 381 students received support. Federal Work-Study, scholarships/grants, and unspecified assistantships available. Support available to part-time students. Financial award applicants required to submit FAFSA. *Unit head:* Kayed Akkawi, Dean, 312-935-6050, Fax: 312-935-6020, E-mail: kakkawi@robertmorris.edu. *Application contact:* Mark Daugherty, Director of Admissions, 312-935-4814, Fax: 312-935-6020, E-mail: mdaugherty@robertmorris.edu.

Roberts Wesleyan College, Health Administration Programs, Rochester, NY 14624-1997. Offers health administration (MS); healthcare informatics administration (MS). *Program availability:* Evening/weekend, online learning. *Degree requirements:* For master's, thesis or alternative. *Entrance requirements:* For master's, minimum GPA of 3.0, verifiable work experience or recommendation.

Rochester Institute of Technology, Graduate Enrollment Services, College of Health Sciences and Technology, Health Sciences Department, Advanced Certificate Program in Health Care Finance, Rochester, NY 14623. Offers Advanced Certificate. *Program availability:* Part-time, evening/weekend, online only, 100% online. *Students:* 1 (woman) part-time. Average age 53. 2 applicants. *Entrance requirements:* For degree, minimum GPA of 3.0 (recommended). Additional exam requirements/recommendations for international students: Required—TOEFL (minimum score 570 paper-based; 88 iBT), IELTS (minimum score 6.5), PTE (minimum score 61). *Application deadline:* Applications are processed on a rolling basis. Application fee: $65. Electronic applications accepted. *Expenses:* $1,035 per credit hour (online study). *Financial support:* Available to part-time students. Applicants required to submit FAFSA. *Faculty research:* Policy and law formation; healthcare economics, innovation, and leadership. *Unit head:* Dr. Carla Stebbins, Graduate Director, 585-475-4761, E-mail: casihst@rit.edu. *Application contact:* Diane Ellison, Senior Associate Vice President, Graduate Enrollment Services, 585-475-2229, Fax: 585-475-7164, E-mail: gradinfo@rit.edu.
Website: http://www.rit.edu/ritonline/program/HLTHFI-ACT

Rochester Institute of Technology, Graduate Enrollment Services, College of Health Sciences and Technology, Health Sciences Department, MS Program in Health Systems Administration, Rochester, NY 14623. Offers MS. *Program availability:* Part-time, evening/weekend, online only, 100% online. *Students:* 3 full-time (all women), 21 part-time (15 women); includes 7 minority (3 Black or African American, non-Hispanic/Latino; 2 Asian, non-Hispanic/Latino; 2 Hispanic/Latino), 1 international. Average age 33. 19 applicants, 32% accepted, 3 enrolled. In 2017, 5 master's awarded. *Degree requirements:* For master's, thesis or alternative, capstone. *Entrance requirements:* For master's, minimum GPA of 3.0 (recommended); related professional work experience. Additional exam requirements/recommendations for international students: Required—TOEFL (minimum score 570 paper-based; 88 iBT), IELTS (minimum score 6.5), PTE (minimum score 61). *Application deadline:* Applications are processed on a rolling basis. Application fee: $65. Electronic applications accepted. *Expenses:* $1,035 per credit hour (online study). *Financial support:* In 2017–18, 3 students received support. Available to part-time students. Applicants required to submit FAFSA. *Faculty research:* Psychological type/MBTI and interpersonal communication, relationship building or leadership; student learning assessment; program evaluation; health care administration education; online/blended programs. *Unit head:* Dr. Carla Stebbins, Graduate Director, 585-475-4761, E-mail: casihst@rit.edu. *Application contact:* Diane Ellison, Senior Associate Vice President, Graduate Enrollment Services, 585-475-2229, Fax: 585-475-7164, E-mail: gradinfo@rit.edu.
Website: http://www.rit.edu/healthsciences/graduate-programs/health-systems-administration

Rockhurst University, Helzberg School of Management, Kansas City, MO 64110-2561. Offers accounting (MBA); business intelligence (MBA, Certificate); business intelligence and analytics (MS); data science (MBA, Certificate); entrepreneurship (MBA); finance (MBA); fundraising leadership (MBA, Certificate); healthcare

management (MBA, Certificate); human capital (Certificate); international business (Certificate); management (MA, MBA, Certificate); nonprofit administration (Certificate); organizational development (Certificate); science leadership (Certificate). *Accreditation:* AACSB. *Program availability:* Part-time, evening/weekend. *Faculty:* 18 full-time (4 women), 20 part-time/adjunct (9 women). *Students:* 99 full-time (30 women), 355 part-time (132 women); includes 95 minority (30 Black or African American, non-Hispanic/Latino; 29 Asian, non-Hispanic/Latino; 25 Hispanic/Latino; 11 Two or more races, non-Hispanic/Latino), 8 international. Average age 32. 249 applicants, 81% accepted, 175 enrolled. In 2017, 145 master's, 17 other advanced degrees awarded. *Entrance requirements:* For master's, GMAT or GRE. Additional exam requirements/recommendations for international students: Required—TOEFL (minimum score 550 paper-based; 79 iBT). *Application deadline:* Applications are processed on a rolling basis. Application fee: $0. Electronic applications accepted. *Financial support:* Applicants required to submit FAFSA. *Faculty research:* Offshoring/outsourcing, systems analysis/synthesis, work teams, multilateral trade, path dependencies/creation. *Unit head:* Cheryl McConnell, Dean, 816-501-4201, Fax: 816-501-4650, E-mail: cheryl.mcconnell@rockhurst.edu. *Application contact:* Jonnae Hill, Director of Graduate Business Advising, 816-501-4823, E-mail: jonnae.hill@rockhurst.edu.
Website: https://www.rockhurst.edu/helzberg

Roger Williams University, School of Justice Studies, Bristol, RI 02809. Offers criminal justice (MS); cybersecurity (MS); leadership (MS), including health care administration (MPA, MS), public management (MPA, MS); public administration (MPA), including health care administration (MPA, MS), public management (MPA, MS); MS/JD. *Program availability:* Part-time, evening/weekend, 100% online, blended/hybrid learning. *Faculty:* 10 full-time (5 women), 7 part-time/adjunct (1 woman). *Students:* 16 full-time (11 women), 114 part-time (57 women); includes 33 minority (14 Black or African American, non-Hispanic/Latino; 1 American Indian or Alaska Native, non-Hispanic/Latino; 1 Asian, non-Hispanic/Latino; 17 Hispanic/Latino), 1 international. Average age 35. 58 applicants, 83% accepted, 33 enrolled. In 2017, 27 master's awarded. *Degree requirements:* For master's, thesis optional. *Entrance requirements:* For master's, 2 letters of recommendation, college transcript, and resume (for MS in leadership and MPA programs); criminal background check (for MS in cybersecurity). Additional exam requirements/recommendations for international students: Required—TOEFL (minimum score 85 iBT), IELTS (minimum score 6.5). *Application deadline:* For fall admission, 8/1 for domestic students; for spring admission, 1/1 for domestic students. Applications are processed on a rolling basis. Application fee: $50. Electronic applications accepted. Application fee is waived when completed online. *Expenses:* Contact institution. *Financial support:* In 2017–18, 1 student received support, including 1 research assistantship (averaging $6,942 per year). Financial award application deadline: 4/1; financial award applicants required to submit FAFSA. *Faculty research:* Opioid addiction and treatment, community policing. *Unit head:* Dr. Eric Bronson, Dean, 401-254-3336, E-mail: ebronson@rwu.edu. *Application contact:* Marcus Hanscom, Director of Graduate Admissions, 401-254-3345, Fax: 401-254-3557, E-mail: gradadmit@rwu.edu.
Website: http://www.rwu.edu/academics/departments/criminaljustice.htm#graduate

Rosalind Franklin University of Medicine and Science, College of Health Professions, Department of Interprofessional Healthcare Studies, Healthcare Administration and Management Program, North Chicago, IL 60064-3095. Offers MS, Certificate. *Program availability:* Part-time, evening/weekend, online learning. *Degree requirements:* For master's, capstone portfolio. *Entrance requirements:* For master's, minimum GPA of 2.75, BS/BA from accredited college or university. Additional exam requirements/recommendations for international students: Required—TOEFL.

Rush University, College of Health Sciences, Department of Health Systems Management, Chicago, IL 60612-3832. Offers MS, PhD. *Accreditation:* CAHME. *Program availability:* Part-time, evening/weekend. *Degree requirements:* For master's, thesis; for doctorate, thesis/dissertation. *Entrance requirements:* For master's, GMAT or GRE General Test, previous undergraduate course work in accounting and statistics; for doctorate, GRE General Test, master's degree preferably in a health discipline. Additional exam requirements/recommendations for international students: Required—TOEFL. *Application deadline:* For fall admission, 2/15 for domestic students, 7/1 for international students. Applications are processed on a rolling basis. Application fee: $50 ($100 for international students). Electronic applications accepted. *Financial support:* Career-related internships or fieldwork, Federal Work-Study, institutionally sponsored loans, scholarships/grants, and traineeships available. Support available to part-time students. Financial award applicants required to submit FAFSA. *Faculty research:* Organizational performance, occupational health, quality of care indicators, leadership development, entrepreneurship, health insurance and disability, managed care. *Unit head:* Peter W. Butler, Chair, 312-942-2169, Fax: 312-942-2055. *Application contact:* Dr. Andrew N. Garman, Director, 312-942-5402, Fax: 312-942-4957, E-mail: andy_n_garman@rush.edu.
Website: http://www.rushu.rush.edu/hsm

Rutgers University–Camden, School of Public Health, Stratford, NJ 08084. Offers general public health (Certificate); health systems and policy (MPH); DO/MPH. *Program availability:* Part-time, evening/weekend. *Degree requirements:* For master's, thesis, internship. *Entrance requirements:* For master's, GRE General Test. Additional exam requirements/recommendations for international students: Required—TOEFL. Electronic applications accepted.

Rutgers University–Newark, Graduate School, Program in Public Administration, Newark, NJ 07102. Offers health care administration (MPA); human resources administration (MPA); public administration (PhD); public management (MPA); public policy analysis (MPA); urban systems and issues (MPA). *Accreditation:* NASPAA (one or more programs are accredited). *Program availability:* Part-time, evening/weekend. *Degree requirements:* For master's, comprehensive exam, thesis or alternative; for doctorate, thesis/dissertation. *Entrance requirements:* For master's, GRE, minimum undergraduate B average; for doctorate, GRE, MPA, minimum B average. Electronic applications accepted. *Faculty research:* Government finance, municipal and state government, public productivity.

Rutgers University–Newark, Rutgers Business School–Newark and New Brunswick, Program in Healthcare Services Management, Newark, NJ 07102. Offers MHSM.

Rutgers University–Newark, School of Health Related Professions, Department of Interdisciplinary Studies, Program in Health Care Management, Newark, NJ 07102. Offers MS. *Program availability:* Part-time, evening/weekend, online learning. *Entrance requirements:* For master's, minimum GPA of 3.0, bachelor's degree, statement of career goals, curriculum vitae, transcript of highest degree. Additional exam requirements/recommendations for international students: Required—TOEFL (minimum score 500 paper-based; 79 iBT). Electronic applications accepted.

Rutgers University–Newark, School of Public Health, Newark, NJ 07107-1709. Offers clinical epidemiology (Certificate); dental public health (MPH); general public health (Certificate); public policy and oral health services administration (Certificate); quantitative methods (MPH); urban health (MPH); DMD/MPH; MD/MPH; MS/MPH. *Program availability:* Part-time, evening/weekend. *Degree requirements:* For master's, thesis, internship. *Entrance requirements:* For master's, GRE General Test. Additional exam requirements/recommendations for international students: Required—TOEFL. Electronic applications accepted.

Rutgers University–New Brunswick, School of Public Health, Piscataway, NJ 08854. Offers biostatistics (MPH, MS, Dr PH, PhD); clinical epidemiology (Certificate); environmental and occupational health (MPH, Dr PH, PhD, Certificate); epidemiology (MPH, Dr PH, PhD); general public health (Certificate); health education and behavioral science (MPH, Dr PH, PhD); health systems and policy (MPH, PhD); public health (MPH, Dr PH, PhD); public health preparedness (Certificate); DO/MPH; JD/MPH; MBA/MPH; MD/MPH; MPH/MBA; MPH/MSPA; MS/MPH; Psy D/MPH. *Accreditation:* CEPH. *Program availability:* Part-time, evening/weekend. *Degree requirements:* For master's, thesis, internship; for doctorate, comprehensive exam, thesis/dissertation. *Entrance requirements:* For master's, GRE General Test; for doctorate, GRE General Test, MPH (Dr PH); MA, MPH, or MS (PhD). Additional exam requirements/recommendations for international students: Required—TOEFL. Electronic applications accepted.

Sage Graduate School, School of Management, Program in Health Services Administration, Troy, NY 12180-4115. Offers gerontology (MS). *Program availability:* Part-time, evening/weekend. *Faculty:* 5 full-time (3 women), 5 part-time/adjunct (1 woman). *Students:* 8 full-time (6 women), 19 part-time (15 women); includes 4 minority (1 Black or African American, non-Hispanic/Latino; 2 Asian, non-Hispanic/Latino; 1 Hispanic/Latino). Average age 31. 26 applicants, 42% accepted, 5 enrolled. In 2017, 14 master's awarded. *Entrance requirements:* For master's, minimum GPA of 2.75, resume, 2 letters of recommendation. Additional exam requirements/recommendations for international students: Required—TOEFL (minimum score 550 paper-based). *Application deadline:* Applications are processed on a rolling basis. Application fee: $30. Electronic applications accepted. Tuition and fees vary according to degree level and program. *Financial support:* Fellowships, research assistantships, and unspecified assistantships available. Financial award application deadline: 3/1; financial award applicants required to submit FAFSA. *Unit head:* Dr. Kimberly Fredericks, Dean, School of Management, 518-292-1782, Fax: 518-292-1964, E-mail: fredek1@sage.edu. *Application contact:* Wendy D. Diefendorf, Director of Graduate and Adult Admission, 518-244-2443, Fax: 518-244-6880, E-mail: diefew@sage.edu.

Saginaw Valley State University, College of Health and Human Services, Program in Health Leadership, University Center, MI 48710. Offers MS. *Program availability:* Part-time, evening/weekend. *Students:* 15 full-time (11 women), 67 part-time (35 women); includes 17 minority (7 Black or African American, non-Hispanic/Latino; 6 Asian, non-Hispanic/Latino; 1 Hispanic/Latino; 3 Two or more races, non-Hispanic/Latino), 8 international. Average age 37. 55 applicants, 80% accepted, 30 enrolled. In 2017, 34 master's awarded. *Entrance requirements:* For master's, minimum GPA of 3.0. Additional exam requirements/recommendations for international students: Required—TOEFL (minimum score 580 paper-based; 92 iBT). *Application deadline:* For fall admission, 7/15 for international students; for winter admission, 11/15 for international students; for spring admission, 4/15 for international students. Applications are processed on a rolling basis. Application fee: $30 ($90 for international students). Electronic applications accepted. *Expenses:* Tuition, state resident: full-time $10,156; part-time $564.20 per credit hour. Tuition, nonresident: full-time $19,336; part-time $1074.20 per credit hour. *Required fees:* $263; $14.60 per credit hour. Tuition and fees vary according to degree level and program. *Financial support:* Federal Work-Study and scholarships/grants available. Support available to part-time students. *Unit head:* Dr. Marilyn Skrocki, Program Coordinator, 989-964-7394, E-mail: mskrocki@svsu.edu. *Application contact:* Jenna Briggs, Director, Graduate and International Admissions, 989-964-6096, Fax: 989-964-2788, E-mail: gradadm@svsu.edu.

St. Ambrose University, College of Business, Program in Business Administration, Davenport, IA 52803-2898. Offers business administration (DBA); health care (MBA); human resources (MBA). *Accreditation:* ACBSP. *Program availability:* Part-time, evening/weekend. *Degree requirements:* For master's, comprehensive exam (for some programs), thesis or alternative, capstone seminar; for doctorate, comprehensive exam, thesis/dissertation, oral and written exams. *Entrance requirements:* For master's, GMAT; for doctorate, GMAT, master's degree. Additional exam requirements/recommendations for international students: Required—TOEFL. Electronic applications accepted. *Expenses:* Contact institution.

St. Catherine University, Graduate Programs, Program in Business Administration, St. Paul, MN 55105. Offers healthcare (MBA); integrated marketing communications (MBA); management (MBA). *Program availability:* Part-time, evening/weekend. *Students:* 62 part-time (54 women); includes 8 minority (4 Black or African American, non-Hispanic/Latino; 2 Asian, non-Hispanic/Latino; 2 Two or more races, non-Hispanic/Latino), 1 international. Average age 33. 28 applicants, 71% accepted, 18 enrolled. In 2017, 31 master's awarded. *Entrance requirements:* For master's, GMAT (if undergraduate GPA is less than 3.0), 2+ years' work or volunteer experience in professional setting(s). Additional exam requirements/recommendations for international students: Required—TOEFL. *Application deadline:* For fall admission, 8/1 priority date for domestic students; for spring admission, 12/15 priority date for domestic students. Application fee: $35. *Expenses:* Contact institution. *Unit head:* Michelle Wieser, Director, 651-690-6355, E-mail: mawieser@stkate.edu.

St. Joseph's College, Long Island Campus, Programs in Health Care Administration, Field in Health Care Management, Patchogue, NY 11772-2399. Offers MBA. *Program availability:* Part-time, evening/weekend, 100% online, blended/hybrid learning. *Faculty:* 15 full-time (7 women), 22 part-time/adjunct (7 women). Application fee: $25. *Expenses: Tuition:* Full-time $17,550; part-time $975 per credit. *Required fees:* $362. *Unit head:* John Sardelis, Associate Chair and Professor, 631-687-1493, E-mail: jsardelis@sjcny.edu.

St. Joseph's College, Long Island Campus, Programs in Management, Field in Health Care Management, Patchogue, NY 11772-2399. Offers MS. *Program availability:* Part-time, evening/weekend, 100% online, blended/hybrid learning. *Faculty:* 15 full-time (7 women), 22 part-time/adjunct (7 women). *Students:* 14 full-time (9 women), 60 part-time (50 women); includes 15 minority (9 Black or African American, non-Hispanic/Latino; 6 Hispanic/Latino). Average age 36. 64 applicants, 59% accepted, 29 enrolled. In 2017, 11 master's awarded. Application fee: $25. *Expenses: Tuition:* Full-time $17,550; part-time $975 per credit. *Required fees:* $362. *Financial support:* In 2017–18, 13 students received support. *Unit head:* Mary A. Chance, Assistant Professor/Interim Director of Graduate Management Studies, 631-687-1297, E-mail: mchance@sjcny.edu.

St. Joseph's College, New York, Programs in Health Care Administration, Field in Health Care Management, Brooklyn, NY 11205-3688. Offers MBA. *Program availability:* Part-time, evening/weekend, 100% online, blended/hybrid learning. *Faculty:* 1 full-time (0 women), 6 part-time/adjunct (4 women). *Students:* 3 full-time (2 women), 1 (woman) part-time; includes 3 minority (2 Black or African American, non-Hispanic/Latino; 1 Hispanic/Latino). Average age 38. In 2017, 2 master's awarded. *Entrance requirements:* For master's, official transcripts, resume, two letters of reference, verification of employment. Additional exam requirements/recommendations for international students: Required—TOEFL (minimum score 80 iBT). *Application deadline:* Applications are processed on a rolling basis. Application fee: $25. Electronic applications accepted. *Expenses: Tuition:* Full-time $17,550; part-time $975 per credit. *Required fees:* $362. *Unit head:* Lauren Pete, Chair, 718-940-5890, E-mail: lpete@sjcny.edu.
Website: https://www.sjcny.edu

St. Joseph's College, New York, Programs in Health Care Administration, Field in Health Care Management - Health Information Systems, Brooklyn, NY 11205-3688. Offers MBA. *Program availability:* Part-time, evening/weekend, 100% online, blended/hybrid learning. *Faculty:* 1 full-time (0 women), 6 part-time/adjunct (4 women). *Students:* 5 full-time (2 women), 9 part-time (7 women); includes 11 minority (6 Black or African American, non-Hispanic/Latino; 4 Asian, non-Hispanic/Latino; 1 Two or more races, non-Hispanic/Latino). Average age 36. 6 applicants, 50% accepted, 2 enrolled. In 2017, 5 master's awarded. *Entrance requirements:* For master's, official transcripts, resume, two letters of reference, verification of employment. Additional exam requirements/recommendations for international students: Required—TOEFL (minimum score 80 iBT). *Application deadline:* Applications are processed on a rolling basis. Application fee: $25. Electronic applications accepted. *Expenses: Tuition:* Full-time $17,550; part-time $975 per credit. *Required fees:* $362. *Financial support:* In 2017–18, 2 students received support. *Unit head:* Lauren Pete, Chair, 718-940-5890, E-mail: lpete@sjcny.edu.

St. Joseph's College, New York, Programs in Management, Field in Health Care Management, Brooklyn, NY 11205-3688. Offers MBA. *Program availability:* Part-time, evening/weekend, 100% online, blended/hybrid learning. *Faculty:* 1 full-time (0 women), 6 part-time/adjunct (4 women). *Students:* 4 full-time (all women), 24 part-time (19 women); includes 20 minority (14 Black or African American, non-Hispanic/Latino; 1 Asian, non-Hispanic/Latino; 5 Hispanic/Latino). Average age 36. 34 applicants, 47% accepted, 14 enrolled. In 2017, 12 master's awarded. *Entrance requirements:* For master's, official transcripts, resume, two letters of reference, verification of employment. Additional exam requirements/recommendations for international students: Required—TOEFL (minimum score 80 iBT). *Application deadline:* Applications are processed on a rolling basis. Application fee: $25. Electronic applications accepted. *Expenses: Tuition:* Full-time $17,550; part-time $975 per credit. *Required fees:* $362. *Financial support:* In 2017–18, 2 students received support. *Unit head:* Lauren Pete, Associate Professor/Chair, 718-940-5890, E-mail: lpete@sjcny.edu.
Website: http://www.sjcny.edu

Saint Joseph's College of Maine, Master of Health Administration Program, Standish, ME 04084. Offers MHA. Degree program is external; available only by correspondence and online. *Program availability:* Part-time, online learning. *Entrance requirements:* For master's, two years of experience in health care. Electronic applications accepted. *Faculty research:* Health care organization, policy, and management; long-term care.

Saint Joseph's University, College of Arts and Sciences, Department of Health Services, Philadelphia, PA 19131-1395. Offers health administration (MS); health informatics (MS); organizations development and leadership (MS). *Program availability:* Part-time, evening/weekend. *Faculty:* 6 full-time (5 women), 29 part-time/adjunct (8 women). *Students:* 35 full-time (25 women), 407 part-time (314 women); includes 171 minority (110 Black or African American, non-Hispanic/Latino; 1 American Indian or Alaska Native, non-Hispanic/Latino; 26 Asian, non-Hispanic/Latino; 28 Hispanic/Latino; 6 Two or more races, non-Hispanic/Latino), 14 international. Average age 32. 157 applicants, 73% accepted, 74 enrolled. In 2017, 219 master's awarded. *Entrance requirements:* For master's, GRE (if GPA less than 2.75), 2 letters of recommendation, resume, personal statement, official transcripts. Additional exam requirements/recommendations for international students: Required—TOEFL (minimum score 550 paper-based; 80 iBT), IELTS (minimum score 6.5). *Application deadline:* For fall admission, 7/15 for international students; for spring admission, 11/1 for international students. Applications are processed on a rolling basis. Application fee: $35. Electronic applications accepted. *Expenses:* Contact institution. *Financial support:* In 2017–18, 12 students received support. Career-related internships or fieldwork and unspecified assistantships available. Financial award application deadline: 5/1; financial award applicants required to submit FAFSA. *Unit head:* Louis D. Horvath, Director, 610-660-3131, E-mail: gradcas@sju.edu. *Application contact:* Graduate Admissions, College of Arts and Sciences, 610-660-3131, E-mail: gradcas@sju.edu.
Website: http://sju.edu/majors-programs/graduate-arts-sciences/masters/health-administration-ms

Saint Joseph's University, Erivan K. Haub School of Business, MBA Program, Philadelphia, PA 19131-1395. Offers accounting (MBA); business intelligence analytics (MBA); finance (MBA); financial analysis reporting (Postbaccalaureate Certificate); general business (MBA); health and medical services administration (MBA); international business (MBA); international marketing (MBA); leading (MBA); marketing (MBA); DO/MBA. DO/MBA offered jointly with Philadelphia College of Osteopathic Medicine. *Program availability:* Part-time-only, evening/weekend, 100% online. *Students:* 85 full-time (36 women), 371 part-time (153 women); includes 74 minority (32 Black or African American, non-Hispanic/Latino; 15 Asian, non-Hispanic/Latino; 19 Hispanic/Latino; 1 Native Hawaiian or other Pacific Islander, non-Hispanic/Latino; 7 Two or more races, non-Hispanic/Latino), 36 international. Average age 30. 247 applicants, 76% accepted, 112 enrolled. In 2017, 163 master's awarded. *Degree requirements:* For master's, minimum GPA of 3.0. *Entrance requirements:* For master's, GMAT or GRE, 2 letters of recommendation, resume, personal statement, official undergraduate and graduate transcripts. Additional exam requirements/recommendations for international students: Required—PTE, TOEFL, IELTS, or PTE. *Application deadline:* For fall admission, 7/15 priority date for domestic students, 5/15 priority date for international students; for spring admission, 11/15 priority date for domestic students, 10/15 priority date for international students; for summer admission, 4/15 priority date for domestic students, 2/15 priority date for international students. Applications are processed on a rolling basis. Application fee: $35. Electronic applications accepted. *Expenses:* Contact institution. *Financial support:* Scholarships/grants and unspecified assistantships available. Financial award application deadline: 5/1; financial award applicants required to submit FAFSA. *Unit head:* Jeannine Lajeunesse, Director, 610-660-1626, Fax: 610-660-1599, E-mail: jlajeune@sju.edu. *Application contact:* Christine Anderson, Assistant Director, 610-660-2252, Fax: 610-660-1599, E-mail: chris.anderson@sju.edu.
Website: http://www.sju.edu/haubmba

Saint Leo University, Graduate Studies in Business, Saint Leo, FL 33574-6665. Offers accounting (M Acc, MBA); cybersecurity (MS); cybersecurity management (MBA); data analytics (MBA); health care management (MBA); human resource management (MBA); international and experiential business administration (MBA); management (MBA, DBA); marketing (MBA); marketing research and social media analytics (MBA); project management (MBA); social media marketing (MBA); sport business (MBA); supply chain global integration management (MBA). *Accreditation:* ACBSP. *Program availability:* Part-time, evening/weekend, 100% online, blended/hybrid learning. *Faculty:* 54 full-time (18 women), 52 part-time/adjunct (18 women). *Students:* 9 full-time (3 women), 1,867 part-time (1,079 women); includes 861 minority (598 Black or African American, non-Hispanic/Latino; 3 American Indian or Alaska Native, non-Hispanic/Latino; 38 Asian, non-Hispanic/Latino; 186 Hispanic/Latino; 3 Native Hawaiian or other Pacific Islander, non-Hispanic/Latino; 33 Two or more races, non-Hispanic/Latino), 68 international. Average age 37. 868 applicants, 63% accepted, 537 enrolled. In 2017, 859 master's, 3 doctorates awarded. *Degree requirements:* For doctorate, comprehensive exam, thesis/dissertation. *Entrance requirements:* For master's, GMAT with minimum score 500 (for M Acc), official transcripts, current resume, 2 professional recommendations, personal statement, bachelor's degree from regionally-accredited university; undergraduate degree in accounting and minimum undergraduate GPA of 3.0 (for M Acc); minimum undergraduate GPA of 3.0 in final 2 years of undergraduate study and 2 years' work experience (for MBA); for doctorate, GMAT (minimum score of 550) if master's GPA is under 3.25, official transcripts, current resume, 2 professional recommendations, personal statement, master's degree from regionally-accredited university with minimum GPA of 3.25, 3 years' work experience, interview. Additional exam requirements/recommendations for international students: Required—TOEFL (minimum score 550 paper-based; 78 iBT). *Application deadline:* For fall admission, 7/1 priority date for domestic and international students; for spring admission, 11/12 priority date for domestic students, 11/1 for international students. Applications are processed on a rolling basis. Application fee: $80. Electronic applications accepted. *Expenses:* Contact institution. *Financial support:* In 2017–18, 106 students received support. Career-related internships or fieldwork, health care benefits, and tuition remission for Saint Leo employees and their dependents available. Financial award application deadline: 3/1; financial award applicants required to submit FAFSA. *Faculty research:* Servant leadership, work/life balance, emotional intelligence, pricing, marketing. *Unit head:* Dr. Charles Hale, Dean, School of Business, 352-588-8599, Fax: 352-588-8912, E-mail: mbaslu@saintleo.edu. *Application contact:* Mark Russum, Assistant Vice President, Enrollment, 800-707-8846, Fax: 352-588-7873, E-mail: grad.admissions@saintleo.edu.
Website: https://www.saintleo.edu/school-of-business

Saint Louis University, Graduate Programs, College for Public Health and Social Justice and Graduate Programs, Department of Health Management and Policy, St. Louis, MO 63103. Offers health administration (MHA); health policy (MPH); public health studies (PhD). *Accreditation:* CAHME. *Program availability:* Part-time. *Degree requirements:* For master's, comprehensive exam, internship. *Entrance requirements:* For master's, GMAT or GRE General Test, LSAT, MCAT, letters of recommendation, resume. Additional exam requirements/recommendations for international students: Required—TOEFL (minimum score 525 paper-based). *Faculty research:* Management of HIV/AIDS, rural health services, prevention of asthma, genetics and health services use, health insurance and access to care.

Saint Mary-of-the-Woods College, Master of Healthcare Administration Program, Saint Mary of the Woods, IN 47876. Offers MHA. *Expenses: Tuition:* Full-time $4260; part-time $3550 per credit hour. Tuition and fees vary according to program.

Saint Mary's University of Minnesota, Schools of Graduate and Professional Programs, Graduate School of Health and Human Services, Health and Human Services Administration Program, Winona, MN 55987-1399. Offers MA. *Unit head:* Susan Doherty, Director, 612-238-4549, E-mail: sdoherty@smumn.edu. *Application contact:* James Callinan, Director of Admissions for Graduate and Professional Programs, 612-728-5158, Fax: 612-728-5121, E-mail: jcallina@smumn.edu.
Website: http://www.smumn.edu/graduate-home/areas-of-study/graduate-school-of-health-human-services/ma-in-health-human-services-administration

St. Norbert College, Master of Business Administration Program, De Pere, WI 54115-2099. Offers business (MBA); health care (MBA); supply chain and manufacturing (MBA). *Program availability:* Part-time-only, evening/weekend. *Faculty:* 10 full-time (3 women), 8 part-time/adjunct (2 women). *Students:* 68 part-time (40 women); includes 5 minority (1 American Indian or Alaska Native, non-Hispanic/Latino; 1 Asian, non-Hispanic/Latino; 2 Hispanic/Latino; 1 Two or more races, non-Hispanic/Latino), 1 international. Average age 33. 15 applicants, 100% accepted, 14 enrolled. In 2017, 12 master's awarded. *Entrance requirements:* For master's, official transcripts, letters of recommendation, professional resume, essay. *Application deadline:* For fall admission, 8/4 for domestic students; for winter admission, 12/15 for domestic students; for spring admission, 3/2 for domestic students; for summer admission, 4/20 for domestic students. Applications are processed on a rolling basis. Application fee: $50. Electronic applications accepted. *Expenses:* $675 per credit tuition, $37.50 per course technology fee. *Financial support:* Federal Work-Study available. Financial award application deadline: 1/1; financial award applicants required to submit FAFSA. *Faculty research:* Urban segregation, religious identity, crisis decision-making, normative ethics, psychological effects of change on individuals and organizations. *Unit head:* Lisa Gray, Coordinator of MBA Program, 920-403-3449, E-mail: lisa.gray@snc.edu. *Application contact:* Brenda Busch, Associate Director of Graduate Recruitment, 920-403-3942, Fax: 920-403-4072, E-mail: brenda.busch@snc.edu.
Website: http://www.snc.edu/mba/

Saint Peter's University, Graduate Business Programs, MBA Program, Jersey City, NJ 07306-5997. Offers finance (MBA); health care administration (MBA); human resource management (MBA); international business (MBA); management (MBA); management information systems (MBA); marketing (MBA); risk management (MBA); MBA/MS. *Program availability:* Part-time, evening/weekend. *Entrance requirements:* Additional exam requirements/recommendations for international students: Required—TOEFL. Electronic applications accepted. *Faculty research:* Finance, health care management, human resource management, international business, management, management information systems, marketing, risk management.

St. Thomas University, School of Business, Department of Management, Miami Gardens, FL 33054-6459. Offers accounting (MBA); general management (MSM, Certificate); health management (MBA, MSM, Certificate); human resource management (MBA, MSM, Certificate); international business (MBA, MIB, MSM, Certificate); justice administration (MSM, Certificate); management accounting (MSM, Certificate); public management (MSM, Certificate); sports administration (MS). *Program availability:* Part-time, evening/weekend. *Degree requirements:* For master's, comprehensive exam. *Entrance requirements:* For master's, interview, minimum GPA of 3.0 or GMAT. Additional exam requirements/recommendations for international students: Required—TOEFL (minimum score 550 paper-based; 79 iBT). Electronic applications accepted.

Saint Xavier University, Graduate Studies, Graham School of Management, Chicago, IL 60655-3105. Offers employee health benefits (Certificate); finance (MBA); financial fraud examination and management (MBA, Certificate); financial planning (MBA, Certificate); generalist/individualized (MBA); health administration (MBA); managed care (Certificate); management (MBA); marketing (MBA); project management (MBA, Certificate); MBA/MS. *Accreditation:* AACSB. *Program availability:* Part-time, evening/weekend. *Entrance requirements:* For master's, GMAT, minimum GPA of 3.0, 2 years of work experience. Electronic applications accepted. *Expenses:* Contact institution.

Salve Regina University, Program in Business Administration, Newport, RI 02840-4192. Offers cybersecurity issues in business (MBA); entrepreneurial enterprise (MBA); health care administration and management (MBA); nonprofit management (MBA); social ventures (MBA). *Program availability:* Part-time, evening/weekend, online learning. *Entrance requirements:* For master's, GMAT, GRE General Test, or MAT, 6 undergraduate credits each in accounting, economics, quantitative analysis and calculus or statistics. Additional exam requirements/recommendations for international students: Required—TOEFL (minimum score 600 paper-based; 100 iBT) or IELTS. Electronic applications accepted.

Salve Regina University, Program in Healthcare Administration and Management, Newport, RI 02840-4192. Offers MS, CGS. *Program availability:* Part-time, evening/weekend, online learning. *Degree requirements:* For master's, internship. *Entrance* *requirements:* For master's, GMAT, GRE General Test, or MAT, health care work experience or 250 internship hours. Additional exam requirements/recommendations for international students: Required—TOEFL (minimum score 600 paper-based; 100 iBT) or IELTS. Electronic applications accepted.

Samford University, School of Public Health, Birmingham, AL 35229. Offers health informatics (MSHI); healthcare administration (MHA); nutrition (MS); public health (MPH); social work (MSW). *Program availability:* Part-time, 100% online. *Faculty:* 17 full-time (12 women), 4 part-time/adjunct (2 women). *Students:* 93 full-time (87 women), 5 part-time (all women); includes 20 minority (14 Black or African American, non-Hispanic/Latino; 2 Asian, non-Hispanic/Latino; 2 Hispanic/Latino; 2 Two or more races, non-Hispanic/Latino), 1 international. Average age 27. 90 applicants, 44% accepted, 32 enrolled. In 2017, 34 master's awarded. *Degree requirements:* For master's, capstone course. *Entrance requirements:* For master's, GRE, MAT, recommendations, resume, personal statement. Additional exam requirements/recommendations for international students: Required—TOEFL (minimum score 550 paper-based); Recommended—IELTS. *Application deadline:* For fall admission, 10/1 for domestic students; for spring admission, 5/1 for domestic students. Application fee: $75. Electronic applications accepted. *Expenses:* $813 per credit hour. *Financial support:* In 2017–18, 32 students received support. Scholarships/grants available. Financial award application deadline: 2/15; financial award applicants required to submit FAFSA. *Faculty research:* Chronic kidney disease, disasters and vulnerable populations, children's health, obesity, metabolism and diabetes, health policy and health care delivery. *Unit head:* Dr. Keith Elder, Dean, School of Public Health, 205-726-4655, E-mail: kelder@samford.edu. *Application contact:* Dr. Marian Carter, Assistant Dean of Enrollment Management and Student Services, 205-726-2611, E-mail: mwcarter@samford.edu.
Website: http://www.samford.edu/publichealth/

San Diego State University, Graduate and Research Affairs, College of Health and Human Services, Graduate School of Public Health, San Diego, CA 92182. Offers environmental health (MPH); epidemiology (MPH, PhD), including biostatistics (MPH); global emergency preparedness and response (MS); global health (PhD); health behavior (PhD); health promotion (MPH); health services administration (MPH); toxicology (MS); MPH/MA; MSW/MPH. *Accreditation:* CAHME (one or more programs are accredited). *Program availability:* Part-time. *Degree requirements:* For master's, comprehensive exam (for some programs), thesis (for some programs); for doctorate, thesis/dissertation. *Entrance requirements:* For master's, GMAT (MPH in health services administration), GRE General Test; for doctorate, GRE General Test. Additional exam requirements/recommendations for international students: Required—TOEFL. *Faculty research:* Evaluation of tobacco, AIDS prevalence and prevention, mammography, infant death project, Alzheimer's in elderly Chinese.

San Francisco State University, Division of Graduate Studies, College of Business, Program in Business Administration, San Francisco, CA 94132-1722. Offers decision sciences/operations research (MBA); ethics and compliance (MBA); finance (MBA); global business and innovation (MBA); healthcare administration (MBA); hospitality and tourism management (MBA); information systems (MBA); leadership (MBA); marketing (MBA); nonprofit and social enterprise leadership (MBA); sustainable business (MBA). *Accreditation:* AACSB. *Program availability:* Part-time, evening/weekend. *Degree requirements:* For master's, thesis, essay test. *Entrance requirements:* For master's, GMAT, minimum GPA of 2.7 in last 60 units. Additional exam requirements/recommendations for international students: Required—TOEFL (minimum score 550 paper-based). *Application deadline:* For fall admission, 5/1 priority date for domestic students, 4/1 for international students; for spring admission, 11/1 for domestic students, 10/15 for international students. Applications are processed on a rolling basis. Application fee: $55. *Financial support:* Application deadline: 3/1. *Unit head:* Dr. Sanjit Sengupta, Faculty Director, 415-817-4366, Fax: 415-817-4340, E-mail: sengupta@sfsu.edu. *Application contact:* Christopher Kingston, Director of Student Advising, 415-817-4322, Fax: 415-817-4340, E-mail: cak@sfsu.edu.
Website: http://cob.sfsu.edu/graduate-programs/mba

Seton Hall University, College of Nursing, South Orange, NJ 07079-2697. Offers advanced practice in primary health care (MSN, DNP), including adult/gerontological nurse practitioner, pediatric nurse practitioner; entry into practice (MSN); health systems administration (MSN, DNP); nursing (PhD); nursing case management (MSN); nursing education (MA); school nurse (MSN); MSN/MA. *Accreditation:* AACN. *Program availability:* Part-time, online learning. *Degree requirements:* For master's, research project; for doctorate, dissertation or scholarly project. *Entrance requirements:* For doctorate, GRE (waived for students with GPA of 3.5 or higher). Additional exam requirements/recommendations for international students: Required—TOEFL. Electronic applications accepted. *Faculty research:* Parent/child, adult, and gerontological nursing; breast cancer; families of children with HIV; parish nursing.

Seton Hill University, MBA Program, Greensburg, PA 15601. Offers entrepreneurship (MBA); forensic accounting and fraud examination (MBA); healthcare administration (MBA); management (MBA). *Program availability:* Part-time, evening/weekend. *Entrance requirements:* For master's, resume, 3 letters of recommendation, personal statement, transcripts. Additional exam requirements/recommendations for international students: Required—TOEFL (minimum score 600 paper-based; 100 iBT), IELTS (minimum score 6.5). *Application deadline:* Applications are processed on a rolling basis. Application fee: $0. Electronic applications accepted. *Expenses: Tuition:* Part-time $734 per credit. Tuition and fees vary according to class time, course level, course load and program. *Financial support:* Federal Work-Study, scholarships/grants, and tuition discounts available. Financial award application deadline: 8/15; financial award applicants required to submit FAFSA. *Unit head:* Dr. Douglas Nelson, Associate Professor, Business/MBA Program Director, E-mail: dnelson@setonhill.edu.
Website: http://www.setonhill.edu/academics/graduate_programs/mba

Shenandoah University, Eleanor Wade Custer School of Nursing, Winchester, VA 22601. Offers adult gerontology primary care nurse practitioner (Graduate Certificate); adult-gerontology primary care nurse practitioner (MSN); family nurse practitioner (MSN, DNP, Graduate Certificate); general (MSN); health systems leadership (DNP); health systems management (MSN, Graduate Certificate); nurse midwifery (MSN); nurse-midwifery (Graduate Certificate); nursing education (Graduate Certificate); nursing practice (DNP); psychiatric mental health nurse practitioner (MSN, DNP, Graduate Certificate). *Accreditation:* AACN; ACNM/ACME. *Faculty:* 17 full-time (all women), 6 part-time/adjunct (all women). *Students:* 30 full-time (26 women), 51 part-time (48 women); includes 19 minority (13 Black or African American, non-Hispanic/Latino; 3 Asian, non-Hispanic/Latino; 2 Hispanic/Latino; 1 Two or more races, non-Hispanic/Latino), 3 international. Average age 37. 52 applicants, 88% accepted, 34 enrolled. In 2017, 18 master's, 1 doctorate, 28 other advanced degrees awarded. *Degree requirements:* For master's, research project, clinical hours; for doctorate, scholarly project, clinical hours; for Graduate Certificate, clinical hours. *Entrance requirements:* For master's, United States RN license; minimum GPA of 3.0; 2080 hours of clinical experience; curriculum vitae; 3 letters of recommendation from former dean, faculty member, or advisor familiar with the applicant, and a former or current supervisor; two-to-three-page essay on a specified topic; for doctorate, MSN, minimum GPA of 3.0, 3 letters of recommendation, interview, BSN, two-to-three page essay on a specific topic, 500-word statement of clinical practice research interest, resume, current U.S. RN license, 2080 clinical hours; for Graduate Certificate, MSN, minimum GPA of 3.0, 2 letters of recommendation, minimum of one year (2080 hours) of clinical nursing experience, interview, two-to-three page essay on a specific topic, resume, current United States RN license. Additional exam requirements/recommendations for international students: Required—TOEFL (minimum score 558 paper-based; 83 iBT). *Application deadline:* For fall admission, 4/15 priority date for domestic and international students; for spring admission, 11/1 for domestic and international students; for summer admission, 3/1 for domestic and international students. Application fee: $30. Electronic applications accepted. *Expenses:* $22,451 tuition, plus $3,579 fees (student services fee, technology fee, and clinical fee). *Financial support:* In 2017–18, 32 students received support. Scholarships/grants and unspecified assistantships available. Financial award applicants required to submit FAFSA. *Faculty research:* Emergency preparedness, workplace environment, maternal child, inter-professional education, health policy. *Total annual research expenditures:* $30,000. *Unit head:* Dr. Kathleen LaSala, RN, Dean, 540-678-4381, Fax: 540-665-5519, E-mail: klasala@su.edu. *Application contact:* Andrew Woodall, Executive Director of Recruitment and Admissions, 540-665-4581, Fax: 540-665-4627, E-mail: admit@su.edu.
Website: http://www.su.edu/nursing/

Shenandoah University, Harry F. Byrd, Jr. School of Business, Winchester, VA 22601-5195. Offers business administration (MBA); business administration essentials (Certificate); healthcare management (Certificate). *Accreditation:* AACSB. *Program availability:* Part-time, evening/weekend. *Faculty:* 16 full-time (8 women), 2 part-time/adjunct (0 women). *Students:* 53 full-time (18 women), 59 part-time (37 women); includes 26 minority (10 Black or African American, non-Hispanic/Latino; 1 American Indian or Alaska Native, non-Hispanic/Latino; 5 Asian, non-Hispanic/Latino; 8 Hispanic/Latino; 2 Two or more races, non-Hispanic/Latino), 28 international. Average age 32. 73 applicants, 93% accepted, 46 enrolled. In 2017, 35 master's awarded. *Entrance requirements:* For master's, transcripts from all institutions of higher learning; minimum GPA of 3.0 in appropriate undergraduate course work; 2 letters of recommendation; resume; interview; brief narrative essay (2-3 pages) of career, professional development and goals, as they relate to the completion of an MBA. Additional exam requirements/recommendations for international students: Required—TOEFL (minimum score 550 paper-based, 79 iBT) or IELTS (6.5). *Application deadline:* For fall admission, 5/1 for domestic students, 4/15 for international students; for spring admission, 11/15 for domestic students, 10/15 for international students; for summer admission, 6/15 for domestic students, 5/1 for international students. Application fee: $30. Electronic applications accepted. *Expenses:* $31,080 tuition, $1,297 fees (technology fee and student services fee). *Financial support:* In 2017–18, 27 students received support. Scholarships/grants and unspecified assistantships available. Financial award applicants required to submit FAFSA. *Faculty research:* Entrepreneurship, sports ethics, healthcare economics, leaderships, sustainability. *Unit head:* Bogdan Daraban, PhD, Associate Dean, School of Business, 540-542-6282, Fax: 540-665-5437, E-mail: bdaraban@su.edu. *Application contact:* Andrew Woodall, Executive Director of Recruitment and Admissions, 540-665-4581, Fax: 540-665-4627, E-mail: admit@su.edu.
Website: http://www.su.edu/business/

Shippensburg University of Pennsylvania, School of Graduate Studies, John L. Grove College of Business, Shippensburg, PA 17257-2299. Offers advanced studies in business (Certificate); advanced supply chain and logistics management (Certificate); business administration (MBA, DBA), including business administration (MBA), business analytics (MBA), finance (MBA), healthcare management (MBA), management information systems (MBA), supply chain management (MBA); finance (Certificate); health care management (Certificate); management information systems (Certificate). *Accreditation:* AACSB. *Program availability:* Part-time, evening/weekend, 100% online, blended/hybrid learning. *Faculty:* 23 full-time (5 women), 1 part-time/adjunct (0 women). *Students:* 46 full-time (14 women), 201 part-time (71 women); includes 35 minority (12 Black or African American, non-Hispanic/Latino; 10 Asian, non-Hispanic/Latino; 11 Hispanic/Latino; 2 Two or more races, non-Hispanic/Latino), 22 international. Average age 32. 169 applicants, 65% accepted, 77 enrolled. In 2017, 105 master's, 82 other advanced degrees awarded. *Degree requirements:* For master's, thesis optional, practicum; for doctorate, comprehensive exam, thesis/dissertation. *Entrance requirements:* For master's, GMAT (minimum score 450 if less than 5 years of mid-level experience, including management experience), current resume; relevant work/classroom experience; 500-word statement of purpose; prerequisites of quantitative analysis, computer usage, and oral and written communications; laptop computer; for doctorate, GMAT (minimum score of 600 if less than 5 years of substantive professional or teaching experience), 2 letters of recommendation from professionals in academia or industry; 2-3 page personal and professional statement; interview; resume. Additional exam requirements/recommendations for international students: Required—TOEFL (minimum score 550 paper-based, 68 iBT) or IELTS (minimum score 6). *Application deadline:* For fall admission, 4/30 for international students; for spring admission, 9/30 for international students. Applications are processed on a rolling basis. Application fee: $45. Electronic applications accepted. *Expenses:* Tuition, state resident: part-time $500 per credit. Tuition, nonresident: part-time $750 per credit. *Required fees:* $145 per credit. *Financial support:* In 2017–18, 14 students received support. Career-related internships or fieldwork, scholarships/grants, unspecified assistantships, and resident hall director and student payroll positions available. Support available to part-time students. Financial award application deadline: 3/1; financial award applicants required to submit FAFSA. *Unit head:* Dr. John G. Kooti, Dean of the College of Business, 717-477-1435, Fax: 717-477-4003, E-mail: jgkooti@ship.edu. *Application contact:* Maya T. Mapp, Director of Admissions, 717-477-1231, Fax: 717-477-4016, E-mail: mtmapp@ship.edu.
Website: http://www.ship.edu/business

Siena Heights University, Graduate College, Adrian, MI 49221-1796. Offers clinical mental health counseling (MA); educational leadership (Specialist); leadership (MA), including health care leadership, organizational leadership; teacher education (MA), including early childhood education, early childhood education: Montessori, education leadership: principal, elementary education: reading K-12, leadership: higher education, secondary education: reading K-12, special education: cognitive impairment, special education: learning disabilities. *Program availability:* Part-time, evening/weekend. *Degree requirements:* For master's, thesis, presentation. *Entrance requirements:* For master's, minimum GPA of 3.0, current resume, essay, all post-secondary transcripts, 3 letters of reference, conviction disclosure form; copy of teaching certificate (for some education programs); for Specialist, master's degree, minimum GPA of 3.0, current resume, essay, all post-secondary transcripts, 3 letters of reference, conviction disclosure form; copy of teaching certificate (for some education programs). Electronic applications accepted.

Simmons College, School of Management, Boston, MA 02115. Offers business administration (MBA); health care (MBA); management (MS, MSM), including communications management (MS), non-profit management (MS); MBA/MSW; MS/MA. *Accreditation:* AACSB. *Program availability:* Part-time, evening/weekend, 100% online, blended/hybrid learning. *Faculty:* 23 full-time (15 women), 5 part-time/adjunct (all women). *Students:* 7 full-time (all women), 130 part-time (118 women); includes 34 minority (14 Black or African American, non-Hispanic/Latino; 8 Asian, non-Hispanic/

Latino; 10 Hispanic/Latino; 2 Two or more races, non-Hispanic/Latino), 1 international. Average age 32. 53 applicants, 68% accepted, 19 enrolled. In 2017, 77 master's awarded. *Entrance requirements:* For master's, GMAT or GRE. Additional exam requirements/recommendations for international students: Required—TOEFL. *Application deadline:* For fall admission, 7/18 priority date for domestic students; for summer admission, 4/24 priority date for domestic students. Applications are processed on a rolling basis. Application fee: $75. Electronic applications accepted. *Expenses:* $1,295 per credit hour, $3,885 per course, $123 activity fee per semester. *Financial support:* Scholarships/grants and unspecified assistantships available. Financial award applicants required to submit FAFSA. *Faculty research:* Gender and organizations, leadership, health care management. *Unit head:* Patricia Deyton, Associate Dean for Graduate Programs, 617-521-3876.
Website: http://www.simmons.edu/som

South Carolina State University, College of Graduate and Professional Studies, School of Business, Orangeburg, SC 29117-0001. Offers agribusiness (MBA); entrepreneurship (MBA); general business administration (MBA); healthcare management (MBA). *Program availability:* Part-time, evening/weekend. *Faculty:* 7 full-time (3 women), 2 part-time/adjunct (0 women). *Students:* 20 full-time (10 women), 11 part-time (7 women); all minorities (all Black or African American, non-Hispanic/Latino). Average age 27. 12 applicants, 92% accepted, 11 enrolled. In 2017, 10 master's awarded. *Degree requirements:* For master's, comprehensive exam, business plan. *Entrance requirements:* For master's, GMAT, minimum GPA of 2.8. Additional exam requirements/recommendations for international students: Required—TOEFL. *Application deadline:* For fall admission, 6/15 for domestic and international students; for spring admission, 11/1 for domestic and international students. Application fee: $25. Electronic applications accepted. *Expenses:* Tuition, state resident: full-time $9388; part-time $607 per credit hour. Tuition, nonresident: full-time $19,968; part-time $1194 per credit hour. *Required fees:* $766; $766 per credit hour. *Financial support:* Fellowships, research assistantships, career-related internships or fieldwork, Federal Work-Study, scholarships/grants, and unspecified assistantships available. Financial award application deadline: 6/1. *Unit head:* Dr. David Jamison, Interim Chair, 803-536-8443, Fax: 803-536-8078, E-mail: djamison@scsu.edu. *Application contact:* Ellen R. Ricoma, MBA Program Director, 803-533-3777, Fax: 803-516-4651, E-mail: ericoma1@scsu.edu.

Southeastern University, Jannetides College of Business and Entrepreneurial Leadership, Lakeland, FL 33801-6099. Offers executive leadership (MBA); global business administration (MBA); healthcare administration (MBA); missional leadership (MBA); organizational leadership (PhD); sport management (MBA); strategic leadership (DSL). *Accreditation:* ACBSP. *Program availability:* Evening/weekend, online learning. *Faculty:* 10 full-time (2 women), 8 part-time/adjunct (1 woman). *Students:* 80 full-time (38 women), 110 part-time (54 women); includes 51 minority (18 Black or African American, non-Hispanic/Latino; 5 Asian, non-Hispanic/Latino; 28 Hispanic/Latino), 7 international. Average age 31. *Entrance requirements:* For master's, GMAT, minimum cumulative GPA of 3.0, writing sample. Application fee: $50. Electronic applications accepted. *Unit head:* Lyle L. Bowlin, Dean, 863-667-5118, E-mail: llbowlin@seu.edu.
Website: http://www.seu.edu/business/

Southern Adventist University, School of Business, Collegedale, TN 37315-0370. Offers accounting (MBA); finance (MBA); healthcare administration (MBA); management (MBA); marketing management (MBA). *Program availability:* Part-time, evening/weekend, 100% online. *Entrance requirements:* For master's, GMAT, minimum cumulative undergraduate GPA of 3.0. Additional exam requirements/recommendations for international students: Required—TOEFL (minimum score 600 paper-based; 100 iBT). *Application deadline:* For fall admission, 7/1 for domestic students, 5/1 for international students; for winter admission, 11/1 for domestic students, 9/1 for international students; for summer admission, 4/1 for domestic students, 2/1 for international students. Applications are processed on a rolling basis. Application fee: $40. Electronic applications accepted. *Expenses: Tuition:* Full-time $11,430; part-time $635 per credit hour. Tuition and fees vary according to degree level and program. *Financial support:* Scholarships/grants and unspecified assistantships available. Financial award application deadline: 9/1; financial award applicants required to submit FAFSA. *Unit head:* Dr. Stephanie Sheehan, Dean, 423-236-2659, Fax: 423-236-1527, E-mail: ssheehan@southern.edu. *Application contact:* Teshia Price, Graduate Studies Coordinator, 423-236-2751, Fax: 423-236-1527, E-mail: tprice@southern.edu.
Website: https://www.southern.edu/academics/business.html

Southern Illinois University Carbondale, School of Law, Program in Legal Studies, Carbondale, IL 62901-4701. Offers general law (MLS); health law and policy (MLS).

Southern Nazarene University, College of Professional and Graduate Studies, School of Business, Bethany, OK 73008. Offers business administration (MBA); health care management (MBA); management (MS Mgt). *Accreditation:* ACBSP. *Program availability:* Part-time, evening/weekend, online learning. *Degree requirements:* For master's, thesis optional. *Entrance requirements:* For master's, resume. Additional exam requirements/recommendations for international students: Required—TOEFL (minimum score 550 paper-based; 80 iBT), IELTS (minimum score 7). Electronic applications accepted.

Southern New Hampshire University, School of Business, Manchester, NH 03106-1045. Offers accounting (MBA, Graduate Certificate); accounting finance (MS); accounting/auditing (MS); accounting/forensic accounting (MS); accounting/management accounting (MS); accounting/taxation (MS); applied economics (MS); athletic administration (MBA, Graduate Certificate); business administration (IMBA, Certificate), including business information systems (Certificate), human resource management (Certificate); business analytics (MBA); business intelligence (MBA); communication (MA), including new media and marketing, public relations; community economic development (MBA); criminal justice (MBA); data analytics (MS); economics (MBA); engineering management (MBA); entrepreneurship (MBA); finance (MBA, MS, Graduate Certificate); finance/corporate finance (MS); finance/investments (MS); forensic accounting (MBA); forensic accounting and fraud examination (Graduate Certificate); healthcare informatics (MBA); healthcare management (MBA); human resource management (MS); human resources (MBA); information technology (MS); information technology management (MBA); international business (PhD); Internet marketing (MBA); leadership (MBA); leadership of nonprofit organizations (Graduate Certificate); management (MS); marketing (MBA, MS, Graduate Certificate); music business (MBA); operations and project management (MS); operations and supply chain management (MBA, Graduate Certificate); organizational leadership (MS); project management (MBA, Graduate Certificate); public administration (MBA, Graduate Certificate); quantitative analysis (MBA); Six Sigma (Graduate Certificate); Six Sigma quality (MBA); social media marketing (MBA, Graduate Certificate); sport management (MBA, MS, Graduate Certificate); sustainability and environmental compliance (MBA); MBA/Certificate. *Accreditation:* ACBSP. *Program availability:* Part-time, evening/weekend, online learning. Terminal master's awarded for partial completion of doctoral program. *Degree requirements:* For master's, one foreign language, comprehensive exam (for some programs), thesis or alternative; for doctorate, one foreign language, comprehensive exam, thesis/dissertation. *Entrance requirements:* For master's, minimum GPA of 2.5; for doctorate, GMAT. Additional exam requirements/recommendations for international students: Required—TOEFL (minimum score 500 paper-based). *Application deadline:* Applications are processed on a rolling basis. Application fee: $40. Electronic applications accepted. *Expenses: Tuition:* Part-time $627 per credit hour. Part-time tuition and fees vary according to campus/location and program. *Financial support:* Career-related internships or fieldwork, Federal Work-Study, institutionally sponsored loans, scholarships/grants, tuition waivers (partial), and unspecified assistantships available. Support available to part-time students. Financial award applicants required to submit FAFSA. *Unit head:* Dr. Bill Lightfoot, Dean, 603-644-3102, Fax: 603-644-3144. *Application contact:* Office of Graduate Admission, 888-327-SNHU, Fax: 603-644-3144, E-mail: enroll@snhu.edu.

South University, Graduate Programs, College of Business, Program in Healthcare Administration, Savannah, GA 31406. Offers MBA.

South University, Program in Business Administration, Royal Palm Beach, FL 33411. Offers business administration (MBA); healthcare administration (MBA).

South University, Program in Healthcare Administration, Columbia, SC 29203. Offers MBA.

South University, Program in Healthcare Administration, Montgomery, AL 36116-1120. Offers MBA.

South University, Program in Healthcare Administration, Tampa, FL 33614. Offers MBA.

Southwest Baptist University, Program in Business, Bolivar, MO 65613-2597. Offers business administration (MBA); health administration (MBA). *Accreditation:* ACBSP. *Program availability:* Part-time, online learning. *Degree requirements:* For master's, comprehensive exam. *Entrance requirements:* For master's, interviews, minimum GPA of 2.75. Additional exam requirements/recommendations for international students: Required—TOEFL (minimum score 550 paper-based).

Stevenson University, Program in Healthcare Management, Owings Mills, MD 21153. Offers project management (MS); quality management and patient safety (MS). *Program availability:* Part-time, online only, 100% online. *Faculty:* 2 full-time (both women), 7 part-time/adjunct (4 women). *Students:* 4 full-time (2 women), 35 part-time (28 women); includes 11 minority (9 Black or African American, non-Hispanic/Latino; 2 Asian, non-Hispanic/Latino). Average age 30. 24 applicants, 71% accepted, 13 enrolled. In 2017, 10 master's awarded. *Degree requirements:* For master's, capstone course. *Entrance requirements:* For master's, official college transcripts from all previous academic work, minimum cumulative GPA of 3.0 in past academic work, minimum grade of B in statistics or an upper-level math and English composition, two professional letters of recommendation with at least one from a current or past supervisor, 250-word personal statement. *Application deadline:* Applications are processed on a rolling basis. Electronic applications accepted. *Expenses:* Contact institution. *Financial support:* Unspecified assistantships available. Financial award applicants required to submit FAFSA. *Unit head:* Sharon Buchbinder, PhD, Coordinator, 443-394-9290, Fax: 443-394-0538, E-mail: sbuchbinder@stevenson.edu. *Application contact:* Amanda Courter, Enrollment Counselor, 443-352-4243, Fax: 443-394-0538, E-mail: acourter@stevenson.edu.
Website: http://www.stevenson.edu

Stony Brook University, State University of New York, Graduate School, College of Business, Program in Business Administration, Stony Brook, NY 11794. Offers accounting (MBA); business administration (MBA); finance (MBA, Certificate); health care management (MBA); human resources (MBA); innovation (MBA); management (MBA); marketing (MBA); operations management (MBA). *Faculty:* 39 full-time (13 women), 14 part-time/adjunct (5 women). *Students:* 181 full-time (98 women), 145 part-time (73 women); includes 68 minority (16 Black or African American, non-Hispanic/Latino; 1 American Indian or Alaska Native, non-Hispanic/Latino; 35 Asian, non-Hispanic/Latino; 11 Hispanic/Latino; 1 Native Hawaiian or other Pacific Islander, non-Hispanic/Latino; 4 Two or more races, non-Hispanic/Latino), 69 international. Average age 29. 154 applicants, 66% accepted, 58 enrolled. In 2017, 105 master's awarded. *Entrance requirements:* For master's, GMAT, 3 letters of recommendation from current or former employers or professors, transcripts, personal statement, resume. Additional exam requirements/recommendations for international students: Required—TOEFL (minimum score 550 paper-based; 90 iBT), IELTS (minimum score 6.5). *Application deadline:* For fall admission, 5/15 for domestic students, 3/15 for international students; for spring admission, 11/15 for domestic students, 10/15 for international students. Application fee: $100. *Expenses:* Contact institution. *Financial support:* Teaching assistantships available. *Total annual research expenditures:* $2,070. *Unit head:* Dr. Manuel London, Dean, 631-632-7159, E-mail: manuel.london@stonybrook.edu. *Application contact:* Dr. Dmytro Holod, Associate Dean for Academic Programs/Graduate Director, 631-632-7183, Fax: 631-632-8181, E-mail: dmytro.holod@stonybrook.edu.
Website: https://www.stonybrook.edu/commcms/business/

Stony Brook University, State University of New York, Stony Brook Medicine, School of Health Technology and Management, Stony Brook, NY 11794. Offers applied health informatics (MS); disability studies (Certificate); health administration (MHA); health and rehabilitation sciences (PhD); health care management (Advanced Certificate); health care policy and management (MS); occupational therapy (MS); physical therapy (DPT); physician assistant (MS). *Accreditation:* APTA. *Faculty:* 62 full-time (42 women), 59 part-time/adjunct (36 women). *Students:* 565 full-time (382 women), 67 part-time (53 women); includes 179 minority (29 Black or African American, non-Hispanic/Latino; 83 Asian, non-Hispanic/Latino; 59 Hispanic/Latino; 2 Native Hawaiian or other Pacific Islander, non-Hispanic/Latino; 6 Two or more races, non-Hispanic/Latino), 14 international. Average age 27. 2,516 applicants, 16% accepted, 266 enrolled. In 2017, 162 master's, 84 doctorates, 39 other advanced degrees awarded. *Degree requirements:* For master's, thesis; for doctorate, thesis/dissertation. *Entrance requirements:* For master's, GRE General Test, minimum GPA of 3.0, work experience in field, references; for doctorate, GRE, three references, essay. Additional exam requirements/recommendations for international students: Required—TOEFL (minimum score 550 paper-based). *Application deadline:* For fall admission, 1/15 for domestic students; for spring admission, 10/1 for domestic students. Application fee: $100. *Expenses:* Contact institution. *Financial support:* Fellowships, research assistantships, teaching assistantships, career-related internships or fieldwork, Federal Work-Study, and institutionally sponsored loans available. Financial award application deadline: 3/15. *Faculty research:* Developmental disabilities, disability studies, health promotion, multiple sclerosis, quality of life program, internal medicine, lung disease, palliative care, respiratory diseases, neuromuscular disorders, orthopedics, physical medicine and rehabilitation, physical therapy, prostheses or implants, advance directives, advocacy alienation, allied health education, allied health occupations, adolescents, adoption, child or adolescent mental health, multiple sclerosis, youth policy. *Total annual research expenditures:* $1.2 million. *Unit head:* Dr. Carlos Vidal, Dean, 631-444-1009, Fax: 631-444-7621, E-mail: carlos.vidal@stonybrook.edu. *Application contact:* Frances Shaw, 631-444-3240, Fax: 631-444-7621, E-mail: frances.shaw@stonybrook.edu.
Website: http://healthtechnology.stonybrookmedicine.edu/

Stratford University, School of Graduate Studies, Falls Church, VA 22043. Offers accounting (MS); business administration (MBA, DBA); cyber security (MS); cyber security leadership and policy (MS); digital forensics (MS); healthcare administration (MS); information systems (MS); information technology (DIT); networking and telecommunications (MS); software engineering (MS). *Program availability:* Part-time, evening/weekend, 100% online, blended/hybrid learning. *Students:* 272 full-time (110 women), 204 part-time (89 women). *Degree requirements:* For master's, comprehensive exam, capstone project. *Entrance requirements:* For master's, GRE or GMAT, baccalaureate degree. Additional exam requirements/recommendations for international students: Required—TOEFL (minimum score 79 iBT), IELTS (minimum score 6.5), PTE (minimum score 5). *Application deadline:* Applications are processed on a rolling basis. Application fee: $50. Electronic applications accepted. *Expenses: Tuition:* Full-time $33,405; part-time $11,135 per credit hour. One-time fee: $385 full-time. Tuition and fees vary according to degree level and program. *Financial support:* Federal Work-Study and scholarships/grants available. Financial award applicants required to submit FAFSA. *Unit head:* Dr. Valarie Trimarchi, Campus President, 703-539-6890, Fax: 703-539-6960. *Application contact:* Lori Smith, Admissions, 214-649-7113, E-mail: lasmith@stratford.edu.

Strayer University, Graduate Studies, Washington, DC 20005-2603. Offers accounting (MS); acquisition (MBA); business administration (MBA); communications technology (MS); educational management (M Ed); finance (MBA); health services administration (MHSA); hospitality and tourism management (MBA); human resource management (MBA); information systems (MS), including computer security management, decision support system management, enterprise resource management, network management, software engineering management, systems development management; management (MBA); management information systems (MS); marketing (MBA); professional accounting (MS), including accounting information systems, controllership, taxation; public administration (MPA); supply chain management (MBA); technology in education (M Ed). Programs also offered at campus locations in Birmingham, AL; Chamblee, GA; Cobb County, GA; Morrow, GA; White Marsh, MD; Charleston, SC; Columbia, SC; Greensboro, NC; Greenville, SC; Lexington, KY; Louisville, KY; Nashville, TN; North Raleigh, NC; Washington, DC. *Accreditation:* ACBSP. *Program availability:* Part-time, evening/weekend, online learning. *Degree requirements:* For master's, thesis. *Entrance requirements:* For master's, GMAT, GRE General Test, bachelor's degree from an accredited college or university, minimum undergraduate GPA of 2.75. Electronic applications accepted.

Suffolk University, Sawyer Business School, Master of Business Administration Program, Boston, MA 02108-2770. Offers accounting (MBA); entrepreneurship (MBA); executive business administration (EMBA); finance (MBA); global business administration (GMBA); health administration (MBA); international business (MBA); marketing (MBA); nonprofit management (MBA); organizational behavior (MBA); strategic management (MBA); supply chain management (MBA); taxation (MBA); JD/MBA; MBA/MHA; MBA/MSA; MBA/MSF; MBA/MST. *Accreditation:* AACSB. *Program availability:* Part-time, evening/weekend, 100% online. *Faculty:* 16 full-time (6 women), 9 part-time/adjunct (1 woman). *Students:* 106 full-time (57 women), 236 part-time (135 women); includes 80 minority (23 Black or African American, non-Hispanic/Latino; 23 Asian, non-Hispanic/Latino; 28 Hispanic/Latino; 6 Two or more races, non-Hispanic/Latino), 41 international. Average age 30. 354 applicants, 69% accepted, 115 enrolled. In 2017, 170 master's awarded. *Entrance requirements:* For master's, GMAT, minimum undergraduate GPA of 2.75 (MBA), 5 years of managerial experience (EMBA). Additional exam requirements/recommendations for international students: Required—TOEFL (minimum score 550 paper-based; 80 iBT). *Application deadline:* For fall admission, 3/15 priority date for domestic students, 10/15 priority date for international students; for spring admission, 10/15 priority date for domestic and international students. Applications are processed on a rolling basis. Application fee: $50. Electronic applications accepted. *Expenses:* $43,980 per year full-time, $1,466 per credit part-time (for MBA); $1,794 per credit part-time (for Executive MBA). *Financial support:* In 2017–18, 198 students received support, including 1 fellowship (averaging $2,325 per year); career-related internships or fieldwork, Federal Work-Study, institutionally sponsored loans, and scholarships/grants also available. Support available to part-time students. Financial award application deadline: 4/1; financial award applicants required to submit FAFSA. *Faculty research:* Foreign investments; career strategies and boundaryless careers; corporate ethics codes; interest rates, inflation, and growth options; innovation and product development performance. *Unit head:* Jodi Detjen, Director of MBA Programs, 617-573-8306, E-mail: jdetjen@suffolk.edu. *Application contact:* Mara Marzocchi, Associate Director of Graduate Admissions, 617-573-8302, Fax: 617-305-1733, E-mail: grad.admission@suffolk.edu.
Website: http://www.suffolk.edu/mba

Suffolk University, Sawyer Business School, Program in Healthcare Administration, Boston, MA 02108-2770. Offers community health (MPA); health (MBAH); healthcare administration (MHA). *Program availability:* Part-time, evening/weekend. *Faculty:* 5 full-time (1 woman), 6 part-time/adjunct (3 women). *Students:* 32 full-time (24 women), 40 part-time (30 women); includes 23 minority (16 Black or African American, non-Hispanic/Latino; 2 Asian, non-Hispanic/Latino; 5 Hispanic/Latino), 7 international. Average age 30. 47 applicants, 77% accepted, 18 enrolled. In 2017, 32 master's awarded. *Entrance requirements:* Additional exam requirements/recommendations for international students: Required—TOEFL (minimum score 550 paper-based; 80 iBT). *Application deadline:* For fall admission, 3/15 priority date for domestic and international students; for spring admission, 10/15 priority date for domestic and international students. Applications are processed on a rolling basis. Application fee: $50. Electronic applications accepted. *Expenses:* $35,130 per year full-time tuition; $1,171 per credit part-time. *Financial support:* In 2017–18, 46 students received support, including 1 fellowship (averaging $6,200 per year); career-related internships or fieldwork, Federal Work-Study, institutionally sponsored loans, scholarships/grants, and health care benefits also available. Support available to part-time students. Financial award application deadline: 4/1; financial award applicants required to submit FAFSA. *Faculty research:* Mental health, federal policy, health care. *Unit head:* Richard Gregg, Director of Programs in Healthcare Administration/Chair of Healthcare Department, 617-994-4246, E-mail: rgregg@suffolk.edu. *Application contact:* Mara Marzocchi, Associate Director of Graduate Admissions, 617-573-8302, Fax: 617-305-1733, E-mail: grad.admission@suffolk.edu.
Website: http://www.suffolk.edu/business/graduate/62398.php

Syracuse University, Maxwell School of Citizenship and Public Affairs, CAS Program in Health Services Management and Policy, Syracuse, NY 13244. Offers CAS. *Program availability:* Part-time. In 2017, 23 CASs awarded. *Entrance requirements:* For degree, 7 years of mid-level professional experience, resume, personal statement, three letters of recommendation, official transcripts. Additional exam requirements/recommendations for international students: Required—TOEFL (minimum score 100 iBT). *Application deadline:* For fall admission, 2/1 for domestic students, 2/1 priority date for international students; for spring admission, 8/15 priority date for domestic and international students. Applications are processed on a rolling basis. Application fee: $75. Electronic applications accepted. *Financial support:* Application deadline: 1/1. *Unit head:* Dr. Thomas H. Dennison, Head, 315-443-9060, Fax: 315-443-9721, E-mail: thdennis@syr.edu. *Application contact:* Margaret Lane, Assistant Director, Executive Education Programs, 315-443-1090, E-mail: melane02@maxwell.syr.edu.
Website: http://www.maxwell.syr.edu/

Temple University, Fox School of Business, MBA Programs, Philadelphia, PA 19122-6096. Offers accounting (MBA); business management (MBA); financial management (MBA); healthcare and life sciences innovation (MBA); human resource management (MBA); international business (IMBA); IT management (MBA); marketing management (MBA); pharmaceutical management (MBA); strategic management (EMBA, MBA). EMBA offered in Philadelphia, PA and Tokyo, Japan. *Accreditation:* AACSB. *Program availability:* Part-time, evening/weekend, online learning. *Entrance requirements:* For master's, GMAT, minimum undergraduate GPA of 3.0. Additional exam requirements/recommendations for international students: Required—TOEFL (minimum score 600 paper-based; 100 iBT), IELTS (minimum score 7.5). *Expenses:* Tuition, state resident: full-time $16,164; part-time $898 per credit hour. Tuition, nonresident: full-time $22,158; part-time $1231 per credit hour. *Required fees:* $890; $445 per semester. Full-time tuition and fees vary according to course load, degree level, campus/location and program.

Texas A&M University, School of Public Health, College Station, TX 77845. Offers biostatistics (MPH, MSPH); environmental health (MPH, MSPH); epidemiology (MPH, MSPH); executive health administration (MHA); health administration (MHA); health policy and management (MPH, MSPH); health promotion and community health sciences (MPH); health services research (PhD); occupational safety and health (MPH). *Program availability:* Part-time, blended/hybrid learning. *Faculty:* 56. *Students:* 279 full-time (196 women), 86 part-time (56 women); includes 153 minority (48 Black or African American, non-Hispanic/Latino; 36 Asian, non-Hispanic/Latino; 62 Hispanic/Latino; 7 Two or more races, non-Hispanic/Latino), 77 international. Average age 29. 179 applicants, 96% accepted, 148 enrolled. In 2017, 124 master's, 8 doctorates awarded. *Entrance requirements:* For master's, GRE General Test, 3 letters of recommendation; statement of purpose; current curriculum vitae or resume; official transcripts; for doctorate, GRE General Test, 3 letters of recommendation; statement of purpose; current curriculum vitae or resume; official transcripts; interview (in some cases). Additional exam requirements/recommendations for international students: Required—TOEFL (minimum score 597 paper-based, 95 iBT) or GRE (minimum verbal score 153). Application fee: $120. Electronic applications accepted. *Expenses:* Contact institution. *Financial support:* In 2017–18, 203 students received support, including 62 research assistantships with tuition reimbursements available (averaging $10,041 per year), 25 teaching assistantships with tuition reimbursements available (averaging $12,913 per year); career-related internships or fieldwork, institutionally sponsored loans, scholarships/grants, traineeships, health care benefits, tuition waivers (full and partial), and unspecified assistantships also available. Support available to part-time students. Financial award applicants required to submit FAFSA. *Unit head:* Dr. Jay Maddock, Dean, 979-436-9322, Fax: 979-458-1878, E-mail: maddock@tamhsc.edu. *Application contact:* Erin E. Schneider, Associate Director of Admissions and Recruitment, 979-436-9380, E-mail: eschneider@sph.tamhsc.edu.
Website: http://sph.tamhsc.edu/

Texas A&M University–Corpus Christi, College of Graduate Studies, College of Business, Corpus Christi, TX 78412. Offers accounting (M Acc); business (MBA); finance (MBA); health care administration (MBA); international business (MBA). *Accreditation:* AACSB. *Program availability:* Part-time, evening/weekend, 100% online, blended/hybrid learning. *Faculty:* 31 full-time (11 women), 2 part-time/adjunct (0 women). *Students:* 107 full-time (50 women), 583 part-time (283 women); includes 259 minority (80 Black or African American, non-Hispanic/Latino; 85 Asian, non-Hispanic/Latino; 83 Hispanic/Latino; 11 Two or more races, non-Hispanic/Latino), 77 international. Average age 34. 485 applicants, 57% accepted, 236 enrolled. In 2017, 310 master's awarded. *Degree requirements:* For master's, 30 to 42 hours (for MBA; varies by concentration area, delivery format, and necessity for foundational courses for students with nonbusiness degrees). *Entrance requirements:* For master's, GMAT, GRE. Additional exam requirements/recommendations for international students: Required—TOEFL (minimum score 550 paper-based; 79 iBT), IELTS (minimum score 6.5). *Application deadline:* For fall admission, 7/15 priority date for domestic students, 5/1 priority date for international students; for spring admission, 11/15 priority date for domestic students, 9/1 priority date for international students; for summer admission, 4/15 priority date for domestic and international students. Applications are processed on a rolling basis. Application fee: $50 ($70 for international students). Electronic applications accepted. *Expenses:* Tuition, state resident: full-time $3568; part-time $198.24 per credit hour. Tuition, nonresident: full-time $11,038; part-time $613.24 per credit hour. *Required fees:* $2129; $1422.58 per semester. Tuition and fees vary according to program. *Financial support:* Research assistantships, teaching assistantships, career-related internships or fieldwork, Federal Work-Study, institutionally sponsored loans, scholarships/grants, health care benefits, and unspecified assistantships available. Support available to part-time students. Financial award application deadline: 3/15; financial award applicants required to submit FAFSA. *Unit head:* Dr. John Gamble, Dean, 361-825-6045, Fax: 361-825-2725, E-mail: john.gamble@tamucc.edu. *Application contact:* Sharon Polansky, Director of Master's Programs, 361-825-3448, Fax: 361-825-2755, E-mail: gradweb@tamucc.edu.
Website: http://cob.tamucc.edu

Texas A&M University–Corpus Christi, College of Graduate Studies, College of Nursing and Health Sciences, Corpus Christi, TX 78412. Offers family nurse practitioner (MSN); leadership in nursing systems (MSN); nurse educator (MSN); nursing practice (DNP). *Accreditation:* AACN. *Program availability:* Part-time, evening/weekend, online only, 100% online. *Faculty:* 17 full-time (16 women), 21 part-time/adjunct (15 women). *Students:* 7 full-time (all women), 364 part-time (307 women); includes 194 minority (25 Black or African American, non-Hispanic/Latino; 26 Asian, non-Hispanic/Latino; 134 Hispanic/Latino; 9 Two or more races, non-Hispanic/Latino). Average age 38. 360 applicants, 33% accepted, 112 enrolled. In 2017, 98 master's awarded. *Degree requirements:* For master's, clinical capstone; for doctorate, capstone/scholarly project. *Entrance requirements:* For master's, essay, resume, 3 letters of recommendation, minimum GPA of 3.0, current valid unencumbered Texas nursing license. Additional exam requirements/recommendations for international students: Required—TOEFL (minimum score 550 paper-based; 79 iBT), IELTS (minimum score 6.5). *Application deadline:* For fall admission, 4/15 for domestic and international students; for spring admission, 1/7 for domestic and international students; for summer admission, 5/27 for domestic and international students. Applications are processed on a rolling basis. Application fee: $50 ($70 for international students). Electronic applications accepted. *Expenses:* Tuition, state resident: full-time $3568; part-time $198.24 per credit hour. Tuition, nonresident: full-time $11,038; part-time $613.24 per credit hour. *Required fees:* $2129; $1422.58 per semester. Tuition and fees vary according to program. *Financial support:* Research assistantships, teaching assistantships, career-related internships or fieldwork, Federal Work-Study, institutionally sponsored loans, scholarships/grants, health care benefits, and unspecified assistantships available. Support available to part-time students. Financial award application deadline: 3/15; financial award applicants required to submit FAFSA. *Unit head:* Dr. Julie Anne Hoff, Dean, 361-825-2275, E-mail: julie.hoff@tamucc.edu. *Application contact:* Graduate Admissions Coordinator, 361-825-2177, Fax: 361-825-2755, E-mail: gradweb@tamucc.edu.
Website: http://conhs.tamucc.edu/

Texas Christian University, Harris College of Nursing and Health Sciences, Master's Program in Nursing, Fort Worth, TX 76129. Offers administration (MSN); clinical nurse

leader (MSN, Certificate); clinical nurse specialist (MSN), including adult/gerontology nursing, pediatrics; nursing education (MSN). *Accreditation:* AACN. *Program availability:* Part-time, online only, 100% online. *Faculty:* 29 full-time (26 women), 2 part-time/adjunct (both women). *Students:* 17 full-time (15 women), 7 part-time (all women); includes 6 minority (1 Black or African American, non-Hispanic/Latino; 2 Asian, non-Hispanic/Latino; 2 Hispanic/Latino; 1 Two or more races, non-Hispanic/Latino). Average age 36. 41 applicants, 49% accepted, 6 enrolled. In 2017, 41 master's awarded. *Degree requirements:* For master's, thesis or alternative, practicum. *Entrance requirements:* For master's, 3 letters of reference, essay, resume, two official transcripts from every institution attended. Additional exam requirements/recommendations for international students: Required—TOEFL. *Application deadline:* For spring admission, 9/1 for domestic and international students; for summer admission, 2/1 for domestic and international students. Application fee: $60. Electronic applications accepted. *Expenses:* $1,555 per credit hour, $125 per course fee, $500 lab fee. *Financial support:* In 2017–18, 20 students received support. Scholarships/grants available. Financial award application deadline: 2/15; financial award applicants required to submit FAFSA. *Faculty research:* Geriatrics, cancer survivorship, health literacy, endothelial cells, clinical simulation outcomes. *Unit head:* Dr. Kathy Ellis, Division Director, Graduate Nursing, 817-257-6726, Fax: 817-257-7944, E-mail: kathryn.ellis@tcu.edu. *Application contact:* Heather Lyon, Academic Program Specialist, 817-257-6726, Fax: 817-257-7944, E-mail: graduatenursing@tcu.edu.
Website: http://www.nursing.tcu.edu/graduate.asp

Texas Health and Science University, Graduate Programs, Austin, TX 78704. Offers acupuncture and Oriental medicine (MS, DAOM); business administration (MBA); healthcare management (MBA). *Accreditation:* ACAOM. *Faculty:* 8 full-time (3 women), 7 part-time/adjunct (5 women). *Students:* 102 full-time (64 women), 9 part-time (8 women); includes 43 minority (1 Black or African American, non-Hispanic/Latino; 1 American Indian or Alaska Native, non-Hispanic/Latino; 35 Asian, non-Hispanic/Latino; 6 Hispanic/Latino). Average age 34. *Entrance requirements:* For master's, 60 hours applicable to bachelor's degree. Additional exam requirements/recommendations for international students: Required—TOEFL (minimum score 500 paper-based), TWE. *Application deadline:* For fall admission, 8/25 priority date for domestic and international students; for spring admission, 12/22 priority date for domestic and international students. Applications are processed on a rolling basis. Application fee: $75 ($300 for international students). Electronic applications accepted. *Expenses: Tuition:* Full-time $11,460. *Required fees:* $600. Tuition and fees vary according to course load, degree level and program. *Financial support:* Teaching assistantships with partial tuition reimbursements, career-related internships or fieldwork, Federal Work-Study, institutionally sponsored loans, scholarships/grants, and tuition waivers (partial) available. Financial award applicants required to submit FAFSA. *Unit head:* Dr. David G. Vequist, IV, Vice President of Academic Affairs, 512-444-8082. *Application contact:* Caleb Li, Admissions Coordinator, 512-444-8082, Fax: 512-444-6345, E-mail: admissions@thsu.edu.

Texas Southern University, College of Pharmacy and Health Sciences, Department of Health Sciences, Houston, TX 77004-4584. Offers health care administration (MS). *Program availability:* Online learning. *Entrance requirements:* For master's, PCAT. Electronic applications accepted.

Texas State University, The Graduate College, College of Health Professions, Program in Healthcare Administration, San Marcos, TX 78666. Offers MHA. *Accreditation:* CAHME. *Program availability:* Part-time, evening/weekend. *Faculty:* 14 full-time (3 women), 6 part-time/adjunct (2 women). *Students:* 43 full-time (32 women), 24 part-time (14 women); includes 33 minority (10 Black or African American, non-Hispanic/Latino; 6 Asian, non-Hispanic/Latino; 15 Hispanic/Latino; 2 Two or more races, non-Hispanic/Latino), 15 international. Average age 28. 83 applicants, 42% accepted, 20 enrolled. In 2017, 39 master's awarded. *Degree requirements:* For master's, comprehensive exam, thesis optional, committee review. *Entrance requirements:* For master's, GRE General Test, baccalaureate degree from regionally-accredited institution; minimum GPA of 2.75 for last 60 hours of undergraduate course work; 3 letters of reference; written statement of purpose; resume; prerequisite courses in statistics, economics, and financial accounting. Additional exam requirements/recommendations for international students: Required—TOEFL (minimum score 550 paper-based; 78 iBT), IELTS (minimum score 6.5). *Application deadline:* For fall admission, 3/1 priority date for domestic and international students. Applications are processed on a rolling basis. Application fee: $40 ($90 for international students). Electronic applications accepted. *Expenses:* Tuition, state resident: full-time $7868; part-time $3934 per semester. Tuition, nonresident: full-time $17,828; part-time $8914 per semester. *Required fees:* $2092; $1435 per semester. Tuition and fees vary according to course load. *Financial support:* In 2017–18, 35 students received support, including 16 teaching assistantships (averaging $12,211 per year); research assistantships, career-related internships or fieldwork, Federal Work-Study, institutionally sponsored loans, scholarships/grants, and unspecified assistantships also available. Support available to part-time students. Financial award application deadline: 3/1; financial award applicants required to submit FAFSA. *Unit head:* Dr. Kimberly Ann Lee, Graduate Advisor, 512-245-3492, Fax: 512-245-8712, E-mail: gradhainterest@txstate.edu. *Application contact:* Dr. Andrea Golato, Dean of Graduate School, 512-245-2581, Fax: 512-245-8365, E-mail: gradcollege@txstate.edu.
Website: http://www.health.txstate.edu/ha/degs-progs/mha.html

Texas Tech University, Rawls College of Business Administration, Lubbock, TX 79409-2101. Offers accounting (MSA, PhD), including audit/financial reporting (MSA), taxation (MSA); data science (MS); finance (PhD); general business (MBA); healthcare management (MS); information systems and operations management (PhD); management (PhD); marketing (PhD); STEM (MBA); JD/MBA; JD/MSA; MBA/M Arch; MBA/MD; MBA/MS; MBA/Pharm D. *Accreditation:* AACSB. *Program availability:* Evening/weekend, 100% online, blended/hybrid learning. *Faculty:* 89 full-time (22 women). *Students:* 660 full-time (252 women); includes 174 minority (30 Black or African American, non-Hispanic/Latino; 3 American Indian or Alaska Native, non-Hispanic/Latino; 20 Asian, non-Hispanic/Latino; 104 Hispanic/Latino; 17 Two or more races, non-Hispanic/Latino), 99 international. Average age 29. 492 applicants, 51% accepted, 148 enrolled. In 2017, 439 master's, 6 doctorates awarded. *Degree requirements:* For master's, thesis (for MS); capstone course; for doctorate, comprehensive exam, thesis/dissertation, qualifying exams. *Entrance requirements:* For master's, GMAT, GRE, MCAT, PCAT, LSAT, or DAT, holistic review of academic credentials, resume, essay, letters of recommendation; for doctorate, GMAT, GRE, holistic review of academic credentials, resume, statement of purpose, letters of recommendation. Additional exam requirements/recommendations for international students: Required—TOEFL (minimum score 550 paper-based; 79 iBT), IELTS (minimum score 6.5), PTE (minimum score 60). *Application deadline:* For fall admission, 7/1 priority date for domestic students, 1/15 for international students; for spring admission, 12/1 priority date for domestic students, 6/15 for international students; for summer admission, 5/1 for domestic students. Applications are processed on a rolling basis. Application fee: $60. Electronic applications accepted. *Expenses:* $5,167.50 full-time; $9,000 per semester (for hybrid MBA). *Financial support:* In 2017–18, 81 students received support, including 1 research assistantship with full tuition reimbursement available (averaging $22,725 per year), 63 teaching assistantships with full tuition reimbursements available (averaging $22,725 per year); career-related internships or fieldwork, Federal Work-Study, scholarships/grants, health care benefits, and unspecified assistantships also available. Financial award application deadline: 3/1; financial award applicants required to submit FAFSA. *Faculty research:* Governmental and nonprofit accounting, securities and options futures, statistical analysis and design, leadership, consumer behavior. *Total annual research expenditures:* $230,000. *Unit head:* Dr. Margaret Williams, Dean, 806-834-2839, Fax: 806-742-1092, E-mail: margaret.l.williams@ttu.edu. *Application contact:* Jennifer Yack, Applications Manager, Graduate and Professional Programs, 806-742-3184, E-mail: rawlsgrad@ttu.edu.
Website: http://www.depts.ttu.edu/rawlsbusiness/graduate/

Texas Tech University Health Sciences Center, School of Health Professions, Program in Healthcare Administration, Lubbock, TX 79430. Offers MS. *Accreditation:* CORE. *Program availability:* Part-time, online only, 100% online. *Faculty:* 4 full-time (2 women), 11 part-time/adjunct (3 women). *Students:* 45 full-time (26 women), 170 part-time (114 women); includes 87 minority (16 Black or African American, non-Hispanic/Latino; 12 Asian, non-Hispanic/Latino; 50 Hispanic/Latino; 2 Native Hawaiian or other Pacific Islander, non-Hispanic/Latino; 7 Two or more races, non-Hispanic/Latino). Average age 34. 250 applicants, 68% accepted, 145 enrolled. In 2017, 61 master's awarded. *Entrance requirements:* Additional exam requirements/recommendations for international students: Required—TOEFL (minimum score 550 paper-based; 79 iBT). *Application deadline:* For fall admission, 7/1 for domestic students; for spring admission, 12/1 for domestic students; for summer admission, 4/1 for domestic students. Applications are processed on a rolling basis. Application fee: $75. Electronic applications accepted. *Financial support:* Institutionally sponsored loans available. Financial award application deadline: 9/1; financial award applicants required to submit FAFSA. *Unit head:* Sharon Hunt, Program Director, 806-743-2262, Fax: 806-743-3244, E-mail: sharon.hunt@ttuhsc.edu. *Application contact:* Lindsay Johnson, Associate Dean for Admissions and Student Affairs, 806-743-3220, Fax: 806-743-2994, E-mail: lindsay.johnson@ttuhsc.edu.
Website: http://www.ttuhsc.edu/health-professions/master-of-science-healthcare-administration/

Texas Woman's University, Graduate School, College of Business, Program in Healthcare Administration, Houston, TX 77030. Offers healthcare administration (MHA), including business analytics. Program offered at Texas Medical Center in Houston. *Accreditation:* CAHME. *Program availability:* Part-time, evening/weekend, blended/hybrid learning. *Faculty:* 5 full-time (2 women), 4 part-time/adjunct (all women). *Students:* 93 full-time (81 women), 62 part-time (52 women); includes 120 minority (48 Black or African American, non-Hispanic/Latino; 2 American Indian or Alaska Native, non-Hispanic/Latino; 43 Asian, non-Hispanic/Latino; 19 Hispanic/Latino; 8 Two or more races, non-Hispanic/Latino), 5 international. Average age 30. 72 applicants, 81% accepted, 36 enrolled. In 2017, 24 master's awarded. *Degree requirements:* For master's, comprehensive exam, thesis or alternative, capstone, portfolio. *Entrance requirements:* For master's, GMAT (preferred minimum score 450) or GRE General Test (preferred minimum scores 150 [450 old version] Verbal, 141 [450 old version] Quantitative), interview, resume, 3 letters of reference, essay, minimum GPA of 3.0 in last 60 hours of undergraduate degree and in all graduate course work. Additional exam requirements/recommendations for international students: Required—TOEFL (minimum score 550 paper-based; 79 iBT); Recommended—IELTS (minimum score 6.5), TSE (minimum score 53). *Application deadline:* For fall admission, 5/30 for domestic students, 3/1 priority date for international students; for spring admission, 9/30 for domestic students, 7/1 priority date for international students; for summer admission, 3/1 for domestic students, 2/1 priority date for international students. Applications are processed on a rolling basis. Application fee: $50 ($75 for international students). Electronic applications accepted. *Expenses:* $7,520 per year full-time in-state; $16,829 per year full-time out-of-state. *Financial support:* In 2017–18, 38 students received support. Career-related internships or fieldwork, Federal Work-Study, institutionally sponsored loans, scholarships/grants, traineeships, health care benefits, and unspecified assistantships available. Support available to part-time students. Financial award application deadline: 3/1; financial award applicants required to submit FAFSA. *Faculty research:* Patient safety and health policy, competition and market structure on health care quality, performance measurement and promotion. *Unit head:* Dr. Gerald Goodman, Director, 940-898-2458, Fax: 940-898-2120, E-mail: mba@twu.edu. *Application contact:* Korie Hawkins, Associate Director of Admissions, Graduate Recruitment, 940-898-3188, Fax: 940-898-3081, E-mail: admissions@twu.edu.
Website: https://www.twu.edu/business/graduate-programs-college-of-business/master-of-healthcare-administration/

Thomas Jefferson University, Jefferson College of Population Health, Program in Healthcare Quality and Safety, Philadelphia, PA 19107. Offers MS, PhD, Certificate. *Program availability:* Part-time, evening/weekend, online learning. *Entrance requirements:* For master's, GRE or other graduate examination, 2 letters of recommendation, interview, curriculum vitae; for doctorate, GRE (within the last 5 years), 3 letters of recommendation, interview, curriculum vitae. Additional exam requirements/recommendations for international students: Required—TOEFL.

Thomas Jefferson University, Jefferson College of Population Health, Program in Health Policy, Philadelphia, PA 19107. Offers MS, PhD, Certificate. *Program availability:* Part-time, evening/weekend, online learning. *Entrance requirements:* For master's, GRE or other graduate exam, two letters of recommendation, curriculum vitae/resume, interview; for doctorate, GRE (taken within the last 5 years), three letters of recommendation, curriculum vitae/resume, interview. Additional exam requirements/recommendations for international students: Required—TOEFL. Electronic applications accepted.

Tiffin University, Program in Business Administration, Tiffin, OH 44883-2161. Offers finance (MBA); general management (MBA); healthcare administration (MBA); human resource management (MBA); international business (MBA); leadership (MBA); marketing (MBA); non-profit management (MBA); sports management (MBA). *Accreditation:* ACBSP. *Program availability:* Part-time, evening/weekend, online learning. *Entrance requirements:* For master's, minimum undergraduate GPA of 2.5, work experience. Additional exam requirements/recommendations for international students: Required—TOEFL (minimum score 550 paper-based; 79 iBT), IELTS. Electronic applications accepted. Application fee is waived when completed online. *Faculty research:* Small business, executive development operations, research and statistical analysis, market research, management information systems.

Towson University, College of Health Professions, Program in Clinician to Administrator Transition, Towson, MD 21252-0001. Offers MS, Postbaccalaureate Certificate. *Students:* 1 full-time (0 women), 8 part-time (6 women); includes 3 minority (all Black or African American, non-Hispanic/Latino), 1 international. *Entrance requirements:* For degree, minimum GPA of 3.0; bachelor's or master's degree in a clinical field; licensure, licensure eligibility, or certificate in a clinical field. *Application deadline:* For fall admission, 1/17 for domestic students, 5/15 for international students; for spring admission, 10/15 for domestic students, 12/1 for international students. Applications are processed on a rolling basis. Application fee: $45. Electronic applications accepted. *Expenses:* Tuition, state resident: full-time $7960; part-time $398 per unit. Tuition, nonresident: full-time $16,480; part-time $824 per unit. *Required fees:*

$2600; $130 per year. $390 per term. *Financial support:* Application deadline: 4/1. *Unit head:* Dr. Marcie Weinstein, Associate Dean, 410-704-4049, E-mail: mweinstein@towson.edu. *Application contact:* Coverley Beidleman, Assistant Director of Graduate Admissions, 410-704-5630, Fax: 410-704-3030, E-mail: cbeidleman@towson.edu. Website: https://www.towson.edu/chp/departments/interprofessional/grad/clinicianadminpbc/index.html

Trevecca Nazarene University, Graduate Business Programs, Nashville, TN 37210-2877. Offers business administration (MBA); health care leadership and innovation (MS); management (MSM). *Program availability:* Evening/weekend, online learning. *Faculty:* 12 full-time (1 woman), 15 part-time/adjunct (8 women). *Students:* 236 full-time (145 women), 50 part-time (29 women); includes 154 minority (128 Black or African American, non-Hispanic/Latino; 1 American Indian or Alaska Native, non-Hispanic/Latino; 4 Asian, non-Hispanic/Latino; 18 Hispanic/Latino; 3 Two or more races, non-Hispanic/Latino), 4 international. Average age 33. In 2017, 55 master's awarded. *Entrance requirements:* For master's, minimum GPA of 2.75, resume, official transcript from regionally accredited institution, minimum math grade of C, minimum English composition grade of C. Additional exam requirements/recommendations for international students: Required—TOEFL (minimum score 550 paper-based; 80 iBT). *Application deadline:* Applications are processed on a rolling basis. Application fee: $0. Electronic applications accepted. *Expenses:* $520 per credit hour. *Financial support:* Applicants required to submit FAFSA. *Unit head:* Dr. Rick Mann, Director of Graduate and Professional Programs for School of Business, 615-248-1529, E-mail: management@trevecca.edu. *Application contact:* 615-248-1529, E-mail: sgcsadmissions@trevecca.edu.
Website: http://www.trevecca.edu/mba

Trident University International, College of Health Sciences, Program in Health Sciences, Cypress, CA 90630. Offers clinical research administration (MS, Certificate); emergency and disaster management (MS, Certificate); environmental health science (Certificate); health care administration (PhD); health care management (MS), including health informatics; health education (MS, Certificate); health informatics (Certificate); health sciences (PhD); international health (MS); international health: educator or researcher option (PhD); international health: practitioner option (PhD); law and expert witness studies (MS, Certificate); public health (MS); quality assurance (Certificate). *Program availability:* Part-time, evening/weekend, online learning. *Degree requirements:* For doctorate, comprehensive exam, thesis/dissertation, defense of dissertation. *Entrance requirements:* For master's, minimum GPA of 2.5 (students with GPA 3.0 or greater may transfer up to 30% of graduate level credits); for doctorate, minimum GPA of 3.4, curriculum vitae, course work in research methods or statistics. Additional exam requirements/recommendations for international students: Required—TOEFL. Electronic applications accepted.

Trinity University, Department of Health Care Administration, San Antonio, TX 78212-7200. Offers MS. *Accreditation:* CAHME. *Program availability:* Part-time, online learning. *Entrance requirements:* For master's, GRE or GMAT, resume or autobiographical sketch; statement of purpose; letters of recommendation; 3-credit hour undergraduate courses each in accounting, economics, and statistics with minimum B grade. *Application deadline:* For fall admission, 6/1 for domestic students. Applications are processed on a rolling basis. Application fee: $50. Electronic applications accepted. *Financial support:* Fellowships, institutionally sponsored loans, scholarships/grants, and unspecified assistantships available. Support available to part-time students. Financial award application deadline: 5/1; financial award applicants required to submit FAFSA. *Unit head:* Dr. Ed Schumacher, Professor/Chair, 210-999-8137, E-mail: hca@trinity.edu. *Application contact:* Dr. Ed Schumacher, Professor/Chair, 210-999-8137, E-mail: hca@trinity.edu.
Website: http://new.trinity.edu/academics/departments/health-care-administration

Trinity Western University, School of Graduate Studies, Program in Leadership, Langley, BC V2Y 1Y1, Canada. Offers business (MA, Certificate); Christian ministry (MA); education (MA, Certificate); healthcare (MA, Certificate); non-profit (MA, Certificate). *Program availability:* Online learning. *Degree requirements:* For master's, major project. *Entrance requirements:* For master's, minimum GPA of 2.7. Additional exam requirements/recommendations for international students: Required—TOEFL (minimum score 620 paper-based; 105 iBT). Electronic applications accepted. *Expenses:* Contact institution. *Faculty research:* Servant leadership.

Troy University, Graduate School, College of Business, Program in Business Administration, Troy, AL 36082. Offers accounting (EMBA, MBA); criminal justice (EMBA); finance (MBA); general management (EMBA, MBA); healthcare management (EMBA); information systems (EMBA, MBA); international economic development (MBA). *Accreditation:* ACBSP. *Program availability:* Part-time, evening/weekend. *Faculty:* 6 full-time (2 women), 1 part-time/adjunct (0 women). *Students:* 43 full-time (22 women), 115 part-time (55 women); includes 50 minority (31 Black or African American, non-Hispanic/Latino; 12 Asian, non-Hispanic/Latino; 6 Hispanic/Latino; 1 Two or more races, non-Hispanic/Latino). Average age 30. 156 applicants, 76% accepted, 36 enrolled. In 2017, 95 master's awarded. *Degree requirements:* For master's, minimum GPA of 3.0, capstone course, research course. *Entrance requirements:* For master's, GMAT (minimum score 500) or GRE (minimum score 900 on old exam or 294 on new exam), bachelor's degree; minimum undergraduate GPA of 2.5 or 3.0 on last 30 semester hours, letter of recommendation. Additional exam requirements/recommendations for international students: Required—TOEFL (minimum score 523 paper-based; 70 iBT), IELTS (minimum score 6). *Application deadline:* Applications are processed on a rolling basis. Application fee: $50. Electronic applications accepted. *Expenses:* Tuition, state resident: part-time $417 per credit hour. Tuition, nonresident: part-time $834 per credit hour. *Required fees:* $42 per credit hour. $50 per semester. Tuition and fees vary according to campus/location. *Financial support:* Fellowships, career-related internships or fieldwork, and scholarships/grants available. Support available to part-time students. Financial award applicants required to submit FAFSA. *Unit head:* Dr. Phillip Mixon, MBA Director, 334-670-3140, Fax: 334-670-3708, E-mail: pamixon@troy.edu. *Application contact:* Jessica A. Kimbro, Director of Graduate Admissions, 334-670-3178, E-mail: jacord@troy.edu.

Tufts University, School of Medicine, Public Health and Professional Degree Programs, Boston, MA 02111. Offers biomedical sciences (MS); health communication (MS, Certificate); pain research, education and policy (MS, Certificate); physician assistant (MS); public health (MPH, Dr PH), including behavioral science (MPH), biostatistics (MPH), epidemiology (MPH), health communication (MPH), health services (MPH), management and policy (MPH), nutrition (MPH); DMD/MPH; DVM/MPH; JD/MPH; MD/MPH; MMS/MPH; MS/MBA; MS/MPH. *Accreditation:* CEPH (one or more programs are accredited). *Program availability:* Part-time, evening/weekend. *Faculty:* 62 full-time (25 women), 50 part-time/adjunct (25 women). *Students:* 449 full-time (280 women), 60 part-time (46 women); includes 188 minority (23 Black or African American, non-Hispanic/Latino; 112 Asian, non-Hispanic/Latino; 35 Hispanic/Latino; 18 Two or more races, non-Hispanic/Latino), 23 international. Average age 27. 1,750 applicants, 46% accepted, 252 enrolled. In 2017, 283 master's awarded. Terminal master's awarded for partial completion of doctoral program. *Degree requirements:* For master's, thesis (for some programs); for doctorate, thesis/dissertation. *Entrance requirements:* For master's, GRE General Test, MCAT, or GMAT; for doctorate, GRE General Test or MCAT. Additional exam requirements/recommendations for international students: Required—TOEFL (minimum score 100 iBT); Recommended—IELTS (minimum score 7). *Application deadline:* For fall admission, 1/15 priority date for domestic and international students; for spring admission, 10/25 priority date for domestic and international students. Applications are processed on a rolling basis. Application fee: $70. Electronic applications accepted. *Expenses:* Contact institution. *Financial support:* In 2017–18, 13 students received support, including 1 fellowship (averaging $3,000 per year), 50 research assistantships (averaging $1,000 per year), 65 teaching assistantships (averaging $2,000 per year); Federal Work-Study and scholarships/grants also available. Financial award application deadline: 2/23; financial award applicants required to submit FAFSA. *Faculty research:* Environmental and occupational health, nutrition, epidemiology, health communication, biostatics, obesity/chronic disease, health policy and health care delivery, global health, health inequality and social determinants of health. *Unit head:* Dr. Aviva Must, Dean, 617-636-0935, Fax: 617-636-0898, E-mail: aviva.must@tufts.edu. *Application contact:* Emily Keily, Director of Admissions, 617-636-0935, Fax: 617-636-0898, E-mail: med-phpd@tufts.edu.
Website: http://publichealth.tufts.edu

Tulane University, School of Public Health and Tropical Medicine, Department of Global Health Management and Policy, New Orleans, LA 70118-5669. Offers MHA, MPH, PhD, Sc D, JD/MHA, MBA/MHA, MD/MPH, MSW/MPH. *Accreditation:* CAHME (one or more programs are accredited). *Degree requirements:* For doctorate, comprehensive exam, thesis/dissertation. *Entrance requirements:* For master's, GMAT, GRE General Test; for doctorate, GRE General Test. Additional exam requirements/recommendations for international students: Required—TOEFL. Electronic applications accepted. *Expenses: Tuition:* Full-time $50,920; part-time $2829 per credit hour. *Required fees:* $2040; $44.50 per credit hour. $580 per term. Tuition and fees vary according to course load, degree level and program. *Faculty research:* Health policy, organizational governance, international health administration.

Uniformed Services University of the Health Sciences, F. Edward Hebert School of Medicine, Graduate Programs in the Biomedical Sciences and Public Health, Bethesda, MD 20814. Offers emerging infectious diseases (PhD); medical and clinical psychology (PhD), including clinical psychology, medical psychology; medicine (MS, PhD), including health professions education; molecular and cell biology (MS, PhD); neuroscience (PhD); preventive medicine and biometrics (MPH, MS, MSPH, MTMH, PhD), including environmental health sciences (PhD), healthcare administration and policy (MS), medical zoology (PhD), public health (MPH, MSPH), tropical medicine and hygiene (MTMH). *Students:* Average age 25. 598 applicants, 17% accepted, 77 enrolled. In 2017, 19 master's, 50 doctorates awarded. Terminal master's awarded for partial completion of doctoral program. *Degree requirements:* For master's, comprehensive exam, thesis or alternative; for doctorate, comprehensive exam, thesis/dissertation, qualifying exam. *Entrance requirements:* For master's, GRE General Test; for doctorate, GRE General Test, minimum GPA of 3.0. *Application deadline:* For fall admission, 12/1 priority date for domestic students. Application fee: $0. Electronic applications accepted. *Expenses:* There are no tuition charges or fees for graduate students at USU. *Financial support:* In 2017–18, 50 fellowships (averaging $43,000 per year) were awarded; research assistantships, career-related internships or fieldwork, scholarships/grants, and health care benefits also available. *Unit head:* Dr. Gregory Mueller, Associate Dean, 301-295-3507, E-mail: gregory.mueller@usuhs.edu. *Application contact:* Tina Finley, Administrative Officer, 301-295-3642, Fax: 301-295-6772, E-mail: netina.finley@usuhs.edu.
Website: http://www.usuhs.mil/graded

Uniformed Services University of the Health Sciences, F. Edward Hebert School of Medicine, Graduate Programs in the Biomedical Sciences and Public Health, Department of Preventive Medicine and Biometrics, Program in Healthcare Administration and Policy, Bethesda, MD 20814-4799. Offers MS.

Union Institute & University, Master of Science Program in Healthcare Leadership, Cincinnati, OH 45206-1925. Offers MS.

Universidad de Ciencias Medicas, Graduate Programs, San Jose, Costa Rica. Offers dermatology (SP); family health (MS); health service center administration (MHA); human anatomy (MS); medical and surgery (MD); occupational medicine (MS); pharmacy (Pharm D). *Program availability:* Part-time. *Degree requirements:* For master's, thesis; for doctorate and SP, comprehensive exam. *Entrance requirements:* For master's, MD or bachelor's degree; for doctorate, admissions test; for SP, admissions test, MD.

Universidad de Iberoamerica, Graduate School, San Jose, Costa Rica. Offers clinical neuropsychology (PhD); clinical psychology (M Psych); educational psychology (M Psych); forensic psychology (M Psych); hospital management (MHA); intensive care nursing (MN); medicine (MD).

Université de Montréal, Faculty of Medicine, Department of Health Administration, Montréal, QC H3C 3J7, Canada. Offers M Sc, DESS. *Accreditation:* CAHME. *Degree requirements:* For master's, thesis. *Entrance requirements:* For master's, proficiency in French. Electronic applications accepted.

University at Albany, State University of New York, Nelson A. Rockefeller College of Public Affairs and Policy, Department of Public Administration and Policy, Albany, NY 12222-0001. Offers financial management and public economics (MPA); financial market regulation (MPA); health policy (MPA); healthcare management (MPA); homeland security (MPA); human resources management (MPA); information strategy and management (MPA); local government management (MPA); nonprofit management (MPA); nonprofit management and leadership (Certificate); organizational behavior and theory (MPA, PhD); planning and policy analysis (CAS); policy analysis (MPA); politics and administration (PhD); public finance (PhD); public management (PhD); public policy (PhD); public sector management (Certificate); women and public policy (Certificate); JD/MPA. JD/MPA offered jointly with Albany Law School. *Accreditation:* NASPAA (one or more programs are accredited). *Faculty:* 21 full-time (7 women), 14 part-time/adjunct (7 women). *Students:* 115 full-time (59 women), 93 part-time (56 women); includes 41 minority (11 Black or African American, non-Hispanic/Latino; 9 Asian, non-Hispanic/Latino; 18 Hispanic/Latino; 3 Two or more races, non-Hispanic/Latino), 32 international. 236 applicants, 69% accepted, 86 enrolled. In 2017, 57 master's, 1 doctorate, 14 other advanced degrees awarded. *Degree requirements:* For doctorate, one foreign language, thesis/dissertation. *Entrance requirements:* For doctorate, GRE General Test. Additional exam requirements/recommendations for international students: Required—TOEFL (minimum score 550 paper-based). *Application deadline:* For fall admission, 2/1 priority date for domestic students, 5/1 for international students; for spring admission, 12/1 for domestic students. Applications are processed on a rolling basis. Application fee: $75. Electronic applications accepted. *Expenses:* Tuition, state resident: full-time $10,870; part-time $453 per credit hour. Tuition, nonresident: full-time $22,210; part-time $925 per credit hour. *Required fees:* $84.68 per credit hour. $508.06 per semester. Part-time tuition and fees vary according to course load and program. *Financial support:* Application deadline: 2/1. *Unit head:* Victor Asal, Chair, 518-591-8729, E-mail: vasal@albany.edu.
Website: http://www.albany.edu/rockefeller/pad.shtml

University at Albany, State University of New York, School of Public Health, Department of Health Policy, Management, and Behavior, Albany, NY 12222-0001. Offers MPH, MS, Dr PH, PhD. *Faculty:* 13 full-time (9 women), 3 part-time/adjunct (2 women). *Students:* 134 full-time (114 women), 129 part-time (88 women); includes 78 minority (36 Black or African American, non-Hispanic/Latino; 17 Asian, non-Hispanic/Latino; 18 Hispanic/Latino; 7 Two or more races, non-Hispanic/Latino), 19 international. 262 applicants, 58% accepted, 117 enrolled. *Degree requirements:* For master's, thesis. *Entrance requirements:* For master's, GRE General Test. Additional exam requirements/recommendations for international students: Required—TOEFL (minimum score 550 paper-based). *Application deadline:* For fall admission, 4/1 for domestic students, 5/1 for international students; for spring admission, 11/30 for domestic students, 11/1 for international students. Applications are processed on a rolling basis. Application fee: $75. Electronic applications accepted. *Expenses:* Tuition, state resident: full-time $10,870; part-time $453 per credit hour. Tuition, nonresident: full-time $22,210; part-time $925 per credit hour. *Required fees:* $84.68 per credit hour. $508.06 per semester. Part-time tuition and fees vary according to course load and program. *Financial support:* Application deadline: 4/1. *Unit head:* Dr. Wendy Weller, Chair, 518-402-0290, E-mail: wweller@albany.edu. *Application contact:* Michael DeRensis, Director, Graduate Admissions, 518-442-3980, Fax: 518-442-3922, E-mail: graduate@albany.edu.

University at Buffalo, the State University of New York, Graduate School, School of Management, Buffalo, NY 14260. Offers accounting (MS); analytics (MBA); business administration (PMBA); consulting (MBA); finance (MBA, MS), including financial risk management (MS), quantitative finance (MS); healthcare (MBA); information assurance (MBA); information systems (MBA); international management (MBA); management (EMBA, PhD); management information systems (MS); marketing (MBA); supply chain and operations (MBA); supply chains and operations management (MS); Au D/MBA; DDS/MBA; JD/MBA; M Arch/MBA; MD/MBA; MPH/MBA; MSW/MBA; Pharm D/MBA. *Accreditation:* AACSB. *Program availability:* Part-time, evening/weekend. *Faculty:* 80 full-time (26 women), 45 part-time/adjunct (12 women). *Students:* 597 full-time (251 women); includes 83 minority (19 Black or African American, non-Hispanic/Latino; 59 Asian, non-Hispanic/Latino; 5 Hispanic/Latino), 306 international. Average age 25. 2,109 applicants, 46% accepted, 376 enrolled. In 2017, 371 master's, 13 doctorates awarded. *Degree requirements:* For master's, capstone courses or projects; for doctorate, comprehensive exam, thesis/dissertation. *Entrance requirements:* For master's, GMAT (for MS in accounting, finance); GRE or GMAT (for MBA, MS in management information systems, supply chains and operations management), essays, letters of recommendation; for doctorate, GMAT or GRE, essays, writing sample, letters of recommendation. Additional exam requirements/recommendations for international students: Required—TOEFL (minimum score 95 iBT) or IELTS (minimum score 6.5); Recommended—TSE (minimum score 73). *Application deadline:* For fall admission, 10/15 priority date for domestic and international students; for winter admission, 2/1 priority date for domestic and international students; for spring admission, 4/15 for domestic students; for summer admission, 5/15 for domestic students. Application fee: $100. Electronic applications accepted. *Expenses:* Varies by program. *Financial support:* Fellowships with full and partial tuition reimbursements, research assistantships with full and partial tuition reimbursements, teaching assistantships with full and partial tuition reimbursements, career-related internships or fieldwork, Federal Work-Study, institutionally sponsored loans, scholarships/grants, health care benefits, and unspecified assistantships available. Financial award application deadline: 2/15. *Faculty research:* Data analytics, accounting and law, rate finance, consumer behavior, supply chain logistics, leadership and team effectiveness. *Total annual research expenditures:* $968,376. *Unit head:* Erin K. O'Brien, Assistant Dean and Director of Graduate Programs, 716-645-3204, Fax: 716-645-2341, E-mail: ekobrien@buffalo.edu. *Application contact:* Meghan Felser, Director of Admissions and Recruiting, 716-645-3204, Fax: 716-645-2341, E-mail: mpwood@buffalo.edu.
Website: http://mgt.buffalo.edu/

The University of Akron, Graduate School, College of Business Administration, Department of Management, Program in Healthcare Management, Akron, OH 44325. Offers MBA. *Students:* 6 full-time (2 women), 10 part-time (4 women); includes 2 minority (1 Black or African American, non-Hispanic/Latino; 1 Asian, non-Hispanic/Latino), 1 international. Average age 30. 6 applicants, 83% accepted, 5 enrolled. In 2017, 11 master's awarded. *Entrance requirements:* For master's, GMAT, GRE, MCAT, LSAT, PCAT, or CAT, minimum GPA of 3.0 (preferred), two letters of recommendation, resume, statement of purpose. Additional exam requirements/recommendations for international students: Required—TOEFL (minimum score 79 iBT), IELTS (minimum score 6.5). *Application deadline:* For fall admission, 7/15 for domestic and international students; for spring admission, 11/15 for domestic and international students; for summer admission, 4/15 for domestic and international students. Application fee: $45 ($75 for international students). Electronic applications accepted. *Unit head:* Dr. Steve Ash, Chair, 330-972-6429, E-mail: ash@uakron.edu. *Application contact:* Dr. William Hauser, Director of Graduate Business Programs, 330-972-7043, Fax: 330-972-6588, E-mail: whauser@uakron.edu.
Website: http://www.uakron.edu/cba/graduate/programs/mba/healthcaremgmt.dot

The University of Alabama at Birmingham, Collat School of Business, Program in Business Administration, Birmingham, AL 35294. Offers business administration (MBA), including finance, health care management, information technology management, marketing; MD/MBA. *Program availability:* Part-time, evening/weekend, 100% online, blended/hybrid learning. *Faculty:* 44 full-time (8 women), 11 part-time/adjunct (4 women). *Students:* 111 full-time (46 women), 308 part-time (136 women); includes 107 minority (73 Black or African American, non-Hispanic/Latino; 21 Asian, non-Hispanic/Latino; 8 Hispanic/Latino; 5 Two or more races, non-Hispanic/Latino), 56 international. Average age 33. 222 applicants, 89% accepted, 143 enrolled. In 2017, 114 master's awarded. *Entrance requirements:* For master's, GMAT. Additional exam requirements/recommendations for international students: Required—TOEFL (minimum score 80 iBT), IELTS (minimum score 6.5). *Application deadline:* For fall admission, 7/1 for domestic and international students; for spring admission, 11/1 for domestic and international students; for summer admission, 4/1 for domestic and international students. Applications are processed on a rolling basis. Application fee: $60 ($75 for international students). Electronic applications accepted. *Faculty research:* Open innovation, workplace issues, leadership, supply chain management, capital markets. *Total annual research expenditures:* $240,000. *Unit head:* Dr. Ken Miller, Executive Director, MBA Programs, 205-934-8855, E-mail: klmiller@uab.edu. *Application contact:* Christy Manning, Coordinator of Graduate Programs in Business, 205-934-8817, E-mail: cmanning@uab.edu.
Website: http://www.uab.edu/business/home/mba

The University of Alabama at Birmingham, School of Education, Community Health and Human Services Program, Birmingham, AL 35294. Offers MA Ed. *Accreditation:* NCATE. *Degree requirements:* For master's, comprehensive exam (for some programs), thesis optional. *Entrance requirements:* For master's, GRE General Test or MAT, minimum GPA of 3.0, references. Electronic applications accepted. *Faculty research:* College student health, minority health disparities/disease, health eating.

The University of Alabama at Birmingham, School of Health Professions, Program in Administration/Health Services, Birmingham, AL 35294. Offers D Sc, PhD. *Degree requirements:* For doctorate, thesis/dissertation. *Entrance requirements:* For doctorate, GRE General Test. Additional exam requirements/recommendations for international students: Required—TOEFL. *Faculty research:* Healthcare strategic management, marketing, organization studies.

The University of Alabama at Birmingham, School of Health Professions, Program in Health Administration, Birmingham, AL 35294. Offers MSHA. *Accreditation:* CAHME. *Faculty:* 21 full-time (12 women), 15 part-time/adjunct (8 women). *Students:* 149 full-time (73 women); includes 37 minority (21 Black or African American, non-Hispanic/Latino; 1 American Indian or Alaska Native, non-Hispanic/Latino; 10 Asian, non-Hispanic/Latino; 5 Hispanic/Latino), 1 international. Average age 29. 141 applicants, 48% accepted, 56 enrolled. In 2017, 59 master's awarded. *Degree requirements:* For master's, administrative residency. *Entrance requirements:* For master's, GMAT or GRE General Test, minimum GPA of 3.0 in final 60 hours of undergraduate course work; 5 years of experience in health care organizations, either as manager or as clinical professional (for executive program). Additional exam requirements/recommendations for international students: Required—TOEFL (minimum score 550 paper-based), TWE. *Application deadline:* For fall admission, 12/1 priority date for domestic students. Applications are processed on a rolling basis. Application fee: $70 ($85 for international students). Electronic applications accepted. *Financial support:* Career-related internships or fieldwork, Federal Work-Study, scholarships/grants, and traineeships available. Financial award application deadline: 5/1; financial award applicants required to submit FAFSA. *Faculty research:* Health care management, organizational behavior of healthcare organizations, health policy, strategic behavior of healthcare organizations, leadership development. *Unit head:* Amy Y. Landry, PhD, Director, 205-996-7767, E-mail: akyarb@uab.edu. *Application contact:* Pamela L. Armstrong, Admissions Coordinator, 205-934-1583, E-mail: parmstrong@uab.edu.
Website: http://www.uab.edu/shp/hsa/msha

The University of Alabama at Birmingham, School of Public Health, Program in Public Health, Birmingham, AL 35294. Offers applied epidemiology and pharmacoepidemiology (MSPH); biostatistics (MPH); clinical and translational science (MSPH); environmental health (MPH); environmental health and toxicology (MSPH); epidemiology (MPH); general theory and practice (MPH); health behavior (MPH); health care organization (MPH); health policy quantitative policy analysis (MPH); industrial hygiene (MPH, MSPH); maternal and child health policy (Dr PH); maternal and child health policy and leadership (MPH); occupational health and safety (MPH); outcomes research (MSPH, Dr PH); public health (PhD); public health management (Dr PH); public health preparedness management (MPH). *Program availability:* Part-time, online learning. *Degree requirements:* For doctorate, comprehensive exam, thesis/dissertation. *Entrance requirements:* For master's and doctorate, GRE. Additional exam requirements/recommendations for international students: Recommended—TOEFL (minimum score 550 paper-based; 79 iBT), IELTS (minimum score 6.5). Electronic applications accepted.

The University of Alabama in Huntsville, School of Graduate Studies, College of Nursing, Huntsville, AL 35899. Offers family nurse practitioner (Certificate); nursing (MSN, DNP), including adult-gerontology acute care nurse practitioner (MSN), adult-gerontology clinical nurse specialist (MSN), family nurse practitioner (MSN), leadership in health care systems (MSN); nursing education (Certificate). DNP offered jointly with The University of Alabama at Birmingham. *Accreditation:* AACN. *Program availability:* Part-time, evening/weekend, online learning. *Degree requirements:* For master's, comprehensive exam, thesis or alternative, oral and written exams. *Entrance requirements:* For master's, MAT or GRE, Alabama RN license, BSN, minimum GPA of 3.0; for doctorate, master's degree in nursing in an advanced practice area; for Certificate, MAT or GRE, minimum GPA of 3.0. Additional exam requirements/recommendations for international students: Required—TOEFL (minimum score 500 paper-based; 80 iBT), IELTS (minimum score 6.5). Electronic applications accepted. *Faculty research:* Health care informatics, chronic illness management, maternal and child health, genetics/genomics, technology and health care.

University of Alaska Anchorage, College of Health, Department of Health Sciences, Anchorage, AK 99508. Offers health administration (MPA); physicians assistant (MS); public health practice (MPH); MSW/MPH. *Accreditation:* CEPH. *Program availability:* Part-time. *Degree requirements:* For master's, comprehensive exam, thesis. *Entrance requirements:* For master's, writing sample. Additional exam requirements/recommendations for international students: Required—TOEFL (minimum score 550 paper-based). *Application deadline:* For fall admission, 3/1 for domestic and international students; for spring admission, 10/1 for domestic and international students. Application fee: $45. *Expenses:* Tuition, state resident: part-time $489 per credit hour. Tuition, nonresident: part-time $1028 per credit hour. *Unit head:* Dr. Rhonda Johnson, Chair, 907-786-6565, E-mail: rhonda.johnson@uaa.alaska.edu. *Application contact:* Elisa Mattison, Director, Graduate School, 907-786-1096, Fax: 907-786-1791, E-mail: esmattison@uaa.alaska.edu.
Website: http://www.uaa.alaska.edu/healthsciences/

University of Alberta, School of Public Health, Department of Public Health Sciences, Edmonton, AB T6G 2E1, Canada. Offers clinical epidemiology (M Sc, MPH); environmental and occupational health (MPH); environmental health sciences (M Sc); epidemiology (M Sc); global health (M Sc, MPH); health policy and management (MPH); health policy research (M Sc); health technology assessment (MPH); occupational health (M Sc); population health (M Sc); public health leadership (MPH); public health sciences (PhD); quantitative methods (MPH). Terminal master's awarded for partial completion of doctoral program. *Degree requirements:* For master's, thesis (for some programs); for doctorate, thesis/dissertation. *Entrance requirements:* For master's, GMAT or GRE General Test. Additional exam requirements/recommendations for international students: Required—TOEFL (minimum score 550 paper-based) or IELTS (minimum score 6). Electronic applications accepted. *Faculty research:* Biostatistics, health promotion and socio-behavioral health science.

University of Arkansas for Medical Sciences, College of Public Health, Little Rock, AR 72205-7199. Offers biostatistics (MPH); environmental and occupational health (MPH, Certificate); epidemiology (MPH, PhD); health behavior and health education (MPH); health policy and management (MPH); health promotion and prevention research (PhD); health services administration (MHSA); health systems research (PhD); public health (Certificate); public health leadership (Dr PH). *Accreditation:* CEPH. *Program availability:* Part-time. *Degree requirements:* For master's, preceptorship, culminating experience, internship; for doctorate, comprehensive exam, capstone. *Entrance requirements:* For master's, GRE, GMAT, LSAT, PCAT, MCAT, DAT; for doctorate, GRE. Additional exam requirements/recommendations for international students: Required—TOEFL (minimum score 80 iBT), IELTS. Electronic applications accepted. *Expenses:* Contact institution. *Faculty research:* Health systems, tobacco prevention control, obesity prevention, environmental and occupational exposure, cancer prevention.

University of Arkansas–Fort Smith, Program in Healthcare Administration, Fort Smith, AR 72913-3649. Offers MS. *Program availability:* Online learning. *Degree requirements:* For master's, project. *Entrance requirements:* For master's, bachelor's degree with minimum GPA of 3.0.

Health Services Management and Hospital Administration

University of Baltimore, Graduate School, College of Public Affairs, Program in Health Systems Management, Baltimore, MD 21201-5779. Offers MS. *Program availability:* Part-time, evening/weekend. *Entrance requirements:* For master's, minimum undergraduate GPA of 3.0. Additional exam requirements/recommendations for international students: Required—TOEFL (minimum score 550 paper-based).

The University of British Columbia, Faculty of Medicine, School of Population and Public Health, Vancouver, BC V6T 1Z3, Canada. Offers health administration (MHA); health sciences (MH Sc); occupational and environmental hygiene (M Sc); population and public health (M Sc, MPH, PhD); MPH/MSN. *Program availability:* Online learning. *Degree requirements:* For master's, thesis (for some programs), major paper (MH Sc), research project (MHA); for doctorate, thesis/dissertation. *Entrance requirements:* For master's, GRE General Test or GMAT, PCAT, MCAT (for MHA), MD or equivalent (for MH Sc); 4-year undergraduate degree from accredited university with minimum B+ overall academic average and in math or statistics course at undergraduate level (for MPH); 4-year undergraduate degree from accredited university with minimum B+ overall academic average plus work experience (for MHA); for doctorate, master's degree from accredited university with minimum B+ overall academic average and in math or statistics course at undergraduate level. Additional exam requirements/recommendations for international students: Required—TOEFL. Electronic applications accepted. *Expenses:* Contact institution. *Faculty research:* Population and public health, clinical epidemiology, epidemiology and biostatistics, global health and vulnerable populations, health care services and systems, occupational and environmental health, public health emerging threats and rapid response, social and life course determinants of health, health administration.

University of California, Berkeley, Graduate Division, School of Public Health, Group in Health Policy, Berkeley, CA 94720-1500. Offers PhD. *Degree requirements:* For doctorate, thesis/dissertation, qualifying exam. *Entrance requirements:* For doctorate, GRE General Test, minimum GPA of 3.0, 3 letters of recommendation. Electronic applications accepted.

University of California, Irvine, The Paul Merage School of Business, Health Care Executive MBA Program, Irvine, CA 92697. Offers MBA. *Students:* 47 full-time (22 women); includes 31 minority (6 American Indian or Alaska Native, non-Hispanic/Latino; 25 Asian, non-Hispanic/Latino), 1 international. Average age 40. 41 applicants, 78% accepted, 24 enrolled. In 2017, 24 master's awarded. Application fee: $105 ($125 for international students). *Unit head:* Anthony Hansford, Senior Assistant Dean, 949-824-3801, E-mail: hansfora@uci.edu. *Application contact:* Jon Masciana, Senior Director, 949-824-0595, E-mail: jmascian@uci.edu.
Website: http://merage.uci.edu/HealthCareExecutiveMBA/Default.aspx

University of California, Los Angeles, Graduate Division, School of Public Health, Department of Health Services, Los Angeles, CA 90095. Offers MPH, MS, Dr PH, PhD, JD/MPH, MBA/MPH, MD/MPH. *Degree requirements:* For master's, comprehensive exam or thesis; for doctorate, thesis/dissertation, oral and written qualifying exams. *Entrance requirements:* For master's, GRE General Test, minimum GPA of 3.0; for doctorate, GRE General Test, minimum undergraduate GPA of 3.0. Electronic applications accepted.

University of California, San Diego, School of Medicine, Program in the Leadership of Healthcare Organizations, La Jolla, CA 92093. Offers MAS. *Program availability:* Part-time, evening/weekend. *Students:* 5 full-time (3 women), 26 part-time (16 women). 21 applicants, 76% accepted, 12 enrolled. In 2017, 9 master's awarded. *Degree requirements:* For master's, independent study project. *Entrance requirements:* For master's, minimum GPA of 3.0, minimum 5 years of professional work/internship in health care or related field, resume or curriculum vitae, 3 letters of recommendation. Additional exam requirements/recommendations for international students: Required—TOEFL (minimum score 550 paper-based; 80 iBT), IELTS (minimum score 7). *Application deadline:* For fall admission, 5/17 for domestic students; for winter admission, 10/18 for domestic students; for spring admission, 1/24 for domestic students. Applications are processed on a rolling basis. Application fee: $105 ($125 for international students). Electronic applications accepted. *Expenses:* Contact institution. *Financial support:* Scholarships/grants available. Financial award applicants required to submit FAFSA. *Unit head:* Todd Gilmer, Chair, 858-534-7596, E-mail: tgilmer@ucsd.edu. *Application contact:* Jessica Nguyen, Graduate Coordinator, 858-534-9162, E-mail: lhco@ucsd.edu.
Website: http://lhco.ucsd.edu/

University of Central Florida, College of Community Innovation and Education, Department of Health Management and Informatics, Orlando, FL 32816. Offers health administration (MHA); health care informatics (MS); health information administration (Certificate). *Accreditation:* CAHME. *Program availability:* Part-time, evening/weekend. *Students:* 167 full-time (111 women), 190 part-time (156 women); includes 226 minority (98 Black or African American, non-Hispanic/Latino; 3 American Indian or Alaska Native, non-Hispanic/Latino; 44 Asian, non-Hispanic/Latino; 70 Hispanic/Latino; 11 Two or more races, non-Hispanic/Latino), 7 international. Average age 29. 281 applicants, 74% accepted, 141 enrolled. In 2017, 125 master's, 1 other advanced degree awarded. *Degree requirements:* For master's, comprehensive exam, thesis or alternative, research report. *Entrance requirements:* For master's, letters of recommendation, resume, goal statement. Additional exam requirements/recommendations for international students: Required—TOEFL. *Application deadline:* For fall admission, 7/15 for domestic students; for spring admission, 12/1 for domestic students. Application fee: $30. Electronic applications accepted. *Expenses:* Tuition, state resident: part-time $288.16 per credit hour. Tuition, nonresident: part-time $1073.31 per credit hour. Tuition and fees vary according to program. *Financial support:* In 2017–18, 4 students received support, including 4 research assistantships with partial tuition reimbursements available (averaging $8,487 per year), 1 teaching assistantship (averaging $4,996 per year); career-related internships or fieldwork, Federal Work-Study, institutionally sponsored loans, and unspecified assistantships also available. Financial award application deadline: 3/1; financial award applicants required to submit FAFSA. *Unit head:* Dr. Reid Oetjen, Interim Chair, 407-823-5668, E-mail: reid.oetjen@ucf.edu. *Application contact:* Associate Director, Graduate Admissions, 407-823-2766, Fax: 407-823-6442, E-mail: gradadmissions@ucf.edu.
Website: https://www.cohpa.ucf.edu/hmi/

University of Chicago, Booth School of Business, Full-Time MBA Program, Chicago, IL 60637. Offers accounting (MBA); analytic finance (MBA); analytic management (MBA); econometrics and statistics (MBA); economics (MBA); entrepreneurship (MBA); finance (MBA); general management (MBA); health administration and policy (Certificate); international business (MBA); managerial and organizational behavior (MBA); marketing analytics (MBA); marketing management (MBA); operations management (MBA); strategic management (MBA); MBA/AM; MBA/JD; MBA/MA; MBA/MD; MBA/MPP. *Accreditation:* AACSB. *Faculty:* 154 full-time (26 women), 61 part-time/adjunct (12 women). *Students:* 1,176 full-time (481 women). In 2017, 586 master's awarded. *Entrance requirements:* For master's, GMAT or GRE, transcripts, resume, 2 letters of recommendation, essays, interview. Additional exam requirements/recommendations for international students: Required—TOEFL, IELTS, or PTE. *Application deadline:* For fall admission, 9/1 for domestic and international students; for winter admission, 1/1 for domestic and international students; for spring admission, 4/1 for domestic and international students. Application fee: $250. Electronic applications accepted. *Expenses:* Contact institution. *Unit head:* Stacey Kole, Deputy Dean for Alumni, Corporate Relations, and the Full-time MBA Program, 773-702-7121. *Application contact:* Kurt Ahlm, Associate Dean for Student Recruitment and Admissions, 773-702-7369, Fax: 773-702-9085, E-mail: admissions@chicagobooth.edu.
Website: https://www.chicagobooth.edu/programs/full-time

University of Colorado Denver, Business School, Master of Business Administration Program, Denver, CO 80217. Offers business administration (MBA); health administration (MBA). *Accreditation:* AACSB. *Program availability:* Part-time, evening/weekend, 100% online, blended/hybrid learning. *Degree requirements:* For master's, 48 semester hours, including 30 of core courses, 3 in international business, and 15 in electives from over 50 other business courses. *Entrance requirements:* For master's, GMAT, resume, official transcripts, essay, two letters of recommendation, financial statements (for international applicants). Additional exam requirements/recommendations for international students: Required—TOEFL (minimum score 560 paper-based; 83 iBT); Recommended—IELTS (minimum score 6.5). *Application deadline:* For fall admission, 4/15 priority date for domestic students, 3/15 priority date for international students; for spring admission, 10/15 priority date for domestic students, 9/15 priority date for international students; for summer admission, 2/15 priority date for domestic students, 1/15 priority date for international students. Applications are processed on a rolling basis. Application fee: $0. Electronic applications accepted. *Expenses:* Contact institution. *Financial support:* Fellowships, research assistantships, teaching assistantships, Federal Work-Study, institutionally sponsored loans, scholarships/grants, traineeships, and unspecified assistantships available. Financial award application deadline: 4/1; financial award applicants required to submit FAFSA. *Faculty research:* Marketing, management, entrepreneurship, finance, health administration. *Unit head:* Woodrow Eckard, MBA Director, 303-315-8470, E-mail: woody.eckard@ucdenver.edu. *Application contact:* Shelly Townley, Admissions Director, Graduate Programs, 303-315-8202, E-mail: shelly.townley@ucdenver.edu.
Website: http://www.ucdenver.edu/academics/colleges/business/degrees/mba/Pages/MBA.aspx

University of Colorado Denver, Business School, Program in Health Administration, Denver, CO 80217. Offers MS. *Accreditation:* CAHME. *Program availability:* Part-time, evening/weekend. *Degree requirements:* For master's, 30 credit hours. *Entrance requirements:* For master's, GMAT, resume, essay, two letters of reference, financial statements (for international applicants). Additional exam requirements/recommendations for international students: Required—TOEFL (minimum score 525 paper-based; 71 iBT); Recommended—IELTS (minimum score 6.5). *Application deadline:* For fall admission, 4/15 priority date for domestic students, 3/15 priority date for international students; for spring admission, 10/15 priority date for domestic students, 9/15 priority date for international students; for summer admission, 2/15 priority date for domestic students, 1/15 priority date for international students. Applications are processed on a rolling basis. Application fee: $0. Electronic applications accepted. *Expenses:* Contact institution. *Financial support:* Fellowships, research assistantships, teaching assistantships, Federal Work-Study, institutionally sponsored loans, scholarships/grants, and traineeships available. Financial award application deadline: 4/1; financial award applicants required to submit FAFSA. *Faculty research:* Cost containment, financial management, governance, rural health-care delivery systems. *Unit head:* Dr. Errol Biggs, Director, 303-315-8851, E-mail: errol.biggs@ucdenver.edu. *Application contact:* Dr. Errol Biggs, Director, 303-315-8851, E-mail: errol.biggs@ucdenver.edu.
Website: http://www.ucdenver.edu/academics/colleges/business/degrees/ms/health-admin/Pages/Health-Administration.aspx

University of Connecticut, Graduate School, School of Business, Storrs, CT 06269. Offers accounting (MS, PhD); business (PhD); business administration (MBA); business analytics and project management (MS); finance (PhD); financial risk management (MS); health care management and insurance studies (MBA); human resource management (MS); management (PhD); management consulting (MBA); marketing (PhD); marketing intelligence (MBA); operations and information management (PhD). *Accreditation:* AACSB. *Degree requirements:* For master's, comprehensive exam; for doctorate, thesis/dissertation. *Entrance requirements:* For master's and doctorate, GMAT. Additional exam requirements/recommendations for international students: Required—TOEFL (minimum score 550 paper-based). Electronic applications accepted.

University of Dallas, Satish and Yasmin Gupta College of Business, Irving, TX 75062-4736. Offers accounting (MBA, MS); business administration (DBA); business analytics (MS); business management (MBA); corporate finance (MBA); cybersecurity (MS); finance (MS); financial services (MBA); global business (MBA, MS); health services management (MBA); human resource management (MBA); information and technology management (MS); information assurance (MBA); information technology (MBA); information technology service management (MBA); marketing management (MBA); organization development (MBA); project management (MBA); sports and entertainment management (MBA); strategic leadership (MBA); supply chain management (MBA). *Accreditation:* AACSB. *Program availability:* Part-time, evening/weekend, online learning. *Entrance requirements:* Additional exam requirements/recommendations for international students: Required—TOEFL. *Application deadline:* Applications are processed on a rolling basis. Application fee: $50. Electronic applications accepted. *Expenses:* Contact institution. *Financial support:* Application deadline: 2/15; applicants required to submit FAFSA. *Unit head:* Brett J.L. Landry, Dean, 972-721-5356, E-mail: blandry@udallas.edu. *Application contact:* Dr. David Sweet, Dean, Braniff Graduate School, 972-721-5288, Fax: 972-721-5280, E-mail: dsweet@udallas.edu.
Website: http://www.udallas.edu/cob/

University of Denver, University College, Denver, CO 80208. Offers arts and culture (MA, Certificate); communication management (MS, Certificate), including translation studies (Certificate), world history and culture (Certificate); environmental policy and management (MS); geographic information systems (MS); global affairs (MA, Certificate), including human capital in organizations (Certificate), philanthropic leadership (Certificate), project management (Certificate), strategic innovation and change (Certificate); healthcare leadership (MS); information communications and technology (MS); leadership and organizations (MS); professional creative writing (MA, Certificate), including emergency planning and response (Certificate), organizational security (Certificate); security management (MS, Certificate); strategic human resources (Certificate). *Program availability:* Part-time, evening/weekend, online learning. *Faculty:* 118 part-time/adjunct (62 women). *Students:* 56 full-time (32 women), 1,287 part-time (707 women); includes 330 minority (99 Black or African American, non-Hispanic/Latino; 7 American Indian or Alaska Native, non-Hispanic/Latino; 43 Asian, non-Hispanic/Latino; 141 Hispanic/Latino; 3 Native Hawaiian or other Pacific Islander, non-Hispanic/Latino; 37 Two or more races, non-Hispanic/Latino), 84 international. Average age 34. 783 applicants, 86% accepted, 420 enrolled. In 2017, 461 master's, 173 other advanced degrees awarded. *Degree requirements:* For master's, capstone project. *Entrance requirements:* For master's, transcripts, two letters of recommendation, personal statement, resume. Additional exam requirements/recommendations for international students: Required—TOEFL (minimum score 550 paper-based; 80 iBT). *Application deadline:* For fall admission, 6/21 priority date for domestic students, 5/1 priority date for

international students; for winter admission, 9/14 priority date for domestic students, 9/19 priority date for international students; for spring admission, 1/11 priority date for domestic students, 12/12 priority date for international students; for summer admission, 3/29 priority date for domestic students, 3/6 priority date for international students. Applications are processed on a rolling basis. Application fee: $75. Electronic applications accepted. *Expenses:* $7,968 per year half-time. *Financial support:* In 2017–18, 29 students received support. Teaching assistantships available. Financial award applicants required to submit FAFSA. *Unit head:* Dr. Michael McGuire, Dean, 303-871-3518, Fax: 303-871-3303, E-mail: mmcguire@du.edu. *Application contact:* Information Contact, 303-871-2291, E-mail: ucoladm@du.edu.
Website: http://universitycollege.du.edu/

University of Detroit Mercy, College of Health Professions, Detroit, MI 48221. Offers clinical nurse leader (MSN); family nurse practitioner (MSN); health services administration (MHSA); health systems management (MSN); nurse anesthesia (MS); nursing (DNP); nursing education (MSN, Certificate); nursing leadership and financial management (Certificate); outcomes performance management (Certificate); physician assistant (MS). *Entrance requirements:* For master's, GRE General Test, minimum GPA of 3.0. *Faculty research:* Research design, respiratory physiology, AIDS prevention, adolescent health, community, low income health education.

University of Evansville, College of Education and Health Sciences, School of Health Sciences, Evansville, IN 47722. Offers athletic training (MSAT); health policy (MPH); health services administration (MS). *Program availability:* Part-time, evening/weekend. *Entrance requirements:* Additional exam requirements/recommendations for international students: Required—TOEFL, IELTS (minimum score 6.5). *Expenses:* Contact institution.

The University of Findlay, Office of Graduate Admissions, Findlay, OH 45840. Offers applied security and analytics (MSAS); athletic training (MAT); business (MBA), including certified management accountant, certified public accountant, health care management, hospitality management; education (MA Ed, Ed D), including children's literature (MA Ed), curriculum and teaching (MA Ed), education (MA Ed), educational administration (MA Ed), human resource development (MA Ed), mathematics (MA Ed), reading (MA Ed), science education (MA Ed), superintendent (Ed D), teaching (Ed D), technology (MA Ed); environmental, safety, and health management (MSEM); health informatics (MS); occupational therapy (MOT); pharmacy (Pharm D); physical therapy (DPT); physician assistant (MPA); rhetoric and writing (MA); teaching English to speakers of other languages (TESOL) and applied linguistics (MA). *Program availability:* Part-time, evening/weekend, 100% online, blended/hybrid learning. *Students:* 688 full-time (430 women), 553 part-time (308 women), 170 international. Average age 28. In 2017, 366 master's, 137 doctorates awarded. *Degree requirements:* For master's, comprehensive exam (for some programs), thesis (for some programs), cumulative project, capstone project; for doctorate, thesis/dissertation (for some programs). *Entrance requirements:* For master's, GRE/GMAT, bachelor's degree from accredited institution, minimum undergraduate GPA of 2.5 in last 64 hours of course work; for doctorate, GRE, MAT, minimum cumulative GPA of 3.0. Additional exam requirements/recommendations for international students: Required—TOEFL (minimum score 79 iBT), IELTS (minimum score 7), PTE (minimum score 61). *Application deadline:* Applications are processed on a rolling basis. Electronic applications accepted. *Financial support:* In 2017–18, 10 research assistantships with partial tuition reimbursements (averaging $7,200 per year), 35 teaching assistantships with partial tuition reimbursements (averaging $7,200 per year) were awarded; Federal Work-Study, institutionally sponsored loans, and unspecified assistantships also available. Financial award applicants required to submit FAFSA. *Unit head:* Christopher M. Harris, Director of Admissions, 419-434-4347, E-mail: harrisc1@findlay.edu. *Application contact:* Madeline Fauser Brennan, Graduate Admissions Counselor, 419-434-4636, Fax: 419-434-4898, E-mail: fauserbrennan@findlay.edu.
Website: http://www.findlay.edu/admissions/graduate/Pages/default.aspx

University of Florida, Graduate School, College of Pharmacy, Graduate Programs in Pharmacy, Department of Pharmaceutical Outcomes and Policy, Gainesville, FL 32611. Offers MSP, PhD. *Program availability:* Part-time, online learning. *Degree requirements:* For doctorate, thesis/dissertation. *Entrance requirements:* For master's and doctorate, GRE General Test, minimum GPA of 3.0. Additional exam requirements/recommendations for international students: Required—TOEFL (minimum score 550 paper-based; 80 iBT), IELTS (minimum score 6). Electronic applications accepted. *Faculty research:* Phamacoepidemiology, patient safety and program evaluation, sociology-behavioral issues in medication use, medication safety, pharmacoeconomics, medication therapy management.

University of Florida, Graduate School, College of Public Health and Health Professions, Department of Health Services Research, Management and Policy, Gainesville, FL 32611. Offers health administration (MHA); health services research (PhD). *Accreditation:* CAHME. *Program availability:* Part-time. *Degree requirements:* For master's, internship. *Entrance requirements:* For master's, GRE General Test (minimum score 300) or GMAT (minimum score 500), minimum GPA of 3.0; for doctorate, GRE General Test, minimum GPA of 3.0. Additional exam requirements/recommendations for international students: Required—TOEFL (minimum score 550 paper-based; 80 iBT), IELTS (minimum score 6). Electronic applications accepted. *Faculty research:* State health policy evaluation, health informatics for pain, family medicine, secondary data analysis, disability, mental health.

University of Florida, Graduate School, Warrington College of Business Administration, Hough Graduate School of Business, Department of Management, Gainesville, FL 32611. Offers health care risk management (MS); international business (MA); management (MS, PhD). *Accreditation:* AACSB. *Program availability:* Online learning. *Degree requirements:* For master's, comprehensive exam, thesis. *Entrance requirements:* For master's, GMAT (minimum score of 465) or GRE General Test, minimum GPA of 3.0. Additional exam requirements/recommendations for international students: Required—TOEFL (minimum score 550 paper-based; 80 iBT), IELTS (minimum score 6). Electronic applications accepted. *Faculty research:* Job attitudes, personality and individual differences, organizational entry and exit, knowledge management, competitive dynamics.

University of Holy Cross, Graduate Programs, New Orleans, LA 70131-7399. Offers biomedical sciences (MS); Catholic theology (MA); counseling (MA, PhD), including community counseling (MA), marriage and family counseling (MA), school counseling (MA); educational leadership (M Ed); executive leadership (Ed D); management (MS), including healthcare management, operations management; teaching and learning (M Ed). *Accreditation:* ACA; NCATE. *Program availability:* Part-time, evening/weekend, online learning. *Faculty:* 7 full-time (4 women), 8 part-time/adjunct (3 women). *Students:* 67 full-time (55 women), 69 part-time (55 women); includes 51 minority (46 Black or African American, non-Hispanic/Latino; 2 American Indian or Alaska Native, non-Hispanic/Latino; 1 Asian, non-Hispanic/Latino; 2 Hispanic/Latino). Average age 30. 20 applicants, 50% accepted. In 2017, 28 degrees awarded. *Degree requirements:* For master's, thesis. *Entrance requirements:* For master's, GRE General Test, minimum GPA of 2.7. *Application deadline:* For fall admission, 9/1 for domestic students. Application fee: $15. *Expenses: Tuition:* Full-time $10,890; part-time $605 per credit hour. *Required fees:* $1624; $812 per semester. One-time fee: $50. *Financial support:* Federal Work-Study and tuition waivers (partial) available. Support available to part-time students. Financial award application deadline: 6/1. *Unit head:* Dr. Myles Seghers, Dean of Humanities, Education, and Counseling, 504-394-7744 Ext. 214, Fax: 504-391-2421, E-mail: mseghers@olhcc.edu. *Application contact:* Anne-Katherine Lene, Director of Student Enrollment, 504-394-7744 Ext. 110, Fax: 504-391-2421, E-mail: aklene@olhcc.edu.

University of Houston–Clear Lake, School of Business, Program in Healthcare Administration, Houston, TX 77058-1002. Offers MHA, MHA/MBA. *Degree requirements:* For master's, thesis optional. *Entrance requirements:* For master's, GMAT. Additional exam requirements/recommendations for international students: Required—TOEFL (minimum score 550 paper-based).

University of Illinois at Chicago, School of Public Health, Division of Health Policy and Administration, Chicago, IL 60607-7128. Offers clinical and translational science (MS); health policy (PhD); health services research (PhD); healthcare administration (MHA); public health policy management (MPH). *Accreditation:* CAHME. *Program availability:* Part-time. Terminal master's awarded for partial completion of doctoral program. *Degree requirements:* For master's, thesis, field practicum; for doctorate, thesis/dissertation, independent research, internship. *Entrance requirements:* For master's and doctorate, GRE General Test, minimum GPA of 2.75. Additional exam requirements/recommendations for international students: Required—TOEFL. Electronic applications accepted. *Expenses:* Contact institution. *Faculty research:* Cancer screening in underserved populations, practices and devices used to reduce firefighter injury, the relationship between communal housing and substance abuse recovery.

University of Illinois at Urbana–Champaign, Graduate College, School of Social Work, Champaign, IL 61820. Offers advocacy, leadership, and social change (MSW); children, youth and family services (MSW); health care (MSW); mental health (MSW); school social work (MSW); social work (PhD). *Accreditation:* CSWE (one or more programs are accredited). *Entrance requirements:* For master's and doctorate, minimum GPA of 3.0.

The University of Iowa, Graduate College, College of Public Health, Department of Health Management and Policy, Iowa City, IA 52242-1316. Offers MHA, PhD, JD/MHA, MBA/MHA, MHA/MA, MHA/MS. *Accreditation:* CAHME (one or more programs are accredited). *Degree requirements:* For doctorate, comprehensive exam, thesis/dissertation. *Entrance requirements:* For master's, GRE General Test or equivalent, minimum GPA of 3.0; for doctorate, GRE General Test, minimum GPA of 3.0. Additional exam requirements/recommendations for international students: Required—TOEFL (minimum score 550 paper-based; 81 iBT). Electronic applications accepted. *Expenses:* Contact institution.

The University of Kansas, University of Kansas Medical Center, School of Medicine, Department of Health Policy and Management, Kansas City, KS 66160. Offers health policy and management (PhD); health services administration (MHSA); JD/MHSA; MD/MHSA; MHSA/MS. *Accreditation:* CAHME. *Program availability:* Part-time. *Faculty:* 16. *Students:* 36 full-time (27 women), 26 part-time (14 women); includes 10 minority (1 Black or African American, non-Hispanic/Latino; 3 Asian, non-Hispanic/Latino; 4 Hispanic/Latino; 2 Two or more races, non-Hispanic/Latino), 2 international. Average age 31. 33 applicants, 70% accepted, 22 enrolled. In 2017, 20 master's, 1 doctorate awarded. *Degree requirements:* For master's, internship or research practicum; for doctorate, comprehensive exam, thesis/dissertation. *Entrance requirements:* For master's, GRE, college-level statistics; for doctorate, GRE, graduate statistics course. Additional exam requirements/recommendations for international students: Required—TOEFL. *Application deadline:* For fall admission, 3/1 priority date for domestic and international students. Applications are processed on a rolling basis. Application fee: $60. Electronic applications accepted. *Financial support:* Fellowships with full tuition reimbursements, research assistantships with partial tuition reimbursements, teaching assistantships with full tuition reimbursements, career-related internships or fieldwork, and scholarships/grants available. Financial award application deadline: 3/1; financial award applicants required to submit FAFSA. *Faculty research:* Impacts of health policy; cancer health services research; health care workforce and occupational health; implementation science and performance improvement; disparities in health outcomes. *Total annual research expenditures:* $183,138. *Unit head:* Dr. Robert H. Lee, Chair, 913-588-2689, Fax: 913-588-8236, E-mail: rlee2@kumc.edu. *Application contact:* Deborah S. Lewis, Student Support Manager, 913-588-3763, Fax: 913-588-8236, E-mail: dlewis4@kumc.edu.
Website: http://www.kumc.edu/school-of-medicine/hpm.html

University of Kentucky, Graduate School, College of Health Sciences, Program in Health Administration, Lexington, KY 40506-0032. Offers MHA. *Accreditation:* CAHME. *Degree requirements:* For master's, comprehensive exam. *Entrance requirements:* For master's, GRE General Test, minimum undergraduate GPA of 2.75. Additional exam requirements/recommendations for international students: Required—TOEFL (minimum score 550 paper-based). Electronic applications accepted. *Faculty research:* Health economy, health finance, health policy.

University of La Verne, College of Business and Public Management, Graduate Programs in Business Administration, La Verne, CA 91750-4443. Offers accounting (MBA, MBA-EP); finance (MBA, MBA-EP); health services management (MBA); information technology (MBA, MBA-EP); international business (MBA, MBA-EP); management and leadership (MBA, MBA-EP); marketing (MBA, MBA-EP); supply chain management (MBA, MBA-EP). *Program availability:* Part-time, evening/weekend. *Faculty:* 24 full-time (11 women), 25 part-time/adjunct (6 women). *Students:* 390 full-time (193 women), 93 part-time (48 women); includes 96 minority (7 Black or African American, non-Hispanic/Latino; 1 American Indian or Alaska Native, non-Hispanic/Latino; 17 Asian, non-Hispanic/Latino; 67 Hispanic/Latino; 1 Native Hawaiian or other Pacific Islander, non-Hispanic/Latino; 3 Two or more races, non-Hispanic/Latino), 336 international. Average age 28. *Entrance requirements:* For master's, GMAT, MAT, or GRE, minimum undergraduate GPA of 3.0, 2 letters of recommendation, resume, statement of purpose. Additional exam requirements/recommendations for international students: Required—TOEFL (minimum score 550 paper-based; 85 iBT). *Application deadline:* Applications are processed on a rolling basis. Application fee: $50. Tuition and fees vary according to program. *Financial support:* Institutionally sponsored loans and scholarships/grants available. Financial award application deadline: 3/2; financial award applicants required to submit FAFSA. *Unit head:* Dr. Abe Helou, Chairperson, 909-448-4455, Fax: 909-392-2704, E-mail: ihelou@laverne.edu. *Application contact:* Rina Lazarian-Chehab, Senior Associate Director of Graduate Admissions, 909-448-4317, Fax: 909-971-2295, E-mail: rlazarian@laverne.edu.
Website: https://business.laverne.edu/mba/

University of La Verne, College of Business and Public Management, Program in Health Administration, La Verne, CA 91750-4443. Offers financial management (MHA); management and leadership (MHA); marketing and business development (MHA). *Program availability:* Part-time. *Faculty:* 4 full-time (3 women), 3 part-time/adjunct (1 woman). *Students:* 35 full-time (28 women), 34 part-time (23 women); includes 34 minority (7 Black or African American, non-Hispanic/Latino; 8 Asian, non-Hispanic/Latino; 19 Hispanic/Latino), 11 international. Average age 30. *Entrance requirements:* For master's, bachelor's degree, experience in health services industry (preferred).

Health Services Management and Hospital Administration

Additional exam requirements/recommendations for international students: Required—TOEFL (minimum score 550 paper-based). *Application deadline:* Applications are processed on a rolling basis. Application fee: $50. *Expenses:* Contact institution. *Financial support:* Federal Work-Study, institutionally sponsored loans, and scholarships/grants available. Financial award application deadline: 3/2; financial award applicants required to submit FAFSA. *Unit head:* Dr. Kathy Duncan, Program Chairperson, 909-448-4415, E-mail: kduncan2@laverne.edu. *Application contact:* Barbara Cox, Associate Director of Graduate Admission, 909-448-4004, Fax: 909-971-2295, E-mail: bcox@laverne.edu.
Website: https://business.laverne.edu/mha/

University of La Verne, Regional and Online Campuses, Graduate Programs, Central Coast/Vandenberg Air Force Base Campuses, La Verne, CA 91750-4443. Offers business administration for experienced professionals (MBA), including health services management, information technology; leadership and management (MS). *Program availability:* Part-time. *Students:* 6 full-time (1 woman), 37 part-time (20 women); includes 9 minority (1 Asian, non-Hispanic/Latino; 8 Hispanic/Latino). Average age 40. In 2017, 20 master's awarded. *Application deadline:* Applications are processed on a rolling basis. Application fee: $50. *Expenses:* Contact institution. *Financial support:* Application deadline: 3/2; applicants required to submit FAFSA. *Unit head:* Kitt Vincent, Director, Vandenberg AFB, 805-788-6202, Fax: 805-788-6201, E-mail: kvincent@laverne.edu. *Application contact:* Admissions, 805-734-6220, Fax: 805-734-6221, E-mail: vafb@laverne.edu.
Website: http://www.laverne.edu/locations

University of La Verne, Regional and Online Campuses, Graduate Programs, Inland Empire Campus, Ontario, CA 91730. Offers business administration (MBA, MBA-EP), including accounting (MBA), finance (MBA), health services management (MBA-EP), information technology (MBA-EP), international business (MBA), managed care (MBA), management and leadership (MBA-EP), marketing (MBA-EP), supply chain management (MBA); leadership and management (MS), including human resource management, nonprofit management, organizational development. *Program availability:* Part-time, evening/weekend. *Faculty:* 5 part-time/adjunct (1 woman). *Students:* 24 full-time (13 women), 72 part-time (44 women); includes 64 minority (12 Black or African American, non-Hispanic/Latino; 13 Asian, non-Hispanic/Latino; 36 Hispanic/Latino; 3 Two or more races, non-Hispanic/Latino). Average age 38. In 2017, 42 master's awarded. *Application deadline:* Applications are processed on a rolling basis. Application fee: $50. *Expenses:* Contact institution. *Financial support:* Application deadline: 3/2; applicants required to submit FAFSA. *Unit head:* Juli Roberts, Campus Director, Inland Empire Regional Campus in Ontario, 760-955-6448, E-mail: jroberts@laverne.edu. *Application contact:* Admissions, 877-468-6858, E-mail: gradadmission@laverne.edu.
Website: https://laverne.edu/locations/

University of La Verne, Regional and Online Campuses, Graduate Programs, Kern County Campus, Bakersfield, CA 93301. Offers business administration for experienced professionals (MBA-EP); education (special emphasis) (M Ed); educational counseling (MS); educational leadership (M Ed); health administration (MHA); leadership and management (MS); mild/moderate education specialist (Credential); multiple subject (elementary) (Credential); organizational leadership (Ed D); preliminary administrative services (Credential); single subject (secondary) (Credential); special education studies (MS). *Program availability:* Part-time, evening/weekend. *Students:* Average age 36. In 2017, 3 master's awarded. *Application deadline:* Applications are processed on a rolling basis. Application fee: $50. *Expenses:* Contact institution. *Financial support:* Institutionally sponsored loans available. Financial award application deadline: 3/2; financial award applicants required to submit FAFSA. *Unit head:* Nora Dominguez, Regional Campus Director, 661-861-6802, E-mail: ndominguez@laverne.edu. *Application contact:* Rebecca Murillo, Associate Director of Admissions, 661-861-6807, E-mail: rmurillo@laverne.edu.
Website: https://laverne.edu/locations/

University of La Verne, Regional and Online Campuses, Graduate Programs, Orange County Campus, Irvine, CA 92840. Offers business administration for experienced professionals (MBA); educational counseling (MS); educational leadership (M Ed); health administration (MHA); leadership and management (MS); preliminary administrative services (Credential); pupil personnel services (Credential). *Program availability:* Part-time. *Students:* 19 full-time (11 women), 51 part-time (30 women); includes 47 minority (12 Black or African American, non-Hispanic/Latino; 2 American Indian or Alaska Native, non-Hispanic/Latino; 12 Asian, non-Hispanic/Latino; 21 Hispanic/Latino). Average age 39. In 2017, 43 master's awarded. *Application deadline:* Applications are processed on a rolling basis. Application fee: $50. *Expenses:* Contact institution. *Financial support:* Application deadline: 3/2; applicants required to submit FAFSA. *Unit head:* Alison Rodriguez-Balles, Interim Campus Director, 714-505-6943, Fax: 909-505-6937, E-mail: arodriguez2@laverne.edu. *Application contact:* 877-468-6858, E-mail: gradadmission@laverne.edu.
Website: https://laverne.edu/locations/

University of Louisville, Graduate School, College of Business, MBA Programs, Louisville, KY 40292-0001. Offers entrepreneurship (MBA); global business (MBA); health sector management (MBA). *Accreditation:* AACSB. *Program availability:* Part-time, evening/weekend. *Students:* 253 full-time (99 women), 21 part-time (6 women); includes 49 minority (25 Black or African American, non-Hispanic/Latino; 1 American Indian or Alaska Native, non-Hispanic/Latino; 10 Asian, non-Hispanic/Latino; 8 Hispanic/Latino; 5 Two or more races, non-Hispanic/Latino), 27 international. Average age 32. 295 applicants, 63% accepted, 155 enrolled. In 2017, 85 master's awarded. *Degree requirements:* For master's, international learning experience. *Entrance requirements:* For master's, GMAT, 2 letters of reference, personal interview, resume, personal statement, college transcript(s). Additional exam requirements/recommendations for international students: Required—TOEFL (minimum score 83 iBT). *Application deadline:* For fall admission, 7/1 for domestic students; for spring admission, 12/1 for domestic students. Applications are processed on a rolling basis. Application fee: $65. *Expenses:* Tuition, state resident: full-time $12,246; part-time $681 per credit hour. Tuition, nonresident: full-time $25,486; part-time $1417 per credit hour. *Required fees:* $196. Tuition and fees vary according to course load, program and reciprocity agreements. *Financial support:* Fellowships with full tuition reimbursements, research assistantships with full tuition reimbursements, health care benefits, and unspecified assistantships available. Financial award application deadline: 3/31; financial award applicants required to submit FAFSA. *Faculty research:* Entrepreneurship, venture capital, retailing/franchising, corporate governance and leadership, supply chain management. *Total annual research expenditures:* $859,000. *Unit head:* Dr. Todd Mooradian, Dean, 502-852-6443, Fax: 502-852-7557, E-mail: todd.mooradian@louisville.edu. *Application contact:* Susan E. Hildebrand, Program Director, 502-852-7257, Fax: 502-852-4901, E-mail: s.hildebrand@louisville.edu.
Website: http://business.louisville.edu/mba

University of Management and Technology, Program in Health Administration, Arlington, VA 22209-1609. Offers MHA.

University of Mary, Gary Tharaldson School of Business, Bismarck, ND 58504-9652. Offers business administration (MBA); energy management (MBA, MS); executive (MBA, MS); health care (MBA, MS); human resource management (MBA); project management (MBA, MPM); virtuous leadership (MBA, MPM, MS). *Program availability:* Part-time, evening/weekend. *Entrance requirements:* For master's, minimum GPA of 2.5. Additional exam requirements/recommendations for international students: Required—TOEFL (minimum score 550 paper-based; 80 iBT). Electronic applications accepted.

University of Maryland, Baltimore County, The Graduate School, College of Arts, Humanities and Social Sciences, Department of Emergency Health Services, Baltimore, MD 21250. Offers emergency health services (MS), including administration, planning, and policy, preventive medicine and epidemiology; emergency management (Postbaccalaureate Certificate); public policy (PhD), including emergency health, emergency management. Some of the required/elective courses within the Preventative Medicine and Epidemiology track are offered in collaboration with the University of Maryland, Baltimore (UMB) and other University System Schools. *Program availability:* Part-time, evening/weekend, 100% online, blended/hybrid learning. *Faculty:* 4 full-time (2 women), 8 part-time/adjunct (3 women). *Students:* 18 full-time (11 women), 4 part-time (3 women); includes 9 minority (6 Black or African American, non-Hispanic/Latino; 1 Asian, non-Hispanic/Latino; 1 Hispanic/Latino; 1 Two or more races, non-Hispanic/Latino). Average age 28. 22 applicants, 91% accepted, 18 enrolled. In 2017, 12 master's awarded. Terminal master's awarded for partial completion of doctoral program. *Degree requirements:* For master's, comprehensive exam (for some programs), capstone project or thesis. *Entrance requirements:* For master's, GRE General Test if GPA is below 3.2, minimum GPA of 3.2. Additional exam requirements/recommendations for international students: Required—TOEFL (minimum score 80 iBT), IELTS, or PTE. *Application deadline:* For fall admission, 6/15 for domestic students, 3/1 for international students; for spring admission, 12/1 for domestic students, 10/1 for international students. Applications are processed on a rolling basis. Application fee: $50. Electronic applications accepted. *Expenses:* $753 per credit hour. *Financial support:* In 2017–18, 6 students received support, including 7 research assistantships with full tuition reimbursements available (averaging $16,875 per year); career-related internships or fieldwork, Federal Work-Study, scholarships/grants, health care benefits, and unspecified assistantships also available. Financial award application deadline: 5/30; financial award applicants required to submit FAFSA. *Faculty research:* EMS management, disaster health services, emergency management, epidemiology, risk profiles, infectious disease control, stress management for care providers, climate change and public health. *Total annual research expenditures:* $715,419. *Unit head:* Dr. J. Lee Jenkins, Department Chair, 410-455-3216, Fax: 410-455-3045, E-mail: jleejenkins@umbc.edu. *Application contact:* Dr. Rick Bissell, Program Director, 410-455-3776, Fax: 410-455-3045, E-mail: bissell@umbc.edu.
Website: http://ehs.umbc.edu/

University of Maryland, Baltimore County, The Graduate School, College of Arts, Humanities and Social Sciences, School of Public Policy, Baltimore, MD 21250. Offers public policy (MPP, PhD), including economics (PhD), educational policy, emergency services (PhD), environmental policy (MPP), evaluation and analytical methods, health policy, policy history (PhD), public management, urban policy. *Program availability:* Part-time, evening/weekend. *Faculty:* 10 full-time (5 women). *Students:* 50 full-time (24 women), 69 part-time (37 women); includes 35 minority (17 Black or African American, non-Hispanic/Latino; 1 American Indian or Alaska Native, non-Hispanic/Latino; 8 Asian, non-Hispanic/Latino; 5 Hispanic/Latino; 1 Native Hawaiian or other Pacific Islander, non-Hispanic/Latino; 3 Two or more races, non-Hispanic/Latino), 6 international. Average age 37. 60 applicants, 68% accepted, 25 enrolled. In 2017, 15 master's, 3 doctorates awarded. Terminal master's awarded for partial completion of doctoral program. *Degree requirements:* For master's, thesis, policy analysis paper, internship for pre-service; for doctorate, comprehensive exam, thesis/dissertation, comprehensive and field qualifying exams. *Entrance requirements:* For master's, GRE General Test, 3 academic letters of reference, resume, official transcripts; for doctorate, GRE General Test, 3 academic letters of reference, resume, research paper, official transcripts. Additional exam requirements/recommendations for international students: Required—TOEFL (minimum score 550 paper-based; 80 iBT), IELTS (minimum score 6.5). *Application deadline:* For fall admission, 1/15 priority date for domestic students, 1/1 priority date for international students; for spring admission, 11/1 priority date for domestic students, 5/1 priority date for international students. Applications are processed on a rolling basis. Application fee: $50. Electronic applications accepted. *Expenses:* $28,061 in-state, $39,356 out-of-state to complete the degree (for MPP); $43,823 in-state, $61,508 out-of-state to complete the degree (for PhD). *Financial support:* In 2017–18, 26 students received support, including 26 research assistantships with full tuition reimbursements available (averaging $20,000 per year); Federal Work-Study, scholarships/grants, health care benefits, and unspecified assistantships also available. Financial award application deadline: 1/1; financial award applicants required to submit FAFSA. *Faculty research:* Education policy, health policy, urban and environmental policy, public management, evaluation and analytical method. *Unit head:* Dr. Susan Sterett, Director, 410-455-2140, Fax: 410-455-1172, E-mail: ssterett@umbc.edu. *Application contact:* Sally F. Helms, Administrator of Academic Affairs, 410-455-3202, Fax: 410-455-1172, E-mail: gradpubpol@umbc.edu.
Website: http://publicpolicy.umbc.edu/

University of Maryland, Baltimore County, The Graduate School, Erickson School of Aging Studies, Baltimore, MD 21228. Offers management of aging services (MA). *Program availability:* Part-time. *Faculty:* 4 full-time (1 woman), 7 part-time/adjunct (1 woman). *Students:* 18 full-time (11 women); includes 9 minority (8 Black or African American, non-Hispanic/Latino; 1 Hispanic/Latino). Average age 30. 23 applicants, 91% accepted, 18 enrolled. In 2017, 13 master's awarded. *Entrance requirements:* For master's, essays. *Application deadline:* For fall admission, 6/1 for domestic students; for spring admission, 12/1 for domestic students. Applications are processed on a rolling basis. Application fee: $50. Electronic applications accepted. *Expenses:* Contact institution. *Financial support:* In 2017–18, 15 students received support, including 1 teaching assistantship with full tuition reimbursement available (averaging $21,600 per year). Financial award applicants required to submit FAFSA. *Faculty research:* Policy implications of entitlement programs, demographic impact of aging population, person-centered care for dementia, changing culture in long-term care. *Unit head:* Bill Holman, Graduate Program Director, 443-543-5603, E-mail: holman1@umbc.edu. *Application contact:* Michelle Howell, Administrative Assistant, 443-543-5607, E-mail: mhowell@umbc.edu.
Website: http://www.umbc.edu/erickson/

University of Maryland, College Park, Academic Affairs, School of Public Health, Department of Health Services Administration, College Park, MD 20742. Offers MHA, PhD.

University of Maryland University College, The Graduate School, Program in Health Care Administration, Adelphi, MD 20783. Offers MS. *Program availability:* Part-time, evening/weekend, online learning. *Students:* 4 full-time (all women), 730 part-time (584 women); includes 460 minority (336 Black or African American, non-Hispanic/Latino; 2 American Indian or Alaska Native, non-Hispanic/Latino; 46 Asian, non-Hispanic/Latino; 46 Hispanic/Latino; 2 Native Hawaiian or other Pacific Islander, non-Hispanic/Latino; 28 Two or more races, non-Hispanic/Latino), 18 international. Average age 35. 196

applicants, 100% accepted, 143 enrolled. In 2017, 182 master's awarded. *Degree requirements:* For master's, thesis or alternative. *Application deadline:* Applications are processed on a rolling basis. Application fee: $50. Electronic applications accepted. *Financial support:* Federal Work-Study and scholarships/grants available. Support available to part-time students. Financial award application deadline: 6/1; financial award applicants required to submit FAFSA. *Application contact:* Coordinator, Graduate Admissions, 800-888-8682, Fax: 240-684-2151, E-mail: newgrad@umuc.edu.
Website: http://www.umuc.edu/academic-programs/masters-degrees/health-care-administration.cfm

University of Massachusetts Amherst, Graduate School, Isenberg School of Management, Program in Management, Amherst, MA 01003. Offers accounting (PhD); business administration (MBA); entrepreneurship (MBA); finance (MBA, PhD); healthcare administration (MBA); hospitality and tourism management (PhD); management science (PhD); marketing (MBA, PhD); organization studies (PhD); sport management (PhD); strategic management (PhD); MBA/MS. *Accreditation:* AACSB. *Program availability:* Part-time, evening/weekend, online learning. Terminal master's awarded for partial completion of doctoral program. *Degree requirements:* For doctorate, comprehensive exam, thesis/dissertation. *Entrance requirements:* For master's and doctorate, GMAT or GRE General Test. Additional exam requirements/recommendations for international students: Required—TOEFL (minimum score 550 paper-based; 80 iBT), IELTS (minimum score 6.5). Electronic applications accepted.

University of Massachusetts Amherst, Graduate School, School of Public Health and Health Sciences, Department of Public Health, Amherst, MA 01003. Offers biostatistics (MPH, MS, PhD); community health education (MPH, MS, PhD); environmental health sciences (MPH, MS, PhD); epidemiology (MPH, MS, PhD); health policy and management (MPH, MS, PhD); nutrition (MPH, PhD); public health practice (MPH); MPH/MPPA. *Program availability:* Part-time, evening/weekend, online learning. Terminal master's awarded for partial completion of doctoral program. *Degree requirements:* For master's, thesis (for some programs); for doctorate, comprehensive exam, thesis/dissertation. *Entrance requirements:* For master's and doctorate, GRE General Test. Additional exam requirements/recommendations for international students: Required—TOEFL (minimum score 550 paper-based; 80 iBT), IELTS (minimum score 6.5). Electronic applications accepted.

University of Massachusetts Dartmouth, Graduate School, Charlton College of Business, Department of Decision and Information Sciences, North Dartmouth, MA 02747-2300. Offers healthcare management (MS); technology management (MS). *Program availability:* Part-time, 100% online, blended/hybrid learning. *Faculty:* 13 full-time (4 women), 4 part-time/adjunct (1 woman). *Students:* 25 full-time (16 women), 26 part-time (16 women); includes 8 minority (3 Black or African American, non-Hispanic/Latino; 2 Asian, non-Hispanic/Latino; 2 Hispanic/Latino; 1 Two or more races, non-Hispanic/Latino), 22 international. Average age 33. 39 applicants, 79% accepted, 21 enrolled. In 2017, 14 master's awarded. *Degree requirements:* For master's, thesis (for some programs), thesis or project (for healthcare management). *Entrance requirements:* For master's, GMAT (or waiver), statement of purpose (minimum 300 words), resume, official transcripts, 2 letters of recommendation. Additional exam requirements/recommendations for international students: Required—TOEFL (minimum score 533 paper-based; 72 iBT), IELTS (minimum score 6). *Application deadline:* For fall admission, 8/1 priority date for domestic students, 7/1 priority date for international students; for spring admission, 11/15 priority date for domestic students, 10/15 priority date for international students. Application fee: $60. Electronic applications accepted. *Expenses:* Tuition, state resident: full-time $15,449; part-time $643.71 per credit. Tuition, nonresident: full-time $27,880; part-time $1161.67 per credit. *Required fees:* $405; $25.88 per credit. Tuition and fees vary according to course load and reciprocity agreements. *Financial support:* Research assistantships, teaching assistantships, tuition waivers, and unspecified assistantships available. Support available to part-time students. Financial award application deadline: 3/1; financial award applicants required to submit FAFSA. *Faculty research:* Project team work processes in project management, technology-mediated learning, the use of IT in organizations, delivery and management of Web-based learning and teaching technologies, end-user training. *Unit head:* Melissa Pacheco, Assistant Dean of Graduate Programs, 508-999-8543, Fax: 508-999-8646, E-mail: mpacheco@umassd.edu. *Application contact:* Steven Briggs, Director of Marketing and Recruitment for Graduate Studies, 508-999-8604, Fax: 508-999-8183, E-mail: graduate@umassd.edu.
Website: http://www.umassd.edu/charlton/programs/graduate

University of Memphis, Graduate School, School of Public Health, Memphis, TN 38152. Offers biostatistics (MPH); environmental health (MPH); epidemiology (MPH, PhD); health systems and policy (PhD); health systems management (MPH); public health (MHA); social and behavioral sciences (MPH, PhD). *Program availability:* Part-time, evening/weekend. *Faculty:* 20 full-time (7 women), 4 part-time/adjunct (1 woman). *Students:* 111 full-time (76 women), 59 part-time (45 women); includes 77 minority (48 Black or African American, non-Hispanic/Latino; 18 Asian, non-Hispanic/Latino; 6 Hispanic/Latino; 5 Two or more races, non-Hispanic/Latino), 23 international. Average age 31. 100 applicants, 91% accepted, 60 enrolled. In 2017, 56 master's, 4 doctorates awarded. *Degree requirements:* For master's, comprehensive exam, thesis (for some programs), practicum/field experience; for doctorate, comprehensive exam, thesis/dissertation, residency. *Entrance requirements:* For master's, GRE or GMAT, letters of recommendation; letter of intent; for doctorate, GRE, letters of recommendation; personal statement. Additional exam requirements/recommendations for international students: Required—TOEFL (minimum score 550 paper-based; 79 iBT). *Application deadline:* For fall admission, 4/1 for domestic students; for spring admission, 11/1 for domestic students. Application fee: $35 ($60 for international students). Electronic applications accepted. *Expenses:* Contact institution. *Financial support:* In 2017–18, 46 students received support, including 8 research assistantships with full tuition reimbursements available (averaging $8,950 per year); Federal Work-Study, scholarships/grants, and unspecified assistantships also available. Financial award application deadline: 2/1; financial award applicants required to submit FAFSA. *Faculty research:* Health and medical savings accounts, adoption rates, health informatics, Telehealth technologies, biostatistics, environmental health, epidemiology, health systems management, social and behavioral sciences. *Unit head:* Dr. Lisa M. Klesges, Dean, 901-678-4501, E-mail: lmklsges@memphis.edu. *Application contact:* Dr. Marian Levy, Assistant Dean, 901-678-4514, Fax: 901-678-5023, E-mail: sph-admin@memphis.edu.
Website: http://www.memphis.edu/sph/

University of Michigan, School of Public Health, Department of Health Management and Policy, Ann Arbor, MI 48109. Offers health management and policy (MHSA, MPH); health services organization and policy (PhD); JD/MHSA; MD/MPH; MHSA/MBA; MHSA/MPP; MHSA/MSIOE; MPH/JD; MPH/MBA; MPH/MPP. PhD and MS offered through the Rackham Graduate School. *Accreditation:* CAHME (one or more programs are accredited). *Program availability:* Evening/weekend. *Degree requirements:* For doctorate, thesis/dissertation, oral defense of dissertation, preliminary exam. *Entrance requirements:* For master's, GMAT, GRE General Test; for doctorate, GRE General Test. Additional exam requirements/recommendations for international students: Required—TOEFL (minimum score 600 paper-based; 100 iBT). Electronic applications accepted. *Expenses:* Tuition, state resident: full-time $22,368; part-time $1201 per credit hour. Tuition, nonresident: full-time $45,156; part-time $2467 per credit hour. *Required fees:* $376 per term. Tuition and fees vary according to course load, degree level and program. *Faculty research:* Health insurance, long-term care and aging, tobacco policy, health information technology, understanding organization.

University of Michigan–Flint, Graduate Programs, Program in Public Administration, Flint, MI 48502-1950. Offers administration of non-profit agencies (MPA); criminal justice administration (MPA); educational administration (MPA); general public administration (MPA); healthcare administration (MPA). *Program availability:* Part-time. *Faculty:* 1 full-time (0 women), 2 part-time/adjunct (both women). *Students:* 13 full-time (6 women), 88 part-time (59 women); includes 38 minority (29 Black or African American, non-Hispanic/Latino; 3 American Indian or Alaska Native, non-Hispanic/Latino; 2 Asian, non-Hispanic/Latino; 4 Two or more races, non-Hispanic/Latino), 3 international. Average age 37. 63 applicants, 81% accepted, 37 enrolled. In 2017, 55 master's awarded. *Degree requirements:* For master's, thesis or alternative, internship. *Entrance requirements:* For master's, bachelor's degree from regionally-accredited institution, minimum overall undergraduate GPA of 3.0. Additional exam requirements/recommendations for international students: Required—TOEFL (minimum score 84 iBT), IELTS (minimum score 6.5). *Application deadline:* For fall admission, 8/1 for domestic students, 5/1 for international students; for winter admission, 11/15 for domestic students, 9/1 for international students; for spring admission, 3/15 for domestic students, 1/1 for international students; for summer admission, 5/15 for domestic students. Applications are processed on a rolling basis. Application fee: $55. Electronic applications accepted. *Expenses:* Contact institution. *Financial support:* Career-related internships or fieldwork, Federal Work-Study, and scholarships/grants available. Support available to part-time students. Financial award application deadline: 3/1; financial award applicants required to submit FAFSA. *Unit head:* Dr. Kathryn Schellenberg, Director, 810-762-3340, E-mail: kathsch@umflint.edu. *Application contact:* Bradley T. Maki, Director of Graduate Admissions, 810-762-3171, Fax: 810-766-6789, E-mail: bmaki@umflint.edu.
Website: http://www.umflint.edu/graduateprograms/public-administration-mpa

University of Michigan–Flint, School of Health Professions and Studies, Program in Public Health, Flint, MI 48502-1950. Offers health administration (MPH); health education (MPH). *Program availability:* Part-time. *Faculty:* 16 full-time (11 women), 36 part-time/adjunct (19 women). *Students:* 14 full-time (11 women), 37 part-time (32 women); includes 15 minority (9 Black or African American, non-Hispanic/Latino; 2 American Indian or Alaska Native, non-Hispanic/Latino; 2 Asian, non-Hispanic/Latino; 2 Two or more races, non-Hispanic/Latino), 7 international. Average age 31. 38 applicants, 50% accepted, 9 enrolled. In 2017, 18 master's awarded. *Degree requirements:* For master's, thesis, public health capstone. *Entrance requirements:* For master's, GRE, bachelor's degree from accredited institution with sufficient preparation in algebra to succeed in epidemiology and biostatistics; minimum overall undergraduate GPA of 3.0. Additional exam requirements/recommendations for international students: Required—TOEFL (minimum score 84 iBT), IELTS (minimum score 6.5). *Application deadline:* For fall admission, 8/1 for domestic students, 5/1 for international students; for winter admission, 11/15 for domestic students, 9/1 for international students; for spring admission, 3/15 for domestic students, 1/1 for international students. Applications are processed on a rolling basis. Application fee: $55. Electronic applications accepted. *Expenses:* Contact institution. *Financial support:* Federal Work-Study, institutionally sponsored loans, scholarships/grants, and unspecified assistantships available. Support available to part-time students. Financial award application deadline: 3/1; financial award applicants required to submit FAFSA. *Unit head:* Dr. Shan Parker, Director, 810-762-3172, E-mail: shanpark@umflint.edu. *Application contact:* Bradley T. Maki, Director of Graduate Admissions, 810-762-3171, Fax: 810-766-6789, E-mail: bmaki@umflint.edu.
Website: http://www.umflint.edu/graduateprograms/public-health-mph

University of Michigan–Flint, School of Management, Program in Business Administration, Flint, MI 48502-1950. Offers accounting (MBA); computer information systems (MBA); finance (MBA, Post-Master's Certificate); general business (Graduate Certificate); general business administration (MBA); health care management (MBA); international business (MBA, Post-Master's Certificate); lean manufacturing (MBA); marketing (Post-Master's Certificate); marketing and innovation management (MBA); organizational leadership (MBA). *Program availability:* Part-time, evening/weekend, mixed mode format. *Faculty:* 32 full-time (5 women), 8 part-time/adjunct (2 women). *Students:* 12 full-time (7 women), 147 part-time (51 women); includes 31 minority (15 Black or African American, non-Hispanic/Latino; 1 American Indian or Alaska Native, non-Hispanic/Latino; 9 Asian, non-Hispanic/Latino; 5 Hispanic/Latino; 1 Two or more races, non-Hispanic/Latino), 18 international. Average age 34. 110 applicants, 52% accepted, 29 enrolled. In 2017, 59 master's, 6 other advanced degrees awarded. *Entrance requirements:* For master's, GMAT or GRE, bachelor's degree in arts, sciences, engineering, or business administration from regionally-accredited college or university with minimum GPA of 3.0; for other advanced degree, bachelor's degree in arts, sciences, engineering, or business administration from regionally-accredited college or university with minimum GPA of 3.0, college-level math, statistics, or quantitative course (for Graduate Certificate); MBA or equivalent degree from regionally-accredited college or university (for Post Master's Certificate). Additional exam requirements/recommendations for international students: Required—TOEFL (minimum score 84 iBT), IELTS (minimum score 6.5). *Application deadline:* For fall admission, 8/1 for domestic students, 5/1 for international students; for winter admission, 11/15 for domestic students, 9/1 for international students; for spring admission, 3/15 for domestic students, 1/1 for international students; for summer admission, 5/15 for domestic students. Applications are processed on a rolling basis. Application fee: $55. Electronic applications accepted. *Expenses:* Contact institution. *Financial support:* Federal Work-Study, scholarships/grants, and unspecified assistantships available. Support available to part-time students. Financial award application deadline: 3/1; financial award applicants required to submit FAFSA. *Unit head:* Dr. Scott Johnson, Dean, School of Management, 810-762-3164, Fax: 810-237-6685, E-mail: scotjohn@umflint.edu. *Application contact:* Bradley T. Maki, Director of Graduate Admissions, 810-762-3171, E-mail: bmaki@umflint.edu.
Website: http://www.umflint.edu/graduateprograms/business-administration-mba

University of Minnesota, Twin Cities Campus, Carlson School of Management, Carlson Full-Time MBA Program, Minneapolis, MN 55455. Offers finance (MBA); information technology (MBA); management (MBA); marketing (MBA); medical industry orientation (MBA); supply chain and operations (MBA); JD/MBA; MBA/MPP; MBA/MSBA; MD/MBA; MHA/MBA; Pharm D/MBA. *Accreditation:* AACSB. *Faculty:* 143 full-time (42 women), 24 part-time/adjunct (6 women). *Students:* 200 full-time (63 women); includes 25 minority (4 Black or African American, non-Hispanic/Latino; 13 Asian, non-Hispanic/Latino; 5 Hispanic/Latino; 3 Two or more races, non-Hispanic/Latino), 41 international. Average age 29. 606 applicants, 45% accepted, 104 enrolled. In 2017, 85 master's awarded. *Entrance requirements:* For master's, GMAT or GRE. Additional exam requirements/recommendations for international students: Required—TOEFL (minimum score 580 paper-based; 84 iBT), IELTS (minimum score 7), PTE. *Application deadline:* For fall admission, 4/1 for domestic students, 2/1 for international students. Application fee: $75. Electronic applications accepted. *Expenses:* $19,104 per semester resident tuition, $24,468 per semester non-resident tuition; $1,138 per semester fees;

$1,050 per semester student health plan; $179 per semester (for international students). *Financial support:* In 2017–18, 147 students received support, including 147 fellowships with tuition reimbursements available (averaging $23,479 per year); research assistantships with partial tuition reimbursements available, teaching assistantships with partial tuition reimbursements available, career-related internships or fieldwork, Federal Work-Study, institutionally sponsored loans, scholarships/grants, health care benefits, and unspecified assistantships also available. Financial award application deadline: 4/1; financial award applicants required to submit FAFSA. *Faculty research:* Market regulation and asset pricing, social networks and data analytics, consumer behavior, innovation and entrepreneurship, workplace wellbeing and labor relationships. *Total annual research expenditures:* $577,440. *Unit head:* Philip J. Miller, Assistant Dean, MBA and MS Programs, 612-625-5555, Fax: 612-625-1012, E-mail: mba@umn.edu. *Application contact:* Linh Gilles, Director of Admissions and Recruiting, 612-625-5555, Fax: 612-625-1012, E-mail: ftmba@umn.edu.
Website: http://www.csom.umn.edu/MBA/full-time/

University of Minnesota, Twin Cities Campus, Carlson School of Management, Carlson Part-Time MBA Program, Minneapolis, MN 55455. Offers finance (MBA); information technology (MBA); management (MBA); marketing (MBA); medical industry orientation (MBA); supply chain and operations (MBA). *Program availability:* Part-time-only, evening/weekend, 100% online, blended/hybrid learning. *Faculty:* 143 full-time (42 women), 26 part-time/adjunct (6 women). *Students:* 919 part-time (291 women); includes 120 minority (14 Black or African American, non-Hispanic/Latino; 2 American Indian or Alaska Native, non-Hispanic/Latino; 55 Asian, non-Hispanic/Latino; 26 Hispanic/Latino; 1 Native Hawaiian or other Pacific Islander, non-Hispanic/Latino; 22 Two or more races, non-Hispanic/Latino), 57 international. Average age 28. 226 applicants, 85% accepted, 167 enrolled. In 2017, 289 master's awarded. *Entrance requirements:* For master's, GMAT or GRE. Additional exam requirements/recommendations for international students: Required—TOEFL (minimum score 580 paper-based; 84 iBT), IELTS (minimum score 7), PTE. *Application deadline:* For fall admission, 5/15 priority date for domestic and international students; for spring admission, 10/15 priority date for domestic and international students. Applications are processed on a rolling basis. Application fee: $75. Electronic applications accepted. *Expenses:* $1,375 per credit tuition, $314 per semester fees. *Financial support:* Applicants required to submit FAFSA. *Faculty research:* Market regulation and asset pricing, social networks and data analytics, consumer behavior, innovation and entrepreneurship, workplace wellbeing and labor relationships. *Total annual research expenditures:* $577,440. *Unit head:* Philip J. Miller, Assistant Dean, MBA and MS Programs, 612-624-2039, Fax: 612-625-1012, E-mail: mba@umn.edu. *Application contact:* Linh Gilles, Director of Admissions and Recruiting, 612-625-5555, Fax: 612-625-1012, E-mail: ptmba@umn.edu.
Website: http://www.carlsonschool.umn.edu/ptmba

University of Minnesota, Twin Cities Campus, School of Public Health, Major in Health Services Research, Policy, and Administration, Minneapolis, MN 55455-0213. Offers MS, PhD, JD/MS, JD/PhD, MD/PhD, MPP/MS. *Program availability:* Part-time. Terminal master's awarded for partial completion of doctoral program. *Degree requirements:* For master's, thesis, internship, final oral exam; for doctorate, thesis/dissertation, teaching experience, written preliminary exam, final oral exam, dissertation. *Entrance requirements:* For master's, GRE General Test, course work in mathematics; for doctorate, GRE General Test, prerequisite courses in calculus and statistics. Additional exam requirements/recommendations for international students: Required—TOEFL (minimum score 600 paper-based; 100 iBT). *Faculty research:* Outcomes, economics and statistics, sociology, health care management.

University of Minnesota, Twin Cities Campus, School of Public Health, Major in Public Health Administration and Policy, Minneapolis, MN 55455-0213. Offers MPH, MPH/JD, MPH/MSN. *Program availability:* Part-time. *Degree requirements:* For master's, thesis, field experience. *Entrance requirements:* For master's, GRE General Test. Additional exam requirements/recommendations for international students: Required—TOEFL. Electronic applications accepted. *Faculty research:* Community health service organizations, nursing services, dental services, the elderly, insurance coverage.

University of Minnesota, Twin Cities Campus, School of Public Health, Program in Healthcare Administration, Minneapolis, MN 55455-0213. Offers MHA. *Accreditation:* AACSB; CAHME. *Program availability:* Part-time, evening/weekend, online learning. *Degree requirements:* For master's, thesis, project. *Entrance requirements:* For master's, GMAT or GRE General Test, minimum GPA of 3.0. Additional exam requirements/recommendations for international students: Required—TOEFL (minimum score 600 paper-based; 100 iBT). Electronic applications accepted. *Expenses:* Contact institution. *Faculty research:* Managed care, physician payment, structure and performance of healthcare systems, long-term care.

University of Missouri, School of Medicine and Office of Research and Graduate Studies, Graduate Programs in Medicine, Columbia, MO 65211. Offers family and community medicine (MS); health administration (MS); medical pharmacology and physiology (MS, PhD); molecular microbiology and immunology (MS, PhD); pathology and anatomical sciences (MS, PhD). *Program availability:* Part-time. *Degree requirements:* For doctorate, thesis/dissertation. *Entrance requirements:* For master's and doctorate, GRE General Test, minimum GPA of 3.0. Additional exam requirements/recommendations for international students: Required—TOEFL. *Application deadline:* Applications are processed on a rolling basis. *Expenses:* Contact institution. *Financial support:* Fellowships, research assistantships, teaching assistantships, career-related internships or fieldwork, and institutionally sponsored loans available.
Website: http://som.missouri.edu/departments.shtml

University of Nebraska Medical Center, Department of Health Services Research and Administration, Omaha, NE 68198-4350. Offers health administration (MHA); health services research, administration, and policy (PhD); public health administration and policy (MPH). *Program availability:* Part-time, 100% online, blended/hybrid learning. *Faculty:* 7 full-time (4 women), 2 part-time/adjunct (0 women). *Students:* 9 full-time (7 women), 1 part-time (0 women); includes 2 minority (both Asian, non-Hispanic/Latino), 6 international. Average age 31. 11 applicants, 55% accepted, 3 enrolled. In 2017, 5 doctorates awarded. *Degree requirements:* For doctorate, comprehensive exam, thesis/dissertation. *Entrance requirements:* For doctorate, GRE, official transcripts, resume or curriculum vitae, three letters of recommendation, statement of intent. Additional exam requirements/recommendations for international students: Required—TOEFL (minimum score 550 paper-based; 80 iBT), IELTS (minimum score 6.5). *Application deadline:* For fall admission, 6/1 for domestic students, 4/1 for international students. Application fee: $60. Electronic applications accepted. *Expenses:* Contact institution. *Financial support:* In 2017–18, 5 students received support. Federal Work-Study, scholarships/grants, and unspecified assistantships available. Financial award application deadline: 2/15; financial award applicants required to submit FAFSA. *Faculty research:* Health services research, health policy. *Unit head:* Dr. Fernando Wilson, Associate Professor, 402-552-6948, E-mail: fernando.wilson@unmc.edu. *Application contact:* Denise Howard, Coordinator, 402-559-5260, E-mail: denise.howard@unmc.edu.
Website: http://www.unmc.edu/publichealth/departments/healthservices/

University of Nevada, Las Vegas, Graduate College, School of Community Health Sciences, Department of Health Care Administration and Policy, Las Vegas, NV 89154-3023. Offers health care administration (Exec MHA, MHA). *Program availability:* Part-time, 100% online, blended/hybrid learning. *Faculty:* 7 full-time (2 women), 5 part-time/adjunct (4 women). *Students:* 35 full-time (24 women), 16 part-time (9 women); includes 22 minority (5 Black or African American, non-Hispanic/Latino; 6 Asian, non-Hispanic/Latino; 7 Hispanic/Latino; 4 Two or more races, non-Hispanic/Latino), 5 international. Average age 33. 29 applicants, 90% accepted, 16 enrolled. In 2017, 11 master's awarded. *Degree requirements:* For master's, thesis (for some programs), capstone course. *Entrance requirements:* For master's, GRE General Test or GMAT, bachelor's degree with minimum GPA 3.0; personal essay; 3 letters of recommendation. Additional exam requirements/recommendations for international students: Required—TOEFL (minimum score 550 paper-based; 80 iBT), IELTS (minimum score 7). *Application deadline:* For fall admission, 4/1 for domestic students; for spring admission, 12/1 for domestic students. Application fee: $60 ($95 for international students). Electronic applications accepted. *Expenses:* $275 per credit, $850 per course, $7,969 per year resident, $22,157 per year non-resident, $7,094 non-resident fee (7 credits or more), $1,307 annual health insurance fee. *Financial support:* In 2017–18, 7 students received support, including 7 research assistantships with partial tuition reimbursements available (averaging $11,636 per year); institutionally sponsored loans, scholarships/grants, health care benefits, and unspecified assistantships also available. Financial award application deadline: 3/15; financial award applicants required to submit FAFSA. *Faculty research:* Effects of the EHR on healthcare outcome, quality and financial performance; patient satisfactions on hospital services; mediation errors, medical home performance, ER use among patients with mental illness. *Unit head:* Dr. Chris Cochran, Chair, 702-895-1400, Fax: 702-895-5573, E-mail: chris.cochran@unlv.edu. *Application contact:* Dr. Jennifer Bonilla, Graduate Coordinator, 702-895-5410, E-mail: jennifer.bonilla@unlv.edu.
Website: http://hca.unlv.edu

University of New England, College of Graduate and Professional Studies, Portland, ME 04005-9526. Offers advanced educational leadership (CAGS); applied nutrition (MS); career and technical education (MS Ed); curriculum and instruction (MS Ed); education (CAGS, Post-Master's Certificate); educational leadership (MS Ed, Ed D); generalist (MS Ed); health informatics (MS, Graduate Certificate); inclusion education (MS Ed); literacy K-12 (MS Ed); medical education leadership (MMEL); public health (MPH); public health (Graduate Certificate); reading specialist (MS Ed); social work (MSW). *Program availability:* Part-time, evening/weekend, online only, 100% online. *Faculty:* 125 part-time/adjunct (94 women). *Students:* 1,403 full-time (1,128 women), 594 part-time (475 women); includes 474 minority (332 Black or African American, non-Hispanic/Latino; 13 American Indian or Alaska Native, non-Hispanic/Latino; 83 Asian, non-Hispanic/Latino; 27 Hispanic/Latino; 11 Native Hawaiian or other Pacific Islander, non-Hispanic/Latino; 8 Two or more races, non-Hispanic/Latino). Average age 35. 3,153 applicants, 41% accepted, 990 enrolled. In 2017, 307 master's, 59 doctorates, 124 other advanced degrees awarded. *Application deadline:* Applications are processed on a rolling basis. Electronic applications accepted. Tuition and fees vary according to degree level, program and student level. *Financial support:* Application deadline: 5/1; applicants required to submit FAFSA. *Unit head:* Dr. Martha Wilson, Associate Provost for Online Worldwide Learning/Dean of the College of Graduate and Professional Studies, 207-221-4985, E-mail: mwilson13@une.edu.
Website: http://online.une.edu

University of New Haven, Graduate School, College of Business, Program in Health Care Administration, West Haven, CT 06516. Offers health care administration (MS, Graduate Certificate); health care marketing (MS); health policy and finance (MS); human resource management (MS); long-term care (MS); long-term health care (Graduate Certificate); managed care (MS); medical group management (MS). *Program availability:* Part-time, evening/weekend. *Students:* 59 full-time (42 women), 78 part-time (58 women); includes 38 minority (28 Black or African American, non-Hispanic/Latino; 6 Asian, non-Hispanic/Latino; 4 Hispanic/Latino), 27 international. Average age 33. 127 applicants, 91% accepted, 53 enrolled. In 2017, 59 master's, 3 other advanced degrees awarded. *Entrance requirements:* Additional exam requirements/recommendations for international students: Required—TOEFL (minimum score 80 iBT), IELTS, PTE. *Application deadline:* Applications are processed on a rolling basis. Application fee: $50. Electronic applications accepted. Application fee is waived when completed online. *Expenses: Tuition:* Full-time $16,020; part-time $890 per credit hour. *Required fees:* $220; $90 per term. *Financial support:* Research assistantships with partial tuition reimbursements, teaching assistantships with partial tuition reimbursements, Federal Work-Study, scholarships/grants, and unspecified assistantships available. Support available to part-time students. Financial award applicants required to submit FAFSA. *Unit head:* Dr. Summer McGee, Associate Professor, 203-479-4104, E-mail: smcgee@newhaven.edu. *Application contact:* Michelle Mason, Director of Graduate Enrollment, 203-932-7067, E-mail: mmason@newhaven.edu.
Website: http://www.newhaven.edu/6848/

University of New Mexico, Graduate Studies, Health Sciences Center, Program in Public Health, Albuquerque, NM 87131-5196. Offers community health (MPH); epidemiology (MPH); health systems, services and policy (MPH). *Program availability:* Part-time, online learning. *Faculty:* 9 full-time (6 women), 1 (woman) part-time/adjunct. *Students:* 23 full-time (20 women), 20 part-time (14 women); includes 15 minority (1 Black or African American, non-Hispanic/Latino; 1 American Indian or Alaska Native, non-Hispanic/Latino; 1 Asian, non-Hispanic/Latino; 12 Hispanic/Latino), 2 international. Average age 32. 34 applicants, 53% accepted, 18 enrolled. In 2017, 13 master's awarded. *Entrance requirements:* For master's, GRE, MCAT, 2 years of experience in health field. Additional exam requirements/recommendations for international students: Required—TOEFL. *Application deadline:* For fall admission, 2/1 for domestic students. Application fee: $50. *Financial support:* Fellowships, research assistantships, and Federal Work-Study available. Financial award application deadline: 12/15; financial award applicants required to submit FAFSA. *Faculty research:* Epidemiology, rural health, environmental health, Native American health issues. *Unit head:* Dr. Kristine Tollestrup, Director, 505-272-4173, Fax: 505-272-4494, E-mail: ktollestrup@salud.unm.edu. *Application contact:* Gayle Garcia, Education Coordinator, 505-272-3982, Fax: 505-272-4494, E-mail: garciag@salud.unm.edu.
Website: http://fcm.unm.edu/

University of New Mexico, Graduate Studies, School of Public Administration, Program in Health Administration, Albuquerque, NM 87131-2039. Offers MHA. *Faculty:* 2 full-time (1 woman), 1 part-time/adjunct (0 women). *Students:* 27 full-time (16 women), 28 part-time (22 women); includes 30 minority (6 Black or African American, non-Hispanic/Latino; 6 American Indian or Alaska Native, non-Hispanic/Latino; 1 Asian, non-Hispanic/Latino; 16 Hispanic/Latino; 1 Two or more races, non-Hispanic/Latino), 3 international. Average age 36. 28 applicants, 89% accepted, 21 enrolled. In 2017, 1 master's awarded. *Entrance requirements:* For master's, baccalaureate degree from accredited college or university with minimum undergraduate GPA of 3.0 for last 60 hours or overall major; letter of intent; three letters of recommendation; resume; official transcripts. *Application deadline:* For fall admission, 4/1 for domestic students, 3/1 for international students. Application fee: $50. Electronic applications accepted. *Unit head:* Dr. Uday Desai, Director, 505-277-1092, Fax: 505-277-2529, E-mail: ucdesai@unm.edu. *Application contact:* Gene V. Henley, Associate Director and Graduate Academic Advisor, 505-277-9196, Fax: 505-277-2529, E-mail: spadvise@unm.edu.
Website: http://spa.unm.edu//mha-graduate-program/

University of New Orleans, Graduate School, College of Business Administration, Program in Health Care Management, New Orleans, LA 70148. Offers MS. *Degree requirements:* For master's, thesis optional. *Entrance requirements:* For master's, GRE or GMAT. Additional exam requirements/recommendations for international students: Required—TOEFL (minimum score 550 paper-based; 79 iBT). *Application deadline:* For fall admission, 7/1 priority date for domestic students, 6/1 for international students; for spring admission, 11/15 priority date for domestic students, 10/1 for international students. Applications are processed on a rolling basis. Application fee: $40. Electronic applications accepted. *Financial support:* Application deadline: 5/15; applicants required to submit FAFSA. *Unit head:* Dr. Walter Lane, Chairperson, 504-280-7145, Fax: 504-280-6397, E-mail: wlane@uno.edu. *Application contact:* Dr. Paul Hensel, Associate Dean, 504-280-6954, Fax: 504-280-6693, E-mail: phensel@uno.edu.

University of North Alabama, College of Business, Florence, AL 35632-0001. Offers business administration (MBA), including accounting, enterprise resource planning systems, executive, finance, health care management, information systems, international business, project management. *Accreditation:* AACSB; ACBSP. *Program availability:* Part-time, 100% online, blended/hybrid learning. *Faculty:* 26 full-time (1 woman), 4 part-time/adjunct (0 women). *Students:* 178 full-time (78 women), 498 part-time (237 women); includes 229 minority (92 Black or African American, non-Hispanic/Latino; 8 American Indian or Alaska Native, non-Hispanic/Latino; 104 Asian, non-Hispanic/Latino; 14 Hispanic/Latino; 11 Two or more races, non-Hispanic/Latino), 53 international. Average age 34. 354 applicants, 71% accepted, 190 enrolled. In 2017, 156 master's awarded. *Entrance requirements:* For master's, GMAT, GRE, minimum GPA of 2.75 in last 60 hours, 2.5 overall (on a 3.0 scale); 27 hours of course work in business and economics. Additional exam requirements/recommendations for international students: Required—TOEFL (minimum score 79 iBT), IELTS (minimum score 6), PTE (minimum score 54). *Application deadline:* Applications are processed on a rolling basis. Application fee: $50 ($100 for international students). Electronic applications accepted. *Expenses:* Tuition, state resident: full-time $7824; part-time $5943 per year. Tuition, nonresident: full-time $15,648; part-time $11,736 per year. *Required fees:* $3064; $2298 per unit. Tuition and fees vary according to course load and reciprocity agreements. *Financial support:* In 2017–18, 114 students received support. Scholarships/grants available. Financial award application deadline: 2/1; financial award applicants required to submit FAFSA. *Total annual research expenditures:* $193,193. *Unit head:* Dr. Gregory A. Carnes, Dean, 256-765-4261, Fax: 256-765-4170, E-mail: gacarnes@una.edu. *Application contact:* Hillary N. Coats, Graduate Admissions Coordinator, 256-765-4447, E-mail: graduate@una.edu.
Website: https://www.una.edu/mba/index.html

The University of North Carolina at Chapel Hill, Graduate School, Gillings School of Global Public Health, Department of Health Policy and Management, Chapel Hill, NC 27599. Offers MHA, MPH, MSPH, Dr PH, PhD, JD/MPH, MBA/MSPH, MHA/MBA, MHA/MCRP, MHA/MSIS, MHA/MSLS, MSPH/MCRP, MSPH/MSIS, MSPH/MSLS. *Accreditation:* CAHME (one or more programs are accredited). *Program availability:* Part-time, blended/hybrid learning. *Faculty:* 30 full-time (16 women), 87 part-time/adjunct (37 women). *Students:* 263 full-time (173 women), 34 part-time (17 women); includes 101 minority (42 Black or African American, non-Hispanic/Latino; 24 Asian, non-Hispanic/Latino; 19 Hispanic/Latino; 16 Two or more races, non-Hispanic/Latino), 28 international. Average age 32. 443 applicants, 43% accepted, 124 enrolled. In 2017, 103 master's, 19 doctorates awarded. *Degree requirements:* For master's, comprehensive exam, capstone course or paper; for doctorate, comprehensive exam, thesis/dissertation. *Entrance requirements:* For master's, GRE General Test or GMAT, 3 letters of recommendation (academic and/or professional), interview; for doctorate, GRE General Test, prior graduate-level degree; UNC MPH Core if not awarded master's degree from accredited school of public health; 3 letters of recommendation (academic and/or professional); interview. Additional exam requirements/recommendations for international students: Required—TOEFL, IELTS. *Application deadline:* For fall admission, 2/13 for domestic and international students. Applications are processed on a rolling basis. Application fee: $85. Electronic applications accepted. *Financial support:* Fellowships with tuition reimbursements, research assistantships with tuition reimbursements, teaching assistantships with tuition reimbursements, career-related internships or fieldwork, Federal Work-Study, institutionally sponsored loans, scholarships/grants, traineeships, health care benefits, and unspecified assistantships available. Financial award application deadline: 12/10; financial award applicants required to submit FAFSA. *Faculty research:* Organizational behavior; human resource management in healthcare; health services finance; mental health economics, service, and research; strategic planning and marketing. *Unit head:* Dr. Morris Weinberger, Chair, 919-966-7385, Fax: 919-966-3671, E-mail: mweinber@email.unc.edu. *Application contact:* Lynnette Jones, Student Services Manager, 919-966-7391, Fax: 919-843-4980, E-mail: lynnette_jones@unc.edu.
Website: https://sph.unc.edu/hpm/health-policy-and-management-home/

The University of North Carolina at Charlotte, College of Health and Human Services, Department of Public Health Sciences, Charlotte, NC 28223-0001. Offers community health (Certificate); health administration (MHA); public health (MPH); public health core concepts (Graduate Certificate); public health sciences (PhD). *Accreditation:* CAHME; CEPH. *Program availability:* Part-time. *Faculty:* 23 full-time (12 women), 3 part-time/adjunct (2 women). *Students:* 94 full-time (74 women), 17 part-time (15 women); includes 49 minority (28 Black or African American, non-Hispanic/Latino; 3 American Indian or Alaska Native, non-Hispanic/Latino; 5 Asian, non-Hispanic/Latino; 6 Hispanic/Latino; 7 Two or more races, non-Hispanic/Latino), 7 international. Average age 25. 169 applicants, 60% accepted, 51 enrolled. In 2017, 44 master's, 2 other advanced degrees awarded. *Degree requirements:* For master's, thesis (for some programs), thesis or project; internship; capstone; for doctorate, thesis/dissertation. *Entrance requirements:* For master's, GRE or MCAT (for MSPH); GRE or GMAT (for MHA), career goal statement, current resume, letters of recommendation; for doctorate, GRE, master's degree in public health or a related field with minimum GPA of 3.5 in all graduate work; statement of purpose detailing why applicant wants to pursue a PhD in public health sciences in the specified concentration at UNC Charlotte; three letters of recommendation (including at least two letters from former professors); for other advanced degree, bachelor's degree from regionally-accredited university; minimum GPA of 2.75 on all post-secondary work attempted; transcripts; personal statement outlining why the applicant seeks admission to the program. Additional exam requirements/recommendations for international students: Required—TOEFL (minimum score 523 paper-based, 70 iBT) or IELTS (6.5). *Application deadline:* For fall admission, 1/10 priority date for domestic and international students; for spring admission, 9/15 priority date for domestic and international students; for summer admission, 4/1 priority date for domestic and international students. Applications are processed on a rolling basis. Application fee: $75. Electronic applications accepted. *Expenses:* Contact institution. *Financial support:* In 2017–18, 26 students received support, including 1 fellowship (averaging $11,869 per year), 22 research assistantships (averaging $7,008 per year), 3 teaching assistantships (averaging $5,176 per year); career-related internships or fieldwork, Federal Work-Study, institutionally sponsored loans, scholarships/grants, and unspecified assistantships also available. Support available to part-time students. Financial award application deadline: 3/1; financial award applicants required to submit FAFSA. *Total annual research expenditures:* $704,999. *Unit head:* Dr. Melinda Forthofer, Chair, 704-687-5682, Fax: 704-687-1644, E-mail: forthofer@uncc.edu. *Application contact:* Kathy B. Giddings, Director of Graduate Admissions, 704-687-5503, Fax: 704-687-1668, E-mail: gradadm@uncc.edu.
Website: http://publichealth.uncc.edu/

The University of North Carolina at Pembroke, The Graduate School, Department of Political Science and Public Administration, Pembroke, NC 28372-1510. Offers criminal justice (MPA); emergency management (MPA); health administration (MPA); public management (MPA). *Program availability:* Part-time, evening/weekend, online learning. *Degree requirements:* For master's, comprehensive exam, thesis optional. *Entrance requirements:* For master's, GRE General Test or MAT, minimum GPA of 3.0 in major, 2.5 overall; interview. Additional exam requirements/recommendations for international students: Required—TOEFL. *Application deadline:* Applications are processed on a rolling basis. Application fee: $45 ($60 for international students). *Financial support:* Application deadline: 4/15; applicants required to submit FAFSA. *Unit head:* Dr. Emily Neff-Sharum, Interim Director, 910-775-4409, E-mail: emily.neffsharum@uncp.edu.

University of Northern Colorado, Graduate School, Monfort College of Business, Greeley, CO 80639. Offers accounting (MA); general business management (MBA); healthcare administration (MBA); human resources management (MBA). *Accreditation:* AACSB.

University of North Texas, Robert B. Toulouse School of Graduate Studies, Denton, TX 76203-5459. Offers accounting (MS); applied anthropology (MA, MS); applied behavior analysis (Certificate); applied geography (MA); applied technology and performance improvement (M Ed, MS); art education (MA); art history (MA); art museum education (Certificate); arts leadership (Certificate); audiology (Au D); behavior analysis (MS); behavioral science (PhD); biochemistry and molecular biology (MS); biology (MA, MS); biomedical engineering (MS); business analysis (MS); chemistry (MS); clinical health psychology (PhD); communication studies (MA, MS); computer engineering (MS); computer science (MS); counseling (M Ed, MS), including clinical mental health counseling (MS), college and university counseling, elementary school counseling, secondary school counseling; creative writing (MA); criminal justice (MS); curriculum and instruction (M Ed); decision sciences (MBA); design (MA, MFA), including fashion design (MFA), innovation studies, interior design (MFA); early childhood studies (MS); economics (MS); educational leadership (M Ed, Ed D); educational psychology (MS, PhD), including family studies (MS), gifted and talented (MS), human development (MS), learning and cognition (MS), research, measurement and evaluation (MS); electrical engineering (MS); emergency management (MPA); engineering technology (MS); English (MA); English as a second language (MA); environmental science (MS); finance (MBA, MS); financial management (MPA); French (MA); health services management (MBA); higher education (M Ed, Ed D); history (MA, MS); hospitality management (MS); human resources management (MPA); information science (MS); information systems (PhD); information technologies (MBA); interdisciplinary studies (MA, MS); international studies (MA); international sustainable tourism (MS); jazz studies (MM); journalism (MA, MJ, Graduate Certificate), including interactive and virtual digital communication (Graduate Certificate), narrative journalism (Graduate Certificate), public relations (Graduate Certificate); kinesiology (MS); linguistics (MA); local government management (MPA); logistics (PhD); logistics and supply chain management (MBA); long-term care, senior housing, and aging services (MA); management (PhD); marketing (MBA); mathematics (MA, MS); mechanical and energy engineering (MS, PhD); music (MA), including ethnomusicology, music theory, musicology, performance; music composition (PhD); music education (MM Ed, PhD); nonprofit management (MPA); operations and supply chain management (MBA); performance (MM, DMA); philosophy (MA); political science (MA); professional and technical communication (MA); radio, television and film (MA, MFA); rehabilitation counseling (Certificate); sociology (MA); Spanish (MA); special education (M Ed); speech-language pathology (MA); strategic management (MBA); studio art (MFA); teaching (M Ed); MBA/MS. *Program availability:* Part-time, evening/weekend, online learning. Terminal master's awarded for partial completion of doctoral program. *Degree requirements:* For master's, variable foreign language requirement, comprehensive exam (for some programs), thesis (for some programs); for doctorate, variable foreign language requirement, comprehensive exam (for some programs), thesis/dissertation; for other advanced degree, variable foreign language requirement, comprehensive exam (for some programs). *Entrance requirements:* For master's and doctorate, GRE, GMAT. Additional exam requirements/recommendations for international students: Required—TOEFL (minimum score 550 paper-based; 79 iBT). Electronic applications accepted.

University of North Texas Health Science Center at Fort Worth, School of Public Health, Fort Worth, TX 76107-2699. Offers biostatistics (MS); epidemiology (MPH, MS, PhD); food security and public health (Graduate Certificate); GIS in public health (Graduate Certificate); global health (Graduate Certificate); global health for medical professionals (Graduate Certificate); health administration (MHA); health behavior research (MS, PhD); maternal and child health (MPH); public health (Graduate Certificate); public health practice (MPH); DO/MPH; MS/MPH. *Accreditation:* CEPH. *Program availability:* Part-time, evening/weekend, 100% online. *Degree requirements:* For master's, thesis or alternative, supervised internship; for doctorate, thesis/dissertation, supervised internship. *Entrance requirements:* For master's, GRE General Test. Additional exam requirements/recommendations for international students: Required—TOEFL. Electronic applications accepted. *Expenses:* Contact institution.

University of Oklahoma, College of Professional and Continuing Studies, Norman, OK 73019. Offers administrative leadership (MA, Graduate Certificate), including government and military leadership (MA), organizational leadership (MA), volunteer and non-profit leadership (MA); corrections management (Graduate Certificate); criminal justice (MS); integrated studies (MA), including human and health services administration, integrated studies; museum studies (MA); prevention science (MPS); restorative justice administration (Graduate Certificate). *Program availability:* Part-time, 100% online, blended/hybrid learning. *Faculty:* 16 full-time (8 women). *Students:* 64 full-time (39 women), 558 part-time (278 women); includes 191 minority (42 Black or African American, non-Hispanic/Latino; 42 American Indian or Alaska Native, non-Hispanic/Latino; 16 Asian, non-Hispanic/Latino; 46 Hispanic/Latino; 1 Native Hawaiian or other Pacific Islander, non-Hispanic/Latino; 44 Two or more races, non-Hispanic/Latino), 4 international. Average age 35. 151 applicants, 95% accepted, 97 enrolled. In 2017, 202 master's, 11 other advanced degrees awarded. *Degree requirements:* For master's, comprehensive exam, thesis optional, 33 credit hours; project/internship (for museum studies program only); for Graduate Certificate, 12 graduate credit hours (for Graduate Certificate). *Entrance requirements:* For master's and Graduate Certificate, minimum GPA of 3.0 in last 60 undergraduate hours; statement of goals; resume. Additional exam requirements/recommendations for international students: Required—TOEFL (minimum score 79 iBT) or IELTS (minimum score 6.5). *Application deadline:* For fall admission, 7/15 for domestic and international students; for winter admission, 12/1 for domestic and international students; for spring admission, 5/1 for domestic and international students. Applications are processed on a rolling basis. Application fee: $50 ($100 for international students). Electronic applications accepted. *Expenses:* Tuition, state resident: full-time $5119; part-time $213.30 per credit hour. Tuition, nonresident: full-time $19,778; part-time $824.10 per credit hour. *Required fees:* $3458; $133.55 per credit hour. $126.50 per semester. *Financial support:* In 2017–18, 92 students received support. Career-

related internships or fieldwork, institutionally sponsored loans, scholarships/grants, health care benefits, and tuition waivers available. Support available to part-time students. Financial award application deadline: 6/1; financial award applicants required to submit FAFSA. *Faculty research:* Change management and leadership; policing and corrections management; neuro-psychology of addiction; disproportionate minority contact; ethnic identity and nationalism. *Unit head:* Dr. Martha L. Banz, Associate Provost for Continuing Education/Interim Dean, College of Professional and Continuing Studies, 405-325-4414, Fax: 405-325-7132, E-mail: mlbanz@ou.edu. *Application contact:* Lindsey Gunderson, Graduate Academic Advisor, 405-325-5827, Fax: 405-325-7132, E-mail: lindsey.gunderson@ou.edu.
Website: https://pacs.ou.edu/

University of Oklahoma Health Sciences Center, Graduate College, College of Public Health, Department of Health Administration and Policy, Oklahoma City, OK 73190. Offers MHA, MPH, MS, Dr PH, PhD, JD/MPH, MBA/MPH. MBA/MPH offered jointly with Oklahoma State University; JD/MPH with University of Oklahoma. *Accreditation:* CAHME. *Program availability:* Part-time. *Degree requirements:* For master's, comprehensive exam, thesis (for some programs); for doctorate, 2 foreign languages, comprehensive exam, thesis/dissertation. *Entrance requirements:* For master's, 3 letters of recommendation, resume; for doctorate, GRE General Test, letters of recommendation. Additional exam requirements/recommendations for international students: Required—TOEFL (minimum score 570 paper-based). *Faculty research:* Public health administration, health institutions management, public policy and the aged, injury control.

University of Ottawa, Faculty of Graduate and Postdoctoral Studies, Telfer School of Management, Health Administration Program, Ottawa, ON K1N 6N5, Canada. Offers MHA. *Program availability:* Part-time. *Degree requirements:* For master's, thesis optional, residency. *Entrance requirements:* For master's, GMAT, bachelor's degree or equivalent, minimum B average. Additional exam requirements/recommendations for international students: Recommended—TOEFL. Electronic applications accepted.

University of Pennsylvania, Wharton School, Health Care Management Department, Philadelphia, PA 19104. Offers MBA, PhD. *Degree requirements:* For doctorate, comprehensive exam, thesis/dissertation. *Entrance requirements:* For master's, GMAT; for doctorate, GMAT or GRE. Electronic applications accepted. *Faculty research:* Health economics, health policy, health care management, health insurance and financing.

University of Phoenix–Bay Area Campus, School of Business, San Jose, CA 95134-1805. Offers accountancy (MS); accounting (MBA); business administration (MBA, DBA); energy management (MBA); global management (MBA); health care management (MBA); human resource management (MBA); human resources management (MM); management (MM); marketing (MBA); organizational leadership (DM); project management (MBA); public administration (MPA); technology management (MBA). *Accreditation:* ACBSP. *Program availability:* Evening/weekend, online learning. *Degree requirements:* For master's, thesis (for some programs). *Entrance requirements:* For master's, minimum undergraduate GPA of 3.0, 3 years of work experience. Additional exam requirements/recommendations for international students: Required—TOEFL (minimum score 550 paper-based; 79 iBT). Electronic applications accepted.

University of Phoenix–Central Valley Campus, College of Nursing, Fresno, CA 93720-1552. Offers education (MHA); gerontology (MHA); health administration (MHA); nursing (MSN); MSN/MBA.

University of Phoenix–Hawaii Campus, College of Nursing, Honolulu, HI 96813-3800. Offers education (MHA); family nurse practitioner (MSN); gerontology (MHA); health administration (MHA); nursing (MSN); nursing/health care education (MSN); MSN/MBA. *Program availability:* Evening/weekend. *Degree requirements:* For master's, thesis (for some programs). *Entrance requirements:* For master's, minimum undergraduate GPA of 2.5, 3 years of work experience, RN license. Additional exam requirements/recommendations for international students: Required—TOEFL (minimum score 550 paper-based; 79 iBT). Electronic applications accepted.

University of Phoenix–Houston Campus, College of Nursing, Houston, TX 77079-2004. Offers health administration (MHA). *Program availability:* Online learning. *Degree requirements:* For master's, thesis (for some programs). *Entrance requirements:* For master's, minimum undergraduate GPA of 2.5, 3 years of work experience. Additional exam requirements/recommendations for international students: Required—TOEFL (minimum score 550 paper-based; 79 iBT). Electronic applications accepted.

University of Phoenix–Online Campus, School of Advanced Studies, Phoenix, AZ 85034-7209. Offers business administration (DBA); education (Ed S); educational leadership (Ed D), including curriculum and instruction, education technology, educational leadership; health administration (DHA); higher education administration (PhD); industrial/organizational psychology (PhD); nursing (PhD); organizational leadership (DM), including information systems and technology, organizational leadership. *Program availability:* Evening/weekend, online learning. *Degree requirements:* For doctorate, thesis/dissertation. *Entrance requirements:* Additional exam requirements/recommendations for international students: Required—TOEFL, TOEIC (Test of English as an International Communication), Berlitz Online English Proficiency Exam, PTE, or IELTS. Electronic applications accepted. *Expenses:* Contact institution.

University of Phoenix–Online Campus, School of Business, Phoenix, AZ 85034-7209. Offers accountancy (MS); accounting (MBA, Certificate); business administration (MBA); energy management (MBA); global management (MBA); health care management (MBA); human resource management (MBA, Certificate); human resources management (MM); management (MM); marketing (MBA, Certificate); project management (MBA, Certificate); public administration (MBA, MM); technology management (MBA). *Program availability:* Evening/weekend, online learning. *Entrance requirements:* Additional exam requirements/recommendations for international students: Required—TOEFL, TOEIC (Test of English as an International Communication), Berlitz Online English Proficiency Exam, PTE, or IELTS. Electronic applications accepted. *Expenses:* Contact institution.

University of Phoenix–Phoenix Campus, School of Business, Tempe, AZ 85282-2371. Offers accounting (MBA, MS, Certificate); business administration (MBA); energy management (MBA); global management (MBA); health care management (MBA); human resource management (MBA, Certificate); management (MM); marketing (MBA); project management (MBA); technology management (MBA). *Program availability:* Evening/weekend, online learning. *Entrance requirements:* Additional exam requirements/recommendations for international students: Required—TOEFL, TOEIC (Test of English as an International Communication), Berlitz Online English Proficiency Exam, PTE, or IELTS. Electronic applications accepted. *Expenses:* Contact institution.

University of Phoenix–Sacramento Valley Campus, College of Nursing, Sacramento, CA 95833-4334. Offers family nurse practitioner (MSN); health administration (MHA); health care education (MSN); nursing (MSN); MSN/MBA. *Program availability:* Evening/weekend. *Degree requirements:* For master's, thesis (for some programs). *Entrance requirements:* For master's, RN license, minimum undergraduate GPA of 2.5, 3 years work experience. Additional exam requirements/recommendations for international students: Required—TOEFL (minimum score 550 paper-based; 79 iBT). Electronic applications accepted.

University of Phoenix–San Antonio Campus, College of Nursing, San Antonio, TX 78230. Offers health administration (MHA).

University of Pikeville, Coleman College of Business, Pikeville, KY 41501. Offers business (MBA); entrepreneurship (MBA); healthcare (MBA). *Program availability:* Part-time, evening/weekend. *Faculty:* 5 part-time/adjunct (2 women). *Students:* 35 full-time (16 women), 2 part-time (both women); includes 3 minority (all Black or African American, non-Hispanic/Latino), 4 international. Average age 29. In 2017, 18 master's awarded. *Degree requirements:* For master's, comprehensive exam (for some programs). *Entrance requirements:* For master's, official transcripts, two professional letters of recommendation, three years of work experience. *Application deadline:* For fall admission, 8/15 for domestic students, 7/1 for international students. Applications are processed on a rolling basis. Application fee: $50. *Expenses:* Contact institution. *Financial support:* Tuition waivers (full) and university employee grants available. Financial award application deadline: 2/15; financial award applicants required to submit FAFSA. *Unit head:* Dr. Howard V. Roberts, Dean, 606-218-5019, Fax: 606-218-5031, E-mail: howardroberts@upike.edu. *Application contact:* Cathy Maynard, Secretary, Business and Economics, 606-218-5020, Fax: 606-218-5031, E-mail: cathymaynard@upike.edu.
Website: http://www.upike.edu/Colleges/CCOB/

University of Pittsburgh, Graduate School of Public Health, Department of Behavioral and Community Health Sciences, Pittsburgh, PA 15261. Offers applied research and leadership in behavioral and community health sciences (Dr PH); applied social and behavioral concepts in public health (MPH); community-based participatory research (Certificate); evaluation of public health programs (Certificate); global health (Certificate); health equity (Certificate); LGBT health and wellness (Certificate); maternal and child health (MPH); MID/MPH; MPH/MPA; MPH/MSW; MPH/PhD. *Accreditation:* CEPH. *Program availability:* Part-time, online learning. *Faculty:* 17 full-time (10 women), 1 (woman) part-time/adjunct. *Students:* 89 full-time (68 women), 22 part-time (17 women); includes 22 minority (12 Black or African American, non-Hispanic/Latino; 7 Hispanic/Latino; 3 Two or more races, non-Hispanic/Latino), 9 international. Average age 29. 186 applicants, 71% accepted, 33 enrolled. In 2017, 32 master's, 7 doctorates awarded. *Degree requirements:* For master's, thesis, 200-contact hour practicum, final paper; for doctorate, comprehensive exam, thesis/dissertation, preliminary exam, dissertation defense. *Entrance requirements:* For master's, GRE, bachelor's degree; for doctorate, GRE, master's degree in public health or related field; for Certificate, GRE. Additional exam requirements/recommendations for international students: Required—TOEFL (minimum score 550 paper-based, 80 iBT) or IELTS (6.5). *Application deadline:* For fall admission, 1/15 for domestic and international students; for winter admission, 9/1 for international students; for spring admission, 10/15 for domestic students, 9/1 for international students; for summer admission, 12/1 for international students. Applications are processed on a rolling basis. Application fee: $135. Electronic applications accepted. *Expenses:* $13,068 per term full-time resident, $21,696 nonresident, $425 per term fees. *Financial support:* In 2017–18, 21 students received support, including 19 fellowships with full tuition reimbursements available (averaging $14,620 per year), 8 research assistantships with full tuition reimbursements available (averaging $14,620 per year). Financial award applicants required to submit FAFSA. *Faculty research:* Health disparities, HIV/AIDS, healthy aging, violence prevention, substance abuse. *Total annual research expenditures:* $4 million. *Unit head:* Dr. Steven M. Albert, Chairman, 412-383-8693, Fax: 412-624-5510, E-mail: smalbert@pitt.edu. *Application contact:* Paul J. Markgraf, Recruitment and Academic Affairs Administrator, 412-624-3107, Fax: 412-624-5510, E-mail: pjm111@pitt.edu.
Website: http://www.bchs.pitt.edu/

University of Pittsburgh, Graduate School of Public Health, Department of Health Policy and Management, Pittsburgh, PA 15261. Offers decision sciences (MS); health policy and economics (MS); health policy and management (MHA, MPH, PhD); JD/MPH. *Accreditation:* CAHME. *Program availability:* Part-time. *Faculty:* 24 full-time (11 women). *Students:* 73 full-time (54 women), 13 part-time (9 women); includes 26 minority (7 Black or African American, non-Hispanic/Latino; 12 Asian, non-Hispanic/Latino; 4 Hispanic/Latino; 3 Two or more races, non-Hispanic/Latino), 12 international. Average age 28. 172 applicants, 72% accepted, 41 enrolled. In 2017, 27 master's, 3 doctorates awarded. Terminal master's awarded for partial completion of doctoral program. *Degree requirements:* For master's, essay, practicum, final paper; comprehensive exam (for MS); for doctorate, comprehensive exam, thesis/dissertation, preliminary exam, dissertation defense. *Entrance requirements:* For master's, GRE, GMAT, LSAT, MCAT, or PCAT, one college-level mathematics or statistics course; at least two courses in the social and behavioral sciences, preferably one in economics; bachelor's degree; recommendations; professional statement; transcripts; minimum QPA of 3.0; minimum of three credits in human biology; for doctorate, GRE, bachelor's degree, recommendations, professional statement, transcripts, college-level calculus course with minimum B grade, minimum QPA of 3.3. Additional exam requirements/recommendations for international students: Required—TOEFL (minimum score 550 paper-based, 80 iBT) or IELTS (minimum score 6.5). *Application deadline:* For fall admission, 1/15 for domestic and international students; for spring admission, 10/15 for domestic and international students. Application fee: $135. Electronic applications accepted. *Expenses:* $13,068 full-time in-state per term, $21,696 out-of-state; $425 full-time fees per term. *Financial support:* Fellowships, research assistantships, teaching assistantships, and tuition waivers available. *Faculty research:* Large database analysis, long-term quality of care, health policy analysis, health system management, health economics. *Total annual research expenditures:* $1.8 million. *Unit head:* Dr. Mark S. Roberts, Chair, 412-383-7049, Fax: 412-624-3146, E-mail: mroberts@pitt.edu. *Application contact:* Tina Micale, Department Administrator, 412-624-2821, Fax: 412-624-3146, E-mail: tina.micale@pitt.edu.
Website: http://www.publichealth.pitt.edu/hpm

University of Pittsburgh, Katz Graduate School of Business, MBA/Master of Health Administration in Health Policy and Management Program, Pittsburgh, PA 15260. Offers MBA/MHA. *Program availability:* Part-time, evening/weekend. *Faculty:* 91 full-time (30 women), 14 part-time/adjunct (4 women). *Students:* 8 full-time (6 women); includes 4 minority (2 Black or African American, non-Hispanic/Latino; 1 Asian, non-Hispanic/Latino; 1 Two or more races, non-Hispanic/Latino). Average age 25. 11 applicants, 73% accepted, 6 enrolled. *Entrance requirements:* Additional exam requirements/recommendations for international students: Required—TOEFL (minimum score 100 iBT), IELTS (minimum score 7). *Application deadline:* For fall admission, 4/1 priority date for domestic students, 2/1 priority date for international students. Application fee: $50. Electronic applications accepted. *Financial support:* Scholarships/grants available. Financial award application deadline: 6/1; financial award applicants required to submit FAFSA. *Faculty research:* Accounting systems/financial reporting, corporate finance, shopper marketing/consumer behavior, management information systems, organizational behavior and entrepreneurship. *Total annual research expenditures:* $475,077. *Unit head:* Dr. Arjang A. Assad, Dean, 412-648-1556, Fax: 412-648-1552, E-mail: aassad@katz.pitt.edu. *Application contact:* Thomas Keller, Director of MBA Admissions, 412-648-1700, Fax: 412-648-1659, E-mail: mba@katz.pitt.edu.
Website: http://www.katz.business.pitt.edu/mba/joint-and-dual/health-administration

University of Pittsburgh, School of Health and Rehabilitation Sciences, Department of Health Information Management, Pittsburgh, PA 15260. Offers health and rehabilitation sciences (MS), including health information systems, healthcare supervision and management. *Accreditation:* APTA. *Program availability:* Part-time. *Faculty:* 7 full-time (4 women). *Students:* 21 full-time (7 women), 13 part-time (7 women); includes 3 minority (2 Black or African American, non-Hispanic/Latino; 1 Asian, non-Hispanic/Latino), 14 international. Average age 28. 51 applicants, 84% accepted, 22 enrolled. In 2017, 25 master's awarded. *Degree requirements:* For master's, comprehensive exam, thesis optional. *Entrance requirements:* For master's, minimum GPA of 3.0. Additional exam requirements/recommendations for international students: Required—TOEFL (minimum score 550 paper-based; 80 iBT), IELTS (minimum score 6.5). *Application deadline:* Applications are processed on a rolling basis. Application fee: $50. Electronic applications accepted. *Financial support:* In 2017–18, 2 research assistantships with full tuition reimbursements (averaging $25,800 per year) were awarded; career-related internships or fieldwork, Federal Work-Study, scholarships/grants, traineeships, and unspecified assistantships also available. *Faculty research:* Effectiveness of technology, mobile health monitoring, independence and self-management using mHealth information and communication technology, telehealth implementation. *Total annual research expenditures:* $1.8 million. *Unit head:* Dr. Mervat Abdelhak, Chair, 412-383-6650, E-mail: abdelhak@pitt.edu. *Application contact:* Jessica Maguire, Director of Admissions, 412-383-6557, Fax: 412-383-6535, E-mail: maguire@pitt.edu.
Website: http://www.shrs.pitt.edu/him

University of Portland, Dr. Robert B. Pamplin, Jr. School of Business, Portland, OR 97203-5798. Offers entrepreneurship (MBA); finance (MBA, MS); health care management (MBA); marketing (MBA); nonprofit management (EMBA); operations and technology management (MBA, MS); sustainability (MBA). *Accreditation:* AACSB. *Program availability:* Part-time, evening/weekend. *Entrance requirements:* For master's, GMAT, minimum GPA of 3.0, resume, 2 letters of recommendation. Additional exam requirements/recommendations for international students: Required—TOEFL (minimum score 570 paper-based; 89 iBT), IELTS (minimum score 7). *Expenses:* Contact institution.

University of Puerto Rico–Medical Sciences Campus, Graduate School of Public Health, Department of Health Services Administration, Program in Health Services Administration, San Juan, PR 00936-5067. Offers MHSA. *Accreditation:* CAHME. *Program availability:* Part-time. *Degree requirements:* For master's, thesis. *Entrance requirements:* For master's, GRE, previous course work in accounting, statistics, economics, algebra, and managerial finance.

University of Regina, Faculty of Graduate Studies and Research, Johnson-Shoyama Graduate School of Public Policy, Regina, SK S4S 0A2, Canada. Offers economic analysis for public policy (Master's Certificate); health administration (MHA); health systems management (Master's Certificate); public management (MPA, Master's Certificate); public policy (MPA, MPP, PhD); public policy analysis (Master's Certificate). *Program availability:* Part-time. *Faculty:* 9 full-time (4 women), 26 part-time/adjunct (10 women). *Students:* 104 full-time (65 women), 189 part-time (123 women). 285 applicants, 52% accepted. In 2017, 30 master's awarded. *Degree requirements:* For master's, thesis (for some programs); for doctorate, thesis/dissertation. *Entrance requirements:* For doctorate, master's degree, intended research program in an area of public policy. Additional exam requirements/recommendations for international students: Required—TOEFL (minimum score 580 paper-based; 80 iBT), IELTS (minimum score 6.5), PTE (minimum score 59). *Application deadline:* For fall admission, 5/1 for domestic and international students; for winter admission, 11/1 for domestic and international students; for spring admission, 3/15 for domestic and international students. Application fee: $100. Electronic applications accepted. *Expenses:* CAD$10,626 per year (for master's degrees); CAD$8,783 per year (for PhD). *Financial support:* In 2017–18, fellowships (averaging $6,059 per year), teaching assistantships (averaging $2,562 per year) were awarded; research assistantships, career-related internships or fieldwork, and scholarships/grants also available. Financial award application deadline: 6/15. *Faculty research:* Governance and administration, public finance, public policy analysis, non-governmental organizations and alternative service delivery, micro-economics for policy analysis. *Unit head:* Dr. Kathleen McNutt, Executive Director, Main Campus, 306-585-4759, Fax: 306-585-5461, E-mail: kathy.mcnutt@uregina.ca. *Application contact:* John Bird, Manager, Main Campus, 306-585-5469, Fax: 306-585-5461, E-mail: john.bird@uregina.ca.
Website: http://www.schoolofpublicpolicy.sk.ca/

University of Rhode Island, Graduate School, College of Business, Kingston, RI 02881. Offers accounting (MS); business administration (MBA, PhD), including finance (MBA), general business (MBA), management (MBA), marketing, operations and supply chain management (PhD), supply chain management (MBA); finance (MBA, MS, PhD); general business (MBA); health care management (MBA); labor research (MS, Graduate Certificate), including labor relations and human resources; management (MBA); marketing (MBA); strategic innovation (MBA); supply chain management (MBA); textiles, fashion merchandising and design (MS, Certificate), including fashion merchandising (Certificate), master seamstress (Certificate), textiles, fashion merchandising and design (MS); MS/JD; Pharm D/MBA. *Accreditation:* AACSB. *Program availability:* Part-time, evening/weekend. *Faculty:* 61 full-time (28 women), 2 part-time/adjunct (1 woman). *Students:* 88 full-time (37 women), 180 part-time (94 women); includes 36 minority (9 Black or African American, non-Hispanic/Latino; 2 American Indian or Alaska Native, non-Hispanic/Latino; 13 Asian, non-Hispanic/Latino; 10 Hispanic/Latino; 2 Two or more races, non-Hispanic/Latino), 20 international. 205 applicants, 68% accepted, 97 enrolled. In 2017, 128 master's, 1 doctorate, 20 other advanced degrees awarded. *Entrance requirements:* Additional exam requirements/recommendations for international students: Required—TOEFL. Application fee: $65. Electronic applications accepted. *Expenses:* Tuition, state resident: full-time $12,706; part-time $786 per credit. Tuition, nonresident: full-time $25,216; part-time $1401 per credit. *Required fees:* $1598; $45 per credit. One-time fee: $30 part-time. *Financial support:* In 2017–18, 19 teaching assistantships with tuition reimbursements (averaging $14,589 per year) were awarded; research assistantships also available. Financial award applicants required to submit FAFSA. *Unit head:* Dr. Maling Ebrahimpour, Dean, 401-874-4348, Fax: 401-874-4312, E-mail: mebrahimpour@uri.edu. *Application contact:* Lisa Lancellotta, Coordinator, MBA Programs, 401-874-4241, Fax: 401-874-4312, E-mail: mba@uri.edu.
Website: https://web.uri.edu/business/

University of Rochester, School of Nursing, Rochester, NY 14642. Offers adult gerontological acute care nurse practitioner (MS); adult gerontological primary care nurse practitioner (MS); clinical nurse leader (MS); family nurse practitioner (MS); family psychiatric mental health nurse practitioner (MS); health care organization management and leadership (MS); nursing (DNP); nursing and health science (PhD); nursing education (MS); pediatric nurse practitioner (MS); pediatric nurse practitioner/neonatal nurse practitioner (MS). *Accreditation:* AACN. *Program availability:* Part-time, 100% online, blended/hybrid learning. *Faculty:* 62 full-time (51 women), 73 part-time/adjunct (63 women). *Students:* 17 full-time (12 women), 306 part-time (252 women); includes 46 minority (16 Black or African American, non-Hispanic/Latino; 1 American Indian or Alaska Native, non-Hispanic/Latino; 7 Asian, non-Hispanic/Latino; 17 Hispanic/Latino; 5 Two or more races, non-Hispanic/Latino), 3 international. Average age 34. 143 applicants, 71% accepted, 87 enrolled. In 2017, 48 master's, 8 doctorates awarded. Terminal master's awarded for partial completion of doctoral program. *Degree requirements:* For master's, comprehensive exam; for doctorate, thesis/dissertation. *Entrance requirements:* For master's, BS in nursing, minimum GPA of 3.0, course work in statistics; for doctorate, GRE General Test (for PhD), MS in nursing, minimum GPA of 3.5. Additional exam requirements/recommendations for international students: Required—TOEFL (minimum score 560 paper-based; 88 iBT) or IELTS (minimum score 6.5) recommended. *Application deadline:* For fall admission, 4/1 for domestic and international students; for spring admission, 9/1 for domestic and international students; for summer admission, 1/2 for domestic and international students. Application fee: $50. Electronic applications accepted. *Financial support:* In 2017–18, 63 students received support, including 2 fellowships with full and partial tuition reimbursements available (averaging $16,000 per year); scholarships/grants, traineeships, health care benefits, tuition waivers (full and partial), and unspecified assistantships also available. Support available to part-time students. Financial award application deadline: 6/30; financial award applicants required to submit CSS PROFILE or FAFSA. *Faculty research:* Symptom science, systems of care, innovations in health technology, promoting healthy behaviors. *Total annual research expenditures:* $2.6 million. *Unit head:* Dr. Kathy H. Rideout, Dean, 585-273-8902, Fax: 585-273-1268, E-mail: kathy_rideout@urmc.rochester.edu. *Application contact:* Elaine Andolina, Director of Admissions, 585-275-2375, Fax: 585-756-8299, E-mail: elaine_andolina@urmc.rochester.edu.
Website: http://www.son.rochester.edu

University of Rochester, Simon Business School, Full-Time Master's Program in Business Administration, Rochester, NY 14627. Offers business systems consulting (MBA); competitive and organizational strategy (MBA); computers and information systems (MBA); corporate accounting (MBA); entrepreneurship (MBA); finance (MBA); health sciences management (MBA); marketing (MBA); operations management (MBA); public accounting (MBA); strategy and organizations (MBA). *Accreditation:* AACSB. *Faculty:* 70 full-time (12 women), 23 part-time/adjunct (6 women). *Students:* 208 full-time (70 women). Average age 28. *Entrance requirements:* For master's, GMAT or GRE. *Application deadline:* For fall admission, 10/15 for domestic and international students; for winter admission, 1/5 for domestic and international students; for spring admission, 3/15 for domestic and international students; for summer admission, 5/15 for domestic and international students. Application fee: $150. *Financial support:* Fellowships, institutionally sponsored loans, scholarships/grants, and tuition waivers (full and partial) available. Financial award application deadline: 1/5; financial award applicants required to submit FAFSA. *Faculty research:* Empirical industrial organization, risk management, financial disclosure and regulation, social media, health care management. *Unit head:* Andrew Ainslie, Dean, 585-275-3316, E-mail: andrew.ainslie@simon.rochester.edu. *Application contact:* Rebekah S. Lewin, Assistant Dean of Admissions and Financial Aid, 585-275-3533, E-mail: admissions@simon.rochester.edu.
Website: http://www.simon.rochester.edu/programs/full-time-mba/index.aspx

University of Rochester, Simon Business School, Part-Time MBA Program, Rochester, NY 14627. Offers business systems consulting (MBA); competitive and organizational strategy (MBA); computers and information systems (MBA); corporate accounting (MBA); entrepreneurship (MBA); finance (MBA); health sciences management (MBA); marketing (MBA), including brand management, marketing strategy, pricing; operations management (MBA); public accounting (MBA). *Program availability:* Part-time-only, evening/weekend. *Faculty:* 70 full-time (12 women), 23 part-time/adjunct (6 women). *Students:* 159 part-time (62 women); includes 25 minority (5 Black or African American, non-Hispanic/Latino; 9 Asian, non-Hispanic/Latino; 9 Hispanic/Latino; 2 Two or more races, non-Hispanic/Latino), 4 international. Average age 32. 39 applicants, 92% accepted, 35 enrolled. In 2017, 59 master's awarded. *Entrance requirements:* For master's, GRE or GMAT. *Application deadline:* For fall admission, 8/1 for domestic students; for spring admission, 2/15 for domestic students. Applications are processed on a rolling basis. Application fee: $150. Electronic applications accepted. *Expenses:* $1,875 per credit, $1,385 fees. *Financial support:* In 2017–18, 69 students received support. Tuition waivers (partial) available. Financial award application deadline: 8/1. *Unit head:* Andrew Ainslie, Dean, 585-275-3316, E-mail: andrew.ainslie@simon.rochester.edu. *Application contact:* Molly Mesko, Executive Director, EMBA and Part-Time Programs, 585-275-4277, E-mail: molly.mesko@simon.rochester.edu.
Website: http://www.simon.rochester.edu/programs/ptmba/index.aspx

University of St. Augustine for Health Sciences, Graduate Programs, Master of Health Administration Program, San Marcos, CA 92069. Offers MHA. *Program availability:* Online learning.

University of St. Augustine for Health Sciences, Graduate Programs, Master of Health Science Program, San Marcos, CA 92069. Offers athletic training (MHS); executive leadership (MHS); informatics (MHS); teaching and learning (MHS). *Program availability:* Online learning. *Degree requirements:* For master's, comprehensive project.

University of Saint Francis, Graduate School, Keith Busse School of Business and Entrepreneurial Leadership, Fort Wayne, IN 46808-3994. Offers business administration (MBA), including sustainability; environmental health (MEH); healthcare administration (MHA); organizational leadership (MOL). *Accreditation:* ACBSP. *Program availability:* Part-time, evening/weekend, online only, 100% online. *Faculty:* 4 full-time (3 women), 11 part-time/adjunct (1 woman). *Students:* 75 full-time (43 women), 108 part-time (59 women); includes 37 minority (21 Black or African American, non-Hispanic/Latino; 1 Asian, non-Hispanic/Latino; 11 Hispanic/Latino; 1 Native Hawaiian or other Pacific Islander, non-Hispanic/Latino; 3 Two or more races, non-Hispanic/Latino). Average age 34. 101 applicants, 98% accepted, 75 enrolled. In 2017, 133 master's awarded. *Entrance requirements:* For master's, GMAT (if cumulative GPA is below 2.75 with less than five years' professional work experience), minimum undergraduate GPA of 2.75; statement of professional goals; resume. Additional exam requirements/recommendations for international students: Required—TOEFL (minimum score 550 paper-based) or IELTS (minimum score 6.5). *Application deadline:* For fall admission, 7/1 for international students; for spring admission, 11/1 for international students; for summer admission, 3/1 for international students. Applications are processed on a rolling basis. Application fee: $0. Electronic applications accepted. *Expenses:* $475 per hour. *Financial support:* Application deadline: 4/15; applicants required to submit FAFSA. *Unit head:* Dr. Robert Lee, Dean, 260-399-7700 Ext. 8304, Fax: 260-399-8174, E-mail: rlee@sf.edu. *Application contact:* Kyle Richardson, Associate Director of Enrollment Services for Adult Learning, 260-399-7700 Ext. 6310, Fax: 260-399-8152, E-mail: krichardson@sf.edu.
Website: https://business.sf.edu/graduate/

University of Saint Mary, Graduate Programs, Program in Business Administration, Leavenworth, KS 66048-5082. Offers enterprise risk management (MBA); finance (MBA); general management (MBA); health care management (MBA); human resource management (MBA); marketing and advertising management (MBA). *Program availability:* Part-time, evening/weekend, 100% online, blended/hybrid learning. *Degree requirements:* For master's, thesis. *Entrance requirements:* For master's, minimum undergraduate GPA of 2.75, official transcripts, two letters of recommendation. Electronic applications accepted. *Expenses:* Contact institution.

University of St. Thomas, Opus College of Business, Health Care UST MBA Program, Minneapolis, MN 55403. Offers MBA. *Accreditation:* CAHME. *Program availability:*

Online learning. *Entrance requirements:* For master's, minimum 5 years of work experience in related field, letters of recommendation, essays, interview. *Application deadline:* For fall admission, 3/1 priority date for domestic students. Applications are processed on a rolling basis. Electronic applications accepted. *Expenses:* Contact institution. *Financial support:* Scholarships/grants available. *Unit head:* Sandy Bauer, Coordinator, 651-962-8800, Fax: 651-962-8810, E-mail: healthcaremba@stthomas.edu. Website: http://www.stthomas.edu/healthcaremba

University of San Francisco, School of Management, Master of Public Administration Program, San Francisco, CA 94117. Offers health services administration (MPA); public administration (MPA). *Program availability:* Part-time, evening/weekend, online learning. *Entrance requirements:* For master's, resume demonstrating minimum of two years of professional work experience, transcripts from each college or university attended, two letters of recommendation, personal statement. Additional exam requirements/recommendations for international students: Required—TOEFL (minimum score 600 paper-based, 100 iBT), IELTS (minimum score 7) or PTE (minimum score 68). Electronic applications accepted. *Expenses:* Contact institution.

University of Saskatchewan, College of Graduate Studies and Research, Edwards School of Business, Program in Business Administration, Saskatoon, SK S7N 5A2, Canada. Offers agribusiness management (MBA); biotechnology management (MBA); health services management (MBA); indigenous management (MBA); international business management (MBA).

The University of Scranton, Kania School of Management, Program in Business Administration, Scranton, PA 18510. Offers accounting (MBA); finance (MBA); general business administration (MBA); health care management (MBA); international business (MBA); management information systems (MBA); marketing (MBA); operations management (MBA). *Accreditation:* AACSB. *Program availability:* Part-time, evening/weekend, 100% online. *Entrance requirements:* For master's, GMAT (for MBA). *Faculty research:* Financial markets, strategic impact of total quality management, internal accounting controls, consumer preference, information systems and the Internet.

The University of Scranton, Panuska College of Professional Studies, Department of Health Administration and Human Resources, Program in Health Administration, Scranton, PA 18510. Offers MHA. *Accreditation:* CAHME. *Program availability:* Part-time, evening/weekend, online only, 100% online.

University of Sioux Falls, Vucurevich School of Business, Sioux Falls, SD 57105-1699. Offers entrepreneurial leadership (MBA); general management (MBA); health care management (MBA); marketing (MBA). *Program availability:* Part-time, evening/weekend. *Degree requirements:* For master's, project. *Entrance requirements:* For master's, minimum GPA of 3.0. Additional exam requirements/recommendations for international students: Required—TOEFL. *Expenses:* Contact institution.

University of South Africa, College of Human Sciences, Pretoria, South Africa. Offers adult education (M Ed); African languages (MA, PhD); African politics (MA, PhD); Afrikaans (MA, PhD); ancient history (MA, PhD); ancient Near Eastern studies (MA, PhD); anthropology (MA, PhD); applied linguistics (MA); Arabic (MA, PhD); archaeology (MA); art history (MA); Biblical archaeology (MA); Biblical studies (M Th, D Th, PhD); Christian spirituality (M Th, D Th); church history (M Th, D Th); classical studies (MA, PhD); clinical psychology (MA); communication (MA, PhD); comparative education (M Ed, Ed D); consulting psychology (D Admin, D Com, PhD); curriculum studies (M Ed, Ed D); development studies (M Admin, MA, D Admin, PhD); didactics (M Ed, Ed D); education (M Tech); education management (M Ed, Ed D); educational psychology (M Ed); English (MA); environmental education (M Ed); French (MA, PhD); German (MA, PhD); Greek (MA); guidance and counseling (M Ed); health studies (MA, PhD), including health sciences education (MA), health services management (MA), medical and surgical nursing science (critical care general) (MA), midwifery and neonatal nursing science (MA), trauma and emergency care (MA); history (MA, PhD); history of education (Ed D); inclusive education (M Ed, Ed D); information and communications technology policy and regulation (MA); information science (MA, MIS, PhD); international politics (MA, PhD); Islamic studies (MA, PhD); Italian (MA, PhD); Judaica (MA, PhD); linguistics (MA, PhD); mathematical education (M Ed); mathematics education (MA); missiology (M Th, D Th); modern Hebrew (MA, PhD); musicology (MA, MMus, D Mus, PhD); natural science education (M Ed); New Testament (M Th, D Th); Old Testament (D Th); pastoral therapy (M Th, D Th); philosophy (MA); philosophy of education (M Ed, Ed D); politics (MA, PhD); Portuguese (MA, PhD); practical theology (M Th, D Th); psychology (MA, MS, PhD); psychology of education (M Ed, Ed D); public health (MA); religious studies (MA, D Th, PhD); Romance languages (MA); Russian (MA, PhD); Semitic languages (MA, PhD); social behavior studies in HIV/AIDS (MA); social science (mental health) (MA); social science in development studies (MA); social science in psychology (MA); social science in social work (MA); social science in sociology (MA); social work (MSW, DSW, PhD); socio-education (M Ed, Ed D); sociolinguistics (MA); sociology (MA, PhD); Spanish (MA, PhD); systematic theology (M Th, D Th); TESOL (teaching English to speakers of other languages) (MA); theological ethics (M Th, D Th); theory of literature (MA, PhD); urban ministries (D Th); urban ministry (M Th).

University of South Carolina, The Graduate School, Arnold School of Public Health, Department of Health Services Policy and Management, Columbia, SC 29208. Offers MHA, MPH, Dr PH, PhD, JD/MHA, MPH/MSN, MSW/MPH. *Accreditation:* CAHME (one or more programs are accredited). *Program availability:* Part-time, evening/weekend. *Degree requirements:* For master's, comprehensive exam, thesis or alternative, internship (MHA); for doctorate, comprehensive exam, thesis/dissertation. *Entrance requirements:* For master's, GMAT (MHA), GRE General Test (MPH); for doctorate, GRE General Test. Additional exam requirements/recommendations for international students: Required—TOEFL (minimum score 570 paper-based). Electronic applications accepted. *Faculty research:* Health systems management, evaluation, and planning; forecast applications in health care; Medicaid process to health care services.

University of South Dakota, Graduate School, Beacom School of Business, Department of Business Administration, Vermillion, SD 57069. Offers business administration (MBA); business analytics (MBA, Graduate Certificate); health services administration (MBA); long term care management (Graduate Certificate); marketing (MBA, Graduate Certificate); operations and supply chain management (MBA, Graduate Certificate); JD/MBA. *Accreditation:* AACSB. *Program availability:* Part-time, blended/hybrid learning. *Degree requirements:* For master's, thesis or alternative. *Entrance requirements:* For master's, GMAT, minimum GPA of 2.7, resume. Additional exam requirements/recommendations for international students: Required—TOEFL (minimum score 550 paper-based; 79 iBT), IELTS (minimum score 6). *Application deadline:* For fall admission, 6/1 priority date for domestic students, 5/1 priority date for international students; for spring admission, 10/1 priority date for domestic students, 9/1 priority date for international students; for summer admission, 3/1 priority date for domestic students. Applications are processed on a rolling basis. Application fee: $35. Electronic applications accepted. *Expenses:* Contact institution. *Financial support:* Research assistantships with partial tuition reimbursements, teaching assistantships with partial tuition reimbursements, career-related internships or fieldwork, Federal Work-Study, and unspecified assistantships available. Financial award applicants required to submit FAFSA. *Application contact:* Graduate School, 605-658-6140, Fax: 605-677-6118, E-mail: grad@usd.edu.
Website: http://www.usd.edu/business/business-administration/graduate

University of South Dakota, Graduate School, College of Arts and Sciences, Program in Administrative Studies, Vermillion, SD 57069. Offers addiction studies (MSA); criminal justice studies (MSA); health services administration (MSA); human resources (MSA); interdisciplinary studies (MSA); long term care administration (MSA); organizational leadership (MSA). *Program availability:* Part-time, evening/weekend, 100% online. *Degree requirements:* For master's, thesis or alternative. *Entrance requirements:* For master's, 3 years of work or experience, minimum GPA of 2.7, resume. Additional exam requirements/recommendations for international students: Required—TOEFL (minimum score 550 paper-based; 79 iBT). *Application deadline:* Applications are processed on a rolling basis. Application fee: $35. Electronic applications accepted. *Financial support:* Teaching assistantships with partial tuition reimbursements available. Financial award applicants required to submit FAFSA. *Application contact:* Graduate School, 605-658-6140, Fax: 605-677-6118, E-mail: grad@usd.edu.
Website: http://www.usd.edu/onlinemsa

University of Southern California, Graduate School, Sol Price School of Public Policy, Executive Master of Health Administration Program, Los Angeles, CA 90089. Offers EMHA. *Program availability:* Part-time, evening/weekend, online learning. *Entrance requirements:* Additional exam requirements/recommendations for international students: Required—TOEFL (minimum score 600 paper-based; 100 iBT). Electronic applications accepted. *Expenses:* Contact institution. *Faculty research:* Health management and policy, health care systems, health care economics and financing, health care access, community health, healthy communities.

University of Southern California, Graduate School, Sol Price School of Public Policy, Master of Health Administration Program, Los Angeles, CA 90089. Offers ambulatory care (Graduate Certificate); health administration (MHA); long-term care (Graduate Certificate); MHA/MS. *Accreditation:* CAHME. *Program availability:* Part-time. *Degree requirements:* For master's, residency placement. *Entrance requirements:* For master's, GRE, GMAT. Additional exam requirements/recommendations for international students: Required—TOEFL (minimum score 600 paper-based; 100 iBT). Electronic applications accepted. *Faculty research:* Health administration, health management and policy, health care economics and financing, health care access, community health, healthy communities.

University of Southern Indiana, Graduate Studies, College of Nursing and Health Professions, Program in Health Administration, Evansville, IN 47712-3590. Offers MHA. *Program availability:* Part-time, 3 required intensives in August (2.5 days), January (2.5 days) and May (2 days). *Faculty:* 3 full-time (1 woman). *Students:* 61 full-time (44 women), 3 part-time (1 woman); includes 8 minority (4 Black or African American, non-Hispanic/Latino; 1 American Indian or Alaska Native, non-Hispanic/Latino; 1 Asian, non-Hispanic/Latino; 2 Hispanic/Latino), 4 international. Average age 33. In 2017, 22 master's awarded. *Entrance requirements:* For master's, GRE, minimum GPA of 3.0, curriculum vitae, letter of intent, three professional references, focused essay(s). Additional exam requirements/recommendations for international students: Required—TOEFL (minimum score 550 paper-based; 79 iBT), IELTS (minimum score 6). *Application deadline:* For fall admission, 6/1 for domestic students, 1/1 priority date for international students. Applications are processed on a rolling basis. Application fee: $40. Electronic applications accepted. *Expenses:* Tuition, state resident: full-time $9394. Tuition, nonresident: full-time $17,917. *Required fees:* $510. *Financial support:* In 2017–18, 3 students received support. Federal Work-Study, scholarships/grants, tuition waivers (full and partial), and unspecified assistantships available. Financial award application deadline: 3/1; financial award applicants required to submit FAFSA. *Unit head:* Dr. Kevin J. Valadares, Program Chair, 812-461-5277, E-mail: kvaladar@usi.edu. *Application contact:* Dr. Mayola Rowser, Director, Graduate Studies, 812-465-7015, Fax: 812-464-1956, E-mail: mrowser@usi.edu.
Website: http://www.usi.edu/health/master-of-health-administration

University of Southern Indiana, Graduate Studies, Romain College of Business, Program in Business Administration, Evansville, IN 47712-3590. Offers accounting (MBA); data analytics (MBA); engineering management (MBA); general business administration (MBA); healthcare administration (MBA); human resource management (MBA). *Accreditation:* AACSB. *Program availability:* Part-time, evening/weekend, 100% online, blended/hybrid learning. *Faculty:* 22 full-time (4 women), 2 part-time/adjunct (0 women). *Students:* 312 full-time (167 women), 148 part-time (56 women); includes 72 minority (43 Black or African American, non-Hispanic/Latino; 8 Asian, non-Hispanic/Latino; 13 Hispanic/Latino; 8 Two or more races, non-Hispanic/Latino), 10 international. Average age 33. In 2017, 34 master's awarded. *Entrance requirements:* For master's, GMAT or GRE, minimum GPA of 2.5, resume, 3 professional references. Additional exam requirements/recommendations for international students: Required—TOEFL (minimum score 550 paper-based; 79 iBT), IELTS (minimum score 6). *Application deadline:* For fall admission, 8/1 for domestic students, 3/1 priority date for international students. Applications are processed on a rolling basis. Application fee: $40. Electronic applications accepted. *Expenses:* Tuition, state resident: full-time $9394. Tuition, nonresident: full-time $17,917. *Required fees:* $510. *Financial support:* In 2017–18, 18 students received support. Federal Work-Study, scholarships/grants, tuition waivers (full and partial), and unspecified assistantships available. Financial award application deadline: 3/1; financial award applicants required to submit FAFSA. *Unit head:* Dr. Jack E. Smothers, Program Director, 812-461-5248, E-mail: jesmothers@usi.edu. *Application contact:* Michelle Simmons, MBA Program Assistant, 812-464-1926, Fax: 812-465-1044, E-mail: masimmons3@usi.edu.
Website: http://www.usi.edu/business/mba

University of Southern Maine, College of Management and Human Service, School of Business, Portland, ME 04104-9300. Offers accounting (MBA); business administration (MBA); finance (MBA); health management and policy (MBA); sustainability (MBA); JD/MBA; MBA/MSA; MBA/MSN; MS/MBA. *Accreditation:* AACSB. *Program availability:* Part-time, evening/weekend. *Entrance requirements:* For master's, GMAT or GRE, minimum AACSB index of 1100. Additional exam requirements/recommendations for international students: Required—TOEFL (minimum score 550 paper-based; 79 iBT). Electronic applications accepted. *Faculty research:* Economic development, management information systems, real options, system dynamics, simulation.

University of Southern Mississippi, College of Health, Department of Public Health, Hattiesburg, MS 39406-0001. Offers epidemiology and biostatistics (MPH); health policy and administration (MPH). *Program availability:* Part-time, evening/weekend. *Students:* 17 full-time (6 women). 42 applicants, 88% accepted, 17 enrolled. In 2017, 2 master's awarded. *Degree requirements:* For master's, comprehensive exam, thesis (for some programs). *Entrance requirements:* For master's, GRE General Test, minimum GPA of 2.75 in last 60 hours. Additional exam requirements/recommendations for international students: Required—TOEFL, IELTS. *Application deadline:* For fall admission, 3/1 priority date for domestic and international students; for spring admission, 1/10 priority date for domestic and international students. Applications are processed on a rolling basis. Application fee: $60. Electronic applications accepted. *Expenses:* Tuition, state resident: full-time $3830. *Financial support:* Research assistantships with full tuition reimbursements, teaching assistantships with full tuition reimbursements, career-related internships or fieldwork, Federal Work-Study, institutionally sponsored loans, scholarships/grants, health care benefits, and unspecified assistantships available. Financial award application deadline: 3/15; financial award applicants required to submit

FAFSA. *Faculty research:* Rural health care delivery, school health, nutrition of pregnant teens, risk factor reduction, sexually transmitted diseases. *Unit head:* Charkarra Anderson-Lewis, Interim Chair, 601-266-5435, Fax: 601-266-5043, E-mail: charkarra.andersonlewis@usm.edu.
Website: http://www.usm.edu/community-public-health-sciences

University of South Florida, College of Public Health, Department of Health Policy and Management, Tampa, FL 33620-9951. Offers MHA, MPH, MSPH, PhD. *Accreditation:* CAHME. *Program availability:* Part-time, evening/weekend. *Degree requirements:* For master's, comprehensive exam, thesis (for some programs); for doctorate, comprehensive exam, thesis/dissertation. *Entrance requirements:* For master's, GRE General Test or GMAT, minimum GPA of 3.0 in upper-level course work, 3 professional letters of recommendation, resume/curriculum vitae; for doctorate, GRE General Test, minimum GPA of 3.0 in upper-level course work, goal statement letter, three professional letters of recommendation, resume/curriculum vitae, writing sample. Additional exam requirements/recommendations for international students: Required—TOEFL (minimum score 550 paper-based; 79 iBT). Electronic applications accepted. *Faculty research:* Tracking community health, inpatient care, discharge policies, stroke education, leadership practices.

University of South Florida, Innovative Education, Tampa, FL 33620-9951. Offers adult, career and higher education (Graduate Certificate), including college teaching, leadership in developing human resources, leadership in higher education; Africana studies (Graduate Certificate), including diasporas and health disparities, genocide and human rights; aging studies (Graduate Certificate), including gerontology; art research (Graduate Certificate), including museum studies; business foundations (Graduate Certificate); chemical and biomedical engineering (Graduate Certificate), including materials science and engineering, water, health and sustainability; child and family studies (Graduate Certificate), including positive behavior support; civil and industrial engineering (Graduate Certificate), including transportation systems analysis; community and family health (Graduate Certificate), including maternal and child health, social marketing and public health, violence and injury: prevention and intervention, women's health; criminology (Graduate Certificate), including criminal justice administration; data science for public administration (Graduate Certificate); digital humanities (Graduate Certificate); educational measurement and research (Graduate Certificate), including evaluation; English (Graduate Certificate), including comparative literary studies, creative writing, professional and technical communication; entrepreneurship (Graduate Certificate); environmental health (Graduate Certificate), including safety management; epidemiology and biostatistics (Graduate Certificate), including applied biostatistics, biostatistics, concepts and tools of epidemiology, epidemiology, epidemiology of infectious diseases; geography, environment and planning (Graduate Certificate), including community development, environmental policy and management, geographical information systems; geology (Graduate Certificate), including hydrogeology; global health (Graduate Certificate), including disaster management, global health and Latin American and Caribbean studies, global health practice, humanitarian assistance, infection control; government and international affairs (Graduate Certificate), including Cuban studies, globalization studies; health policy and management (Graduate Certificate), including health management and leadership, public health policy and programs; hearing specialist: early intervention (Graduate Certificate); industrial and management systems engineering (Graduate Certificate), including systems engineering, technology management; information studies (Graduate Certificate), including school library media specialist; information systems/decision sciences (Graduate Certificate), including analytics and business intelligence; instructional technology (Graduate Certificate), including distance education, Florida digital/virtual educator, instructional design, multimedia design, Web design; internal medicine, bioethics and medical humanities (Graduate Certificate), including biomedical ethics; Latin American and Caribbean studies (Graduate Certificate); leadership for coastal resiliency planning (Graduate Certificate); mass communications (Graduate Certificate), including multimedia journalism; mathematics and statistics (Graduate Certificate), including mathematics; medicine (Graduate Certificate), including aging and neuroscience, bioinformatics, biotechnology, brain fitness and memory management, clinical investigation, hand and upper limb rehabilitation, health informatics, health sciences, integrative weight management, intellectual property, medicine and gender, metabolic and nutritional medicine, metabolic cardiology, pharmacy sciences; national and competitive intelligence (Graduate Certificate); nursing (Graduate Certificate), including simulation based academic fellowship in advanced pain management; psychological and social foundations (Graduate Certificate), including career counseling, college teaching, diversity in education, mental health counseling, school counseling; public affairs (Graduate Certificate), including nonprofit management, public management, research administration; public health (Graduate Certificate), including assessing chemical toxicity and public health risks, health equity, pharmacoepidemiology, public health generalist, toxicology, translational research in adolescent behavioral health; public health practices (Graduate Certificate), including planning for healthy communities; rehabilitation and mental health counseling (Graduate Certificate), including integrative mental health care, marriage and family therapy, rehabilitation technology; secondary education (Graduate Certificate), including ESOL, foreign language education: culture and content, foreign language education: professional; social work (Graduate Certificate), including geriatric social work/clinical gerontology; special education (Graduate Certificate), including autism spectrum disorder, disabilities education: severe/profound; world languages (Graduate Certificate), including teaching English as a second language (TESL) or foreign language. *Unit head:* Dr. Cynthia DeLuca, Associate Vice President and Assistant Vice Provost, 813-974-3077, Fax: 813-974-7061, E-mail: deluca@usf.edu. *Application contact:* Owen Hooper, Director, Summer and Alternative Calendar Programs, 813-974-6917, E-mail: hooper@usf.edu.
Website: http://www.usf.edu/innovative-education/

The University of Tennessee, Graduate School, College of Education, Health and Human Sciences, Program in Public Health, Knoxville, TN 37996. Offers community health education (MPH); gerontology (MPH); health planning/administration (MPH); MS/MPH. *Accreditation:* CEPH. *Degree requirements:* For master's, thesis optional. *Entrance requirements:* For master's, minimum GPA of 2.7. Additional exam requirements/recommendations for international students: Required—TOEFL. Electronic applications accepted.

The University of Texas at Arlington, Graduate School, College of Business, Program in Health Care Administration, Arlington, TX 76019. Offers MS. *Program availability:* Part-time, evening/weekend. *Degree requirements:* For master's, one foreign language, thesis optional. *Entrance requirements:* For master's, GRE General Test or GMAT, minimum GPA of 3.0, official undergraduate and graduate transcripts, current professional resume, personal statement, three letters of recommendation. Additional exam requirements/recommendations for international students: Required—TOEFL (minimum score 550 paper-based; 79 iBT).

The University of Texas at Dallas, Naveen Jindal School of Management, Program in Organizations, Strategy and International Management, Richardson, TX 75080. Offers business administration (MBA); executive business administration (EMBA); global leadership (EMBA); healthcare leadership and management (MS); healthcare management (EMBA); innovation and entrepreneurship (MS); international management studies (MS, PhD); management science (MS, PhD); project management (EMBA); systems engineering and management (MS); MS/MBA. *Program availability:* Part-time, evening/weekend. *Faculty:* 18 full-time (6 women), 17 part-time/adjunct (2 women). *Students:* 608 full-time (232 women), 711 part-time (326 women); includes 446 minority (93 Black or African American, non-Hispanic/Latino; 3 American Indian or Alaska Native, non-Hispanic/Latino; 212 Asian, non-Hispanic/Latino; 107 Hispanic/Latino; 31 Two or more races, non-Hispanic/Latino), 339 international. Average age 32. 1,665 applicants, 36% accepted, 398 enrolled. In 2017, 473 master's, 14 doctorates awarded. *Degree requirements:* For doctorate, thesis/dissertation. *Entrance requirements:* For master's and doctorate, GMAT. Additional exam requirements/recommendations for international students: Required—TOEFL (minimum score 550 paper-based). *Application deadline:* For fall admission, 7/15 for domestic students, 5/1 priority date for international students; for spring admission, 11/15 for domestic students, 9/1 priority date for international students. Applications are processed on a rolling basis. Application fee: $50 ($100 for international students). Electronic applications accepted. *Expenses:* Tuition, state resident: full-time $12,916; part-time $718 per credit hour. Tuition, nonresident: full-time $25,252; part-time $1403 per credit hour. *Financial support:* In 2017–18, 369 students received support, including 22 research assistantships with partial tuition reimbursements available (averaging $36,554 per year), 88 teaching assistantships with partial tuition reimbursements available (averaging $25,176 per year); Federal Work-Study, institutionally sponsored loans, scholarships/grants, and unspecified assistantships also available. Support available to part-time students. Financial award application deadline: 4/30; financial award applicants required to submit FAFSA. *Faculty research:* International accounting, international trade and finance, economic development, international economics. *Unit head:* Dr. Erik W.K. Tsang, Area Coordinator, 972-883-4386, Fax: 972-883-5977, E-mail: ewktsang@utdallas.edu.
Website: http://jindal.utdallas.edu/osim/

The University of Texas at El Paso, Graduate School, School of Nursing, El Paso, TX 79968-0001. Offers family nurse practitioner (MSN); health care leadership and management (Certificate); interdisciplinary health sciences (PhD); nursing (DNP); nursing education (MSN, Certificate); nursing systems management (MSN). *Accreditation:* AACN. *Program availability:* Online learning. *Degree requirements:* For master's, thesis optional; for doctorate, thesis/dissertation. *Entrance requirements:* For master's, minimum GPA of 3.0, resume; for doctorate, GRE, letters of reference, relevant personal/professional experience; master's degree in nursing (for DNP); for Certificate, bachelor's degree in nursing. Additional exam requirements/recommendations for international students: Required—TOEFL; Recommended—IELTS. *Application deadline:* For fall admission, 8/1 for domestic students, 3/1 for international students; for spring admission, 11/1 for domestic students, 9/1 for international students. Applications are processed on a rolling basis. Application fee: $45 ($80 for international students). Electronic applications accepted. *Financial support:* Fellowships with partial tuition reimbursements, research assistantships with partial tuition reimbursements, teaching assistantships with partial tuition reimbursements, institutionally sponsored loans, scholarships/grants, health care benefits, tuition waivers (partial), and unspecified assistantships available. Support available to part-time students. Financial award application deadline: 3/15; financial award applicants required to submit FAFSA. *Unit head:* Dr. Elias Provencio-Vasquez, Dean, 915-747-8194, Fax: 915-747-8266, E-mail: eprovenciovasquez@utep.edu. *Application contact:* Dr. Benjamin Flores, Interim Dean of the Graduate School, 915-747-5491, Fax: 915-747-5788, E-mail: bflores@utep.edu.
Website: http://nursing.utep.edu/

The University of Texas at Tyler, College of Business and Technology, Program in Business Administration, Tyler, TX 75799-0001. Offers cyber security (MBA); engineering management (MBA); general management (MBA); healthcare management (MBA); internal assurance and consulting (MBA); marketing (MBA); oil, gas and energy (MBA); organizational development (MBA); quality management (MBA). *Accreditation:* AACSB. *Program availability:* Part-time, online learning. *Entrance requirements:* Additional exam requirements/recommendations for international students: Required—TOEFL (minimum score 550 paper-based). *Faculty research:* General business, inventory control, institutional markets, service marketing, product distribution, accounting fraud, financial reporting and recognition.

The University of Texas Health Science Center at Houston, School of Public Health, Houston, TX 77030. Offers behavioral science (PhD); biostatistics (MPH, MS, PhD); environmental health (MPH); epidemiology (MPH, MS, PhD); general public health (Certificate); genomics and bioinformatics (Certificate); health disparities (Certificate); health promotion/health education (MPH, Dr PH); healthcare management (Certificate); management, policy and community health (MPH, Dr PH, PhD); maternal and child health (Certificate); public health informatics (Certificate); DDS/MPH; JD/MPH; MBA/MPH; MD/MPH; MGPS/MPH; MP Aff/MPH; MS/MPH; MSN/MPH; MSW/MPH; PhD/MPH. Specific programs are offered at each of our six campuses in Texas (Austin, Brownsville, Dallas, El Paso, Houston, and San Antonio). *Accreditation:* CEPH. *Program availability:* Part-time. *Faculty:* 140 full-time (74 women), 23 part-time/adjunct (14 women). *Students:* 604 full-time (446 women), 534 part-time (384 women); includes 504 minority (106 Black or African American, non-Hispanic/Latino; 177 Asian, non-Hispanic/Latino; 88 Hispanic/Latino; 1 Native Hawaiian or other Pacific Islander, non-Hispanic/Latino; 132 Two or more races, non-Hispanic/Latino). Average age 31. 1,425 applicants, 58% accepted, 423 enrolled. In 2017, 315 master's, 68 doctorates awarded. *Degree requirements:* For master's, thesis (for some programs); for doctorate, comprehensive exam, thesis/dissertation. *Entrance requirements:* For master's and doctorate, GRE General Test. Additional exam requirements/recommendations for international students: Required—TOEFL (minimum score 600 paper-based, 100 iBT) or IELTS (7.5). *Application deadline:* For fall admission, 3/1 for domestic and international students; for spring admission, 10/1 for domestic and international students; for summer admission, 3/1 for domestic students. Applications are processed on a rolling basis. Application fee: $135. Electronic applications accepted. *Expenses:* $233 per semester credit hour resident tuition, $980 per semester credit hour non-resident tuition. *Financial support:* Fellowships, research assistantships, teaching assistantships, career-related internships or fieldwork, institutionally sponsored loans, scholarships/grants, traineeships, health care benefits, and unspecified assistantships available. Support available to part-time students. Financial award application deadline: 5/5; financial award applicants required to submit FAFSA. *Faculty research:* Chronic and infectious disease epidemiology; health promotion and health education; applied and theoretical biostatistics; healthcare management, policy and economics; environmental and occupational health. *Total annual research expenditures:* $47.8 million. *Unit head:* Dr. Susan Emery, Senior Associate Dean of Academic and Research Affairs. *Application contact:* Elvis Parada, Manager of Admissions and Recruitment, 713-500-9028, Fax: 713-500-9068, E-mail: elvis.a.parada@uth.tmc.edu.
Website: https://sph.uth.edu

The University of Texas Rio Grande Valley, College of Health Affairs, Department of Health and Biomedical Sciences, Brownville, TX 78520. Offers clinical laboratory sciences (MSHS); health care administration (MSHS); nutrition (MSHS). *Faculty:* 2 full-time (both women), 10 part-time/adjunct (all women). *Students:* 129 part-time (94 women); includes 103 minority (8 Black or African American, non-Hispanic/Latino; 4 Asian, non-Hispanic/Latino; 90 Hispanic/Latino; 1 Two or more races, non-Hispanic/Latino), 6 international. 51 applicants, 96% accepted, 49 enrolled. *Application deadline:* For fall admission, 7/20 for domestic and international students; for spring admission,

12/2 for domestic students, 12/1 for international students. Application fee: $50 ($100 for international students). *Expenses:* Tuition, state resident: full-time $5550; part-time $417 per credit hour. Tuition, nonresident: full-time $13,020; part-time $832 per credit hour. *Required fees:* $1169. *Faculty research:* Health disparities, post-menopausal osteoporosis bone loss and bone density, alternative medicine and nutritional supplements, health informatics competencies, online learning and quality matters, health literacy. *Unit head:* Dr. Saraswathy Nair, Associate Professor and Chair, Health and Biomedical, 956-882-5108, Fax: 956-882-6835, E-mail: saraswathy.nair@utrgv.edu. *Application contact:* Kim Garcia, Lecturer III/Associate Chair, Health and Biomedical Sciences, 956-665-4781, E-mail: kim.garcia@utrgv.edu.
Website: http://www.utrgv.edu/hbs/

University of the Incarnate Word, School of Professional Studies, San Antonio, TX 78209-6397. Offers communication arts (MAA), including applied administration, communication arts, healthcare administration, industrial and organizational psychology, organizational development; organizational development and leadership (MS); professional studies (DBA). *Program availability:* Part-time, evening/weekend, 100% online, blended/hybrid learning. *Faculty:* 9 full-time (3 women), 25 part-time/adjunct (10 women). *Students:* 528 full-time (263 women), 348 part-time (141 women); includes 543 minority (122 Black or African American, non-Hispanic/Latino; 3 American Indian or Alaska Native, non-Hispanic/Latino; 26 Asian, non-Hispanic/Latino; 365 Hispanic/Latino; 6 Native Hawaiian or other Pacific Islander, non-Hispanic/Latino; 21 Two or more races, non-Hispanic/Latino). In 2017, 377 master's, 10 doctorates awarded. *Degree requirements:* For master's, comprehensive exam (for some programs), thesis or alternative. *Entrance requirements:* For master's, GMAT, GRE, official transcripts from all other colleges attended. Additional exam requirements/recommendations for international students: Required—TOEFL (minimum score 560 paper-based; 83 iBT). *Application deadline:* Applications are processed on a rolling basis. Electronic applications accepted. *Expenses:* $915 per credit hour (for master's programs); $940 per credit hour (for doctoral program). *Financial support:* Scholarships/grants and unspecified assistantships available. Financial award applicants required to submit FAFSA. *Unit head:* Dr. Cyndi Porter, Vice President, 877-603-1130, E-mail: porter@uiwtx.edu. *Application contact:* Julie Weber, Director of Marketing and Recruitment, 210-318-1876, Fax: 210-829-2756, E-mail: eapadmission@uiwtx.edu.
Website: http://sps.uiw.edu/

University of the Sciences, Program in Health Policy, Philadelphia, PA 19104-4495. Offers MS, PhD. *Program availability:* Part-time, evening/weekend, online learning. *Degree requirements:* For doctorate, comprehensive exam, thesis/dissertation. *Entrance requirements:* For master's and doctorate, GRE General Test. Additional exam requirements/recommendations for international students: Required—TOEFL, TWE. *Expenses:* Contact institution.

The University of Toledo, College of Graduate Studies, College of Languages, Literature and Social Sciences, Department of Political Science and Public Administration, Toledo, OH 43606-3390. Offers health care policy and administration (Certificate); management of non-profit organizations (Certificate); municipal administration (Certificate); political science (MA); public administration (MPA); JD/MPA. *Program availability:* Part-time. *Degree requirements:* For master's, comprehensive exam (for some programs), thesis. *Entrance requirements:* For master's, GRE General Test, minimum cumulative point-hour ratio of 2.7 (3.0 for MPA) for all previous academic work, three letters of recommendation, statement of purpose, transcripts from all prior institutions attended; for Certificate, minimum cumulative point-hour ratio of 2.7 for all previous academic work, three letters of recommendation, statement of purpose, transcripts from all prior institutions attended. Additional exam requirements/recommendations for international students: Required—TOEFL (minimum score 550 paper-based; 80 iBT). Electronic applications accepted. *Faculty research:* Economic development, health care, Third World, criminal justice, Eastern Europe.

The University of Toledo, College of Graduate Studies, College of Medicine and Life Sciences, Department of Public Health and Preventative Medicine, Toledo, OH 43606-3390. Offers biostatistics and epidemiology (Certificate); contemporary gerontological practice (Certificate); environmental and occupational health and safety (MPH); epidemiology (Certificate); global public health (Certificate); health promotion and education (MPH); industrial hygiene (MSOH); medical and health science teaching and learning (Certificate); occupational health (Certificate); public health administration (MPH); public health and emergency response (Certificate); public health epidemiology (MPH); public health nutrition (MPH); MD/MPH. *Program availability:* Part-time, evening/weekend. *Degree requirements:* For master's, thesis or alternative. *Entrance requirements:* For master's, GRE, minimum undergraduate GPA of 3.0, three letters of recommendation, statement of purpose, transcripts from all prior institutions attended, resume; for Certificate, minimum undergraduate GPA of 3.0, three letters of recommendation, statement of purpose, transcripts from all prior institutions attended, resume. Additional exam requirements/recommendations for international students: Required—TOEFL (minimum score 550 paper-based; 80 iBT), IELTS (minimum score 6.5). Electronic applications accepted.

University of Toronto, Faculty of Medicine, Institute of Health Policy, Management and Evaluation, Program in Health Administration, Toronto, ON M5S 1A1, Canada. Offers MH Sc. *Accreditation:* CAHME. *Entrance requirements:* For master's, minimum B+ average on each of the last two years of a four-year undergraduate program, minimum of three years relevant clinical or management experience. Additional exam requirements/recommendations for international students: Required—TOEFL (minimum score 580 paper-based; 93 iBT), TWE (minimum score 5). Electronic applications accepted.

University of Utah, Graduate School, College of Pharmacy, Department of Pharmacotherapy, Salt Lake City, UT 84112. Offers health system pharmacy administration (MS); outcomes research and health policy (PhD). *Faculty:* 5 full-time (3 women), 18 part-time/adjunct (13 women). *Students:* 2 full-time (0 women), 4 part-time (3 women), 1 international. Average age 28. 26 applicants, 19% accepted, 4 enrolled. In 2017, 5 master's, 2 doctorates awarded. Terminal master's awarded for partial completion of doctoral program. *Degree requirements:* For master's, comprehensive exam, thesis or alternative, project; for doctorate, comprehensive exam, thesis/dissertation. *Entrance requirements:* For doctorate, GRE. Additional exam requirements/recommendations for international students: Required—TOEFL (minimum score 550 paper-based; 80 iBT). *Application deadline:* For fall admission, 1/10 for domestic students, 12/15 for international students. Application fee: $55 ($65 for international students). *Financial support:* In 2017–18, 7 students received support, including 9 research assistantships with full tuition reimbursements available (averaging $21,400 per year); health care benefits also available. Financial award application deadline: 12/15. *Faculty research:* Outcomes in pharmacy, pharmacotherapy. *Total annual research expenditures:* $131,217. *Unit head:* Dr. Diana I. Brixner, Department Chair and Professor, 801-581-6731, E-mail: diana.brixner@utah.edu. *Application contact:* Ashley Weisman, Manager, Administration, 801-581-5984, Fax: 801-585-6160, E-mail: ashley.weisman@pharm.utah.edu.
Website: http://www.pharmacy.utah.edu/pharmacotherapy/

University of Utah, Graduate School, David Eccles School of Business, Master in Healthcare Administration Program, Salt Lake City, UT 84112. Offers MHA, MBA/MHA, MHA/MPA, MPH/MHA, PMBA/MHA. *Accreditation:* CAHME. *Program availability:* Part-time, evening/weekend. *Students:* 29 full-time (9 women); includes 5 minority (3 Hispanic/Latino; 2 Two or more races, non-Hispanic/Latino). Average age 27. 51 applicants, 55% accepted, 12 enrolled. In 2017, 18 master's awarded. *Degree requirements:* For master's, administrative internship. *Entrance requirements:* For master's, GMAT, GRE, statistics course with minimum B grade; minimum undergraduate GPA of 3.0. Additional exam requirements/recommendations for international students: Required—TOEFL (minimum score 600 paper-based; 100 iBT), IELTS (minimum score 7). *Application deadline:* Applications are processed on a rolling basis. Application fee: $55 ($65 for international students). Electronic applications accepted. *Expenses:* Contact institution. *Financial support:* In 2017–18, 31 students received support. Scholarships/grants, tuition waivers (partial), and unspecified assistantships available. Financial award application deadline: 5/15; financial award applicants required to submit FAFSA. *Faculty research:* Healthcare leadership, problem-solving, primary care delivery redesign, patient engagement, patient-reported outcomes. *Unit head:* Dr. Debra Scammon, Professor, 801-581-4754, Fax: 801-581-3666, E-mail: debra.scammon@business.utah.edu. *Application contact:* Aislynn Schultz, Graduate Admissions Specialist, 801-581-7785, Fax: 801-581-7785, E-mail: mastersinfo@business.utah.edu.

University of Vermont, The Robert Larner, MD College of Medicine and Graduate College, Graduate Programs in Medicine, Program in Public Health, Burlington, VT 05405. Offers epidemiology (Graduate Certificate); global and environmental health (Graduate Certificate); healthcare management and policy (Graduate Certificate); public health (MPH). *Program availability:* Online only, 100% online. *Students:* 96. 73 applicants, 88% accepted, 41 enrolled. In 2017, 6 master's, 6 other advanced degrees awarded. *Entrance requirements:* For master's and Graduate Certificate, resume/curriculum vitae. Additional exam requirements/recommendations for international students: Required—TOEFL (minimum iBT score of 90) or IELTS (6.5). *Application deadline:* For fall admission, 7/1 for domestic and international students; for spring admission, 11/15 for domestic and international students; for summer admission, 4/1 for domestic and international students. Application fee: $65. Electronic applications accepted. *Expenses:* $646 per credit in-state, $970 per credit out-of-state. *Unit head:* Dr. Jan Carney, Coordinator, 802-656-2085, E-mail: public.health@uvm.edu.
Website: https://learn.uvm.edu/program/master-of-public-health/

University of Virginia, School of Medicine, Department of Public Health Sciences, Charlottesville, VA 22903. Offers clinical research (MS), including clinical investigation and patient-oriented research, informatics in medicine; public health (MPH); MPP/MPH. *Program availability:* Part-time. *Faculty:* 51 full-time (27 women), 7 part-time/adjunct (2 women). *Students:* 59 full-time (42 women), 19 part-time (13 women); includes 30 minority (9 Black or African American, non-Hispanic/Latino; 12 Asian, non-Hispanic/Latino; 5 Hispanic/Latino; 4 Two or more races, non-Hispanic/Latino), 5 international. Average age 26. 152 applicants, 78% accepted, 53 enrolled. In 2017, 54 master's awarded. *Entrance requirements:* For master's, GRE General Test or MCAT. Additional exam requirements/recommendations for international students: Required—TOEFL. *Application deadline:* Applications are processed on a rolling basis. Application fee: $60. Electronic applications accepted. *Financial support:* Career-related internships or fieldwork available. Financial award applicants required to submit FAFSA. *Unit head:* Ruth Gaare Bernheim, Chair, 434-924-8430, Fax: 434-924-8437, E-mail: rg3r@virginia.edu. *Application contact:* Tracey C. Brookman, Academic Programs Administrator, 434-924-8430, Fax: 434-924-8437, E-mail: phsdegrees@virginia.edu.
Website: http://www.medicine.virginia.edu/clinical/departments/phs

University of Washington, Graduate School, School of Public Health, Programs in Health Administration, Seattle, WA 98195. Offers EMHA, MHA, JD/MHA, MHA/MBA, MHA/MD, MHA/MPA. *Accreditation:* CAHME. *Program availability:* Part-time. *Students:* 113 full-time (69 women), 2 part-time (1 woman); includes 34 minority (4 Black or African American, non-Hispanic/Latino; 2 American Indian or Alaska Native, non-Hispanic/Latino; 22 Asian, non-Hispanic/Latino; 5 Hispanic/Latino; 1 Native Hawaiian or other Pacific Islander, non-Hispanic/Latino), 2 international. Average age 33. 145 applicants, 60% accepted, 55 enrolled. In 2017, 58 master's awarded. Electronic applications accepted. *Expenses:* Contact institution. *Financial support:* Scholarships/grants and unspecified assistantships available. Financial award applicants required to submit FAFSA. *Faculty research:* Health economics, health information management, research design in health services, health policy, clinical effectiveness. *Unit head:* Dennis Stillman, Director, 206-221-7234, Fax: 206-543-3964, E-mail: stillman@uw.edu.
Website: https://www.mha.uw.edu/

The University of Western Ontario, Richard Ivey School of Business, London, ON N6A 3K7, Canada. Offers business (EMBA, PhD); corporate strategy and leadership elective (MBA); entrepreneurship elective (MBA); finance elective (MBA); health sector stream (MBA); international management elective (MBA); marketing elective (MBA); JD/MBA. *Degree requirements:* For master's, thesis (for some programs); for doctorate, thesis/dissertation. *Entrance requirements:* For master's, GMAT, 2 years of full-time work experience, interview. Additional exam requirements/recommendations for international students: Required—TOEFL (minimum score 100 iBT) or IELTS (minimum score 6). Electronic applications accepted. *Faculty research:* Strategy, organizational behavior, international business, finance, operations management.

University of West Florida, Usha Kundu, MD College of Health, Department of Health Sciences and Administration, Pensacola, FL 32514-5750. Offers healthcare administration (MHA). *Program availability:* Part-time, evening/weekend, online learning. *Entrance requirements:* For master's, GRE General Test, letter of intent, names of references. Additional exam requirements/recommendations for international students: Required—TOEFL (minimum score 550 paper-based).

University of West Georgia, Tanner Health System School of Nursing, Carrollton, GA 30118. Offers health systems leadership (Post-Master's Certificate); nursing (MSN); nursing education (Ed D, Post-Master's Certificate). *Accreditation:* AACN. *Program availability:* Part-time, evening/weekend, 100% online, blended/hybrid learning. *Faculty:* 13 full-time (all women). *Students:* 64 full-time (63 women), 78 part-time (74 women); includes 34 minority (27 Black or African American, non-Hispanic/Latino; 1 Asian, non-Hispanic/Latino; 5 Hispanic/Latino; 1 Two or more races, non-Hispanic/Latino). Average age 41. 92 applicants, 88% accepted, 61 enrolled. In 2017, 36 master's, 7 doctorates, 1 other advanced degree awarded. *Entrance requirements:* Additional exam requirements/recommendations for international students: Required—TOEFL (minimum score 523 paper-based; 69 iBT); Recommended—IELTS (minimum score 6.5). *Application deadline:* For fall admission, 2/1 priority date for domestic and international students. Applications are processed on a rolling basis. Application fee: $40. Electronic applications accepted. *Expenses:* Contact institution. *Financial support:* Fellowships, research assistantships, teaching assistantships, career-related internships or fieldwork, Federal Work-Study, institutionally sponsored loans, scholarships/grants, and unspecified assistantships available. Support available to part-time students. Financial award application deadline: 4/1; financial award applicants required to submit FAFSA. *Unit head:* Dr. Jennifer Schuessler, Dean of the School of Nursing, 678-839-5640, Fax: 678-839-6553, E-mail: jschuess@westga.edu. *Application contact:* Dr. Toby Ziglar, Assistant Dean of the Graduate School, 678-839-1390, Fax: 678-839-1395, E-mail: graduate@westga.edu.
Website: https://www.westga.edu/nursing

University of Wisconsin–Milwaukee, Graduate School, College of Engineering and Applied Science, Biomedical and Health Informatics Program, Milwaukee, WI 53201-

0413. Offers health information systems (PhD); health services management and policy (PhD); knowledge based systems (PhD); medical imaging and instrumentation (PhD); public health informatics (PhD). *Students:* 8 full-time (3 women), 14 part-time (6 women); includes 3 minority (2 Black or African American, non-Hispanic/Latino; 1 Asian, non-Hispanic/Latino), 9 international. Average age 37. 18 applicants, 56% accepted, 4 enrolled. *Degree requirements:* For doctorate, comprehensive exam, thesis/dissertation. *Entrance requirements:* For doctorate, GRE, GMAT or MCAT. Additional exam requirements/recommendations for international students: Required—TOEFL (minimum score 600 paper-based; 79 iBT), IELTS (minimum score 6.5). Application fee: $56 ($96 for international students). Electronic applications accepted. *Financial support:* Fellowships, research assistantships, teaching assistantships, and project assistantships available. *Unit head:* Devendra Misra, PhD, Chair, 414-229-3327, E-mail: misra@uwm.edu. *Application contact:* Betty Warras, Engineering and Computer Science Graduate Programs, 414-229-6169, E-mail: ceas-graduate@uwm.edu.
Website: http://uwm.edu/engineering/academics-2/departments/biomedical-engineering/

University of Wisconsin–Milwaukee, Graduate School, College of Health Sciences, Department of Health Informatics and Administration, Milwaukee, WI 53201-0413. Offers health care informatics (MS); healthcare administration (MHA). *Students:* 38 full-time (28 women), 17 part-time (12 women); includes 12 minority (3 Black or African American, non-Hispanic/Latino; 5 Asian, non-Hispanic/Latino; 4 Two or more races, non-Hispanic/Latino), 7 international. Average age 31. 42 applicants, 71% accepted, 15 enrolled. In 2017, 6 master's awarded. *Degree requirements:* For master's, comprehensive exam, thesis optional. *Entrance requirements:* For master's, GRE General Test. Additional exam requirements/recommendations for international students: Required—TOEFL (minimum score 550 paper-based; 79 iBT), IELTS (minimum score 6.5). Application fee: $56 ($96 for international students). *Financial support:* Fellowships, research assistantships, and teaching assistantships available. *Unit head:* Priya Nambisan, Department Chair, 414-229-7136, Fax: 414-229-3373, E-mail: nambisap@uwm.edu. *Application contact:* Kathleen M. Olewinski, Educational Coordinator, 414-229-7110, Fax: 414-229-3373, E-mail: kmo@uwm.edu.
Website: http://uwm.edu/healthsciences/academics/health-informatics-administration/

University of Wisconsin–Milwaukee, Graduate School, College of Health Sciences, Program in Health Sciences, Milwaukee, WI 53201-0413. Offers health sciences (PhD), including diagnostic and biomedical sciences, disability and rehabilitation, health administration and policy, human movement sciences, population health. *Students:* 17 full-time (10 women), 7 part-time (4 women); includes 6 minority (1 Black or African American, non-Hispanic/Latino; 3 Asian, non-Hispanic/Latino; 2 Two or more races, non-Hispanic/Latino), 11 international. Average age 33. 7 applicants, 43% accepted, 3 enrolled. In 2017, 1 doctorate awarded. *Degree requirements:* For doctorate, comprehensive exam, thesis/dissertation. *Entrance requirements:* For doctorate, GRE. Additional exam requirements/recommendations for international students: Required—TOEFL (minimum score 600 paper-based), IELTS (minimum score 6.5). Application fee: $56 ($96 for international students). *Financial support:* Fellowships, research assistantships, teaching assistantships, and project assistantships available. *Application contact:* Susan Cashin, PhD, Assistant Dean, 414-229-3303, E-mail: scashin@uwm.edu.
Website: http://uwm.edu/healthsciences/academics/phd-health-sciences/

University of Wisconsin–Oshkosh, Graduate Studies, College of Letters and Science, Department of Public Administration, Oshkosh, WI 54901. Offers general agency (MPA); health care (MPA). *Program availability:* Part-time, evening/weekend. *Degree requirements:* For master's, thesis or alternative. *Entrance requirements:* For master's, public service-related experience, resume, sample of written work. Additional exam requirements/recommendations for international students: Required—TOEFL (minimum score 550 paper-based; 79 iBT). Electronic applications accepted. *Faculty research:* Drug policy, local government state revenues and expenditures, health care regulation.

University of Wyoming, College of Health Sciences, School of Pharmacy, Laramie, WY 82071. Offers health services administration (MS); pharmacy (Pharm D). *Accreditation:* ACPE (one or more programs are accredited). *Program availability:* Online learning. *Entrance requirements:* For doctorate, PCAT. Additional exam requirements/recommendations for international students: Required—TOEFL.

Ursuline College, School of Graduate and Professional Studies, Program in Business Administration, Pepper Pike, OH 44124-4398. Offers ethical and entrepreneurial leadership (MBA); financial planning and accounting (MBA); health services management (MBA); management (MBA); management and leadership (MBA); marketing and communications management (MBA). *Program availability:* Part-time. *Faculty:* 3 full-time (2 women), 3 part-time/adjunct (2 women). *Students:* 3 full-time (all women), 26 part-time (23 women); includes 13 minority (12 Black or African American, non-Hispanic/Latino; 1 Two or more races, non-Hispanic/Latino). Average age 38. 13 applicants, 85% accepted, 6 enrolled. In 2017, 11 master's awarded. *Degree requirements:* For master's, comprehensive exam (for some programs). *Entrance requirements:* For master's, GRE. Additional exam requirements/recommendations for international students: Required—TOEFL (minimum score 500 paper-based) or GRE. *Application deadline:* Applications are processed on a rolling basis. Application fee: $25. Electronic applications accepted. *Expenses:* $842 per credit hour. *Financial support:* In 2017–18, 3 students received support. Scholarships/grants available. Financial award application deadline: 8/1; financial award applicants required to submit FAFSA. *Faculty research:* Gift economy; sharing economy; cooperative business models; collaborative leadership; corporate social responsibility and the triple bottom line, defined as the three P's: people, planet and profit. *Unit head:* Dr. Anthony Caffarelli, Associate Professor, 440-646-8134, Fax: 440-684-6088, E-mail: tcafarelli@ursuline.edu. *Application contact:* Melanie Steele, Director of Graduate Admission, 440-646-8146, Fax: 440-684-6138, E-mail: graduateadmissions@ursuline.edu.

Utica College, Program in Health Care Administration, Utica, NY 13502-4892. Offers MS. *Program availability:* Part-time, evening/weekend, online learning. *Faculty:* 2 full-time (both women), 11 part-time/adjunct (4 women). *Students:* 15 full-time (12 women), 186 part-time (147 women); includes 52 minority (29 Black or African American, non-Hispanic/Latino; 9 Asian, non-Hispanic/Latino; 11 Hispanic/Latino; 3 Two or more races, non-Hispanic/Latino), 1 international. Average age 33. 67 applicants, 93% accepted, 60 enrolled. In 2017, 56 master's awarded. *Degree requirements:* For master's, capstone (internship or research/program development project). *Entrance requirements:* For master's, BS, minimum GPA of 3.0, 2 recommendation letters, personal essay. Additional exam requirements/recommendations for international students: Required—TOEFL (minimum score 525 paper-based). *Application deadline:* Applications are processed on a rolling basis. Application fee: $50. Electronic applications accepted. *Expenses:* Contact institution. *Financial support:* Application deadline: 3/15; applicants required to submit FAFSA. *Unit head:* Dr. Jamie Cuda, Program Director, 315-792-3540, E-mail: jlcuda@utica.edu. *Application contact:* John D. Rowe, Director of Graduate Admissions, 315-792-3824, Fax: 315-792-3003, E-mail: jrowe@utica.edu.

Valdosta State University, Langdale College of Business, Valdosta, GA 31698. Offers accountancy (M Acc); business administration (MBA); healthcare administration (MBA). MBA program is a member of the Georgia WebMBA. *Accreditation:* AACSB. *Program availability:* Part-time, evening/weekend, 100% online, blended/hybrid learning. *Degree requirements:* For master's, comprehensive written and/or oral exams. *Entrance requirements:* For master's, GMAT or GRE, minimum GPA of 2.75. Additional exam requirements/recommendations for international students: Required—TOEFL (minimum score 523 paper-based); Recommended—IELTS. *Application deadline:* For fall admission, 7/1 for domestic and international students; for spring admission, 11/1 for domestic and international students. Applications are processed on a rolling basis. Application fee: $45. Electronic applications accepted. *Expenses:* Contact institution. *Financial support:* Research assistantships with full tuition reimbursements, institutionally sponsored loans, and scholarships/grants available. Support available to part-time students. Financial award application deadline: 7/1; financial award applicants required to submit FAFSA. *Unit head:* Dr. Mel Schnake, Director, 229-245-2233, Fax: 229-245-2795, E-mail: mschnake@valdosta.edu. *Application contact:* Jessica Powers, Admission Specialist, 229-333-5694, Fax: 229-245-3853, E-mail: jldevane@valdosta.edu.
Website: http://www.valdosta.edu/academics/graduate-school/our-programs/business-administration.php

Valparaiso University, Graduate School and Continuing Education, Program in Health Administration, Valparaiso, IN 46383. Offers health administration (MHA); health care administration (MS). *Program availability:* Part-time, evening/weekend. *Degree requirements:* For master's, practicum, internship. *Entrance requirements:* For master's, minimum overall GPA of 3.0 or 5 years of work experience in the field; basic course in statistics; official transcripts; two letters of recommendation; essay. Additional exam requirements/recommendations for international students: Required—TOEFL (minimum score 550 paper-based; 80 iBT), IELTS (minimum score 6). Electronic applications accepted. *Expenses: Tuition:* Full-time $11,340; part-time $630 per credit hour. *Required fees:* $520; $250 per year. $125 per semester. Tuition and fees vary according to program and reciprocity agreements.

Vanderbilt University, Vanderbilt University Owen Graduate School of Management, Master of Management in Health Care Program, Nashville, TN 37203. Offers MM. *Entrance requirements:* For master's, GMAT or GRE (recommended), undergraduate transcript, five years of relevant work experience, interview. Electronic applications accepted. *Expenses:* Contact institution.

Vanderbilt University, Vanderbilt University Owen Graduate School of Management, Vanderbilt MBA Program, Nashville, TN 37203. Offers accounting (MBA); finance (MBA); general management (MBA); health care (MBA); human and organizational performance (MBA); marketing (MBA); operations (MBA); strategy (MBA); MBA/JD; MBA/M Div; MBA/MD; MBA/MSN; MBA/MTS; MBA/PhD. *Accreditation:* AACSB. *Degree requirements:* For master's, 62 credit hours of coursework; completion of ethics course; minimum GPA of 3.0. *Entrance requirements:* For master's, GMAT (preferred) or GRE, 2 years of work experience (recommended). Additional exam requirements/recommendations for international students: Required—TOEFL (minimum score 100 iBT). Electronic applications accepted. *Expenses:* Contact institution. *Faculty research:* Accounting and finance, business strategy and economics, marketing, operations management, organization studies.

Villanova University, Villanova School of Business, MBA - The Fast Track Program, Villanova, PA 19085. Offers finance (MBA); healthcare (MBA); international business (MBA); strategic management (MBA). *Accreditation:* AACSB. *Program availability:* Part-time, evening/weekend. *Faculty:* 68 full-time (22 women), 65 part-time/adjunct (11 women). *Students:* 128 part-time (55 women); includes 11 minority (3 Black or African American, non-Hispanic/Latino; 4 Asian, non-Hispanic/Latino; 4 Hispanic/Latino), 4 international. Average age 30. 79 applicants, 96% accepted, 64 enrolled. In 2017, 58 master's awarded. *Degree requirements:* For master's, minimum GPA of 3.0. *Entrance requirements:* For master's, GMAT or GRE, work experience, 2 letters of recommendation, 2 essays, resume, official transcripts, interview. Additional exam requirements/recommendations for international students: Required—TOEFL (minimum score 550 paper-based; 100 iBT). *Application deadline:* For fall admission, 6/30 for domestic and international students. Applications are processed on a rolling basis. Application fee: $65. Electronic applications accepted. *Expenses:* $56,016 per year tuition, $1,167 per credit; $50 semester fee. *Financial support:* Scholarships/grants available. Financial award application deadline: 6/30; financial award applicants required to submit FAFSA. *Faculty research:* Business analytics; creativity, innovation and entrepreneurship; global leadership; real estate; church management; business ethics; marketing and consumer insights. *Unit head:* Dr. Joyce Russell, Dean of Villanova School of Business, 610-519-5424, Fax: 610-519-6273, E-mail: joyce.russell@villanova.edu. *Application contact:* Kimberly Kane, Manager of Admissions, 610-519-3701, Fax: 610-519-6273, E-mail: kimberly.kane@villanova.edu.
Website: http://www1.villanova.edu/villanova/business/graduate/mba.html

Villanova University, Villanova School of Business, MBA - The Flex Track Program, Villanova, PA 19085. Offers healthcare (MBA); international business (MBA); marketing (MBA); real estate (MBA); strategic management (MBA); JD/MBA. *Accreditation:* AACSB. *Program availability:* Part-time, evening/weekend, online learning. *Faculty:* 68 full-time (22 women), 65 part-time/adjunct (11 women). *Students:* 13 full-time (4 women), 410 part-time (137 women); includes 105 minority (28 Black or African American, non-Hispanic/Latino; 1 American Indian or Alaska Native, non-Hispanic/Latino; 41 Asian, non-Hispanic/Latino; 29 Hispanic/Latino; 6 Two or more races, non-Hispanic/Latino), 13 international. Average age 31. 94 applicants, 94% accepted, 79 enrolled. In 2017, 201 master's awarded. *Degree requirements:* For master's, minimum GPA of 3.0. *Entrance requirements:* For master's, GMAT or GRE, work experience, 2 letters of recommendation, 2 essays, resume, official transcript. Additional exam requirements/recommendations for international students: Required—TOEFL (minimum score 550 paper-based; 100 iBT). *Application deadline:* For fall admission, 6/30 for domestic and international students; for spring admission, 11/15 for domestic and international students; for summer admission, 3/31 for domestic and international students. Applications are processed on a rolling basis. Application fee: $65. Electronic applications accepted. *Expenses:* $50,016 per year tuition, $1,167 per credit; $50 semester fee. *Financial support:* In 2017–18, 19 research assistantships with full tuition reimbursements (averaging $16,245 per year) were awarded; scholarships/grants also available. Financial award application deadline: 6/30; financial award applicants required to submit FAFSA. *Faculty research:* Business analytics; creativity, innovation and entrepreneurship; global leadership; real estate; church management; business ethics. *Unit head:* Dr. Joyce Russell, Dean of Villanova School of Business, 610-519-5424, Fax: 610-519-6273, E-mail: joyce.russell@villanova.edu. *Application contact:* Claire Bruno, Director of Recruitment and Enrollment Management, 610-519-4336, Fax: 610-519-6273, E-mail: claire.bruno@villanova.edu.
Website: http://www1.villanova.edu/villanova/business/graduate/mba.html

Virginia Commonwealth University, Graduate School, School of Allied Health Professions, Department of Health Administration, Doctoral Program in Health Services Organization and Research, Richmond, VA 23284-9005. Offers PhD. *Degree requirements:* For doctorate, thesis/dissertation, residency. *Entrance requirements:* For doctorate, GMAT or GRE General Test, minimum graduate GPA of 3.0. Additional exam requirements/recommendations for international students: Required—TOEFL (minimum score 600 paper-based; 100 iBT). Electronic applications accepted. *Faculty research:* Organizational studies, theory, associated analytical techniques.

Health Services Management and Hospital Administration

Virginia Commonwealth University, Graduate School, School of Allied Health Professions, Department of Health Administration, Master's Program in Health Administration, Richmond, VA 23284-9005. Offers MHA, JD/MHA, MHA/MD, MHA/MSIS. *Accreditation:* CAHME. *Degree requirements:* For master's, residency. *Entrance requirements:* For master's, GMAT or GRE General Test (preferred minimum score of 5.0 on analytical writing), course work in accounting, economics, and statistics; minimum GPA of 3.0. Additional exam requirements/recommendations for international students: Required—TOEFL (minimum score 600 paper-based; 100 iBT). Electronic applications accepted.

Virginia Commonwealth University, Graduate School, School of Allied Health Professions, Department of Health Administration, Professional Online Master of Science in Health Administration Program, Richmond, VA 23284-9005. Offers MSHA. *Accreditation:* CAHME. *Program availability:* Online learning. *Degree requirements:* For master's, residency. *Entrance requirements:* For master's, GMAT or GRE General Test. Additional exam requirements/recommendations for international students: Required—TOEFL (minimum score 600 paper-based; 100 iBT). Electronic applications accepted.

Virginia Commonwealth University, Graduate School, School of Allied Health Professions, Doctoral Program in Health Related Sciences, Richmond, VA 23284-9005. Offers clinical laboratory sciences (PhD); gerontology (PhD); health administration (PhD); nurse anesthesia (PhD); occupational therapy (PhD); physical therapy (PhD); radiation sciences (PhD); rehabilitation leadership (PhD). *Entrance requirements:* For doctorate, GRE General Test or MAT, minimum GPA of 3.3 in master's degree. Additional exam requirements/recommendations for international students: Required—TOEFL (minimum score 600 paper-based; 100 iBT); Recommended—IELTS (minimum score 6.5). Electronic applications accepted.

Virginia Commonwealth University, Medical College of Virginia-Professional Programs, School of Medicine, Graduate Programs in Medicine, Department of Health Behavior and Policy, Richmond, VA 23284-9005. Offers healthcare policy and research (PhD); social and behavioral sciences (PhD). *Entrance requirements:* For doctorate, GRE General Test. Additional exam requirements/recommendations for international students: Required—TOEFL (minimum score 600 paper-based; 100 iBT). Electronic applications accepted. *Faculty research:* Evaluation of healthcare services and systems to enhance quality of care and patient safety outcomes; examination of chronic disease (e.g. cancer, HIV/AIDS) policies and practices to improve health outcomes and economic efficiency; impact of the uninsured, public insurance (such as Medicaid) and the safety net on access to care and the health of low-income, underserved, and foreign-born populations; the study of labor supply and healthcare coverage in response to health behaviors and shocks.

Virginia International University, School of Business, Fairfax, VA 22030. Offers accounting (MBA, MS); entrepreneurship (MBA); executive management (Graduate Certificate); global logistics (MBA); health care management (MBA); hospitality and tourism management (MBA); human resources management (MBA); international business management (MBA); international finance (MBA); marketing management (MBA); mass media and public relations (MBA); project management (MBA, MS). *Program availability:* Part-time, online learning. *Entrance requirements:* For master's and Graduate Certificate, bachelor's degree. Additional exam requirements/recommendations for international students: Required—TOEFL (minimum score 550 paper-based; 80 iBT), IELTS (minimum score 6). Electronic applications accepted.

Viterbo University, Master of Business Administration Program, La Crosse, WI 54601-4797. Offers general business administration (MBA); health care management (MBA); international business (MBA); leadership (MBA); project management (MBA). *Accreditation:* ACBSP. *Program availability:* Part-time, evening/weekend. *Degree requirements:* For master's, 34 semester credits. *Entrance requirements:* For master's, bachelor's degree, transcripts, minimum undergraduate cumulative GPA of 3.0, 2 letters of reference, 3-5 page essay. Additional exam requirements/recommendations for international students: Recommended—TOEFL (minimum score 550 paper-based). Electronic applications accepted. *Expenses:* Contact institution.

Walden University, Graduate Programs, School of Health Sciences, Minneapolis, MN 55401. Offers clinical research administration (MS, Graduate Certificate); health education and promotion (MS, PhD), including behavioral health (PhD), disease surveillance (PhD), emergency preparedness (MS), general (MHA, MS), global health (PhD), health policy (PhD), health policy and advocacy (MS), population health (PhD); health informatics (MS); health services (PhD), including community health, healthcare administration, leadership, public health policy, self-designed; healthcare administration (MHA, DHA), including general (MHA, MS); leadership and organizational development (MHA); public health (MPH, Dr PH, PhD, Graduate Certificate), including community health education (PhD), epidemiology (PhD); systems policy (MHA). *Program availability:* Part-time, evening/weekend, online only, 100% online. *Degree requirements:* For doctorate, thesis/dissertation, residency. *Entrance requirements:* For master's, bachelor's degree or higher; minimum GPA of 2.5; official transcripts; goal statement (for some programs); access to computer and Internet; for doctorate, master's degree or higher; three years of related professional or academic experience (preferred); minimum GPA of 3.0; goal statement and current resume (for select programs); official transcripts; access to computer and Internet; for Graduate Certificate, relevant work experience; access to computer and Internet. Additional exam requirements/recommendations for international students: Required—TOEFL (minimum score 550 paper-based, 79 iBT), IELTS (minimum score 6.5), Michigan English Language Assessment Battery (minimum score 82), or PTE (minimum score 53). Electronic applications accepted.

Walden University, Graduate Programs, School of Management, Minneapolis, MN 55401. Offers accounting (MBA, MS, DBA), including accounting for the professional (MS), accounting with CPA emphasis (MS), self-designed (MS); advanced project management (Graduate Certificate); applied project management (Graduate Certificate); auditing (Graduate Certificate); bridge to business administration (Post-Doctoral Certificate); bridge to management (Post-Doctoral Certificate); business management (Graduate Certificate); communication (MBA); corporate finance (MBA); digital marketing (Graduate Certificate); entrepreneurship (DBA); entrepreneurship and small business (MBA); finance (MS, DBA), including finance for the professional (MS), finance with CFA/investment (MS), finance with CPA emphasis (MS); global supply chain management (DBA); healthcare management (MBA, DBA); human resource management (MBA, MS, Graduate Certificate), including functional human resource management (MS), general program (MS), integrating functional and strategic human resource management (MS), organizational strategy (MS); human resources management (DBA); information systems management (DBA); international business (MBA, DBA); leadership (MBA, MS, DBA, Graduate Certificate), including general program (MS), human resource leadership (MS), leader development (MS), self-designed (MS); management (MS, PhD), including communications (MS), finance (PhD), general program (MS), healthcare management (MS), human resource management (MS), human resources management (PhD), information systems management (PhD), international business (MS), leadership (MS), leadership and organizational change (PhD), marketing (MS), project management (MS), strategy and operations (MS); managerial accounting (Graduate Certificate); marketing (MBA, MS, DBA); project management (MBA, MS, DBA); self-designed (MBA, DBA); social impact management (DBA); technology entrepreneurship (DBA). *Accreditation:* ACBSP. *Program availability:* Part-time, evening/weekend, online only, 100% online. *Degree requirements:* For master's, thesis (for some programs), residency (for EMBA); for doctorate, thesis/dissertation (for some programs), residency. *Entrance requirements:* For master's, bachelor's degree or higher; minimum GPA of 2.5; official transcripts; goal statement (for some programs); access to computer and Internet; for doctorate, master's degree or higher; three years of related professional or academic experience (preferred); minimum GPA of 3.0; goal statement and current resume (for select programs); official transcripts; access to computer and Internet; for other advanced degree, relevant work experience; access to computer and Internet. Additional exam requirements/recommendations for international students: Required—TOEFL (minimum score 550 paper-based, 79 iBT), IELTS (minimum score 6.5), Michigan English Language Assessment Battery (minimum score 82), or PTE (minimum score 53). Electronic applications accepted.

Walden University, Graduate Programs, School of Nursing, Minneapolis, MN 55401. Offers adult-gerontology acute care nurse practitioner (MSN); adult-gerontology nurse practitioner (MSN); education (MSN); family nurse practitioner (MSN); informatics (MSN); leadership and management (MSN); nursing (PhD, Post-Master's Certificate), including education (PhD), healthcare administration (PhD), interdisciplinary health (PhD), leadership (PhD), nursing education (Post-Master's Certificate), nursing informatics (Post-Master's Certificate), nursing leadership and management (Post-Master's Certificate), public health policy (PhD); nursing practice (DNP); psychiatric mental health (MSN). *Accreditation:* AACN. *Program availability:* Part-time, evening/weekend, online only, 100% online. *Degree requirements:* For doctorate, thesis/dissertation (for some programs), residency (for some programs), field experience (for some programs). *Entrance requirements:* For master's, bachelor's degree or equivalent in related field or RN; minimum GPA of 2.5; official transcripts; goal statement (for some programs); access to computer and Internet; for doctorate, master's degree or higher; RN; three years of related professional or academic experience; goal statement; access to computer and Internet; for Post-Master's Certificate, relevant work experience; access to computer and Internet. Additional exam requirements/recommendations for international students: Required—TOEFL (minimum score 550 paper-based, 79 iBT), IELTS (minimum score 6.5), Michigan English Language Assessment Battery (minimum score 82), or PTE (minimum score 53). Electronic applications accepted.

Walden University, Graduate Programs, School of Public Policy and Administration, Minneapolis, MN 55401. Offers criminal justice (MPA, MPP, MS, Graduate Certificate), including emergency management (MS, PhD), general program (MS), global leadership (MS, PhD), homeland security and policy coordination (MS, PhD), law and public policy (MS, PhD), policy analysis (MS, PhD), public management and leadership (MS, PhD), self-designed (MS), terrorism, mediation, and peace (MS, PhD); criminal justice and executive management (MS), including global leadership (MS, PhD); criminal justice leadership and executive management (MS), including emergency management (MS, PhD), general program, homeland security and policy coordination (MS, PhD), law and public policy (MS, PhD), policy analysis (MS, PhD), public management and leadership (MS, PhD), self-designed, terrorism, mediation, and peace (MS, PhD); emergency management (MPA, MPP, MS), including criminal justice (MS, PhD), general program (MS), homeland security (MS), public management and leadership (MS, PhD), terrorism and emergency management (MS); general program (MPA, MPP); global leadership (MPA, MPP); government management (Graduate Certificate); health policy (MPA, MPP); homeland security (Graduate Certificate); homeland security and policy coordination (MPA, MPP); international nongovernmental organizations (MPA, MPP); law and public policy (MPA, MPP); local government management for sustainable communities (MPA, MPP); nonprofit management (Graduate Certificate); nonprofit management and leadership (MPA, MPP, MS), including global leadership (MS, PhD), international nongovernmental organization (MS), local government for sustainable communities (MS), self designed (MS); online teaching in higher education (Post-Master's Certificate); policy analysis (MPA); public management and leadership (MPA, MPP, Graduate Certificate); public policy (Graduate Certificate); public policy and administration (PhD), including criminal justice (MS, PhD), emergency management (MS, PhD), global leadership (MS, PhD), health policy, homeland security and policy coordination (MS, PhD), international nongovernmental organizations, law and public policy (MS, PhD), local government management for sustainable communities, nonprofit management and leadership, policy analysis (MS, PhD), public management and leadership (MS, PhD), terrorism, mediation, and peace (MS, PhD); strategic planning and public policy (Graduate Certificate); terrorism, mediation, and peace (MPA, MPP). *Program availability:* Part-time, evening/weekend, online only, 100% online. *Degree requirements:* For doctorate, thesis/dissertation, residency. *Entrance requirements:* For master's, bachelor's degree or higher; minimum GPA of 2.5; official transcripts; goal statement (for some programs); access to computer and Internet; for doctorate, master's degree or higher; three years of related professional or academic experience (preferred); minimum GPA of 3.0; goal statement and current resume (for select programs); official transcripts; access to computer and Internet; for other advanced degree, relevant work experience; access to computer and Internet. Additional exam requirements/recommendations for international students: Required—TOEFL (minimum score 550 paper-based, 79 iBT), IELTS (minimum score 6.5), Michigan English Language Assessment Battery (minimum score 82), or PTE (minimum score 53). Electronic applications accepted.

Walsh University, Graduate Programs, MBA Program, North Canton, OH 44720-3396. Offers healthcare management (MBA); management (MBA); marketing (MBA). *Program availability:* Part-time, evening/weekend, online only, 100% online. *Degree requirements:* For master's, capstone course in strategic management. *Entrance requirements:* For master's, GMAT (minimum score of 490), minimum GPA of 3.0. Additional exam requirements/recommendations for international students: Required—TOEFL (minimum score 500 paper-based; 61 iBT). Electronic applications accepted. Application fee is waived when completed online. *Expenses:* Contact institution. *Faculty research:* Medical tourism, familial influence in financial fitness, pedagogy in finance courses, sociocultural aspects of women entrepreneurs, patient satisfaction.

Washington Adventist University, Program in Health Care Administration, Takoma Park, MD 20912. Offers MA. *Program availability:* Part-time. *Students:* 7 full-time (4 women), 18 part-time (12 women); includes 15 minority (10 Black or African American, non-Hispanic/Latino; 5 Asian, non-Hispanic/Latino), 8 international. Average age 33. In 2017, 8 master's awarded. *Entrance requirements:* Additional exam requirements/recommendations for international students: Required—TOEFL (minimum score 550 paper-based; 80 iBT), IELTS (minimum score 6.5). *Application deadline:* For fall admission, 8/26 for domestic students; for spring admission, 1/6 for domestic students; for summer admission, 5/11 for domestic students. Applications are processed on a rolling basis. Application fee: $25. Electronic applications accepted. *Expenses: Tuition:* Part-time $625 per credit. *Financial support:* Applicants required to submit FAFSA. *Unit head:* Dr. Patrick Williams, Associate Provost, 301-891-4116, E-mail: pawillia@wau.edu. *Application contact:* Jessica Ritchie, Program Coordinator, 301-891-4086, E-mail: jritchie@wau.edu.
Website: http://www.wau.edu/index.php?option-com_content&view-article&id-1007temid-964

Washington State University, College of Pharmacy, Department of Health Policy and Administration, Spokane, WA 99210. Offers MHPA. Programs offered at the Spokane campus. *Accreditation:* CAHME. *Program availability:* Part-time, evening/weekend. *Degree requirements:* For master's, comprehensive exam (for some programs), thesis (for some programs), oral exam. *Entrance requirements:* For master's, GRE General Test or GMAT, minimum GPA of 3.0, 3 letters of recommendation. Additional exam requirements/recommendations for international students: Required—TOEFL (minimum score 550 paper-based) or IELTS (minimum score 7).

Wayland Baptist University, Graduate Programs, Programs in Business Administration/Management, Plainview, TX 79072-6998. Offers accounting (MBA); general business (MBA); health care administration (MAM, MBA); human resource management (MAM, MBA); international management (MBA); management (MBA, D Mgt); management information systems (MBA); organization management (MAM); project management (MBA). *Program availability:* Part-time, evening/weekend, online learning. *Faculty:* 30 full-time (5 women), 38 part-time/adjunct (9 women). *Students:* 42 full-time (20 women), 538 part-time (253 women); includes 311 minority (98 Black or African American, non-Hispanic/Latino; 4 American Indian or Alaska Native, non-Hispanic/Latino; 16 Asian, non-Hispanic/Latino; 153 Hispanic/Latino; 11 Native Hawaiian or other Pacific Islander, non-Hispanic/Latino; 29 Two or more races, non-Hispanic/Latino), 6 international. Average age 40. 100 applicants, 96% accepted, 60 enrolled. In 2017, 216 master's awarded. *Degree requirements:* For master's, capstone course. *Entrance requirements:* For master's, GMAT, GRE or MAT. Additional exam requirements/recommendations for international students: Required—TOEFL (minimum score 500 paper-based; 61 iBT). *Application deadline:* Applications are processed on a rolling basis. Application fee: $50. Electronic applications accepted. *Expenses: Tuition:* Full-time $11,250; part-time $625 per credit hour. *Required fees:* $1200. *Financial support:* Federal Work-Study, institutionally sponsored loans, and scholarships/grants available. Support available to part-time students. Financial award application deadline: 5/1; financial award applicants required to submit FAFSA. *Unit head:* Dr. Kelly Warren, Chairman, 806-291-1020, Fax: 806-291-1957, E-mail: warrenk@wbu.edu. *Application contact:* Amanda Stanton, Graduate Studies, 806-291-3423, Fax: 806-291-1950, E-mail: stanton@wbu.edu.

Waynesburg University, Graduate and Professional Studies, Canonsburg, PA 15370. Offers business (MBA), including energy management, finance, health systems, human resources, leadership, market development; counseling (MA), including addictions counseling, clinical mental health; counselor education and supervision (PhD); criminal investigation (MA); education (M Ed), including autism, curriculum and instruction, educational leadership, online teaching; nursing (MSN), including administration, education, informatics; nursing practice (DNP); special education (M Ed); technology (M Ed); MSN/MBA. *Accreditation:* AACN. *Program availability:* Part-time, evening/weekend. *Degree requirements:* For doctorate, thesis/dissertation. *Entrance requirements:* Additional exam requirements/recommendations for international students: Required—TOEFL. Electronic applications accepted.

Wayne State University, College of Liberal Arts and Sciences, Department of Political Science, Detroit, MI 48202. Offers political science (MA, PhD); public administration (MPA), including economic development policy and management, health and human services policy and management, human and fiscal resource management, nonprofit policy and management, organizational behavior and management, urban and metropolitan policy and management; JD/MA. *Accreditation:* NASPAA. *Faculty:* 18. *Students:* 48 full-time (20 women), 68 part-time (36 women); includes 37 minority (26 Black or African American, non-Hispanic/Latino; 3 Asian, non-Hispanic/Latino; 2 Hispanic/Latino; 6 Two or more races, non-Hispanic/Latino), 6 international. Average age 32. 105 applicants, 39% accepted, 20 enrolled. In 2017, 17 master's, 3 doctorates awarded. *Degree requirements:* For master's, comprehensive exam (for some programs), thesis (for some programs); for doctorate, thesis/dissertation. *Entrance requirements:* For master's, GRE General Test, substantial undergraduate preparation in the social sciences, minimum upper-division undergraduate GPA of 3.0, two letters of recommendation, personal statement; for doctorate, GRE General Test, 3 letters of recommendation; personal statement; interview. Additional exam requirements/recommendations for international students: Required—TOEFL (minimum score 550 paper-based; 79 iBT), TWE (minimum score 5.5), Michigan English Language Assessment Battery (minimum score 85); Recommended—IELTS (minimum score 6.5). *Application deadline:* For fall admission, 5/15 for domestic students, 5/1 priority date for international students; for winter admission, 10/15 for domestic students, 9/1 priority date for international students. Applications are processed on a rolling basis. Application fee: $50. Electronic applications accepted. *Expenses:* Contact institution. *Financial support:* In 2017–18, 44 students received support, including 6 fellowships with tuition reimbursements available (averaging $11,698 per year), 12 teaching assistantships with tuition reimbursements available (averaging $18,534 per year); research assistantships with tuition reimbursements available, scholarships/grants, health care benefits, and unspecified assistantships also available. Financial award applicants required to submit FAFSA. *Faculty research:* American government and politics, comparative politics, political methodology, political theory, public administration, public law, public policy, world politics/international relations, formal theory/modeling, gender and politics, international law, peace research, political economy, political psychology, politics of developing countries, race, religion, and ethnicity, urban politics. *Unit head:* Dr. Daniel Geller, Professor and Chair, 313-577-6328, E-mail: dgeller@wayne.edu. *Application contact:* Dr. Sharon Lean, Graduate Director, 313-577-2630, E-mail: gradpolisci@wayne.edu.
Website: http://clas.wayne.edu/politicalscience/

Weber State University, Dumke College of Health Professions, Master of Health Administration Program, Ogden, UT 84408-1001. Offers MHA. *Accreditation:* CAHME. *Program availability:* Part-time, evening/weekend. *Faculty:* 5 full-time (2 women). *Students:* 69 full-time (26 women), 15 part-time (5 women); includes 3 minority (1 Black or African American, non-Hispanic/Latino; 2 Hispanic/Latino), 1 international. Average age 33. In 2017, 32 master's awarded. *Entrance requirements:* For master's, GMAT or GRE. Additional exam requirements/recommendations for international students: Required—TOEFL (minimum score 550 paper-based). *Application deadline:* For fall admission, 3/15 for domestic students, 2/20 for international students. Application fee: $60 ($95 for international students). Electronic applications accepted. *Expenses:* Tuition, state resident: full-time $7283. Tuition, nonresident: full-time $17,166. *Required fees:* $898. Tuition and fees vary according to program. *Financial support:* In 2017–18, 14 students received support. Scholarships/grants available. Financial award application deadline: 4/1; financial award applicants required to submit FAFSA. *Unit head:* Pat Shaw, Associate Professor/Chair, Health Administrative Services, 801-626-7989, Fax: 801-626-6475, E-mail: pshaw@weber.edu. *Application contact:* Cory Moss, Assistant Professor, 801-626-7237, Fax: 801-626-6475, E-mail: cmoss@weber.edu.
Website: http://www.weber.edu/MHA/

Webster University, George Herbert Walker School of Business and Technology, Department of Management, St. Louis, MO 63119-3194. Offers business and organizational security management (MA); digital marketing management (Graduate Certificate); government contracting (Graduate Certificate); health administration (MHA); health care management (MA); health services management (MA); human resources development (MA); human resources management (MA); information technology management (MA, MS); management (D Mgt); management and leadership (MA); marketing (MA); nonprofit leadership (MA); nonprofit revenue development (Graduate Certificate); organizational development (Graduate Certificate); procurement and acquisitions management (MA); public administration (MPA); space systems operations management (MS). *Program availability:* Part-time, evening/weekend, online learning. *Degree requirements:* For master's, thesis (for some programs); for doctorate, thesis/dissertation, written exam. *Entrance requirements:* For doctorate, GMAT, 3 years of work experience, MBA. Additional exam requirements/recommendations for international students: Required—TOEFL.

West Chester University of Pennsylvania, College of Health Sciences, Department of Health, West Chester, PA 19383. Offers health care management (Certificate); integrative health (Certificate); public health (MPH). *Accreditation:* CEPH. *Program availability:* Part-time, evening/weekend, 100% online. *Students:* 99 full-time (78 women), 72 part-time (57 women); includes 78 minority (60 Black or African American, non-Hispanic/Latino; 11 Asian, non-Hispanic/Latino; 5 Hispanic/Latino; 2 Two or more races, non-Hispanic/Latino), 11 international. Average age 29. 108 applicants, 90% accepted, 63 enrolled. In 2017, 75 master's, 13 other advanced degrees awarded. *Degree requirements:* For master's, minimum GPA of 3.0, completion of major project and practicum (for MPH). *Entrance requirements:* For master's, undergraduate introduction to statistics course. Additional exam requirements/recommendations for international students: Required—TOEFL or IELTS. *Application deadline:* For fall admission, 5/15 for international students; for spring admission, 10/15 for international students. Applications are processed on a rolling basis. Application fee: $50. Electronic applications accepted. *Expenses:* Tuition, state resident: full-time $9000; part-time $500 per credit. Tuition, nonresident: full-time $13,500; part-time $750 per credit. *Required fees:* $2959; $149.79 per credit. *Financial support:* Scholarships/grants and unspecified assistantships available. Financial award application deadline: 2/15; financial award applicants required to submit FAFSA. *Faculty research:* Healthy communities, community health issues and evidence-based programs, environment and health, current issues in health care management and integrative health. *Unit head:* Dr. James W. Brenner, Chair, 610-436-2931, E-mail: jbrenner@wcupa.edu. *Application contact:* Dr. Lynn Carson, Graduate Coordinator, 610-436-2138, E-mail: lcarson@wcupa.edu.
Website: http://www.wcupa.edu/HealthSciences/health/

West Coast University, Graduate Programs, North Hollywood, CA 91606. Offers advanced generalist (MSN); family nurse practitioner (MSN); health administration (MHA); occupational therapy (MS); pharmacy (Pharm D); physical therapy (DPT).

Western Carolina University, Graduate School, College of Health and Human Sciences, School of Health Sciences, Cullowhee, NC 28723. Offers MHS. *Program availability:* Part-time, evening/weekend. *Degree requirements:* For master's, thesis or alternative. *Entrance requirements:* For master's, GRE General Test, appropriate undergraduate degree with minimum GPA of 3.0, 3 letters of recommendation. Additional exam requirements/recommendations for international students: Required—TOEFL (minimum score 550 paper-based; 79 iBT). *Expenses:* Tuition, state resident: full-time $4436. Tuition, nonresident: full-time $14,842. *Required fees:* $2926. *Faculty research:* Epidemiology, dietetics, public health, environmental technology, water quality, occupational health.

Western Connecticut State University, Division of Graduate Studies, Ancell School of Business, Program in Health Administration, Danbury, CT 06810-6885. Offers MHA. *Program availability:* Part-time. *Degree requirements:* For master's, comprehensive exam, completion of program within 6 years. *Entrance requirements:* For master's, GMAT, GRE, or MAT, minimum GPA of 2.5. Additional exam requirements/recommendations for international students: Recommended—TOEFL (minimum score 550 paper-based; 79 iBT), IELTS (minimum score 6). *Expenses:* Tuition, state resident: full-time $6757; part-time $374 per credit hour. Tuition, nonresident: full-time $18,102; part-time $374 per credit hour. *Required fees:* $4994; $190 per credit hour. $60 per term. Tuition and fees vary according to degree level and program. *Faculty research:* Organizational behavior, human resource management, health delivery systems, health services financial management, managing health services organizations, health services quality management, health policy and strategic management for health services, long-term care administration, health services marketing, health care law.

Western Governors University, College of Health Professions, Salt Lake City, UT 84107. Offers healthcare management (MBA); leadership and management (MSN); nursing education (MSN); nursing informatics (MSN). *Program availability:* Evening/weekend, online learning. *Degree requirements:* For master's, capstone project. *Entrance requirements:* For master's, transcripts. Additional exam requirements/recommendations for international students: Required—TOEFL (minimum score 450 paper-based; 80 iBT). *Application deadline:* Applications are processed on a rolling basis. Application fee: $65. Electronic applications accepted. Application fee is waived when completed online. *Financial support:* Tuition waivers (partial) available. Financial award applicants required to submit FAFSA. *Unit head:* Dr. Jan Jones-Schenk, Director. *Application contact:* Enrollment Department, 866-225-5948, Fax: 801-274-3306, E-mail: info@wgu.edu.
Website: https://www.wgu.edu/online-nursing-health-degrees.html#

Western Kentucky University, Graduate Studies, College of Health and Human Services, Department of Public Health, Bowling Green, KY 42101. Offers healthcare administration (MHA); public health (MPH). *Program availability:* Part-time, evening/weekend. *Degree requirements:* For master's, comprehensive exam, thesis or alternative. *Entrance requirements:* For master's, GRE General Test, minimum GPA of 2.75. Additional exam requirements/recommendations for international students: Required—TOEFL (minimum score 555 paper-based; 79 iBT). *Faculty research:* Health education training, driver traffic safety, community readiness, occupational injuries, local health departments.

Western Michigan University, Graduate College, College of Arts and Sciences, School of Public Affairs and Administration, Kalamazoo, MI 49008. Offers health care administration (MPA, Graduate Certificate); nonprofit leadership and administration (Graduate Certificate); public administration (PhD). *Accreditation:* NASPAA (one or more programs are accredited). *Degree requirements:* For doctorate, thesis/dissertation.

Widener University, School of Business Administration, Program in Health and Medical Services Administration, Chester, PA 19013-5792. Offers MBA, MHA, MD/MBA, MD/MHA, Psy D/MBA, Psy D/MHA. *Accreditation:* CAHME (one or more programs are accredited). *Program availability:* Part-time, evening/weekend, 100% online, blended/hybrid learning. *Faculty:* 3 full-time (1 woman), 6 part-time/adjunct (1 woman). *Students:* 7 full-time (5 women), 28 part-time (19 women); includes 16 minority (7 Black or African American, non-Hispanic/Latino; 3 Asian, non-Hispanic/Latino; 5 Hispanic/Latino; 1 Native Hawaiian or other Pacific Islander, non-Hispanic/Latino), 2 international. Average age 31. 30 applicants, 80% accepted. In 2017, 1 master's awarded. *Degree requirements:* For master's, clerkship, residency. *Entrance requirements:* For master's, GMAT, interview, minimum GPA of 2.5. *Application deadline:* For fall admission, 8/1 priority date for domestic students; for spring admission, 12/1 for domestic students. Applications are processed on a rolling basis. Application fee: $25 ($300 for international students). Electronic applications accepted. *Financial support:* Research

assistantships, career-related internships or fieldwork, and traineeships available. Support available to part-time students. Financial award application deadline: 5/1. *Faculty research:* Cost containment in health care, reimbursement of hospitals, strategic behavior. *Unit head:* Dr. Jose Proenca, Director, 610-499-4330. *Application contact:* Ann Seltzer, Graduate Enrollment Administrator, 610-499-4305, E-mail: apseltzer@widener.edu.
Website: http://www.widener.edu

Widener University, School of Human Service Professions, Institute for Graduate Clinical Psychology, Program in Clinical Psychology and Health and Medical Services Administration, Chester, PA 19013-5792. Offers Psy D/MBA, Psy D/MHA. *Accreditation:* APA (one or more programs are accredited); CAHME. *Faculty:* 15 full-time (6 women), 18 part-time/adjunct (10 women). *Students:* 7 full-time (5 women); includes 1 minority (Black or African American, non-Hispanic/Latino). Average age 28. *Application deadline:* For fall admission, 12/31 for domestic students. Application fee: $75. Electronic applications accepted. *Financial support:* Career-related internships or fieldwork, Federal Work-Study, and institutionally sponsored loans available. Financial award application deadline: 5/31. *Faculty research:* Psychosocial competence, family systems, medical care systems and financing. *Unit head:* Dr. Hal Shorey, Director, 610-499-4598, Fax: 610-499-4625.

Wilkes University, College of Graduate and Professional Studies, Jay S. Sidhu School of Business and Leadership, Wilkes-Barre, PA 18766-0002. Offers accounting (MBA); entrepreneurship (MBA); finance (MBA); health care administration (MBA); human resource management (MBA); international business (MBA); operations management (MBA); organizational leadership and development (MBA). *Accreditation:* ACBSP. *Program availability:* Part-time, evening/weekend. *Students:* 37 full-time (18 women), 87 part-time (45 women); includes 17 minority (4 Black or African American, non-Hispanic/Latino; 5 Asian, non-Hispanic/Latino; 6 Hispanic/Latino; 2 Two or more races, non-Hispanic/Latino), 14 international. Average age 30. In 2017, 77 master's awarded. *Entrance requirements:* For master's, GMAT. Additional exam requirements/recommendations for international students: Required—TOEFL (minimum score 550 paper-based; 79 iBT). *Application deadline:* Applications are processed on a rolling basis. Application fee: $45 ($65 for international students). Electronic applications accepted. *Expenses:* Contact institution. *Financial support:* Unspecified assistantships available. Financial award application deadline: 3/1; financial award applicants required to submit FAFSA. *Unit head:* Dr. Abel Adekola, Dean, 570-408-4701, Fax: 570-408-7846, E-mail: abel.adekola@wilkes.edu. *Application contact:* Kristin Donati, Associate Director of Graduate Admissions, 570-408-3338, Fax: 570-408-7846, E-mail: kristin.donati@wilkes.edu.
Website: http://www.wilkes.edu/academics/colleges/sidhu-school-of-business-leadership/index.aspx

William Woods University, Graduate and Adult Studies, Fulton, MO 65251-1098. Offers administration (M Ed, Ed S); athletic/activities administration (M Ed); curriculum and instruction (M Ed, Ed S); educational leadership (Ed D); equestrian education (M Ed); health management (MBA); human resources (MBA); leadership (MBA); marketing, advertising, and public relations (MBA); teaching and technology (M Ed). *Program availability:* Part-time, evening/weekend. *Degree requirements:* For master's, capstone course (MBA), action research (M Ed); for Ed S, field experience. *Entrance requirements:* Additional exam requirements/recommendations for international students: Required—TOEFL (minimum score 550 paper-based). Electronic applications accepted. *Expenses:* Contact institution.

Wilmington University, College of Business, New Castle, DE 19720-6491. Offers accounting (MBA, MS); business administration (MBA, DBA); environmental stewardship (MBA); finance (MBA); health care administration (MBA, MSM); homeland security (MBA, MSM); human resource management (MSM); management information systems (MBA, MSN); marketing (MSM); marketing management (MBA); military leadership (MSM); organizational leadership (MBA, MSM); public administration (MSM). *Program availability:* Part-time, evening/weekend. *Faculty:* 16 full-time (8 women), 106 part-time/adjunct (49 women). *Students:* 525 full-time (294 women), 1,212 part-time (780 women); includes 557 minority (412 Black or African American, non-Hispanic/Latino; 14 American Indian or Alaska Native, non-Hispanic/Latino; 55 Asian, non-Hispanic/Latino; 25 Hispanic/Latino; 3 Native Hawaiian or other Pacific Islander, non-Hispanic/Latino; 48 Two or more races, non-Hispanic/Latino), 157 international. Average age 35. 1,484 applicants, 70% accepted, 685 enrolled. In 2017, 543 master's, 16 doctorates awarded. *Entrance requirements:* Additional exam requirements/recommendations for international students: Required—TOEFL (minimum score 500 paper-based). *Application deadline:* Applications are processed on a rolling basis. Application fee: $35. Electronic applications accepted. *Expenses: Tuition:* Part-time $466 per credit. *Required fees:* $25 per semester. Tuition and fees vary according to degree level and campus/location. *Financial support:* Applicants required to submit FAFSA. *Unit head:* Dr. Kathy S. Kennedy Ratajack, Dean, 302-356-2481. *Application contact:* Laura Morris, Director of Admissions, 877-967-5456, E-mail: infocenter@wilmu.edu.
Website: http://www.wilmu.edu/business/

Wilson College, Graduate Programs, Chambersburg, PA 17201-1285. Offers accounting (M Acc); choreography and visual art (MFA); education (M Ed); educational technology (MET); healthcare administration (MHA); humanities (MA), including art and culture, critical/cultural theory, English language and literature, women's studies; management (MSM); nursing (MSN), including nursing education, nursing leadership and management; special education (MSE). *Program availability:* Evening/weekend. *Degree requirements:* For master's, project. *Entrance requirements:* For master's, PRAXIS, minimum undergraduate cumulative GPA of 3.0, 2 letters of recommendation, current certification for eligibility to teach in grades K-12, resume, personal interview. Electronic applications accepted.

Wingate University, Porter B. Byrum School of Business, Wingate, NC 28174. Offers accounting (MAC); corporate innovation (MBA); finance (MBA); general management (MBA); healthcare management (MBA); marketing (MBA); project management (MBA). *Accreditation:* ACBSP. *Program availability:* Part-time, evening/weekend. *Entrance requirements:* For master's, GMAT, work experience, 2 letters of recommendation. Electronic applications accepted. *Expenses:* Contact institution. *Faculty research:* Stochastic processes, business ethics, regional economic development, municipal finance, consumer behavior.

Winston-Salem State University, Program in Health Administration, Winston-Salem, NC 27110-0003. Offers MHA. *Entrance requirements:* For master's, baccalaureate degree, minimum cumulative undergraduate GPA of 3.0, personal statement, three letters of recommendation, interview.

Worcester State University, Graduate School, Program in Health Care Administration, Worcester, MA 01602-2597. Offers MS. *Program availability:* Part-time. *Faculty:* 2 full-time. *Students:* 2 full-time (1 woman), 15 part-time (7 women); includes 4 minority (3 Black or African American, non-Hispanic/Latino; 1 Asian, non-Hispanic/Latino), 5 international. Average age 39. 23 applicants, 39% accepted, 7 enrolled. In 2017, 7 master's awarded. *Degree requirements:* For master's, comprehensive exam (for some programs), thesis optional, capstone. *Entrance requirements:* For master's, GMAT (preferred), GRE. Additional exam requirements/recommendations for international students: Required—TOEFL (minimum score 550 paper-based; 79 iBT). *Application deadline:* For fall admission, 6/15 for domestic and international students; for spring admission, 11/1 for domestic and international students; for summer admission, 4/1 for domestic and international students. Applications are processed on a rolling basis. Application fee: $50. Electronic applications accepted. *Expenses:* Tuition, state resident: full-time $3042; part-time $169 per credit hour. Tuition, nonresident: full-time $3042; part-time $169 per credit hour. *Required fees:* $2754; $153 per credit hour. *Financial support:* Career-related internships or fieldwork, scholarships/grants, and unspecified assistantships available. Financial award application deadline: 3/1; financial award applicants required to submit FAFSA. *Unit head:* Dr. Robert Holmes, Coordinator, 508-929-8343, E-mail: rholmes3@worcester.edu. *Application contact:* Sara Grady, Associate Dean, Graduate Studies and Professional Development, 508-929-8130, E-mail: sara.grady@worcester.edu.

Xavier University, College of Social Sciences, Health and Education, Department of Health Services Administration, Cincinnati, OH 45207. Offers MHSA, MHSA/MBA. *Accreditation:* CAHME. *Program availability:* Part-time. *Degree requirements:* For master's, thesis, residency, project. *Entrance requirements:* For master's, GMAT or GRE, resume, two letters of recommendation, statement of intent, official transcripts, interview, minimum accounting and statistics grade of C. Additional exam requirements/recommendations for international students: Required—TOEFL (minimum score 550 paper-based; 80 iBT). Electronic applications accepted. Application fee is waived when completed online. *Expenses:* Contact institution. *Faculty research:* Success factors of ethics committees in health care, early hospital readmission and quality, health and labor economics, clinical emergency medicine and uncompensated care.

See Display on the next page and Close-Up on page 557.

Xavier University, Williams College of Business, Master of Business Administration Program, Cincinnati, OH 45207. Offers business administration (Exec MBA, MBA); business intelligence (MBA); finance (MBA); health industry (MBA); international business (MBA); marketing (MBA); values-based leadership (MBA); MBA/MHSA; MSN/MBA. *Accreditation:* AACSB. *Program availability:* Part-time, evening/weekend. *Degree requirements:* For master's, capstone course. *Entrance requirements:* For master's, GMAT or GRE, official transcript; resume. Additional exam requirements/recommendations for international students: Required—TOEFL (minimum score 550 paper-based; 79 iBT). Electronic applications accepted. Application fee is waived when completed online. *Expenses:* Contact institution.

Yale University, Yale School of Medicine, Yale School of Public Health, New Haven, CT 06520. Offers applied biostatistics and epidemiology (APMPH); biostatistics (MPH, MS, PhD), including global health (MPH); chronic disease epidemiology (MPH, PhD), including global health (MPH); environmental health sciences (MPH, PhD), including global health (MPH); epidemiology of microbial diseases (MPH, PhD), including global health (MPH); global health (APMPH); health management (MPH), including global health; health policy (MPH), including global health; health policy and administration (APMPH, PhD); occupational and environmental medicine (APMPH); preventive medicine (APMPH); social and behavioral sciences (APMPH, MPH), including global health (MPH); JD/MPH; M Div/MPH; MBA/MPH; MD/MPH; MEM/MPH; MFS/MPH; MM Sc/MPH; MPH/MA; MSN/MPH. MS and PhD offered through the Graduate School. *Accreditation:* CEPH. *Program availability:* Part-time. Terminal master's awarded for partial completion of doctoral program. *Degree requirements:* For master's, thesis, summer internship; for doctorate, comprehensive exam, thesis/dissertation, residency. *Entrance requirements:* For master's, GMAT, GRE, or MCAT, two years of undergraduate coursework in math and science; for doctorate, GRE General Test. Additional exam requirements/recommendations for international students: Required—TOEFL (minimum score 100 iBT). Electronic applications accepted. *Expenses:* Contact institution. *Faculty research:* Genetic and emerging infections epidemiology, virology, cost/quality, vector biology, quantitative methods, aging, asthma, cancer.

York College of Pennsylvania, Graham School of Business, York, PA 17403-3651. Offers accounting (M Acc); business (MBA); continuous improvement (MBA); financial management (MBA); health care management (MBA); management (MBA); marketing (MBA); self-designed (MBA). *Accreditation:* ACBSP. *Program availability:* Part-time, evening/weekend. *Faculty:* 9 full-time (2 women), 3 part-time/adjunct (0 women). *Students:* 3 full-time (2 women), 72 part-time (33 women); includes 14 minority (7 Black or African American, non-Hispanic/Latino; 3 Asian, non-Hispanic/Latino; 1 Hispanic/Latino; 3 Two or more races, non-Hispanic/Latino). Average age 35. 68 applicants, 76% accepted, 28 enrolled. In 2017, 17 master's awarded. *Degree requirements:* For master's, directed study. *Entrance requirements:* For master's, GMAT. Additional exam requirements/recommendations for international students: Required—TOEFL (minimum score 530 paper-based; 72 iBT), IELTS (minimum score 6). *Application deadline:* For fall admission, 7/15 priority date for domestic students, 5/1 for international students; for spring admission, 11/15 priority date for domestic students, 9/1 for international students; for summer admission, 4/15 priority date for domestic students. Applications are processed on a rolling basis. Application fee: $0. Electronic applications accepted. *Expenses:* $795 per credit. *Financial support:* In 2017–18, 3 students received support. Scholarships/grants available. Financial award applicants required to submit FAFSA. *Unit head:* Nicole Cornell Sadowski, MBA Director, 717-815-1491, Fax: 717-600-3999, E-mail: ncornell@ycp.edu. *Application contact:* MBA Office, 717-815-1491, Fax: 717-600-3999, E-mail: mba@ycp.edu.
Website: http://www.ycp.edu/mba

Youngstown State University, Graduate School, Bitonte College of Health and Human Services, Department of Health Professions, Youngstown, OH 44555-0001. Offers health and human services (MHHS); public health (MPH). *Accreditation:* NAACLS. *Program availability:* Part-time, evening/weekend. *Degree requirements:* For master's, thesis optional. *Entrance requirements:* For master's, GRE General Test, minimum GPA of 3.0. Additional exam requirements/recommendations for international students: Required—TOEFL. *Faculty research:* Drug prevention, multiskilling in health care, organizational behavior, health care management, health behaviors, research management.

Health Services Research

Albany College of Pharmacy and Health Sciences, School of Arts and Sciences, Albany, NY 12208. Offers clinical laboratory sciences (MS); cytotechnology and molecular cytology (MS); health outcomes research (MS); molecular biosciences (MS). *Degree requirements:* For master's, thesis. *Entrance requirements:* For master's, GRE, minimum GPA of 3.0. Additional exam requirements/recommendations for international students: Required—TOEFL (minimum score 84 iBT). Electronic applications accepted.

Albany College of Pharmacy and Health Sciences, School of Pharmacy and Pharmaceutical Sciences, Albany, NY 12208. Offers health outcomes research (MS); pharmaceutical sciences (MS), including pharmaceutics, pharmacology; pharmacy (Pharm D). *Accreditation:* ACPE. *Degree requirements:* For master's, thesis; for doctorate, practice experience. *Entrance requirements:* For master's, GRE, minimum GPA of 3.0; for doctorate, PCAT, minimum GPA of 2.5. Additional exam requirements/recommendations for international students: Required—TOEFL (minimum score 84 iBT). Electronic applications accepted. *Faculty research:* Therapeutic use of drugs, pharmacokinetics, drug delivery and design.

American University of Beirut, Graduate Programs, Faculty of Health Sciences, 1107 2020, Lebanon. Offers environmental sciences (MS), including environmental health; epidemiology (MS, PhD); epidemiology and biostatistics (MPH); health care leadership (EMHCL); health management and policy (MPH), including health service administration; health promotion and community health (MPH); health research (MS); public health nutrition (MS). *Program availability:* Part-time. *Faculty:* 33 full-time (22 women), 5 part-time/adjunct (2 women). *Students:* 75 full-time (60 women), 78 part-time (67 women). Average age 27. 274 applicants, 56% accepted, 47 enrolled. In 2017, 63 master's awarded. *Degree requirements:* For master's, one foreign language, comprehensive exam (for some programs), thesis (for MS); for doctorate, one foreign language, comprehensive exam, thesis/dissertation. *Entrance requirements:* For master's, 2 letters of recommendations, personal statement, transcript; for doctorate, GRE, 3 letters of recommendations, personal statement, interview. Additional exam requirements/recommendations for international students: Required—TOEFL (minimum score 583 paper-based; 97 iBT), IELTS (minimum score 7). *Application deadline:* For fall admission, 4/4 for domestic and international students; for spring admission, 11/3 for domestic and international students. Application fee: $50. Electronic applications accepted. *Expenses:* Contact institution. *Financial support:* In 2017–18, 75 students received support. Scholarships/grants, health care benefits, and unspecified assistantships available. Financial award application deadline: 4/4. *Faculty research:* Reproductive and sexual health; occupational and environmental health; conflict and health; mental health; quality in health care delivery, tobacco control. *Total annual research expenditures:* $2 million. *Unit head:* Prof. Iman Adel Nuwayhid, Dean/Professor, 961-1-759683 Ext. 4600, Fax: 961-1-744470, E-mail: nuwayhid@aub.edu.lb. *Application contact:* Mitra Tauk, Administrative Coordinator, 961-1-350000 Ext. 4687, E-mail: mt12@aub.edu.lb.
Website: http://www.aub.edu.lb/fhs/fhs_home/Pages/index.aspx

Boston University, School of Public Health, Health Law, Policy and Management Department, Boston, MA 02215. Offers health law, policy and management (MPH); health services and systems research (MS); health services research (PhD). *Accreditation:* CAHME. *Program availability:* Part-time, evening/weekend. *Degree requirements:* For master's, comprehensive exam (for some programs), thesis (for some programs); for doctorate, comprehensive exam, thesis/dissertation. *Entrance requirements:* For master's, GRE, MCAT, GMAT; for doctorate, GRE. Additional exam requirements/recommendations for international students: Required—TOEFL (minimum score 600 paper-based; 100 iBT), IELTS (minimum score 7). Electronic applications accepted. *Faculty research:* Health policy, health law and ethics, human rights, healthcare management.

Brown University, Graduate School, Division of Biology and Medicine, School of Public Health, Department of Health Services, Policy and Practice, Providence, RI 02912. Offers PhD.

Clarkson University, School of Arts and Sciences, Program in Basic Science, Potsdam, NY 13699. Offers basic science (MS), including biology. *Students:* 3 full-time (1 woman), 1 (woman) part-time; includes 2 minority (both Asian, non-Hispanic/Latino), 1 international. 6 applicants, 67% accepted, 2 enrolled. In 2017, 2 master's awarded. *Entrance requirements:* For master's, GRE. Additional exam requirements/recommendations for international students: Required—TOEFL (minimum score 550 paper-based, 80 iBT) or IELTS (6.5). *Application deadline:* Applications are processed on a rolling basis. Application fee: $50. Electronic applications accepted. *Expenses: Tuition:* Full-time $24,210; part-time $1345 per credit hour. Tuition and fees vary according to campus/location and program. *Financial support:* Scholarships/grants and unspecified assistantships available. *Unit head:* Dr. Charles Thorpe, Interim Dean of Arts and Sciences, 315-268-6544. *Application contact:* Dan Capogna, Director of Graduate Admissions, 518-631-9910, E-mail: graduate@clarkson.edu.
Website: https://www.clarkson.edu/academics/graduate

Dartmouth College, The Dartmouth Institute, Hanover, NH 03755. Offers MPH, MS, PhD. *Program availability:* Part-time. *Faculty:* 51 full-time (26 women), 95 part-time/adjunct (41 women). *Students:* 77 full-time (39 women), 59 part-time (40 women); includes 20 minority (3 Black or African American, non-Hispanic/Latino; 2 American Indian or Alaska Native, non-Hispanic/Latino; 11 Asian, non-Hispanic/Latino; 1 Hispanic/Latino; 3 Two or more races, non-Hispanic/Latino), 7 international. Average age 33. 331 applicants, 54% accepted, 83 enrolled. *Degree requirements:* For master's, research project or practicum; for doctorate, thesis/dissertation. *Entrance requirements:* For master's, GRE, GMAT or MCAT, 2 letters of recommendation, current resume or curriculum vitae; for doctorate, GRE, 3 letters of recommendation, current resume or curriculum vitae. *Application deadline:* For fall admission, 1/15 for domestic students. Application fee: $135. *Financial support:* In 2017–18, fellowships with full tuition reimbursements (averaging $28,200 per year) were awarded; scholarships/grants also available. *Unit head:* Dr. Elliot S. Fisher, Director, 603-653-0802. *Application contact:* Marc Aquila, Senior Director of Recruitment and Admissions, 603-650-1539.
Website: http://tdi.dartmouth.edu/

Emory University, Rollins School of Public Health, Department of Health Policy and Management, Atlanta, GA 30322-1100. Offers health policy (MPH); health policy research (MSPH); health services management (MPH); health services research and health policy (PhD). *Program availability:* Part-time. *Degree requirements:* For master's, thesis (for some programs), practicum, capstone course. *Entrance requirements:* For master's, GRE General Test. Additional exam requirements/recommendations for international students: Required—TOEFL (minimum score 550 paper-based; 80 iBT). Electronic applications accepted. *Faculty research:* U.S. health policy and financing, healthcare organization and financing.

Health Services Research

Florida Agricultural and Mechanical University, Division of Graduate Studies, Research, and Continuing Education, College of Pharmacy and Pharmaceutical Sciences, Graduate Programs in Pharmaceutical Sciences, Tallahassee, FL 32307-3200. Offers environmental toxicology (PhD); health outcomes research and pharmacoeconomics (PhD); medicinal chemistry (MS, PhD); pharmaceutics (MS, PhD); pharmacology/toxicology (MS, PhD); pharmacy administration (MS). *Accreditation:* CEPH. *Degree requirements:* For master's, comprehensive exam, thesis, publishable paper; for doctorate, comprehensive exam, thesis/dissertation, publishable paper. *Entrance requirements:* For master's and doctorate, GRE General Test, minimum GPA of 3.0 in last 60 hours. Additional exam requirements/recommendations for international students: Required—TOEFL. *Faculty research:* Anticancer agents, anti-inflammatory drugs, chronopharmacology, neuroendocrinology, microbiology.

George Mason University, College of Health and Human Services, Department of Health Administration and Policy, Fairfax, VA 22030. Offers health and medical policy (MS); health informatics (MS); health informatics and data analytics (Certificate); health services research (PhD); health systems management (MHA); quality improvement and outcomes management in health care systems (Certificate). *Accreditation:* CAHME. *Program availability:* Part-time, evening/weekend, 100% online. *Faculty:* 16 full-time (7 women), 29 part-time/adjunct (12 women). *Students:* 68 full-time (52 women), 97 part-time (73 women); includes 64 minority (22 Black or African American, non-Hispanic/Latino; 31 Asian, non-Hispanic/Latino; 10 Hispanic/Latino; 1 Two or more races, non-Hispanic/Latino), 37 international. Average age 32. 124 applicants, 73% accepted, 41 enrolled. In 2017, 63 master's, 18 other advanced degrees awarded. *Degree requirements:* For master's, comprehensive exam, internship; for doctorate, thesis/dissertation. *Entrance requirements:* For master's, GRE recommended if undergraduate GPA is below 3.0 (for MS in health and medical policy), 2 official transcripts; expanded goals statement; 3 letters of recommendation; resume; 1 year of work experience (for MHA in health systems management); minimum GPA of 3.25 preferred (for MS in health informatics); for doctorate, GRE, professional and volunteer experience, evidence of ability to write and conduct research at the doctoral level, master's degree or equivalent; for Certificate, 2 official transcripts; expanded goals statement; 3 letters of recommendation; resume. Additional exam requirements/recommendations for international students: Required—TOEFL (minimum score 575 paper-based; 88 iBT), IELTS (minimum score 6.5), PTE (minimum score 59). *Application deadline:* For fall admission, 4/1 for domestic and international students; for spring admission, 11/1 for domestic and international students. Application fee: $75 ($80 for international students). Electronic applications accepted. *Expenses:* $978 per credit (MHA); $900 per credit (MHI). *Financial support:* In 2017–18, 22 students received support, including 18 research assistantships with tuition reimbursements available (averaging $18,018 per year), 5 teaching assistantships (averaging $4,804 per year); career-related internships or fieldwork, Federal Work-Study, scholarships/grants, unspecified assistantships, and health care benefits (for full-time research or teaching assistantship recipients) also available. Support available to part-time students. Financial award application deadline: 3/1; financial award applicants required to submit FAFSA. *Faculty research:* Universal health care, publications, relationships between malpractice pressure and rates of Cesarean section and VBAC, seniors and Wii gaming, relationships between changes in physician's incomes and practice settings and their care to Medicaid and charity patients. *Total annual research expenditures:* $396,087. *Unit head:* Dr. P.J. Maddox, Chair, 703-993-1982, Fax: 703-993-1953, E-mail: pmaddox@gmu.edu. *Application contact:* Tracy Shevlin, Department Manager, 703-993-1929, Fax: 703-993-1953, E-mail: tshevlin@gmu.edu.
Website: http://chhs.gmu.edu/hap/index

The George Washington University, School of Medicine and Health Sciences, Health Sciences Programs, Washington, DC 20052. Offers clinical practice management (MSHS); clinical research administration (MSHS); emergency services management (MSHS); end-of-life care (MSHS); immunohematology (MSHS); immunohematology and biotechnology (MSHS); physical therapy (DPT); physician assistant (MSHS). *Program availability:* Online learning. *Faculty:* 31 full-time (23 women), 4 part-time/adjunct (2 women). *Students:* 304 full-time (233 women), 321 part-time (248 women); includes 212 minority (70 Black or African American, non-Hispanic/Latino; 1 American Indian or Alaska Native, non-Hispanic/Latino; 64 Asian, non-Hispanic/Latino; 59 Hispanic/Latino; 3 Native Hawaiian or other Pacific Islander, non-Hispanic/Latino; 15 Two or more races, non-Hispanic/Latino), 18 international. Average age 33. 2,366 applicants, 19% accepted, 246 enrolled. In 2017, 159 master's, 49 doctorates, 2 other advanced degrees awarded. *Entrance requirements:* Additional exam requirements/recommendations for international students: Required—TOEFL (minimum score 550 paper-based). *Application deadline:* Applications are processed on a rolling basis. Application fee: $75. *Expenses:* Contact institution. *Unit head:* Jean E. Johnson, Senior Associate Dean, 202-994-3725, E-mail: jejohns@gwu.edu. *Application contact:* Joke Ogundiran, Director of Admission, 202-994-1668, Fax: 202-994-0870, E-mail: jokeogun@gwu.edu.

Lakehead University, Graduate Studies, Faculty of Social Sciences and Humanities, Department of Sociology, Thunder Bay, ON P7B 5E1, Canada. Offers gerontology (MA); health services and policy research (MA); sociology (MA); women's studies (MA). *Program availability:* Part-time, evening/weekend. *Degree requirements:* For master's, research project or thesis. *Entrance requirements:* For master's, minimum B average. Additional exam requirements/recommendations for international students: Required—TOEFL. *Faculty research:* Sociology of medicine, cultural and social change, health human resources, gerontology, women's studies.

McMaster University, Faculty of Health Sciences and School of Graduate Studies, Program in Health Research Methodology, Hamilton, ON L8S 4M2, Canada. Offers M Sc, PhD. *Program availability:* Part-time. *Degree requirements:* For doctorate, comprehensive exam. *Entrance requirements:* For master's, honors degree, minimum B+ average in last year of undergraduate course work; for doctorate, M Sc, minimum B+ average. Additional exam requirements/recommendations for international students: Required—TOEFL (minimum score 580 paper-based; 92 iBT).

Northwestern University, Feinberg School of Medicine and Interdepartmental Programs, Driskill Graduate Program in Life Sciences, Chicago, IL 60611. Offers biostatistics (PhD); epidemiology (PhD); health and biomedical informatics (PhD); health services and outcomes research (PhD); healthcare quality and patient safety (PhD); translational outcomes in science (PhD). *Degree requirements:* For doctorate, comprehensive exam, thesis/dissertation, written and oral qualifying exams. *Entrance requirements:* For doctorate, GRE General Test. Additional exam requirements/recommendations for international students: Required—TOEFL (minimum score 600 paper-based). Electronic applications accepted.

Old Dominion University, College of Health Sciences, Program in Health Services Research, Norfolk, VA 23529. Offers PhD. *Faculty:* 14 full-time (9 women), 10 part-time/adjunct (5 women). *Students:* 7 full-time (6 women), 14 part-time (12 women); includes 5 minority (2 Black or African American, non-Hispanic/Latino; 3 Asian, non-Hispanic/Latino), 4 international. Average age 35. 16 applicants, 31% accepted, 4 enrolled. In 2017, 6 doctorates awarded. *Degree requirements:* For doctorate, comprehensive exam, thesis/dissertation, oral presentation of dissertation. *Entrance requirements:* For doctorate, GRE, minimum GPA of 3.25, master's degree, degree in health profession or health services, interview. Additional exam requirements/recommendations for international students: Required—TOEFL (minimum score 550 paper-based; 79 iBT). *Application deadline:* For fall admission, 3/1 for domestic students, 2/1 for international students. Applications are processed on a rolling basis. Application fee: $50. Electronic applications accepted. *Expenses:* $29,760 resident full-time, $74,940 nonresident full-time. *Financial support:* In 2017–18, 8 students received support, including 6 fellowships (averaging $9,000 per year), 1 research assistantship with full tuition reimbursement available (averaging $15,000 per year), 1 teaching assistantship (averaging $15,000 per year); unspecified assistantships also available. Financial award application deadline: 7/1; financial award applicants required to submit FAFSA. *Faculty research:* Access to health services, women's health, domestic violence, health policy and planning, economics of obesity, substance abuse, health disparities, global health, injury prevention, curricular impact. *Unit head:* Dr. Bonnie Van Lunen, Graduate Program Director, 757-683-3516, Fax: 757-683-4410, E-mail: bvanlune@odu.edu. *Application contact:* William Heffelfinger, Director of Graduate Admissions, 757-683-5554, Fax: 757-683-3255, E-mail: gradadmit@odu.edu.
Website: http://hs.odu.edu/commhealth/academics/phd/

Penn State Hershey Medical Center, College of Medicine, Graduate School Programs in the Biomedical Sciences, Graduate Program in Public Health Sciences, Hershey, PA 17033. Offers MS. *Program availability:* Part-time. *Students:* 26 applicants, 12% accepted, 3 enrolled. *Entrance requirements:* For master's, GRE General Test. Additional exam requirements/recommendations for international students: Required—TOEFL (minimum score 81 iBT). *Application deadline:* For fall admission, 1/31 priority date for domestic students, 2/1 priority date for international students. Applications are processed on a rolling basis. Application fee: $65. Electronic applications accepted. *Financial support:* Applicants required to submit FAFSA. *Faculty research:* Clinical trials, statistical methods in genetic epidemiology, genetic factors in nicotine dependence and dementia syndromes, health economics, cancer. *Unit head:* Dr. Kristen Kjerulff, Chair, 717-531-7178, Fax: 717-531-5779, E-mail: hes-grad-hmc@psu.edu. *Application contact:* Mardi Sawyer, Program Administrator, 717-531-7178, Fax: 717-531-5779, E-mail: hes-grad-hmc@psu.edu.
Website: http://med.psu.edu

Stanford University, School of Medicine, Graduate Programs in Medicine, Department of Health Research and Policy, Stanford, CA 94305-2004. Offers biostatistics (PhD); epidemiology and clinical research (MS, PhD); health policy (MS, PhD). *Degree requirements:* For master's, thesis. Electronic applications accepted. *Expenses: Tuition:* Full-time $48,987; part-time $10,620 per quarter. One-time fee: $400. Tuition and fees vary according to program. *Faculty research:* Cost and quality of life in cardiovascular disease, technology assessment, physician decision-making.

Texas A&M University, School of Public Health, College Station, TX 77845. Offers biostatistics (MPH, MSPH); environmental health (MPH, MSPH); epidemiology (MPH, MSPH); executive health administration (MHA); health administration (MHA); health policy and management (MPH, MSPH); health promotion and community health sciences (MPH); health services research (PhD); occupational safety and health (MPH). *Program availability:* Part-time, blended/hybrid learning. *Faculty:* 56. *Students:* 279 full-time (196 women), 86 part-time (56 women); includes 153 minority (48 Black or African American, non-Hispanic/Latino; 36 Asian, non-Hispanic/Latino; 62 Hispanic/Latino; 7 Two or more races, non-Hispanic/Latino), 77 international. Average age 29. 179 applicants, 96% accepted, 148 enrolled. In 2017, 124 master's, 8 doctorates awarded. *Entrance requirements:* For master's, GRE General Test, 3 letters of recommendation; statement of purpose; current curriculum vitae or resume; official transcripts; for doctorate, GRE General Test, 3 letters of recommendation; statement of purpose; current curriculum vitae or resume; official transcripts; interview (in some cases). Additional exam requirements/recommendations for international students: Required—TOEFL (minimum score 597 paper-based, 95 iBT) or GRE (minimum verbal score 153). Application fee: $120. Electronic applications accepted. *Expenses:* Contact institution. *Financial support:* In 2017–18, 203 students received support, including 62 research assistantships with tuition reimbursements available (averaging $10,041 per year), 25 teaching assistantships with tuition reimbursements available (averaging $12,913 per year); career-related internships or fieldwork, institutionally sponsored loans, scholarships/grants, traineeships, health care benefits, tuition waivers (full and partial), and unspecified assistantships also available. Support available to part-time students. Financial award applicants required to submit FAFSA. *Unit head:* Dr. Jay Maddock, Dean, 979-436-9322, Fax: 979-458-1878, E-mail: maddock@tamhsc.edu. *Application contact:* Erin E. Schneider, Associate Director of Admissions and Recruitment, 979-436-9380, E-mail: eschneider@sph.tamhsc.edu.
Website: http://sph.tamhsc.edu/

Thomas Jefferson University, Jefferson College of Biomedical Sciences, Certificate Program in Patient-Centered Research, Philadelphia, PA 19107. Offers Certificate. *Program availability:* Part-time. *Faculty:* 43 full-time (16 women), 28 part-time/adjunct (9 women). *Students:* 3 part-time (2 women); includes 2 minority (both Two or more races, non-Hispanic/Latino). *Entrance requirements:* For degree, GRE General Test (recommended). Additional exam requirements/recommendations for international students: Required—TOEFL, IELTS (minimum score 7). *Application deadline:* For fall admission, 8/1 priority date for domestic students, 3/1 priority date for international students; for winter admission, 12/1 priority date for domestic students, 6/1 priority date for international students; for spring admission, 4/1 priority date for domestic students. Applications are processed on a rolling basis. Application fee: $50. *Financial support:* Federal Work-Study and institutionally sponsored loans available. Support available to part-time students. Financial award application deadline: 5/1; financial award applicants required to submit FAFSA. *Unit head:* Dr. Carol L. Beck, Associate Dean/Program Director, 215-503-6539, Fax: 215-503-3433, E-mail: carol.beck@jefferson.edu. *Application contact:* Marc E. Stearns, Senior Associate Director of Admissions, 215-503-0155, Fax: 215-503-3433, E-mail: jgsbs-info@jefferson.edu.
Website: http://www.jefferson.edu/university/biomedical-sciences/degrees-programs/graduate-certificate.html

Thomas Jefferson University, Jefferson College of Population Health, Philadelphia, PA 19107. Offers applied health economics and outcomes research (MS, PhD, Certificate); behavioral health science (PhD); health policy (MS, Certificate); healthcare quality and safety (MS, PhD); population health (Certificate); public health (MPH, Certificate). *Program availability:* Part-time, evening/weekend, online learning. Terminal master's awarded for partial completion of doctoral program. *Degree requirements:* For master's, thesis; for doctorate, comprehensive exam, thesis/dissertation. *Entrance requirements:* For master's, GRE or other graduate entrance exam (MCAT, LSAT, DAT, etc.), two letters of recommendation, curriculum vitae, transcripts from all undergraduate and graduate institutions; for doctorate, GRE (taken within the last 5 years), three letters of recommendation, curriculum vitae, transcripts from all undergraduate and graduate institutions. Additional exam requirements/recommendations for international students: Required—TOEFL. Electronic applications accepted. *Faculty research:* Applied health economics and outcomes research, behavioral and health sciences, chronic disease management, health policy, healthcare quality and patient safety, wellness and prevention.

The University of Alabama at Birmingham, School of Public Health, Program in Public Health, Birmingham, AL 35294. Offers applied epidemiology and pharmacoepidemiology (MSPH); biostatistics (MPH); clinical and translational science (MSPH); environmental health (MPH); environmental health and toxicology (MSPH); epidemiology (MPH); general theory and practice (MPH); health behavior (MPH); health care organization (MPH); health policy quantitative policy analysis (MPH); industrial hygiene (MPH, MSPH); maternal and child health policy (Dr PH); maternal and child health policy and leadership (MPH); occupational health and safety (MPH); outcomes research (MSPH, Dr PH); public health (PhD); public health management (Dr PH); public health preparedness management (MPH). *Program availability:* Part-time, online learning. *Degree requirements:* For doctorate, comprehensive exam, thesis/dissertation. *Entrance requirements:* For master's and doctorate, GRE. Additional exam requirements/recommendations for international students: Recommended—TOEFL (minimum score 550 paper-based; 79 iBT), IELTS (minimum score 6.5). Electronic applications accepted.

University of Alberta, School of Public Health, Department of Public Health Sciences, Edmonton, AB T6G 2E1, Canada. Offers clinical epidemiology (M Sc, MPH); environmental and occupational health (MPH); environmental health sciences (M Sc); epidemiology (M Sc); global health (M Sc, MPH); health policy and management (MPH); health policy research (M Sc); health technology assessment (MPH); occupational health (M Sc); population health (M Sc); public health leadership (MPH); public health sciences (PhD); quantitative methods (MPH). Terminal master's awarded for partial completion of doctoral program. *Degree requirements:* For master's, thesis (for some programs); for doctorate, thesis/dissertation. *Entrance requirements:* For master's, GMAT or GRE General Test. Additional exam requirements/recommendations for international students: Required—TOEFL (minimum score 550 paper-based) or IELTS (minimum score 6). Electronic applications accepted. *Faculty research:* Biostatistics, health promotion and socio-behavioral health science.

University of Arkansas for Medical Sciences, College of Public Health, Little Rock, AR 72205-7199. Offers biostatistics (MPH); environmental and occupational health (MPH, Certificate); epidemiology (MPH, PhD); health behavior and health education (MPH); health policy and management (MPH); health promotion and prevention research (PhD); health services administration (MHSA); health systems research (PhD); public health (Certificate); public health leadership (Dr PH). *Accreditation:* CEPH. *Program availability:* Part-time. *Degree requirements:* For master's, preceptorship, culminating experience, internship; for doctorate, comprehensive exam, capstone. *Entrance requirements:* For master's, GRE, GMAT, LSAT, PCAT, MCAT, DAT; for doctorate, GRE. Additional exam requirements/recommendations for international students: Required—TOEFL (minimum score 80 iBT), IELTS. Electronic applications accepted. *Expenses:* Contact institution. *Faculty research:* Health systems, tobacco prevention control, obesity prevention, environmental and occupational exposure, cancer prevention.

University of Cincinnati, Graduate School, College of Medicine, Graduate Programs in Biomedical Sciences, Program in Biomedical Research, Cincinnati, OH 45221. Offers MS. *Expenses: Tuition, area resident:* Full-time $14,468. Tuition, state resident: full-time $14,968; part-time $754 per credit hour. Tuition, nonresident: full-time $24,210; part-time $1311 per credit hour. *International tuition:* $26,460 full-time. *Required fees:* $3958; $84 per credit hour. One-time fee: $85 full-time. Tuition and fees vary according to course load, degree level and program.

University of Colorado Denver, Colorado School of Public Health, Health Services Research Program, Aurora, CO 80045. Offers MS, PhD. *Program availability:* Part-time. *Entrance requirements:* For doctorate, GRE, MCAT, or MA, MS or PhD from an accredited school, minimum undergraduate GPA of 3.0. Application fee: $0. *Faculty research:* Drug safety and risk management, health care financing and cost, health interaction with environmental factors, quality improvement and strategic research, cardiovascular health promotion. *Unit head:* Dr. Adam Atherly, Chair, 303-724-4471, E-mail: adam.atherly@ucdenver.edu. *Application contact:* Mary Baitinger, Departmental Assistant, 303-724-6698, E-mail: mary.baitinger@ucdenver.edu.
Website: http://www.ucdenver.edu/academics/colleges/PublicHealth/departments/HealthSystems/Pages/welcome.aspx

University of Colorado Denver, School of Medicine, Clinical Science Graduate Program, Aurora, CO 80045. Offers clinical investigation (PhD); clinical sciences (MS); health information technology (PhD); health services research (PhD). *Students:* 46 full-time (31 women), 26 part-time (15 women); includes 7 minority (2 Black or African American, non-Hispanic/Latino; 4 Asian, non-Hispanic/Latino; 1 Hispanic/Latino). Average age 37. 18 applicants, 67% accepted, 11 enrolled. In 2017, 21 master's, 1 doctorate awarded. *Degree requirements:* For master's, thesis, minimum of 30 credit hours, defense/final exam of thesis or publishable paper; for doctorate, comprehensive exam, thesis/dissertation, at least 30 credit hours of thesis work. *Entrance requirements:* For master's, GRE General Test or MCAT (waived if candidate has earned MS/MA or PhD from accredited U.S. school), minimum undergraduate GPA of 3.0, 3-4 letters of recommendation; for doctorate, GRE General Test or MCAT (waived if candidate has earned MS/MA or PhD from accredited U.S. school), health care graduate, professional degree, or graduate degree related to health sciences; minimum GPA of 3.0; 3-4 letters of recommendation. Additional exam requirements/recommendations for international students: Required—TOEFL (minimum score 550 paper-based; 80 iBT). *Application deadline:* For fall admission, 2/1 for domestic students, 1/15 priority date for international students; for spring admission, 10/1 for domestic students. Application fee: $50 ($75 for international students). Electronic applications accepted. *Unit head:* Dr. Lisa Cicutto, Program Director, 303-398-1539, E-mail: cicuttol@njhealth.org. *Application contact:* Galit Mankin, Program Administrator, 720-848-6249, Fax: 303-848-7381, E-mail: galit.mankin@ucdenver.edu.
Website: http://www.ucdenver.edu/research/CCTSI/education-training/clsc/Pages/default.aspx

University of Florida, Graduate School, College of Public Health and Health Professions, Department of Health Services Research, Management and Policy, Gainesville, FL 32611. Offers health administration (MHA); health services research (PhD). *Accreditation:* CAHME. *Program availability:* Part-time. *Degree requirements:* For master's, internship. *Entrance requirements:* For master's, GRE General Test (minimum score 300) or GMAT (minimum score 500), minimum GPA of 3.0; for doctorate, GRE General Test, minimum GPA of 3.0. Additional exam requirements/recommendations for international students: Required—TOEFL (minimum score 550 paper-based; 80 iBT), IELTS (minimum score 6). Electronic applications accepted. *Faculty research:* State health policy evaluation, health informatics for pain, family medicine, secondary data analysis, disability, mental health.

University of Illinois at Chicago, School of Public Health, Division of Health Policy and Administration, Chicago, IL 60607-7128. Offers clinical and translational science (MS); health policy (PhD); health services research (PhD); healthcare administration (MHA); public health policy management (MPH). *Accreditation:* CAHME. *Program availability:* Part-time. Terminal master's awarded for partial completion of doctoral program. *Degree requirements:* For master's, thesis, field practicum; for doctorate, thesis/dissertation, independent research, internship. *Entrance requirements:* For master's and doctorate, GRE General Test, minimum GPA of 2.75. Additional exam requirements/recommendations for international students: Required—TOEFL. Electronic applications accepted. *Expenses:* Contact institution. *Faculty research:* Cancer screening in underserved populations, practices and devices used to reduce firefighter injury, the relationship between communal housing and substance abuse recovery.

University of La Verne, College of Business and Public Management, Program in Health Administration, La Verne, CA 91750-4443. Offers financial management (MHA); management and leadership (MHA); marketing and business development (MHA). *Program availability:* Part-time. *Faculty:* 4 full-time (3 women), 3 part-time/adjunct (1 woman). *Students:* 35 full-time (28 women), 34 part-time (23 women); includes 34 minority (7 Black or African American, non-Hispanic/Latino; 8 Asian, non-Hispanic/Latino; 19 Hispanic/Latino), 11 international. Average age 30. *Entrance requirements:* For master's, bachelor's degree, experience in health services industry (preferred). Additional exam requirements/recommendations for international students: Required—TOEFL (minimum score 550 paper-based). *Application deadline:* Applications are processed on a rolling basis. Application fee: $50. *Expenses:* Contact institution. *Financial support:* Federal Work-Study, institutionally sponsored loans, and scholarships/grants available. Financial award application deadline: 3/2; financial award applicants required to submit FAFSA. *Unit head:* Dr. Kathy Duncan, Program Chairperson, 909-448-4415, E-mail: kduncan2@laverne.edu. *Application contact:* Barbara Cox, Associate Director of Graduate Admission, 909-448-4004, Fax: 909-971-2295, E-mail: bcox@laverne.edu.
Website: https://business.laverne.edu/mha/

University of Maryland, Baltimore, Graduate School, Graduate Programs in Pharmacy, Department of Pharmaceutical Health Service Research, Baltimore, MD 21201. Offers epidemiology (MS); pharmacy administration (PhD); Pharm D/PhD. *Degree requirements:* For doctorate, comprehensive exam, thesis/dissertation. *Entrance requirements:* For doctorate, GRE General Test. Additional exam requirements/recommendations for international students: Required—TOEFL, IELTS. Electronic applications accepted. *Expenses:* Tuition, state resident: full-time $13,990; part-time $661 per credit. Tuition, nonresident: full-time $30,484; part-time $1310 per credit. *Required fees:* $1894; $94 per credit. $415 per semester. Part-time tuition and fees vary according to course load, degree level and program. *Faculty research:* Pharmacoeconomics, outcomes research, public health policy, drug therapy and aging.

University of Massachusetts Medical School, Graduate School of Biomedical Sciences, Worcester, MA 01655-0115. Offers biomedical sciences (PhD), including biochemistry and molecular pharmacology, bioinformatics and computational biology, cancer biology, immunology and microbiology, interdisciplinary, neuroscience, translational science; biomedical sciences (millennium program) (PhD); clinical and population health research (PhD); clinical investigation (MS). *Faculty:* 1,316 full-time (526 women), 357 part-time/adjunct (229 women). *Students:* 347 full-time (180 women); includes 61 minority (10 Black or African American, non-Hispanic/Latino; 1 American Indian or Alaska Native, non-Hispanic/Latino; 35 Asian, non-Hispanic/Latino; 15 Hispanic/Latino), 130 international. Average age 29. 608 applicants, 28% accepted, 54 enrolled. In 2017, 6 master's, 51 doctorates awarded. Terminal master's awarded for partial completion of doctoral program. *Degree requirements:* For master's, comprehensive exam, thesis; for doctorate, comprehensive exam, thesis/dissertation. *Entrance requirements:* For master's, MD, PhD, DVM, or PharmD; for doctorate, GRE General Test, bachelor's degree. Additional exam requirements/recommendations for international students: Required—TOEFL (minimum score 90 iBT) or IELTS (minimum score 7.0). *Application deadline:* For fall admission, 12/15 for domestic and international students. Applications are processed on a rolling basis. Application fee: $80. Electronic applications accepted. Application fee is waived when completed online. *Expenses:* $14,883 in-state tuition and mandatory fees; $31,486 out-of-state. *Financial support:* In 2017–18, 15 fellowships with partial tuition reimbursements (averaging $29,000 per year), 296 research assistantships with full tuition reimbursements (averaging $31,212 per year) were awarded; institutionally sponsored loans and scholarships/grants also available. Financial award application deadline: 5/15. *Faculty research:* RNA biology, molecular/cell/developmental/metabolic biology, bioinformatics and computational biology, clinical/translational research, infectious disease and immunology. *Total annual research expenditures:* $279 million. *Unit head:* Dr. Mary Ellen Lane, Dean, 508-856-4018, E-mail: maryellen.lane@umassmed.edu. *Application contact:* Dr. Kendall Knight, Assistant Vice Provost for Admissions, 508-856-5628, Fax: 508-856-3659, E-mail: kendall.knight@umassmed.edu.
Website: http://www.umassmed.edu/gsbs/

University of Minnesota, Twin Cities Campus, School of Public Health, Major in Health Services Research, Policy, and Administration, Minneapolis, MN 55455-0213. Offers MS, PhD, JD/MS, JD/PhD, MD/PhD, MPP/MS. *Program availability:* Part-time. Terminal master's awarded for partial completion of doctoral program. *Degree requirements:* For master's, thesis, internship, final oral exam; for doctorate, thesis/dissertation, teaching experience, written preliminary exam, final oral exam, dissertation. *Entrance requirements:* For master's, GRE General Test, course work in mathematics; for doctorate, GRE General Test, prerequisite courses in calculus and statistics. Additional exam requirements/recommendations for international students: Required—TOEFL (minimum score 600 paper-based; 100 iBT). *Faculty research:* Outcomes, economics and statistics, sociology, health care management.

University of Nebraska Medical Center, Department of Health Services Research and Administration, Omaha, NE 68198-4350. Offers health administration (MHA); health services research, administration, and policy (PhD); public health administration and policy (MPH). *Program availability:* Part-time, 100% online, blended/hybrid learning. *Faculty:* 7 full-time (4 women), 2 part-time/adjunct (0 women). *Students:* 9 full-time (7 women), 1 part-time (0 women); includes 2 minority (both Asian, non-Hispanic/Latino), 6 international. Average age 31. 11 applicants, 55% accepted, 3 enrolled. In 2017, 5 doctorates awarded. *Degree requirements:* For doctorate, comprehensive exam, thesis/dissertation. *Entrance requirements:* For doctorate, GRE, official transcripts, resume or curriculum vitae, three letters of recommendation, statement of intent. Additional exam requirements/recommendations for international students: Required—TOEFL (minimum score 550 paper-based; 80 iBT), IELTS (minimum score 6.5). *Application deadline:* For fall admission, 6/1 for domestic students, 4/1 for international students. Application fee: $60. Electronic applications accepted. *Expenses:* Contact institution. *Financial support:* In 2017–18, 5 students received support. Federal Work-Study, scholarships/grants, and unspecified assistantships available. Financial award application deadline: 2/15; financial award applicants required to submit FAFSA. *Faculty research:* Health services research, health policy. *Unit head:* Dr. Fernando Wilson, Associate Professor, 402-552-6948, E-mail: fernando.wilson@unmc.edu. *Application contact:* Denise Howard, Coordinator, 402-559-5260, E-mail: denise.howard@unmc.edu.
Website: http://www.unmc.edu/publichealth/departments/healthservices/

University of New Brunswick Fredericton, School of Graduate Studies, Applied Health Services Research Program, Fredericton, NB E3B 5A3, Canada. Offers MAHSR. *Program availability:* Part-time, online learning. *Degree requirements:* For master's, thesis. *Entrance requirements:* For master's, honors BA, minimum GPA of 3.0. Additional exam requirements/recommendations for international students: Required—TWE (minimum score 4), TOEFL (minimum score 600 paper-based; 100 iBT) or IELTS (minimum score 7). Electronic applications accepted. *Faculty research:* Applied health services research.

Health Services Research

The University of North Carolina at Charlotte, College of Health and Human Services, Program in Health Services Research, Charlotte, NC 28223-0001. Offers PhD. *Program availability:* Part-time. *Students:* 12 full-time (8 women), 11 part-time (3 women); includes 6 minority (1 Asian, non-Hispanic/Latino; 4 Hispanic/Latino; 1 Two or more races, non-Hispanic/Latino), 4 international. Average age 42. 8 applicants, 25% accepted, 1 enrolled. In 2017, 4 doctorates awarded. *Degree requirements:* For doctorate, thesis/dissertation. *Entrance requirements:* For doctorate, GRE (minimum score of 153 verbal, 144 quantitative, 4.0 analytical), master's or doctoral degree from regionally-accredited university in a health-related field, including, but not limited to, public health, nursing, medicine, social work, kinesiology, health psychology, public administration, business administration, and nutrition; minimum graduate GPA of 3.5, essay, curriculum vitae, interviews, reference letters. Additional exam requirements/recommendations for international students: Required—TOEFL (minimum score 523 paper-based, 70 iBT) or IELTS (6.5). *Application deadline:* For fall admission, 2/1 for domestic and international students. Applications are processed on a rolling basis. Application fee: $75. Electronic applications accepted. *Expenses:* Tuition, state resident: full-time $4337. Tuition, nonresident: full-time $17,771. *Required fees:* $3211. Tuition and fees vary according to course load and program. *Financial support:* Career-related internships or fieldwork, institutionally sponsored loans, scholarships/grants, and unspecified assistantships available. Support available to part-time students. Financial award application deadline: 3/1; financial award applicants required to submit FAFSA. *Unit head:* Dr. Nancy Fey-Yensan, Dean, 704-687-7917, E-mail: fey-yensan@uncc.edu. *Application contact:* Kathy B. Giddings, Director of Graduate Admissions, 704-687-5503, Fax: 704-687-1668, E-mail: gradadm@uncc.edu.
Website: https://health.uncc.edu/academic-programs/hsr-phd-overview

University of North Texas Health Science Center at Fort Worth, School of Public Health, Fort Worth, TX 76107-2699. Offers biostatistics (MS); epidemiology (MPH, MS, PhD); food security and public health (Graduate Certificate); GIS in public health (Graduate Certificate); global health (Graduate Certificate); global health for medical professionals (Graduate Certificate); health administration (MHA); health behavior research (MS, PhD); maternal and child health (MPH); public health (Graduate Certificate); public health practice (MPH); DO/MPH; MS/MPH. *Accreditation:* CEPH. *Program availability:* Part-time, evening/weekend, 100% online. *Degree requirements:* For master's, thesis or alternative, supervised internship; for doctorate, thesis/dissertation, supervised internship. *Entrance requirements:* For master's, GRE General Test. Additional exam requirements/recommendations for international students: Required—TOEFL. Electronic applications accepted. *Expenses:* Contact institution.

University of Ottawa, Faculty of Graduate and Postdoctoral Studies, Interdisciplinary Programs, Ottawa, ON K1N 6N5, Canada. Offers e-business (Certificate); e-commerce (Certificate); finance (Certificate); health services and policies research (Diploma); population health (PhD); population health risk assessment and management (Certificate); public management and governance (Certificate); systems science (Certificate).

University of Pennsylvania, Perelman School of Medicine, Program in Health Policy Research, Philadelphia, PA 19104. Offers MSHP, MD/MSHP. *Program availability:* Part-time. *Faculty:* 23 full-time (14 women). *Students:* 46 full-time (28 women); includes 22 minority (7 Black or African American, non-Hispanic/Latino; 12 Asian, non-Hispanic/Latino; 3 Hispanic/Latino). Average age 33. 31 applicants, 81% accepted, 22 enrolled. In 2017, 18 master's awarded. *Degree requirements:* For master's, thesis. *Entrance requirements:* For master's, MCAT/GRE (depending on applicant's terminal degree). Additional exam requirements/recommendations for international students: Required—TOEFL. *Application deadline:* For fall admission, 11/30 for domestic and international students. *Financial support:* In 2017–18, 34 fellowships with full tuition reimbursements were awarded; research assistantships, teaching assistantships, scholarships/grants, traineeships, and tuition waivers also available. Financial award application deadline: 11/30. *Faculty research:* Disparities in health care; cost effectiveness analysis; outcomes research; biological, clinical, behavioral and environmental factors in health care; diffusion of health care innovation; medical ethics; innovation; lay support with peer mentors and community health workers; evaluating medical homes; quality improvement research, health literacy, health numeracy, medical decision-making. *Unit head:* Dr. Judy Shea, Co-Director, 215-573-5111, E-mail: sheaja@mail.med.upenn.edu. *Application contact:* Suzanne Mosko, E-mail: suzannej@mail.med.upenn.edu.
Website: http://www.med.upenn.edu/mshp/

University of Pittsburgh, School of Law, Master of Studies in Law Program, Pittsburgh, PA 15260. Offers biomedical and health services research (MSL); business law (MSL), including commercial law, corporate law, general business law, international business, tax law; Constitutional law (MSL); criminal law and justice (MSL); disability law (MSL); elder and estate planning law (MSL); employment and labor law (MSL); energy law (MSL); environmental and real estate law (MSL); family law (MSL); health law (MSL); intellectual property and technology law (MSL); international and human rights law (MSL); jurisprudence (MSL); regulatory law (MSL); self-designed (MSL). *Program availability:* Part-time. *Faculty:* 47 full-time (22 women), 116 part-time/adjunct (29 women). *Students:* 4 full-time (2 women), 17 part-time (12 women); includes 6 minority (5 Black or African American, non-Hispanic/Latino; 1 Hispanic/Latino). Average age 26. 28 applicants, 75% accepted, 15 enrolled. In 2017, 15 master's awarded. *Entrance requirements:* Additional exam requirements/recommendations for international students: Required—TOEFL (minimum score 600 paper-based; 100 iBT), IELTS (minimum score 7). *Application deadline:* For fall admission, 6/30 for domestic students, 5/1 for international students. Applications are processed on a rolling basis. Application fee: $0. *Faculty research:* Law, health law, business law, contracts, intellectual property, environmental law. *Unit head:* Prof. Alan Meisel, Director, 412-648-1384, Fax: 412-648-2649, E-mail: meisel@pitt.edu. *Application contact:* Beth Ann Pischke, Administrative Coordinator, 412-648-7120, Fax: 412-648-2649, E-mail: pischke@pitt.edu.
Website: http://www.law.pitt.edu/msl

University of Puerto Rico–Medical Sciences Campus, Graduate School of Public Health, Department of Health Services Administration, Program in Evaluative Research of Health Systems, San Juan, PR 00936-5067. Offers MS. *Program availability:* Part-time. *Degree requirements:* For master's, thesis. *Entrance requirements:* For master's, GRE, previous course work in algebra and statistics. *Expenses:* Contact institution.

University of Rochester, School of Medicine and Dentistry, Graduate Programs in Medicine and Dentistry, Department of Community and Preventive Medicine, Program in Health Services Research and Policy, Rochester, NY 14627. Offers PhD, MPH/PhD. *Degree requirements:* For doctorate, thesis/dissertation, qualifying exam. *Entrance requirements:* For doctorate, GRE General Test.

University of Southern California, Keck School of Medicine and Graduate School, Graduate Programs in Medicine, Department of Preventive Medicine, Program in Health Behavior Research, Los Angeles, CA 90032. Offers PhD. *Faculty:* 24 full-time (15 women), 1 (woman) part-time/adjunct. *Students:* 33 full-time (23 women), 3 part-time (2 women); includes 16 minority (9 Asian, non-Hispanic/Latino; 5 Hispanic/Latino; 2 Two or more races, non-Hispanic/Latino), 4 international. Average age 31. 58 applicants, 22% accepted, 9 enrolled. In 2017, 7 doctorates awarded. *Degree requirements:* For doctorate, comprehensive exam, thesis/dissertation. *Entrance requirements:* For doctorate, GRE General Test (minimum preferred score for combined Verbal and Quantitative of 311), minimum GPA of 3.0 (3.5 preferred). Additional exam requirements/recommendations for international students: Required—TOEFL (minimum score 600 paper-based; 100 iBT). *Application deadline:* For fall admission, 12/1 priority date for domestic and international students. Application fee: $95. Electronic applications accepted. *Financial support:* In 2017–18, 31 students received support, including 13 fellowships with full tuition reimbursements available (averaging $33,000 per year), 7 research assistantships with full tuition reimbursements available (averaging $33,000 per year), 11 teaching assistantships with full tuition reimbursements available (averaging $33,000 per year); institutionally sponsored loans, scholarships/grants, traineeships, health care benefits, and unspecified assistantships also available. Financial award application deadline: 6/30; financial award applicants required to submit CSS PROFILE or FAFSA. *Faculty research:* Obesity prevention; etiology and prevention of substance abuse, other addictive behaviors, and chronic diseases; health disparities; translational research. *Unit head:* Dr. Jennifer Unger, Director, 323-442-8234, E-mail: unger@usc.edu. *Application contact:* Marny Barovich, Program Manager, 323-442-8299, E-mail: barovich@hsc.usc.edu.
Website: http://phdhbr.usc.edu

The University of Tennessee Health Science Center, College of Graduate Health Sciences, Memphis, TN 38163. Offers biomedical engineering (MS, PhD); biomedical sciences (PhD); dental sciences (MDS); epidemiology (MS); health outcomes and policy research (PhD); laboratory research and management (MS); nursing science (PhD); pharmaceutical sciences (PhD); pharmacology (MS); speech and hearing science (PhD); DDS/PhD; DNP/PhD; MD/PhD; Pharm D/PhD. MS and PhD programs in biomedical engineering offered jointly with University of Memphis. *Faculty:* 528 full-time (176 women). *Students:* 258 full-time (130 women); includes 87 minority (14 Black or African American, non-Hispanic/Latino; 68 Asian, non-Hispanic/Latino; 5 Hispanic/Latino). Average age 28. 673 applicants, 17% accepted, 102 enrolled. In 2017, 23 master's, 30 doctorates awarded. Terminal master's awarded for partial completion of doctoral program. *Degree requirements:* For master's, comprehensive exam, thesis; for doctorate, thesis/dissertation, oral and written preliminary and comprehensive exams. *Entrance requirements:* For master's and doctorate, GRE General Test, minimum GPA of 3.0. Additional exam requirements/recommendations for international students: Recommended—TOEFL (minimum score 79 iBT), IELTS (minimum score 6.5). *Application deadline:* For winter admission, 1/1 for domestic and international students; for spring admission, 3/1 for domestic and international students. Applications are processed on a rolling basis. Application fee: $0. Electronic applications accepted. *Expenses:* Contact institution. *Financial support:* In 2017–18, 150 students received support, including 150 research assistantships (averaging $25,000 per year); fellowships, institutionally sponsored loans, scholarships/grants, health care benefits, and tuition waivers (full and partial) also available. Support available to part-time students. *Faculty research:* Cell biology, epidemiology, biomedical engineering, speech and hearing science, health policy, pharmaceutical sciences, dental sciences, nursing science, pharmacology. *Unit head:* Dr. Donald B. Thomason, Dean, 901-448-5538, E-mail: dthomaso@uthsc.edu. *Application contact:* Dr. Isaac O. Donkor, Associate Dean for Student Affairs, 901-448-5538, E-mail: idonkor@uthsc.edu.
Website: http://grad.uthsc.edu/

University of Utah, Graduate School, College of Pharmacy, Department of Pharmacotherapy, Salt Lake City, UT 84112. Offers health system pharmacy administration (MS); outcomes research and health policy (PhD). *Faculty:* 5 full-time (3 women), 18 part-time/adjunct (13 women). *Students:* 2 full-time (0 women), 4 part-time (3 women), 1 international. Average age 28. 26 applicants, 19% accepted, 4 enrolled. In 2017, 5 master's, 2 doctorates awarded. Terminal master's awarded for partial completion of doctoral program. *Degree requirements:* For master's, comprehensive exam, thesis or alternative, project; for doctorate, comprehensive exam, thesis/dissertation. *Entrance requirements:* For doctorate, GRE. Additional exam requirements/recommendations for international students: Required—TOEFL (minimum score 550 paper-based; 80 iBT). *Application deadline:* For fall admission, 1/10 for domestic students, 12/15 for international students. Application fee: $55 ($65 for international students). *Financial support:* In 2017–18, 7 students received support, including 9 research assistantships with full tuition reimbursements available (averaging $21,400 per year); health care benefits also available. Financial award application deadline: 12/15. *Faculty research:* Outcomes in pharmacy, pharmacotherapy. *Total annual research expenditures:* $131,217. *Unit head:* Dr. Diana I. Brixner, Department Chair and Professor, 801-581-6731, E-mail: diana.brixner@utah.edu. *Application contact:* Ashley Weisman, Manager, Administration, 801-581-5984, Fax: 801-585-6160, E-mail: ashley.weisman@pharm.utah.edu.
Website: http://www.pharmacy.utah.edu/pharmacotherapy/

University of Virginia, School of Medicine, Department of Public Health Sciences, Charlottesville, VA 22903. Offers clinical research (MS), including clinical investigation and patient-oriented research, informatics in medicine; public health (MPH); MPP/MPH. *Program availability:* Part-time. *Faculty:* 51 full-time (27 women), 7 part-time/adjunct (2 women). *Students:* 59 full-time (42 women), 19 part-time (13 women); includes 30 minority (9 Black or African American, non-Hispanic/Latino; 12 Asian, non-Hispanic/Latino; 5 Hispanic/Latino; 4 Two or more races, non-Hispanic/Latino), 5 international. Average age 26. 152 applicants, 78% accepted, 53 enrolled. In 2017, 54 master's awarded. *Entrance requirements:* For master's, GRE General Test or MCAT. Additional exam requirements/recommendations for international students: Required—TOEFL. *Application deadline:* Applications are processed on a rolling basis. Application fee: $60. Electronic applications accepted. *Financial support:* Career-related internships or fieldwork available. Financial award applicants required to submit FAFSA. *Unit head:* Ruth Gaare Bernheim, Chair, 434-924-8430, Fax: 434-924-8437, E-mail: rg3r@virginia.edu. *Application contact:* Tracey C. Brookman, Academic Programs Administrator, 434-924-8430, Fax: 434-924-8437, E-mail: phsdegrees@virginia.edu.
Website: http://www.medicine.virginia.edu/clinical/departments/phs

University of Washington, Graduate School, School of Public Health, Department of Health Services, Seattle, WA 98195. Offers community-oriented public health practice (MPH); health services (MPH, MS, PhD); health systems and policy (MPH); maternal and child health (MPH); social and behavioral sciences (MPH); MPH/JD; MPH/MD; MPH/MN; MPH/MPA; MPH/MS; MPH/MSD; MPH/MSW; MPH/PhD. *Program availability:* Online learning. *Faculty:* 51 full-time (24 women), 69 part-time/adjunct (36 women). *Students:* 156 full-time (133 women), 9 part-time (all women); includes 58 minority (12 Black or African American, non-Hispanic/Latino; 4 American Indian or Alaska Native, non-Hispanic/Latino; 25 Asian, non-Hispanic/Latino; 16 Hispanic/Latino; 1 Native Hawaiian or other Pacific Islander, non-Hispanic/Latino), 5 international. Average age 30. 288 applicants, 64% accepted, 82 enrolled. In 2017, 69 master's, 5 doctorates awarded. Terminal master's awarded for partial completion of doctoral program. Electronic applications accepted. *Expenses:* Contact institution. *Financial support:* Fellowships, research assistantships, teaching assistantships, institutionally sponsored loans, traineeships, and health care benefits available. Financial award applicants required to submit FAFSA. *Faculty research:* Public health practice, health promotion and disease prevention, maternal and child health, organizational behavior and culture, health policy. *Unit head:* Dr. Larry Kessler, Chair, 206-543-2703. *Application contact:* Programs Manager, 206-616-2926, Fax: 206-543-3964, E-mail: hservmph@u.washington.edu.
Website: http://depts.washington.edu/hserv/

Virginia Commonwealth University, Graduate School, School of Allied Health Professions, Department of Health Administration, Doctoral Program in Health Services Organization and Research, Richmond, VA 23284-9005. Offers PhD. *Degree requirements:* For doctorate, thesis/dissertation, residency. *Entrance requirements:* For doctorate, GMAT or GRE General Test, minimum graduate GPA of 3.0. Additional exam requirements/recommendations for international students: Required—TOEFL (minimum score 600 paper-based; 100 iBT). Electronic applications accepted. *Faculty research:* Organizational studies, theory, associated analytical techniques.

Virginia Commonwealth University, Medical College of Virginia-Professional Programs, School of Medicine, Graduate Programs in Medicine, Department of Health Behavior and Policy, Richmond, VA 23284-9005. Offers healthcare policy and research (PhD); social and behavioral sciences (PhD). *Entrance requirements:* For doctorate, GRE General Test. Additional exam requirements/recommendations for international students: Required—TOEFL (minimum score 600 paper-based; 100 iBT). Electronic applications accepted. *Faculty research:* Evaluation of healthcare services and systems to enhance quality of care and patient safety outcomes; examination of chronic disease (e.g. cancer, HIV/AIDS) policies and practices to improve health outcomes and economic efficiency; impact of the uninsured, public insurance (such as Medicaid) and the safety net on access to care and the health of low-income, underserved, and foreign-born populations; the study of labor supply and healthcare coverage in response to health behaviors and shocks.

Wake Forest University, School of Medicine and Graduate School of Arts and Sciences, Graduate Programs in Medicine, Program in Health Sciences Research, Winston-Salem, NC 27109. Offers MS. *Degree requirements:* For master's, thesis. *Entrance requirements:* For master's, GRE General Test. Additional exam requirements/recommendations for international students: Required—TOEFL. Electronic applications accepted. *Faculty research:* Research methodologies, statistical methods, measurement of health outcomes, health economics.

Washington University in St. Louis, School of Medicine, Program in Applied Health Behavior Research, St. Louis, MO 63110. Offers applied health behavior research (MS); health behavior planning and evaluation (Graduate Certificate). *Program availability:* Part-time, evening/weekend. *Entrance requirements:* For master's and Graduate Certificate, baccalaureate degree in psychology, biology, social work, public health, anthropology, allied health, sciences, or other related fields. Electronic applications accepted. *Faculty research:* Health behavior, health disparities, health education, program management, program evaluation.

Wayne State University, College of Liberal Arts and Sciences, Department of Economics, Detroit, MI 48202. Offers applied macroeconomics (MA, PhD); health economics (MA, PhD); industrial organization (MA, PhD); international economics (MA, PhD); labor and human resources (MA, PhD); JD/MA. *Faculty:* 11. *Students:* 34 full-time (8 women), 9 part-time (3 women); includes 5 minority (4 Black or African American, non-Hispanic/Latino; 1 Asian, non-Hispanic/Latino), 17 international. Average age 30. 90 applicants, 30% accepted, 13 enrolled. In 2017, 10 master's, 6 doctorates awarded. *Degree requirements:* For master's, comprehensive exam; for doctorate, comprehensive exam, thesis/dissertation, oral examination on research, completion of course work in quantitative methods, final lecture. *Entrance requirements:* For master's, minimum upper-division GPA of 3.0; prior coursework in intermediate microeconomic and macroeconomic theory, statistics, and elementary calculus; for doctorate, GRE, minimum upper-division GPA of 3.0, prior coursework in intermediate microeconomic and macroeconomic theory, statistics, two courses in calculus, three letters of recommendation from officials or teaching staff at institution(s) most recently attended, statement of purpose. Additional exam requirements/recommendations for international students: Required—TOEFL (minimum score 550 paper-based; 79 iBT), TWE (minimum score 5.5), Michigan English Language Assessment Battery (minimum score 85); Recommended—IELTS (minimum score 6.5). *Application deadline:* For fall admission, 5/1 for domestic and international students; for winter admission, 10/1 priority date for domestic students, 9/1 priority date for international students; for spring admission, 1/1 priority date for domestic and international students. Applications are processed on a rolling basis. Application fee: $50. Electronic applications accepted. *Expenses:* Tuition, state resident: full-time $10,224; part-time $638.98 per credit hour. Tuition, nonresident: full-time $22,145; part-time $1384.04 per credit hour. Tuition and fees vary according to course load and program. *Financial support:* In 2017–18, 25 students received support, including 2 fellowships with tuition reimbursements available (averaging $16,000 per year), 17 teaching assistantships with tuition reimbursements available (averaging $18,534 per year); research assistantships with tuition reimbursements available, scholarships/grants, health care benefits, and unspecified assistantships also available. Support available to part-time students. Financial award applicants required to submit FAFSA. *Faculty research:* Health economics, international economics, macroeconomics, urban and labor economics, econometrics. *Unit head:* Dr. Kevin Cotter, Interim Chair, 313-577-3345, E-mail: kevin.cotter@wayne.edu. *Application contact:* Dr. Li Way Lee, Professor and Director of Graduate Studies, 313-577-3345, E-mail: aa1313@wayne.edu.
Website: http://clas.wayne.edu/economics/

Weill Cornell Medicine, Weill Cornell Graduate School of Medical Sciences, Program in Clinical Epidemiology and Health Services Research, New York, NY 10021. Offers MS. *Degree requirements:* For master's, thesis. *Entrance requirements:* For master's, 3 years of work experience, MD or RN certificate. *Faculty research:* Research methodology, biostatistical techniques, data management, decision analysis, health economics.

XAVIER UNIVERSITY

Graduate Program in Health Services Administration

★ For more information, visit http://petersons.to/xavier-healthservices

Programs of Study

The Xavier University graduate program in Health Services Administration, the only program in the country to have received inaugural CAHME awards two years in a row, offers a rigorous curriculum that integrates both theory and practical experience. This combination fully equips its students to hold management, executive, and other leadership positions in a wide range of fields in the health services industry, including hospitals, health systems, group practice, insurance, consulting, government, and the military. Xavier's Master of Health Services Administration (M.H.S.A.) program is accredited by the Commission on the Accreditation of Healthcare Management Education (CAHME) and is one of only a handful of M.H.S.A. programs still requiring the eight to twelve month paid residency. As one of the nation's oldest accredited health administration programs, the M.H.S.A. degree from Xavier has a tradition of excellence recognized throughout the healthcare industry since 1958.

The M.H.S.A. program offers both full-time and Executive M.H.S.A. degree options, both of which can be completed in three years. The program also offers a concurrent degree with M.B.A.

The M.H.S.A. full-time day program prepares students for administrative and executive positions in healthcare organizations. This option consists of four semesters of on-campus coursework over a two year period. After completing this coursework, students begin the required eight to twelve month paid residency (the average stipend in 2018 is $43,000) at a healthcare organization. With more than 150 approved residency sites across the country, the residency provides students with the opportunity to apply the knowledge and skills from their coursework to a real-world setting under the guidance of a senior manager.

The Executive M.H.S.A. evening program enables individuals who are already working in health care to learn the administrative skills needed to progress in their careers and increase their value to their employers. This track consists of nine consecutive semesters of part-time, on-campus coursework. During this time, students will also complete a practicum, which is a guided field experience conducted within the student's place of employment in a healthcare setting.

The concurrent degree option provides an opportunity for students to pursue a business (M.B.A.) degree in addition to an M.H.S.A. degree. Students in this track must apply and be accepted into both programs. An M.B.A. may be earned over a two-year period by pursuing additional hours of M.B.A. graduate-level course work in the Williams College of Business at Xavier. The concurrent degree is designed to be completed within three years.

Research Facilities

The McDonald Library at Xavier University contains most of the library's collections, including archives and special collections. Connected to this building is the Conaton Learning Commons (CLC), which hosts the "Connection Center," an integrated service point, blending library and help desk services. The library and CLC both provide study, lounge, conference, and instruction space along with access to photocopiers, computer workstations, and printers. The library emphasizes individual study while the CLC focuses on collaboration, housing thirteen group study rooms; nine of these rooms have plasma screen projection with Internet access. A food kiosk, vending machines, and kitchenette are available for students. The Connection Center in the CLC brings together at one desk circulation, traditional reserves, research, computer technology, and classroom support services. Other student support services in the CLC include the Learning Assistance Center, Writing Center, Language Resource Center, Academic Advising, and Digital Media Lab.

Financial Aid

Internal scholarships are available from M.H.S.A. endowed funds. These awards are granted to students based on academic merit or a scholarship application. When available, graduate assistantships are awarded which may include tuition remission and an hourly rate for work as determined by the University. Students who file a FAFSA and enroll at least half time may qualify for a Direct Loan, which is a long-term, low-interest loan. These students may also apply for a Graduate PLUS loan, which is credit-based. Various alternative loans are available for students who need additional assistance. Further information is available from the Financial Aid Office (phone: 513-745-3142) or by e-mailing hellkampal@xavier.edu.

Cost of Study

Tuition for 2018–19 is $650 per credit hour. There is a $175 admissions fee for all M.H.S.A. students upon acceptance. Textbooks are an additional cost.

Living and Housing Costs

Xavier University does not provide graduate-specific housing on campus, as most graduate students live in neighboring areas of Cincinnati at affordable prices. Information regarding apartments located on campus is available at http://liveatustation.com.

Student Group

There are between 20 and 30 students in each of the three full-time cohorts, while the part-time program consists of 6 to 10 students per cohort. The average age is 24 for full-time students and 32 for part-time students.

Location

Xavier is located just north of downtown Cincinnati, Ohio which was named one of America's most livable cities (according to *Places Rated Almanac*). Cincinnati is known for great restaurants, shops, a major amusement park, and culture with Broadway theater, museums, a zoo, and aquarium. The city is home to major sports teams: the Cincinnati Reds, the Cincinnati Bengals, and FC Cincinnati.

The University

Founded in 1831, Xavier is a private, coed university. As one of 28 Jesuit colleges/universities in the U.S., Xavier provides an education in the Jesuit Catholic tradition of preparing the whole person, developing knowledge, values, spiritual growth, and responsibility for others. The University's focus on ethics and values helps students ready themselves for moral decisions they must make in their lives and careers. Xavier has 4,485 undergraduate students and 2,165 graduate students.

The Faculty

M.H.S.A. Full-Time Faculty

- Nancy Linenkugel, Department Chair and Program Director; D.M., OSF, Weatherhead School of Management, 1999.
- Rick Browne, Assistant Professor; Ph.D., Indiana University, 2002.
- Dwight Ellingwood, Assistant Professor; M.S., University of Utah, 1980.
- Lin Guo, Associate Professor; Ph.D., University of Cincinnati, 1995.
- Edmond Hooker, Associate Professor; M.D., Eastern Virginia Medical School, 1985.
- Thomas Ruthemeyer, Clinical Professor; M.B.A., Xavier University, 1984.
- France Weaver, Assistant Professor; Ph.D., University of North Carolina, 2005.

M.H.S.A. Adjunct Faculty

- Matthew Arend, Adjunct Faculty; J.D., Notre Dame Law School, 2005.
- Leslie Barden, Adjunct Faculty; M.H.S.A., Xavier University, 1986.
- Chris Boue, Adjunct Faculty; M.B.A., Florida Metropolitan University, 1993.
- Donald Brannen, Adjunct Faculty; Ph.D., Walden University, 2013.
- Adam Colvin, Adjunct Faculty; J.D., UCLA School of Law.
- Spencer Hale, Adjunct Faculty; M.B.A., Xavier University, 2012; M.H.S.A., Xavier University, 2016.
- Gayle Heintzelman, Adjunct Faculty; M.Ed., Xavier University, 2008.
- Arvind Joshi, Adjunct Faculty; M.B.A., Wright State University, 2003.
- Jennifer Mitchell, Adjunct Faculty; J.D., The University of Akron, 1998.
- Karen Tepe, Adjunct Faculty; M.H.S.A., Xavier University, 1999; M.B.A., Xavier University, 2004.
- Tamara Ward, Adjunct Faculty; M.B.A., Miami University, 2014.

Applying

M.H.S.A. students matriculate in the fall each year. Deadlines to apply are January 1 for international students and June 1 for domestic students of the year in which they plan to enroll. Application requirements include a completed online application form, two recommendation letters, a statement of intent, resume, official transcripts from all previous college work, and GRE or GMAT scores. Prerequisites include accounting and statistics. An on-campus interview is required for admission. Additional documents are required for international students.

Correspondence and Information

Amy Hellkamp
Recruitment and Marketing Coordinator
Xavier University
Department of Health Services Administration
3800 Victory Parkway
Cincinnati, Ohio 45207-5141
Phone: 513-745-3687
E-mail: hellkampal@xavier.edu
Website: http://www.xavier.edu/mhsa/

Hinkle Hall, Xavier University.

Gallagher Student Center, Xavier University Green Space.

Section 23
Nursing

This section contains a directory of institutions offering graduate work in nursing, followed by in-depth entries submitted by institutions that chose to prepare detailed program descriptions. Additional information about programs listed in the directory but not augmented by an in-depth entry may be obtained by writing directly to the dean of a graduate school or chair of a department at the address given in the directory.

For programs offering related work, see also in this book *Health Services* and *Public Health.* In another guide in this series:

Graduate Programs in the Humanities, Arts & Social Sciences
See *Family and Consumer Sciences (Gerontology)*

CONTENTS

Program Directories

Featured Schools: Displays and Close-Ups

Nursing—General

Abilene Christian University, College of Graduate and Professional Studies, Program in Nursing Practice, Abilene, TX 79699. Offers advanced practice nurse (DNP); executive nursing leadership (DNP); nursing education (DNP). *Program availability:* Part-time, online only, blended/hybrid learning. *Faculty:* 3 full-time (2 women), 3 part-time/adjunct (2 women). *Students:* 45 full-time (38 women), 3 part-time (all women); includes 17 minority (14 Black or African American, non-Hispanic/Latino; 3 Asian, non-Hispanic/Latino). 73 applicants, 59% accepted, 28 enrolled. *Entrance requirements:* For doctorate, master's degree in nursing, official transcripts, minimum graduate nursing cumulative GPA of 3.0, two recommendation letters, 500-word statement of purpose, professional curriculum vitae or resume. Additional exam requirements/recommendations for international students: Required—TOEFL (minimum score 80 iBT), IELTS (minimum score 6). *Application deadline:* For fall admission, 8/15 for domestic students; for winter admission, 10/1 for domestic students; for spring admission, 12/15 for domestic students; for summer admission, 4/1 for domestic students. Applications are processed on a rolling basis. Application fee: $50. Electronic applications accepted. *Expenses:* $1,000 per hour. *Financial support:* Application deadline: 4/1; applicants required to submit FAFSA. *Unit head:* Dr. Tonya Sawyer-McGee, Program Director, 214-305-9500, E-mail: tcs15b@acu.edu. *Application contact:* Graduate Advisor, 855-219-7300, E-mail: gradonline@acu.edu.
Website: http://www.acu.edu/online/academics/doctor-of-nursing-practice.html

Adelphi University, College of Nursing and Public Health, PhD in Nursing Program, Garden City, NY 11530-0701. Offers PhD. *Students:* 42 part-time (39 women); includes 19 minority (10 Black or African American, non-Hispanic/Latino; 4 Asian, non-Hispanic/Latino; 4 Hispanic/Latino; 1 Two or more races, non-Hispanic/Latino), 1 international. Average age 51. 13 applicants, 62% accepted, 5 enrolled. In 2017, 6 doctorates awarded. *Entrance requirements:* Additional exam requirements/recommendations for international students: Required—TOEFL (minimum score 550 paper-based; 80 iBT), IELTS (minimum score 6.5). Application fee: $50. *Expenses:* Contact institution. *Financial support:* Research assistantships, teaching assistantships, career-related internships or fieldwork, institutionally sponsored loans, scholarships/grants, traineeships, and unspecified assistantships available. Support available to part-time students. *Unit head:* Patricia Donohue-Porter, Director, 516-877-4532, E-mail: donohue-porter@adelphi.edu. *Application contact:* E-mail: graduateadmissions@adelphi.edu.

Albany State University, Darton College of Health Professions, Albany, GA 31705-2717. Offers nursing (MSN), including family nurse practitioner, nurse educator. *Accreditation:* ACEN. *Program availability:* Part-time, evening/weekend, online learning. *Degree requirements:* For master's, comprehensive exam, thesis. *Entrance requirements:* For master's, GRE or MAT, official transcript, letters of recommendation, pre-medical/certificate of immunizations. Electronic applications accepted.

Alcorn State University, School of Graduate Studies, School of Nursing, Natchez, MS 39122-8399. Offers rural nursing (MSN). *Accreditation:* ACEN.

Allen College, Graduate Programs, Waterloo, IA 50703. Offers adult-gerontology acute care nurse practitioner (MSN); community/public health nursing (MSN); education (MSN); family nurse practitioner (MSN); health sciences (Ed D); leadership in health care delivery (MSN); leadership in health care informatics (MSN); nursing (DNP); occupational therapy (MS); psychiatric mental health nurse practitioner (MSN). MSN in leadership in healthcare informatics offered in partnership with University of Minnesota. *Accreditation:* AACN; ACEN. *Program availability:* Part-time, 100% online, blended/hybrid learning. *Faculty:* 24 full-time (all women), 8 part-time/adjunct (7 women). *Students:* 106 full-time (91 women), 187 part-time (164 women); includes 22 minority (12 Black or African American, non-Hispanic/Latino; 1 American Indian or Alaska Native, non-Hispanic/Latino; 2 Asian, non-Hispanic/Latino; 3 Hispanic/Latino; 4 Two or more races, non-Hispanic/Latino), 2 international. Average age 33. 352 applicants, 56% accepted, 131 enrolled. In 2017, 73 master's, 2 doctorates awarded. *Entrance requirements:* For master's, minimum GPA of 3.0 in the last 60 hours of undergraduate coursework; for doctorate, minimum GPA of 3.25 in graduate coursework. *Application deadline:* For fall admission, 2/1 priority date for domestic students; for spring admission, 9/1 priority date for domestic students. Applications are processed on a rolling basis. Application fee: $50. Electronic applications accepted. *Expenses:* $17,860 per year. *Financial support:* In 2017–18, 97 students received support. Federal Work-Study, institutionally sponsored loans, scholarships/grants, and traineeships available. Support available to part-time students. Financial award application deadline: 8/1; financial award applicants required to submit FAFSA. *Faculty research:* Poverty. *Unit head:* Dr. Nancy Kramer, Vice Chancellor for Academic Affairs, 319-226-2040, Fax: 319-226-2070, E-mail: nancy.kramer@allencollege.edu. *Application contact:* Molly Quinn, Director of Admissions, 319-226-2001, Fax: 319-226-2010, E-mail: molly.quinn@allencollege.edu.
Website: http://www.allencollege.edu/

Alvernia University, School of Graduate Studies, Department of Nursing, Reading, PA 19607-1799. Offers adult gerontology nurse practitioner (DNP); family nurse practitioner (DNP); nursing education (MSN); nursing leadership (Graduate Certificate); nursing leadership and healthcare administration (MSN).

Alverno College, JoAnn McGrath School of Nursing and Health Professions, Milwaukee, WI 53234-3922. Offers clinical nurse specialist (MSN); family nurse practitioner (MSN); nursing practice (DNP); psychiatric mental health nurse practitioner (MSN). *Accreditation:* AACN. *Program availability:* Part-time, evening/weekend. *Faculty:* 10 full-time (all women), 7 part-time/adjunct (4 women). *Students:* 119 full-time (107 women), 103 part-time (101 women); includes 53 minority (22 Black or African American, non-Hispanic/Latino; 1 American Indian or Alaska Native, non-Hispanic/Latino; 11 Asian, non-Hispanic/Latino; 15 Hispanic/Latino; 4 Two or more races, non-Hispanic/Latino), 1 international. Average age 35. 80 applicants, 99% accepted, 56 enrolled. In 2017, 47 master's awarded. *Degree requirements:* For master's, 500 clinical hours, capstone; for doctorate, 1,000 post-BSN clinical hours. *Entrance requirements:* For master's, BSN, current license; for doctorate, MSN, nursing license. Additional exam requirements/recommendations for international students: Required—TOEFL. *Application deadline:* For fall admission, 7/15 priority date for domestic and international students; for spring admission, 12/15 priority date for domestic and international students. Applications are processed on a rolling basis. Application fee: $0. Electronic applications accepted. *Expenses:* Contact institution. *Financial support:* Federal Work-Study and scholarships/grants available. Support available to part-time students. Financial award applicants required to submit FAFSA. *Faculty research:* International practicum experience and impact on future practice decision-making of family nurse practitioners; comparative health policy; improvement of HPV vaccination rates; use of language/words by healthcare practitioners and their effect on health outcomes. *Unit head:* Margaret Rauschenberger, Dean, 414-382-6276, Fax: 414-382-6354, E-mail: margaret.rauschenberger@alverno.edu. *Application contact:* Karin Wasiullah, Associate Dean, Master of Science in Nursing, 414-382-6275, Fax: 414-382-6354, E-mail: karin.wasiullah@alverno.edu.
Website: http://www.alverno.edu/academics/academicdepartments/joannmcgrathschoolofnursing/

American Public University System, AMU/APU Graduate Programs, Charles Town, WV 25414. Offers accounting (MS); applied business analytics (MS); business administration (MBA); criminal justice (MA); cybersecurity studies (MS); educational leadership (M Ed); environmental policy and management (MS); global security (DGS); health information management (MS); history (MA), including American military history, American Revolution, civil war, war since 1945, World War II; information technology (MS); international relations and conflict resolution (MA), including American politics and government, comparative government and development, general, international relations, public policy; national security studies (MA); nursing (MSN); political science (MA); public policy (MPP); reverse logistics management (MA), including comparative and security issues, conflict resolution, international and transnational security issues, peacekeeping; space studies (MS); sports management (MS); strategic intelligence (DSI); teaching (M Ed), including secondary social studies; transportation and logistics management (MA). *Program availability:* Part-time, evening/weekend, online only, 100% online. *Students:* 455 full-time (227 women), 7,939 part-time (3,353 women); includes 2,793 minority (1,429 Black or African American, non-Hispanic/Latino; 48 American Indian or Alaska Native, non-Hispanic/Latino; 205 Asian, non-Hispanic/Latino; 766 Hispanic/Latino; 62 Native Hawaiian or other Pacific Islander, non-Hispanic/Latino; 283 Two or more races, non-Hispanic/Latino), 101 international. Average age 37. In 2017, 2,977 master's awarded. *Degree requirements:* For master's, comprehensive exam or practicum. *Entrance requirements:* For master's, official transcript showing earned bachelor's degree from institution accredited by recognized accrediting body. Additional exam requirements/recommendations for international students: Required—TOEFL (minimum score 550 paper-based), IELTS (minimum score 6.5). *Application deadline:* Applications are processed on a rolling basis. Application fee: $0. Electronic applications accepted. *Expenses: Tuition:* Full-time $6300; part-time $350 per credit. *Required fees:* $300; $50 per course. *Financial support:* Scholarships/grants available. Financial award applicants required to submit FAFSA. *Unit head:* Dr. Wallace Boston, President, 877-468-6268, Fax: 304-728-2348, E-mail: president@apus.edu. *Application contact:* Yoci Deal, Associate Vice President, Graduate and International Admissions, 877-468-6268, Fax: 304-724-3764, E-mail: info@apus.edu.
Website: http://www.apus.edu

American Sentinel University, Graduate Programs, Aurora, CO 80014. Offers business administration (MBA); business intelligence (MS); computer science (MSCS); health information management (MS); healthcare (MBA); information systems (MSIS); nursing (MSN). *Program availability:* Part-time, evening/weekend, online learning. *Entrance requirements:* Additional exam requirements/recommendations for international students: Required—TOEFL (minimum score 600 paper-based). Electronic applications accepted.

American University of Beirut, Graduate Programs, Rafic Hariri School of Nursing, Beirut, Lebanon. Offers adult gerontology clinical nurse specialist (MSN); community and public health nursing (MSN); nursing administration and management (MSN); psychiatric mental health clinical nurse specialist (MSN). *Accreditation:* AACN. *Faculty:* 13 full-time (12 women), 23 part-time/adjunct (18 women). *Students:* 4 full-time (3 women), 40 part-time (34 women). Average age 28. 32 applicants, 81% accepted, 9 enrolled. In 2017, 18 master's awarded. *Degree requirements:* For master's, comprehensive exam, residency and project or thesis. *Entrance requirements:* For master's, minimum cumulative average of 80, minimum of 1 year of work experience. Additional exam requirements/recommendations for international students: Required—TOEFL (minimum score 583 paper-based; 97 iBT); Recommended—IELTS (minimum score 7). *Application deadline:* For fall admission, 4/4 for domestic students. Applications are processed on a rolling basis. Application fee: $50. Electronic applications accepted. *Expenses:* $810 per credit. *Financial support:* In 2017–18, 7 students received support. Teaching assistantships, scholarships/grants, traineeships, and unspecified assistantships available. Financial award application deadline: 12/20. *Faculty research:* Pain management and palliative care, postwar PTSD, depression, anxiety, and social support, cardiovascular care, vitamin D and cognitive function, nursing workforce and health systems research. *Total annual research expenditures:* $305,241. *Unit head:* Dr. Huda Abu-Saad Huijer, Director of the Hariri School of Nursing, 961-1-350000 Ext. 5953, Fax: 961-1-744476, E-mail: hh35@aub.edu.lb. *Application contact:* Nisreen Ghalayini, Administrative Assistant, 961-1-350000 Ext. 5951, E-mail: ng28@aub.edu.lb.
Website: http://www.aub.edu.lb/hson

Anderson University, College of Health Professions, Anderson, SC 29621-4035. Offers advanced practice (DNP); executive leadership (MSN, DNP); family nurse practitioner (MSN, DNP); nurse educator (MSN); psychiatric mental health nurse practitioner (MSN, DNP). *Program availability:* Online learning. *Expenses: Tuition:* Full-time $24,290; part-time $650 per credit hour. Full-time tuition and fees vary according to degree level and program. *Unit head:* Dr. Donald M. Peace, Dean, 864-231-5513, E-mail: dpeace@andersonuniversity.edu. *Application contact:* Chris Woodlief, Associate Director of Adult and Graduate Programs, 864-231-5531, E-mail: cwoodlief@andersonuniversity.edu.
Website: http://www.andersonuniversity.edu/health-professions

Andrews University, School of Health Professions, Department of Nursing, Berrien Springs, MI 49104. Offers MS, DNP. *Accreditation:* ACEN. *Program availability:* Part-time, evening/weekend. *Faculty:* 3 full-time (all women), 1 (woman) part-time/adjunct. *Students:* 1 (woman) full-time, 28 part-time (27 women); includes 23 minority (20 Black or African American, non-Hispanic/Latino; 1 American Indian or Alaska Native, non-Hispanic/Latino; 1 Asian, non-Hispanic/Latino; 1 Hispanic/Latino). Average age 45. 20 applicants, 70% accepted, 13 enrolled. *Degree requirements:* For master's, thesis. *Entrance requirements:* For master's, GRE, minimum GPA of 2.5, 1 year of nursing experience, RN license. Additional exam requirements/recommendations for international students: Required—TOEFL (minimum score 550 paper-based). *Application deadline:* Applications are processed on a rolling basis. Application fee: $40. *Financial support:* Institutionally sponsored loans available. *Faculty research:* Theory for nursing, salary equitability. *Unit head:* Dr. Jochebed Ade-Oshifogun, Chairperson, 269-471-3364. *Application contact:* Justina Clayburn, Supervisor of Graduate Admission, 800-253-2874, Fax: 269-471-6321, E-mail: graduate@andrews.edu.
Website: http://www.andrews.edu/shp/nursing/

Angelo State University, College of Graduate Studies and Research, Archer College of Health and Human Services, Department of Nursing, San Angelo, TX 76909. Offers

family nurse practitioner (MSN); nurse educator (MSN). *Accreditation:* AACN; ACEN. *Program availability:* Part-time, evening/weekend, online learning. *Students:* 35 full-time (28 women), 55 part-time (49 women); includes 26 minority (4 Black or African American, non-Hispanic/Latino; 2 Asian, non-Hispanic/Latino; 18 Hispanic/Latino; 2 Two or more races, non-Hispanic/Latino). Average age 34. *Degree requirements:* For master's, comprehensive exam. *Entrance requirements:* For master's, essay, three letters of recommendation. Additional exam requirements/recommendations for international students: Required—TOEFL or IELTS. *Application deadline:* For fall admission, 4/1 priority date for domestic students, 6/10 for international students; for spring admission, 9/1 priority date for domestic students, 11/1 for international students. Applications are processed on a rolling basis. Application fee: $40 ($50 for international students). Electronic applications accepted. *Expenses:* Tuition, state resident: full-time $3856. Tuition, nonresident: full-time $11,324. *Required fees:* $2650. *Financial support:* Research assistantships, career-related internships or fieldwork, Federal Work-Study, and scholarships/grants available. Support available to part-time students. Financial award application deadline: 3/1. *Unit head:* Dr. Wrennah L. Gabbert, Chair, 325-942-2224, Fax: 325-942-2236, E-mail: wrennah.gabbert@angelo.edu. *Application contact:* Dr. Molly J. Walker, Graduate Advisor, 325-486-6872, Fax: 325-942-2236, E-mail: molly.walker@angelo.edu.
Website: http://www.angelo.edu/dept/nursing/

Arizona State University at the Tempe campus, College of Nursing and Health Innovation, Phoenix, AZ 85004. Offers advanced nursing practice (DNP); clinical research management (MS); community and public health practice (Graduate Certificate); family mental health nurse practitioner (Graduate Certificate); family nurse practitioner (Graduate Certificate); geriatric nursing (Graduate Certificate); healthcare innovation (MHI); nurse education in academic and practice settings (Graduate Certificate); nurse educator (MS); nursing and healthcare innovation (PhD). *Accreditation:* AACN. *Program availability:* Online learning. *Degree requirements:* For master's, comprehensive exam (for some programs), thesis (for some programs), interactive Program of Study (iPOS) submitted before completing 50 percent of required credit hours; for doctorate, comprehensive exam, thesis/dissertation, interactive Program of Study (iPOS) submitted before completing 50 percent of required credit hours. *Entrance requirements:* For master's and doctorate, GRE, minimum GPA of 3.0 or equivalent in last 2 years of work leading to bachelor's degree. Additional exam requirements/recommendations for international students: Required—TOEFL, IELTS, or PTE. Electronic applications accepted. *Expenses:* Contact institution.

Arkansas State University, Graduate School, College of Nursing and Health Professions, School of Nursing, State University, AR 72467. Offers aging studies (Graduate Certificate); health care management (Graduate Certificate); health sciences (MS); health sciences education (Graduate Certificate); nurse anesthesia (MSN); nursing (MSN); nursing practice (DNP). *Accreditation:* AANA/CANAEP (one or more programs are accredited); ACEN. *Program availability:* Part-time. *Degree requirements:* For master's and Graduate Certificate, comprehensive exam, thesis or alternative; for doctorate, comprehensive exam, thesis/dissertation. *Entrance requirements:* For master's, GRE General Test or MAT, appropriate bachelor's degree, current Arkansas nursing license, CPR certification, physical examination, professional liability insurance, critical care experience, ACLS Certification, PALS Certification, interview, immunization records, personal goal statement, health assessment; for doctorate, GRE or MAT, NCLEX-RN Exam, appropriate master's degree, current Arkansas nursing license, CPR certification, physical examination, professional liability insurance, critical care experience, ACLS Certification, PALS Certification, interview, immunization records, personal goal statement, health assessment, TB skin test, background check; for Graduate Certificate, GRE or MAT, appropriate bachelor's degree, official transcripts, immunization records, proof of employment in healthcare, TB Skin Test, TB Mask Fit Test, CPR Certification. Additional exam requirements/recommendations for international students: Required—TOEFL (minimum score 550 paper-based; 79 iBT), IELTS (minimum score 6), PTE (minimum score 56). Electronic applications accepted. *Expenses:* Contact institution.

Arkansas Tech University, College of Natural and Health Sciences, Russellville, AR 72801. Offers fisheries and wildlife biology (MS); health informatics (MS); nursing (MSN). *Program availability:* Part-time, evening/weekend, 100% online, blended/hybrid learning. *Students:* 6 full-time (3 women), 53 part-time (36 women); includes 14 minority (9 Black or African American, non-Hispanic/Latino; 1 Asian, non-Hispanic/Latino; 3 Hispanic/Latino; 1 Two or more races, non-Hispanic/Latino), 1 international. Average age 35. In 2017, 16 master's awarded. *Degree requirements:* For master's, thesis (for some programs), project. *Entrance requirements:* Additional exam requirements/recommendations for international students: Required—TOEFL (minimum score 550 paper-based; 79 iBT), IELTS (minimum score 6.5), PTE (minimum score 58). *Application deadline:* For fall admission, 3/1 priority date for domestic students, 5/1 priority date for international students; for spring admission, 10/1 priority date for domestic and international students. Applications are processed on a rolling basis. Application fee: $40 ($90 for international students). Electronic applications accepted. *Expenses:* Tuition, state resident: full-time $6816; part-time $284 per credit hour. Tuition, nonresident: full-time $13,632; part-time $568 per credit hour. *Required fees:* $420 per semester. Tuition and fees vary according to course load. *Financial support:* In 2017–18, research assistantships with full and partial tuition reimbursements (averaging $4,800 per year), teaching assistantships with full and partial tuition reimbursements (averaging $4,800 per year) were awarded; career-related internships or fieldwork, Federal Work-Study, scholarships/grants, health care benefits, and unspecified assistantships also available. Support available to part-time students. Financial award application deadline: 4/15; financial award applicants required to submit FAFSA. *Unit head:* Dr. Jeff Robertson, Dean, 479-968-0498, E-mail: jrobertson@atu.edu. *Application contact:* Dr. Mary B. Gunter, Dean of Graduate College, 479-968-0398, Fax: 479-964-0542, E-mail: gradcollege@atu.edu.
Website: http://www.atu.edu/nhs/

Ashland University, Dwight Schar College of Nursing and Health Sciences, Department of Nursing, Ashland, OH 44805-3702. Offers family nurse practitioner (DNP). *Entrance requirements:* For doctorate, minimum GPA of 3.0, one year of clinical practice experience, 2-3 page paper, undergraduate- or graduate-level statistics course, interview. Additional exam requirements/recommendations for international students: Recommended—TOEFL, IELTS, TSE. *Application deadline:* Applications are processed on a rolling basis. Electronic applications accepted. *Expenses: Tuition:* Full-time $9621; part-time $4707 per credit hour. *Required fees:* $15 per semester. *Unit head:* Dr. Juanita Reese Kline, Chair, 419-521-6811, E-mail: jkline6@ashland.edu. *Application contact:* Bernie Bannin, Director, Graduate, Online, and Adult Admissions, 419-289-5291, E-mail: grad-admissions@ashland.edu.
Website: http://www.ashland.edu/conhs/nursing

Aspen University, Program in Nursing, Denver, CO 80246-1930. Offers forensic nursing (MSN); informatics (MSN); nursing (MSN); nursing administration and management (MSN); nursing education (MSN); public health (MSN).

Athabasca University, Faculty of Health Disciplines, Athabasca, AB T9S 3A3, Canada. Offers advanced nursing practice (MN, Advanced Diploma); generalist (MN); health studies (MHS). *Program availability:* Part-time, online learning. *Degree requirements:* For master's, comprehensive exam (for some programs). *Entrance requirements:* For master's, bachelor's degree in health-related field and 2 years of professional health service experience (MHS); bachelor's degree in nursing and 2 years' nursing experience (MN); minimum GPA of 3.0 in final 30 credits; for Advanced Diploma, RN license, 2 years of health care experience. Electronic applications accepted. *Expenses:* Contact institution.

Auburn University, Graduate School, School of Nursing, Auburn University, AL 36849. Offers nursing educator (MSN); primary care practitioner (MSN). *Accreditation:* AACN. *Faculty:* 26 full-time (24 women). *Students:* 9 full-time (all women), 116 part-time (105 women); includes 25 minority (18 Black or African American, non-Hispanic/Latino; 1 American Indian or Alaska Native, non-Hispanic/Latino; 3 Hispanic/Latino; 3 Two or more races, non-Hispanic/Latino). Average age 33. 67 applicants, 81% accepted, 43 enrolled. In 2017, 55 master's awarded. *Expenses:* Tuition, state resident: full-time $10,974; part-time $519 per credit hour. Tuition, nonresident: full-time $29,658; part-time $1557 per credit hour. *Required fees:* $816 per semester. Tuition and fees vary according to degree level and program. *Unit head:* Dr. Gregg Newschwander, Dean, 334-844-3658, E-mail: gen0002@auburn.edu. *Application contact:* Dr. George Flowers, Dean of the Graduate School, 334-844-4700, E-mail: gradadm@auburn.edu.
Website: https://cws.auburn.edu/nursing/

Auburn University at Montgomery, College of Nursing and Health Sciences, Montgomery, AL 36124-4023. Offers family nurse practitioner (MSN); nurse educator for interprofessional practice (MSN). Programs offered jointly with Auburn University. *Accreditation:* AACN. *Students:* 23 full-time (14 women), 19 part-time (9 women); includes 10 minority (9 Black or African American, non-Hispanic/Latino; 1 Hispanic/Latino), 2 international. *Entrance requirements:* Additional exam requirements/recommendations for international students: Recommended—TOEFL (minimum score 500 paper-based; 61 iBT), IELTS (minimum score 5.5), TSE (minimum score 44). *Application deadline:* For fall admission, 7/1 for domestic students; for spring admission, 10/1 for domestic students; for summer admission, 3/1 for domestic students. Applications are processed on a rolling basis. Application fee: $25 ($0 for international students). Electronic applications accepted. *Expenses:* Tuition, state resident: full-time $6930; part-time $385 per credit hour. Tuition, nonresident: full-time $15,588; part-time $866 per credit hour. *Required fees:* $640. *Unit head:* Dr. Jean Leuner, Dean, 334-244-3658, E-mail: jleuner@aum.edu. *Application contact:* Dr. Barbara Wilder, Graduate Program Director, 334-844-6766, E-mail: wildebf@auburn.edu.
Website: http://conhs.aum.edu/

Augsburg University, Programs in Nursing, Minneapolis, MN 55454-1351. Offers MA, DNP. *Accreditation:* AACN. *Degree requirements:* For master's, thesis or alternative.

Augusta University, College of Nursing, Doctor of Nursing Practice Program, Augusta, GA 30912. Offers adult gerontology acute care nurse practitioner (DNP); family nurse practitioner (DNP); nurse executive (DNP); nursing (DNP); nursing anesthesia (DNP); pediatric nurse practitioner (DNP); psychiatric mental health nurse practitioner (DNP). *Accreditation:* AACN; AANA/CANAEP. *Degree requirements:* For doctorate, thesis/dissertation or alternative. *Entrance requirements:* For doctorate, GRE General Test or MAT, master's degree in nursing or related field, current professional nurse licensure. Additional exam requirements/recommendations for international students: Required—TOEFL (minimum score 600 paper-based; 100 iBT). Electronic applications accepted.

Augusta University, College of Nursing, Nursing PhD Program, Augusta, GA 30912. Offers PhD. *Degree requirements:* For doctorate, thesis/dissertation. *Entrance requirements:* For doctorate, GRE General Test, current GA nurse licensure. Additional exam requirements/recommendations for international students: Required—TOEFL (minimum score 550 paper-based; 79 iBT). Electronic applications accepted.

Austin Peay State University, College of Graduate Studies, College of Behavioral and Health Sciences, School of Nursing, Clarksville, TN 37044. Offers family nurse practitioner (MSN); nursing administration (MSN); nursing education (MSN); nursing informatics (MSN). *Program availability:* Part-time, online learning. *Faculty:* 8 full-time (all women), 8 part-time/adjunct (all women). *Students:* 12 full-time (11 women), 139 part-time (128 women); includes 19 minority (11 Black or African American, non-Hispanic/Latino; 1 Asian, non-Hispanic/Latino; 5 Hispanic/Latino; 2 Two or more races, non-Hispanic/Latino). Average age 35. 36 applicants, 86% accepted, 20 enrolled. In 2017, 67 master's awarded. *Degree requirements:* For master's, comprehensive exam. *Entrance requirements:* For master's, minimum GPA of 3.0, RN license eligibility, 3 letters of recommendation. Additional exam requirements/recommendations for international students: Required—TOEFL (minimum score 500 paper-based). *Application deadline:* For fall admission, 8/8 priority date for domestic students. Applications are processed on a rolling basis. Application fee: $45 ($55 for international students). Electronic applications accepted. *Expenses:* Tuition, state resident: full-time $7686; part-time $427 per credit hour. Tuition, nonresident: full-time $20,268; part-time $1126 per credit hour. *Required fees:* $1529; $76.45 per credit hour. *Financial support:* Research assistantships with full tuition reimbursements, career-related internships or fieldwork, Federal Work-Study, institutionally sponsored loans, scholarships/grants, and unspecified assistantships available. Support available to part-time students. Financial award application deadline: 4/1; financial award applicants required to submit FAFSA. *Unit head:* Dr. Rebecca Corvey, Director of Nursing, 931-221-7710, Fax: 931-221-7595, E-mail: corveyr@apsu.edu. *Application contact:* Megan Mitchell, Coordinator of Graduate Admissions, 931-221-6189, Fax: 931-221-7641, E-mail: mitchellm@apsu.edu.
Website: http://www.apsu.edu/nursing

Azusa Pacific University, School of Nursing, Azusa, CA 91702-7000. Offers adult clinical nurse specialist (MSN); adult-gerontology nurse practitioner (MSN); family nurse practitioner (MSN); healthcare administration and leadership (MSN); nursing (MSN, DNP, PhD); nursing education (MSN); parent-child clinical nurse specialist (MSN); psychiatric mental health nurse practitioner (MSN). *Accreditation:* AACN. *Program availability:* Part-time, evening/weekend. *Degree requirements:* For master's, thesis optional. *Entrance requirements:* For master's, BSN.

Ball State University, Graduate School, College of Health, School of Nursing, Muncie, IN 47304. Offers adult/gerontology nurse practitioner (Post Master's Certificate); evidence-based clinical practice (Postbaccalaureate Certificate); family nurse practitioner (Post Master's Certificate); nurse educator (Post Master's Certificate); nursing (MS), including family nurse practitioner, nurse administrator, nurse educator; nursing education (Postbaccalaureate Certificate); nursing practice (DNP). *Accreditation:* AACN. *Program availability:* Part-time-only, online only, 100% online. *Faculty:* 10 full-time (all women), 9 part-time/adjunct (all women). *Students:* 9 full-time (8 women), 325 part-time (299 women); includes 26 minority (13 Black or African American, non-Hispanic/Latino; 3 Asian, non-Hispanic/Latino; 7 Hispanic/Latino; 3 Two or more races, non-Hispanic/Latino). Average age 33. 190 applicants, 37% accepted, 66 enrolled. In 2017, 88 master's, 2 doctorates awarded. *Entrance requirements:* For master's, bachelor's degree in nursing, minimum GPA of 3.0, minimum C grade in at least 2 quarter or semester hours in an undergraduate research course, unencumbered license as a registered nurse in state of practice; for doctorate, advanced practice nurse (nurse practitioner, clinical nurse specialist, nurse midwife); master's degree in nursing from accredited program with minimum GPA of 3.2; graduate-level statistics, nursing research, and health assessment courses; unencumbered license as registered nurse in

state of practice. Additional exam requirements/recommendations for international students: Required—TOEFL (minimum score 550 paper-based; 79 iBT), IELTS (minimum score 6.5). *Application deadline:* For fall admission, 2/9 for domestic students; for spring admission, 8/9 for domestic students. Applications are processed on a rolling basis. Application fee: $60. Electronic applications accepted. *Expenses:* Contact institution. *Financial support:* Application deadline: 3/1; applicants required to submit FAFSA. *Unit head:* Dr. Linda Siktberg, Director, 765-285-8718, Fax: 765-285-2169, E-mail: lsiktberg@bsu.edu. *Application contact:* Shantelle Estes, Graduate Advisor, 765-285-9130, Fax: 765-285-2169, E-mail: smestes@bsu.edu.
Website: http://www.bsu.edu/nursing/

Barry University, School of Adult and Continuing Education, Division of Nursing, Miami Shores, FL 33161-6695. Offers MSN, PhD, Certificate, MSN/MBA. *Program availability:* Part-time, evening/weekend. *Degree requirements:* For master's, research project or thesis; for doctorate, thesis/dissertation. *Entrance requirements:* For master's, GRE General Test or MAT, BSN, minimum GPA of 3.0, course work in statistics and research, Florida RN license; for doctorate, GRE General Test or MAT, minimum GPA of 3.3, MSN. Electronic applications accepted. *Faculty research:* Adult education, nurse practitioner, stress reduction in pregnancy, prevention of cardiac problems, in children, level of school age children.

Baylor University, Graduate School, Louise Herrington School of Nursing, Dallas, TX 76798. Offers family nurse practitioner (MSN); neonatal nurse practitioner (MSN); nurse-midwifery (DNP). *Accreditation:* AACN. *Program availability:* Part-time, online learning. *Faculty:* 11 full-time (all women), 3 part-time/adjunct (2 women). *Students:* 35 full-time (34 women), 11 part-time (all women); includes 21 minority (5 Black or African American, non-Hispanic/Latino; 1 American Indian or Alaska Native, non-Hispanic/Latino; 5 Asian, non-Hispanic/Latino; 8 Hispanic/Latino; 2 Two or more races, non-Hispanic/Latino). Average age 35. 47 applicants, 70% accepted, 26 enrolled. In 2017, 13 master's, 4 doctorates awarded. *Degree requirements:* For doctorate, comprehensive exam (for some programs), capstone project. *Entrance requirements:* For master's, GRE General Test or MAT; for doctorate, GRE General Test. Additional exam requirements/recommendations for international students: Required—TOEFL. *Application deadline:* For fall admission, 2/1 for domestic students. Application fee: $50. Electronic applications accepted. *Financial support:* In 2017–18, 66 students received support. Teaching assistantships, Federal Work-Study, scholarships/grants, and unspecified assistantships available. Support available to part-time students. Financial award application deadline: 6/30; financial award applicants required to submit FAFSA. *Faculty research:* Women and strokes, obesity and pregnancy, educational environmental factors, international undeserved populations, midwifery. *Total annual research expenditures:* $5,000. *Unit head:* Dr. Barbara Camune, Graduate Program Director, 214-367-3754, Fax: 214-820-3375, E-mail: barbara_camune@baylor.edu. *Application contact:* Elaine Lark, Coordinator of Recruitment and Enrollment, 214-818-7839, Fax: 214-820-3835, E-mail: elaine_lark@baylor.edu.
Website: http://www.baylor.edu/nursing/

Bellarmine University, College of Health Professions, Donna and Allan Lansing School of Nursing and Clinical Sciences, Louisville, KY 40205. Offers family nurse practitioner (MSN); health science (MHS); nursing administration (MSN); nursing education (MSN); nursing practice (DNP). *Accreditation:* AACN; APTA. *Program availability:* Part-time, evening/weekend. *Faculty:* 20 full-time (17 women), 7 part-time/adjunct (6 women). *Students:* 10 full-time (6 women), 101 part-time (89 women); includes 10 minority (5 Black or African American, non-Hispanic/Latino; 2 Asian, non-Hispanic/Latino; 1 Hispanic/Latino; 2 Two or more races, non-Hispanic/Latino), 1 international. Average age 34. In 2017, 42 master's, 5 doctorates awarded. *Degree requirements:* For master's, comprehensive exam, thesis (for some programs); for doctorate, comprehensive exam, thesis/dissertation. *Entrance requirements:* For master's, GRE General Test, minimum GPA of 3.0, interview, resume; BSN from CCNE- or ACEN-accredited program, professional references, goal statement, and RN license (for MSN); bachelor's degree with exposure to health issues and grade of C or better in math/science courses (for MHS); for doctorate, GRE General Test, MSN from CCNE- or ACEN-accredited program; minimum GPA of 3.5 in graduate coursework; professional references; goal statement; current curriculum vitae or resume; RN license; verification of post-baccalaureate clinical and practice hours. Additional exam requirements/recommendations for international students: Required—TOEFL (minimum iBT score of 83, 26 on speaking test), IELTS (minimum score 7, speaking band score of 8), or language training at an approved center. *Application deadline:* Applications are processed on a rolling basis. Application fee: $40. Electronic applications accepted. *Expenses:* Contact institution. *Financial support:* Career-related internships or fieldwork and scholarships/grants available. Financial award applicants required to submit FAFSA. *Faculty research:* Nursing: pain, empathy, leadership styles, control; physical therapy: service-learning; exercise in chronic and pre-operative conditions, athletes; women's health; aging. *Unit head:* Dr. Nancy York, Dean, 502-272-8639, E-mail: nyork@bellarmine.edu. *Application contact:* Julie Armstrong-Binnix, Health Science Recruiter, 800-274-4723 Ext. 8364, E-mail: julieab@bellarmine.edu.
Website: http://www.bellarmine.edu/lansing

Bellin College, School of Nursing, Green Bay, WI 54305. Offers family nurse practitioner (MSN); nurse educator (MSN). *Accreditation:* AACN. *Faculty:* 10 part-time/adjunct (all women). *Students:* 13 full-time (12 women), 29 part-time (27 women). *Expenses: Tuition:* Part-time $728 per credit. *Unit head:* Dr. Amber B. Carriveau, Graduate Program Director, 920-433-6694, Fax: 920-433-1921, E-mail: amber.carriveau@bellincollege.edu.

Belmont University, College of Health Sciences, Nashville, TN 37212. Offers nursing (MSN, DNP); occupational therapy (MSOT, OTD); physical therapy (DPT). *Program availability:* Part-time, blended/hybrid learning. *Faculty:* 29 full-time (25 women), 16 part-time/adjunct (11 women). *Students:* 394 full-time (330 women), 9 part-time (8 women); includes 34 minority (9 Black or African American, non-Hispanic/Latino; 12 Asian, non-Hispanic/Latino; 7 Hispanic/Latino; 6 Two or more races, non-Hispanic/Latino). Average age 26. In 2017, 52 master's, 79 doctorates awarded. *Degree requirements:* For master's, comprehensive exam, thesis; for doctorate, comprehensive exam. *Entrance requirements:* For master's, GRE, BSN, minimum GPA of 3.0. Additional exam requirements/recommendations for international students: Required—TOEFL (minimum score 550 paper-based). *Application deadline:* Applications are processed on a rolling basis. Application fee: $50. Electronic applications accepted. *Expenses:* Contact institution. *Financial support:* Teaching assistantships with full tuition reimbursements, career-related internships or fieldwork, scholarships/grants, and traineeships available. Financial award application deadline: 3/1; financial award applicants required to submit FAFSA. *Unit head:* Dr. Cathy Taylor, Dean, 615-460-6916, Fax: 615-460-6750. *Application contact:* Bill Nichols, Director of Enrollment Services, 615-460-6107, E-mail: bill.nichols@belmont.edu.
Website: http://www.belmont.edu/healthsciences/

Benedictine University, Graduate Programs, Program in Nursing, Lisle, IL 60532. Offers MSN. *Accreditation:* AACN.

Bethel College, Adult and Graduate Programs, Program in Nursing, Mishawaka, IN 46545-5591. Offers MSN. *Accreditation:* ACEN. *Program availability:* Part-time, evening/weekend, 100% online, blended/hybrid learning. *Faculty:* 3 full-time (all women). *Students:* 12 part-time (all women); includes 1 minority (Two or more races, non-Hispanic/Latino), 1 international. Average age 35. 3 applicants, 33% accepted. In 2017, 4 master's awarded. *Degree requirements:* For master's, thesis. *Entrance requirements:* Additional exam requirements/recommendations for international students: Required—TOEFL (minimum score 540 paper-based). *Application deadline:* For fall admission, 8/15 for domestic students, 5/1 for international students; for spring admission, 10/1 for international students. Electronic applications accepted. Tuition and fees vary according to program. *Financial support:* Career-related internships or fieldwork available. Financial award applicants required to submit FAFSA. *Unit head:* Dr. Deborah Gillum, Dean of Nursing, 574-807-7015, E-mail: deborah.gillum@bethelcollege.edu. *Application contact:* Tanya Sobaski, Program Director for Master of Science in Nursing, 574-807-7343, E-mail: tanya.sobaski@bethelcollege.edu.

Binghamton University, State University of New York, Graduate School, Decker School of Nursing, Binghamton, NY 13902-6000. Offers adult-gerontological nursing (MS, DNP, Certificate); community health nursing (MS, DNP, Certificate); family health nursing (MS, DNP, Certificate); family psychiatric mental health nursing (MS, DNP, Certificate); nursing (PhD). *Accreditation:* AACN. *Program availability:* Part-time, evening/weekend. *Faculty:* 52 full-time (45 women). *Students:* 94 full-time (79 women), 109 part-time (94 women); includes 43 minority (21 Black or African American, non-Hispanic/Latino; 10 Asian, non-Hispanic/Latino; 7 Hispanic/Latino; 5 Two or more races, non-Hispanic/Latino), 13 international. Average age 36. 111 applicants, 95% accepted, 63 enrolled. In 2017, 53 master's, 5 doctorates, 20 other advanced degrees awarded. Terminal master's awarded for partial completion of doctoral program. *Degree requirements:* For master's, comprehensive exam, thesis; for doctorate, comprehensive exam (for some programs), thesis/dissertation. *Entrance requirements:* For master's and doctorate, GRE General Test, nursing licensure. Additional exam requirements/recommendations for international students: Required—TOEFL (minimum score 90 iBT). Application fee: $75. Electronic applications accepted. *Expenses:* Contact institution. *Financial support:* In 2017–18, 33 students received support, including 1 fellowship with partial tuition reimbursement available (averaging $16,500 per year), research assistantships with full tuition reimbursements available (averaging $12,500 per year), 1 teaching assistantship with full tuition reimbursement available (averaging $16,500 per year); career-related internships or fieldwork, Federal Work-Study, institutionally sponsored loans, traineeships, health care benefits, tuition waivers (full and partial), and unspecified assistantships also available. Financial award applicants required to submit FAFSA. *Unit head:* Dr. Mario R. Ortiz, Dean, 607-777-2311, E-mail: mortiz@binghamton.edu. *Application contact:* Ben Balkaya, Assistant Dean and Director, 607-777-2151, Fax: 607-777-2501, E-mail: balkaya@binghamton.edu.
Website: http://www.binghamton.edu/dson/

Blessing-Rieman College of Nursing & Health Sciences, Master of Science in Nursing Program, Quincy, IL 62305-7005. Offers nursing education (MSN); nursing leadership (MSN). *Program availability:* Part-time-only, evening/weekend, online only, 100% online. *Faculty:* 7 full-time (all women). *Students:* 16 part-time (14 women). Average age 35. *Degree requirements:* For master's, thesis or project. *Entrance requirements:* Additional exam requirements/recommendations for international students: Required—TOEFL (minimum score 500 paper-based; 80 iBT). *Application deadline:* Applications are processed on a rolling basis. Electronic applications accepted. *Expenses: Tuition:* Part-time $500 per credit hour. *Required fees:* $300 per unit. $150 per semester. One-time fee: $20 part-time. *Financial support:* Scholarships/grants available. Financial award application deadline: 4/30; financial award applicants required to submit FAFSA. *Unit head:* Dr. Karen Mayville, Administrative Coordinator, Assessment, 217-228-5520 Ext. 6968, Fax: 217-223-1781, E-mail: kmayville@brcn.edu. *Application contact:* Heather Mutter, Admissions Counselor, 217-228-5520 Ext. 6964, Fax: 217-223-4661, E-mail: hmutter@brcn.edu.
Website: https://www.brcn.edu/programs/msn-online

Bloomsburg University of Pennsylvania, School of Graduate Studies, College of Science and Technology, Department of Nursing, Bloomsburg, PA 17815-1301. Offers adult and family nurse practitioner (MSN); community health (MSN); nurse anesthesia (MSN); nursing (MSN, DNP); nursing administration (MSN). *Accreditation:* AACN. *Degree requirements:* For master's, thesis (for some programs), clinical experience. *Entrance requirements:* For master's, minimum QPA of 3.0, personal statement, 2 letters of recommendation, nursing license. Additional exam requirements/recommendations for international students: Required—TOEFL, IELTS. Electronic applications accepted. *Expenses:* Contact institution.

Boise State University, College of Health Sciences, School of Nursing, Boise, ID 83725-0399. Offers acute care adult gerontology (Graduate Certificate); adult gerontology acute care (MSN); adult gerontology primary care (MSN); healthcare simulation (Graduate Certificate); nursing practice (DNP); primary care adult gerontology (Graduate Certificate). *Accreditation:* AACN. *Students:* 1 (woman) full-time, 91 part-time (73 women); includes 11 minority (5 Black or African American, non-Hispanic/Latino; 2 Asian, non-Hispanic/Latino; 3 Hispanic/Latino; 1 Native Hawaiian or other Pacific Islander, non-Hispanic/Latino). Average age 43. 32 applicants, 44% accepted, 12 enrolled. In 2017, 3 master's awarded. *Entrance requirements:* For master's, minimum GPA of 3.0. Additional exam requirements/recommendations for international students: Required—TOEFL (minimum score 550 paper-based; 80 iBT), IELTS (minimum score 6). *Application deadline:* For spring admission, 10/15 priority date for domestic and international students. Applications are processed on a rolling basis. Application fee: $65 ($95 for international students). Electronic applications accepted. *Expenses:* Tuition, state resident: full-time $6471; part-time $390 per credit. Tuition, nonresident: full-time $21,787; part-time $685 per credit. *Required fees:* $2283; $100 per term. Part-time tuition and fees vary according to course load and program. *Financial support:* Scholarships/grants and unspecified assistantships available. Financial award application deadline: 10/15; financial award applicants required to submit FAFSA. *Unit head:* Dr. Ann Hubbert, Director, 208-426-3404, E-mail: annhubbert@boisestate.edu. *Application contact:* Dr. Nancy Loftus, Program Coordinator, 208-426-3819, E-mail: nancyloftus@boisestate.edu.
Website: http://hs.boisestate.edu/nursing/

Boston College, William F. Connell School of Nursing, Chestnut Hill, MA 02467. Offers adult-gerontology primary care nurse practitioner (MS); family health nursing (MS); nurse anesthesia (MS); nursing (PhD); pediatric primary care nurse practitioner (MS), including pediatric and women's health; psychiatric-mental health nursing (MS); women's health nursing (MS); MBA/MS; MS/MA; MS/PhD. MS/MBA offered jointly with Carroll School of Management, MS/MA with School of Theology and Ministry. *Accreditation:* AACN; AANA/CANAEP (one or more programs are accredited). *Program availability:* Part-time. *Faculty:* 54 full-time (48 women). *Students:* 170 full-time (153 women), 90 part-time (83 women); includes 39 minority (8 Black or African American, non-Hispanic/Latino; 10 Asian, non-Hispanic/Latino; 12 Hispanic/Latino; 9 Two or more races, non-Hispanic/Latino), 3 international. Average age 28. 360 applicants, 56% accepted, 94 enrolled. In 2017, 104 master's, 5 doctorates awarded. *Degree requirements:* For master's, comprehensive exam; for doctorate, comprehensive exam, thesis/dissertation, computer literacy exam or foreign language. *Entrance requirements:* For master's, bachelor's degree in nursing; for doctorate, GRE General Test, MS in nursing. Additional exam requirements/recommendations for international students:

Required—TOEFL (minimum score 600 paper-based; 100 iBT), IELTS (minimum score 7.5). *Application deadline:* For fall admission, 9/30 for domestic and international students; for winter admission, 1/15 for domestic and international students; for spring admission, 3/15 for domestic and international students. Application fee: $40. Electronic applications accepted. *Expenses:* $1,350 per credit tuition. *Financial support:* In 2017–18, 152 students received support, including 11 fellowships with full tuition reimbursements available (averaging $24,504 per year), 29 teaching assistantships (averaging $3,768 per year), scholarships/grants, health care benefits, tuition waivers (partial), and unspecified assistantships also available. Support available to part-time students. Financial award application deadline: 4/18; financial award applicants required to submit FAFSA. *Faculty research:* Sexual and reproductive health, health promotion/illness prevention, aging, eating disorders, symptom management. *Total annual research expenditures:* $879,812. *Unit head:* Dr. Susan Gennaro, Dean, 617-552-4251, Fax: 617-552-0931, E-mail: susan.gennaro@bc.edu. *Application contact:* Sean Sendall, Assistant Dean, Graduate Enrollment and Data Analytics, 617-552-4745, Fax: 617-552-2121, E-mail: sean.sendall@bc.edu.
Website: http://www.bc.edu/cson

Bowie State University, Graduate Programs, Department of Nursing, Bowie, MD 20715-9465. Offers administration of nursing services (MS); family nurse practitioner (MS); nursing education (MS). *Accreditation:* ACEN. *Program availability:* Part-time. *Faculty:* 7 full-time (4 women), 15 part-time/adjunct (10 women). *Students:* 29 full-time (25 women), 30 part-time (24 women); includes 42 minority (35 Black or African American, non-Hispanic/Latino; 1 Asian, non-Hispanic/Latino; 6 Hispanic/Latino), 8 international. Average age 42. 9 applicants, 89% accepted, 7 enrolled. In 2017, 30 master's awarded. *Degree requirements:* For master's, comprehensive exam, thesis, research paper. *Entrance requirements:* For master's, minimum GPA of 2.5. *Application deadline:* For fall admission, 5/15 for domestic students. Applications are processed on a rolling basis. Application fee: $40. Electronic applications accepted. *Financial support:* Institutionally sponsored loans and traineeships available. Financial award application deadline: 4/1. *Faculty research:* Minority health, women's health, gerontology, leadership management. *Unit head:* Dr. Bonita Jenkins, Acting Chairperson, 301-860-3210, E-mail: mccaskill@bowiestate.edu. *Application contact:* Angela Issac, Information Contact, 301-860-4000.

Bradley University, The Graduate School, College of Education and Health Sciences, Department of Nursing, Peoria, IL 61625-0002. Offers family nurse practitioner (MSN, DNP, Certificate); leadership (DNP); nursing administration (MSN); nursing education (MSN, Certificate). *Accreditation:* AACN; ACEN. *Program availability:* Part-time, evening/weekend. *Degree requirements:* For master's, comprehensive exam, thesis optional. *Entrance requirements:* For master's, GRE General Test or MAT, interview, Illinois RN license, advanced cardiac life support certification, pediatric advanced life support certification, 3 letters of recommendation. Additional exam requirements/recommendations for international students: Required—TOEFL (minimum score 550 paper-based; 79 iBT), IELTS (minimum score 6.5). Electronic applications accepted.

Brandman University, Marybelle and S. Paul Musco School of Nursing and Health Professions, Irvine, CA 92618. Offers nursing (DNP). *Accreditation:* AACN. *Expenses: Tuition:* Part-time $640 per credit hour. Tuition and fees vary according to degree level and program. *Unit head:* Dr. Tyke Hanisch, Dean, 949-341-9815. *Application contact:* Dr. Tyke Hanisch, Dean, 949-341-9815.
Website: https://www.brandman.edu/academic-programs/nursing-and-health-professions

Briar Cliff University, Graduate Nursing Programs, Sioux City, IA 51104-0100. Offers MSN, DNP, Post-Master's Certificate. *Accreditation:* AACN. *Program availability:* Part-time, online only, 100% online, blended/hybrid learning. *Degree requirements:* For master's, thesis optional. *Entrance requirements:* For master's, minimum undergraduate GPA of 3.0 for last 60 credits from accredited institution, current RN license, current CPR certification, 2000 hours of nursing experience, 2 letters of recommendation, personal development statement, official transcripts from all undergraduate institutions attended; for doctorate, minimum undergraduate GPA of 3.0 for last 60 credits from accredited institution, current RN license, current CPR certification, 2000 hours of nursing experience, 2 letters of recommendation, personal development statement, official transcripts from all undergraduate institutions attended, clinical hours completed from earned MSN. Additional exam requirements/recommendations for international students: Recommended—TOEFL. Electronic applications accepted. *Expenses:* Contact institution. *Faculty research:* Process/experience of trying something new (or change), experience of taking a risk.

Brigham Young University, Graduate Studies, College of Nursing, Provo, UT 84602. Offers family nurse practitioner (MS). *Accreditation:* AACN. *Faculty:* 17 full-time (11 women). *Students:* 29 full-time (20 women); includes 1 minority (Hispanic/Latino). Average age 33. 40 applicants, 45% accepted, 14 enrolled. In 2017, 14 master's awarded. *Degree requirements:* For master's, thesis. *Entrance requirements:* For master's, GRE, minimum cumulative undergraduate GPA of 3.0, baccalaureate degree in nursing from school with national nursing accreditation, interview, current RN license in Utah, pathophysiology and statistics classes, 3 letters of recommendation. Additional exam requirements/recommendations for international students: Required—TOEFL (minimum score 580 paper-based; 85 iBT). *Application deadline:* For spring admission, 12/1 for domestic and international students. Application fee: $50. Electronic applications accepted. *Expenses:* Contact institution. *Financial support:* In 2017–18, 27 students received support, including 1 research assistantship (averaging $12,800 per year); teaching assistantships, institutionally sponsored loans, and scholarships/grants also available. Financial award application deadline: 4/13; financial award applicants required to submit FAFSA. *Faculty research:* End-of-life, childhood immunizations, global health nursing, exercise outcomes on health, sexual violence, critical care, diabetes. *Unit head:* Dr. Patricia Ravert, Dean, 801-422-1167, Fax: 801-422-0536, E-mail: patricia_ravert@byu.edu. *Application contact:* Cherie Top, Graduate Secretary, 801-422-4142, Fax: 801-422-0538, E-mail: cherie-top@byu.edu.
Website: http://nursing.byu.edu/

Brookline College, Nursing Programs, Phoenix, AZ 85021. Offers health systems administration (MSN); nursing (MSN). *Program availability:* Part-time, online learning.

California Baptist University, Doctor of Nursing Practice Program, Riverside, CA 92504-3206. Offers DNP. *Program availability:* Part-time. *Faculty:* 6 full-time (5 women). *Students:* 1 full-time (0 women), 5 part-time (3 women); includes 4 minority (1 Black or African American, non-Hispanic/Latino; 1 American Indian or Alaska Native, non-Hispanic/Latino; 2 Hispanic/Latino). Average age 49. 4 applicants, 100% accepted, 3 enrolled. *Degree requirements:* For doctorate, thesis/dissertation or alternative, translational capstone project. *Entrance requirements:* For doctorate, MA in nursing, minimum cumulative GPA of 3.3, current California RN license, interview, official transcripts, three references, written statement about potential project, professional resume or curriculum vitae, writing sample. Additional exam requirements/recommendations for international students: Required—TOEFL (minimum score 80 iBT). *Application deadline:* For fall admission, 8/1 priority date for domestic students, 7/1 priority date for international students; for spring admission, 12/1 priority date for domestic students, 11/1 priority date for international students. Applications are processed on a rolling basis. Application fee: $45. Electronic applications accepted. *Expenses:* Contact institution. *Financial support:* Federal Work-Study and scholarships/grants available. Financial award applicants required to submit CSS PROFILE or FAFSA. *Faculty research:* Community health, pediatric nursing, interprofessional education, global healthcare technology, male health. *Unit head:* Dr. Geneva Oaks, Dean, School of Nursing, 951-343-4702, E-mail: goaks@calbaptist.edu. *Application contact:* Dr. Lisa Bursch, DNP Program Director, 951-343-4940, E-mail: lbursch@calbaptist.edu.
Website: http://www.calbaptist.edu/academics/schools-colleges/school-nursing/doctor-nursing-practice/

California Baptist University, Program in Nursing, Riverside, CA 92504-3206. Offers clinical nurse specialist (MSN); family nurse practitioner (MSN); healthcare systems management (MSN); teaching-learning (MSN). *Accreditation:* AACN. *Program availability:* Part-time. *Faculty:* 19 full-time (18 women), 12 part-time/adjunct (11 women). *Students:* 78 full-time (59 women), 130 part-time (106 women); includes 114 minority (25 Black or African American, non-Hispanic/Latino; 3 American Indian or Alaska Native, non-Hispanic/Latino; 34 Asian, non-Hispanic/Latino; 47 Hispanic/Latino; 2 Native Hawaiian or other Pacific Islander, non-Hispanic/Latino; 3 Two or more races, non-Hispanic/Latino), 2 international. Average age 32. 25 applicants, 84% accepted, 14 enrolled. In 2017, 49 master's awarded. *Degree requirements:* For master's, comprehensive exam or directed project thesis; capstone practicum. *Entrance requirements:* For master's, GRE or California Critical Thinking Skills Test; Test of Essential Academic Skills (TEAS), minimum undergraduate GPA of 3.0; completion of prerequisite courses with minimum grade of C; CPR certification; background check clearance; health clearance; drug testing; proof of health insurance; proof of motor vehicle insurance; three letters of recommendation; 1000-word essay; interview. Additional exam requirements/recommendations for international students: Required—TOEFL (minimum score 80 iBT). *Application deadline:* For fall admission, 8/1 priority date for domestic students, 7/1 for international students; for spring admission, 12/1 priority date for domestic students, 11/1 for international students. Applications are processed on a rolling basis. Application fee: $45. Electronic applications accepted. *Expenses:* Contact institution. *Financial support:* In 2017–18, 38 students received support. Federal Work-Study and scholarships/grants available. Financial award applicants required to submit CSS PROFILE or FAFSA. *Faculty research:* Qualitative research using Parse methodology, gerontology, disaster preparedness, medical-surgical nursing, maternal-child nursing. *Unit head:* Dr. Geneva Oaks, Dean, School of Nursing, 951-343-4702, E-mail: goaks@calbaptist.edu. *Application contact:* Tamakia King, Graduate Admissions Counselor, 951-552-8138, Fax: 951-343-5095, E-mail: tking@calbaptist.edu.
Website: http://www.calbaptist.edu/explore-cbu/schools-colleges/school-nursing/master-science-nursing/

California State University, Bakersfield, Division of Graduate Studies, School of Natural Sciences, Mathematics, and Engineering, Program in Nursing, Bakersfield, CA 93311. Offers family nurse practitioner (MSN). Applications accepted every other year. *Faculty:* 2 full-time (both women), 2 part-time/adjunct (both women). *Students:* 17 full-time (13 women); includes 12 minority (2 Black or African American, non-Hispanic/Latino; 5 Asian, non-Hispanic/Latino; 5 Hispanic/Latino). Average age 32. 75 applicants, 27% accepted, 17 enrolled. In 2017, 15 master's awarded. *Degree requirements:* For master's, thesis, project. *Entrance requirements:* For master's, BSN from ACEN-accredited program, 1 year of full-time nursing experience. *Application deadline:* Applications are processed on a rolling basis. Application fee: $55. Electronic applications accepted. *Expenses:* Tuition, state resident: full-time $7176; part-time $4164 per year. *Financial support:* In 2017–18, fellowships (averaging $1,850 per year) were awarded; Federal Work-Study, scholarships/grants, and tuition waivers (full and partial) also available. Financial award application deadline: 3/2; financial award applicants required to submit FAFSA. *Faculty research:* AIDS, gerontological nursing, cultural health beliefs. *Unit head:* Dr. Heidi He, Director, Graduate Program, 661-654-3112, Fax: 661-654-6437, E-mail: hhe@csub.edu. *Application contact:* Fatima Ramos, Program Advisor, 661-654-2610, E-mail: framos12@csub.edu.
Website: http://www.csub.edu/nursing/

California State University, Chico, Office of Graduate Studies, College of Natural Sciences, School of Nursing, Chico, CA 95929. Offers MSN. *Accreditation:* AACN. *Program availability:* Part-time, online learning. *Degree requirements:* For master's, project or thesis and oral exam. *Entrance requirements:* For master's, GRE, statement of purpose, course work in statistics in the last seven years, BSN, California nursing license. Additional exam requirements/recommendations for international students: Required—TOEFL (minimum score 550 paper-based; 80 iBT), IELTS (minimum score 6.5), PTE (minimum score 59). Electronic applications accepted.

California State University, Dominguez Hills, College of Health, Human Services and Nursing, Program in Nursing, Carson, CA 90747-0001. Offers MSN. *Accreditation:* AACN. *Program availability:* Part-time, online learning. *Degree requirements:* For master's, comprehensive exam. *Entrance requirements:* For master's, minimum GPA of 2.5, 3.0 in prior coursework in statistics, research, pathophysiology and assessment. Additional exam requirements/recommendations for international students: Required—TOEFL. Electronic applications accepted. *Faculty research:* AIDS/HIV, health promotion, elderly.

California State University, Fresno, Division of Research and Graduate Studies, College of Health and Human Services, School of Nursing, Fresno, CA 93740-8027. Offers nursing (MS, DNP), including clinical nurse specialist (MS). DNP offered in collaboration with San Jose State University. *Accreditation:* AACN. *Program availability:* Part-time, evening/weekend. *Degree requirements:* For master's, thesis or alternative. *Entrance requirements:* For master's, GRE General Test, 1 year of clinical practice, previous course work in statistics, BSN, minimum GPA of 3.0 in nursing. Additional exam requirements/recommendations for international students: Required—TOEFL. Electronic applications accepted. *Faculty research:* Training grant, HIV assessment.

California State University, Fullerton, Graduate Studies, College of Health and Human Development, School of Nursing, Fullerton, CA 92831-3599. Offers leadership (MS); nurse anesthesia (MS); nurse educator (MS); nursing (DNP); school nursing (MS); women's health care (MS). *Accreditation:* AACN. *Program availability:* Part-time. *Faculty:* 27 full-time (23 women), 11 part-time/adjunct (all women). *Students:* 136 full-time (107 women), 116 part-time (96 women); includes 142 minority (9 Black or African American, non-Hispanic/Latino; 81 Asian, non-Hispanic/Latino; 37 Hispanic/Latino; 1 Native Hawaiian or other Pacific Islander, non-Hispanic/Latino; 14 Two or more races, non-Hispanic/Latino), 2 international. Average age 36. 235 applicants, 59% accepted, 117 enrolled. Application fee: $55. *Financial support:* Career-related internships or fieldwork, Federal Work-Study, institutionally sponsored loans, scholarships/grants, and traineeships available. Support available to part-time students. Financial award application deadline: 3/1; financial award applicants required to submit FAFSA. *Unit head:* Dr. Cindy Greenberg, Chair, 657-278-3336. *Application contact:* Admissions/Applications, 657-278-2371.
Website: http://nursing.fullerton.edu/

California State University, Long Beach, Graduate Studies, College of Health and Human Services, School of Nursing, Long Beach, CA 90840. Offers MSN, DNP, Graduate Certificate. DNP offered jointly with California State University, Fullerton and

Nursing—General

California State University, Los Angeles. *Accreditation:* AACN. *Program availability:* Part-time. *Degree requirements:* For master's, thesis optional. *Entrance requirements:* For master's, minimum GPA of 3.0. Electronic applications accepted. *Faculty research:* Newborns of drug-dependent mothers, abuse of residents in nursing homes, interventions in care of Alzheimer's patients.

California State University, Los Angeles, Graduate Studies, College of Health and Human Services, School of Nursing, Los Angeles, CA 90032-8530. Offers MS, Post Master's Certificate. *Accreditation:* AACN. *Program availability:* Part-time, evening/weekend. *Degree requirements:* For master's, comprehensive exam, project or thesis. *Entrance requirements:* For master's, minimum GPA of 3.0 in nursing, course work in nursing and statistics. Additional exam requirements/recommendations for international students: Required—TOEFL (minimum score 500 paper-based). *Faculty research:* Family stress, geripsychiatric nursing, self-care counseling, holistic nursing, adult health.

California State University, Sacramento, College of Health and Human Services, Division of Nursing, Sacramento, CA 95819-6096. Offers MS. *Accreditation:* AACN. *Program availability:* Part-time. *Students:* 70 full-time (65 women), 84 part-time (79 women); includes 41 minority (5 Black or African American, non-Hispanic/Latino; 2 American Indian or Alaska Native, non-Hispanic/Latino; 23 Asian, non-Hispanic/Latino; 11 Hispanic/Latino). Average age 40. 41 applicants, 93% accepted, 32 enrolled. In 2017, 43 master's awarded. *Degree requirements:* For master's, comprehensive exam, thesis or project, writing proficiency exam. *Entrance requirements:* For master's, bachelor's degree in nursing, minimum GPA of 3.0. Additional exam requirements/recommendations for international students: Required—TOEFL (minimum score 550 paper-based; 80 iBT); Recommended—IELTS, TSE. *Application deadline:* For fall admission, 3/1 for domestic and international students; for spring admission, 12/1 for domestic and international students. Applications are processed on a rolling basis. Application fee: $55. Electronic applications accepted. *Expenses:* Contact institution. *Financial support:* Teaching assistantships, career-related internships or fieldwork, Federal Work-Study, and scholarships/grants available. Support available to part-time students. Financial award application deadline: 3/1; financial award applicants required to submit FAFSA. *Unit head:* Dr. Tanya Altmann, Chair, 916-278-1504, E-mail: altmannt@csus.edu. *Application contact:* Jose Martinez, Graduate Admissions Supervisor, 916-278-7871, E-mail: martinj@skymail.csus.edu.
Website: http://www.csus.edu/hhs/nrs/index.html

California State University, San Bernardino, Graduate Studies, College of Natural Sciences, Program in Nursing, San Bernardino, CA 92407. Offers MSN. *Accreditation:* AACN. *Faculty:* 2 full-time (both women), 3 part-time/adjunct (2 women). *Students:* 7 full-time (4 women), 8 part-time (7 women); includes 10 minority (3 Black or African American, non-Hispanic/Latino; 3 Asian, non-Hispanic/Latino; 4 Hispanic/Latino), 1 international. Average age 42. 22 applicants, 45% accepted, 4 enrolled. In 2017, 11 master's awarded. *Degree requirements:* For master's, thesis optional. *Entrance requirements:* Additional exam requirements/recommendations for international students: Required—TOEFL. *Application deadline:* For fall admission, 7/16 for domestic students; for winter admission, 10/16 for domestic students; for spring admission, 1/22 for domestic students. Application fee: $55. *Unit head:* Teresa Dodd-Butera, MSN Coordinator, 909-537-5448, Fax: 909-537-7089, E-mail: tdbutera@csusb.edu. *Application contact:* Dr. Dorota Huizinga, Dean of Graduate Studies, 909-537-3064, E-mail: dorota.huizinga@csusb.edu.

California State University, San Marcos, College of Education, Health and Human Services, School of Nursing, San Marcos, CA 92096-0001. Offers advanced practice nursing (MSN), including clinical nurse specialist, family nurse practitioner, psychiatric mental health nurse practitioner; clinical nurse leader (MSN); nursing education (MSN). *Expenses:* Tuition, state resident: full-time $7176. Tuition, nonresident: full-time $9504. *Unit head:* Lorna Kendrick, Director, 760-750-7580, E-mail: lkendrick@csusm.edu.
Website: http://www.csusm.edu/nursing/

California State University, Stanislaus, College of Science, Master's in Nursing Program, Turlock, CA 95382. Offers gerontological nursing (MS); nursing education (MS). *Accreditation:* AACN. *Program availability:* Part-time. *Degree requirements:* For master's, comprehensive exam, thesis or alternative. *Entrance requirements:* For master's, GRE or MAT, minimum GPA of 3.0, 3 letters of reference, RN. Additional exam requirements/recommendations for international students: Required—TOEFL (minimum score 550 paper-based). Electronic applications accepted.

California University of Pennsylvania, School of Graduate Studies and Research, Eberly College of Science and Technology, Department of Nursing, California, PA 15419-1394. Offers nursing administration and leadership (MSN); nursing education (MSN).

Capella University, School of Public Service Leadership, Doctoral Programs in Nursing, Minneapolis, MN 55402. Offers nursing education (PhD); nursing practice (DNP).

Capella University, School of Public Service Leadership, Master's Programs in Nursing, Minneapolis, MN 55402. Offers diabetes nursing (MSN); general nursing (MSN); gerontology nursing (MSN); health information management (MS); nurse educator (MSN); nursing leadership and administration (MSN). *Accreditation:* AACN.

Capital University, School of Nursing, Columbus, OH 43209-2394. Offers administration (MSN); legal studies (MSN); theological studies (MSN); JD/MSN; MBA/MSN; MSN/MTS. *Accreditation:* AACN. *Program availability:* Part-time, evening/weekend. *Degree requirements:* For master's, thesis or alternative. *Entrance requirements:* For master's, BSN, current RN license, minimum GPA of 3.0, undergraduate courses in statistics and research. Additional exam requirements/recommendations for international students: Required—TOEFL (minimum score 550 paper-based). *Expenses:* Contact institution. *Faculty research:* Bereavement, wellness/health promotion, emergency cardiac care, critical thinking, complementary and alternative healthcare.

Cardinal Stritch University, Ruth S. Coleman College of Nursing and Health Sciences, Milwaukee, WI 53217-3985. Offers MSN. *Accreditation:* ACEN. *Program availability:* Part-time, evening/weekend. *Students:* 17 applicants, 100% accepted. In 2017, 8 master's awarded. *Degree requirements:* For master's, thesis. *Entrance requirements:* For master's, interview; minimum GPA of 3.0; RN license; 3 letters of recommendation; undergraduate coursework in statistics and nursing research; computer literacy; curriculum vitae. Additional exam requirements/recommendations for international students: Required—TOEFL (minimum score 79 iBT), IELTS (minimum score 6.5). *Application deadline:* For fall admission, 6/15 priority date for domestic students; for spring admission, 11/15 priority date for domestic students. Applications are processed on a rolling basis. Electronic applications accepted. *Expenses:* *Tuition:* Full-time $9520; part-time $680 per credit. Tuition and fees vary according to course load, degree level, program and student's religious affiliation. *Financial support:* Federal Work-Study and scholarships/grants available. Financial award applicants required to submit FAFSA. *Unit head:* Dr. Kelly J. Dries, Dean, 414-410-4397, E-mail: kjdries@stritch.edu. *Application contact:* Graduate Admissions, 800-347-8822 Ext. 4042, E-mail: admissions@stritch.edu.

Carlow University, College of Health and Wellness, Doctor of Nursing Practice Program, Pittsburgh, PA 15213-3165. Offers DNP. *Accreditation:* AACN. *Program availability:* Part-time, evening/weekend, low-residency. *Students:* 24 full-time (20 women), 17 part-time (15 women); includes 2 minority (1 Black or African American, non-Hispanic/Latino; 1 Asian, non-Hispanic/Latino). Average age 43. 41 applicants, 93% accepted, 21 enrolled. In 2017, 16 doctorates awarded. *Degree requirements:* For doctorate, 3-semester scholarly inquiry. *Entrance requirements:* For doctorate, master's degree with minimum GPA of 3.0; BSN; current RN license; official transcripts from all undergraduate and graduate institutions; copy of RN license; current curriculum vitae; two letters of academic and/or professional recommendation; reflective essay describing career goals and expectations for education. Additional exam requirements/recommendations for international students: Required—TOEFL (minimum score 550 paper-based). *Application deadline:* For fall admission, 4/1 priority date for domestic students. Applications are processed on a rolling basis. Electronic applications accepted. *Expenses:* Contact institution. *Financial support:* Application deadline: 4/1; applicants required to submit FAFSA. *Unit head:* Dr. Renee Ingel, Director, DNP Program, 412-578-6103, Fax: 412-578-6114, E-mail: rmingel@carlow.edu.
Website: http://www.carlow.edu/Nursing_Doctoral_Offering.aspx

Carlow University, College of Health and Wellness, MSN-MBA Dual Degree Program, Pittsburgh, PA 15213-3165. Offers MSN/MBA. *Program availability:* Part-time, 100% online, blended/hybrid learning. *Students:* 31 full-time (24 women), 7 part-time (all women); includes 2 minority (both Black or African American, non-Hispanic/Latino). Average age 35. 9 applicants, 100% accepted, 7 enrolled. *Entrance requirements:* Additional exam requirements/recommendations for international students: Required—TOEFL (minimum score 550 paper-based). *Application deadline:* Applications are processed on a rolling basis. Electronic applications accepted. *Expenses:* *Tuition:* Full-time $12,103; part-time $825 per credit hour. Tuition and fees vary according to program. *Financial support:* Application deadline: 4/1; applicants required to submit FAFSA. *Unit head:* Dr. Renee Ingel, Program Director, 412-578-6103, E-mail: rmingel@carlow.edu. *Application contact:* E-mail: gradstudies@carlow.edu.
Website: http://www.carlow.edu/MSN-MBA_Dual_Degree.aspx

Carson-Newman University, Department of Nursing, Jefferson City, TN 37760. Offers family nurse practitioner (MSN); nurse educator (MSN). *Accreditation:* AACN. *Program availability:* Part-time. *Faculty:* 4 full-time (3 women). *Students:* 7 full-time (6 women), 33 part-time (30 women), 2 international. Average age 33. 18 applicants, 100% accepted, 13 enrolled. In 2017, 14 master's awarded. *Degree requirements:* For master's, comprehensive exam, thesis optional. *Entrance requirements:* For master's, GRE (minimum score of 290 within ten years of application), minimum GPA of 3.0 for all undergraduate work. Additional exam requirements/recommendations for international students: Recommended—TOEFL (minimum score 79 iBT), IELTS (minimum score 6.5), TSE (minimum score 53). *Application deadline:* For fall admission, 3/15 for domestic students; for spring admission, 10/15 for domestic students. Applications are processed on a rolling basis. Application fee: $50. *Expenses:* *Tuition:* Full-time $10,516; part-time $478 per credit hour. *Required fees:* $240; $120 per semester. One-time fee: $150. *Financial support:* Federal Work-Study and tuition waivers (full and partial) available. Financial award applicants required to submit FAFSA. *Unit head:* Dr. Kimberly Bolton, Director, 865-471-4056, E-mail: kbolton@cn.edu. *Application contact:* Nilma Stewart, Graduate Admissions and Services Adviser, 865-471-3230, Fax: 865-471-3875, E-mail: adults@cn.edu.
Website: http://www.cn.edu/adult-graduate-studies/programs/new/nursing

Case Western Reserve University, Frances Payne Bolton School of Nursing, Doctor of Nursing Practice Program, Cleveland, OH 44106. Offers educational leadership (DNP); practice leadership (DNP). *Accreditation:* AACN. *Program availability:* Part-time. *Faculty:* 51 full-time (44 women). *Students:* 63 full-time (56 women), 72 part-time (63 women); includes 33 minority (18 Black or African American, non-Hispanic/Latino; 10 Asian, non-Hispanic/Latino; 4 Hispanic/Latino; 1 Native Hawaiian or other Pacific Islander, non-Hispanic/Latino), 9 international. Average age 52. 55 applicants, 89% accepted, 38 enrolled. In 2017, 42 doctorates awarded. *Degree requirements:* For doctorate, thesis/dissertation, log of 1000 practicum hours. *Entrance requirements:* Additional exam requirements/recommendations for international students: Required—TOEFL (minimum score 577 paper-based; 90 iBT), IELTS (minimum score 7). *Application deadline:* For fall admission, 6/1 for domestic and international students; for spring admission, 10/1 for domestic and international students; for summer admission, 3/1 for domestic and international students. Applications are processed on a rolling basis. Application fee: $75. Electronic applications accepted. *Expenses:* Contact institution. *Financial support:* In 2017–18, 76 students received support. Research assistantships, teaching assistantships, scholarships/grants, and nurse faculty loan program available. Support available to part-time students. Financial award application deadline: 5/15; financial award applicants required to submit FAFSA. *Faculty research:* Symptom science, family/community care, aging across the lifespan, self-management of health and illness, neuroscience. *Unit head:* Dr. Patricia Higgins, Interim Director, 216-368-8850, E-mail: pxg3@case.edu. *Application contact:* Jackie Tepale, Admissions Coordinator, 216-368-5253, Fax: 216-368-0124, E-mail: yyd@case.edu.
Website: https://case.edu/nursing/dnp/

Case Western Reserve University, Frances Payne Bolton School of Nursing, Master's Programs in Nursing, Cleveland, OH 44106. Offers nurse anesthesia (MSN); nurse education (MSN); nurse midwifery (MSN); nurse practitioner (MSN), including acute care pediatric nurse practitioner, acute care/cardiovascular nursing, acute care/flight nurse, adult gerontology acute care nurse practitioner, adult gerontology nurse practitioner, adult gerontology primary care nurse practitioner, family nurse practitioner, family systems psychiatric mental health nursing, neonatal nurse practitioner, palliative care, pediatric nurse practitioner, women's health nurse practitioner; nursing (MN). *Accreditation:* ACEN. *Program availability:* Part-time. *Faculty:* 67 full-time (60 women), 29 part-time/adjunct (26 women). *Students:* 140 full-time (108 women), 155 part-time (124 women); includes 62 minority (24 Black or African American, non-Hispanic/Latino; 20 Asian, non-Hispanic/Latino; 9 Hispanic/Latino; 1 Native Hawaiian or other Pacific Islander, non-Hispanic/Latino; 8 Two or more races, non-Hispanic/Latino), 9 international. Average age 33. 250 applicants, 63% accepted, 94 enrolled. In 2017, 134 master's awarded. *Degree requirements:* For master's, thesis optional, minimum GPA of 3.0, Typhon log of clinical hours corresponding to requirements to sit for certification exam. *Entrance requirements:* For master's, GRE General Test or MAT, CCRN certification (for nurse anesthesia). Additional exam requirements/recommendations for international students: Required—TOEFL (minimum score 577 paper-based; 90 iBT), IELTS (minimum score 7). *Application deadline:* For fall admission, 3/1 for domestic and international students; for spring admission, 10/1 for domestic and international students; for summer admission, 3/1 for domestic and international students. Applications are processed on a rolling basis. Application fee: $75. Electronic applications accepted. *Expenses:* $2,011 per credit hour; $215 lab fee; $15 activity fee. *Financial support:* In 2017–18, 22 students received support. Scholarships/grants available. Financial award application deadline: 5/15; financial award applicants required to submit FAFSA. *Faculty research:* Symptom science, family/community care, aging across the lifespan, self-management of health and illness, neuroscience. *Unit head:* Dr. Latina Brooks, Director, 216-368-1196, Fax: 215-368-3542, E-mail: lmb3@case.edu. *Application contact:* Jackie Tepale, Admissions Coordinator, 216-368-5253, Fax: 216-368-0124, E-mail: yyd@case.edu.
Website: https://case.edu/nursing/msn/

Case Western Reserve University, Frances Payne Bolton School of Nursing, PhD in Nursing Program, Cleveland, OH 44106. Offers PhD. *Program availability:* Part-time. *Faculty:* 30 full-time (24 women). *Students:* 53 full-time (46 women), 5 part-time (3 women); includes 9 minority (4 Black or African American, non-Hispanic/Latino; 2 Asian, non-Hispanic/Latino; 3 Two or more races, non-Hispanic/Latino), 20 international. Average age 36. 23 applicants, 57% accepted, 9 enrolled. In 2017, 9 doctorates awarded. *Degree requirements:* For doctorate, comprehensive exam, thesis/dissertation, 240 hour research practicum. *Entrance requirements:* Additional exam requirements/recommendations for international students: Required—TOEFL (minimum score 577 paper-based, 90 iBT) or IELTS (minimum score 7.0). *Application deadline:* For fall admission, 2/1 for domestic and international students; for spring admission, 10/1 for domestic and international students. Applications are processed on a rolling basis. Application fee: $50. Electronic applications accepted. *Expenses:* $1,827 per credit hour; $15.00 activity fee; $17.00 Graduate Council fee. *Financial support:* In 2017–18, 29 students received support, including 10 fellowships with full tuition reimbursements available (averaging $10,598 per year), 7 research assistantships with partial tuition reimbursements available (averaging $16,674 per year); scholarships/grants and nurse faculty loan program also available. Financial award application deadline: 5/15; financial award applicants required to submit FAFSA. *Faculty research:* Neuroscience, self-management, symptom science, aging across the lifespan, and family/community care. *Unit head:* Dr. Jaclene A. Zauszniewski, Director, 216-368-3612, Fax: 215-368-3542, E-mail: jaz@case.edu. *Application contact:* Jackie Tepale, Admissions Coordinator, Graduate Programs, 216-368-5253, Fax: 216-368-0124, E-mail: yyd@case.edu.
Website: http://fpb.cwru.edu/PhD/

The Catholic University of America, School of Nursing, Washington, DC 20064. Offers MSN, DNP, PhD, Certificate. *Accreditation:* AACN. *Program availability:* Part-time, 100% online. *Faculty:* 21 full-time (all women), 42 part-time/adjunct (36 women). *Students:* 22 full-time (all women), 177 part-time (162 women); includes 67 minority (40 Black or African American, non-Hispanic/Latino; 6 Asian, non-Hispanic/Latino; 7 Hispanic/Latino; 14 Two or more races, non-Hispanic/Latino), 13 international. Average age 42. 125 applicants, 72% accepted, 49 enrolled. In 2017, 47 master's, 9 doctorates, 3 other advanced degrees awarded. *Degree requirements:* For master's, comprehensive exam, thesis optional; for doctorate, comprehensive exam, thesis/dissertation, minimum GPA of 3.0, oral proposal defense. *Entrance requirements:* For master's, GRE General Test, 3 letters of recommendation, BA in nursing, RN registration, official copies of academic transcripts, some post-baccalaureate nursing experience; for doctorate, GRE General Test, BA in nursing, professional portfolio (including statements, resume, copy of RN license, 3 letters of recommendation, narrative description of clinical practice), copy of research/scholarly paper related to clinical nursing; for Certificate, GRE General Test. Additional exam requirements/recommendations for international students: Required—TOEFL (minimum score 550 paper-based; 80 iBT). *Application deadline:* For fall admission, 7/15 priority date for domestic students, 7/1 for international students; for spring admission, 11/15 priority date for domestic students, 11/1 for international students. Applications are processed on a rolling basis. Application fee: $55. Electronic applications accepted. *Expenses:* Contact institution. *Financial support:* Fellowships, research assistantships, teaching assistantships, Federal Work-Study, scholarships/grants, tuition waivers (full and partial), and unspecified assistantships available. Financial award application deadline: 2/1; financial award applicants required to submit FAFSA. *Faculty research:* Community involvement in health care services, primary health care services, pediatrics, chronic illness, cardiovascular disease. *Total annual research expenditures:* $276,695. *Unit head:* Dr. Patricia McMullen, Dean, 202-319-5403, Fax: 202-319-6485, E-mail: mcmullep@cua.edu. *Application contact:* Dr. Steven Brown, Director of Graduate Admissions, 202-319-5057, Fax: 202-319-6533, E-mail: cua-admissions@cua.edu.
Website: https://nursing.catholic.edu/

Cedar Crest College, Program in Nursing, Allentown, PA 18104-6196. Offers nursing administration (MS); nursing education (MS). *Program availability:* Part-time. *Faculty:* 4 full-time (3 women), 2 part-time/adjunct (1 woman). *Students:* 25 part-time (23 women); includes 7 minority (2 Black or African American, non-Hispanic/Latino; 2 Asian, non-Hispanic/Latino; 3 Hispanic/Latino). Average age 36. In 2017, 8 master's awarded. *Application deadline:* Applications are processed on a rolling basis. Electronic applications accepted. *Expenses:* Contact institution. *Unit head:* Dr. Wendy Robb, Director, 610-606-4666, E-mail: wjrobb@cedarcrest.edu. *Application contact:* Nancy Wunderly, Director of School of Adult and Graduate Education, 610-606-4666, E-mail: sage@cedarcrest.edu.
Website: http://sage.cedarcrest.edu/degrees/graduate/nursing-science/

Central Connecticut State University, School of Graduate Studies, School of Education and Professional Studies, Department of Nursing, New Britain, CT 06050-4010. Offers hospice and palliative care (MSN). *Program availability:* Part-time, evening/weekend. *Faculty:* 2 full-time (both women). *Students:* 5 part-time (all women). Average age 44. 9 applicants, 78% accepted, 5 enrolled. *Degree requirements:* For master's, thesis, nursing capstone. *Entrance requirements:* For master's, minimum undergraduate GPA of 2.7, essay, letter of reference, minimum grade of C+ in an undergraduate statistics course. Additional exam requirements/recommendations for international students: Required—TOEFL (minimum score 550 paper-based; 79 iBT); Recommended—IELTS (minimum score 6.5). *Application deadline:* For summer admission, 3/1 for domestic and international students. Application fee: $50. *Expenses:* *Tuition, area resident:* Full-time $6757. Tuition, state resident: full-time $9750; part-time $374 per credit. Tuition, nonresident: full-time $18,102; part-time $374 per credit. *Required fees:* $4635; $255 per credit. *Financial support:* Application deadline: 3/1; applicants required to submit FAFSA. *Unit head:* Dr. Catherine Thomas, Acting Chair, 860-832-0032, E-mail: csthomas@ccsu.edu. *Application contact:* Patricia Gardner, Associate Director of Graduate Studies, 860-832-2350, Fax: 860-832-2362.
Website: http://www.ccsu.edu/nursing

Central Methodist University, College of Graduate and Extended Studies, Fayette, MO 65248-1198. Offers clinical counseling (MS); clinical nurse leader (MSN); education (M Ed); music education (MME); nurse educator (MSN). *Program availability:* Part-time, evening/weekend, online learning. *Degree requirements:* For master's, thesis. *Entrance requirements:* For master's, GRE General Test, minimum GPA of 2.75. Electronic applications accepted.

Chatham University, Nursing Programs, Pittsburgh, PA 15232-2826. Offers education/leadership (MSN); nursing (DNP). *Accreditation:* AACN. *Program availability:* Online learning. *Faculty:* 12 full-time (all women), 12 part-time/adjunct (10 women). *Students:* 49 full-time (41 women), 95 part-time (80 women); includes 68 minority (51 Black or African American, non-Hispanic/Latino; 7 Asian, non-Hispanic/Latino; 8 Hispanic/Latino; 2 Two or more races, non-Hispanic/Latino), 11 international. Average age 42. 209 applicants, 51% accepted, 76 enrolled. In 2017, 13 master's, 82 doctorates awarded. *Entrance requirements:* For master's, RN license, BSN, minimum GPA of 3.0; for doctorate, RN license, MSN. Additional exam requirements/recommendations for international students: Required—TOEFL (minimum score 600 paper-based; 100 iBT), IELTS (minimum score 6.5), TWE. *Application deadline:* For fall admission, 5/1 priority date for domestic and international students. Applications are processed on a rolling basis. Application fee: $35. Electronic applications accepted. Application fee is waived when completed online. *Expenses:* Contact institution. *Financial support:* Application deadline: 8/1; applicants required to submit FAFSA. *Unit head:* Dr. Diane Hunker, Director, 412-365-1738, E-mail: dhunker@chatham.edu. *Application contact:* Patricia Golla, Assistant Director of Graduate Admissions, 412-365-1386, Fax: 412-365-1720, E-mail: pgolla@chatham.edu.
Website: http://www.chatham.edu/nursing

Chicago State University, School of Graduate and Professional Studies, College of Health Sciences, Department of Nursing, Chicago, IL 60628. Offers MSN. *Unit head:* Dr. Lisa A. Young, Interim Chairperson, 773-995-3901, Fax: 773-821-2438, E-mail: lyoung24@csu.edu. *Application contact:* Daphne G. Townsend, Admissions and Records Officer II, 773-995-2404, Fax: 773-995-3671, E-mail: g-studies1@csu.edu.
Website: http://www.csu.edu/Nursing/

Clarion University of Pennsylvania, College of Health and Human Services, Doctor of Nursing Practice Program, Clarion, PA 16214. Offers DNP. Program offered jointly with Edinboro University of Pennsylvania. *Program availability:* Part-time-only, evening/weekend, online only, 100% online. *Faculty:* 3 part-time/adjunct (all women). *Students:* 10 part-time (7 women); includes 2 minority (both Black or African American, non-Hispanic/Latino). Average age 42. 26 applicants, 62% accepted, 8 enrolled. In 2017, 7 doctorates awarded. *Degree requirements:* For doctorate, thesis/dissertation, portfolio. *Entrance requirements:* Additional exam requirements/recommendations for international students: Required—TOEFL (minimum score 550 paper-based, 80 iBT) or IELTS (7). *Application deadline:* For summer admission, 4/1 priority date for domestic students, 1/1 priority date for international students. Applications are processed on a rolling basis. Application fee: $40. Electronic applications accepted. *Expenses:* $861 per credit. *Financial support:* Career-related internships or fieldwork, scholarships/grants, and unspecified assistantships available. Support available to part-time students. Financial award application deadline: 3/1; financial award applicants required to submit FAFSA. *Unit head:* Dr. Deborah Kelly, Department Chair, 814-393-1251 Ext. 1258, E-mail: dkelly@clarion.edu. *Application contact:* Dana Bearer, Associate Director for Transfer, Adult and Graduate Admissions, 814-393-2337, Fax: 814-393-2772, E-mail: gradstudies@clarion.edu.
Website: http://www.clarion.edu/academics/degrees-programs/sohs/nursing/index.html#doctor-of-nursing-practice

Clarion University of Pennsylvania, College of Health and Human Services, Master of Science in Nursing Program, Clarion, PA 16214. Offers family nurse practitioner (MSN). *Accreditation:* ACEN. *Program availability:* Part-time, online only, 100% online. *Faculty:* 10 full-time (9 women), 6 part-time/adjunct (all women). *Students:* 54 part-time (51 women); includes 5 minority (2 Black or African American, non-Hispanic/Latino; 2 Asian, non-Hispanic/Latino; 1 Hispanic/Latino). Average age 35. 73 applicants, 70% accepted, 33 enrolled. In 2017, 35 master's awarded. *Degree requirements:* For master's, comprehensive exam, thesis, portfolio. *Entrance requirements:* For master's, minimum QPA of 2.75. Additional exam requirements/recommendations for international students: Required—TOEFL (minimum score 550 paper-based, 80 iBT) or IELTS (7). *Application deadline:* For fall admission, 10/1 for domestic students, 7/1 priority date for international students. Applications are processed on a rolling basis. Application fee: $40. Electronic applications accepted. *Expenses:* $712 per credit. *Financial support:* Career-related internships or fieldwork, scholarships/grants, and unspecified assistantships available. Support available to part-time students. Financial award application deadline: 3/1; financial award applicants required to submit FAFSA. *Unit head:* Dr. Deborah J. Kelly, Chair and Nurse Administrator, 814-393-1258, E-mail: dkelly@clarion.edu. *Application contact:* Dana Bearer, Associate Director for Transfer, Adult, and Graduate Programs, 814-393-2337, Fax: 814-393-2772, E-mail: gradstudies@clarion.edu.
Website: http://www.clarion.edu/admissions/graduate/index.html

Clarke University, Department of Nursing and Health, Dubuque, IA 52001-3198. Offers family nurse practitioner (DNP); health leadership and practice (DNP); psychiatric mental health nurse practitioner (DNP). *Accreditation:* AACN. *Program availability:* Part-time. *Faculty:* 6 full-time (all women). *Students:* 55 full-time (54 women), 11 part-time (10 women); includes 3 minority (1 Black or African American, non-Hispanic/Latino; 1 Asian, non-Hispanic/Latino; 1 Two or more races, non-Hispanic/Latino). Average age 32. 62 applicants, 40% accepted, 22 enrolled. In 2017, 36 doctorates awarded. *Degree requirements:* For doctorate, comprehensive exam, thesis/dissertation. *Entrance requirements:* For doctorate, GRE (if GPA under 3.0), bachelor's degree from accredited nursing program and accredited college or university; minimum GPA of 3.0; minimum C grade on undergraduate prerequisite courses; three recommendation forms; curriculum vitae; statement of goals; transcripts; copy of nursing license; proof of health insurance; interview. Additional exam requirements/recommendations for international students: Required—TOEFL (minimum score 550 paper-based; 80 iBT), IELTS (minimum score 6.5). *Application deadline:* For fall admission, 2/1 priority date for domestic students. Application fee: $35. Electronic applications accepted. *Expenses:* $850 per credit. *Financial support:* Applicants required to submit FAFSA. *Faculty research:* Narrative pedagogy, ethics, end-of-life care, pedagogy, family systems, simulation. *Unit head:* Dr. Jan Lee, Chair, 563-588-6339, E-mail: jan.lee@clarke.edu. *Application contact:* Kimberly Roush, Director of Admission, Graduate and Adult Programs, 563-588-6539, Fax: 563-552-7994, E-mail: graduate@clarke.edu.
Website: https://www.clarke.edu/academics/doctor-of-nursing-practice/

Clarkson College, Master of Science in Nursing Program, Omaha, NE 68131. Offers adult nurse practitioner (MSN, Post-Master's Certificate); family nurse practitioner (MSN, Post-Master's Certificate); nursing education (MSN, Post-Master's Certificate); nursing health care leadership (MSN, Post-Master's Certificate). *Accreditation:* AANA/CANAEP; ACEN. *Program availability:* Part-time, evening/weekend, online learning. *Degree requirements:* For master's, on-campus skills assessment (family nurse practitioner, adult nurse practitioner), comprehensive exam or thesis. *Entrance requirements:* For master's, minimum GPA of 3.0, 2 references, resume. Additional exam requirements/recommendations for international students: Required—TOEFL (minimum score 600 paper-based; 100 iBT). Electronic applications accepted.

Clayton State University, School of Graduate Studies, College of Health, Program in Nursing, Morrow, GA 30260-0285. Offers family nurse practitioner (MSN). *Accreditation:* AACN. *Degree requirements:* For master's, thesis. *Entrance requirements:* For master's, GRE, official transcript, 3 letters of recommendation, statement of purpose, on-campus interview, 1-2 years of clinical nursing experience (preferred). Additional exam requirements/recommendations for international students: Required—TOEFL (minimum score 550 paper-based; 80 iBT). Electronic applications accepted. *Expenses:* Contact institution.

Clemson University, Graduate School, College of Behavioral, Social and Health Sciences, School of Nursing, Clemson, SC 29634. Offers clinical and translational research (PhD); global health (Certificate), including low resource countries; healthcare genetics (PhD); nursing (MS, DNP), including adult/gerontology nurse practitioner (MS), family nurse practitioner (MS). *Accreditation:* AACN. *Program availability:* Part-time, 100% online, blended/hybrid learning. *Faculty:* 37 full-time (35 women). *Students:* 130 full-time (118 women), 195 part-time (170 women); includes 50 minority (23 Black or African American, non-Hispanic/Latino; 5 Asian, non-Hispanic/Latino; 16 Hispanic/Latino; 6 Two or more races, non-Hispanic/Latino), 14 international. Average age 34. 71 applicants, 66% accepted, 33 enrolled. In 2017, 88 master's, 2 doctorates, 10 other

advanced degrees awarded. *Degree requirements:* For master's, comprehensive exam, thesis or alternative; for doctorate, comprehensive exam, thesis/dissertation. *Entrance requirements:* For master's, GRE General Test, South Carolina RN license, unofficial transcripts, resume, letters of recommendation; for doctorate, GRE General Test, unofficial transcripts, MS/MA thesis or publications, curriculum vitae, statement of career goals, letters of recommendation. Additional exam requirements/recommendations for international students: Required—TOEFL (minimum score 80 iBT), IELTS (minimum score 6.5), PTE (minimum score 54). *Application deadline:* For fall admission, 3/1 priority date for domestic and international students; for spring admission, 10/1 priority date for domestic and international students. Application fee: $80 ($90 for international students). Electronic applications accepted. *Expenses:* Contact institution. *Financial support:* In 2017–18, 41 students received support, including 46 teaching assistantships with partial tuition reimbursements available (averaging $4,919 per year); career-related internships or fieldwork and unspecified assistantships also available. Financial award application deadline: 3/1. *Faculty research:* Breast cancer, healthcare, genetics, international healthcare, educational innovation and technology. *Total annual research expenditures:* $371,674. *Unit head:* Dr. Kathleen Valentine, Director and Associate College Dean, 864-656-4758, E-mail: klvalen@clemson.edu. *Application contact:* Dr. Stephanie Davis, Graduate Studies Coordinator, 864-656-2588, E-mail: stephad@clemson.edu.
Website: http://www.clemson.edu/cbshs/departments/nursing/

Cleveland State University, College of Graduate Studies, School of Nursing, Cleveland, OH 44115. Offers MSN, PhD, MSN/MBA. *Accreditation:* AACN. *Program availability:* Part-time, 100% online. *Faculty:* 7 full-time (all women). *Students:* 10 full-time (9 women), 57 part-time (51 women); includes 15 minority (10 Black or African American, non-Hispanic/Latino; 2 Asian, non-Hispanic/Latino; 3 Hispanic/Latino). Average age 36. 60 applicants, 62% accepted, 26 enrolled. In 2017, 14 master's awarded. *Degree requirements:* For master's, thesis optional, portfolio, capstone practicum project; for doctorate, comprehensive exam, thesis/dissertation. *Entrance requirements:* For master's, RN license in the U.S., BSN with minimum cumulative GPA of 3.0, recent (within last 5 years) course work in statistics; for doctorate, GRE, MSN with minimum cumulative GPA of 3.25. Additional exam requirements/recommendations for international students: Required—TOEFL (minimum score 550 paper-based; 78 iBT), IELTS (minimum score 6). *Application deadline:* For fall admission, 3/1 priority date for domestic and international students. Application fee: $55. Electronic applications accepted. *Financial support:* Tuition waivers (full) and unspecified assistantships available. Financial award application deadline: 5/1; financial award applicants required to submit FAFSA. *Faculty research:* Diabetes management, African-American elders medication compliance, risk in home visiting, suffering, COPD and stress, nursing education, disaster health preparedness. *Total annual research expenditures:* $330,000. *Unit head:* Dr. Vida Lock, Dean, 216-523-7237, Fax: 216-687-3556, E-mail: v.lock@csuohio.edu. *Application contact:* Maureen Mitchell, Assistant Professor and Graduate Program Director, 216-523-7128, Fax: 216-687-3556, E-mail: m.m.mitchell1@csuohio.edu.
Website: http://www.csuohio.edu/nursing/

College of Mount Saint Vincent, School of Professional and Graduate Studies, Department of Nursing, Riverdale, NY 10471-1093. Offers family nurse practitioner (MSN, PMC); nurse educator (PMC); nursing administration (MSN); nursing education (MSN). *Accreditation:* AACN. *Program availability:* Part-time. *Entrance requirements:* For master's, BSN, interview, RN license, minimum GPA of 3.0, letters of reference. Additional exam requirements/recommendations for international students: Required—TOEFL. *Expenses:* Contact institution.

The College of New Jersey, Office of Graduate and Advancing Education, School of Nursing, Health, and Exercise Science, Program in Nursing, Ewing, NJ 08628. Offers MSN, Certificate. *Accreditation:* AACN. *Program availability:* Part-time. *Degree requirements:* For master's, comprehensive exam. *Entrance requirements:* For master's, GRE, minimum GPA of 3.0 in field or 2.75 overall. Additional exam requirements/recommendations for international students: Required—TOEFL. Electronic applications accepted.

The College of New Rochelle, Graduate School, Program in Nursing, New Rochelle, NY 10805-2308. Offers acute care nurse practitioner (MS, Certificate); clinical specialist in holistic nursing (MS, Certificate); family nurse practitioner (MS, Certificate); nursing and health care management (MS); nursing education (Certificate). *Accreditation:* AACN. *Program availability:* Part-time. *Entrance requirements:* For master's, GRE General Test or MAT, BSN, malpractice insurance, minimum GPA of 3.0, RN license. Electronic applications accepted. *Expenses: Tuition:* Full-time $17,406. *Required fees:* $1120.

College of Saint Elizabeth, Department of Nursing, Morristown, NJ 07960-6989. Offers MSN. *Accreditation:* ACEN. *Program availability:* Part-time. *Faculty:* 3 full-time (all women), 1 (woman) part-time/adjunct. *Students:* 1 (woman) full-time, 26 part-time (23 women); includes 9 minority (1 Black or African American, non-Hispanic/Latino; 3 Asian, non-Hispanic/Latino; 5 Hispanic/Latino). Average age 41. 10 applicants, 100% accepted, 7 enrolled. In 2017, 19 master's awarded. *Degree requirements:* For master's, thesis. *Entrance requirements:* Additional exam requirements/recommendations for international students: Required—TOEFL (minimum score 550 paper-based; 79 iBT), IELTS (minimum score 6.5). *Application deadline:* For fall admission, 5/1 for international students. Applications are processed on a rolling basis. Application fee: $35. Electronic applications accepted. Application fee is waived when completed online. *Financial support:* Career-related internships or fieldwork, scholarships/grants, tuition waivers (partial), and unspecified assistantships available. Financial award applicants required to submit FAFSA. *Unit head:* Dr. Sarah Arnold, Interim Nursing Administrator, 973-290-4037, E-mail: sarnold@cse.edu. *Application contact:* Lori J. Fragoso, Director of Graduate and Continuing Studies Admissions, 973-290-4413, Fax: 973-290-4710, E-mail: apply@cse.edu.
Website: http://www.cse.edu/academics/prof-studies/nursing/ms-in-nursing

College of Saint Mary, Program in Nursing, Omaha, NE 68106. Offers MSN. *Accreditation:* ACEN. *Program availability:* Part-time. *Entrance requirements:* For master's, bachelor's degree in nursing, Nebraska RN license, essay or scholarly writing, minimum cumulative GPA of 3.0, 2 references. Additional exam requirements/recommendations for international students: Required—TOEFL.

The College of St. Scholastica, Graduate Studies, Department of Nursing, Duluth, MN 55811-4199. Offers MA, PMC. *Accreditation:* AACN. *Program availability:* Part-time, online learning. *Degree requirements:* For master's, thesis. *Entrance requirements:* For master's, GRE General Test. Additional exam requirements/recommendations for international students: Required—TOEFL (minimum score 550 paper-based; 79 iBT). Electronic applications accepted. *Faculty research:* Critical thinking and professional development, social organization of responsibility, rural health HIV/AIDS prevention, Web-based instruction in nursing.

College of Staten Island of the City University of New York, Graduate Programs, School of Health Sciences, DNP Program in Adult-Gerontological Health Nursing, Staten Island, NY 10314-6600. Offers DNP. *Program availability:* Part-time. *Students:* 3. *Degree requirements:* For doctorate, 75 credits with minimum of 1,000 supervised hours toward development of clinical competencies for primary care of the adult-gerontological population and implementation of an integrative practice project in the clinical setting. *Entrance requirements:* For doctorate, GRE taken within last five years, bachelor's degree from regionally-accredited college with minimum GPA of 3.25 and at least one year of experience in nursing or bachelor's degree in another field with three years of clinical experience; RN license in NY state. Additional exam requirements/recommendations for international students: Required—TOEFL (minimum score 550 paper-based; 79 iBT), IELTS (minimum score 6.5). *Application deadline:* For fall admission, 12/1 for domestic and international students. Applications are processed on a rolling basis. Application fee: $125. Electronic applications accepted. *Expenses:* Contact institution. *Financial support:* Applicants required to submit FAFSA. *Faculty research:* LGBTQ Healthcare; smoking cessation; caregivers of persons with autism; end of life decision-making/compassionate care; burn survivors. *Unit head:* Prof. Catherine Paradiso, 718-982-3838, E-mail: catherine.paradiso@csi.cuny.edu. *Application contact:* Sasha Spence, Associate Director for Graduate Admissions, 718-982-2019, Fax: 718-982-2500, E-mail: sasha.spence@csi.cuny.edu.
Website: https://www.csi.cuny.edu/sites/default/files/pdf/admissions/grad/pdf/DNP%20Nursing%20Fact%20Sheet.pdf

Colorado Mesa University, Department of Health Sciences, Grand Junction, CO 81501-3122. Offers advanced nursing practice (MSN); family nurse practitioner (DNP); health information technology systems (Graduate Certificate); nursing education (MSN). *Accreditation:* AACN. *Program availability:* Part-time, evening/weekend, 100% online, blended/hybrid learning. *Degree requirements:* For master's and doctorate, capstone. *Entrance requirements:* For master's and doctorate, minimum GPA of 3.0 in BSN program. Additional exam requirements/recommendations for international students: Required—TOEFL (minimum score 550 paper-based). Electronic applications accepted.

Colorado State University–Pueblo, College of Education, Engineering and Professional Studies, Nursing Department, Pueblo, CO 81001-4901. Offers MS. *Accreditation:* ACEN. *Degree requirements:* For master's, comprehensive exam or thesis. *Entrance requirements:* Additional exam requirements/recommendations for international students: Required—TOEFL.

Columbia College of Nursing, Graduate Program, Glendale, WI 53212. Offers MSN. *Entrance requirements:* For master's, bachelor's degree, minimum cumulative GPA of 3.0, undergraduate or graduate statistics course, unencumbered Wisconsin RN license.

Columbia University, School of Nursing, New York, NY 10032. Offers MS, DNP, PhD, Adv C, MBA/MS, MPH/MS. *Accreditation:* AACN. *Degree requirements:* For master's, comprehensive exam; for doctorate, thesis/dissertation. *Entrance requirements:* For master's, GRE General Test, bachelor's degree, 1 year of clinical experience (preferred for most, required for some); for doctorate, GRE General Test. Additional exam requirements/recommendations for international students: Required—TOEFL (minimum score 100 iBT). Electronic applications accepted. *Expenses:* Contact institution. *Faculty research:* HIV/AIDS, health promotion/disease prevention, health policies, advanced practice, urban health.

Columbus State University, Graduate Studies, College of Education and Health Professions, School of Nursing, Columbus, GA 31907-5645. Offers family nurse practitioner (MSN); nursing (MSN), including nurse educator, nurse informatics, nurse leader. Program offered in collaboration with Georgia Southwestern StateUniversity. *Program availability:* Part-time, online only, 100% online. *Faculty:* 7 full-time (all women), 2 part-time/adjunct (both women). *Students:* 43 full-time (40 women), 134 part-time (121 women); includes 88 minority (65 Black or African American, non-Hispanic/Latino; 7 Asian, non-Hispanic/Latino; 10 Hispanic/Latino; 6 Two or more races, non-Hispanic/Latino). Average age 35. 141 applicants, 49% accepted, 12 enrolled. In 2017, 28 master's awarded. *Entrance requirements:* For master's, GRE, BSN, minimum undergraduate GPA of 3.0. Additional exam requirements/recommendations for international students: Required—TOEFL (minimum score 550 paper-based; 79 iBT). *Application deadline:* For fall admission, 5/1 for domestic and international students; for spring admission, 11/1 for domestic and international students; for summer admission, 3/1 for domestic and international students. Applications are processed on a rolling basis. Application fee: $50. Electronic applications accepted. *Expenses:* Contact institution. *Financial support:* In 2017–18, 3 students received support. Institutionally sponsored loans available. Financial award application deadline: 5/1; financial award applicants required to submit FAFSA. *Unit head:* Latonya Santo, Director, 706-507-8576, E-mail: santo_latonya@columbusstate.edu. *Application contact:* Catrina Smith-Edmond, Assistant Director for Graduate and Global Admission, 706-507-8824, Fax: 706-568-5091, E-mail: smithedmond_catrina@columbusstate.edu.
Website: http://nursing.columbusstate.edu/

Concordia University Irvine, School of Professional Studies, Irvine, CA 92612-3299. Offers healthcare administration (MHA); international studies (MAIS), including Africa, China; nursing (MSN).

Concordia University Wisconsin, Graduate Programs, School of Nursing, Mequon, WI 53097-2402. Offers family nurse practitioner (MSN). *Accreditation:* AACN. *Program availability:* Online learning. *Degree requirements:* For master's, comprehensive exam, thesis or alternative. *Entrance requirements:* Additional exam requirements/recommendations for international students: Required—TOEFL. *Expenses:* Contact institution.

Coppin State University, Division of Graduate Studies, Helene Fuld School of Nursing, Baltimore, MD 21216-3698. Offers family nurse practitioner (PMC); nursing (MSN). *Accreditation:* AACN; ACEN. *Program availability:* Part-time, evening/weekend. *Degree requirements:* For master's, comprehensive exam, thesis, clinical internship. *Entrance requirements:* For master's, GRE, bachelor's degree in nursing, interview, minimum GPA of 3.0, RN license. Additional exam requirements/recommendations for international students: Required—TOEFL (minimum score 550 paper-based).

Cox College, Programs in Nursing, Springfield, MO 65802. Offers clinical nurse leader (MSN); family nurse practitioner (MSN); nurse educator (MSN). *Accreditation:* AACN. *Entrance requirements:* For master's, RN license, essay, 2 letters of recommendation, official transcripts. Electronic applications accepted.

Creighton University, College of Nursing, Omaha, NE 68178-0001. Offers adult gerontology acute care nurse practitioner (DNP, Post-Master's Certificate); adult gerontology nurse practitioner (DNP); clinical nurse leader (MSN, Post-Graduate Certificate); clinical systems administration (MSN, DNP); family nurse practitioner (DNP, Post-Master's Certificate); neonatal nurse practitioner (DNP, Post-Master's Certificate); nursing (Post-Graduate Certificate); pediatric acute care nurse practitioner (DNP, Post-Master's Certificate); psychiatric mental health nurse practitioner (DNP). *Accreditation:* AACN. *Program availability:* Part-time, blended/hybrid learning. *Degree requirements:* For master's, capstone project; for doctorate, scholarly project. *Entrance requirements:* For master's and doctorate, BSN from ACEN- or CCNE-accredited nursing school, minimum cumulative GPA of 3.0, personal statement, active unencumbered RN license with NE eligibility, undergraduate statistics course, physical assessment course or equivalent, three recommendation letters; for other advanced degree, MSN or MS in nursing from ACEN- or CCNE-accredited nursing school, minimum cumulative GPA of 3.0, active unencumbered RN license with NE eligibility. Additional exam requirements/recommendations for international students: Required—TOEFL (minimum score 600 paper-based, 100 iBT) or IELTS. Electronic applications accepted. *Expenses:* Contact institution. *Faculty research:* School health report card, obesity prevention in children, simulated clinical experience evaluation, vitamin D3 and calcium and cancer risk reduction education, online support and education to reduce stress for prenatal patients on bed rest, health literacy, immunization research.

Curry College, Graduate Studies, Program in Nursing, Milton, MA 02186-9984. Offers MSN. *Accreditation:* AACN.

Daemen College, Department of Nursing, Amherst, NY 14226-3592. Offers adult nurse practitioner (MS, Post Master's Certificate); nurse executive leadership (Post Master's Certificate); nursing education (MS, Post Master's Certificate); nursing executive leadership (MS); nursing practice (DNP); palliative care nursing (Post Master's Certificate). *Accreditation:* ACEN. *Program availability:* Part-time. *Degree requirements:* For master's, thesis or alternative, degree completed in 4 years; minimum GPA of 3.0; for doctorate, degree completed in 5 years; 500 post-master's clinical hours. *Entrance requirements:* For master's, BN, 1 year medical/surgical experience, RN license and state registration, statistics course with minimum C grade, 3 letters of recommendation, minimum GPA of 3.25, interview; for doctorate, MS in advance nursing practice; New York state RN license; goal statement; resume; interview; statistics course with minimum grade of 'C'; for Post Master's Certificate, master's degree in clinical area; RN license and current registration; one year of clinical experience; statistics course with minimum grade of 'C'; 3 letters of recommendation; interview; letter of intent. Additional exam requirements/recommendations for international students: Required—TOEFL (minimum score 500 paper-based; 63 iBT), IELTS (minimum score 5.5). Electronic applications accepted. *Faculty research:* Professional stress, client behavior, drug therapy, treatment modalities and pulmonary cancers, chemical dependency.

Dalhousie University, Faculty of Health Professions, School of Nursing, Halifax, NS B3H 3J5, Canada. Offers MN, PhD, MN/MHSA. *Program availability:* Part-time, online learning. *Degree requirements:* For master's, thesis optional. *Entrance requirements:* For master's, minimum GPA of 3.0; for doctorate, written support of faculty member who has agreed to be thesis supervisor. Additional exam requirements/recommendations for international students: Required—TOEFL, IELTS, CANTEST, CAEL, or Michigan English Language Assessment Battery. Electronic applications accepted. *Faculty research:* Coping, social support, health promotion, aging, feminist studies.

Delaware State University, Graduate Programs, College of Education, Health and Public Policy, Department of Nursing, Dover, DE 19901-2277. Offers MS. *Entrance requirements:* Additional exam requirements/recommendations for international students: Required—TOEFL (minimum score 550 paper-based). Electronic applications accepted.

Delta State University, Graduate Programs, Robert E. Smith School of Nursing, Cleveland, MS 38733. Offers family nurse practitioner (MSN); nurse administrator (MSN); nurse educator (MSN). *Accreditation:* AACN. *Program availability:* Part-time. *Degree requirements:* For master's, thesis optional. *Entrance requirements:* For master's, GRE General Test. Electronic applications accepted.

DePaul University, College of Science and Health, Chicago, IL 60604. Offers applied mathematics (MS); applied statistics (MA, MS); biological sciences (MA, MS); chemistry (MS); environmental science (MS); mathematics education (MA); mathematics for teaching (MS); nursing (MS); nursing practice (DNP); physics (MS); polymer and coatings science (MS); psychology (MS); pure mathematics (MS); science education (MS); MA/PhD. *Accreditation:* AACN. *Application deadline:* Applications are processed on a rolling basis. Application fee: $40. Electronic applications accepted. *Financial support:* Applicants required to submit FAFSA. *Unit head:* Dr. Gerald P. Koocher, Dean, 773-325-8300. *Application contact:* Ann Spittle, Director of Graduate Admission, 773-325-7315, Fax: 312-476-3244, E-mail: graddepaul@depaul.edu.
Website: http://csh.depaul.edu/

DeSales University, Division of Healthcare, Center Valley, PA 18034-9568. Offers adult-gerontology acute care (Post Master's Certificate); adult-gerontology acute care nurse practitioner (MSN); adult-gerontology acute certified nurse practitioner (Post Master's Certificate); adult-gerontology clinical nurse specialist (MSN, Post Master's Certificate); clinical leadership (DNP); family nurse practitioner (MSN, Post Master's Certificate); general nursing practice (DNP); nurse anesthetist (MSN); nurse educator (Post Master's Certificate, Postbaccalaureate Certificate); nurse midwife (MSN); nurse practitioner (MSN); psychiatric-mental health nurse practitioner (MSN, Post Master's Certificate); DNP/MBA. *Accreditation:* ACEN. *Program availability:* Part-time. *Faculty:* 26 full-time (20 women), 30 part-time/adjunct (19 women). *Students:* 282 full-time (210 women), 101 part-time (85 women); includes 39 minority (12 Black or African American, non-Hispanic/Latino; 11 Asian, non-Hispanic/Latino; 12 Hispanic/Latino; 4 Two or more races, non-Hispanic/Latino), 1 international. Average age 29. 2,884 applicants, 5% accepted, 114 enrolled. In 2017, 76 master's, 6 doctorates awarded. *Degree requirements:* For master's, minimum GPA of 3.0, portfolio; for doctorate, minimum GPA of 3.0, scholarly capstone project. *Entrance requirements:* For master's, GRE or MAT (waived if applicant has an undergraduate GPA of 3.0 or higher), BSN from ACEN- or CCNE-accredited program, minimum undergraduate GPA of 3.0, active RN license or eligibility, two letters of recommendation, essay, health care experience, personal interview; for doctorate, BSN or MSN from ACEN- or CCNE-accredited institution, minimum GPA of 3.3 in graduate program, current licensure as an RN. Additional exam requirements/recommendations for international students: Required—TOEFL (minimum score 104 iBT). *Application deadline:* Applications are processed on a rolling basis. Application fee: $50. Electronic applications accepted. *Expenses:* Contact institution. *Financial support:* Applicants required to submit FAFSA. *Unit head:* Ronald Nordone, Dean of Graduate Education, 610-282-1100 Ext. 1289, E-mail: ronald.nordone@desales.edu. *Application contact:* Julia Ferraro, Director of Graduate Admissions, 610-282-1100 Ext. 1768, E-mail: gradadmissions@desales.edu.

Drexel University, College of Nursing and Health Professions, Division of Graduate Nursing, Philadelphia, PA 19104-2875. Offers adult acute care (MSN); adult psychiatric/mental health (MSN); advanced practice nursing (MSN); clinical trials research (MSN); family nurse practitioner (MSN); leadership in health systems management (MSN); nursing education (MSN); pediatric primary care (MSN); women's health (MSN). *Accreditation:* AACN. Electronic applications accepted.

Drexel University, College of Nursing and Health Professions, Doctor of Nursing Practice Program, Philadelphia, PA 19104-2875. Offers Dr NP. *Accreditation:* AACN.

Duke University, School of Nursing, PhD Program in Nursing, Durham, NC 27708-0586. Offers PhD. *Faculty:* 31 full-time (24 women). *Students:* 38 full-time (33 women); includes 13 minority (11 Black or African American, non-Hispanic/Latino; 1 Asian, non-Hispanic/Latino; 1 Hispanic/Latino), 15 international. Average age 32. 26 applicants, 46% accepted, 10 enrolled. In 2017, 9 doctorates awarded. *Degree requirements:* For doctorate, comprehensive exam, thesis/dissertation. *Entrance requirements:* For doctorate, GRE General Test, resume, personal statement, minimum cumulative undergraduate GPA of 3.2, recommendations, previous work in nursing, research course, graduate-level statistics course. Additional exam requirements/recommendations for international students: Required—TOEFL (minimum score 577 paper-based; 90 iBT), IELTS (minimum score 7). *Application deadline:* For fall admission, 12/1 priority date for domestic and international students. Application fee: $80. Electronic applications accepted. *Expenses:* Contact institution. *Financial support:* Fellowships, institutionally sponsored loans, scholarships/grants, health care benefits, and stipends, summer research fellowships available. *Faculty research:* Nursing management practices, adolescents and families undergoing intense treatments, psychosocial and chronic disease. *Unit head:* Dr. Janice C. Humphreys, Interim Director for the PhD in Nursing Program/Associate Dean for Academic Affairs, 919-613-7162, Fax: 919-681-8899, E-mail: janice.humphreys@duke.edu. *Application contact:* Revonda P. Huppert, Senior Program Coordinator, 919-668-4797, Fax: 919-681-8899, E-mail: revonda.huppert@duke.edu.
Website: http://nursing.duke.edu/academics/programs/phd/phd-program

Duquesne University, School of Nursing, Doctor of Nursing Practice Program, Pittsburgh, PA 15282-0001. Offers DNP. *Program availability:* Part-time, evening/weekend, 100% online. *Faculty:* 7 full-time (6 women). *Students:* 6 full-time (all women), 11 part-time (all women); includes 4 minority (2 Black or African American, non-Hispanic/Latino; 1 Hispanic/Latino; 1 Two or more races, non-Hispanic/Latino). Average age 46. 22 applicants, 86% accepted, 10 enrolled. In 2017, 14 doctorates awarded. *Entrance requirements:* For doctorate, current RN license; BSN; master's degree with minimum GPA of 3.5; current certifications; phone interview. Additional exam requirements/recommendations for international students: Required—TOEFL (minimum score 600 paper-based; 100 iBT). *Application deadline:* For fall admission, 7/10 for domestic and international students; for spring admission, 11/29 for domestic and international students; for summer admission, 4/2 for domestic and international students. Application fee: $0. Electronic applications accepted. *Expenses:* $1,312 per credit. *Financial support:* In 2017–18, 5 students received support, including 5 teaching assistantships with partial tuition reimbursements available (averaging $7,560 per year); institutionally sponsored loans, scholarships/grants, traineeships, tuition waivers (partial), and unspecified assistantships also available. Support available to part-time students. Financial award application deadline: 5/1; financial award applicants required to submit FAFSA. *Faculty research:* Vulnerable populations, cultural competence, health disparities, wellness, technology. *Total annual research expenditures:* $650,096. *Unit head:* Dr. Alison Colbert, Associate Professor/Associate Dean of Academic Affairs, 412-396-1511, Fax: 412-396-1821, E-mail: colberta@duq.edu. *Application contact:* Susan Hardner, Nurse Recruiter, 412-396-4945, Fax: 412-396-6346, E-mail: nursing@duq.edu.
Website: http://www.duq.edu/academics/schools/nursing/graduate-programs/doctor-of-nursing-practice

Duquesne University, School of Nursing, Doctor of Philosophy in Nursing Program, Pittsburgh, PA 15282-0001. Offers nursing (PhD); nursing ethics (PhD). *Program availability:* Part-time, evening/weekend, minimal on-campus study. *Faculty:* 8 full-time (6 women). *Students:* 27 full-time (all women), 31 part-time (28 women); includes 13 minority (7 Black or African American, non-Hispanic/Latino; 5 Hispanic/Latino; 1 Two or more races, non-Hispanic/Latino). Average age 48. 35 applicants, 43% accepted, 12 enrolled. In 2017, 9 doctorates awarded. *Degree requirements:* For doctorate, thesis/dissertation, preliminary exam. *Entrance requirements:* For doctorate, current RN license; BSN; master's degree with minimum GPA of 3.5. Additional exam requirements/recommendations for international students: Required—TOEFL (minimum score 600 paper-based; 100 iBT). *Application deadline:* For fall admission, 2/1 for domestic and international students. Application fee: $0. Electronic applications accepted. *Expenses:* $1,312 per credit. *Financial support:* In 2017–18, 16 students received support, including 16 teaching assistantships with partial tuition reimbursements available (averaging $5,333 per year); institutionally sponsored loans, scholarships/grants, traineeships, tuition waivers (partial), and unspecified assistantships also available. Support available to part-time students. Financial award application deadline: 5/1; financial award applicants required to submit FAFSA. *Faculty research:* Vulnerable populations, cultural competence, health disparities, wellness, technology. *Total annual research expenditures:* $650,096. *Unit head:* Dr. Alison Colbert, Associate Professor/Associate Dean of Academic Affairs, 412-396-1511, Fax: 412-396-1821, E-mail: colberta@duq.edu. *Application contact:* Susan Hardner, Nurse Recruiter, 412-396-4945, Fax: 412-396-6346, E-mail: nursing@duq.edu.
Website: http://www.duq.edu/academics/schools/nursing/graduate-programs/phd-in-nursing

Duquesne University, School of Nursing, Master of Science in Nursing Program, Pittsburgh, PA 15282-0001. Offers family (individual across the life span) nurse practitioner (MSN); forensic nursing (MSN); nursing education and faculty role (MSN). *Accreditation:* AACN. *Program availability:* Part-time, evening/weekend, minimal on-campus study. *Faculty:* 26 full-time (21 women), 3 part-time/adjunct (all women). *Students:* 132 full-time (118 women), 54 part-time (49 women); includes 25 minority (7 Black or African American, non-Hispanic/Latino; 2 American Indian or Alaska Native, non-Hispanic/Latino; 5 Asian, non-Hispanic/Latino; 7 Hispanic/Latino; 4 Two or more races, non-Hispanic/Latino), 1 international. Average age 33. 160 applicants, 73% accepted, 87 enrolled. In 2017, 50 master's awarded. *Entrance requirements:* For master's, current RN license; BSN with minimum GPA of 3.0; minimum of 1 year of full-time work experience as RN prior to registration in clinical or specialty course. Additional exam requirements/recommendations for international students: Required—TOEFL (minimum score 600 paper-based; 100 iBT). *Application deadline:* For fall admission, 7/16 for domestic and international students; for spring admission, 11/29 for domestic and international students; for summer admission, 4/1 for domestic and international students. Application fee: $0. Electronic applications accepted. *Expenses:* $1,312 per credit. *Financial support:* In 2017–18, 10 students received support, including 10 teaching assistantships with partial tuition reimbursements available (averaging $3,297 per year); institutionally sponsored loans, scholarships/grants, traineeships, tuition waivers (partial), and unspecified assistantships also available. Support available to part-time students. Financial award application deadline: 5/1; financial award applicants required to submit FAFSA. *Faculty research:* Vulnerable populations, cultural competence, health disparities, wellness, technology. *Total annual research expenditures:* $650,096. *Unit head:* Dr. Alison Colbert, Associate Professor/Associate Dean of Academic Affairs, 412-396-1511, Fax: 412-396-1821, E-mail: colberta@duq.edu. *Application contact:* Susan Hardner, Nurse Recruiter, 412-396-4945, Fax: 412-396-6346, E-mail: nursing@duq.edu.
Website: http://www.duq.edu/academics/schools/nursing/graduate-programs/master-science-nursing

Duquesne University, School of Nursing, Post Master's Certificate Program, Pittsburgh, PA 15282-0001. Offers family (individual across the life span) nurse practitioner (Post-Master's Certificate); forensic nursing (Post-Master's Certificate); nursing education and faculty role (Post-Master's Certificate). *Program availability:* Part-time, evening/weekend, minimal on-campus study. *Faculty:* 8 full-time (6 women), 2 part-time/adjunct (both women). *Students:* 14 full-time (all women), 6 part-time (all women); includes 3 minority (2 Black or African American, non-Hispanic/Latino; 1 American Indian or Alaska Native, non-Hispanic/Latino). Average age 43. 27 applicants, 78% accepted, 10 enrolled. In 2017, 6 Post-Master's Certificates awarded. *Entrance requirements:* For degree, current RN license, BSN, MSN. Additional exam requirements/recommendations for international students: Required—TOEFL (minimum score 600 paper-based; 100 iBT). *Application deadline:* For fall admission, 7/16 for domestic and international students; for spring admission, 11/29 for domestic and

international students; for summer admission, 4/1 for domestic and international students. Application fee: $0. Electronic applications accepted. *Expenses:* $1,312 per credit. *Financial support:* Teaching assistantships with partial tuition reimbursements, institutionally sponsored loans, scholarships/grants, traineeships, and tuition waivers (partial) available. Support available to part-time students. Financial award application deadline: 5/1; financial award applicants required to submit FAFSA. *Faculty research:* Vulnerable populations, cultural competence, health disparities, wellness, technology. *Total annual research expenditures:* $650,096. *Unit head:* Dr. Alison Colbert, Associate Professor/Associate Dean of Academic Affairs, 412-396-1511, Fax: 412-396-1821, E-mail: colberta@duq.edu. *Application contact:* Susan Hardner, Nurse Recruiter, 412-396-4945, Fax: 412-396-6346, E mail: nursing@duq.edu.
Website: http://www.duq.edu/academics/schools/nursing/graduate-programs/post-masters-certificates

D'Youville College, School of Nursing, Buffalo, NY 14201-1084. Offers advanced practice nursing (DNP); family nurse practitioner (MSN, Certificate); nursing and health-related professions education (Certificate). *Accreditation:* AACN. *Program availability:* Part-time. *Degree requirements:* For master's, thesis or alternative. *Entrance requirements:* For master's, BS in nursing, minimum GPA of 3.0, course work in statistics and computers; for doctorate, BS in nursing, MS in advanced practice nursing specialty, minimum GPA of 3.25. Additional exam requirements/recommendations for international students: Required—TOEFL (minimum score 500 paper-based). Electronic applications accepted. *Faculty research:* Nursing curriculum, nursing theory-testing, wellness research, communication and socialization patterns.

East Carolina University, Graduate School, College of Nursing, Greenville, NC 27858-4353. Offers MSN, DNP, PhD. *Accreditation:* AACN; AANA/CANAEP (one or more programs are accredited); ACNM/ACME (one or more programs are accredited). *Program availability:* Part-time. *Students:* 163 full-time (147 women), 391 part-time (363 women); includes 115 minority (78 Black or African American, non-Hispanic/Latino; 5 American Indian or Alaska Native, non-Hispanic/Latino; 13 Asian, non-Hispanic/Latino; 11 Hispanic/Latino; 1 Native Hawaiian or other Pacific Islander, non-Hispanic/Latino; 7 Two or more races, non-Hispanic/Latino), 2 international. Average age 38. 234 applicants, 79% accepted, 162 enrolled. In 2017, 119 master's, 47 doctorates awarded. *Degree requirements:* For master's, comprehensive exam, thesis optional; for doctorate, comprehensive exam, thesis/dissertation. *Entrance requirements:* For master's, GRE General Test or MAT, bachelor's degree in nursing, professional license, minimum B average in nursing. *Application deadline:* For fall admission, 3/15 priority date for domestic students; for spring admission, 10/15 priority date for domestic students. Applications are processed on a rolling basis. Application fee: $70. *Expenses:* Tuition, state resident: full-time $4749; part-time $297 per credit hour. Tuition, nonresident: full-time $17,898; part-time $1119 per credit hour. *Required fees:* $2691; $224 per credit hour. Part-time tuition and fees vary according to course load and program. *Financial support:* Research assistantships with partial tuition reimbursements, teaching assistantships with partial tuition reimbursements, and Federal Work-Study available. Support available to part-time students. Financial award application deadline: 6/1. *Unit head:* Dr. Sylvia Brown, Dean, 252-744-6372, E-mail: brownsy@ecu.edu.
Website: http://www.ecu.edu/nursing/

Eastern Kentucky University, The Graduate School, College of Health Sciences, Department of Nursing, Richmond, KY 40475-3102. Offers rural community health care (MSN); rural health family nurse practitioner (MSN). *Accreditation:* AACN. *Entrance requirements:* For master's, GRE General Test, minimum GPA of 2.75.

Eastern Mennonite University, Program in Nursing, Harrisonburg, VA 22802-2462. Offers leadership and management (MSN); leadership and school nursing (MSN); nursing management (DNP). *Accreditation:* AACN. *Program availability:* Part-time, online learning. *Degree requirements:* For master's, leadership project. *Entrance requirements:* For master's, RN license, one year of full-time work experience as RN, minimum GPA of 3.0. Additional exam requirements/recommendations for international students: Required—TOEFL. *Application deadline:* For fall admission, 6/1 for domestic students. Applications are processed on a rolling basis. Application fee: $25. Application fee is waived when completed online. *Financial support:* Federal Work-Study and scholarships/grants available. Financial award applicants required to submit FAFSA. *Faculty research:* Community health, international health, effectiveness of the nursing school environment, development of caring ability in nursing students, international nursing students. *Unit head:* Ann Hershberger, Coordinator, 540-432-4192, E-mail: hershbea@emu.edu. *Application contact:* Don A. Yoder, Director of Seminary and Graduate Admissions, 540-432-4257, Fax: 540-432-4598, E-mail: yoderda@emu.edu.

Eastern New Mexico University, Graduate School, College of Liberal Arts and Sciences, Department of Health and Human Services, Portales, NM 88130. Offers communicative disorders (MS); nursing (MSN). *Accreditation:* ASHA. *Program availability:* Part-time, online learning. *Degree requirements:* For master's, thesis optional, oral and written comprehensive exam, oral presentation of professional portfolio. *Entrance requirements:* For master's, GRE, three letters of recommendation, resume, two essays. Additional exam requirements/recommendations for international students: Required—TOEFL (minimum score 550 paper-based; 79 iBT), IELTS (minimum score 6). *Application deadline:* For fall admission, 3/1 priority date for domestic and international students. Applications are processed on a rolling basis. Application fee: $10. Electronic applications accepted. *Financial support:* Applicants required to submit FAFSA. *Unit head:* Dr. Suzanne Swift, Chair/Interim Graduate Coordinator, 575-562-2724, Fax: 575-562-2380, E-mail: suzanne.swift@enmu.edu. *Application contact:* Wendy Turner, Department Secretary, 575-562-2156, Fax: 575-562-2380, E-mail: wendy.turner@enmu.edu.
Website: http://liberal-arts.enmu.edu/health/cdis/graduate-cdis.shtml

East Tennessee State University, School of Graduate Studies, College of Nursing, Johnson City, TN 37614. Offers acute care nurse practitioner (DNP); adult-gerontology primary care nurse practitioner (DNP); adult/gerontological nurse practitioner (Postbaccalaureate Certificate); executive leadership in nursing (DNP, Postbaccalaureate Certificate); family nurse practitioner (MSN, DNP, Post-Master's Certificate, Postbaccalaureate Certificate); nursing (PhD); nursing administration (MSN); nursing education (MSN); pediatric primary care nurse practitioner (DNP); psychiatric mental health nurse practitioner (Postbaccalaureate Certificate); psychiatric/mental health nurse practitioner (MSN, DNP, Post-Master's Certificate); women's health care nurse practitioner (DNP). *Accreditation:* AACN. *Program availability:* Part-time, evening/weekend, online learning. In 2017, 126 master's, 30 doctorates, 4 other advanced degrees awarded. *Degree requirements:* For master's and other advanced degree, comprehensive exam, practicum; for doctorate, comprehensive exam, thesis/dissertation (for some programs), practicum, internship, evidence of professional malpractice insurance, CPR certification. *Entrance requirements:* For master's, bachelor's degree, minimum GPA of 3.0, current RN license and eligibility to practice, resume, three letters of recommendation; for doctorate, GRE General Test, MSN (for PhD), BSN or MSN (for DNP), current RN license and eligibility to practice, 2 years of full-time registered nurse work experience or equivalent, three letters of recommendation, resume or curriculum vitae, interview, writing sample; for other advanced degree, MSN, minimum GPA of 3.0, current RN license and eligibility to practice, three letters of recommendation, resume or curriculum vitae; DNP with designated concentration in advanced clinical practice or nursing administration (for select programs). Additional exam requirements/recommendations for international students: Required—TOEFL (minimum score 600 paper-based; 79 iBT). *Application deadline:* For fall admission, 4/15 priority date for domestic and international students; for spring admission, 10/15 priority date for domestic and international students; for summer admission, 2/1 for domestic and international students. Application fee: $55 ($65 for international students). Electronic applications accepted. *Financial support:* Research assistantships with tuition reimbursements, teaching assistantships, career-related internships or fieldwork, institutionally sponsored loans, scholarships/grants, and unspecified assistantships available. Financial award application deadline: 7/1; financial award applicants required to submit FAFSA. *Faculty research:* Improving health of rural and underserved populations (low income elders living in public housing, rural caregivers, Hispanic populations), health services and systems research (quality outcomes of nurse-managed primary care, in-home, and rural health care), nursing education (experiences of second-degree BSN students, well-being of BSN students). *Unit head:* Dr. Wendy Nehring, Dean, 423-439-7051, Fax: 423-439-4543, E-mail: nursing@etsu.edu. *Application contact:* Dr. Myra Clark, Director of Graduate Programs, 423-439-4396, Fax: 423-439-4100, E-mail: clarkml2@etsu.edu.
Website: http://www.etsu.edu/nursing/

Edgewood College, Henry Predolin School of Nursing, Madison, WI 53711-1997. Offers MSN, DNP. *Accreditation:* AACN. *Degree requirements:* For master's, practicum, research project; for doctorate, practicum, capstone project. *Entrance requirements:* For master's, minimum GPA of 3.0, 2 letters of reference, current RN license. Additional exam requirements/recommendations for international students: Required—TOEFL. *Application deadline:* For fall admission, 8/15 priority date for domestic students, 5/1 for international students; for spring admission, 1/8 priority date for domestic students, 11/1 for international students. Applications are processed on a rolling basis. Application fee: $30. Electronic applications accepted. *Expenses: Tuition:* Part-time $930 per credit. *Unit head:* Dr. Margaret Noreuil, Dean, 608-663-2820, Fax: 608-663-3291, E-mail: mnoreuil@edgewood.edu.
Website: https://www.edgewood.edu/academics/schools/henry-predolin-school-of-nursing

Edinboro University of Pennsylvania, Department of Nursing, Edinboro, PA 16444. Offers advanced practice nursing (DNP); family nurse practitioner (MSN); nurse educator (MSN). *Program availability:* Part-time, evening/weekend. *Degree requirements:* For master's, thesis, competency exam. *Entrance requirements:* For master's, GRE or MAT, minimum QPA of 2.5. Electronic applications accepted.

EDP University of Puerto Rico–San Sebastian, Graduate School, San Sebastian, PR 00685. Offers nursing science (MS).

Elmhurst College, Graduate Programs, Nursing Master's Entry Program, Elmhurst, IL 60126-3296. Offers MS. *Faculty:* 8 full-time (all women). *Students:* 37 full-time (34 women); includes 6 minority (1 Black or African American, non-Hispanic/Latino; 1 Asian, non-Hispanic/Latino; 4 Hispanic/Latino). Average age 27. 165 applicants, 26% accepted, 22 enrolled. In 2017, 12 master's awarded. *Entrance requirements:* For master's, baccalaureate degree in any field from regionally-accredited institution with minimum cumulative GPA of 3.2. Additional exam requirements/recommendations for international students: Required—TOEFL (minimum score 550 paper-based; 79 iBT), IELTS (minimum score 6.5). *Application deadline:* Applications are processed on a rolling basis. Application fee: $0. Electronic applications accepted. *Expenses:* Contact institution. *Financial support:* In 2017–18, 24 students received support. Scholarships/grants available. Financial award application deadline: 3/1; financial award applicants required to submit FAFSA. *Unit head:* Dr. Elizabeth Davis, Director, 630-617-3549, E-mail: elizabeth.davis@elmhurst.edu. *Application contact:* Timothy J. Panfil, Director of Enrollment Management, 630-617-3300 Ext. 3256, Fax: 630-617-6471, E-mail: panfilt@elmhurst.edu.
Website: http://www.elmhurst.edu/nursing_masters_entry

Elmhurst College, Graduate Programs, Program in Nursing, Elmhurst, IL 60126-3296. Offers MSN. *Accreditation:* AACN. *Program availability:* Part-time, evening/weekend. *Faculty:* 8 full-time (all women). *Students:* 1 (woman) full-time, 67 part-time (64 women); includes 15 minority (2 Asian, non-Hispanic/Latino; 13 Hispanic/Latino), 1 international. Average age 34. 60 applicants, 75% accepted, 40 enrolled. In 2017, 9 master's awarded. *Entrance requirements:* For master's, 3 recommendations, resume, statement of purpose, current RN licensure in Illinois, interview. Additional exam requirements/recommendations for international students: Required—TOEFL (minimum score 550 paper-based; 79 iBT). *Application deadline:* Applications are processed on a rolling basis. Application fee: $0. Electronic applications accepted. *Expenses:* Contact institution. *Financial support:* In 2017–18, 2 students received support. Scholarships/grants available. Support available to part-time students. Financial award application deadline: 3/1; financial award applicants required to submit FAFSA. *Unit head:* Dr. Becky Hulett, Director, 630-617-3506, E-mail: becky.hulett@elmhurst.edu. *Application contact:* Timothy J. Panfil, Director of Enrollment Management, 630-617-3300 Ext. 3256, Fax: 630-617-6471, E-mail: panfilt@elmhurst.edu.
Website: http://www.elmhurst.edu/nrs

Elms College, School of Nursing, Chicopee, MA 01013-2839. Offers adult-gerontology acute care nurse practitioner (DNP); family nurse practitioner (DNP); health systems innovation and leadership (DNP); nursing and health services management (MSN); nursing education (MSN). *Accreditation:* AACN. *Program availability:* Part-time, evening/weekend. *Faculty:* 5 full-time (all women), 9 part-time/adjunct (6 women). *Students:* 20 full-time (16 women), 79 part-time (70 women); includes 12 minority (2 Black or African American, non-Hispanic/Latino; 2 American Indian or Alaska Native, non-Hispanic/Latino; 8 Hispanic/Latino). Average age 40. 33 applicants, 94% accepted, 28 enrolled. In 2017, 14 master's, 30 doctorates awarded. *Entrance requirements:* Additional exam requirements/recommendations for international students: Required—TOEFL. *Application deadline:* For fall admission, 7/1 priority date for domestic students; for spring admission, 11/1 priority date for domestic students. Applications are processed on a rolling basis. Application fee: $30. *Expenses: Tuition:* Full-time $13,860; part-time $770 per credit hour. *Required fees:* $200. Tuition and fees vary according to degree level and program. *Financial support:* Applicants required to submit FAFSA. *Unit head:* Dr. Kathleen Scoble, Dean, School of Nursing, 413-265-2204, E-mail: scoblek@elms.edu. *Application contact:* Dr. Cynthia L. Dakin, Director of Graduate Nursing Studies, 413-265-2455, Fax: 413-265-2335, E-mail: dakinc@elms.edu.

Emmanuel College, Graduate and Professional Programs, Graduate Program in Nursing, Boston, MA 02115. Offers education (MSN, Graduate Certificate); management (MSN, Graduate Certificate). *Accreditation:* AACN. *Program availability:* Part-time, evening/weekend. *Faculty:* 3 full-time (all women), 4 part-time/adjunct (all women). *Students:* 35 part-time (33 women); includes 6 minority (3 Black or African American, non-Hispanic/Latino; 3 Hispanic/Latino). Average age 42. 26 applicants, 27% accepted, 3 enrolled. In 2017, 7 master's awarded. *Degree requirements:* For master's, 36 credits, including 6-credit practicum. *Entrance requirements:* For master's, transcripts from all regionally-accredited institutions attended (showing proof of bachelor's degree completion), proof of RN license, 2 letters of recommendation, essay, resume; for Graduate Certificate, transcripts from all regionally-accredited institutions attended (showing proof of master's degree completion), proof of RN license, 2 letters of

recommendation, essay, resume. Additional exam requirements/recommendations for international students: Required—TOEFL. *Application deadline:* Applications are processed on a rolling basis. Electronic applications accepted. *Expenses:* $28,391 (for MSN); $10,324 (for Graduate Certificate). *Financial support:* Application deadline: 2/15; applicants required to submit FAFSA. *Unit head:* Diane Shea, Associate Dean for Nursing/Professor of Nursing Practice, 617-732-1604, E-mail: shead@emmanuel.edu. *Application contact:* Helen Muterperl, Director of Graduate and Professional Programs, 617-735-9700, Fax: 617-507-0434, E-mail: gpp@emmanuel.edu.
Website: http://www.emmanuel.edu/graduate-professional-programs/academics/nursing.html

Emory University, Laney Graduate School, Program in Nursing, Atlanta, GA 30322-1100. Offers PhD. *Accreditation:* AACN. *Degree requirements:* For doctorate, comprehensive exam, thesis/dissertation. *Entrance requirements:* For doctorate, GRE General Test. Additional exam requirements/recommendations for international students: Required—TOEFL. Electronic applications accepted. *Faculty research:* Symptoms, self management, care-giving, biobehavioral approaches, women's health.

Emory University, Nell Hodgson Woodruff School of Nursing, Atlanta, GA 30322-1100. Offers adult nurse practitioner (MSN); emergency nurse practitioner (MSN); family nurse practitioner (MSN); family nurse-midwife (MSN); health systems leadership (MSN); nurse-midwifery (MSN); pediatric nurse practitioner acute and primary care (MSN); women's health care (Title X) (MSN); women's health nurse practitioner (MSN); MSN/MPH. *Accreditation:* AACN; ACNM/ACME (one or more programs are accredited). *Program availability:* Part-time. *Entrance requirements:* For master's, GRE General Test or MAT, minimum GPA of 3.0, BS in nursing from an accredited institution, RN license and additional course work, 3 letters of recommendation. Additional exam requirements/recommendations for international students: Required—TOEFL (minimum score 600 paper-based; 100 iBT). Electronic applications accepted. *Expenses:* Contact institution. *Faculty research:* Older adult falls and injuries, minority health issues, cardiac symptoms and quality of life, bio-ethics and decision-making, menopausal issues.

Endicott College, Van Loan School of Graduate and Professional Studies, Program in Nursing, Beverly, MA 01915-2096. Offers family nurse practitioner (MSN, Post-Master's Certificate); global health (MSN); nursing administration (MSN); nursing administrator (Post-Master's Certificate); nursing educator (MSN, Post-Master's Certificate). *Program availability:* Part-time, evening/weekend. *Faculty:* 5 full-time (4 women), 14 part-time/adjunct (12 women). *Students:* 43 full-time (41 women), 57 part-time (51 women); includes 8 minority (5 Black or African American, non-Hispanic/Latino; 3 Hispanic/Latino), 1 international. Average age 37. 41 applicants, 100% accepted, 38 enrolled. In 2017, 33 master's awarded. *Degree requirements:* For master's, thesis, practicum. *Entrance requirements:* For master's, MAT or GRE, statement of professional goals, official transcripts of all undergraduate and graduate course work, two letters of recommendation, photocopy of current and unrestricted RN license, basic statistics course, interview. Additional exam requirements/recommendations for international students: Required—TOEFL. *Application deadline:* Applications are processed on a rolling basis. Application fee: $50. Electronic applications accepted. *Expenses:* Contact institution. *Financial support:* Applicants required to submit FAFSA. *Unit head:* Dr. Kelly Fisher, Dean, 978-232-2328, Fax: 978-232-3000, E-mail: kfisher@endicott.edu. *Application contact:* Ian Menchini, Director, Graduate Enrollment and Advising, 978-232-5292, Fax: 978-232-3000, E-mail: imenchin@endicott.edu.
Website: https://vanloan.endicott.edu/programs-of-study/masters-programs/nursing-programs

Excelsior College, School of Nursing, Albany, NY 12203-5159. Offers nursing (MS); nursing education (MS); nursing informatics (MS); nursing leadership and administration of health care systems (MS). *Accreditation:* ACEN. *Program availability:* Part-time, evening/weekend, online learning. *Faculty:* 12 part-time/adjunct (9 women). *Students:* 388 part-time (313 women); includes 122 minority (63 Black or African American, non-Hispanic/Latino; 4 American Indian or Alaska Native, non-Hispanic/Latino; 18 Asian, non-Hispanic/Latino; 28 Hispanic/Latino; 2 Native Hawaiian or other Pacific Islander, non-Hispanic/Latino; 7 Two or more races, non-Hispanic/Latino). Average age 44. In 2017, 173 master's awarded. *Entrance requirements:* For master's, RN license. *Application deadline:* Applications are processed on a rolling basis. Application fee: $50. Electronic applications accepted. *Expenses: Tuition:* Part-time $645 per credit. *Required fees:* $265 per credit. *Financial support:* Scholarships/grants available. *Unit head:* Dr. Mary Lee Pollard, Dean, School of Nursing, 518-464-8500, Fax: 518-464-8777, E-mail: msn@excelsior.edu. *Application contact:* Admissions Counselor, 888-647-2388, Fax: 518-464-8777, E-mail: gradadmissions@excelsior.edu.
Website: http://www.excelsior.edu/programs/nursing

Fairfield University, Marion Peckham Egan School of Nursing and Health Studies, Fairfield, CT 06824. Offers advanced practice (DNP); family nurse practitioner (MSN, DNP); nurse anesthesia (DNP); nursing leadership (MSN); psychiatric nurse practitioner (MSN, DNP). *Accreditation:* AACN; AANA/CANAEP. *Program availability:* Part-time, evening/weekend. *Faculty:* 9 full-time (all women), 11 part-time/adjunct (8 women). *Students:* 50 full-time (42 women), 153 part-time (140 women); includes 48 minority (15 Black or African American, non-Hispanic/Latino; 1 American Indian or Alaska Native, non-Hispanic/Latino; 10 Asian, non-Hispanic/Latino; 19 Hispanic/Latino; 3 Two or more races, non-Hispanic/Latino), 2 international. Average age 34. 160 applicants, 50% accepted, 55 enrolled. In 2017, 26 master's, 36 doctorates awarded. *Degree requirements:* For master's, capstone project. *Entrance requirements:* For master's, minimum QPA of 3.0, RN license, resume, 2 recommendations; for doctorate, MSN (minimum QPA of 3.2) or BSN (minimum QPA of 3.0); critical care nursing experience (for nurse anesthesia DNP candidates). Additional exam requirements/recommendations for international students: Required—TOEFL (minimum score 550 paper-based; 80 iBT) or IELTS (minimum score 6.5). *Application deadline:* For fall admission, 5/15 for international students; for spring admission, 10/15 for international students. Applications are processed on a rolling basis. Application fee: $60. Electronic applications accepted. *Expenses:* $850 per credit hour (for MSN); $1,000 per credit hour (for DNP). *Financial support:* In 2017–18, 45 students received support. Scholarships/grants and unspecified assistantships available. Financial award applicants required to submit FAFSA. *Faculty research:* Aging, spiritual care, palliative and end of life care, psychiatric mental health, pediatric trauma. *Unit head:* Dr. Meredith Wallace Kazer, Dean, 203-254-4000 Ext. 2701, Fax: 203-254-4126, E-mail: mkazer@fairfield.edu. *Application contact:* Marianne Gumpper, Director of Graduate and Continuing Studies Admission, 203-254-4184, Fax: 203-254-4073, E-mail: gradadmis@fairfield.edu.
Website: http://fairfield.edu/son

Fairleigh Dickinson University, Florham Campus, University College: Arts, Sciences, and Professional Studies, The Henry P. Becton School of Nursing and Allied Health, Madison, NJ 07940-1099. Offers adult gerontology primary care nurse practitioner (MSN); family psychiatric/mental health nurse practitioner (MSN). *Program availability:* Part-time, evening/weekend. *Entrance requirements:* For master's, BSN, minimum undergraduate GPA of 3.0, courses in statistics and nursing research at the undergraduate level, NJ Registered Nurse licensure, minimum of 1 year of clinical nursing experience, two letters of recommendation. *Expenses: Tuition:* Full-time $22,410; part-time $1245 per credit. *Required fees:* $888; $414 per unit. Tuition and fees vary according to course load, degree level and program.

Fairleigh Dickinson University, Metropolitan Campus, University College: Arts, Sciences, and Professional Studies, Henry P. Becton School of Nursing and Allied Health, Program in Nursing, Teaneck, NJ 07666-1914. Offers MSN, Certificate. *Accreditation:* AACN. *Expenses: Tuition:* Full-time $22,410; part-time $1245 per credit. *Required fees:* $888; $414 per unit. Tuition and fees vary according to course load, degree level and program.

Fairleigh Dickinson University, Metropolitan Campus, University College: Arts, Sciences, and Professional Studies, Henry P. Becton School of Nursing and Allied Health, Program in Nursing Practice, Teaneck, NJ 07666-1914. Offers DNP. *Accreditation:* AACN. *Expenses: Tuition:* Full-time $22,410; part-time $1245 per credit. *Required fees:* $888; $414 per unit. Tuition and fees vary according to course load, degree level and program.

Felician University, Doctor of Nursing Practice Program, Lodi, NJ 07644-2117. Offers advanced practice (DNP); executive leadership (DNP). *Accreditation:* AACN. *Program availability:* Evening/weekend, online only, 100% online, blended/hybrid learning. *Faculty:* 4 full-time (all women). *Students:* 9 part-time (all women); includes 4 minority (2 Black or African American, non-Hispanic/Latino; 2 Hispanic/Latino). Average age 55. 3 applicants, 67% accepted. In 2017, 2 doctorates awarded. *Degree requirements:* For doctorate, thesis/dissertation, scholarly project. *Entrance requirements:* For doctorate, 2 letters of recommendation; national certification as nurse executive/administrator (preferred); interview; minimum GPA of 3.0. Additional exam requirements/recommendations for international students: Required—TOEFL (minimum score 550 paper-based; 79 iBT), IELTS (minimum score 6.5), PTE (minimum score 56). *Application deadline:* Applications are processed on a rolling basis. Application fee: $40. Electronic applications accepted. Application fee is waived when completed online. *Expenses:* Contact institution. *Financial support:* Federal Work-Study and scholarships/grants available. Financial award applicants required to submit FAFSA. *Faculty research:* Quality improvement, health promotion in populations, student attitudes towards aging. *Unit head:* Dr. Ann Tritak, Associate Dean of Graduate Nursing, 201-559-6151, E-mail: tritaka@felician.edu. *Application contact:* Michael Szarek, Assistant Vice-President of Graduate Admissions, 201-355-1450, E-mail: szarekm@felician.edu.

Felician University, Master of Science in Nursing Program, Lodi, NJ 07644-2117. Offers adult-gerontology nurse practitioner (MSN, PMC); executive leadership (MSN, PMC); family nurse practitioner (MSN, PMC); nursing education (MSN, PMC). *Accreditation:* AACN. *Program availability:* Evening/weekend, online only, 100% online, blended/hybrid learning. *Faculty:* 9 full-time (8 women), 1 (woman) part-time/adjunct. *Students:* 90 part-time (90 women); includes 40 minority (17 Black or African American, non-Hispanic/Latino; 1 American Indian or Alaska Native, non-Hispanic/Latino; 16 Asian, non-Hispanic/Latino; 12 Hispanic/Latino; 1 Native Hawaiian or other Pacific Islander, non-Hispanic/Latino; 1 Two or more races, non-Hispanic/Latino). Average age 37. 49 applicants, 86% accepted, 23 enrolled. In 2017, 35 master's, 3 other advanced degrees awarded. *Degree requirements:* For master's, thesis, clinical presentation; for PMC, thesis, education project. *Entrance requirements:* For master's, BSN; minimum GPA of 3.0; 2 letters of recommendation; NJ RN license; personal statement; for PMC, RN license, minimum GPA of 3.0. Additional exam requirements/recommendations for international students: Required—TOEFL (minimum score 550 paper-based; 79 iBT), IELTS (minimum score 6.5), PTE (minimum score 56). *Application deadline:* Applications are processed on a rolling basis. Application fee: $40. Electronic applications accepted. Application fee is waived when completed online. *Expenses:* Contact institution. *Financial support:* Federal Work-Study, scholarships/grants, and traineeships available. Financial award applicants required to submit FAFSA. *Faculty research:* Anxiety and fear, curriculum innovation, health promotion and populations, attitudes of college students towards aging. *Unit head:* Dr. Ann Tritak, Associate Dean of Graduate Nursing, 201-559-6151, E-mail: tritaka@felician.edu. *Application contact:* Michael Szarek, Assistant Vice-President, Graduate Admissions, 201-355-1450, E-mail: szarekm@felician.edu.

Ferris State University, College of Health Professions, School of Nursing, Big Rapids, MI 49307. Offers nursing (MSN); nursing administration (MSN); nursing education (MSN); nursing informatics (MSN). *Accreditation:* ACEN. *Program availability:* Part-time, evening/weekend, online only, 100% online. *Faculty:* 7 full-time (all women), 2 part-time/adjunct (both women). *Students:* 3 full-time (all women), 104 part-time (95 women); includes 15 minority (3 Black or African American, non-Hispanic/Latino; 5 American Indian or Alaska Native, non-Hispanic/Latino; 2 Asian, non-Hispanic/Latino; 3 Hispanic/Latino; 1 Native Hawaiian or other Pacific Islander, non-Hispanic/Latino; 1 Two or more races, non-Hispanic/Latino). Average age 40. 36 applicants, 92% accepted, 31 enrolled. In 2017, 25 master's awarded. *Degree requirements:* For master's, practicum, practicum project. *Entrance requirements:* For master's, BS in nursing (for nursing education track); BS in nursing or related field (for nursing administration and nursing informatics tracks); registered nurse license, writing sample, letters of reference, 2 years' clinical experience (recommended). Additional exam requirements/recommendations for international students: Required—TOEFL (minimum score 550 paper-based; 61 iBT). *Application deadline:* For fall admission, 4/15 priority date for domestic students; for spring admission, 10/15 for domestic students. Application fee: $0. Electronic applications accepted. *Financial support:* In 2017–18, 3 students received support. Career-related internships or fieldwork and scholarships/grants available. Financial award application deadline: 4/15; financial award applicants required to submit FAFSA. *Faculty research:* Nursing education, end of life, leadership/education introverts in nursing, complementary and alternative medicine therapies. *Unit head:* Dr. Susan Owens, Chair, School of Nursing, 231-591-2267, Fax: 231-591-2325, E-mail: owenss3@ferris.edu. *Application contact:* Sharon Colley, MSN Program Coordinator, 231-591-2288, Fax: 231-591-2325, E-mail: colleys@ferris.edu.
Website: http://www.ferris.edu/htmls/colleges/alliedhe/Nursing/homepage.htm

Florida Agricultural and Mechanical University, Division of Graduate Studies, Research, and Continuing Education, School of Nursing, Tallahassee, FL 32307-3200. Offers MSN, PhD. *Accreditation:* ACEN. *Entrance requirements:* Additional exam requirements/recommendations for international students: Required—TOEFL.

Florida Atlantic University, Christine E. Lynn College of Nursing, Boca Raton, FL 33431. Offers administrative and financial leadership in nursing and health care (Post Master's Certificate); nursing (MSN, PhD); nursing practice (DNP). *Accreditation:* AACN. *Program availability:* Part-time. *Faculty:* 32 full-time (31 women), 7 part-time/adjunct (6 women). *Students:* 61 full-time (57 women), 443 part-time (405 women); includes 265 minority (133 Black or African American, non-Hispanic/Latino; 33 Asian, non-Hispanic/Latino; 87 Hispanic/Latino; 1 Native Hawaiian or other Pacific Islander, non-Hispanic/Latino; 11 Two or more races, non-Hispanic/Latino), 6 international. Average age 37. 569 applicants, 28% accepted, 128 enrolled. In 2017, 131 master's, 28 doctorates awarded. *Degree requirements:* For master's, thesis or alternative; for doctorate, comprehensive exam, thesis/dissertation. *Entrance requirements:* For master's, GRE General Test or MAT, bachelor's degree in nursing, Florida RN license, minimum GPA of 3.0, resume/curriculum vitae, letter of recommendation; for doctorate, GRE General Test or MAT, curriculum vitae, Florida RN license, minimum GPA of 3.5, master's degree in nursing, three letters of recommendation. *Application deadline:* For fall admission, 6/1 for domestic students, 2/15 for international students; for spring admission, 10/1 for domestic students, 7/15 for international students. Applications are

processed on a rolling basis. Application fee: $30. *Expenses:* Tuition, state resident: full-time $7400; part-time $369.82 per credit. Tuition, nonresident: full-time $20,496; part-time $1042.81 per credit. *Financial support:* Research assistantships with partial tuition reimbursements, teaching assistantships with partial tuition reimbursements, career-related internships or fieldwork, Federal Work-Study, institutionally sponsored loans, scholarships/grants, and traineeships available. Support available to part-time students. *Faculty research:* Econometrics of nurse-patient relationship, Alzheimer's disease, community-based programs, falls, self-healing. *Unit head:* Marlaine Smith, Dean, 561-297-3206, E-mail: msmit230@health.fau.edu.
Website: http://nursing.fau.edu/

Florida International University, Nicole Wertheim College of Nursing and Health Sciences, Nursing Program, Miami, FL 33199. Offers adult health nursing (MSN); family health (MSN); nurse anesthetist (MSN); nursing practice (DNP); nursing science research (PhD); pediatric nurse (MSN); psychiatric and mental health nursing (MSN); registered nurse (MSN). *Accreditation:* AACN; AANA/CANAEP. *Program availability:* Part-time, evening/weekend. *Faculty:* 40 full-time (33 women), 79 part-time/adjunct (69 women). *Students:* 330 full-time (233 women), 89 part-time (73 women); includes 326 minority (92 Black or African American, non-Hispanic/Latino; 1 American Indian or Alaska Native, non-Hispanic/Latino; 33 Asian, non-Hispanic/Latino; 195 Hispanic/Latino; 2 Native Hawaiian or other Pacific Islander, non-Hispanic/Latino; 3 Two or more races, non-Hispanic/Latino), 9 international. Average age 33. 304 applicants, 50% accepted, 148 enrolled. In 2017, 144 master's, 8 doctorates awarded. *Degree requirements:* For master's, thesis or alternative; for doctorate, comprehensive exam, thesis/dissertation. *Entrance requirements:* For master's, bachelor's degree in nursing, minimum undergraduate GPA of 3.0 in upper-level coursework, letters of recommendation; for doctorate, GRE, letters of recommendation, minimum undergraduate GPA of 3.0 in upper-level coursework, interview. Additional exam requirements/recommendations for international students: Required—TOEFL (minimum score 550 paper-based; 80 iBT). *Application deadline:* For fall admission, 6/1 for domestic students, 4/1 for international students; for spring admission, 10/1 for domestic students, 9/1 for international students. Applications are processed on a rolling basis. Application fee: $30. Electronic applications accepted. *Expenses:* Tuition, state resident: full-time $8912; part-time $446 per credit hour. Tuition, nonresident: full-time $21,393; part-time $992 per credit hour. *Required fees:* $390; $195 per semester. *Financial support:* Institutionally sponsored loans and scholarships/grants available. Financial award application deadline: 3/1; financial award applicants required to submit FAFSA. *Faculty research:* Adult health nursing. *Unit head:* Dr. Yhovana Gordon, Chair, 305-348-7733, Fax: 305-348-7051, E-mail: gordony@fiu.edu. *Application contact:* Nanett Rojas, Manager, Admissions Operations, 305-348-7464, Fax: 305-348-7441, E-mail: gradadm@fiu.edu.
Website: http://cnhs.fiu.edu/

Florida National University, Program in Nursing, Hialeah, FL 33012. Offers family nurse practitioner (MSN); nurse educator (MSN); nurse leadership and management (MSN). *Program availability:* 100% online, blended/hybrid learning. *Degree requirements:* For master's, practicum. *Entrance requirements:* For master's, active registered nurse license, BSN from accredited institution. *Expenses: Tuition:* Full-time $15,600. *Required fees:* $650.
Website: https://www.fnu.edu/prospective-students/our-programs/select-a-program/master-of-business-administration/nursing-msn-master/

Florida Southern College, Program in Nursing, Lakeland, FL 33801-5698. Offers adult gerontology clinical nurse specialist (MSN); adult gerontology primary care nurse practitioner (MSN); family nurse practitioner (MSN); nurse educator (MSN); nursing administration (MSN). *Accreditation:* AACN. *Program availability:* Part-time. *Faculty:* 5 full-time (all women), 2 part-time/adjunct (both women). *Students:* 142 full-time (126 women), 9 part-time (all women); includes 70 minority (39 Black or African American, non-Hispanic/Latino; 1 American Indian or Alaska Native, non-Hispanic/Latino; 11 Asian, non-Hispanic/Latino; 13 Hispanic/Latino; 1 Native Hawaiian or other Pacific Islander, non-Hispanic/Latino; 5 Two or more races, non-Hispanic/Latino), 1 international. Average age 40. 83 applicants, 93% accepted, 72 enrolled. In 2017, 41 master's awarded. *Degree requirements:* For master's, 780 clinical practice hours. *Entrance requirements:* For master's, GMAT or GRE General Test, Florida RN license, 3 letters of recommendation, personal statement, minimum GPA of 3.0, resume. Additional exam requirements/recommendations for international students: Required—TOEFL (minimum score 550 paper-based; 79 iBT), IELTS (minimum score 6.5). *Application deadline:* For fall admission, 6/1 for domestic and international students; for spring admission, 10/1 for domestic and international students. Applications are processed on a rolling basis. Application fee: $30. Electronic applications accepted. *Expenses:* $585 per credit hour, $100 required fees. *Financial support:* In 2017–18, 1 student received support. Scholarships/grants and traineeships available. Support available to part-time students. Financial award applicants required to submit FAFSA. *Faculty research:* End of life care, dementia, health promotion. *Unit head:* Dr. Linda Comer, Dean, 863-680-4310, Fax: 863-680-3872, E-mail: lcomer@flsouthern.edu. *Application contact:* Kathy Connelly, Evening Program Assistant Director, 863-680-4205, Fax: 863-680-3872, E-mail: kconnelly@flsouthern.edu.

Florida State University, The Graduate School, College of Nursing, Tallahassee, FL 32306-4310. Offers family nurse practitioner (DNP); psychiatric mental health (Certificate). *Accreditation:* AACN; AANA/CANAEP. *Program availability:* Part-time, 100% online. *Faculty:* 20 full-time (19 women), 3 part-time/adjunct (all women). *Students:* 82 full-time (72 women), 26 part-time (25 women); includes 29 minority (9 Black or African American, non-Hispanic/Latino; 8 Asian, non-Hispanic/Latino; 10 Hispanic/Latino; 2 Two or more races, non-Hispanic/Latino). Average age 38. 123 applicants, 48% accepted, 41 enrolled. In 2017, 20 doctorates awarded. *Degree requirements:* For doctorate, thesis/dissertation, evidence-based project. *Entrance requirements:* For doctorate, GRE General Test, MAT, minimum GPA of 3.0, BSN or MSN, Florida RN license. Additional exam requirements/recommendations for international students: Required—TOEFL (minimum score 550 paper-based). *Application deadline:* For fall admission, 4/1 for domestic and international students. Application fee: $30. Electronic applications accepted. *Expenses:* Contact institution. *Financial support:* In 2017–18, 29 students received support, including fellowships with partial tuition reimbursements available (averaging $6,300 per year), research assistantships with partial tuition reimbursements available (averaging $3,000 per year), 3 teaching assistantships with partial tuition reimbursements available (averaging $3,000 per year); career-related internships or fieldwork, Federal Work-Study, institutionally sponsored loans, scholarships/grants, traineeships, and tuition waivers (partial) also available. Financial award application deadline: 4/1; financial award applicants required to submit FAFSA. *Faculty research:* Cardiac, women's health, health promotion and prevention, educational strategies, infectious diseases, health disparities. *Unit head:* Dr. Judith McFetridge-Durdle, Dean, 850-644-6846, Fax: 850-644-7660, E-mail: jdurdle@nursing.fsu.edu. *Application contact:* Carlos Urrutia, Assistant Director for Student Services, 850-644-5638, Fax: 850-645-7249, E-mail: currutia@fsu.edu.
Website: http://nursing.fsu.edu/

Fort Hays State University, Graduate School, College of Health and Life Sciences, Department of Nursing, Hays, KS 67601-4099. Offers MSN. *Accreditation:* AACN. *Degree requirements:* For master's, comprehensive exam, thesis optional. *Entrance requirements:* For master's, GRE General Test or MAT. Additional exam requirements/recommendations for international students: Required—TOEFL (minimum score 550 paper-based). Electronic applications accepted.

Framingham State University, Graduate Studies, Program in Nursing, Framingham, MA 01701-9101. Offers nursing education (MSN); nursing leadership (MSN). *Accreditation:* AACN. *Entrance requirements:* For master's, BSN; minimum cumulative undergraduate GPA of 3.0, 3.25 in nursing courses; coursework in statistics; 2 letters of recommendation; interview. *Application deadline:* For fall admission, 7/1 for domestic students. Application fee: $50. Electronic applications accepted. *Unit head:* Dr. Cynthia Bechtel, Program Coordinator, 508-626-4997, Fax: 508-626-4030, E-mail: cbechtel@framingham.edu. *Application contact:* Dr. Scott Greenberg, Associate Vice President of Academic Affairs and Dean of Continuing Education, 508-626-4603, E-mail: sgreenberg@framingham.edu.

Franciscan Missionaries of Our Lady University, School of Nursing, Baton Rouge, LA 70808. Offers MSN, DNP. *Accreditation:* ACEN. *Unit head:* Dr. Amy M. Hall, RN, Dean, 225-768-1753. *Application contact:* Dr. Amy M. Hall, RN, Dean, 225-768-1753.
Website: https://www.franu.edu/academics/schools/school-of-nursing

Franciscan University of Steubenville, Graduate Programs, Department of Nursing, Steubenville, OH 43952-1763. Offers MSN. *Accreditation:* ACEN. *Program availability:* Part-time, evening/weekend. *Degree requirements:* For master's, thesis. *Entrance requirements:* For master's, GRE General Test, MAT. Additional exam requirements/recommendations for international students: Required—TOEFL. Electronic applications accepted. Application fee is waived when completed online. *Expenses: Tuition:* Full-time $9000; part-time $500 per semester hour. *Required fees:* $16 per semester hour. Tuition and fees vary according to program.

Francis Marion University, Graduate Programs, Department of Nursing, Florence, SC 29502-0547. Offers family nurse practitioner (MSN); family nurse practitioner with nurse educator certificate (MSN); nurse educator (MSN). *Program availability:* Part-time. *Entrance requirements:* For master's, GRE, official transcripts, two letters of recommendation from professional associates or former professors, written statement of applicant's career goals, current nursing license. Additional exam requirements/recommendations for international students: Required—TOEFL (minimum score 550 paper-based; 79 iBT). Electronic applications accepted. *Expenses:* Contact institution.

Fresno Pacific University, Graduate Programs, Program in Nursing, Fresno, CA 93702-4709. Offers family nurse practitioner (MSN). *Entrance requirements:* For master's, official transcripts verifying BSN from accredited nursing program; minimum cumulative GPA of 3.0; three reference forms; statement of intent; resume or curriculum vitae; personal interview; active California RN license; completion of statistics, chemistry and upper-division writing. *Expenses:* Contact institution.

Frontier Nursing University, Graduate Programs, Hyden, KY 41749. Offers family nurse practitioner (MSN, DNP, Post Master's Certificate); nurse-midwifery (MSN, DNP, Post Master's Certificate); psychiatric-mental health nurse practitioner (MSN, DNP, Post Master's Certificate); women's health care nurse practitioner (MSN, DNP, Post Master's Certificate). *Accreditation:* ACEN. *Degree requirements:* For doctorate, capstone project, practicum.

See Display on the next page and Close-Up on page 761.

Frostburg State University, College of Liberal Arts and Sciences, Department of Nursing, Frostburg, MD 21532. Offers nursing administration (MSN); nursing education (MSN). *Program availability:* Part-time, online learning. *Faculty:* 6 full-time (all women). *Students:* 1 (woman) full-time, 22 part-time (all women); includes 3 minority (2 Black or African American, non-Hispanic/Latino; 1 Hispanic/Latino). Average age 35. 10 applicants, 80% accepted, 5 enrolled. In 2017, 12 master's awarded. *Entrance requirements:* For master's, current unrestricted RN license; BSN from a nursing program accredited by CCNE or ACEN. Additional exam requirements/recommendations for international students: Required—TOEFL. *Application deadline:* For spring admission, 11/1 for domestic students. Application fee: $45. *Expenses:* Tuition, state resident: part-time $433 per credit hour. Tuition, nonresident: part-time $557 per credit hour. *Required fees:* $121 per credit hour. $27 per term. *Financial support:* Unspecified assistantships available. Financial award application deadline: 4/1. *Unit head:* Dr. Heather Gable, Department Chair, 301-687-4894, E-mail: hagable@frostburg.edu. *Application contact:* Vickie Mazer, Director, Graduate Services, 301-687-7053, Fax: 301-687-4597, E-mail: vmmazer@frostburg.edu.
Website: http://www.frostburg.edu/nursing/

Gannon University, School of Graduate Studies, Morosky College of Health Professions and Sciences, Villa Maria School of Nursing, Program in Nursing Practice, Erie, PA 16541-0001. Offers DNP. *Program availability:* Part-time, evening/weekend, online only, 100% online. *Entrance requirements:* For doctorate, MSN; nurse practitioner, nurse midwife, or nurse anesthetist certification; transcripts; 3 letters of recommendation; portfolio; minimum GPA of 3.5. Additional exam requirements/recommendations for international students: Required—TOEFL (minimum score 79 iBT). Electronic applications accepted. Application fee is waived when completed online. *Expenses:* Contact institution.

Gardner-Webb University, Graduate School, School of Nursing, Boiling Springs, NC 28017. Offers family nurse practitioner (MSN, DNP). *Accreditation:* ACEN. *Program availability:* Part-time, online learning. *Faculty:* 13 full-time (11 women), 8 part-time/adjunct (all women). *Students:* 1 (woman) full-time, 223 part-time (206 women); includes 41 minority (31 Black or African American, non-Hispanic/Latino; 2 American Indian or Alaska Native, non-Hispanic/Latino; 4 Asian, non-Hispanic/Latino; 2 Hispanic/Latino; 2 Two or more races, non-Hispanic/Latino), 2 international. Average age 37. *Entrance requirements:* For master's, GRE or MAT, minimum undergraduate GPA of 2.7; unrestricted licensure to practice as an RN. *Expenses:* Contact institution. *Unit head:* Nicole Waters, Dean, 704-406-4358, Fax: 704-406-4329, E-mail: gradschool@gardner-webb.edu. *Application contact:* Office of Graduate Admissions, 877-498-4723, Fax: 704-406-3895, E-mail: gradinfo@gardner-webb.edu.

George Mason University, College of Health and Human Services, School of Nursing, Fairfax, VA 22030. Offers adult gerontology (DNP); adult/gerontological nurse practitioner (MSN); family nurse practitioner (MSN, DNP); nurse educator (MSN); nursing (PhD); nursing administration (MSN, DNP); nursing education (Certificate); psychiatric mental health (DNP). *Accreditation:* AACN. *Program availability:* Part-time, evening/weekend, blended/hybrid learning. *Faculty:* 28 full-time (27 women), 51 part-time/adjunct (47 women). *Students:* 51 full-time (40 women), 182 part-time (162 women); includes 110 minority (59 Black or African American, non-Hispanic/Latino; 1 American Indian or Alaska Native, non-Hispanic/Latino; 36 Asian, non-Hispanic/Latino; 10 Hispanic/Latino; 4 Two or more races, non-Hispanic/Latino), 8 international. Average age 37. 159 applicants, 70% accepted, 73 enrolled. In 2017, 33 master's, 24 doctorates, 1 other advanced degree awarded. *Degree requirements:* For master's, comprehensive exam (for some programs), thesis in clinical classes; for doctorate, comprehensive exam (for some programs), thesis/dissertation (for some programs). *Entrance requirements:* For master's, 2 official transcripts; expanded goals statement; resume; BSN from accredited institution; minimum GPA of 3.0 in last 60 credits of undergraduate work; 2 letters of recommendation; completion of undergraduate statistics and graduate-level

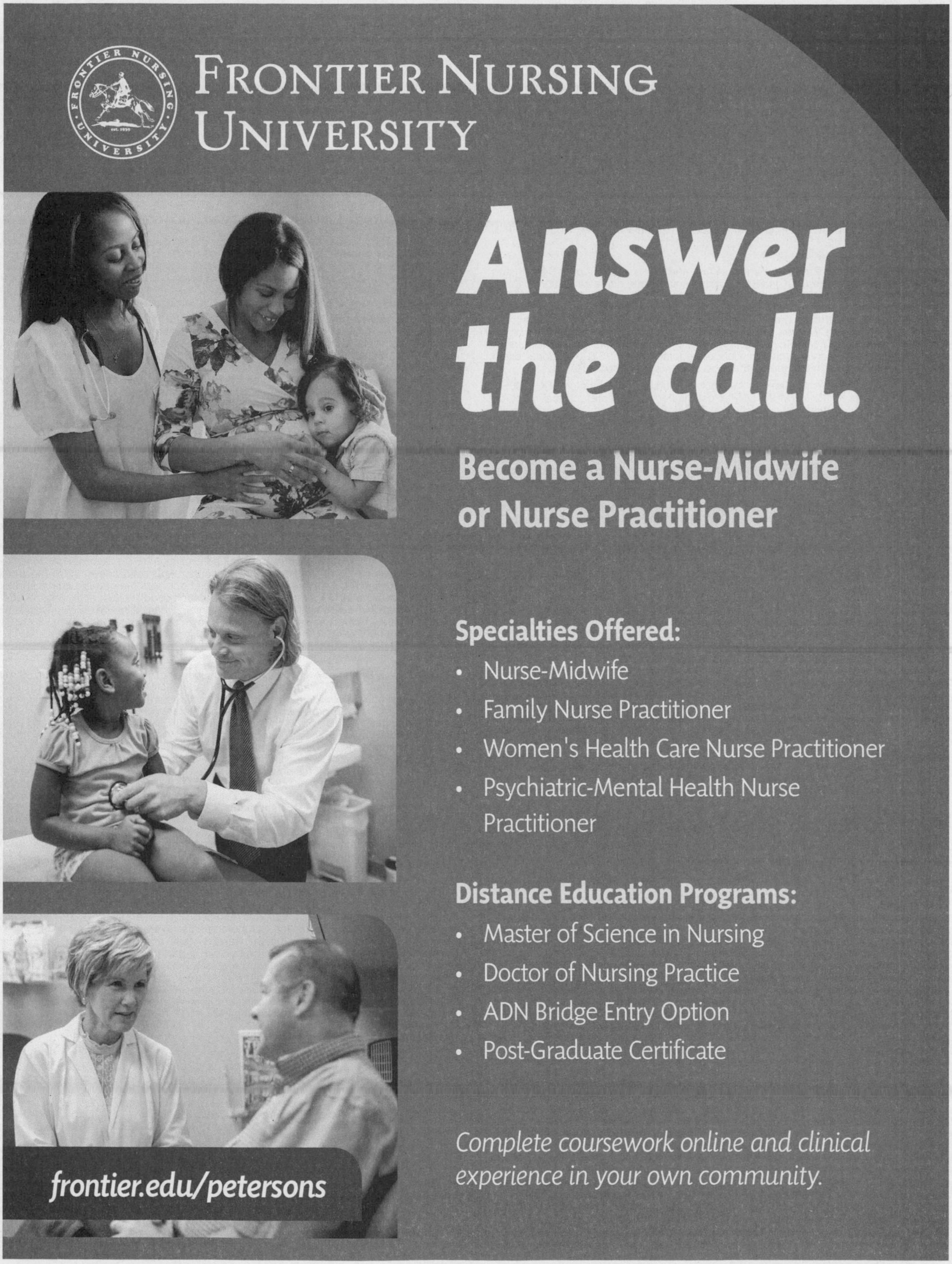
FRONTIER NURSING
UNIVERSITY
FRONTIER NURSING UNIVERSITY
est. 1939
Answer
the call.
Become a Nurse-Midwife
or Nurse Practitioner
Specialties Offered:
• Nurse-Midwife
• Family Nurse Practitioner
• Women's Health Care Nurse Practitioner
• Psychiatric-Mental Health Nurse Practitioner
Distance Education Programs:
• Master of Science in Nursing
• Doctor of Nursing Practice
• ADN Bridge Entry Option
• Post-Graduate Certificate
Complete coursework online and clinical experience in your own community.
frontier.edu/petersons

bivariate statistics; certification in professional CPR; for doctorate, GRE, 2 official transcripts; expanded goals statement; resume; 2 recommendation letters; nursing license; at least 1 year of work experience as an RN; interview; writing sample; evidence of graduate-level course in applied statistics; master's degree in nursing with minimum GPA of 3.5; for Certificate, 2 official transcripts; expanded goals statement; resume; master's degree from accredited institution or currently enrolled with minimum GPA of 3.0. Additional exam requirements/recommendations for international students: Required—TOEFL (minimum score 570 paper-based; 88 iBT), IELTS (minimum score 6.5), PTE (minimum score 59). *Application deadline:* For fall admission, 2/1 for domestic and international students. Application fee: $75 ($80 for international students). Electronic applications accepted. *Expenses:* Contact institution. *Financial support:* In 2017–18, 7 students received support, including 5 research assistantships with tuition reimbursements available (averaging $20,500 per year), 2 teaching assistantships; career-related internships or fieldwork, Federal Work-Study, scholarships/grants, unspecified assistantships, and health care benefits (for full-time research or teaching assistantship recipients) also available. Financial award application deadline: 3/1; financial award applicants required to submit FAFSA. *Faculty research:* Health care, nursing science. *Total annual research expenditures:* $1.6 million. *Unit head:* Carol Urban, Director, 703-993-2991, Fax: 703-993-1949, E-mail: curban@gmu.edu. *Application contact:* Susan Eckis, Office Manager, 703-993-1938, Fax: 703-993-1949, E-mail: seckis@gmu.edu.
Website: http://chhs.gmu.edu/nursing

Georgetown University, Graduate School of Arts and Sciences, School of Nursing and Health Studies, Washington, DC 20057. Offers acute care nurse practitioner (MS); clinical nurse specialist (MS); family nurse practitioner (MS); nurse anesthesia (MS); nurse-midwifery (MS); nursing (DNP); nursing education (MS). *Accreditation:* AACN; AANA/CANAEP (one or more programs are accredited); ACNM/ACME (one or more programs are accredited). *Degree requirements:* For master's, thesis optional. *Entrance requirements:* For master's, GRE General Test or MAT, bachelor's degree in nursing from ACEN-accredited school, minimum undergraduate GPA of 3.0. Additional exam requirements/recommendations for international students: Required—TOEFL.

The George Washington University, School of Nursing, Washington, DC 20052. Offers adult nurse practitioner (MSN, DNP, Post-Master's Certificate); clinical research administration (MSN); family nurse practitioner (MSN, Post-Master's Certificate); health care quality (MSN, Post-Master's Certificate); nursing leadership and management (MSN); nursing practice (DNP), including nursing education; palliative care nurse practitioner (Post-Master's Certificate). *Accreditation:* AACN. *Faculty:* 58 full-time (56 women), 119 part-time/adjunct (111 women). *Students:* 38 full-time (34 women), 570 part-time (510 women); includes 197 minority (92 Black or African American, non-Hispanic/Latino; 2 American Indian or Alaska Native, non-Hispanic/Latino; 63 Asian, non-Hispanic/Latino; 28 Hispanic/Latino; 1 Native Hawaiian or other Pacific Islander, non-Hispanic/Latino; 11 Two or more races, non-Hispanic/Latino), 2 international. Average age 31. 507 applicants, 76% accepted, 185 enrolled. In 2017, 155 master's, 32 doctorates awarded. *Expenses: Tuition:* Full-time $28,800; part-time $1655 per credit hour. *Required fees:* $45; $2.75 per credit hour. *Unit head:* Pamela R. Jeffries, Dean, 202-994-3725, E-mail: pjeffries@gwu.edu. *Application contact:* Kristin Williams, Associate Provost for Graduate Enrollment Management, 202-994-0467, Fax: 202-994-0371, E-mail: ksw@gwu.edu.
Website: http://nursing.gwumc.edu/

Georgia College & State University, Graduate School, College of Health Sciences, Graduate Nursing Program, Milledgeville, GA 31061. Offers nursing (MSN, Post-MSN Certificate); nursing practice (DNP). *Accreditation:* AACN; ACEN. *Program availability:* Part-time, evening/weekend, blended/hybrid learning. *Students:* 16 full-time (all women), 125 part-time (116 women); includes 57 minority (43 Black or African American, non-Hispanic/Latino; 5 Asian, non-Hispanic/Latino; 8 Hispanic/Latino; 1 Two or more races, non-Hispanic/Latino). Average age 39. 19 applicants, 100% accepted, 18 enrolled. In 2017, 27 master's, 3 doctorates, 5 other advanced degrees awarded. *Degree requirements:* For master's, comprehensive exam, minimum GPA of 3.0, electronic portfolio, completion of requirements within a period of 7 years; for doctorate, capstone project, complete all required courses within a period of 7 years; for Post-MSN Certificate, practicum. *Entrance requirements:* For master's, GRE (taken within last 5 years), bachelor's degree in nursing, RN license, 1 year of clinical experience, minimum GPA of 2.75 on last 60 undergraduate hours required in nursing major, statistics course, interview, 3 letters of reference, transcript, resume; for doctorate, master's degree in nursing or anesthesia, minimum graduate GPA of 3.2 in MSN program, unencumbered RN licensure, 500 faculty-supervised clinical hours in master's program, interview, computer access, resume; for Post-MSN Certificate, RN licensure, MSN with minimum GPA of 3.2, transcript, 2 letters of reference, resume, statement of professional goals. *Application deadline:* For fall admission, 1/1 priority date for domestic students. Applications are processed on a rolling basis. Application fee: $40. Electronic applications accepted. *Expenses:* Contact institution. *Financial support:* In 2017–18, 5 students received support. Unspecified assistantships available. Financial award applicants required to submit FAFSA. *Unit head:* Dr. Deborah MacMillan, School of Nursing Programs Director, 478-445-5122, E-mail: debby.macmillan@gcsu.edu.

Georgia Southern University, Jack N. Averitt College of Graduate Studies, College of Health and Human Sciences, School of Nursing, Program in Nursing Science, Statesboro, GA 30460. Offers DNP. *Program availability:* Part-time, online learning. *Students:* 42 full-time (32 women), 60 part-time (55 women); includes 29 minority (20 Black or African American, non-Hispanic/Latino; 3 Asian, non-Hispanic/Latino; 5 Hispanic/Latino; 1 Two or more races, non-Hispanic/Latino). Average age 37. 118 applicants, 47% accepted, 37 enrolled. *Degree requirements:* For doctorate, comprehensive exam (for some programs), thesis/dissertation (for some programs). *Entrance requirements:* Additional exam requirements/recommendations for international students: Required—TOEFL (minimum score 550 paper-based; 80 iBT), IELTS (minimum score 6). *Application deadline:* For fall admission, 6/1 priority date for domestic and international students; for spring admission, 10/1 priority date for domestic students, 10/1 for international students. Applications are processed on a rolling basis. Application fee: $50. Electronic applications accepted. *Expenses:* Tuition, state resident: full-time $4986; part-time $3324 per year. Tuition, nonresident: full-time $21,982; part-time $15,352 per year. *Required fees:* $2092; $1802 per credit hour. $901 per semester. Tuition and fees vary according to course load, campus/location and program. *Financial support:* In 2017–18, 45 students received support. Career-related internships or fieldwork, Federal Work-Study, scholarships/grants, traineeships, and tuition waivers available. Support available to part-time students. Financial award application deadline: 4/15; financial award applicants required to submit FAFSA. *Faculty research:* Vulnerable populations, breast cancer, diabetes, mellitus, advanced practice nursing issues. *Unit head:* Dr. Deborah Allen, Chair, 912-478-5770, Fax: 912-478-0536, E-mail: debbieallen@georgiasouthern.edu.

Georgia Southern University–Armstrong Campus, College of Graduate Studies, School of Nursing, Savannah, GA 31419-1997. Offers adult-gerontological acute care nurse practitioner (Certificate); adult-gerontological clinical nurse specialist (Certificate); adult-gerontological primary care nurse practitioner (Certificate); family nurse practitioner (MSN). *Accreditation:* AACN. *Program availability:* Part-time, evening/weekend. *Faculty:* 12 full-time (all women). *Students:* 36 full-time (30 women), 22 part-time (21 women); includes 17 minority (7 Black or African American, non-Hispanic/Latino; 2 Asian, non-Hispanic/Latino; 4 Hispanic/Latino; 4 Two or more races, non-Hispanic/Latino), 1 international. Average age 32. 59 applicants, 32% accepted, 18 enrolled. In 2017, 10 master's awarded. *Degree requirements:* For master's, comprehensive exam, project or thesis. *Entrance requirements:* For master's, GRE General Test or MAT, minimum GPA of 3.0, letter of recommendation, letter of intent. Additional exam requirements/recommendations for international students: Required—TOEFL (minimum score 523 paper-based; 70 iBT). *Application deadline:* For fall admission, 2/28 for domestic and international students; for spring admission, 11/15 for domestic students, 9/15 for international students. Applications are processed on a rolling basis. Application fee: $30. Electronic applications accepted. *Expenses:* Tuition, state resident: part-time $211 per credit hour. Tuition, nonresident: part-time $782 per credit hour. *Required fees:* $737 per semester. Tuition and fees vary according to course load, degree level, campus/location and program. *Financial support:* In 2017–18, research assistantships with full tuition reimbursements (averaging $5,000 per year) were awarded; Federal Work-Study, scholarships/grants, and unspecified assistantships also available. Support available to part-time students. Financial award application deadline: 3/1; financial award applicants required to submit FAFSA. *Faculty research:* Midwifery, mental health, nursing simulation, smoking cessation during pregnancy, asthma education, vulnerable populations, geriatrics, disaster nursing, complementary and alternative modalities, nephrology. *Unit head:* Dr. Catherine Gilbert, Department Head, 912-344-3145, E-mail: catherine.gilbert@armstrong.edu. *Application contact:* McKenzie Peterman, Graduate Admissions Specialist, 912-478-5678, Fax: 912-478-0740, E-mail: mpeterman@georgiasouthern.edu.
Website: https://www.armstrong.edu/degree-programs/nursing-msn

Georgia Southwestern State University, College of Nursing and Health Sciences, Americus, GA 31709-4693. Offers family nurse practitioner (MSN); health informatics (Postbaccalaureate Certificate); nurse educator (Post Master's Certificate); nursing educator (MSN); nursing informatics (MSN); nursing leadership (MSN). MSN program offered by the Georgia Intercollegiate Consortium for Graduate Nursing Education, a partnership with Columbus State University. *Program availability:* Part-time, online only, all theory courses are offered online. *Faculty:* 10 full-time, 5 part-time/adjunct. *Students:* 23 full-time (22 women), 106 part-time (92 women); includes 41 minority (all Black or African American, non-Hispanic/Latino). Average age 35. 95 applicants, 63% accepted, 30 enrolled. In 2017, 17 master's awarded. *Degree requirements:* For master's, comprehensive exam (for some programs), thesis (for some programs), minimum cumulative GPA of 3.0; maximum of 6 credit hours with C grade and no D grades; degree completed within 7 calendar years from initial enrollment date in graduate courses; for other advanced degree, minimum cumulative GPA of 3.0; maximum of 6 credit hours with C grade and no D grades; degree completed within 7 calendar years from initial enrollment date in graduate courses. *Entrance requirements:* For master's and other advanced degree, baccalaureate degree in nursing from regionally-accredited institution and nationally-accredited nursing program with minimum GPA of 3.0; three professional letters of recommendation; current unencumbered RN license in state where clinical course requirements will be met; background check/drug test; proof of immunizations. *Application deadline:* For fall admission, 1/15 for domestic students; for spring admission, 10/15 for domestic students. Application fee: $25. Electronic applications accepted. *Expenses:* $385 per credit hour, plus fees, which vary according to enrolled credit hours. *Financial support:* Application deadline: 6/1; applicants required to submit FAFSA. *Unit head:* Dr. Sandra Daniel, Dean, 229-931-2275. *Application contact:* Whitney Ford, Admissions Specialist, Office of Graduate Admissions, 800-338-0082, Fax: 229-931-2983, E-mail: graduateadmissions@gsw.edu.
Website: https://gsw.edu/Academics/Schools-and-Departments/School-of-Nursing/index

Georgia State University, Byrdine F. Lewis School of Nursing, Atlanta, GA 30303. Offers adult health clinical nurse specialist/nurse practitioner (MS, Certificate); child health clinical nurse specialist/pediatric nurse practitioner (MS, Certificate); family nurse practitioner (MS, Certificate); family psychiatric mental health nurse practitioner (MS, Certificate); nursing (PhD); nursing leadership in healthcare innovations (MS), including nursing administration, nursing informatics; nutrition (MS); perinatal clinical nurse specialist/women's health nurse practitioner (MS, Certificate); physical therapy (DPT); respiratory therapy (MS). *Accreditation:* AACN. *Program availability:* Part-time, blended/hybrid learning. *Faculty:* 69 full-time (52 women). *Students:* 322 full-time (248 women), 481 part-time (466 women); includes 186 minority (112 Black or African American, non-Hispanic/Latino; 44 Asian, non-Hispanic/Latino; 20 Hispanic/Latino; 10 Two or more races, non-Hispanic/Latino), 18 international. Average age 31. 370 applicants, 56% accepted, 148 enrolled. In 2017, 131 master's, 49 doctorates, 11 other advanced degrees awarded. *Degree requirements:* For doctorate, comprehensive exam, thesis/dissertation. *Entrance requirements:* For doctorate, GRE. Additional exam requirements/recommendations for international students: Required—TOEFL. *Application deadline:* For fall admission, 2/1 priority date for domestic and international students; for spring admission, 9/15 for domestic and international students. Applications are processed on a rolling basis. Application fee: $50. Electronic applications accepted. *Expenses:* Contact institution. *Financial support:* In 2017–18, research assistantships with tuition reimbursements (averaging $1,666 per year), teaching assistantships with tuition reimbursements (averaging $1,920 per year) were awarded; scholarships/grants, tuition waivers (full and partial), and unspecified assistantships also available. Support available to part-time students. Financial award application deadline: 8/1; financial award applicants required to submit FAFSA. *Faculty research:* Stroke intervention for caregivers, stroke prevention in African-Americans; relationships between psychological distress and health outcomes in parents with a medically ill infant; medically fragile children; nursing expertise and patient outcomes. *Unit head:* Nancy Kropf, Dean of Nursing, 404-413-1101, Fax: 404-413-1090, E-mail: nkropf@gsu.edu.
Website: http://nursing.gsu.edu/

Goldfarb School of Nursing at Barnes-Jewish College, Graduate Programs, St. Louis, MO 63110. Offers adult-gerontology (MSN), including primary care nurse practitioner; adult-gerontology (MSN), including acute care nurse practitioner; health systems and population health leadership (MSN); nurse anesthesia (MSN). *Accreditation:* AACN; AANA/CANAEP. *Program availability:* Part-time, online learning. *Faculty:* 42 full-time (39 women), 6 part-time/adjunct (all women). *Students:* 61 full-time (49 women), 3 part-time (2 women); includes 13 minority (8 Black or African American, non-Hispanic/Latino; 2 Asian, non-Hispanic/Latino; 1 Hispanic/Latino; 2 Two or more races, non-Hispanic/Latino). *Degree requirements:* For master's, thesis or alternative. *Entrance requirements:* For master's, 2 references, personal statement, curriculum vitae or resume. Additional exam requirements/recommendations for international students: Required—TOEFL (minimum score 575 paper-based; 85 iBT). *Application deadline:* Applications are processed on a rolling basis. Application fee: $50. *Expenses: Tuition:* Full-time $11,910; part-time $794 per credit hour. *Required fees:* $30; $15 per term. Full-time tuition and fees vary according to program. *Financial support:* Research assistantships, Federal Work-Study, institutionally sponsored loans, scholarships/grants, and traineeships available. Support available to part-time students. Financial award applicants required to submit FAFSA. *Faculty research:* HIV stigma, HIV symptom management, palliative care with children and

their families, heart disease prevention in Hispanic women, depression in the well elderly, alternative therapies in pre-term infants. *Unit head:* Dr. Gretchen Drinkard, Associate Dean for Academic Affairs, 314-454-7540, Fax: 314-362-9222, E-mail: gdrinkard@bjc.org. *Application contact:* Karen Sartorius, Admission Specialist, 314-454-7057, Fax: 314-362-9250, E-mail: karen.sartorius@bjc.org.
Website: http://www.barnesjewishcollege.edu/

Gonzaga University, School of Nursing and Human Physiology, Spokane, WA 99258. Offers MSN, DNP, DNP-A. *Accreditation:* AACN; AANA/CANAEP. *Program availability:* Part-time, evening/weekend, 100% online, immersion weekends. *Faculty:* 10 full-time (all women), 57 part-time/adjunct (48 women). *Students:* 34 full-time (22 women), 673 part-time (566 women); includes 106 minority (18 Black or African American, non-Hispanic/Latino; 4 American Indian or Alaska Native, non-Hispanic/Latino; 29 Asian, non-Hispanic/Latino; 28 Hispanic/Latino; 1 Native Hawaiian or other Pacific Islander, non-Hispanic/Latino; 26 Two or more races, non-Hispanic/Latino), 3 international. Average age 38. 454 applicants, 38% accepted, 130 enrolled. In 2017, 180 master's, 4 doctorates awarded. *Entrance requirements:* For master's, MAT or GRE within the last 5 years if GPA is lower than 3.0, official transcripts, two letters of recommendation, statement of purpose, current resume/curriculum vitae, current registered nurse license. Additional exam requirements/recommendations for international students: Required—TOEFL (minimum score 88 iBT) or IELTS (minimum score 6.5). *Application deadline:* For spring admission, 9/1 for domestic students; for summer admission, 3/28 for domestic students. Applications are processed on a rolling basis. Application fee: $50. Electronic applications accepted. *Expenses:* $955 per credit. *Financial support:* In 2017–18, 28 students received support. Scholarships/grants, traineeships, and unspecified assistantships available. Support available to part-time students. Financial award applicants required to submit FAFSA. *Unit head:* Dr. Lin Murphy, Interim Dean, 509-313-3569, E-mail: murpheyl1@gonzaga.edu. *Application contact:* Shannon Zaranski, Assistant to the Dean, 509-313-3569, E-mail: zaranski@gonzaga.edu.
Website: https://www.gonzaga.edu/school-of-nursing-human-physiology

Goshen College, Program in Nursing, Goshen, IN 46526-4794. Offers family nurse practitioner (MSN). *Accreditation:* AACN. *Program availability:* Part-time, evening/weekend. *Faculty:* 5 full-time (4 women), 1 (woman) part-time/adjunct. *Students:* 55 full-time (48 women), 1 (woman) part-time; includes 10 minority (3 Black or African American, non-Hispanic/Latino; 2 Asian, non-Hispanic/Latino; 4 Hispanic/Latino; 1 Two or more races, non-Hispanic/Latino), 1 international. Average age 35. *Degree requirements:* For master's, comprehensive exam (for some programs). *Entrance requirements:* For master's, minimum GPA of 3.0, curriculum vitae, bachelor's degree in nursing, active RN license in Indiana or Michigan, three professional references, essay, one year of clinical experience, statistics course, interview with program director. Additional exam requirements/recommendations for international students: Required—TOEFL (minimum score 600 paper-based; 100 iBT), IELTS (minimum score 6.5). *Application deadline:* For fall admission, 3/15 priority date for domestic students. Electronic applications accepted. *Expenses: Tuition:* Full-time $13,356; part-time $742 per credit hour. Tuition and fees vary according to degree level, campus/location and program. *Financial support:* Scholarships/grants available. *Unit head:* Ruth Stoltzfus, Director, 574-535-7973, E-mail: ruthas@goshen.edu. *Application contact:* Natalie Shields, Admissions Counselor for Graduate and Continuing Studies, 574-535-7458, E-mail: nshields@goshen.edu.
Website: http://www.goshen.edu/graduate/nursing/

Governors State University, College of Health and Human Services, Program in Nursing, University Park, IL 60484. Offers MSN. *Accreditation:* ACEN. *Program availability:* Part-time. *Faculty:* 11 full-time (all women), 14 part-time/adjunct (13 women). *Students:* 4 full-time (all women), 124 part-time (108 women); includes 93 minority (64 Black or African American, non-Hispanic/Latino; 1 American Indian or Alaska Native, non-Hispanic/Latino; 12 Asian, non-Hispanic/Latino; 14 Hispanic/Latino; 1 Native Hawaiian or other Pacific Islander, non-Hispanic/Latino; 1 Two or more races, non-Hispanic/Latino). Average age 40. 122 applicants, 36% accepted, 22 enrolled. In 2017, 58 master's awarded. *Application deadline:* For fall admission, 4/1 for domestic students. Applications are processed on a rolling basis. Application fee: $50. Electronic applications accepted. *Expenses:* Contact institution. *Financial support:* Application deadline: 5/1; applicants required to submit FAFSA. *Unit head:* Nancy MacMullen, Chair, Department of Nursing, 708-534-5000 Ext. 4043, E-mail: nmacmullen@govst.edu.

Graceland University, School of Nursing, Independence, MO 64050-3434. Offers adult and gerontology acute care (MSN, PMC); family nurse practitioner (MSN, PMC); nurse educator (MSN, PMC); organizational leadership (DNP). *Accreditation:* AACN. *Program availability:* Part-time, online learning. *Faculty:* 13 full-time (11 women), 24 part-time/adjunct (all women). *Students:* 338 full-time (294 women), 311 part-time (282 women); includes 102 minority (33 Black or African American, non-Hispanic/Latino; 8 American Indian or Alaska Native, non-Hispanic/Latino; 18 Asian, non-Hispanic/Latino; 29 Hispanic/Latino; 1 Native Hawaiian or other Pacific Islander, non-Hispanic/Latino; 13 Two or more races, non-Hispanic/Latino), 2 international. Average age 36. 119 applicants, 86% accepted, 95 enrolled. In 2017, 158 master's, 2 doctorates awarded. *Degree requirements:* For master's, comprehensive exam (for some programs), thesis optional, scholarly project; for doctorate, capstone project. *Entrance requirements:* For master's, BSN from nationally-accredited program, RN license, minimum GPA of 3.0, satisfactory criminal background check, three professional reference letters, professional goals statement of 150 words or less; for doctorate, MSN from nationally-accredited program, RN license, minimum GPA of 3.2, criminal background check. Additional exam requirements/recommendations for international students: Required—TOEFL (minimum score 550 paper-based; 79 iBT). *Application deadline:* For fall admission, 6/1 priority date for domestic students; for winter admission, 10/1 priority date for domestic students; for spring admission, 10/1 priority date for domestic students; for summer admission, 2/1 for domestic students. Application fee: $50. Electronic applications accepted. *Expenses:* $775 per credit hour tuition, $1,800 practicum fees, $480 research fees, $846 university technology fees, $655 lab fees, $300 program support fees. *Financial support:* In 2017–18, 14 students received support. Institutionally sponsored loans available. Support available to part-time students. Financial award application deadline: 6/1; financial award applicants required to submit FAFSA. *Faculty research:* International nursing, family care-giving, health promotion, mental health nursing. *Unit head:* Dr. Claudia D. Horton, Interim Vice President for Independence Campus/Dean, 816-423-4670, Fax: 816-423-4753, E-mail: horton@graceland.edu. *Application contact:* Admissions Representative, 816-423-4717, Fax: 816-833-2990, E-mail: distancelearning@graceland.edu.
Website: http://www.graceland.edu/nursing

The Graduate Center, City University of New York, Graduate Studies, Program in Nursing, New York, NY 10016-4039. Offers PhD. *Faculty:* 22 full-time (21 women). *Students:* 46 full-time (41 women); includes 21 minority (12 Black or African American, non-Hispanic/Latino; 5 Asian, non-Hispanic/Latino; 4 Hispanic/Latino), 4 international. Average age 49. 16 applicants, 56% accepted, 7 enrolled. In 2017, 7 doctorates awarded. *Degree requirements:* For doctorate, thesis/dissertation, exams. *Entrance requirements:* For doctorate, GRE, 2 letters of recommendation, personal statement. Additional exam requirements/recommendations for international students: Required—TOEFL. *Application deadline:* For fall admission, 12/1 for domestic students. Application fee: $125. Electronic applications accepted. *Financial support:* In 2017–18, 2 students received support. *Unit head:* Prof. Donna Nickitas, Executive Officer, 212-817-7978, E-mail: dnickitas@gc.cuny.edu. *Application contact:* Les Gribben, Director of Admissions, 212-817-7470, Fax: 212-817-1624, E-mail: lgribben@gc.cuny.edu.
Website: http://web.gc.cuny.edu/ClinicalDoctoral/nursing/

Grambling State University, School of Graduate Studies and Research, College of Professional Studies, School of Nursing, Grambling, LA 71245. Offers family nurse practitioner (PMC); nursing (MSN). *Accreditation:* ACEN. *Program availability:* Part-time. *Degree requirements:* For master's, comprehensive exam (for some programs), thesis (for some programs). *Entrance requirements:* For master's, GRE, minimum GPA of 3.0 on last degree, interview, 2 years of experience as RN. Additional exam requirements/recommendations for international students: Required—TOEFL (minimum score 500 paper-based; 62 iBT). Electronic applications accepted.

Grand Canyon University, College of Nursing and Health Care Professions, Phoenix, AZ 85017-1097. Offers acute care nurse practitioner (MSN, PMC); family nurse practitioner (MSN, PMC); health care administration (MS); health care informatics (MS, MSN); leadership in health care systems (MSN); nursing (DNP); nursing education (MSN, PMC); public health (MPH, MSN); MBA/MSN. *Accreditation:* AACN. *Program availability:* Part-time, evening/weekend, online learning. *Degree requirements:* For master's and PMC, comprehensive exam (for some programs). *Entrance requirements:* For master's, minimum cumulative and science course undergraduate GPA of 3.0. Additional exam requirements/recommendations for international students: Required—TOEFL (minimum score 575 paper-based; 90 iBT), IELTS (minimum score 7).

Grand Valley State University, Kirkhof College of Nursing, Allendale, MI 49503-3314. Offers advanced practice (MSN); case management (MSN); nursing administration (MSN); nursing education (MSN); nursing practice (DNP); MSN/MBA. *Accreditation:* AACN. *Program availability:* Part-time. *Faculty:* 17 full-time (all women), 5 part-time/adjunct (4 women). *Students:* 44 full-time (40 women), 74 part-time (63 women); includes 15 minority (7 Black or African American, non-Hispanic/Latino; 4 Asian, non-Hispanic/Latino; 3 Hispanic/Latino; 1 Two or more races, non-Hispanic/Latino), 4 international. Average age 33. 34 applicants, 100% accepted, 23 enrolled. In 2017, 8 master's, 22 doctorates awarded. *Degree requirements:* For master's, thesis optional; for doctorate, thesis/dissertation optional. *Entrance requirements:* For master's, GRE, minimum upper-division GPA of 3.0, course work in statistics, Michigan RN license, writing sample, interview, criminal background check and drug screen, health records; for doctorate, minimum GPA of 3.0 in master's-level coursework, writing sample, interview, RN in Michigan, criminal background check and drug screen, health records. Additional exam requirements/recommendations for international students: Required—TOEFL (minimum iBT score of 80), IELTS (6.5), or Michigan English Language Assessment Battery (77). *Application deadline:* For fall admission, 3/15 priority date for domestic students. Applications are processed on a rolling basis. Application fee: $30. Electronic applications accepted. *Expenses:* $686 per credit hour (for MSN); $770 per credit hour (for DNP). *Financial support:* In 2017–18, 34 students received support, including 10 fellowships, 30 research assistantships with partial tuition reimbursements available (averaging $4,000 per year); career-related internships or fieldwork, Federal Work-Study, institutionally sponsored loans, and traineeships also available. Financial award application deadline: 2/15. *Faculty research:* Multigenerational health promotion, chronic disease prevention, end-of-life issues, nursing workload, family caregiver health. *Total annual research expenditures:* $36,000. *Unit head:* Dr. Cynthia McCurren, Dean, 616-331-3558, Fax: 616-331-2510, E-mail: mccurrec@gvsu.edu. *Application contact:* Dr. Karen Burritt, Associate Dean for Graduate Programs, 616-331-5585, Fax: 616-331-2510, E-mail: burritka@gvsu.edu.
Website: http://www.gvsu.edu/kcon/

Grantham University, College of Nursing and Allied Health, Lenexa, KS 66219. Offers case management (MSN); health systems management (MS); healthcare administration (MHA); nursing education (MSN); nursing informatics (MSN); nursing management and organizational leadership (MSN). *Program availability:* Part-time, evening/weekend, online only, 100% online. *Faculty:* 2 full-time, 34 part-time/adjunct. *Students:* 198 full-time (144 women), 113 part-time (83 women); includes 170 minority (118 Black or African American, non-Hispanic/Latino; 3 American Indian or Alaska Native, non-Hispanic/Latino; 27 Asian, non-Hispanic/Latino; 11 Hispanic/Latino; 2 Native Hawaiian or other Pacific Islander, non-Hispanic/Latino; 9 Two or more races, non-Hispanic/Latino). Average age 41. 95 applicants, 89% accepted, 72 enrolled. In 2017, 123 master's awarded. *Entrance requirements:* For master's, BSN from state-approved nursing program with minimum cumulative GPA of 2.5 from institution accredited by agency recognized by U.S. DOE or foreign equivalent; unencumbered and current RN license. Additional exam requirements/recommendations for international students: Required—TOEFL (minimum score 530 paper-based; 71 iBT), IELTS (minimum score 6.5), PTE (minimum score 50). *Application deadline:* Applications are processed on a rolling basis. Application fee: $0. Electronic applications accepted. *Expenses:* $325 per credit hour. *Financial support:* Scholarships/grants available. Financial award applicants required to submit FAFSA. *Faculty research:* Compassion in caring improving incivility in the ICU setting, get well network technology in enhancing patient education, opioid use and abuse in postpartum women. *Unit head:* Dr. Cheryl Rules, Dean of the College of Nursing and Allied Health, 913-309-4783, Fax: 844-897-6490, E-mail: crules@grantham.edu. *Application contact:* Jared Parlette, Vice President of Student Enrollment, 800-955-2527 Ext. 803, Fax: 866-914-4557, E-mail: admissions@grantham.edu.
Website: http://www.grantham.edu/nursing-and-allied-health/

Gwynedd Mercy University, Frances M. Maguire School of Nursing and Health Professions, Gwynedd Valley, PA 19437-0901. Offers clinical nurse specialist (MSN), including gerontology, oncology, pediatrics; nurse educator (MSN); nurse practitioner (MSN), including adult health, pediatric health; nursing (DNP). *Accreditation:* ACEN. *Program availability:* Part-time, blended/hybrid learning. *Faculty:* 4 full-time (all women), 1 (woman) part-time/adjunct. *Students:* 28 full-time (25 women), 48 part-time (43 women); includes 28 minority (15 Black or African American, non-Hispanic/Latino; 11 Asian, non-Hispanic/Latino; 1 Hispanic/Latino; 1 Two or more races, non-Hispanic/Latino). Average age 37. 72 applicants, 25% accepted, 16 enrolled. In 2017, 7 master's awarded. *Degree requirements:* For master's, thesis optional; for doctorate, evidence-based scholarly project. *Entrance requirements:* For master's, GRE General Test or MAT, current nursing experience, physical assessment, course work in statistics, BSN from ACEN-accredited program, 2 letters of recommendation, personal interview. Additional exam requirements/recommendations for international students: Required—TOEFL (minimum score 575 paper-based). *Application deadline:* For fall admission, 8/1 priority date for domestic students; for winter admission, 12/1 priority date for domestic students. Applications are processed on a rolling basis. Electronic applications accepted. *Expenses:* $825 per credit (non-doctoral degrees), $930 per credit (doctoral); $17 part-time fee, $165 graduation fee. *Financial support:* In 2017–18, 5 students received support. Scholarships/grants, traineeships, and unspecified assistantships available. Financial award application deadline: 8/30. *Faculty research:* Critical thinking, primary care, domestic violence, multiculturalism, nursing centers. *Unit head:* Dr. Andrea D. Hollingsworth, Dean, 215-646-7300 Ext. 539, Fax: 215-641-5517, E-mail: hollingsworth.a@gmc.edu. *Application contact:* Dr. Barbara A. Jones, Director, 215-646-7300 Ext. 407, Fax: 215-641-5564, E-mail: jones.b@gmc.edu.
Website: http://www.gmercyu.edu/academics/graduate-programs/nursing

Nursing—General

Hampton University, School of Nursing, Hampton, VA 23668. Offers community health nursing (MS); family nurse practitioner (MS); family research (PhD); nursing administration (MS); nursing education (MS). *Accreditation:* AACN. *Program availability:* Part-time, online learning. *Students:* 6 full-time (all women), 28 part-time (25 women); includes 31 minority (29 Black or African American, non-Hispanic/Latino; 2 Hispanic/Latino). Average age 48. 7 applicants, 14% accepted. In 2017, 3 master's, 4 doctorates awarded. *Degree requirements:* For master's, comprehensive exam, thesis optional; for doctorate, comprehensive exam, thesis/dissertation. *Entrance requirements:* For master's, GRE General Test. *Application deadline:* For fall admission, 6/1 priority date for domestic students, 4/1 priority date for international students; for spring admission, 11/1 priority date for domestic students, 9/1 priority date for international students; for summer admission, 4/1 priority date for domestic students, 2/1 priority date for international students. Applications are processed on a rolling basis. Application fee: $35. Electronic applications accepted. *Expenses: Tuition:* Full-time $22,630; part-time $575 per semester hour. *Required fees:* $70. Tuition and fees vary according to program. *Financial support:* In 2017–18, 2 students received support. Fellowships, research assistantships, teaching assistantships, career-related internships or fieldwork, Federal Work-Study, institutionally sponsored loans, and scholarships/grants available. Support available to part-time students. Financial award application deadline: 6/30; financial award applicants required to submit FAFSA. *Faculty research:* African-American stress, HIV education, pediatric obesity, hypertension, breast cancer. *Unit head:* Dr. Shevallanie Lott, Dean, 757-727-5654, E-mail: shevellanie.lott@hamptonu.edu.
Website: http://nursing.hamptonu.edu

Hardin-Simmons University, Graduate School, Patty Hanks Shelton School of Nursing, Abilene, TX 79698-0001. Offers education (MSN); family nurse practitioner (MSN). Programs offered jointly with McMurry University. *Accreditation:* AACN. *Program availability:* Part-time. *Faculty:* 2 full-time (both women), 1 (woman) part-time/adjunct. *Students:* 17 part-time (8 women); includes 5 minority (1 Black or African American, non-Hispanic/Latino; 1 Asian, non-Hispanic/Latino; 3 Hispanic/Latino), 1 international. Average age 36. In 2017, 7 master's awarded. *Degree requirements:* For master's, comprehensive exam, thesis or alternative. *Entrance requirements:* For master's, GRE, minimum undergraduate GPA of 3.0; interview; upper-level course work in statistics; CPR certification; letters of recommendation. Additional exam requirements/recommendations for international students: Required—TOEFL (minimum score 550 paper-based; 75 iBT). *Application deadline:* For fall admission, 8/15 priority date for domestic students, 4/1 for international students; for spring admission, 1/5 priority date for domestic students, 9/1 for international students. Applications are processed on a rolling basis. Application fee: $50 ($150 for international students). Electronic applications accepted. *Expenses:* Contact institution. *Financial support:* In 2017–18, 10 students received support. Career-related internships or fieldwork and scholarships/grants available. Support available to part-time students. Financial award application deadline: 6/30; financial award applicants required to submit FAFSA. *Faculty research:* Child abuse, alternative medicine, pediatric chronic disease, health promotion. *Unit head:* Dr. Nina Ouimette, Dean, 325-671-2357, Fax: 325-671-2386, E-mail: nouimette@phssn.edu. *Application contact:* Dr. Nancy Kucinski, Dean of Graduate Studies, 325-670-1298, Fax: 325-670-1564, E-mail: gradoff@hsutx.edu.
Website: http://www.phssn.edu/

Hawai`i Pacific University, College of Health and Society, Program in Nursing, Honolulu, HI 96813. Offers MSN, DNP. *Accreditation:* AACN. *Program availability:* Part-time, evening/weekend, 100% online, blended/hybrid learning. *Faculty:* 3 full-time (all women), 5 part-time/adjunct (4 women). *Students:* 46 full-time (33 women), 24 part-time (21 women); includes 42 minority (6 Black or African American, non-Hispanic/Latino; 17 Asian, non-Hispanic/Latino; 8 Hispanic/Latino; 11 Two or more races, non-Hispanic/Latino), 5 international. Average age 37. 39 applicants, 87% accepted, 24 enrolled. In 2017, 9 master's awarded. *Entrance requirements:* For master's, BN with minimum GPA of 3.0, proof of valid Hawai'i RN license; for doctorate, minimum graduate GPA of 3.0, U.S. State RN license, prerequisite or transfer equivalent coursework in statistics, curriculum vitae or resume, personal interview (phone/video conference) with DNP Program Coordinator and Graduate Program Chair, MSN with national certification in field of study, 2 letters of recommendation. Additional exam requirements/recommendations for international students: Recommended—TOEFL (minimum score 550 paper-based; 80 iBT), IELTS (minimum score 6), TWE (minimum score 5). *Application deadline:* For fall admission, 1/15 priority date for domestic students; for spring admission, 10/15 priority date for domestic students. Applications are processed on a rolling basis. Application fee: $50. Electronic applications accepted. *Expenses:* Contact institution. *Financial support:* In 2017–18, 4 students received support. Research assistantships, career-related internships or fieldwork, Federal Work-Study, scholarships/grants, tuition waivers (partial), and unspecified assistantships available. Financial award application deadline: 3/1; financial award applicants required to submit FAFSA. *Unit head:* Michelle Johnson, Chief Nurse Administrator and Associate Professor, 808-236-5815, E-mail: mjohnson@hpu.edu. *Application contact:* Danny Lam, Assistant Director of Graduate Admissions, 808-544-1135, E-mail: graduate@hpu.edu.
Website: https://www.hpu.edu/chs/nursing/index.html

Herzing University Online, Program in Nursing, Menomonee Falls, WI 53051. Offers nursing (MSN); nursing education (MSN); nursing management (MSN). *Accreditation:* AACN. *Program availability:* Online learning.

Hofstra University, Hofstra Northwell School of Graduate Nursing and Physician Assistant Studies, Programs in Nursing, Hempstead, NY 11549. Offers adult-gerontology acute care nurse practitioner (MS); family nurse practitioner (MS); psychiatric-mental health nurse practitioner (MS). *Students:* 29 full-time (23 women), 107 part-time (89 women); includes 62 minority (16 Black or African American, non-Hispanic/Latino; 21 Asian, non-Hispanic/Latino; 25 Hispanic/Latino). Average age 35. 122 applicants, 62% accepted, 62 enrolled. *Degree requirements:* For master's, comprehensive exam, minimum GPA of 3.0. *Entrance requirements:* For master's, bachelor's degree in biology or equivalent, 2 letters of recommendation, essay, minimum GPA of 3.0. Additional exam requirements/recommendations for international students: Required—TOEFL (minimum score 550 paper-based; 80 iBT). *Application deadline:* For fall admission, 11/1 for domestic students. Application fee: $75. Electronic applications accepted. *Expenses: Tuition:* Full-time $1292. *Required fees:* $970. Tuition and fees vary according to program. *Financial support:* In 2017–18, 4 students received support, including 4 fellowships with full and partial tuition reimbursements available (averaging $16,205 per year); research assistantships with full and partial tuition reimbursements available, career-related internships or fieldwork, Federal Work-Study, institutionally sponsored loans, scholarships/grants, traineeships, tuition waivers (full and partial), and unspecified assistantships also available. Support available to part-time students. Financial award applicants required to submit FAFSA. *Faculty research:* Innovative educational pedagogies; simulation science; problem (case) based learning; chronic disease management; evidence based practice. *Unit head:* Dr. Kathleen Gallo, Dean, 516-463-7475, Fax: 516-463-7495, E-mail: kathleen.gallo@hofstra.edu. *Application contact:* Sunil Samuel, Assistant Vice President of Admissions, 516-463-4723, Fax: 516-463-4664, E-mail: graduateadmission@hofstra.edu.

Holy Family University, Graduate and Professional Programs, School of Nursing and Allied Health Professions, Philadelphia, PA 19114. Offers nursing administration (MSN); nursing education (MSN). *Accreditation:* AACN. *Program availability:* Part-time, evening/weekend. *Degree requirements:* For master's, thesis or alternative, comprehensive portfolio, clinical practicum. *Entrance requirements:* For master's, BSN or RN from appropriately-accredited program, minimum GPA of 3.0, professional references, official transcripts of all college or university work, essay/personal statement, current resume, completion of one undergraduate statistics course with minimum grade of C. Additional exam requirements/recommendations for international students: Required—TOEFL (minimum score 550 paper-based; 79 iBT), IELTS (minimum score 6), or PTE (minimum score 54). Electronic applications accepted. *Expenses: Tuition:* Full-time $13,518; part-time $9012 per credit hour. Tuition and fees vary according to degree level and program.

Holy Names University, Graduate Division, Department of Nursing, Oakland, CA 94619-1699. Offers administration/management (MSN, PMC); care transition management (MSN); family nurse practitioner (MSN, PMC); informatics (MSN); nurse educator (PMC); MSN/MBA. *Accreditation:* AACN. *Program availability:* Part-time, evening/weekend. *Entrance requirements:* For master's, bachelor's degree in nursing or related field; California RN license or eligibility; minimum cumulative GPA of 2.8, 3.0 in nursing courses from baccalaureate program; courses in pathophysiology, statistics, and research at the undergraduate level. Additional exam requirements/recommendations for international students: Required—TOEFL (minimum score 500 paper-based; 79 iBT). Electronic applications accepted. Application fee is waived when completed online. *Faculty research:* Women's reproductive health, gerontology, attitudes about aging, schizophrenic families, international health issues.

Howard University, College of Nursing and Allied Health Sciences, Division of Nursing, Washington, DC 20059-0002. Offers family nurse practitioner (MSN); nurse educator (MSN). *Accreditation:* AACN. *Program availability:* Part-time. *Degree requirements:* For master's, comprehensive exam, thesis optional. *Entrance requirements:* For master's, RN license, minimum GPA of 3.0, BS in nursing. *Faculty research:* Urinary incontinence, breast cancer prevention, depression in the elderly, adolescent pregnancy.

Hunter College of the City University of New York, Graduate School, Hunter-Bellevue School of Nursing, New York, NY 10010. Offers MS, DNP, AC. *Accreditation:* AACN. *Program availability:* Part-time. *Degree requirements:* For master's, practicum, portfolio. *Entrance requirements:* For master's, BSN, minimum GPA of 3.0, New York RN license, course work in basic statistics, resume; for AC, MSN, minimum GPA of 3.0. Additional exam requirements/recommendations for international students: Required—TOEFL. *Faculty research:* Aging, high-risk mothers and babies, adolescent health, care of HIV/AIDS clients, critical care nursing.

Husson University, Graduate Nursing Program, Bangor, ME 04401-2999. Offers educational leadership (MSN); family and community nurse practitioner (MSN, PMC); psychiatric mental health nurse practitioner (MSN, PMC). *Accreditation:* AACN. *Program availability:* Part-time, evening/weekend. *Faculty:* 4 full-time (all women), 4 part-time/adjunct (all women). *Students:* 1 full-time (0 women), 62 part-time (54 women); includes 3 minority (2 Black or African American, non-Hispanic/Latino; 1 Hispanic/Latino), 1 international. Average age 36. 62 applicants, 55% accepted, 26 enrolled. In 2017, 9 master's awarded. *Degree requirements:* For master's, comprehensive exam (for some programs), research project. *Entrance requirements:* For master's, proof of RN licensure. Additional exam requirements/recommendations for international students: Required—TOEFL (minimum score 550 paper-based; 80 iBT), IELTS (minimum score 6.5). *Application deadline:* For fall admission, 7/15 for domestic students; for spring admission, 10/30 for domestic students. Application fee: $50. Electronic applications accepted. *Expenses:* $577 per credit; $110 to $480 yearly fee depending on credit load. *Financial support:* In 2017–18, 1 student received support. Federal Work-Study, institutionally sponsored loans, traineeships, and unspecified assistantships available. Financial award application deadline: 3/31; financial award applicants required to submit FAFSA. *Faculty research:* Health disparities and methods to better identify and provide healthcare services to those most in need. *Unit head:* Prof. Mary Jude, Director, Graduate Nursing, 207-941-7769, Fax: 207-941-7198, E-mail: judem@husson.edu. *Application contact:* Kristen Card, Director of Graduate Admissions, 207-404-5660, Fax: 207-941-7935, E-mail: cardk@husson.edu.
Website: http://www.husson.edu/college-of-health-and-education/school-of-nursing/graduate-nursing/

Idaho State University, Office of Graduate Studies, School of Nursing, Pocatello, ID 83209-8101. Offers MS, DNP, PhD. *Accreditation:* AACN. *Program availability:* Part-time. *Degree requirements:* For master's, comprehensive exam, thesis optional, practicum and/or clinical hours. *Entrance requirements:* For master's, GRE General Test, interview, 3 letters of reference, active RN license. Additional exam requirements/recommendations for international students: Required—TOEFL (minimum score 600 paper-based). Electronic applications accepted. *Faculty research:* Health promotions, health of homeless, exercise and elderly, student stress, midwifery.

Illinois State University, Graduate School, Mennonite College of Nursing, Normal, IL 61790. Offers family nurse practitioner (PMC); nursing (MSN, PhD). *Accreditation:* AACN. *Faculty research:* Expanding the teaching-nursing home culture in the state of Illinois, advanced education nursing traineeship program, collaborative doctoral program-caring for older adults.

Immaculata University, College of Graduate Studies, Division of Nursing, Immaculata, PA 19345. Offers nursing administration (MSN); nursing education (MSN). *Accreditation:* AACN. *Program availability:* Part-time, evening/weekend. *Entrance requirements:* For master's, MAT or GRE, BSN, minimum undergraduate GPA of 3.0. Additional exam requirements/recommendations for international students: Required—TOEFL.

Independence University, Program in Nursing, Salt Lake City, UT 84107. Offers community health (MSN); gerontology (MSN); nursing administration (MSN); wellness promotion (MSN).

Indiana State University, College of Graduate and Professional Studies, College of Health and Human Services, Department of Advanced Practice Nursing, Terre Haute, IN 47809. Offers advanced practice nursing (DNP); family nurse practitioner (MS); nursing administration (MS); nursing education (MS). *Accreditation:* ACEN. *Program availability:* Part-time. *Degree requirements:* For master's, thesis or alternative. *Entrance requirements:* For master's, BSN, RN license, minimum undergraduate GPA of 3.0. Electronic applications accepted. *Faculty research:* Nursing faculty-student interactions, clinical evaluation, program evaluation, sexual dysfunction, faculty attitudes.

Indiana University East, School of Nursing, Richmond, IN 47374-1289. Offers MSN.

Indiana University Kokomo, School of Nursing, Kokomo, IN 46904. Offers family nurse practitioner (MSN); nurse administrator (MSN); nurse educator (MSN). Electronic applications accepted. *Expenses:* Contact institution.

Indiana University of Pennsylvania, School of Graduate Studies and Research, College of Health and Human Services, Department of Nursing and Allied Health Professions, Nursing DNP to PhD Pathway Program, Indiana, PA 15705. Offers PhD. *Program availability:* Part-time, evening/weekend. *Faculty:* 12 full-time (11 women), 1 (woman) part-time/adjunct. *Students:* 3 part-time (2 women). Average age 49. 14

applicants, 79% accepted. In 2017, 1 doctorate awarded. *Degree requirements:* For doctorate, comprehensive exam, thesis/dissertation. *Entrance requirements:* For doctorate, nursing license. *Application deadline:* Applications are processed on a rolling basis. Application fee: $50. Electronic applications accepted. *Expenses:* Tuition, state resident: full-time $12,000; part-time $500 per credit. Tuition, nonresident: full-time $18,000; part-time $750 per credit. *Required fees:* $4073; $165.55 per credit. $64 per term. *Financial support:* Fellowships with full tuition reimbursements, career-related internships or fieldwork, Federal Work-Study, scholarships/grants, and unspecified assistantships available. Financial award application deadline: 4/15; financial award applicants required to submit FAFSA. *Unit head:* Dr. Susan Poorman, Doctoral Coordinator, 724-357-3258, E-mail: susan.poorman@iup.edu.

Indiana University of Pennsylvania, School of Graduate Studies and Research, College of Health and Human Services, Department of Nursing and Allied Health Professions, PhD in Nursing Program, Indiana, PA 15705. Offers PhD. *Program availability:* Part-time. *Faculty:* 12 full-time (11 women), 1 (woman) part-time/adjunct. *Students:* 37 part-time (35 women); includes 2 minority (1 Asian, non-Hispanic/Latino; 1 Hispanic/Latino). Average age 43. 2 applicants, 100% accepted. In 2017, 3 doctorates awarded. *Degree requirements:* For doctorate, comprehensive exam, thesis/dissertation. *Entrance requirements:* For doctorate, GRE. Additional exam requirements/recommendations for international students: Required—TOEFL (minimum score 540 paper-based). *Application deadline:* Applications are processed on a rolling basis. Application fee: $50. Electronic applications accepted. *Expenses:* Contact institution. *Financial support:* Fellowships with full tuition reimbursements, research assistantships, teaching assistantships with partial tuition reimbursements, career-related internships or fieldwork, Federal Work-Study, scholarships/grants, and unspecified assistantships available. Financial award application deadline: 4/15; financial award applicants required to submit FAFSA. *Unit head:* Dr. Susan Poorman, Doctoral Coordinator, 724-357-3258, E-mail: susan.poorman@iup.edu.
Website: http://www.iup.edu/grad/nursingphd/default.aspx

Indiana University–Purdue University Fort Wayne, College of Health and Human Services, Department of Nursing, Fort Wayne, IN 46805-1499. Offers adult-gerontology primary care nurse practitioner (MS); family nurse practitioner (MS); nurse executive (MS); nursing administration (Certificate); nursing education (MS). *Accreditation:* ACEN. *Program availability:* Part-time. *Entrance requirements:* For master's, GRE Writing Test (if GPA below 3.0), BS in nursing, eligibility for Indiana RN license, minimum GPA of 3.0, essay, copy of resume, three references, undergraduate course work in research and statistics within last 5 years. Additional exam requirements/recommendations for international students: Required—TOEFL (minimum score 550 paper-based; 79 iBT); Recommended—TWE. Electronic applications accepted. *Faculty research:* Community engagement, cervical screening, evidence-based practice.

Indiana University–Purdue University Indianapolis, School of Nursing, Doctor of Nursing Practice Program, Indianapolis, IN 46202. Offers executive leadership (DNP). *Accreditation:* AACN. *Program availability:* Blended/hybrid learning. *Entrance requirements:* For doctorate, MSN from ACEN- or CCNE-accredited program with minimum cumulative GPA of 3.3, documentation of supervised practice hours from accredited MSN program, unencumbered RN license, graduate-level course in statistics, three references indicating ability to succeed in DNP program. Additional exam requirements/recommendations for international students: Required—TOEFL (minimum score 550 paper-based; 79 iBT). Electronic applications accepted. *Expenses:* Contact institution. *Faculty research:* Quality of life, symptom management, cancer prevention and control, heart failure, pediatric oncology.

Indiana University–Purdue University Indianapolis, School of Nursing, MSN Program in Nursing, Indianapolis, IN 46202. Offers adult/gerontology acute care nurse practitioner (MSN); adult/gerontology clinical nurse specialist (MSN); adult/gerontology primary care nurse practitioner (MSN); family nurse practitioner (MSN); nursing education (MSN); nursing leadership in health systems (MSN); pediatric clinical nurse specialist (MSN); pediatric nurse practitioner (MSN). *Accreditation:* AACN. *Program availability:* Part-time, blended/hybrid learning. *Degree requirements:* For master's, thesis. *Entrance requirements:* For master's, BSN from ACEN- or CCNE-accredited program, minimum undergraduate GPA of 3.0 (preferred), professional resume or curriculum vitae, essay stating career goals and objectives, current unencumbered RN license, three references from individuals with knowledge of ability to succeed in graduate program. Additional exam requirements/recommendations for international students: Required—TOEFL (minimum score 550 paper-based; 79 iBT). Electronic applications accepted. *Expenses:* Contact institution. *Faculty research:* Quality of life, symptom management, cancer prevention and control, heart failure, pediatric oncology.

Indiana University–Purdue University Indianapolis, School of Nursing, PhD Program in Nursing Science, Indianapolis, IN 46202. Offers clinical nursing science (PhD); health systems (PhD). *Program availability:* Part-time, blended/hybrid learning. *Degree requirements:* For doctorate, comprehensive exam, thesis/dissertation. *Entrance requirements:* For doctorate, GRE General Test, BSN or MSN from ACEN- or CCNE-accredited program; minimum baccalaureate cumulative GPA of 3.0 or master's degree 3.5. Additional exam requirements/recommendations for international students: Required—TOEFL (minimum score 550 paper-based; 79 iBT). Electronic applications accepted. *Expenses:* Contact institution. *Faculty research:* Quality of life, symptom management, cancer prevention and control, heart failure, pediatric oncology.

Indiana University South Bend, Vera Z. Dwyer College of Health Sciences, School of Nursing, South Bend, IN 46615. Offers family nurse practitioner (MSN). *Accreditation:* AACN. *Program availability:* Part-time, evening/weekend. *Entrance requirements:* For master's, GRE General Test, minimum GPA of 3.0. *Expenses:* Contact institution.

Indiana Wesleyan University, Graduate School, School of Nursing, Marion, IN 46953-4974. Offers nursing administration (MS); nursing education (MS); primary care nursing (MS); MSN/MBA. *Accreditation:* AACN. *Program availability:* Part-time, online learning. *Degree requirements:* For master's, capstone project or thesis. *Entrance requirements:* For master's, writing sample, RN license, 1 year of related experience, graduate statistics course. Additional exam requirements/recommendations for international students: Required—TOEFL. *Expenses:* Contact institution. *Faculty research:* Primary health care with international emphasis, international nursing.

Inter American University of Puerto Rico, Arecibo Campus, Program in Nursing, Arecibo, PR 00614-4050. Offers critical care nursing (MSN); surgical nursing (MSN). *Entrance requirements:* For master's, EXADEP or GRE General Test or MAT, 2 letters of recommendation, bachelor's degree in nursing, minimum GPA of 2.5 in last 60 credits, minimum 1 year nursing experience, nursing license.

Inter American University of Puerto Rico, Barranquitas Campus, Program in Nursing, Barranquitas, PR 00794. Offers critical care nursing (MSN); medical surgical nursing (MSN). *Program availability:* Part-time, evening/weekend. *Faculty:* 2 full-time (both women). *Students:* 30 part-time (24 women); all minorities (all Hispanic/Latino). Average age 31. 30 applicants, 97% accepted, 29 enrolled. *Degree requirements:* For master's, 2 foreign languages, comprehensive exam (for some programs), thesis optional, minimum grade of B on all courses, integration seminar. *Entrance requirements:* For master's, bachelor's degree in nursing from accredited institution, minimum GPA of 2.5, provisional or permanent nursing license for practicing nursing in Puerto Rico, official academic transcript from institution that conferred bachelor's degree, two recommendations letters. *Application deadline:* Applications are processed on a rolling basis. Application fee: $31. Electronic applications accepted. *Expenses:* $3,392 full-time tuition plus $652 fees. *Financial support:* Applicants required to submit FAFSA. *Unit head:* Juan A. Negron-Berrios, PhD, Chancellor, 787-857-3600 Ext. 2002, Fax: 787-857-2125, E-mail: janegron@br.inter.edu. *Application contact:* Aramilda Cartagena-Santiago, Dean of Students, 787-857-3600 Ext. 2009, Fax: 787-857-2125, E-mail: aramildacartagena@br.inter.edu.

Jacksonville State University, College of Graduate Studies and Continuing Education, College of Nursing, Jacksonville, AL 36265-1602. Offers MSN. *Accreditation:* AACN. *Program availability:* Part-time, evening/weekend. *Degree requirements:* For master's, comprehensive exam, thesis (for some programs). *Entrance requirements:* For master's, GRE General Test or MAT. Additional exam requirements/recommendations for international students: Required—TOEFL (minimum score 500 paper-based; 61 iBT). Electronic applications accepted.

Jacksonville University, Brooks Rehabilitation College of Healthcare Sciences, Keigwin School of Nursing, Doctor of Nursing Practice Program, Jacksonville, FL 32211. Offers DNP. *Program availability:* Part-time, blended/hybrid learning. *Faculty:* 6 full-time (all women), 3 part-time/adjunct (all women). *Students:* 20 full-time (17 women), 93 part-time (82 women); includes 33 minority (18 Black or African American, non-Hispanic/Latino; 5 Asian, non-Hispanic/Latino; 6 Hispanic/Latino; 1 Native Hawaiian or other Pacific Islander, non-Hispanic/Latino; 3 Two or more races, non-Hispanic/Latino). Average age 39. 40 applicants, 50% accepted, 16 enrolled. In 2017, 9 doctorates awarded. *Degree requirements:* For doctorate, thesis/dissertation. *Entrance requirements:* For doctorate, official transcripts from all colleges/universities attended; MSN from ACEN- or CCNE-accredited program; licensure as RN or ARNP; 3 letters of reference (2 clinical, 1 professional/academic); curriculum vitae; graded essay. Additional exam requirements/recommendations for international students: Required—TOEFL (minimum score 650 paper-based; 114 iBT), IELTS (minimum score 8). *Application deadline:* For fall admission, 2/1 for domestic and international students. Applications are processed on a rolling basis. Application fee: $50. Electronic applications accepted. *Expenses:* $630 per credit hour (for DNP); $950 per credit hour (for OTD). *Financial support:* Federal Work-Study, institutionally sponsored loans, scholarships/grants, and health care benefits available. Support available to part-time students. Financial award application deadline: 3/15; financial award applicants required to submit FAFSA. *Unit head:* Dr. Hilary Morgan, Director, Graduate Nursing Programs/Associate Professor, 904-256-7601, E-mail: hmorgan@ju.edu. *Application contact:* Stephanie Bloom, Assistant Director, Enrollment and Advanced Graduate Nursing, 904-256-7286, E-mail: sstrick4@ju.edu.
Website: https://www.ju.edu/nursing/graduate/doctor-nursing-practice/

Jacksonville University, Brooks Rehabilitation College of Healthcare Sciences, Keigwin School of Nursing, Master of Science in Nursing Program, Jacksonville, FL 32211. Offers clinical nurse educator (MSN); family nurse practitioner (MSN); family nurse practitioner/emergency nurse practitioner (MSN); leadership in the healthcare system (MSN); nursing informatics (MSN); psychiatric nurse practitioner (MSN); MSN/MBA. *Program availability:* Part-time, 100% online, blended/hybrid learning. *Faculty:* 8 full-time (all women), 8 part-time/adjunct (6 women). *Students:* 41 full-time (36 women), 456 part-time (415 women); includes 169 minority (102 Black or African American, non-Hispanic/Latino; 4 American Indian or Alaska Native, non-Hispanic/Latino; 24 Asian, non-Hispanic/Latino; 33 Hispanic/Latino; 1 Native Hawaiian or other Pacific Islander, non-Hispanic/Latino; 5 Two or more races, non-Hispanic/Latino), 1 international. Average age 39. 232 applicants, 59% accepted, 110 enrolled. In 2017, 87 master's awarded. *Degree requirements:* For master's, thesis. *Entrance requirements:* For master's, GRE General Test or undergraduate GPA above 3.0, BSN from ACEN- or CCNE-accredited program; course work in statistics and physical assessment within last 5 years; Florida nursing license; CPR/BLS certification; 3 recommendations, 2 of which are professional references; statement of intent; resume. Additional exam requirements/recommendations for international students: Required—TOEFL (minimum score 650 paper-based; 114 iBT), IELTS (minimum score 8). *Application deadline:* For fall admission, 2/1 for domestic and international students. Applications are processed on a rolling basis. Application fee: $50. Electronic applications accepted. *Expenses:* $620 per credit hour, $455 per credit hour off-campus, $720 per credit hour online. *Financial support:* Federal Work-Study, institutionally sponsored loans, scholarships/grants, and health care benefits available. Support available to part-time students. Financial award application deadline: 3/15; financial award applicants required to submit FAFSA. *Faculty research:* Treatment of anxiety. *Unit head:* Dr. Hilary Morgan, Director, Graduate Nursing Programs/Associate Professor, 904-256-7601, E-mail: hmorgan@ju.edu. *Application contact:* Stephanie Bloom, Assistant Director, Enrollment and Advanced Graduate Nursing, 904-256-7286, E-mail: sstrick4@ju.edu.
Website: https://www.ju.edu/nursing/graduate/master-science-nursing/index.php

James Madison University, The Graduate School, College of Health and Behavioral Studies, Program in Nursing, Harrisonburg, VA 22807. Offers adult/gerontology primary care nurse practitioner (MSN); clinical nurse leader (MSN); family nurse practitioner (MSN); nurse administrator (MSN); nurse midwifery (MSN); nursing (MSN, DNP); psychiatric mental health nurse practitioner (MSN). *Accreditation:* AACN. *Program availability:* Part-time, 100% online, blended/hybrid learning. *Students:* 10 full-time (9 women), 77 part-time (71 women); includes 10 minority (2 Black or African American, non-Hispanic/Latino; 5 Asian, non-Hispanic/Latino; 1 Hispanic/Latino; 2 Two or more races, non-Hispanic/Latino). Average age 30. In 2017, 27 master's awarded. Application fee: $55. Electronic applications accepted. *Expenses:* Tuition, state resident: full-time $10,512; part-time $438 per credit hour. Tuition, nonresident: full-time $28,358; part-time $1162 per credit hour. *Required fees:* $1128. *Financial support:* In 2017–18, 2 students received support. Federal Work-Study and 2 assistantships (averaging $7911) available. Financial award application deadline: 3/1; financial award applicants required to submit FAFSA. *Unit head:* Dr. Julie T. Sanford, Department Head, 540-568-6314, E-mail: sanforjt@jmu.edu. *Application contact:* Lynette D. Michael, Director of Graduate Admissions, 540-568-6131 Ext. 6395, Fax: 540-568-7860, E-mail: michaeld@jmu.edu.
Website: http://www.nursing.jmu.edu

Jefferson College of Health Sciences, Program in Nursing, Roanoke, VA 24013. Offers nursing education (MSN); nursing management (MSN). *Accreditation:* AACN. *Program availability:* Part-time. *Degree requirements:* For master's, project. *Entrance requirements:* For master's, MAT. Additional exam requirements/recommendations for international students: Required—TOEFL (minimum score 550 paper-based; 80 iBT). Electronic applications accepted. *Faculty research:* Nursing, teaching and learning techniques, cultural competence, spirituality and nursing.

Johns Hopkins University, School of Nursing, Certificate Programs in Nursing, Baltimore, MD 21205. Offers nursing education (Certificate); pediatric acute care nurse practitioner (Certificate); psychiatric mental health nurse practitioner (Certificate). *Program availability:* Part-time-only, online only, 100% online. *Faculty:* 62 full-time (46 women), 160 part-time/adjunct (all women). *Students:* 39 part-time (35 women); includes 14 minority (5 Black or African American, non-Hispanic/Latino; 2 Asian, non-Hispanic/Latino; 4 Hispanic/Latino; 3 Two or more races, non-Hispanic/Latino). Average age 44. 159 applicants, 33% accepted, 45 enrolled. In 2017, 18 Certificates awarded.

Entrance requirements: For degree, minimum GPA of 3.0, goal statement/essay, resume, letters of recommendation, official transcripts from all post-secondary institutions, MSN, RN license, NP license. Additional exam requirements/recommendations for international students: Required—TOEFL (minimum score 600 paper-based; 100 iBT), IELTS (minimum score 7). *Application deadline:* For fall admission, 1/1 priority date for domestic students; for spring admission, 11/1 priority date for domestic students. Application fee: $70. Electronic applications accepted. *Expenses:* $1,591 per credit. *Financial support:* Application deadline: 3/1; applicants required to submit FAFSA. *Faculty research:* Palliative care, cardiovascular health, disease prevention and risk reduction, women's health, palliative and end-of-life care. *Unit head:* Dr. Patricia M. Davidson, Dean, 410-955-7544, Fax: 410-955-4890, E-mail: sondeansoffice@jhu.edu. *Application contact:* Cathy Wilson, Director of Admissions, 410-955-7548, Fax: 410-614-7086, E-mail: jhuson@jhu.edu.
Website: http://nursing.jhu.edu/

See Display on next page and Close-Up on page 763.

Johns Hopkins University, School of Nursing, Doctoral Programs in Nursing, Baltimore, MD 21205. Offers adult/gerontological primary care nurse practitioner (PhD); nursing (PhD); nursing practice (DNP); DNP/PhD. *Program availability:* Blended/hybrid learning. *Faculty:* 62 full-time (46 women), 160 part-time/adjunct (all women). *Students:* 110 full-time (100 women), 69 part-time (62 women); includes 79 minority (30 Black or African American, non-Hispanic/Latino; 1 American Indian or Alaska Native, non-Hispanic/Latino; 25 Asian, non-Hispanic/Latino; 17 Hispanic/Latino; 6 Two or more races, non-Hispanic/Latino), 10 international. Average age 38. 228 applicants, 52% accepted, 74 enrolled. In 2017, 23 doctorates awarded. *Degree requirements:* For doctorate, comprehensive exam (for some programs), thesis/dissertation (for some programs). *Entrance requirements:* For doctorate, minimum GPA of 3.0, goal statement/essay, resume, letters of recommendation, official transcripts from all post-secondary institutions attended; BSN and RN license (for DNP); writing sample (for PhD). Additional exam requirements/recommendations for international students: Required—TOEFL (minimum score 600 paper-based; 100 iBT), IELTS (minimum score 7). *Application deadline:* For fall admission, 11/1 priority date for domestic and international students; for summer admission, 11/1 priority date for domestic and international students. Application fee: $70. Electronic applications accepted. *Expenses:* $2,310 per credit (for PhD); $1,671 per credit (for DNP). *Financial support:* In 2017–18, 101 students received support, including 18 research assistantships, 18 teaching assistantships; Federal Work-Study, scholarships/grants, and tuition waivers (partial) also available. Support available to part-time students. Financial award application deadline: 3/1; financial award applicants required to submit FAFSA. *Faculty research:* Cardiovascular health, disease prevention and risk reduction, women's health, palliative and end-of-life care, community-based health promotion. *Unit head:* Dr. Patricia M. Davidson, Dean, 410-955-7544, Fax: 410-955-4890, E-mail: sondeansoffice@jhu.edu. *Application contact:* Cathy Wilson, Director of Admissions, 410-955-7548, Fax: 410-614-7086, E-mail: jhuson@jhu.edu.
Website: http://nursing.jhu.edu/

See Display on next page and Close-Up on page 763.

Johns Hopkins University, School of Nursing, Master's Programs in Nursing, Baltimore, MD 21205. Offers MSN, MSN/MBA, MSN/MPH. MSN/MPH offered jointly with Bloomberg School of Public Health, MSN/MBA with Carey Business School. *Accreditation:* AACN. *Program availability:* 100% online, blended/hybrid learning. *Faculty:* 62 full-time (46 women), 160 part-time/adjunct (all women). *Students:* 398 full-time (344 women), 173 part-time (160 women); includes 200 minority (78 Black or African American, non-Hispanic/Latino; 59 Asian, non-Hispanic/Latino; 46 Hispanic/Latino; 1 Native Hawaiian or other Pacific Islander, non-Hispanic/Latino; 16 Two or more races, non-Hispanic/Latino), 7 international. Average age 29. 396 applicants, 71% accepted, 160 enrolled. In 2017, 215 master's awarded. *Entrance requirements:* For master's, minimum GPA of 3.0, goal statement/essay, resume, letters of recommendation, official transcripts from all post-secondary institutions attended, BSN and RN license (for advanced practice tracks). Additional exam requirements/recommendations for international students: Required—TOEFL (minimum score 600 paper-based; 100 iBT), IELTS (minimum score 7). *Application deadline:* For fall admission, 11/1 priority date for domestic and international students; for spring admission, 7/1 priority date for domestic and international students. Application fee: $70. Electronic applications accepted. *Expenses:* $1,591 per credit. *Financial support:* In 2017–18, 3 students received support. Federal Work-Study and scholarships/grants available. Support available to part-time students. Financial award application deadline: 3/1; financial award applicants required to submit FAFSA. *Faculty research:* Cardiovascular health, disease prevention and risk reduction, women's health, palliative and end-of-life care, community-based health promotion. *Unit head:* Dr. Patricia M. Davidson, Dean, 410-955-7544, Fax: 410-955-4890, E-mail: sondeansoffice@jhu.edu. *Application contact:* Cathy Wilson, Director of Admissions, 410-955-7548, Fax: 410-614-7086, E-mail: jhuson@jhu.edu.
Website: http://nursing.jhu.edu/

See Display on next page and Close-Up on page 763.

Johns Hopkins University, School of Nursing, MSN: Entry into Nursing Practice Program, Baltimore, MD 21218. Offers MSN. *Faculty:* 56 full-time (53 women). *Students:* 367 full-time (319 women), 2 part-time (both women); includes 142 minority (54 Black or African American, non-Hispanic/Latino; 38 Asian, non-Hispanic/Latino; 34 Hispanic/Latino; 1 Native Hawaiian or other Pacific Islander, non-Hispanic/Latino; 15 Two or more races, non-Hispanic/Latino), 5 international. Average age 31. 370 applicants, 71% accepted, 146 enrolled. In 2017, 106 master's awarded. *Entrance requirements:* For master's, bachelor's degree (in a discipline other than nursing), minimum GPA of 3.0, essays, resume, letters of recommendation, official transcripts from all post-secondary institutions attended. Additional exam requirements/recommendations for international students: Required—TOEFL (minimum score 600 paper-based; 100 iBT), IELTS (minimum score 7). *Application deadline:* For fall admission, 11/1 priority date for domestic and international students; for spring admission, 7/1 priority date for domestic and international students. Application fee: $50. Electronic applications accepted. *Expenses:* $1,591 per credit. *Financial support:* In 2017–18, 397 students received support. Federal Work-Study, institutionally sponsored loans, and scholarships/grants available. Financial award application deadline: 3/1; financial award applicants required to submit FAFSA. *Faculty research:* Cardiovascular health; disease prevention and risk reduction; women's health; care at end of life; community-based health promotion. *Unit head:* Dr. Kathleen M. White, Director, 410-614-4664, E-mail: kwhite2@jhu.edu. *Application contact:* Cathy Wilson, Director of Admissions, 410-955-7548, Fax: 410-614-7086, E-mail: jhuson@jhu.edu.
Website: http://nursing.jhu.edu/academics/programs/pre-licensure/masters-entry/

See Display on next page and Close-Up on page 763.

Kean University, College of Natural, Applied and Health Sciences, Program in Nursing, Union, NJ 07083. Offers clinical management (MSN); community health nursing (MSN). *Accreditation:* ACEN. *Program availability:* Part-time. *Faculty:* 12 full-time (all women). *Students:* 7 full-time (all women), 50 part-time (46 women); includes 34 minority (23 Black or African American, non-Hispanic/Latino; 8 Asian, non-Hispanic/Latino; 2 Hispanic/Latino; 1 Two or more races, non-Hispanic/Latino). Average age 47. 15 applicants, 53% accepted, 4 enrolled. In 2017, 51 master's awarded. *Degree requirements:* For master's, thesis or alternative, clinical field experience. *Entrance requirements:* For master's, minimum GPA of 3.0; BS in nursing; RN license; 2 letters of recommendation; interview; official transcripts from all institutions attended. Additional exam requirements/recommendations for international students: Required—TOEFL (minimum score 550 paper-based; 79 iBT), IELTS (minimum score 6.5). *Application deadline:* For fall admission, 6/30 for domestic and international students; for spring admission, 12/1 for domestic and international students. Applications are processed on a rolling basis. Application fee: $75. Electronic applications accepted. *Expenses:* Tuition, state resident: full-time $13,419; part-time $653 per credit. Tuition, nonresident: full-time $18,188; part-time $801 per credit. *Required fees:* $3382; $154 per credit. Tuition and fees vary according to course level, course load, degree level and program. *Financial support:* Scholarships/grants and unspecified assistantships available. Financial award applicants required to submit FAFSA. *Unit head:* Dr. Joan Valas, Program Coordinator, 908-737-6210, E-mail: nursing@kean.edu. *Application contact:* Pedro Lopes, Admissions Counselor, 908-737-7100, E-mail: gradadmissions@kean.edu.
Website: http://grad.kean.edu/masters-programs/nursing-clinical-management

Keiser University, Master of Science in Nursing Program, Fort Lauderdale, FL 33309. Offers family nurse practitioner (MSN); nursing (MSN).
Website: http://www.keiseruniversity.edu/graduateschool/nursing-program-overview.php

Kennesaw State University, WellStar College of Health and Human Services, Doctor of Nursing Science Program, Kennesaw, GA 30144. Offers DNS. *Program availability:* Part-time. *Degree requirements:* For doctorate, comprehensive exam, thesis/dissertation. *Entrance requirements:* For doctorate, GRE, master's degree in nursing, RN licensure. Additional exam requirements/recommendations for international students: Required—TOEFL (minimum score 550 paper-based; 80 iBT), IELTS (minimum score 6.5). *Application deadline:* For fall admission, 3/1 for domestic and international students. Applications are processed on a rolling basis. Application fee: $60. Electronic applications accepted. *Financial support:* Research assistantships with full tuition reimbursements available. Financial award application deadline: 4/1; financial award applicants required to submit FAFSA. *Unit head:* Yvonne Eaves, Director, 470-578-6061, E-mail: yeaves@kennesaw.edu. *Application contact:* Jerryl Morris, Admissions Counselor, 470-578-2030, Fax: 470-578-9172, E-mail: ksugrad@kennesaw.edu.
Website: http://wellstarcollege.kennesaw.edu/nursing/doctor-nursing-science/overview.php

Kennesaw State University, WellStar College of Health and Human Services, Program in Primary Care Nurse Practitioner, Kennesaw, GA 30144. Offers MSN. *Accreditation:* AACN. *Program availability:* Part-time, evening/weekend. *Entrance requirements:* For master's, GRE General Test, minimum GPA of 2.5, RN license, 3 years of professional experience. Additional exam requirements/recommendations for international students: Required—TOEFL (minimum score 550 paper-based), IELTS (minimum score 6.5). *Application deadline:* For fall admission, 3/1 for domestic and international students. Application fee: $60. Electronic applications accepted. *Financial support:* Research assistantships with full tuition reimbursements, Federal Work-Study, and unspecified assistantships available. Support available to part-time students. Financial award application deadline: 4/1; financial award applicants required to submit FAFSA. *Unit head:* Deborah King, Coordinator, 470-578-6172, E-mail: dking4@kennesaw.edu. *Application contact:* Jerryl Morris, Admissions Counselor, 470-578-2030, Fax: 470-578-9172, E-mail: ksugrad@kennesaw.edu.
Website: http://wellstarcollege.kennesaw.edu/nursing/master-science-nursing/primary-nurse-practitioner.php

Kent State University, College of Nursing, Kent, OH 44242. Offers advanced nursing practice (DNP), including adult/gerontology acute care nurse practitioner (MSN, DNP); nursing (MSN, PhD), including adult/gerontology acute care nurse practitioner (MSN, DNP), adult/gerontology clinical nurse specialist (MSN), adult/gerontology primary care nurse practitioner (MSN), family nurse practitioner (MSN), nurse educator (MSN), nursing and healthcare management (MSN), pediatric primary care nurse practitioner (MSN), psychiatric/mental health nurse practitioner (MSN); MBA/MSN. PhD program offered jointly with The University of Akron. *Accreditation:* AACN. *Program availability:* Part-time, online learning. *Faculty:* 29 full-time (28 women), 15 part-time/adjunct (12 women). *Students:* 167 full-time (142 women), 405 part-time (359 women); includes 70 minority (39 Black or African American, non-Hispanic/Latino; 11 Asian, non-Hispanic/Latino; 18 Hispanic/Latino; 2 Two or more races, non-Hispanic/Latino), 13 international. Average age 35. 272 applicants, 74% accepted, 166 enrolled. In 2017, 144 master's, 8 doctorates awarded. *Degree requirements:* For master's, thesis optional; for doctorate, comprehensive exam, thesis/dissertation. *Entrance requirements:* For master's, GRE or GMAT, minimum GPA of 3.0, active RN license, statement of purpose, 3 letters of reference, undergraduate level statistics class, baccalaureate or graduate-level nursing degree, curriculum vitae/resume; for doctorate, GRE, minimum GPA of 3.0, transcripts, 3 letters of reference, interview, active unrestricted Ohio RN license, statement of purpose, writing sample, curriculum vitae/resume, baccalaureate and master's degrees in nursing or DNP. Additional exam requirements/recommendations for international students: Required—TOEFL (minimum score 560 paper-based; 83 iBT), IELTS (minimum score 6.5), PTE (minimum score 55), Michigan English Language Assessment Battery (minimum score 78). *Application deadline:* For fall admission, 3/1 for domestic and international students; for spring admission, 10/1 for domestic and international students. Applications are processed on a rolling basis. Application fee: $45 ($70 for international students). Electronic applications accepted. *Expenses:* Tuition, state resident: full-time $11,310; part-time $515 per credit hour. Tuition, nonresident: full-time $20,396; part-time $928 per credit hour. *International tuition:* $18,544 full-time. *Financial support:* Scholarships/grants available. Financial award application deadline: 5/4. *Unit head:* Dr. Barbara Broome, Dean, 330-672-3777, E-mail: bbroome1@kent.edu. *Application contact:* Dr. Wendy A. Umberger, Associate Dean for Graduate Programs/Professor, 330-672-8813, E-mail: wlewando@kent.edu.
Website: http://www.kent.edu/nursing/

Kentucky State University, College of Professional Studies, Frankfort, KY 40601. Offers nursing (DNP); public administration (MPA), including human resource management; special education (MA). *Program availability:* Part-time, evening/weekend, 100% online, blended/hybrid learning. *Faculty:* 9 full-time (7 women), 3 part-time/adjunct (all women). *Students:* 29 full-time (18 women), 29 part-time (24 women); includes 42 minority (40 Black or African American, non-Hispanic/Latino; 1 Asian, non-Hispanic/Latino; 1 Two or more races, non-Hispanic/Latino). Average age 35. 17 applicants, 53% accepted, 7 enrolled. In 2017, 11 master's, 4 doctorates awarded. *Degree requirements:* For master's, comprehensive exam, thesis optional; for doctorate, comprehensive exam, thesis/dissertation optional, 180 clinical hours. *Entrance requirements:* For master's, GMAT, GRE, transcript, essay, letters of recommendation; for doctorate, RN license; resume; graduate research and statistics courses (strongly recommended). Additional exam requirements/recommendations for international

JOHNS HOPKINS
SCHOOL of NURSING
Leading the Way
in education, research and practice - locally and globally
BEST
GRAD SCHOOLS
U.S.News & WORLD REPORT
NURSING
MASTER'S DEGREE
2017
MSN: Entry into Nursing
Public Health Nursing
Health Systems Management
Advanced Specialty DNP
Executive DNP
PhD
nursing.jhu.edu/nursingcareer
#1 Ranked Graduate School
U.S. News & World Report 2017
Ranked #2 DNP
U.S. News & World Report 2017
Ranked #2 by
QS Quacquarelli Symonds
#1
College Choice
#1 Most Innovative
Best Master of Science
in Nursing Degrees
#1 Ranked Online
U.S. News & World Report 2017
HEED Award
Insight into Diversity

students: Required—TOEFL (minimum score 525 paper-based, 41 iBT) or IELTS (minimum score 4). *Application deadline:* For fall admission, 7/1 for domestic students, 4/1 for international students; for spring admission, 11/15 for domestic students, 8/15 for international students; for summer admission, 5/1 for domestic students, 2/1 for international students. Applications are processed on a rolling basis. Application fee: $30 ($100 for international students). Electronic applications accepted. *Expenses:* Contact institution. *Financial support:* In 2017–18, 54 students received support, including 1 research assistantship (averaging $1,350 per year); scholarships/grants, tuition waivers (partial), and unspecified assistantships also available. Financial award application deadline: 4/15; financial award applicants required to submit FAFSA. *Faculty research:* Risk assessment and failure modeling for the public sector implication of property rights on economic development, the social stability of communities, civil peace of nations. *Total annual research expenditures:* $414,831. *Unit head:* Dr. Kristen Broady, Assistant Vice President and Dean of Graduate Programs, 502-597-6386, E-mail: kristen.broady@kysu.edu. *Application contact:* Dr. James Obielodan, Director of Graduate Studies, 502-597-4723, E-mail: james.obielodan@kysu.edu.
Website: http://kysu.edu/academics/college-of-professional-studies/

Keuka College, Program in Nursing, Keuka Park, NY 14478. Offers adult gerontology (MS); nursing education (MS). *Accreditation:* AACN. *Degree requirements:* For master's, exam or thesis. *Entrance requirements:* For master's, bachelor's degree from accredited institution, minimum GPA of 3.0, unencumbered NY State license, and current registration as RN (for nursing); currently full-time or part-time working RN and 2 clinical letters of recommendation (for adult gerontology nurse practitioner). Additional exam requirements/recommendations for international students: Required—TOEFL (minimum score 550 paper-based). Electronic applications accepted. *Expenses:* Contact institution. *Faculty research:* Endocrinology and diabetes management of adults, insulin pump efficacy in those with type 2 diabetes; primary care for all ages, addiction, and substance abuse prevention and treatment; music therapy for those with chronic lung disease; maternal child health nursing; parish nursing; nursing education; homeopathy and wellness, pediatric health; effects of infant feeding experiences.

King University, School of Nursing, Bristol, TN 37620-2699. Offers family nurse practitioner (MSN); nurse educator (MSN); nursing (DNP); nursing administration (MSN); pediatric nurse practitioner (MSN).

Lamar University, College of Graduate Studies, College of Arts and Sciences, JoAnne Gay Dishman Department of Nursing, Beaumont, TX 77701. Offers nursing administration (MSN); nursing education (MSN); MSN/MBA. *Accreditation:* ACEN. *Program availability:* Part-time, evening/weekend, online learning. *Faculty:* 35 full-time (33 women), 3 part-time/adjunct (2 women). *Students:* 92 part-time (85 women); includes 43 minority (27 Black or African American, non-Hispanic/Latino; 7 Asian, non-Hispanic/Latino; 9 Hispanic/Latino). Average age 38. 68 applicants, 88% accepted, 18 enrolled. In 2017, 15 master's awarded. *Degree requirements:* For master's, comprehensive exam, practicum project presentation, evidence-based project. *Entrance requirements:* For master's, GRE General Test, MAT, criminal background check, RN license, ACEN-accredited BSN, college course work in statistics in past 5 years, letters of recommendation, minimum undergraduate GPA of 3.0. Additional exam requirements/recommendations for international students: Required—TOEFL (minimum score 550 paper-based; 79 iBT), IELTS (minimum score 6.5). *Application deadline:* For fall admission, 8/10 for domestic students, 7/1 for international students; for spring admission, 1/5 for domestic students, 12/1 for international students. Applications are processed on a rolling basis. Application fee: $25 ($50 for international students). Electronic applications accepted. *Expenses:* Contact institution. *Financial support:* In 2017–18, 2 teaching assistantships (averaging $24,000 per year) were awarded; scholarships/grants and traineeships also available. Financial award application deadline: 4/1; financial award applicants required to submit FAFSA. *Faculty research:* Student retention, theory, care giving, online course and research. *Unit head:* Cynthia Stinson, Interim Chair, 409-880-8817, Fax: 409-880-8698. *Application contact:* Deidre Mayer, Interim Director, Admissions and Academic Services, 409-880-8888, Fax: 409-880-7419, E-mail: gradmissions@lamar.edu.
Website: http://artssciences.lamar.edu/nursing

Lander University, Graduate Studies, Greenwood, SC 29649-2099. Offers clinical nurse leader (MSN); emergency management (MS); Montessori education (M Ed); teaching and learning (M Ed). *Accreditation:* NCATE. *Program availability:* Part-time, online learning. *Degree requirements:* For master's, comprehensive exam, thesis or alternative. *Entrance requirements:* For master's, GRE General Test. Additional exam requirements/recommendations for international students: Required—TOEFL (minimum score 550 paper-based). Electronic applications accepted.

La Roche College, School of Graduate Studies and Adult Education, Program in Nursing, Pittsburgh, PA 15237-5898. Offers clinical nurse leader (MSN); nursing education (MSN); nursing management (MSN). *Accreditation:* ACEN. *Program availability:* Part-time, evening/weekend, online only, 100% online. *Faculty:* 3 full-time (all women), 2 part-time/adjunct (1 woman). *Students:* 17 full-time (15 women), 9 part-time (all women), 1 international. Average age 35. 16 applicants, 75% accepted, 10 enrolled. In 2017, 11 master's awarded. *Degree requirements:* For master's, thesis optional, internship, practicum. *Entrance requirements:* For master's, GRE General Test, BSN, nursing license, work experience. Additional exam requirements/recommendations for international students: Recommended—TOEFL (minimum score 550 paper-based). *Application deadline:* For fall admission, 8/15 priority date for domestic students, 8/15 for international students; for spring admission, 12/15 priority date for domestic students, 12/15 for international students. Applications are processed on a rolling basis. Application fee: $50. Electronic applications accepted. *Expenses:* Contact institution. *Financial support:* Application deadline: 3/31; applicants required to submit FAFSA. *Faculty research:* Patient education, perception. *Unit head:* Dr. Terri Liberto, Division Chair, 412-847-1813, Fax: 412-536-1175, E-mail: terri.liberto@laroche.edu. *Application contact:* Hope Schiffgens, Director of Graduate Studies and Adult Education, 412-536-1266, Fax: 412-536-1283, E-mail: schombh1@laroche.edu.

La Salle University, School of Nursing and Health Sciences, Program in Nursing, Philadelphia, PA 19141-1199. Offers adult gerontology primary care nurse practitioner (MSN, Certificate); adult health and illness clinical nurse specialist (MSN); adult-gerontology clinical nurse specialist (MSN, Certificate); clinical nurse leader (MSN); family primary care nurse practitioner (MSN, Certificate); gerontology (Certificate); nurse anesthetist (MSN, Certificate); nursing (MSN, Certificate); nursing administration (MSN, Certificate); nursing education (Certificate); nursing practice (DNP); nursing service administration (MSN); public health nursing (MSN, Certificate); school nursing (Certificate); MSN/MBA; MSN/MPH. *Accreditation:* AACN. *Program availability:* Part-time, evening/weekend, 100% online. *Faculty:* 12 full-time (11 women), 14 part-time/adjunct (11 women). *Students:* 1 (woman) full-time, 277 part-time (220 women); includes 72 minority (36 Black or African American, non-Hispanic/Latino; 1 American Indian or Alaska Native, non-Hispanic/Latino; 18 Asian, non-Hispanic/Latino; 10 Hispanic/Latino; 1 Native Hawaiian or other Pacific Islander, non-Hispanic/Latino; 6 Two or more races, non-Hispanic/Latino), 1 international. Average age 36. 70 applicants, 56% accepted, 24 enrolled. In 2017, 81 master's, 4 doctorates, 13 other advanced degrees awarded. *Degree requirements:* For doctorate, minimum of 1,000 hours of post baccalaureate clinical practice supervised by preceptors. *Entrance requirements:* For master's, GRE, MAT, or GMAT (for students with BSN GPA of less than 3.2), baccalaureate degree in nursing from ACEN- or CCNE-accredited program or an MSN Bridge program; Pennsylvania RN license; 2 letters of reference; resume; statement of philosophy articulating professional values and future educational goal; 1 year of work experience as a registered nurse; for doctorate, GRE (waived for applicants with MSN cumulative GPA of 3.7 or above), MSN, master's degree, MBA or MHA from nationally-accredited program; resume or curriculum vitae; 2 letters of reference; interview; for Certificate, GRE, MAT, or GMAT (for students with BSN GPA of less than 3.2, baccalaureate degree in nursing from ACEN- or CCNE-accredited program or an MSN Bridge program; Pennsylvania RN license; 2 letters of reference; resume; statement of philosophy articulating professional values and future educational goal; 1 year of work experience as a registered nurse. Additional exam requirements/recommendations for international students: Required—TOEFL. *Application deadline:* For fall admission, 8/15 priority date for domestic students, 7/15 for international students; for spring admission, 12/15 priority date for domestic students, 11/15 for international students; for summer admission, 4/15 priority date for domestic students, 3/15 for international students. Applications are processed on a rolling basis. Application fee: $35. Electronic applications accepted. Application fee is waived when completed online. *Expenses:* Contact institution. *Financial support:* In 2017–18, 7 students received support. Scholarships/grants and traineeships available. Support available to part-time students. Financial award application deadline: 8/31; financial award applicants required to submit FAFSA. *Unit head:* Dr. Patricia M. Dillon, Director, 215-951-1322, Fax: 215-951-1896, E-mail: msnapn@lasalle.edu. *Application contact:* Elizabeth Heenan, Director, Graduate and Adult Enrollment, 215-951-1100, Fax: 215-951-1462, E-mail: heenan@lasalle.edu.
Website: http://www.lasalle.edu/nursing/program-options/

Laurentian University, School of Graduate Studies and Research, Programme in Nursing, Sudbury, ON P3E 2C6, Canada. Offers M Sc N.

Lehman College of the City University of New York, School of Health Sciences, Human Services and Nursing, Department of Nursing, Bronx, NY 10468-1589. Offers adult health nursing (MS); nursing of older adults (MS); parent-child nursing (MS); pediatric nurse practitioner (MS). *Accreditation:* AACN. *Program availability:* Part-time, evening/weekend. *Entrance requirements:* For master's, bachelor's degree in nursing, New York RN license.

Le Moyne College, Department of Nursing, Syracuse, NY 13214. Offers family nurse practitioner (MS, CAS); informatics (MS, CAS); nursing administration (MS, CAS); nursing education (MS, CAS). *Accreditation:* AACN. *Program availability:* Part-time, evening/weekend. *Faculty:* 3 full-time (all women), 5 part-time/adjunct (all women). *Students:* 27 full-time (20 women), 51 part-time (47 women); includes 10 minority (4 Black or African American, non-Hispanic/Latino; 1 Asian, non-Hispanic/Latino; 4 Hispanic/Latino; 1 Two or more races, non-Hispanic/Latino). Average age 32. 39 applicants, 95% accepted, 31 enrolled. In 2017, 20 master's, 2 other advanced degrees awarded. *Degree requirements:* For master's, scholarly project. *Entrance requirements:* For master's, bachelor's degree, interview, minimum GPA of 3.0, New York RN license, 2 letters of recommendation, writing sample, transcripts. *Application deadline:* For fall admission, 8/1 priority date for domestic students, 8/1 for international students; for spring admission, 12/15 priority date for domestic students, 12/15 for international students; for summer admission, 5/1 priority date for domestic students, 5/1 for international students. Applications are processed on a rolling basis. Application fee: $50. Electronic applications accepted. *Expenses:* $700 per credit hour. *Financial support:* In 2017–18, 2 students received support. Career-related internships or fieldwork, scholarships/grants, health care benefits, and unspecified assistantships available. Support available to part-time students. Financial award applicants required to submit FAFSA. *Faculty research:* Inter-profession education, gerontology, utilization of free healthcare services by the insured, health promotion education, innovative undergraduate nursing education models, patient and family education, horizontal violence. *Unit head:* Dr. Margaret M. Wells, Professor/Chair of Nursing, 315-445-5435, Fax: 315-445-6024, E-mail: wellsmm@lemoyne.edu. *Application contact:* Kristen P. Richards, Senior Director of Enrollment Management, 315-445-5444, Fax: 315-445-6092, E-mail: trapaskp@lemoyne.edu.
Website: http://www.lemoyne.edu/nursing

Lenoir-Rhyne University, Graduate Programs, School of Nursing, Program in Nursing, Hickory, NC 28601. Offers nursing administration (MSN); nursing education (MSN). *Accreditation:* AACN. *Program availability:* Online learning. *Degree requirements:* For master's, comprehensive exam, thesis optional. *Entrance requirements:* For master's, official transcripts, two recommendations, essay, resume, unrestricted RN license, criminal background check. Additional exam requirements/recommendations for international students: Required—TOEFL (minimum score 600 paper-based). Electronic applications accepted. *Expenses:* Contact institution.

Lewis University, College of Nursing and Health Professions, Program in Nursing, Romeoville, IL 60446. Offers adult gerontology acute care nurse practitioner (MSN); adult gerontology clinical nurse specialist (MSN); adult gerontology primary care nurse practitioner (MSN); family nurse practitioner (MSN); healthcare systems leadership (MSN); nursing (DNP); nursing education (MSN); school nurse (MSN). *Accreditation:* AACN. *Program availability:* Part-time, evening/weekend, 100% online, blended/hybrid learning. *Students:* 14 full-time (11 women), 361 part-time (336 women); includes 100 minority (27 Black or African American, non-Hispanic/Latino; 33 Asian, non-Hispanic/Latino; 35 Hispanic/Latino; 5 Two or more races, non-Hispanic/Latino), 1 international. Average age 37. *Degree requirements:* For master's, clinical practicum. *Entrance requirements:* For master's, minimum undergraduate GPA of 3.0, degree in nursing, RN license, letter of recommendation, interview, resume or curriculum vitae. Additional exam requirements/recommendations for international students: Required—TOEFL (minimum score 550 paper-based; 80 iBT). *Application deadline:* For fall admission, 5/1 priority date for international students; for spring admission, 11/15 priority date for international students. Applications are processed on a rolling basis. Application fee: $40. Electronic applications accepted. Tuition and fees vary according to program. *Financial support:* Federal Work-Study, scholarships/grants, tuition waivers (full and partial), and unspecified assistantships available. Financial award application deadline: 5/1; financial award applicants required to submit FAFSA. *Faculty research:* Cancer prevention, phenomenological methods, public policy analysis. *Total annual research expenditures:* $1,000. *Unit head:* 815-836-5610. *Application contact:* Nancy Wiksten, Adult Admission Counselor, 815-836-5628, Fax: 815-836-5578, E-mail: wikstena@lewisu.edu.

Lewis University, College of Nursing and Health Professions and College of Business, Program in Nursing/Business, Romeoville, IL 60446. Offers MSN/MBA. *Program availability:* Part-time, evening/weekend. *Students:* 3 full-time (all women), 27 part-time (23 women); includes 10 minority (4 Black or African American, non-Hispanic/Latino; 2 Asian, non-Hispanic/Latino; 4 Hispanic/Latino). Average age 38. *Entrance requirements:* Additional exam requirements/recommendations for international students: Required—TOEFL (minimum score 550 paper-based; 80 iBT). *Application deadline:* For fall admission, 4/2 priority date for domestic students, 5/1 priority date for international students; for spring admission, 11/15 priority date for international students. Applications are processed on a rolling basis. Electronic applications accepted. Tuition and fees vary according to program. *Financial support:* Scholarships/grants, tuition waivers (full and partial), and unspecified assistantships available. Financial award application deadline: 5/1; financial award applicants required to submit FAFSA. *Faculty research:* Cancer prevention, phenomenological methods, public policy analysis. *Total annual research expenditures:* $1,000. *Unit head:* Dr. Suling Li, Associate Dean and Director, Graduate Studies in Nursing, 815-838-0500 Ext. 5878, E-mail: lisu@lewisu.edu. *Application contact:* Nancy Wiksten, Adult Admission Counselor, 815-838-0500 Ext. 5628, Fax: 815-836-5578, E-mail: wikstena@lewisu.edu.

Liberty University, School of Nursing, Lynchburg, VA 24515. Offers family nurse practitioner (DNP); nurse educator (MSN); nursing administration (MSN); nursing informatics (MSN). *Accreditation:* AACN. *Program availability:* Part-time, online learning. *Students:* 148 full-time (131 women), 461 part-time (421 women); includes 103 minority (58 Black or African American, non-Hispanic/Latino; 4 American Indian or Alaska Native, non-Hispanic/Latino; 15 Asian, non-Hispanic/Latino; 11 Hispanic/Latino; 3 Native Hawaiian or other Pacific Islander, non-Hispanic/Latino; 12 Two or more races, non-Hispanic/Latino), 8 international. Average age 39. 536 applicants, 30% accepted, 105 enrolled. In 2017, 100 master's, 13 doctorates awarded. *Entrance requirements:* For master's, minimum cumulative undergraduate GPA of 3.0; for doctorate, minimum GPA of 3.25 in most current nursing program completed. Additional exam requirements/recommendations for international students: Recommended—TOEFL. *Application deadline:* Applications are processed on a rolling basis. Application fee: $50. Electronic applications accepted. *Financial support:* Applicants required to submit FAFSA. *Unit head:* Dr. Deanna Britt, Dean, 434-582-2519, E-mail: dbritt@liberty.edu. *Application contact:* Jay Bridge, Director of Admissions, 800-424-9595, Fax: 800-628-7977, E-mail: gradadmissions@liberty.edu.

Lincoln Memorial University, Caylor School of Nursing, Harrogate, TN 37752-1901. Offers family nurse practitioner (MSN); nurse anesthesia (MSN); psychiatric mental health nurse practitioner (MSN). *Accreditation:* AANA/CANAEP; ACEN. *Program availability:* Part-time. *Entrance requirements:* For master's, GRE.

Lindenwood University, Graduate Programs, School of Health Sciences, St. Charles, MO 63301-1695. Offers human performance (MS); nursing (MS). *Program availability:* Part-time, blended/hybrid learning. *Faculty:* 9 full-time (4 women), 4 part-time/adjunct (3 women). *Students:* 24 full-time (12 women), 57 part-time (51 women); includes 13 minority (7 Black or African American, non-Hispanic/Latino; 5 Hispanic/Latino; 1 Two or more races, non-Hispanic/Latino), 4 international. Average age 35. 65 applicants, 49% accepted, 22 enrolled. In 2017, 24 master's awarded. *Degree requirements:* For master's, minimum cumulative GPA of 3.0. *Entrance requirements:* For master's, BSN with 1 year of clinical experience as an RN, minimum cumulative GPA of 3.0. Additional exam requirements/recommendations for international students: Required—TOEFL (minimum score 550 paper-based; 80 iBT); Recommended—IELTS (minimum score 6.5). *Application deadline:* For fall admission, 8/27 priority date for domestic and international students; for spring admission, 1/14 priority date for domestic and international students; for summer admission, 6/4 priority date for domestic and international students. Applications are processed on a rolling basis. Application fee: $30 ($100 for international students). Electronic applications accepted. *Expenses: Tuition:* Full-time $16,300; part-time $460 per credit. *Required fees:* $660; $330 per credit. Tuition and fees vary according to degree level and program. *Financial support:* In 2017–18, 79 students received support. Career-related internships or fieldwork, Federal Work-Study, institutionally sponsored loans, scholarships/grants, tuition waivers (partial), and unspecified assistantships available. Financial award application deadline: 6/30; financial award applicants required to submit FAFSA. *Unit head:* Dr. Cynthia Schroeder, Dean, School of Health Sciences, 636-949-4318, E-mail: cschroeder@lindenwood.edu. *Application contact:* Kara Schilli, Director, Evening and Graduate Admissions, 636-949-4349, Fax: 636-949-4109, E-mail: adultadmissions@lindenwood.edu.
Website: http://www.lindenwood.edu/academics/academic-schools/school-of-health-sciences/

Loma Linda University, School of Nursing, Program in Nursing, Loma Linda, CA 92350. Offers DNP, PhD. *Accreditation:* AACN. *Program availability:* Part-time. *Entrance requirements:* Additional exam requirements/recommendations for international students: Required—TOEFL. Electronic applications accepted. *Faculty research:* Family coping in chronic illness; women, identity, and career/family issues.

Long Island University–LIU Brooklyn, Harriet Rothkopf Heilbrunn School of Nursing, Brooklyn, NY 11201. Offers adult nurse practitioner (MS, Advanced Certificate); family nurse practitioner (MS, Advanced Certificate); nurse educator (MS). *Accreditation:* AACN. *Program availability:* Part-time, evening/weekend, blended/hybrid learning. *Faculty:* 9 full-time (7 women), 6 part-time/adjunct (4 women). *Students:* 5 full-time (all women), 195 part-time (174 women); includes 117 minority (70 Black or African American, non-Hispanic/Latino; 28 Asian, non-Hispanic/Latino; 17 Hispanic/Latino; 2 Two or more races, non-Hispanic/Latino), 1 international. Average age 37. 168 applicants, 60% accepted, 73 enrolled. In 2017, 69 master's, 2 other advanced degrees awarded. *Entrance requirements:* Additional exam requirements/recommendations for international students: Required—TOEFL or IELTS. *Application deadline:* Applications are processed on a rolling basis. Application fee: $50. Electronic applications accepted. *Expenses: Tuition:* Full-time $21,618; part-time $1201 per credit. *Required fees:* $1840; $920 per term. Tuition and fees vary according to course load. *Financial support:* In 2017–18, 15 students received support. Career-related internships or fieldwork, Federal Work-Study, scholarships/grants, and unspecified assistantships available. Support available to part-time students. Financial award application deadline: 2/15; financial award applicants required to submit FAFSA. *Faculty research:* Clinical and health outcomes in managed care; attitudes of nurses towards people with disabilities; adherence to CPAP in obstructive sleep apnea; diabetes and treatment compliance; chronic neurological disease management outside facilities. *Unit head:* Peggy Tallier, Interim Dean, 718-780-3367, E-mail: peggy.tallier@liu.edu. *Application contact:* Luis Santiago, Dean of Admissions, 718-488-1011, Fax: 718-780-6110, E-mail: bkln-admissions@liu.edu.
Website: http://www.liu.edu/Brooklyn/Academics/Harriet-Rothkopf-Heilbrunn-School-of-Nursing

Louisiana State University Health Sciences Center, School of Nursing, New Orleans, LA 70112. Offers adult gerontology acute care nurse practitioner (DNP, Post-Master's Certificate); adult gerontology clinical nurse specialist (DNP, Post-Master's Certificate); adult gerontology primary care nurse practitioner (DNP, Post-Master's Certificate); clinical nurse leader (MSN); executive nurse leader (DNP, Post-Master's Certificate); neonatal nurse practitioner (DNP, Post-Master's Certificate); nurse anesthesia (DNP, Post-Master's Certificate); nurse educator (MSN); nursing (DNS); primary care family nurse practitioner (DNP, Post-Master's Certificate); public/community health nursing (DNP, Post-Master's Certificate). *Accreditation:* AACN; AANA/CANAEP (one or more programs are accredited). *Program availability:* Part-time. *Faculty:* 29 full-time (26 women), 20 part-time/adjunct (8 women). *Students:* 184 full-time (132 women), 41 part-time (35 women); includes 69 minority (45 Black or African American, non-Hispanic/Latino; 11 Asian, non-Hispanic/Latino; 12 Hispanic/Latino; 1 Two or more races, non-Hispanic/Latino), 1 international. Average age 30. 162 applicants, 42% accepted, 68 enrolled. In 2017, 52 master's, 46 doctorates awarded. *Degree requirements:* For master's, thesis optional; for doctorate, thesis/dissertation. *Entrance requirements:* For master's, GRE, minimum GPA of 3.0; for doctorate, GRE, minimum GPA of 3.0 (for DNP), 3.5 (for DNS). Additional exam requirements/recommendations for international students: Required—TOEFL (minimum score 550 paper-based; 79 iBT). *Application deadline:* Applications are processed on a rolling basis. Application fee: $100. Electronic applications accepted. *Expenses:* Contact institution. *Financial support:* Federal Work-Study, institutionally sponsored loans, scholarships/grants, and traineeships available. Financial award applicants required to submit FAFSA. *Faculty research:* Advanced clinical practice, nursing education, interprofessional education, nursing administration, culturally competent care. *Unit head:* Dr. Demetrius James Porche, Dean, 504-568-4106, Fax: 504-599-0573, E-mail: dporch@lsuhsc.edu. *Application contact:* Tracie Gravolet, Director, Office of Student Affairs, 504-568-4114, Fax: 504-568-5711, E-mail: tgravo@lsuhsc.edu.
Website: http://nursing.lsuhsc.edu/

Loyola University Chicago, Graduate School, Marcella Niehoff School of Nursing, Maywood, IL 60141. Offers adult clinical nurse specialist (MSN, Certificate); adult nurse practitioner (Certificate); dietetics (MS); family nurse practitioner (Certificate); family, adult, and women's health nurse practitioner (MSN); health systems leadership (MSN); healthcare quality using education in safety and technology (DNP); infection prevention (MSN, DNP); nursing science (PhD); women's health clinical nurse specialist (Certificate). *Accreditation:* AACN. *Program availability:* Part-time, blended/hybrid learning. *Faculty:* 24 full-time (22 women), 21 part-time/adjunct (19 women). *Students:* 188 full-time (178 women), 222 part-time (208 women); includes 105 minority (23 Black or African American, non-Hispanic/Latino; 40 Asian, non-Hispanic/Latino; 30 Hispanic/Latino; 2 Native Hawaiian or other Pacific Islander, non-Hispanic/Latino; 10 Two or more races, non-Hispanic/Latino), 4 international. Average age 36. 197 applicants, 55% accepted, 80 enrolled. In 2017, 94 master's, 17 doctorates, 26 other advanced degrees awarded. *Degree requirements:* For master's, comprehensive exam; for doctorate, thesis/dissertation, qualifying examination (for PhD); capstone project (for DNP). *Entrance requirements:* For master's, BSN, minimum nursing GPA of 3.0, Illinois RN license, 3 letters of recommendation, 1000 hours of experience in area of specialty prior to starting clinical rotations, personal statement; for doctorate, BSN or MSN, minimum GPA of 3.0, professional nursing license, 3 letters of recommendation, personal statement. Additional exam requirements/recommendations for international students: Required—TOEFL (minimum score 550 paper-based; 79 iBT), IELTS (minimum score 6.5). *Application deadline:* For fall admission, 6/1 priority date for domestic and international students; for spring admission, 11/15 priority date for domestic and international students; for summer admission, 3/15 priority date for domestic and international students. Applications are processed on a rolling basis. Application fee: $50. Electronic applications accepted. Application fee is waived when completed online. *Expenses:* Contact institution. *Financial support:* In 2017–18, 10 students received support, including 3 research assistantships with full tuition reimbursements available (averaging $18,000 per year), 1 teaching assistantship with full tuition reimbursement available (averaging $18,000 per year); scholarships/grants, unspecified assistantships, and nurse faculty loan program also available. Financial award application deadline: 5/1; financial award applicants required to submit FAFSA. *Faculty research:* Epigenetics and social determinants of health; women's health; vitamin D; health equity; interprofessional education; prevention and self-management of chronic disease; body mass in oncology patients. *Total annual research expenditures:* $1.4 million. *Unit head:* Dr. Vickie Keough, Dean, 708-216-5448, Fax: 708-216-9555, E-mail: vkeough@luc.edu. *Application contact:* Toni Topalova, Enrollment Advisor, 708-216-3751, Fax: 708-216-9555, E-mail: atopalova@luc.edu.
Website: http://www.luc.edu/nursing/

Loyola University New Orleans, College of Nursing and Health, School of Nursing, New Orleans, LA 70118. Offers family nurse practitioner (DNP); nursing (MSN). *Accreditation:* AACN; ACEN. *Program availability:* Part-time, evening/weekend, online learning. *Faculty:* 13 full-time (10 women), 5 part-time/adjunct (all women). *Students:* 35 full-time (all women), 265 part-time (245 women); includes 102 minority (69 Black or African American, non-Hispanic/Latino; 2 American Indian or Alaska Native, non-Hispanic/Latino; 12 Asian, non-Hispanic/Latino; 15 Hispanic/Latino; 2 Native Hawaiian or other Pacific Islander, non-Hispanic/Latino; 2 Two or more races, non-Hispanic/Latino). Average age 41. 191 applicants, 54% accepted, 83 enrolled. In 2017, 126 master's, 20 doctorates awarded. *Degree requirements:* For master's, practicum; for doctorate, capstone project. *Entrance requirements:* For master's, BSN, unencumbered RN license, 1 year of work experience in clinical nursing, interview, resume, 3 recommendations, statement of purpose. Additional exam requirements/recommendations for international students: Recommended—TOEFL (minimum score 550 paper-based; 79 iBT), IELTS. *Application deadline:* For fall admission, 8/1 priority date for domestic and international students; for winter admission, 12/15 priority date for domestic and international students; for spring admission, 5/15 priority date for domestic and international students. Applications are processed on a rolling basis. Application fee: $40. Electronic applications accepted. *Expenses:* $818 per hour tuition; $738 per semester full-time fees, $376.50 part-time. *Financial support:* Traineeships and Incumbent Workers Training Program grants available. Financial award application deadline: 5/1; financial award applicants required to submit FAFSA. *Faculty research:* Increasing compliance with treatment, patient satisfaction with care provided by nurse practitioners. *Unit head:* Dr. Laurie Ann Ferguson, Interim Director, 504-865-2880, Fax: 504-865-3254, E-mail: nursing@loyno.edu. *Application contact:* Elizabeth Wadsworth, Executive Assistant to the Director, 504-865-2307, Fax: 504-865-3254, E-mail: edwadswo@loyno.edu.
Website: http://gps.loyno.edu/nursing

Madonna University, Program in Nursing, Livonia, MI 48150-1173. Offers adult health: chronic health conditions (MSN); adult nurse practitioner (MSN); nursing administration (MSN); MSN/MSBA. *Accreditation:* AACN. *Program availability:* Part-time. *Degree requirements:* For master's, thesis or alternative. *Entrance requirements:* For master's, GRE General Test, Michigan nursing license. Electronic applications accepted. *Faculty research:* Coping, caring.

Malone University, Graduate Program in Nursing, Canton, OH 44709. Offers family nurse practitioner (MSN). *Accreditation:* AACN. *Program availability:* Part-time, evening/weekend. *Degree requirements:* For master's, thesis. *Entrance requirements:* For master's, minimum GPA of 3.0 from BSN program, interview, Ohio RN license. Additional exam requirements/recommendations for international students: Required—TOEFL (minimum score 550 paper-based; 79 iBT). *Expenses:* Contact institution. *Faculty research:* Home heath care and geriatrics, community settings, culture, Hispanics, tuberculosis, geriatrics, Neuman Systems Model, nursing education.

Mansfield University of Pennsylvania, Graduate Studies, Program in Nursing, Mansfield, PA 16933. Offers MSN. *Accreditation:* ACEN. *Program availability:* Part-time, evening/weekend, online learning. *Degree requirements:* For master's, comprehensive exam, thesis optional. *Entrance requirements:* For master's, minimum GPA of 3.0. Additional exam requirements/recommendations for international students: Required—TOEFL (minimum score 550 paper-based). Electronic applications accepted. *Faculty research:* Women's health, gyniatrics, art therapy, nursing empowerment.

Marian University, Leighton School of Nursing, Indianapolis, IN 46222-1997. Offers family nurse practitioner (DNP); nurse anesthesia (DNP); nursing education (MSN).

Program availability: Part-time. *Faculty:* 6 full-time (all women), 2 part-time/adjunct (both women). *Students:* 23 full-time (20 women), 1 (woman) part-time; includes 7 minority (5 Black or African American, non-Hispanic/Latino; 1 Asian, non-Hispanic/Latino; 1 Hispanic/Latino). Average age 36. 69 applicants, 35% accepted, 5 enrolled. *Degree requirements:* For master's, 38 credits, designed to be completed in 2 years; 225-hour practicum including a culminating project; for doctorate, 70 credit hours (for family nurse practitioner track); 85 credits (for nurse anesthesia track); minimum of 1000 hours of supervised practice. *Entrance requirements:* For master's, degree in nursing from NLNAC- or CCNE-accredited program; current, valid RN license in State of Indiana; minimum undergraduate GPA of 3.0; 3 recommendations; interview with admissions committee; current resume; 500-word essay describing career goals; for doctorate, BSN from NSNAC- or CCNE-accredited program; minimum undergraduate GPA of 3.0; cureent, valid RN license; current resume or curriculum vitae; 500-word essay addressing career goals; 3 letters of recommendation; interview with Admissions Committee. Additional exam requirements/recommendations for international students: Required—TOEFL (minimum score 550 paper-based; 79 iBT). *Application deadline:* For fall admission, 2/15 for domestic and international students. Applications are processed on a rolling basis. Application fee: $40. Electronic applications accepted. Application fee is waived when completed online. *Expenses:* Contact institution. *Financial support:* Application deadline: 4/15; applicants required to submit FAFSA. *Unit head:* Dr. Dorothy A. Gomez, RN, Dean, 317-955-6159, E-mail: dgomez@marian.edu. *Application contact:* Bryan Moody, Executive Director of Graduate Admission, 317-955-6284, E-mail: bmoody@marian.edu.
Website: http://www.marian.edu/school-of-nursing

Marian University, School of Nursing and Health Professions, Fond du Lac, WI 54935-4699. Offers adult nurse practitioner (MSN); nurse educator (MSN); thanatology (MS). *Accreditation:* AACN. *Program availability:* Part-time, evening/weekend. *Degree requirements:* For master's, thesis, 675 clinical practicum hours. *Entrance requirements:* For master's, 3 letters of professional recommendation; undergraduate work in nursing research, statistics, health assessment. Additional exam requirements/recommendations for international students: Required—TOEFL (minimum score 525 paper-based; 70 iBT). Electronic applications accepted. *Expenses:* Contact institution.

Marquette University, Graduate School, College of Nursing, Milwaukee, WI 53201-1881. Offers acute care nurse practitioner (Certificate); adult clinical nurse specialist (Certificate); adult nurse practitioner (Certificate); advanced practice nursing (MSN, DNP), including adult-older adult acute care (DNP), adults (MSN), adults-older adults (DNP), clinical nurse leader (MSN), health care systems leadership (DNP), nurse-midwifery (MSN), older adults (MSN), pediatrics-acute care, pediatrics-primary care, primary care (DNP), systems leadership and healthcare quality (MSN); family nurse practitioner (Certificate); nurse-midwifery (Certificate); nursing (PhD); pediatric acute care (Certificate); pediatric primary care (Certificate); systems leadership and healthcare quality (Certificate). *Accreditation:* AACN. Terminal master's awarded for partial completion of doctoral program. *Degree requirements:* For master's, comprehensive exam, thesis or alternative. *Entrance requirements:* For master's, GRE General Test, BSN, Wisconsin RN license, official transcripts from all current and previous colleges/universities except Marquette, three completed recommendation forms, resume, written statement of professional goals; for doctorate, GRE General Test, official transcripts from all current and previous colleges/universities except Marquette, three letters of recommendation, resume, written statement of professional goals, sample of scholarly writing. Additional exam requirements/recommendations for international students: Required—TOEFL (minimum score 530 paper-based). Electronic applications accepted. *Faculty research:* Psychosocial adjustment to chronic illness, gerontology, reminiscence, health policy: uninsured and access, hospital care delivery systems.

Marshall University, Academic Affairs Division, College of Health Professions, Department of Nursing, Huntington, WV 25755. Offers MSN, Certificate. *Students:* 8 full-time (all women), 106 part-time (96 women); includes 5 minority (2 Black or African American, non-Hispanic/Latino; 1 American Indian or Alaska Native, non-Hispanic/Latino; 1 Asian, non-Hispanic/Latino; 1 Hispanic/Latino). Average age 32. In 2017, 35 master's awarded. *Entrance requirements:* For master's, GRE General Test. Application fee: $40. *Unit head:* Dr. Diana Stotts, Associate Dean, 304-696-2623, E-mail: stotts@marshall.edu. *Application contact:* Information Contact, 304-746-1900, Fax: 304-746-1902, E-mail: services@marshall.edu.

Marymount University, Malek School of Health Professions, Program in Nursing, Arlington, VA 22207-4299. Offers family nurse practitioner (MSN, Certificate); nursing (DNP). *Accreditation:* AACN. *Program availability:* Part-time, evening/weekend. *Faculty:* 7 full-time (all women), 2 part-time/adjunct (both women). *Students:* 20 full-time (19 women), 43 part-time (40 women); includes 29 minority (18 Black or African American, non-Hispanic/Latino; 6 Asian, non-Hispanic/Latino; 4 Hispanic/Latino; 1 Two or more races, non-Hispanic/Latino), 2 international. Average age 38. 34 applicants, 56% accepted, 13 enrolled. In 2017, 21 master's, 1 doctorate, 3 other advanced degrees awarded. *Degree requirements:* For master's, comprehensive exam, clinical practicum; for doctorate, thesis/dissertation, research presentation/residency. *Entrance requirements:* For master's, 2 letters of recommendation, interview, resume, RN license, personal statement, minimum GPA of 3.0; for doctorate, 2 letters of recommendation, interview, resume, RN license, minimum MSN GPA of 3.5 or BSN 3.3, APN certification, personal statement; for Certificate, interview, master's degree in nursing with minimum of GPA of 3.3, current RN licensure. Additional exam requirements/recommendations for international students: Required—TOEFL (minimum score 600 paper-based; 96 iBT), IELTS (minimum score 6.5). *Application deadline:* For fall admission, 3/1 priority date for domestic and international students; for spring admission, 11/1 priority date for domestic and international students. Application fee: $40. Electronic applications accepted. *Expenses: Tuition:* Full-time $17,550; part-time $975 per credit hour. *Required fees:* $198; $11 per credit hour. One-time fee: $250. Tuition and fees vary according to program. *Financial support:* In 2017–18, 4 students received support, including 1 teaching assistantship with full and partial tuition reimbursement available (averaging $5,850 per year); career-related internships or fieldwork, Federal Work-Study, scholarships/grants, and unspecified assistantships also available. Support available to part-time students. Financial award application deadline: 3/1; financial award applicants required to submit FAFSA. *Unit head:* Colleen Sanders, Program Director, 703-284-6886, Fax: 703-284-3819, E-mail: colleen.sanders@marymount.edu. *Application contact:* Francesca Reed, Director, Graduate Admissions, 703-284-5901, Fax: 703-527-3815, E-mail: grad.admissions@marymount.edu.
Website: http://www.marymount.edu/Academics/Malek-School-of-Health-Professions/Graduate-Programs/Nursing-(M-S-N-)

Maryville University of Saint Louis, Myrtle E. and Earl E. Walker College of Health Professions, The Catherine McAuley School of Nursing, St. Louis, MO 63141-7299. Offers acute care nurse practitioner (MSN); adult gerontology nurse practitioner (MSN); advanced practice nursing (DNP); family nurse practitioner (MSN); pediatric nurse practitioner (MSN). *Accreditation:* AACN. *Program availability:* 100% online, blended/hybrid learning. *Faculty:* 15 full-time (all women), 142 part-time/adjunct (123 women). *Students:* 49 full-time (42 women), 2,999 part-time (2,645 women); includes 773 minority (375 Black or African American, non-Hispanic/Latino; 51 American Indian or Alaska Native, non-Hispanic/Latino; 135 Asian, non-Hispanic/Latino; 149 Hispanic/Latino; 63 Two or more races, non-Hispanic/Latino), 21 international. Average age 36. In 2017, 843 master's, 42 doctorates awarded. *Degree requirements:* For master's, practicum. *Entrance requirements:* For master's, BSN, current licensure, minimum GPA of 3.0, 3 letters of recommendation, curriculum vitae. Additional exam requirements/recommendations for international students: Required—TOEFL (minimum score 550 paper-based). *Application deadline:* Applications are processed on a rolling basis. Electronic applications accepted. *Expenses:* Contact institution. *Financial support:* Federal Work-Study and campus employment available. Support available to part-time students. Financial award application deadline: 4/1; financial award applicants required to submit FAFSA. *Unit head:* Dr. Elizabeth Buck, Assistant Dean/Director of Online Nursing, 314-529-9453, Fax: 314-529-9139, E-mail: ebuck@maryville.edu. *Application contact:* Jeannie DeLuca, Director of Admissions and Advising, 314-929-9355, Fax: 314-529-9927, E-mail: cjacobsmeyer@maryville.edu.
Website: http://www.maryville.edu/hp/nursing/

McGill University, Faculty of Graduate and Postdoctoral Studies, Faculty of Medicine, School of Nursing, Montréal, QC H3A 2T5, Canada. Offers nurse practitioner (Graduate Diploma); nursing (M Sc A, PhD). PhD offered jointly with Université du Québec à Montréal.

McKendree University, Graduate Programs, Master of Science in Nursing Program, Lebanon, IL 62254-1299. Offers nursing education (MSN); nursing management/administration (MSN). *Accreditation:* AACN. *Program availability:* Part-time, evening/weekend, online learning. *Degree requirements:* For master's, research project or thesis. *Entrance requirements:* For master's, resume, references, valid Professional Registered Nurse license. Additional exam requirements/recommendations for international students: Required—TOEFL. Electronic applications accepted.

McMaster University, Faculty of Health Sciences and School of Graduate Studies, Program in Nursing (course-based), Hamilton, ON L8S 4M2, Canada. Offers M Sc. *Degree requirements:* For master's, scholarly paper. *Entrance requirements:* For master's, 4 year honors BSCN, minimum B+ average in last 60 units. Additional exam requirements/recommendations for international students: Required—TOEFL (minimum score 580 paper-based; 92 iBT).

McMaster University, Faculty of Health Sciences and School of Graduate Studies, Program in Nursing (thesis), Hamilton, ON L8S 4M2, Canada. Offers M Sc, PhD. *Degree requirements:* For master's, thesis; for doctorate, comprehensive exam, thesis/dissertation. *Entrance requirements:* For master's, honors B Sc N, B+ average in last 60 units; for doctorate, M Sc, minimum B+ average. Additional exam requirements/recommendations for international students: Required—TOEFL (minimum score 580 paper-based; 92 iBT).

McMurry University, Graduate Studies, Abilene, TX 79697. Offers education (MSN); family nurse practitioner (MSN).

McNeese State University, Doré School of Graduate Studies, College of Nursing and Health Professions, Lake Charles, LA 70609. Offers MSN, PMC. *Accreditation:* AACN. *Entrance requirements:* For master's, GRE, eligibility for unencumbered licensure as RN in Louisiana. *Application deadline:* For fall admission, 5/15 priority date for domestic and international students; for spring admission, 10/15 priority date for domestic and international students. Applications are processed on a rolling basis. Application fee: $20 ($30 for international students). *Financial support:* Application deadline: 5/1. *Unit head:* Dr. Peggy L. Wolfe, Dean, 337-475-5820, Fax: 337-475-5924, E-mail: pwolfe@mcneese.edu. *Application contact:* Dr. Ann Warner, Co-Coordinator, 337-475-5831, Fax: 337-475-5702, E-mail: awarner@mcneese.edu.
Website: http://www.mcneese.edu/nursing

MCPHS University, Graduate Studies, Program in Nursing, Boston, MA 02115-5896. Offers MS. *Accreditation:* AACN. *Program availability:* Part-time, online learning. *Entrance requirements:* For master's, BSN. Additional exam requirements/recommendations for international students: Required—TOEFL (minimum score 550 paper-based; 79 iBT). Electronic applications accepted.

Medical University of South Carolina, College of Nursing, PhD in Nursing Program, Charleston, SC 29425. Offers PhD. *Accreditation:* AACN. *Program availability:* Part-time, online learning. *Degree requirements:* For doctorate, comprehensive exam, thesis/dissertation, mentored teaching and research seminar. *Entrance requirements:* For doctorate, BSN or MSN from accredited ACEN or CCNE program, minimum GPA of 3.5, documentation of RN license from state of residence, curriculum vitae, personal statement, 3 references, interview, evidence of computer literacy. Additional exam requirements/recommendations for international students: Required—TOEFL (minimum score 550 paper-based; 80 iBT). Electronic applications accepted. *Faculty research:* Rare diseases, vascular ulcer prevention, health disparities, community engagement, health services.

Medical University of South Carolina, College of Nursing, Post-MSN Doctor of Nursing Practice Program, Charleston, SC 29425. Offers advanced practice nursing (DNP). *Accreditation:* AACN. *Program availability:* Part-time, online learning. *Degree requirements:* For doctorate, final project. *Entrance requirements:* For doctorate, BSN and MSN from nationally-accredited program, minimum cumulative GPA of 3.0 for undergraduate and graduate coursework, active APRN License and specialty certification, 3 confidential references, current curriculum vitae or resume, statement of goals. Additional exam requirements/recommendations for international students: Required—TOEFL (minimum score 550 paper-based; 80 iBT). Electronic applications accepted. *Faculty research:* Women's health cardiovascular, hospital roles, HPV, guidelines implementation, adolescent family obesity.

Memorial University of Newfoundland, School of Graduate Studies, School of Nursing, St. John's, NL A1C 5S7, Canada. Offers MN, PhD. *Program availability:* Part-time. *Degree requirements:* For master's, thesis optional. *Entrance requirements:* For master's, bachelor's degree in nursing, 1 year of experience in nursing practice, practicing license. Electronic applications accepted. *Faculty research:* Women's health, infant feeding practices, nursing management, care of the elderly, children's health.

Mercer University, Graduate Studies, Cecil B. Day Campus, Georgia Baptist College of Nursing, Atlanta, GA 30341. Offers adult gerontology acute care nurse practitioner (MSN, Certificate); family nurse practitioner (MSN, Certificate); nursing (PhD); nursing practice (DNP), including adult gerontology acute care nurse practitioner. *Accreditation:* AACN. *Program availability:* Part-time, blended/hybrid learning. *Faculty:* 10 full-time (9 women), 4 part-time/adjunct (3 women). *Students:* 72 full-time (70 women), 33 part-time (29 women); includes 44 minority (29 Black or African American, non-Hispanic/Latino; 9 Asian, non-Hispanic/Latino; 3 Hispanic/Latino; 3 Two or more races, non-Hispanic/Latino), 1 international. Average age 36. 65 applicants, 66% accepted, 30 enrolled. In 2017, 27 master's, 9 doctorates awarded. *Degree requirements:* For master's, thesis or alternative, capstone; for doctorate, comprehensive exam (for some programs), scholarly project (for DNP); dissertation (for PhD). *Entrance requirements:* For master's, MAT or GRE, bachelor's degree from accredited nursing program, registered unencumbered GA nursing license, essay, three professional references; for doctorate, GRE (for PhD), master's degree from accredited nursing program, RN licensure, graduate statistics course, three professional references. Additional exam requirements/recommendations for international students: Required—TOEFL (minimum score 100

iBT). *Application deadline:* For fall admission, 5/1 for domestic students, 3/1 for international students; for winter admission, 11/1 for domestic students, 9/1 for international students; for spring admission, 11/1 for domestic students, 10/1 for international students; for summer admission, 3/1 for domestic and international students. Applications are processed on a rolling basis. Application fee: $50. Electronic applications accepted. *Expenses:* $32,000. *Financial support:* In 2017–18, 23 students received support, including 1 research assistantship (averaging $6,000 per year); scholarships/grants also available. Financial award application deadline: 6/30; financial award applicants required to submit FAFSA. *Faculty research:* Cognitive competence, cancer survivorship, interprofessional education, cultural competence, clopidogrel adherence, high fidelity simulation, self-awareness practices, simulation. *Unit head:* Dr. Linda Streit, Dean/Professor, 678-547-6793, Fax: 678-547-6796, E-mail: streit_la@mercer.edu. *Application contact:* Janda Anderson, Director of Admissions, 678-547-6700, Fax: 678-547-6794, E-mail: anderson_j@mercer.edu.
Website: http://www.mercer.edu/nursing

Mercy College, School of Health and Natural Sciences, Programs in Nursing, Dobbs Ferry, NY 10522-1189. Offers nursing administration (MS); nursing education (MS). *Accreditation:* AACN. *Program availability:* Part-time, evening/weekend, blended/hybrid learning. *Students:* 4 full-time (all women), 136 part-time (128 women); includes 83 minority (54 Black or African American, non-Hispanic/Latino; 14 Asian, non-Hispanic/Latino; 12 Hispanic/Latino; 3 Native Hawaiian or other Pacific Islander, non-Hispanic/Latino). Average age 33. 80 applicants, 70% accepted, 38 enrolled. In 2017, 42 master's awarded. *Degree requirements:* For master's, comprehensive exam (for some programs), written comprehensive exam or the production of a comprehensive project. *Entrance requirements:* For master's, interview, two letters of reference, bachelor's degree, RN registration in the U.S. Additional exam requirements/recommendations for international students: Required—TOEFL (minimum score 600 paper-based; 100 iBT), IELTS (minimum score 8). *Application deadline:* For fall admission, 8/1 for international students. Applications are processed on a rolling basis. Application fee: $62. Electronic applications accepted. *Expenses: Tuition:* Full-time $15,426; part-time $857 per credit hour. *Required fees:* $630; $158 per term. Tuition and fees vary according to course load, degree level and program. *Financial support:* Career-related internships or fieldwork, Federal Work-Study, scholarships/grants, and unspecified assistantships available. Support available to part-time students. Financial award applicants required to submit FAFSA. *Unit head:* Dr. Joan Toglia, Dean, School of Health and Natural Sciences, 914-674-7837, E-mail: jtoglia@mercy.edu. *Application contact:* Allison Gurdineer, Senior Director of Admissions, 877-637-2946, Fax: 914-674-7382, E-mail: admissions@mercy.edu.
Website: https://www.mercy.edu/health-and-natural-sciences/graduate

Mercy College of Ohio, Program in Nursing, Toledo, OH 43604. Offers MSN. *Program availability:* Part-time-only, online only. *Students:* 12 part-time (11 women). *Entrance requirements:* For master's, degree in nursing at bachelor's level or higher from regionally-accredited institution and professionally-accredited (ACEN or CCNE) program; minimum overall GPA of 3.0 on undergraduate and graduate course work; proof of active RN license with no restrictions. Application fee: $50. Electronic applications accepted. *Expenses: Tuition:* Part-time $600 per credit hour. *Required fees:* $450 per semester. One-time fee: $250 part-time. *Financial support:* Applicants required to submit FAFSA. *Unit head:* Deborah Karns, MSN Program Director, 419-251-1718, E-mail: deborah.karns@mercycollege.edu.
Website: https://www.mercycollege.edu/program/nursing-master-of-science

Metropolitan State University, College of Nursing and Health Sciences, St. Paul, MN 55106-5000. Offers advanced dental therapy (MS); leadership and management (MSN); nurse educator (MSN); nursing (DNP). *Accreditation:* AACN. *Program availability:* Part-time. *Degree requirements:* For master's, thesis or alternative; for doctorate, thesis/dissertation or alternative. *Entrance requirements:* For master's, GRE General Test, minimum GPA of 3.0, RN license, BS/BA; for doctorate, minimum GPA of 3.0, RN license, MSN. Additional exam requirements/recommendations for international students: Required—TOEFL (minimum score 550 paper-based). *Application deadline:* For fall admission, 1/15 for domestic and international students; for winter admission, 1/15 for international students. Application fee: $20. *Expenses:* Tuition, state resident: part-time $388.55 per credit. Tuition, nonresident: part-time $777.11 per credit. *Required fees:* $35.11 per credit. Part-time tuition and fees vary according to campus/location and program. *Financial support:* Fellowships, career-related internships or fieldwork, Federal Work-Study, institutionally sponsored loans, and traineeships available. Financial award applicants required to submit FAFSA. *Faculty research:* Women's health, gerontology.
Website: https://www.metrostate.edu/academics/nursing-and-health-sciences

MGH Institute of Health Professions, School of Nursing, Boston, MA 02129. Offers advanced practice nursing (MSN); gerontological nursing (MSN); nursing (DNP); pediatric nursing (MSN); psychiatric nursing (MSN); teaching and learning for health care education (Certificate); women's health nursing (MSN). *Accreditation:* AACN. *Degree requirements:* For master's, thesis or alternative. *Entrance requirements:* For master's, GRE General Test, bachelor's degree from regionally-accredited college or university. Additional exam requirements/recommendations for international students: Required—TOEFL (minimum score 550 paper-based; 80 iBT). Electronic applications accepted. *Faculty research:* Biobehavioral nursing, HIV/AIDS, gerontological nursing, women's health, vulnerable populations, health systems.

Miami Regional University, School of Nursing and Health Sciences, Miami Springs, FL 33166. Offers nursing (MSN); nursing education (MSN); nursing leadership (MSN).

Michigan State University, The Graduate School, College of Nursing, East Lansing, MI 48824. Offers MSN, PhD. *Accreditation:* AACN; AANA/CANAEP. *Program availability:* Part-time, online learning. *Entrance requirements:* Additional exam requirements/recommendations for international students: Required—TOEFL (minimum score 580 paper-based), Michigan State University ELT (minimum score 85), Michigan English Language Assessment Battery (minimum score 83). Electronic applications accepted. *Faculty research:* Hormone replacement therapy, end of life research, human-animal bond, chronic disease, family home care for cancer.

MidAmerica Nazarene University, School of Nursing and Health Science, Olathe, KS 66062. Offers healthcare administration (MSN); healthcare quality management (MSN); nursing education (MSN); public health (MSN); MSN/MBA. *Accreditation:* AACN. *Program availability:* Part-time, evening/weekend, 100% online, blended/hybrid learning. *Entrance requirements:* For master's, BSN, minimum GPA of 3.0, active unencumbered RN license, undergraduate statistics course. Additional exam requirements/recommendations for international students: Required—TOEFL. Electronic applications accepted. *Expenses:* Contact institution. *Faculty research:* Technology in education, minority recruitment and retention in nursing programs, faculty views and attitudes on culturally competency, innovative nursing program development, spirituality and holistic health.

Middle Tennessee State University, College of Graduate Studies, College of Behavioral and Health Sciences, School of Nursing, Murfreesboro, TN 37132. Offers MSN, Graduate Certificate. *Program availability:* Part-time, evening/weekend, online learning. *Entrance requirements:* Additional exam requirements/recommendations for international students: Required—TOEFL (minimum score 525 paper-based; 71 iBT) or IELTS (minimum score 6). Electronic applications accepted.

Midwestern State University, Billie Doris McAda Graduate School, Robert D. and Carol Gunn College of Health Sciences and Human Services, Wilson School of Nursing, Wichita Falls, TX 76308. Offers family nurse practitioner (MSN); family psychiatric mental health nurse practitioner (MSN); nurse educator (MSN). *Accreditation:* AACN. *Program availability:* Part-time, evening/weekend. *Degree requirements:* For master's, comprehensive exam, thesis optional. *Entrance requirements:* For master's, GRE General Test or MAT. Additional exam requirements/recommendations for international students: Required—TOEFL (minimum score 550 paper-based). Electronic applications accepted. *Faculty research:* Infant feeding, musculoskeletal disorders, diabetes, community health education, water quality reporting.

Millersville University of Pennsylvania, College of Graduate Studies and Adult Learning, College of Science and Technology, Department of Nursing, Program in Nursing Practice, Millersville, PA 17551-0302. Offers DNP. *Program availability:* Part-time-only, evening/weekend, blended/hybrid learning. *Faculty:* 5 full-time (all women), 8 part-time/adjunct (7 women). *Students:* 3 part-time (2 women). Average age 38. *Degree requirements:* For doctorate, thesis/dissertation, scholarly project, clinical hours. *Entrance requirements:* For doctorate, current RN license, goal statement, 3- to 5-page writing sample (APA 6th Ed.) defining a specific issue or problem in nursing practices, current resume/curriculum vitae, verification of MSN clinical hours, MSN or MPH with minimum GPA of 3.5. Additional exam requirements/recommendations for international students: Required—TOEFL (minimum score 80 iBT), IELTS (minimum score 6.5), PTE (minimum score 60). *Application deadline:* For summer admission, 3/1 priority date for domestic students. Applications are processed on a rolling basis. Application fee: $40. Electronic applications accepted. *Expenses:* $550 per credit resident tuition, $825 per credit non-resident tuition; $115 fees. *Financial support:* Unspecified assistantships available. Financial award application deadline: 3/15; financial award applicants required to submit FAFSA. *Faculty research:* Family nurse practitioner, nurse education, primary care, health promotion, health administration, health technology. *Unit head:* Dr. Kelly A. Kuhns, Chairperson and DNP Coordinator, 717-871-5276, Fax: 717-871-4877, E-mail: kelly.kuhns@millersville.edu. *Application contact:* Dr. Victor S. DeSantis, Dean of College of Graduate Studies and Adult Learning/Associate Provost for Civic and Community Engagement, 717-871-7619, Fax: 717-871-7954, E-mail: victor.desantis@millersville.edu.
Website: http://www.millersville.edu/nursing/dnp.php

Millikin University, School of Nursing, Decatur, IL 62522-2084. Offers entry into nursing practice (MSN); family nurse practitioner (DNP); nurse anesthesia (DNP); nurse educator (MSN). *Accreditation:* AACN. *Program availability:* Part-time. *Faculty:* 19 full-time (17 women), 7 part-time/adjunct (6 women). *Students:* 42 full-time (30 women), 20 part-time (17 women); includes 12 minority (8 Black or African American, non-Hispanic/Latino; 2 Asian, non-Hispanic/Latino; 2 Hispanic/Latino). Average age 30. 114 applicants, 36% accepted, 23 enrolled. In 2017, 3 master's, 13 doctorates awarded. *Degree requirements:* For master's, thesis or alternative, scholarly project; for doctorate, thesis/dissertation or alternative, scholarly project. *Entrance requirements:* For master's, GRE (if undergraduate cumulative GPA is below 3.0 for nurse educator, 3.25 for entry into nursing practice), official academic transcript(s), written statement, resume/vitae, 3 letters of recommendation, RN license; for doctorate, GRE (if undergraduate cumulative GPA is below 3.0), official academic transcript(s), written statement, resume/vitae, 3 letters of recommendation, RN or APRN license. Additional exam requirements/recommendations for international students: Required—TOEFL (minimum score 550 paper-based; 79 iBT), IELTS (minimum score 6.5). *Application deadline:* For spring admission, 7/1 priority date for domestic and international students; for summer admission, 11/1 priority date for domestic and international students. Applications are processed on a rolling basis. Application fee: $0. Electronic applications accepted. *Expenses:* $832 per credit hour (for MSN); $950 per credit hour (for DNP). *Financial support:* Traineeships and unspecified assistantships available. Financial award applicants required to submit FAFSA. *Faculty research:* Quality of life, teaching/learning strategies, clinical simulation. *Unit head:* Dr. Pamela Lindsey, Director, 217-424-6348, Fax: 217-420-6731, E-mail: plindsey@millikin.edu. *Application contact:* Bonnie Niemeyer, Administrative Assistant, 800-373-7733 Ext. 5034, Fax: 217-420-6731, E-mail: bniemeyer@millikin.edu.
Website: http://www.millikin.edu/grad-nursing

Minnesota State University Mankato, College of Graduate Studies and Research, College of Allied Health and Nursing, School of Nursing, Mankato, MN 56001. Offers family nurse practitioner (MSN), including family nurse practitioner; nurse educator (MSN); nursing (DNP). *Accreditation:* AACN. *Degree requirements:* For master's, comprehensive exam, internships, research project or thesis; for doctorate, capstone project. *Entrance requirements:* For master's, GRE General Test or on-campus essay, minimum GPA of 3.0 during previous 2 years, BSN or equivalent references; for doctorate, master's degree in nursing. Additional exam requirements/recommendations for international students: Required—TOEFL. Electronic applications accepted. *Faculty research:* Psychosocial nursing, computers in nursing, family adaptation.

Minnesota State University Moorhead, Graduate Studies, College of Science, Health and the Environment, Moorhead, MN 56563. Offers healthcare administration (MHA); nursing (MS); school psychology (MS, Psy S). *Program availability:* Part-time. *Faculty:* 24. *Students:* 34 full-time (25 women), 104 part-time (84 women). Average age 32. 42 applicants, 74% accepted. In 2017, 34 master's, 11 other advanced degrees awarded. *Degree requirements:* For master's, comprehensive exam (for some programs), thesis, final oral defense. *Entrance requirements:* For master's, GRE (for school psychology program), minimum GPA of 3.0, essay, letters of reference. Additional exam requirements/recommendations for international students: Required—TOEFL (minimum score 550 paper-based). *Application deadline:* Applications are processed on a rolling basis. Application fee: $20. Electronic applications accepted. *Expenses:* Tuition, state resident: full-time $9000; part-time $374 per credit. Tuition, nonresident: full-time $18,000; part-time $748 per credit. *Required fees:* $1055; $43.96 per credit. Tuition and fees vary according to degree level, program and reciprocity agreements. *Financial support:* Federal Work-Study and unspecified assistantships available. Financial award application deadline: 10/1; financial award applicants required to submit FAFSA. *Unit head:* Dr. Jeffrey Bodwin, Dean, 218-477-5892, E-mail: jeffrey.bodwin@mnstate.edu. *Application contact:* Karla Wenger, Graduate Studies Office Manager, 218-477-2344, Fax: 218-477-2482, E-mail: wengerk@mnstate.edu.
Website: http://www.mnstate.edu/cshe/

Misericordia University, College of Health Sciences and Education, Department of Nursing, Dallas, PA 18612-1098. Offers MSN, DNP. *Accreditation:* AACN. *Program availability:* Part-time, evening/weekend, blended/hybrid learning. *Degree requirements:* For master's, thesis optional, practicum. *Entrance requirements:* For master's, interview, minimum GPA of 3.0; for doctorate, official transcripts of all previous college work, MSN from CCNE- or ACEN-accredited institution, copy of unencumbered RN license, license to practice as an advanced practice nurse, minimum graduate GPA of 3.0, two letters of reference, 500-word statement/writing sample of personal and professional goals, telephone interview. Additional exam requirements/recommendations for international students: Required—TOEFL. Electronic applications accepted. *Expenses:* Contact institution. *Faculty research:* Quality of life, maternal-child, spirituality, critical thinking, adult health.

Nursing—General

Mississippi University for Women, Graduate School, College of Nursing and Health Sciences, Columbus, MS 39701-9998. Offers nursing (MSN, DNP, PMC); public health education (MPH); speech-language pathology (MS). *Accreditation:* AACN; ASHA. *Program availability:* Part-time. *Degree requirements:* For master's, comprehensive exam, thesis. *Entrance requirements:* For master's, GRE General Test, bachelor's degree in nursing, previous course work in statistics, proficiency in English.

Missouri Southern State University, Program in Nursing, Joplin, MO 64801-1595. Offers MSN. Program offered jointly with University of Missouri–Kansas City. *Accreditation:* AACN. *Program availability:* Part-time. *Entrance requirements:* For master's, minimum cumulative GPA of 3.2 for the last 60 hours of the BSN program, resume, RN licensure, CPR certification, course work in statistics and health assessment. Electronic applications accepted.

Missouri State University, Graduate College, College of Health and Human Services, Department of Nursing, Springfield, MO 65897. Offers nursing (MSN), including family nurse practitioner, nurse educator; nursing practice (DNP). *Accreditation:* AACN. *Program availability:* 100% online, blended/hybrid learning. *Faculty:* 9 full-time (all women), 16 part-time/adjunct (13 women). *Students:* 30 full-time (26 women), 47 part-time (41 women); includes 13 minority (6 Black or African American, non-Hispanic/Latino; 1 American Indian or Alaska Native, non-Hispanic/Latino; 3 Asian, non-Hispanic/Latino; 1 Native Hawaiian or other Pacific Islander, non-Hispanic/Latino; 2 Two or more races, non-Hispanic/Latino). Average age 27. 12 applicants, 33% accepted, 1 enrolled. In 2017, 6 master's, 16 doctorates awarded. *Degree requirements:* For master's, comprehensive exam, thesis or alternative. *Entrance requirements:* For master's, GRE General Test, minimum GPA of 3.0, RN license (for MSN), 1 year of work experience (for MPH). Additional exam requirements/recommendations for international students: Required—TOEFL (minimum score 550 paper-based; 79 iBT), IELTS (minimum score 6). *Application deadline:* For fall admission, 12/1 priority date for domestic students, 5/1 for international students. Applications are processed on a rolling basis. Application fee: $35 ($50 for international students). Electronic applications accepted. *Expenses:* Tuition, state resident: full-time $2915; part-time $2021 per credit hour. Tuition, nonresident: full-time $5354; part-time $3647 per credit hour. *International tuition:* $11,992 full-time. *Required fees:* $173; $173 per credit hour. Tuition and fees vary according to class time, course level, course load, degree level, campus/location and program. *Financial support:* In 2017–18, 2 teaching assistantships with partial tuition reimbursements (averaging $8,772 per year) were awarded; Federal Work-Study, institutionally sponsored loans, scholarships/grants, and unspecified assistantships also available. Financial award application deadline: 3/31; financial award applicants required to submit FAFSA. *Faculty research:* Preconceptual health, women's health, nursing satisfaction, nursing education. *Unit head:* Dr. Stephen Stapleton, Department Head, 417-836-5310, Fax: 417-836-5484, E-mail: nursing@missouristate.edu. *Application contact:* Stephanie Praschan, Director, Graduate Enrollment Management, 417-836-5330, Fax: 417-836-6200, E-mail: stephaniepraschan@missouristate.edu.
Website: http://www.missouristate.edu/nursing/

Missouri Western State University, Program in Nursing, St. Joseph, MO 64507-2294. Offers health care leadership (MSN); nurse educator (MSN, Graduate Certificate). *Program availability:* Part-time. *Students:* 1 (woman) full-time, 40 part-time (38 women); includes 2 minority (1 Black or African American, non-Hispanic/Latino; 1 Hispanic/Latino), 2 international. Average age 36. 9 applicants, 100% accepted, 9 enrolled. In 2017, 8 master's awarded. *Entrance requirements:* For master's, minimum cumulative GPA of 2.75, statement of interest, current and unencumbered RN license. Additional exam requirements/recommendations for international students: Recommended—TOEFL (minimum score 79 iBT), IELTS (minimum score 6). *Application deadline:* For fall admission, 7/15 for domestic and international students; for spring admission, 10/1 for domestic and international students; for summer admission, 3/15 for domestic students. Applications are processed on a rolling basis. Application fee: $45 ($50 for international students). Electronic applications accepted. *Expenses:* Tuition, state resident: full-time $6391; part-time $336 per credit hour. Tuition, nonresident: full-time $11,483; part-time $604 per credit hour. *Required fees:* $542; $99 per credit hour. $176 per semester. One-time fee: $45. Tuition and fees vary according to course load and program. *Financial support:* Scholarships/grants and unspecified assistantships available. Support available to part-time students. *Unit head:* Dr. Carolyn Brose, Associate Professor, 816-271-5912, E-mail: brose@missouriwestern.edu. *Application contact:* Dr. Benjamin D. Caldwell, Dean of the Graduate School, 816-271-4394, Fax: 816-271-4525, E-mail: graduate@missouriwestern.edu.
Website: https://www.missouriwestern.edu/nursing/msn/

Molloy College, The Barbara H. Hagan School of Nursing, Rockville Centre, NY 11571-5002. Offers adult - gerontology nurse practitioner (MS); adult-gerontology clinical nurse specialist (DNP); adult-gerontology nurse practitioner (DNP); clinical nurse specialist: adult - gerontology (MS); family nurse practitioner (MS, DNP); family psychiatric/mental health nurse practitioner (MS, DNP); nursing (PhD, Advanced Certificate); nursing administration with informatics (MS); nursing education (MS); pediatric nurse practitioner (MS, DNP). *Accreditation:* AACN. *Program availability:* Part-time, evening/weekend. *Faculty:* 28 full-time (all women), 7 part-time/adjunct (6 women). *Students:* 19 full-time (14 women), 574 part-time (527 women); includes 336 minority (179 Black or African American, non-Hispanic/Latino; 2 American Indian or Alaska Native, non-Hispanic/Latino; 107 Asian, non-Hispanic/Latino; 42 Hispanic/Latino; 1 Native Hawaiian or other Pacific Islander, non-Hispanic/Latino; 5 Two or more races, non-Hispanic/Latino), 4 international. Average age 44. 292 applicants, 65% accepted, 147 enrolled. In 2017, 135 master's, 9 doctorates, 5 other advanced degrees awarded. *Degree requirements:* For master's, thesis optional. *Entrance requirements:* For master's, 3 letters of reference, BS in nursing, minimum undergraduate GPA of 3.0; for Advanced Certificate, 3 letters of reference, master's degree in nursing. Additional exam requirements/recommendations for international students: Required—TOEFL (minimum score 550 paper-based; 79 iBT). *Application deadline:* For fall admission, 9/2 priority date for domestic students; for spring admission, 1/20 priority date for domestic students. Applications are processed on a rolling basis. Application fee: $60. Electronic applications accepted. *Expenses: Tuition:* Full-time $19,980; part-time $1110 per credit. *Required fees:* $1040. Tuition and fees vary according to course load and degree level. *Financial support:* Research assistantships with partial tuition reimbursements, teaching assistantships with partial tuition reimbursements, institutionally sponsored loans, scholarships/grants, and unspecified assistantships available. Support available to part-time students. Financial award application deadline: 3/1; financial award applicants required to submit FAFSA. *Faculty research:* Workplace violence involving nurses and psychiatric patients; moral distress in nursing; primary care of veterans; the role of service immersion programs in graduate nursing education; academic integrity. *Unit head:* Dr. Marcia R. Gardner, Dean, The Barbara H. Hagan School of Nursing, 516-323-3651, E-mail: mgardner@molloy.edu. *Application contact:* Jaclyn Machowicz, Assistant Director for Admissions, 516-323-4010, E-mail: jmachowicz@molloy.edu.

Monmouth University, Graduate Studies, Marjorie K. Unterberg School of Nursing and Health Studies, West Long Branch, NJ 07764-1898. Offers adult-gerontological primary care nurse practitioner (MSN, Post-Master's Certificate); family nurse practitioner (MSN, Post-Master's Certificate); forensic nursing (MSN, Certificate); nursing (MSN); nursing administration (MSN); nursing education (MSN, Post-Master's Certificate); nursing practice (DNP); physician assistant (MS); psychiatric and mental health nurse practitioner (MSN, Post-Master's Certificate); school nursing (MSN, Certificate). *Accreditation:* AACN. *Program availability:* Part-time, evening/weekend, 100% online, blended/hybrid learning. *Faculty:* 12 full-time (all women), 20 part-time/adjunct (12 women). *Students:* 90 full-time (66 women), 329 part-time (302 women); includes 129 minority (51 Black or African American, non-Hispanic/Latino; 43 Asian, non-Hispanic/Latino; 31 Hispanic/Latino; 1 Native Hawaiian or other Pacific Islander, non-Hispanic/Latino; 3 Two or more races, non-Hispanic/Latino), 1 international. Average age 36. In 2017, 85 master's, 4 other advanced degrees awarded. *Degree requirements:* For master's, practicum (for some tracks); for doctorate, practicum, capstone course. *Entrance requirements:* For master's, GRE General Test (waived for MSN applicants with minimum B grade in each of the first four courses and for MS applicants with master's degree), BSN with minimum GPA of 2.75, current RN license, proof of liability and malpractice policy, personal statement, two letters of recommendation, college course work in health assessment, resume; CASPA application (for MS); for doctorate, accredited master's nursing program degree with minimum GPA of 3.2, active RN license, national certification as nurse practitioner or nurse administrator, working knowledge of statistics, statement of goals and vision for change, 2 letters of recommendation (professional or academic), resume, interview. Additional exam requirements/recommendations for international students: Required—TOEFL (minimum score 550 paper-based; 79 iBT), IELTS (minimum score 6) or Michigan English Language Assessment Battery (minimum score 77). *Application deadline:* For fall admission, 7/15 priority date for domestic students, 6/1 for international students; for spring admission, 12/1 priority date for domestic students, 11/1 for international students; for summer admission, 5/1 for domestic students. Applications are processed on a rolling basis. Application fee: $50. Electronic applications accepted. *Expenses:* Contact institution. *Financial support:* In 2017–18, 197 students received support. Institutionally sponsored loans, scholarships/grants, and unspecified assistantships available. Support available to part-time students. Financial award applicants required to submit FAFSA. *Faculty research:* School nursing, health policy, and smoking cessation in teens; Multiple Sclerosis; adherence and self-efficacy; aging issues and geriatric care. *Unit head:* Dr. Janet Mahoney, Dean, 732-571-3443, Fax: 732-263-5131, E-mail: jmahoney@monmouth.edu. *Application contact:* Lucia Fedele, Graduate Admission Counselor, 732-571-3452, Fax: 732-263-5123, E-mail: gradadm@monmouth.edu.
Website: https://www.monmouth.edu/graduate/nursing-programs-of-study/

Montana State University, The Graduate School, College of Nursing, Bozeman, MT 59717. Offers clinical nurse leader (MN); family and individual nurse practitioner (DNP); family nurse practitioner (MN, Post-Master's Certificate); nursing education (Certificate, Post-Master's Certificate); psychiatric mental health nurse practitioner (MN); psychiatric/mental health nurse practitioner (DNP). *Accreditation:* AACN. *Program availability:* Part-time, online learning. *Degree requirements:* For master's, comprehensive exam, thesis (for some programs); for doctorate, thesis/dissertation, 1,125 hours in clinical settings. *Entrance requirements:* For master's, GRE General Test, minimum GPA of 3.0 for undergraduate and post-baccalaureate work. Additional exam requirements/recommendations for international students: Required—TOEFL (minimum score 580 paper-based). Electronic applications accepted. *Faculty research:* Rural nursing, health disparities, environmental/public health, oral health, resilience.

Moravian College, Graduate and Continuing Studies, Helen S. Breidegam School of Nursing, Bethlehem, PA 18018-6650. Offers clinical nurse leader (MS); nurse administrator (MS); nurse educator (MS); nurse practitioner - acute care (MS); nurse practitioner - primary care (MS). *Accreditation:* AACN. *Program availability:* Part-time, evening/weekend. *Faculty:* 5 full-time (all women), 4 part-time/adjunct (2 women). *Students:* 4 full-time (all women), 64 part-time (60 women); includes 9 minority (3 Black or African American, non-Hispanic/Latino; 2 Asian, non-Hispanic/Latino; 4 Hispanic/Latino), 1 international. Average age 38. 34 applicants, 85% accepted, 20 enrolled. In 2017, 24 master's awarded. *Degree requirements:* For master's, comprehensive exam (for some programs), evidence-based practice project. *Entrance requirements:* For master's, BSN with minimum GPA of 3.0, active RN license, statistics course with minimum C grade, 2 professional references, written statement of goals, professional resume, interview, official transcripts. Additional exam requirements/recommendations for international students: Required—TOEFL (minimum score 550 paper-based; 90 iBT), IELTS (minimum score 6.5). *Application deadline:* For fall admission, 8/1 priority date for domestic and international students; for spring admission, 1/1 priority date for domestic and international students; for summer admission, 5/1 priority date for domestic and international students. Applications are processed on a rolling basis. Electronic applications accepted. *Expenses:* Contact institution. *Financial support:* Applicants required to submit FAFSA. *Faculty research:* College binge drinking, obesity, underrepresented minorities in nursing, education needs of nursing preceptors, delirium superimposed on dementia. *Unit head:* Dr. Kerry Cheever, Professor/Chairperson, 610-861-1412, Fax: 610-861-1466, E-mail: nursing@moravian.edu. *Application contact:* Caroline Febbo, Student Experience Mentor, 610-861-1400, Fax: 610-861-1466, E-mail: graduate@moravian.edu.

Morgan State University, School of Graduate Studies, School of Community Health and Policy, Program in Nursing, Baltimore, MD 21251. Offers MS, PhD. *Accreditation:* AACN. *Expenses:* Tuition, state resident: part-time $433 per credit. Tuition, nonresident: part-time $851 per credit. *Required fees:* $81.50 per credit. *Unit head:* Dr. Maija Anderson, Program Director, 443-885-4144, E-mail: maija.anderson@morgan.edu. *Application contact:* Dr. Dean Campbell, Graduate Recruitment Specialist, 443-885-3185, Fax: 443-885-8226, E-mail: dean.campbell@morgan.edu.

Morningside College, Graduate Programs, Nylen School of Nursing, Sioux City, IA 51106. Offers adult gerontology primary care nurse practitioner (MSN); clinical nurse leader (MSN); family primary care nurse practitioner (MSN). *Program availability:* Part-time, online only, 100% online. *Faculty:* 3 full-time (all women), 4 part-time/adjunct (all women). *Students:* 7 full-time (3 women), 86 part-time (81 women); includes 8 minority (1 American Indian or Alaska Native, non-Hispanic/Latino; 3 Asian, non-Hispanic/Latino; 4 Hispanic/Latino). Average age 32. 37 applicants, 100% accepted, 37 enrolled. In 2017, 19 master's awarded. *Application deadline:* Applications are processed on a rolling basis. Application fee: $65. Electronic applications accepted. *Expenses:* Contact institution. *Financial support:* In 2017–18, 67 students received support. Scholarships/grants and tuition waivers (partial) available. Financial award application deadline: 3/1; financial award applicants required to submit FAFSA. *Unit head:* Dr. Jackie Barber, Dean of Graduate Nursing, 712-274-5297, E-mail: barber@morningside.edu.

Mount Carmel College of Nursing, Nursing Program, Columbus, OH 43222. Offers adult gerontology acute care nurse practitioner (MS); adult health clinical nurse specialist (MS); family nurse practitioner (MS); nursing (DNP); nursing administration (MS); nursing education (MS). *Accreditation:* AACN. *Program availability:* Part-time. *Faculty:* 11 full-time (all women), 5 part-time/adjunct (4 women). *Students:* 112 full-time (93 women), 72 part-time (65 women); includes 35 minority (20 Black or African American, non-Hispanic/Latino; 4 Asian, non-Hispanic/Latino; 3 Hispanic/Latino; 8 Two or more races, non-Hispanic/Latino). Average age 35. 135 applicants, 65% accepted, 68 enrolled. In 2017, 64 master's awarded. *Degree requirements:* For master's, professional manuscript; for doctorate, practicum. *Entrance requirements:* For master's, letters of recommendation, statement of purpose, current resume, baccalaureate degree in nursing, current Ohio RN license, minimum cumulative GPA of 3.0; for doctorate, master's degree in nursing from program accredited by either ACEN or CCNE. Additional exam requirements/recommendations for international students: Required—TOEFL (minimum score 550 paper-based; 80 iBT). *Application deadline:* For fall admission, 2/1 priority date for domestic students; for spring admission, 11/1 priority date for domestic students. Applications are processed on a rolling basis. Application fee: $30. Electronic applications accepted. *Expenses: Tuition:* Full-time $11,403; part-time $543 per credit. *Required fees:* $50; $50 per year. *Financial support:* In 2017–18, 3 students received support. Institutionally sponsored loans and scholarships/grants available. Financial award application deadline: 3/1; financial award applicants required to submit FAFSA. *Unit head:* Dr. Jill Kilanowski, Associate Dean, 614-234-5237, Fax: 614-234-2875, E-mail: jkilanowski@mccn.edu. *Application contact:* Dr. Kim Campbell, Director of Recruitment and Admissions, 614-234-5144, Fax: 614-234-5427, E-mail: kcampbell@mccn.edu.

Mount Marty College, Graduate Studies Division, Yankton, SD 57078-3724. Offers business administration (MBA); nurse anesthesia (MS); nursing (MSN); pastoral ministries (MPM). *Accreditation:* AANA/CANAEP (one or more programs are accredited). *Degree requirements:* For master's, thesis or alternative. *Entrance requirements:* For master's, GRE General Test, minimum GPA of 3.0. Electronic applications accepted. *Faculty research:* Clinical anesthesia, professional characteristics, motivations of applicants.

Mount Mercy University, Program in Nursing, Cedar Rapids, IA 52402-4797. Offers health advocacy (MSN); nurse administration (MSN); nurse education (MSN). *Accreditation:* AACN. *Program availability:* Evening/weekend. *Degree requirements:* For master's, project/practicum.

Mount St. Joseph University, Doctor of Nursing Practice Program, Cincinnati, OH 45233-1670. Offers health systems leadership (DNP). *Accreditation:* AACN. *Program availability:* Part-time-only. *Faculty:* 9 full-time (all women), 15 part-time/adjunct (all women). *Students:* 53 part-time (50 women); includes 4 minority (all Black or African American, non-Hispanic/Latino). Average age 48. In 2017, 1 doctorate awarded. *Degree requirements:* For doctorate, capstone, minimum cumulative GPA of 3.0, completion of program within 5 years of enrollment, minimum of 75% of credits earned at Mount St. Joseph University, 1000 practicum hours between prior master's degree and DNP programs, minimum of 400 practicum hours in the DNP program. *Entrance requirements:* For doctorate, essay; MSN from regionally-accredited university; minimum graduate GPA of 3.0; professional resume; two professional references; interview, 2 years of clinical nursing experience; active RN license; minimum C grade in an undergraduate statistics course; official documentation of practicum hours post-BSN. Additional exam requirements/recommendations for international students: Required—TOEFL (minimum score 560 paper-based; 83 iBT). *Application deadline:* Applications are processed on a rolling basis. Application fee: $50. Electronic applications accepted. *Expenses:* $635 per credit hour. *Financial support:* Applicants required to submit FAFSA. *Unit head:* Dr. Nancy Hinzman, Assistant Dean of Nursing, 513-244-4325, Fax: 513-451-2547, E-mail: nancy.hinzman@msj.edu. *Application contact:* Autumn Richards, Admission Counselor for Graduate Studies, 513-244-4228, Fax: 513-244-4629, E-mail: autumn.richards@msj.edu.
Website: http://www.msj.edu/academics/graduate-programs/doctor-of-nursing-practice/

Mount St. Joseph University, Master of Science in Nursing Program, Cincinnati, OH 45233-1670. Offers administration (MSN); clinical nurse leader (MSN); education (MSN). *Accreditation:* AACN. *Program availability:* Part-time. *Faculty:* 9 full-time (all women), 15 part-time/adjunct (all women). *Students:* 122 part-time (113 women); includes 3 minority (2 Black or African American, non-Hispanic/Latino; 1 Two or more races, non-Hispanic/Latino). Average age 40. In 2017, 8 master's awarded. *Entrance requirements:* For master's, essay; BSN from regionally-accredited university; minimum undergraduate GPA of 3.25 or GRE; professional resume; three professional references; interview; 2 years of clinical nursing experience; active RN license; criminal background check. Additional exam requirements/recommendations for international students: Required—TOEFL (minimum score 560 paper-based; 83 iBT). *Application deadline:* Applications are processed on a rolling basis. Application fee: $50. Electronic applications accepted. *Expenses:* $610 per credit hour. *Financial support:* Applicants required to submit FAFSA. *Unit head:* Dr. Nancy Hinzman, MSN/DNP Director, 513-244-4325, E-mail: nancy.hinzman@msj.edu. *Application contact:* Mary Brigham, Assistant Director for Graduate Recruitment, 513-244-4233, Fax: 513-244-4629, E-mail: mary.brigham@msj.edu.
Website: http://www.msj.edu/academics/graduate-programs/master-of-science-in-nursing/

Mount St. Joseph University, Master's Graduate Entry-Level into Nursing (MAGELIN) Program, Cincinnati, OH 45233-1670. Offers MSN. *Accreditation:* AACN. *Faculty:* 9 full-time (all women), 15 part-time/adjunct (all women). *Students:* 81 full-time (65 women), 3 part-time (2 women); includes 22 minority (16 Black or African American, non-Hispanic/Latino; 1 Asian, non-Hispanic/Latino; 2 Hispanic/Latino; 3 Two or more races, non-Hispanic/Latino), 1 international. Average age 27. In 2017, 58 master's awarded. *Degree requirements:* For master's, evidence-based project, preceptorship. *Entrance requirements:* For master's, GRE or minimum GPA of 3.0, interview; course work in chemistry, anatomy, physiology, microbiology, psychology, sociology, statistics, life span development, and nutrition; non-nursing bachelor's degree; statement of goals; transcripts; criminal background check. Additional exam requirements/recommendations for international students: Required—TOEFL (minimum score 560 paper-based; 83 iBT). *Application deadline:* Applications are processed on a rolling basis. Application fee: $50. Electronic applications accepted. *Expenses:* $610 per credit hour plus a clinical fee. *Financial support:* In 2017–18, 1 student received support. Scholarships/grants available. Financial award applicants required to submit FAFSA. *Faculty research:* Utilizing technology in learning, assessment of student learning, critical thinking, women's health and nursing education. *Unit head:* Donna Glankler, Program Director, 513-244-4321, Fax: 513-451-2547, E-mail: donna.glankler@msj.edu. *Application contact:* Mary Brigham, Assistant Director of Graduate Recruitment, 513-244-4233, Fax: 513-244-4629, E-mail: mary.brigham@msj.edu.
Website: http://www.msj.edu/academics/graduate-programs/magelin-masters-graduate-entry-level-into-nursing/

Mount Saint Mary College, School of Nursing, Newburgh, NY 12550-3494. Offers adult nurse practitioner (MS, Advanced Certificate), including nursing education (MS), nursing management (MS); family nurse practitioner (Advanced Certificate); nursing education (Advanced Certificate). *Accreditation:* AACN. *Program availability:* Part-time, evening/weekend, blended/hybrid learning. *Faculty:* 7 full-time (all women), 5 part-time/adjunct (all women). *Students:* 3 full-time (1 woman), 153 part-time (143 women); includes 42 minority (22 Black or African American, non-Hispanic/Latino; 1 American Indian or Alaska Native, non-Hispanic/Latino; 6 Asian, non-Hispanic/Latino; 11 Hispanic/Latino; 1 Native Hawaiian or other Pacific Islander, non-Hispanic/Latino; 1 Two or more races, non-Hispanic/Latino). Average age 38. 34 applicants, 91% accepted, 28 enrolled. In 2017, 30 master's, 5 other advanced degrees awarded. *Degree requirements:* For master's, research utilization project. *Entrance requirements:* For master's, BSN, minimum GPA of 3.0, RN license. Additional exam requirements/recommendations for international students: Required—TOEFL (minimum score 80 iBT). *Application deadline:* For fall admission, 6/3 priority date for domestic students; for spring admission, 10/31 priority date for domestic students. Applications are processed on a rolling basis. Application fee: $45. Electronic applications accepted. Application fee is waived when completed online. *Expenses: Tuition:* Full-time $14,454; part-time $803 per credit. *Required fees:* $172; $86 per semester. *Financial support:* In 2017–18, 8 students received support. Unspecified assistantships available. Financial award application deadline: 4/15; financial award applicants required to submit FAFSA. *Unit head:* Christine Berte, Graduate Coordinator, 845-569-3141, Fax: 845-562-6762, E-mail: christine.berte@msmc.edu. *Application contact:* Lisa Alvarez, Director of Admissions for Graduate Programs and Adult Degree Completion, 845-569-3166, Fax: 845-569-3450, E-mail: lisa.gallina@msmc.edu.
Website: http://www.msmc.edu/Academics/Graduate_Programs/Master_of_Science_in_Nursing

Mount Saint Mary's University, Graduate Division, Los Angeles, CA 90049. Offers business administration (MBA); counseling psychology (MS); creative writing (MFA); education (MS, Certificate); film and television (MFA); health policy and management (MS); humanities (MA); nursing (MSN, Certificate); physical therapy (DPT); religious studies (MA). *Program availability:* Part-time, evening/weekend. *Faculty:* 50 full-time (35 women), 110 part-time/adjunct (81 women). *Students:* 670 full-time (518 women), 147 part-time (116 women); includes 414 minority (73 Black or African American, non-Hispanic/Latino; 4 American Indian or Alaska Native, non-Hispanic/Latino; 60 Asian, non-Hispanic/Latino; 259 Hispanic/Latino; 7 Native Hawaiian or other Pacific Islander, non-Hispanic/Latino; 11 Two or more races, non-Hispanic/Latino), 4 international. Average age 32. 1,398 applicants, 21% accepted, 242 enrolled. In 2017, 170 master's, 28 doctorates, 35 other advanced degrees awarded. *Entrance requirements:* Additional exam requirements/recommendations for international students: Required—TOEFL. *Application deadline:* For fall admission, 6/30 priority date for domestic and international students; for spring admission, 10/30 priority date for domestic and international students; for summer admission, 3/30 priority date for domestic and international students. Applications are processed on a rolling basis. Application fee: $50. Electronic applications accepted. *Expenses: Tuition:* Part-time $905 per unit. One-time fee: $155 part-time. Tuition and fees vary according to degree level and program. *Financial support:* Career-related internships or fieldwork, Federal Work-Study, institutionally sponsored loans, and tuition waivers (full and partial) available. Support available to part-time students. Financial award application deadline: 3/15; financial award applicants required to submit FAFSA. *Unit head:* Albert Ramos, Director of Graduate Admissions, 213-477-2800, E-mail: gradprograms@msmu.edu. *Application contact:* Shawn Peters, Graduate Admission Counselor, 213-477-2070, E-mail: gradprograms@msmu.edu.
Website: http://www.msmu.edu/graduate-programs/

Murray State University, School of Nursing and Health Professions, Department of Nursing, Murray, KY 42071. Offers family nurse practitioner (DNP); nurse anesthetist (DNP). *Accreditation:* AACN; AANA/CANAEP. *Program availability:* Evening/weekend, 100% online, blended/hybrid learning. *Faculty:* 7 full-time (6 women), 1 part-time/adjunct (0 women). *Students:* 63 full-time (45 women), 21 part-time (17 women); includes 12 minority (8 Black or African American, non-Hispanic/Latino; 3 Asian, non-Hispanic/Latino; 1 Two or more races, non-Hispanic/Latino). Average age 33. 85 applicants, 35% accepted, 21 enrolled. In 2017, 26 doctorates awarded. *Entrance requirements:* For doctorate, GRE, minimum university GPA of 2.75. Additional exam requirements/recommendations for international students: Required—TOEFL (minimum score 527 paper-based; 71 iBT). *Application deadline:* Applications are processed on a rolling basis. Application fee: $30. Electronic applications accepted. *Expenses:* Tuition, state resident: full-time $9504. Tuition, nonresident: full-time $26,811. *International tuition:* $14,400 full-time. Tuition and fees vary according to course load, degree level and reciprocity agreements. *Financial support:* Federal Work-Study, scholarships/grants, and unspecified assistantships available. Financial award applicants required to submit FAFSA. *Unit head:* Dr. Marcia Hobbs, Dean, School of Nursing and Health Professions, 270-809-3196, Fax: 270-809-6662, E-mail: mhobbs4@murraystate.edu. *Application contact:* Kaitlyn Burzynski, Interim Assistant Director for Graduate Admission and Records, 270-809-5732, Fax: 270-809-3780, E-mail: msu.graduateadmissions@murraystate.edu.

Nebraska Methodist College, Program in Nursing, Omaha, NE 68114. Offers nurse educator (MSN); nurse executive (MSN). *Accreditation:* AACN. *Program availability:* Evening/weekend, online learning. *Degree requirements:* For master's, thesis or alternative, Evidence Based Practice (EBP) project. *Entrance requirements:* For master's, interview. Additional exam requirements/recommendations for international students: Required—TOEFL (minimum score 550 paper-based; 80 iBT). *Faculty research:* Spirituality, student outcomes, service-learning, leadership and administration, women's issues.

Nebraska Wesleyan University, University College, Program in Nursing, Lincoln, NE 68504-2796. Offers MSN. *Accreditation:* AACN; ACEN. *Program availability:* Part-time.

Neumann University, Graduate Program in Nursing, Aston, PA 19014. Offers adult-gerontology nurse practitioner (MS, Certificate). *Accreditation:* ACEN. *Program availability:* Part-time, evening/weekend. *Faculty:* 2 full-time (both women), 4 part-time/adjunct (3 women). *Students:* 37 part-time (35 women); includes 11 minority (5 Black or African American, non-Hispanic/Latino; 2 Asian, non-Hispanic/Latino; 2 Hispanic/Latino; 2 Two or more races, non-Hispanic/Latino). Average age 41. 15 applicants, 47% accepted, 7 enrolled. In 2017, 11 master's awarded. *Entrance requirements:* For master's, official transcripts from all institutions attended, resume, letter of intent, current registered nursing license, two letters of reference; for Certificate, BSN, MSN, official transcripts from all institutions attended, resume, letter of intent, current registered nursing license, two official letters of reference. Additional exam requirements/recommendations for international students: Required—TOEFL (minimum score 84 iBT). *Application deadline:* Applications are processed on a rolling basis. Application fee: $0. Electronic applications accepted. *Expenses: Tuition:* Part-time $700 per credit hour. Tuition and fees vary according to degree level, campus/location and program. *Financial support:* Scholarships/grants, traineeships, and health care benefits available. Support available to part-time students. Financial award application deadline: 3/15; financial award applicants required to submit FAFSA. *Unit head:* Dr. Kathleen Hoover, Dean, Division of Nursing and Health Sciences, 610-558-5560, Fax: 610-361-5265, E-mail: hooverk@neumann.edu. *Application contact:* Dr. Erika K. Davis, Director of Adult and Graduate Admissions, 800-9-NEUMANN Ext. 5208, Fax: 610-361-2548, E-mail: gradadultadmiss@neumann.edu.

New Mexico State University, College of Health and Social Services, School of Nursing, Las Cruces, NM 88003. Offers family nurse practitioner (DNP, Graduate Certificate); nursing administration (MSN); nursing science (PhD); psychiatric/mental health nurse practitioner (DNP, Graduate Certificate). *Accreditation:* AACN. *Program availability:* Part-time, blended/hybrid learning. *Faculty:* 11 full-time (all women). *Students:* 29 full-time (26 women), 68 part-time (57 women); includes 46 minority (10 Black or African American, non-Hispanic/Latino; 6 Asian, non-Hispanic/Latino; 29 Hispanic/Latino; 1 Two or more races, non-Hispanic/Latino), 1 international. Average age 42. 47 applicants, 81% accepted, 25 enrolled. In 2017, 3 master's, 9 doctorates, 5 other advanced degrees awarded. *Degree requirements:* For master's, comprehensive

exam, thesis optional, clinical practicum; for doctorate, comprehensive exam, thesis/dissertation. *Entrance requirements:* For master's, NCLEX exam, BSN, minimum GPA of 3.0, course work in statistics, 3 letters of reference, writing sample, RN license, CPR certification, proof of liability, immunizations, criminal background check; for doctorate, NCLEX exam, MSN, minimum GPA of 3.0, 3 letters of reference, writing sample, RN license, CPR certification, proof of liability, immunizations, criminal background check, statistics course. Additional exam requirements/recommendations for international students: Required—TOEFL (minimum score 550 paper-based; 79 iBT), IELTS (minimum score 6.5). *Application deadline:* For fall admission, 2/1 priority date for domestic students, 2/1 for international students. Application fee: $40 ($50 for international students). Electronic applications accepted. *Expenses:* Tuition, state resident: full-time $4390. Tuition, nonresident: full-time $15,309. *Required fees:* $853. *Financial support:* In 2017–18, 22 students received support, including 5 teaching assistantships (averaging $11,249 per year); career-related internships or fieldwork, Federal Work-Study, scholarships/grants, traineeships, health care benefits, and unspecified assistantships also available. Support available to part-time students. Financial award application deadline: 3/1. *Faculty research:* Women's health, community health, health disparities, nursing informatics and health care technologies, health care and nursing administration, nursing education, adolescent mental health, addiction and substance abuse. *Total annual research expenditures:* $1,321. *Unit head:* Dr. Alexa Doig, Director, 575-646-3812, Fax: 575-646-2167, E-mail: adoig@nmsu.edu. *Application contact:* Alyce Kolenovsky, 575-646-3812, Fax: 575-646-2167, E-mail: nursing@nmsu.edu.
Website: http://schoolofnursing.nmsu.edu

New York University, Rory Meyers College of Nursing, Doctor of Nursing Practice Program, New York, NY 10012-1019. Offers nursing (DNP), including adult-gerontology acute care nurse practitioner, adult-gerontology primary care nurse practitioner, family nurse practitioner, nurse-midwifery, pediatrics nurse practitioner, psychiatric-mental health nurse practitioner. *Accreditation:* AACN. *Program availability:* Part-time, evening/weekend. *Faculty:* 16 full-time (all women), 1 (woman) part-time/adjunct. *Students:* 48 part-time (43 women); includes 11 minority (5 Black or African American, non-Hispanic/Latino; 5 Asian, non-Hispanic/Latino; 1 Hispanic/Latino). Average age 28. 20 applicants, 75% accepted, 10 enrolled. In 2017, 8 doctorates awarded. *Degree requirements:* For doctorate, thesis/dissertation, project. *Entrance requirements:* For doctorate, MS, RN license, interview, Nurse Practitioner Certification, writing sample. Additional exam requirements/recommendations for international students: Required—TOEFL (minimum score 100 iBT), IELTS (minimum score 7). *Application deadline:* For fall admission, 3/1 priority date for domestic and international students. Applications are processed on a rolling basis. Application fee: $80. Electronic applications accepted. *Expenses:* Contact institution. *Financial support:* In 2017–18, 13 students received support. Scholarships/grants available. Support available to part-time students. Financial award application deadline: 2/1; financial award applicants required to submit FAFSA. *Faculty research:* Workforce determinants of healthcare quality, genomics, health literacy and health outcomes, health policy. *Unit head:* Dr. Mary Jo Vetter, Director, DNP Program, 212-998-5165, E-mail: mjv5@nyu.edu. *Application contact:* Matthew Burke, Assistant Director, Graduate Student Affairs and Admissions, 212-998-7397, E-mail: mb6060@nyu.edu.

New York University, Rory Meyers College of Nursing, Doctor of Philosophy in Nursing Program, New York, NY 10012-1019. Offers nursing research and theory development (PhD). *Program availability:* Part-time. *Faculty:* 35 full-time (29 women). *Students:* 21 full-time (19 women), 14 part-time (12 women); includes 8 minority (1 Black or African American, non-Hispanic/Latino; 5 Asian, non-Hispanic/Latino; 2 Hispanic/Latino), 4 international. Average age 39. 20 applicants, 50% accepted, 7 enrolled. In 2017, 10 doctorates awarded. *Degree requirements:* For doctorate, thesis/dissertation, candidacy exam. *Entrance requirements:* For doctorate, GRE General Test, interview. Additional exam requirements/recommendations for international students: Required—TOEFL (minimum score 100 iBT), IELTS (minimum score 7). *Application deadline:* For fall admission, 12/15 for domestic students, 1/15 for international students. Application fee: $80. Electronic applications accepted. *Expenses:* Contact institution. *Financial support:* In 2017–18, 14 students received support, including 9 research assistantships with full tuition reimbursements available (averaging $27,000 per year); scholarships/grants and unspecified assistantships also available. Financial award application deadline: 2/1; financial award applicants required to submit FAFSA. *Faculty research:* Geriatrics, infectious diseases/global public health, chronic disease prevention and management, nursing workforce, technology. *Unit head:* Dr. Deborah Chyun, Executive Associate Dean, 212-998-5264, E-mail: dc116@nyu.edu. *Application contact:* Matthew Burke, Assistant Director, Graduate Student Affairs and Admissions, 212-998-7397, Fax: 212-995-4302, E-mail: mb6060@nyu.edu.

New York University, Rory Meyers College of Nursing, Programs in Advanced Practice Nursing, New York, NY 10012-1019. Offers adult-gerontology acute care nurse practitioner (MS, Advanced Certificate); adult-gerontology primary care nurse practitioner (MS, Advanced Certificate); family nurse practitioner (MS, Advanced Certificate); gerontology nurse practitioner (Advanced Certificate); nurse-midwifery (MS, Advanced Certificate); nursing administration (MS, Advanced Certificate); nursing education (MS, Advanced Certificate); nursing informatics (MS, Advanced Certificate); pediatrics nurse practitioner (MS, Advanced Certificate); psychiatric-mental health nurse practitioner (MS, Advanced Certificate); MS/MPH. *Accreditation:* AACN; ACNM/ACME. *Program availability:* Part-time, evening/weekend. *Faculty:* 23 full-time (all women), 62 part-time/adjunct (56 women). *Students:* 50 full-time (46 women), 557 part-time (509 women); includes 234 minority (58 Black or African American, non-Hispanic/Latino; 1 American Indian or Alaska Native, non-Hispanic/Latino; 116 Asian, non-Hispanic/Latino; 43 Hispanic/Latino; 1 Native Hawaiian or other Pacific Islander, non-Hispanic/Latino; 15 Two or more races, non-Hispanic/Latino), 23 international. Average age 32. 391 applicants, 59% accepted, 149 enrolled. In 2017, 187 master's, 5 other advanced degrees awarded. *Degree requirements:* For master's, thesis (for some programs), capstone. *Entrance requirements:* For master's, BS in nursing, AS in nursing with another BS/BA, interview, RN license, 1 year of clinical experience (3 for the MS in nursing education program); for Advanced Certificate, master's degree in nursing. Additional exam requirements/recommendations for international students: Required—TOEFL (minimum score 100 iBT), IELTS (minimum score 7). *Application deadline:* For fall admission, 3/1 priority date for domestic and international students; for spring admission, 11/1 priority date for domestic and international students; for summer admission, 3/1 for domestic and international students. Application fee: $80. Electronic applications accepted. *Expenses:* Contact institution. *Financial support:* In 2017–18, 130 students received support. Career-related internships or fieldwork, Federal Work-Study, and scholarships/grants available. Support available to part-time students. Financial award application deadline: 3/1; financial award applicants required to submit FAFSA. *Faculty research:* Vaccine hesitancy in pregnant women and mothers, palliative care and midwifery, diabetes education, curriculum development, workforce training, education and development, geriatrics. *Unit head:* Dr. James Pace, Senior Associate Dean for Academic Programs, 212-992-7343, E-mail: james.pace@nyu.edu. *Application contact:* Matthew Burke, Assistant Director, Graduate Student Affairs and Admissions, 212-998-7397, Fax: 212-995-4302, E-mail: mb6060@nyu.edu.

Nicholls State University, Graduate Studies, College of Nursing and Allied Health, Thibodaux, LA 70310. Offers family nurse practitioner (MSN); nurse executive (MSN); nursing education (MSN); psychiatric/mental health nurse practitioner (MSN).

North Dakota State University, College of Graduate and Interdisciplinary Studies, College of Health Professions, School of Nursing, Fargo, ND 58102. Offers DNP. *Accreditation:* AACN. *Program availability:* Part-time, online learning. *Degree requirements:* For doctorate, thesis/dissertation or alternative, oral defense. *Entrance requirements:* For doctorate, bachelor's or master's degree with a nursing major, minimum GPA of 3.0 in nursing courses, RN license. Additional exam requirements/recommendations for international students: Required—TOEFL, IELTS. *Application deadline:* For fall admission, 5/1 priority date for domestic students; for spring admission, 11/1 priority date for domestic students. Applications are processed on a rolling basis. Application fee: $35. Electronic applications accepted. *Expenses:* Contact institution. *Financial support:* Application deadline: 8/15; applicants required to submit CSS PROFILE or FAFSA. *Faculty research:* Prevention of farmers' hearing loss, breast cancer in Native American women, colon cancer, quality improvement in a wellness center. *Unit head:* Dr. Carla Gross, Chair, 701-231-7772, Fax: 701-231-7606, E-mail: carla.gross@ndsu.edu. *Application contact:* Dr. Carla Gross, Chair, 701-231-7772, Fax: 701-231-7606, E-mail: carla.gross@ndsu.edu.
Website: http://www.ndsu.edu/nursing/

Northeastern University, Bouvé College of Health Sciences, Boston, MA 02115-5096. Offers applied behavior analysis (MS); audiology (Au D); counseling psychology (MS, PhD, CAGS); exercise science (MS); nursing (MS, PhD, CAGS), including administration (MS), adult-gerontology acute care nurse practitioner (MS, CAGS), adult-gerontology primary care nurse practitioner (MS, CAGS), anesthesia (MS), family nurse practitioner (MS, CAGS), neonatal nurse practitioner (MS, CAGS), pediatric nurse practitioner (MS, CAGS), psychiatric mental health nurse practitioner (MS, CAGS); nursing practice (DNP); pharmaceutical sciences (MS, PhD), including interdisciplinary concentration, pharmaceutics and drug delivery systems; pharmacology (MS); pharmacy (Pharm D); school psychology (PhD); speech-language pathology (MS); urban health (MPH); MS/MBA. *Accreditation:* ACPE (one or more programs are accredited). *Program availability:* Part-time, evening/weekend, online learning. *Faculty:* 192 full-time. *Students:* 1,685. In 2017, 352 master's, 312 doctorates, 25 other advanced degrees awarded. *Degree requirements:* For doctorate, thesis/dissertation (for some programs); for CAGS, comprehensive exam. Application fee: $75. Electronic applications accepted. *Expenses:* Contact institution. *Financial support:* Fellowships, research assistantships, teaching assistantships, career-related internships or fieldwork, scholarships/grants, health care benefits, tuition waivers, and unspecified assistantships available. Support available to part-time students. Financial award applicants required to submit FAFSA. *Unit head:* Susan L. Parish, Dean, Bouve College of Health Sciences, 617-373-3321, Fax: 617-373-3030, E-mail: s.parish@northeastern.edu. *Application contact:* 617-373-2708, Fax: 617-373-4701, E-mail: bouvegrad@northeastern.edu.
Website: https://www.northeastern.edu/bouve/

Northern Arizona University, College of Health and Human Services, School of Nursing, Flagstaff, AZ 86011. Offers family nurse practitioner (Certificate); nursing (MS), including family nurse practitioner, generalist; nursing practice (DNP). *Accreditation:* AACN. *Program availability:* Part-time, 100% online, blended/hybrid learning. *Faculty:* 50 full-time (45 women), 26 part-time/adjunct (21 women). *Students:* 12 full-time (10 women), 175 part-time (151 women); includes 57 minority (5 Black or African American, non-Hispanic/Latino; 9 American Indian or Alaska Native, non-Hispanic/Latino; 8 Asian, non-Hispanic/Latino; 32 Hispanic/Latino; 1 Native Hawaiian or other Pacific Islander, non-Hispanic/Latino; 2 Two or more races, non-Hispanic/Latino). Average age 39. 66 applicants, 83% accepted, 52 enrolled. In 2017, 60 master's, 5 doctorates, 4 other advanced degrees awarded. *Degree requirements:* For master's, variable foreign language requirement, comprehensive exam (for some programs), thesis (for some programs); for doctorate, variable foreign language requirement, comprehensive exam (for some programs), thesis/dissertation (for some programs), oral defense, individualized research. *Entrance requirements:* For master's, bachelor's degree in nursing from accredited program or associate's degree in nursing from accredited program with bachelor's degree in another field; minimum GPA of 3.0 in all nursing coursework; current RN license in good standing; for doctorate, master's degree in nursing from regionally-accredited university and nationally-accredited nursing program; minimum cumulative GPA of 3.0 in all nursing coursework of master's degree program; current RN license in good standing to practice. Additional exam requirements/recommendations for international students: Required—TOEFL (minimum score 80 iBT), IELTS (minimum score 6.5). *Application deadline:* For fall admission, 3/1 for domestic and international students; for spring admission, 10/1 for domestic and international students. Applications are processed on a rolling basis. Application fee: $65. Electronic applications accepted. *Expenses:* Tuition, state resident: full-time $9240; part-time $458 per credit hour. Tuition, nonresident: full-time $21,588; part-time $1199 per credit hour. *Required fees:* $1021; $14 per credit hour. $646 per semester. Tuition and fees vary according to course load, campus/location and program. *Financial support:* Institutionally sponsored loans and tuition waivers (full and partial) available. Financial award application deadline: 2/1; financial award applicants required to submit FAFSA. *Unit head:* Pamela Stetina, Director, 928-523-2671, Fax: 928-523-7171, E-mail: pamela.stetina@nau.edu. *Application contact:* Penny Walior, Student Academic Specialist, 928-523-6770, Fax: 928-523-9155, E-mail: graduatenursing@nau.edu.
Website: https://nau.edu/chhs/nursing/

Northern Illinois University, Graduate School, College of Health and Human Sciences, School of Nursing, De Kalb, IL 60115-2854. Offers MS, DNP. *Accreditation:* AACN. *Program availability:* Part-time. *Faculty:* 12 full-time (11 women), 1 (woman) part-time/adjunct. *Students:* 10 full-time (all women), 112 part-time (100 women); includes 37 minority (8 Black or African American, non-Hispanic/Latino; 17 Asian, non-Hispanic/Latino; 8 Hispanic/Latino; 4 Two or more races, non-Hispanic/Latino), 1 international. Average age 35. 54 applicants, 46% accepted, 18 enrolled. In 2017, 73 master's awarded. *Degree requirements:* For master's, thesis optional, internship. *Entrance requirements:* For master's, minimum GPA of 3.0 in last 60 hours, BA in nursing, nursing license. Additional exam requirements/recommendations for international students: Required—TOEFL (minimum score 550 paper-based). *Application deadline:* For fall admission, 6/1 for domestic students, 5/1 for international students; for spring admission, 11/1 for domestic students, 10/1 for international students. Applications are processed on a rolling basis. Application fee: $40. Electronic applications accepted. *Financial support:* In 2017–18, 1 research assistantship with full tuition reimbursement, 16 teaching assistantships with full tuition reimbursements were awarded; fellowships with full tuition reimbursements, career-related internships or fieldwork, Federal Work-Study, scholarships/grants, tuition waivers (full), and unspecified assistantships also available. Support available to part-time students. Financial award applicants required to submit FAFSA. *Faculty research:* Neonatal intensive care, stress and coping, refugee and immigrant issues, older adults, autoimmune disorders. *Unit head:* Dr. Janice Strom, Chair, 815-753-6550, Fax: 815-753-0814, E-mail: jstrom@niu.edu. *Application contact:* Graduate School Office, 815-753-0395, E-mail: gradsch@niu.edu.
Website: http://www.chhs.niu.edu/nursing/

Northern Kentucky University, Office of Graduate Programs, School of Nursing and Health Professions, Online Doctor of Nursing Practice Program, Highland Heights, KY 41099. Offers DNP. *Program availability:* Part-time, online learning. *Degree requirements:* For doctorate, thesis/dissertation. *Entrance requirements:* For doctorate, RN license, master's degree in nursing, minimum GPA of 3.25, course in upper-division statistics, course in informatics, 3 professional recommendations (2 from nurses), resume or curriculum vitae, all official transcripts, graduate paper of intent, interview. Additional exam requirements/recommendations for international students: Required—TOEFL (minimum score 79 iBT); Recommended—IELTS (minimum score 6.5). *Expenses:* Contact institution. *Faculty research:* Pathways to nursing degree, lead poisoning in children, predictors for NCLEX success in BSN and ABSN programs, work-life balance and deans of baccalaureate nursing programs, heart failure self management.

Northern Kentucky University, Office of Graduate Programs, School of Nursing and Health Professions, Program in Nursing, Highland Heights, KY 41099. Offers MSHS, MSN, Certificate, Post-Master's Certificate. *Accreditation:* ACEN. *Program availability:* Part-time, evening/weekend, online learning. *Degree requirements:* For master's, comprehensive exam, thesis optional. *Entrance requirements:* For master's, BS in nursing, letter from employer on letterhead indicating a minimum of 1,000 clinical hours of RN practice, updated resume, letter of purpose, official transcripts, proof of current licensure, minimum GPA of 3.0, two electronic letters of reference, successful completion of elementary statistics. Additional exam requirements/recommendations for international students: Required—TOEFL (minimum score 550 paper-based; 79 iBT); Recommended—IELTS (minimum score 6.5). Electronic applications accepted. *Faculty research:* Career planning for middle school students, technology skills for workforce, diabetes, factors affecting NCLEX scores.

Northern Michigan University, Office of Graduate Education and Research, College of Health Sciences and Professional Studies, School of Nursing, Marquette, MI 49855-5301. Offers DNP. *Accreditation:* AACN. *Program availability:* Part-time, online learning. *Entrance requirements:* For doctorate, Michigan RN license; minimum undergraduate GPA of 3.0; 3 letters of recommendation; written personal goal statement. Additional exam requirements/recommendations for international students: Required—TOEFL (minimum score 550 paper-based; 79 iBT), IELTS (minimum score 6.5). *Application deadline:* For fall admission, 4/15 for domestic and international students; for winter admission, 11/15 for domestic students; for spring admission, 3/17 for domestic students. Application fee: $50. Electronic applications accepted. *Expenses:* Tuition, state resident: full-time $9417; part-time $542 per credit hour. Tuition, nonresident: full-time $12,873; part-time $758 per credit hour. Tuition and fees vary according to course load, degree level and program. *Financial support:* Teaching assistantships with full tuition reimbursements, Federal Work-Study, institutionally sponsored loans, and unspecified assistantships available. Financial award application deadline: 3/1; financial award applicants required to submit FAFSA. *Faculty research:* Grief experiences in Alzheimer's caregivers, nursing students attitudes towards the elderly, using Facebook as a means of simulation and educational means for pediatric undergraduate nursing students, use of a nurse practitioner student educational intervention to reduce sugar sweetened beverage consumption in rural adolescents. *Unit head:* Kristi Robinia, Interim Associate Dean and Director, 906-227-2042, E-mail: krobinia@nmu.edu. *Application contact:* Dr. Melissa Romero, Associate Professor and Graduate Program Coordinator, 906-227-2488, Fax: 906-227-1658, E-mail: mromero@nmu.edu.
Website: http://www.nmu.edu/nursing/

North Park University, School of Nursing and Health Sciences, Chicago, IL 60625-4895. Offers advanced practice nursing (MS); leadership and management (MS); MBA/MS; MM/MSN; MS/MHR; MS/MNA. *Accreditation:* AACN. *Program availability:* Part-time, evening/weekend. *Degree requirements:* For master's, thesis. *Entrance requirements:* For master's, GMAT, MAT. *Faculty research:* Aging, consultation roles, critical thinking skills, family breakdown, science of caring.

Northwestern State University of Louisiana, Graduate Studies and Research, College of Nursing and School of Allied Health, Shreveport, LA 71101-4653. Offers MS, MSN. *Accreditation:* AACN. *Program availability:* Part-time. *Degree requirements:* For master's, comprehensive exam, thesis or alternative. *Entrance requirements:* For master's, GRE General Test, 6 months of clinical nursing experience, BS in nursing, minimum GPA of 3.0. Additional exam requirements/recommendations for international students: Required—TOEFL. Electronic applications accepted.

Norwich University, College of Graduate and Continuing Studies, Master of Science in Nursing Program, Northfield, VT 05663. Offers nursing administration (MSN); nursing education (MSN). *Accreditation:* AACN. *Program availability:* Evening/weekend, online only, mostly all online with a week-long residency requirement. *Entrance requirements:* For master's, minimum undergraduate GPA of 3.0. Additional exam requirements/recommendations for international students: Required—TOEFL (minimum score 550 paper-based; 80 iBT), IELTS (minimum score 6.5). Electronic applications accepted. *Expenses:* Contact institution.

Nova Southeastern University, Ron and Kathy Assaf College of Nursing, Fort Lauderdale, FL 33314-7796. Offers advanced practice registered nurse (MSN), including adult-gerontology acute care nurse practitioner, family nurse practitioner, psychiatric mental health nurse practitioner; executive nurse leadership (MSN); nursing (PhD), including nursing education; nursing education (MSN); nursing informatics (MSN); nursing practice (DNP). *Accreditation:* AACN. *Program availability:* Part-time, evening/weekend, 100% online, blended/hybrid learning, annual one-week summer institute delivered face-to-face on main campus. *Faculty:* 9 full-time (all women), 47 part-time/adjunct (43 women). *Students:* 658 full-time (599 women); includes 414 minority (175 Black or African American, non-Hispanic/Latino; 37 Asian, non-Hispanic/Latino; 179 Hispanic/Latino; 1 Native Hawaiian or other Pacific Islander, non-Hispanic/Latino; 22 Two or more races, non-Hispanic/Latino), 3 international. Average age 38. 179 applicants, 100% accepted, 163 enrolled. In 2017, 161 master's, 16 doctorates awarded. *Degree requirements:* For doctorate, comprehensive exam, thesis/dissertation. *Entrance requirements:* For master's, minimum GPA of 3.0, RN, BSN, BS or BA; for doctorate, minimum GPA of 3.5, MSN, RN. Additional exam requirements/recommendations for international students: Recommended—TOEFL. *Application deadline:* For fall admission, 3/1 priority date for domestic students, 3/1 for international students; for winter admission, 11/1 for domestic and international students. Applications are processed on a rolling basis. Application fee: $50. Electronic applications accepted. *Expenses:* Contact institution. *Financial support:* Application deadline: 4/15; applicants required to submit FAFSA. *Faculty research:* Nursing education, curriculum, clinical research, interdisciplinary research. *Total annual research expenditures:* $9,500. *Unit head:* Dr. Marcella M. Rutherford, Dean, 954-262-1963, E-mail: rmarcell@nova.edu. *Application contact:* Dianna Murphey, Director of Operations, 954-262-1975, E-mail: dgardner1@nova.edu.
Website: http://www.nova.edu/nursing/

Oakland University, Graduate Study and Lifelong Learning, School of Nursing, Rochester, MI 48309-4401. Offers MSN, DNP, PMC. *Accreditation:* AACN. *Program availability:* Part-time, evening/weekend. *Entrance requirements:* For master's, GRE General Test, minimum GPA of 3.0. Electronic applications accepted. *Expenses:* Tuition, state resident: full-time $16,950; part-time $706.25 per credit. Tuition, nonresident: full-time $24,648; part-time $1027 per credit.

The Ohio State University, Graduate School, College of Nursing, Columbus, OH 43210. Offers MHI, MS, DNP, PhD. *Accreditation:* AACN; ACNM/ACME. *Program availability:* Part-time. *Faculty:* 60. *Students:* 589 full-time (494 women), 280 part-time (237 women); includes 129 minority (53 Black or African American, non-Hispanic/Latino; 26 Asian, non-Hispanic/Latino; 22 Hispanic/Latino; 28 Two or more races, non-Hispanic/Latino), 4 international. Average age 32. In 2017, 232 master's, 11 doctorates awarded. *Degree requirements:* For master's, thesis optional; for doctorate, thesis/dissertation. *Entrance requirements:* For doctorate, GRE (for PhD). Additional exam requirements/recommendations for international students: Required—TOEFL (minimum score 600 paper-based; 100 iBT); Recommended—IELTS (minimum score 8). *Application deadline:* For fall admission, 12/13 priority date for domestic students, 11/30 priority date for international students; for summer admission, 10/12 for domestic and international students. Applications are processed on a rolling basis. Application fee: $60 ($70 for international students). Electronic applications accepted. *Financial support:* Fellowships, research assistantships, teaching assistantships, Federal Work-Study, institutionally sponsored loans, and unspecified assistantships available. Support available to part-time students. *Unit head:* Dr. Bernadette M. Melnyk, Dean, 614-292-4844, Fax: 614-292-4535, E-mail: melnyk.15@osu.edu. *Application contact:* Graduate and Professional Admissions, 614-292-9444, Fax: 614-292-3895, E-mail: gpadmissions@osu.edu.
Website: http://nursing.osu.edu/

Ohio University, Graduate College, College of Health Sciences and Professions, School of Nursing, Athens, OH 45701-2979. Offers advanced clinical practice (DNP); executive practice (DNP); family nurse practitioner (MSN); nurse educator (MSN). *Accreditation:* AACN. *Degree requirements:* For master's, capstone project. *Entrance requirements:* For master's, GRE, bachelor's degree in nursing from accredited college or university, minimum overall undergraduate GPA of 3.0, official transcripts, statement of goals and objectives, resume, 3 letters of recommendation. Additional exam requirements/recommendations for international students: Required—TOEFL (minimum score 550 paper-based; 80 iBT) or IELTS (minimum score 6.5). Electronic applications accepted.

Oklahoma Baptist University, Program in Nursing, Shawnee, OK 74804. Offers global nursing (MSN); nursing education (MSN). *Accreditation:* AACN.

Oklahoma City University, Kramer School of Nursing, Oklahoma City, OK 73106-1402. Offers clinical nurse leader (MSN); nursing (DNP, PhD); nursing education (MSN). *Accreditation:* ACEN. *Program availability:* Part-time, evening/weekend, online learning. *Faculty:* 10 full-time (all women), 8 part-time/adjunct (all women). *Students:* 111 full-time (100 women), 25 part-time (all women); includes 48 minority (16 Black or African American, non-Hispanic/Latino; 9 American Indian or Alaska Native, non-Hispanic/Latino; 9 Asian, non-Hispanic/Latino; 4 Hispanic/Latino; 10 Two or more races, non-Hispanic/Latino), 8 international. Average age 37. 68 applicants, 72% accepted, 35 enrolled. In 2017, 10 master's, 34 doctorates awarded. *Degree requirements:* For master's, thesis, minimum GPA of 3.0; for doctorate, comprehensive exam, thesis/dissertation, minimum GPA of 3.0. *Entrance requirements:* For master's, registered nurse licensure, minimum undergraduate GPA of 3.0, BSN from nationally-accredited nursing program, completion of courses in health assessment and statistics; for doctorate, GRE, current RN licensure; bachelor's and master's degrees from accredited programs (at least one of which must be in nursing); minimum graduate GPA of 3.5; personal essay; approved scholarly paper or published article/paper in a refereed journal. Additional exam requirements/recommendations for international students: Required—TOEFL (minimum score 550 paper-based; 80 iBT), IELTS (minimum score 6). *Application deadline:* Applications are processed on a rolling basis. Application fee: $50. Electronic applications accepted. *Expenses:* $13,320. *Financial support:* In 2017–18, 89 students received support. Federal Work-Study, institutionally sponsored loans, scholarships/grants, and tuition waivers (full and partial) available. Support available to part-time students. Financial award application deadline: 3/1; financial award applicants required to submit FAFSA. *Unit head:* Dr. Lois Salmeron, Dean, Kramer School of Nursing, 405-208-5900, Fax: 405-208-5914, E-mail: lsalmeron@okcu.edu. *Application contact:* Michael Harrington, Director of Graduate Admissions, 800-633-7242, Fax: 405-208-5916, E-mail: gadmissions@okcu.edu.
Website: http://www.okcu.edu/nursing/

Old Dominion University, College of Health Sciences, School of Nursing, Doctor of Nursing Practice Program, Norfolk, VA 23529. Offers advanced practice (DNP); nurse executive (DNP). *Accreditation:* AACN. *Program availability:* Part-time, blended/hybrid learning. *Faculty:* 4 full-time (all women), 3 part-time/adjunct (2 women). *Students:* 21 full-time (20 women), 35 part-time (31 women); includes 23 minority (15 Black or African American, non-Hispanic/Latino; 3 Asian, non-Hispanic/Latino; 3 Hispanic/Latino; 2 Two or more races, non-Hispanic/Latino). Average age 43. 71 applicants, 77% accepted, 36 enrolled. In 2017, 30 doctorates awarded. Terminal master's awarded for partial completion of doctoral program. *Degree requirements:* For doctorate, thesis/dissertation, capstone project. *Entrance requirements:* For doctorate, 3 letters of recommendation, essay, resume, transcripts. Additional exam requirements/recommendations for international students: Required—TOEFL. *Application deadline:* For spring admission, 9/15 priority date for domestic students, 4/15 priority date for international students. Application fee: $50. Electronic applications accepted. *Expenses:* $469 per credit. *Financial support:* In 2017–18, 1 teaching assistantship with partial tuition reimbursement (averaging $16,000 per year) was awarded; unspecified assistantships also available. *Faculty research:* Cultural competency, sleep disorders, self-care in HIV positive African-American women, ethical decision-making in pediatric cases. *Unit head:* Dr. Carolyn M. Rutledge, Associate Chair of Graduate Program, 757-683-5009, Fax: 757-683-5253, E-mail: crutledg@odu.edu. *Application contact:* Sue Parker, Graduate Program Coordinator, 757-683-4298, Fax: 757-683-5253, E-mail: sparker@odu.edu.
Website: http://www.odu.edu/academics/programs/doctoral/nursing-practice

Olivet Nazarene University, Graduate School, Department of Nursing, Bourbonnais, IL 60914. Offers family nurse practitioner (MSN); nursing (MSN).

Oregon Health & Science University, School of Nursing, Portland, OR 97239-2941. Offers MN, DNP, PhD, Post Master's Certificate. *Accreditation:* AACN; ACNM/ACME (one or more programs are accredited). *Program availability:* Part-time, 100% online, blended/hybrid learning. *Degree requirements:* For master's, thesis optional; for doctorate, thesis/dissertation (for some programs). *Entrance requirements:* For master's, GRE General Test, bachelor's degree in nursing, minimum undergraduate GPA of 3.0, previous course work in statistics; for doctorate, GRE General Test, master's degree in nursing; minimum undergraduate GPA of 3.0, 3.5 graduate; for Post Master's Certificate, master's degree in nursing. Additional exam requirements/recommendations for international students: Required—TOEFL (minimum score 83 iBT). Electronic applications accepted. *Expenses:* Contact institution. *Faculty research:* Palliative care and end-of-life care for older adults with chronic illness, cancer symptom management and cancer survivorship, decreasing non-evidence based cesarean delivery, data science and information technology, rural community-based approaches to childhood obesity.

Otterbein University, Department of Nursing, Westerville, OH 43081. Offers advanced practice nurse educator (Certificate); clinical nurse leader (MSN); family nurse practitioner (MSN, Certificate); nurse anesthesia (MSN, Certificate); nursing (DNP);

nursing service administration (MSN). *Accreditation:* AACN; AANA/CANAEP; ACEN. *Program availability:* Part-time, evening/weekend, online learning. *Degree requirements:* For master's, comprehensive exam (for some programs), thesis (for some programs). *Entrance requirements:* For master's, 2 reference forms, resume; for Certificate, official transcripts, 2 reference forms, essay, resumé. Additional exam requirements/recommendations for international students: Required—TOEFL (minimum score 550 paper-based; 79 iBT). *Faculty research:* Patient education, women's health, trauma curriculum development, administration.

Pace University, College of Health Professions, Lienhard School of Nursing, New York, NY 10038. Offers adult acute care nurse practitioner (MS, CAGS); family nurse practitioner (MS, CAGS); nursing (DNP, PhD); professional nursing leadership (MS, CAGS). *Accreditation:* AACN. *Program availability:* Part-time. *Faculty:* 11 full-time (10 women), 31 part-time/adjunct (27 women). *Students:* 11 full-time (all women), 515 part-time (459 women); includes 277 minority (145 Black or African American, non-Hispanic/Latino; 1 American Indian or Alaska Native, non-Hispanic/Latino; 88 Asian, non-Hispanic/Latino; 34 Hispanic/Latino; 9 Two or more races, non-Hispanic/Latino), 1 international. Average age 35. 289 applicants, 74% accepted, 138 enrolled. In 2017, 483 master's, 45 doctorates, 27 other advanced degrees awarded. Terminal master's awarded for partial completion of doctoral program. *Degree requirements:* For master's and CAGS, thesis. *Entrance requirements:* For master's, RN license, resume, personal statement, 2 letters of recommendation, official transcripts, minimum GPA of 3.0, undergraduate statistics; for doctorate, RN license, resume, personal statement, 2 letters of recommendation, official transcripts, accredited master's degree in nursing, minimum GPA of 3.3, state certification and board eligibility as FNP or ANP; for CAGS, RN license, resume, personal statement, 2 letters of recommendation, official transcripts, minimum GPA of 3.0, undergraduate statistics, completion of 2nd degree in nursing. Additional exam requirements/recommendations for international students: Required—TOEFL (minimum score 100 iBT), IELTS or PTE. *Application deadline:* For fall admission, 3/1 for domestic and international students. Applications are processed on a rolling basis. Application fee: $70. Electronic applications accepted. *Expenses:* Contact institution. *Financial support:* Research assistantships, teaching assistantships, career-related internships or fieldwork, Federal Work-Study, institutionally sponsored loans, tuition waivers (partial), and unspecified assistantships available. Support available to part-time students. Financial award application deadline: 2/15; financial award applicants required to submit FAFSA. *Unit head:* Dr. Harriet R. Feldman, Dean, College of Health Professions, 914-773-3341, E-mail: hfeldman@pace.edu. *Application contact:* Susan Ford-Goldschein, Director of Graduate Admissions, 212-346-1531, Fax: 212-346-1585, E-mail: graduateadmission@pace.edu.
Website: http://www.pace.edu/lienhard

Pacific Lutheran University, School of Nursing, Tacoma, WA 98447. Offers MSN, DNP. *Accreditation:* AACN. *Degree requirements:* For master's, thesis or alternative. *Entrance requirements:* For master's, GRE General Test, minimum undergraduate GPA of 3.0. Additional exam requirements/recommendations for international students: Required—TOEFL (minimum score 550 paper-based; 86 iBT). Electronic applications accepted. *Expenses:* Contact institution.

Palm Beach Atlantic University, School of Nursing, West Palm Beach, FL 33416-4708. Offers family nurse practitioner (DNP); health systems leadership (MSN). *Accreditation:* AACN. *Program availability:* Part-time. *Entrance requirements:* For master's, minimum GPA of 3.0; active RN license; personal interview; for doctorate, minimum GPA of 3.0; one year of experience as an RN; personal interview. Additional exam requirements/recommendations for international students: Required—TOEFL (minimum score 550 paper-based; 79 iBT). Electronic applications accepted. *Expenses:* Contact institution. *Faculty research:* Elder care, nursing education theory.

Penn State University Park, Graduate School, College of Nursing, University Park, PA 16802. Offers nursing (MSN). *Accreditation:* AACN; ACEN. *Program availability:* Part-time, evening/weekend. *Students:* 51 full-time (42 women), 53 part-time (47 women). Average age 32. 50 applicants, 56% accepted, 26 enrolled. In 2017, 41 master's, 4 doctorates awarded. *Entrance requirements:* Additional exam requirements/recommendations for international students: Required—TOEFL (minimum score 550 paper-based; 80 iBT), IELTS. *Application deadline:* Applications are processed on a rolling basis. Application fee: $65. Electronic applications accepted. *Expenses:* Contact institution. *Financial support:* Fellowships, research assistantships, teaching assistantships, career-related internships or fieldwork, Federal Work-Study, scholarships/grants, traineeships, health care benefits, and unspecified assistantships available. Support available to part-time students. Financial award application deadline: 2/15; financial award applicants required to submit FAFSA. *Unit head:* Dr. Janice L. Penrod, Dean, 814-863-0245, Fax: 814-865-3779. *Application contact:* Lori Hawn, Director, Graduate Student Services, 814-865-1795, Fax: 814-863-4627, E-mail: l-gswww@lists.psu.edu.
Website: http://nursing.psu.edu/

Pensacola Christian College, Graduate Studies, Pensacola, FL 32503-2267. Offers business administration (MBA); curriculum and instruction (MS, Ed D, Ed S); dramatics (MFA); educational leadership (MS, Ed D, Ed S); graphic design (MA, MFA); music (MA); nursing (MSN); performance studies (MA); studio art (MA, MFA).

Pittsburg State University, Graduate School, College of Arts and Sciences, Irene Ransom Bailey School of Nursing, Pittsburg, KS 66762. Offers nursing (DNP); nursing education (MSN). *Accreditation:* AACN. *Program availability:* Part-time. *Students:* 48 (42 women); includes 11 minority (1 American Indian or Alaska Native, non-Hispanic/Latino; 2 Hispanic/Latino; 8 Two or more races, non-Hispanic/Latino). In 2017, 7 master's, 13 doctorates awarded. *Degree requirements:* For master's, thesis optional; for doctorate, thesis/dissertation optional. *Entrance requirements:* For master's, GRE General Test. Additional exam requirements/recommendations for international students: Required—TOEFL (minimum score 550 paper-based; 79 iBT), IELTS (minimum score 6.5), PTE (minimum score 53). *Application deadline:* For fall admission, 7/15 for domestic students, 6/1 for international students; for spring admission, 12/15 for domestic students, 10/15 for international students; for summer admission, 5/15 for domestic students, 4/1 for international students. Applications are processed on a rolling basis. Application fee: $35 ($60 for international students). Electronic applications accepted. *Expenses:* Contact institution. *Financial support:* In 2017–18, 3 teaching assistantships with full tuition reimbursements (averaging $5,500 per year) were awarded. Financial award application deadline: 2/1; financial award applicants required to submit FAFSA. *Unit head:* Dr. Chyerl Giefer, Chairperson, 620-235-4438, E-mail: cgiefer@pittstate.edu. *Application contact:* Lisa Allen, Assistant Director of Graduate and Continuing Studies, 620-235-4223, Fax: 620-235-4219, E-mail: lallen@pittstate.edu.

Point Loma Nazarene University, School of Nursing, Doctorate of Nursing Practice Program, San Diego, CA 92106-2899. Offers DNP. *Program availability:* Online learning. *Students:* 12 part-time (all women); includes 9 minority (2 Black or African American, non-Hispanic/Latino; 3 Asian, non-Hispanic/Latino; 1 Hispanic/Latino; 1 Native Hawaiian or other Pacific Islander, non-Hispanic/Latino; 2 Two or more races, non-Hispanic/Latino). Average age 45. 13 applicants, 100% accepted, 12 enrolled. *Unit head:* Dr. Barb Taylor, Dean of the School of Nursing, 619-849-2766, E-mail: bataylor@pointloma.edu. *Application contact:* Joanie Joy, Senior Director of Enrollment Management, 619-329-6785, E-mail: gradinfo@pointloma.edu.
Website: https://www.pointloma.edu/graduate-studies/programs/doctorate-nursing-practice

Point Loma Nazarene University, School of Nursing, MS in Nursing Program, San Diego, CA 92106-2899. Offers adult-gerontology (MSN); family individual health (MSN); pediatrics (MSN). *Program availability:* Part-time. *Students:* 59 part-time (49 women); includes 28 minority (4 Black or African American, non-Hispanic/Latino; 1 American Indian or Alaska Native, non-Hispanic/Latino; 4 Asian, non-Hispanic/Latino; 9 Hispanic/Latino; 4 Native Hawaiian or other Pacific Islander, non-Hispanic/Latino; 6 Two or more races, non-Hispanic/Latino), 1 international. Average age 36. 23 applicants, 96% accepted, 18 enrolled. In 2017, 21 master's awarded. *Entrance requirements:* For master's, NCLEX exam, ADN or BSN in nursing, interview, RN license, essay, letters of recommendation, interview. *Application deadline:* For fall admission, 7/5 priority date for domestic students; for spring admission, 11/1 priority date for domestic students; for summer admission, 3/22 priority date for domestic students. Applications are processed on a rolling basis. Electronic applications accepted. *Expenses:* Contact institution. *Financial support:* Scholarships/grants available. Financial award applicants required to submit FAFSA. *Unit head:* Dr. Barb Taylor, Dean of the School of Nursing, 619-849-2766, E-mail: bataylor@pointloma.edu. *Application contact:* Joanie Joy, Senior Director of Enrollment Management, 619-329-6785, E-mail: gradinfo@pointloma.edu.
Website: https://www.pointloma.edu/graduate-studies/programs/nursing-ms

Point Loma Nazarene University, School of Nursing, Post-MSN Clinical Nurse Specialist Certificate Program, San Diego, CA 92106-2899. Offers Post-MSN Certificate. *Students:* 4 part-time (all women). Average age 43. 3 applicants, 67% accepted, 1 enrolled. *Unit head:* Dr. Barb Taylor, Dean of the School of Nursing, 619-849-2766, E-mail: bataylor@pointloma.edu. *Application contact:* Joanie Joy, Senior Director of Enrollment Management, 619-329-6785, E-mail: gradinfo@pointloma.edu.
Website: https://www.pointloma.edu/graduate-studies/programs/post-msn-cns-certificate

Pontifical Catholic University of Puerto Rico, College of Sciences, Department of Nursing, Ponce, PR 00717-0777. Offers medical-surgical nursing (MSN); mental health and psychiatric nursing (MSN). *Accreditation:* ACEN. *Program availability:* Part-time, evening/weekend. *Degree requirements:* For master's, comprehensive exam (for some programs), thesis, clinical research paper. *Entrance requirements:* For master's, GRE General Test, 2 letters of recommendation, interview, minimum GPA of 2.5. Electronic applications accepted.

Prairie View A&M University, College of Nursing, Houston, TX 77030. Offers MSN, DNP. *Accreditation:* AACN; ACEN. *Program availability:* Part-time, evening/weekend. *Faculty:* 11 full-time (all women), 2 part-time/adjunct (1 woman). *Students:* 37 full-time (30 women), 60 part-time (53 women); includes 92 minority (70 Black or African American, non-Hispanic/Latino; 17 Asian, non-Hispanic/Latino; 5 Hispanic/Latino), 2 international. Average age 35. 39 applicants, 95% accepted, 34 enrolled. In 2017, 74 master's, 1 doctorate awarded. *Degree requirements:* For master's, comprehensive exam, thesis. *Entrance requirements:* For master's, MAT or GRE, BS in nursing; minimum 1 year of experience as registered nurse; minimum GPA of 2.75; 3 letters of recommendation from professional nurses; for doctorate, GRE, minimum GPA of 3.0 undergraduate, 3.3 graduate; 3 letters of recommendation from professional nurses. Additional exam requirements/recommendations for international students: Required—TOEFL (minimum score 550 paper-based; 79 iBT). *Application deadline:* For fall admission, 5/1 priority date for domestic and international students; for spring admission, 10/1 priority date for domestic students, 9/1 priority date for international students; for summer admission, 3/1 priority date for domestic students, 2/1 priority date for international students. Applications are processed on a rolling basis. Application fee: $50. Electronic applications accepted. *Expenses:* Tuition, state resident: part-time $242 per credit. Tuition, nonresident: part-time $695 per credit. *Required fees:* $149 per credit. *Financial support:* Career-related internships or fieldwork, Federal Work-Study, institutionally sponsored loans, scholarships/grants, and traineeships available. Support available to part-time students. Financial award application deadline: 4/1; financial award applicants required to submit FAFSA. *Faculty research:* Software development and violence prevention, health promotion and disease prevention. *Unit head:* Dr. Betty N. Adams, Dean, 713-797-7009, Fax: 713-797-7013, E-mail: bnadams@pvamu.edu. *Application contact:* Dr. Forest Smith, Director of Student Services and Admissions, 713-797-7031, Fax: 713-797-7012, E-mail: fdsmith@pvamu.edu.
Website: http://www.pvamu.edu/nursing/

Purdue University, Graduate School, College of Health and Human Sciences, School of Nursing, West Lafayette, IN 47907. Offers adult gerontology primary care nurse practitioner (MS, Post Master's Certificate); nursing (DNP, PhD); primary care family nurse practitioner (MS, Post Master's Certificate); primary care pediatric nurse practitioner (MS, Post Master's Certificate). *Faculty:* 31 full-time (30 women), 2 part-time/adjunct (both women). *Students:* 41 full-time (39 women), 33 part-time (32 women); includes 10 minority (5 Black or African American, non-Hispanic/Latino; 1 American Indian or Alaska Native, non-Hispanic/Latino; 1 Asian, non-Hispanic/Latino; 2 Hispanic/Latino; 1 Two or more races, non-Hispanic/Latino), 2 international. Average age 35. 36 applicants, 78% accepted, 16 enrolled. In 2017, 13 master's, 5 doctorates, 2 other advanced degrees awarded. *Unit head:* Jane M. Kirkpatrick, Head of the Graduate Program, 765-494-6644, E-mail: jmkirk@purdue.edu. *Application contact:* Reanne Hall, Graduate Contact, 765-494-9248, E-mail: gradnursing@purdue.edu.
Website: http://www.purdue.edu/hhs/nur/

Purdue University Global, School of Nursing, Davenport, IA 52807. Offers nurse administrator (MS); nurse educator (MS). *Program availability:* Part-time, evening/weekend, online learning. *Entrance requirements:* For master's, RN. Additional exam requirements/recommendations for international students: Required—TOEFL (minimum score 550 paper-based).

Purdue University Northwest, Graduate Studies Office, School of Nursing, Hammond, IN 46323-2094. Offers adult health clinical nurse specialist (MS); critical care clinical nurse specialist (MS); family nurse practitioner (MS); nurse executive (MS). *Accreditation:* ACEN. *Program availability:* Part-time, online learning. *Entrance requirements:* For master's, BSN. Additional exam requirements/recommendations for international students: Required—TOEFL. Electronic applications accepted. *Faculty research:* Adult health, cardiovascular and pulmonary nursing.

Queen's University at Kingston, School of Graduate Studies, Faculty of Health Sciences, School of Nursing, Kingston, ON K7L 3N6, Canada. Offers health and chronic illness (M Sc); nurse scientist (PhD); primary health care nurse practitioner (Certificate); women's and children's health (M Sc). *Degree requirements:* For master's, thesis. *Entrance requirements:* For master's, RN license. Additional exam requirements/recommendations for international students: Required—TOEFL. *Faculty research:* Women and children's health, health and chronic illness.

Queens University of Charlotte, Presbyterian School of Nursing, Charlotte, NC 28274-0002. Offers clinical nurse leader (MSN); nurse educator (MSN); nursing administrator (MSN). *Accreditation:* AACN. *Degree requirements:* For master's, research project. *Entrance requirements:* For master's, minimum GPA of 3.0. Additional exam requirements/recommendations for international students: Required—TOEFL. Electronic applications accepted. *Expenses:* Contact institution.

Quinnipiac University, School of Nursing, Hamden, CT 06518-1940. Offers DNP. *Accreditation:* AACN. *Faculty:* 18 full-time (17 women), 11 part-time/adjunct (8 women).

Students: 57 full-time (47 women), 231 part-time (205 women); includes 84 minority (40 Black or African American, non-Hispanic/Latino; 1 American Indian or Alaska Native, non-Hispanic/Latino; 23 Asian, non-Hispanic/Latino; 17 Hispanic/Latino; 3 Two or more races, non-Hispanic/Latino), 3 international. 225 applicants, 64% accepted, 104 enrolled. In 2017, 71 doctorates awarded. *Entrance requirements:* Additional exam requirements/recommendations for international students: Required—TOEFL (minimum score 575 paper-based; 90 iBT), IELTS (minimum score 6.5). *Application deadline:* Applications are processed on a rolling basis. Application fee: $45. Electronic applications accepted. *Financial support:* Federal Work-Study, scholarships/grants, and unspecified assistantships available. Financial award application deadline: 6/1; financial award applicants required to submit FAFSA. *Faculty research:* Decreasing social isolation of older adults, high fidelity simulation as a teaching method, teaching end of life care to nursing students, nurses with disabilities and practice roles, improving depression care of older home care patients, determining hip labral tears with new physical examination technique.
Website: http://www.qu.edu/gradnursing

Radford University, College of Graduate Studies and Research, Program in Nursing Practice, Radford, VA 24142. Offers DNP. *Accreditation:* AACN. *Program availability:* Part-time, evening/weekend, online learning. *Faculty:* 10 full-time (9 women), 2 part-time/adjunct (both women). *Students:* 23 full-time (18 women), 27 part-time (22 women); includes 16 minority (11 Black or African American, non-Hispanic/Latino; 1 Asian, non-Hispanic/Latino; 3 Hispanic/Latino; 1 Two or more races, non-Hispanic/Latino). Average age 36. 24 applicants, 83% accepted, 16 enrolled. In 2017, 14 doctorates awarded. *Degree requirements:* For doctorate, thesis/dissertation. *Entrance requirements:* For doctorate, GRE, current license to practice as RN; minimum undergraduate GPA of 3.0, graduate 3.5; 3-5 page essay; professional writing sample; three letters of reference; personal interview; resume or curriculum vitae; official transcripts; 2,000 hours of RN clinical experience; certification in BLS or ACLS; BSN. Additional exam requirements/recommendations for international students: Required—TOEFL (minimum score 550 paper-based; 79 iBT), IELTS (minimum score 6.5). *Application deadline:* For fall admission, 4/1 priority date for domestic students, 12/1 for international students; for spring admission, 10/1 for domestic students, 7/1 for international students. Applications are processed on a rolling basis. Application fee: $50. Electronic applications accepted. *Expenses:* Contact institution. *Financial support:* In 2017–18, 44 students received support, including 1 teaching assistantship (averaging $10,000 per year); career-related internships or fieldwork, scholarships/grants, and unspecified assistantships also available. Support available to part-time students. Financial award application deadline: 3/1; financial award applicants required to submit FAFSA. *Unit head:* Dr. Iris Mullins, Coordinator, 540-831-7656, Fax: 540-831-7716, E-mail: imullins@radford.edu.
Website: http://www.radford.edu/content/wchs/home/dnp.html

Ramapo College of New Jersey, Master of Science in Nursing Program, Mahwah, NJ 07430-1680. Offers family nurse practitioner (MSN); nursing administrator (MSN); nursing education (MSN). *Accreditation:* ACEN. *Program availability:* Part-time. *Faculty:* 4 full-time (all women), 2 part-time/adjunct (1 woman). *Students:* 79 part-time (70 women); includes 28 minority (4 Black or African American, non-Hispanic/Latino; 18 Asian, non-Hispanic/Latino; 5 Hispanic/Latino; 1 Two or more races, non-Hispanic/Latino). Average age 33. 84 applicants, 67% accepted, 37 enrolled. In 2017, 9 master's awarded. *Entrance requirements:* For master's, official transcript; personal statement; 2 letters of recommendation; resume; current licensure as a Registered Nurse, or eligibility for licensure; evidence of one year of recent experience as RN prior to entry into clinical practicum courses; evidence of undergraduate statistics course; criminal background check. Additional exam requirements/recommendations for international students: Required—TOEFL (minimum score 550 paper-based; 90 iBT); Recommended—IELTS (minimum score 6). *Application deadline:* For fall admission, 5/1 for domestic and international students; for spring admission, 12/1 for domestic and international students. Applications are processed on a rolling basis. Application fee: $65. Electronic applications accepted. *Expenses:* $690.60 per credit tuition, $56.95 per credit fees. *Financial support:* Career-related internships or fieldwork available. Financial award application deadline: 3/1; financial award applicants required to submit FAFSA. *Faculty research:* Learning styles and critical thinking, evidence-based education, outcomes measurement. *Unit head:* Dr. Kathleen M. Burke, Assistant Dean of Nursing Programs/Professor, 201-684-7737, Fax: 201-684-7954, E-mail: kmburke@ramapo.edu. *Application contact:* Anthony Dovi, Associate Director of Admissions, Adult Learners and Graduate Programs, 201-684-7305, Fax: 201-684-7964, E-mail: adovi@ramapo.edu.
Website: http://www.ramapo.edu/msn/

Regis College, Nursing and Health Sciences School, Weston, MA 02493. Offers applied behavior analysis (MS); counseling psychology (MA); health administration (MS); nurse practitioner (Certificate); nursing (MS, DNP); nursing education (Certificate); occupational therapy (MS). *Accreditation:* ACEN. *Program availability:* Part-time, evening/weekend, 100% online, blended/hybrid learning. *Degree requirements:* For doctorate, thesis/dissertation. *Entrance requirements:* For master's, GRE General Test or MAT, minimum GPA of 3.0, official transcripts, recommendations, personal statement, resume/curriculum vitae, interview; for doctorate, MAT or GRE if GPA from master's lower than 3.5. Additional exam requirements/recommendations for international students: Required—TOEFL (minimum score 560 paper-based; 79 iBT); Recommended—IELTS (minimum score 6.5). *Application deadline:* Applications are processed on a rolling basis. Application fee: $75. Electronic applications accepted. *Financial support:* Federal Work-Study, scholarships/grants, traineeships, and unspecified assistantships available. Support available to part-time students. Financial award applicants required to submit FAFSA. *Faculty research:* Global public health, health policy, education, aging, job satisfaction, psychiatric nursing, critical thinking. *Application contact:* Hillary Lyons, Graduate Admission Counselor, 781-768-7746, E-mail: hillary.lyons@regiscollege.edu.

Research College of Nursing, Nursing Program, Kansas City, MO 64132. Offers adult-gerontological nurse practitioner (MSN); executive practice and healthcare leadership (MSN); family nurse practitioner (MSN). *Accreditation:* AACN. *Program availability:* Part-time-only, 100% online. *Faculty:* 10 full-time (all women), 4 part-time/adjunct (2 women). *Students:* 1 (woman) full-time, 150 part-time (125 women); includes 14 minority (7 Black or African American, non-Hispanic/Latino; 1 American Indian or Alaska Native, non-Hispanic/Latino; 2 Asian, non-Hispanic/Latino; 2 Hispanic/Latino; 1 Native Hawaiian or other Pacific Islander, non-Hispanic/Latino; 1 Two or more races, non-Hispanic/Latino). *Degree requirements:* For master's, research project. *Entrance requirements:* For master's, 3 letters of recommendation, official transcripts, resume, personal statement/writing sample. *Application deadline:* Applications are processed on a rolling basis. Application fee: $65. Electronic applications accepted. *Expenses: Tuition:* Part-time $550 per credit hour. *Financial support:* Applicants required to submit FAFSA. *Unit head:* Dr. Thad Wilson, President, 816-995-2815, Fax: 816-995-2817, E-mail: thad.wilson@researchcollege.edu. *Application contact:* Leslie Burry, Director of Transfer and Graduate Recruitment, 816-995-2820, Fax: 816-995-2813, E-mail: leslie.burry@researchcollege.edu.

Resurrection University, Nursing Program, Chicago, IL 60622. Offers MSN. *Accreditation:* AACN. *Entrance requirements:* For master's, letter of recommendation.

Rhode Island College, School of Graduate Studies, School of Nursing, Providence, RI 02908-1991. Offers MSN, DNP. *Accreditation:* AACN; AANA/CANAEP. *Program availability:* Part-time. *Students:* 21 full-time (15 women), 69 part-time (54 women); includes 11 minority (2 Black or African American, non-Hispanic/Latino; 5 Asian, non-Hispanic/Latino; 2 Hispanic/Latino; 1 Native Hawaiian or other Pacific Islander, non-Hispanic/Latino; 1 Two or more races, non-Hispanic/Latino). Average age 37. In 2017, 28 master's awarded. *Entrance requirements:* For master's, GRE, undergraduate transcripts; minimum undergraduate GPA of 3.0; 3 letters of recommendation; evidence of current unrestricted Rhode Island RN licensure; professional resume; letter of intent. Additional exam requirements/recommendations for international students: Recommended—TOEFL (minimum score 550 paper-based; 79 iBT). *Application deadline:* For fall admission, 2/15 for domestic students. Applications are processed on a rolling basis. Application fee: $50. Electronic applications accepted. *Expenses:* Tuition, state resident: full-time $9768; part-time $407 per credit. Tuition, nonresident: full-time $19,008; part-time $792 per credit. *Required fees:* $696; $29 per credit. One-time fee: $200 full-time; $100 part-time. Tuition and fees vary according to course load. *Financial support:* In 2017–18, 9 teaching assistantships with full tuition reimbursements (averaging $1,583 per year) were awarded; Federal Work-Study, scholarships/grants, health care benefits, and unspecified assistantships also available. Support available to part-time students. Financial award application deadline: 5/15; financial award applicants required to submit FAFSA. *Unit head:* Dr. Debra Servello, Interim Dean, 401-456-8013, Fax: 401-456-8206.
Website: http://www.ric.edu/nursing/

Rivier University, School of Graduate Studies, Division of Nursing and Health Professions, Nashua, NH 03060. Offers family nurse practitioner (MS); leadership in health systems management (MS); nursing education (MS); nursing practice (DNP); psychiatric/mental health nurse practitioner (MS); public health (MPH). *Accreditation:* ACEN. *Program availability:* Part-time, evening/weekend. *Entrance requirements:* For master's, GRE, MAT. Electronic applications accepted.

Robert Morris University, School of Nursing and Health Sciences, Moon Township, PA 15108-1189. Offers MSN, DNP. *Accreditation:* AACN. *Program availability:* Part-time, evening/weekend. *Faculty:* 13 full-time (11 women), 7 part-time/adjunct (all women). *Students:* 234 part-time (202 women); includes 25 minority (19 Black or African American, non-Hispanic/Latino; 2 Asian, non-Hispanic/Latino; 2 Hispanic/Latino; 2 Two or more races, non-Hispanic/Latino). Average age 35. 130 applicants, 72% accepted, 65 enrolled. In 2017, 46 master's, 32 doctorates awarded. *Entrance requirements:* For master's, letters of recommendation. Additional exam requirements/recommendations for international students: Required—TOEFL (minimum score 550 paper-based; 79 iBT). *Application deadline:* For fall admission, 7/1 priority date for domestic and international students; for spring admission, 11/1 priority date for domestic and international students. Applications are processed on a rolling basis. Application fee: $35. Electronic applications accepted. *Expenses:* Contact institution. *Financial support:* Federal Work-Study, institutionally sponsored loans, and unspecified assistantships available. Financial award application deadline: 5/1; financial award applicants required to submit FAFSA. *Unit head:* Dr. Valerie M. Howard, Dean, 412-397-6801, Fax: 412-397-3277, E-mail: howardv@rmu.edu.
Website: http://snhs.rmu.edu/

Roberts Wesleyan College, Department of Nursing, Rochester, NY 14624-1997. Offers nursing education (MSN); nursing informatics (MSN); nursing leadership and administration (MSN). *Accreditation:* AACN. *Program availability:* Evening/weekend, online learning. *Degree requirements:* For master's, thesis. *Entrance requirements:* For master's, minimum GPA of 3.0; BS in nursing; interview; RN license; resume; course work in statistics. Additional exam requirements/recommendations for international students: Required—TOEFL (minimum score 90 iBT), IELTS (minimum score 6.5). Electronic applications accepted.

Rowan University, Graduate School, College of Science and Mathematics, Department of Nursing, Glassboro, NJ 08028-1701. Offers MS. *Accreditation:* AACN. Electronic applications accepted. *Expenses:* Tuition, state resident: full-time $15,020; part-time $751 per semester hour. Tuition, nonresident: full-time $15,020; part-time $751 per semester hour. *Required fees:* $3158; $157.90 per semester hour. Tuition and fees vary according to course load, campus/location and program.

Rush University, College of Nursing, PhD in Nursing Science Program, Chicago, IL 60612. Offers PhD. *Program availability:* Part-time, online only, 100% online. *Students:* 4 full-time (all women), 20 part-time (all women); includes 8 minority (3 Black or African American, non-Hispanic/Latino; 3 Asian, non-Hispanic/Latino; 2 Hispanic/Latino). 8 applicants, 63% accepted, 3 enrolled. In 2017, 4 doctorates awarded. *Degree requirements:* For doctorate, thesis/dissertation. *Entrance requirements:* For doctorate, GRE General Test, interview, 3 letters of recommendation, personal statement, current resume. Additional exam requirements/recommendations for international students: Required—TOEFL (minimum score 94 iBT). *Application deadline:* For fall admission, 1/2 for domestic students. Applications are processed on a rolling basis. Application fee: $110. Electronic applications accepted. *Expenses:* Contact institution. *Financial support:* Research assistantships, teaching assistantships, Federal Work-Study, scholarships/grants, and health care benefits available. Support available to part-time students. Financial award application deadline: 3/1; financial award applicants required to submit FAFSA. *Unit head:* Dr. Barbara Swanson, Assistant Dean, 312-942-7117, E-mail: barbara_a_swanson@rush.edu. *Application contact:* Jennifer Thorndyke, Director of Admissions, 312-563-7526, E-mail: jennifer_thorndyke@rush.edu.
Website: https://www.rushu.rush.edu/college-nursing/programs-admissions/nursing-science-phd

Rutgers University–Camden, School of Nursing–Camden, Camden, NJ 08102-1401. Offers adult gerontology primary care nurse practitioner (DNP); family nurse practitioner (DNP). *Degree requirements:* For doctorate, minimum of 1,000 clinical residency hours, evidence-based clinical project.

Rutgers University–Newark, Rutgers School of Nursing, Newark, NJ 07107-3001. Offers adult health (MSN); adult occupational health (MSN); advanced practice nursing (MSN, Post Master's Certificate); family nurse practitioner (MSN); nurse anesthesia (MSN); nursing (MSN); nursing informatics (MSN); urban health (PhD); women's health practitioner (MSN). *Accreditation:* AANA/CANAEP. *Program availability:* Part-time. *Entrance requirements:* For master's, GRE, RN license; basic life support, statistics, and health assessment experience. Additional exam requirements/recommendations for international students: Required—TOEFL. Electronic applications accepted. *Expenses:* Contact institution. *Faculty research:* HIV/AIDS, diabetes education, learned helplessness, nursing science, psychoeducation.

Sacred Heart University, Graduate Programs, College of Nursing, Fairfield, CT 06825. Offers clinical (DNP); clinical nurse leader (MSN); family nurse practitioner (MSN, Post-Master's Certificate); leadership (DNP); nursing education (MSN); nursing management and executive leadership (MSN). *Accreditation:* AACN. *Program availability:* Part-time, evening/weekend, 100% online, blended/hybrid learning. *Faculty:* 17 full-time (all women), 29 part-time/adjunct (26 women). *Students:* 21 full-time (20 women), 692 part-time (650 women); includes 136 minority (52 Black or African American, non-Hispanic/Latino; 2 American Indian or Alaska Native, non-Hispanic/Latino; 29 Asian, non-

Hispanic/Latino; 46 Hispanic/Latino; 7 Two or more races, non-Hispanic/Latino). Average age 37. 70 applicants, 69% accepted, 32 enrolled. In 2017, 260 master's, 16 doctorates awarded. *Degree requirements:* For master's, thesis, 500 clinical hours; for doctorate, capstone. *Entrance requirements:* For master's, minimum GPA of 3.0, BSN or RN plus BS (for MSN); for doctorate, minimum GPA of 3.0, MSN or BSN plus MS in related field (for DNP). Additional exam requirements/recommendations for international students: Required—TOEFL (minimum score 570 paper-based, 80 iBT), TWE, or IELTS (6.5). *Application deadline:* For fall admission, 2/15 for domestic and international students. Applications are processed on a rolling basis. Application fee: $75. Electronic applications accepted. *Expenses:* Contact institution. *Financial support:* Unspecified assistantships available. Financial award applicants required to submit FAFSA. *Unit head:* Mary Alice Donius, Dean of Nursing, 203-365-4508, E-mail: doniusm@sacredheart.edu. *Application contact:* Tara Chudy, Executive Director of Graduate Admissions, 203-365-4735, Fax: 203-365-4732, E-mail: chudyt@sacredheart.edu.
Website: http://www.sacredheart.edu/academics/collegeofhealthprofessions/academicprograms/nursing/nursingprograms/graduateprograms/

Sage Graduate School, School of Health Sciences, Department of Nursing, Troy, NY 12180-4115. Offers MS, DNS, Certificate, Post Master's Certificate. *Accreditation:* AACN. *Program availability:* Part-time, evening/weekend. *Faculty:* 6 full-time (all women), 11 part-time/adjunct (10 women). *Students:* 36 full-time (30 women), 195 part-time (180 women); includes 48 minority (21 Black or African American, non-Hispanic/Latino; 3 American Indian or Alaska Native, non-Hispanic/Latino; 11 Asian, non-Hispanic/Latino; 8 Hispanic/Latino; 5 Two or more races, non-Hispanic/Latino), 2 international. Average age 39. 250 applicants, 40% accepted, 59 enrolled. In 2017, 57 master's, 5 doctorates, 4 other advanced degrees awarded. *Degree requirements:* For master's, thesis or alternative. *Entrance requirements:* For master's, currently licensed as registered professional nurse in state of practice; baccalaureate degree in nursing from nationally-accredited program or its international equivalent. Additional exam requirements/recommendations for international students: Required—TOEFL (minimum score 550 paper-based). *Application deadline:* Applications are processed on a rolling basis. Application fee: $30. Electronic applications accepted. Tuition and fees vary according to degree level and program. *Financial support:* Fellowships, research assistantships, scholarships/grants, and unspecified assistantships available. Financial award application deadline: 3/1; financial award applicants required to submit FAFSA. *Unit head:* Dr. Theresa Hand, Dean, School of Health Sciences, 518-244-2064, Fax: 518-244-4571, E-mail: handt@sage.edu. *Application contact:* Dr. Carol Braungart, Co-Director, Graduate Nursing Program, 518-244-2459, Fax: 518-244-2009, E-mail: braunc@sage.edu.

Saginaw Valley State University, College of Health and Human Services, Program in Clinical Nurse Specialist, University Center, MI 48710. Offers MSN. *Accreditation:* AACN. *Program availability:* Part-time, evening/weekend. *Degree requirements:* For master's, thesis optional. *Entrance requirements:* Additional exam requirements/recommendations for international students: Required—TOEFL (minimum score 580 paper-based; 92 iBT). *Application deadline:* For fall admission, 7/15 for international students; for winter admission, 11/15 for international students; for spring admission, 4/15 for international students. Applications are processed on a rolling basis. Application fee: $30 ($90 for international students). Electronic applications accepted. *Expenses:* Tuition, state resident: full-time $10,156; part-time $564.20 per credit hour. Tuition, nonresident: full-time $19,336; part-time $1074.20 per credit hour. *Required fees:* $263; $14.60 per credit hour. Tuition and fees vary according to degree level and program. *Financial support:* Federal Work-Study and scholarships/grants available. Support available to part-time students. Financial award application deadline: 4/1; financial award applicants required to submit FAFSA. *Unit head:* Dr. Karen Brown-Fackler, Associate Professor of Nursing, 989-964-2185, Fax: 989-964-4925, E-mail: kmbrown4@svsu.edu. *Application contact:* Jenna Briggs, Director, Graduate and International Admissions, 989-964-6096, Fax: 989-964-2788, E-mail: gradadm@svsu.edu.

Saginaw Valley State University, College of Health and Human Services, Program in Nursing, University Center, MI 48710. Offers MSN. *Accreditation:* AACN. *Program availability:* Part-time, evening/weekend. *Students:* 9 part-time (all women); includes 3 minority (1 Black or African American, non-Hispanic/Latino; 1 Hispanic/Latino; 1 Two or more races, non-Hispanic/Latino). Average age 38. 1 applicant, 100% accepted, 1 enrolled. In 2017, 1 master's awarded. *Entrance requirements:* For master's, GRE, minimum GPA of 3.0. Additional exam requirements/recommendations for international students: Required—TOEFL (minimum score 580 paper-based; 92 iBT). *Application deadline:* For fall admission, 7/15 for international students; for winter admission, 11/15 for international students; for spring admission, 4/15 for international students. Applications are processed on a rolling basis. Application fee: $30 ($90 for international students). Electronic applications accepted. *Expenses:* Tuition, state resident: full-time $10,156; part-time $564.20 per credit hour. Tuition, nonresident: full-time $19,336; part-time $1074.20 per credit hour. *Required fees:* $263; $14.60 per credit hour. Tuition and fees vary according to degree level and program. *Financial support:* Federal Work-Study and scholarships/grants available. Support available to part-time students. *Unit head:* Dr. Karen Brown-Fackler, Coordinator, 989-964-2185, Fax: 989-964-4925, E-mail: kmbrown4@svsu.edu. *Application contact:* Jenna Briggs, Director, Graduate and International Admissions, 989-964-6096, Fax: 989-964-2788, E-mail: gradadm@svsu.edu.

Saint Anthony College of Nursing, Graduate Program, Rockford, IL 61114. Offers MSN. *Accreditation:* AACN. *Program availability:* Part-time.

St. Catherine University, Graduate Programs, Program in Nursing, St. Paul, MN 55105. Offers adult-gerontological nurse practitioner (MS); nurse educator (MS); nursing (DNP); nursing: entry-level (MS); pediatric nurse practitioner (MS). *Accreditation:* ACEN. *Program availability:* Part-time, evening/weekend. *Degree requirements:* For master's, thesis; for doctorate, portfolio, systems change project. *Entrance requirements:* For master's, GRE General Test, bachelor's degree in nursing, current nursing license, 2 years of recent clinical practice; for doctorate, master's degree in nursing, RN license, advanced nursing position. Additional exam requirements/recommendations for international students: Required—TOEFL (minimum score 600 paper-based; 100 iBT). *Application deadline:* For fall admission, 1/15 priority date for domestic students. Application fee: $35. *Expenses:* Contact institution. *Financial support:* Career-related internships or fieldwork and institutionally sponsored loans available. Support available to part-time students. Financial award application deadline: 4/1; financial award applicants required to submit FAFSA. *Unit head:* Margaret Dexheimer-Pharris, Professor/Associate Dean for Nursing, 651-690-6572, Fax: 651-690-6941, E-mail: mdpharris@stkate.edu. *Application contact:* Kristin Chalberg, Associate Director of Non-Traditional Admissions, 651-690-6868, Fax: 651-690-6064.

Saint Francis Medical Center College of Nursing, Graduate Programs, Peoria, IL 61603-3783. Offers adult gerontology (MSN); clinical nurse leader (MSN); family nurse practitioner (MSN, Post-Graduate Certificate); family psychiatric mental health nurse practitioner (MSN); neonatal nurse practitioner (MSN); nurse clinician (Post-Graduate Certificate); nurse educator (MSN, Post-Graduate Certificate); nursing (DNP); nursing management leadership (MSN). *Accreditation:* ACEN. *Program availability:* Part-time, online only, 100% online, blended/hybrid learning. *Faculty:* 11 full-time (all women), 7 part-time/adjunct (all women). *Students:* 4 full-time (all women), 239 part-time (209 women); includes 24 minority (12 Black or African American, non-Hispanic/Latino; 3 Asian, non-Hispanic/Latino; 4 Hispanic/Latino; 5 Two or more races, non-Hispanic/Latino). Average age 37. 105 applicants, 83% accepted, 60 enrolled. In 2017, 52 master's, 8 doctorates awarded. *Degree requirements:* For master's, research experience, portfolio, practicum; for doctorate, practicum. *Entrance requirements:* For master's, nursing research, health assessment, graduate course work in statistics, RN license; for doctorate, master's degree in nursing, professional portfolio, graduate statistics, transcripts, RN license. Additional exam requirements/recommendations for international students: Required—TOEFL (minimum score 550 paper-based; 79 iBT). *Application deadline:* For fall admission, 6/1 priority date for domestic and international students; for spring admission, 11/15 priority date for domestic and international students. Applications are processed on a rolling basis. Application fee: $50. *Expenses:* Contact institution. *Financial support:* In 2017–18, 13 students received support. Scholarships/grants and tuition waivers (partial) available. Support available to part-time students. Financial award application deadline: 6/15; financial award applicants required to submit FAFSA. *Faculty research:* Outcome and curriculum planning, health promotion, NCLEX-RN results, decision-making program evaluation. *Unit head:* Dr. Patti A. Stockert, President of the College, 309-655-4124, Fax: 309-624-8973, E-mail: patricia.a.stockert@osfhealthcare.org. *Application contact:* Dr. Kim A. Mitchell, Dean, Graduate Program, 309-655-2201, Fax: 309-624-8973, E-mail: kim.a.mitchell@osfhealthcare.org.
Website: http://www.sfmccon.edu/graduate-programs/

Saint Francis University, Nursing Program, Loretto, PA 15940-0600. Offers leadership/education (MSN). *Program availability:* Part-time, online only, blended/hybrid learning. *Faculty:* 2 full-time (both women), 4 part-time/adjunct (all women). *Students:* 12 part-time (all women). Average age 37. 5 applicants, 100% accepted, 4 enrolled. *Entrance requirements:* Additional exam requirements/recommendations for international students: Required—TOEFL. Application fee: $30. Electronic applications accepted. *Expenses:* $2,572.50 per course, $857.50 per credit, $55 technology fee per semester part-time, $111 technology fee per semester full-time. *Financial support:* Applicants required to submit FAFSA. *Unit head:* Dr. Camille Wendekier, RN, Coordinator, E-mail: cwendekier@francis.edu. *Application contact:* Dr. Peter Raymond Skoner, Associate Provost, 814-472-3085, Fax: 814-472-3365, E-mail: pskoner@francis.edu.
Website: https://www.francis.edu/Nursing-Masters/

St. John Fisher College, Wegmans School of Nursing, Advanced Practice Nursing Program, Rochester, NY 14618-3597. Offers MS, Certificate. *Accreditation:* AACN. *Program availability:* Part-time, evening/weekend. *Faculty:* 13 full-time (12 women), 4 part-time/adjunct (3 women). *Students:* 5 full-time (3 women), 193 part-time (170 women); includes 30 minority (16 Black or African American, non-Hispanic/Latino; 1 American Indian or Alaska Native, non-Hispanic/Latino; 3 Asian, non-Hispanic/Latino; 9 Hispanic/Latino; 1 Two or more races, non-Hispanic/Latino). Average age 31. 133 applicants, 51% accepted, 50 enrolled. In 2017, 39 master's awarded. *Degree requirements:* For master's, clinical practice, project; for Certificate, clinical practice. *Entrance requirements:* For master's, BSN; undergraduate course work in statistics, health assessment, and nursing research; current New York State RN license; 2 letters of recommendation; current resume. Additional exam requirements/recommendations for international students: Required—TOEFL (minimum score 575 paper-based; 80 iBT). *Application deadline:* Applications are processed on a rolling basis. Application fee: $30. Electronic applications accepted. *Expenses:* Contact institution. *Financial support:* Scholarships/grants and traineeships available. Financial award applicants required to submit FAFSA. *Faculty research:* Chronic illness, pediatric injury, women's health, public health policy, health care teams. *Unit head:* Dr. Colleen Donegan, Graduate Director, 585-899-3788, Fax: 585-385-8466, E-mail: cdonegan@sjfc.edu. *Application contact:* Michelle Gosier, Director of Transfer and Graduate Admissions, 585-385-8064, E-mail: mgosier@sjfc.edu.
Website: https://www.sjfc.edu/graduate-programs/ms-in-nursing-programs/

St. John Fisher College, Wegmans School of Nursing, Doctor of Nursing Practice Program, Rochester, NY 14618-3597. Offers DNP. *Accreditation:* AACN. *Program availability:* Part-time, evening/weekend. *Faculty:* 3 full-time (2 women), 2 part-time/adjunct (1 woman). *Students:* 10 full-time (9 women), 8 part-time (7 women); includes 5 minority (3 Black or African American, non-Hispanic/Latino; 2 Asian, non-Hispanic/Latino). Average age 36. 3 applicants, 67% accepted, 2 enrolled. In 2017, 5 doctorates awarded. *Degree requirements:* For doctorate, 1,000 hours of clinical practice, clinical scholarship project. *Entrance requirements:* For doctorate, New York State RN license; New York State Certificate as advanced practice nurse (APN) or eligibility and National Professional Certification in APN specialty; currently practicing as APN; 2 letters of recommendation; writing sample. *Application deadline:* For fall admission, 8/1 for domestic students; for spring admission, 12/1 for domestic students. Applications are processed on a rolling basis. Application fee: $0. Electronic applications accepted. *Expenses:* Contact institution. *Financial support:* Scholarships/grants available. Financial award applicants required to submit FAFSA. *Unit head:* Dr. John Kirchgessner, Program Director, 585-899-3739, E-mail: jKirchgessner@sjfc.edu. *Application contact:* Michelle Gosier, Director of Transfer and Graduate Admissions, 585-385-8064, E-mail: mgosier@sjfc.edu.
Website: https://www.sjfc.edu/graduate-programs/doctor-of-nursing-practice-dnp/

St. Joseph's College, Long Island Campus, Program in Nursing, Patchogue, NY 11772-2399. Offers adult-gerontology clinical nurse specialist (MS); adult-gerontology primary care nurse practitioner (MS); nursing education (MS). *Program availability:* Part-time, evening/weekend. *Faculty:* 4 full-time (all women), 1 (woman) part-time/adjunct. *Students:* 1 (woman) full-time, 40 part-time (36 women); includes 15 minority (7 Black or African American, non-Hispanic/Latino; 3 Asian, non-Hispanic/Latino; 5 Hispanic/Latino). Average age 41. 39 applicants, 69% accepted, 21 enrolled. In 2017, 6 master's awarded. *Entrance requirements:* For master's, one year of professional clinical practice prior to admission, proof of New York State RN license and current professional registration, curriculum vitae, personal statement, two letters of reference, official college transcripts, proof of malpractice insurance. Additional exam requirements/recommendations for international students: Required—TOEFL (minimum score 550 paper-based; 80 iBT). *Application deadline:* Applications are processed on a rolling basis. Application fee: $25. Electronic applications accepted. *Expenses: Tuition:* Full-time $17,550; part-time $975 per credit. *Required fees:* $362. *Financial support:* In 2017–18, 23 students received support. *Unit head:* Dr. Maria Fletcher, RN, Director/Associate Professor, 631-687-5180, E-mail: mfletcher@sjcny.edu.
Website: http://www.sjcny.edu/long-island

St. Joseph's College, New York, Program in Nursing, Brooklyn, NY 11205-3688. Offers adult-gerontology clinical nurse specialist (MS); adult-gerontology primary care nurse practitioner (MS); nursing education (MS). *Accreditation:* ACEN. *Program availability:* Part-time, evening/weekend. *Faculty:* 4 full-time (all women), 1 (woman) part-time/adjunct. *Students:* 47 part-time (46 women); includes 38 minority (35 Black or African American, non-Hispanic/Latino; 1 Asian, non-Hispanic/Latino; 2 Two or more races, non-Hispanic/Latino). Average age 45. 51 applicants, 71% accepted, 20 enrolled. In 2017, 7 master's awarded. *Entrance requirements:* For master's, one year of

professional clinical practice, proof of NY State RN license and current professional registration, curriculum vitae, personal statement, 2 letters of reference, official transcripts, malpractice insurance. Additional exam requirements/recommendations for international students: Required—TOEFL (minimum score 80 iBT). *Application deadline:* Applications are processed on a rolling basis. Application fee: $25. Electronic applications accepted. *Expenses: Tuition:* Full-time $17,550; part-time $975 per credit. *Required fees:* $362. *Financial support:* In 2017–18, 7 students received support. *Unit head:* Maria Fletcher, Associate Professor/Director, 718-940-5891, E-mail: mfletcher@sjcny.edu.
Website: http://www.sjcny.edu

Saint Joseph's College of Maine, Master of Science in Nursing Program, Standish, ME 04084. Offers administration (MSN); education (MSN); family nurse practitioner (MSN); nursing administration and leadership (Certificate); nursing and health care education (Certificate). *Accreditation:* AACN. *Program availability:* Part-time, online learning. *Entrance requirements:* For master's, MAT. Electronic applications accepted.

Saint Louis University, Graduate Programs, School of Nursing, St. Louis, MO 63104-1099. Offers MSN, DNP, PhD, Certificate. *Accreditation:* AACN. *Program availability:* Part-time, online learning. *Degree requirements:* For master's, comprehensive exam, thesis optional; for doctorate, comprehensive exam, thesis/dissertation, preliminary exams. *Entrance requirements:* For master's, 3 letters of recommendation, resumé, transcripts; for doctorate, GRE General Test, 3 letters of recommendation, curriculum vitae; for Certificate, 3 letters of recommendation, resumé, transcripts, copy of RN license, personal statement. Additional exam requirements/recommendations for international students: Required—TOEFL (minimum score 525 paper-based). Electronic applications accepted. *Faculty research:* Sensory enhancement to the elderly, fall prevention in elderly, tube feeding placement and gastroenterology, patient outcomes, exercise behavior in the older adult.

Saint Mary-of-the-Woods College, Master of Science in Nursing Program, Saint Mary of the Woods, IN 47876. Offers MSN. *Expenses: Tuition:* Full-time $4260; part-time $3550 per credit hour. Tuition and fees vary according to program.

Saint Mary's College, Graduate Programs, Doctor of Nursing Practice Program, Notre Dame, IN 46556. Offers adult - gerontology acute care (DNP); adult - gerontology primary care (DNP); family nurse practitioner (DNP). *Program availability:* Part-time-only. *Faculty:* 7 full-time (all women), 4 part-time/adjunct (3 women). *Students:* 39 part-time (37 women); includes 12 minority (4 Black or African American, non-Hispanic/Latino; 5 Asian, non-Hispanic/Latino; 3 Hispanic/Latino). Average age 31. 36 applicants, 60% accepted, 20 enrolled. *Degree requirements:* For doctorate, comprehensive exam, thesis/dissertation. *Entrance requirements:* For doctorate, BSN or MSN, unencumbered RN license or eligibility for RN licensure, official transcripts from previously-attended institutions, 3 letters of recommendation, personal statement, resume or curriculum vitae. Additional exam requirements/recommendations for international students: Recommended—TOEFL (minimum score 80 iBT), IELTS (minimum score 6.5). *Application deadline:* For fall admission, 6/15 priority date for domestic and international students. Applications are processed on a rolling basis. Application fee: $65. Electronic applications accepted. *Expenses:* $5,382 per semester. *Financial support:* Application deadline: 3/1; applicants required to submit FAFSA. *Faculty research:* Suicide prevention, infant death prevention, delirium management, teaching methodologies, nurses' perceptions of care. *Unit head:* Linda Paskiewicz, Director of the Department of Nursing Science, 574-284-4679, E-mail: lpaskie@saintmarys.edu. *Application contact:* Melissa Fruscione, Graduate Admission, 574-284-5098, E-mail: graduateadmission@saintmarys.edu.
Website: https://grad.saintmarys.edu/academic-programs/doctor-nursing-practice

Saint Peter's University, School of Nursing, Nursing Program, Jersey City, NJ 07306-5997. Offers adult nurse practitioner (MSN, Certificate); advanced practice (DNP); case management (MSN, DNP). *Accreditation:* AACN. *Program availability:* Part-time, evening/weekend. *Entrance requirements:* Additional exam requirements/recommendations for international students: Required—TOEFL. Electronic applications accepted.

Saint Xavier University, Graduate Studies, School of Nursing, Chicago, IL 60655-3105. Offers MSN, Certificate, MBA/MS. *Accreditation:* AACN. *Program availability:* Part-time, evening/weekend. *Entrance requirements:* For master's, GRE General Test or MAT, minimum GPA of 3.0, RN license.

Salem State University, School of Graduate Studies, Program in Nursing, Salem, MA 01970-5353. Offers adult-gerontology primary care nursing (MSN); nursing administration (MSN); nursing education (MSN); MBA/MSN. *Accreditation:* AACN. *Program availability:* Part-time, evening/weekend. *Entrance requirements:* For master's, GRE or MAT. Additional exam requirements/recommendations for international students: Required—TOEFL (minimum score 550 paper-based; 80 iBT) or IELTS (minimum score 5.5).

Salisbury University, DNP Program, Salisbury, MD 21801. Offers family nurse practitioner (DNP); nursing leadership (DNP). *Accreditation:* AACN. *Program availability:* Part-time. *Faculty:* 10 full-time (all women). *Students:* 35 full-time (32 women), 4 part-time (all women); includes 8 minority (all Black or African American, non-Hispanic/Latino). Average age 33. 21 applicants, 43% accepted, 9 enrolled. In 2017, 1 doctorate awarded. Terminal master's awarded for partial completion of doctoral program. *Degree requirements:* For doctorate, thesis/dissertation. *Entrance requirements:* For doctorate, three letters of reference; transcripts from colleges and universities attended; nursing degree; personal statement; minimum GPA of 3.0; U.S. RN license; resume. Additional exam requirements/recommendations for international students: Required—TOEFL (minimum score 550 paper-based; 79 iBT), IELTS (minimum score 6.5). *Application deadline:* For fall admission, 3/1 priority date for domestic and international students. Applications are processed on a rolling basis. Application fee: $65. Electronic applications accepted. *Expenses:* $640 per credit hour resident; $807 per credit hour non-resident; $92 per credit hour fees. *Financial support:* In 2017–18, 3 students received support. Career-related internships or fieldwork and scholarships/grants available. Support available to part-time students. Financial award application deadline: 3/1; financial award applicants required to submit FAFSA. *Faculty research:* Simulation education; chronic disease management; palliative care; gerontology; mental illness. *Unit head:* Dr. Lisa Seldomridge, Graduate Program Director, Nursing DNP, 410-543-6413, E-mail: laseldomridge@salisbury.edu.
Website: http://www.salisbury.edu/gsr/gradstudies/DNPpage.html

Salisbury University, MS in Nursing Program, Salisbury, MD 21801-6837. Offers nursing (MS), including clinical nurse educator, health care leadership. *Accreditation:* AACN. *Program availability:* Part-time. *Faculty:* 4 full-time (3 women), 2 part-time/adjunct (both women). *Students:* 3 part-time (all women); includes 1 minority (Black or African American, non-Hispanic/Latino). Average age 40. In 2017, 1 master's awarded. *Degree requirements:* For master's, thesis. *Entrance requirements:* For master's, two letters of recommendation; transcripts from colleges and universities attended; BSN with minimum cumulative GPA of 3.0; personal statement; current U.S. RN license; resume. Additional exam requirements/recommendations for international students: Required—TOEFL (minimum score 550 paper-based; 79 iBT), IELTS (minimum score 6.5). *Application deadline:* For fall admission, 3/1 for domestic and international students. Application fee: $65. Electronic applications accepted. *Expenses:* $640 per credit hour resident; $807 per credit hour non-resident; $92 per credit hour fees. *Financial support:* Career-related internships or fieldwork and scholarships/grants available. Support available to part-time students. Financial award application deadline: 3/1; financial award applicants required to submit FAFSA. *Faculty research:* Gerontology; simulation education; palliative care; chronic disease management; mental illness. *Unit head:* Dr. Lisa Seldomridge, Graduate Program Director, Nursing MS, 410-543-6413, E-mail: laseldomridge@salisbury.edu.
Website: http://www.salisbury.edu/gsr/gradstudies/MSNpage.html

Salve Regina University, Program in Nursing, Newport, RI 02840-4192. Offers DNP. *Program availability:* Part-time, evening/weekend. *Entrance requirements:* For doctorate, BS in nursing with minimum cumulative GPA of 3.0, unencumbered license or eligibility for RN licensure in the state of Rhode Island, clear criminal background check, course in statistics. Electronic applications accepted. *Expenses:* Contact institution.

Samford University, Ida Moffett School of Nursing, Birmingham, AL 35229. Offers administration (DNP); advanced practice (DNP); dual nurse practitioner (family/emergency) (DNP); family nurse practitioner (MSN, DNP); nurse anesthesia (MSN, DNP); nursing administration (DNP), including health systems and administration, informatics, transformation of care. *Accreditation:* AACN; AANA/CANAEP. *Program availability:* Part-time, evening/weekend, blended/hybrid learning. *Faculty:* 20 full-time (19 women), 3 part-time/adjunct (0 women). *Students:* 296 full-time (240 women), 41 part-time (38 women); includes 67 minority (43 Black or African American, non-Hispanic/Latino; 2 American Indian or Alaska Native, non-Hispanic/Latino; 6 Asian, non-Hispanic/Latino; 8 Hispanic/Latino; 8 Two or more races, non-Hispanic/Latino). Average age 35. 79 applicants, 71% accepted, 29 enrolled. In 2017, 117 master's, 39 doctorates awarded. *Degree requirements:* For doctorate, project with poster presentation. *Entrance requirements:* For master's, GRE within the past five years (for nurse anesthesia), RN, minimum nursing GPA of 3.0, undergraduate course in nursing research with minimum C grade, undergraduate health assessment course with minimum B grade; interview, 1 year full-time critical care as RN, 3 letters of recommendation, undergraduate courses in general chemistry and research with minimum B grade for both (for nurse anesthesia); for doctorate, unencumbered licensure as registered nurse; master's degree from CCNE-, CNEA-, or ACEN-accredited program in the area of advanced practice or administration; minimum master's degree cumulative GPA of 3.5; video interview submission. Additional exam requirements/recommendations for international students: Required—TOEFL (minimum score 575 paper-based; 90 iBT); Recommended—IELTS (minimum score 6.5). *Application deadline:* For fall admission, 4/1 for domestic and international students; for spring admission, 8/1 for domestic and international students; for summer admission, 1/1 for domestic and international students. Application fee: $50. Electronic applications accepted. *Expenses:* $809 per credit (for DNP and MSN); $9,737 per semester (for MSN in nurse anesthesia). *Financial support:* In 2017–18, 63 students received support. Application deadline: 2/15; applicants required to submit FAFSA. *Unit head:* Dr. Nena F. Sanders, Vice Provost, College of Health Sciences/Ida Moffett School of Nursing Dean/Professor, 205-726-2612, E-mail: nfsander@samford.edu. *Application contact:* Allyson Maddox, Director of Graduate Student Services, 205-726-2047, E-mail: amaddox@samford.edu.
Website: http://samford.edu/nursing

Samuel Merritt University, School of Nursing, Oakland, CA 94609-3108. Offers case management (MSN); family nurse practitioner (MSN, DNP, Certificate); nurse anesthetist (MSN, Certificate); nursing (DNP). *Accreditation:* AACN; AANA/CANAEP (one or more programs are accredited). *Program availability:* Part-time, evening/weekend, 100% online, blended/hybrid learning. *Faculty:* 57 full-time (49 women), 90 part-time/adjunct (77 women). *Students:* 401 full-time (322 women), 267 part-time (202 women); includes 438 minority (52 Black or African American, non-Hispanic/Latino; 4 American Indian or Alaska Native, non-Hispanic/Latino; 224 Asian, non-Hispanic/Latino; 108 Hispanic/Latino; 9 Native Hawaiian or other Pacific Islander, non-Hispanic/Latino; 41 Two or more races, non-Hispanic/Latino). 788 applicants, 54% accepted, 306 enrolled. In 2017, 176 master's, 6 doctorates, 7 other advanced degrees awarded. *Degree requirements:* For master's, thesis or alternative; for doctorate, project. *Entrance requirements:* For master's, GRE General Test (for nurse anesthetist program), minimum GPA of 2.5 in science, 3.0 overall; previous course work in statistics; current RN license; for doctorate and Certificate, minimum GPA of 2.5 in science, 3.0 overall; previous course work in statistics; current RN license. Additional exam requirements/recommendations for international students: Required—TOEFL (minimum score 100 iBT). *Application deadline:* For fall admission, 7/1 priority date for domestic students; for spring admission, 11/1 priority date for domestic students; for summer admission, 3/1 priority date for domestic students. Applications are processed on a rolling basis. Application fee: $65. Electronic applications accepted. *Expenses:* $1,394 per unit tuition (for MSN); $1,208 per unit tuition (for DNP). *Financial support:* Career-related internships or fieldwork, Federal Work-Study, scholarships/grants, and traineeships available. Support available to part-time students. Financial award applicants required to submit FAFSA. *Faculty research:* Gerontology, community health, maternal-child health, sexually transmitted diseases, substance abuse, oncology. *Unit head:* Dr. Audrey Berman, Dean of Nursing, 510-869-6733, Fax: 510-869-6525. *Application contact:* Timothy Cranford, Dean of Admission, 510-869-6576, Fax: 510-869-6525, E-mail: admission@samuelmerritt.edu.
Website: http://www.samuelmerritt.edu/nursing

San Diego State University, Graduate and Research Affairs, College of Health and Human Services, School of Nursing, San Diego, CA 92182. Offers MS. *Accreditation:* AACN; ACNM/ACME. *Program availability:* Part-time, evening/weekend. *Entrance requirements:* For master's, GRE General Test, previous course work in statistics and physical assessment, 3 letters of recommendation, California RN license. Additional exam requirements/recommendations for international students: Required—TOEFL. Electronic applications accepted. *Faculty research:* Health promotion, nursing systems and leadership, maternal-child nursing, advanced practice nursing, child oral health.

San Francisco State University, Division of Graduate Studies, College of Health and Social Sciences, School of Nursing, San Francisco, CA 94132-1722. Offers adult acute care (MS); clinical nurse specialist (MS); community/public health nursing (MS); family nurse practitioner (Certificate); nursing administration (MS); pediatrics (MS); women's health (MS). *Accreditation:* AACN. *Program availability:* Part-time. *Application deadline:* Applications are processed on a rolling basis. *Financial support:* Career-related internships or fieldwork available. *Unit head:* Connie Carr, Assistant Director of Graduate Programs, 415-338-6856, Fax: 415-338-0555, E-mail: ccarr@sfsu.edu.
Website: http://nursing.sfsu.edu

San Jose State University, Graduate Studies and Research, College of Health and Human Sciences, San Jose, CA 95192-0049. Offers criminology (MS), including global criminology, law and justice; justice studies (MS); kinesiology (MA), including athletic training, exercise physiology, interdisciplinary, sport studies, sports management; library and information science (MLIS); mass communications (MS); nursing (MS), including family nurse practitioner; nutritional science (MS); occupational therapy (MS); public health (MPH); social work (MSW); MD/M Div. *Program availability:* Part-time, 100% online, blended/hybrid learning. *Faculty:* 15 full-time (7 women), 6 part-time/adjunct (3

women). *Students:* 517 full-time (407 women), 405 part-time (302 women); includes 523 minority (39 Black or African American, non-Hispanic/Latino; 2 American Indian or Alaska Native, non-Hispanic/Latino; 141 Asian, non-Hispanic/Latino; 226 Hispanic/Latino; 2 Native Hawaiian or other Pacific Islander, non-Hispanic/Latino; 113 Two or more races, non-Hispanic/Latino), 14 international. Average age 32. 1,250 applicants, 45% accepted, 375 enrolled. In 2017, 808 master's awarded. *Degree requirements:* For master's, thesis (for some programs), graduate writing assessment. *Entrance requirements:* Additional exam requirements/recommendations for international students: Required—TOEFL (minimum score 550 paper-based; 80 iBT), IELTS (minimum score 6.5), PTE (minimum score 53). *Application deadline:* For fall admission, 2/1 for domestic and international students. Applications are processed on a rolling basis. Application fee: $55. Electronic applications accepted. *Expenses:* Tuition, state resident: full-time $7176. Tuition, nonresident: full-time $16,680. Tuition and fees vary according to course load and program. *Financial support:* Fellowships, research assistantships, teaching assistantships, career-related internships or fieldwork, Federal Work-Study, scholarships/grants, and tuition waivers (full and partial) available. Support available to part-time students. Financial award application deadline: 4/24; financial award applicants required to submit FAFSA. *Unit head:* Dr. Mary Schutten, Dean, College of Health and Human Sciences, 408-924-2900, Fax: 408-924-2901, E-mail: mary.schutten@sjsu.edu.
Website: http://www.sjsu.edu/casa/

Seattle Pacific University, MS in Nursing Program, Seattle, WA 98119-1997. Offers administration (MSN); adult/gerontology nurse practitioner (MSN); clinical nurse specialist (MSN); family nurse practitioner (MSN, Certificate); informatics (MSN); nurse educator (MSN). *Accreditation:* AACN. *Program availability:* Part-time. *Students:* 22 full-time (17 women), 40 part-time (35 women); includes 13 minority (4 Black or African American, non-Hispanic/Latino; 1 American Indian or Alaska Native, non-Hispanic/Latino; 7 Asian, non-Hispanic/Latino; 1 Two or more races, non-Hispanic/Latino). Average age 36. 52 applicants, 73% accepted, 22 enrolled. In 2017, 23 master's awarded. *Degree requirements:* For master's, thesis. *Entrance requirements:* For master's, personal statement, transcripts, undergraduate nursing degree, proof of undergraduate statistics course with minimum GPA of 2.0, 2 recommendations. *Application deadline:* For fall admission, 1/15 priority date for domestic students; for spring admission, 1/15 for domestic students. Applications are processed on a rolling basis. Application fee: $50. Electronic applications accepted. *Expenses:* Contact institution. *Financial support:* Fellowships and scholarships/grants available. Financial award applicants required to submit FAFSA. *Unit head:* Dr. Christine Hoyle, Associate Dean, 206-281-2469, E-mail: hoylec@spu.edu.
Website: http://spu.edu/academics/school-of-health-sciences/undergraduate-programs/nursing

Seattle University, College of Nursing, Doctor of Nursing Practice Program, Seattle, WA 98122-1090. Offers DNP. *Accreditation:* AACN. *Program availability:* Evening/weekend. *Faculty:* 29 full-time (25 women), 20 part-time/adjunct (18 women). *Students:* 5 full-time (4 women), 21 part-time (18 women); includes 4 minority (1 Asian, non-Hispanic/Latino; 2 Hispanic/Latino; 1 Two or more races, non-Hispanic/Latino). Average age 41. In 2017, 10 doctorates awarded. *Degree requirements:* For doctorate, capstone project. *Entrance requirements:* For doctorate, letter of intent. *Application deadline:* For fall admission, 11/1 priority date for domestic students. *Expenses:* *Tuition:* Full-time $12,960. *Required fees:* $570. Tuition and fees vary according to program. *Financial support:* In 2017–18, 6 students received support. *Unit head:* Dr. Kristen Swanson, Dean, 206-296-5670, E-mail: swansonk@seattleu.edu. *Application contact:* Janet Shandley, Director of Graduate Admissions, 206-296-5900, Fax: 206-298-5656, E-mail: grad_admissions@seattleu.edu.
Website: https://www.seattleu.edu/nursing/dnp/

Seton Hall University, College of Nursing, South Orange, NJ 07079-2697. Offers advanced practice in primary health care (MSN, DNP), including adult/gerontological nurse practitioner, pediatric nurse practitioner; entry into practice (MSN); health systems administration (MSN, DNP); nursing (PhD); nursing case management (MSN); nursing education (MA); school nurse (MSN); MSN/MA. *Accreditation:* AACN. *Program availability:* Part-time, online learning. *Degree requirements:* For master's, research project; for doctorate, dissertation or scholarly project. *Entrance requirements:* For doctorate, GRE (waived for students with GPA of 3.5 or higher). Additional exam requirements/recommendations for international students: Required—TOEFL. Electronic applications accepted. *Faculty research:* Parent/child, adult, and gerontological nursing; breast cancer; families of children with HIV; parish nursing.

Shenandoah University, Eleanor Wade Custer School of Nursing, Winchester, VA 22601. Offers adult gerontology primary care nurse practitioner (Graduate Certificate); adult-gerontology primary care nurse practitioner (MSN); family nurse practitioner (MSN, DNP, Graduate Certificate); general (MSN); health systems leadership (DNP); health systems management (MSN, Graduate Certificate); nurse midwifery (MSN); nurse-midwifery (Graduate Certificate); nursing education (Graduate Certificate); nursing practice (DNP); psychiatric mental health nurse practitioner (MSN, DNP, Graduate Certificate). *Accreditation:* AACN; ACNM/ACME. *Faculty:* 17 full-time (all women), 6 part-time/adjunct (all women). *Students:* 30 full-time (26 women), 51 part-time (48 women); includes 19 minority (13 Black or African American, non-Hispanic/Latino; 3 Asian, non-Hispanic/Latino; 2 Hispanic/Latino; 1 Two or more races, non-Hispanic/Latino), 3 international. Average age 37. 52 applicants, 88% accepted, 34 enrolled. In 2017, 18 master's, 1 doctorate, 28 other advanced degrees awarded. *Degree requirements:* For master's, research project, clinical hours; for doctorate, scholarly project, clinical hours; for Graduate Certificate, clinical hours. *Entrance requirements:* For master's, United States RN license; minimum GPA of 3.0; 2080 hours of clinical experience; curriculum vitae; 3 letters of recommendation from former dean, faculty member, or advisor familiar with the applicant, and a former or current supervisor; two-to-three-page essay on a specified topic; for doctorate, MSN, minimum GPA of 3.0, 3 letters of recommendation, interview, BSN, two-to-three page essay on a specific topic, 500-word statement of clinical practice research interest, resume, current U.S. RN license, 2080 clinical hours; for Graduate Certificate, MSN, minimum GPA of 3.0, 2 letters of recommendation, minimum of one year (2080 hours) of clinical nursing experience, interview, two-to-three page essay on a specific topic, resume, current United States RN license. Additional exam requirements/recommendations for international students: Required—TOEFL (minimum score 558 paper-based; 83 iBT). *Application deadline:* For fall admission, 4/15 priority date for domestic and international students; for spring admission, 11/1 for domestic and international students; for summer admission, 3/1 for domestic and international students. Application fee: $30. Electronic applications accepted. *Expenses:* $22,451 tuition, plus $3,579 fees (student services fee, technology fee, and clinical fee). *Financial support:* In 2017–18, 32 students received support. Scholarships/grants and unspecified assistantships available. Financial award applicants required to submit FAFSA. *Faculty research:* Emergency preparedness, workplace environment, maternal child, inter-professional education, health policy. *Total annual research expenditures:* $30,000. *Unit head:* Dr. Kathleen LaSala, RN, Dean, 540-678-4381, Fax: 540-665-5519, E-mail: klasala@su.edu. *Application contact:* Andrew Woodall, Executive Director of Recruitment and Admissions, 540-665-4581, Fax: 540-665-4627, E-mail: admit@su.edu.
Website: http://www.su.edu/nursing/

Simmons College, School of Nursing and Health Sciences, Boston, MA 02115. Offers didactic dietetics (Certificate); dietetic internship (Certificate); health professions education (PhD, CAGS); nursing (MS, MSN), including family nurse practitioner (MS); nursing practice (DNP); nutrition and health promotion (MS); physical therapy (DPT); sports nutrition (Certificate). *Accreditation:* AACN. *Program availability:* Part-time, 100% online, blended/hybrid learning. *Faculty:* 34 full-time (28 women), 44 part-time/adjunct (40 women). *Students:* 390 full-time (350 women), 1,286 part-time (1,169 women); includes 346 minority (131 Black or African American, non-Hispanic/Latino; 6 American Indian or Alaska Native, non-Hispanic/Latino; 75 Asian, non-Hispanic/Latino; 91 Hispanic/Latino; 3 Native Hawaiian or other Pacific Islander, non-Hispanic/Latino; 40 Two or more races, non-Hispanic/Latino), 9 international. Average age 34. 1,219 applicants, 74% accepted, 481 enrolled. In 2017, 423 master's, 39 doctorates, 55 other advanced degrees awarded. *Entrance requirements:* For doctorate, GRE. Additional exam requirements/recommendations for international students: Required—TOEFL (minimum score 570 paper-based; 88 iBT). *Application deadline:* For fall admission, 6/1 for international students. Application fee: $50. Electronic applications accepted. *Expenses:* $1,278 per credit, $116 activity fee per semester. *Financial support:* In 2017–18, 15 research assistantships with partial tuition reimbursements were awarded; scholarships/grants and unspecified assistantships also available. Financial award applicants required to submit FAFSA. *Unit head:* Dr. Judy Beal, Dean, 617-521-2139. *Application contact:* Brett DiMarzo, Director of Graduate Admission, 617-521-2651, Fax: 617-521-3137, E-mail: brett.dimarzo@simmons.edu.
Website: http://www.simmons.edu/snhs/

Sonoma State University, School of Science and Technology, Family Nurse Practitioner Program, Rohnert Park, CA 94928. Offers MSN. *Accreditation:* ACEN. *Program availability:* Part-time. *Degree requirements:* For master's, comprehensive exam, thesis or alternative, oral exams. *Entrance requirements:* For master's, GRE General Test, BSN, minimum GPA of 3.0, course work in statistics, physical assessment, RN license. Additional exam requirements/recommendations for international students: Required—TOEFL (minimum score 500 paper-based). *Application deadline:* For fall admission, 11/30 for domestic students. Application fee: $55. *Financial support:* Traineeships available. Financial award applicants required to submit FAFSA. *Faculty research:* Neonatal ethics. *Unit head:* Dr. Mary Ellen Wilkosz, Chair, 707-664-2297, E-mail: mark.wilkosz@sonoma.edu. *Application contact:* Dr. Wendy Smith, Assistant Director, 707-664-2276, E-mail: wendy.smith@sonoma.edu.
Website: http://www.sonoma.edu/nursing/fnpp/

South Dakota State University, Graduate School, College of Nursing, Brookings, SD 57007. Offers MS, PhD. *Accreditation:* AACN. *Program availability:* Part-time, evening/weekend, online learning. *Degree requirements:* For master's, comprehensive exam, thesis (for some programs), oral exam. *Entrance requirements:* For master's, nurse registration; for doctorate, nurse registration, MS. Additional exam requirements/recommendations for international students: Required—TOEFL (minimum score 525 paper-based; 71 iBT). *Expenses:* Contact institution. *Faculty research:* Rural health, aging, health promotion, Native American health, woman's health, underserved populations, quality of life.

Southeastern Louisiana University, College of Nursing and Health Sciences, School of Nursing, Hammond, LA 70402. Offers nursing (MSN); nursing practice (DNP). *Accreditation:* AACN. *Program availability:* Part-time. *Faculty:* 17 full-time (16 women), 2 part-time/adjunct (1 woman). *Students:* 29 full-time (26 women), 133 part-time (111 women); includes 29 minority (14 Black or African American, non-Hispanic/Latino; 2 Asian, non-Hispanic/Latino; 12 Hispanic/Latino; 1 Two or more races, non-Hispanic/Latino), 1 international. Average age 35. 68 applicants, 49% accepted, 23 enrolled. In 2017, 45 master's, 13 doctorates awarded. *Degree requirements:* For master's, thesis. *Entrance requirements:* For master's, GRE, evidence of valid, unencumbered Louisiana Registered Nurse license; documentation of physical assessment skills for the following roles: nurse practitioner and nurse educator. Additional exam requirements/recommendations for international students: Required—TOEFL (minimum score 500 paper-based; 61 iBT). *Application deadline:* For fall admission, 7/15 priority date for domestic students, 6/1 priority date for international students; for spring admission, 12/1 priority date for domestic students, 10/1 priority date for international students. Applications are processed on a rolling basis. Application fee: $20 ($30 for international students). Electronic applications accepted. *Expenses:* Tuition, state resident: full-time $6684. Tuition, nonresident: full-time $19,162. *Required fees:* $2088. *Financial support:* In 2017–18, 23 students received support. Federal Work-Study, institutionally sponsored loans, scholarships/grants, traineeships, tuition waivers (full), and unspecified assistantships available. Support available to part-time students. Financial award application deadline: 5/1; financial award applicants required to submit FAFSA. *Faculty research:* Men's health, stem cell research, pediatric obesity, nursing informatics. *Unit head:* Dr. Eileen Creel, Department Head, School of Nursing, 985-549-2156, Fax: 985-549-2869, E-mail: eileen.creel@southeastern.edu. *Application contact:* Sandra Meyers, Graduate Admissions Analyst, 985-549-5620, Fax: 985-549-5632, E-mail: admissions@southeastern.edu.
Website: http://www.southeastern.edu/acad_research/depts/nurs/about/index.html

Southeast Missouri State University, School of Graduate Studies, Department of Nursing, Cape Girardeau, MO 63701-4799. Offers MSN. *Accreditation:* AACN. *Faculty:* 9 full-time (all women), 1 (woman) part-time/adjunct. *Students:* 11 full-time (all women), 15 part-time (12 women); includes 2 minority (1 Black or African American, non-Hispanic/Latino; 1 Asian, non-Hispanic/Latino). Average age 31. 19 applicants, 68% accepted, 12 enrolled. In 2017, 9 master's awarded. *Degree requirements:* For master's, comprehensive exam, scholarly paper. *Entrance requirements:* For master's, baccalaureate degree with upper-division major in nursing from program accredited by the National League for Nursing or the Commission on Collegiate Nursing Education; minimum GPA of 3.25; current Missouri license as registered professional nurse; evidence of professional liability insurance. Additional exam requirements/recommendations for international students: Required—TOEFL (minimum score 550 paper-based; 79 iBT), IELTS (minimum score 6), PTE (minimum score 53). *Application deadline:* For fall admission, 4/1 for domestic and international students; for spring admission, 11/21 for domestic students, 10/1 for international students. Applications are processed on a rolling basis. Application fee: $30 ($40 for international students). Electronic applications accepted. *Expenses:* $270.35 per credit hour in-state tuition, $33.40 per credit hour fees. *Financial support:* In 2017–18, 5 students received support, including 5 teaching assistantships with full tuition reimbursements available; career-related internships or fieldwork, Federal Work-Study, scholarships/grants, traineeships, tuition waivers (full), and unspecified assistantships also available. Financial award application deadline: 6/30; financial award applicants required to submit FAFSA. *Faculty research:* Rural health, domestic abuse, substance abuse, use of simulation for nursing education, student retention and success. *Unit head:* Dr. Gloria Green, Chair, 573-651-5961, Fax: 573-651-2141, E-mail: gjgreen@semo.edu. *Application contact:* Dr. Elaine Jackson, Graduate Program Coordinator, 573-651-2871, Fax: 573-651-2141, E-mail: ejackson@semo.edu.
Website: http://www.semo.edu/nursing/

Southern Adventist University, School of Nursing, Collegedale, TN 37315-0370. Offers adult/gerontology acute care nurse practitioner (MSN, DNP); adult/gerontology

nurse practitioner (MSN); family nurse practitioner (MSN, DNP); lifestyle therapeutics (DNP); nurse educator (MSN, DNP); psychiatric mental health nurse practitioner (MSN, DNP); MSN/MBA. *Accreditation:* ACEN. *Program availability:* Part-time. *Degree requirements:* For master's, thesis or project. *Entrance requirements:* For master's, RN license. Additional exam requirements/recommendations for international students: Required—TOEFL (minimum score 600 paper-based). *Application deadline:* For fall admission, 7/1 for domestic and international students; for winter admission, 12/1 for domestic and international students. Applications are processed on a rolling basis. Application fee: $40. Electronic applications accepted. *Expenses: Tuition:* Full-time $11,430; part-time $635 per credit hour. Tuition and fees vary according to degree level and program. *Financial support:* Teaching assistantships with partial tuition reimbursements available. *Faculty research:* Pain management, ethics, corporate wellness, caring spirituality, stress. *Unit head:* Dr. Barbara James, Dean, 423-236-2942, Fax: 423-236-1940, E-mail: bjames@southern.edu. *Application contact:* Sylvia Mayer, RN, Director of Nursing Admissions, 423-236-2941, Fax: 423-236-1940, E-mail: smayer@southern.edu.
Website: https://www.southern.edu/academics/nursing.html

Southern Connecticut State University, School of Graduate Studies, School of Health and Human Services, Department of Nursing, New Haven, CT 06515-1355. Offers family nurse practitioner (MSN); nursing (Ed D); nursing education (MSN). *Accreditation:* AACN. *Program availability:* Part-time, evening/weekend. *Degree requirements:* For master's, thesis. *Entrance requirements:* For master's, GRE, MAT, interview, minimum QPA of 2.8, RN license, minimum 1 year of professional nursing experience. Electronic applications accepted.

Southern Illinois University Edwardsville, Graduate School, School of Nursing, Edwardsville, IL 62026. Offers MS, DNP, Post-Master's Certificate. *Accreditation:* AACN; AANA/CANAEP. *Program availability:* Part-time, evening/weekend. *Degree requirements:* For master's, comprehensive exam (for some programs), thesis or alternative; for doctorate, thesis/dissertation or alternative, project. *Entrance requirements:* For master's, appropriate bachelor's degree, RN license; for Post-Master's Certificate, minimum graduate nursing GPA of 3.0, completion of graduate-level statistics and epidemiology courses with minimum B grade, current unencumbered RN licensure. Additional exam requirements/recommendations for international students: Required—TOEFL (minimum score 550 paper-based; 79 iBT), IELTS (minimum score 6.5). Electronic applications accepted.

Southern Nazarene University, College of Professional and Graduate Studies, School of Nursing, Bethany, OK 73008. Offers nursing education (MS), nursing leadership (MS). *Accreditation:* AACN. *Program availability:* Part-time, evening/weekend. *Degree requirements:* For master's, thesis. *Entrance requirements:* For master's, minimum undergraduate cumulative GPA of 3.0; baccalaureate degree in nursing from nationally-accredited program; current unencumbered registered nurse licensure in Oklahoma or eligibility for same; documentation of basic computer skills; basic statistics course; statement of professional goals; three letters of recommendation. Additional exam requirements/recommendations for international students: Required—TOEFL (minimum score 550 paper-based).

Southern New Hampshire University, Program in Nursing, Manchester, NH 03106-1045. Offers clinical nurse leader (MSN); nurse educator (MSN); nursing (MSN); patient safety and quality (MSN, Post Master's Certificate). *Program availability:* Online only, 100% online. *Entrance requirements:* For master's, undergraduate transcripts, active unencumbered license, bachelor's degree with minimum cumulative GPA of 3.0. *Application deadline:* Applications are processed on a rolling basis. Application fee: $40. Electronic applications accepted. *Expenses: Tuition:* Part-time $627 per credit hour. Part-time tuition and fees vary according to campus/location and program. *Application contact:* Office of Graduate Admission, 888-327-SNHU, Fax: 603-644-3144, E-mail: enroll@snhu.edu.
Website: https://www.snhu.edu/online-degrees/nursing

Southern University and Agricultural and Mechanical College, College of Nursing and Allied Health, School of Nursing, Baton Rouge, LA 70813. Offers educator/administrator (PhD); family health nursing (MSN); family nurse practitioner (Post Master's Certificate); geriatric nurse practitioner/gerontology (PhD); nursing (DNP). *Accreditation:* AACN. *Program availability:* Part-time. *Degree requirements:* For master's, comprehensive exam, thesis; for doctorate, comprehensive exam, thesis/dissertation. *Entrance requirements:* For master's, GRE General Test, BSN, minimum GPA of 2.7; for doctorate, GRE General Test; for Post Master's Certificate, MSN. Additional exam requirements/recommendations for international students: Required—TOEFL (minimum score 525 paper-based). *Faculty research:* Health promotions, vulnerable populations, (community-based) cardiovascular participating research, health disparities chronic diseases, care of the elderly.

South University, Graduate Programs, College of Nursing, Savannah, GA 31406. Offers nurse educator (MS). *Accreditation:* AACN.

South University, Program in Nursing, Tampa, FL 33614. Offers adult health nurse practitioner (MS); family nurse practitioner (MS); nurse educator (MS).

South University, Program in Nursing, Royal Palm Beach, FL 33411. Offers family nurse practitioner (MS).

South University, Program in Nursing, Montgomery, AL 36116-1120. Offers MSN.

South University, Program in Nursing, Columbia, SC 29203. Offers MSN.

South University, Program in Nursing, Glen Allen, VA 23060. Offers MSN.

South University, Program in Nursing, Virginia Beach, VA 23452. Offers family nurse practitioner (MSN).

Spalding University, Graduate Studies, Kosair College of Health and Natural Sciences, School of Nursing, Louisville, KY 40203-2188. Offers adult nurse practitioner (MSN); family nurse practitioner (MSN); leadership in nursing and healthcare (MSN); nurse educator (Post-Master's Certificate); nurse practitioner (Post-Master's Certificate); pediatric nurse practitioner (MSN). *Accreditation:* AACN. *Program availability:* Part-time, evening/weekend. *Degree requirements:* For master's, comprehensive exam (for some programs), thesis. *Entrance requirements:* For master's, GRE General Test, BSN or bachelor's degree in related field, RN licensure, autobiographical statement, transcripts, letters of recommendation. Additional exam requirements/recommendations for international students: Required—TOEFL (minimum score 535 paper-based). *Faculty research:* Nurse educational administration, gerontology, bioterrorism, healthcare ethics, leadership.

Spring Arbor University, School of Human Services, Spring Arbor, MI 49283-9799. Offers counseling (MAC); family studies (MAFS); nursing (MSN). *Program availability:* Part-time, evening/weekend, online learning. *Entrance requirements:* For master's, bachelor's degree from regionally-accredited college or university, minimum GPA of 3.0 for at least the last two years of the bachelor's degree, at least two recommendations from professional/academic individuals. Additional exam requirements/recommendations for international students: Required—TOEFL (minimum score 600 paper-based). Electronic applications accepted.

Spring Hill College, Graduate Programs, Program in Nursing, Mobile, AL 36608-1791. Offers MSN, Post-Master's Certificate. *Accreditation:* AACN. *Program availability:* Part-time, evening/weekend, online only, 100% online. *Faculty:* 1 (woman) full-time, 1 (woman) part-time/adjunct. *Students:* 3 part-time (2 women). Average age 50. In 2017, 5 master's awarded. *Degree requirements:* For master's, comprehensive exam, capstone courses, completion of program within 6 calendar years; for Post-Master's Certificate, 460 clinical integration hours. *Entrance requirements:* For master's, RN license in state where practicing nursing; 1 year of clinical nursing experience; work in clinical setting or access to health care facility for clinical integration/research; 3 written references; employer verification; resume; 500-word essay explaining how becoming a CNL will help applicant achieve personal and professional goals; for Post-Master's Certificate, RN license; master's degree in nursing. Additional exam requirements/recommendations for international students: Required—TOEFL (minimum score 550 paper-based; 80 iBT), IELTS (minimum score 6.5), CPE or CAE (minimum score C), Michigan English Language Assessment Battery (minimum score 90). *Application deadline:* For fall admission, 8/1 priority date for domestic and international students; for spring admission, 12/1 priority date for domestic and international students. Applications are processed on a rolling basis. Application fee: $25 ($35 for international students). Electronic applications accepted. *Expenses:* Contact institution. *Financial support:* Applicants required to submit FAFSA. *Unit head:* Dr. Terran Mathers, Director, 251-380-4485, Fax: 251-460-4495, E-mail: tmathers@shc.edu. *Application contact:* Robert Stewart, Vice President of Enrollment, 251-380-3030, Fax: 251-460-2186, E-mail: rstewart@shc.edu.
Website: http://ug.shc.edu/graduate-degrees/master-science-nursing/

Stanbridge University, Program in Nursing, Irvine, CA 92612. Offers MSN. *Program availability:* Online learning.

State University of New York College of Technology at Delhi, Program in Nursing, Delhi, NY 13753. Offers nursing administration (MS); nursing education (MS). *Program availability:* Online only, 100% online. *Faculty:* 6 full-time (all women), 1 (woman) part-time/adjunct. *Students:* 6 full-time (all women), 35 part-time (32 women). *Expenses:* $462 per credit hour in-state tuition, $944 per credit hour out-of-state, $555 online. *Application contact:* Misty Fields, Associate Director of Admission, 607-746-4546, E-mail: fieldsmr@delhi.edu.

State University of New York Downstate Medical Center, College of Nursing, Graduate Programs in Nursing, Brooklyn, NY 11203-2098. Offers clinical nurse specialist (MS, Post Master's Certificate); nurse anesthesia (MS); nurse midwifery (MS, Post Master's Certificate); nurse practitioner (MS, Post Master's Certificate); nursing (MS). *Accreditation:* AACN. *Program availability:* Part-time. *Degree requirements:* For master's, thesis optional, clinical research project. *Entrance requirements:* For master's, GRE, BSN; minimum GPA of 3.0; previous undergraduate course work in statistics, health assessment, and nursing research; RN license; for Post Master's Certificate, BSN; minimum GPA of 3.0; RN license; previous undergraduate course work in statistics, health assessment, and nursing research. *Faculty research:* AIDS, continuity of care, case management, self-care.

State University of New York Upstate Medical University, College of Nursing, Syracuse, NY 13210. Offers nurse practitioner (Post Master's Certificate); nursing (MS). *Accreditation:* AACN. *Program availability:* Part-time, online learning. *Degree requirements:* For master's, thesis or alternative. *Entrance requirements:* For master's, 3 years of work experience. Electronic applications accepted.

Stevenson University, Program in Nursing, Owings Mills, MD 21153. Offers nursing education (MS); nursing leadership/management (MS); population-based care coordination (MS). *Accreditation:* AACN. *Program availability:* Part-time, blended/hybrid learning. *Faculty:* 4 full-time (all women), 12 part-time/adjunct (all women). *Students:* 174 part-time (167 women); includes 53 minority (40 Black or African American, non-Hispanic/Latino; 5 Asian, non-Hispanic/Latino; 8 Two or more races, non-Hispanic/Latino). Average age 40. 45 applicants, 100% accepted, 38 enrolled. In 2017, 47 master's awarded. *Degree requirements:* For master's, capstone course. *Entrance requirements:* For master's, bachelor's degree from regionally-accredited institution, current registered nurse's license in good standing, official college transcripts from all previous academic work, minimum cumulative GPA of 3.0 in past academic work, personal statement (250-350 words), two professional letters of recommendation, resume. *Application deadline:* Applications are processed on a rolling basis. Application fee: $0. Electronic applications accepted. *Expenses:* Contact institution. *Financial support:* Unspecified assistantships available. Financial award applicants required to submit FAFSA. *Unit head:* Judith Feustle, PhD, Associate Dean, 443-352-4292, Fax: 443-394-0538, E-mail: jfeustle@stevenson.edu. *Application contact:* Amanda Courter, Enrollment Counselor, 443-352-4243, Fax: 443-394-0538, E-mail: acourter@stevenson.edu.
Website: http://www.stevenson.edu

Stockton University, Office of Graduate Studies, Program in Nursing, Galloway, NJ 08205-9441. Offers MSN. *Accreditation:* AACN. *Program availability:* Part-time. *Faculty:* 5 full-time (3 women), 3 part-time/adjunct (2 women). *Students:* 1 (woman) full-time, 38 part-time (28 women); includes 8 minority (1 Black or African American, non-Hispanic/Latino; 3 Asian, non-Hispanic/Latino; 2 Hispanic/Latino; 1 Native Hawaiian or other Pacific Islander, non-Hispanic/Latino; 1 Two or more races, non-Hispanic/Latino). Average age 38. 32 applicants, 69% accepted, 13 enrolled. In 2017, 9 master's awarded. *Entrance requirements:* For master's, CPR certification, minimum GPA of 3.0, RN license. Additional exam requirements/recommendations for international students: Required—TOEFL. *Application deadline:* For fall admission, 5/1 for domestic and international students; for spring admission, 12/1 for domestic students, 11/1 for international students. Applications are processed on a rolling basis. Application fee: $50. Electronic applications accepted. *Expenses:* Contact institution. *Financial support:* Fellowships, research assistantships, career-related internships or fieldwork, Federal Work-Study, scholarships/grants, and unspecified assistantships available. Support available to part-time students. Financial award application deadline: 3/1; financial award applicants required to submit FAFSA. *Faculty research:* Psychoneuroimmunology, relationship of nutrition and disease, mental health as affected by chronic disease states, home care for elderly relatives. *Unit head:* Dr. Lori Prol, Program Director, 609-626-3640, E-mail: edward.walton@stockton.edu. *Application contact:* Tara Williams, Associate Director of Admissions, 609-626-3640, Fax: 609-626-6050, E-mail: gradschool@stockton.edu.

Stony Brook University, State University of New York, Stony Brook Medicine, School of Nursing, Stony Brook, NY 11794. Offers MS, DNP, PhD, Certificate. *Accreditation:* AACN; ACNM/ACME. *Program availability:* Blended/hybrid learning. *Faculty:* 36 full-time (33 women), 48 part-time/adjunct (42 women). *Students:* 36 full-time (33 women), 928 part-time (833 women); includes 343 minority (130 Black or African American, non-Hispanic/Latino; 6 American Indian or Alaska Native, non-Hispanic/Latino; 102 Asian, non-Hispanic/Latino; 88 Hispanic/Latino; 1 Native Hawaiian or other Pacific Islander, non-Hispanic/Latino; 16 Two or more races, non-Hispanic/Latino). Average age 36. 860 applicants, 49% accepted, 344 enrolled. In 2017, 237 master's, 21 doctorates, 21 other advanced degrees awarded. *Degree requirements:* For master's, thesis; for doctorate, thesis/dissertation. *Entrance requirements:* For master's, BSN, minimum GPA of 3.0, course work in statistics; for doctorate, GRE General Test (for PhD). Additional exam

requirements/recommendations for international students: Required—TOEFL (minimum iBT score of 90, 22 on each section). *Application deadline:* For fall admission, 4/15 for domestic students, 3/15 for international students. Application fee: $100. Electronic applications accepted. *Expenses:* Contact institution. *Financial support:* Fellowships, research assistantships, teaching assistantships, career-related internships or fieldwork, Federal Work-Study, institutionally sponsored loans, and traineeships available. Financial award application deadline: 3/15. *Total annual research expenditures:* $1.7 million. *Unit head:* Dr. Lee Anne Xippolitos, Dean, 631-444-3200, Fax: 631-444-3136, E-mail: lee.xippolitos@stonybrook.edu. *Application contact:* Karen Allard, Admissions Coordinator, 631-444-6628, Fax: 631-444-3136, E-mail: karen.allard@stonybrook.edu.
Website: http://www.nursing.stonybrookmedicine.edu/

Tarleton State University, College of Graduate Studies, College of Health Sciences and Human Services, Department of Nursing, Stephenville, TX 76402. Offers nursing administration (MSN); nursing education (MSN). *Accreditation:* AACN. *Program availability:* Part-time, evening/weekend. *Faculty:* 5 full-time (all women), 1 (woman) part-time/adjunct. *Students:* 1 (woman) full-time, 19 part-time (16 women); includes 6 minority (5 Black or African American, non-Hispanic/Latino; 1 Hispanic/Latino), 1 international. Average age 38. 15 applicants, 87% accepted, 10 enrolled. *Degree requirements:* For master's, comprehensive exam. *Entrance requirements:* For master's, GRE General Test, minimum GPA of 3.0. Additional exam requirements/recommendations for international students: Required—TOEFL (minimum score 550 paper-based; 80 iBT), IELTS (minimum score 6). *Application deadline:* For fall admission, 8/15 priority date for domestic students; for spring admission, 1/7 for domestic students. Applications are processed on a rolling basis. Application fee: $45 ($145 for international students). Electronic applications accepted. *Expenses:* Contact institution. *Financial support:* Career-related internships or fieldwork, Federal Work-Study, and institutionally sponsored loans available. Support available to part-time students. Financial award applicants required to submit FAFSA. *Unit head:* Dr. Mary Winton, Department Head, 254-968-9139, E-mail: mwinton@tarleton.edu. *Application contact:* Information Contact, 254-968-9104, Fax: 254-968-9670, E-mail: gradoffice@tarleton.edu.
Website: http://www.tarleton.edu/nursing/degrees_grad.html

Temple University, College of Public Health, Department of Nursing, Philadelphia, PA 19122. Offers adult-gerontology primary care (DNP); family-individual across the lifespan (DNP); nursing (DNP). *Accreditation:* AACN. *Program availability:* Part-time. *Faculty:* 12 full-time (all women). *Students:* 5 full-time (4 women), 53 part-time (46 women); includes 31 minority (13 Black or African American, non-Hispanic/Latino; 12 Asian, non-Hispanic/Latino; 5 Hispanic/Latino; 1 Two or more races, non-Hispanic/Latino). 11 applicants, 18% accepted. In 2017, 17 doctorates awarded. *Degree requirements:* For doctorate, evidence-based practice project. *Entrance requirements:* For doctorate, GRE General Test or MAT, 2 letters of reference, RN license, interview, statement of purpose, resume. Additional exam requirements/recommendations for international students: Required—TOEFL (minimum score 600 paper-based; 100 iBT). *Application deadline:* For fall admission, 2/15 priority date for domestic students, 1/15 for international students; for spring admission, 10/15 for domestic students, 9/15 for international students. Applications are processed on a rolling basis. Application fee: $60. Electronic applications accepted. *Expenses:* Contact institution. *Financial support:* Federal Work-Study, scholarships/grants, traineeships, and tuition waivers available. Support available to part-time students. Financial award application deadline: 1/15. *Faculty research:* Health promotion, chronic illness, family support systems, primary care, health policy, community health services, evidence-based practice. *Unit head:* Dolores Zygmont, Graduate Director, 215-707-3789, E-mail: zygmont@temple.edu. *Application contact:* Audrey Scriven, Academic Coordinator, Graduate Program, 215-707-4618, E-mail: tunurse@temple.edu.
Website: https://cph.temple.edu/nursing/home

Tennessee State University, The School of Graduate Studies and Research, College of Health Sciences, School of Nursing, Nashville, TN 37209-1561. Offers family nurse practitioner (MSN, Certificate); holistic nurse practitioner (MSN); holistic nursing (Certificate); nursing education (MSN, Certificate). *Accreditation:* ACEN. *Entrance requirements:* For master's, GRE General Test or MAT, BSN, current RN license, minimum GPA of 3.0.

Tennessee Technological University, Whitson-Hester School of Nursing, Cookeville, TN 38505. Offers MSN, DNP. *Program availability:* Part-time, evening/weekend, online learning. *Students:* 22 full-time (17 women), 88 part-time (74 women); includes 5 minority (2 Black or African American, non-Hispanic/Latino; 2 Hispanic/Latino; 1 Two or more races, non-Hispanic/Latino). 62 applicants, 58% accepted, 30 enrolled. In 2017, 41 master's awarded. *Degree requirements:* For master's, comprehensive exam, thesis or alternative. *Entrance requirements:* Additional exam requirements/recommendations for international students: Required—TOEFL (minimum score 600 paper-based; 100 iBT), IELTS (minimum score 5.5), PTE, or TOEIC (Test of English as an International Communication). *Application deadline:* For fall admission, 7/1 for domestic students, 5/1 for international students; for spring admission, 11/1 for domestic students, 10/1 for international students; for summer admission, 5/1 for domestic students, 2/1 for international students. Applications are processed on a rolling basis. Application fee: $35 ($40 for international students). Electronic applications accepted. *Expenses:* Tuition, state resident: full-time $9925; part-time $565 per credit hour. Tuition, nonresident: full-time $22,993; part-time $1291 per credit hour. *Financial support:* Teaching assistantships available. Financial award application deadline: 4/1. *Unit head:* Dr. Kim Hanna, Dean, 931-372-3547, Fax: 931-372-6244, E-mail: khanna@tntech.edu. *Application contact:* Shelia K. Kendrick, Coordinator of Graduate Studies, 931-372-3808, Fax: 931-372-3497, E-mail: skendrick@tntech.edu.

Texas A&M International University, Office of Graduate Studies and Research, College of Nursing and Health Sciences, Laredo, TX 78041. Offers family nurse practitioner (MSN). *Accreditation:* ACEN. *Entrance requirements:* Additional exam requirements/recommendations for international students: Required—TOEFL (minimum score 550 paper-based; 79 iBT).

Texas A&M University, College of Nursing, Bryan, TX 77807. Offers family nurse practitioner (MSN); forensic nursing (MSN); nursing education (MSN). *Faculty:* 19. *Students:* 9 full-time (all women), 47 part-time (all women); includes 14 minority (2 Asian, non-Hispanic/Latino; 12 Hispanic/Latino). Average age 34. In 2017, 27 master's awarded. *Expenses:* Contact institution. *Financial support:* In 2017–18, 8 students received support, including 2 fellowships (averaging $4,300 per year); career-related internships or fieldwork, institutionally sponsored loans, scholarships/grants, traineeships, health care benefits, tuition waivers (full and partial), and unspecified assistantships also available. Support available to part-time students. Financial award applicants required to submit FAFSA. *Unit head:* Dr. Sharon A. Wilkerson, Founding Dean, 979-436-0111, Fax: 979-436-0098, E-mail: wilkerson@tamhsc.edu. *Application contact:* Jennifer Frank, Program Coordinator for Recruitment and Admission, 979-436-0110, E-mail: conadmissions@tamhsc.edu.
Website: http://nursing.tamhsc.edu/

Texas A&M University–Corpus Christi, College of Graduate Studies, College of Nursing and Health Sciences, Corpus Christi, TX 78412. Offers family nurse practitioner (MSN); leadership in nursing systems (MSN); nurse educator (MSN); nursing practice (DNP). *Accreditation:* AACN. *Program availability:* Part-time, evening/weekend, online only, 100% online. *Faculty:* 17 full-time (16 women), 21 part-time/adjunct (15 women). *Students:* 7 full-time (all women), 364 part-time (307 women); includes 194 minority (25 Black or African American, non-Hispanic/Latino; 26 Asian, non-Hispanic/Latino; 134 Hispanic/Latino; 9 Two or more races, non-Hispanic/Latino). Average age 38. 360 applicants, 33% accepted, 112 enrolled. In 2017, 98 master's awarded. *Degree requirements:* For master's, clinical capstone; for doctorate, capstone/scholarly project. *Entrance requirements:* For master's, essay, resume, 3 letters of recommendation, minimum GPA of 3.0, current valid unencumbered Texas nursing license. Additional exam requirements/recommendations for international students: Required—TOEFL (minimum score 550 paper-based; 79 iBT), IELTS (minimum score 6.5). *Application deadline:* For fall admission, 4/15 for domestic and international students; for spring admission, 1/7 for domestic and international students; for summer admission, 5/27 for domestic and international students. Applications are processed on a rolling basis. Application fee: $50 ($70 for international students). Electronic applications accepted. *Expenses:* Tuition, state resident: full-time $3568; part-time $198.24 per credit hour. Tuition, nonresident: full-time $11,038; part-time $613.24 per credit hour. *Required fees:* $2129; $1422.58 per semester. Tuition and fees vary according to program. *Financial support:* Research assistantships, teaching assistantships, career-related internships or fieldwork, Federal Work-Study, institutionally sponsored loans, scholarships/grants, health care benefits, and unspecified assistantships available. Support available to part-time students. Financial award application deadline: 3/15; financial award applicants required to submit FAFSA. *Unit head:* Dr. Julie Anne Hoff, Dean, 361-825-2275, E-mail: julie.hoff@tamucc.edu. *Application contact:* Graduate Admissions Coordinator, 361-825-2177, Fax: 361-825-2755, E-mail: gradweb@tamucc.edu.
Website: http://conhs.tamucc.edu/

Texas Christian University, Harris College of Nursing and Health Sciences, Doctor of Nursing Practice Program, Fort Worth, TX 76129. Offers clinical nurse specialist - adult/gerontology nursing (DNP); clinical nurse specialist - pediatrics (DNP); family nurse practitioner (DNP); general (DNP); nursing administration (DNP). *Accreditation:* AACN. *Program availability:* Part-time. *Faculty:* 29 full-time (26 women), 2 part-time/adjunct (both women). *Students:* 51 full-time (45 women), 10 part-time (9 women); includes 16 minority (6 Black or African American, non-Hispanic/Latino; 2 Asian, non-Hispanic/Latino; 6 Hispanic/Latino; 2 Two or more races, non-Hispanic/Latino). Average age 41. 59 applicants, 64% accepted, 24 enrolled. In 2017, 23 doctorates awarded. *Degree requirements:* For doctorate, thesis/dissertation or alternative, practicum. *Entrance requirements:* For doctorate, three reference letters, essay, resume, two official transcripts from each institution attended, APRN recognition or MSN with experience in nursing administration. Additional exam requirements/recommendations for international students: Required—TOEFL. *Application deadline:* For summer admission, 11/15 for domestic and international students. Application fee: $60. Electronic applications accepted. *Expenses:* $1,555 per credit hour, $125 per course fee, $500 lab fee. *Financial support:* In 2017–18, 14 students received support. Scholarships/grants available. Financial award application deadline: 2/15; financial award applicants required to submit FAFSA. *Faculty research:* Geriatrics, cancer survivorship, health literacy, endothelial cells, clinical simulation outcomes. *Unit head:* Dr. Kathy Ellis, Division Director, Graduate Nursing, 817-257-6726, Fax: 817-257-7944, E-mail: kathryn.ellis@tcu.edu. *Application contact:* Heather Lyon, Academic Program Specialist, 817-257-6726, Fax: 817-257-7944, E-mail: graduatenursing@tcu.edu.
Website: http://dnp.tcu.edu/

Texas Christian University, Harris College of Nursing and Health Sciences, Master's Program in Nursing, Fort Worth, TX 76129. Offers administration (MSN); clinical nurse leader (MSN, Certificate); clinical nurse specialist (MSN), including adult/gerontology nursing, pediatrics; nursing education (MSN). *Accreditation:* AACN. *Program availability:* Part-time, online only, 100% online. *Faculty:* 29 full-time (26 women), 2 part-time/adjunct (both women). *Students:* 17 full-time (15 women), 7 part-time (all women); includes 6 minority (1 Black or African American, non-Hispanic/Latino; 2 Asian, non-Hispanic/Latino; 2 Hispanic/Latino; 1 Two or more races, non-Hispanic/Latino). Average age 36. 41 applicants, 49% accepted, 6 enrolled. In 2017, 41 master's awarded. *Degree requirements:* For master's, thesis or alternative, practicum. *Entrance requirements:* For master's, 3 letters of reference, essay, resume, two official transcripts from every institution attended. Additional exam requirements/recommendations for international students: Required—TOEFL. *Application deadline:* For spring admission, 9/1 for domestic and international students; for summer admission, 2/1 for domestic and international students. Application fee: $60. Electronic applications accepted. *Expenses:* $1,555 per credit hour, $125 per course fee, $500 lab fee. *Financial support:* In 2017–18, 20 students received support. Scholarships/grants available. Financial award application deadline: 2/15; financial award applicants required to submit FAFSA. *Faculty research:* Geriatrics, cancer survivorship, health literacy, endothelial cells, clinical simulation outcomes. *Unit head:* Dr. Kathy Ellis, Division Director, Graduate Nursing, 817-257-6726, Fax: 817-257-7944, E-mail: kathryn.ellis@tcu.edu. *Application contact:* Heather Lyon, Academic Program Specialist, 817-257-6726, Fax: 817-257-7944, E-mail: graduatenursing@tcu.edu.
Website: http://www.nursing.tcu.edu/graduate.asp

Texas Tech University Health Sciences Center, School of Nursing, Lubbock, TX 79430. Offers acute care nurse practitioner (MSN, Certificate); administration (MSN); advanced practice (DNP); education (MSN); executive leadership (DNP); family nurse practitioner (MSN, Certificate); geriatric nurse practitioner (MSN, Certificate); pediatric nurse practitioner (MSN, Certificate). *Accreditation:* AACN. *Program availability:* Part-time, online learning. *Degree requirements:* For master's, thesis optional. *Entrance requirements:* For master's, minimum GPA of 3.0, 3 letters of reference, BSN, RN license; for Certificate, minimum GPA of 3.0, 3 letters of reference, RN license. Additional exam requirements/recommendations for international students: Required—TOEFL (minimum score 550 paper-based). *Faculty research:* Diabetes/obesity, nurse competency, disease management, intervention and measurements, health disparities.

Texas Tech University Health Sciences Center El Paso, Gayle Greve Hunt School of Nursing, El Paso, TX 79905. Offers MSN.

Texas Woman's University, Graduate School, College of Nursing, Denton, TX 76204. Offers adult health clinical nurse specialist (MS); adult health nurse practitioner (MS); adult/gerontology acute care nurse practitioner (MS); child health clinical nurse specialist (MS); clinical nurse leader (MS); family nurse practitioner (MS); health systems management (MS); nursing education (MS); nursing practice (DNP); nursing science (PhD); pediatric nurse practitioner (MS); women's health clinical nurse specialist (MS); women's health nurse practitioner (MS). *Accreditation:* AACN. *Program availability:* Part-time, 100% online, blended/hybrid learning. *Faculty:* 48 full-time (47 women), 44 part-time/adjunct (37 women). *Students:* 23 full-time (22 women), 816 part-time (750 women); includes 475 minority (188 Black or African American, non-Hispanic/Latino; 4 American Indian or Alaska Native, non-Hispanic/Latino; 171 Asian, non-Hispanic/Latino; 83 Hispanic/Latino; 3 Native Hawaiian or other Pacific Islander, non-Hispanic/Latino; 26 Two or more races, non-Hispanic/Latino), 12 international. Average age 37. 201 applicants, 88% accepted, 123 enrolled. In 2017, 232 master's, 17 doctorates awarded. *Degree requirements:* For master's, comprehensive exam, thesis or alternative, 6-year time limit for completion of degree, professional or clinical project; for doctorate, comprehensive

exam, thesis/dissertation, 10-year time limit for completion of degree. *Entrance requirements:* For master's, GRE or MAT, minimum GPA of 3.0 on last 60 hours in undergraduate nursing degree and overall, RN license, BS in nursing, basic statistics course, 1 year of clinical experience; for doctorate, GRE (preferred minimum score 153 [500 old version] Verbal, 144 [500 old version] Quantitative, 4 Analytical), MS in nursing, minimum preferred GPA of 3.5, RN license, statistics course, 2 letters of reference, curriculum vitae, graduate nursing-theory course, graduate research course, statement of professional goals and research interests. Additional exam requirements/ recommendations for international students: Required—TOEFL (minimum score 550 paper-based; 79 iBT); Recommended—IELTS (minimum score 6.5), TSE (minimum score 53). *Application deadline:* For fall admission, 5/1 for domestic students, 3/1 priority date for international students; for spring admission, 9/15 for domestic students, 7/1 priority date for international students; for summer admission, 2/1 for domestic and international students. Applications are processed on a rolling basis. Application fee: $50 ($75 for international students). Electronic applications accepted. *Expenses:* $8,510 per year full-time in-state, $17,810 per year full-time out-of-state. *Financial support:* In 2017–18, 146 students received support, including 7 teaching assistantships (averaging $28,195 per year); research assistantships, career-related internships or fieldwork, Federal Work-Study, institutionally sponsored loans, scholarships/grants, traineeships, health care benefits, and unspecified assistantships also available. Support available to part-time students. Financial award application deadline: 3/1; financial award applicants required to submit FAFSA. *Faculty research:* Women's health, nurse staffing and satisfaction in health systems, perinatal safety, chronic illness, pediatric health. *Total annual research expenditures:* $380,388. *Unit head:* Dr. Anita G. Hufft, Dean, 940-898-2401, Fax: 940-898-2437, E-mail: nursing@twu.edu. *Application contact:* Korie Hawkins, Associate Director of Admissions, Graduate Recruitment, 940-898-3188, Fax: 940-898-3081, E-mail: admissions@twu.edu.
Website: http://www.twu.edu/nursing/

Thomas Edison State University, W. Cary Edwards School of Nursing, Doctor of Nursing Practice Program, Trenton, NJ 08608. Offers systems-level leadership (DNP). *Accreditation:* AACN. *Program availability:* Part-time, 100% online. *Entrance requirements:* Additional exam requirements/recommendations for international students: Required—TOEFL (minimum score 550 paper-based; 79 iBT). Electronic applications accepted.

Thomas Edison State University, W. Cary Edwards School of Nursing, Master of Science in Nursing Program, Trenton, NJ 08608. Offers nurse educator (MSN); nursing administration (MSN); nursing informatics (MSN). *Accreditation:* AACN; ACEN. *Program availability:* Part-time, online learning. *Degree requirements:* For master's, nursing education seminar, onground practicum, online practicum. *Entrance requirements:* For master's, BSN. Additional exam requirements/recommendations for international students: Required—TOEFL (minimum score 550 paper-based; 79 iBT). Electronic applications accepted.

Thomas Jefferson University, Jefferson College of Nursing, Philadelphia, PA 19107. Offers MS, DNP. *Accreditation:* AACN; AANA/CANAEP. *Program availability:* Part-time, online only, 100% online, blended/hybrid learning. *Degree requirements:* For master's, thesis; for doctorate, thesis/dissertation. *Entrance requirements:* For doctorate, GRE (only for those under 3.2 GPA). Electronic applications accepted. *Faculty research:* Neonatal abstinence, diabetes, infection control, opioid use in geriatric patients, geriatric pain.

Thomas University, Department of Nursing, Thomasville, GA 31792-7499. Offers MSN. *Accreditation:* ACEN. *Program availability:* Part-time. *Entrance requirements:* For master's, resume, 3 academic/professional references. Additional exam requirements/ recommendations for international students: Required—TOEFL (minimum score 600 paper-based). Electronic applications accepted.

Towson University, College of Health Professions, Program in Nursing, Towson, MD 21252-0001. Offers nursing education (Postbaccalaureate Certificate). *Accreditation:* AACN. *Program availability:* Part-time. *Students:* 3 full-time (2 women), 30 part-time (26 women); includes 11 minority (9 Black or African American, non-Hispanic/Latino; 1 Asian, non-Hispanic/Latino; 1 Hispanic/Latino), 1 international. *Entrance requirements:* For degree, minimum GPA of 3.0, copy of current nursing license, current resume or curriculum vitae, bachelor's degree, completion of an elementary statistics and/or nursing research course, completion of an approved physical assessment course, personal statement. *Application deadline:* For fall admission, 1/17 for domestic students, 5/15 for international students; for spring admission, 10/15 for domestic students, 12/1 for international students. Applications are processed on a rolling basis. Application fee: $45. Electronic applications accepted. *Expenses:* Tuition, state resident: full-time $7960; part-time $398 per unit. Tuition, nonresident: full-time $16,480; part-time $824 per unit. *Required fees:* $2600; $130 per year. $390 per term. *Financial support:* Application deadline: 4/1. *Unit head:* Dr. Kathy Ogle, Graduate Program Director, 410-704-4389, E-mail: nursinggradprogram@towson.edu. *Application contact:* Coverley Beidleman, Assistant Director of Graduate Admissions, 410-704-5630, Fax: 410-704-3030, E-mail: cbeidleman@towson.edu.
Website: http://www.towson.edu/chp/departments/nursing/grad/

Trinity Western University, School of Graduate Studies, School of Nursing, Langley, BC V2Y 1Y1, Canada. Offers MSN.

Troy University, Graduate School, College of Health and Human Services, Program in Nursing, Troy, AL 36082. Offers adult health (MSN); family nurse practitioner (DNP); maternal infant (MSN); nursing informatics specialist (MSN). *Accreditation:* ACEN. *Program availability:* Part-time, evening/weekend. *Faculty:* 15 full-time (14 women), 8 part-time/adjunct (all women). *Students:* 58 full-time (52 women), 207 part-time (184 women); includes 53 minority (40 Black or African American, non-Hispanic/Latino; 1 American Indian or Alaska Native, non-Hispanic/Latino; 1 Asian, non-Hispanic/Latino; 6 Hispanic/Latino; 5 Two or more races, non-Hispanic/Latino). Average age 36. 66 applicants, 100% accepted, 49 enrolled. In 2017, 113 master's, 14 doctorates awarded. *Degree requirements:* For master's, comprehensive exam, minimum GPA of 3.0, candidacy; for doctorate, minimum GPA of 3.0, submission of approved comprehensive e-portfolio, completion of residency synthesis project, minimum of 1000 hours of clinical practice, qualifying exam. *Entrance requirements:* For master's, GRE (minimum score of 850 on old exam or 290 on new exam) or MAT (minimum score of 396), minimum GPA of 3.0, BSN, current RN licensure, 2 letters of reference, undergraduate health assessment course; for doctorate, GRE (minimum score of 850 on old exam or 294 on new exam), BSN or MSN, minimum GPA of 3.0, 2 letters of reference, current RN licensure, essay. Additional exam requirements/recommendations for international students: Required—TOEFL (minimum score 523 paper-based; 70 iBT), IELTS (minimum score 6). *Application deadline:* Applications are processed on a rolling basis. Application fee: $50. Electronic applications accepted. *Expenses:* Tuition, state resident: part-time $417 per credit hour. Tuition, nonresident: part-time $834 per credit hour. *Required fees:* $42 per credit hour. $50 per semester. Tuition and fees vary according to campus/location. *Financial support:* Fellowships, career-related internships or fieldwork, and scholarships/grants available. Support available to part-time students. Financial award applicants required to submit FAFSA. *Unit head:* Dr. Denise Green, Director, School of Nursing, 334-670-5864, Fax: 334-670-3745, E-mail: dmgreen@troy.edu. *Application contact:* Crystal G. Bishop, Director of Graduate Admissions, School of Nursing, 334-241-8631, E-mail: cdgodwin@troy.edu.

Tusculum College, Program in Nursing, Greeneville, TN 37743-9997. Offers family nurse practitioner (MSN). *Program availability:* Part-time. *Entrance requirements:* For master's, GRE. Additional exam requirements/recommendations for international students: Required—TOEFL. *Application deadline:* For spring admission, 12/10 for domestic students. Application fee: $25. *Application contact:* Lindsey Seal, Director of Enrollment, 423-636-7300 Ext. 5006, E-mail: lseal@tusculum.edu.

Uniformed Services University of the Health Sciences, Daniel K. Inouye Graduate School of Nursing, Bethesda, MD 20814. Offers adult-gerontology clinical nurse specialist (MSN, DNP); family nurse practitioner (DNP); nurse anesthesia (DNP); nursing science (PhD); psychiatric mental health nurse practitioner (DNP); women's health nurse practitioner (DNP). *Accreditation:* AACN; AANA/CANAEP. *Faculty:* 42 full-time (28 women), 2 part-time/adjunct (1 woman). *Students:* 170 full-time (98 women); includes 51 minority (21 Black or African American, non-Hispanic/Latino; 17 Asian, non-Hispanic/ Latino; 11 Hispanic/Latino; 2 Native Hawaiian or other Pacific Islander, non-Hispanic/ Latino). Average age 34. 88 applicants, 75% accepted, 66 enrolled. In 2017, 55 doctorates awarded. *Degree requirements:* For master's, thesis, scholarly project; for doctorate, dissertation (for PhD); project (for DNP). *Entrance requirements:* For master's, GRE, BSN, clinical experience, minimum GPA of 3.0, previous course work in science; for doctorate, GRE, BSN, minimum GPA of 3.0, undergraduate/graduate science course within past 5 years, writing example, interview (for some programs), and 3 letters of reference (for DNP); master's degree, minimum GPA of 3.0 in nursing or related field, personal statement, 3 references, and interview (for PhD). *Application deadline:* For winter admission, 2/15 for domestic students; for summer admission, 8/15 for domestic students. Application fee: $0. Electronic applications accepted. *Expenses:* There are no tuition costs or fees; students incur obligated service according to the requirements of their sponsoring organization. *Faculty research:* Military health care, military readiness, women's health, family, behavioral health. *Total annual research expenditures:* $100,000. *Unit head:* Dr. Diane C. Seibert, Associate Dean for Academic Affairs, 301-295-1080, Fax: 301-295-1707, E-mail: diane.seibert@usuhs.edu. *Application contact:* Maureen Jackson, Registrar, 301-295-1055, Fax: 301-295-1707, E-mail: maureen.jackson.ctr@usuhs.edu.
Website: http://www.usuhs.edu/gsn/

Union University, School of Nursing, Jackson, TN 38305-3697. Offers executive leadership (DNP); nurse anesthesia (DNP); nurse practitioner (DNP); nursing education (MSN, PMC). *Accreditation:* AACN; AANA/CANAEP. *Degree requirements:* For master's, thesis or alternative. *Entrance requirements:* For master's, GRE, 3 letters of reference, bachelor's degree in nursing, minimum GPA of 3.0. Additional exam requirements/recommendations for international students: Required—TOEFL (minimum score 560 paper-based). Electronic applications accepted. *Faculty research:* Children's health, occupational rehabilitation, informatics, health promotion.

Universidad Metropolitana, School of Health Sciences, Department of Nursing, San Juan, PR 00928-1150. Offers case management (Certificate); nursing (MSN); oncology nursing (Certificate). *Accreditation:* ACEN.

Université de Montréal, Faculty of Nursing, Montréal, QC H3C 3J7, Canada. Offers M Sc, PhD, Certificate, DESS. PhD offered jointly with McGill University. *Program availability:* Part-time. *Degree requirements:* For master's, one foreign language, thesis optional; for doctorate, thesis/dissertation, general exam; for other advanced degree, one foreign language. *Entrance requirements:* For master's, doctorate, and other advanced degree, proficiency in French. Electronic applications accepted. *Faculty research:* Mental and physical care of chronic patients, care of the hospitalized aged, cancer nursing, home care of caregivers, AIDS patients.

Université du Québec à Rimouski, Graduate Programs, Program in Nursing Studies, Rimouski, QC G5L 3A1, Canada. Offers M Sc, Diploma. Programs offered jointly with Université du Québec à Chicoutimi, Université du Québec à Trois-Rivières, and Université du Québec en Outaouais.

Université du Québec à Trois-Rivières, Graduate Programs, Program in Nursing Sciences, Trois-Rivières, QC G9A 5H7, Canada. Offers M Sc, DESS. *Program availability:* Part-time.

Université du Québec en Outaouais, Graduate Programs, Program in Nursing, Gatineau, QC J8X 3X7, Canada. Offers M Sc, DESS, Diploma. *Program availability:* Part-time, evening/weekend. *Degree requirements:* For master's, thesis (for some programs). *Entrance requirements:* For master's, appropriate bachelor's degree, proficiency in French.

Université Laval, Faculty of Nursing, Programs in Nursing, Québec, QC G1K 7P4, Canada. Offers M Sc, PhD, DESS, Diploma. *Degree requirements:* For master's, thesis (for some programs). *Entrance requirements:* For master's, French exam, knowledge of English; for other advanced degree, knowledge of French. Electronic applications accepted.

University at Buffalo, the State University of New York, Graduate School, School of Nursing, Buffalo, NY 14260. Offers adult gerontology nurse practitioner (DNP); family nurse practitioner (DNP); health care systems and leadership (MS); nurse anesthetist (DNP); nursing (PhD); nursing education (Certificate); psychiatric/mental health nurse practitioner (DNP). *Accreditation:* AACN; AANA/CANAEP (one or more programs are accredited). *Program availability:* Part-time, 100% online. *Faculty:* 41 full-time (36 women), 15 part-time/adjunct (all women). *Students:* 64 full-time (39 women), 136 part-time (120 women); includes 32 minority (13 Black or African American, non-Hispanic/Latino; 1 American Indian or Alaska Native, non-Hispanic/Latino; 18 Asian, non-Hispanic/Latino). Average age 34. 182 applicants, 39% accepted, 50 enrolled. In 2017, 3 master's, 32 doctorates, 2 other advanced degrees awarded. *Degree requirements:* For master's, thesis optional; for doctorate, comprehensive exam (for some programs), capstone (for DNP), dissertation (for PhD). *Entrance requirements:* For master's, GRE or MAT; for doctorate, GRE or MAT, minimum GPA of 3.0 (for DNP), 3.25 (for PhD); RN license; BS or MS in nursing; 3 references; writing sample; resume; personal statement; for Certificate, interview, minimum GPA of 3.0 or GRE General Test, RN license, MS in nursing, professional certification. Additional exam requirements/recommendations for international students: Required—TOEFL (minimum score 550 paper-based; 79 iBT), IELTS (minimum score 6.5). *Application deadline:* For fall admission, 4/1 for domestic students, 2/1 for international students; for spring admission, 1/15 for domestic students, 10/1 for international students; for summer admission, 4/1 for domestic students. Applications are processed on a rolling basis. Application fee: $75. Electronic applications accepted. *Expenses:* Contact institution. *Financial support:* In 2017–18, 80 students received support, including 2 fellowships with tuition reimbursements available (averaging $17,000 per year), 4 research assistantships with tuition reimbursements available (averaging $10,600 per year), 7 teaching assistantships with tuition reimbursements available (averaging $10,600 per year); scholarships/grants, traineeships, health care benefits, and unspecified assistantships also available. Financial award application deadline: 4/1; financial award applicants required to submit FAFSA. *Faculty research:* Oncology, palliative care, gerontology, addictions, mental health, community wellness, sleep, workforce, care of underserved populations, quality and safety, person-centered care, adolescent health. *Total annual research expenditures:* $1.4 million. *Unit head:* Dr. Marsha L. Lewis, Dean and Professor, 716-829-2533, Fax: 716-829-2566, E-mail: ubnursingdean@buffalo.edu. *Application contact:* Jennifer H. Schreier, Director of Graduate Student Services, 716-829-3311, Fax: 716-829-2067, E-mail: jhv2@buffalo.edu.
Website: http://nursing.buffalo.edu/

Nursing—General

The University of Akron, Graduate School, College of Health Professions, School of Nursing, Akron, OH 44325-3701. Offers nursing (MSN, PhD); nursing practice (DNP); public health (MPH). PhD offered jointly with Kent State University. *Accreditation:* AACN; AANA/CANAEP (one or more programs are accredited). *Program availability:* Part-time. *Faculty:* 14 full-time (all women), 15 part-time/adjunct (13 women). *Students:* 39 full-time (22 women), 246 part-time (179 women); includes 29 minority (12 Black or African American, non-Hispanic/Latino; 8 Asian, non-Hispanic/Latino; 6 Hispanic/Latino; 3 Two or more races, non-Hispanic/Latino), 6 international. Average age 31. 110 applicants, 75% accepted, 70 enrolled. In 2017, 90 master's, 6 doctorates awarded. *Degree requirements:* For doctorate, one foreign language, thesis/dissertation, qualifying exam. *Entrance requirements:* For master's, current Ohio state license as registered nurse, three letters of reference, 300-word essay, interview with program coordinator; for doctorate, GRE, minimum GPA of 3.0, MSN, nursing license or eligibility for licensure, writing sample, letters of recommendation, interview, resume, personal statement of research interests and career goals. Additional exam requirements/recommendations for international students: Required—TOEFL (minimum score 79 iBT), IELTS (minimum score 6.5). *Application deadline:* For fall admission, 7/15 for domestic and international students. Applications are processed on a rolling basis. Application fee: $45 ($70 for international students). Electronic applications accepted. *Financial support:* In 2017–18, 3 teaching assistantships with full tuition reimbursements were awarded. *Faculty research:* Health promotion and chronic disease prevention, mental health and psychosocial resilience, erotological health, trauma and violence, gut oxygenation during shock and trauma, simulation and the pedagogy of teaching and learning. *Total annual research expenditures:* $476,886. *Unit head:* Dr. Marlene Huff, Director, 330-972-5930, E-mail: mhuff@uakron.edu. *Application contact:* Dr. Linda Shanks, Assistant Director, Graduate Programs, 330-972-6699, E-mail: shanks@uakron.edu.
Website: http://www.uakron.edu/nursing/

The University of Alabama, Graduate School, Capstone College of Nursing, Tuscaloosa, AL 35487. Offers MSN, DNP. *Accreditation:* AACN. *Program availability:* Part-time, online learning. *Faculty:* 29 full-time (26 women), 6 part-time/adjunct (5 women). *Students:* 151 full-time (131 women), 197 part-time (170 women); includes 124 minority (98 Black or African American, non-Hispanic/Latino; 3 American Indian or Alaska Native, non-Hispanic/Latino; 3 Asian, non-Hispanic/Latino; 15 Hispanic/Latino; 1 Native Hawaiian or other Pacific Islander, non-Hispanic/Latino; 4 Two or more races, non-Hispanic/Latino), 1 international. Average age 40. 352 applicants, 55% accepted, 150 enrolled. In 2017, 53 master's, 61 doctorates awarded. *Degree requirements:* For master's, thesis optional; for doctorate, comprehensive exam, thesis/dissertation, scholarly practice project. *Entrance requirements:* For master's, GRE or MAT (if GPA is below 3.0), minimum GPA of 3.0 overall and/or last 60 hours; BSN; current unencumbered RN licensure in the U.S.; drug and background screen deemed acceptable by university officials; statement of purpose; resume; 2 recommendation letters; for doctorate, GRE or MAT (if GPA is below 3.0), current RN license; master's degree in advanced nursing practice area with minimum GPA of 3.0; advanced practice national certification or certification exam prior to completing first 12 hours; background and drug screen checks; statement of purpose; resume; 2 recommendation letters; verification of post baccalaureate clinical hours; writing sample. Additional exam requirements/recommendations for international students: Required—TOEFL (minimum score 550 paper-based; 79 iBT), IELTS (minimum score 6.5), PTE (minimum score 59). *Application deadline:* For fall admission, 3/1 priority date for domestic students. Applications are processed on a rolling basis. Application fee: $50 ($60 for international students). Electronic applications accepted. *Financial support:* Scholarships/grants available. Financial award application deadline: 6/15; financial award applicants required to submit FAFSA. *Faculty research:* Diabetes education, childhood asthma, HIV/AIDS prevention and care, breast cancer in rural minority women, nursing labor cost, nursing case management, sleep, gerontology, health disparities of rural children. *Total annual research expenditures:* $70,873. *Unit head:* Dr. Suzanne Prevost, Dean, 205-348-1040, Fax: 205-348-5559, E-mail: sprevost@ua.edu. *Application contact:* Vickie L. Samuel, Graduate Recruitment and Retention Liaison, 205-348-8163, Fax: 205-348-6674, E-mail: vsamuel@ua.edu.
Website: http://nursing.ua.edu/

The University of Alabama at Birmingham, School of Nursing, Birmingham, AL 35294-1210. Offers clinical nurse leader (MSN); nurse anesthesia (DNP); nurse practitioner (MSN, DNP), including adult-gerontology acute care (MSN), adult-gerontology primary care (MSN), family (MSN), pediatric (MSN), psychiatric/mental health (MSN), women's health (MSN); nursing (MSN, DNP, PhD); nursing health systems administration (MSN); nursing informatics (MSN). *Accreditation:* AACN; AANA/CANAEP. *Program availability:* Part-time, online only, blended/hybrid learning. Terminal master's awarded for partial completion of doctoral program. *Degree requirements:* For master's, comprehensive exam; for doctorate, comprehensive exam, thesis/dissertation, research mentorship experience (for PhD); scholarly project (for DNP). *Entrance requirements:* For master's, GRE, GMAT, or MAT, minimum cumulative undergraduate GPA of 3.0 or on last 60 semesters hours; letters of recommendation; for doctorate, GRE General Test, computer literacy, course work in statistics, interview, minimum GPA of 3.0, MS in nursing, references, writing sample. Additional exam requirements/recommendations for international students: Required—TOEFL (minimum score 500 paper-based, 80 iBT) or IELTS (5.5). Electronic applications accepted. *Expenses:* Contact institution. *Faculty research:* Palliative care; oncology; aging; HIV/AIDS; nursing work environments.

The University of Alabama in Huntsville, School of Graduate Studies, College of Nursing, Huntsville, AL 35899. Offers family nurse practitioner (Certificate); nursing (MSN, DNP), including adult-gerontology acute care nurse practitioner (MSN), adult-gerontology clinical nurse specialist (MSN), family nurse practitioner (MSN), leadership in health care systems (MSN); nursing education (Certificate). DNP offered jointly with The University of Alabama at Birmingham. *Accreditation:* AACN. *Program availability:* Part-time, evening/weekend, online learning. *Degree requirements:* For master's, comprehensive exam, thesis or alternative, oral and written exams. *Entrance requirements:* For master's, MAT or GRE, Alabama RN license, BSN, minimum GPA of 3.0; for doctorate, master's degree in nursing in an advanced practice area; for Certificate, MAT or GRE, minimum GPA of 3.0. Additional exam requirements/recommendations for international students: Required—TOEFL (minimum score 500 paper-based; 80 iBT), IELTS (minimum score 6.5). Electronic applications accepted. *Faculty research:* Health care informatics, chronic illness management, maternal and child health, genetics/genomics, technology and health care.

University of Alberta, Faculty of Graduate Studies and Research, Faculty of Nursing, Edmonton, AB T6G 2E1, Canada. Offers MN, PhD. *Program availability:* Part-time. *Degree requirements:* For master's, thesis optional, clinical practice; for doctorate, thesis/dissertation. *Entrance requirements:* For master's, B Sc N, 1 year of clinical nursing experience in specialty area; for doctorate, MN. Additional exam requirements/recommendations for international students: Required—TOEFL (minimum score 550 paper-based). *Faculty research:* Symptom management, healthy human development, health policy, teaching excellence and information.

The University of Arizona, College of Nursing, Tucson, AZ 85721. Offers health care informatics (Certificate); nurse practitioner (MS); nursing (DNP, PhD). *Accreditation:* AACN; AANA/CANAEP. *Program availability:* Part-time, online learning. Terminal master's awarded for partial completion of doctoral program. *Degree requirements:* For master's, thesis optional; for doctorate, comprehensive exam, thesis/dissertation. *Entrance requirements:* For master's, BSN, eligibility for RN license; for doctorate, BSN; for Certificate, GRE General Test, Arizona RN license, BSN, minimum GPA of 3.0. Additional exam requirements/recommendations for international students: Required—TOEFL (minimum score 550 paper-based; 79 iBT). Electronic applications accepted. *Expenses:* Contact institution. *Faculty research:* Vulnerable populations, injury mechanisms and biobehavioral responses, health care systems, informatics, rural health.

University of Arkansas, Graduate School, College of Education and Health Professions, Eleanor Mann School of Nursing, Fayetteville, AR 72701. Offers MSN. *Accreditation:* AACN. *Program availability:* Online learning. In 2017, 3 master's awarded. *Application deadline:* For fall admission, 8/1 for domestic students, 4/1 for international students; for spring admission, 12/1 for domestic students, 10/1 for international students; for summer admission, 4/15 for domestic students, 3/1 for international students. Applications are processed on a rolling basis. Application fee: $60. Electronic applications accepted. *Expenses:* Tuition, state resident: full-time $3782. Tuition, nonresident: full-time $10,238. *Financial support:* Fellowships, research assistantships, and teaching assistantships available. *Unit head:* Dr. Susan Kane Patton, Interim Director, 479-575-3907, Fax: 479-575-3218, E-mail: skpatton@uark.edu. *Application contact:* Dr. Martha Butler, Graduate Admissions, 479-575-4914, E-mail: mrbutler@uark.edu.
Website: http://nurs.uark.edu/

University of Arkansas for Medical Sciences, College of Nursing, Little Rock, AR 72205-7199. Offers PhD. *Accreditation:* AACN. *Program availability:* Part-time. *Entrance requirements:* For doctorate, GRE. Additional exam requirements/recommendations for international students: Required—TOEFL. *Expenses:* Contact institution.

The University of British Columbia, Faculty of Applied Science, School of Nursing, Vancouver, BC V6T 2B5, Canada. Offers nurse practitioner (MN); nursing (MSN, PhD). *Program availability:* Part-time. *Degree requirements:* For doctorate, comprehensive exam, thesis/dissertation. *Entrance requirements:* Additional exam requirements/recommendations for international students: Required—TOEFL. Electronic applications accepted. *Expenses:* Contact institution. *Faculty research:* Women and children, aging, critical care, cross-cultural, health leadership and policy.

University of Calgary, Faculty of Graduate Studies, Faculty of Nursing, Calgary, AB T2N 1N4, Canada. Offers MN, PhD, PMD. *Program availability:* Part-time. *Degree requirements:* For master's, comprehensive exam (for some programs), thesis (for some programs); for doctorate, thesis/dissertation; for PMD, comprehensive exam. *Entrance requirements:* For master's and PMD, nursing experience, nursing registration; for doctorate, nursing registration. Additional exam requirements/recommendations for international students: Required—TOEFL (minimum score 600 paper-based), IELTS (minimum score 7), Michigan English Language Assessment Battery. Electronic applications accepted. *Expenses:* Contact institution. *Faculty research:* Health outcomes across multiple populations and multiple settings including patients and families with chronic health problems, culturally diverse, and vulnerable populations; family health; core processes; professional, educational and health services delivery.

University of California, Irvine, Programs in Health Sciences, Program in Nursing Science, Irvine, CA 92697. Offers MSN. *Accreditation:* AACN. *Students:* 46 full-time (43 women); includes 32 minority (16 Asian, non-Hispanic/Latino; 12 Hispanic/Latino; 4 Two or more races, non-Hispanic/Latino). Average age 32. 227 applicants, 13% accepted, 24 enrolled. In 2017, 18 master's awarded. Application fee: $105 ($125 for international students). *Unit head:* Adey Nyamathi, Dean, 949-824-1514, E-mail: anyamath@uci.edu. *Application contact:* Julie Aird, Director, Student Affairs and Support Services, 949-824-1514, E-mail: jaird@uci.edu.
Website: http://www.nursing.uci.edu/

University of California, Los Angeles, Graduate Division, School of Nursing, Los Angeles, CA 90095. Offers MSN, PhD, MBA/MSN. *Accreditation:* AACN. *Degree requirements:* For master's, comprehensive exam; for doctorate, thesis/dissertation, oral and written qualifying exams. *Entrance requirements:* For master's, bachelor's degree in nursing; minimum undergraduate GPA of 3.0 (or its equivalent if letter grade system not used); for doctorate, bachelor's degree in nursing; minimum undergraduate GPA of 3.5 (or its equivalent if letter grade system not used); writing sample. Additional exam requirements/recommendations for international students: Required—TOEFL. Electronic applications accepted. *Expenses:* Contact institution.

University of California, San Francisco, Graduate Division, School of Nursing, Program in Nursing, San Francisco, CA 94143. Offers MS, PhD. *Accreditation:* AACN; ACNM/ACME (one or more programs are accredited). *Degree requirements:* For master's, comprehensive exam, thesis or alternative; for doctorate, thesis/dissertation. *Entrance requirements:* For master's and doctorate, GRE General Test. *Expenses:* Contact institution.

University of Central Arkansas, Graduate School, College of Health and Behavioral Sciences, Department of Nursing, Conway, AR 72035-0001. Offers adult nurse practitioner (PMC); clinical nurse leader (PMC); clinical nurse specialist (MSN); family nurse practitioner (PMC); nurse educator (PMC); nurse practitioner (MSN). *Accreditation:* AACN. *Program availability:* Part-time, evening/weekend, online learning. *Degree requirements:* For master's, comprehensive exam, thesis optional, clinicals. *Entrance requirements:* For master's, GRE General Test, minimum GPA of 2.7. Additional exam requirements/recommendations for international students: Required—TOEFL (minimum score 550 paper-based; 80 iBT). *Application deadline:* For fall admission, 3/1 priority date for domestic students; for spring admission, 10/1 for domestic students. Applications are processed on a rolling basis. Application fee: $25 ($50 for international students). Electronic applications accepted. *Expenses:* Contact institution. *Financial support:* Federal Work-Study, traineeships, and unspecified assistantships available. Financial award application deadline: 2/15; financial award applicants required to submit FAFSA.
Website: http://www.uca.edu/divisions/academic/chas/nurse2ab.asp

University of Central Florida, College of Nursing, Orlando, FL 32816. Offers adult-gerontology acute care nurse practitioner (Certificate); adult-gerontology primary care nurse practitioner (Certificate); family nurse practitioner (Certificate); nursing (MSN, PhD); nursing education (Post-Master's Certificate); nursing practice (DNP). *Accreditation:* AACN. *Program availability:* Part-time, evening/weekend. *Faculty:* 57 full-time (49 women), 70 part-time/adjunct (68 women). *Students:* 63 full-time (58 women), 327 part-time (297 women); includes 131 minority (40 Black or African American, non-Hispanic/Latino; 1 American Indian or Alaska Native, non-Hispanic/Latino; 16 Asian, non-Hispanic/Latino; 62 Hispanic/Latino; 12 Two or more races, non-Hispanic/Latino), 1 international. Average age 38. 303 applicants, 64% accepted, 129 enrolled. In 2017, 87 master's, 5 doctorates, 4 other advanced degrees awarded. *Degree requirements:* For master's, thesis or alternative; for doctorate, comprehensive exam, thesis/dissertation. *Entrance requirements:* For master's, essay, curriculum vitae; for doctorate, GRE General Test, letters of recommendation, resume, essay. Additional exam requirements/recommendations for international students: Required—TOEFL. *Application deadline:*

For fall admission, 3/15 for domestic students; for spring admission, 10/15 for domestic students. Application fee: $30. Electronic applications accepted. *Expenses:* Tuition, state resident: part-time $288.16 per credit hour. Tuition, nonresident: part-time $1073.31 per credit hour. Tuition and fees vary according to program. *Financial support:* In 2017–18, 3 students received support, including 2 fellowships with partial tuition reimbursements available (averaging $7,377 per year), 1 research assistantship with partial tuition reimbursement available (averaging $11,952 per year); career-related internships or fieldwork, Federal Work-Study, institutionally sponsored loans, traineeships, and unspecified assistantships also available. Financial award application deadline: 3/1; financial award applicants required to submit FAFSA. *Unit head:* Dr. Mary Lou Sole, Dean, 407-823-5496, Fax: 407-823-5675, E-mail: mary.sole@ucf.edu. *Application contact:* Associate Director, Graduate Admissions, 407-823-2766, Fax: 407-823-6442, E-mail: gradadmissions@ucf.edu.
Website: http://nursing.ucf.edu/

University of Central Missouri, The Graduate School, Warrensburg, MO 64093. Offers accountancy (MA); accounting (MBA); applied mathematics (MS); aviation safety (MA); biology (MS); business administration (MBA); career and technical education leadership (MS); college student personnel administration (MS); communication (MA); computer science (MS); counseling (MS); criminal justice (MS), educational leadership (Ed D); educational technology (MS); elementary and early childhood education (MSE); English (MA); environmental studies (MA); finance (MBA); history (MA); human services/educational technology (Ed S); human services/learning resources (Ed S); human services/professional counseling (Ed S); industrial hygiene (MS); industrial management (MS); information systems (MBA); information technology (MS); kinesiology (MS); library science and information services (MS); literacy education (MSE); marketing (MBA); mathematics (MS); music (MA); occupational safety management (MS); psychology (MS); rural family nursing (MS); school administration (MSE); social gerontology (MS); sociology (MA); special education (MSE); speech language pathology (MS); superintendency (Ed S); teaching (MAT); teaching English as a second language (MA); technology (MS); technology management (PhD); theatre (MA). *Program availability:* Part-time, 100% online, blended/hybrid learning. *Faculty:* 337 full-time (145 women), 41 part-time/adjunct (28 women). *Students:* 785 full-time (398 women), 1,633 part-time (1,063 women); includes 231 minority (102 Black or African American, non-Hispanic/Latino; 4 American Indian or Alaska Native, non-Hispanic/Latino; 16 Asian, non-Hispanic/Latino; 52 Hispanic/Latino; 57 Two or more races, non-Hispanic/Latino), 692 international. Average age 30. In 2017, 2,605 master's, 122 other advanced degrees awarded. *Degree requirements:* For master's and Ed S, comprehensive exam (for some programs), thesis (for some programs). *Entrance requirements:* Additional exam requirements/recommendations for international students: Required—TOEFL (minimum score 550 paper-based; 79 iBT). *Application deadline:* For fall admission, 6/1 priority date for domestic and international students; for spring admission, 10/1 priority date for domestic and international students; for summer admission, 4/1 priority date for domestic and international students. Applications are processed on a rolling basis. Application fee: $30 ($75 for international students). Electronic applications accepted. *Expenses:* Tuition, state resident: full-time $8771; part-time $292.35 per credit hour. Tuition, nonresident: full-time $17,541; part-time $584.70 per credit hour. *Required fees:* $372; $24.78 per credit hour. *Financial support:* In 2017–18, 99 students received support. Research assistantships, teaching assistantships, career-related internships or fieldwork, Federal Work-Study, scholarships/grants, and administrative and laboratory assistantships available. Support available to part-time students. Financial award application deadline: 3/1; financial award applicants required to submit FAFSA. *Unit head:* Shellie Hewitt, Director of Graduate and International Student Services, 660-543-4621, Fax: 660-543-4778, E-mail: hewitt@ucmo.edu. *Application contact:* 660-543-4621, E-mail: admit_intl@ucmo.edu.
Website: http://www.ucmo.edu/graduate/

University of Central Oklahoma, The Jackson College of Graduate Studies, College of Mathematics and Science, Department of Nursing, Edmond, OK 73034-5209. Offers MS. *Accreditation:* AACN. *Program availability:* Part-time. *Faculty:* 6 full-time (all women). *Students:* 14 full-time (12 women), 13 part-time (all women); includes 4 minority (all Black or African American, non-Hispanic/Latino), 8 international. Average age 37. 22 applicants, 68% accepted, 6 enrolled. In 2017, 14 master's awarded. *Degree requirements:* For master's, thesis (for some programs). *Entrance requirements:* For master's, minimum undergraduate GPA of 3.0 in nursing; bachelor's degree in nursing; RN license (preferred). Additional exam requirements/recommendations for international students: Required—TOEFL (minimum score 550 paper-based; 79 iBT), IELTS (minimum score 6.5). *Application deadline:* For fall admission, 7/15 for international students; for spring admission, 11/15 for international students. Applications are processed on a rolling basis. Application fee: $60. Electronic applications accepted. *Expenses:* Contact institution. *Financial support:* In 2017–18, 7 students received support, including 5 teaching assistantships with partial tuition reimbursements available (averaging $10,050 per year); research assistantships, scholarships/grants, and tuition waivers (partial) also available. Financial award application deadline: 3/31; financial award applicants required to submit FAFSA. *Unit head:* Dr. Linda Rider, Chair, 405-974-2461, Fax: 405-974-3824. *Application contact:* Dr. Barbara Arnold, Graduate Advisor, 405-974-5191, Fax: 405-974-3824, E-mail: gradcoll@uco.edu.
Website: https://sites.uco.edu/cms/nursing/

University of Cincinnati, Graduate School, College of Nursing, Cincinnati, OH 45221-0038. Offers nurse midwifery (MSN); nurse practitioner (MSN, DNP), including acute care pediatrics (DNP), adult-gerontology acute care, adult-gerontology primary care, anesthesia (DNP), family (MSN), leadership (DNP), neonatal (MSN), women's health (MSN); nursing (MSN, PhD), including occupational health (MSN). *Accreditation:* AACN; AANA/CANAEP (one or more programs are accredited); ACNM/ACME. *Program availability:* Part-time, 100% online, blended/hybrid learning. *Faculty:* 74 full-time (69 women), 112 part-time/adjunct (105 women). *Students:* 323 full-time (261 women), 1,084 part-time (949 women); includes 311 minority (113 Black or African American, non-Hispanic/Latino; 4 American Indian or Alaska Native, non-Hispanic/Latino; 56 Asian, non-Hispanic/Latino; 108 Hispanic/Latino; 1 Native Hawaiian or other Pacific Islander, non-Hispanic/Latino; 29 Two or more races, non-Hispanic/Latino), 12 international. Average age 34. 582 applicants, 64% accepted, 314 enrolled. In 2017, 579 master's, 18 doctorates awarded. *Degree requirements:* For master's, thesis or alternative; for doctorate, comprehensive exam (for some programs), thesis/dissertation (for some programs). *Entrance requirements:* For doctorate, GRE General Test. Additional exam requirements/recommendations for international students: Required—TOEFL (minimum score 600 paper-based; 100 iBT); Recommended—IELTS (minimum score 7). *Application deadline:* For fall admission, 5/1 priority date for domestic students, 5/1 for international students; for spring admission, 10/1 for domestic students; for summer admission, 3/1 priority date for domestic students. Applications are processed on a rolling basis. Application fee: $130 ($70 for international students). Electronic applications accepted. *Expenses:* $14,668 annual full-time in-state tuition, $707 annual fees. *Financial support:* In 2017–18, 123 students received support, including 8 fellowships with full tuition reimbursements available (averaging $30,423 per year), 7 research assistantships with full tuition reimbursements available (averaging $17,971 per year), 5 teaching assistantships with full tuition reimbursements available (averaging $17,971 per year); Federal Work-Study, institutionally sponsored loans, scholarships/grants, traineeships, health care benefits, tuition waivers (partial), and unspecified assistantships also available. Support available to part-time students. Financial award application deadline: 5/1; financial award applicants required to submit FAFSA. *Faculty research:* Vulnerable populations, education, violence, chronicity/aging, cancer. *Total annual research expenditures:* $575,576. *Unit head:* Dr. Greer Glazer, Dean, 513-558-

5330, Fax: 513-558-9030, E-mail: greer.glazer@uc.edu. *Application contact:* Office of Student Recruitment, 513-558-8400, Fax: 513-558-5012, E-mail: nursingbearcats@uc.edu.
Website: https://nursing.uc.edu/

University of Colorado Colorado Springs, Helen and Arthur E. Johnson Beth-El College of Nursing and Health Sciences, Colorado Springs, CO 80918. Offers nursing practice (DNP); primary care nurse practitioner (MSN). *Accreditation:* AACN. *Program availability:* Part-time, 100% online, blended/hybrid learning. *Faculty:* 11 full-time (10 women), 13 part-time/adjunct (12 women). *Students:* 7 full-time (6 women), 213 part-time (192 women); includes 50 minority (8 Black or African American, non-Hispanic/Latino; 1 American Indian or Alaska Native, non-Hispanic/Latino; 11 Asian, non-Hispanic/Latino; 23 Hispanic/Latino; 1 Native Hawaiian or other Pacific Islander, non-Hispanic/Latino; 6 Two or more races, non-Hispanic/Latino). Average age 37. 125 applicants, 66% accepted, 57 enrolled. In 2017, 47 master's, 10 doctorates awarded. *Degree requirements:* For master's, comprehensive exam, thesis optional; for doctorate, capstone project. *Entrance requirements:* For master's, GRE General Test or MAT, minimum overall GPA of 2.75 for all undergraduate course work, minimum BSN GPA of 3.3; for doctorate, interview; active RN license; MA; minimum GPA of 3.3; National Certification as nurse practitioner or clinical nurse specialist; portfolio. Additional exam requirements/recommendations for international students: Required—TOEFL (minimum score 550 paper-based; 80 iBT). *Application deadline:* For fall admission, 3/15 priority date for domestic students, 3/15 for international students; for spring admission, 8/15 for domestic and international students. Applications are processed on a rolling basis. Application fee: $60 ($100 for international students). Electronic applications accepted. *Expenses:* $12,241 per year resident tuition, $21,511 nonresident, $13,869 nonresidential online; annual costs vary depending on program, course-load, and residency status. *Financial support:* In 2017–18, 28 students received support. Research assistantships, career-related internships or fieldwork, Federal Work-Study, and scholarships/grants available. Support available to part-time students. Financial award application deadline: 3/1; financial award applicants required to submit FAFSA. *Faculty research:* Behavioral interventions to reduce stroke risk factors in older adults, interprofessional models of health promotion for older adults, nurse practitioner education, practice and policy, cardiology, cardiac and pulmonary rehab, heart failure and stroke, community health prevention, veterans studies, anger management, sports medicine, sports nutrition. *Total annual research expenditures:* $580,217. *Unit head:* Dr. Deborah Pollard, Nursing Department Chair, 719-255-3577, Fax: 719-255-4416, E-mail: dpollard@uccs.edu. *Application contact:* Diane Busch, Program Assistant II, 719-255-4424, Fax: 719-255-4416, E-mail: dbusch@uccs.edu.
Website: http://www.uccs.edu/bethel/index.html

University of Colorado Denver, College of Nursing, Aurora, CO 80045. Offers adult clinical nurse specialist (MS); adult nurse practitioner (MS); family nurse practitioner (MS); family psychiatric mental health nurse practitioner (MS); health care informatics (MS); nurse-midwifery (MS); nursing (DNP, PhD); nursing leadership and health care systems (MS); pediatric nurse practitioner (MS); women's health (MS); MS/PhD. *Accreditation:* ACNM/ACME (one or more programs are accredited). *Program availability:* Part-time, evening/weekend, online learning. *Students:* 297 applicants, 55% accepted, 141 enrolled. In 2017, 138 master's, 18 doctorates awarded. Terminal master's awarded for partial completion of doctoral program. *Degree requirements:* For master's, thesis optional; for doctorate, comprehensive exam, thesis/dissertation, 42 credits of coursework. *Entrance requirements:* For master's, GRE if cumulative undergraduate GPA is less than 3.0, undergraduate nursing degree from ACEN- or CCNE-accredited school or university; completion of research and statistics courses with minimum grade of C; copy of current and unencumbered nursing license; for doctorate, GRE, bachelor's and/or master's degrees in nursing from ACEN- or CCNE-accredited institution; portfolio; minimum undergraduate GPA of 3.0, graduate 3.5; graduate-level intermediate statistics and master's-level nursing theory courses with minimum B grade; interview. Additional exam requirements/recommendations for international students: Required—TOEFL (minimum score 560 paper-based; 83 iBT). *Application deadline:* For fall admission, 2/15 for domestic students, 1/15 for international students; for spring admission, 7/1 for domestic students, 6/1 for international students. Application fee: $50 ($75 for international students). Electronic applications accepted. *Unit head:* Dr. Sarah Thompson, Dean, 303-724-1679, E-mail: sarah.a.thompson@ucdenver.edu. *Application contact:* Judy Campbell, Graduate Programs Coordinator, 303-724-8503, E-mail: judy.campbell@ucdenver.edu.
Website: http://www.ucdenver.edu/academics/colleges/nursing/Pages/default.aspx

★ **University of Connecticut,** Graduate School, School of Nursing, Doctorate of Nursing Practice Program, Storrs, CT 06269. Offers DNP. *Program availability:* Part-time, online learning. *Entrance requirements:* For doctorate, current licensure as registered professional nurse; minimum GPA of 3.0; three reference letters; personal statement; personal interview; master's degree from accredited college or university. Additional exam requirements/recommendations for international students: Required—TOEFL (minimum score 550 paper-based). Electronic applications accepted.

See Display on the previous page and Close-Up on page 767.

★ **University of Connecticut,** Graduate School, School of Nursing, PhD Program in Nursing, Storrs, CT 06269. Offers PhD.

See Display below and Close-Up on page 765.

★ **University of Connecticut,** Graduate School, School of Nursing, Post-Master's Certificate Programs, Storrs, CT 06269. Offers adult gerontology acute care nurse practitioner (Post-Master's Certificate); adult gerontology primary care nurse practitioner (Post-Master's Certificate); neonatal nurse practitioner (Post-Master's Certificate). *Entrance requirements:* For degree, minimum graduate GPA of 3.0, current Connecticut RN license, three letters of recommendation, current resume/curriculum vitae.

See Display below and Close-Up on page 767.

University of Delaware, College of Health Sciences, School of Nursing, Newark, DE 19716. Offers adult nurse practitioner (MSN, PMC); cardiopulmonary clinical nurse specialist (MSN, PMC); cardiopulmonary clinical nurse specialist/adult nurse practitioner (MSN, PMC); family nurse practitioner (MSN, PMC); gerontology clinical nurse specialist (MSN, PMC); gerontology clinical nurse specialist geriatric nurse practitioner (PMC); gerontology clinical nurse specialist/geriatric nurse practitioner (MSN); health services administration (MSN, PMC); nursing of children clinical nurse specialist (MSN, PMC); nursing of children clinical nurse specialist/pediatric nurse practitioner (MSN, PMC); oncology/immune deficiency clinical nurse specialist (MSN, PMC); oncology/immune deficiency clinical nurse specialist/adult nurse practitioner (MSN, PMC); perinatal/women's health clinical nurse specialist (MSN, PMC); perinatal/women's health clinical nurse specialist/women's health nurse practitioner (MSN, PMC); psychiatric nursing clinical nurse specialist (MSN, PMC). *Accreditation:* AACN. *Program availability:* Part-time, evening/weekend, online learning. *Degree requirements:* For master's, thesis optional. *Entrance requirements:* For master's, BSN, interview, RN license. Electronic applications accepted. *Faculty research:* Marriage and chronic illness, health promotion, congestive heart failure patient outcomes, school nursing, diabetes in children, culture, health disparities, cardiovascular, prison nursing, oncology, public policy, child obesity, smoking and teen pregnancy, blood pressure measurements, men's health.

University of Detroit Mercy, College of Health Professions, Detroit, MI 48221. Offers clinical nurse leader (MSN); family nurse practitioner (MSN); health services administration (MHSA); health systems management (MSN); nurse anesthesia (MS); nursing (DNP); nursing education (MSN, Certificate); nursing leadership and financial management (Certificate); outcomes performance management (Certificate); physician assistant (MS). *Entrance requirements:* For master's, GRE General Test, minimum GPA of 3.0. *Faculty research:* Research design, respiratory physiology, AIDS prevention, adolescent health, community, low income health education.

University of Florida, Graduate School, College of Nursing, Gainesville, FL 32611. Offers clinical and translational science (PhD); clinical nursing (DNP); nursing (MSN); nursing sciences (PhD). *Accreditation:* AACN; ACNM/ACME (one or more programs are accredited). *Program availability:* Part-time. *Degree requirements:* For master's, thesis optional; for doctorate, thesis/dissertation. *Entrance requirements:* For master's and doctorate, GRE General Test, minimum GPA of 3.0. Additional exam requirements/ recommendations for international students: Required—TOEFL (minimum score 550 paper-based; 80 iBT), IELTS (minimum score 6). Electronic applications accepted. *Faculty research:* Aging and health: cancer survivorship, interventions to promote healthy aging, and symptom management; women's health, fetal and infant development; biobehavioral interventions: interrelationships among the biological, behavioral, psychological, social and spiritual factors that influence wellness and disease; health policy: influence of local and national policy on physical and psychological health.

University of Hartford, College of Education, Nursing, and Health Professions, Program in Nursing, West Hartford, CT 06117-1599. Offers community/public health nursing (MSN); nursing education (MSN); nursing management (MSN). *Accreditation:* AACN. *Program availability:* Part-time, evening/weekend. *Degree requirements:* For master's, research project. *Entrance requirements:* For master's, BSN, Connecticut RN license. Additional exam requirements/recommendations for international students: Required—TOEFL (minimum score 550 paper-based). Electronic applications accepted. *Expenses:* Contact institution. *Faculty research:* Child development, women in doctoral study, applying feminist theory in teaching methods, near death experience, grandmothers as primary care providers.

University of Hawaii at Hilo, Program in Nursing Practice, Hilo, HI 96720-4091. Offers DNP. *Accreditation:* AACN. *Entrance requirements:* Additional exam requirements/ recommendations for international students: Required—TOEFL, IELTS. Electronic applications accepted.

University of Hawaii at Manoa, Office of Graduate Education, School of Nursing and Dental Hygiene, Honolulu, HI 96822. Offers clinical nurse specialist (MS), including adult health, community mental health; nurse practitioner (MS), including adult health, community mental health, family nurse practitioner; nursing (PhD, Graduate Certificate); nursing administration (MS). *Accreditation:* AACN. *Program availability:* Part-time, online learning. *Degree requirements:* For master's, thesis optional; for doctorate, comprehensive exam, thesis/dissertation. *Entrance requirements:* For master's, Hawaii RN license. Additional exam requirements/recommendations for international students: Required—TOEFL (minimum score 580 paper-based; 92 iBT), IELTS (minimum score 5). *Expenses:* Contact institution.

University of Houston, College of Nursing, Sugar Land, TX 77479. Offers family nurse practitioner (MSN); nursing administration (MSN); nursing education (MSN). *Accreditation:* AACN. *Faculty:* 13 full-time (12 women). *Students:* 29 full-time (24 women); includes 15 minority (6 Black or African American, non-Hispanic/Latino; 5 Asian, non-Hispanic/Latino; 4 Hispanic/Latino), 3 international. Average age 37. 36 applicants, 61% accepted, 15 enrolled. In 2017, 14 master's awarded. *Entrance requirements:* For master's, GRE or MAT, minimum GPA of 3.0 in last 60 hours of academic course work, valid Texas RN licensure, 2 letters of recommendation, essay, resume, interview. Additional exam requirements/recommendations for international students: Required—TOEFL. *Application deadline:* For fall admission, 7/1 for domestic students, 6/1 for international students; for spring admission, 12/1 for domestic students, 10/1 for international students. Application fee: $75. Electronic applications accepted. *Financial support:* In 2017–18, 19 students received support. Federal Work-Study, scholarships/grants, and unspecified assistantships available. Support available to part-time students. Financial award application deadline: 5/1; financial award applicants required to submit FAFSA. *Unit head:* Dr. Kathryn Tart, Dean, 832-842-8200, E-mail: kmtart@uh.edu. *Application contact:* Tammy N. Whatley, Student Affairs Director, 832-842-8220, E-mail: tnwhatley@uh.edu.
Website: http://www.uh.edu/nursing

University of Illinois at Chicago, College of Nursing, Chicago, IL 60607-7128. Offers MS, DNP, PhD, Certificate, MBA/MS, MPH/MS. *Accreditation:* AACN. *Program availability:* Part-time. *Degree requirements:* For master's, thesis or alternative; for doctorate, thesis/dissertation. *Entrance requirements:* For master's and doctorate, GRE General Test, minimum GPA of 2.75. Additional exam requirements/recommendations for international students: Required—TOEFL. Electronic applications accepted. *Expenses:* Contact institution. *Faculty research:* Health promotion and disease prevention, quality of life and symptom management, end-of-life, health disparities and health equity, pregnancy outcomes.

University of Indianapolis, Graduate Programs, School of Nursing, Indianapolis, IN 46227-3697. Offers advanced practice nursing (DNP); family nurse practitioner (MSN); gerontological nurse practitioner (MSN); neonatal nurse practitioner (MSN); nurse-midwifery (MSN); nursing (MSN); nursing and health systems leadership (MSN); nursing education (MSN); women's health nurse practitioner (MSN); MBA/MSN. *Accreditation:* AACN. *Entrance requirements:* For master's, minimum GPA of 3.0, interview, letters of recommendation, resume, IN nursing license, 1 year of professional practice; for doctorate, graduate of ACEN- or CCNE-accredited nursing program; MSN or MA with nursing major and minimum cumulative GPA of 3.25; unencumbered RN license with eligibility for licensure in Indiana; completion of graduate-level statistics course within last 5 years with minimum grade of B; resume; essay; official transcripts from all academic institutions. Additional exam requirements/recommendations for international students: Required—TOEFL (minimum score 550 paper-based). Electronic applications accepted.

The University of Iowa, Graduate College, College of Nursing, Iowa City, IA 52242-1316. Offers MSN, DNP, PhD. *Accreditation:* AACN; AANA/CANAEP (one or more programs are accredited). *Degree requirements:* For master's, thesis optional, portfolio, project; for doctorate, comprehensive exam, thesis/dissertation. *Entrance requirements:* For master's, minimum GPA of 3.0; for doctorate, GRE General Test, minimum GPA of 3.0. Additional exam requirements/recommendations for international students: Required—TOEFL (minimum score 550 paper-based; 81 iBT). Electronic applications accepted. *Expenses:* Contact institution.

The University of Kansas, University of Kansas Medical Center, School of Nursing, Kansas City, KS 66160. Offers adult/gerontological clinical nurse specialist (PMC); adult/gerontological nurse practitioner (PMC); health care informatics (PMC); health professions educator (PMC); nurse midwife (PMC); nursing (MS, DNP, PhD); organizational leadership (PMC); psychiatric/mental health nurse practitioner (PMC); public health nursing (PMC). *Accreditation:* AACN; ACNM/ACME. *Program availability:* Part-time, 100% online, blended/hybrid learning. *Faculty:* 56. *Students:* 48 full-time (44 women), 260 part-time (235 women); includes 50 minority (12 Black or African American, non-Hispanic/Latino; 2 American Indian or Alaska Native, non-Hispanic/ Latino; 16 Asian, non-Hispanic/Latino; 8 Hispanic/Latino; 12 Two or more races, non-Hispanic/Latino). Average age 36. 87 applicants, 95% accepted, 61 enrolled. In 2017, 37 master's, 18 doctorates, 3 other advanced degrees awarded. Terminal master's awarded for partial completion of doctoral program. *Degree requirements:* For master's, comprehensive exam, thesis (for some programs), general oral exam; for doctorate, thesis/dissertation or alternative, comprehensive oral exam (for DNP); comprehensive written and oral exam, or three publications (for PhD). *Entrance requirements:* For master's, bachelor's degree in nursing, minimum GPA of 3.0, 1 year of clinical experience, RN license in KS and MO; for doctorate, GRE General Test (for PhD only), bachelor's degree in nursing, minimum GPA of 3.5, RN license in KS and MO. Additional exam requirements/recommendations for international students: Required—TOEFL. *Application deadline:* For fall admission, 4/1 for domestic and international students; for spring admission, 9/1 for domestic and international students. Application fee: $75. Electronic applications accepted. *Financial support:* In 2017–18, 5 research assistantships with tuition reimbursements (averaging $20,000 per year), 30 teaching assistantships with tuition reimbursements (averaging $20,000 per year) were awarded; scholarships/grants and traineeships also available. Financial award application deadline: 3/1; financial award applicants required to submit FAFSA. *Faculty research:* Breastfeeding practices of teen mothers, national database of nursing quality indicators, caregiving of families of patients using technology in the home, simulation in nursing education, diaphragm fatigue. *Total annual research expenditures:* $1.4 million. *Unit head:* Dr. Sally Maliski, Dean, 913-588-1601, Fax: 913-588-1660, E-mail: smaliski@kumc.edu. *Application contact:* Dr. Pamela K. Barnes, Associate Dean, Student Affairs, 913-588-1619, Fax: 913-588-1615, E-mail: pbarnes2@kumc.edu.
Website: http://nursing.kumc.edu

University of Kentucky, Graduate School, College of Nursing, Lexington, KY 40506-0032. Offers DNP, PhD. *Accreditation:* AACN. *Degree requirements:* For doctorate, comprehensive exam, thesis/dissertation. *Entrance requirements:* For doctorate, GRE General Test, minimum undergraduate GPA of 3.0. Additional exam requirements/ recommendations for international students: Required—TOEFL (minimum score 550 paper-based). Electronic applications accepted.

University of Lethbridge, School of Graduate Studies, Lethbridge, AB T1K 3M4, Canada. Offers addictions counseling (M Sc); agricultural biotechnology (M Sc); agricultural studies (M Sc, MA); anthropology (MA); archaeology (M Sc, MA); art (MA, MFA); biochemistry (M Sc); biological sciences (M Sc); biomolecular science (PhD); biosystems and biodiversity (PhD); Canadian studies (MA); chemistry (M Sc); computer science (M Sc); computer science and geographical information science (M Sc); counseling (MC); counseling psychology (M Ed); dramatic arts (MA); earth, space, and physical science (PhD); economics (MA); education (MA, PhD); educational leadership (M Ed); English (MA); environmental science (M Sc); evolution and behavior (PhD); exercise science (M Sc); French (MA); French/German (MA); French/Spanish (MA); general education (M Ed); geography (M Sc, MA); German (MA); health sciences (M Sc); individualized multidisciplinary (M Sc, MA); kinesiology (M Sc, MA); management (M Sc), including accounting, finance, human resource management and labor relations, information systems, international management, marketing, policy and strategy; mathematics (M Sc); music (M Mus, MA); Native American studies (MA); neuroscience (M Sc, PhD); new media (MA, MFA); nursing (M Sc, MN); philosophy (MA); physics (M Sc); political science (MA); psychology (M Sc, MA); religious studies (MA); sociology (MA); theatre and dramatic arts (MFA); theoretical and computational science (PhD); urban and regional studies (MA); women and gender studies (MA). *Program availability:* Part-time, evening/weekend. *Degree requirements:* For master's, thesis (for some programs); for doctorate, comprehensive exam, thesis/dissertation. *Entrance requirements:* For master's, GMAT (for M Sc in management), bachelor's degree in related field, minimum GPA of 3.0 during previous 20 graded semester courses, 2 years' teaching or related experience (M Ed); for doctorate, master's degree, minimum graduate GPA of 3.5. Additional exam requirements/recommendations for international students: Required—TOEFL (minimum score 580 paper-based; 93 iBT). Electronic applications accepted. *Faculty research:* Movement and brain plasticity, gibberellin physiology, photosynthesis, carbon cycling, molecular properties of main-group ring components.

University of Louisiana at Lafayette, College of Nursing and Allied Health Professions, Lafayette, LA 70504. Offers family nurse practitioner (MSN); nurse executive curriculum (MSN); nursing and allied health professions (DNP). Program offered jointly with Southern Louisiana University, McNeese State University, Southern University and Agricultural and Mechanical College. *Accreditation:* AACN. *Entrance requirements:* For master's, GRE General Test, minimum GPA of 2.75. Additional exam requirements/recommendations for international students: Required—TOEFL (minimum score 550 paper-based). *Application deadline:* For fall admission, 5/15 for domestic and international students; for spring admission, 10/1 for domestic students. Applications are processed on a rolling basis. Application fee: $25 ($30 for international students). Electronic applications accepted. *Unit head:* Dr. Lisa Broussard, Department Head, 337-482-5654, E-mail: lisabroussard@louisiana.edu. *Application contact:* Dr. Carolyn P. Delahoussaye, Graduate Coordinator, 337-482-5617, Fax: 337-482-5649, E-mail: cgp6303@louisiana.edu.
Website: http://nursing.louisiana.edu

University of Louisville, Graduate School, School of Nursing, Louisville, KY 40202. Offers adult gerontology nurse practitioner (MSN, DNP); education and administration (MSN); family nurse practitioner (MSN, DNP); neonatal nurse practitioner (MSN, DNP); nursing research (PhD); psychiatric/mental health nurse practitioner (MSN, DNP); women's health nurse practitioner (MSN). *Accreditation:* AACN. *Program availability:* Part-time. *Faculty:* 44 full-time (40 women), 45 part-time/adjunct (41 women). *Students:* 130 full-time (107 women), 30 part-time (25 women); includes 33 minority (16 Black or African American, non-Hispanic/Latino; 7 Asian, non-Hispanic/Latino; 5 Hispanic/Latino; 5 Two or more races, non-Hispanic/Latino), 2 international. Average age 33. 61 applicants, 67% accepted, 36 enrolled. In 2017, 54 master's awarded. *Degree requirements:* For doctorate, comprehensive exam (for some programs), thesis/ dissertation (for some programs). *Entrance requirements:* For master's, bachelor's degree from nationally-accredited college, completion of 6 prerequisite courses, minimum undergraduate GPA of 3.0; for doctorate, GRE with minimum score of 156 Verbal, 146 Quantitative, 4.0 Analytic (for PhD), 3 letters of professional reference; minimum GPA of 3.0 with BSN, 3.25 with MSN; written statement of career goals, areas of expertise, and reasons for pursuing doctoral degree; resume including RN license. Additional exam requirements/recommendations for international students: Recommended—TOEFL (minimum score 560 paper-based), IELTS (minimum score 6.5). *Application deadline:* For fall admission, 1/15 priority date for domestic students, 1/ 15 for international students; for summer admission, 10/15 priority date for domestic students. Application fee: $65. Electronic applications accepted. *Expenses:* Tuition, state resident: full-time $12,246; part-time $681 per credit hour. Tuition, nonresident: full-time $25,486; part-time $1417 per credit hour. *Required fees:* $196. Tuition and fees vary according to course load, program and reciprocity agreements. *Financial support:* In 2017–18, 8 research assistantships with full tuition reimbursements (averaging

$20,000 per year), 4 teaching assistantships with full tuition reimbursements (averaging $15,000 per year) were awarded; fellowships with full tuition reimbursements, scholarships/grants, and unspecified assistantships also available. Financial award application deadline: 10/1; financial award applicants required to submit FAFSA. *Faculty research:* Environmental health, health services research, women's mental health, self-management of chronic illness in adults and children, health disparities. *Total annual research expenditures:* $762,266. *Unit head:* Dr. Marcia J. Hern, RN, Dean and Professor, 502-852-8300, Fax: 502-852-8783, E-mail: m.hern@louisville.edu. *Application contact:* Trish Hart, Assistant Dean for Student Affairs, 502-852-5825, Fax: 502-852-8783, E-mail: trish.hart@louisville.edu.
Website: http://www.louisville.edu/nursing/

University of Maine, Graduate School, College of Natural Sciences, Forestry, and Agriculture, School of Nursing, Orono, ME 04469. Offers individualized (MS); nursing education (CGS); rural health family nurse practitioner (MS, CAS). *Accreditation:* AACN. *Faculty:* 6 full-time (all women), 6 part-time/adjunct (4 women). *Students:* 22 full-time (19 women), 14 part-time (12 women); includes 3 minority (1 American Indian or Alaska Native, non-Hispanic/Latino; 1 Asian, non-Hispanic/Latino; 1 Two or more races, non-Hispanic/Latino), 1 international. Average age 35. 22 applicants, 100% accepted, 17 enrolled. In 2017, 10 master's, 2 other advanced degrees awarded. *Entrance requirements:* For master's, GRE General Test; for other advanced degree, master's degree. Additional exam requirements/recommendations for international students: Required—TOEFL. *Application deadline:* For fall admission, 7/1 for domestic students; for spring admission, 12/15 for domestic students; for summer admission, 4/15 for domestic students. Applications are processed on a rolling basis. Application fee: $65. Electronic applications accepted. *Expenses:* Tuition, state resident: full-time $7722; part-time $429 per credit hour. Tuition, nonresident: full-time $25,146; part-time $1397 per credit hour. *Required fees:* $1162; $581 per credit hour. *Financial support:* Career-related internships or fieldwork, Federal Work-Study, institutionally sponsored loans, tuition waivers (full and partial), and unspecified assistantships available. Support available to part-time students. Financial award application deadline: 3/1. *Faculty research:* Population health, health disparities, infectious waste management, domestic violence older adults. *Total annual research expenditures:* $249,000. *Unit head:* Dr. Nancy Fishwick, Director, 207-581-2505, Fax: 207-581-2585. *Application contact:* Scott G. Delcourt, Assistant Vice President for Graduate Studies and Senior Associate Dean, 207-581-3291, Fax: 207-581-3232, E-mail: graduate@maine.edu.
Website: http://umaine.edu/nursing/

The University of Manchester, School of Nursing, Midwifery and Social Work, Manchester, United Kingdom. Offers nursing (M Phil, PhD); social work (M Phil, PhD).

University of Manitoba, Faculty of Graduate Studies, College of Nursing, Winnipeg, MB R3T 2N2, Canada. Offers cancer nursing (MN); nursing (MN). *Degree requirements:* For master's, thesis.

University of Mary, School of Health Sciences, Division of Nursing, Bismarck, ND 58504-9652. Offers family nurse practitioner (DNP); nurse administrator (MSN); nursing educator (MSN); MSN/MBA. *Accreditation:* AACN. *Program availability:* Part-time, evening/weekend, online learning. *Degree requirements:* For master's, comprehensive exam (for some programs), thesis (for some programs), internship (family nurse practitioner), teaching practice. *Entrance requirements:* For master's, minimum GPA of 2.75 in nursing, interview, letters of recommendation, criminal background check, immunizations, statement of professional goals. Additional exam requirements/recommendations for international students: Required—TOEFL (minimum score 500 paper-based; 71 iBT). Electronic applications accepted. *Faculty research:* Gerontology issues, rural nursing, health policy, primary care, women's health.

University of Mary Hardin-Baylor, Graduate Studies in Nursing, Belton, TX 76513. Offers family nurse practitioner (MSN, Post-Master's Certificate); nursing education (MSN); nursing practice (DNP). *Accreditation:* AACN. *Program availability:* Evening/weekend. *Faculty:* 6 full-time (all women), 8 part-time/adjunct (7 women). *Students:* 44 full-time (40 women), 10 part-time (9 women); includes 19 minority (10 Black or African American, non-Hispanic/Latino; 7 Hispanic/Latino; 2 Two or more races, non-Hispanic/Latino). Average age 34. 47 applicants, 83% accepted, 31 enrolled. In 2017, 44 master's, 2 other advanced degrees awarded. *Degree requirements:* For master's, comprehensive exam, practicum; for doctorate, scholarly project. *Entrance requirements:* For master's, baccalaureate degree in nursing, current licensure as Registered Nurse in the state of Texas, minimum GPA of 3.0 in last 60 hours of undergraduate program, two letters of recommendation, full-time RN for 1 year, personal interview with director of MSN program; for doctorate, master's degree as an advanced practice nurse, nurse leader or nurse educator; three letters of recommendation; current RN license and approval to practice as an advanced practice nurse; essay; curriculum vitae; interview. Additional exam requirements/recommendations for international students: Required—TOEFL (minimum score 60 iBT), IELTS (minimum score 4.5). *Application deadline:* For fall admission, 6/1 for domestic students, 4/30 priority date for international students; for spring admission, 11/1 for domestic students, 9/30 priority date for international students. Applications are processed on a rolling basis. Application fee: $35 ($135 for international students). Electronic applications accepted. *Expenses:* $920 per credit hour. *Financial support:* In 2017–18, 34 students received support. Federal Work-Study, unspecified assistantships, and scholarships for some active duty military personnel available. Support available to part-time students. Financial award applicants required to submit FAFSA. *Faculty research:* Grief counseling, identifying escalating patients. *Unit head:* Dr. Sharon Souter, Dean, College of Nursing/MSN and DNP Programs Director, 254-295-4662, E-mail: ssouter@umhb.edu. *Application contact:* Sharon Aguilera, Assistant Director, Graduate Admissions, 254-295-4835, E-mail: saguilera@umhb.edu.
Website: https://go.umhb.edu/graduate/nursing/home

University of Maryland, Baltimore, School of Nursing, Baltimore, MD 21201. Offers adult-gerontology acute care nurse practitioner (DNP); adult-gerontology primary care nurse practitioner (DNP); clinical nurse leader (MS); community/public health nursing (MS); family nurse practitioner (DNP); global health (Postbaccalaureate Certificate); health services leadership and management (MS); neonatal nurse practitioner (DNP); nurse anesthesia (DNP); nursing (PhD); nursing informatics (MS, Postbaccalaureate Certificate); pediatric acute/primary care nurse practitioner (DNP); psychiatric mental health nurse practitioner (DNP); teaching in nursing and health professions (Postbaccalaureate Certificate); MS/MBA. MS/MBA offered jointly with University of Baltimore. *Program availability:* Part-time. *Faculty:* 130 full-time (117 women), 125 part-time/adjunct (114 women). *Students:* 504 full-time (442 women), 532 part-time (482 women); includes 443 minority (249 Black or African American, non-Hispanic/Latino; 1 American Indian or Alaska Native, non-Hispanic/Latino; 115 Asian, non-Hispanic/Latino; 48 Hispanic/Latino; 2 Native Hawaiian or other Pacific Islander, non-Hispanic/Latino; 28 Two or more races, non-Hispanic/Latino), 15 international. Average age 33. 935 applicants, 62% accepted, 394 enrolled. In 2017, 182 master's, 57 doctorates awarded. *Degree requirements:* For master's and Postbaccalaureate Certificate, thesis (for some programs); for doctorate, comprehensive exam, thesis/dissertation. *Entrance requirements:* Additional exam requirements/recommendations for international students: Required—TOEFL (minimum score 550 paper-based; 79 iBT); Recommended—IELTS (minimum score 7). *Application deadline:* For fall admission, 11/1 for domestic and international students; for spring admission, 8/1 for domestic and international students. Application fee: $75. Electronic applications accepted. *Expenses:* Contact institution. *Financial support:* In 2017–18, 22 research assistantships with full and partial tuition reimbursements (averaging $21,523 per year), 41 teaching assistantships with full and partial tuition reimbursements (averaging $13,439 per year) were awarded; fellowships and scholarships/grants also available. Financial award application deadline: 3/1; financial award applicants required to submit FAFSA. *Unit head:* Dr. Jane Kirschling, Dean, 410-706-4359, E-mail: kirschling@umaryland.edu. *Application contact:* Larry Fillian, Associate Dean of Student and Academic Services, 410-706-6298, E-mail: lfillian@umaryland.edu.
Website: http://www.nursing.umaryland.edu/

University of Massachusetts Amherst, Graduate School, College of Nursing, Amherst, MA 01003. Offers adult gerontology primary care nurse practitioner (DNP); clinical nurse leader (MS); family nurse practitioner (DNP); nursing (PhD); public health nurse leader (DNP). *Accreditation:* AACN. *Program availability:* Part-time, online learning. Terminal master's awarded for partial completion of doctoral program. *Degree requirements:* For master's, thesis optional; for doctorate, comprehensive exam, thesis/dissertation. *Entrance requirements:* Additional exam requirements/recommendations for international students: Required—TOEFL (minimum score 550 paper-based; 80 iBT), IELTS (minimum score 6.5). Electronic applications accepted. *Faculty research:* Health of older adults and their caretakers, mental health of individuals and families, health of children and adolescents, power and decision-making, transcultural health.

University of Massachusetts Boston, College of Nursing and Health Sciences, Program in Nursing, Boston, MA 02125-3393. Offers MS, PhD. PhD offered jointly with University of Massachusetts Lowell. *Program availability:* Part-time, evening/weekend. *Faculty:* 34 full-time (32 women), 85 part-time/adjunct (78 women). *Students:* 51 full-time (45 women), 166 part-time (154 women); includes 51 minority (24 Black or African American, non-Hispanic/Latino; 10 Asian, non-Hispanic/Latino; 16 Hispanic/Latino; 1 Two or more races, non-Hispanic/Latino), 16 international. Average age 34. 68 applicants, 76% accepted, 32 enrolled. In 2017, 56 master's, 4 doctorates awarded. *Entrance requirements:* For master's, GRE General Test, minimum GPA of 2.75, RN license; for doctorate, GRE General Test, master's degree, minimum GPA of 3.3, RN license or eligibility. *Application deadline:* For fall admission, 3/1 for domestic students; for spring admission, 11/1 for domestic students. *Expenses:* Tuition, state resident: full-time $17,375. Tuition, nonresident: full-time $33,915. *Required fees:* $355. *Financial support:* Research assistantships, teaching assistantships, career-related internships or fieldwork, Federal Work-Study, and unspecified assistantships available. Support available to part-time students. Financial award application deadline: 3/1; financial award applicants required to submit FAFSA. *Unit head:* Dr. Patricia Halon, 617-287-7500, E-mail: pat.halon@umb.edu. *Application contact:* Graduate Admissions Coordinator, 617-287-6400, Fax: 617-287-6236, E-mail: bos.gadm@dpc.umassp.edu.

University of Massachusetts Boston, College of Nursing and Health Sciences, Program in Nursing Practice, Boston, MA 02125-3393. Offers DNP. *Students:* 3 full-time (all women), 33 part-time (31 women); includes 10 minority (4 Black or African American, non-Hispanic/Latino; 2 Asian, non-Hispanic/Latino; 1 Hispanic/Latino; 3 Two or more races, non-Hispanic/Latino), 2 international. Average age 41. 16 applicants, 44% accepted, 4 enrolled. In 2017, 9 doctorates awarded. *Expenses:* Tuition, state resident: full-time $17,375. Tuition, nonresident: full-time $33,915. *Required fees:* $355. *Unit head:* Dr. Linda Thompson, Dean, 617-287-5000, E-mail: linda.thompson@umb.edu. *Application contact:* Graduate Admissions Coordinator, 617-287-6400, Fax: 617-287-6236, E-mail: bos.gadm@dpc.umassp.edu.

University of Massachusetts Dartmouth, Graduate School, College of Nursing, North Dartmouth, MA 02747-2300. Offers MS, DNP, PhD. *Accreditation:* AACN. *Program availability:* Part-time, 100% online, blended/hybrid learning. *Faculty:* 32 full-time (all women), 37 part-time/adjunct (36 women). *Students:* 112 part-time (100 women); includes 21 minority (12 Black or African American, non-Hispanic/Latino; 4 Asian, non-Hispanic/Latino; 4 Hispanic/Latino; 1 Two or more races, non-Hispanic/Latino). Average age 38. 51 applicants, 94% accepted, 37 enrolled. In 2017, 5 master's, 17 doctorates awarded. Terminal master's awarded for partial completion of doctoral program. *Degree requirements:* For master's, capstone project; for doctorate, project (for DNP); dissertation (for PhD). *Entrance requirements:* For master's, statement of purpose (minimum of 300 words), resume, 2 letters of recommendation, official transcripts, copy of RN license or license number; for doctorate, statement of purpose (minimum of 300 words), resume, 3 letters of recommendation, official transcripts, copy of RN license, minimum 10-page scholarly writing sample (for PhD program only). Additional exam requirements/recommendations for international students: Required—TOEFL (minimum score 533 paper-based; 72 iBT), IELTS (minimum score 6). *Application deadline:* For fall admission, 2/15 priority date for domestic students, 1/15 priority date for international students. Application fee: $60. Electronic applications accepted. *Expenses:* Tuition, state resident: full-time $15,449; part-time $643.71 per credit. Tuition, nonresident: full-time $27,880; part-time $1161.67 per credit. *Required fees:* $405; $25.88 per credit. Tuition and fees vary according to course load and reciprocity agreements. *Financial support:* In 2017–18, 1 fellowship (averaging $24,000 per year), 10 teaching assistantships (averaging $9,801 per year) were awarded; tuition waivers (full and partial) also available. Support available to part-time students. Financial award application deadline: 3/1; financial award applicants required to submit FAFSA. *Faculty research:* Disparities in health/healthcare, global community health, vulnerable populations, chronic illness, symptom management, living with traumatic spinal cord injury, nursing theory, symptom clusters in SCI, Family caregivers, nursing philosophy, chronic cardiac illness, self-care, health disparities. *Total annual research expenditures:* $143,000. *Unit head:* June Horowitz, Associate Dean for Graduate Programs and Research, 508-910-6487, E-mail: jhorowitz@umassd.edu. *Application contact:* Steven Briggs, Director of Marketing and Recruitment for Graduate Studies, 508-999-8604, Fax: 508-999-8183, E-mail: graduate@umassd.edu.
Website: http://www.umassd.edu/nursing/

University of Massachusetts Lowell, College of Health Sciences, School of Nursing, Lowell, MA 01854. Offers adult/gerontological nursing (MS); family health nursing (MS); nursing (DNP, PhD). *Accreditation:* AACN. *Degree requirements:* For master's, thesis optional; for doctorate, thesis/dissertation. *Entrance requirements:* For master's and doctorate, GRE General Test. *Faculty research:* Gerontology, women's health issues, long-term care, alcoholism, health promotion.

University of Massachusetts Medical School, Graduate School of Nursing, Worcester, MA 01655-0115. Offers adult gerontological acute care nurse practitioner (DNP, Post Master's Certificate); adult gerontological primary care nurse practitioner (DNP, Post Master's Certificate); family nursing practitioner (DNP); nurse administrator (DNP); nurse educator (MS, Post Master's Certificate); nursing (PhD). *Accreditation:* AACN. *Faculty:* 31 full-time (28 women), 39 part-time/adjunct (34 women). *Students:* 129 full-time (111 women), 31 part-time (30 women); includes 35 minority (17 Black or African American, non-Hispanic/Latino; 10 Asian, non-Hispanic/Latino; 7 Hispanic/Latino; 1 Native Hawaiian or other Pacific Islander, non-Hispanic/Latino), 1 international. Average age 32. 124 applicants, 55% accepted, 59 enrolled. In 2017, 48 master's, 10 doctorates, 2 other advanced degrees awarded. *Degree requirements:* For doctorate, thesis/dissertation (for some programs), comprehensive exam and manuscript (for PhD); capstone project and manuscript (for DNP). *Entrance requirements:* For master's, GRE General Test, bachelor's degree in nursing, course work in statistics, unrestricted Massachusetts license as registered nurse; for doctorate, GRE General Test, bachelor's or master's degree; for

Post Master's Certificate, GRE General Test, MS in nursing. Additional exam requirements/recommendations for international students: Required—TOEFL (minimum score 400 paper-based; 81 iBT). *Application deadline:* For fall admission, 12/1 priority date for domestic students. Applications are processed on a rolling basis. Application fee: $60. Electronic applications accepted. *Expenses:* $14,778 in-state tuition and mandatory fees; $19,728 out-of-state. *Financial support:* In 2017–18, 6 students received support. Scholarships/grants available. Support available to part-time students. Financial award application deadline: 5/15; financial award applicants required to submit FAFSA. *Faculty research:* Health literacy, social justice, HIV prevention, cancer-related decision making, nursing education, diabetes care and education, family-focused interventions for children with type 1 diabetes. *Total annual research expenditures:* $874,000. *Unit head:* Dr. Joan Vitello-Cicciu, Dean, 508-856-5081, Fax: 508-856-6552, E-mail: joan.vitello@umassmed.edu. *Application contact:* Diane Brescia, Admissions Coordinator, 508-856-3488, Fax: 508-856-5851, E-mail: diane.brescia@umassmed.edu.
Website: http://www.umassmed.edu/gsn/

University of Memphis, Loewenberg College of Nursing, Memphis, TN 38152. Offers advanced practice nursing (Graduate Certificate); executive leadership (MSN); family nurse practitioner (MSN); nursing administration (MSN, Graduate Certificate); nursing education (MSN, Graduate Certificate). *Accreditation:* AACN. *Program availability:* Part-time, evening/weekend, online learning. *Faculty:* 15 full-time (14 women), 3 part-time/adjunct (all women). *Students:* 16 full-time (15 women), 225 part-time (201 women); includes 90 minority (72 Black or African American, non-Hispanic/Latino; 1 American Indian or Alaska Native, non-Hispanic/Latino; 9 Asian, non-Hispanic/Latino; 5 Hispanic/Latino; 1 Native Hawaiian or other Pacific Islander, non-Hispanic/Latino; 2 Two or more races, non-Hispanic/Latino). Average age 35. 168 applicants, 53% accepted, 55 enrolled. In 2017, 120 master's, 6 other advanced degrees awarded. *Degree requirements:* For master's, comprehensive exam, thesis optional, scholarly project; clinical practicum hours. *Entrance requirements:* For master's, NCLEX exam, minimum undergraduate GPA of 2.8, letter of interest, letters of recommendation, interview, resume, nursing licensure; for Graduate Certificate, unrestricted license to practice as RN in TN, current CPR certification, evidence of vaccination, annual flu shot, evidence of current professional malpractice insurance, letters of recommendation, letter of intent, resume. Additional exam requirements/recommendations for international students: Required—TOEFL (minimum score 550 paper-based; 79 iBT). *Application deadline:* For fall admission, 2/15 for domestic and international students; for spring admission, 10/1 for domestic and international students. Application fee: $35 ($60 for international students). *Expenses:* Contact institution. *Financial support:* In 2017–18, 147 students received support. Federal Work-Study and scholarships/grants available. Financial award application deadline: 2/1; financial award applicants required to submit FAFSA. *Faculty research:* Technology in nursing, nurse retention, cultural competence, health policy, health access. *Total annual research expenditures:* $560,619. *Unit head:* Dr. Lin Zhan, Dean, 901-678-2003, Fax: 901-678-4907, E-mail: lzhan@memphis.edu. *Application contact:* Dr. Shirleatha Lee, Associate Dean for Academic Programs, 901-678-2036, Fax: 901-678-5023, E-mail: sntaylr1@memphis.edu.
Website: http://www.memphis.edu/nursing

University of Miami, Graduate School, School of Nursing and Health Studies, Coral Gables, FL 33124. Offers acute care (MSN), including acute care nurse practitioner, nurse anesthesia; nursing (PhD); primary care (MSN), including adult nurse practitioner, family nurse practitioner, nurse midwifery, women's health practitioner. *Accreditation:* AACN; AANA/CANAEP; ACNM/ACME (one or more programs are accredited). *Program availability:* Part-time. *Degree requirements:* For master's, thesis optional; for doctorate, thesis/dissertation. *Entrance requirements:* For master's, GRE General Test, BSN, minimum GPA of 3.0, Florida RN license; for doctorate, GRE General Test, BSN or MSN, minimum GPA of 3.0. Additional exam requirements/recommendations for international students: Required—TOEFL (minimum score 550 paper-based). Electronic applications accepted. *Faculty research:* Transcultural nursing, exercise and depression in Alzheimer's disease, infectious diseases/HIV–AIDS, postpartum depression, outcomes assessment.

University of Michigan, Rackham Graduate School, School of Nursing, Ann Arbor, MI 48109. Offers acute care pediatric nurse practitioner (MS); nursing (DNP, PhD, Post Master's Certificate). *Accreditation:* AACN; ACNM/ACME (one or more programs are accredited). *Program availability:* Part-time, online learning. Terminal master's awarded for partial completion of doctoral program. *Degree requirements:* For doctorate, thesis/dissertation. *Expenses:* Tuition, state resident: full-time $22,368; part-time $1201 per credit hour. Tuition, nonresident: full-time $45,156; part-time $2467 per credit hour. *Required fees:* $376 per term. Tuition and fees vary according to course load, degree level and program. *Faculty research:* Preparation of clinical nurse researchers, biobehavior, women's health, health promotion, substance abuse, psychobiology of menopause, fertility, obesity, health care systems.

University of Michigan–Flint, School of Nursing, Flint, MI 48502-1950. Offers adult-gerontology acute care (DNP); adult-gerontology primary care (DNP); family nurse practitioner (DNP); nursing (MSN); psychiatric mental health (DNP); psychiatric mental health nurse practitioner (Certificate). *Accreditation:* AACN. *Program availability:* Part-time, evening/weekend, 100% online. *Faculty:* 36 full-time (35 women), 66 part-time/adjunct (61 women). *Students:* 159 full-time (143 women), 148 part-time (126 women); includes 80 minority (36 Black or African American, non-Hispanic/Latino; 5 American Indian or Alaska Native, non-Hispanic/Latino; 14 Asian, non-Hispanic/Latino; 14 Hispanic/Latino; 2 Native Hawaiian or other Pacific Islander, non-Hispanic/Latino; 9 Two or more races, non-Hispanic/Latino), 3 international. Average age 37. 86 applicants, 78% accepted, 41 enrolled. In 2017, 12 master's, 42 doctorates, 9 other advanced degrees awarded. *Entrance requirements:* For master's, BSN from regionally-accredited college; minimum GPA of 3.2; current unencumbered RN license in the United States; three or more credits in college-level chemistry or statistics with minimum C grade; for doctorate, BSN or MSN (with APRN certification) from regionally-accredited college or university with minimum overall undergraduate GPA of 3.2; college-level statistics with minimum C grade; for Certificate, completion of nurse practitioner program with MS from regionally-accredited college or university with minimum overall GPA of 3.2; current unencumbered RN license in the United States; current unencumbered license as nurse practitioner; current certification as nurse practitioner in specialty other than discipline of study. Additional exam requirements/recommendations for international students: Required—TOEFL (minimum score 84 iBT), IELTS (minimum score 6.5). *Application deadline:* For fall admission, 7/1 for domestic students, 5/1 for international students; for winter admission, 11/1 for domestic students, 9/1 for international students; for spring admission, 3/15 for domestic students, 1/1 for international students. Applications are processed on a rolling basis. Application fee: $55. Electronic applications accepted. *Expenses:* Contact institution. *Financial support:* Federal Work-Study, scholarships/grants, and unspecified assistantships available. Support available to part-time students. Financial award application deadline: 3/1; financial award applicants required to submit FAFSA. *Faculty research:* Family system stress, self breast exam, family roads evaluation, causal model testing for psycho social development, basic needs, nurse preparation training. *Unit head:* Dr. Constance J. Creech, Director, 810-762-3420, Fax: 810-766-6851, E-mail: ccreech@umflint.edu. *Application contact:* Bradley T. Maki, Director of Graduate Admissions, 810-762-3171, Fax: 810-766-6789, E-mail: bmaki@umflint.edu.
Website: https://www.umflint.edu/nursing/graduate-nursing-programs

University of Minnesota, Twin Cities Campus, Graduate School, School of Nursing, Minneapolis, MN 55455-0213. Offers adult/gerontological clinical nurse specialist (DNP); adult/gerontological primary care nurse practitioner (DNP); family nurse practitioner (DNP); health innovation and leadership (DNP); integrative health and healing (DNP); nurse anesthesia (DNP); nurse midwifery (DNP); nursing (MN, PhD); nursing informatics (DNP); pediatric clinical nurse specialist (DNP); primary care certified pediatric nurse practitioner (DNP); psychiatric/mental health nurse practitioner (DNP); women's health nurse practitioner (DNP). *Accreditation:* AACN; AANA/CANAEP; ACNM/ACME (one or more programs are accredited). *Program availability:* Part-time, online learning. Terminal master's awarded for partial completion of doctoral program. *Degree requirements:* For master's, final oral exam, project or thesis; for doctorate, thesis/dissertation. *Entrance requirements:* For master's and doctorate, GRE General Test. Additional exam requirements/recommendations for international students: Required—TOEFL (minimum score 586 paper-based). *Expenses:* Contact institution. *Faculty research:* Child and family health promotion, nursing research on elders.

University of Mississippi Medical Center, School of Nursing, Jackson, MS 39216-4505. Offers MSN, DNP, PhD. *Accreditation:* AACN. *Program availability:* Part-time, evening/weekend, online learning. *Degree requirements:* For master's, thesis optional; for doctorate, comprehensive exam, thesis/dissertation, publishable paper. *Entrance requirements:* For master's, GRE, 1 year of clinical experience (acute care nurse practitioner only), RN license; for doctorate, GRE, RN license, professional nursing experience. Additional exam requirements/recommendations for international students: Required—TOEFL (minimum score 550 paper-based; 79 iBT). Electronic applications accepted. *Expenses:* Contact institution. *Faculty research:* Predictive biomarkers for head and neck cancer; cellular events in response to demyelization in diseases; health care disparities (various diseases); childhood obesity; psychosocial adaptations to pregnancy and birth.

University of Missouri, Office of Research and Graduate Studies, Sinclair School of Nursing, Columbia, MO 65211. Offers adult-gerontology clinical nurse specialist (DNP, Certificate); family nurse practitioner (DNP); family psychiatric and mental health nurse practitioner (DNP); nursing (MS, PhD); nursing leadership and innovations in health care (DNP); pediatric clinical nurse specialist (DNP, Certificate); pediatric nurse practitioner (DNP). *Accreditation:* AACN. *Program availability:* Part-time. *Degree requirements:* For master's, thesis optional, oral exam; for doctorate, thesis/dissertation. *Entrance requirements:* For master's, GRE General Test, BSN, minimum GPA of 3.0 during last 60 hours, nursing license. Additional exam requirements/recommendations for international students: Required—TOEFL, IELTS. *Application deadline:* Applications are processed on a rolling basis. Electronic applications accepted. *Expenses:* Tuition, state resident: full-time $6480. Tuition, nonresident: full-time $17,744. *Required fees:* $1108. Tuition and fees vary according to course load, campus/location and program. *Financial support:* Fellowships, research assistantships, teaching assistantships, career-related internships or fieldwork, institutionally sponsored loans, scholarships/grants, traineeships, health care benefits, tuition waivers (full), and unspecified assistantships available. Support available to part-time students.
Website: http://nursing.missouri.edu/

University of Missouri–Kansas City, School of Nursing and Health Studies, Kansas City, MO 64110-2499. Offers adult clinical nurse specialist (MSN), including adult nurse practitioner, women's health nurse practitioner (MSN, DNP); adult clinical nursing practice (DNP), including adult gerontology nurse practitioner, women's health nurse practitioner (MSN, DNP); clinical nursing practice (DNP), including family nurse practitioner; neonatal nurse practitioner (MSN); nurse educator (MSN); nurse executive (MSN); nursing practice (DNP); pediatric clinical nursing practice (DNP), including pediatric nurse practitioner; pediatric nurse practitioner (MSN). *Accreditation:* AACN. *Program availability:* Part-time, online learning. *Degree requirements:* For master's, thesis or alternative. *Entrance requirements:* For master's, minimum undergraduate GPA of 3.2; for doctorate, GRE, 3 letters of reference. Additional exam requirements/recommendations for international students: Required—TOEFL (minimum score 550 paper-based; 80 iBT). *Faculty research:* Geriatrics/gerontology, children's pain, neonatology, Alzheimer's care, cancer caregivers.

University of Missouri–St. Louis, College of Nursing, St. Louis, MO 63121. Offers adult/geriatric nurse practitioner (Post Master's Certificate); family nurse practitioner (Post Master's Certificate); nursing (DNP, PhD); pediatric acute care nurse practitioner (Post Master's Certificate); pediatric nurse practitioner (Post Master's Certificate); psychiatric-mental health nurse practitioner (Post Master's Certificate); women's health nurse practitioner (Post Master's Certificate). *Accreditation:* AACN. *Program availability:* Part-time. *Faculty:* 24 full-time (22 women), 12 part-time/adjunct (11 women). *Students:* 47 full-time (44 women), 162 part-time (152 women); includes 53 minority (37 Black or African American, non-Hispanic/Latino; 10 Asian, non-Hispanic/Latino; 4 Hispanic/Latino; 2 Two or more races, non-Hispanic/Latino), 3 international. 112 applicants, 93% accepted, 70 enrolled. *Degree requirements:* For doctorate, comprehensive exam, thesis/dissertation; for Post Master's Certificate, thesis. *Entrance requirements:* For doctorate, GRE, 2 letters of recommendation, MSN, minimum GPA of 3.2, course in differential/inferential statistics; for Post Master's Certificate, 2 recommendation letters; MSN; advanced practice certificate; minimum GPA of 3.0; essay. Additional exam requirements/recommendations for international students: Recommended—TOEFL (minimum score 550 paper-based; 79 iBT), IELTS (minimum score 6.5). *Application deadline:* For fall admission, 2/15 for domestic and international students. Application fee: $50 ($40 for international students). Electronic applications accepted. *Expenses:* Tuition, state resident: part-time $476.50 per credit hour. Tuition, nonresident: part-time $1169.70 per credit hour. *Financial support:* Research assistantships with tuition reimbursements available. Financial award application deadline: 4/1; financial award applicants required to submit FAFSA. *Faculty research:* Health promotion and restoration, family disruption, violence, abuse, battered women, health survey methods. *Unit head:* Sue Dean-Baar, Dean, 314-516-6066. *Application contact:* 314-516-5458, Fax: 314-516-6996, E-mail: gradadm@umsl.edu.
Website: http://www.umsl.edu/divisions/nursing/

University of Mobile, Graduate Studies, Program in Nursing, Mobile, AL 36613. Offers education/administration (MSN); nurse practitioner (DNP). *Accreditation:* AACN. *Program availability:* Part-time, evening/weekend. *Degree requirements:* For master's, comprehensive exam, thesis or alternative. *Entrance requirements:* For master's, GRE. Additional exam requirements/recommendations for international students: Required—TOEFL (minimum score 550 paper-based; 80 iBT). *Application deadline:* For fall admission, 8/3 priority date for domestic and international students; for spring admission, 12/23 priority date for domestic and international students. Applications are processed on a rolling basis. Application fee: $40 ($50 for international students). Electronic applications accepted. *Financial support:* Application deadline: 8/1; applicants required to submit FAFSA. *Faculty research:* Nursing management, transcultural nursing, spiritual aspects, educational expectations. *Unit head:* Dr. Kathryn Sheppard, Dean, School of Nursing, 251-442-2343, Fax: 251-442-2520, E-mail: ksheppard@umobile.edu. *Application contact:* Brian Boyle, Director of Recruitment, 251-442-2727, Fax: 251-442-2523.

University of Mount Olive, Graduate Programs, Mount Olive, NC 28365. Offers business (MBA); education (M Ed); nursing (MSN). *Program availability:* Online learning.

Nursing—General

University of Nebraska Medical Center, PhD in Nursing Program, Omaha, NE 68198-5330. Offers PhD. *Accreditation:* AACN. *Program availability:* Part-time, blended/hybrid learning. *Faculty:* 19 full-time (13 women), 13 part-time/adjunct (all women). *Students:* 15 full-time (14 women), 6 part-time (all women); includes 3 minority (1 Black or African American, non-Hispanic/Latino; 1 Asian, non-Hispanic/Latino; 1 Hispanic/Latino). Average age 42. 6 applicants, 100% accepted, 6 enrolled. In 2017, 5 doctorates awarded. *Degree requirements:* For doctorate, comprehensive exam, thesis/dissertation. *Entrance requirements:* For doctorate, GRE General Test, minimum GPA of 3.2. Additional exam requirements/recommendations for international students: Required—TOEFL (minimum score 550 paper-based; 80 iBT), IELTS (minimum score 7). *Application deadline:* For spring admission, 1/15 for domestic and international students. Application fee: $65. Electronic applications accepted. *Expenses:* $548.50 per credit hour. *Financial support:* In 2017–18, 10 students received support. Scholarships/grants and unspecified assistantships available. Financial award application deadline: 2/1; financial award applicants required to submit FAFSA. *Faculty research:* Health promotion, sleep and fatigue in cancer patients, symptoms management in cardiovascular disease, prevention of osteoporosis, self-management and chronic illness, health systems and care quality. *Total annual research expenditures:* $55,679. *Unit head:* Dr. Carol Pullen, Professor, 402-559-6548, E-mail: chpullen@unmc.edu. *Application contact:* Rolee Kelly, Graduate Coordinator, Student Services, 402-559-4120, E-mail: rolee.kelly@unmc.edu.
Website: http://www.unmc.edu/nursing/

University of Nevada, Las Vegas, Graduate College, School of Nursing, Las Vegas, NV 89154-3018. Offers biobehavioral nursing (Advanced Certificate); family nurse practitioner (Advanced Certificate); nursing (MS, DNP, PhD); nursing education (Advanced Certificate). *Accreditation:* AACN. *Program availability:* Part-time, 100% online, blended/hybrid learning. *Faculty:* 11 full-time (9 women), 10 part-time/adjunct (all women). *Students:* 46 full-time (40 women), 78 part-time (73 women); includes 43 minority (6 Black or African American, non-Hispanic/Latino; 16 Asian, non-Hispanic/Latino; 12 Hispanic/Latino; 9 Two or more races, non-Hispanic/Latino). Average age 37. 185 applicants, 38% accepted, 54 enrolled. In 2017, 35 master's, 9 doctorates, 3 other advanced degrees awarded. *Degree requirements:* For master's, comprehensive exam, thesis; for doctorate, comprehensive exam (for some programs), thesis/dissertation, project defense (for DNP). *Entrance requirements:* For master's, bachelor's degree with minimum GPA 3.0; 2 letters of recommendation; valid RN license; statement of purpose; for doctorate, GRE General Test, bachelor's degree; statement of purpose; 3 letters of recommendation; for Advanced Certificate, 2 letters of recommendation; statement of purpose; valid RN license. Additional exam requirements/recommendations for international students: Recommended—TOEFL (minimum score 550 paper-based; 80 iBT), IELTS (minimum score 7). *Application deadline:* For fall admission, 2/1 for domestic students. Application fee: $60 ($95 for international students). Electronic applications accepted. *Expenses:* Contact institution. *Financial support:* In 2017–18, 3 students received support, including 1 research assistantship with partial tuition reimbursement available (averaging $20,250 per year), 2 teaching assistantships with partial tuition reimbursements available (averaging $20,250 per year); institutionally sponsored loans, scholarships/grants, health care benefits, and unspecified assistantships also available. Financial award application deadline: 3/15; financial award applicants required to submit FAFSA. *Faculty research:* Skeletal muscle injury; chronic diseases and health promotion in diabetes, cardiovascular disease, pain, trauma, and obesity; nursing education; sexual assault. *Total annual research expenditures:* $500,875. *Unit head:* Dr. Carolyn Yucha, Dean, 702-895-3906, Fax: 702-895-4807, E-mail: carolyn.yucha@unlv.edu.
Website: http://nursing.unlv.edu/

University of Nevada, Reno, Graduate School, Division of Health Sciences, Orvis School of Nursing, Reno, NV 89557. Offers MSN, DNP, MPH/MSN. *Accreditation:* AACN. *Degree requirements:* For master's, thesis optional. *Entrance requirements:* For master's, minimum GPA of 3.0 in bachelor's degree from accredited school. Additional exam requirements/recommendations for international students: Required—TOEFL (minimum score 500 paper-based; 61 iBT), IELTS (minimum score 6). Electronic applications accepted. *Faculty research:* Analysis and evaluation of nursing theory, strategies for nursing applications.

University of New Brunswick Fredericton, School of Graduate Studies, Faculty of Nursing, Fredericton, NB E3B 5A3, Canada. Offers nurse educator (MN); nurse practitioner (MN); nursing (MN). *Program availability:* Part-time, online learning. *Degree requirements:* For master's, comprehensive exam (for some programs), thesis (for some programs). *Entrance requirements:* For master's, undergraduate coursework in statistics and nursing research, minimum GPA of 3.3, registration as a nurse (or eligibility) in New Brunswick. Additional exam requirements/recommendations for international students: Required—TOEFL (minimum score 600 paper-based). Electronic applications accepted. *Faculty research:* Intimate partner violence; abuse; healthy child development, chronic illness and addiction; rural populations' access to health care and primary healthcare; teaching and learning in the classroom, clinical lab, and by distance; Aboriginal nursing; workplace bullying; eating disorders; women's health; lesbian health; nurse managed primary care clinics; HIV/AIDS; returning to work after depression; adolescent mental health; cancer survivorship.

University of New Hampshire, Graduate School, College of Health and Human Services, Department of Nursing, Durham, NH 03824. Offers family nurse practitioner (Postbaccalaureate Certificate); nursing (MS, DNP); psychiatric mental health (Postbaccalaureate Certificate). *Accreditation:* AACN. *Program availability:* Part-time, online learning. *Students:* 40 full-time (32 women), 107 part-time (91 women); includes 8 minority (2 Black or African American, non-Hispanic/Latino; 2 Asian, non-Hispanic/Latino; 2 Hispanic/Latino; 2 Two or more races, non-Hispanic/Latino). Average age 35. 83 applicants, 58% accepted, 30 enrolled. In 2017, 38 master's, 1 doctorate, 5 other advanced degrees awarded. *Entrance requirements:* Additional exam requirements/recommendations for international students: Required—TOEFL (minimum score 550 paper-based; 80 iBT). *Application deadline:* For fall admission, 4/1 priority date for domestic students, 4/1 for international students; for spring admission, 11/1 for domestic students. Application fee: $65. Electronic applications accepted. *Financial support:* In 2017–18, 15 students received support, including 2 teaching assistantships; fellowships, research assistantships, Federal Work-Study, scholarships/grants, and tuition waivers (full and partial) also available. Financial award application deadline: 2/15. *Unit head:* Dr. Gene Harkless, Chair, 603-862-2285. *Application contact:* Jane Dufresne, Administrative Assistant, 603-862-2299, E-mail: nursing.department@unh.edu.
Website: https://chhs.unh.edu/nursing/graduate-program-nursing

University of New Mexico, Graduate Studies, Health Sciences Center, Program in Nursing, Albuquerque, NM 87131. Offers MSN, DNP, PhD. *Accreditation:* AACN; ACNM/ACME (one or more programs are accredited). *Program availability:* Part-time, online learning. *Faculty:* 19 full-time (18 women), 2 part-time/adjunct (both women). *Students:* 72 full-time (66 women), 70 part-time (62 women); includes 61 minority (7 Black or African American, non-Hispanic/Latino; 7 American Indian or Alaska Native, non-Hispanic/Latino; 4 Asian, non-Hispanic/Latino; 37 Hispanic/Latino; 6 Two or more races, non-Hispanic/Latino), 2 international. Average age 40. 6 applicants, 67% accepted, 4 enrolled. In 2017, 70 master's, 8 doctorates awarded. *Degree requirements:* For master's, comprehensive exam, thesis optional; for doctorate, comprehensive exam, thesis/dissertation. *Entrance requirements:* For master's, minimum GPA of 3.0, course work in statistics (recommended), interview (for some concentrations), BSN or RN with BA; for doctorate, interview, minimum GPA of 3.0, writing sample, MSN or BSN with MA. Additional exam requirements/recommendations for international students: Required—TOEFL. Application fee: $60. Electronic applications accepted. *Financial support:* Fellowships, research assistantships with partial tuition reimbursements, teaching assistantships with partial tuition reimbursements, institutionally sponsored loans, scholarships/grants, and unspecified assistantships available. Support available to part-time students. Financial award application deadline: 3/1; financial award applicants required to submit FAFSA. *Faculty research:* Women's and children's health, pregnancy prevention in teens, vulnerable populations, nursing education, chronic illness, symptom appraisal and management. *Unit head:* Dr. Nancy Ridenour, Dean, 505-272-6284, Fax: 505-272-4343, E-mail: nridenour@salud.unm.edu. *Application contact:* Nissane Capps, Senior Academic Advisor, 505-272-4223, Fax: 505-272-3970, E-mail: ncapps@salud.unm.edu.
Website: http://nursing.unm.edu/

University of North Alabama, Anderson College of Nursing, Florence, AL 35632-0001. Offers MSN. *Accreditation:* AACN. *Program availability:* Part-time, online only, 100% online, blended/hybrid learning. *Faculty:* 14 full-time (all women). *Students:* 42 full-time (39 women), 56 part-time (49 women); includes 25 minority (21 Black or African American, non-Hispanic/Latino; 1 Asian, non-Hispanic/Latino; 1 Hispanic/Latino; 2 Two or more races, non-Hispanic/Latino). Average age 34. 53 applicants, 77% accepted, 32 enrolled. In 2017, 37 master's awarded. *Entrance requirements:* For master's, one year of clinical practice as registered nurse. Additional exam requirements/recommendations for international students: Required—TOEFL (minimum score 550 paper-based; 79 iBT), IELTS (minimum score 6), PTE (minimum score 54). *Application deadline:* Applications are processed on a rolling basis. Application fee: $50 ($100 for international students). Electronic applications accepted. *Expenses:* Tuition, state resident: full-time $7824; part-time $5943 per year. Tuition, nonresident: full-time $15,648; part-time $11,736 per year. *Required fees:* $3064; $2298 per unit. Tuition and fees vary according to course load and reciprocity agreements. *Financial support:* In 2017–18, 4 students received support. Scholarships/grants available. Financial award application deadline: 2/1; financial award applicants required to submit FAFSA. *Total annual research expenditures:* $580,795. *Unit head:* Dr. Vicky G. Pierce, Dean, 256-765-4311, E-mail: vgpierce@una.edu. *Application contact:* Hillary N. Coats, Graduate Admissions Coordinator, 256-465-4447, E-mail: graduate@una.edu.
Website: http://www.una.edu/nursing/

The University of North Carolina at Chapel Hill, School of Nursing, Chapel Hill, NC 27599-7460. Offers advanced practice registered nurse (DNP); nursing (MSN, PhD, PMC), including administration (MSN), adult gerontology primary care nurse practitioner (MSN), clinical nurse leader (MSN), education (MSN), health care systems (PMC), informatics (MSN, PMC), nursing leadership (PMC), outcomes management (MSN), primary care family nurse practitioner (MSN), primary care pediatric nurse practitioner (MSN), psychiatric/mental health nurse practitioner (MSN, PMC). *Accreditation:* AACN; ACEN (one or more programs are accredited). *Program availability:* Part-time. *Faculty:* 86 full-time (78 women), 44 part-time/adjunct (40 women). *Students:* 208 full-time (186 women), 128 part-time (116 women); includes 100 minority (49 Black or African American, non-Hispanic/Latino; 4 American Indian or Alaska Native, non-Hispanic/Latino; 23 Asian, non-Hispanic/Latino; 7 Hispanic/Latino; 17 Two or more races, non-Hispanic/Latino), 17 international. Average age 33. 624 applicants, 25% accepted, 150 enrolled. In 2017, 91 master's, 14 doctorates awarded. *Degree requirements:* For master's, comprehensive exam, thesis; for doctorate, thesis/dissertation, 3 exams; for PMC, thesis. *Entrance requirements:* Additional exam requirements/recommendations for international students: Required—TOEFL (minimum score 575 paper-based; 89 iBT), IELTS (minimum score 8). *Application deadline:* For fall admission, 12/15 for domestic and international students. Application fee: $88. Electronic applications accepted. *Financial support:* In 2017–18, 8 fellowships with full tuition reimbursements, 6 research assistantships with partial tuition reimbursements (averaging $8,000 per year), 10 teaching assistantships with partial tuition reimbursements (averaging $8,000 per year) were awarded; scholarships/grants, traineeships, health care benefits, and unspecified assistantships also available. Support available to part-time students. Financial award application deadline: 3/1; financial award applicants required to submit FAFSA. *Faculty research:* Preventing and managing chronic illness, reducing health disparities, Improving healthcare quality and patient outcomes, understanding biobehavioral and genetic bases of health and illness, developing innovative ways to enhance science and its clinical translation. *Unit head:* Dr. Nilda Peragallo Montano, Dean/Professor, 919-966-3731, Fax: 919-966-3540, E-mail: npm@email.unc.edu. *Application contact:* Emily Sayed, Assistant Director, Graduate Admissions, 919-966-4260, Fax: 919-966-3540, E-mail: sayed@unc.edu.
Website: http://nursing.unc.edu

The University of North Carolina at Charlotte, College of Health and Human Services, School of Nursing, Charlotte, NC 28223-0001. Offers adult-gerontology acute care nurse practitioner (Post-Master's Certificate); advanced clinical nursing (MSN), including adult psychiatric mental health, adult-gerontology acute care nurse practitioner, family nurse practitioner across the lifespan; family nurse practitioner across the lifespan (Post-Master's Certificate); nurse anesthesia (MSN), including nurse anesthesia across the lifespan; nurse anesthesia across the lifespan (Post-Master's Certificate); nursing (DNP); nursing administration (Graduate Certificate); nursing education (Graduate Certificate); systems/population nursing (MSN), including community/public health nursing, nurse administrator, nurse educator. *Accreditation:* AACN; AANA/CANAEP. *Program availability:* Part-time, blended/hybrid learning. *Faculty:* 24 full-time (22 women), 6 part-time/adjunct (4 women). *Students:* 113 full-time (84 women), 163 part-time (150 women); includes 63 minority (47 Black or African American, non-Hispanic/Latino; 2 American Indian or Alaska Native, non-Hispanic/Latino; 6 Asian, non-Hispanic/Latino; 3 Hispanic/Latino; 5 Two or more races, non-Hispanic/Latino). Average age 37. 443 applicants, 31% accepted, 113 enrolled. In 2017, 83 master's, 8 doctorates, 8 other advanced degrees awarded. Terminal master's awarded for partial completion of doctoral program. *Degree requirements:* For doctorate, thesis/dissertation or alternative, residency; for other advanced degree, practicum. *Entrance requirements:* For master's, GRE General Test, current unrestricted license as Registered Nurse in North Carolina; BSN from nationally-accredited program; one year of professional nursing practice in acute/critical care; minimum overall GPA of 3.0 in last degree; completion of undergraduate statistics course with minimum grade of C; statement of purpose; for doctorate, GRE or MAT, master's degree in nursing in an advanced nursing practice specialty from nationally-accredited program; minimum overall GPA of 3.5 in MSN program; current RN licensure in U.S. at time of application with eligibility for NC licensure; essay; resume/curriculum vitae; professional recommendations; clinical hours; for other advanced degree, GRE. Additional exam requirements/recommendations for international students: Required—TOEFL (minimum score 523 paper-based, 70 iBT) or IELTS (6.5). *Application deadline:* For fall admission, 1/10 for domestic and international students; for spring admission, 9/10 for domestic and international students; for summer admission, 4/1 for domestic and international students. Applications are processed on a rolling basis. Application fee: $75. Electronic

applications accepted. *Expenses:* Contact institution. *Financial support:* In 2017–18, 6 students received support, including 4 research assistantships (averaging $6,338 per year), 2 teaching assistantships (averaging $6,250 per year); career-related internships or fieldwork, institutionally sponsored loans, scholarships/grants, traineeships, and unspecified assistantships also available. Support available to part-time students. Financial award application deadline: 3/1; financial award applicants required to submit FAFSA. *Total annual research expenditures:* $800,072. *Unit head:* Dr. Dena Evans, Director, 704-687-7974, E-mail: devans37@uncc.edu. *Application contact:* Kathy B. Giddings, Director of Graduate Admissions, 704-687-5503, Fax: 704-687-1668, E-mail: gradadm@uncc.edu.
Website: http://nursing.uncc.edu/

The University of North Carolina at Greensboro, Graduate School, School of Nursing, Greensboro, NC 27412-5001. Offers adult clinical nurse specialist (MSN, PMC); adult/gerontological nurse practitioner (MSN, PMC); nurse anesthesia (MSN, PMC); nursing (PhD); nursing administration (MSN); nursing education (MSN); MSN/MBA. *Accreditation:* ACEN. *Degree requirements:* For master's, thesis or alternative. *Entrance requirements:* For master's, GRE General Test or MAT, BSN, clinical experience, liability insurance, RN license; for PMC, liability insurance, MSN, RN license. Additional exam requirements/recommendations for international students: Required—TOEFL. Electronic applications accepted.

The University of North Carolina at Pembroke, The Graduate School, Department of Nursing, Pembroke, NC 28372-1510. Offers clinical nurse leader (MSN); nurse educator (MSN); rural case manager (MSN). *Accreditation:* AACN. *Program availability:* Part-time. Application fee: $45 ($60 for international students). *Unit head:* Julie Harrison-Swartz, Director of Graduate Programs, 910-775-4509, E-mail: julie.harrison-swartz@uncp.edu.
Website: http://www.uncp.edu/nursing/

The University of North Carolina Wilmington, School of Nursing, Wilmington, NC 28403-3297. Offers clinical research and product development (MS); family nurse practitioner (Post-Master's Certificate); nurse educator (Post-Master's Certificate); nursing (MSN); nursing practice (DNP). *Accreditation:* AACN; ACEN. *Program availability:* Part-time, 100% online. *Faculty:* 44 full-time (38 women). *Students:* 160 full-time (148 women), 237 part-time (213 women); includes 79 minority (55 Black or African American, non-Hispanic/Latino; 3 American Indian or Alaska Native, non-Hispanic/Latino; 6 Asian, non-Hispanic/Latino; 9 Hispanic/Latino; 6 Two or more races, non-Hispanic/Latino). Average age 36. 287 applicants, 71% accepted, 167 enrolled. In 2017, 40 master's awarded. *Degree requirements:* For master's, thesis or alternative, research project, presentation; for doctorate, clinical scholarly project, 1000 clinical hours. *Entrance requirements:* For master's, GRE General Test, 3 recommendations, statement of interest, resume, writing sample, RN experience, RN license (for MSN), bachelor's degree in related field; for doctorate, 3 recommendations, Advanced Practice Registered Nurse with current unrestricted RN license in state in which practice will occur, minimum GPA of 3.0, essay, resume or curriculum vitae, interview, criminal background check and 12-panel drug screening. Additional exam requirements/recommendations for international students: Required—TOEFL (minimum score 550 paper-based; 79 iBT), IELTS (minimum score 6.5). *Application deadline:* For fall admission, 3/1 for domestic students. Applications are processed on a rolling basis. Application fee: $75. Electronic applications accepted. *Expenses:* $318.15 per credit hour in-state, $965.60 per credit hour out-of-state (for DNP). *Financial support:* Application deadline: 1/1; applicants required to submit FAFSA. *Unit head:* Dr. Laurie Badzek, Director, 910-962-7410, Fax: 910-962-3723, E-mail: badzekl@uncw.edu. *Application contact:* Dr. Micah Scott, MSN Graduate Coordinator, 910-962-7534, E-mail: scottmi@uncw.edu.
Website: https://www.uncw.edu/son/academicprograms.html

University of North Dakota, Graduate School, College of Nursing and Professional Disciplines, Department of Nursing, Grand Forks, ND 58202. Offers adult-gerontological nurse practitioner (MS); advanced public health nurse (MS); family nurse practitioner (MS); nurse anesthesia (MS); nurse educator (MS); nursing (PhD, Post-Master's Certificate); nursing practice (DNP); psychiatric and mental health nurse practitioner (MS).

University of Northern Colorado, Graduate School, College of Natural and Health Sciences, School of Nursing, Greeley, CO 80639. Offers adult-gerontology acute care nurse practitioner (MSN, DNP); family nurse practitioner (MSN, DNP); nursing education (PhD); nursing practice (DNP). *Accreditation:* AACN. *Program availability:* Online learning. *Degree requirements:* For master's, comprehensive exam, thesis or alternative; for doctorate, comprehensive exam, thesis/dissertation. *Entrance requirements:* For master's and doctorate, GRE General Test, minimum GPA of 3.0 in last 60 hours, BS in nursing, 2 letters of recommendation. Electronic applications accepted.

University of North Florida, Brooks College of Health, School of Nursing, Jacksonville, FL 32224. Offers family nurse practitioner (Certificate); nurse anesthetist (MSN). *Accreditation:* AACN; AANA/CANAEP. *Program availability:* Part-time. *Degree requirements:* For master's, thesis optional. *Entrance requirements:* For master's, GRE General Test, minimum GPA of 3.0 in last 60 hours of course work, BSN, clinical experience, resume; for doctorate, GRE, master's degree in nursing specialty from nationally-accredited program; national certification in one of the following APRN roles: CNE, CNM, CNS, CRNA, CNP; minimum graduate GPA of 3.3; three letters of reference which address academic ability and clinical skills; active license as registered nurse or advanced practice registered nurse. Additional exam requirements/recommendations for international students: Required—TOEFL (minimum score 500 paper-based; 61 iBT). Electronic applications accepted. *Faculty research:* Teen pregnancy, diabetes, ethical decision-making, family caregivers.

University of Oklahoma Health Sciences Center, Graduate College, College of Nursing, Oklahoma City, OK 73190. Offers MS, MS/MBA. MS/MBA offered jointly with Oklahoma State University and University of Oklahoma. *Accreditation:* AACN; ACEN. *Program availability:* Part-time. *Degree requirements:* For master's, comprehensive exam, thesis optional. *Entrance requirements:* For master's, 3 letters of recommendation, Oklahoma RN license, statistics course, research methods, computer course or completion of a computer literacy test. *Faculty research:* Parenting and Native Americans, elderly reminiscence, diabetes in Native Americans.

University of Ottawa, Faculty of Graduate and Postdoctoral Studies, Faculty of Health Sciences, School of Nursing, Ottawa, ON K1N 6N5, Canada. Offers nurse practitioner (Certificate); nursing (M Sc, PhD); nursing/primary health care (M Sc). *Program availability:* Part-time, evening/weekend. *Degree requirements:* For master's, thesis or alternative. *Entrance requirements:* For master's, honors degree or equivalent, minimum B average. Electronic applications accepted. *Faculty research:* Decision making in nursing, evaluating complete nursing interventions.

University of Pennsylvania, School of Nursing, Philadelphia, PA 19104. Offers MSN, PhD, Certificate, MBA/MSN, MBA/PhD, MSN/PhD. *Accreditation:* AACN; AANA/CANAEP. *Program availability:* Part-time, online learning. *Faculty:* 52 full-time (46 women), 35 part-time/adjunct (31 women). *Students:* 247 full-time (208 women), 452 part-time (410 women); includes 166 minority (47 Black or African American, non-Hispanic/Latino; 1 American Indian or Alaska Native, non-Hispanic/Latino; 62 Asian, non-Hispanic/Latino; 36 Hispanic/Latino; 1 Native Hawaiian or other Pacific Islander, non-Hispanic/Latino; 19 Two or more races, non-Hispanic/Latino), 11 international. Average age 32. 728 applicants, 57% accepted, 373 enrolled. In 2017, 320 master's, 15 doctorates awarded. Terminal master's awarded for partial completion of doctoral program. *Unit head:* Dr. Christina Costanzo Clark, Assistant Dean for Admissions and Academic Affairs, 215-898-4271, Fax: 215-573-8439, E-mail: costanzo@nursing.upenn.edu. *Application contact:* Sylvia English, Enrollment Management Coordinator, 215-898-8439, Fax: 215-573-8439, E-mail: sylviaj@nursing.upenn.edu.
Website: http://www.nursing.upenn.edu/

University of Phoenix–Bay Area Campus, College of Nursing, San Jose, CA 95134-1805. Offers education (MHA); gerontology (MHA); health administration (MHA, DHA); informatics (MHA, MSN); nursing (MSN, PhD); nursing/health care education (MSN); MSN/MBA. *Program availability:* Evening/weekend, online learning. *Degree requirements:* For master's, thesis (for some programs). *Entrance requirements:* For master's, minimum undergraduate GPA of 2.5, 3 years of work experience, RN license. Additional exam requirements/recommendations for international students: Required—TOEFL (minimum score 550 paper-based; 79 iBT). Electronic applications accepted.

University of Phoenix–Central Valley Campus, College of Nursing, Fresno, CA 93720-1552. Offers education (MHA); gerontology (MHA); health administration (MHA); nursing (MSN); MSN/MBA.

University of Phoenix–Hawaii Campus, College of Nursing, Honolulu, HI 96813-3800. Offers education (MHA); family nurse practitioner (MSN); gerontology (MHA); health administration (MHA); nursing (MSN); nursing/health care education (MSN); MSN/MBA. *Program availability:* Evening/weekend. *Degree requirements:* For master's, thesis (for some programs). *Entrance requirements:* For master's, minimum undergraduate GPA of 2.5, 3 years of work experience, RN license. Additional exam requirements/recommendations for international students: Required—TOEFL (minimum score 550 paper-based; 79 iBT). Electronic applications accepted.

University of Phoenix–Houston Campus, College of Nursing, Houston, TX 77079-2004. Offers health administration (MHA). *Program availability:* Online learning. *Degree requirements:* For master's, thesis (for some programs). *Entrance requirements:* For master's, minimum undergraduate GPA of 2.5, 3 years of work experience. Additional exam requirements/recommendations for international students: Required—TOEFL (minimum score 550 paper-based; 79 iBT). Electronic applications accepted.

University of Phoenix–Online Campus, College of Health Sciences and Nursing, Phoenix, AZ 85034-7209. Offers family nurse practitioner (Certificate); health care (Certificate); health care education (Certificate); health care informatics (Certificate); informatics (MSN); nursing (MSN); nursing and health care education (MSN); MSN/MBA; MSN/MHA. *Accreditation:* AACN. *Program availability:* Evening/weekend, online learning. *Entrance requirements:* Additional exam requirements/recommendations for international students: Required—TOEFL, TOEIC (Test of English as an International Communication), Berlitz Online English Proficiency Exam, PTE, or IELTS. Electronic applications accepted. *Expenses:* Contact institution.

University of Phoenix–Online Campus, School of Advanced Studies, Phoenix, AZ 85034-7209. Offers business administration (DBA); education (Ed S); educational leadership (Ed D), including curriculum and instruction, education technology, educational leadership; health administration (DHA); higher education administration (PhD); industrial/organizational psychology (PhD); nursing (PhD); organizational leadership (DM), including information systems and technology, organizational leadership. *Program availability:* Evening/weekend, online learning. *Degree requirements:* For doctorate, thesis/dissertation. *Entrance requirements:* Additional exam requirements/recommendations for international students: Required—TOEFL, TOEIC (Test of English as an International Communication), Berlitz Online English Proficiency Exam, PTE, or IELTS. Electronic applications accepted. *Expenses:* Contact institution.

University of Phoenix–Phoenix Campus, College of Health Sciences and Nursing, Tempe, AZ 85282-2371. Offers family nurse practitioner (MSN, Certificate); gerontology health care (Certificate); health care education (MSN, Certificate); health care informatics (Certificate); informatics (MSN); nursing (MSN); MSN/MHA. *Program availability:* Evening/weekend, online learning. *Entrance requirements:* Additional exam requirements/recommendations for international students: Required—TOEFL, TOEIC (Test of English as an International Communication), Berlitz Online English Proficiency Exam, PTE, or IELTS. Electronic applications accepted. *Expenses:* Contact institution.

University of Phoenix–Sacramento Valley Campus, College of Nursing, Sacramento, CA 95833-4334. Offers family nurse practitioner (MSN); health administration (MHA); health care education (MSN); nursing (MSN); MSN/MBA. *Program availability:* Evening/weekend. *Degree requirements:* For master's, thesis (for some programs). *Entrance requirements:* For master's, RN license, minimum undergraduate GPA of 2.5, 3 years work experience. Additional exam requirements/recommendations for international students: Required—TOEFL (minimum score 550 paper-based; 79 iBT). Electronic applications accepted.

University of Phoenix–San Antonio Campus, College of Nursing, San Antonio, TX 78230. Offers health administration (MHA).

University of Phoenix–San Diego Campus, College of Nursing, San Diego, CA 92123. Offers health care education (MSN); nursing (MSN); MSN/MBA. *Program availability:* Evening/weekend. *Degree requirements:* For master's, thesis (for some programs). *Entrance requirements:* For master's, minimum undergraduate GPA of 2.5, 3 years work experience, RN license. Additional exam requirements/recommendations for international students: Required—TOEFL (minimum score 550 paper-based; 79 iBT). Electronic applications accepted.

University of Pittsburgh, School of Nursing, Clinical Nurse Specialist Program, Pittsburgh, PA 15260. Offers clinical nurse specialist (DNP), including adult gerontology. *Accreditation:* AACN. *Program availability:* Part-time. *Faculty:* 1 (woman) full-time. *Students:* 6 full-time (5 women), 2 part-time (both women). Average age 46. 4 applicants, 75% accepted, 3 enrolled. In 2017, 2 doctorates awarded. *Entrance requirements:* For doctorate, GRE, BSN, RN license, minimum GPA of 3.5, 3 letters of recommendation, relevant nursing experience, resume, course work in statistics. Additional exam requirements/recommendations for international students: Required—TOEFL (minimum score 600 paper-based; 100 IBT) or IELTS (minimum score 7.0). *Application deadline:* For fall admission, 5/1 priority date for domestic students, 2/15 priority date for international students. Application fee: $50. Electronic applications accepted. *Expenses:* $13,068 per term full-time resident tuition, $1,064 per credit part-time; $15,270 per term full-time non-resident tuition, $1,247 per credit part-time; $437 per term full-time fees; $282 per term part-time fees. *Financial support:* In 2017–18, 6 students received support, including 4 fellowships (averaging $19,180 per year); scholarships/grants also available. Financial award applicants required to submit FAFSA. *Faculty research:* Behavioral management of chronic disorders, patient management in critical care, consumer informatics, genetic applications (molecular genetics and psychosocial implications), technology for nurses and patients to improve care. *Unit head:* Dr. Sandra Engberg, Associate Dean for Clinical Education, 412-624-3835, Fax: 412-624-8521, E-mail: sje1@pitt.edu. *Application contact:* Laurie Lapsley, Graduate Administrator, 412-624-9670, Fax: 412-624-2409, E-mail: lapsleyl@pitt.edu.

Nursing—General

University of Pittsburgh, School of Nursing, PhD Program in Nursing, Pittsburgh, PA 15261. Offers PhD. *Program availability:* Part-time. *Faculty:* 21 full-time (16 women), 1 (woman) part-time/adjunct. *Students:* 25 full-time (23 women), 3 part-time (all women); includes 3 minority (1 Black or African American, non-Hispanic/Latino; 1 Asian, non-Hispanic/Latino; 1 Hispanic/Latino), 12 international. Average age 33. 10 applicants, 20% accepted, 2 enrolled. In 2017, 4 doctorates awarded. *Degree requirements:* For doctorate, comprehensive exam, thesis/dissertation. *Entrance requirements:* For doctorate, GRE General Test, BSN/MSN, 3 letters of recommendation, resume, course work in statistics. Additional exam requirements/recommendations for international students: Required—TOEFL (minimum score 600 paper-based; 100 IBT) or IELTS (minimum score 7.0). *Application deadline:* For fall admission, 5/1 for domestic students, 2/1 priority date for international students. Application fee: $50. Electronic applications accepted. *Expenses:* $13,068 per term full-time resident tuition, $1,064 per credit part-time; $15,270 per term full-time non-resident tuition, $1,247 per credit part-time; $437 per term full-time fees; $282 per term part-time fees. *Financial support:* In 2017–18, 24 students received support, including 7 fellowships (averaging $14,385 per year), 8 research assistantships (averaging $11,530 per year), 1 teaching assistantship (averaging $27,675 per year); scholarships/grants and unspecified assistantships also available. Financial award applicants required to submit FAFSA. *Faculty research:* Behavioral management of chronic disorders, patient management in critical care, consumer informatics, genetic applications, technology. *Unit head:* Dr. Marilyn Hravnak, Director, PhD Program, 412-383-5148, Fax: 412-624-2401, E-mail: mhra@pitt.edu. *Application contact:* Laurie Lapsley, Graduate Administrator, 412-624-9670, Fax: 412-624-2409, E-mail: lapsleyl@pitt.edu.
Website: http://www.nursing.pitt.edu/

University of Portland, School of Nursing, Portland, OR 97203. Offers clinical nurse leader (MS); family nurse practitioner (DNP); nurse educator (MS). *Accreditation:* AACN. *Program availability:* Part-time, evening/weekend, online learning. *Entrance requirements:* For master's, GRE General Test or MAT, Oregon RN license, BSN, course work in statistics, resume, letters of recommendation, writing sample; for doctorate, GRE General Test or MAT, Oregon RN license, BSN or MSN, 2 letters of recommendation, resume, writing sample, official transcripts. Additional exam requirements/recommendations for international students: Required—TOEFL (minimum score 550 paper-based; 80 iBT), IELTS (minimum score 7). *Expenses:* Contact institution.

University of Puerto Rico–Medical Sciences Campus, School of Nursing, San Juan, PR 00936-5067. Offers adult and elderly nursing (MSN); child and adolescent nursing (MSN); critical care nursing (MSN); family and community nursing (MSN); family nurse practitioner (MSN); maternity nursing (MSN); mental health and psychiatric nursing (MSN). *Accreditation:* AACN; AANA/CANAEP. *Entrance requirements:* For master's, GRE or EXADEP, interview, Puerto Rico RN license or professional license for international students, general and specific point average, article analysis. Electronic applications accepted. *Faculty research:* HIV, health disparities, teen violence, women and violence, neurological disorders.

University of Regina, Faculty of Graduate Studies and Research, Faculty of Nursing, Regina, SK S4S 0A2, Canada. Offers nurse practitioner clinical nurse specialist (MN); nursing (M Sc, PhD). *Faculty:* 18 full-time (14 women), 9 part-time/adjunct (all women). *Students:* 14 full-time (13 women), 40 part-time (37 women). 44 applicants, 50% accepted. In 2017, 10 master's awarded. *Entrance requirements:* For master's, proof of licensure or registration as an RN including registration number in a Canadian province or territory, 2 years of clinical practice within last 5 years, essay, minimum overall GPA of 75% in all 3rd- and 4th-year nursing courses taken at a Canadian-accredited or provincially-approved baccalaureate nursing education program. Additional exam requirements/recommendations for international students: Required—TOEFL (minimum score 580 paper-based; 80 iBT), IELTS (minimum score 6.5), PTE (minimum score 59). *Application deadline:* For fall admission, 3/15 for domestic and international students. Application fee: $100. Electronic applications accepted. *Expenses:* CAD$11,159 per year (for master's degrees); CAD$9,930 per year (for PhD). *Financial support:* In 2017–18, fellowships (averaging $6,000 per year), teaching assistantships (averaging $2,652 per year) were awarded; scholarships/grants also available. Financial award application deadline: 6/15. *Unit head:* Dr. Glenn Donnelly, Associate Dean, Graduate Programs and Research, 306-337-8544, Fax: 306-337-8493, E-mail: glenn.donnelly@uregina.ca. *Application contact:* Gillian Borys, Graduate Program Assistant, 306-337-3355, Fax: 306-337-8493, E-mail: gillian.borys@uregina.ca.
Website: http://www.uregina.ca/nursing/

University of Rhode Island, Graduate School, College of Nursing, Kingston, RI 02881. Offers acute care nurse practitioner (adult-gerontology focus) (Post Master's Certificate); adult gerontology nurse practitioner/clinical nurse specialist (Post Master's Certificate); adult-gerontological acute care nurse practitioner (MS); adult-gerontological nurse practitioner/clinical nurse specialist (MS); family nurse practitioner (MS, Post Master's Certificate); nursing (DNP, PhD); nursing education (MS, Post Master's Certificate). *Accreditation:* AACN; ACNM/ACME (one or more programs are accredited). *Program availability:* Part-time, evening/weekend, 100% online, blended/hybrid learning. *Faculty:* 31 full-time (30 women). *Students:* 42 full-time (36 women), 86 part-time (79 women); includes 12 minority (3 Black or African American, non-Hispanic/Latino; 3 Asian, non-Hispanic/Latino; 3 Hispanic/Latino; 1 Native Hawaiian or other Pacific Islander, non-Hispanic/Latino; 2 Two or more races, non-Hispanic/Latino), 3 international. 33 applicants, 79% accepted, 23 enrolled. In 2017, 25 master's, 8 doctorates, 2 other advanced degrees awarded. *Entrance requirements:* For master's, GRE or MAT, 2 letters of recommendation, scholarly papers; for doctorate, GRE, 3 letters of recommendation, scholarly papers. Additional exam requirements/recommendations for international students: Required—TOEFL. *Application deadline:* For fall admission, 2/15 for domestic students, 2/1 for international students; for spring admission, 10/15 for domestic students, 7/15 for international students. Application fee: $65. Electronic applications accepted. *Expenses:* Tuition, state resident: full-time $12,706; part-time $786 per credit. Tuition, nonresident: full-time $25,216; part-time $1401 per credit. *Required fees:* $1598; $45 per credit. One-time fee: $30 part-time. *Financial support:* In 2017–18, 1 research assistantship with tuition reimbursement (averaging $18,080 per year), 5 teaching assistantships with tuition reimbursements (averaging $10,133 per year) were awarded. Financial award application deadline: 2/1; financial award applicants required to submit FAFSA. *Unit head:* Dr. Barbara Wolfe, Dean, 401-874-5324, E-mail: bwolfe@uri.edu. *Application contact:* Dr. Denise Coppa, Associate Professor/Interim Associate Dean for Graduate Programs, 401-874-5036, E-mail: dcoppa@uri.edu.
Website: http://www.uri.edu/nursing/

University of Rochester, School of Nursing, Rochester, NY 14642. Offers adult gerontological acute care nurse practitioner (MS); adult gerontological primary care nurse practitioner (MS); clinical nurse leader (MS); family nurse practitioner (MS); family psychiatric mental health nurse practitioner (MS); health care organization management and leadership (MS); nursing (DNP); nursing and health science (PhD); nursing education (MS); pediatric nurse practitioner (MS); pediatric nurse practitioner/neonatal nurse practitioner (MS). *Accreditation:* AACN. *Program availability:* Part-time, 100% online, blended/hybrid learning. *Faculty:* 62 full-time (51 women), 73 part-time/adjunct (63 women). *Students:* 17 full-time (12 women), 306 part-time (252 women); includes 46 minority (16 Black or African American, non-Hispanic/Latino; 1 American Indian or Alaska Native, non-Hispanic/Latino; 7 Asian, non-Hispanic/Latino; 17 Hispanic/Latino; 5 Two or more races, non-Hispanic/Latino), 3 international. Average age 34. 143 applicants, 71% accepted, 87 enrolled. In 2017, 48 master's, 8 doctorates awarded. Terminal master's awarded for partial completion of doctoral program. *Degree requirements:* For master's, comprehensive exam; for doctorate, thesis/dissertation. *Entrance requirements:* For master's, BS in nursing, minimum GPA of 3.0, course work in statistics; for doctorate, GRE General Test (for PhD), MS in nursing, minimum GPA of 3.5. Additional exam requirements/recommendations for international students: Required—TOEFL (minimum score 560 paper-based; 88 iBT) or IELTS (minimum score 6.5) recommended. *Application deadline:* For fall admission, 4/1 for domestic and international students; for spring admission, 9/1 for domestic and international students; for summer admission, 1/2 for domestic and international students. Application fee: $50. Electronic applications accepted. *Financial support:* In 2017–18, 63 students received support, including 2 fellowships with full and partial tuition reimbursements available (averaging $16,000 per year); scholarships/grants, traineeships, health care benefits, tuition waivers (full and partial), and unspecified assistantships also available. Support available to part-time students. Financial award application deadline: 6/30; financial award applicants required to submit CSS PROFILE or FAFSA. *Faculty research:* Symptom science, systems of care, innovations in health technology, promoting healthy behaviors. *Total annual research expenditures:* $2.6 million. *Unit head:* Dr. Kathy H. Rideout, Dean, 585-273-8902, Fax: 585-273-1268, E-mail: kathy_rideout@urmc.rochester.edu. *Application contact:* Elaine Andolina, Director of Admissions, 585-275-2375, Fax: 585-756-8299, E-mail: elaine_andolina@urmc.rochester.edu.
Website: http://www.son.rochester.edu

University of St. Augustine for Health Sciences, Graduate Programs, Doctor of Nursing Practice Program, San Marcos, CA 92069. Offers DNP.

University of St. Augustine for Health Sciences, Graduate Programs, Master of Science in Nursing Program, San Marcos, CA 92069. Offers nurse educator (MSN); nurse executive (MSN); nurse informatics (MSN). *Program availability:* Part-time, online learning.

University of Saint Francis, Graduate School, Department of Nursing, Fort Wayne, IN 46808. Offers family nurse practitioner (MSN, Post Master's Certificate); nurse anesthesia (DNP); nursing practice (DNP). *Accreditation:* AACN. *Program availability:* Part-time, blended/hybrid learning. *Faculty:* 8 full-time (7 women), 12 part-time/adjunct (10 women). *Students:* 44 full-time (36 women), 72 part-time (65 women); includes 10 minority (4 Black or African American, non-Hispanic/Latino; 1 Asian, non-Hispanic/Latino; 2 Hispanic/Latino; 3 Two or more races, non-Hispanic/Latino). Average age 32. 48 applicants, 71% accepted, 29 enrolled. In 2017, 30 master's, 2 other advanced degrees awarded. *Degree requirements:* For doctorate, comprehensive exam. *Entrance requirements:* For master's, GRE (if undergraduate GPA is less than 3.0), minimum undergraduate GPA of 3.2; ASN, BSN, or MSN from regionally-accredited U.S. institution; current license as registered nurse; graduate or undergraduate statistics course within last five years; for doctorate, BSN from ACEN- or CCNE-accredited nursing program; minimum cumulative undergraduate GPA of 3.2; 2 courses in chemistry and 1 statistics course with minimum B grade; official transcripts; resume; 1 year of continuous full-time critical care experience; current Indiana RN license; 3 professional letters of recommendation; essay; interview; for Post Master's Certificate, GRE (if undergraduate GPA is less than 3.0), minimum undergraduate GPA of 3.2; MSN from regionally-accredited U.S. institution; current license as registered nurse; graduate or undergraduate statistics course within last five years. Additional exam requirements/recommendations for international students: Required—TOEFL (minimum score 550 paper-based; 100 iBT), IELTS (minimum score 6.5), TWE (minimum score 5). *Application deadline:* For fall admission, 7/1 for international students; for spring admission, 11/1 for international students; for summer admission, 3/1 for international students. Applications are processed on a rolling basis. Application fee: $0. Electronic applications accepted. *Expenses:* $905 per hour (for MSN); $1,055 per hour (for DNP). *Financial support:* In 2017–18, 21 students received support. Federal Work-Study, scholarships/grants, and unspecified assistantships available. Financial award application deadline: 4/15; financial award applicants required to submit FAFSA. *Unit head:* Dr. Wendy Clark, Program Director, Master of Science in Nursing, 260-399-7700 Ext. 8534, Fax: 260-399-8167, E-mail: wclark@sf.edu. *Application contact:* Kyle Richardson, Associate Director of Enrollment Services for Adult Learning, 260-399-7700 Ext. 6310, Fax: 260-399-8152, E-mail: krichardson@sf.edu.
Website: https://nursing.sf.edu/

University of St. Francis, Leach College of Nursing, Joliet, IL 60435-6169. Offers family nurse practitioner (MSN, Post-Master's Certificate); nursing administration (MSN); nursing education (MSN); nursing practice (DNP); psychology/mental health nurse practitioner (MSN, Post-Master's Certificate); teaching in nursing (Certificate). *Accreditation:* AACN. *Program availability:* Part-time, evening/weekend, 100% online. *Faculty:* 9 full-time (all women), 12 part-time/adjunct (11 women). *Students:* 66 full-time (61 women), 292 part-time (262 women); includes 136 minority (67 Black or African American, non-Hispanic/Latino; 2 American Indian or Alaska Native, non-Hispanic/Latino; 25 Asian, non-Hispanic/Latino; 29 Hispanic/Latino; 3 Native Hawaiian or other Pacific Islander, non-Hispanic/Latino; 10 Two or more races, non-Hispanic/Latino). Average age 40. 280 applicants, 34% accepted, 81 enrolled. In 2017, 117 master's, 5 doctorates, 12 other advanced degrees awarded. *Degree requirements:* For master's, comprehensive exam. *Entrance requirements:* Additional exam requirements/recommendations for international students: Required—TOEFL (minimum score 550 paper-based; 79 iBT), IELTS (minimum score 6). *Application deadline:* Applications are processed on a rolling basis. Application fee: $30. Electronic applications accepted. Application fee is waived when completed online. *Expenses:* $775 per credit hour. *Financial support:* In 2017–18, 115 students received support. Scholarships/grants available. Support available to part-time students. Financial award applicants required to submit FAFSA. *Unit head:* Dr. Carol Wilson, Dean, 815-740-3840, Fax: 815-740-4243, E-mail: cwilson@stfrancis.edu. *Application contact:* Sandra Sloka, Director of Admissions for Graduate and Degree Completion Programs, 800-735-7500, Fax: 815-740-3431, E-mail: ssloka@stfrancis.edu.
Website: http://www.stfrancis.edu/academics/college-of-nursing/

University of Saint Joseph, Department of Nursing, West Hartford, CT 06117-2700. Offers family nurse practitioner (MS); nurse educator (MS); nursing practice (DNP); psychiatric/mental health nurse practitioner (MS). *Accreditation:* AACN. *Program availability:* Part-time, evening/weekend. *Degree requirements:* For master's, thesis. *Entrance requirements:* For master's, 2 letters of recommendation. *Application deadline:* Applications are processed on a rolling basis. Application fee: $50. Electronic applications accepted. Application fee is waived when completed online. *Financial support:* Career-related internships or fieldwork and unspecified assistantships available. Support available to part-time students. Financial award applicants required to submit FAFSA.
Website: http://www.usj.edu/academics/schools/school-of-health-natural-sciences/nursing/

University of Saint Mary, Graduate Programs, Program in Nursing, Leavenworth, KS 66048-5082. Offers nurse administrator (MSN); nurse educator (MSN). *Accreditation:* AACN. *Program availability:* Part-time, online only, 100% online. *Degree requirements:* For master's, practicum. *Entrance requirements:* For master's, BSN from CCNE- or ACEN-accredited baccalaureate nursing program at regionally-accredited institution. Electronic applications accepted. *Expenses:* Contact institution.

University of San Diego, Hahn School of Nursing and Health Science, San Diego, CA 92110-2492. Offers adult-gerontology clinical nurse specialist (MSN); adult-gerontology nurse practitioner/family nurse practitioner (MSN); clinical nurse leader (MSN); executive nurse leader (MSN); family nurse practitioner (MSN); healthcare informatics (MS, MSN); nursing (PhD); nursing practice (DNP); pediatric/family nurse practitioner (MSN); psychiatric-mental health nurse practitioner (MSN). *Accreditation:* AACN. *Program availability:* Part-time, evening/weekend. *Faculty:* 26 full-time (21 women), 36 part-time/adjunct (29 women). *Students:* 238 full-time (198 women), 230 part-time (167 women); includes 230 minority (32 Black or African American, non-Hispanic/Latino; 104 Asian, non-Hispanic/Latino; 75 Hispanic/Latino; 19 Two or more races, non-Hispanic/Latino), 12 international. Average age 35. In 2017, 93 master's, 44 doctorates awarded. *Degree requirements:* For doctorate, thesis/dissertation (for some programs), residency (DNP). *Entrance requirements:* For master's, GRE General Test (for entry-level nursing), BSN, current California RN licensure (except for entry-level nursing), minimum GPA of 3.0; for doctorate, minimum GPA of 3.5, MSN, current California RN licensure. Additional exam requirements/recommendations for international students: Required—TOEFL (minimum score 580 paper-based; 83 iBT), TWE. *Application deadline:* Applications are processed on a rolling basis. Application fee: $45. Electronic applications accepted. *Financial support:* In 2017–18, 242 students received support. Scholarships/grants and traineeships available. Support available to part-time students. Financial award application deadline: 4/1; financial award applicants required to submit FAFSA. *Faculty research:* Maternal/neonatal health, palliative and end of life care, adolescent obesity, health disparities, cognitive dysfunction. *Unit head:* Dr. Janes Georges, Interim Dean, 619-260-4550, Fax: 619-260-6814, E-mail: nursing@sandiego.edu. *Application contact:* Monica Mahon, Associate Director of Graduate Admissions, 619-260-4524, Fax: 619-260-4158, E-mail: grads@sandiego.edu.
Website: http://www.sandiego.edu/nursing/

University of San Francisco, School of Nursing and Health Professions, Doctor of Nursing Practice Program, San Francisco, CA 94117-1080. Offers DNP.

University of Saskatchewan, College of Graduate Studies and Research, College of Nursing, Saskatoon, SK S7N 5E5, Canada. Offers MN. *Program availability:* Part-time. *Entrance requirements:* Additional exam requirements/recommendations for international students: Required—TOEFL.

The University of Scranton, Panuska College of Professional Studies, Department of Nursing, Scranton, PA 18510-4595. Offers family nurse practitioner (MSN, PMC); nurse anesthesia (MSN, PMC); nursing leadership (DNP). Applicants accepted in odd-numbered years only. *Accreditation:* AACN; AANA/CANAEP. *Program availability:* Part-time, evening/weekend. *Degree requirements:* For master's, comprehensive exam (for some programs), thesis (for some programs), capstone experience. *Entrance requirements:* For master's, minimum GPA of 3.0, three letters of reference; for doctorate, RN licensure and evidence of certification in advanced practice nursing specialty. Additional exam requirements/recommendations for international students: Required—TOEFL (minimum score 500 paper-based; 80 iBT), IELTS (minimum score 6.5). Electronic applications accepted. *Faculty research:* Home care, doctoral education, health care of women and children, pain, health promotion and adolescence.

University of South Alabama, College of Nursing, Mobile, AL 36688. Offers nursing (MSN, DNP); nursing administration (Certificate); nursing education (Certificate); nursing practice (Certificate). *Accreditation:* AACN. *Program availability:* Part-time, online learning. *Faculty:* 73 full-time (67 women), 112 part-time/adjunct (103 women). *Students:* 2,163 full-time (1,905 women), 714 part-time (619 women); includes 882 minority (566 Black or African American, non-Hispanic/Latino; 26 American Indian or Alaska Native, non-Hispanic/Latino; 117 Asian, non-Hispanic/Latino; 102 Hispanic/Latino; 7 Native Hawaiian or other Pacific Islander, non-Hispanic/Latino; 64 Two or more races, non-Hispanic/Latino), 6 international. Average age 35. 918 applicants, 77% accepted, 522 enrolled. In 2017, 791 master's, 96 doctorates, 95 other advanced degrees awarded. *Degree requirements:* For master's, thesis optional; for doctorate, final project. *Entrance requirements:* For master's, BSN, RN licensure, minimum GPA of 3.0, resume documenting clinical experience, background check, drug screening; for doctorate, MSN, RN licensure, minimum GPA of 3.0; for Certificate, MSN/DN/DNP, RN licensure, minimum GPA of 3.0, resume documenting clinical experience, background check, drug screening. Additional exam requirements/recommendations for international students: Required—TOEFL. *Application deadline:* For fall admission, 2/15 for domestic students; for spring admission, 7/15 priority date for domestic students; for summer admission, 11/15 priority date for domestic students. Applications are processed on a rolling basis. Application fee: $100. Electronic applications accepted. *Expenses:* Tuition, state resident: full-time $10,104; part-time $421 per semester hour. Tuition, nonresident: full-time $20,208; part-time $842 per semester hour. *Financial support:* Fellowships, research assistantships, teaching assistantships, career-related internships or fieldwork, Federal Work-Study, institutionally sponsored loans, scholarships/grants, and unspecified assistantships available. Support available to part-time students. Financial award application deadline: 3/31; financial award applicants required to submit FAFSA. *Unit head:* Dr. Heather Hall, Interim Dean, College of Nursing, 251-445-9400, Fax: 251-445-9416, E-mail: heatherhall@southalabama.edu. *Application contact:* Brenda Mosley, Academic Advisor II, 251-445-9400, Fax: 251-445-9416, E-mail: bmosley@southalabama.edu.
Website: http://www.southalabama.edu/colleges/con/index.html

University of South Carolina, The Graduate School, College of Nursing, Program in Advanced Practice Clinical Nursing, Columbia, SC 29208. Offers acute care nurse practitioner (Certificate); advanced practice clinical nursing (MSN). *Accreditation:* AACN. *Program availability:* Part-time, online learning. *Entrance requirements:* For master's, master's degree in nursing, RN license; for Certificate, MSN. Additional exam requirements/recommendations for international students: Required—TOEFL (minimum score 570 paper-based). Electronic applications accepted. *Faculty research:* Systems research, evidence based practice, breast cancer, violence.

University of South Carolina, The Graduate School, College of Nursing, Program in Advanced Practice Nursing in Primary Care, Columbia, SC 29208. Offers MSN, Certificate. *Accreditation:* AACN. *Entrance requirements:* For master's, master's degree in nursing, RN license; for Certificate, MSN. Additional exam requirements/recommendations for international students: Required—TOEFL (minimum score 570 paper-based). Electronic applications accepted. *Faculty research:* Systems research, evidence based practice, breast cancer, violence.

University of Southern Indiana, Graduate Studies, College of Nursing and Health Professions, Program in Nursing, Evansville, IN 47712-3590. Offers adult-gerontology acute care nurse practitioner (MSN, PMC); adult-gerontology clinical nurse specialist (MSN, PMC); adult-gerontology primary care nurse practitioner (MSN, PMC); advanced nursing practice (DNP); family nurse practiioner (MSN); family nurse practitioner (PMC); nursing education (MSN, PMC); nursing management and leadership (MSN, PMC); organizational and systems leadership (DNP); psychiatric mental health nurse practitioner (MSN, PMC). *Accreditation:* AACN. *Program availability:* Part-time, online learning. *Faculty:* 9 full-time (8 women), 2 part-time/adjunct (both women). *Students:* 73 full-time (59 women), 370 part-time (314 women); includes 47 minority (18 Black or African American, non-Hispanic/Latino; 2 American Indian or Alaska Native, non-Hispanic/Latino; 10 Asian, non-Hispanic/Latino; 12 Hispanic/Latino; 1 Native Hawaiian or other Pacific Islander, non-Hispanic/Latino; 4 Two or more races, non-Hispanic/Latino), 1 international. Average age 36. In 2017, 91 master's, 10 doctorates, 18 other advanced degrees awarded. *Entrance requirements:* For master's, BSN from nationally-accredited school; minimum cumulative GPA of 3.0; satisfactory completion of a course in undergraduate statistics (minimum grade C); one year of full-time experience or 2,000 hours of clinical practice as an RN (recommended); unencumbered U.S. RN license; for doctorate, minimum GPA of 3.0, completion of graduate research course with minimum B grade, unencumbered RN license, resume/curriculum vitae, three professional references, 1-2 page narrative of practice experience and professional goals, Capstone Project Information form. Additional exam requirements/recommendations for international students: Required—TOEFL (minimum score 550 paper-based; 79 iBT), IELTS (minimum score 6). *Application deadline:* For fall admission, 2/1 for domestic students, 1/1 priority date for international students. Applications are processed on a rolling basis. Application fee: $40. Electronic applications accepted. *Expenses:* Contact institution. *Financial support:* In 2017–18, 1 student received support. Federal Work-Study, scholarships/grants, tuition waivers (full and partial), and unspecified assistantships available. Financial award application deadline: 3/1; financial award applicants required to submit FAFSA. *Unit head:* Dr. Mellisa A. Hall, Chair of the Master of Science in Nursing Program, 812-465-1168, E-mail: mhall@usi.edu. *Application contact:* Dr. Mayola Rowser, Director, Graduate Studies, 812-465-7015, Fax: 812-464-1956, E-mail: mrowser@usi.edu.
Website: https://www.usi.edu/health/nursing/

University of Southern Maine, College of Science, Technology, and Health, School of Nursing, Portland, ME 04103. Offers adult-gerontology primary care nurse practitioner (MS, PMC); education (MS); family nurse practitioner (MS, PMC); family psychiatric/mental health nurse practitioner (MS); management (MS); nursing (CAS, CGS); psychiatric-mental health nurse practitioner (PMC). *Accreditation:* AACN. *Program availability:* Part-time. *Degree requirements:* For master's, thesis optional. *Entrance requirements:* For master's, GRE General Test or MAT, minimum GPA of 3.0; for doctorate, GRE. Additional exam requirements/recommendations for international students: Required—TOEFL (minimum score 550 paper-based). Electronic applications accepted. *Faculty research:* Women's health, nursing history, weight control, community services, substance abuse.

University of Southern Mississippi, College of Nursing, Hattiesburg, MS 39406-0001. Offers MSN, DNP, PhD, Graduate Certificate. *Accreditation:* AACN; AANA/CANAEP. *Program availability:* Part-time, evening/weekend. *Students:* 51 full-time (42 women), 2 part-time (both women). 134 applicants, 64% accepted, 51 enrolled. In 2017, 1 master's, 1 doctorate, 2 other advanced degrees awarded. *Degree requirements:* For master's, comprehensive exam, thesis optional; for doctorate, comprehensive exam, thesis/dissertation. *Entrance requirements:* For master's, GRE General Test, minimum GPA of 2.75 during last 60 hours, nursing license, BS in nursing; for doctorate, GRE General Test, master's degree in nursing, minimum GPA of 3.5. Additional exam requirements/recommendations for international students: Required—TOEFL, IELTS. *Application deadline:* For fall admission, 3/15 priority date for domestic students, 5/1 for international students; for spring admission, 1/10 priority date for domestic and international students. Applications are processed on a rolling basis. Application fee: $60. Electronic applications accepted. *Expenses:* Tuition, state resident: full-time $3830. *Financial support:* Research assistantships with full tuition reimbursements, teaching assistantships, Federal Work-Study, institutionally sponsored loans, scholarships/grants, traineeships, health care benefits, and unspecified assistantships available. Financial award application deadline: 3/15; financial award applicants required to submit FAFSA. *Faculty research:* Gerontology, caregivers, HIV, bereavement, pain, nursing leadership. *Unit head:* Dr. Kathleen Masters, Interim Dean, 601-266-6485, Fax: 601-266-5927, E-mail: kathleen.masters@usm.edu. *Application contact:* Dr. Sandra Bishop, Graduate Coordinator, 601-266-5500, Fax: 601-266-5927.
Website: https://www.usm.edu/nursing

University of South Florida, College of Nursing, Tampa, FL 33612. Offers nurse anesthesia (DNP); nursing (MS, DNP), including adult-gerontology acute care nursing, adult-gerontology primary care nursing, family health nursing, nurse anesthesia (MS), nursing education (MS), occupational health nursing/adult-gerontology primary care nursing, oncology nursing/adult-gerontology primary care nursing (DNP), pediatric health nursing; nursing education (Post Master's Certificate); nursing science (PhD); simulation based academic fellowship in advanced pain management (Graduate Certificate). *Accreditation:* AACN; AANA/CANAEP. *Program availability:* Part-time. *Faculty:* 37 full-time (32 women), 2 part-time/adjunct (1 woman). *Students:* 224 full-time (178 women), 669 part-time (577 women); includes 309 minority (105 Black or African American, non-Hispanic/Latino; 2 American Indian or Alaska Native, non-Hispanic/Latino; 53 Asian, non-Hispanic/Latino; 122 Hispanic/Latino; 1 Native Hawaiian or other Pacific Islander, non-Hispanic/Latino; 26 Two or more races, non-Hispanic/Latino), 6 international. Average age 32. 949 applicants, 47% accepted, 382 enrolled. In 2017, 264 master's, 39 doctorates awarded. *Degree requirements:* For master's, comprehensive exam, thesis optional; for doctorate, comprehensive exam, thesis/dissertation. *Entrance requirements:* For master's, GRE General Test, bachelor's degree from accredited program with minimum GPA of 3.0 in all upper-division coursework; current license as Registered Nurse; 3 letters of recommendation; personal statement of goals; resume or curriculum vitae; personal interview; for doctorate, GRE General Test (recommended), bachelor's degree in nursing from ACEN or CCNE regionally-accredited institution with minimum GPA of 3.0 in all coursework or in all upper-division coursework; current license as Registered Nurse in Florida; undergraduate statistics course with minimum B grade; 3 letters of recommendation; statement of goals; resume; interview. Additional exam requirements/recommendations for international students: Required—TOEFL (minimum score 550 paper-based; 79 iBT). *Application deadline:* For fall admission, 10/15 for domestic and international students; for spring admission, 10/1 for domestic students, 9/15 for international students. Application fee: $30. Electronic applications accepted. *Financial support:* In 2017–18, 132 students received support, including 7 research assistantships with tuition reimbursements available (averaging $18,935 per year), 29 teaching assistantships with tuition reimbursements available (averaging $30,814 per year); tuition waivers (partial) and unspecified assistantships also available. Financial award application deadline: 2/1; financial award applicants required to submit FAFSA. *Faculty research:* Women's health, palliative and end-of-life care, cardiac rehabilitation, complementary therapies for chronic illness and cancer. *Total annual research expenditures:* $3.2 million. *Unit head:* Dr. Victoria Rich, Dean, College of Nursing, 813-974-8939, Fax: 813-974-5418, E-mail: victoriarich@health.usf.edu. *Application contact:* Dr. Brian Graves, Assistant Professor/Assistant Dean, 813-974-8054, Fax: 813-974-5418, E-mail: bgraves1@health.usf.edu.
Website: http://health.usf.edu/nursing/index.htm

Nursing—General

The University of Tampa, Program in Nursing, Tampa, FL 33606-1490. Offers adult nursing practitioner (MSN); family nursing practitioner (MSN); nursing (MS). *Accreditation:* ACEN. *Program availability:* Part-time, evening/weekend. *Faculty:* 7 full-time (6 women), 6 part-time/adjunct (all women). *Students:* 4 full-time (all women), 166 part-time (148 women); includes 29 minority (15 Black or African American, non-Hispanic/Latino; 8 Asian, non-Hispanic/Latino; 6 Two or more races, non-Hispanic/Latino), 2 international. Average age 33. 132 applicants, 64% accepted, 51 enrolled. In 2017, 45 master's awarded. *Degree requirements:* For master's, comprehensive exam, oral exam, practicum. *Entrance requirements:* For master's, GMAT or GRE, current licensure as registered nurse in state of Florida; minimum GPA of 3.0 in last 60 credit hours; minimum of one year of direct patient care experience within the past five years (recommended). Additional exam requirements/recommendations for international students: Required—TOEFL (minimum score 577 paper-based; 90 iBT), IELTS (minimum score 7.5). *Application deadline:* Applications are processed on a rolling basis. Application fee: $40. Electronic applications accepted. *Expenses:* Contact institution. *Financial support:* In 2017–18, 9 students received support. Career-related internships or fieldwork, scholarships/grants, and unspecified assistantships available. Financial award applicants required to submit FAFSA. *Faculty research:* Vaccinations and public health, osteoporosis, cultural diversity, ethics, nursing practice. *Unit head:* Michele Wolf, Director, 813-257-3179, E-mail: mwolf@ut.edu. *Application contact:* Chanelle Cox, Staff Assistant, Admissions for Graduate and Continuing Studies, 813-253-6249, E-mail: ccox@ut.edu.
Website: http://www.ut.edu/msn/

The University of Tennessee, Graduate School, College of Nursing, Knoxville, TN 37996. Offers MSN, PhD. *Accreditation:* AACN; AANA/CANAEP. *Program availability:* Part-time. *Degree requirements:* For master's, thesis or alternative; for doctorate, thesis/dissertation. *Entrance requirements:* For master's and doctorate, GRE General Test, minimum GPA of 2.7. Additional exam requirements/recommendations for international students: Required—TOEFL. Electronic applications accepted.

The University of Tennessee at Chattanooga, School of Nursing, Chattanooga, TN 37403. Offers certified nurse anesthetist (Post-Master's Certificate); family nurse practitioner (MSN, Post-Master's Certificate); gerontology acute care (MSN, Post-Master's Certificate); nurse anesthesia (MSN); nurse education (Post-Master's Certificate); nursing (DNP). *Accreditation:* AACN; AANA/CANAEP (one or more programs are accredited). *Students:* 62 full-time (33 women), 69 part-time (61 women); includes 24 minority (11 Black or African American, non-Hispanic/Latino; 1 American Indian or Alaska Native, non-Hispanic/Latino; 5 Asian, non-Hispanic/Latino; 3 Hispanic/Latino; 4 Two or more races, non-Hispanic/Latino). Average age 34. 47 applicants, 100% accepted, 45 enrolled. In 2017, 33 master's, 14 doctorates, 7 other advanced degrees awarded. *Degree requirements:* For master's, thesis optional, qualifying exams, professional project; for doctorate, professional project; for Post-Master's Certificate, thesis or alternative, practicum, seminar. *Entrance requirements:* For master's, GRE General Test, MAT, BSN, minimum GPA of 3.0, eligibility for Tennessee RN license, 1 year of direct patient care experience; for doctorate, GRE General Test or MAT (if applicant does not have MSN), minimum GPA of 3.0 for highest degree earned; for Post-Master's Certificate, GRE General Test, MAT, MSN, minimum GPA of 3.0, eligibility for Tennessee RN license, one year of direct patient care experience. Additional exam requirements/recommendations for international students: Required—TOEFL (minimum score 550 paper-based; 79 iBT), IELTS (minimum score 6). *Application deadline:* For fall admission, 6/15 priority date for domestic students, 7/1 for international students; for spring admission, 11/1 priority date for domestic students, 11/1 for international students. Applications are processed on a rolling basis. Application fee: $35 ($40 for international students). Electronic applications accepted. *Expenses:* Contact institution. *Financial support:* Teaching assistantships, career-related internships or fieldwork, and scholarships/grants available. Support available to part-time students. Financial award application deadline: 7/1; financial award applicants required to submit FAFSA. *Faculty research:* Diabetes in women, health care for elderly, alternative medicine, hypertension, nurse anesthesia. *Total annual research expenditures:* $985,388. *Unit head:* Dr. Chris Smith, Director, 423-425-1741, Fax: 423-425-4668, E-mail: chris-smith@utc.edu. *Application contact:* Dr. Joanne Romagni, Dean of the Graduate School, 423-425-4478, Fax: 423-425-5223, E-mail: joanne-romagni@utc.edu.
Website: http://www.utc.edu/nursing/

The University of Tennessee Health Science Center, College of Graduate Health Sciences, Memphis, TN 38163. Offers biomedical engineering (MS, PhD); biomedical sciences (PhD); dental sciences (MDS); epidemiology (MS); health outcomes and policy research (PhD); laboratory research and management (MS); nursing science (PhD); pharmaceutical sciences (PhD); pharmacology (MS); speech and hearing science (PhD); DDS/PhD; DNP/PhD; MD/PhD; Pharm D/PhD. MS and PhD programs in biomedical engineering offered jointly with University of Memphis. *Faculty:* 528 full-time (176 women). *Students:* 258 full-time (130 women); includes 87 minority (14 Black or African American, non-Hispanic/Latino; 68 Asian, non-Hispanic/Latino; 5 Hispanic/Latino). Average age 28. 673 applicants, 17% accepted, 102 enrolled. In 2017, 23 master's, 30 doctorates awarded. Terminal master's awarded for partial completion of doctoral program. *Degree requirements:* For master's, comprehensive exam, thesis; for doctorate, thesis/dissertation, oral and written preliminary and comprehensive exams. *Entrance requirements:* For master's and doctorate, GRE General Test, minimum GPA of 3.0. Additional exam requirements/recommendations for international students: Recommended—TOEFL (minimum score 79 iBT), IELTS (minimum score 6.5). *Application deadline:* For winter admission, 1/1 for domestic and international students; for spring admission, 3/1 for domestic and international students. Applications are processed on a rolling basis. Application fee: $0. Electronic applications accepted. *Expenses:* Contact institution. *Financial support:* In 2017–18, 150 students received support, including 150 research assistantships (averaging $25,000 per year); fellowships, institutionally sponsored loans, scholarships/grants, health care benefits, and tuition waivers (full and partial) also available. Support available to part-time students. *Faculty research:* Cell biology, epidemiology, biomedical engineering, speech and hearing science, health policy, pharmaceutical sciences, dental sciences, nursing science, pharmacology. *Unit head:* Dr. Donald B. Thomason, Dean, 901-448-5538, E-mail: dthomaso@uthsc.edu. *Application contact:* Dr. Isaac O. Donkor, Associate Dean for Student Affairs, 901-448-5538, E-mail: idonkor@uthsc.edu.
Website: http://grad.uthsc.edu/

The University of Tennessee Health Science Center, College of Nursing, Memphis, TN 38163. Offers adult-gerontology acute care nurse practitioner (Post Master's Certificate); advance practice nursing (DNP); family nurse practitioner (Post-Doctoral Certificate); pediatric acute care nurse practitioner (Post-Doctoral Certificate); pediatric primary care nurse practitioner (Post-Doctoral Certificate); psychiatric/mental health nurse practitioner (Post-Doctoral Certificate); registered nurse first assistant (Certificate). *Accreditation:* AACN; AANA/CANAEP. *Program availability:* Part-time, blended/hybrid learning. *Faculty:* 52 full-time (47 women), 11 part-time/adjunct (4 women). *Students:* 262 full-time (228 women), 13 part-time (12 women); includes 83 minority (71 Black or African American, non-Hispanic/Latino; 6 Asian, non-Hispanic/Latino; 6 Hispanic/Latino). Average age 32. 215 applicants, 49% accepted, 79 enrolled. In 2017, 78 doctorates, 2 Certificates awarded. *Degree requirements:* For doctorate, project. *Entrance requirements:* For doctorate, RN license, minimum GPA of 3.0; for other advanced degree, MSN, APN license, minimum GPA of 3.0. Additional exam requirements/recommendations for international students: Required—TOEFL (minimum score 550 paper-based; 80 iBT). *Application deadline:* For fall admission, 1/15 for domestic students; for spring admission, 8/15 for domestic students. Application fee: $70. Electronic applications accepted. *Expenses:* $13,420 in-state tuition and fees; $17,222 out-of-state tuition and fees. *Financial support:* In 2017–18, 112 students received support, including 9 research assistantships (averaging $24,783 per year); Federal Work-Study, institutionally sponsored loans, scholarships/grants, and tuition waivers (partial) also available. Financial award application deadline: 3/15; financial award applicants required to submit FAFSA. *Faculty research:* Efficacy of a cognitive behavioral group intervention and its influence on symptoms of depression and anxiety as well as caregiver function; quality of life and sexual function in women who undergo vulvar surgeries; influence of prenatal and early childhood environments on health and developmental trajectories across childhood; interaction between physical activity, diet, genetics, insulin resistance, and obesity. *Total annual research expenditures:* $1.2 million. *Unit head:* Dr. Wendy Likes, Dean, 901-448-6135, Fax: 901-448-4121, E-mail: wlikes@uthsc.edu. *Application contact:* Jamie Overton, Director, Student Affairs, 901-448-6139, Fax: 901-448-4121, E-mail: joverton@uthsc.edu.
Website: http://uthsc.edu/nursing/

The University of Texas at Arlington, Graduate School, College of Nursing and Health Innovation, Arlington, TX 76019. Offers athletic training (MS); exercise science (MS); kinesiology (PhD); nurse practitioner (MSN); nursing (PhD); nursing administration (MSN); nursing education (MSN); nursing practice (DNP). *Accreditation:* AACN. *Program availability:* Part-time, evening/weekend, online learning. *Degree requirements:* For master's, practicum course; for doctorate, comprehensive exam (for some programs), thesis/dissertation (for some programs), proposal defense dissertation (for PhD); scholarship project (for DNP). *Entrance requirements:* For master's, GRE General Test if GPA less than 3.0, minimum GPA of 3.0, Texas nursing license, minimum C grade in undergraduate statistics course; for doctorate, GRE General Test (waived for MSN-to-PhD applicants), minimum undergraduate, graduate and statistics GPA of 3.0; Texas RN license; interview; written statement of goals. Additional exam requirements/recommendations for international students: Required—TOEFL (minimum score 550 paper-based), IELTS (minimum score 7). *Faculty research:* Simulation in clinical education and practice, cultural diversity, vulnerable populations, substance abuse.

The University of Texas at Austin, Graduate School, School of Nursing, Austin, TX 78712-1111. Offers adult - gerontology clinical nurse specialist (MSN); child health (MSN), including administration, public health nursing, teaching; family nurse practitioner (MSN); family psychiatric/mental health nurse practitioner (MSN); holistic adult health (MSN), including administration, teaching; maternity (MSN), including administration, public health nursing, teaching; nursing (PhD); nursing administration and healthcare systems management (MSN); nursing practice (DNP); pediatric nurse practitioner (MSN); public health nursing (MSN). *Accreditation:* AACN. *Program availability:* Part-time. *Degree requirements:* For master's, thesis optional; for doctorate, thesis/dissertation. *Entrance requirements:* For master's and doctorate, GRE General Test. Additional exam requirements/recommendations for international students: Required—TOEFL (minimum score 550 paper-based). Electronic applications accepted. *Faculty research:* Chronic illness management, memory and aging, health promotion, women's health, adolescent health.

The University of Texas at El Paso, Graduate School, School of Nursing, El Paso, TX 79968-0001. Offers family nurse practitioner (MSN); health care leadership and management (Certificate); interdisciplinary health sciences (PhD); nursing (DNP); nursing education (MSN, Certificate); nursing systems management (MSN). *Accreditation:* AACN. *Program availability:* Online learning. *Degree requirements:* For master's, thesis optional; for doctorate, thesis/dissertation. *Entrance requirements:* For master's, minimum GPA of 3.0, resume; for doctorate, GRE, letters of reference, relevant personal/professional experience; master's degree in nursing (for DNP); for Certificate, bachelor's degree in nursing. Additional exam requirements/recommendations for international students: Required—TOEFL; Recommended—IELTS. *Application deadline:* For fall admission, 8/1 for domestic students, 3/1 for international students; for spring admission, 11/1 for domestic students, 9/1 for international students. Applications are processed on a rolling basis. Application fee: $45 ($80 for international students). Electronic applications accepted. *Financial support:* Fellowships with partial tuition reimbursements, research assistantships with partial tuition reimbursements, teaching assistantships with partial tuition reimbursements, institutionally sponsored loans, scholarships/grants, health care benefits, tuition waivers (partial), and unspecified assistantships available. Support available to part-time students. Financial award application deadline: 3/15; financial award applicants required to submit FAFSA. *Unit head:* Dr. Elias Provencio-Vasquez, Dean, 915-747-8194, Fax: 915-747-8266, E-mail: eprovenciovasquez@utep.edu. *Application contact:* Dr. Benjamin Flores, Interim Dean of the Graduate School, 915-747-5491, Fax: 915-747-5788, E-mail: bflores@utep.edu.
Website: http://nursing.utep.edu/

The University of Texas at Tyler, College of Nursing and Health Sciences, Program in Nursing, Tyler, TX 75799-0001. Offers nurse practitioner (MSN); nursing (PhD); nursing administration (MSN); nursing education (MSN); MSN/MBA. *Accreditation:* AACN. *Program availability:* Part-time, evening/weekend, online learning. *Degree requirements:* For master's, comprehensive exam (for some programs), thesis (for some programs); for doctorate, thesis/dissertation. *Entrance requirements:* For master's, GRE General Test or MAT, GMAT, minimum undergraduate GPA of 3.0, course work in statistics, RN license, BSN. Additional exam requirements/recommendations for international students: Required—TOEFL. Electronic applications accepted. *Faculty research:* Psychosocial adjustment, aging, support/commitment of caregivers, psychological abuse and violence, hope/hopelessness, professional values, end of life care, suicidology, clinical supervision, workforce retention and issues, global health issues, health promotion.

The University of Texas Health Science Center at Houston, Cizik School of Nursing, Houston, TX 77030. Offers MSN, DNP, PhD, MSN/MPH. *Accreditation:* AACN; AANA/CANAEP. *Program availability:* Part-time. *Degree requirements:* For master's, thesis, research project, or clinical project; for doctorate, thesis/dissertation. *Entrance requirements:* For master's, GRE or MAT, BSN, Texas RN license, related work experience, interview, writing sample; for doctorate, GRE, interview, Texas RN license, portfolio, master's degree. Additional exam requirements/recommendations for international students: Required—TOEFL (minimum score 550 paper-based; 86 iBT). Electronic applications accepted. *Faculty research:* Malnutrition in institutionalized elderly, defining nursing, sensitive outcome measures, substance abuse in mothers during pregnancy, psychoeducational intervention among caregivers of stroke patients.

The University of Texas Health Science Center at San Antonio, Graduate School of Biomedical Sciences, Program in Nursing Science, San Antonio, TX 78229-3900. Offers PhD.

The University of Texas Health Science Center at San Antonio, School of Nursing, San Antonio, TX 78229-3900. Offers administrative management (MSN); adult-gerontology acute care nurse practitioner (PGC); advanced practice leadership (DNP);

clinical nurse leader (MSN); executive administrative management (DNP); family nurse practitioner (MSN, PGC); nursing (MSN, PhD); nursing education (MSN, PGC); pediatric nurse practitioner primary care (PGC); psychiatric mental health nurse practitioner (PGC); public health nurse leader (DNP). *Accreditation:* AACN. *Program availability:* Part-time. Terminal master's awarded for partial completion of doctoral program. *Degree requirements:* For master's, thesis optional; for doctorate, comprehensive exam, thesis/dissertation.

The University of Texas Medical Branch, Graduate School of Biomedical Sciences, Doctoral Program in Nursing, Galveston, TX 77555. Offers PhD. *Degree requirements:* For doctorate, comprehensive exam, thesis/dissertation. *Entrance requirements:* For doctorate, GRE General Test, minimum GPA of 3.0, BSN and MSN or equivalent advanced degree, 2 writing samples, 3 letters of reference, curriculum vitae or resume. Additional exam requirements/recommendations for international students: Required—TOEFL (minimum score 550 paper-based). Electronic applications accepted.

The University of Texas Medical Branch, School of Nursing, Master's Program in Nursing, Galveston, TX 77555. Offers MSN. *Accreditation:* AACN. *Program availability:* Part-time, online learning. *Entrance requirements:* For master's, GRE General Test or MAT, minimum BSN GPA of 3.0, 3 references, interview, 1 year nursing experience. Additional exam requirements/recommendations for international students: Required—TOEFL (minimum score 550 paper-based).

The University of Texas Rio Grande Valley, College of Health Affairs, School of Nursing, Edinburg, TX 78539. Offers adult health nursing (MSN); family nurse practitioner (MSN); nursing administration (MSN); nursing education (MSN); psychiatric mental health nursing (Post Master's Certificate). *Accreditation:* AACN. *Program availability:* Part-time, evening/weekend. *Faculty:* 7 full-time (all women), 5 part-time/adjunct (3 women). *Students:* 48 full-time, 5 part-time; includes 43 minority (5 Black or African American, non-Hispanic/Latino; 38 Hispanic/Latino). Average age 31. 61 applicants. In 2017, 46 master's awarded. *Degree requirements:* For master's, thesis optional. *Entrance requirements:* For master's, Texas RN licensure, undergraduate physical statistic course. Additional exam requirements/recommendations for international students: Required—TOEFL (minimum score 550 paper-based). *Application deadline:* For fall admission, 7/1 priority date for domestic and international students; for spring admission, 10/1 priority date for domestic and international students. Applications are processed on a rolling basis. Application fee: $50. Electronic applications accepted. *Expenses:* Contact institution. *Financial support:* Scholarships/grants and traineeships available. Financial award application deadline: 9/1; financial award applicants required to submit FAFSA. *Faculty research:* Health promotion, adolescent pregnancy, herbal and nontraditional approaches, healing touch stress. *Unit head:* Dr. Eloisa G. Tamez, Professor/Chief Nursing Administrator, 956-665-3616, Fax: 956-665-5252, E-mail: eloisa.tamez@utrgv.edu. *Application contact:* Dr. Beatriz Bautista, Clinical Professor, 956-665-3497, Fax: 956-665-3491, E-mail: beatriz.bautista@utrgv.edu.
Website: http://www.utrgv.edu/nursing/

University of the Incarnate Word, Ila Faye Miller School of Nursing and Health Professions, San Antonio, TX 78209-6397. Offers kinesiology (MS); nursing (MSN, DNP); sport management (MS). *Program availability:* Part-time, evening/weekend. *Faculty:* 18 full-time (14 women). *Students:* 48 full-time (26 women), 75 part-time (62 women); includes 86 minority (22 Black or African American, non-Hispanic/Latino; 1 American Indian or Alaska Native, non-Hispanic/Latino; 8 Asian, non-Hispanic/Latino; 53 Hispanic/Latino; 2 Two or more races, non-Hispanic/Latino), 3 international. In 2017, 31 master's, 10 doctorates awarded. *Degree requirements:* For master's, comprehensive exam (for some programs), thesis or alternative, capstone. *Entrance requirements:* For master's, GRE General Test, MAT, baccalaureate degree in ACEN- or CCNE-accredited nursing program with health assessment and statistics; minimum cumulative GPA of 2.5 (3.0 in upper-division courses); three professional references; Texas State license or multi-state compact. Additional exam requirements/recommendations for international students: Required—TOEFL (minimum score 560 paper-based; 83 iBT). *Application deadline:* Applications are processed on a rolling basis. Application fee: $20. Electronic applications accepted. *Expenses:* $905 per credit hour (for DNP); $915 per credit hour (for master's-level porgrams). *Financial support:* Research assistantships, Federal Work-Study, scholarships/grants, tuition waivers (partial), and unspecified assistantships available. Financial award applicants required to submit FAFSA. *Faculty research:* Pediatric oncology, military pregnancy and the family, diabetes prevention, substance abuse and addictions, nursing of vulnerable populations. *Unit head:* Dr. Mary Hoke, Dean, 210-829-3982, Fax: 210-829-3174, E-mail: mhoke@uiwtx.edu. *Application contact:* Johnny Garcia, Graduate Admissions Counselor, 210-805-3554, Fax: 210-829-3921, E-mail: admis@uiwtx.edu.
Website: http://uiw.edu/snhp/

The University of Toledo, College of Graduate Studies, College of Nursing, Toledo, OH 43614. Offers MSN, DNP, Certificate. *Accreditation:* AACN. *Program availability:* Part-time, online learning. *Degree requirements:* For master's, thesis or scholarly project; for doctorate, thesis/dissertation or alternative, evidence-based project. *Entrance requirements:* For master's, GRE, BS in nursing, minimum undergraduate GPA of 3.0, statement of purpose, two letters of recommendation, transcripts from all prior institutions attended, resume, Nursing CAS application, UT supplemental application; for doctorate, minimum undergraduate GPA of 3.0, statement of purpose, three letters of recommendation, transcripts from all prior institutions attended, resume, Nursing CAS application, UT supplemental application. Additional exam requirements/recommendations for international students: Required—TOEFL (minimum score 550 paper-based; 80 iBT). Electronic applications accepted. *Expenses:* Contact institution. *Faculty research:* Sexuality issues, prenatal testing, health care of homeless, nursing education, chronic/acute pain, eating disorders, low birth weight infants.

University of Toronto, School of Graduate Studies, Department of Nursing Science, Toronto, ON M5S 1A1, Canada. Offers MN, PhD, MHSc/MN. *Program availability:* Part-time. *Degree requirements:* For doctorate, thesis/dissertation, departmental and final oral exam/thesis defense. *Entrance requirements:* For master's, B Sc N or equivalent, minimum B average in next-to-final year, resume, 3 letters of reference; for doctorate, minimum B+ average, master's degree in nursing or a related area, resume, 2 letters of recommendation. Additional exam requirements/recommendations for international students: Required—TOEFL (minimum score 580 paper-based; 93 iBT), TWE (minimum score 5). Electronic applications accepted. *Expenses:* Contact institution.

The University of Tulsa, Graduate School, Oxley College of Health Sciences, School of Nursing, Tulsa, OK 74104-3189. Offers adult-gerontology acute care nurse practitioner (DNP); family nurse practitioner (DNP). Summer enrollment only. *Faculty:* 18 full-time (16 women), 6 part-time/adjunct (5 women). *Students:* 27 full-time (23 women); includes 6 minority (1 Black or African American, non-Hispanic/Latino; 1 Asian, non-Hispanic/Latino; 3 Hispanic/Latino; 1 Two or more races, non-Hispanic/Latino). Average age 36. 42 applicants, 57% accepted, 21 enrolled. *Degree requirements:* For doctorate, comprehensive exam, thesis/dissertation. *Entrance requirements:* Additional exam requirements/recommendations for international students: Required—TOEFL (minimum score 550 paper-based; 91 iBT), IELTS (minimum score 6.5). Application fee: $55. Electronic applications accepted. *Expenses:* $1,040 per credit hour tuition. *Unit head:* Robin Ploeger, Interim Dean, 918-631-3170, E-mail: robin-ploeger@utulsa.edu. *Application contact:* Dr. Sheryl Stansifer, Department Chair, 918-631-3125, Fax: 918-631-2156, E-mail: sheryl-stansifer@utulsa.edu.
Website: https://healthsciences.utulsa.edu/departments-schools/nursing/nursing-graduate-programs/

University of Utah, Graduate School, College of Nursing, Program in Nursing, Salt Lake City, UT 84112. Offers MS, DNP, PhD. *Accreditation:* AACN. *Program availability:* Part-time, evening/weekend, online learning. *Faculty:* 92 full-time (82 women), 35 part-time/adjunct (30 women). *Students:* 294 full-time (226 women), 78 part-time (63 women); includes 64 minority (10 Black or African American, non-Hispanic/Latino; 1 American Indian or Alaska Native, non-Hispanic/Latino; 16 Asian, non-Hispanic/Latino; 21 Hispanic/Latino; 1 Native Hawaiian or other Pacific Islander, non-Hispanic/Latino; 15 Two or more races, non-Hispanic/Latino), 8 international. Average age 27. 262 applicants, 56% accepted, 122 enrolled. In 2017, 9 master's, 98 doctorates awarded. *Entrance requirements:* For master's, GRE General Test (if cumulative GPA less than 3.2), RN licensure in one of the jurisdictions of the National Council of State Boards of Nursing, goal statement, professional references; for doctorate, GRE General Test, interview, curriculum vitae/resume, goal statement, professional and academic references, writing sample. Additional exam requirements/recommendations for international students: Required—TOEFL (minimum score 500 paper-based; 85 iBT). Application fee: $55 ($65 for international students). Electronic applications accepted. *Expenses:* Contact institution. *Financial support:* Fellowships, research assistantships, teaching assistantships, scholarships/grants, traineeships, health care benefits, and unspecified assistantships available. Support available to part-time students. Financial award application deadline: 1/15; financial award applicants required to submit FAFSA. *Faculty research:* Symptom management, patient-provider communication, patient safety/informatics, gerontology/geriatric nursing, end-of-life bereavement. *Total annual research expenditures:* $2.2 million. *Unit head:* Patricia Morton, PhD, Dean, 801-581-8262, Fax: 801-581-4642, E-mail: patricia.morton@nurs.utah.edu. *Application contact:* Carrie Radmall, Program Administrator, 801-581-8798, Fax: 801-585-3414, E-mail: carrie.radmall@nurs.utah.edu.
Website: http://www.nursing.utah.edu/

University of Vermont, Graduate College, College of Nursing and Health Sciences, Department of Nursing, Burlington, VT 05405. Offers MS, DNP, Post-Graduate Certificate. *Accreditation:* AACN. *Students:* 87 full-time (75 women); includes 6 minority (1 Asian, non-Hispanic/Latino; 3 Hispanic/Latino; 2 Two or more races, non-Hispanic/Latino), 1 international. 96 applicants, 51% accepted, 24 enrolled. In 2017, 19 master's, 2 doctorates awarded. *Entrance requirements:* For master's, GRE General Test; for doctorate, GRE. Additional exam requirements/recommendations for international students: Required—TOEFL (minimum iBT score of 90) or IELTS (6.5). *Application deadline:* For fall admission, 4/3 for domestic and international students. Application fee: $65. Electronic applications accepted. *Expenses:* $646 per credit in-state, $1,100 per credit out-of-state. *Financial support:* Scholarships/grants available. Financial award application deadline: 3/1. *Unit head:* Dr. Carol Buck-Rolland, Graduate Program Director, 802-656-3381, E-mail: carol.buck-rolland@med.uvm.edu. *Application contact:* Kristen Cella, Admissions Specialist, 802-656-3858, E-mail: cnhsgrad@uvm.edu.
Website: https://www.uvm.edu/cnhs/nursing

University of Victoria, Faculty of Graduate Studies, Faculty of Human and Social Development, School of Nursing, Victoria, BC V8W 2Y2, Canada. Offers advanced nursing practice (advanced practice leadership option) (MN); advanced nursing practice (nurse educator option) (MN); advanced nursing practice (nurse practitioner option) (MN); nursing (PhD). *Program availability:* Part-time, online learning. *Entrance requirements:* Additional exam requirements/recommendations for international students: Required—TOEFL (minimum score 575 paper-based), IELTS (minimum score 7). Electronic applications accepted.

University of Virginia, School of Nursing, Charlottesville, VA 22903. Offers acute and specialty care (MSN); acute care nurse practitioner (MSN); clinical nurse leadership (MSN); community-public health leadership (MSN); nursing (DNP, PhD); psychiatric mental health counseling (MSN); MSN/MBA. *Accreditation:* AACN. *Program availability:* Part-time. *Faculty:* 51 full-time (44 women), 17 part-time/adjunct (16 women). *Students:* 202 full-time (168 women), 139 part-time (114 women); includes 78 minority (32 Black or African American, non-Hispanic/Latino; 2 American Indian or Alaska Native, non-Hispanic/Latino; 14 Asian, non-Hispanic/Latino; 17 Hispanic/Latino; 1 Native Hawaiian or other Pacific Islander, non-Hispanic/Latino; 12 Two or more races, non-Hispanic/Latino), 9 international. Average age 34. 183 applicants, 68% accepted, 98 enrolled. In 2017, 105 master's, 27 doctorates awarded. *Degree requirements:* For doctorate, comprehensive exam (for some programs), capstone project (DNP), dissertation (PhD). *Entrance requirements:* For master's, GRE General Test, MAT; for doctorate, GRE General Test. Additional exam requirements/recommendations for international students: Required—TOEFL, IELTS. *Application deadline:* Applications are processed on a rolling basis. Application fee: $60. Electronic applications accepted. *Financial support:* Fellowships, research assistantships, teaching assistantships, Federal Work-Study, and scholarships/grants available. Financial award applicants required to submit FAFSA. *Unit head:* Dorrie K. Fontaine, Dean, 434-924-0141, Fax: 434-982-1809, E-mail: dkf2u@virginia.edu. *Application contact:* Teresa Carroll, Senior Assistant Dean for Academic and Student Services, 434-924-0141, Fax: 434-982-1809, E-mail: nur-osa@virginia.edu.
Website: http://www.nursing.virginia.edu/

University of Washington, Graduate School, School of Nursing, Seattle, WA 98195. Offers MN, MS, DNP, PhD, Graduate Certificate, MN/MPH. *Accreditation:* AACN; ACNM/ACME (one or more programs are accredited). *Program availability:* Part-time. *Degree requirements:* For master's, thesis (for some programs); for doctorate, thesis/dissertation. *Entrance requirements:* For master's, GRE, minimum GPA of 3.0, resume; for doctorate, GRE, minimum GPA of 3.0. Additional exam requirements/recommendations for international students: Required—TOEFL. *Faculty research:* High risk youth, pain management, women's health, oncology, sleep.

University of Washington, Bothell, Program in Nursing, Bothell, WA 98011. Offers MN. *Program availability:* Part-time. *Degree requirements:* For master's, scholarly project. *Entrance requirements:* For master's, BSN (or other bachelor's degree with additional prerequisite work); current license as registered nurse in Washington state; minimum GPA of 3.0 in last 90 college credits, 2.0 in college statistics course. Additional exam requirements/recommendations for international students: Required—TOEFL (minimum score 580 paper-based). Electronic applications accepted. *Expenses:* Contact institution. *Faculty research:* Health of special populations, nursing education, higher education technology, healing through patient's narratives, women's health care issues, end of life issues in nursing.

University of Washington, Tacoma, Graduate Programs, Program in Nursing, Tacoma, WA 98402-3100. Offers communities, populations and health (MN); leadership in healthcare (MN); nurse educator (MN). *Program availability:* Part-time. *Degree requirements:* For master's, thesis (for some programs), advance fieldwork. *Entrance requirements:* For master's, Washington State NCLEX exam, minimum GPA of 3.0. Additional exam requirements/recommendations for international students: Required—TOEFL (minimum score 580 paper-based; 70 iBT); Recommended—IELTS (minimum score 7). *Faculty research:* Hospice and palliative care; clinical trial decision-making; minority nurse retention; asthma and public health; injustice, suffering, difference: Linking Them to Us; adolescent health.

Nursing—General

The University of Western Ontario, Faculty of Graduate Studies, Health Sciences Division, School of Nursing, London, ON N6A 5B8, Canada. Offers M Sc N, MN NP, PhD. *Program availability:* Part-time. *Degree requirements:* For master's, thesis; for doctorate, thesis/dissertation. *Entrance requirements:* Additional exam requirements/recommendations for international students: Required—TOEFL. *Faculty research:* Empowerment, self-efficacy, family health, community health, gerontology.

University of West Florida, Usha Kundu, MD College of Health, School of Nursing, Pensacola, FL 32514-5750. Offers MSN. *Accreditation:* AACN. *Program availability:* Part-time, evening/weekend. *Entrance requirements:* For master's, GRE or MAT, letter of intent; current curriculum vitae/resume. Additional exam requirements/recommendations for international students: Required—TOEFL (minimum score 550 paper-based).

University of West Georgia, Tanner Health System School of Nursing, Carrollton, GA 30118. Offers health systems leadership (Post-Master's Certificate); nursing (MSN); nursing education (Ed D, Post-Master's Certificate). *Accreditation:* AACN. *Program availability:* Part-time, evening/weekend, 100% online, blended/hybrid learning. *Faculty:* 13 full-time (all women). *Students:* 64 full-time (63 women), 78 part-time (74 women); includes 34 minority (27 Black or African American, non-Hispanic/Latino; 1 Asian, non-Hispanic/Latino; 5 Hispanic/Latino; 1 Two or more races, non-Hispanic/Latino). Average age 41. 92 applicants, 88% accepted, 61 enrolled. In 2017, 36 master's, 7 doctorates, 1 other advanced degree awarded. *Entrance requirements:* Additional exam requirements/recommendations for international students: Required—TOEFL (minimum score 523 paper-based; 69 iBT); Recommended—IELTS (minimum score 6.5). *Application deadline:* For fall admission, 2/1 priority date for domestic and international students. Applications are processed on a rolling basis. Application fee: $40. Electronic applications accepted. *Expenses:* Contact institution. *Financial support:* Fellowships, research assistantships, teaching assistantships, career-related internships or fieldwork, Federal Work-Study, institutionally sponsored loans, scholarships/grants, and unspecified assistantships available. Support available to part-time students. Financial award application deadline: 4/1; financial award applicants required to submit FAFSA. *Unit head:* Dr. Jennifer Schuessler, Dean of the School of Nursing, 678-839-5640, Fax: 678-839-6553, E-mail: jschuess@westga.edu. *Application contact:* Dr. Toby Ziglar, Assistant Dean of the Graduate School, 678-839-1390, Fax: 678-839-1395, E-mail: graduate@westga.edu. Website: https://www.westga.edu/nursing

University of Windsor, Faculty of Graduate Studies, Faculty of Nursing, Windsor, ON N9B 3P4, Canada. Offers M Sc, MN. *Degree requirements:* For master's, thesis or alternative. *Entrance requirements:* For master's, minimum B average, certificate of competence (nurse registration). Additional exam requirements/recommendations for international students: Required—TOEFL (minimum score 560 paper-based). Electronic applications accepted.

University of Wisconsin–Eau Claire, College of Nursing and Health Sciences, Program in Nursing, Eau Claire, WI 54702-4004. Offers adult-gerontological administration (DNP); adult-gerontological clinical nurse specialist (DNP); adult-gerontological education (MSN); adult-gerontological primary care nurse practitioner (DNP); family health administration (DNP); family health in education (MSN); family health nurse practitioner (DNP); nursing (MSN); nursing practice (DNP). *Accreditation:* AACN. *Program availability:* Part-time. Terminal master's awarded for partial completion of doctoral program. *Degree requirements:* For master's, thesis optional, 500-600 hours clinical practicum, oral and written exams. *Entrance requirements:* For master's, Wisconsin RN license, minimum GPA of 3.0, undergraduate statistics, course work in health assessment. Additional exam requirements/recommendations for international students: Required—TOEFL (minimum score 79 iBT). *Expenses:* Contact institution.

University of Wisconsin–Madison, School of Nursing, Madison, WI 53706-1380. Offers adult/gerontology (DNP); nursing (PhD); pediatrics (DNP); psychiatric mental health (DNP); MS/MPH. *Accreditation:* AACN. *Program availability:* Part-time. *Degree requirements:* For doctorate, comprehensive exam, thesis/dissertation. *Entrance requirements:* For doctorate, GRE General Test, 2 samples of scholarly written work, BS in nursing from an accredited program, minimum undergraduate GPA of 3.0 in last 60 credits (for PhD); licensure as professional nurse (for DNP). Additional exam requirements/recommendations for international students: Required—TOEFL (minimum score 600 paper-based; 100 iBT). Electronic applications accepted. *Faculty research:* Nursing informatics to promote self-care and disease management skills among patients and caregivers; quality of care to frail, vulnerable, and chronically ill populations; study of health-related and health-seeking behaviors; eliminating health disparities; pain and symptom management for patients with cancer.

University of Wisconsin–Milwaukee, Graduate School, College of Nursing, Milwaukee, WI 53201. Offers clinical nurse specialist (Graduate Certificate); family nurse practitioner (Graduate Certificate); nursing (MN, DNP, PhD); sustainable peacebuilding (MSP). *Accreditation:* AACN. *Program availability:* Part-time. *Students:* 181 full-time (153 women), 128 part-time (117 women); includes 73 minority (23 Black or African American, non-Hispanic/Latino; 1 American Indian or Alaska Native, non-Hispanic/Latino; 17 Asian, non-Hispanic/Latino; 3 Hispanic/Latino; 29 Two or more races, non-Hispanic/Latino), 11 international. Average age 36. 154 applicants, 59% accepted, 60 enrolled. In 2017, 26 master's, 54 doctorates, 2 other advanced degrees awarded. *Entrance requirements:* For master's, GRE General Test or MAT, autobiographical sketch; for doctorate, GRE, minimum GPA of 3.2. Additional exam requirements/recommendations for international students: Required—TOEFL (minimum score 550 paper-based; 79 iBT), IELTS (minimum score 6.5). *Application deadline:* For fall admission, 1/1 priority date for domestic students; for spring admission, 9/1 for domestic students. Application fee: $56 ($96 for international students). Electronic applications accepted. *Financial support:* Fellowships, research assistantships, teaching assistantships, career-related internships or fieldwork, Federal Work-Study, health care benefits, unspecified assistantships, and project assistantships available. Support available to part-time students. Financial award application deadline: 4/15; financial award applicants required to submit FAFSA. *Unit head:* Dr. Kim Litwack, Interim Dean, 414-229-4189, E-mail: litwack@uwm.edu. *Application contact:* Student Affairs Office, 414-229-5047, E-mail: uwmnurse@uwm.edu. Website: http://uwm.edu/nursing/

See Display below and Close-Up on page 769.

University of Wisconsin–Oshkosh, Graduate Studies, College of Nursing, Oshkosh, WI 54901. Offers adult health and illness (MSN); family nurse practitioner (MSN). *Accreditation:* AACN. *Program availability:* Part-time. *Degree requirements:* For master's, thesis or alternative, clinical paper. *Entrance requirements:* For master's, RN license, BSN, previous course work in statistics and health assessment, minimum undergraduate GPA of 3.0, letters of recommendation. Additional exam requirements/recommendations for international students: Required—TOEFL (minimum score 550 paper-based; 79 iBT). Electronic applications accepted. *Faculty research:* Adult health and illness, nurse practitioners practice, health care service, advanced practitioner roles, natural alternative complementary healthcare.

University of Wyoming, College of Health Sciences, Fay W. Whitney School of Nursing, Laramie, WY 82071. Offers MS. *Accreditation:* AACN. *Program availability:* Part-time, online learning. *Degree requirements:* For master's, thesis. *Entrance requirements:* For master's, GRE General Test, BSN from CCNE or NCN-accredited school, minimum GPA of 3.0. Additional exam requirements/recommendations for international students: Required—TOEFL. *Faculty research:* Support systems for the elderly, fetal alcohol syndrome, teen pregnancy, rehabilitation with chronic mental illness, global peace building among women.

Urbana University–A Branch Campus of Franklin University, College of Nursing and Allied Health, Urbana, OH 43078-2091. Offers nursing (MSN). *Accreditation:* AACN. *Entrance requirements:* For master's, baccalaureate degree in nursing with minimum cumulative undergraduate GPA of 3.0, official transcripts, Ohio RN license, background check, statement of goals and objectives, resume, 3 letters of recommendation, interview.

Ursuline College, School of Graduate and Professional Studies, Programs in Nursing, Pepper Pike, OH 44124-4398. Offers acute-care nurse practitioner (MSN); adult nurse practitioner (MSN); adult-gerontology acute care nurse practitioner (MSN); adult-gerontology clinical nurse specialist (MSN); adult-gerontology nurse practitioner (MSN); care management (MSN); clinical nurse specialist (MSN); family nurse practitioner (MSN); nursing (DNP); nursing education (MSN); palliative care (MSN). *Accreditation:* AACN. *Program availability:* Part-time. *Faculty:* 6 full-time (all women), 25 part-time/adjunct (23 women). *Students:* 136 applicants, 89% accepted, 85 enrolled. In 2017, 85 master's, 6 doctorates awarded. *Degree requirements:* For master's, comprehensive exam; for doctorate, thesis/dissertation. *Entrance requirements:* For master's, minimum undergraduate GPA of 3.0, bachelor's degree in nursing, eligibility for or current Ohio RN license. Additional exam requirements/recommendations for international students: Required—TOEFL (minimum score 500 paper-based). *Application deadline:* For fall admission, 8/1 priority date for domestic students. Applications are processed on a rolling basis. Application fee: $25. Electronic applications accepted. *Expenses:* $1,094 per credit hour. *Financial support:* In 2017–18, 6 students received support. Scholarships/grants available. Financial award application deadline: 3/1; financial award applicants required to submit FAFSA. *Faculty research:* Core Determinants of Health (CDH) screening tool and accompanying education, academic-practice partnerships, active learning/teaching strategies, innovative clinical education models, competency development and testing, health care policy and clinical competence. *Total annual research expenditures:* $864,511. *Unit head:* Dr. Janet Baker, Associate Dean of Graduate Nursing, 440-864-8172, Fax: 440-684-6053, E-mail: jbaker@ursuline.edu. *Application contact:* Melanie Steele, Director, Graduate Admission, 440-646-8119, Fax: 440-684-6138, E-mail: graduateadmissions@ursuline.edu.

Utah Valley University, Program in Nursing, Orem, UT 84058-5999. Offers MSN. *Accreditation:* ACEN. *Program availability:* Part-time, online learning. Terminal master's awarded for partial completion of doctoral program. *Degree requirements:* For master's, project or thesis. *Entrance requirements:* For master's, GRE, baccalaureate degree in nursing, nurse licensure, undergraduate course in statistics, minimum undergraduate GPA of 3.2 overall or in last 60 semester hours of coursework, 3 letters of recommendation. Additional exam requirements/recommendations for international students: Required—TOEFL (minimum score 83 iBT). Electronic applications accepted. *Expenses:* Contact institution.

Valdosta State University, College of Nursing and Health Sciences, Valdosta, GA 31698. Offers adult gerontology nurse practitioner (MSN); exercise physiology (MS); family nurse practitioner (MSN); family psychiatric mental health nurse practitioner (MSN). *Accreditation:* AACN. *Program availability:* Part-time, online learning. *Degree requirements:* For master's, thesis (for some programs), comprehensive written and/or oral exams. *Entrance requirements:* For master's, minimum GPA of 2.8. Additional exam requirements/recommendations for international students: Required—TOEFL (minimum score 523 paper-based). *Application deadline:* For fall admission, 7/1 for domestic and international students; for spring admission, 11/15 for domestic and international students. Applications are processed on a rolling basis. Application fee: $45. Electronic applications accepted. *Financial support:* Research assistantships with full tuition reimbursements, institutionally sponsored loans, scholarships/grants, and unspecified assistantships available. Support available to part-time students. Financial award application deadline: 7/1; financial award applicants required to submit FAFSA. *Faculty research:* Nutrition, children's health beliefs, alternative treatment modalities, job satisfaction, leadership. *Unit head:* Sheri Noviello, Dean, 229-333-5959, E-mail: srnoviello@valdosta.edu. *Application contact:* Sheri Noviello, Dean, 229-333-5959, E-mail: srnoviello@valdosta.edu.
Website: https://www.valdosta.edu/colleges/nursing-and-health-sciences/

Valparaiso University, Graduate School and Continuing Education, College of Nursing and Health Professions, Valparaiso, IN 46383. Offers nursing (DNP); nursing education (MSN, Certificate); physician assistant (MSPA); public health (MPH); MSN/MHA. *Accreditation:* AACN. *Program availability:* Part-time, evening/weekend, online learning. *Entrance requirements:* For master's, minimum GPA of 3.0, undergraduate major in nursing, Indiana registered nursing license, undergraduate courses in research and statistics. Additional exam requirements/recommendations for international students: Required—TOEFL (minimum score 550 paper-based; 80 iBT), IELTS (minimum score 6). Electronic applications accepted. *Expenses:* Contact institution.

Vanderbilt University, Program in Nursing Science, Nashville, TN 37240-1001. Offers PhD. *Faculty:* 23 full-time (20 women), 4 part-time/adjunct (2 women). *Students:* 24 full-time (20 women), 4 part-time (2 women); includes 7 minority (1 Black or African American, non-Hispanic/Latino; 3 Hispanic/Latino; 1 Native Hawaiian or other Pacific Islander, non-Hispanic/Latino; 2 Two or more races, non-Hispanic/Latino). Average age 36. 41 applicants, 20% accepted, 7 enrolled. In 2017, 4 doctorates awarded. *Degree requirements:* For doctorate, comprehensive exam, thesis/dissertation, final and qualifying exams. *Entrance requirements:* For doctorate, GRE General Test. Additional exam requirements/recommendations for international students: Required—TOEFL (minimum score 570 paper-based; 88 iBT). *Application deadline:* For fall admission, 1/15 for domestic and international students. Electronic applications accepted. *Financial support:* Fellowships with full tuition reimbursements, research assistantships with full tuition reimbursements, teaching assistantships with full tuition reimbursements, career-related internships or fieldwork, Federal Work-Study, institutionally sponsored loans, scholarships/grants, health care benefits, and tuition waivers (full and partial) available. Financial award application deadline: 1/15; financial award applicants required to submit CSS PROFILE or FAFSA. *Faculty research:* Adaptation to chronic illness/conditions, health problems related to stress and coping, vulnerable childbearing and child rearing families. *Unit head:* Sheila Ridner, Director of Graduate Studies, 615-322-3800, Fax: 615-343-5898, E-mail: sheila.ridner@vanderbilt.edu. *Application contact:* Judy Vesterfelt, Program Manager, 615-322-7410, E-mail: judy.vesterfelt@vanderbilt.edu.
Website: http://www.nursing.vanderbilt.edu/

Vanderbilt University, Vanderbilt University School of Nursing, Nashville, TN 37240. Offers adult-gerontology acute care nurse practitioner (MSN), including hospitalist, intensivist; adult-gerontology primary care nurse practitioner (MSN); emergency nurse practitioner (MSN); family nurse practitioner (MSN); healthcare leadership (MSN); neonatal nurse practitioner (MSN); nurse midwifery (MSN); nurse midwifery/family nurse practitioner (MSN); nursing (Post-Master's Certificate); nursing informatics (MSN); nursing practice (DNP); nursing science (PhD); pediatric acute care nurse practitioner (MSN); pediatric primary care nurse practitioner (MSN); psychiatric-mental health nurse practitioner (MSN); women's health nurse practitioner (MSN); women's health nurse practitioner/adult gerontology primary care nurse practitioner (MSN); MSN/M Div; MSN/MTS. *Accreditation:* AACN; ACEN (one or more programs are accredited); ACNM/ACME. *Program availability:* Part-time, 100% online, blended/hybrid learning. *Faculty:* 292 full-time (267 women), 321 part-time/adjunct (253 women). *Students:* 501 full-time (435 women), 387 part-time (355 women); includes 153 minority (40 Black or African American, non-Hispanic/Latino; 1 American Indian or Alaska Native, non-Hispanic/Latino; 27 Asian, non-Hispanic/Latino; 48 Hispanic/Latino; 4 Native Hawaiian or other Pacific Islander, non-Hispanic/Latino; 33 Two or more races, non-Hispanic/Latino), 9 international. Average age 31. 1,210 applicants, 57% accepted, 473 enrolled. In 2017, 319 master's, 47 doctorates awarded. *Degree requirements:* For doctorate, comprehensive exam, thesis/dissertation. *Entrance requirements:* For master's, GRE General Test (taken within the past 5 years), minimum B average in undergraduate course work, 3 letters of recommendation; for doctorate, GRE General Test, interview, 3 letters of recommendation from doctorally-prepared faculty, MSN, essay. Additional exam requirements/recommendations for international students: Required—TOEFL (minimum score 570 paper-based), IELTS (minimum score 6.5). *Application deadline:* For fall admission, 11/1 priority date for domestic and international students. Applications are processed on a rolling basis. Application fee: $50. Electronic applications accepted. *Expenses:* Contact institution. *Financial support:* In 2017–18, 627 students received support. Scholarships/grants available. Financial award application deadline: 3/1; financial award applicants required to submit FAFSA. *Faculty research:* Lymphedema, palliative care and bereavement, health services research including workforce, safety and quality of care, gerontology, better birth outcomes including nutrition. *Total annual research expenditures:* $2 million. *Unit head:* Dr. Linda Norman, Dean, 615-343-8876, Fax: 615-343-7711, E-mail: linda.norman@vanderbilt.edu. *Application contact:* Patricia Peerman, Assistant Dean for Enrollment Management, 615-322-3800, Fax: 615-343-0333, E-mail: vusn-admissions@vanderbilt.edu.
Website: http://www.nursing.vanderbilt.edu

Vanguard University of Southern California, Graduate Program in Nursing, Costa Mesa, CA 92626. Offers MSN. *Accreditation:* AACN. *Program availability:* Part-time, evening/weekend, blended/hybrid learning. *Degree requirements:* For master's, thesis, two 55-hour practicums. *Entrance requirements:* For master's, free and clear RN license in California. *Application deadline:* For fall admission, 3/1 priority date for domestic students; for spring admission, 10/1 priority date for domestic students. Application fee: $45. *Expenses:* Contact institution. *Financial support:* Federal Work-Study available. *Unit head:* Director, 714-668-6101, Fax: 714-966-6306. *Application contact:* Karen Benitez, Director of Admissions, 714-966-5499, Fax: 714-966-5471, E-mail: karen.benitez@vanguard.edu.
Website: https://www.vanguard.edu/academics/academic-programs/nursing

Villanova University, M. Louise Fitzpatrick College of Nursing, Villanova, PA 19085. Offers adult-gerontology primary care nurse practitioner (MSN, Post Master's Certificate); family primary care nurse practitioner (MSN, Post Master's Certificate); nurse anesthesia (DNP); nursing (PhD); nursing education (MSN, Post Master's Certificate); nursing practice (DNP); pediatric primary care nurse practitioner (MSN, Post Master's Certificate). *Accreditation:* AACN; AANA/CANAEP. *Program availability:* Part-time, online learning. *Students:* 151 full-time, 199 part-time; includes 42 minority (18 Black or African American, non-Hispanic/Latino; 12 Asian, non-Hispanic/Latino; 8 Hispanic/Latino; 4 Two or more races, non-Hispanic/Latino), 10 international. 274 applicants, 43% accepted, 92 enrolled. In 2017, 70 master's, 15 doctorates awarded. *Entrance requirements:* Additional exam requirements/recommendations for international students: Required—TOEFL, IELTS. *Application deadline:* For fall admission, 7/1 for domestic and international students; for spring admission, 10/1 for domestic and international students; for summer admission, 4/1 for domestic and international students. Application fee: $50. Electronic applications accepted. *Financial support:* Fellowships, research assistantships, teaching assistantships, scholarships/grants, traineeships, and tuition waivers available. *Unit head:* Dr. Marguerite K. Schlag, Associate Professor, Assistant Dean and Director of Graduate Nursing Program, 610-519-4907, Fax: 610-519-7650, E-mail: marguerite.schlag@villanova.edu. *Application contact:* Kathleen Geibel, Assistant to Graduate Program, 610-519-4934, Fax: 610-519-7650, E-mail: kathleen.geibel@villanova.edu.
Website: http://www.nursing.villanova.edu

Virginia Commonwealth University, Graduate School, School of Nursing, Richmond, VA 23284-9005. Offers adult health acute nursing (MS); adult health primary nursing (MS); biobehavioral clinical research (PhD); child health nursing (MS); clinical nurse leader (MS); family health nursing (MS); nurse educator (MS); nurse practitioner (MS); nursing (Certificate); nursing administration (MS), including clinical nurse manager; psychiatric-mental health nursing (MS); quality and safety in health care (DNP); women's health nursing (MS). *Accreditation:* AACN; ACEN (one or more programs are accredited). *Program availability:* Part-time, evening/weekend, online learning. *Degree requirements:* For master's, thesis optional; for doctorate, thesis/dissertation. *Entrance requirements:* For master's, GRE General Test, BSN, minimum GPA of 2.8; for doctorate, GRE General Test. Additional exam requirements/recommendations for international students: Required—TOEFL (minimum score 600 paper-based; 100 iBT). Electronic applications accepted.

Viterbo University, Graduate Program in Nursing, La Crosse, WI 54601-4797. Offers DNP. *Accreditation:* AACN. *Program availability:* Part-time. *Degree requirements:* For doctorate, project. *Entrance requirements:* For doctorate, GRE General Test or MAT, bachelor's degree in nursing, minimum GPA of 3.0, RN license, one year of practice as an RN prior to beginning classes. Electronic applications accepted. *Expenses:* Contact institution. *Faculty research:* Mild cognitive impairment, education pedagogy.

Wagner College, Division of Graduate Studies, Evelyn L. Spiro School of Nursing, Staten Island, NY 10301-4495. Offers family nurse practitioner (MS, Certificate); nurse educator (MS); nursing (DNP). *Accreditation:* ACEN (one or more programs are accredited). *Program availability:* Part-time, evening/weekend. *Faculty:* 6 full-time (all women), 6 part-time/adjunct (5 women). *Students:* 15 full-time (13 women), 223 part-time (197 women); includes 75 minority (20 Black or African American, non-Hispanic/Latino; 29 Asian, non-Hispanic/Latino; 21 Hispanic/Latino; 5 Two or more races, non-Hispanic/Latino). Average age 35. 126 applicants, 75% accepted, 69 enrolled. In 2017, 52 master's, 11 doctorates, 2 other advanced degrees awarded. *Degree requirements:* For master's, thesis optional. *Entrance requirements:* For master's, BS in nursing, current clinical experience, minimum GPA of 3.3; for Certificate, master's degree in nursing from an NLN-accredited program, minimum GPA of 3.0. Additional exam requirements/recommendations for international students: Required—TOEFL (minimum score 550 paper-based; 79 iBT), IELTS (minimum score 6.5). *Application deadline:* For fall admission, 2/1 priority date for domestic students, 2/1 for international students. Application fee: $60. Electronic applications accepted. *Financial support:* In 2017–18, 62 students received support. Traineeships, unspecified assistantships, and alumni fellowship grants available. Financial award application deadline: 2/15; financial award applicants required to submit FAFSA. *Unit head:* Dr. Patricia Tooker, Dean, 718-390-3452, Fax: 718-420-4009, E-mail: ptooker@wagner.edu. *Application contact:* Patricia Clancy, Assistant Director, 718-420-4464, Fax: 718-390-3105, E-mail: patricia.clancy@wagner.edu.
Website: http://wagner.edu/nursing/

Walden University, Graduate Programs, School of Nursing, Minneapolis, MN 55401. Offers adult-gerontology acute care nurse practitioner (MSN); adult-gerontology nurse practitioner (MSN); education (MSN); family nurse practitioner (MSN); informatics (MSN); leadership and management (MSN); nursing (PhD, Post-Master's Certificate), including education (PhD), healthcare administration (PhD), interdisciplinary health (PhD), leadership (PhD), nursing education (Post-Master's Certificate), nursing informatics (Post-Master's Certificate), nursing leadership and management (Post-Master's Certificate), public health policy (PhD); nursing practice (DNP); psychiatric mental health (MSN). *Accreditation:* AACN. *Program availability:* Part-time, evening/weekend, online only, 100% online. *Degree requirements:* For doctorate, thesis/dissertation (for some programs), residency (for some programs), field experience (for some programs). *Entrance requirements:* For master's, bachelor's degree or equivalent in related field or RN; minimum GPA of 2.5; official transcripts; goal statement (for some programs); access to computer and Internet; for doctorate, master's degree or higher; RN; three years of related professional or academic experience; goal statement; access to computer and Internet; for Post-Master's Certificate, relevant work experience; access to computer and Internet. Additional exam requirements/recommendations for international students: Required—TOEFL (minimum score 550 paper-based, 79 iBT), IELTS (minimum score 6.5), Michigan English Language Assessment Battery (minimum score 82), or PTE (minimum score 53). Electronic applications accepted.

Walsh University, Graduate Programs, Gary and Linda Byers School of Nursing, North Canton, OH 44720-3396. Offers academic nurse educator (MSN); adult acute care nurse practitioner (MSN); clinical nurse leader (MSN); nursing practice (DNP). *Accreditation:* AACN. *Program availability:* Part-time, evening/weekend, online only, 100% online. *Degree requirements:* For doctorate, scholarly project; residency practicum. *Entrance requirements:* For master's, undergraduate nursing degree, current unencumbered RN license, completion of an undergraduate or graduate statistics course, essay, interview, recommendations; for doctorate, BSN; master's degree; statistics and research courses; essay; interview. Additional exam requirements/recommendations for international students: Required—TOEFL. Electronic applications accepted. *Expenses:* Contact institution. *Faculty research:* Self-efficacy, Newman theory, curriculum development and assessment on family nurse practitioner (FNP) practice, DNP online rubrics.

Washburn University, School of Nursing, Topeka, KS 66621. Offers clinical nurse leader (MSN); nursing (DNP); psychiatric mental health nurse practitioner (Post-Graduate Certificate). *Accreditation:* AACN. *Program availability:* Part-time. *Entrance requirements:* Additional exam requirements/recommendations for international students: Required—TOEFL (minimum score 550 paper-based).

Washington Adventist University, Program in Nursing - Business Leadership, Takoma Park, MD 20912. Offers MSN. *Program availability:* Part-time. *Students:* 5 full-time (1 woman), 3 part-time (all women); includes 4 minority (all Black or African American, non-Hispanic/Latino), 3 international. Average age 44. In 2017, 6 master's awarded. *Entrance requirements:* Additional exam requirements/recommendations for international students: Required—TOEFL (minimum score 550 paper-based), IELTS (minimum score 5). *Application deadline:* Applications are processed on a rolling basis. *Expenses: Tuition:* Part-time $625 per credit. *Financial support:* Applicants required to submit FAFSA. *Unit head:* Dr. Patrick Williams, Associate Provost, 301-891-4092, E-mail: jeedward@wau.edu. *Application contact:* Jessica Ritchie, Program Coordinator, 301-891-4086, Fax: 301-891-4023, E-mail: jritchie@wau.edu.
Website: http://www.wau.edu/index.php?option-com_content&view-article&id-408temid-965

Washington State University, College of Nursing, Spokane, WA 99210. Offers advanced population health (MN, DNP); family nurse practitioner (MN, DNP); nursing (PhD); psychiatric/mental health nurse practitioner (DNP); psychiatric/mental health practitioner (MN). Programs offered at the Spokane, Tri-Cities, and Vancouver campuses. *Accreditation:* AACN. *Degree requirements:* For master's, comprehensive exam (for some programs), thesis (for some programs), oral exam, research project. *Entrance requirements:* For master's, minimum GPA of 3.0, Washington state RN license, physical assessment skills, course work in statistics, recommendations, written interview (for nurse practitioner). *Faculty research:* Cardiovascular and Type 2 diabetes in children, evaluation of strategies to increase physical activity in sedentary people.

Waynesburg University, Graduate and Professional Studies, Canonsburg, PA 15370. Offers business (MBA), including energy management, finance, health systems, human resources, leadership, market development; counseling (MA), including addictions counseling, clinical mental health; counselor education and supervision (PhD); criminal investigation (MA); education (M Ed), including autism, curriculum and instruction, educational leadership, online teaching; nursing (MSN), including administration, education, informatics; nursing practice (DNP); special education (M Ed); technology (M Ed); MSN/MBA. *Accreditation:* AACN. *Program availability:* Part-time, evening/weekend. *Degree requirements:* For doctorate, thesis/dissertation. *Entrance requirements:* Additional exam requirements/recommendations for international students: Required—TOEFL. Electronic applications accepted.

Wayne State University, College of Nursing, Detroit, MI 48202. Offers adult gerontology acute care nurse practitioner (MSN); adult gerontology primary care nurse practitioner (MSN); advanced public health nursing (MSN); infant and mental health (DNP, PhD); neonatal nurse practitioner (MSN); nurse-midwifery (MSN); pediatric acute care nurse practitioner (MSN); pediatric primary care nurse practitioner (MSN); psychiatric mental health nurse practitioner (MSN); women's health nurse practitioner (MSN). Doctoral program admits for fall only. *Accreditation:* AACN. *Program availability:* Part-time. *Faculty:* 30. *Students:* 133 full-time (120 women), 184 part-time (167 women); includes 85 minority (57 Black or African American, non-Hispanic/Latino; 16 Asian, non-Hispanic/Latino; 4 Hispanic/Latino; 8 Two or more races, non-Hispanic/Latino), 22 international. Average age 34. 318 applicants, 39% accepted, 94 enrolled. In 2017, 51 master's, 29 doctorates awarded. *Degree requirements:* For doctorate, thesis/dissertation (for some programs). *Entrance requirements:* For master's, BSN from ACEN- or CCNE-accredited program with minimum GPA of 3.0; three references; current RN license; personal statement; for doctorate, resume or curriculum vitae; goals statement; bachelor's or master's degree in nursing from ACEN- or CCNE-accredited program with minimum GPA of 3.0; current RN license, writing sample and interview (for DNP); reference letters (3 for PhD, 2 for DNP). Additional exam requirements/recommendations for international students: Required—TOEFL (minimum score 101 iBT), TWE (minimum score 6), Michigan English Language Assessment Battery (minimum score 85); Recommended—IELTS (minimum score 7). Application fee: $50. Electronic applications accepted. *Expenses:* Contact institution. *Financial support:* In 2017–18, 92 students received support, including 16 fellowships with tuition reimbursements available (averaging $8,285 per year), 5 teaching assistantships with tuition reimbursements available (averaging $25,000 per year); scholarships/grants, health care benefits, and unspecified assistantships also available. Support available to part-time students. Financial award applicants required to submit FAFSA. *Faculty research:* Bridging transitions and technology to promote asthma care in the community, chronic wound care for persons who injected drugs, decreasing at-risk parenting to reduce child maltreatment and trauma, dementia symptoms (cognition, behavior, function), determining readiness to engage in end of life/palliative care conversations with adolescents and young adults living with advanced cancer, dyspnea assessment and treatment at the end of life. *Unit head:* Dr. Laurie Lauzon Clabo, Dean, College of Nursing, 313-577-4082, E-mail: laurie.lauzon.clabo@wayne.edu. *Application contact:* 313-577-4082, Fax: 313-577-6949, E-mail: nursinginfo@wayne.edu.
Website: http://nursing.wayne.edu/

Weber State University, Dumke College of Health Professions, School of Nursing, Ogden, UT 84408-1001. Offers educator (MSN); executive (MSN); nurse practitioner (MSN). *Program availability:* Part-time, evening/weekend, 100% online. *Faculty:* 11 full-time (all women), 3 part-time/adjunct (all women). *Students:* 88 full-time (70 women), 5 part-time (all women); includes 2 minority (both Hispanic/Latino), 1 international. Average age 38. In 2017, 29 master's awarded. *Entrance requirements:* For master's, bachelor's degree in nursing from ACEN- or CCNE-accredited program. *Application deadline:* For fall admission, 4/1 priority date for domestic students. Application fee: $60 ($90 for international students). Electronic applications accepted. *Expenses:* Tuition, state resident: full-time $7283. Tuition, nonresident: full-time $17,166. *Required fees:* $898. Tuition and fees vary according to program. *Financial support:* In 2017–18, 26 students received support. Scholarships/grants available. Financial award application deadline: 4/1; financial award applicants required to submit FAFSA. *Unit head:* Dr. Melissa Neville, MSN Program Director, 801-626-6204, Fax: 801-626-6397, E-mail: mneville@weber.edu. *Application contact:* Robert Holt, Director of Enrollment, 801-626-7774, Fax: 801-626-6397, E-mail: rholt@weber.edu.
Website: http://www.weber.edu/nursing

Webster University, College of Arts and Sciences, Department of Nursing, St. Louis, MO 63119-3194. Offers nurse educator (MSN). *Accreditation:* ACEN. *Degree requirements:* For master's, comprehensive exam. *Entrance requirements:* For master's, 1 year of clinical experience, BSN, interview, minimum C+ average in statistics and physical assessment, minimum GPA of 3.0, RN license. Additional exam requirements/recommendations for international students: Required—TOEFL. *Faculty research:* Health teaching.

Wesley College, Nursing Program, Dover, DE 19901-3875. Offers MSN. *Accreditation:* ACEN. *Program availability:* Part-time, evening/weekend. *Degree requirements:* For master's, thesis optional, portfolio. *Entrance requirements:* For master's, GRE or MAT. Electronic applications accepted. *Faculty research:* Childhood obesity, organizational behavior, health promotion and wellness.

West Chester University of Pennsylvania, College of Health Sciences, Department of Nursing, West Chester, PA 19383. Offers adult-gerontology clinical nurse specialist (MSN); nursing (DNP); nursing education (MSN); school nurse (Certificate). *Accreditation:* AACN. *Program availability:* Part-time, evening/weekend, 2-day on-campus residency requirement (for DNP). *Students:* 1 full-time (0 women), 102 part-time (94 women); includes 16 minority (12 Black or African American, non-Hispanic/Latino; 1 Asian, non-Hispanic/Latino; 2 Hispanic/Latino; 1 Two or more races, non-Hispanic/Latino). Average age 42. 57 applicants, 82% accepted, 38 enrolled. In 2017, 1 master's, 21 doctorates, 9 other advanced degrees awarded. *Entrance requirements:* For master's, goals statement; official academic transcript(s) from all colleges and universities attended, demonstrating minimum cumulative undergraduate GPA of 2.8, with successful completion of BSN and courses in statistics and physical assessment; documentation of current clinical experience and current RN; for doctorate, master's degree in nursing in an advanced nursing specialty, minimum master's GPA of 3.0, licensed Registered Nurse in state of practice, prerequisite graduate-level research course and statistics course, two letters of reference, telephone or in-person interview with program coordinator. Additional exam requirements/recommendations for international students: Required—TOEFL or IELTS. *Application deadline:* For fall admission, 5/15 for international students; for spring admission, 10/15 for international students. Applications are processed on a rolling basis. Application fee: $50. Electronic applications accepted. *Expenses:* Tuition, state resident: full-time $9000; part-time $500 per credit. Tuition, nonresident: full-time $13,500; part-time $750 per credit. *Required fees:* $2959; $149.79 per credit. *Financial support:* Scholarships/grants and unspecified assistantships available. Financial award application deadline: 2/15; financial award applicants required to submit FAFSA. *Unit head:* Dr. Megan Infanti Mraz, Chair, 610-436-2219, Fax: 610-436-3083, E-mail: mmraz@wcupa.edu. *Application contact:* Dr. Cheryl Schlamb, Graduate Coordinator, 610-436-2219, E-mail: cschlamb@wcupa.edu.
Website: http://www.wcupa.edu/healthsciences/nursing/

West Coast University, Graduate Programs, North Hollywood, CA 91606. Offers advanced generalist (MSN); family nurse practitioner (MSN); health administration (MHA); occupational therapy (MS); pharmacy (Pharm D); physical therapy (DPT).

Western Carolina University, Graduate School, College of Health and Human Sciences, School of Nursing, Cullowhee, NC 28723. Offers MS, DNP, Post-Master's Certificate, Postbaccalaureate Certificate. *Accreditation:* AACN; AANA/CANAEP. *Program availability:* Part-time, evening/weekend. *Degree requirements:* For master's, comprehensive exam, thesis or alternative. *Entrance requirements:* For master's, GRE General Test, BSN with minimum GPA of 3.0, 3 references, 1 year of clinical experience. Additional exam requirements/recommendations for international students: Required—TOEFL (minimum score 550 paper-based; 79 iBT). *Expenses:* Tuition, state resident: full-time $4436. Tuition, nonresident: full-time $14,842. *Required fees:* $2926.

Western Connecticut State University, Division of Graduate Studies, School of Professional Studies, Nursing Department, Danbury, CT 06810-6885. Offers adult gerontology clinical nurse specialist (MSN); adult gerontology nurse practitioner (MSN); nursing education (Ed D). *Accreditation:* AACN. *Program availability:* Part-time. *Degree requirements:* For master's, clinical component, thesis or research project, completion of program in 6 years. *Entrance requirements:* For master's, MAT (if GPA less than 3.0), bachelor's degree in nursing, minimum GPA of 3.0, previous course work in statistics and nursing research, RN license. Additional exam requirements/recommendations for international students: Recommended—TOEFL (minimum score 550 paper-based; 79 iBT), IELTS (minimum score 6). *Expenses:* Contact institution. *Faculty research:* Evaluating effectiveness of Reiki and acupressure on stress reduction.

Western Kentucky University, Graduate Studies, College of Health and Human Services, School of Nursing, Bowling Green, KY 42101. Offers MSN. *Accreditation:* AACN. *Program availability:* Part-time, evening/weekend. *Degree requirements:* For master's, comprehensive exam, thesis optional. *Entrance requirements:* For master's, GRE General Test, minimum GPA of 2.75. Additional exam requirements/recommendations for international students: Required—TOEFL (minimum score 555 paper-based; 79 iBT). *Faculty research:* Folic acid, disease and injury prevention, rural mobile health, mental health issues.

Western Michigan University, Graduate College, College of Health and Human Services, Bronson School of Nursing, Kalamazoo, MI 49008. Offers MSN. *Accreditation:* AACN.

Western University of Health Sciences, College of Graduate Nursing, Doctor of Nursing Practice Program, Pomona, CA 91766-1854. Offers DNP. *Accreditation:* AACN. *Program availability:* Part-time, blended/hybrid learning. *Faculty:* 5 full-time (4 women), 3 part-time/adjunct (2 women). *Students:* 16 full-time (13 women), 20 part-time (19 women); includes 21 minority (4 Black or African American, non-Hispanic/Latino; 11 Asian, non-Hispanic/Latino; 5 Hispanic/Latino; 1 Two or more races, non-Hispanic/Latino). Average age 50. 16 applicants, 81% accepted, 13 enrolled. In 2017, 10 doctorates awarded. *Degree requirements:* For doctorate, thesis/dissertation, dissertation project. *Entrance requirements:* For doctorate, MSN from ACEN- or CCNE-accredited program, personal statement, curriculum vitae, 3 reference forms, official transcripts of all schools attended, example of scholarly writing. Additional exam

requirements/recommendations for international students: Required—TOEFL (minimum score 80 iBT). *Application deadline:* For fall admission, 3/1 for domestic and international students. Application fee: $60. Electronic applications accepted. Application fee is waived when completed online. *Expenses:* $1,075 per unit. *Financial support:* In 2017–18, 2 students received support. Fellowships, research assistantships, and scholarships/grants available. Support available to part-time students. Financial award application deadline: 3/2; financial award applicants required to submit FAFSA. *Unit head:* Dr. Mary Lopez, Dean, 909-706-3860, Fax: 909-469-5521, E-mail: mlopez@westernu.edu. *Application contact:* Kathryn Ford, Director of Admissions/International Student Advisor, 909-469-5335, Fax: 909-469-5570, E-mail: admissions@westernu.edu.
Website: http://www.westernu.edu/nursing-dnp

Western University of Health Sciences, College of Graduate Nursing, Master of Science in Nursing Program, Pomona, CA 91766-1854. Offers administrative nurse leader (MSN); clinical nurse leader (MSN); nursing (MSN). *Accreditation:* AACN. *Program availability:* Part-time, blended/hybrid learning. *Faculty:* 15 full-time (13 women), 20 part-time/adjunct (13 women). *Students:* 220 full-time (181 women), 15 part-time (all women); includes 164 minority (5 Black or African American, non-Hispanic/Latino; 1 American Indian or Alaska Native, non-Hispanic/Latino; 67 Asian, non-Hispanic/Latino; 64 Hispanic/Latino; 1 Native Hawaiian or other Pacific Islander, non-Hispanic/Latino; 26 Two or more races, non-Hispanic/Latino), 2 international. Average age 30. 454 applicants, 41% accepted, 129 enrolled. In 2017, 87 master's awarded. *Degree requirements:* For master's, comprehensive exam (for some programs), thesis (for some programs), project. *Entrance requirements:* For master's, personal statement, BSN, minimum GPA of 3.0, 3 letters of recommendation, resume/curriculum vitae, official transcripts of all schools attended. Additional exam requirements/recommendations for international students: Required—TOEFL (minimum score 80 iBT). *Application deadline:* For fall admission, 10/1 for domestic and international students. Application fee: $60. Electronic applications accepted. Application fee is waived when completed online. *Expenses:* $50,525 first year, $1,075 per unit. *Financial support:* In 2017–18, 25 students received support. Fellowships, research assistantships, teaching assistantships, and scholarships/grants available. Support available to part-time students. Financial award application deadline: 3/2; financial award applicants required to submit FAFSA. *Unit head:* Dr. Mary Lopez, Dean, 909-706-3860, Fax: 909-469-5521, E-mail: mlopez@westernu.edu. *Application contact:* Kathryn Ford, Director of Admissions/International Student Advisor, 909-469-5335, Fax: 909-469-5570, E-mail: admissions@westernu.edu.

Westminster College, School of Nursing and Health Sciences, Salt Lake City, UT 84105-3697. Offers family nurse practitioner (MSN); nurse anesthesia (MSNA); public health (MPH). *Accreditation:* AACN; AANA/CANAEP. *Faculty:* 9 full-time (5 women), 10 part-time/adjunct (5 women). *Students:* 130 full-time (81 women), 1 (woman) part-time; includes 18 minority (2 Black or African American, non-Hispanic/Latino; 1 American Indian or Alaska Native, non-Hispanic/Latino; 5 Asian, non-Hispanic/Latino; 4 Hispanic/Latino; 2 Native Hawaiian or other Pacific Islander, non-Hispanic/Latino; 4 Two or more races, non-Hispanic/Latino), 3 international. Average age 33. 149 applicants, 51% accepted, 62 enrolled. In 2017, 49 master's awarded. *Degree requirements:* For master's, clinical practicum, 504 clinical practice hours. *Entrance requirements:* For master's, GRE (can be waived in select cases), personal statement, resume, 3 professional recommendations, copy of unrestricted Utah license to practice professional nursing, background check, minimum cumulative GPA of 3.0, documentation of current immunizations, physical and mental health certificate signed by primary care provider. Additional exam requirements/recommendations for international students: Required—TOEFL (minimum score 84 iBT), IELTS (minimum score 7). Application fee: $50. Electronic applications accepted. *Expenses:* Contact institution. *Financial support:* In 2017–18, 7 students received support. Career-related internships or fieldwork, scholarships/grants, unspecified assistantships, and tuition remission available. Financial award applicants required to submit FAFSA. *Faculty research:* Intellectual empathy, professional boundaries, learned optimism, collaborative testing in nursing: student outcomes and perspectives, implementing new educational paradigms into pre-licensure nursing curricula. *Unit head:* Dr. Sheryl Steadman, Dean, 801-832-2164, Fax: 801-832-3110, E-mail: ssteadman@westminstercollege.edu. *Application contact:* Collin Bess, Enrollment Coordinator/Admissions Recruiter, 801-832-2207, Fax: 801-832-3101, E-mail: cbess@westminstercollege.edu.
Website: https://www.westminstercollege.edu/graduate/programs

West Texas A&M University, College of Nursing and Health Sciences, Department of Nursing, Canyon, TX 79015. Offers family nurse practitioner (MSN); nursing (MSN). *Accreditation:* AACN. *Program availability:* Part-time, online learning. *Degree requirements:* For master's, comprehensive exam, thesis optional. *Entrance requirements:* For master's, GRE General Test, bachelor's degree in nursing, minimum GPA of 3.0 in last 60 hours. Additional exam requirements/recommendations for international students: Required—TOEFL (minimum score 550 paper-based). Electronic applications accepted. *Faculty research:* Family-focused nursing, nursing traineeship, professional nursing.

West Virginia University, School of Nursing, Morgantown, WV 26506-9600. Offers nurse practitioner (Certificate); nursing (MSN, DNP, PhD). *Accreditation:* AACN. *Program availability:* Part-time, online learning. *Students:* 22 full-time (20 women), 175 part-time (155 women); includes 54 minority (16 Black or African American, non-Hispanic/Latino; 4 Asian, non-Hispanic/Latino; 29 Hispanic/Latino; 5 Two or more races, non-Hispanic/Latino). *Degree requirements:* For master's, thesis or alternative; for doctorate, comprehensive exam, thesis/dissertation. *Entrance requirements:* For master's, GRE General Test, minimum GPA of 3.0, current U.S. RN license, BSN, course work in statistics and physical assessment; for doctorate, GRE General Test (for PhD), minimum graduate GPA of 3.0, minimum grade of B in graduate statistics course work. Additional exam requirements/recommendations for international students: Required—TOEFL (minimum score 550 paper-based). *Application deadline:* For fall admission, 6/1 for domestic students. Application fee: $60. Electronic applications accepted. *Expenses:* Contact institution. *Financial support:* Teaching assistantships, Federal Work-Study, institutionally sponsored loans, health care benefits, tuition waivers (partial), and administrative assistantships available. Financial award application deadline: 2/1; financial award applicants required to submit FAFSA. *Faculty research:* Rural primary health/health promotion, parent/child/women's health, cardiovascular risk reduction, complementary health modalities, breast cancer detection-care. *Unit head:* Dr. Tara Hulsey, Dean, 304-293-6521, Fax: 304-293-6826, E-mail: tmhulsey@hsc.wvu.edu. *Application contact:* Brandy Sue Toothman, Program Assistant III, 304-293-4298, Fax: 304-293-2546, E-mail: btoothman@hsc.wvu.edu.
Website: https://nursing.hsc.wvu.edu

West Virginia Wesleyan College, Department of Nursing, Buckhannon, WV 26201. Offers family nurse practitioner (MS, Post Master's Certificate); nurse administrator (MS); nurse educator (MS); nurse-midwifery (MS); nursing administration (Post Master's Certificate); nursing education (Post Master's Certificate); psychiatric mental health nurse practitioner (MS); MSN/MBA. *Accreditation:* ACEN.

Wheeling Jesuit University, Department of Nursing, Wheeling, WV 26003-6295. Offers MSN. *Accreditation:* AACN. *Program availability:* Part-time, evening/weekend, online learning. *Degree requirements:* For master's, comprehensive exam (for some programs), thesis (for some programs). *Entrance requirements:* For master's, GRE General Test or MAT, BSN, minimum GPA of 3.0, course work in research and statistics, U.S. nursing license. Additional exam requirements/recommendations for international students: Required—TOEFL (minimum score 600 paper-based; 100 iBT). Electronic applications accepted. Application fee is waived when completed online. *Faculty research:* Obesity in women, underserved populations, spirituality.

Wichita State University, Graduate School, College of Health Professions, School of Nursing, Wichita, KS 67260. Offers nursing (MSN); nursing practice (DNP). *Accreditation:* AACN. *Program availability:* Part-time, 100% online, blended/hybrid learning. *Unit head:* Dr. Victoria Mosack, Chairperson, 316-978-3610, Fax: 316-978-3025, E-mail: victoria.mosack@wichita.edu. *Application contact:* Jordan Oleson, Admissions Coordinator, 316-978-3095, Fax: 316-978-3253, E-mail: jordan.oleson@wichita.edu.
Website: http://www.wichita.edu/nursing

Widener University, School of Nursing, Chester, PA 19013-5792. Offers MSN, DN Sc, PhD, PMC. *Accreditation:* AACN. *Program availability:* Part-time, evening/weekend. *Faculty:* 12 full-time (all women), 4 part-time/adjunct (3 women). *Students:* 43 full-time (39 women), 179 part-time (167 women); includes 90 minority (59 Black or African American, non-Hispanic/Latino; 1 American Indian or Alaska Native, non-Hispanic/Latino; 22 Asian, non-Hispanic/Latino; 6 Hispanic/Latino; 2 Two or more races, non-Hispanic/Latino), 7 international. Average age 39. 139 applicants, 38% accepted, 43 enrolled. In 2017, 64 master's, 12 doctorates awarded. *Degree requirements:* For doctorate, thesis/dissertation. *Entrance requirements:* For master's, GRE General Test, BSN, undergraduate course in statistics; for doctorate, GRE General Test, MSN, undergraduate course in statistics. *Application deadline:* For fall admission, 7/1 for domestic students; for winter admission, 3/1 for domestic students; for spring admission, 11/1 for domestic students. Applications are processed on a rolling basis. Application fee: $25 ($300 for international students). Electronic applications accepted. *Expenses:* Contact institution. *Financial support:* Career-related internships or fieldwork, Federal Work-Study, and traineeships available. Support available to part-time students. Financial award application deadline: 4/1. *Faculty research:* Women's health leadership, nursing education, research utilization, program evaluation, health promotion. *Unit head:* Dr. Laura Dzurec, Dean, 610-499-4214, E-mail: lcdzurec@widener.edu.

Wilkes University, College of Graduate and Professional Studies, Passan School of Nursing, Wilkes-Barre, PA 18766-0002. Offers MSN, DNP, PhD. *Accreditation:* AACN. *Program availability:* Part-time, online only, 100% online. *Students:* [illegible] full-time ([illegible] women), 793 part-time (706 women); includes 260 minority (167 Black or African American, non-Hispanic/Latino; 1 American Indian or Alaska Native, non-Hispanic/Latino; 42 Asian, non-Hispanic/Latino; 35 Hispanic/Latino; 3 Native Hawaiian or other Pacific Islander, non-Hispanic/Latino; 12 Two or more races, non-Hispanic/Latino). Average age 43. In 2017, 49 master's, 30 doctorates awarded. *Entrance requirements:* Additional exam requirements/recommendations for international students: Required—TOEFL (minimum score 550 paper-based; 79 iBT). *Application deadline:* Applications are processed on a rolling basis. Application fee: $45. Electronic applications accepted. *Financial support:* Unspecified assistantships available. Financial award application deadline: 3/1; financial award applicants required to submit FAFSA. *Unit head:* Dr. Deborah Zbegner, Dean, 570-408-4086, Fax: 570-408-7807, E-mail: deborah.zbegner@wilkes.edu. *Application contact:* Director of Graduate Enrollment, 570-408-4234, Fax: 570-408-7846.
Website: http://www.wilkes.edu/academics/colleges/school-of-nursing/index.aspx

William Carey University, School of Nursing, Hattiesburg, MS 39401. Offers MSN. *Accreditation:* AACN. *Program availability:* Part-time. *Degree requirements:* For master's, thesis or alternative. *Entrance requirements:* For master's, GRE, minimum GPA of 3.0, RN license. Additional exam requirements/recommendations for international students: Required—TOEFL (minimum score 500 paper-based).

William Paterson University of New Jersey, College of Science and Health, Wayne, NJ 07470-8420. Offers adult gerontology nurse practitioner (Certificate); biology (MS); biotechnology (MS); communication disorders (MS); exercise and sport studies (MS); materials chemistry (MS); nurse practitioner (Certificate); nursing (MSN); nursing education (Certificate); nursing practice (DNP); school nurse (Certificate). *Program availability:* Part-time. *Faculty:* 29 full-time (15 women), 25 part-time/adjunct (24 women). *Students:* 66 full-time (56 women), 197 part-time (163 women); includes 104 minority (15 Black or African American, non-Hispanic/Latino; 45 Asian, non-Hispanic/Latino; 38 Hispanic/Latino; 6 Two or more races, non-Hispanic/Latino), 3 international. Average age 33. 387 applicants, 34% accepted, 77 enrolled. In 2017, 87 master's, 5 doctorates awarded. *Degree requirements:* For master's, comprehensive exam (for some programs), thesis (for some programs), non-thesis internship/practicum (for some programs). *Entrance requirements:* For master's, GRE/MAT, minimum GPA of 3.0; 2-3 letters of recommendation; personal statement; work experience (for some programs); for doctorate, GRE/MAT, minimum GPA of 3.3; work experience; 3 letters of recommendation; interview; master's degree in nursing. Additional exam requirements/recommendations for international students: Required—TOEFL (minimum score 550 paper-based; 79 iBT), IELTS (minimum score 6). *Application deadline:* For fall admission, 6/1 for domestic students, 3/1 for international students; for spring admission, 11/1 for domestic students, 10/1 for international students. Applications are processed on a rolling basis. Application fee: $50. Electronic applications accepted. *Expenses:* Tuition, state resident: full-time $13,920; part-time $6264 per year. Tuition, nonresident: full-time $21,700; part-time $9765 per year. *Required fees:* $80; $36 per year. Tuition and fees vary according to course load, degree level and program. *Financial support:* In 2017–18, 9,800 students received support. Career-related internships or fieldwork, Federal Work-Study, scholarships/grants, and unspecified assistantships available. Support available to part-time students. Financial award application deadline: 3/15; financial award applicants required to submit FAFSA. *Faculty research:* Behaviors of American long-eared bats, postpartum fatigue, methodologies for coating carbon nano-tubes, paleoclimatology, and pre-linguistic gestures in children with language disorders. *Total annual research expenditures:* $291,600. *Unit head:* Dr. Venkat Sharma, Dean, 973-720-2194, Fax: 973-720-3414, E-mail: sharmav@wpunj.edu. *Application contact:* Christina Aiello, Assistant Director, Graduate Admissions, 973-720-2506, Fax: 973-720-2035, E-mail: aielloc@wpunj.edu.
Website: http://www.wpunj.edu/cosh

Wilmington University, College of Health Professions, New Castle, DE 19720-6491. Offers adult nurse practitioner (MSN); family nurse practitioner (MSN); gerontology nurse practitioner (MSN); nursing (MSN); nursing leadership (MSN); nursing practice (DNP). *Accreditation:* AACN. *Program availability:* Part-time. *Faculty:* 10 full-time (9 women), 59 part-time/adjunct (50 women). *Students:* 164 full-time (154 women), 662 part-time (604 women); includes 178 minority (129 Black or African American, non-Hispanic/Latino; 5 American Indian or Alaska Native, non-Hispanic/Latino; 23 Asian, non-Hispanic/Latino; 7 Hispanic/Latino; 3 Native Hawaiian or other Pacific Islander, non-Hispanic/Latino; 11 Two or more races, non-Hispanic/Latino), 6 international. Average age 39. 770 applicants, 63% accepted, 361 enrolled. In 2017, 259 master's, 22 doctorates awarded. *Degree requirements:* For master's, thesis. *Entrance requirements:* For master's, BSN, RN license, interview, 3 letters of recommendation. Additional exam

requirements/recommendations for international students: Required—TOEFL (minimum score 500 paper-based). *Application deadline:* For fall admission, 4/1 for domestic students; for spring admission, 9/1 for domestic students. Applications are processed on a rolling basis. Application fee: $35. Electronic applications accepted. *Expenses: Tuition:* Part-time $466 per credit. *Required fees:* $25 per semester. Tuition and fees vary according to degree level and campus/location. *Financial support:* Fellowships with tuition reimbursements and traineeships available. Financial award applicants required to submit FAFSA. *Faculty research:* Outcomes assessment, student writing ability. *Unit head:* Denise Z. Westbrook, Dean, 302-356-6915. *Application contact:* Laura Morris, Director of Admissions, 877-967-5464, E-mail: infocenter@wilmu.edu.
Website: http://www.wilmu.edu/health/

Wilson College, Graduate Programs, Chambersburg, PA 17201-1285. Offers accounting (M Acc); choreography and visual art (MFA); education (M Ed); educational technology (MET); healthcare administration (MHA); humanities (MA), including art and culture, critical/cultural theory, English language and literature, women's studies; management (MSM); nursing (MSN), including nursing education, nursing leadership and management; special education (MSE). *Program availability:* Evening/weekend. *Degree requirements:* For master's, project. *Entrance requirements:* For master's, PRAXIS, minimum undergraduate cumulative GPA of 3.0, 2 letters of recommendation, current certification for eligibility to teach in grades K-12, resume, personal interview. Electronic applications accepted.

Winona State University, College of Nursing and Health Sciences, Winona, MN 55987. Offers adult-gerontology acute care nurse practitioner (MS, DNP, Post Master's Certificate); adult-gerontology clinical nurse specialist (MS, DNP, Post Master's Certificate); adult-gerontology primary care nurse practitioner (MS, DNP, Post Master's Certificate); family nurse practitioner (MS, DNP, Post Master's Certificate); nurse educator (MS); nursing and organizational leadership (MS, DNP, Post Master's Certificate); practice and leadership innovations (DNP, Post Master's Certificate). *Accreditation:* AACN. *Program availability:* Part-time, online learning. *Degree requirements:* For master's, thesis; for doctorate, capstone. *Entrance requirements:* For master's, GRE (if GPA less than 3.0). Additional exam requirements/recommendations for international students: Required—TOEFL (minimum score 550 paper-based).

Winston-Salem State University, Program in Nursing, Winston-Salem, NC 27110-0003. Offers advanced nurse educator (MSN); family nurse practitioner (MSN); nursing (DNP). *Accreditation:* AACN. *Program availability:* Part-time, evening/weekend, online learning. *Entrance requirements:* For master's, GRE, MAT, resume, NC or state compact license, 3 letters of recommendation. Electronic applications accepted. *Faculty research:* Elimination of health care disparities.

Wright State University, Graduate School, College of Nursing and Health, Program in Nursing, Dayton, OH 45435. Offers administration of nursing and health care systems (MS); adult gerontology clinical nurse specialist (MS); adult-gerontology acute care nurse practitioner (MS); family nurse practitioner (MS); neonatal nurse practitioner (MS); pediatric nurse practitioner-acute care (MS); pediatric nurse practitioner-primary care (MS); psychiatric mental health nurse practitioner (MS); school nurse (MS). *Accreditation:* AACN. *Program availability:* Part-time, evening/weekend. *Degree requirements:* For master's, thesis or alternative. *Entrance requirements:* For master's, GRE General Test, BSN from ACEN-accredited college, Ohio RN license. Additional exam requirements/recommendations for international students: Required—TOEFL. *Faculty research:* Clinical nursing and health, teaching, caring, pain administration, informatics and technology.

Xavier University, College of Social Sciences, Health and Education, School of Nursing, Cincinnati, OH 45207. Offers MSN, DNP, PMC, MSN/M Ed, MSN/MBA, MSN/MS. *Accreditation:* AACN. *Program availability:* Part-time, evening/weekend. *Degree requirements:* For master's, thesis, scholarly project; for doctorate, thesis/dissertation, scholarly project; for PMC, practicum. *Entrance requirements:* For master's, GRE, resume; statement of purpose and/or portfolio; RN licensure or bachelor's degree; official transcript; 3 references/recommendations; for doctorate, MSN from CCNE- or ACEN-accredited school or master's degree in other field (must have BSN from a CCNE-, ACEN-, or regionally-accredited institution); basic statistics course; one year of professional nursing work experience; RN licensure; official transcript; 1-3 page personal statement; published work or paper; resume; 3 professional references; for PMC, RN licensure; master's degree in nursing; licensed in state where participating in clinical experiences; official transcript. Additional exam requirements/recommendations for international students: Required—TOEFL (minimum score 550 paper-based; 79 iBT). Electronic applications accepted. Application fee is waived when completed online. *Expenses:* Contact institution. *Faculty research:* Clinical nurse leader, simulation, employment satisfaction, nontraditional students, holistic nursing.

Yale University, School of Nursing, West Haven, CT 06516. Offers MSN, DNP, PhD, Post Master's Certificate, MAR/MSN, MSN/M Div, MSN/MPH. *Accreditation:* AACN. *Program availability:* Part-time, online learning. Terminal master's awarded for partial completion of doctoral program. *Degree requirements:* For master's, thesis; for doctorate, comprehensive exam, thesis/dissertation. *Entrance requirements:* For master's, GRE General Test, bachelor's degree; for doctorate, GRE General Test, MSN; for Post Master's Certificate, MSN. Additional exam requirements/recommendations for international students: Required—TOEFL or IELTS. Electronic applications accepted. *Expenses:* Contact institution. *Faculty research:* Family-based care, chronic illness, primary care, development, policy.

York College of Pennsylvania, The Stabler Department of Nursing, York, PA 17403-3651. Offers adult gerontology clinical nurse specialist (MS); nurse anesthetist (MS). *Accreditation:* AACN; AANA/CANAEP. *Program availability:* Part-time. *Faculty:* 7 full-time (all women), 8 part-time/adjunct (5 women). *Students:* 41 full-time (30 women), 40 part-time (38 women); includes 9 minority (1 Black or African American, non-Hispanic/Latino; 3 Asian, non-Hispanic/Latino; 1 Hispanic/Latino; 4 Two or more races, non-Hispanic/Latino), 1 international. Average age 35. 96 applicants, 31% accepted, 29 enrolled. In 2017, 24 master's awarded. *Entrance requirements:* For master's, bachelor's degree in nursing, minimum GPA of 3.0. Additional exam requirements/recommendations for international students: Required—TOEFL (minimum score 530 paper-based; 72 iBT). Application fee: $0. Electronic applications accepted. *Expenses:* $795 per credit. *Financial support:* In 2017–18, 1 student received support. Scholarships/grants available. Financial award applicants required to submit FAFSA. *Faculty research:* Adults with intellectual disabilities, healthy work environment, perinatal bereavement, palliative care. *Unit head:* Dr. Kimberly Fenstermacher, Graduate Program Director, 717-815-1383, Fax: 717-849-1651, E-mail: kfenster@ycp.edu. *Application contact:* Allison Malachosky, Administrative Assistant, 717-815-1243, E-mail: amalacho@ycp.edu.
Website: http://www.ycp.edu/academics/academic-departments/nursing/

York University, Faculty of Graduate Studies, Faculty of Health, Program in Nursing, Toronto, ON M3J 1P3, Canada. Offers M Sc N.

Youngstown State University, Graduate School, Bitonte College of Health and Human Services, Department of Nursing, Youngstown, OH 44555-0001. Offers MSN. *Accreditation:* ACEN. *Program availability:* Part-time, evening/weekend. *Degree requirements:* For master's, thesis optional. *Entrance requirements:* For master's, GRE General Test, BSN, CPR certification. Additional exam requirements/recommendations for international students: Required—TOEFL.

Acute Care/Critical Care Nursing

Augusta University, College of Nursing, Doctor of Nursing Practice Program, Augusta, GA 30912. Offers adult gerontology acute care nurse practitioner (DNP); family nurse practitioner (DNP); nurse executive (DNP); nursing (DNP); nursing anesthesia (DNP); pediatric nurse practitioner (DNP); psychiatric mental health nurse practitioner (DNP). *Accreditation:* AACN; AANA/CANAEP. *Degree requirements:* For doctorate, thesis/dissertation or alternative. *Entrance requirements:* For doctorate, GRE General Test or MAT, master's degree in nursing or related field, current professional nurse licensure. Additional exam requirements/recommendations for international students: Required—TOEFL (minimum score 600 paper-based; 100 iBT). Electronic applications accepted.

Barry University, School of Adult and Continuing Education, Division of Nursing, Program in Nurse Practitioner, Miami Shores, FL 33161-6695. Offers acute care nurse practitioner (MSN); family nurse practitioner (MSN); nurse practitioner (Certificate). *Accreditation:* AACN. *Program availability:* Part-time, evening/weekend. *Degree requirements:* For master's, research project or thesis. *Entrance requirements:* For master's, GRE General Test or MAT, BSN, minimum GPA of 3.0, course work in statistics. Electronic applications accepted. *Faculty research:* Child abuse, health beliefs, teenage pregnancy, cultural and clinical studies across the lifespan.

Case Western Reserve University, Frances Payne Bolton School of Nursing, Master's Programs in Nursing, Nurse Practitioner Program, Cleveland, OH 44106. Offers acute care pediatric nurse practitioner (MSN); acute care/cardiovascular nursing (MSN); acute care/flight nurse (MSN); adult gerontology acute care nurse practitioner (MSN); adult gerontology primary care nurse practitioner (MSN); family nurse practitioner (MSN); family systems psychiatric mental health nursing (MSN); neonatal nurse practitioner (MSN); palliative care (MSN); pediatric nurse practitioner (MSN); women's health nurse practitioner (MSN). *Accreditation:* ACEN. *Program availability:* Part-time. *Faculty:* 30 full-time (26 women), 5 part-time/adjunct (3 women). *Students:* 34 full-time (28 women), 97 part-time (73 women); includes 24 minority (5 Black or African American, non-Hispanic/Latino; 9 Asian, non-Hispanic/Latino; 6 Hispanic/Latino; 4 Two or more races, non-Hispanic/Latino), 4 international. Average age 33. 56 applicants, 82% accepted, 29 enrolled. In 2017, 68 master's awarded. *Degree requirements:* For master's, minimum GPA of 3.0, clinical hours corresponding to requirements to sit for certification exam, portfolio. *Entrance requirements:* For master's, GRE General Test or MAT. Additional exam requirements/recommendations for international students: Required—TOEFL (minimum score 577 paper-based; 90 iBT), IELTS (minimum score 7). *Application deadline:* For fall admission, 5/1 for domestic and international students; for spring admission, 10/1 for domestic and international students; for summer admission, 3/1 for domestic and international students. Applications are processed on a rolling basis. Application fee: $75. Electronic applications accepted. *Expenses:* $2,011 per credit tuition; $15 nursing activity fee; $17 activity fee. *Financial support:* In 2017–18, 86 students received support, including 19 teaching assistantships with partial tuition reimbursements available (averaging $18,100 per year); scholarships/grants and traineeships also available. Support available to part-time students. Financial award application deadline: 5/15; financial award applicants required to submit FAFSA. *Faculty research:* Symptom science, family/community care, aging across the lifespan, self-management of health and illness, neuroscience. *Unit head:* Dr. Latina Brooks, Director, 216-368-1196, Fax: 216-368-3542, E-mail: lmb3@case.edu. *Application contact:* Jackie Tepale, Admissions Coordinator, 216-368-5253, Fax: 216-368-0124, E-mail: yyd@case.edu.
Website: http://fpb.cwru.edu/MSN/majors.shtm

The College of New Rochelle, Graduate School, Program in Nursing, New Rochelle, NY 10805-2308. Offers acute care nurse practitioner (MS, Certificate); clinical specialist in holistic nursing (MS, Certificate); family nurse practitioner (MS, Certificate); nursing and health care management (MS); nursing education (Certificate). *Accreditation:* AACN. *Program availability:* Part-time. *Entrance requirements:* For master's, GRE General Test or MAT, BSN, malpractice insurance, minimum GPA of 3.0, RN license. Electronic applications accepted. *Expenses: Tuition:* Full-time $17,406. *Required fees:* $1120.

Columbia University, School of Nursing, Program in Adult-Gerontology Acute Care Nurse Practitioner, New York, NY 10032. Offers MS, Adv C. *Accreditation:* AACN. *Program availability:* Part-time. *Entrance requirements:* For master's, GRE General Test, NCLEX, 1 year of clinical experience, BSN; for Adv C, MSN. Additional exam requirements/recommendations for international students: Required—TOEFL (minimum score 100 iBT). Electronic applications accepted. *Expenses: Tuition:* Full-time $44,864; part-time $1704 per credit. *Required fees:* $2370 per semester. One-time fee: $105.

Drexel University, College of Nursing and Health Professions, Division of Graduate Nursing, Philadelphia, PA 19104-2875. Offers adult acute care (MSN); adult psychiatric/mental health (MSN); advanced practice nursing (MSN); clinical trials research (MSN); family nurse practitioner (MSN); leadership in health systems management (MSN); nursing education (MSN); pediatric primary care (MSN); women's health (MSN). *Accreditation:* AACN. Electronic applications accepted.

Duke University, School of Nursing, Durham, NC 27708-0586. Offers acute care pediatric nurse practitioner (MSN, Post-Graduate Certificate); adult-gerontology nurse practitioner (MSN, Post-Graduate Certificate), including acute care, primary care; family nurse practitioner (MSN, Post-Graduate Certificate); neonatal nurse practitioner (MSN, Post-Graduate Certificate); nurse anesthesia (DNP); nurse practitioner (DNP); nursing (PhD); nursing and health care leadership (MSN, Post-Graduate Certificate); nursing education (MSN, Post-Graduate Certificate); nursing informatics (MSN, Post-Graduate Certificate); pediatric nurse practitioner (MSN, Post-Graduate Certificate), including primary care; psychiatric mental health nurse practitioner (MSN, Post-Graduate Certificate); women's health nurse practitioner (MSN, Post-Graduate Certificate).

Accreditation: AACN; AANA/CANAEP. *Program availability:* Part-time, evening/weekend, online with on-campus intensives. *Faculty:* 72 full-time (61 women). *Students:* 155 full-time (137 women), 613 part-time (548 women); includes 177 minority (64 Black or African American, non-Hispanic/Latino; 2 American Indian or Alaska Native, non-Hispanic/Latino; 47 Asian, non-Hispanic/Latino; 34 Hispanic/Latino; 30 Two or more races, non-Hispanic/Latino), 10 international. Average age 34. 631 applicants, 47% accepted, 211 enrolled. In 2017, 221 master's, 71 doctorates, 26 other advanced degrees awarded. Terminal master's awarded for partial completion of doctoral program. *Degree requirements:* For master's, thesis optional; for doctorate, capstone project. *Entrance requirements:* For master's, GRE General Test (waived if undergraduate GPA of 3.4 or higher), 1 year of nursing experience (recommended), BSN, minimum GPA of 3.0, previous course work in statistics; for doctorate, GRE General Test (waived if undergraduate GPA of 3.4 or higher), BSN or MSN, minimum GPA of 3.0, resume, personal statement, undergraduate statistics course, current licensure as a registered nurse, transcripts from all post-secondary institutions; for Post-Graduate Certificate, MSN, licensure or eligibility as a professional nurse, transcripts from all post-secondary institutions, previous course work in statistics. Additional exam requirements/recommendations for international students: Required—TOEFL (minimum score 100 iBT), IELTS (minimum score 7). *Application deadline:* For fall admission, 12/1 for domestic and international students; for spring admission, 5/1 for domestic and international students. Application fee: $50. Electronic applications accepted. *Expenses:* Contact institution. *Financial support:* Institutionally sponsored loans, scholarships/grants, and traineeships available. Support available to part-time students. Financial award applicants required to submit FAFSA. *Faculty research:* Cardiovascular disease, caregiver skill training, data mining, prostate cancer, neonatal immune system. *Unit head:* Dr. Marion E. Broome, Dean/Vice Chancellor for Nursing Affairs/Associate Vice President for Academic Affairs for Nursing, 919-684-9446, Fax: 919-684-9414, E-mail: marion.broome@duke.edu. *Application contact:* Dr. Ernie Rushing, Director of Admissions and Recruitment, 919-668-6274, Fax: 919-668-4693, E-mail: ernie.rushing@dm.duke.edu.
Website: http://www.nursing.duke.edu/

Elms College, School of Nursing, Chicopee, MA 01013-2839. Offers adult-gerontology acute care nurse practitioner (DNP); family nurse practitioner (DNP); health systems innovation and leadership (DNP); nursing and health services management (MSN); nursing education (MSN). *Accreditation:* AACN. *Program availability:* Part-time, evening/weekend. *Faculty:* 5 full-time (all women), 9 part-time/adjunct (6 women). *Students:* 20 full-time (16 women), 79 part-time (70 women); includes 12 minority (2 Black or African American, non-Hispanic/Latino; 2 American Indian or Alaska Native, non-Hispanic/Latino; 8 Hispanic/Latino). Average age 40. 33 applicants, 94% accepted, 28 enrolled. In 2017, 14 master's, 30 doctorates awarded. *Entrance requirements:* Additional exam requirements/recommendations for international students: Required—TOEFL. *Application deadline:* For fall admission, 7/1 priority date for domestic students; for spring admission, 11/1 priority date for domestic students. Applications are processed on a rolling basis. Application fee: $30. *Expenses: Tuition:* Full-time $13,860; part-time $770 per credit hour. *Required fees:* $200. Tuition and fees vary according to degree level and program. *Financial support:* Applicants required to submit FAFSA. *Unit head:* Dr. Kathleen Scoble, Dean, School of Nursing, 413-265-2204, E-mail: scoblek@elms.edu. *Application contact:* Dr. Cynthia L. Dakin, Director of Graduate Nursing Studies, 413-265-2455, Fax: 413-265-2335, E-mail: dakinc@elms.edu.

Georgetown University, Graduate School of Arts and Sciences, School of Nursing and Health Studies, Washington, DC 20057. Offers acute care nurse practitioner (MS); clinical nurse specialist (MS); family nurse practitioner (MS); nurse anesthesia (MS); nurse-midwifery (MS); nursing (DNP); nursing education (MS). *Accreditation:* AACN; AANA/CANAEP (one or more programs are accredited); ACNM/ACME (one or more programs are accredited). *Degree requirements:* For master's, thesis optional. *Entrance requirements:* For master's, GRE General Test or MAT, bachelor's degree in nursing from ACEN-accredited school, minimum undergraduate GPA of 3.0. Additional exam requirements/recommendations for international students: Required—TOEFL.

Goldfarb School of Nursing at Barnes-Jewish College, Graduate Programs, St. Louis, MO 63110. Offers adult-gerontology (MSN), including primary care nurse practitioner; adult-gerontology (MSN), including acute care nurse practitioner; health systems and population health leadership (MSN); nurse anesthesia (MSN). *Accreditation:* AACN; AANA/CANAEP. *Program availability:* Part-time, online learning. *Faculty:* 42 full-time (39 women), 6 part-time/adjunct (all women). *Students:* 61 full-time (49 women), 3 part-time (2 women); includes 13 minority (8 Black or African American, non-Hispanic/Latino; 2 Asian, non-Hispanic/Latino; 1 Hispanic/Latino; 2 Two or more races, non-Hispanic/Latino). *Degree requirements:* For master's, thesis or alternative. *Entrance requirements:* For master's, 2 references, personal statement, curriculum vitae or resume. Additional exam requirements/recommendations for international students: Required—TOEFL (minimum score 575 paper-based; 85 iBT). *Application deadline:* Applications are processed on a rolling basis. Application fee: $50. *Expenses: Tuition:* Full-time $11,910; part-time $794 per credit hour. *Required fees:* $30; $15 per term. Full-time tuition and fees vary according to program. *Financial support:* Research assistantships, Federal Work-Study, institutionally sponsored loans, scholarships/grants, and traineeships available. Support available to part-time students. Financial award applicants required to submit FAFSA. *Faculty research:* HIV stigma, HIV symptom management, palliative care with children and their families, heart disease prevention in Hispanic women, depression in the well elderly, alternative therapies in pre-term infants. *Unit head:* Dr. Gretchen Drinkard, Associate Dean for Academic Affairs, 314-454-7540, Fax: 314-362-9222, E-mail: gdrinkard@bjc.org. *Application contact:* Karen Sartorius, Admission Specialist, 314-454-7057, Fax: 314-362-9250, E-mail: karen.sartorius@bjc.org.
Website: http://www.barnesjewishcollege.edu/

Grand Canyon University, College of Nursing and Health Care Professions, Phoenix, AZ 85017-1097. Offers acute care nurse practitioner (MSN, PMC); family nurse practitioner (MSN, PMC); health care administration (MS); health care informatics (MS, MSN); leadership in health care systems (MSN); nursing (DNP); nursing education (MSN, PMC); public health (MPH, MSN); MBA/MSN. *Accreditation:* AACN. *Program availability:* Part-time, evening/weekend, online learning. *Degree requirements:* For master's and PMC, comprehensive exam (for some programs). *Entrance requirements:* For master's, minimum cumulative and science course undergraduate GPA of 3.0. Additional exam requirements/recommendations for international students: Required—TOEFL (minimum score 575 paper-based; 90 iBT), IELTS (minimum score 7).

Indiana University–Purdue University Indianapolis, School of Nursing, MSN Program in Nursing, Indianapolis, IN 46202. Offers adult/gerontology acute care nurse practitioner (MSN); adult/gerontology clinical nurse specialist (MSN); adult/gerontology primary care nurse practitioner (MSN); family nurse practitioner (MSN); nursing education (MSN); nursing leadership in health systems (MSN); pediatric clinical nurse specialist (MSN); pediatric nurse practitioner (MSN). *Accreditation:* AACN. *Program availability:* Part-time, blended/hybrid learning. *Degree requirements:* For master's, thesis. *Entrance requirements:* For master's, BSN from ACEN- or CCNE-accredited program, minimum undergraduate GPA of 3.0 (preferred), professional resume or curriculum vitae, essay stating career goals and objectives, current unencumbered RN license, three references from individuals with knowledge of ability to succeed in graduate program. Additional exam requirements/recommendations for international students: Required—TOEFL (minimum score 550 paper-based; 79 iBT). Electronic applications accepted. *Expenses:* Contact institution. *Faculty research:* Quality of life, symptom management, cancer prevention and control, heart failure, pediatric oncology.

Inter American University of Puerto Rico, Arecibo Campus, Program in Nursing, Arecibo, PR 00614-4050. Offers critical care nursing (MSN); surgical nursing (MSN). *Entrance requirements:* For master's, EXADEP or GRE General Test or MAT, 2 letters of recommendation, bachelor's degree in nursing, minimum GPA of 2.5 in last 60 credits, minimum 1 year nursing experience, nursing license.

Inter American University of Puerto Rico, Barranquitas Campus, Program in Nursing, Barranquitas, PR 00794. Offers critical care nursing (MSN); medical surgical nursing (MSN). *Program availability:* Part-time, evening/weekend. *Faculty:* 2 full-time (both women). *Students:* 30 part-time (24 women); all minorities (all Hispanic/Latino). Average age 31. 30 applicants, 97% accepted, 29 enrolled. *Degree requirements:* For master's, 2 foreign languages, comprehensive exam (for some programs), thesis optional, minimum grade of B on all courses, integration seminar. *Entrance requirements:* For master's, bachelor's degree in nursing from accredited institution, minimum GPA of 2.5, provisional or permanent nursing license for practicing nursing in Puerto Rico, official academic transcript from institution that conferred bachelor's degree, two recommendations letters. *Application deadline:* Applications are processed on a rolling basis. Application fee: $31. Electronic applications accepted. *Expenses:* $3,392 full-time tuition plus $652 fees. *Financial support:* Applicants required to submit FAFSA. *Unit head:* Juan A. Negron-Berrios, PhD, Chancellor, 787-857-3600 Ext. 2002, Fax: 787-857-2125, E-mail: janegron@br.inter.edu. *Application contact:* Aramilda Cartagena-Santiago, Dean of Students, 787-857-3600 Ext. 2009, Fax: 787-857-2125, E-mail: aramildacartagena@br.inter.edu.

Marquette University, Graduate School, College of Nursing, Milwaukee, WI 53201-1881. Offers acute care nurse practitioner (Certificate); adult clinical nurse specialist (Certificate); adult nurse practitioner (Certificate); advanced practice nursing (MSN, DNP), including adult-older adult acute care (DNP), adults (MSN), adults-older adults (DNP), clinical nurse leader (MSN), health care systems leadership (DNP), nurse-midwifery (MSN), older adults (MSN), pediatrics-acute care, pediatrics-primary care, primary care (DNP), systems leadership and healthcare quality (MSN); family nurse practitioner (Certificate); nurse-midwifery (Certificate); nursing (PhD); pediatric acute care (Certificate); pediatric primary care (Certificate); systems leadership and healthcare quality (Certificate). *Accreditation:* AACN. Terminal master's awarded for partial completion of doctoral program. *Degree requirements:* For master's, comprehensive exam, thesis or alternative. *Entrance requirements:* For master's, GRE General Test, BSN, Wisconsin RN license, official transcripts from all current and previous colleges/universities except Marquette, three completed recommendation forms, resume, written statement of professional goals; for doctorate, GRE General Test, official transcripts from all current and previous colleges/universities except Marquette, three letters of recommendation, resume, written statement of professional goals, sample of scholarly writing. Additional exam requirements/recommendations for international students: Required—TOEFL (minimum score 530 paper-based). Electronic applications accepted. *Faculty research:* Psychosocial adjustment to chronic illness, gerontology, reminiscence, health policy: uninsured and access, hospital care delivery systems.

Maryville University of Saint Louis, Myrtle E. and Earl E. Walker College of Health Professions, The Catherine McAuley School of Nursing, St. Louis, MO 63141-7299. Offers acute care nurse practitioner (MSN); adult gerontology nurse practitioner (MSN); advanced practice nursing (DNP); family nurse practitioner (MSN); pediatric nurse practitioner (MSN). *Accreditation:* AACN. *Program availability:* 100% online, blended/hybrid learning. *Faculty:* 15 full-time (all women), 142 part-time/adjunct (123 women). *Students:* 49 full-time (42 women), 2,999 part-time (2,645 women); includes 773 minority (375 Black or African American, non-Hispanic/Latino; 51 American Indian or Alaska Native, non-Hispanic/Latino; 135 Asian, non-Hispanic/Latino; 149 Hispanic/Latino; 63 Two or more races, non-Hispanic/Latino), 21 international. Average age 36. In 2017, 843 master's, 42 doctorates awarded. *Degree requirements:* For master's, practicum. *Entrance requirements:* For master's, BSN, current licensure, minimum GPA of 3.0, 3 letters of recommendation, curriculum vitae. Additional exam requirements/recommendations for international students: Required—TOEFL (minimum score 550 paper-based). *Application deadline:* Applications are processed on a rolling basis. Electronic applications accepted. *Expenses:* Contact institution. *Financial support:* Federal Work-Study and campus employment available. Support available to part-time students. Financial award application deadline: 4/1; financial award applicants required to submit FAFSA. *Unit head:* Dr. Elizabeth Buck, Assistant Dean/Director of Online Nursing, 314-529-9453, Fax: 314-529-9139, E-mail: ebuck@maryville.edu. *Application contact:* Jeannie DeLuca, Director of Admissions and Advising, 314-929-9355, Fax: 314-529-9927, E-mail: cjacobsmeyer@maryville.edu.
Website: http://www.maryville.edu/hp/nursing/

Moravian College, Graduate and Continuing Studies, Helen S. Breidegam School of Nursing, Bethlehem, PA 18018-6650. Offers clinical nurse leader (MS); nurse administrator (MS); nurse educator (MS); nurse practitioner - acute care (MS); nurse practitioner - primary care (MS). *Accreditation:* AACN. *Program availability:* Part-time, evening/weekend. *Faculty:* 5 full-time (all women), 4 part-time/adjunct (2 women). *Students:* 4 full-time (all women), 64 part-time (60 women); includes 9 minority (3 Black or African American, non-Hispanic/Latino; 2 Asian, non-Hispanic/Latino; 4 Hispanic/Latino), 1 international. Average age 38. 34 applicants, 85% accepted, 20 enrolled. In 2017, 24 master's awarded. *Degree requirements:* For master's, comprehensive exam (for some programs), evidence-based practice project. *Entrance requirements:* For master's, BSN with minimum GPA of 3.0, active RN license, statistics course with minimum C grade, 2 professional references, written statement of goals, professional resume, interview, official transcripts. Additional exam requirements/recommendations for international students: Required—TOEFL (minimum score 550 paper-based; 90 iBT), IELTS (minimum score 6.5). *Application deadline:* For fall admission, 8/1 priority date for domestic and international students; for spring admission, 1/1 priority date for domestic and international students; for summer admission, 5/1 priority date for domestic and international students. Applications are processed on a rolling basis. Electronic applications accepted. *Expenses:* Contact institution. *Financial support:* Applicants required to submit FAFSA. *Faculty research:* College binge drinking, obesity, underrepresented minorities in nursing, education needs of nursing preceptors, delirium superimposed on dementia. *Unit head:* Dr. Kerry Cheever, Professor/Chairperson, 610-861-1412, Fax: 610-861-1466, E-mail: nursing@moravian.edu. *Application contact:* Caroline Febbo, Student Experience Mentor, 610-861-1400, Fax: 610-861-1466, E-mail: graduate@moravian.edu.

Mount Carmel College of Nursing, Nursing Program, Columbus, OH 43222. Offers adult gerontology acute care nurse practitioner (MS); adult health clinical nurse specialist (MS); family nurse practitioner (MS); nursing (DNP); nursing administration (MS); nursing education (MS). *Accreditation:* AACN. *Program availability:* Part-time. *Faculty:* 11 full-time (all women), 5 part-time/adjunct (4 women). *Students:* 112 full-time (93 women), 72 part-time (65 women); includes 35 minority (20 Black or African American, non-Hispanic/Latino; 4 Asian, non-Hispanic/Latino; 3 Hispanic/Latino; 8 Two or more races, non-Hispanic/Latino). Average age 35. 135 applicants, 65% accepted, 68 enrolled. In 2017, 64 master's awarded. *Degree requirements:* For master's, professional manuscript; for doctorate, practicum. *Entrance requirements:* For master's, letters of recommendation, statement of purpose, current resume, baccalaureate degree in nursing, current Ohio RN license, minimum cumulative GPA of 3.0; for doctorate, master's degree in nursing from program accredited by either ACEN or CCNE. Additional exam requirements/recommendations for international students: Required—TOEFL (minimum score 550 paper-based; 80 iBT). *Application deadline:* For fall admission, 2/1 priority date for domestic students; for spring admission, 11/1 priority date for domestic students. Applications are processed on a rolling basis. Application fee: $30. Electronic applications accepted. *Expenses: Tuition:* Full-time $11,403; part-time $543 per credit. *Required fees:* $50; $50 per year. *Financial support:* In 2017–18, 3 students received support. Institutionally sponsored loans and scholarships/grants available. Financial award application deadline: 3/1; financial award applicants required to submit FAFSA. *Unit head:* Dr. Jill Kilanowski, Associate Dean, 614-234-5237, Fax: 614-234-2875, E-mail: jkilanowski@mccn.edu. *Application contact:* Dr. Kim Campbell, Director of Recruitment and Admissions, 614-234-5144, Fax: 614-234-5427, E-mail: kcampbell@mccn.edu.

New York University, Rory Meyers College of Nursing, Doctor of Nursing Practice Program, New York, NY 10012-1019. Offers nursing (DNP), including adult-gerontology acute care nurse practitioner, adult-gerontology primary care nurse practitioner, family nurse practitioner, nurse-midwifery, pediatrics nurse practitioner, psychiatric-mental health nurse practitioner. *Accreditation:* AACN. *Program availability:* Part-time, evening/weekend. *Faculty:* 16 full-time (all women), 1 (woman) part-time/adjunct. *Students:* 48 part-time (43 women); includes 11 minority (5 Black or African American, non-Hispanic/Latino; 5 Asian, non-Hispanic/Latino; 1 Hispanic/Latino). Average age 28. 20 applicants, 75% accepted, 10 enrolled. In 2017, 8 doctorates awarded. *Degree requirements:* For doctorate, thesis/dissertation, project. *Entrance requirements:* For doctorate, MS, RN license, interview, Nurse Practitioner Certification, writing sample. Additional exam requirements/recommendations for international students: Required—TOEFL (minimum score 100 iBT), IELTS (minimum score 7). *Application deadline:* For fall admission, 3/1 priority date for domestic and international students. Applications are processed on a rolling basis. Application fee: $80. Electronic applications accepted. *Expenses:* Contact institution. *Financial support:* In 2017–18, 13 students received support. Scholarships/grants available. Support available to part-time students. Financial award application deadline: 2/1; financial award applicants required to submit FAFSA. *Faculty research:* Workforce determinants of healthcare quality, genomics, health literacy and health outcomes, health policy. *Unit head:* Dr. Mary Jo Vetter, Director, DNP Program, 212-998-5165, E-mail: mjv5@nyu.edu. *Application contact:* Matthew Burke, Assistant Director, Graduate Student Affairs and Admissions, 212-998-7397, E-mail: mb6060@nyu.edu.

New York University, Rory Meyers College of Nursing, Programs in Advanced Practice Nursing, New York, NY 10012-1019. Offers adult-gerontology acute care nurse practitioner (MS, Advanced Certificate); adult-gerontology primary care nurse practitioner (MS, Advanced Certificate); family nurse practitioner (MS, Advanced Certificate); gerontology nurse practitioner (Advanced Certificate); nurse-midwifery (MS, Advanced Certificate); nursing administration (MS, Advanced Certificate); nursing education (MS, Advanced Certificate); nursing informatics (MS, Advanced Certificate); pediatrics nurse practitioner (MS, Advanced Certificate); psychiatric-mental health nurse practitioner (MS, Advanced Certificate); MS/MPH. *Accreditation:* AACN; ACNM/ACME. *Program availability:* Part-time, evening/weekend. *Faculty:* 23 full-time (all women), 62 part-time/adjunct (56 women). *Students:* 50 full-time (46 women), 557 part-time (509 women); includes 234 minority (58 Black or African American, non-Hispanic/Latino; 1 American Indian or Alaska Native, non-Hispanic/Latino; 116 Asian, non-Hispanic/Latino; 43 Hispanic/Latino; 1 Native Hawaiian or other Pacific Islander, non-Hispanic/Latino; 15 Two or more races, non-Hispanic/Latino), 23 international. Average age 32. 391 applicants, 59% accepted, 149 enrolled. In 2017, 187 master's, 5 other advanced degrees awarded. *Degree requirements:* For master's, thesis (for some programs), capstone. *Entrance requirements:* For master's, BS in nursing, AS in nursing with another BS/BA, interview, RN license, 1 year of clinical experience (3 for the MS in nursing education program); for Advanced Certificate, master's degree in nursing. Additional exam requirements/recommendations for international students: Required—TOEFL (minimum score 100 iBT), IELTS (minimum score 7). *Application deadline:* For fall admission, 3/1 priority date for domestic and international students; for spring admission, 11/1 priority date for domestic and international students; for summer admission, 3/1 for domestic and international students. Application fee: $80. Electronic applications accepted. *Expenses:* Contact institution. *Financial support:* In 2017–18, 130 students received support. Career-related internships or fieldwork, Federal Work-Study, and scholarships/grants available. Support available to part-time students. Financial award application deadline: 3/1; financial award applicants required to submit FAFSA. *Faculty research:* Vaccine hesitancy in pregnant women and mothers, palliative care and midwifery, diabetes education, curriculum development, workforce training, education and development, geriatrics. *Unit head:* Dr. James Pace, Senior Associate Dean for Academic Programs, 212-992-7343, E-mail: james.pace@nyu.edu. *Application contact:* Matthew Burke, Assistant Director, Graduate Student Affairs and Admissions, 212-998-7397, Fax: 212-995-4302, E-mail: mb6060@nyu.edu.

Northeastern University, Bouvé College of Health Sciences, Boston, MA 02115-5096. Offers applied behavior analysis (MS); audiology (Au D); counseling psychology (MS, PhD, CAGS); exercise science (MS); nursing (MS, PhD, CAGS), including administration (MS), adult-gerontology acute care nurse practitioner (MS, CAGS), adult-gerontology primary care nurse practitioner (MS, CAGS), anesthesia (MS), family nurse practitioner (MS, CAGS), neonatal nurse practitioner (MS, CAGS), pediatric nurse practitioner (MS, CAGS), psychiatric mental health nurse practitioner (MS, CAGS); nursing practice (DNP); pharmaceutical sciences (MS, PhD), including interdisciplinary concentration, pharmaceutics and drug delivery systems; pharmacology (MS); pharmacy (Pharm D); school psychology (PhD); speech-language pathology (MS); urban health (MPH); MS/MBA. *Accreditation:* ACPE (one or more programs are accredited). *Program availability:* Part-time, evening/weekend, online learning. *Faculty:* 192 full-time. *Students:* 1,685. In 2017, 352 master's, 312 doctorates, 25 other advanced degrees awarded. *Degree requirements:* For doctorate, thesis/dissertation (for some programs); for CAGS, comprehensive exam. Application fee: $75. Electronic applications accepted. *Expenses:* Contact institution. *Financial support:* Fellowships, research assistantships, teaching assistantships, career-related internships or fieldwork, scholarships/grants, health care benefits, tuition waivers, and unspecified assistantships available. Support available to part-time students. Financial award applicants required to submit FAFSA. *Unit head:* Susan L. Parish, Dean, Bouve College of Health Sciences, 617-373-3321, Fax: 617-373-3030, E-mail: s.parish@northeastern.edu. *Application contact:* 617-373-2708, Fax: 617-373-4701, E-mail: bouvegrad@northeastern.edu.
Website: https://www.northeastern.edu/bouve/

Point Loma Nazarene University, School of Nursing, MS in Nursing Program, San Diego, CA 92106-2899. Offers adult-gerontology (MSN); family individual health (MSN); pediatrics (MSN). *Program availability:* Part-time. *Students:* 59 part-time (49 women); includes 28 minority (4 Black or African American, non-Hispanic/Latino; 1 American Indian or Alaska Native, non-Hispanic/Latino; 4 Asian, non-Hispanic/Latino; 9 Hispanic/Latino; 4 Native Hawaiian or other Pacific Islander, non-Hispanic/Latino; 6 Two or more races, non-Hispanic/Latino), 1 international. Average age 36. 23 applicants, 96% accepted, 18 enrolled. In 2017, 21 master's awarded. *Entrance requirements:* For master's, NCLEX exam, ADN or BSN in nursing, interview, RN license, essay, letters of recommendation, interview. *Application deadline:* For fall admission, 7/5 priority date for domestic students; for spring admission, 11/1 priority date for domestic students; for summer admission, 3/22 priority date for domestic students. Applications are processed on a rolling basis. Electronic applications accepted. *Expenses:* Contact institution. *Financial support:* Scholarships/grants available. Financial award applicants required to submit FAFSA. *Unit head:* Dr. Barb Taylor, Dean of the School of Nursing, 619-849-2766, E-mail: bataylor@pointloma.edu. *Application contact:* Joanie Joy, Senior Director of Enrollment Management, 619-329-6785, E-mail: gradinfo@pointloma.edu.
Website: https://www.pointloma.edu/graduate-studies/programs/nursing-ms

Purdue University Northwest, Graduate Studies Office, School of Nursing, Hammond, IN 46323-2094. Offers adult health clinical nurse specialist (MS); critical care clinical nurse specialist (MS); family nurse practitioner (MS); nurse executive (MS). *Accreditation:* ACEN. *Program availability:* Part-time, online learning. *Entrance requirements:* For master's, BSN. Additional exam requirements/recommendations for international students: Required—TOEFL. Electronic applications accepted. *Faculty research:* Adult health, cardiovascular and pulmonary nursing.

San Francisco State University, Division of Graduate Studies, College of Health and Social Sciences, School of Nursing, San Francisco, CA 94132-1722. Offers adult acute care (MS); clinical nurse specialist (MS); community/public health nursing (MS); family nurse practitioner (Certificate); nursing administration (MS); pediatrics (MS); women's health (MS). *Accreditation:* AACN. *Program availability:* Part-time. *Application deadline:* Applications are processed on a rolling basis. *Financial support:* Career-related internships or fieldwork available. *Unit head:* Connie Carr, Assistant Director of Graduate Programs, 415-338-6856, Fax: 415-338-0555, E-mail: ccarr@sfsu.edu.
Website: http://nursing.sfsu.edu

Southern Adventist University, School of Nursing, Collegedale, TN 37315-0370. Offers adult/gerontology acute care nurse practitioner (MSN, DNP); adult/gerontology nurse practitioner (MSN); family nurse practitioner (MSN, DNP); lifestyle therapeutics (DNP); nurse educator (MSN, DNP); psychiatric mental health nurse practitioner (MSN, DNP); MSN/MBA. *Accreditation:* ACEN. *Program availability:* Part-time. *Degree requirements:* For master's, thesis or project. *Entrance requirements:* For master's, RN license. Additional exam requirements/recommendations for international students: Required—TOEFL (minimum score 600 paper-based). *Application deadline:* For fall admission, 7/1 for domestic and international students; for winter admission, 12/1 for domestic and international students. Applications are processed on a rolling basis. Application fee: $40. Electronic applications accepted. *Expenses: Tuition:* Full-time $11,430; part-time $635 per credit hour. Tuition and fees vary according to degree level and program. *Financial support:* Teaching assistantships with partial tuition reimbursements available. *Faculty research:* Pain management, ethics, corporate wellness, caring spirituality, stress. *Unit head:* Dr. Barbara James, Dean, 423-236-2942, Fax: 423-236-1940, E-mail: bjames@southern.edu. *Application contact:* Sylvia Mayer, RN, Director of Nursing Admissions, 423-236-2941, Fax: 423-236-1940, E-mail: smayer@southern.edu.
Website: https://www.southern.edu/academics/nursing.html

Tennessee Technological University, Whitson-Hester School of Nursing, DNP Program, Cookeville, TN 38505. Offers adult-gerontology acute care nurse practitioner (DNP); executive leadership in nursing (DNP); family nurse practitioner (DNP); pediatric nurse practitioner-primary care (DNP); psychiatric/mental health nurse practitioner (DNP); women's health care nurse practitioner (DNP). *Program availability:* Part-time. *Students:* 10 part-time (all women). 14 applicants, 86% accepted, 10 enrolled. *Application deadline:* For fall admission, 7/1 for domestic students, 5/1 for international students; for spring admission, 12/1 for domestic students, 10/1 for international students; for summer admission, 5/1 for domestic students, 2/1 for international students. Applications are processed on a rolling basis. Application fee: $35 ($40 for international students). Electronic applications accepted. *Expenses:* Tuition, state resident: full-time $9925; part-time $565 per credit hour. Tuition, nonresident: full-time $22,993; part-time $1291 per credit hour. *Financial support:* Application deadline: 4/1; applicants required to submit FAFSA. *Unit head:* Dr. Bedelia Russell, Program Director, Fax: 931-372-6244, E-mail: bhrussell@tntech.edu. *Application contact:* Shelia K. Kendrick, Coordinator of Graduate Studies, 931-372-3808, Fax: 931-372-3497, E-mail: skendrick@tntech.edu.
Website: https://www.tntech.edu/nursing/doctor-of-nursing-practice/

Texas Tech University Health Sciences Center, School of Nursing, Lubbock, TX 79430. Offers acute care nurse practitioner (MSN, Certificate); administration (MSN); advanced practice (DNP); education (MSN); executive leadership (DNP); family nurse practitioner (MSN, Certificate); geriatric nurse practitioner (MSN, Certificate); pediatric nurse practitioner (MSN, Certificate). *Accreditation:* AACN. *Program availability:* Part-time, online learning. *Degree requirements:* For master's, thesis optional. *Entrance requirements:* For master's, minimum GPA of 3.0, 3 letters of reference, BSN, RN license; for Certificate, minimum GPA of 3.0, 3 letters of reference, RN license. Additional exam requirements/recommendations for international students: Required—TOEFL (minimum score 550 paper-based). *Faculty research:* Diabetes/obesity, nurse competency, disease management, intervention and measurements, health disparities.

Texas Woman's University, Graduate School, College of Nursing, Denton, TX 76204. Offers adult health clinical nurse specialist (MS); adult health nurse practitioner (MS); adult/gerontology acute care nurse practitioner (MS); child health clinical nurse specialist (MS); clinical nurse leader (MS); family nurse practitioner (MS); health systems management (MS); nursing education (MS); nursing practice (DNP); nursing science (PhD); pediatric nurse practitioner (MS); women's health clinical nurse specialist (MS); women's health nurse practitioner (MS). *Accreditation:* AACN. *Program availability:* Part-time, 100% online, blended/hybrid learning. *Faculty:* 48 full-time (47 women), 44 part-time/adjunct (37 women). *Students:* 23 full-time (22 women), 816 part-time (750 women); includes 475 minority (188 Black or African American, non-Hispanic/Latino; 4 American Indian or Alaska Native, non-Hispanic/Latino; 171 Asian, non-Hispanic/Latino; 83 Hispanic/Latino; 3 Native Hawaiian or other Pacific Islander, non-Hispanic/Latino; 26 Two or more races, non-Hispanic/Latino), 12 international. Average age 37. 201 applicants, 88% accepted, 123 enrolled. In 2017, 232 master's, 17 doctorates awarded. *Degree requirements:* For master's, comprehensive exam, thesis or alternative, 6-year time limit for completion of degree, professional or clinical project; for doctorate, comprehensive exam, thesis/dissertation, 10-year time limit for completion of degree. *Entrance requirements:* For master's, GRE or MAT, minimum GPA of 3.0 on last 60 hours in undergraduate nursing degree and overall, RN license, BS in nursing, basic statistics course, 1 year of clinical experience; for doctorate, GRE (preferred minimum score 153 [500 old version] Verbal, 144 [500 old version] Quantitative, 4 Analytical), MS in nursing, minimum preferred GPA of 3.5, RN license, statistics course, 2 letters of reference, curriculum vitae, graduate nursing-theory course, graduate research course, statement of professional goals and research interests. Additional exam requirements/recommendations for international students: Required—TOEFL (minimum score 550 paper-based; 79 iBT); Recommended—IELTS (minimum score

6.5), TSE (minimum score 53). *Application deadline:* For fall admission, 5/1 for domestic students, 3/1 priority date for international students; for spring admission, 9/15 for domestic students, 7/1 priority date for international students; for summer admission, 2/1 for domestic and international students. Applications are processed on a rolling basis. Application fee: $50 ($75 for international students). Electronic applications accepted. *Expenses:* $8,510 per year full-time in-state, $17,810 per year full-time out-of-state. *Financial support:* In 2017–18, 146 students received support, including 7 teaching assistantships (averaging $28,195 per year); research assistantships, career-related internships or fieldwork, Federal Work-Study, institutionally sponsored loans, scholarships/grants, traineeships, health care benefits, and unspecified assistantships also available. Support available to part-time students. Financial award application deadline: 3/1; financial award applicants required to submit FAFSA. *Faculty research:* Women's health, nurse staffing and satisfaction in health systems, perinatal safety, chronic illness, pediatric health. *Total annual research expenditures:* $380,388. *Unit head:* Dr. Anita G. Hufft, Dean, 940-898-2401, Fax: 940-898-2437, E-mail: nursing@twu.edu. *Application contact:* Korie Hawkins, Associate Director of Admissions, Graduate Recruitment, 940-898-3188, Fax: 940-898-3081, E-mail: admissions@twu.edu.
Website: http://www.twu.edu/nursing/

Universidad de Iberoamerica, Graduate School, San Jose, Costa Rica. Offers clinical neuropsychology (PhD); clinical psychology (M Psych); educational psychology (M Psych); forensic psychology (M Psych); hospital management (MHA); intensive care nursing (MN); medicine (MD).

The University of Alabama in Huntsville, School of Graduate Studies, College of Nursing, Huntsville, AL 35899. Offers family nurse practitioner (Certificate); nursing (MSN, DNP), including adult-gerontology acute care nurse practitioner (MSN), adult-gerontology clinical nurse specialist (MSN), family nurse practitioner (MSN), leadership in health care systems (MSN); nursing education (Certificate). DNP offered jointly with The University of Alabama at Birmingham. *Accreditation:* AACN. *Program availability:* Part-time, evening/weekend, online learning. *Degree requirements:* For master's, comprehensive exam, thesis or alternative, oral and written exams. *Entrance requirements:* For master's, MAT or GRE, Alabama RN license, BSN, minimum GPA of 3.0; for doctorate, master's degree in nursing in an advanced practice area; for Certificate, MAT or GRE, minimum GPA of 3.0. Additional exam requirements/recommendations for international students: Required—TOEFL (minimum score 500 paper-based; 80 iBT), IELTS (minimum score 6.5). Electronic applications accepted. *Faculty research:* Health care informatics, chronic illness management, maternal and child health, genetics/genomics, technology and health care.

University of Central Florida, College of Nursing, Orlando, FL 32816. Offers adult-gerontology acute care nurse practitioner (Certificate); adult-gerontology primary care nurse practitioner (Certificate); family nurse practitioner (Certificate); nursing (MSN, PhD); nursing education (Post-Master's Certificate); nursing practice (DNP). *Accreditation:* AACN. *Program availability:* Part-time, evening/weekend. *Faculty:* 57 full-time (49 women), 70 part-time/adjunct (68 women). *Students:* 63 full-time (58 women), 327 part-time (297 women); includes 131 minority (40 Black or African American, non-Hispanic/Latino; 1 American Indian or Alaska Native, non-Hispanic/Latino; 16 Asian, non-Hispanic/Latino; 62 Hispanic/Latino; 12 Two or more races, non-Hispanic/Latino), 1 international. Average age 38. 303 applicants, 64% accepted, 129 enrolled. In 2017, 87 master's, 5 doctorates, 4 other advanced degrees awarded. *Degree requirements:* For master's, thesis or alternative; for doctorate, comprehensive exam, thesis/dissertation. *Entrance requirements:* For master's, essay, curriculum vitae; for doctorate, GRE General Test, letters of recommendation, resume, essay. Additional exam requirements/recommendations for international students: Required—TOEFL. *Application deadline:* For fall admission, 3/15 for domestic students; for spring admission, 10/15 for domestic students. Application fee: $30. Electronic applications accepted. *Expenses:* Tuition, state resident: part-time $288.16 per credit hour. Tuition, nonresident: part-time $1073.31 per credit hour. Tuition and fees vary according to program. *Financial support:* In 2017–18, 3 students received support, including 2 fellowships with partial tuition reimbursements available (averaging $7,377 per year), 1 research assistantship with partial tuition reimbursement available (averaging $11,952 per year); career-related internships or fieldwork, Federal Work-Study, institutionally sponsored loans, traineeships, and unspecified assistantships also available. Financial award application deadline: 3/1; financial award applicants required to submit FAFSA. *Unit head:* Dr. Mary Lou Sole, Dean, 407-823-5496, Fax: 407-823-5675, E-mail: mary.sole@ucf.edu. *Application contact:* Associate Director, Graduate Admissions, 407-823-2766, Fax: 407-823-6442, E-mail: gradadmissions@ucf.edu.
Website: http://nursing.ucf.edu/

University of Cincinnati, Graduate School, College of Nursing, Cincinnati, OH 45221-0038. Offers nurse midwifery (MSN); nurse practitioner (MSN, DNP), including acute care pediatrics (DNP), adult-gerontology acute care, adult-gerontology primary care, anesthesia (DNP), family (MSN), leadership (DNP), neonatal (MSN), women's health (MSN); nursing (MSN, PhD), including occupational health (MSN). *Accreditation:* AACN; AANA/CANAEP (one or more programs are accredited); ACNM/ACME. *Program availability:* Part-time, 100% online, blended/hybrid learning. *Faculty:* 74 full-time (69 women), 112 part-time/adjunct (105 women). *Students:* 323 full-time (261 women), 1,084 part-time (949 women); includes 311 minority (113 Black or African American, non-Hispanic/Latino; 4 American Indian or Alaska Native, non-Hispanic/Latino; 56 Asian, non-Hispanic/Latino; 108 Hispanic/Latino; 1 Native Hawaiian or other Pacific Islander, non-Hispanic/Latino; 29 Two or more races, non-Hispanic/Latino), 12 international. Average age 34. 582 applicants, 64% accepted, 314 enrolled. In 2017, 579 master's, 18 doctorates awarded. *Degree requirements:* For master's, thesis or alternative; for doctorate, comprehensive exam (for some programs), thesis/dissertation (for some programs). *Entrance requirements:* For doctorate, GRE General Test. Additional exam requirements/recommendations for international students: Required—TOEFL (minimum score 600 paper-based; 100 iBT); Recommended—IELTS (minimum score 7). *Application deadline:* For fall admission, 5/1 priority date for domestic students, 5/1 for international students; for spring admission, 10/1 for domestic students; for summer admission, 3/1 priority date for domestic students. Applications are processed on a rolling basis. Application fee: $130 ($70 for international students). Electronic applications accepted. *Expenses:* $14,668 annual full-time in-state tuition, $707 annual fees. *Financial support:* In 2017–18, 123 students received support, including 8 fellowships with full tuition reimbursements available (averaging $30,423 per year), 7 research assistantships with full tuition reimbursements available (averaging $17,971 per year), 5 teaching assistantships with full tuition reimbursements available (averaging $17,971 per year); Federal Work-Study, institutionally sponsored loans, scholarships/grants, traineeships, health care benefits, tuition waivers (partial), and unspecified assistantships also available. Support available to part-time students. Financial award application deadline: 5/1; financial award applicants required to submit FAFSA. *Faculty research:* Vulnerable populations, education, violence, chronicity/aging, cancer. *Total annual research expenditures:* $575,576. *Unit head:* Dr. Greer Glazer, Dean, 513-558-5330, Fax: 513-558-9030, E-mail: greer.glazer@uc.edu. *Application contact:* Office of Student Recruitment, 513-558-8400, Fax: 513-558-5012, E-mail: nursingbearcats@uc.edu.
Website: https://nursing.uc.edu/

University of Guelph, Ontario Veterinary College and Graduate Studies, Graduate Programs in Veterinary Sciences, Department of Clinical Studies, Guelph, ON N1G 2W1, Canada. Offers anesthesiology (M Sc, DV Sc); cardiology (DV Sc, Diploma); clinical studies (Diploma); dermatology (M Sc); diagnostic imaging (M Sc, DV Sc); emergency/critical care (M Sc, DV Sc, Diploma); medicine (M Sc, DV Sc); neurology (M Sc, DV Sc); ophthalmology (M Sc, DV Sc); surgery (M Sc, DV Sc). *Degree requirements:* For master's, thesis; for doctorate, comprehensive exam, thesis/dissertation. *Entrance requirements:* Additional exam requirements/recommendations for international students: Required—TOEFL (minimum score 550 paper-based), IELTS (minimum score 6.5). Electronic applications accepted. *Faculty research:* Orthopedics, respirology, oncology, exercise physiology, cardiology.

University of Illinois at Chicago, College of Nursing, Program in Nursing, Chicago, IL 60607-7128. Offers acute care clinical nurse specialist (MS); administrative nursing leadership (Certificate); adult nurse practitioner (MS); adult/geriatric nurse practitioner (MS); advanced community health nurse specialist (MS); family nurse practitioner (MS); geriatric clinical nurse specialist (MS); geriatric nurse practitioner (MS); nurse midwifery (MS); occupational health/advanced community health nurse specialist (MS); occupational health/family nurse practitioner (MS); pediatric nurse practitioner (MS); perinatal clinical nurse specialist (MS); school/advanced community health nurse specialist (MS); school/family nurse practitioner (MS); women's health nurse practitioner (MS). *Accreditation:* AACN. *Program availability:* Part-time. *Degree requirements:* For master's, thesis or alternative. *Entrance requirements:* For master's, GRE General Test, minimum GPA of 2.75. Additional exam requirements/recommendations for international students: Required—TOEFL. Electronic applications accepted.

University of Miami, Graduate School, School of Nursing and Health Studies, Coral Gables, FL 33124. Offers acute care (MSN), including acute care nurse practitioner, nurse anesthesia; nursing (PhD); primary care (MSN), including adult nurse practitioner, family nurse practitioner, nurse midwifery, women's health practitioner. *Accreditation:* AACN; AANA/CANAEP; ACNM/ACME (one or more programs are accredited). *Program availability:* Part-time. *Degree requirements:* For master's, thesis optional; for doctorate, thesis/dissertation. *Entrance requirements:* For master's, GRE General Test, BSN, minimum GPA of 3.0, Florida RN license; for doctorate, GRE General Test, BSN or MSN, minimum GPA of 3.0. Additional exam requirements/recommendations for international students: Required—TOEFL (minimum score 550 paper-based). Electronic applications accepted. *Faculty research:* Transcultural nursing, exercise and depression in Alzheimer's disease, infectious diseases/HIV–AIDS, postpartum depression, outcomes assessment.

The University of North Carolina at Charlotte, College of Health and Human Services, School of Nursing, Charlotte, NC 28223-0001. Offers adult-gerontology acute care nurse practitioner (Post-Master's Certificate); advanced clinical nursing (MSN), including adult psychiatric mental health, adult-gerontology acute care nurse practitioner, family nurse practitioner across the lifespan; family nurse practitioner across the lifespan (Post-Master's Certificate); nurse anesthesia (MSN), including nurse anesthesia across the lifespan; nurse anesthesia across the lifespan (Post-Master's Certificate); nursing (DNP); nursing administration (Graduate Certificate); nursing education (Graduate Certificate); systems/population nursing (MSN), including community/public health nursing, nurse administrator, nurse educator. *Accreditation:* AACN; AANA/CANAEP. *Program availability:* Part-time, blended/hybrid learning. *Faculty:* 24 full-time (22 women), 6 part-time/adjunct (4 women). *Students:* 113 full-time (84 women), 163 part-time (150 women); includes 63 minority (47 Black or African American, non-Hispanic/Latino; 2 American Indian or Alaska Native, non-Hispanic/Latino; 6 Asian, non-Hispanic/Latino; 3 Hispanic/Latino; 5 Two or more races, non-Hispanic/Latino). Average age 37. 443 applicants, 31% accepted, 113 enrolled. In 2017, 83 master's, 8 doctorates, 8 other advanced degrees awarded. Terminal master's awarded for partial completion of doctoral program. *Degree requirements:* For doctorate, thesis/dissertation or alternative, residency; for other advanced degree, practicum. *Entrance requirements:* For master's, GRE General Test, current unrestricted license as Registered Nurse in North Carolina; BSN from nationally-accredited program; one year of professional nursing practice in acute/critical care; minimum overall GPA of 3.0 in last degree; completion of undergraduate statistics course with minimum grade of C; statement of purpose; for doctorate, GRE or MAT, master's degree in nursing in an advanced nursing practice specialty from nationally-accredited program; minimum overall GPA of 3.5 in MSN program; current RN licensure in U.S. at time of application with eligibility for NC licensure; essay; resume/curriculum vitae; professional recommendations; clinical hours; for other advanced degree, GRE. Additional exam requirements/recommendations for international students: Required—TOEFL (minimum score 523 paper-based, 70 iBT) or IELTS (6.5). *Application deadline:* For fall admission, 1/10 for domestic and international students; for spring admission, 9/10 for domestic and international students; for summer admission, 4/1 for domestic and international students. Applications are processed on a rolling basis. Application fee: $75. Electronic applications accepted. *Expenses:* Contact institution. *Financial support:* In 2017–18, 6 students received support, including 4 research assistantships (averaging $6,338 per year), 2 teaching assistantships (averaging $6,250 per year); career-related internships or fieldwork, institutionally sponsored loans, scholarships/grants, traineeships, and unspecified assistantships also available. Support available to part-time students. Financial award application deadline: 3/1; financial award applicants required to submit FAFSA. *Total annual research expenditures:* $800,072. *Unit head:* Dr. Dena Evans, Director, 704-687-7974, E-mail: devans37@uncc.edu. *Application contact:* Kathy B. Giddings, Director of Graduate Admissions, 704-687-5503, Fax: 704-687-1668, E-mail: gradadm@uncc.edu.
Website: http://nursing.uncc.edu/

University of Northern Colorado, Graduate School, College of Natural and Health Sciences, School of Nursing, Greeley, CO 80639. Offers adult-gerontology acute care nurse practitioner (MSN, DNP); family nurse practitioner (MSN, DNP); nursing education (PhD); nursing practice (DNP). *Accreditation:* AACN. *Program availability:* Online learning. *Degree requirements:* For master's, comprehensive exam, thesis or alternative; for doctorate, comprehensive exam, thesis/dissertation. *Entrance requirements:* For master's and doctorate, GRE General Test, minimum GPA of 3.0 in last 60 hours, BS in nursing, 2 letters of recommendation. Electronic applications accepted.

University of Pennsylvania, School of Nursing, Adult-Gerontology Acute Care Nurse Practitioner Program, Philadelphia, PA 19104. Offers MSN. *Accreditation:* AACN. *Program availability:* Part-time, online learning. *Students:* 19 full-time (17 women), 174 part-time (155 women); includes 46 minority (11 Black or African American, non-Hispanic/Latino; 27 Asian, non-Hispanic/Latino; 8 Hispanic/Latino), 3 international. Average age 35. 245 applicants, 74% accepted, 163 enrolled. In 2017, 116 master's awarded. *Entrance requirements:* For master's, GRE General Test. Application fee: $80. *Financial support:* Application deadline: 4/1. *Faculty research:* Post-injury disability, bereavement and attributions in fire survivors, stress in staff nurses. *Unit head:* Assistant Dean of Admissions and Financial Aid, 866-867-6877, Fax: 215-573-8439, E-mail: admissions@nursing.upenn.edu. *Application contact:* Deborah Becker, Program Director, 215-898-0432, E-mail: debecker@nursing.upenn.edu.
Website: http://www.nursing.upenn.edu/

Acute Care/Critical Care Nursing

University of Pennsylvania, School of Nursing, Pediatric Acute Care Nurse Practitioner Program, Philadelphia, PA 19104. Offers MSN. *Accreditation:* AACN. *Program availability:* Part-time, online learning. *Students:* 15 full-time (all women), 41 part-time (all women); includes 10 minority (1 Black or African American, non-Hispanic/Latino; 7 Asian, non-Hispanic/Latino; 2 Two or more races, non-Hispanic/Latino). Average age 27. 49 applicants, 67% accepted, 33 enrolled. In 2017, 31 master's awarded. Application fee: $80.

University of Pittsburgh, School of Nursing, Nurse Practitioner Program, Pittsburgh, PA 15261. Offers adult-gerontology acute care (DNP); adult-gerontology primary care (DNP); family (individual across the lifespan) (DNP); neonatal (MSN, DNP); pediatric primary care (DNP); psychiatric mental health (DNP). *Accreditation:* AACN. *Program availability:* Part-time. *Faculty:* 17 full-time (14 women), 3 part-time/adjunct (2 women). *Students:* 50 full-time (47 women), 43 part-time (36 women); includes 9 minority (1 Black or African American, non-Hispanic/Latino; 1 American Indian or Alaska Native, non-Hispanic/Latino; 7 Asian, non-Hispanic/Latino), 1 international. Average age 31. 77 applicants, 40% accepted, 25 enrolled. In 2017, 6 master's, 35 doctorates awarded. *Degree requirements:* For master's, comprehensive exam, thesis optional. *Entrance requirements:* For master's, GRE General Test, BSN, RN license, 3 letters of recommendation, resume, course work in statistics, relevant nursing experience; for doctorate, GRE General Test, BSN, RN license, minimum GPA of 3.5, 3 letters of recommendation, relevant nursing experience, resume, course work in statistics. Additional exam requirements/recommendations for international students: Required—TOEFL (minimum score 600 paper-based; 100 IBT) or IELTS (minimum score 7.0). *Application deadline:* For fall admission, 5/1 priority date for domestic students, 2/15 priority date for international students. Application fee: $50. Electronic applications accepted. *Expenses:* $13,068 per term full-time resident tuition, $1,064 per credit part-time; $15,270 per term full-time non-resident tuition, $1,247 per credit part-time; $437 per term full-time fees; $282 per term part-time fees. *Financial support:* In 2017–18, 58 students received support, including 7 fellowships (averaging $15,755 per year), 15 teaching assistantships (averaging $12,454 per year); scholarships/grants, tuition waivers, and unspecified assistantships also available. Financial award applicants required to submit FAFSA. *Faculty research:* Behavioral management of chronic disorders, patient management in critical care, consumer informatics, genetic applications (molecular genetics and psychosocial implications), technology for nurses and patients to improve care. *Unit head:* Dr. Sandra Engberg, Associate Dean for Clinical Education, 412-624-3835, Fax: 412-624-8521, E-mail: sje1@pitt.edu. *Application contact:* Laurie Lapsley, Graduate Administrator, 412-624-9670, Fax: 412-624-2409, E-mail: lapsleyl@pitt.edu.
Website: http://www.nursing.pitt.edu

University of Puerto Rico–Medical Sciences Campus, School of Nursing, San Juan, PR 00936-5067. Offers adult and elderly nursing (MSN); child and adolescent nursing (MSN); critical care nursing (MSN); family and community nursing (MSN); family nurse practitioner (MSN); maternity nursing (MSN); mental health and psychiatric nursing (MSN). *Accreditation:* AACN; AANA/CANAEP. *Entrance requirements:* For master's, GRE or EXADEP, interview, Puerto Rico RN license or professional license for international students, general and specific point average, article analysis. Electronic applications accepted. *Faculty research:* HIV, health disparities, teen violence, women and violence, neurological disorders.

University of Rhode Island, Graduate School, College of Nursing, Kingston, RI 02881. Offers acute care nurse practitioner (adult-gerontology focus) (Post Master's Certificate); adult gerontology nurse practitioner/clinical nurse specialist (Post Master's Certificate); adult-gerontological acute care nurse practitioner (MS); adult-gerontological nurse practitioner/clinical nurse specialist (MS); family nurse practitioner (MS, Post Master's Certificate); nursing (DNP, PhD); nursing education (MS, Post Master's Certificate). *Accreditation:* AACN; ACNM/ACME (one or more programs are accredited). *Program availability:* Part-time, evening/weekend, 100% online, blended/hybrid learning. *Faculty:* 31 full-time (30 women). *Students:* 42 full-time (36 women), 86 part-time (79 women); includes 12 minority (3 Black or African American, non-Hispanic/Latino; 3 Asian, non-Hispanic/Latino; 3 Hispanic/Latino; 1 Native Hawaiian or other Pacific Islander, non-Hispanic/Latino; 2 Two or more races, non-Hispanic/Latino), 3 international. 33 applicants, 79% accepted, 23 enrolled. In 2017, 25 master's, 8 doctorates, 2 other advanced degrees awarded. *Entrance requirements:* For master's, GRE or MAT, 2 letters of recommendation, scholarly papers; for doctorate, GRE, 3 letters of recommendation, scholarly papers. Additional exam requirements/recommendations for international students: Required—TOEFL. *Application deadline:* For fall admission, 2/15 for domestic students, 2/1 for international students; for spring admission, 10/15 for domestic students, 7/15 for international students. Application fee: $65. Electronic applications accepted. *Expenses:* Tuition, state resident: full-time $12,706; part-time $786 per credit. Tuition, nonresident: full-time $25,216; part-time $1401 per credit. *Required fees:* $1598; $45 per credit. One-time fee: $30 part-time. *Financial support:* In 2017–18, 1 research assistantship with tuition reimbursement (averaging $18,080 per year), 5 teaching assistantships with tuition reimbursements (averaging $10,133 per year) were awarded. Financial award application deadline: 2/1; financial award applicants required to submit FAFSA. *Unit head:* Dr. Barbara Wolfe, Dean, 401-874-5324, E-mail: bwolfe@uri.edu. *Application contact:* Dr. Denise Coppa, Associate Professor/Interim Associate Dean for Graduate Programs, 401-874-5036, E-mail: dcoppa@uri.edu.
Website: http://www.uri.edu/nursing/

University of Rochester, School of Nursing, Rochester, NY 14642. Offers adult gerontological acute care nurse practitioner (MS); adult gerontological primary care nurse practitioner (MS); clinical nurse leader (MS); family nurse practitioner (MS); family psychiatric mental health nurse practitioner (MS); health care organization management and leadership (MS); nursing (DNP); nursing and health science (PhD); nursing education (MS); pediatric nurse practitioner (MS); pediatric nurse practitioner/neonatal nurse practitioner (MS). *Accreditation:* AACN. *Program availability:* Part-time, 100% online, blended/hybrid learning. *Faculty:* 62 full-time (51 women), 73 part-time/adjunct (63 women). *Students:* 17 full-time (12 women), 306 part-time (252 women); includes 46 minority (16 Black or African American, non-Hispanic/Latino; 1 American Indian or Alaska Native, non-Hispanic/Latino; 7 Asian, non-Hispanic/Latino; 17 Hispanic/Latino; 5 Two or more races, non-Hispanic/Latino), 3 international. Average age 34. 143 applicants, 71% accepted, 87 enrolled. In 2017, 48 master's, 8 doctorates awarded. Terminal master's awarded for partial completion of doctoral program. *Degree requirements:* For master's, comprehensive exam; for doctorate, thesis/dissertation. *Entrance requirements:* For master's, BS in nursing, minimum GPA of 3.0, course work in statistics; for doctorate, GRE General Test (for PhD), MS in nursing, minimum GPA of 3.5. Additional exam requirements/recommendations for international students: Required—TOEFL (minimum score 560 paper-based; 88 iBT) or IELTS (minimum score 6.5) recommended. *Application deadline:* For fall admission, 4/1 for domestic and international students; for spring admission, 9/1 for domestic and international students; for summer admission, 1/2 for domestic and international students. Application fee: $50. Electronic applications accepted. *Financial support:* In 2017–18, 63 students received support, including 2 fellowships with full and partial tuition reimbursements available (averaging $16,000 per year); scholarships/grants, traineeships, health care benefits, tuition waivers (full and partial), and unspecified assistantships also available. Support available to part-time students. Financial award application deadline: 6/30; financial award applicants required to submit CSS PROFILE or FAFSA. *Faculty research:* Symptom science, systems of care, innovations in health technology, promoting healthy behaviors. *Total annual research expenditures:* $2.6 million. *Unit head:* Dr. Kathy H. Rideout, Dean, 585-273-8902, Fax: 585-273-1268, E-mail: kathy_rideout@urmc.rochester.edu. *Application contact:* Elaine Andolina, Director of Admissions, 585-275-2375, Fax: 585-756-8299, E-mail: elaine_andolina@urmc.rochester.edu.
Website: http://www.son.rochester.edu

University of South Africa, College of Human Sciences, Pretoria, South Africa. Offers adult education (M Ed); African languages (MA, PhD); African politics (MA, PhD); Afrikaans (MA, PhD); ancient history (MA, PhD); ancient Near Eastern studies (MA, PhD); anthropology (MA, PhD); applied linguistics (MA); Arabic (MA, PhD); archaeology (MA); art history (MA); Biblical archaeology (MA); Biblical studies (M Th, D Th, PhD); Christian spirituality (M Th, D Th); church history (M Th, D Th); classical studies (MA, PhD); clinical psychology (MA); communication (MA, PhD); comparative education (M Ed, Ed D); consulting psychology (D Admin, D Com, PhD); curriculum studies (M Ed, Ed D); development studies (M Admin, MA, D Admin, PhD); didactics (M Ed, Ed D); education (M Tech); education management (M Ed, Ed D); educational psychology (M Ed); English (MA); environmental education (M Ed); French (MA, PhD); German (MA, PhD); Greek (MA); guidance and counseling (M Ed); health studies (MA, PhD), including health sciences education (MA), health services management (MA), medical and surgical nursing science (critical care general) (MA), midwifery and neonatal nursing science (MA), trauma and emergency care (MA); history (MA, PhD); history of education (Ed D); inclusive education (M Ed, Ed D); information and communications technology policy and regulation (MA); information science (MA, MIS, PhD); international politics (MA, PhD); Islamic studies (MA, PhD); Italian (MA, PhD); Judaica (MA, PhD); linguistics (MA, PhD); mathematical education (M Ed); mathematics education (MA); missiology (M Th, D Th); modern Hebrew (MA, PhD); musicology (MA, MMus, D Mus, PhD); natural science education (M Ed); New Testament (M Th, D Th); Old Testament (D Th); pastoral therapy (M Th, D Th); philosophy (MA); philosophy of education (M Ed, Ed D); politics (MA, PhD); Portuguese (MA, PhD); practical theology (M Th, D Th); psychology (MA, MS, PhD); psychology of education (M Ed, Ed D); public health (MA); religious studies (MA, D Th, PhD); Romance languages (MA); Russian (MA, PhD); Semitic languages (MA, PhD); social behavior studies in HIV/AIDS (MA); social science (mental health) (MA); social science in development studies (MA); social science in psychology (MA); social science in social work (MA); social science in sociology (MA); social work (MSW, DSW, PhD); socio-education (M Ed, Ed D); sociolinguistics (MA); sociology (MA, PhD); Spanish (MA, PhD); systematic theology (M Th, D Th); TESOL (teaching English to speakers of other languages) (MA); theological ethics (M Th, D Th); theory of literature (MA, PhD); urban ministries (D Th); urban ministry (M Th).

University of South Carolina, The Graduate School, College of Nursing, Program in Advanced Practice Clinical Nursing, Columbia, SC 29208. Offers acute care nurse practitioner (Certificate); advanced practice clinical nursing (MSN). *Accreditation:* AACN. *Program availability:* Part-time, online learning. *Entrance requirements:* For master's, master's degree in nursing, RN license; for Certificate, MSN. Additional exam requirements/recommendations for international students: Required—TOEFL (minimum score 570 paper-based). Electronic applications accepted. *Faculty research:* Systems research, evidence based practice, breast cancer, violence.

University of South Carolina, The Graduate School, College of Nursing, Program in Clinical Nursing, Columbia, SC 29208. Offers acute care clinical specialist (MSN); acute care nurse practitioner (MSN); women's health nurse practitioner (MSN). *Accreditation:* AACN. *Program availability:* Part-time. *Degree requirements:* For master's, thesis or alternative. *Entrance requirements:* For master's, GRE General Test or MAT, BS in nursing, RN licensure. Additional exam requirements/recommendations for international students: Required—TOEFL (minimum score 570 paper-based). Electronic applications accepted. *Faculty research:* Systems research, evidence based practice, breast cancer, violence.

University of South Florida, College of Nursing, Tampa, FL 33612. Offers nurse anesthesia (DNP); nursing (MS, DNP), including adult-gerontology acute care nursing, adult-gerontology primary care nursing, family health nursing, nurse anesthesia (MS), nursing education (MS), occupational health nursing/adult-gerontology primary care nursing, oncology nursing/adult-gerontology primary care nursing (DNP), pediatric health nursing; nursing education (Post Master's Certificate); nursing science (PhD); simulation based academic fellowship in advanced pain management (Graduate Certificate). *Accreditation:* AACN; AANA/CANAEP. *Program availability:* Part-time. *Faculty:* 37 full-time (32 women), 2 part-time/adjunct (1 woman). *Students:* 224 full-time (178 women), 669 part-time (577 women); includes 309 minority (105 Black or African American, non-Hispanic/Latino; 2 American Indian or Alaska Native, non-Hispanic/Latino; 53 Asian, non-Hispanic/Latino; 122 Hispanic/Latino; 1 Native Hawaiian or other Pacific Islander, non-Hispanic/Latino; 26 Two or more races, non-Hispanic/Latino), 6 international. Average age 32. 949 applicants, 47% accepted, 382 enrolled. In 2017, 264 master's, 39 doctorates awarded. *Degree requirements:* For master's, comprehensive exam, thesis optional; for doctorate, comprehensive exam, thesis/dissertation. *Entrance requirements:* For master's, GRE General Test, bachelor's degree from accredited program with minimum GPA of 3.0 in all upper-division coursework; current license as Registered Nurse; 3 letters of recommendation; personal statement of goals; resume or curriculum vitae; personal interview; for doctorate, GRE General Test (recommended), bachelor's degree in nursing from ACEN or CCNE regionally-accredited institution with minimum GPA of 3.0 in all coursework or in all upper-division coursework; current license as Registered Nurse in Florida; undergraduate statistics course with minimum B grade; 3 letters of recommendation; statement of goals; resume; interview. Additional exam requirements/recommendations for international students: Required—TOEFL (minimum score 550 paper-based; 79 iBT). *Application deadline:* For fall admission, 12/15 for domestic and international students; for spring admission, 10/1 for domestic students, 9/15 for international students. Application fee: $30. Electronic applications accepted. *Financial support:* In 2017–18, 132 students received support, including 7 research assistantships with tuition reimbursements available (averaging $18,935 per year), 29 teaching assistantships with tuition reimbursements available (averaging $30,814 per year); tuition waivers (partial) and unspecified assistantships also available. Financial award application deadline: 2/1; financial award applicants required to submit FAFSA. *Faculty research:* Women's health, palliative and end-of-life care, cardiac rehabilitation, complementary therapies for chronic illness and cancer. *Total annual research expenditures:* $3.2 million. *Unit head:* Dr. Victoria Rich, Dean, College of Nursing, 813-974-8939, Fax: 813-974-5418, E-mail: victoriarich@health.usf.edu. *Application contact:* Dr. Brian Graves, Assistant Professor/Assistant Dean, 813-974-8054, Fax: 813-974-5418, E-mail: bgraves1@health.usf.edu.
Website: http://health.usf.edu/nursing/index.htm

The University of Texas Health Science Center at San Antonio, School of Nursing, San Antonio, TX 78229-3900. Offers administrative management (MSN); adult-gerontology acute care nurse practitioner (PGC); advanced practice leadership (DNP); clinical nurse leader (MSN); executive administrative management (DNP); family nurse practitioner (MSN, PGC); nursing (MSN, PhD); nursing education (MSN, PGC); pediatric nurse practitioner primary care (PGC); psychiatric mental health nurse practitioner (PGC); public health nurse leader (DNP). *Accreditation:* AACN. *Program availability:* Part-time. Terminal master's awarded for partial completion of doctoral program. *Degree requirements:* For master's, thesis optional; for doctorate, comprehensive exam, thesis/dissertation.

University of Virginia, School of Nursing, Charlottesville, VA 22903. Offers acute and specialty care (MSN); acute care nurse practitioner (MSN); clinical nurse leadership (MSN); community-public health leadership (MSN); nursing (DNP, PhD); psychiatric mental health counseling (MSN); MSN/MBA. *Accreditation:* AACN. *Program availability:* Part-time. *Faculty:* 51 full-time (44 women), 17 part-time/adjunct (16 women). *Students:* 202 full-time (168 women), 139 part-time (114 women); includes 78 minority (32 Black or African American, non-Hispanic/Latino; 2 American Indian or Alaska Native, non-Hispanic/Latino; 14 Asian, non-Hispanic/Latino; 17 Hispanic/Latino; 1 Native Hawaiian or other Pacific Islander, non-Hispanic/Latino; 12 Two or more races, non-Hispanic/Latino), 9 international. Average age 34. 183 applicants, 68% accepted, 98 enrolled. In 2017, 105 master's, 27 doctorates awarded. *Degree requirements:* For doctorate, comprehensive exam (for some programs), capstone project (DNP), dissertation (PhD). *Entrance requirements:* For master's, GRE General Test, MAT; for doctorate, GRE General Test. Additional exam requirements/recommendations for international students: Required—TOEFL, IELTS. *Application deadline:* Applications are processed on a rolling basis. Application fee: $60. Electronic applications accepted. *Financial support:* Fellowships, research assistantships, teaching assistantships, Federal Work-Study, and scholarships/grants available. Financial award applicants required to submit FAFSA. *Unit head:* Dorrie K. Fontaine, Dean, 434-924-0141, Fax: 434-982-1809, E-mail: dkf2u@virginia.edu. *Application contact:* Teresa Carroll, Senior Assistant Dean for Academic and Student Services, 434-924-0141, Fax: 434-982-1809, E-mail: nur-osa@virginia.edu.
Website: http://www.nursing.virginia.edu/

Vanderbilt University, Vanderbilt University School of Nursing, Nashville, TN 37240. Offers adult-gerontology acute care nurse practitioner (MSN), including hospitalist, intensivist; adult-gerontology primary care nurse practitioner (MSN); emergency nurse practitioner (MSN); family nurse practitioner (MSN); healthcare leadership (MSN); neonatal nurse practitioner (MSN); nurse midwifery (MSN); nurse midwifery/family nurse practitioner (MSN); nursing (Post-Master's Certificate); nursing informatics (MSN); nursing practice (DNP); nursing science (PhD); pediatric acute care nurse practitioner (MSN); pediatric primary care nurse practitioner (MSN); psychiatric-mental health nurse practitioner (MSN); women's health nurse practitioner (MSN); women's health nurse practitioner/adult gerontology primary care nurse practitioner (MSN); MSN/M Div; MSN/MTS. *Accreditation:* AACN; ACEN (one or more programs are accredited); ACNM/ACME. *Program availability:* Part-time, 100% online, blended/hybrid learning. *Faculty:* 292 full-time (267 women), 321 part-time/adjunct (253 women). *Students:* 501 full-time (435 women), 387 part-time (355 women); includes 153 minority (40 Black or African American, non-Hispanic/Latino; 1 American Indian or Alaska Native, non-Hispanic/Latino; 27 Asian, non-Hispanic/Latino; 48 Hispanic/Latino; 4 Native Hawaiian or other Pacific Islander, non-Hispanic/Latino; 33 Two or more races, non-Hispanic/Latino), 9 international. Average age 31. 1,210 applicants, 57% accepted, 473 enrolled. In 2017, 319 master's, 47 doctorates awarded. *Degree requirements:* For doctorate, comprehensive exam, thesis/dissertation. *Entrance requirements:* For master's, GRE General Test (taken within the past 5 years), minimum B average in undergraduate course work, 3 letters of recommendation; for doctorate, GRE General Test, interview, 3 letters of recommendation from doctorally-prepared faculty, MSN, essay. Additional exam requirements/recommendations for international students: Required—TOEFL (minimum score 570 paper-based), IELTS (minimum score 6.5). *Application deadline:* For fall admission, 11/1 priority date for domestic and international students. Applications are processed on a rolling basis. Application fee: $50. Electronic applications accepted. *Expenses:* Contact institution. *Financial support:* In 2017–18, 627 students received support. Scholarships/grants available. Financial award application deadline: 3/1; financial award applicants required to submit FAFSA. *Faculty research:* Lymphedema, palliative care and bereavement, health services research including workforce, safety and quality of care, gerontology, better birth outcomes including nutrition. *Total annual research expenditures:* $2 million. *Unit head:* Dr. Linda Norman, Dean, 615-343-8876, Fax: 615-343-7711, E-mail: linda.norman@vanderbilt.edu. *Application contact:* Patricia Peerman, Assistant Dean for Enrollment Management, 615-322-3800, Fax: 615-343-0333, E-mail: vusn-admissions@vanderbilt.edu.
Website: http://www.nursing.vanderbilt.edu

Wayne State University, College of Nursing, Detroit, MI 48202. Offers adult gerontology acute care nurse practitioner (MSN); adult gerontology primary care nurse practitioner (MSN); advanced public health nursing (MSN); infant and mental health (DNP, PhD); neonatal nurse practitioner (MSN); nurse-midwifery (MSN); pediatric acute care nurse practitioner (MSN); pediatric primary care nurse practitioner (MSN); psychiatric mental health nurse practitioner (MSN); women's health nurse practitioner (MSN). Doctoral program admits for fall only. *Accreditation:* AACN. *Program availability:* Part-time. *Faculty:* 30. *Students:* 133 full-time (120 women), 184 part-time (167 women); includes 85 minority (57 Black or African American, non-Hispanic/Latino; 16 Asian, non-Hispanic/Latino; 4 Hispanic/Latino; 8 Two or more races, non-Hispanic/Latino), 22 international. Average age 34. 318 applicants, 39% accepted, 94 enrolled. In 2017, 51 master's, 29 doctorates awarded. *Degree requirements:* For doctorate, thesis/dissertation (for some programs). *Entrance requirements:* For master's, BSN from ACEN- or CCNE-accredited program with minimum GPA of 3.0; three references; current RN license; personal statement; for doctorate, resume or curriculum vitae; goals statement; bachelor's or master's degree in nursing from ACEN- or CCNE-accredited program with minimum GPA of 3.0; current RN license, writing sample and interview (for DNP); reference letters (3 for PhD, 2 for DNP). Additional exam requirements/recommendations for international students: Required—TOEFL (minimum score 101 iBT), TWE (minimum score 6), Michigan English Language Assessment Battery (minimum score 85); Recommended—IELTS (minimum score 7). Application fee: $50. Electronic applications accepted. *Expenses:* Contact institution. *Financial support:* In 2017–18, 92 students received support, including 16 fellowships with tuition reimbursements available (averaging $8,285 per year), 5 teaching assistantships with tuition reimbursements available (averaging $25,000 per year); scholarships/grants, health care benefits, and unspecified assistantships also available. Support available to part-time students. Financial award applicants required to submit FAFSA. *Faculty research:* Bridging transitions and technology to promote asthma care in the community, chronic wound care for persons who injected drugs, decreasing at-risk parenting to reduce child maltreatment and trauma, dementia symptoms (cognition, behavior, function), determining readiness to engage in end of life/palliative care conversations with adolescents and young adults living with advanced cancer, dyspnea assessment and treatment at the end of life. *Unit head:* Dr. Laurie Lauzon Clabo, Dean, College of Nursing, 313-577-4082, E-mail: laurie.lauzon.clabo@wayne.edu. *Application contact:* 313-577-4082, Fax: 313-577-6949, E-mail: nursinginfo@wayne.edu.
Website: http://nursing.wayne.edu/

Winona State University, College of Nursing and Health Sciences, Winona, MN 55987. Offers adult-gerontology acute care nurse practitioner (MS, DNP, Post Master's Certificate); adult-gerontology clinical nurse specialist (MS, DNP, Post Master's Certificate); adult-gerontology primary care nurse practitioner (MS, DNP, Post Master's Certificate); family nurse practitioner (MS, DNP, Post Master's Certificate); nurse educator (MS); nursing and organizational leadership (MS, DNP, Post Master's Certificate); practice and leadership innovations (DNP, Post Master's Certificate). *Accreditation:* AACN. *Program availability:* Part-time, online learning. *Degree requirements:* For master's, thesis; for doctorate, capstone. *Entrance requirements:* For master's, GRE (if GPA less than 3.0). Additional exam requirements/recommendations for international students: Required—TOEFL (minimum score 550 paper-based).

Wright State University, Graduate School, College of Nursing and Health, Program in Nursing, Dayton, OH 45435. Offers administration of nursing and health care systems (MS); adult gerontology clinical nurse specialist (MS); adult-gerontology acute care nurse practitioner (MS); family nurse practitioner (MS); neonatal nurse practitioner (MS); pediatric nurse practitioner-acute care (MS); pediatric nurse practitioner-primary care (MS); psychiatric mental health nurse practitioner (MS); school nurse (MS). *Accreditation:* AACN. *Program availability:* Part-time, evening/weekend. *Degree requirements:* For master's, thesis or alternative. *Entrance requirements:* For master's, GRE General Test, BSN from ACEN-accredited college, Ohio RN license. Additional exam requirements/recommendations for international students: Required—TOEFL. *Faculty research:* Clinical nursing and health, teaching, caring, pain administration, informatics and technology.

Adult Nursing

Adelphi University, College of Nursing and Public Health, Program in Adult Health Nurse, Garden City, NY 11530-0701. Offers MS. *Students:* 143 part-time (127 women); includes 96 minority (42 Black or African American, non-Hispanic/Latino; 33 Asian, non-Hispanic/Latino; 14 Hispanic/Latino; 7 Two or more races, non-Hispanic/Latino). Average age 36. 127 applicants, 57% accepted, 47 enrolled. In 2017, 33 master's awarded. *Entrance requirements:* Additional exam requirements/recommendations for international students: Required—TOEFL (minimum score 550 paper-based; 80 iBT), IELTS (minimum score 6.5). Application fee: $50. *Expenses:* Contact institution. *Financial support:* Research assistantships, teaching assistantships, career-related internships or fieldwork, institutionally sponsored loans, scholarships/grants, traineeships, and unspecified assistantships available. Support available to part-time students. *Unit head:* Maryann Forbes, Chair, 516-877-3597, E-mail: forbes@adelphi.edu. *Application contact:* Christine Murphy, Director of Admissions, 516-877-3050, Fax: 516-877-3039, E-mail: graduateadmissions@adelphi.edu.

Allen College, Graduate Programs, Waterloo, IA 50703. Offers adult-gerontology acute care nurse practitioner (MSN); community/public health nursing (MSN); education (MSN); family nurse practitioner (MSN); health sciences (Ed D); leadership in health care delivery (MSN); leadership in health care informatics (MSN); nursing (DNP); occupational therapy (MS); psychiatric mental health nurse practitioner (MSN). MSN in leadership in healthcare informatics offered in partnership with University of Minnesota. *Accreditation:* AACN; ACEN. *Program availability:* Part-time, 100% online, blended/hybrid learning. *Faculty:* 24 full-time (all women), 8 part-time/adjunct (7 women). *Students:* 106 full-time (91 women), 187 part-time (164 women); includes 22 minority (12 Black or African American, non-Hispanic/Latino; 1 American Indian or Alaska Native, non-Hispanic/Latino; 2 Asian, non-Hispanic/Latino; 3 Hispanic/Latino; 4 Two or more races, non-Hispanic/Latino), 2 international. Average age 33. 352 applicants, 56% accepted, 131 enrolled. In 2017, 73 master's, 2 doctorates awarded. *Entrance requirements:* For master's, minimum GPA of 3.0 in the last 60 hours of undergraduate coursework; for doctorate, minimum GPA of 3.25 in graduate coursework. *Application deadline:* For fall admission, 2/1 priority date for domestic students; for spring admission, 9/1 priority date for domestic students. Applications are processed on a rolling basis. Application fee: $50. Electronic applications accepted. *Expenses:* $17,860 per year. *Financial support:* In 2017–18, 97 students received support. Federal Work-Study, institutionally sponsored loans, scholarships/grants, and traineeships available. Support available to part-time students. Financial award application deadline: 8/1; financial award applicants required to submit FAFSA. *Faculty research:* Poverty. *Unit head:* Dr. Nancy Kramer, Vice Chancellor for Academic Affairs, 319-226-2040, Fax: 319-226-2070, E-mail: nancy.kramer@allencollege.edu. *Application contact:* Molly Quinn, Director of Admissions, 319-226-2001, Fax: 319-226-2010, E-mail: molly.quinn@allencollege.edu.
Website: http://www.allencollege.edu/

Azusa Pacific University, School of Nursing, Azusa, CA 91702-7000. Offers adult clinical nurse specialist (MSN); adult-gerontology nurse practitioner (MSN); family nurse practitioner (MSN); healthcare administration and leadership (MSN); nursing (MSN, DNP, PhD); nursing education (MSN); parent-child clinical nurse specialist (MSN); psychiatric mental health nurse practitioner (MSN). *Accreditation:* AACN. *Program availability:* Part-time, evening/weekend. *Degree requirements:* For master's, thesis optional. *Entrance requirements:* For master's, BSN.

Bloomsburg University of Pennsylvania, School of Graduate Studies, College of Science and Technology, Department of Nursing, Bloomsburg, PA 17815-1301. Offers adult and family nurse practitioner (MSN); community health (MSN); nurse anesthesia (MSN); nursing (MSN, DNP); nursing administration (MSN). *Accreditation:* AACN. *Degree requirements:* For master's, thesis (for some programs), clinical experience. *Entrance requirements:* For master's, minimum QPA of 3.0, personal statement, 2 letters of recommendation, nursing license. Additional exam requirements/recommendations for international students: Required—TOEFL, IELTS. Electronic applications accepted. *Expenses:* Contact institution.

Boston College, William F. Connell School of Nursing, Chestnut Hill, MA 02467. Offers adult-gerontology primary care nurse practitioner (MS); family health nursing (MS); nurse anesthesia (MS); nursing (PhD); pediatric primary care nurse practitioner (MS), including pediatric and women's health; psychiatric-mental health nursing (MS); women's health nursing (MS); MBA/MS; MS/MA; MS/PhD. MS/MBA offered jointly with Carroll School of Management, MS/MA with School of Theology and Ministry. *Accreditation:* AACN; AANA/CANAEP (one or more programs are accredited). *Program availability:* Part-time. *Faculty:* 54 full-time (48 women). *Students:* 170 full-time (153 women), 90 part-time (83 women); includes 39 minority (8 Black or African American, non-Hispanic/Latino; 10 Asian, non-Hispanic/Latino; 12 Hispanic/Latino; 9 Two or more

races, non-Hispanic/Latino), 3 international. Average age 28. 360 applicants, 56% accepted, 94 enrolled. In 2017, 104 master's, 5 doctorates awarded. *Degree requirements:* For master's, comprehensive exam; for doctorate, comprehensive exam, thesis/dissertation, computer literacy exam or foreign language. *Entrance requirements:* For master's, bachelor's degree in nursing; for doctorate, GRE General Test, MS in nursing. Additional exam requirements/recommendations for international students: Required—TOEFL (minimum score 600 paper-based; 100 iBT), IELTS (minimum score 7.5). *Application deadline:* For fall admission, 9/30 for domestic and international students; for winter admission, 1/15 for domestic and international students; for spring admission, 3/15 for domestic and international students. Application fee: $40. Electronic applications accepted. *Expenses:* $1,350 per credit tuition. *Financial support:* In 2017–18, 152 students received support, including 11 fellowships with full tuition reimbursements available (averaging $24,504 per year), 29 teaching assistantships (averaging $3,768 per year); scholarships/grants, health care benefits, tuition waivers (partial), and unspecified assistantships also available. Support available to part-time students. Financial award application deadline: 4/18; financial award applicants required to submit FAFSA. *Faculty research:* Sexual and reproductive health, health promotion/illness prevention, aging, eating disorders, symptom management. *Total annual research expenditures:* $879,812. *Unit head:* Dr. Susan Gennaro, Dean, 617-552-4251, Fax: 617-552-0931, E-mail: susan.gennaro@bc.edu. *Application contact:* Sean Sendall, Assistant Dean, Graduate Enrollment and Data Analytics, 617-552-4745, Fax: 617-552-2121, E-mail: sean.sendall@bc.edu.
Website: http://www.bc.edu/cson

California Baptist University, Program in Nursing, Riverside, CA 92504-3206. Offers clinical nurse specialist (MSN); family nurse practitioner (MSN); healthcare systems management (MSN); teaching-learning (MSN). *Accreditation:* AACN. *Program availability:* Part-time. *Faculty:* 19 full-time (18 women), 12 part-time/adjunct (11 women). *Students:* 78 full-time (59 women), 130 part-time (106 women); includes 114 minority (25 Black or African American, non-Hispanic/Latino; 3 American Indian or Alaska Native, non-Hispanic/Latino; 34 Asian, non-Hispanic/Latino; 47 Hispanic/Latino; 2 Native Hawaiian or other Pacific Islander, non-Hispanic/Latino; 3 Two or more races, non-Hispanic/Latino), 2 international. Average age 32. 25 applicants, 84% accepted, 14 enrolled. In 2017, 49 master's awarded. *Degree requirements:* For master's, comprehensive exam or directed project thesis; capstone practicum. *Entrance requirements:* For master's, GRE or California Critical Thinking Skills Test; Test of Essential Academic Skills (TEAS), minimum undergraduate GPA of 3.0; completion of prerequisite courses with minimum grade of C; CPR certification; background check clearance; health clearance; drug testing; proof of health insurance; proof of motor vehicle insurance; three letters of recommendation; 1000-word essay; interview. Additional exam requirements/recommendations for international students: Required—TOEFL (minimum score 80 iBT). *Application deadline:* For fall admission, 8/1 priority date for domestic students, 7/1 for international students; for spring admission, 12/1 priority date for domestic students, 11/1 for international students. Applications are processed on a rolling basis. Application fee: $45. Electronic applications accepted. *Expenses:* Contact institution. *Financial support:* In 2017–18, 38 students received support. Federal Work-Study and scholarships/grants available. Financial award applicants required to submit CSS PROFILE or FAFSA. *Faculty research:* Qualitative research using Parse methodology, gerontology, disaster preparedness, medical-surgical nursing, maternal-child nursing. *Unit head:* Dr. Geneva Oaks, Dean, School of Nursing, 951-343-4702, E-mail: goaks@calbaptist.edu. *Application contact:* Tamakia King, Graduate Admissions Counselor, 951-552-8138, Fax: 951-343-5095, E-mail: tking@calbaptist.edu.
Website: http://www.calbaptist.edu/explore-cbu/schools-colleges/school-nursing/master-science-nursing/

Clarkson College, Master of Science in Nursing Program, Omaha, NE 68131. Offers adult nurse practitioner (MSN, Post-Master's Certificate); family nurse practitioner (MSN, Post-Master's Certificate); nursing education (MSN, Post-Master's Certificate); nursing health care leadership (MSN, Post-Master's Certificate). *Accreditation:* AANA/CANAEP; ACEN. *Program availability:* Part-time, evening/weekend, online learning. *Degree requirements:* For master's, on-campus skills assessment (family nurse practitioner, adult nurse practitioner), comprehensive exam or thesis. *Entrance requirements:* For master's, minimum GPA of 3.0, 2 references, resume. Additional exam requirements/recommendations for international students: Required—TOEFL (minimum score 600 paper-based; 100 iBT). Electronic applications accepted.

College of Staten Island of the City University of New York, Graduate Programs, School of Health Sciences, DNP Program in Adult-Gerontological Health Nursing, Staten Island, NY 10314-6600. Offers DNP. *Program availability:* Part-time. *Students:* 3. *Degree requirements:* For doctorate, 75 credits with minimum of 1,000 supervised hours toward development of clinical competencies for primary care of the adult-gerontological population and implementation of an integrative practice project in the clinical setting. *Entrance requirements:* For doctorate, GRE taken within last five years, bachelor's degree from regionally-accredited college with minimum GPA of 3.25 and at least one year of experience in nursing or bachelor's degree in another field with three years of clinical experience; RN license in NY state. Additional exam requirements/recommendations for international students: Required—TOEFL (minimum score 550 paper-based; 79 iBT), IELTS (minimum score 6.5). *Application deadline:* For fall admission, 12/1 for domestic and international students. Applications are processed on a rolling basis. Application fee: $125. Electronic applications accepted. *Expenses:* Contact institution. *Financial support:* Applicants required to submit FAFSA. *Faculty research:* LGBTQ Healthcare; smoking cessation; caregivers of persons with autism; end of life decision-making/compassionate care; burn survivors. *Unit head:* Prof. Catherine Paradiso, 718-982-3838, E-mail: catherine.paradiso@csi.cuny.edu. *Application contact:* Sasha Spence, Associate Director for Graduate Admissions, 718-982-2019, Fax: 718-982-2500, E-mail: sasha.spence@csi.cuny.edu.
Website: https://www.csi.cuny.edu/sites/default/files/pdf/admissions/grad/pdf/DNP%20Nursing%20Fact%20Sheet.pdf

College of Staten Island of the City University of New York, Graduate Programs, School of Health Sciences, Program in Adult-Gerontological Nursing, Staten Island, NY 10314-6600. Offers adult-gerontological nursing (MS, Post Master's Certificate), including clinical nurse specialist, nurse practitioner. *Program availability:* Part-time, evening/weekend. *Faculty:* 6 full-time, 3 part-time/adjunct. *Students:* 48. 1 applicant, 100% accepted, 1 enrolled. In 2017, 19 master's, 6 other advanced degrees awarded. *Degree requirements:* For master's, thesis optional, 42 credits with minimum of 500 supervised hours toward development of clinical competencies for primary care of the adult-gerontological population (15 core credits, advanced practice core of nine credits, specialty courses of 12 credits, and six credits of elective courses); for Post Master's Certificate, 12-21 credits with minimum of 500 supervised hours toward development of Clinical Nurse Specialist or Nurse Practitioner competencies. *Entrance requirements:* For master's, bachelor's degree in nursing with minimum GPA of 3.0 in nursing major, two letters of recommendation, personal statement, current New York State RN license, minimum of one year of full-time experience as registered nurse, three years of appropriate full-time clinical experience in nursing; for Post Master's Certificate, master's degree in nursing; master's-level courses in pathophysiology, health assessment and pharmacology. Additional exam requirements/recommendations for international students: Required—TOEFL (minimum score 550 paper-based; 79 iBT), IELTS (minimum score 6.5). *Application deadline:* For spring admission, 10/15 priority date for domestic and international students. Applications are processed on a rolling basis. Application fee: $125. Electronic applications accepted. *Expenses:* Tuition, state resident: full-time $10,450; part-time $440 per credit. Tuition, nonresident: full-time $19,320; part-time $440 per credit. *Required fees:* $181.10 per semester. Tuition and fees vary according to program. *Faculty research:* Perceptions and attitudes about behavioral health; type 2 diabetes/obesity; instrument development and role stress; cancer prevention and survivorship; older adults and end of life: decision making, dying, palliative and hospice care. *Unit head:* Prof. Catherine Paradiso, 718-982-3838, E-mail: catherine.paradiso@csi.cuny.edu. *Application contact:* Sasha Spence, Associate Director for Graduate Admissions, 718-982-2019, Fax: 718-982-2500, E-mail: sasha.spence@csi.cuny.edu.
Website: http://www.csi.cuny.edu/nursing/graduate.html

Columbia University, School of Nursing, Program in Adult-Gerontology Primary Care Nurse Practitioner, New York, NY 10032. Offers MS, Adv C. *Accreditation:* AACN. *Program availability:* Part-time. *Entrance requirements:* For master's, GRE General Test, NCLEX, BSN, 1 year of clinical experience (preferred); for Adv C, MSN. Additional exam requirements/recommendations for international students: Required—TOEFL (minimum score 100 iBT). Electronic applications accepted. *Expenses: Tuition:* Full-time $44,864; part-time $1704 per credit. *Required fees:* $2370 per semester. One-time fee: $105.

Creighton University, College of Nursing, Omaha, NE 68178-0001. Offers adult gerontology acute care nurse practitioner (DNP, Post-Master's Certificate); adult gerontology nurse practitioner (DNP); clinical nurse leader (MSN, Post-Graduate Certificate); clinical systems administration (MSN, DNP); family nurse practitioner (DNP, Post-Master's Certificate); neonatal nurse practitioner (DNP, Post-Master's Certificate); nursing (Post-Graduate Certificate); pediatric acute care nurse practitioner (DNP, Post-Master's Certificate); psychiatric mental health nurse practitioner (DNP). *Accreditation:* AACN. *Program availability:* Part-time, blended/hybrid learning. *Degree requirements:* For master's, capstone project; for doctorate, scholarly project. *Entrance requirements:* For master's and doctorate, BSN from ACEN- or CCNE-accredited nursing school, minimum cumulative GPA of 3.0, personal statement, active unencumbered RN license with NE eligibility, undergraduate statistics course, physical assessment course or equivalent, three recommendation letters; for other advanced degree, MSN or MS in nursing from ACEN- or CCNE-accredited nursing school, minimum cumulative GPA of 3.0, active unencumbered RN license with NE eligibility. Additional exam requirements/recommendations for international students: Required—TOEFL (minimum score 600 paper-based, 100 iBT) or IELTS. Electronic applications accepted. *Expenses:* Contact institution. *Faculty research:* School health report card, obesity prevention in children, simulated clinical experience evaluation, vitamin D3 and calcium and cancer risk reduction education, online support and education to reduce stress for prenatal patients on bed rest, health literacy, immunization research.

Daemen College, Department of Nursing, Amherst, NY 14226-3592. Offers adult nurse practitioner (MS, Post Master's Certificate); nurse executive leadership (Post Master's Certificate); nursing education (MS, Post Master's Certificate); nursing executive leadership (MS); nursing practice (DNP); palliative care nursing (Post Master's Certificate). *Accreditation:* ACEN. *Program availability:* Part-time. *Degree requirements:* For master's, thesis or alternative, degree completed in 4 years; minimum GPA of 3.0; for doctorate, degree completed in 5 years; 500 post-master's clinical hours. *Entrance requirements:* For master's, BN, 1 year medical/surgical experience, RN license and state registration, statistics course with minimum C grade, 3 letters of recommendation, minimum GPA of 3.25, interview; for doctorate, MS in advance nursing practice; New York state RN license; goal statement; resume; interview; statistics course with minimum grade of 'C'; for Post Master's Certificate, master's degree in clinical area; RN license and current registration; one year of clinical experience; statistics course with minimum grade of 'C'; 3 letters of recommendation; interview; letter of intent. Additional exam requirements/recommendations for international students: Required—TOEFL (minimum score 500 paper-based; 63 iBT), IELTS (minimum score 5.5). Electronic applications accepted. *Faculty research:* Professional stress, client behavior, drug therapy, treatment modalities and pulmonary cancers, chemical dependency.

Duke University, School of Nursing, Durham, NC 27708-0586. Offers acute care pediatric nurse practitioner (MSN, Post-Graduate Certificate); adult-gerontology nurse practitioner (MSN, Post-Graduate Certificate), including acute care, primary care; family nurse practitioner (MSN, Post-Graduate Certificate); neonatal nurse practitioner (MSN, Post-Graduate Certificate); nurse anesthesia (DNP); nurse practitioner (DNP); nursing (PhD); nursing and health care leadership (MSN, Post-Graduate Certificate); nursing education (MSN, Post-Graduate Certificate); nursing informatics (MSN, Post-Graduate Certificate); pediatric nurse practitioner (MSN, Post-Graduate Certificate), including primary care; psychiatric mental health nurse practitioner (MSN, Post-Graduate Certificate); women's health nurse practitioner (MSN, Post-Graduate Certificate). *Accreditation:* AACN; AANA/CANAEP. *Program availability:* Part-time, evening/weekend, online with on-campus intensives. *Faculty:* 72 full-time (61 women). *Students:* 155 full-time (137 women), 613 part-time (548 women); includes 177 minority (64 Black or African American, non-Hispanic/Latino; 2 American Indian or Alaska Native, non-Hispanic/Latino; 47 Asian, non-Hispanic/Latino; 34 Hispanic/Latino; 30 Two or more races, non-Hispanic/Latino), 10 international. Average age 34. 631 applicants, 47% accepted, 211 enrolled. In 2017, 221 master's, 71 doctorates, 26 other advanced degrees awarded. Terminal master's awarded for partial completion of doctoral program. *Degree requirements:* For master's, thesis optional; for doctorate, capstone project. *Entrance requirements:* For master's, GRE General Test (waived if undergraduate GPA of 3.4 or higher), 1 year of nursing experience (recommended), BSN, minimum GPA of 3.0, previous course work in statistics; for doctorate, GRE General Test (waived if undergraduate GPA of 3.4 or higher), BSN or MSN, minimum GPA of 3.0, resume, personal statement, undergraduate statistics course, current licensure as a registered nurse, transcripts from all post-secondary institutions; for Post-Graduate Certificate, MSN, licensure or eligibility as a professional nurse, transcripts from all post-secondary institutions, previous course work in statistics. Additional exam requirements/recommendations for international students: Required—TOEFL (minimum score 100 iBT), IELTS (minimum score 7). *Application deadline:* For fall admission, 12/1 for domestic and international students; for spring admission, 5/1 for domestic and international students. Application fee: $50. Electronic applications accepted. *Expenses:* Contact institution. *Financial support:* Institutionally sponsored loans, scholarships/grants, and traineeships available. Support available to part-time students. Financial award applicants required to submit FAFSA. *Faculty research:* Cardiovascular disease, caregiver skill training, data mining, prostate cancer, neonatal immune system. *Unit head:* Dr. Marion E. Broome, Dean/Vice Chancellor for Nursing Affairs/Associate Vice President for Academic Affairs for Nursing, 919-684-9446, Fax: 919-684-9414, E-mail: marion.broome@duke.edu. *Application contact:* Dr. Ernie Rushing, Director of Admissions and Recruitment, 919-668-6274, Fax: 919-668-4693, E-mail: ernie.rushing@dm.duke.edu.
Website: http://www.nursing.duke.edu/

Eastern Michigan University, Graduate School, College of Health and Human Services, School of Nursing, Ypsilanti, MI 48197. Offers nursing (MSN); teaching in health care systems (MSN, Graduate Certificate). *Accreditation:* AACN. *Program availability:* Part-time, evening/weekend, online learning. *Faculty:* 25 full-time (22 women). *Students:* 20 full-time (18 women), 21 part-time (17 women); includes 12 minority (8 Black or African American, non-Hispanic/Latino; 2 Asian, non-Hispanic/Latino; 2 Hispanic/Latino), 1 international. Average age 38. 20 applicants, 55% accepted, 1 enrolled. In 2017, 12 master's, 1 other advanced degree awarded. *Degree requirements:* For master's, thesis optional. *Entrance requirements:* For master's, GRE General Test, Michigan RN license. Additional exam requirements/recommendations for international students: Required—TOEFL. *Application deadline:* Applications are processed on a rolling basis. Application fee: $45. *Financial support:* Fellowships, research assistantships with full tuition reimbursements, teaching assistantships with full tuition reimbursements, career-related internships or fieldwork, Federal Work-Study, institutionally sponsored loans, scholarships/grants, tuition waivers (partial), and unspecified assistantships available. Support available to part-time students. Financial award applicants required to submit FAFSA. *Unit head:* Dr. Michael Williams, Director, 734-487-2310, Fax: 734-487-6946, E-mail: mwilliams@emich.edu. *Application contact:* Roberta Towne, Coordinator, School of Nursing, 734-487-2340, Fax: 734-487-6946, E-mail: rtowne1@emich.edu.
Website: http://www.emich.edu/nursing

Emory University, Nell Hodgson Woodruff School of Nursing, Atlanta, GA 30322-1100. Offers adult nurse practitioner (MSN); emergency nurse practitioner (MSN); family nurse practitioner (MSN); family nurse-midwife (MSN); health systems leadership (MSN); nurse-midwifery (MSN); pediatric nurse practitioner acute and primary care (MSN); women's health care (Title X) (MSN); women's health nurse practitioner (MSN); MSN/MPH. *Accreditation:* AACN; ACNM/ACME (one or more programs are accredited). *Program availability:* Part-time. *Entrance requirements:* For master's, GRE General Test or MAT, minimum GPA of 3.0, BS in nursing from an accredited institution, RN license and additional course work, 3 letters of recommendation. Additional exam requirements/recommendations for international students: Required—TOEFL (minimum score 600 paper-based; 100 iBT). Electronic applications accepted. *Expenses:* Contact institution. *Faculty research:* Older adult falls and injuries, minority health issues, cardiac symptoms and quality of life, bio-ethics and decision-making, menopausal issues.

Felician University, Master of Science in Nursing Program, Lodi, NJ 07644-2117. Offers adult-gerontology nurse practitioner (MSN, PMC); executive leadership (MSN, PMC); family nurse practitioner (MSN, PMC); nursing education (MSN, PMC). *Accreditation:* AACN. *Program availability:* Evening/weekend, online only, 100% online, blended/hybrid learning. *Faculty:* 9 full-time (8 women), 1 (woman) part-time/adjunct. *Students:* 96 part-time (90 women); includes 48 minority (17 Black or African American, non-Hispanic/Latino; 1 American Indian or Alaska Native, non-Hispanic/Latino; 16 Asian, non-Hispanic/Latino; 12 Hispanic/Latino; 1 Native Hawaiian or other Pacific Islander, non-Hispanic/Latino; 1 Two or more races, non-Hispanic/Latino). Average age 37. 49 applicants, 86% accepted, 23 enrolled. In 2017, 35 master's, 3 other advanced degrees awarded. *Degree requirements:* For master's, thesis, clinical presentation; for PMC, thesis, education project. *Entrance requirements:* For master's, BSN; minimum GPA of 3.0; 2 letters of recommendation; NJ RN license; personal statement; for PMC, RN license, minimum GPA of 3.0. Additional exam requirements/recommendations for international students: Required—TOEFL (minimum score 550 paper-based; 79 iBT), IELTS (minimum score 6.5), PTE (minimum score 56). *Application deadline:* Applications are processed on a rolling basis. Application fee: $40. Electronic applications accepted. Application fee is waived when completed online. *Expenses:* Contact institution. *Financial support:* Federal Work-Study, scholarships/grants, and traineeships available. Financial award applicants required to submit FAFSA. *Faculty research:* Anxiety and fear, curriculum innovation, health promotion and populations, attitudes of college students towards aging. *Unit head:* Dr. Ann Tritak, Associate Dean of Graduate Nursing, 201-559-6151, E-mail: tritaka@felician.edu. *Application contact:* Michael Szarek, Assistant Vice-President, Graduate Admissions, 201-355-1450, E-mail: szarekm@felician.edu.

Florida International University, Nicole Wertheim College of Nursing and Health Sciences, Nursing Program, Miami, FL 33199. Offers adult health nursing (MSN); family health (MSN); nurse anesthetist (MSN); nursing practice (DNP); nursing science research (PhD); pediatric nurse (MSN); psychiatric and mental health nursing (MSN); registered nurse (MSN). *Accreditation:* AACN; AANA/CANAEP. *Program availability:* Part-time, evening/weekend. *Faculty:* 40 full-time (33 women), 79 part-time/adjunct (69 women). *Students:* 330 full-time (233 women), 89 part-time (73 women); includes 326 minority (92 Black or African American, non-Hispanic/Latino; 1 American Indian or Alaska Native, non-Hispanic/Latino; 33 Asian, non-Hispanic/Latino; 195 Hispanic/Latino; 2 Native Hawaiian or other Pacific Islander, non-Hispanic/Latino; 3 Two or more races, non-Hispanic/Latino), 9 international. Average age 33. 304 applicants, 50% accepted, 148 enrolled. In 2017, 144 master's, 8 doctorates awarded. *Degree requirements:* For master's, thesis or alternative; for doctorate, comprehensive exam, thesis/dissertation. *Entrance requirements:* For master's, bachelor's degree in nursing, minimum undergraduate GPA of 3.0 in upper-level coursework, letters of recommendation; for doctorate, GRE, letters of recommendation, minimum undergraduate GPA of 3.0 in upper-level coursework, interview. Additional exam requirements/recommendations for international students: Required—TOEFL (minimum score 550 paper-based; 80 iBT). *Application deadline:* For fall admission, 6/1 for domestic students, 4/1 for international students; for spring admission, 10/1 for domestic students, 9/1 for international students. Applications are processed on a rolling basis. Application fee: $30. Electronic applications accepted. *Expenses:* Tuition, state resident: full-time $8912; part-time $446 per credit hour. Tuition, nonresident: full-time $21,393; part-time $992 per credit hour. *Required fees:* $390; $195 per semester. *Financial support:* Institutionally sponsored loans and scholarships/grants available. Financial award application deadline: 3/1; financial award applicants required to submit FAFSA. *Faculty research:* Adult health nursing. *Unit head:* Dr. Yhovana Gordon, Chair, 305-348-7733, Fax: 305-348-7051, E-mail: gordony@fiu.edu. *Application contact:* Nanett Rojas, Manager, Admissions Operations, 305-348-7464, Fax: 305-348-7441, E-mail: gradadm@fiu.edu.
Website: http://cnhs.fiu.edu/

Florida Southern College, Program in Nursing, Lakeland, FL 33801-5698. Offers adult gerontology clinical nurse specialist (MSN); adult gerontology primary care nurse practitioner (MSN); family nurse practitioner (MSN); nurse educator (MSN); nursing administration (MSN). *Accreditation:* AACN. *Program availability:* Part-time. *Faculty:* 5 full-time (all women), 2 part-time/adjunct (both women). *Students:* 142 full-time (126 women), 9 part-time (all women); includes 70 minority (39 Black or African American, non-Hispanic/Latino; 1 American Indian or Alaska Native, non-Hispanic/Latino; 11 Asian, non-Hispanic/Latino; 13 Hispanic/Latino; 1 Native Hawaiian or other Pacific Islander, non-Hispanic/Latino; 5 Two or more races, non-Hispanic/Latino), 1 international. Average age 40. 83 applicants, 93% accepted, 72 enrolled. In 2017, 41 master's awarded. *Degree requirements:* For master's, 780 clinical practice hours. *Entrance requirements:* For master's, GMAT or GRE General Test, Florida RN license, 3 letters of recommendation, personal statement, minimum GPA of 3.0, resume. Additional exam requirements/recommendations for international students: Required—TOEFL (minimum score 550 paper-based; 79 iBT), IELTS (minimum score 6.5). *Application deadline:* For fall admission, 6/1 for domestic and international students; for spring admission, 10/1 for domestic and international students. Applications are processed on a rolling basis. Application fee: $30. Electronic applications accepted. *Expenses:* $585 per credit hour, $100 required fees. *Financial support:* In 2017–18, 1 student received support. Scholarships/grants and traineeships available. Support available to part-time students. Financial award applicants required to submit FAFSA. *Faculty research:* End of life care, dementia, health promotion. *Unit head:* Dr. Linda Comer, Dean, 863-680-4310, Fax: 863-680-3872, E-mail: lcomer@flsouthern.edu. *Application contact:* Kathy Connelly, Evening Program Assistant Director, 863-680-4205, Fax: 863-680-3872, E-mail: kconnelly@flsouthern.edu.

George Mason University, College of Health and Human Services, School of Nursing, Fairfax, VA 22030. Offers adult gerontology (DNP); adult/gerontological nurse practitioner (MSN); family nurse practitioner (MSN, DNP); nurse educator (MSN); nursing (PhD); nursing administration (MSN, DNP); nursing education (Certificate); psychiatric mental health (DNP). *Accreditation:* AACN. *Program availability:* Part-time, evening/weekend, blended/hybrid learning. *Faculty:* 28 full-time (27 women), 51 part-time/adjunct (47 women). *Students:* 51 full-time (40 women), 182 part-time (162 women); includes 110 minority (59 Black or African American, non-Hispanic/Latino; 1 American Indian or Alaska Native, non-Hispanic/Latino; 36 Asian, non Hispanic/Latino; 10 Hispanic/Latino; 4 Two or more races, non-Hispanic/Latino), 8 international. Average age 37. 159 applicants, 70% accepted, 73 enrolled. In 2017, 33 master's, 24 doctorates, 1 other advanced degree awarded. *Degree requirements:* For master's, comprehensive exam (for some programs), thesis in clinical classes; for doctorate, comprehensive exam (for some programs), thesis/dissertation (for some programs). *Entrance requirements:* For master's, 2 official transcripts; expanded goals statement; resume; BSN from accredited institution; minimum GPA of 3.0 in last 60 credits of undergraduate work; 2 letters of recommendation; completion of undergraduate statistics and graduate-level bivariate statistics; certification in professional CPR; for doctorate, GRE, 2 official transcripts; expanded goals statement; resume; 2 recommendation letters; nursing license; at least 1 year of work experience as an RN; interview; writing sample; evidence of graduate-level course in applied statistics; master's degree in nursing with minimum GPA of 3.5; for Certificate, 2 official transcripts; expanded goals statement; resume; master's degree from accredited institution or currently enrolled with minimum GPA of 3.0. Additional exam requirements/recommendations for international students: Required—TOEFL (minimum score 570 paper-based; 88 iBT), IELTS (minimum score 6.5), PTE (minimum score 59). *Application deadline:* For fall admission, 2/1 for domestic and international students. Application fee: $75 ($80 for international students). Electronic applications accepted. *Expenses:* Contact institution. *Financial support:* In 2017–18, 7 students received support, including 5 research assistantships with tuition reimbursements available (averaging $20,500 per year), 2 teaching assistantships; career-related internships or fieldwork, Federal Work-Study, scholarships/grants, unspecified assistantships, and health care benefits (for full-time research or teaching assistantship recipients) also available. Financial award application deadline: 3/1; financial award applicants required to submit FAFSA. *Faculty research:* Health care, nursing science. *Total annual research expenditures:* $1.6 million. *Unit head:* Carol Urban, Director, 703-993-2991, Fax: 703-993-1949, E-mail: curban@gmu.edu. *Application contact:* Susan Eckis, Office Manager, 703-993-1938, Fax: 703-993-1949, E-mail: seckis@gmu.edu.
Website: http://chhs.gmu.edu/nursing

The George Washington University, School of Nursing, Washington, DC 20052. Offers adult nurse practitioner (MSN, DNP, Post-Master's Certificate); clinical research administration (MSN); family nurse practitioner (MSN, Post-Master's Certificate); health care quality (MSN, Post-Master's Certificate); nursing leadership and management (MSN); nursing practice (DNP), including nursing education; palliative care nurse practitioner (Post-Master's Certificate). *Accreditation:* AACN. *Faculty:* 58 full-time (56 women), 119 part-time/adjunct (111 women). *Students:* 38 full-time (34 women), 570 part-time (510 women); includes 197 minority (92 Black or African American, non-Hispanic/Latino; 2 American Indian or Alaska Native, non-Hispanic/Latino; 63 Asian, non-Hispanic/Latino; 28 Hispanic/Latino; 1 Native Hawaiian or other Pacific Islander, non-Hispanic/Latino; 11 Two or more races, non-Hispanic/Latino), 2 international. Average age 31. 507 applicants, 76% accepted, 185 enrolled. In 2017, 155 master's, 32 doctorates awarded. *Expenses:* *Tuition:* Full-time $28,800; part-time $1655 per credit hour. *Required fees:* $45; $2.75 per credit hour. *Unit head:* Pamela R. Jeffries, Dean, 202-994-3725, E-mail: pjeffries@gwu.edu. *Application contact:* Kristin Williams, Associate Provost for Graduate Enrollment Management, 202-994-0467, Fax: 202-994-0371, E-mail: ksw@gwu.edu.
Website: http://nursing.gwumc.edu/

Georgia Southern University–Armstrong Campus, College of Graduate Studies, School of Nursing, Savannah, GA 31419-1997. Offers adult-gerontological acute care nurse practitioner (Certificate); adult-gerontological clinical nurse specialist (Certificate); adult-gerontological primary care nurse practitioner (Certificate); family nurse practitioner (MSN). *Accreditation:* AACN. *Program availability:* Part-time, evening/weekend. *Faculty:* 12 full-time (all women). *Students:* 36 full-time (30 women), 22 part-time (21 women); includes 17 minority (7 Black or African American, non-Hispanic/Latino; 2 Asian, non-Hispanic/Latino; 4 Hispanic/Latino; 4 Two or more races, non-Hispanic/Latino), 1 international. Average age 32. 59 applicants, 32% accepted, 18 enrolled. In 2017, 10 master's awarded. *Degree requirements:* For master's, comprehensive exam, project or thesis. *Entrance requirements:* For master's, GRE General Test or MAT, minimum GPA of 3.0, letter of recommendation, letter of intent. Additional exam requirements/recommendations for international students: Required—TOEFL (minimum score 523 paper-based; 70 iBT). *Application deadline:* For fall admission, 2/28 for domestic and international students; for spring admission, 11/15 for domestic students, 9/15 for international students. Applications are processed on a rolling basis. Application fee: $30. Electronic applications accepted. *Expenses:* Tuition, state resident: part-time $211 per credit hour. Tuition, nonresident: part-time $782 per credit hour. *Required fees:* $737 per semester. Tuition and fees vary according to course load, degree level, campus/location and program. *Financial support:* In 2017–18, research assistantships with full tuition reimbursements (averaging $5,000 per year) were awarded; Federal Work-Study, scholarships/grants, and unspecified assistantships also available. Support available to part-time students. Financial award application deadline: 3/1; financial award applicants required to submit FAFSA. *Faculty research:* Midwifery, mental health, nursing simulation, smoking cessation during pregnancy, asthma education, vulnerable populations, geriatrics, disaster nursing, complementary and alternative modalities, nephrology. *Unit head:* Dr. Catherine Gilbert, Department Head, 912-344-3145, E-mail: catherine.gilbert@armstrong.edu. *Application contact:* McKenzie Peterman, Graduate Admissions Specialist, 912-478-5678, Fax: 912-478-0740, E-mail: mpeterman@georgiasouthern.edu.
Website: https://www.armstrong.edu/degree-programs/nursing-msn

Georgia State University, Byrdine F. Lewis School of Nursing, Atlanta, GA 30303. Offers adult health clinical nurse specialist/nurse practitioner (MS, Certificate); child health clinical nurse specialist/pediatric nurse practitioner (MS, Certificate); family nurse practitioner (MS, Certificate); family psychiatric mental health nurse practitioner (MS, Certificate); nursing (PhD); nursing leadership in healthcare innovations (MS), including nursing administration, nursing informatics; nutrition (MS); perinatal clinical nurse

specialist/women's health nurse practitioner (MS, Certificate); physical therapy (DPT); respiratory therapy (MS). *Accreditation:* AACN. *Program availability:* Part-time, blended/hybrid learning. *Faculty:* 69 full-time (52 women). *Students:* 322 full-time (248 women), 481 part-time (466 women); includes 186 minority (112 Black or African American, non-Hispanic/Latino; 44 Asian, non-Hispanic/Latino; 20 Hispanic/Latino; 10 Two or more races, non-Hispanic/Latino), 18 international. Average age 31. 370 applicants, 56% accepted, 148 enrolled. In 2017, 131 master's, 49 doctorates, 11 other advanced degrees awarded. *Degree requirements:* For doctorate, comprehensive exam, thesis/dissertation. *Entrance requirements:* For doctorate, GRE. Additional exam requirements/recommendations for international students: Required—TOEFL. *Application deadline:* For fall admission, 2/1 priority date for domestic and international students; for spring admission, 9/15 for domestic and international students. Applications are processed on a rolling basis. Application fee: $50. Electronic applications accepted. *Expenses:* Contact institution. *Financial support:* In 2017–18, research assistantships with tuition reimbursements (averaging $1,666 per year), teaching assistantships with tuition reimbursements (averaging $1,920 per year) were awarded; scholarships/grants, tuition waivers (full and partial), and unspecified assistantships also available. Support available to part-time students. Financial award application deadline: 8/1; financial award applicants required to submit FAFSA. *Faculty research:* Stroke intervention for caregivers, stroke prevention in African-Americans; relationships between psychological distress and health outcomes in parents with a medically ill infant; medically fragile children; nursing expertise and patient outcomes. *Unit head:* Nancy Kropf, Dean of Nursing, 404-413-1101, Fax: 404-413-1090, E-mail: nkropf@gsu.edu.
Website: http://nursing.gsu.edu/

Gwynedd Mercy University, Frances M. Maguire School of Nursing and Health Professions, Gwynedd Valley, PA 19437-0901. Offers clinical nurse specialist (MSN), including gerontology, oncology, pediatrics; nurse educator (MSN); nurse practitioner (MSN), including adult health, pediatric health; nursing (DNP). *Accreditation:* ACEN. *Program availability:* Part-time, blended/hybrid learning. *Faculty:* 4 full-time (all women), 1 (woman) part-time/adjunct. *Students:* 28 full-time (25 women), 48 part-time (43 women); includes 28 minority (15 Black or African American, non-Hispanic/Latino; 11 Asian, non-Hispanic/Latino; 1 Hispanic/Latino; 1 Two or more races, non-Hispanic/Latino). Average age 37. 72 applicants, 25% accepted, 16 enrolled. In 2017, 7 master's awarded. *Degree requirements:* For master's, thesis optional; for doctorate, evidence-based scholarly project. *Entrance requirements:* For master's, GRE General Test or MAT, current nursing experience, physical assessment, course work in statistics, BSN from ACEN-accredited program, 2 letters of recommendation, personal interview. Additional exam requirements/recommendations for international students: Required—TOEFL (minimum score 575 paper-based). *Application deadline:* For fall admission, 8/1 priority date for domestic students; for winter admission, 12/1 priority date for domestic students. Applications are processed on a rolling basis. Electronic applications accepted. *Expenses:* $825 per credit (non-doctoral degrees), $930 per credit (doctoral); $17 part-time fee, $165 graduation fee. *Financial support:* In 2017–18, 5 students received support. Scholarships/grants, traineeships, and unspecified assistantships available. Financial award application deadline: 8/30. *Faculty research:* Critical thinking, primary care, domestic violence, multiculturalism, nursing centers. *Unit head:* Dr. Andrea D. Hollingsworth, Dean, 215-646-7300 Ext. 539, Fax: 215-641-5517, E-mail: hollingsworth.a@gmc.edu. *Application contact:* Dr. Barbara A. Jones, Director, 215-646-7300 Ext. 407, Fax: 215-641-5564, E-mail: jones.b@gmc.edu.
Website: http://www.gmercyu.edu/academics/graduate-programs/nursing

Hunter College of the City University of New York, Graduate School, Hunter-Bellevue School of Nursing, Gerontological/Adult Nurse Practitioner Program, New York, NY 10065-5085. Offers MS. *Accreditation:* AACN. *Program availability:* Part-time. *Degree requirements:* For master's, practicum. *Entrance requirements:* For master's, minimum GPA of 3.0, New York RN license, 2 years of professional practice experience, BSN. Additional exam requirements/recommendations for international students: Required—TOEFL.

Hunter College of the City University of New York, Graduate School, Hunter-Bellevue School of Nursing, Program in Adult-Gerontology Clinical Nurse Specialist, New York, NY 10065-5085. Offers MS. *Accreditation:* AACN. *Degree requirements:* For master's, practicum. *Entrance requirements:* For master's, minimum GPA of 3.0, New York RN license, 2 years of professional practice experience, BSN. Additional exam requirements/recommendations for international students: Required—TOEFL.

Indiana University–Purdue University Fort Wayne, College of Health and Human Services, Department of Nursing, Fort Wayne, IN 46805-1499. Offers adult-gerontology primary care nurse practitioner (MS); family nurse practitioner (MS); nurse executive (MS); nursing administration (Certificate); nursing education (MS). *Accreditation:* ACEN. *Program availability:* Part-time. *Entrance requirements:* For master's, GRE Writing Test (if GPA below 3.0), BS in nursing, eligibility for Indiana RN license, minimum GPA of 3.0, essay, copy of resume, three references, undergraduate course work in research and statistics within last 5 years. Additional exam requirements/recommendations for international students: Required—TOEFL (minimum score 550 paper-based; 79 iBT); Recommended—TWE. Electronic applications accepted. *Faculty research:* Community engagement, cervical screening, evidence-based practice.

Jacksonville University, Brooks Rehabilitation College of Healthcare Sciences, Keigwin School of Nursing, Jacksonville, FL 32211. Offers adult gerontology acute care nurse practitioner (MSN), including clinical nurse educator, family nurse practitioner, family nurse practitioner/emergency nurse practitioner, leadership in the healthcare system, nursing informatics, psychiatric nurse practitioner; adult-gerontology acute care nurse practitioner (Certificate); clinical nurse educator (Certificate); emergency nurse practitioner (Certificate); family nurse practitioner (Certificate); family nurse practitioner/emergency nurse practitioner (Certificate); leadership in healthcare systems (Certificate); nursing informatics (MSN, Certificate); nursing practice (DNP); psychiatric mental health nurse practitioner (Certificate); MSN/MBA. *Accreditation:* AACN. *Program availability:* Part-time, 100% online, blended/hybrid learning. *Faculty:* 18 full-time (all women), 11 part-time/adjunct (9 women). *Students:* 61 full-time (53 women), 549 part-time (497 women); includes 202 minority (120 Black or African American, non-Hispanic/Latino; 4 American Indian or Alaska Native, non-Hispanic/Latino; 29 Asian, non-Hispanic/Latino; 39 Hispanic/Latino; 2 Native Hawaiian or other Pacific Islander, non-Hispanic/Latino; 8 Two or more races, non-Hispanic/Latino), 1 international. Average age 40. 272 applicants, 58% accepted, 126 enrolled. In 2017, 293 master's, 9 doctorates awarded. *Degree requirements:* For master's, thesis; for doctorate, thesis/dissertation. *Entrance requirements:* For master's, GRE General Test or undergraduate GPA above 3.0, BSN from ACEN- or CCNE-accredited program; course work in statistics and physical assessment within last 5 years; Florida nursing license; CPR/BLS certification; 3 recommendations, 2 of which are professional references; statement of intent; resume; for doctorate, official transcripts from all colleges/universities attended; MSN from ACEN- or CCNE-accredited program; licensure as RN or ARNP; 3 letters of reference (2 clinical, 1 professional/academic); curriculum vitae; graded essay; for Certificate, GRE (minimum score of 290, waived if undergraduate nursing GPA is 3.0 or higher), official transcripts from MSN; minimum graduate nursing GPA of 3.0; graduation from CCNE- or ACEN-accredited MSN program; 3 recommendations, 2 of which are professional references; 2 years of work experience in critical care setting; statement of intent; resume. Additional exam requirements/recommendations for international students: Required—TOEFL (minimum score 650 paper-based; 114 iBT), IELTS (minimum score 8). *Application deadline:* For fall admission, 2/1 for domestic and international students. Applications are processed on a rolling basis. Application fee: $50. Electronic applications accepted. *Expenses:* Contact institution. *Financial support:* Federal Work-Study, institutionally sponsored loans, scholarships/grants, and health care benefits available. Support available to part-time students. Financial award application deadline: 3/15; financial award applicants required to submit FAFSA. *Faculty research:* Treatment of anxiety. *Unit head:* Dr. Hilary Morgan, Director, Graduate Nursing Programs/Associate Professor, 904-256-7601, E-mail: hmorgan@ju.edu. *Application contact:* Stephanie Bloom, Assistant Director, Enrollment and Advanced Graduate Nursing, 904-256-7286, E-mail: sstrick4@ju.edu.
Website: http://www.ju.edu/chs/nursing/

Kent State University, College of Nursing, Kent, OH 44242. Offers advanced nursing practice (DNP), including adult/gerontology acute care nurse practitioner (MSN, DNP); nursing (MSN, PhD), including adult/gerontology acute care nurse practitioner (MSN, DNP), adult/gerontology clinical nurse specialist (MSN), adult/gerontology primary care nurse practitioner (MSN), family nurse practitioner (MSN), nurse educator (MSN), nursing and healthcare management (MSN), pediatric primary care nurse practitioner (MSN), psychiatric/mental health nurse practitioner (MSN); MBA/MSN. PhD program offered jointly with The University of Akron. *Accreditation:* AACN. *Program availability:* Part-time, online learning. *Faculty:* 29 full-time (28 women), 15 part-time/adjunct (12 women). *Students:* 167 full-time (142 women), 405 part-time (359 women); includes 70 minority (39 Black or African American, non-Hispanic/Latino; 11 Asian, non-Hispanic/Latino; 18 Hispanic/Latino; 2 Two or more races, non-Hispanic/Latino), 13 international. Average age 35. 272 applicants, 74% accepted, 166 enrolled. In 2017, 144 master's, 8 doctorates awarded. *Degree requirements:* For master's, thesis optional; for doctorate, comprehensive exam, thesis/dissertation. *Entrance requirements:* For master's, GRE or GMAT, minimum GPA of 3.0, active RN license, statement of purpose, 3 letters of reference, undergraduate level statistics class, baccalaureate or graduate-level nursing degree, curriculum vitae/resume; for doctorate, GRE, minimum GPA of 3.0, transcripts, 3 letters of reference, interview, active unrestricted Ohio RN license, statement of purpose, writing sample, curriculum vitae/resume, baccalaureate and master's degrees in nursing or DNP. Additional exam requirements/recommendations for international students: Required—TOEFL (minimum score 560 paper-based; 83 iBT), IELTS (minimum score 6.5), PTE (minimum score 55), Michigan English Language Assessment Battery (minimum score 78). *Application deadline:* For fall admission, 3/1 for domestic and international students; for spring admission, 10/1 for domestic and international students. Applications are processed on a rolling basis. Application fee: $45 ($70 for international students). Electronic applications accepted. *Expenses:* Tuition, state resident: full-time $11,310; part-time $515 per credit hour. Tuition, nonresident: full-time $20,396; part-time $928 per credit hour. *International tuition:* $18,544 full-time. *Financial support:* Scholarships/grants available. Financial award application deadline: 5/4. *Unit head:* Dr. Barbara Broome, Dean, 330-672-3777, E-mail: bbroome1@kent.edu. *Application contact:* Dr. Wendy A. Umberger, Associate Dean for Graduate Programs/Professor, 330-672-8813, E-mail: wlewando@kent.edu.
Website: http://www.kent.edu/nursing/

La Salle University, School of Nursing and Health Sciences, Program in Nursing, Philadelphia, PA 19141-1199. Offers adult gerontology primary care nurse practitioner (MSN, Certificate); adult health and illness clinical nurse specialist (MSN); adult-gerontology clinical nurse specialist (MSN, Certificate); clinical nurse leader (MSN); family primary care nurse practitioner (MSN, Certificate); gerontology (Certificate); nurse anesthetist (MSN, Certificate); nursing (MSN, Certificate); nursing administration (MSN, Certificate); nursing education (Certificate); nursing practice (DNP); nursing service administration (MSN); public health nursing (MSN, Certificate); school nursing (Certificate); MSN/MBA; MSN/MPH. *Accreditation:* AACN. *Program availability:* Part-time, evening/weekend, 100% online. *Faculty:* 12 full-time (11 women), 14 part-time/adjunct (11 women). *Students:* 1 (woman) full-time, 277 part-time (220 women); includes 72 minority (36 Black or African American, non-Hispanic/Latino; 1 American Indian or Alaska Native, non-Hispanic/Latino; 18 Asian, non-Hispanic/Latino; 10 Hispanic/Latino; 1 Native Hawaiian or other Pacific Islander, non-Hispanic/Latino; 6 Two or more races, non-Hispanic/Latino), 1 international. Average age 36. 70 applicants, 56% accepted, 24 enrolled. In 2017, 81 master's, 4 doctorates, 13 other advanced degrees awarded. *Degree requirements:* For doctorate, minimum of 1,000 hours of post baccalaureate clinical practice supervised by preceptors. *Entrance requirements:* For master's, GRE, MAT, or GMAT (for students with BSN GPA of less than 3.2), baccalaureate degree in nursing from ACEN- or CCNE-accredited program or an MSN Bridge program; Pennsylvania RN license; 2 letters of reference; resume; statement of philosophy articulating professional values and future educational goal; 1 year of work experience as a registered nurse; for doctorate, GRE (waived for applicants with MSN cumulative GPA of 3.7 or above), MSN, master's degree, MBA or MHA from nationally-accredited program; resume or curriculum vitae; 2 letters of reference; interview; for Certificate, GRE, MAT, or GMAT (for students with BSN GPA of less than 3.2, baccalaureate degree in nursing from ACEN- or CCNE-accredited program or an MSN Bridge program; Pennsylvania RN license; 2 letters of reference; resume; statement of philosophy articulating professional values and future educational goal; 1 year of work experience as a registered nurse. Additional exam requirements/recommendations for international students: Required—TOEFL. *Application deadline:* For fall admission, 8/15 priority date for domestic students, 7/15 for international students; for spring admission, 12/15 priority date for domestic students, 11/15 for international students; for summer admission, 4/15 priority date for domestic students, 3/15 for international students. Applications are processed on a rolling basis. Application fee: $35. Electronic applications accepted. Application fee is waived when completed online. *Expenses:* Contact institution. *Financial support:* In 2017–18, 7 students received support. Scholarships/grants and traineeships available. Support available to part-time students. Financial award application deadline: 8/31; financial award applicants required to submit FAFSA. *Unit head:* Dr. Patricia M. Dillon, Director, 215-951-1322, Fax: 215-951-1896, E-mail: msnapn@lasalle.edu. *Application contact:* Elizabeth Heenan, Director, Graduate and Adult Enrollment, 215-951-1100, Fax: 215-951-1462, E-mail: heenan@lasalle.edu.
Website: http://www.lasalle.edu/nursing/program-options/

Lehman College of the City University of New York, School of Health Sciences, Human Services and Nursing, Department of Nursing, Bronx, NY 10468-1589. Offers adult health nursing (MS); nursing of older adults (MS); parent-child nursing (MS); pediatric nurse practitioner (MS). *Accreditation:* AACN. *Program availability:* Part-time, evening/weekend. *Entrance requirements:* For master's, bachelor's degree in nursing, New York RN license.

Lewis University, College of Nursing and Health Professions, Program in Nursing, Romeoville, IL 60446. Offers adult gerontology acute care nurse practitioner (MSN); adult gerontology clinical nurse specialist (MSN); adult gerontology primary care nurse practitioner (MSN); family nurse practitioner (MSN); healthcare systems leadership (MSN); nursing (DNP); nursing education (MSN); school nurse (MSN). *Accreditation:* AACN. *Program availability:* Part-time, evening/weekend, 100% online, blended/hybrid learning. *Students:* 14 full-time (11 women), 361 part-time (336 women); includes 100 minority (27 Black or African American, non-Hispanic/Latino; 33 Asian, non-Hispanic/Latino; 35 Hispanic/Latino; 5 Two or more races, non-Hispanic/Latino), 1 international. Average age 37. *Degree requirements:* For master's, clinical practicum. *Entrance requirements:* For master's, minimum undergraduate GPA of 3.0, degree in nursing, RN license, letter of recommendation, interview, resume or curriculum vitae. Additional exam requirements/recommendations for international students: Required—TOEFL (minimum score 550 paper-based; 80 iBT). *Application deadline:* For fall admission, 5/1 priority date for international students; for spring admission, 11/15 priority date for international students. Applications are processed on a rolling basis. Application fee: $40. Electronic applications accepted. Tuition and fees vary according to program. *Financial support:* Federal Work-Study, scholarships/grants, tuition waivers (full and partial), and unspecified assistantships available. Financial award application deadline: 5/1; financial award applicants required to submit FAFSA. *Faculty research:* Cancer prevention, phenomenological methods, public policy analysis. *Total annual research expenditures:* $1,000. *Unit head:* 815-836-5610. *Application contact:* Nancy Wiksten, Adult Admission Counselor, 815-836-5628, Fax: 815-836-5578, E-mail: wikstena@lewisu.edu.

Loma Linda University, School of Nursing, Program in Nurse Educator, Loma Linda, CA 92350. Offers adult/gerontology (MS); obstetrics-pediatrics (MS). *Accreditation:* AACN. *Program availability:* Part-time. *Degree requirements:* For master's, thesis or alternative. *Entrance requirements:* For master's, GRE General Test, BSN, minimum GPA of 3.0, RN license. Additional exam requirements/recommendations for international students: Required—TOEFL. Electronic applications accepted. *Faculty research:* Coping, integration of research.

Long Island University–LIU Brooklyn, Harriet Rothkopf Heilbrunn School of Nursing, Brooklyn, NY 11201. Offers adult nurse practitioner (MS, Advanced Certificate); family nurse practitioner (MS, Advanced Certificate); nurse educator (MS). *Accreditation:* AACN. *Program availability:* Part-time, evening/weekend, blended/hybrid learning. *Faculty:* 9 full-time (7 women), 6 part-time/adjunct (4 women). *Students:* 5 full-time (all women), 195 part-time (174 women); includes 117 minority (70 Black or African American, non-Hispanic/Latino; 28 Asian, non-Hispanic/Latino; 17 Hispanic/Latino; 2 Two or more races, non-Hispanic/Latino), 1 international. Average age 37. 168 applicants, 60% accepted, 73 enrolled. In 2017, 69 master's, 2 other advanced degrees awarded. *Entrance requirements:* Additional exam requirements/recommendations for international students: Required—TOEFL or IELTS. *Application deadline:* Applications are processed on a rolling basis. Application fee: $50. Electronic applications accepted. *Expenses: Tuition:* Full-time $21,618; part-time $1201 per credit. *Required fees:* $1840; $920 per term. Tuition and fees vary according to course load. *Financial support:* In 2017–18, 15 students received support. Career-related internships or fieldwork, Federal Work-Study, scholarships/grants, and unspecified assistantships available. Support available to part-time students. Financial award application deadline: 2/15; financial award applicants required to submit FAFSA. *Faculty research:* Clinical and health outcomes in managed care; attitudes of nurses towards people with disabilities; adherence to CPAP in obstructive sleep apnea; diabetes and treatment compliance; chronic neurological disease management outside facilities. *Unit head:* Peggy Tallier, Interim Dean, 718-780-3367, E-mail: peggy.tallier@liu.edu. *Application contact:* Luis Santiago, Dean of Admissions, 718-488-1011, Fax: 718-780-6110, E-mail: bkln-admissions@liu.edu.
Website: http://www.liu.edu/Brooklyn/Academics/Harriet-Rothkopf-Heilbrunn-School-of-Nursing

Loyola University Chicago, Graduate School, Marcella Niehoff School of Nursing, Maywood, IL 60141. Offers adult clinical nurse specialist (MSN, Certificate); adult nurse practitioner (Certificate); dietetics (MS); family nurse practitioner (Certificate); family, adult, and women's health nurse practitioner (MSN); health systems leadership (MSN); healthcare quality using education in safety and technology (DNP); infection prevention (MSN, DNP); nursing science (PhD); women's health clinical nurse specialist (Certificate). *Accreditation:* AACN. *Program availability:* Part-time, blended/hybrid learning. *Faculty:* 24 full-time (22 women), 21 part-time/adjunct (19 women). *Students:* 188 full-time (178 women), 222 part-time (208 women); includes 105 minority (23 Black or African American, non-Hispanic/Latino; 40 Asian, non-Hispanic/Latino; 30 Hispanic/Latino; 2 Native Hawaiian or other Pacific Islander, non-Hispanic/Latino; 10 Two or more races, non-Hispanic/Latino), 4 international. Average age 36. 197 applicants, 55% accepted, 80 enrolled. In 2017, 94 master's, 17 doctorates, 26 other advanced degrees awarded. *Degree requirements:* For master's, comprehensive exam; for doctorate, thesis/dissertation, qualifying examination (for PhD); capstone project (for DNP). *Entrance requirements:* For master's, BSN, minimum nursing GPA of 3.0, Illinois RN license, 3 letters of recommendation, 1000 hours of experience in area of specialty prior to starting clinical rotations, personal statement; for doctorate, BSN or MSN, minimum GPA of 3.0, professional nursing license, 3 letters of recommendation, personal statement. Additional exam requirements/recommendations for international students: Required—TOEFL (minimum score 550 paper-based; 79 iBT), IELTS (minimum score 6.5). *Application deadline:* For fall admission, 6/1 priority date for domestic and international students; for spring admission, 11/15 priority date for domestic and international students; for summer admission, 3/15 priority date for domestic and international students. Applications are processed on a rolling basis. Application fee: $50. Electronic applications accepted. Application fee is waived when completed online. *Expenses:* Contact institution. *Financial support:* In 2017–18, 10 students received support, including 3 research assistantships with full tuition reimbursements available (averaging $18,000 per year), 1 teaching assistantship with full tuition reimbursement available (averaging $18,000 per year); scholarships/grants, unspecified assistantships, and nurse faculty loan program also available. Financial award application deadline: 5/1; financial award applicants required to submit FAFSA. *Faculty research:* Epigenetics and social determinants of health; women's health; vitamin D; health equity; interprofessional education; prevention and self-management of chronic disease; body mass in oncology patients. *Total annual research expenditures:* $1.4 million. *Unit head:* Dr. Vickie Keough, Dean, 708-216-5448, Fax: 708-216-9555, E-mail: vkeough@luc.edu. *Application contact:* Toni Topalova, Enrollment Advisor, 708-216-3751, Fax: 708-216-9555, E-mail: atopalova@luc.edu.
Website: http://www.luc.edu/nursing/

Madonna University, Program in Nursing, Livonia, MI 48150-1173. Offers adult health: chronic health conditions (MSN); adult nurse practitioner (MSN); nursing administration (MSN); MSN/MSBA. *Accreditation:* AACN. *Program availability:* Part-time. *Degree requirements:* For master's, thesis or alternative. *Entrance requirements:* For master's, GRE General Test, Michigan nursing license. Electronic applications accepted. *Faculty research:* Coping, caring.

Marian University, School of Nursing and Health Professions, Fond du Lac, WI 54935-4699. Offers adult nurse practitioner (MSN); nurse educator (MSN); thanatology (MS). *Accreditation:* AACN. *Program availability:* Part-time, evening/weekend. *Degree requirements:* For master's, thesis, 675 clinical practicum hours. *Entrance requirements:* For master's, 3 letters of professional recommendation; undergraduate work in nursing research, statistics, health assessment. Additional exam requirements/recommendations for international students: Required—TOEFL (minimum score 525 paper-based; 70 iBT). Electronic applications accepted. *Expenses:* Contact institution.

Marquette University, Graduate School, College of Nursing, Milwaukee, WI 53201-1881. Offers acute care nurse practitioner (Certificate); adult clinical nurse specialist (Certificate); adult nurse practitioner (Certificate); advanced practice nursing (MSN, DNP), including adult-older adult acute care (DNP), adults (MSN), adults-older adults (DNP), clinical nurse leader (MSN), health care systems leadership (DNP), nurse-midwifery (MSN), older adults (MSN), pediatrics-acute care, pediatrics-primary care, primary care (DNP), systems leadership and healthcare quality (MSN); family nurse practitioner (Certificate); nurse-midwifery (Certificate); nursing (PhD); pediatric acute care (Certificate); pediatric primary care (Certificate); systems leadership and healthcare quality (Certificate). *Accreditation:* AACN. Terminal master's awarded for partial completion of doctoral program. *Degree requirements:* For master's, comprehensive exam, thesis or alternative. *Entrance requirements:* For master's, GRE General Test, BSN, Wisconsin RN license, official transcripts from all current and previous colleges/universities except Marquette, three completed recommendation forms, resume, written statement of professional goals; for doctorate, GRE General Test, official transcripts from all current and previous colleges/universities except Marquette, three letters of recommendation, resume, written statement of professional goals, sample of scholarly writing. Additional exam requirements/recommendations for international students: Required—TOEFL (minimum score 530 paper-based). Electronic applications accepted. *Faculty research:* Psychosocial adjustment to chronic illness, gerontology, reminiscence, health policy: uninsured and access, hospital care delivery systems.

Maryville University of Saint Louis, Myrtle E. and Earl E. Walker College of Health Professions, The Catherine McAuley School of Nursing, St. Louis, MO 63141-7299. Offers acute care nurse practitioner (MSN); adult gerontology nurse practitioner (MSN); advanced practice nursing (DNP); family nurse practitioner (MSN); pediatric nurse practitioner (MSN). *Accreditation:* AACN. *Program availability:* 100% online, blended/hybrid learning. *Faculty:* 15 full-time (all women), 142 part-time/adjunct (123 women). *Students:* 49 full-time (42 women), 2,999 part-time (2,645 women); includes 773 minority (375 Black or African American, non-Hispanic/Latino; 51 American Indian or Alaska Native, non-Hispanic/Latino; 135 Asian, non-Hispanic/Latino; 149 Hispanic/Latino; 63 Two or more races, non-Hispanic/Latino), 21 international. Average age 36. In 2017, 843 master's, 42 doctorates awarded. *Degree requirements:* For master's, practicum. *Entrance requirements:* For master's, BSN, current licensure, minimum GPA of 3.0, 3 letters of recommendation, curriculum vitae. Additional exam requirements/recommendations for international students: Required—TOEFL (minimum score 550 paper-based). *Application deadline:* Applications are processed on a rolling basis. Electronic applications accepted. *Expenses:* Contact institution. *Financial support:* Federal Work-Study and campus employment available. Support available to part-time students. Financial award application deadline: 4/1; financial award applicants required to submit FAFSA. *Unit head:* Dr. Elizabeth Buck, Assistant Dean/Director of Online Nursing, 314-529-9453, Fax: 314-529-9139, E-mail: ebuck@maryville.edu. *Application contact:* Jeannie DeLuca, Director of Admissions and Advising, 314-929-9355, Fax: 314-529-9927, E-mail: cjacobsmeyer@maryville.edu.
Website: http://www.maryville.edu/hp/nursing/

Medical University of South Carolina, College of Nursing, Adult-Gerontology Health Nurse Practitioner Program, Charleston, SC 29425. Offers MSN, DNP. *Program availability:* Part-time, online learning. *Degree requirements:* For master's, comprehensive exam (for some programs), thesis optional; for doctorate, final project. *Entrance requirements:* For master's, BSN from nationally-accredited program, minimum nursing and cumulative GPA of 3.0, undergraduate-level statistics course, active RN License, 3 confidential references, current curriculum vitae or resume, essay; for doctorate, BSN from nationally-accredited program, minimum nursing and cumulative GPA of 3.0, undergraduate-level statistics course, active RN License, 3 confidential references, current curriculum vitae or resume, personal essay (for DNP). Additional exam requirements/recommendations for international students: Required—TOEFL (minimum score 550 paper-based; 80 iBT). Electronic applications accepted. *Faculty research:* Palliative care, dementia, hospital acquired infections, diabetes, advance practice nurse utilization.

Monmouth University, Graduate Studies, Marjorie K. Unterberg School of Nursing and Health Studies, West Long Branch, NJ 07764-1898. Offers adult-gerontological primary care nurse practitioner (MSN, Post-Master's Certificate); family nurse practitioner (MSN, Post-Master's Certificate); forensic nursing (MSN, Certificate); nursing (MSN); nursing administration (MSN); nursing education (MSN, Post-Master's Certificate); nursing practice (DNP); physician assistant (MS); psychiatric and mental health nurse practitioner (MSN, Post-Master's Certificate); school nursing (MSN, Certificate). *Accreditation:* AACN. *Program availability:* Part-time, evening/weekend, 100% online, blended/hybrid learning. *Faculty:* 12 full-time (all women), 20 part-time/adjunct (12 women). *Students:* 90 full-time (66 women), 329 part-time (302 women); includes 129 minority (51 Black or African American, non-Hispanic/Latino; 43 Asian, non-Hispanic/Latino; 31 Hispanic/Latino; 1 Native Hawaiian or other Pacific Islander, non-Hispanic/Latino; 3 Two or more races, non-Hispanic/Latino), 1 international. Average age 36. In 2017, 85 master's, 4 other advanced degrees awarded. *Degree requirements:* For master's, practicum (for some tracks); for doctorate, practicum, capstone course. *Entrance requirements:* For master's, GRE General Test (waived for MSN applicants with minimum B grade in each of the first four courses and for MS applicants with master's degree), BSN with minimum GPA of 2.75, current RN license, proof of liability and malpractice policy, personal statement, two letters of recommendation, college course work in health assessment, resume; CASPA application (for MS); for doctorate, accredited master's nursing program degree with minimum GPA of 3.2, active RN license, national certification as nurse practitioner or nurse administrator, working knowledge of statistics, statement of goals and vision for change, 2 letters of recommendation (professional or academic), resume, interview. Additional exam requirements/recommendations for international students: Required—TOEFL (minimum score 550 paper-based; 79 iBT), IELTS (minimum score 6) or Michigan English Language Assessment Battery (minimum score 77). *Application deadline:* For fall admission, 7/15 priority date for domestic students, 6/1 for international students; for spring admission, 12/1 priority date for domestic students, 11/1 for international students; for summer admission, 5/1 for domestic students. Applications are processed on a rolling basis. Application fee: $50. Electronic applications accepted. *Expenses:* Contact institution. *Financial support:* In 2017–18, 197 students received support. Institutionally sponsored loans, scholarships/grants, and unspecified assistantships available. Support available to part-time students. Financial award applicants required to submit FAFSA. *Faculty research:* School nursing, health policy, and smoking cessation in teens; Multiple Sclerosis; adherence and self-efficacy; aging issues and geriatric care. *Unit head:* Dr. Janet Mahoney, Dean, 732-571-3443, Fax: 732-263-5131, E-mail: jmahoney@monmouth.edu. *Application contact:* Lucia Fedele, Graduate Admission Counselor, 732-571-3452, Fax: 732-263-5123, E-mail: gradadm@monmouth.edu.
Website: https://www.monmouth.edu/graduate/nursing-programs-of-study/

Mount Carmel College of Nursing, Nursing Program, Columbus, OH 43222. Offers adult gerontology acute care nurse practitioner (MS); adult health clinical nurse specialist (MS); family nurse practitioner (MS); nursing (DNP); nursing administration (MS); nursing education (MS). *Accreditation:* AACN. *Program availability:* Part-time. *Faculty:* 11 full-time (all women), 5 part-time/adjunct (4 women). *Students:* 112 full-time (93 women), 72 part-time (65 women); includes 35 minority (20 Black or African

American, non-Hispanic/Latino; 4 Asian, non-Hispanic/Latino; 3 Hispanic/Latino; 8 Two or more races, non-Hispanic/Latino). Average age 35. 135 applicants, 65% accepted, 68 enrolled. In 2017, 64 master's awarded. *Degree requirements:* For master's, professional manuscript; for doctorate, practicum. *Entrance requirements:* For master's, letters of recommendation, statement of purpose, current resume, baccalaureate degree in nursing, current Ohio RN license, minimum cumulative GPA of 3.0; for doctorate, master's degree in nursing from program accredited by either ACEN or CCNE. Additional exam requirements/recommendations for international students: Required—TOEFL (minimum score 550 paper-based; 80 iBT). *Application deadline:* For fall admission, 2/1 priority date for domestic students; for spring admission, 11/1 priority date for domestic students. Applications are processed on a rolling basis. Application fee: $30. Electronic applications accepted. *Expenses: Tuition:* Full-time $11,403; part-time $543 per credit. *Required fees:* $50; $50 per year. *Financial support:* In 2017–18, 3 students received support. Institutionally sponsored loans and scholarships/grants available. Financial award application deadline: 3/1; financial award applicants required to submit FAFSA. *Unit head:* Dr. Jill Kilanowski, Associate Dean, 614-234-5237, Fax: 614-234-2875, E-mail: jkilanowski@mccn.edu. *Application contact:* Dr. Kim Campbell, Director of Recruitment and Admissions, 614-234-5144, Fax: 614-234-5427, E-mail: kcampbell@mccn.edu.

Mount Saint Mary College, School of Nursing, Newburgh, NY 12550-3494. Offers adult nurse practitioner (MS, Advanced Certificate), including nursing education (MS), nursing management (MS); family nurse practitioner (Advanced Certificate); nursing education (Advanced Certificate). *Accreditation:* AACN. *Program availability:* Part-time, evening/weekend, blended/hybrid learning. *Faculty:* 7 full-time (all women), 5 part-time/adjunct (all women). *Students:* 3 full-time (1 woman), 153 part-time (143 women); includes 42 minority (22 Black or African American, non-Hispanic/Latino; 1 American Indian or Alaska Native, non-Hispanic/Latino; 6 Asian, non-Hispanic/Latino; 11 Hispanic/Latino; 1 Native Hawaiian or other Pacific Islander, non-Hispanic/Latino; 1 Two or more races, non-Hispanic/Latino). Average age 38. 34 applicants, 91% accepted, 28 enrolled. In 2017, 30 master's, 5 other advanced degrees awarded. *Degree requirements:* For master's, research utilization project. *Entrance requirements:* For master's, BSN, minimum GPA of 3.0, RN license. Additional exam requirements/recommendations for international students: Required—TOEFL (minimum score 80 iBT). *Application deadline:* For fall admission, 6/3 priority date for domestic students; for spring admission, 10/31 priority date for domestic students. Applications are processed on a rolling basis. Application fee: $45. Electronic applications accepted. Application fee is waived when completed online. *Expenses: Tuition:* Full-time $14,454; part-time $803 per credit. *Required fees:* $172; $86 per semester. *Financial support:* In 2017–18, 8 students received support. Unspecified assistantships available. Financial award application deadline: 4/15; financial award applicants required to submit FAFSA. *Unit head:* Christine Berte, Graduate Coordinator, 845-569-3141, Fax: 845-562-6762, E-mail: christine.berte@msmc.edu. *Application contact:* Lisa Alvarez, Director of Admissions for Graduate Programs and Adult Degree Completion, 845-569-3166, Fax: 845-569-3450, E-mail: lisa.gallina@msmc.edu.
Website: http://www.msmc.edu/Academics/Graduate_Programs/Master_of_Science_in_Nursing

Neumann University, Graduate Program in Nursing, Aston, PA 19014. Offers adult-gerontology nurse practitioner (MS, Certificate). *Accreditation:* ACEN. *Program availability:* Part-time, evening/weekend. *Faculty:* 2 full-time (both women), 4 part-time/adjunct (3 women). *Students:* 37 part-time (35 women); includes 11 minority (5 Black or African American, non-Hispanic/Latino; 2 Asian, non-Hispanic/Latino; 2 Hispanic/Latino; 2 Two or more races, non-Hispanic/Latino). Average age 41. 15 applicants, 47% accepted, 7 enrolled. In 2017, 11 master's awarded. *Entrance requirements:* For master's, official transcripts from all institutions attended, resume, letter of intent, current registered nursing license, two letters of reference; for Certificate, BSN, MSN, official transcripts from all institutions attended, resume, letter of intent, current registered nursing license, two official letters of reference. Additional exam requirements/recommendations for international students: Required—TOEFL (minimum score 84 iBT). *Application deadline:* Applications are processed on a rolling basis. Application fee: $0. Electronic applications accepted. *Expenses: Tuition:* Part-time $700 per credit hour. Tuition and fees vary according to degree level, campus/location and program. *Financial support:* Scholarships/grants, traineeships, and health care benefits available. Support available to part-time students. Financial award application deadline: 3/15; financial award applicants required to submit FAFSA. *Unit head:* Dr. Kathleen Hoover, Dean, Division of Nursing and Health Sciences, 610-558-5560, Fax: 610-361-5265, E-mail: hooverk@neumann.edu. *Application contact:* Dr. Erika K. Davis, Director of Adult and Graduate Admissions, 800-9-NEUMANN Ext. 5208, Fax: 610-361-2548, E-mail: gradadultadmiss@neumann.edu.

New York University, Rory Meyers College of Nursing, Doctor of Nursing Practice Program, New York, NY 10012-1019. Offers nursing (DNP), including adult-gerontology acute care nurse practitioner, adult-gerontology primary care nurse practitioner, family nurse practitioner, nurse-midwifery, pediatrics nurse practitioner, psychiatric-mental health nurse practitioner. *Accreditation:* AACN. *Program availability:* Part-time, evening/weekend. *Faculty:* 16 full-time (all women), 1 (woman) part-time/adjunct. *Students:* 48 part-time (43 women); includes 11 minority (5 Black or African American, non-Hispanic/Latino; 5 Asian, non-Hispanic/Latino; 1 Hispanic/Latino). Average age 28. 20 applicants, 75% accepted, 10 enrolled. In 2017, 8 doctorates awarded. *Degree requirements:* For doctorate, thesis/dissertation, project. *Entrance requirements:* For doctorate, MS, RN license, interview, Nurse Practitioner Certification, writing sample. Additional exam requirements/recommendations for international students: Required—TOEFL (minimum score 100 iBT), IELTS (minimum score 7). *Application deadline:* For fall admission, 3/1 priority date for domestic and international students. Applications are processed on a rolling basis. Application fee: $80. Electronic applications accepted. *Expenses:* Contact institution. *Financial support:* In 2017–18, 13 students received support. Scholarships/grants available. Support available to part-time students. Financial award application deadline: 2/1; financial award applicants required to submit FAFSA. *Faculty research:* Workforce determinants of healthcare quality, genomics, health literacy and health outcomes, health policy. *Unit head:* Dr. Mary Jo Vetter, Director, DNP Program, 212-998-5165, E-mail: mjv5@nyu.edu. *Application contact:* Matthew Burke, Assistant Director, Graduate Student Affairs and Admissions, 212-998-7397, E-mail: mb6060@nyu.edu.

New York University, Rory Meyers College of Nursing, Programs in Advanced Practice Nursing, New York, NY 10012-1019. Offers adult-gerontology acute care nurse practitioner (MS, Advanced Certificate); adult-gerontology primary care nurse practitioner (MS, Advanced Certificate); family nurse practitioner (MS, Advanced Certificate); gerontology nurse practitioner (Advanced Certificate); nurse-midwifery (MS, Advanced Certificate); nursing administration (MS, Advanced Certificate); nursing education (MS, Advanced Certificate); nursing informatics (MS, Advanced Certificate); pediatrics nurse practitioner (MS, Advanced Certificate); psychiatric-mental health nurse practitioner (MS, Advanced Certificate); MS/MPH. *Accreditation:* AACN; ACNM/ACME. *Program availability:* Part-time, evening/weekend. *Faculty:* 23 full-time (all women), 62 part-time/adjunct (56 women). *Students:* 50 full-time (46 women), 557 part-time (509 women); includes 234 minority (58 Black or African American, non-Hispanic/Latino; 1 American Indian or Alaska Native, non-Hispanic/Latino; 116 Asian, non-Hispanic/Latino; 43 Hispanic/Latino; 1 Native Hawaiian or other Pacific Islander, non-Hispanic/Latino; 15 Two or more races, non-Hispanic/Latino), 23 international. Average age 32. 391 applicants, 59% accepted, 149 enrolled. In 2017, 187 master's, 5 other advanced degrees awarded. *Degree requirements:* For master's, thesis (for some programs), capstone. *Entrance requirements:* For master's, BS in nursing, AS in nursing with another BS/BA, interview, RN license, 1 year of clinical experience (3 for the MS in nursing education program); for Advanced Certificate, master's degree in nursing. Additional exam requirements/recommendations for international students: Required—TOEFL (minimum score 100 iBT), IELTS (minimum score 7). *Application deadline:* For fall admission, 3/1 priority date for domestic and international students; for spring admission, 11/1 priority date for domestic and international students; for summer admission, 3/1 for domestic and international students. Application fee: $80. Electronic applications accepted. *Expenses:* Contact institution. *Financial support:* In 2017–18, 130 students received support. Career-related internships or fieldwork, Federal Work-Study, and scholarships/grants available. Support available to part-time students. Financial award application deadline: 3/1; financial award applicants required to submit FAFSA. *Faculty research:* Vaccine hesitancy in pregnant women and mothers, palliative care and midwifery, diabetes education, curriculum development, workforce training, education and development, geriatrics. *Unit head:* Dr. James Pace, Senior Associate Dean for Academic Programs, 212-992-7343, E-mail: james.pace@nyu.edu. *Application contact:* Matthew Burke, Assistant Director, Graduate Student Affairs and Admissions, 212-998-7397, Fax: 212-995-4302, E-mail: mb6060@nyu.edu.

North Park University, School of Nursing and Health Sciences, Chicago, IL 60625-4895. Offers advanced practice nursing (MS); leadership and management (MS); MBA/MS; MM/MSN; MS/MHR; MS/MNA. *Accreditation:* AACN. *Program availability:* Part-time, evening/weekend. *Degree requirements:* For master's, thesis. *Entrance requirements:* For master's, GMAT, MAT. *Faculty research:* Aging, consultation roles, critical thinking skills, family breakdown, science of caring.

Nova Southeastern University, Ron and Kathy Assaf College of Nursing, Fort Lauderdale, FL 33314-7796. Offers advanced practice registered nurse (MSN), including adult-gerontology acute care nurse practitioner, family nurse practitioner, psychiatric mental health nurse practitioner; executive nurse leadership (MSN); nursing (PhD), including nursing education; nursing education (MSN); nursing informatics (MSN); nursing practice (DNP). *Accreditation:* AACN. *Program availability:* Part-time, evening/weekend, 100% online, blended/hybrid learning, annual one-week summer institute delivered face-to-face on main campus. *Faculty:* 9 full-time (all women), 47 part-time/adjunct (43 women). *Students:* 658 full-time (599 women); includes 414 minority (175 Black or African American, non-Hispanic/Latino; 37 Asian, non-Hispanic/Latino; 179 Hispanic/Latino; 1 Native Hawaiian or other Pacific Islander, non-Hispanic/Latino; 22 Two or more races, non-Hispanic/Latino), 3 international. Average age 38. 179 applicants, 100% accepted, 163 enrolled. In 2017, 161 master's, 16 doctorates awarded. *Degree requirements:* For doctorate, comprehensive exam, thesis/dissertation. *Entrance requirements:* For master's, minimum GPA of 3.0, RN, BSN, BS or BA; for doctorate, minimum GPA of 3.5, MSN, RN. Additional exam requirements/recommendations for international students: Recommended—TOEFL. *Application deadline:* For fall admission, 3/1 priority date for domestic students, 3/1 for international students; for winter admission, 11/1 for domestic and international students. Applications are processed on a rolling basis. Application fee: $50. Electronic applications accepted. *Expenses:* Contact institution. *Financial support:* Application deadline: 4/15; applicants required to submit FAFSA. *Faculty research:* Nursing education, curriculum, clinical research, interdisciplinary research. *Total annual research expenditures:* $9,500. *Unit head:* Dr. Marcella M. Rutherford, Dean, 954-262-1963, E-mail: rmarcell@nova.edu. *Application contact:* Dianna Murphey, Director of Operations, 954-262-1975, E-mail: dgardner1@nova.edu.
Website: http://www.nova.edu/nursing/

Old Dominion University, College of Health Sciences, School of Nursing, Adult Gerontology Nursing Emphasis, Norfolk, VA 23529. Offers adult gerontology clinical nurse specialist/administrator (MSN); adult gerontology clinical nurse specialist/educator (MSN); advanced practice (DNP); neonatal clinical nurse specialist (MSN); pediatric clinical nurse specialist (MSN). *Program availability:* Part-time, online only, blended/hybrid learning. *Faculty:* 2 full-time (both women), 2 part-time/adjunct (both women). *Students:* 9 full-time (all women), 10 part-time (9 women); includes 10 minority (8 Black or African American, non-Hispanic/Latino; 2 Asian, non-Hispanic/Latino). Average age 37. 27 applicants, 96% accepted, 12 enrolled. In 2017, 5 master's awarded. *Degree requirements:* For master's, comprehensive exam, internship, practicum. *Entrance requirements:* For master's, GRE or MAT (waived with a GPA above 3.5), undergraduate health/physical assessment course, statistics, 3 letters of recommendation, essay, resume, transcripts. Additional exam requirements/recommendations for international students: Required—TOEFL. *Application deadline:* For fall admission, 6/1 priority date for domestic students, 4/15 priority date for international students. Applications are processed on a rolling basis. Application fee: $50. Electronic applications accepted. *Expenses:* $469 per credit; $450 School of Nursing fee per semester. *Financial support:* Unspecified assistantships available. Financial award applicants required to submit FAFSA. *Unit head:* Dr. Tina Haney, Program Director, 757-683-5428, Fax: 757-683-5253, E-mail: thaney@odu.edu. *Application contact:* Sue Parker, Graduate Program Coordinator, 757-683-4298, Fax: 757-683-5253, E-mail: sparker@odu.edu.

Purdue University Northwest, Graduate Studies Office, School of Nursing, Hammond, IN 46323-2094. Offers adult health clinical nurse specialist (MS); critical care clinical nurse specialist (MS); family nurse practitioner (MS); nurse executive (MS). *Accreditation:* ACEN. *Program availability:* Part-time, online learning. *Entrance requirements:* For master's, BSN. Additional exam requirements/recommendations for international students: Required—TOEFL. Electronic applications accepted. *Faculty research:* Adult health, cardiovascular and pulmonary nursing.

Quinnipiac University, School of Nursing, Adult Nurse Practitioner Track, Hamden, CT 06518-1940. Offers DNP. *Accreditation:* ACEN. *Program availability:* Part-time. *Faculty:* 18 full-time (17 women), 11 part-time/adjunct (8 women). *Students:* 11 full-time (10 women), 32 part-time (28 women); includes 13 minority (8 Black or African American, non-Hispanic/Latino; 3 Asian, non-Hispanic/Latino; 1 Hispanic/Latino; 1 Two or more races, non-Hispanic/Latino). 23 applicants, 87% accepted, 14 enrolled. In 2017, 36 doctorates awarded. *Entrance requirements:* Additional exam requirements/recommendations for international students: Required—TOEFL (minimum score 575 paper-based; 90 iBT), IELTS (minimum score 6.5). *Application deadline:* For fall admission, 5/1 priority date for domestic students, 4/30 for international students. Applications are processed on a rolling basis. Application fee: $45. Electronic applications accepted. *Financial support:* Federal Work-Study, scholarships/grants, and unspecified assistantships available. Financial award application deadline: 6/1; financial award applicants required to submit FAFSA. *Unit head:* Laima Karosas, Program Director, 203-582-5366, E-mail: graduate@qu.edu. *Application contact:* Office of Graduate Admissions, 203-582-8672, Fax: 203-582-3443, E-mail: graduate@qu.edu.
Website: http://www.qu.edu/gradnursing

Research College of Nursing, Nursing Program, Kansas City, MO 64132. Offers adult-gerontological nurse practitioner (MSN); executive practice and healthcare leadership

(MSN); family nurse practitioner (MSN). *Accreditation:* AACN. *Program availability:* Part-time-only, 100% online. *Faculty:* 10 full-time (all women), 4 part-time/adjunct (2 women). *Students:* 1 (woman) full-time, 150 part-time (125 women); includes 14 minority (7 Black or African American, non-Hispanic/Latino; 1 American Indian or Alaska Native, non-Hispanic/Latino; 2 Asian, non-Hispanic/Latino; 2 Hispanic/Latino; 1 Native Hawaiian or other Pacific Islander, non-Hispanic/Latino; 1 Two or more races, non-Hispanic/Latino). *Degree requirements:* For master's, research project. *Entrance requirements:* For master's, 3 letters of recommendation, official transcripts, resume, personal statement/writing sample. *Application deadline:* Applications are processed on a rolling basis. Application fee: $65. Electronic applications accepted. *Expenses:* *Tuition:* Part-time $550 per credit hour. *Financial support:* Applicants required to submit FAFSA. *Unit head:* Dr. Thad Wilson, President, 816-995-2815, Fax: 816-995-2817, E-mail: thad.wilson@researchcollege.edu. *Application contact:* Leslie Burry, Director of Transfer and Graduate Recruitment, 816-995-2820, Fax: 816-995-2813, E-mail: leslie.burry@researchcollege.edu.

Rush University, College of Nursing, Department of Adult Health and Gerontological Nursing, Chicago, IL 60612. Offers adult gerontology acute care clinical nurse specialist (DNP); adult gerontology acute care nurse practitioner (DNP, Post-Graduate Certificate); adult gerontology primary care nurse practitioner (DNP); nurse anesthesia (DNP). *Accreditation:* AACN; AANA/CANAEP (one or more programs are accredited). *Program availability:* Part-time. *Students:* 98 full-time (68 women), 155 part-time (17 women); includes 48 minority (7 Black or African American, non-Hispanic/Latino; 22 Asian, non-Hispanic/Latino; 14 Hispanic/Latino; 5 Two or more races, non-Hispanic/Latino). 170 applicants, 54% accepted, 69 enrolled. In 2017, 51 doctorates awarded. *Degree requirements:* For doctorate, scholarly project. *Entrance requirements:* For doctorate, GRE General Test (for nurse anesthesia; waived for other DNPs if cumulative GPA is 3.25 or greater, nursing GPA is 3.0 or greater, or a completed graduate program GPA is 3.5 or greater), interview, 3 letters of recommendation, personal statement, current resume; for Post-Graduate Certificate, MSN in a clinical discipline, 3 letters of recommendation, personal statement, current resume, interview. Additional exam requirements/recommendations for international students: Required—TOEFL (minimum score 94 iBT). *Application deadline:* For fall admission, 1/2 for domestic students; for spring admission, 8/1 for domestic students; for summer admission, 12/1 for domestic students. Applications are processed on a rolling basis. Application fee: $110. Electronic applications accepted. *Expenses:* Contact institution. *Financial support:* Research assistantships, teaching assistantships, Federal Work-Study, institutionally sponsored loans, scholarships/grants, traineeships, and health care benefits available. Support available to part-time students. Financial award application deadline: 3/1; financial award applicants required to submit FAFSA. *Faculty research:* Physical activity; prevention; cardiovascular risk; caregivers; gerontology. *Unit head:* Dr. Elizabeth Carlson, Chairperson, 312-942-7117, E-mail: elizabeth_carlson@rush.edu. *Application contact:* Jennifer Thorndyke, Director of Admissions, 312-563-7526, E-mail: jennifer_thorndyke@rush.edu.
Website: https://www.rushu.rush.edu/college-nursing/departments-college-nursing/department-adult-health-and-gerontological-nursing

Rutgers University–Newark, Rutgers School of Nursing, Newark, NJ 07107-3001. Offers adult health (MSN); adult occupational health (MSN); advanced practice nursing (MSN, Post Master's Certificate); family nurse practitioner (MSN); nurse anesthesia (MSN); nursing (MSN); nursing informatics (MSN); urban health (PhD); women's health practitioner (MSN). *Accreditation:* AANA/CANAEP. *Program availability:* Part-time. *Entrance requirements:* For master's, GRE, RN license; basic life support, statistics, and health assessment experience. Additional exam requirements/recommendations for international students: Required—TOEFL. Electronic applications accepted. *Expenses:* Contact institution. *Faculty research:* HIV/AIDS, diabetes education, learned helplessness, nursing science, psychoeducation.

St. Catherine University, Graduate Programs, Program in Nursing, St. Paul, MN 55105. Offers adult-gerontological nurse practitioner (MS); nurse educator (MS); nursing (DNP); nursing: entry-level (MS); pediatric nurse practitioner (MS). *Accreditation:* ACEN. *Program availability:* Part-time, evening/weekend. *Degree requirements:* For master's, thesis; for doctorate, portfolio, systems change project. *Entrance requirements:* For master's, GRE General Test, bachelor's degree in nursing, current nursing license, 2 years of recent clinical practice; for doctorate, master's degree in nursing, RN license, advanced nursing position. Additional exam requirements/recommendations for international students: Required—TOEFL (minimum score 600 paper-based; 100 iBT). *Application deadline:* For fall admission, 1/15 priority date for domestic students. Application fee: $35. *Expenses:* Contact institution. *Financial support:* Career-related internships or fieldwork and institutionally sponsored loans available. Support available to part-time students. Financial award application deadline: 4/1; financial award applicants required to submit FAFSA. *Unit head:* Margaret Dexheimer-Pharris, Professor/Associate Dean for Nursing, 651-690-6572, Fax: 651-690-6941, E-mail: mdpharris@stkate.edu. *Application contact:* Kristin Chalberg, Associate Director of Non-Traditional Admissions, 651-690-6868, Fax: 651-690-6064.

St. Joseph's College, Long Island Campus, Program in Nursing, Patchogue, NY 11772-2399. Offers adult-gerontology clinical nurse specialist (MS); adult-gerontology primary care nurse practitioner (MS); nursing education (MS). *Program availability:* Part-time, evening/weekend. *Faculty:* 4 full-time (all women), 1 (woman) part-time/adjunct. *Students:* 1 (woman) full-time, 40 part-time (36 women); includes 15 minority (7 Black or African American, non-Hispanic/Latino; 3 Asian, non-Hispanic/Latino; 5 Hispanic/Latino). Average age 41. 39 applicants, 69% accepted, 21 enrolled. In 2017, 6 master's awarded. *Entrance requirements:* For master's, one year of professional clinical practice prior to admission, proof of New York State RN license and current professional registration, curriculum vitae, personal statement, two letters of reference, official college transcripts, proof of malpractice insurance. Additional exam requirements/recommendations for international students: Required—TOEFL (minimum score 550 paper-based; 80 iBT). *Application deadline:* Applications are processed on a rolling basis. Application fee: $25. Electronic applications accepted. *Expenses:* *Tuition:* Full-time $17,550; part-time $975 per credit. *Required fees:* $362. *Financial support:* In 2017–18, 23 students received support. *Unit head:* Dr. Maria Fletcher, RN, Director/Associate Professor, 631-687-5180, E-mail: mfletcher@sjcny.edu.
Website: http://www.sjcny.edu/long-island

St. Joseph's College, New York, Program in Nursing, Brooklyn, NY 11205-3688. Offers adult-gerontology clinical nurse specialist (MS); adult-gerontology primary care nurse practitioner (MS); nursing education (MS). *Accreditation:* ACEN. *Program availability:* Part-time, evening/weekend. *Faculty:* 4 full-time (all women), 1 (woman) part-time/adjunct. *Students:* 47 part-time (46 women); includes 38 minority (35 Black or African American, non-Hispanic/Latino; 1 Asian, non-Hispanic/Latino; 2 Two or more races, non-Hispanic/Latino). Average age 45. 51 applicants, 71% accepted, 20 enrolled. In 2017, 7 master's awarded. *Entrance requirements:* For master's, one year of professional clinical practice, proof of NY State RN license and current professional registration, curriculum vitae, personal statement, 2 letters of reference, official transcripts, malpractice insurance. Additional exam requirements/recommendations for international students: Required—TOEFL (minimum score 80 iBT). *Application deadline:* Applications are processed on a rolling basis. Application fee: $25. Electronic applications accepted. *Expenses:* *Tuition:* Full-time $17,550; part-time $975 per credit. *Required fees:* $362. *Financial support:* In 2017–18, 7 students received support. *Unit head:* Maria Fletcher, Associate Professor/Director, 718-940-5891, E-mail: mfletcher@sjcny.edu.
Website: http://www.sjcny.edu

Saint Mary's College, Graduate Programs, Doctor of Nursing Practice Program, Notre Dame, IN 46556. Offers adult - gerontology acute care (DNP); adult - gerontology primary care (DNP); family nurse practitioner (DNP). *Program availability:* Part-time-only. *Faculty:* 7 full-time (all women), 4 part-time/adjunct (3 women). *Students:* 39 part-time (37 women); includes 12 minority (4 Black or African American, non-Hispanic/Latino; 5 Asian, non-Hispanic/Latino; 3 Hispanic/Latino). Average age 31. 36 applicants, 83% accepted, 26 enrolled. *Degree requirements:* For doctorate, comprehensive exam, thesis/dissertation. *Entrance requirements:* For doctorate, BSN or MSN, unencumbered RN license or eligibility for RN licensure, official transcripts from previously-attended institutions, 3 letters of recommendation, personal statement, resume or curriculum vitae. Additional exam requirements/recommendations for international students: Recommended—TOEFL (minimum score 80 iBT), IELTS (minimum score 6.5). *Application deadline:* For fall admission, 6/15 priority date for domestic and international students. Applications are processed on a rolling basis. Application fee: $65. Electronic applications accepted. *Expenses:* $5,382 per semester. *Financial support:* Application deadline: 3/1; applicants required to submit FAFSA. *Faculty research:* Suicide prevention, infant death prevention, delirium management, teaching methodologies, nurses' perceptions of care. *Unit head:* Linda Paskiewicz, Director of the Department of Nursing Science, 574-284-4679, E-mail: lpaskie@saintmarys.edu. *Application contact:* Melissa Fruscione, Graduate Admission, 574-284-5098, E-mail: graduateadmission@saintmarys.edu.
Website: https://grad.saintmarys.edu/academic-programs/doctor-nursing-practice

Saint Peter's University, School of Nursing, Nursing Program, Jersey City, NJ 07306-5997. Offers adult nurse practitioner (MSN, Certificate); advanced practice (DNP); case management (MSN, DNP). *Accreditation:* AACN. *Program availability:* Part-time, evening/weekend. *Entrance requirements:* Additional exam requirements/recommendations for international students: Required—TOEFL. Electronic applications accepted.

Seattle Pacific University, MS in Nursing Program, Seattle, WA 98119-1997. Offers administration (MSN); adult/gerontology nurse practitioner (MSN); clinical nurse specialist (MSN), family nurse practitioner (MSN, Certificate), informatics (MSN), nurse educator (MSN). *Accreditation:* AACN. *Program availability:* Part-time. *Students:* 22 full-time (17 women), 40 part-time (35 women); includes 13 minority (4 Black or African American, non-Hispanic/Latino; 1 American Indian or Alaska Native, non-Hispanic/Latino; 7 Asian, non-Hispanic/Latino; 1 Two or more races, non-Hispanic/Latino). Average age 36. 52 applicants, 73% accepted, 22 enrolled. In 2017, 23 master's awarded. *Degree requirements:* For master's, thesis. *Entrance requirements:* For master's, personal statement, transcripts, undergraduate nursing degree, proof of undergraduate statistics course with minimum GPA of 2.0, 2 recommendations. *Application deadline:* For fall admission, 1/15 priority date for domestic students; for spring admission, 1/15 for domestic students. Applications are processed on a rolling basis. Application fee: $50. Electronic applications accepted. *Expenses:* Contact institution. *Financial support:* Fellowships and scholarships/grants available. Financial award applicants required to submit FAFSA. *Unit head:* Dr. Christine Hoyle, Associate Dean, 206-281-2469, E-mail: hoylec@spu.edu.
Website: http://spu.edu/academics/school-of-health-sciences/undergraduate-programs/nursing

Seton Hall University, College of Nursing, South Orange, NJ 07079-2697. Offers advanced practice in primary health care (MSN, DNP), including adult/gerontological nurse practitioner, pediatric nurse practitioner; entry into practice (MSN); health systems administration (MSN, DNP); nursing (PhD); nursing case management (MSN); nursing education (MA); school nurse (MSN); MSN/MA. *Accreditation:* AACN. *Program availability:* Part-time, online learning. *Degree requirements:* For master's, research project; for doctorate, dissertation or scholarly project. *Entrance requirements:* For doctorate, GRE (waived for students with GPA of 3.5 or higher). Additional exam requirements/recommendations for international students: Required—TOEFL. Electronic applications accepted. *Faculty research:* Parent/child, adult, and gerontological nursing; breast cancer; families of children with HIV; parish nursing.

Shenandoah University, Eleanor Wade Custer School of Nursing, Winchester, VA 22601. Offers adult gerontology primary care nurse practitioner (Graduate Certificate); adult-gerontology primary care nurse practitioner (MSN); family nurse practitioner (MSN, DNP, Graduate Certificate); general (MSN); health systems leadership (DNP); health systems management (MSN, Graduate Certificate); nurse midwifery (MSN); nurse-midwifery (Graduate Certificate); nursing education (Graduate Certificate); nursing practice (DNP); psychiatric mental health nurse practitioner (MSN, DNP, Graduate Certificate). *Accreditation:* AACN; ACNM/ACME. *Faculty:* 17 full-time (all women), 6 part-time/adjunct (all women). *Students:* 30 full-time (26 women), 51 part-time (48 women); includes 19 minority (13 Black or African American, non-Hispanic/Latino; 3 Asian, non-Hispanic/Latino; 2 Hispanic/Latino; 1 Two or more races, non-Hispanic/Latino), 3 international. Average age 37. 52 applicants, 88% accepted, 34 enrolled. In 2017, 18 master's, 1 doctorate, 28 other advanced degrees awarded. *Degree requirements:* For master's, research project, clinical hours; for doctorate, scholarly project, clinical hours; for Graduate Certificate, clinical hours. *Entrance requirements:* For master's, United States RN license; minimum GPA of 3.0; 2080 hours of clinical experience; curriculum vitae; 3 letters of recommendation from former dean, faculty member, or advisor familiar with the applicant, and a former or current supervisor; two-to-three-page essay on a specified topic; for doctorate, MSN, minimum GPA of 3.0, 3 letters of recommendation, interview, BSN, two-to-three page essay on a specific topic, 500-word statement of clinical practice research interest, resume, current U.S. RN license, 2080 clinical hours; for Graduate Certificate, MSN, minimum GPA of 3.0, 2 letters of recommendation, minimum of one year (2080 hours) of clinical nursing experience, interview, two-to-three page essay on a specific topic, resume, current United States RN license. Additional exam requirements/recommendations for international students: Required—TOEFL (minimum score 558 paper-based; 83 iBT). *Application deadline:* For fall admission, 4/15 priority date for domestic and international students; for spring admission, 11/1 for domestic and international students; for summer admission, 3/1 for domestic and international students. Application fee: $30. Electronic applications accepted. *Expenses:* $22,451 tuition, plus $3,579 fees (student services fee, technology fee, and clinical fee). *Financial support:* In 2017–18, 32 students received support. Scholarships/grants and unspecified assistantships available. Financial award applicants required to submit FAFSA. *Faculty research:* Emergency preparedness, workplace environment, maternal child, inter-professional education, health policy. *Total annual research expenditures:* $30,000. *Unit head:* Dr. Kathleen LaSala, RN, Dean, 540-678-4381, Fax: 540-665-5519, E-mail: klasala@su.edu. *Application contact:* Andrew Woodall, Executive Director of Recruitment and Admissions, 540-665-4581, Fax: 540-665-4627, E-mail: admit@su.edu.
Website: http://www.su.edu/nursing/

Adult Nursing

Southern Adventist University, School of Nursing, Collegedale, TN 37315-0370. Offers adult/gerontology acute care nurse practitioner (MSN, DNP); adult/gerontology nurse practitioner (MSN); family nurse practitioner (MSN, DNP); lifestyle therapeutics (DNP); nurse educator (MSN, DNP); psychiatric mental health nurse practitioner (MSN, DNP); MSN/MBA. *Accreditation:* ACEN. *Program availability:* Part-time. *Degree requirements:* For master's, thesis or project. *Entrance requirements:* For master's, RN license. Additional exam requirements/recommendations for international students: Required—TOEFL (minimum score 600 paper-based). *Application deadline:* For fall admission, 7/1 for domestic and international students; for winter admission, 12/1 for domestic and international students. Applications are processed on a rolling basis. Application fee: $40. Electronic applications accepted. *Expenses: Tuition:* Full-time $11,430; part-time $635 per credit hour. Tuition and fees vary according to degree level and program. *Financial support:* Teaching assistantships with partial tuition reimbursements available. *Faculty research:* Pain management, ethics, corporate wellness, caring spirituality, stress. *Unit head:* Dr. Barbara James, Dean, 423-236-2942, Fax: 423-236-1940, E-mail: bjames@southern.edu. *Application contact:* Sylvia Mayer, RN, Director of Nursing Admissions, 423-236-2941, Fax: 423-236-1940, E-mail: smayer@southern.edu.
Website: https://www.southern.edu/academics/nursing.html

South University, Program in Nursing, Tampa, FL 33614. Offers adult health nurse practitioner (MS); family nurse practitioner (MS); nurse educator (MS).

Spalding University, Graduate Studies, Kosair College of Health and Natural Sciences, School of Nursing, Louisville, KY 40203-2188. Offers adult nurse practitioner (MSN); family nurse practitioner (MSN); leadership in nursing and healthcare (MSN); nurse educator (Post-Master's Certificate); nurse practitioner (Post-Master's Certificate); pediatric nurse practitioner (MSN). *Accreditation:* AACN. *Program availability:* Part-time, evening/weekend. *Degree requirements:* For master's, comprehensive exam (for some programs), thesis. *Entrance requirements:* For master's, GRE General Test, BSN or bachelor's degree in related field, RN licensure, autobiographical statement, transcripts, letters of recommendation. Additional exam requirements/recommendations for international students: Required—TOEFL (minimum score 535 paper-based). *Faculty research:* Nurse educational administration, gerontology, bioterrorism, healthcare ethics, leadership.

Stony Brook University, State University of New York, Stony Brook Medicine, School of Nursing, Adult-Gerontology Primary Care Nurse Practitioner Program, Stony Brook, NY 11794. Offers adult health nurse practitioner (Certificate); adult health/primary care nursing (MS, DNP). *Accreditation:* AACN. *Program availability:* Part-time, blended/hybrid learning. *Students:* 13 full-time (all women), 194 part-time (165 women); includes 75 minority (21 Black or African American, non-Hispanic/Latino; 1 American Indian or Alaska Native, non-Hispanic/Latino; 29 Asian, non-Hispanic/Latino; 20 Hispanic/Latino; 4 Two or more races, non-Hispanic/Latino). 169 applicants, 37% accepted, 59 enrolled. In 2017, 78 master's, 14 doctorates, 3 other advanced degrees awarded. *Degree requirements:* For master's, thesis; for doctorate, thesis/dissertation. *Entrance requirements:* For master's, BSN, minimum GPA of 3.0, course work in statistics. Additional exam requirements/recommendations for international students: Required—TOEFL (minimum score 90 iBT). *Application deadline:* For fall admission, 1/18 for domestic students. Application fee: $100. *Expenses:* Contact institution. *Financial support:* Application deadline: 3/15. *Unit head:* Justin M. Waryold, Program Director, 631-444-3074, Fax: 631-444-3074, E-mail: justin.waryold@stonybrook.edu. *Application contact:* Dr. Dolores Bilges, Senior Staff Assistant, 631-444-2644, Fax: 631-444-3136, E-mail: anp.nursing@stonybrook.edu.
Website: https://nursing.stonybrookmedicine.edu/graduate

Temple University, College of Public Health, Department of Nursing, Philadelphia, PA 19122. Offers adult-gerontology primary care (DNP); family-individual across the lifespan (DNP); nursing (DNP). *Accreditation:* AACN. *Program availability:* Part-time. *Faculty:* 12 full-time (all women). *Students:* 5 full-time (4 women), 53 part-time (46 women); includes 31 minority (13 Black or African American, non-Hispanic/Latino; 12 Asian, non-Hispanic/Latino; 5 Hispanic/Latino; 1 Two or more races, non-Hispanic/Latino). 11 applicants, 18% accepted. In 2017, 17 doctorates awarded. *Degree requirements:* For doctorate, evidence-based practice project. *Entrance requirements:* For doctorate, GRE General Test or MAT, 2 letters of reference, RN license, interview, statement of purpose, resume. Additional exam requirements/recommendations for international students: Required—TOEFL (minimum score 600 paper-based; 100 iBT). *Application deadline:* For fall admission, 2/15 priority date for domestic students, 1/15 for international students; for spring admission, 10/15 for domestic students, 9/15 for international students. Applications are processed on a rolling basis. Application fee: $60. Electronic applications accepted. *Expenses:* Contact institution. *Financial support:* Federal Work-Study, scholarships/grants, traineeships, and tuition waivers available. Support available to part-time students. Financial award application deadline: 1/15. *Faculty research:* Health promotion, chronic illness, family support systems, primary care, health policy, community health services, evidence-based practice. *Unit head:* Dolores Zygmont, Graduate Director, 215-707-3789, E-mail: zygmont@temple.edu. *Application contact:* Audrey Scriven, Academic Coordinator, Graduate Program, 215-707-4618, E-mail: tunurse@temple.edu.
Website: https://cph.temple.edu/nursing/home

Texas Christian University, Harris College of Nursing and Health Sciences, Master's Program in Nursing, Fort Worth, TX 76129. Offers administration (MSN); clinical nurse leader (MSN, Certificate); clinical nurse specialist (MSN), including adult/gerontology nursing, pediatrics; nursing education (MSN). *Accreditation:* AACN. *Program availability:* Part-time, online only, 100% online. *Faculty:* 29 full-time (26 women), 2 part-time/adjunct (both women). *Students:* 17 full-time (15 women), 7 part-time (all women); includes 6 minority (1 Black or African American, non-Hispanic/Latino; 2 Asian, non-Hispanic/Latino; 2 Hispanic/Latino; 1 Two or more races, non-Hispanic/Latino). Average age 36. 41 applicants, 49% accepted, 6 enrolled. In 2017, 41 master's awarded. *Degree requirements:* For master's, thesis or alternative, practicum. *Entrance requirements:* For master's, 3 letters of reference, essay, resume, two official transcripts from every institution attended. Additional exam requirements/recommendations for international students: Required—TOEFL. *Application deadline:* For spring admission, 9/1 for domestic and international students; for summer admission, 2/1 for domestic and international students. Application fee: $60. Electronic applications accepted. *Expenses:* $1,555 per credit hour, $125 per course fee, $500 lab fee. *Financial support:* In 2017–18, 20 students received support. Scholarships/grants available. Financial award application deadline: 2/15; financial award applicants required to submit FAFSA. *Faculty research:* Geriatrics, cancer survivorship, health literacy, endothelial cells, clinical simulation outcomes. *Unit head:* Dr. Kathy Ellis, Division Director, Graduate Nursing, 817-257-6726, Fax: 817-257-7944, E-mail: kathryn.ellis@tcu.edu. *Application contact:* Heather Lyon, Academic Program Specialist, 817-257-6726, Fax: 817-257-7944, E-mail: graduatenursing@tcu.edu.
Website: http://www.nursing.tcu.edu/graduate.asp

Texas Woman's University, Graduate School, College of Nursing, Denton, TX 76204. Offers adult health clinical nurse specialist (MS); adult health nurse practitioner (MS); adult/gerontology acute care nurse practitioner (MS); child health clinical nurse specialist (MS); clinical nurse leader (MS); family nurse practitioner (MS); health systems management (MS); nursing education (MS); nursing practice (DNP); nursing science (PhD); pediatric nurse practitioner (MS); women's health clinical nurse specialist (MS); women's health nurse practitioner (MS). *Accreditation:* AACN. *Program availability:* Part-time, 100% online, blended/hybrid learning. *Faculty:* 48 full-time (47 women), 44 part-time/adjunct (37 women). *Students:* 23 full-time (22 women), 816 part-time (750 women); includes 475 minority (188 Black or African American, non-Hispanic/Latino; 4 American Indian or Alaska Native, non-Hispanic/Latino; 171 Asian, non-Hispanic/Latino; 83 Hispanic/Latino; 3 Native Hawaiian or other Pacific Islander, non-Hispanic/Latino; 26 Two or more races, non-Hispanic/Latino), 12 international. Average age 37. 201 applicants, 88% accepted, 123 enrolled. In 2017, 232 master's, 17 doctorates awarded. *Degree requirements:* For master's, comprehensive exam, thesis or alternative, 6-year time limit for completion of degree, professional or clinical project; for doctorate, comprehensive exam, thesis/dissertation, 10-year time limit for completion of degree. *Entrance requirements:* For master's, GRE or MAT, minimum GPA of 3.0 on last 60 hours in undergraduate nursing degree and overall, RN license, BS in nursing, basic statistics course, 1 year of clinical experience; for doctorate, GRE (preferred minimum score 153 [500 old version] Verbal, 144 [500 old version] Quantitative, 4 Analytical), MS in nursing, minimum preferred GPA of 3.5, RN license, statistics course, 2 letters of reference, curriculum vitae, graduate nursing-theory course, graduate research course, statement of professional goals and research interests. Additional exam requirements/recommendations for international students: Required—TOEFL (minimum score 550 paper-based; 79 iBT); Recommended—IELTS (minimum score 6.5), TSE (minimum score 53). *Application deadline:* For fall admission, 5/1 for domestic students, 3/1 priority date for international students; for spring admission, 9/15 for domestic students, 7/1 priority date for international students; for summer admission, 2/1 for domestic and international students. Applications are processed on a rolling basis. Application fee: $50 ($75 for international students). Electronic applications accepted. *Expenses:* $8,510 per year full-time in-state, $17,810 per year full-time out-of-state. *Financial support:* In 2017–18, 146 students received support, including 7 teaching assistantships (averaging $28,195 per year); research assistantships, career-related internships or fieldwork, Federal Work-Study, institutionally sponsored loans, scholarships/grants, traineeships, health care benefits, and unspecified assistantships also available. Support available to part-time students. Financial award application deadline: 3/1; financial award applicants required to submit FAFSA. *Faculty research:* Women's health, nurse staffing and satisfaction in health systems, perinatal safety, chronic illness, pediatric health. *Total annual research expenditures:* $380,388. *Unit head:* Dr. Anita G. Hufft, Dean, 940-898-2401, Fax: 940-898-2437, E-mail: nursing@twu.edu. *Application contact:* Korie Hawkins, Associate Director of Admissions, Graduate Recruitment, 940-898-3188, Fax: 940-898-3081, E-mail: admissions@twu.edu.
Website: http://www.twu.edu/nursing/

Troy University, Graduate School, College of Health and Human Services, Program in Nursing, Troy, AL 36082. Offers adult health (MSN); family nurse practitioner (DNP); maternal infant (MSN); nursing informatics specialist (MSN). *Accreditation:* ACEN. *Program availability:* Part-time, evening/weekend. *Faculty:* 15 full-time (14 women), 8 part-time/adjunct (all women). *Students:* 58 full-time (52 women), 207 part-time (184 women); includes 53 minority (40 Black or African American, non-Hispanic/Latino; 1 American Indian or Alaska Native, non-Hispanic/Latino; 1 Asian, non-Hispanic/Latino; 6 Hispanic/Latino; 5 Two or more races, non-Hispanic/Latino). Average age 36. 66 applicants, 100% accepted, 49 enrolled. In 2017, 113 master's, 14 doctorates awarded. *Degree requirements:* For master's, comprehensive exam, minimum GPA of 3.0, candidacy; for doctorate, minimum GPA of 3.0, submission of approved comprehensive e-portfolio, completion of residency synthesis project, minimum of 1000 hours of clinical practice, qualifying exam. *Entrance requirements:* For master's, GRE (minimum score of 850 on old exam or 290 on new exam) or MAT (minimum score of 396), minimum GPA of 3.0, BSN, current RN licensure, 2 letters of reference, undergraduate health assessment course; for doctorate, GRE (minimum score of 850 on old exam or 294 on new exam), BSN or MSN, minimum GPA of 3.0, 2 letters of reference, current RN licensure, essay. Additional exam requirements/recommendations for international students: Required—TOEFL (minimum score 523 paper-based; 70 iBT), IELTS (minimum score 6). *Application deadline:* Applications are processed on a rolling basis. Application fee: $50. Electronic applications accepted. *Expenses:* Tuition, state resident: part-time $417 per credit hour. Tuition, nonresident: part-time $834 per credit hour. *Required fees:* $42 per credit hour. $50 per semester. Tuition and fees vary according to campus/location. *Financial support:* Fellowships, career-related internships or fieldwork, and scholarships/grants available. Support available to part-time students. Financial award applicants required to submit FAFSA. *Unit head:* Dr. Denise Green, Director, School of Nursing, 334-670-5864, Fax: 334-670-3745, E-mail: dmgreen@troy.edu. *Application contact:* Crystal G. Bishop, Director of Graduate Admissions, School of Nursing, 334-241-8631, E-mail: cdgodwin@troy.edu.

Universidad del Turabo, Graduate Programs, School of Health Sciences, Programs in Nursing, Program in Family Nurse Practitioner - Adult Nursing, Gurabo, PR 00778-3030. Offers MSN, Certificate. *Entrance requirements:* For master's, GRE, EXADEP or GMAT, interview, essay, official transcript, recommendation letters. Electronic applications accepted.

University at Buffalo, the State University of New York, Graduate School, School of Nursing, Buffalo, NY 14260. Offers adult gerontology nurse practitioner (DNP); family nurse practitioner (DNP); health care systems and leadership (MS); nurse anesthetist (DNP); nursing (PhD); nursing education (Certificate); psychiatric/mental health nurse practitioner (DNP). *Accreditation:* AACN; AANA/CANAEP (one or more programs are accredited). *Program availability:* Part-time, 100% online. *Faculty:* 41 full-time (36 women), 15 part-time/adjunct (all women). *Students:* 64 full-time (39 women), 136 part-time (120 women); includes 32 minority (13 Black or African American, non-Hispanic/Latino; 1 American Indian or Alaska Native, non-Hispanic/Latino; 18 Asian, non-Hispanic/Latino). Average age 34. 182 applicants, 39% accepted, 50 enrolled. In 2017, 3 master's, 32 doctorates, 2 other advanced degrees awarded. *Degree requirements:* For master's, thesis optional; for doctorate, comprehensive exam (for some programs), capstone (for DNP), dissertation (for PhD). *Entrance requirements:* For master's, GRE or MAT; for doctorate, GRE or MAT, minimum GPA of 3.0 (for DNP), 3.25 (for PhD); RN license; BS or MS in nursing; 3 references; writing sample; resume; personal statement; for Certificate, interview, minimum GPA of 3.0 or GRE General Test, RN license, MS in nursing, professional certification. Additional exam requirements/recommendations for international students: Required—TOEFL (minimum score 550 paper-based; 79 iBT), IELTS (minimum score 6.5). *Application deadline:* For fall admission, 4/1 for domestic students, 2/1 for international students; for spring admission, 1/15 for domestic students, 10/1 for international students; for summer admission, 4/1 for domestic students. Applications are processed on a rolling basis. Application fee: $75. Electronic applications accepted. *Expenses:* Contact institution. *Financial support:* In 2017–18, 80 students received support, including 2 fellowships with tuition reimbursements available (averaging $17,000 per year), 4 research assistantships with tuition reimbursements available (averaging $10,600 per year), 7 teaching assistantships with tuition reimbursements available (averaging $10,600 per year); scholarships/grants, traineeships, health care benefits, and unspecified assistantships also available. Financial award application deadline: 4/1; financial award applicants required to submit

FAFSA. *Faculty research:* Oncology, palliative care, gerontology, addictions, mental health, community wellness, sleep, workforce, care of underserved populations, quality and safety, person-centered care, adolescent health. *Total annual research expenditures:* $1.4 million. *Unit head:* Dr. Marsha L. Lewis, Dean and Professor, 716-829-2533, Fax: 716-829-2566, E-mail: ubnursingdean@buffalo.edu. *Application contact:* Jennifer H. Schreier, Director of Graduate Student Services, 716-829-3311, Fax: 716-829-2067, E-mail: jhv2@buffalo.edu.
Website: http://nursing.buffalo.edu/

The University of Alabama at Birmingham, School of Nursing, Birmingham, AL 35294-1210. Offers clinical nurse leader (MSN); nurse anesthesia (DNP); nurse practitioner (MSN, DNP), including adult-gerontology acute care (MSN), adult-gerontology primary care (MSN), family (MSN), pediatric (MSN), psychiatric/mental health (MSN), women's health (MSN); nursing (MSN, DNP, PhD); nursing health systems administration (MSN); nursing informatics (MSN). *Accreditation:* AACN; AANA/CANAEP. *Program availability:* Part-time, online only, blended/hybrid learning. Terminal master's awarded for partial completion of doctoral program. *Degree requirements:* For master's, comprehensive exam; for doctorate, comprehensive exam, thesis/dissertation, research mentorship experience (for PhD); scholarly project (for DNP). *Entrance requirements:* For master's, GRE, GMAT, or MAT, minimum cumulative undergraduate GPA of 3.0 or on last 60 semesters hours; letters of recommendation; for doctorate, GRE General Test, computer literacy, course work in statistics, interview, minimum GPA of 3.0, MS in nursing, references, writing sample. Additional exam requirements/recommendations for international students: Required—TOEFL (minimum score 500 paper-based, 80 iBT) or IELTS (5.5). Electronic applications accepted. *Expenses:* Contact institution. *Faculty research:* Palliative care; oncology; aging; HIV/AIDS; nursing work environments.

University of Central Arkansas, Graduate School, College of Health and Behavioral Sciences, Department of Nursing, Conway, AR 72035-0001. Offers adult nurse practitioner (PMC); clinical nurse leader (PMC); clinical nurse specialist (MSN); family nurse practitioner (PMC); nurse educator (PMC); nurse practitioner (MSN). *Accreditation:* AACN. *Program availability:* Part-time, evening/weekend, online learning. *Degree requirements:* For master's, comprehensive exam, thesis optional, clinicals. *Entrance requirements:* For master's, GRE General Test, minimum GPA of 2.7. Additional exam requirements/recommendations for international students: Required—TOEFL (minimum score 550 paper-based; 80 iBT). *Application deadline:* For fall admission, 3/1 priority date for domestic students; for spring admission, 10/1 for domestic students. Applications are processed on a rolling basis. Application fee: $25 ($50 for international students). Electronic applications accepted. *Expenses:* Contact institution. *Financial support:* Federal Work-Study, traineeships, and unspecified assistantships available. Financial award application deadline: 2/15; financial award applicants required to submit FAFSA.
Website: http://www.uca.edu/divisions/academic/chas/nurse2ab.asp

University of Cincinnati, Graduate School, College of Nursing, Cincinnati, OH 45221-0038. Offers nurse midwifery (MSN); nurse practitioner (MSN, DNP), including acute care pediatrics (DNP), adult-gerontology acute care, adult-gerontology primary care, anesthesia (DNP), family (MSN), leadership (DNP), neonatal (MSN), women's health (MSN); nursing (MSN, PhD), including occupational health (MSN). *Accreditation:* AACN; AANA/CANAEP (one or more programs are accredited); ACNM/ACME. *Program availability:* Part-time, 100% online, blended/hybrid learning. *Faculty:* 74 full-time (69 women), 112 part-time/adjunct (105 women). *Students:* 323 full-time (261 women), 1,084 part-time (949 women); includes 311 minority (113 Black or African American, non-Hispanic/Latino; 4 American Indian or Alaska Native, non-Hispanic/Latino; 56 Asian, non-Hispanic/Latino; 108 Hispanic/Latino; 1 Native Hawaiian or other Pacific Islander, non-Hispanic/Latino; 29 Two or more races, non-Hispanic/Latino), 12 international. Average age 34. 582 applicants, 64% accepted, 314 enrolled. In 2017, 579 master's, 18 doctorates awarded. *Degree requirements:* For master's, thesis or alternative; for doctorate, comprehensive exam (for some programs), thesis/dissertation (for some programs). *Entrance requirements:* For doctorate, GRE General Test. Additional exam requirements/recommendations for international students: Required—TOEFL (minimum score 600 paper-based; 100 iBT); Recommended—IELTS (minimum score 7). *Application deadline:* For fall admission, 5/1 priority date for domestic students, 5/1 for international students; for spring admission, 10/1 for domestic students; for summer admission, 3/1 priority date for domestic students. Applications are processed on a rolling basis. Application fee: $130 ($70 for international students). Electronic applications accepted. *Expenses:* $14,668 annual full-time in-state tuition, $707 annual fees. *Financial support:* In 2017–18, 123 students received support, including 8 fellowships with full tuition reimbursements available (averaging $30,423 per year), 7 research assistantships with full tuition reimbursements available (averaging $17,971 per year), 5 teaching assistantships with full tuition reimbursements available (averaging $17,971 per year); Federal Work-Study, institutionally sponsored loans, scholarships/grants, traineeships, health care benefits, tuition waivers (partial), and unspecified assistantships also available. Support available to part-time students. Financial award application deadline: 5/1; financial award applicants required to submit FAFSA. *Faculty research:* Vulnerable populations, education, violence, chronicity/aging, cancer. *Total annual research expenditures:* $575,576. *Unit head:* Dr. Greer Glazer, Dean, 513-558-5330, Fax: 513-558-9030, E-mail: greer.glazer@uc.edu. *Application contact:* Office of Student Recruitment, 513-558-8400, Fax: 513-558-5012, E-mail: nursingbearcats@uc.edu.
Website: https://nursing.uc.edu/

University of Colorado Colorado Springs, Helen and Arthur E. Johnson Beth-El College of Nursing and Health Sciences, Colorado Springs, CO 80918. Offers nursing practice (DNP); primary care nurse practitioner (MSN). *Accreditation:* AACN. *Program availability:* Part-time, 100% online, blended/hybrid learning. *Faculty:* 11 full-time (10 women), 13 part-time/adjunct (12 women). *Students:* 7 full-time (6 women), 213 part-time (192 women); includes 50 minority (8 Black or African American, non-Hispanic/Latino; 1 American Indian or Alaska Native, non-Hispanic/Latino; 11 Asian, non-Hispanic/Latino; 23 Hispanic/Latino; 1 Native Hawaiian or other Pacific Islander, non-Hispanic/Latino; 6 Two or more races, non-Hispanic/Latino). Average age 37. 125 applicants, 66% accepted, 57 enrolled. In 2017, 47 master's, 10 doctorates awarded. *Degree requirements:* For master's, comprehensive exam, thesis optional; for doctorate, capstone project. *Entrance requirements:* For master's, GRE General Test or MAT, minimum overall GPA of 2.75 for all undergraduate course work, minimum BSN GPA of 3.3; for doctorate, interview; active RN license; MA; minimum GPA of 3.3; National Certification as nurse practitioner or clinical nurse specialist; portfolio. Additional exam requirements/recommendations for international students: Required—TOEFL (minimum score 550 paper-based; 80 iBT). *Application deadline:* For fall admission, 3/15 priority date for domestic students, 3/15 for international students; for spring admission, 8/15 for domestic and international students. Applications are processed on a rolling basis. Application fee: $60 ($100 for international students). Electronic applications accepted. *Expenses:* $12,241 per year resident tuition, $21,511 nonresident, $13,869 nonresidential online; annual costs vary depending on program, course-load, and residency status. *Financial support:* In 2017–18, 28 students received support. Research assistantships, career-related internships or fieldwork, Federal Work-Study, and scholarships/grants available. Support available to part-time students. Financial award application deadline: 3/1; financial award applicants required to submit FAFSA. *Faculty research:* Behavioral interventions to reduce stroke risk factors in older adults, interprofessional models of health promotion for older adults, nurse practitioner education, practice and policy, cardiology, cardiac and pulmonary rehab, heart failure and stroke, community health prevention, veterans studies, anger management, sports medicine, sports nutrition. *Total annual research expenditures:* $580,217. *Unit head:* Dr. Deborah Pollard, Nursing Department Chair, 719-255-3577, Fax: 719-255-4416, E-mail: dpollard@uccs.edu. *Application contact:* Diane Busch, Program Assistant II, 719-255-4424, Fax: 719-255-4416, E-mail: dbusch@uccs.edu.
Website: http://www.uccs.edu/bethel/index.html

University of Colorado Denver, College of Nursing, Aurora, CO 80045. Offers adult clinical nurse specialist (MS); adult nurse practitioner (MS); family nurse practitioner (MS); family psychiatric mental health nurse practitioner (MS); health care informatics (MS); nurse-midwifery (MS); nursing (DNP, PhD); nursing leadership and health care systems (MS); pediatric nurse practitioner (MS); women's health (MS); MS/PhD. *Accreditation:* ACNM/ACME (one or more programs are accredited). *Program availability:* Part-time, evening/weekend, online learning. *Students:* 297 applicants, 55% accepted, 141 enrolled. In 2017, 138 master's, 18 doctorates awarded. Terminal master's awarded for partial completion of doctoral program. *Degree requirements:* For master's, thesis optional; for doctorate, comprehensive exam, thesis/dissertation, 42 credits of coursework. *Entrance requirements:* For master's, GRE if cumulative undergraduate GPA is less than 3.0, undergraduate nursing degree from ACEN- or CCNE-accredited school or university; completion of research and statistics courses with minimum grade of C; copy of current and unencumbered nursing license; for doctorate, GRE, bachelor's and/or master's degrees in nursing from ACEN- or CCNE-accredited institution; portfolio; minimum undergraduate GPA of 3.0, graduate 3.5; graduate-level intermediate statistics and master's-level nursing theory courses with minimum B grade; interview. Additional exam requirements/recommendations for international students: Required—TOEFL (minimum score 560 paper-based; 83 iBT). *Application deadline:* For fall admission, 2/15 for domestic students, 1/15 for international students; for spring admission, 7/1 for domestic students, 6/1 for international students. Application fee: $50 ($75 for international students). Electronic applications accepted. *Unit head:* Dr. Sarah Thompson, Dean, 303-724-1679, E-mail: sarah.a.thompson@ucdenver.edu. *Application contact:* Judy Campbell, Graduate Programs Coordinator, 303-724-8503, E-mail: judy.campbell@ucdenver.edu.
Website: http://www.ucdenver.edu/academics/colleges/nursing/Pages/default.aspx

University of Delaware, College of Health Sciences, School of Nursing, Newark, DE 19716. Offers adult nurse practitioner (MSN, PMC); cardiopulmonary clinical nurse specialist (MSN, PMC); cardiopulmonary clinical nurse specialist/adult nurse practitioner (MSN, PMC); family nurse practitioner (MSN, PMC); gerontology clinical nurse specialist (MSN, PMC); gerontology clinical nurse specialist geriatric nurse practitioner (PMC); gerontology clinical nurse specialist/geriatric nurse practitioner (MSN); health services administration (MSN, PMC); nursing of children clinical nurse specialist (MSN, PMC); nursing of children clinical nurse specialist/pediatric nurse practitioner (MSN, PMC); oncology/immune deficiency clinical nurse specialist (MSN, PMC); oncology/immune deficiency clinical nurse specialist/adult nurse practitioner (MSN, PMC); perinatal/women's health clinical nurse specialist (MSN, PMC); perinatal/women's health clinical nurse specialist/women's health nurse practitioner (MSN, PMC); psychiatric nursing clinical nurse specialist (MSN, PMC). *Accreditation:* AACN. *Program availability:* Part-time, evening/weekend, online learning. *Degree requirements:* For master's, thesis optional. *Entrance requirements:* For master's, BSN, interview, RN license. Electronic applications accepted. *Faculty research:* Marriage and chronic illness, health promotion, congestive heart failure patient outcomes, school nursing, diabetes in children, culture, health disparities, cardiovascular, prison nursing, oncology, public policy, child obesity, smoking and teen pregnancy, blood pressure measurements, men's health.

University of Hawaii at Manoa, Office of Graduate Education, School of Nursing and Dental Hygiene, Honolulu, HI 96822. Offers clinical nurse specialist (MS), including adult health, community mental health; nurse practitioner (MS), including adult health, community mental health, family nurse practitioner; nursing (PhD, Graduate Certificate); nursing administration (MS). *Accreditation:* AACN. *Program availability:* Part-time, online learning. *Degree requirements:* For master's, thesis optional; for doctorate, comprehensive exam, thesis/dissertation. *Entrance requirements:* For master's, Hawaii RN license. Additional exam requirements/recommendations for international students: Required—TOEFL (minimum score 580 paper-based; 92 iBT), IELTS (minimum score 5). *Expenses:* Contact institution.

University of Illinois at Chicago, College of Nursing, Program in Nursing, Chicago, IL 60607-7128. Offers acute care clinical nurse specialist (MS); administrative nursing leadership (Certificate); adult nurse practitioner (MS); adult/geriatric nurse practitioner (MS); advanced community health nurse specialist (MS); family nurse practitioner (MS); geriatric clinical nurse specialist (MS); geriatric nurse practitioner (MS); nurse midwifery (MS); occupational health/advanced community health nurse specialist (MS); occupational health/family nurse practitioner (MS); pediatric nurse practitioner (MS); perinatal clinical nurse specialist (MS); school/advanced community health nurse specialist (MS); school/family nurse practitioner (MS); women's health nurse practitioner (MS). *Accreditation:* AACN. *Program availability:* Part-time. *Degree requirements:* For master's, thesis or alternative. *Entrance requirements:* For master's, GRE General Test, minimum GPA of 2.75. Additional exam requirements/recommendations for international students: Required—TOEFL. Electronic applications accepted.

The University of Kansas, University of Kansas Medical Center, School of Nursing, Kansas City, KS 66160. Offers adult/gerontological clinical nurse specialist (PMC); adult/gerontological nurse practitioner (PMC); health care informatics (PMC); health professions educator (PMC); nurse midwife (PMC); nursing (MS, DNP, PhD); organizational leadership (PMC); psychiatric/mental health nurse practitioner (PMC); public health nursing (PMC). *Accreditation:* AACN; ACNM/ACME. *Program availability:* Part-time, 100% online, blended/hybrid learning. *Faculty:* 56. *Students:* 48 full-time (44 women), 260 part-time (235 women); includes 50 minority (12 Black or African American, non-Hispanic/Latino; 2 American Indian or Alaska Native, non-Hispanic/Latino; 16 Asian, non-Hispanic/Latino; 8 Hispanic/Latino; 12 Two or more races, non-Hispanic/Latino). Average age 36. 87 applicants, 95% accepted, 61 enrolled. In 2017, 37 master's, 18 doctorates, 3 other advanced degrees awarded. Terminal master's awarded for partial completion of doctoral program. *Degree requirements:* For master's, comprehensive exam, thesis (for some programs), general oral exam; for doctorate, thesis/dissertation or alternative, comprehensive oral exam (for DNP); comprehensive written and oral exam, or three publications (for PhD). *Entrance requirements:* For master's, bachelor's degree in nursing, minimum GPA of 3.0, 1 year of clinical experience, RN license in KS and MO; for doctorate, GRE General Test (for PhD only), bachelor's degree in nursing, minimum GPA of 3.5, RN license in KS and MO. Additional exam requirements/recommendations for international students: Required—TOEFL. *Application deadline:* For fall admission, 4/1 for domestic and international students; for spring admission, 9/1 for domestic and international students. Application fee: $75. Electronic applications accepted. *Financial support:* In 2017–18, 5 research assistantships with tuition reimbursements (averaging $20,000 per year), 30 teaching assistantships with tuition reimbursements (averaging $20,000 per year) were awarded;

scholarships/grants and traineeships also available. Financial award application deadline: 3/1; financial award applicants required to submit FAFSA. *Faculty research:* Breastfeeding practices of teen mothers, national database of nursing quality indicators, caregiving of families of patients using technology in the home, simulation in nursing education, diaphragm fatigue. *Total annual research expenditures:* $1.4 million. *Unit head:* Dr. Sally Maliski, Dean, 913-588-1601, Fax: 913-588-1660, E-mail: smaliski@kumc.edu. *Application contact:* Dr. Pamela K. Barnes, Associate Dean, Student Affairs, 913-588-1619, Fax: 913-588-1615, E-mail: pbarnes2@kumc.edu.
Website: http://nursing.kumc.edu

University of Massachusetts Amherst, Graduate School, College of Nursing, Amherst, MA 01003. Offers adult gerontology primary care nurse practitioner (DNP); clinical nurse leader (MS); family nurse practitioner (DNP); nursing (PhD); public health nurse leader (DNP). *Accreditation:* AACN. *Program availability:* Part-time, online learning. Terminal master's awarded for partial completion of doctoral program. *Degree requirements:* For master's, thesis optional; for doctorate, comprehensive exam, thesis/dissertation. *Entrance requirements:* Additional exam requirements/recommendations for international students: Required—TOEFL (minimum score 550 paper-based; 80 iBT), IELTS (minimum score 6.5). Electronic applications accepted. *Faculty research:* Health of older adults and their caretakers, mental health of individuals and families, health of children and adolescents, power and decision-making, transcultural health.

University of Massachusetts Medical School, Graduate School of Nursing, Worcester, MA 01655-0115. Offers adult gerontological acute care nurse practitioner (DNP, Post Master's Certificate); adult gerontological primary care nurse practitioner (DNP, Post Master's Certificate); family nursing practitioner (DNP); nurse administrator (DNP); nurse educator (MS, Post Master's Certificate); nursing (PhD). *Accreditation:* AACN. *Faculty:* 31 full-time (28 women), 39 part-time/adjunct (34 women). *Students:* 129 full-time (111 women), 31 part-time (30 women); includes 35 minority (17 Black or African American, non-Hispanic/Latino; 10 Asian, non-Hispanic/Latino; 7 Hispanic/Latino; 1 Native Hawaiian or other Pacific Islander, non-Hispanic/Latino), 1 international. Average age 32. 124 applicants, 55% accepted, 59 enrolled. In 2017, 48 master's, 10 doctorates, 2 other advanced degrees awarded. *Degree requirements:* For doctorate, thesis/dissertation (for some programs), comprehensive exam and manuscript (for PhD); capstone project and manuscript (for DNP). *Entrance requirements:* For master's, GRE General Test, bachelor's degree in nursing, course work in statistics, unrestricted Massachusetts license as registered nurse; for doctorate, GRE General Test, bachelor's or master's degree; for Post Master's Certificate, GRE General Test, MS in nursing. Additional exam requirements/recommendations for international students: Required—TOEFL (minimum score 400 paper-based; 81 iBT). *Application deadline:* For fall admission, 12/1 priority date for domestic students. Applications are processed on a rolling basis. Application fee: $60. Electronic applications accepted. *Expenses:* $14,778 in-state tuition and mandatory fees; $19,728 out-of-state. *Financial support:* In 2017–18, 6 students received support. Scholarships/grants available. Support available to part-time students. Financial award application deadline: 5/15; financial award applicants required to submit FAFSA. *Faculty research:* Health literacy, social justice, HIV prevention, cancer-related decision making, nursing education, diabetes care and education, family-focused interventions for children with type 1 diabetes. *Total annual research expenditures:* $874,000. *Unit head:* Dr. Joan Vitello-Cicciu, Dean, 508-856-5081, Fax: 508-856-6552, E-mail: joan.vitello@umassmed.edu. *Application contact:* Diane Brescia, Admissions Coordinator, 508-856-3488, Fax: 508-856-5851, E-mail: diane.brescia@umassmed.edu.
Website: http://www.umassmed.edu/gsn/

University of Miami, Graduate School, School of Nursing and Health Studies, Coral Gables, FL 33124. Offers acute care (MSN), including acute care nurse practitioner, nurse anesthesia; nursing (PhD); primary care (MSN), including adult nurse practitioner, family nurse practitioner, nurse midwifery, women's health practitioner. *Accreditation:* AACN; AANA/CANAEP; ACNM/ACME (one or more programs are accredited). *Program availability:* Part-time. *Degree requirements:* For master's, thesis optional; for doctorate, thesis/dissertation. *Entrance requirements:* For master's, GRE General Test, BSN, minimum GPA of 3.0, Florida RN license; for doctorate, GRE General Test, BSN or MSN, minimum GPA of 3.0. Additional exam requirements/recommendations for international students: Required—TOEFL (minimum score 550 paper-based). Electronic applications accepted. *Faculty research:* Transcultural nursing, exercise and depression in Alzheimer's disease, infectious diseases/HIV–AIDS, postpartum depression, outcomes assessment.

University of Missouri, Office of Research and Graduate Studies, Sinclair School of Nursing, Columbia, MO 65211. Offers adult-gerontology clinical nurse specialist (DNP, Certificate); family nurse practitioner (DNP); family psychiatric and mental health nurse practitioner (DNP); nursing (MS, PhD); nursing leadership and innovations in health care (DNP); pediatric clinical nurse specialist (DNP, Certificate); pediatric nurse practitioner (DNP). *Accreditation:* AACN. *Program availability:* Part-time. *Degree requirements:* For master's, thesis optional, oral exam; for doctorate, thesis/dissertation. *Entrance requirements:* For master's, GRE General Test, BSN, minimum GPA of 3.0 during last 60 hours, nursing license. Additional exam requirements/recommendations for international students: Required—TOEFL, IELTS. *Application deadline:* Applications are processed on a rolling basis. Electronic applications accepted. *Expenses:* Tuition, state resident: full-time $6480. Tuition, nonresident: full-time $17,744. *Required fees:* $1108. Tuition and fees vary according to course load, campus/location and program. *Financial support:* Fellowships, research assistantships, teaching assistantships, career-related internships or fieldwork, institutionally sponsored loans, scholarships/grants, traineeships, health care benefits, tuition waivers (full), and unspecified assistantships available. Support available to part-time students.
Website: http://nursing.missouri.edu/

University of Missouri–Kansas City, School of Nursing and Health Studies, Kansas City, MO 64110-2499. Offers adult clinical nurse specialist (MSN), including adult nurse practitioner, women's health nurse practitioner (MSN, DNP); adult clinical nursing practice (DNP), including adult gerontology nurse practitioner, women's health nurse practitioner (MSN, DNP); clinical nursing practice (DNP), including family nurse practitioner; neonatal nurse practitioner (MSN); nurse educator (MSN); nurse executive (MSN); nursing practice (DNP); pediatric clinical nursing practice (DNP), including pediatric nurse practitioner; pediatric nurse practitioner (MSN). *Accreditation:* AACN. *Program availability:* Part-time, online learning. *Degree requirements:* For master's, thesis or alternative. *Entrance requirements:* For master's, minimum undergraduate GPA of 3.2; for doctorate, GRE, 3 letters of reference. Additional exam requirements/recommendations for international students: Required—TOEFL (minimum score 550 paper-based; 80 iBT). *Faculty research:* Geriatrics/gerontology, children's pain, neonatology, Alzheimer's care, cancer caregivers.

University of Missouri–St. Louis, College of Nursing, St. Louis, MO 63121. Offers adult/geriatric nurse practitioner (Post Master's Certificate); family nurse practitioner (Post Master's Certificate); nursing (DNP, PhD); pediatric acute care nurse practitioner (Post Master's Certificate); pediatric nurse practitioner (Post Master's Certificate); psychiatric-mental health nurse practitioner (Post Master's Certificate); women's health nurse practitioner (Post Master's Certificate). *Accreditation:* AACN. *Program availability:* Part-time. *Faculty:* 24 full-time (22 women), 12 part-time/adjunct (11 women). *Students:* 47 full-time (44 women), 162 part-time (152 women); includes 53 minority (37 Black or African American, non-Hispanic/Latino; 10 Asian, non-Hispanic/Latino; 4 Hispanic/Latino; 2 Two or more races, non-Hispanic/Latino), 3 international. 112 applicants, 93% accepted, 70 enrolled. *Degree requirements:* For doctorate, comprehensive exam, thesis/dissertation; for Post Master's Certificate, thesis. *Entrance requirements:* For doctorate, GRE, 2 letters of recommendation, MSN, minimum GPA of 3.2, course in differential/inferential statistics; for Post Master's Certificate, 2 recommendation letters; MSN; advanced practice certificate; minimum GPA of 3.0; essay. Additional exam requirements/recommendations for international students: Recommended—TOEFL (minimum score 550 paper-based; 79 iBT), IELTS (minimum score 6.5). *Application deadline:* For fall admission, 2/15 for domestic and international students. Application fee: $50 ($40 for international students). Electronic applications accepted. *Expenses:* Tuition, state resident: part-time $476.50 per credit hour. Tuition, nonresident: part-time $1169.70 per credit hour. *Financial support:* Research assistantships with tuition reimbursements available. Financial award application deadline: 4/1; financial award applicants required to submit FAFSA. *Faculty research:* Health promotion and restoration, family disruption, violence, abuse, battered women, health survey methods. *Unit head:* Sue Dean-Baar, Dean, 314-516-6066. *Application contact:* 314-516-5458, Fax: 314-516-6996, E-mail: gradadm@umsl.edu.
Website: http://www.umsl.edu/divisions/nursing/

The University of North Carolina at Chapel Hill, School of Nursing, Chapel Hill, NC 27599-7460. Offers advanced practice registered nurse (DNP); nursing (MSN, PhD, PMC), including administration (MSN), adult gerontology primary care nurse practitioner (MSN), clinical nurse leader (MSN), education (MSN), health care systems (PMC), informatics (MSN, PMC), nursing leadership (PMC), outcomes management (MSN), primary care family nurse practitioner (MSN), primary care pediatric nurse practitioner (MSN), psychiatric/mental health nurse practitioner (MSN, PMC). *Accreditation:* AACN; ACEN (one or more programs are accredited). *Program availability:* Part-time. *Faculty:* 86 full-time (78 women), 44 part-time/adjunct (40 women). *Students:* 208 full-time (186 women), 128 part-time (116 women); includes 100 minority (49 Black or African American, non-Hispanic/Latino; 4 American Indian or Alaska Native, non-Hispanic/Latino; 23 Asian, non-Hispanic/Latino; 7 Hispanic/Latino; 17 Two or more races, non-Hispanic/Latino), 17 international. Average age 33. 624 applicants, 25% accepted, 150 enrolled. In 2017, 91 master's, 14 doctorates awarded. *Degree requirements:* For master's, comprehensive exam, thesis; for doctorate, thesis/dissertation, 3 exams; for PMC, thesis. *Entrance requirements:* Additional exam requirements/recommendations for international students: Required—TOEFL (minimum score 575 paper-based; 89 iBT), IELTS (minimum score 8). *Application deadline:* For fall admission, 12/15 for domestic and international students. Application fee: $88. Electronic applications accepted. *Financial support:* In 2017–18, 8 fellowships with full tuition reimbursements, 6 research assistantships with partial tuition reimbursements (averaging $8,000 per year), 10 teaching assistantships with partial tuition reimbursements (averaging $8,000 per year) were awarded; scholarships/grants, traineeships, health care benefits, and unspecified assistantships also available. Support available to part-time students. Financial award application deadline: 3/1; financial award applicants required to submit FAFSA. *Faculty research:* Preventing and managing chronic illness, reducing health disparities, Improving healthcare quality and patient outcomes, understanding biobehavioral and genetic bases of health and illness, developing innovative ways to enhance science and its clinical translation. *Unit head:* Dr. Nilda Peragallo Montano, Dean/Professor, 919-966-3731, Fax: 919-966-3540, E-mail: npm@email.unc.edu. *Application contact:* Emily Sayed, Assistant Director, Graduate Admissions, 919-966-4260, Fax: 919-966-3540, E-mail: sayed@unc.edu.
Website: http://nursing.unc.edu

The University of North Carolina at Greensboro, Graduate School, School of Nursing, Greensboro, NC 27412-5001. Offers adult clinical nurse specialist (MSN, PMC); adult/gerontological nurse practitioner (MSN, PMC); nurse anesthesia (MSN, PMC); nursing (PhD); nursing administration (MSN); nursing education (MSN); MSN/MBA. *Accreditation:* ACEN. *Degree requirements:* For master's, thesis or alternative. *Entrance requirements:* For master's, GRE General Test or MAT, BSN, clinical experience, liability insurance, RN license; for PMC, liability insurance, MSN, RN license. Additional exam requirements/recommendations for international students: Required—TOEFL. Electronic applications accepted.

University of Pennsylvania, School of Nursing, Adult-Gerontology Acute Care Nurse Practitioner Program, Philadelphia, PA 19104. Offers MSN. *Accreditation:* AACN. *Program availability:* Part-time, online learning. *Students:* 19 full-time (17 women), 174 part-time (155 women); includes 46 minority (11 Black or African American, non-Hispanic/Latino; 27 Asian, non-Hispanic/Latino; 8 Hispanic/Latino), 3 international. Average age 35. 245 applicants, 74% accepted, 163 enrolled. In 2017, 116 master's awarded. *Entrance requirements:* For master's, GRE General Test. Application fee: $80. *Financial support:* Application deadline: 4/1. *Faculty research:* Post-injury disability, bereavement and attributions in fire survivors, stress in staff nurses. *Unit head:* Assistant Dean of Admissions and Financial Aid, 866-867-6877, Fax: 215-573-8439, E-mail: admissions@nursing.upenn.edu. *Application contact:* Deborah Becker, Program Director, 215-898-0432, E-mail: debecker@nursing.upenn.edu.
Website: http://www.nursing.upenn.edu/

University of Puerto Rico–Medical Sciences Campus, School of Nursing, San Juan, PR 00936-5067. Offers adult and elderly nursing (MSN); child and adolescent nursing (MSN); critical care nursing (MSN); family and community nursing (MSN); family nurse practitioner (MSN); maternity nursing (MSN); mental health and psychiatric nursing (MSN). *Accreditation:* AACN; AANA/CANAEP. *Entrance requirements:* For master's, GRE or EXADEP, interview, Puerto Rico RN license or professional license for international students, general and specific point average, article analysis. Electronic applications accepted. *Faculty research:* HIV, health disparities, teen violence, women and violence, neurological disorders.

University of Rhode Island, Graduate School, College of Nursing, Kingston, RI 02881. Offers acute care nurse practitioner (adult-gerontology focus) (Post Master's Certificate); adult gerontology nurse practitioner/clinical nurse specialist (Post Master's Certificate); adult-gerontological acute care nurse practitioner (MS); adult-gerontological nurse practitioner/clinical nurse specialist (MS); family nurse practitioner (MS, Post Master's Certificate); nursing (DNP, PhD); nursing education (MS, Post Master's Certificate). *Accreditation:* AACN; ACNM/ACME (one or more programs are accredited). *Program availability:* Part-time, evening/weekend, 100% online, blended/hybrid learning. *Faculty:* 31 full-time (30 women). *Students:* 42 full-time (36 women), 86 part-time (79 women); includes 12 minority (3 Black or African American, non-Hispanic/Latino; 3 Asian, non-Hispanic/Latino; 3 Hispanic/Latino; 1 Native Hawaiian or other Pacific Islander, non-Hispanic/Latino; 2 Two or more races, non-Hispanic/Latino), 3 international. 33 applicants, 79% accepted, 23 enrolled. In 2017, 25 master's, 8 doctorates, 2 other advanced degrees awarded. *Entrance requirements:* For master's, GRE or MAT, 2 letters of recommendation, scholarly papers; for doctorate, GRE, 3 letters of recommendation, scholarly papers. Additional exam requirements/recommendations for international students: Required—TOEFL. *Application deadline:* For fall admission, 2/15 for domestic students, 2/1 for international students; for spring admission, 10/15 for domestic students, 7/15 for international students. Application fee: $65. Electronic

applications accepted. *Expenses:* Tuition, state resident: full-time $12,706; part-time $786 per credit. Tuition, nonresident: full-time $25,216; part-time $1401 per credit. *Required fees:* $1598; $45 per credit. One-time fee: $30 part-time. *Financial support:* In 2017–18, 1 research assistantship with tuition reimbursement (averaging $18,080 per year), 5 teaching assistantships with tuition reimbursements (averaging $10,133 per year) were awarded. Financial award application deadline: 2/1; financial award applicants required to submit FAFSA. *Unit head:* Dr. Barbara Wolfe, Dean, 401-874-5324, E-mail: bwolfe@uri.edu. *Application contact:* Dr. Denise Coppa, Associate Professor/Interim Associate Dean for Graduate Programs, 401-874-5036, E-mail: dcoppa@uri.edu.
Website: http://www.uri.edu/nursing/

University of Rochester, School of Nursing, Rochester, NY 14642. Offers adult gerontological acute care nurse practitioner (MS); adult gerontological primary care nurse practitioner (MS); clinical nurse leader (MS); family nurse practitioner (MS); family psychiatric mental health nurse practitioner (MS); health care organization management and leadership (MS); nursing (DNP); nursing and health science (PhD); nursing education (MS); pediatric nurse practitioner (MS); pediatric nurse practitioner/neonatal nurse practitioner (MS). *Accreditation:* AACN. *Program availability:* Part-time, 100% online, blended/hybrid learning. *Faculty:* 62 full-time (51 women), 73 part-time/adjunct (63 women). *Students:* 17 full-time (12 women), 306 part-time (252 women); includes 46 minority (16 Black or African American, non-Hispanic/Latino; 1 American Indian or Alaska Native, non-Hispanic/Latino; 7 Asian, non-Hispanic/Latino; 17 Hispanic/Latino; 5 Two or more races, non-Hispanic/Latino), 3 international. Average age 34. 143 applicants, 71% accepted, 87 enrolled. In 2017, 48 master's, 8 doctorates awarded. Terminal master's awarded for partial completion of doctoral program. *Degree requirements:* For master's, comprehensive exam; for doctorate, thesis/dissertation. *Entrance requirements:* For master's, BS in nursing, minimum GPA of 3.0, course work in statistics; for doctorate, GRE General Test (for PhD), MS in nursing, minimum GPA of 3.5. Additional exam requirements/recommendations for international students: Required—TOEFL (minimum score 560 paper-based; 88 iBT) or IELTS (minimum score 6.5) recommended. *Application deadline:* For fall admission, 4/1 for domestic and international students; for spring admission, 9/1 for domestic and international students; for summer admission, 1/2 for domestic and international students. Application fee: $50. Electronic applications accepted. *Financial support:* In 2017–18, 63 students received support, including 2 fellowships with full and partial tuition reimbursements available (averaging $16,000 per year); scholarships/grants, traineeships, health care benefits, tuition waivers (full and partial), and unspecified assistantships also available. Support available to part-time students. Financial award application deadline: 6/30; financial award applicants required to submit CSS PROFILE or FAFSA. *Faculty research:* Symptom science, systems of care, innovations in health technology, promoting healthy behaviors. *Total annual research expenditures:* $2.6 million. *Unit head:* Dr. Kathy H. Rideout, Dean, 585-273-8902, Fax: 585-273-1268, E-mail: kathy_rideout@urmc.rochester.edu. *Application contact:* Elaine Andolina, Director of Admissions, 585-275-2375, Fax: 585-756-8299, E-mail: elaine_andolina@urmc.rochester.edu.
Website: http://www.son.rochester.edu

University of San Diego, Hahn School of Nursing and Health Science, San Diego, CA 92110-2492. Offers adult-gerontology clinical nurse specialist (MSN); adult-gerontology nurse practitioner/family nurse practitioner (MSN); clinical nurse leader (MSN); executive nurse leader (MSN); family nurse practitioner (MSN); healthcare informatics (MS, MSN); nursing (PhD); nursing practice (DNP); pediatric/family nurse practitioner (MSN); psychiatric-mental health nurse practitioner (MSN). *Accreditation:* AACN. *Program availability:* Part-time, evening/weekend. *Faculty:* 26 full-time (21 women), 36 part-time/adjunct (29 women). *Students:* 238 full-time (198 women), 230 part-time (167 women); includes 230 minority (32 Black or African American, non-Hispanic/Latino; 104 Asian, non-Hispanic/Latino; 75 Hispanic/Latino; 19 Two or more races, non-Hispanic/Latino), 12 international. Average age 35. In 2017, 93 master's, 44 doctorates awarded. *Degree requirements:* For doctorate, thesis/dissertation (for some programs), residency (DNP). *Entrance requirements:* For master's, GRE General Test (for entry-level nursing), BSN, current California RN licensure (except for entry-level nursing), minimum GPA of 3.0; for doctorate, minimum GPA of 3.5, MSN, current California RN licensure. Additional exam requirements/recommendations for international students: Required—TOEFL (minimum score 580 paper-based; 83 iBT), TWE. *Application deadline:* Applications are processed on a rolling basis. Application fee: $45. Electronic applications accepted. *Financial support:* In 2017–18, 242 students received support. Scholarships/grants and traineeships available. Support available to part-time students. Financial award application deadline: 4/1; financial award applicants required to submit FAFSA. *Faculty research:* Maternal/neonatal health, palliative and end of life care, adolescent obesity, health disparities, cognitive dysfunction. *Unit head:* Dr. Janes Georges, Interim Dean, 619-260-4550, Fax: 619-260-6814, E-mail: nursing@sandiego.edu. *Application contact:* Monica Mahon, Associate Director of Graduate Admissions, 619-260-4524, Fax: 619-260-4158, E-mail: grads@sandiego.edu.
Website: http://www.sandiego.edu/nursing/

University of South Carolina, The Graduate School, College of Nursing, Program in Health Nursing, Columbia, SC 29208. Offers adult nurse practitioner (MSN); community/public health clinical nurse specialist (MSN); family nurse practitioner (MSN); pediatric nurse practitioner (MSN). *Accreditation:* AACN. *Program availability:* Part-time. *Degree requirements:* For master's, thesis or alternative. *Entrance requirements:* For master's, GRE General Test or MAT, BS in nursing, nursing license. Additional exam requirements/recommendations for international students: Required—TOEFL (minimum score 570 paper-based). Electronic applications accepted. *Faculty research:* System research, evidence based practice, breast cancer, violence.

University of Southern Maine, College of Science, Technology, and Health, School of Nursing, Portland, ME 04103. Offers adult-gerontology primary care nurse practitioner (MS, PMC); education (MS); family nurse practitioner (MS, PMC); family psychiatric/mental health nurse practitioner (MS); management (MS); nursing (CAS, CGS); psychiatric-mental health nurse practitioner (PMC). *Accreditation:* AACN. *Program availability:* Part-time. *Degree requirements:* For master's, thesis optional. *Entrance requirements:* For master's, GRE General Test or MAT, minimum GPA of 3.0; for doctorate, GRE. Additional exam requirements/recommendations for international students: Required—TOEFL (minimum score 550 paper-based). Electronic applications accepted. *Faculty research:* Women's health, nursing history, weight control, community services, substance abuse.

University of South Florida, College of Nursing, Tampa, FL 33612. Offers nurse anesthesia (DNP); nursing (MS, DNP), including adult-gerontology acute care nursing, adult-gerontology primary care nursing, family health nursing, nurse anesthesia (MS), nursing education (MS), occupational health nursing/adult-gerontology primary care nursing, oncology nursing/adult-gerontology primary care nursing (DNP), pediatric health nursing; nursing education (Post Master's Certificate); nursing science (PhD); simulation based academic fellowship in advanced pain management (Graduate Certificate). *Accreditation:* AACN; AANA/CANAEP. *Program availability:* Part-time. *Faculty:* 37 full-time (32 women), 2 part-time/adjunct (1 woman). *Students:* 224 full-time (178 women), 669 part-time (577 women); includes 309 minority (105 Black or African American, non-Hispanic/Latino; 2 American Indian or Alaska Native, non-Hispanic/Latino; 53 Asian, non-Hispanic/Latino; 122 Hispanic/Latino; 1 Native Hawaiian or other Pacific Islander, non-Hispanic/Latino; 26 Two or more races, non-Hispanic/Latino), 6 international. Average age 32. 949 applicants, 47% accepted, 382 enrolled. In 2017, 264 master's, 39 doctorates awarded. *Degree requirements:* For master's, comprehensive exam, thesis optional; for doctorate, comprehensive exam, thesis/dissertation. *Entrance requirements:* For master's, GRE General Test, bachelor's degree from accredited program with minimum GPA of 3.0 in all upper-division coursework; current license as Registered Nurse; 3 letters of recommendation; personal statement of goals; resume or curriculum vitae; personal interview; for doctorate, GRE General Test (recommended), bachelor's degree in nursing from ACEN or CCNE regionally-accredited institution with minimum GPA of 3.0 in all coursework or in all upper-division coursework; current license as Registered Nurse in Florida; undergraduate statistics course with minimum B grade; 3 letters of recommendation; statement of goals; resume; interview. Additional exam requirements/recommendations for international students: Required—TOEFL (minimum score 550 paper-based; 79 iBT). *Application deadline:* For fall admission, 12/15 for domestic and international students; for spring admission, 10/1 for domestic students, 9/15 for international students. Application fee: $30. Electronic applications accepted. *Financial support:* In 2017–18, 132 students received support, including 7 research assistantships with tuition reimbursements available (averaging $18,935 per year), 29 teaching assistantships with tuition reimbursements available (averaging $30,814 per year); tuition waivers (partial) and unspecified assistantships also available. Financial award application deadline: 2/1; financial award applicants required to submit FAFSA. *Faculty research:* Women's health, palliative and end-of-life care, cardiac rehabilitation, complementary therapies for chronic illness and cancer. *Total annual research expenditures:* $3.2 million. *Unit head:* Dr. Victoria Rich, Dean, College of Nursing, 813-974-8939, Fax: 813-974-5418, E-mail: victoriarich@health.usf.edu. *Application contact:* Dr. Brian Graves, Assistant Professor/Assistant Dean, 813-974-8054, Fax: 813-974-5418, E-mail: bgraves1@health.usf.edu.
Website: http://health.usf.edu/nursing/index.htm

The University of Tampa, Program in Nursing, Tampa, FL 33606-1490. Offers adult nursing practitioner (MSN); family nursing practitioner (MSN); nursing (MS). *Accreditation:* ACEN. *Program availability:* Part-time, evening/weekend. *Faculty:* 7 full-time (6 women), 6 part-time/adjunct (all women). *Students:* 4 full-time (all women), 166 part-time (148 women); includes 29 minority (15 Black or African American, non-Hispanic/Latino; 8 Asian, non-Hispanic/Latino; 6 Two or more races, non-Hispanic/Latino), 2 international. Average age 33. 132 applicants, 64% accepted, 51 enrolled. In 2017, 45 master's awarded. *Degree requirements:* For master's, comprehensive exam, oral exam, practicum. *Entrance requirements:* For master's, GMAT or GRE, current licensure as registered nurse in state of Florida; minimum GPA of 3.0 in last 60 credit hours; minimum of one year of direct patient care experience within the past five years (recommended). Additional exam requirements/recommendations for international students: Required—TOEFL (minimum score 577 paper-based; 90 iBT), IELTS (minimum score 7.5). *Application deadline:* Applications are processed on a rolling basis. Application fee: $40. Electronic applications accepted. *Expenses:* Contact institution. *Financial support:* In 2017–18, 9 students received support. Career-related internships or fieldwork, scholarships/grants, and unspecified assistantships available. Financial award applicants required to submit FAFSA. *Faculty research:* Vaccinations and public health, osteoporosis, cultural diversity, ethics, nursing practice. *Unit head:* Michele Wolf, Director, 813-257-3179, E-mail: mwolf@ut.edu. *Application contact:* Chanelle Cox, Staff Assistant, Admissions for Graduate and Continuing Studies, 813-253-6249, E-mail: ccox@ut.edu.
Website: http://www.ut.edu/msn/

The University of Texas at Austin, Graduate School, School of Nursing, Austin, TX 78712-1111. Offers adult - gerontology clinical nurse specialist (MSN); child health (MSN), including administration, public health nursing, teaching; family nurse practitioner (MSN); family psychiatric/mental health nurse practitioner (MSN); holistic adult health (MSN), including administration, teaching; maternity (MSN), including administration, public health nursing, teaching; nursing (PhD); nursing administration and healthcare systems management (MSN); nursing practice (DNP); pediatric nurse practitioner (MSN); public health nursing (MSN). *Accreditation:* AACN. *Program availability:* Part-time. *Degree requirements:* For master's, thesis optional; for doctorate, thesis/dissertation. *Entrance requirements:* For master's and doctorate, GRE General Test. Additional exam requirements/recommendations for international students: Required—TOEFL (minimum score 550 paper-based). Electronic applications accepted. *Faculty research:* Chronic illness management, memory and aging, health promotion, women's health, adolescent health.

The University of Texas Rio Grande Valley, College of Health Affairs, School of Nursing, Edinburg, TX 78539. Offers adult health nursing (MSN); family nurse practitioner (MSN); nursing administration (MSN); nursing education (MSN); psychiatric mental health nursing (Post Master's Certificate). *Accreditation:* AACN. *Program availability:* Part-time, evening/weekend. *Faculty:* 7 full-time (all women), 5 part-time/adjunct (3 women). *Students:* 48 full-time, 5 part-time; includes 43 minority (5 Black or African American, non-Hispanic/Latino; 38 Hispanic/Latino). Average age 31. 61 applicants. In 2017, 46 master's awarded. *Degree requirements:* For master's, thesis optional. *Entrance requirements:* For master's, Texas RN licensure, undergraduate physical statistic course. Additional exam requirements/recommendations for international students: Required—TOEFL (minimum score 550 paper-based). *Application deadline:* For fall admission, 7/1 priority date for domestic and international students; for spring admission, 10/1 priority date for domestic and international students. Applications are processed on a rolling basis. Application fee: $50. Electronic applications accepted. *Expenses:* Contact institution. *Financial support:* Scholarships/grants and traineeships available. Financial award application deadline: 9/1; financial award applicants required to submit FAFSA. *Faculty research:* Health promotion, adolescent pregnancy, herbal and nontraditional approaches, healing touch stress. *Unit head:* Dr. Eloisa G. Tamez, Professor/Chief Nursing Administrator, 956-665-3616, Fax: 956-665-5252, E-mail: eloisa.tamez@utrgv.edu. *Application contact:* Dr. Beatriz Bautista, Clinical Professor, 956-665-3497, Fax: 956-665-3491, E-mail: beatriz.bautista@utrgv.edu.
Website: http://www.utrgv.edu/nursing/

University of Wisconsin–Eau Claire, College of Nursing and Health Sciences, Program in Nursing, Eau Claire, WI 54702-4004. Offers adult-gerontological administration (DNP); adult-gerontological clinical nurse specialist (DNP); adult-gerontological education (MSN); adult-gerontological primary care nurse practitioner (DNP); family health administration (DNP); family health in education (MSN); family health nurse practitioner (DNP); nursing (MSN); nursing practice (DNP). *Accreditation:* AACN. *Program availability:* Part-time. Terminal master's awarded for partial completion of doctoral program. *Degree requirements:* For master's, thesis optional, 500-600 hours clinical practicum, oral and written exams. *Entrance requirements:* For master's, Wisconsin RN license, minimum GPA of 3.0, undergraduate statistics, course work in health assessment. Additional exam requirements/recommendations for international students: Required—TOEFL (minimum score 79 iBT). *Expenses:* Contact institution.

University of Wisconsin–Madison, School of Nursing, Madison, WI 53706-1380. Offers adult/gerontology (DNP); nursing (PhD); pediatrics (DNP); psychiatric mental health (DNP); MS/MPH. *Accreditation:* AACN. *Program availability:* Part-time. *Degree requirements:* For doctorate, comprehensive exam, thesis/dissertation. *Entrance requirements:* For doctorate, GRE General Test, 2 samples of scholarly written work, BS in nursing from an accredited program, minimum undergraduate GPA of 3.0 in last 60 credits (for PhD); licensure as professional nurse (for DNP). Additional exam requirements/recommendations for international students: Required—TOEFL (minimum score 600 paper-based; 100 iBT). Electronic applications accepted. *Faculty research:* Nursing informatics to promote self-care and disease management skills among patients and caregivers; quality of care to frail, vulnerable, and chronically ill populations; study of health-related and health-seeking behaviors; eliminating health disparities; pain and symptom management for patients with cancer.

University of Wisconsin–Oshkosh, Graduate Studies, College of Nursing, Oshkosh, WI 54901. Offers adult health and illness (MSN); family nurse practitioner (MSN). *Accreditation:* AACN. *Program availability:* Part-time. *Degree requirements:* For master's, thesis or alternative, clinical paper. *Entrance requirements:* For master's, RN license, BSN, previous course work in statistics and health assessment, minimum undergraduate GPA of 3.0, letters of recommendation. Additional exam requirements/recommendations for international students: Required—TOEFL (minimum score 550 paper-based; 79 iBT). Electronic applications accepted. *Faculty research:* Adult health and illness, nurse practitioners practice, health care service, advanced practitioner roles, natural alternative complementary healthcare.

Ursuline College, School of Graduate and Professional Studies, Programs in Nursing, Pepper Pike, OH 44124-4398. Offers acute-care nurse practitioner (MSN); adult nurse practitioner (MSN); adult-gerontology acute care nurse practitioner (MSN); adult-gerontology clinical nurse specialist (MSN); adult-gerontology nurse practitioner (MSN); care management (MSN); clinical nurse specialist (MSN); family nurse practitioner (MSN); nursing (DNP); nursing education (MSN); palliative care (MSN). *Accreditation:* AACN. *Program availability:* Part-time. *Faculty:* 6 full-time (all women), 25 part-time/adjunct (23 women). *Students:* 136 applicants, 89% accepted, 85 enrolled. In 2017, 85 master's, 6 doctorates awarded. *Degree requirements:* For master's, comprehensive exam; for doctorate, thesis/dissertation. *Entrance requirements:* For master's, minimum undergraduate GPA of 3.0, bachelor's degree in nursing, eligibility for or current Ohio RN license. Additional exam requirements/recommendations for international students: Required—TOEFL (minimum score 500 paper-based). *Application deadline:* For fall admission, 8/1 priority date for domestic students. Applications are processed on a rolling basis. Application fee: $25. Electronic applications accepted. *Expenses:* $1,094 per credit hour. *Financial support:* In 2017–18, 6 students received support. Scholarships/grants available. Financial award application deadline: 3/1; financial award applicants required to submit FAFSA. *Faculty research:* Core Determinants of Health (CDH) screening tool and accompanying education, academic-practice partnerships, active learning/teaching strategies, innovative clinical education models, competency development and testing, health care policy and cultural competence. *Total annual research expenditures:* $864,511. *Unit head:* Dr. Janet Baker, Associate Dean of Graduate Nursing, 440-864-8172, Fax: 440-684-6053, E-mail: jbaker@ursuline.edu. *Application contact:* Melanie Steele, Director, Graduate Admission, 440-646-8119, Fax: 440-684-6138, E-mail: graduateadmissions@ursuline.edu.

Vanderbilt University, Vanderbilt University School of Nursing, Nashville, TN 37240. Offers adult-gerontology acute care nurse practitioner (MSN), including hospitalist, intensivist; adult-gerontology primary care nurse practitioner (MSN); emergency nurse practitioner (MSN); family nurse practitioner (MSN); healthcare leadership (MSN); neonatal nurse practitioner (MSN); nurse midwifery (MSN); nurse midwifery/family nurse practitioner (MSN); nursing (Post-Master's Certificate); nursing informatics (MSN); nursing practice (DNP); nursing science (PhD); pediatric acute care nurse practitioner (MSN); pediatric primary care nurse practitioner (MSN); psychiatric-mental health nurse practitioner (MSN); women's health nurse practitioner (MSN); women's health nurse practitioner/adult gerontology primary care nurse practitioner (MSN); MSN/M Div; MSN/MTS. *Accreditation:* AACN; ACEN (one or more programs are accredited); ACNM/ACME. *Program availability:* Part-time, 100% online, blended/hybrid learning. *Faculty:* 292 full-time (267 women), 321 part-time/adjunct (253 women). *Students:* 501 full-time (435 women), 387 part-time (355 women); includes 153 minority (40 Black or African American, non-Hispanic/Latino; 1 American Indian or Alaska Native, non-Hispanic/Latino; 27 Asian, non-Hispanic/Latino; 48 Hispanic/Latino; 4 Native Hawaiian or other Pacific Islander, non-Hispanic/Latino; 33 Two or more races, non-Hispanic/Latino), 9 international. Average age 31. 1,210 applicants, 57% accepted, 473 enrolled. In 2017, 319 master's, 47 doctorates awarded. *Degree requirements:* For doctorate, comprehensive exam, thesis/dissertation. *Entrance requirements:* For master's, GRE General Test (taken within the past 5 years), minimum B average in undergraduate course work, 3 letters of recommendation; for doctorate, GRE General Test, interview, 3 letters of recommendation from doctorally-prepared faculty, MSN, essay. Additional exam requirements/recommendations for international students: Required—TOEFL (minimum score 570 paper-based), IELTS (minimum score 6.5). *Application deadline:* For fall admission, 11/1 priority date for domestic and international students. Applications are processed on a rolling basis. Application fee: $50. Electronic applications accepted. *Expenses:* Contact institution. *Financial support:* In 2017–18, 627 students received support. Scholarships/grants available. Financial award application deadline: 3/1; financial award applicants required to submit FAFSA. *Faculty research:* Lymphedema, palliative care and bereavement, health services research including workforce, safety and quality of care, gerontology, better birth outcomes including nutrition. *Total annual research expenditures:* $2 million. *Unit head:* Dr. Linda Norman, Dean, 615-343-8876, Fax: 615-343-7711, E-mail: linda.norman@vanderbilt.edu. *Application contact:* Patricia Peerman, Assistant Dean for Enrollment Management, 615-322-3800, Fax: 615-343-0333, E-mail: vusn-admissions@vanderbilt.edu.
Website: http://www.nursing.vanderbilt.edu

Villanova University, M. Louise Fitzpatrick College of Nursing, Villanova, PA 19085. Offers adult-gerontology primary care nurse practitioner (MSN, Post Master's Certificate); family primary care nurse practitioner (MSN, Post Master's Certificate); nurse anesthesia (DNP); nursing (PhD); nursing education (MSN, Post Master's Certificate); nursing practice (DNP); pediatric primary care nurse practitioner (MSN, Post Master's Certificate). *Accreditation:* AACN; AANA/CANAEP. *Program availability:* Part-time, online learning. *Students:* 151 full-time, 199 part-time; includes 42 minority (18 Black or African American, non-Hispanic/Latino; 12 Asian, non-Hispanic/Latino; 8 Hispanic/Latino; 4 Two or more races, non-Hispanic/Latino), 10 international. 274 applicants, 43% accepted, 92 enrolled. In 2017, 70 master's, 15 doctorates awarded. *Entrance requirements:* Additional exam requirements/recommendations for international students: Required—TOEFL, IELTS. *Application deadline:* For fall admission, 7/1 for domestic and international students; for spring admission, 10/1 for domestic and international students; for summer admission, 4/1 for domestic and international students. Application fee: $50. Electronic applications accepted. *Financial support:* Fellowships, research assistantships, teaching assistantships, scholarships/grants, traineeships, and tuition waivers available. *Unit head:* Dr. Marguerite K. Schlag, Associate Professor, Assistant Dean and Director of Graduate Nursing Program, 610-519-4907, Fax: 610-519-7650, E-mail: marguerite.schlag@villanova.edu. *Application contact:* Kathleen Geibel, Assistant to Graduate Program, 610-519-4934, Fax: 610-519-7650, E-mail: kathleen.geibel@villanova.edu.
Website: http://www.nursing.villanova.edu

Virginia Commonwealth University, Graduate School, School of Nursing, Richmond, VA 23284-9005. Offers adult health acute nursing (MS); adult health primary nursing (MS); biobehavioral clinical research (PhD); child health nursing (MS); clinical nurse leader (MS); family health nursing (MS); nurse educator (MS); nurse practitioner (MS); nursing (Certificate); nursing administration (MS), including clinical nurse manager; psychiatric-mental health nursing (MS); quality and safety in health care (DNP); women's health nursing (MS). *Accreditation:* AACN; ACEN (one or more programs are accredited). *Program availability:* Part-time, evening/weekend, online learning. *Degree requirements:* For master's, thesis optional; for doctorate, thesis/dissertation. *Entrance requirements:* For master's, GRE General Test, BSN, minimum GPA of 2.8; for doctorate, GRE General Test. Additional exam requirements/recommendations for international students: Required—TOEFL (minimum score 600 paper-based; 100 iBT). Electronic applications accepted.

Walden University, Graduate Programs, School of Nursing, Minneapolis, MN 55401. Offers adult-gerontology acute care nurse practitioner (MSN); adult-gerontology nurse practitioner (MSN); education (MSN); family nurse practitioner (MSN); informatics (MSN); leadership and management (MSN); nursing (PhD, Post-Master's Certificate), including education (PhD), healthcare administration (PhD), interdisciplinary health (PhD), leadership (PhD), nursing education (Post-Master's Certificate), nursing informatics (Post-Master's Certificate), nursing leadership and management (Post-Master's Certificate), public health policy (PhD); nursing practice (DNP); psychiatric mental health (MSN). *Accreditation:* AACN. *Program availability:* Part-time, evening/weekend, online only, 100% online. *Degree requirements:* For doctorate, thesis/dissertation (for some programs), residency (for some programs), field experience (for some programs). *Entrance requirements:* For master's, bachelor's degree or equivalent in related field or RN; minimum GPA of 2.5; official transcripts; goal statement (for some programs); access to computer and Internet; for doctorate, master's degree or higher; RN; three years of related professional or academic experience; goal statement; access to computer and Internet; for Post-Master's Certificate, relevant work experience; access to computer and Internet. Additional exam requirements/recommendations for international students: Required—TOEFL (minimum score 550 paper-based, 79 iBT), IELTS (minimum score 6.5), Michigan English Language Assessment Battery (minimum score 82), or PTE (minimum score 53). Electronic applications accepted.

Walsh University, Graduate Programs, Gary and Linda Byers School of Nursing, North Canton, OH 44720-3396. Offers academic nurse educator (MSN); adult acute care nurse practitioner (MSN); clinical nurse leader (MSN); nursing practice (DNP). *Accreditation:* AACN. *Program availability:* Part-time, evening/weekend, online only, 100% online. *Degree requirements:* For doctorate, scholarly project; residency practicum. *Entrance requirements:* For master's, undergraduate nursing degree, current unencumbered RN license, completion of an undergraduate or graduate statistics course, essay, interview, recommendations; for doctorate, BSN; master's degree; statistics and research courses; essay; interview. Additional exam requirements/recommendations for international students: Required—TOEFL. Electronic applications accepted. *Expenses:* Contact institution. *Faculty research:* Self-efficacy, Newman theory, curriculum development and assessment on family nurse practitioner (FNP) practice, DNP online rubrics.

Wayne State University, College of Nursing, Detroit, MI 48202. Offers adult gerontology acute care nurse practitioner (MSN); adult gerontology primary care nurse practitioner (MSN); advanced public health nursing (MSN); infant and mental health (DNP, PhD); neonatal nurse practitioner (MSN); nurse-midwifery (MSN); pediatric acute care nurse practitioner (MSN); pediatric primary care nurse practitioner (MSN); psychiatric mental health nurse practitioner (MSN); women's health nurse practitioner (MSN). Doctoral program admits for fall only. *Accreditation:* AACN. *Program availability:* Part-time. *Faculty:* 30. *Students:* 133 full-time (120 women), 184 part-time (167 women); includes 85 minority (57 Black or African American, non-Hispanic/Latino; 16 Asian, non-Hispanic/Latino; 4 Hispanic/Latino; 8 Two or more races, non-Hispanic/Latino), 22 international. Average age 34. 318 applicants, 39% accepted, 94 enrolled. In 2017, 51 master's, 29 doctorates awarded. *Degree requirements:* For doctorate, thesis/dissertation (for some programs). *Entrance requirements:* For master's, BSN from ACEN- or CCNE-accredited program with minimum GPA of 3.0; three references; current RN license; personal statement; for doctorate, resume or curriculum vitae; goals statement; bachelor's or master's degree in nursing from ACEN- or CCNE-accredited program with minimum GPA of 3.0; current RN license, writing sample and interview (for DNP); reference letters (3 for PhD, 2 for DNP). Additional exam requirements/recommendations for international students: Required—TOEFL (minimum score 101 iBT), TWE (minimum score 6), Michigan English Language Assessment Battery (minimum score 85); Recommended—IELTS (minimum score 7). Application fee: $50. Electronic applications accepted. *Expenses:* Contact institution. *Financial support:* In 2017–18, 92 students received support, including 16 fellowships with tuition reimbursements available (averaging $8,285 per year), 5 teaching assistantships with tuition reimbursements available (averaging $25,000 per year); scholarships/grants, health care benefits, and unspecified assistantships also available. Support available to part-time students. Financial award applicants required to submit FAFSA. *Faculty research:* Bridging transitions and technology to promote asthma care in the community, chronic wound care for persons who injected drugs, decreasing at-risk parenting to reduce child maltreatment and trauma, dementia symptoms (cognition, behavior, function), determining readiness to engage in end of life/palliative care conversations with adolescents and young adults living with advanced cancer, dyspnea assessment and treatment at the end of life. *Unit head:* Dr. Laurie Lauzon Clabo, Dean, College of Nursing, 313-577-4082, E-mail: laurie.lauzon.clabo@wayne.edu. *Application contact:* 313-577-4082, Fax: 313-577-6949, E-mail: nursinginfo@wayne.edu.
Website: http://nursing.wayne.edu/

Western Connecticut State University, Division of Graduate Studies, School of Professional Studies, Nursing Department, Danbury, CT 06810-6885. Offers adult gerontology clinical nurse specialist (MSN); adult gerontology nurse practitioner (MSN); nursing education (Ed D). *Accreditation:* AACN. *Program availability:* Part-time. *Degree requirements:* For master's, clinical component, thesis or research project, completion of program in 6 years. *Entrance requirements:* For master's, MAT (if GPA less than 3.0), bachelor's degree in nursing, minimum GPA of 3.0, previous course work in statistics and nursing research, RN license. Additional exam requirements/recommendations for international students: Recommended—TOEFL (minimum score 550 paper-based; 79 iBT), IELTS (minimum score 6). *Expenses:* Contact institution. *Faculty research:* Evaluating effectiveness of Reiki and acupressure on stress reduction.

William Paterson University of New Jersey, College of Science and Health, Wayne, NJ 07470-8420. Offers adult gerontology nurse practitioner (Certificate); biology (MS); biotechnology (MS); communication disorders (MS); exercise and sport studies (MS); materials chemistry (MS); nurse practitioner (Certificate); nursing (MSN); nursing education (Certificate); nursing practice (DNP); school nurse (Certificate). *Program availability:* Part-time. *Faculty:* 29 full-time (15 women), 25 part-time/adjunct (24 women). *Students:* 66 full-time (56 women), 197 part-time (163 women); includes 104 minority (15 Black or African American, non-Hispanic/Latino; 45 Asian, non-Hispanic/Latino; 38 Hispanic/Latino; 6 Two or more races, non-Hispanic/Latino), 3 international. Average age 33. 387 applicants, 34% accepted, 77 enrolled. In 2017, 87 master's, 5

doctorates awarded. *Degree requirements:* For master's, comprehensive exam (for some programs), thesis (for some programs), non-thesis internship/practicum (for some programs). *Entrance requirements:* For master's, GRE/MAT, minimum GPA of 3.0; 2-3 letters of recommendation; personal statement; work experience (for some programs); for doctorate, GRE/MAT, minimum GPA of 3.3; work experience; 3 letters of recommendation; interview; master's degree in nursing. Additional exam requirements/recommendations for international students: Required—TOEFL (minimum score 550 paper-based; 79 iBT), IELTS (minimum score 6). *Application deadline:* For fall admission, 6/1 for domestic students, 3/1 for international students; for spring admission, 11/1 for domestic students, 10/1 for international students. Applications are processed on a rolling basis. Application fee: $50. Electronic applications accepted. *Expenses:* Tuition, state resident: full-time $13,920; part-time $6264 per year. Tuition, nonresident: full-time $21,700; part-time $9765 per year. *Required fees:* $80; $36 per year. Tuition and fees vary according to course load, degree level and program. *Financial support:* In 2017–18, 9,800 students received support. Career-related internships or fieldwork, Federal Work-Study, scholarships/grants, and unspecified assistantships available. Support available to part-time students. Financial award application deadline: 3/15; financial award applicants required to submit FAFSA. *Faculty research:* Behaviors of American long-eared bats, postpartum fatigue, methodologies for coating carbon nano-tubes, paleoclimatology, and pre-linguistic gestures in children with language disorders. *Total annual research expenditures:* $291,600. *Unit head:* Dr. Venkat Sharma, Dean, 973-720-2194, Fax: 973-720-3414, E-mail: sharmav@wpunj.edu. *Application contact:* Christina Aiello, Assistant Director, Graduate Admissions, 973-720-2506, Fax: 973-720-2035, E-mail: aielloc@wpunj.edu.
Website: http://www.wpunj.edu/cosh

Wilmington University, College of Health Professions, New Castle, DE 19720-6491. Offers adult nurse practitioner (MSN); family nurse practitioner (MSN); gerontology nurse practitioner (MSN); nursing (MSN); nursing leadership (MSN); nursing practice (DNP). *Accreditation:* AACN. *Program availability:* Part-time. *Faculty:* 10 full-time (9 women), 59 part-time/adjunct (50 women). *Students:* 164 full-time (154 women), 662 part-time (604 women); includes 178 minority (129 Black or African American, non-Hispanic/Latino; 5 American Indian or Alaska Native, non-Hispanic/Latino; 23 Asian, non-Hispanic/Latino; 7 Hispanic/Latino; 3 Native Hawaiian or other Pacific Islander, non-Hispanic/Latino; 11 Two or more races, non-Hispanic/Latino), 6 international. Average age 39. 770 applicants, 63% accepted, 361 enrolled. In 2017, 259 master's, 22 doctorates awarded. *Degree requirements:* For master's, thesis. *Entrance requirements:* For master's, BSN, RN license, interview, 3 letters of recommendation. Additional exam requirements/recommendations for international students: Required—TOEFL (minimum score 500 paper-based). *Application deadline:* For fall admission, 4/1 for domestic students; for spring admission, 9/1 for domestic students. Applications are processed on a rolling basis. Application fee: $35. Electronic applications accepted. *Expenses: Tuition:* Part-time $466 per credit. *Required fees:* $25 per semester. Tuition and fees vary according to degree level and campus/location. *Financial support:* Fellowships with tuition reimbursements and traineeships available. Financial award applicants required to submit FAFSA. *Faculty research:* Outcomes assessment, student writing ability. *Unit head:* Denise Z. Westbrook, Dean, 302-356-6915. *Application contact:* Laura Morris, Director of Admissions, 877-967-5464, E-mail: infocenter@wilmu.edu.
Website: http://www.wilmu.edu/health/

Winona State University, College of Nursing and Health Sciences, Winona, MN 55987. Offers adult-gerontology acute care nurse practitioner (MS, DNP, Post Master's Certificate); adult-gerontology clinical nurse specialist (MS, DNP, Post Master's Certificate); adult-gerontology primary care nurse practitioner (MS, DNP, Post Master's Certificate); family nurse practitioner (MS, DNP, Post Master's Certificate); nurse educator (MS); nursing and organizational leadership (MS, DNP, Post Master's Certificate); practice and leadership innovations (DNP, Post Master's Certificate). *Accreditation:* AACN. *Program availability:* Part-time, online learning. *Degree requirements:* For master's, thesis; for doctorate, capstone. *Entrance requirements:* For master's, GRE (if GPA less than 3.0). Additional exam requirements/recommendations for international students: Required—TOEFL (minimum score 550 paper-based).

Wright State University, Graduate School, College of Nursing and Health, Program in Nursing, Dayton, OH 45435. Offers administration of nursing and health care systems (MS); adult gerontology clinical nurse specialist (MS); adult-gerontology acute care nurse practitioner (MS); family nurse practitioner (MS); neonatal nurse practitioner (MS); pediatric nurse practitioner-acute care (MS); pediatric nurse practitioner-primary care (MS); psychiatric mental health nurse practitioner (MS); school nurse (MS). *Accreditation:* AACN. *Program availability:* Part-time, evening/weekend. *Degree requirements:* For master's, thesis or alternative. *Entrance requirements:* For master's, GRE General Test, BSN from ACEN-accredited college, Ohio RN license. Additional exam requirements/recommendations for international students: Required—TOEFL. *Faculty research:* Clinical nursing and health, teaching, caring, pain administration, informatics and technology.

Community Health Nursing

Allen College, Graduate Programs, Waterloo, IA 50703. Offers adult-gerontology acute care nurse practitioner (MSN); community/public health nursing (MSN); education (MSN); family nurse practitioner (MSN); health sciences (Ed D); leadership in health care delivery (MSN); leadership in health care informatics (MSN); nursing (DNP); occupational therapy (MS); psychiatric mental health nurse practitioner (MSN). MSN in leadership in healthcare informatics offered in partnership with University of Minnesota. *Accreditation:* AACN; ACEN. *Program availability:* Part-time, 100% online, blended/hybrid learning. *Faculty:* 24 full-time (all women), 8 part-time/adjunct (7 women). *Students:* 106 full-time (91 women), 187 part-time (164 women); includes 22 minority (12 Black or African American, non-Hispanic/Latino; 1 American Indian or Alaska Native, non-Hispanic/Latino; 2 Asian, non-Hispanic/Latino; 3 Hispanic/Latino; 4 Two or more races, non-Hispanic/Latino), 2 international. Average age 33. 352 applicants, 56% accepted, 131 enrolled. In 2017, 73 master's, 2 doctorates awarded. *Entrance requirements:* For master's, minimum GPA of 3.0 in the last 60 hours of undergraduate coursework; for doctorate, minimum GPA of 3.25 in graduate coursework. *Application deadline:* For fall admission, 2/1 priority date for domestic students; for spring admission, 9/1 priority date for domestic students. Applications are processed on a rolling basis. Application fee: $50. Electronic applications accepted. *Expenses:* $17,860 per year. *Financial support:* In 2017–18, 97 students received support. Federal Work-Study, institutionally sponsored loans, scholarships/grants, and traineeships available. Support available to part-time students. Financial award application deadline: 8/1; financial award applicants required to submit FAFSA. *Faculty research:* Poverty. *Unit head:* Dr. Nancy Kramer, Vice Chancellor for Academic Affairs, 319-226-2040, Fax: 319-226-2070, E-mail: nancy.kramer@allencollege.edu. *Application contact:* Molly Quinn, Director of Admissions, 319-226-2001, Fax: 319-226-2010, E-mail: molly.quinn@allencollege.edu.
Website: http://www.allencollege.edu/

American University of Beirut, Graduate Programs, Rafic Hariri School of Nursing, Beirut, Lebanon. Offers adult gerontology clinical nurse specialist (MSN); community and public health nursing (MSN); nursing administration and management (MSN); psychiatric mental health clinical nurse specialist (MSN). *Accreditation:* AACN. *Faculty:* 13 full-time (12 women), 23 part-time/adjunct (18 women). *Students:* 4 full-time (3 women), 40 part-time (34 women). Average age 28. 32 applicants, 81% accepted, 9 enrolled. In 2017, 18 master's awarded. *Degree requirements:* For master's, comprehensive exam, residency and project or thesis. *Entrance requirements:* For master's, minimum cumulative average of 80, minimum of 1 year of work experience. Additional exam requirements/recommendations for international students: Required—TOEFL (minimum score 583 paper-based; 97 iBT); Recommended—IELTS (minimum score 7). *Application deadline:* For fall admission, 4/4 for domestic students. Applications are processed on a rolling basis. Application fee: $50. Electronic applications accepted. *Expenses:* $810 per credit. *Financial support:* In 2017–18, 7 students received support. Teaching assistantships, scholarships/grants, traineeships, and unspecified assistantships available. Financial award application deadline: 12/20. *Faculty research:* Pain management and palliative care, postwar PTSD, depression, anxiety, and social support, cardiovascular care, vitamin D and cognitive function, nursing workforce and health systems research. *Total annual research expenditures:* $305,241. *Unit head:* Dr. Huda Abu-Saad Huijer, Director of the Hariri School of Nursing, 961-1-350000 Ext. 5953, Fax: 961-1-744476, E-mail: hh35@aub.edu.lb. *Application contact:* Nisreen Ghalayini, Administrative Assistant, 961-1-350000 Ext. 5951, E-mail: ng28@aub.edu.lb.
Website: http://www.aub.edu.lb/hson

Binghamton University, State University of New York, Graduate School, Decker School of Nursing, Binghamton, NY 13902-6000. Offers adult-gerontological nursing (MS, DNP, Certificate); community health nursing (MS, DNP, Certificate); family health nursing (MS, DNP, Certificate); family psychiatric mental health nursing (MS, DNP, Certificate); nursing (PhD). *Accreditation:* AACN. *Program availability:* Part-time, evening/weekend. *Faculty:* 52 full-time (45 women). *Students:* 94 full-time (79 women), 109 part-time (94 women); includes 43 minority (21 Black or African American, non-Hispanic/Latino; 10 Asian, non-Hispanic/Latino; 7 Hispanic/Latino; 5 Two or more races, non-Hispanic/Latino), 13 international. Average age 36. 111 applicants, 95% accepted, 63 enrolled. In 2017, 53 master's, 5 doctorates, 20 other advanced degrees awarded. Terminal master's awarded for partial completion of doctoral program. *Degree requirements:* For master's, comprehensive exam, thesis; for doctorate, comprehensive exam (for some programs), thesis/dissertation. *Entrance requirements:* For master's and doctorate, GRE General Test, nursing licensure. Additional exam requirements/recommendations for international students: Required—TOEFL (minimum score 90 iBT). Application fee: $75. Electronic applications accepted. *Expenses:* Contact institution. *Financial support:* In 2017–18, 33 students received support, including 1 fellowship with partial tuition reimbursement available (averaging $16,500 per year), research assistantships with full tuition reimbursements available (averaging $12,500 per year), 1 teaching assistantship with full tuition reimbursement available (averaging $16,500 per year); career-related internships or fieldwork, Federal Work-Study, institutionally sponsored loans, traineeships, health care benefits, tuition waivers (full and partial), and unspecified assistantships also available. Financial award applicants required to submit FAFSA. *Unit head:* Dr. Mario R. Ortiz, Dean, 607-777-2311, E-mail: mortiz@binghamton.edu. *Application contact:* Ben Balkaya, Assistant Dean and Director, 607-777-2151, Fax: 607-777-2501, E-mail: balkaya@binghamton.edu.
Website: http://www.binghamton.edu/dson/

Hampton University, School of Nursing, Hampton, VA 23668. Offers community health nursing (MS); family nurse practitioner (MS); family research (PhD); nursing administration (MS); nursing education (MS). *Accreditation:* AACN. *Program availability:* Part-time, online learning. *Students:* 6 full-time (all women), 28 part-time (25 women); includes 31 minority (29 Black or African American, non-Hispanic/Latino; 2 Hispanic/Latino). Average age 48. 7 applicants, 14% accepted. In 2017, 3 master's, 4 doctorates awarded. *Degree requirements:* For master's, comprehensive exam, thesis optional; for doctorate, comprehensive exam, thesis/dissertation. *Entrance requirements:* For master's, GRE General Test. *Application deadline:* For fall admission, 6/1 priority date for domestic students, 4/1 priority date for international students; for spring admission, 11/1 priority date for domestic students, 9/1 priority date for international students; for summer admission, 4/1 priority date for domestic students, 2/1 priority date for international students. Applications are processed on a rolling basis. Application fee: $35. Electronic applications accepted. *Expenses: Tuition:* Full-time $22,630; part-time $575 per semester hour. *Required fees:* $70. Tuition and fees vary according to program. *Financial support:* In 2017–18, 2 students received support. Fellowships, research assistantships, teaching assistantships, career-related internships or fieldwork, Federal Work-Study, institutionally sponsored loans, and scholarships/grants available. Support available to part-time students. Financial award application deadline: 6/30; financial award applicants required to submit FAFSA. *Faculty research:* African-American stress, HIV education, pediatric obesity, hypertension, breast cancer. *Unit head:* Dr. Shevallanie Lott, Dean, 757-727-5654, E-mail: shevellanie.lott@hamptonu.edu.
Website: http://nursing.hamptonu.edu

Hunter College of the City University of New York, Graduate School, Hunter-Bellevue School of Nursing, Community/Public Health Nursing Program, New York, NY 10065-5085. Offers MS. *Accreditation:* AACN. *Program availability:* Part-time. *Degree requirements:* For master's, practicum. *Entrance requirements:* For master's, minimum GPA of 3.0, New York RN license, BSN. Additional exam requirements/recommendations for international students: Required—TOEFL. *Faculty research:* HIV/AIDS, health promotion with vulnerable populations.

Husson University, Graduate Nursing Program, Bangor, ME 04401-2999. Offers educational leadership (MSN); family and community nurse practitioner (MSN, PMC); psychiatric mental health nurse practitioner (MSN, PMC). *Accreditation:* AACN. *Program availability:* Part-time, evening/weekend. *Faculty:* 4 full-time (all women), 4 part-time/adjunct (all women). *Students:* 1 full-time (0 women), 62 part-time (54 women); includes 3 minority (2 Black or African American, non-Hispanic/Latino; 1 Hispanic/Latino), 1

international. Average age 36. 62 applicants, 55% accepted, 26 enrolled. In 2017, 9 master's awarded. *Degree requirements:* For master's, comprehensive exam (for some programs), research project. *Entrance requirements:* For master's, proof of RN licensure. Additional exam requirements/recommendations for international students: Required—TOEFL (minimum score 550 paper-based; 80 iBT), IELTS (minimum score 6.5). *Application deadline:* For fall admission, 7/15 for domestic students; for spring admission, 10/30 for domestic students. Application fee: $50. Electronic applications accepted. *Expenses:* $577 per credit; $110 to $480 yearly fee depending on credit load. *Financial support:* In 2017–18, 1 student received support. Federal Work-Study, institutionally sponsored loans, traineeships, and unspecified assistantships available. Financial award application deadline: 3/31; financial award applicants required to submit FAFSA. *Faculty research:* Health disparities and methods to better identify and provide healthcare services to those most in need. *Unit head:* Prof. Mary Jude, Director, Graduate Nursing, 207-941-7769, Fax: 207-941-7198, E-mail: judem@husson.edu. *Application contact:* Kristen Card, Director of Graduate Admissions, 207-404-5660, Fax: 207-941-7935, E-mail: cardk@husson.edu.
Website: http://www.husson.edu/college-of-health-and-education/school-of-nursing/graduate-nursing/

Independence University, Program in Nursing, Salt Lake City, UT 84107. Offers community health (MSN); gerontology (MSN); nursing administration (MSN); wellness promotion (MSN).

Johns Hopkins University, School of Nursing and Bloomberg School of Public Health, Joint Degree Program in Nursing and Public Health, Baltimore, MD 21205. Offers MSN/MPH. Program offered jointly with Bloomberg School of Public Health. *Accreditation:* AACN; CEPH. *Program availability:* Part-time. *Faculty:* 4 full-time (all women), 2 part-time/adjunct (both women). *Students:* 10 full-time (9 women), 11 part-time (10 women); includes 5 minority (1 Black or African American, non-Hispanic/Latino; 4 Asian, non-Hispanic/Latino). Average age 29. 13 applicants, 46% accepted, 5 enrolled. *Entrance requirements:* Additional exam requirements/recommendations for international students: Required—TOEFL (minimum score 600 paper-based; 100 iBT), IELTS (minimum score 7). *Application deadline:* For summer admission, 11/1 priority date for domestic and international students. Application fee: $70. Electronic applications accepted. *Expenses:* $1,636 per credit. *Financial support:* In 2017–18, 4 students received support. Federal Work-Study and scholarships/grants available. Support available to part-time students. Financial award application deadline: 3/1; financial award applicants required to submit FAFSA. *Faculty research:* Asthma, tuberculosis control, injury, violence, international health, women's health, substance abuse. *Unit head:* Dr. Patricia M. Davidson, Dean, 410-955-7544, Fax: 410-955-4890, E-mail: sondeansoffice@jhu.edu. *Application contact:* Cathy Wilson, Director of Admissions, 410-955-7548, Fax: 410-614-7086, E-mail: jhuson@jhu.edu.
Website: http://www.nursing.jhu.edu

See Display on page 576 and Close-Up on page 763.

Kean University, College of Natural, Applied and Health Sciences, Program in Nursing, Union, NJ 07083. Offers clinical management (MSN); community health nursing (MSN). *Accreditation:* ACEN. *Program availability:* Part-time. *Faculty:* 12 full-time (all women). *Students:* 7 full-time (all women), 50 part-time (46 women); includes 34 minority (23 Black or African American, non-Hispanic/Latino; 8 Asian, non-Hispanic/Latino; 2 Hispanic/Latino; 1 Two or more races, non-Hispanic/Latino). Average age 47. 15 applicants, 53% accepted, 4 enrolled. In 2017, 51 master's awarded. *Degree requirements:* For master's, thesis or alternative, clinical field experience. *Entrance requirements:* For master's, minimum GPA of 3.0; BS in nursing; RN license; 2 letters of recommendation; interview; official transcripts from all institutions attended. Additional exam requirements/recommendations for international students: Required—TOEFL (minimum score 550 paper-based; 79 iBT), IELTS (minimum score 6.5). *Application deadline:* For fall admission, 6/30 for domestic and international students; for spring admission, 12/1 for domestic and international students. Applications are processed on a rolling basis. Application fee: $75. Electronic applications accepted. *Expenses:* Tuition, state resident: full-time $13,419; part-time $653 per credit. Tuition, nonresident: full-time $18,188; part-time $801 per credit. *Required fees:* $3382; $154 per credit. Tuition and fees vary according to course level, course load, degree level and program. *Financial support:* Scholarships/grants and unspecified assistantships available. Financial award applicants required to submit FAFSA. *Unit head:* Dr. Joan Valas, Program Coordinator, 908-737-6210, E-mail: nursing@kean.edu. *Application contact:* Pedro Lopes, Admissions Counselor, 908-737-7100, E-mail: gradadmissions@kean.edu.
Website: http://grad.kean.edu/masters-programs/nursing-clinical-management

La Salle University, School of Nursing and Health Sciences, Program in Nursing, Philadelphia, PA 19141-1199. Offers adult gerontology primary care nurse practitioner (MSN, Certificate); adult health and illness clinical nurse specialist (MSN); adult-gerontology clinical nurse specialist (MSN, Certificate); clinical nurse leader (MSN); family primary care nurse practitioner (MSN, Certificate); gerontology (Certificate); nurse anesthetist (MSN, Certificate); nursing (MSN, Certificate); nursing administration (MSN, Certificate); nursing education (Certificate); nursing practice (DNP); nursing service administration (MSN); public health nursing (MSN, Certificate); school nursing (Certificate); MSN/MBA; MSN/MPH. *Accreditation:* AACN. *Program availability:* Part-time, evening/weekend, 100% online. *Faculty:* 12 full-time (11 women), 14 part-time/adjunct (11 women). *Students:* 1 (woman) full-time, 277 part-time (220 women); includes 72 minority (36 Black or African American, non-Hispanic/Latino; 1 American Indian or Alaska Native, non-Hispanic/Latino; 18 Asian, non-Hispanic/Latino; 10 Hispanic/Latino; 1 Native Hawaiian or other Pacific Islander, non-Hispanic/Latino; 6 Two or more races, non-Hispanic/Latino), 1 international. Average age 36. 70 applicants, 56% accepted, 24 enrolled. In 2017, 81 master's, 4 doctorates, 13 other advanced degrees awarded. *Degree requirements:* For doctorate, minimum of 1,000 hours of post baccalaureate clinical practice supervised by preceptors. *Entrance requirements:* For master's, GRE, MAT, or GMAT (for students with BSN GPA of less than 3.2), baccalaureate degree in nursing from ACEN- or CCNE-accredited program or an MSN Bridge program; Pennsylvania RN license; 2 letters of reference; resume; statement of philosophy articulating professional values and future educational goal; 1 year of work experience as a registered nurse; for doctorate, GRE (waived for applicants with MSN cumulative GPA of 3.7 or above), MSN, master's degree, MBA or MHA from nationally-accredited program; resume or curriculum vitae; 2 letters of reference; interview; for Certificate, GRE, MAT, or GMAT (for students with BSN GPA of less than 3.2, baccalaureate degree in nursing from ACEN- or CCNE-accredited program or an MSN Bridge program; Pennsylvania RN license; 2 letters of reference; resume; statement of philosophy articulating professional values and future educational goal; 1 year of work experience as a registered nurse. Additional exam requirements/recommendations for international students: Required—TOEFL. *Application deadline:* For fall admission, 8/15 priority date for domestic students, 7/15 for international students; for spring admission, 12/15 priority date for domestic students, 11/15 for international students; for summer admission, 4/15 priority date for domestic students, 3/15 for international students. Applications are processed on a rolling basis. Application fee: $35. Electronic applications accepted. Application fee is waived when completed online. *Expenses:* Contact institution. *Financial support:* In 2017–18, 7 students received support. Scholarships/grants and traineeships available. Support available to part-time students. Financial award application deadline: 8/31; financial award applicants required to submit FAFSA. *Unit head:* Dr. Patricia M. Dillon, Director, 215-951-1322, Fax: 215-951-1896, E-mail: msnapn@lasalle.edu. *Application contact:* Elizabeth Heenan, Director, Graduate and Adult Enrollment, 215-951-1100, Fax: 215-951-1462, E-mail: heenan@lasalle.edu.
Website: http://www.lasalle.edu/nursing/program-options/

Louisiana State University Health Sciences Center, School of Nursing, New Orleans, LA 70112. Offers adult gerontology acute care nurse practitioner (DNP, Post-Master's Certificate); adult gerontology clinical nurse specialist (DNP, Post-Master's Certificate); adult gerontology primary care nurse practitioner (DNP, Post-Master's Certificate); clinical nurse leader (MSN); executive nurse leader (DNP, Post-Master's Certificate); neonatal nurse practitioner (DNP, Post-Master's Certificate); nurse anesthesia (DNP, Post-Master's Certificate); nurse educator (MSN); nursing (DNS); primary care family nurse practitioner (DNP, Post-Master's Certificate); public/community health nursing (DNP, Post-Master's Certificate). *Accreditation:* AACN; AANA/CANAEP (one or more programs are accredited). *Program availability:* Part-time. *Faculty:* 29 full-time (26 women), 20 part-time/adjunct (8 women). *Students:* 184 full-time (132 women), 41 part-time (35 women); includes 69 minority (45 Black or African American, non-Hispanic/Latino; 11 Asian, non-Hispanic/Latino; 12 Hispanic/Latino; 1 Two or more races, non-Hispanic/Latino), 1 international. Average age 30. 162 applicants, 42% accepted, 68 enrolled. In 2017, 52 master's, 46 doctorates awarded. *Degree requirements:* For master's, thesis optional; for doctorate, thesis/dissertation. *Entrance requirements:* For master's, GRE, minimum GPA of 3.0; for doctorate, GRE, minimum GPA of 3.0 (for DNP), 3.5 (for DNS). Additional exam requirements/recommendations for international students: Required—TOEFL (minimum score 550 paper-based; 79 iBT). *Application deadline:* Applications are processed on a rolling basis. Application fee: $100. Electronic applications accepted. *Expenses:* Contact institution. *Financial support:* Federal Work-Study, institutionally sponsored loans, scholarships/grants, and traineeships available. Financial award applicants required to submit FAFSA. *Faculty research:* Advanced clinical practice, nursing education, interprofessional education, nursing administration, culturally competent care. *Unit head:* Dr. Demetrius James Porche, Dean, 504-568-4106, Fax: 504-599-0573, E-mail: dporch@lsuhsc.edu. *Application contact:* Tracie Gravolet, Director, Office of Student Affairs, 504-568-4114, Fax: 504-568-5711, E-mail: tgravo@lsuhsc.edu.
Website: http://nursing.lsuhsc.edu/

Oregon Health & Science University, School of Nursing, Program in Nursing Education, Portland, OR 97239-3098. Offers MN, Post Master's Certificate. *Program availability:* Part-time, online only, 100% online. *Entrance requirements:* For master's, minimum cumulative GPA of 3.0, 3 letters of recommendation, essay, RN license or eligibility, BS with major in nursing or BSN, statistics taken in last 5 years with minimum B- grade; for Post Master's Certificate, minimum cumulative GPA of 3.0, 3 letters of recommendation, essay, RN license or eligibility, master's degree in nursing, statistics taken in last 5 years with minimum B- grade. Additional exam requirements/recommendations for international students: Required—TOEFL (minimum score 83 iBT). Electronic applications accepted. *Expenses:* Contact institution. *Faculty research:* Quality of end-of-life care in long-term settings, ethical issues in studying dying people and their families, strategies for improving clinical judgement.

Rush University, College of Nursing, Department of Community, Systems, and Mental Health Nursing, Chicago, IL 60612. Offers advanced public health nursing (DNP); family nurse practitioner (DNP); psychiatric mental health nurse practitioner (DNP); transformative leadership: population health (DNP). *Accreditation:* AACN. *Program availability:* Part-time, 100% online, blended/hybrid learning. *Students:* 23 full-time (21 women), 264 part-time (245 women); includes 83 minority (36 Black or African American, non-Hispanic/Latino; 1 American Indian or Alaska Native, non-Hispanic/Latino; 16 Asian, non-Hispanic/Latino; 24 Hispanic/Latino; 6 Two or more races, non-Hispanic/Latino). 176 applicants, 56% accepted, 79 enrolled. In 2017, 64 doctorates awarded. *Degree requirements:* For doctorate, scholarly project. *Entrance requirements:* For doctorate, GRE General Test (waived for DNP if cumulative GPA is 3.25 or greater, nursing GPA is 3.0 or greater, or a completed graduate program GPA is 3.5 or greater), interview, 3 letters of recommendation, personal statement, current resume. Additional exam requirements/recommendations for international students: Required—TOEFL (minimum score 94 iBT). *Application deadline:* For fall admission, 1/2 for domestic students; for spring admission, 8/1 for domestic students; for summer admission, 12/1 for domestic students. Applications are processed on a rolling basis. Application fee: $110. Electronic applications accepted. *Expenses:* Contact institution. *Financial support:* Research assistantships, teaching assistantships, Federal Work-Study, scholarships/grants, traineeships, and health care benefits available. Support available to part-time students. Financial award application deadline: 3/1; financial award applicants required to submit FAFSA. *Faculty research:* Health behaviors; caregivers; psychiatric services; disabilities; population health. *Unit head:* Dr. Mona Shattell, Chairperson, 312-942-7117, E-mail: mona_shattell@rush.edu. *Application contact:* Jennifer Thorndyke, Director of Admissions, 312-563-7526, E-mail: jennifer_thorndyke@rush.edu.
Website: https://www.rushu.rush.edu/college-nursing/departments-college-nursing/department-community-systems-and-mental-health-nursing

San Francisco State University, Division of Graduate Studies, College of Health and Social Sciences, School of Nursing, San Francisco, CA 94132-1722. Offers adult acute care (MS); clinical nurse specialist (MS); community/public health nursing (MS); family nurse practitioner (Certificate); nursing administration (MS); pediatrics (MS); women's health (MS). *Accreditation:* AACN. *Program availability:* Part-time. *Application deadline:* Applications are processed on a rolling basis. *Financial support:* Career-related internships or fieldwork available. *Unit head:* Connie Carr, Assistant Director of Graduate Programs, 415-338-6856, Fax: 415-338-0555, E-mail: ccarr@sfsu.edu.
Website: http://nursing.sfsu.edu

University of Hartford, College of Education, Nursing, and Health Professions, Program in Nursing, West Hartford, CT 06117-1599. Offers community/public health nursing (MSN); nursing education (MSN); nursing management (MSN). *Accreditation:* AACN. *Program availability:* Part-time, evening/weekend. *Degree requirements:* For master's, research project. *Entrance requirements:* For master's, BSN, Connecticut RN license. Additional exam requirements/recommendations for international students: Required—TOEFL (minimum score 550 paper-based). Electronic applications accepted. *Expenses:* Contact institution. *Faculty research:* Child development, women in doctoral study, applying feminist theory in teaching methods, near death experience, grandmothers as primary care providers.

University of Hawaii at Manoa, Office of Graduate Education, School of Nursing and Dental Hygiene, Honolulu, HI 96822. Offers clinical nurse specialist (MS), including adult health, community mental health; nurse practitioner (MS), including adult health, community mental health, family nurse practitioner; nursing (PhD, Graduate Certificate); nursing administration (MS). *Accreditation:* AACN. *Program availability:* Part-time, online learning. *Degree requirements:* For master's, thesis optional; for doctorate, comprehensive exam, thesis/dissertation. *Entrance requirements:* For master's, Hawaii RN license. Additional exam requirements/recommendations for international students: Required—TOEFL (minimum score 580 paper-based; 92 iBT), IELTS (minimum score 5). *Expenses:* Contact institution.

University of Illinois at Chicago, College of Nursing, Program in Nursing, Chicago, IL 60607-7128. Offers acute care clinical nurse specialist (MS); administrative nursing leadership (Certificate); adult nurse practitioner (MS); adult/geriatric nurse practitioner (MS); advanced community health nurse specialist (MS); family nurse practitioner (MS); geriatric clinical nurse specialist (MS); geriatric nurse practitioner (MS); nurse midwifery (MS); occupational health/advanced community health nurse specialist (MS); occupational health/family nurse practitioner (MS); pediatric nurse practitioner (MS); perinatal clinical nurse specialist (MS); school/advanced community health nurse specialist (MS); school/family nurse practitioner (MS); women's health nurse practitioner (MS). *Accreditation:* AACN. *Program availability:* Part-time. *Degree requirements:* For master's, thesis or alternative. *Entrance requirements:* For master's, GRE General Test, minimum GPA of 2.75. Additional exam requirements/recommendations for international students: Required—TOEFL. Electronic applications accepted.

The University of Kansas, University of Kansas Medical Center, School of Nursing, Kansas City, KS 66160. Offers adult/gerontological clinical nurse specialist (PMC); adult/gerontological nurse practitioner (PMC); health care informatics (PMC); health professions educator (PMC); nurse midwife (PMC); nursing (MS, DNP, PhD); organizational leadership (PMC); psychiatric/mental health nurse practitioner (PMC); public health nursing (PMC). *Accreditation:* AACN; ACNM/ACME. *Program availability:* Part-time, 100% online, blended/hybrid learning. *Faculty:* 56. *Students:* 48 full-time (44 women), 260 part-time (235 women); includes 50 minority (12 Black or African American, non-Hispanic/Latino; 2 American Indian or Alaska Native, non-Hispanic/Latino; 16 Asian, non-Hispanic/Latino; 8 Hispanic/Latino; 12 Two or more races, non-Hispanic/Latino). Average age 36. 87 applicants, 95% accepted, 61 enrolled. In 2017, 37 master's, 18 doctorates, 3 other advanced degrees awarded. Terminal master's awarded for partial completion of doctoral program. *Degree requirements:* For master's, comprehensive exam, thesis (for some programs), general oral exam; for doctorate, thesis/dissertation or alternative, comprehensive oral exam (for DNP); comprehensive written and oral exam, or three publications (for PhD). *Entrance requirements:* For master's, bachelor's degree in nursing, minimum GPA of 3.0, 1 year of clinical experience, RN license in KS and MO; for doctorate, GRE General Test (for PhD only), bachelor's degree in nursing, minimum GPA of 3.5, RN license in KS and MO. Additional exam requirements/recommendations for international students: Required—TOEFL. *Application deadline:* For fall admission, 4/1 for domestic and international students; for spring admission, 9/1 for domestic and international students. Application fee: $75. Electronic applications accepted. *Financial support:* In 2017–18, 5 research assistantships with tuition reimbursements (averaging $20,000 per year), 30 teaching assistantships with tuition reimbursements (averaging $20,000 per year) were awarded; scholarships/grants and traineeships also available. Financial award application deadline: 3/1; financial award applicants required to submit FAFSA. *Faculty research:* Breastfeeding practices of teen mothers, national database of nursing quality indicators, caregiving of families of patients using technology in the home, simulation in nursing education, diaphragm fatigue. *Total annual research expenditures:* $1.4 million. *Unit head:* Dr. Sally Maliski, Dean, 913-588-1601, Fax: 913-588-1660, E-mail: smaliski@kumc.edu. *Application contact:* Dr. Pamela K. Barnes, Associate Dean, Student Affairs, 913-588-1619, Fax: 913-588-1615, E-mail: pbarnes2@kumc.edu.
Website: http://nursing.kumc.edu

University of Maryland, Baltimore, School of Nursing, Baltimore, MD 21201. Offers adult-gerontology acute care nurse practitioner (DNP); adult-gerontology primary care nurse practitioner (DNP); clinical nurse leader (MS); community/public health nursing (MS); family nurse practitioner (DNP); global health (Postbaccalaureate Certificate); health services leadership and management (MS); neonatal nurse practitioner (DNP); nurse anesthesia (DNP); nursing (PhD); nursing informatics (MS, Postbaccalaureate Certificate); pediatric acute/primary care nurse practitioner (DNP); psychiatric mental health nurse practitioner (DNP); teaching in nursing and health professions (Postbaccalaureate Certificate); MS/MBA. MS/MBA offered jointly with University of Baltimore. *Program availability:* Part-time. *Faculty:* 130 full-time (117 women), 125 part-time/adjunct (114 women). *Students:* 504 full-time (442 women), 532 part-time (482 women); includes 443 minority (249 Black or African American, non-Hispanic/Latino; 1 American Indian or Alaska Native, non-Hispanic/Latino; 115 Asian, non-Hispanic/Latino; 48 Hispanic/Latino; 2 Native Hawaiian or other Pacific Islander, non-Hispanic/Latino; 28 Two or more races, non-Hispanic/Latino), 15 international. Average age 33. 935 applicants, 62% accepted, 394 enrolled. In 2017, 182 master's, 57 doctorates awarded. *Degree requirements:* For master's and Postbaccalaureate Certificate, thesis (for some programs); for doctorate, comprehensive exam, thesis/dissertation. *Entrance requirements:* Additional exam requirements/recommendations for international students: Required—TOEFL (minimum score 550 paper-based; 79 iBT); Recommended—IELTS (minimum score 7). *Application deadline:* For fall admission, 11/1 for domestic and international students; for spring admission, 8/1 for domestic and international students. Application fee: $75. Electronic applications accepted. *Expenses:* Contact institution. *Financial support:* In 2017–18, 22 research assistantships with full and partial tuition reimbursements (averaging $21,523 per year), 41 teaching assistantships with full and partial tuition reimbursements (averaging $13,439 per year) were awarded; fellowships and scholarships/grants also available. Financial award application deadline: 3/1; financial award applicants required to submit FAFSA. *Unit head:* Dr. Jane Kirschling, Dean, 410-706-4359, E-mail: kirschling@umaryland.edu. *Application contact:* Larry Fillian, Associate Dean of Student and Academic Services, 410-706-6298, E-mail: lfillian@umaryland.edu.
Website: http://www.nursing.umaryland.edu/

University of Massachusetts Amherst, Graduate School, College of Nursing, Amherst, MA 01003. Offers adult gerontology primary care nurse practitioner (DNP); clinical nurse leader (MS); family nurse practitioner (DNP); nursing (PhD); public health nurse leader (DNP). *Accreditation:* AACN. *Program availability:* Part-time, online learning. Terminal master's awarded for partial completion of doctoral program. *Degree requirements:* For master's, thesis optional; for doctorate, comprehensive exam, thesis/dissertation. *Entrance requirements:* Additional exam requirements/recommendations for international students: Required—TOEFL (minimum score 550 paper-based; 80 iBT), IELTS (minimum score 6.5). Electronic applications accepted. *Faculty research:* Health of older adults and their caretakers, mental health of individuals and families, health of children and adolescents, power and decision-making, transcultural health.

University of Massachusetts Dartmouth, Graduate School, College of Nursing, North Dartmouth, MA 02747-2300. Offers MS, DNP, PhD. *Accreditation:* AACN. *Program availability:* Part-time, 100% online, blended/hybrid learning. *Faculty:* 32 full-time (all women), 37 part-time/adjunct (36 women). *Students:* 112 part-time (100 women); includes 21 minority (12 Black or African American, non-Hispanic/Latino; 4 Asian, non-Hispanic/Latino; 4 Hispanic/Latino; 1 Two or more races, non-Hispanic/Latino). Average age 38. 51 applicants, 94% accepted, 37 enrolled. In 2017, 5 master's, 17 doctorates awarded. Terminal master's awarded for partial completion of doctoral program. *Degree requirements:* For master's, capstone project; for doctorate, project (for DNP); dissertation (for PhD). *Entrance requirements:* For master's, statement of purpose (minimum of 300 words), resume, 2 letters of recommendation, official transcripts, copy of RN license or license number; for doctorate, statement of purpose (minimum of 300 words), resume, 3 letters of recommendation, official transcripts, copy of RN license, minimum 10-page scholarly writing sample (for PhD program only). Additional exam requirements/recommendations for international students: Required—TOEFL (minimum score 533 paper-based; 72 iBT), IELTS (minimum score 6). *Application deadline:* For fall admission, 2/15 priority date for domestic students, 1/15 priority date for international students. Application fee: $60. Electronic applications accepted. *Expenses:* Tuition, state resident: full-time $15,449; part-time $643.71 per credit. Tuition, nonresident: full-time $27,880; part-time $1161.67 per credit. *Required fees:* $405; $25.88 per credit. Tuition and fees vary according to course load and reciprocity agreements. *Financial support:* In 2017–18, 1 fellowship (averaging $24,000 per year), 10 teaching assistantships (averaging $9,801 per year) were awarded; tuition waivers (full and partial) also available. Support available to part-time students. Financial award application deadline: 3/1; financial award applicants required to submit FAFSA. *Faculty research:* Disparities in health/healthcare, global community health, vulnerable populations, chronic illness, symptom management, living with traumatic spinal cord injury, nursing theory, symptom clusters in SCI, Family caregivers, nursing philosophy, chronic cardiac illness, self-care, health disparities. *Total annual research expenditures:* $143,000. *Unit head:* June Horowitz, Associate Dean for Graduate Programs and Research, 508-910-6487, E-mail: jhorowitz@umassd.edu. *Application contact:* Steven Briggs, Director of Marketing and Recruitment for Graduate Studies, 508-999-8604, Fax: 508-999-8183, E-mail: graduate@umassd.edu.
Website: http://www.umassd.edu/nursing/

University of North Dakota, Graduate School, College of Nursing and Professional Disciplines, Department of Nursing, Grand Forks, ND 58202. Offers adult-gerontological nurse practitioner (MS); advanced public health nurse (MS); family nurse practitioner (MS); nurse anesthesia (MS); nurse educator (MS); nursing (PhD, Post-Master's Certificate); nursing practice (DNP); psychiatric and mental health nurse practitioner (MS).

University of Puerto Rico–Medical Sciences Campus, School of Nursing, San Juan, PR 00936-5067. Offers adult and elderly nursing (MSN); child and adolescent nursing (MSN); critical care nursing (MSN); family and community nursing (MSN); family nurse practitioner (MSN); maternity nursing (MSN); mental health and psychiatric nursing (MSN). *Accreditation:* AACN; AANA/CANAEP. *Entrance requirements:* For master's, GRE or EXADEP, interview, Puerto Rico RN license or professional license for international students, general and specific point average, article analysis. Electronic applications accepted. *Faculty research:* HIV, health disparities, teen violence, women and violence, neurological disorders.

University of South Carolina, The Graduate School, College of Nursing, Program in Health Nursing, Columbia, SC 29208. Offers adult nurse practitioner (MSN); community/public health clinical nurse specialist (MSN); family nurse practitioner (MSN); pediatric nurse practitioner (MSN). *Accreditation:* AACN. *Program availability:* Part-time. *Degree requirements:* For master's, thesis or alternative. *Entrance requirements:* For master's, GRE General Test or MAT, BS in nursing, nursing license. Additional exam requirements/recommendations for international students: Required—TOEFL (minimum score 570 paper-based). Electronic applications accepted. *Faculty research:* System research, evidence based practice, breast cancer, violence.

University of South Carolina, The Graduate School, College of Nursing, Program in Nursing and Public Health, Columbia, SC 29208. Offers MPH/MSN. *Accreditation:* AACN; CEPH. *Program availability:* Part-time. *Entrance requirements:* Additional exam requirements/recommendations for international students: Required—TOEFL (minimum score 570 paper-based). Electronic applications accepted. *Faculty research:* System research, evidence based practice, breast cancer, violence.

The University of Texas at Austin, Graduate School, School of Nursing, Austin, TX 78712-1111. Offers adult - gerontology clinical nurse specialist (MSN); child health (MSN), including administration, public health nursing, teaching; family nurse practitioner (MSN); family psychiatric/mental health nurse practitioner (MSN); holistic adult health (MSN), including administration, teaching; maternity (MSN), including administration, public health nursing, teaching; nursing (PhD); nursing administration and healthcare systems management (MSN); nursing practice (DNP); pediatric nurse practitioner (MSN); public health nursing (MSN). *Accreditation:* AACN. *Program availability:* Part-time. *Degree requirements:* For master's, thesis optional; for doctorate, thesis/dissertation. *Entrance requirements:* For master's and doctorate, GRE General Test. Additional exam requirements/recommendations for international students: Required—TOEFL (minimum score 550 paper-based). Electronic applications accepted. *Faculty research:* Chronic illness management, memory and aging, health promotion, women's health, adolescent health.

The University of Texas Health Science Center at San Antonio, School of Nursing, San Antonio, TX 78229-3900. Offers administrative management (MSN); adult-gerontology acute care nurse practitioner (PGC); advanced practice leadership (DNP); clinical nurse leader (MSN); executive administrative management (DNP); family nurse practitioner (MSN, PGC); nursing (MSN, PhD); nursing education (MSN, PGC); pediatric nurse practitioner primary care (PGC); psychiatric mental health nurse practitioner (PGC); public health nurse leader (DNP). *Accreditation:* AACN. *Program availability:* Part-time. Terminal master's awarded for partial completion of doctoral program. *Degree requirements:* For master's, thesis optional; for doctorate, comprehensive exam, thesis/dissertation.

The University of Toledo, College of Graduate Studies, College of Nursing, Department of Population and Community Care, Toledo, OH 43606-3390. Offers clinical nurse leader (MSN); family nurse practitioner (MSN, Certificate); nurse educator (MSN, Certificate); pediatric nurse practitioner (MSN, Certificate). *Program availability:* Part-time. *Degree requirements:* For master's, thesis or alternative. *Entrance requirements:* For master's, GRE, BS in nursing, minimum undergraduate GPA of 3.0, statement of purpose, three letters of recommendation, transcripts from all prior institutions attended, Nursing CAS application, UT supplemental application; for Certificate, BS in nursing, minimum undergraduate GPA of 3.0, statement of purpose, three letters of recommendation, transcripts from all prior institutions attended. Additional exam requirements/recommendations for international students: Required—TOEFL (minimum score 550 paper-based; 80 iBT). Electronic applications accepted.

University of Washington, Tacoma, Graduate Programs, Program in Nursing, Tacoma, WA 98402-3100. Offers communities, populations and health (MN); leadership in healthcare (MN); nurse educator (MN). *Program availability:* Part-time. *Degree requirements:* For master's, thesis (for some programs), advance fieldwork. *Entrance requirements:* For master's, Washington State NCLEX exam, minimum GPA of 3.0. Additional exam requirements/recommendations for international students: Required—TOEFL (minimum score 580 paper-based; 70 iBT); Recommended—IELTS (minimum score 7). *Faculty research:* Hospice and palliative care; clinical trial decision-making; minority nurse retention; asthma and public health; injustice, suffering, difference: Linking Them to Us; adolescent health.

Wayne State University, College of Nursing, Detroit, MI 48202. Offers adult gerontology acute care nurse practitioner (MSN); adult gerontology primary care nurse practitioner (MSN); advanced public health nursing (MSN); infant and mental health (DNP, PhD); neonatal nurse practitioner (MSN); nurse-midwifery (MSN); pediatric acute care nurse practitioner (MSN); pediatric primary care nurse practitioner (MSN); psychiatric mental health nurse practitioner (MSN); women's health nurse practitioner (MSN). Doctoral program admits for fall only. *Accreditation:* AACN. *Program availability:* Part-time. *Faculty:* 30. *Students:* 133 full-time (120 women), 184 part-time (167 women); includes 85 minority (57 Black or African American, non-Hispanic/Latino; 16 Asian, non-Hispanic/Latino; 4 Hispanic/Latino; 8 Two or more races, non-Hispanic/Latino), 22 international. Average age

34. 318 applicants, 39% accepted, 94 enrolled. In 2017, 51 master's, 29 doctorates awarded. *Degree requirements:* For doctorate, thesis/dissertation (for some programs). *Entrance requirements:* For master's, BSN from ACEN- or CCNE-accredited program with minimum GPA of 3.0; three references; current RN license; personal statement; for doctorate, resume or curriculum vitae; goals statement; bachelor's or master's degree in nursing from ACEN- or CCNE-accredited program with minimum GPA of 3.0; current RN license, writing sample and interview (for DNP); reference letters (3 for PhD, 2 for DNP). Additional exam requirements/recommendations for international students: Required—TOEFL (minimum score 101 iBT), TWE (minimum score 6), Michigan English Language Assessment Battery (minimum score 85); Recommended—IELTS (minimum score 7). Application fee: $50. Electronic applications accepted. *Expenses:* Contact institution. *Financial support:* In 2017–18, 92 students received support, including 16 fellowships with tuition reimbursements available (averaging $8,285 per year), 5 teaching assistantships with tuition reimbursements available (averaging $25,000 per year); scholarships/grants, health care benefits, and unspecified assistantships also available. Support available to part-time students. Financial award applicants required to submit FAFSA. *Faculty research:* Bridging transitions and technology to promote asthma care in the community, chronic wound care for persons who injected drugs, decreasing at-risk parenting to reduce child maltreatment and trauma, dementia symptoms (cognition, behavior, function), determining readiness to engage in end of life/palliative care conversations with adolescents and young adults living with advanced cancer, dyspnea assessment and treatment at the end of life. *Unit head:* Dr. Laurie Lauzon Clabo, Dean, College of Nursing, 313-577-4082, E-mail: laurie.lauzon.clabo@wayne.edu. *Application contact:* 313-577-4082, Fax: 313-577-6949, E-mail: nursinginfo@wayne.edu.
Website: http://nursing.wayne.edu/

Worcester State University, Graduate School, Department of Nursing, Program in Community and Public Health Nursing, Worcester, MA 01602-2597. Offers MSN. *Accreditation:* AACN. *Program availability:* Part-time. *Students:* 3 full-time (all women), 34 part-time (30 women); includes 7 minority (5 Black or African American, non-Hispanic/Latino; 1 Hispanic/Latino; 1 Two or more races, non-Hispanic/Latino). Average age 42. 15 applicants, 93% accepted, 9 enrolled. In 2017, 8 master's awarded. *Degree requirements:* For master's, final project, practicum. *Entrance requirements:* For master's, unencumbered license to practice as a Registered Nurse in Massachusetts. Additional exam requirements/recommendations for international students: Required—TOEFL (minimum score 500 paper-based; 79 iBT). *Application deadline:* For fall admission, 6/15 for domestic and international students; for spring admission, 11/1 for domestic and international students; for summer admission, 4/1 for domestic and international students. Applications are processed on a rolling basis. Application fee: $50. Electronic applications accepted. *Expenses:* Tuition, state resident: full-time $3042; part-time $169 per credit hour. Tuition, nonresident: full-time $3042; part-time $169 per credit hour. *Required fees:* $2754; $153 per credit hour. *Financial support:* Career-related internships or fieldwork, scholarships/grants, and unspecified assistantships available. Financial award application deadline: 3/1; financial award applicants required to submit FAFSA. *Unit head:* Dr. Stephanie Chalupka, Coordinator, 508-929-8680, E-mail: schalupka@worcester.edu. *Application contact:* Sara Grady, Associate Dean of Graduate Studies and Professional Development, 508-929-8130, Fax: 508-929-8100, E-mail: sara.grady@worcester.edu.

Family Nurse Practitioner Studies

Albany State University, Darton College of Health Professions, Albany, GA 31705-2717. Offers nursing (MSN), including family nurse practitioner, nurse educator. *Accreditation:* ACEN. *Program availability:* Part-time, evening/weekend, online learning. *Degree requirements:* For master's, comprehensive exam, thesis. *Entrance requirements:* For master's, GRE or MAT, official transcript, letters of recommendation, pre-medical/certificate of immunizations. Electronic applications accepted.

Allen College, Graduate Programs, Waterloo, IA 50703. Offers adult-gerontology acute care nurse practitioner (MSN); community/public health nursing (MSN); education (MSN); family nurse practitioner (MSN); health sciences (Ed D); leadership in health care delivery (MSN); leadership in health care informatics (MSN); nursing (DNP); occupational therapy (MS); psychiatric mental health nurse practitioner (MSN). MSN in leadership in healthcare informatics offered in partnership with University of Minnesota. *Accreditation:* AACN; ACEN. *Program availability:* Part-time, 100% online, blended/hybrid learning. *Faculty:* 24 full-time (all women), 8 part-time/adjunct (7 women). *Students:* 106 full-time (91 women), 187 part-time (164 women); includes 22 minority (12 Black or African American, non-Hispanic/Latino; 1 American Indian or Alaska Native, non-Hispanic/Latino; 2 Asian, non-Hispanic/Latino; 3 Hispanic/Latino; 4 Two or more races, non-Hispanic/Latino), 2 international. Average age 33. 352 applicants, 56% accepted, 131 enrolled. In 2017, 73 master's, 2 doctorates awarded. *Entrance requirements:* For master's, minimum GPA of 3.0 in the last 60 hours of undergraduate coursework; for doctorate, minimum GPA of 3.25 in graduate coursework. *Application deadline:* For fall admission, 2/1 priority date for domestic students; for spring admission, 9/1 priority date for domestic students. Applications are processed on a rolling basis. Application fee: $50. Electronic applications accepted. *Expenses:* $17,860 per year. *Financial support:* In 2017–18, 97 students received support. Federal Work-Study, institutionally sponsored loans, scholarships/grants, and traineeships available. Support available to part-time students. Financial award application deadline: 8/1; financial award applicants required to submit FAFSA. *Faculty research:* Poverty. *Unit head:* Dr. Nancy Kramer, Vice Chancellor for Academic Affairs, 319-226-2040, Fax: 319-226-2070, E-mail: nancy.kramer@allencollege.edu. *Application contact:* Molly Quinn, Director of Admissions, 319-226-2001, Fax: 319-226-2010, E-mail: molly.quinn@allencollege.edu.
Website: http://www.allencollege.edu/

Alvernia University, School of Graduate Studies, Department of Nursing, Reading, PA 19607-1799. Offers adult gerontology nurse practitioner (DNP); family nurse practitioner (DNP); nursing education (MSN); nursing leadership (Graduate Certificate); nursing leadership and healthcare administration (MSN).

Alverno College, JoAnn McGrath School of Nursing and Health Professions, Milwaukee, WI 53234-3922. Offers clinical nurse specialist (MSN); family nurse practitioner (MSN); nursing practice (DNP); psychiatric mental health nurse practitioner (MSN). *Accreditation:* AACN. *Program availability:* Part-time, evening/weekend. *Faculty:* 10 full-time (all women), 7 part-time/adjunct (4 women). *Students:* 119 full-time (107 women), 103 part-time (101 women); includes 53 minority (22 Black or African American, non-Hispanic/Latino; 1 American Indian or Alaska Native, non-Hispanic/Latino; 11 Asian, non-Hispanic/Latino; 15 Hispanic/Latino; 4 Two or more races, non-Hispanic/Latino), 1 international. Average age 35. 80 applicants, 99% accepted, 56 enrolled. In 2017, 47 master's awarded. *Degree requirements:* For master's, 500 clinical hours, capstone; for doctorate, 1,000 post-BSN clinical hours. *Entrance requirements:* For master's, BSN, current license; for doctorate, MSN, nursing license. Additional exam requirements/recommendations for international students: Required—TOEFL. *Application deadline:* For fall admission, 7/15 priority date for domestic and international students; for spring admission, 12/15 priority date for domestic and international students. Applications are processed on a rolling basis. Application fee: $0. Electronic applications accepted. *Expenses:* Contact institution. *Financial support:* Federal Work-Study and scholarships/grants available. Support available to part-time students. Financial award applicants required to submit FAFSA. *Faculty research:* International practicum experience and impact on future practice decision-making of family nurse practitioners; comparative health policy; improvement of HPV vaccination rates; use of language/words by healthcare practitioners and their effect on health outcomes. *Unit head:* Margaret Rauschenberger, Dean, 414-382-6276, Fax: 414-382-6354, E-mail: margaret.rauschenberger@alverno.edu. *Application contact:* Karin Wasiullah, Associate Dean, Master of Science in Nursing, 414-382-6275, Fax: 414-382-6354, E-mail: karin.wasiullah@alverno.edu.
Website: http://www.alverno.edu/academics/academicdepartments/joannmcgrathschoolofnursing/

American International College, School of Health Sciences, Springfield, MA 01109-3189. Offers exercise science (MS); family nurse practitioner (MSN, Post-Master's Certificate); nursing administrator (MSN); nursing educator (MSN); occupational therapy (MSOT, OTD); physical therapy (DPT). *Program availability:* Part-time, 100% online. *Faculty:* 14 full-time (13 women), 10 part-time/adjunct (all women). *Students:* 286 full-time (220 women), 11 part-time (9 women); includes 75 minority (30 Black or African American, non-Hispanic/Latino; 21 Asian, non-Hispanic/Latino; 19 Hispanic/Latino; 5 Two or more races, non-Hispanic/Latino), 2 international. Average age 27. 652 applicants, 49% accepted, 109 enrolled. In 2017, 48 master's, 28 doctorates, 2 other advanced degrees awarded. *Degree requirements:* For master's, practicum; for doctorate, thesis/dissertation, practicum. *Entrance requirements:* For master's, 3 letters of recommendation, personal goal statement; minimum GPA of 3.2, interview, BS or BA, and 2 clinical PT observations (for DPT); minimum GPA of 3.0, MSOT, OT licensen, and 2 clinical OT observations (for OTD); for doctorate, personal goal statement, 2 letters of recommendation; minimum GPA of 3.0, BS or BA, 2 clinical OT observations (for MSOT); RN license and minimum GPA of 3.0 (for MSN). Additional exam requirements/recommendations for international students: Required—TOEFL (minimum score 577 paper-based; 91 iBT). *Application deadline:* For fall admission, 12/1 priority date for domestic and international students; for spring admission, 11/15 priority date for domestic and international students. Application fee: $50. Electronic applications accepted. *Expenses:* Contact institution. *Faculty research:* Teaching simulation, ergonomics, orthopedics, use of social media in health care. *Unit head:* Dr. Cesarina Thompson, Dean, 413-205-3056, Fax: 413-654-1430, E-mail: cesarina.thompson@aic.edu. *Application contact:* Kerry Barnes, Director of Graduate Admissions, 413-205-3703, Fax: 413-205-3051, E-mail: kerry.barnes@aic.edu.
Website: http://www.aic.edu/academics/hs

Anderson University, College of Health Professions, Anderson, SC 29621-4035. Offers advanced practice (DNP); executive leadership (MSN, DNP); family nurse practitioner (MSN, DNP); nurse educator (MSN); psychiatric mental health nurse practitioner (MSN, DNP). *Program availability:* Online learning. *Expenses: Tuition:* Full-time $24,290; part-time $650 per credit hour. Full-time tuition and fees vary according to degree level and program. *Unit head:* Dr. Donald M. Peace, Dean, 864-231-5513, E-mail: dpeace@andersonuniversity.edu. *Application contact:* Chris Woodlief, Associate Director of Adult and Graduate Programs, 864-231-5531, E-mail: cwoodlief@andersonuniversity.edu.
Website: http://www.andersonuniversity.edu/health-professions

Angelo State University, College of Graduate Studies and Research, Archer College of Health and Human Services, Department of Nursing, San Angelo, TX 76909. Offers family nurse practitioner (MSN); nurse educator (MSN). *Accreditation:* AACN; ACEN. *Program availability:* Part-time, evening/weekend, online learning. *Students:* 35 full-time (28 women), 55 part-time (49 women); includes 26 minority (4 Black or African American, non-Hispanic/Latino; 2 Asian, non-Hispanic/Latino; 18 Hispanic/Latino; 2 Two or more races, non-Hispanic/Latino). Average age 34. *Degree requirements:* For master's, comprehensive exam. *Entrance requirements:* For master's, essay, three letters of recommendation. Additional exam requirements/recommendations for international students: Required—TOEFL or IELTS. *Application deadline:* For fall admission, 4/1 priority date for domestic students, 6/10 for international students; for spring admission, 9/1 priority date for domestic students, 11/1 for international students. Applications are processed on a rolling basis. Application fee: $40 ($50 for international students). Electronic applications accepted. *Expenses:* Tuition, state resident: full-time $3856. Tuition, nonresident: full-time $11,324. *Required fees:* $2650. *Financial support:* Research assistantships, career-related internships or fieldwork, Federal Work-Study, and scholarships/grants available. Support available to part-time students. Financial award application deadline: 3/1. *Unit head:* Dr. Wrennah L. Gabbert, Chair, 325-942-2224, Fax: 325-942-2236, E-mail: wrennah.gabbert@angelo.edu. *Application contact:* Dr. Molly J. Walker, Graduate Advisor, 325-486-6872, Fax: 325-942-2236, E-mail: molly.walker@angelo.edu.
Website: http://www.angelo.edu/dept/nursing/

Arizona State University at the Tempe campus, College of Nursing and Health Innovation, Phoenix, AZ 85004. Offers advanced nursing practice (DNP); clinical research management (MS); community and public health practice (Graduate Certificate); family mental health nurse practitioner (Graduate Certificate); family nurse practitioner (Graduate Certificate); geriatric nursing (Graduate Certificate); healthcare innovation (MHI); nurse education in academic and practice settings (Graduate Certificate); nurse educator (MS); nursing and healthcare innovation (PhD). *Accreditation:* AACN. *Program availability:* Online learning. *Degree requirements:* For master's, comprehensive exam (for some programs), thesis (for some programs), interactive Program of Study (iPOS) submitted before completing 50 percent of required credit hours; for doctorate, comprehensive exam, thesis/dissertation, interactive Program of Study (iPOS) submitted before completing 50 percent of required credit hours. *Entrance requirements:* For master's and doctorate, GRE, minimum GPA of 3.0 or equivalent in last 2 years of work leading to bachelor's degree. Additional exam requirements/recommendations for international students: Required—TOEFL, IELTS, or PTE. Electronic applications accepted. *Expenses:* Contact institution.

Ashland University, Dwight Schar College of Nursing and Health Sciences, Department of Nursing, Ashland, OH 44805-3702. Offers family nurse practitioner (DNP). *Entrance requirements:* For doctorate, minimum GPA of 3.0, one year of clinical practice experience, 2-3 page paper, undergraduate- or graduate-level statistics course, interview. Additional exam requirements/recommendations for international students: Recommended—TOEFL, IELTS, TSE. *Application deadline:* Applications are processed on a rolling basis. Electronic applications accepted. *Expenses: Tuition:* Full-time $9621; part-time $4707 per credit hour. *Required fees:* $15 per semester. *Unit head:* Dr. Juanita Reese Kline, Chair, 419-521-6811, E-mail: jkline6@ashland.edu. *Application contact:* Bernie Bannin, Director, Graduate, Online, and Adult Admissions, 419-289-5291, E-mail: grad-admissions@ashland.edu.
Website: http://www.ashland.edu/conhs/nursing

Auburn University at Montgomery, College of Nursing and Health Sciences, Montgomery, AL 36124-4023. Offers family nurse practitioner (MSN); nurse educator for interprofessional practice (MSN). Programs offered jointly with Auburn University. *Accreditation:* AACN. *Students:* 23 full-time (14 women), 19 part-time (9 women); includes 10 minority (9 Black or African American, non-Hispanic/Latino; 1 Hispanic/ Latino), 2 international. *Entrance requirements:* Additional exam requirements/ recommendations for international students: Recommended—TOEFL (minimum score 500 paper-based; 61 iBT), IELTS (minimum score 5.5), TSE (minimum score 44). *Application deadline:* For fall admission, 7/1 for domestic students; for spring admission, 10/1 for domestic students; for summer admission, 3/1 for domestic students. Applications are processed on a rolling basis. Application fee: $25 ($0 for international students). Electronic applications accepted. *Expenses:* Tuition, state resident: full-time $6930; part-time $385 per credit hour. Tuition, nonresident: full-time $15,588; part-time $866 per credit hour. *Required fees:* $640. *Unit head:* Dr. Jean Leuner, Dean, 334-244-3658, E-mail: jleuner@aum.edu. *Application contact:* Dr. Barbara Wilder, Graduate Program Director, 334-844-6766, E-mail: wildebf@auburn.edu.
Website: http://conhs.aum.edu/

Augsburg University, Programs in Nursing, Minneapolis, MN 55454-1351. Offers MA, DNP. *Accreditation:* AACN. *Degree requirements:* For master's, thesis or alternative.

Augusta University, College of Nursing, Doctor of Nursing Practice Program, Augusta, GA 30912. Offers adult gerontology acute care nurse practitioner (DNP); family nurse practitioner (DNP); nurse executive (DNP); nursing (DNP); nursing anesthesia (DNP); pediatric nurse practitioner (DNP); psychiatric mental health nurse practitioner (DNP). *Accreditation:* AACN; AANA/CANAEP. *Degree requirements:* For doctorate, thesis/ dissertation or alternative. *Entrance requirements:* For doctorate, GRE General Test or MAT, master's degree in nursing or related field, current professional nurse licensure. Additional exam requirements/recommendations for international students: Required—TOEFL (minimum score 600 paper-based; 100 iBT). Electronic applications accepted.

Austin Peay State University, College of Graduate Studies, College of Behavioral and Health Sciences, School of Nursing, Clarksville, TN 37044. Offers family nurse practitioner (MSN); nursing administration (MSN); nursing education (MSN); nursing informatics (MSN). *Program availability:* Part-time, online learning. *Faculty:* 8 full-time (all women), 8 part-time/adjunct (all women). *Students:* 12 full-time (11 women), 139 part-time (128 women); includes 19 minority (11 Black or African American, non-Hispanic/Latino; 1 Asian, non-Hispanic/Latino; 5 Hispanic/Latino; 2 Two or more races, non-Hispanic/Latino). Average age 35. 36 applicants, 86% accepted, 20 enrolled. In 2017, 67 master's awarded. *Degree requirements:* For master's, comprehensive exam. *Entrance requirements:* For master's, minimum GPA of 3.0, RN license eligibility, 3 letters of recommendation. Additional exam requirements/recommendations for international students: Required—TOEFL (minimum score 500 paper-based). *Application deadline:* For fall admission, 8/8 priority date for domestic students. Applications are processed on a rolling basis. Application fee: $45 ($55 for international students). Electronic applications accepted. *Expenses:* Tuition, state resident: full-time $7686; part-time $427 per credit hour. Tuition, nonresident: full-time $20,268; part-time $1126 per credit hour. *Required fees:* $1529; $76.45 per credit hour. *Financial support:* Research assistantships with full tuition reimbursements, career-related internships or fieldwork, Federal Work-Study, institutionally sponsored loans, scholarships/grants, and unspecified assistantships available. Support available to part-time students. Financial award application deadline: 4/1; financial award applicants required to submit FAFSA. *Unit head:* Dr. Rebecca Corvey, Director of Nursing, 931-221-7710, Fax: 931-221-7595, E-mail: corveyr@apsu.edu. *Application contact:* Megan Mitchell, Coordinator of Graduate Admissions, 931-221-6189, Fax: 931-221-7641, E-mail: mitchellm@apsu.edu.
Website: http://www.apsu.edu/nursing

Azusa Pacific University, School of Nursing, Azusa, CA 91702-7000. Offers adult clinical nurse specialist (MSN); adult-gerontology nurse practitioner (MSN); family nurse practitioner (MSN); healthcare administration and leadership (MSN); nursing (MSN, DNP, PhD); nursing education (MSN); parent-child clinical nurse specialist (MSN); psychiatric mental health nurse practitioner (MSN). *Accreditation:* AACN. *Program availability:* Part-time, evening/weekend. *Degree requirements:* For master's, thesis optional. *Entrance requirements:* For master's, BSN.

Ball State University, Graduate School, College of Health, School of Nursing, Muncie, IN 47304. Offers adult/gerontology nurse practitioner (Post Master's Certificate); evidence-based clinical practice (Postbaccalaureate Certificate); family nurse practitioner (Post Master's Certificate); nurse educator (Post Master's Certificate); nursing (MS), including family nurse practitioner, nurse administrator, nurse educator; nursing education (Postbaccalaureate Certificate); nursing practice (DNP). *Accreditation:* AACN. *Program availability:* Part-time-only, online only, 100% online. *Faculty:* 10 full-time (all women), 9 part-time/adjunct (all women). *Students:* 9 full-time (8 women), 325 part-time (299 women); includes 26 minority (13 Black or African American, non-Hispanic/Latino; 3 Asian, non-Hispanic/Latino; 7 Hispanic/Latino; 3 Two or more races, non-Hispanic/Latino). Average age 33. 190 applicants, 37% accepted, 66 enrolled. In 2017, 88 master's, 2 doctorates awarded. *Entrance requirements:* For master's, bachelor's degree in nursing, minimum GPA of 3.0, minimum C grade in at least 2 quarter or semester hours in an undergraduate research course, unencumbered license as a registered nurse in state of practice; for doctorate, advanced practice nurse (nurse practitioner, clinical nurse specialist, nurse midwife); master's degree in nursing from accredited program with minimum GPA of 3.2; graduate-level statistics, nursing research, and health assessment courses; unencumbered license as registered nurse in state of practice. Additional exam requirements/recommendations for international students: Required—TOEFL (minimum score 550 paper-based; 79 iBT), IELTS (minimum score 6.5). *Application deadline:* For fall admission, 2/9 for domestic students; for spring admission, 8/9 for domestic students. Applications are processed on a rolling basis. Application fee: $60. Electronic applications accepted. *Expenses:* Contact institution. *Financial support:* Application deadline: 3/1; applicants required to submit FAFSA. *Unit head:* Dr. Linda Siktberg, Director, 765-285-8718, Fax: 765-285-2169, E-mail: lsiktberg@bsu.edu. *Application contact:* Shantelle Estes, Graduate Advisor, 765-285-9130, Fax: 765-285-2169, E-mail: smestes@bsu.edu.
Website: http://www.bsu.edu/nursing/

Barry University, School of Adult and Continuing Education, Division of Nursing, Program in Nurse Practitioner, Miami Shores, FL 33161-6695. Offers acute care nurse practitioner (MSN); family nurse practitioner (MSN); nurse practitioner (Certificate). *Accreditation:* AACN. *Program availability:* Part-time, evening/weekend. *Degree requirements:* For master's, research project or thesis. *Entrance requirements:* For master's, GRE General Test or MAT, BSN, minimum GPA of 3.0, course work in statistics. Electronic applications accepted. *Faculty research:* Child abuse, health beliefs, teenage pregnancy, cultural and clinical studies across the lifespan.

Baylor University, Graduate School, Louise Herrington School of Nursing, Dallas, TX 76798. Offers family nurse practitioner (MSN); neonatal nurse practitioner (MSN); nurse-midwifery (DNP). *Accreditation:* AACN. *Program availability:* Part-time, online learning. *Faculty:* 11 full-time (all women), 3 part-time/adjunct (2 women). *Students:* 35 full-time (34 women), 11 part-time (all women); includes 21 minority (5 Black or African American, non-Hispanic/Latino; 1 American Indian or Alaska Native, non-Hispanic/ Latino; 5 Asian, non-Hispanic/Latino; 8 Hispanic/Latino; 2 Two or more races, non-Hispanic/Latino). Average age 35. 47 applicants, 70% accepted, 26 enrolled. In 2017, 13 master's, 4 doctorates awarded. *Degree requirements:* For doctorate, comprehensive exam (for some programs), capstone project. *Entrance requirements:* For master's, GRE General Test or MAT; for doctorate, GRE General Test. Additional exam requirements/recommendations for international students: Required—TOEFL. *Application deadline:* For fall admission, 2/1 for domestic students. Application fee: $50. Electronic applications accepted. *Financial support:* In 2017–18, 66 students received support. Teaching assistantships, Federal Work-Study, scholarships/grants, and unspecified assistantships available. Support available to part-time students. Financial award application deadline: 6/30; financial award applicants required to submit FAFSA. *Faculty research:* Women and strokes, obesity and pregnancy, educational environmental factors, international undeserved populations, midwifery. *Total annual research expenditures:* $5,000. *Unit head:* Dr. Barbara Camune, Graduate Program Director, 214-367-3754, Fax: 214-820-3375, E-mail: barbara_camune@baylor.edu. *Application contact:* Elaine Lark, Coordinator of Recruitment and Enrollment, 214-818-7839, Fax: 214-820-3835, E-mail: elaine_lark@baylor.edu.
Website: http://www.baylor.edu/nursing/

Bellarmine University, College of Health Professions, Donna and Allan Lansing School of Nursing and Clinical Sciences, Louisville, KY 40205. Offers family nurse practitioner (MSN); health science (MHS); nursing administration (MSN); nursing education (MSN); nursing practice (DNP). *Accreditation:* AACN; APTA. *Program availability:* Part-time, evening/weekend. *Faculty:* 20 full-time (17 women), 7 part-time/adjunct (6 women). *Students:* 10 full-time (6 women), 101 part-time (89 women); includes 10 minority (5 Black or African American, non-Hispanic/Latino; 2 Asian, non-Hispanic/Latino; 1 Hispanic/Latino; 2 Two or more races, non-Hispanic/Latino), 1 international. Average age 34. In 2017, 42 master's, 5 doctorates awarded. *Degree requirements:* For master's, comprehensive exam, thesis (for some programs); for doctorate, comprehensive exam, thesis/dissertation. *Entrance requirements:* For master's, GRE General Test, minimum GPA of 3.0, interview, resume; BSN from CCNE- or ACEN-accredited program, professional references, goal statement, and RN license (for MSN); bachelor's degree with exposure to health issues and grade of C or better in math/ science courses (for MHS); for doctorate, GRE General Test, MSN from CCNE- or ACEN-accredited program; minimum GPA of 3.5 in graduate coursework; professional references; goal statement; current curriculum vitae or resume; RN license; verification of post-baccalaureate clinical and practice hours. Additional exam requirements/ recommendations for international students: Required—TOEFL (minimum iBT score of 83, 26 on speaking test), IELTS (minimum score 7, speaking band score of 8), or language training at an approved center. *Application deadline:* Applications are processed on a rolling basis. Application fee: $40. Electronic applications accepted. *Expenses:* Contact institution. *Financial support:* Career-related internships or fieldwork and scholarships/grants available. Financial award applicants required to submit FAFSA. *Faculty research:* Nursing: pain, empathy, leadership styles, control; physical therapy: service-learning; exercise in chronic and pre-operative conditions, athletes; women's health; aging. *Unit head:* Dr. Nancy York, Dean, 502-272-8639, E-mail: nyork@bellarmine.edu. *Application contact:* Julie Armstrong-Binnix, Health Science Recruiter, 800-274-4723 Ext. 8364, E-mail: julieab@bellarmine.edu.
Website: http://www.bellarmine.edu/lansing

Bellin College, School of Nursing, Green Bay, WI 54305. Offers family nurse practitioner (MSN); nurse educator (MSN). *Accreditation:* AACN. *Faculty:* 10 part-time/ adjunct (all women). *Students:* 13 full-time (12 women), 29 part-time (27 women). *Expenses: Tuition:* Part-time $728 per credit. *Unit head:* Dr. Amber B. Carriveau, Graduate Program Director, 920-433-6694, Fax: 920-433-1921, E-mail: amber.carriveau@bellincollege.edu.

Binghamton University, State University of New York, Graduate School, Decker School of Nursing, Binghamton, NY 13902-6000. Offers adult-gerontological nursing (MS, DNP, Certificate); community health nursing (MS, DNP, Certificate); family health nursing (MS, DNP, Certificate); family psychiatric mental health nursing (MS, DNP, Certificate); nursing (PhD). *Accreditation:* AACN. *Program availability:* Part-time, evening/weekend. *Faculty:* 52 full-time (45 women). *Students:* 94 full-time (79 women), 109 part-time (94 women); includes 43 minority (21 Black or African American, non-Hispanic/Latino; 10 Asian, non-Hispanic/Latino; 7 Hispanic/Latino; 5 Two or more races, non-Hispanic/Latino), 13 international. Average age 36. 111 applicants, 95% accepted, 63 enrolled. In 2017, 53 master's, 5 doctorates, 20 other advanced degrees awarded. Terminal master's awarded for partial completion of doctoral program. *Degree requirements:* For master's, comprehensive exam, thesis; for doctorate, comprehensive exam (for some programs), thesis/dissertation. *Entrance requirements:* For master's and doctorate, GRE General Test, nursing licensure. Additional exam requirements/ recommendations for international students: Required—TOEFL (minimum score 90 iBT). Application fee: $75. Electronic applications accepted. *Expenses:* Contact institution. *Financial support:* In 2017–18, 33 students received support, including 1 fellowship with partial tuition reimbursement available (averaging $16,500 per year), research assistantships with full tuition reimbursements available (averaging $12,500 per year), 1 teaching assistantship with full tuition reimbursement available (averaging $16,500 per year); career-related internships or fieldwork, Federal Work-Study, institutionally sponsored loans, traineeships, health care benefits, tuition waivers (full and partial), and unspecified assistantships also available. Financial award applicants required to submit FAFSA. *Unit head:* Dr. Mario R. Ortiz, Dean, 607-777-2311, E-mail: mortiz@binghamton.edu. *Application contact:* Ben Balkaya, Assistant Dean and Director, 607-777-2151, Fax: 607-777-2501, E-mail: balkaya@binghamton.edu.
Website: http://www.binghamton.edu/dson/

Bloomsburg University of Pennsylvania, School of Graduate Studies, College of Science and Technology, Department of Nursing, Bloomsburg, PA 17815-1301. Offers adult and family nurse practitioner (MSN); community health (MSN); nurse anesthesia (MSN); nursing (MSN, DNP); nursing administration (MSN). *Accreditation:* AACN. *Degree requirements:* For master's, thesis (for some programs), clinical experience. *Entrance requirements:* For master's, minimum QPA of 3.0, personal statement, 2 letters of recommendation, nursing license. Additional exam requirements/ recommendations for international students: Required—TOEFL, IELTS. Electronic applications accepted. *Expenses:* Contact institution.

Bowie State University, Graduate Programs, Department of Nursing, Bowie, MD 20715-9465. Offers administration of nursing services (MS); family nurse practitioner

(MS); nursing education (MS). *Accreditation:* ACEN. *Program availability:* Part-time. *Faculty:* 7 full-time (4 women), 15 part-time/adjunct (10 women). *Students:* 29 full-time (25 women), 30 part-time (24 women); includes 42 minority (35 Black or African American, non-Hispanic/Latino; 1 Asian, non-Hispanic/Latino; 6 Hispanic/Latino), 8 international. Average age 42. 9 applicants, 89% accepted, 7 enrolled. In 2017, 30 master's awarded. *Degree requirements:* For master's, comprehensive exam, thesis, research paper. *Entrance requirements:* For master's, minimum GPA of 2.5. *Application deadline:* For fall admission, 5/15 for domestic students. Applications are processed on a rolling basis. Application fee: $40. Electronic applications accepted. *Financial support:* Institutionally sponsored loans and traineeships available. Financial award application deadline: 4/1. *Faculty research:* Minority health, women's health, gerontology, leadership management. *Unit head:* Dr. Bonita Jenkins, Acting Chairperson, 301-860-3210, E-mail: mccaskill@bowiestate.edu. *Application contact:* Angela Issac, Information Contact, 301-860-4000.

Bradley University, The Graduate School, College of Education and Health Sciences, Department of Nursing, Peoria, IL 61625-0002. Offers family nurse practitioner (MSN, DNP, Certificate); leadership (DNP); nursing administration (MSN); nursing education (MSN, Certificate). *Accreditation:* AACN; ACEN. *Program availability:* Part-time, evening/weekend. *Degree requirements:* For master's, comprehensive exam, thesis optional. *Entrance requirements:* For master's, GRE General Test or MAT, interview, Illinois RN license, advanced cardiac life support certification, pediatric advanced life support certification, 3 letters of recommendation. Additional exam requirements/recommendations for international students: Required—TOEFL (minimum score 550 paper-based; 79 iBT), IELTS (minimum score 6.5). Electronic applications accepted.

Brenau University, Sydney O. Smith Graduate School, College of Health Sciences, Gainesville, GA 30501. Offers family nurse practitioner (MSN); nurse educator (MSN); nursing management (MSN); occupational therapy (MS); psychology (MS). *Accreditation:* AOTA. *Program availability:* Part-time, evening/weekend. *Degree requirements:* For master's, comprehensive exam (for some programs), thesis (for some programs), clinical practicum hours. *Entrance requirements:* For master's, GRE General Test or MAT (for some programs), interview, writing sample, references (for some programs). Additional exam requirements/recommendations for international students: Required—TOEFL (minimum score 500 paper-based; 61 iBT); Recommended—IELTS (minimum score 5). Electronic applications accepted. *Expenses:* Contact institution.

Brigham Young University, Graduate Studies, College of Nursing, Provo, UT 84602. Offers family nurse practitioner (MS). *Accreditation:* AACN. *Faculty:* 17 full-time (11 women). *Students:* 29 full-time (20 women); includes 1 minority (Hispanic/Latino). Average age 33. 40 applicants, 45% accepted, 14 enrolled. In 2017, 14 master's awarded. *Degree requirements:* For master's, thesis. *Entrance requirements:* For master's, GRE, minimum cumulative undergraduate GPA of 3.0, baccalaureate degree in nursing from school with national nursing accreditation, interview, current RN license in Utah, pathophysiology and statistics classes, 3 letters of recommendation. Additional exam requirements/recommendations for international students: Required—TOEFL (minimum score 580 paper-based; 85 iBT). *Application deadline:* For spring admission, 12/1 for domestic and international students. Application fee: $50. Electronic applications accepted. *Expenses:* Contact institution. *Financial support:* In 2017–18, 27 students received support, including 1 research assistantship (averaging $12,800 per year); teaching assistantships, institutionally sponsored loans, and scholarships/grants also available. Financial award application deadline: 4/13; financial award applicants required to submit FAFSA. *Faculty research:* End-of-life, childhood immunizations, global health nursing, exercise outcomes on health, sexual violence, critical care, diabetes. *Unit head:* Dr. Patricia Ravert, Dean, 801-422-1167, Fax: 801-422-0536, E-mail: patricia_ravert@byu.edu. *Application contact:* Cherie Top, Graduate Secretary, 801-422-4142, Fax: 801-422-0538, E-mail: cherie-top@byu.edu.
Website: http://nursing.byu.edu/

California Baptist University, Program in Nursing, Riverside, CA 92504-3206. Offers clinical nurse specialist (MSN); family nurse practitioner (MSN); healthcare systems management (MSN); teaching-learning (MSN). *Accreditation:* AACN. *Program availability:* Part-time. *Faculty:* 19 full-time (18 women), 12 part-time/adjunct (11 women). *Students:* 78 full-time (59 women), 130 part-time (106 women); includes 114 minority (25 Black or African American, non-Hispanic/Latino; 3 American Indian or Alaska Native, non-Hispanic/Latino; 34 Asian, non-Hispanic/Latino; 47 Hispanic/Latino; 2 Native Hawaiian or other Pacific Islander, non-Hispanic/Latino; 3 Two or more races, non-Hispanic/Latino), 2 international. Average age 32. 25 applicants, 84% accepted, 14 enrolled. In 2017, 49 master's awarded. *Degree requirements:* For master's, comprehensive exam or directed project thesis; capstone practicum. *Entrance requirements:* For master's, GRE or California Critical Thinking Skills Test; Test of Essential Academic Skills (TEAS), minimum undergraduate GPA of 3.0; completion of prerequisite courses with minimum grade of C; CPR certification; background check clearance; health clearance; drug testing; proof of health insurance; proof of motor vehicle insurance; three letters of recommendation; 1000-word essay; interview. Additional exam requirements/recommendations for international students: Required—TOEFL (minimum score 80 iBT). *Application deadline:* For fall admission, 8/1 priority date for domestic students, 7/1 for international students; for spring admission, 12/1 priority date for domestic students, 11/1 for international students. Applications are processed on a rolling basis. Application fee: $45. Electronic applications accepted. *Expenses:* Contact institution. *Financial support:* In 2017–18, 38 students received support. Federal Work-Study and scholarships/grants available. Financial award applicants required to submit CSS PROFILE or FAFSA. *Faculty research:* Qualitative research using Parse methodology, gerontology, disaster preparedness, medical-surgical nursing, maternal-child nursing. *Unit head:* Dr. Geneva Oaks, Dean, School of Nursing, 951-343-4702, E-mail: goaks@calbaptist.edu. *Application contact:* Tamakia King, Graduate Admissions Counselor, 951-552-8138, Fax: 951-343-5095, E-mail: tking@calbaptist.edu.
Website: http://www.calbaptist.edu/explore-cbu/schools-colleges/school-nursing/master-science-nursing/

California State University, Bakersfield, Division of Graduate Studies, School of Natural Sciences, Mathematics, and Engineering, Program in Nursing, Bakersfield, CA 93311. Offers family nurse practitioner (MSN). Applications accepted every other year. *Faculty:* 2 full-time (both women), 2 part-time/adjunct (both women). *Students:* 17 full-time (13 women); includes 12 minority (2 Black or African American, non-Hispanic/Latino; 5 Asian, non-Hispanic/Latino; 5 Hispanic/Latino). Average age 32. 75 applicants, 27% accepted, 17 enrolled. In 2017, 15 master's awarded. *Degree requirements:* For master's, thesis, project. *Entrance requirements:* For master's, BSN from ACEN-accredited program, 1 year of full-time nursing experience. *Application deadline:* Applications are processed on a rolling basis. Application fee: $55. Electronic applications accepted. *Expenses:* Tuition, state resident: full-time $7176; part-time $4164 per year. *Financial support:* In 2017–18, fellowships (averaging $1,850 per year) were awarded; Federal Work-Study, scholarships/grants, and tuition waivers (full and partial) also available. Financial award application deadline: 3/2; financial award applicants required to submit FAFSA. *Faculty research:* AIDS, gerontological nursing, cultural health beliefs. *Unit head:* Dr. Heidi He, Director, Graduate Program, 661-654-3112, Fax: 661-654-6437, E-mail: hhe@csub.edu. *Application contact:* Fatima Ramos, Program Advisor, 661-654-2610, E-mail: framos12@csub.edu.
Website: http://www.csub.edu/nursing/

California State University, San Marcos, College of Education, Health and Human Services, School of Nursing, San Marcos, CA 92096-0001. Offers advanced practice nursing (MSN), including clinical nurse specialist, family nurse practitioner, psychiatric mental health nurse practitioner; clinical nurse leader (MSN); nursing education (MSN). *Expenses:* Tuition, state resident: full-time $7176. Tuition, nonresident: full-time $9504. *Unit head:* Lorna Kendrick, Director, 760-750-7580, E-mail: lkendrick@csusm.edu.
Website: http://www.csusm.edu/nursing/

Carlow University, College of Health and Wellness, Program in Family Nurse Practitioner, Pittsburgh, PA 15213-3165. Offers MSN, Certificate. *Program availability:* Part-time. *Students:* 140 full-time (125 women), 58 part-time (55 women); includes 19 minority (8 Black or African American, non-Hispanic/Latino; 1 American Indian or Alaska Native, non-Hispanic/Latino; 6 Asian, non-Hispanic/Latino; 3 Hispanic/Latino; 1 Two or more races, non-Hispanic/Latino). Average age 33. 70 applicants, 99% accepted, 52 enrolled. In 2017, 75 master's, 4 other advanced degrees awarded. *Entrance requirements:* For master's, minimum undergraduate GPA of 3.0 from accredited BSN program; current license as RN in Pennsylvania; at least one year of recent clinical (bedside) nursing experience; course in statistics in past 6 years with a minimum grade of C; two recommendations; personal statement; personal interview. Additional exam requirements/recommendations for international students: Required—TOEFL (minimum score 550 paper-based). *Application deadline:* Applications are processed on a rolling basis. Electronic applications accepted. *Expenses:* Contact institution. *Financial support:* Application deadline: 4/1; applicants required to submit FAFSA. *Unit head:* Dr. Deborah Mitchum, Director, Family Nurse Practitioner Program, 412-578-6586, Fax: 412-578-6114, E-mail: dlmitchum@carlow.edu. *Application contact:* E-mail: gradstudies@carlow.edu.
Website: http://www.carlow.edu/Master_of_Science_in_Nursing_Family_Nurse_Practitioner.aspx

Carson-Newman University, Department of Nursing, Jefferson City, TN 37760. Offers family nurse practitioner (MSN); nurse educator (MSN). *Accreditation:* AACN. *Program availability:* Part-time. *Faculty:* 4 full-time (3 women). *Students:* 7 full-time (6 women), 33 part-time (30 women), 2 international. Average age 33. 18 applicants, 100% accepted, 13 enrolled. In 2017, 14 master's awarded. *Degree requirements:* For master's, comprehensive exam, thesis optional. *Entrance requirements:* For master's, GRE (minimum score of 290 within ten years of application), minimum GPA of 3.0 for all undergraduate work. Additional exam requirements/recommendations for international students: Recommended—TOEFL (minimum score 79 iBT), IELTS (minimum score 6.5), TSE (minimum score 53). *Application deadline:* For fall admission, 3/15 for domestic students; for spring admission, 10/15 for domestic students. Applications are processed on a rolling basis. Application fee: $50. *Expenses: Tuition:* Full-time $10,516; part-time $478 per credit hour. *Required fees:* $240; $120 per semester. One-time fee: $150. *Financial support:* Federal Work-Study and tuition waivers (full and partial) available. Financial award applicants required to submit FAFSA. *Unit head:* Dr. Kimberly Bolton, Director, 865-471-4056, E-mail: kbolton@cn.edu. *Application contact:* Nilma Stewart, Graduate Admissions and Services Adviser, 865-471-3230, Fax: 865-471-3875, E-mail: adults@cn.edu.
Website: http://www.cn.edu/adult-graduate-studies/programs/new/nursing

Case Western Reserve University, Frances Payne Bolton School of Nursing, Master's Programs in Nursing, Nurse Practitioner Program, Cleveland, OH 44106. Offers acute care pediatric nurse practitioner (MSN); acute care/cardiovascular nursing (MSN); acute care/flight nurse (MSN); adult gerontology acute care nurse practitioner (MSN); adult gerontology primary care nurse practitioner (MSN); family nurse practitioner (MSN); family systems psychiatric mental health nursing (MSN); neonatal nurse practitioner (MSN); palliative care (MSN); pediatric nurse practitioner (MSN); women's health nurse practitioner (MSN). *Accreditation:* ACEN. *Program availability:* Part-time. *Faculty:* 30 full-time (26 women), 5 part-time/adjunct (3 women). *Students:* 34 full-time (28 women), 97 part-time (73 women); includes 24 minority (5 Black or African American, non-Hispanic/Latino; 9 Asian, non-Hispanic/Latino; 6 Hispanic/Latino; 4 Two or more races, non-Hispanic/Latino), 4 international. Average age 33. 56 applicants, 82% accepted, 29 enrolled. In 2017, 68 master's awarded. *Degree requirements:* For master's, minimum GPA of 3.0, clinical hours corresponding to requirements to sit for certification exam, portfolio. *Entrance requirements:* For master's, GRE General Test or MAT. Additional exam requirements/recommendations for international students: Required—TOEFL (minimum score 577 paper-based; 90 iBT), IELTS (minimum score 7). *Application deadline:* For fall admission, 5/1 for domestic and international students; for spring admission, 10/1 for domestic and international students; for summer admission, 3/1 for domestic and international students. Applications are processed on a rolling basis. Application fee: $75. Electronic applications accepted. *Expenses:* $2,011 per credit tuition; $15 nursing activity fee; $17 activity fee. *Financial support:* In 2017–18, 86 students received support, including 19 teaching assistantships with partial tuition reimbursements available (averaging $18,100 per year); scholarships/grants and traineeships also available. Support available to part-time students. Financial award application deadline: 5/15; financial award applicants required to submit FAFSA. *Faculty research:* Symptom science, family/community care, aging across the lifespan, self-management of health and illness, neuroscience. *Unit head:* Dr. Latina Brooks, Director, 216-368-1196, Fax: 216-368-3542, E-mail: lmb3@case.edu. *Application contact:* Jackie Tepale, Admissions Coordinator, 216-368-5253, Fax: 216-368-0124, E-mail: yyd@case.edu.
Website: http://fpb.cwru.edu/MSN/majors.shtm

Cedarville University, Graduate Programs, Cedarville, OH 45314. Offers business administration (MBA); family nurse practitioner (MSN); global ministry (M Div); global public health nursing (MSN); healthcare administration (MBA); ministry (M Min); nurse educator (MSN); operations management (MBA); pharmacy (Pharm D). *Program availability:* Part-time, evening/weekend, 100% online, blended/hybrid learning. *Faculty:* 23 full-time (9 women), 48 part-time/adjunct (21 women). *Students:* 202 full-time (123 women), 146 part-time (96 women); includes 63 minority (39 Black or African American, non-Hispanic/Latino; 3 American Indian or Alaska Native, non-Hispanic/Latino; 15 Asian, non-Hispanic/Latino; 2 Hispanic/Latino; 1 Native Hawaiian or other Pacific Islander, non-Hispanic/Latino; 3 Two or more races, non-Hispanic/Latino), 3 international. Average age 24. 345 applicants, 37% accepted, 91 enrolled. In 2017, 53 master's, 47 doctorates awarded. *Degree requirements:* For master's, portfolio; for doctorate, comprehensive exam. *Entrance requirements:* For master's, GRE, 2 professional recommendations; for doctorate, PCAT, professional recommendation from a practicing pharmacist or current employer/supervisor, resume, essay, interview. Additional exam requirements/recommendations for international students: Required—TOEFL (minimum score 550 paper-based; 80 iBT). *Application deadline:* For fall admission, 5/1 priority date for domestic and international students; for spring admission, 11/1 priority date for domestic and international students. Applications are processed on a rolling basis. Application fee: $0. Electronic applications accepted. *Expenses: Tuition:* Full-time $12,594; part-time $566 per credit. One-time fee: $100 full-time. Tuition and fees vary according to degree level and program. *Financial support:* Scholarships/grants and unspecified assistantships available. Support available to part-time students. Financial award application deadline: 1/30; financial award applicants required to submit FAFSA. *Faculty research:* Establishing competencies of clinical reasoning for nursing students in Taiwan, social determinants of health in pediatric

primary care, meeting needs of palliative care populations, natural product utility in cancer, monoclonal antibodies directed at angiogenesis regulation. *Total annual research expenditures:* $3,800. *Unit head:* Dr. Janice Supplee, Dean of Graduate Studies, 937-766-7700, E-mail: suppleej@cedarville.edu. *Application contact:* Jim Amstutz, Director of Graduate Admissions, 937-766-7878, Fax: 937-766-7575, E-mail: amstutzj@cedarville.edu.
Website: https://www.cedarville.edu/Admissions/Graduate/Graduate-Programs.aspx

Clarion University of Pennsylvania, College of Health and Human Services, Master of Science in Nursing Program, Clarion, PA 16214. Offers family nurse practitioner (MSN). *Accreditation:* ACEN. *Program availability:* Part-time, online only, 100% online. *Faculty:* 10 full-time (9 women), 3 part-time/adjunct (all women). *Students:* 94 part-time (81 women); includes 5 minority (2 Black or African American, non-Hispanic/Latino; 2 Asian, non-Hispanic/Latino; 1 Hispanic/Latino). Average age 35. 73 applicants, 70% accepted, 33 enrolled. In 2017, 35 master's awarded. *Degree requirements:* For master's, comprehensive exam, thesis, portfolio. *Entrance requirements:* For master's, minimum QPA of 2.75. Additional exam requirements/recommendations for international students: Required—TOEFL (minimum score 550 paper-based, 80 iBT) or IELTS (7). *Application deadline:* For fall admission, 10/1 for domestic students, 7/1 priority date for international students. Applications are processed on a rolling basis. Application fee: $40. Electronic applications accepted. *Expenses:* $712 per credit. *Financial support:* Career-related internships or fieldwork, scholarships/grants, and unspecified assistantships available. Support available to part-time students. Financial award application deadline: 3/1; financial award applicants required to submit FAFSA. *Unit head:* Dr. Deborah J. Kelly, Chair and Nurse Administrator, 814-393-1258, E-mail: dkelly@clarion.edu. *Application contact:* Dana Bearer, Associate Director for Transfer, Adult, and Graduate Programs, 814-393-2337, Fax: 814-393-2772, E-mail: gradstudies@clarion.edu.
Website: http://www.clarion.edu/admissions/graduate/index.html

Clarke University, Department of Nursing and Health, Dubuque, IA 52001-3198. Offers family nurse practitioner (DNP); health leadership and practice (DNP); psychiatric mental health nurse practitioner (DNP). *Accreditation:* AACN. *Program availability:* Part-time. *Faculty:* 6 full-time (all women). *Students:* 55 full-time (54 women), 11 part-time (10 women); includes 3 minority (1 Black or African American, non-Hispanic/Latino; 1 Asian, non-Hispanic/Latino; 1 Two or more races, non-Hispanic/Latino). Average age 32. 62 applicants, 40% accepted, 22 enrolled. In 2017, 36 doctorates awarded. *Degree requirements:* For doctorate, comprehensive exam, thesis/dissertation. *Entrance requirements:* For doctorate, GRE (if GPA under 3.0), bachelor's degree from accredited nursing program and accredited college or university; minimum GPA of 3.0; minimum C grade on undergraduate prerequisite courses; three recommendation forms; curriculum vitae; statement of goals; transcripts; copy of nursing license; proof of health insurance; interview. Additional exam requirements/recommendations for international students: Required—TOEFL (minimum score 550 paper-based; 80 iBT), IELTS (minimum score 6.5). *Application deadline:* For fall admission, 2/1 priority date for domestic students. Application fee: $35. Electronic applications accepted. *Expenses:* $850 per credit. *Financial support:* Applicants required to submit FAFSA. *Faculty research:* Narrative pedagogy, ethics, end-of-life care, pedagogy, family systems, simulation. *Unit head:* Dr. Jan Lee, Chair, 563-588-6339, E-mail: jan.lee@clarke.edu. *Application contact:* Kimberly Roush, Director of Admission, Graduate and Adult Programs, 563-588-6539, Fax: 563-552-7994, E-mail: graduate@clarke.edu.
Website: https://www.clarke.edu/academics/doctor-of-nursing-practice/

Clarkson College, Master of Science in Nursing Program, Omaha, NE 68131. Offers adult nurse practitioner (MSN, Post-Master's Certificate); family nurse practitioner (MSN, Post-Master's Certificate); nursing education (MSN, Post-Master's Certificate); nursing health care leadership (MSN, Post-Master's Certificate). *Accreditation:* AANA/CANAEP; ACEN. *Program availability:* Part-time, evening/weekend, online learning. *Degree requirements:* For master's, on-campus skills assessment (family nurse practitioner, adult nurse practitioner), comprehensive exam or thesis. *Entrance requirements:* For master's, minimum GPA of 3.0, 2 references, resume. Additional exam requirements/recommendations for international students: Required—TOEFL (minimum score 600 paper-based; 100 iBT). Electronic applications accepted.

Clayton State University, School of Graduate Studies, College of Health, Program in Nursing, Morrow, GA 30260-0285. Offers family nurse practitioner (MSN). *Accreditation:* AACN. *Degree requirements:* For master's, thesis. *Entrance requirements:* For master's, GRE, official transcript, 3 letters of recommendation, statement of purpose, on-campus interview, 1-2 years of clinical nursing experience (preferred). Additional exam requirements/recommendations for international students: Required—TOEFL (minimum score 550 paper-based; 80 iBT). Electronic applications accepted. *Expenses:* Contact institution.

Clemson University, Graduate School, College of Behavioral, Social and Health Sciences, School of Nursing, Clemson, SC 29634. Offers clinical and translational research (PhD); global health (Certificate), including low resource countries; healthcare genetics (PhD); nursing (MS, DNP), including adult/gerontology nurse practitioner (MS), family nurse practitioner (MS). *Accreditation:* AACN. *Program availability:* Part-time, 100% online, blended/hybrid learning. *Faculty:* 37 full-time (35 women). *Students:* 130 full-time (118 women), 195 part-time (170 women); includes 50 minority (23 Black or African American, non-Hispanic/Latino; 5 Asian, non-Hispanic/Latino; 16 Hispanic/Latino; 6 Two or more races, non-Hispanic/Latino), 14 international. Average age 34. 71 applicants, 66% accepted, 33 enrolled. In 2017, 88 master's, 2 doctorates, 10 other advanced degrees awarded. *Degree requirements:* For master's, comprehensive exam, thesis or alternative; for doctorate, comprehensive exam, thesis/dissertation. *Entrance requirements:* For master's, GRE General Test, South Carolina RN license, unofficial transcripts, resume, letters of recommendation; for doctorate, GRE General Test, unofficial transcripts, MS/MA thesis or publications, curriculum vitae, statement of career goals, letters of recommendation. Additional exam requirements/recommendations for international students: Required—TOEFL (minimum score 80 iBT), IELTS (minimum score 6.5), PTE (minimum score 54). *Application deadline:* For fall admission, 3/1 priority date for domestic and international students; for spring admission, 10/1 priority date for domestic and international students. Application fee: $80 ($90 for international students). Electronic applications accepted. *Expenses:* Contact institution. *Financial support:* In 2017–18, 41 students received support, including 46 teaching assistantships with partial tuition reimbursements available (averaging $4,919 per year); career-related internships or fieldwork and unspecified assistantships also available. Financial award application deadline: 3/1. *Faculty research:* Breast cancer, healthcare, genetics, international healthcare, educational innovation and technology. *Total annual research expenditures:* $371,674. *Unit head:* Dr. Kathleen Valentine, Director and Associate College Dean, 864-656-4758, E-mail: klvalen@clemson.edu. *Application contact:* Dr. Stephanie Davis, Graduate Studies Coordinator, 864-656-2588, E-mail: stephad@clemson.edu.
Website: http://www.clemson.edu/cbshs/departments/nursing/

College of Mount Saint Vincent, School of Professional and Graduate Studies, Department of Nursing, Riverdale, NY 10471-1093. Offers family nurse practitioner (MSN, PMC); nurse educator (PMC); nursing administration (MSN); nursing education (MSN). *Accreditation:* AACN. *Program availability:* Part-time. *Entrance requirements:* For master's, BSN, interview, RN license, minimum GPA of 3.0, letters of reference. Additional exam requirements/recommendations for international students: Required—TOEFL. *Expenses:* Contact institution.

The College of New Rochelle, Graduate School, Program in Nursing, New Rochelle, NY 10805-2308. Offers acute care nurse practitioner (MS, Certificate); clinical specialist in holistic nursing (MS, Certificate); family nurse practitioner (MS, Certificate); nursing and health care management (MS); nursing education (Certificate). *Accreditation:* AACN. *Program availability:* Part-time. *Entrance requirements:* For master's, GRE General Test or MAT, BSN, malpractice insurance, minimum GPA of 3.0, RN license. Electronic applications accepted. *Expenses: Tuition:* Full-time $17,406. *Required fees:* $1120.

Colorado Mesa University, Department of Health Sciences, Grand Junction, CO 81501-3122. Offers advanced nursing practice (MSN); family nurse practitioner (DNP); health information technology systems (Graduate Certificate); nursing education (MSN). *Accreditation:* AACN. *Program availability:* Part-time, evening/weekend, 100% online, blended/hybrid learning. *Degree requirements:* For master's and doctorate, capstone. *Entrance requirements:* For master's and doctorate, minimum GPA of 3.0 in BSN program. Additional exam requirements/recommendations for international students: Required—TOEFL (minimum score 550 paper-based). Electronic applications accepted.

Columbia University, School of Nursing, Program in Family Nurse Practitioner, New York, NY 10032. Offers MS, Adv C. *Accreditation:* AACN. *Program availability:* Part-time. *Entrance requirements:* For master's, GRE General Test, NCLEX, BSN, 1 year of clinical experience (preferred); for Adv C, MSN. Additional exam requirements/recommendations for international students: Required—TOEFL (minimum score 100 iBT). Electronic applications accepted. *Expenses: Tuition:* Full-time $44,864; part-time $1704 per credit. *Required fees:* $2370 per semester. One-time fee: $105.

Columbus State University, Graduate Studies, College of Education and Health Professions, School of Nursing, Columbus, GA 31907-5645. Offers family nurse practitioner (MSN); nursing (MSN), including nurse educator, nurse informatics, nurse leader. Program offered in collaboration with Georgia Southwestern StateUniversity. *Program availability:* Part-time, online only, 100% online. *Faculty:* 7 full-time (all women), 2 part-time/adjunct (both women). *Students:* 43 full-time (40 women), 134 part-time (121 women); includes 88 minority (65 Black or African American, non-Hispanic/Latino; 7 Asian, non-Hispanic/Latino; 10 Hispanic/Latino; 6 Two or more races, non-Hispanic/Latino). Average age 35. 141 applicants, 49% accepted, 12 enrolled. In 2017, 28 master's awarded. *Entrance requirements:* For master's, GRE, BSN, minimum undergraduate GPA of 3.0. Additional exam requirements/recommendations for international students: Required—TOEFL (minimum score 550 paper-based; 79 iBT). *Application deadline:* For fall admission, 5/1 for domestic and international students; for spring admission, 11/1 for domestic and international students; for summer admission, 3/1 for domestic and international students. Applications are processed on a rolling basis. Application fee: $50. Electronic applications accepted. *Expenses:* Contact institution. *Financial support:* In 2017–18, 3 students received support. Institutionally sponsored loans available. Financial award application deadline: 5/1; financial award applicants required to submit FAFSA. *Unit head:* Latonya Santo, Director, 706-507-8576, E-mail: santo_latonya@columbusstate.edu. *Application contact:* Catrina Smith-Edmond, Assistant Director for Graduate and Global Admission, 706-507-8824, Fax: 706-568-5091, E-mail: smithedmond_catrina@columbusstate.edu.
Website: http://nursing.columbusstate.edu/

Concordia University Wisconsin, Graduate Programs, School of Nursing, Mequon, WI 53097-2402. Offers family nurse practitioner (MSN). *Accreditation:* AACN. *Program availability:* Online learning. *Degree requirements:* For master's, comprehensive exam, thesis or alternative. *Entrance requirements:* Additional exam requirements/recommendations for international students: Required—TOEFL. *Expenses:* Contact institution.

Coppin State University, Division of Graduate Studies, Helene Fuld School of Nursing, Baltimore, MD 21216-3698. Offers family nurse practitioner (PMC); nursing (MSN). *Accreditation:* AACN; ACEN. *Program availability:* Part-time, evening/weekend. *Degree requirements:* For master's, comprehensive exam, thesis, clinical internship. *Entrance requirements:* For master's, GRE, bachelor's degree in nursing, interview, minimum GPA of 3.0, RN license. Additional exam requirements/recommendations for international students: Required—TOEFL (minimum score 550 paper-based).

Cox College, Programs in Nursing, Springfield, MO 65802. Offers clinical nurse leader (MSN); family nurse practitioner (MSN); nurse educator (MSN). *Accreditation:* AACN. *Entrance requirements:* For master's, RN license, essay, 2 letters of recommendation, official transcripts. Electronic applications accepted.

Creighton University, College of Nursing, Omaha, NE 68178-0001. Offers adult gerontology acute care nurse practitioner (DNP, Post-Master's Certificate); adult gerontology nurse practitioner (DNP); clinical nurse leader (MSN, Post-Graduate Certificate); clinical systems administration (MSN, DNP); family nurse practitioner (DNP, Post-Master's Certificate); neonatal nurse practitioner (DNP, Post-Master's Certificate); nursing (Post-Graduate Certificate); pediatric acute care nurse practitioner (DNP, Post-Master's Certificate); psychiatric mental health nurse practitioner (DNP). *Accreditation:* AACN. *Program availability:* Part-time, blended/hybrid learning. *Degree requirements:* For master's, capstone project; for doctorate, scholarly project. *Entrance requirements:* For master's and doctorate, BSN from ACEN- or CCNE-accredited nursing school, minimum cumulative GPA of 3.0, personal statement, active unencumbered RN license with NE eligibility, undergraduate statistics course, physical assessment course or equivalent, three recommendation letters; for other advanced degree, MSN or MS in nursing from ACEN- or CCNE-accredited nursing school, minimum cumulative GPA of 3.0, active unencumbered RN license with NE eligibility. Additional exam requirements/recommendations for international students: Required—TOEFL (minimum score 600 paper-based, 100 iBT) or IELTS. Electronic applications accepted. *Expenses:* Contact institution. *Faculty research:* School health report card, obesity prevention in children, simulated clinical experience evaluation, vitamin D3 and calcium and cancer risk reduction education, online support and education to reduce stress for prenatal patients on bed rest, health literacy, immunization research.

Delta State University, Graduate Programs, Robert E. Smith School of Nursing, Cleveland, MS 38733. Offers family nurse practitioner (MSN); nurse administrator (MSN); nurse educator (MSN). *Accreditation:* AACN. *Program availability:* Part-time. *Degree requirements:* For master's, thesis optional. *Entrance requirements:* For master's, GRE General Test. Electronic applications accepted.

DePaul University, College of Science and Health, Chicago, IL 60604. Offers applied mathematics (MS); applied statistics (MS); biological sciences (MA, MS); chemistry (MS); environmental science (MS); mathematics education (MA); mathematics for teaching (MS); nursing (MS); nursing practice (DNP); physics (MS); polymer and coatings science (MS); psychology (MS); pure mathematics (MS); science education (MS); MA/PhD. *Accreditation:* AACN. *Application deadline:* Applications are processed on a rolling basis. Application fee: $40. Electronic applications accepted. *Financial support:* Applicants required to submit FAFSA. *Unit head:* Dr. Gerald P. Koocher, Dean, 773-325-8300. *Application contact:* Ann Spittle, Director of Graduate Admission, 773-325-7315, Fax: 312-476-3244, E-mail: graddepaul@depaul.edu.
Website: http://csh.depaul.edu/

DeSales University, Division of Healthcare, Center Valley, PA 18034-9568. Offers adult-gerontology acute care (Post Master's Certificate); adult-gerontology acute care nurse practitioner (MSN); adult-gerontology acute certified nurse practitioner (Post Master's Certificate); adult-gerontology clinical nurse specialist (MSN, Post Master's Certificate); clinical leadership (DNP); family nurse practitioner (MSN, Post Master's Certificate); general nursing practice (DNP); nurse anesthetist (MSN); nurse educator (Post Master's Certificate, Postbaccalaureate Certificate); nurse midwife (MSN); nurse practitioner (MSN); psychiatric-mental health nurse practitioner (MSN, Post Master's Certificate); DNP/MBA. *Accreditation:* ACEN. *Program availability:* Part-time. *Faculty:* 26 full-time (20 women), 30 part-time/adjunct (19 women). *Students:* 282 full-time (210 women), 101 part-time (85 women); includes 39 minority (12 Black or African American, non-Hispanic/Latino; 11 Asian, non-Hispanic/Latino; 12 Hispanic/Latino; 4 Two or more races, non-Hispanic/Latino), 1 international. Average age 29. 2,884 applicants, 5% accepted, 114 enrolled. In 2017, 76 master's, 6 doctorates awarded. *Degree requirements:* For master's, minimum GPA of 3.0, portfolio; for doctorate, minimum GPA of 3.0, scholarly capstone project. *Entrance requirements:* For master's, GRE or MAT (waived if applicant has an undergraduate GPA of 3.0 or higher), BSN from ACEN- or CCNE-accredited program, minimum undergraduate GPA of 3.0, active RN license or eligibility, two letters of recommendation, essay, health care experience, personal interview; for doctorate, BSN or MSN from ACEN- or CCNE-accredited institution, minimum GPA of 3.3 in graduate program, current licensure as an RN. Additional exam requirements/recommendations for international students: Required—TOEFL (minimum score 104 iBT). *Application deadline:* Applications are processed on a rolling basis. Application fee: $50. Electronic applications accepted. *Expenses:* Contact institution. *Financial support:* Applicants required to submit FAFSA. *Unit head:* Ronald Nordone, Dean of Graduate Education, 610-282-1100 Ext. 1289, E-mail: ronald.nordone@desales.edu. *Application contact:* Julia Ferraro, Director of Graduate Admissions, 610-282-1100 Ext. 1768, E-mail: gradadmissions@desales.edu.

Dominican College, Division of Nursing, Orangeburg, NY 10962-1210. Offers MSN, DNP. *Accreditation:* AACN. *Program availability:* Part-time, evening/weekend. *Faculty:* 1 (woman) full-time. *Students:* 19 full-time (18 women), 94 part-time (84 women); includes 59 minority (17 Black or African American, non-Hispanic/Latino; 20 Asian, non-Hispanic/Latino; 20 Hispanic/Latino; 2 Two or more races, non-Hispanic/Latino), 2 international. In 2017, 16 master's, 7 doctorates awarded. *Degree requirements:* For master's, guided research project, 750 hours of clinical practice with a final written project. *Entrance requirements:* For master's, RN license with 1 year of experience; minimum undergraduate GPA of 3.0; 3 letters of recommendation. Additional exam requirements/recommendations for international students: Required—TOEFL (minimum score 550 paper-based; 90 iBT). *Application deadline:* Applications are processed on a rolling basis. Application fee: $50. Electronic applications accepted. *Expenses: Tuition:* Part-time $900 per credit. One-time fee: $200. Tuition and fees vary according to degree level and program. *Financial support:* Application deadline: 2/1; applicants required to submit FAFSA. *Unit head:* Dr. Nancy DiDona, Director, 845-848-6051, Fax: 845-398-4891, E-mail: nancy.didona@dc.edu. *Application contact:* Heather Bergling, Assistant Director of Graduate Admissions, 845-848-7908, Fax: 845-365-3150, E-mail: admissions@dc.edu.

Drexel University, College of Nursing and Health Professions, Division of Graduate Nursing, Philadelphia, PA 19104-2875. Offers adult acute care (MSN); adult psychiatric/mental health (MSN); advanced practice nursing (MSN); clinical trials research (MSN); family nurse practitioner (MSN); leadership in health systems management (MSN); nursing education (MSN); pediatric primary care (MSN); women's health (MSN). *Accreditation:* AACN. Electronic applications accepted.

Duke University, School of Nursing, Durham, NC 27708-0586. Offers acute care pediatric nurse practitioner (MSN, Post-Graduate Certificate); adult-gerontology nurse practitioner (MSN, Post-Graduate Certificate), including acute care, primary care; family nurse practitioner (MSN, Post-Graduate Certificate); neonatal nurse practitioner (MSN, Post-Graduate Certificate); nurse anesthesia (DNP); nurse practitioner (DNP); nursing (PhD); nursing and health care leadership (MSN, Post-Graduate Certificate); nursing education (MSN, Post-Graduate Certificate); nursing informatics (MSN, Post-Graduate Certificate); pediatric nurse practitioner (MSN, Post-Graduate Certificate), including primary care; psychiatric mental health nurse practitioner (MSN, Post-Graduate Certificate); women's health nurse practitioner (MSN, Post-Graduate Certificate). *Accreditation:* AACN; AANA/CANAEP. *Program availability:* Part-time, evening/weekend, online with on-campus intensives. *Faculty:* 72 full-time (61 women). *Students:* 155 full-time (137 women), 613 part-time (548 women); includes 177 minority (64 Black or African American, non-Hispanic/Latino; 2 American Indian or Alaska Native, non-Hispanic/Latino; 47 Asian, non-Hispanic/Latino; 34 Hispanic/Latino; 30 Two or more races, non-Hispanic/Latino), 10 international. Average age 34. 631 applicants, 47% accepted, 211 enrolled. In 2017, 221 master's, 71 doctorates, 26 other advanced degrees awarded. Terminal master's awarded for partial completion of doctoral program. *Degree requirements:* For master's, thesis optional; for doctorate, capstone project. *Entrance requirements:* For master's, GRE General Test (waived if undergraduate GPA of 3.4 or higher), 1 year of nursing experience (recommended), BSN, minimum GPA of 3.0, previous course work in statistics; for doctorate, GRE General Test (waived if undergraduate GPA of 3.4 or higher), BSN or MSN, minimum GPA of 3.0, resume, personal statement, undergraduate statistics course, current licensure as a registered nurse, transcripts from all post-secondary institutions; for Post-Graduate Certificate, MSN, licensure or eligibility as a professional nurse, transcripts from all post-secondary institutions, previous course work in statistics. Additional exam requirements/recommendations for international students: Required—TOEFL (minimum score 100 iBT), IELTS (minimum score 7). *Application deadline:* For fall admission, 12/1 for domestic and international students; for spring admission, 5/1 for domestic and international students. Application fee: $50. Electronic applications accepted. *Expenses:* Contact institution. *Financial support:* Institutionally sponsored loans, scholarships/grants, and traineeships available. Support available to part-time students. Financial award applicants required to submit FAFSA. *Faculty research:* Cardiovascular disease, caregiver skill training, data mining, prostate cancer, neonatal immune system. *Unit head:* Dr. Marion E. Broome, Dean/Vice Chancellor for Nursing Affairs/Associate Vice President for Academic Affairs for Nursing, 919-684-9446, Fax: 919-684-9414, E-mail: marion.broome@duke.edu. *Application contact:* Dr. Ernie Rushing, Director of Admissions and Recruitment, 919-668-6274, Fax: 919-668-4693, E-mail: ernie.rushing@dm.duke.edu.
Website: http://www.nursing.duke.edu/

Duquesne University, School of Nursing, Master of Science in Nursing Program, Pittsburgh, PA 15282-0001. Offers family (individual across the life span) nurse practitioner (MSN); forensic nursing (MSN); nursing education and faculty role (MSN). *Accreditation:* AACN. *Program availability:* Part-time, evening/weekend, minimal on-campus study. *Faculty:* 26 full-time (21 women), 3 part-time/adjunct (all women). *Students:* 132 full-time (118 women), 54 part-time (49 women); includes 25 minority (7 Black or African American, non-Hispanic/Latino; 2 American Indian or Alaska Native, non-Hispanic/Latino; 5 Asian, non-Hispanic/Latino; 7 Hispanic/Latino; 4 Two or more races, non-Hispanic/Latino), 1 international. Average age 33. 160 applicants, 73% accepted, 87 enrolled. In 2017, 50 master's awarded. *Entrance requirements:* For master's, current RN license; BSN with minimum GPA of 3.0; minimum of 1 year of full-time work experience as RN prior to registration in clinical or specialty course. Additional exam requirements/recommendations for international students: Required—TOEFL (minimum score 600 paper-based; 100 iBT). *Application deadline:* For fall admission, 7/16 for domestic and international students; for spring admission, 11/29 for domestic and international students; for summer admission, 4/1 for domestic and international students. Application fee: $0. Electronic applications accepted. *Expenses:* $1,312 per credit. *Financial support:* In 2017–18, 10 students received support, including 10 teaching assistantships with partial tuition reimbursements available (averaging $3,297 per year); institutionally sponsored loans, scholarships/grants, traineeships, tuition waivers (partial), and unspecified assistantships also available. Support available to part-time students. Financial award application deadline: 5/1; financial award applicants required to submit FAFSA. *Faculty research:* Vulnerable populations, cultural competence, health disparities, wellness, technology. *Total annual research expenditures:* $650,096. *Unit head:* Dr. Alison Colbert, Associate Professor/Associate Dean of Academic Affairs, 412-396-1511, Fax: 412-396-1821, E-mail: colberta@duq.edu. *Application contact:* Susan Hardner, Nurse Recruiter, 412-396-4945, Fax: 412-396-6346, E-mail: nursing@duq.edu.
Website: http://www.duq.edu/academics/schools/nursing/graduate-programs/master-science-nursing

Duquesne University, School of Nursing, Post Master's Certificate Program, Pittsburgh, PA 15282-0001. Offers family (individual across the life span) nurse practitioner (Post-Master's Certificate); forensic nursing (Post-Master's Certificate); nursing education and faculty role (Post-Master's Certificate). *Program availability:* Part-time, evening/weekend, minimal on-campus study. *Faculty:* 8 full-time (6 women), 2 part-time/adjunct (both women). *Students:* 14 full-time (all women), 6 part-time (all women); includes 3 minority (2 Black or African American, non-Hispanic/Latino; 1 American Indian or Alaska Native, non-Hispanic/Latino). Average age 43. 27 applicants, 78% accepted, 10 enrolled. In 2017, 6 Post-Master's Certificates awarded. *Entrance requirements:* For degree, current RN license, BSN, MSN. Additional exam requirements/recommendations for international students: Required—TOEFL (minimum score 600 paper-based; 100 iBT). *Application deadline:* For fall admission, 7/16 for domestic and international students; for spring admission, 11/29 for domestic and international students; for summer admission, 4/1 for domestic and international students. Application fee: $0. Electronic applications accepted. *Expenses:* $1,312 per credit. *Financial support:* Teaching assistantships with partial tuition reimbursements, institutionally sponsored loans, scholarships/grants, traineeships, and tuition waivers (partial) available. Support available to part-time students. Financial award application deadline: 5/1; financial award applicants required to submit FAFSA. *Faculty research:* Vulnerable populations, cultural competence, health disparities, wellness, technology. *Total annual research expenditures:* $650,096. *Unit head:* Dr. Alison Colbert, Associate Professor/Associate Dean of Academic Affairs, 412-396-1511, Fax: 412-396-1821, E-mail: colberta@duq.edu. *Application contact:* Susan Hardner, Nurse Recruiter, 412-396-4945, Fax: 412-396-6346, E-mail: nursing@duq.edu.
Website: http://www.duq.edu/academics/schools/nursing/graduate-programs/post-masters-certificates

D'Youville College, School of Nursing, Buffalo, NY 14201-1084. Offers advanced practice nursing (DNP); family nurse practitioner (MSN, Certificate); nursing and health-related professions education (Certificate). *Accreditation:* AACN. *Program availability:* Part-time. *Degree requirements:* For master's, thesis or alternative. *Entrance requirements:* For master's, BS in nursing, minimum GPA of 3.0, course work in statistics and computers; for doctorate, BS in nursing, MS in advanced practice nursing specialty, minimum GPA of 3.25. Additional exam requirements/recommendations for international students: Required—TOEFL (minimum score 500 paper-based). Electronic applications accepted. *Faculty research:* Nursing curriculum, nursing theory-testing, wellness research, communication and socialization patterns.

Eastern Kentucky University, The Graduate School, College of Health Sciences, Department of Nursing, Richmond, KY 40475-3102. Offers rural community health care (MSN); rural health family nurse practitioner (MSN). *Accreditation:* AACN. *Entrance requirements:* For master's, GRE General Test, minimum GPA of 2.75.

East Tennessee State University, School of Graduate Studies, College of Nursing, Johnson City, TN 37614. Offers acute care nurse practitioner (DNP); adult-gerontology primary care nurse practitioner (DNP); adult/gerontological nurse practitioner (Postbaccalaureate Certificate); executive leadership in nursing (DNP, Postbaccalaureate Certificate); family nurse practitioner (MSN, DNP, Post-Master's Certificate, Postbaccalaureate Certificate); nursing (PhD); nursing administration (MSN); nursing education (MSN); pediatric primary care nurse practitioner (DNP); psychiatric mental health nurse practitioner (Postbaccalaureate Certificate); psychiatric/mental health nurse practitioner (MSN, DNP, Post-Master's Certificate); women's health care nurse practitioner (DNP). *Accreditation:* AACN. *Program availability:* Part-time, evening/weekend, online learning. In 2017, 126 master's, 30 doctorates, 4 other advanced degrees awarded. *Degree requirements:* For master's and other advanced degree, comprehensive exam, practicum; for doctorate, comprehensive exam, thesis/dissertation (for some programs), practicum, internship, evidence of professional malpractice insurance, CPR certification. *Entrance requirements:* For master's, bachelor's degree, minimum GPA of 3.0, current RN license and eligibility to practice, resume, three letters of recommendation; for doctorate, GRE General Test, MSN (for PhD), BSN or MSN (for DNP), current RN license and eligibility to practice, 2 years of full-time registered nurse work experience or equivalent, three letters of recommendation, resume or curriculum vitae, interview, writing sample; for other advanced degree, MSN, minimum GPA of 3.0, current RN license and eligibility to practice, three letters of recommendation, resume or curriculum vitae; DNP with designated concentration in advanced clinical practice or nursing administration (for select programs). Additional exam requirements/recommendations for international students: Required—TOEFL (minimum score 600 paper-based; 79 iBT). *Application deadline:* For fall admission, 4/15 priority date for domestic and international students; for spring admission, 10/15 priority date for domestic and international students; for summer admission, 2/1 for domestic and international students. Application fee: $55 ($65 for international students). Electronic applications accepted. *Financial support:* Research assistantships with tuition reimbursements, teaching assistantships, career-related internships or fieldwork, institutionally sponsored loans, scholarships/grants, and unspecified assistantships available. Financial award application deadline: 7/1; financial award applicants required to submit FAFSA. *Faculty research:* Improving health of rural and underserved populations (low income elders living in public housing, rural caregivers, Hispanic populations), health services and systems research (quality outcomes of nurse-managed primary care, in-home, and rural health care), nursing education (experiences of second-degree BSN students, well-being of BSN students). *Unit head:* Dr. Wendy Nehring, Dean, 423-439-7051, Fax: 423-439-4543, E-mail: nursing@etsu.edu. *Application contact:* Dr. Myra Clark, Director of Graduate Programs, 423-439-4396, Fax: 423-439-4100, E-mail: clarkml2@etsu.edu.
Website: http://www.etsu.edu/nursing/

Edinboro University of Pennsylvania, Department of Nursing, Edinboro, PA 16444. Offers advanced practice nursing (DNP); family nurse practitioner (MSN); nurse educator (MSN). *Program availability:* Part-time, evening/weekend. *Degree requirements:* For master's, thesis, competency exam. *Entrance requirements:* For master's, GRE or MAT, minimum QPA of 2.5. Electronic applications accepted.

Elms College, School of Nursing, Chicopee, MA 01013-2839. Offers adult-gerontology acute care nurse practitioner (DNP); family nurse practitioner (DNP); health systems innovation and leadership (DNP); nursing and health services management (MSN); nursing education (MSN). *Accreditation:* AACN. *Program availability:* Part-time, evening/weekend. *Faculty:* 5 full-time (all women), 9 part-time/adjunct (6 women). *Students:* 20 full-time (16 women), 79 part-time (70 women); includes 12 minority (2 Black or African American, non-Hispanic/Latino; 2 American Indian or Alaska Native, non-Hispanic/Latino; 8 Hispanic/Latino). Average age 40. 33 applicants, 94% accepted, 28 enrolled. In 2017, 14 master's, 30 doctorates awarded. *Entrance requirements:* Additional exam requirements/recommendations for international students: Required—TOEFL. *Application deadline:* For fall admission, 7/1 priority date for domestic students; for spring admission, 11/1 priority date for domestic students. Applications are processed on a rolling basis. Application fee: $30. *Expenses: Tuition:* Full-time $13,860; part-time $770 per credit hour. *Required fees:* $200. Tuition and fees vary according to degree level and program. *Financial support:* Applicants required to submit FAFSA. *Unit head:* Dr. Kathleen Scoble, Dean, School of Nursing, 413-265-2204, E-mail: scoblek@elms.edu. *Application contact:* Dr. Cynthia L. Dakin, Director of Graduate Nursing Studies, 413-265-2455, Fax: 413-265-2335, E-mail: dakinc@elms.edu.

Emory University, Nell Hodgson Woodruff School of Nursing, Atlanta, GA 30322-1100. Offers adult nurse practitioner (MSN); emergency nurse practitioner (MSN); family nurse practitioner (MSN); family nurse-midwife (MSN); health systems leadership (MSN); nurse-midwifery (MSN); pediatric nurse practitioner acute and primary care (MSN); women's health care (Title X) (MSN); women's health nurse practitioner (MSN); MSN/MPH. *Accreditation:* AACN; ACNM/ACME (one or more programs are accredited). *Program availability:* Part-time. *Entrance requirements:* For master's, GRE General Test or MAT, minimum GPA of 3.0, BS in nursing from an accredited institution, RN license and additional course work, 3 letters of recommendation. Additional exam requirements/recommendations for international students: Required—TOEFL (minimum score 600 paper-based; 100 iBT). Electronic applications accepted. *Expenses:* Contact institution. *Faculty research:* Older adult falls and injuries, minority health issues, cardiac symptoms and quality of life, bio-ethics and decision-making, menopausal issues.

Endicott College, Van Loan School of Graduate and Professional Studies, Program in Nursing, Beverly, MA 01915-2096. Offers family nurse practitioner (MSN, Post-Master's Certificate); global health (MSN); nursing administration (MSN); nursing administrator (Post-Master's Certificate); nursing educator (MSN, Post-Master's Certificate). *Program availability:* Part-time, evening/weekend. *Faculty:* 5 full-time (4 women), 14 part-time/adjunct (12 women). *Students:* 43 full-time (41 women), 57 part-time (51 women); includes 9 minority (6 Black or African American, non-Hispanic/Latino; 3 Hispanic/Latino), 1 international. Average age 37. 41 applicants, 100% accepted, 38 enrolled. In 2017, 33 master's awarded. *Degree requirements:* For master's, thesis, practicum. *Entrance requirements:* For master's, MAT or GRE, statement of professional goals, official transcripts of all undergraduate and graduate course work, two letters of recommendation, photocopy of current and unrestricted RN license, basic statistics course, interview. Additional exam requirements/recommendations for international students: Required—TOEFL. *Application deadline:* Applications are processed on a rolling basis. Application fee: $50. Electronic applications accepted. *Expenses:* Contact institution. *Financial support:* Applicants required to submit FAFSA. *Unit head:* Dr. Kelly Fisher, Dean, 978-232-2328, Fax: 978-232-3000, E-mail: kfisher@endicott.edu. *Application contact:* Ian Menchini, Director, Graduate Enrollment and Advising, 978-232-5292, Fax: 978-232-3000, E-mail: imenchin@endicott.edu.
Website: https://vanloan.endicott.edu/programs-of-study/masters-programs/nursing-programs

Fairfield University, Marion Peckham Egan School of Nursing and Health Studies, Fairfield, CT 06824. Offers advanced practice (DNP); family nurse practitioner (MSN, DNP); nurse anesthesia (DNP); nursing leadership (MSN); psychiatric nurse practitioner (MSN, DNP). *Accreditation:* AACN; AANA/CANAEP. *Program availability:* Part-time, evening/weekend. *Faculty:* 9 full-time (all women), 11 part-time/adjunct (8 women). *Students:* 50 full-time (42 women), 153 part-time (140 women); includes 48 minority (15 Black or African American, non-Hispanic/Latino; 1 American Indian or Alaska Native, non-Hispanic/Latino; 10 Asian, non-Hispanic/Latino; 19 Hispanic/Latino; 3 Two or more races, non-Hispanic/Latino), 2 international. Average age 34. 160 applicants, 50% accepted, 55 enrolled. In 2017, 26 master's, 36 doctorates awarded. *Degree requirements:* For master's, capstone project. *Entrance requirements:* For master's, minimum QPA of 3.0, RN license, resume, 2 recommendations; for doctorate, MSN (minimum QPA of 3.2) or BSN (minimum QPA of 3.0); critical care nursing experience (for nurse anesthesia DNP candidates). Additional exam requirements/recommendations for international students: Required—TOEFL (minimum score 550 paper-based; 80 iBT) or IELTS (minimum score 6.5). *Application deadline:* For fall admission, 5/15 for international students; for spring admission, 10/15 for international students. Applications are processed on a rolling basis. Application fee: $60. Electronic applications accepted. *Expenses:* $850 per credit hour (for MSN); $1,000 per credit hour (for DNP). *Financial support:* In 2017–18, 45 students received support. Scholarships/grants and unspecified assistantships available. Financial award applicants required to submit FAFSA. *Faculty research:* Aging, spiritual care, palliative and end of life care, psychiatric mental health, pediatric trauma. *Unit head:* Dr. Meredith Wallace Kazer, Dean, 203-254-4000 Ext. 2701, Fax: 203-254-4126, E-mail: mkazer@fairfield.edu. *Application contact:* Marianne Gumpper, Director of Graduate and Continuing Studies Admission, 203-254-4184, Fax: 203-254-4073, E-mail: gradadmis@fairfield.edu.
Website: http://fairfield.edu/son

Felician University, Master of Science in Nursing Program, Lodi, NJ 07644-2117. Offers adult-gerontology nurse practitioner (MSN, PMC); executive leadership (MSN, PMC); family nurse practitioner (MSN, PMC); nursing education (MSN, PMC). *Accreditation:* AACN. *Program availability:* Evening/weekend, online only, 100% online, blended/hybrid learning. *Faculty:* 9 full-time (8 women), 1 (woman) part-time/adjunct. *Students:* 96 part-time (90 women); includes 48 minority (17 Black or African American, non-Hispanic/Latino; 1 American Indian or Alaska Native, non-Hispanic/Latino; 16 Asian, non-Hispanic/Latino; 12 Hispanic/Latino; 1 Native Hawaiian or other Pacific Islander, non-Hispanic/Latino; 1 Two or more races, non-Hispanic/Latino). Average age 37. 49 applicants, 86% accepted, 23 enrolled. In 2017, 35 master's, 3 other advanced degrees awarded. *Degree requirements:* For master's, thesis, clinical presentation; for PMC, thesis, education project. *Entrance requirements:* For master's, BSN; minimum GPA of 3.0; 2 letters of recommendation; NJ RN license; personal statement; for PMC, RN license, minimum GPA of 3.0. Additional exam requirements/recommendations for international students: Required—TOEFL (minimum score 550 paper-based; 79 iBT), IELTS (minimum score 6.5), PTE (minimum score 56). *Application deadline:* Applications are processed on a rolling basis. Application fee: $40. Electronic applications accepted. Application fee is waived when completed online. *Expenses:* Contact institution. *Financial support:* Federal Work-Study, scholarships/grants, and traineeships available. Financial award applicants required to submit FAFSA. *Faculty research:* Anxiety and fear, curriculum innovation, health promotion and populations, attitudes of college students towards aging. *Unit head:* Dr. Ann Tritak, Associate Dean of Graduate Nursing, 201-559-6151, E-mail: tritaka@felician.edu. *Application contact:* Michael Szarek, Assistant Vice-President, Graduate Admissions, 201-355-1450, E-mail: szarekm@felician.edu.

Florida National University, Program in Nursing, Hialeah, FL 33012. Offers family nurse practitioner (MSN); nurse educator (MSN); nurse leadership and management (MSN). *Program availability:* 100% online, blended/hybrid learning. *Degree requirements:* For master's, practicum. *Entrance requirements:* For master's, active registered nurse license, BSN from accredited institution. *Expenses: Tuition:* Full-time $15,600. *Required fees:* $650.
Website: https://www.fnu.edu/prospective-students/our-programs/select-a-program/master-of-business-administration/nursing-msn-master/

Florida Southern College, Program in Nursing, Lakeland, FL 33801-5698. Offers adult gerontology clinical nurse specialist (MSN); adult gerontology primary care nurse practitioner (MSN); family nurse practitioner (MSN); nurse educator (MSN); nursing administration (MSN). *Accreditation:* AACN. *Program availability:* Part-time. *Faculty:* 5 full-time (all women), 2 part-time/adjunct (both women). *Students:* 142 full-time (126 women), 9 part-time (all women); includes 70 minority (39 Black or African American, non-Hispanic/Latino; 1 American Indian or Alaska Native, non-Hispanic/Latino; 11 Asian, non-Hispanic/Latino; 13 Hispanic/Latino; 1 Native Hawaiian or other Pacific Islander, non-Hispanic/Latino; 5 Two or more races, non-Hispanic/Latino), 1 international. Average age 40. 83 applicants, 93% accepted, 72 enrolled. In 2017, 41 master's awarded. *Degree requirements:* For master's, 780 clinical practice hours. *Entrance requirements:* For master's, GMAT or GRE General Test, Florida RN license, 3 letters of recommendation, personal statement, minimum GPA of 3.0, resume. Additional exam requirements/recommendations for international students: Required—TOEFL (minimum score 550 paper-based; 79 iBT), IELTS (minimum score 6.5). *Application deadline:* For fall admission, 6/1 for domestic and international students; for spring admission, 10/1 for domestic and international students. Applications are processed on a rolling basis. Application fee: $30. Electronic applications accepted. *Expenses:* $585 per credit hour, $100 required fees. *Financial support:* In 2017–18, 1 student received support. Scholarships/grants and traineeships available. Support available to part-time students. Financial award applicants required to submit FAFSA. *Faculty research:* End of life care, dementia, health promotion. *Unit head:* Dr. Linda Comer, Dean, 863-680-4310, Fax: 863-680-3872, E-mail: lcomer@flsouthern.edu. *Application contact:* Kathy Connelly, Evening Program Assistant Director, 863-680-4205, Fax: 863-680-3872, E-mail: kconnelly@flsouthern.edu.

Florida State University, The Graduate School, College of Nursing, Tallahassee, FL 32306-4310. Offers family nurse practitioner (DNP); psychiatric mental health (Certificate). *Accreditation:* AACN; AANA/CANAEP. *Program availability:* Part-time, 100% online. *Faculty:* 20 full-time (19 women), 3 part-time/adjunct (all women). *Students:* 82 full-time (72 women), 26 part-time (25 women); includes 29 minority (9 Black or African American, non-Hispanic/Latino; 8 Asian, non-Hispanic/Latino; 10 Hispanic/Latino; 2 Two or more races, non-Hispanic/Latino). Average age 38. 123 applicants, 48% accepted, 41 enrolled. In 2017, 20 doctorates awarded. *Degree requirements:* For doctorate, thesis/dissertation, evidence-based project. *Entrance requirements:* For doctorate, GRE General Test, MAT, minimum GPA of 3.0, BSN or MSN, Florida RN license. Additional exam requirements/recommendations for international students: Required—TOEFL (minimum score 550 paper-based). *Application deadline:* For fall admission, 4/1 for domestic and international students. Application fee: $30. Electronic applications accepted. *Expenses:* Contact institution. *Financial support:* In 2017–18, 29 students received support, including fellowships with partial tuition reimbursements available (averaging $6,300 per year), research assistantships with partial tuition reimbursements available (averaging $3,000 per year), 3 teaching assistantships with partial tuition reimbursements available (averaging $3,000 per year); career-related internships or fieldwork, Federal Work-Study, institutionally sponsored loans, scholarships/grants, traineeships, and tuition waivers (partial) also available. Financial award application deadline: 4/1; financial award applicants required to submit FAFSA. *Faculty research:* Cardiac, women's health, health promotion and prevention, educational strategies, infectious diseases, health disparities. *Unit head:* Dr. Judith McFetridge-Durdle, Dean, 850-644-6846, Fax: 850-644-7660, E-mail: jdurdle@nursing.fsu.edu. *Application contact:* Carlos Urrutia, Assistant Director for Student Services, 850-644-5638, Fax: 850-645-7249, E-mail: currutia@fsu.edu.
Website: http://nursing.fsu.edu/

Franciscan Missionaries of Our Lady University, School of Nursing, Program in Nursing, Baton Rouge, LA 70808. Offers family nurse practitioner (MSN). *Program availability:* Part-time. *Degree requirements:* For master's, capstone project. *Entrance requirements:* For master's, GRE within the last five years, BSN with minimum GPA of 3.0 during the last 60 hours of undergraduate work, 1 year of full-time experience as a registered nurse, current licensure or eligibility to practice as registered nurse in Louisiana, 3 professional letters of recommendation. *Application deadline:* For fall admission, 5/15 for domestic students; for spring admission, 9/15 for domestic students. *Unit head:* Dr. Kristin Martin, Director, 225-490-1677, E-mail: kristin.martin@franu.edu. *Application contact:* Dr. Kristin Martin, Director, 225-490-1677, E-mail: kristin.martin@franu.edu.
Website: https://www.franu.edu/academics/academic-programs/family-nurse-practitioner

Francis Marion University, Graduate Programs, Department of Nursing, Florence, SC 29502-0547. Offers family nurse practitioner (MSN); family nurse practitioner with nurse educator certificate (MSN); nurse educator (MSN). *Program availability:* Part-time. *Entrance requirements:* For master's, GRE, official transcripts, two letters of recommendation from professional associates or former professors, written statement of applicant's career goals, current nursing license. Additional exam requirements/recommendations for international students: Required—TOEFL (minimum score 550 paper-based; 79 iBT). Electronic applications accepted. *Expenses:* Contact institution.

Fresno Pacific University, Graduate Programs, Program in Nursing, Fresno, CA 93702-4709. Offers family nurse practitioner (MSN). *Entrance requirements:* For master's, official transcripts verifying BSN from accredited nursing program; minimum cumulative GPA of 3.0; three reference forms; statement of intent; resume or curriculum vitae; personal interview; active California RN license; completion of statistics, chemistry and upper-division writing. *Expenses:* Contact institution.

Frontier Nursing University, Graduate Programs, Hyden, KY 41749. Offers family nurse practitioner (MSN, DNP, Post Master's Certificate); nurse-midwifery (MSN, DNP, Post Master's Certificate); psychiatric-mental health nurse practitioner (MSN, DNP, Post Master's Certificate); women's health care nurse practitioner (MSN, DNP, Post Master's Certificate). *Accreditation:* ACEN. *Degree requirements:* For doctorate, capstone project, practicum.

See Display on page 570 and Close-Up on page 761.

Gannon University, School of Graduate Studies, Morosky College of Health Professions and Sciences, Villa Maria School of Nursing, Program in Family Nurse Practitioner, Erie, PA 16541-0001. Offers MSN, Certificate. *Program availability:* Part-time, evening/weekend. *Degree requirements:* For master's, thesis (for some programs), practicum. *Entrance requirements:* For master's, GRE, BS with major in nursing from accredited program, transcripts, three letters of recommendation, evidence of fulfillment of legal requirements for practice of nursing in the United States; for Certificate, GRE, interview. Additional exam requirements/recommendations for international students: Required—TOEFL (minimum score 79 iBT). Electronic applications accepted.

Family Nurse Practitioner Studies

Gardner-Webb University, Graduate School, School of Nursing, Boiling Springs, NC 28017. Offers family nurse practitioner (MSN, DNP). *Accreditation:* ACEN. *Program availability:* Part-time, online learning. *Faculty:* 13 full-time (11 women), 8 part-time/adjunct (all women). *Students:* 1 (woman) full-time, 223 part-time (206 women); includes 41 minority (31 Black or African American, non-Hispanic/Latino; 2 American Indian or Alaska Native, non-Hispanic/Latino; 4 Asian, non-Hispanic/Latino; 2 Hispanic/Latino; 2 Two or more races, non-Hispanic/Latino), 2 international. Average age 37. *Entrance requirements:* For master's, GRE or MAT, minimum undergraduate GPA of 2.7; unrestricted licensure to practice as an RN. *Expenses:* Contact institution. *Unit head:* Nicole Waters, Dean, 704-406-4358, Fax: 704-406-4329, E-mail: gradschool@gardner-webb.edu. *Application contact:* Office of Graduate Admissions, 877-498-4723, Fax: 704-406-3895, E-mail: gradinfo@gardner-webb.edu.

George Mason University, College of Health and Human Services, School of Nursing, Fairfax, VA 22030. Offers adult gerontology (DNP); adult/gerontological nurse practitioner (MSN); family nurse practitioner (MSN, DNP); nurse educator (MSN); nursing (PhD); nursing administration (MSN, DNP); nursing education (Certificate); psychiatric mental health (DNP). *Accreditation:* AACN. *Program availability:* Part-time, evening/weekend, blended/hybrid learning. *Faculty:* 28 full-time (27 women), 51 part-time/adjunct (47 women). *Students:* 51 full-time (40 women), 182 part-time (162 women); includes 110 minority (59 Black or African American, non-Hispanic/Latino; 1 American Indian or Alaska Native, non-Hispanic/Latino; 36 Asian, non-Hispanic/Latino; 10 Hispanic/Latino; 4 Two or more races, non-Hispanic/Latino), 8 international. Average age 37. 159 applicants, 70% accepted, 73 enrolled. In 2017, 33 master's, 24 doctorates, 1 other advanced degree awarded. *Degree requirements:* For master's, comprehensive exam (for some programs), thesis in clinical classes; for doctorate, comprehensive exam (for some programs), thesis/dissertation (for some programs). *Entrance requirements:* For master's, 2 official transcripts; expanded goals statement; resume; BSN from accredited institution; minimum GPA of 3.0 in last 60 credits of undergraduate work; 2 letters of recommendation; completion of undergraduate statistics and graduate-level bivariate statistics; certification in professional CPR; for doctorate, GRE, 2 official transcripts; expanded goals statement; resume; 2 recommendation letters; nursing license; at least 1 year of work experience as an RN; interview; writing sample; evidence of graduate-level course in applied statistics; master's degree in nursing with minimum GPA of 3.5; for Certificate, 2 official transcripts; expanded goals statement; resume; master's degree from accredited institution or currently enrolled with minimum GPA of 3.0. Additional exam requirements/recommendations for international students: Required—TOEFL (minimum score 570 paper-based; 88 iBT), IELTS (minimum score 6.5), PTE (minimum score 59). *Application deadline:* For fall admission, 2/1 for domestic and international students. Application fee: $75 ($80 for international students). Electronic applications accepted. *Expenses:* Contact institution. *Financial support:* In 2017–18, 7 students received support, including 5 research assistantships with tuition reimbursements available (averaging $20,500 per year), 2 teaching assistantships; career-related internships or fieldwork, Federal Work-Study, scholarships/grants, unspecified assistantships, and health care benefits (for full-time research or teaching assistantship recipients) also available. Financial award application deadline: 3/1; financial award applicants required to submit FAFSA. *Faculty research:* Health care, nursing science. *Total annual research expenditures:* $1.6 million. *Unit head:* Carol Urban, Director, 703-993-2991, Fax: 703-993-1949, E-mail: curban@gmu.edu. *Application contact:* Susan Eckis, Office Manager, 703-993-1938, Fax: 703-993-1949, E-mail: seckis@gmu.edu.
Website: http://chhs.gmu.edu/nursing

Georgetown University, Graduate School of Arts and Sciences, School of Nursing and Health Studies, Washington, DC 20057. Offers acute care nurse practitioner (MS); clinical nurse specialist (MS); family nurse practitioner (MS); nurse anesthesia (MS); nurse-midwifery (MS); nursing (DNP); nursing education (MS). *Accreditation:* AACN; AANA/CANAEP (one or more programs are accredited); ACNM/ACME (one or more programs are accredited). *Degree requirements:* For master's, thesis optional. *Entrance requirements:* For master's, GRE General Test or MAT, bachelor's degree in nursing from ACEN-accredited school, minimum undergraduate GPA of 3.0. Additional exam requirements/recommendations for international students: Required—TOEFL.

The George Washington University, School of Nursing, Washington, DC 20052. Offers adult nurse practitioner (MSN, DNP, Post-Master's Certificate); clinical research administration (MSN); family nurse practitioner (MSN, Post-Master's Certificate); health care quality (MSN, Post-Master's Certificate); nursing leadership and management (MSN); nursing practice (DNP), including nursing education; palliative care nurse practitioner (Post-Master's Certificate). *Accreditation:* AACN. *Faculty:* 58 full-time (56 women), 119 part-time/adjunct (111 women). *Students:* 38 full-time (34 women), 570 part-time (510 women); includes 197 minority (92 Black or African American, non-Hispanic/Latino; 2 American Indian or Alaska Native, non-Hispanic/Latino; 63 Asian, non-Hispanic/Latino; 28 Hispanic/Latino; 1 Native Hawaiian or other Pacific Islander, non-Hispanic/Latino; 11 Two or more races, non-Hispanic/Latino), 2 international. Average age 31. 507 applicants, 76% accepted, 185 enrolled. In 2017, 155 master's, 32 doctorates awarded. *Expenses: Tuition:* Full-time $28,800; part-time $1655 per credit hour. *Required fees:* $45; $2.75 per credit hour. *Unit head:* Pamela R. Jeffries, Dean, 202-994-3725, E-mail: pjeffries@gwu.edu. *Application contact:* Kristin Williams, Associate Provost for Graduate Enrollment Management, 202-994-0467, Fax: 202-994-0371, E-mail: ksw@gwu.edu.
Website: http://nursing.gwumc.edu/

Georgia Southern University, Jack N. Averitt College of Graduate Studies, College of Health and Human Sciences, School of Nursing, Program in Nurse Practitioner, Statesboro, GA 30458. Offers family nurse practitioner (MSN); psychiatric mental health nurse practitioner (MSN). *Program availability:* Part-time, blended/hybrid learning. *Students:* 2 part-time (both women); includes 1 minority (Black or African American, non-Hispanic/Latino). Average age 43. 3 applicants, 33% accepted. In 2017, 12 master's awarded. *Entrance requirements:* For master's, minimum GPA of 3.0, Georgia nursing license, 2 years of clinical experience, CPR certification. Additional exam requirements/recommendations for international students: Required—TOEFL (minimum score 550 paper-based; 80 iBT), IELTS (minimum score 6). *Application deadline:* For fall admission, 7/31 priority date for domestic and international students; for spring admission, 11/30 priority date for domestic students, 11/30 for international students; for summer admission, 3/31 for domestic and international students. Applications are processed on a rolling basis. Application fee: $50. Electronic applications accepted. *Expenses:* Tuition, state resident: full-time $4986; part-time $3324 per year. Tuition, nonresident: full-time $21,982; part-time $15,352 per year. *Required fees:* $2092; $1802 per credit hour. $901 per semester. Tuition and fees vary according to course load, campus/location and program. *Financial support:* In 2017–18, 1 student received support, including 5 fellowships with full tuition reimbursements available (averaging $7,750 per year); career-related internships or fieldwork, Federal Work-Study, scholarships/grants, traineeships, tuition waivers (full), and unspecified assistantships also available. Support available to part-time students. Financial award application deadline: 4/15; financial award applicants required to submit FAFSA. *Faculty research:* Vulnerable populations, breast cancer, diabetes, mellitus, advanced practice nursing issues. *Unit head:* Dr. Sharon Radzyminski, Department Chair, 912-478-5455, Fax: 912-478-5036, E-mail: sradzyminski@georgiasouthern.edu.

Georgia Southern University–Armstrong Campus, College of Graduate Studies, School of Nursing, Savannah, GA 31419-1997. Offers adult-gerontological acute care nurse practitioner (Certificate); adult-gerontological clinical nurse specialist (Certificate); adult-gerontological primary care nurse practitioner (Certificate); family nurse practitioner (MSN). *Accreditation:* AACN. *Program availability:* Part-time, evening/weekend. *Faculty:* 12 full-time (all women). *Students:* 36 full-time (30 women), 22 part-time (21 women); includes 17 minority (7 Black or African American, non-Hispanic/Latino; 2 Asian, non-Hispanic/Latino; 4 Hispanic/Latino; 4 Two or more races, non-Hispanic/Latino), 1 international. Average age 32. 59 applicants, 32% accepted, 18 enrolled. In 2017, 10 master's awarded. *Degree requirements:* For master's, comprehensive exam, project or thesis. *Entrance requirements:* For master's, GRE General Test or MAT, minimum GPA of 3.0, letter of recommendation, letter of intent. Additional exam requirements/recommendations for international students: Required—TOEFL (minimum score 523 paper-based; 70 iBT). *Application deadline:* For fall admission, 2/28 for domestic and international students; for spring admission, 11/15 for domestic students, 9/15 for international students. Applications are processed on a rolling basis. Application fee: $30. Electronic applications accepted. *Expenses:* Tuition, state resident: part-time $211 per credit hour. Tuition, nonresident: part-time $782 per credit hour. *Required fees:* $737 per semester. Tuition and fees vary according to course load, degree level, campus/location and program. *Financial support:* In 2017–18, research assistantships with full tuition reimbursements (averaging $5,000 per year) were awarded; Federal Work-Study, scholarships/grants, and unspecified assistantships also available. Support available to part-time students. Financial award application deadline: 3/1; financial award applicants required to submit FAFSA. *Faculty research:* Midwifery, mental health, nursing simulation, smoking cessation during pregnancy, asthma education, vulnerable populations, geriatrics, disaster nursing, complementary and alternative modalities, nephrology. *Unit head:* Dr. Catherine Gilbert, Department Head, 912-344-3145, E-mail: catherine.gilbert@armstrong.edu. *Application contact:* McKenzie Peterman, Graduate Admissions Specialist, 912-478-5678, Fax: 912-478-0740, E-mail: mpeterman@georgiasouthern.edu.
Website: https://www.armstrong.edu/degree-programs/nursing-msn

Georgia Southwestern State University, College of Nursing and Health Sciences, Americus, GA 31709-4693. Offers family nurse practitioner (MSN); health informatics (Postbaccalaureate Certificate); nurse educator (Post Master's Certificate); nursing educator (MSN); nursing informatics (MSN); nursing leadership (MSN). MSN program offered by the Georgia Intercollegiate Consortium for Graduate Nursing Education, a partnership with Columbus State University. *Program availability:* Part-time, online only, all theory courses are offered online. *Faculty:* 10 full-time, 5 part-time/adjunct. *Students:* 23 full-time (22 women), 106 part-time (92 women); includes 41 minority (all Black or African American, non-Hispanic/Latino). Average age 35. 95 applicants, 63% accepted, 30 enrolled. In 2017, 17 master's awarded. *Degree requirements:* For master's, comprehensive exam (for some programs), thesis (for some programs), minimum cumulative GPA of 3.0; maximum of 6 credit hours with C grade and no D grades; degree completed within 7 calendar years from initial enrollment date in graduate courses; for other advanced degree, minimum cumulative GPA of 3.0; maximum of 6 credit hours with C grade and no D grades; degree completed within 7 calendar years from initial enrollment date in graduate courses. *Entrance requirements:* For master's and other advanced degree, baccalaureate degree in nursing from regionally-accredited institution and nationally-accredited nursing program with minimum GPA of 3.0; three professional letters of recommendation; current unencumbered RN license in state where clinical course requirements will be met; background check/drug test; proof of immunizations. *Application deadline:* For fall admission, 1/15 for domestic students; for spring admission, 10/15 for domestic students. Application fee: $25. Electronic applications accepted. *Expenses:* $385 per credit hour, plus fees, which vary according to enrolled credit hours. *Financial support:* Application deadline: 6/1; applicants required to submit FAFSA. *Unit head:* Dr. Sandra Daniel, Dean, 229-931-2275. *Application contact:* Whitney Ford, Admissions Specialist, Office of Graduate Admissions, 800-338-0082, Fax: 229-931-2983, E-mail: graduateadmissions@gsw.edu.
Website: https://gsw.edu/Academics/Schools-and-Departments/School-of-Nursing/index

Georgia State University, Byrdine F. Lewis School of Nursing, Atlanta, GA 30303. Offers adult health clinical nurse specialist/nurse practitioner (MS, Certificate); child health clinical nurse specialist/pediatric nurse practitioner (MS, Certificate); family nurse practitioner (MS, Certificate); family psychiatric mental health nurse practitioner (MS, Certificate); nursing (PhD); nursing leadership in healthcare innovations (MS), including nursing administration, nursing informatics; nutrition (MS); perinatal clinical nurse specialist/women's health nurse practitioner (MS, Certificate); physical therapy (DPT); respiratory therapy (MS). *Accreditation:* AACN. *Program availability:* Part-time, blended/hybrid learning. *Faculty:* 69 full-time (52 women). *Students:* 322 full-time (248 women), 481 part-time (466 women); includes 186 minority (112 Black or African American, non-Hispanic/Latino; 44 Asian, non-Hispanic/Latino; 20 Hispanic/Latino; 10 Two or more races, non-Hispanic/Latino), 18 international. Average age 31. 370 applicants, 56% accepted, 148 enrolled. In 2017, 131 master's, 49 doctorates, 11 other advanced degrees awarded. *Degree requirements:* For doctorate, comprehensive exam, thesis/dissertation. *Entrance requirements:* For doctorate, GRE. Additional exam requirements/recommendations for international students: Required—TOEFL. *Application deadline:* For fall admission, 2/1 priority date for domestic and international students; for spring admission, 9/15 for domestic and international students. Applications are processed on a rolling basis. Application fee: $50. Electronic applications accepted. *Expenses:* Contact institution. *Financial support:* In 2017–18, research assistantships with tuition reimbursements (averaging $1,666 per year), teaching assistantships with tuition reimbursements (averaging $1,920 per year) were awarded; scholarships/grants, tuition waivers (full and partial), and unspecified assistantships also available. Support available to part-time students. Financial award application deadline: 8/1; financial award applicants required to submit FAFSA. *Faculty research:* Stroke intervention for caregivers, stroke prevention in African-Americans; relationships between psychological distress and health outcomes in parents with a medically ill infant; medically fragile children; nursing expertise and patient outcomes. *Unit head:* Nancy Kropf, Dean of Nursing, 404-413-1101, Fax: 404-413-1090, E-mail: nkropf@gsu.edu.
Website: http://nursing.gsu.edu/

Goshen College, Program in Nursing, Goshen, IN 46526-4794. Offers family nurse practitioner (MSN). *Accreditation:* AACN. *Program availability:* Part-time, evening/weekend. *Faculty:* 5 full-time (4 women), 1 (woman) part-time/adjunct. *Students:* 55 full-time (48 women), 1 (woman) part-time; includes 10 minority (3 Black or African American, non-Hispanic/Latino; 2 Asian, non-Hispanic/Latino; 4 Hispanic/Latino; 1 Two or more races, non-Hispanic/Latino), 1 international. Average age 35. *Degree requirements:* For master's, comprehensive exam (for some programs). *Entrance requirements:* For master's, minimum GPA of 3.0, curriculum vitae, bachelor's degree in nursing, active RN license in Indiana or Michigan, three professional references, essay, one year of clinical experience, statistics course, interview with program director. Additional exam requirements/recommendations for international students: Required—TOEFL (minimum score 600 paper-based; 100 iBT), IELTS (minimum score 6.5). *Application deadline:* For fall admission, 3/15 priority date for domestic students.

Electronic applications accepted. *Expenses: Tuition:* Full-time $13,356; part-time $742 per credit hour. Tuition and fees vary according to degree level, campus/location and program. *Financial support:* Scholarships/grants available. *Unit head:* Ruth Stoltzfus, Director, 574-535-7973, E-mail: ruthas@goshen.edu. *Application contact:* Natalie Shields, Admissions Counselor for Graduate and Continuing Studies, 574-535-7458, E-mail: nshields@goshen.edu.
Website: http://www.goshen.edu/graduate/nursing/

Graceland University, School of Nursing, Independence, MO 64050-3434. Offers adult and gerontology acute care (MSN, PMC); family nurse practitioner (MSN, PMC); nurse educator (MSN, PMC); organizational leadership (DNP). *Accreditation:* AACN. *Program availability:* Part-time, online learning. *Faculty:* 13 full-time (11 women), 24 part-time/adjunct (all women). *Students:* 338 full-time (294 women), 311 part-time (282 women); includes 102 minority (33 Black or African American, non-Hispanic/Latino; 8 American Indian or Alaska Native, non-Hispanic/Latino; 18 Asian, non-Hispanic/Latino; 29 Hispanic/Latino; 1 Native Hawaiian or other Pacific Islander, non-Hispanic/Latino; 13 Two or more races, non-Hispanic/Latino), 2 international. Average age 36. 119 applicants, 86% accepted, 95 enrolled. In 2017, 158 master's, 2 doctorates awarded. *Degree requirements:* For master's, comprehensive exam (for some programs), thesis optional, scholarly project; for doctorate, capstone project. *Entrance requirements:* For master's, BSN from nationally-accredited program, RN license, minimum GPA of 3.0, satisfactory criminal background check, three professional reference letters, professional goals statement of 150 words or less; for doctorate, MSN from nationally-accredited program, RN license, minimum GPA of 3.2, criminal background check. Additional exam requirements/recommendations for international students: Required—TOEFL (minimum score 550 paper-based; 79 iBT). *Application deadline:* For fall admission, 6/1 priority date for domestic students; for winter admission, 10/1 priority date for domestic students; for spring admission, 10/1 priority date for domestic students; for summer admission, 2/1 for domestic students. Application fee: $50. Electronic applications accepted. *Expenses:* $775 per credit hour tuition, $1,800 practicum fees, $480 research fees, $846 university technology fees, $655 lab fees, $300 program support fees. *Financial support:* In 2017–18, 14 students received support. Institutionally sponsored loans available. Support available to part-time students. Financial award application deadline: 6/1; financial award applicants required to submit FAFSA. *Faculty research:* International nursing, family care-giving, health promotion, mental health nursing. *Unit head:* Dr. Claudia D. Horton, Interim Vice President for Independence Campus/Dean, 816-423-4670, Fax: 816-423-4753, E-mail: horton@graceland.edu. *Application contact:* Admissions Representative, 816-423-4717, Fax: 816-833-2990, E-mail: distancelearning@graceland.edu.
Website: http://www.graceland.edu/nursing

Grambling State University, School of Graduate Studies and Research, College of Professional Studies, School of Nursing, Grambling, LA 71245. Offers family nurse practitioner (PMC); nursing (MSN). *Accreditation:* ACEN. *Program availability:* Part-time. *Degree requirements:* For master's, comprehensive exam (for some programs), thesis (for some programs). *Entrance requirements:* For master's, GRE, minimum GPA of 3.0 on last degree, interview, 2 years of experience as RN. Additional exam requirements/recommendations for international students: Required—TOEFL (minimum score 500 paper-based; 62 iBT). Electronic applications accepted.

Grand Canyon University, College of Nursing and Health Care Professions, Phoenix, AZ 85017-1097. Offers acute care nurse practitioner (MSN, PMC); family nurse practitioner (MSN, PMC); health care administration (MS); health care informatics (MS, MSN); leadership in health care systems (MSN); nursing (DNP); nursing education (MSN, PMC); public health (MPH, MSN); MBA/MSN. *Accreditation:* AACN. *Program availability:* Part-time, evening/weekend, online learning. *Degree requirements:* For master's and PMC, comprehensive exam (for some programs). *Entrance requirements:* For master's, minimum cumulative and science course undergraduate GPA of 3.0. Additional exam requirements/recommendations for international students: Required—TOEFL (minimum score 575 paper-based; 90 iBT), IELTS (minimum score 7).

Gwynedd Mercy University, Frances M. Maguire School of Nursing and Health Professions, Gwynedd Valley, PA 19437-0901. Offers clinical nurse specialist (MSN), including gerontology, oncology, pediatrics; nurse educator (MSN); nurse practitioner (MSN), including adult health, pediatric health; nursing (DNP). *Accreditation:* ACEN. *Program availability:* Part-time, blended/hybrid learning. *Faculty:* 4 full-time (all women), 1 (woman) part-time/adjunct. *Students:* 28 full-time (25 women), 48 part-time (43 women); includes 28 minority (15 Black or African American, non-Hispanic/Latino; 11 Asian, non-Hispanic/Latino; 1 Hispanic/Latino; 1 Two or more races, non-Hispanic/Latino). Average age 37. 72 applicants, 25% accepted, 16 enrolled. In 2017, 7 master's awarded. *Degree requirements:* For master's, thesis optional; for doctorate, evidence-based scholarly project. *Entrance requirements:* For master's, GRE General Test or MAT, current nursing experience, physical assessment, course work in statistics, BSN from ACEN-accredited program, 2 letters of recommendation, personal interview. Additional exam requirements/recommendations for international students: Required—TOEFL (minimum score 575 paper-based). *Application deadline:* For fall admission, 8/1 priority date for domestic students; for winter admission, 12/1 priority date for domestic students. Applications are processed on a rolling basis. Electronic applications accepted. *Expenses:* $825 per credit (non-doctoral degrees), $930 per credit (doctoral); $17 part-time fee, $165 graduation fee. *Financial support:* In 2017–18, 5 students received support. Scholarships/grants, traineeships, and unspecified assistantships available. Financial award application deadline: 8/30. *Faculty research:* Critical thinking, primary care, domestic violence, multiculturalism, nursing centers. *Unit head:* Dr. Andrea D. Hollingsworth, Dean, 215-646-7300 Ext. 539, Fax: 215-641-5517, E-mail: hollingsworth.a@gmc.edu. *Application contact:* Dr. Barbara A. Jones, Director, 215-646-7300 Ext. 407, Fax: 215-641-5564, E-mail: jones.b@gmc.edu.
Website: http://www.gmercyu.edu/academics/graduate-programs/nursing

Hampton University, School of Nursing, Hampton, VA 23668. Offers community health nursing (MS); family nurse practitioner (MS); family research (PhD); nursing administration (MS); nursing education (MS). *Accreditation:* AACN. *Program availability:* Part-time, online learning. *Students:* 6 full-time (all women), 28 part-time (25 women); includes 31 minority (29 Black or African American, non-Hispanic/Latino; 2 Hispanic/Latino). Average age 48. 7 applicants, 14% accepted. In 2017, 3 master's, 4 doctorates awarded. *Degree requirements:* For master's, comprehensive exam, thesis optional; for doctorate, comprehensive exam, thesis/dissertation. *Entrance requirements:* For master's, GRE General Test. *Application deadline:* For fall admission, 6/1 priority date for domestic students, 4/1 priority date for international students; for spring admission, 11/1 priority date for domestic students, 9/1 priority date for international students; for summer admission, 4/1 priority date for domestic students, 2/1 priority date for international students. Applications are processed on a rolling basis. Application fee: $35. Electronic applications accepted. *Expenses: Tuition:* Full-time $22,630; part-time $575 per semester hour. *Required fees:* $70. Tuition and fees vary according to program. *Financial support:* In 2017–18, 2 students received support. Fellowships, research assistantships, teaching assistantships, career-related internships or fieldwork, Federal Work-Study, institutionally sponsored loans, and scholarships/grants available. Support available to part-time students. Financial award application deadline: 6/30; financial award applicants required to submit FAFSA. *Faculty research:* African-American stress, HIV education, pediatric obesity, hypertension, breast cancer. *Unit head:* Dr. Shevallanie Lott, Dean, 757-727-5654, E-mail: shevellanie.lott@hamptonu.edu.
Website: http://nursing.hamptonu.edu

Hardin-Simmons University, Graduate School, Patty Hanks Shelton School of Nursing, Abilene, TX 79698-0001. Offers education (MSN); family nurse practitioner (MSN). Programs offered jointly with McMurry University. *Accreditation:* AACN. *Program availability:* Part-time. *Faculty:* 2 full-time (both women), 1 (woman) part-time/adjunct. *Students:* 17 part-time (8 women); includes 5 minority (1 Black or African American, non-Hispanic/Latino; 1 Asian, non-Hispanic/Latino; 3 Hispanic/Latino), 1 international. Average age 36. In 2017, 7 master's awarded. *Degree requirements:* For master's, comprehensive exam, thesis or alternative. *Entrance requirements:* For master's, GRE, minimum undergraduate GPA of 3.0; interview; upper-level course work in statistics; CPR certification; letters of recommendation. Additional exam requirements/recommendations for international students: Required—TOEFL (minimum score 550 paper-based; 75 iBT). *Application deadline:* For fall admission, 8/15 priority date for domestic students, 4/1 for international students; for spring admission, 1/5 priority date for domestic students, 9/1 for international students. Applications are processed on a rolling basis. Application fee: $50 ($150 for international students). Electronic applications accepted. *Expenses:* Contact institution. *Financial support:* In 2017–18, 10 students received support. Career-related internships or fieldwork and scholarships/grants available. Support available to part-time students. Financial award application deadline: 6/30; financial award applicants required to submit FAFSA. *Faculty research:* Child abuse, alternative medicine, pediatric chronic disease, health promotion. *Unit head:* Dr. Nina Ouimette, Dean, 325-671-2357, Fax: 325-671-2386, E-mail: nouimette@phssn.edu. *Application contact:* Dr. Nancy Kucinski, Dean of Graduate Studies, 325-670-1298, Fax: 325-670-1564, E-mail: gradoff@hsutx.edu.
Website: http://www.phssn.edu/

Hofstra University, Hofstra Northwell School of Graduate Nursing and Physician Assistant Studies, Programs in Nursing, Hempstead, NY 11549. Offers adult-gerontology acute care nurse practitioner (MS); family nurse practitioner (MS); psychiatric-mental health nurse practitioner (MS). *Students:* 29 full-time (23 women), 107 part-time (89 women); includes 62 minority (16 Black or African American, non-Hispanic/Latino; 21 Asian, non-Hispanic/Latino; 25 Hispanic/Latino). Average age 35. 122 applicants, 62% accepted, 62 enrolled. *Degree requirements:* For master's, comprehensive exam, minimum GPA of 3.0. *Entrance requirements:* For master's, bachelor's degree in biology or equivalent, 2 letters of recommendation, essay, minimum GPA of 3.0. Additional exam requirements/recommendations for international students: Required—TOEFL (minimum score 550 paper-based; 80 iBT). *Application deadline:* For fall admission, 11/1 for domestic students. Application fee: $75. Electronic applications accepted. *Expenses: Tuition:* Full-time $1292. *Required fees:* $970. Tuition and fees vary according to program. *Financial support:* In 2017–18, 4 students received support, including 4 fellowships with full and partial tuition reimbursements available (averaging $16,205 per year); research assistantships with full and partial tuition reimbursements available, career-related internships or fieldwork, Federal Work-Study, institutionally sponsored loans, scholarships/grants, traineeships, tuition waivers (full and partial), and unspecified assistantships also available. Support available to part-time students. Financial award applicants required to submit FAFSA. *Faculty research:* Innovative educational pedagogies; simulation science; problem (case) based learning; chronic disease management; evidence based practice. *Unit head:* Dr. Kathleen Gallo, Dean, 516-463-7475, Fax: 516-463-7495, E-mail: kathleen.gallo@hofstra.edu. *Application contact:* Sunil Samuel, Assistant Vice President of Admissions, 516-463-4723, Fax: 516-463-4664, E-mail: graduateadmission@hofstra.edu.

Holy Names University, Graduate Division, Department of Nursing, Oakland, CA 94619-1699. Offers administration/management (MSN, PMC); care transition management (MSN); family nurse practitioner (MSN, PMC); informatics (MSN); nurse educator (PMC); MSN/MBA. *Accreditation:* AACN. *Program availability:* Part-time, evening/weekend. *Entrance requirements:* For master's, bachelor's degree in nursing or related field; California RN license or eligibility; minimum cumulative GPA of 2.8, 3.0 in nursing courses from baccalaureate program; courses in pathophysiology, statistics, and research at the undergraduate level. Additional exam requirements/recommendations for international students: Required—TOEFL (minimum score 500 paper-based; 79 iBT). Electronic applications accepted. Application fee is waived when completed online. *Faculty research:* Women's reproductive health, gerontology, attitudes about aging, schizophrenic families, international health issues.

Howard University, College of Nursing and Allied Health Sciences, Division of Nursing, Washington, DC 20059-0002. Offers family nurse practitioner (MSN); nurse educator (MSN). *Accreditation:* AACN. *Program availability:* Part-time. *Degree requirements:* For master's, comprehensive exam, thesis optional. *Entrance requirements:* For master's, RN license, minimum GPA of 3.0, BS in nursing. *Faculty research:* Urinary incontinence, breast cancer prevention, depression in the elderly, adolescent pregnancy.

Hunter College of the City University of New York, Graduate School, Hunter-Bellevue School of Nursing, Doctor of Nursing Practice Program, New York, NY 10065-5085. Offers adult-gerontology nurse practitioner (DNP); family nurse practitioner (DNP); psychiatric-mental health nurse practitioner (DNP).

Husson University, Graduate Nursing Program, Bangor, ME 04401-2999. Offers educational leadership (MSN); family and community nurse practitioner (MSN, PMC); psychiatric mental health nurse practitioner (MSN, PMC). *Accreditation:* AACN. *Program availability:* Part-time, evening/weekend. *Faculty:* 4 full-time (all women), 4 part-time/adjunct (all women). *Students:* 1 full-time (0 women), 62 part-time (54 women); includes 3 minority (2 Black or African American, non-Hispanic/Latino; 1 Hispanic/Latino), 1 international. Average age 36. 62 applicants, 55% accepted, 26 enrolled. In 2017, 9 master's awarded. *Degree requirements:* For master's, comprehensive exam (for some programs), research project. *Entrance requirements:* For master's, proof of RN licensure. Additional exam requirements/recommendations for international students: Required—TOEFL (minimum score 550 paper-based; 80 iBT), IELTS (minimum score 6.5). *Application deadline:* For fall admission, 7/15 for domestic students; for spring admission, 10/30 for domestic students. Application fee: $50. Electronic applications accepted. *Expenses:* $577 per credit; $110 to $480 yearly fee depending on credit load. *Financial support:* In 2017–18, 1 student received support. Federal Work-Study, institutionally sponsored loans, traineeships, and unspecified assistantships available. Financial award application deadline: 3/31; financial award applicants required to submit FAFSA. *Faculty research:* Health disparities and methods to better identify and provide healthcare services to those most in need. *Unit head:* Prof. Mary Jude, Director, Graduate Nursing, 207-941-7769, Fax: 207-941-7198, E-mail: judem@husson.edu. *Application contact:* Kristen Card, Director of Graduate Admissions, 207-404-5660, Fax: 207-941-7935, E-mail: cardk@husson.edu.
Website: http://www.husson.edu/college-of-health-and-education/school-of-nursing/graduate-nursing/

Illinois State University, Graduate School, Mennonite College of Nursing, Normal, IL 61790. Offers family nurse practitioner (PMC); nursing (MSN, PhD). *Accreditation:* AACN. *Faculty research:* Expanding the teaching-nursing home culture in the state of Illinois, advanced education nursing traineeship program, collaborative doctoral program-caring for older adults.

Family Nurse Practitioner Studies

Indiana State University, College of Graduate and Professional Studies, College of Health and Human Services, Department of Advanced Practice Nursing, Terre Haute, IN 47809. Offers advanced practice nursing (DNP); family nurse practitioner (MS); nursing administration (MS); nursing education (MS). *Accreditation:* ACEN. *Program availability:* Part-time. *Degree requirements:* For master's, thesis or alternative. *Entrance requirements:* For master's, BSN, RN license, minimum undergraduate GPA of 3.0. Electronic applications accepted. *Faculty research:* Nursing faculty-student interactions, clinical evaluation, program evaluation, sexual dysfunction, faculty attitudes.

Indiana University Kokomo, School of Nursing, Kokomo, IN 46904. Offers family nurse practitioner (MSN); nurse administrator (MSN); nurse educator (MSN). Electronic applications accepted. *Expenses:* Contact institution.

Indiana University–Purdue University Fort Wayne, College of Health and Human Services, Department of Nursing, Fort Wayne, IN 46805-1499. Offers adult-gerontology primary care nurse practitioner (MS); family nurse practitioner (MS); nurse executive (MS); nursing administration (Certificate); nursing education (MS). *Accreditation:* ACEN. *Program availability:* Part-time. *Entrance requirements:* For master's, GRE Writing Test (if GPA below 3.0), BS in nursing, eligibility for Indiana RN license, minimum GPA of 3.0, essay, copy of resume, three references, undergraduate course work in research and statistics within last 5 years. Additional exam requirements/recommendations for international students: Required—TOEFL (minimum score 550 paper-based; 79 iBT); Recommended—TWE. Electronic applications accepted. *Faculty research:* Community engagement, cervical screening, evidence-based practice.

Indiana University–Purdue University Indianapolis, School of Nursing, MSN Program in Nursing, Indianapolis, IN 46202. Offers adult/gerontology acute care nurse practitioner (MSN); adult/gerontology clinical nurse specialist (MSN); adult/gerontology primary care nurse practitioner (MSN); family nurse practitioner (MSN); nursing education (MSN); nursing leadership in health systems (MSN); pediatric clinical nurse specialist (MSN); pediatric nurse practitioner (MSN). *Accreditation:* AACN. *Program availability:* Part-time, blended/hybrid learning. *Degree requirements:* For master's, thesis. *Entrance requirements:* For master's, BSN from ACEN- or CCNE-accredited program, minimum undergraduate GPA of 3.0 (preferred), professional resume or curriculum vitae, essay stating career goals and objectives, current unencumbered RN license, three references from individuals with knowledge of ability to succeed in graduate program. Additional exam requirements/recommendations for international students: Required—TOEFL (minimum score 550 paper-based; 79 iBT). Electronic applications accepted. *Expenses:* Contact institution. *Faculty research:* Quality of life, symptom management, cancer prevention and control, heart failure, pediatric oncology.

Indiana University South Bend, Vera Z. Dwyer College of Health Sciences, School of Nursing, South Bend, IN 46615. Offers family nurse practitioner (MSN). *Accreditation:* AACN. *Program availability:* Part-time, evening/weekend. *Entrance requirements:* For master's, GRE General Test, minimum GPA of 3.0. *Expenses:* Contact institution.

Jacksonville University, Brooks Rehabilitation College of Healthcare Sciences, Keigwin School of Nursing, Master of Science in Nursing Program, Jacksonville, FL 32211. Offers clinical nurse educator (MSN); family nurse practitioner (MSN); family nurse practitioner/emergency nurse practitioner (MSN); leadership in the healthcare system (MSN); nursing informatics (MSN); psychiatric nurse practitioner (MSN); MSN/MBA. *Program availability:* Part-time, 100% online, blended/hybrid learning. *Faculty:* 8 full-time (all women), 8 part-time/adjunct (6 women). *Students:* 41 full-time (36 women), 456 part-time (415 women); includes 169 minority (102 Black or African American, non-Hispanic/Latino; 4 American Indian or Alaska Native, non-Hispanic/Latino; 24 Asian, non-Hispanic/Latino; 33 Hispanic/Latino; 1 Native Hawaiian or other Pacific Islander, non-Hispanic/Latino; 5 Two or more races, non-Hispanic/Latino), 1 international. Average age 39. 232 applicants, 59% accepted, 110 enrolled. In 2017, 87 master's awarded. *Degree requirements:* For master's, thesis. *Entrance requirements:* For master's, GRE General Test or undergraduate GPA above 3.0, BSN from ACEN- or CCNE-accredited program; course work in statistics and physical assessment within last 5 years; Florida nursing license; CPR/BLS certification; 3 recommendations, 2 of which are professional references; statement of intent; resume. Additional exam requirements/recommendations for international students: Required—TOEFL (minimum score 650 paper-based; 114 iBT), IELTS (minimum score 8). *Application deadline:* For fall admission, 2/1 for domestic and international students. Applications are processed on a rolling basis. Application fee: $50. Electronic applications accepted. *Expenses:* $620 per credit hour, $455 per credit hour off-campus, $720 per credit hour online. *Financial support:* Federal Work-Study, institutionally sponsored loans, scholarships/grants, and health care benefits available. Support available to part-time students. Financial award application deadline: 3/15; financial award applicants required to submit FAFSA. *Faculty research:* Treatment of anxiety. *Unit head:* Dr. Hilary Morgan, Director, Graduate Nursing Programs/Associate Professor, 904-256-7601, E-mail: hmorgan@ju.edu. *Application contact:* Stephanie Bloom, Assistant Director, Enrollment and Advanced Graduate Nursing, 904-256-7286, E-mail: sstrick4@ju.edu.
Website: https://www.ju.edu/nursing/graduate/master-science-nursing/index.php

James Madison University, The Graduate School, College of Health and Behavioral Studies, Program in Nursing, Harrisonburg, VA 22807. Offers adult/gerontology primary care nurse practitioner (MSN); clinical nurse leader (MSN); family nurse practitioner (MSN); nurse administrator (MSN); nurse midwifery (MSN); nursing (MSN, DNP); psychiatric mental health nurse practitioner (MSN). *Accreditation:* AACN. *Program availability:* Part-time, 100% online, blended/hybrid learning. *Students:* 10 full-time (9 women), 77 part-time (71 women); includes 10 minority (2 Black or African American, non-Hispanic/Latino; 5 Asian, non-Hispanic/Latino; 1 Hispanic/Latino; 2 Two or more races, non-Hispanic/Latino). Average age 30. In 2017, 27 master's awarded. Application fee: $55. Electronic applications accepted. *Expenses:* Tuition, state resident: full-time $10,512; part-time $438 per credit hour. Tuition, nonresident: full-time $28,358; part-time $1162 per credit hour. *Required fees:* $1128. *Financial support:* In 2017–18, 2 students received support. Federal Work-Study and 2 assistantships (averaging $7911) available. Financial award application deadline: 3/1; financial award applicants required to submit FAFSA. *Unit head:* Dr. Julie T. Sanford, Department Head, 540-568-6314, E-mail: sanforjt@jmu.edu. *Application contact:* Lynette D. Michael, Director of Graduate Admissions, 540-568-6131 Ext. 6395, Fax: 540-568-7860, E-mail: michaeld@jmu.edu.
Website: http://www.nursing.jmu.edu

Johns Hopkins University, School of Nursing, Nurse Practitioner Program, Baltimore, MD 21205. Offers adult/gerontological acute care nurse practitioner (DNP); adult/gerontological primary care nurse practitioner (DNP); family primary care nurse practitioner (DNP); pediatric primary care nurse practitioner (DNP). *Accreditation:* AACN. *Program availability:* Part-time. *Faculty:* 9 full-time (all women), 10 part-time/adjunct (all women). *Students:* 52 full-time (46 women), 173 part-time (160 women); includes 77 minority (28 Black or African American, non-Hispanic/Latino; 26 Asian, non-Hispanic/Latino; 18 Hispanic/Latino; 5 Two or more races, non-Hispanic/Latino), 2 international. Average age 33. 157 applicants, 55% accepted, 52 enrolled. *Entrance requirements:* For doctorate, GRE, minimum GPA of 3.0, goal statement/essay, resume, letters of recommendation, official transcripts from all post-secondary institutions attended; BSN; RN license; writing sample. Additional exam requirements/recommendations for international students: Required—TOEFL (minimum score 600 paper-based; 100 iBT), IELTS (minimum score 7). *Application deadline:* For fall admission, 11/1 priority date for domestic and international students. Application fee: $70. Electronic applications accepted. *Expenses:* $1,671 per credit. *Financial support:* In 2017–18, 28 students received support. Federal Work-Study and scholarships/grants available. Support available to part-time students. Financial award application deadline: 3/1; financial award applicants required to submit FAFSA. *Faculty research:* Community outreach, primary care of underserved populations, substance-abusing individuals, childhood violence, women's health. *Unit head:* Dr. Patricia M. Davidson, Dean, 410-955-7544, Fax: 410-955-4890, E-mail: sondeansoffice@jhu.edu. *Application contact:* Cathy Wilson, Director of Admissions, 410-955-7548, Fax: 410-614-7086, E-mail: jhuson@jhu.edu.
Website: http://www.nursing.jhu.edu

See Display on page 576 and Close-Up on page 763.

Keiser University, Master of Science in Nursing Program, Fort Lauderdale, FL 33309. Offers family nurse practitioner (MSN); nursing (MSN).
Website: http://www.keiseruniversity.edu/graduateschool/nursing-program-overview.php

Kent State University, College of Nursing, Kent, OH 44242. Offers advanced nursing practice (DNP), including adult/gerontology acute care nurse practitioner (MSN, DNP); nursing (MSN, PhD), including adult/gerontology acute care nurse practitioner (MSN, DNP), adult/gerontology clinical nurse specialist (MSN), adult/gerontology primary care nurse practitioner (MSN), family nurse practitioner (MSN), nurse educator (MSN), nursing and healthcare management (MSN), pediatric primary care nurse practitioner (MSN), psychiatric/mental health nurse practitioner (MSN); MBA/MSN. PhD program offered jointly with The University of Akron. *Accreditation:* AACN. *Program availability:* Part-time, online learning. *Faculty:* 29 full-time (28 women), 15 part-time/adjunct (12 women). *Students:* 167 full-time (142 women), 405 part-time (359 women); includes 70 minority (39 Black or African American, non-Hispanic/Latino; 11 Asian, non-Hispanic/Latino; 18 Hispanic/Latino; 2 Two or more races, non-Hispanic/Latino), 13 international. Average age 35. 272 applicants, 74% accepted, 166 enrolled. In 2017, 144 master's, 8 doctorates awarded. *Degree requirements:* For master's, thesis optional; for doctorate, comprehensive exam, thesis/dissertation. *Entrance requirements:* For master's, GRE or GMAT, minimum GPA of 3.0, active RN license, statement of purpose, 3 letters of reference, undergraduate level statistics class, baccalaureate or graduate-level nursing degree, curriculum vitae/resume; for doctorate, GRE, minimum GPA of 3.0, transcripts, 3 letters of reference, interview, active unrestricted Ohio RN license, statement of purpose, writing sample, curriculum vitae/resume, baccalaureate and master's degrees in nursing or DNP. Additional exam requirements/recommendations for international students: Required—TOEFL (minimum score 560 paper-based; 83 iBT), IELTS (minimum score 6.5), PTE (minimum score 55), Michigan English Language Assessment Battery (minimum score 78). *Application deadline:* For fall admission, 3/1 for domestic and international students; for spring admission, 10/1 for domestic and international students. Applications are processed on a rolling basis. Application fee: $45 ($70 for international students). Electronic applications accepted. *Expenses:* Tuition, state resident: full-time $11,310; part-time $515 per credit hour. Tuition, nonresident: full-time $20,396; part-time $928 per credit hour. *International tuition:* $18,544 full-time. *Financial support:* Scholarships/grants available. Financial award application deadline: 5/4. *Unit head:* Dr. Barbara Broome, Dean, 330-672-3777, E-mail: bbroome1@kent.edu. *Application contact:* Dr. Wendy A. Umberger, Associate Dean for Graduate Programs/Professor, 330-672-8813, E-mail: wlewando@kent.edu.
Website: http://www.kent.edu/nursing/

King University, School of Nursing, Bristol, TN 37620-2699. Offers family nurse practitioner (MSN); nurse educator (MSN); nursing (DNP); nursing administration (MSN); pediatric nurse practitioner (MSN).

La Salle University, School of Nursing and Health Sciences, Program in Nursing, Philadelphia, PA 19141-1199. Offers adult gerontology primary care nurse practitioner (MSN, Certificate); adult health and illness clinical nurse specialist (MSN); adult-gerontology clinical nurse specialist (MSN, Certificate); clinical nurse leader (MSN); family primary care nurse practitioner (MSN, Certificate); gerontology (Certificate); nurse anesthetist (MSN, Certificate); nursing (MSN, Certificate); nursing administration (MSN, Certificate); nursing education (Certificate); nursing practice (DNP); nursing service administration (MSN); public health nursing (MSN, Certificate); school nursing (Certificate); MSN/MBA; MSN/MPH. *Accreditation:* AACN. *Program availability:* Part-time, evening/weekend, 100% online. *Faculty:* 12 full-time (11 women), 14 part-time/adjunct (11 women). *Students:* 1 (woman) full-time, 277 part-time (220 women); includes 72 minority (36 Black or African American, non-Hispanic/Latino; 1 American Indian or Alaska Native, non-Hispanic/Latino; 18 Asian, non-Hispanic/Latino; 10 Hispanic/Latino; 1 Native Hawaiian or other Pacific Islander, non-Hispanic/Latino; 6 Two or more races, non-Hispanic/Latino), 1 international. Average age 36. 70 applicants, 56% accepted, 24 enrolled. In 2017, 81 master's, 4 doctorates, 13 other advanced degrees awarded. *Degree requirements:* For doctorate, minimum of 1,000 hours of post baccalaureate clinical practice supervised by preceptors. *Entrance requirements:* For master's, GRE, MAT, or GMAT (for students with BSN GPA of less than 3.2), baccalaureate degree in nursing from ACEN- or CCNE-accredited program or an MSN Bridge program; Pennsylvania RN license; 2 letters of reference; resume; statement of philosophy articulating professional values and future educational goal; 1 year of work experience as a registered nurse; for doctorate, GRE (waived for applicants with MSN cumulative GPA of 3.7 or above), MSN, master's degree, MBA or MHA from nationally-accredited program; resume or curriculum vitae; 2 letters of reference; interview; for Certificate, GRE, MAT, or GMAT (for students with BSN GPA of less than 3.2, baccalaureate degree in nursing from ACEN- or CCNE-accredited program or an MSN Bridge program; Pennsylvania RN license; 2 letters of reference; resume; statement of philosophy articulating professional values and future educational goal; 1 year of work experience as a registered nurse. Additional exam requirements/recommendations for international students: Required—TOEFL. *Application deadline:* For fall admission, 8/15 priority date for domestic students, 7/15 for international students; for spring admission, 12/15 priority date for domestic students, 11/15 for international students; for summer admission, 4/15 priority date for domestic students, 3/15 for international students. Applications are processed on a rolling basis. Application fee: $35. Electronic applications accepted. Application fee is waived when completed online. *Expenses:* Contact institution. *Financial support:* In 2017–18, 7 students received support. Scholarships/grants and traineeships available. Support available to part-time students. Financial award application deadline: 8/31; financial award applicants required to submit FAFSA. *Unit head:* Dr. Patricia M. Dillon, Director, 215-951-1322, Fax: 215-951-1896, E-mail: msnapn@lasalle.edu. *Application contact:* Elizabeth Heenan, Director, Graduate and Adult Enrollment, 215-951-1100, Fax: 215-951-1462, E-mail: heenan@lasalle.edu.
Website: http://www.lasalle.edu/nursing/program-options/

Le Moyne College, Department of Nursing, Syracuse, NY 13214. Offers family nurse practitioner (MS, CAS); informatics (MS, CAS); nursing administration (MS, CAS); nursing education (MS, CAS). *Accreditation:* AACN. *Program availability:* Part-time, evening/weekend. *Faculty:* 3 full-time (all women), 5 part-time/adjunct (all women). *Students:* 27 full-time (20 women), 51 part-time (47 women); includes 10 minority (4 Black or African American, non-Hispanic/Latino; 1 Asian, non-Hispanic/Latino; 4 Hispanic/Latino; 1 Two or more races, non-Hispanic/Latino). Average age 32. 39

applicants, 95% accepted, 31 enrolled. In 2017, 20 master's, 2 other advanced degrees awarded. *Degree requirements:* For master's, scholarly project. *Entrance requirements:* For master's, bachelor's degree, interview, minimum GPA of 3.0, New York RN license, 2 letters of recommendation, writing sample, transcripts. *Application deadline:* For fall admission, 8/1 priority date for domestic students, 8/1 for international students; for spring admission, 12/15 priority date for domestic students, 12/15 for international students; for summer admission, 5/1 priority date for domestic students, 5/1 for international students. Applications are processed on a rolling basis. Application fee: $50. Electronic applications accepted. *Expenses:* $700 per credit hour. *Financial support:* In 2017–18, 2 students received support. Career-related internships or fieldwork, scholarships/grants, health care benefits, and unspecified assistantships available. Support available to part-time students. Financial award applicants required to submit FAFSA. *Faculty research:* Inter-profession education, gerontology, utilization of free healthcare services by the insured, health promotion education, innovative undergraduate nursing education models, patient and family education, horizontal violence. *Unit head:* Dr. Margaret M. Wells, Professor/Chair of Nursing, 315-445-5435, Fax: 315-445-6024, E-mail: wellsmm@lemoyne.edu. *Application contact:* Kristen P. Richards, Senior Director of Enrollment Management, 315-445-5444, Fax: 315-445-6092, E-mail: trapaskp@lemoyne.edu.
Website: http://www.lemoyne.edu/nursing

Lewis University, College of Nursing and Health Professions, Program in Nursing, Romeoville, IL 60446. Offers adult gerontology acute care nurse practitioner (MSN); adult gerontology clinical nurse specialist (MSN); adult gerontology primary care nurse practitioner (MSN); family nurse practitioner (MSN); healthcare systems leadership (MSN); nursing (DNP); nursing education (MSN); school nurse (MSN). *Accreditation:* AACN. *Program availability:* Part-time, evening/weekend, 100% online, blended/hybrid learning. *Students:* 14 full-time (11 women), 361 part-time (336 women); includes 100 minority (27 Black or African American, non-Hispanic/Latino; 33 Asian, non-Hispanic/Latino; 35 Hispanic/Latino; 5 Two or more races, non-Hispanic/Latino), 1 international. Average age 37. *Degree requirements:* For master's, clinical practicum. *Entrance requirements:* For master's, minimum undergraduate GPA of 3.0, degree in nursing, RN license, letter of recommendation, interview, resume or curriculum vitae. Additional exam requirements/recommendations for international students: Required—TOEFL (minimum score 550 paper-based; 80 iBT). *Application deadline:* For fall admission, 5/1 priority date for international students; for spring admission, 11/15 priority date for international students. Applications are processed on a rolling basis. Application fee: $40. Electronic applications accepted. Tuition and fees vary according to program. *Financial support:* Federal Work-Study, scholarships/grants, tuition waivers (full and partial), and unspecified assistantships available. Financial award application deadline: 5/1; financial award applicants required to submit FAFSA. *Faculty research:* Cancer prevention, phenomenological methods, public policy analysis. *Total annual research expenditures:* $1,000. *Unit head:* 815-836-5610. *Application contact:* Nancy Wiksten, Adult Admission Counselor, 815-836-5628, Fax: 815-836-5578, E-mail: wikstena@lewisu.edu.

Liberty University, School of Nursing, Lynchburg, VA 24515. Offers family nurse practitioner (DNP); nurse educator (MSN); nursing administration (MSN); nursing informatics (MSN). *Accreditation:* AACN. *Program availability:* Part-time, online learning. *Students:* 148 full-time (131 women), 461 part-time (421 women); includes 103 minority (58 Black or African American, non-Hispanic/Latino; 4 American Indian or Alaska Native, non-Hispanic/Latino; 15 Asian, non-Hispanic/Latino; 11 Hispanic/Latino; 3 Native Hawaiian or other Pacific Islander, non-Hispanic/Latino; 12 Two or more races, non-Hispanic/Latino), 8 international. Average age 39. 536 applicants, 30% accepted, 105 enrolled. In 2017, 100 master's, 13 doctorates awarded. *Entrance requirements:* For master's, minimum cumulative undergraduate GPA of 3.0; for doctorate, minimum GPA of 3.25 in most current nursing program completed. Additional exam requirements/recommendations for international students: Recommended—TOEFL. *Application deadline:* Applications are processed on a rolling basis. Application fee: $50. Electronic applications accepted. *Financial support:* Applicants required to submit FAFSA. *Unit head:* Dr. Deanna Britt, Dean, 434-582-2519, E-mail: dbritt@liberty.edu. *Application contact:* Jay Bridge, Director of Admissions, 800-424-9595, Fax: 800-628-7977, E-mail: gradadmissions@liberty.edu.

Lincoln Memorial University, Caylor School of Nursing, Harrogate, TN 37752-1901. Offers family nurse practitioner (MSN); nurse anesthesia (MSN); psychiatric mental health nurse practitioner (MSN). *Accreditation:* AANA/CANAEP; ACEN. *Program availability:* Part-time. *Entrance requirements:* For master's, GRE.

Long Island University–Brentwood Campus, Graduate Programs, Brentwood, NY 11717. Offers childhood education (MS), including grades 1-6; childhood education/literacy B-6 (MS); childhood education/special education (grades 1-6) (MS); clinical mental health counseling (MS, Advanced Certificate); criminal justice (MS); early childhood education (MS); educational leadership (MS Ed); family nurse practitioner (MS, Advanced Certificate); health administration (MPA); library and information science (MS); literacy (B-6) (MS Ed); school counselor (MS, Advanced Certificate); social work (MSW); special education (MS Ed); students with disabilities generalist (grades 7-12) (Advanced Certificate). *Program availability:* Part-time. *Faculty:* 14 full-time (9 women), 22 part-time/adjunct (11 women). *Students:* 111 full-time (89 women), 47 part-time (34 women); includes 35 minority (8 Black or African American, non-Hispanic/Latino; 1 American Indian or Alaska Native, non-Hispanic/Latino; 3 Asian, non-Hispanic/Latino; 22 Hispanic/Latino; 1 Two or more races, non-Hispanic/Latino), 1 international. Average age 30. 110 applicants, 82% accepted, 63 enrolled. In 2017, 58 master's, 5 other advanced degrees awarded. *Entrance requirements:* For master's and Advanced Certificate, GRE. Additional exam requirements/recommendations for international students: Required—TOEFL or IELTS. *Application deadline:* Applications are processed on a rolling basis. Application fee: $50. Electronic applications accepted. *Expenses: Tuition:* Full-time $21,168; part-time $1201 per credit. *Required fees:* $1840; $920 per term. Tuition and fees vary according to course load. *Financial support:* In 2017–18, 121 students received support. Scholarships/grants available. Support available to part-time students. Financial award application deadline: 2/15; financial award applicants required to submit FAFSA. *Unit head:* Dr. Abby Van Vlerah, Dean and Chief Operating Officer, 631-299-3831, E-mail: abagail.vanvlerah@liu.edu. *Application contact:* Scott Aug, Associate Director of Enrollment Management, 631-287-8506, E-mail: scott.aug@liu.edu.
Website: http://liu.edu/brentwood

Long Island University–LIU Brooklyn, Harriet Rothkopf Heilbrunn School of Nursing, Brooklyn, NY 11201. Offers adult nurse practitioner (MS, Advanced Certificate); family nurse practitioner (MS, Advanced Certificate); nurse educator (MS). *Accreditation:* AACN. *Program availability:* Part-time, evening/weekend, blended/hybrid learning. *Faculty:* 9 full-time (7 women), 6 part-time/adjunct (4 women). *Students:* 5 full-time (all women), 195 part-time (174 women); includes 117 minority (70 Black or African American, non-Hispanic/Latino; 28 Asian, non-Hispanic/Latino; 17 Hispanic/Latino; 2 Two or more races, non-Hispanic/Latino), 1 international. Average age 37. 168 applicants, 60% accepted, 73 enrolled. In 2017, 69 master's, 2 other advanced degrees awarded. *Entrance requirements:* Additional exam requirements/recommendations for international students: Required—TOEFL or IELTS. *Application deadline:* Applications are processed on a rolling basis. Application fee: $50. Electronic applications accepted. *Expenses: Tuition:* Full-time $21,618; part-time $1201 per credit. *Required fees:* $1840; $920 per term. Tuition and fees vary according to course load. *Financial support:* In 2017–18, 15 students received support. Career-related internships or fieldwork, Federal Work-Study, scholarships/grants, and unspecified assistantships available. Support available to part-time students. Financial award application deadline: 2/15; financial award applicants required to submit FAFSA. *Faculty research:* Clinical and health outcomes in managed care; attitudes of nurses towards people with disabilities; adherence to CPAP in obstructive sleep apnea; diabetes and treatment compliance; chronic neurological disease management outside facilities. *Unit head:* Peggy Tallier, Interim Dean, 718-780-3367, E-mail: peggy.tallier@liu.edu. *Application contact:* Luis Santiago, Dean of Admissions, 718-488-1011, Fax: 718-780-6110, E-mail: bkln-admissions@liu.edu.
Website: http://www.liu.edu/Brooklyn/Academics/Harriet-Rothkopf-Heilbrunn-School-of-Nursing

Long Island University–LIU Post, School of Health Professions and Nursing, Brookville, NY 11548-1300. Offers biomedical science (MS); cardiovascular perfusion (MS); clinical lab sciences (MS); clinical laboratory management (MS); dietetic internship (Advanced Certificate); family nurse practitioner (MS, Advanced Certificate); forensic social work (Advanced Certificate); gerontology (Advanced Certificate); health administration (MPA); non-profit management (Advanced Certificate); nursing education (MS); nutrition (MS); public administration (MPA); social work (MSW). *Program availability:* Part-time, blended/hybrid learning. *Faculty:* 23 full-time (17 women), 33 part-time/adjunct (19 women). *Students:* 228 full-time (174 women), 227 part-time (185 women); includes 172 minority (76 Black or African American, non-Hispanic/Latino; 1 American Indian or Alaska Native, non-Hispanic/Latino; 44 Asian, non-Hispanic/Latino; 48 Hispanic/Latino; 3 Two or more races, non-Hispanic/Latino), 60 international. Average age 31. 392 applicants, 67% accepted, 138 enrolled. In 2017, 180 master's, 26 other advanced degrees awarded. *Degree requirements:* For master's, comprehensive exam (for some programs), thesis (for some programs). *Entrance requirements:* Additional exam requirements/recommendations for international students: Required—TOEFL (minimum score 85 iBT) or IELTS (7.5). *Application deadline:* Applications are processed on a rolling basis. Application fee: $50. Electronic applications accepted. *Expenses: Tuition:* Full-time $21,618; part-time $1201 per credit. *Required fees:* $1840; $920 per term. Tuition and fees vary according to course load. *Financial support:* In 2017–18, 102 students received support. Research assistantships, teaching assistantships, career-related internships or fieldwork, Federal Work-Study, scholarships/grants, and unspecified assistantships available. Support available to part-time students. Financial award application deadline: 2/15; financial award applicants required to submit FAFSA. *Faculty research:* Antibiotic resistance, evidence-based practice, family care, interprofessional learning, simulation learning. *Unit head:* Dr. Stacy Gropack, Dean, 516-299-2485, Fax: 516-299-2527, E-mail: post-shpn@liu.edu. *Application contact:* Kathy Riley, Associate Director of Graduate Admissions, 516-299-2900, Fax: 516-299-2137, E-mail: post-enroll@liu.edu.
Website: http://liu.edu/post/health

Louisiana State University Health Sciences Center, School of Nursing, New Orleans, LA 70112. Offers adult gerontology acute care nurse practitioner (DNP, Post-Master's Certificate); adult gerontology clinical nurse specialist (DNP, Post-Master's Certificate); adult gerontology primary care nurse practitioner (DNP, Post-Master's Certificate); clinical nurse leader (MSN); executive nurse leader (DNP, Post-Master's Certificate); neonatal nurse practitioner (DNP, Post-Master's Certificate); nurse anesthesia (DNP, Post-Master's Certificate); nurse educator (MSN); nursing (DNS); primary care family nurse practitioner (DNP, Post-Master's Certificate); public/community health nursing (DNP, Post-Master's Certificate). *Accreditation:* AACN, AANA/CANAEP (one or more programs are accredited). *Program availability:* Part-time. *Faculty:* 29 full-time (26 women), 20 part-time/adjunct (8 women). *Students:* 184 full-time (132 women), 41 part-time (35 women); includes 69 minority (45 Black or African American, non-Hispanic/Latino; 11 Asian, non-Hispanic/Latino; 12 Hispanic/Latino; 1 Two or more races, non-Hispanic/Latino), 1 international. Average age 30. 162 applicants, 42% accepted, 68 enrolled. In 2017, 52 master's, 46 doctorates awarded. *Degree requirements:* For master's, thesis optional; for doctorate, thesis/dissertation. *Entrance requirements:* For master's, GRE, minimum GPA of 3.0; for doctorate, GRE, minimum GPA of 3.0 (for DNP), 3.5 (for DNS). Additional exam requirements/recommendations for international students: Required—TOEFL (minimum score 550 paper-based; 79 iBT). *Application deadline:* Applications are processed on a rolling basis. Application fee: $100. Electronic applications accepted. *Expenses:* Contact institution. *Financial support:* Federal Work-Study, institutionally sponsored loans, scholarships/grants, and traineeships available. Financial award applicants required to submit FAFSA. *Faculty research:* Advanced clinical practice, nursing education, interprofessional education, nursing administration, culturally competent care. *Unit head:* Dr. Demetrius James Porche, Dean, 504-568-4106, Fax: 504-599-0573, E-mail: dporch@lsuhsc.edu. *Application contact:* Tracie Gravolet, Director, Office of Student Affairs, 504-568-4114, Fax: 504-568-5711, E-mail: tgravo@lsuhsc.edu.
Website: http://nursing.lsuhsc.edu/

Loyola University Chicago, Graduate School, Marcella Niehoff School of Nursing, Maywood, IL 60141. Offers adult clinical nurse specialist (MSN, Certificate); adult nurse practitioner (Certificate); dietetics (MS); family nurse practitioner (Certificate); family, adult, and women's health nurse practitioner (MSN); health systems leadership (MSN); healthcare quality using education in safety and technology (DNP); infection prevention (MSN, DNP); nursing science (PhD); women's health clinical nurse specialist (Certificate). *Accreditation:* AACN. *Program availability:* Part-time, blended/hybrid learning. *Faculty:* 24 full-time (22 women), 21 part-time/adjunct (19 women). *Students:* 188 full-time (178 women), 222 part-time (208 women); includes 105 minority (23 Black or African American, non-Hispanic/Latino; 40 Asian, non-Hispanic/Latino; 30 Hispanic/Latino; 2 Native Hawaiian or other Pacific Islander, non-Hispanic/Latino; 10 Two or more races, non-Hispanic/Latino), 4 international. Average age 36. 197 applicants, 55% accepted, 80 enrolled. In 2017, 94 master's, 17 doctorates, 26 other advanced degrees awarded. *Degree requirements:* For master's, comprehensive exam; for doctorate, thesis/dissertation, qualifying examination (for PhD); capstone project (for DNP). *Entrance requirements:* For master's, BSN, minimum nursing GPA of 3.0, Illinois RN license, 3 letters of recommendation, 1000 hours of experience in area of specialty prior to starting clinical rotations, personal statement; for doctorate, BSN or MSN, minimum GPA of 3.0, professional nursing license, 3 letters of recommendation, personal statement. Additional exam requirements/recommendations for international students: Required—TOEFL (minimum score 550 paper-based; 79 iBT), IELTS (minimum score 6.5). *Application deadline:* For fall admission, 6/1 priority date for domestic and international students; for spring admission, 11/15 priority date for domestic and international students; for summer admission, 3/15 priority date for domestic and international students. Applications are processed on a rolling basis. Application fee: $50. Electronic applications accepted. Application fee is waived when completed online. *Expenses:* Contact institution. *Financial support:* In 2017–18, 10 students received support, including 3 research assistantships with full tuition reimbursements available (averaging $18,000 per year), 1 teaching assistantship with full tuition reimbursement available (averaging $18,000 per year); scholarships/grants, unspecified assistantships,

and nurse faculty loan program also available. Financial award application deadline: 5/1; financial award applicants required to submit FAFSA. *Faculty research:* Epigenetics and social determinants of health; women's health; vitamin D; health equity; interprofessional education; prevention and self-management of chronic disease; body mass in oncology patients. *Total annual research expenditures:* $1.4 million. *Unit head:* Dr. Vickie Keough, Dean, 708-216-5448, Fax: 708-216-9555, E-mail: vkeough@luc.edu. *Application contact:* Toni Topalova, Enrollment Advisor, 708-216-3751, Fax: 708-216-9555, E-mail: atopalova@luc.edu.
Website: http://www.luc.edu/nursing/

Loyola University New Orleans, College of Nursing and Health, School of Nursing, New Orleans, LA 70118. Offers family nurse practitioner (DNP); nursing (MSN). *Accreditation:* AACN; ACEN. *Program availability:* Part-time, evening/weekend, online learning. *Faculty:* 13 full-time (10 women), 5 part-time/adjunct (all women). *Students:* 35 full-time (all women), 265 part-time (245 women); includes 102 minority (69 Black or African American, non-Hispanic/Latino; 2 American Indian or Alaska Native, non-Hispanic/Latino; 12 Asian, non-Hispanic/Latino; 15 Hispanic/Latino; 2 Native Hawaiian or other Pacific Islander, non-Hispanic/Latino; 2 Two or more races, non-Hispanic/Latino). Average age 41. 191 applicants, 54% accepted, 83 enrolled. In 2017, 126 master's, 20 doctorates awarded. *Degree requirements:* For master's, practicum; for doctorate, capstone project. *Entrance requirements:* For master's, BSN, unencumbered RN license, 1 year of work experience in clinical nursing, interview, resume, 3 recommendations, statement of purpose. Additional exam requirements/recommendations for international students: Recommended—TOEFL (minimum score 550 paper-based; 79 iBT), IELTS. *Application deadline:* For fall admission, 8/1 priority date for domestic and international students; for winter admission, 12/15 priority date for domestic and international students; for spring admission, 5/15 priority date for domestic and international students. Applications are processed on a rolling basis. Application fee: $40. Electronic applications accepted. *Expenses:* $818 per hour tuition; $738 per semester full-time fees, $376.50 part-time. *Financial support:* Traineeships and Incumbent Workers Training Program grants available. Financial award application deadline: 5/1; financial award applicants required to submit FAFSA. *Faculty research:* Increasing compliance with treatment, patient satisfaction with care provided by nurse practitioners. *Unit head:* Dr. Laurie Ann Ferguson, Interim Director, 504-865-2880, Fax: 504-865-3254, E-mail: nursing@loyno.edu. *Application contact:* Elizabeth Wadsworth, Executive Assistant to the Director, 504-865-2307, Fax: 504-865-3254, E-mail: edwadswo@loyno.edu.
Website: http://gps.loyno.edu/nursing

Malone University, Graduate Program in Nursing, Canton, OH 44709. Offers family nurse practitioner (MSN). *Accreditation:* AACN. *Program availability:* Part-time, evening/weekend. *Degree requirements:* For master's, thesis. *Entrance requirements:* For master's, minimum GPA of 3.0 from BSN program, interview, Ohio RN license. Additional exam requirements/recommendations for international students: Required—TOEFL (minimum score 550 paper-based; 79 iBT). *Expenses:* Contact institution. *Faculty research:* Home heath care and geriatrics, community settings, culture, Hispanics, tuberculosis, geriatrics, Neuman Systems Model, nursing education.

Marian University, Leighton School of Nursing, Indianapolis, IN 46222-1997. Offers family nurse practitioner (DNP); nurse anesthesia (DNP); nursing education (MSN). *Program availability:* Part-time. *Faculty:* 6 full-time (all women), 2 part-time/adjunct (both women). *Students:* 23 full-time (20 women), 1 (woman) part-time; includes 7 minority (5 Black or African American, non-Hispanic/Latino; 1 Asian, non-Hispanic/Latino; 1 Hispanic/Latino). Average age 36. 69 applicants, 35% accepted, 5 enrolled. *Degree requirements:* For master's, 38 credits, designed to be completed in 2 years; 225-hour practicum including a culminating project; for doctorate, 70 credit hours (for family nurse practitioner track); 85 credits (for nurse anesthesia track); minimum of 1000 hours of supervised practice. *Entrance requirements:* For master's, degree in nursing from NLNAC- or CCNE-accredited program; current, valid RN license in State of Indiana; minimum undergraduate GPA of 3.0; 3 recommendations; interview with admissions committee; current resume; 500-word essay describing career goals; for doctorate, BSN from NSNAC- or CCNE-accredited program; minimum undergraduate GPA of 3.0; cureent, valid RN license; current resume or curriculum vitae; 500-word essay addressing career goals; 3 letters of recommendation; interview with Admissions Committee. Additional exam requirements/recommendations for international students: Required—TOEFL (minimum score 550 paper-based; 79 iBT). *Application deadline:* For fall admission, 2/15 for domestic and international students. Applications are processed on a rolling basis. Application fee: $40. Electronic applications accepted. Application fee is waived when completed online. *Expenses:* Contact institution. *Financial support:* Application deadline: 4/15; applicants required to submit FAFSA. *Unit head:* Dr. Dorothy A. Gomez, RN, Dean, 317-955-6159, E-mail: dgomez@marian.edu. *Application contact:* Bryan Moody, Executive Director of Graduate Admission, 317-955-6284, E-mail: bmoody@marian.edu.
Website: http://www.marian.edu/school-of-nursing

Marquette University, Graduate School, College of Nursing, Milwaukee, WI 53201-1881. Offers acute care nurse practitioner (Certificate); adult clinical nurse specialist (Certificate); adult nurse practitioner (Certificate); advanced practice nursing (MSN, DNP), including adult-older adult acute care (DNP), adults (MSN), adults-older adults (DNP), clinical nurse leader (MSN), health care systems leadership (DNP), nurse-midwifery (MSN), older adults (MSN), pediatrics-acute care, pediatrics-primary care, primary care (DNP), systems leadership and healthcare quality (MSN); family nurse practitioner (Certificate); nurse-midwifery (Certificate); nursing (PhD); pediatric acute care (Certificate); pediatric primary care (Certificate); systems leadership and healthcare quality (Certificate). *Accreditation:* AACN. Terminal master's awarded for partial completion of doctoral program. *Degree requirements:* For master's, comprehensive exam, thesis or alternative. *Entrance requirements:* For master's, GRE General Test, BSN, Wisconsin RN license, official transcripts from all current and previous colleges/universities except Marquette, three completed recommendation forms, resume, written statement of professional goals; for doctorate, GRE General Test, official transcripts from all current and previous colleges/universities except Marquette, three letters of recommendation, resume, written statement of professional goals, sample of scholarly writing. Additional exam requirements/recommendations for international students: Required—TOEFL (minimum score 530 paper-based). Electronic applications accepted. *Faculty research:* Psychosocial adjustment to chronic illness, gerontology, reminiscence, health policy: uninsured and access, hospital care delivery systems.

Marymount University, Malek School of Health Professions, Program in Nursing, Arlington, VA 22207-4299. Offers family nurse practitioner (MSN, Certificate); nursing (DNP). *Accreditation:* AACN. *Program availability:* Part-time, evening/weekend. *Faculty:* 7 full-time (all women), 2 part-time/adjunct (both women). *Students:* 20 full-time (19 women), 43 part-time (40 women); includes 29 minority (18 Black or African American, non-Hispanic/Latino; 6 Asian, non-Hispanic/Latino; 4 Hispanic/Latino; 1 Two or more races, non-Hispanic/Latino), 2 international. Average age 38. 34 applicants, 56% accepted, 13 enrolled. In 2017, 21 master's, 1 doctorate, 3 other advanced degrees awarded. *Degree requirements:* For master's, comprehensive exam, clinical practicum; for doctorate, thesis/dissertation, research presentation/residency. *Entrance requirements:* For master's, 2 letters of recommendation, interview, resume, RN license, personal statement, minimum GPA of 3.0; for doctorate, 2 letters of recommendation, interview, resume, RN license, minimum MSN GPA of 3.5 or BSN 3.3, APN certification, personal statement; for Certificate, interview, master's degree in nursing with minimum of GPA of 3.3, current RN licensure. Additional exam requirements/recommendations for international students: Required—TOEFL (minimum score 600 paper-based; 96 iBT), IELTS (minimum score 6.5). *Application deadline:* For fall admission, 3/1 priority date for domestic and international students; for spring admission, 11/1 priority date for domestic and international students. Application fee: $40. Electronic applications accepted. *Expenses: Tuition:* Full-time $17,550; part-time $975 per credit hour. *Required fees:* $198; $11 per credit hour. One-time fee: $250. Tuition and fees vary according to program. *Financial support:* In 2017–18, 4 students received support, including 1 teaching assistantship with full and partial tuition reimbursement available (averaging $5,850 per year); career-related internships or fieldwork, Federal Work-Study, scholarships/grants, and unspecified assistantships also available. Support available to part-time students. Financial award application deadline: 3/1; financial award applicants required to submit FAFSA. *Unit head:* Colleen Sanders, Program Director, 703-284-6886, Fax: 703-284-3819, E-mail: colleen.sanders@marymount.edu. *Application contact:* Francesca Reed, Director, Graduate Admissions, 703-284-5901, Fax: 703-527-3815, E-mail: grad.admissions@marymount.edu.
Website: http://www.marymount.edu/Academics/Malek-School-of-Health-Professions/Graduate-Programs/Nursing-(M-S-N-)

Maryville University of Saint Louis, Myrtle E. and Earl E. Walker College of Health Professions, The Catherine McAuley School of Nursing, St. Louis, MO 63141-7299. Offers acute care nurse practitioner (MSN); adult gerontology nurse practitioner (MSN); advanced practice nursing (DNP); family nurse practitioner (MSN); pediatric nurse practitioner (MSN). *Accreditation:* AACN. *Program availability:* 100% online, blended/hybrid learning. *Faculty:* 15 full-time (all women), 142 part-time/adjunct (123 women). *Students:* 49 full-time (42 women), 2,999 part-time (2,645 women); includes 773 minority (375 Black or African American, non-Hispanic/Latino; 51 American Indian or Alaska Native, non-Hispanic/Latino; 135 Asian, non-Hispanic/Latino; 149 Hispanic/Latino; 63 Two or more races, non-Hispanic/Latino), 21 international. Average age 36. In 2017, 843 master's, 42 doctorates awarded. *Degree requirements:* For master's, practicum. *Entrance requirements:* For master's, BSN, current licensure, minimum GPA of 3.0, 3 letters of recommendation, curriculum vitae. Additional exam requirements/recommendations for international students: Required—TOEFL (minimum score 550 paper-based). *Application deadline:* Applications are processed on a rolling basis. Electronic applications accepted. *Expenses:* Contact institution. *Financial support:* Federal Work-Study and campus employment available. Support available to part-time students. Financial award application deadline: 4/1; financial award applicants required to submit FAFSA. *Unit head:* Dr. Elizabeth Buck, Assistant Dean/Director of Online Nursing, 314-529-9453, Fax: 314-529-9139, E-mail: ebuck@maryville.edu. *Application contact:* Jeannie DeLuca, Director of Admissions and Advising, 314-929-9355, Fax: 314-529-9927, E-mail: cjacobsmeyer@maryville.edu.
Website: http://www.maryville.edu/hp/nursing/

McGill University, Faculty of Graduate and Postdoctoral Studies, Faculty of Medicine, School of Nursing, Montréal, QC H3A 2T5, Canada. Offers nurse practitioner (Graduate Diploma); nursing (M Sc A, PhD). PhD offered jointly with Université du Québec à Montréal.

McMurry University, Graduate Studies, Abilene, TX 79697. Offers education (MSN); family nurse practitioner (MSN).

McNeese State University, Doré School of Graduate Studies, College of Nursing and Health Professions, MSN Program, Lake Charles, LA 70609. Offers family nurse practitioner (MSN); nurse educator (MSN); psychiatric/mental health nurse practitioner (MSN). *Entrance requirements:* For master's, GRE, baccalaureate degree in nursing, minimum overall GPA of 2.7 for all undergraduate coursework, eligibility for unencumbered licensure as Registered Nurse in Louisiana or Texas, course in introductory statistics with minimum C grade, physical assessment skills, two letters of professional reference, 500-word essay, current resume. *Application deadline:* For fall admission, 5/15 priority date for domestic and international students; for spring admission, 10/15 priority date for domestic and international students. Applications are processed on a rolling basis. Application fee: $20 ($30 for international students). *Financial support:* Application deadline: 5/1. *Unit head:* Dr. Sattaria Dilks, Co-Coordinator, 337-475-5840, Fax: 337-475-5924, E-mail: tdilks@mcneese.edu. *Application contact:* Dr. Ann Warner, Co-Coordinator, 337-475-5831, Fax: 337-475-5702, E-mail: awarner@mcneese.edu.
Website: http://www.mcneese.edu/nursing/graduate

Medical University of South Carolina, College of Nursing, Family Nurse Practitioner Program, Charleston, SC 29425. Offers MSN, DNP. *Program availability:* Part-time, online learning. *Degree requirements:* For master's, thesis optional; for doctorate, final project. *Entrance requirements:* For master's, BSN from nationally-accredited program, minimum nursing and cumulative GPA of 3.0, undergraduate-level statistics course, active RN License, 3 confidential references, current curriculum vitae or resume, essay; for doctorate, BSN from nationally-accredited program, minimum nursing and cumulative GPA of 3.0, undergraduate-level statistics course, active RN License, 3 confidential references, current curriculum vitae or resume, personal essay (for DNP). Additional exam requirements/recommendations for international students: Required—TOEFL (minimum score 550 paper-based; 80 iBT). Electronic applications accepted. *Faculty research:* Primary care, smoking cessation, patient navigation, informatics, depression.

Mercer University, Graduate Studies, Cecil B. Day Campus, Georgia Baptist College of Nursing, Atlanta, GA 30341. Offers adult gerontology acute care nurse practitioner (MSN, Certificate); family nurse practitioner (MSN, Certificate); nursing (PhD); nursing practice (DNP), including adult gerontology acute care nurse practitioner. *Accreditation:* AACN. *Program availability:* Part-time, blended/hybrid learning. *Faculty:* 10 full-time (9 women), 4 part-time/adjunct (3 women). *Students:* 72 full-time (70 women), 33 part-time (29 women); includes 44 minority (29 Black or African American, non-Hispanic/Latino; 9 Asian, non-Hispanic/Latino; 3 Hispanic/Latino; 3 Two or more races, non-Hispanic/Latino), 1 international. Average age 36. 65 applicants, 66% accepted, 30 enrolled. In 2017, 27 master's, 9 doctorates awarded. *Degree requirements:* For master's, thesis or alternative, capstone; for doctorate, comprehensive exam (for some programs), scholarly project (for DNP); dissertation (for PhD). *Entrance requirements:* For master's, MAT or GRE, bachelor's degree from accredited nursing program, registered unencumbered GA nursing license, essay, three professional references; for doctorate, GRE (for PhD), master's degree from accredited nursing program, RN licensure, graduate statistics course, three professional references. Additional exam requirements/recommendations for international students: Required—TOEFL (minimum score 100 iBT). *Application deadline:* For fall admission, 5/1 for domestic students, 3/1 for international students; for winter admission, 11/1 for domestic students, 9/1 for international students; for spring admission, 11/1 for domestic students, 10/1 for international students; for summer admission, 3/1 for domestic and international students. Applications are processed on a rolling basis. Application fee: $50. Electronic applications accepted. *Expenses:* $32,000. *Financial support:* In 2017–18, 23 students received support, including 1 research assistantship (averaging $6,000 per year);

scholarships/grants also available. Financial award application deadline: 6/30; financial award applicants required to submit FAFSA. *Faculty research:* Cognitive competence, cancer survivorship, interprofessional education, cultural competence, clopidogrel adherence, high fidelity simulation, self-awareness practices, simulation. *Unit head:* Dr. Linda Streit, Dean/Professor, 678-547-6793, Fax: 678-547-6796, E-mail: streit_la@mercer.edu. *Application contact:* Janda Anderson, Director of Admissions, 678-547-6700, Fax: 678-547-6794, E-mail: anderson_j@mercer.edu.
Website: http://www.mercer.edu/nursing

Middle Tennessee State University, College of Graduate Studies, College of Behavioral and Health Sciences, School of Nursing, Program in Family Nurse Practitioner, Murfreesboro, TN 37132. Offers MSN, Graduate Certificate. *Program availability:* Part-time, evening/weekend, online learning. *Entrance requirements:* Additional exam requirements/recommendations for international students: Required—TOEFL (minimum score 525 paper-based; 71 iBT) or IELTS (minimum score 6). Electronic applications accepted.

Midwestern State University, Billie Doris McAda Graduate School, Robert D. and Carol Gunn College of Health Sciences and Human Services, Wilson School of Nursing, Wichita Falls, TX 76308. Offers family nurse practitioner (MSN); family psychiatric mental health nurse practitioner (MSN); nurse educator (MSN). *Accreditation:* AACN. *Program availability:* Part-time, evening/weekend. *Degree requirements:* For master's, comprehensive exam, thesis optional. *Entrance requirements:* For master's, GRE General Test or MAT. Additional exam requirements/recommendations for international students: Required—TOEFL (minimum score 550 paper-based). Electronic applications accepted. *Faculty research:* Infant feeding, musculoskeletal disorders, diabetes, community health education, water quality reporting.

Millersville University of Pennsylvania, College of Graduate Studies and Adult Learning, College of Science and Technology, Department of Nursing, Program in Family Nurse Practitioner, Millersville, PA 17551-0302. Offers MSN, Post-Master's Certificate. *Program availability:* Part-time, evening/weekend. *Faculty:* 5 full-time (all women), 8 part-time/adjunct (7 women). *Students:* 93 part-time (76 women); includes 14 minority (5 Black or African American, non-Hispanic/Latino; 1 American Indian or Alaska Native, non-Hispanic/Latino; 3 Asian, non-Hispanic/Latino; 5 Hispanic/Latino), 1 international. Average age 36. 44 applicants, 84% accepted, 24 enrolled. In 2017, 20 master's awarded. *Degree requirements:* For master's, internship, scholarly project. *Entrance requirements:* For master's, resume, copy of RN license, minimum GPA of 3.0, all transfer transcripts, interview, three academic and/or professional references, completion of undergraduate statistics and health assessment course, minimum one year of clinical experience in nursing. Additional exam requirements/recommendations for international students: Required—TOEFL (minimum score 80 iBT), IELTS (minimum score 6.5), PTE (minimum score 60). *Application deadline:* For fall admission, 1/15 for domestic students; for spring admission, 8/1 for domestic students. Application fee: $40. Electronic applications accepted. *Expenses:* $500 per credit resident tuition and fees; $750 per credit non-resident tuition and fees; $114.75 per credit general fee (maximum of 12 credits); technology fee $27 per credit (resident), $39 per credit (non-resident). *Financial support:* In 2017–18, 3 students received support. Unspecified assistantships available. Financial award application deadline: 3/15; financial award applicants required to submit FAFSA. *Faculty research:* Family nurse practitioner, nurse education, primary care, health promotion, college health, breast health, immunizations. *Unit head:* Dr. Jenny Monn, Graduate Program Coordinator, 717-871-7454, E-mail: jenny.monn@millersville.edu. *Application contact:* Dr. Victor S. DeSantis, Dean of College of Graduate Studies and Adult Learning/Associate Provost for Civic and Community Engagement, 717-871-7619, Fax: 717-871-7954, E-mail: victor.desantis@millersville.edu.
Website: http://www.millersville.edu/nursing/msn/nurse-practitioner.php

Millikin University, School of Nursing, Decatur, IL 62522-2084. Offers entry into nursing practice (MSN); family nurse practitioner (DNP); nurse anesthesia (DNP); nurse educator (MSN). *Accreditation:* AACN. *Program availability:* Part-time. *Faculty:* 19 full-time (17 women), 7 part-time/adjunct (6 women). *Students:* 42 full-time (30 women), 20 part-time (17 women); includes 12 minority (8 Black or African American, non-Hispanic/Latino; 2 Asian, non-Hispanic/Latino; 2 Hispanic/Latino). Average age 30. 114 applicants, 36% accepted, 23 enrolled. In 2017, 3 master's, 13 doctorates awarded. *Degree requirements:* For master's, thesis or alternative, scholarly project; for doctorate, thesis/dissertation or alternative, scholarly project. *Entrance requirements:* For master's, GRE (if undergraduate cumulative GPA is below 3.0 for nurse educator, 3.25 for entry into nursing practice), official academic transcript(s), written statement, resume/vitae, 3 letters of recommendation, RN license; for doctorate, GRE (if undergraduate cumulative GPA is below 3.0), official academic transcript(s), written statement, resume/vitae, 3 letters of recommendation, RN or APRN license. Additional exam requirements/recommendations for international students: Required—TOEFL (minimum score 550 paper-based; 79 iBT), IELTS (minimum score 6.5). *Application deadline:* For spring admission, 7/1 priority date for domestic and international students; for summer admission, 11/1 priority date for domestic and international students. Applications are processed on a rolling basis. Application fee: $0. Electronic applications accepted. *Expenses:* $832 per credit hour (for MSN); $950 per credit hour (for DNP). *Financial support:* Traineeships and unspecified assistantships available. Financial award applicants required to submit FAFSA. *Faculty research:* Quality of life, teaching/learning strategies, clinical simulation. *Unit head:* Dr. Pamela Lindsey, Director, 217-424-6348, Fax: 217-420-6731, E-mail: plindsey@millikin.edu. *Application contact:* Bonnie Niemeyer, Administrative Assistant, 800-373-7733 Ext. 5034, Fax: 217-420-6731, E-mail: bniemeyer@millikin.edu.
Website: http://www.millikin.edu/grad-nursing

Minnesota State University Mankato, College of Graduate Studies and Research, College of Allied Health and Nursing, School of Nursing, Mankato, MN 56001. Offers family nurse practitioner (MSN), including family nurse practitioner; nurse educator (MSN); nursing (DNP). *Accreditation:* AACN. *Degree requirements:* For master's, comprehensive exam, internships, research project or thesis; for doctorate, capstone project. *Entrance requirements:* For master's, GRE General Test or on-campus essay, minimum GPA of 3.0 during previous 2 years, BSN or equivalent references; for doctorate, master's degree in nursing. Additional exam requirements/recommendations for international students: Required—TOEFL. Electronic applications accepted. *Faculty research:* Psychosocial nursing, computers in nursing, family adaptation.

Missouri State University, Graduate College, College of Health and Human Services, Department of Nursing, Springfield, MO 65897. Offers nursing (MSN), including family nurse practitioner, nurse educator; nursing practice (DNP). *Accreditation:* AACN. *Program availability:* 100% online, blended/hybrid learning. *Faculty:* 9 full-time (all women), 16 part-time/adjunct (13 women). *Students:* 30 full-time (26 women), 47 part-time (41 women); includes 13 minority (6 Black or African American, non-Hispanic/Latino; 1 American Indian or Alaska Native, non-Hispanic/Latino; 3 Asian, non-Hispanic/Latino; 1 Native Hawaiian or other Pacific Islander, non-Hispanic/Latino; 2 Two or more races, non-Hispanic/Latino). Average age 27. 12 applicants, 33% accepted, 1 enrolled. In 2017, 6 master's, 16 doctorates awarded. *Degree requirements:* For master's, comprehensive exam, thesis or alternative. *Entrance requirements:* For master's, GRE General Test, minimum GPA of 3.0, RN license (for MSN), 1 year of work experience (for MPH). Additional exam requirements/recommendations for international students: Required—TOEFL (minimum score 550 paper-based; 79 iBT), IELTS (minimum score 6). *Application deadline:* For fall admission, 12/1 priority date for domestic students, 5/1 for international students. Applications are processed on a rolling basis. Application fee: $35 ($50 for international students). Electronic applications accepted. *Expenses:* Tuition, state resident: full-time $2915; part-time $2021 per credit hour. Tuition, nonresident: full-time $5354; part-time $3647 per credit hour. *International tuition:* $11,992 full-time. *Required fees:* $173; $173 per credit hour. Tuition and fees vary according to class time, course level, course load, degree level, campus/location and program. *Financial support:* In 2017–18, 2 teaching assistantships with partial tuition reimbursements (averaging $8,772 per year) were awarded; Federal Work-Study, institutionally sponsored loans, scholarships/grants, and unspecified assistantships also available. Financial award application deadline: 3/31; financial award applicants required to submit FAFSA. *Faculty research:* Preconceptual health, women's health, nursing satisfaction, nursing education. *Unit head:* Dr. Stephen Stapleton, Department Head, 417-836-5310, Fax: 417-836-5484, E-mail: nursing@missouristate.edu. *Application contact:* Stephanie Praschan, Director, Graduate Enrollment Management, 417-836-5330, Fax: 417-836-6200, E-mail: stephaniepraschan@missouristate.edu.
Website: http://www.missouristate.edu/nursing/

Molloy College, The Barbara H. Hagan School of Nursing, Rockville Centre, NY 11571-5002. Offers adult - gerontology nurse practitioner (MS); adult-gerontology clinical nurse specialist (DNP); adult-gerontology nurse practitioner (DNP); clinical nurse specialist: adult - gerontology (MS); family nurse practitioner (MS, DNP); family psychiatric/mental health nurse practitioner (MS, DNP); nursing (PhD, Advanced Certificate); nursing administration with informatics (MS); nursing education (MS); pediatric nurse practitioner (MS, DNP). *Accreditation:* AACN. *Program availability:* Part-time, evening/weekend. *Faculty:* 28 full-time (all women), 7 part-time/adjunct (6 women). *Students:* 19 full-time (14 women), 574 part-time (527 women); includes 336 minority (179 Black or African American, non-Hispanic/Latino; 2 American Indian or Alaska Native, non-Hispanic/Latino; 107 Asian, non-Hispanic/Latino; 42 Hispanic/Latino; 1 Native Hawaiian or other Pacific Islander, non-Hispanic/Latino; 5 Two or more races, non-Hispanic/Latino), 4 international. Average age 44. 292 applicants, 65% accepted, 147 enrolled. In 2017, 135 master's, 9 doctorates, 5 other advanced degrees awarded. *Degree requirements:* For master's, thesis optional. *Entrance requirements:* For master's, 3 letters of reference, BS in nursing, minimum undergraduate GPA of 3.0; for Advanced Certificate, 3 letters of reference, master's degree in nursing. Additional exam requirements/recommendations for international students: Required—TOEFL (minimum score 550 paper-based; 79 iBT). *Application deadline:* For fall admission, 9/2 priority date for domestic students; for spring admission, 1/20 priority date for domestic students. Applications are processed on a rolling basis. Application fee: $60. Electronic applications accepted. *Expenses: Tuition:* Full-time $19,980; part-time $1110 per credit. *Required fees:* $1040. Tuition and fees vary according to course load and degree level. *Financial support:* Research assistantships with partial tuition reimbursements, teaching assistantships with partial tuition reimbursements, institutionally sponsored loans, scholarships/grants, and unspecified assistantships available. Support available to part-time students. Financial award application deadline: 3/1; financial award applicants required to submit FAFSA. *Faculty research:* Workplace violence involving nurses and psychiatric patients; moral distress in nursing; primary care of veterans; the role of service immersion programs in graduate nursing education; academic integrity. *Unit head:* Dr. Marcia R. Gardner, Dean, The Barbara H. Hagan School of Nursing, 516-323-3651, E-mail: mgardner@molloy.edu. *Application contact:* Jaclyn Machowicz, Assistant Director for Admissions, 516-323-4010, E-mail: jmachowicz@molloy.edu.

Monmouth University, Graduate Studies, Marjorie K. Unterberg School of Nursing and Health Studies, West Long Branch, NJ 07764-1898. Offers adult-gerontological primary care nurse practitioner (MSN, Post-Master's Certificate); family nurse practitioner (MSN, Post-Master's Certificate); forensic nursing (MSN, Certificate); nursing (MSN); nursing administration (MSN); nursing education (MSN, Post-Master's Certificate); nursing practice (DNP); physician assistant (MS); psychiatric and mental health nurse practitioner (MSN, Post-Master's Certificate); school nursing (MSN, Certificate). *Accreditation:* AACN. *Program availability:* Part-time, evening/weekend, 100% online, blended/hybrid learning. *Faculty:* 12 full-time (all women), 20 part-time/adjunct (12 women). *Students:* 90 full-time (66 women), 329 part-time (302 women); includes 129 minority (51 Black or African American, non-Hispanic/Latino; 43 Asian, non-Hispanic/Latino; 31 Hispanic/Latino; 1 Native Hawaiian or other Pacific Islander, non-Hispanic/Latino; 3 Two or more races, non-Hispanic/Latino), 1 international. Average age 36. In 2017, 85 master's, 4 other advanced degrees awarded. *Degree requirements:* For master's, practicum (for some tracks); for doctorate, practicum, capstone course. *Entrance requirements:* For master's, GRE General Test (waived for MSN applicants with minimum B grade in each of the first four courses and for MS applicants with master's degree), BSN with minimum GPA of 2.75, current RN license, proof of liability and malpractice policy, personal statement, two letters of recommendation, college course work in health assessment, resume; CASPA application (for MS); for doctorate, accredited master's nursing program degree with minimum GPA of 3.2, active RN license, national certification as nurse practitioner or nurse administrator, working knowledge of statistics, statement of goals and vision for change, 2 letters of recommendation (professional or academic), resume, interview. Additional exam requirements/recommendations for international students: Required—TOEFL (minimum score 550 paper-based; 79 iBT), IELTS (minimum score 6) or Michigan English Language Assessment Battery (minimum score 77). *Application deadline:* For fall admission, 7/15 priority date for domestic students, 6/1 for international students; for spring admission, 12/1 priority date for domestic students, 11/1 for international students; for summer admission, 5/1 for domestic students. Applications are processed on a rolling basis. Application fee: $50. Electronic applications accepted. *Expenses:* Contact institution. *Financial support:* In 2017–18, 197 students received support. Institutionally sponsored loans, scholarships/grants, and unspecified assistantships available. Support available to part-time students. Financial award applicants required to submit FAFSA. *Faculty research:* School nursing, health policy, and smoking cessation in teens; Multiple Sclerosis; adherence and self-efficacy; aging issues and geriatric care. *Unit head:* Dr. Janet Mahoney, Dean, 732-571-3443, Fax: 732-263-5131, E-mail: jmahoney@monmouth.edu. *Application contact:* Lucia Fedele, Graduate Admission Counselor, 732-571-3452, Fax: 732-263-5123, E-mail: gradadm@monmouth.edu.
Website: https://www.monmouth.edu/graduate/nursing-programs-of-study/

Montana State University, The Graduate School, College of Nursing, Bozeman, MT 59717. Offers clinical nurse leader (MN); family and individual nurse practitioner (DNP); family nurse practitioner (MN, Post-Master's Certificate); nursing education (Certificate, Post-Master's Certificate); psychiatric mental health nurse practitioner (MN); psychiatric/mental health nurse practitioner (DNP). *Accreditation:* AACN. *Program availability:* Part-time, online learning. *Degree requirements:* For master's, comprehensive exam, thesis (for some programs); for doctorate, thesis/dissertation, 1,125 hours in clinical settings. *Entrance requirements:* For master's, GRE General Test, minimum GPA of 3.0 for undergraduate and post-baccalaureate work. Additional exam requirements/recommendations for international students: Required—TOEFL (minimum score 580 paper-based). Electronic applications accepted. *Faculty research:* Rural nursing, health disparities, environmental/public health, oral health, resilience.

Morningside College, Graduate Programs, Nylen School of Nursing, Sioux City, IA 51106. Offers adult gerontology primary care nurse practitioner (MSN); clinical nurse leader (MSN); family primary care nurse practitioner (MSN). *Program availability:* Part-time, online only, 100% online. *Faculty:* 3 full-time (all women), 4 part-time/adjunct (all women). *Students:* 7 full-time (3 women), 86 part-time (81 women); includes 8 minority (1 American Indian or Alaska Native, non-Hispanic/Latino; 3 Asian, non-Hispanic/Latino; 4 Hispanic/Latino). Average age 32. 37 applicants, 100% accepted, 37 enrolled. In 2017, 19 master's awarded. *Application deadline:* Applications are processed on a rolling basis. Application fee: $65. Electronic applications accepted. *Expenses:* Contact institution. *Financial support:* In 2017–18, 67 students received support. Scholarships/grants and tuition waivers (partial) available. Financial award application deadline: 3/1; financial award applicants required to submit FAFSA. *Unit head:* Dr. Jackie Barber, Dean of Graduate Nursing, 712-274-5297, E-mail: barber@morningside.edu.

Mount Carmel College of Nursing, Nursing Program, Columbus, OH 43222. Offers adult gerontology acute care nurse practitioner (MS); adult health clinical nurse specialist (MS); family nurse practitioner (MS); nursing (DNP); nursing administration (MS); nursing education (MS). *Accreditation:* AACN. *Program availability:* Part-time. *Faculty:* 11 full-time (all women), 5 part-time/adjunct (4 women). *Students:* 112 full-time (93 women), 72 part-time (65 women); includes 35 minority (20 Black or African American, non-Hispanic/Latino; 4 Asian, non-Hispanic/Latino; 3 Hispanic/Latino; 8 Two or more races, non-Hispanic/Latino). Average age 35. 135 applicants, 65% accepted, 68 enrolled. In 2017, 64 master's awarded. *Degree requirements:* For master's, professional manuscript; for doctorate, practicum. *Entrance requirements:* For master's, letters of recommendation, statement of purpose, current resume, baccalaureate degree in nursing, current Ohio RN license, minimum cumulative GPA of 3.0; for doctorate, master's degree in nursing from program accredited by either ACEN or CCNE. Additional exam requirements/recommendations for international students: Required—TOEFL (minimum score 550 paper-based; 80 iBT). *Application deadline:* For fall admission, 2/1 priority date for domestic students; for spring admission, 11/1 priority date for domestic students. Applications are processed on a rolling basis. Application fee: $30. Electronic applications accepted. *Expenses: Tuition:* Full-time $11,403; part-time $543 per credit. *Required fees:* $50; $50 per year. *Financial support:* In 2017–18, 3 students received support. Institutionally sponsored loans and scholarships/grants available. Financial award application deadline: 3/1; financial award applicants required to submit FAFSA. *Unit head:* Dr. Jill Kilanowski, Associate Dean, 614-234-5237, Fax: 614-234-2875, E-mail: jkilanowski@mccn.edu. *Application contact:* Dr. Kim Campbell, Director of Recruitment and Admissions, 614-234-5144, Fax: 614-234-5427, E-mail: kcampbell@mccn.edu.

Mount Saint Mary College, School of Nursing, Newburgh, NY 12550-3494. Offers adult nurse practitioner (MS, Advanced Certificate), including nursing education (MS), nursing management (MS); family nurse practitioner (Advanced Certificate); nursing education (Advanced Certificate). *Accreditation:* AACN. *Program availability:* Part-time, evening/weekend, blended/hybrid learning. *Faculty:* 7 full-time (all women), 5 part-time/adjunct (all women). *Students:* 3 full-time (1 woman), 153 part-time (143 women); includes 42 minority (22 Black or African American, non-Hispanic/Latino; 1 American Indian or Alaska Native, non-Hispanic/Latino; 6 Asian, non-Hispanic/Latino; 11 Hispanic/Latino; 1 Native Hawaiian or other Pacific Islander, non-Hispanic/Latino; 1 Two or more races, non-Hispanic/Latino). Average age 38. 34 applicants, 91% accepted, 28 enrolled. In 2017, 30 master's, 5 other advanced degrees awarded. *Degree requirements:* For master's, research utilization project. *Entrance requirements:* For master's, BSN, minimum GPA of 3.0, RN license. Additional exam requirements/recommendations for international students: Required—TOEFL (minimum score 80 iBT). *Application deadline:* For fall admission, 6/3 priority date for domestic students; for spring admission, 10/31 priority date for domestic students. Applications are processed on a rolling basis. Application fee: $45. Electronic applications accepted. Application fee is waived when completed online. *Expenses: Tuition:* Full-time $14,454; part-time $803 per credit. *Required fees:* $172; $86 per semester. *Financial support:* In 2017–18, 8 students received support. Unspecified assistantships available. Financial award application deadline: 4/15; financial award applicants required to submit FAFSA. *Unit head:* Christine Berte, Graduate Coordinator, 845-569-3141, Fax: 845-562-6762, E-mail: christine.berte@msmc.edu. *Application contact:* Lisa Alvarez, Director of Admissions for Graduate Programs and Adult Degree Completion, 845-569-3166, Fax: 845-569-3450, E-mail: lisa.gallina@msmc.edu.
Website: http://www.msmc.edu/Academics/Graduate_Programs/Master_of_Science_in_Nursing

Murray State University, School of Nursing and Health Professions, Department of Nursing, Murray, KY 42071. Offers family nurse practitioner (DNP); nurse anesthetist (DNP). *Accreditation:* AACN; AANA/CANAEP. *Program availability:* Evening/weekend, 100% online, blended/hybrid learning. *Faculty:* 7 full-time (6 women), 1 part-time/adjunct (0 women). *Students:* 63 full-time (45 women), 21 part-time (17 women); includes 12 minority (8 Black or African American, non-Hispanic/Latino; 3 Asian, non-Hispanic/Latino; 1 Two or more races, non-Hispanic/Latino). Average age 33. 85 applicants, 35% accepted, 21 enrolled. In 2017, 26 doctorates awarded. *Entrance requirements:* For doctorate, GRE, minimum university GPA of 2.75. Additional exam requirements/recommendations for international students: Required—TOEFL (minimum score 527 paper-based; 71 iBT). *Application deadline:* Applications are processed on a rolling basis. Application fee: $30. Electronic applications accepted. *Expenses:* Tuition, state resident: full-time $9504. Tuition, nonresident: full-time $26,811. *International tuition:* $14,400 full-time. Tuition and fees vary according to course load, degree level and reciprocity agreements. *Financial support:* Federal Work-Study, scholarships/grants, and unspecified assistantships available. Financial award applicants required to submit FAFSA. *Unit head:* Dr. Marcia Hobbs, Dean, School of Nursing and Health Professions, 270-809-3196, Fax: 270-809-6662, E-mail: mhobbs4@murraystate.edu. *Application contact:* Kaitlyn Burzynski, Interim Assistant Director for Graduate Admission and Records, 270-809-5732, Fax: 270-809-3780, E-mail: msu.graduateadmissions@murraystate.edu.

National University, School of Health and Human Services, La Jolla, CA 92037-1011. Offers clinical affairs (MS); clinical regulatory affairs (MS); complementary and integrative healthcare (MS); family nurse practitioner (MSN); health and life science analytics (MS); health informatics (MS, Certificate); healthcare administration (MHA); nurse anesthesia (MSNA); nursing administration (MSN); nursing informatics (MSN); psychiatric-mental health nurse practitioner (MSN); public health (MPH), including health promotion, healthcare administration, mental health. *Program availability:* Part-time, evening/weekend, 100% online, blended/hybrid learning. *Degree requirements:* For master's, thesis (for some programs). *Entrance requirements:* For master's, interview, minimum GPA of 2.5. Additional exam requirements/recommendations for international students: Required—TOEFL (minimum score 550 paper-based; 79 iBT), IELTS (minimum score 6). *Application deadline:* Applications are processed on a rolling basis. Application fee: $60 ($65 for international students). Electronic applications accepted. *Expenses: Tuition:* Part-time $430 per quarter hour. *Financial support:* Career-related internships or fieldwork, institutionally sponsored loans, scholarships/grants, and tuition waivers (partial) available. Support available to part-time students. Financial award application deadline: 6/30; financial award applicants required to submit FAFSA. *Faculty research:* Nursing education, obesity prevention, workforce diversity. *Unit head:* Dr. Gloria J. McNeal, Dean, 858-309-3473, E-mail: shhs@nu.edu. *Application contact:* Brandon Jouganatos, Vice President for Enrollment Services, 800-628-8648, E-mail: advisor@nu.edu.
Website: http://www.nu.edu/OurPrograms/SchoolOfHealthAndHumanServices.html

New Mexico State University, College of Health and Social Services, School of Nursing, Las Cruces, NM 88003. Offers family nurse practitioner (DNP, Graduate Certificate); nursing administration (MSN); nursing science (PhD); psychiatric/mental health nurse practitioner (DNP, Graduate Certificate). *Accreditation:* AACN. *Program availability:* Part-time, blended/hybrid learning. *Faculty:* 11 full-time (all women). *Students:* 29 full-time (26 women), 68 part-time (57 women); includes 46 minority (10 Black or African American, non-Hispanic/Latino; 6 Asian, non-Hispanic/Latino; 29 Hispanic/Latino; 1 Two or more races, non-Hispanic/Latino), 1 international. Average age 42. 47 applicants, 81% accepted, 25 enrolled. In 2017, 3 master's, 9 doctorates, 5 other advanced degrees awarded. *Degree requirements:* For master's, comprehensive exam, thesis optional, clinical practicum; for doctorate, comprehensive exam, thesis/dissertation. *Entrance requirements:* For master's, NCLEX exam, BSN, minimum GPA of 3.0, course work in statistics, 3 letters of reference, writing sample, RN license, CPR certification, proof of liability, immunizations, criminal background check; for doctorate, NCLEX exam, MSN, minimum GPA of 3.0, 3 letters of reference, writing sample, RN license, CPR certification, proof of liability, immunizations, criminal background check, statistics course. Additional exam requirements/recommendations for international students: Required—TOEFL (minimum score 550 paper-based; 79 iBT), IELTS (minimum score 6.5). *Application deadline:* For fall admission, 2/1 priority date for domestic students, 2/1 for international students. Application fee: $40 ($50 for international students). Electronic applications accepted. *Expenses:* Tuition, state resident: full-time $4390. Tuition, nonresident: full-time $15,309. *Required fees:* $853. *Financial support:* In 2017–18, 22 students received support, including 5 teaching assistantships (averaging $11,249 per year); career-related internships or fieldwork, Federal Work-Study, scholarships/grants, traineeships, health care benefits, and unspecified assistantships also available. Support available to part-time students. Financial award application deadline: 3/1. *Faculty research:* Women's health, community health, health disparities, nursing informatics and health care technologies, health care and nursing administration, nursing education, adolescent mental health, addiction and substance abuse. *Total annual research expenditures:* $1,321. *Unit head:* Dr. Alexa Doig, Director, 575-646-3812, Fax: 575-646-2167, E-mail: adoig@nmsu.edu. *Application contact:* Alyce Kolenovsky, 575-646-3812, Fax: 575-646-2167, E-mail: nursing@nmsu.edu.
Website: http://schoolofnursing.nmsu.edu

New York University, Rory Meyers College of Nursing, Doctor of Nursing Practice Program, New York, NY 10012-1019. Offers nursing (DNP), including adult-gerontology acute care nurse practitioner, adult-gerontology primary care nurse practitioner, family nurse practitioner, nurse-midwifery, pediatrics nurse practitioner, psychiatric-mental health nurse practitioner. *Accreditation:* AACN. *Program availability:* Part-time, evening/weekend. *Faculty:* 16 full-time (all women), 1 (woman) part-time/adjunct. *Students:* 48 part-time (43 women); includes 11 minority (5 Black or African American, non-Hispanic/Latino; 5 Asian, non-Hispanic/Latino; 1 Hispanic/Latino). Average age 28. 20 applicants, 75% accepted, 10 enrolled. In 2017, 8 doctorates awarded. *Degree requirements:* For doctorate, thesis/dissertation, project. *Entrance requirements:* For doctorate, MS, RN license, interview, Nurse Practitioner Certification, writing sample. Additional exam requirements/recommendations for international students: Required—TOEFL (minimum score 100 iBT), IELTS (minimum score 7). *Application deadline:* For fall admission, 3/1 priority date for domestic and international students. Applications are processed on a rolling basis. Application fee: $80. Electronic applications accepted. *Expenses:* Contact institution. *Financial support:* In 2017–18, 13 students received support. Scholarships/grants available. Support available to part-time students. Financial award application deadline: 2/1; financial award applicants required to submit FAFSA. *Faculty research:* Workforce determinants of healthcare quality, genomics, health literacy and health outcomes, health policy. *Unit head:* Dr. Mary Jo Vetter, Director, DNP Program, 212-998-5165, E-mail: mjv5@nyu.edu. *Application contact:* Matthew Burke, Assistant Director, Graduate Student Affairs and Admissions, 212-998-7397, E-mail: mb6060@nyu.edu.

New York University, Rory Meyers College of Nursing, Programs in Advanced Practice Nursing, New York, NY 10012-1019. Offers adult-gerontology acute care nurse practitioner (MS, Advanced Certificate); adult-gerontology primary care nurse practitioner (MS, Advanced Certificate); family nurse practitioner (MS, Advanced Certificate); gerontology nurse practitioner (Advanced Certificate); nurse-midwifery (MS, Advanced Certificate); nursing administration (MS, Advanced Certificate); nursing education (MS, Advanced Certificate); nursing informatics (MS, Advanced Certificate); pediatrics nurse practitioner (MS, Advanced Certificate); psychiatric-mental health nurse practitioner (MS, Advanced Certificate); MS/MPH. *Accreditation:* AACN; ACNM/ACME. *Program availability:* Part-time, evening/weekend. *Faculty:* 23 full-time (all women), 62 part-time/adjunct (56 women). *Students:* 50 full-time (46 women), 557 part-time (509 women); includes 234 minority (58 Black or African American, non-Hispanic/Latino; 1 American Indian or Alaska Native, non-Hispanic/Latino; 116 Asian, non-Hispanic/Latino; 43 Hispanic/Latino; 1 Native Hawaiian or other Pacific Islander, non-Hispanic/Latino; 15 Two or more races, non-Hispanic/Latino), 23 international. Average age 32. 391 applicants, 59% accepted, 149 enrolled. In 2017, 187 master's, 5 other advanced degrees awarded. *Degree requirements:* For master's, thesis (for some programs), capstone. *Entrance requirements:* For master's, BS in nursing, AS in nursing with another BS/BA, interview, RN license, 1 year of clinical experience (3 for the MS in nursing education program); for Advanced Certificate, master's degree in nursing. Additional exam requirements/recommendations for international students: Required—TOEFL (minimum score 100 iBT), IELTS (minimum score 7). *Application deadline:* For fall admission, 3/1 priority date for domestic and international students; for spring admission, 11/1 priority date for domestic and international students; for summer admission, 3/1 for domestic and international students. Application fee: $80. Electronic applications accepted. *Expenses:* Contact institution. *Financial support:* In 2017–18, 130 students received support. Career-related internships or fieldwork, Federal Work-Study, and scholarships/grants available. Support available to part-time students. Financial award application deadline: 3/1; financial award applicants required to submit FAFSA. *Faculty research:* Vaccine hesitancy in pregnant women and mothers, palliative care and midwifery, diabetes education, curriculum development, workforce training, education and development, geriatrics. *Unit head:* Dr. James Pace, Senior Associate Dean for Academic Programs, 212-992-7343, E-mail: james.pace@nyu.edu. *Application contact:* Matthew Burke, Assistant Director, Graduate Student Affairs and Admissions, 212-998-7397, Fax: 212-995-4302, E-mail: mb6060@nyu.edu.

Nicholls State University, Graduate Studies, College of Nursing and Allied Health, Thibodaux, LA 70310. Offers family nurse practitioner (MSN); nurse executive (MSN); nursing education (MSN); psychiatric/mental health nurse practitioner (MSN).

Northeastern University, Bouvé College of Health Sciences, Boston, MA 02115-5096. Offers applied behavior analysis (MS); audiology (Au D); counseling psychology (MS, PhD, CAGS); exercise science (MS); nursing (MS, PhD, CAGS), including administration (MS), adult-gerontology acute care nurse practitioner (MS, CAGS), adult-

gerontology primary care nurse practitioner (MS, CAGS), anesthesia (MS), family nurse practitioner (MS, CAGS), neonatal nurse practitioner (MS, CAGS), pediatric nurse practitioner (MS, CAGS), psychiatric mental health nurse practitioner (MS, CAGS); nursing practice (DNP); pharmaceutical sciences (MS, PhD), including interdisciplinary concentration, pharmaceutics and drug delivery systems; pharmacology (MS); pharmacy (Pharm D); school psychology (PhD); speech-language pathology (MS); urban health (MPH); MS/MBA. *Accreditation:* ACPE (one or more programs are accredited). *Program availability:* Part-time, evening/weekend, online learning. *Faculty:* 192 full-time. *Students:* 1,685. In 2017, 352 master's, 312 doctorates, 25 other advanced degrees awarded. *Degree requirements:* For doctorate, thesis/dissertation (for some programs); for CAGS, comprehensive exam. Application fee: $75. Electronic applications accepted. *Expenses:* Contact institution. *Financial support:* Fellowships, research assistantships, teaching assistantships, career-related internships or fieldwork, scholarships/grants, health care benefits, tuition waivers, and unspecified assistantships available. Support available to part-time students. Financial award applicants required to submit FAFSA. *Unit head:* Susan L. Parish, Dean, Bouve College of Health Sciences, 617-373-3321, Fax: 617-373-3030, E-mail: s.parish@northeastern.edu. *Application contact:* 617-373-2708, Fax: 617-373-4701, E-mail: bouvegrad@northeastern.edu.
Website: https://www.northeastern.edu/bouve/

Northern Arizona University, College of Health and Human Services, School of Nursing, Flagstaff, AZ 86011. Offers family nurse practitioner (Certificate); nursing (MS), including family nurse practitioner, generalist; nursing practice (DNP). *Accreditation:* AACN. *Program availability:* Part-time, 100% online, blended/hybrid learning. *Faculty:* 50 full-time (45 women), 26 part-time/adjunct (21 women). *Students:* 12 full-time (10 women), 175 part-time (151 women); includes 57 minority (5 Black or African American, non-Hispanic/Latino; 9 American Indian or Alaska Native, non-Hispanic/Latino; 8 Asian, non-Hispanic/Latino; 32 Hispanic/Latino; 1 Native Hawaiian or other Pacific Islander, non-Hispanic/Latino; 2 Two or more races, non-Hispanic/Latino). Average age 39. 66 applicants, 83% accepted, 52 enrolled. In 2017, 60 master's, 5 doctorates, 4 other advanced degrees awarded. *Degree requirements:* For master's, variable foreign language requirement, comprehensive exam (for some programs), thesis (for some programs); for doctorate, variable foreign language requirement, comprehensive exam (for some programs), thesis/dissertation (for some programs), oral defense, individualized research. *Entrance requirements:* For master's, bachelor's degree in nursing from accredited program or associate's degree in nursing from accredited program with bachelor's degree in another field; minimum GPA of 3.0 in all nursing coursework; current RN license in good standing; for doctorate, master's degree in nursing from regionally-accredited university and nationally-accredited nursing program; minimum cumulative GPA of 3.0 in all nursing coursework of master's degree program; current RN license in good standing to practice. Additional exam requirements/recommendations for international students: Required—TOEFL (minimum score 80 iBT), IELTS (minimum score 6.5). *Application deadline:* For fall admission, 3/1 for domestic and international students; for spring admission, 10/1 for domestic and international students. Applications are processed on a rolling basis. Application fee: $65. Electronic applications accepted. *Expenses:* Tuition, state resident: full-time $9240; part-time $458 per credit hour. Tuition, nonresident: full-time $21,588; part-time $1199 per credit hour. *Required fees:* $1021; $14 per credit hour. $646 per semester. Tuition and fees vary according to course load, campus/location and program. *Financial support:* Institutionally sponsored loans and tuition waivers (full and partial) available. Financial award application deadline: 2/1; financial award applicants required to submit FAFSA. *Unit head:* Pamela Stetina, Director, 928-523-2671, Fax: 928-523-7171, E-mail: pamela.stetina@nau.edu. *Application contact:* Penny Walior, Student Academic Specialist, 928-523-6770, Fax: 928-523-9155, E-mail: graduatenursing@nau.edu.
Website: https://nau.edu/chhs/nursing/

Nova Southeastern University, Ron and Kathy Assaf College of Nursing, Fort Lauderdale, FL 33314-7796. Offers advanced practice registered nurse (MSN), including adult-gerontology acute care nurse practitioner, family nurse practitioner, psychiatric mental health nurse practitioner; executive nurse leadership (MSN); nursing (PhD), including nursing education; nursing education (MSN); nursing informatics (MSN); nursing practice (DNP). *Accreditation:* AACN. *Program availability:* Part-time, evening/weekend, 100% online, blended/hybrid learning, annual one-week summer institute delivered face-to-face on main campus. *Faculty:* 9 full-time (all women), 47 part-time/adjunct (43 women). *Students:* 658 full-time (599 women); includes 414 minority (175 Black or African American, non-Hispanic/Latino; 37 Asian, non-Hispanic/Latino; 179 Hispanic/Latino; 1 Native Hawaiian or other Pacific Islander, non-Hispanic/Latino; 22 Two or more races, non-Hispanic/Latino), 3 international. Average age 38. 179 applicants, 100% accepted, 163 enrolled. In 2017, 161 master's, 16 doctorates awarded. *Degree requirements:* For doctorate, comprehensive exam, thesis/dissertation. *Entrance requirements:* For master's, minimum GPA of 3.0, RN, BSN, BS or BA; for doctorate, minimum GPA of 3.5, MSN, RN. Additional exam requirements/recommendations for international students: Recommended—TOEFL. *Application deadline:* For fall admission, 3/1 priority date for domestic students, 3/1 for international students; for winter admission, 11/1 for domestic and international students. Applications are processed on a rolling basis. Application fee: $50. Electronic applications accepted. *Expenses:* Contact institution. *Financial support:* Application deadline: 4/15; applicants required to submit FAFSA. *Faculty research:* Nursing education, curriculum, clinical research, interdisciplinary research. *Total annual research expenditures:* $9,500. *Unit head:* Dr. Marcella M. Rutherford, Dean, 954-262-1963, E-mail: rmarcell@nova.edu. *Application contact:* Dianna Murphey, Director of Operations, 954-262-1975, E-mail: dgardner1@nova.edu.
Website: http://www.nova.edu/nursing/

Oakland University, Graduate Study and Lifelong Learning, School of Nursing, Program in Family Nurse Practitioner, Rochester, MI 48309-4401. Offers MSN, PMC. *Accreditation:* AACN. *Degree requirements:* For master's, thesis. *Entrance requirements:* For master's, GRE General Test, minimum GPA of 3.0. Additional exam requirements/recommendations for international students: Required—TOEFL (minimum score 550 paper-based). Electronic applications accepted. *Expenses:* Contact institution.

Ohio University, Graduate College, College of Health Sciences and Professions, School of Nursing, Athens, OH 45701-2979. Offers advanced clinical practice (DNP); executive practice (DNP); family nurse practitioner (MSN); nurse educator (MSN). *Accreditation:* AACN. *Degree requirements:* For master's, capstone project. *Entrance requirements:* For master's, GRE, bachelor's degree in nursing from accredited college or university, minimum overall undergraduate GPA of 3.0, official transcripts, statement of goals and objectives, resume, 3 letters of recommendation. Additional exam requirements/recommendations for international students: Required—TOEFL (minimum score 550 paper-based; 80 iBT) or IELTS (minimum score 6.5). Electronic applications accepted.

Old Dominion University, College of Health Sciences, School of Nursing, Family Nurse Practitioner Emphasis, Norfolk, VA 23529. Offers MSN. *Program availability:* Blended/hybrid learning. *Faculty:* 3 full-time (all women), 9 part-time/adjunct (all women). *Students:* 57 full-time (51 women), 6 part-time (all women); includes 17 minority (8 Black or African American, non-Hispanic/Latino; 1 Asian, non-Hispanic/Latino; 5 Hispanic/Latino; 3 Two or more races, non-Hispanic/Latino). Average age 36. 111 applicants, 42% accepted, 31 enrolled. In 2017, 24 master's awarded. *Degree requirements:* For master's, comprehensive exam. *Entrance requirements:* For master's, GRE or MAT (waived with a GPA above 3.5), 3 letters of recommendation, essay, resume, transcripts. Additional exam requirements/recommendations for international students: Required—TOEFL. *Application deadline:* For fall admission, 3/1 priority date for domestic students, 4/15 priority date for international students. Application fee: $50. Electronic applications accepted. *Expenses:* $469 per credit; $450 School of Nursing fee per semester. *Financial support:* Traineeships available. Financial award application deadline: 3/1. *Faculty research:* Military families, nurse practitioner student reaching modalities, gerontology, pediatrics, ethics. *Unit head:* Dr. Deborah Gray, FNP Program Director, 757-683-5093, Fax: 757-683-5253, E-mail: dcgray@odu.edu. *Application contact:* Sue Parker, Graduate Program Coordinator, 757-683-4298, Fax: 757-683-5253, E-mail: sparker@odu.edu.
Website: http://catalog.odu.edu/graduate/collegeofhealthsciences/schoolofnursing/#masterofscienceinnursing013familynursepractitionerrole

Olivet Nazarene University, Graduate School, Department of Nursing, Bourbonnais, IL 60914. Offers family nurse practitioner (MSN); nursing (MSN).

Oregon Health & Science University, School of Nursing, Family Nurse Practitioner Program, Portland, OR 97239-2941. Offers MN. *Program availability:* Blended/hybrid learning. *Entrance requirements:* For master's, GRE General Test, bachelor's degree in nursing, minimum cumulative and science GPA of 3.0, 3 letters of recommendation, essay, statistics taken within last 5 years. Additional exam requirements/recommendations for international students: Required—TOEFL (minimum score 83 iBT). Electronic applications accepted. *Expenses:* Contact institution. *Faculty research:* Data science, information technology, mind/body interventions to optimize symptom management in chronic pain, health disparities, childhood obesity.

Otterbein University, Department of Nursing, Westerville, OH 43081. Offers advanced practice nurse educator (Certificate); clinical nurse leader (MSN); family nurse practitioner (MSN, Certificate); nurse anesthesia (MSN, Certificate); nursing (DNP); nursing service administration (MSN). *Accreditation:* AACN; AANA/CANAEP; ACEN. *Program availability:* Part-time, evening/weekend, online learning. *Degree requirements:* For master's, comprehensive exam (for some programs), thesis (for some programs). *Entrance requirements:* For master's, 2 reference forms, resume; for Certificate, official transcripts, 2 reference forms, essay, resumé. Additional exam requirements/recommendations for international students: Required—TOEFL (minimum score 550 paper-based; 79 iBT). *Faculty research:* Patient education, women's health, trauma curriculum development, administration.

Pace University, College of Health Professions, Lienhard School of Nursing, New York, NY 10038. Offers adult acute care nurse practitioner (MS, CAGS); family nurse practitioner (MS, CAGS); nursing (DNP, PhD); professional nursing leadership (MS, CAGS). *Accreditation:* AACN. *Program availability:* Part-time. *Faculty:* 11 full-time (10 women), 31 part-time/adjunct (27 women). *Students:* 11 full-time (all women), 515 part-time (459 women); includes 277 minority (145 Black or African American, non-Hispanic/Latino; 1 American Indian or Alaska Native, non-Hispanic/Latino; 88 Asian, non-Hispanic/Latino; 34 Hispanic/Latino; 9 Two or more races, non-Hispanic/Latino), 1 international. Average age 35. 289 applicants, 74% accepted, 138 enrolled. In 2017, 483 master's, 45 doctorates, 27 other advanced degrees awarded. Terminal master's awarded for partial completion of doctoral program. *Degree requirements:* For master's and CAGS, thesis. *Entrance requirements:* For master's, RN license, resume, personal statement, 2 letters of recommendation, official transcripts, minimum GPA of 3.0, undergraduate statistics; for doctorate, RN license, resume, personal statement, 2 letters of recommendation, official transcripts, accredited master's degree in nursing, minimum GPA of 3.3, state certification and board eligibility as FNP or ANP; for CAGS, RN license, resume, personal statement, 2 letters of recommendation, official transcripts, minimum GPA of 3.0, undergraduate statistics, completion of 2nd degree in nursing. Additional exam requirements/recommendations for international students: Required—TOEFL (minimum score 100 iBT), IELTS or PTE. *Application deadline:* For fall admission, 3/1 for domestic and international students. Applications are processed on a rolling basis. Application fee: $70. Electronic applications accepted. *Expenses:* Contact institution. *Financial support:* Research assistantships, teaching assistantships, career-related internships or fieldwork, Federal Work-Study, institutionally sponsored loans, tuition waivers (partial), and unspecified assistantships available. Support available to part-time students. Financial award application deadline: 2/15; financial award applicants required to submit FAFSA. *Unit head:* Dr. Harriet R. Feldman, Dean, College of Health Professions, 914-773-3341, E-mail: hfeldman@pace.edu. *Application contact:* Susan Ford-Goldschein, Director of Graduate Admissions, 212-346-1531, Fax: 212-346-1585, E-mail: graduateadmission@pace.edu.
Website: http://www.pace.edu/lienhard

Pacific Lutheran University, School of Nursing, DNP Program, Tacoma, WA 98447. Offers DNP. Program designed for the working nurse; classes typically held Thursday evenings and all day Friday. *Accreditation:* AACN. *Entrance requirements:* Additional exam requirements/recommendations for international students: Required—TOEFL (minimum score 550 paper-based; 86 iBT). Electronic applications accepted. *Expenses:* Contact institution.

Palm Beach Atlantic University, School of Nursing, West Palm Beach, FL 33416-4708. Offers family nurse practitioner (DNP); health systems leadership (MSN). *Accreditation:* AACN. *Program availability:* Part-time. *Entrance requirements:* For master's, minimum GPA of 3.0; active RN license; personal interview; for doctorate, minimum GPA of 3.0; one year of experience as an RN; personal interview. Additional exam requirements/recommendations for international students: Required—TOEFL (minimum score 550 paper-based; 79 iBT). Electronic applications accepted. *Expenses:* Contact institution. *Faculty research:* Elder care, nursing education theory.

Point Loma Nazarene University, School of Nursing, MS in Nursing Program, San Diego, CA 92106-2899. Offers adult-gerontology (MSN); family individual health (MSN); pediatrics (MSN). *Program availability:* Part-time. *Students:* 59 part-time (49 women); includes 28 minority (4 Black or African American, non-Hispanic/Latino; 1 American Indian or Alaska Native, non-Hispanic/Latino; 4 Asian, non-Hispanic/Latino; 9 Hispanic/Latino; 4 Native Hawaiian or other Pacific Islander, non-Hispanic/Latino; 6 Two or more races, non-Hispanic/Latino), 1 international. Average age 36. 23 applicants, 96% accepted, 18 enrolled. In 2017, 21 master's awarded. *Entrance requirements:* For master's, NCLEX exam, ADN or BSN in nursing, interview, RN license, essay, letters of recommendation, interview. *Application deadline:* For fall admission, 7/5 priority date for domestic students; for spring admission, 11/1 priority date for domestic students; for summer admission, 3/22 priority date for domestic students. Applications are processed on a rolling basis. Electronic applications accepted. *Expenses:* Contact institution. *Financial support:* Scholarships/grants available. Financial award applicants required to submit FAFSA. *Unit head:* Dr. Barb Taylor, Dean of the School of Nursing, 619-849-2766, E-mail: bataylor@pointloma.edu. *Application contact:* Joanie Joy, Senior Director of Enrollment Management, 619-329-6785, E-mail: gradinfo@pointloma.edu.
Website: https://www.pointloma.edu/graduate-studies/programs/nursing-ms

Family Nurse Practitioner Studies

Purdue University, Graduate School, College of Health and Human Sciences, School of Nursing, West Lafayette, IN 47907. Offers adult gerontology primary care nurse practitioner (MS, Post Master's Certificate); nursing (DNP, PhD); primary care family nurse practitioner (MS, Post Master's Certificate); primary care pediatric nurse practitioner (MS, Post Master's Certificate). *Faculty:* 31 full-time (30 women), 2 part-time/adjunct (both women). *Students:* 41 full-time (39 women), 33 part-time (32 women); includes 10 minority (5 Black or African American, non-Hispanic/Latino; 1 American Indian or Alaska Native, non-Hispanic/Latino; 1 Asian, non-Hispanic/Latino; 2 Hispanic/Latino; 1 Two or more races, non-Hispanic/Latino), 2 international. Average age 35. 36 applicants, 78% accepted, 16 enrolled. In 2017, 13 master's, 5 doctorates, 2 other advanced degrees awarded. *Unit head:* Jane M. Kirkpatrick, Head of the Graduate Program, 765-494-6644, E-mail: jmkirk@purdue.edu. *Application contact:* Reanne Hall, Graduate Contact, 765-494-9248, E-mail: gradnursing@purdue.edu.
Website: http://www.purdue.edu/hhs/nur/

Purdue University Northwest, Graduate Studies Office, School of Nursing, Hammond, IN 46323-2094. Offers adult health clinical nurse specialist (MS); critical care clinical nurse specialist (MS); family nurse practitioner (MS); nurse executive (MS). *Accreditation:* ACEN. *Program availability:* Part-time, online learning. *Entrance requirements:* For master's, BSN. Additional exam requirements/recommendations for international students: Required—TOEFL. Electronic applications accepted. *Faculty research:* Adult health, cardiovascular and pulmonary nursing.

Queen's University at Kingston, School of Graduate Studies, Faculty of Health Sciences, School of Nursing, Kingston, ON K7L 3N6, Canada. Offers health and chronic illness (M Sc); nurse scientist (PhD); primary health care nurse practitioner (Certificate); women's and children's health (M Sc). *Degree requirements:* For master's, thesis. *Entrance requirements:* For master's, RN license. Additional exam requirements/recommendations for international students: Required—TOEFL. *Faculty research:* Women and children's health, health and chronic illness.

Quinnipiac University, School of Nursing, Family Nurse Practitioner Track, Hamden, CT 06518-1940. Offers DNP. *Accreditation:* ACEN. *Faculty:* 18 full-time (17 women), 11 part-time/adjunct (8 women). *Students:* 24 full-time (21 women), 46 part-time (40 women); includes 20 minority (7 Black or African American, non-Hispanic/Latino; 7 Asian, non-Hispanic/Latino; 6 Hispanic/Latino). 53 applicants, 60% accepted, 23 enrolled. In 2017, 37 doctorates awarded. *Entrance requirements:* Additional exam requirements/recommendations for international students: Required—TOEFL (minimum score 575 paper-based; 90 iBT), IELTS (minimum score 6.5). *Application deadline:* For fall admission, 5/1 for domestic students, 4/30 for international students. Applications are processed on a rolling basis. Application fee: $45. Electronic applications accepted. *Financial support:* Federal Work-Study, scholarships/grants, and unspecified assistantships available. Financial award application deadline: 6/1; financial award applicants required to submit FAFSA. *Unit head:* Laima Karosas, Program Director, 203-582-5366, E-mail: graduate@qu.edu. *Application contact:* Office of Graduate Admissions, 800-462-1944, Fax: 203-582-3443, E-mail: graduate@qu.edu.
Website: http://www.qu.edu/gradnursing

Ramapo College of New Jersey, Master of Science in Nursing Program, Mahwah, NJ 07430-1680. Offers family nurse practitioner (MSN); nursing administrator (MSN); nursing education (MSN). *Accreditation:* ACEN. *Program availability:* Part-time. *Faculty:* 4 full-time (all women), 2 part-time/adjunct (1 woman). *Students:* 79 part-time (70 women); includes 28 minority (4 Black or African American, non-Hispanic/Latino; 18 Asian, non-Hispanic/Latino; 5 Hispanic/Latino; 1 Two or more races, non-Hispanic/Latino). Average age 33. 84 applicants, 67% accepted, 37 enrolled. In 2017, 9 master's awarded. *Entrance requirements:* For master's, official transcript; personal statement; 2 letters of recommendation; resume; current licensure as a Registered Nurse, or eligibility for licensure; evidence of one year of recent experience as RN prior to entry into clinical practicum courses; evidence of undergraduate statistics course; criminal background check. Additional exam requirements/recommendations for international students: Required—TOEFL (minimum score 550 paper-based; 90 iBT); Recommended—IELTS (minimum score 6). *Application deadline:* For fall admission, 5/1 for domestic and international students; for spring admission, 12/1 for domestic and international students. Applications are processed on a rolling basis. Application fee: $65. Electronic applications accepted. *Expenses:* $690.60 per credit tuition, $56.95 per credit fees. *Financial support:* Career-related internships or fieldwork available. Financial award application deadline: 3/1; financial award applicants required to submit FAFSA. *Faculty research:* Learning styles and critical thinking, evidence-based education, outcomes measurement. *Unit head:* Dr. Kathleen M. Burke, Assistant Dean of Nursing Programs/Professor, 201-684-7737, Fax: 201-684-7954, E-mail: kmburke@ramapo.edu. *Application contact:* Anthony Dovi, Associate Director of Admissions, Adult Learners and Graduate Programs, 201-684-7305, Fax: 201-684-7964, E-mail: adovi@ramapo.edu.
Website: http://www.ramapo.edu/msn/

Regis College, Nursing and Health Sciences School, Weston, MA 02493. Offers applied behavior analysis (MS); counseling psychology (MA); health administration (MS); nurse practitioner (Certificate); nursing (MS, DNP); nursing education (Certificate); occupational therapy (MS). *Accreditation:* ACEN. *Program availability:* Part-time, evening/weekend, 100% online, blended/hybrid learning. *Degree requirements:* For doctorate, thesis/dissertation. *Entrance requirements:* For master's, GRE General Test or MAT, minimum GPA of 3.0, official transcripts, recommendations, personal statement, resume/curriculum vitae, interview; for doctorate, MAT or GRE if GPA from master's lower than 3.5. Additional exam requirements/recommendations for international students: Required—TOEFL (minimum score 560 paper-based; 79 iBT); Recommended—IELTS (minimum score 6.5). *Application deadline:* Applications are processed on a rolling basis. Application fee: $75. Electronic applications accepted. *Financial support:* Federal Work-Study, scholarships/grants, traineeships, and unspecified assistantships available. Support available to part-time students. Financial award applicants required to submit FAFSA. *Faculty research:* Global public health, health policy, education, aging, job satisfaction, psychiatric nursing, critical thinking. *Application contact:* Hillary Lyons, Graduate Admission Counselor, 781-768-7746, E-mail: hillary.lyons@regiscollege.edu.

Research College of Nursing, Nursing Program, Kansas City, MO 64132. Offers adult-gerontological nurse practitioner (MSN); executive practice and healthcare leadership (MSN); family nurse practitioner (MSN). *Accreditation:* AACN. *Program availability:* Part-time-only, 100% online. *Faculty:* 10 full-time (all women), 4 part-time/adjunct (2 women). *Students:* 1 (woman) full-time, 150 part-time (125 women); includes 14 minority (7 Black or African American, non-Hispanic/Latino; 1 American Indian or Alaska Native, non-Hispanic/Latino; 2 Asian, non-Hispanic/Latino; 2 Hispanic/Latino; 1 Native Hawaiian or other Pacific Islander, non-Hispanic/Latino; 1 Two or more races, non-Hispanic/Latino). *Degree requirements:* For master's, research project. *Entrance requirements:* For master's, 3 letters of recommendation, official transcripts, resume, personal statement/writing sample. *Application deadline:* Applications are processed on a rolling basis. Application fee: $65. Electronic applications accepted. *Expenses: Tuition:* Part-time $550 per credit hour. *Financial support:* Applicants required to submit FAFSA. *Unit head:* Dr. Thad Wilson, President, 816-995-2815, Fax: 816-995-2817, E-mail: thad.wilson@researchcollege.edu. *Application contact:* Leslie Burry, Director of Transfer and Graduate Recruitment, 816-995-2820, Fax: 816-995-2813, E-mail: leslie.burry@researchcollege.edu.

Rivier University, School of Graduate Studies, Division of Nursing and Health Professions, Nashua, NH 03060. Offers family nurse practitioner (MS); leadership in health systems management (MS); nursing education (MS); nursing practice (DNP); psychiatric/mental health nurse practitioner (MS); public health (MPH). *Accreditation:* ACEN. *Program availability:* Part-time, evening/weekend. *Entrance requirements:* For master's, GRE, MAT. Electronic applications accepted.

Rocky Mountain University of Health Professions, Doctor of Nursing Practice Program, Provo, UT 84606. Offers DNP. *Accreditation:* AACN.

Rush University, College of Nursing, Department of Community, Systems, and Mental Health Nursing, Chicago, IL 60612. Offers advanced public health nursing (DNP); family nurse practitioner (DNP); psychiatric mental health nurse practitioner (DNP); transformative leadership: population health (DNP). *Accreditation:* AACN. *Program availability:* Part-time, 100% online, blended/hybrid learning. *Students:* 23 full-time (21 women), 264 part-time (245 women); includes 83 minority (36 Black or African American, non-Hispanic/Latino; 1 American Indian or Alaska Native, non-Hispanic/Latino; 16 Asian, non-Hispanic/Latino; 24 Hispanic/Latino; 6 Two or more races, non-Hispanic/Latino). 176 applicants, 56% accepted, 79 enrolled. In 2017, 64 doctorates awarded. *Degree requirements:* For doctorate, scholarly project. *Entrance requirements:* For doctorate, GRE General Test (waived for DNP if cumulative GPA is 3.25 or greater, nursing GPA is 3.0 or greater, or a completed graduate program GPA is 3.5 or greater), interview, 3 letters of recommendation, personal statement, current resume. Additional exam requirements/recommendations for international students: Required—TOEFL (minimum score 94 iBT). *Application deadline:* For fall admission, 1/2 for domestic students; for spring admission, 8/1 for domestic students; for summer admission, 12/1 for domestic students. Applications are processed on a rolling basis. Application fee: $110. Electronic applications accepted. *Expenses:* Contact institution. *Financial support:* Research assistantships, teaching assistantships, Federal Work-Study, scholarships/grants, traineeships, and health care benefits available. Support available to part-time students. Financial award application deadline: 3/1; financial award applicants required to submit FAFSA. *Faculty research:* Health behaviors; caregivers; psychiatric services; disabilities; population health. *Unit head:* Dr. Mona Shattell, Chairperson, 312-942-7117, E-mail: mona_shattell@rush.edu. *Application contact:* Jennifer Thorndyke, Director of Admissions, 312-563-7526, E-mail: jennifer_thorndyke@rush.edu.
Website: https://www.rushu.rush.edu/college-nursing/departments-college-nursing/department-community-systems-and-mental-health-nursing

Rutgers University–Camden, School of Nursing–Camden, Camden, NJ 08102-1401. Offers adult gerontology primary care nurse practitioner (DNP); family nurse practitioner (DNP). *Degree requirements:* For doctorate, minimum of 1,000 clinical residency hours, evidence-based clinical project.

Rutgers University–Newark, Rutgers School of Nursing, Newark, NJ 07107-3001. Offers adult health (MSN); adult occupational health (MSN); advanced practice nursing (MSN, Post Master's Certificate); family nurse practitioner (MSN); nurse anesthesia (MSN); nursing (MSN); nursing informatics (MSN); urban health (PhD); women's health practitioner (MSN). *Accreditation:* AANA/CANAEP. *Program availability:* Part-time. *Entrance requirements:* For master's, GRE, RN license; basic life support, statistics, and health assessment experience. Additional exam requirements/recommendations for international students: Required—TOEFL. Electronic applications accepted. *Expenses:* Contact institution. *Faculty research:* HIV/AIDS, diabetes education, learned helplessness, nursing science, psychoeducation.

Sacred Heart University, Graduate Programs, College of Nursing, Fairfield, CT 06825. Offers clinical (DNP); clinical nurse leader (MSN); family nurse practitioner (MSN, Post-Master's Certificate); leadership (DNP); nursing education (MSN); nursing management and executive leadership (MSN). *Accreditation:* AACN. *Program availability:* Part-time, evening/weekend, 100% online, blended/hybrid learning. *Faculty:* 17 full-time (all women), 29 part-time/adjunct (26 women). *Students:* 21 full-time (20 women), 692 part-time (650 women); includes 136 minority (52 Black or African American, non-Hispanic/Latino; 2 American Indian or Alaska Native, non-Hispanic/Latino; 29 Asian, non-Hispanic/Latino; 46 Hispanic/Latino; 7 Two or more races, non-Hispanic/Latino). Average age 37. 70 applicants, 69% accepted, 32 enrolled. In 2017, 260 master's, 16 doctorates awarded. *Degree requirements:* For master's, thesis, 500 clinical hours; for doctorate, capstone. *Entrance requirements:* For master's, minimum GPA of 3.0, BSN or RN plus BS (for MSN); for doctorate, minimum GPA of 3.0, MSN or BSN plus MS in related field (for DNP). Additional exam requirements/recommendations for international students: Required—TOEFL (minimum score 570 paper-based, 80 iBT), TWE, or IELTS (6.5). *Application deadline:* For fall admission, 2/15 for domestic and international students. Applications are processed on a rolling basis. Application fee: $75. Electronic applications accepted. *Expenses:* Contact institution. *Financial support:* Unspecified assistantships available. Financial award applicants required to submit FAFSA. *Unit head:* Mary Alice Donius, Dean of Nursing, 203-365-4508, E-mail: doniusm@sacredheart.edu. *Application contact:* Tara Chudy, Executive Director of Graduate Admissions, 203-365-4735, Fax: 203-365-4732, E-mail: chudyt@sacredheart.edu.
Website: http://www.sacredheart.edu/academics/collegeofhealthprofessions/academicprograms/nursing/nursingprograms/graduateprograms/

Sage Graduate School, School of Health Sciences, Department of Nursing, Program in Family Nurse Practitioner, Troy, NY 12180-4115. Offers MS. *Accreditation:* AACN. *Program availability:* Part-time, evening/weekend. *Faculty:* 6 full-time (all women), 11 part-time/adjunct (10 women). *Students:* 23 full-time (20 women), 96 part-time (90 women); includes 32 minority (13 Black or African American, non-Hispanic/Latino; 2 American Indian or Alaska Native, non-Hispanic/Latino; 7 Asian, non-Hispanic/Latino; 7 Hispanic/Latino; 3 Two or more races, non-Hispanic/Latino). Average age 34. 144 applicants, 41% accepted, 32 enrolled. In 2017, 37 master's awarded. *Degree requirements:* For master's, thesis or alternative. *Entrance requirements:* For master's, currently licensed as registered professional nurse in state of practice; baccalaureate degree in nursing from nationally-accredited program or its international equivalent. Additional exam requirements/recommendations for international students: Required—TOEFL (minimum score 550 paper-based). *Application deadline:* Applications are processed on a rolling basis. Application fee: $30. Electronic applications accepted. Tuition and fees vary according to degree level and program. *Financial support:* Fellowships, research assistantships, scholarships/grants, and unspecified assistantships available. Financial award application deadline: 3/1; financial award applicants required to submit FAFSA. *Unit head:* Dr. Theresa Hand, Dean, School of Health Sciences, 518-244-2264, Fax: 518-244-4571, E-mail: handt@sage.edu. *Application contact:* Dr. Carol Braungart, Co-Director, Graduate Nursing Program, 518-244-2459, Fax: 518-244-2009, E-mail: braunc@sage.edu.

Saginaw Valley State University, College of Health and Human Services, Program in Nurse Practitioner, University Center, MI 48710. Offers MSN, DNP. *Accreditation:* AACN. *Program availability:* Part-time, evening/weekend, online learning. *Students:* 6 full-time (4 women), 86 part-time (74 women); includes 10 minority (6 Black or African American, non-Hispanic/Latino; 2 Asian, non-Hispanic/Latino; 2 Two or more races, non-Hispanic/Latino), 5 international. Average age 32. 28 applicants, 93% accepted, 23 enrolled. In 2017, 7 master's, 7 doctorates awarded. *Degree requirements:* For master's, thesis optional. *Entrance requirements:* For master's, GRE, minimum GPA of 3.0, license to practice nursing in MI; for doctorate, GRE, minimum GPA of 3.3, college chemistry with minimum C grade, college statistics with minimum B grade, employed as RN with current license in MI. Additional exam requirements/recommendations for international students: Required—TOEFL (minimum score 580 paper-based; 92 iBT). *Application deadline:* For fall admission, 7/15 for international students; for winter admission, 11/15 for international students; for spring admission, 4/15 for international students. Applications are processed on a rolling basis. Application fee: $30 ($90 for international students). Electronic applications accepted. *Expenses:* Tuition, state resident: full-time $10,156; part-time $564.20 per credit hour. Tuition, nonresident: full-time $19,336; part-time $1074.20 per credit hour. *Required fees:* $263; $14.60 per credit hour. Tuition and fees vary according to degree level and program. *Financial support:* Federal Work-Study and scholarships/grants available. Support available to part-time students. Financial award application deadline: 4/1; financial award applicants required to submit FAFSA. *Unit head:* Dr. Karen Brown-Fackler, Coordinator, 989-964-2185, Fax: 989-964-4925, E-mail: kmbrown4@svsu.edu. *Application contact:* Jenna Briggs, Director, Graduate and International Admissions, 989-964-6096, Fax: 989-964-2788, E-mail: gradadm@svsu.edu.

Saint Francis Medical Center College of Nursing, Graduate Programs, Peoria, IL 61603-3783. Offers adult gerontology (MSN); clinical nurse leader (MSN); family nurse practitioner (MSN, Post-Graduate Certificate); family psychiatric mental health nurse practitioner (MSN); neonatal nurse practitioner (MSN); nurse clinician (Post-Graduate Certificate); nurse educator (MSN, Post-Graduate Certificate); nursing (DNP); nursing management leadership (MSN). *Accreditation:* ACEN. *Program availability:* Part-time, online only, 100% online, blended/hybrid learning. *Faculty:* 11 full-time (all women), 7 part-time/adjunct (all women). *Students:* 4 full-time (all women), 239 part-time (209 women); includes 24 minority (12 Black or African American, non-Hispanic/Latino; 3 Asian, non-Hispanic/Latino; 4 Hispanic/Latino; 5 Two or more races, non-Hispanic/Latino). Average age 37. 105 applicants, 83% accepted, 60 enrolled. In 2017, 52 master's, 8 doctorates awarded. *Degree requirements:* For master's, research experience, portfolio, practicum; for doctorate, practicum. *Entrance requirements:* For master's, nursing research, health assessment, graduate course work in statistics, RN license; for doctorate, master's degree in nursing, professional portfolio, graduate statistics, transcripts, RN license. Additional exam requirements/recommendations for international students: Required—TOEFL (minimum score 550 paper-based; 79 iBT). *Application deadline:* For fall admission, 6/1 priority date for domestic and international students; for spring admission, 11/15 priority date for domestic and international students. Applications are processed on a rolling basis. Application fee: $50. *Expenses:* Contact institution. *Financial support:* In 2017–18, 13 students received support. Scholarships/grants and tuition waivers (partial) available. Support available to part-time students. Financial award application deadline: 6/15; financial award applicants required to submit FAFSA. *Faculty research:* Outcome and curriculum planning, health promotion, NCLEX-RN results, decision-making program evaluation. *Unit head:* Dr. Patti A. Stockert, President of the College, 309-655-4124, Fax: 309-624-8973, E-mail: patricia.a.stockert@osfhealthcare.org. *Application contact:* Dr. Kim A. Mitchell, Dean, Graduate Program, 309-655-2201, Fax: 309-624-8973, E-mail: kim.a.mitchell@osfhealthcare.org.
Website: http://www.sfmccon.edu/graduate-programs/

Saint Joseph's College of Maine, Master of Science in Nursing Program, Standish, ME 04084. Offers administration (MSN); education (MSN); family nurse practitioner (MSN); nursing administration and leadership (Certificate); nursing and health care education (Certificate). *Accreditation:* AACN. *Program availability:* Part-time, online learning. *Entrance requirements:* For master's, MAT. Electronic applications accepted.

Saint Mary's College, Graduate Programs, Doctor of Nursing Practice Program, Notre Dame, IN 46556. Offers adult - gerontology acute care (DNP); adult - gerontology primary care (DNP); family nurse practitioner (DNP). *Program availability:* Part-time-only. *Faculty:* 7 full-time (all women), 4 part-time/adjunct (3 women). *Students:* 39 part-time (37 women); includes 12 minority (4 Black or African American, non-Hispanic/Latino; 5 Asian, non-Hispanic/Latino; 3 Hispanic/Latino). Average age 31. 36 applicants, 83% accepted, 26 enrolled. *Degree requirements:* For doctorate, comprehensive exam, thesis/dissertation. *Entrance requirements:* For doctorate, BSN or MSN, unencumbered RN license or eligibility for RN licensure, official transcripts from previously-attended institutions, 3 letters of recommendation, personal statement, resume or curriculum vitae. Additional exam requirements/recommendations for international students: Recommended—TOEFL (minimum score 80 iBT), IELTS (minimum score 6.5). *Application deadline:* For fall admission, 6/15 priority date for domestic and international students. Applications are processed on a rolling basis. Application fee: $65. Electronic applications accepted. *Expenses:* $5,382 per semester. *Financial support:* Application deadline: 3/1; applicants required to submit FAFSA. *Faculty research:* Suicide prevention, infant death prevention, delirium management, teaching methodologies, nurses' perceptions of care. *Unit head:* Linda Paskiewicz, Director of the Department of Nursing Science, 574-284-4679, E-mail: lpaskie@saintmarys.edu. *Application contact:* Melissa Fruscione, Graduate Admission, 574-284-5098, E-mail: graduateadmission@saintmarys.edu.
Website: https://grad.saintmarys.edu/academic-programs/doctor-nursing-practice

Salisbury University, DNP Program, Salisbury, MD 21801. Offers family nurse practitioner (DNP); nursing leadership (DNP). *Accreditation:* AACN. *Program availability:* Part-time. *Faculty:* 10 full-time (all women). *Students:* 35 full-time (32 women), 4 part-time (all women); includes 8 minority (all Black or African American, non-Hispanic/Latino). Average age 33. 21 applicants, 43% accepted, 9 enrolled. In 2017, 1 doctorate awarded. Terminal master's awarded for partial completion of doctoral program. *Degree requirements:* For doctorate, thesis/dissertation. *Entrance requirements:* For doctorate, three letters of reference; transcripts from colleges and universities attended; nursing degree; personal statement; minimum GPA of 3.0; U.S. RN license; resume. Additional exam requirements/recommendations for international students: Required—TOEFL (minimum score 550 paper-based; 79 iBT), IELTS (minimum score 6.5). *Application deadline:* For fall admission, 3/1 priority date for domestic and international students. Applications are processed on a rolling basis. Application fee: $65. Electronic applications accepted. *Expenses:* $640 per credit hour resident; $807 per credit hour non-resident; $92 per credit hour fees. *Financial support:* In 2017–18, 3 students received support. Career-related internships or fieldwork and scholarships/grants available. Support available to part-time students. Financial award application deadline: 3/1; financial award applicants required to submit FAFSA. *Faculty research:* Simulation education; chronic disease management; palliative care; gerontology; mental illness. *Unit head:* Dr. Lisa Seldomridge, Graduate Program Director, Nursing DNP, 410-543-6413, E-mail: laseldomridge@salisbury.edu.
Website: http://www.salisbury.edu/gsr/gradstudies/DNPpage.html

Samford University, Ida Moffett School of Nursing, Birmingham, AL 35229. Offers administration (DNP); advanced practice (DNP); dual nurse practitioner (family/emergency) (DNP); family nurse practitioner (MSN, DNP); nurse anesthesia (MSN, DNP); nursing administration (DNP), including health systems and administration, informatics, transformation of care. *Accreditation:* AACN; AANA/CANAEP. *Program availability:* Part-time, evening/weekend, blended/hybrid learning. *Faculty:* 20 full-time (19 women), 3 part-time/adjunct (0 women). *Students:* 296 full-time (240 women), 41 part-time (38 women); includes 67 minority (43 Black or African American, non-Hispanic/Latino; 2 American Indian or Alaska Native, non-Hispanic/Latino; 6 Asian, non-Hispanic/Latino; 8 Hispanic/Latino; 8 Two or more races, non-Hispanic/Latino). Average age 35. 79 applicants, 71% accepted, 29 enrolled. In 2017, 117 master's, 39 doctorates awarded. *Degree requirements:* For doctorate, project with poster presentation. *Entrance requirements:* For master's, GRE within the past five years (for nurse anesthesia), RN, minimum nursing GPA of 3.0, undergraduate course in nursing research with minimum C grade, undergraduate health assessment course with minimum B grade; interview, 1 year full time critical care as RN, 3 letters of recommendation, undergraduate courses in general chemistry and research with minimum B grade for both (for nurse anesthesia); for doctorate, unencumbered licensure as registered nurse; master's degree from CCNE-, CNEA-, or ACEN-accredited program in the area of advanced practice or administration; minimum master's degree cumulative GPA of 3.5; video interview submission. Additional exam requirements/recommendations for international students: Required—TOEFL (minimum score 575 paper-based; 90 iBT); Recommended—IELTS (minimum score 6.5). *Application deadline:* For fall admission, 4/1 for domestic and international students; for spring admission, 8/1 for domestic and international students; for summer admission, 1/1 for domestic and international students. Application fee: $50. Electronic applications accepted. *Expenses:* $809 per credit (for DNP and MSN); $9,737 per semester (for MSN in nurse anesthesia). *Financial support:* In 2017–18, 63 students received support. Application deadline: 2/15; applicants required to submit FAFSA. *Unit head:* Dr. Nena F. Sanders, Vice Provost, College of Health Sciences/Ida Moffett School of Nursing Dean/Professor, 205-726-2612, E-mail: nfsander@samford.edu. *Application contact:* Allyson Maddox, Director of Graduate Student Services, 205-726-2047, E-mail: amaddox@samford.edu.
Website: http://samford.edu/nursing

Samuel Merritt University, School of Nursing, Oakland, CA 94609-3108. Offers case management (MSN); family nurse practitioner (MSN, DNP, Certificate); nurse anesthetist (MSN, Certificate); nursing (DNP). *Accreditation:* AACN; AANA/CANAEP (one or more programs are accredited). *Program availability:* Part-time, evening/weekend, 100% online, blended/hybrid learning. *Faculty:* 57 full-time (49 women), 90 part-time/adjunct (77 women). *Students:* 401 full-time (322 women), 267 part-time (202 women); includes 438 minority (52 Black or African American, non-Hispanic/Latino; 4 American Indian or Alaska Native, non-Hispanic/Latino; 224 Asian, non-Hispanic/Latino; 108 Hispanic/Latino; 9 Native Hawaiian or other Pacific Islander, non-Hispanic/Latino; 41 Two or more races, non-Hispanic/Latino). 788 applicants, 54% accepted, 306 enrolled. In 2017, 176 master's, 6 doctorates, 7 other advanced degrees awarded. *Degree requirements:* For master's, thesis or alternative; for doctorate, project. *Entrance requirements:* For master's, GRE General Test (for nurse anesthetist program), minimum GPA of 2.5 in science, 3.0 overall; previous course work in statistics; current RN license; for doctorate and Certificate, minimum GPA of 2.5 in science, 3.0 overall; previous course work in statistics; current RN license. Additional exam requirements/recommendations for international students: Required—TOEFL (minimum score 100 iBT). *Application deadline:* For fall admission, 7/1 priority date for domestic students; for spring admission, 11/1 priority date for domestic students; for summer admission, 3/1 priority date for domestic students. Applications are processed on a rolling basis. Application fee: $65. Electronic applications accepted. *Expenses:* $1,394 per unit tuition (for MSN); $1,208 per unit tuition (for DNP). *Financial support:* Career-related internships or fieldwork, Federal Work-Study, scholarships/grants, and traineeships available. Support available to part-time students. Financial award applicants required to submit FAFSA. *Faculty research:* Gerontology, community health, maternal-child health, sexually transmitted diseases, substance abuse, oncology. *Unit head:* Dr. Audrey Berman, Dean of Nursing, 510-869-6733, Fax: 510-869-6525. *Application contact:* Timothy Cranford, Dean of Admission, 510-869-6576, Fax: 510-869-6525, E-mail: admission@samuelmerritt.edu.
Website: http://www.samuelmerritt.edu/nursing

San Francisco State University, Division of Graduate Studies, College of Health and Social Sciences, School of Nursing, San Francisco, CA 94132-1722. Offers adult acute care (MS); clinical nurse specialist (MS); community/public health nursing (MS); family nurse practitioner (Certificate); nursing administration (MS); pediatrics (MS); women's health (MS). *Accreditation:* AACN. *Program availability:* Part-time. *Application deadline:* Applications are processed on a rolling basis. *Financial support:* Career-related internships or fieldwork available. *Unit head:* Connie Carr, Assistant Director of Graduate Programs, 415-338-6856, Fax: 415-338-0555, E-mail: ccarr@sfsu.edu.
Website: http://nursing.sfsu.edu

San Jose State University, Graduate Studies and Research, College of Health and Human Sciences, San Jose, CA 95192-0049. Offers criminology (MS), including global criminology, law and justice; justice studies (MS); kinesiology (MA), including athletic training, exercise physiology, interdisciplinary, sport studies, sports management; library and information science (MLIS); mass communications (MS); nursing (MS), including family nurse practitioner; nutritional science (MS); occupational therapy (MS); public health (MPH); social work (MSW); MD/M Div. *Program availability:* Part-time, 100% online, blended/hybrid learning. *Faculty:* 15 full-time (7 women), 6 part-time/adjunct (3 women). *Students:* 517 full-time (407 women), 405 part-time (302 women); includes 523 minority (39 Black or African American, non-Hispanic/Latino; 2 American Indian or Alaska Native, non-Hispanic/Latino; 141 Asian, non-Hispanic/Latino; 226 Hispanic/Latino; 2 Native Hawaiian or other Pacific Islander, non-Hispanic/Latino; 113 Two or more races, non-Hispanic/Latino), 14 international. Average age 32. 1,250 applicants, 45% accepted, 375 enrolled. In 2017, 808 master's awarded. *Degree requirements:* For master's, thesis (for some programs), graduate writing assessment. *Entrance requirements:* Additional exam requirements/recommendations for international students: Required—TOEFL (minimum score 550 paper-based; 80 iBT), IELTS (minimum score 6.5), PTE (minimum score 53). *Application deadline:* For fall admission, 2/1 for domestic and international students. Applications are processed on a rolling basis. Application fee: $55. Electronic applications accepted. *Expenses:* Tuition, state resident: full-time $7176. Tuition, nonresident: full-time $16,680. Tuition and fees vary according to course load and program. *Financial support:* Fellowships, research assistantships, teaching assistantships, career-related internships or fieldwork, Federal Work-Study, scholarships/grants, and tuition waivers (full and partial) available. Support available to part-time students. Financial award application deadline: 4/24; financial award applicants required to submit FAFSA. *Unit head:* Dr. Mary Schutten, Dean, College of Health and Human Sciences, 408-924-2900, Fax: 408-924-2901, E-mail: mary.schutten@sjsu.edu.
Website: http://www.sjsu.edu/casa/

Seattle Pacific University, MS in Nursing Program, Seattle, WA 98119-1997. Offers administration (MSN); adult/gerontology nurse practitioner (MSN); clinical nurse specialist (MSN); family nurse practitioner (MSN, Certificate); informatics (MSN); nurse educator (MSN). *Accreditation:* AACN. *Program availability:* Part-time. *Students:* 22 full-time (17 women), 40 part-time (35 women); includes 13 minority (4 Black or African American, non-Hispanic/Latino; 1 American Indian or Alaska Native, non-Hispanic/Latino; 7 Asian, non-Hispanic/Latino; 1 Two or more races, non-Hispanic/Latino). Average age 36. 52 applicants, 73% accepted, 22 enrolled. In 2017, 23 master's awarded. *Degree requirements:* For master's, thesis. *Entrance requirements:* For master's, personal statement, transcripts, undergraduate nursing degree, proof of

undergraduate statistics course with minimum GPA of 2.0, 2 recommendations. *Application deadline:* For fall admission, 1/15 priority date for domestic students; for spring admission, 1/15 for domestic students. Applications are processed on a rolling basis. Application fee: $50. Electronic applications accepted. *Expenses:* Contact institution. *Financial support:* Fellowships and scholarships/grants available. Financial award applicants required to submit FAFSA. *Unit head:* Dr. Christine Hoyle, Associate Dean, 206-281-2469, E-mail: hoylec@spu.edu.
Website: http://spu.edu/academics/school-of-health-sciences/undergraduate-programs/nursing

Shenandoah University, Eleanor Wade Custer School of Nursing, Winchester, VA 22601. Offers adult gerontology primary care nurse practitioner (Graduate Certificate); adult-gerontology primary care nurse practitioner (MSN); family nurse practitioner (MSN, DNP, Graduate Certificate); general (MSN); health systems leadership (DNP); health systems management (MSN, Graduate Certificate); nurse midwifery (MSN); nurse-midwifery (Graduate Certificate); nursing education (Graduate Certificate); nursing practice (DNP); psychiatric mental health nurse practitioner (MSN, DNP, Graduate Certificate). *Accreditation:* AACN; ACNM/ACME. *Faculty:* 17 full-time (all women), 6 part-time/adjunct (all women). *Students:* 30 full-time (26 women), 51 part-time (48 women); includes 19 minority (13 Black or African American, non-Hispanic/Latino; 3 Asian, non-Hispanic/Latino; 2 Hispanic/Latino; 1 Two or more races, non-Hispanic/Latino), 3 international. Average age 37. 52 applicants, 88% accepted, 34 enrolled. In 2017, 18 master's, 1 doctorate, 28 other advanced degrees awarded. *Degree requirements:* For master's, research project, clinical hours; for doctorate, scholarly project, clinical hours; for Graduate Certificate, clinical hours. *Entrance requirements:* For master's, United States RN license; minimum GPA of 3.0; 2080 hours of clinical experience; curriculum vitae; 3 letters of recommendation from former dean, faculty member, or advisor familiar with the applicant, and a former or current supervisor; two-to-three-page essay on a specified topic; for doctorate, MSN, minimum GPA of 3.0, 3 letters of recommendation, interview, BSN, two-to-three page essay on a specific topic, 500-word statement of clinical practice research interest, resume, current U.S. RN license, 2080 clinical hours; for Graduate Certificate, MSN, minimum GPA of 3.0, 2 letters of recommendation, minimum of one year (2080 hours) of clinical nursing experience, interview, two-to-three page essay on a specific topic, resume, current United States RN license. Additional exam requirements/recommendations for international students: Required—TOEFL (minimum score 558 paper-based; 83 iBT). *Application deadline:* For fall admission, 4/15 priority date for domestic and international students; for spring admission, 11/1 for domestic and international students; for summer admission, 3/1 for domestic and international students. Application fee: $30. Electronic applications accepted. *Expenses:* $22,451 tuition, plus $3,579 fees (student services fee, technology fee, and clinical fee). *Financial support:* In 2017–18, 32 students received support. Scholarships/grants and unspecified assistantships available. Financial award applicants required to submit FAFSA. *Faculty research:* Emergency preparedness, workplace environment, maternal child, inter-professional education, health policy. *Total annual research expenditures:* $30,000. *Unit head:* Dr. Kathleen LaSala, RN, Dean, 540-678-4381, Fax: 540-665-5519, E-mail: klasala@su.edu. *Application contact:* Andrew Woodall, Executive Director of Recruitment and Admissions, 540-665-4581, Fax: 540-665-4627, E-mail: admit@su.edu.
Website: http://www.su.edu/nursing/

Simmons College, School of Nursing and Health Sciences, Boston, MA 02115. Offers didactic dietetics (Certificate); dietetic internship (Certificate); health professions education (PhD, CAGS); nursing (MS, MSN), including family nurse practitioner (MS); nursing practice (DNP); nutrition and health promotion (MS); physical therapy (DPT); sports nutrition (Certificate). *Accreditation:* AACN. *Program availability:* Part-time, 100% online, blended/hybrid learning. *Faculty:* 34 full-time (28 women), 44 part-time/adjunct (40 women). *Students:* 390 full-time (350 women), 1,286 part-time (1,169 women); includes 346 minority (131 Black or African American, non-Hispanic/Latino; 6 American Indian or Alaska Native, non-Hispanic/Latino; 75 Asian, non-Hispanic/Latino; 91 Hispanic/Latino; 3 Native Hawaiian or other Pacific Islander, non-Hispanic/Latino; 40 Two or more races, non-Hispanic/Latino), 9 international. Average age 34. 1,219 applicants, 74% accepted, 481 enrolled. In 2017, 423 master's, 39 doctorates, 55 other advanced degrees awarded. *Entrance requirements:* For doctorate, GRE. Additional exam requirements/recommendations for international students: Required—TOEFL (minimum score 570 paper-based; 88 iBT). *Application deadline:* For fall admission, 6/1 for international students. Application fee: $50. Electronic applications accepted. *Expenses:* $1,278 per credit, $116 activity fee per semester. *Financial support:* In 2017–18, 15 research assistantships with partial tuition reimbursements were awarded; scholarships/grants and unspecified assistantships also available. Financial award applicants required to submit FAFSA. *Unit head:* Dr. Judy Beal, Dean, 617-521-2139. *Application contact:* Brett DiMarzo, Director of Graduate Admission, 617-521-2651, Fax: 617-521-3137, E-mail: brett.dimarzo@simmons.edu.
Website: http://www.simmons.edu/snhs/

Sonoma State University, School of Science and Technology, Family Nurse Practitioner Program, Rohnert Park, CA 94928. Offers MSN. *Accreditation:* ACEN. *Program availability:* Part-time. *Degree requirements:* For master's, comprehensive exam, thesis or alternative, oral exams. *Entrance requirements:* For master's, GRE General Test, BSN, minimum GPA of 3.0, course work in statistics, physical assessment, RN license. Additional exam requirements/recommendations for international students: Required—TOEFL (minimum score 500 paper-based). *Application deadline:* For fall admission, 11/30 for domestic students. Application fee: $55. *Financial support:* Traineeships available. Financial award applicants required to submit FAFSA. *Faculty research:* Neonatal ethics. *Unit head:* Dr. Mary Ellen Wilkosz, Chair, 707-664-2297, E-mail: mark.wilkosz@sonoma.edu. *Application contact:* Dr. Wendy Smith, Assistant Director, 707-664-2276, E-mail: wendy.smith@sonoma.edu.
Website: http://www.sonoma.edu/nursing/fnpp/

Southern Adventist University, School of Nursing, Collegedale, TN 37315-0370. Offers adult/gerontology acute care nurse practitioner (MSN, DNP); adult/gerontology nurse practitioner (MSN); family nurse practitioner (MSN, DNP); lifestyle therapeutics (DNP); nurse educator (MSN, DNP); psychiatric mental health nurse practitioner (MSN, DNP); MSN/MBA. *Accreditation:* ACEN. *Program availability:* Part-time. *Degree requirements:* For master's, thesis or project. *Entrance requirements:* For master's, RN license. Additional exam requirements/recommendations for international students: Required—TOEFL (minimum score 600 paper-based). *Application deadline:* For fall admission, 7/1 for domestic and international students; for winter admission, 12/1 for domestic and international students. Applications are processed on a rolling basis. Application fee: $40. Electronic applications accepted. *Expenses: Tuition:* Full-time $11,430; part-time $635 per credit hour. Tuition and fees vary according to degree level and program. *Financial support:* Teaching assistantships with partial tuition reimbursements available. *Faculty research:* Pain management, ethics, corporate wellness, caring spirituality, stress. *Unit head:* Dr. Barbara James, Dean, 423-236-2942, Fax: 423-236-1940, E-mail: bjames@southern.edu. *Application contact:* Sylvia Mayer, RN, Director of Nursing Admissions, 423-236-2941, Fax: 423-236-1940, E-mail: smayer@southern.edu.
Website: https://www.southern.edu/academics/nursing.html

Southern Connecticut State University, School of Graduate Studies, School of Health and Human Services, Department of Nursing, New Haven, CT 06515-1355. Offers family nurse practitioner (MSN); nursing (Ed D); nursing education (MSN). *Accreditation:* AACN. *Program availability:* Part-time, evening/weekend. *Degree requirements:* For master's, thesis. *Entrance requirements:* For master's, GRE, MAT, interview, minimum QPA of 2.8, RN license, minimum 1 year of professional nursing experience. Electronic applications accepted.

Southern Illinois University Edwardsville, Graduate School, School of Nursing, Doctor of Nursing Practice Program, Edwardsville, IL 62026. Offers family nurse practitioner (DNP); nurse anesthesia (DNP); nursing (DNP). *Accreditation:* AACN. *Program availability:* Part-time, evening/weekend. *Degree requirements:* For doctorate, thesis/dissertation or alternative, project. *Entrance requirements:* Additional exam requirements/recommendations for international students: Required—TOEFL (minimum score 550 paper-based; 79 iBT), IELTS (minimum score 6.5). Electronic applications accepted.

Southern Illinois University Edwardsville, Graduate School, School of Nursing, Program in Family Nurse Practitioner, Edwardsville, IL 62026. Offers MS, Post-Master's Certificate. *Accreditation:* AACN. *Program availability:* Part-time, evening/weekend. *Degree requirements:* For master's, comprehensive exam. *Entrance requirements:* For master's, appropriate bachelor's degree, RN license. Additional exam requirements/recommendations for international students: Required—TOEFL (minimum score 550 paper-based; 79 iBT), IELTS (minimum score 6.5). Electronic applications accepted.

Southern University and Agricultural and Mechanical College, College of Nursing and Allied Health, School of Nursing, Baton Rouge, LA 70813. Offers educator/administrator (PhD); family health nursing (MSN); family nurse practitioner (Post Master's Certificate); geriatric nurse practitioner/gerontology (PhD); nursing (DNP). *Accreditation:* AACN. *Program availability:* Part-time. *Degree requirements:* For master's, comprehensive exam, thesis; for doctorate, comprehensive exam, thesis/dissertation. *Entrance requirements:* For master's, GRE General Test, BSN, minimum GPA of 2.7; for doctorate, GRE General Test; for Post Master's Certificate, MSN. Additional exam requirements/recommendations for international students: Required—TOEFL (minimum score 525 paper-based). *Faculty research:* Health promotions, vulnerable populations, (community-based) cardiovascular participating research, health disparities chronic diseases, care of the elderly.

South University, Program in Nursing, Tampa, FL 33614. Offers adult health nurse practitioner (MS); family nurse practitioner (MS); nurse educator (MS).

South University, Program in Nursing, Royal Palm Beach, FL 33411. Offers family nurse practitioner (MS).

South University, Program in Nursing, Virginia Beach, VA 23452. Offers family nurse practitioner (MSN).

Spalding University, Graduate Studies, Kosair College of Health and Natural Sciences, School of Nursing, Louisville, KY 40203-2188. Offers adult nurse practitioner (MSN); family nurse practitioner (MSN); leadership in nursing and healthcare (MSN); nurse educator (Post-Master's Certificate); nurse practitioner (Post-Master's Certificate); pediatric nurse practitioner (MSN). *Accreditation:* AACN. *Program availability:* Part-time, evening/weekend. *Degree requirements:* For master's, comprehensive exam (for some programs), thesis. *Entrance requirements:* For master's, GRE General Test, BSN or bachelor's degree in related field, RN licensure, autobiographical statement, transcripts, letters of recommendation. Additional exam requirements/recommendations for international students: Required—TOEFL (minimum score 535 paper-based). *Faculty research:* Nurse educational administration, gerontology, bioterrorism, healthcare ethics, leadership.

State University of New York Downstate Medical Center, College of Nursing, Graduate Programs in Nursing, Nurse Practitioner Program, Brooklyn, NY 11203-2098. Offers MS, Post Master's Certificate. *Accreditation:* AACN. *Program availability:* Part-time. *Degree requirements:* For master's, thesis optional. *Entrance requirements:* For master's, GRE, BSN; minimum GPA of 3.0; previous undergraduate course work in statistics, health assessment, and nursing research; RN license; for Post Master's Certificate, BSN; minimum GPA of 3.0; RN license; previous undergraduate course work in statistics, health assessment, and nursing research. *Faculty research:* Women's health.

State University of New York Polytechnic Institute, Program in Family Nurse Practitioner, Utica, NY 13502. Offers MS, CAS. *Accreditation:* AACN. *Program availability:* Part-time. *Faculty:* 1 (woman) full-time, 18 part-time/adjunct (17 women). *Students:* 64 full-time (59 women), 117 part-time (108 women); includes 22 minority (6 Black or African American, non-Hispanic/Latino; 1 American Indian or Alaska Native, non-Hispanic/Latino; 6 Asian, non-Hispanic/Latino; 6 Hispanic/Latino; 3 Two or more races, non-Hispanic/Latino). Average age 36. 197 applicants, 58% accepted, 92 enrolled. In 2017, 40 master's awarded. *Degree requirements:* For master's, clinical hours. *Application deadline:* For fall admission, 7/1 for domestic and international students. Application fee: $60. *Expenses:* Tuition, state resident: full-time $8154; part-time $2718 per year. Tuition, nonresident: full-time $16,650; part-time $5550 per year. *Required fees:* $993; $331 per unit. Tuition and fees vary according to course load, degree level, campus/location and program. *Financial support:* Fellowships and scholarships/grants available. Financial award application deadline: 6/1; financial award applicants required to submit FAFSA. *Faculty research:* Cardiology, medication reconciliation, health beliefs, international and under-served populations, nutrition knowledge among practicing family nurse practitioners. *Unit head:* Kathleen Maroll, RN, Program Coordinator, E-mail: marollk@sunyit.edu. *Application contact:* Alicia Foster, Director of Graduate Admissions, E-mail: alicia.foster@sunyit.edu.
Website: https://sunypoly.edu/academics/majors-and-programs/ms-family-nurse-practitioner.html

State University of New York Upstate Medical University, College of Nursing, Syracuse, NY 13210. Offers nurse practitioner (Post Master's Certificate); nursing (MS). *Accreditation:* AACN. *Program availability:* Part-time, online learning. *Degree requirements:* For master's, thesis or alternative. *Entrance requirements:* For master's, 3 years of work experience. Electronic applications accepted.

Stony Brook University, State University of New York, Stony Brook Medicine, School of Nursing, Program in Family Nurse Practitioner, Stony Brook, NY 11794. Offers MS, DNP, Certificate. *Accreditation:* AACN. *Program availability:* Part-time, blended/hybrid learning. *Students:* 5 full-time (all women), 190 part-time (165 women); includes 73 minority (27 Black or African American, non-Hispanic/Latino; 2 American Indian or Alaska Native, non-Hispanic/Latino; 25 Asian, non-Hispanic/Latino; 17 Hispanic/Latino; 2 Two or more races, non-Hispanic/Latino). 288 applicants, 25% accepted, 59 enrolled. In 2017, 22 master's, 3 doctorates, 1 other advanced degree awarded. *Degree requirements:* For master's, thesis; for doctorate, thesis/dissertation. *Entrance requirements:* For master's, BSN, minimum GPA of 3.0, course work in statistics. Additional exam requirements/recommendations for international students: Required—TOEFL (minimum score 90 iBT). *Application deadline:* For fall admission, 12/7 for domestic students. Application fee: $100. *Expenses:* Contact institution. *Financial support:* Application deadline: 3/15. *Unit head:* Dr. Cheryl Meddles-Torres, Program

Director, 631-444-6334, Fax: 631-444-3136, E-mail: cheryl.meddles-torres@stonybrook.edu. *Application contact:* Anita Defranco, Staff Assistant, 631-444-3276, Fax: 631-444-3136, E-mail: fnp.nursing@stonybrook.edu.
Website: http://www.nursing.stonybrookmedicine.edu/about

Stony Brook University, State University of New York, Stony Brook Medicine, School of Nursing, Program in Perinatal Women's Health Nursing, Stony Brook, NY 11794. Offers MS, DNP, Certificate. *Accreditation:* AACN. *Program availability:* Blended/hybrid learning. *Students:* 7 part-time (all women); includes 1 minority (American Indian or Alaska Native, non-Hispanic/Latino). In 2017, 4 master's, 1 other advanced degree awarded. *Degree requirements:* For master's, thesis; for doctorate, thesis/dissertation. *Entrance requirements:* For master's, BSN, minimum GPA of 3.0, course work in statistics. Additional exam requirements/recommendations for international students: Required—TOEFL (minimum score 90 iBT). *Application deadline:* For fall admission, 3/8 for domestic students. Application fee: $100. *Expenses:* Contact institution. *Financial support:* Application deadline: 3/15. *Unit head:* Dr. Elizabeth Collins, Program Director, 631-444-3296, Fax: 631-444-3136, E-mail: elizabeth.collins@stonybrook.edu. *Application contact:* Linda Sacino, Staff Assistant, 631-632-3262, Fax: 631-444-3136, E-mail: elizabeth.collins@stonybrook.edu.
Website: http://www.nursing.stonybrookmedicine.edu/

Temple University, College of Public Health, Department of Nursing, Philadelphia, PA 19122. Offers adult-gerontology primary care (DNP); family-individual across the lifespan (DNP); nursing (DNP). *Accreditation:* AACN. *Program availability:* Part-time. *Faculty:* 12 full-time (all women). *Students:* 5 full-time (4 women), 53 part-time (46 women); includes 31 minority (13 Black or African American, non-Hispanic/Latino; 12 Asian, non-Hispanic/Latino; 5 Hispanic/Latino; 1 Two or more races, non-Hispanic/Latino). 11 applicants, 18% accepted. In 2017, 17 doctorates awarded. *Degree requirements:* For doctorate, evidence-based practice project. *Entrance requirements:* For doctorate, GRE General Test or MAT, 2 letters of reference, RN license, interview, statement of purpose, resume. Additional exam requirements/recommendations for international students: Required—TOEFL (minimum score 600 paper-based; 100 iBT). *Application deadline:* For fall admission, 2/15 priority date for domestic students, 1/15 for international students; for spring admission, 10/15 for domestic students, 9/15 for international students. Applications are processed on a rolling basis. Application fee: $60. Electronic applications accepted. *Expenses:* Contact institution. *Financial support:* Federal Work-Study, scholarships/grants, traineeships, and tuition waivers available. Support available to part-time students. Financial award application deadline: 1/15. *Faculty research:* Health promotion, chronic illness, family support systems, primary care, health policy, community health services, evidence-based practice. *Unit head:* Dolores Zygmont, Graduate Director, 215-707-3789, E-mail: zygmont@temple.edu. *Application contact:* Audrey Scriven, Academic Coordinator, Graduate Program, 215-707-4618, E-mail: tunurse@temple.edu.
Website: https://cph.temple.edu/nursing/home

Tennessee State University, The School of Graduate Studies and Research, College of Health Sciences, School of Nursing, Nashville, TN 37209-1561. Offers family nurse practitioner (MSN, Certificate); holistic nurse practitioner (MSN); holistic nursing (Certificate); nursing education (MSN, Certificate). *Accreditation:* ACEN. *Entrance requirements:* For master's, GRE General Test or MAT, BSN, current RN license, minimum GPA of 3.0.

Tennessee Technological University, Whitson-Hester School of Nursing, DNP Program, Cookeville, TN 38505. Offers adult-gerontology acute care nurse practitioner (DNP); executive leadership in nursing (DNP); family nurse practitioner (DNP); pediatric nurse practitioner-primary care (DNP); psychiatric/mental health nurse practitioner (DNP); women's health care nurse practitioner (DNP). *Program availability:* Part-time. *Students:* 10 part-time (all women). 14 applicants, 86% accepted, 10 enrolled. *Application deadline:* For fall admission, 7/1 for domestic students, 5/1 for international students; for spring admission, 12/1 for domestic students, 10/1 for international students; for summer admission, 5/1 for domestic students, 2/1 for international students. Applications are processed on a rolling basis. Application fee: $35 ($40 for international students). Electronic applications accepted. *Expenses:* Tuition, state resident: full-time $9925; part-time $565 per credit hour. Tuition, nonresident: full-time $22,993; part-time $1291 per credit hour. *Financial support:* Application deadline: 4/1; applicants required to submit FAFSA. *Unit head:* Dr. Bedelia Russell, Program Director, Fax: 931-372-6244, E-mail: bhrussell@tntech.edu. *Application contact:* Shelia K. Kendrick, Coordinator of Graduate Studies, 931-372-3808, Fax: 931-372-3497, E-mail: skendrick@tntech.edu.
Website: https://www.tntech.edu/nursing/doctor-of-nursing-practice/

Tennessee Technological University, Whitson-Hester School of Nursing, MSN Programs, Cookeville, TN 38505. Offers family nurse practitioner (MSN); nursing administration (MSN); nursing education (MSN). *Program availability:* Part-time. *Students:* 22 full-time (17 women), 78 part-time (64 women); includes 5 minority (2 Black or African American, non-Hispanic/Latino; 2 Hispanic/Latino; 1 Two or more races, non-Hispanic/Latino). 48 applicants, 50% accepted, 20 enrolled. In 2017, 41 master's awarded. *Application deadline:* For fall admission, 7/1 for domestic students, 5/1 for international students; for spring admission, 12/1 for domestic students, 10/1 for international students; for summer admission, 5/1 for domestic students, 2/1 for international students. Applications are processed on a rolling basis. Application fee: $35 ($40 for international students). Electronic applications accepted. *Expenses:* Tuition, state resident: full-time $9925; part-time $565 per credit hour. Tuition, nonresident: full-time $22,993; part-time $1291 per credit hour. *Financial support:* Application deadline: 4/1; applicants required to submit FAFSA. *Unit head:* Dr. Kim Hanna, Interim Dean, Fax: 931-372-6244, E-mail: khanna@tntech.edu. *Application contact:* Shelia K. Kendrick, Coordinator of Graduate Studies, 931-372-3808, Fax: 931-372-3497, E-mail: skendrick@tntech.edu.
Website: https://www.tntech.edu/nursing/masters/

Texas A&M International University, Office of Graduate Studies and Research, College of Nursing and Health Sciences, Laredo, TX 78041. Offers family nurse practitioner (MSN). *Accreditation:* ACEN. *Entrance requirements:* Additional exam requirements/recommendations for international students: Required—TOEFL (minimum score 550 paper-based; 79 iBT).

Texas A&M University, College of Nursing, Bryan, TX 77807. Offers family nurse practitioner (MSN); forensic nursing (MSN); nursing education (MSN). *Faculty:* 19. *Students:* 9 full-time (all women), 47 part-time (all women); includes 14 minority (2 Asian, non-Hispanic/Latino; 12 Hispanic/Latino). Average age 34. In 2017, 27 master's awarded. *Expenses:* Contact institution. *Financial support:* In 2017–18, 8 students received support, including 2 fellowships (averaging $4,300 per year); career-related internships or fieldwork, institutionally sponsored loans, scholarships/grants, traineeships, health care benefits, tuition waivers (full and partial), and unspecified assistantships also available. Support available to part-time students. Financial award applicants required to submit FAFSA. *Unit head:* Dr. Sharon A. Wilkerson, Founding Dean, 979-436-0111, Fax: 979-436-0098, E-mail: wilkerson@tamhsc.edu. *Application contact:* Jennifer Frank, Program Coordinator for Recruitment and Admission, 979-436-0110, E-mail: conadmissions@tamhsc.edu.
Website: http://nursing.tamhsc.edu/

Texas A&M University–Corpus Christi, College of Graduate Studies, College of Nursing and Health Sciences, Corpus Christi, TX 78412. Offers family nurse practitioner (MSN); leadership in nursing systems (MSN); nurse educator (MSN); nursing practice (DNP). *Accreditation:* AACN. *Program availability:* Part-time, evening/weekend, online only, 100% online. *Faculty:* 17 full-time (16 women), 21 part-time/adjunct (15 women). *Students:* 7 full-time (all women), 364 part-time (307 women); includes 194 minority (25 Black or African American, non-Hispanic/Latino; 26 Asian, non-Hispanic/Latino; 134 Hispanic/Latino; 9 Two or more races, non-Hispanic/Latino). Average age 38. 360 applicants, 33% accepted, 112 enrolled. In 2017, 98 master's awarded. *Degree requirements:* For master's, clinical capstone; for doctorate, capstone/scholarly project. *Entrance requirements:* For master's, essay, resume, 3 letters of recommendation, minimum GPA of 3.0, current valid unencumbered Texas nursing license. Additional exam requirements/recommendations for international students: Required—TOEFL (minimum score 550 paper-based; 79 iBT), IELTS (minimum score 6.5). *Application deadline:* For fall admission, 4/15 for domestic and international students; for spring admission, 1/7 for domestic and international students; for summer admission, 5/27 for domestic and international students. Applications are processed on a rolling basis. Application fee: $50 ($70 for international students). Electronic applications accepted. *Expenses:* Tuition, state resident: full-time $3568; part-time $198.24 per credit hour. Tuition, nonresident: full-time $11,038; part-time $613.24 per credit hour. *Required fees:* $2129; $1422.58 per semester. Tuition and fees vary according to program. *Financial support:* Research assistantships, teaching assistantships, career-related internships or fieldwork, Federal Work-Study, institutionally sponsored loans, scholarships/grants, health care benefits, and unspecified assistantships available. Support available to part-time students. Financial award application deadline: 3/15; financial award applicants required to submit FAFSA. *Unit head:* Dr. Julie Anne Hoff, Dean, 361-825-2275, E-mail: julie.hoff@tamucc.edu. *Application contact:* Graduate Admissions Coordinator, 361-825-2177, Fax: 361-825-2755, E-mail: gradweb@tamucc.edu.
Website: http://conhs.tamucc.edu/

Texas Christian University, Harris College of Nursing and Health Sciences, Doctor of Nursing Practice Program, Fort Worth, TX 76129. Offers clinical nurse specialist - adult/gerontology nursing (DNP); clinical nurse specialist - pediatrics (DNP); family nurse practitioner (DNP); general (DNP); nursing administration (DNP). *Accreditation:* AACN. *Program availability:* Part-time. *Faculty:* 29 full-time (26 women), 2 part-time/adjunct (both women). *Students:* 51 full-time (45 women), 10 part-time (9 women); includes 16 minority (6 Black or African American, non-Hispanic/Latino; 2 Asian, non-Hispanic/Latino; 6 Hispanic/Latino; 2 Two or more races, non-Hispanic/Latino). Average age 41. 59 applicants, 64% accepted, 24 enrolled. In 2017, 23 doctorates awarded. *Degree requirements:* For doctorate, thesis/dissertation or alternative, practicum. *Entrance requirements:* For doctorate, three reference letters, essay, resume, two official transcripts from each institution attended, APRN recognition or MSN with experience in nursing administration. Additional exam requirements/recommendations for international students: Required—TOEFL. *Application deadline:* For summer admission, 11/15 for domestic and international students. Application fee: $60. Electronic applications accepted. *Expenses:* $1,555 per credit hour, $125 per course fee, $500 lab fee. *Financial support:* In 2017–18, 14 students received support. Scholarships/grants available. Financial award application deadline: 2/15; financial award applicants required to submit FAFSA. *Faculty research:* Geriatrics, cancer survivorship, health literacy, endothelial cells, clinical simulation outcomes. *Unit head:* Dr. Kathy Ellis, Division Director, Graduate Nursing, 817-257-6726, Fax: 817-257-7944, E-mail: kathryn.ellis@tcu.edu. *Application contact:* Heather Lyon, Academic Program Specialist, 817-257-6726, Fax: 817-257-7944, E-mail: graduatenursing@tcu.edu.
Website: http://dnp.tcu.edu/

Texas State University, The Graduate College, College of Health Professions, Family Nurse Practitioner Program, San Marcos, TX 78666. Offers MSN. *Accreditation:* CAHME. *Program availability:* Part-time, evening/weekend, blended/hybrid learning. *Faculty:* 6 full-time (all women), 7 part-time/adjunct (5 women). *Students:* 74 full-time (67 women); includes 27 minority (1 Black or African American, non-Hispanic/Latino; 5 Asian, non-Hispanic/Latino; 20 Hispanic/Latino; 1 Two or more races, non-Hispanic/Latino). Average age 33. 121 applicants, 49% accepted, 36 enrolled. In 2017, 30 master's awarded. *Degree requirements:* For master's, comprehensive exam. *Entrance requirements:* For master's, BSN from institution accredited by nationally-recognized nursing education accrediting body (i.e., ACEN, CCNE) with minimum GPA of 3.0 in nursing courses and last 60 hours of undergraduate course work; current valid unencumbered RN license or multi-state privilege to practice as a registered nurse. Additional exam requirements/recommendations for international students: Required—TOEFL (minimum score 550 paper-based; 78 iBT), IELTS (minimum score 6). *Application deadline:* For fall admission, 1/15 for domestic and international students. Applications are processed on a rolling basis. Application fee: $40 ($90 for international students). Electronic applications accepted. *Expenses:* Tuition, state resident: full-time $7868; part-time $3934 per semester. Tuition, nonresident: full-time $17,828; part-time $8914 per semester. *Required fees:* $2092; $1435 per semester. Tuition and fees vary according to course load. *Financial support:* In 2017–18, 26 students received support. Research assistantships, teaching assistantships, career-related internships or fieldwork, Federal Work-Study, institutionally sponsored loans, scholarships/grants, and unspecified assistantships available. Support available to part-time students. Financial award application deadline: 3/1; financial award applicants required to submit FAFSA. *Faculty research:* Nursing and allied health. *Total annual research expenditures:* $12,975. *Unit head:* Dr. Shirley Levenson, Program Director, 512-716-2957, Fax: 512-716-2911, E-mail: sal111@txstate.edu. *Application contact:* Dr. Andrea Golato, Dean of Graduate School, 512-245-2581, Fax: 512-245-8365, E-mail: gradcollege@txstate.edu.
Website: http://www.nursing.txstate.edu/prospective-nursing-students/msn-admission.html

Texas Tech University Health Sciences Center, School of Nursing, Lubbock, TX 79430. Offers acute care nurse practitioner (MSN, Certificate); administration (MSN); advanced practice (DNP); education (MSN); executive leadership (DNP); family nurse practitioner (MSN, Certificate); geriatric nurse practitioner (MSN, Certificate); pediatric nurse practitioner (MSN, Certificate). *Accreditation:* AACN. *Program availability:* Part-time, online learning. *Degree requirements:* For master's, thesis optional. *Entrance requirements:* For master's, minimum GPA of 3.0, 3 letters of reference, BSN, RN license; for Certificate, minimum GPA of 3.0, 3 letters of reference, RN license. Additional exam requirements/recommendations for international students: Required—TOEFL (minimum score 550 paper-based). *Faculty research:* Diabetes/obesity, nurse competency, disease management, intervention and measurements, health disparities.

Texas Woman's University, Graduate School, College of Nursing, Denton, TX 76204. Offers adult health clinical nurse specialist (MS); adult health nurse practitioner (MS); adult/gerontology acute care nurse practitioner (MS); child health clinical nurse specialist (MS); clinical nurse leader (MS); family nurse practitioner (MS); health systems management (MS); nursing education (MS); nursing practice (DNP); nursing science (PhD); pediatric nurse practitioner (MS); women's health clinical nurse specialist (MS); women's health nurse practitioner (MS). *Accreditation:* AACN. *Program availability:* Part-time, 100% online, blended/hybrid learning. *Faculty:* 48 full-time (47 women), 44 part-time/adjunct (37 women). *Students:* 23 full-time (22 women), 816 part-time (750 women); includes 475 minority (188 Black or African American, non-Hispanic/

Latino; 4 American Indian or Alaska Native, non-Hispanic/Latino; 171 Asian, non-Hispanic/Latino; 83 Hispanic/Latino; 3 Native Hawaiian or other Pacific Islander, non-Hispanic/Latino; 26 Two or more races, non-Hispanic/Latino), 12 international. Average age 37. 201 applicants, 88% accepted, 123 enrolled. In 2017, 232 master's, 17 doctorates awarded. *Degree requirements:* For master's, comprehensive exam, thesis or alternative, 6-year time limit for completion of degree, professional or clinical project; for doctorate, comprehensive exam, thesis/dissertation, 10-year time limit for completion of degree. *Entrance requirements:* For master's, GRE or MAT, minimum GPA of 3.0 on last 60 hours in undergraduate nursing degree and overall, RN license, BS in nursing, basic statistics course, 1 year of clinical experience; for doctorate, GRE (preferred minimum score 153 [500 old version] Verbal, 144 [500 old version] Quantitative, 4 Analytical), MS in nursing, minimum preferred GPA of 3.5, RN license, statistics course, 2 letters of reference, curriculum vitae, graduate nursing-theory course, graduate research course, statement of professional goals and research interests. Additional exam requirements/recommendations for international students: Required—TOEFL (minimum score 550 paper-based; 79 iBT); Recommended—IELTS (minimum score 6.5), TSE (minimum score 53). *Application deadline:* For fall admission, 5/1 for domestic students, 3/1 priority date for international students; for spring admission, 9/15 for domestic students, 7/1 priority date for international students; for summer admission, 2/1 for domestic and international students. Applications are processed on a rolling basis. Application fee: $50 ($75 for international students). Electronic applications accepted. *Expenses:* $8,510 per year full-time in-state, $17,810 per year full-time out-of-state. *Financial support:* In 2017–18, 146 students received support, including 7 teaching assistantships (averaging $28,195 per year); research assistantships, career-related internships or fieldwork, Federal Work-Study, institutionally sponsored loans, scholarships/grants, traineeships, health care benefits, and unspecified assistantships also available. Support available to part-time students. Financial award application deadline: 3/1; financial award applicants required to submit FAFSA. *Faculty research:* Women's health, nurse staffing and satisfaction in health systems, perinatal safety, chronic illness, pediatric health. *Total annual research expenditures:* $380,388. *Unit head:* Dr. Anita G. Hufft, Dean, 940-898-2401, Fax: 940-898-2437, E-mail: nursing@twu.edu. *Application contact:* Korie Hawkins, Associate Director of Admissions, Graduate Recruitment, 940-898-3188, Fax: 940-898-3081, E-mail: admissions@twu.edu.
Website: http://www.twu.edu/nursing/

Troy University, Graduate School, College of Health and Human Services, Program in Nursing, Troy, AL 36082. Offers adult health (MSN); family nurse practitioner (DNP); maternal infant (MSN); nursing informatics specialist (MSN). *Accreditation:* ACEN. *Program availability:* Part-time, evening/weekend. *Faculty:* 15 full-time (14 women), 8 part-time/adjunct (all women). *Students:* 58 full-time (52 women), 207 part-time (184 women); includes 53 minority (40 Black or African American, non-Hispanic/Latino; 1 American Indian or Alaska Native, non-Hispanic/Latino; 1 Asian, non-Hispanic/Latino; 6 Hispanic/Latino; 5 Two or more races, non-Hispanic/Latino). Average age 36. 66 applicants, 100% accepted, 49 enrolled. In 2017, 113 master's, 14 doctorates awarded. *Degree requirements:* For master's, comprehensive exam, minimum GPA of 3.0, candidacy; for doctorate, minimum GPA of 3.0, submission of approved comprehensive e-portfolio, completion of residency synthesis project, minimum of 1000 hours of clinical practice, qualifying exam. *Entrance requirements:* For master's, GRE (minimum score of 850 on old exam or 290 on new exam) or MAT (minimum score of 396), minimum GPA of 3.0, BSN, current RN licensure, 2 letters of reference, undergraduate health assessment course; for doctorate, GRE (minimum score of 850 on old exam or 294 on new exam), BSN or MSN, minimum GPA of 3.0, 2 letters of reference, current RN licensure, essay. Additional exam requirements/recommendations for international students: Required—TOEFL (minimum score 523 paper-based; 70 iBT), IELTS (minimum score 6). *Application deadline:* Applications are processed on a rolling basis. Application fee: $50. Electronic applications accepted. *Expenses:* Tuition, state resident: part-time $417 per credit hour. Tuition, nonresident: part-time $834 per credit hour. *Required fees:* $42 per credit hour. $50 per semester. Tuition and fees vary according to campus/location. *Financial support:* Fellowships, career-related internships or fieldwork, and scholarships/grants available. Support available to part-time students. Financial award applicants required to submit FAFSA. *Unit head:* Dr. Denise Green, Director, School of Nursing, 334-670-5864, Fax: 334-670-3745, E-mail: dmgreen@troy.edu. *Application contact:* Crystal G. Bishop, Director of Graduate Admissions, School of Nursing, 334-241-8631, E-mail: cdgodwin@troy.edu.

Tusculum College, Program in Nursing, Greeneville, TN 37743-9997. Offers family nurse practitioner (MSN). *Program availability:* Part-time. *Entrance requirements:* For master's, GRE. Additional exam requirements/recommendations for international students: Required—TOEFL. *Application deadline:* For spring admission, 12/10 for domestic students. Application fee: $25. *Application contact:* Lindsey Seal, Director of Enrollment, 423-636-7300 Ext. 5006, E-mail: lseal@tusculum.edu.

Uniformed Services University of the Health Sciences, Daniel K. Inouye Graduate School of Nursing, Bethesda, MD 20814. Offers adult-gerontology clinical nurse specialist (MSN, DNP); family nurse practitioner (DNP); nurse anesthesia (DNP); nursing science (PhD); psychiatric mental health nurse practitioner (DNP); women's health nurse practitioner (DNP). *Accreditation:* AACN; AANA/CANAEP. *Faculty:* 42 full-time (28 women), 2 part-time/adjunct (1 woman). *Students:* 170 full-time (98 women); includes 51 minority (21 Black or African American, non-Hispanic/Latino; 17 Asian, non-Hispanic/Latino; 11 Hispanic/Latino; 2 Native Hawaiian or other Pacific Islander, non-Hispanic/Latino). Average age 34. 88 applicants, 75% accepted, 66 enrolled. In 2017, 55 doctorates awarded. *Degree requirements:* For master's, thesis, scholarly project; for doctorate, dissertation (for PhD); project (for DNP). *Entrance requirements:* For master's, GRE, BSN, clinical experience, minimum GPA of 3.0, previous course work in science; for doctorate, GRE, BSN, minimum GPA of 3.0, undergraduate/graduate science course within past 5 years, writing example, interview (for some programs), and 3 letters of reference (for DNP); master's degree, minimum GPA of 3.0 in nursing or related field, personal statement, 3 references, and interview (for PhD). *Application deadline:* For winter admission, 2/15 for domestic students; for summer admission, 8/15 for domestic students. Application fee: $0. Electronic applications accepted. *Expenses:* There are no tuition costs or fees; students incur obligated service according to the requirements of their sponsoring organization. *Faculty research:* Military health care, military readiness, women's health, family, behavioral health. *Total annual research expenditures:* $100,000. *Unit head:* Dr. Diane C. Seibert, Associate Dean for Academic Affairs, 301-295-1080, Fax: 301-295-1707, E-mail: diane.seibert@usuhs.edu. *Application contact:* Maureen Jackson, Registrar, 301-295-1055, Fax: 301-295-1707, E-mail: maureen.jackson.ctr@usuhs.edu.
Website: http://www.usuhs.edu/gsn/

Union University, School of Nursing, Jackson, TN 38305-3697. Offers executive leadership (DNP); nurse anesthesia (DNP); nurse practitioner (DNP); nursing education (MSN, PMC). *Accreditation:* AACN; AANA/CANAEP. *Degree requirements:* For master's, thesis or alternative. *Entrance requirements:* For master's, GRE, 3 letters of reference, bachelor's degree in nursing, minimum GPA of 3.0. Additional exam requirements/recommendations for international students: Required—TOEFL (minimum score 560 paper-based). Electronic applications accepted. *Faculty research:* Children's health, occupational rehabilitation, informatics, health promotion.

United States University, Family Nurse Practitioner Program, San Diego, CA 92108. Offers MSN. *Degree requirements:* For master's, project. *Entrance requirements:* For master's, RN license, minimum cumulative undergraduate GPA of 2.5, background check, official transcripts, personal goal statement. Additional exam requirements/recommendations for international students: Required—TOEFL (minimum score 550 paper-based; 80 iBT).

Universidad del Turabo, Graduate Programs, School of Health Sciences, Programs in Nursing, Program in Family Nurse Practitioner, Gurabo, PR 00778-3030. Offers MSN, Certificate. *Entrance requirements:* For master's, GMAT, EXADEP or GRE, interview, essay, official transcript, recommendation letters. Electronic applications accepted.

University at Buffalo, the State University of New York, Graduate School, School of Nursing, Buffalo, NY 14260. Offers adult gerontology nurse practitioner (DNP); family nurse practitioner (DNP); health care systems and leadership (MS); nurse anesthetist (DNP); nursing (PhD); nursing education (Certificate); psychiatric/mental health nurse practitioner (DNP). *Accreditation:* AACN; AANA/CANAEP (one or more programs are accredited). *Program availability:* Part-time, 100% online. *Faculty:* 41 full-time (36 women), 15 part-time/adjunct (all women). *Students:* 64 full-time (39 women), 136 part-time (120 women); includes 32 minority (13 Black or African American, non-Hispanic/Latino; 1 American Indian or Alaska Native, non-Hispanic/Latino; 18 Asian, non-Hispanic/Latino). Average age 34. 182 applicants, 39% accepted, 50 enrolled. In 2017, 3 master's, 32 doctorates, 2 other advanced degrees awarded. *Degree requirements:* For master's, thesis optional; for doctorate, comprehensive exam (for some programs), capstone (for DNP), dissertation (for PhD). *Entrance requirements:* For master's, GRE or MAT; for doctorate, GRE or MAT, minimum GPA of 3.0 (for DNP), 3.25 (for PhD); RN license; BS or MS in nursing; 3 references; writing sample; resume; personal statement; for Certificate, interview, minimum GPA of 3.0 or GRE General Test, RN license, MS in nursing, professional certification. Additional exam requirements/recommendations for international students: Required—TOEFL (minimum score 550 paper-based; 79 iBT), IELTS (minimum score 6.5). *Application deadline:* For fall admission, 4/1 for domestic students, 2/1 for international students; for spring admission, 1/15 for domestic students, 10/1 for international students; for summer admission, 4/1 for domestic students. Applications are processed on a rolling basis. Application fee: $75. Electronic applications accepted. *Expenses:* Contact institution. *Financial support:* In 2017–18, 80 students received support, including 2 fellowships with tuition reimbursements available (averaging $17,000 per year), 4 research assistantships with tuition reimbursements available (averaging $10,600 per year), 7 teaching assistantships with tuition reimbursements available (averaging $10,600 per year); scholarships/grants, traineeships, health care benefits, and unspecified assistantships also available. Financial award application deadline: 4/1; financial award applicants required to submit FAFSA. *Faculty research:* Oncology, palliative care, gerontology, addictions, mental health, community wellness, sleep, workforce, care of underserved populations, quality and safety, person-centered care, adolescent health. *Total annual research expenditures:* $1.4 million. *Unit head:* Dr. Marsha L. Lewis, Dean and Professor, 716-829-2533, Fax: 716-829-2566, E-mail: ubnursingdean@buffalo.edu. *Application contact:* Jennifer H. Schreier, Director of Graduate Student Services, 716-829-3311, Fax: 716-829-2067, E-mail: jhv2@buffalo.edu.
Website: http://nursing.buffalo.edu/

The University of Alabama at Birmingham, School of Nursing, Birmingham, AL 35294-1210. Offers clinical nurse leader (MSN); nurse anesthesia (DNP); nurse practitioner (MSN, DNP), including adult-gerontology acute care (MSN), adult-gerontology primary care (MSN), family (MSN), pediatric (MSN), psychiatric/mental health (MSN), women's health (MSN); nursing (MSN, DNP, PhD); nursing health systems administration (MSN); nursing informatics (MSN). *Accreditation:* AACN; AANA/CANAEP. *Program availability:* Part-time, online only, blended/hybrid learning. Terminal master's awarded for partial completion of doctoral program. *Degree requirements:* For master's, comprehensive exam; for doctorate, comprehensive exam, thesis/dissertation, research mentorship experience (for PhD); scholarly project (for DNP). *Entrance requirements:* For master's, GRE, GMAT, or MAT, minimum cumulative undergraduate GPA of 3.0 or on last 60 semesters hours; letters of recommendation; for doctorate, GRE General Test, computer literacy, course work in statistics, interview, minimum GPA of 3.0, MS in nursing, references, writing sample. Additional exam requirements/recommendations for international students: Required—TOEFL (minimum score 500 paper-based, 80 iBT) or IELTS (5.5). Electronic applications accepted. *Expenses:* Contact institution. *Faculty research:* Palliative care; oncology; aging; HIV/AIDS; nursing work environments.

The University of Alabama in Huntsville, School of Graduate Studies, College of Nursing, Huntsville, AL 35899. Offers family nurse practitioner (Certificate); nursing (MSN, DNP), including adult-gerontology acute care nurse practitioner (MSN), adult-gerontology clinical nurse specialist (MSN), family nurse practitioner (MSN), leadership in health care systems (MSN); nursing education (Certificate). DNP offered jointly with The University of Alabama at Birmingham. *Accreditation:* AACN. *Program availability:* Part-time, evening/weekend, online learning. *Degree requirements:* For master's, comprehensive exam, thesis or alternative, oral and written exams. *Entrance requirements:* For master's, MAT or GRE, Alabama RN license, BSN, minimum GPA of 3.0; for doctorate, master's degree in nursing in an advanced practice area; for Certificate, MAT or GRE, minimum GPA of 3.0. Additional exam requirements/recommendations for international students: Required—TOEFL (minimum score 500 paper-based; 80 iBT), IELTS (minimum score 6.5). Electronic applications accepted. *Faculty research:* Health care informatics, chronic illness management, maternal and child health, genetics/genomics, technology and health care.

The University of Arizona, College of Nursing, Tucson, AZ 85721. Offers health care informatics (Certificate); nurse practitioner (MS); nursing (DNP, PhD). *Accreditation:* AACN; AANA/CANAEP. *Program availability:* Part-time, online learning. Terminal master's awarded for partial completion of doctoral program. *Degree requirements:* For master's, thesis optional; for doctorate, comprehensive exam, thesis/dissertation. *Entrance requirements:* For master's, BSN, eligibility for RN license; for doctorate, BSN; for Certificate, GRE General Test, Arizona RN license, BSN, minimum GPA of 3.0. Additional exam requirements/recommendations for international students: Required—TOEFL (minimum score 550 paper-based; 79 iBT). Electronic applications accepted. *Expenses:* Contact institution. *Faculty research:* Vulnerable populations, injury mechanisms and biobehavioral responses, health care systems, informatics, rural health.

University of Central Arkansas, Graduate School, College of Health and Behavioral Sciences, Department of Nursing, Conway, AR 72035-0001. Offers adult nurse practitioner (PMC); clinical nurse leader (PMC); clinical nurse specialist (MSN); family nurse practitioner (PMC); nurse educator (PMC); nurse practitioner (MSN). *Accreditation:* AACN. *Program availability:* Part-time, evening/weekend, online learning. *Degree requirements:* For master's, comprehensive exam, thesis optional, clinicals. *Entrance requirements:* For master's, GRE General Test, minimum GPA of 2.7. Additional exam requirements/recommendations for international students: Required—TOEFL (minimum score 550 paper-based; 80 iBT). *Application deadline:* For fall admission, 3/1 priority date for domestic students; for spring admission, 10/1 for domestic students. Applications are processed on a rolling basis. Application fee: $25

($50 for international students). Electronic applications accepted. *Expenses:* Contact institution. *Financial support:* Federal Work-Study, traineeships, and unspecified assistantships available. Financial award application deadline: 2/15; financial award applicants required to submit FAFSA.
Website: http://www.uca.edu/divisions/academic/chas/nurse2ab.asp

University of Central Florida, College of Nursing, Orlando, FL 32816. Offers adult-gerontology acute care nurse practitioner (Certificate); adult-gerontology primary care nurse practitioner (Certificate); family nurse practitioner (Certificate); nursing (MSN, PhD); nursing education (Post-Master's Certificate); nursing practice (DNP). *Accreditation:* AACN. *Program availability:* Part-time, evening/weekend. *Faculty:* 57 full-time (49 women), 70 part-time/adjunct (68 women). *Students:* 63 full-time (58 women), 327 part-time (297 women); includes 131 minority (40 Black or African American, non-Hispanic/Latino; 1 American Indian or Alaska Native, non-Hispanic/Latino; 16 Asian, non-Hispanic/Latino; 62 Hispanic/Latino; 12 Two or more races, non-Hispanic/Latino), 1 international. Average age 38. 303 applicants, 64% accepted, 129 enrolled. In 2017, 87 master's, 5 doctorates, 4 other advanced degrees awarded. *Degree requirements:* For master's, thesis or alternative; for doctorate, comprehensive exam, thesis/dissertation. *Entrance requirements:* For master's, essay, curriculum vitae; for doctorate, GRE General Test, letters of recommendation, resume, essay. Additional exam requirements/recommendations for international students: Required—TOEFL. *Application deadline:* For fall admission, 3/15 for domestic students; for spring admission, 10/15 for domestic students. Application fee: $30. Electronic applications accepted. *Expenses:* Tuition, state resident: part-time $288.16 per credit hour. Tuition, nonresident: part-time $1073.31 per credit hour. Tuition and fees vary according to program. *Financial support:* In 2017–18, 3 students received support, including 2 fellowships with partial tuition reimbursements available (averaging $7,377 per year), 1 research assistantship with partial tuition reimbursement available (averaging $11,952 per year); career-related internships or fieldwork, Federal Work-Study, institutionally sponsored loans, traineeships, and unspecified assistantships also available. Financial award application deadline: 3/1; financial award applicants required to submit FAFSA. *Unit head:* Dr. Mary Lou Sole, Dean, 407-823-5496, Fax: 407-823-5675, E-mail: mary.sole@ucf.edu. *Application contact:* Associate Director, Graduate Admissions, 407-823-2766, Fax: 407-823-6442, E-mail: gradadmissions@ucf.edu.
Website: http://nursing.ucf.edu/

University of Colorado Denver, College of Nursing, Aurora, CO 80045. Offers adult clinical nurse specialist (MS); adult nurse practitioner (MS); family nurse practitioner (MS); family psychiatric mental health nurse practitioner (MS); health care informatics (MS); nurse-midwifery (MS); nursing (DNP, PhD); nursing leadership and health care systems (MS); pediatric nurse practitioner (MS); women's health (MS); MS/PhD. *Accreditation:* ACNM/ACME (one or more programs are accredited). *Program availability:* Part-time, evening/weekend, online learning. *Students:* 297 applicants, 55% accepted, 141 enrolled. In 2017, 138 master's, 18 doctorates awarded. Terminal master's awarded for partial completion of doctoral program. *Degree requirements:* For master's, thesis optional; for doctorate, comprehensive exam, thesis/dissertation, 42 credits of coursework. *Entrance requirements:* For master's, GRE if cumulative undergraduate GPA is less than 3.0, undergraduate nursing degree from ACEN- or CCNE-accredited school or university; completion of research and statistics courses with minimum grade of C; copy of current and unencumbered nursing license; for doctorate, GRE, bachelor's and/or master's degrees in nursing from ACEN- or CCNE-accredited institution; portfolio; minimum undergraduate GPA of 3.0, graduate 3.5; graduate-level intermediate statistics and master's-level nursing theory courses with minimum B grade; interview. Additional exam requirements/recommendations for international students: Required—TOEFL (minimum score 560 paper-based; 83 iBT). *Application deadline:* For fall admission, 2/15 for domestic students, 1/15 for international students; for spring admission, 7/1 for domestic students, 6/1 for international students. Application fee: $50 ($75 for international students). Electronic applications accepted. *Unit head:* Dr. Sarah Thompson, Dean, 303-724-1679, E-mail: sarah.a.thompson@ucdenver.edu. *Application contact:* Judy Campbell, Graduate Programs Coordinator, 303-724-8503, E-mail: judy.campbell@ucdenver.edu.
Website: http://www.ucdenver.edu/academics/colleges/nursing/Pages/default.aspx

University of Delaware, College of Health Sciences, School of Nursing, Newark, DE 19716. Offers adult nurse practitioner (MSN, PMC); cardiopulmonary clinical nurse specialist (MSN, PMC); cardiopulmonary clinical nurse specialist/adult nurse practitioner (MSN, PMC); family nurse practitioner (MSN, PMC); gerontology clinical nurse specialist (MSN, PMC); gerontology clinical nurse specialist geriatric nurse practitioner (PMC); gerontology clinical nurse specialist/geriatric nurse practitioner (MSN); health services administration (MSN, PMC); nursing of children clinical nurse specialist (MSN, PMC); nursing of children clinical nurse specialist/pediatric nurse practitioner (MSN, PMC); oncology/immune deficiency clinical nurse specialist (MSN, PMC); oncology/immune deficiency clinical nurse specialist/adult nurse practitioner (MSN, PMC); perinatal/women's health clinical nurse specialist (MSN, PMC); perinatal/women's health clinical nurse specialist/women's health nurse practitioner (MSN, PMC); psychiatric nursing clinical nurse specialist (MSN, PMC). *Accreditation:* AACN. *Program availability:* Part-time, evening/weekend, online learning. *Degree requirements:* For master's, thesis optional. *Entrance requirements:* For master's, BSN, interview, RN license. Electronic applications accepted. *Faculty research:* Marriage and chronic illness, health promotion, congestive heart failure patient outcomes, school nursing, diabetes in children, culture, health disparities, cardiovascular, prison nursing, oncology, public policy, child obesity, smoking and teen pregnancy, blood pressure measurements, men's health.

University of Detroit Mercy, College of Health Professions, Detroit, MI 48221. Offers clinical nurse leader (MSN); family nurse practitioner (MSN); health services administration (MHSA); health systems management (MSN); nurse anesthesia (MS); nursing (DNP); nursing education (MSN, Certificate); nursing leadership and financial management (Certificate); outcomes performance management (Certificate); physician assistant (MS). *Entrance requirements:* For master's, GRE General Test, minimum GPA of 3.0. *Faculty research:* Research design, respiratory physiology, AIDS prevention, adolescent health, community, low income health education.

University of Hawaii at Manoa, Office of Graduate Education, School of Nursing and Dental Hygiene, Honolulu, HI 96822. Offers clinical nurse specialist (MS), including adult health, community mental health; nurse practitioner (MS), including adult health, community mental health, family nurse practitioner; nursing (PhD, Graduate Certificate); nursing administration (MS). *Accreditation:* AACN. *Program availability:* Part-time, online learning. *Degree requirements:* For master's, thesis optional; for doctorate, comprehensive exam, thesis/dissertation. *Entrance requirements:* For master's, Hawaii RN license. Additional exam requirements/recommendations for international students: Required—TOEFL (minimum score 580 paper-based; 92 iBT), IELTS (minimum score 5). *Expenses:* Contact institution.

University of Houston, College of Nursing, Sugar Land, TX 77479. Offers family nurse practitioner (MSN); nursing administration (MSN); nursing education (MSN). *Accreditation:* AACN. *Faculty:* 13 full-time (12 women). *Students:* 29 full-time (24 women); includes 15 minority (6 Black or African American, non-Hispanic/Latino; 5 Asian, non-Hispanic/Latino; 4 Hispanic/Latino), 3 international. Average age 37. 36 applicants, 61% accepted, 15 enrolled. In 2017, 14 master's awarded. *Entrance requirements:* For master's, GRE or MAT, minimum GPA of 3.0 in last 60 hours of academic course work, valid Texas RN licensure, 2 letters of recommendation, essay, resume, interview. Additional exam requirements/recommendations for international students: Required—TOEFL. *Application deadline:* For fall admission, 7/1 for domestic students, 6/1 for international students; for spring admission, 12/1 for domestic students, 10/1 for international students. Application fee: $75. Electronic applications accepted. *Financial support:* In 2017–18, 19 students received support. Federal Work-Study, scholarships/grants, and unspecified assistantships available. Support available to part-time students. Financial award application deadline: 5/1; financial award applicants required to submit FAFSA. *Unit head:* Dr. Kathryn Tart, Dean, 832-842-8200, E-mail: kmtart@uh.edu. *Application contact:* Tammy N. Whatley, Student Affairs Director, 832-842-8220, E-mail: tnwhatley@uh.edu.
Website: http://www.uh.edu/nursing

University of Illinois at Chicago, College of Nursing, Program in Nursing, Chicago, IL 60607-7128. Offers acute care clinical nurse specialist (MS); administrative nursing leadership (Certificate); adult nurse practitioner (MS); adult/geriatric nurse practitioner (MS); advanced community health nurse specialist (MS); family nurse practitioner (MS); geriatric clinical nurse specialist (MS); geriatric nurse practitioner (MS); nurse midwifery (MS); occupational health/advanced community health nurse specialist (MS); occupational health/family nurse practitioner (MS); pediatric nurse practitioner (MS); perinatal clinical nurse specialist (MS); school/advanced community health nurse specialist (MS); school/family nurse practitioner (MS); women's health nurse practitioner (MS). *Accreditation:* AACN. *Program availability:* Part-time. *Degree requirements:* For master's, thesis or alternative. *Entrance requirements:* For master's, GRE General Test, minimum GPA of 2.75. Additional exam requirements/recommendations for international students: Required—TOEFL. Electronic applications accepted.

University of Indianapolis, Graduate Programs, School of Nursing, Indianapolis, IN 46227-3697. Offers advanced practice nursing (DNP); family nurse practitioner (MSN); gerontological nurse practitioner (MSN); neonatal nurse practitioner (MSN); nurse-midwifery (MSN); nursing (MSN); nursing and health systems leadership (MSN); nursing education (MSN); women's health nurse practitioner (MSN); MBA/MSN. *Accreditation:* AACN. *Entrance requirements:* For master's, minimum GPA of 3.0, interview, letters of recommendation, resume, IN nursing license, 1 year of professional practice; for doctorate, graduate of ACEN- or CCNE-accredited nursing program; MSN or MA with nursing major and minimum cumulative GPA of 3.25; unencumbered RN license with eligibility for licensure in Indiana; completion of graduate-level statistics course within last 5 years with minimum grade of B; resume; essay; official transcripts from all academic institutions. Additional exam requirements/recommendations for international students: Required—TOEFL (minimum score 550 paper-based). Electronic applications accepted.

University of Louisiana at Lafayette, College of Nursing and Allied Health Professions, Lafayette, LA 70504. Offers family nurse practitioner (MSN); nurse executive curriculum (MSN); nursing and allied health professions (DNP). Program offered jointly with Southern Louisiana University, McNeese State University, Southern University and Agricultural and Mechanical College. *Accreditation:* AACN. *Entrance requirements:* For master's, GRE General Test, minimum GPA of 2.75. Additional exam requirements/recommendations for international students: Required—TOEFL (minimum score 550 paper-based). *Application deadline:* For fall admission, 5/15 for domestic and international students; for spring admission, 10/1 for domestic students. Applications are processed on a rolling basis. Application fee: $25 ($30 for international students). Electronic applications accepted. *Unit head:* Dr. Lisa Broussard, Department Head, 337-482-5654, E-mail: lisabroussard@louisiana.edu. *Application contact:* Dr. Carolyn P. Delahoussaye, Graduate Coordinator, 337-482-5617, Fax: 337-482-5649, E-mail: cgp6303@louisiana.edu.
Website: http://nursing.louisiana.edu

University of Louisville, Graduate School, School of Nursing, Louisville, KY 40202. Offers adult gerontology nurse practitioner (MSN, DNP); education and administration (MSN); family nurse practitioner (MSN, DNP); neonatal nurse practitioner (MSN, DNP); nursing research (PhD); psychiatric/mental health nurse practitioner (MSN, DNP); women's health nurse practitioner (MSN). *Accreditation:* AACN. *Program availability:* Part-time. *Faculty:* 44 full-time (40 women), 45 part-time/adjunct (41 women). *Students:* 130 full-time (107 women), 30 part-time (25 women); includes 33 minority (16 Black or African American, non-Hispanic/Latino; 7 Asian, non-Hispanic/Latino; 5 Hispanic/Latino; 5 Two or more races, non-Hispanic/Latino), 2 international. Average age 33. 61 applicants, 67% accepted, 36 enrolled. In 2017, 54 master's awarded. *Degree requirements:* For doctorate, comprehensive exam (for some programs), thesis/dissertation (for some programs). *Entrance requirements:* For master's, bachelor's degree from nationally-accredited college, completion of 6 prerequisite courses, minimum undergraduate GPA of 3.0; for doctorate, GRE with minimum score of 156 Verbal, 146 Quantitative, 4.0 Analytic (for PhD), 3 letters of professional reference; minimum GPA of 3.0 with BSN, 3.25 with MSN; written statement of career goals, areas of expertise, and reasons for pursuing doctoral degree; resume including RN license. Additional exam requirements/recommendations for international students: Recommended—TOEFL (minimum score 560 paper-based), IELTS (minimum score 6.5). *Application deadline:* For fall admission, 1/15 priority date for domestic students, 1/15 for international students; for summer admission, 10/15 priority date for domestic students. Application fee: $65. Electronic applications accepted. *Expenses:* Tuition, state resident: full-time $12,246; part-time $681 per credit hour. Tuition, nonresident: full-time $25,486; part-time $1417 per credit hour. *Required fees:* $196. Tuition and fees vary according to course load, program and reciprocity agreements. *Financial support:* In 2017–18, 8 research assistantships with full tuition reimbursements (averaging $20,000 per year), 4 teaching assistantships with full tuition reimbursements (averaging $15,000 per year) were awarded; fellowships with full tuition reimbursements, scholarships/grants, and unspecified assistantships also available. Financial award application deadline: 10/1; financial award applicants required to submit FAFSA. *Faculty research:* Environmental health, health services research, women's mental health, self-management of chronic illness in adults and children, health disparities. *Total annual research expenditures:* $762,266. *Unit head:* Dr. Marcia J. Hern, RN, Dean and Professor, 502-852-8300, Fax: 502-852-8783, E-mail: m.hern@louisville.edu. *Application contact:* Trish Hart, Assistant Dean for Student Affairs, 502-852-5825, Fax: 502-852-8783, E-mail: trish.hart@louisville.edu.
Website: http://www.louisville.edu/nursing/

University of Maine, Graduate School, College of Natural Sciences, Forestry, and Agriculture, School of Nursing, Orono, ME 04469. Offers individualized (MS); nursing education (CGS); rural health family nurse practitioner (MS, CAS). *Accreditation:* AACN. *Faculty:* 6 full-time (all women), 6 part-time/adjunct (4 women). *Students:* 22 full-time (19 women), 14 part-time (12 women); includes 3 minority (1 American Indian or Alaska Native, non-Hispanic/Latino; 1 Asian, non-Hispanic/Latino; 1 Two or more races, non-Hispanic/Latino), 1 international. Average age 35. 22 applicants, 100% accepted, 17 enrolled. In 2017, 10 master's, 2 other advanced degrees awarded. *Entrance requirements:* For master's, GRE General Test; for other advanced degree, master's degree. Additional exam requirements/recommendations for international students: Required—TOEFL. *Application deadline:* For fall admission, 7/1 for domestic students;

for spring admission, 12/15 for domestic students; for summer admission, 4/15 for domestic students. Applications are processed on a rolling basis. Application fee: $65. Electronic applications accepted. *Expenses:* Tuition, state resident: full-time $7722; part-time $429 per credit hour. Tuition, nonresident: full-time $25,146; part-time $1397 per credit hour. *Required fees:* $1162; $581 per credit hour. *Financial support:* Career-related internships or fieldwork, Federal Work-Study, institutionally sponsored loans, tuition waivers (full and partial), and unspecified assistantships available. Support available to part-time students. Financial award application deadline: 3/1. *Faculty research:* Population health, health disparities, infectious waste management, domestic violence older adults. *Total annual research expenditures:* $249,000. *Unit head:* Dr. Nancy Fishwick, Director, 207-581-2505, Fax: 207-581-2585. *Application contact:* Scott G. Delcourt, Assistant Vice President for Graduate Studies and Senior Associate Dean, 207-581-3291, Fax: 207-581-3232, E-mail: graduate@maine.edu.
Website: http://umaine.edu/nursing/

University of Mary, School of Health Sciences, Division of Nursing, Bismarck, ND 58504-9652. Offers family nurse practitioner (DNP); nurse administrator (MSN); nursing educator (MSN); MSN/MBA. *Accreditation:* AACN. *Program availability:* Part-time, evening/weekend, online learning. *Degree requirements:* For master's, comprehensive exam (for some programs), thesis (for some programs), internship (family nurse practitioner), teaching practice. *Entrance requirements:* For master's, minimum GPA of 2.75 in nursing, interview, letters of recommendation, criminal background check, immunizations, statement of professional goals. Additional exam requirements/recommendations for international students: Required—TOEFL (minimum score 500 paper-based; 71 iBT). Electronic applications accepted. *Faculty research:* Gerontology issues, rural nursing, health policy, primary care, women's health.

University of Mary Hardin-Baylor, Graduate Studies in Nursing, Belton, TX 76513. Offers family nurse practitioner (MSN, Post-Master's Certificate); nursing education (MSN); nursing practice (DNP). *Accreditation:* AACN. *Program availability:* Evening/weekend. *Faculty:* 6 full-time (all women), 8 part-time/adjunct (7 women). *Students:* 44 full-time (40 women), 10 part-time (9 women); includes 19 minority (10 Black or African American, non-Hispanic/Latino; 7 Hispanic/Latino; 2 Two or more races, non-Hispanic/Latino). Average age 34. 47 applicants, 83% accepted, 31 enrolled. In 2017, 44 master's, 2 other advanced degrees awarded. *Degree requirements:* For master's, comprehensive exam, practicum; for doctorate, scholarly project. *Entrance requirements:* For master's, baccalaureate degree in nursing, current licensure as Registered Nurse in the state of Texas, minimum GPA of 3.0 in last 60 hours of undergraduate program, two letters of recommendation, full-time RN for 1 year, personal interview with director of MSN program; for doctorate, master's degree as an advanced practice nurse, nurse leader or nurse educator; three letters of recommendation; current RN license and approval to practice as an advanced practice nurse; essay; curriculum vitae; interview. Additional exam requirements/recommendations for international students: Required—TOEFL (minimum score 60 iBT), IELTS (minimum score 4.5). *Application deadline:* For fall admission, 6/1 for domestic students, 4/30 priority date for international students; for spring admission, 11/1 for domestic students, 9/30 priority date for international students. Applications are processed on a rolling basis. Application fee: $35 ($135 for international students). Electronic applications accepted. *Expenses:* $920 per credit hour. *Financial support:* In 2017–18, 34 students received support. Federal Work-Study, unspecified assistantships, and scholarships for some active duty military personnel available. Support available to part-time students. Financial award applicants required to submit FAFSA. *Faculty research:* Grief counseling, identifying escalating patients. *Unit head:* Dr. Sharon Souter, Dean, College of Nursing/MSN and DNP Programs Director, 254-295-4662, E-mail: ssouter@umhb.edu. *Application contact:* Sharon Aguilera, Assistant Director, Graduate Admissions, 254-295-4835, E-mail: saguilera@umhb.edu.
Website: https://go.umhb.edu/graduate/nursing/home

University of Maryland, Baltimore, School of Nursing, Baltimore, MD 21201. Offers adult-gerontology acute care nurse practitioner (DNP); adult-gerontology primary care nurse practitioner (DNP); clinical nurse leader (MS); community/public health nursing (MS); family nurse practitioner (DNP); global health (Postbaccalaureate Certificate); health services leadership and management (MS); neonatal nurse practitioner (DNP); nurse anesthesia (DNP); nursing (PhD); nursing informatics (MS, Postbaccalaureate Certificate); pediatric acute/primary care nurse practitioner (DNP); psychiatric mental health nurse practitioner (DNP); teaching in nursing and health professions (Postbaccalaureate Certificate); MS/MBA. MS/MBA offered jointly with University of Baltimore. *Program availability:* Part-time. *Faculty:* 130 full-time (117 women), 125 part-time/adjunct (114 women). *Students:* 504 full-time (442 women), 532 part-time (482 women); includes 443 minority (249 Black or African American, non-Hispanic/Latino; 1 American Indian or Alaska Native, non-Hispanic/Latino; 115 Asian, non-Hispanic/Latino; 48 Hispanic/Latino; 2 Native Hawaiian or other Pacific Islander, non-Hispanic/Latino; 28 Two or more races, non-Hispanic/Latino), 15 international. Average age 33. 935 applicants, 62% accepted, 394 enrolled. In 2017, 182 master's, 57 doctorates awarded. *Degree requirements:* For master's and Postbaccalaureate Certificate, thesis (for some programs); for doctorate, comprehensive exam, thesis/dissertation. *Entrance requirements:* Additional exam requirements/recommendations for international students: Required—TOEFL (minimum score 550 paper-based; 79 iBT); Recommended—IELTS (minimum score 7). *Application deadline:* For fall admission, 11/1 for domestic and international students; for spring admission, 8/1 for domestic and international students. Application fee: $75. Electronic applications accepted. *Expenses:* Contact institution. *Financial support:* In 2017–18, 22 research assistantships with full and partial tuition reimbursements (averaging $21,523 per year), 41 teaching assistantships with full and partial tuition reimbursements (averaging $13,439 per year) were awarded; fellowships and scholarships/grants also available. Financial award application deadline: 3/1; financial award applicants required to submit FAFSA. *Unit head:* Dr. Jane Kirschling, Dean, 410-706-4359, E-mail: kirschling@umaryland.edu. *Application contact:* Larry Fillian, Associate Dean of Student and Academic Services, 410-706-6298, E-mail: lfillian@umaryland.edu.
Website: http://www.nursing.umaryland.edu/

University of Massachusetts Amherst, Graduate School, College of Nursing, Amherst, MA 01003. Offers adult gerontology primary care nurse practitioner (DNP); clinical nurse leader (MS); family nurse practitioner (DNP); nursing (PhD); public health nurse leader (DNP). *Accreditation:* AACN. *Program availability:* Part-time, online learning. Terminal master's awarded for partial completion of doctoral program. *Degree requirements:* For master's, thesis optional; for doctorate, comprehensive exam, thesis/dissertation. *Entrance requirements:* Additional exam requirements/recommendations for international students: Required—TOEFL (minimum score 550 paper-based; 80 iBT), IELTS (minimum score 6.5). Electronic applications accepted. *Faculty research:* Health of older adults and their caretakers, mental health of individuals and families, health of children and adolescents, power and decision-making, transcultural health.

University of Massachusetts Lowell, College of Health Sciences, School of Nursing, Program in Family Health Nursing, Lowell, MA 01854. Offers MS. *Accreditation:* AACN. *Degree requirements:* For master's, thesis optional. *Entrance requirements:* For master's, GRE General Test, minimum GPA of 3.0, MA nursing license, interview, 3 letters of recommendation.

University of Massachusetts Medical School, Graduate School of Nursing, Worcester, MA 01655-0115. Offers adult gerontological acute care nurse practitioner (DNP, Post Master's Certificate); adult gerontological primary care nurse practitioner (DNP, Post Master's Certificate); family nursing practitioner (DNP); nurse administrator (DNP); nurse educator (MS, Post Master's Certificate); nursing (PhD). *Accreditation:* AACN. *Faculty:* 31 full-time (28 women), 39 part-time/adjunct (34 women). *Students:* 129 full-time (111 women), 31 part-time (30 women); includes 35 minority (17 Black or African American, non-Hispanic/Latino; 10 Asian, non-Hispanic/Latino; 7 Hispanic/Latino; 1 Native Hawaiian or other Pacific Islander, non-Hispanic/Latino), 1 international. Average age 32. 124 applicants, 55% accepted, 59 enrolled. In 2017, 48 master's, 10 doctorates, 2 other advanced degrees awarded. *Degree requirements:* For doctorate, thesis/dissertation (for some programs), comprehensive exam and manuscript (for PhD); capstone project and manuscript (for DNP). *Entrance requirements:* For master's, GRE General Test, bachelor's degree in nursing, course work in statistics, unrestricted Massachusetts license as registered nurse; for doctorate, GRE General Test, bachelor's or master's degree; for Post Master's Certificate, GRE General Test, MS in nursing. Additional exam requirements/recommendations for international students: Required—TOEFL (minimum score 400 paper-based; 81 iBT). *Application deadline:* For fall admission, 12/1 priority date for domestic students. Applications are processed on a rolling basis. Application fee: $60. Electronic applications accepted. *Expenses:* $14,778 in-state tuition and mandatory fees; $19,728 out-of-state. *Financial support:* In 2017–18, 6 students received support. Scholarships/grants available. Support available to part-time students. Financial award application deadline: 5/15; financial award applicants required to submit FAFSA. *Faculty research:* Health literacy, social justice, HIV prevention, cancer-related decision making, nursing education, diabetes care and education, family-focused interventions for children with type 1 diabetes. *Total annual research expenditures:* $874,000. *Unit head:* Dr. Joan Vitello-Cicciu, Dean, 508-856-5081, Fax: 508-856-6552, E-mail: joan.vitello@umassmed.edu. *Application contact:* Diane Brescia, Admissions Coordinator, 508-856-3488, Fax: 508-856-5851, E-mail: diane.brescia@umassmed.edu.
Website: http://www.umassmed.edu/gsn/

University of Memphis, Loewenberg College of Nursing, Memphis, TN 38152. Offers advanced practice nursing (Graduate Certificate); executive leadership (MSN); family nurse practitioner (MSN); nursing administration (MSN, Graduate Certificate); nursing education (MSN, Graduate Certificate). *Accreditation:* AACN. *Program availability:* Part-time, evening/weekend, online learning. *Faculty:* 15 full-time (14 women), 3 part-time/adjunct (all women). *Students:* 16 full-time (15 women), 225 part-time (201 women); includes 90 minority (72 Black or African American, non-Hispanic/Latino; 1 American Indian or Alaska Native, non-Hispanic/Latino; 9 Asian, non-Hispanic/Latino; 5 Hispanic/Latino; 1 Native Hawaiian or other Pacific Islander, non-Hispanic/Latino; 2 Two or more races, non-Hispanic/Latino). Average age 35. 168 applicants, 53% accepted, 55 enrolled. In 2017, 120 master's, 6 other advanced degrees awarded. *Degree requirements:* For master's, comprehensive exam, thesis optional, scholarly project; clinical practicum hours. *Entrance requirements:* For master's, NCLEX exam, minimum undergraduate GPA of 2.8, letter of interest, letters of recommendation, interview, resume, nursing licensure; for Graduate Certificate, unrestricted license to practice as RN in TN, current CPR certification, evidence of vaccination, annual flu shot, evidence of current professional malpractice insurance, letters of recommendation, letter of intent, resume. Additional exam requirements/recommendations for international students: Required—TOEFL (minimum score 550 paper-based; 79 iBT). *Application deadline:* For fall admission, 2/15 for domestic and international students; for spring admission, 10/1 for domestic and international students. Application fee: $35 ($60 for international students). *Expenses:* Contact institution. *Financial support:* In 2017–18, 147 students received support. Federal Work-Study and scholarships/grants available. Financial award application deadline: 2/1; financial award applicants required to submit FAFSA. *Faculty research:* Technology in nursing, nurse retention, cultural competence, health policy, health access. *Total annual research expenditures:* $560,619. *Unit head:* Dr. Lin Zhan, Dean, 901-678-2003, Fax: 901-678-4907, E-mail: lzhan@memphis.edu. *Application contact:* Dr. Shirleatha Lee, Associate Dean for Academic Programs, 901-678-2036, Fax: 901-678-5023, E-mail: sntaylr1@memphis.edu.
Website: http://www.memphis.edu/nursing

University of Miami, Graduate School, School of Nursing and Health Studies, Coral Gables, FL 33124. Offers acute care (MSN), including acute care nurse practitioner, nurse anesthesia; nursing (PhD); primary care (MSN), including adult nurse practitioner, family nurse practitioner, nurse midwifery, women's health practitioner. *Accreditation:* AACN; AANA/CANAEP; ACNM/ACME (one or more programs are accredited). *Program availability:* Part-time. *Degree requirements:* For master's, thesis optional; for doctorate, thesis/dissertation. *Entrance requirements:* For master's, GRE General Test, BSN, minimum GPA of 3.0, Florida RN license; for doctorate, GRE General Test, BSN or MSN, minimum GPA of 3.0. Additional exam requirements/recommendations for international students: Required—TOEFL (minimum score 550 paper-based). Electronic applications accepted. *Faculty research:* Transcultural nursing, exercise and depression in Alzheimer's disease, infectious diseases/HIV–AIDS, postpartum depression, outcomes assessment.

University of Michigan–Flint, School of Nursing, Flint, MI 48502-1950. Offers adult-gerontology acute care (DNP); adult-gerontology primary care (DNP); family nurse practitioner (DNP); nursing (MSN); psychiatric mental health (DNP); psychiatric mental health nurse practitioner (Certificate). *Accreditation:* AACN. *Program availability:* Part-time, evening/weekend, 100% online. *Faculty:* 36 full-time (35 women), 66 part-time/adjunct (61 women). *Students:* 159 full-time (143 women), 148 part-time (126 women); includes 80 minority (36 Black or African American, non-Hispanic/Latino; 5 American Indian or Alaska Native, non-Hispanic/Latino; 14 Asian, non-Hispanic/Latino; 14 Hispanic/Latino; 2 Native Hawaiian or other Pacific Islander, non-Hispanic/Latino; 9 Two or more races, non-Hispanic/Latino), 3 international. Average age 37. 86 applicants, 78% accepted, 41 enrolled. In 2017, 12 master's, 42 doctorates, 9 other advanced degrees awarded. *Entrance requirements:* For master's, BSN from regionally-accredited college; minimum GPA of 3.2; current unencumbered RN license in the United States; three or more credits in college-level chemistry or statistics with minimum C grade; for doctorate, BSN or MSN (with APRN certification) from regionally-accredited college or university with minimum overall undergraduate GPA of 3.2; college-level statistics with minimum C grade; for Certificate, completion of nurse practitioner program with MS from regionally-accredited college or university with minimum overall GPA of 3.2; current unencumbered RN license in the United States; current unencumbered license as nurse practitioner; current certification as nurse practitioner in specialty other than discipline of study. Additional exam requirements/recommendations for international students: Required—TOEFL (minimum score 84 iBT), IELTS (minimum score 6.5). *Application deadline:* For fall admission, 7/1 for domestic students, 5/1 for international students; for winter admission, 11/1 for domestic students, 9/1 for international students; for spring admission, 3/15 for domestic students, 1/1 for international students. Applications are processed on a rolling basis. Application fee: $55. Electronic applications accepted. *Expenses:* Contact institution. *Financial support:* Federal Work-Study, scholarships/grants, and unspecified assistantships available. Support available to part-time students. Financial award application deadline: 3/1; financial award applicants required to submit FAFSA. *Faculty research:* Family system stress, self breast exam, family roads

evaluation, causal model testing for psycho social development, basic needs, nurse preparation training. *Unit head:* Dr. Constance J. Creech, Director, 810-762-3420, Fax: 810-766-6851, E-mail: ccreech@umflint.edu. *Application contact:* Bradley T. Maki, Director of Graduate Admissions, 810-762-3171, Fax: 810-766-6789, E-mail: bmaki@umflint.edu.
Website: https://www.umflint.edu/nursing/graduate-nursing-programs

University of Minnesota, Twin Cities Campus, Graduate School, School of Nursing, Minneapolis, MN 55455-0213. Offers adult/gerontological clinical nurse specialist (DNP); adult/gerontological primary care nurse practitioner (DNP); family nurse practitioner (DNP); health innovation and leadership (DNP); integrative health and healing (DNP); nurse anesthesia (DNP); nurse midwifery (DNP); nursing (MN, PhD); nursing informatics (DNP); pediatric clinical nurse specialist (DNP); primary care certified pediatric nurse practitioner (DNP); psychiatric/mental health nurse practitioner (DNP); women's health nurse practitioner (DNP). *Accreditation:* AACN; AANA/CANAEP; ACNM/ACME (one or more programs are accredited). *Program availability:* Part-time, online learning. Terminal master's awarded for partial completion of doctoral program. *Degree requirements:* For master's, final oral exam, project or thesis; for doctorate, thesis/dissertation. *Entrance requirements:* For master's and doctorate, GRE General Test. Additional exam requirements/recommendations for international students: Required—TOEFL (minimum score 586 paper-based). *Expenses:* Contact institution. *Faculty research:* Child and family health promotion, nursing research on elders.

University of Missouri, Office of Research and Graduate Studies, Sinclair School of Nursing, Columbia, MO 65211. Offers adult-gerontology clinical nurse specialist (DNP, Certificate); family nurse practitioner (DNP); family psychiatric and mental health nurse practitioner (DNP); nursing (MS, PhD); nursing leadership and innovations in health care (DNP); pediatric clinical nurse specialist (DNP, Certificate); pediatric nurse practitioner (DNP). *Accreditation:* AACN. *Program availability:* Part-time. *Degree requirements:* For master's, thesis optional, oral exam; for doctorate, thesis/dissertation. *Entrance requirements:* For master's, GRE General Test, BSN, minimum GPA of 3.0 during last 60 hours, nursing license. Additional exam requirements/recommendations for international students: Required—TOEFL, IELTS. *Application deadline:* Applications are processed on a rolling basis. Electronic applications accepted. *Expenses:* Tuition, state resident: full-time $6480. Tuition, nonresident: full-time $17,744. *Required fees:* $1108. Tuition and fees vary according to course load, campus/location and program. *Financial support:* Fellowships, research assistantships, teaching assistantships, career-related internships or fieldwork, institutionally sponsored loans, scholarships/grants, traineeships, health care benefits, tuition waivers (full), and unspecified assistantships available. Support available to part-time students.
Website: http://nursing.missouri.edu/

University of Missouri–Kansas City, School of Nursing and Health Studies, Kansas City, MO 64110-2499. Offers adult clinical nurse specialist (MSN), including adult nurse practitioner, women's health nurse practitioner (MSN, DNP); adult clinical nursing practice (DNP), including adult gerontology nurse practitioner, women's health nurse practitioner (MSN, DNP); clinical nursing practice (DNP), including family nurse practitioner; neonatal nurse practitioner (MSN); nurse educator (MSN); nurse executive (MSN); nursing practice (DNP); pediatric clinical nursing practice (DNP), including pediatric nurse practitioner; pediatric nurse practitioner (MSN). *Accreditation:* AACN. *Program availability:* Part-time, online learning. *Degree requirements:* For master's, thesis or alternative. *Entrance requirements:* For master's, minimum undergraduate GPA of 3.2; for doctorate, GRE, 3 letters of reference. Additional exam requirements/recommendations for international students: Required—TOEFL (minimum score 550 paper-based; 80 iBT). *Faculty research:* Geriatrics/gerontology, children's pain, neonatology, Alzheimer's care, cancer caregivers.

University of Missouri–St. Louis, College of Nursing, St. Louis, MO 63121. Offers adult/geriatric nurse practitioner (Post Master's Certificate); family nurse practitioner (Post Master's Certificate); nursing (DNP, PhD); pediatric acute care nurse practitioner (Post Master's Certificate); pediatric nurse practitioner (Post Master's Certificate); psychiatric-mental health nurse practitioner (Post Master's Certificate); women's health nurse practitioner (Post Master's Certificate). *Accreditation:* AACN. *Program availability:* Part-time. *Faculty:* 24 full-time (22 women), 12 part-time/adjunct (11 women). *Students:* 47 full-time (44 women), 162 part-time (152 women); includes 53 minority (37 Black or African American, non-Hispanic/Latino; 10 Asian, non-Hispanic/Latino; 4 Hispanic/Latino; 2 Two or more races, non-Hispanic/Latino), 3 international. 112 applicants, 93% accepted, 70 enrolled. *Degree requirements:* For doctorate, comprehensive exam, thesis/dissertation; for Post Master's Certificate, thesis. *Entrance requirements:* For doctorate, GRE, 2 letters of recommendation, MSN, minimum GPA of 3.2, course in differential/inferential statistics; for Post Master's Certificate, 2 recommendation letters; MSN; advanced practice certificate; minimum GPA of 3.0; essay. Additional exam requirements/recommendations for international students: Recommended—TOEFL (minimum score 550 paper-based; 79 iBT), IELTS (minimum score 6.5). *Application deadline:* For fall admission, 2/15 for domestic and international students. Application fee: $50 ($40 for international students). Electronic applications accepted. *Expenses:* Tuition, state resident: part-time $476.50 per credit hour. Tuition, nonresident: part-time $1169.70 per credit hour. *Financial support:* Research assistantships with tuition reimbursements available. Financial award application deadline: 4/1; financial award applicants required to submit FAFSA. *Faculty research:* Health promotion and restoration, family disruption, violence, abuse, battered women, health survey methods. *Unit head:* Sue Dean-Baar, Dean, 314-516-6066. *Application contact:* 314-516-5458, Fax: 314-516-6996, E-mail: gradadm@umsl.edu.
Website: http://www.umsl.edu/divisions/nursing/

University of Nevada, Las Vegas, Graduate College, School of Nursing, Las Vegas, NV 89154-3018. Offers biobehavioral nursing (Advanced Certificate); family nurse practitioner (Advanced Certificate); nursing (MS, DNP, PhD); nursing education (Advanced Certificate). *Accreditation:* AACN. *Program availability:* Part-time, 100% online, blended/hybrid learning. *Faculty:* 11 full-time (9 women), 10 part-time/adjunct (all women). *Students:* 46 full-time (40 women), 78 part-time (73 women); includes 43 minority (6 Black or African American, non-Hispanic/Latino; 16 Asian, non-Hispanic/Latino; 12 Hispanic/Latino; 9 Two or more races, non-Hispanic/Latino). Average age 37. 185 applicants, 38% accepted, 54 enrolled. In 2017, 35 master's, 9 doctorates, 3 other advanced degrees awarded. *Degree requirements:* For master's, comprehensive exam, thesis; for doctorate, comprehensive exam (for some programs), thesis/dissertation, project defense (for DNP). *Entrance requirements:* For master's, bachelor's degree with minimum GPA 3.0; 2 letters of recommendation; valid RN license; statement of purpose; for doctorate, GRE General Test, bachelor's degree; statement of purpose; 3 letters of recommendation; for Advanced Certificate, 2 letters of recommendation; statement of purpose; valid RN license. Additional exam requirements/recommendations for international students: Recommended—TOEFL (minimum score 550 paper-based; 80 iBT), IELTS (minimum score 7). *Application deadline:* For fall admission, 2/1 for domestic students. Application fee: $60 ($95 for international students). Electronic applications accepted. *Expenses:* Contact institution. *Financial support:* In 2017–18, 3 students received support, including 1 research assistantship with partial tuition reimbursement available (averaging $20,250 per year), 2 teaching assistantships with partial tuition reimbursements available (averaging $20,250 per year); institutionally sponsored loans, scholarships/grants, health care benefits, and unspecified assistantships also available. Financial award application deadline: 3/15; financial award applicants required to submit FAFSA. *Faculty research:* Skeletal muscle injury; chronic diseases and health promotion in diabetes, cardiovascular disease, pain, trauma, and obesity; nursing education; sexual assault. *Total annual research expenditures:* $500,875. *Unit head:* Dr. Carolyn Yucha, Dean, 702-895-3906, Fax: 702-895-4807, E-mail: carolyn.yucha@unlv.edu.
Website: http://nursing.unlv.edu/

University of New Hampshire, Graduate School, College of Health and Human Services, Department of Nursing, Durham, NH 03824. Offers family nurse practitioner (Postbaccalaureate Certificate); nursing (MS, DNP); psychiatric mental health (Postbaccalaureate Certificate). *Accreditation:* AACN. *Program availability:* Part-time, online learning. *Students:* 40 full-time (32 women), 107 part-time (91 women); includes 8 minority (2 Black or African American, non-Hispanic/Latino; 2 Asian, non-Hispanic/Latino; 2 Hispanic/Latino; 2 Two or more races, non-Hispanic/Latino). Average age 35. 83 applicants, 58% accepted, 30 enrolled. In 2017, 38 master's, 1 doctorate, 5 other advanced degrees awarded. *Entrance requirements:* Additional exam requirements/recommendations for international students: Required—TOEFL (minimum score 550 paper-based; 80 iBT). *Application deadline:* For fall admission, 4/1 priority date for domestic students, 4/1 for international students; for spring admission, 11/1 for domestic students. Application fee: $65. Electronic applications accepted. *Financial support:* In 2017–18, 15 students received support, including 2 teaching assistantships; fellowships, research assistantships, Federal Work-Study, scholarships/grants, and tuition waivers (full and partial) also available. Financial award application deadline: 2/15. *Unit head:* Dr. Gene Harkless, Chair, 603-862-2285. *Application contact:* Jane Dufresne, Administrative Assistant, 603-862-2299, E-mail: nursing.department@unh.edu.
Website: https://chhs.unh.edu/nursing/graduate-program-nursing

The University of North Carolina at Chapel Hill, School of Nursing, Chapel Hill, NC 27599-7460. Offers advanced practice registered nurse (DNP); nursing (MSN, PhD, PMC), including administration (MSN), adult gerontology primary care nurse practitioner (MSN), clinical nurse leader (MSN), education (MSN), health care systems (PMC), informatics (MSN, PMC), nursing leadership (PMC), outcomes management (MSN), primary care family nurse practitioner (MSN), primary care pediatric nurse practitioner (MSN), psychiatric/mental health nurse practitioner (MSN, PMC). *Accreditation:* AACN; ACEN (one or more programs are accredited). *Program availability:* Part-time. *Faculty:* 86 full-time (78 women), 44 part-time/adjunct (40 women). *Students:* 208 full-time (186 women), 128 part-time (116 women); includes 100 minority (49 Black or African American, non-Hispanic/Latino; 4 American Indian or Alaska Native, non-Hispanic/Latino; 23 Asian, non-Hispanic/Latino; 7 Hispanic/Latino; 17 Two or more races, non-Hispanic/Latino), 17 international. Average age 33. 624 applicants, 25% accepted, 150 enrolled. In 2017, 91 master's, 14 doctorates awarded. *Degree requirements:* For master's, comprehensive exam, thesis; for doctorate, thesis/dissertation, 3 exams; for PMC, thesis. *Entrance requirements:* Additional exam requirements/recommendations for international students: Required—TOEFL (minimum score 575 paper-based; 89 iBT), IELTS (minimum score 8). *Application deadline:* For fall admission, 12/15 for domestic and international students. Application fee: $88. Electronic applications accepted. *Financial support:* In 2017–18, 8 fellowships with full tuition reimbursements, 6 research assistantships with partial tuition reimbursements (averaging $8,000 per year), 10 teaching assistantships with partial tuition reimbursements (averaging $8,000 per year) were awarded; scholarships/grants, traineeships, health care benefits, and unspecified assistantships also available. Support available to part-time students. Financial award application deadline: 3/1; financial award applicants required to submit FAFSA. *Faculty research:* Preventing and managing chronic illness, reducing health disparities, improving healthcare quality and patient outcomes, understanding biobehavioral and genetic bases of health and illness, developing innovative ways to enhance science and its clinical translation. *Unit head:* Dr. Nilda Peragallo Montano, Dean/Professor, 919-966-3731, Fax: 919-966-3540, E-mail: npm@email.unc.edu. *Application contact:* Emily Sayed, Assistant Director, Graduate Admissions, 919-966-4260, Fax: 919-966-3540, E-mail: sayed@unc.edu.
Website: http://nursing.unc.edu

The University of North Carolina at Charlotte, College of Health and Human Services, School of Nursing, Charlotte, NC 28223-0001. Offers adult-gerontology acute care nurse practitioner (Post-Master's Certificate); advanced clinical nursing (MSN), including adult psychiatric mental health, adult-gerontology acute care nurse practitioner, family nurse practitioner across the lifespan; family nurse practitioner across the lifespan (Post-Master's Certificate); nurse anesthesia (MSN), including nurse anesthesia across the lifespan; nurse anesthesia across the lifespan (Post-Master's Certificate); nursing (DNP); nursing administration (Graduate Certificate); nursing education (Graduate Certificate); systems/population nursing (MSN), including community/public health nursing, nurse administrator, nurse educator. *Accreditation:* AACN; AANA/CANAEP. *Program availability:* Part-time, blended/hybrid learning. *Faculty:* 24 full-time (22 women), 6 part-time/adjunct (4 women). *Students:* 113 full-time (84 women), 163 part-time (150 women); includes 63 minority (47 Black or African American, non-Hispanic/Latino; 2 American Indian or Alaska Native, non-Hispanic/Latino; 6 Asian, non-Hispanic/Latino; 3 Hispanic/Latino; 5 Two or more races, non-Hispanic/Latino). Average age 37. 443 applicants, 31% accepted, 113 enrolled. In 2017, 83 master's, 8 doctorates, 8 other advanced degrees awarded. Terminal master's awarded for partial completion of doctoral program. *Degree requirements:* For doctorate, thesis/dissertation or alternative, residency; for other advanced degree, practicum. *Entrance requirements:* For master's, GRE General Test, current unrestricted license as Registered Nurse in North Carolina; BSN from nationally-accredited program; one year of professional nursing practice in acute/critical care; minimum overall GPA of 3.0 in last degree; completion of undergraduate statistics course with minimum grade of C; statement of purpose; for doctorate, GRE or MAT, master's degree in nursing in an advanced nursing practice specialty from nationally-accredited program; minimum overall GPA of 3.5 in MSN program; current RN licensure in U.S. at time of application with eligibility for NC licensure; essay; resume/curriculum vitae; professional recommendations; clinical hours; for other advanced degree, GRE. Additional exam requirements/recommendations for international students: Required—TOEFL (minimum score 523 paper-based, 70 iBT) or IELTS (6.5). *Application deadline:* For fall admission, 1/10 for domestic and international students; for spring admission, 9/10 for domestic and international students; for summer admission, 4/1 for domestic and international students. Applications are processed on a rolling basis. Application fee: $75. Electronic applications accepted. *Expenses:* Contact institution. *Financial support:* In 2017–18, 6 students received support, including 4 research assistantships (averaging $6,338 per year), 2 teaching assistantships (averaging $6,250 per year); career-related internships or fieldwork, institutionally sponsored loans, scholarships/grants, traineeships, and unspecified assistantships also available. Support available to part-time students. Financial award application deadline: 3/1; financial award applicants required to submit FAFSA. *Total annual research expenditures:* $800,072. *Unit head:* Dr. Dena Evans, Director, 704-687-7974, E-mail: devans37@uncc.edu. *Application contact:* Kathy B. Giddings, Director of Graduate Admissions, 704-687-5503, Fax: 704-687-1668, E-mail: gradadm@uncc.edu.
Website: http://nursing.uncc.edu/

Family Nurse Practitioner Studies

The University of North Carolina Wilmington, School of Nursing, Wilmington, NC 28403-3297. Offers clinical research and product development (MS); family nurse practitioner (Post-Master's Certificate); nurse educator (Post-Master's Certificate); nursing (MSN); nursing practice (DNP). *Accreditation:* AACN; ACEN. *Program availability:* Part-time, 100% online. *Faculty:* 44 full-time (38 women). *Students:* 160 full-time (148 women), 237 part-time (213 women); includes 79 minority (55 Black or African American, non-Hispanic/Latino; 3 American Indian or Alaska Native, non-Hispanic/Latino; 6 Asian, non-Hispanic/Latino; 9 Hispanic/Latino; 6 Two or more races, non-Hispanic/Latino). Average age 36. 287 applicants, 71% accepted, 167 enrolled. In 2017, 40 master's awarded. *Degree requirements:* For master's, thesis or alternative, research project, presentation; for doctorate, clinical scholarly project, 1000 clinical hours. *Entrance requirements:* For master's, GRE General Test, 3 recommendations, statement of interest, resume, writing sample, RN experience, RN license (for MSN), bachelor's degree in related field; for doctorate, 3 recommendations, Advanced Practice Registered Nurse with current unrestricted RN license in state in which practice will occur, minimum GPA of 3.0, essay, resume or curriculum vitae, interview, criminal background check and 12-panel drug screening. Additional exam requirements/recommendations for international students: Required—TOEFL (minimum score 550 paper-based; 79 iBT), IELTS (minimum score 6.5). *Application deadline:* For fall admission, 3/1 for domestic students. Applications are processed on a rolling basis. Application fee: $75. Electronic applications accepted. *Expenses:* $318.15 per credit hour in-state, $965.60 per credit hour out-of-state (for DNP). *Financial support:* Application deadline: 1/1; applicants required to submit FAFSA. *Unit head:* Dr. Laurie Badzek, Director, 910-962-7410, Fax: 910-962-3723, E-mail: badzekl@uncw.edu. *Application contact:* Dr. Micah Scott, MSN Graduate Coordinator, 910-962-7534, E-mail: scottmi@uncw.edu.
Website: https://www.uncw.edu/son/academicprograms.html

University of North Dakota, Graduate School, College of Nursing and Professional Disciplines, Department of Nursing, Grand Forks, ND 58202. Offers adult-gerontological nurse practitioner (MS); advanced public health nurse (MS); family nurse practitioner (MS); nurse anesthesia (MS); nurse educator (MS); nursing (PhD, Post-Master's Certificate); nursing practice (DNP); psychiatric and mental health nurse practitioner (MS).

University of Northern Colorado, Graduate School, College of Natural and Health Sciences, School of Nursing, Greeley, CO 80639. Offers adult-gerontology acute care nurse practitioner (MSN, DNP); family nurse practitioner (MSN, DNP); nursing education (PhD); nursing practice (DNP). *Accreditation:* AACN. *Program availability:* Online learning. *Degree requirements:* For master's, comprehensive exam, thesis or alternative; for doctorate, comprehensive exam, thesis/dissertation. *Entrance requirements:* For master's and doctorate, GRE General Test, minimum GPA of 3.0 in last 60 hours, BS in nursing, 2 letters of recommendation. Electronic applications accepted.

University of North Florida, Brooks College of Health, School of Nursing, Jacksonville, FL 32224. Offers family nurse practitioner (Certificate); nurse anesthetist (MSN). *Accreditation:* AACN; AANA/CANAEP. *Program availability:* Part-time. *Degree requirements:* For master's, thesis optional. *Entrance requirements:* For master's, GRE General Test, minimum GPA of 3.0 in last 60 hours of course work, BSN, clinical experience, resume; for doctorate, GRE, master's degree in nursing specialty from nationally-accredited program; national certification in one of the following APRN roles: CNE, CNM, CNS, CRNA, CNP; minimum graduate GPA of 3.3; three letters of reference which address academic ability and clinical skills; active license as registered nurse or advanced practice registered nurse. Additional exam requirements/recommendations for international students: Required—TOEFL (minimum score 500 paper-based; 61 iBT). Electronic applications accepted. *Faculty research:* Teen pregnancy, diabetes, ethical decision-making, family caregivers.

University of North Georgia, Program in Family Nurse Practitioner, Dahlonega, GA 30597. Offers MS, Certificate. *Program availability:* Part-time. *Students:* 50 part-time (47 women); includes 12 minority (5 Black or African American, non-Hispanic/Latino; 5 Asian, non-Hispanic/Latino; 2 Two or more races, non-Hispanic/Latino). Average age 36. 2 applicants, 100% accepted, 2 enrolled. In 2017, 29 master's, 1 other advanced degree awarded. *Degree requirements:* For master's, comprehensive exam, clinical primary care thesis/research project. *Entrance requirements:* For master's, BSN with minimum GPA of 3.0, 1-2 years of post licensure clinical experience, GA registered nurse, professional resume. Additional exam requirements/recommendations for international students: Required—TOEFL (minimum score 550 paper-based; 79 iBT), IELTS (minimum score 6.5). *Application deadline:* For summer admission, 2/28 for domestic students. Application fee: $40. Electronic applications accepted. *Expenses:* Contact institution. *Financial support:* Application deadline: 3/17; applicants required to submit FAFSA. *Unit head:* Dr. Kim Hudson-Gallogly, Department Head, 706-864-1934, E-mail: kim.hudson-gallogly@ung.edu. *Application contact:* Melinda Maxwell, Director of Graduate Admissions, 706-864-1543, E-mail: melinda.maxwell@ung.edu.
Website: https://ung.edu/nursing/graduate/ms-family-nurse-practitioner.php

University of Pennsylvania, School of Nursing, Family Nurse Practitioner Program, Philadelphia, PA 19104. Offers MSN, Certificate. *Accreditation:* AACN. *Program availability:* Part-time. *Students:* Average age 28. 97 applicants, 41% accepted, 33 enrolled. In 2017, 22 master's awarded. *Financial support:* Application deadline: 4/1.

University of Phoenix–Hawaii Campus, College of Nursing, Honolulu, HI 96813-3800. Offers education (MHA); family nurse practitioner (MSN); gerontology (MHA); health administration (MHA); nursing (MSN); nursing/health care education (MSN); MSN/MBA. *Program availability:* Evening/weekend. *Degree requirements:* For master's, thesis (for some programs). *Entrance requirements:* For master's, minimum undergraduate GPA of 2.5, 3 years of work experience, RN license. Additional exam requirements/recommendations for international students: Required—TOEFL (minimum score 550 paper-based; 79 iBT). Electronic applications accepted.

University of Phoenix–Online Campus, College of Health Sciences and Nursing, Phoenix, AZ 85034-7209. Offers family nurse practitioner (Certificate); health care (Certificate); health care education (Certificate); health care informatics (Certificate); informatics (MSN); nursing (MSN); nursing and health care education (MSN); MSN/MBA; MSN/MHA. *Accreditation:* AACN. *Program availability:* Evening/weekend, online learning. *Entrance requirements:* Additional exam requirements/recommendations for international students: Required—TOEFL, TOEIC (Test of English as an International Communication), Berlitz Online English Proficiency Exam, PTE, or IELTS. Electronic applications accepted. *Expenses:* Contact institution.

University of Phoenix–Phoenix Campus, College of Health Sciences and Nursing, Tempe, AZ 85282-2371. Offers family nurse practitioner (MSN, Certificate); gerontology health care (Certificate); health care education (MSN, Certificate); health care informatics (Certificate); informatics (MSN); nursing (MSN); MSN/MHA. *Program availability:* Evening/weekend, online learning. *Entrance requirements:* Additional exam requirements/recommendations for international students: Required—TOEFL, TOEIC (Test of English as an International Communication), Berlitz Online English Proficiency Exam, PTE, or IELTS. Electronic applications accepted. *Expenses:* Contact institution.

University of Phoenix–Sacramento Valley Campus, College of Nursing, Sacramento, CA 95833-4334. Offers family nurse practitioner (MSN); health administration (MHA); health care education (MSN); nursing (MSN); MSN/MBA. *Program availability:* Evening/weekend. *Degree requirements:* For master's, thesis (for some programs). *Entrance requirements:* For master's, RN license, minimum undergraduate GPA of 2.5, 3 years work experience. Additional exam requirements/recommendations for international students: Required—TOEFL (minimum score 550 paper-based; 79 iBT). Electronic applications accepted.

University of Pittsburgh, School of Nursing, Nurse Practitioner Program, Pittsburgh, PA 15261. Offers adult-gerontology acute care (DNP); adult-gerontology primary care (DNP); family (individual across the lifespan) (DNP); neonatal (MSN, DNP); pediatric primary care (DNP); psychiatric mental health (DNP). *Accreditation:* AACN. *Program availability:* Part-time. *Faculty:* 17 full-time (14 women), 3 part-time/adjunct (2 women). *Students:* 50 full-time (47 women), 43 part-time (36 women); includes 9 minority (1 Black or African American, non-Hispanic/Latino; 1 American Indian or Alaska Native, non-Hispanic/Latino; 7 Asian, non-Hispanic/Latino), 1 international. Average age 31. 77 applicants, 40% accepted, 25 enrolled. In 2017, 6 master's, 35 doctorates awarded. *Degree requirements:* For master's, comprehensive exam, thesis optional. *Entrance requirements:* For master's, GRE General Test, BSN, RN license, 3 letters of recommendation, resume, course work in statistics, relevant nursing experience; for doctorate, GRE General Test, BSN, RN license, minimum GPA of 3.5, 3 letters of recommendation, relevant nursing experience, resume, course work in statistics. Additional exam requirements/recommendations for international students: Required—TOEFL (minimum score 600 paper-based; 100 IBT) or IELTS (minimum score 7.0). *Application deadline:* For fall admission, 5/1 priority date for domestic students, 2/15 priority date for international students. Application fee: $50. Electronic applications accepted. *Expenses:* $13,068 per term full-time resident tuition, $1,064 per credit part-time; $15,270 per term full-time non-resident tuition, $1,247 per credit part-time; $437 per term full-time fees; $282 per term part-time fees. *Financial support:* In 2017–18, 58 students received support, including 7 fellowships (averaging $15,755 per year), 15 teaching assistantships (averaging $12,454 per year); scholarships/grants, tuition waivers, and unspecified assistantships also available. Financial award applicants required to submit FAFSA. *Faculty research:* Behavioral management of chronic disorders, patient management in critical care, consumer informatics, genetic applications (molecular genetics and psychosocial implications), technology for nurses and patients to improve care. *Unit head:* Dr. Sandra Engberg, Associate Dean for Clinical Education, 412-624-3835, Fax: 412-624-8521, E-mail: sje1@pitt.edu. *Application contact:* Laurie Lapsley, Graduate Administrator, 412-624-9670, Fax: 412-624-2409, E-mail: lapsleyl@pitt.edu.
Website: http://www.nursing.pitt.edu

University of Portland, School of Nursing, Portland, OR 97203. Offers clinical nurse leader (MS); family nurse practitioner (DNP); nurse educator (MS). *Accreditation:* AACN. *Program availability:* Part-time, evening/weekend, online learning. *Entrance requirements:* For master's, GRE General Test or MAT, Oregon RN license, BSN, course work in statistics, resume, letters of recommendation, writing sample; for doctorate, GRE General Test or MAT, Oregon RN license, BSN or MSN, 2 letters of recommendation, resume, writing sample, official transcripts. Additional exam requirements/recommendations for international students: Required—TOEFL (minimum score 550 paper-based; 80 iBT), IELTS (minimum score 7). *Expenses:* Contact institution.

University of Puerto Rico–Medical Sciences Campus, School of Nursing, San Juan, PR 00936-5067. Offers adult and elderly nursing (MSN); child and adolescent nursing (MSN); critical care nursing (MSN); family and community nursing (MSN); family nurse practitioner (MSN); maternity nursing (MSN); mental health and psychiatric nursing (MSN). *Accreditation:* AACN; AANA/CANAEP. *Entrance requirements:* For master's, GRE or EXADEP, interview, Puerto Rico RN license or professional license for international students, general and specific point average, article analysis. Electronic applications accepted. *Faculty research:* HIV, health disparities, teen violence, women and violence, neurological disorders.

University of Rhode Island, Graduate School, College of Nursing, Kingston, RI 02881. Offers acute care nurse practitioner (adult-gerontology focus) (Post Master's Certificate); adult gerontology nurse practitioner/clinical nurse specialist (Post Master's Certificate); adult-gerontological acute care nurse practitioner (MS); adult-gerontological nurse practitioner/clinical nurse specialist (MS); family nurse practitioner (MS, Post Master's Certificate); nursing (DNP, PhD); nursing education (MS, Post Master's Certificate). *Accreditation:* AACN; ACNM/ACME (one or more programs are accredited). *Program availability:* Part-time, evening/weekend, 100% online, blended/hybrid learning. *Faculty:* 31 full-time (30 women). *Students:* 42 full-time (36 women), 86 part-time (79 women); includes 12 minority (3 Black or African American, non-Hispanic/Latino; 3 Asian, non-Hispanic/Latino; 3 Hispanic/Latino; 1 Native Hawaiian or other Pacific Islander, non-Hispanic/Latino; 2 Two or more races, non-Hispanic/Latino), 3 international. 33 applicants, 79% accepted, 23 enrolled. In 2017, 25 master's, 8 doctorates, 2 other advanced degrees awarded. *Entrance requirements:* For master's, GRE or MAT, 2 letters of recommendation, scholarly papers; for doctorate, GRE, 3 letters of recommendation, scholarly papers. Additional exam requirements/recommendations for international students: Required—TOEFL. *Application deadline:* For fall admission, 2/15 for domestic students, 2/1 for international students; for spring admission, 10/15 for domestic students, 7/15 for international students. Application fee: $65. Electronic applications accepted. *Expenses:* Tuition, state resident: full-time $12,706; part-time $786 per credit. Tuition, nonresident: full-time $25,216; part-time $1401 per credit. *Required fees:* $1598; $45 per credit. One-time fee: $30 part-time. *Financial support:* In 2017–18, 1 research assistantship with tuition reimbursement (averaging $18,080 per year), 5 teaching assistantships with tuition reimbursements (averaging $10,133 per year) were awarded. Financial award application deadline: 2/1; financial award applicants required to submit FAFSA. *Unit head:* Dr. Barbara Wolfe, Dean, 401-874-5324, E-mail: bwolfe@uri.edu. *Application contact:* Dr. Denise Coppa, Associate Professor/Interim Associate Dean for Graduate Programs, 401-874-5036, E-mail: dcoppa@uri.edu.
Website: http://www.uri.edu/nursing/

University of Rochester, School of Nursing, Rochester, NY 14642. Offers adult gerontological acute care nurse practitioner (MS); adult gerontological primary care nurse practitioner (MS); clinical nurse leader (MS); family nurse practitioner (MS); family psychiatric mental health nurse practitioner (MS); health care organization management and leadership (MS); nursing (DNP); nursing and health science (PhD); nursing education (MS); pediatric nurse practitioner (MS); pediatric nurse practitioner/neonatal nurse practitioner (MS). *Accreditation:* AACN. *Program availability:* Part-time, 100% online, blended/hybrid learning. *Faculty:* 62 full-time (51 women), 73 part-time/adjunct (63 women). *Students:* 17 full-time (12 women), 306 part-time (252 women); includes 46 minority (16 Black or African American, non-Hispanic/Latino; 1 American Indian or Alaska Native, non-Hispanic/Latino; 7 Asian, non-Hispanic/Latino; 17 Hispanic/Latino; 5 Two or more races, non-Hispanic/Latino), 3 international. Average age 34. 143 applicants, 71% accepted, 87 enrolled. In 2017, 48 master's, 8 doctorates awarded. Terminal master's awarded for partial completion of doctoral program. *Degree*

requirements: For master's, comprehensive exam; for doctorate, thesis/dissertation. *Entrance requirements:* For master's, BS in nursing, minimum GPA of 3.0, course work in statistics; for doctorate, GRE General Test (for PhD), MS in nursing, minimum GPA of 3.5. Additional exam requirements/recommendations for international students: Required—TOEFL (minimum score 560 paper-based; 88 iBT) or IELTS (minimum score 6.5) recommended. *Application deadline:* For fall admission, 4/1 for domestic and international students; for spring admission, 9/1 for domestic and international students; for summer admission, 1/2 for domestic and international students. Application fee: $50. Electronic applications accepted. *Financial support:* In 2017–18, 63 students received support, including 2 fellowships with full and partial tuition reimbursements available (averaging $16,000 per year); scholarships/grants, traineeships, health care benefits, tuition waivers (full and partial), and unspecified assistantships also available. Support available to part-time students. Financial award application deadline: 6/30; financial award applicants required to submit CSS PROFILE or FAFSA. *Faculty research:* Symptom science, systems of care, innovations in health technology, promoting healthy behaviors. *Total annual research expenditures:* $2.6 million. *Unit head:* Dr. Kathy H. Rideout, Dean, 585-273-8902, Fax: 585-273-1268, E-mail: kathy_rideout@urmc.rochester.edu. *Application contact:* Elaine Andolina, Director of Admissions, 585-275-2375, Fax: 585-756-8299, E-mail: elaine_andolina@urmc.rochester.edu.
Website: http://www.son.rochester.edu

University of Saint Francis, Graduate School, Department of Nursing, Fort Wayne, IN 46808. Offers family nurse practitioner (MSN, Post Master's Certificate); nurse anesthesia (DNP); nursing practice (DNP). *Accreditation:* AACN. *Program availability:* Part-time, blended/hybrid learning. *Faculty:* 8 full-time (7 women), 12 part-time/adjunct (10 women). *Students:* 44 full-time (36 women), 72 part-time (65 women); includes 10 minority (4 Black or African American, non-Hispanic/Latino; 1 Asian, non-Hispanic/Latino; 2 Hispanic/Latino; 3 Two or more races, non-Hispanic/Latino). Average age 32. 48 applicants, 71% accepted, 29 enrolled. In 2017, 30 master's, 2 other advanced degrees awarded. *Degree requirements:* For doctorate, comprehensive exam. *Entrance requirements:* For master's, GRE (if undergraduate GPA is less than 3.0), minimum undergraduate GPA of 3.2; ASN, BSN, or MSN from regionally-accredited U.S. institution; current license as registered nurse; graduate or undergraduate statistics course within last five years; for doctorate, BSN from ACEN- or CCNE-accredited nursing program; minimum cumulative undergraduate GPA of 3.2; 2 courses in chemistry and 1 statistics course with minimum B grade; official transcripts; resume; 1 year of continuous full-time critical care experience; current Indiana RN license; 3 professional letters of recommendation; essay; interview; for Post Master's Certificate, GRE (if undergraduate GPA is less than 3.0), minimum undergraduate GPA of 3.2; MSN from regionally-accredited U.S. institution; current license as registered nurse; graduate or undergraduate statistics course within last five years. Additional exam requirements/recommendations for international students: Required—TOEFL (minimum score 550 paper-based; 100 iBT), IELTS (minimum score 6.5), TWE (minimum score 5). *Application deadline:* For fall admission, 7/1 for international students; for spring admission, 11/1 for international students; for summer admission, 3/1 for international students. Applications are processed on a rolling basis. Application fee: $0. Electronic applications accepted. *Expenses:* $905 per hour (for MSN); $1,055 per hour (for DNP). *Financial support:* In 2017–18, 21 students received support. Federal Work-Study, scholarships/grants, and unspecified assistantships available. Financial award application deadline: 4/15; financial award applicants required to submit FAFSA. *Unit head:* Dr. Wendy Clark, Program Director, Master of Science in Nursing, 260-399-7700 Ext. 8534, Fax: 260-399-8167, E-mail: wclark@sf.edu. *Application contact:* Kyle Richardson, Associate Director of Enrollment Services for Adult Learning, 260-399-7700 Ext. 6310, Fax: 260-399-8152, E-mail: krichardson@sf.edu.
Website: https://nursing.sf.edu/

University of St. Francis, Leach College of Nursing, Joliet, IL 60435-6169. Offers family nurse practitioner (MSN, Post-Master's Certificate); nursing administration (MSN); nursing education (MSN); nursing practice (DNP); psychology/mental health nurse practitioner (MSN, Post-Master's Certificate); teaching in nursing (Certificate). *Accreditation:* AACN. *Program availability:* Part-time, evening/weekend, 100% online. *Faculty:* 9 full-time (all women), 12 part-time/adjunct (11 women). *Students:* 66 full-time (61 women), 292 part-time (262 women); includes 136 minority (67 Black or African American, non-Hispanic/Latino; 2 American Indian or Alaska Native, non-Hispanic/Latino; 25 Asian, non-Hispanic/Latino; 29 Hispanic/Latino; 3 Native Hawaiian or other Pacific Islander, non-Hispanic/Latino; 10 Two or more races, non-Hispanic/Latino). Average age 40. 280 applicants, 34% accepted, 81 enrolled. In 2017, 117 master's, 5 doctorates, 12 other advanced degrees awarded. *Degree requirements:* For master's, comprehensive exam. *Entrance requirements:* Additional exam requirements/recommendations for international students: Required—TOEFL (minimum score 550 paper-based; 79 iBT), IELTS (minimum score 6). *Application deadline:* Applications are processed on a rolling basis. Application fee: $30. Electronic applications accepted. Application fee is waived when completed online. *Expenses:* $775 per credit hour. *Financial support:* In 2017–18, 115 students received support. Scholarships/grants available. Support available to part-time students. Financial award applicants required to submit FAFSA. *Unit head:* Dr. Carol Wilson, Dean, 815-740-3840, Fax: 815-740-4243, E-mail: cwilson@stfrancis.edu. *Application contact:* Sandra Sloka, Director of Admissions for Graduate and Degree Completion Programs, 800-735-7500, Fax: 815-740-3431, E-mail: ssloka@stfrancis.edu.
Website: http://www.stfrancis.edu/academics/college-of-nursing/

University of Saint Joseph, Department of Nursing, West Hartford, CT 06117-2700. Offers family nurse practitioner (MS); nurse educator (MS); nursing practice (DNP); psychiatric/mental health nurse practitioner (MS). *Accreditation:* AACN. *Program availability:* Part-time, evening/weekend. *Degree requirements:* For master's, thesis. *Entrance requirements:* For master's, 2 letters of recommendation. *Application deadline:* Applications are processed on a rolling basis. Application fee: $50. Electronic applications accepted. Application fee is waived when completed online. *Financial support:* Career-related internships or fieldwork and unspecified assistantships available. Support available to part-time students. Financial award applicants required to submit FAFSA.
Website: http://www.usj.edu/academics/schools/school-of-health-natural-sciences/nursing/

University of San Diego, Hahn School of Nursing and Health Science, San Diego, CA 92110-2492. Offers adult-gerontology clinical nurse specialist (MSN); adult-gerontology nurse practitioner/family nurse practitioner (MSN); clinical nurse leader (MSN); executive nurse leader (MSN); family nurse practitioner (MSN); healthcare informatics (MS, MSN); nursing (PhD); nursing practice (DNP); pediatric/family nurse practitioner (MSN); psychiatric-mental health nurse practitioner (MSN). *Accreditation:* AACN. *Program availability:* Part-time, evening/weekend. *Faculty:* 26 full-time (21 women), 36 part-time/adjunct (29 women). *Students:* 238 full-time (198 women), 230 part-time (167 women); includes 230 minority (32 Black or African American, non-Hispanic/Latino; 104 Asian, non-Hispanic/Latino; 75 Hispanic/Latino; 19 Two or more races, non-Hispanic/Latino), 12 international. Average age 35. In 2017, 93 master's, 44 doctorates awarded. *Degree requirements:* For doctorate, thesis/dissertation (for some programs), residency (DNP). *Entrance requirements:* For master's, GRE General Test (for entry-level nursing), BSN, current California RN licensure (except for entry-level nursing), minimum GPA of 3.0; for doctorate, minimum GPA of 3.5, MSN, current California RN licensure. Additional exam requirements/recommendations for international students: Required—TOEFL (minimum score 580 paper-based; 83 iBT), TWE. *Application deadline:* Applications are processed on a rolling basis. Application fee: $45. Electronic applications accepted. *Financial support:* In 2017–18, 242 students received support. Scholarships/grants and traineeships available. Support available to part-time students. Financial award application deadline: 4/1; financial award applicants required to submit FAFSA. *Faculty research:* Maternal/neonatal health, palliative and end of life care, adolescent obesity, health disparities, cognitive dysfunction. *Unit head:* Dr. Janes Georges, Interim Dean, 619-260-4550, Fax: 619-260-6814, E-mail: nursing@sandiego.edu. *Application contact:* Monica Mahon, Associate Director of Graduate Admissions, 619-260-4524, Fax: 619-260-4158, E-mail: grads@sandiego.edu.
Website: http://www.sandiego.edu/nursing/

The University of Scranton, Panuska College of Professional Studies, Department of Nursing, Scranton, PA 18510-4595. Offers family nurse practitioner (MSN, PMC); nurse anesthesia (MSN, PMC); nursing leadership (DNP). Applicants accepted in odd-numbered years only. *Accreditation:* AACN; AANA/CANAEP. *Program availability:* Part-time, evening/weekend. *Degree requirements:* For master's, comprehensive exam (for some programs), thesis (for some programs), capstone experience. *Entrance requirements:* For master's, minimum GPA of 3.0, three letters of reference; for doctorate, RN licensure and evidence of certification in advanced practice nursing specialty. Additional exam requirements/recommendations for international students: Required—TOEFL (minimum score 500 paper-based; 80 iBT), IELTS (minimum score 6.5). Electronic applications accepted. *Faculty research:* Home care, doctoral education, health care of women and children, pain, health promotion and adolescence.

University of South Carolina, The Graduate School, College of Nursing, Program in Health Nursing, Columbia, SC 29208. Offers adult nurse practitioner (MSN); community/public health clinical nurse specialist (MSN); family nurse practitioner (MSN); pediatric nurse practitioner (MSN). *Accreditation:* AACN. *Program availability:* Part-time. *Degree requirements:* For master's, thesis or alternative. *Entrance requirements:* For master's, GRE General Test or MAT, BS in nursing, nursing license. Additional exam requirements/recommendations for international students: Required—TOEFL (minimum score 570 paper-based). Electronic applications accepted. *Faculty research:* System research, evidence based practice, breast cancer, violence.

University of Southern Indiana, Graduate Studies, College of Nursing and Health Professions, Program in Nursing, Evansville, IN 47712-3590. Offers adult-gerontology acute care nurse practitioner (MSN, PMC); adult-gerontology clinical nurse specialist (MSN, PMC); adult-gerontology primary care nurse practitioner (MSN, PMC); advanced nursing practice (DNP); family nurse practiioner (MSN); family nurse practitioner (PMC); nursing education (MSN, PMC); nursing management and leadership (MSN, PMC); organizational and systems leadership (DNP); psychiatric mental health nurse practitioner (MSN, PMC). *Accreditation:* AACN. *Program availability:* Part-time, online learning. *Faculty:* 9 full-time (8 women), 2 part-time/adjunct (both women). *Students:* 73 full-time (59 women), 370 part-time (314 women); includes 47 minority (18 Black or African American, non-Hispanic/Latino; 2 American Indian or Alaska Native, non-Hispanic/Latino; 10 Asian, non-Hispanic/Latino; 12 Hispanic/Latino; 1 Native Hawaiian or other Pacific Islander, non-Hispanic/Latino; 4 Two or more races, non-Hispanic/Latino), 1 international. Average age 36. In 2017, 91 master's, 10 doctorates, 18 other advanced degrees awarded. *Entrance requirements:* For master's, BSN from nationally-accredited school; minimum cumulative GPA of 3.0; satisfactory completion of a course in undergraduate statistics (minimum grade C); one year of full-time experience or 2,000 hours of clinical practice as an RN (recommended); unencumbered U.S. RN license; for doctorate, minimum GPA of 3.0, completion of graduate research course with minimum B grade, unencumbered RN license, resume/curriculum vitae, three professional references, 1-2 page narrative of practice experience and professional goals, Capstone Project Information form. Additional exam requirements/recommendations for international students: Required—TOEFL (minimum score 550 paper-based; 79 iBT), IELTS (minimum score 6). *Application deadline:* For fall admission, 2/1 for domestic students, 1/1 priority date for international students. Applications are processed on a rolling basis. Application fee: $40. Electronic applications accepted. *Expenses:* Contact institution. *Financial support:* In 2017–18, 1 student received support. Federal Work-Study, scholarships/grants, tuition waivers (full and partial), and unspecified assistantships available. Financial award application deadline: 3/1; financial award applicants required to submit FAFSA. *Unit head:* Dr. Mellisa A. Hall, Chair of the Master of Science in Nursing Program, 812-465-1168, E-mail: mhall@usi.edu. *Application contact:* Dr. Mayola Rowser, Director, Graduate Studies, 812-465-7015, Fax: 812-464-1956, E-mail: mrowser@usi.edu.
Website: https://www.usi.edu/health/nursing/

University of Southern Maine, College of Science, Technology, and Health, School of Nursing, Portland, ME 04103. Offers adult-gerontology primary care nurse practitioner (MS, PMC); education (MS); family nurse practitioner (MS, PMC); family psychiatric/mental health nurse practitioner (MS); management (MS); nursing (CAS, CGS); psychiatric-mental health nurse practitioner (PMC). *Accreditation:* AACN. *Program availability:* Part-time. *Degree requirements:* For master's, thesis optional. *Entrance requirements:* For master's, GRE General Test or MAT, minimum GPA of 3.0; for doctorate, GRE. Additional exam requirements/recommendations for international students: Required—TOEFL (minimum score 550 paper-based). Electronic applications accepted. *Faculty research:* Women's health, nursing history, weight control, community services, substance abuse.

University of South Florida, College of Nursing, Tampa, FL 33612. Offers nurse anesthesia (DNP); nursing (MS, DNP), including adult-gerontology acute care nursing, adult-gerontology primary care nursing, family health nursing, nurse anesthesia (MS), nursing education (MS), occupational health nursing/adult-gerontology primary care nursing, oncology nursing/adult-gerontology primary care nursing (DNP), pediatric health nursing; nursing education (Post Master's Certificate); nursing science (PhD); simulation based academic fellowship in advanced pain management (Graduate Certificate). *Accreditation:* AACN; AANA/CANAEP. *Program availability:* Part-time. *Faculty:* 37 full-time (32 women), 2 part-time/adjunct (1 woman). *Students:* 224 full-time (178 women), 669 part-time (577 women); includes 309 minority (105 Black or African American, non-Hispanic/Latino; 2 American Indian or Alaska Native, non-Hispanic/Latino; 53 Asian, non-Hispanic/Latino; 122 Hispanic/Latino; 1 Native Hawaiian or other Pacific Islander, non-Hispanic/Latino; 26 Two or more races, non-Hispanic/Latino), 6 international. Average age 32. 949 applicants, 47% accepted, 382 enrolled. In 2017, 264 master's, 39 doctorates awarded. *Degree requirements:* For master's, comprehensive exam, thesis optional; for doctorate, comprehensive exam, thesis/dissertation. *Entrance requirements:* For master's, GRE General Test, bachelor's degree from accredited program with minimum GPA of 3.0 in all upper-division coursework; current license as Registered Nurse; 3 letters of recommendation; personal statement of goals; resume or curriculum vitae; personal interview; for doctorate, GRE General Test (recommended), bachelor's degree in nursing from ACEN or CCNE regionally-accredited institution with minimum GPA of 3.0 in all coursework or in all upper-division coursework; current license as Registered Nurse in Florida; undergraduate statistics course with minimum B grade; 3 letters of recommendation; statement of goals; resume; interview. Additional

exam requirements/recommendations for international students: Required—TOEFL (minimum score 550 paper-based; 79 iBT). *Application deadline:* For fall admission, 12/15 for domestic and international students; for spring admission, 10/1 for domestic students, 9/15 for international students. Application fee: $30. Electronic applications accepted. *Financial support:* In 2017–18, 132 students received support, including 7 research assistantships with tuition reimbursements available (averaging $18,935 per year), 29 teaching assistantships with tuition reimbursements available (averaging $30,814 per year); tuition waivers (partial) and unspecified assistantships also available. Financial award application deadline: 2/1; financial award applicants required to submit FAFSA. *Faculty research:* Women's health, palliative and end-of-life care, cardiac rehabilitation, complementary therapies for chronic illness and cancer. *Total annual research expenditures:* $3.2 million. *Unit head:* Dr. Victoria Rich, Dean, College of Nursing, 813-974-8939, Fax: 813-974-5418, E-mail: victoriarich@health.usf.edu. *Application contact:* Dr. Brian Graves, Assistant Professor/Assistant Dean, 813-974-8054, Fax: 813-974-5418, E-mail: bgraves1@health.usf.edu.
Website: http://health.usf.edu/nursing/index.htm

The University of Tampa, Program in Nursing, Tampa, FL 33606-1490. Offers adult nursing practitioner (MSN); family nursing practitioner (MSN); nursing (MS). *Accreditation:* ACEN. *Program availability:* Part-time, evening/weekend. *Faculty:* 7 full-time (6 women), 6 part-time/adjunct (all women). *Students:* 4 full-time (all women), 166 part-time (148 women); includes 29 minority (15 Black or African American, non-Hispanic/Latino; 8 Asian, non-Hispanic/Latino; 6 Two or more races, non-Hispanic/Latino), 2 international. Average age 33. 132 applicants, 64% accepted, 51 enrolled. In 2017, 45 master's awarded. *Degree requirements:* For master's, comprehensive exam, oral exam, practicum. *Entrance requirements:* For master's, GMAT or GRE, current licensure as registered nurse in state of Florida; minimum GPA of 3.0 in last 60 credit hours; minimum of one year of direct patient care experience within the past five years (recommended). Additional exam requirements/recommendations for international students: Required—TOEFL (minimum score 577 paper-based; 90 iBT), IELTS (minimum score 7.5). *Application deadline:* Applications are processed on a rolling basis. Application fee: $40. Electronic applications accepted. *Expenses:* Contact institution. *Financial support:* In 2017–18, 9 students received support. Career-related internships or fieldwork, scholarships/grants, and unspecified assistantships available. Financial award applicants required to submit FAFSA. *Faculty research:* Vaccinations and public health, osteoporosis, cultural diversity, ethics, nursing practice. *Unit head:* Michele Wolf, Director, 813-257-3179, E-mail: mwolf@ut.edu. *Application contact:* Chanelle Cox, Staff Assistant, Admissions for Graduate and Continuing Studies, 813-253-6249, E-mail: ccox@ut.edu.
Website: http://www.ut.edu/msn/

The University of Tennessee at Chattanooga, School of Nursing, Chattanooga, TN 37403. Offers certified nurse anesthetist (Post-Master's Certificate); family nurse practitioner (MSN, Post-Master's Certificate); gerontology acute care (MSN, Post-Master's Certificate); nurse anesthesia (MSN); nurse education (Post-Master's Certificate); nursing (DNP). *Accreditation:* AACN; AANA/CANAEP (one or more programs are accredited). *Students:* 62 full-time (33 women), 69 part-time (61 women); includes 24 minority (11 Black or African American, non-Hispanic/Latino; 1 American Indian or Alaska Native, non-Hispanic/Latino; 5 Asian, non-Hispanic/Latino; 3 Hispanic/Latino; 4 Two or more races, non-Hispanic/Latino). Average age 34. 47 applicants, 100% accepted, 45 enrolled. In 2017, 33 master's, 14 doctorates, 7 other advanced degrees awarded. *Degree requirements:* For master's, thesis optional, qualifying exams, professional project; for doctorate, professional project; for Post-Master's Certificate, thesis or alternative, practicum, seminar. *Entrance requirements:* For master's, GRE General Test, MAT, BSN, minimum GPA of 3.0, eligibility for Tennessee RN license, 1 year of direct patient care experience; for doctorate, GRE General Test or MAT (if applicant does not have MSN), minimum GPA of 3.0 for highest degree earned; for Post-Master's Certificate, GRE General Test, MAT, MSN, minimum GPA of 3.0, eligibility for Tennessee RN license, one year of direct patient care experience. Additional exam requirements/recommendations for international students: Required—TOEFL (minimum score 550 paper-based; 79 iBT), IELTS (minimum score 6). *Application deadline:* For fall admission, 6/15 priority date for domestic students, 7/1 for international students; for spring admission, 11/1 priority date for domestic students, 11/1 for international students. Applications are processed on a rolling basis. Application fee: $35 ($40 for international students). Electronic applications accepted. *Expenses:* Contact institution. *Financial support:* Teaching assistantships, career-related internships or fieldwork, and scholarships/grants available. Support available to part-time students. Financial award application deadline: 7/1; financial award applicants required to submit FAFSA. *Faculty research:* Diabetes in women, health care for elderly, alternative medicine, hypertension, nurse anesthesia. *Total annual research expenditures:* $985,388. *Unit head:* Dr. Chris Smith, Director, 423-425-1741, Fax: 423-425-4668, E-mail: chris-smith@utc.edu. *Application contact:* Dr. Joanne Romagni, Dean of the Graduate School, 423-425-4478, Fax: 423-425-5223, E-mail: joanne-romagni@utc.edu.
Website: http://www.utc.edu/nursing/

The University of Tennessee Health Science Center, College of Nursing, Memphis, TN 38163. Offers adult-gerontology acute care nurse practitioner (Post Master's Certificate); advance practice nursing (DNP); family nurse practitioner (Post-Doctoral Certificate); pediatric acute care nurse practitioner (Post-Doctoral Certificate); pediatric primary care nurse practitioner (Post-Doctoral Certificate); psychiatric/mental health nurse practitioner (Post-Doctoral Certificate); registered nurse first assistant (Certificate). *Accreditation:* AACN; AANA/CANAEP. *Program availability:* Part-time, blended/hybrid learning. *Faculty:* 52 full-time (47 women), 11 part-time/adjunct (4 women). *Students:* 262 full-time (228 women), 13 part-time (12 women); includes 83 minority (71 Black or African American, non-Hispanic/Latino; 6 Asian, non-Hispanic/Latino; 6 Hispanic/Latino). Average age 32. 215 applicants, 49% accepted, 79 enrolled. In 2017, 78 doctorates, 2 Certificates awarded. *Degree requirements:* For doctorate, project. *Entrance requirements:* For doctorate, RN license, minimum GPA of 3.0; for other advanced degree, MSN, APN license, minimum GPA of 3.0. Additional exam requirements/recommendations for international students: Required—TOEFL (minimum score 550 paper-based; 80 iBT). *Application deadline:* For fall admission, 1/15 for domestic students; for spring admission, 8/15 for domestic students. Application fee: $70. Electronic applications accepted. *Expenses:* $13,420 in-state tuition and fees; $17,222 out-of-state tuition and fees. *Financial support:* In 2017–18, 112 students received support, including 9 research assistantships (averaging $24,783 per year); Federal Work-Study, institutionally sponsored loans, scholarships/grants, and tuition waivers (partial) also available. Financial award application deadline: 3/15; financial award applicants required to submit FAFSA. *Faculty research:* Efficacy of a cognitive behavioral group intervention and its influence on symptoms of depression and anxiety as well as caregiver function; quality of life and sexual function in women who undergo vulvar surgeries; influence of prenatal and early childhood environments on health and developmental trajectories across childhood; interaction between physical activity, diet, genetics, insulin resistance, and obesity. *Total annual research expenditures:* $1.2 million. *Unit head:* Dr. Wendy Likes, Dean, 901-448-6135, Fax: 901-448-4121, E-mail: wlikes@uthsc.edu. *Application contact:* Jamie Overton, Director, Student Affairs, 901-448-6139, Fax: 901-448-4121, E-mail: joverton@uthsc.edu.
Website: http://uthsc.edu/nursing/

The University of Texas at Arlington, Graduate School, College of Nursing and Health Innovation, Arlington, TX 76019. Offers athletic training (MS); exercise science (MS); kinesiology (PhD); nurse practitioner (MSN); nursing (PhD); nursing administration (MSN); nursing education (MSN); nursing practice (DNP). *Accreditation:* AACN. *Program availability:* Part-time, evening/weekend, online learning. *Degree requirements:* For master's, practicum course; for doctorate, comprehensive exam (for some programs), thesis/dissertation (for some programs), proposal defense dissertation (for PhD); scholarship project (for DNP). *Entrance requirements:* For master's, GRE General Test if GPA less than 3.0, minimum GPA of 3.0, Texas nursing license, minimum C grade in undergraduate statistics course; for doctorate, GRE General Test (waived for MSN-to-PhD applicants), minimum undergraduate, graduate and statistics GPA of 3.0; Texas RN license; interview; written statement of goals. Additional exam requirements/recommendations for international students: Required—TOEFL (minimum score 550 paper-based), IELTS (minimum score 7). *Faculty research:* Simulation in clinical education and practice, cultural diversity, vulnerable populations, substance abuse.

The University of Texas at Austin, Graduate School, School of Nursing, Austin, TX 78712-1111. Offers adult - gerontology clinical nurse specialist (MSN); child health (MSN), including administration, public health nursing, teaching; family nurse practitioner (MSN); family psychiatric/mental health nurse practitioner (MSN); holistic adult health (MSN), including administration, teaching; maternity (MSN), including administration, public health nursing, teaching; nursing (PhD); nursing administration and healthcare systems management (MSN); nursing practice (DNP); pediatric nurse practitioner (MSN); public health nursing (MSN). *Accreditation:* AACN. *Program availability:* Part-time. *Degree requirements:* For master's, thesis optional; for doctorate, thesis/dissertation. *Entrance requirements:* For master's and doctorate, GRE General Test. Additional exam requirements/recommendations for international students: Required—TOEFL (minimum score 550 paper-based). Electronic applications accepted. *Faculty research:* Chronic illness management, memory and aging, health promotion, women's health, adolescent health.

The University of Texas at El Paso, Graduate School, School of Nursing, El Paso, TX 79968-0001. Offers family nurse practitioner (MSN); health care leadership and management (Certificate); interdisciplinary health sciences (PhD); nursing (DNP); nursing education (MSN, Certificate); nursing systems management (MSN). *Accreditation:* AACN. *Program availability:* Online learning. *Degree requirements:* For master's, thesis optional; for doctorate, thesis/dissertation. *Entrance requirements:* For master's, minimum GPA of 3.0, resume; for doctorate, GRE, letters of reference, relevant personal/professional experience; master's degree in nursing (for DNP); for Certificate, bachelor's degree in nursing. Additional exam requirements/recommendations for international students: Required—TOEFL; Recommended—IELTS. *Application deadline:* For fall admission, 8/1 for domestic students, 3/1 for international students; for spring admission, 11/1 for domestic students, 9/1 for international students. Applications are processed on a rolling basis. Application fee: $45 ($80 for international students). Electronic applications accepted. *Financial support:* Fellowships with partial tuition reimbursements, research assistantships with partial tuition reimbursements, teaching assistantships with partial tuition reimbursements, institutionally sponsored loans, scholarships/grants, health care benefits, tuition waivers (partial), and unspecified assistantships available. Support available to part-time students. Financial award application deadline: 3/15; financial award applicants required to submit FAFSA. *Unit head:* Dr. Elias Provencio-Vasquez, Dean, 915-747-8194, Fax: 915-747-8266, E-mail: eprovenciovasquez@utep.edu. *Application contact:* Dr. Benjamin Flores, Interim Dean of the Graduate School, 915-747-5491, Fax: 915-747-5788, E-mail: bflores@utep.edu.
Website: http://nursing.utep.edu/

The University of Texas at Tyler, College of Nursing and Health Sciences, Program in Nursing, Tyler, TX 75799-0001. Offers nurse practitioner (MSN); nursing (PhD); nursing administration (MSN); nursing education (MSN); MSN/MBA. *Accreditation:* AACN. *Program availability:* Part-time, evening/weekend, online learning. *Degree requirements:* For master's, comprehensive exam (for some programs), thesis (for some programs); for doctorate, thesis/dissertation. *Entrance requirements:* For master's, GRE General Test or MAT, GMAT, minimum undergraduate GPA of 3.0, course work in statistics, RN license, BSN. Additional exam requirements/recommendations for international students: Required—TOEFL. Electronic applications accepted. *Faculty research:* Psychosocial adjustment, aging, support/commitment of caregivers, psychological abuse and violence, hope/hopelessness, professional values, end of life care, suicidology, clinical supervision, workforce retention and issues, global health issues, health promotion.

The University of Texas Health Science Center at San Antonio, School of Nursing, San Antonio, TX 78229-3900. Offers administrative management (MSN); adult-gerontology acute care nurse practitioner (PGC); advanced practice leadership (DNP); clinical nurse leader (MSN); executive administrative management (DNP); family nurse practitioner (MSN, PGC); nursing (MSN, PhD); nursing education (MSN, PGC); pediatric nurse practitioner primary care (PGC); psychiatric mental health nurse practitioner (PGC); public health nurse leader (DNP). *Accreditation:* AACN. *Program availability:* Part-time. Terminal master's awarded for partial completion of doctoral program. *Degree requirements:* For master's, thesis optional; for doctorate, comprehensive exam, thesis/dissertation.

The University of Texas Rio Grande Valley, College of Health Affairs, School of Nursing, Edinburg, TX 78539. Offers adult health nursing (MSN); family nurse practitioner (MSN); nursing administration (MSN); nursing education (MSN); psychiatric mental health nursing (Post Master's Certificate). *Accreditation:* AACN. *Program availability:* Part-time, evening/weekend. *Faculty:* 7 full-time (all women), 5 part-time/adjunct (3 women). *Students:* 48 full-time, 5 part-time; includes 43 minority (5 Black or African American, non-Hispanic/Latino; 38 Hispanic/Latino). Average age 31. 61 applicants. In 2017, 46 master's awarded. *Degree requirements:* For master's, thesis optional. *Entrance requirements:* For master's, Texas RN licensure, undergraduate physical statistic course. Additional exam requirements/recommendations for international students: Required—TOEFL (minimum score 550 paper-based). *Application deadline:* For fall admission, 7/1 priority date for domestic and international students; for spring admission, 10/1 priority date for domestic and international students. Applications are processed on a rolling basis. Application fee: $50. Electronic applications accepted. *Expenses:* Contact institution. *Financial support:* Scholarships/grants and traineeships available. Financial award application deadline: 9/1; financial award applicants required to submit FAFSA. *Faculty research:* Health promotion, adolescent pregnancy, herbal and nontraditional approaches, healing touch stress. *Unit head:* Dr. Eloisa G. Tamez, Professor/Chief Nursing Administrator, 956-665-3616, Fax: 956-665-5252, E-mail: eloisa.tamez@utrgv.edu. *Application contact:* Dr. Beatriz Bautista, Clinical Professor, 956-665-3497, Fax: 956-665-3491, E-mail: beatriz.bautista@utrgv.edu.
Website: http://www.utrgv.edu/nursing/

The University of Toledo, College of Graduate Studies, College of Nursing, Department of Population and Community Care, Toledo, OH 43606-3390. Offers clinical nurse leader (MSN); family nurse practitioner (MSN, Certificate); nurse educator (MSN, Certificate); pediatric nurse practitioner (MSN, Certificate). *Program availability:* Part-time. *Degree requirements:* For master's, thesis or alternative. *Entrance requirements:*

For master's, GRE, BS in nursing, minimum undergraduate GPA of 3.0, statement of purpose, three letters of recommendation, transcripts from all prior institutions attended, Nursing CAS application, UT supplemental application; for Certificate, BS in nursing, minimum undergraduate GPA of 3.0, statement of purpose, three letters of recommendation, transcripts from all prior institutions attended. Additional exam requirements/recommendations for international students: Required—TOEFL (minimum score 550 paper-based; 80 iBT). Electronic applications accepted.

The University of Tulsa, Graduate School, Oxley College of Health Sciences, School of Nursing, Tulsa, OK 74104-3189. Offers adult-gerontology acute care nurse practitioner (DNP); family nurse practitioner (DNP). Summer enrollment only. *Faculty:* 18 full-time (16 women), 6 part-time/adjunct (5 women). *Students:* 27 full-time (23 women); includes 6 minority (1 Black or African American, non-Hispanic/Latino; 1 Asian, non-Hispanic/Latino; 3 Hispanic/Latino; 1 Two or more races, non-Hispanic/Latino). Average age 36. 42 applicants, 57% accepted, 21 enrolled. *Degree requirements:* For doctorate, comprehensive exam, thesis/dissertation. *Entrance requirements:* Additional exam requirements/recommendations for international students: Required—TOEFL (minimum score 550 paper-based; 91 iBT), IELTS (minimum score 6.5). Application fee: $55. Electronic applications accepted. *Expenses:* $1,040 per credit hour tuition. *Unit head:* Robin Ploeger, Interim Dean, 918-631-3170, E-mail: robin-ploeger@utulsa.edu. *Application contact:* Dr. Sheryl Stansifer, Department Chair, 918-631-3125, Fax: 918-631-2156, E-mail: sheryl-stansifer@utulsa.edu.
Website: https://healthsciences.utulsa.edu/departments-schools/nursing/nursing-graduate-programs/

University of Victoria, Faculty of Graduate Studies, Faculty of Human and Social Development, School of Nursing, Victoria, BC V8W 2Y2, Canada. Offers advanced nursing practice (advanced practice leadership option) (MN); advanced nursing practice (nurse educator option) (MN); advanced nursing practice (nurse practitioner option) (MN); nursing (PhD). *Program availability:* Part-time, online learning. *Entrance requirements:* Additional exam requirements/recommendations for international students: Required—TOEFL (minimum score 575 paper-based), IELTS (minimum score 7). Electronic applications accepted.

University of Wisconsin–Eau Claire, College of Nursing and Health Sciences, Program in Nursing, Eau Claire, WI 54702-4004. Offers adult-gerontological administration (DNP); adult-gerontological clinical nurse specialist (DNP); adult-gerontological education (MSN); adult-gerontological primary care nurse practitioner (DNP); family health administration (DNP); family health in education (MSN); family health nurse practitioner (DNP); nursing (MSN); nursing practice (DNP). *Accreditation:* AACN. *Program availability:* Part-time. Terminal master's awarded for partial completion of doctoral program. *Degree requirements:* For master's, thesis optional, 500-600 hours clinical practicum, oral and written exams. *Entrance requirements:* For master's, Wisconsin RN license, minimum GPA of 3.0, undergraduate statistics, course work in health assessment. Additional exam requirements/recommendations for international students: Required—TOEFL (minimum score 79 iBT). *Expenses:* Contact institution.

University of Wisconsin–Milwaukee, Graduate School, College of Nursing, Milwaukee, WI 53201. Offers clinical nurse specialist (Graduate Certificate); family nurse practitioner (Graduate Certificate); nursing (MN, DNP, PhD); sustainable peacebuilding (MSP). *Accreditation:* AACN. *Program availability:* Part-time. *Students:* 181 full-time (153 women), 128 part-time (117 women); includes 73 minority (23 Black or African American, non-Hispanic/Latino; 1 American Indian or Alaska Native, non-Hispanic/Latino; 17 Asian, non-Hispanic/Latino; 3 Hispanic/Latino; 29 Two or more races, non-Hispanic/Latino), 11 international. Average age 36. 154 applicants, 59% accepted, 60 enrolled. In 2017, 26 master's, 54 doctorates, 2 other advanced degrees awarded. *Entrance requirements:* For master's, GRE General Test or MAT, autobiographical sketch; for doctorate, GRE, minimum GPA of 3.2. Additional exam requirements/recommendations for international students: Required—TOEFL (minimum score 550 paper-based; 79 iBT), IELTS (minimum score 6.5). *Application deadline:* For fall admission, 1/1 priority date for domestic students; for spring admission, 9/1 for domestic students. Application fee: $56 ($96 for international students). Electronic applications accepted. *Financial support:* Fellowships, research assistantships, teaching assistantships, career-related internships or fieldwork, Federal Work-Study, health care benefits, unspecified assistantships, and project assistantships available. Support available to part-time students. Financial award application deadline: 4/15; financial award applicants required to submit FAFSA. *Unit head:* Dr. Kim Litwack, Interim Dean, 414-229-4189, E-mail: litwack@uwm.edu. *Application contact:* Student Affairs Office, 414-229-5047, E-mail: uwmnurse@uwm.edu.
Website: http://uwm.edu/nursing/

See Display on page 606 and Close-Up on page 769.

University of Wisconsin–Oshkosh, Graduate Studies, College of Nursing, Oshkosh, WI 54901. Offers adult health and illness (MSN); family nurse practitioner (MSN). *Accreditation:* AACN. *Program availability:* Part-time. *Degree requirements:* For master's, thesis or alternative, clinical paper. *Entrance requirements:* For master's, RN license, BSN, previous course work in statistics and health assessment, minimum undergraduate GPA of 3.0, letters of recommendation. Additional exam requirements/recommendations for international students: Required—TOEFL (minimum score 550 paper-based; 79 iBT). Electronic applications accepted. *Faculty research:* Adult health and illness, nurse practitioners practice, health care service, advanced practitioner roles, natural alternative complementary healthcare.

Ursuline College, School of Graduate and Professional Studies, Programs in Nursing, Pepper Pike, OH 44124-4398. Offers acute-care nurse practitioner (MSN); adult nurse practitioner (MSN); adult-gerontology acute care nurse practitioner (MSN); adult-gerontology clinical nurse specialist (MSN); adult-gerontology nurse practitioner (MSN); care management (MSN); clinical nurse specialist (MSN); family nurse practitioner (MSN); nursing (DNP); nursing education (MSN); palliative care (MSN). *Accreditation:* AACN. *Program availability:* Part-time. *Faculty:* 6 full-time (all women), 25 part-time/adjunct (23 women). *Students:* 136 applicants, 89% accepted, 85 enrolled. In 2017, 85 master's, 6 doctorates awarded. *Degree requirements:* For master's, comprehensive exam; for doctorate, thesis/dissertation. *Entrance requirements:* For master's, minimum undergraduate GPA of 3.0, bachelor's degree in nursing, eligibility for or current Ohio RN license. Additional exam requirements/recommendations for international students: Required—TOEFL (minimum score 500 paper-based). *Application deadline:* For fall admission, 8/1 priority date for domestic students. Applications are processed on a rolling basis. Application fee: $25. Electronic applications accepted. *Expenses:* $1,094 per credit hour. *Financial support:* In 2017–18, 6 students received support. Scholarships/grants available. Financial award application deadline: 3/1; financial award applicants required to submit FAFSA. *Faculty research:* Core Determinants of Health (CDH) screening tool and accompanying education, academic-practice partnerships, active learning/teaching strategies, innovative clinical education models, competency development and testing, health care policy and cultural competence. *Total annual research expenditures:* $864,511. *Unit head:* Dr. Janet Baker, Associate Dean of Graduate Nursing, 440-864-8172, Fax: 440-684-6053, E-mail: jbaker@ursuline.edu. *Application contact:* Melanie Steele, Director, Graduate Admission, 440-646-8119, Fax: 440-684-6138, E-mail: graduateadmissions@ursuline.edu.

Valdosta State University, College of Nursing and Health Sciences, Valdosta, GA 31698. Offers adult gerontology nurse practitioner (MSN); exercise physiology (MS); family nurse practitioner (MSN); family psychiatric mental health nurse practitioner (MSN). *Accreditation:* AACN. *Program availability:* Part-time, online learning. *Degree requirements:* For master's, thesis (for some programs), comprehensive written and/or oral exams. *Entrance requirements:* For master's, minimum GPA of 2.8. Additional exam requirements/recommendations for international students: Required—TOEFL (minimum score 523 paper-based). *Application deadline:* For fall admission, 7/1 for domestic and international students; for spring admission, 11/15 for domestic and international students. Applications are processed on a rolling basis. Application fee: $45. Electronic applications accepted. *Financial support:* Research assistantships with full tuition reimbursements, institutionally sponsored loans, scholarships/grants, and unspecified assistantships available. Support available to part-time students. Financial award application deadline: 7/1; financial award applicants required to submit FAFSA. *Faculty research:* Nutrition, children's health beliefs, alternative treatment modalities, job satisfaction, leadership. *Unit head:* Sheri Noviello, Dean, 229-333-5959, E-mail: srnoviello@valdosta.edu. *Application contact:* Sheri Noviello, Dean, 229-333-5959, E-mail: srnoviello@valdosta.edu.
Website: https://www.valdosta.edu/colleges/nursing-and-health-sciences/

Vanderbilt University, Vanderbilt University School of Nursing, Nashville, TN 37240. Offers adult-gerontology acute care nurse practitioner (MSN), including hospitalist, intensivist; adult-gerontology primary care nurse practitioner (MSN); emergency nurse practitioner (MSN); family nurse practitioner (MSN); healthcare leadership (MSN); neonatal nurse practitioner (MSN); nurse midwifery (MSN); nurse midwifery/family nurse practitioner (MSN); nursing (Post-Master's Certificate); nursing informatics (MSN); nursing practice (DNP); nursing science (PhD); pediatric acute care nurse practitioner (MSN); pediatric primary care nurse practitioner (MSN); psychiatric-mental health nurse practitioner (MSN); women's health nurse practitioner (MSN); women's health nurse practitioner/adult gerontology primary care nurse practitioner (MSN); MSN/M Div; MSN/MTS. *Accreditation:* AACN; ACEN (one or more programs are accredited); ACNM/ACME. *Program availability:* Part-time, 100% online, blended/hybrid learning. *Faculty:* 292 full-time (267 women), 321 part-time/adjunct (253 women). *Students:* 501 full-time (435 women), 387 part-time (355 women); includes 153 minority (40 Black or African American, non-Hispanic/Latino; 1 American Indian or Alaska Native, non-Hispanic/Latino; 27 Asian, non-Hispanic/Latino; 48 Hispanic/Latino; 4 Native Hawaiian or other Pacific Islander, non-Hispanic/Latino; 33 Two or more races, non-Hispanic/Latino), 9 international. Average age 31. 1,210 applicants, 57% accepted, 473 enrolled. In 2017, 319 master's, 47 doctorates awarded. *Degree requirements:* For doctorate, comprehensive exam, thesis/dissertation. *Entrance requirements:* For master's, GRE General Test (taken within the past 5 years), minimum B average in undergraduate course work, 3 letters of recommendation; for doctorate, GRE General Test, interview, 3 letters of recommendation from doctorally-prepared faculty, MSN, essay. Additional exam requirements/recommendations for international students: Required—TOEFL (minimum score 570 paper-based), IELTS (minimum score 6.5). *Application deadline:* For fall admission, 11/1 priority date for domestic and international students. Applications are processed on a rolling basis. Application fee: $50. Electronic applications accepted. *Expenses:* Contact institution. *Financial support:* In 2017–18, 627 students received support. Scholarships/grants available. Financial award application deadline: 3/1; financial award applicants required to submit FAFSA. *Faculty research:* Lymphedema, palliative care and bereavement, health services research including workforce, safety and quality of care, gerontology, better birth outcomes including nutrition. *Total annual research expenditures:* $2 million. *Unit head:* Dr. Linda Norman, Dean, 615-343-8876, Fax: 615-343-7711, E-mail: linda.norman@vanderbilt.edu. *Application contact:* Patricia Peerman, Assistant Dean for Enrollment Management, 615-322-3800, Fax: 615-343-0333, E-mail: vusn-admissions@vanderbilt.edu.
Website: http://www.nursing.vanderbilt.edu

Villanova University, M. Louise Fitzpatrick College of Nursing, Villanova, PA 19085. Offers adult-gerontology primary care nurse practitioner (MSN, Post Master's Certificate); family primary care nurse practitioner (MSN, Post Master's Certificate); nurse anesthesia (DNP); nursing (PhD); nursing education (MSN, Post Master's Certificate); nursing practice (DNP); pediatric primary care nurse practitioner (MSN, Post Master's Certificate). *Accreditation:* AACN; AANA/CANAEP. *Program availability:* Part-time, online learning. *Students:* 151 full-time, 199 part-time; includes 42 minority (18 Black or African American, non-Hispanic/Latino; 12 Asian, non-Hispanic/Latino; 8 Hispanic/Latino; 4 Two or more races, non-Hispanic/Latino), 10 international. 274 applicants, 43% accepted, 92 enrolled. In 2017, 70 master's, 15 doctorates awarded. *Entrance requirements:* Additional exam requirements/recommendations for international students: Required—TOEFL, IELTS. *Application deadline:* For fall admission, 7/1 for domestic and international students; for spring admission, 10/1 for domestic and international students; for summer admission, 4/1 for domestic and international students. Application fee: $50. Electronic applications accepted. *Financial support:* Fellowships, research assistantships, teaching assistantships, scholarships/grants, traineeships, and tuition waivers available. *Unit head:* Dr. Marguerite K. Schlag, Associate Professor, Assistant Dean and Director of Graduate Nursing Program, 610-519-4907, Fax: 610-519-7650, E-mail: marguerite.schlag@villanova.edu. *Application contact:* Kathleen Geibel, Assistant to Graduate Program, 610-519-4934, Fax: 610-519-7650, E-mail: kathleen.geibel@villanova.edu.
Website: http://www.nursing.villanova.edu

Virginia Commonwealth University, Graduate School, School of Nursing, Nurse Practitioner Program, Richmond, VA 23284-9005. Offers MS. *Program availability:* Part-time. *Entrance requirements:* For master's, GRE General Test, minimum GPA of 2.8. Additional exam requirements/recommendations for international students: Required—TOEFL (minimum score 600 paper-based; 100 iBT). Electronic applications accepted.

Wagner College, Division of Graduate Studies, Evelyn L. Spiro School of Nursing, Staten Island, NY 10301-4495. Offers family nurse practitioner (MS, Certificate); nurse educator (MS); nursing (DNP). *Accreditation:* ACEN (one or more programs are accredited). *Program availability:* Part-time, evening/weekend. *Faculty:* 6 full-time (all women), 6 part-time/adjunct (5 women). *Students:* 15 full-time (13 women), 223 part-time (197 women); includes 75 minority (20 Black or African American, non-Hispanic/Latino; 29 Asian, non-Hispanic/Latino; 21 Hispanic/Latino; 5 Two or more races, non-Hispanic/Latino). Average age 35. 126 applicants, 75% accepted, 69 enrolled. In 2017, 52 master's, 11 doctorates, 2 other advanced degrees awarded. *Degree requirements:* For master's, thesis optional. *Entrance requirements:* For master's, BS in nursing, current clinical experience, minimum GPA of 3.3; for Certificate, master's degree in nursing from an NLN-accredited program, minimum GPA of 3.0. Additional exam requirements/recommendations for international students: Required—TOEFL (minimum score 550 paper-based; 79 iBT), IELTS (minimum score 6.5). *Application deadline:* For fall admission, 2/1 priority date for domestic students, 2/1 for international students. Application fee: $60. Electronic applications accepted. *Financial support:* In 2017–18, 62 students received support. Traineeships, unspecified assistantships, and alumni fellowship grants available. Financial award application deadline: 2/15; financial award applicants required to submit FAFSA. *Unit head:* Dr. Patricia Tooker, Dean, 718-390-3452, Fax: 718-420-4009, E-mail: ptooker@wagner.edu. *Application contact:* Patricia Clancy, Assistant Director, 718-420-4464, Fax: 718-390-3105, E-mail: patricia.clancy@wagner.edu.
Website: http://wagner.edu/nursing/

Walden University, Graduate Programs, School of Nursing, Minneapolis, MN 55401. Offers adult-gerontology acute care nurse practitioner (MSN); adult-gerontology nurse practitioner (MSN); education (MSN); family nurse practitioner (MSN); informatics (MSN); leadership and management (MSN); nursing (PhD, Post-Master's Certificate), including education (PhD), healthcare administration (PhD), interdisciplinary health (PhD), leadership (PhD), nursing education (Post-Master's Certificate), nursing informatics (Post-Master's Certificate), nursing leadership and management (Post-Master's Certificate), public health policy (PhD); nursing practice (DNP); psychiatric mental health (MSN). *Accreditation:* AACN. *Program availability:* Part-time, evening/weekend, online only, 100% online. *Degree requirements:* For doctorate, thesis/dissertation (for some programs), residency (for some programs), field experience (for some programs). *Entrance requirements:* For master's, bachelor's degree or equivalent in related field or RN; minimum GPA of 2.5; official transcripts; goal statement (for some programs); access to computer and Internet; for doctorate, master's degree or higher; RN; three years of related professional or academic experience; goal statement; access to computer and Internet; for Post-Master's Certificate, relevant work experience; access to computer and Internet. Additional exam requirements/recommendations for international students: Required—TOEFL (minimum score 550 paper-based, 79 iBT), IELTS (minimum score 6.5), Michigan English Language Assessment Battery (minimum score 82), or PTE (minimum score 53). Electronic applications accepted.

Washington State University, College of Nursing, Spokane, WA 99210. Offers advanced population health (MN, DNP); family nurse practitioner (MN, DNP); nursing (PhD); psychiatric/mental health nurse practitioner (DNP); psychiatric/mental health practitioner (MN). Programs offered at the Spokane, Tri-Cities, and Vancouver campuses. *Accreditation:* AACN. *Degree requirements:* For master's, comprehensive exam (for some programs), thesis (for some programs), oral exam, research project. *Entrance requirements:* For master's, minimum GPA of 3.0, Washington state RN license, physical assessment skills, course work in statistics, recommendations, written interview (for nurse practitioner). *Faculty research:* Cardiovascular and Type 2 diabetes in children, evaluation of strategies to increase physical activity in sedentary people.

West Coast University, Graduate Programs, North Hollywood, CA 91606. Offers advanced generalist (MSN); family nurse practitioner (MSN); health administration (MHA); occupational therapy (MS); pharmacy (Pharm D); physical therapy (DPT).

Westminster College, School of Nursing and Health Sciences, Salt Lake City, UT 84105-3697. Offers family nurse practitioner (MSN); nurse anesthesia (MSNA); public health (MPH). *Accreditation:* AACN; AANA/CANAEP. *Faculty:* 9 full-time (5 women), 10 part-time/adjunct (5 women). *Students:* 130 full-time (81 women), 1 (woman) part-time; includes 18 minority (2 Black or African American, non-Hispanic/Latino; 1 American Indian or Alaska Native, non-Hispanic/Latino; 5 Asian, non-Hispanic/Latino; 4 Hispanic/Latino; 2 Native Hawaiian or other Pacific Islander, non-Hispanic/Latino; 4 Two or more races, non-Hispanic/Latino), 3 international. Average age 33. 149 applicants, 51% accepted, 62 enrolled. In 2017, 49 master's awarded. *Degree requirements:* For master's, clinical practicum, 504 clinical practice hours. *Entrance requirements:* For master's, GRE (can be waived in select cases), personal statement, resume, 3 professional recommendations, copy of unrestricted Utah license to practice professional nursing, background check, minimum cumulative GPA of 3.0, documentation of current immunizations, physical and mental health certificate signed by primary care provider. Additional exam requirements/recommendations for international students: Required—TOEFL (minimum score 84 iBT), IELTS (minimum score 7). Application fee: $50. Electronic applications accepted. *Expenses:* Contact institution. *Financial support:* In 2017–18, 7 students received support. Career-related internships or fieldwork, scholarships/grants, unspecified assistantships, and tuition remission available. Financial award applicants required to submit FAFSA. *Faculty research:* Intellectual empathy, professional boundaries, learned optimism, collaborative testing in nursing: student outcomes and perspectives, implementing new educational paradigms into pre-licensure nursing curricula. *Unit head:* Dr. Sheryl Steadman, Dean, 801-832-2164, Fax: 801-832-3110, E-mail: ssteadman@westminstercollege.edu. *Application contact:* Collin Bess, Enrollment Coordinator/Admissions Recruiter, 801-832-2207, Fax: 801-832-3101, E-mail: cbess@westminstercollege.edu.
Website: https://www.westminstercollege.edu/graduate/programs

West Texas A&M University, College of Nursing and Health Sciences, Department of Nursing, Canyon, TX 79015. Offers family nurse practitioner (MSN); nursing (MSN). *Accreditation:* AACN. *Program availability:* Part-time, online learning. *Degree requirements:* For master's, comprehensive exam, thesis optional. *Entrance requirements:* For master's, GRE General Test, bachelor's degree in nursing, minimum GPA of 3.0 in last 60 hours. Additional exam requirements/recommendations for international students: Required—TOEFL (minimum score 550 paper-based). Electronic applications accepted. *Faculty research:* Family-focused nursing, nursing traineeship, professional nursing.

West Virginia Wesleyan College, Department of Nursing, Buckhannon, WV 26201. Offers family nurse practitioner (MS, Post Master's Certificate); nurse administrator (MS); nurse educator (MS); nurse-midwifery (MS); nursing administration (Post Master's Certificate); nursing education (Post Master's Certificate); psychiatric mental health nurse practitioner (MS); MSN/MBA. *Accreditation:* ACEN.

Wilmington University, College of Health Professions, New Castle, DE 19720-6491. Offers adult nurse practitioner (MSN); family nurse practitioner (MSN); gerontology nurse practitioner (MSN); nursing (MSN); nursing leadership (MSN); nursing practice (DNP). *Accreditation:* AACN. *Program availability:* Part-time. *Faculty:* 10 full-time (9 women), 59 part-time/adjunct (50 women). *Students:* 164 full-time (154 women), 662 part-time (604 women); includes 178 minority (129 Black or African American, non-Hispanic/Latino; 5 American Indian or Alaska Native, non-Hispanic/Latino; 23 Asian, non-Hispanic/Latino; 7 Hispanic/Latino; 3 Native Hawaiian or other Pacific Islander, non-Hispanic/Latino; 11 Two or more races, non-Hispanic/Latino), 6 international. Average age 39. 770 applicants, 63% accepted, 361 enrolled. In 2017, 259 master's, 22 doctorates awarded. *Degree requirements:* For master's, thesis. *Entrance requirements:* For master's, BSN, RN license, interview, 3 letters of recommendation. Additional exam requirements/recommendations for international students: Required—TOEFL (minimum score 500 paper-based). *Application deadline:* For fall admission, 4/1 for domestic students; for spring admission, 9/1 for domestic students. Applications are processed on a rolling basis. Application fee: $35. Electronic applications accepted. *Expenses: Tuition:* Part-time $466 per credit. *Required fees:* $25 per semester. Tuition and fees vary according to degree level and campus/location. *Financial support:* Fellowships with tuition reimbursements and traineeships available. Financial award applicants required to submit FAFSA. *Faculty research:* Outcomes assessment, student writing ability. *Unit head:* Denise Z. Westbrook, Dean, 302-356-6915. *Application contact:* Laura Morris, Director of Admissions, 877-967-5464, E-mail: infocenter@wilmu.edu.
Website: http://www.wilmu.edu/health/

Winona State University, College of Nursing and Health Sciences, Winona, MN 55987. Offers adult-gerontology acute care nurse practitioner (MS, DNP, Post Master's Certificate); adult-gerontology clinical nurse specialist (MS, DNP, Post Master's Certificate); adult-gerontology primary care nurse practitioner (MS, DNP, Post Master's Certificate); family nurse practitioner (MS, DNP, Post Master's Certificate); nurse educator (MS); nursing and organizational leadership (MS, DNP, Post Master's Certificate); practice and leadership innovations (DNP, Post Master's Certificate). *Accreditation:* AACN. *Program availability:* Part-time, online learning. *Degree requirements:* For master's, thesis; for doctorate, capstone. *Entrance requirements:* For master's, GRE (if GPA less than 3.0). Additional exam requirements/recommendations for international students: Required—TOEFL (minimum score 550 paper-based).

Winston-Salem State University, Program in Nursing, Winston-Salem, NC 27110-0003. Offers advanced nurse educator (MSN); family nurse practitioner (MSN); nursing (DNP). *Accreditation:* AACN. *Program availability:* Part-time, evening/weekend, online learning. *Entrance requirements:* For master's, GRE, MAT, resume, NC or state compact license, 3 letters of recommendation. Electronic applications accepted. *Faculty research:* Elimination of health care disparities.

Wright State University, Graduate School, College of Nursing and Health, Program in Nursing, Dayton, OH 45435. Offers administration of nursing and health care systems (MS); adult gerontology clinical nurse specialist (MS); adult-gerontology acute care nurse practitioner (MS); family nurse practitioner (MS); neonatal nurse practitioner (MS); pediatric nurse practitioner-acute care (MS); pediatric nurse practitioner-primary care (MS); psychiatric mental health nurse practitioner (MS); school nurse (MS). *Accreditation:* AACN. *Program availability:* Part-time, evening/weekend. *Degree requirements:* For master's, thesis or alternative. *Entrance requirements:* For master's, GRE General Test, BSN from ACEN-accredited college, Ohio RN license. Additional exam requirements/recommendations for international students: Required—TOEFL. *Faculty research:* Clinical nursing and health, teaching, caring, pain administration, informatics and technology.

Forensic Nursing

Aspen University, Program in Nursing, Denver, CO 80246-1930. Offers forensic nursing (MSN); informatics (MSN); nursing (MSN); nursing administration and management (MSN); nursing education (MSN); public health (MSN).

Duquesne University, School of Nursing, Master of Science in Nursing Program, Pittsburgh, PA 15282-0001. Offers family (individual across the life span) nurse practitioner (MSN); forensic nursing (MSN); nursing education and faculty role (MSN). *Accreditation:* AACN. *Program availability:* Part-time, evening/weekend, minimal on-campus study. *Faculty:* 26 full-time (21 women), 3 part-time/adjunct (all women). *Students:* 132 full-time (118 women), 54 part-time (49 women); includes 25 minority (7 Black or African American, non-Hispanic/Latino; 2 American Indian or Alaska Native, non-Hispanic/Latino; 5 Asian, non-Hispanic/Latino; 7 Hispanic/Latino; 4 Two or more races, non-Hispanic/Latino), 1 international. Average age 33. 160 applicants, 73% accepted, 87 enrolled. In 2017, 50 master's awarded. *Entrance requirements:* For master's, current RN license; BSN with minimum GPA of 3.0; minimum of 1 year of full-time work experience as RN prior to registration in clinical or specialty course. Additional exam requirements/recommendations for international students: Required—TOEFL (minimum score 600 paper-based; 100 iBT). *Application deadline:* For fall admission, 7/16 for domestic and international students; for spring admission, 11/29 for domestic and international students; for summer admission, 4/1 for domestic and international students. Application fee: $0. Electronic applications accepted. *Expenses:* $1,312 per credit. *Financial support:* In 2017–18, 10 students received support, including 10 teaching assistantships with partial tuition reimbursements available (averaging $3,297 per year); institutionally sponsored loans, scholarships/grants, traineeships, tuition waivers (partial), and unspecified assistantships also available. Support available to part-time students. Financial award application deadline: 5/1; financial award applicants required to submit FAFSA. *Faculty research:* Vulnerable populations, cultural competence, health disparities, wellness, technology. *Total annual research expenditures:* $650,096. *Unit head:* Dr. Alison Colbert, Associate Professor/Associate Dean of Academic Affairs, 412-396-1511, Fax: 412-396-1821, E-mail: colberta@duq.edu. *Application contact:* Susan Hardner, Nurse Recruiter, 412-396-4945, Fax: 412-396-6346, E-mail: nursing@duq.edu.
Website: http://www.duq.edu/academics/schools/nursing/graduate-programs/master-science-nursing

Duquesne University, School of Nursing, Post Master's Certificate Program, Pittsburgh, PA 15282-0001. Offers family (individual across the life span) nurse practitioner (Post-Master's Certificate); forensic nursing (Post-Master's Certificate); nursing education and faculty role (Post-Master's Certificate). *Program availability:* Part-time, evening/weekend, minimal on-campus study. *Faculty:* 8 full-time (6 women), 2 part-time/adjunct (both women). *Students:* 14 full-time (all women), 6 part-time (all women); includes 3 minority (2 Black or African American, non-Hispanic/Latino; 1 American Indian or Alaska Native, non-Hispanic/Latino). Average age 43. 27 applicants, 78% accepted, 10 enrolled. In 2017, 6 Post-Master's Certificates awarded. *Entrance requirements:* For degree, current RN license, BSN, MSN. Additional exam requirements/recommendations for international students: Required—TOEFL (minimum score 600 paper-based; 100 iBT). *Application deadline:* For fall admission, 7/16 for domestic and international students; for spring admission, 11/29 for domestic and international students; for summer admission, 4/1 for domestic and international students. Application fee: $0. Electronic applications accepted. *Expenses:* $1,312 per credit. *Financial support:* Teaching assistantships with partial tuition reimbursements, institutionally sponsored loans, scholarships/grants, traineeships, and tuition waivers (partial) available. Support available to part-time students. Financial award application deadline: 5/1; financial award applicants required to submit FAFSA. *Faculty research:* Vulnerable populations, cultural competence, health disparities, wellness, technology. *Total annual research expenditures:* $650,096. *Unit head:* Dr. Alison Colbert, Associate Professor/Associate Dean of Academic Affairs, 412-396-1511, Fax: 412-396-1821, E-mail: colberta@duq.edu. *Application contact:* Susan Hardner, Nurse Recruiter, 412-396-4945, Fax: 412-396-6346, E-mail: nursing@duq.edu.
Website: http://www.duq.edu/academics/schools/nursing/graduate-programs/post-masters-certificates

Fitchburg State University, Division of Graduate and Continuing Education, Program in Forensic Nursing, Fitchburg, MA 01420-2697. Offers MS, Certificate. *Accreditation:* AACN. *Program availability:* Part-time, evening/weekend, online only, 100% online. *Faculty:* 4 full-time (2 women), 4 part-time/adjunct (all women). *Students:* 27 full-time (24 women), 31 part-time (all women); includes 13 minority (4 Black or African American, non-Hispanic/Latino; 2 American Indian or Alaska Native, non-Hispanic/Latino; 4 Hispanic/Latino; 1 Native Hawaiian or other Pacific Islander, non-Hispanic/Latino; 2 Two or more races, non-Hispanic/Latino). Average age 30. 24 applicants, 100% accepted, 22 enrolled. In 2017, 13 master's awarded. *Entrance requirements:* Additional exam requirements/recommendations for international students: Required—TOEFL (minimum score 550 paper-based; 79 iBT). *Application deadline:* For fall admission, 7/15 for international students; for spring admission, 12/1 for international students. Applications are processed on a rolling basis. Application fee: $50. Electronic applications accepted. *Expenses:* Contact institution. *Financial support:* In 2017–18, research assistantships with partial tuition reimbursements (averaging $5,500 per year) were awarded; Federal Work-Study, scholarships/grants, and unspecified assistantships also available. Support available to part-time students. Financial award application deadline: 3/1; financial award applicants required to submit FAFSA. *Unit head:* Dr. Deborah Stone, Chair, 978-665-3426, Fax: 978-665-3658, E-mail: gce@fitchburgstate.edu. *Application contact:* Jinawa McNeil, Director of Admissions, 978-665-3140, Fax: 978-665-4540, E-mail: admissions@fitchburgstate.edu.
Website: http://www.fitchburgstate.edu/

Monmouth University, Graduate Studies, Marjorie K. Unterberg School of Nursing and Health Studies, West Long Branch, NJ 07764-1898. Offers adult-gerontological primary care nurse practitioner (MSN, Post-Master's Certificate); family nurse practitioner (MSN, Post-Master's Certificate); forensic nursing (MSN, Certificate); nursing (MSN); nursing administration (MSN); nursing education (MSN, Post-Master's Certificate); nursing practice (DNP); physician assistant (MS); psychiatric and mental health nurse practitioner (MSN, Post-Master's Certificate); school nursing (MSN, Certificate). *Accreditation:* AACN. *Program availability:* Part-time, evening/weekend, 100% online, blended/hybrid learning. *Faculty:* 12 full-time (all women), 20 part-time/adjunct (12 women). *Students:* 90 full-time (66 women), 329 part-time (302 women); includes 129 minority (51 Black or African American, non-Hispanic/Latino; 43 Asian, non-Hispanic/Latino; 31 Hispanic/Latino; 1 Native Hawaiian or other Pacific Islander, non-Hispanic/Latino; 3 Two or more races, non-Hispanic/Latino), 1 international. Average age 36. In 2017, 85 master's, 4 other advanced degrees awarded. *Degree requirements:* For master's, practicum (for some tracks); for doctorate, practicum, capstone course. *Entrance requirements:* For master's, GRE General Test (waived for MSN applicants with minimum B grade in each of the first four courses and for MS applicants with master's degree), BSN with minimum GPA of 2.75, current RN license, proof of liability and malpractice policy, personal statement, two letters of recommendation, college course work in health assessment, resume; CASPA application (for MS); for doctorate, accredited master's nursing program degree with minimum GPA of 3.2, active RN license, national certification as nurse practitioner or nurse administrator, working knowledge of statistics, statement of goals and vision for change, 2 letters of recommendation (professional or academic), resume, interview. Additional exam requirements/recommendations for international students: Required—TOEFL (minimum score 550 paper-based; 79 iBT), IELTS (minimum score 6) or Michigan English Language Assessment Battery (minimum score 77). *Application deadline:* For fall admission, 7/15 priority date for domestic students, 6/1 for international students; for spring admission, 12/1 priority date for domestic students, 11/1 for international students; for summer admission, 5/1 for domestic students. Applications are processed on a rolling basis. Application fee: $50. Electronic applications accepted. *Expenses:* Contact institution. *Financial support:* In 2017–18, 197 students received support. Institutionally sponsored loans, scholarships/grants, and unspecified assistantships available. Support available to part-time students. Financial award applicants required to submit FAFSA. *Faculty research:* School nursing, health policy, and smoking cessation in teens; Multiple Sclerosis; adherence and self-efficacy; aging issues and geriatric care. *Unit head:* Dr. Janet Mahoney, Dean, 732-571-3443, Fax: 732-263-5131, E-mail: jmahoney@monmouth.edu. *Application contact:* Lucia Fedele, Graduate Admission Counselor, 732-571-3452, Fax: 732-263-5123, E-mail: gradadm@monmouth.edu.
Website: https://www.monmouth.edu/graduate/nursing-programs-of-study/

Texas A&M University, College of Nursing, Bryan, TX 77807. Offers family nurse practitioner (MSN); forensic nursing (MSN); nursing education (MSN). *Faculty:* 19. *Students:* 9 full-time (all women), 47 part-time (all women); includes 14 minority (2 Asian, non-Hispanic/Latino; 12 Hispanic/Latino). Average age 34. In 2017, 27 master's awarded. *Expenses:* Contact institution. *Financial support:* In 2017–18, 8 students received support, including 2 fellowships (averaging $4,300 per year); career-related internships or fieldwork, institutionally sponsored loans, scholarships/grants, traineeships, health care benefits, tuition waivers (full and partial), and unspecified assistantships also available. Support available to part-time students. Financial award applicants required to submit FAFSA. *Unit head:* Dr. Sharon A. Wilkerson, Founding Dean, 979-436-0111, Fax: 979-436-0098, E-mail: wilkerson@tamhsc.edu. *Application contact:* Jennifer Frank, Program Coordinator for Recruitment and Admission, 979-436-0110, E-mail: conadmissions@tamhsc.edu.
Website: http://nursing.tamhsc.edu/

Gerontological Nursing

Allen College, Graduate Programs, Waterloo, IA 50703. Offers adult-gerontology acute care nurse practitioner (MSN); community/public health nursing (MSN); education (MSN); family nurse practitioner (MSN); health sciences (Ed D); leadership in health care delivery (MSN); leadership in health care informatics (MSN); nursing (DNP); occupational therapy (MS); psychiatric mental health nurse practitioner (MSN). MSN in leadership in healthcare informatics offered in partnership with University of Minnesota. *Accreditation:* AACN; ACEN. *Program availability:* Part-time, 100% online, blended/hybrid learning. *Faculty:* 24 full-time (all women), 8 part-time/adjunct (7 women). *Students:* 106 full-time (91 women), 187 part-time (164 women); includes 22 minority (12 Black or African American, non-Hispanic/Latino; 1 American Indian or Alaska Native, non-Hispanic/Latino; 2 Asian, non-Hispanic/Latino; 3 Hispanic/Latino; 4 Two or more races, non-Hispanic/Latino), 2 international. Average age 33. 352 applicants, 56% accepted, 131 enrolled. In 2017, 73 master's, 2 doctorates awarded. *Entrance requirements:* For master's, minimum GPA of 3.0 in the last 60 hours of undergraduate coursework; for doctorate, minimum GPA of 3.25 in graduate coursework. *Application deadline:* For fall admission, 2/1 priority date for domestic students; for spring admission, 9/1 priority date for domestic students. Applications are processed on a rolling basis. Application fee: $50. Electronic applications accepted. *Expenses:* $17,860 per year. *Financial support:* In 2017–18, 97 students received support. Federal Work-Study, institutionally sponsored loans, scholarships/grants, and traineeships available. Support available to part-time students. Financial award application deadline: 8/1; financial award applicants required to submit FAFSA. *Faculty research:* Poverty. *Unit head:* Dr. Nancy Kramer, Vice Chancellor for Academic Affairs, 319-226-2040, Fax: 319-226-2070, E-mail: nancy.kramer@allencollege.edu. *Application contact:* Molly Quinn, Director of Admissions, 319-226-2001, Fax: 319-226-2010, E-mail: molly.quinn@allencollege.edu.
Website: http://www.allencollege.edu/

Alvernia University, School of Graduate Studies, Department of Nursing, Reading, PA 19607-1799. Offers adult gerontology nurse practitioner (DNP); family nurse practitioner (DNP); nursing education (MSN); nursing leadership (Graduate Certificate); nursing leadership and healthcare administration (MSN).

American University of Beirut, Graduate Programs, Rafic Hariri School of Nursing, Beirut, Lebanon. Offers adult gerontology clinical nurse specialist (MSN); community and public health nursing (MSN); nursing administration and management (MSN); psychiatric mental health clinical nurse specialist (MSN). *Accreditation:* AACN. *Faculty:* 13 full-time (12 women), 23 part-time/adjunct (18 women). *Students:* 4 full-time (3 women), 40 part-time (34 women). Average age 28. 32 applicants, 81% accepted, 9 enrolled. In 2017, 18 master's awarded. *Degree requirements:* For master's, comprehensive exam, residency and project or thesis. *Entrance requirements:* For master's, minimum cumulative average of 80, minimum of 1 year of work experience. Additional exam requirements/recommendations for international students: Required—TOEFL (minimum score 583 paper-based; 97 iBT); Recommended—IELTS (minimum score 7). *Application deadline:* For fall admission, 4/4 for domestic students. Applications are processed on a rolling basis. Application fee: $50. Electronic applications accepted. *Expenses:* $810 per credit. *Financial support:* In 2017–18, 7 students received support. Teaching assistantships, scholarships/grants, traineeships, and unspecified assistantships available. Financial award application deadline: 12/20. *Faculty research:* Pain management and palliative care, postwar PTSD, depression, anxiety, and social support, cardiovascular care, vitamin D and cognitive function, nursing workforce and health systems research. *Total annual research expenditures:* $305,241. *Unit head:* Dr. Huda Abu-Saad Huijer, Director of the Hariri School of Nursing, 961-1-350000 Ext. 5953, Fax: 961-1-744476, E-mail: hh35@aub.edu.lb. *Application contact:* Nisreen Ghalayini, Administrative Assistant, 961-1-350000 Ext. 5951, E-mail: ng28@aub.edu.lb.
Website: http://www.aub.edu.lb/hson

Arizona State University at the Tempe campus, College of Nursing and Health Innovation, Phoenix, AZ 85004. Offers advanced nursing practice (DNP); clinical research management (MS); community and public health practice (Graduate Certificate); family mental health nurse practitioner (Graduate Certificate); family nurse practitioner (Graduate Certificate); geriatric nursing (Graduate Certificate); healthcare innovation (MHI); nurse education in academic and practice settings (Graduate Certificate); nurse educator (MS); nursing and healthcare innovation (PhD). *Accreditation:* AACN. *Program availability:* Online learning. *Degree requirements:* For master's, comprehensive exam (for some programs), thesis (for some programs), interactive Program of Study (iPOS) submitted before completing 50 percent of required credit hours; for doctorate, comprehensive exam, thesis/dissertation, interactive Program of Study (iPOS) submitted before completing 50 percent of required credit hours. *Entrance requirements:* For master's and doctorate, GRE, minimum GPA of 3.0 or equivalent in last 2 years of work leading to bachelor's degree. Additional exam requirements/recommendations for international students: Required—TOEFL, IELTS, or PTE. Electronic applications accepted. *Expenses:* Contact institution.

Augusta University, College of Nursing, Doctor of Nursing Practice Program, Augusta, GA 30912. Offers adult gerontology acute care nurse practitioner (DNP); family nurse practitioner (DNP); nurse executive (DNP); nursing (DNP); nursing anesthesia (DNP); pediatric nurse practitioner (DNP); psychiatric mental health nurse practitioner (DNP). *Accreditation:* AACN; AANA/CANAEP. *Degree requirements:* For doctorate, thesis/dissertation or alternative. *Entrance requirements:* For doctorate, GRE General Test or MAT, master's degree in nursing or related field, current professional nurse licensure. Additional exam requirements/recommendations for international students: Required—TOEFL (minimum score 600 paper-based; 100 iBT). Electronic applications accepted.

Azusa Pacific University, School of Nursing, Azusa, CA 91702-7000. Offers adult clinical nurse specialist (MSN); adult-gerontology nurse practitioner (MSN); family nurse practitioner (MSN); healthcare administration and leadership (MSN); nursing (MSN, DNP, PhD); nursing education (MSN); parent-child clinical nurse specialist (MSN); psychiatric mental health nurse practitioner (MSN). *Accreditation:* AACN. *Program availability:* Part-time, evening/weekend. *Degree requirements:* For master's, thesis optional. *Entrance requirements:* For master's, BSN.

Ball State University, Graduate School, College of Health, School of Nursing, Muncie, IN 47304. Offers adult/gerontology nurse practitioner (Post Master's Certificate); evidence-based clinical practice (Postbaccalaureate Certificate); family nurse practitioner (Post Master's Certificate); nurse educator (Post Master's Certificate); nursing (MS), including family nurse practitioner, nurse administrator, nurse educator; nursing education (Postbaccalaureate Certificate); nursing practice (DNP). *Accreditation:* AACN. *Program availability:* Part-time-only, online only, 100% online. *Faculty:* 10 full-time (all women), 9 part-time/adjunct (all women). *Students:* 9 full-time (8 women), 325 part-time (299 women); includes 26 minority (13 Black or African American, non-Hispanic/Latino; 3 Asian, non-Hispanic/Latino; 7 Hispanic/Latino; 3 Two or more races, non-Hispanic/Latino). Average age 33. 190 applicants, 37% accepted, 66 enrolled. In 2017, 88 master's, 2 doctorates awarded. *Entrance requirements:* For master's, bachelor's degree in nursing, minimum GPA of 3.0, minimum C grade in at least 2 quarter or semester hours in an undergraduate research course, unencumbered license as a registered nurse in state of practice; for doctorate, advanced practice nurse (nurse practitioner, clinical nurse specialist, nurse midwife); master's degree in nursing from accredited program with minimum GPA of 3.2; graduate-level statistics, nursing research, and health assessment courses; unencumbered license as registered nurse in state of practice. Additional exam requirements/recommendations for international students: Required—TOEFL (minimum score 550 paper-based; 79 iBT), IELTS (minimum score 6.5). *Application deadline:* For fall admission, 2/9 for domestic students; for spring admission, 8/9 for domestic students. Applications are processed on a rolling basis. Application fee: $60. Electronic applications accepted. *Expenses:* Contact

institution. *Financial support:* Application deadline: 3/1; applicants required to submit FAFSA. *Unit head:* Dr. Linda Siktberg, Director, 765-285-8718, Fax: 765-285-2169, E-mail: lsiktberg@bsu.edu. *Application contact:* Shantelle Estes, Graduate Advisor, 765-285-9130, Fax: 765-285-2169, E-mail: smestes@bsu.edu.
Website: http://www.bsu.edu/nursing/

Binghamton University, State University of New York, Graduate School, Decker School of Nursing, Binghamton, NY 13902-6000. Offers adult-gerontological nursing (MS, DNP, Certificate); community health nursing (MS, DNP, Certificate); family health nursing (MS, DNP, Certificate); family psychiatric mental health nursing (MS, DNP, Certificate); nursing (PhD). *Accreditation:* AACN. *Program availability:* Part-time, evening/weekend. *Faculty:* 52 full-time (45 women). *Students:* 94 full-time (79 women), 109 part-time (94 women); includes 43 minority (21 Black or African American, non-Hispanic/Latino; 10 Asian, non-Hispanic/Latino; 7 Hispanic/Latino; 5 Two or more races, non-Hispanic/Latino), 13 international. Average age 36. 111 applicants, 95% accepted, 63 enrolled. In 2017, 53 master's, 5 doctorates, 20 other advanced degrees awarded. Terminal master's awarded for partial completion of doctoral program. *Degree requirements:* For master's, comprehensive exam, thesis; for doctorate, comprehensive exam (for some programs), thesis/dissertation. *Entrance requirements:* For master's and doctorate, GRE General Test, nursing licensure. Additional exam requirements/recommendations for international students: Required—TOEFL (minimum score 90 iBT). Application fee: $75. Electronic applications accepted. *Expenses:* Contact institution. *Financial support:* In 2017–18, 33 students received support, including 1 fellowship with partial tuition reimbursement available (averaging $16,500 per year), research assistantships with full tuition reimbursements available (averaging $12,500 per year), 1 teaching assistantship with full tuition reimbursement available (averaging $16,500 per year); career-related internships or fieldwork, Federal Work-Study, institutionally sponsored loans, traineeships, health care benefits, tuition waivers (full and partial), and unspecified assistantships also available. Financial award applicants required to submit FAFSA. *Unit head:* Dr. Mario R. Ortiz, Dean, 607-777-2311, E-mail: mortiz@binghamton.edu. *Application contact:* Ben Balkaya, Assistant Dean and Director, 607-777-2151, Fax: 607-777-2501, E-mail: balkaya@binghamton.edu.
Website: http://www.binghamton.edu/dson/

Boise State University, College of Health Sciences, School of Nursing, Boise, ID 83725-0399. Offers acute care adult gerontology (Graduate Certificate); adult gerontology acute care (MSN); adult gerontology primary care (MSN); healthcare simulation (Graduate Certificate); nursing practice (DNP); primary care adult gerontology (Graduate Certificate). *Accreditation:* AACN. *Students:* 1 (woman) full-time, 91 part-time (73 women); includes 11 minority (5 Black or African American, non-Hispanic/Latino; 2 Asian, non-Hispanic/Latino; 3 Hispanic/Latino; 1 Native Hawaiian or other Pacific Islander, non-Hispanic/Latino). Average age 43. 32 applicants, 44% accepted, 12 enrolled. In 2017, 3 master's awarded. *Entrance requirements:* For master's, minimum GPA of 3.0. Additional exam requirements/recommendations for international students: Required—TOEFL (minimum score 550 paper-based; 80 iBT), IELTS (minimum score 6). *Application deadline:* For spring admission, 10/15 priority date for domestic and international students. Applications are processed on a rolling basis. Application fee: $65 ($95 for international students). Electronic applications accepted. *Expenses:* Tuition, state resident: full-time $6471; part-time $390 per credit. Tuition, nonresident: full-time $21,787; part-time $685 per credit. *Required fees:* $2283; $100 per term. Part-time tuition and fees vary according to course load and program. *Financial support:* Scholarships/grants and unspecified assistantships available. Financial award application deadline: 10/15; financial award applicants required to submit FAFSA. *Unit head:* Dr. Ann Hubbert, Director, 208-426-3404, E-mail: annhubbert@boisestate.edu. *Application contact:* Dr. Nancy Loftus, Program Coordinator, 208-426-3819, E-mail: nancyloftus@boisestate.edu.
Website: http://hs.boisestate.edu/nursing/

Boston College, William F. Connell School of Nursing, Chestnut Hill, MA 02467. Offers adult-gerontology primary care nurse practitioner (MS); family health nursing (MS); nurse anesthesia (MS); nursing (PhD); pediatric primary care nurse practitioner (MS), including pediatric and women's health; psychiatric-mental health nursing (MS); women's health nursing (MS); MBA/MS; MS/MA; MS/PhD. MS/MBA offered jointly with Carroll School of Management, MS/MA with School of Theology and Ministry. *Accreditation:* AACN; AANA/CANAEP (one or more programs are accredited). *Program availability:* Part-time. *Faculty:* 54 full-time (48 women). *Students:* 170 full-time (153 women), 90 part-time (83 women); includes 39 minority (8 Black or African American, non-Hispanic/Latino; 10 Asian, non-Hispanic/Latino; 12 Hispanic/Latino; 9 Two or more races, non-Hispanic/Latino), 3 international. Average age 28. 360 applicants, 56% accepted, 94 enrolled. In 2017, 104 master's, 5 doctorates awarded. *Degree requirements:* For master's, comprehensive exam; for doctorate, comprehensive exam, thesis/dissertation, computer literacy exam or foreign language. *Entrance requirements:* For master's, bachelor's degree in nursing; for doctorate, GRE General Test, MS in nursing. Additional exam requirements/recommendations for international students: Required—TOEFL (minimum score 600 paper-based; 100 iBT), IELTS (minimum score 7.5). *Application deadline:* For fall admission, 9/30 for domestic and international students; for winter admission, 1/15 for domestic and international students; for spring admission, 3/15 for domestic and international students. Application fee: $40. Electronic applications accepted. *Expenses:* $1,350 per credit tuition. *Financial support:* In 2017–18, 152 students received support, including 11 fellowships with full tuition reimbursements available (averaging $24,504 per year), 29 teaching assistantships (averaging $3,768 per year); scholarships/grants, health care benefits, tuition waivers (partial), and unspecified assistantships also available. Support available to part-time students. Financial award application deadline: 4/18; financial award applicants required to submit FAFSA. *Faculty research:* Sexual and reproductive health, health promotion/illness prevention, aging, eating disorders, symptom management. *Total annual research expenditures:* $879,812. *Unit head:* Dr. Susan Gennaro, Dean, 617-552-4251, Fax: 617-552-0931, E-mail: susan.gennaro@bc.edu. *Application contact:* Sean Sendall, Assistant Dean, Graduate Enrollment and Data Analytics, 617-552-4745, Fax: 617-552-2121, E-mail: sean.sendall@bc.edu.
Website: http://www.bc.edu/cson

California State University, Stanislaus, College of Science, Master's in Nursing Program, Turlock, CA 95382. Offers gerontological nursing (MS); nursing education (MS). *Accreditation:* AACN. *Program availability:* Part-time. *Degree requirements:* For master's, comprehensive exam, thesis or alternative. *Entrance requirements:* For master's, GRE or MAT, minimum GPA of 3.0, 3 letters of reference, RN. Additional exam requirements/recommendations for international students: Required—TOEFL (minimum score 550 paper-based). Electronic applications accepted.

Capella University, School of Public Service Leadership, Master's Programs in Nursing, Minneapolis, MN 55402. Offers diabetes nursing (MSN); general nursing (MSN); gerontology nursing (MSN); health information management (MS); nurse educator (MSN); nursing leadership and administration (MSN). *Accreditation:* AACN.

Caribbean University, Graduate School, Bayamón, PR 00960-0493. Offers administration and supervision (MA Ed); criminal justice (MA); curriculum and instruction (MA Ed, PhD), including elementary education (MA Ed), English education (MA Ed), history education (MA Ed), mathematics education (MA Ed), primary education (MA Ed), science education (MA Ed), Spanish education (MA Ed); educational technology in instructional systems (MA Ed); gerontology (MSN); human resources (MBA); museology, archiving and art history (MA Ed); neonatal pediatrics (MSN); physical education (MA Ed); special education (MA Ed). *Entrance requirements:* For master's, interview, minimum GPA of 2.5.

Case Western Reserve University, Frances Payne Bolton School of Nursing, Master's Programs in Nursing, Nurse Practitioner Program, Cleveland, OH 44106. Offers acute care pediatric nurse practitioner (MSN); acute care/cardiovascular nursing (MSN); acute care/flight nurse (MSN); adult gerontology acute care nurse practitioner (MSN); adult gerontology primary care nurse practitioner (MSN); family nurse practitioner (MSN); family systems psychiatric mental health nursing (MSN); neonatal nurse practitioner (MSN); palliative care (MSN); pediatric nurse practitioner (MSN); women's health nurse practitioner (MSN). *Accreditation:* ACEN. *Program availability:* Part-time. *Faculty:* 30 full-time (26 women), 5 part-time/adjunct (3 women). *Students:* 34 full-time (28 women), 97 part-time (73 women); includes 24 minority (5 Black or African American, non-Hispanic/Latino; 9 Asian, non-Hispanic/Latino; 6 Hispanic/Latino; 4 Two or more races, non-Hispanic/Latino), 4 international. Average age 33. 56 applicants, 82% accepted, 29 enrolled. In 2017, 68 master's awarded. *Degree requirements:* For master's, minimum GPA of 3.0, clinical hours corresponding to requirements to sit for certification exam, portfolio. *Entrance requirements:* For master's, GRE General Test or MAT. Additional exam requirements/recommendations for international students: Required—TOEFL (minimum score 577 paper-based; 90 iBT), IELTS (minimum score 7). *Application deadline:* For fall admission, 5/1 for domestic and international students; for spring admission, 10/1 for domestic and international students; for summer admission, 3/1 for domestic and international students. Applications are processed on a rolling basis. Application fee: $75. Electronic applications accepted. *Expenses:* $2,011 per credit tuition; $15 nursing activity fee; $17 activity fee. *Financial support:* In 2017–18, 86 students received support, including 19 teaching assistantships with partial tuition reimbursements available (averaging $18,100 per year); scholarships/grants and traineeships also available. Support available to part-time students. Financial award application deadline: 5/15; financial award applicants required to submit FAFSA. *Faculty research:* Symptom science, family/community care, aging across the lifespan, self-management of health and illness, neuroscience. *Unit head:* Dr. Latina Brooks, Director, 216-368-1196, Fax: 216-368-3542, E-mail: lmb3@case.edu. *Application contact:* Jackie Tepale, Admissions Coordinator, 216-368-5253, Fax: 216-368-0124, E-mail: yyd@case.edu.
Website: http://fpb.cwru.edu/MSN/majors.shtm

Clemson University, Graduate School, College of Behavioral, Social and Health Sciences, School of Nursing, Clemson, SC 29634. Offers clinical and translational research (PhD); global health (Certificate), including low resource countries; healthcare genetics (PhD); nursing (MS, DNP), including adult/gerontology nurse practitioner (MS), family nurse practitioner (MS). *Accreditation:* AACN. *Program availability:* Part-time, 100% online, blended/hybrid learning. *Faculty:* 37 full-time (35 women). *Students:* 130 full-time (118 women), 195 part-time (170 women); includes 50 minority (23 Black or African American, non-Hispanic/Latino; 5 Asian, non-Hispanic/Latino; 16 Hispanic/Latino; 6 Two or more races, non-Hispanic/Latino), 14 international. Average age 34. 71 applicants, 66% accepted, 33 enrolled. In 2017, 88 master's, 2 doctorates, 10 other advanced degrees awarded. *Degree requirements:* For master's, comprehensive exam, thesis or alternative; for doctorate, comprehensive exam, thesis/dissertation. *Entrance requirements:* For master's, GRE General Test, South Carolina RN license, unofficial transcripts, resume, letters of recommendation; for doctorate, GRE General Test, unofficial transcripts, MS/MA thesis or publications, curriculum vitae, statement of career goals, letters of recommendation. Additional exam requirements/recommendations for international students: Required—TOEFL (minimum score 80 iBT), IELTS (minimum score 6.5), PTE (minimum score 54). *Application deadline:* For fall admission, 3/1 priority date for domestic and international students; for spring admission, 10/1 priority date for domestic and international students. Application fee: $80 ($90 for international students). Electronic applications accepted. *Expenses:* Contact institution. *Financial support:* In 2017–18, 41 students received support, including 46 teaching assistantships with partial tuition reimbursements available (averaging $4,919 per year); career-related internships or fieldwork and unspecified assistantships also available. Financial award application deadline: 3/1. *Faculty research:* Breast cancer, healthcare, genetics, international healthcare, educational innovation and technology. *Total annual research expenditures:* $371,674. *Unit head:* Dr. Kathleen Valentine, Director and Associate College Dean, 864-656-4758, E-mail: klvalen@clemson.edu. *Application contact:* Dr. Stephanie Davis, Graduate Studies Coordinator, 864-656-2588, E-mail: stephad@clemson.edu.
Website: http://www.clemson.edu/cbshs/departments/nursing/

College of Staten Island of the City University of New York, Graduate Programs, School of Health Sciences, DNP Program in Adult-Gerontological Health Nursing, Staten Island, NY 10314-6600. Offers DNP. *Program availability:* Part-time. *Students:* 3. *Degree requirements:* For doctorate, 75 credits with minimum of 1,000 supervised hours toward development of clinical competencies for primary care of the adult-gerontological population and implementation of an integrative practice project in the clinical setting. *Entrance requirements:* For doctorate, GRE taken within last five years, bachelor's degree from regionally-accredited college with minimum GPA of 3.25 and at least one year of experience in nursing or bachelor's degree in another field with three years of clinical experience; RN license in NY state. Additional exam requirements/recommendations for international students: Required—TOEFL (minimum score 550 paper-based; 79 iBT), IELTS (minimum score 6.5). *Application deadline:* For fall admission, 12/1 for domestic and international students. Applications are processed on a rolling basis. Application fee: $125. Electronic applications accepted. *Expenses:* Contact institution. *Financial support:* Applicants required to submit FAFSA. *Faculty research:* LGBTQ Healthcare; smoking cessation; caregivers of persons with autism; end of life decision-making/compassionate care; burn survivors. *Unit head:* Prof. Catherine Paradiso, 718-982-3838, E-mail: catherine.paradiso@csi.cuny.edu. *Application contact:* Sasha Spence, Associate Director for Graduate Admissions, 718-982-2019, Fax: 718-982-2500, E-mail: sasha.spence@csi.cuny.edu.
Website: https://www.csi.cuny.edu/sites/default/files/pdf/admissions/grad/pdf/DNP%20Nursing%20Fact%20Sheet.pdf

College of Staten Island of the City University of New York, Graduate Programs, School of Health Sciences, Program in Adult-Gerontological Nursing, Staten Island, NY 10314-6600. Offers adult-gerontological nursing (MS, Post Master's Certificate), including clinical nurse specialist, nurse practitioner. *Program availability:* Part-time, evening/weekend. *Faculty:* 6 full-time, 3 part-time/adjunct. *Students:* 48. 1 applicant, 100% accepted, 1 enrolled. In 2017, 19 master's, 6 other advanced degrees awarded. *Degree requirements:* For master's, thesis optional, 42 credits with minimum of 500 supervised hours toward development of clinical competencies for primary care of the adult-gerontological population (15 core credits, advanced practice core of nine credits, specialty courses of 12 credits, and six credits of elective courses); for Post Master's Certificate, 12-21 credits with minimum of 500 supervised hours toward development of Clinical Nurse Specialist or Nurse Practitioner competencies. *Entrance requirements:* For master's, bachelor's degree in nursing with minimum GPA of 3.0 in nursing major, two letters of recommendation, personal statement, current New York State RN license,

minimum of one year of full-time experience as registered nurse, three years of appropriate full-time clinical experience in nursing; for Post Master's Certificate, master's degree in nursing; master's-level courses in pathophysiology, health assessment and pharmacology. Additional exam requirements/recommendations for international students: Required—TOEFL (minimum score 550 paper-based; 79 iBT), IELTS (minimum score 6.5). *Application deadline:* For spring admission, 10/15 priority date for domestic and international students. Applications are processed on a rolling basis. Application fee: $125. Electronic applications accepted. *Expenses:* Tuition, state resident: full-time $10,450; part-time $440 per credit. Tuition, nonresident: full-time $19,320; part-time $440 per credit. *Required fees:* $181.10 per semester. Tuition and fees vary according to program. *Faculty research:* Perceptions and attitudes about behavioral health; type 2 diabetes/obesity; instrument development and role stress; cancer prevention and survivorship; older adults and end of life: decision making, dying, palliative and hospice care. *Unit head:* Prof. Catherine Paradiso, 718-982-3838, E-mail: catherine.paradiso@csi.cuny.edu. *Application contact:* Sasha Spence, Associate Director for Graduate Admissions, 718-982-2019, Fax: 718-982-2500, E-mail: sasha.spence@csi.cuny.edu.
Website: http://www.csi.cuny.edu/nursing/graduate.html

Columbia University, School of Nursing, Program in Adult-Gerontology Primary Care Nurse Practitioner, New York, NY 10032. Offers MS, Adv C. *Accreditation:* AACN. *Program availability:* Part-time. *Entrance requirements:* For master's, GRE General Test, NCLEX, BSN, 1 year of clinical experience (preferred); for Adv C, MSN. Additional exam requirements/recommendations for international students: Required—TOEFL (minimum score 100 iBT). Electronic applications accepted. *Expenses: Tuition:* Full-time $44,864; part-time $1704 per credit. *Required fees:* $2370 per semester. One-time fee: $105.

Creighton University, College of Nursing, Omaha, NE 68178-0001. Offers adult gerontology acute care nurse practitioner (DNP, Post-Master's Certificate); adult gerontology nurse practitioner (DNP); clinical nurse leader (MSN, Post-Graduate Certificate); clinical systems administration (MSN, DNP); family nurse practitioner (DNP, Post-Master's Certificate); neonatal nurse practitioner (DNP, Post-Master's Certificate); nursing (Post-Graduate Certificate); pediatric acute care nurse practitioner (DNP, Post-Master's Certificate); psychiatric mental health nurse practitioner (DNP). *Accreditation:* AACN. *Program availability:* Part-time, blended/hybrid learning. *Degree requirements:* For master's, capstone project; for doctorate, scholarly project. *Entrance requirements:* For master's and doctorate, BSN from ACEN- or CCNE-accredited nursing school, minimum cumulative GPA of 3.0, personal statement, active unencumbered RN license with NE eligibility, undergraduate statistics course, physical assessment course or equivalent, three recommendation letters; for other advanced degree, MSN or MS in nursing from ACEN- or CCNE-accredited nursing school, minimum cumulative GPA of 3.0, active unencumbered RN license with NE eligibility. Additional exam requirements/recommendations for international students: Required—TOEFL (minimum score 600 paper-based, 100 iBT) or IELTS. Electronic applications accepted. *Expenses:* Contact institution. *Faculty research:* School health report card, obesity prevention in children, simulated clinical experience evaluation, vitamin D3 and calcium and cancer risk reduction education, online support and education to reduce stress for prenatal patients on bed rest, health literacy, immunization research.

Duke University, School of Nursing, Durham, NC 27708-0586. Offers acute care pediatric nurse practitioner (MSN, Post-Graduate Certificate); adult-gerontology nurse practitioner (MSN, Post-Graduate Certificate), including acute care, primary care; family nurse practitioner (MSN, Post-Graduate Certificate); neonatal nurse practitioner (MSN, Post-Graduate Certificate); nurse anesthesia (DNP); nurse practitioner (DNP); nursing (PhD), nursing and health care leadership (MSN, Post Graduate Certificate); nursing education (MSN, Post-Graduate Certificate); nursing informatics (MSN, Post-Graduate Certificate); pediatric nurse practitioner (MSN, Post-Graduate Certificate), including primary care; psychiatric mental health nurse practitioner (MSN, Post-Graduate Certificate); women's health nurse practitioner (MSN, Post-Graduate Certificate). *Accreditation:* AACN; AANA/CANAEP. *Program availability:* Part-time, evening/weekend, online with on-campus intensives. *Faculty:* 72 full-time (61 women). *Students:* 155 full-time (137 women), 613 part-time (548 women); includes 177 minority (64 Black or African American, non-Hispanic/Latino; 2 American Indian or Alaska Native, non-Hispanic/Latino; 47 Asian, non-Hispanic/Latino; 34 Hispanic/Latino; 30 Two or more races, non-Hispanic/Latino), 10 international. Average age 34. 631 applicants, 47% accepted, 211 enrolled. In 2017, 221 master's, 71 doctorates, 26 other advanced degrees awarded. Terminal master's awarded for partial completion of doctoral program. *Degree requirements:* For master's, thesis optional; for doctorate, capstone project. *Entrance requirements:* For master's, GRE General Test (waived if undergraduate GPA of 3.4 or higher), 1 year of nursing experience (recommended), BSN, minimum GPA of 3.0, previous course work in statistics; for doctorate, GRE General Test (waived if undergraduate GPA of 3.4 or higher), BSN or MSN, minimum GPA of 3.0, resume, personal statement, undergraduate statistics course, current licensure as a registered nurse, transcripts from all post-secondary institutions; for Post-Graduate Certificate, MSN, licensure or eligibility as a professional nurse, transcripts from all post-secondary institutions, previous course work in statistics. Additional exam requirements/recommendations for international students: Required—TOEFL (minimum score 100 iBT), IELTS (minimum score 7). *Application deadline:* For fall admission, 12/1 for domestic and international students; for spring admission, 5/1 for domestic and international students. Application fee: $50. Electronic applications accepted. *Expenses:* Contact institution. *Financial support:* Institutionally sponsored loans, scholarships/grants, and traineeships available. Support available to part-time students. Financial award applicants required to submit FAFSA. *Faculty research:* Cardiovascular disease, caregiver skill training, data mining, prostate cancer, neonatal immune system. *Unit head:* Dr. Marion E. Broome, Dean/Vice Chancellor for Nursing Affairs/Associate Vice President for Academic Affairs for Nursing, 919-684-9446, Fax: 919-684-9414, E-mail: marion.broome@duke.edu. *Application contact:* Dr. Ernie Rushing, Director of Admissions and Recruitment, 919-668-6274, Fax: 919-668-4693, E-mail: ernie.rushing@dm.duke.edu.
Website: http://www.nursing.duke.edu/

East Tennessee State University, School of Graduate Studies, College of Nursing, Johnson City, TN 37614. Offers acute care nurse practitioner (DNP); adult-gerontology primary care nurse practitioner (DNP); adult/gerontological nurse practitioner (Postbaccalaureate Certificate); executive leadership in nursing (DNP, Postbaccalaureate Certificate); family nurse practitioner (MSN, DNP, Post-Master's Certificate, Postbaccalaureate Certificate); nursing (PhD); nursing administration (MSN); nursing education (MSN); pediatric primary care nurse practitioner (DNP); psychiatric mental health nurse practitioner (Postbaccalaureate Certificate); psychiatric/mental health nurse practitioner (MSN, DNP, Post-Master's Certificate); women's health care nurse practitioner (DNP). *Accreditation:* AACN. *Program availability:* Part-time, evening/weekend, online learning. In 2017, 126 master's, 30 doctorates, 4 other advanced degrees awarded. *Degree requirements:* For master's and other advanced degree, comprehensive exam, practicum; for doctorate, comprehensive exam, thesis/dissertation (for some programs), practicum, internship, evidence of professional malpractice insurance, CPR certification. *Entrance requirements:* For master's, bachelor's degree, minimum GPA of 3.0, current RN license and eligibility to practice, resume, three letters of recommendation; for doctorate, GRE General Test, MSN (for PhD), BSN or MSN (for DNP), current RN license and eligibility to practice, 2 years of full-time registered nurse work experience or equivalent, three letters of recommendation, resume or curriculum vitae, interview, writing sample; for other advanced degree, MSN, minimum GPA of 3.0, current RN license and eligibility to practice, three letters of recommendation, resume or curriculum vitae; DNP with designated concentration in advanced clinical practice or nursing administration (for select programs). Additional exam requirements/recommendations for international students: Required—TOEFL (minimum score 600 paper-based; 79 iBT). *Application deadline:* For fall admission, 4/15 priority date for domestic and international students; for spring admission, 10/15 priority date for domestic and international students; for summer admission, 2/1 for domestic and international students. Application fee: $55 ($65 for international students). Electronic applications accepted. *Financial support:* Research assistantships with tuition reimbursements, teaching assistantships, career-related internships or fieldwork, institutionally sponsored loans, scholarships/grants, and unspecified assistantships available. Financial award application deadline: 7/1; financial award applicants required to submit FAFSA. *Faculty research:* Improving health of rural and underserved populations (low income elders living in public housing, rural caregivers, Hispanic populations), health services and systems research (quality outcomes of nurse-managed primary care, in-home, and rural health care), nursing education (experiences of second-degree BSN students, well-being of BSN students). *Unit head:* Dr. Wendy Nehring, Dean, 423-439-7051, Fax: 423-439-4543, E-mail: nursing@etsu.edu. *Application contact:* Dr. Myra Clark, Director of Graduate Programs, 423-439-4396, Fax: 423-439-4100, E-mail: clarkml2@etsu.edu.
Website: http://www.etsu.edu/nursing/

Elms College, School of Nursing, Chicopee, MA 01013-2839. Offers adult-gerontology acute care nurse practitioner (DNP); family nurse practitioner (DNP); health systems innovation and leadership (DNP); nursing and health services management (MSN); nursing education (MSN). *Accreditation:* AACN. *Program availability:* Part-time, evening/weekend. *Faculty:* 5 full-time (all women), 9 part-time/adjunct (6 women). *Students:* 20 full-time (16 women), 79 part-time (70 women); includes 12 minority (2 Black or African American, non-Hispanic/Latino; 2 American Indian or Alaska Native, non-Hispanic/Latino; 8 Hispanic/Latino). Average age 40. 33 applicants, 94% accepted, 28 enrolled. In 2017, 14 master's, 30 doctorates awarded. *Entrance requirements:* Additional exam requirements/recommendations for international students: Required—TOEFL. *Application deadline:* For fall admission, 7/1 priority date for domestic students; for spring admission, 11/1 priority date for domestic students. Applications are processed on a rolling basis. Application fee: $30. *Expenses: Tuition:* Full-time $13,860; part-time $770 per credit hour. *Required fees:* $200. Tuition and fees vary according to degree level and program. *Financial support:* Applicants required to submit FAFSA. *Unit head:* Dr. Kathleen Scoble, Dean, School of Nursing, 413-265-2204, E-mail: scoblek@elms.edu. *Application contact:* Dr. Cynthia L. Dakin, Director of Graduate Nursing Studies, 413-265-2455, Fax: 413-265-2335, E-mail: dakinc@elms.edu.

Fairleigh Dickinson University, Florham Campus, University College: Arts, Sciences, and Professional Studies, The Henry P. Becton School of Nursing and Allied Health, Madison, NJ 07940-1099. Offers adult gerontology primary care nurse practitioner (MSN); family psychiatric/mental health nurse practitioner (MSN). *Program availability:* Part-time, evening/weekend. *Entrance requirements:* For master's, BSN, minimum undergraduate GPA of 3.0, courses in statistics and nursing research at the undergraduate level, NJ Registered Nurse licensure, minimum of 1 year of clinical nursing experience, two letters of recommendation. *Expenses: Tuition:* Full-time $22,410; part-time $1245 per credit. *Required fees:* $888; $414 per unit. Tuition and fees vary according to course load, degree level and program.

Felician University, Master of Science in Nursing Program, Lodi, NJ 07644-2117. Offers adult-gerontology nurse practitioner (MSN, PMC); executive leadership (MSN, PMC); family nurse practitioner (MSN, PMC); nursing education (MSN, PMC). *Accreditation:* AACN. *Program availability:* Evening/weekend, online only, 100% online, blended/hybrid learning. *Faculty:* 9 full-time (8 women), 1 (woman) part-time/adjunct. *Students:* 96 part-time (90 women); includes 48 minority (17 Black or African American, non-Hispanic/Latino; 1 American Indian or Alaska Native, non-Hispanic/Latino; 16 Asian, non-Hispanic/Latino; 12 Hispanic/Latino; 1 Native Hawaiian or other Pacific Islander, non-Hispanic/Latino; 1 Two or more races, non-Hispanic/Latino). Average age 37. 49 applicants, 86% accepted, 23 enrolled. In 2017, 35 master's, 3 other advanced degrees awarded. *Degree requirements:* For master's, thesis, clinical presentation; for PMC, thesis, education project. *Entrance requirements:* For master's, BSN; minimum GPA of 3.0; 2 letters of recommendation; NJ RN license; personal statement; for PMC, RN license, minimum GPA of 3.0. Additional exam requirements/recommendations for international students: Required—TOEFL (minimum score 550 paper-based; 79 iBT), IELTS (minimum score 6.5), PTE (minimum score 56). *Application deadline:* Applications are processed on a rolling basis. Application fee: $40. Electronic applications accepted. Application fee is waived when completed online. *Expenses:* Contact institution. *Financial support:* Federal Work-Study, scholarships/grants, and traineeships available. Financial award applicants required to submit FAFSA. *Faculty research:* Anxiety and fear, curriculum innovation, health promotion and populations, attitudes of college students towards aging. *Unit head:* Dr. Ann Tritak, Associate Dean of Graduate Nursing, 201-559-6151, E-mail: tritaka@felician.edu. *Application contact:* Michael Szarek, Assistant Vice-President, Graduate Admissions, 201-355-1450, E-mail: szarekm@felician.edu.

Florida Southern College, Program in Nursing, Lakeland, FL 33801-5698. Offers adult gerontology clinical nurse specialist (MSN); adult gerontology primary care nurse practitioner (MSN); family nurse practitioner (MSN); nurse educator (MSN); nursing administration (MSN). *Accreditation:* AACN. *Program availability:* Part-time. *Faculty:* 5 full-time (all women), 2 part-time/adjunct (both women). *Students:* 142 full-time (126 women), 9 part-time (all women); includes 70 minority (39 Black or African American, non-Hispanic/Latino; 1 American Indian or Alaska Native, non-Hispanic/Latino; 11 Asian, non-Hispanic/Latino; 13 Hispanic/Latino; 1 Native Hawaiian or other Pacific Islander, non-Hispanic/Latino; 5 Two or more races, non-Hispanic/Latino), 1 international. Average age 40. 83 applicants, 93% accepted, 72 enrolled. In 2017, 41 master's awarded. *Degree requirements:* For master's, 780 clinical practice hours. *Entrance requirements:* For master's, GMAT or GRE General Test, Florida RN license, 3 letters of recommendation, personal statement, minimum GPA of 3.0, resume. Additional exam requirements/recommendations for international students: Required—TOEFL (minimum score 550 paper-based; 79 iBT), IELTS (minimum score 6.5). *Application deadline:* For fall admission, 6/1 for domestic and international students; for spring admission, 10/1 for domestic and international students. Applications are processed on a rolling basis. Application fee: $30. Electronic applications accepted. *Expenses:* $585 per credit hour, $100 required fees. *Financial support:* In 2017–18, 1 student received support. Scholarships/grants and traineeships available. Support available to part-time students. Financial award applicants required to submit FAFSA. *Faculty research:* End of life care, dementia, health promotion. *Unit head:* Dr. Linda Comer, Dean, 863-680-4310, Fax: 863-680-3872, E-mail: lcomer@flsouthern.edu. *Application contact:* Kathy Connelly, Evening Program Assistant Director, 863-680-4205, Fax: 863-680-3872, E-mail: kconnelly@flsouthern.edu.

Gerontological Nursing

George Mason University, College of Health and Human Services, School of Nursing, Fairfax, VA 22030. Offers adult gerontology (DNP); adult/gerontological nurse practitioner (MSN); family nurse practitioner (MSN, DNP); nurse educator (MSN); nursing (PhD); nursing administration (MSN, DNP); nursing education (Certificate); psychiatric mental health (DNP). *Accreditation:* AACN. *Program availability:* Part-time, evening/weekend, blended/hybrid learning. *Faculty:* 28 full-time (27 women), 51 part-time/adjunct (47 women). *Students:* 51 full-time (40 women), 182 part-time (162 women); includes 110 minority (59 Black or African American, non-Hispanic/Latino; 1 American Indian or Alaska Native, non-Hispanic/Latino; 36 Asian, non-Hispanic/Latino; 10 Hispanic/Latino; 4 Two or more races, non-Hispanic/Latino), 8 international. Average age 37. 159 applicants, 70% accepted, 73 enrolled. In 2017, 33 master's, 24 doctorates, 1 other advanced degree awarded. *Degree requirements:* For master's, comprehensive exam (for some programs), thesis in clinical classes; for doctorate, comprehensive exam (for some programs), thesis/dissertation (for some programs). *Entrance requirements:* For master's, 2 official transcripts; expanded goals statement; resume; BSN from accredited institution; minimum GPA of 3.0 in last 60 credits of undergraduate work; 2 letters of recommendation; completion of undergraduate statistics and graduate-level bivariate statistics; certification in professional CPR; for doctorate, GRE, 2 official transcripts; expanded goals statement; resume; 2 recommendation letters; nursing license; at least 1 year of work experience as an RN; interview; writing sample; evidence of graduate-level course in applied statistics; master's degree in nursing with minimum GPA of 3.5; for Certificate, 2 official transcripts; expanded goals statement; resume; master's degree from accredited institution or currently enrolled with minimum GPA of 3.0. Additional exam requirements/recommendations for international students: Required—TOEFL (minimum score 570 paper-based; 88 iBT), IELTS (minimum score 6.5), PTE (minimum score 59). *Application deadline:* For fall admission, 2/1 for domestic and international students. Application fee: $75 ($80 for international students). Electronic applications accepted. *Expenses:* Contact institution. *Financial support:* In 2017–18, 7 students received support, including 5 research assistantships with tuition reimbursements available (averaging $20,500 per year), 2 teaching assistantships; career-related internships or fieldwork, Federal Work-Study, scholarships/grants, unspecified assistantships, and health care benefits (for full-time research or teaching assistantship recipients) also available. Financial award application deadline: 3/1; financial award applicants required to submit FAFSA. *Faculty research:* Health care, nursing science. *Total annual research expenditures:* $1.6 million. *Unit head:* Carol Urban, Director, 703-993-2991, Fax: 703-993-1949, E-mail: curban@gmu.edu. *Application contact:* Susan Eckis, Office Manager, 703-993-1938, Fax: 703-993-1949, E-mail: seckis@gmu.edu.
Website: http://chhs.gmu.edu/nursing

Georgia Southern University–Armstrong Campus, College of Graduate Studies, School of Nursing, Savannah, GA 31419-1997. Offers adult-gerontological acute care nurse practitioner (Certificate); adult-gerontological clinical nurse specialist (Certificate); adult-gerontological primary care nurse practitioner (Certificate); family nurse practitioner (MSN). *Accreditation:* AACN. *Program availability:* Part-time, evening/weekend. *Faculty:* 12 full-time (all women). *Students:* 36 full-time (30 women), 22 part-time (21 women); includes 17 minority (7 Black or African American, non-Hispanic/Latino; 2 Asian, non-Hispanic/Latino; 4 Hispanic/Latino; 4 Two or more races, non-Hispanic/Latino), 1 international. Average age 32. 59 applicants, 32% accepted, 18 enrolled. In 2017, 10 master's awarded. *Degree requirements:* For master's, comprehensive exam, project or thesis. *Entrance requirements:* For master's, GRE General Test or MAT, minimum GPA of 3.0, letter of recommendation, letter of intent. Additional exam requirements/recommendations for international students: Required—TOEFL (minimum score 523 paper-based; 70 iBT). *Application deadline:* For fall admission, 2/28 for domestic and international students; for spring admission, 11/15 for domestic students, 9/15 for international students. Applications are processed on a rolling basis. Application fee: $30. Electronic applications accepted. *Expenses:* Tuition, state resident: part-time $211 per credit hour. Tuition, nonresident: part-time $782 per credit hour. *Required fees:* $737 per semester. Tuition and fees vary according to course load, degree level, campus/location and program. *Financial support:* In 2017–18, research assistantships with full tuition reimbursements (averaging $5,000 per year) were awarded; Federal Work-Study, scholarships/grants, and unspecified assistantships also available. Support available to part-time students. Financial award application deadline: 3/1; financial award applicants required to submit FAFSA. *Faculty research:* Midwifery, mental health, nursing simulation, smoking cessation during pregnancy, asthma education, vulnerable populations, geriatrics, disaster nursing, complementary and alternative modalities, nephrology. *Unit head:* Dr. Catherine Gilbert, Department Head, 912-344-3145, E-mail: catherine.gilbert@armstrong.edu. *Application contact:* McKenzie Peterman, Graduate Admissions Specialist, 912-478-5678, Fax: 912-478-0740, E-mail: mpeterman@georgiasouthern.edu.
Website: https://www.armstrong.edu/degree-programs/nursing-msn

Goldfarb School of Nursing at Barnes-Jewish College, Graduate Programs, St. Louis, MO 63110. Offers adult-gerontology (MSN), including primary care nurse practitioner; adult-gerontology (MSN), including acute care nurse practitioner; health systems and population health leadership (MSN); nurse anesthesia (MSN). *Accreditation:* AACN; AANA/CANAEP. *Program availability:* Part-time, online learning. *Faculty:* 42 full-time (39 women), 6 part-time/adjunct (all women). *Students:* 61 full-time (49 women), 3 part-time (2 women); includes 13 minority (8 Black or African American, non-Hispanic/Latino; 2 Asian, non-Hispanic/Latino; 1 Hispanic/Latino; 2 Two or more races, non-Hispanic/Latino). *Degree requirements:* For master's, thesis or alternative. *Entrance requirements:* For master's, 2 references, personal statement, curriculum vitae or resume. Additional exam requirements/recommendations for international students: Required—TOEFL (minimum score 575 paper-based; 85 iBT). *Application deadline:* Applications are processed on a rolling basis. Application fee: $50. *Expenses: Tuition:* Full-time $11,910; part-time $794 per credit hour. *Required fees:* $30; $15 per term. Full-time tuition and fees vary according to program. *Financial support:* Research assistantships, Federal Work-Study, institutionally sponsored loans, scholarships/grants, and traineeships available. Support available to part-time students. Financial award applicants required to submit FAFSA. *Faculty research:* HIV stigma, HIV symptom management, palliative care with children and their families, heart disease prevention in Hispanic women, depression in the well elderly, alternative therapies in pre-term infants. *Unit head:* Dr. Gretchen Drinkard, Associate Dean for Academic Affairs, 314-454-7540, Fax: 314-362-9222, E-mail: gdrinkard@bjc.org. *Application contact:* Karen Sartorius, Admission Specialist, 314-454-7057, Fax: 314-362-9250, E-mail: karen.sartorius@bjc.org.
Website: http://www.barnesjewishcollege.edu/

Graceland University, School of Nursing, Independence, MO 64050-3434. Offers adult and gerontology acute care (MSN, PMC); family nurse practitioner (MSN, PMC); nurse educator (MSN, PMC); organizational leadership (DNP). *Accreditation:* AACN. *Program availability:* Part-time, online learning. *Faculty:* 13 full-time (11 women), 24 part-time/adjunct (all women). *Students:* 338 full-time (294 women), 311 part-time (282 women); includes 102 minority (33 Black or African American, non-Hispanic/Latino; 8 American Indian or Alaska Native, non-Hispanic/Latino; 18 Asian, non-Hispanic/Latino; 29 Hispanic/Latino; 1 Native Hawaiian or other Pacific Islander, non-Hispanic/Latino; 13 Two or more races, non-Hispanic/Latino), 2 international. Average age 36. 119 applicants, 86% accepted, 95 enrolled. In 2017, 158 master's, 2 doctorates awarded. *Degree requirements:* For master's, comprehensive exam (for some programs), thesis optional, scholarly project; for doctorate, capstone project. *Entrance requirements:* For master's, BSN from nationally-accredited program, RN license, minimum GPA of 3.0, satisfactory criminal background check, three professional reference letters, professional goals statement of 150 words or less; for doctorate, MSN from nationally-accredited program, RN license, minimum GPA of 3.2, criminal background check. Additional exam requirements/recommendations for international students: Required—TOEFL (minimum score 550 paper-based; 79 iBT). *Application deadline:* For fall admission, 6/1 priority date for domestic students; for winter admission, 10/1 priority date for domestic students; for spring admission, 10/1 priority date for domestic students; for summer admission, 2/1 for domestic students. Application fee: $50. Electronic applications accepted. *Expenses:* $775 per credit hour tuition, $1,800 practicum fees, $480 research fees, $846 university technology fees, $655 lab fees, $300 program support fees. *Financial support:* In 2017–18, 14 students received support. Institutionally sponsored loans available. Support available to part-time students. Financial award application deadline: 6/1; financial award applicants required to submit FAFSA. *Faculty research:* International nursing, family care-giving, health promotion, mental health nursing. *Unit head:* Dr. Claudia D. Horton, Interim Vice President for Independence Campus/Dean, 816-423-4670, Fax: 816-423-4753, E-mail: horton@graceland.edu. *Application contact:* Admissions Representative, 816-423-4717, Fax: 816-833-2990, E-mail: distancelearning@graceland.edu.
Website: http://www.graceland.edu/nursing

Gwynedd Mercy University, Frances M. Maguire School of Nursing and Health Professions, Gwynedd Valley, PA 19437-0901. Offers clinical nurse specialist (MSN), including gerontology, oncology, pediatrics; nurse educator (MSN); nurse practitioner (MSN), including adult health, pediatric health; nursing (DNP). *Accreditation:* ACEN. *Program availability:* Part-time, blended/hybrid learning. *Faculty:* 4 full-time (all women), 1 (woman) part-time/adjunct. *Students:* 28 full-time (25 women), 48 part-time (43 women); includes 28 minority (15 Black or African American, non-Hispanic/Latino; 11 Asian, non-Hispanic/Latino; 1 Hispanic/Latino; 1 Two or more races, non-Hispanic/Latino). Average age 37. 72 applicants, 25% accepted, 16 enrolled. In 2017, 7 master's awarded. *Degree requirements:* For master's, thesis optional; for doctorate, evidence-based scholarly project. *Entrance requirements:* For master's, GRE General Test or MAT, current nursing experience, physical assessment, course work in statistics, BSN from ACEN-accredited program, 2 letters of recommendation, personal interview. Additional exam requirements/recommendations for international students: Required—TOEFL (minimum score 575 paper-based). *Application deadline:* For fall admission, 8/1 priority date for domestic students; for winter admission, 12/1 priority date for domestic students. Applications are processed on a rolling basis. Electronic applications accepted. *Expenses:* $825 per credit (non-doctoral degrees), $930 per credit (doctoral); $17 part-time fee, $165 graduation fee. *Financial support:* In 2017–18, 5 students received support. Scholarships/grants, traineeships, and unspecified assistantships available. Financial award application deadline: 8/30. *Faculty research:* Critical thinking, primary care, domestic violence, multiculturalism, nursing centers. *Unit head:* Dr. Andrea D. Hollingsworth, Dean, 215-646-7300 Ext. 539, Fax: 215-641-5517, E-mail: hollingsworth.a@gmc.edu. *Application contact:* Dr. Barbara A. Jones, Director, 215-646-7300 Ext. 407, Fax: 215-641-5564, E-mail: jones.b@gmc.edu.
Website: http://www.gmercyu.edu/academics/graduate-programs/nursing

Hofstra University, Hofstra Northwell School of Graduate Nursing and Physician Assistant Studies, Programs in Nursing, Hempstead, NY 11549. Offers adult-gerontology acute care nurse practitioner (MS); family nurse practitioner (MS); psychiatric-mental health nurse practitioner (MS). *Students:* 29 full-time (23 women), 107 part-time (89 women); includes 62 minority (16 Black or African American, non-Hispanic/Latino; 21 Asian, non-Hispanic/Latino; 25 Hispanic/Latino). Average age 35. 122 applicants, 62% accepted, 62 enrolled. *Degree requirements:* For master's, comprehensive exam, minimum GPA of 3.0. *Entrance requirements:* For master's, bachelor's degree in biology or equivalent, 2 letters of recommendation, essay, minimum GPA of 3.0. Additional exam requirements/recommendations for international students: Required—TOEFL (minimum score 550 paper-based; 80 iBT). *Application deadline:* For fall admission, 11/1 for domestic students. Application fee: $75. Electronic applications accepted. *Expenses: Tuition:* Full-time $1292. *Required fees:* $970. Tuition and fees vary according to program. *Financial support:* In 2017–18, 4 students received support, including 4 fellowships with full and partial tuition reimbursements available (averaging $16,205 per year); research assistantships with full and partial tuition reimbursements available, career-related internships or fieldwork, Federal Work-Study, institutionally sponsored loans, scholarships/grants, traineeships, tuition waivers (full and partial), and unspecified assistantships also available. Support available to part-time students. Financial award applicants required to submit FAFSA. *Faculty research:* Innovative educational pedagogies; simulation science; problem (case) based learning; chronic disease management; evidence based practice. *Unit head:* Dr. Kathleen Gallo, Dean, 516-463-7475, Fax: 516-463-7495, E-mail: kathleen.gallo@hofstra.edu. *Application contact:* Sunil Samuel, Assistant Vice President of Admissions, 516-463-4723, Fax: 516-463-4664, E-mail: graduateadmission@hofstra.edu.

Hunter College of the City University of New York, Graduate School, Hunter-Bellevue School of Nursing, Doctor of Nursing Practice Program, New York, NY 10065-5085. Offers adult-gerontology nurse practitioner (DNP); family nurse practitioner (DNP); psychiatric-mental health nurse practitioner (DNP).

Hunter College of the City University of New York, Graduate School, Hunter-Bellevue School of Nursing, Gerontological/Adult Nurse Practitioner Program, New York, NY 10065-5085. Offers MS. *Accreditation:* AACN. *Program availability:* Part-time. *Degree requirements:* For master's, practicum. *Entrance requirements:* For master's, minimum GPA of 3.0, New York RN license, 2 years of professional practice experience, BSN. Additional exam requirements/recommendations for international students: Required—TOEFL.

Hunter College of the City University of New York, Graduate School, Hunter-Bellevue School of Nursing, Program in Adult-Gerontology Clinical Nurse Specialist, New York, NY 10065-5085. Offers MS. *Accreditation:* AACN. *Degree requirements:* For master's, practicum. *Entrance requirements:* For master's, minimum GPA of 3.0, New York RN license, 2 years of professional practice experience, BSN. Additional exam requirements/recommendations for international students: Required—TOEFL.

Independence University, Program in Nursing, Salt Lake City, UT 84107. Offers community health (MSN); gerontology (MSN); nursing administration (MSN); wellness promotion (MSN).

Indiana University–Purdue University Fort Wayne, College of Health and Human Services, Department of Nursing, Fort Wayne, IN 46805-1499. Offers adult-gerontology primary care nurse practitioner (MS); family nurse practitioner (MS); nurse executive (MS); nursing administration (Certificate); nursing education (MS). *Accreditation:* ACEN. *Program availability:* Part-time. *Entrance requirements:* For master's, GRE Writing Test (if GPA below 3.0), BS in nursing, eligibility for Indiana RN license, minimum GPA of 3.0, essay, copy of resume, three references, undergraduate course work in research and statistics within last 5 years. Additional exam requirements/recommendations for international students: Required—TOEFL (minimum score 550 paper-based; 79 iBT); Recommended—TWE. Electronic applications accepted. *Faculty research:* Community engagement, cervical screening, evidence-based practice.

Indiana University–Purdue University Indianapolis, School of Nursing, MSN Program in Nursing, Indianapolis, IN 46202. Offers adult/gerontology acute care nurse practitioner (MSN); adult/gerontology clinical nurse specialist (MSN); adult/gerontology primary care nurse practitioner (MSN); family nurse practitioner (MSN); nursing education (MSN); nursing leadership in health systems (MSN); pediatric clinical nurse specialist (MSN); pediatric nurse practitioner (MSN). *Accreditation:* AACN. *Program availability:* Part-time, blended/hybrid learning. *Degree requirements:* For master's, thesis. *Entrance requirements:* For master's, BSN from ACEN- or CCNE-accredited program, minimum undergraduate GPA of 3.0 (preferred), professional resume or curriculum vitae, essay stating career goals and objectives, current unencumbered RN license, three references from individuals with knowledge of ability to succeed in graduate program. Additional exam requirements/recommendations for international students: Required—TOEFL (minimum score 550 paper-based; 79 iBT). Electronic applications accepted. *Expenses:* Contact institution. *Faculty research:* Quality of life, symptom management, cancer prevention and control, heart failure, pediatric oncology.

Jacksonville University, Brooks Rehabilitation College of Healthcare Sciences, Keigwin School of Nursing, Jacksonville, FL 32211. Offers adult gerontology acute care nurse practitioner (MSN), including clinical nurse educator, family nurse practitioner, family nurse practitioner/emergency nurse practitioner, leadership in the healthcare system, nursing informatics, psychiatric nurse practitioner; adult-gerontology acute care nurse practitioner (Certificate); clinical nurse educator (Certificate); emergency nurse practitioner (Certificate); family nurse practitioner (Certificate); family nurse practitioner/emergency nurse practitioner (Certificate); leadership in healthcare systems (Certificate); nursing informatics (MSN, Certificate); nursing practice (DNP); psychiatric mental health nurse practitioner (Certificate); MSN/MBA. *Accreditation:* AACN. *Program availability:* Part-time, 100% online, blended/hybrid learning. *Faculty:* 18 full-time (all women), 11 part-time/adjunct (9 women). *Students:* 61 full-time (53 women), 549 part-time (497 women); includes 202 minority (120 Black or African American, non-Hispanic/Latino; 4 American Indian or Alaska Native, non-Hispanic/Latino; 29 Asian, non-Hispanic/Latino; 39 Hispanic/Latino; 2 Native Hawaiian or other Pacific Islander, non-Hispanic/Latino; 8 Two or more races, non-Hispanic/Latino), 1 international. Average age 40. 272 applicants, 58% accepted, 126 enrolled. In 2017, 293 master's, 9 doctorates awarded. *Degree requirements:* For master's, thesis; for doctorate, thesis/dissertation. *Entrance requirements:* For master's, GRE General Test or undergraduate GPA above 3.0, BSN from ACEN- or CCNE-accredited program; course work in statistics and physical assessment within last 5 years; Florida nursing license; CPR/BLS certification; 3 recommendations, 2 of which are professional references; statement of intent; resume; for doctorate, official transcripts from all colleges/universities attended; MSN from ACEN- or CCNE-accredited program; licensure as RN or ARNP; 3 letters of reference (2 clinical, 1 professional/academic); curriculum vitae; graded essay; for Certificate, GRE (minimum score of 290, waived if undergraduate nursing GPA is 3.0 or higher), official transcripts from MSN; minimum graduate nursing GPA of 3.0; graduation from CCNE- or ACEN-accredited MSN program; 3 recommendations, 2 of which are professional references; 2 years of work experience in critical care setting; statement of intent; resume. Additional exam requirements/recommendations for international students: Required—TOEFL (minimum score 650 paper-based; 114 iBT), IELTS (minimum score 8). *Application deadline:* For fall admission, 2/1 for domestic and international students. Applications are processed on a rolling basis. Application fee: $50. Electronic applications accepted. *Expenses:* Contact institution. *Financial support:* Federal Work-Study, institutionally sponsored loans, scholarships/grants, and health care benefits available. Support available to part-time students. Financial award application deadline: 3/15; financial award applicants required to submit FAFSA. *Faculty research:* Treatment of anxiety. *Unit head:* Dr. Hilary Morgan, Director, Graduate Nursing Programs/Associate Professor, 904-256-7601, E-mail: hmorgan@ju.edu. *Application contact:* Stephanie Bloom, Assistant Director, Enrollment and Advanced Graduate Nursing, 904-256-7286, E-mail: sstrick4@ju.edu.
Website: http://www.ju.edu/chs/nursing/

James Madison University, The Graduate School, College of Health and Behavioral Studies, Program in Nursing, Harrisonburg, VA 22807. Offers adult/gerontology primary care nurse practitioner (MSN); clinical nurse leader (MSN); family nurse practitioner (MSN); nurse administrator (MSN); nurse midwifery (MSN); nursing (MSN, DNP); psychiatric mental health nurse practitioner (MSN). *Accreditation:* AACN. *Program availability:* Part-time, 100% online, blended/hybrid learning. *Students:* 10 full-time (9 women), 77 part-time (71 women); includes 10 minority (2 Black or African American, non-Hispanic/Latino; 5 Asian, non-Hispanic/Latino; 1 Hispanic/Latino; 2 Two or more races, non-Hispanic/Latino). Average age 30. In 2017, 27 master's awarded. Application fee: $55. Electronic applications accepted. *Expenses:* Tuition, state resident: full-time $10,512; part-time $438 per credit hour. Tuition, nonresident: full-time $28,358; part-time $1162 per credit hour. *Required fees:* $1128. *Financial support:* In 2017–18, 2 students received support. Federal Work-Study and 2 assistantships (averaging $7911) available. Financial award application deadline: 3/1; financial award applicants required to submit FAFSA. *Unit head:* Dr. Julie T. Sanford, Department Head, 540-568-6314, E-mail: sanforjt@jmu.edu. *Application contact:* Lynette D. Michael, Director of Graduate Admissions, 540-568-6131 Ext. 6395, Fax: 540-568-7860, E-mail: michaeld@jmu.edu.
Website: http://www.nursing.jmu.edu

Johns Hopkins University, School of Nursing, Doctoral Programs in Nursing, Baltimore, MD 21205. Offers adult/gerontological primary care nurse practitioner (PhD); nursing (PhD); nursing practice (DNP); DNP/PhD. *Program availability:* Blended/hybrid learning. *Faculty:* 62 full-time (46 women), 160 part-time/adjunct (all women). *Students:* 110 full-time (100 women), 69 part-time (62 women); includes 79 minority (30 Black or African American, non-Hispanic/Latino; 1 American Indian or Alaska Native, non-Hispanic/Latino; 25 Asian, non-Hispanic/Latino; 17 Hispanic/Latino; 6 Two or more races, non-Hispanic/Latino), 10 international. Average age 38. 228 applicants, 52% accepted, 74 enrolled. In 2017, 23 doctorates awarded. *Degree requirements:* For doctorate, comprehensive exam (for some programs), thesis/dissertation (for some programs). *Entrance requirements:* For doctorate, minimum GPA of 3.0, goal statement/essay, resume, letters of recommendation, official transcripts from all post-secondary institutions attended; BSN and RN license (for DNP); writing sample (for PhD). Additional exam requirements/recommendations for international students: Required—TOEFL (minimum score 600 paper-based; 100 iBT), IELTS (minimum score 7). *Application deadline:* For fall admission, 11/1 priority date for domestic and international students; for summer admission, 11/1 priority date for domestic and international students. Application fee: $70. Electronic applications accepted. *Expenses:* $2,310 per credit (for PhD); $1,671 per credit (for DNP). *Financial support:* In 2017–18, 101 students received support, including 18 research assistantships, 18 teaching assistantships; Federal Work-Study, scholarships/grants, and tuition waivers (partial) also available. Support available to part-time students. Financial award application deadline: 3/1; financial award applicants required to submit FAFSA. *Faculty research:* Cardiovascular health, disease prevention and risk reduction, women's health, palliative and end-of-life care, community-based health promotion. *Unit head:* Dr. Patricia M. Davidson, Dean, 410-955-7544, Fax: 410-955-4890, E-mail: sondeansoffice@jhu.edu. *Application contact:* Cathy Wilson, Director of Admissions, 410-955-7548, Fax: 410-614-7086, E-mail: jhuson@jhu.edu.
Website: http://nursing.jhu.edu/

See Display on page 576 and Close-Up on page 763.

Johns Hopkins University, School of Nursing, Nurse Practitioner Program, Baltimore, MD 21205. Offers adult/gerontological acute care nurse practitioner (DNP); adult/gerontological primary care nurse practitioner (DNP); family primary care nurse practitioner (DNP); pediatric primary care nurse practitioner (DNP). *Accreditation:* AACN. *Program availability:* Part-time. *Faculty:* 9 full-time (all women), 10 part-time/adjunct (all women). *Students:* 52 full-time (46 women), 173 part-time (160 women); includes 77 minority (28 Black or African American, non-Hispanic/Latino; 26 Asian, non-Hispanic/Latino; 18 Hispanic/Latino; 5 Two or more races, non-Hispanic/Latino), 2 international. Average age 33. 157 applicants, 55% accepted, 52 enrolled. *Entrance requirements:* For doctorate, GRE, minimum GPA of 3.0, goal statement/essay, resume, letters of recommendation, official transcripts from all post-secondary institutions attended; BSN; RN license; writing sample. Additional exam requirements/recommendations for international students: Required—TOEFL (minimum score 600 paper-based; 100 iBT), IELTS (minimum score 7). *Application deadline:* For fall admission, 11/1 priority date for domestic and international students. Application fee: $70. Electronic applications accepted. *Expenses:* $1,671 per credit. *Financial support:* In 2017–18, 28 students received support. Federal Work-Study and scholarships/grants available. Support available to part-time students. Financial award application deadline: 3/1; financial award applicants required to submit FAFSA. *Faculty research:* Community outreach, primary care of underserved populations, substance-abusing individuals, childhood violence, women's health. *Unit head:* Dr. Patricia M. Davidson, Dean, 410-955-7544, Fax: 410-955-4890, E-mail: sondeansoffice@jhu.edu. *Application contact:* Cathy Wilson, Director of Admissions, 410-955-7548, Fax: 410-614-7086, E-mail: jhuson@jhu.edu.
Website: http://www.nursing.jhu.edu

See Display on page 576 and Close-Up on page 763.

Johns Hopkins University, School of Nursing, Program in Clinical Nurse Specialist, Baltimore, MD 21205. Offers adult/gerontological critical care clinical nurse specialist (DNP); adult/gerontological health clinical nurse specialist (DNP); pediatric critical care clinical nurse specialist (DNP). *Accreditation:* AACN. *Program availability:* Part-time, 100% online, blended/hybrid learning. *Faculty:* 3 full-time (2 women). *Students:* 13 full-time (all women), 15 part-time (13 women); includes 11 minority (1 Black or African American, non-Hispanic/Latino; 1 American Indian or Alaska Native, non-Hispanic/Latino; 2 Asian, non-Hispanic/Latino; 6 Hispanic/Latino; 1 Two or more races, non-Hispanic/Latino). Average age 32. 32 applicants, 63% accepted, 14 enrolled. *Entrance requirements:* For doctorate, GRE, minimum GPA of 3.0, goal statement/essay, resume, letters of recommendation, official transcripts from all post-secondary institutions attended; BSN; RN license; writing sample. Additional exam requirements/recommendations for international students: Required—TOEFL (minimum score 600 paper-based; 100 iBT), IELTS (minimum score 7). *Application deadline:* For fall admission, 11/1 priority date for domestic and international students. Application fee: $70. Electronic applications accepted. *Expenses:* $1,671 per credit. *Financial support:* In 2017–18, 8 students received support. Federal Work-Study and scholarships/grants available. Support available to part-time students. Financial award application deadline: 3/1; financial award applicants required to submit FAFSA. *Faculty research:* Maternal child health, symptom management, cardiovascular risk reduction, asthma, hypertension. *Unit head:* Dr. Patricia M. Davidson, Dean, 410-955-7544, Fax: 410-955-4890, E-mail: sondeansoffice@jhu.edu. *Application contact:* Cathy Wilson, Director of Admissions, 410-955-7548, Fax: 410-614-7086, E-mail: jhuson@jhu.edu.
Website: http://www.nursing.jhu.edu

See Display on page 576 and Close-Up on page 763.

Kent State University, College of Nursing, Kent, OH 44242. Offers advanced nursing practice (DNP), including adult/gerontology acute care nurse practitioner (MSN, DNP); nursing (MSN, PhD), including adult/gerontology acute care nurse practitioner (MSN, DNP), adult/gerontology clinical nurse specialist (MSN), adult/gerontology primary care nurse practitioner (MSN), family nurse practitioner (MSN), nurse educator (MSN), nursing and healthcare management (MSN), pediatric primary care nurse practitioner (MSN), psychiatric/mental health nurse practitioner (MSN); MBA/MSN. PhD program offered jointly with The University of Akron. *Accreditation:* AACN. *Program availability:* Part-time, online learning. *Faculty:* 29 full-time (28 women), 15 part-time/adjunct (12 women). *Students:* 167 full-time (142 women), 405 part-time (359 women); includes 70 minority (39 Black or African American, non-Hispanic/Latino; 11 Asian, non-Hispanic/Latino; 18 Hispanic/Latino; 2 Two or more races, non-Hispanic/Latino), 13 international. Average age 35. 272 applicants, 74% accepted, 166 enrolled. In 2017, 144 master's, 8 doctorates awarded. *Degree requirements:* For master's, thesis optional; for doctorate, comprehensive exam, thesis/dissertation. *Entrance requirements:* For master's, GRE or GMAT, minimum GPA of 3.0, active RN license, statement of purpose, 3 letters of reference, undergraduate level statistics class, baccalaureate or graduate-level nursing degree, curriculum vitae/resume; for doctorate, GRE, minimum GPA of 3.0, transcripts, 3 letters of reference, interview, active unrestricted Ohio RN license, statement of purpose, writing sample, curriculum vitae/resume, baccalaureate and master's degrees in nursing or DNP. Additional exam requirements/recommendations for international students: Required—TOEFL (minimum score 560 paper-based; 83 iBT), IELTS (minimum score 6.5), PTE (minimum score 55), Michigan English Language Assessment Battery (minimum score 78). *Application deadline:* For fall admission, 3/1 for domestic and international students; for spring admission, 10/1 for domestic and international students. Applications are processed on a rolling basis. Application fee: $45 ($70 for international students). Electronic applications accepted. *Expenses:* Tuition, state resident: full-time $11,310; part-time $515 per credit hour. Tuition, nonresident: full-time $20,396; part-time $928 per credit hour. *International tuition:* $18,544 full-time. *Financial support:* Scholarships/grants available. Financial award application deadline: 5/4. *Unit head:* Dr. Barbara Broome, Dean, 330-672-3777, E-mail: bbroome1@kent.edu. *Application contact:* Dr. Wendy A. Umberger, Associate Dean for Graduate Programs/Professor, 330-672-8813, E-mail: wlewando@kent.edu.
Website: http://www.kent.edu/nursing/

Keuka College, Program in Nursing, Keuka Park, NY 14478. Offers adult gerontology (MS); nursing education (MS). *Accreditation:* AACN. *Degree requirements:* For master's, exam or thesis. *Entrance requirements:* For master's, bachelor's degree from accredited institution, minimum GPA of 3.0, unencumbered NY State license, and current registration as RN (for nursing); currently full-time or part-time working RN and 2 clinical letters of recommendation (for adult gerontology nurse practitioner). Additional exam requirements/recommendations for international students: Required—TOEFL (minimum score 550 paper-based). Electronic applications accepted. *Expenses:* Contact institution. *Faculty research:* Endocrinology and diabetes management of adults, insulin pump efficacy in those with type 2 diabetes; primary care for all ages, addiction, and substance abuse prevention and treatment; music therapy for those with chronic lung disease; maternal child health nursing; parish nursing; nursing education; homeopathy and wellness, pediatric health; effects of infant feeding experiences.

La Salle University, School of Nursing and Health Sciences, Program in Nursing, Philadelphia, PA 19141-1199. Offers adult gerontology primary care nurse practitioner (MSN, Certificate); adult health and illness clinical nurse specialist (MSN); adult-gerontology clinical nurse specialist (MSN, Certificate); clinical nurse leader (MSN);

family primary care nurse practitioner (MSN, Certificate); gerontology (Certificate); nurse anesthetist (MSN, Certificate); nursing (MSN, Certificate); nursing administration (MSN, Certificate); nursing education (Certificate); nursing practice (DNP); nursing service administration (MSN); public health nursing (MSN, Certificate); school nursing (Certificate); MSN/MBA; MSN/MPH. *Accreditation:* AACN. *Program availability:* Part-time, evening/weekend, 100% online. *Faculty:* 12 full-time (11 women), 14 part-time/adjunct (11 women). *Students:* 1 (woman) full-time, 277 part-time (220 women); includes 72 minority (36 Black or African American, non-Hispanic/Latino; 1 American Indian or Alaska Native, non-Hispanic/Latino; 18 Asian, non-Hispanic/Latino; 10 Hispanic/Latino; 1 Native Hawaiian or other Pacific Islander, non-Hispanic/Latino; 6 Two or more races, non-Hispanic/Latino), 1 international. Average age 36. 70 applicants, 56% accepted, 24 enrolled. In 2017, 81 master's, 4 doctorates, 13 other advanced degrees awarded. *Degree requirements:* For doctorate, minimum of 1,000 hours of post baccalaureate clinical practice supervised by preceptors. *Entrance requirements:* For master's, GRE, MAT, or GMAT (for students with BSN GPA of less than 3.2), baccalaureate degree in nursing from ACEN- or CCNE-accredited program or an MSN Bridge program; Pennsylvania RN license; 2 letters of reference; resume; statement of philosophy articulating professional values and future educational goal; 1 year of work experience as a registered nurse; for doctorate, GRE (waived for applicants with MSN cumulative GPA of 3.7 or above), MSN, master's degree, MBA or MHA from nationally-accredited program; resume or curriculum vitae; 2 letters of reference; interview; for Certificate, GRE, MAT, or GMAT (for students with BSN GPA of less than 3.2, baccalaureate degree in nursing from ACEN- or CCNE-accredited program or an MSN Bridge program; Pennsylvania RN license; 2 letters of reference; resume; statement of philosophy articulating professional values and future educational goal; 1 year of work experience as a registered nurse. Additional exam requirements/recommendations for international students: Required—TOEFL. *Application deadline:* For fall admission, 8/15 priority date for domestic students, 7/15 for international students; for spring admission, 12/15 priority date for domestic students, 11/15 for international students; for summer admission, 4/15 priority date for domestic students, 3/15 for international students. Applications are processed on a rolling basis. Application fee: $35. Electronic applications accepted. Application fee is waived when completed online. *Expenses:* Contact institution. *Financial support:* In 2017–18, 7 students received support. Scholarships/grants and traineeships available. Support available to part-time students. Financial award application deadline: 8/31; financial award applicants required to submit FAFSA. *Unit head:* Dr. Patricia M. Dillon, Director, 215-951-1322, Fax: 215-951-1896, E-mail: msnapn@lasalle.edu. *Application contact:* Elizabeth Heenan, Director, Graduate and Adult Enrollment, 215-951-1100, Fax: 215-951-1462, E-mail: heenan@lasalle.edu.
Website: http://www.lasalle.edu/nursing/program-options/

Lehman College of the City University of New York, School of Health Sciences, Human Services and Nursing, Department of Nursing, Bronx, NY 10468-1589. Offers adult health nursing (MS); nursing of older adults (MS); parent-child nursing (MS); pediatric nurse practitioner (MS). *Accreditation:* AACN. *Program availability:* Part-time, evening/weekend. *Entrance requirements:* For master's, bachelor's degree in nursing, New York RN license.

Loma Linda University, School of Nursing, Program in Nurse Educator, Loma Linda, CA 92350. Offers adult/gerontology (MS); obstetrics-pediatrics (MS). *Accreditation:* AACN. *Program availability:* Part-time. *Degree requirements:* For master's, thesis or alternative. *Entrance requirements:* For master's, GRE General Test, BSN, minimum GPA of 3.0, RN license. Additional exam requirements/recommendations for international students: Required—TOEFL. Electronic applications accepted. *Faculty research:* Coping, integration of research.

Louisiana State University Health Sciences Center, School of Nursing, New Orleans, LA 70112. Offers adult gerontology acute care nurse practitioner (DNP, Post-Master's Certificate); adult gerontology clinical nurse specialist (DNP, Post-Master's Certificate); adult gerontology primary care nurse practitioner (DNP, Post-Master's Certificate); clinical nurse leader (MSN); executive nurse leader (DNP, Post-Master's Certificate); neonatal nurse practitioner (DNP, Post-Master's Certificate); nurse anesthesia (DNP, Post-Master's Certificate); nurse educator (MSN); nursing (DNS); primary care family nurse practitioner (DNP, Post-Master's Certificate); public/community health nursing (DNP, Post-Master's Certificate). *Accreditation:* AACN; AANA/CANAEP (one or more programs are accredited). *Program availability:* Part-time. *Faculty:* 29 full-time (26 women), 20 part-time/adjunct (8 women). *Students:* 184 full-time (132 women), 41 part-time (35 women); includes 69 minority (45 Black or African American, non-Hispanic/Latino; 11 Asian, non-Hispanic/Latino; 12 Hispanic/Latino; 1 Two or more races, non-Hispanic/Latino), 1 international. Average age 30. 162 applicants, 42% accepted, 68 enrolled. In 2017, 52 master's, 46 doctorates awarded. *Degree requirements:* For master's, thesis optional; for doctorate, thesis/dissertation. *Entrance requirements:* For master's, GRE, minimum GPA of 3.0; for doctorate, GRE, minimum GPA of 3.0 (for DNP), 3.5 (for DNS). Additional exam requirements/recommendations for international students: Required—TOEFL (minimum score 550 paper-based; 79 iBT). *Application deadline:* Applications are processed on a rolling basis. Application fee: $100. Electronic applications accepted. *Expenses:* Contact institution. *Financial support:* Federal Work-Study, institutionally sponsored loans, scholarships/grants, and traineeships available. Financial award applicants required to submit FAFSA. *Faculty research:* Advanced clinical practice, nursing education, interprofessional education, nursing administration, culturally competent care. *Unit head:* Dr. Demetrius James Porche, Dean, 504-568-4106, Fax: 504-599-0573, E-mail: dporch@lsuhsc.edu. *Application contact:* Tracie Gravolet, Director, Office of Student Affairs, 504-568-4114, Fax: 504-568-5711, E-mail: tgravo@lsuhsc.edu.
Website: http://nursing.lsuhsc.edu/

Marquette University, Graduate School, College of Nursing, Milwaukee, WI 53201-1881. Offers acute care nurse practitioner (Certificate); adult clinical nurse specialist (Certificate); adult nurse practitioner (Certificate); advanced practice nursing (MSN, DNP), including adult-older adult acute care (DNP), adults (MSN), adults-older adults (DNP), clinical nurse leader (MSN), health care systems leadership (DNP), nurse-midwifery (MSN), older adults (MSN), pediatrics-acute care, pediatrics-primary care, primary care (DNP), systems leadership and healthcare quality (MSN); family nurse practitioner (Certificate); nurse-midwifery (Certificate); nursing (PhD); pediatric acute care (Certificate); pediatric primary care (Certificate); systems leadership and healthcare quality (Certificate). *Accreditation:* AACN. Terminal master's awarded for partial completion of doctoral program. *Degree requirements:* For master's, comprehensive exam, thesis or alternative. *Entrance requirements:* For master's, GRE General Test, BSN, Wisconsin RN license, official transcripts from all current and previous colleges/universities except Marquette, three completed recommendation forms, resume, written statement of professional goals; for doctorate, GRE General Test, official transcripts from all current and previous colleges/universities except Marquette, three letters of recommendation, resume, written statement of professional goals, sample of scholarly writing. Additional exam requirements/recommendations for international students: Required—TOEFL (minimum score 530 paper-based). Electronic applications accepted. *Faculty research:* Psychosocial adjustment to chronic illness, gerontology, reminiscence, health policy: uninsured and access, hospital care delivery systems.

Maryville University of Saint Louis, Myrtle E. and Earl E. Walker College of Health Professions, The Catherine McAuley School of Nursing, St. Louis, MO 63141-7299. Offers acute care nurse practitioner (MSN); adult gerontology nurse practitioner (MSN); advanced practice nursing (DNP); family nurse practitioner (MSN); pediatric nurse practitioner (MSN). *Accreditation:* AACN. *Program availability:* 100% online, blended/hybrid learning. *Faculty:* 15 full-time (all women), 142 part-time/adjunct (123 women). *Students:* 49 full-time (42 women), 2,999 part-time (2,645 women); includes 773 minority (375 Black or African American, non-Hispanic/Latino; 51 American Indian or Alaska Native, non-Hispanic/Latino; 135 Asian, non-Hispanic/Latino; 149 Hispanic/Latino; 63 Two or more races, non-Hispanic/Latino), 21 international. Average age 36. In 2017, 843 master's, 42 doctorates awarded. *Degree requirements:* For master's, practicum. *Entrance requirements:* For master's, BSN, current licensure, minimum GPA of 3.0, 3 letters of recommendation, curriculum vitae. Additional exam requirements/recommendations for international students: Required—TOEFL (minimum score 550 paper-based). *Application deadline:* Applications are processed on a rolling basis. Electronic applications accepted. *Expenses:* Contact institution. *Financial support:* Federal Work-Study and campus employment available. Support available to part-time students. Financial award application deadline: 4/1; financial award applicants required to submit FAFSA. *Unit head:* Dr. Elizabeth Buck, Assistant Dean/Director of Online Nursing, 314-529-9453, Fax: 314-529-9139, E-mail: ebuck@maryville.edu. *Application contact:* Jeannie DeLuca, Director of Admissions and Advising, 314-929-9355, Fax: 314-529-9927, E-mail: cjacobsmeyer@maryville.edu.
Website: http://www.maryville.edu/hp/nursing/

Medical University of South Carolina, College of Nursing, Adult-Gerontology Health Nurse Practitioner Program, Charleston, SC 29425. Offers MSN, DNP. *Program availability:* Part-time, online learning. *Degree requirements:* For master's, comprehensive exam (for some programs), thesis optional; for doctorate, final project. *Entrance requirements:* For master's, BSN from nationally-accredited program, minimum nursing and cumulative GPA of 3.0, undergraduate-level statistics course, active RN License, 3 confidential references, current curriculum vitae or resume, essay; for doctorate, BSN from nationally-accredited program, minimum nursing and cumulative GPA of 3.0, undergraduate-level statistics course, active RN License, 3 confidential references, current curriculum vitae or resume, personal essay (for DNP). Additional exam requirements/recommendations for international students: Required—TOEFL (minimum score 550 paper-based; 80 iBT). Electronic applications accepted. *Faculty research:* Palliative care, dementia, hospital acquired infections, diabetes, advance practice nurse utilization.

Mercer University, Graduate Studies, Cecil B. Day Campus, Georgia Baptist College of Nursing, Atlanta, GA 30341. Offers adult gerontology acute care nurse practitioner (MSN, Certificate); family nurse practitioner (MSN, Certificate); nursing (PhD); nursing practice (DNP), including adult gerontology acute care nurse practitioner. *Accreditation:* AACN. *Program availability:* Part-time, blended/hybrid learning. *Faculty:* 10 full-time (9 women), 4 part-time/adjunct (3 women). *Students:* 72 full-time (70 women), 33 part-time (29 women); includes 44 minority (29 Black or African American, non-Hispanic/Latino; 9 Asian, non-Hispanic/Latino; 3 Hispanic/Latino; 3 Two or more races, non-Hispanic/Latino), 1 international. Average age 36. 65 applicants, 66% accepted, 30 enrolled. In 2017, 27 master's, 9 doctorates awarded. *Degree requirements:* For master's, thesis or alternative, capstone; for doctorate, comprehensive exam (for some programs), scholarly project (for DNP); dissertation (for PhD). *Entrance requirements:* For master's, MAT or GRE, bachelor's degree from accredited nursing program, registered unencumbered GA nursing license, essay, three professional references; for doctorate, GRE (for PhD), master's degree from accredited nursing program, RN licensure, graduate statistics course, three professional references. Additional exam requirements/recommendations for international students: Required—TOEFL (minimum score 100 iBT). *Application deadline:* For fall admission, 5/1 for domestic students, 3/1 for international students; for winter admission, 11/1 for domestic students, 9/1 for international students; for spring admission, 11/1 for domestic students, 10/1 for international students; for summer admission, 3/1 for domestic and international students. Applications are processed on a rolling basis. Application fee: $50. Electronic applications accepted. *Expenses:* $32,000. *Financial support:* In 2017–18, 23 students received support, including 1 research assistantship (averaging $6,000 per year); scholarships/grants also available. Financial award application deadline: 6/30; financial award applicants required to submit FAFSA. *Faculty research:* Cognitive competence, cancer survivorship, interprofessional education, cultural competence, clopidogrel adherence, high fidelity simulation, self-awareness practices, simulation. *Unit head:* Dr. Linda Streit, Dean/Professor, 678-547-6793, Fax: 678-547-6796, E-mail: streit_la@mercer.edu. *Application contact:* Janda Anderson, Director of Admissions, 678-547-6700, Fax: 678-547-6794, E-mail: anderson_j@mercer.edu.
Website: http://www.mercer.edu/nursing

MGH Institute of Health Professions, School of Nursing, Boston, MA 02129. Offers advanced practice nursing (MSN); gerontological nursing (MSN); nursing (DNP); pediatric nursing (MSN); psychiatric nursing (MSN); teaching and learning for health care education (Certificate); women's health nursing (MSN). *Accreditation:* AACN. *Degree requirements:* For master's, thesis or alternative. *Entrance requirements:* For master's, GRE General Test, bachelor's degree from regionally-accredited college or university. Additional exam requirements/recommendations for international students: Required—TOEFL (minimum score 550 paper-based; 80 iBT). Electronic applications accepted. *Faculty research:* Biobehavioral nursing, HIV/AIDS, gerontological nursing, women's health, vulnerable populations, health systems.

Middle Georgia State University, Office of Graduate Studies, Macon, GA 31206. Offers adult/gerontology acute care nurse practitioner (MSN); information technology (MS), including health informatics, information security and digital forensics, software development. *Entrance requirements:* For master's, GRE. Additional exam requirements/recommendations for international students: Required—TOEFL (minimum score 523 paper-based; 69 iBT). *Expenses:* Contact institution.

Molloy College, The Barbara H. Hagan School of Nursing, Rockville Centre, NY 11571-5002. Offers adult - gerontology nurse practitioner (MS); adult-gerontology clinical nurse specialist (DNP); adult-gerontology nurse practitioner (DNP); clinical nurse specialist: adult - gerontology (MS); family nurse practitioner (MS, DNP); family psychiatric/mental health nurse practitioner (MS, DNP); nursing (PhD, Advanced Certificate); nursing administration with informatics (MS); nursing education (MS); pediatric nurse practitioner (MS, DNP). *Accreditation:* AACN. *Program availability:* Part-time, evening/weekend. *Faculty:* 28 full-time (all women), 7 part-time/adjunct (6 women). *Students:* 19 full-time (14 women), 574 part-time (527 women); includes 336 minority (179 Black or African American, non-Hispanic/Latino; 2 American Indian or Alaska Native, non-Hispanic/Latino; 107 Asian, non-Hispanic/Latino; 42 Hispanic/Latino; 1 Native Hawaiian or other Pacific Islander, non-Hispanic/Latino; 5 Two or more races, non-Hispanic/Latino), 4 international. Average age 44. 292 applicants, 65% accepted, 147 enrolled. In 2017, 135 master's, 9 doctorates, 5 other advanced degrees awarded. *Degree requirements:* For master's, thesis optional. *Entrance requirements:* For master's, 3 letters of reference, BS in nursing, minimum undergraduate GPA of 3.0; for Advanced Certificate, 3 letters of reference, master's degree in nursing. Additional exam requirements/recommendations for international students: Required—TOEFL (minimum score 550 paper-based; 79 iBT).

Application deadline: For fall admission, 9/2 priority date for domestic students; for spring admission, 1/20 priority date for domestic students. Applications are processed on a rolling basis. Application fee: $60. Electronic applications accepted. *Expenses: Tuition:* Full-time $19,980; part-time $1110 per credit. *Required fees:* $1040. Tuition and fees vary according to course load and degree level. *Financial support:* Research assistantships with partial tuition reimbursements, teaching assistantships with partial tuition reimbursements, institutionally sponsored loans, scholarships/grants, and unspecified assistantships available. Support available to part-time students. Financial award application deadline: 3/1; financial award applicants required to submit FAFSA. *Faculty research:* Workplace violence involving nurses and psychiatric patients; moral distress in nursing; primary care of veterans; the role of service immersion programs in graduate nursing education; academic integrity. *Unit head:* Dr. Marcia R. Gardner, Dean, The Barbara H. Hagan School of Nursing, 516-323-3651, E-mail: mgardner@molloy.edu. *Application contact:* Jaclyn Machowicz, Assistant Director for Admissions, 516-323-4010, E-mail: jmachowicz@molloy.edu.

Monmouth University, Graduate Studies, Marjorie K. Unterberg School of Nursing and Health Studies, West Long Branch, NJ 07764-1898. Offers adult-gerontological primary care nurse practitioner (MSN, Post-Master's Certificate); family nurse practitioner (MSN, Post-Master's Certificate); forensic nursing (MSN, Certificate); nursing (MSN); nursing administration (MSN); nursing education (MSN, Post-Master's Certificate); nursing practice (DNP); physician assistant (MS); psychiatric and mental health nurse practitioner (MSN, Post-Master's Certificate); school nursing (MSN, Certificate). *Accreditation:* AACN. *Program availability:* Part-time, evening/weekend, 100% online, blended/hybrid learning. *Faculty:* 12 full-time (all women), 20 part-time/adjunct (12 women). *Students:* 90 full-time (66 women), 329 part-time (302 women); includes 129 minority (51 Black or African American, non-Hispanic/Latino; 43 Asian, non-Hispanic/Latino; 31 Hispanic/Latino; 1 Native Hawaiian or other Pacific Islander, non-Hispanic/Latino; 3 Two or more races, non-Hispanic/Latino), 1 international. Average age 36. In 2017, 85 master's, 4 other advanced degrees awarded. *Degree requirements:* For master's, practicum (for some tracks); for doctorate, practicum, capstone course. *Entrance requirements:* For master's, GRE General Test (waived for MSN applicants with minimum B grade in each of the first four courses and for MS applicants with master's degree), BSN with minimum GPA of 2.75, current RN license, proof of liability and malpractice policy, personal statement, two letters of recommendation, college course work in health assessment, resume; CASPA application (for MS); for doctorate, accredited master's nursing program degree with minimum GPA of 3.2, active RN license, national certification as nurse practitioner or nurse administrator, working knowledge of statistics, statement of goals and vision for change, 2 letters of recommendation (professional or academic), resume, interview. Additional exam requirements/recommendations for international students: Required—TOEFL (minimum score 550 paper-based; 79 iBT), IELTS (minimum score 6) or Michigan English Language Assessment Battery (minimum score 77). *Application deadline:* For fall admission, 7/15 priority date for domestic students, 6/1 for international students; for spring admission, 12/1 priority date for domestic students, 11/1 for international students; for summer admission, 5/1 for domestic students. Applications are processed on a rolling basis. Application fee: $50. Electronic applications accepted. *Expenses:* Contact institution. *Financial support:* In 2017–18, 197 students received support. Institutionally sponsored loans, scholarships/grants, and unspecified assistantships available. Support available to part-time students. Financial award applicants required to submit FAFSA. *Faculty research:* School nursing, health policy, and smoking cessation in teens; Multiple Sclerosis; adherence and self-efficacy; aging issues and geriatric care. *Unit head:* Dr. Janet Mahoney, Dean, 732-571-3443, Fax: 732-263-5131, E-mail: jmahoney@monmouth.edu. *Application contact:* Lucia Fedele, Graduate Admission Counselor, 732-571-3452, Fax: 732-263-5123, E-mail: gradadm@monmouth.edu. Website: https://www.monmouth.edu/graduate/nursing-programs-of-study/

Morningside College, Graduate Programs, Nylen School of Nursing, Sioux City, IA 51106. Offers adult gerontology primary care nurse practitioner (MSN); clinical nurse leader (MSN); family primary care nurse practitioner (MSN). *Program availability:* Part-time, online only, 100% online. *Faculty:* 3 full-time (all women), 4 part-time/adjunct (all women). *Students:* 7 full-time (3 women), 86 part-time (81 women); includes 8 minority (1 American Indian or Alaska Native, non-Hispanic/Latino; 3 Asian, non-Hispanic/Latino; 4 Hispanic/Latino). Average age 32. 37 applicants, 100% accepted, 37 enrolled. In 2017, 19 master's awarded. *Application deadline:* Applications are processed on a rolling basis. Application fee: $65. Electronic applications accepted. *Expenses:* Contact institution. *Financial support:* In 2017–18, 67 students received support. Scholarships/grants and tuition waivers (partial) available. Financial award application deadline: 3/1; financial award applicants required to submit FAFSA. *Unit head:* Dr. Jackie Barber, Dean of Graduate Nursing, 712-274-5297, E-mail: barber@morningside.edu.

Mount Carmel College of Nursing, Nursing Program, Columbus, OH 43222. Offers adult gerontology acute care nurse practitioner (MS); adult health clinical nurse specialist (MS); family nurse practitioner (MS); nursing (DNP); nursing administration (MS); nursing education (MS). *Accreditation:* AACN. *Program availability:* Part-time. *Faculty:* 11 full-time (all women), 5 part-time/adjunct (4 women). *Students:* 112 full-time (93 women), 72 part-time (65 women); includes 35 minority (20 Black or African American, non-Hispanic/Latino; 4 Asian, non-Hispanic/Latino; 3 Hispanic/Latino; 8 Two or more races, non-Hispanic/Latino). Average age 35. 135 applicants, 65% accepted, 68 enrolled. In 2017, 64 master's awarded. *Degree requirements:* For master's, professional manuscript; for doctorate, practicum. *Entrance requirements:* For master's, letters of recommendation, statement of purpose, current resume, baccalaureate degree in nursing, current Ohio RN license, minimum cumulative GPA of 3.0; for doctorate, master's degree in nursing from program accredited by either ACEN or CCNE. Additional exam requirements/recommendations for international students: Required—TOEFL (minimum score 550 paper-based; 80 iBT). *Application deadline:* For fall admission, 2/1 priority date for domestic students; for spring admission, 11/1 priority date for domestic students. Applications are processed on a rolling basis. Application fee: $30. Electronic applications accepted. *Expenses: Tuition:* Full-time $11,403; part-time $543 per credit. *Required fees:* $50; $50 per year. *Financial support:* In 2017–18, 3 students received support. Institutionally sponsored loans and scholarships/grants available. Financial award application deadline: 3/1; financial award applicants required to submit FAFSA. *Unit head:* Dr. Jill Kilanowski, Associate Dean, 614-234-5237, Fax: 614-234-2875, E-mail: jkilanowski@mccn.edu. *Application contact:* Dr. Kim Campbell, Director of Recruitment and Admissions, 614-234-5144, Fax: 614-234-5427, E-mail: kcampbell@mccn.edu.

Neumann University, Graduate Program in Nursing, Aston, PA 19014. Offers adult-gerontology nurse practitioner (MS, Certificate). *Accreditation:* ACEN. *Program availability:* Part-time, evening/weekend. *Faculty:* 2 full-time (both women), 4 part-time/adjunct (3 women). *Students:* 37 part-time (35 women); includes 11 minority (5 Black or African American, non-Hispanic/Latino; 2 Asian, non-Hispanic/Latino; 2 Hispanic/Latino; 2 Two or more races, non-Hispanic/Latino). Average age 41. 15 applicants, 47% accepted, 7 enrolled. In 2017, 11 master's awarded. *Entrance requirements:* For master's, official transcripts from all institutions attended, resume, letter of intent, current registered nursing license, two letters of reference; for Certificate, BSN, MSN, official transcripts from all institutions attended, resume, letter of intent, current registered nursing license, two official letters of reference. Additional exam requirements/recommendations for international students: Required—TOEFL (minimum score 84 iBT). *Application deadline:* Applications are processed on a rolling basis. Application fee: $0. Electronic applications accepted. *Expenses: Tuition:* Part-time $700 per credit hour. Tuition and fees vary according to degree level, campus/location and program. *Financial support:* Scholarships/grants, traineeships, and health care benefits available. Support available to part-time students. Financial award application deadline: 3/15; financial award applicants required to submit FAFSA. *Unit head:* Dr. Kathleen Hoover, Dean, Division of Nursing and Health Sciences, 610-558-5560, Fax: 610-361-5265, E-mail: hooverk@neumann.edu. *Application contact:* Dr. Erika K. Davis, Director of Adult and Graduate Admissions, 800-9-NEUMANN Ext. 5208, Fax: 610-361-2548, E-mail: gradadultadmiss@neumann.edu.

New York University, Rory Meyers College of Nursing, Doctor of Nursing Practice Program, New York, NY 10012-1019. Offers nursing (DNP), including adult-gerontology acute care nurse practitioner, adult-gerontology primary care nurse practitioner, family nurse practitioner, nurse-midwifery, pediatrics nurse practitioner, psychiatric-mental health nurse practitioner. *Accreditation:* AACN. *Program availability:* Part-time, evening/weekend. *Faculty:* 16 full-time (all women), 1 (woman) part-time/adjunct. *Students:* 48 part-time (43 women); includes 11 minority (5 Black or African American, non-Hispanic/Latino; 5 Asian, non-Hispanic/Latino; 1 Hispanic/Latino). Average age 28. 20 applicants, 75% accepted, 10 enrolled. In 2017, 8 doctorates awarded. *Degree requirements:* For doctorate, thesis/dissertation, project. *Entrance requirements:* For doctorate, MS, RN license, interview, Nurse Practitioner Certification, writing sample. Additional exam requirements/recommendations for international students: Required—TOEFL (minimum score 100 iBT), IELTS (minimum score 7). *Application deadline:* For fall admission, 3/1 priority date for domestic and international students. Applications are processed on a rolling basis. Application fee: $80. Electronic applications accepted. *Expenses:* Contact institution. *Financial support:* In 2017–18, 13 students received support. Scholarships/grants available. Support available to part-time students. Financial award application deadline: 2/1; financial award applicants required to submit FAFSA. *Faculty research:* Workforce determinants of healthcare quality, genomics, health literacy and health outcomes, health policy. *Unit head:* Dr. Mary Jo Vetter, Director, DNP Program, 212-998-5165, E-mail: mjv5@nyu.edu. *Application contact:* Matthew Burke, Assistant Director, Graduate Student Affairs and Admissions, 212-998-7397, E-mail: mb6060@nyu.edu.

New York University, Rory Meyers College of Nursing, Programs in Advanced Practice Nursing, New York, NY 10012-1019. Offers adult-gerontology acute care nurse practitioner (MS, Advanced Certificate); adult-gerontology primary care nurse practitioner (MS, Advanced Certificate), family nurse practitioner (MS, Advanced Certificate); gerontology nurse practitioner (Advanced Certificate); nurse-midwifery (MS, Advanced Certificate); nursing administration (MS, Advanced Certificate); nursing education (MS, Advanced Certificate); nursing informatics (MS, Advanced Certificate); pediatrics nurse practitioner (MS, Advanced Certificate); psychiatric-mental health nurse practitioner (MS, Advanced Certificate); MS/MPH. *Accreditation:* AACN; ACNM/ACME. *Program availability:* Part-time, evening/weekend. *Faculty:* 23 full-time (all women), 62 part-time/adjunct (56 women). *Students:* 50 full-time (46 women), 557 part-time (509 women); includes 234 minority (58 Black or African American, non-Hispanic/Latino; 1 American Indian or Alaska Native, non-Hispanic/Latino; 116 Asian, non-Hispanic/Latino; 43 Hispanic/Latino; 1 Native Hawaiian or other Pacific Islander, non-Hispanic/Latino; 15 Two or more races, non-Hispanic/Latino), 23 international. Average age 32. 391 applicants, 59% accepted, 149 enrolled. In 2017, 187 master's, 5 other advanced degrees awarded. *Degree requirements:* For master's, thesis (for some programs), capstone. *Entrance requirements:* For master's, BS in nursing, AS in nursing with another BS/BA, interview, RN license, 1 year of clinical experience (3 for the MS in nursing education program); for Advanced Certificate, master's degree in nursing. Additional exam requirements/recommendations for international students: Required—TOEFL (minimum score 100 iBT), IELTS (minimum score 7). *Application deadline:* For fall admission, 3/1 priority date for domestic and international students; for spring admission, 11/1 priority date for domestic and international students; for summer admission, 3/1 for domestic and international students. Application fee: $80. Electronic applications accepted. *Expenses:* Contact institution. *Financial support:* In 2017–18, 130 students received support. Career-related internships or fieldwork, Federal Work-Study, and scholarships/grants available. Support available to part-time students. Financial award application deadline: 3/1; financial award applicants required to submit FAFSA. *Faculty research:* Vaccine hesitancy in pregnant women and mothers, palliative care and midwifery, diabetes education, curriculum development, workforce training, education and development, geriatrics. *Unit head:* Dr. James Pace, Senior Associate Dean for Academic Programs, 212-992-7343, E-mail: james.pace@nyu.edu. *Application contact:* Matthew Burke, Assistant Director, Graduate Student Affairs and Admissions, 212-998-7397, Fax: 212-995-4302, E-mail: mb6060@nyu.edu.

Northeastern University, Bouvé College of Health Sciences, Boston, MA 02115-5096. Offers applied behavior analysis (MS); audiology (Au D); counseling psychology (MS, PhD, CAGS); exercise science (MS); nursing (MS, PhD, CAGS), including administration (MS), adult-gerontology acute care nurse practitioner (MS, CAGS), adult-gerontology primary care nurse practitioner (MS, CAGS), anesthesia (MS), family nurse practitioner (MS, CAGS), neonatal nurse practitioner (MS, CAGS), pediatric nurse practitioner (MS, CAGS), psychiatric mental health nurse practitioner (MS, CAGS); nursing practice (DNP); pharmaceutical sciences (MS, PhD), including interdisciplinary concentration, pharmaceutics and drug delivery systems; pharmacology (MS); pharmacy (Pharm D); school psychology (PhD); speech-language pathology (MS); urban health (MPH); MS/MBA. *Accreditation:* ACPE (one or more programs are accredited). *Program availability:* Part-time, evening/weekend, online learning. *Faculty:* 192 full-time. *Students:* 1,685. In 2017, 352 master's, 312 doctorates, 25 other advanced degrees awarded. *Degree requirements:* For doctorate, thesis/dissertation (for some programs); for CAGS, comprehensive exam. Application fee: $75. Electronic applications accepted. *Expenses:* Contact institution. *Financial support:* Fellowships, research assistantships, teaching assistantships, career-related internships or fieldwork, scholarships/grants, health care benefits, tuition waivers, and unspecified assistantships available. Support available to part-time students. Financial award applicants required to submit FAFSA. *Unit head:* Susan L. Parish, Dean, Bouve College of Health Sciences, 617-373-3321, Fax: 617-373-3030, E-mail: s.parish@northeastern.edu. *Application contact:* 617-373-2708, Fax: 617-373-4701, E-mail: bouvegrad@northeastern.edu. Website: https://www.northeastern.edu/bouve/

Nova Southeastern University, Ron and Kathy Assaf College of Nursing, Fort Lauderdale, FL 33314-7796. Offers advanced practice registered nurse (MSN), including adult-gerontology acute care nurse practitioner, family nurse practitioner, psychiatric mental health nurse practitioner; executive nurse leadership (MSN); nursing (PhD), including nursing education; nursing education (MSN); nursing informatics (MSN); nursing practice (DNP). *Accreditation:* AACN. *Program availability:* Part-time, evening/weekend, 100% online, blended/hybrid learning, annual one-week summer institute delivered face-to-face on main campus. *Faculty:* 9 full-time (all women), 47 part-time/adjunct (43 women). *Students:* 658 full-time (599 women); includes 414 minority (175 Black or African American, non-Hispanic/Latino; 37 Asian, non-Hispanic/Latino; 179 Hispanic/Latino; 1 Native Hawaiian or other Pacific Islander, non-Hispanic/Latino; 22 Two or more races, non-Hispanic/Latino), 3 international. Average age 38. 179

applicants, 100% accepted, 163 enrolled. In 2017, 161 master's, 16 doctorates awarded. *Degree requirements:* For doctorate, comprehensive exam, thesis/dissertation. *Entrance requirements:* For master's, minimum GPA of 3.0, RN, BSN, BS or BA; for doctorate, minimum GPA of 3.5, MSN, RN. Additional exam requirements/recommendations for international students: Recommended—TOEFL. *Application deadline:* For fall admission, 3/1 priority date for domestic students, 3/1 for international students; for winter admission, 11/1 for domestic and international students. Applications are processed on a rolling basis. Application fee: $50. Electronic applications accepted. *Expenses:* Contact institution. *Financial support:* Application deadline: 4/15; applicants required to submit FAFSA. *Faculty research:* Nursing education, curriculum, clinical research, interdisciplinary research. *Total annual research expenditures:* $9,500. *Unit head:* Dr. Marcella M. Rutherford, Dean, 954-262-1963, E-mail: rmarcell@nova.edu. *Application contact:* Dianna Murphey, Director of Operations, 954-262-1975, E-mail: dgardner1@nova.edu.
Website: http://www.nova.edu/nursing/

Oakland University, Graduate Study and Lifelong Learning, School of Nursing, Adult Gerontological Nurse Practitioner Program, Rochester, MI 48309-4401. Offers MSN, PMC. *Expenses:* Tuition, state resident: full-time $16,950; part-time $706.25 per credit. Tuition, nonresident: full-time $24,648; part-time $1027 per credit.

Old Dominion University, College of Health Sciences, School of Nursing, Adult Gerontology Nursing Emphasis, Norfolk, VA 23529. Offers adult gerontology clinical nurse specialist/administrator (MSN); adult gerontology clinical nurse specialist/educator (MSN); advanced practice (DNP); neonatal clinical nurse specialist (MSN); pediatric clinical nurse specialist (MSN). *Program availability:* Part-time, online only, blended/hybrid learning. *Faculty:* 2 full-time (both women), 2 part-time/adjunct (both women). *Students:* 9 full-time (all women), 10 part-time (9 women); includes 10 minority (8 Black or African American, non-Hispanic/Latino; 2 Asian, non-Hispanic/Latino). Average age 37. 27 applicants, 96% accepted, 12 enrolled. In 2017, 5 master's awarded. *Degree requirements:* For master's, comprehensive exam, internship, practicum. *Entrance requirements:* For master's, GRE or MAT (waived with a GPA above 3.5), undergraduate health/physical assessment course, statistics, 3 letters of recommendation, essay, resume, transcripts. Additional exam requirements/recommendations for international students: Required—TOEFL. *Application deadline:* For fall admission, 6/1 priority date for domestic students, 4/15 priority date for international students. Applications are processed on a rolling basis. Application fee: $50. Electronic applications accepted. *Expenses:* $469 per credit; $450 School of Nursing fee per semester. *Financial support:* Unspecified assistantships available. Financial award applicants required to submit FAFSA. *Unit head:* Dr. Tina Haney, Program Director, 757-683-5428, Fax: 757-683-5253, E-mail: thaney@odu.edu. *Application contact:* Sue Parker, Graduate Program Coordinator, 757-683-4298, Fax: 757-683-5253, E-mail: sparker@odu.edu.

Oregon Health & Science University, School of Nursing, Program in Adult Gerontology Acute Care Nurse Practitioner, Portland, OR 97239-2941. Offers MN. *Entrance requirements:* For master's, minimum cumulative and science GPA of 3.0, 3 letters of recommendation, essay, statistics within last 5 years. Additional exam requirements/recommendations for international students: Required—TOEFL (minimum score 83 iBT). Electronic applications accepted. *Expenses:* Contact institution. *Faculty research:* Weight loss and cachexia in head and neck cancer patients, clinical outcomes in the ICU, metabolic dysfunction in heart failure.

Point Loma Nazarene University, School of Nursing, MS in Nursing Program, San Diego, CA 92106-2899. Offers adult-gerontology (MSN); family individual health (MSN); pediatrics (MSN). *Program availability:* Part-time. *Students:* 59 part-time (49 women); includes 28 minority (4 Black or African American, non-Hispanic/Latino; 1 American Indian or Alaska Native, non-Hispanic/Latino; 4 Asian, non-Hispanic/Latino; 9 Hispanic/Latino; 4 Native Hawaiian or other Pacific Islander, non-Hispanic/Latino; 6 Two or more races, non-Hispanic/Latino), 1 international. Average age 36. 23 applicants, 96% accepted, 18 enrolled. In 2017, 21 master's awarded. *Entrance requirements:* For master's, NCLEX exam, ADN or BSN in nursing, interview, RN license, essay, letters of recommendation, interview. *Application deadline:* For fall admission, 7/5 priority date for domestic students; for spring admission, 11/1 priority date for domestic students; for summer admission, 3/22 priority date for domestic students. Applications are processed on a rolling basis. Electronic applications accepted. *Expenses:* Contact institution. *Financial support:* Scholarships/grants available. Financial award applicants required to submit FAFSA. *Unit head:* Dr. Barb Taylor, Dean of the School of Nursing, 619-849-2766, E-mail: bataylor@pointloma.edu. *Application contact:* Joanie Joy, Senior Director of Enrollment Management, 619-329-6785, E-mail: gradinfo@pointloma.edu.
Website: https://www.pointloma.edu/graduate-studies/programs/nursing-ms

Purdue University, Graduate School, College of Health and Human Sciences, School of Nursing, West Lafayette, IN 47907. Offers adult gerontology primary care nurse practitioner (MS, Post Master's Certificate); nursing (DNP, PhD); primary care family nurse practitioner (MS, Post Master's Certificate); primary care pediatric nurse practitioner (MS, Post Master's Certificate). *Faculty:* 31 full-time (30 women), 2 part-time/adjunct (both women). *Students:* 41 full-time (39 women), 33 part-time (32 women); includes 10 minority (5 Black or African American, non-Hispanic/Latino; 1 American Indian or Alaska Native, non-Hispanic/Latino; 1 Asian, non-Hispanic/Latino; 2 Hispanic/Latino; 1 Two or more races, non-Hispanic/Latino), 2 international. Average age 35. 36 applicants, 78% accepted, 16 enrolled. In 2017, 13 master's, 5 doctorates, 2 other advanced degrees awarded. *Unit head:* Jane M. Kirkpatrick, Head of the Graduate Program, 765-494-6644, E-mail: jmkirk@purdue.edu. *Application contact:* Reanne Hall, Graduate Contact, 765-494-9248, E-mail: gradnursing@purdue.edu.
Website: http://www.purdue.edu/hhs/nur/

Research College of Nursing, Nursing Program, Kansas City, MO 64132. Offers adult-gerontological nurse practitioner (MSN); executive practice and healthcare leadership (MSN); family nurse practitioner (MSN). *Accreditation:* AACN. *Program availability:* Part-time-only, 100% online. *Faculty:* 10 full-time (all women), 4 part-time/adjunct (2 women). *Students:* 1 (woman) full-time, 150 part-time (125 women); includes 14 minority (7 Black or African American, non-Hispanic/Latino; 1 American Indian or Alaska Native, non-Hispanic/Latino; 2 Asian, non-Hispanic/Latino; 2 Hispanic/Latino; 1 Native Hawaiian or other Pacific Islander, non-Hispanic/Latino; 1 Two or more races, non-Hispanic/Latino). *Degree requirements:* For master's, research project. *Entrance requirements:* For master's, 3 letters of recommendation, official transcripts, resume, personal statement/writing sample. *Application deadline:* Applications are processed on a rolling basis. Application fee: $65. Electronic applications accepted. *Expenses: Tuition:* Part-time $550 per credit hour. *Financial support:* Applicants required to submit FAFSA. *Unit head:* Dr. Thad Wilson, President, 816-995-2815, Fax: 816-995-2817, E-mail: thad.wilson@researchcollege.edu. *Application contact:* Leslie Burry, Director of Transfer and Graduate Recruitment, 816-995-2820, Fax: 816-995-2813, E-mail: leslie.burry@researchcollege.edu.

Rush University, College of Nursing, Department of Adult Health and Gerontological Nursing, Chicago, IL 60612. Offers adult gerontology acute care clinical nurse specialist (DNP); adult gerontology acute care nurse practitioner (DNP, Post-Graduate Certificate); adult gerontology primary care nurse practitioner (DNP); nurse anesthesia (DNP). *Accreditation:* AACN; AANA/CANAEP (one or more programs are accredited). *Program availability:* Part-time. *Students:* 98 full-time (68 women), 155 part-time (17 women); includes 48 minority (7 Black or African American, non-Hispanic/Latino; 22 Asian, non-Hispanic/Latino; 14 Hispanic/Latino; 5 Two or more races, non-Hispanic/Latino). 170 applicants, 54% accepted, 69 enrolled. In 2017, 51 doctorates awarded. *Degree requirements:* For doctorate, scholarly project. *Entrance requirements:* For doctorate, GRE General Test (for nurse anesthesia; waived for other DNPs if cumulative GPA is 3.25 or greater, nursing GPA is 3.0 or greater, or a completed graduate program GPA is 3.5 or greater), interview, 3 letters of recommendation, personal statement, current resume; for Post-Graduate Certificate, MSN in a clinical discipline, 3 letters of recommendation, personal statement, current resume, interview. Additional exam requirements/recommendations for international students: Required—TOEFL (minimum score 94 iBT). *Application deadline:* For fall admission, 1/2 for domestic students; for spring admission, 8/1 for domestic students; for summer admission, 12/1 for domestic students. Applications are processed on a rolling basis. Application fee: $110. Electronic applications accepted. *Expenses:* Contact institution. *Financial support:* Research assistantships, teaching assistantships, Federal Work-Study, institutionally sponsored loans, scholarships/grants, traineeships, and health care benefits available. Support available to part-time students. Financial award application deadline: 3/1; financial award applicants required to submit FAFSA. *Faculty research:* Physical activity; prevention; cardiovascular risk; caregivers; gerontology. *Unit head:* Dr. Elizabeth Carlson, Chairperson, 312-942-7117, E-mail: elizabeth_carlson@rush.edu. *Application contact:* Jennifer Thorndyke, Director of Admissions, 312-563-7526, E-mail: jennifer_thorndyke@rush.edu.
Website: https://www.rushu.rush.edu/college-nursing/departments-college-nursing/department-adult-health-and-gerontological-nursing

Rutgers University–Camden, School of Nursing–Camden, Camden, NJ 08102-1401. Offers adult gerontology primary care nurse practitioner (DNP); family nurse practitioner (DNP). *Degree requirements:* For doctorate, minimum of 1,000 clinical residency hours, evidence-based clinical project.

Sage Graduate School, School of Health Sciences, Department of Nursing, Program in Adult Gerontology Nurse Practitioner, Troy, NY 12180-4115. Offers MS, Certificate. *Program availability:* Part-time, evening/weekend. *Faculty:* 6 full-time (all women), 11 part-time/adjunct (10 women). *Students:* 1 (woman) full-time, 20 part-time (18 women); includes 4 minority (3 Asian, non-Hispanic/Latino; 1 Two or more races, non-Hispanic/Latino). Average age 43. 15 applicants, 27% accepted, 2 enrolled. In 2017, 3 master's awarded. *Entrance requirements:* For master's, currently licensed as registered professional nurse in state of practice; baccalaureate degree in nursing from nationally-accredited program or its international equivalent. Additional exam requirements/recommendations for international students: Required—TOEFL (minimum score 550 paper-based). *Application deadline:* Applications are processed on a rolling basis. Application fee: $30. Electronic applications accepted. Tuition and fees vary according to degree level and program. *Financial support:* Fellowships, research assistantships, scholarships/grants, and unspecified assistantships available. Financial award application deadline: 3/1; financial award applicants required to submit FAFSA. *Unit head:* Dr. Theresa Hand, Dean, School of Health Sciences, 518-244-2264, Fax: 518-244-4571, E-mail: handt@sage.edu. *Application contact:* Dr. Carol Braungart, Co-Director, Graduate Program in Nursing, 518-244-2459, Fax: 518-244-2009, E-mail: braunc@sage.edu.

St. Catherine University, Graduate Programs, Program in Nursing, St. Paul, MN 55105. Offers adult-gerontological nurse practitioner (MS); nurse educator (MS); nursing (DNP); nursing: entry-level (MS); pediatric nurse practitioner (MS). *Accreditation:* ACEN. *Program availability:* Part-time, evening/weekend. *Degree requirements:* For master's, thesis; for doctorate, portfolio, systems change project. *Entrance requirements:* For master's, GRE General Test, bachelor's degree in nursing, current nursing license, 2 years of recent clinical practice; for doctorate, master's degree in nursing, RN license, advanced nursing position. Additional exam requirements/recommendations for international students: Required—TOEFL (minimum score 600 paper-based; 100 iBT). *Application deadline:* For fall admission, 1/15 priority date for domestic students. Application fee: $35. *Expenses:* Contact institution. *Financial support:* Career-related internships or fieldwork and institutionally sponsored loans available. Support available to part-time students. Financial award application deadline: 4/1; financial award applicants required to submit FAFSA. *Unit head:* Margaret Dexheimer-Pharris, Professor/Associate Dean for Nursing, 651-690-6572, Fax: 651-690-6941, E-mail: mdpharris@stkate.edu. *Application contact:* Kristin Chalberg, Associate Director of Non-Traditional Admissions, 651-690-6868, Fax: 651-690-6064.

Saint Francis Medical Center College of Nursing, Graduate Programs, Peoria, IL 61603-3783. Offers adult gerontology (MSN); clinical nurse leader (MSN); family nurse practitioner (MSN, Post-Graduate Certificate); family psychiatric mental health nurse practitioner (MSN); neonatal nurse practitioner (MSN); nurse clinician (Post-Graduate Certificate); nurse educator (MSN, Post-Graduate Certificate); nursing (DNP); nursing management leadership (MSN). *Accreditation:* ACEN. *Program availability:* Part-time, online only, 100% online, blended/hybrid learning. *Faculty:* 11 full-time (all women), 7 part-time/adjunct (all women). *Students:* 4 full-time (all women), 239 part-time (209 women); includes 24 minority (12 Black or African American, non-Hispanic/Latino; 3 Asian, non-Hispanic/Latino; 4 Hispanic/Latino; 5 Two or more races, non-Hispanic/Latino). Average age 37. 105 applicants, 83% accepted, 60 enrolled. In 2017, 52 master's, 8 doctorates awarded. *Degree requirements:* For master's, research experience, portfolio, practicum; for doctorate, practicum. *Entrance requirements:* For master's, nursing research, health assessment, graduate course work in statistics, RN license; for doctorate, master's degree in nursing, professional portfolio, graduate statistics, transcripts, RN license. Additional exam requirements/recommendations for international students: Required—TOEFL (minimum score 550 paper-based; 79 iBT). *Application deadline:* For fall admission, 6/1 priority date for domestic and international students; for spring admission, 11/15 priority date for domestic and international students. Applications are processed on a rolling basis. Application fee: $50. *Expenses:* Contact institution. *Financial support:* In 2017–18, 13 students received support. Scholarships/grants and tuition waivers (partial) available. Support available to part-time students. Financial award application deadline: 6/15; financial award applicants required to submit FAFSA. *Faculty research:* Outcome and curriculum planning, health promotion, NCLEX-RN results, decision-making program evaluation. *Unit head:* Dr. Patti A. Stockert, President of the College, 309-655-4124, Fax: 309-624-8973, E-mail: patricia.a.stockert@osfhealthcare.org. *Application contact:* Dr. Kim A. Mitchell, Dean, Graduate Program, 309-655-2201, Fax: 309-624-8973, E-mail: kim.a.mitchell@osfhealthcare.org.
Website: http://www.sfmccon.edu/graduate-programs/

St. Joseph's College, Long Island Campus, Program in Nursing, Patchogue, NY 11772-2399. Offers adult-gerontology clinical nurse specialist (MS); adult-gerontology primary care nurse practitioner (MS); nursing education (MS). *Program availability:* Part-time, evening/weekend. *Faculty:* 4 full-time (all women), 1 (woman) part-time/adjunct. *Students:* 1 (woman) full-time, 40 part-time (36 women); includes 15 minority (7 Black or African American, non-Hispanic/Latino; 3 Asian, non-Hispanic/Latino; 5 Hispanic/Latino). Average age 41. 39 applicants, 69% accepted, 21 enrolled. In 2017, 6 master's awarded. *Entrance requirements:* For master's, one year of professional clinical practice

prior to admission, proof of New York State RN license and current professional registration, curriculum vitae, personal statement, two letters of reference, official college transcripts, proof of malpractice insurance. Additional exam requirements/recommendations for international students: Required—TOEFL (minimum score 550 paper-based; 80 iBT). *Application deadline:* Applications are processed on a rolling basis. Application fee: $25. Electronic applications accepted. *Expenses: Tuition:* Full-time $17,550; part-time $975 per credit. *Required fees:* $362. *Financial support:* In 2017–18, 23 students received support. *Unit head:* Dr. Maria Fletcher, RN, Director/Associate Professor, 631-687-5180, E-mail: mfletcher@sjcny.edu.
Website: http://www.sjcny.edu/long-island

St. Joseph's College, New York, Program in Nursing, Brooklyn, NY 11205-3688. Offers adult-gerontology clinical nurse specialist (MS); adult-gerontology primary care nurse practitioner (MS); nursing education (MS). *Accreditation:* ACEN. *Program availability:* Part-time, evening/weekend. *Faculty:* 4 full-time (all women), 1 (woman) part-time/adjunct. *Students:* 47 part-time (46 women); includes 38 minority (35 Black or African American, non-Hispanic/Latino; 1 Asian, non-Hispanic/Latino; 2 Two or more races, non-Hispanic/Latino). Average age 45. 51 applicants, 71% accepted, 20 enrolled. In 2017, 7 master's awarded. *Entrance requirements:* For master's, one year of professional clinical practice, proof of NY State RN license and current professional registration, curriculum vitae, personal statement, 2 letters of reference, official transcripts, malpractice insurance. Additional exam requirements/recommendations for international students: Required—TOEFL (minimum score 80 iBT). *Application deadline:* Applications are processed on a rolling basis. Application fee: $25. Electronic applications accepted. *Expenses: Tuition:* Full-time $17,550; part-time $975 per credit. *Required fees:* $362. *Financial support:* In 2017–18, 7 students received support. *Unit head:* Maria Fletcher, Associate Professor/Director, 718-940-5891, E-mail: mfletcher@sjcny.edu.
Website: http://www.sjcny.edu

Saint Mary's College, Graduate Programs, Doctor of Nursing Practice Program, Notre Dame, IN 46556. Offers adult - gerontology acute care (DNP); adult - gerontology primary care (DNP); family nurse practitioner (DNP). *Program availability:* Part-time-only. *Faculty:* 7 full-time (all women), 4 part-time/adjunct (3 women). *Students:* 39 part-time (37 women); includes 12 minority (4 Black or African American, non-Hispanic/Latino; 5 Asian, non-Hispanic/Latino; 3 Hispanic/Latino). Average age 31. 36 applicants, 83% accepted, 26 enrolled. *Degree requirements:* For doctorate, comprehensive exam, thesis/dissertation. *Entrance requirements:* For doctorate, BSN or MSN, unencumbered RN license or eligibility for RN licensure, official transcripts from previously-attended institutions, 3 letters of recommendation, personal statement, resume or curriculum vitae. Additional exam requirements/recommendations for international students: Recommended—TOEFL (minimum score 80 iBT), IELTS (minimum score 6.5). *Application deadline:* For fall admission, 6/15 priority date for domestic and international students. Applications are processed on a rolling basis. Application fee: $65. Electronic applications accepted. *Expenses:* $5,382 per semester. *Financial support:* Application deadline: 3/1; applicants required to submit FAFSA. *Faculty research:* Suicide prevention, infant death prevention, delirium management, teaching methodologies, nurses' perceptions of care. *Unit head:* Linda Paskiewicz, Director of the Department of Nursing Science, 574-284-4679, E-mail: lpaskie@saintmarys.edu. *Application contact:* Melissa Fruscione, Graduate Admission, 574-284-5098, E-mail: graduateadmission@saintmarys.edu.
Website: https://grad.saintmarys.edu/academic-programs/doctor-nursing-practice

Salem State University, School of Graduate Studies, Program in Nursing, Salem, MA 01970-5353. Offers adult-gerontology primary care nursing (MSN); nursing administration (MSN); nursing education (MSN); MBA/MSN. *Accreditation:* AACN. *Program availability:* Part-time, evening/weekend. *Entrance requirements:* For master's, GRE or MAT. Additional exam requirements/recommendations for international students: Required—TOEFL (minimum score 550 paper-based; 80 iBT) or IELTS (minimum score 5.5).

Seattle Pacific University, MS in Nursing Program, Seattle, WA 98119-1997. Offers administration (MSN); adult/gerontology nurse practitioner (MSN); clinical nurse specialist (MSN); family nurse practitioner (MSN, Certificate); informatics (MSN); nurse educator (MSN). *Accreditation:* AACN. *Program availability:* Part-time. *Students:* 22 full-time (17 women), 40 part-time (35 women); includes 13 minority (4 Black or African American, non-Hispanic/Latino; 1 American Indian or Alaska Native, non-Hispanic/Latino; 7 Asian, non-Hispanic/Latino; 1 Two or more races, non-Hispanic/Latino). Average age 36. 52 applicants, 73% accepted, 22 enrolled. In 2017, 23 master's awarded. *Degree requirements:* For master's, thesis. *Entrance requirements:* For master's, personal statement, transcripts, undergraduate nursing degree, proof of undergraduate statistics course with minimum GPA of 2.0, 2 recommendations. *Application deadline:* For fall admission, 1/15 priority date for domestic students; for spring admission, 1/15 for domestic students. Applications are processed on a rolling basis. Application fee: $50. Electronic applications accepted. *Expenses:* Contact institution. *Financial support:* Fellowships and scholarships/grants available. Financial award applicants required to submit FAFSA. *Unit head:* Dr. Christine Hoyle, Associate Dean, 206-281-2469, E-mail: hoylec@spu.edu.
Website: http://spu.edu/academics/school-of-health-sciences/undergraduate-programs/nursing

Seton Hall University, College of Nursing, South Orange, NJ 07079-2697. Offers advanced practice in primary health care (MSN, DNP), including adult/gerontological nurse practitioner, pediatric nurse practitioner; entry into practice (MSN); health systems administration (MSN, DNP); nursing (PhD); nursing case management (MSN); nursing education (MA); school nurse (MSN); MSN/MA. *Accreditation:* AACN. *Program availability:* Part-time, online learning. *Degree requirements:* For master's, research project; for doctorate, dissertation or scholarly project. *Entrance requirements:* For doctorate, GRE (waived for students with GPA of 3.5 or higher). Additional exam requirements/recommendations for international students: Required—TOEFL. Electronic applications accepted. *Faculty research:* Parent/child, adult, and gerontological nursing; breast cancer; families of children with HIV; parish nursing.

Shenandoah University, Eleanor Wade Custer School of Nursing, Winchester, VA 22601. Offers adult gerontology primary care nurse practitioner (Graduate Certificate); adult-gerontology primary care nurse practitioner (MSN); family nurse practitioner (MSN, DNP, Graduate Certificate); general (MSN); health systems leadership (DNP); health systems management (MSN, Graduate Certificate); nurse midwifery (MSN); nurse-midwifery (Graduate Certificate); nursing education (Graduate Certificate); nursing practice (DNP); psychiatric mental health nurse practitioner (MSN, DNP, Graduate Certificate). *Accreditation:* AACN; ACNM/ACME. *Faculty:* 17 full-time (all women), 6 part-time/adjunct (all women). *Students:* 30 full-time (26 women), 51 part-time (48 women); includes 19 minority (13 Black or African American, non-Hispanic/Latino; 3 Asian, non-Hispanic/Latino; 2 Hispanic/Latino; 1 Two or more races, non-Hispanic/Latino), 3 international. Average age 37. 52 applicants, 88% accepted, 34 enrolled. In 2017, 18 master's, 1 doctorate, 28 other advanced degrees awarded. *Degree requirements:* For master's, research project, clinical hours; for doctorate, scholarly project, clinical hours; for Graduate Certificate, clinical hours. *Entrance requirements:* For master's, United States RN license; minimum GPA of 3.0; 2080 hours of clinical experience; curriculum vitae; 3 letters of recommendation from former dean, faculty member, or advisor familiar with the applicant, and a former or current supervisor; two-to-three-page essay on a specified topic; for doctorate, MSN, minimum GPA of 3.0, 3 letters of recommendation, interview, BSN, two-to-three page essay on a specific topic, 500-word statement of clinical practice research interest, resume, current U.S. RN license, 2080 clinical hours; for Graduate Certificate, MSN, minimum GPA of 3.0, 2 letters of recommendation, minimum of one year (2080 hours) of clinical nursing experience, interview, two-to-three page essay on a specific topic, resume, current United States RN license. Additional exam requirements/recommendations for international students: Required—TOEFL (minimum score 558 paper-based; 83 iBT). *Application deadline:* For fall admission, 4/15 priority date for domestic and international students; for spring admission, 11/1 for domestic and international students; for summer admission, 3/1 for domestic and international students. Application fee: $30. Electronic applications accepted. *Expenses:* $22,451 tuition, plus $3,579 fees (student services fee, technology fee, and clinical fee). *Financial support:* In 2017–18, 32 students received support. Scholarships/grants and unspecified assistantships available. Financial award applicants required to submit FAFSA. *Faculty research:* Emergency preparedness, workplace environment, maternal child, inter-professional education, health policy. *Total annual research expenditures:* $30,000. *Unit head:* Dr. Kathleen LaSala, RN, Dean, 540-678-4381, Fax: 540-665-5519, E-mail: klasala@su.edu. *Application contact:* Andrew Woodall, Executive Director of Recruitment and Admissions, 540-665-4581, Fax: 540-665-4627, E-mail: admit@su.edu.
Website: http://www.su.edu/nursing/

Southern Adventist University, School of Nursing, Collegedale, TN 37315-0370. Offers adult/gerontology acute care nurse practitioner (MSN, DNP); adult/gerontology nurse practitioner (MSN); family nurse practitioner (MSN, DNP); lifestyle therapeutics (DNP); nurse educator (MSN, DNP); psychiatric mental health nurse practitioner (MSN, DNP); MSN/MBA. *Accreditation:* ACEN. *Program availability:* Part-time. *Degree requirements:* For master's, thesis or project. *Entrance requirements:* For master's, RN license. Additional exam requirements/recommendations for international students: Required—TOEFL (minimum score 600 paper-based). *Application deadline:* For fall admission, 7/1 for domestic and international students; for winter admission, 12/1 for domestic and international students. Applications are processed on a rolling basis. Application fee: $40. Electronic applications accepted. *Expenses: Tuition:* Full-time $11,430; part-time $635 per credit hour. Tuition and fees vary according to degree level and program. *Financial support:* Teaching assistantships with partial tuition reimbursements available. *Faculty research:* Pain management, ethics, corporate wellness, caring spirituality, stress. *Unit head:* Dr. Barbara James, Dean, 423-236-2942, Fax: 423-236-1940, E-mail: bjames@southern.edu. *Application contact:* Sylvia Mayer, RN, Director of Nursing Admissions, 423-236-2941, Fax: 423-236-1940, E-mail: smayer@southern.edu.
Website: https://www.southern.edu/academics/nursing.html

Southern University and Agricultural and Mechanical College, College of Nursing and Allied Health, School of Nursing, Baton Rouge, LA 70813. Offers educator/administrator (PhD); family health nursing (MSN); family nurse practitioner (Post Master's Certificate); geriatric nurse practitioner/gerontology (PhD); nursing (DNP). *Accreditation:* AACN. *Program availability:* Part-time. *Degree requirements:* For master's, comprehensive exam, thesis; for doctorate, comprehensive exam, thesis/dissertation. *Entrance requirements:* For master's, GRE General Test, BSN, minimum GPA of 2.7; for doctorate, GRE General Test; for Post Master's Certificate, MSN. Additional exam requirements/recommendations for international students: Required—TOEFL (minimum score 525 paper-based). *Faculty research:* Health promotions, vulnerable populations, (community-based) cardiovascular participating research, health disparities chronic diseases, care of the elderly.

Stony Brook University, State University of New York, Stony Brook Medicine, School of Nursing, Adult-Gerontology Primary Care Nurse Practitioner Program, Stony Brook, NY 11794. Offers adult health nurse practitioner (Certificate); adult health/primary care nursing (MS, DNP). *Accreditation:* AACN. *Program availability:* Part-time, blended/hybrid learning. *Students:* 13 full-time (all women), 194 part-time (165 women); includes 75 minority (21 Black or African American, non-Hispanic/Latino; 1 American Indian or Alaska Native, non-Hispanic/Latino; 29 Asian, non-Hispanic/Latino; 20 Hispanic/Latino; 4 Two or more races, non-Hispanic/Latino). 169 applicants, 37% accepted, 59 enrolled. In 2017, 78 master's, 14 doctorates, 3 other advanced degrees awarded. *Degree requirements:* For master's, thesis; for doctorate, thesis/dissertation. *Entrance requirements:* For master's, BSN, minimum GPA of 3.0, course work in statistics. Additional exam requirements/recommendations for international students: Required—TOEFL (minimum score 90 iBT). *Application deadline:* For fall admission, 1/18 for domestic students. Application fee: $100. *Expenses:* Contact institution. *Financial support:* Application deadline: 3/15. *Unit head:* Justin M. Waryold, Program Director, 631-444-3074, Fax: 631-444-3074, E-mail: justin.waryold@stonybrook.edu. *Application contact:* Dr. Dolores Bilges, Senior Staff Assistant, 631-444-2644, Fax: 631-444-3136, E-mail: anp.nursing@stonybrook.edu.
Website: https://nursing.stonybrookmedicine.edu/graduate

Tennessee Technological University, Whitson-Hester School of Nursing, DNP Program, Cookeville, TN 38505. Offers adult-gerontology acute care nurse practitioner (DNP); executive leadership in nursing (DNP); family nurse practitioner (DNP); pediatric nurse practitioner-primary care (DNP); psychiatric/mental health nurse practitioner (DNP); women's health care nurse practitioner (DNP). *Program availability:* Part-time. *Students:* 10 part-time (all women). 14 applicants, 86% accepted, 10 enrolled. *Application deadline:* For fall admission, 7/1 for domestic students, 5/1 for international students; for spring admission, 12/1 for domestic students, 10/1 for international students; for summer admission, 5/1 for domestic students, 2/1 for international students. Applications are processed on a rolling basis. Application fee: $35 ($40 for international students). Electronic applications accepted. *Expenses:* Tuition, state resident: full-time $9925; part-time $565 per credit hour. Tuition, nonresident: full-time $22,993; part-time $1291 per credit hour. *Financial support:* Application deadline: 4/1; applicants required to submit FAFSA. *Unit head:* Dr. Bedelia Russell, Program Director, Fax: 931-372-6244, E-mail: bhrussell@tntech.edu. *Application contact:* Shelia K. Kendrick, Coordinator of Graduate Studies, 931-372-3808, Fax: 931-372-3497, E-mail: skendrick@tntech.edu.
Website: https://www.tntech.edu/nursing/doctor-of-nursing-practice/

Texas Christian University, Harris College of Nursing and Health Sciences, Master's Program in Nursing, Fort Worth, TX 76129. Offers administration (MSN); clinical nurse leader (MSN, Certificate); clinical nurse specialist (MSN), including adult/gerontology nursing, pediatrics; nursing education (MSN). *Accreditation:* AACN. *Program availability:* Part-time, online only, 100% online. *Faculty:* 29 full-time (26 women), 2 part-time/adjunct (both women). *Students:* 17 full-time (15 women), 7 part-time (all women); includes 6 minority (1 Black or African American, non-Hispanic/Latino; 2 Asian, non-Hispanic/Latino; 2 Hispanic/Latino; 1 Two or more races, non-Hispanic/Latino). Average age 36. 41 applicants, 49% accepted, 6 enrolled. In 2017, 41 master's awarded. *Degree requirements:* For master's, thesis or alternative, practicum. *Entrance requirements:* For master's, 3 letters of reference, essay, resume, two official transcripts from every institution attended. Additional exam requirements/recommendations for international

students: Required—TOEFL. *Application deadline:* For spring admission, 9/1 for domestic and international students; for summer admission, 2/1 for domestic and international students. Application fee: $60. Electronic applications accepted. *Expenses:* $1,555 per credit hour, $125 per course fee, $500 lab fee. *Financial support:* In 2017–18, 20 students received support. Scholarships/grants available. Financial award application deadline: 2/15; financial award applicants required to submit FAFSA. *Faculty research:* Geriatrics, cancer survivorship, health literacy, endothelial cells, clinical simulation outcomes. *Unit head:* Dr. Kathy Ellis, Division Director, Graduate Nursing, 817-257-6726, Fax: 817-257-7944, E-mail: kathryn.ellis@tcu.edu. *Application contact:* Heather Lyon, Academic Program Specialist, 817-257-6726, Fax: 817-257-7944, E-mail: graduatenursing@tcu.edu.
Website: http://www.nursing.tcu.edu/graduate.asp

Texas Tech University Health Sciences Center, School of Nursing, Lubbock, TX 79430. Offers acute care nurse practitioner (MSN, Certificate); administration (MSN); advanced practice (DNP); education (MSN); executive leadership (DNP); family nurse practitioner (MSN, Certificate); geriatric nurse practitioner (MSN, Certificate); pediatric nurse practitioner (MSN, Certificate). *Accreditation:* AACN. *Program availability:* Part-time, online learning. *Degree requirements:* For master's, thesis optional. *Entrance requirements:* For master's, minimum GPA of 3.0, 3 letters of reference, BSN, RN license; for Certificate, minimum GPA of 3.0, 3 letters of reference, RN license. Additional exam requirements/recommendations for international students: Required—TOEFL (minimum score 550 paper-based). *Faculty research:* Diabetes/obesity, nurse competency, disease management, intervention and measurements, health disparities.

Texas Woman's University, Graduate School, College of Nursing, Denton, TX 76204. Offers adult health clinical nurse specialist (MS); adult health nurse practitioner (MS); adult/gerontology acute care nurse practitioner (MS); child health clinical nurse specialist (MS); clinical nurse leader (MS); family nurse practitioner (MS); health systems management (MS); nursing education (MS); nursing practice (DNP); nursing science (PhD); pediatric nurse practitioner (MS); women's health clinical nurse specialist (MS); women's health nurse practitioner (MS). *Accreditation:* AACN. *Program availability:* Part-time, 100% online, blended/hybrid learning. *Faculty:* 48 full-time (47 women), 44 part-time/adjunct (37 women). *Students:* 23 full-time (22 women), 816 part-time (750 women); includes 475 minority (188 Black or African American, non-Hispanic/Latino; 4 American Indian or Alaska Native, non-Hispanic/Latino; 171 Asian, non-Hispanic/Latino; 83 Hispanic/Latino; 3 Native Hawaiian or other Pacific Islander, non-Hispanic/Latino; 26 Two or more races, non-Hispanic/Latino), 12 international. Average age 37. 201 applicants, 88% accepted, 123 enrolled. In 2017, 232 master's, 17 doctorates awarded. *Degree requirements:* For master's, comprehensive exam, thesis or alternative, 6-year time limit for completion of degree, professional or clinical project; for doctorate, comprehensive exam, thesis/dissertation, 10-year time limit for completion of degree. *Entrance requirements:* For master's, GRE or MAT, minimum GPA of 3.0 on last 60 hours in undergraduate nursing degree and overall, RN license, BS in nursing, basic statistics course, 1 year of clinical experience; for doctorate, GRE (preferred minimum score 153 [500 old version] Verbal, 144 [500 old version] Quantitative, 4 Analytical), MS in nursing, minimum preferred GPA of 3.5, RN license, statistics course, 2 letters of reference, curriculum vitae, graduate nursing-theory course, graduate research course, statement of professional goals and research interests. Additional exam requirements/recommendations for international students: Required—TOEFL (minimum score 550 paper-based; 79 iBT); Recommended—IELTS (minimum score 6.5), TSE (minimum score 53). *Application deadline:* For fall admission, 5/1 for domestic students, 3/1 priority date for international students; for spring admission, 9/15 for domestic students, 7/1 priority date for international students; for summer admission, 2/1 for domestic and international students. Applications are processed on a rolling basis. Application fee: $50 ($75 for international students). Electronic applications accepted. *Expenses:* $8,510 per year full-time in-state, $17,810 per year full-time out-of-state. *Financial support:* In 2017–18, 146 students received support, including 7 teaching assistantships (averaging $28,195 per year); research assistantships, career-related internships or fieldwork, Federal Work-Study, institutionally sponsored loans, scholarships/grants, traineeships, health care benefits, and unspecified assistantships also available. Support available to part-time students. Financial award application deadline: 3/1; financial award applicants required to submit FAFSA. *Faculty research:* Women's health, nurse staffing and satisfaction in health systems, perinatal safety, chronic illness, pediatric health. *Total annual research expenditures:* $380,388. *Unit head:* Dr. Anita G. Hufft, Dean, 940-898-2401, Fax: 940-898-2437, E-mail: nursing@twu.edu. *Application contact:* Korie Hawkins, Associate Director of Admissions, Graduate Recruitment, 940-898-3188, Fax: 940-898-3081, E-mail: admissions@twu.edu.
Website: http://www.twu.edu/nursing/

Uniformed Services University of the Health Sciences, Daniel K. Inouye Graduate School of Nursing, Bethesda, MD 20814. Offers adult-gerontology clinical nurse specialist (MSN, DNP); family nurse practitioner (DNP); nurse anesthesia (DNP); nursing science (PhD); psychiatric mental health nurse practitioner (DNP); women's health nurse practitioner (DNP). *Accreditation:* AACN; AANA/CANAEP. *Faculty:* 42 full-time (28 women), 2 part-time/adjunct (1 woman). *Students:* 170 full-time (98 women); includes 51 minority (21 Black or African American, non-Hispanic/Latino; 17 Asian, non-Hispanic/Latino; 11 Hispanic/Latino; 2 Native Hawaiian or other Pacific Islander, non-Hispanic/Latino). Average age 34. 88 applicants, 75% accepted, 66 enrolled. In 2017, 55 doctorates awarded. *Degree requirements:* For master's, thesis, scholarly project; for doctorate, dissertation (for PhD); project (for DNP). *Entrance requirements:* For master's, GRE, BSN, clinical experience, minimum GPA of 3.0, previous course work in science; for doctorate, GRE, BSN, minimum GPA of 3.0, undergraduate/graduate science course within past 5 years, writing example, interview (for some programs), and 3 letters of reference (for DNP); master's degree, minimum GPA of 3.0 in nursing or related field, personal statement, 3 references, and interview (for PhD). *Application deadline:* For winter admission, 2/15 for domestic students; for summer admission, 8/15 for domestic students. Application fee: $0. Electronic applications accepted. *Expenses:* There are no tuition costs or fees; students incur obligated service according to the requirements of their sponsoring organization. *Faculty research:* Military health care, military readiness, women's health, family, behavioral health. *Total annual research expenditures:* $100,000. *Unit head:* Dr. Diane C. Seibert, Associate Dean for Academic Affairs, 301-295-1080, Fax: 301-295-1707, E-mail: diane.seibert@usuhs.edu. *Application contact:* Maureen Jackson, Registrar, 301-295-1055, Fax: 301-295-1707, E-mail: maureen.jackson.ctr@usuhs.edu.
Website: http://www.usuhs.edu/gsn/

University at Buffalo, the State University of New York, Graduate School, School of Nursing, Buffalo, NY 14260. Offers adult gerontology nurse practitioner (DNP); family nurse practitioner (DNP); health care systems and leadership (MS); nurse anesthetist (DNP); nursing (PhD); nursing education (Certificate); psychiatric/mental health nurse practitioner (DNP). *Accreditation:* AACN; AANA/CANAEP (one or more programs are accredited). *Program availability:* Part-time, 100% online. *Faculty:* 41 full-time (36 women), 15 part-time/adjunct (all women). *Students:* 64 full-time (39 women), 136 part-time (120 women); includes 32 minority (13 Black or African American, non-Hispanic/Latino; 1 American Indian or Alaska Native, non-Hispanic/Latino; 18 Asian, non-Hispanic/Latino). Average age 34. 182 applicants, 39% accepted, 50 enrolled. In 2017, 3 master's, 32 doctorates, 2 other advanced degrees awarded. *Degree requirements:* For master's, thesis optional; for doctorate, comprehensive exam (for some programs), capstone (for DNP), dissertation (for PhD). *Entrance requirements:* For master's, GRE or MAT; for doctorate, GRE or MAT, minimum GPA of 3.0 (for DNP), 3.25 (for PhD); RN license; BS or MS in nursing; 3 references; writing sample; resume; personal statement; for Certificate, interview, minimum GPA of 3.0 or GRE General Test, RN license, MS in nursing, professional certification. Additional exam requirements/recommendations for international students: Required—TOEFL (minimum score 550 paper-based; 79 iBT), IELTS (minimum score 6.5). *Application deadline:* For fall admission, 4/1 for domestic students, 2/1 for international students; for spring admission, 1/15 for domestic students, 10/1 for international students; for summer admission, 4/1 for domestic students. Applications are processed on a rolling basis. Application fee: $75. Electronic applications accepted. *Expenses:* Contact institution. *Financial support:* In 2017–18, 80 students received support, including 2 fellowships with tuition reimbursements available (averaging $17,000 per year), 4 research assistantships with tuition reimbursements available (averaging $10,600 per year), 7 teaching assistantships with tuition reimbursements available (averaging $10,600 per year); scholarships/grants, traineeships, health care benefits, and unspecified assistantships also available. Financial award application deadline: 4/1; financial award applicants required to submit FAFSA. *Faculty research:* Oncology, palliative care, gerontology, addictions, mental health, community wellness, sleep, workforce, care of underserved populations, quality and safety, person-centered care, adolescent health. *Total annual research expenditures:* $1.4 million. *Unit head:* Dr. Marsha L. Lewis, Dean and Professor, 716-829-2533, Fax: 716-829-2566, E-mail: ubnursingdean@buffalo.edu. *Application contact:* Jennifer H. Schreier, Director of Graduate Student Services, 716-829-3311, Fax: 716-829-2067, E-mail: jhv2@buffalo.edu.
Website: http://nursing.buffalo.edu/

The University of Alabama at Birmingham, School of Nursing, Birmingham, AL 35294-1210. Offers clinical nurse leader (MSN); nurse anesthesia (DNP); nurse practitioner (MSN, DNP), including adult-gerontology acute care (MSN), adult-gerontology primary care (MSN), family (MSN), pediatric (MSN), psychiatric/mental health (MSN), women's health (MSN); nursing (MSN, DNP, PhD); nursing health systems administration (MSN); nursing informatics (MSN). *Accreditation:* AACN; AANA/CANAEP. *Program availability:* Part-time, online only, blended/hybrid learning. Terminal master's awarded for partial completion of doctoral program. *Degree requirements:* For master's, comprehensive exam; for doctorate, comprehensive exam, thesis/dissertation, research mentorship experience (for PhD); scholarly project (for DNP). *Entrance requirements:* For master's, GRE, GMAT, or MAT, minimum cumulative undergraduate GPA of 3.0 or on last 60 semesters hours; letters of recommendation; for doctorate, GRE General Test, computer literacy, course work in statistics, interview, minimum GPA of 3.0, MS in nursing, references, writing sample. Additional exam requirements/recommendations for international students: Required—TOEFL (minimum score 500 paper-based, 80 iBT) or IELTS (5.5). Electronic applications accepted. *Expenses:* Contact institution. *Faculty research:* Palliative care; oncology; aging; HIV/AIDS; nursing work environments.

The University of Alabama in Huntsville, School of Graduate Studies, College of Nursing, Huntsville, AL 35899. Offers family nurse practitioner (Certificate); nursing (MSN, DNP), including adult-gerontology acute care nurse practitioner (MSN), adult-gerontology clinical nurse specialist (MSN), family nurse practitioner (MSN), leadership in health care systems (MSN); nursing education (Certificate). DNP offered jointly with The University of Alabama at Birmingham. *Accreditation:* AACN. *Program availability:* Part-time, evening/weekend, online learning. *Degree requirements:* For master's, comprehensive exam, thesis or alternative, oral and written exams. *Entrance requirements:* For master's, MAT or GRE, Alabama RN license, BSN, minimum GPA of 3.0; for doctorate, master's degree in nursing in an advanced practice area; for Certificate, MAT or GRE, minimum GPA of 3.0. Additional exam requirements/recommendations for international students: Required—TOEFL (minimum score 500 paper-based; 80 iBT), IELTS (minimum score 6.5). Electronic applications accepted. *Faculty research:* Health care informatics, chronic illness management, maternal and child health, genetics/genomics, technology and health care.

University of Central Florida, College of Nursing, Orlando, FL 32816. Offers adult-gerontology acute care nurse practitioner (Certificate); adult-gerontology primary care nurse practitioner (Certificate); family nurse practitioner (Certificate); nursing (MSN, PhD); nursing education (Post-Master's Certificate); nursing practice (DNP). *Accreditation:* AACN. *Program availability:* Part-time, evening/weekend. *Faculty:* 57 full-time (49 women), 70 part-time/adjunct (68 women). *Students:* 63 full-time (58 women), 327 part-time (297 women); includes 131 minority (40 Black or African American, non-Hispanic/Latino; 1 American Indian or Alaska Native, non-Hispanic/Latino; 16 Asian, non-Hispanic/Latino; 62 Hispanic/Latino; 12 Two or more races, non-Hispanic/Latino), 1 international. Average age 38. 303 applicants, 64% accepted, 129 enrolled. In 2017, 87 master's, 5 doctorates, 4 other advanced degrees awarded. *Degree requirements:* For master's, thesis or alternative; for doctorate, comprehensive exam, thesis/dissertation. *Entrance requirements:* For master's, essay, curriculum vitae; for doctorate, GRE General Test, letters of recommendation, resume, essay. Additional exam requirements/recommendations for international students: Required—TOEFL. *Application deadline:* For fall admission, 3/15 for domestic students; for spring admission, 10/15 for domestic students. Application fee: $30. Electronic applications accepted. *Expenses:* Tuition, state resident: part-time $288.16 per credit hour. Tuition, nonresident: part-time $1073.31 per credit hour. Tuition and fees vary according to program. *Financial support:* In 2017–18, 3 students received support, including 2 fellowships with partial tuition reimbursements available (averaging $7,377 per year), 1 research assistantship with partial tuition reimbursement available (averaging $11,952 per year); career-related internships or fieldwork, Federal Work-Study, institutionally sponsored loans, traineeships, and unspecified assistantships also available. Financial award application deadline: 3/1; financial award applicants required to submit FAFSA. *Unit head:* Dr. Mary Lou Sole, Dean, 407-823-5496, Fax: 407-823-5675, E-mail: mary.sole@ucf.edu. *Application contact:* Associate Director, Graduate Admissions, 407-823-2766, Fax: 407-823-6442, E-mail: gradadmissions@ucf.edu.
Website: http://nursing.ucf.edu/

University of Cincinnati, Graduate School, College of Nursing, Cincinnati, OH 45221-0038. Offers nurse midwifery (MSN); nurse practitioner (MSN, DNP), including acute care pediatrics (DNP), adult-gerontology acute care, adult-gerontology primary care, anesthesia (DNP), family (MSN), leadership (DNP), neonatal (MSN), women's health (MSN); nursing (MSN, PhD), including occupational health (MSN). *Accreditation:* AACN; AANA/CANAEP (one or more programs are accredited); ACNM/ACME. *Program availability:* Part-time, 100% online, blended/hybrid learning. *Faculty:* 74 full-time (69 women), 112 part-time/adjunct (105 women). *Students:* 323 full-time (261 women), 1,084 part-time (949 women); includes 311 minority (113 Black or African American, non-Hispanic/Latino; 4 American Indian or Alaska Native, non-Hispanic/Latino; 56 Asian, non-Hispanic/Latino; 108 Hispanic/Latino; 1 Native Hawaiian or other Pacific Islander, non-Hispanic/Latino; 29 Two or more races, non-Hispanic/Latino), 12 international. Average age 34. 582 applicants, 64% accepted, 314 enrolled. In 2017, 579 master's, 18 doctorates awarded. *Degree requirements:* For master's, thesis or alternative; for doctorate, comprehensive exam (for some programs), thesis/dissertation

(for some programs). *Entrance requirements:* For doctorate, GRE General Test. Additional exam requirements/recommendations for international students: Required—TOEFL (minimum score 600 paper-based; 100 iBT); Recommended—IELTS (minimum score 7). *Application deadline:* For fall admission, 5/1 priority date for domestic students, 5/1 for international students; for spring admission, 10/1 for domestic students; for summer admission, 3/1 priority date for domestic students. Applications are processed on a rolling basis. Application fee: $130 ($70 for international students). Electronic applications accepted. *Expenses:* $14,668 annual full-time in-state tuition, $707 annual fees. *Financial support:* In 2017–18, 123 students received support, including 8 fellowships with full tuition reimbursements available (averaging $30,423 per year), 7 research assistantships with full tuition reimbursements available (averaging $17,971 per year), 5 teaching assistantships with full tuition reimbursements available (averaging $17,971 per year); Federal Work-Study, institutionally sponsored loans, scholarships/grants, traineeships, health care benefits, tuition waivers (partial), and unspecified assistantships also available. Support available to part-time students. Financial award application deadline: 5/1; financial award applicants required to submit FAFSA. *Faculty research:* Vulnerable populations, education, violence, chronicity/aging, cancer. *Total annual research expenditures:* $575,576. *Unit head:* Dr. Greer Glazer, Dean, 513-558-5330, Fax: 513-558-9030, E-mail: greer.glazer@uc.edu. *Application contact:* Office of Student Recruitment, 513-558-8400, Fax: 513-558-5012, E-mail: nursingbearcats@uc.edu.
Website: https://nursing.uc.edu/

University of Colorado Colorado Springs, Helen and Arthur E. Johnson Beth-El College of Nursing and Health Sciences, Colorado Springs, CO 80918. Offers nursing practice (DNP); primary care nurse practitioner (MSN). *Accreditation:* AACN. *Program availability:* Part-time, 100% online, blended/hybrid learning. *Faculty:* 11 full-time (10 women), 13 part-time/adjunct (12 women). *Students:* 7 full-time (6 women), 213 part-time (192 women); includes 50 minority (8 Black or African American, non-Hispanic/Latino; 1 American Indian or Alaska Native, non-Hispanic/Latino; 11 Asian, non-Hispanic/Latino; 23 Hispanic/Latino; 1 Native Hawaiian or other Pacific Islander, non-Hispanic/Latino; 6 Two or more races, non-Hispanic/Latino). Average age 37. 125 applicants, 66% accepted, 57 enrolled. In 2017, 47 master's, 10 doctorates awarded. *Degree requirements:* For master's, comprehensive exam, thesis optional; for doctorate, capstone project. *Entrance requirements:* For master's, GRE General Test or MAT, minimum overall GPA of 2.75 for all undergraduate course work, minimum BSN GPA of 3.3; for doctorate, interview; active RN license; MA; minimum GPA of 3.3; National Certification as nurse practitioner or clinical nurse specialist; portfolio. Additional exam requirements/recommendations for international students: Required—TOEFL (minimum score 550 paper-based; 80 iBT). *Application deadline:* For fall admission, 3/15 priority date for domestic students, 3/15 for international students; for spring admission, 8/15 for domestic and international students. Applications are processed on a rolling basis. Application fee: $60 ($100 for international students). Electronic applications accepted. *Expenses:* $12,241 per year resident tuition, $21,511 nonresident, $13,869 nonresidential online; annual costs vary depending on program, course-load, and residency status. *Financial support:* In 2017–18, 28 students received support. Research assistantships, career-related internships or fieldwork, Federal Work-Study, and scholarships/grants available. Support available to part-time students. Financial award application deadline: 3/1; financial award applicants required to submit FAFSA. *Faculty research:* Behavioral interventions to reduce stroke risk factors in older adults, interprofessional models of health promotion for older adults, nurse practitioner education, practice and policy, cardiology, cardiac and pulmonary rehab, heart failure and stroke, community health prevention, veterans studies, anger management, sports medicine, sports nutrition. *Total annual research expenditures:* $580,217. *Unit head:* Dr. Deborah Pollard, Nursing Department Chair, 719-255-3577, Fax: 719-255-4416, E-mail: dpollard@uccs.edu. *Application contact:* Diane Busch, Program Assistant II, 719-255-4424, Fax: 719-255-4416, E-mail: dbusch@uccs.edu.
Website: http://www.uccs.edu/bethel/index.html

★ **University of Connecticut,** Graduate School, School of Nursing, Post-Master's Certificate Programs, Storrs, CT 06269. Offers adult gerontology acute care nurse practitioner (Post-Master's Certificate); adult gerontology primary care nurse practitioner (Post-Master's Certificate); neonatal nurse practitioner (Post-Master's Certificate). *Entrance requirements:* For degree, minimum graduate GPA of 3.0, current Connecticut RN license, three letters of recommendation, current resume/curriculum vitae.

See Display on page 596 and Close-Up on page 767.

University of Delaware, College of Health Sciences, School of Nursing, Newark, DE 19716. Offers adult nurse practitioner (MSN, PMC); cardiopulmonary clinical nurse specialist (MSN, PMC); cardiopulmonary clinical nurse specialist/adult nurse practitioner (MSN, PMC); family nurse practitioner (MSN, PMC); gerontology clinical nurse specialist (MSN, PMC); gerontology clinical nurse specialist geriatric nurse practitioner (PMC); gerontology clinical nurse specialist/geriatric nurse practitioner (MSN); health services administration (MSN, PMC); nursing of children clinical nurse specialist (MSN, PMC); nursing of children clinical nurse specialist/pediatric nurse practitioner (MSN, PMC); oncology/immune deficiency clinical nurse specialist (MSN, PMC); oncology/immune deficiency clinical nurse specialist/adult nurse practitioner (MSN, PMC); perinatal/women's health clinical nurse specialist (MSN, PMC); perinatal/women's health clinical nurse specialist/women's health nurse practitioner (MSN, PMC); psychiatric nursing clinical nurse specialist (MSN, PMC). *Accreditation:* AACN. *Program availability:* Part-time, evening/weekend, online learning. *Degree requirements:* For master's, thesis optional. *Entrance requirements:* For master's, BSN, interview, RN license. Electronic applications accepted. *Faculty research:* Marriage and chronic illness, health promotion, congestive heart failure patient outcomes, school nursing, diabetes in children, culture, health disparities, cardiovascular, prison nursing, oncology, public policy, child obesity, smoking and teen pregnancy, blood pressure measurements, men's health.

University of Illinois at Chicago, College of Nursing, Program in Nursing, Chicago, IL 60607-7128. Offers acute care clinical nurse specialist (MS); administrative nursing leadership (Certificate); adult nurse practitioner (MS); adult/geriatric nurse practitioner (MS); advanced community health nurse specialist (MS); family nurse practitioner (MS); geriatric clinical nurse specialist (MS); geriatric nurse practitioner (MS); nurse midwifery (MS); occupational health/advanced community health nurse specialist (MS); occupational health/family nurse practitioner (MS); pediatric nurse practitioner (MS); perinatal clinical nurse specialist (MS); school/advanced community health nurse specialist (MS); school/family nurse practitioner (MS); women's health nurse practitioner (MS). *Accreditation:* AACN. *Program availability:* Part-time. *Degree requirements:* For master's, thesis or alternative. *Entrance requirements:* For master's, GRE General Test, minimum GPA of 2.75. Additional exam requirements/recommendations for international students: Required—TOEFL. Electronic applications accepted.

The University of Kansas, University of Kansas Medical Center, School of Nursing, Kansas City, KS 66160. Offers adult/gerontological clinical nurse specialist (PMC); adult/gerontological nurse practitioner (PMC); health care informatics (PMC); health professions educator (PMC); nurse midwife (PMC); nursing (MS, DNP, PhD); organizational leadership (PMC); psychiatric/mental health nurse practitioner (PMC); public health nursing (PMC). *Accreditation:* AACN; ACNM/ACME. *Program availability:* Part-time, 100% online, blended/hybrid learning. *Faculty:* 56. *Students:* 48 full-time (44 women), 260 part-time (235 women); includes 50 minority (12 Black or African American, non-Hispanic/Latino; 2 American Indian or Alaska Native, non-Hispanic/Latino; 16 Asian, non-Hispanic/Latino; 8 Hispanic/Latino; 12 Two or more races, non-Hispanic/Latino). Average age 36. 87 applicants, 95% accepted, 61 enrolled. In 2017, 37 master's, 18 doctorates, 3 other advanced degrees awarded. Terminal master's awarded for partial completion of doctoral program. *Degree requirements:* For master's, comprehensive exam, thesis (for some programs), general oral exam; for doctorate, thesis/dissertation or alternative, comprehensive oral exam (for DNP); comprehensive written and oral exam, or three publications (for PhD). *Entrance requirements:* For master's, bachelor's degree in nursing, minimum GPA of 3.0, 1 year of clinical experience, RN license in KS and MO; for doctorate, GRE General Test (for PhD only), bachelor's degree in nursing, minimum GPA of 3.5, RN license in KS and MO. Additional exam requirements/recommendations for international students: Required—TOEFL. *Application deadline:* For fall admission, 4/1 for domestic and international students; for spring admission, 9/1 for domestic and international students. Application fee: $75. Electronic applications accepted. *Financial support:* In 2017–18, 5 research assistantships with tuition reimbursements (averaging $20,000 per year), 30 teaching assistantships with tuition reimbursements (averaging $20,000 per year) were awarded; scholarships/grants and traineeships also available. Financial award application deadline: 3/1; financial award applicants required to submit FAFSA. *Faculty research:* Breastfeeding practices of teen mothers, national database of nursing quality indicators, caregiving of families of patients using technology in the home, simulation in nursing education, diaphragm fatigue. *Total annual research expenditures:* $1.4 million. *Unit head:* Dr. Sally Maliski, Dean, 913-588-1601, Fax: 913-588-1660, E-mail: smaliski@kumc.edu. *Application contact:* Dr. Pamela K. Barnes, Associate Dean, Student Affairs, 913-588-1619, Fax: 913-588-1615, E-mail: pbarnes2@kumc.edu.
Website: http://nursing.kumc.edu

University of Louisville, Graduate School, School of Nursing, Louisville, KY 40202. Offers adult gerontology nurse practitioner (MSN, DNP); education and administration (MSN); family nurse practitioner (MSN, DNP); neonatal nurse practitioner (MSN, DNP); nursing research (PhD); psychiatric/mental health nurse practitioner (MSN, DNP); women's health nurse practitioner (MSN). *Accreditation:* AACN. *Program availability:* Part-time. *Faculty:* 44 full-time (40 women), 45 part-time/adjunct (41 women). *Students:* 130 full-time (107 women), 30 part-time (25 women); includes 33 minority (16 Black or African American, non-Hispanic/Latino; 7 Asian, non-Hispanic/Latino; 5 Hispanic/Latino; 5 Two or more races, non-Hispanic/Latino), 2 international. Average age 33. 61 applicants, 67% accepted, 36 enrolled. In 2017, 54 master's awarded. *Degree requirements:* For doctorate, comprehensive exam (for some programs), thesis/dissertation (for some programs). *Entrance requirements:* For master's, bachelor's degree from nationally-accredited college, completion of 6 prerequisite courses, minimum undergraduate GPA of 3.0; for doctorate, GRE with minimum score of 156 Verbal, 146 Quantitative, 4.0 Analytic (for PhD), 3 letters of professional reference; minimum GPA of 3.0 with BSN, 3.25 with MSN; written statement of career goals, areas of expertise, and reasons for pursuing doctoral degree; resume including RN license. Additional exam requirements/recommendations for international students: Recommended—TOEFL (minimum score 560 paper-based), IELTS (minimum score 6.5). *Application deadline:* For fall admission, 1/15 priority date for domestic students, 1/15 for international students; for summer admission, 10/15 priority date for domestic students. Application fee: $65. Electronic applications accepted. *Expenses:* Tuition, state resident: full-time $12,246; part-time $681 per credit hour. Tuition, nonresident: full-time $25,486; part-time $1417 per credit hour. *Required fees:* $196. Tuition and fees vary according to course load, program and reciprocity agreements. *Financial support:* In 2017–18, 8 research assistantships with full tuition reimbursements (averaging $20,000 per year), 4 teaching assistantships with full tuition reimbursements (averaging $15,000 per year) were awarded; fellowships with full tuition reimbursements, scholarships/grants, and unspecified assistantships also available. Financial award application deadline: 10/1; financial award applicants required to submit FAFSA. *Faculty research:* Environmental health, health services research, women's mental health, self-management of chronic illness in adults and children, health disparities. *Total annual research expenditures:* $762,266. *Unit head:* Dr. Marcia J. Hern, RN, Dean and Professor, 502-852-8300, Fax: 502-852-8783, E-mail: m.hern@louisville.edu. *Application contact:* Trish Hart, Assistant Dean for Student Affairs, 502-852-5825, Fax: 502-852-8783, E-mail: trish.hart@louisville.edu.
Website: http://www.louisville.edu/nursing/

University of Maryland, Baltimore, School of Nursing, Baltimore, MD 21201. Offers adult-gerontology acute care nurse practitioner (DNP); adult-gerontology primary care nurse practitioner (DNP); clinical nurse leader (MS); community/public health nursing (MS); family nurse practitioner (DNP); global health (Postbaccalaureate Certificate); health services leadership and management (MS); neonatal nurse practitioner (DNP); nurse anesthesia (DNP); nursing (PhD); nursing informatics (MS, Postbaccalaureate Certificate); pediatric acute/primary care nurse practitioner (DNP); psychiatric mental health nurse practitioner (DNP); teaching in nursing and health professions (Postbaccalaureate Certificate); MS/MBA. MS/MBA offered jointly with University of Baltimore. *Program availability:* Part-time. *Faculty:* 130 full-time (117 women), 125 part-time/adjunct (114 women). *Students:* 504 full-time (442 women), 532 part-time (482 women); includes 443 minority (249 Black or African American, non-Hispanic/Latino; 1 American Indian or Alaska Native, non-Hispanic/Latino; 115 Asian, non-Hispanic/Latino; 48 Hispanic/Latino; 2 Native Hawaiian or other Pacific Islander, non-Hispanic/Latino; 28 Two or more races, non-Hispanic/Latino), 15 international. Average age 33. 935 applicants, 62% accepted, 394 enrolled. In 2017, 182 master's, 57 doctorates awarded. *Degree requirements:* For master's and Postbaccalaureate Certificate, thesis (for some programs); for doctorate, comprehensive exam, thesis/dissertation. *Entrance requirements:* Additional exam requirements/recommendations for international students: Required—TOEFL (minimum score 550 paper-based; 79 iBT); Recommended—IELTS (minimum score 7). *Application deadline:* For fall admission, 11/1 for domestic and international students; for spring admission, 8/1 for domestic and international students. Application fee: $75. Electronic applications accepted. *Expenses:* Contact institution. *Financial support:* In 2017–18, 22 research assistantships with full and partial tuition reimbursements (averaging $21,523 per year), 41 teaching assistantships with full and partial tuition reimbursements (averaging $13,439 per year) were awarded; fellowships and scholarships/grants also available. Financial award application deadline: 3/1; financial award applicants required to submit FAFSA. *Unit head:* Dr. Jane Kirschling, Dean, 410-706-4359, E-mail: kirschling@umaryland.edu. *Application contact:* Larry Fillian, Associate Dean of Student and Academic Services, 410-706-6298, E-mail: lfillian@umaryland.edu.
Website: http://www.nursing.umaryland.edu/

University of Massachusetts Amherst, Graduate School, College of Nursing, Amherst, MA 01003. Offers adult gerontology primary care nurse practitioner (DNP); clinical nurse leader (MS); family nurse practitioner (DNP); nursing (PhD); public health nurse leader (DNP). *Accreditation:* AACN. *Program availability:* Part-time, online learning. Terminal master's awarded for partial completion of doctoral program. *Degree requirements:* For master's, thesis optional; for doctorate, comprehensive exam, thesis/dissertation. *Entrance requirements:* Additional exam requirements/recommendations for international students: Required—TOEFL (minimum score 550 paper-based; 80 iBT), IELTS (minimum score 6.5). Electronic applications accepted. *Faculty research:* Health of older adults and their caretakers, mental health of individuals and families, health of children and adolescents, power and decision-making, transcultural health.

University of Massachusetts Lowell, College of Health Sciences, School of Nursing, Program in Adult/Gerontological Nursing, Lowell, MA 01854. Offers MS. *Accreditation:* AACN. *Degree requirements:* For master's, thesis optional. *Entrance requirements:* For master's, GRE General Test, minimum GPA of 3.0, MA nursing license, interview, 3 letters of recommendation.

University of Massachusetts Medical School, Graduate School of Nursing, Worcester, MA 01655-0115. Offers adult gerontological acute care nurse practitioner (DNP, Post Master's Certificate); adult gerontological primary care nurse practitioner (DNP, Post Master's Certificate); family nursing practitioner (DNP); nurse administrator (DNP); nurse educator (MS, Post Master's Certificate); nursing (PhD). *Accreditation:* AACN. *Faculty:* 31 full-time (28 women), 39 part-time/adjunct (34 women). *Students:* 129 full-time (111 women), 31 part-time (30 women); includes 35 minority (17 Black or African American, non-Hispanic/Latino; 10 Asian, non-Hispanic/Latino; 7 Hispanic/Latino; 1 Native Hawaiian or other Pacific Islander, non-Hispanic/Latino), 1 international. Average age 32. 124 applicants, 55% accepted, 59 enrolled. In 2017, 48 master's, 10 doctorates, 2 other advanced degrees awarded. *Degree requirements:* For doctorate, thesis/dissertation (for some programs), comprehensive exam and manuscript (for PhD); capstone project and manuscript (for DNP). *Entrance requirements:* For master's, GRE General Test, bachelor's degree in nursing, course work in statistics, unrestricted Massachusetts license as registered nurse; for doctorate, GRE General Test, bachelor's or master's degree; for Post Master's Certificate, GRE General Test, MS in nursing. Additional exam requirements/recommendations for international students: Required—TOEFL (minimum score 400 paper-based; 81 iBT). *Application deadline:* For fall admission, 12/1 priority date for domestic students. Applications are processed on a rolling basis. Application fee: $60. Electronic applications accepted. *Expenses:* $14,778 in-state tuition and mandatory fees; $19,728 out-of-state. *Financial support:* In 2017–18, 6 students received support. Scholarships/grants available. Support available to part-time students. Financial award application deadline: 5/15; financial award applicants required to submit FAFSA. *Faculty research:* Health literacy, social justice, HIV prevention, cancer-related decision making, nursing education, diabetes care and education, family-focused interventions for children with type 1 diabetes. *Total annual research expenditures:* $874,000. *Unit head:* Dr. Joan Vitello-Cicciu, Dean, 508-856-5081, Fax: 508-856-6552, E-mail: joan.vitello@umassmed.edu. *Application contact:* Diane Brescia, Admissions Coordinator, 508-856-3488, Fax: 508-856-5851, E-mail: diane.brescia@umassmed.edu.
Website: http://www.umassmed.edu/gsn/

University of Minnesota, Twin Cities Campus, Graduate School, School of Nursing, Minneapolis, MN 55455-0213. Offers adult/gerontological clinical nurse specialist (DNP); adult/gerontological primary care nurse practitioner (DNP); family nurse practitioner (DNP); health innovation and leadership (DNP); integrative health and healing (DNP); nurse anesthesia (DNP); nurse midwifery (DNP); nursing (MN, PhD); nursing informatics (DNP); pediatric clinical nurse specialist (DNP); primary care certified pediatric nurse practitioner (DNP); psychiatric/mental health nurse practitioner (DNP); women's health nurse practitioner (DNP). *Accreditation:* AACN; AANA/CANAEP; ACNM/ACME (one or more programs are accredited). *Program availability:* Part-time, online learning. Terminal master's awarded for partial completion of doctoral program. *Degree requirements:* For master's, final oral exam, project or thesis; for doctorate, thesis/dissertation. *Entrance requirements:* For master's and doctorate, GRE General Test. Additional exam requirements/recommendations for international students: Required—TOEFL (minimum score 586 paper-based). *Expenses:* Contact institution. *Faculty research:* Child and family health promotion, nursing research on elders.

University of Missouri, Office of Research and Graduate Studies, Sinclair School of Nursing, Columbia, MO 65211. Offers adult-gerontology clinical nurse specialist (DNP, Certificate); family nurse practitioner (DNP); family psychiatric and mental health nurse practitioner (DNP); nursing (MS, PhD); nursing leadership and innovations in health care (DNP); pediatric clinical nurse specialist (DNP, Certificate); pediatric nurse practitioner (DNP). *Accreditation:* AACN. *Program availability:* Part-time. *Degree requirements:* For master's, thesis optional, oral exam; for doctorate, thesis/dissertation. *Entrance requirements:* For master's, GRE General Test, BSN, minimum GPA of 3.0 during last 60 hours, nursing license. Additional exam requirements/recommendations for international students: Required—TOEFL, IELTS. *Application deadline:* Applications are processed on a rolling basis. Electronic applications accepted. *Expenses:* Tuition, state resident: full-time $6480. Tuition, nonresident: full-time $17,744. *Required fees:* $1108. Tuition and fees vary according to course load, campus/location and program. *Financial support:* Fellowships, research assistantships, teaching assistantships, career-related internships or fieldwork, institutionally sponsored loans, scholarships/grants, traineeships, health care benefits, tuition waivers (full), and unspecified assistantships available. Support available to part-time students.
Website: http://nursing.missouri.edu/

University of Missouri–Kansas City, School of Nursing and Health Studies, Kansas City, MO 64110-2499. Offers adult clinical nurse specialist (MSN), including adult nurse practitioner, women's health nurse practitioner (MSN, DNP); adult clinical nursing practice (DNP), including adult gerontology nurse practitioner, women's health nurse practitioner (MSN, DNP); clinical nursing practice (DNP), including family nurse practitioner; neonatal nurse practitioner (MSN); nurse educator (MSN); nurse executive (MSN); nursing practice (DNP); pediatric clinical nursing practice (DNP), including pediatric nurse practitioner; pediatric nurse practitioner (MSN). *Accreditation:* AACN. *Program availability:* Part-time, online learning. *Degree requirements:* For master's, thesis or alternative. *Entrance requirements:* For master's, minimum undergraduate GPA of 3.2; for doctorate, GRE, 3 letters of reference. Additional exam requirements/recommendations for international students: Required—TOEFL (minimum score 550 paper-based; 80 iBT). *Faculty research:* Geriatrics/gerontology, children's pain, neonatology, Alzheimer's care, cancer caregivers.

University of Missouri–St. Louis, College of Nursing, St. Louis, MO 63121. Offers adult/geriatric nurse practitioner (Post Master's Certificate); family nurse practitioner (Post Master's Certificate); nursing (DNP, PhD); pediatric acute care nurse practitioner (Post Master's Certificate); pediatric nurse practitioner (Post Master's Certificate); psychiatric-mental health nurse practitioner (Post Master's Certificate); women's health nurse practitioner (Post Master's Certificate). *Accreditation:* AACN. *Program availability:* Part-time. *Faculty:* 24 full-time (22 women), 12 part-time/adjunct (11 women). *Students:* 47 full-time (44 women), 162 part-time (152 women); includes 53 minority (37 Black or African American, non-Hispanic/Latino; 10 Asian, non-Hispanic/Latino; 4 Hispanic/Latino; 2 Two or more races, non-Hispanic/Latino), 3 international. 112 applicants, 93% accepted, 70 enrolled. *Degree requirements:* For doctorate, comprehensive exam, thesis/dissertation; for Post Master's Certificate, thesis. *Entrance requirements:* For doctorate, GRE, 2 letters of recommendation, MSN, minimum GPA of 3.2, course in differential/inferential statistics; for Post Master's Certificate, 2 recommendation letters; MSN; advanced practice certificate; minimum GPA of 3.0; essay. Additional exam requirements/recommendations for international students: Recommended—TOEFL (minimum score 550 paper-based; 79 iBT), IELTS (minimum score 6.5). *Application deadline:* For fall admission, 2/15 for domestic and international students. Application fee: $50 ($40 for international students). Electronic applications accepted. *Expenses:* Tuition, state resident: part-time $476.50 per credit hour. Tuition, nonresident: part-time $1169.70 per credit hour. *Financial support:* Research assistantships with tuition reimbursements available. Financial award application deadline: 4/1; financial award applicants required to submit FAFSA. *Faculty research:* Health promotion and restoration, family disruption, violence, abuse, battered women, health survey methods. *Unit head:* Sue Dean-Baar, Dean, 314-516-6066. *Application contact:* 314-516-5458, Fax: 314-516-6996, E-mail: gradadm@umsl.edu.
Website: http://www.umsl.edu/divisions/nursing/

The University of North Carolina at Chapel Hill, School of Nursing, Chapel Hill, NC 27599-7460. Offers advanced practice registered nurse (DNP); nursing (MSN, PhD, PMC), including administration (MSN), adult gerontology primary care nurse practitioner (MSN), clinical nurse leader (MSN), education (MSN), health care systems (PMC), informatics (MSN, PMC), nursing leadership (PMC), outcomes management (MSN), primary care family nurse practitioner (MSN), primary care pediatric nurse practitioner (MSN), psychiatric/mental health nurse practitioner (MSN, PMC). *Accreditation:* AACN; ACEN (one or more programs are accredited). *Program availability:* Part-time. *Faculty:* 86 full-time (78 women), 44 part-time/adjunct (40 women). *Students:* 208 full-time (186 women), 128 part-time (116 women); includes 100 minority (49 Black or African American, non-Hispanic/Latino; 4 American Indian or Alaska Native, non-Hispanic/Latino; 23 Asian, non-Hispanic/Latino; 7 Hispanic/Latino; 17 Two or more races, non-Hispanic/Latino), 17 international. Average age 33. 624 applicants, 25% accepted, 150 enrolled. In 2017, 91 master's, 14 doctorates awarded. *Degree requirements:* For master's, comprehensive exam, thesis; for doctorate, thesis/dissertation, 3 exams; for PMC, thesis. *Entrance requirements:* Additional exam requirements/recommendations for international students: Required—TOEFL (minimum score 575 paper-based; 89 iBT), IELTS (minimum score 8). *Application deadline:* For fall admission, 12/15 for domestic and international students. Application fee: $88. Electronic applications accepted. *Financial support:* In 2017–18, 8 fellowships with full tuition reimbursements, 6 research assistantships with partial tuition reimbursements (averaging $8,000 per year), 10 teaching assistantships with partial tuition reimbursements (averaging $8,000 per year) were awarded; scholarships/grants, traineeships, health care benefits, and unspecified assistantships also available. Support available to part-time students. Financial award application deadline: 3/1; financial award applicants required to submit FAFSA. *Faculty research:* Preventing and managing chronic illness, reducing health disparities, Improving healthcare quality and patient outcomes, understanding biobehavioral and genetic bases of health and illness, developing innovative ways to enhance science and its clinical translation. *Unit head:* Dr. Nilda Peragallo Montano, Dean/Professor, 919-966-3731, Fax: 919-966-3540, E-mail: npm@email.unc.edu. *Application contact:* Emily Sayed, Assistant Director, Graduate Admissions, 919-966-4260, Fax: 919-966-3540, E-mail: sayed@unc.edu.
Website: http://nursing.unc.edu

The University of North Carolina at Charlotte, College of Health and Human Services, School of Nursing, Charlotte, NC 28223-0001. Offers adult-gerontology acute care nurse practitioner (Post-Master's Certificate); advanced clinical nursing (MSN), including adult psychiatric mental health, adult-gerontology acute care nurse practitioner, family nurse practitioner across the lifespan; family nurse practitioner across the lifespan (Post-Master's Certificate); nurse anesthesia (MSN), including nurse anesthesia across the lifespan; nurse anesthesia across the lifespan (Post-Master's Certificate); nursing (DNP); nursing administration (Graduate Certificate); nursing education (Graduate Certificate); systems/population nursing (MSN), including community/public health nursing, nurse administrator, nurse educator. *Accreditation:* AACN; AANA/CANAEP. *Program availability:* Part-time, blended/hybrid learning. *Faculty:* 24 full-time (22 women), 6 part-time/adjunct (4 women). *Students:* 113 full-time (84 women), 163 part-time (150 women); includes 63 minority (47 Black or African American, non-Hispanic/Latino; 2 American Indian or Alaska Native, non-Hispanic/Latino; 6 Asian, non-Hispanic/Latino; 3 Hispanic/Latino; 5 Two or more races, non-Hispanic/Latino). Average age 37. 443 applicants, 31% accepted, 113 enrolled. In 2017, 83 master's, 8 doctorates, 8 other advanced degrees awarded. Terminal master's awarded for partial completion of doctoral program. *Degree requirements:* For doctorate, thesis/dissertation or alternative, residency; for other advanced degree, practicum. *Entrance requirements:* For master's, GRE General Test, current unrestricted license as Registered Nurse in North Carolina; BSN from nationally-accredited program; one year of professional nursing practice in acute/critical care; minimum overall GPA of 3.0 in last degree; completion of undergraduate statistics course with minimum grade of C; statement of purpose; for doctorate, GRE or MAT, master's degree in nursing in an advanced nursing practice specialty from nationally-accredited program; minimum overall GPA of 3.5 in MSN program; current RN licensure in U.S. at time of application with eligibility for NC licensure; essay; resume/curriculum vitae; professional recommendations; clinical hours; for other advanced degree, GRE. Additional exam requirements/recommendations for international students: Required—TOEFL (minimum score 523 paper-based, 70 iBT) or IELTS (6.5). *Application deadline:* For fall admission, 1/10 for domestic and international students; for spring admission, 9/10 for domestic and international students; for summer admission, 4/1 for domestic and international students. Applications are processed on a rolling basis. Application fee: $75. Electronic applications accepted. *Expenses:* Contact institution. *Financial support:* In 2017–18, 6 students received support, including 4 research assistantships (averaging $6,338 per year), 2 teaching assistantships (averaging $6,250 per year); career-related internships or fieldwork, institutionally sponsored loans, scholarships/grants, traineeships, and unspecified assistantships also available. Support available to part-time students. Financial award application deadline: 3/1; financial award applicants required to submit FAFSA. *Total annual research expenditures:* $800,072. *Unit head:* Dr. Dena Evans, Director, 704-687-7974, E-mail: devans37@uncc.edu. *Application contact:* Kathy B. Giddings, Director of Graduate Admissions, 704-687-5503, Fax: 704-687-1668, E-mail: gradadm@uncc.edu.
Website: http://nursing.uncc.edu/

The University of North Carolina at Greensboro, Graduate School, School of Nursing, Greensboro, NC 27412-5001. Offers adult clinical nurse specialist (MSN, PMC); adult/gerontological nurse practitioner (MSN, PMC); nurse anesthesia (MSN, PMC); nursing (PhD); nursing administration (MSN); nursing education (MSN); MSN/MBA. *Accreditation:* ACEN. *Degree requirements:* For master's, thesis or alternative. *Entrance requirements:* For master's, GRE General Test or MAT, BSN, clinical experience, liability insurance, RN license; for PMC, liability insurance, MSN, RN license. Additional exam requirements/recommendations for international students: Required—TOEFL. Electronic applications accepted.

University of North Dakota, Graduate School, College of Nursing and Professional Disciplines, Department of Nursing, Grand Forks, ND 58202. Offers adult-gerontological nurse practitioner (MS); advanced public health nurse (MS); family nurse practitioner (MS); nurse anesthesia (MS); nurse educator (MS); nursing (PhD, Post-Master's Certificate); nursing practice (DNP); psychiatric and mental health nurse practitioner (MS).

University of Pennsylvania, School of Nursing, Adult Gerontology Clinical Nurse Specialist Program, Philadelphia, PA 19104. Offers MSN. *Students:* 5 part-time (4 women); includes 3 minority (1 Black or African American, non-Hispanic/Latino; 1 Hispanic/Latino; 1 Two or more races, non-Hispanic/Latino). Average age 30. In 2017, 3 master's awarded. Application fee: $80.
Website: http://www.nursing.upenn.edu/ahcns/

University of Pennsylvania, School of Nursing, Adult Gerontology Primary Care Nurse Practitioner Program, Philadelphia, PA 19104. Offers MSN. *Program availability:* Part-time. *Students:* 17 full-time (all women), 62 part-time (58 women); includes 24 minority (8 Black or African American, non-Hispanic/Latino; 7 Asian, non-Hispanic/Latino; 7 Hispanic/Latino; 2 Two or more races, non-Hispanic/Latino), 1 international. Average age 29. In 2017, 17 master's awarded. Application fee: $80.

University of Phoenix–Bay Area Campus, College of Nursing, San Jose, CA 95134-1805. Offers education (MHA); gerontology (MHA); health administration (MHA, DHA); informatics (MHA, MSN); nursing (MSN, PhD); nursing/health care education (MSN); MSN/MBA. *Program availability:* Evening/weekend, online learning. *Degree requirements:* For master's, thesis (for some programs). *Entrance requirements:* For master's, minimum undergraduate GPA of 2.5, 3 years of work experience, RN license. Additional exam requirements/recommendations for international students: Required—TOEFL (minimum score 550 paper-based; 79 iBT). Electronic applications accepted.

University of Phoenix–Phoenix Campus, College of Health Sciences and Nursing, Tempe, AZ 85282-2371. Offers family nurse practitioner (MSN, Certificate); gerontology health care (Certificate); health care education (MSN, Certificate); health care informatics (Certificate); informatics (MSN); nursing (MSN); MSN/MHA. *Program availability:* Evening/weekend, online learning. *Entrance requirements:* Additional exam requirements/recommendations for international students: Required—TOEFL, TOEIC (Test of English as an International Communication), Berlitz Online English Proficiency Exam, PTE, or IELTS. Electronic applications accepted. *Expenses:* Contact institution.

University of Pittsburgh, School of Nursing, Clinical Nurse Specialist Program, Pittsburgh, PA 15260. Offers clinical nurse specialist (DNP), including adult gerontology. *Accreditation:* AACN. *Program availability:* Part-time. *Faculty:* 1 (woman) full-time. *Students:* 6 full-time (5 women), 2 part-time (both women). Average age 46. 4 applicants, 75% accepted, 3 enrolled. In 2017, 2 doctorates awarded. *Entrance requirements:* For doctorate, GRE, BSN, RN license, minimum GPA of 3.5, 3 letters of recommendation, relevant nursing experience, resume, course work in statistics. Additional exam requirements/recommendations for international students: Required—TOEFL (minimum score 600 paper-based; 100 IBT) or IELTS (minimum score 7.0). *Application deadline:* For fall admission, 5/1 priority date for domestic students, 2/15 priority date for international students. Application fee: $50. Electronic applications accepted. *Expenses:* $13,068 per term full-time resident tuition, $1,064 per credit part-time; $15,270 per term full-time non-resident tuition, $1,247 per credit part-time; $437 per term full-time fees; $282 per term part-time fees. *Financial support:* In 2017–18, 6 students received support, including 4 fellowships (averaging $19,180 per year); scholarships/grants also available. Financial award applicants required to submit FAFSA. *Faculty research:* Behavioral management of chronic disorders, patient management in critical care, consumer informatics, genetic applications (molecular genetics and psychosocial implications), technology for nurses and patients to improve care. *Unit head:* Dr. Sandra Engberg, Associate Dean for Clinical Education, 412-624-3835, Fax: 412-624-8521, E-mail: sje1@pitt.edu. *Application contact:* Laurie Lapsley, Graduate Administrator, 412-624-9670, Fax: 412-624-2409, E-mail: lapsleyl@pitt.edu.

University of Pittsburgh, School of Nursing, Nurse Practitioner Program, Pittsburgh, PA 15261. Offers adult-gerontology acute care (DNP); adult-gerontology primary care (DNP); family (individual across the lifespan) (DNP); neonatal (MSN, DNP); pediatric primary care (DNP); psychiatric mental health (DNP). *Accreditation:* AACN. *Program availability:* Part-time. *Faculty:* 17 full-time (14 women), 3 part-time/adjunct (2 women). *Students:* 50 full-time (47 women), 43 part-time (36 women); includes 9 minority (1 Black or African American, non-Hispanic/Latino; 1 American Indian or Alaska Native, non-Hispanic/Latino; 7 Asian, non-Hispanic/Latino), 1 international. Average age 31. 77 applicants, 40% accepted, 25 enrolled. In 2017, 6 master's, 35 doctorates awarded. *Degree requirements:* For master's, comprehensive exam, thesis optional. *Entrance requirements:* For master's, GRE General Test, BSN, RN license, 3 letters of recommendation, resume, course work in statistics, relevant nursing experience; for doctorate, GRE General Test, BSN, RN license, minimum GPA of 3.5, 3 letters of recommendation, relevant nursing experience, resume, course work in statistics. Additional exam requirements/recommendations for international students: Required—TOEFL (minimum score 600 paper-based; 100 IBT) or IELTS (minimum score 7.0). *Application deadline:* For fall admission, 5/1 priority date for domestic students, 2/15 priority date for international students. Application fee: $50. Electronic applications accepted. *Expenses:* $13,068 per term full-time resident tuition, $1,064 per credit part-time; $15,270 per term full-time non-resident tuition, $1,247 per credit part-time; $437 per term full-time fees; $282 per term part-time fees. *Financial support:* In 2017–18, 58 students received support, including 7 fellowships (averaging $15,755 per year), 15 teaching assistantships (averaging $12,454 per year); scholarships/grants, tuition waivers, and unspecified assistantships also available. Financial award applicants required to submit FAFSA. *Faculty research:* Behavioral management of chronic disorders, patient management in critical care, consumer informatics, genetic applications (molecular genetics and psychosocial implications), technology for nurses and patients to improve care. *Unit head:* Dr. Sandra Engberg, Associate Dean for Clinical Education, 412-624-3835, Fax: 412-624-8521, E-mail: sje1@pitt.edu. *Application contact:* Laurie Lapsley, Graduate Administrator, 412-624-9670, Fax: 412-624-2409, E-mail: lapsleyl@pitt.edu.
Website: http://www.nursing.pitt.edu

University of Puerto Rico–Medical Sciences Campus, School of Nursing, San Juan, PR 00936-5067. Offers adult and elderly nursing (MSN); child and adolescent nursing (MSN); critical care nursing (MSN); family and community nursing (MSN); family nurse practitioner (MSN); maternity nursing (MSN); mental health and psychiatric nursing (MSN). *Accreditation:* AACN; AANA/CANAEP. *Entrance requirements:* For master's, GRE or EXADEP, interview, Puerto Rico RN license or professional license for international students, general and specific point average, article analysis. Electronic applications accepted. *Faculty research:* HIV, health disparities, teen violence, women and violence, neurological disorders.

University of Rhode Island, Graduate School, College of Nursing, Kingston, RI 02881. Offers acute care nurse practitioner (adult-gerontology focus) (Post Master's Certificate); adult gerontology nurse practitioner/clinical nurse specialist (Post Master's Certificate); adult-gerontological acute care nurse practitioner (MS); adult-gerontological nurse practitioner/clinical nurse specialist (MS); family nurse practitioner (MS, Post Master's Certificate); nursing (DNP, PhD); nursing education (MS, Post Master's Certificate). *Accreditation:* AACN; ACNM/ACME (one or more programs are accredited). *Program availability:* Part-time, evening/weekend, 100% online, blended/hybrid learning. *Faculty:* 31 full-time (30 women). *Students:* 42 full-time (36 women), 86 part-time (79 women); includes 12 minority (3 Black or African American, non-Hispanic/Latino; 3 Asian, non-Hispanic/Latino; 3 Hispanic/Latino; 1 Native Hawaiian or other Pacific Islander, non-Hispanic/Latino; 2 Two or more races, non-Hispanic/Latino), 3 international. 33 applicants, 79% accepted, 23 enrolled. In 2017, 25 master's, 8 doctorates, 2 other advanced degrees awarded. *Entrance requirements:* For master's, GRE or MAT, 2 letters of recommendation, scholarly papers; for doctorate, GRE, 3 letters of recommendation, scholarly papers. Additional exam requirements/recommendations for international students: Required—TOEFL. *Application deadline:* For fall admission, 2/15 for domestic students, 2/1 for international students; for spring admission, 10/15 for domestic students, 7/15 for international students. Application fee: $65. Electronic applications accepted. *Expenses:* Tuition, state resident: full-time $12,706; part-time $786 per credit. Tuition, nonresident: full-time $25,216; part-time $1401 per credit. *Required fees:* $1598; $45 per credit. One-time fee: $30 part-time. *Financial support:* In 2017–18, 1 research assistantship with tuition reimbursement (averaging $18,080 per year), 5 teaching assistantships with tuition reimbursements (averaging $10,133 per year) were awarded. Financial award application deadline: 2/1; financial award applicants required to submit FAFSA. *Unit head:* Dr. Barbara Wolfe, Dean, 401-874-5324, E-mail: bwolfe@uri.edu. *Application contact:* Dr. Denise Coppa, Associate Professor/Interim Associate Dean for Graduate Programs, 401-874-5036, E-mail: dcoppa@uri.edu.
Website: http://www.uri.edu/nursing/

University of Rochester, School of Nursing, Rochester, NY 14642. Offers adult gerontological acute care nurse practitioner (MS); adult gerontological primary care nurse practitioner (MS); clinical nurse leader (MS); family nurse practitioner (MS); family psychiatric mental health nurse practitioner (MS); health care organization management and leadership (MS); nursing (DNP); nursing and health science (PhD); nursing education (MS); pediatric nurse practitioner (MS); pediatric nurse practitioner/neonatal nurse practitioner (MS). *Accreditation:* AACN. *Program availability:* Part-time, 100% online, blended/hybrid learning. *Faculty:* 62 full-time (51 women), 73 part-time/adjunct (63 women). *Students:* 17 full-time (12 women), 306 part-time (252 women); includes 46 minority (16 Black or African American, non-Hispanic/Latino; 1 American Indian or Alaska Native, non-Hispanic/Latino; 7 Asian, non-Hispanic/Latino; 17 Hispanic/Latino; 5 Two or more races, non-Hispanic/Latino), 3 international. Average age 34. 143 applicants, 71% accepted, 87 enrolled. In 2017, 48 master's, 8 doctorates awarded. Terminal master's awarded for partial completion of doctoral program. *Degree requirements:* For master's, comprehensive exam; for doctorate, thesis/dissertation. *Entrance requirements:* For master's, BS in nursing, minimum GPA of 3.0, course work in statistics; for doctorate, GRE General Test (for PhD), MS in nursing, minimum GPA of 3.5. Additional exam requirements/recommendations for international students: Required—TOEFL (minimum score 560 paper-based; 88 iBT) or IELTS (minimum score 6.5) recommended. *Application deadline:* For fall admission, 4/1 for domestic and international students; for spring admission, 9/1 for domestic and international students; for summer admission, 1/2 for domestic and international students. Application fee: $50. Electronic applications accepted. *Financial support:* In 2017–18, 63 students received support, including 2 fellowships with full and partial tuition reimbursements available (averaging $16,000 per year); scholarships/grants, traineeships, health care benefits, tuition waivers (full and partial), and unspecified assistantships also available. Support available to part-time students. Financial award application deadline: 6/30; financial award applicants required to submit CSS PROFILE or FAFSA. *Faculty research:* Symptom science, systems of care, innovations in health technology, promoting healthy behaviors. *Total annual research expenditures:* $2.6 million. *Unit head:* Dr. Kathy H. Rideout, Dean, 585-273-8902, Fax: 585-273-1268, E-mail: kathy_rideout@urmc.rochester.edu. *Application contact:* Elaine Andolina, Director of Admissions, 585-275-2375, Fax: 585-756-8299, E-mail: elaine_andolina@urmc.rochester.edu.
Website: http://www.son.rochester.edu

University of San Diego, Hahn School of Nursing and Health Science, San Diego, CA 92110-2492. Offers adult-gerontology clinical nurse specialist (MSN); adult-gerontology nurse practitioner/family nurse practitioner (MSN); clinical nurse leader (MSN); executive nurse leader (MSN); family nurse practitioner (MSN); healthcare informatics (MS, MSN); nursing (PhD); nursing practice (DNP); pediatric/family nurse practitioner (MSN); psychiatric-mental health nurse practitioner (MSN). *Accreditation:* AACN. *Program availability:* Part-time, evening/weekend. *Faculty:* 26 full-time (21 women), 36 part-time/adjunct (29 women). *Students:* 238 full-time (198 women), 230 part-time (167 women); includes 230 minority (32 Black or African American, non-Hispanic/Latino; 104 Asian, non-Hispanic/Latino; 75 Hispanic/Latino; 19 Two or more races, non-Hispanic/Latino), 12 international. Average age 35. In 2017, 93 master's, 44 doctorates awarded. *Degree requirements:* For doctorate, thesis/dissertation (for some programs), residency (DNP). *Entrance requirements:* For master's, GRE General Test (for entry-level nursing), BSN, current California RN licensure (except for entry-level nursing), minimum GPA of 3.0; for doctorate, minimum GPA of 3.5, MSN, current California RN licensure. Additional exam requirements/recommendations for international students: Required—TOEFL (minimum score 580 paper-based; 83 iBT), TWE. *Application deadline:* Applications are processed on a rolling basis. Application fee: $45. Electronic applications accepted. *Financial support:* In 2017–18, 242 students received support. Scholarships/grants and traineeships available. Support available to part-time students. Financial award application deadline: 4/1; financial award applicants required to submit FAFSA. *Faculty research:* Maternal/neonatal health, palliative and end of life care, adolescent obesity, health disparities, cognitive dysfunction. *Unit head:* Dr. Janes Georges, Interim Dean, 619-260-4550, Fax: 619-260-6814, E-mail: nursing@sandiego.edu. *Application contact:* Monica Mahon, Associate Director of Graduate Admissions, 619-260-4524, Fax: 619-260-4158, E-mail: grads@sandiego.edu.
Website: http://www.sandiego.edu/nursing/

University of Southern Maine, College of Science, Technology, and Health, School of Nursing, Portland, ME 04103. Offers adult-gerontology primary care nurse practitioner (MS, PMC); education (MS); family nurse practitioner (MS, PMC); family psychiatric/mental health nurse practitioner (MS); management (MS); nursing (CAS, CGS); psychiatric-mental health nurse practitioner (PMC). *Accreditation:* AACN. *Program availability:* Part-time. *Degree requirements:* For master's, thesis optional. *Entrance requirements:* For master's, GRE General Test or MAT, minimum GPA of 3.0; for doctorate, GRE. Additional exam requirements/recommendations for international students: Required—TOEFL (minimum score 550 paper-based). Electronic applications accepted. *Faculty research:* Women's health, nursing history, weight control, community services, substance abuse.

University of South Florida, College of Nursing, Tampa, FL 33612. Offers nurse anesthesia (DNP); nursing (MS, DNP), including adult-gerontology acute care nursing, adult-gerontology primary care nursing, family health nursing, nurse anesthesia (MS), nursing education (MS), occupational health nursing/adult-gerontology primary care nursing, oncology nursing/adult-gerontology primary care nursing (DNP), pediatric health nursing; nursing education (Post Master's Certificate); nursing science (PhD); simulation based academic fellowship in advanced pain management (Graduate Certificate). *Accreditation:* AACN; AANA/CANAEP. *Program availability:* Part-time. *Faculty:* 37 full-time (32 women), 2 part-time/adjunct (1 woman). *Students:* 224 full-time (178 women), 669 part-time (577 women); includes 309 minority (105 Black or African American, non-Hispanic/Latino; 2 American Indian or Alaska Native, non-Hispanic/Latino; 53 Asian, non-Hispanic/Latino; 122 Hispanic/Latino; 1 Native Hawaiian or other Pacific Islander, non-Hispanic/Latino; 26 Two or more races, non-Hispanic/Latino), 6 international. Average age 32. 949 applicants, 47% accepted, 382 enrolled. In 2017, 264

master's, 39 doctorates awarded. *Degree requirements:* For master's, comprehensive exam, thesis optional; for doctorate, comprehensive exam, thesis/dissertation. *Entrance requirements:* For master's, GRE General Test, bachelor's degree from accredited program with minimum GPA of 3.0 in all upper-division coursework; current license as Registered Nurse; 3 letters of recommendation; personal statement of goals; resume or curriculum vitae; personal interview; for doctorate, GRE General Test (recommended), bachelor's degree in nursing from ACEN or CCNE regionally-accredited institution with minimum GPA of 3.0 in all coursework or in all upper-division coursework; current license as Registered Nurse in Florida; undergraduate statistics course with minimum B grade; 3 letters of recommendation; statement of goals; resume; interview. Additional exam requirements/recommendations for international students: Required—TOEFL (minimum score 550 paper-based; 79 iBT). *Application deadline:* For fall admission, 12/15 for domestic and international students; for spring admission, 10/1 for domestic students, 9/15 for international students. Application fee: $30. Electronic applications accepted. *Financial support:* In 2017–18, 132 students received support, including 7 research assistantships with tuition reimbursements available (averaging $18,935 per year), 29 teaching assistantships with tuition reimbursements available (averaging $30,814 per year); tuition waivers (partial) and unspecified assistantships also available. Financial award application deadline: 2/1; financial award applicants required to submit FAFSA. *Faculty research:* Women's health, palliative and end-of-life care, cardiac rehabilitation, complementary therapies for chronic illness and cancer. *Total annual research expenditures:* $3.2 million. *Unit head:* Dr. Victoria Rich, Dean, College of Nursing, 813-974-8939, Fax: 813-974-5418, E-mail: victoriarich@health.usf.edu. *Application contact:* Dr. Brian Graves, Assistant Professor/Assistant Dean, 813-974-8054, Fax: 813-974-5418, E-mail: bgraves1@health.usf.edu.
Website: http://health.usf.edu/nursing/index.htm

The University of Tennessee at Chattanooga, School of Nursing, Chattanooga, TN 37403. Offers certified nurse anesthetist (Post-Master's Certificate); family nurse practitioner (MSN, Post-Master's Certificate); gerontology acute care (MSN, Post-Master's Certificate); nurse anesthesia (MSN); nurse education (Post-Master's Certificate); nursing (DNP). *Accreditation:* AACN; AANA/CANAEP (one or more programs are accredited). *Students:* 62 full-time (33 women), 69 part-time (61 women); includes 24 minority (11 Black or African American, non-Hispanic/Latino; 1 American Indian or Alaska Native, non-Hispanic/Latino; 5 Asian, non-Hispanic/Latino; 3 Hispanic/Latino; 4 Two or more races, non-Hispanic/Latino). Average age 34. 47 applicants, 100% accepted, 45 enrolled. In 2017, 33 master's, 14 doctorates, 7 other advanced degrees awarded. *Degree requirements:* For master's, thesis optional, qualifying exams, professional project; for doctorate, professional project; for Post-Master's Certificate, thesis or alternative, practicum, seminar. *Entrance requirements:* For master's, GRE General Test, MAT, BSN, minimum GPA of 3.0, eligibility for Tennessee RN license, 1 year of direct patient care experience; for doctorate, GRE General Test or MAT (if applicant does not have MSN), minimum GPA of 3.0 for highest degree earned; for Post-Master's Certificate, GRE General Test, MAT, MSN, minimum GPA of 3.0, eligibility for Tennessee RN license, one year of direct patient care experience. Additional exam requirements/recommendations for international students: Required—TOEFL (minimum score 550 paper-based; 79 iBT), IELTS (minimum score 6). *Application deadline:* For fall admission, 6/15 priority date for domestic students, 7/1 for international students; for spring admission, 11/1 priority date for domestic students, 11/1 for international students. Applications are processed on a rolling basis. Application fee: $35 ($40 for international students). Electronic applications accepted. *Expenses:* Contact institution. *Financial support:* Teaching assistantships, career-related internships or fieldwork, and scholarships/grants available. Support available to part-time students. Financial award application deadline: 7/1; financial award applicants required to submit FAFSA. *Faculty research:* Diabetes in women, health care for elderly, alternative medicine, hypertension, nurse anesthesia. *Total annual research expenditures:* $985,388. *Unit head:* Dr. Chris Smith, Director, 423-425-1741, Fax: 423-425-4668, E-mail: chris-smith@utc.edu. *Application contact:* Dr. Joanne Romagni, Dean of the Graduate School, 423-425-4478, Fax: 423-425-5223, E-mail: joanne-romagni@utc.edu.
Website: http://www.utc.edu/nursing/

The University of Tennessee Health Science Center, College of Nursing, Memphis, TN 38163. Offers adult-gerontology acute care nurse practitioner (Post Master's Certificate); advance practice nursing (DNP); family nurse practitioner (Post-Doctoral Certificate); pediatric acute care nurse practitioner (Post-Doctoral Certificate); pediatric primary care nurse practitioner (Post-Doctoral Certificate); psychiatric/mental health nurse practitioner (Post-Doctoral Certificate); registered nurse first assistant (Certificate). *Accreditation:* AACN; AANA/CANAEP. *Program availability:* Part-time, blended/hybrid learning. *Faculty:* 52 full-time (47 women), 11 part-time/adjunct (4 women). *Students:* 262 full-time (228 women), 13 part-time (12 women); includes 83 minority (71 Black or African American, non-Hispanic/Latino; 6 Asian, non-Hispanic/Latino; 6 Hispanic/Latino). Average age 32. 215 applicants, 49% accepted, 79 enrolled. In 2017, 78 doctorates, 2 Certificates awarded. *Degree requirements:* For doctorate, project. *Entrance requirements:* For doctorate, RN license, minimum GPA of 3.0; for other advanced degree, MSN, APN license, minimum GPA of 3.0. Additional exam requirements/recommendations for international students: Required—TOEFL (minimum score 550 paper-based; 80 iBT). *Application deadline:* For fall admission, 1/15 for domestic students; for spring admission, 8/15 for domestic students. Application fee: $70. Electronic applications accepted. *Expenses:* $13,420 in-state tuition and fees; $17,222 out-of-state tuition and fees. *Financial support:* In 2017–18, 112 students received support, including 9 research assistantships (averaging $24,783 per year); Federal Work-Study, institutionally sponsored loans, scholarships/grants, and tuition waivers (partial) also available. Financial award application deadline: 3/15; financial award applicants required to submit FAFSA. *Faculty research:* Efficacy of a cognitive behavioral group intervention and its influence on symptoms of depression and anxiety as well as caregiver function; quality of life and sexual function in women who undergo vulvar surgeries; influence of prenatal and early childhood environments on health and developmental trajectories across childhood; interaction between physical activity, diet, genetics, insulin resistance, and obesity. *Total annual research expenditures:* $1.2 million. *Unit head:* Dr. Wendy Likes, Dean, 901-448-6135, Fax: 901-448-4121, E-mail: wlikes@uthsc.edu. *Application contact:* Jamie Overton, Director, Student Affairs, 901-448-6139, Fax: 901-448-4121, E-mail: joverton@uthsc.edu.
Website: http://uthsc.edu/nursing/

The University of Texas at Austin, Graduate School, School of Nursing, Austin, TX 78712-1111. Offers adult - gerontology clinical nurse specialist (MSN); child health (MSN), including administration, public health nursing, teaching; family nurse practitioner (MSN); family psychiatric/mental health nurse practitioner (MSN); holistic adult health (MSN), including administration, teaching; maternity (MSN), including administration, public health nursing, teaching; nursing (PhD); nursing administration and healthcare systems management (MSN); nursing practice (DNP); pediatric nurse practitioner (MSN); public health nursing (MSN). *Accreditation:* AACN. *Program availability:* Part-time. *Degree requirements:* For master's, thesis optional; for doctorate, thesis/dissertation. *Entrance requirements:* For master's and doctorate, GRE General Test. Additional exam requirements/recommendations for international students: Required—TOEFL (minimum score 550 paper-based). Electronic applications accepted. *Faculty research:* Chronic illness management, memory and aging, health promotion, women's health, adolescent health.

The University of Texas Health Science Center at San Antonio, School of Nursing, San Antonio, TX 78229-3900. Offers administrative management (MSN); adult-gerontology acute care nurse practitioner (PGC); advanced practice leadership (DNP); clinical nurse leader (MSN); executive administrative management (DNP); family nurse practitioner (MSN, PGC); nursing (MSN, PhD); nursing education (MSN, PGC); pediatric nurse practitioner primary care (PGC); psychiatric mental health nurse practitioner (PGC); public health nurse leader (DNP). *Accreditation:* AACN. *Program availability:* Part-time. Terminal master's awarded for partial completion of doctoral program. *Degree requirements:* For master's, thesis optional; for doctorate, comprehensive exam, thesis/dissertation.

The University of Tulsa, Graduate School, Oxley College of Health Sciences, School of Nursing, Tulsa, OK 74104-3189. Offers adult-gerontology acute care nurse practitioner (DNP); family nurse practitioner (DNP). Summer enrollment only. *Faculty:* 18 full-time (16 women), 6 part-time/adjunct (5 women). *Students:* 27 full-time (23 women); includes 6 minority (1 Black or African American, non-Hispanic/Latino; 1 Asian, non-Hispanic/Latino; 3 Hispanic/Latino; 1 Two or more races, non-Hispanic/Latino). Average age 36. 42 applicants, 57% accepted, 21 enrolled. *Degree requirements:* For doctorate, comprehensive exam, thesis/dissertation. *Entrance requirements:* Additional exam requirements/recommendations for international students: Required—TOEFL (minimum score 550 paper-based; 91 iBT), IELTS (minimum score 6.5). Application fee: $55. Electronic applications accepted. *Expenses:* $1,040 per credit hour tuition. *Unit head:* Robin Ploeger, Interim Dean, 918-631-3170, E-mail: robin-ploeger@utulsa.edu. *Application contact:* Dr. Sheryl Stansifer, Department Chair, 918-631-3125, Fax: 918-631-2156, E-mail: sheryl-stansifer@utulsa.edu.
Website: https://healthsciences.utulsa.edu/departments-schools/nursing/nursing-graduate-programs/

University of Utah, Graduate School, College of Nursing, Gerontology Interdisciplinary Program, Salt Lake City, UT 84112. Offers MS, Certificate. *Program availability:* Part-time, evening/weekend, online only, 100% online, blended/hybrid learning. *Faculty:* 9 full-time (8 women). *Students:* 2 full-time (both women), 4 part-time (all women). Average age 34. 5 applicants, 100% accepted, 4 enrolled. In 2017, 3 master's awarded. *Degree requirements:* For master's, thesis or project. *Entrance requirements:* For master's, GRE General Test (if cumulative GPA is less than 3.2), minimum undergraduate GPA of 3.0. Additional exam requirements/recommendations for international students: Required—TOEFL (minimum score 500 paper-based; 85 iBT). *Application deadline:* For fall admission, 1/15 for domestic and international students. Application fee: $55 ($65 for international students). Electronic applications accepted. *Expenses:* $12,018.08. *Financial support:* In 2017–18, 8 students received support, including 4 fellowships with full tuition reimbursements available (averaging $7,500 per year); teaching assistantships, scholarships/grants, and health care benefits also available. Support available to part-time students. Financial award application deadline: 1/15; financial award applicants required to submit FAFSA. *Faculty research:* Spousal bereavement, family caregiving, health promotion and self-care, geriatric care management, technology and aging. *Unit head:* Dr. Jackie Eaton, Director, 801-587-9638, Fax: 801-587-7697, E-mail: jacqueline.eaton@nurs.utah.edu. *Application contact:* Arminka Zeljkovic, Program Manager, 801-581-8198, Fax: 801-585-9705, E-mail: arminka.zeljkovic@nurs.utah.edu.
Website: http://www.nursing.utah.edu/gerontology/

University of Wisconsin–Eau Claire, College of Nursing and Health Sciences, Program in Nursing, Eau Claire, WI 54702-4004. Offers adult-gerontological administration (DNP); adult-gerontological clinical nurse specialist (DNP); adult-gerontological education (MSN); adult-gerontological primary care nurse practitioner (DNP); family health administration (DNP); family health in education (MSN); family health nurse practitioner (DNP); nursing (MSN); nursing practice (DNP). *Accreditation:* AACN. *Program availability:* Part-time. Terminal master's awarded for partial completion of doctoral program. *Degree requirements:* For master's, thesis optional, 500-600 hours clinical practicum, oral and written exams. *Entrance requirements:* For master's, Wisconsin RN license, minimum GPA of 3.0, undergraduate statistics, course work in health assessment. Additional exam requirements/recommendations for international students: Required—TOEFL (minimum score 79 iBT). *Expenses:* Contact institution.

University of Wisconsin–Madison, School of Nursing, Madison, WI 53706-1380. Offers adult/gerontology (DNP); nursing (PhD); pediatrics (DNP); psychiatric mental health (DNP); MS/MPH. *Accreditation:* AACN. *Program availability:* Part-time. *Degree requirements:* For doctorate, comprehensive exam, thesis/dissertation. *Entrance requirements:* For doctorate, GRE General Test, 2 samples of scholarly written work, BS in nursing from an accredited program, minimum undergraduate GPA of 3.0 in last 60 credits (for PhD); licensure as professional nurse (for DNP). Additional exam requirements/recommendations for international students: Required—TOEFL (minimum score 600 paper-based; 100 iBT). Electronic applications accepted. *Faculty research:* Nursing informatics to promote self-care and disease management skills among patients and caregivers; quality of care to frail, vulnerable, and chronically ill populations; study of health-related and health-seeking behaviors; eliminating health disparities; pain and symptom management for patients with cancer.

Ursuline College, School of Graduate and Professional Studies, Programs in Nursing, Pepper Pike, OH 44124-4398. Offers acute-care nurse practitioner (MSN); adult nurse practitioner (MSN); adult-gerontology acute care nurse practitioner (MSN); adult-gerontology clinical nurse specialist (MSN); adult-gerontology nurse practitioner (MSN); care management (MSN); clinical nurse specialist (MSN); family nurse practitioner (MSN); nursing (DNP); nursing education (MSN); palliative care (MSN). *Accreditation:* AACN. *Program availability:* Part-time. *Faculty:* 6 full-time (all women), 25 part-time/adjunct (23 women). *Students:* 136 applicants, 89% accepted, 85 enrolled. In 2017, 85 master's, 6 doctorates awarded. *Degree requirements:* For master's, comprehensive exam; for doctorate, thesis/dissertation. *Entrance requirements:* For master's, minimum undergraduate GPA of 3.0, bachelor's degree in nursing, eligibility for or current Ohio RN license. Additional exam requirements/recommendations for international students: Required—TOEFL (minimum score 500 paper-based). *Application deadline:* For fall admission, 8/1 priority date for domestic students. Applications are processed on a rolling basis. Application fee: $25. Electronic applications accepted. *Expenses:* $1,094 per credit hour. *Financial support:* In 2017–18, 6 students received support. Scholarships/grants available. Financial award application deadline: 3/1; financial award applicants required to submit FAFSA. *Faculty research:* Core Determinants of Health (CDH) screening tool and accompanying education, academic-practice partnerships, active learning/teaching strategies, innovative clinical education models, competency development and testing, health care policy and cultural competence. *Total annual research expenditures:* $864,511. *Unit head:* Dr. Janet Baker, Associate Dean of Graduate Nursing, 440-864-8172, Fax: 440-684-6053, E-mail: jbaker@ursuline.edu. *Application contact:* Melanie Steele, Director, Graduate Admission, 440-646-8119, Fax: 440-684-6138, E-mail: graduateadmissions@ursuline.edu.

Valdosta State University, College of Nursing and Health Sciences, Valdosta, GA 31698. Offers adult gerontology nurse practitioner (MSN); exercise physiology (MS); family nurse practitioner (MSN); family psychiatric mental health nurse practitioner (MSN). *Accreditation:* AACN. *Program availability:* Part-time, online learning. *Degree requirements:* For master's, thesis (for some programs), comprehensive written and/or

oral exams. *Entrance requirements:* For master's, minimum GPA of 2.8. Additional exam requirements/recommendations for international students: Required—TOEFL (minimum score 523 paper-based). *Application deadline:* For fall admission, 7/1 for domestic and international students; for spring admission, 11/15 for domestic and international students. Applications are processed on a rolling basis. Application fee: $45. Electronic applications accepted. *Financial support:* Research assistantships with full tuition reimbursements, institutionally sponsored loans, scholarships/grants, and unspecified assistantships available. Support available to part-time students. Financial award application deadline: 7/1; financial award applicants required to submit FAFSA. *Faculty research:* Nutrition, children's health beliefs, alternative treatment modalities, job satisfaction, leadership. *Unit head:* Sheri Noviello, Dean, 229-333-5959, E-mail: srnoviello@valdosta.edu. *Application contact:* Sheri Noviello, Dean, 229-333-5959, E-mail: srnoviello@valdosta.edu.
Website: https://www.valdosta.edu/colleges/nursing-and-health-sciences/

Vanderbilt University, Vanderbilt University School of Nursing, Nashville, TN 37240. Offers adult-gerontology acute care nurse practitioner (MSN), including hospitalist, intensivist; adult-gerontology primary care nurse practitioner (MSN); emergency nurse practitioner (MSN); family nurse practitioner (MSN); healthcare leadership (MSN); neonatal nurse practitioner (MSN); nurse midwifery (MSN); nurse midwifery/family nurse practitioner (MSN); nursing (Post-Master's Certificate); nursing informatics (MSN); nursing practice (DNP); nursing science (PhD); pediatric acute care nurse practitioner (MSN); pediatric primary care nurse practitioner (MSN); psychiatric-mental health nurse practitioner (MSN); women's health nurse practitioner (MSN); women's health nurse practitioner/adult gerontology primary care nurse practitioner (MSN); MSN/M Div; MSN/MTS. *Accreditation:* AACN; ACEN (one or more programs are accredited); ACNM/ACME. *Program availability:* Part-time, 100% online, blended/hybrid learning. *Faculty:* 292 full-time (267 women), 321 part-time/adjunct (253 women). *Students:* 501 full-time (435 women), 387 part-time (355 women); includes 153 minority (40 Black or African American, non-Hispanic/Latino; 1 American Indian or Alaska Native, non-Hispanic/Latino; 27 Asian, non-Hispanic/Latino; 48 Hispanic/Latino; 4 Native Hawaiian or other Pacific Islander, non-Hispanic/Latino; 33 Two or more races, non-Hispanic/Latino), 9 international. Average age 31. 1,210 applicants, 57% accepted, 473 enrolled. In 2017, 319 master's, 47 doctorates awarded. *Degree requirements:* For doctorate, comprehensive exam, thesis/dissertation. *Entrance requirements:* For master's, GRE General Test (taken within the past 5 years), minimum B average in undergraduate course work, 3 letters of recommendation; for doctorate, GRE General Test, interview, 3 letters of recommendation from doctorally-prepared faculty, MSN, essay. Additional exam requirements/recommendations for international students: Required—TOEFL (minimum score 570 paper-based), IELTS (minimum score 6.5). *Application deadline:* For fall admission, 11/1 priority date for domestic and international students. Applications are processed on a rolling basis. Application fee: $50. Electronic applications accepted. *Expenses:* Contact institution. *Financial support:* In 2017–18, 627 students received support. Scholarships/grants available. Financial award application deadline: 3/1; financial award applicants required to submit FAFSA. *Faculty research:* Lymphedema, palliative care and bereavement, health services research including workforce, safety and quality of care, gerontology, better birth outcomes including nutrition. *Total annual research expenditures:* $2 million. *Unit head:* Dr. Linda Norman, Dean, 615-343-8876, Fax: 615-343-7711, E-mail: linda.norman@vanderbilt.edu. *Application contact:* Patricia Peerman, Assistant Dean for Enrollment Management, 615-322-3800, Fax: 615-343-0333, E-mail: vusn-admissions@vanderbilt.edu.
Website: http://www.nursing.vanderbilt.edu

Villanova University, M. Louise Fitzpatrick College of Nursing, Villanova, PA 19085. Offers adult gerontology primary care nurse practitioner (MSN, Post Master's Certificate); family primary care nurse practitioner (MSN, Post Master's Certificate); nurse anesthesia (DNP); nursing (PhD); nursing education (MSN, Post Master's Certificate); nursing practice (DNP); pediatric primary care nurse practitioner (MSN, Post Master's Certificate). *Accreditation:* AACN; AANA/CANAEP. *Program availability:* Part-time, online learning. *Students:* 151 full-time, 199 part-time; includes 42 minority (18 Black or African American, non-Hispanic/Latino; 12 Asian, non-Hispanic/Latino; 8 Hispanic/Latino; 4 Two or more races, non-Hispanic/Latino), 10 international. 274 applicants, 43% accepted, 92 enrolled. In 2017, 70 master's, 15 doctorates awarded. *Entrance requirements:* Additional exam requirements/recommendations for international students: Required—TOEFL, IELTS. *Application deadline:* For fall admission, 7/1 for domestic and international students; for spring admission, 10/1 for domestic and international students; for summer admission, 4/1 for domestic and international students. Application fee: $50. Electronic applications accepted. *Financial support:* Fellowships, research assistantships, teaching assistantships, scholarships/grants, traineeships, and tuition waivers available. *Unit head:* Dr. Marguerite K. Schlag, Associate Professor, Assistant Dean and Director of Graduate Nursing Program, 610-519-4907, Fax: 610-519-7650, E-mail: marguerite.schlag@villanova.edu. *Application contact:* Kathleen Geibel, Assistant to Graduate Program, 610-519-4934, Fax: 610-519-7650, E-mail: kathleen.geibel@villanova.edu.
Website: http://www.nursing.villanova.edu

Walden University, Graduate Programs, School of Nursing, Minneapolis, MN 55401. Offers adult-gerontology acute care nurse practitioner (MSN); adult-gerontology nurse practitioner (MSN); education (MSN); family nurse practitioner (MSN); informatics (MSN); leadership and management (MSN); nursing (PhD, Post-Master's Certificate), including education (PhD), healthcare administration (PhD), interdisciplinary health (PhD), leadership (PhD), nursing education (Post-Master's Certificate), nursing informatics (Post-Master's Certificate), nursing leadership and management (Post-Master's Certificate), public health policy (PhD); nursing practice (DNP); psychiatric mental health (MSN). *Accreditation:* AACN. *Program availability:* Part-time, evening/weekend, online only, 100% online. *Degree requirements:* For doctorate, thesis/dissertation (for some programs), residency (for some programs), field experience (for some programs). *Entrance requirements:* For master's, bachelor's degree or equivalent in related field or RN; minimum GPA of 2.5; official transcripts; goal statement (for some programs); access to computer and Internet; for doctorate, master's degree or higher; RN; three years of related professional or academic experience; goal statement; access to computer and Internet; for Post-Master's Certificate, relevant work experience; access to computer and Internet. Additional exam requirements/recommendations for international students: Required—TOEFL (minimum score 550 paper-based, 79 iBT), IELTS (minimum score 6.5), Michigan English Language Assessment Battery (minimum score 82), or PTE (minimum score 53). Electronic applications accepted.

Wayne State University, College of Nursing, Detroit, MI 48202. Offers adult gerontology acute care nurse practitioner (MSN); adult gerontology primary care nurse practitioner (MSN); advanced public health nursing (MSN); infant and mental health (DNP, PhD); neonatal nurse practitioner (MSN); nurse-midwifery (MSN); pediatric acute care nurse practitioner (MSN); pediatric primary care nurse practitioner (MSN); psychiatric mental health nurse practitioner (MSN); women's health nurse practitioner (MSN). Doctoral program admits for fall only. *Accreditation:* AACN. *Program availability:* Part-time. *Faculty:* 30. *Students:* 133 full-time (120 women), 184 part-time (167 women); includes 85 minority (57 Black or African American, non-Hispanic/Latino; 16 Asian, non-Hispanic/Latino; 4 Hispanic/Latino; 8 Two or more races, non-Hispanic/Latino), 22 international. Average age 34. 318 applicants, 39% accepted, 94 enrolled. In 2017, 51 master's, 29 doctorates awarded. *Degree requirements:* For doctorate, thesis/dissertation (for some programs). *Entrance requirements:* For master's, BSN from ACEN- or CCNE-accredited program with minimum GPA of 3.0; three references; current RN license; personal statement; for doctorate, resume or curriculum vitae; goals statement; bachelor's or master's degree in nursing from ACEN- or CCNE-accredited program with minimum GPA of 3.0; current RN license, writing sample and interview (for DNP); reference letters (3 for PhD, 2 for DNP). Additional exam requirements/recommendations for international students: Required—TOEFL (minimum score 101 iBT), TWE (minimum score 6), Michigan English Language Assessment Battery (minimum score 85); Recommended—IELTS (minimum score 7). Application fee: $50. Electronic applications accepted. *Expenses:* Contact institution. *Financial support:* In 2017–18, 92 students received support, including 16 fellowships with tuition reimbursements available (averaging $8,285 per year), 5 teaching assistantships with tuition reimbursements available (averaging $25,000 per year); scholarships/grants, health care benefits, and unspecified assistantships also available. Support available to part-time students. Financial award applicants required to submit FAFSA. *Faculty research:* Bridging transitions and technology to promote asthma care in the community, chronic wound care for persons who injected drugs, decreasing at-risk parenting to reduce child maltreatment and trauma, dementia symptoms (cognition, behavior, function), determining readiness to engage in end of life/palliative care conversations with adolescents and young adults living with advanced cancer, dyspnea assessment and treatment at the end of life. *Unit head:* Dr. Laurie Lauzon Clabo, Dean, College of Nursing, 313-577-4082, E-mail: laurie.lauzon.clabo@wayne.edu. *Application contact:* 313-577-4082, Fax: 313-577-6949, E-mail: nursinginfo@wayne.edu.
Website: http://nursing.wayne.edu/

West Chester University of Pennsylvania, College of Health Sciences, Department of Nursing, West Chester, PA 19383. Offers adult-gerontology clinical nurse specialist (MSN); nursing (DNP); nursing education (MSN); school nurse (Certificate). *Accreditation:* AACN. *Program availability:* Part-time, evening/weekend, 2-day on-campus residency requirement (for DNP). *Students:* 1 full-time (0 women), 102 part-time (94 women); includes 16 minority (12 Black or African American, non-Hispanic/Latino; 1 Asian, non-Hispanic/Latino; 2 Hispanic/Latino; 1 Two or more races, non-Hispanic/Latino). Average age 42. 57 applicants, 82% accepted, 38 enrolled. In 2017, 1 master's, 21 doctorates, 9 other advanced degrees awarded. *Entrance requirements:* For master's, goals statement; official academic transcript(s) from all colleges and universities attended, demonstrating minimum cumulative undergraduate GPA of 2.8, with successful completion of BSN and courses in statistics and physical assessment; documentation of current clinical experience and current RN; for doctorate, master's degree in nursing in an advanced nursing specialty, minimum master's GPA of 3.0, licensed Registered Nurse in state of practice, prerequisite graduate-level research course and statistics course, two letters of reference, telephone or in-person interview with program coordinator. Additional exam requirements/recommendations for international students: Required—TOEFL or IELTS. *Application deadline:* For fall admission, 5/15 for international students; for spring admission, 10/15 for international students. Applications are processed on a rolling basis. Application fee: $50. Electronic applications accepted. *Expenses:* Tuition, state resident: full-time $9000; part-time $500 per credit. Tuition, nonresident: full-time $13,500; part-time $750 per credit. *Required fees:* $2959; $149.79 per credit. *Financial support:* Scholarships/grants and unspecified assistantships available. Financial award application deadline: 2/15; financial award applicants required to submit FAFSA. *Unit head:* Dr. Megan Infanti Mraz, Chair, 610-436-2219, Fax: 610-436-3083, E-mail: mmraz@wcupa.edu. *Application contact:* Dr. Cheryl Schlamb, Graduate Coordinator, 610-436-2219, E-mail: cschlamb@wcupa.edu.
Website: http://www.wcupa.edu/healthsciences/nursing/

Western Connecticut State University, Division of Graduate Studies, School of Professional Studies, Nursing Department, Danbury, CT 06810-6885. Offers adult gerontology clinical nurse specialist (MSN); adult gerontology nurse practitioner (MSN); nursing education (Ed D). *Accreditation:* AACN. *Program availability:* Part-time. *Degree requirements:* For master's, clinical component, thesis or research project, completion of program in 6 years. *Entrance requirements:* For master's, MAT (if GPA less than 3.0), bachelor's degree in nursing, minimum GPA of 3.0, previous course work in statistics and nursing research, RN license. Additional exam requirements/recommendations for international students: Recommended—TOEFL (minimum score 550 paper-based; 79 iBT), IELTS (minimum score 6). *Expenses:* Contact institution. *Faculty research:* Evaluating effectiveness of Reiki and acupressure on stress reduction.

William Paterson University of New Jersey, College of Science and Health, Wayne, NJ 07470-8420. Offers adult gerontology nurse practitioner (Certificate); biology (MS); biotechnology (MS); communication disorders (MS); exercise and sport studies (MS); materials chemistry (MS); nurse practitioner (Certificate); nursing (MSN); nursing education (Certificate); nursing practice (DNP); school nurse (Certificate). *Program availability:* Part-time. *Faculty:* 29 full-time (15 women), 25 part-time/adjunct (24 women). *Students:* 66 full-time (56 women), 197 part-time (163 women); includes 104 minority (15 Black or African American, non-Hispanic/Latino; 45 Asian, non-Hispanic/Latino; 38 Hispanic/Latino; 6 Two or more races, non-Hispanic/Latino), 3 international. Average age 33. 387 applicants, 34% accepted, 77 enrolled. In 2017, 87 master's, 5 doctorates awarded. *Degree requirements:* For master's, comprehensive exam (for some programs), thesis (for some programs), non-thesis internship/practicum (for some programs). *Entrance requirements:* For master's, GRE/MAT, minimum GPA of 3.0; 2-3 letters of recommendation; personal statement; work experience (for some programs); for doctorate, GRE/MAT, minimum GPA of 3.3; work experience; 3 letters of recommendation; interview; master's degree in nursing. Additional exam requirements/recommendations for international students: Required—TOEFL (minimum score 550 paper-based; 79 iBT), IELTS (minimum score 6). *Application deadline:* For fall admission, 6/1 for domestic students, 3/1 for international students; for spring admission, 11/1 for domestic students, 10/1 for international students. Applications are processed on a rolling basis. Application fee: $50. Electronic applications accepted. *Expenses:* Tuition, state resident: full-time $13,920; part-time $6264 per year. Tuition, nonresident: full-time $21,700; part-time $9765 per year. *Required fees:* $80; $36 per year. Tuition and fees vary according to course load, degree level and program. *Financial support:* In 2017–18, 9,800 students received support. Career-related internships or fieldwork, Federal Work-Study, scholarships/grants, and unspecified assistantships available. Support available to part-time students. Financial award application deadline: 3/15; financial award applicants required to submit FAFSA. *Faculty research:* Behaviors of American long-eared bats, postpartum fatigue, methodologies for coating carbon nano-tubes, paleoclimatology, and pre-linguistic gestures in children with language disorders. *Total annual research expenditures:* $291,600. *Unit head:* Dr. Venkat Sharma, Dean, 973-720-2194, Fax: 973-720-3414, E-mail: sharmav@wpunj.edu. *Application contact:* Christina Aiello, Assistant Director, Graduate Admissions, 973-720-2506, Fax: 973-720-2035, E-mail: aielloc@wpunj.edu.
Website: http://www.wpunj.edu/cosh

Wilmington University, College of Health Professions, New Castle, DE 19720-6491. Offers adult nurse practitioner (MSN); family nurse practitioner (MSN); gerontology nurse practitioner (MSN); nursing (MSN); nursing leadership (MSN); nursing practice (DNP). *Accreditation:* AACN. *Program availability:* Part-time. *Faculty:* 10 full-time (9

women), 59 part-time/adjunct (50 women). *Students:* 164 full-time (154 women), 662 part-time (604 women); includes 178 minority (129 Black or African American, non-Hispanic/Latino; 5 American Indian or Alaska Native, non-Hispanic/Latino; 23 Asian, non-Hispanic/Latino; 7 Hispanic/Latino; 3 Native Hawaiian or other Pacific Islander, non-Hispanic/Latino; 11 Two or more races, non-Hispanic/Latino), 6 international. Average age 39. 770 applicants, 63% accepted, 361 enrolled. In 2017, 259 master's, 22 doctorates awarded. *Degree requirements:* For master's, thesis. *Entrance requirements:* For master's, BSN, RN license, interview, 3 letters of recommendation. Additional exam requirements/recommendations for international students: Required—TOEFL (minimum score 500 paper-based). *Application deadline:* For fall admission, 4/1 for domestic students; for spring admission, 9/1 for domestic students. Applications are processed on a rolling basis. Application fee: $35. Electronic applications accepted. *Expenses: Tuition:* Part-time $466 per credit. *Required fees:* $25 per semester. Tuition and fees vary according to degree level and campus/location. *Financial support:* Fellowships with tuition reimbursements and traineeships available. Financial award applicants required to submit FAFSA. *Faculty research:* Outcomes assessment, student writing ability. *Unit head:* Denise Z. Westbrook, Dean, 302-356-6915. *Application contact:* Laura Morris, Director of Admissions, 877-967-5464, E-mail: infocenter@wilmu.edu.
Website: http://www.wilmu.edu/health/

Winona State University, College of Nursing and Health Sciences, Winona, MN 55987. Offers adult-gerontology acute care nurse practitioner (MS, DNP, Post Master's Certificate); adult-gerontology clinical nurse specialist (MS, DNP, Post Master's Certificate); adult-gerontology primary care nurse practitioner (MS, DNP, Post Master's Certificate); family nurse practitioner (MS, DNP, Post Master's Certificate); nurse educator (MS); nursing and organizational leadership (MS, DNP, Post Master's Certificate); practice and leadership innovations (DNP, Post Master's Certificate). *Accreditation:* AACN. *Program availability:* Part-time, online learning. *Degree requirements:* For master's, thesis; for doctorate, capstone. *Entrance requirements:* For master's, GRE (if GPA less than 3.0). Additional exam requirements/recommendations for international students: Required—TOEFL (minimum score 550 paper-based).

Wright State University, Graduate School, College of Nursing and Health, Program in Nursing, Dayton, OH 45435. Offers administration of nursing and health care systems (MS); adult gerontology clinical nurse specialist (MS); adult-gerontology acute care nurse practitioner (MS); family nurse practitioner (MS); neonatal nurse practitioner (MS); pediatric nurse practitioner-acute care (MS); pediatric nurse practitioner-primary care (MS); psychiatric mental health nurse practitioner (MS); school nurse (MS). *Accreditation:* AACN. *Program availability:* Part-time, evening/weekend. *Degree requirements:* For master's, thesis or alternative. *Entrance requirements:* For master's, GRE General Test, BSN from ACEN-accredited college, Ohio RN license. Additional exam requirements/recommendations for international students: Required—TOEFL. *Faculty research:* Clinical nursing and health, teaching, caring, pain administration, informatics and technology.

York College of Pennsylvania, The Stabler Department of Nursing, York, PA 17403-3651. Offers adult gerontology clinical nurse specialist (MS); nurse anesthetist (MS). *Accreditation:* AACN; AANA/CANAEP. *Program availability:* Part-time. *Faculty:* 7 full-time (all women), 8 part-time/adjunct (5 women). *Students:* 41 full-time (30 women), 40 part-time (38 women); includes 9 minority (1 Black or African American, non-Hispanic/Latino; 3 Asian, non-Hispanic/Latino; 1 Hispanic/Latino; 4 Two or more races, non-Hispanic/Latino), 1 international. Average age 35. 96 applicants, 31% accepted, 29 enrolled. In 2017, 24 master's awarded. *Entrance requirements:* For master's, bachelor's degree in nursing, minimum GPA of 3.0. Additional exam requirements/recommendations for international students: Required—TOEFL (minimum score 530 paper-based; 72 iBT). Application fee: $0. Electronic applications accepted. *Expenses:* $795 per credit. *Financial support:* In 2017–18, 1 student received support. Scholarships/grants available. Financial award applicants required to submit FAFSA. *Faculty research:* Adults with intellectual disabilities, healthy work environment, perinatal bereavement, palliative care. *Unit head:* Dr. Kimberly Fenstermacher, Graduate Program Director, 717-815-1383, Fax: 717-849-1651, E-mail: kfenster@ycp.edu. *Application contact:* Allison Malachosky, Administrative Assistant, 717-815-1243, E-mail: amalacho@ycp.edu.
Website: http://www.ycp.edu/academics/academic-departments/nursing/

HIV/AIDS Nursing

University of Delaware, College of Health Sciences, School of Nursing, Newark, DE 19716. Offers adult nurse practitioner (MSN, PMC); cardiopulmonary clinical nurse specialist (MSN, PMC); cardiopulmonary clinical nurse specialist/adult nurse practitioner (MSN, PMC); family nurse practitioner (MSN, PMC); gerontology clinical nurse specialist (MSN, PMC); gerontology clinical nurse specialist geriatric nurse practitioner (PMC); gerontology clinical nurse specialist/geriatric nurse practitioner (MSN); health services administration (MSN, PMC); nursing of children clinical nurse specialist (MSN, PMC); nursing of children clinical nurse specialist/pediatric nurse practitioner (MSN, PMC); oncology/immune deficiency clinical nurse specialist (MSN, PMC); oncology/immune deficiency clinical nurse specialist/adult nurse practitioner (MSN, PMC); perinatal/women's health clinical nurse specialist (MSN, PMC); perinatal/women's health clinical nurse specialist/women's health nurse practitioner (MSN, PMC); psychiatric nursing clinical nurse specialist (MSN, PMC). *Accreditation:* AACN. *Program availability:* Part-time, evening/weekend, online learning. *Degree requirements:* For master's, thesis optional. *Entrance requirements:* For master's, BSN, interview, RN license. Electronic applications accepted. *Faculty research:* Marriage and chronic illness, health promotion, congestive heart failure patient outcomes, school nursing, diabetes in children, culture, health disparities, cardiovascular, prison nursing, oncology, public policy, child obesity, smoking and teen pregnancy, blood pressure measurements, men's health.

Hospice Nursing

Central Connecticut State University, School of Graduate Studies, School of Education and Professional Studies, Department of Nursing, New Britain, CT 06050-4010. Offers hospice and palliative care (MSN). *Program availability:* Part-time, evening/weekend. *Faculty:* 2 full-time (both women). *Students:* 5 part-time (all women). Average age 44. 9 applicants, 78% accepted, 5 enrolled. *Degree requirements:* For master's, thesis, nursing capstone. *Entrance requirements:* For master's, minimum undergraduate GPA of 2.7, essay, letter of reference, minimum grade of C+ in an undergraduate statistics course. Additional exam requirements/recommendations for international students: Required—TOEFL (minimum score 550 paper-based; 79 iBT); Recommended—IELTS (minimum score 6.5). *Application deadline:* For summer admission, 3/1 for domestic and international students. Application fee: $50. *Expenses: Tuition, area resident:* Full-time $6757. Tuition, state resident: full-time $9750; part-time $374 per credit. Tuition, nonresident: full-time $18,102; part-time $374 per credit. *Required fees:* $4635; $255 per credit. *Financial support:* Application deadline: 3/1; applicants required to submit FAFSA. *Unit head:* Dr. Catherine Thomas, Acting Chair, 860-832-0032, E-mail: csthomas@ccsu.edu. *Application contact:* Patricia Gardner, Associate Director of Graduate Studies, 860-832-2350, Fax: 860-832-2362.
Website: http://www.ccsu.edu/nursing

Madonna University, Program in Hospice, Livonia, MI 48150-1173. Offers MSH. *Program availability:* Part-time, evening/weekend. *Degree requirements:* For master's, thesis or alternative. *Entrance requirements:* For master's, GRE General Test, minimum undergraduate GPA of 3.0, 2 letters of recommendation, interview. Electronic applications accepted.

Maternal and Child/Neonatal Nursing

Baylor University, Graduate School, Louise Herrington School of Nursing, Dallas, TX 76798. Offers family nurse practitioner (MSN); neonatal nurse practitioner (MSN); nurse-midwifery (DNP). *Accreditation:* AACN. *Program availability:* Part-time, online learning. *Faculty:* 11 full-time (all women), 3 part-time/adjunct (2 women). *Students:* 35 full-time (34 women), 11 part-time (all women); includes 21 minority (5 Black or African American, non-Hispanic/Latino; 1 American Indian or Alaska Native, non-Hispanic/Latino; 5 Asian, non-Hispanic/Latino; 8 Hispanic/Latino; 2 Two or more races, non-Hispanic/Latino). Average age 35. 47 applicants, 70% accepted, 26 enrolled. In 2017, 13 master's, 4 doctorates awarded. *Degree requirements:* For doctorate, comprehensive exam (for some programs), capstone project. *Entrance requirements:* For master's, GRE General Test or MAT; for doctorate, GRE General Test. Additional exam requirements/recommendations for international students: Required—TOEFL. *Application deadline:* For fall admission, 2/1 for domestic students. Application fee: $50. Electronic applications accepted. *Financial support:* In 2017–18, 66 students received support. Teaching assistantships, Federal Work-Study, scholarships/grants, and unspecified assistantships available. Support available to part-time students. Financial award application deadline: 6/30; financial award applicants required to submit FAFSA. *Faculty research:* Women and strokes, obesity and pregnancy, educational environmental factors, international undeserved populations, midwifery. *Total annual research expenditures:* $5,000. *Unit head:* Dr. Barbara Camune, Graduate Program Director, 214-367-3754, Fax: 214-820-3375, E-mail: barbara_camune@baylor.edu. *Application contact:* Elaine Lark, Coordinator of Recruitment and Enrollment, 214-818-7839, Fax: 214-820-3835, E-mail: elaine_lark@baylor.edu.
Website: http://www.baylor.edu/nursing/

Boston College, William F. Connell School of Nursing, Chestnut Hill, MA 02467. Offers adult-gerontology primary care nurse practitioner (MS); family health nursing (MS); nurse anesthesia (MS); nursing (PhD); pediatric primary care nurse practitioner (MS), including pediatric and women's health; psychiatric-mental health nursing (MS); women's health nursing (MS); MBA/MS; MS/MA; MS/PhD. MS/MBA offered jointly with Carroll School of Management, MS/MA with School of Theology and Ministry. *Accreditation:* AACN; AANA/CANAEP (one or more programs are accredited). *Program availability:* Part-time. *Faculty:* 54 full-time (48 women). *Students:* 170 full-time (153 women), 90 part-time (83 women); includes 39 minority (8 Black or African American, non-Hispanic/Latino; 10 Asian, non-Hispanic/Latino; 12 Hispanic/Latino; 9 Two or more races, non-Hispanic/Latino), 3 international. Average age 28. 360 applicants, 56% accepted, 94 enrolled. In 2017, 104 master's, 5 doctorates awarded. *Degree requirements:* For master's, comprehensive exam; for doctorate, comprehensive exam, thesis/dissertation, computer literacy exam or foreign language. *Entrance requirements:* For master's, bachelor's degree in nursing; for doctorate, GRE General Test, MS in nursing. Additional exam requirements/recommendations for international students: Required—TOEFL (minimum score 600 paper-based; 100 iBT), IELTS (minimum score

7.5). *Application deadline:* For fall admission, 9/30 for domestic and international students; for winter admission, 1/15 for domestic and international students; for spring admission, 3/15 for domestic and international students. Application fee: $40. Electronic applications accepted. *Expenses:* $1,350 per credit tuition. *Financial support:* In 2017–18, 152 students received support, including 11 fellowships with full tuition reimbursements available (averaging $24,504 per year), 29 teaching assistantships (averaging $3,768 per year); scholarships/grants, health care benefits, tuition waivers (partial), and unspecified assistantships also available. Support available to part-time students. Financial award application deadline: 4/18; financial award applicants required to submit FAFSA. *Faculty research:* Sexual and reproductive health, health promotion/illness prevention, aging, eating disorders, symptom management. *Total annual research expenditures:* $879,812. *Unit head:* Dr. Susan Gennaro, Dean, 617-552-4251, Fax: 617-552-0931, E-mail: susan.gennaro@bc.edu. *Application contact:* Sean Sendall, Assistant Dean, Graduate Enrollment and Data Analytics, 617-552-4745, Fax: 617-552-2121, E-mail: sean.sendall@bc.edu.
Website: http://www.bc.edu/cson

Case Western Reserve University, Frances Payne Bolton School of Nursing, Master's Programs in Nursing, Nurse Practitioner Program, Cleveland, OH 44106. Offers acute care pediatric nurse practitioner (MSN); acute care/cardiovascular nursing (MSN); acute care/flight nurse (MSN); adult gerontology acute care nurse practitioner (MSN); adult gerontology primary care nurse practitioner (MSN); family nurse practitioner (MSN); family systems psychiatric mental health nursing (MSN); neonatal nurse practitioner (MSN); palliative care (MSN); pediatric nurse practitioner (MSN); women's health nurse practitioner (MSN). *Accreditation:* ACEN. *Program availability:* Part-time. *Faculty:* 30 full-time (26 women), 5 part-time/adjunct (3 women). *Students:* 34 full-time (28 women), 97 part-time (73 women); includes 24 minority (5 Black or African American, non-Hispanic/Latino; 9 Asian, non-Hispanic/Latino; 6 Hispanic/Latino; 4 Two or more races, non-Hispanic/Latino), 4 international. Average age 33. 56 applicants, 82% accepted, 29 enrolled. In 2017, 68 master's awarded. *Degree requirements:* For master's, minimum GPA of 3.0, clinical hours corresponding to requirements to sit for certification exam, portfolio. *Entrance requirements:* For master's, GRE General Test or MAT. Additional exam requirements/recommendations for international students: Required—TOEFL (minimum score 577 paper-based; 90 iBT), IELTS (minimum score 7). *Application deadline:* For fall admission, 5/1 for domestic and international students; for spring admission, 10/1 for domestic and international students; for summer admission, 3/1 for domestic and international students. Applications are processed on a rolling basis. Application fee: $75. Electronic applications accepted. *Expenses:* $2,011 per credit tuition; $15 nursing activity fee; $17 activity fee. *Financial support:* In 2017–18, 86 students received support, including 19 teaching assistantships with partial tuition reimbursements available (averaging $18,100 per year); scholarships/grants and traineeships also available. Support available to part-time students. Financial award application deadline: 5/15; financial award applicants required to submit FAFSA. *Faculty research:* Symptom science, family/community care, aging across the lifespan, self-management of health and illness, neuroscience. *Unit head:* Dr. Latina Brooks, Director, 216-368-1196, Fax: 216-368-3542, E-mail: lmb3@case.edu. *Application contact:* Jackie Tepale, Admissions Coordinator, 216-368-5253, Fax: 216-368-0124, E-mail: yyd@case.edu.
Website: http://fpb.cwru.edu/MSN/majors.shtm

Creighton University, College of Nursing, Omaha, NE 68178-0001. Offers adult gerontology acute care nurse practitioner (DNP, Post-Master's Certificate); adult gerontology nurse practitioner (DNP); clinical nurse leader (MSN, Post-Graduate Certificate); clinical systems administration (MSN, DNP); family nurse practitioner (DNP, Post-Master's Certificate); neonatal nurse practitioner (DNP, Post-Master's Certificate); nursing (Post-Graduate Certificate); pediatric acute care nurse practitioner (DNP, Post-Master's Certificate); psychiatric mental health nurse practitioner (DNP). *Accreditation:* AACN. *Program availability:* Part-time, blended/hybrid learning. *Degree requirements:* For master's, capstone project; for doctorate, scholarly project. *Entrance requirements:* For master's and doctorate, BSN from ACEN- or CCNE-accredited nursing school, minimum cumulative GPA of 3.0, personal statement, active unencumbered RN license with NE eligibility, undergraduate statistics course, physical assessment course or equivalent, three recommendation letters; for other advanced degree, MSN or MS in nursing from ACEN- or CCNE-accredited nursing school, minimum cumulative GPA of 3.0, active unencumbered RN license with NE eligibility. Additional exam requirements/recommendations for international students: Required—TOEFL (minimum score 600 paper-based, 100 iBT) or IELTS. Electronic applications accepted. *Expenses:* Contact institution. *Faculty research:* School health report card, obesity prevention in children, simulated clinical experience evaluation, vitamin D3 and calcium and cancer risk reduction education, online support and education to reduce stress for prenatal patients on bed rest, health literacy, immunization research.

Duke University, School of Nursing, Durham, NC 27708-0586. Offers acute care pediatric nurse practitioner (MSN, Post-Graduate Certificate); adult-gerontology nurse practitioner (MSN, Post-Graduate Certificate), including acute care, primary care; family nurse practitioner (MSN, Post-Graduate Certificate); neonatal nurse practitioner (MSN, Post-Graduate Certificate); nurse anesthesia (DNP); nurse practitioner (DNP); nursing (PhD); nursing and health care leadership (MSN, Post-Graduate Certificate); nursing education (MSN, Post-Graduate Certificate); nursing informatics (MSN, Post-Graduate Certificate); pediatric nurse practitioner (MSN, Post-Graduate Certificate), including primary care; psychiatric mental health nurse practitioner (MSN, Post-Graduate Certificate); women's health nurse practitioner (MSN, Post-Graduate Certificate). *Accreditation:* AACN; AANA/CANAEP. *Program availability:* Part-time, evening/weekend, online with on-campus intensives. *Faculty:* 72 full-time (61 women). *Students:* 155 full-time (137 women), 613 part-time (548 women); includes 177 minority (64 Black or African American, non-Hispanic/Latino; 2 American Indian or Alaska Native, non-Hispanic/Latino; 47 Asian, non-Hispanic/Latino; 34 Hispanic/Latino; 30 Two or more races, non-Hispanic/Latino), 10 international. Average age 34. 631 applicants, 47% accepted, 211 enrolled. In 2017, 221 master's, 71 doctorates, 26 other advanced degrees awarded. Terminal master's awarded for partial completion of doctoral program. *Degree requirements:* For master's, thesis optional; for doctorate, capstone project. *Entrance requirements:* For master's, GRE General Test (waived if undergraduate GPA of 3.4 or higher), 1 year of nursing experience (recommended), BSN, minimum GPA of 3.0, previous course work in statistics; for doctorate, GRE General Test (waived if undergraduate GPA of 3.4 or higher), BSN or MSN, minimum GPA of 3.0, resume, personal statement, undergraduate statistics course, current licensure as a registered nurse, transcripts from all post-secondary institutions; for Post-Graduate Certificate, MSN, licensure or eligibility as a professional nurse, transcripts from all post-secondary institutions, previous course work in statistics. Additional exam requirements/recommendations for international students: Required—TOEFL (minimum score 100 iBT), IELTS (minimum score 7). *Application deadline:* For fall admission, 12/1 for domestic and international students; for spring admission, 5/1 for domestic and international students. Application fee: $50. Electronic applications accepted. *Expenses:* Contact institution. *Financial support:* Institutionally sponsored loans, scholarships/grants, and traineeships available. Support available to part-time students. Financial award applicants required to submit FAFSA. *Faculty research:* Cardiovascular disease, caregiver skill training, data mining, prostate cancer, neonatal immune system. *Unit head:* Dr. Marion E. Broome, Dean/Vice Chancellor for Nursing Affairs/Associate Vice President for Academic Affairs for Nursing, 919-684-9446, Fax: 919-684-9414, E-mail: marion.broome@duke.edu. *Application contact:* Dr. Ernie Rushing, Director of Admissions and Recruitment, 919-668-6274, Fax: 919-668-4693, E-mail: ernie.rushing@dm.duke.edu.
Website: http://www.nursing.duke.edu/

Hardin-Simmons University, Graduate School, Patty Hanks Shelton School of Nursing, Abilene, TX 79698-0001. Offers education (MSN); family nurse practitioner (MSN). Programs offered jointly with McMurry University. *Accreditation:* AACN. *Program availability:* Part-time. *Faculty:* 2 full-time (both women), 1 (woman) part-time/adjunct. *Students:* 17 part-time (8 women); includes 5 minority (1 Black or African American, non-Hispanic/Latino; 1 Asian, non-Hispanic/Latino; 3 Hispanic/Latino), 1 international. Average age 36. In 2017, 7 master's awarded. *Degree requirements:* For master's, comprehensive exam, thesis or alternative. *Entrance requirements:* For master's, GRE, minimum undergraduate GPA of 3.0; interview; upper-level course work in statistics; CPR certification; letters of recommendation. Additional exam requirements/recommendations for international students: Required—TOEFL (minimum score 550 paper-based; 75 iBT). *Application deadline:* For fall admission, 8/15 priority date for domestic students, 4/1 for international students; for spring admission, 1/5 priority date for domestic students, 9/1 for international students. Applications are processed on a rolling basis. Application fee: $50 ($150 for international students). Electronic applications accepted. *Expenses:* Contact institution. *Financial support:* In 2017–18, 10 students received support. Career-related internships or fieldwork and scholarships/grants available. Support available to part-time students. Financial award application deadline: 6/30; financial award applicants required to submit FAFSA. *Faculty research:* Child abuse, alternative medicine, pediatric chronic disease, health promotion. *Unit head:* Dr. Nina Ouimette, Dean, 325-671-2357, Fax: 325-671-2386, E-mail: nouimette@phssn.edu. *Application contact:* Dr. Nancy Kucinski, Dean of Graduate Studies, 325-670-1298, Fax: 325-670-1564, E-mail: gradoff@hsutx.edu.
Website: http://www.phssn.edu/

Lehman College of the City University of New York, School of Health Sciences, Human Services and Nursing, Department of Nursing, Bronx, NY 10468-1589. Offers adult health nursing (MS); nursing of older adults (MS); parent-child nursing (MS); pediatric nurse practitioner (MS). *Accreditation:* AACN. *Program availability:* Part-time, evening/weekend. *Entrance requirements:* For master's, bachelor's degree in nursing, New York RN license.

Louisiana State University Health Sciences Center, School of Nursing, New Orleans, LA 70112. Offers adult gerontology acute care nurse practitioner (DNP, Post-Master's Certificate); adult gerontology clinical nurse specialist (DNP, Post-Master's Certificate); adult gerontology primary care nurse practitioner (DNP, Post-Master's Certificate); clinical nurse leader (MSN); executive nurse leader (DNP, Post-Master's Certificate); neonatal nurse practitioner (DNP, Post-Master's Certificate); nurse anesthesia (DNP, Post-Master's Certificate); nurse educator (MSN); nursing (DNS); primary care family nurse practitioner (DNP, Post-Master's Certificate); public/community health nursing (DNP, Post-Master's Certificate). *Accreditation:* AACN; AANA/CANAEP (one or more programs are accredited). *Program availability:* Part-time. *Faculty:* 29 full-time (26 women), 20 part-time/adjunct (8 women). *Students:* 184 full-time (132 women), 41 part-time (35 women); includes 69 minority (45 Black or African American, non-Hispanic/Latino; 11 Asian, non-Hispanic/Latino; 12 Hispanic/Latino; 1 Two or more races, non-Hispanic/Latino), 1 international. Average age 30. 162 applicants, 42% accepted, 68 enrolled. In 2017, 52 master's, 46 doctorates awarded. *Degree requirements:* For master's, thesis optional; for doctorate, thesis/dissertation. *Entrance requirements:* For master's, GRE, minimum GPA of 3.0; for doctorate, GRE, minimum GPA of 3.0 (for DNP), 3.5 (for DNS). Additional exam requirements/recommendations for international students: Required—TOEFL (minimum score 550 paper-based; 79 iBT). *Application deadline:* Applications are processed on a rolling basis. Application fee: $100. Electronic applications accepted. *Expenses:* Contact institution. *Financial support:* Federal Work-Study, institutionally sponsored loans, scholarships/grants, and traineeships available. Financial award applicants required to submit FAFSA. *Faculty research:* Advanced clinical practice, nursing education, interprofessional education, nursing administration, culturally competent care. *Unit head:* Dr. Demetrius James Porche, Dean, 504-568-4106, Fax: 504-599-0573, E-mail: dporch@lsuhsc.edu. *Application contact:* Tracie Gravolet, Director, Office of Student Affairs, 504-568-4114, Fax: 504-568-5711, E-mail: tgravo@lsuhsc.edu.
Website: http://nursing.lsuhsc.edu/

Medical University of South Carolina, College of Nursing, Pediatric Nurse Practitioner Program, Charleston, SC 29425. Offers MSN, DNP. *Accreditation:* AACN. *Program availability:* Part-time, online learning. *Degree requirements:* For master's, comprehensive exam (for some programs), thesis optional; for doctorate, final project. *Entrance requirements:* For master's, BSN from nationally-accredited program, minimum nursing and cumulative GPA of 3.0, undergraduate-level statistics course, active RN License, 3 confidential references, current curriculum vitae or resume, essay; for doctorate, BSN from nationally-accredited program, minimum nursing and cumulative GPA of 3.0, undergraduate-level statistics course, active RN License, 3 confidential references, current curriculum vitae or resume, personal essay (for DNP). Additional exam requirements/recommendations for international students: Required—TOEFL (minimum score 550 paper-based; 80 iBT). Electronic applications accepted. *Faculty research:* School based clinics, epilepsy, caregiver burden, ADD/ADHD, developmental disorders.

Northeastern University, Bouvé College of Health Sciences, Boston, MA 02115-5096. Offers applied behavior analysis (MS); audiology (Au D); counseling psychology (MS, PhD, CAGS); exercise science (MS); nursing (MS, PhD, CAGS), including administration (MS), adult-gerontology acute care nurse practitioner (MS, CAGS), adult-gerontology primary care nurse practitioner (MS, CAGS), anesthesia (MS), family nurse practitioner (MS, CAGS), neonatal nurse practitioner (MS, CAGS), pediatric nurse practitioner (MS, CAGS), psychiatric mental health nurse practitioner (MS, CAGS); nursing practice (DNP); pharmaceutical sciences (MS, PhD), including interdisciplinary concentration, pharmaceutics and drug delivery systems, pharmacology (MS), pharmacy (Pharm D); school psychology (PhD); speech-language pathology (MS); urban health (MPH); MS/MBA. *Accreditation:* ACPE (one or more programs are accredited). *Program availability:* Part-time, evening/weekend, online learning. *Faculty:* 192 full-time. *Students:* 1,685. In 2017, 352 master's, 312 doctorates, 25 other advanced degrees awarded. *Degree requirements:* For doctorate, thesis/dissertation (for some programs); for CAGS, comprehensive exam. Application fee: $75. Electronic applications accepted. *Expenses:* Contact institution. *Financial support:* Fellowships, research assistantships, teaching assistantships, career-related internships or fieldwork, scholarships/grants, health care benefits, tuition waivers, and unspecified assistantships available. Support available to part-time students. Financial award applicants required to submit FAFSA. *Unit head:* Susan L. Parish, Dean, Bouve College of Health Sciences, 617-373-3321, Fax: 617-373-3030, E-mail: s.parish@northeastern.edu. *Application contact:* 617-373-2708, Fax: 617-373-4701, E-mail: bouvegrad@northeastern.edu.
Website: https://www.northeastern.edu/bouve/

Maternal and Child/Neonatal Nursing

Old Dominion University, College of Health Sciences, School of Nursing, Adult Gerontology Nursing Emphasis, Norfolk, VA 23529. Offers adult gerontology clinical nurse specialist/administrator (MSN); adult gerontology clinical nurse specialist/educator (MSN); advanced practice (DNP); neonatal clinical nurse specialist (MSN); pediatric clinical nurse specialist (MSN). *Program availability:* Part-time, online only, blended/hybrid learning. *Faculty:* 2 full-time (both women), 2 part-time/adjunct (both women). *Students:* 9 full-time (all women), 10 part-time (9 women); includes 10 minority (8 Black or African American, non-Hispanic/Latino; 2 Asian, non-Hispanic/Latino). Average age 37. 27 applicants, 96% accepted, 12 enrolled. In 2017, 5 master's awarded. *Degree requirements:* For master's, comprehensive exam, internship, practicum. *Entrance requirements:* For master's, GRE or MAT (waived with a GPA above 3.5), undergraduate health/physical assessment course, statistics, 3 letters of recommendation, essay, resume, transcripts. Additional exam requirements/recommendations for international students: Required—TOEFL. *Application deadline:* For fall admission, 6/1 priority date for domestic students, 4/15 priority date for international students. Applications are processed on a rolling basis. Application fee: $50. Electronic applications accepted. *Expenses:* $469 per credit; $450 School of Nursing fee per semester. *Financial support:* Unspecified assistantships available. Financial award applicants required to submit FAFSA. *Unit head:* Dr. Tina Haney, Program Director, 757-683-5428, Fax: 757-683-5253, E-mail: thaney@odu.edu. *Application contact:* Sue Parker, Graduate Program Coordinator, 757-683-4298, Fax: 757-683-5253, E-mail: sparker@odu.edu.

Old Dominion University, College of Health Sciences, School of Nursing, Neonatal Nurse Practitioner Program, Norfolk, VA 23529. Offers advanced practice (DNP); neonatal clinical nurse specialist (MSN); neonatal nurse practitioner (MSN). *Program availability:* Part-time, online only, blended/hybrid learning. *Faculty:* 1 (woman) full-time. *Students:* 5 full-time (4 women), 9 part-time (all women); includes 3 minority (2 Black or African American, non-Hispanic/Latino; 1 Asian, non-Hispanic/Latino), 1 international. Average age 34. 11 applicants, 91% accepted, 10 enrolled. *Degree requirements:* For master's, comprehensive exam. *Entrance requirements:* For master's, current unencumbered license as a registered nurse (RN), baccalaureate degree in nursing or related science field with minimum GPA of 3.0, three letters of recommendation, undergraduate courses in statistics and health/physical assessment, two years' recent clinical practice experience working in an NICU. Additional exam requirements/recommendations for international students: Required—TOEFL. *Application deadline:* For fall admission, 6/1 priority date for domestic students, 4/15 for international students. Applications are processed on a rolling basis. Application fee: $50. Electronic applications accepted. *Expenses:* $469 per credit; $450 School of Nursing fee per semester. *Faculty research:* Fetal origins of adult diseases, overuse injuries in elite adolescent divers. *Unit head:* Dr. Susan Braid, Program Director, 757-683-4563, Fax: 757-683-5253, E-mail: sbraid@odu.edu. *Application contact:* Sue Parker, Graduate Program Coordinator, 757-683-4298, Fax: 757-683-5253, E-mail: sparker@odu.edu.

Regis University, Rueckert-Hartman College for Health Professions, Denver, CO 80221-1099. Offers advanced practice nurse (DNP); counseling (MA); counseling children and adolescents (Post-Graduate Certificate); counseling military families (Post-Graduate Certificate); depth psychotherapy (Post-Graduate Certificate); fellowship in orthopedic manual physical therapy (Certificate); health care business management (Certificate); health care quality and patient safety (Certificate); health industry leadership (MBA); health services administration (MS); marriage and family therapy (MA, Post-Graduate Certificate); neonatal nurse practitioner (MSN); nursing education (MSN); nursing leadership (MSN); occupational therapy (OTD); pharmacy (Pharm D); physical therapy (DPT). *Program availability:* Part-time, evening/weekend, 100% online, blended/hybrid learning. *Degree requirements:* For master's, thesis (for some programs), internship. *Entrance requirements:* For master's, official transcript reflecting baccalaureate degree awarded from regionally-accredited college or university. Additional exam requirements/recommendations for international students: Required—TOEFL (minimum score 550 paper-based; 82 iBT). Electronic applications accepted. *Expenses:* Contact institution. *Faculty research:* Normal and pathological balance and gait research, normal/pathological upper limb motor control/biomechanics, exercise energy/metabolism research, optical treatment protocols for therapeutic modalities.

Rush University, College of Nursing, Department of Women, Children, and Family Nursing, Chicago, IL 60612. Offers neonatal clinical nurse specialist (DNP); neonatal nurse practitioner (DNP, Post-Graduate Certificate); pediatric acute care nurse practitioner (DNP, Post-Graduate Certificate); pediatric clinical nurse specialist (DNP); pediatric primary care nurse practitioner (DNP); transformative leadership: systems (DNP). *Accreditation:* AACN. *Program availability:* Part-time, 100% online. *Students:* 3 full-time (all women), 219 part-time (208 women); includes 35 minority (7 Black or African American, non-Hispanic/Latino; 8 Asian, non-Hispanic/Latino; 18 Hispanic/Latino; 2 Two or more races, non-Hispanic/Latino). 119 applicants, 69% accepted, 59 enrolled. In 2017, 71 doctorates, 12 Post-Graduate Certificates awarded. *Degree requirements:* For doctorate, scholarly project. *Entrance requirements:* For doctorate, GRE General Test (waived for DNP if cumulative GPA is 3.25 or greater, nursing GPA is 3.0 or greater, or a completed graduate program GPA is 3.5 or greater), interview, 3 letters of recommendation, personal statement, current resume; for Post-Graduate Certificate, MSN in a clinical discipline, 3 letters of recommendation, personal statement, current resume, interview. Additional exam requirements/recommendations for international students: Required—TOEFL (minimum score 94 iBT). *Application deadline:* For fall admission, 1/2 for domestic students; for spring admission, 8/1 for domestic students; for summer admission, 12/1 for domestic students. Applications are processed on a rolling basis. Application fee: $110. Electronic applications accepted. *Expenses:* Contact institution. *Financial support:* Research assistantships, teaching assistantships with tuition reimbursements, Federal Work-Study, scholarships/grants, traineeships, and health care benefits available. Support available to part-time students. Financial award application deadline: 3/1; financial award applicants required to submit FAFSA. *Faculty research:* Health disparities; parenting and grandparenting; child and adolescent health; women's health, fatherhood and men's health. *Unit head:* Dr. Wrenetha Julion, Chairperson, 312-942-7117, E-mail: wrenetha_a_julion@rush.edu. *Application contact:* Jennifer Thorndyke, Director of Admissions, 312-563-7526, E-mail: jennifer_thorndyke@rush.edu.
Website: https://www.rushu.rush.edu/college-nursing/departments-college-nursing/department-women-children-and-family-nursing

Saint Francis Medical Center College of Nursing, Graduate Programs, Peoria, IL 61603-3783. Offers adult gerontology (MSN); clinical nurse leader (MSN); family nurse practitioner (MSN, Post-Graduate Certificate); family psychiatric mental health nurse practitioner (MSN); neonatal nurse practitioner (MSN); nurse clinician (Post-Graduate Certificate); nurse educator (MSN, Post-Graduate Certificate); nursing (DNP); nursing management leadership (MSN). *Accreditation:* ACEN. *Program availability:* Part-time, online only, 100% online, blended/hybrid learning. *Faculty:* 11 full-time (all women), 7 part-time/adjunct (all women). *Students:* 4 full-time (all women), 239 part-time (209 women); includes 24 minority (12 Black or African American, non-Hispanic/Latino; 3 Asian, non-Hispanic/Latino; 4 Hispanic/Latino; 5 Two or more races, non-Hispanic/Latino). Average age 37. 105 applicants, 83% accepted, 60 enrolled. In 2017, 52 master's, 8 doctorates awarded. *Degree requirements:* For master's, research experience, portfolio, practicum; for doctorate, practicum. *Entrance requirements:* For master's, nursing research, health assessment, graduate course work in statistics, RN license; for doctorate, master's degree in nursing, professional portfolio, graduate statistics, transcripts, RN license. Additional exam requirements/recommendations for international students: Required—TOEFL (minimum score 550 paper-based; 79 iBT). *Application deadline:* For fall admission, 6/1 priority date for domestic and international students; for spring admission, 11/15 priority date for domestic and international students. Applications are processed on a rolling basis. Application fee: $50. *Expenses:* Contact institution. *Financial support:* In 2017–18, 13 students received support. Scholarships/grants and tuition waivers (partial) available. Support available to part-time students. Financial award application deadline: 6/15; financial award applicants required to submit FAFSA. *Faculty research:* Outcome and curriculum planning, health promotion, NCLEX-RN results, decision-making program evaluation. *Unit head:* Dr. Patti A. Stockert, President of the College, 309-655-4124, Fax: 309-624-8973, E-mail: patricia.a.stockert@osfhealthcare.org. *Application contact:* Dr. Kim A. Mitchell, Dean, Graduate Program, 309-655-2201, Fax: 309-624-8973, E-mail: kim.a.mitchell@osfhealthcare.org.
Website: http://www.sfmccon.edu/graduate-programs/

Stony Brook University, State University of New York, Stony Brook Medicine, School of Nursing, Program in Neonatal Nursing, Stony Brook, NY 11794. Offers neonatal nurse practitioner (Certificate); neonatal nursing (MS, DNP). *Accreditation:* AACN. *Program availability:* Part-time, blended/hybrid learning. *Students:* 1 (woman) full-time, 42 part-time (41 women); includes 19 minority (6 Black or African American, non-Hispanic/Latino; 7 Asian, non-Hispanic/Latino; 6 Hispanic/Latino). 33 applicants, 88% accepted, 15 enrolled. In 2017, 13 master's, 1 doctorate, 2 other advanced degrees awarded. *Degree requirements:* For master's, thesis; for doctorate, thesis/dissertation. *Entrance requirements:* For master's, BSN, minimum GPA of 3.0, course work in statistics. Additional exam requirements/recommendations for international students: Required—TOEFL (minimum score 90 iBT). *Application deadline:* For fall admission, 3/8 for domestic students. Application fee: $100. *Expenses:* Contact institution. *Financial support:* Application deadline: 3/15. *Unit head:* Paula M. Timoney, Program Director, 631-444-3298, Fax: 631-444-3136, E-mail: paula.timoney@stonybrook.edu. *Application contact:* Linda Sacino, Staff Assistant, 631-632-3262, Fax: 631-444-3136, E-mail: nnp.nursing@stonybrook.edu.
Website: http://www.nursing.stonybrookmedicine.edu/

Stony Brook University, State University of New York, Stony Brook Medicine, School of Nursing, Program in Perinatal Women's Health Nursing, Stony Brook, NY 11794. Offers MS, DNP, Certificate. *Accreditation:* AACN. *Program availability:* Blended/hybrid learning. *Students:* 7 part-time (all women); includes 1 minority (American Indian or Alaska Native, non-Hispanic/Latino). In 2017, 4 master's, 1 other advanced degree awarded. *Degree requirements:* For master's, thesis; for doctorate, thesis/dissertation. *Entrance requirements:* For master's, BSN, minimum GPA of 3.0, course work in statistics. Additional exam requirements/recommendations for international students: Required—TOEFL (minimum score 90 iBT). *Application deadline:* For fall admission, 3/8 for domestic students. Application fee: $100. *Expenses:* Contact institution. *Financial support:* Application deadline: 3/15. *Unit head:* Dr. Elizabeth Collins, Program Director, 631-444-3296, Fax: 631-444-3136, E-mail: elizabeth.collins@stonybrook.edu. *Application contact:* Linda Sacino, Staff Assistant, 631-632-3262, Fax: 631-444-3136, E-mail: elizabeth.collins@stonybrook.edu.
Website: http://www.nursing.stonybrookmedicine.edu/

University of Alberta, Faculty of Medicine and Dentistry and Faculty of Graduate Studies and Research, Graduate Programs in Medicine, Department of Obstetrics and Gynecology, Edmonton, AB T6G 2E1, Canada. Offers MD. *Entrance requirements:* Additional exam requirements/recommendations for international students: Required—TOEFL. *Faculty research:* Parturition, fetal/neonatal lung development, nitric oxide, vascular reactivity, pre-eclampsia gestational diabetes.

University of Cincinnati, Graduate School, College of Nursing, Cincinnati, OH 45221-0038. Offers nurse midwifery (MSN); nurse practitioner (MSN, DNP), including acute care pediatrics (DNP), adult-gerontology acute care, adult-gerontology primary care, anesthesia (DNP), family (MSN), leadership (DNP), neonatal (MSN), women's health (MSN); nursing (MSN, PhD), including occupational health (MSN). *Accreditation:* AACN; AANA/CANAEP (one or more programs are accredited); ACNM/ACME. *Program availability:* Part-time, 100% online, blended/hybrid learning. *Faculty:* 74 full-time (69 women), 112 part-time/adjunct (105 women). *Students:* 323 full-time (261 women), 1,084 part-time (949 women); includes 311 minority (113 Black or African American, non-Hispanic/Latino; 4 American Indian or Alaska Native, non-Hispanic/Latino; 56 Asian, non-Hispanic/Latino; 108 Hispanic/Latino; 1 Native Hawaiian or other Pacific Islander, non-Hispanic/Latino; 29 Two or more races, non-Hispanic/Latino), 12 international. Average age 34. 582 applicants, 64% accepted, 314 enrolled. In 2017, 579 master's, 18 doctorates awarded. *Degree requirements:* For master's, thesis or alternative; for doctorate, comprehensive exam (for some programs), thesis/dissertation (for some programs). *Entrance requirements:* For doctorate, GRE General Test. Additional exam requirements/recommendations for international students: Required—TOEFL (minimum score 600 paper-based; 100 iBT); Recommended—IELTS (minimum score 7). *Application deadline:* For fall admission, 5/1 priority date for domestic students, 5/1 for international students; for spring admission, 10/1 for domestic students; for summer admission, 3/1 priority date for domestic students. Applications are processed on a rolling basis. Application fee: $130 ($70 for international students). Electronic applications accepted. *Expenses:* $14,668 annual full-time in-state tuition, $707 annual fees. *Financial support:* In 2017–18, 123 students received support, including 8 fellowships with full tuition reimbursements available (averaging $30,423 per year), 7 research assistantships with full tuition reimbursements available (averaging $17,971 per year), 5 teaching assistantships with full tuition reimbursements available (averaging $17,971 per year); Federal Work-Study, institutionally sponsored loans, scholarships/grants, traineeships, health care benefits, tuition waivers (partial), and unspecified assistantships also available. Support available to part-time students. Financial award application deadline: 5/1; financial award applicants required to submit FAFSA. *Faculty research:* Vulnerable populations, education, violence, chronicity/aging, cancer. *Total annual research expenditures:* $575,576. *Unit head:* Dr. Greer Glazer, Dean, 513-558-5330, Fax: 513-558-9030, E-mail: greer.glazer@uc.edu. *Application contact:* Office of Student Recruitment, 513-558-8400, Fax: 513-558-5012, E-mail: nursingbearcats@uc.edu.
Website: https://nursing.uc.edu/

★ **University of Connecticut,** Graduate School, School of Nursing, Post-Master's Certificate Programs, Storrs, CT 06269. Offers adult gerontology acute care nurse practitioner (Post-Master's Certificate); adult gerontology primary care nurse practitioner (Post-Master's Certificate); neonatal nurse practitioner (Post-Master's Certificate). *Entrance requirements:* For degree, minimum graduate GPA of 3.0, current Connecticut RN license, three letters of recommendation, current resume/curriculum vitae.

See Display on page 596 and Close-Up on page 767.

University of Delaware, College of Health Sciences, School of Nursing, Newark, DE 19716. Offers adult nurse practitioner (MSN, PMC); cardiopulmonary clinical nurse specialist (MSN, PMC); cardiopulmonary clinical nurse specialist/adult nurse practitioner (MSN, PMC); family nurse practitioner (MSN, PMC); gerontology clinical nurse specialist (MSN, PMC); gerontology clinical nurse specialist geriatric nurse practitioner (PMC); gerontology clinical nurse specialist/geriatric nurse practitioner (MSN); health services administration (MSN, PMC); nursing of children clinical nurse specialist (MSN, PMC); nursing of children clinical nurse specialist/pediatric nurse practitioner (MSN, PMC); oncology/immune deficiency clinical nurse specialist (MSN, PMC); oncology/immune deficiency clinical nurse specialist/adult nurse practitioner (MSN, PMC); perinatal/women's health clinical nurse specialist (MSN, PMC); perinatal/women's health clinical nurse specialist/women's health nurse practitioner (MSN, PMC); psychiatric nursing clinical nurse specialist (MSN, PMC). *Accreditation:* AACN. *Program availability:* Part-time, evening/weekend, online learning. *Degree requirements:* For master's, thesis optional. *Entrance requirements:* For master's, BSN, interview, RN license. Electronic applications accepted. *Faculty research:* Marriage and chronic illness, health promotion, congestive heart failure patient outcomes, school nursing, diabetes in children, culture, health disparities, cardiovascular, prison nursing, oncology, public policy, child obesity, smoking and teen pregnancy, blood pressure measurements, men's health.

University of Illinois at Chicago, College of Nursing, Program in Nursing, Chicago, IL 60607-7128. Offers acute care clinical nurse specialist (MS); administrative nursing leadership (Certificate); adult nurse practitioner (MS); adult/geriatric nurse practitioner (MS); advanced community health nurse specialist (MS); family nurse practitioner (MS); geriatric clinical nurse specialist (MS); geriatric nurse practitioner (MS); nurse midwifery (MS); occupational health/advanced community health nurse specialist (MS); occupational health/family nurse practitioner (MS); pediatric nurse practitioner (MS); perinatal clinical nurse specialist (MS); school/advanced community health nurse specialist (MS); school/family nurse practitioner (MS); women's health nurse practitioner (MS). *Accreditation:* AACN. *Program availability:* Part-time. *Degree requirements:* For master's, thesis or alternative. *Entrance requirements:* For master's, GRE General Test, minimum GPA of 2.75. Additional exam requirements/recommendations for international students: Required—TOEFL. Electronic applications accepted.

University of Indianapolis, Graduate Programs, School of Nursing, Indianapolis, IN 46227-3697. Offers advanced practice nursing (DNP); family nurse practitioner (MSN); gerontological nurse practitioner (MSN); neonatal nurse practitioner (MSN); nurse-midwifery (MSN); nursing (MSN); nursing and health systems leadership (MSN); nursing education (MSN); women's health nurse practitioner (MSN); MBA/MSN. *Accreditation:* AACN. *Entrance requirements:* For master's, minimum GPA of 3.0, interview, letters of recommendation, resume, IN nursing license, 1 year of professional practice; for doctorate, graduate of ACEN- or CCNE-accredited nursing program; MSN or MA with nursing major and minimum cumulative GPA of 3.25; unencumbered RN license with eligibility for licensure in Indiana; completion of graduate-level statistics course within last 5 years with minimum grade of B; resume; essay; official transcripts from all academic institutions. Additional exam requirements/recommendations for international students: Required—TOEFL (minimum score 550 paper-based). Electronic applications accepted.

University of Louisville, Graduate School, School of Nursing, Louisville, KY 40202. Offers adult gerontology nurse practitioner (MSN, DNP); education and administration (MSN); family nurse practitioner (MSN, DNP); neonatal nurse practitioner (MSN, DNP); nursing research (PhD); psychiatric/mental health nurse practitioner (MSN, DNP); women's health nurse practitioner (MSN). *Accreditation:* AACN. *Program availability:* Part-time. *Faculty:* 44 full-time (40 women), 45 part-time/adjunct (41 women). *Students:* 130 full-time (107 women), 30 part-time (25 women); includes 33 minority (16 Black or African American, non-Hispanic/Latino; 7 Asian, non-Hispanic/Latino; 5 Hispanic/Latino; 5 Two or more races, non-Hispanic/Latino), 2 international. Average age 33. 61 applicants, 67% accepted, 36 enrolled. In 2017, 54 master's awarded. *Degree requirements:* For doctorate, comprehensive exam (for some programs), thesis/dissertation (for some programs). *Entrance requirements:* For master's, bachelor's degree from nationally-accredited college, completion of 6 prerequisite courses, minimum undergraduate GPA of 3.0; for doctorate, GRE with minimum score of 156 Verbal, 146 Quantitative, 4.0 Analytic (for PhD), 3 letters of professional reference; minimum GPA of 3.0 with BSN, 3.25 with MSN; written statement of career goals, areas of expertise, and reasons for pursuing doctoral degree; resume including RN license. Additional exam requirements/recommendations for international students: Recommended—TOEFL (minimum score 560 paper-based), IELTS (minimum score 6.5). *Application deadline:* For fall admission, 1/15 priority date for domestic students, 1/15 for international students; for summer admission, 10/15 priority date for domestic students. Application fee: $65. Electronic applications accepted. *Expenses:* Tuition, state resident: full-time $12,246; part-time $681 per credit hour. Tuition, nonresident: full-time $25,486; part-time $1417 per credit hour. *Required fees:* $196. Tuition and fees vary according to course load, program and reciprocity agreements. *Financial support:* In 2017–18, 8 research assistantships with full tuition reimbursements (averaging $20,000 per year), 4 teaching assistantships with full tuition reimbursements (averaging $15,000 per year) were awarded; fellowships with full tuition reimbursements, scholarships/grants, and unspecified assistantships also available. Financial award application deadline: 10/1; financial award applicants required to submit FAFSA. *Faculty research:* Environmental health, health services research, women's mental health, self-management of chronic illness in adults and children, health disparities. *Total annual research expenditures:* $762,266. *Unit head:* Dr. Marcia J. Hern, RN, Dean and Professor, 502-852-8300, Fax: 502-852-8783, E-mail: m.hern@louisville.edu. *Application contact:* Trish Hart, Assistant Dean for Student Affairs, 502-852-5825, Fax: 502-852-8783, E-mail: trish.hart@louisville.edu.
Website: http://www.louisville.edu/nursing/

University of Maryland, Baltimore, School of Nursing, Baltimore, MD 21201. Offers adult-gerontology acute care nurse practitioner (DNP); adult-gerontology primary care nurse practitioner (DNP); clinical nurse leader (MS); community/public health nursing (MS); family nurse practitioner (DNP); global health (Postbaccalaureate Certificate); health services leadership and management (MS); neonatal nurse practitioner (DNP); nurse anesthesia (DNP); nursing (PhD); nursing informatics (MS, Postbaccalaureate Certificate); pediatric acute/primary care nurse practitioner (DNP); psychiatric mental health nurse practitioner (DNP); teaching in nursing and health professions (Postbaccalaureate Certificate); MS/MBA. MS/MBA offered jointly with University of Baltimore. *Program availability:* Part-time. *Faculty:* 130 full-time (117 women), 125 part-time/adjunct (114 women). *Students:* 504 full-time (442 women), 532 part-time (482 women); includes 443 minority (249 Black or African American, non-Hispanic/Latino; 1 American Indian or Alaska Native, non-Hispanic/Latino; 115 Asian, non-Hispanic/Latino; 48 Hispanic/Latino; 2 Native Hawaiian or other Pacific Islander, non-Hispanic/Latino; 28 Two or more races, non-Hispanic/Latino), 15 international. Average age 33. 935 applicants, 62% accepted, 394 enrolled. In 2017, 182 master's, 57 doctorates awarded. *Degree requirements:* For master's and Postbaccalaureate Certificate, thesis (for some programs); for doctorate, comprehensive exam, thesis/dissertation. *Entrance requirements:* Additional exam requirements/recommendations for international students: Required—TOEFL (minimum score 550 paper-based; 79 iBT); Recommended—IELTS (minimum score 7). *Application deadline:* For fall admission, 11/1 for domestic and international students; for spring admission, 8/1 for domestic and international students. Application fee: $75. Electronic applications accepted. *Expenses:* Contact institution. *Financial support:* In 2017–18, 22 research assistantships with full and partial tuition reimbursements (averaging $21,523 per year), 41 teaching assistantships with full and partial tuition reimbursements (averaging $13,439 per year) were awarded; fellowships and scholarships/grants also available. Financial award application deadline: 3/1; financial award applicants required to submit FAFSA. *Unit head:* Dr. Jane Kirschling, Dean, 410-706-4359, E-mail: kirschling@umaryland.edu. *Application contact:* Larry Fillian, Associate Dean of Student and Academic Services, 410-706-6298, E-mail: lfillian@umaryland.edu.
Website: http://www.nursing.umaryland.edu/

University of Missouri–Kansas City, School of Nursing and Health Studies, Kansas City, MO 64110-2499. Offers adult clinical nurse specialist (MSN), including adult nurse practitioner, women's health nurse practitioner (MSN, DNP); adult clinical nursing practice (DNP), including adult gerontology nurse practitioner, women's health nurse practitioner (MSN, DNP); clinical nursing practice (DNP), including family nurse practitioner; neonatal nurse practitioner (MSN); nurse educator (MSN); nurse executive (MSN); nursing practice (DNP); pediatric clinical nursing practice (DNP), including pediatric nurse practitioner; pediatric nurse practitioner (MSN). *Accreditation:* AACN. *Program availability:* Part-time, online learning. *Degree requirements:* For master's, thesis or alternative. *Entrance requirements:* For master's, minimum undergraduate GPA of 3.2; for doctorate, GRE, 3 letters of reference. Additional exam requirements/recommendations for international students: Required—TOEFL (minimum score 550 paper-based; 80 iBT). *Faculty research:* Geriatrics/gerontology, children's pain, neonatology, Alzheimer's care, cancer caregivers.

University of Pennsylvania, School of Nursing, Neonatal Clinical Nurse Specialist Program, Philadelphia, PA 19104. Offers MSN. *Program availability:* Part-time. *Students:* 2 part-time (both women). Average age 31. In 2017, 2 master's awarded. Application fee: $80.

University of Pennsylvania, School of Nursing, Neonatal Nurse Practitioner Program, Philadelphia, PA 19104. Offers MSN. *Accreditation:* AACN. *Program availability:* Part-time. *Students:* 2 part-time (both women). Average age 31. 10 applicants, 70% accepted, 2 enrolled. In 2017, 6 master's awarded. Application fee: $80.

University of Pittsburgh, School of Nursing, Nurse Practitioner Program, Pittsburgh, PA 15261. Offers adult-gerontology acute care (DNP); adult-gerontology primary care (DNP); family (individual across the lifespan) (DNP); neonatal (MSN, DNP); pediatric primary care (DNP); psychiatric mental health (DNP). *Accreditation:* AACN. *Program availability:* Part-time. *Faculty:* 17 full-time (14 women), 3 part-time/adjunct (2 women). *Students:* 50 full-time (47 women), 43 part-time (36 women); includes 9 minority (1 Black or African American, non-Hispanic/Latino; 1 American Indian or Alaska Native, non-Hispanic/Latino; 7 Asian, non-Hispanic/Latino), 1 international. Average age 31. 77 applicants, 40% accepted, 25 enrolled. In 2017, 6 master's, 35 doctorates awarded. *Degree requirements:* For master's, comprehensive exam, thesis optional. *Entrance requirements:* For master's, GRE General Test, BSN, RN license, 3 letters of recommendation, resume, course work in statistics, relevant nursing experience; for doctorate, GRE General Test, BSN, RN license, minimum GPA of 3.5, 3 letters of recommendation, relevant nursing experience, resume, course work in statistics. Additional exam requirements/recommendations for international students: Required—TOEFL (minimum score 600 paper-based; 100 IBT) or IELTS (minimum score 7.0). *Application deadline:* For fall admission, 5/1 priority date for domestic students, 2/15 priority date for international students. Application fee: $50. Electronic applications accepted. *Expenses:* $13,068 per term full-time resident tuition, $1,064 per credit part-time; $15,270 per term full-time non-resident tuition, $1,247 per credit part-time; $437 per term full-time fees; $282 per term part-time fees. *Financial support:* In 2017–18, 58 students received support, including 7 fellowships (averaging $15,755 per year), 15 teaching assistantships (averaging $12,454 per year); scholarships/grants, tuition waivers, and unspecified assistantships also available. Financial award applicants required to submit FAFSA. *Faculty research:* Behavioral management of chronic disorders, patient management in critical care, consumer informatics, genetic applications (molecular genetics and psychosocial implications), technology for nurses and patients to improve care. *Unit head:* Dr. Sandra Engberg, Associate Dean for Clinical Education, 412-624-3835, Fax: 412-624-8521, E-mail: sje1@pitt.edu. *Application contact:* Laurie Lapsley, Graduate Administrator, 412-624-9670, Fax: 412-624-2409, E-mail: lapsleyl@pitt.edu.
Website: http://www.nursing.pitt.edu

University of Puerto Rico–Medical Sciences Campus, School of Nursing, San Juan, PR 00936-5067. Offers adult and elderly nursing (MSN); child and adolescent nursing (MSN); critical care nursing (MSN); family and community nursing (MSN); family nurse practitioner (MSN); maternity nursing (MSN); mental health and psychiatric nursing (MSN). *Accreditation:* AACN; AANA/CANAEP. *Entrance requirements:* For master's, GRE or EXADEP, interview, Puerto Rico RN license or professional license for international students, general and specific point average, article analysis. Electronic applications accepted. *Faculty research:* HIV, health disparities, teen violence, women and violence, neurological disorders.

University of Rochester, School of Nursing, Rochester, NY 14642. Offers adult gerontological acute care nurse practitioner (MS); adult gerontological primary care nurse practitioner (MS); clinical nurse leader (MS); family nurse practitioner (MS); family psychiatric mental health nurse practitioner (MS); health care organization management and leadership (MS); nursing (DNP); nursing and health science (PhD); nursing education (MS); pediatric nurse practitioner (MS); pediatric nurse practitioner/neonatal nurse practitioner (MS). *Accreditation:* AACN. *Program availability:* Part-time, 100% online, blended/hybrid learning. *Faculty:* 62 full-time (51 women), 73 part-time/adjunct (63 women). *Students:* 17 full-time (12 women), 306 part-time (252 women); includes 46 minority (16 Black or African American, non-Hispanic/Latino; 1 American Indian or Alaska Native, non-Hispanic/Latino; 7 Asian, non-Hispanic/Latino; 17 Hispanic/Latino; 5 Two or more races, non-Hispanic/Latino), 3 international. Average age 34. 143 applicants, 71% accepted, 87 enrolled. In 2017, 48 master's, 8 doctorates awarded. Terminal master's awarded for partial completion of doctoral program. *Degree requirements:* For master's, comprehensive exam; for doctorate, thesis/dissertation. *Entrance requirements:* For master's, BS in nursing, minimum GPA of 3.0, course work in statistics; for doctorate, GRE General Test (for PhD), MS in nursing, minimum GPA of 3.5. Additional exam requirements/recommendations for international students: Required—TOEFL (minimum score 560 paper-based; 88 iBT) or IELTS (minimum score 6.5) recommended. *Application deadline:* For fall admission, 4/1 for domestic and international students; for spring admission, 9/1 for domestic and international students; for summer admission, 1/2 for domestic and international students. Application fee: $50. Electronic applications accepted. *Financial support:* In 2017–18, 63 students received support, including 2 fellowships with full and partial tuition reimbursements available (averaging $16,000 per year); scholarships/grants, traineeships, health care benefits, tuition waivers (full and partial), and unspecified assistantships also available. Support available to part-time students. Financial award application deadline: 6/30; financial award applicants required to submit CSS PROFILE or FAFSA. *Faculty research:* Symptom science, systems of care, innovations in health technology, promoting healthy behaviors. *Total annual research expenditures:* $2.6 million. *Unit head:* Dr. Kathy H. Rideout, Dean, 585-273-8902, Fax: 585-273-1268, E-mail: kathy_rideout@urmc.rochester.edu. *Application contact:* Elaine Andolina, Director of Admissions, 585-275-2375, Fax: 585-756-8299, E-mail: elaine_andolina@urmc.rochester.edu.
Website: http://www.son.rochester.edu

University of South Africa, College of Human Sciences, Pretoria, South Africa. Offers adult education (M Ed); African languages (MA, PhD); African politics (MA, PhD); Afrikaans (MA, PhD); ancient history (MA, PhD); ancient Near Eastern studies (MA, PhD); anthropology (MA, PhD); applied linguistics (MA); Arabic (MA, PhD); archaeology (MA); art history (MA); Biblical archaeology (MA); Biblical studies (M Th, D Th, PhD); Christian spirituality (M Th, D Th); church history (M Th, D Th); classical studies (MA, PhD); clinical psychology (MA); communication (MA, PhD); comparative education (M Ed, Ed D); consulting psychology (D Admin, D Com, PhD); curriculum studies (M Ed, Ed D); development studies (M Admin, MA, D Admin, PhD); didactics (M Ed, Ed D); education (M Tech); education management (M Ed, Ed D); educational psychology (M Ed); English (MA); environmental education (M Ed); French (MA, PhD); German (MA, PhD); Greek (MA); guidance and counseling (M Ed); health studies (MA, PhD), including health sciences education (MA), health services management (MA), medical and surgical nursing science (critical care general) (MA), midwifery and neonatal nursing science (MA), trauma and emergency care (MA); history (MA, PhD); history of education (Ed D); inclusive education (M Ed, Ed D); information and communications technology policy and regulation (MA); information science (MA, MIS, PhD); international politics (MA, PhD); Islamic studies (MA, PhD); Italian (MA, PhD); Judaica (MA, PhD); linguistics (MA, PhD); mathematical education (M Ed); mathematics education (MA); missiology (M Th, D Th); modern Hebrew (MA, PhD); musicology (MA, MMus, D Mus, PhD); natural science education (M Ed); New Testament (M Th, D Th); Old Testament (D Th); pastoral therapy (M Th, D Th); philosophy (MA); philosophy of education (M Ed, Ed D); politics (MA, PhD); Portuguese (MA, PhD); practical theology (M Th, D Th); psychology (MA, MS, PhD); psychology of education (M Ed, Ed D); public health (MA); religious studies (MA, D Th, PhD); Romance languages (MA); Russian (MA, PhD); Semitic languages (MA, PhD); social behavior studies in HIV/AIDS (MA); social science (mental health) (MA); social science in development studies (MA); social science in psychology (MA); social science in social work (MA); social science in sociology (MA); social work (MSW, DSW, PhD); socio-education (M Ed, Ed D); sociolinguistics (MA); sociology (MA, PhD); Spanish (MA, PhD); systematic theology (M Th, D Th); TESOL (teaching English to speakers of other languages) (MA); theological ethics (M Th, D Th); theory of literature (MA, PhD); urban ministries (D Th); urban ministry (M Th).

The University of Texas at Austin, Graduate School, School of Nursing, Austin, TX 78712-1111. Offers adult - gerontology clinical nurse specialist (MSN); child health (MSN), including administration, public health nursing, teaching; family nurse practitioner (MSN); family psychiatric/mental health nurse practitioner (MSN); holistic adult health (MSN), including administration, teaching; maternity (MSN), including administration, public health nursing, teaching; nursing (PhD); nursing administration and healthcare systems management (MSN); nursing practice (DNP); pediatric nurse practitioner (MSN); public health nursing (MSN). *Accreditation:* AACN. *Program availability:* Part-time. *Degree requirements:* For master's, thesis optional; for doctorate, thesis/dissertation. *Entrance requirements:* For master's and doctorate, GRE General Test. Additional exam requirements/recommendations for international students: Required—TOEFL (minimum score 550 paper-based). Electronic applications accepted. *Faculty research:* Chronic illness management, memory and aging, health promotion, women's health, adolescent health.

Vanderbilt University, Vanderbilt University School of Nursing, Nashville, TN 37240. Offers adult-gerontology acute care nurse practitioner (MSN), including hospitalist, intensivist; adult-gerontology primary care nurse practitioner (MSN); emergency nurse practitioner (MSN); family nurse practitioner (MSN); healthcare leadership (MSN); neonatal nurse practitioner (MSN); nurse midwifery (MSN); nurse midwifery/family nurse practitioner (MSN); nursing (Post-Master's Certificate); nursing informatics (MSN); nursing practice (DNP); nursing science (PhD); pediatric acute care nurse practitioner (MSN); pediatric primary care nurse practitioner (MSN); psychiatric-mental health nurse practitioner (MSN); women's health nurse practitioner (MSN); women's health nurse practitioner/adult gerontology primary care nurse practitioner (MSN); MSN/M Div; MSN/MTS. *Accreditation:* AACN; ACEN (one or more programs are accredited); ACNM/ACME. *Program availability:* Part-time, 100% online, blended/hybrid learning. *Faculty:* 292 full-time (267 women), 321 part-time/adjunct (253 women). *Students:* 501 full-time (435 women), 387 part-time (355 women); includes 153 minority (40 Black or African American, non-Hispanic/Latino; 1 American Indian or Alaska Native, non-Hispanic/Latino; 27 Asian, non-Hispanic/Latino; 48 Hispanic/Latino; 4 Native Hawaiian or other Pacific Islander, non-Hispanic/Latino; 33 Two or more races, non-Hispanic/Latino), 9 international. Average age 31. 1,210 applicants, 57% accepted, 473 enrolled. In 2017, 319 master's, 47 doctorates awarded. *Degree requirements:* For doctorate, comprehensive exam, thesis/dissertation. *Entrance requirements:* For master's, GRE General Test (taken within the past 5 years), minimum B average in undergraduate course work, 3 letters of recommendation; for doctorate, GRE General Test, interview, 3 letters of recommendation from doctorally-prepared faculty, MSN, essay. Additional exam requirements/recommendations for international students: Required—TOEFL (minimum score 570 paper-based), IELTS (minimum score 6.5). *Application deadline:* For fall admission, 11/1 priority date for domestic and international students. Applications are processed on a rolling basis. Application fee: $50. Electronic applications accepted. *Expenses:* Contact institution. *Financial support:* In 2017–18, 627 students received support. Scholarships/grants available. Financial award application deadline: 3/1; financial award applicants required to submit FAFSA. *Faculty research:* Lymphedema, palliative care and bereavement, health services research including workforce, safety and quality of care, gerontology, better birth outcomes including nutrition. *Total annual research expenditures:* $2 million. *Unit head:* Dr. Linda Norman, Dean, 615-343-8876, Fax: 615-343-7711, E-mail: linda.norman@vanderbilt.edu. *Application contact:* Patricia Peerman, Assistant Dean for Enrollment Management, 615-322-3800, Fax: 615-343-0333, E-mail: vusn-admissions@vanderbilt.edu.
Website: http://www.nursing.vanderbilt.edu

Wayne State University, College of Nursing, Detroit, MI 48202. Offers adult gerontology acute care nurse practitioner (MSN); adult gerontology primary care nurse practitioner (MSN); advanced public health nursing (MSN); infant and mental health (DNP, PhD); neonatal nurse practitioner (MSN); nurse-midwifery (MSN); pediatric acute care nurse practitioner (MSN); pediatric primary care nurse practitioner (MSN); psychiatric mental health nurse practitioner (MSN); women's health nurse practitioner (MSN). Doctoral program admits for fall only. *Accreditation:* AACN. *Program availability:* Part-time. *Faculty:* 30. *Students:* 133 full-time (120 women), 184 part-time (167 women); includes 85 minority (57 Black or African American, non-Hispanic/Latino; 16 Asian, non-Hispanic/Latino; 4 Hispanic/Latino; 8 Two or more races, non-Hispanic/Latino), 22 international. Average age 34. 318 applicants, 39% accepted, 94 enrolled. In 2017, 51 master's, 29 doctorates awarded. *Degree requirements:* For doctorate, thesis/dissertation (for some programs). *Entrance requirements:* For master's, BSN from ACEN- or CCNE-accredited program with minimum GPA of 3.0; three references; current RN license; personal statement; for doctorate, resume or curriculum vitae; goals statement; bachelor's or master's degree in nursing from ACEN- or CCNE-accredited program with minimum GPA of 3.0; current RN license, writing sample and interview (for DNP); reference letters (3 for PhD, 2 for DNP). Additional exam requirements/recommendations for international students: Required—TOEFL (minimum score 101 iBT), TWE (minimum score 6), Michigan English Language Assessment Battery (minimum score 85); Recommended—IELTS (minimum score 7). Application fee: $50. Electronic applications accepted. *Expenses:* Contact institution. *Financial support:* In 2017–18, 92 students received support, including 16 fellowships with tuition reimbursements available (averaging $8,285 per year), 5 teaching assistantships with tuition reimbursements available (averaging $25,000 per year); scholarships/grants, health care benefits, and unspecified assistantships also available. Support available to part-time students. Financial award applicants required to submit FAFSA. *Faculty research:* Bridging transitions and technology to promote asthma care in the community, chronic wound care for persons who injected drugs, decreasing at-risk parenting to reduce child maltreatment and trauma, dementia symptoms (cognition, behavior, function), determining readiness to engage in end of life/palliative care conversations with adolescents and young adults living with advanced cancer, dyspnea assessment and treatment at the end of life. *Unit head:* Dr. Laurie Lauzon Clabo, Dean, College of Nursing, 313-577-4082, E-mail: laurie.lauzon.clabo@wayne.edu. *Application contact:* 313-577-4082, Fax: 313-577-6949, E-mail: nursinginfo@wayne.edu.
Website: http://nursing.wayne.edu/

Wright State University, Graduate School, College of Nursing and Health, Program in Nursing, Dayton, OH 45435. Offers administration of nursing and health care systems (MS); adult gerontology clinical nurse specialist (MS); adult-gerontology acute care nurse practitioner (MS); family nurse practitioner (MS); neonatal nurse practitioner (MS); pediatric nurse practitioner-acute care (MS); pediatric nurse practitioner-primary care (MS); psychiatric mental health nurse practitioner (MS); school nurse (MS). *Accreditation:* AACN. *Program availability:* Part-time, evening/weekend. *Degree requirements:* For master's, thesis or alternative. *Entrance requirements:* For master's, GRE General Test, BSN from ACEN-accredited college, Ohio RN license. Additional exam requirements/recommendations for international students: Required—TOEFL. *Faculty research:* Clinical nursing and health, teaching, caring, pain administration, informatics and technology.

Medical/Surgical Nursing

Case Western Reserve University, Frances Payne Bolton School of Nursing, Master's Programs in Nursing, Nurse Practitioner Program, Cleveland, OH 44106. Offers acute care pediatric nurse practitioner (MSN); acute care/cardiovascular nursing (MSN); acute care/flight nurse (MSN); adult gerontology acute care nurse practitioner (MSN); adult gerontology primary care nurse practitioner (MSN); family nurse practitioner (MSN); family systems psychiatric mental health nursing (MSN); neonatal nurse practitioner (MSN); palliative care (MSN); pediatric nurse practitioner (MSN); women's health nurse practitioner (MSN). *Accreditation:* ACEN. *Program availability:* Part-time. *Faculty:* 30 full-time (26 women), 5 part-time/adjunct (3 women). *Students:* 34 full-time (28 women), 97 part-time (73 women); includes 24 minority (5 Black or African American, non-Hispanic/Latino; 9 Asian, non-Hispanic/Latino; 6 Hispanic/Latino; 4 Two or more races, non-Hispanic/Latino), 4 international. Average age 33. 56 applicants, 82% accepted, 29 enrolled. In 2017, 68 master's awarded. *Degree requirements:* For master's, minimum GPA of 3.0, clinical hours corresponding to requirements to sit for certification exam, portfolio. *Entrance requirements:* For master's, GRE General Test or MAT. Additional exam requirements/recommendations for international students: Required—TOEFL (minimum score 577 paper-based; 90 iBT), IELTS (minimum score 7). *Application deadline:* For fall admission, 5/1 for domestic and international students; for spring admission, 10/1 for domestic and international students; for summer admission, 3/1 for domestic and international students. Applications are processed on a rolling basis. Application fee: $75. Electronic applications accepted. *Expenses:* $2,011 per credit tuition; $15 nursing activity fee; $17 activity fee. *Financial support:* In 2017–18, 86 students received support, including 19 teaching assistantships with partial tuition reimbursements available (averaging $18,100 per year); scholarships/grants and traineeships also available. Support available to part-time students. Financial award application deadline: 5/15; financial award applicants required to submit FAFSA. *Faculty research:* Symptom science, family/community care, aging across the lifespan, self-management of health and illness, neuroscience. *Unit head:* Dr. Latina Brooks, Director, 216-368-1196, Fax: 216-368-3542, E-mail: lmb3@case.edu. *Application contact:* Jackie Tepale, Admissions Coordinator, 216-368-5253, Fax: 216-368-0124, E-mail: yyd@case.edu.
Website: http://fpb.cwru.edu/MSN/majors.shtm

Daemen College, Department of Nursing, Amherst, NY 14226-3592. Offers adult nurse practitioner (MS, Post Master's Certificate); nurse executive leadership (Post Master's Certificate); nursing education (MS, Post Master's Certificate); nursing executive leadership (MS); nursing practice (DNP); palliative care nursing (Post Master's Certificate). *Accreditation:* ACEN. *Program availability:* Part-time. *Degree requirements:* For master's, thesis or alternative, degree completed in 4 years; minimum GPA of 3.0; for doctorate, degree completed in 5 years; 500 post-master's clinical hours. *Entrance requirements:* For master's, BN, 1 year medical/surgical experience, RN license and state registration, statistics course with minimum C grade, 3 letters of recommendation, minimum GPA of 3.25, interview; for doctorate, MS in advance nursing practice; New York state RN license; goal statement; resume; interview; statistics course with minimum grade of 'C'; for Post Master's Certificate, master's degree in clinical area; RN license and current registration; one year of clinical experience; statistics course with minimum grade of 'C'; 3 letters of recommendation; interview; letter of intent. Additional exam requirements/recommendations for international students: Required—TOEFL (minimum score 500 paper-based; 63 iBT), IELTS (minimum score 5.5). Electronic applications accepted. *Faculty research:* Professional stress, client behavior, drug therapy, treatment modalities and pulmonary cancers, chemical dependency.

Eastern Virginia Medical School, Master of Surgical Assisting Program, Norfolk, VA 23501-1980. Offers MSA. Electronic applications accepted. *Expenses:* Contact institution.

Inter American University of Puerto Rico, Arecibo Campus, Program in Nursing, Arecibo, PR 00614-4050. Offers critical care nursing (MSN); surgical nursing (MSN).

Entrance requirements: For master's, EXADEP or GRE General Test or MAT, 2 letters of recommendation, bachelor's degree in nursing, minimum GPA of 2.5 in last 60 credits, minimum 1 year nursing experience, nursing license.

Inter American University of Puerto Rico, Barranquitas Campus, Program in Nursing, Barranquitas, PR 00794. Offers critical care nursing (MSN); medical surgical nursing (MSN). *Program availability:* Part-time, evening/weekend. *Faculty:* 2 full-time (both women). *Students:* 30 part-time (24 women); all minorities (all Hispanic/Latino). Average age 31. 30 applicants, 97% accepted, 29 enrolled. *Degree requirements:* For master's, 2 foreign languages, comprehensive exam (for some programs), thesis optional, minimum grade of B on all courses, integration seminar. *Entrance requirements:* For master's, bachelor's degree in nursing from accredited institution, minimum GPA of 2.5, provisional or permanent nursing license for practicing nursing in Puerto Rico, official academic transcript from institution that conferred bachelor's degree, two recommendations letters. *Application deadline:* Applications are processed on a rolling basis. Application fee: $31. Electronic applications accepted. *Expenses:* $3,392 full-time tuition plus $652 fees. *Financial support:* Applicants required to submit FAFSA. *Unit head:* Juan A. Negron-Berrios, PhD, Chancellor, 787-857-3600 Ext. 2002, Fax: 787-857-2125, E-mail: janegron@br.inter.edu. *Application contact:* Aramilda Cartagena-Santiago, Dean of Students, 787-857-3600 Ext. 2009, Fax: 787-857-2125, E-mail: aramildacartagena@br.inter.edu.

Pontifical Catholic University of Puerto Rico, College of Sciences, Department of Nursing, Program in Medical-Surgical Nursing, Ponce, PR 00717-0777. Offers MSN. *Program availability:* Part-time, evening/weekend. *Degree requirements:* For master's, comprehensive exam (for some programs), thesis, clinical research paper. *Entrance requirements:* For master's, GRE General Test, 2 letters of recommendation, interview, minimum GPA of 2.75. Electronic applications accepted.

Saint Francis Medical Center College of Nursing, Graduate Programs, Peoria, IL 61603-3783. Offers adult gerontology (MSN); clinical nurse leader (MSN); family nurse practitioner (MSN, Post-Graduate Certificate); family psychiatric mental health nurse practitioner (MSN); neonatal nurse practitioner (MSN); nurse clinician (Post-Graduate Certificate); nurse educator (MSN, Post-Graduate Certificate); nursing (DNP); nursing management leadership (MSN). *Accreditation:* ACEN. *Program availability:* Part-time, online only, 100% online, blended/hybrid learning. *Faculty:* 11 full-time (all women), 7 part-time/adjunct (all women). *Students:* 4 full-time (all women), 239 part-time (209 women); includes 24 minority (12 Black or African American, non-Hispanic/Latino; 3 Asian, non-Hispanic/Latino; 4 Hispanic/Latino; 5 Two or more races, non-Hispanic/Latino). Average age 37. 105 applicants, 83% accepted, 60 enrolled. In 2017, 52 master's, 8 doctorates awarded. *Degree requirements:* For master's, research experience, portfolio, practicum; for doctorate, practicum. *Entrance requirements:* For master's, nursing research, health assessment, graduate course work in statistics, RN license; for doctorate, master's degree in nursing, professional portfolio, graduate statistics, transcripts, RN license. Additional exam requirements/recommendations for international students: Required—TOEFL (minimum score 550 paper-based; 79 iBT). *Application deadline:* For fall admission, 6/1 priority date for domestic and international students; for spring admission, 11/15 priority date for domestic and international students. Applications are processed on a rolling basis. Application fee: $50. *Expenses:* Contact institution. *Financial support:* In 2017–18, 13 students received support. Scholarships/grants and tuition waivers (partial) available. Support available to part-time students. Financial award application deadline: 6/15; financial award applicants required to submit FAFSA. *Faculty research:* Outcome and curriculum planning, health promotion, NCLEX-RN results, decision-making program evaluation. *Unit head:* Dr. Patti A. Stockert, President of the College, 309-655-4124, Fax: 309-624-8973, E-mail: patricia.a.stockert@osfhealthcare.org. *Application contact:* Dr. Kim A. Mitchell, Dean, Graduate Program, 309-655-2201, Fax: 309-624-8973, E-mail: kim.a.mitchell@osfhealthcare.org.
Website: http://www.sfmccon.edu/graduate-programs/

State University of New York Downstate Medical Center, College of Nursing, Graduate Programs in Nursing, Program in Clinical Nurse Specialist, Brooklyn, NY 11203-2098. Offers MS, Post Master's Certificate.

Universidad Adventista de las Antillas, EGECED Department, Mayagüez, PR 00681-0118. Offers curriculum and instruction (M Ed); medical surgical nursing (MN); school administration and supervision (M Ed). *Degree requirements:* For master's, comprehensive exam (for some programs), thesis (for some programs). *Entrance requirements:* For master's, EXADEP or GRE General Test, recommendations. Electronic applications accepted.

University of South Africa, College of Human Sciences, Pretoria, South Africa. Offers adult education (M Ed); African languages (MA, PhD); African politics (MA, PhD); Afrikaans (MA, PhD); ancient history (MA, PhD); ancient Near Eastern studies (MA, PhD); anthropology (MA, PhD); applied linguistics (MA); Arabic (MA, PhD); archaeology (MA); art history (MA); Biblical archaeology (MA); Biblical studies (M Th, D Th, PhD); Christian spirituality (M Th, D Th); church history (M Th, D Th); classical studies (MA, PhD); clinical psychology (MA); communication (MA, PhD); comparative education (M Ed, Ed D); consulting psychology (D Admin, D Com, PhD); curriculum studies (M Ed, Ed D); development studies (M Admin, MA, D Admin, PhD); didactics (M Ed, Ed D); education (M Tech); education management (M Ed, Ed D); educational psychology (M Ed); English (MA); environmental education (M Ed); French (MA, PhD); German (MA, PhD); Greek (MA); guidance and counseling (M Ed); health studies (MA, PhD), including health sciences education (MA), health services management (MA), medical and surgical nursing science (critical care general) (MA), midwifery and neonatal nursing science (MA), trauma and emergency care (MA); history (MA, PhD); history of education (Ed D); inclusive education (M Ed, Ed D); information and communications technology policy and regulation (MA); information science (MA, MIS, PhD); international politics (MA, PhD); Islamic studies (MA, PhD); Italian (MA, PhD); Judaica (MA, PhD); linguistics (MA, PhD); mathematical education (M Ed); mathematics education (MA); missiology (M Th, D Th); modern Hebrew (MA, PhD); musicology (MA, MMus, D Mus, PhD); natural science education (M Ed); New Testament (M Th, D Th); Old Testament (D Th); pastoral therapy (M Th, D Th); philosophy (MA); philosophy of education (M Ed, Ed D); politics (MA, PhD); Portuguese (MA, PhD); practical theology (M Th, D Th); psychology (MA, MS, PhD); psychology of education (M Ed, Ed D); public health (MA); religious studies (MA, D Th, PhD); Romance languages (MA); Russian (MA, PhD); Semitic languages (MA, PhD); social behavior studies in HIV/AIDS (MA); social science (mental health) (MA); social science in development studies (MA); social science in psychology (MA); social science in social work (MA); social science in sociology (MA); social work (MSW, DSW, PhD); socio-education (M Ed, Ed D); sociolinguistics (MA); sociology (MA, PhD); Spanish (MA, PhD); systematic theology (M Th, D Th); TESOL (teaching English to speakers of other languages) (MA); theological ethics (M Th, D Th); theory of literature (MA, PhD); urban ministries (D Th); urban ministry (M Th).

University of South Carolina, The Graduate School, College of Nursing, Program in Clinical Nursing, Columbia, SC 29208. Offers acute care clinical specialist (MSN); acute care nurse practitioner (MSN); women's health nurse practitioner (MSN). *Accreditation:* AACN. *Program availability:* Part-time. *Degree requirements:* For master's, thesis or alternative. *Entrance requirements:* For master's, GRE General Test or MAT, BS in nursing, RN licensure. Additional exam requirements/recommendations for international students: Required—TOEFL (minimum score 570 paper-based). Electronic applications accepted. *Faculty research:* Systems research, evidence based practice, breast cancer, violence.

Ursuline College, School of Graduate and Professional Studies, Programs in Nursing, Pepper Pike, OH 44124-4398. Offers acute-care nurse practitioner (MSN); adult nurse practitioner (MSN); adult-gerontology acute care nurse practitioner (MSN); adult-gerontology clinical nurse specialist (MSN); adult-gerontology nurse practitioner (MSN); care management (MSN); clinical nurse specialist (MSN); family nurse practitioner (MSN); nursing (DNP); nursing education (MSN); palliative care (MSN). *Accreditation:* AACN. *Program availability:* Part-time. *Faculty:* 6 full-time (all women), 25 part-time/adjunct (23 women). *Students:* 136 applicants, 89% accepted, 85 enrolled. In 2017, 85 master's, 6 doctorates awarded. *Degree requirements:* For master's, comprehensive exam; for doctorate, thesis/dissertation. *Entrance requirements:* For master's, minimum undergraduate GPA of 3.0, bachelor's degree in nursing, eligibility for or current Ohio RN license. Additional exam requirements/recommendations for international students: Required—TOEFL (minimum score 500 paper-based). *Application deadline:* For fall admission, 8/1 priority date for domestic students. Applications are processed on a rolling basis. Application fee: $25. Electronic applications accepted. *Expenses:* $1,094 per credit hour. *Financial support:* In 2017–18, 6 students received support. Scholarships/grants available. Financial award application deadline: 3/1; financial award applicants required to submit FAFSA. *Faculty research:* Core Determinants of Health (CDH) screening tool and accompanying education, academic-practice partnerships, active learning/teaching strategies, innovative clinical education models, competency development and testing, health care policy and cultural competence. *Total annual research expenditures:* $864,511. *Unit head:* Dr. Janet Baker, Associate Dean of Graduate Nursing, 440-864-8172, Fax: 440-684-6053, E-mail: jbaker@ursuline.edu. *Application contact:* Melanie Steele, Director, Graduate Admission, 440-646-8119, Fax: 440-684-6138, E-mail: graduateadmissions@ursuline.edu.

Nurse Anesthesia

Adventist University of Health Sciences, Program in Nurse Anesthesia, Orlando, FL 32803. Offers MS. *Accreditation:* AANA/CANAEP. *Entrance requirements:* For master's, GRE or MAT, minimum undergraduate cumulative GPA of 3.0, 1 year of intensive critical care nursing experience, 3 recommendations, interview.

Albany Medical College, Center for Nurse Anesthesiology, Albany, NY 12208. Offers anesthesia (MS). *Accreditation:* AANA/CANAEP. *Degree requirements:* For master's, thesis, thesis proposal/clinical research. *Entrance requirements:* For master's, GRE General Test, BSN or appropriate bachelor's degree, current RN license, critical care experience, organic chemistry, research methods. Electronic applications accepted. *Expenses:* Contact institution.

Arkansas State University, Graduate School, College of Nursing and Health Professions, School of Nursing, State University, AR 72467. Offers aging studies (Graduate Certificate); health care management (Graduate Certificate); health sciences (MS); health sciences education (Graduate Certificate); nurse anesthesia (MSN); nursing (MSN); nursing practice (DNP). *Accreditation:* AANA/CANAEP (one or more programs are accredited); ACEN. *Program availability:* Part-time. *Degree requirements:* For master's and Graduate Certificate, comprehensive exam, thesis or alternative; for doctorate, comprehensive exam, thesis/dissertation. *Entrance requirements:* For master's, GRE General Test or MAT, appropriate bachelor's degree, current Arkansas nursing license, CPR certification, physical examination, professional liability insurance, critical care experience, ACLS Certification, PALS Certification, interview, immunization records, personal goal statement, health assessment; for doctorate, GRE or MAT, NCLEX-RN Exam, appropriate master's degree, current Arkansas nursing license, CPR certification, physical examination, professional liability insurance, critical care experience, ACLS Certification, PALS Certification, interview, immunization records, personal goal statement, health assessment, TB skin test, background check; for Graduate Certificate, GRE or MAT, appropriate bachelor's degree, official transcripts, immunization records, proof of employment in healthcare, TB Skin Test, TB Mask Fit Test, CPR Certification. Additional exam requirements/recommendations for international students: Required—TOEFL (minimum score 550 paper-based; 79 iBT), IELTS (minimum score 6), PTE (minimum score 56). Electronic applications accepted. *Expenses:* Contact institution.

Augusta University, College of Nursing, Doctor of Nursing Practice Program, Augusta, GA 30912. Offers adult gerontology acute care nurse practitioner (DNP); family nurse practitioner (DNP); nurse executive (DNP); nursing (DNP); nursing anesthesia (DNP); pediatric nurse practitioner (DNP); psychiatric mental health nurse practitioner (DNP). *Accreditation:* AACN; AANA/CANAEP. *Degree requirements:* For doctorate, thesis/dissertation or alternative. *Entrance requirements:* For doctorate, GRE General Test or MAT, master's degree in nursing or related field, current professional nurse licensure. Additional exam requirements/recommendations for international students: Required—TOEFL (minimum score 600 paper-based; 100 iBT). Electronic applications accepted.

Barry University, College of Health Sciences, Program in Anesthesiology, Miami Shores, FL 33161-6695. Offers MS. *Accreditation:* AANA/CANAEP. *Degree requirements:* For master's, comprehensive exam. *Entrance requirements:* For master's, GRE General Test, minimum GPA of 3.0; 2 courses in chemistry (1 with lab); minimum 1 year critical care experience; BSN or RN; 4-year bachelor's degree in health sciences, nursing, biology, or chemistry. Electronic applications accepted. *Faculty research:* Use of computers in education, psychological well-bring of health care providers.

Baylor College of Medicine, School of Allied Health Sciences, Graduate Program in Nurse Anesthesia, Houston, TX 77030-3498. Offers DNP. *Accreditation:* AANA/CANAEP. *Degree requirements:* For doctorate, comprehensive exam, thesis/dissertation. *Entrance requirements:* For doctorate, GRE General Test, Texas nursing license, 1 year of work experience in critical care nursing, minimum GPA of 3.0, BSN, statistics, organic chemistry. Electronic applications accepted. *Expenses:* Contact institution. *Faculty research:* Education, simulation.

Nurse Anesthesia

Bloomsburg University of Pennsylvania, School of Graduate Studies, College of Science and Technology, Department of Nursing, Bloomsburg, PA 17815-1301. Offers adult and family nurse practitioner (MSN); community health (MSN); nurse anesthesia (MSN); nursing (MSN, DNP); nursing administration (MSN). *Accreditation:* AACN. *Degree requirements:* For master's, thesis (for some programs), clinical experience. *Entrance requirements:* For master's, minimum QPA of 3.0, personal statement, 2 letters of recommendation, nursing license. Additional exam requirements/recommendations for international students: Required—TOEFL, IELTS. Electronic applications accepted. *Expenses:* Contact institution.

Boston College, William F. Connell School of Nursing, Chestnut Hill, MA 02467. Offers adult-gerontology primary care nurse practitioner (MS); family health nursing (MS); nurse anesthesia (MS); nursing (PhD); pediatric primary care nurse practitioner (MS), including pediatric and women's health; psychiatric-mental health nursing (MS); women's health nursing (MS); MBA/MS; MS/MA; MS/PhD. MS/MBA offered jointly with Carroll School of Management, MS/MA with School of Theology and Ministry. *Accreditation:* AACN; AANA/CANAEP (one or more programs are accredited). *Program availability:* Part-time. *Faculty:* 54 full-time (48 women). *Students:* 170 full-time (153 women), 90 part-time (83 women); includes 39 minority (8 Black or African American, non-Hispanic/Latino; 10 Asian, non-Hispanic/Latino; 12 Hispanic/Latino; 9 Two or more races, non-Hispanic/Latino), 3 international. Average age 28. 360 applicants, 56% accepted, 94 enrolled. In 2017, 104 master's, 5 doctorates awarded. *Degree requirements:* For master's, comprehensive exam; for doctorate, comprehensive exam, thesis/dissertation, computer literacy exam or foreign language. *Entrance requirements:* For master's, bachelor's degree in nursing; for doctorate, GRE General Test, MS in nursing. Additional exam requirements/recommendations for international students: Required—TOEFL (minimum score 600 paper-based; 100 iBT), IELTS (minimum score 7.5). *Application deadline:* For fall admission, 9/30 for domestic and international students; for winter admission, 1/15 for domestic and international students; for spring admission, 3/15 for domestic and international students. Application fee: $40. Electronic applications accepted. *Expenses:* $1,350 per credit tuition. *Financial support:* In 2017–18, 152 students received support, including 11 fellowships with full tuition reimbursements available (averaging $24,504 per year), 29 teaching assistantships (averaging $3,768 per year); scholarships/grants, health care benefits, tuition waivers (partial), and unspecified assistantships also available. Support available to part-time students. Financial award application deadline: 4/18; financial award applicants required to submit FAFSA. *Faculty research:* Sexual and reproductive health, health promotion/illness prevention, aging, eating disorders, symptom management. *Total annual research expenditures:* $879,812. *Unit head:* Dr. Susan Gennaro, Dean, 617-552-4251, Fax: 617-552-0931, E-mail: susan.gennaro@bc.edu. *Application contact:* Sean Sendall, Assistant Dean, Graduate Enrollment and Data Analytics, 617-552-4745, Fax: 617-552-2121, E-mail: sean.sendall@bc.edu.
Website: http://www.bc.edu/cson

Bryan College of Health Sciences, School of Nurse Anesthesia, Lincoln, NE 68506-1398. Offers MS. *Accreditation:* AANA/CANAEP.

California State University, Fullerton, Graduate Studies, College of Health and Human Development, School of Nursing, Fullerton, CA 92831-3599. Offers leadership (MS); nurse anesthesia (MS); nurse educator (MS); nursing (DNP); school nursing (MS); women's health care (MS). *Accreditation:* AACN. *Program availability:* Part-time. *Faculty:* 27 full-time (23 women), 11 part-time/adjunct (all women). *Students:* 136 full-time (107 women), 116 part-time (96 women); includes 142 minority (9 Black or African American, non-Hispanic/Latino; 81 Asian, non-Hispanic/Latino; 37 Hispanic/Latino; 1 Native Hawaiian or other Pacific Islander, non-Hispanic/Latino; 14 Two or more races, non-Hispanic/Latino), 2 international. Average age 36. 235 applicants, 59% accepted, 117 enrolled. Application fee: $55. *Financial support:* Career-related internships or fieldwork, Federal Work-Study, institutionally sponsored loans, scholarships/grants, and traineeships available. Support available to part-time students. Financial award application deadline: 3/1; financial award applicants required to submit FAFSA. *Unit head:* Dr. Cindy Greenberg, Chair, 657-278-3336. *Application contact:* Admissions/Applications, 657-278-2371.
Website: http://nursing.fullerton.edu/

Case Western Reserve University, Frances Payne Bolton School of Nursing, Master's Programs in Nursing, Program in Nurse Anesthesia, Cleveland, OH 44106. Offers MSN. *Accreditation:* AANA/CANAEP. *Faculty:* 23 full-time (20 women), 1 part-time/adjunct (0 women). *Students:* 27 full-time (all women), 59 part-time (32 women); includes 12 minority (6 Black or African American, non-Hispanic/Latino; 2 Asian, non-Hispanic/Latino; 1 Hispanic/Latino; 1 Native Hawaiian or other Pacific Islander, non-Hispanic/Latino; 2 Two or more races, non-Hispanic/Latino). Average age 32. 84 applicants, 42% accepted, 30 enrolled. In 2017, 28 master's awarded. *Degree requirements:* For master's, minimum GPA of 3.0, clinical hours corresponding to requirements to sit for certification exam, portfolio. *Entrance requirements:* For master's, GRE General Test or MAT, CCRN certification. Additional exam requirements/recommendations for international students: Required—TOEFL (minimum score 577 paper-based; 90 iBT), IELTS (minimum score 7). *Application deadline:* For summer admission, 6/1 for domestic and international students. Applications are processed on a rolling basis. Application fee: $75. Electronic applications accepted. *Expenses:* Contact institution. *Financial support:* In 2017–18, 85 students received support. Scholarships/grants and traineeships available. Financial award application deadline: 5/15; financial award applicants required to submit FAFSA. *Faculty research:* Mechanical ventilation antioxidant trial, intravenous function and mechanical ventilation, impact of taxane on peripheral nerve function. *Unit head:* Dr. Sonya Moore, Director, 216-368-6659, Fax: 216-368-3542, E-mail: sdm37@case.edu. *Application contact:* Jackie Tepale, Admissions Coordinator, 216-368-5253, Fax: 216-368-0124, E-mail: yyd@case.edu.
Website: http://fpb.cwru.edu/MSN/anesthesia.shtm

Columbia University, School of Nursing, Program in Nurse Anesthesia, New York, NY 10032. Offers MS, Adv C. *Accreditation:* AACN; AANA/CANAEP. *Entrance requirements:* For master's, GRE General Test, NCLEX, BSN, 1 year of intensive care unit experience; for Adv C, MSN, 1 year of intensive care unit experience. Additional exam requirements/recommendations for international students: Required—TOEFL (minimum score 100 iBT). Electronic applications accepted. *Expenses: Tuition:* Full-time $44,864; part-time $1704 per credit. *Required fees:* $2370 per semester. One-time fee: $105.

DeSales University, Division of Healthcare, Center Valley, PA 18034-9568. Offers adult-gerontology acute care (Post Master's Certificate); adult-gerontology acute care nurse practitioner (MSN); adult-gerontology acute certified nurse practitioner (Post Master's Certificate); adult-gerontology clinical nurse specialist (MSN, Post Master's Certificate); clinical leadership (DNP); family nurse practitioner (MSN, Post Master's Certificate); general nursing practice (DNP); nurse anesthetist (MSN); nurse educator (Post Master's Certificate, Postbaccalaureate Certificate); nurse midwife (MSN); nurse practitioner (MSN); psychiatric-mental health nurse practitioner (MSN, Post Master's Certificate); DNP/MBA. *Accreditation:* ACEN. *Program availability:* Part-time. *Faculty:* 26 full-time (20 women), 30 part-time/adjunct (19 women). *Students:* 282 full-time (210 women), 101 part-time (85 women); includes 39 minority (12 Black or African American, non-Hispanic/Latino; 11 Asian, non-Hispanic/Latino; 12 Hispanic/Latino; 4 Two or more races, non-Hispanic/Latino), 1 international. Average age 29. 2,884 applicants, 5% accepted, 114 enrolled. In 2017, 76 master's, 6 doctorates awarded. *Degree requirements:* For master's, minimum GPA of 3.0, portfolio; for doctorate, minimum GPA of 3.0, scholarly capstone project. *Entrance requirements:* For master's, GRE or MAT (waived if applicant has an undergraduate GPA of 3.0 or higher), BSN from ACEN- or CCNE-accredited program, minimum undergraduate GPA of 3.0, active RN license or eligibility, two letters of recommendation, essay, health care experience, personal interview; for doctorate, BSN or MSN from ACEN- or CCNE-accredited institution, minimum GPA of 3.3 in graduate program, current licensure as an RN. Additional exam requirements/recommendations for international students: Required—TOEFL (minimum score 104 iBT). *Application deadline:* Applications are processed on a rolling basis. Application fee: $50. Electronic applications accepted. *Expenses:* Contact institution. *Financial support:* Applicants required to submit FAFSA. *Unit head:* Ronald Nordone, Dean of Graduate Education, 610-282-1100 Ext. 1289, E-mail: ronald.nordone@desales.edu. *Application contact:* Julia Ferraro, Director of Graduate Admissions, 610-282-1100 Ext. 1768, E-mail: gradadmissions@desales.edu.

Drexel University, College of Nursing and Health Professions, Department of Nurse Anesthesia, Philadelphia, PA 19104-2875. Offers MSN. *Accreditation:* AACN; AANA/CANAEP. Electronic applications accepted.

Duke University, School of Nursing, Durham, NC 27708-0586. Offers acute care pediatric nurse practitioner (MSN, Post-Graduate Certificate); adult-gerontology nurse practitioner (MSN, Post-Graduate Certificate), including acute care, primary care; family nurse practitioner (MSN, Post-Graduate Certificate); neonatal nurse practitioner (MSN, Post-Graduate Certificate); nurse anesthesia (DNP); nurse practitioner (DNP); nursing (PhD); nursing and health care leadership (MSN, Post-Graduate Certificate); nursing education (MSN, Post-Graduate Certificate); nursing informatics (MSN, Post-Graduate Certificate); pediatric nurse practitioner (MSN, Post-Graduate Certificate), including primary care; psychiatric mental health nurse practitioner (MSN, Post-Graduate Certificate); women's health nurse practitioner (MSN, Post-Graduate Certificate). *Accreditation:* AACN; AANA/CANAEP. *Program availability:* Part-time, evening/weekend, online with on-campus intensives. *Faculty:* 72 full-time (61 women). *Students:* 155 full-time (137 women), 613 part-time (548 women); includes 177 minority (64 Black or African American, non-Hispanic/Latino; 2 American Indian or Alaska Native, non-Hispanic/Latino; 47 Asian, non-Hispanic/Latino; 34 Hispanic/Latino; 30 Two or more races, non-Hispanic/Latino), 10 international. Average age 34. 631 applicants, 47% accepted, 211 enrolled. In 2017, 221 master's, 71 doctorates, 26 other advanced degrees awarded. Terminal master's awarded for partial completion of doctoral program. *Degree requirements:* For master's, thesis optional; for doctorate, capstone project. *Entrance requirements:* For master's, GRE General Test (waived if undergraduate GPA of 3.4 or higher), 1 year of nursing experience (recommended), BSN, minimum GPA of 3.0, previous course work in statistics; for doctorate, GRE General Test (waived if undergraduate GPA of 3.4 or higher), BSN or MSN, minimum GPA of 3.0, resume, personal statement, undergraduate statistics course, current licensure as a registered nurse, transcripts from all post-secondary institutions; for Post-Graduate Certificate, MSN, licensure or eligibility as a professional nurse, transcripts from all post-secondary institutions, previous course work in statistics. Additional exam requirements/recommendations for international students: Required—TOEFL (minimum score 100 iBT), IELTS (minimum score 7). *Application deadline:* For fall admission, 12/1 for domestic and international students; for spring admission, 5/1 for domestic and international students. Application fee: $50. Electronic applications accepted. *Expenses:* Contact institution. *Financial support:* Institutionally sponsored loans, scholarships/grants, and traineeships available. Support available to part-time students. Financial award applicants required to submit FAFSA. *Faculty research:* Cardiovascular disease, caregiver skill training, data mining, prostate cancer, neonatal immune system. *Unit head:* Dr. Marion E. Broome, Dean/Vice Chancellor for Nursing Affairs/Associate Vice President for Academic Affairs for Nursing, 919-684-9446, Fax: 919-684-9414, E-mail: marion.broome@duke.edu. *Application contact:* Dr. Ernie Rushing, Director of Admissions and Recruitment, 919-668-6274, Fax: 919-668-4693, E-mail: ernie.rushing@dm.duke.edu.
Website: http://www.nursing.duke.edu/

Fairfield University, Marion Peckham Egan School of Nursing and Health Studies, Fairfield, CT 06824. Offers advanced practice (DNP); family nurse practitioner (MSN, DNP); nurse anesthesia (DNP); nursing leadership (MSN); psychiatric nurse practitioner (MSN, DNP). *Accreditation:* AACN; AANA/CANAEP. *Program availability:* Part-time, evening/weekend. *Faculty:* 9 full-time (all women), 11 part-time/adjunct (8 women). *Students:* 50 full-time (42 women), 153 part-time (140 women); includes 48 minority (15 Black or African American, non-Hispanic/Latino; 1 American Indian or Alaska Native, non-Hispanic/Latino; 10 Asian, non-Hispanic/Latino; 19 Hispanic/Latino; 3 Two or more races, non-Hispanic/Latino), 2 international. Average age 34. 160 applicants, 50% accepted, 55 enrolled. In 2017, 26 master's, 36 doctorates awarded. *Degree requirements:* For master's, capstone project. *Entrance requirements:* For master's, minimum QPA of 3.0, RN license, resume, 2 recommendations; for doctorate, MSN (minimum QPA of 3.2) or BSN (minimum QPA of 3.0); critical care nursing experience (for nurse anesthesia DNP candidates). Additional exam requirements/recommendations for international students: Required—TOEFL (minimum score 550 paper-based; 80 iBT) or IELTS (minimum score 6.5). *Application deadline:* For fall admission, 5/15 for international students; for spring admission, 10/15 for international students. Applications are processed on a rolling basis. Application fee: $60. Electronic applications accepted. *Expenses:* $850 per credit hour (for MSN); $1,000 per credit hour (for DNP). *Financial support:* In 2017–18, 45 students received support. Scholarships/grants and unspecified assistantships available. Financial award applicants required to submit FAFSA. *Faculty research:* Aging, spiritual care, palliative and end of life care, psychiatric mental health, pediatric trauma. *Unit head:* Dr. Meredith Wallace Kazer, Dean, 203-254-4000 Ext. 2701, Fax: 203-254-4126, E-mail: mkazer@fairfield.edu. *Application contact:* Marianne Gumpper, Director of Graduate and Continuing Studies Admission, 203-254-4184, Fax: 203-254-4073, E-mail: gradadmis@fairfield.edu.
Website: http://fairfield.edu/son

Florida Gulf Coast University, Elaine Nicpon Marieb College of Health and Human Services, Program in Nurse Anesthesia, Fort Myers, FL 33965-6565. Offers MSN. *Accreditation:* AACN; AANA/CANAEP. *Program availability:* Part-time. *Faculty:* 71 full-time (49 women), 49 part-time/adjunct (32 women). *Students:* 31 full-time (15 women); includes 7 minority (1 Black or African American, non-Hispanic/Latino; 2 Asian, non-Hispanic/Latino; 4 Hispanic/Latino). Average age 32. 2 applicants. In 2017, 14 master's awarded. *Degree requirements:* For master's, thesis or alternative. *Entrance requirements:* For master's, GRE General Test, MAT, minimum GPA of 3.0. Additional exam requirements/recommendations for international students: Required—TOEFL (minimum score 550 paper-based). *Application deadline:* For spring admission, 5/15 priority date for domestic students. Applications are processed on a rolling basis. Application fee: $30. Electronic applications accepted. *Expenses:* Tuition, state resident: part-time $290 per credit hour. Tuition, nonresident: part-time $1173 per credit hour. *Required fees:* $127 per credit hour. Tuition and fees vary according to course load. *Financial support:* In 2017–18, 10 students received support. Application deadline: 6/30; applicants required to submit FAFSA. *Faculty research:* Gerontology, community health, ethical and legal aspects of health care, critical care. *Unit head:* Dr. Gretchen Warn, Graduate Program Assistant, 239-590-7505, E-mail: gwarn@fgcu.edu. *Application contact:* MeLinda Coffey, Administrative Assistant, 239-590-7530, Fax: 239-590-7474, E-mail: mcoffey@fgcu.edu.

Florida International University, Nicole Wertheim College of Nursing and Health Sciences, Nursing Program, Miami, FL 33199. Offers adult health nursing (MSN); family health (MSN); nurse anesthetist (MSN); nursing practice (DNP); nursing science research (PhD); pediatric nurse (MSN); psychiatric and mental health nursing (MSN); registered nurse (MSN). *Accreditation:* AACN; AANA/CANAEP. *Program availability:* Part-time, evening/weekend. *Faculty:* 40 full-time (33 women), 79 part-time/adjunct (69 women). *Students:* 330 full-time (233 women), 89 part-time (73 women); includes 326 minority (92 Black or African American, non-Hispanic/Latino; 1 American Indian or Alaska Native, non-Hispanic/Latino; 33 Asian, non-Hispanic/Latino; 195 Hispanic/Latino; 2 Native Hawaiian or other Pacific Islander, non-Hispanic/Latino; 3 Two or more races, non-Hispanic/Latino), 9 international. Average age 33. 304 applicants, 50% accepted, 148 enrolled. In 2017, 144 master's, 8 doctorates awarded. *Degree requirements:* For master's, thesis or alternative; for doctorate, comprehensive exam, thesis/dissertation. *Entrance requirements:* For master's, bachelor's degree in nursing, minimum undergraduate GPA of 3.0 in upper-level coursework, letters of recommendation; for doctorate, GRE, letters of recommendation, minimum undergraduate GPA of 3.0 in upper-level coursework, interview. Additional exam requirements/recommendations for international students: Required—TOEFL (minimum score 550 paper-based; 80 iBT). *Application deadline:* For fall admission, 6/1 for domestic students, 4/1 for international students; for spring admission, 10/1 for domestic students, 9/1 for international students. Applications are processed on a rolling basis. Application fee: $30. Electronic applications accepted. *Expenses:* Tuition, state resident: full-time $8912; part-time $446 per credit hour. Tuition, nonresident: full-time $21,393; part-time $992 per credit hour. *Required fees:* $390; $195 per semester. *Financial support:* Institutionally sponsored loans and scholarships/grants available. Financial award application deadline: 3/1; financial award applicants required to submit FAFSA. *Faculty research:* Adult health nursing. *Unit head:* Dr. Yhovana Gordon, Chair, 305-348-7733, Fax: 305-348-7051, E-mail: gordony@fiu.edu. *Application contact:* Nanett Rojas, Manager, Admissions Operations, 305-348-7464, Fax: 305-348-7441, E-mail: gradadm@fiu.edu.
Website: http://cnhs.fiu.edu/

Franciscan Missionaries of Our Lady University, School of Nursing, Program in Nurse Anesthesia, Baton Rouge, LA 70808. Offers DNP. *Accreditation:* AANA/CANAEP. *Entrance requirements:* For doctorate, GRE, current RN license; baccalaureate degree in nursing; 1 year of full-time experience (2 years preferred) as RN in adult intensive care unit; minimum cumulative GPA of 3.0; three professional letters of recommendation. Additional exam requirements/recommendations for international students: Required—TOEFL. *Application deadline:* For fall admission, 7/1 for domestic students. *Financial support:* Applicants required to submit FAFSA. *Unit head:* Phyllis Pedersen, Assistant Director, 225-214-6979, E-mail: phyllis.pedersen@franu.edu. *Application contact:* Phyllis Pedersen, Assistant Director, 225-214-6979, E-mail: phyllis.pedersen@franu.edu.
Website: https://www.franu.edu/academics/academic-programs/nurse-anesthesia

Gannon University, School of Graduate Studies, Morosky College of Health Professions and Sciences, Villa Maria School of Nursing, Program in Nurse Anesthesia, Erie, PA 16541-0001. Offers MSN, Certificate. *Program availability:* Part-time, evening/weekend. *Degree requirements:* For master's, thesis (for some programs), practicum. *Entrance requirements:* For master's and Certificate, GRE, BSN from accredited program, transcripts, evidence of fulfillment of legal requirements for practice of nursing in the United States, minimum cumulative GPA of 3.0 for undergraduate math and science courses and for last 60 hours of undergraduate nursing studies, four letters of recommendation, two years of clinical experience. Additional exam requirements/recommendations for international students: Required—TOEFL (minimum score 79 iBT). Electronic applications accepted.

Georgetown University, Graduate School of Arts and Sciences, School of Nursing and Health Studies, Washington, DC 20057. Offers acute care nurse practitioner (MS); clinical nurse specialist (MS); family nurse practitioner (MS); nurse anesthesia (MS); nurse-midwifery (MS); nursing (DNP); nursing education (MS). *Accreditation:* AACN; AANA/CANAEP (one or more programs are accredited); ACNM/ACME (one or more programs are accredited). *Degree requirements:* For master's, thesis optional. *Entrance requirements:* For master's, GRE General Test or MAT, bachelor's degree in nursing from ACEN-accredited school, minimum undergraduate GPA of 3.0. Additional exam requirements/recommendations for international students: Required—TOEFL.

Goldfarb School of Nursing at Barnes-Jewish College, Graduate Programs, St. Louis, MO 63110. Offers adult-gerontology (MSN), including primary care nurse practitioner; adult-gerontology (MSN), including acute care nurse practitioner; health systems and population health leadership (MSN); nurse anesthesia (MSN). *Accreditation:* AACN; AANA/CANAEP. *Program availability:* Part-time, online learning. *Faculty:* 42 full-time (39 women), 6 part-time/adjunct (all women). *Students:* 61 full-time (49 women), 3 part-time (2 women); includes 13 minority (8 Black or African American, non-Hispanic/Latino; 2 Asian, non-Hispanic/Latino; 1 Hispanic/Latino; 2 Two or more races, non-Hispanic/Latino). *Degree requirements:* For master's, thesis or alternative. *Entrance requirements:* For master's, 2 references, personal statement, curriculum vitae or resume. Additional exam requirements/recommendations for international students: Required—TOEFL (minimum score 575 paper-based; 85 iBT). *Application deadline:* Applications are processed on a rolling basis. Application fee: $50. *Expenses: Tuition:* Full-time $11,910; part-time $794 per credit hour. *Required fees:* $30; $15 per term. Full-time tuition and fees vary according to program. *Financial support:* Research assistantships, Federal Work-Study, institutionally sponsored loans, scholarships/grants, and traineeships available. Support available to part-time students. Financial award applicants required to submit FAFSA. *Faculty research:* HIV stigma, HIV symptom management, palliative care with children and their families, heart disease prevention in Hispanic women, depression in the well elderly, alternative therapies in pre-term infants. *Unit head:* Dr. Gretchen Drinkard, Associate Dean for Academic Affairs, 314-454-7540, Fax: 314-362-9222, E-mail: gdrinkard@bjc.org. *Application contact:* Karen Sartorius, Admission Specialist, 314-454-7057, Fax: 314-362-9250, E-mail: karen.sartorius@bjc.org.
Website: http://www.barnesjewishcollege.edu/

Inter American University of Puerto Rico, Arecibo Campus, Program in Anesthesia, Arecibo, PR 00614-4050. Offers MS. *Accreditation:* AANA/CANAEP. *Degree requirements:* For master's, comprehensive exam, thesis optional. *Entrance requirements:* For master's, GRE, EXADEP, 2 letters of recommendation, bachelor's degree in nursing, interview, minimum GPA of 3.0 in last 60 credits, minimum 1 year experience.

La Roche College, School of Graduate Studies and Adult Education, Program in Nurse Anesthesia, Pittsburgh, PA 15237-5898. Offers MS, DNAP. *Accreditation:* AANA/CANAEP. *Faculty:* 1 full-time (0 women), 3 part-time/adjunct (1 woman). *Students:* 36 full-time (23 women), 2 part-time (both women); includes 1 minority (Asian, non-Hispanic/Latino). Average age 31. 19 applicants, 100% accepted, 19 enrolled. In 2017, 12 master's awarded. *Degree requirements:* For master's, thesis optional. *Entrance requirements:* For master's, GRE General Test, prior acceptance to the Allegheny Valley School of Anesthesia. *Application deadline:* For fall admission, 12/31 for domestic students. Application fee: $50. Electronic applications accepted. *Expenses: Tuition:* Part-time $715 per credit hour. *Required fees:* $80 per credit hour. *Financial support:* Application deadline: 3/31; applicants required to submit FAFSA. *Unit head:* Dr. Don Fujito, Coordinator, 412-536-1157, Fax: 412-536-1175, E-mail: fujitod1@laroche.edu. *Application contact:* Hope Schiffgens, Director of Graduate Studies and Adult Education, 412-536-1266, Fax: 412-536-1283, E-mail: schombh1@laroche.edu.

La Salle University, School of Nursing and Health Sciences, Program in Nursing, Philadelphia, PA 19141-1199. Offers adult gerontology primary care nurse practitioner (MSN, Certificate); adult health and illness clinical nurse specialist (MSN); adult-gerontology clinical nurse specialist (MSN, Certificate); clinical nurse leader (MSN); family primary care nurse practitioner (MSN, Certificate); gerontology (Certificate); nurse anesthetist (MSN, Certificate); nursing (MSN, Certificate); nursing administration (MSN, Certificate); nursing education (Certificate); nursing practice (DNP); nursing service administration (MSN); public health nursing (MSN, Certificate); school nursing (Certificate); MSN/MBA; MSN/MPH. *Accreditation:* AACN. *Program availability:* Part-time, evening/weekend, 100% online. *Faculty:* 12 full-time (11 women), 14 part-time/adjunct (11 women). *Students:* 1 (woman) full-time, 277 part-time (220 women); includes 72 minority (36 Black or African American, non-Hispanic/Latino; 1 American Indian or Alaska Native, non-Hispanic/Latino; 18 Asian, non-Hispanic/Latino; 10 Hispanic/Latino; 1 Native Hawaiian or other Pacific Islander, non-Hispanic/Latino; 6 Two or more races, non-Hispanic/Latino), 1 international. Average age 36. 70 applicants, 56% accepted, 24 enrolled. In 2017, 81 master's, 4 doctorates, 13 other advanced degrees awarded. *Degree requirements:* For doctorate, minimum of 1,000 hours of post baccalaureate clinical practice supervised by preceptors. *Entrance requirements:* For master's, GRE, MAT, or GMAT (for students with BSN GPA of less than 3.2), baccalaureate degree in nursing from ACEN- or CCNE-accredited program or an MSN Bridge program; Pennsylvania RN license; 2 letters of reference; resume; statement of philosophy articulating professional values and future educational goal; 1 year of work experience as a registered nurse; for doctorate, GRE (waived for applicants with MSN cumulative GPA of 3.7 or above), MSN, master's degree, MBA or MHA from nationally-accredited program; resume or curriculum vitae; 2 letters of reference; interview; for Certificate, GRE, MAT, or GMAT (for students with BSN GPA of less than 3.2, baccalaureate degree in nursing from ACEN- or CCNE-accredited program or an MSN Bridge program; Pennsylvania RN license; 2 letters of reference; resume; statement of philosophy articulating professional values and future educational goal; 1 year of work experience as a registered nurse. Additional exam requirements/recommendations for international students: Required—TOEFL. *Application deadline:* For fall admission, 8/15 priority date for domestic students, 7/15 for international students; for spring admission, 12/15 priority date for domestic students, 11/15 for international students; for summer admission, 4/15 priority date for domestic students, 3/15 for international students. Applications are processed on a rolling basis. Application fee: $35. Electronic applications accepted. Application fee is waived when completed online. *Expenses:* Contact institution. *Financial support:* In 2017–18, 7 students received support. Scholarships/grants and traineeships available. Support available to part-time students. Financial award application deadline: 8/31; financial award applicants required to submit FAFSA. *Unit head:* Dr. Patricia M. Dillon, Director, 215-951-1322, Fax: 215-951-1896, E-mail: msnapn@lasalle.edu. *Application contact:* Elizabeth Heenan, Director, Graduate and Adult Enrollment, 215-951-1100, Fax: 215-951-1462, E-mail: heenan@lasalle.edu.
Website: http://www.lasalle.edu/nursing/program-options/

Lincoln Memorial University, Caylor School of Nursing, Harrogate, TN 37752-1901. Offers family nurse practitioner (MSN); nurse anesthesia (MSN); psychiatric mental health nurse practitioner (MSN). *Accreditation:* AANA/CANAEP; ACEN. *Program availability:* Part-time. *Entrance requirements:* For master's, GRE.

Louisiana State University Health Sciences Center, School of Nursing, New Orleans, LA 70112. Offers adult gerontology acute care nurse practitioner (DNP, Post-Master's Certificate); adult gerontology clinical nurse specialist (DNP, Post-Master's Certificate); adult gerontology primary care nurse practitioner (DNP, Post-Master's Certificate); clinical nurse leader (MSN); executive nurse leader (DNP, Post-Master's Certificate); neonatal nurse practitioner (DNP, Post-Master's Certificate); nurse anesthesia (DNP, Post-Master's Certificate); nurse educator (MSN); nursing (DNS); primary care family nurse practitioner (DNP, Post-Master's Certificate); public/community health nursing (DNP, Post-Master's Certificate). *Accreditation:* AACN; AANA/CANAEP (one or more programs are accredited). *Program availability:* Part-time. *Faculty:* 29 full-time (26 women), 20 part-time/adjunct (8 women). *Students:* 184 full-time (132 women), 41 part-time (35 women); includes 69 minority (45 Black or African American, non-Hispanic/Latino; 11 Asian, non-Hispanic/Latino; 12 Hispanic/Latino; 1 Two or more races, non-Hispanic/Latino), 1 international. Average age 30. 162 applicants, 42% accepted, 68 enrolled. In 2017, 52 master's, 46 doctorates awarded. *Degree requirements:* For master's, thesis optional; for doctorate, thesis/dissertation. *Entrance requirements:* For master's, GRE, minimum GPA of 3.0; for doctorate, GRE, minimum GPA of 3.0 (for DNP), 3.5 (for DNS). Additional exam requirements/recommendations for international students: Required—TOEFL (minimum score 550 paper-based; 79 iBT). *Application deadline:* Applications are processed on a rolling basis. Application fee: $100. Electronic applications accepted. *Expenses:* Contact institution. *Financial support:* Federal Work-Study, institutionally sponsored loans, scholarships/grants, and traineeships available. Financial award applicants required to submit FAFSA. *Faculty research:* Advanced clinical practice, nursing education, interprofessional education, nursing administration, culturally competent care. *Unit head:* Dr. Demetrius James Porche, Dean, 504-568-4106, Fax: 504-599-0573, E-mail: dporch@lsuhsc.edu. *Application contact:* Tracie Gravolet, Director, Office of Student Affairs, 504-568-4114, Fax: 504-568-5711, E-mail: tgravo@lsuhsc.edu.
Website: http://nursing.lsuhsc.edu/

Lourdes University, Graduate School, Sylvania, OH 43560-2898. Offers business (MBA); leadership (M Ed); nurse anesthesia (MSN); nurse educator (MSN); nurse leader (MSN); organizational leadership (MOL); reading (M Ed); teaching and curriculum (M Ed); theology (MA). *Program availability:* Evening/weekend. *Entrance requirements:* Additional exam requirements/recommendations for international students: Required—TOEFL.

Marian University, Leighton School of Nursing, Indianapolis, IN 46222-1997. Offers family nurse practitioner (DNP); nurse anesthesia (DNP); nursing education (MSN). *Program availability:* Part-time. *Faculty:* 6 full-time (all women), 2 part-time/adjunct (both women). *Students:* 23 full-time (20 women), 1 (woman) part-time; includes 7 minority (5 Black or African American, non-Hispanic/Latino; 1 Asian, non-Hispanic/Latino; 1 Hispanic/Latino). Average age 36. 69 applicants, 35% accepted, 5 enrolled. *Degree requirements:* For master's, 38 credits, designed to be completed in 2 years; 225-hour practicum including a culminating project; for doctorate, 70 credit hours (for family nurse practitioner track); 85 credits (for nurse anesthesia track); minimum of 1000 hours of supervised practice. *Entrance requirements:* For master's, degree in nursing from NLNAC- or CCNE-accredited program; current, valid RN license in State of Indiana; minimum undergraduate GPA of 3.0; 3 recommendations; interview with admissions committee; current resume; 500-word essay describing career goals; for doctorate, BSN from NSNAC- or CCNE-accredited program; minimum undergraduate GPA of 3.0; cureent, valid RN license; current resume or curriculum vitae; 500-word essay addressing career goals; 3 letters of recommendation; interview with Admissions Committee. Additional exam requirements/recommendations for international students:

Required—TOEFL (minimum score 550 paper-based; 79 iBT). *Application deadline:* For fall admission, 2/15 for domestic and international students. Applications are processed on a rolling basis. Application fee: $40. Electronic applications accepted. Application fee is waived when completed online. *Expenses:* Contact institution. *Financial support:* Application deadline: 4/15; applicants required to submit FAFSA. *Unit head:* Dr. Dorothy A. Gomez, RN, Dean, 317-955-6159, E-mail: dgomez@marian.edu. *Application contact:* Bryan Moody, Executive Director of Graduate Admission, 317-955-6284, E-mail: bmoody@marian.edu.
Website: http://www.marian.edu/school-of-nursing

Marshall University, Academic Affairs Division, College of Business, Program in Nurse Anesthesia, Huntington, WV 25755. Offers DMPNA. Program offered jointly with Charleston Area Medical Center. *Students:* 77 full-time (44 women); includes 11 minority (2 Black or African American, non-Hispanic/Latino; 2 Asian, non-Hispanic/Latino; 4 Hispanic/Latino; 3 Two or more races, non-Hispanic/Latino). Average age 31. In 2017, 28 doctorates awarded. *Unit head:* Dr. Nancy Tierney, Director, 304-388-9950, E-mail: nancy.tierney@camc.org. *Application contact:* Information Contact, Graduate Admissions, 304-746-1900, Fax: 304-746-1902, E-mail: services@marshall.edu.
Website: http://camcinstitute.org/anesthesia/

Mayo Clinic School of Health Sciences, Doctor of Nurse Anesthesia Practice Program, Rochester, MN 55905. Offers DNAP. *Accreditation:* AANA/CANAEP. *Degree requirements:* For doctorate, comprehensive exam, research project. *Entrance requirements:* For doctorate, GRE General Test, official transcripts, three references, essay, RN license. Additional exam requirements/recommendations for international students: Required—TOEFL. *Application deadline:* For fall admission, 8/1 for domestic students. Application fee: $50. Electronic applications accepted. *Expenses:* Contact institution. *Financial support:* Institutionally sponsored loans, scholarships/grants, health care benefits, and stipends available. Financial award applicants required to submit FAFSA. *Unit head:* Dr. Mary E. Marienau, Director, 507-284-8331, Fax: 507-284-2818, E-mail: marienau.mary@mayo.edu. *Application contact:* Julie Predmore, Administrative Assistant, 507-286-4163, Fax: 507-284-2818, E-mail: predmore.julie@mayo.edu.

Medical University of South Carolina, College of Health Professions, Anesthesia for Nurses Program, Charleston, SC 29425. Offers MSNA. *Accreditation:* AANA/CANAEP. *Degree requirements:* For master's, comprehensive exam, research project, clinical practica. *Entrance requirements:* For master's, GRE General Test, interview, minimum GPA of 3.0, 2 years of RN (ICU) experience, RN license. Additional exam requirements/recommendations for international students: Required—TOEFL (minimum score 600 paper-based). Electronic applications accepted. *Faculty research:* Stress in nurse anesthesia, economic changes and continuing education.

Middle Tennessee School of Anesthesia, Graduate Programs, Madison, TN 37116. Offers MS, DNAP. *Accreditation:* AANA/CANAEP. *Degree requirements:* For master's, project; for doctorate, capstone project. *Entrance requirements:* For master's, GRE General Test, RN license, 1 year of critical-care nursing experience, BSN, general chemistry (minimum of 3 semester hours).

Midwestern University, Glendale Campus, College of Health Sciences, Arizona Campus, Program in Nurse Anesthesia, Glendale, AZ 85308. Offers MS. *Accreditation:* AANA/CANAEP. Application fee: $50. *Expenses:* Contact institution.
Website: http://www.midwestern.edu/course-catalog-home/glendale-az-campus-/college-of-health-sciences/nurse-anesthesia-program.html

Millikin University, School of Nursing, Decatur, IL 62522-2084. Offers entry into nursing practice (MSN); family nurse practitioner (DNP); nurse anesthesia (DNP); nurse educator (MSN). *Accreditation:* AACN. *Program availability:* Part-time. *Faculty:* 19 full-time (17 women), 7 part-time/adjunct (6 women). *Students:* 42 full-time (30 women), 20 part-time (17 women); includes 12 minority (8 Black or African American, non-Hispanic/Latino; 2 Asian, non-Hispanic/Latino; 2 Hispanic/Latino). Average age 30. 114 applicants, 36% accepted, 23 enrolled. In 2017, 3 master's, 13 doctorates awarded. *Degree requirements:* For master's, thesis or alternative, scholarly project; for doctorate, thesis/dissertation or alternative, scholarly project. *Entrance requirements:* For master's, GRE (if undergraduate cumulative GPA is below 3.0 for nurse educator, 3.25 for entry into nursing practice), official academic transcript(s), written statement, resume/vitae, 3 letters of recommendation, RN license; for doctorate, GRE (if undergraduate cumulative GPA is below 3.0), official academic transcript(s), written statement, resume/vitae, 3 letters of recommendation, RN or APRN license. Additional exam requirements/recommendations for international students: Required—TOEFL (minimum score 550 paper-based; 79 iBT), IELTS (minimum score 6.5). *Application deadline:* For spring admission, 7/1 priority date for domestic and international students; for summer admission, 11/1 priority date for domestic and international students. Applications are processed on a rolling basis. Application fee: $0. Electronic applications accepted. *Expenses:* $832 per credit hour (for MSN); $950 per credit hour (for DNP). *Financial support:* Traineeships and unspecified assistantships available. Financial award applicants required to submit FAFSA. *Faculty research:* Quality of life, teaching/learning strategies, clinical simulation. *Unit head:* Dr. Pamela Lindsey, Director, 217-424-6348, Fax: 217-420-6731, E-mail: plindsey@millikin.edu. *Application contact:* Bonnie Niemeyer, Administrative Assistant, 800-373-7733 Ext. 5034, Fax: 217-420-6731, E-mail: bniemeyer@millikin.edu.
Website: http://www.millikin.edu/grad-nursing

Missouri State University, Graduate College, College of Health and Human Services, Department of Biomedical Sciences, Program in Nurse Anesthesia, Springfield, MO 65897. Offers DNAP. *Accreditation:* AANA/CANAEP. *Faculty:* 27 full-time (19 women), 3 part-time/adjunct (0 women). *Students:* 85 full-time (42 women), 49 part-time (30 women); includes 23 minority (11 Black or African American, non-Hispanic/Latino; 6 Asian, non-Hispanic/Latino; 4 Hispanic/Latino; 1 Native Hawaiian or other Pacific Islander, non-Hispanic/Latino; 1 Two or more races, non-Hispanic/Latino). Average age 28. 22 applicants, 95% accepted, 19 enrolled. In 2017, 42 doctorates awarded. *Entrance requirements:* Additional exam requirements/recommendations for international students: Required—TOEFL (minimum score 550 paper-based; 79 iBT), IELTS (minimum score 6). *Application deadline:* For fall admission, 11/1 for domestic and international students; for spring admission, 7/1 for domestic and international students. Application fee: $35 ($50 for international students). Electronic applications accepted. *Expenses:* Tuition, state resident: full-time $2915; part-time $2021 per credit hour. Tuition, nonresident: full-time $5354; part-time $3647 per credit hour. *International tuition:* $11,992 full-time. *Required fees:* $173; $173 per credit hour. Tuition and fees vary according to class time, course level, course load, degree level, campus/location and program. *Financial support:* In 2017–18, 2 teaching assistantships with full tuition reimbursements (averaging $8,772 per year) were awarded; career-related internships or fieldwork and institutionally sponsored loans also available. Support available to part-time students. Financial award application deadline: 3/31; financial award applicants required to submit FAFSA. *Unit head:* Monika Feeney, Program Director, 417-838-5603, Fax: 417-836-5588, E-mail: monikafeeney@missouristate.edu. *Application contact:* Stephanie Praschan, Director, Graduate Enrollment Management, 417-836-5330, Fax: 417-836-6200, E-mail: stephaniepraschan@missouristate.edu.

Mount Marty College, Graduate Studies Division, Yankton, SD 57078-3724. Offers business administration (MBA); nurse anesthesia (MS); nursing (MSN); pastoral ministries (MPM). *Accreditation:* AANA/CANAEP (one or more programs are accredited). *Degree requirements:* For master's, thesis or alternative. *Entrance requirements:* For master's, GRE General Test, minimum GPA of 3.0. Electronic applications accepted. *Faculty research:* Clinical anesthesia, professional characteristics, motivations of applicants.

Murray State University, School of Nursing and Health Professions, Department of Nursing, Murray, KY 42071. Offers family nurse practitioner (DNP); nurse anesthetist (DNP). *Accreditation:* AACN; AANA/CANAEP. *Program availability:* Evening/weekend, 100% online, blended/hybrid learning. *Faculty:* 7 full-time (6 women), 1 part-time/adjunct (0 women). *Students:* 63 full-time (45 women), 21 part-time (17 women); includes 12 minority (8 Black or African American, non-Hispanic/Latino; 3 Asian, non-Hispanic/Latino; 1 Two or more races, non-Hispanic/Latino). Average age 33. 85 applicants, 35% accepted, 21 enrolled. In 2017, 26 doctorates awarded. *Entrance requirements:* For doctorate, GRE, minimum university GPA of 2.75. Additional exam requirements/recommendations for international students: Required—TOEFL (minimum score 527 paper-based; 71 iBT). *Application deadline:* Applications are processed on a rolling basis. Application fee: $30. Electronic applications accepted. *Expenses:* Tuition, state resident: full-time $9504. Tuition, nonresident: full-time $26,811. *International tuition:* $14,400 full-time. Tuition and fees vary according to course load, degree level and reciprocity agreements. *Financial support:* Federal Work-Study, scholarships/grants, and unspecified assistantships available. Financial award applicants required to submit FAFSA. *Unit head:* Dr. Marcia Hobbs, Dean, School of Nursing and Health Professions, 270-809-3196, Fax: 270-809-6662, E-mail: mhobbs4@murraystate.edu. *Application contact:* Kaitlyn Burzynski, Interim Assistant Director for Graduate Admission and Records, 270-809-5732, Fax: 270-809-3780, E-mail: msu.graduateadmissions@murraystate.edu.

National University, School of Health and Human Services, La Jolla, CA 92037-1011. Offers clinical affairs (MS); clinical regulatory affairs (MS); complementary and integrative healthcare (MS); family nurse practitioner (MSN); health and life science analytics (MS); health informatics (MS, Certificate); healthcare administration (MHA); nurse anesthesia (MSNA); nursing administration (MSN); nursing informatics (MSN); psychiatric-mental health nurse practitioner (MSN); public health (MPH), including health promotion, healthcare administration, mental health. *Program availability:* Part-time, evening/weekend, 100% online, blended/hybrid learning. *Degree requirements:* For master's, thesis (for some programs). *Entrance requirements:* For master's, interview, minimum GPA of 2.5. Additional exam requirements/recommendations for international students: Required—TOEFL (minimum score 550 paper-based; 79 iBT), IELTS (minimum score 6). *Application deadline:* Applications are processed on a rolling basis. Application fee: $60 ($65 for international students). Electronic applications accepted. *Expenses:* Tuition: Part-time $430 per quarter hour. *Financial support:* Career-related internships or fieldwork, institutionally sponsored loans, scholarships/grants, and tuition waivers (partial) available. Support available to part-time students. Financial award application deadline: 6/30; financial award applicants required to submit FAFSA. *Faculty research:* Nursing education, obesity prevention, workforce diversity. *Unit head:* Dr. Gloria J. McNeal, Dean, 858-309-3473, E-mail: shhs@nu.edu. *Application contact:* Brandon Jouganatos, Vice President for Enrollment Services, 800-628-8648, E-mail: advisor@nu.edu.
Website: http://www.nu.edu/OurPrograms/SchoolOfHealthAndHumanServices.html

Newman University, School of Nursing and Allied Health, Wichita, KS 67213-2097. Offers nurse anesthesia (MS). *Accreditation:* AANA/CANAEP. *Degree requirements:* For master's, thesis optional. *Entrance requirements:* For master's, GRE General Test, registered professional nursing license in Kansas, 3 professional recommendations, 1-page letter detailing professional and educational goals, BSN, statistics course, 1 year of employment, interview. Additional exam requirements/recommendations for international students: Required—TOEFL (minimum score 600 paper-based; 100 iBT). Electronic applications accepted. *Expenses:* Contact institution.

Oakland University, Graduate Study and Lifelong Learning, School of Nursing, Program in Nurse Anesthetist, Rochester, MI 48309-4401. Offers nurse anesthesia (MSN, PMC). Programs offered jointly with Beaumont Hospital Corporation. *Accreditation:* AACN; AANA/CANAEP. *Degree requirements:* For master's, thesis (for some programs). *Entrance requirements:* For master's, GRE General Test. Additional exam requirements/recommendations for international students: Required—TOEFL (minimum score 550 paper-based). Electronic applications accepted. *Expenses:* Contact institution.

Old Dominion University, College of Health Sciences, School of Nursing, Nurse Anesthesia Program, Virginia Beach, VA 23452. Offers DNP. *Accreditation:* AANA/CANAEP. *Faculty:* 2 full-time (1 woman), 2 part-time/adjunct (1 woman). *Students:* 36 full-time (26 women); includes 7 minority (1 Black or African American, non-Hispanic/Latino; 1 American Indian or Alaska Native, non-Hispanic/Latino; 3 Asian, non-Hispanic/Latino; 1 Hispanic/Latino; 1 Two or more races, non-Hispanic/Latino). Average age 31. 45 applicants, 42% accepted, 18 enrolled. *Degree requirements:* For doctorate, comprehensive exam, thesis/dissertation. *Entrance requirements:* For doctorate, GRE. *Application deadline:* For fall admission, 9/15 priority date for domestic students. Application fee: $50. Electronic applications accepted. *Expenses:* Contact institution. *Financial support:* Traineeships available. Financial award application deadline: 5/7; financial award applicants required to submit FAFSA. *Faculty research:* Wellness, pain, anesthesia, handoff. *Unit head:* Dr. Nathaniel Michael Apatov, Graduate Program Director, 757-368-4174, Fax: 757-386-4176, E-mail: napatov@odu.edu. *Application contact:* Sue Parker, Coordinator, Graduate Student Services, 757-683-4298, Fax: 757-683-5253, E-mail: sparker@odu.edu.
Website: http://catalog.odu.edu/graduate/collegeofhealthsciences/schoolofnursing/#masterofscienceinnursing013nurseanesthesiarole

Oregon Health & Science University, School of Nursing, Program in Nurse Anesthesia, Portland, OR 97239-3098. Offers MN. *Accreditation:* AANA/CANAEP. *Entrance requirements:* For master's, GRE, BS with major in nursing or BSN, licensed in state of Oregon, at least one year of adult or pediatric critical care ICU experience, statistics in last 5 years with minimum B- grade, three letters of reference. Additional exam requirements/recommendations for international students: Required—TOEFL (minimum score 83 iBT). Electronic applications accepted. *Expenses:* Contact institution. *Faculty research:* Anesthesia-related issues; traumatic brain injury patients.

Otterbein University, Department of Nursing, Westerville, OH 43081. Offers advanced practice nurse educator (Certificate); clinical nurse leader (MSN); family nurse practitioner (MSN, Certificate); nurse anesthesia (MSN, Certificate); nursing (DNP); nursing service administration (MSN). *Accreditation:* AACN; AANA/CANAEP; ACEN. *Program availability:* Part-time, evening/weekend, online learning. *Degree requirements:* For master's, comprehensive exam (for some programs), thesis (for some programs). *Entrance requirements:* For master's, 2 reference forms, resume; for Certificate, official transcripts, 2 reference forms, essay, resumé. Additional exam requirements/recommendations for international students: Required—TOEFL (minimum score 550 paper-based; 79 iBT). *Faculty research:* Patient education, women's health, trauma curriculum development, administration.

Quinnipiac University, School of Nursing, Post-Bachelor's Nurse Anesthesia Track, Hamden, CT 06518-1940. Offers DNP. *Faculty:* 18 full-time (17 women), 11 part-time/adjunct (8 women). *Students:* 19 full-time (14 women), 10 part-time (8 women); includes 7 minority (2 Black or African American, non-Hispanic/Latino; 3 Asian, non-Hispanic/Latino; 2 Hispanic/Latino). 60 applicants, 27% accepted, 9 enrolled. In 2017, 5 doctorates awarded. *Entrance requirements:* For doctorate, bachelor's degree in nursing or appropriate science, RN license, minimum GPA of 3.0, specific core science courses completed within the last 10 years, critical care experience within the last 5 years. *Application deadline:* For summer admission, 10/15 for domestic students. Applications are processed on a rolling basis. Application fee: $45. Electronic applications accepted. *Financial support:* Federal Work-Study, scholarships/grants, and unspecified assistantships available. Financial award application deadline: 4/30; financial award applicants required to submit FAFSA. *Unit head:* Judy Thompson, Program Director, 203-582-8875, E-mail: graduate@qu.edu. *Application contact:* Office of Graduate Admissions, 800-462-1944, Fax: 203-582-3443, E-mail: graduate@qu.edu.
Website: http://www.qu.edu/gradnursing

Quinnipiac University, School of Nursing, Post-Master's Nurse Anesthesia Track, Hamden, CT 06518-1940. Offers DNP. *Accreditation:* AANA/CANAEP. *Program availability:* Part-time-only, evening/weekend, online only. *Faculty:* 17 full-time (16 women), 10 part-time/adjunct (6 women). *Students:* 24 part-time (21 women); includes 11 minority (5 Black or African American, non-Hispanic/Latino; 3 Asian, non-Hispanic/Latino; 3 Hispanic/Latino). 21 applicants, 95% accepted, 20 enrolled. In 2017, 3 doctorates awarded. *Entrance requirements:* For doctorate, bachelor's degree in nursing or another field; minimum GPA of 3.0; current BCLS, ACLS and CRNA certifications. *Application deadline:* Applications are processed on a rolling basis. Application fee: $45. Electronic applications accepted. *Expenses:* Contact institution. *Financial support:* Federal Work-Study and scholarships/grants available. Financial award application deadline: 6/1; financial award applicants required to submit FAFSA. *Unit head:* Judy Thompson, Assistant Professor, 203-582-8875, E-mail: quonlineadmissions@qu.edu. *Application contact:* Quinnipiac University Online Admissions Office, 203-582-3918, E-mail: quonlineadmissions@qu.edu.
Website: https://quonline.quinnipiac.edu/online-programs/online-doctorate-programs/doctor-of-nursing-practice/nurse-anesthesia-track/

Rosalind Franklin University of Medicine and Science, College of Health Professions, Nurse Anesthesia Department, North Chicago, IL 60064-3095. Offers DNAP. *Accreditation:* AANA/CANAEP. *Entrance requirements:* For doctorate, interview. Additional exam requirements/recommendations for international students: Required—TOEFL. Electronic applications accepted. *Faculty research:* Patient safety, pediatric anesthesia, instructional technology.

Rush University, College of Nursing, Department of Adult Health and Gerontological Nursing, Chicago, IL 60612. Offers adult gerontology acute care clinical nurse specialist (DNP); adult gerontology acute care nurse practitioner (DNP, Post-Graduate Certificate); adult gerontology primary care nurse practitioner (DNP); nurse anesthesia (DNP). *Accreditation:* AACN; AANA/CANAEP (one or more programs are accredited). *Program availability:* Part-time. *Students:* 98 full-time (68 women), 155 part-time (17 women); includes 48 minority (7 Black or African American, non-Hispanic/Latino; 22 Asian, non-Hispanic/Latino; 14 Hispanic/Latino; 5 Two or more races, non-Hispanic/Latino). 170 applicants, 54% accepted, 69 enrolled. In 2017, 51 doctorates awarded. *Degree requirements:* For doctorate, scholarly project. *Entrance requirements:* For doctorate, GRE General Test (for nurse anesthesia; waived for other DNPs if cumulative GPA is 3.25 or greater, nursing GPA is 3.0 or greater, or a completed graduate program GPA is 3.5 or greater), interview, 3 letters of recommendation, personal statement, current resume; for Post-Graduate Certificate, MSN in a clinical discipline, 3 letters of recommendation, personal statement, current resume, interview. Additional exam requirements/recommendations for international students: Required—TOEFL (minimum score 94 iBT). *Application deadline:* For fall admission, 1/2 for domestic students; for spring admission, 8/1 for domestic students; for summer admission, 12/1 for domestic students. Applications are processed on a rolling basis. Application fee: $110. Electronic applications accepted. *Expenses:* Contact institution. *Financial support:* Research assistantships, teaching assistantships, Federal Work-Study, institutionally sponsored loans, scholarships/grants, traineeships, and health care benefits available. Support available to part-time students. Financial award application deadline: 3/1; financial award applicants required to submit FAFSA. *Faculty research:* Physical activity; prevention; cardiovascular risk; caregivers; gerontology. *Unit head:* Dr. Elizabeth Carlson, Chairperson, 312-942-7117, E-mail: elizabeth_carlson@rush.edu. *Application contact:* Jennifer Thorndyke, Director of Admissions, 312-563-7526, E-mail: jennifer_thorndyke@rush.edu.
Website: https://www.rushu.rush.edu/college-nursing/departments-college-nursing/department-adult-health-and-gerontological-nursing

Rutgers University–Newark, Rutgers School of Nursing, Newark, NJ 07107-3001. Offers adult health (MSN); adult occupational health (MSN); advanced practice nursing (MSN, Post Master's Certificate); family nurse practitioner (MSN); nurse anesthesia (MSN); nursing (MSN); nursing informatics (MSN); urban health (PhD); women's health practitioner (MSN). *Accreditation:* AANA/CANAEP. *Program availability:* Part-time. *Entrance requirements:* For master's, GRE, RN license; basic life support, statistics, and health assessment experience. Additional exam requirements/recommendations for international students: Required—TOEFL. Electronic applications accepted. *Expenses:* Contact institution. *Faculty research:* HIV/AIDS, diabetes education, learned helplessness, nursing science, psychoeducation.

Saint Mary's University of Minnesota, Schools of Graduate and Professional Programs, Graduate School of Health and Human Services, Nurse Anesthesia Program, Winona, MN 55987-1399. Offers MS. Program offered jointly with the Minneapolis School of Anesthesia. *Accreditation:* AANA/CANAEP. *Unit head:* Merri Moody, Director, 612-728-5133. *Application contact:* James Callinan, Director of Admissions for Graduate and Professional Programs, 612-728-5158, Fax: 612-728-5121, E-mail: jcallina@smumn.edu.
Website: http://www.smumn.edu/graduate-home/areas-of-study/graduate-school-of-health-human-services/ms-in-nurse-anesthesia

Saint Vincent College, Program in Health Science, Latrobe, PA 15650-2690. Offers nurse anesthesia (MS).

Samford University, Ida Moffett School of Nursing, Birmingham, AL 35229. Offers administration (DNP); advanced practice (DNP); dual nurse practitioner (family/emergency) (DNP); family nurse practitioner (MSN, DNP); nurse anesthesia (MSN, DNP); nursing administration (DNP), including health systems and administration, informatics, transformation of care. *Accreditation:* AACN; AANA/CANAEP. *Program availability:* Part-time, evening/weekend, blended/hybrid learning. *Faculty:* 20 full-time (19 women), 3 part-time/adjunct (0 women). *Students:* 296 full-time (240 women), 41 part-time (38 women); includes 67 minority (43 Black or African American, non-Hispanic/Latino; 2 American Indian or Alaska Native, non-Hispanic/Latino; 6 Asian, non-Hispanic/Latino; 8 Hispanic/Latino; 8 Two or more races, non-Hispanic/Latino). Average age 35. 79 applicants, 71% accepted, 29 enrolled. In 2017, 117 master's, 39 doctorates awarded. *Degree requirements:* For doctorate, project with poster presentation. *Entrance requirements:* For master's, GRE within the past five years (for nurse anesthesia), RN, minimum nursing GPA of 3.0, undergraduate course in nursing research with minimum C grade, undergraduate health assessment course with minimum B grade; interview, 1 year full-time critical care as RN, 3 letters of recommendation, undergraduate courses in general chemistry and research with minimum B grade for both (for nurse anesthesia); for doctorate, unencumbered licensure as registered nurse; master's degree from CCNE-, CNEA-, or ACEN-accredited program in the area of advanced practice or administration; minimum master's degree cumulative GPA of 3.5; video interview submission. Additional exam requirements/recommendations for international students: Required—TOEFL (minimum score 575 paper-based; 90 iBT); Recommended—IELTS (minimum score 6.5). *Application deadline:* For fall admission, 4/1 for domestic and international students; for spring admission, 8/1 for domestic and international students; for summer admission, 1/1 for domestic and international students. Application fee: $50. Electronic applications accepted. *Expenses:* $809 per credit (for DNP and MSN); $9,737 per semester (for MSN in nurse anesthesia). *Financial support:* In 2017–18, 63 students received support. Application deadline: 2/15; applicants required to submit FAFSA. *Unit head:* Dr. Nena F. Sanders, Vice Provost, College of Health Sciences/Ida Moffett School of Nursing Dean/Professor, 205-726-2612, E-mail: nfsander@samford.edu. *Application contact:* Allyson Maddox, Director of Graduate Student Services, 205-726-2047, E-mail: amaddox@samford.edu.
Website: http://samford.edu/nursing

Samuel Merritt University, School of Nursing, Oakland, CA 94609-3108. Offers case management (MSN); family nurse practitioner (MSN, DNP, Certificate); nurse anesthetist (MSN, Certificate); nursing (DNP). *Accreditation:* AACN; AANA/CANAEP (one or more programs are accredited). *Program availability:* Part-time, evening/weekend, 100% online, blended/hybrid learning. *Faculty:* 57 full-time (49 women), 90 part-time/adjunct (77 women). *Students:* 401 full-time (322 women), 267 part-time (202 women); includes 438 minority (52 Black or African American, non-Hispanic/Latino; 4 American Indian or Alaska Native, non-Hispanic/Latino; 224 Asian, non-Hispanic/Latino; 108 Hispanic/Latino; 9 Native Hawaiian or other Pacific Islander, non-Hispanic/Latino; 41 Two or more races, non-Hispanic/Latino). 788 applicants, 54% accepted, 306 enrolled. In 2017, 176 master's, 6 doctorates, 7 other advanced degrees awarded. *Degree requirements:* For master's, thesis or alternative; for doctorate, project. *Entrance requirements:* For master's, GRE General Test (for nurse anesthetist program), minimum GPA of 2.5 in science, 3.0 overall; previous course work in statistics; current RN license; for doctorate and Certificate, minimum GPA of 2.5 in science, 3.0 overall; previous course work in statistics; current RN license. Additional exam requirements/recommendations for international students: Required—TOEFL (minimum score 100 iBT). *Application deadline:* For fall admission, 7/1 priority date for domestic students; for spring admission, 11/1 priority date for domestic students; for summer admission, 3/1 priority date for domestic students. Applications are processed on a rolling basis. Application fee: $65. Electronic applications accepted. *Expenses:* $1,394 per unit tuition (for MSN); $1,208 per unit tuition (for DNP). *Financial support:* Career-related internships or fieldwork, Federal Work-Study, scholarships/grants, and traineeships available. Support available to part-time students. Financial award applicants required to submit FAFSA. *Faculty research:* Gerontology, community health, maternal-child health, sexually transmitted diseases, substance abuse, oncology. *Unit head:* Dr. Audrey Berman, Dean of Nursing, 510-869-6733, Fax: 510-869-6525. *Application contact:* Timothy Cranford, Dean of Admission, 510-869-6576, Fax: 510-869-6525, E-mail: admission@samuelmerritt.edu.
Website: http://www.samuelmerritt.edu/nursing

Southern Illinois University Edwardsville, Graduate School, School of Nursing, Doctor of Nursing Practice Program, Edwardsville, IL 62026. Offers family nurse practitioner (DNP); nurse anesthesia (DNP); nursing (DNP). *Accreditation:* AACN. *Program availability:* Part-time, evening/weekend. *Degree requirements:* For doctorate, thesis/dissertation or alternative, project. *Entrance requirements:* Additional exam requirements/recommendations for international students: Required—TOEFL (minimum score 550 paper-based; 79 iBT), IELTS (minimum score 6.5). Electronic applications accepted.

State University of New York Downstate Medical Center, College of Nursing, Graduate Programs in Nursing, Program in Nurse Anesthesia, Brooklyn, NY 11203-2098. Offers MS. *Accreditation:* AACN; AANA/CANAEP. *Degree requirements:* For master's, thesis optional. *Entrance requirements:* For master's, GRE, BSN; minimum GPA of 3.0; previous undergraduate course work in statistics, health assessment, and nursing research; RN license.

Texas Christian University, Harris College of Nursing and Health Sciences, School of Nurse Anesthesia, Fort Worth, TX 76129. Offers DNP-A. *Accreditation:* AANA/CANAEP. *Faculty:* 10 full-time (5 women), 3 part-time/adjunct (2 women). *Students:* 164 full-time (99 women); includes 25 minority (4 Black or African American, non-Hispanic/Latino; 7 Asian, non-Hispanic/Latino; 8 Hispanic/Latino; 1 Native Hawaiian or other Pacific Islander, non-Hispanic/Latino; 5 Two or more races, non-Hispanic/Latino). Average age 30. 201 applicants, 36% accepted, 66 enrolled. In 2017, 58 doctorates awarded. *Entrance requirements:* For doctorate, GRE General Test, writing sample. Additional exam requirements/recommendations for international students: Required—TOEFL (minimum score 600 paper-based; 94 iBT). *Application deadline:* For fall and spring admission, 7/1 for domestic and international students. Applications are processed on a rolling basis. Application fee: $60. Electronic applications accepted. *Expenses:* Contact institution. *Financial support:* In 2017–18, 3 students received support. Scholarships/grants available. Financial award application deadline: 7/1; financial award applicants required to submit FAFSA. *Faculty research:* Anesthesia, genetics. *Unit head:* Dr. Kay K. Sanders, Director, 817-257-7887, Fax: 817-257-5472, E-mail: k.sanders@tcu.edu. *Application contact:* Stephanie Morton Dwight, Administrative Assistant, 817-257-7887, Fax: 817-257-5472, E-mail: s.m.dwight@tcu.edu.
Website: http://www.crna.tcu.edu/

Texas Wesleyan University, Graduate Programs, Programs in Nurse Anesthesia, Fort Worth, TX 76105. Offers MHS, MSNA, DNAP. *Accreditation:* AANA/CANAEP (one or more programs are accredited). *Faculty:* 19 full-time (10 women), 14 part-time/adjunct (10 women). *Students:* 375 full-time (201 women); includes 115 minority (27 Black or African American, non-Hispanic/Latino; 3 American Indian or Alaska Native, non-Hispanic/Latino; 27 Asian, non-Hispanic/Latino; 42 Hispanic/Latino; 2 Native Hawaiian or other Pacific Islander, non-Hispanic/Latino; 14 Two or more races, non-Hispanic/Latino), 1 international. Average age 33. 448 applicants, 38% accepted, 133 enrolled. In 2017, 107 master's, 21 doctorates awarded. *Entrance requirements:* For master's, GRE General Test, bachelor's degree, minimum GPA of 3.0, college-level chemistry within three years of start date, current unrestricted RN license valid in one of the 50 states or U.S. territories, minimum of one year of full-time critical care, current ACLS and PALS certifications; for doctorate, master's degree, RN license, CRNA certification/recertification, minimum GPA of 3.0 overall or on last 60 hours, graduate-level research course with minimum grade of B, current curriculum vitae. *Application deadline:* For fall admission, 10/15 priority date for domestic students. Applications are processed on a rolling basis. Electronic applications accepted. *Expenses:* Contact institution. *Financial support:* Federal Work-Study, institutionally sponsored loans, scholarships/grants, and tuition waivers (full and partial) available. Support available to part-time students.

Financial award application deadline: 3/15; financial award applicants required to submit FAFSA. *Faculty research:* Life support device validation and performance, efficacious implementation of evidence-based interventions such as clinical practice guidelines, thermoregulation in the perioperative clinical simulation. *Unit head:* Dr. Heidi Taylor, Dean, School of Health Professions, 817-531-4257, Fax: 817-531-6508, E-mail: htaylor@txwes.edu. *Application contact:* Tommie Kates, Coordinator, 817-531-4279, Fax: 817-531-6508, E-mail: tkates@txwes.edu.
Website: http://www.txwes.edu/academics/gpna

Uniformed Services University of the Health Sciences, Daniel K. Inouye Graduate School of Nursing, Bethesda, MD 20814. Offers adult-gerontology clinical nurse specialist (MSN, DNP); family nurse practitioner (DNP); nurse anesthesia (DNP); nursing science (PhD); psychiatric mental health nurse practitioner (DNP); women's health nurse practitioner (DNP). *Accreditation:* AACN; AANA/CANAEP. *Faculty:* 42 full-time (28 women), 2 part-time/adjunct (1 woman). *Students:* 170 full-time (98 women); includes 51 minority (21 Black or African American, non-Hispanic/Latino; 17 Asian, non-Hispanic/Latino; 11 Hispanic/Latino; 2 Native Hawaiian or other Pacific Islander, non-Hispanic/Latino). Average age 34. 88 applicants, 75% accepted, 66 enrolled. In 2017, 55 doctorates awarded. *Degree requirements:* For master's, thesis, scholarly project; for doctorate, dissertation (for PhD); project (for DNP). *Entrance requirements:* For master's, GRE, BSN, clinical experience, minimum GPA of 3.0, previous course work in science; for doctorate, GRE, BSN, minimum GPA of 3.0, undergraduate/graduate science course within past 5 years, writing example, interview (for some programs), and 3 letters of reference (for DNP); master's degree, minimum GPA of 3.0 in nursing or related field, personal statement, 3 references, and interview (for PhD). *Application deadline:* For winter admission, 2/15 for domestic students; for summer admission, 8/15 for domestic students. Application fee: $0. Electronic applications accepted. *Expenses:* There are no tuition costs or fees; students incur obligated service according to the requirements of their sponsoring organization. *Faculty research:* Military health care, military readiness, women's health, family, behavioral health. *Total annual research expenditures:* $100,000. *Unit head:* Dr. Diane C. Seibert, Associate Dean for Academic Affairs, 301-295-1080, Fax: 301-295-1707, E-mail: diane.seibert@usuhs.edu. *Application contact:* Maureen Jackson, Registrar, 301-295-1055, Fax: 301-295-1707, E-mail: maureen.jackson.ctr@usuhs.edu.
Website: http://www.usuhs.edu/gsn/

Union University, School of Nursing, Jackson, TN 38305-3697. Offers executive leadership (DNP); nurse anesthesia (DNP); nurse practitioner (DNP); nursing education (MSN, PMC). *Accreditation:* AACN; AANA/CANAEP. *Degree requirements:* For master's, thesis or alternative. *Entrance requirements:* For master's, GRE, 3 letters of reference, bachelor's degree in nursing, minimum GPA of 3.0. Additional exam requirements/recommendations for international students: Required—TOEFL (minimum score 560 paper-based). Electronic applications accepted. *Faculty research:* Children's health, occupational rehabilitation, informatics, health promotion.

University at Buffalo, the State University of New York, Graduate School, School of Nursing, Buffalo, NY 14260. Offers adult gerontology nurse practitioner (DNP); family nurse practitioner (DNP); health care systems and leadership (MS); nurse anesthetist (DNP); nursing (PhD); nursing education (Certificate); psychiatric/mental health nurse practitioner (DNP). *Accreditation:* AACN; AANA/CANAEP (one or more programs are accredited). *Program availability:* Part-time, 100% online. *Faculty:* 41 full-time (36 women), 15 part-time/adjunct (all women). *Students:* 64 full-time (39 women), 136 part-time (120 women); includes 32 minority (13 Black or African American, non-Hispanic/Latino; 1 American Indian or Alaska Native, non-Hispanic/Latino; 18 Asian, non-Hispanic/Latino). Average age 34. 182 applicants, 39% accepted, 50 enrolled. In 2017, 3 master's, 32 doctorates, 2 other advanced degrees awarded. *Degree requirements:* For master's, thesis optional; for doctorate, comprehensive exam (for some programs), capstone (for DNP), dissertation (for PhD). *Entrance requirements:* For master's, GRE or MAT; for doctorate, GRE or MAT, minimum GPA of 3.0 (for DNP), 3.25 (for PhD); RN license; BS or MS in nursing; 3 references; writing sample; resume; personal statement; for Certificate, interview, minimum GPA of 3.0 or GRE General Test, RN license, MS in nursing, professional certification. Additional exam requirements/recommendations for international students: Required—TOEFL (minimum score 550 paper-based; 79 iBT), IELTS (minimum score 6.5). *Application deadline:* For fall admission, 4/1 for domestic students, 2/1 for international students; for spring admission, 1/15 for domestic students, 10/1 for international students; for summer admission, 4/1 for domestic students. Applications are processed on a rolling basis. Application fee: $75. Electronic applications accepted. *Expenses:* Contact institution. *Financial support:* In 2017–18, 80 students received support, including 2 fellowships with tuition reimbursements available (averaging $17,000 per year), 4 research assistantships with tuition reimbursements available (averaging $10,600 per year), 7 teaching assistantships with tuition reimbursements available (averaging $10,600 per year); scholarships/grants, traineeships, health care benefits, and unspecified assistantships also available. Financial award application deadline: 4/1; financial award applicants required to submit FAFSA. *Faculty research:* Oncology, palliative care, gerontology, addictions, mental health, community wellness, sleep, workforce, care of underserved populations, quality and safety, person-centered care, adolescent health. *Total annual research expenditures:* $1.4 million. *Unit head:* Dr. Marsha L. Lewis, Dean and Professor, 716-829-2533, Fax: 716-829-2566, E-mail: ubnursingdean@buffalo.edu. *Application contact:* Jennifer H. Schreier, Director of Graduate Student Services, 716-829-3311, Fax: 716-829-2067, E-mail: jhv2@buffalo.edu.
Website: http://nursing.buffalo.edu/

The University of Alabama at Birmingham, School of Nursing, Birmingham, AL 35294-1210. Offers clinical nurse leader (MSN); nurse anesthesia (DNP); nurse practitioner (MSN, DNP), including adult-gerontology acute care (MSN), adult-gerontology primary care (MSN), family (MSN), pediatric (MSN), psychiatric/mental health (MSN), women's health (MSN); nursing (MSN, DNP, PhD); nursing health systems administration (MSN); nursing informatics (MSN). *Accreditation:* AACN; AANA/CANAEP. *Program availability:* Part-time, online only, blended/hybrid learning. Terminal master's awarded for partial completion of doctoral program. *Degree requirements:* For master's, comprehensive exam; for doctorate, comprehensive exam, thesis/dissertation, research mentorship experience (for PhD); scholarly project (for DNP). *Entrance requirements:* For master's, GRE, GMAT, or MAT, minimum cumulative undergraduate GPA of 3.0 or on last 60 semesters hours; letters of recommendation; for doctorate, GRE General Test, computer literacy, course work in statistics, interview, minimum GPA of 3.0, MS in nursing, references, writing sample. Additional exam requirements/recommendations for international students: Required—TOEFL (minimum score 500 paper-based, 80 iBT) or IELTS (5.5). Electronic applications accepted. *Expenses:* Contact institution. *Faculty research:* Palliative care; oncology; aging; HIV/AIDS; nursing work environments.

University of Cincinnati, Graduate School, College of Nursing, Cincinnati, OH 45221-0038. Offers nurse midwifery (MSN); nurse practitioner (MSN, DNP), including acute care pediatrics (DNP), adult-gerontology acute care, adult-gerontology primary care, anesthesia (DNP), family (MSN), leadership (DNP), neonatal (MSN), women's health (MSN); nursing (MSN, PhD), including occupational health (MSN). *Accreditation:* AACN; AANA/CANAEP (one or more programs are accredited); ACNM/ACME. *Program availability:* Part-time, 100% online, blended/hybrid learning. *Faculty:* 74 full-time (69 women), 112 part-time/adjunct (105 women). *Students:* 323 full-time (261 women), 1,084 part-time (949 women); includes 311 minority (113 Black or African American, non-Hispanic/Latino; 4 American Indian or Alaska Native, non-Hispanic/Latino; 56 Asian, non-Hispanic/Latino; 108 Hispanic/Latino; 1 Native Hawaiian or other Pacific Islander, non-Hispanic/Latino; 29 Two or more races, non-Hispanic/Latino), 12 international. Average age 34. 582 applicants, 64% accepted, 314 enrolled. In 2017, 579 master's, 18 doctorates awarded. *Degree requirements:* For master's, thesis or alternative; for doctorate, comprehensive exam (for some programs), thesis/dissertation (for some programs). *Entrance requirements:* For doctorate, GRE General Test. Additional exam requirements/recommendations for international students: Required—TOEFL (minimum score 600 paper-based; 100 iBT); Recommended—IELTS (minimum score 7). *Application deadline:* For fall admission, 5/1 priority date for domestic students, 5/1 for international students; for spring admission, 10/1 for domestic students; for summer admission, 3/1 priority date for domestic students. Applications are processed on a rolling basis. Application fee: $130 ($70 for international students). Electronic applications accepted. *Expenses:* $14,668 annual full-time in-state tuition, $707 annual fees. *Financial support:* In 2017–18, 123 students received support, including 8 fellowships with full tuition reimbursements available (averaging $30,423 per year), 7 research assistantships with full tuition reimbursements available (averaging $17,971 per year), 5 teaching assistantships with full tuition reimbursements available (averaging $17,971 per year); Federal Work-Study, institutionally sponsored loans, scholarships/grants, traineeships, health care benefits, tuition waivers (partial), and unspecified assistantships also available. Support available to part-time students. Financial award application deadline: 5/1; financial award applicants required to submit FAFSA. *Faculty research:* Vulnerable populations, education, violence, chronicity/aging, cancer. *Total annual research expenditures:* $575,576. *Unit head:* Dr. Greer Glazer, Dean, 513-558-5330, Fax: 513-558-9030, E-mail: greer.glazer@uc.edu. *Application contact:* Office of Student Recruitment, 513-558-8400, Fax: 513-558-5012, E-mail: nursingbearcats@uc.edu.
Website: https://nursing.uc.edu/

University of Detroit Mercy, College of Health Professions, Detroit, MI 48221. Offers clinical nurse leader (MSN); family nurse practitioner (MSN); health services administration (MHSA); health systems management (MSN); nurse anesthesia (MS); nursing (DNP); nursing education (MSN, Certificate); nursing leadership and financial management (Certificate); outcomes performance management (Certificate); physician assistant (MS). *Entrance requirements:* For master's, GRE General Test, minimum GPA of 3.0. *Faculty research:* Research design, respiratory physiology, AIDS prevention, adolescent health, community, low income health education.

The University of Kansas, University of Kansas Medical Center, School of Health Professions, Department of Nurse Anesthesia Education, Kansas City, KS 66160. Offers DNAP. *Accreditation:* AANA/CANAEP. *Faculty:* 17. *Students:* 70 full-time (37 women), 1 part-time (0 women); includes 10 minority (3 Black or African American, non-Hispanic/Latino; 1 American Indian or Alaska Native, non-Hispanic/Latino; 2 Asian, non-Hispanic/Latino; 2 Hispanic/Latino; 2 Two or more races, non-Hispanic/Latino). Average age 30. 107 applicants, 30% accepted, 24 enrolled. In 2017, 25 doctorates awarded. *Degree requirements:* For doctorate, comprehensive exam, thesis/dissertation or alternative. *Entrance requirements:* For doctorate, bachelor's degree in nursing or related field, RN license, 2 years of experience as an RN including 1 year of experience in ICU; five science classes (human anatomy, human physiology, microbiology and 2 chemistry) and statistics; ACLS/BLS/PALS certification; minimum GPA of 3.0 on overall college course work and in the five science prerequisites. Additional exam requirements/recommendations for international students: Required—TOEFL. *Application deadline:* For summer admission, 7/15 for domestic and international students. Application fee: $60. Electronic applications accepted. *Expenses:* Contact institution. *Financial support:* Scholarships/grants available. Financial award application deadline: 3/1; financial award applicants required to submit FAFSA. *Faculty research:* Simulation training, cognitive aids, patient safety initiatives, international outreach (GHANA project, Peru project). *Total annual research expenditures:* $35,214. *Unit head:* Dr. Donna S. Nyght, Chair, 913-588-6612, Fax: 913-588-3334, E-mail: dnyght@kumc.edu. *Application contact:* Kelli Highfill, Program Coordinator, 913-588-6612, Fax: 913-588-3334, E-mail: na@kumc.edu.
Website: http://www.kumc.edu/school-of-health-professions/nurse-anesthesia-education.html

University of Maryland, Baltimore, School of Nursing, Baltimore, MD 21201. Offers adult-gerontology acute care nurse practitioner (DNP); adult-gerontology primary care nurse practitioner (DNP); clinical nurse leader (MS); community/public health nursing (MS); family nurse practitioner (DNP); global health (Postbaccalaureate Certificate); health services leadership and management (MS); neonatal nurse practitioner (DNP); nurse anesthesia (DNP); nursing (PhD); nursing informatics (MS, Postbaccalaureate Certificate); pediatric acute/primary care nurse practitioner (DNP); psychiatric mental health nurse practitioner (DNP); teaching in nursing and health professions (Postbaccalaureate Certificate); MS/MBA. MS/MBA offered jointly with University of Baltimore. *Program availability:* Part-time. *Faculty:* 130 full-time (117 women), 125 part-time/adjunct (114 women). *Students:* 504 full-time (442 women), 532 part-time (482 women); includes 443 minority (249 Black or African American, non-Hispanic/Latino; 1 American Indian or Alaska Native, non-Hispanic/Latino; 115 Asian, non-Hispanic/Latino; 48 Hispanic/Latino; 2 Native Hawaiian or other Pacific Islander, non-Hispanic/Latino; 28 Two or more races, non-Hispanic/Latino), 15 international. Average age 33. 935 applicants, 62% accepted, 394 enrolled. In 2017, 182 master's, 57 doctorates awarded. *Degree requirements:* For master's and Postbaccalaureate Certificate, thesis (for some programs); for doctorate, comprehensive exam, thesis/dissertation. *Entrance requirements:* Additional exam requirements/recommendations for international students: Required—TOEFL (minimum score 550 paper-based; 79 iBT); Recommended—IELTS (minimum score 7). *Application deadline:* For fall admission, 11/1 for domestic and international students; for spring admission, 8/1 for domestic and international students. Application fee: $75. Electronic applications accepted. *Expenses:* Contact institution. *Financial support:* In 2017–18, 22 research assistantships with full and partial tuition reimbursements (averaging $21,523 per year), 41 teaching assistantships with full and partial tuition reimbursements (averaging $13,439 per year) were awarded; fellowships and scholarships/grants also available. Financial award application deadline: 3/1; financial award applicants required to submit FAFSA. *Unit head:* Dr. Jane Kirschling, Dean, 410-706-4359, E-mail: kirschling@umaryland.edu. *Application contact:* Larry Fillian, Associate Dean of Student and Academic Services, 410-706-6298, E-mail: lfillian@umaryland.edu.
Website: http://www.nursing.umaryland.edu/

University of Miami, Graduate School, School of Nursing and Health Studies, Coral Gables, FL 33124. Offers acute care (MSN), including acute care nurse practitioner, nurse anesthesia; nursing (PhD); primary care (MSN), including adult nurse practitioner, family nurse practitioner, nurse midwifery, women's health practitioner. *Accreditation:* AACN; AANA/CANAEP; ACNM/ACME (one or more programs are accredited). *Program availability:* Part-time. *Degree requirements:* For master's, thesis optional; for doctorate, thesis/dissertation. *Entrance requirements:* For master's, GRE General Test, BSN, minimum GPA of 3.0, Florida RN license; for doctorate, GRE General Test, BSN or

MSN, minimum GPA of 3.0. Additional exam requirements/recommendations for international students: Required—TOEFL (minimum score 550 paper-based). Electronic applications accepted. *Faculty research:* Transcultural nursing, exercise and depression in Alzheimer's disease, infectious diseases/HIV–AIDS, postpartum depression, outcomes assessment.

University of Michigan–Flint, School of Health Professions and Studies, Program in Anesthesia, Flint, MI 48502-1950. Offers DNAP. *Accreditation:* AACN; AANA/CANAEP. *Program availability:* Part-time, evening/weekend, 100% online. *Faculty:* 10 full-time (11 women), 36 part-time/adjunct (19 women). *Students:* 41 full-time (16 women), 31 part-time (21 women); includes 11 minority (2 Black or African American, non-Hispanic/Latino; 1 American Indian or Alaska Native, non-Hispanic/Latino; 4 Asian, non-Hispanic/Latino; 2 Hispanic/Latino; 2 Two or more races, non-Hispanic/Latino). Average age 35. 100 applicants, 30% accepted, 25 enrolled. In 2017, 11 doctorates awarded. *Entrance requirements:* For doctorate, master's degree in science, biology, or nursing with focus on nurse anesthesia, or post-master's certificate from program accredited by Council on Accreditation (COA) of Nurse Anesthesia Educational Programs; minimum overall master's degree GPA of 3.2 (5.0 on U-M 9.0 scale); current, unrestricted RN license; CRNA certification. Additional exam requirements/recommendations for international students: Required—TOEFL (minimum score 84 iBT), IELTS (minimum score 6.5). *Application deadline:* For fall admission, 2/1 for domestic students, 12/1 for international students. Applications are processed on a rolling basis. Application fee: $55. Electronic applications accepted. *Expenses:* Contact institution. *Financial support:* Federal Work-Study, scholarships/grants, and unspecified assistantships available. Support available to part-time students. Financial award application deadline: 3/1; financial award applicants required to submit FAFSA. *Faculty research:* CRNA expected retirement patterns, factors of importance in CENA selection of first job, lidocaine 4% in ETT cuff and reducing in coughing on emergence, orientation of spinal needle benel, length of time to discharge outpatients. *Unit head:* Dr. Shawn Fryzel, Director of Anesthesia Programs, 810-262-9264, Fax: 810-760-0839, E-mail: sfryzel1@hurleymc.com. *Application contact:* Bradley T. Maki, Director of Graduate Admissions, 810-762-3171, Fax: 810-766-6789, E-mail: bmaki@umflint.edu.
Website: https://www.umflint.edu/pubhealth/graduate-degrees

University of Minnesota, Twin Cities Campus, Graduate School, School of Nursing, Minneapolis, MN 55455-0213. Offers adult/gerontological clinical nurse specialist (DNP); adult/gerontological primary care nurse practitioner (DNP); family nurse practitioner (DNP); health innovation and leadership (DNP); integrative health and healing (DNP); nurse anesthesia (DNP); nurse midwifery (DNP); nursing (MN, PhD); nursing informatics (DNP); pediatric clinical nurse specialist (DNP); primary care certified pediatric nurse practitioner (DNP); psychiatric/mental health nurse practitioner (DNP); women's health nurse practitioner (DNP). *Accreditation:* AACN; AANA/CANAEP; ACNM/ACME (one or more programs are accredited). *Program availability:* Part-time, online learning. Terminal master's awarded for partial completion of doctoral program. *Degree requirements:* For master's, final oral exam, project or thesis; for doctorate, thesis/dissertation. *Entrance requirements:* For master's and doctorate, GRE General Test. Additional exam requirements/recommendations for international students: Required—TOEFL (minimum score 586 paper-based). *Expenses:* Contact institution. *Faculty research:* Child and family health promotion, nursing research on elders.

University of New England, Westbrook College of Health Professions, Biddeford, ME 04005-9526. Offers nurse anesthesia (MSNA); occupational therapy (MS); physical therapy (DPT); physician assistant (MS); social work (MSW). *Program availability:* Part-time. *Faculty:* 43 full-time (30 women), 26 part-time/adjunct (19 women). *Students:* 527 full-time (401 women), 5 part-time (4 women); includes 50 minority (11 Black or African American, non-Hispanic/Latino; 1 American Indian or Alaska Native, non-Hispanic/Latino; 24 Asian, non-Hispanic/Latino; 5 Hispanic/Latino; 1 Native Hawaiian or other Pacific Islander, non-Hispanic/Latino; 8 Two or more races, non-Hispanic/Latino), 1 international. Average age 27. 2,499 applicants, 18% accepted, 226 enrolled. In 2017, 440 master's, 71 doctorates awarded. *Application deadline:* Applications are processed on a rolling basis. Electronic applications accepted. Tuition and fees vary according to degree level, program and student level. *Financial support:* Application deadline: 5/1; applicants required to submit FAFSA. *Unit head:* Dr. Elizabeth Francis- Connolly, Dean, Westbrook College of Health Professions, 207-221-4523, E-mail: efrancisconnonlly@une.edu. *Application contact:* Scott Steinberg, Dean of University Admission, 207-221-4225, Fax: 207-523-1925, E-mail: ssteinberg@une.edu.
Website: http://www.une.edu/wchp/index.cfm

The University of North Carolina at Charlotte, College of Health and Human Services, School of Nursing, Charlotte, NC 28223-0001. Offers adult-gerontology acute care nurse practitioner (Post-Master's Certificate); advanced clinical nursing (MSN), including adult psychiatric mental health, adult-gerontology acute care nurse practitioner, family nurse practitioner across the lifespan; family nurse practitioner across the lifespan (Post-Master's Certificate); nurse anesthesia (MSN), including nurse anesthesia across the lifespan; nurse anesthesia across the lifespan (Post-Master's Certificate); nursing (DNP); nursing administration (Graduate Certificate); nursing education (Graduate Certificate); systems/population nursing (MSN), including community/public health nursing, nurse administrator, nurse educator. *Accreditation:* AACN; AANA/CANAEP. *Program availability:* Part-time, blended/hybrid learning. *Faculty:* 24 full-time (22 women), 6 part-time/adjunct (4 women). *Students:* 113 full-time (84 women), 163 part-time (150 women); includes 63 minority (47 Black or African American, non-Hispanic/Latino; 2 American Indian or Alaska Native, non-Hispanic/Latino; 6 Asian, non-Hispanic/Latino; 3 Hispanic/Latino; 5 Two or more races, non-Hispanic/Latino). Average age 37. 443 applicants, 31% accepted, 113 enrolled. In 2017, 83 master's, 8 doctorates, 8 other advanced degrees awarded. Terminal master's awarded for partial completion of doctoral program. *Degree requirements:* For doctorate, thesis/dissertation or alternative, residency; for other advanced degree, practicum. *Entrance requirements:* For master's, GRE General Test, current unrestricted license as Registered Nurse in North Carolina; BSN from nationally-accredited program; one year of professional nursing practice in acute/critical care; minimum overall GPA of 3.0 in last degree; completion of undergraduate statistics course with minimum grade of C; statement of purpose; for doctorate, GRE or MAT, master's degree in nursing in an advanced nursing practice specialty from nationally-accredited program; minimum overall GPA of 3.5 in MSN program; current RN licensure in U.S. at time of application with eligibility for NC licensure; essay; resume/curriculum vitae; professional recommendations; clinical hours; for other advanced degree, GRE. Additional exam requirements/recommendations for international students: Required—TOEFL (minimum score 523 paper-based, 70 iBT) or IELTS (6.5). *Application deadline:* For fall admission, 1/10 for domestic and international students; for spring admission, 9/10 for domestic and international students; for summer admission, 4/1 for domestic and international students. Applications are processed on a rolling basis. Application fee: $75. Electronic applications accepted. *Expenses:* Contact institution. *Financial support:* In 2017–18, 6 students received support, including 4 research assistantships (averaging $6,338 per year), 2 teaching assistantships (averaging $6,250 per year); career-related internships or fieldwork, institutionally sponsored loans, scholarships/grants, traineeships, and unspecified assistantships also available. Support available to part-time students. Financial award application deadline: 3/1; financial award applicants required to submit FAFSA. *Total annual research expenditures:* $800,072. *Unit head:* Dr. Dena Evans, Director, 704-687-7974, E-mail: devans37@uncc.edu. *Application contact:* Kathy B. Giddings, Director of Graduate Admissions, 704-687-5503, Fax: 704-687-1668, E-mail: gradadm@uncc.edu.
Website: http://nursing.uncc.edu/

The University of North Carolina at Greensboro, Graduate School, School of Nursing, Greensboro, NC 27412-5001. Offers adult clinical nurse specialist (MSN, PMC); adult/gerontological nurse practitioner (MSN, PMC); nurse anesthesia (MSN, PMC); nursing (PhD); nursing administration (MSN); nursing education (MSN); MSN/MBA. *Accreditation:* ACEN. *Degree requirements:* For master's, thesis or alternative. *Entrance requirements:* For master's, GRE General Test or MAT, BSN, clinical experience, liability insurance, RN license; for PMC, liability insurance, MSN, RN license. Additional exam requirements/recommendations for international students: Required—TOEFL. Electronic applications accepted.

University of North Dakota, Graduate School, College of Nursing and Professional Disciplines, Department of Nursing, Grand Forks, ND 58202. Offers adult-gerontological nurse practitioner (MS); advanced public health nurse (MS); family nurse practitioner (MS); nurse anesthesia (MS); nurse educator (MS); nursing (PhD, Post-Master's Certificate); nursing practice (DNP); psychiatric and mental health nurse practitioner (MS).

University of North Florida, Brooks College of Health, School of Nursing, Jacksonville, FL 32224. Offers family nurse practitioner (Certificate); nurse anesthetist (MSN). *Accreditation:* AACN; AANA/CANAEP. *Program availability:* Part-time. *Degree requirements:* For master's, thesis optional. *Entrance requirements:* For master's, GRE General Test, minimum GPA of 3.0 in last 60 hours of course work, BSN, clinical experience, resume; for doctorate, GRE, master's degree in nursing specialty from nationally-accredited program; national certification in one of the following APRN roles: CNE, CNM, CNS, CRNA, CNP; minimum graduate GPA of 3.3; three letters of reference which address academic ability and clinical skills; active license as registered nurse or advanced practice registered nurse. Additional exam requirements/recommendations for international students: Required—TOEFL (minimum score 500 paper-based; 61 iBT). Electronic applications accepted. *Faculty research:* Teen pregnancy, diabetes, ethical decision-making, family caregivers.

University of Pennsylvania, School of Nursing, Nurse Anesthesia Program, Philadelphia, PA 19104. Offers MSN. *Accreditation:* AANA/CANAEP. *Program availability:* Online learning. *Students:* 44 full-time (30 women), 3 part-time (all women); includes 18 minority (1 Black or African American, non-Hispanic/Latino; 9 Asian, non-Hispanic/Latino; 1 Hispanic/Latino; 1 Two or more races, non-Hispanic/Latino). Average age 29. 120 applicants, 38% accepted, 42 enrolled. In 2017, 23 master's awarded. Application fee: $80.

University of Pittsburgh, School of Nursing, Nurse Anesthesia Program, Pittsburgh, PA 15260. Offers DNP. *Accreditation:* AACN; AANA/CANAEP. *Faculty:* 5 full-time (2 women), 2 part-time/adjunct (both women). *Students:* 110 full-time (73 women), 14 part-time (8 women); includes 21 minority (6 Black or African American, non-Hispanic/Latino; 15 Asian, non-Hispanic/Latino), 1 international. Average age 29. 145 applicants, 32% accepted, 44 enrolled. In 2017, 7 doctorates awarded. *Entrance requirements:* For doctorate, GRE, BSN, RN license, minimum GPA of 3.5, 3 letters of recommendation, relevant nursing experience, resume, course work in statistics. Additional exam requirements/recommendations for international students: Required—TOEFL (minimum score 600 paper-based; 100 IBT) or IELTS (minimum score 7.0). Application fee: $50. Electronic applications accepted. *Expenses:* $13,068 per term full-time resident tuition, $1,064 per credit part-time; $15,270 per term full-time non-resident tuition, $1,247 per credit part-time; $437 per term full-time fees; $282 per term part-time fees. *Financial support:* In 2017–18, 36 students received support, including 4 teaching assistantships (averaging $8,072 per year); scholarships/grants and unspecified assistantships also available. Financial award applicants required to submit FAFSA. *Faculty research:* Behavioral management of chronic disorders, patient management in critical care, consumer informatics, genetic applications (molecular genetics and psychosocial implications), technology for nurses and patients to improve care. *Unit head:* John O'Donnell, Director, 412-624-4860, Fax: 412-624-2401, E-mail: jod01@pitt.edu. *Application contact:* Laurie Lapsley, Graduate Administrator, 412-624-9670, Fax: 412-624-2409, E-mail: lapsleyl@pitt.edu.
Website: http://www.nursing.pitt.edu/

University of Saint Francis, Graduate School, Department of Nursing, Fort Wayne, IN 46808. Offers family nurse practitioner (MSN, Post Master's Certificate); nurse anesthesia (DNP); nursing practice (DNP). *Accreditation:* AACN. *Program availability:* Part-time, blended/hybrid learning. *Faculty:* 8 full-time (7 women), 12 part-time/adjunct (10 women). *Students:* 44 full-time (36 women), 72 part-time (65 women); includes 10 minority (4 Black or African American, non-Hispanic/Latino; 1 Asian, non-Hispanic/Latino; 2 Hispanic/Latino; 3 Two or more races, non-Hispanic/Latino). Average age 32. 48 applicants, 71% accepted, 29 enrolled. In 2017, 30 master's, 2 other advanced degrees awarded. *Degree requirements:* For doctorate, comprehensive exam. *Entrance requirements:* For master's, GRE (if undergraduate GPA is less than 3.0), minimum undergraduate GPA of 3.2; ASN, BSN, or MSN from regionally-accredited U.S. institution; current license as registered nurse; graduate or undergraduate statistics course within last five years; for doctorate, BSN from ACEN- or CCNE-accredited nursing program; minimum cumulative undergraduate GPA of 3.2; 2 courses in chemistry and 1 statistics course with minimum B grade; official transcripts; resume; 1 year of continuous full-time critical care experience; current Indiana RN license; 3 professional letters of recommendation; essay; interview; for Post Master's Certificate, GRE (if undergraduate GPA is less than 3.0), minimum undergraduate GPA of 3.2; MSN from regionally-accredited U.S. institution; current license as registered nurse; graduate or undergraduate statistics course within last five years. Additional exam requirements/recommendations for international students: Required—TOEFL (minimum score 550 paper-based; 100 iBT), IELTS (minimum score 6.5), TWE (minimum score 5). *Application deadline:* For fall admission, 7/1 for international students; for spring admission, 11/1 for international students; for summer admission, 3/1 for international students. Applications are processed on a rolling basis. Application fee: $0. Electronic applications accepted. *Expenses:* $905 per hour (for MSN); $1,055 per hour (for DNP). *Financial support:* In 2017–18, 21 students received support. Federal Work-Study, scholarships/grants, and unspecified assistantships available. Financial award application deadline: 4/15; financial award applicants required to submit FAFSA. *Unit head:* Dr. Wendy Clark, Program Director, Master of Science in Nursing, 260-399-7700 Ext. 8534, Fax: 260-399-8167, E-mail: wclark@sf.edu. *Application contact:* Kyle Richardson, Associate Director of Enrollment Services for Adult Learning, 260-399-7700 Ext. 6310, Fax: 260-399-8152, E-mail: krichardson@sf.edu.
Website: https://nursing.sf.edu/

The University of Scranton, Panuska College of Professional Studies, Department of Nursing, Scranton, PA 18510-4595. Offers family nurse practitioner (MSN, PMC); nurse anesthesia (MSN, PMC); nursing leadership (DNP). Applicants accepted in odd-numbered years only. *Accreditation:* AACN; AANA/CANAEP. *Program availability:* Part-time, evening/weekend. *Degree requirements:* For master's, comprehensive exam (for some programs), thesis (for some programs), capstone experience. *Entrance requirements:* For master's, minimum GPA of 3.0, three letters of reference; for doctorate, RN licensure and evidence of certification in advanced practice nursing specialty. Additional exam requirements/recommendations for international students: Required—TOEFL (minimum score 500 paper-based; 80 iBT), IELTS (minimum score 6.5). Electronic applications accepted. *Faculty research:* Home care, doctoral education, health care of women and children, pain, health promotion and adolescence.

University of South Carolina, School of Medicine and The Graduate School, Graduate Programs in Medicine, Program in Nurse Anesthesia, Columbia, SC 29208. Offers MNA. *Accreditation:* AACN. *Degree requirements:* For master's, comprehensive exam, practicum. *Entrance requirements:* For master's, GRE, 1 year of critical care experience, RN license. Electronic applications accepted. *Expenses:* Contact institution. *Faculty research:* Neuroscience, cardiovascular, hormones, stress, homeostasis.

University of Southern California, Keck School of Medicine, Doctor of Nurse Anesthesia Practice Program, Los Angeles, CA 90089. Offers DNAP. *Faculty:* 3 full-time (all women), 11 part-time/adjunct (5 women). *Students:* 36 full-time (24 women); includes 14 minority (1 Black or African American, non-Hispanic/Latino; 10 Asian, non-Hispanic/Latino; 3 Hispanic/Latino). Average age 28. 95 applicants, 20 enrolled. *Degree requirements:* For doctorate, comprehensive exam, capstone project. *Entrance requirements:* For doctorate, GRE, interview; minimum GPA of 3.0; minimum of one year of critical care or emergency department experience in a high acuity setting and shadow experience of CRNAs or anesthesiologists. *Application deadline:* For fall admission, 12/1 for domestic students. Application fee: $85. Electronic applications accepted. *Unit head:* Dr. Michele E. Gold, Director, 323-442-2037.
Website: http://keck.usc.edu/nurse-anesthesia-program/

University of South Florida, College of Nursing, Tampa, FL 33612. Offers nurse anesthesia (DNP); nursing (MS, DNP), including adult-gerontology acute care nursing, adult-gerontology primary care nursing, family health nursing, nurse anesthesia (MS), nursing education (MS), occupational health nursing/adult-gerontology primary care nursing, oncology nursing/adult-gerontology primary care nursing (DNP), pediatric health nursing; nursing education (Post Master's Certificate); nursing science (PhD); simulation based academic fellowship in advanced pain management (Graduate Certificate). *Accreditation:* AACN; AANA/CANAEP. *Program availability:* Part-time. *Faculty:* 37 full-time (32 women), 2 part-time/adjunct (1 woman). *Students:* 224 full-time (178 women), 669 part-time (577 women); includes 309 minority (105 Black or African American, non-Hispanic/Latino; 2 American Indian or Alaska Native, non-Hispanic/Latino; 53 Asian, non-Hispanic/Latino; 122 Hispanic/Latino; 1 Native Hawaiian or other Pacific Islander, non-Hispanic/Latino; 26 Two or more races, non-Hispanic/Latino), 6 international. Average age 32. 949 applicants, 47% accepted, 382 enrolled. In 2017, 264 master's, 39 doctorates awarded. *Degree requirements:* For master's, comprehensive exam, thesis optional; for doctorate, comprehensive exam, thesis/dissertation. *Entrance requirements:* For master's, GRE General Test, bachelor's degree from accredited program with minimum GPA of 3.0 in all upper-division coursework; current license as Registered Nurse; 3 letters of recommendation; personal statement of goals; resume or curriculum vitae; personal interview; for doctorate, GRE General Test (recommended), bachelor's degree in nursing from ACEN or CCNE regionally-accredited institution with minimum GPA of 3.0 in all coursework or in all upper-division coursework; current license as Registered Nurse in Florida; undergraduate statistics course with minimum B grade; 3 letters of recommendation; statement of goals; resume; interview. Additional exam requirements/recommendations for international students: Required—TOEFL (minimum score 550 paper-based; 79 iBT). *Application deadline:* For fall admission, 12/15 for domestic and international students; for spring admission, 10/1 for domestic students, 9/15 for international students. Application fee: $30. Electronic applications accepted. *Financial support:* In 2017–18, 132 students received support, including 7 research assistantships with tuition reimbursements available (averaging $18,935 per year), 29 teaching assistantships with tuition reimbursements available (averaging $30,814 per year); tuition waivers (partial) and unspecified assistantships also available. Financial award application deadline: 2/1; financial award applicants required to submit FAFSA. *Faculty research:* Women's health, palliative and end-of-life care, cardiac rehabilitation, complementary therapies for chronic illness and cancer. *Total annual research expenditures:* $3.2 million. *Unit head:* Dr. Victoria Rich, Dean, College of Nursing, 813-974-8939, Fax: 813-974-5418, E-mail: victoriarich@health.usf.edu. *Application contact:* Dr. Brian Graves, Assistant Professor/Assistant Dean, 813-974-8054, Fax: 813-974-5418, E-mail: bgraves1@health.usf.edu.
Website: http://health.usf.edu/nursing/index.htm

The University of Tennessee at Chattanooga, School of Nursing, Chattanooga, TN 37403. Offers certified nurse anesthetist (Post-Master's Certificate); family nurse practitioner (MSN, Post-Master's Certificate); gerontology acute care (MSN, Post-Master's Certificate); nurse anesthesia (MSN); nurse education (Post-Master's Certificate); nursing (DNP). *Accreditation:* AACN; AANA/CANAEP (one or more programs are accredited). *Students:* 62 full-time (33 women), 69 part-time (61 women); includes 24 minority (11 Black or African American, non-Hispanic/Latino; 1 American Indian or Alaska Native, non-Hispanic/Latino; 5 Asian, non-Hispanic/Latino; 3 Hispanic/Latino; 4 Two or more races, non-Hispanic/Latino). Average age 34. 47 applicants, 100% accepted, 45 enrolled. In 2017, 33 master's, 14 doctorates, 7 other advanced degrees awarded. *Degree requirements:* For master's, thesis optional, qualifying exams, professional project; for doctorate, professional project; for Post-Master's Certificate, thesis or alternative, practicum, seminar. *Entrance requirements:* For master's, GRE General Test, MAT, BSN, minimum GPA of 3.0, eligibility for Tennessee RN license, 1 year of direct patient care experience; for doctorate, GRE General Test or MAT (if applicant does not have MSN), minimum GPA of 3.0 for highest degree earned; for Post-Master's Certificate, GRE General Test, MAT, MSN, minimum GPA of 3.0, eligibility for Tennessee RN license, one year of direct patient care experience. Additional exam requirements/recommendations for international students: Required—TOEFL (minimum score 550 paper-based; 79 iBT), IELTS (minimum score 6). *Application deadline:* For fall admission, 6/15 priority date for domestic students, 7/1 for international students; for spring admission, 11/1 priority date for domestic students, 11/1 for international students. Applications are processed on a rolling basis. Application fee: $35 ($40 for international students). Electronic applications accepted. *Expenses:* Contact institution. *Financial support:* Teaching assistantships, career-related internships or fieldwork, and scholarships/grants available. Support available to part-time students. Financial award application deadline: 7/1; financial award applicants required to submit FAFSA. *Faculty research:* Diabetes in women, health care for elderly, alternative medicine, hypertension, nurse anesthesia. *Total annual research expenditures:* $985,388. *Unit head:* Dr. Chris Smith, Director, 423-425-1741, Fax: 423-425-4668, E-mail: chris-smith@utc.edu. *Application contact:* Dr. Joanne Romagni, Dean of the Graduate School, 423-425-4478, Fax: 423-425-5223, E-mail: joanne-romagni@utc.edu.
Website: http://www.utc.edu/nursing/

University of Wisconsin–La Crosse, College of Science and Health, Department of Biology, La Crosse, WI 54601-3742. Offers aquatic sciences (MS); biology (MS); cellular and molecular biology (MS); clinical microbiology (MS); microbiology (MS); nurse anesthesia (MS); physiology (MS). *Accreditation:* AANA/CANAEP. *Program availability:* Part-time. *Students:* 11 full-time (2 women), 29 part-time (14 women); includes 1 minority (Two or more races, non-Hispanic/Latino). Average age 30. 67 applicants, 28% accepted, 18 enrolled. In 2017, 24 master's awarded. *Degree requirements:* For master's, comprehensive exam, thesis. *Entrance requirements:* For master's, GRE General Test, minimum GPA of 2.85. Additional exam requirements/recommendations for international students: Required—TOEFL (minimum score 550 paper-based; 79 iBT). *Application deadline:* For fall admission, 2/1 priority date for domestic and international students; for spring admission, 1/4 priority date for domestic and international students. Applications are processed on a rolling basis. Electronic applications accepted. *Financial support:* Research assistantships with partial tuition reimbursements, Federal Work-Study, scholarships/grants, health care benefits, and tuition waivers (partial) available. Support available to part-time students. Financial award application deadline: 3/15; financial award applicants required to submit FAFSA. *Unit head:* Dr. Mark Sandheinrich, Department Chair, 608-785-8261, E-mail: msandheinrich@uwlax.edu. *Application contact:* Brandon Schaller, Senior Graduate Student Status Examiner, 608-785-8941, E-mail: admissions@uwlax.edu.
Website: http://uwlax.edu/biology/

Villanova University, M. Louise Fitzpatrick College of Nursing, Villanova, PA 19085. Offers adult-gerontology primary care nurse practitioner (MSN, Post Master's Certificate); family primary care nurse practitioner (MSN, Post Master's Certificate); nurse anesthesia (DNP); nursing (PhD); nursing education (MSN, Post Master's Certificate); nursing practice (DNP); pediatric primary care nurse practitioner (MSN, Post Master's Certificate). *Accreditation:* AACN; AANA/CANAEP. *Program availability:* Part-time, online learning. *Students:* 151 full-time, 199 part-time; includes 42 minority (18 Black or African American, non-Hispanic/Latino; 12 Asian, non-Hispanic/Latino; 8 Hispanic/Latino; 4 Two or more races, non-Hispanic/Latino), 10 international. 274 applicants, 43% accepted, 92 enrolled. In 2017, 70 master's, 15 doctorates awarded. *Entrance requirements:* Additional exam requirements/recommendations for international students: Required—TOEFL, IELTS. *Application deadline:* For fall admission, 7/1 for domestic and international students; for spring admission, 10/1 for domestic and international students; for summer admission, 4/1 for domestic and international students. Application fee: $50. Electronic applications accepted. *Financial support:* Fellowships, research assistantships, teaching assistantships, scholarships/grants, traineeships, and tuition waivers available. *Unit head:* Dr. Marguerite K. Schlag, Associate Professor, Assistant Dean and Director of Graduate Nursing Program, 610-519-4907, Fax: 610-519-7650, E-mail: marguerite.schlag@villanova.edu. *Application contact:* Kathleen Geibel, Assistant to Graduate Program, 610-519-4934, Fax: 610-519-7650, E-mail: kathleen.geibel@villanova.edu.
Website: http://www.nursing.villanova.edu

Virginia Commonwealth University, Graduate School, School of Allied Health Professions, Department of Nurse Anesthesia, Richmond, VA 23284-9005. Offers MSNA, DNAP. *Accreditation:* AANA/CANAEP. *Degree requirements:* For master's, thesis. *Entrance requirements:* For master's, GRE General Test, 1 year of experience in acute critical care nursing, current state RN license, minimum GPA of 3.0; for doctorate, GRE General Test, accredited MSNA, CCNA certification, minimum GPA of 3.0. Additional exam requirements/recommendations for international students: Required—TOEFL (minimum score 600 paper-based; 100 iBT); Recommended—IELTS (minimum score 6.5). Electronic applications accepted. *Faculty research:* Obstetrical anesthesia, ambulatory anesthesia, regional anesthesia, practice profiles, clinical practice.

Virginia Commonwealth University, Graduate School, School of Allied Health Professions, Doctoral Program in Health Related Sciences, Richmond, VA 23284-9005. Offers clinical laboratory sciences (PhD); gerontology (PhD); health administration (PhD); nurse anesthesia (PhD); occupational therapy (PhD); physical therapy (PhD); radiation sciences (PhD); rehabilitation leadership (PhD). *Entrance requirements:* For doctorate, GRE General Test or MAT, minimum GPA of 3.3 in master's degree. Additional exam requirements/recommendations for international students: Required—TOEFL (minimum score 600 paper-based; 100 iBT); Recommended—IELTS (minimum score 6.5). Electronic applications accepted.

Wake Forest University, School of Medicine and Graduate School of Arts and Sciences, Graduate Programs in Medicine, Nurse Anesthesia Program, Winston-Salem, NC 27109. Offers MS.

Wayne State University, Eugene Applebaum College of Pharmacy and Health Sciences, Department of Health Care Sciences, Program in Nurse Anesthesia, Detroit, MI 48202. Offers anesthesia (MS); nurse anesthesia practice (DNP-A); pediatric anesthesia (Certificate). *Accreditation:* AACN; AANA/CANAEP. *Faculty:* 7. *Students:* 38 full-time (27 women); includes 7 minority (3 Black or African American, non-Hispanic/Latino; 3 Asian, non-Hispanic/Latino; 1 Hispanic/Latino). Average age 30. In 2017, 20 master's awarded. *Entrance requirements:* For master's, bachelor's degree in nursing or related science with minimum GPA of 3.0 overall and in science, current RN license, CCRN certification, one year of full-time experience in adult ICU, ACLS certification, PALS certification, hospital shadow experience (arranged by department); for Certificate, MS in anesthesia from accredited program, meeting with course coordinators from Children's Hospital of Michigan. Additional exam requirements/recommendations for international students: Required—TOEFL (minimum score 550 paper-based; 79 iBT), Michigan English Language Assessment Battery (minimum score 85); Recommended—IELTS (minimum score 6.5), TWE (minimum score 5.5). *Application deadline:* For fall admission, 7/1 for domestic and international students. Application fee: $50. Electronic applications accepted. *Expenses:* Contact institution. *Financial support:* In 2017–18, 17 students received support. Scholarships/grants available. Financial award applicants required to submit FAFSA. *Faculty research:* Music therapy in pain management, student success/students perspective, pacemaker management-safety, airway devices. *Unit head:* Dr. Prudentia A. Worth, Program Director, 313-993-7168, E-mail: aa1635@wayne.edu.
Website: http://cphs.wayne.edu/nurse-anesthesia/

Webster University, College of Arts and Sciences, Department of Nurse Anesthesia, St. Louis, MO 63119-3194. Offers DNAP. *Accreditation:* AANA/CANAEP. *Program availability:* Online learning. *Entrance requirements:* Additional exam requirements/recommendations for international students: Required—TOEFL. *Faculty research:* Clinical anesthesia, substance abuse education in the health professions, technology and education, clinical pharmacology.

Westminster College, School of Nursing and Health Sciences, Salt Lake City, UT 84105-3697. Offers family nurse practitioner (MSN); nurse anesthesia (MSNA); public health (MPH). *Accreditation:* AACN; AANA/CANAEP. *Faculty:* 9 full-time (5 women), 10 part-time/adjunct (5 women). *Students:* 130 full-time (81 women), 1 (woman) part-time; includes 18 minority (2 Black or African American, non-Hispanic/Latino; 1 American Indian or Alaska Native, non-Hispanic/Latino; 5 Asian, non-Hispanic/Latino; 4 Hispanic/Latino; 2 Native Hawaiian or other Pacific Islander, non-Hispanic/Latino; 4 Two or more races, non-Hispanic/Latino), 3 international. Average age 33. 149 applicants, 51% accepted, 62 enrolled. In 2017, 49 master's awarded. *Degree requirements:* For master's, clinical practicum, 504 clinical practice hours. *Entrance requirements:* For master's, GRE (can be waived in select cases), personal statement, resume, 3 professional recommendations, copy of unrestricted Utah license to practice professional nursing, background check, minimum cumulative GPA of 3.0, documentation of current immunizations, physical and mental health certificate signed by primary care provider. Additional exam requirements/recommendations for

international students: Required—TOEFL (minimum score 84 iBT), IELTS (minimum score 7). Application fee: $50. Electronic applications accepted. *Expenses:* Contact institution. *Financial support:* In 2017–18, 7 students received support. Career-related internships or fieldwork, scholarships/grants, unspecified assistantships, and tuition remission available. Financial award applicants required to submit FAFSA. *Faculty research:* Intellectual empathy, professional boundaries, learned optimism, collaborative testing in nursing: student outcomes and perspectives, implementing new educational paradigms into pre licensure nursing curricula. *Unit head:* Dr. Sheryl Steadman, Dean, 801-832-2164, Fax: 801-832-3110, E-mail: ssteadman@westminstercollege.edu. *Application contact:* Collin Bess, Enrollment Coordinator/Admissions Recruiter, 801-832-2207, Fax: 801-832-3101, E-mail: cbess@westminstercollege.edu.
Website: https://www.westminstercollege.edu/graduate/programs

Wolford College, Graduate Programs, Naples, FL 34108. Offers MSNA, DNAP.

York College of Pennsylvania, The Stabler Department of Nursing, York, PA 17403-3651. Offers adult gerontology clinical nurse specialist (MS); nurse anesthetist (MS). *Accreditation:* AACN; AANA/CANAEP. *Program availability:* Part-time. *Faculty:* 7 full-time (all women), 8 part-time/adjunct (5 women). *Students:* 41 full-time (30 women), 40 part-time (38 women); includes 9 minority (1 Black or African American, non-Hispanic/Latino; 3 Asian, non-Hispanic/Latino; 1 Hispanic/Latino; 4 Two or more races, non-Hispanic/Latino), 1 international. Average age 35. 96 applicants, 31% accepted, 29 enrolled. In 2017, 24 master's awarded. *Entrance requirements:* For master's, bachelor's degree in nursing, minimum GPA of 3.0. Additional exam requirements/recommendations for international students: Required—TOEFL (minimum score 530 paper-based; 72 IBT). Application fee: $0. Electronic applications accepted. *Expenses:* $795 per credit. *Financial support:* In 2017–18, 1 student received support. Scholarships/grants available. Financial award applicants required to submit FAFSA. *Faculty research:* Adults with intellectual disabilities, healthy work environment, perinatal bereavement, palliative care. *Unit head:* Dr. Kimberly Fenstermacher, Graduate Program Director, 717-815-1383, Fax: 717-849-1651, E-mail: kfenster@ycp.edu. *Application contact:* Allison Malachosky, Administrative Assistant, 717-815-1243, E-mail: amalacho@ycp.edu.
Website: http://www.ycp.edu/academics/academic-departments/nursing/

Nurse Midwifery

Bastyr University, School of Natural Health Arts and Sciences, Kenmore, WA 98028-4966. Offers counseling psychology (MA); maternal-child health systems (MA); midwifery (MS); nutrition (Certificate); nutrition and clinical health psychology (MS); nutrition and wellness (MS). *Accreditation:* AND. *Program availability:* Part-time. *Degree requirements:* For master's, thesis optional. *Entrance requirements:* For master's, 1-2 years' basic sciences course work (depending on program). Additional exam requirements/recommendations for international students: Required—TOEFL (minimum score 550 paper-based; 79 iBT). *Application deadline:* For fall admission, 3/15 priority date for domestic and international students. Applications are processed on a rolling basis. Application fee: $75. *Expenses: Tuition:* Part-time $714 per credit hour. *Required fees:* $75. *Financial support:* Career-related internships or fieldwork, Federal Work-Study, and scholarships/grants available. Support available to part-time students. Financial award application deadline: 4/15; financial award applicants required to submit FAFSA. *Faculty research:* Whole-food nutrition for type 2 diabetes; meditation in end-of-life care; stress management; Qi Gong, Tai Chi and yoga for older adults; Echinacea and immunology. *Unit head:* Dr. Lynelle Golden, Dean, 425-602-3110, Fax: 425-823-6222, E-mail: lgolden@bastyr.edu. *Application contact:* Admissions Office, 425-602-3330, Fax: 425-602-3090, E-mail: admissions@bastyr.edu.
Website: http://www.bastyr.edu/academics/schools-departments/school-natural-health-arts-sciences

Baylor University, Graduate School, Louise Herrington School of Nursing, Dallas, TX 76798. Offers family nurse practitioner (MSN); neonatal nurse practitioner (MSN); nurse-midwifery (DNP). *Accreditation:* AACN. *Program availability:* Part-time, online learning. *Faculty:* 11 full-time (all women), 3 part-time/adjunct (2 women). *Students:* 35 full-time (34 women), 11 part-time (all women); includes 21 minority (5 Black or African American, non-Hispanic/Latino; 1 American Indian or Alaska Native, non-Hispanic/Latino; 5 Asian, non-Hispanic/Latino; 8 Hispanic/Latino; 2 Two or more races, non-Hispanic/Latino). Average age 35. 47 applicants, 70% accepted, 26 enrolled. In 2017, 13 master's, 4 doctorates awarded. *Degree requirements:* For doctorate, comprehensive exam (for some programs), capstone project. *Entrance requirements:* For master's, GRE General Test or MAT; for doctorate, GRE General Test. Additional exam requirements/recommendations for international students: Required—TOEFL. *Application deadline:* For fall admission, 2/1 for domestic students. Application fee: $50. Electronic applications accepted. *Financial support:* In 2017–18, 66 students received support. Teaching assistantships, Federal Work-Study, scholarships/grants, and unspecified assistantships available. Support available to part-time students. Financial award application deadline: 6/30; financial award applicants required to submit FAFSA. *Faculty research:* Women and strokes, obesity and pregnancy, educational environmental factors, international undeserved populations, midwifery. *Total annual research expenditures:* $5,000. *Unit head:* Dr. Barbara Camune, Graduate Program Director, 214-367-3754, Fax: 214-820-3375, E-mail: barbara_camune@baylor.edu. *Application contact:* Elaine Lark, Coordinator of Recruitment and Enrollment, 214-818-7839, Fax: 214-820-3835, E-mail: elaine_lark@baylor.edu.
Website: http://www.baylor.edu/nursing/

Bethel University, Graduate School, St. Paul, MN 55112-6999. Offers business administration (MBA); classroom management (Certificate); counseling (MA); K-12 education (MA); leadership (Ed D); leadership foundations (Certificate); nurse educator (MS, Certificate); nurse-midwifery (MS); physician assistant (MS); special education (MA); strategic leadership (MA); teaching (MA); teaching and learning (Certificate). *Program availability:* Part-time, evening/weekend, 100% online, blended/hybrid learning. *Faculty:* 22 full-time (16 women), 70 part-time/adjunct (44 women). *Students:* 611 full-time (431 women), 393 part-time (249 women); includes 176 minority (82 Black or African American, non-Hispanic/Latino; 4 American Indian or Alaska Native, non-Hispanic/Latino; 31 Asian, non-Hispanic/Latino; 39 Hispanic/Latino; 2 Native Hawaiian or other Pacific Islander, non-Hispanic/Latino; 18 Two or more races, non-Hispanic/Latino), 9 international. Average age 36. 668 applicants, 42% accepted, 223 enrolled. In 2017, 287 master's, 30 doctorates, 172 other advanced degrees awarded. *Degree requirements:* For master's, comprehensive exam (for some programs), thesis (for some programs); for doctorate, comprehensive exam, thesis/dissertation. *Entrance requirements:* Additional exam requirements/recommendations for international students: Required—TOEFL (minimum score 550 paper-based, 80 iBT) or IELTS. *Application deadline:* Applications are processed on a rolling basis. Application fee: $0. Electronic applications accepted. *Expenses:* Contact institution. *Financial support:* Teaching assistantships, career-related internships or fieldwork, and scholarships/grants available. Support available to part-time students. Financial award applicants required to submit FAFSA. *Unit head:* Dr. Randy Bergen, Associate Provost, 651-635-8000, Fax: 651-635-8004, E-mail: r-bergen@bethel.edu. *Application contact:* Director of Admissions, 651-635-8000, Fax: 651-635-8004, E-mail: gs@bethel.edu.
Website: https://www.bethel.edu/graduate/

Case Western Reserve University, Frances Payne Bolton School of Nursing, Master's Programs in Nursing, Program in Nurse Midwifery, Cleveland, OH 44106. Offers MSN. *Accreditation:* ACNM/ACME. *Program availability:* Part-time. *Faculty:* 18 full-time (17 women), 3 part-time/adjunct (2 women). *Students:* 3 full-time (2 women), 11 part-time (all women); includes 5 minority (4 Black or African American, non-Hispanic/Latino; 1 Two or more races, non-Hispanic/Latino). Average age 33. 7 applicants, 57% accepted, 3 enrolled. In 2017, 6 master's awarded. *Degree requirements:* For master's, minimum GPA of 3.0, clinical hours corresponding to requirements to sit for certification exam, portfolio. *Entrance requirements:* For master's, GRE General Test or MAT. Additional exam requirements/recommendations for international students: Required—TOEFL (minimum score 577 paper-based, 90 IBT) or IELTS (minimum score 7.0). *Application deadline:* For fall admission, 5/1 for domestic and international students; for spring admission, 10/1 for domestic and international students; for summer admission, 3/1 for domestic and international students. Applications are processed on a rolling basis. Application fee: $75. Electronic applications accepted. *Expenses:* Contact institution. *Financial support:* In 2017–18, 1 student received support, including 1 teaching assistantship with partial tuition reimbursement available (averaging $18,100 per year); scholarships/grants and traineeships also available. Financial award application deadline: 5/15; financial award applicants required to submit FAFSA. *Faculty research:* Clinical nursing, normal childbearing, descriptive studies of care, high risk pregnancy, side effects of bed rest, strengthening and expanding nursing services. *Unit head:* Dr. Kimberly Garcia, Head, 216-368-0671, E-mail: ksg11@case.edu. *Application contact:* Jackie Tepale, Admissions Coordinator, 216-368-5253, Fax: 216-368-0124, E-mail: yyd@case.edu.
Website: http://fpb.case.edu/MSN/midwifery.shtm

Columbia University, School of Nursing, Program in Nurse Midwifery, New York, NY 10032. Offers MS. *Accreditation:* AACN; ACNM/ACME. *Program availability:* Part-time. *Entrance requirements:* For master's, GRE General Test, NCLEX, BSN, 1 year of clinical experience (preferred). Additional exam requirements/recommendations for international students: Required—TOEFL (minimum score 100 iBT). Electronic applications accepted. *Expenses: Tuition:* Full-time $44,864; part-time $1704 per credit. *Required fees:* $2370 per semester. One-time fee: $105.

DeSales University, Division of Healthcare, Center Valley, PA 18034-9568. Offers adult-gerontology acute care (Post Master's Certificate); adult-gerontology acute care nurse practitioner (MSN); adult-gerontology acute certified nurse practitioner (Post Master's Certificate); adult-gerontology clinical nurse specialist (MSN, Post Master's Certificate); clinical leadership (DNP); family nurse practitioner (MSN, Post Master's Certificate); general nursing practice (DNP); nurse anesthetist (MSN); nurse educator (Post Master's Certificate, Postbaccalaureate Certificate); nurse midwife (MSN); nurse practitioner (MSN); psychiatric-mental health nurse practitioner (MSN, Post Master's Certificate); DNP/MBA. *Accreditation:* ACEN. *Program availability:* Part-time. *Faculty:* 26 full-time (20 women), 30 part-time/adjunct (19 women). *Students:* 282 full-time (210 women), 101 part-time (85 women); includes 39 minority (12 Black or African American, non-Hispanic/Latino; 11 Asian, non-Hispanic/Latino; 12 Hispanic/Latino; 4 Two or more races, non-Hispanic/Latino), 1 international. Average age 29. 2,884 applicants, 5% accepted, 114 enrolled. In 2017, 76 master's, 6 doctorates awarded. *Degree requirements:* For master's, minimum GPA of 3.0, portfolio; for doctorate, minimum GPA of 3.0, scholarly capstone project. *Entrance requirements:* For master's, GRE or MAT (waived if applicant has an undergraduate GPA of 3.0 or higher), BSN from ACEN- or CCNE-accredited program, minimum undergraduate GPA of 3.0, active RN license or eligibility, two letters of recommendation, essay, health care experience, personal interview; for doctorate, BSN or MSN from ACEN- or CCNE-accredited institution, minimum GPA of 3.3 in graduate program, current licensure as an RN. Additional exam requirements/recommendations for international students: Required—TOEFL (minimum score 104 iBT). *Application deadline:* Applications are processed on a rolling basis. Application fee: $50. Electronic applications accepted. *Expenses:* Contact institution. *Financial support:* Applicants required to submit FAFSA. *Unit head:* Ronald Nordone, Dean of Graduate Education, 610-282-1100 Ext. 1289, E-mail: ronald.nordone@desales.edu. *Application contact:* Julia Ferraro, Director of Graduate Admissions, 610-282-1100 Ext. 1768, E-mail: gradadmissions@desales.edu.

Emory University, Nell Hodgson Woodruff School of Nursing, Atlanta, GA 30322-1100. Offers adult nurse practitioner (MSN); emergency nurse practitioner (MSN); family nurse practitioner (MSN); family nurse-midwife (MSN); health systems leadership (MSN); nurse-midwifery (MSN); pediatric nurse practitioner acute and primary care (MSN); women's health care (Title X) (MSN); women's health nurse practitioner (MSN); MSN/MPH. *Accreditation:* AACN; ACNM/ACME (one or more programs are accredited). *Program availability:* Part-time. *Entrance requirements:* For master's, GRE General Test or MAT, minimum GPA of 3.0, BS in nursing from an accredited institution, RN license and additional course work, 3 letters of recommendation. Additional exam requirements/recommendations for international students: Required—TOEFL (minimum score 600 paper-based; 100 iBT). Electronic applications accepted. *Expenses:* Contact institution. *Faculty research:* Older adult falls and injuries, minority health issues, cardiac symptoms and quality of life, bio-ethics and decision-making, menopausal issues.

Frontier Nursing University, Graduate Programs, Hyden, KY 41749. Offers family nurse practitioner (MSN, DNP, Post Master's Certificate); nurse-midwifery (MSN, DNP, Post Master's Certificate); psychiatric-mental health nurse practitioner (MSN, DNP, Post Master's Certificate); women's health care nurse practitioner (MSN, DNP, Post Master's Certificate). *Accreditation:* ACEN. *Degree requirements:* For doctorate, capstone project, practicum.

See Display on page 570 and Close-Up on page 761.

Georgetown University, Graduate School of Arts and Sciences, School of Nursing and Health Studies, Washington, DC 20057. Offers acute care nurse practitioner (MS); clinical nurse specialist (MS); family nurse practitioner (MS); nurse anesthesia (MS); nurse-midwifery (MS); nursing (DNP); nursing education (MS). *Accreditation:* AACN;

Nurse Midwifery

AANA/CANAEP (one or more programs are accredited); ACNM/ACME (one or more programs are accredited). *Degree requirements:* For master's, thesis optional. *Entrance requirements:* For master's, GRE General Test or MAT, bachelor's degree in nursing from ACEN-accredited school, minimum undergraduate GPA of 3.0. Additional exam requirements/recommendations for international students: Required—TOEFL.

James Madison University, The Graduate School, College of Health and Behavioral Studies, Program in Nursing, Harrisonburg, VA 22807. Offers adult/gerontology primary care nurse practitioner (MSN); clinical nurse leader (MSN); family nurse practitioner (MSN); nurse administrator (MSN); nurse midwifery (MSN); nursing (MSN, DNP); psychiatric mental health nurse practitioner (MSN). *Accreditation:* AACN. *Program availability:* Part-time, 100% online, blended/hybrid learning. *Students:* 10 full-time (9 women), 77 part-time (71 women); includes 10 minority (2 Black or African American, non-Hispanic/Latino; 5 Asian, non-Hispanic/Latino; 1 Hispanic/Latino; 2 Two or more races, non-Hispanic/Latino). Average age 30. In 2017, 27 master's awarded. Application fee: $55. Electronic applications accepted. *Expenses:* Tuition, state resident: full-time $10,512; part-time $438 per credit hour. Tuition, nonresident: full-time $28,358; part-time $1162 per credit hour. *Required fees:* $1128. *Financial support:* In 2017–18, 2 students received support. Federal Work-Study and 2 assistantships (averaging $7911) available. Financial award application deadline: 3/1; financial award applicants required to submit FAFSA. *Unit head:* Dr. Julie T. Sanford, Department Head, 540-568-6314, E-mail: sanforjt@jmu.edu. *Application contact:* Lynette D. Michael, Director of Graduate Admissions, 540-568-6131 Ext. 6395, Fax: 540-568-7860, E-mail: michaeld@jmu.edu.
Website: http://www.nursing.jmu.edu

Marquette University, Graduate School, College of Nursing, Milwaukee, WI 53201-1881. Offers acute care nurse practitioner (Certificate); adult clinical nurse specialist (Certificate); adult nurse practitioner (Certificate); advanced practice nursing (MSN, DNP), including adult-older adult acute care (DNP), adults (MSN), adults-older adults (DNP), clinical nurse leader (MSN), health care systems leadership (DNP), nurse-midwifery (MSN), older adults (MSN), pediatrics-acute care, pediatrics-primary care, primary care (DNP), systems leadership and healthcare quality (MSN); family nurse practitioner (Certificate); nurse-midwifery (Certificate); nursing (PhD); pediatric acute care (Certificate); pediatric primary care (Certificate); systems leadership and healthcare quality (Certificate). *Accreditation:* AACN. Terminal master's awarded for partial completion of doctoral program. *Degree requirements:* For master's, comprehensive exam, thesis or alternative. *Entrance requirements:* For master's, GRE General Test, BSN, Wisconsin RN license, official transcripts from all current and previous colleges/universities except Marquette, three completed recommendation forms, resume, written statement of professional goals; for doctorate, GRE General Test, official transcripts from all current and previous colleges/universities except Marquette, three letters of recommendation, resume, written statement of professional goals, sample of scholarly writing. Additional exam requirements/recommendations for international students: Required—TOEFL (minimum score 530 paper-based). Electronic applications accepted. *Faculty research:* Psychosocial adjustment to chronic illness, gerontology, reminiscence, health policy: uninsured and access, hospital care delivery systems.

Midwives College of Utah, Graduate Program, Salt Lake City, UT 84106. Offers MS. *Accreditation:* MEAC. *Program availability:* Part-time. *Faculty:* 6. *Students:* 5 (all women); includes 1 minority (Hispanic/Latino). In 2017, 2 master's awarded. *Degree requirements:* For master's, comprehensive exam, thesis. *Entrance requirements:* Additional exam requirements/recommendations for international students: Required—TOEFL (minimum score 88 iBT). *Application deadline:* For fall admission, 3/15 for domestic and international students; for winter admission, 7/9 for domestic and international students; for summer admission, 11/6 for domestic and international students. Application fee: $60. Electronic applications accepted. *Financial support:* Applicants required to submit FAFSA. *Faculty research:* Interprofessional collaboration; health equity; evidence-informed practice; outcomes of midwifery care. *Unit head:* Courtney L. Everson, Dean of Graduate Studies, 801-649-5230 Ext. 806, Fax: 866-207-2024, E-mail: graduatedean@midwifery.edu.

National College of Midwifery, Graduate Programs, Taos, NM 87571. Offers MS, PhD. *Accreditation:* MEAC. *Program availability:* Part-time, evening/weekend, online learning. *Degree requirements:* For master's, thesis, publication; for doctorate, thesis/dissertation, presentation, publication. *Entrance requirements:* For master's and doctorate, midwifery license or certification. Electronic applications accepted.

New York University, Rory Meyers College of Nursing, Doctor of Nursing Practice Program, New York, NY 10012-1019. Offers nursing (DNP), including adult-gerontology acute care nurse practitioner, adult-gerontology primary care nurse practitioner, family nurse practitioner, nurse-midwifery, pediatrics nurse practitioner, psychiatric-mental health nurse practitioner. *Accreditation:* AACN. *Program availability:* Part-time, evening/weekend. *Faculty:* 16 full-time (all women), 1 (woman) part-time/adjunct. *Students:* 48 part-time (43 women); includes 11 minority (5 Black or African American, non-Hispanic/Latino; 5 Asian, non-Hispanic/Latino; 1 Hispanic/Latino). Average age 28. 20 applicants, 75% accepted, 10 enrolled. In 2017, 8 doctorates awarded. *Degree requirements:* For doctorate, thesis/dissertation, project. *Entrance requirements:* For doctorate, MS, RN license, interview, Nurse Practitioner Certification, writing sample. Additional exam requirements/recommendations for international students: Required—TOEFL (minimum score 100 iBT), IELTS (minimum score 7). *Application deadline:* For fall admission, 3/1 priority date for domestic and international students. Applications are processed on a rolling basis. Application fee: $80. Electronic applications accepted. *Expenses:* Contact institution. *Financial support:* In 2017–18, 13 students received support. Scholarships/grants available. Support available to part-time students. Financial award application deadline: 2/1; financial award applicants required to submit FAFSA. *Faculty research:* Workforce determinants of healthcare quality, genomics, health literacy and health outcomes, health policy. *Unit head:* Dr. Mary Jo Vetter, Director, DNP Program, 212-998-5165, E-mail: mjv5@nyu.edu. *Application contact:* Matthew Burke, Assistant Director, Graduate Student Affairs and Admissions, 212-998-7397, E-mail: mb6060@nyu.edu.

New York University, Rory Meyers College of Nursing, Programs in Advanced Practice Nursing, New York, NY 10012-1019. Offers adult-gerontology acute care nurse practitioner (MS, Advanced Certificate); adult-gerontology primary care nurse practitioner (MS, Advanced Certificate); family nurse practitioner (MS, Advanced Certificate); gerontology nurse practitioner (Advanced Certificate); nurse-midwifery (MS, Advanced Certificate); nursing administration (MS, Advanced Certificate); nursing education (MS, Advanced Certificate); nursing informatics (MS, Advanced Certificate); pediatrics nurse practitioner (MS, Advanced Certificate); psychiatric-mental health nurse practitioner (MS, Advanced Certificate); MS/MPH. *Accreditation:* AACN; ACNM/ACME. *Program availability:* Part-time, evening/weekend. *Faculty:* 23 full-time (all women), 62 part-time/adjunct (56 women). *Students:* 50 full-time (46 women), 557 part-time (509 women); includes 234 minority (58 Black or African American, non-Hispanic/Latino; 1 American Indian or Alaska Native, non-Hispanic/Latino; 116 Asian, non-Hispanic/Latino; 43 Hispanic/Latino; 1 Native Hawaiian or other Pacific Islander, non-Hispanic/Latino; 15 Two or more races, non-Hispanic/Latino), 23 international. Average age 32. 391 applicants, 59% accepted, 149 enrolled. In 2017, 187 master's, 5 other advanced degrees awarded. *Degree requirements:* For master's, thesis (for some programs), capstone. *Entrance requirements:* For master's, BS in nursing, AS in nursing with another BS/BA, interview, RN license, 1 year of clinical experience (3 for the MS in nursing education program); for Advanced Certificate, master's degree in nursing. Additional exam requirements/recommendations for international students: Required—TOEFL (minimum score 100 iBT), IELTS (minimum score 7). *Application deadline:* For fall admission, 3/1 priority date for domestic and international students; for spring admission, 11/1 priority date for domestic and international students; for summer admission, 3/1 for domestic and international students. Application fee: $80. Electronic applications accepted. *Expenses:* Contact institution. *Financial support:* In 2017–18, 130 students received support. Career-related internships or fieldwork, Federal Work-Study, and scholarships/grants available. Support available to part-time students. Financial award application deadline: 3/1; financial award applicants required to submit FAFSA. *Faculty research:* Vaccine hesitancy in pregnant women and mothers, palliative care and midwifery, diabetes education, curriculum development, workforce training, education and development, geriatrics. *Unit head:* Dr. James Pace, Senior Associate Dean for Academic Programs, 212-992-7343, E-mail: james.pace@nyu.edu. *Application contact:* Matthew Burke, Assistant Director, Graduate Student Affairs and Admissions, 212-998-7397, Fax: 212-995-4302, E-mail: mb6060@nyu.edu.

Oregon Health & Science University, School of Nursing, Program in Nurse Midwifery, Portland, OR 97239-3098. Offers MN. *Accreditation:* AACN; ACNM/ACME. *Degree requirements:* For master's, thesis optional. *Entrance requirements:* For master's, GRE General Test, minimum cumulative and science GPA of 3.0, 3 letters of recommendation, essay, statistics in last 5 years with minimum B- grade, BS with major in nursing or BSN. Additional exam requirements/recommendations for international students: Required—TOEFL (minimum score 83 iBT). Electronic applications accepted. *Expenses:* Contact institution. *Faculty research:* Vaginal birth after cesarean, lactation outcomes, promotion of physiologic birth, post partum hemorrhage, decreasing non-evidence based cesarean delivery; establishing new evidence for labor dystocia.

Shenandoah University, Eleanor Wade Custer School of Nursing, Winchester, VA 22601. Offers adult gerontology primary care nurse practitioner (Graduate Certificate); adult-gerontology primary care nurse practitioner (MSN); family nurse practitioner (MSN, DNP, Graduate Certificate); general (MSN); health systems leadership (DNP); health systems management (MSN, Graduate Certificate); nurse midwifery (MSN); nurse-midwifery (Graduate Certificate); nursing education (Graduate Certificate); nursing practice (DNP); psychiatric mental health nurse practitioner (MSN, DNP, Graduate Certificate). *Accreditation:* AACN; ACNM/ACME. *Faculty:* 17 full-time (all women), 6 part-time/adjunct (all women). *Students:* 30 full-time (26 women), 51 part-time (48 women); includes 19 minority (13 Black or African American, non-Hispanic/Latino; 3 Asian, non-Hispanic/Latino; 2 Hispanic/Latino; 1 Two or more races, non-Hispanic/Latino), 3 international. Average age 37. 52 applicants, 88% accepted, 34 enrolled. In 2017, 18 master's, 1 doctorate, 28 other advanced degrees awarded. *Degree requirements:* For master's, research project, clinical hours; for doctorate, scholarly project, clinical hours; for Graduate Certificate, clinical hours. *Entrance requirements:* For master's, United States RN license; minimum GPA of 3.0; 2080 hours of clinical experience; curriculum vitae; 3 letters of recommendation from former dean, faculty member, or advisor familiar with the applicant, and a former or current supervisor; two-to-three-page essay on a specified topic; for doctorate, MSN, minimum GPA of 3.0, 3 letters of recommendation, interview, BSN, two-to-three page essay on a specific topic, 500-word statement of clinical practice research interest, resume, current U.S. RN license, 2080 clinical hours; for Graduate Certificate, MSN, minimum GPA of 3.0, 2 letters of recommendation, minimum of one year (2080 hours) of clinical nursing experience, interview, two-to-three page essay on a specific topic, resume, current United States RN license. Additional exam requirements/recommendations for international students: Required—TOEFL (minimum score 558 paper-based; 83 iBT). *Application deadline:* For fall admission, 4/15 priority date for domestic and international students; for spring admission, 11/1 for domestic and international students; for summer admission, 3/1 for domestic and international students. Application fee: $30. Electronic applications accepted. *Expenses:* $22,451 tuition, plus $3,579 fees (student services fee, technology fee, and clinical fee). *Financial support:* In 2017–18, 32 students received support. Scholarships/grants and unspecified assistantships available. Financial award applicants required to submit FAFSA. *Faculty research:* Emergency preparedness, workplace environment, maternal child, inter-professional education, health policy. *Total annual research expenditures:* $30,000. *Unit head:* Dr. Kathleen LaSala, RN, Dean, 540-678-4381, Fax: 540-665-5519, E-mail: klasala@su.edu. *Application contact:* Andrew Woodall, Executive Director of Recruitment and Admissions, 540-665-4581, Fax: 540-665-4627, E-mail: admit@su.edu.
Website: http://www.su.edu/nursing/

State University of New York Downstate Medical Center, College of Nursing, Graduate Programs in Nursing, Program in Nurse Midwifery, Brooklyn, NY 11203-2098. Offers MS, Post Master's Certificate. *Accreditation:* ACNM/ACME.

Stony Brook University, State University of New York, Stony Brook Medicine, School of Nursing, Program in Nurse Midwifery, Stony Brook, NY 11794. Offers MS, DNP, Certificate. *Accreditation:* AACN; ACNM/ACME. *Program availability:* Part-time, blended/hybrid learning. *Students:* 2 full-time (both women), 37 part-time (all women); includes 12 minority (5 Black or African American, non-Hispanic/Latino; 1 American Indian or Alaska Native, non-Hispanic/Latino; 2 Asian, non-Hispanic/Latino; 4 Hispanic/Latino). 44 applicants, 45% accepted, 12 enrolled. In 2017, 6 master's, 3 other advanced degrees awarded. *Degree requirements:* For master's, thesis. *Entrance requirements:* For master's, BSN, minimum GPA of 3.0, course work in statistics. Additional exam requirements/recommendations for international students: Required—TOEFL (minimum score 90 iBT). *Application deadline:* For fall admission, 3/3 for domestic students. Application fee: $100. *Expenses:* Contact institution. *Financial support:* Fellowships, research assistantships, and teaching assistantships available. Financial award application deadline: 3/15. *Unit head:* Heather Findletar-Hines, Program Director, 631-444-1491, Fax: 631-444-3136, E-mail: heather.finlander@stonybrook.edu. *Application contact:* Crystal Garcia, Staff Assistant, 631-632-3392, Fax: 631-444-3136, E-mail: crystal.garcia@stonybrook.edu.
Website: http://www.nursing.stonybrookmedicine.edu/

Thomas Jefferson University, College of Science, Health and the Liberal Arts, Program in Midwifery, Philadelphia, PA 19107. Offers MS. *Program availability:* Part-time, evening/weekend, online learning. *Entrance requirements:* For master's, GRE or MAT. Additional exam requirements/recommendations for international students: Required—TOEFL (minimum score 550 paper-based; 79 iBT). Electronic applications accepted.

University of Cincinnati, Graduate School, College of Nursing, Cincinnati, OH 45221-0038. Offers nurse midwifery (MSN); nurse practitioner (MSN, DNP), including acute care pediatrics (DNP), adult-gerontology acute care, adult-gerontology primary care, anesthesia (DNP), family (MSN), leadership (DNP), neonatal (MSN), women's health (MSN); nursing (MSN, PhD), including occupational health (MSN). *Accreditation:* AACN; AANA/CANAEP (one or more programs are accredited); ACNM/ACME. *Program availability:* Part-time, 100% online, blended/hybrid learning. *Faculty:* 74 full-time (69 women), 112 part-time/adjunct (105 women). *Students:* 323 full-time (261 women), 1,084 part-time (949 women); includes 311 minority (113 Black or African American, non-Hispanic/Latino; 4 American Indian or Alaska Native, non-Hispanic/Latino; 56

Asian, non-Hispanic/Latino; 108 Hispanic/Latino; 1 Native Hawaiian or other Pacific Islander, non-Hispanic/Latino; 29 Two or more races, non-Hispanic/Latino), 12 international. Average age 34. 582 applicants, 64% accepted, 314 enrolled. In 2017, 579 master's, 18 doctorates awarded. *Degree requirements:* For master's, thesis or alternative; for doctorate, comprehensive exam (for some programs), thesis/dissertation (for some programs). *Entrance requirements:* For doctorate, GRE General Test. Additional exam requirements/recommendations for international students: Required—TOEFL (minimum score 600 paper-based; 100 iBT); Recommended—IELTS (minimum score 7). *Application deadline:* For fall admission, 5/1 priority date for domestic students, 5/1 for international students; for spring admission, 10/1 for domestic students; for summer admission, 3/1 priority date for domestic students. Applications are processed on a rolling basis. Application fee: $130 ($70 for international students). Electronic applications accepted. *Expenses:* $14,668 annual full-time in-state tuition, $707 annual fees. *Financial support:* In 2017–18, 123 students received support, including 8 fellowships with full tuition reimbursements available (averaging $30,423 per year), 7 research assistantships with full tuition reimbursements available (averaging $17,971 per year), 5 teaching assistantships with full tuition reimbursements available (averaging $17,971 per year); Federal Work-Study, institutionally sponsored loans, scholarships/grants, traineeships, health care benefits, tuition waivers (partial), and unspecified assistantships also available. Support available to part-time students. Financial award application deadline: 5/1; financial award applicants required to submit FAFSA. *Faculty research:* Vulnerable populations, education, violence, chronicity/aging, cancer. *Total annual research expenditures:* $575,576. *Unit head:* Dr. Greer Glazer, Dean, 513-558-5330, Fax: 513-558-9030, E-mail: greer.glazer@uc.edu. *Application contact:* Office of Student Recruitment, 513-558-8400, Fax: 513-558-5012, E-mail: nursingbearcats@uc.edu.
Website: https://nursing.uc.edu/

University of Colorado Denver, College of Nursing, Aurora, CO 80045. Offers adult clinical nurse specialist (MS); adult nurse practitioner (MS); family nurse practitioner (MS); family psychiatric mental health nurse practitioner (MS); health care informatics (MS); nurse-midwifery (MS); nursing (DNP, PhD); nursing leadership and health care systems (MS); pediatric nurse practitioner (MS); women's health (MS); MS/PhD. *Accreditation:* ACNM/ACME (one or more programs are accredited). *Program availability:* Part-time, evening/weekend, online learning. *Students:* 297 applicants, 55% accepted, 141 enrolled. In 2017, 138 master's, 18 doctorates awarded. Terminal master's awarded for partial completion of doctoral program. *Degree requirements:* For master's, thesis optional; for doctorate, comprehensive exam, thesis/dissertation, 42 credits of coursework. *Entrance requirements:* For master's, GRE if cumulative undergraduate GPA is less than 3.0, undergraduate nursing degree from ACEN- or CCNE-accredited school or university; completion of research and statistics courses with minimum grade of C; copy of current and unencumbered nursing license; for doctorate, GRE, bachelor's and/or master's degrees in nursing from ACEN- or CCNE-accredited institution; portfolio; minimum undergraduate GPA of 3.0, graduate 3.5; graduate-level intermediate statistics and master's-level nursing theory courses with minimum B grade; interview. Additional exam requirements/recommendations for international students: Required—TOEFL (minimum score 560 paper-based; 83 iBT). *Application deadline:* For fall admission, 2/15 for domestic students, 1/15 for international students; for spring admission, 7/1 for domestic students, 6/1 for international students. Application fee: $50 ($75 for international students). Electronic applications accepted. *Unit head:* Dr. Sarah Thompson, Dean, 303-724-1679, E-mail: sarah.a.thompson@ucdenver.edu. *Application contact:* Judy Campbell, Graduate Programs Coordinator, 303-724-8503, E-mail: judy.campbell@ucdenver.edu.
Website: http://www.ucdenver.edu/academics/colleges/nursing/Pages/default.aspx

University of Illinois at Chicago, College of Nursing, Program in Nursing, Chicago, IL 60607-7128. Offers acute care clinical nurse specialist (MS); administrative nursing leadership (Certificate); adult nurse practitioner (MS); adult/geriatric nurse practitioner (MS); advanced community health nurse specialist (MS); family nurse practitioner (MS); geriatric clinical nurse specialist (MS); geriatric nurse practitioner (MS); nurse midwifery (MS); occupational health/advanced community health nurse specialist (MS); occupational health/family nurse practitioner (MS); pediatric nurse practitioner (MS); perinatal clinical nurse specialist (MS); school/advanced community health nurse specialist (MS); school/family nurse practitioner (MS); women's health nurse practitioner (MS). *Accreditation:* AACN. *Program availability:* Part-time. *Degree requirements:* For master's, thesis or alternative. *Entrance requirements:* For master's, GRE General Test, minimum GPA of 2.75. Additional exam requirements/recommendations for international students: Required—TOEFL. Electronic applications accepted.

University of Indianapolis, Graduate Programs, School of Nursing, Indianapolis, IN 46227-3697. Offers advanced practice nursing (DNP); family nurse practitioner (MSN); gerontological nurse practitioner (MSN); neonatal nurse practitioner (MSN); nurse-midwifery (MSN); nursing (MSN); nursing and health systems leadership (MSN); nursing education (MSN); women's health nurse practitioner (MSN); MBA/MSN. *Accreditation:* AACN. *Entrance requirements:* For master's, minimum GPA of 3.0, interview, letters of recommendation, resume, IN nursing license, 1 year of professional practice; for doctorate, graduate of ACEN- or CCNE-accredited nursing program; MSN or MA with nursing major and minimum cumulative GPA of 3.25; unencumbered RN license with eligibility for licensure in Indiana; completion of graduate-level statistics course within last 5 years with minimum grade of B; resume; essay; official transcripts from all academic institutions. Additional exam requirements/recommendations for international students: Required—TOEFL (minimum score 550 paper-based). Electronic applications accepted.

The University of Kansas, University of Kansas Medical Center, School of Nursing, Kansas City, KS 66160. Offers adult/gerontological clinical nurse specialist (PMC); adult/gerontological nurse practitioner (PMC); health care informatics (PMC); health professions educator (PMC); nurse midwife (PMC); nursing (MS, DNP, PhD); organizational leadership (PMC); psychiatric/mental health nurse practitioner (PMC); public health nursing (PMC). *Accreditation:* AACN; ACNM/ACME. *Program availability:* Part-time, 100% online, blended/hybrid learning. *Faculty:* 56. *Students:* 48 full-time (44 women), 260 part-time (235 women); includes 50 minority (12 Black or African American, non-Hispanic/Latino; 2 American Indian or Alaska Native, non-Hispanic/Latino; 16 Asian, non-Hispanic/Latino; 8 Hispanic/Latino; 12 Two or more races, non-Hispanic/Latino). Average age 36. 87 applicants, 95% accepted, 61 enrolled. In 2017, 37 master's, 18 doctorates, 3 other advanced degrees awarded. Terminal master's awarded for partial completion of doctoral program. *Degree requirements:* For master's, comprehensive exam, thesis (for some programs), general oral exam; for doctorate, thesis/dissertation or alternative, comprehensive oral exam (for DNP); comprehensive written and oral exam, or three publications (for PhD). *Entrance requirements:* For master's, bachelor's degree in nursing, minimum GPA of 3.0, 1 year of clinical experience, RN license in KS and MO; for doctorate, GRE General Test (for PhD only), bachelor's degree in nursing, minimum GPA of 3.5, RN license in KS and MO. Additional exam requirements/recommendations for international students: Required—TOEFL. *Application deadline:* For fall admission, 4/1 for domestic and international students; for spring admission, 9/1 for domestic and international students. Application fee: $75. Electronic applications accepted. *Financial support:* In 2017–18, 5 research assistantships with tuition reimbursements (averaging $20,000 per year), 30 teaching assistantships with tuition reimbursements (averaging $20,000 per year) were awarded; scholarships/grants and traineeships also available. Financial award application deadline: 3/1; financial award applicants required to submit FAFSA. *Faculty research:* Breastfeeding practices of teen mothers, national database of nursing quality indicators, caregiving of families of patients using technology in the home, simulation in nursing education, diaphragm fatigue. *Total annual research expenditures:* $1.4 million. *Unit head:* Dr. Sally Maliski, Dean, 913-588-1601, Fax: 913-588-1660, E-mail: smaliski@kumc.edu. *Application contact:* Dr. Pamela K. Barnes, Associate Dean, Student Affairs, 913-588-1619, Fax: 913-588-1615, E-mail: pbarnes2@kumc.edu.
Website: http://nursing.kumc.edu

The University of Manchester, School of Nursing, Midwifery and Social Work, Manchester, United Kingdom. Offers nursing (M Phil, PhD); social work (M Phil, PhD).

University of Miami, Graduate School, School of Nursing and Health Studies, Coral Gables, FL 33124. Offers acute care (MSN), including acute care nurse practitioner, nurse anesthesia; nursing (PhD); primary care (MSN), including adult nurse practitioner, family nurse practitioner, nurse midwifery, women's health practitioner. *Accreditation:* AACN; AANA/CANAEP; ACNM/ACME (one or more programs are accredited). *Program availability:* Part-time. *Degree requirements:* For master's, thesis optional; for doctorate, thesis/dissertation. *Entrance requirements:* For master's, GRE General Test, BSN, minimum GPA of 3.0, Florida RN license; for doctorate, GRE General Test, BSN or MSN, minimum GPA of 3.0. Additional exam requirements/recommendations for international students: Required—TOEFL (minimum score 550 paper-based). Electronic applications accepted. *Faculty research:* Transcultural nursing, exercise and depression in Alzheimer's disease, infectious diseases/HIV–AIDS, postpartum depression, outcomes assessment.

University of Minnesota, Twin Cities Campus, Graduate School, School of Nursing, Minneapolis, MN 55455-0213. Offers adult/gerontological clinical nurse specialist (DNP); adult/gerontological primary care nurse practitioner (DNP); family nurse practitioner (DNP); health innovation and leadership (DNP); integrative health and healing (DNP); nurse anesthesia (DNP); nurse midwifery (DNP); nursing (MN, PhD); nursing informatics (DNP); pediatric clinical nurse specialist (DNP); primary care certified pediatric nurse practitioner (DNP); psychiatric/mental health nurse practitioner (DNP); women's health nurse practitioner (DNP). *Accreditation:* AACN; AANA/CANAEP; ACNM/ACME (one or more programs are accredited). *Program availability:* Part-time, online learning. Terminal master's awarded for partial completion of doctoral program. *Degree requirements:* For master's, final oral exam, project or thesis; for doctorate, thesis/dissertation. *Entrance requirements:* For master's and doctorate, GRE General Test. Additional exam requirements/recommendations for international students: Required—TOEFL (minimum score 586 paper-based). *Expenses:* Contact institution. *Faculty research:* Child and family health promotion, nursing research on elders.

University of Pennsylvania, School of Nursing, Program in Nurse Midwifery, Philadelphia, PA 19104. Offers MSN. *Accreditation:* AACN; ACNM/ACME. *Program availability:* Part-time. *Students:* 30 full-time (all women), 16 part-time (all women); includes 8 minority (1 Black or African American, non-Hispanic/Latino; 4 Asian, non-Hispanic/Latino; 2 Hispanic/Latino; 1 Two or more races, non-Hispanic/Latino). Average age 30. 33 applicants, 30% accepted, 10 enrolled. In 2017, 20 master's awarded. Application fee: $80.

University of Pittsburgh, School of Nursing, Nurse-Midwife Program, Pittsburgh, PA 15260. Offers DNP. *Program availability:* Part-time. *Faculty:* 3 full-time (all women), 1 (woman) part-time/adjunct. *Students:* 2 full-time (both women), 4 part-time (all women); includes 1 minority (Black or African American, non-Hispanic/Latino). Average age 27. 5 applicants, 40% accepted, 2 enrolled. *Entrance requirements:* For doctorate, GRE General Test, BSN, RN license, minimum GPA of 3.5, 3 letters of recommendation, resume, personal essay, course work in statistics. Additional exam requirements/recommendations for international students: Required—TOEFL (minimum score 600 paper-based; 100 IBT) or IELTS (minimum score 7.0). Application fee: $50. Electronic applications accepted. *Expenses:* $13,068 per term full-time resident tuition, $1,064 per credit part-time; $15,270 per term full-time non-resident tuition, $1,247 per credit part-time; $437 per term full-time fees; $282 per term part-time fees. *Financial support:* In 2017–18, 4 students received support, including 1 teaching assistantship (averaging $27,675 per year); scholarships/grants also available. Financial award applicants required to submit FAFSA. *Unit head:* Dr. Sandra Engberg, Associate Dean for Clinical Education, 412-624-3835, Fax: 412-624-8521, E-mail: sje1@pitt.edu. *Application contact:* Laurie Lapsley, Administrator of Graduate Student Services, 412-624-9670, Fax: 412-624-2409, E-mail: lapsleyl@pitt.edu.

University of Puerto Rico–Medical Sciences Campus, Graduate School of Public Health, Department of Human Development, Program in Nurse Midwifery, San Juan, PR 00936-5067. Offers MPH, Certificate. *Program availability:* Part-time. *Entrance requirements:* For master's, GRE, previous course work in algebra.

University of South Africa, College of Human Sciences, Pretoria, South Africa. Offers adult education (M Ed); African languages (MA, PhD); African politics (MA, PhD); Afrikaans (MA, PhD); ancient history (MA, PhD); ancient Near Eastern studies (MA, PhD); anthropology (MA, PhD); applied linguistics (MA); Arabic (MA, PhD); archaeology (MA); art history (MA); Biblical archaeology (MA); Biblical studies (M Th, D Th, PhD); Christian spirituality (M Th, D Th); church history (M Th, D Th); classical studies (MA, PhD); clinical psychology (MA); communication (MA, PhD); comparative education (M Ed, Ed D); consulting psychology (D Admin, D Com, PhD); curriculum studies (M Ed, Ed D); development studies (M Admin, MA, D Admin, PhD); didactics (M Ed, Ed D); education (M Tech); education management (M Ed, Ed D); educational psychology (M Ed); English (MA); environmental education (M Ed); French (MA, PhD); German (MA, PhD); Greek (MA); guidance and counseling (M Ed); health studies (MA, PhD), including health sciences education (MA), health services management (MA), medical and surgical nursing science (critical care general) (MA), midwifery and neonatal nursing science (MA), trauma and emergency care (MA); history (MA, PhD); history of education (Ed D); inclusive education (M Ed, Ed D); information and communications technology policy and regulation (MA); information science (MA, MIS, PhD); international politics (MA, PhD); Islamic studies (MA, PhD); Italian (MA, PhD); Judaica (MA, PhD); linguistics (MA, PhD); mathematical education (M Ed); mathematics education (MA); missiology (M Th, D Th); modern Hebrew (MA, PhD); musicology (MA, MMus, D Mus, PhD); natural science education (M Ed); New Testament (M Th, D Th); Old Testament (D Th); pastoral therapy (M Th, D Th); philosophy (MA); philosophy of education (M Ed, Ed D); politics (MA, PhD); Portuguese (MA, PhD); practical theology (M Th, D Th); psychology (MA, MS, PhD); psychology of education (M Ed, Ed D); public health (MA); religious studies (MA, D Th, PhD); Romance languages (MA); Russian (MA, PhD); Semitic languages (MA, PhD); social behavior studies in HIV/AIDS (MA); social science (mental health) (MA); social science in development studies (MA); social science in psychology (MA); social science in social work (MA); social science in sociology (MA); social work (MSW, DSW, PhD); socio-education (M Ed, Ed D); sociolinguistics (MA); sociology (MA, PhD); Spanish (MA, PhD); systematic theology (M Th, D Th); TESOL (teaching English to speakers of other languages) (MA); theological ethics (M Th, D Th); theory of literature (MA, PhD); urban ministries (D Th); urban ministry (M Th).

Vanderbilt University, Vanderbilt University School of Nursing, Nashville, TN 37240. Offers adult-gerontology acute care nurse practitioner (MSN), including hospitalist, intensivist; adult-gerontology primary care nurse practitioner (MSN); emergency nurse practitioner (MSN); family nurse practitioner (MSN); healthcare leadership (MSN); neonatal nurse practitioner (MSN); nurse midwifery (MSN); nurse midwifery/family nurse practitioner (MSN); nursing (Post-Master's Certificate); nursing informatics (MSN); nursing practice (DNP); nursing science (PhD); pediatric acute care nurse practitioner (MSN); pediatric primary care nurse practitioner (MSN); psychiatric-mental health nurse practitioner (MSN); women's health nurse practitioner (MSN); women's health nurse practitioner/adult gerontology primary care nurse practitioner (MSN); MSN/M Div; MSN/MTS. *Accreditation:* AACN; ACEN (one or more programs are accredited); ACNM/ACME. *Program availability:* Part-time, 100% online, blended/hybrid learning. *Faculty:* 292 full-time (267 women), 321 part-time/adjunct (253 women). *Students:* 501 full-time (435 women), 387 part-time (355 women); includes 153 minority (40 Black or African American, non-Hispanic/Latino; 1 American Indian or Alaska Native, non-Hispanic/Latino; 27 Asian, non-Hispanic/Latino; 48 Hispanic/Latino; 4 Native Hawaiian or other Pacific Islander, non-Hispanic/Latino; 33 Two or more races, non-Hispanic/Latino), 9 international. Average age 31. 1,210 applicants, 57% accepted, 473 enrolled. In 2017, 319 master's, 47 doctorates awarded. *Degree requirements:* For doctorate, comprehensive exam, thesis/dissertation. *Entrance requirements:* For master's, GRE General Test (taken within the past 5 years), minimum B average in undergraduate course work, 3 letters of recommendation; for doctorate, GRE General Test, interview, 3 letters of recommendation from doctorally-prepared faculty, MSN, essay. Additional exam requirements/recommendations for international students: Required—TOEFL (minimum score 570 paper-based), IELTS (minimum score 6.5). *Application deadline:* For fall admission, 11/1 priority date for domestic and international students. Applications are processed on a rolling basis. Application fee: $50. Electronic applications accepted. *Expenses:* Contact institution. *Financial support:* In 2017–18, 627 students received support. Scholarships/grants available. Financial award application deadline: 3/1; financial award applicants required to submit FAFSA. *Faculty research:* Lymphedema, palliative care and bereavement, health services research including workforce, safety and quality of care, gerontology, better birth outcomes including nutrition. *Total annual research expenditures:* $2 million. *Unit head:* Dr. Linda Norman, Dean, 615-343-8876, Fax: 615-343-7711, E-mail: linda.norman@vanderbilt.edu. *Application contact:* Patricia Peerman, Assistant Dean for Enrollment Management, 615-322-3800, Fax: 615-343-0333, E-mail: vusn-admissions@vanderbilt.edu.
Website: http://www.nursing.vanderbilt.edu

Wayne State University, College of Nursing, Detroit, MI 48202. Offers adult gerontology acute care nurse practitioner (MSN); adult gerontology primary care nurse practitioner (MSN); advanced public health nursing (MSN); infant and mental health (DNP, PhD); neonatal nurse practitioner (MSN); nurse-midwifery (MSN); pediatric acute care nurse practitioner (MSN); pediatric primary care nurse practitioner (MSN); psychiatric mental health nurse practitioner (MSN); women's health nurse practitioner (MSN). Doctoral program admits for fall only. *Accreditation:* AACN. *Program availability:* Part-time. *Faculty:* 30. *Students:* 133 full-time (120 women), 184 part-time (167 women); includes 85 minority (57 Black or African American, non-Hispanic/Latino; 16 Asian, non-Hispanic/Latino; 4 Hispanic/Latino; 8 Two or more races, non-Hispanic/Latino), 22 international. Average age 34. 318 applicants, 39% accepted, 94 enrolled. In 2017, 51 master's, 29 doctorates awarded. *Degree requirements:* For doctorate, thesis/dissertation (for some programs). *Entrance requirements:* For master's, BSN from ACEN- or CCNE-accredited program with minimum GPA of 3.0; three references; current RN license; personal statement; for doctorate, resume or curriculum vitae; goals statement; bachelor's or master's degree in nursing from ACEN- or CCNE-accredited program with minimum GPA of 3.0; current RN license, writing sample and interview (for DNP); reference letters (3 for PhD, 2 for DNP). Additional exam requirements/recommendations for international students: Required—TOEFL (minimum score 101 iBT), TWE (minimum score 6), Michigan English Language Assessment Battery (minimum score 85); Recommended—IELTS (minimum score 7). Application fee: $50. Electronic applications accepted. *Expenses:* Contact institution. *Financial support:* In 2017–18, 92 students received support, including 16 fellowships with tuition reimbursements available (averaging $8,285 per year), 5 teaching assistantships with tuition reimbursements available (averaging $25,000 per year); scholarships/grants, health care benefits, and unspecified assistantships also available. Support available to part-time students. Financial award applicants required to submit FAFSA. *Faculty research:* Bridging transitions and technology to promote asthma care in the community, chronic wound care for persons who injected drugs, decreasing at-risk parenting to reduce child maltreatment and trauma, dementia symptoms (cognition, behavior, function), determining readiness to engage in end of life/palliative care conversations with adolescents and young adults living with advanced cancer, dyspnea assessment and treatment at the end of life. *Unit head:* Dr. Laurie Lauzon Clabo, Dean, College of Nursing, 313-577-4082, E-mail: laurie.lauzon.clabo@wayne.edu. *Application contact:* 313-577-4082, Fax: 313-577-6949, E-mail: nursinginfo@wayne.edu.
Website: http://nursing.wayne.edu/

West Virginia Wesleyan College, Department of Nursing, Buckhannon, WV 26201. Offers family nurse practitioner (MS, Post Master's Certificate); nurse administrator (MS); nurse educator (MS); nurse-midwifery (MS); nursing administration (Post Master's Certificate); nursing education (Post Master's Certificate); psychiatric mental health nurse practitioner (MS); MSN/MBA. *Accreditation:* ACEN.

Nursing and Healthcare Administration

Abilene Christian University, College of Graduate and Professional Studies, Program in Nursing Practice, Abilene, TX 79699. Offers advanced practice nurse (DNP); executive nursing leadership (DNP); nursing education (DNP). *Program availability:* Part-time, online only, blended/hybrid learning. *Faculty:* 3 full-time (2 women), 3 part-time/adjunct (2 women). *Students:* 45 full-time (38 women), 3 part-time (all women); includes 17 minority (14 Black or African American, non-Hispanic/Latino; 3 Asian, non-Hispanic/Latino). 73 applicants, 59% accepted, 28 enrolled. *Entrance requirements:* For doctorate, master's degree in nursing, official transcripts, minimum graduate nursing cumulative GPA of 3.0, two recommendation letters, 500-word statement of purpose, professional curriculum vitae or resume. Additional exam requirements/recommendations for international students: Required—TOEFL (minimum score 80 iBT), IELTS (minimum score 6). *Application deadline:* For fall admission, 8/15 for domestic students; for winter admission, 10/1 for domestic students; for spring admission, 12/15 for domestic students; for summer admission, 4/1 for domestic students. Applications are processed on a rolling basis. Application fee: $50. Electronic applications accepted. *Expenses:* $1,000 per hour. *Financial support:* Application deadline: 4/1; applicants required to submit FAFSA. *Unit head:* Dr. Tonya Sawyer-McGee, Program Director, 214-305-9500, E-mail: tcs15b@acu.edu. *Application contact:* Graduate Advisor, 855-219-7300, E-mail: gradonline@acu.edu.
Website: http://www.acu.edu/online/academics/doctor-of-nursing-practice.html

Adelphi University, College of Nursing and Public Health, Program in Nursing Administration, Garden City, NY 11530-0701. Offers MS, Certificate. *Students:* 20 part-time (18 women); includes 15 minority (9 Black or African American, non-Hispanic/Latino; 2 Asian, non-Hispanic/Latino; 2 Hispanic/Latino; 2 Two or more races, non-Hispanic/Latino). Average age 40. 17 applicants, 24% accepted, 3 enrolled. *Entrance requirements:* Additional exam requirements/recommendations for international students: Required—TOEFL (minimum score 550 paper-based; 80 iBT), IELTS (minimum score 6.5). Application fee: $50. *Expenses:* Contact institution. *Financial support:* Research assistantships, teaching assistantships, career-related internships or fieldwork, institutionally sponsored loans, scholarships/grants, traineeships, and unspecified assistantships available. Support available to part-time students. *Unit head:* Joan Valas, Director, 516-877-4571, E-mail: valas@adelphi.edu. *Application contact:* E-mail: graduateadmissions@adelphi.edu.

Allen College, Graduate Programs, Waterloo, IA 50703. Offers adult-gerontology acute care nurse practitioner (MSN); community/public health nursing (MSN); education (MSN); family nurse practitioner (MSN); health sciences (Ed D); leadership in health care delivery (MSN); leadership in health care informatics (MSN); nursing (DNP); occupational therapy (MS); psychiatric mental health nurse practitioner (MSN). MSN in leadership in healthcare informatics offered in partnership with University of Minnesota. *Accreditation:* AACN; ACEN. *Program availability:* Part-time, 100% online, blended/hybrid learning. *Faculty:* 24 full-time (all women), 8 part-time/adjunct (7 women). *Students:* 106 full-time (91 women), 187 part-time (164 women); includes 22 minority (12 Black or African American, non-Hispanic/Latino; 1 American Indian or Alaska Native, non-Hispanic/Latino; 2 Asian, non-Hispanic/Latino; 3 Hispanic/Latino; 4 Two or more races, non-Hispanic/Latino), 2 international. Average age 33. 352 applicants, 56% accepted, 131 enrolled. In 2017, 73 master's, 2 doctorates awarded. *Entrance requirements:* For master's, minimum GPA of 3.0 in the last 60 hours of undergraduate coursework; for doctorate, minimum GPA of 3.25 in graduate coursework. *Application deadline:* For fall admission, 2/1 priority date for domestic students; for spring admission, 9/1 priority date for domestic students. Applications are processed on a rolling basis. Application fee: $50. Electronic applications accepted. *Expenses:* $17,860 per year. *Financial support:* In 2017–18, 97 students received support. Federal Work-Study, institutionally sponsored loans, scholarships/grants, and traineeships available. Support available to part-time students. Financial award application deadline: 8/1; financial award applicants required to submit FAFSA. *Faculty research:* Poverty. *Unit head:* Dr. Nancy Kramer, Vice Chancellor for Academic Affairs, 319-226-2040, Fax: 319-226-2070, E-mail: nancy.kramer@allencollege.edu. *Application contact:* Molly Quinn, Director of Admissions, 319-226-2001, Fax: 319-226-2010, E-mail: molly.quinn@allencollege.edu.
Website: http://www.allencollege.edu/

Alvernia University, School of Graduate Studies, Department of Nursing, Reading, PA 19607-1799. Offers adult gerontology nurse practitioner (DNP); family nurse practitioner (DNP); nursing education (MSN); nursing leadership (Graduate Certificate); nursing leadership and healthcare administration (MSN).

American International College, School of Health Sciences, Springfield, MA 01109-3189. Offers exercise science (MS); family nurse practitioner (MSN, Post-Master's Certificate); nursing administrator (MSN); nursing educator (MSN); occupational therapy (MSOT, OTD); physical therapy (DPT). *Program availability:* Part-time, 100% online. *Faculty:* 14 full-time (13 women), 10 part-time/adjunct (all women). *Students:* 286 full-time (220 women), 11 part-time (9 women); includes 75 minority (30 Black or African American, non-Hispanic/Latino; 21 Asian, non-Hispanic/Latino; 19 Hispanic/Latino; 5 Two or more races, non-Hispanic/Latino), 2 international. Average age 27. 652 applicants, 49% accepted, 109 enrolled. In 2017, 48 master's, 28 doctorates, 2 other advanced degrees awarded. *Degree requirements:* For master's, practicum; for doctorate, thesis/dissertation, practicum. *Entrance requirements:* For master's, 3 letters of recommendation, personal goal statement; minimum GPA of 3.2, interview, BS or BA, and 2 clinical PT observations (for DPT); minimum GPA of 3.0, MSOT, OT licensen, and 2 clinical OT observations (for OTD); for doctorate, personal goal statement, 2 letters of recommendation; minimum GPA of 3.0, BS or BA, 2 clinical OT observations (for MSOT); RN license and minimum GPA of 3.0 (for MSN). Additional exam requirements/recommendations for international students: Required—TOEFL (minimum score 577 paper-based; 91 iBT). *Application deadline:* For fall admission, 12/1 priority date for domestic and international students; for spring admission, 11/15 priority date for domestic and international students. Application fee: $50. Electronic applications accepted. *Expenses:* Contact institution. *Faculty research:* Teaching simulation, ergonomics, orthopedics, use of social media in health care. *Unit head:* Dr. Cesarina Thompson, Dean, 413-205-3056, Fax: 413-654-1430, E-mail: cesarina.thompson@aic.edu. *Application contact:* Kerry Barnes, Director of Graduate Admissions, 413-205-3703, Fax: 413-205-3051, E-mail: kerry.barnes@aic.edu.
Website: http://www.aic.edu/academics/hs

American University of Beirut, Graduate Programs, Rafic Hariri School of Nursing, Beirut, Lebanon. Offers adult gerontology clinical nurse specialist (MSN); community and public health nursing (MSN); nursing administration and management (MSN); psychiatric mental health clinical nurse specialist (MSN). *Accreditation:* AACN. *Faculty:* 13 full-time (12 women), 23 part-time/adjunct (18 women). *Students:* 4 full-time (3 women), 40 part-time (34 women). Average age 28. 32 applicants, 81% accepted, 9 enrolled. In 2017, 18 master's awarded. *Degree requirements:* For master's, comprehensive exam, residency and project or thesis. *Entrance requirements:* For master's, minimum cumulative average of 80, minimum of 1 year of work experience. Additional exam requirements/recommendations for international students: Required—TOEFL (minimum score 583 paper-based; 97 iBT); Recommended—IELTS (minimum score 7). *Application deadline:* For fall admission, 4/4 for domestic students. Applications are processed on a rolling basis. Application fee: $50. Electronic applications accepted. *Expenses:* $810 per credit. *Financial support:* In 2017–18, 7 students received support. Teaching assistantships, scholarships/grants, traineeships, and unspecified assistantships available. Financial award application deadline: 12/20. *Faculty research:* Pain management and palliative care, postwar PTSD, depression,

anxiety, and social support, cardiovascular care, vitamin D and cognitive function, nursing workforce and health systems research. *Total annual research expenditures:* $305,241. *Unit head:* Dr. Huda Abu-Saad Huijer, Director of the Hariri School of Nursing, 961-1-350000 Ext. 5953, Fax: 961-1-744476, E-mail: hh35@aub.edu.lb. *Application contact:* Nisreen Ghalayini, Administrative Assistant, 961-1-350000 Ext. 5951, E-mail: ng28@aub.edu.lb.
Website: http://www.aub.edu.lb/hson

Anderson University, College of Health Professions, Anderson, SC 29621-4035. Offers advanced practice (DNP); executive leadership (MSN, DNP); family nurse practitioner (MSN, DNP); nurse educator (MSN); psychiatric mental health nurse practitioner (MSN, DNP). *Program availability:* Online learning. *Expenses: Tuition:* Full-time $24,290; part-time $650 per credit hour. Full-time tuition and fees vary according to degree level and program. *Unit head:* Dr. Donald M. Peace, Dean, 864-231-5513, E-mail: dpeace@andersonuniversity.edu. *Application contact:* Chris Woodlief, Associate Director of Adult and Graduate Programs, 864-231-5531, E-mail: cwoodlief@andersonuniversity.edu.
Website: http://www.andersonuniversity.edu/health-professions

Arizona State University at the Tempe campus, College of Nursing and Health Innovation, Phoenix, AZ 85004. Offers advanced nursing practice (DNP); clinical research management (MS); community and public health practice (Graduate Certificate); family mental health nurse practitioner (Graduate Certificate); family nurse practitioner (Graduate Certificate); geriatric nursing (Graduate Certificate); healthcare innovation (MHI); nurse education in academic and practice settings (Graduate Certificate); nurse educator (MS); nursing and healthcare innovation (PhD). *Accreditation:* AACN. *Program availability:* Online learning. *Degree requirements:* For master's, comprehensive exam (for some programs), thesis (for some programs), interactive Program of Study (iPOS) submitted before completing 50 percent of required credit hours; for doctorate, comprehensive exam, thesis/dissertation, interactive Program of Study (iPOS) submitted before completing 50 percent of required credit hours. *Entrance requirements:* For master's and doctorate, GRE, minimum GPA of 3.0 or equivalent in last 2 years of work leading to bachelor's degree. Additional exam requirements/recommendations for international students: Required—TOEFL, IELTS, or PTE. Electronic applications accepted. *Expenses:* Contact institution.

Aspen University, Program in Nursing, Denver, CO 80246-1930. Offers forensic nursing (MSN); informatics (MSN); nursing (MSN); nursing administration and management (MSN); nursing education (MSN); public health (MSN).

Athabasca University, Faculty of Health Disciplines, Athabasca, AB T9S 3A3, Canada. Offers advanced nursing practice (MN, Advanced Diploma); generalist (MN); health studies (MHS). *Program availability:* Part-time, online learning. *Degree requirements:* For master's, comprehensive exam (for some programs). *Entrance requirements:* For master's, bachelor's degree in health-related field and 2 years of professional health service experience (MHS); bachelor's degree in nursing and 2 years' nursing experience (MN); minimum GPA of 3.0 in final 30 credits; for Advanced Diploma, RN license, 2 years of health care experience. Electronic applications accepted. *Expenses:* Contact institution.

Augusta University, College of Nursing, Clinical Nurse Leader Program, Augusta, GA 30912. Offers MSN. *Entrance requirements:* For master's, GRE (minimum score of 290 combined Verbal and Quantitative sections) or MAT (minimum score of 400) within last five years, bachelor's degree or higher in non-nursing discipline, minimum undergraduate cumulative GPA of 3.0. Additional exam requirements/recommendations for international students: Required—TOEFL (minimum score 600 paper-based). Electronic applications accepted. *Expenses:* Contact institution.

Augusta University, College of Nursing, Doctor of Nursing Practice Program, Augusta, GA 30912. Offers adult gerontology acute care nurse practitioner (DNP); family nurse practitioner (DNP); nurse executive (DNP); nursing (DNP); nursing anesthesia (DNP); pediatric nurse practitioner (DNP); psychiatric mental health nurse practitioner (DNP). *Accreditation:* AACN; AANA/CANAEP. *Degree requirements:* For doctorate, thesis/dissertation or alternative. *Entrance requirements:* For doctorate, GRE General Test or MAT, master's degree in nursing or related field, current professional nurse licensure. Additional exam requirements/recommendations for international students: Required—TOEFL (minimum score 600 paper-based; 100 iBT). Electronic applications accepted.

Austin Peay State University, College of Graduate Studies, College of Behavioral and Health Sciences, School of Nursing, Clarksville, TN 37044. Offers family nurse practitioner (MSN); nursing administration (MSN); nursing education (MSN); nursing informatics (MSN). *Program availability:* Part-time, online learning. *Faculty:* 8 full-time (all women), 8 part-time/adjunct (all women). *Students:* 12 full-time (11 women), 139 part-time (128 women); includes 19 minority (11 Black or African American, non-Hispanic/Latino; 1 Asian, non-Hispanic/Latino; 5 Hispanic/Latino; 2 Two or more races, non-Hispanic/Latino). Average age 35. 36 applicants, 86% accepted, 20 enrolled. In 2017, 67 master's awarded. *Degree requirements:* For master's, comprehensive exam. *Entrance requirements:* For master's, minimum GPA of 3.0, RN license eligibility, 3 letters of recommendation. Additional exam requirements/recommendations for international students: Required—TOEFL (minimum score 500 paper-based). *Application deadline:* For fall admission, 8/8 priority date for domestic students. Applications are processed on a rolling basis. Application fee: $45 ($55 for international students). Electronic applications accepted. *Expenses:* Tuition, state resident: full-time $7686; part-time $427 per credit hour. Tuition, nonresident: full-time $20,268; part-time $1126 per credit hour. *Required fees:* $1529; $76.45 per credit hour. *Financial support:* Research assistantships with full tuition reimbursements, career-related internships or fieldwork, Federal Work-Study, institutionally sponsored loans, scholarships/grants, and unspecified assistantships available. Support available to part-time students. Financial award application deadline: 4/1; financial award applicants required to submit FAFSA. *Unit head:* Dr. Rebecca Corvey, Director of Nursing, 931-221-7710, Fax: 931-221-7595, E-mail: corveyr@apsu.edu. *Application contact:* Megan Mitchell, Coordinator of Graduate Admissions, 931-221-6189, Fax: 931-221-7641, E-mail: mitchellm@apsu.edu.
Website: http://www.apsu.edu/nursing

Azusa Pacific University, School of Nursing, Azusa, CA 91702-7000. Offers adult clinical nurse specialist (MSN); adult-gerontology nurse practitioner (MSN); family nurse practitioner (MSN); healthcare administration and leadership (MSN); nursing (MSN, DNP, PhD); nursing education (MSN); parent-child clinical nurse specialist (MSN); psychiatric mental health nurse practitioner (MSN). *Accreditation:* AACN. *Program availability:* Part-time, evening/weekend. *Degree requirements:* For master's, thesis optional. *Entrance requirements:* For master's, BSN.

Barry University, School of Adult and Continuing Education, Division of Nursing, Program in Nursing Administration, Miami Shores, FL 33161-6695. Offers MSN, PhD, Certificate. *Accreditation:* AACN. *Program availability:* Part-time, evening/weekend. *Degree requirements:* For master's, research project or thesis. *Entrance requirements:* For master's, GRE General Test or MAT, BSN, minimum GPA of 3.0, course work in statistics. Electronic applications accepted. *Faculty research:* Power/empowerment, health delivery systems, managed care, employee health and well being.

Barry University, School of Adult and Continuing Education, Division of Nursing and Andreas School of Business, Program in Nursing Administration and Business Administration, Miami Shores, FL 33161-6695. Offers MSN/MBA. *Accreditation:* AACN. *Program availability:* Part-time, evening/weekend. Electronic applications accepted. *Faculty research:* Power/empowerment, health delivery systems, managed care, employee health well-being.

Bellarmine University, College of Health Professions, Donna and Allan Lansing School of Nursing and Clinical Sciences, Louisville, KY 40205. Offers family nurse practitioner (MSN); health science (MHS); nursing administration (MSN); nursing education (MSN); nursing practice (DNP). *Accreditation:* AACN; APTA. *Program availability:* Part-time, evening/weekend. *Faculty:* 20 full-time (17 women), 7 part-time/adjunct (6 women). *Students:* 10 full-time (6 women), 101 part-time (89 women); includes 10 minority (5 Black or African American, non-Hispanic/Latino; 2 Asian, non-Hispanic/Latino; 1 Hispanic/Latino; 2 Two or more races, non-Hispanic/Latino), 1 international. Average age 34. In 2017, 42 master's, 5 doctorates awarded. *Degree requirements:* For master's, comprehensive exam, thesis (for some programs); for doctorate, comprehensive exam, thesis/dissertation. *Entrance requirements:* For master's, GRE General Test, minimum GPA of 3.0, interview, resume; BSN from CCNE- or ACEN-accredited program, professional references, goal statement, and RN license (for MSN); bachelor's degree with exposure to health issues and grade of C or better in math/science courses (for MHS); for doctorate, GRE General Test, MSN from CCNE- or ACEN-accredited program; minimum GPA of 3.5 in graduate coursework; professional references; goal statement; current curriculum vitae or resume; RN license; verification of post-baccalaureate clinical and practice hours. Additional exam requirements/recommendations for international students: Required—TOEFL (minimum iBT score of 83, 26 on speaking test), IELTS (minimum score 7, speaking band score of 8), or language training at an approved center. *Application deadline:* Applications are processed on a rolling basis. Application fee: $40. Electronic applications accepted. *Expenses:* Contact institution. *Financial support:* Career-related internships or fieldwork and scholarships/grants available. Financial award applicants required to submit FAFSA. *Faculty research:* Nursing: pain, empathy, leadership styles, control; physical therapy: service-learning; exercise in chronic and pre-operative conditions, athletes; women's health; aging. *Unit head:* Dr. Nancy York, Dean, 502-272-8639, E-mail: nyork@bellarmine.edu. *Application contact:* Julie Armstrong-Binnix, Health Science Recruiter, 800-274-4723 Ext. 8364, E-mail: julieab@bellarmine.edu.
Website: http://www.bellarmine.edu/lansing

Blessing-Rieman College of Nursing & Health Sciences, Master of Science in Nursing Program, Quincy, IL 62305-7005. Offers nursing education (MSN); nursing leadership (MSN). *Program availability:* Part-time-only, evening/weekend, online only, 100% online. *Faculty:* 7 full-time (all women). *Students:* 16 part-time (14 women). Average age 35. *Degree requirements:* For master's, thesis or project. *Entrance requirements:* Additional exam requirements/recommendations for international students: Required—TOEFL (minimum score 500 paper-based; 80 iBT). *Application deadline:* Applications are processed on a rolling basis. Electronic applications accepted. *Expenses: Tuition:* Part-time $500 per credit hour. *Required fees:* $300 per unit. $150 per semester. One-time fee: $20 part-time. *Financial support:* Scholarships/grants available. Financial award application deadline: 4/30; financial award applicants required to submit FAFSA. *Unit head:* Dr. Karen Mayville, Administrative Coordinator, Assessment, 217-228-5520 Ext. 6968, Fax: 217-223-1781, E-mail: kmayville@brcn.edu. *Application contact:* Heather Mutter, Admissions Counselor, 217-228-5520 Ext. 6964, Fax: 217-223-4661, E-mail: hmutter@brcn.edu.
Website: https://www.brcn.edu/programs/msn-online

Bloomsburg University of Pennsylvania, School of Graduate Studies, College of Science and Technology, Department of Nursing, Bloomsburg, PA 17815-1301. Offers adult and family nurse practitioner (MSN); community health (MSN); nurse anesthesia (MSN); nursing (MSN, DNP); nursing administration (MSN). *Accreditation:* AACN. *Degree requirements:* For master's, thesis (for some programs), clinical experience. *Entrance requirements:* For master's, minimum QPA of 3.0, personal statement, 2 letters of recommendation, nursing license. Additional exam requirements/recommendations for international students: Required—TOEFL, IELTS. Electronic applications accepted. *Expenses:* Contact institution.

Bowie State University, Graduate Programs, Department of Nursing, Bowie, MD 20715-9465. Offers administration of nursing services (MS); family nurse practitioner (MS); nursing education (MS). *Accreditation:* ACEN. *Program availability:* Part-time. *Faculty:* 7 full-time (4 women), 15 part-time/adjunct (10 women). *Students:* 29 full-time (25 women), 30 part-time (24 women); includes 42 minority (35 Black or African American, non-Hispanic/Latino; 1 Asian, non-Hispanic/Latino; 6 Hispanic/Latino), 8 international. Average age 42. 9 applicants, 89% accepted, 7 enrolled. In 2017, 30 master's awarded. *Degree requirements:* For master's, comprehensive exam, thesis, research paper. *Entrance requirements:* For master's, minimum GPA of 2.5. *Application deadline:* For fall admission, 5/15 for domestic students. Applications are processed on a rolling basis. Application fee: $40. Electronic applications accepted. *Financial support:* Institutionally sponsored loans and traineeships available. Financial award application deadline: 4/1. *Faculty research:* Minority health, women's health, gerontology, leadership management. *Unit head:* Dr. Bonita Jenkins, Acting Chairperson, 301-860-3210, E-mail: mccaskill@bowiestate.edu. *Application contact:* Angela Issac, Information Contact, 301-860-4000.

Bradley University, The Graduate School, College of Education and Health Sciences, Department of Nursing, Peoria, IL 61625-0002. Offers family nurse practitioner (MSN, DNP, Certificate); leadership (DNP); nursing administration (MSN); nursing education (MSN, Certificate). *Accreditation:* AACN; ACEN. *Program availability:* Part-time, evening/weekend. *Degree requirements:* For master's, comprehensive exam, thesis optional. *Entrance requirements:* For master's, GRE General Test or MAT, interview, Illinois RN license, advanced cardiac life support certification, pediatric advanced life support certification, 3 letters of recommendation. Additional exam requirements/recommendations for international students: Required—TOEFL (minimum score 550 paper-based; 79 iBT), IELTS (minimum score 6.5). Electronic applications accepted.

Brenau University, Sydney O. Smith Graduate School, College of Health Sciences, Gainesville, GA 30501. Offers family nurse practitioner (MSN); nurse educator (MSN); nursing management (MSN); occupational therapy (MS); psychology (MS). *Accreditation:* AOTA. *Program availability:* Part-time, evening/weekend. *Degree requirements:* For master's, comprehensive exam (for some programs), thesis (for some programs), clinical practicum hours. *Entrance requirements:* For master's, GRE General Test or MAT (for some programs), interview, writing sample, references (for some programs). Additional exam requirements/recommendations for international students: Required—TOEFL (minimum score 500 paper-based; 61 iBT); Recommended—IELTS (minimum score 5). Electronic applications accepted. *Expenses:* Contact institution.

Brookline College, Nursing Programs, Phoenix, AZ 85021. Offers health systems administration (MSN); nursing (MSN). *Program availability:* Part-time, online learning.

California Baptist University, Program in Nursing, Riverside, CA 92504-3206. Offers clinical nurse specialist (MSN); family nurse practitioner (MSN); healthcare systems management (MSN); teaching-learning (MSN). *Accreditation:* AACN. *Program availability:* Part-time. *Faculty:* 19 full-time (18 women), 12 part-time/adjunct (11 women). *Students:* 78 full-time (59 women), 130 part-time (106 women); includes 114

minority (25 Black or African American, non-Hispanic/Latino; 3 American Indian or Alaska Native, non-Hispanic/Latino; 34 Asian, non-Hispanic/Latino; 47 Hispanic/Latino; 2 Native Hawaiian or other Pacific Islander, non-Hispanic/Latino; 3 Two or more races, non-Hispanic/Latino), 2 international. Average age 32. 25 applicants, 84% accepted, 14 enrolled. In 2017, 49 master's awarded. *Degree requirements:* For master's, comprehensive exam or directed project thesis; capstone practicum. *Entrance requirements:* For master's, GRE or California Critical Thinking Skills Test; Test of Essential Academic Skills (TEAS), minimum undergraduate GPA of 3.0; completion of prerequisite courses with minimum grade of C; CPR certification; background check clearance; health clearance; drug testing; proof of health insurance; proof of motor vehicle insurance; three letters of recommendation; 1000-word essay; interview. Additional exam requirements/recommendations for international students: Required—TOEFL (minimum score 80 iBT). *Application deadline:* For fall admission, 8/1 priority date for domestic students, 7/1 for international students; for spring admission, 12/1 priority date for domestic students, 11/1 for international students. Applications are processed on a rolling basis. Application fee: $45. Electronic applications accepted. *Expenses:* Contact institution. *Financial support:* In 2017–18, 38 students received support. Federal Work-Study and scholarships/grants available. Financial award applicants required to submit CSS PROFILE or FAFSA. *Faculty research:* Qualitative research using Parse methodology, gerontology, disaster preparedness, medical-surgical nursing, maternal-child nursing. *Unit head:* Dr. Geneva Oaks, Dean, School of Nursing, 951-343-4702, E-mail: goaks@calbaptist.edu. *Application contact:* Tamakia King, Graduate Admissions Counselor, 951-552-8138, Fax: 951-343-5095, E-mail: tking@calbaptist.edu.
Website: http://www.calbaptist.edu/explore-cbu/schools-colleges/school-nursing/master-science-nursing/

California State University, Fullerton, Graduate Studies, College of Health and Human Development, School of Nursing, Fullerton, CA 92831-3599. Offers leadership (MS); nurse anesthesia (MS); nurse educator (MS); nursing (DNP); school nursing (MS); women's health care (MS). *Accreditation:* AACN. *Program availability:* Part-time. *Faculty:* 27 full-time (23 women), 11 part-time/adjunct (all women). *Students:* 136 full-time (107 women), 116 part-time (96 women); includes 142 minority (9 Black or African American, non-Hispanic/Latino; 81 Asian, non-Hispanic/Latino; 37 Hispanic/Latino; 1 Native Hawaiian or other Pacific Islander, non-Hispanic/Latino; 14 Two or more races, non-Hispanic/Latino), 2 international. Average age 36. 235 applicants, 59% accepted, 117 enrolled. Application fee: $55. *Financial support:* Career-related internships or fieldwork, Federal Work-Study, institutionally sponsored loans, scholarships/grants, and traineeships available. Support available to part-time students. Financial award application deadline: 3/1; financial award applicants required to submit FAFSA. *Unit head:* Dr. Cindy Greenberg, Chair, 657-278-3336. *Application contact:* Admissions/Applications, 657-278-2371.
Website: http://nursing.fullerton.edu/

California State University, San Marcos, College of Education, Health and Human Services, School of Nursing, San Marcos, CA 92096-0001. Offers advanced practice nursing (MSN), including clinical nurse specialist, family nurse practitioner, psychiatric mental health nurse practitioner; clinical nurse leader (MSN); nursing education (MSN). *Expenses:* Tuition, state resident: full-time $7176. Tuition, nonresident: full-time $9504. *Unit head:* Lorna Kendrick, Director, 760-750-7580, E-mail: lkendrick@csusm.edu.
Website: http://www.csusm.edu/nursing/

California University of Pennsylvania, School of Graduate Studies and Research, Eberly College of Science and Technology, Department of Nursing, California, PA 15419-1394. Offers nursing administration and leadership (MSN); nursing education (MSN).

Capella University, School of Public Service Leadership, Master's Programs in Nursing, Minneapolis, MN 55402. Offers diabetes nursing (MSN); general nursing (MSN); gerontology nursing (MSN); health information management (MS); nurse educator (MSN); nursing leadership and administration (MSN). *Accreditation:* AACN.

Capital University, School of Nursing, Columbus, OH 43209-2394. Offers administration (MSN); legal studies (MSN); theological studies (MSN); JD/MSN; MBA/MSN; MSN/MTS. *Accreditation:* AACN. *Program availability:* Part-time, evening/weekend. *Degree requirements:* For master's, thesis or alternative. *Entrance requirements:* For master's, BSN, current RN license, minimum GPA of 3.0, undergraduate courses in statistics and research. Additional exam requirements/recommendations for international students: Required—TOEFL (minimum score 550 paper-based). *Expenses:* Contact institution. *Faculty research:* Bereavement, wellness/health promotion, emergency cardiac care, critical thinking, complementary and alternative healthcare.

Carlow University, College of Health and Wellness, Program in Nursing Leadership and Education, Pittsburgh, PA 15213-3165. Offers MSN. *Program availability:* Part-time, evening/weekend, 100% online, blended/hybrid learning. *Students:* 35 full-time (34 women), 17 part-time (all women); includes 3 minority (1 Black or African American, non-Hispanic/Latino; 2 Hispanic/Latino). Average age 36. 12 applicants, 92% accepted, 6 enrolled. In 2017, 20 master's awarded. *Degree requirements:* For master's, internship. *Entrance requirements:* For master's, minimum undergraduate GPA of 3.0 from accredited BSN program; current license as RN in Pennsylvania; statistics class within past 6 years with minimum C grade; two professional recommendations; reflective essay of 300 words or less describing career goals and expectations for education. Additional exam requirements/recommendations for international students: Required—TOEFL (minimum score 550 paper-based). *Application deadline:* Applications are processed on a rolling basis. Electronic applications accepted. *Expenses: Tuition:* Full-time $12,103; part-time $825 per credit hour. Tuition and fees vary according to program. *Financial support:* Application deadline: 4/1; applicants required to submit FAFSA. *Unit head:* Dr. Renee Ingel, Director, Nursing Leadership and DNP Programs, 412-578-6103, Fax: 412-578-6114, E-mail: rmingel@carlow.edu.
Website: http://www.carlow.edu/Master_of_Science_in_Nursing_Concentration_in_Education_and_Leadership.aspx

Cedar Crest College, Program in Nursing, Allentown, PA 18104-6196. Offers nursing administration (MS); nursing education (MS). *Program availability:* Part-time. *Faculty:* 4 full-time (3 women), 2 part-time/adjunct (1 woman). *Students:* 25 part-time (23 women); includes 7 minority (2 Black or African American, non-Hispanic/Latino; 2 Asian, non-Hispanic/Latino; 3 Hispanic/Latino). Average age 36. In 2017, 8 master's awarded. *Application deadline:* Applications are processed on a rolling basis. Electronic applications accepted. *Expenses:* Contact institution. *Unit head:* Dr. Wendy Robb, Director, 610-606-4666, E-mail: wjrobb@cedarcrest.edu. *Application contact:* Nancy Wunderly, Director of School of Adult and Graduate Education, 610-606-4666, E-mail: sage@cedarcrest.edu.
Website: http://sage.cedarcrest.edu/degrees/graduate/nursing-science/

Central Methodist University, College of Graduate and Extended Studies, Fayette, MO 65248-1198. Offers clinical counseling (MS); clinical nurse leader (MSN); education (M Ed); music education (MME); nurse educator (MSN). *Program availability:* Part-time, evening/weekend, online learning. *Degree requirements:* For master's, thesis. *Entrance requirements:* For master's, GRE General Test, minimum GPA of 2.75. Electronic applications accepted.

Chatham University, Nursing Programs, Pittsburgh, PA 15232-2826. Offers education/leadership (MSN); nursing (DNP). *Accreditation:* AACN. *Program availability:* Online learning. *Faculty:* 12 full-time (all women), 12 part-time/adjunct (10 women). *Students:* 49 full-time (41 women), 95 part-time (80 women); includes 68 minority (51 Black or African American, non-Hispanic/Latino; 7 Asian, non-Hispanic/Latino; 8 Hispanic/Latino; 2 Two or more races, non-Hispanic/Latino), 11 international. Average age 42. 209 applicants, 51% accepted, 76 enrolled. In 2017, 13 master's, 82 doctorates awarded. *Entrance requirements:* For master's, RN license, BSN, minimum GPA of 3.0; for doctorate, RN license, MSN. Additional exam requirements/recommendations for international students: Required—TOEFL (minimum score 600 paper-based; 100 iBT), IELTS (minimum score 6.5), TWE. *Application deadline:* For fall admission, 5/1 priority date for domestic and international students. Applications are processed on a rolling basis. Application fee: $35. Electronic applications accepted. Application fee is waived when completed online. *Expenses:* Contact institution. *Financial support:* Application deadline: 8/1; applicants required to submit FAFSA. *Unit head:* Dr. Diane Hunker, Director, 412-365-1738, E-mail: dhunker@chatham.edu. *Application contact:* Patricia Golla, Assistant Director of Graduate Admissions, 412-365-1386, Fax: 412-365-1720, E-mail: pgolla@chatham.edu.
Website: http://www.chatham.edu/nursing

Clarke University, Department of Nursing and Health, Dubuque, IA 52001-3198. Offers family nurse practitioner (DNP); health leadership and practice (DNP); psychiatric mental health nurse practitioner (DNP). *Accreditation:* AACN. *Program availability:* Part-time. *Faculty:* 6 full-time (all women). *Students:* 55 full-time (54 women), 11 part-time (10 women); includes 3 minority (1 Black or African American, non-Hispanic/Latino; 1 Asian, non-Hispanic/Latino; 1 Two or more races, non-Hispanic/Latino). Average age 32. 62 applicants, 40% accepted, 22 enrolled. In 2017, 36 doctorates awarded. *Degree requirements:* For doctorate, comprehensive exam, thesis/dissertation. *Entrance requirements:* For doctorate, GRE (if GPA under 3.0), bachelor's degree from accredited nursing program and accredited college or university; minimum GPA of 3.0; minimum C grade on undergraduate prerequisite courses; three recommendation forms; curriculum vitae; statement of goals; transcripts; copy of nursing license; proof of health insurance; interview. Additional exam requirements/recommendations for international students: Required—TOEFL (minimum score 550 paper-based; 80 iBT), IELTS (minimum score 6.5). *Application deadline:* For fall admission, 2/1 priority date for domestic students. Application fee: $35. Electronic applications accepted. *Expenses:* $850 per credit. *Financial support:* Applicants required to submit FAFSA. *Faculty research:* Narrative pedagogy, ethics, end-of-life care, pedagogy, family systems, simulation. *Unit head:* Dr. Jan Lee, Chair, 563-588-6339, E-mail: jan.lee@clarke.edu. *Application contact:* Kimberly Roush, Director of Admission, Graduate and Adult Programs, 563-588-6539, Fax: 563-552-7994, E-mail: graduate@clarke.edu.
Website: https://www.clarke.edu/academics/doctor-of-nursing-practice/

Clarkson College, Master of Science in Nursing Program, Omaha, NE 68131. Offers adult nurse practitioner (MSN, Post-Master's Certificate); family nurse practitioner (MSN, Post-Master's Certificate); nursing education (MSN, Post-Master's Certificate); nursing health care leadership (MSN, Post-Master's Certificate). *Accreditation:* AANA/CANAEP; ACEN. *Program availability:* Part-time, evening/weekend, online learning. *Degree requirements:* For master's, on-campus skills assessment (family nurse practitioner, adult nurse practitioner), comprehensive exam or thesis. *Entrance requirements:* For master's, minimum GPA of 3.0, 2 references, resume. Additional exam requirements/recommendations for international students: Required—TOEFL (minimum score 600 paper-based; 100 iBT). Electronic applications accepted.

Clarkson College, Program in Health Care Administration, Omaha, NE 68131-2739. Offers MHCA. *Program availability:* Part-time, evening/weekend, online learning. *Entrance requirements:* For master's, minimum GPA of 3.0, resume, references. Additional exam requirements/recommendations for international students: Required—TOEFL (minimum score 600 paper-based; 100 iBT). Electronic applications accepted.

Clarkson University, David D. Reh School of Business, Master's Programs in Healthcare Management and Leadership, Schenectady, NY 12308. Offers clinical leadership in healthcare management (MS); healthcare data analytics (MS); healthcare management (MBA, Advanced Certificate). *Program availability:* Part-time, evening/weekend, blended/hybrid learning. *Faculty:* 20 full-time (5 women), 13 part-time/adjunct (3 women). *Students:* 43 full-time (23 women), 35 part-time (21 women); includes 12 minority (4 Black or African American, non-Hispanic/Latino; 6 Asian, non-Hispanic/Latino; 2 Hispanic/Latino), 5 international. 64 applicants, 55% accepted, 28 enrolled. In 2017, 41 master's, 3 other advanced degrees awarded. *Entrance requirements:* For master's, GRE or GMAT. Additional exam requirements/recommendations for international students: Required—TOEFL (minimum score 550 paper-based, 80 iBT) or IELTS (6.5). *Application deadline:* Applications are processed on a rolling basis. Application fee: $50. Electronic applications accepted. *Expenses: Tuition:* Full-time $24,210; part-time $1345 per credit hour. Tuition and fees vary according to campus/location and program. *Financial support:* Scholarships/grants available. *Unit head:* Dr. John Huppertz, Director of Healthcare Management, 518-631-9892, E-mail: jhuppert@clarkson.edu. *Application contact:* Dan Capogna, Director of Graduate Admissions, 518-631-9910, E-mail: graduate@clarkson.edu.
Website: https://www.clarkson.edu/academics/graduate

College of Mount Saint Vincent, School of Professional and Graduate Studies, Department of Nursing, Riverdale, NY 10471-1093. Offers family nurse practitioner (MSN, PMC); nurse educator (PMC); nursing administration (MSN); nursing education (MSN). *Accreditation:* AACN. *Program availability:* Part-time. *Entrance requirements:* For master's, BSN, interview, RN license, minimum GPA of 3.0, letters of reference. Additional exam requirements/recommendations for international students: Required—TOEFL. *Expenses:* Contact institution.

The College of New Rochelle, Graduate School, Program in Nursing, New Rochelle, NY 10805-2308. Offers acute care nurse practitioner (MS, Certificate); clinical specialist in holistic nursing (MS, Certificate); family nurse practitioner (MS, Certificate); nursing and health care management (MS); nursing education (Certificate). *Accreditation:* AACN. *Program availability:* Part-time. *Entrance requirements:* For master's, GRE General Test or MAT, BSN, malpractice insurance, minimum GPA of 3.0, RN license. Electronic applications accepted. *Expenses: Tuition:* Full-time $17,406. *Required fees:* $1120.

Columbus State University, Graduate Studies, College of Education and Health Professions, School of Nursing, Columbus, GA 31907-5645. Offers family nurse practitioner (MSN); nursing (MSN), including nurse educator, nurse informatics, nurse leader. Program offered in collaboration with Georgia Southwestern StateUniversity. *Program availability:* Part-time, online only, 100% online. *Faculty:* 7 full-time (all women), 2 part-time/adjunct (both women). *Students:* 43 full-time (40 women), 134 part-time (121 women); includes 88 minority (65 Black or African American, non-Hispanic/Latino; 7 Asian, non-Hispanic/Latino; 10 Hispanic/Latino; 6 Two or more races, non-Hispanic/Latino). Average age 35. 141 applicants, 49% accepted, 12 enrolled. In 2017, 28 master's awarded. *Entrance requirements:* For master's, GRE, BSN, minimum undergraduate GPA of 3.0. Additional exam requirements/recommendations for international students: Required—TOEFL (minimum score 550 paper-based; 79 iBT). *Application deadline:* For fall admission, 5/1 for domestic and international students; for

spring admission, 11/1 for domestic and international students; for summer admission, 3/1 for domestic and international students. Applications are processed on a rolling basis. Application fee: $50. Electronic applications accepted. *Expenses:* Contact institution. *Financial support:* In 2017–18, 3 students received support. Institutionally sponsored loans available. Financial award application deadline: 5/1; financial award applicants required to submit FAFSA. *Unit head:* Latonya Santo, Director, 706-507-8576, E-mail: santo_latonya@columbusstate.edu. *Application contact:* Catrina Smith-Edmond, Assistant Director for Graduate and Global Admission, 706-507-8821, Fax: 706-568-5091, E-mail: smithedmond_catrina@columbusstate.edu.
Website: http://nursing.columbusstate.edu/

Cox College, Programs in Nursing, Springfield, MO 65802. Offers clinical nurse leader (MSN); family nurse practitioner (MSN); nurse educator (MSN). *Accreditation:* AACN. *Entrance requirements:* For master's, RN license, essay, 2 letters of recommendation, official transcripts. Electronic applications accepted.

Creighton University, College of Nursing, Omaha, NE 68178-0001. Offers adult gerontology acute care nurse practitioner (DNP, Post-Master's Certificate); adult gerontology nurse practitioner (DNP); clinical nurse leader (MSN, Post-Graduate Certificate); clinical systems administration (MSN, DNP); family nurse practitioner (DNP, Post-Master's Certificate); neonatal nurse practitioner (DNP, Post-Master's Certificate); nursing (Post-Graduate Certificate); pediatric acute care nurse practitioner (DNP, Post-Master's Certificate); psychiatric mental health nurse practitioner (DNP). *Accreditation:* AACN. *Program availability:* Part-time, blended/hybrid learning. *Degree requirements:* For master's, capstone project; for doctorate, scholarly project. *Entrance requirements:* For master's and doctorate, BSN from ACEN- or CCNE-accredited nursing school, minimum cumulative GPA of 3.0, personal statement, active unencumbered RN license with NE eligibility, undergraduate statistics course, physical assessment course or equivalent, three recommendation letters; for other advanced degree, MSN or MS in nursing from ACEN- or CCNE-accredited nursing school, minimum cumulative GPA of 3.0, active unencumbered RN license with NE eligibility. Additional exam requirements/recommendations for international students: Required—TOEFL (minimum score 600 paper-based, 100 iBT) or IELTS. Electronic applications accepted. *Expenses:* Contact institution. *Faculty research:* School health report card, obesity prevention in children, simulated clinical experience evaluation, vitamin D3 and calcium and cancer risk reduction education, online support and education to reduce stress for prenatal patients on bed rest, health literacy, immunization research.

Daemen College, Department of Nursing, Amherst, NY 14226-3592. Offers adult nurse practitioner (MS, Post Master's Certificate); nurse executive leadership (Post Master's Certificate); nursing education (MS, Post Master's Certificate); nursing executive leadership (MS); nursing practice (DNP); palliative care nursing (Post Master's Certificate). *Accreditation:* ACEN. *Program availability:* Part-time. *Degree requirements:* For master's, thesis or alternative, degree completed in 4 years; minimum GPA of 3.0; for doctorate, degree completed in 5 years; 500 post-master's clinical hours. *Entrance requirements:* For master's, BN, 1 year medical/surgical experience, RN license and state registration, statistics course with minimum C grade, 3 letters of recommendation, minimum GPA of 3.25, interview; for doctorate, MS in advance nursing practice; New York state RN license; goal statement; resume; interview; statistics course with minimum grade of 'C'; for Post Master's Certificate, master's degree in clinical area; RN license and current registration; one year of clinical experience; statistics course with minimum grade of 'C'; 3 letters of recommendation; interview; letter of intent. Additional exam requirements/recommendations for international students: Required—TOEFL (minimum score 500 paper-based; 63 iBT), IELTS (minimum score 5.5). Electronic applications accepted. *Faculty research:* Professional stress, client behavior, drug therapy, treatment modalities and pulmonary cancers, chemical dependency.

DeSales University, Division of Healthcare, Center Valley, PA 18034-9568. Offers adult-gerontology acute care (Post Master's Certificate); adult-gerontology acute care nurse practitioner (MSN); adult-gerontology acute certified nurse practitioner (Post Master's Certificate); adult-gerontology clinical nurse specialist (MSN, Post Master's Certificate); clinical leadership (DNP); family nurse practitioner (MSN, Post Master's Certificate); general nursing practice (DNP); nurse anesthetist (MSN); nurse educator (Post Master's Certificate, Postbaccalaureate Certificate); nurse midwife (MSN); nurse practitioner (MSN); psychiatric-mental health nurse practitioner (MSN, Post Master's Certificate); DNP/MBA. *Accreditation:* ACEN. *Program availability:* Part-time. *Faculty:* 26 full-time (20 women), 30 part-time/adjunct (19 women). *Students:* 282 full-time (210 women), 101 part-time (85 women); includes 39 minority (12 Black or African American, non-Hispanic/Latino; 11 Asian, non-Hispanic/Latino; 12 Hispanic/Latino; 4 Two or more races, non-Hispanic/Latino), 1 international. Average age 29. 2,884 applicants, 5% accepted, 114 enrolled. In 2017, 76 master's, 6 doctorates awarded. *Degree requirements:* For master's, minimum GPA of 3.0, portfolio; for doctorate, minimum GPA of 3.0, scholarly capstone project. *Entrance requirements:* For master's, GRE or MAT (waived if applicant has an undergraduate GPA of 3.0 or higher), BSN from ACEN- or CCNE-accredited program, minimum undergraduate GPA of 3.0, active RN license or eligibility, two letters of recommendation, essay, health care experience, personal interview; for doctorate, BSN or MSN from ACEN- or CCNE-accredited institution, minimum GPA of 3.3 in graduate program, current licensure as an RN. Additional exam requirements/recommendations for international students: Required—TOEFL (minimum score 104 iBT). *Application deadline:* Applications are processed on a rolling basis. Application fee: $50. Electronic applications accepted. *Expenses:* Contact institution. *Financial support:* Applicants required to submit FAFSA. *Unit head:* Ronald Nordone, Dean of Graduate Education, 610-282-1100 Ext. 1289, E-mail: ronald.nordone@desales.edu. *Application contact:* Julia Ferraro, Director of Graduate Admissions, 610-282-1100 Ext. 1768, E-mail: gradadmissions@desales.edu.

Drexel University, College of Nursing and Health Professions, Division of Graduate Nursing, Philadelphia, PA 19104-2875. Offers adult acute care (MSN); adult psychiatric/mental health (MSN); advanced practice nursing (MSN); clinical trials research (MSN); family nurse practitioner (MSN); leadership in health systems management (MSN); nursing education (MSN); pediatric primary care (MSN); women's health (MSN). *Accreditation:* AACN. Electronic applications accepted.

Duke University, School of Nursing, Durham, NC 27708-0586. Offers acute care pediatric nurse practitioner (MSN, Post-Graduate Certificate); adult-gerontology nurse practitioner (MSN, Post-Graduate Certificate), including acute care, primary care; family nurse practitioner (MSN, Post-Graduate Certificate); neonatal nurse practitioner (MSN, Post-Graduate Certificate); nurse anesthesia (DNP); nurse practitioner (DNP); nursing (PhD); nursing and health care leadership (MSN, Post-Graduate Certificate); nursing education (MSN, Post-Graduate Certificate); nursing informatics (MSN, Post-Graduate Certificate); pediatric nurse practitioner (MSN, Post-Graduate Certificate), including primary care; psychiatric mental health nurse practitioner (MSN, Post-Graduate Certificate); women's health nurse practitioner (MSN, Post-Graduate Certificate). *Accreditation:* AACN; AANA/CANAEP. *Program availability:* Part-time, evening/weekend, online with on-campus intensives. *Faculty:* 72 full-time (61 women). *Students:* 155 full-time (137 women), 613 part-time (548 women); includes 177 minority (64 Black or African American, non-Hispanic/Latino; 2 American Indian or Alaska Native, non-Hispanic/Latino; 47 Asian, non-Hispanic/Latino; 34 Hispanic/Latino; 30 Two or more races, non-Hispanic/Latino), 10 international. Average age 34. 631 applicants, 47% accepted, 211 enrolled. In 2017, 221 master's, 71 doctorates, 26 other advanced degrees awarded. Terminal master's awarded for partial completion of doctoral program. *Degree requirements:* For master's, thesis optional; for doctorate, capstone project. *Entrance requirements:* For master's, GRE General Test (waived if undergraduate GPA of 3.4 or higher), 1 year of nursing experience (recommended), BSN, minimum GPA of 3.0, previous course work in statistics; for doctorate, GRE General Test (waived if undergraduate GPA of 3.4 or higher), BSN or MSN, minimum GPA of 3.0, resume, personal statement, undergraduate statistics course, current licensure as a registered nurse, transcripts from all post-secondary institutions; for Post-Graduate Certificate, MSN, licensure or eligibility as a professional nurse, transcripts from all post-secondary institutions, previous course work in statistics. Additional exam requirements/recommendations for international students: Required—TOEFL (minimum score 100 iBT), IELTS (minimum score 7). *Application deadline:* For fall admission, 12/1 for domestic and international students; for spring admission, 5/1 for domestic and international students. Application fee: $50. Electronic applications accepted. *Expenses:* Contact institution. *Financial support:* Institutionally sponsored loans, scholarships/grants, and traineeships available. Support available to part-time students. Financial award applicants required to submit FAFSA. *Faculty research:* Cardiovascular disease, caregiver skill training, data mining, prostate cancer, neonatal immune system. *Unit head:* Dr. Marion E. Broome, Dean/Vice Chancellor for Nursing Affairs/Associate Vice President for Academic Affairs for Nursing, 919-684-9446, Fax: 919-684-9414, E-mail: marion.broome@duke.edu. *Application contact:* Dr. Ernie Rushing, Director of Admissions and Recruitment, 919-668-6274, Fax: 919-668-4693, E-mail: ernie.rushing@dm.duke.edu.
Website: http://www.nursing.duke.edu/

Eastern Mennonite University, Program in Nursing, Harrisonburg, VA 22802-2462. Offers leadership and management (MSN); leadership and school nursing (MSN); nursing management (DNP). *Accreditation:* AACN. *Program availability:* Part-time, online learning. *Degree requirements:* For master's, leadership project. *Entrance requirements:* For master's, RN license, one year of full-time work experience as RN, minimum GPA of 3.0. Additional exam requirements/recommendations for international students: Required—TOEFL. *Application deadline:* For fall admission, 6/1 for domestic students. Applications are processed on a rolling basis. Application fee: $25. Application fee is waived when completed online. *Financial support:* Federal Work-Study and scholarships/grants available. Financial award applicants required to submit FAFSA. *Faculty research:* Community health, international health, effectiveness of the nursing school environment, development of caring ability in nursing students, international nursing students. *Unit head:* Ann Hershberger, Coordinator, 540-432-4192, E-mail: hershbea@emu.edu. *Application contact:* Don A. Yoder, Director of Seminary and Graduate Admissions, 540-432-4257, Fax: 540-432-4598, E-mail: yoderda@emu.edu.

Eastern Michigan University, Graduate School, College of Health and Human Services, School of Health Sciences, Programs in Clinical Research Administration, Ypsilanti, MI 48197. Offers MS, Graduate Certificate. *Program availability:* Part-time, evening/weekend, online learning. *Students:* 4 full-time (all women), 16 part-time (12 women); includes 2 minority (1 Black or African American, non-Hispanic/Latino; 1 Asian, non-Hispanic/Latino), 7 international. Average age 34. 26 applicants, 85% accepted, 9 enrolled. In 2017, 10 master's, 1 other advanced degree awarded. *Entrance requirements:* Additional exam requirements/recommendations for international students: Required—TOEFL. *Application deadline:* Applications are processed on a rolling basis. Application fee: $45. *Financial support:* Fellowships, research assistantships with full tuition reimbursements, teaching assistantships with full tuition reimbursements, career-related internships or fieldwork, Federal Work-Study, institutionally sponsored loans, scholarships/grants, tuition waivers (partial), and unspecified assistantships available. Support available to part-time students. Financial award applicants required to submit FAFSA. *Application contact:* Dr. Jean Rowan, Program Director, 734-487-1238, Fax: 734-487-4095, E-mail: jrowan3@emich.edu.

East Tennessee State University, School of Graduate Studies, College of Nursing, Johnson City, TN 37614. Offers acute care nurse practitioner (DNP); adult-gerontology primary care nurse practitioner (DNP); adult/gerontological nurse practitioner (Postbaccalaureate Certificate); executive leadership in nursing (DNP, Postbaccalaureate Certificate); family nurse practitioner (MSN, DNP, Post-Master's Certificate, Postbaccalaureate Certificate); nursing (PhD); nursing administration (MSN); nursing education (MSN); pediatric primary care nurse practitioner (DNP); psychiatric mental health nurse practitioner (Postbaccalaureate Certificate); psychiatric/mental health nurse practitioner (MSN, DNP, Post-Master's Certificate); women's health care nurse practitioner (DNP). *Accreditation:* AACN. *Program availability:* Part-time, evening/weekend, online learning. In 2017, 126 master's, 30 doctorates, 4 other advanced degrees awarded. *Degree requirements:* For master's and other advanced degree, comprehensive exam, practicum; for doctorate, comprehensive exam, thesis/dissertation (for some programs), practicum, internship, evidence of professional malpractice insurance, CPR certification. *Entrance requirements:* For master's, bachelor's degree, minimum GPA of 3.0, current RN license and eligibility to practice, resume, three letters of recommendation; for doctorate, GRE General Test, MSN (for PhD), BSN or MSN (for DNP), current RN license and eligibility to practice, 2 years of full-time registered nurse work experience or equivalent, three letters of recommendation, resume or curriculum vitae, interview, writing sample; for other advanced degree, MSN, minimum GPA of 3.0, current RN license and eligibility to practice, three letters of recommendation, resume or curriculum vitae; DNP with designated concentration in advanced clinical practice or nursing administration (for select programs). Additional exam requirements/recommendations for international students: Required—TOEFL (minimum score 600 paper-based; 79 iBT). *Application deadline:* For fall admission, 4/15 priority date for domestic and international students; for spring admission, 10/15 priority date for domestic and international students; for summer admission, 2/1 for domestic and international students. Application fee: $55 ($65 for international students). Electronic applications accepted. *Financial support:* Research assistantships with tuition reimbursements, teaching assistantships, career-related internships or fieldwork, institutionally sponsored loans, scholarships/grants, and unspecified assistantships available. Financial award application deadline: 7/1; financial award applicants required to submit FAFSA. *Faculty research:* Improving health of rural and underserved populations (low income elders living in public housing, rural caregivers, Hispanic populations), health services and systems research (quality outcomes of nurse-managed primary care, in-home, and rural health care), nursing education (experiences of second-degree BSN students, well-being of BSN students). *Unit head:* Dr. Wendy Nehring, Dean, 423-439-7051, Fax: 423-439-4543, E-mail: nursing@etsu.edu. *Application contact:* Dr. Myra Clark, Director of Graduate Programs, 423-439-4396, Fax: 423-439-4100, E-mail: clarkml2@etsu.edu.
Website: http://www.etsu.edu/nursing/

Elms College, School of Nursing, Chicopee, MA 01013-2839. Offers adult-gerontology acute care nurse practitioner (DNP); family nurse practitioner (DNP); health systems innovation and leadership (DNP); nursing and health services management (MSN); nursing education (MSN). *Accreditation:* AACN. *Program availability:* Part-time, evening/weekend. *Faculty:* 5 full-time (all women), 9 part-time/adjunct (6 women). *Students:* 20 full-time (16 women), 79 part-time (70 women); includes 12 minority (2 Black or African American, non-Hispanic/Latino; 2 American Indian or Alaska Native, non-Hispanic/

Latino; 8 Hispanic/Latino). Average age 40. 33 applicants, 94% accepted, 28 enrolled. In 2017, 14 master's, 30 doctorates awarded. *Entrance requirements:* Additional exam requirements/recommendations for international students: Required—TOEFL. *Application deadline:* For fall admission, 7/1 priority date for domestic students; for spring admission, 11/1 priority date for domestic students. Applications are processed on a rolling basis. Application fee: $30. *Expenses: Tuition:* Full-time $13,860; part-time $770 per credit hour. *Required fees:* $200. Tuition and fees vary according to degree level and program. *Financial support:* Applicants required to submit FAFSA. *Unit head:* Dr. Kathleen Scoble, Dean, School of Nursing, 413-265-2204, E-mail: scoblek@elms.edu. *Application contact:* Dr. Cynthia L. Dakin, Director of Graduate Nursing Studies, 413-265-2455, Fax: 413-265-2335, E-mail: dakinc@elms.edu.

Emmanuel College, Graduate and Professional Programs, Graduate Program in Nursing, Boston, MA 02115. Offers education (MSN, Graduate Certificate); management (MSN, Graduate Certificate). *Accreditation:* AACN. *Program availability:* Part-time, evening/weekend. *Faculty:* 3 full-time (all women), 4 part-time/adjunct (all women). *Students:* 35 part-time (33 women); includes 6 minority (3 Black or African American, non-Hispanic/Latino; 3 Hispanic/Latino). Average age 42. 26 applicants, 27% accepted, 3 enrolled. In 2017, 7 master's awarded. *Degree requirements:* For master's, 36 credits, including 6-credit practicum. *Entrance requirements:* For master's, transcripts from all regionally-accredited institutions attended (showing proof of bachelor's degree completion), proof of RN license, 2 letters of recommendation, essay, resume; for Graduate Certificate, transcripts from all regionally-accredited institutions attended (showing proof of master's degree completion), proof of RN license, 2 letters of recommendation, essay, resume. Additional exam requirements/recommendations for international students: Required—TOEFL. *Application deadline:* Applications are processed on a rolling basis. Electronic applications accepted. *Expenses:* $28,391 (for MSN); $10,324 (for Graduate Certificate). *Financial support:* Application deadline: 2/15; applicants required to submit FAFSA. *Unit head:* Diane Shea, Associate Dean for Nursing/Professor of Nursing Practice, 617-732-1604, E-mail: shead@emmanuel.edu. *Application contact:* Helen Muterperl, Director of Graduate and Professional Programs, 617-735-9700, Fax: 617-507-0434, E-mail: gpp@emmanuel.edu.
Website: http://www.emmanuel.edu/graduate-professional-programs/academics/nursing.html

Emory University, Nell Hodgson Woodruff School of Nursing, Atlanta, GA 30322-1100. Offers adult nurse practitioner (MSN); emergency nurse practitioner (MSN); family nurse practitioner (MSN); family nurse-midwife (MSN); health systems leadership (MSN); nurse-midwifery (MSN); pediatric nurse practitioner acute and primary care (MSN); women's health care (Title X) (MSN); women's health nurse practitioner (MSN); MSN/MPH. *Accreditation:* AACN; ACNM/ACME (one or more programs are accredited). *Program availability:* Part-time. *Entrance requirements:* For master's, GRE General Test or MAT, minimum GPA of 3.0, BS in nursing from an accredited institution, RN license and additional course work, 3 letters of recommendation. Additional exam requirements/recommendations for international students: Required—TOEFL (minimum score 600 paper-based; 100 iBT). Electronic applications accepted. *Expenses:* Contact institution. *Faculty research:* Older adult falls and injuries, minority health issues, cardiac symptoms and quality of life, bio-ethics and decision-making, menopausal issues.

Endicott College, Van Loan School of Graduate and Professional Studies, Program in Nursing, Beverly, MA 01915-2096. Offers family nurse practitioner (MSN, Post-Master's Certificate); global health (MSN); nursing administration (MSN); nursing administrator (Post-Master's Certificate); nursing educator (MSN, Post-Master's Certificate). *Program availability:* Part-time, evening/weekend. *Faculty:* 5 full-time (4 women), 14 part-time/adjunct (12 women). *Students:* 43 full-time (41 women), 57 part-time (51 women); includes 8 minority (5 Black or African American, non-Hispanic/Latino; 3 Hispanic/Latino), 1 international. Average age 37. 41 applicants, 100% accepted, 38 enrolled. In 2017, 33 master's awarded. *Degree requirements:* For master's, thesis, practicum. *Entrance requirements:* For master's, MAT or GRE, statement of professional goals, official transcripts of all undergraduate and graduate course work, two letters of recommendation, photocopy of current and unrestricted RN license, basic statistics course, interview. Additional exam requirements/recommendations for international students: Required—TOEFL. *Application deadline:* Applications are processed on a rolling basis. Application fee: $50. Electronic applications accepted. *Expenses:* Contact institution. *Financial support:* Applicants required to submit FAFSA. *Unit head:* Dr. Kelly Fisher, Dean, 978-232-2328, Fax: 978-232-3000, E-mail: kfisher@endicott.edu. *Application contact:* Ian Menchini, Director, Graduate Enrollment and Advising, 978-232-5292, Fax: 978-232-3000, E-mail: imenchin@endicott.edu.
Website: https://vanloan.endicott.edu/programs-of-study/masters-programs/nursing-programs

Excelsior College, School of Health Sciences, Albany, NY 12203-5159. Offers health care administration (MS); health professions education (MSHS); healthcare informatics (MS); organizational development (MS); public health (MSHS). *Program availability:* Part-time, evening/weekend, online learning. *Faculty:* 4 part-time/adjunct (all women). *Students:* 133 part-time (92 women); includes 84 minority (49 Black or African American, non-Hispanic/Latino; 4 American Indian or Alaska Native, non-Hispanic/Latino; 8 Asian, non-Hispanic/Latino; 13 Hispanic/Latino; 2 Native Hawaiian or other Pacific Islander, non-Hispanic/Latino; 8 Two or more races, non-Hispanic/Latino). Average age 40. In 2017, 38 master's awarded. *Application deadline:* Applications are processed on a rolling basis. Application fee: $50. Electronic applications accepted. *Expenses: Tuition:* Part-time $645 per credit. *Required fees:* $265 per credit. *Financial support:* Scholarships/grants available. *Unit head:* Dr. Barbara Pieper, Dean, 518-464-8500, Fax: 518-464-8777. *Application contact:* Admissions Counselor, 518-464-8500, Fax: 518-464-8777, E-mail: gradadmissions@excelsior.edu.

Excelsior College, School of Nursing, Albany, NY 12203-5159. Offers nursing (MS); nursing education (MS); nursing informatics (MS); nursing leadership and administration of health care systems (MS). *Accreditation:* ACEN. *Program availability:* Part-time, evening/weekend, online learning. *Faculty:* 12 part-time/adjunct (9 women). *Students:* 388 part-time (313 women); includes 122 minority (63 Black or African American, non-Hispanic/Latino; 4 American Indian or Alaska Native, non-Hispanic/Latino; 18 Asian, non-Hispanic/Latino; 28 Hispanic/Latino; 2 Native Hawaiian or other Pacific Islander, non-Hispanic/Latino; 7 Two or more races, non-Hispanic/Latino). Average age 44. In 2017, 173 master's awarded. *Entrance requirements:* For master's, RN license. *Application deadline:* Applications are processed on a rolling basis. Application fee: $50. Electronic applications accepted. *Expenses: Tuition:* Part-time $645 per credit. *Required fees:* $265 per credit. *Financial support:* Scholarships/grants available. *Unit head:* Dr. Mary Lee Pollard, Dean, School of Nursing, 518-464-8500, Fax: 518-464-8777, E-mail: msn@excelsior.edu. *Application contact:* Admissions Counselor, 888-647-2388, Fax: 518-464-8777, E-mail: gradadmissions@excelsior.edu.
Website: http://www.excelsior.edu/programs/nursing

Fairfield University, Marion Peckham Egan School of Nursing and Health Studies, Fairfield, CT 06824. Offers advanced practice (DNP); family nurse practitioner (MSN, DNP); nurse anesthesia (DNP); nursing leadership (MSN); psychiatric nurse practitioner (MSN, DNP). *Accreditation:* AACN; AANA/CANAEP. *Program availability:* Part-time, evening/weekend. *Faculty:* 9 full-time (all women), 11 part-time/adjunct (8 women). *Students:* 50 full-time (42 women), 153 part-time (140 women); includes 48 minority (15 Black or African American, non-Hispanic/Latino; 1 American Indian or Alaska Native, non-Hispanic/Latino; 10 Asian, non-Hispanic/Latino; 19 Hispanic/Latino; 3 Two or more races, non-Hispanic/Latino), 2 international. Average age 34. 160 applicants, 50% accepted, 55 enrolled. In 2017, 26 master's, 36 doctorates awarded. *Degree requirements:* For master's, capstone project. *Entrance requirements:* For master's, minimum QPA of 3.0, RN license, resume, 2 recommendations; for doctorate, MSN (minimum QPA of 3.2) or BSN (minimum QPA of 3.0); critical care nursing experience (for nurse anesthesia DNP candidates). Additional exam requirements/recommendations for international students: Required—TOEFL (minimum score 550 paper-based; 80 iBT) or IELTS (minimum score 6.5). *Application deadline:* For fall admission, 5/15 for international students; for spring admission, 10/15 for international students. Applications are processed on a rolling basis. Application fee: $60. Electronic applications accepted. *Expenses:* $850 per credit hour (for MSN); $1,000 per credit hour (for DNP). *Financial support:* In 2017–18, 45 students received support. Scholarships/grants and unspecified assistantships available. Financial award applicants required to submit FAFSA. *Faculty research:* Aging, spiritual care, palliative and end of life care, psychiatric mental health, pediatric trauma. *Unit head:* Dr. Meredith Wallace Kazer, Dean, 203-254-4000 Ext. 2701, Fax: 203-254-4126, E-mail: mkazer@fairfield.edu. *Application contact:* Marianne Gumpper, Director of Graduate and Continuing Studies Admission, 203-254-4184, Fax: 203-254-4073, E-mail: gradadmis@fairfield.edu.
Website: http://fairfield.edu/son

Felician University, Doctor of Nursing Practice Program, Lodi, NJ 07644-2117. Offers advanced practice (DNP); executive leadership (DNP). *Accreditation:* AACN. *Program availability:* Evening/weekend, online only, 100% online, blended/hybrid learning. *Faculty:* 4 full-time (all women). *Students:* 9 part-time (all women); includes 4 minority (2 Black or African American, non-Hispanic/Latino; 2 Hispanic/Latino). Average age 55. 3 applicants, 67% accepted. In 2017, 2 doctorates awarded. *Degree requirements:* For doctorate, thesis/dissertation, scholarly project. *Entrance requirements:* For doctorate, 2 letters of recommendation; national certification as nurse executive/administrator (preferred); interview; minimum GPA of 3.0. Additional exam requirements/recommendations for international students: Required—TOEFL (minimum score 550 paper-based; 79 iBT), IELTS (minimum score 6.5), PTE (minimum score 56). *Application deadline:* Applications are processed on a rolling basis. Application fee: $40. Electronic applications accepted. Application fee is waived when completed online. *Expenses:* Contact institution. *Financial support:* Federal Work-Study and scholarships/grants available. Financial award applicants required to submit FAFSA. *Faculty research:* Quality improvement, health promotion in populations, student attitudes towards aging. *Unit head:* Dr. Ann Tritak, Associate Dean of Graduate Nursing, 201-559-6151, E-mail: tritaka@felician.edu. *Application contact:* Michael Szarek, Assistant Vice-President of Graduate Admissions, 201-355-1450, E-mail: szarekm@felician.edu.

Felician University, Master of Science in Nursing Program, Lodi, NJ 07644-2117. Offers adult-gerontology nurse practitioner (MSN, PMC); executive leadership (MSN, PMC); family nurse practitioner (MSN, PMC); nursing education (MSN, PMC). *Accreditation:* AACN. *Program availability:* Evening/weekend, online only, 100% online, blended/hybrid learning. *Faculty:* 9 full-time (8 women), 1 (woman) part-time/adjunct. *Students:* 96 part-time (90 women); includes 48 minority (17 Black or African American, non-Hispanic/Latino; 1 American Indian or Alaska Native, non-Hispanic/Latino; 16 Asian, non-Hispanic/Latino; 12 Hispanic/Latino; 1 Native Hawaiian or other Pacific Islander, non-Hispanic/Latino; 1 Two or more races, non-Hispanic/Latino). Average age 37. 49 applicants, 86% accepted, 23 enrolled. In 2017, 35 master's, 3 other advanced degrees awarded. *Degree requirements:* For master's, thesis, clinical presentation; for PMC, thesis, education project. *Entrance requirements:* For master's, BSN; minimum GPA of 3.0; 2 letters of recommendation; NJ RN license; personal statement; for PMC, RN license, minimum GPA of 3.0. Additional exam requirements/recommendations for international students: Required—TOEFL (minimum score 550 paper-based; 79 iBT), IELTS (minimum score 6.5), PTE (minimum score 56). *Application deadline:* Applications are processed on a rolling basis. Application fee: $40. Electronic applications accepted. Application fee is waived when completed online. *Expenses:* Contact institution. *Financial support:* Federal Work-Study, scholarships/grants, and traineeships available. Financial award applicants required to submit FAFSA. *Faculty research:* Anxiety and fear, curriculum innovation, health promotion and populations, attitudes of college students towards aging. *Unit head:* Dr. Ann Tritak, Associate Dean of Graduate Nursing, 201-559-6151, E-mail: tritaka@felician.edu. *Application contact:* Michael Szarek, Assistant Vice-President, Graduate Admissions, 201-355-1450, E-mail: szarekm@felician.edu.

Ferris State University, College of Health Professions, School of Nursing, Big Rapids, MI 49307. Offers nursing (MSN); nursing administration (MSN); nursing education (MSN); nursing informatics (MSN). *Accreditation:* ACEN. *Program availability:* Part-time, evening/weekend, online only, 100% online. *Faculty:* 7 full-time (all women), 2 part-time/adjunct (both women). *Students:* 3 full-time (all women), 104 part-time (95 women); includes 15 minority (3 Black or African American, non-Hispanic/Latino; 5 American Indian or Alaska Native, non-Hispanic/Latino; 2 Asian, non-Hispanic/Latino; 3 Hispanic/Latino; 1 Native Hawaiian or other Pacific Islander, non-Hispanic/Latino; 1 Two or more races, non-Hispanic/Latino). Average age 40. 36 applicants, 92% accepted, 31 enrolled. In 2017, 25 master's awarded. *Degree requirements:* For master's, practicum, practicum project. *Entrance requirements:* For master's, BS in nursing (for nursing education track); BS in nursing or related field (for nursing administration and nursing informatics tracks); registered nurse license, writing sample, letters of reference, 2 years' clinical experience (recommended). Additional exam requirements/recommendations for international students: Required—TOEFL (minimum score 550 paper-based; 61 iBT). *Application deadline:* For fall admission, 4/15 priority date for domestic students; for spring admission, 10/15 for domestic students. Application fee: $0. Electronic applications accepted. *Financial support:* In 2017–18, 3 students received support. Career-related internships or fieldwork and scholarships/grants available. Financial award application deadline: 4/15; financial award applicants required to submit FAFSA. *Faculty research:* Nursing education, end of life, leadership/education introverts in nursing, complementary and alternative medicine therapies. *Unit head:* Dr. Susan Owens, Chair, School of Nursing, 231-591-2267, Fax: 231-591-2325, E-mail: owenss3@ferris.edu. *Application contact:* Sharon Colley, MSN Program Coordinator, 231-591-2288, Fax: 231-591-2325, E-mail: colleys@ferris.edu.
Website: http://www.ferris.edu/htmls/colleges/alliedhe/Nursing/homepage.htm

Florida Agricultural and Mechanical University, Division of Graduate Studies, Research, and Continuing Education, School of Allied Health Sciences, Tallahassee, FL 32307-3200. Offers health administration (MS); occupational therapy (MOT); physical therapy (DPT). *Degree requirements:* For master's, thesis (for some programs). *Entrance requirements:* For master's, GRE General Test or GMAT, minimum GPA of 3.0. Additional exam requirements/recommendations for international students: Required—TOEFL (minimum score 550 paper-based).

Florida Atlantic University, Christine E. Lynn College of Nursing, Boca Raton, FL 33431. Offers administrative and financial leadership in nursing and health care (Post Master's Certificate); nursing (MSN, PhD); nursing practice (DNP). *Accreditation:* AACN. *Program availability:* Part-time. *Faculty:* 32 full-time (31 women), 7 part-time/adjunct (6 women). *Students:* 61 full-time (57 women), 443 part-time (405 women); includes 265

minority (133 Black or African American, non-Hispanic/Latino; 33 Asian, non-Hispanic/Latino; 87 Hispanic/Latino; 1 Native Hawaiian or other Pacific Islander, non-Hispanic/Latino; 11 Two or more races, non-Hispanic/Latino), 6 international. Average age 37. 569 applicants, 28% accepted, 128 enrolled. In 2017, 131 master's, 28 doctorates awarded. *Degree requirements:* For master's, thesis or alternative; for doctorate, comprehensive exam, thesis/dissertation. *Entrance requirements:* For master's, GRE General Test or MAT, bachelor's degree in nursing, Florida RN license, minimum GPA of 3.0, resume/curriculum vitae, letter of recommendation; for doctorate, GRE General Test or MAT, curriculum vitae, Florida RN license, minimum GPA of 3.5, master's degree in nursing, three letters of recommendation. *Application deadline:* For fall admission, 6/1 for domestic students, 2/15 for international students; for spring admission, 10/1 for domestic students, 7/15 for international students. Applications are processed on a rolling basis. Application fee: $30. *Expenses:* Tuition, state resident: full-time $7400; part-time $369.82 per credit. Tuition, nonresident: full-time $20,496; part-time $1042.81 per credit. *Financial support:* Research assistantships with partial tuition reimbursements, teaching assistantships with partial tuition reimbursements, career-related internships or fieldwork, Federal Work-Study, institutionally sponsored loans, scholarships/grants, and traineeships available. Support available to part-time students. *Faculty research:* Econometrics of nurse-patient relationship, Alzheimer's disease, community-based programs, falls, self-healing. *Unit head:* Marlaine Smith, Dean, 561-297-3206, E-mail: msmit230@health.fau.edu.
Website: http://nursing.fau.edu/

Florida National University, Program in Nursing, Hialeah, FL 33012. Offers family nurse practitioner (MSN); nurse educator (MSN); nurse leadership and management (MSN). *Program availability:* 100% online, blended/hybrid learning. *Degree requirements:* For master's, practicum. *Entrance requirements:* For master's, active registered nurse license, BSN from accredited institution. *Expenses: Tuition:* Full-time $15,600. *Required fees:* $650.
Website: https://www.fnu.edu/prospective-students/our-programs/select-a-program/master-of-business-administration/nursing-msn-master/

Florida Southern College, Program in Nursing, Lakeland, FL 33801-5698. Offers adult gerontology clinical nurse specialist (MSN); adult gerontology primary care nurse practitioner (MSN); family nurse practitioner (MSN); nurse educator (MSN); nursing administration (MSN). *Accreditation:* AACN. *Program availability:* Part-time. *Faculty:* 5 full-time (all women), 2 part-time/adjunct (both women). *Students:* 142 full-time (126 women), 9 part-time (all women); includes 70 minority (39 Black or African American, non-Hispanic/Latino; 1 American Indian or Alaska Native, non-Hispanic/Latino; 11 Asian, non-Hispanic/Latino; 13 Hispanic/Latino; 1 Native Hawaiian or other Pacific Islander, non-Hispanic/Latino; 5 Two or more races, non-Hispanic/Latino), 1 international. Average age 40. 83 applicants, 93% accepted, 72 enrolled. In 2017, 41 master's awarded. *Degree requirements:* For master's, 780 clinical practice hours. *Entrance requirements:* For master's, GMAT or GRE General Test, Florida RN license, 3 letters of recommendation, personal statement, minimum GPA of 3.0, resume. Additional exam requirements/recommendations for international students: Required—TOEFL (minimum score 550 paper-based; 79 iBT), IELTS (minimum score 6.5). *Application deadline:* For fall admission, 6/1 for domestic and international students; for spring admission, 10/1 for domestic and international students. Applications are processed on a rolling basis. Application fee: $30. Electronic applications accepted. *Expenses:* $585 per credit hour, $100 required fees. *Financial support:* In 2017–18, 1 student received support. Scholarships/grants and traineeships available. Support available to part-time students. Financial award applicants required to submit FAFSA. *Faculty research:* End of life care, dementia, health promotion. *Unit head:* Dr. Linda Comer, Dean, 863-680-4310, Fax: 863-680-3872, E-mail: lcomer@flsouthern.edu. *Application contact:* Kathy Connelly, Evening Program Assistant Director, 863-680-4205, Fax: 863-680-3872, E-mail: kconnelly@flsouthern.edu.

Framingham State University, Graduate Studies, Program in Nursing, Framingham, MA 01701-9101. Offers nursing education (MSN); nursing leadership (MSN). *Accreditation:* AACN. *Entrance requirements:* For master's, BSN; minimum cumulative undergraduate GPA of 3.0, 3.25 in nursing courses; coursework in statistics; 2 letters of recommendation; interview. *Application deadline:* For fall admission, 7/1 for domestic students. Application fee: $50. Electronic applications accepted. *Unit head:* Dr. Cynthia Bechtel, Program Coordinator, 508-626-4997, Fax: 508-626-4030, E-mail: cbechtel@framingham.edu. *Application contact:* Dr. Scott Greenberg, Associate Vice President of Academic Affairs and Dean of Continuing Education, 508-626-4603, E-mail: sgreenberg@framingham.edu.

Franklin Pierce University, Graduate and Professional Studies, Rindge, NH 03461-0060. Offers curriculum and instruction (M Ed); elementary education (MS Ed); emerging network technologies (Graduate Certificate); energy and sustainability studies (MBA, Graduate Certificate); health administration (MBA, Graduate Certificate); human resource management (MBA, Graduate Certificate); information technology (MBA); leadership (MBA); nursing education (MS); nursing leadership (MS); physical therapy (DPT); physician assistant studies (MPAS); special education (M Ed); sports management (MBA). *Accreditation:* APTA. *Program availability:* Part-time, 100% online, blended/hybrid learning. *Degree requirements:* For master's, concentrated original research projects; student teaching; fieldwork and/or internship; leadership project; PRAXIS I and II (for M Ed); for doctorate, concentrated original research projects, clinical fieldwork and/or internship, leadership project. *Entrance requirements:* For master's, minimum GPA of 2.5, 3 letters of recommendation; competencies in accounting, economics, statistics, and computer skills through life experience or undergraduate coursework (for MBA); certification/e-portfolio, minimum C grade in all education courses (for M Ed); license to practice as RN (for MS); for doctorate, GRE, 80 hours of observation/work in PT settings; completion of anatomy, chemistry, physics, and statistics; minimum GPA of 3.0. Additional exam requirements/recommendations for international students: Required—TOEFL (minimum score 550 paper-based; 61 iBT). Electronic applications accepted. *Faculty research:* Evidence-based practice in sports physical therapy, human resource management in economic crisis, leadership in nursing, innovation in sports facility management, differentiated learning and understanding by design.

Frostburg State University, College of Liberal Arts and Sciences, Department of Nursing, Frostburg, MD 21532. Offers nursing administration (MSN); nursing education (MSN). *Program availability:* Part-time, online learning. *Faculty:* 6 full-time (all women). *Students:* 1 (woman) full-time, 22 part-time (all women); includes 3 minority (2 Black or African American, non-Hispanic/Latino; 1 Hispanic/Latino). Average age 35. 10 applicants, 80% accepted, 5 enrolled. In 2017, 12 master's awarded. *Entrance requirements:* For master's, current unrestricted RN license; BSN from a nursing program accredited by CCNE or ACEN. Additional exam requirements/recommendations for international students: Required—TOEFL. *Application deadline:* For spring admission, 11/1 for domestic students. Application fee: $45. *Expenses:* Tuition, state resident: part-time $433 per credit hour. Tuition, nonresident: part-time $557 per credit hour. *Required fees:* $121 per credit hour. $27 per term. *Financial support:* Unspecified assistantships available. Financial award application deadline: 4/1. *Unit head:* Dr. Heather Gable, Department Chair, 301-687-4894, E-mail: hagable@frostburg.edu. *Application contact:* Vickie Mazer, Director, Graduate Services, 301-687-7053, Fax: 301-687-4597, E-mail: vmmazer@frostburg.edu.
Website: http://www.frostburg.edu/nursing/

Gannon University, School of Graduate Studies, Morosky College of Health Professions and Sciences, Villa Maria School of Nursing, Program in Nursing Administration, Erie, PA 16541-0001. Offers MSN. *Program availability:* Part-time, evening/weekend. *Degree requirements:* For master's, thesis (for some programs), practicum. *Entrance requirements:* For master's, GRE, RN, transcripts, 3 letters of recommendation, evidence of the fulfillment of legal requirements for the practice of nursing in the United States. Additional exam requirements/recommendations for international students: Required—TOEFL (minimum score 79 iBT). Electronic applications accepted.

The George Washington University, School of Nursing, Washington, DC 20052. Offers adult nurse practitioner (MSN, DNP, Post-Master's Certificate); clinical research administration (MSN); family nurse practitioner (MSN, Post-Master's Certificate); health care quality (MSN, Post-Master's Certificate); nursing leadership and management (MSN); nursing practice (DNP), including nursing education; palliative care nurse practitioner (Post-Master's Certificate). *Accreditation:* AACN. *Faculty:* 58 full-time (56 women), 119 part-time/adjunct (111 women). *Students:* 38 full-time (34 women), 570 part-time (510 women); includes 197 minority (92 Black or African American, non-Hispanic/Latino; 2 American Indian or Alaska Native, non-Hispanic/Latino; 63 Asian, non-Hispanic/Latino; 28 Hispanic/Latino; 1 Native Hawaiian or other Pacific Islander, non-Hispanic/Latino; 11 Two or more races, non-Hispanic/Latino), 2 international. Average age 31. 507 applicants, 76% accepted, 185 enrolled. In 2017, 155 master's, 32 doctorates awarded. *Expenses: Tuition:* Full-time $28,800; part-time $1655 per credit hour. *Required fees:* $45; $2.75 per credit hour. *Unit head:* Pamela R. Jeffries, Dean, 202-994-3725, E-mail: pjeffries@gwu.edu. *Application contact:* Kristin Williams, Associate Provost for Graduate Enrollment Management, 202-994-0467, Fax: 202-994-0371, E-mail: ksw@gwu.edu.
Website: http://nursing.gwumc.edu/

Georgia Southwestern State University, College of Nursing and Health Sciences, Americus, GA 31709-4693. Offers family nurse practitioner (MSN); health informatics (Postbaccalaureate Certificate); nurse educator (Post Master's Certificate); nursing educator (MSN); nursing informatics (MSN); nursing leadership (MSN). MSN program offered by the Georgia Intercollegiate Consortium for Graduate Nursing Education, a partnership with Columbus State University. *Program availability:* Part-time, online only, all theory courses are offered online. *Faculty:* 10 full-time, 5 part-time/adjunct. *Students:* 23 full-time (22 women), 106 part-time (92 women); includes 41 minority (all Black or African American, non-Hispanic/Latino). Average age 35. 95 applicants, 63% accepted, 30 enrolled. In 2017, 17 master's awarded. *Degree requirements:* For master's, comprehensive exam (for some programs), thesis (for some programs), minimum cumulative GPA of 3.0; maximum of 6 credit hours with C grade and no D grades; degree completed within 7 calendar years from initial enrollment date in graduate courses; for other advanced degree, minimum cumulative GPA of 3.0; maximum of 6 credit hours with C grade and no D grades; degree completed within 7 calendar years from initial enrollment date in graduate courses. *Entrance requirements:* For master's and other advanced degree, baccalaureate degree in nursing from regionally-accredited institution and nationally-accredited nursing program with minimum GPA of 3.0; three professional letters of recommendation; current unencumbered RN license in state where clinical course requirements will be met; background check/drug test; proof of immunizations. *Application deadline:* For fall admission, 1/15 for domestic students; for spring admission, 10/15 for domestic students. Application fee: $25. Electronic applications accepted. *Expenses:* $385 per credit hour, plus fees, which vary according to enrolled credit hours. *Financial support:* Application deadline: 6/1; applicants required to submit FAFSA. *Unit head:* Dr. Sandra Daniel, Dean, 229-931-2275. *Application contact:* Whitney Ford, Admissions Specialist, Office of Graduate Admissions, 800-338-0082, Fax: 229-931-2983, E-mail: graduateadmissions@gsw.edu.
Website: https://gsw.edu/Academics/Schools-and-Departments/School-of-Nursing/index

Georgia State University, Byrdine F. Lewis School of Nursing, Atlanta, GA 30303. Offers adult health clinical nurse specialist/nurse practitioner (MS, Certificate); child health clinical nurse specialist/pediatric nurse practitioner (MS, Certificate); family nurse practitioner (MS, Certificate); family psychiatric mental health nurse practitioner (MS, Certificate); nursing (PhD); nursing leadership in healthcare innovations (MS), including nursing administration, nursing informatics; nutrition (MS); perinatal clinical nurse specialist/women's health nurse practitioner (MS, Certificate); physical therapy (DPT); respiratory therapy (MS). *Accreditation:* AACN. *Program availability:* Part-time, blended/hybrid learning. *Faculty:* 69 full-time (52 women). *Students:* 322 full-time (248 women), 481 part-time (466 women); includes 186 minority (112 Black or African American, non-Hispanic/Latino; 44 Asian, non-Hispanic/Latino; 20 Hispanic/Latino; 10 Two or more races, non-Hispanic/Latino), 18 international. Average age 31. 370 applicants, 56% accepted, 148 enrolled. In 2017, 131 master's, 49 doctorates, 11 other advanced degrees awarded. *Degree requirements:* For doctorate, comprehensive exam, thesis/dissertation. *Entrance requirements:* For doctorate, GRE. Additional exam requirements/recommendations for international students: Required—TOEFL. *Application deadline:* For fall admission, 2/1 priority date for domestic and international students; for spring admission, 9/15 for domestic and international students. Applications are processed on a rolling basis. Application fee: $50. Electronic applications accepted. *Expenses:* Contact institution. *Financial support:* In 2017–18, research assistantships with tuition reimbursements (averaging $1,666 per year), teaching assistantships with tuition reimbursements (averaging $1,920 per year) were awarded; scholarships/grants, tuition waivers (full and partial), and unspecified assistantships also available. Support available to part-time students. Financial award application deadline: 8/1; financial award applicants required to submit FAFSA. *Faculty research:* Stroke intervention for caregivers, stroke prevention in African-Americans; relationships between psychological distress and health outcomes in parents with a medically ill infant; medically fragile children; nursing expertise and patient outcomes. *Unit head:* Nancy Kropf, Dean of Nursing, 404-413-1101, Fax: 404-413-1090, E-mail: nkropf@gsu.edu.
Website: http://nursing.gsu.edu/

Goldfarb School of Nursing at Barnes-Jewish College, Graduate Programs, St. Louis, MO 63110. Offers adult-gerontology (MSN), including primary care nurse practitioner; adult-gerontology (MSN), including acute care nurse practitioner; health systems and population health leadership (MSN); nurse anesthesia (MSN). *Accreditation:* AACN; AANA/CANAEP. *Program availability:* Part-time, online learning. *Faculty:* 42 full-time (39 women), 6 part-time/adjunct (all women). *Students:* 61 full-time (49 women), 3 part-time (2 women); includes 13 minority (8 Black or African American, non-Hispanic/Latino; 2 Asian, non-Hispanic/Latino; 1 Hispanic/Latino; 2 Two or more races, non-Hispanic/Latino). *Degree requirements:* For master's, thesis or alternative. *Entrance requirements:* For master's, 2 references, personal statement, curriculum vitae or resume. Additional exam requirements/recommendations for international students: Required—TOEFL (minimum score 575 paper-based; 85 iBT). *Application deadline:* Applications are processed on a rolling basis. Application fee: $50. *Expenses: Tuition:* Full-time $11,910; part-time $794 per credit hour. *Required fees:* $30; $15 per term. Full-time tuition and fees vary according to program. *Financial support:* Research assistantships, Federal Work-Study, institutionally sponsored loans, scholarships/grants, and traineeships available. Support available to part-time students. Financial

award applicants required to submit FAFSA. *Faculty research:* HIV stigma, HIV symptom management, palliative care with children and their families, heart disease prevention in Hispanic women, depression in the well elderly, alternative therapies in pre-term infants. *Unit head:* Dr. Gretchen Drinkard, Associate Dean for Academic Affairs, 314-454-7540, Fax: 314-362-9222, E-mail: gdrinkard@bjc.org. *Application contact:* Karen Sartorius, Admission Specialist, 314-454-7057, Fax: 314-362-9250, E-mail: karen.sartorius@bjc.org.
Website: http://www.barnesjewishcollege.edu/

Grand Valley State University, Kirkhof College of Nursing, Allendale, MI 49503-3314. Offers advanced practice (MSN); case management (MSN); nursing administration (MSN); nursing education (MSN); nursing practice (DNP); MSN/MBA. *Accreditation:* AACN. *Program availability:* Part-time. *Faculty:* 17 full-time (all women), 5 part-time/adjunct (4 women). *Students:* 44 full-time (40 women), 74 part-time (63 women); includes 15 minority (7 Black or African American, non-Hispanic/Latino; 4 Asian, non-Hispanic/Latino; 3 Hispanic/Latino; 1 Two or more races, non-Hispanic/Latino), 4 international. Average age 33. 34 applicants, 100% accepted, 23 enrolled. In 2017, 8 master's, 22 doctorates awarded. *Degree requirements:* For master's, thesis optional; for doctorate, thesis/dissertation optional. *Entrance requirements:* For master's, GRE, minimum upper-division GPA of 3.0, course work in statistics, Michigan RN license, writing sample, interview, criminal background check and drug screen, health records; for doctorate, minimum GPA of 3.0 in master's-level coursework, writing sample, interview, RN in Michigan, criminal background check and drug screen, health records. Additional exam requirements/recommendations for international students: Required—TOEFL (minimum iBT score of 80), IELTS (6.5), or Michigan English Language Assessment Battery (77). *Application deadline:* For fall admission, 3/15 priority date for domestic students. Applications are processed on a rolling basis. Application fee: $30. Electronic applications accepted. *Expenses:* $686 per credit hour (for MSN); $770 per credit hour (for DNP). *Financial support:* In 2017–18, 34 students received support, including 10 fellowships, 30 research assistantships with partial tuition reimbursements available (averaging $4,000 per year); career-related internships or fieldwork, Federal Work-Study, institutionally sponsored loans, and traineeships also available. Financial award application deadline: 2/15. *Faculty research:* Multigenerational health promotion, chronic disease prevention, end-of-life issues, nursing workload, family caregiver health. *Total annual research expenditures:* $36,000. *Unit head:* Dr. Cynthia McCurren, Dean, 616-331-3558, Fax: 616-331-2510, E-mail: mccurrec@gvsu.edu. *Application contact:* Dr. Karen Burritt, Associate Dean for Graduate Programs, 616-331-5585, Fax: 616-331-2510, E-mail: burritka@gvsu.edu.
Website: http://www.gvsu.edu/kcon/

Grand View University, Graduate Studies, Des Moines, IA 50316-1599. Offers athletic training (MS); clinical nurse leader (MSN, Post Master's Certificate); nursing education (MSN, Post Master's Certificate); organizational leadership (MS); sport management (MS); teacher leadership (M Ed); urban education (M Ed). *Program availability:* Part-time, evening/weekend. *Degree requirements:* For master's, completion of all required coursework in common core and selected track with minimum cumulative GPA of 3.0 and no more than two grades of C. *Entrance requirements:* For master's, GRE, GMAT, or essay, minimum undergraduate GPA of 3.0, professional resume, 3 letters of recommendation, interview. Additional exam requirements/recommendations for international students: Required—TOEFL (minimum score 550 paper-based). Electronic applications accepted.

Grantham University, College of Nursing and Allied Health, Lenexa, KS 66219. Offers case management (MSN); health systems management (MS); healthcare administration (MHA); nursing education (MSN); nursing informatics (MSN); nursing management and organizational leadership (MSN). *Program availability:* Part-time, evening/weekend, online only, 100% online. *Faculty:* 2 full-time, 34 part-time/adjunct. *Students:* 198 full-time (144 women), 113 part-time (83 women); includes 170 minority (118 Black or African American, non-Hispanic/Latino; 3 American Indian or Alaska Native, non-Hispanic/Latino; 27 Asian, non-Hispanic/Latino; 11 Hispanic/Latino; 2 Native Hawaiian or other Pacific Islander, non-Hispanic/Latino; 9 Two or more races, non-Hispanic/Latino). Average age 41. 95 applicants, 89% accepted, 72 enrolled. In 2017, 123 master's awarded. *Entrance requirements:* For master's, BSN from state-approved nursing program with minimum cumulative GPA of 2.5 from institution accredited by agency recognized by U.S. DOE or foreign equivalent; unencumbered and current RN license. Additional exam requirements/recommendations for international students: Required—TOEFL (minimum score 530 paper-based; 71 iBT), IELTS (minimum score 6.5), PTE (minimum score 50). *Application deadline:* Applications are processed on a rolling basis. Application fee: $0. Electronic applications accepted. *Expenses:* $325 per credit hour. *Financial support:* Scholarships/grants available. Financial award applicants required to submit FAFSA. *Faculty research:* Compassion in caring improving incivility in the ICU setting, get well network technology in enhancing patient education, opioid use and abuse in postpartum women. *Unit head:* Dr. Cheryl Rules, Dean of the College of Nursing and Allied Health, 913-309-4783, Fax: 844-897-6490, E-mail: crules@grantham.edu. *Application contact:* Jared Parlette, Vice President of Student Enrollment, 800-955-2527 Ext. 803, Fax: 866-914-4557, E-mail: admissions@grantham.edu.
Website: http://www.grantham.edu/nursing-and-allied-health/

Hampton University, School of Nursing, Hampton, VA 23668. Offers community health nursing (MS); family nurse practitioner (MS); family research (PhD); nursing administration (MS); nursing education (MS). *Accreditation:* AACN. *Program availability:* Part-time, online learning. *Students:* 6 full-time (all women), 28 part-time (25 women); includes 31 minority (29 Black or African American, non-Hispanic/Latino; 2 Hispanic/Latino). Average age 48. 7 applicants, 14% accepted. In 2017, 3 master's, 4 doctorates awarded. *Degree requirements:* For master's, comprehensive exam, thesis optional; for doctorate, comprehensive exam, thesis/dissertation. *Entrance requirements:* For master's, GRE General Test. *Application deadline:* For fall admission, 6/1 priority date for domestic students, 4/1 priority date for international students; for spring admission, 11/1 priority date for domestic students, 9/1 priority date for international students; for summer admission, 4/1 priority date for domestic students, 2/1 priority date for international students. Applications are processed on a rolling basis. Application fee: $35. Electronic applications accepted. *Expenses: Tuition:* Full-time $22,630; part-time $575 per semester hour. *Required fees:* $70. Tuition and fees vary according to program. *Financial support:* In 2017–18, 2 students received support. Fellowships, research assistantships, teaching assistantships, career-related internships or fieldwork, Federal Work-Study, institutionally sponsored loans, and scholarships/grants available. Support available to part-time students. Financial award application deadline: 6/30; financial award applicants required to submit FAFSA. *Faculty research:* African-American stress, HIV education, pediatric obesity, hypertension, breast cancer. *Unit head:* Dr. Shevallanie Lott, Dean, 757-727-5654, E-mail: shevellanie.lott@hamptonu.edu.
Website: http://nursing.hamptonu.edu

Herzing University Online, Program in Nursing, Menomonee Falls, WI 53051. Offers nursing (MSN); nursing education (MSN); nursing management (MSN). *Accreditation:* AACN. *Program availability:* Online learning.

Hofstra University, School of Education, Specialized Programs in Education, Hempstead, NY 11549. Offers applied behavior analysis (Advanced Certificate); childhood special education (MS Ed); early childhood special education (MS Ed, Advanced Certificate); educational and policy leadership (Ed D); educational leadership (Advanced Certificate), including school building leader/school district business leader; educational leadership and policy studies (MS Ed), including K-12; elementary special education (MS Ed); gifted education (Advanced Certificate), including school building leader/school district business leader; health education (MS); health professions pedagogy and leadership (MS); higher education leadership and policy studies (MS Ed); inclusive early childhood special education (MS Ed); inclusive elementary special education (MS Ed); inclusive secondary special education (MS Ed); literacy studies (MA, MS Ed, Ed D, Advanced Certificate), including birth-grade 6 (MS Ed, Advanced Certificate), grades 5-12 (MS Ed, Advanced Certificate), literacy studies (Ed D); pedagogy for health professions (Advanced Certificate); physical education (MS); school district business leader (Advanced Certificate); secondary education generalist - students with disabilities 7-12 (MS Ed), including students with disabilities 7-12; secondary special education generalist (MS Ed), including extension in secondary education; special education (MS Ed, Advanced Certificate); special education assessment and diagnosis (Advanced Certificate); special education early childhood intervention (MS Ed); special education: international perspectives (MS Ed); teaching students with severe or multiple disabilities (Advanced Certificate). *Program availability:* Part-time, evening/weekend, blended/hybrid learning. *Students:* 148 full-time (110 women), 249 part-time (188 women); includes 105 minority (54 Black or African American, non-Hispanic/Latino; 1 American Indian or Alaska Native, non-Hispanic/Latino; 13 Asian, non-Hispanic/Latino; 35 Hispanic/Latino; 1 Native Hawaiian or other Pacific Islander, non-Hispanic/Latino; 1 Two or more races, non-Hispanic/Latino), 1 international. Average age 32. 228 applicants, 93% accepted, 132 enrolled. In 2017, 97 master's, 22 doctorates, 31 other advanced degrees awarded. *Degree requirements:* For master's, one foreign language, comprehensive exam (for some programs), thesis (for some programs), electronic portfolio, capstone course, internship, practicum, student teaching, seminars, minimum GPA of 3.0; for doctorate, one foreign language, comprehensive exam, thesis/dissertation, qualifying hearing. *Entrance requirements:* For master's, GRE, interview, letters of recommendation, portfolio, essay, certification; for doctorate, GRE or MAT, interview, resume, essay, master's degree, 3 letters of recommendation, writing sample; for Advanced Certificate, GRE, interview, letters of recommendation, essay, professional experience, resume, master's degree. Additional exam requirements/recommendations for international students: Required—TOEFL (minimum score 550 paper-based; 80 iBT). *Application deadline:* Applications are processed on a rolling basis. Application fee: $75. Electronic applications accepted. *Expenses: Tuition:* Full-time $1292. *Required fees:* $970. Tuition and fees vary according to program. *Financial support:* In 2017–18, 225 students received support, including 118 fellowships with full and partial tuition reimbursements available (averaging $3,887 per year), 12 research assistantships with full and partial tuition reimbursements available (averaging $7,215 per year); career-related internships or fieldwork, Federal Work-Study, institutionally sponsored loans, scholarships/grants, traineeships, tuition waivers (full and partial), and unspecified assistantships also available. Support available to part-time students. Financial award applicants required to submit FAFSA. *Faculty research:* Collaborative teaching and learning; language and culture; new media literacies; applied behavior analysis; K-12 leadership development. *Unit head:* Dr. Elfreda Blue, Chairperson, 516-463-5762, Fax: 516-463-6184, E-mail: elfreda.blue@hofstra.edu. *Application contact:* Sunil Samuel, Assistant Vice President of Admissions, 516-463-4723, Fax: 516-463-4664, E-mail: graduateadmission@hofstra.edu.
Website: http://www.hofstra.edu/education/

Holy Family University, Graduate and Professional Programs, School of Nursing and Allied Health Professions, Philadelphia, PA 19114. Offers nursing administration (MSN); nursing education (MSN). *Accreditation:* AACN. *Program availability:* Part-time, evening/weekend. *Degree requirements:* For master's, thesis or alternative, comprehensive portfolio, clinical practicum. *Entrance requirements:* For master's, BSN or RN from appropriately-accredited program, minimum GPA of 3.0, professional references, official transcripts of all college or university work, essay/personal statement, current resume, completion of one undergraduate statistics course with minimum grade of C. Additional exam requirements/recommendations for international students: Required—TOEFL (minimum score 550 paper-based; 79 iBT), IELTS (minimum score 6), or PTE (minimum score 54). Electronic applications accepted. *Expenses: Tuition:* Full-time $13,518; part-time $9012 per credit hour. Tuition and fees vary according to degree level and program.

Holy Names University, Graduate Division, Department of Nursing, Oakland, CA 94619-1699. Offers administration/management (MSN, PMC); care transition management (MSN); family nurse practitioner (MSN, PMC); informatics (MSN); nurse educator (PMC); MSN/MBA. *Accreditation:* AACN. *Program availability:* Part-time, evening/weekend. *Entrance requirements:* For master's, bachelor's degree in nursing or related field; California RN license or eligibility; minimum cumulative GPA of 2.8, 3.0 in nursing courses from baccalaureate program; courses in pathophysiology, statistics, and research at the undergraduate level. Additional exam requirements/recommendations for international students: Required—TOEFL (minimum score 500 paper-based; 79 iBT). Electronic applications accepted. Application fee is waived when completed online. *Faculty research:* Women's reproductive health, gerontology, attitudes about aging, schizophrenic families, international health issues.

Immaculata University, College of Graduate Studies, Division of Nursing, Immaculata, PA 19345. Offers nursing administration (MSN); nursing education (MSN). *Accreditation:* AACN. *Program availability:* Part-time, evening/weekend. *Entrance requirements:* For master's, MAT or GRE, BSN, minimum undergraduate GPA of 3.0. Additional exam requirements/recommendations for international students: Required—TOEFL.

Independence University, Program in Nursing, Salt Lake City, UT 84107. Offers community health (MSN); gerontology (MSN); nursing administration (MSN); wellness promotion (MSN).

Indiana State University, College of Graduate and Professional Studies, College of Health and Human Services, Department of Advanced Practice Nursing, Terre Haute, IN 47809. Offers advanced practice nursing (DNP); family nurse practitioner (MS); nursing administration (MS); nursing education (MS). *Accreditation:* ACEN. *Program availability:* Part-time. *Degree requirements:* For master's, thesis or alternative. *Entrance requirements:* For master's, BSN, RN license, minimum undergraduate GPA of 3.0. Electronic applications accepted. *Faculty research:* Nursing faculty-student interactions, clinical evaluation, program evaluation, sexual dysfunction, faculty attitudes.

Indiana University Kokomo, School of Nursing, Kokomo, IN 46904. Offers family nurse practitioner (MSN); nurse administrator (MSN); nurse educator (MSN). Electronic applications accepted. *Expenses:* Contact institution.

Indiana University of Pennsylvania, School of Graduate Studies and Research, College of Health and Human Services, Department of Nursing and Allied Health Professions, Program in Nursing Administration, Indiana, PA 15705. Offers MS. *Accreditation:* AACN. *Program availability:* Part-time. *Faculty:* 12 full-time (11 women), 1 (woman) part-time/adjunct. *Students:* 11 full-time (all women), 19 part-time (14 women); includes 1 minority (Hispanic/Latino), 17 international. Average age 32. 16 applicants, 75% accepted, 7 enrolled. In 2017, 18 master's awarded. *Degree requirements:* For master's, thesis optional, practicum. *Entrance requirements:* Additional exam requirements/recommendations for international students: Required—TOEFL (minimum score 540 paper-based). *Application deadline:* Applications are processed on a rolling

basis. Application fee: $50. Electronic applications accepted. *Expenses:* Tuition, state resident: full-time $12,000; part-time $500 per credit. Tuition, nonresident: full-time $18,000; part-time $750 per credit. *Required fees:* $4073; $165.55 per credit. $64 per term. *Financial support:* In 2017–18, 3 research assistantships with tuition reimbursements (averaging $2,147 per year) were awarded; career-related internships or fieldwork, Federal Work-Study, scholarships/grants, and unspecified assistantships also available. Financial award application deadline: 4/15; financial award applicants required to submit FAFSA. *Unit head:* Dr. Nashat Zuraikat, Graduate Coordinator, 724-357-3262, E-mail: zuraikat@iup.edu.
Website: http://www.iup.edu/grad/nursing/default.aspx

Indiana University–Purdue University Fort Wayne, College of Health and Human Services, Department of Nursing, Fort Wayne, IN 46805-1499. Offers adult-gerontology primary care nurse practitioner (MS); family nurse practitioner (MS); nurse executive (MS); nursing administration (Certificate); nursing education (MS). *Accreditation:* ACEN. *Program availability:* Part-time. *Entrance requirements:* For master's, GRE Writing Test (if GPA below 3.0), BS in nursing, eligibility for Indiana RN license, minimum GPA of 3.0, essay, copy of resume, three references, undergraduate course work in research and statistics within last 5 years. Additional exam requirements/recommendations for international students: Required—TOEFL (minimum score 550 paper-based; 79 iBT); Recommended—TWE. Electronic applications accepted. *Faculty research:* Community engagement, cervical screening, evidence-based practice.

Indiana University–Purdue University Indianapolis, School of Nursing, Doctor of Nursing Practice Program, Indianapolis, IN 46202. Offers executive leadership (DNP). *Accreditation:* AACN. *Program availability:* Blended/hybrid learning. *Entrance requirements:* For doctorate, MSN from ACEN- or CCNE-accredited program with minimum cumulative GPA of 3.3, documentation of supervised practice hours from accredited MSN program, unencumbered RN license, graduate-level course in statistics, three references indicating ability to succeed in DNP program. Additional exam requirements/recommendations for international students: Required—TOEFL (minimum score 550 paper-based; 79 iBT). Electronic applications accepted. *Expenses:* Contact institution. *Faculty research:* Quality of life, symptom management, cancer prevention and control, heart failure, pediatric oncology.

Indiana University–Purdue University Indianapolis, School of Nursing, MSN Program in Nursing, Indianapolis, IN 46202. Offers adult/gerontology acute care nurse practitioner (MSN); adult/gerontology clinical nurse specialist (MSN); adult/gerontology primary care nurse practitioner (MSN); family nurse practitioner (MSN); nursing education (MSN); nursing leadership in health systems (MSN), pediatric clinical nurse specialist (MSN); pediatric nurse practitioner (MSN). *Accreditation:* AACN. *Program availability:* Part-time, blended/hybrid learning. *Degree requirements:* For master's, thesis. *Entrance requirements:* For master's, BSN from ACEN- or CCNE-accredited program, minimum undergraduate GPA of 3.0 (preferred), professional resume or curriculum vitae, essay stating career goals and objectives, current unencumbered RN license, three references from individuals with knowledge of ability to succeed in graduate program. Additional exam requirements/recommendations for international students: Required—TOEFL (minimum score 550 paper-based; 79 iBT). Electronic applications accepted. *Expenses:* Contact institution. *Faculty research:* Quality of life, symptom management, cancer prevention and control, heart failure, pediatric oncology.

Indiana Wesleyan University, Graduate School, School of Nursing, Marion, IN 46953-4974. Offers nursing administration (MS); nursing education (MS); primary care nursing (MS); MSN/MBA. *Accreditation:* AACN. *Program availability:* Part-time, online learning. *Degree requirements:* For master's, capstone project or thesis. *Entrance requirements:* For master's, writing sample, RN license, 1 year of related experience, graduate statistics course. Additional exam requirements/recommendations for international students: Required—TOEFL. *Expenses:* Contact institution. *Faculty research:* Primary health care with international emphasis, international nursing.

Jacksonville University, Brooks Rehabilitation College of Healthcare Sciences, Keigwin School of Nursing, Master of Science in Nursing Program, Jacksonville, FL 32211. Offers clinical nurse educator (MSN); family nurse practitioner (MSN); family nurse practitioner/emergency nurse practitioner (MSN); leadership in the healthcare system (MSN); nursing informatics (MSN); psychiatric nurse practitioner (MSN); MSN/MBA. *Program availability:* Part-time, 100% online, blended/hybrid learning. *Faculty:* 8 full-time (all women), 8 part-time/adjunct (6 women). *Students:* 41 full-time (36 women), 456 part-time (415 women); includes 169 minority (102 Black or African American, non-Hispanic/Latino; 4 American Indian or Alaska Native, non-Hispanic/Latino; 24 Asian, non-Hispanic/Latino; 33 Hispanic/Latino; 1 Native Hawaiian or other Pacific Islander, non-Hispanic/Latino; 5 Two or more races, non-Hispanic/Latino), 1 international. Average age 39. 232 applicants, 59% accepted, 110 enrolled. In 2017, 87 master's awarded. *Degree requirements:* For master's, thesis. *Entrance requirements:* For master's, GRE General Test or undergraduate GPA above 3.0, BSN from ACEN- or CCNE-accredited program, course work in statistics and physical assessment within last 5 years; Florida nursing license; CPR/BLS certification; 3 recommendations, 2 of which are professional references; statement of intent; resume. Additional exam requirements/recommendations for international students: Required—TOEFL (minimum score 650 paper-based; 114 iBT), IELTS (minimum score 8). *Application deadline:* For fall admission, 2/1 for domestic and international students. Applications are processed on a rolling basis. Application fee: $50. Electronic applications accepted. *Expenses:* $620 per credit hour, $455 per credit hour off-campus, $720 per credit hour online. *Financial support:* Federal Work-Study, institutionally sponsored loans, scholarships/grants, and health care benefits available. Support available to part-time students. Financial award application deadline: 3/15; financial award applicants required to submit FAFSA. *Faculty research:* Treatment of anxiety. *Unit head:* Dr. Hilary Morgan, Director, Graduate Nursing Programs/Associate Professor, 904-256-7601, E-mail: hmorgan@ju.edu. *Application contact:* Stephanie Bloom, Assistant Director, Enrollment and Advanced Graduate Nursing, 904-256-7286, E-mail: sstrick4@ju.edu.
Website: https://www.ju.edu/nursing/graduate/master-science-nursing/index.php

James Madison University, The Graduate School, College of Health and Behavioral Studies, Program in Nursing, Harrisonburg, VA 22807. Offers adult/gerontology primary care nurse practitioner (MSN); clinical nurse leader (MSN); family nurse practitioner (MSN); nurse administrator (MSN); nurse midwifery (MSN); nursing (MSN, DNP), psychiatric mental health nurse practitioner (MSN). *Accreditation:* AACN. *Program availability:* Part-time, 100% online, blended/hybrid learning. *Students:* 10 full-time (9 women), 77 part-time (71 women); includes 10 minority (2 Black or African American, non-Hispanic/Latino; 5 Asian, non-Hispanic/Latino; 1 Hispanic/Latino; 2 Two or more races, non-Hispanic/Latino). Average age 30. In 2017, 27 master's awarded. Application fee: $55. Electronic applications accepted. *Expenses:* Tuition, state resident: full-time $10,512; part-time $438 per credit hour. Tuition, nonresident: full-time $28,358; part-time $1162 per credit hour. *Required fees:* $1128. *Financial support:* In 2017–18, 2 students received support. Federal Work-Study and 2 assistantships (averaging $7911) available. Financial award application deadline: 3/1; financial award applicants required to submit FAFSA. *Unit head:* Dr. Julie T. Sanford, Department Head, 540-568-6314, E-mail: sanforjt@jmu.edu. *Application contact:* Lynette D. Michael, Director of Graduate Admissions, 540-568-6131 Ext. 6395, Fax: 540-568-7860, E-mail: michaeld@jmu.edu.
Website: http://www.nursing.jmu.edu

Jefferson College of Health Sciences, Program in Nursing, Roanoke, VA 24013. Offers nursing education (MSN); nursing management (MSN). *Accreditation:* AACN. *Program availability:* Part-time. *Degree requirements:* For master's, project. *Entrance requirements:* For master's, MAT. Additional exam requirements/recommendations for international students: Required—TOEFL (minimum score 550 paper-based; 80 iBT). Electronic applications accepted. *Faculty research:* Nursing, teaching and learning techniques, cultural competence, spirituality and nursing.

Johns Hopkins University, School of Nursing, Program in Clinical Nurse Specialist, Baltimore, MD 21205. Offers adult/gerontological critical care clinical nurse specialist (DNP); adult/gerontological health clinical nurse specialist (DNP); pediatric critical care clinical nurse specialist (DNP). *Accreditation:* AACN. *Program availability:* Part-time, 100% online, blended/hybrid learning. *Faculty:* 3 full-time (2 women). *Students:* 13 full-time (all women), 15 part-time (13 women); includes 11 minority (1 Black or African American, non-Hispanic/Latino; 1 American Indian or Alaska Native, non-Hispanic/Latino; 2 Asian, non-Hispanic/Latino; 6 Hispanic/Latino; 1 Two or more races, non-Hispanic/Latino). Average age 32. 32 applicants, 63% accepted, 14 enrolled. *Entrance requirements:* For doctorate, GRE, minimum GPA of 3.0, goal statement/essay, resume, letters of recommendation, official transcripts from all post-secondary institutions attended; BSN; RN license; writing sample. Additional exam requirements/recommendations for international students: Required—TOEFL (minimum score 600 paper-based; 100 iBT), IELTS (minimum score 7). *Application deadline:* For fall admission, 11/1 priority date for domestic and international students. Application fee: $70. Electronic applications accepted. *Expenses:* $1,671 per credit. *Financial support:* In 2017–18, 8 students received support. Federal Work-Study and scholarships/grants available. Support available to part-time students. Financial award application deadline: 3/1; financial award applicants required to submit FAFSA. *Faculty research:* Maternal child health, symptom management, cardiovascular risk reduction, asthma, hypertension. *Unit head:* Dr. Patricia M. Davidson, Dean, 410-955-7544, Fax: 410-955-4890, E-mail: sondeansoffice@jhu.edu. *Application contact:* Cathy Wilson, Director of Admissions, 410-955-7548, Fax: 410-614-7086, E-mail: jhuson@jhu.edu.
Website: http://www.nursing.jhu.edu

See Display on page 576 and Close-Up on page 763.

Johns Hopkins University, School of Nursing, Program in Health Systems Management, Baltimore, MD 21205. Offers MSN. *Accreditation:* AACN. *Program availability:* Part-time, 100% online, blended/hybrid learning. *Faculty:* 2 full-time (both women), 2 part-time/adjunct (1 woman). *Students:* 3 full-time (1 woman), 18 part-time (17 women); includes 7 minority (3 Black or African American, non-Hispanic/Latino; 3 Asian, non-Hispanic/Latino; 1 Hispanic/Latino). Average age 36. 26 applicants, 69% accepted, 14 enrolled. In 2017, 4 master's awarded. *Degree requirements:* For master's, thesis optional, scholarly project or portfolio. *Entrance requirements:* For master's, minimum GPA of 3.0, goal statement/essay, resume, letters of recommendation, official transcripts from all post-secondary institutions attended, BSN, RN license. Additional exam requirements/recommendations for international students: Required—TOEFL (minimum score 600 paper-based; 100 iBT), IELTS (minimum score 7). *Application deadline:* For fall admission, 1/1 priority date for domestic students; for spring admission, 11/15 priority date for domestic students. Application fee: $70. Electronic applications accepted. *Expenses:* $1,591 per credit. *Financial support:* Federal Work-Study available. Financial award application deadline: 3/1; financial award applicants required to submit FAFSA. *Faculty research:* Program evaluation, program development, staff satisfaction, quality and safety. *Unit head:* Dr. Patricia M. Davidson, Dean, 410-955-7844, Fax: 410-955-4890, E-mail: sondeansoffice@jhu.edu. *Application contact:* Cathy Wilson, Director of Admissions, 410-955-7548, Fax: 410-614-7086, E-mail: jhuson@jhu.edu.
Website: http://www.nursing.jhu.edu

See Display on page 576 and Close-Up on page 763.

Kean University, College of Natural, Applied and Health Sciences, Doctorate Program in Nursing Educational Leadership, Union, NJ 07083. Offers educational leadership (PhD). *Accreditation:* ACEN. *Faculty:* 12 full-time (all women). *Students:* 1 (woman) full-time, 19 part-time (17 women); includes 6 minority (5 Black or African American, non-Hispanic/Latino; 1 Asian, non-Hispanic/Latino). Average age 53. *Degree requirements:* For doctorate, comprehensive exam, thesis/dissertation. *Entrance requirements:* For doctorate, GRE, MSN, minimum cumulative GPA of 3.2 in last degree obtained, official transcripts from all institutions attended, valid RN license, three letters of recommendation, professional resume/curriculum vitae, personal statement. Additional exam requirements/recommendations for international students: Required—TOEFL (minimum score 550 paper-based; 79 iBT), IELTS (minimum score 6.5). *Application deadline:* For fall admission, 5/1 for domestic students; for spring admission, 12/1 for domestic and international students. Application fee: $75. Electronic applications accepted. *Expenses:* Contact institution. *Financial support:* Scholarships/grants and unspecified assistantships available. *Unit head:* Dr. Joan Valas, Program Coordinator, 908-737-6210, E-mail: nursing@kean.edu. *Application contact:* Pedro Lopes, Admissions Counselor, 908-737-7100, E-mail: gradadmissions@kean.edu.
Website: http://grad.kean.edu/doctoral-programs/doctor-nursing-educational-leadership

Kean University, College of Natural, Applied and Health Sciences, Program in Nursing, Union, NJ 07083. Offers clinical management (MSN); community health nursing (MSN). *Accreditation:* ACEN. *Program availability:* Part-time. *Faculty:* 12 full-time (all women). *Students:* 7 full-time (all women), 50 part-time (46 women); includes 34 minority (23 Black or African American, non-Hispanic/Latino; 8 Asian, non-Hispanic/Latino; 2 Hispanic/Latino; 1 Two or more races, non-Hispanic/Latino). Average age 47. 15 applicants, 53% accepted, 4 enrolled. In 2017, 51 master's awarded. *Degree requirements:* For master's, thesis or alternative, clinical field experience. *Entrance requirements:* For master's, minimum GPA of 3.0; BS in nursing; RN license; 2 letters of recommendation; interview; official transcripts from all institutions attended. Additional exam requirements/recommendations for international students: Required—TOEFL (minimum score 550 paper-based; 79 iBT), IELTS (minimum score 6.5). *Application deadline:* For fall admission, 6/30 for domestic and international students; for spring admission, 12/1 for domestic and international students. Applications are processed on a rolling basis. Application fee: $75. Electronic applications accepted. *Expenses:* Tuition, state resident: full-time $13,419; part-time $653 per credit. Tuition, nonresident: full-time $18,188; part-time $801 per credit. *Required fees:* $3382; $154 per credit. Tuition and fees vary according to course level, course load, degree level and program. *Financial support:* Scholarships/grants and unspecified assistantships available. Financial award applicants required to submit FAFSA. *Unit head:* Dr. Joan Valas, Program Coordinator, 908-737-6210, E-mail: nursing@kean.edu. *Application contact:* Pedro Lopes, Admissions Counselor, 908-737-7100, E-mail: gradadmissions@kean.edu.
Website: http://grad.kean.edu/masters-programs/nursing-clinical-management

Kennesaw State University, WellStar College of Health and Human Services, Program in Leadership in Nursing, Kennesaw, GA 30144. Offers nursing administration (MSN); nursing education (MSN). *Program availability:* Part-time, evening/weekend, online learning. *Entrance requirements:* For master's, GRE General Test, minimum GPA of 3.0, RN license. Additional exam requirements/recommendations for international

students: Required—TOEFL (minimum score 550 paper-based; 80 iBT), IELTS (minimum score 6.5). *Application deadline:* For fall admission, 6/1 for domestic and international students. Application fee: $60. Electronic applications accepted. *Financial support:* Research assistantships with tuition reimbursements and unspecified assistantships available. Financial award application deadline: 4/1; financial award applicants required to submit FAFSA. *Unit head:* Yvonne Eaves, Director, 470-578-6061, E-mail: yeaves@kennesaw.edu. *Application contact:* Jerryl Morris, Admissions Counselor, 470-578-2030, Fax: 470-578-9172, E-mail: ksugrad@kennesaw.edu.
Website: http://wellstarcollege.kennesaw.edu/nursing/master-science-nursing/leadership-in-nursing.php

Kent State University, College of Nursing, Kent, OH 44242. Offers advanced nursing practice (DNP), including adult/gerontology acute care nurse practitioner (MSN, DNP); nursing (MSN, PhD), including adult/gerontology acute care nurse practitioner (MSN, DNP), adult/gerontology clinical nurse specialist (MSN), adult/gerontology primary care nurse practitioner (MSN), family nurse practitioner (MSN), nurse educator (MSN), nursing and healthcare management (MSN), pediatric primary care nurse practitioner (MSN), psychiatric/mental health nurse practitioner (MSN); MBA/MSN. PhD program offered jointly with The University of Akron. *Accreditation:* AACN. *Program availability:* Part-time, online learning. *Faculty:* 29 full-time (28 women), 15 part-time/adjunct (12 women). *Students:* 167 full-time (142 women), 405 part-time (359 women); includes 70 minority (39 Black or African American, non-Hispanic/Latino; 11 Asian, non-Hispanic/Latino; 18 Hispanic/Latino; 2 Two or more races, non-Hispanic/Latino), 13 international. Average age 35. 272 applicants, 74% accepted, 166 enrolled. In 2017, 144 master's, 8 doctorates awarded. *Degree requirements:* For master's, thesis optional; for doctorate, comprehensive exam, thesis/dissertation. *Entrance requirements:* For master's, GRE or GMAT, minimum GPA of 3.0, active RN license, statement of purpose, 3 letters of reference, undergraduate level statistics class, baccalaureate or graduate-level nursing degree, curriculum vitae/resume; for doctorate, GRE, minimum GPA of 3.0, transcripts, 3 letters of reference, interview, active unrestricted Ohio RN license, statement of purpose, writing sample, curriculum vitae/resume, baccalaureate and master's degrees in nursing or DNP. Additional exam requirements/recommendations for international students: Required—TOEFL (minimum score 560 paper-based; 83 iBT), IELTS (minimum score 6.5), PTE (minimum score 55), Michigan English Language Assessment Battery (minimum score 78). *Application deadline:* For fall admission, 3/1 for domestic and international students; for spring admission, 10/1 for domestic and international students. Applications are processed on a rolling basis. Application fee: $45 ($70 for international students). Electronic applications accepted. *Expenses:* Tuition, state resident: full-time $11,310; part-time $515 per credit hour. Tuition, nonresident: full-time $20,396; part-time $928 per credit hour. *International tuition:* $18,544 full-time. *Financial support:* Scholarships/grants available. Financial award application deadline: 5/4. *Unit head:* Dr. Barbara Broome, Dean, 330-672-3777, E-mail: bbroome1@kent.edu. *Application contact:* Dr. Wendy A. Umberger, Associate Dean for Graduate Programs/Professor, 330-672-8813, E-mail: wlewando@kent.edu.
Website: http://www.kent.edu/nursing/

King University, School of Nursing, Bristol, TN 37620-2699. Offers family nurse practitioner (MSN); nurse educator (MSN); nursing (DNP); nursing administration (MSN); pediatric nurse practitioner (MSN).

Lamar University, College of Graduate Studies, College of Arts and Sciences, JoAnne Gay Dishman Department of Nursing, Beaumont, TX 77701. Offers nursing administration (MSN); nursing education (MSN); MSN/MBA. *Accreditation:* ACEN. *Program availability:* Part-time, evening/weekend, online learning. *Faculty:* 35 full-time (33 women), 3 part-time/adjunct (2 women). *Students:* 92 part-time (85 women); includes 43 minority (27 Black or African American, non-Hispanic/Latino; 7 Asian, non-Hispanic/Latino; 9 Hispanic/Latino). Average age 38. 68 applicants, 88% accepted, 18 enrolled. In 2017, 15 master's awarded. *Degree requirements:* For master's, comprehensive exam, practicum project presentation, evidence-based project. *Entrance requirements:* For master's, GRE General Test, MAT, criminal background check, RN license, ACEN-accredited BSN, college course work in statistics in past 5 years, letters of recommendation, minimum undergraduate GPA of 3.0. Additional exam requirements/recommendations for international students: Required—TOEFL (minimum score 550 paper-based; 79 iBT), IELTS (minimum score 6.5). *Application deadline:* For fall admission, 8/10 for domestic students, 7/1 for international students; for spring admission, 1/5 for domestic students, 12/1 for international students. Applications are processed on a rolling basis. Application fee: $25 ($50 for international students). Electronic applications accepted. *Expenses:* Contact institution. *Financial support:* In 2017–18, 2 teaching assistantships (averaging $24,000 per year) were awarded; scholarships/grants and traineeships also available. Financial award application deadline: 4/1; financial award applicants required to submit FAFSA. *Faculty research:* Student retention, theory, care giving, online course and research. *Unit head:* Cynthia Stinson, Interim Chair, 409-880-8817, Fax: 409-880-8698. *Application contact:* Deidre Mayer, Interim Director, Admissions and Academic Services, 409-880-8888, Fax: 409-880-7419, E-mail: gradmissions@lamar.edu.
Website: http://artssciences.lamar.edu/nursing

La Roche College, School of Graduate Studies and Adult Education, Program in Nursing, Pittsburgh, PA 15237-5898. Offers clinical nurse leader (MSN); nursing education (MSN); nursing management (MSN). *Accreditation:* ACEN. *Program availability:* Part-time, evening/weekend, online only, 100% online. *Faculty:* 3 full-time (all women), 2 part-time/adjunct (1 woman). *Students:* 17 full-time (15 women), 9 part-time (all women), 1 international. Average age 35. 16 applicants, 75% accepted, 10 enrolled. In 2017, 11 master's awarded. *Degree requirements:* For master's, thesis optional, internship, practicum. *Entrance requirements:* For master's, GRE General Test, BSN, nursing license, work experience. Additional exam requirements/recommendations for international students: Recommended—TOEFL (minimum score 550 paper-based). *Application deadline:* For fall admission, 8/15 priority date for domestic students, 8/15 for international students; for spring admission, 12/15 priority date for domestic students, 12/15 for international students. Applications are processed on a rolling basis. Application fee: $50. Electronic applications accepted. *Expenses:* Contact institution. *Financial support:* Application deadline: 3/31; applicants required to submit FAFSA. *Faculty research:* Patient education, perception. *Unit head:* Dr. Terri Liberto, Division Chair, 412-847-1813, Fax: 412-536-1175, E-mail: terri.liberto@laroche.edu. *Application contact:* Hope Schiffgens, Director of Graduate Studies and Adult Education, 412-536-1266, Fax: 412-536-1283, E-mail: schombh1@laroche.edu.

La Salle University, School of Nursing and Health Sciences, Program in Nursing, Philadelphia, PA 19141-1199. Offers adult gerontology primary care nurse practitioner (MSN, Certificate); adult health and illness clinical nurse specialist (MSN); adult-gerontology clinical nurse specialist (MSN, Certificate); clinical nurse leader (MSN); family primary care nurse practitioner (MSN, Certificate); gerontology (Certificate); nurse anesthetist (MSN, Certificate); nursing (MSN, Certificate); nursing administration (MSN, Certificate); nursing education (Certificate); nursing practice (DNP); nursing service administration (MSN); public health nursing (MSN, Certificate); school nursing (Certificate); MSN/MBA; MSN/MPH. *Accreditation:* AACN. *Program availability:* Part-time, evening/weekend, 100% online. *Faculty:* 12 full-time (11 women), 14 part-time/adjunct (11 women). *Students:* 1 (woman) full-time, 277 part-time (220 women); includes 72 minority (36 Black or African American, non-Hispanic/Latino; 1 American Indian or Alaska Native, non-Hispanic/Latino; 18 Asian, non-Hispanic/Latino; 10 Hispanic/Latino; 1 Native Hawaiian or other Pacific Islander, non-Hispanic/Latino; 6 Two or more races, non-Hispanic/Latino), 1 international. Average age 36. 70 applicants, 56% accepted, 24 enrolled. In 2017, 81 master's, 4 doctorates, 13 other advanced degrees awarded. *Degree requirements:* For doctorate, minimum of 1,000 hours of post baccalaureate clinical practice supervised by preceptors. *Entrance requirements:* For master's, GRE, MAT, or GMAT (for students with BSN GPA of less than 3.2), baccalaureate degree in nursing from ACEN- or CCNE-accredited program or an MSN Bridge program; Pennsylvania RN license; 2 letters of reference; resume; statement of philosophy articulating professional values and future educational goal; 1 year of work experience as a registered nurse; for doctorate, GRE (waived for applicants with MSN cumulative GPA of 3.7 or above), MSN, master's degree, MBA or MHA from nationally-accredited program; resume or curriculum vitae; 2 letters of reference; interview; for Certificate, GRE, MAT, or GMAT (for students with BSN GPA of less than 3.2, baccalaureate degree in nursing from ACEN- or CCNE-accredited program or an MSN Bridge program; Pennsylvania RN license; 2 letters of reference; resume; statement of philosophy articulating professional values and future educational goal; 1 year of work experience as a registered nurse. Additional exam requirements/recommendations for international students: Required—TOEFL. *Application deadline:* For fall admission, 8/15 priority date for domestic students, 7/15 for international students; for spring admission, 12/15 priority date for domestic students, 11/15 for international students; for summer admission, 4/15 priority date for domestic students, 3/15 for international students. Applications are processed on a rolling basis. Application fee: $35. Electronic applications accepted. Application fee is waived when completed online. *Expenses:* Contact institution. *Financial support:* In 2017–18, 7 students received support. Scholarships/grants and traineeships available. Support available to part-time students. Financial award application deadline: 8/31; financial award applicants required to submit FAFSA. *Unit head:* Dr. Patricia M. Dillon, Director, 215-951-1322, Fax: 215-951-1896, E-mail: msnapn@lasalle.edu. *Application contact:* Elizabeth Heenan, Director, Graduate and Adult Enrollment, 215-951-1100, Fax: 215-951-1462, E-mail: heenan@lasalle.edu.
Website: http://www.lasalle.edu/nursing/program-options/

Le Moyne College, Department of Nursing, Syracuse, NY 13214. Offers family nurse practitioner (MS, CAS); informatics (MS, CAS); nursing administration (MS, CAS); nursing education (MS, CAS). *Accreditation:* AACN. *Program availability:* Part-time, evening/weekend. *Faculty:* 3 full-time (all women), 5 part-time/adjunct (all women). *Students:* 27 full-time (20 women), 51 part-time (47 women); includes 10 minority (4 Black or African American, non-Hispanic/Latino; 1 Asian, non-Hispanic/Latino; 4 Hispanic/Latino; 1 Two or more races, non-Hispanic/Latino). Average age 32. 39 applicants, 95% accepted, 31 enrolled. In 2017, 20 master's, 2 other advanced degrees awarded. *Degree requirements:* For master's, scholarly project. *Entrance requirements:* For master's, bachelor's degree, interview, minimum GPA of 3.0, New York RN license, 2 letters of recommendation, writing sample, transcripts. *Application deadline:* For fall admission, 8/1 priority date for domestic students, 8/1 for international students; for spring admission, 12/15 priority date for domestic students, 12/15 for international students; for summer admission, 5/1 priority date for domestic students, 5/1 for international students. Applications are processed on a rolling basis. Application fee: $50. Electronic applications accepted. *Expenses:* $700 per credit hour. *Financial support:* In 2017–18, 2 students received support. Career-related internships or fieldwork, scholarships/grants, health care benefits, and unspecified assistantships available. Support available to part-time students. Financial award applicants required to submit FAFSA. *Faculty research:* Inter-profession education, gerontology, utilization of free healthcare services by the insured, health promotion education, innovative undergraduate nursing education models, patient and family education, horizontal violence. *Unit head:* Dr. Margaret M. Wells, Professor/Chair of Nursing, 315-445-5435, Fax: 315-445-6024, E-mail: wellsmm@lemoyne.edu. *Application contact:* Kristen P. Richards, Senior Director of Enrollment Management, 315-445-5444, Fax: 315-445-6092, E-mail: trapaskp@lemoyne.edu.
Website: http://www.lemoyne.edu/nursing

Lenoir-Rhyne University, Graduate Programs, School of Nursing, Program in Nursing, Hickory, NC 28601. Offers nursing administration (MSN); nursing education (MSN). *Accreditation:* AACN. *Program availability:* Online learning. *Degree requirements:* For master's, comprehensive exam, thesis optional. *Entrance requirements:* For master's, official transcripts, two recommendations, essay, resume, unrestricted RN license, criminal background check. Additional exam requirements/recommendations for international students: Required—TOEFL (minimum score 600 paper-based). Electronic applications accepted. *Expenses:* Contact institution.

Lewis University, College of Nursing and Health Professions, Program in Nursing, Romeoville, IL 60446. Offers adult gerontology acute care nurse practitioner (MSN); adult gerontology clinical nurse specialist (MSN); adult gerontology primary care nurse practitioner (MSN); family nurse practitioner (MSN); healthcare systems leadership (MSN); nursing (DNP); nursing education (MSN); school nurse (MSN). *Accreditation:* AACN. *Program availability:* Part-time, evening/weekend, 100% online, blended/hybrid learning. *Students:* 14 full-time (11 women), 361 part-time (336 women); includes 100 minority (27 Black or African American, non-Hispanic/Latino; 33 Asian, non-Hispanic/Latino; 35 Hispanic/Latino; 5 Two or more races, non-Hispanic/Latino), 1 international. Average age 37. *Degree requirements:* For master's, clinical practicum. *Entrance requirements:* For master's, minimum undergraduate GPA of 3.0, degree in nursing, RN license, letter of recommendation, interview, resume or curriculum vitae. Additional exam requirements/recommendations for international students: Required—TOEFL (minimum score 550 paper-based; 80 iBT). *Application deadline:* For fall admission, 5/1 priority date for international students; for spring admission, 11/15 priority date for international students. Applications are processed on a rolling basis. Application fee: $40. Electronic applications accepted. Tuition and fees vary according to program. *Financial support:* Federal Work-Study, scholarships/grants, tuition waivers (full and partial), and unspecified assistantships available. Financial award application deadline: 5/1; financial award applicants required to submit FAFSA. *Faculty research:* Cancer prevention, phenomenological methods, public policy analysis. *Total annual research expenditures:* $1,000. *Unit head:* 815-836-5610. *Application contact:* Nancy Wiksten, Adult Admission Counselor, 815-836-5628, Fax: 815-836-5578, E-mail: wikstena@lewisu.edu.

Liberty University, Helms School of Government, Lynchburg, VA 24515. Offers criminal justice (MS), including forensic psychology, homeland security, public administration (MA, MS); international relations (MS); political science (MS); public administration (MPA), including business and government, healthcare, law and public policy, public and non-profit management; public policy (MA), including campaigns and elections, international affairs, Middle East affairs, public administration (MA, MS). *Program availability:* Part-time, online learning. *Students:* 287 full-time (148 women), 639 part-time (248 women); includes 231 minority (173 Black or African American, non-Hispanic/Latino; 4 American Indian or Alaska Native, non-Hispanic/Latino; 8 Asian, non-Hispanic/Latino; 20 Hispanic/Latino; 1 Native Hawaiian or other Pacific Islander, non-Hispanic/Latino; 25 Two or more races, non-Hispanic/Latino), 7 international. Average age 35. 876 applicants, 64% accepted, 277 enrolled. In 2017, 211 master's awarded. *Entrance requirements:* For master's, minimum undergraduate GPA of 3.0. Additional exam requirements/recommendations for international students: Required—TOEFL (minimum score 600 paper-based; 100 iBT). *Application deadline:* Applications are processed on a rolling basis. Application fee: $50. Electronic applications accepted. *Unit head:* Shawn D. Akers, Dean, 434-592-4986. *Application contact:* Jay Bridge, Director of Admissions, 800-424-9595, Fax: 800-628-7977, E-mail: gradadmissions@liberty.edu.

Liberty University, School of Nursing, Lynchburg, VA 24515. Offers family nurse practitioner (DNP); nurse educator (MSN); nursing administration (MSN); nursing informatics (MSN). *Accreditation:* AACN. *Program availability:* Part-time, online learning. *Students:* 148 full-time (131 women), 461 part-time (421 women); includes 103 minority (58 Black or African American, non-Hispanic/Latino; 4 American Indian or Alaska Native, non-Hispanic/Latino; 15 Asian, non-Hispanic/Latino; 11 Hispanic/Latino; 3 Native Hawaiian or other Pacific Islander, non-Hispanic/Latino; 12 Two or more races, non-Hispanic/Latino), 8 international. Average age 39. 536 applicants, 30% accepted, 105 enrolled. In 2017, 100 master's, 13 doctorates awarded. *Entrance requirements:* For master's, minimum cumulative undergraduate GPA of 3.0; for doctorate, minimum GPA of 3.25 in most current nursing program completed. Additional exam requirements/recommendations for international students: Recommended—TOEFL. *Application deadline:* Applications are processed on a rolling basis. Application fee: $50. Electronic applications accepted. *Financial support:* Applicants required to submit FAFSA. *Unit head:* Dr. Deanna Britt, Dean, 434-582-2519, E-mail: dbritt@liberty.edu. *Application contact:* Jay Bridge, Director of Admissions, 800-424-9595, Fax: 800-628-7977, E-mail: gradadmissions@liberty.edu.

Loma Linda University, School of Nursing, Program in Nursing Administration, Loma Linda, CA 92350. Offers MS. *Accreditation:* AACN. *Program availability:* Part-time. *Degree requirements:* For master's, thesis or alternative. *Entrance requirements:* For master's, GRE General Test, BSN, minimum GPA of 3.0, RN license. Additional exam requirements/recommendations for international students: Required—TOEFL. Electronic applications accepted. *Faculty research:* Job aspects contributing to satisfaction among leaders in health care institutions, leadership content significant to RN graduates.

Louisiana State University Health Sciences Center, School of Nursing, New Orleans, LA 70112. Offers adult gerontology acute care nurse practitioner (DNP, Post-Master's Certificate); adult gerontology clinical nurse specialist (DNP, Post-Master's Certificate); adult gerontology primary care nurse practitioner (DNP, Post-Master's Certificate); clinical nurse leader (MSN); executive nurse leader (DNP, Post-Master's Certificate); neonatal nurse practitioner (DNP, Post-Master's Certificate); nurse anesthesia (DNP, Post-Master's Certificate); nurse educator (MSN); nursing (DNS); primary care family nurse practitioner (DNP, Post-Master's Certificate); public/community health nursing (DNP, Post-Master's Certificate). *Accreditation:* AACN; AANA/CANAEP (one or more programs are accredited). *Program availability:* Part-time. *Faculty:* 29 full-time (26 women), 20 part-time/adjunct (8 women). *Students:* 184 full-time (132 women), 41 part-time (35 women); includes 69 minority (45 Black or African American, non-Hispanic/Latino; 11 Asian, non-Hispanic/Latino; 12 Hispanic/Latino; 1 Two or more races, non-Hispanic/Latino), 1 international. Average age 30. 162 applicants, 42% accepted, 68 enrolled. In 2017, 52 master's, 46 doctorates awarded. *Degree requirements:* For master's, thesis optional; for doctorate, thesis/dissertation. *Entrance requirements:* For master's, GRE, minimum GPA of 3.0; for doctorate, GRE, minimum GPA of 3.0 (for DNP), 3.5 (for DNS). Additional exam requirements/recommendations for international students: Required—TOEFL (minimum score 550 paper-based; 79 iBT). *Application deadline:* Applications are processed on a rolling basis. Application fee: $100. Electronic applications accepted. *Expenses:* Contact institution. *Financial support:* Federal Work-Study, institutionally sponsored loans, scholarships/grants, and traineeships available. Financial award applicants required to submit FAFSA. *Faculty research:* Advanced clinical practice, nursing education, interprofessional education, nursing administration, culturally competent care. *Unit head:* Dr. Demetrius James Porche, Dean, 504-568-4106, Fax: 504-599-0573, E-mail: dporch@lsuhsc.edu. *Application contact:* Tracie Gravolet, Director, Office of Student Affairs, 504-568-4114, Fax: 504-568-5711, E-mail: tgravo@lsuhsc.edu.
Website: http://nursing.lsuhsc.edu/

Lourdes University, Graduate School, Sylvania, OH 43560-2898. Offers business (MBA); leadership (M Ed); nurse anesthesia (MSN); nurse educator (MSN); nurse leader (MSN); organizational leadership (MOL); reading (M Ed); teaching and curriculum (M Ed); theology (MA). *Program availability:* Evening/weekend. *Entrance requirements:* Additional exam requirements/recommendations for international students: Required—TOEFL.

Loyola University Chicago, Graduate School, Marcella Niehoff School of Nursing, Maywood, IL 60141. Offers adult clinical nurse specialist (MSN, Certificate); adult nurse practitioner (Certificate); dietetics (MS); family nurse practitioner (Certificate); family, adult, and women's health nurse practitioner (MSN); health systems leadership (MSN); healthcare quality using education in safety and technology (DNP); infection prevention (MSN, DNP); nursing science (PhD); women's health clinical nurse specialist (Certificate). *Accreditation:* AACN. *Program availability:* Part-time, blended/hybrid learning. *Faculty:* 24 full-time (22 women), 21 part-time/adjunct (19 women). *Students:* 188 full-time (178 women), 222 part-time (208 women); includes 105 minority (23 Black or African American, non-Hispanic/Latino; 40 Asian, non-Hispanic/Latino; 30 Hispanic/Latino; 2 Native Hawaiian or other Pacific Islander, non-Hispanic/Latino; 10 Two or more races, non-Hispanic/Latino), 4 international. Average age 36. 197 applicants, 55% accepted, 80 enrolled. In 2017, 94 master's, 17 doctorates, 26 other advanced degrees awarded. *Degree requirements:* For master's, comprehensive exam; for doctorate, thesis/dissertation, qualifying examination (for PhD); capstone project (for DNP). *Entrance requirements:* For master's, BSN, minimum nursing GPA of 3.0, Illinois RN license, 3 letters of recommendation, 1000 hours of experience in area of specialty prior to starting clinical rotations, personal statement; for doctorate, BSN or MSN, minimum GPA of 3.0, professional nursing license, 3 letters of recommendation, personal statement. Additional exam requirements/recommendations for international students: Required—TOEFL (minimum score 550 paper-based; 79 iBT), IELTS (minimum score 6.5). *Application deadline:* For fall admission, 6/1 priority date for domestic and international students; for spring admission, 11/15 priority date for domestic and international students; for summer admission, 3/15 priority date for domestic and international students. Applications are processed on a rolling basis. Application fee: $50. Electronic applications accepted. Application fee is waived when completed online. *Expenses:* Contact institution. *Financial support:* In 2017–18, 10 students received support, including 3 research assistantships with full tuition reimbursements available (averaging $18,000 per year), 1 teaching assistantship with full tuition reimbursement available (averaging $18,000 per year); scholarships/grants, unspecified assistantships, and nurse faculty loan program also available. Financial award application deadline: 5/1; financial award applicants required to submit FAFSA. *Faculty research:* Epigenetics and social determinants of health; women's health; vitamin D; health equity; interprofessional education; prevention and self-management of chronic disease; body mass in oncology patients. *Total annual research expenditures:* $1.4 million. *Unit head:* Dr. Vickie Keough, Dean, 708-216-5448, Fax: 708-216-9555, E-mail: vkeough@luc.edu. *Application contact:* Toni Topalova, Enrollment Advisor, 708-216-3751, Fax: 708-216-9555, E-mail: atopalova@luc.edu.
Website: http://www.luc.edu/nursing/

Madonna University, Program in Nursing, Livonia, MI 48150-1173. Offers adult health: chronic health conditions (MSN); adult nurse practitioner (MSN); nursing administration (MSN); MSN/MSBA. *Accreditation:* AACN. *Program availability:* Part-time. *Degree requirements:* For master's, thesis or alternative. *Entrance requirements:* For master's, GRE General Test, Michigan nursing license. Electronic applications accepted. *Faculty research:* Coping, caring.

Marquette University, Graduate School, College of Nursing, Milwaukee, WI 53201-1881. Offers acute care nurse practitioner (Certificate); adult clinical nurse specialist (Certificate); adult nurse practitioner (Certificate); advanced practice nursing (MSN, DNP), including adult-older adult acute care (DNP), adults (MSN), adults-older adults (DNP), clinical nurse leader (MSN), health care systems leadership (DNP), nurse-midwifery (MSN), older adults (MSN), pediatrics-acute care, pediatrics-primary care, primary care (DNP), systems leadership and healthcare quality (MSN); family nurse practitioner (Certificate); nurse-midwifery (Certificate); nursing (PhD); pediatric acute care (Certificate); pediatric primary care (Certificate); systems leadership and healthcare quality (Certificate). *Accreditation:* AACN. Terminal master's awarded for partial completion of doctoral program. *Degree requirements:* For master's, comprehensive exam, thesis or alternative. *Entrance requirements:* For master's, GRE General Test, BSN, Wisconsin RN license, official transcripts from all current and previous colleges/universities except Marquette, three completed recommendation forms, resume, written statement of professional goals; for doctorate, GRE General Test, official transcripts from all current and previous colleges/universities except Marquette, three letters of recommendation, resume, written statement of professional goals, sample of scholarly writing. Additional exam requirements/recommendations for international students: Required—TOEFL (minimum score 530 paper-based). Electronic applications accepted. *Faculty research:* Psychosocial adjustment to chronic illness, gerontology, reminiscence, health policy: uninsured and access, hospital care delivery systems.

McKendree University, Graduate Programs, Master of Science in Nursing Program, Lebanon, IL 62254-1299. Offers nursing education (MSN); nursing management/administration (MSN). *Accreditation:* AACN. *Program availability:* Part-time, evening/weekend, online learning. *Degree requirements:* For master's, research project or thesis. *Entrance requirements:* For master's, resume, references, valid Professional Registered Nurse license. Additional exam requirements/recommendations for international students: Required—TOEFL. Electronic applications accepted.

Medical University of South Carolina, College of Nursing, Nurse Administrator Program, Charleston, SC 29425. Offers MSN. *Accreditation:* AACN. *Program availability:* Part-time, online learning. *Degree requirements:* For master's, thesis optional. *Entrance requirements:* For master's, BSN, nursing license, minimum GPA of 3.0, current curriculum vitae, essay, three references. Additional exam requirements/recommendations for international students: Required—TOEFL (minimum score 600 paper-based). Electronic applications accepted. *Faculty research:* Hospital billing for nursing intensity.

Mercer University, Graduate Studies, Cecil B. Day Campus, Penfield College, Atlanta, GA 30341. Offers certified rehabilitation counseling (MS); clinical mental health (MS); counselor education and supervision (PhD); criminal justice and public safety leadership (MS); health informatics (MS); human services (MS), including child and adolescent services, gerontology services; organizational leadership (MS), including leadership for the health care professional, leadership for the nonprofit organization, organizational development and change; school counseling (MS). *Program availability:* Part-time, evening/weekend, 100% online, blended/hybrid learning. *Faculty:* 17 full-time (10 women), 27 part-time/adjunct (24 women). *Students:* 199 full-time (165 women), 266 part-time (218 women); includes 268 minority (226 Black or African American, non-Hispanic/Latino; 1 American Indian or Alaska Native, non-Hispanic/Latino; 19 Asian, non-Hispanic/Latino; 19 Hispanic/Latino; 3 Two or more races, non-Hispanic/Latino). Average age 32. 300 applicants, 45% accepted, 114 enrolled. In 2017, 101 master's, 5 doctorates awarded. *Degree requirements:* For master's, comprehensive exam (for some programs), thesis (for some programs); for doctorate, thesis/dissertation. *Entrance requirements:* For master's, GRE or MAT, Georgia Professional Standards Commission (GPSC) Certification at the SC-5 level; for doctorate, GRE or MAT. Additional exam requirements/recommendations for international students: Recommended—TOEFL (minimum score 550 paper-based; 80 iBT), IELTS (minimum score 6.5). *Application deadline:* For fall admission, 7/1 priority date for domestic and international students; for spring admission, 11/1 priority date for domestic and international students; for summer admission, 4/1 priority date for domestic and international students. Application fee: $35. Electronic applications accepted. Application fee is waived when completed online. *Expenses:* $637 per credit. *Financial support:* In 2017–18, 32 students received support. Federal Work-Study, scholarships/grants, and unspecified assistantships available. Financial award applicants required to submit FAFSA. *Faculty research:* Marriage and families issues, leadership and ethics, cyber-bullying, trauma, narrative counseling and theory. *Total annual research expenditures:* $85,000. *Unit head:* Dr. Priscilla R. Danheiser, Dean, 678-547-6028, Fax: 678-547-6008, E-mail: danheiser_p@mercer.edu. *Application contact:* Dr. Melissa McCants Cruz, Director of Graduate Admissions, 678-547-6024, E-mail: penfield.admissions@mercer.edu.
Website: http://penfield.mercer.edu/programs/graduate-professional/

Mercy College, School of Health and Natural Sciences, Programs in Nursing, Dobbs Ferry, NY 10522-1189. Offers nursing administration (MS); nursing education (MS). *Accreditation:* AACN. *Program availability:* Part-time, evening/weekend, blended/hybrid learning. *Students:* 4 full-time (all women), 136 part-time (128 women); includes 83 minority (54 Black or African American, non-Hispanic/Latino; 14 Asian, non-Hispanic/Latino; 12 Hispanic/Latino; 3 Native Hawaiian or other Pacific Islander, non-Hispanic/Latino). Average age 33. 80 applicants, 70% accepted, 38 enrolled. In 2017, 42 master's awarded. *Degree requirements:* For master's, comprehensive exam (for some programs), written comprehensive exam or the production of a comprehensive project. *Entrance requirements:* For master's, interview, two letters of reference, bachelor's degree, RN registration in the U.S. Additional exam requirements/recommendations for international students: Required—TOEFL (minimum score 600 paper-based; 100 iBT), IELTS (minimum score 8). *Application deadline:* For fall admission, 8/1 for domestic students. Applications are processed on a rolling basis. Application fee: $62. Electronic applications accepted. *Expenses: Tuition:* Full-time $15,426; part-time $857 per credit hour. *Required fees:* $630; $158 per term. Tuition and fees vary according to course load, degree level and program. *Financial support:* Career-related internships or fieldwork, Federal Work-Study, scholarships/grants, and unspecified assistantships available. Support available to part-time students. Financial award applicants required to submit FAFSA. *Unit head:* Dr. Joan Toglia, Dean, School of Health and Natural Sciences, 914-674-7837, E-mail: jtoglia@mercy.edu. *Application contact:* Allison Gurdineer, Senior Director of Admissions, 877-637-2946, Fax: 914-674-7382, E-mail: admissions@mercy.edu.
Website: https://www.mercy.edu/health-and-natural-sciences/graduate

Metropolitan State University, College of Nursing and Health Sciences, St. Paul, MN 55106-5000. Offers advanced dental therapy (MS); leadership and management (MSN); nurse educator (MSN); nursing (DNP). *Accreditation:* AACN. *Program availability:* Part-time. *Degree requirements:* For master's, thesis or alternative; for doctorate, thesis/dissertation or alternative. *Entrance requirements:* For master's, GRE General Test,

minimum GPA of 3.0, RN license, BS/BA; for doctorate, minimum GPA of 3.0, RN license, MSN. Additional exam requirements/recommendations for international students: Required—TOEFL (minimum score 550 paper-based). *Application deadline:* For fall admission, 1/15 for domestic and international students; for winter admission, 1/15 for international students. Application fee: $20. *Expenses:* Tuition, state resident: part-time $388.55 per credit. Tuition, nonresident: part-time $777.11 per credit. *Required fees:* $35.11 per credit. Part-time tuition and fees vary according to campus/location and program. *Financial support:* Fellowships, career-related internships or fieldwork, Federal Work-Study, institutionally sponsored loans, and traineeships available. Financial award applicants required to submit FAFSA. *Faculty research:* Women's health, gerontology.
Website: https://www.metrostate.edu/academics/nursing-and-health-sciences

Miami Regional University, School of Nursing and Health Sciences, Miami Springs, FL 33166. Offers nursing (MSN); nursing education (MSN); nursing leadership (MSN).

MidAmerica Nazarene University, School of Nursing and Health Science, Olathe, KS 66062. Offers healthcare administration (MSN); healthcare quality management (MSN); nursing education (MSN); public health (MSN); MSN/MBA. *Accreditation:* AACN. *Program availability:* Part-time, evening/weekend, 100% online, blended/hybrid learning. *Entrance requirements:* For master's, BSN, minimum GPA of 3.0, active unencumbered RN license, undergraduate statistics course. Additional exam requirements/recommendations for international students: Required—TOEFL. Electronic applications accepted. *Expenses:* Contact institution. *Faculty research:* Technology in education, minority recruitment and retention in nursing programs, faculty views and attitudes on culturally competency, innovative nursing program development, spirituality and holistic health.

Middle Tennessee State University, College of Graduate Studies, University College, Murfreesboro, TN 37132. Offers advanced studies in teaching and learning (M Ed); human resources leadership (MPS); nursing administration (MSN); nursing education (MSN); strategic leadership (MPS); training and development (MPS). *Program availability:* Part-time, evening/weekend, online learning. *Entrance requirements:* Additional exam requirements/recommendations for international students: Required—TOEFL (minimum score 525 paper-based; 71 iBT) or IELTS (minimum score 6).

Milwaukee School of Engineering, MS Program in Nursing - Leadership and Management, Milwaukee, WI 53202-3109. Offers MSN. *Program availability:* Part-time, evening/weekend, 100% online, blended/hybrid learning. *Students:* 5 full-time (all women), 1 (woman) part-time; includes 2 minority (1 Asian, non-Hispanic/Latino; 1 Hispanic/Latino). Average age 31. 5 applicants, 60% accepted, 3 enrolled. In 2017, 3 master's awarded. *Entrance requirements:* For master's, GRE General Test or GMAT if undergraduate GPA less than 3.0, 2 letters of recommendation; BSN from accredited institution; current unrestricted licensure as a Registered Nurse. Additional exam requirements/recommendations for international students: Required—TOEFL (minimum score 90 iBT), IELTS (minimum score 7). *Application deadline:* Applications are processed on a rolling basis. Application fee: $0. Electronic applications accepted. *Expenses: Tuition:* Part-time $814 per credit hour. *Required fees:* $12.50 per credit hour. *Financial support:* In 2017–18, 2 students received support. Scholarships/grants available. Financial award application deadline: 3/15; financial award applicants required to submit FAFSA. *Unit head:* Dr. Debra Jenks, Program Director, 414-277-4516, E-mail: jenks@msoe.edu. *Application contact:* Brian Rutz, Graduate Admission Counselor, 414-277-7200, E-mail: rutz@msoe.edu.
Website: https://www.msoe.edu/academics/graduate-degrees/health/nursing/

Missouri Western State University, Program in Nursing, St. Joseph, MO 64507-2294. Offers health care leadership (MSN); nurse educator (MSN, Graduate Certificate). *Program availability:* Part-time. *Students:* 1 (woman) full-time, 40 part-time (38 women); includes 2 minority (1 Black or African American, non-Hispanic/Latino; 1 Hispanic/Latino), 2 international. Average age 36. 9 applicants, 100% accepted, 9 enrolled. In 2017, 8 master's awarded. *Entrance requirements:* For master's, minimum cumulative GPA of 2.75, statement of interest, current and unencumbered RN license. Additional exam requirements/recommendations for international students: Recommended—TOEFL (minimum score 79 iBT), IELTS (minimum score 6). *Application deadline:* For fall admission, 7/15 for domestic and international students; for spring admission, 10/1 for domestic and international students; for summer admission, 3/15 for domestic students. Applications are processed on a rolling basis. Application fee: $45 ($50 for international students). Electronic applications accepted. *Expenses:* Tuition, state resident: full-time $6391; part-time $336 per credit hour. Tuition, nonresident: full-time $11,483; part-time $604 per credit hour. *Required fees:* $542; $99 per credit hour. $176 per semester. One-time fee: $45. Tuition and fees vary according to course load and program. *Financial support:* Scholarships/grants and unspecified assistantships available. Support available to part-time students. *Unit head:* Dr. Carolyn Brose, Associate Professor, 816-271-5912, E-mail: brose@missouriwestern.edu. *Application contact:* Dr. Benjamin D. Caldwell, Dean of the Graduate School, 816-271-4394, Fax: 816-271-4525, E-mail: graduate@missouriwestern.edu.
Website: https://www.missouriwestern.edu/nursing/msn/

Monmouth University, Graduate Studies, Marjorie K. Unterberg School of Nursing and Health Studies, West Long Branch, NJ 07764-1898. Offers adult-gerontological primary care nurse practitioner (MSN, Post-Master's Certificate); family nurse practitioner (MSN, Post-Master's Certificate); forensic nursing (MSN, Certificate); nursing (MSN); nursing administration (MSN); nursing education (MSN, Post-Master's Certificate); nursing practice (DNP); physician assistant (MS); psychiatric and mental health nurse practitioner (MSN, Post-Master's Certificate); school nursing (MSN, Certificate). *Accreditation:* AACN. *Program availability:* Part-time, evening/weekend, 100% online, blended/hybrid learning. *Faculty:* 12 full-time (all women), 20 part-time/adjunct (12 women). *Students:* 90 full-time (66 women), 329 part-time (302 women); includes 129 minority (51 Black or African American, non-Hispanic/Latino; 43 Asian, non-Hispanic/Latino; 31 Hispanic/Latino; 1 Native Hawaiian or other Pacific Islander, non-Hispanic/Latino; 3 Two or more races, non-Hispanic/Latino), 1 international. Average age 36. In 2017, 85 master's, 4 other advanced degrees awarded. *Degree requirements:* For master's, practicum (for some tracks); for doctorate, practicum, capstone course. *Entrance requirements:* For master's, GRE General Test (waived for MSN applicants with minimum B grade in each of the first four courses and for MS applicants with master's degree), BSN with minimum GPA of 2.75, current RN license, proof of liability and malpractice policy, personal statement, two letters of recommendation, college course work in health assessment, resume; CASPA application (for MS); for doctorate, accredited master's nursing program degree with minimum GPA of 3.2, active RN license, national certification as nurse practitioner or nurse administrator, working knowledge of statistics, statement of goals and vision for change, 2 letters of recommendation (professional or academic), resume, interview. Additional exam requirements/recommendations for international students: Required—TOEFL (minimum score 550 paper-based; 79 iBT), IELTS (minimum score 6) or Michigan English Language Assessment Battery (minimum score 77). *Application deadline:* For fall admission, 7/15 priority date for domestic students, 6/1 for international students; for spring admission, 12/1 priority date for domestic students, 11/1 for international students; for summer admission, 5/1 for domestic students. Applications are processed on a rolling basis. Application fee: $50. Electronic applications accepted. *Expenses:* Contact institution. *Financial support:* In 2017–18, 197 students received support. Institutionally sponsored loans, scholarships/grants, and unspecified assistantships available. Support available to part-time students. Financial award applicants required to submit FAFSA. *Faculty research:* School nursing, health policy, and smoking cessation in teens; Multiple Sclerosis; adherence and self-efficacy; aging issues and geriatric care. *Unit head:* Dr. Janet Mahoney, Dean, 732-571-3443, Fax: 732-263-5131, E-mail: jmahoney@monmouth.edu. *Application contact:* Lucia Fedele, Graduate Admission Counselor, 732-571-3452, Fax: 732-263-5123, E-mail: gradadm@monmouth.edu.
Website: https://www.monmouth.edu/graduate/nursing-programs-of-study/

Montana State University, The Graduate School, College of Nursing, Bozeman, MT 59717. Offers clinical nurse leader (MN); family and individual nurse practitioner (DNP); family nurse practitioner (MN, Post-Master's Certificate); nursing education (Certificate, Post-Master's Certificate); psychiatric mental health nurse practitioner (MN); psychiatric/mental health nurse practitioner (DNP). *Accreditation:* AACN. *Program availability:* Part-time, online learning. *Degree requirements:* For master's, comprehensive exam, thesis (for some programs); for doctorate, thesis/dissertation, 1,125 hours in clinical settings. *Entrance requirements:* For master's, GRE General Test, minimum GPA of 3.0 for undergraduate and post-baccalaureate work. Additional exam requirements/recommendations for international students: Required—TOEFL (minimum score 580 paper-based). Electronic applications accepted. *Faculty research:* Rural nursing, health disparities, environmental/public health, oral health, resilience.

Moravian College, Graduate and Continuing Studies, Helen S. Breidegam School of Nursing, Bethlehem, PA 18018-6650. Offers clinical nurse leader (MS); nurse administrator (MS); nurse educator (MS); nurse practitioner - acute care (MS); nurse practitioner - primary care (MS). *Accreditation:* AACN. *Program availability:* Part-time, evening/weekend. *Faculty:* 5 full-time (all women), 4 part-time/adjunct (2 women). *Students:* 4 full-time (all women), 64 part-time (60 women); includes 9 minority (3 Black or African American, non-Hispanic/Latino; 2 Asian, non-Hispanic/Latino; 4 Hispanic/Latino), 1 international. Average age 38. 34 applicants, 85% accepted, 20 enrolled. In 2017, 24 master's awarded. *Degree requirements:* For master's, comprehensive exam (for some programs), evidence-based practice project. *Entrance requirements:* For master's, BSN with minimum GPA of 3.0, active RN license, statistics course with minimum C grade, 2 professional references, written statement of goals, professional resume, interview, official transcripts. Additional exam requirements/recommendations for international students: Required—TOEFL (minimum score 550 paper-based; 90 iBT), IELTS (minimum score 6.5). *Application deadline:* For fall admission, 8/1 priority date for domestic and international students; for spring admission, 1/1 priority date for domestic and international students; for summer admission, 5/1 priority date for domestic and international students. Applications are processed on a rolling basis. Electronic applications accepted. *Expenses:* Contact institution. *Financial support:* Applicants required to submit FAFSA. *Faculty research:* College binge drinking, obesity, underrepresented minorities in nursing, education needs of nursing preceptors, delirium superimposed on dementia. *Unit head:* Dr. Kerry Cheever, Professor/Chairperson, 610-861-1412, Fax: 610-861-1466, E-mail: nursing@moravian.edu. *Application contact:* Caroline Febbo, Student Experience Mentor, 610-861-1400, Fax: 610-861-1466, E-mail: graduate@moravian.edu.

Mount Carmel College of Nursing, Nursing Program, Columbus, OH 43222. Offers adult gerontology acute care nurse practitioner (MS); adult health clinical nurse specialist (MS); family nurse practitioner (MS); nursing (DNP); nursing administration (MS); nursing education (MS). *Accreditation:* AACN. *Program availability:* Part-time. *Faculty:* 11 full-time (all women), 5 part-time/adjunct (4 women). *Students:* 112 full-time (93 women), 72 part-time (65 women); includes 35 minority (20 Black or African American, non-Hispanic/Latino; 4 Asian, non-Hispanic/Latino; 3 Hispanic/Latino; 8 Two or more races, non-Hispanic/Latino). Average age 35. 135 applicants, 65% accepted, 68 enrolled. In 2017, 64 master's awarded. *Degree requirements:* For master's, professional manuscript; for doctorate, practicum. *Entrance requirements:* For master's, letters of recommendation, statement of purpose, current resume, baccalaureate degree in nursing, current Ohio RN license, minimum cumulative GPA of 3.0; for doctorate, master's degree in nursing from program accredited by either ACEN or CCNE. Additional exam requirements/recommendations for international students: Required—TOEFL (minimum score 550 paper-based; 80 iBT). *Application deadline:* For fall admission, 2/1 priority date for domestic students; for spring admission, 11/1 priority date for domestic students. Applications are processed on a rolling basis. Application fee: $30. Electronic applications accepted. *Expenses: Tuition:* Full-time $11,403; part-time $543 per credit. *Required fees:* $50; $50 per year. *Financial support:* In 2017–18, 3 students received support. Institutionally sponsored loans and scholarships/grants available. Financial award application deadline: 3/1; financial award applicants required to submit FAFSA. *Unit head:* Dr. Jill Kilanowski, Associate Dean, 614-234-5237, Fax: 614-234-2875, E-mail: jkilanowski@mccn.edu. *Application contact:* Dr. Kim Campbell, Director of Recruitment and Admissions, 614-234-5144, Fax: 614-234-5427, E-mail: kcampbell@mccn.edu.

Mount Mary University, Graduate Programs, Program in Business Administration, Milwaukee, WI 53222-4597. Offers general management (MBA); health systems leadership (MBA). *Program availability:* Part-time, evening/weekend. *Degree requirements:* For master's, terminal project. *Entrance requirements:* For master's, minimum GPA of 2.75. Additional exam requirements/recommendations for international students: Required—TOEFL (minimum score 550 paper-based; 80 iBT); Recommended—IELTS (minimum score 6.5). Electronic applications accepted. *Expenses:* Contact institution. *Faculty research:* Economics, quantitative analysis, accounting, finance.

Mount Mercy University, Program in Nursing, Cedar Rapids, IA 52402-4797. Offers health advocacy (MSN); nurse administration (MSN); nurse education (MSN). *Accreditation:* AACN. *Program availability:* Evening/weekend. *Degree requirements:* For master's, project/practicum.

Mount St. Joseph University, Master of Science in Nursing Program, Cincinnati, OH 45233-1670. Offers administration (MSN); clinical nurse leader (MSN); education (MSN). *Accreditation:* AACN. *Program availability:* Part-time. *Faculty:* 9 full-time (all women), 15 part-time/adjunct (all women). *Students:* 122 part-time (113 women); includes 3 minority (2 Black or African American, non-Hispanic/Latino; 1 Two or more races, non-Hispanic/Latino). Average age 40. In 2017, 8 master's awarded. *Entrance requirements:* For master's, essay; BSN from regionally-accredited university; minimum undergraduate GPA of 3.25 or GRE; professional resume; three professional references; interview; 2 years of clinical nursing experience; active RN license; criminal background check. Additional exam requirements/recommendations for international students: Required—TOEFL (minimum score 560 paper-based; 83 iBT). *Application deadline:* Applications are processed on a rolling basis. Application fee: $50. Electronic applications accepted. *Expenses:* $610 per credit hour. *Financial support:* Applicants required to submit FAFSA. *Unit head:* Dr. Nancy Hinzman, MSN/DNP Director, 513-244-4325, E-mail: nancy.hinzman@msj.edu. *Application contact:* Mary Brigham, Assistant Director for Graduate Recruitment, 513-244-4233, Fax: 513-244-4629, E-mail: mary.brigham@msj.edu.
Website: http://www.msj.edu/academics/graduate-programs/master-of-science-in-nursing/

Mount Saint Mary College, School of Nursing, Newburgh, NY 12550-3494. Offers adult nurse practitioner (MS, Advanced Certificate), including nursing education (MS), nursing management (MS); family nurse practitioner (Advanced Certificate); nursing education (Advanced Certificate). *Accreditation:* AACN. *Program availability:* Part-time, evening/weekend, blended/hybrid learning. *Faculty:* 7 full-time (all women), 5 part-time/adjunct (all women). *Students:* 3 full-time (1 woman), 153 part-time (143 women); includes 42 minority (22 Black or African American, non-Hispanic/Latino; 1 American Indian or Alaska Native, non-Hispanic/Latino; 6 Asian, non-Hispanic/Latino; 11 Hispanic/Latino; 1 Native Hawaiian or other Pacific Islander, non-Hispanic/Latino; 1 Two or more races, non-Hispanic/Latino). Average age 38. 34 applicants, 91% accepted, 28 enrolled. In 2017, 30 master's, 5 other advanced degrees awarded. *Degree requirements:* For master's, research utilization project. *Entrance requirements:* For master's, BSN, minimum GPA of 3.0, RN license. Additional exam requirements/recommendations for international students: Required—TOEFL (minimum score 80 iBT). *Application deadline:* For fall admission, 6/3 priority date for domestic students; for spring admission, 10/31 priority date for domestic students. Applications are processed on a rolling basis. Application fee: $45. Electronic applications accepted. Application fee is waived when completed online. *Expenses: Tuition:* Full-time $14,454; part-time $803 per credit. *Required fees:* $172; $86 per semester. *Financial support:* In 2017–18, 8 students received support. Unspecified assistantships available. Financial award application deadline: 4/15; financial award applicants required to submit FAFSA. *Unit head:* Christine Berte, Graduate Coordinator, 845-569-3141, Fax: 845-562-6762, E-mail: christine.berte@msmc.edu. *Application contact:* Lisa Alvarez, Director of Admissions for Graduate Programs and Adult Degree Completion, 845-569-3166, Fax: 845-569-3450, E-mail: lisa.gallina@msmc.edu.
Website: http://www.msmc.edu/Academics/Graduate_Programs/Master_of_Science_in_Nursing

National American University, Roueche Graduate Center, Austin, TX 78731. Offers accounting (MBA); aviation management (MBA, MM); care coordination (MSN); community college leadership (Ed D); criminal justice (MM); e-marketing (MBA, MM); health care administration (MBA, MM); higher education (MM); human resources management (MBA, MM); information technology management (MBA, MM); international business (MBA); leadership (EMBA); management (MBA); nursing administration (MSN); nursing education (MSN); nursing informatics (MSN); operations and configuration management (MBA, MM); project and process management (MBA, MM). Master's programs offered online through the Harold D. Buckingham Graduate School. *Program availability:* Part-time, evening/weekend, online learning. *Entrance requirements:* For master's, minimum undergraduate GPA of 2.75. Additional exam requirements/recommendations for international students: Required—TOEFL, TWE. Electronic applications accepted. *Faculty research:* Tourism, finance, marketing.

National University, School of Health and Human Services, La Jolla, CA 92037-1011. Offers clinical affairs (MS); clinical regulatory affairs (MS); complementary and integrative healthcare (MS); family nurse practitioner (MSN); health and life science analytics (MS); health informatics (MS, Certificate); healthcare administration (MHA); nurse anesthesia (MSNA); nursing administration (MSN); nursing informatics (MSN); psychiatric-mental health nurse practitioner (MSN); public health (MPH), including health promotion, healthcare administration, mental health. *Program availability:* Part-time, evening/weekend, 100% online, blended/hybrid learning. *Degree requirements:* For master's, thesis (for some programs). *Entrance requirements:* For master's, interview, minimum GPA of 2.5. Additional exam requirements/recommendations for international students: Required—TOEFL (minimum score 550 paper-based; 79 iBT), IELTS (minimum score 6). *Application deadline:* Applications are processed on a rolling basis. Application fee: $60 ($65 for international students). Electronic applications accepted. *Expenses: Tuition:* Part-time $430 per quarter hour. *Financial support:* Career-related internships or fieldwork, institutionally sponsored loans, scholarships/grants, and tuition waivers (partial) available. Support available to part-time students. Financial award application deadline: 6/30; financial award applicants required to submit FAFSA. *Faculty research:* Nursing education, obesity prevention, workforce diversity. *Unit head:* Dr. Gloria J. McNeal, Dean, 858-309-3473, E-mail: shhs@nu.edu. *Application contact:* Brandon Jouganatos, Vice President for Enrollment Services, 800-628-8648, E-mail: advisor@nu.edu.
Website: http://www.nu.edu/OurPrograms/SchoolOfHealthAndHumanServices.html

Nebraska Methodist College, Program in Nursing, Omaha, NE 68114. Offers nurse educator (MSN); nurse executive (MSN). *Accreditation:* AACN. *Program availability:* Evening/weekend, online learning. *Degree requirements:* For master's, thesis or alternative, Evidence Based Practice (EBP) project. *Entrance requirements:* For master's, interview. Additional exam requirements/recommendations for international students: Required—TOEFL (minimum score 550 paper-based; 80 iBT). *Faculty research:* Spirituality, student outcomes, service-learning, leadership and administration, women's issues.

New Mexico State University, College of Health and Social Services, School of Nursing, Las Cruces, NM 88003. Offers family nurse practitioner (DNP, Graduate Certificate); nursing administration (MSN); nursing science (PhD); psychiatric/mental health nurse practitioner (DNP, Graduate Certificate). *Accreditation:* AACN. *Program availability:* Part-time, blended/hybrid learning. *Faculty:* 11 full-time (all women). *Students:* 29 full-time (26 women), 68 part-time (57 women); includes 46 minority (10 Black or African American, non-Hispanic/Latino; 6 Asian, non-Hispanic/Latino; 29 Hispanic/Latino; 1 Two or more races, non-Hispanic/Latino), 1 international. Average age 42. 47 applicants, 81% accepted, 25 enrolled. In 2017, 3 master's, 9 doctorates, 5 other advanced degrees awarded. *Degree requirements:* For master's, comprehensive exam, thesis optional, clinical practicum; for doctorate, comprehensive exam, thesis/dissertation. *Entrance requirements:* For master's, NCLEX exam, BSN, minimum GPA of 3.0, course work in statistics, 3 letters of reference, writing sample, RN license, CPR certification, proof of liability, immunizations, criminal background check; for doctorate, NCLEX exam, MSN, minimum GPA of 3.0, 3 letters of reference, writing sample, RN license, CPR certification, proof of liability, immunizations, criminal background check, statistics course. Additional exam requirements/recommendations for international students: Required—TOEFL (minimum score 550 paper-based; 79 iBT), IELTS (minimum score 6.5). *Application deadline:* For fall admission, 2/1 priority date for domestic students, 2/1 for international students. Application fee: $40 ($50 for international students). Electronic applications accepted. *Expenses:* Tuition, state resident: full-time $4390. Tuition, nonresident: full-time $15,309. *Required fees:* $853. *Financial support:* In 2017–18, 22 students received support, including 5 teaching assistantships (averaging $11,249 per year); career-related internships or fieldwork, Federal Work-Study, scholarships/grants, traineeships, health care benefits, and unspecified assistantships also available. Support available to part-time students. Financial award application deadline: 3/1. *Faculty research:* Women's health, community health, health disparities, nursing informatics and health care technologies, health care and nursing administration, nursing education, adolescent mental health, addiction and substance abuse. *Total annual research expenditures:* $1,321. *Unit head:* Dr. Alexa Doig, Director, 575-646-3812, Fax: 575-646-2167, E-mail: adoig@nmsu.edu. *Application contact:* Alyce Kolenovsky, 575-646-3812, Fax: 575-646-2167, E-mail: nursing@nmsu.edu.
Website: http://schoolofnursing.nmsu.edu

New York University, Rory Meyers College of Nursing, Programs in Advanced Practice Nursing, New York, NY 10012-1019. Offers adult-gerontology acute care nurse practitioner (MS, Advanced Certificate); adult-gerontology primary care nurse practitioner (MS, Advanced Certificate); family nurse practitioner (MS, Advanced Certificate); gerontology nurse practitioner (Advanced Certificate); nurse-midwifery (MS, Advanced Certificate); nursing administration (MS, Advanced Certificate); nursing education (MS, Advanced Certificate); nursing informatics (MS, Advanced Certificate); pediatrics nurse practitioner (MS, Advanced Certificate); psychiatric-mental health nurse practitioner (MS, Advanced Certificate); MS/MPH. *Accreditation:* AACN; ACNM/ACME. *Program availability:* Part-time, evening/weekend. *Faculty:* 23 full-time (all women), 62 part-time/adjunct (56 women). *Students:* 50 full-time (46 women), 557 part-time (509 women); includes 234 minority (58 Black or African American, non-Hispanic/Latino; 1 American Indian or Alaska Native, non-Hispanic/Latino; 116 Asian, non-Hispanic/Latino; 43 Hispanic/Latino; 1 Native Hawaiian or other Pacific Islander, non-Hispanic/Latino; 15 Two or more races, non-Hispanic/Latino), 23 international. Average age 32. 391 applicants, 59% accepted, 149 enrolled. In 2017, 187 master's, 5 other advanced degrees awarded. *Degree requirements:* For master's, thesis (for some programs), capstone. *Entrance requirements:* For master's, BS in nursing, AS in nursing with another BS/BA, interview, RN license, 1 year of clinical experience (3 for the MS in nursing education program); for Advanced Certificate, master's degree in nursing. Additional exam requirements/recommendations for international students: Required—TOEFL (minimum score 100 iBT), IELTS (minimum score 7). *Application deadline:* For fall admission, 3/1 priority date for domestic and international students; for spring admission, 11/1 priority date for domestic and international students; for summer admission, 3/1 for domestic and international students. Application fee: $80. Electronic applications accepted. *Expenses:* Contact institution. *Financial support:* In 2017–18, 130 students received support. Career-related internships or fieldwork, Federal Work-Study, and scholarships/grants available. Support available to part-time students. Financial award application deadline: 3/1; financial award applicants required to submit FAFSA. *Faculty research:* Vaccine hesitancy in pregnant women and mothers, palliative care and midwifery, diabetes education, curriculum development, workforce training, education and development, geriatrics. *Unit head:* Dr. James Pace, Senior Associate Dean for Academic Programs, 212-992-7343, E-mail: james.pace@nyu.edu. *Application contact:* Matthew Burke, Assistant Director, Graduate Student Affairs and Admissions, 212-998-7397, Fax: 212-995-4302, E-mail: mb6060@nyu.edu.

Nicholls State University, Graduate Studies, College of Nursing and Allied Health, Thibodaux, LA 70310. Offers family nurse practitioner (MSN); nurse executive (MSN); nursing education (MSN); psychiatric/mental health nurse practitioner (MSN).

Northeastern State University, College of Science and Health Professions, Department of Health Professions, Program in Nursing Education, Muskogee, OK 74401. Offers nursing (MSN). *Faculty:* 1 (woman) full-time. *Students:* 7 part-time (all women); includes 2 minority (1 American Indian or Alaska Native, non-Hispanic/Latino; 1 Two or more races, non-Hispanic/Latino). Average age 40. In 2017, 9 master's awarded. *Application deadline:* Applications are processed on a rolling basis. Application fee: $25. Electronic applications accepted. *Expenses:* Tuition, state resident: part-time $222 per credit hour. Tuition, nonresident: part-time $501.75 per credit hour. *Required fees:* $37.40 per credit hour. Tuition and fees vary according to degree level. *Unit head:* Dr. Heather Fenton, Program Coordinator, 918-444-5221, E-mail: fentonh@nsuok.edu. *Application contact:* Josh McCollum, Graduate Coordinator, 918-444-2093, E-mail: mccolluj@nsuok.edu.
Website: http://academics.nsuok.edu/healthprofessions/DegreePrograms/Graduate/NursingEducationMSN.aspx

Northeastern University, Bouvé College of Health Sciences, Boston, MA 02115-5096. Offers applied behavior analysis (MS); audiology (Au D); counseling psychology (MS, PhD, CAGS); exercise science (MS); nursing (MS, PhD, CAGS), including administration (MS), adult-gerontology acute care nurse practitioner (MS, CAGS), adult-gerontology primary care nurse practitioner (MS, CAGS), anesthesia (MS), family nurse practitioner (MS, CAGS), neonatal nurse practitioner (MS, CAGS), pediatric nurse practitioner (MS, CAGS), psychiatric mental health nurse practitioner (MS, CAGS); nursing practice (DNP); pharmaceutical sciences (MS, PhD), including interdisciplinary concentration, pharmaceutics and drug delivery systems; pharmacology (MS); pharmacy (Pharm D); school psychology (PhD); speech-language pathology (MS); urban health (MPH); MS/MBA. *Accreditation:* ACPE (one or more programs are accredited). *Program availability:* Part-time, evening/weekend, online learning. *Faculty:* 192 full-time. *Students:* 1,685. In 2017, 352 master's, 312 doctorates, 25 other advanced degrees awarded. *Degree requirements:* For doctorate, thesis/dissertation (for some programs); for CAGS, comprehensive exam. Application fee: $75. Electronic applications accepted. *Expenses:* Contact institution. *Financial support:* Fellowships, research assistantships, teaching assistantships, career-related internships or fieldwork, scholarships/grants, health care benefits, tuition waivers, and unspecified assistantships available. Support available to part-time students. Financial award applicants required to submit FAFSA. *Unit head:* Susan L. Parish, Dean, Bouve College of Health Sciences, 617-373-3321, Fax: 617-373-3030, E-mail: s.parish@northeastern.edu. *Application contact:* 617-373-2708, Fax: 617-373-4701, E-mail: bouvegrad@northeastern.edu.
Website: https://www.northeastern.edu/bouve/

North Park University, School of Nursing and Health Sciences, Chicago, IL 60625-4895. Offers advanced practice nursing (MS); leadership and management (MS); MBA/MS; MM/MSN; MS/MHR; MS/MNA. *Accreditation:* AACN. *Program availability:* Part-time, evening/weekend. *Degree requirements:* For master's, thesis. *Entrance requirements:* For master's, GMAT, MAT. *Faculty research:* Aging, consultation roles, critical thinking skills, family breakdown, science of caring.

Northwest Nazarene University, Program in Nursing, Nampa, ID 83686-5897. Offers MSN. *Accreditation:* AACN. *Program availability:* Online learning. *Students:* Average age 40. 24 applicants, 88% accepted, 12 enrolled. In 2017, 10 master's awarded. Application fee: $50. *Unit head:* Dr. Leonie Sutherland, Director, 208-467-8679, E-mail: lsutherland@nnu.edu. *Application contact:* Sandy Blom, Graduate Nursing Coordinator, 208-467-8642, Fax: 208-467-8651, E-mail: sblom@nnu.edu.
Website: http://www.nnu.edu/msn

Norwich University, College of Graduate and Continuing Studies, Master of Science in Nursing Program, Northfield, VT 05663. Offers nursing administration (MSN); nursing education (MSN). *Accreditation:* AACN. *Program availability:* Evening/weekend, online only, mostly all online with a week-long residency requirement. *Entrance requirements:* For master's, minimum undergraduate GPA of 3.0. Additional exam requirements/recommendations for international students: Required—TOEFL (minimum score 550 paper-based; 80 iBT), IELTS (minimum score 6.5). Electronic applications accepted. *Expenses:* Contact institution.

Ohio University, Graduate College, College of Health Sciences and Professions, School of Nursing, Athens, OH 45701-2979. Offers advanced clinical practice (DNP); executive practice (DNP); family nurse practitioner (MSN); nurse educator (MSN). *Accreditation:* AACN. *Degree requirements:* For master's, capstone project. *Entrance requirements:* For master's, GRE, bachelor's degree in nursing from accredited college or university, minimum overall undergraduate GPA of 3.0, official transcripts, statement of goals and objectives, resume, 3 letters of recommendation. Additional exam requirements/recommendations for international students: Required—TOEFL (minimum score 550 paper-based; 80 iBT) or IELTS (minimum score 6.5). Electronic applications accepted.

Nursing and Healthcare Administration

Oklahoma Wesleyan University, Professional Studies Division, Bartlesville, OK 74006-6299. Offers nursing administration (MSN); nursing education (MSN); strategic leadership (MS); theology and apologetics (MA).

Old Dominion University, College of Health Sciences, School of Nursing, Adult Gerontology Nursing Emphasis, Norfolk, VA 23529. Offers adult gerontology clinical nurse specialist/administrator (MSN); adult gerontology clinical nurse specialist/educator (MSN); advanced practice (DNP); neonatal clinical nurse specialist (MSN); pediatric clinical nurse specialist (MSN). *Program availability:* Part-time, online only, blended/hybrid learning. *Faculty:* 2 full-time (both women), 2 part-time/adjunct (both women). *Students:* 9 full-time (all women), 10 part-time (9 women); includes 10 minority (8 Black or African American, non-Hispanic/Latino; 2 Asian, non-Hispanic/Latino). Average age 37. 27 applicants, 96% accepted, 12 enrolled. In 2017, 5 master's awarded. *Degree requirements:* For master's, comprehensive exam, internship, practicum. *Entrance requirements:* For master's, GRE or MAT (waived with a GPA above 3.5), undergraduate health/physical assessment course, statistics, 3 letters of recommendation, essay, resume, transcripts. Additional exam requirements/recommendations for international students: Required—TOEFL. *Application deadline:* For fall admission, 6/1 priority date for domestic students, 4/15 priority date for international students. Applications are processed on a rolling basis. Application fee: $50. Electronic applications accepted. *Expenses:* $469 per credit; $450 School of Nursing fee per semester. *Financial support:* Unspecified assistantships available. Financial award applicants required to submit FAFSA. *Unit head:* Dr. Tina Haney, Program Director, 757-683-5428, Fax: 757-683-5253, E-mail: thaney@odu.edu. *Application contact:* Sue Parker, Graduate Program Coordinator, 757-683-4298, Fax: 757-683-5253, E-mail: sparker@odu.edu.

Old Dominion University, College of Health Sciences, School of Nursing, Nurse Administrator Emphasis, Norfolk, VA 23529. Offers nurse administrator (MSN); nurse executive (DNP). *Program availability:* Part-time, blended/hybrid learning. *Faculty:* 1 (woman) full-time, 3 part-time/adjunct (2 women). *Students:* 7 full-time (all women), 6 part-time (all women); includes 4 minority (3 Black or African American, non-Hispanic/Latino; 1 Asian, non-Hispanic/Latino), 1 international. Average age 38. 11 applicants, 100% accepted, 8 enrolled. In 2017, 4 master's awarded. *Degree requirements:* For master's, comprehensive exam; for doctorate, capstone project. *Entrance requirements:* For master's, GRE or MAT if GPA is below 3.5, 3 letters of recommendation, essay, resume, transcripts. Additional exam requirements/recommendations for international students: Required—TOEFL. *Application deadline:* For fall admission, 4/15 priority date for international students; for spring admission, 8/1 priority date for domestic students. Application fee: $50. Electronic applications accepted. *Expenses:* Contact institution. *Financial support:* Application deadline: 4/1. *Faculty research:* Telehealth, vulnerable populations. *Unit head:* Dr. Nancy L. Sweeney, Nurse Executive DNP Program Director, 757-683-4303, Fax: 757-683-5253, E-mail: nsweeney@odu.edu. *Application contact:* Sue Parker, Graduate Program Coordinator, 757-683-4298, Fax: 757-683-5253, E-mail: sparker@odu.edu.
Website: http://catalog.odu.edu/graduate/collegeofhealthsciences/schoolofnursing/#doctorofnursingpracticednp-advancedpracticepostmasters

Oregon Health & Science University, School of Nursing, Program in Health Systems and Organizational Leadership, Portland, OR 97239-3098. Offers MN. *Program availability:* Part-time, online only, 100% online. *Entrance requirements:* For master's, GRE General Test, 3 letters of recommendation, essay, statistics within last 5 years with minimum B- grade, BS in nursing, RN license. Additional exam requirements/recommendations for international students: Required—TOEFL (minimum score 83 iBT). Electronic applications accepted. *Expenses:* Contact institution. *Faculty research:* Immune response in acute ischemic stroke and influences on infection and neurological outcomes.

Otterbein University, Department of Nursing, Westerville, OH 43081. Offers advanced practice nurse educator (Certificate); clinical nurse leader (MSN); family nurse practitioner (MSN, Certificate); nurse anesthesia (MSN, Certificate); nursing (DNP); nursing service administration (MSN). *Accreditation:* AACN; AANA/CANAEP; ACEN. *Program availability:* Part-time, evening/weekend, online learning. *Degree requirements:* For master's, comprehensive exam (for some programs), thesis (for some programs). *Entrance requirements:* For master's, 2 reference forms, resume; for Certificate, official transcripts, 2 reference forms, essay, resumé. Additional exam requirements/recommendations for international students: Required—TOEFL (minimum score 550 paper-based; 79 iBT). *Faculty research:* Patient education, women's health, trauma curriculum development, administration.

Pace University, College of Health Professions, Lienhard School of Nursing, New York, NY 10038. Offers adult acute care nurse practitioner (MS, CAGS); family nurse practitioner (MS, CAGS); nursing (DNP, PhD); professional nursing leadership (MS, CAGS). *Accreditation:* AACN. *Program availability:* Part-time. *Faculty:* 11 full-time (10 women), 31 part-time/adjunct (27 women). *Students:* 11 full-time (all women), 515 part-time (459 women); includes 277 minority (145 Black or African American, non-Hispanic/Latino; 1 American Indian or Alaska Native, non-Hispanic/Latino; 88 Asian, non-Hispanic/Latino; 34 Hispanic/Latino; 9 Two or more races, non-Hispanic/Latino), 1 international. Average age 35. 289 applicants, 74% accepted, 138 enrolled. In 2017, 483 master's, 45 doctorates, 27 other advanced degrees awarded. Terminal master's awarded for partial completion of doctoral program. *Degree requirements:* For master's and CAGS, thesis. *Entrance requirements:* For master's, RN license, resume, personal statement, 2 letters of recommendation, official transcripts, minimum GPA of 3.0, undergraduate statistics; for doctorate, RN license, resume, personal statement, 2 letters of recommendation, official transcripts, accredited master's degree in nursing, minimum GPA of 3.3, state certification and board eligibility as FNP or ANP; for CAGS, RN license, resume, personal statement, 2 letters of recommendation, official transcripts, minimum GPA of 3.0, undergraduate statistics, completion of 2nd degree in nursing. Additional exam requirements/recommendations for international students: Required—TOEFL (minimum score 100 iBT), IELTS or PTE. *Application deadline:* For fall admission, 3/1 for domestic and international students. Applications are processed on a rolling basis. Application fee: $70. Electronic applications accepted. *Expenses:* Contact institution. *Financial support:* Research assistantships, teaching assistantships, career-related internships or fieldwork, Federal Work-Study, institutionally sponsored loans, tuition waivers (partial), and unspecified assistantships available. Support available to part-time students. Financial award application deadline: 2/15; financial award applicants required to submit FAFSA. *Unit head:* Dr. Harriet R. Feldman, Dean, College of Health Professions, 914-773-3341, E-mail: hfeldman@pace.edu. *Application contact:* Susan Ford-Goldschein, Director of Graduate Admissions, 212-346-1531, Fax: 212-346-1585, E-mail: graduateadmission@pace.edu.
Website: http://www.pace.edu/lienhard

Palm Beach Atlantic University, School of Nursing, West Palm Beach, FL 33416-4708. Offers family nurse practitioner (DNP); health systems leadership (MSN). *Accreditation:* AACN. *Program availability:* Part-time. *Entrance requirements:* For master's, minimum GPA of 3.0; active RN license; personal interview; for doctorate, minimum GPA of 3.0; one year of experience as an RN; personal interview. Additional exam requirements/recommendations for international students: Required—TOEFL (minimum score 550 paper-based; 79 iBT). Electronic applications accepted. *Expenses:* Contact institution. *Faculty research:* Elder care, nursing education theory.

Pennsylvania College of Health Sciences, Graduate Programs, Lancaster, PA 17601. Offers administration (MSN); education (MSHS, MSN); healthcare administration (MHA). *Degree requirements:* For master's, internship (for MHA, MSN in administration); practicum (for MSHS, MSN in education).

Purdue University Global, School of Nursing, Davenport, IA 52807. Offers nurse administrator (MS); nurse educator (MS). *Program availability:* Part-time, evening/weekend, online learning. *Entrance requirements:* For master's, RN. Additional exam requirements/recommendations for international students: Required—TOEFL (minimum score 550 paper-based).

Purdue University Northwest, Graduate Studies Office, School of Nursing, Hammond, IN 46323-2094. Offers adult health clinical nurse specialist (MS); critical care clinical nurse specialist (MS); family nurse practitioner (MS); nurse executive (MS). *Accreditation:* ACEN. *Program availability:* Part-time, online learning. *Entrance requirements:* For master's, BSN. Additional exam requirements/recommendations for international students: Required—TOEFL. Electronic applications accepted. *Faculty research:* Adult health, cardiovascular and pulmonary nursing.

Queens University of Charlotte, Presbyterian School of Nursing, Charlotte, NC 28274-0002. Offers clinical nurse leader (MSN); nurse educator (MSN); nursing administrator (MSN). *Accreditation:* AACN. *Degree requirements:* For master's, research project. *Entrance requirements:* For master's, minimum GPA of 3.0. Additional exam requirements/recommendations for international students: Required—TOEFL. Electronic applications accepted. *Expenses:* Contact institution.

Quinnipiac University, School of Nursing, Nursing Leadership Track, Hamden, CT 06518-1940. Offers DNP. *Program availability:* Part-time-only, evening/weekend, online only. *Faculty:* 17 full-time (16 women), 10 part-time/adjunct (6 women). *Students:* 31 part-time (30 women); includes 9 minority (6 Black or African American, non-Hispanic/Latino; 1 Asian, non-Hispanic/Latino; 2 Hispanic/Latino). 34 applicants, 97% accepted, 19 enrolled. *Application deadline:* For fall admission, 7/1 for domestic students. Applications are processed on a rolling basis. Application fee: $45. Electronic applications accepted. *Expenses:* Contact institution. *Financial support:* Federal Work-Study and unspecified assistantships available. Financial award application deadline: 6/1; financial award applicants required to submit FAFSA. *Application contact:* Quinnipiac University Online Admissions, 203-582-3918, E-mail: quonlineadmissions@qu.edu.
Website: https://quonline.quinnipiac.edu/online-programs/online-doctorate-programs/doctor-of-nursing-practice/nursing-leadership-track.php

Ramapo College of New Jersey, Master of Science in Nursing Program, Mahwah, NJ 07430-1680. Offers family nurse practitioner (MSN); nursing administrator (MSN); nursing education (MSN). *Accreditation:* ACEN. *Program availability:* Part-time. *Faculty:* 4 full-time (all women), 2 part-time/adjunct (1 woman). *Students:* 79 part-time (70 women); includes 28 minority (4 Black or African American, non-Hispanic/Latino; 18 Asian, non-Hispanic/Latino; 5 Hispanic/Latino; 1 Two or more races, non-Hispanic/Latino). Average age 33. 84 applicants, 67% accepted, 37 enrolled. In 2017, 9 master's awarded. *Entrance requirements:* For master's, official transcript; personal statement; 2 letters of recommendation; resume; current licensure as a Registered Nurse, or eligibility for licensure; evidence of one year of recent experience as RN prior to entry into clinical practicum courses; evidence of undergraduate statistics course; criminal background check. Additional exam requirements/recommendations for international students: Required—TOEFL (minimum score 550 paper-based; 90 iBT); Recommended—IELTS (minimum score 6). *Application deadline:* For fall admission, 5/1 for domestic and international students; for spring admission, 12/1 for domestic and international students. Applications are processed on a rolling basis. Application fee: $65. Electronic applications accepted. *Expenses:* $690.60 per credit tuition, $56.95 per credit fees. *Financial support:* Career-related internships or fieldwork available. Financial award application deadline: 3/1; financial award applicants required to submit FAFSA. *Faculty research:* Learning styles and critical thinking, evidence-based education, outcomes measurement. *Unit head:* Dr. Kathleen M. Burke, Assistant Dean of Nursing Programs/Professor, 201-684-7737, Fax: 201-684-7954, E-mail: kmburke@ramapo.edu. *Application contact:* Anthony Dovi, Associate Director of Admissions, Adult Learners and Graduate Programs, 201-684-7305, Fax: 201-684-7964, E-mail: adovi@ramapo.edu.
Website: http://www.ramapo.edu/msn/

Regis University, Rueckert-Hartman College for Health Professions, Denver, CO 80221-1099. Offers advanced practice nurse (DNP); counseling (MA); counseling children and adolescents (Post-Graduate Certificate); counseling military families (Post-Graduate Certificate); depth psychotherapy (Post-Graduate Certificate); fellowship in orthopedic manual physical therapy (Certificate); health care business management (Certificate); health care quality and patient safety (Certificate); health industry leadership (MBA); health services administration (MS); marriage and family therapy (MA, Post-Graduate Certificate); neonatal nurse practitioner (MSN); nursing education (MSN); nursing leadership (MSN); occupational therapy (OTD); pharmacy (Pharm D); physical therapy (DPT). *Program availability:* Part-time, evening/weekend, 100% online, blended/hybrid learning. *Degree requirements:* For master's, thesis (for some programs), internship. *Entrance requirements:* For master's, official transcript reflecting baccalaureate degree awarded from regionally-accredited college or university. Additional exam requirements/recommendations for international students: Required—TOEFL (minimum score 550 paper-based; 82 iBT). Electronic applications accepted. *Expenses:* Contact institution. *Faculty research:* Normal and pathological balance and gait research, normal/pathological upper limb motor control/biomechanics, exercise energy/metabolism research, optical treatment protocols for therapeutic modalities.

Research College of Nursing, Nursing Program, Kansas City, MO 64132. Offers adult-gerontological nurse practitioner (MSN); executive practice and healthcare leadership (MSN); family nurse practitioner (MSN). *Accreditation:* AACN. *Program availability:* Part-time-only, 100% online. *Faculty:* 10 full-time (all women), 4 part-time/adjunct (2 women). *Students:* 1 (woman) full-time, 150 part-time (125 women); includes 14 minority (7 Black or African American, non-Hispanic/Latino; 1 American Indian or Alaska Native, non-Hispanic/Latino; 2 Asian, non-Hispanic/Latino; 2 Hispanic/Latino; 1 Native Hawaiian or other Pacific Islander, non-Hispanic/Latino; 1 Two or more races, non-Hispanic/Latino). *Degree requirements:* For master's, research project. *Entrance requirements:* For master's, 3 letters of recommendation, official transcripts, resume, personal statement/writing sample. *Application deadline:* Applications are processed on a rolling basis. Application fee: $65. Electronic applications accepted. *Expenses: Tuition:* Part-time $550 per credit hour. *Financial support:* Applicants required to submit FAFSA. *Unit head:* Dr. Thad Wilson, President, 816-995-2815, Fax: 816-995-2817, E-mail: thad.wilson@researchcollege.edu. *Application contact:* Leslie Burry, Director of Transfer and Graduate Recruitment, 816-995-2820, Fax: 816-995-2813, E-mail: leslie.burry@researchcollege.edu.

Rivier University, School of Graduate Studies, Division of Nursing and Health Professions, Nashua, NH 03060. Offers family nurse practitioner (MS); leadership in health systems management (MS); nursing education (MS); nursing practice (DNP); psychiatric/mental health nurse practitioner (MS); public health (MPH). *Accreditation:* ACEN. *Program availability:* Part-time, evening/weekend. *Entrance requirements:* For master's, GRE, MAT. Electronic applications accepted.

Roberts Wesleyan College, Department of Nursing, Rochester, NY 14624-1997. Offers nursing education (MSN); nursing informatics (MSN); nursing leadership and administration (MSN). *Accreditation:* AACN. *Program availability:* Evening/weekend, online learning. *Degree requirements:* For master's, thesis. *Entrance requirements:* For master's, minimum GPA of 3.0; BS in nursing; interview; RN license; resume; course work in statistics. Additional exam requirements/recommendations for international students: Required—TOEFL (minimum score 90 iBT), IELTS (minimum score 6.5). Electronic applications accepted.

Rush University, College of Nursing, Master's Entry in Nursing (MSN) for Non-Nurses: Generalist Entry Master's Clinical Nurse Leader Program, Chicago, IL 60612. Offers MSN. *Students:* 289 full-time (237 women); includes 93 minority (23 Black or African American, non-Hispanic/Latino; 25 Asian, non-Hispanic/Latino; 34 Hispanic/Latino; 11 Two or more races, non-Hispanic/Latino). 293 applicants, 39% accepted, 78 enrolled. In 2017, 133 master's awarded. *Degree requirements:* For master's, comprehensive exam, capstone project. *Entrance requirements:* For master's, GRE General Test (waived if cumulative GPA is 3.25 or greater), interview, 3 letters of recommendation, personal statement, current resume. Additional exam requirements/recommendations for international students: Required—TOEFL (minimum score 94 iBT). *Application deadline:* For fall admission, 1/2 for domestic students; for spring admission, 8/13 for domestic students. Application fee: $90. Electronic applications accepted. *Expenses:* Contact institution. *Financial support:* Research assistantships, Federal Work-Study, scholarships/grants, and health care benefits available. Support available to part-time students. Financial award application deadline: 3/1; financial award applicants required to submit FAFSA. *Unit head:* Dr. Rebekah Hamilton, Director for Generalist Education/Assistant Dean for Academic Affairs, 312-942-7111, E-mail: rebekah_hamilton@rush.edu. *Application contact:* Molly Spurlock, Director of Prelicensure Advancement, 312-942-6222, E-mail: molly_spurlock@rush.edu.
Website: https://www.rushu.rush.edu/college-nursing/programs-admissions/masters-entry-nursing-msn-non-nurses

Rush University, College of Nursing, MSN for RN's: Clinical Nurse Leader (CNL) Program, Chicago, IL 60612. Offers MSN. *Program availability:* Part-time-only, online only, 100% online. *Students:* 43 part-time (39 women); includes 9 minority (2 Black or African American, non-Hispanic/Latino; 5 Asian, non-Hispanic/Latino; 2 Hispanic/Latino). 12 applicants, 92% accepted, 8 enrolled. In 2017, 21 master's awarded. *Degree requirements:* For master's, clinical project. *Entrance requirements:* For master's, GRE (waived if cumulative GPA is 3.25 or greater or if nursing GPA is 3.0 or greater), interview, 3 letters of recommendation, personal statement, current resume. Additional exam requirements/recommendations for international students: Required—TOEFL (minimum score 94 iBT). *Application deadline:* For fall admission, 1/1 for domestic students; for spring admission, 8/1 for domestic students; for summer admission, 12/1 for domestic students. Applications are processed on a rolling basis. Application fee: $110. Electronic applications accepted. *Expenses:* Contact institution. *Financial support:* Research assistantships, Federal Work-Study, scholarships/grants, and health care benefits available. Support available to part-time students. Financial award application deadline: 3/1; financial award applicants required to submit FAFSA. *Unit head:* Dr. Rebekah Hamilton, Director of Generalist Education/Assistant Dean for Academic Affairs, 312-942-5587, E-mail: rebekah_hamilton@rush.edu. *Application contact:* Monica Degenhardt, Admissions Specialist, 312-942-6986, E-mail: monica_degenhardt@rush.edu.
Website: https://www.rushu.rush.edu/college-nursing/programs-admissions/online-clinical-nurse-leader-program-rns-msn

Sacred Heart University, Graduate Programs, College of Nursing, Fairfield, CT 06825. Offers clinical (DNP); clinical nurse leader (MSN); family nurse practitioner (MSN, Post-Master's Certificate); leadership (DNP); nursing education (MSN); nursing management and executive leadership (MSN). *Accreditation:* AACN. *Program availability:* Part-time, evening/weekend, 100% online, blended/hybrid learning. *Faculty:* 17 full-time (all women), 29 part-time/adjunct (26 women). *Students:* 21 full-time (20 women), 692 part-time (650 women); includes 136 minority (52 Black or African American, non-Hispanic/Latino; 2 American Indian or Alaska Native, non-Hispanic/Latino; 29 Asian, non-Hispanic/Latino; 46 Hispanic/Latino; 7 Two or more races, non-Hispanic/Latino). Average age 37. 70 applicants, 69% accepted, 32 enrolled. In 2017, 260 master's, 16 doctorates awarded. *Degree requirements:* For master's, thesis, 500 clinical hours; for doctorate, capstone. *Entrance requirements:* For master's, minimum GPA of 3.0, BSN or RN plus BS (for MSN); for doctorate, minimum GPA of 3.0, MSN or BSN plus MS in related field (for DNP). Additional exam requirements/recommendations for international students: Required—TOEFL (minimum score 570 paper-based, 80 iBT), TWE, or IELTS (6.5). *Application deadline:* For fall admission, 2/15 for domestic and international students. Applications are processed on a rolling basis. Application fee: $75. Electronic applications accepted. *Expenses:* Contact institution. *Financial support:* Unspecified assistantships available. Financial award applicants required to submit FAFSA. *Unit head:* Mary Alice Donius, Dean of Nursing, 203-365-4508, E-mail: doniusm@sacredheart.edu. *Application contact:* Tara Chudy, Executive Director of Graduate Admissions, 203-365-4735, Fax: 203-365-4732, E-mail: chudyt@sacredheart.edu.
Website: http://www.sacredheart.edu/academics/collegeofhealthprofessions/academicprograms/nursing/nursingprograms/graduateprograms/

Saint Francis Medical Center College of Nursing, Graduate Programs, Peoria, IL 61603-3783. Offers adult gerontology (MSN); clinical nurse leader (MSN); family nurse practitioner (MSN, Post-Graduate Certificate); family psychiatric mental health nurse practitioner (MSN); neonatal nurse practitioner (MSN); nurse clinician (Post-Graduate Certificate); nurse educator (MSN, Post-Graduate Certificate); nursing (DNP); nursing management leadership (MSN). *Accreditation:* ACEN. *Program availability:* Part-time, online only, 100% online, blended/hybrid learning. *Faculty:* 11 full-time (all women), 7 part-time/adjunct (all women). *Students:* 4 full-time (all women), 239 part-time (209 women); includes 24 minority (12 Black or African American, non-Hispanic/Latino; 3 Asian, non-Hispanic/Latino; 4 Hispanic/Latino; 5 Two or more races, non-Hispanic/Latino). Average age 37. 105 applicants, 83% accepted, 60 enrolled. In 2017, 52 master's, 8 doctorates awarded. *Degree requirements:* For master's, research experience, portfolio, practicum; for doctorate, practicum. *Entrance requirements:* For master's, nursing research, health assessment, graduate course work in statistics, RN license; for doctorate, master's degree in nursing, professional portfolio, graduate statistics, transcripts, RN license. Additional exam requirements/recommendations for international students: Required—TOEFL (minimum score 550 paper-based; 79 iBT). *Application deadline:* For fall admission, 6/1 priority date for domestic and international students; for spring admission, 11/15 priority date for domestic and international students. Applications are processed on a rolling basis. Application fee: $50. *Expenses:* Contact institution. *Financial support:* In 2017–18, 13 students received support. Scholarships/grants and tuition waivers (partial) available. Support available to part-time students. Financial award application deadline: 6/15; financial award applicants required to submit FAFSA. *Faculty research:* Outcome and curriculum planning, health promotion, NCLEX-RN results, decision-making program evaluation. *Unit head:* Dr. Patti A. Stockert, President of the College, 309-655-4124, Fax: 309-624-8973, E-mail: patricia.a.stockert@osfhealthcare.org. *Application contact:* Dr. Kim A. Mitchell, Dean, Graduate Program, 309-655-2201, Fax: 309-624-8973, E-mail: kim.a.mitchell@osfhealthcare.org.
Website: http://www.sfmccon.edu/graduate-programs/

Saint Francis University, Nursing Program, Loretto, PA 15940-0600. Offers leadership/education (MSN). *Program availability:* Part-time, online only, blended/hybrid learning. *Faculty:* 2 full-time (both women), 4 part-time/adjunct (all women). *Students:* 12 part-time (all women). Average age 37. 5 applicants, 100% accepted, 4 enrolled. *Entrance requirements:* Additional exam requirements/recommendations for international students: Required—TOEFL. Application fee: $30. Electronic applications accepted. *Expenses:* $2,572.50 per course, $857.50 per credit, $55 technology fee per semester part-time, $111 technology fee per semester full-time. *Financial support:* Applicants required to submit FAFSA. *Unit head:* Dr. Camille Wendekier, RN, Coordinator, E-mail: cwendekier@francis.edu. *Application contact:* Dr. Peter Raymond Skoner, Associate Provost, 814-472-3085, Fax: 814-472-3365, E-mail: pskoner@francis.edu.
Website: https://www.francis.edu/Nursing-Masters/

Saint Joseph's College of Maine, Master of Science in Nursing Program, Standish, ME 04084. Offers administration (MSN); education (MSN); family nurse practitioner (MSN); nursing administration and leadership (Certificate); nursing and health care education (Certificate). *Accreditation:* AACN. *Program availability:* Part-time, online learning. *Entrance requirements:* For master's, MAT. Electronic applications accepted.

Saint Peter's University, School of Nursing, Nursing Program, Jersey City, NJ 07306-5997. Offers adult nurse practitioner (MSN, Certificate); advanced practice (DNP); case management (MSN, DNP). *Accreditation:* AACN. *Program availability:* Part-time, evening/weekend. *Entrance requirements:* Additional exam requirements/recommendations for international students: Required—TOEFL. Electronic applications accepted.

Salem State University, School of Graduate Studies, Program in Nursing, Salem, MA 01970-5353. Offers adult-gerontology primary care nursing (MSN); nursing administration (MSN); nursing education (MSN); MBA/MSN. *Accreditation:* AACN. *Program availability:* Part-time, evening/weekend. *Entrance requirements:* For master's, GRE or MAT. Additional exam requirements/recommendations for international students: Required—TOEFL (minimum score 550 paper-based; 80 iBT) or IELTS (minimum score 5.5).

Salisbury University, DNP Program, Salisbury, MD 21801. Offers family nurse practitioner (DNP); nursing leadership (DNP). *Accreditation:* AACN. *Program availability:* Part-time. *Faculty:* 10 full-time (all women). *Students:* 35 full-time (32 women), 4 part-time (all women); includes 8 minority (all Black or African American, non-Hispanic/Latino). Average age 33. 21 applicants, 43% accepted, 9 enrolled. In 2017, 1 doctorate awarded. Terminal master's awarded for partial completion of doctoral program. *Degree requirements:* For doctorate, thesis/dissertation. *Entrance requirements:* For doctorate, three letters of reference; transcripts from colleges and universities attended; nursing degree; personal statement; minimum GPA of 3.0; U.S. RN license; resume. Additional exam requirements/recommendations for international students: Required—TOEFL (minimum score 550 paper-based; 79 iBT), IELTS (minimum score 6.5). *Application deadline:* For fall admission, 3/1 priority date for domestic and international students. Applications are processed on a rolling basis. Application fee: $65. Electronic applications accepted. *Expenses:* $640 per credit hour resident; $807 per credit hour non-resident; $92 per credit hour fees. *Financial support:* In 2017–18, 3 students received support. Career-related internships or fieldwork and scholarships/grants available. Support available to part-time students. Financial award application deadline: 3/1; financial award applicants required to submit FAFSA. *Faculty research:* Simulation education; chronic disease management; palliative care; gerontology; mental illness. *Unit head:* Dr. Lisa Seldomridge, Graduate Program Director, Nursing DNP, 410-543-6413, E-mail: laseldomridge@salisbury.edu.
Website: http://www.salisbury.edu/gsr/gradstudies/DNPpage.html

Salisbury University, MS in Nursing Program, Salisbury, MD 21801-6837. Offers nursing (MS), including clinical nurse educator, health care leadership. *Accreditation:* AACN. *Program availability:* Part-time. *Faculty:* 4 full-time (3 women), 2 part-time/adjunct (both women). *Students:* 3 part-time (all women); includes 1 minority (Black or African American, non-Hispanic/Latino). Average age 40. In 2017, 1 master's awarded. *Degree requirements:* For master's, thesis. *Entrance requirements:* For master's, two letters of recommendation; transcripts from colleges and universities attended; BSN with minimum cumulative GPA of 3.0; personal statement; current U.S. RN license; resume. Additional exam requirements/recommendations for international students: Required—TOEFL (minimum score 550 paper-based; 79 iBT), IELTS (minimum score 6.5). *Application deadline:* For fall admission, 3/1 for domestic and international students. Application fee: $65. Electronic applications accepted. *Expenses:* $640 per credit hour resident; $807 per credit hour non-resident; $92 per credit hour fees. *Financial support:* Career-related internships or fieldwork and scholarships/grants available. Support available to part-time students. Financial award application deadline: 3/1; financial award applicants required to submit FAFSA. *Faculty research:* Gerontology; simulation education; palliative care; chronic disease management; mental illness. *Unit head:* Dr. Lisa Seldomridge, Graduate Program Director, Nursing MS, 410-543-6413, E-mail: laseldomridge@salisbury.edu.
Website: http://www.salisbury.edu/gsr/gradstudies/MSNpage.html

Samford University, Ida Moffett School of Nursing, Birmingham, AL 35229. Offers administration (DNP); advanced practice (DNP); dual nurse practitioner (family/emergency) (DNP); family nurse practitioner (MSN, DNP); nurse anesthesia (MSN, DNP); nursing administration (DNP), including health systems and administration, informatics, transformation of care. *Accreditation:* AACN; AANA/CANAEP. *Program availability:* Part-time, evening/weekend, blended/hybrid learning. *Faculty:* 20 full-time (19 women), 3 part-time/adjunct (0 women). *Students:* 296 full-time (240 women), 41 part-time (38 women); includes 67 minority (43 Black or African American, non-Hispanic/Latino; 2 American Indian or Alaska Native, non-Hispanic/Latino; 6 Asian, non-Hispanic/Latino; 8 Hispanic/Latino; 8 Two or more races, non-Hispanic/Latino). Average age 35. 79 applicants, 71% accepted, 29 enrolled. In 2017, 117 master's, 39 doctorates awarded. *Degree requirements:* For doctorate, project with poster presentation. *Entrance requirements:* For master's, GRE within the past five years (for nurse anesthesia), RN, minimum nursing GPA of 3.0, undergraduate course in nursing research with minimum C grade, undergraduate health assessment course with minimum B grade; interview, 1 year full-time critical care as RN, 3 letters of recommendation, undergraduate courses in general chemistry and research with minimum B grade for both (for nurse anesthesia); for doctorate, unencumbered licensure as registered nurse, master's degree from CCNE, ONCA, or ACEN accredited program in the area of advanced practice or administration; minimum master's degree cumulative GPA of 3.5; video interview submission. Additional exam requirements/recommendations for international students: Required—TOEFL (minimum score 575 paper-based; 90 iBT); Recommended—IELTS (minimum score 6.5). *Application deadline:* For fall admission, 4/1 for domestic and international students; for spring admission, 8/1 for domestic and international students; for summer admission, 1/1 for domestic and international students. Application fee: $50. Electronic applications accepted. *Expenses:* $809 per credit (for DNP and MSN); $9,737 per semester (for MSN in nurse anesthesia). *Financial support:* In 2017–18, 63 students received support. Application deadline: 2/15; applicants required to submit FAFSA. *Unit head:* Dr. Nena F. Sanders, Vice Provost, College of Health Sciences/Ida Moffett School of Nursing Dean/Professor, 205-726-2612, E-mail: nfsander@samford.edu. *Application contact:* Allyson Maddox, Director of Graduate Student Services, 205-726-2047, E-mail: amaddox@samford.edu.
Website: http://samford.edu/nursing

Samuel Merritt University, School of Nursing, Oakland, CA 94609-3108. Offers case management (MSN); family nurse practitioner (MSN, DNP, Certificate); nurse anesthetist (MSN, Certificate); nursing (DNP). *Accreditation:* AACN; AANA/CANAEP (one or more programs are accredited). *Program availability:* Part-time, evening/weekend, 100% online, blended/hybrid learning. *Faculty:* 57 full-time (49 women), 90 part-time/adjunct (77 women). *Students:* 401 full-time (322 women), 267 part-time (202 women); includes 438 minority (52 Black or African American, non-Hispanic/Latino; 4 American Indian or Alaska Native, non-Hispanic/Latino; 224 Asian, non-Hispanic/Latino; 108 Hispanic/Latino; 9 Native Hawaiian or other Pacific Islander, non-Hispanic/Latino; 41 Two or more races, non-Hispanic/Latino). 788 applicants, 54% accepted, 306 enrolled. In 2017, 176 master's, 6 doctorates, 7 other advanced degrees awarded. *Degree requirements:* For master's, thesis or alternative; for doctorate, project. *Entrance requirements:* For master's, GRE General Test (for nurse anesthetist program), minimum GPA of 2.5 in science, 3.0 overall; previous course work in statistics; current RN license; for doctorate and Certificate, minimum GPA of 2.5 in science, 3.0 overall; previous course work in statistics; current RN license. Additional exam requirements/recommendations for international students: Required—TOEFL (minimum score 100 iBT). *Application deadline:* For fall admission, 7/1 priority date for domestic students; for spring admission, 11/1 priority date for domestic students; for summer admission, 3/1 priority date for domestic students. Applications are processed on a rolling basis. Application fee: $65. Electronic applications accepted. *Expenses:* $1,394 per unit tuition (for MSN); $1,208 per unit tuition (for DNP). *Financial support:* Career-related internships or fieldwork, Federal Work-Study, scholarships/grants, and traineeships available. Support available to part-time students. Financial award applicants required to submit FAFSA. *Faculty research:* Gerontology, community health, maternal-child health, sexually transmitted diseases, substance abuse, oncology. *Unit head:* Dr. Audrey Berman, Dean of Nursing, 510-869-6733, Fax: 510-869-6525. *Application contact:* Timothy Cranford, Dean of Admission, 510-869-6576, Fax: 510-869-6525, E-mail: admission@samuelmerritt.edu.
Website: http://www.samuelmerritt.edu/nursing

San Francisco State University, Division of Graduate Studies, College of Health and Social Sciences, School of Nursing, San Francisco, CA 94132-1722. Offers adult acute care (MS); clinical nurse specialist (MS); community/public health nursing (MS); family nurse practitioner (Certificate); nursing administration (MS); pediatrics (MS); women's health (MS). *Accreditation:* AACN. *Program availability:* Part-time. *Application deadline:* Applications are processed on a rolling basis. *Financial support:* Career-related internships or fieldwork available. *Unit head:* Connie Carr, Assistant Director of Graduate Programs, 415-338-6856, Fax: 415-338-0555, E-mail: ccarr@sfsu.edu.
Website: http://nursing.sfsu.edu

Seattle Pacific University, MS in Nursing Program, Seattle, WA 98119-1997. Offers administration (MSN); adult/gerontology nurse practitioner (MSN); clinical nurse specialist (MSN); family nurse practitioner (MSN, Certificate); informatics (MSN); nurse educator (MSN). *Accreditation:* AACN. *Program availability:* Part-time. *Students:* 22 full-time (17 women), 40 part-time (35 women); includes 13 minority (4 Black or African American, non-Hispanic/Latino; 1 American Indian or Alaska Native, non-Hispanic/Latino; 7 Asian, non-Hispanic/Latino; 1 Two or more races, non-Hispanic/Latino). Average age 36. 52 applicants, 73% accepted, 22 enrolled. In 2017, 23 master's awarded. *Degree requirements:* For master's, thesis. *Entrance requirements:* For master's, personal statement, transcripts, undergraduate nursing degree, proof of undergraduate statistics course with minimum GPA of 2.0, 2 recommendations. *Application deadline:* For fall admission, 1/15 priority date for domestic students; for spring admission, 1/15 for domestic students. Applications are processed on a rolling basis. Application fee: $50. Electronic applications accepted. *Expenses:* Contact institution. *Financial support:* Fellowships and scholarships/grants available. Financial award applicants required to submit FAFSA. *Unit head:* Dr. Christine Hoyle, Associate Dean, 206-281-2469, E-mail: hoylec@spu.edu.
Website: http://spu.edu/academics/school-of-health-sciences/undergraduate-programs/nursing

Seton Hall University, College of Nursing, South Orange, NJ 07079-2697. Offers advanced practice in primary health care (MSN, DNP), including adult/gerontological nurse practitioner, pediatric nurse practitioner; entry into practice (MSN); health systems administration (MSN, DNP); nursing (PhD); nursing case management (MSN); nursing education (MA); school nurse (MSN); MSN/MA. *Accreditation:* AACN. *Program availability:* Part-time, online learning. *Degree requirements:* For master's, research project; for doctorate, dissertation or scholarly project. *Entrance requirements:* For doctorate, GRE (waived for students with GPA of 3.5 or higher). Additional exam requirements/recommendations for international students: Required—TOEFL. Electronic applications accepted. *Faculty research:* Parent/child, adult, and gerontological nursing; breast cancer; families of children with HIV; parish nursing.

Shenandoah University, Eleanor Wade Custer School of Nursing, Winchester, VA 22601. Offers adult gerontology primary care nurse practitioner (Graduate Certificate); adult-gerontology primary care nurse practitioner (MSN); family nurse practitioner (MSN, DNP, Graduate Certificate); general (MSN); health systems leadership (DNP); health systems management (MSN, Graduate Certificate); nurse midwifery (MSN); nurse-midwifery (Graduate Certificate); nursing education (Graduate Certificate); nursing practice (DNP); psychiatric mental health nurse practitioner (MSN, DNP, Graduate Certificate). *Accreditation:* AACN; ACNM/ACME. *Faculty:* 17 full-time (all women), 6 part-time/adjunct (all women). *Students:* 30 full-time (26 women), 51 part-time (48 women); includes 19 minority (13 Black or African American, non-Hispanic/Latino; 3 Asian, non-Hispanic/Latino; 2 Hispanic/Latino; 1 Two or more races, non-Hispanic/Latino), 3 international. Average age 37. 52 applicants, 88% accepted, 34 enrolled. In 2017, 18 master's, 1 doctorate, 28 other advanced degrees awarded. *Degree requirements:* For master's, research project, clinical hours; for doctorate, scholarly project, clinical hours; for Graduate Certificate, clinical hours. *Entrance requirements:* For master's, United States RN license; minimum GPA of 3.0; 2080 hours of clinical experience; curriculum vitae; 3 letters of recommendation from former dean, faculty member, or advisor familiar with the applicant, and a former or current supervisor; two-to-three-page essay on a specified topic; for doctorate, MSN, minimum GPA of 3.0, 3 letters of recommendation, interview, BSN, two-to-three page essay on a specific topic, 500-word statement of clinical practice research interest, resume, current U.S. RN license, 2080 clinical hours; for Graduate Certificate, MSN, minimum GPA of 3.0, 2 letters of recommendation, minimum of one year (2080 hours) of clinical nursing experience, interview, two-to-three page essay on a specific topic, resume, current United States RN license. Additional exam requirements/recommendations for international students: Required—TOEFL (minimum score 558 paper-based; 83 iBT). *Application deadline:* For fall admission, 4/15 priority date for domestic and international students; for spring admission, 11/1 for domestic and international students; for summer admission, 3/1 for domestic and international students. Application fee: $30. Electronic applications accepted. *Expenses:* $22,451 tuition, plus $3,579 fees (student services fee, technology fee, and clinical fee). *Financial support:* In 2017–18, 32 students received support. Scholarships/grants and unspecified assistantships available. Financial award applicants required to submit FAFSA. *Faculty research:* Emergency preparedness, workplace environment, maternal child, inter-professional education, health policy. *Total annual research expenditures:* $30,000. *Unit head:* Dr. Kathleen LaSala, RN, Dean, 540-678-4381, Fax: 540-665-5519, E-mail: klasala@su.edu. *Application contact:* Andrew Woodall, Executive Director of Recruitment and Admissions, 540-665-4581, Fax: 540-665-4627, E-mail: admit@su.edu.
Website: http://www.su.edu/nursing/

Southern Illinois University Edwardsville, Graduate School, School of Nursing, Program in Health Care and Nursing Administration, Edwardsville, IL 62026. Offers MS, Post-Master's Certificate. *Program availability:* Part-time. *Degree requirements:* For master's, comprehensive exam. *Entrance requirements:* For master's, RN licensure, minimum undergraduate nursing GPA of 3.0, BS from CCNE- or ACEN-accredited program. Additional exam requirements/recommendations for international students: Required—TOEFL (minimum score 550 paper-based; 79 iBT), IELTS (minimum score 6.5). Electronic applications accepted.

Southern Nazarene University, College of Professional and Graduate Studies, School of Nursing, Bethany, OK 73008. Offers nursing education (MS); nursing leadership (MS). *Accreditation:* AACN. *Program availability:* Part-time, evening/weekend. *Degree requirements:* For master's, thesis. *Entrance requirements:* For master's, minimum undergraduate cumulative GPA of 3.0; baccalaureate degree in nursing from nationally-accredited program; current unencumbered registered nurse licensure in Oklahoma or eligibility for same; documentation of basic computer skills; basic statistics course; statement of professional goals; three letters of recommendation. Additional exam requirements/recommendations for international students: Required—TOEFL (minimum score 550 paper-based).

Southern New Hampshire University, Program in Nursing, Manchester, NH 03106-1045. Offers clinical nurse leader (MSN); nurse educator (MSN); nursing (MSN); patient safety and quality (MSN, Post Master's Certificate). *Program availability:* Online only, 100% online. *Entrance requirements:* For master's, undergraduate transcripts, active unencumbered license, bachelor's degree with minimum cumulative GPA of 3.0. *Application deadline:* Applications are processed on a rolling basis. Application fee: $40. Electronic applications accepted. *Expenses:* Tuition: Part-time $627 per credit hour. Part-time tuition and fees vary according to campus/location and program. *Application contact:* Office of Graduate Admission, 888-327-SNHU, Fax: 603-644-3144, E-mail: enroll@snhu.edu.
Website: https://www.snhu.edu/online-degrees/nursing

Southern University and Agricultural and Mechanical College, College of Nursing and Allied Health, School of Nursing, Baton Rouge, LA 70813. Offers educator/administrator (PhD); family health nursing (MSN); family nurse practitioner (Post Master's Certificate); geriatric nurse practitioner/gerontology (PhD); nursing (DNP). *Accreditation:* AACN. *Program availability:* Part-time. *Degree requirements:* For master's, comprehensive exam, thesis; for doctorate, comprehensive exam, thesis/dissertation. *Entrance requirements:* For master's, GRE General Test, BSN, minimum GPA of 2.7; for doctorate, GRE General Test; for Post Master's Certificate, MSN. Additional exam requirements/recommendations for international students: Required—TOEFL (minimum score 525 paper-based). *Faculty research:* Health promotions, vulnerable populations, (community-based) cardiovascular participating research, health disparities chronic diseases, care of the elderly.

Spalding University, Graduate Studies, Kosair College of Health and Natural Sciences, School of Nursing, Louisville, KY 40203-2188. Offers adult nurse practitioner (MSN); family nurse practitioner (MSN); leadership in nursing and healthcare (MSN); nurse educator (Post-Master's Certificate); nurse practitioner (Post-Master's Certificate); pediatric nurse practitioner (MSN). *Accreditation:* AACN. *Program availability:* Part-time, evening/weekend. *Degree requirements:* For master's, comprehensive exam (for some programs), thesis. *Entrance requirements:* For master's, GRE General Test, BSN or bachelor's degree in related field, RN licensure, autobiographical statement, transcripts, letters of recommendation. Additional exam requirements/recommendations for international students: Required—TOEFL (minimum score 535 paper-based). *Faculty research:* Nurse educational administration, gerontology, bioterrorism, healthcare ethics, leadership.

Spring Hill College, Graduate Programs, Program in Nursing, Mobile, AL 36608-1791. Offers MSN, Post-Master's Certificate. *Accreditation:* AACN. *Program availability:* Part-time, evening/weekend, online only, 100% online. *Faculty:* 1 (woman) full-time, 1 (woman) part-time/adjunct. *Students:* 3 part-time (2 women). Average age 50. In 2017, 5 master's awarded. *Degree requirements:* For master's, comprehensive exam, capstone courses, completion of program within 6 calendar years; for Post-Master's Certificate, 460 clinical integration hours. *Entrance requirements:* For master's, RN license in state where practicing nursing; 1 year of clinical nursing experience; work in clinical setting or access to health care facility for clinical integration/research; 3 written references; employer verification; resume; 500-word essay explaining how becoming a CNL will help applicant achieve personal and professional goals; for Post-Master's Certificate, RN license; master's degree in nursing. Additional exam requirements/recommendations for international students: Required—TOEFL (minimum score 550 paper-based; 80 iBT), IELTS (minimum score 6.5), CPE or CAE (minimum score C), Michigan English Language Assessment Battery (minimum score 90). *Application deadline:* For fall admission, 8/1 priority date for domestic and international students; for spring admission, 12/1 priority date for domestic and international students. Applications are processed on a rolling basis. Application fee: $25 ($35 for international students). Electronic applications accepted. *Expenses:* Contact institution. *Financial support:* Applicants required to submit FAFSA. *Unit head:* Dr. Terran Mathers, Director, 251-380-4485, Fax: 251-460-4495, E-mail: tmathers@shc.edu. *Application contact:* Robert Stewart, Vice President of Enrollment, 251-380-3030, Fax: 251-460-2186, E-mail: rstewart@shc.edu.
Website: http://ug.shc.edu/graduate-degrees/master-science-nursing/

State University of New York College of Technology at Delhi, Program in Nursing, Delhi, NY 13753. Offers nursing administration (MS); nursing education (MS). *Program availability:* Online only, 100% online. *Faculty:* 6 full-time (all women), 1 (woman) part-time/adjunct. *Students:* 6 full-time (all women), 35 part-time (32 women). *Expenses:* $462 per credit hour in-state tuition, $944 per credit hour out-of-state, $555 online. *Application contact:* Misty Fields, Associate Director of Admission, 607-746-4546, E-mail: fieldsmr@delhi.edu.

Stevenson University, Program in Nursing, Owings Mills, MD 21153. Offers nursing education (MS); nursing leadership/management (MS); population-based care coordination (MS). *Accreditation:* AACN. *Program availability:* Part-time, blended/hybrid learning. *Faculty:* 4 full-time (all women), 12 part-time/adjunct (all women). *Students:* 174 part-time (167 women); includes 53 minority (40 Black or African American, non-Hispanic/Latino; 5 Asian, non-Hispanic/Latino; 8 Two or more races, non-Hispanic/Latino). Average age 40. 45 applicants, 100% accepted, 38 enrolled. In 2017, 47 master's awarded. *Degree requirements:* For master's, capstone course. *Entrance requirements:* For master's, bachelor's degree from regionally-accredited institution, current registered nurse's license in good standing, official college transcripts from all previous academic work, minimum cumulative GPA of 3.0 in past academic work, personal statement (250-350 words), two professional letters of recommendation, resume. *Application deadline:* Applications are processed on a rolling basis. Application fee: $0. Electronic applications accepted. *Expenses:* Contact institution. *Financial*

support: Unspecified assistantships available. Financial award applicants required to submit FAFSA. *Unit head:* Judith Feustle, PhD, Associate Dean, 443-352-4292, Fax: 443-394-0538, E-mail: jfeustle@stevenson.edu. *Application contact:* Amanda Courter, Enrollment Counselor, 443-352-4243, Fax: 443-394-0538, E-mail: acourter@stevenson.edu.
Website: http://www.stevenson.edu

Stony Brook University, State University of New York, Stony Brook Medicine, School of Nursing, Program in Nursing Leadership, Stony Brook, NY 11794. Offers MS, Certificate. *Program availability:* Part-time, blended/hybrid learning. *Students:* 155 part-time (146 women); includes 46 minority (16 Black or African American, non-Hispanic/Latino; 11 Asian, non-Hispanic/Latino; 15 Hispanic/Latino; 1 Native Hawaiian or other Pacific Islander, non-Hispanic/Latino; 3 Two or more races, non-Hispanic/Latino). 80 applicants, 100% accepted, 65 enrolled. In 2017, 44 master's awarded. *Entrance requirements:* Additional exam requirements/recommendations for international students: Required—TOEFL (minimum score 90 iBT). *Application deadline:* For fall admission, 3/8 for domestic students. Application fee: $100. *Expenses:* Contact institution. *Unit head:* Paula M Timoney, Program Director, 631-444-3298, Fax: 631-444-3136, E-mail: paula.timoney@stonybrook.edu. *Application contact:* Silvana Jara, Staff Assistant, 631-444-3392, Fax: 631-444-3136, E-mail: silvana.jara@stonybrook.edu.

Stony Brook University, State University of New York, Stony Brook Medicine, School of Nursing, Program in Nursing Practice, Stony Brook, NY 11794. Offers DNP. *Program availability:* Part-time, blended/hybrid learning. *Students:* 20 full-time (all women), 20 part-time (all women); includes 17 minority (6 Black or African American, non-Hispanic/Latino; 1 American Indian or Alaska Native, non-Hispanic/Latino; 6 Asian, non-Hispanic/Latino; 4 Hispanic/Latino). Average age 41. 36 applicants, 61% accepted, 16 enrolled. In 2017, 21 doctorates awarded. *Degree requirements:* For doctorate, thesis/dissertation, project. *Entrance requirements:* For doctorate, minimum GPA of 3.0. Additional exam requirements/recommendations for international students: Required—TOEFL (minimum score 90 iBT). *Application deadline:* For fall admission, 3/3 for domestic and international students. Application fee: $100. *Expenses:* Contact institution. *Unit head:* Dr. Corrine Jurgens, Program Director, 631-444-3236, Fax: 631-444-3136, E-mail: corrine.jurgens@stonybroko.edu. *Application contact:* Dr. Dolores Bilges, Senior Staff Assistant, 631-444-2644, Fax: 631-444-3136, E-mail: dnp.nursing@stonybrook.edu.
Website: http://www.nursing.stonybrookmedicine.edu/

Tarleton State University, College of Graduate Studies, College of Health Sciences and Human Services, Department of Nursing, Stephenville, TX 76402. Offers nursing administration (MSN); nursing education (MSN). *Accreditation:* AACN. *Program availability:* Part-time, evening/weekend. *Faculty:* 5 full-time (all women), 1 (woman) part-time/adjunct. *Students:* 1 (woman) full-time, 19 part-time (16 women); includes 6 minority (5 Black or African American, non-Hispanic/Latino; 1 Hispanic/Latino), 1 international. Average age 38. 15 applicants, 87% accepted, 10 enrolled. *Degree requirements:* For master's, comprehensive exam. *Entrance requirements:* For master's, GRE General Test, minimum GPA of 3.0. Additional exam requirements/recommendations for international students: Required—TOEFL (minimum score 550 paper-based; 80 iBT), IELTS (minimum score 6). *Application deadline:* For fall admission, 8/15 priority date for domestic students; for spring admission, 1/7 for domestic students. Applications are processed on a rolling basis. Application fee: $45 ($145 for international students). Electronic applications accepted. *Expenses:* Contact institution. *Financial support:* Career-related internships or fieldwork, Federal Work-Study, and institutionally sponsored loans available. Support available to part-time students. Financial award applicants required to submit FAFSA. *Unit head:* Dr. Mary Winton, Department Head, 254-968-9139, E-mail: mwinton@tarleton.edu. *Application contact:* Information Contact, 254-968-9104, Fax: 254-968-9670, E-mail: gradoffice@tarleton.edu.
Website: http://www.tarleton.edu/nursing/degrees_grad.html

Teachers College, Columbia University, Department of Organization and Leadership, New York, NY 10027-6696. Offers adult education guided intensive study (Ed D); adult learning and leadership (Ed M, MA, Ed D); educational leadership (Ed D); higher and postsecondary education (MA, Ed D); leadership, policy and politics (Ed D); nurse executive (MA, Ed D), including administration studies (MA), professorial studies (MA); private school leadership (Ed M, MA); public school building leadership (Ed M, MA); social and organizational psychology (MA); urban education leaders (Ed D); MA/MBA. *Program availability:* Part-time, evening/weekend. *Students:* 342 full-time (244 women), 378 part-time (256 women); includes 288 minority (106 Black or African American, non-Hispanic/Latino; 69 Asian, non-Hispanic/Latino; 92 Hispanic/Latino; 21 Two or more races, non-Hispanic/Latino), 86 international. Average age 33. 1,063 applicants, 59% accepted, 405 enrolled. *Degree requirements:* For doctorate, thesis/dissertation. *Unit head:* Prof. Bill Baldwin, Chair, E-mail: wjb12@tc.columbia.edu. *Application contact:* David Estrella, Director of Admission, 212-678-3305, E-mail: estrella@tc.columbia.edu.

Tennessee Technological University, College of Graduate Studies, College of Interdisciplinary Studies, School of Professional Studies, Cookeville, TN 38505. Offers health care administration (MPS); human resources leadership (MPS); public safety (MPS); strategic leadership (MPS); teaching English to speakers of other languages (MPS); training and development (MPS). *Program availability:* Part-time, evening/weekend, online learning. *Students:* 20 full-time (11 women), 74 part-time (46 women); includes 18 minority (11 Black or African American, non-Hispanic/Latino; 1 Hispanic/Latino; 1 Native Hawaiian or other Pacific Islander, non-Hispanic/Latino; 5 Two or more races, non-Hispanic/Latino), 1 international. 50 applicants, 82% accepted, 29 enrolled. In 2017, 23 master's awarded. *Degree requirements:* For master's, comprehensive exam, thesis or alternative. *Entrance requirements:* For master's, GRE. Additional exam requirements/recommendations for international students: Required—TOEFL (minimum score 527 paper-based; 71 iBT), IELTS (minimum score 5.5), PTE (minimum score 48), or TOEIC (Test of English as an International Communication). *Application deadline:* For fall admission, 7/1 for domestic students, 5/1 for international students; for spring admission, 11/1 for domestic students, 10/1 for international students; for summer admission, 5/1 for domestic students, 2/1 for international students. Applications are processed on a rolling basis. Application fee: $35 ($40 for international students). Electronic applications accepted. *Expenses:* Tuition, state resident: full-time $9925; part-time $565 per credit hour. Tuition, nonresident: full-time $22,993; part-time $1291 per credit hour. *Financial support:* Application deadline: 4/1. *Unit head:* Dr. Joseph Roberts, Interim Director, School of Professional Studies, 931-372-6223, E-mail: jmroberts@tntech.edu. *Application contact:* Shelia K. Kendrick, Coordinator of Graduate Studies, 931-372-3808, Fax: 931-372-3497, E-mail: skendrick@tntech.edu.
Website: https://www.tntech.edu/is/sps/

Tennessee Technological University, Whitson-Hester School of Nursing, DNP Program, Cookeville, TN 38505. Offers adult-gerontology acute care nurse practitioner (DNP); executive leadership in nursing (DNP); family nurse practitioner (DNP); pediatric nurse practitioner-primary care (DNP); psychiatric/mental health nurse practitioner (DNP); women's health care nurse practitioner (DNP). *Program availability:* Part-time. *Students:* 10 part-time (all women). 14 applicants, 86% accepted, 10 enrolled. *Application deadline:* For fall admission, 7/1 for domestic students, 5/1 for international students; for spring admission, 12/1 for domestic students, 10/1 for international students; for summer admission, 5/1 for domestic students, 2/1 for international students. Applications are processed on a rolling basis. Application fee: $35 ($40 for international students). Electronic applications accepted. *Expenses:* Tuition, state resident: full-time $9925; part-time $565 per credit hour. Tuition, nonresident: full-time $22,993; part-time $1291 per credit hour. *Financial support:* Application deadline: 4/1; applicants required to submit FAFSA. *Unit head:* Dr. Bedelia Russell, Program Director, Fax: 931-372-6244, E-mail: bhrussell@tntech.edu. *Application contact:* Shelia K. Kendrick, Coordinator of Graduate Studies, 931-372-3808, Fax: 931-372-3497, E-mail: skendrick@tntech.edu.
Website: https://www.tntech.edu/nursing/doctor-of-nursing-practice/

Tennessee Technological University, Whitson-Hester School of Nursing, MSN Programs, Cookeville, TN 38505. Offers family nurse practitioner (MSN); nursing administration (MSN); nursing education (MSN). *Program availability:* Part-time. *Students:* 22 full-time (17 women), 78 part-time (64 women); includes 5 minority (2 Black or African American, non-Hispanic/Latino; 2 Hispanic/Latino; 1 Two or more races, non-Hispanic/Latino). 48 applicants, 50% accepted, 20 enrolled. In 2017, 41 master's awarded. *Application deadline:* For fall admission, 7/1 for domestic students, 5/1 for international students; for spring admission, 12/1 for domestic students, 10/1 for international students; for summer admission, 5/1 for domestic students, 2/1 for international students. Applications are processed on a rolling basis. Application fee: $35 ($40 for international students). Electronic applications accepted. *Expenses:* Tuition, state resident: full-time $9925; part-time $565 per credit hour. Tuition, nonresident: full-time $22,993; part-time $1291 per credit hour. *Financial support:* Application deadline: 4/1; applicants required to submit FAFSA. *Unit head:* Dr. Kim Hanna, Interim Dean, Fax: 931-372-6244, E-mail: khanna@tntech.edu. *Application contact:* Shelia K. Kendrick, Coordinator of Graduate Studies, 931-372-3808, Fax: 931-372-3497, E-mail: skendrick@tntech.edu.
Website: https://www.tntech.edu/nursing/masters/

Texas A&M University, School of Public Health, College Station, TX 77845. Offers biostatistics (MPH, MSPH); environmental health (MPH, MSPH); epidemiology (MPH, MSPH); executive health administration (MHA); health administration (MHA); health policy and management (MPH, MSPH); health promotion and community health sciences (MPH); health services research (PhD); occupational safety and health (MPH). *Program availability:* Part-time, blended/hybrid learning. *Faculty:* 56. *Students:* 279 full-time (196 women), 86 part-time (56 women); includes 153 minority (48 Black or African American, non-Hispanic/Latino; 36 Asian, non-Hispanic/Latino; 62 Hispanic/Latino; 7 Two or more races, non-Hispanic/Latino), 77 international. Average age 29. 179 applicants, 96% accepted, 148 enrolled. In 2017, 124 master's, 8 doctorates awarded. *Entrance requirements:* For master's, GRE General Test, 3 letters of recommendation; statement of purpose; current curriculum vitae or resume; official transcripts; for doctorate, GRE General Test, 3 letters of recommendation; statement of purpose; current curriculum vitae or resume; official transcripts; interview (in some cases). Additional exam requirements/recommendations for international students: Required—TOEFL (minimum score 597 paper-based, 95 iBT) or GRE (minimum verbal score 153). Application fee: $120. Electronic applications accepted. *Expenses:* Contact institution. *Financial support:* In 2017–18, 203 students received support, including 62 research assistantships with tuition reimbursements available (averaging $10,041 per year), 25 teaching assistantships with tuition reimbursements available (averaging $12,913 per year); career-related internships or fieldwork, institutionally sponsored loans, scholarships/grants, traineeships, health care benefits, tuition waivers (full and partial), and unspecified assistantships also available. Support available to part-time students. Financial award applicants required to submit FAFSA. *Unit head:* Dr. Jay Maddock, Dean, 979-436-9322, Fax: 979-458-1878, E-mail: maddock@tamhsc.edu. *Application contact:* Erin E. Schneider, Associate Director of Admissions and Recruitment, 979-436-9380, E-mail: eschneider@sph.tamhsc.edu.
Website: http://sph.tamhsc.edu/

Texas A&M University–Corpus Christi, College of Graduate Studies, College of Nursing and Health Sciences, Corpus Christi, TX 78412. Offers family nurse practitioner (MSN); leadership in nursing systems (MSN); nurse educator (MSN); nursing practice (DNP). *Accreditation:* AACN. *Program availability:* Part-time, evening/weekend, online only, 100% online. *Faculty:* 17 full-time (16 women), 21 part-time/adjunct (15 women). *Students:* 7 full-time (all women), 364 part-time (307 women); includes 194 minority (25 Black or African American, non-Hispanic/Latino; 26 Asian, non-Hispanic/Latino; 134 Hispanic/Latino; 9 Two or more races, non-Hispanic/Latino). Average age 38. 360 applicants, 33% accepted, 112 enrolled. In 2017, 98 master's awarded. *Degree requirements:* For master's, clinical capstone; for doctorate, capstone/scholarly project. *Entrance requirements:* For master's, essay, resume, 3 letters of recommendation, minimum GPA of 3.0, current valid unencumbered Texas nursing license. Additional exam requirements/recommendations for international students: Required—TOEFL (minimum score 550 paper-based; 79 iBT), IELTS (minimum score 6.5). *Application deadline:* For fall admission, 4/15 for domestic and international students; for spring admission, 1/7 for domestic and international students; for summer admission, 5/27 for domestic and international students. Applications are processed on a rolling basis. Application fee: $50 ($70 for international students). Electronic applications accepted. *Expenses:* Tuition, state resident: full-time $3568; part-time $198.24 per credit hour. Tuition, nonresident: full-time $11,038; part-time $613.24 per credit hour. *Required fees:* $2129; $1422.58 per semester. Tuition and fees vary according to program. *Financial support:* Research assistantships, teaching assistantships, career-related internships or fieldwork, Federal Work-Study, institutionally sponsored loans, scholarships/grants, health care benefits, and unspecified assistantships available. Support available to part-time students. Financial award application deadline: 3/15; financial award applicants required to submit FAFSA. *Unit head:* Dr. Julie Anne Hoff, Dean, 361-825-2275, E-mail: julie.hoff@tamucc.edu. *Application contact:* Graduate Admissions Coordinator, 361-825-2177, Fax: 361-825-2755, E-mail: gradweb@tamucc.edu.
Website: http://conhs.tamucc.edu/

Texas Christian University, Harris College of Nursing and Health Sciences, Doctor of Nursing Practice Program, Fort Worth, TX 76129. Offers clinical nurse specialist - adult/gerontology nursing (DNP); clinical nurse specialist - pediatrics (DNP); family nurse practitioner (DNP); general (DNP); nursing administration (DNP). *Accreditation:* AACN. *Program availability:* Part-time. *Faculty:* 29 full-time (26 women), 2 part-time/adjunct (both women). *Students:* 51 full-time (45 women), 10 part-time (9 women); includes 16 minority (6 Black or African American, non-Hispanic/Latino; 2 Asian, non-Hispanic/Latino; 6 Hispanic/Latino; 2 Two or more races, non-Hispanic/Latino). Average age 41. 59 applicants, 64% accepted, 24 enrolled. In 2017, 23 doctorates awarded. *Degree requirements:* For doctorate, thesis/dissertation or alternative, practicum. *Entrance requirements:* For doctorate, three reference letters, essay, resume, two official transcripts from each institution attended, APRN recognition or MSN with experience in nursing administration. Additional exam requirements/recommendations for international students: Required—TOEFL. *Application deadline:* For summer admission, 11/15 for domestic and international students. Application fee: $60. Electronic applications accepted. *Expenses:* $1,555 per credit hour, $125 per course fee, $500 lab fee. *Financial support:* In 2017–18, 14 students received support. Scholarships/grants available. Financial award application deadline: 2/15; financial award applicants required to submit FAFSA. *Faculty research:* Geriatrics, cancer survivorship, health literacy,

endothelial cells, clinical simulation outcomes. *Unit head:* Dr. Kathy Ellis, Division Director, Graduate Nursing, 817-257-6726, Fax: 817-257-7944, E-mail: kathryn.ellis@tcu.edu. *Application contact:* Heather Lyon, Academic Program Specialist, 817-257-6726, Fax: 817-257-7944, E-mail: graduatenursing@tcu.edu.
Website: http://dnp.tcu.edu/

Texas Christian University, Harris College of Nursing and Health Sciences, Master's Program in Nursing, Fort Worth, TX 76129. Offers administration (MSN); clinical nurse leader (MSN, Certificate); clinical nurse specialist (MSN), including adult/gerontology nursing, pediatrics; nursing education (MSN). *Accreditation:* AACN. *Program availability:* Part-time, online only, 100% online. *Faculty:* 29 full-time (26 women), 2 part-time/adjunct (both women). *Students:* 17 full-time (15 women), 7 part-time (all women); includes 6 minority (1 Black or African American, non-Hispanic/Latino; 2 Asian, non-Hispanic/Latino; 2 Hispanic/Latino; 1 Two or more races, non-Hispanic/Latino). Average age 36. 41 applicants, 49% accepted, 6 enrolled. In 2017, 41 master's awarded. *Degree requirements:* For master's, thesis or alternative, practicum. *Entrance requirements:* For master's, 3 letters of reference, essay, resume, two official transcripts from every institution attended. Additional exam requirements/recommendations for international students: Required—TOEFL. *Application deadline:* For spring admission, 9/1 for domestic and international students; for summer admission, 2/1 for domestic and international students. Application fee: $60. Electronic applications accepted. *Expenses:* $1,555 per credit hour, $125 per course fee, $500 lab fee. *Financial support:* In 2017–18, 20 students received support. Scholarships/grants available. Financial award application deadline: 2/15; financial award applicants required to submit FAFSA. *Faculty research:* Geriatrics, cancer survivorship, health literacy, endothelial cells, clinical simulation outcomes. *Unit head:* Dr. Kathy Ellis, Division Director, Graduate Nursing, 817-257-6726, Fax: 817-257-7944, E-mail: kathryn.ellis@tcu.edu. *Application contact:* Heather Lyon, Academic Program Specialist, 817-257-6726, Fax: 817-257-7944, E-mail: graduatenursing@tcu.edu.
Website: http://www.nursing.tcu.edu/graduate.asp

Texas Tech University Health Sciences Center, School of Nursing, Lubbock, TX 79430. Offers acute care nurse practitioner (MSN, Certificate); administration (MSN); advanced practice (DNP); education (MSN); executive leadership (DNP); family nurse practitioner (MSN, Certificate); geriatric nurse practitioner (MSN, Certificate); pediatric nurse practitioner (MSN, Certificate). *Accreditation:* AACN. *Program availability:* Part-time, online learning. *Degree requirements:* For master's, thesis optional. *Entrance requirements:* For master's, minimum GPA of 3.0, 3 letters of reference, BSN, RN license; for Certificate, minimum GPA of 3.0, 3 letters of reference, RN license. Additional exam requirements/recommendations for international students: Required—TOEFL (minimum score 550 paper-based). *Faculty research:* Diabetes/obesity, nurse competency, disease management, intervention and measurements, health disparities.

Texas Woman's University, Graduate School, College of Nursing, Denton, TX 76204. Offers adult health clinical nurse specialist (MS); adult health nurse practitioner (MS); adult/gerontology acute care nurse practitioner (MS); child health clinical nurse specialist (MS); clinical nurse leader (MS); family nurse practitioner (MS); health systems management (MS); nursing education (MS); nursing practice (DNP); nursing science (PhD); pediatric nurse practitioner (MS); women's health clinical nurse specialist (MS); women's health nurse practitioner (MS). *Accreditation:* AACN. *Program availability:* Part-time, 100% online, blended/hybrid learning. *Faculty:* 48 full-time (47 women), 44 part-time/adjunct (37 women). *Students:* 23 full-time (22 women), 816 part-time (750 women); includes 475 minority (188 Black or African American, non-Hispanic/Latino; 4 American Indian or Alaska Native, non-Hispanic/Latino; 171 Asian, non-Hispanic/Latino; 83 Hispanic/Latino; 3 Native Hawaiian or other Pacific Islander, non-Hispanic/Latino; 26 Two or more races, non-Hispanic/Latino), 12 international. Average age 37. 201 applicants, 88% accepted, 123 enrolled. In 2017, 232 master's, 17 doctorates awarded. *Degree requirements:* For master's, comprehensive exam, thesis or alternative, 6-year time limit for completion of degree, professional or clinical project; for doctorate, comprehensive exam, thesis/dissertation, 10-year time limit for completion of degree. *Entrance requirements:* For master's, GRE or MAT, minimum GPA of 3.0 on last 60 hours in undergraduate nursing degree and overall, RN license, BS in nursing, basic statistics course, 1 year of clinical experience; for doctorate, GRE (preferred minimum score 153 [500 old version] Verbal, 144 [500 old version] Quantitative, 4 Analytical), MS in nursing, minimum preferred GPA of 3.5, RN license, statistics course, 2 letters of reference, curriculum vitae, graduate nursing-theory course, graduate research course, statement of professional goals and research interests. Additional exam requirements/recommendations for international students: Required—TOEFL (minimum score 550 paper-based; 79 iBT); Recommended—IELTS (minimum score 6.5), TSE (minimum score 53). *Application deadline:* For fall admission, 5/1 for domestic students, 3/1 priority date for international students; for spring admission, 9/15 for domestic students, 7/1 priority date for international students; for summer admission, 2/1 for domestic and international students. Applications are processed on a rolling basis. Application fee: $50 ($75 for international students). Electronic applications accepted. *Expenses:* $8,510 per year full-time in-state, $17,810 per year full-time out-of-state. *Financial support:* In 2017–18, 146 students received support, including 7 teaching assistantships (averaging $28,195 per year); research assistantships, career-related internships or fieldwork, Federal Work-Study, institutionally sponsored loans, scholarships/grants, traineeships, health care benefits, and unspecified assistantships also available. Support available to part-time students. Financial award application deadline: 3/1; financial award applicants required to submit FAFSA. *Faculty research:* Women's health, nurse staffing and satisfaction in health systems, perinatal safety, chronic illness, pediatric health. *Total annual research expenditures:* $380,388. *Unit head:* Dr. Anita G. Hufft, Dean, 940-898-2401, Fax: 940-898-2437, E-mail: nursing@twu.edu. *Application contact:* Korie Hawkins, Associate Director of Admissions, Graduate Recruitment, 940-898-3188, Fax: 940-898-3081, E-mail: admissions@twu.edu.
Website: http://www.twu.edu/nursing/

Thomas Edison State University, W. Cary Edwards School of Nursing, Master of Science in Nursing Program, Trenton, NJ 08608. Offers nurse educator (MSN); nursing administration (MSN); nursing informatics (MSN). *Accreditation:* AACN; ACEN. *Program availability:* Part-time, online learning. *Degree requirements:* For master's, nursing education seminar, onground practicum, online practicum. *Entrance requirements:* For master's, BSN. Additional exam requirements/recommendations for international students: Required—TOEFL (minimum score 550 paper-based; 79 iBT). Electronic applications accepted.

Union University, School of Nursing, Jackson, TN 38305-3697. Offers executive leadership (DNP); nurse anesthesia (DNP); nurse practitioner (DNP); nursing education (MSN, PMC). *Accreditation:* AACN; AANA/CANAEP. *Degree requirements:* For master's, thesis or alternative. *Entrance requirements:* For master's, GRE, 3 letters of reference, bachelor's degree in nursing, minimum GPA of 3.0. Additional exam requirements/recommendations for international students: Required—TOEFL (minimum score 560 paper-based). Electronic applications accepted. *Faculty research:* Children's health, occupational rehabilitation, informatics, health promotion.

Universidad Metropolitana, School of Health Sciences, Department of Nursing, San Juan, PR 00928-1150. Offers case management (Certificate); nursing (MSN); oncology nursing (Certificate). *Accreditation:* ACEN.

University at Buffalo, the State University of New York, Graduate School, School of Nursing, Buffalo, NY 14260. Offers adult gerontology nurse practitioner (DNP); family nurse practitioner (DNP); health care systems and leadership (MS); nurse anesthetist (DNP); nursing (PhD); nursing education (Certificate); psychiatric/mental health nurse practitioner (DNP). *Accreditation:* AACN; AANA/CANAEP (one or more programs are accredited). *Program availability:* Part-time, 100% online. *Faculty:* 41 full-time (36 women), 15 part-time/adjunct (all women). *Students:* 64 full-time (39 women), 136 part-time (120 women); includes 32 minority (13 Black or African American, non-Hispanic/Latino; 1 American Indian or Alaska Native, non-Hispanic/Latino; 18 Asian, non-Hispanic/Latino). Average age 34. 182 applicants, 39% accepted, 50 enrolled. In 2017, 3 master's, 32 doctorates, 2 other advanced degrees awarded. *Degree requirements:* For master's, thesis optional; for doctorate, comprehensive exam (for some programs), capstone (for DNP), dissertation (for PhD). *Entrance requirements:* For master's, GRE or MAT; for doctorate, GRE or MAT, minimum GPA of 3.0 (for DNP), 3.25 (for PhD); RN license; BS or MS in nursing; 3 references; writing sample; resume; personal statement; for Certificate, interview, minimum GPA of 3.0 or GRE General Test, RN license, MS in nursing, professional certification. Additional exam requirements/recommendations for international students: Required—TOEFL (minimum score 550 paper-based; 79 iBT), IELTS (minimum score 6.5). *Application deadline:* For fall admission, 4/1 for domestic students, 2/1 for international students; for spring admission, 1/15 for domestic students, 10/1 for international students; for summer admission, 4/1 for domestic students. Applications are processed on a rolling basis. Application fee: $75. Electronic applications accepted. *Expenses:* Contact institution. *Financial support:* In 2017–18, 80 students received support, including 2 fellowships with tuition reimbursements available (averaging $17,000 per year), 4 research assistantships with tuition reimbursements available (averaging $10,600 per year), 7 teaching assistantships with tuition reimbursements available (averaging $10,600 per year); scholarships/grants, traineeships, health care benefits, and unspecified assistantships also available. Financial award application deadline: 4/1; financial award applicants required to submit FAFSA. *Faculty research:* Oncology, palliative care, gerontology, addictions, mental health, community wellness, sleep, workforce, care of underserved populations, quality and safety, person-centered care, adolescent health. *Total annual research expenditures:* $1.4 million. *Unit head:* Dr. Marsha L. Lewis, Dean and Professor, 716-829-2533, Fax: 716-829-2566, E-mail: ubnursingdean@buffalo.edu. *Application contact:* Jennifer H. Schreier, Director of Graduate Student Services, 716-829-3311, Fax: 716-829-2067, E-mail: jhv2@buffalo.edu.
Website: http://nursing.buffalo.edu/

The University of Alabama at Birmingham, School of Nursing, Birmingham, AL 35294-1210. Offers clinical nurse leader (MSN); nurse anesthesia (DNP); nurse practitioner (MSN, DNP), including adult-gerontology acute care (MSN), adult-gerontology primary care (MSN), family (MSN), pediatric (MSN), psychiatric/mental health (MSN), women's health (MSN); nursing (MSN, DNP, PhD); nursing health systems administration (MSN); nursing informatics (MSN). *Accreditation:* AACN; AANA/CANAEP. *Program availability:* Part-time, online only, blended/hybrid learning. Terminal master's awarded for partial completion of doctoral program. *Degree requirements:* For master's, comprehensive exam; for doctorate, comprehensive exam, thesis/dissertation, research mentorship experience (for PhD); scholarly project (for DNP). *Entrance requirements:* For master's, GRE, GMAT, or MAT, minimum cumulative undergraduate GPA of 3.0 or on last 60 semesters hours; letters of recommendation; for doctorate, GRE General Test, computer literacy, course work in statistics, interview, minimum GPA of 3.0, MS in nursing, references, writing sample. Additional exam requirements/recommendations for international students: Required—TOEFL (minimum score 500 paper-based, 80 iBT) or IELTS (5.5). Electronic applications accepted. *Expenses:* Contact institution. *Faculty research:* Palliative care; oncology; aging; HIV/AIDS; nursing work environments.

University of Central Arkansas, Graduate School, College of Health and Behavioral Sciences, Department of Nursing, Conway, AR 72035-0001. Offers adult nurse practitioner (PMC); clinical nurse leader (PMC); clinical nurse specialist (MSN); family nurse practitioner (PMC); nurse educator (PMC); nurse practitioner (MSN). *Accreditation:* AACN. *Program availability:* Part-time, evening/weekend, online learning. *Degree requirements:* For master's, comprehensive exam, thesis optional, clinicals. *Entrance requirements:* For master's, GRE General Test, minimum GPA of 2.7. Additional exam requirements/recommendations for international students: Required—TOEFL (minimum score 550 paper-based; 80 iBT). *Application deadline:* For fall admission, 3/1 priority date for domestic students; for spring admission, 10/1 for domestic students. Applications are processed on a rolling basis. Application fee: $25 ($50 for international students). Electronic applications accepted. *Expenses:* Contact institution. *Financial support:* Federal Work-Study, traineeships, and unspecified assistantships available. Financial award application deadline: 2/15; financial award applicants required to submit FAFSA.
Website: http://www.uca.edu/divisions/academic/chas/nurse2ab.asp

University of Cincinnati, Graduate School, College of Nursing, Cincinnati, OH 45221-0038. Offers nurse midwifery (MSN); nurse practitioner (MSN, DNP), including acute care pediatrics (DNP), adult-gerontology acute care, adult-gerontology primary care, anesthesia (DNP), family (MSN), leadership (DNP), neonatal (MSN), women's health (MSN); nursing (MSN, PhD), including occupational health (MSN). *Accreditation:* AACN; AANA/CANAEP (one or more programs are accredited); ACNM/ACME. *Program availability:* Part-time, 100% online, blended/hybrid learning. *Faculty:* 74 full-time (69 women), 112 part-time/adjunct (105 women). *Students:* 323 full-time (261 women), 1,084 part-time (949 women); includes 311 minority (113 Black or African American, non-Hispanic/Latino; 4 American Indian or Alaska Native, non-Hispanic/Latino; 56 Asian, non-Hispanic/Latino; 108 Hispanic/Latino; 1 Native Hawaiian or other Pacific Islander, non-Hispanic/Latino; 29 Two or more races, non-Hispanic/Latino), 12 international. Average age 34. 582 applicants, 64% accepted, 314 enrolled. In 2017, 579 master's, 18 doctorates awarded. *Degree requirements:* For master's, thesis or alternative; for doctorate, comprehensive exam (for some programs), thesis/dissertation (for some programs). *Entrance requirements:* For doctorate, GRE General Test. Additional exam requirements/recommendations for international students: Required—TOEFL (minimum score 600 paper-based; 100 iBT); Recommended—IELTS (minimum score 7). *Application deadline:* For fall admission, 5/1 priority date for domestic students, 5/1 for international students; for spring admission, 10/1 for domestic students; for summer admission, 3/1 priority date for domestic students. Applications are processed on a rolling basis. Application fee: $130 ($70 for international students). Electronic applications accepted. *Expenses:* $14,668 annual full-time in-state tuition, $707 annual fees. *Financial support:* In 2017–18, 123 students received support, including 8 fellowships with full tuition reimbursements available (averaging $30,423 per year), 7 research assistantships with full tuition reimbursements available (averaging $17,971 per year), 5 teaching assistantships with full tuition reimbursements available (averaging $17,971 per year); Federal Work-Study, institutionally sponsored loans, scholarships/grants, traineeships, health care benefits, tuition waivers (partial), and unspecified assistantships also available. Support available to part-time students. Financial award

application deadline: 5/1; financial award applicants required to submit FAFSA. *Faculty research:* Vulnerable populations, education, violence, chronicity/aging, cancer. *Total annual research expenditures:* $575,576. *Unit head:* Dr. Greer Glazer, Dean, 513-558-5330, Fax: 513-558-9030, E-mail: greer.glazer@uc.edu. *Application contact:* Office of Student Recruitment, 513-558-8400, Fax: 513-558-5012, E-mail: nursingbearcats@uc.edu.
Website: https://nursing.uc.edu/

University of Colorado Denver, College of Nursing, Aurora, CO 80045. Offers adult clinical nurse specialist (MS); adult nurse practitioner (MS); family nurse practitioner (MS); family psychiatric mental health nurse practitioner (MS); health care informatics (MS); nurse-midwifery (MS); nursing (DNP, PhD); nursing leadership and health care systems (MS); pediatric nurse practitioner (MS); women's health (MS); MS/PhD. *Accreditation:* ACNM/ACME (one or more programs are accredited). *Program availability:* Part-time, evening/weekend, online learning. *Students:* 297 applicants, 55% accepted, 141 enrolled. In 2017, 138 master's, 18 doctorates awarded. Terminal master's awarded for partial completion of doctoral program. *Degree requirements:* For master's, thesis optional; for doctorate, comprehensive exam, thesis/dissertation, 42 credits of coursework. *Entrance requirements:* For master's, GRE if cumulative undergraduate GPA is less than 3.0, undergraduate nursing degree from ACEN- or CCNE-accredited school or university; completion of research and statistics courses with minimum grade of C; copy of current and unencumbered nursing license; for doctorate, GRE, bachelor's and/or master's degrees in nursing from ACEN- or CCNE-accredited institution; portfolio; minimum undergraduate GPA of 3.0, graduate 3.5; graduate-level intermediate statistics and master's-level nursing theory courses with minimum B grade; interview. Additional exam requirements/recommendations for international students: Required—TOEFL (minimum score 560 paper-based; 83 iBT). *Application deadline:* For fall admission, 2/15 for domestic students, 1/15 for international students; for spring admission, 7/1 for domestic students, 6/1 for international students. Application fee: $50 ($75 for international students). Electronic applications accepted. *Unit head:* Dr. Sarah Thompson, Dean, 303-724-1679, E-mail: sarah.a.thompson@ucdenver.edu. *Application contact:* Judy Campbell, Graduate Programs Coordinator, 303-724-8503, E-mail: judy.campbell@ucdenver.edu.
Website: http://www.ucdenver.edu/academics/colleges/nursing/Pages/default.aspx

University of Delaware, College of Health Sciences, School of Nursing, Newark, DE 19716. Offers adult nurse practitioner (MSN, PMC); cardiopulmonary clinical nurse specialist (MSN, PMC); cardiopulmonary clinical nurse specialist/adult nurse practitioner (MSN, PMC); family nurse practitioner (MSN, PMC); gerontology clinical nurse specialist (MSN, PMC); gerontology clinical nurse specialist geriatric nurse practitioner (PMC); gerontology clinical nurse specialist/geriatric nurse practitioner (MSN); health services administration (MSN, PMC); nursing of children clinical nurse specialist (MSN, PMC); nursing of children clinical nurse specialist/pediatric nurse practitioner (MSN, PMC); oncology/immune deficiency clinical nurse specialist (MSN, PMC); oncology/immune deficiency clinical nurse specialist/adult nurse practitioner (MSN, PMC); perinatal/women's health clinical nurse specialist (MSN, PMC); perinatal/women's health clinical nurse specialist/women's health nurse practitioner (MSN, PMC); psychiatric nursing clinical nurse specialist (MSN, PMC). *Accreditation:* AACN. *Program availability:* Part-time, evening/weekend, online learning. *Degree requirements:* For master's, thesis optional. *Entrance requirements:* For master's, BSN, interview, RN license. Electronic applications accepted. *Faculty research:* Marriage and chronic illness, health promotion, congestive heart failure patient outcomes, school nursing, diabetes in children, culture, health disparities, cardiovascular, prison nursing, oncology, public policy, child obesity, smoking and teen pregnancy, blood pressure measurements, men's health.

University of Hawaii at Manoa, Office of Graduate Education, School of Nursing and Dental Hygiene, Honolulu, HI 96822. Offers clinical nurse specialist (MS), including adult health, community mental health; nurse practitioner (MS), including adult health, community mental health, family nurse practitioner; nursing (PhD, Graduate Certificate); nursing administration (MS). *Accreditation:* AACN. *Program availability:* Part-time, online learning. *Degree requirements:* For master's, thesis optional; for doctorate, comprehensive exam, thesis/dissertation. *Entrance requirements:* For master's, Hawaii RN license. Additional exam requirements/recommendations for international students: Required—TOEFL (minimum score 580 paper-based; 92 iBT), IELTS (minimum score 5). *Expenses:* Contact institution.

University of Houston, College of Nursing, Sugar Land, TX 77479. Offers family nurse practitioner (MSN); nursing administration (MSN); nursing education (MSN). *Accreditation:* AACN. *Faculty:* 13 full-time (12 women). *Students:* 29 full-time (24 women); includes 15 minority (6 Black or African American, non-Hispanic/Latino; 5 Asian, non-Hispanic/Latino; 4 Hispanic/Latino), 3 international. Average age 37. 36 applicants, 61% accepted, 15 enrolled. In 2017, 14 master's awarded. *Entrance requirements:* For master's, GRE or MAT, minimum GPA of 3.0 in last 60 hours of academic course work, valid Texas RN licensure, 2 letters of recommendation, essay, resume, interview. Additional exam requirements/recommendations for international students: Required—TOEFL. *Application deadline:* For fall admission, 7/1 for domestic students, 6/1 for international students; for spring admission, 12/1 for domestic students, 10/1 for international students. Application fee: $75. Electronic applications accepted. *Financial support:* In 2017–18, 19 students received support. Federal Work-Study, scholarships/grants, and unspecified assistantships available. Support available to part-time students. Financial award application deadline: 5/1; financial award applicants required to submit FAFSA. *Unit head:* Dr. Kathryn Tart, Dean, 832-842-8200, E-mail: kmtart@uh.edu. *Application contact:* Tammy N. Whatley, Student Affairs Director, 832-842-8220, E-mail: tnwhatley@uh.edu.
Website: http://www.uh.edu/nursing

University of Illinois at Chicago, College of Nursing, Program in Nursing, Chicago, IL 60607-7128. Offers acute care clinical nurse specialist (MS); administrative nursing leadership (Certificate); adult nurse practitioner (MS); adult/geriatric nurse practitioner (MS); advanced community health nurse specialist (MS); family nurse practitioner (MS); geriatric clinical nurse specialist (MS); geriatric nurse practitioner (MS); nurse midwifery (MS); occupational health/advanced community health nurse specialist (MS); occupational health/family nurse practitioner (MS); pediatric nurse practitioner (MS); perinatal clinical nurse specialist (MS); school/advanced community health nurse specialist (MS); school/family nurse practitioner (MS); women's health nurse practitioner (MS). *Accreditation:* AACN. *Program availability:* Part-time. *Degree requirements:* For master's, thesis or alternative. *Entrance requirements:* For master's, GRE General Test, minimum GPA of 2.75. Additional exam requirements/recommendations for international students: Required—TOEFL. Electronic applications accepted.

University of Indianapolis, Graduate Programs, School of Nursing, Indianapolis, IN 46227-3697. Offers advanced practice nursing (DNP); family nurse practitioner (MSN); gerontological nurse practitioner (MSN); neonatal nurse practitioner (MSN); nurse-midwifery (MSN); nursing (MSN); nursing and health systems leadership (MSN); nursing education (MSN); women's health nurse practitioner (MSN); MBA/MSN. *Accreditation:* AACN. *Entrance requirements:* For master's, minimum GPA of 3.0, interview, letters of recommendation, resume, IN nursing license, 1 year of professional practice; for doctorate, graduate of ACEN- or CCNE-accredited nursing program; MSN or MA with nursing major and minimum cumulative GPA of 3.25; unencumbered RN license with eligibility for licensure in Indiana; completion of graduate-level statistics course within last 5 years with minimum grade of B; resume; essay; official transcripts from all academic institutions. Additional exam requirements/recommendations for international students: Required—TOEFL (minimum score 550 paper-based). Electronic applications accepted.

University of Louisiana at Lafayette, BI Moody III College of Business Administration MBA Program, Lafayette, LA 70504. Offers accounting (MS); business administration (MBA); entrepreneurship (MBA); finance (MBA); global management (MBA); health care administration (MBA); hospitality management (MBA); human resource management (MBA); project management (MBA); sales leadership (MBA). *Accreditation:* AACSB. *Program availability:* Part-time, evening/weekend. *Entrance requirements:* For master's, GRE General Test. Additional exam requirements/recommendations for international students: Required—TOEFL (minimum score 550 paper-based). *Application deadline:* For fall admission, 5/15 for domestic students. Application fee: $25 ($30 for international students). *Unit head:* P. Robert Viguerie, Jr., Graduate Coordinator, 337-482-5882, E-mail: MBADirector@louisiana.edu. *Application contact:* Dr. C. E. Palmer, Dean, 337-482-6965, Fax: 337-482-1333, E-mail: palmer@louisiana.edu.
Website: http://moody.louisiana.edu

University of Louisville, Graduate School, School of Nursing, Louisville, KY 40202. Offers adult gerontology nurse practitioner (MSN, DNP); education and administration (MSN); family nurse practitioner (MSN, DNP); neonatal nurse practitioner (MSN, DNP); nursing research (PhD); psychiatric/mental health nurse practitioner (MSN, DNP); women's health nurse practitioner (MSN). *Accreditation:* AACN. *Program availability:* Part-time. *Faculty:* 44 full-time (40 women), 45 part-time/adjunct (41 women). *Students:* 130 full-time (107 women), 30 part-time (25 women); includes 33 minority (16 Black or African American, non-Hispanic/Latino; 7 Asian, non-Hispanic/Latino; 5 Hispanic/Latino; 5 Two or more races, non-Hispanic/Latino), 2 international. Average age 33. 61 applicants, 67% accepted, 36 enrolled. In 2017, 54 master's awarded. *Degree requirements:* For doctorate, comprehensive exam (for some programs), thesis/dissertation (for some programs). *Entrance requirements:* For master's, bachelor's degree from nationally-accredited college, completion of 6 prerequisite courses, minimum undergraduate GPA of 3.0; for doctorate, GRE with minimum score of 156 Verbal, 146 Quantitative, 4.0 Analytic (for PhD), 3 letters of professional reference; minimum GPA of 3.0 with BSN, 3.25 with MSN; written statement of career goals, areas of expertise, and reasons for pursuing doctoral degree; resume including RN license. Additional exam requirements/recommendations for international students: Recommended—TOEFL (minimum score 560 paper-based), IELTS (minimum score 6.5). *Application deadline:* For fall admission, 1/15 priority date for domestic students, 1/15 for international students; for summer admission, 10/15 priority date for domestic students. Application fee: $65. Electronic applications accepted. *Expenses:* Tuition, state resident: full-time $12,246; part-time $681 per credit hour. Tuition, nonresident: full-time $25,486; part-time $1417 per credit hour. *Required fees:* $196. Tuition and fees vary according to course load, program and reciprocity agreements. *Financial support:* In 2017–18, 8 research assistantships with full tuition reimbursements (averaging $20,000 per year), 4 teaching assistantships with full tuition reimbursements (averaging $15,000 per year) were awarded; fellowships with full tuition reimbursements, scholarships/grants, and unspecified assistantships also available. Financial award application deadline: 10/1; financial award applicants required to submit FAFSA. *Faculty research:* Environmental health, health services research, women's mental health, self-management of chronic illness in adults and children, health disparities. *Total annual research expenditures:* $762,266. *Unit head:* Dr. Marcia J. Hern, RN, Dean and Professor, 502-852-8300, Fax: 502-852-8783, E-mail: m.hern@louisville.edu. *Application contact:* Trish Hart, Assistant Dean for Student Affairs, 502-852-5825, Fax: 502-852-8783, E-mail: trish.hart@louisville.edu.
Website: http://www.louisville.edu/nursing/

University of Mary, School of Health Sciences, Division of Nursing, Bismarck, ND 58504-9652. Offers family nurse practitioner (DNP); nurse administrator (MSN); nursing educator (MSN); MSN/MBA. *Accreditation:* AACN. *Program availability:* Part-time, evening/weekend, online learning. *Degree requirements:* For master's, comprehensive exam (for some programs), thesis (for some programs), internship (family nurse practitioner), teaching practice. *Entrance requirements:* For master's, minimum GPA of 2.75 in nursing, interview, letters of recommendation, criminal background check, immunizations, statement of professional goals. Additional exam requirements/recommendations for international students: Required—TOEFL (minimum score 500 paper-based; 71 iBT). Electronic applications accepted. *Faculty research:* Gerontology issues, rural nursing, health policy, primary care, women's health.

University of Maryland, Baltimore, School of Nursing, Baltimore, MD 21201. Offers adult-gerontology acute care nurse practitioner (DNP); adult-gerontology primary care nurse practitioner (DNP); clinical nurse leader (MS); community/public health nursing (MS); family nurse practitioner (DNP); global health (Postbaccalaureate Certificate); health services leadership and management (MS); neonatal nurse practitioner (DNP); nurse anesthesia (DNP); nursing (PhD); nursing informatics (MS, Postbaccalaureate Certificate); pediatric acute/primary care nurse practitioner (DNP); psychiatric mental health nurse practitioner (DNP); teaching in nursing and health professions (Postbaccalaureate Certificate); MS/MBA. MS/MBA offered jointly with University of Baltimore. *Program availability:* Part-time. *Faculty:* 130 full-time (117 women), 125 part-time/adjunct (114 women). *Students:* 504 full-time (442 women), 532 part-time (482 women); includes 443 minority (249 Black or African American, non-Hispanic/Latino; 1 American Indian or Alaska Native, non-Hispanic/Latino; 115 Asian, non-Hispanic/Latino; 48 Hispanic/Latino; 2 Native Hawaiian or other Pacific Islander, non-Hispanic/Latino; 28 Two or more races, non-Hispanic/Latino), 15 international. Average age 33. 935 applicants, 62% accepted, 394 enrolled. In 2017, 182 master's, 57 doctorates awarded. *Degree requirements:* For master's and Postbaccalaureate Certificate, thesis (for some programs); for doctorate, comprehensive exam, thesis/dissertation. *Entrance requirements:* Additional exam requirements/recommendations for international students: Required—TOEFL (minimum score 550 paper-based; 79 iBT); Recommended—IELTS (minimum score 7). *Application deadline:* For fall admission, 11/1 for domestic and international students; for spring admission, 8/1 for domestic and international students. Application fee: $75. Electronic applications accepted. *Expenses:* Contact institution. *Financial support:* In 2017–18, 22 research assistantships with full and partial tuition reimbursements (averaging $21,523 per year), 41 teaching assistantships with full and partial tuition reimbursements (averaging $13,439 per year) were awarded; fellowships and scholarships/grants also available. Financial award application deadline: 3/1; financial award applicants required to submit FAFSA. *Unit head:* Dr. Jane Kirschling, Dean, 410-706-4359, E-mail: kirschling@umaryland.edu. *Application contact:* Larry Fillian, Associate Dean of Student and Academic Services, 410-706-6298, E-mail: lfillian@umaryland.edu.
Website: http://www.nursing.umaryland.edu/

University of Massachusetts Amherst, Graduate School, College of Nursing, Amherst, MA 01003. Offers adult gerontology primary care nurse practitioner (DNP); clinical nurse leader (MS); family nurse practitioner (DNP); nursing (PhD); public health nurse leader (DNP). *Accreditation:* AACN. *Program availability:* Part-time, online learning. Terminal master's awarded for partial completion of doctoral program. *Degree* *requirements:* For master's, thesis optional; for doctorate, comprehensive exam, thesis/dissertation. *Entrance requirements:* Additional exam requirements/recommendations for international students: Required—TOEFL (minimum score 550 paper-based; 80 iBT), IELTS (minimum score 6.5). Electronic applications accepted. *Faculty research:* Health of older adults and their caretakers, mental health of individuals and families, health of children and adolescents, power and decision-making, transcultural health.

University of Massachusetts Medical School, Graduate School of Nursing, Worcester, MA 01655-0115. Offers adult gerontological acute care nurse practitioner (DNP, Post Master's Certificate); adult gerontological primary care nurse practitioner (DNP, Post Master's Certificate); family nursing practitioner (DNP); nurse administrator (DNP); nurse educator (MS, Post Master's Certificate); nursing (PhD). *Accreditation:* AACN. *Faculty:* 31 full-time (28 women), 39 part-time/adjunct (34 women). *Students:* 129 full-time (111 women), 31 part-time (30 women); includes 35 minority (17 Black or African American, non-Hispanic/Latino; 10 Asian, non-Hispanic/Latino; 7 Hispanic/Latino; 1 Native Hawaiian or other Pacific Islander, non-Hispanic/Latino), 1 international. Average age 32. 124 applicants, 55% accepted, 59 enrolled. In 2017, 48 master's, 10 doctorates, 2 other advanced degrees awarded. *Degree requirements:* For doctorate, thesis/dissertation (for some programs), comprehensive exam and manuscript (for PhD); capstone project and manuscript (for DNP). *Entrance requirements:* For master's, GRE General Test, bachelor's degree in nursing, course work in statistics, unrestricted Massachusetts license as registered nurse; for doctorate, GRE General Test, bachelor's or master's degree; for Post Master's Certificate, GRE General Test, MS in nursing. Additional exam requirements/recommendations for international students: Required—TOEFL (minimum score 400 paper-based; 81 iBT). *Application deadline:* For fall admission, 12/1 priority date for domestic students. Applications are processed on a rolling basis. Application fee: $60. Electronic applications accepted. *Expenses:* $14,778 in-state tuition and mandatory fees; $19,728 out-of-state. *Financial support:* In 2017–18, 6 students received support. Scholarships/grants available. Support available to part-time students. Financial award application deadline: 5/15; financial award applicants required to submit FAFSA. *Faculty research:* Health literacy, social justice, HIV prevention, cancer-related decision making, nursing education, diabetes care and education, family-focused interventions for children with type 1 diabetes. *Total annual research expenditures:* $874,000. *Unit head:* Dr. Joan Vitello-Cicciu, Dean, 508-856-5081, Fax: 508-856-6552, E-mail: joan.vitello@umassmed.edu. *Application contact:* Diane Brescia, Admissions Coordinator, 508-856-3488, Fax: 508-856-5851, E-mail: diane.brescia@umassmed.edu.
Website: http://www.umassmed.edu/gsn/

University of Memphis, Loewenberg College of Nursing, Memphis, TN 38152. Offers advanced practice nursing (Graduate Certificate); executive leadership (MSN); family nurse practitioner (MSN); nursing administration (MSN, Graduate Certificate); nursing education (MSN, Graduate Certificate). *Accreditation:* AACN. *Program availability:* Part-time, evening/weekend, online learning. *Faculty:* 15 full-time (14 women), 3 part-time/adjunct (all women). *Students:* 16 full-time (15 women), 225 part-time (201 women); includes 90 minority (72 Black or African American, non-Hispanic/Latino; 1 American Indian or Alaska Native, non-Hispanic/Latino; 9 Asian, non-Hispanic/Latino; 5 Hispanic/Latino; 1 Native Hawaiian or other Pacific Islander, non-Hispanic/Latino; 2 Two or more races, non-Hispanic/Latino). Average age 35. 168 applicants, 53% accepted, 55 enrolled. In 2017, 120 master's, 6 other advanced degrees awarded. *Degree requirements:* For master's, comprehensive exam, thesis optional, scholarly project; clinical practicum hours. *Entrance requirements:* For master's, NCLEX exam, minimum undergraduate GPA of 2.8, letter of interest, letters of recommendation, interview, resume, nursing licensure; for Graduate Certificate, unrestricted license to practice as RN in TN, current CPR certification, evidence of vaccination, annual flu shot, evidence of current professional malpractice insurance, letters of recommendation, letter of intent, resume. Additional exam requirements/recommendations for international students: Required—TOEFL (minimum score 550 paper-based; 79 iBT). *Application deadline:* For fall admission, 2/15 for domestic and international students; for spring admission, 10/1 for domestic and international students. Application fee: $35 ($60 for international students). *Expenses:* Contact institution. *Financial support:* In 2017–18, 147 students received support. Federal Work-Study and scholarships/grants available. Financial award application deadline: 2/1; financial award applicants required to submit FAFSA. *Faculty research:* Technology in nursing, nurse retention, cultural competence, health policy, health access. *Total annual research expenditures:* $560,619. *Unit head:* Dr. Lin Zhan, Dean, 901-678-2003, Fax: 901-678-4907, E-mail: lzhan@memphis.edu. *Application contact:* Dr. Shirleatha Lee, Associate Dean for Academic Programs, 901-678-2036, Fax: 901-678-5023, E-mail: sntaylr1@memphis.edu.
Website: http://www.memphis.edu/nursing

University of Minnesota, Twin Cities Campus, Graduate School, School of Nursing, Minneapolis, MN 55455-0213. Offers adult/gerontological clinical nurse specialist (DNP); adult/gerontological primary care nurse practitioner (DNP); family nurse practitioner (DNP); health innovation and leadership (DNP); integrative health and healing (DNP); nurse anesthesia (DNP); nurse midwifery (DNP); nursing (MN, PhD); nursing informatics (DNP); pediatric clinical nurse specialist (DNP); primary care certified pediatric nurse practitioner (DNP); psychiatric/mental health nurse practitioner (DNP); women's health nurse practitioner (DNP). *Accreditation:* AACN; AANA/CANAEP; ACNM/ACME (one or more programs are accredited). *Program availability:* Part-time, online learning. Terminal master's awarded for partial completion of doctoral program. *Degree requirements:* For master's, final oral exam, project or thesis; for doctorate, thesis/dissertation. *Entrance requirements:* For master's and doctorate, GRE General Test. Additional exam requirements/recommendations for international students: Required—TOEFL (minimum score 586 paper-based). *Expenses:* Contact institution. *Faculty research:* Child and family health promotion, nursing research on elders.

University of Missouri, Office of Research and Graduate Studies, Sinclair School of Nursing, Columbia, MO 65211. Offers adult-gerontology clinical nurse specialist (DNP, Certificate); family nurse practitioner (DNP); family psychiatric and mental health nurse practitioner (DNP); nursing (MS, PhD); nursing leadership and innovations in health care (DNP); pediatric clinical nurse specialist (DNP, Certificate); pediatric nurse practitioner (DNP). *Accreditation:* AACN. *Program availability:* Part-time. *Degree requirements:* For master's, thesis optional, oral exam; for doctorate, thesis/dissertation. *Entrance requirements:* For master's, GRE General Test, BSN, minimum GPA of 3.0 during last 60 hours, nursing license. Additional exam requirements/recommendations for international students: Required—TOEFL, IELTS. *Application deadline:* Applications are processed on a rolling basis. Electronic applications accepted. *Expenses:* Tuition, state resident: full-time $6480. Tuition, nonresident: full-time $17,744. *Required fees:* $1108. Tuition and fees vary according to course load, campus/location and program. *Financial support:* Fellowships, research assistantships, teaching assistantships, career-related internships or fieldwork, institutionally sponsored loans, scholarships/grants, traineeships, health care benefits, tuition waivers (full), and unspecified assistantships available. Support available to part-time students.
Website: http://nursing.missouri.edu/

University of Missouri–Kansas City, School of Nursing and Health Studies, Kansas City, MO 64110-2499. Offers adult clinical nurse specialist (MSN), including adult nurse practitioner, women's health nurse practitioner (MSN, DNP); adult clinical nursing practice (DNP), including adult gerontology nurse practitioner, women's health nurse practitioner (MSN, DNP); clinical nursing practice (DNP), including family nurse practitioner; neonatal nurse practitioner (MSN); nurse educator (MSN); nurse executive (MSN); nursing practice (DNP); pediatric clinical nursing practice (DNP), including pediatric nurse practitioner; pediatric nurse practitioner (MSN). *Accreditation:* AACN. *Program availability:* Part-time, online learning. *Degree requirements:* For master's, thesis or alternative. *Entrance requirements:* For master's, minimum undergraduate GPA of 3.2; for doctorate, GRE, 3 letters of reference. Additional exam requirements/recommendations for international students: Required—TOEFL (minimum score 550 paper-based; 80 iBT). *Faculty research:* Geriatrics/gerontology, children's pain, neonatology, Alzheimer's care, cancer caregivers.

University of Mobile, Graduate Studies, Program in Nursing, Mobile, AL 36613. Offers education/administration (MSN); nurse practitioner (DNP). *Accreditation:* AACN. *Program availability:* Part-time, evening/weekend. *Degree requirements:* For master's, comprehensive exam, thesis or alternative. *Entrance requirements:* For master's, GRE. Additional exam requirements/recommendations for international students: Required—TOEFL (minimum score 550 paper-based; 80 iBT). *Application deadline:* For fall admission, 8/3 priority date for domestic and international students; for spring admission, 12/23 priority date for domestic and international students. Applications are processed on a rolling basis. Application fee: $40 ($50 for international students). Electronic applications accepted. *Financial support:* Application deadline: 8/1; applicants required to submit FAFSA. *Faculty research:* Nursing management, transcultural nursing, spiritual aspects, educational expectations. *Unit head:* Dr. Kathryn Sheppard, Dean, School of Nursing, 251-442-2343, Fax: 251-442-2520, E-mail: ksheppard@umobile.edu. *Application contact:* Brian Boyle, Director of Recruitment, 251-442-2727, Fax: 251-442-2523.

The University of North Carolina at Chapel Hill, School of Nursing, Chapel Hill, NC 27599-7460. Offers advanced practice registered nurse (DNP); nursing (MSN, PhD, PMC), including administration (MSN), adult gerontology primary care nurse practitioner (MSN), clinical nurse leader (MSN), education (MSN), health care systems (PMC), informatics (MSN, PMC), nursing leadership (PMC), outcomes management (MSN), primary care family nurse practitioner (MSN), primary care pediatric nurse practitioner (MSN), psychiatric/mental health nurse practitioner (MSN, PMC). *Accreditation:* AACN; ACEN (one or more programs are accredited). *Program availability:* Part-time. *Faculty:* 86 full-time (78 women), 44 part-time/adjunct (40 women). *Students:* 208 full-time (186 women), 128 part-time (116 women); includes 100 minority (49 Black or African American, non-Hispanic/Latino; 4 American Indian or Alaska Native, non-Hispanic/Latino; 23 Asian, non-Hispanic/Latino; 7 Hispanic/Latino; 17 Two or more races, non-Hispanic/Latino), 17 international. Average age 33. 624 applicants, 25% accepted, 150 enrolled. In 2017, 91 master's, 14 doctorates awarded. *Degree requirements:* For master's, comprehensive exam, thesis; for doctorate, thesis/dissertation, 3 exams; for PMC, thesis. *Entrance requirements:* Additional exam requirements/recommendations for international students: Required—TOEFL (minimum score 575 paper-based; 89 iBT), IELTS (minimum score 8). *Application deadline:* For fall admission, 12/15 for domestic and international students. Application fee: $88. Electronic applications accepted. *Financial support:* In 2017–18, 8 fellowships with full tuition reimbursements, 6 research assistantships with partial tuition reimbursements (averaging $8,000 per year), 10 teaching assistantships with partial tuition reimbursements (averaging $8,000 per year) were awarded; scholarships/grants, traineeships, health care benefits, and unspecified assistantships also available. Support available to part-time students. Financial award application deadline: 3/1; financial award applicants required to submit FAFSA. *Faculty research:* Preventing and managing chronic illness, reducing health disparities, Improving healthcare quality and patient outcomes, understanding biobehavioral and genetic bases of health and illness, developing innovative ways to enhance science and its clinical translation. *Unit head:* Dr. Nilda Peragallo Montano, Dean/Professor, 919-966-3731, Fax: 919-966-3540, E-mail: npm@email.unc.edu. *Application contact:* Emily Sayed, Assistant Director, Graduate Admissions, 919-966-4260, Fax: 919-966-3540, E-mail: sayed@unc.edu.
Website: http://nursing.unc.edu

The University of North Carolina at Charlotte, College of Health and Human Services, School of Nursing, Charlotte, NC 28223-0001. Offers adult-gerontology acute care nurse practitioner (Post-Master's Certificate); advanced clinical nursing (MSN), including adult psychiatric mental health, adult-gerontology acute care nurse practitioner, family nurse practitioner across the lifespan; family nurse practitioner across the lifespan (Post-Master's Certificate); nurse anesthesia (MSN), including nurse anesthesia across the lifespan; nurse anesthesia across the lifespan (Post-Master's Certificate); nursing (DNP); nursing administration (Graduate Certificate); nursing education (Graduate Certificate); systems/population nursing (MSN), including community/public health nursing, nurse administrator, nurse educator. *Accreditation:* AACN; AANA/CANAEP. *Program availability:* Part-time, blended/hybrid learning. *Faculty:* 24 full-time (22 women), 6 part-time/adjunct (4 women). *Students:* 113 full-time (84 women), 163 part-time (150 women); includes 63 minority (47 Black or African American, non-Hispanic/Latino; 2 American Indian or Alaska Native, non-Hispanic/Latino; 6 Asian, non-Hispanic/Latino; 3 Hispanic/Latino; 5 Two or more races, non-Hispanic/Latino). Average age 37. 443 applicants, 31% accepted, 113 enrolled. In 2017, 83 master's, 8 doctorates, 8 other advanced degrees awarded. Terminal master's awarded for partial completion of doctoral program. *Degree requirements:* For doctorate, thesis/dissertation or alternative, residency; for other advanced degree, practicum. *Entrance requirements:* For master's, GRE General Test, current unrestricted license as Registered Nurse in North Carolina; BSN from nationally-accredited program; one year of professional nursing practice in acute/critical care; minimum overall GPA of 3.0 in last degree; completion of undergraduate statistics course with minimum grade of C; statement of purpose; for doctorate, GRE or MAT, master's degree in nursing in an advanced nursing practice specialty from nationally-accredited program; minimum overall GPA of 3.5 in MSN program; current RN licensure in U.S. at time of application with eligibility for NC licensure; essay; resume/curriculum vitae; professional recommendations; clinical hours; for other advanced degree, GRE. Additional exam requirements/recommendations for international students: Required—TOEFL (minimum score 523 paper-based, 70 iBT) or IELTS (6.5). *Application deadline:* For fall admission, 1/10 for domestic and international students; for spring admission, 9/10 for domestic and international students; for summer admission, 4/1 for domestic and international students. Applications are processed on a rolling basis. Application fee: $75. Electronic applications accepted. *Expenses:* Contact institution. *Financial support:* In 2017–18, 6 students received support, including 4 research assistantships (averaging $6,338 per year), 2 teaching assistantships (averaging $6,250 per year); career-related internships or fieldwork, institutionally sponsored loans, scholarships/grants, traineeships, and unspecified assistantships also available. Support available to part-time students. Financial award application deadline: 3/1; financial award applicants required to submit FAFSA. *Total annual research expenditures:* $800,072. *Unit head:* Dr. Dena Evans, Director, 704-687-7974, E-mail: devans37@uncc.edu. *Application contact:* Kathy B. Giddings, Director of Graduate Admissions, 704-687-5503, Fax: 704-687-1668, E-mail: gradadm@uncc.edu.
Website: http://nursing.uncc.edu/

The University of North Carolina at Greensboro, Graduate School, School of Nursing, Greensboro, NC 27412-5001. Offers adult clinical nurse specialist (MSN, PMC); adult/gerontological nurse practitioner (MSN, PMC); nurse anesthesia (MSN, PMC); nursing (PhD); nursing administration (MSN); nursing education (MSN); MSN/MBA. *Accreditation:* ACEN. *Degree requirements:* For master's, thesis or alternative. *Entrance requirements:* For master's, GRE General Test or MAT, BSN, clinical experience, liability insurance, RN license; for PMC, liability insurance, MSN, RN license. Additional exam requirements/recommendations for international students: Required—TOEFL. Electronic applications accepted.

The University of North Carolina at Pembroke, The Graduate School, Department of Nursing, Pembroke, NC 28372-1510. Offers clinical nurse leader (MSN); nurse educator (MSN); rural case manager (MSN). *Accreditation:* AACN. *Program availability:* Part-time. Application fee: $45 ($60 for international students). *Unit head:* Julie Harrison-Swartz, Director of Graduate Programs, 910-775-4509, E-mail: julie.harrison-swartz@uncp.edu. Website: http://www.uncp.edu/nursing/

University of Pennsylvania, School of Nursing, Health Leadership Program, Philadelphia, PA 19104. Offers MSN. *Accreditation:* AACN. *Program availability:* Part-time. *Students:* 4 full-time (all women), 20 part-time (18 women); includes 3 minority (2 Hispanic/Latino; 1 Two or more races, non-Hispanic/Latino), 1 international. Average age 34. 7 applicants, 71% accepted, 5 enrolled. In 2017, 4 master's awarded. Application fee: $80. *Financial support:* Application deadline: 4/1.

University of Pennsylvania, School of Nursing, Program in Nursing and Health Care Administration, Philadelphia, PA 19104. Offers MSN, PhD, MBA/MSN. *Accreditation:* AACN. *Program availability:* Part-time. *Students:* 6 full-time (all women), 20 part-time (14 women); includes 5 minority (1 Black or African American, non-Hispanic/Latino; 1 Asian, non-Hispanic/Latino; 1 Hispanic/Latino; 2 Two or more races, non-Hispanic/Latino). Average age 28. 14 applicants, 57% accepted, 7 enrolled. In 2017, 8 master's awarded. Terminal master's awarded for partial completion of doctoral program. Application fee: $80.

University of Phoenix–Bay Area Campus, College of Nursing, San Jose, CA 95134-1805. Offers education (MHA); gerontology (MHA); health administration (MHA, DHA); informatics (MHA, MSN); nursing (MSN, PhD); nursing/health care education (MSN); MSN/MBA. *Program availability:* Evening/weekend, online learning. *Degree requirements:* For master's, thesis (for some programs). *Entrance requirements:* For master's, minimum undergraduate GPA of 2.5, 3 years of work experience, RN license. Additional exam requirements/recommendations for international students: Required—TOEFL (minimum score 550 paper-based; 79 iBT). Electronic applications accepted.

University of Pittsburgh, School of Nursing, Nurse Specialty Role Program, Pittsburgh, PA 15260. Offers clinical nurse leader (MSN); health systems executive leadership (DNP); nursing informatics (MSN). *Accreditation:* AACN. *Program availability:* Part-time. *Faculty:* 9 full-time (8 women), 1 (woman) part-time/adjunct. *Students:* 5 full-time (4 women), 60 part-time (53 women); includes 8 minority (3 Black or African American, non-Hispanic/Latino; 5 Asian, non-Hispanic/Latino), 1 international. Average age 37. 43 applicants, 72% accepted, 26 enrolled. In 2017, 15 master's, 4 doctorates awarded. *Degree requirements:* For master's, comprehensive exam, thesis optional. *Entrance requirements:* For master's, GRE, BSN, RN license, 3 letters of recommendation, personal essay, resume, course work in statistics, relevant nursing experience; for doctorate, GRE, BSN/MSN, RN license, minimum GPA of 3.5, 3 letters of recommendation, personal essay, resume, course work in statistics, relevant nursing experience. Additional exam requirements/recommendations for international students: Required—TOEFL (minimum score 600 paper-based; 100 IBT) or IELTS (minimum score 7.0). *Application deadline:* For fall admission, 5/1 priority date for domestic students, 2/15 priority date for international students. Application fee: $50. Electronic applications accepted. *Expenses:* $13,068 per term full-time resident tuition, $1,064 per credit part-time; $15,270 per term full-time non-resident tuition, $1,247 per credit part-time; $437 per term full-time fees; $282 per term part-time fees. *Financial support:* In 2017–18, 37 students received support. Scholarships/grants and tuition waivers available. Financial award applicants required to submit FAFSA. *Faculty research:* Behavioral management of chronic disorders, patient management in critical care, consumer informatics, genetic applications (molecular genetics and psychosocial implications), technology for nurses and patients to improve care. *Unit head:* Dr. Sandra Engberg, Associate Dean for Clinical Education, 412-624-3835, Fax: 412-624-8521, E-mail: sje1@pitt.edu. *Application contact:* Laurie Lapsley, Graduate Administrator, 412-624-9670, Fax: 412-624-2409, E-mail: lapsleyl@pitt.edu.
Website: http://www.nursing.pitt.edu/

University of Rochester, School of Nursing, Rochester, NY 14642. Offers adult gerontological acute care nurse practitioner (MS); adult gerontological primary care nurse practitioner (MS); clinical nurse leader (MS); family nurse practitioner (MS); family psychiatric mental health nurse practitioner (MS); health care organization management and leadership (MS); nursing (DNP); nursing and health science (PhD); nursing education (MS); pediatric nurse practitioner (MS); pediatric nurse practitioner/neonatal nurse practitioner (MS). *Accreditation:* AACN. *Program availability:* Part-time, 100% online, blended/hybrid learning. *Faculty:* 62 full-time (51 women), 73 part-time/adjunct (63 women). *Students:* 17 full-time (12 women), 306 part-time (252 women); includes 46 minority (16 Black or African American, non-Hispanic/Latino; 1 American Indian or Alaska Native, non-Hispanic/Latino; 7 Asian, non-Hispanic/Latino; 17 Hispanic/Latino; 5 Two or more races, non-Hispanic/Latino), 3 international. Average age 34. 143 applicants, 71% accepted, 87 enrolled. In 2017, 48 master's, 8 doctorates awarded. Terminal master's awarded for partial completion of doctoral program. *Degree requirements:* For master's, comprehensive exam; for doctorate, thesis/dissertation. *Entrance requirements:* For master's, BS in nursing, minimum GPA of 3.0, course work in statistics; for doctorate, GRE General Test (for PhD), MS in nursing, minimum GPA of 3.5. Additional exam requirements/recommendations for international students: Required—TOEFL (minimum score 560 paper-based; 88 iBT) or IELTS (minimum score 6.5) recommended. *Application deadline:* For fall admission, 4/1 for domestic and international students; for spring admission, 9/1 for domestic and international students; for summer admission, 1/2 for domestic and international students. Application fee: $50. Electronic applications accepted. *Financial support:* In 2017–18, 63 students received support, including 2 fellowships with full and partial tuition reimbursements available (averaging $16,000 per year); scholarships/grants, traineeships, health care benefits, tuition waivers (full and partial), and unspecified assistantships also available. Support available to part-time students. Financial award application deadline: 6/30; financial award applicants required to submit CSS PROFILE or FAFSA. *Faculty research:* Symptom science, systems of care, innovations in health technology, promoting healthy behaviors. *Total annual research expenditures:* $2.6 million. *Unit head:* Dr. Kathy H. Rideout, Dean, 585-273-8902, Fax: 585-273-1268, E-mail: kathy_rideout@urmc.rochester.edu. *Application contact:* Elaine Andolina, Director of Admissions, 585-275-2375, Fax: 585-756-8299, E-mail: elaine_andolina@urmc.rochester.edu.
Website: http://www.son.rochester.edu

University of St. Augustine for Health Sciences, Graduate Programs, Master of Science in Nursing Program, San Marcos, CA 92069. Offers nurse educator (MSN); nurse executive (MSN); nurse informatics (MSN). *Program availability:* Part-time, online learning.

University of St. Francis, Leach College of Nursing, Joliet, IL 60435-6169. Offers family nurse practitioner (MSN, Post-Master's Certificate); nursing administration (MSN); nursing education (MSN); nursing practice (DNP); psychology/mental health nurse practitioner (MSN, Post-Master's Certificate); teaching in nursing (Certificate). *Accreditation:* AACN. *Program availability:* Part-time, evening/weekend, 100% online. *Faculty:* 9 full-time (all women), 12 part-time/adjunct (11 women). *Students:* 66 full-time (61 women), 292 part-time (262 women); includes 136 minority (67 Black or African American, non-Hispanic/Latino; 2 American Indian or Alaska Native, non-Hispanic/Latino; 25 Asian, non-Hispanic/Latino; 29 Hispanic/Latino; 3 Native Hawaiian or other Pacific Islander, non-Hispanic/Latino; 10 Two or more races, non-Hispanic/Latino). Average age 40. 280 applicants, 34% accepted, 81 enrolled. In 2017, 117 master's, 5 doctorates, 12 other advanced degrees awarded. *Degree requirements:* For master's, comprehensive exam. *Entrance requirements:* Additional exam requirements/recommendations for international students: Required—TOEFL (minimum score 550 paper-based; 79 iBT), IELTS (minimum score 6). *Application deadline:* Applications are processed on a rolling basis. Application fee: $30. Electronic applications accepted. Application fee is waived when completed online. *Expenses:* $775 per credit hour. *Financial support:* In 2017–18, 115 students received support. Scholarships/grants available. Support available to part-time students. Financial award applicants required to submit FAFSA. *Unit head:* Dr. Carol Wilson, Dean, 815-740-3840, Fax: 815-740-4243, E-mail: cwilson@stfrancis.edu. *Application contact:* Sandra Sloka, Director of Admissions for Graduate and Degree Completion Programs, 800-735-7500, Fax: 815-740-3431, E-mail: ssloka@stfrancis.edu.
Website: http://www.stfrancis.edu/academics/college-of-nursing/

University of Saint Mary, Graduate Programs, Program in Nursing, Leavenworth, KS 66048-5082. Offers nurse administrator (MSN); nurse educator (MSN). *Accreditation:* AACN. *Program availability:* Part-time, online only, 100% online. *Degree requirements:* For master's, practicum. *Entrance requirements:* For master's, BSN from CCNE- or ACEN-accredited baccalaureate nursing program at regionally-accredited institution. Electronic applications accepted. *Expenses:* Contact institution.

University of San Diego, Hahn School of Nursing and Health Science, San Diego, CA 92110-2492. Offers adult-gerontology clinical nurse specialist (MSN); adult-gerontology nurse practitioner/family nurse practitioner (MSN); clinical nurse leader (MSN); executive nurse leader (MSN); family nurse practitioner (MSN); healthcare informatics (MS, MSN); nursing (PhD); nursing practice (DNP); pediatric/family nurse practitioner (MSN); psychiatric-mental health nurse practitioner (MSN). *Accreditation:* AACN. *Program availability:* Part-time, evening/weekend. *Faculty:* 36 full-time (31 women), 36 part-time/adjunct (29 women). *Students:* 238 full-time (198 women), 230 part-time (167 women); includes 230 minority (32 Black or African American, non-Hispanic/Latino; 104 Asian, non-Hispanic/Latino; 75 Hispanic/Latino; 19 Two or more races, non-Hispanic/Latino), 12 international. Average age 35. In 2017, 93 master's, 44 doctorates awarded. *Degree requirements:* For doctorate, thesis/dissertation (for some programs), residency (DNP). *Entrance requirements:* For master's, GRE General Test (for entry-level nursing), BSN, current California RN licensure (except for entry-level nursing), minimum GPA of 3.0; for doctorate, minimum GPA of 3.5, MSN, current California RN licensure. Additional exam requirements/recommendations for international students: Required—TOEFL (minimum score 580 paper-based; 83 iBT), TWE. *Application deadline:* Applications are processed on a rolling basis. Application fee: $45. Electronic applications accepted. *Financial support:* In 2017–18, 242 students received support. Scholarships/grants and traineeships available. Support available to part-time students. Financial award application deadline: 4/1; financial award applicants required to submit FAFSA. *Faculty research:* Maternal/neonatal health, palliative and end of life care, adolescent obesity, health disparities, cognitive dysfunction. *Unit head:* Dr. Janes Georges, Interim Dean, 619-260-4550, Fax: 619-260-6814, E-mail: nursing@sandiego.edu. *Application contact:* Monica Mahon, Associate Director of Graduate Admissions, 619-260-4524, Fax: 619-260-4158, E-mail: grads@sandiego.edu.
Website: http://www.sandiego.edu/nursing/

The University of Scranton, Panuska College of Professional Studies, Department of Nursing, Scranton, PA 18510-4595. Offers family nurse practitioner (MSN, PMC); nurse anesthesia (MSN, PMC); nursing leadership (DNP). Applicants accepted in odd-numbered years only. *Accreditation:* AACN; AANA/CANAEP. *Program availability:* Part-time, evening/weekend. *Degree requirements:* For master's, comprehensive exam (for some programs), thesis (for some programs), capstone experience. *Entrance requirements:* For master's, minimum GPA of 3.0, three letters of reference; for doctorate, RN licensure and evidence of certification in advanced practice nursing specialty. Additional exam requirements/recommendations for international students: Required—TOEFL (minimum score 500 paper-based; 80 iBT), IELTS (minimum score 6.5). Electronic applications accepted. *Faculty research:* Home care, doctoral education, health care of women and children, pain, health promotion and adolescence.

University of South Alabama, College of Nursing, Mobile, AL 36688. Offers nursing (MSN, DNP); nursing administration (Certificate); nursing education (Certificate); nursing practice (Certificate). *Accreditation:* AACN. *Program availability:* Part-time, online learning. *Faculty:* 73 full-time (67 women), 112 part-time/adjunct (103 women). *Students:* 2,163 full-time (1,905 women), 714 part-time (619 women); includes 882 minority (566 Black or African American, non-Hispanic/Latino; 26 American Indian or Alaska Native, non-Hispanic/Latino; 117 Asian, non-Hispanic/Latino; 102 Hispanic/Latino; 7 Native Hawaiian or other Pacific Islander, non-Hispanic/Latino; 64 Two or more races, non-Hispanic/Latino), 6 international. Average age 35. 918 applicants, 77% accepted, 522 enrolled. In 2017, 791 master's, 96 doctorates, 95 other advanced degrees awarded. *Degree requirements:* For master's, thesis optional; for doctorate, final project. *Entrance requirements:* For master's, BSN, RN licensure, minimum GPA of 3.0, resume documenting clinical experience, background check, drug screening; for doctorate, MSN, RN licensure, minimum GPA of 3.0; for Certificate, MSN/DN/DNP, RN licensure, minimum GPA of 3.0, resume documenting clinical experience, background check, drug screening. Additional exam requirements/recommendations for international students: Required—TOEFL. *Application deadline:* For fall admission, 2/15 for domestic students; for spring admission, 7/15 priority date for domestic students; for summer admission, 11/15 priority date for domestic students. Applications are processed on a rolling basis. Application fee: $100. Electronic applications accepted. *Expenses:* Tuition, state resident: full-time $10,104; part-time $421 per semester hour. Tuition, nonresident: full-time $20,208; part-time $842 per semester hour. *Financial support:* Fellowships, research assistantships, teaching assistantships, career-related internships or fieldwork, Federal Work-Study, institutionally sponsored loans, scholarships/grants, and unspecified assistantships available. Support available to part-time students. Financial award application deadline: 3/31; financial award applicants required to submit FAFSA. *Unit head:* Dr. Heather Hall, Interim Dean, College of Nursing, 251-445-9400, Fax: 251-445-9416, E-mail: heatherhall@southalabama.edu. *Application contact:* Brenda Mosley, Academic Advisor II, 251-445-9400, Fax: 251-445-9416, E-mail: bmosley@southalabama.edu.
Website: http://www.southalabama.edu/colleges/con/index.html

University of South Carolina, The Graduate School, College of Nursing, Program in Nursing Administration, Columbia, SC 29208. Offers MSN. *Accreditation:* AACN. *Program availability:* Part-time. *Degree requirements:* For master's, thesis or alternative.

Entrance requirements: For master's, GRE General Test or MAT, BS in nursing, nursing license. Additional exam requirements/recommendations for international students: Required—TOEFL (minimum score 570 paper-based). Electronic applications accepted. *Faculty research:* System research, evidence based practice, breast cancer, violence.

University of Southern Indiana, Graduate Studies, College of Nursing and Health Professions, Program in Nursing, Evansville, IN 47712-3590. Offers adult-gerontology acute care nurse practitioner (MSN, PMC); adult-gerontology clinical nurse specialist (MSN, PMC); adult-gerontology primary care nurse practitioner (MSN, PMC); advanced nursing practice (DNP); family nurse practiioner (MSN); family nurse practitioner (PMC); nursing education (MSN, PMC); nursing management and leadership (MSN, PMC); organizational and systems leadership (DNP); psychiatric mental health nurse practitioner (MSN, PMC). *Accreditation:* AACN. *Program availability:* Part-time, online learning. *Faculty:* 9 full-time (8 women), 2 part-time/adjunct (both women). *Students:* 73 full-time (59 women), 370 part-time (314 women); includes 47 minority (18 Black or African American, non-Hispanic/Latino; 2 American Indian or Alaska Native, non-Hispanic/Latino; 10 Asian, non-Hispanic/Latino; 12 Hispanic/Latino; 1 Native Hawaiian or other Pacific Islander, non-Hispanic/Latino; 4 Two or more races, non-Hispanic/Latino), 1 international. Average age 36. In 2017, 91 master's, 10 doctorates, 18 other advanced degrees awarded. *Entrance requirements:* For master's, BSN from nationally-accredited school; minimum cumulative GPA of 3.0; satisfactory completion of a course in undergraduate statistics (minimum grade C); one year of full-time experience or 2,000 hours of clinical practice as an RN (recommended); unencumbered U.S. RN license; for doctorate, minimum GPA of 3.0, completion of graduate research course with minimum B grade, unencumbered RN license, resume/curriculum vitae, three professional references, 1-2 page narrative of practice experience and professional goals, Capstone Project Information form. Additional exam requirements/recommendations for international students: Required—TOEFL (minimum score 550 paper-based; 79 iBT), IELTS (minimum score 6). *Application deadline:* For fall admission, 2/1 for domestic students, 1/1 priority date for international students. Applications are processed on a rolling basis. Application fee: $40. Electronic applications accepted. *Expenses:* Contact institution. *Financial support:* In 2017–18, 1 student received support. Federal Work-Study, scholarships/grants, tuition waivers (full and partial), and unspecified assistantships available. Financial award application deadline: 3/1; financial award applicants required to submit FAFSA. *Unit head:* Dr. Mellisa A. Hall, Chair of the Master of Science in Nursing Program, 812-465-1168, E-mail: mhall@usi.edu. *Application contact:* Dr. Mayola Rowser, Director, Graduate Studies, 812-465-7015, Fax: 812-464-1956, E-mail: mrowser@usi.edu.
Website: https://www.usi.edu/health/nursing/

University of Southern Maine, College of Science, Technology, and Health, School of Nursing, Portland, ME 04103. Offers adult-gerontology primary care nurse practitioner (MS, PMC); education (MS); family nurse practitioner (MS, PMC); family psychiatric/mental health nurse practitioner (MS); management (MS); nursing (CAS, CGS); psychiatric-mental health nurse practitioner (PMC). *Accreditation:* AACN. *Program availability:* Part-time. *Degree requirements:* For master's, thesis optional. *Entrance requirements:* For master's, GRE General Test or MAT, minimum GPA of 3.0; for doctorate, GRE. Additional exam requirements/recommendations for international students: Required—TOEFL (minimum score 550 paper-based). Electronic applications accepted. *Faculty research:* Women's health, nursing history, weight control, community services, substance abuse.

The University of Texas at Arlington, Graduate School, College of Nursing and Health Innovation, Arlington, TX 76019. Offers athletic training (MS); exercise science (MS); kinesiology (PhD); nurse practitioner (MSN); nursing (PhD); nursing administration (MSN); nursing education (MSN); nursing practice (DNP). *Accreditation:* AACN. *Program availability:* Part-time, evening/weekend, online learning. *Degree requirements:* For master's, practicum course; for doctorate, comprehensive exam (for some programs), thesis/dissertation (for some programs), proposal defense dissertation (for PhD); scholarship project (for DNP). *Entrance requirements:* For master's, GRE General Test if GPA less than 3.0, minimum GPA of 3.0, Texas nursing license, minimum C grade in undergraduate statistics course; for doctorate, GRE General Test (waived for MSN-to-PhD applicants), minimum undergraduate, graduate and statistics GPA of 3.0; Texas RN license; interview; written statement of goals. Additional exam requirements/recommendations for international students: Required—TOEFL (minimum score 550 paper-based), IELTS (minimum score 7). *Faculty research:* Simulation in clinical education and practice, cultural diversity, vulnerable populations, substance abuse.

The University of Texas at Austin, Graduate School, School of Nursing, Austin, TX 78712-1111. Offers adult - gerontology clinical nurse specialist (MSN); child health (MSN), including administration, public health nursing, teaching; family nurse practitioner (MSN); family psychiatric/mental health nurse practitioner (MSN); holistic adult health (MSN), including administration, teaching; maternity (MSN), including administration, public health nursing, teaching; nursing (PhD); nursing administration and healthcare systems management (MSN); nursing practice (DNP); pediatric nurse practitioner (MSN); public health nursing (MSN). *Accreditation:* AACN. *Program availability:* Part-time. *Degree requirements:* For master's, thesis optional; for doctorate, thesis/dissertation. *Entrance requirements:* For master's and doctorate, GRE General Test. Additional exam requirements/recommendations for international students: Required—TOEFL (minimum score 550 paper-based). Electronic applications accepted. *Faculty research:* Chronic illness management, memory and aging, health promotion, women's health, adolescent health.

The University of Texas at El Paso, Graduate School, School of Nursing, El Paso, TX 79968-0001. Offers family nurse practitioner (MSN); health care leadership and management (Certificate); interdisciplinary health sciences (PhD); nursing (DNP); nursing education (MSN, Certificate); nursing systems management (MSN). *Accreditation:* AACN. *Program availability:* Online learning. *Degree requirements:* For master's, thesis optional; for doctorate, thesis/dissertation. *Entrance requirements:* For master's, minimum GPA of 3.0, resume; for doctorate, GRE, letters of reference, relevant personal/professional experience; master's degree in nursing (for DNP); for Certificate, bachelor's degree in nursing. Additional exam requirements/recommendations for international students: Required—TOEFL; Recommended—IELTS. *Application deadline:* For fall admission, 8/1 for domestic students, 3/1 for international students; for spring admission, 11/1 for domestic students, 9/1 for international students. Applications are processed on a rolling basis. Application fee: $45 ($80 for international students). Electronic applications accepted. *Financial support:* Fellowships with partial tuition reimbursements, research assistantships with partial tuition reimbursements, teaching assistantships with partial tuition reimbursements, institutionally sponsored loans, scholarships/grants, health care benefits, tuition waivers (partial), and unspecified assistantships available. Support available to part-time students. Financial award application deadline: 3/15; financial award applicants required to submit FAFSA. *Unit head:* Dr. Elias Provencio-Vasquez, Dean, 915-747-8194, Fax: 915-747-8266, E-mail: eprovenciovasquez@utep.edu. *Application contact:* Dr. Benjamin Flores, Interim Dean of the Graduate School, 915-747-5491, Fax: 915-747-5788, E-mail: bflores@utep.edu.
Website: http://nursing.utep.edu/

The University of Texas at Tyler, College of Nursing and Health Sciences, Program in Nursing, Tyler, TX 75799-0001. Offers nurse practitioner (MSN); nursing (PhD); nursing administration (MSN); nursing education (MSN); MSN/MBA. *Accreditation:* AACN. *Program availability:* Part-time, evening/weekend, online learning. *Degree requirements:* For master's, comprehensive exam (for some programs), thesis (for some programs); for doctorate, thesis/dissertation. *Entrance requirements:* For master's, GRE General Test or MAT, GMAT, minimum undergraduate GPA of 3.0, course work in statistics, RN license, BSN. Additional exam requirements/recommendations for international students: Required—TOEFL. Electronic applications accepted. *Faculty research:* Psychosocial adjustment, aging, support/commitment of caregivers, psychological abuse and violence, hope/hopelessness, professional values, end of life care, suicidology, clinical supervision, workforce retention and issues, global health issues, health promotion.

The University of Texas Health Science Center at San Antonio, School of Nursing, San Antonio, TX 78229-3900. Offers administrative management (MSN); adult-gerontology acute care nurse practitioner (PGC); advanced practice leadership (DNP); clinical nurse leader (MSN); executive administrative management (DNP); family nurse practitioner (MSN, PGC); nursing (MSN, PhD); nursing education (MSN, PGC); pediatric nurse practitioner primary care (PGC); psychiatric mental health nurse practitioner (PGC); public health nurse leader (DNP). *Accreditation:* AACN. *Program availability:* Part-time. Terminal master's awarded for partial completion of doctoral program. *Degree requirements:* For master's, thesis optional; for doctorate, comprehensive exam, thesis/dissertation.

The University of Texas Rio Grande Valley, College of Health Affairs, School of Nursing, Edinburg, TX 78539. Offers adult health nursing (MSN); family nurse practitioner (MSN); nursing administration (MSN); nursing education (MSN); psychiatric mental health nursing (Post Master's Certificate). *Accreditation:* AACN. *Program availability:* Part-time, evening/weekend. *Faculty:* 7 full-time (all women), 5 part-time/adjunct (3 women). *Students:* 48 full-time, 5 part-time; includes 43 minority (5 Black or African American, non-Hispanic/Latino; 38 Hispanic/Latino). Average age 31. 61 applicants. In 2017, 46 master's awarded. *Degree requirements:* For master's, thesis optional. *Entrance requirements:* For master's, Texas RN licensure, undergraduate physical statistic course. Additional exam requirements/recommendations for international students: Required—TOEFL (minimum score 550 paper-based). *Application deadline:* For fall admission, 7/1 priority date for domestic and international students; for spring admission, 10/1 priority date for domestic and international students. Applications are processed on a rolling basis. Application fee: $50. Electronic applications accepted. *Expenses:* Contact institution. *Financial support:* Scholarships/grants and traineeships available. Financial award application deadline: 9/1; financial award applicants required to submit FAFSA. *Faculty research:* Health promotion, adolescent pregnancy, herbal and nontraditional approaches, healing touch stress. *Unit head:* Dr. Eloisa G. Tamez, Professor/Chief Nursing Administrator, 956-665-3616, Fax: 956-665-5252, E-mail: eloisa.tamez@utrgv.edu. *Application contact:* Dr. Beatriz Bautista, Clinical Professor, 956-665-3497, Fax: 956-665-3491, E-mail: beatriz.bautista@utrgv.edu.
Website: http://www.utrgv.edu/nursing/

The University of Toledo, College of Graduate Studies, College of Nursing, Department of Population and Community Care, Toledo, OH 43606-3390. Offers clinical nurse leader (MSN); family nurse practitioner (MSN, Certificate); nurse educator (MSN, Certificate); pediatric nurse practitioner (MSN, Certificate). *Program availability:* Part-time. *Degree requirements:* For master's, thesis or alternative. *Entrance requirements:* For master's, GRE, BS in nursing, minimum undergraduate GPA of 3.0, statement of purpose, three letters of recommendation, transcripts from all prior institutions attended, Nursing CAS application, UT supplemental application; for Certificate, BS in nursing, minimum undergraduate GPA of 3.0, statement of purpose, three letters of recommendation, transcripts from all prior institutions attended. Additional exam requirements/recommendations for international students: Required—TOEFL (minimum score 550 paper-based; 80 iBT). Electronic applications accepted.

University of Victoria, Faculty of Graduate Studies, Faculty of Human and Social Development, School of Nursing, Victoria, BC V8W 2Y2, Canada. Offers advanced nursing practice (advanced practice leadership option) (MN); advanced nursing practice (nurse educator option) (MN); advanced nursing practice (nurse practitioner option) (MN); nursing (PhD). *Program availability:* Part-time, online learning. *Entrance requirements:* Additional exam requirements/recommendations for international students: Required—TOEFL (minimum score 575 paper-based), IELTS (minimum score 7). Electronic applications accepted.

University of Virginia, School of Nursing, Charlottesville, VA 22903. Offers acute and specialty care (MSN); acute care nurse practitioner (MSN); clinical nurse leadership (MSN); community-public health leadership (MSN); nursing (DNP, PhD); psychiatric mental health counseling (MSN); MSN/MBA. *Accreditation:* AACN. *Program availability:* Part-time. *Faculty:* 51 full-time (44 women), 17 part-time/adjunct (16 women). *Students:* 202 full-time (168 women), 139 part-time (114 women); includes 78 minority (32 Black or African American, non-Hispanic/Latino; 2 American Indian or Alaska Native, non-Hispanic/Latino; 14 Asian, non-Hispanic/Latino; 17 Hispanic/Latino; 1 Native Hawaiian or other Pacific Islander, non-Hispanic/Latino; 12 Two or more races, non-Hispanic/Latino), 9 international. Average age 34. 183 applicants, 68% accepted, 98 enrolled. In 2017, 105 master's, 27 doctorates awarded. *Degree requirements:* For doctorate, comprehensive exam (for some programs), capstone project (DNP), dissertation (PhD). *Entrance requirements:* For master's, GRE General Test, MAT; for doctorate, GRE General Test. Additional exam requirements/recommendations for international students: Required—TOEFL, IELTS. *Application deadline:* Applications are processed on a rolling basis. Application fee: $60. Electronic applications accepted. *Financial support:* Fellowships, research assistantships, teaching assistantships, Federal Work-Study, and scholarships/grants available. Financial award applicants required to submit FAFSA. *Unit head:* Dorrie K. Fontaine, Dean, 434-924-0141, Fax: 434-982-1809, E-mail: dkf2u@virginia.edu. *Application contact:* Teresa Carroll, Senior Assistant Dean for Academic and Student Services, 434-924-0141, Fax: 434-982-1809, E-mail: nur-osa@virginia.edu.
Website: http://www.nursing.virginia.edu/

University of Washington, Tacoma, Graduate Programs, Program in Nursing, Tacoma, WA 98402-3100. Offers communities, populations and health (MN); leadership in healthcare (MN); nurse educator (MN). *Program availability:* Part-time. *Degree requirements:* For master's, thesis (for some programs), advance fieldwork. *Entrance requirements:* For master's, Washington State NCLEX exam, minimum GPA of 3.0. Additional exam requirements/recommendations for international students: Required—TOEFL (minimum score 580 paper-based; 70 iBT); Recommended—IELTS (minimum score 7). *Faculty research:* Hospice and palliative care; clinical trial decision-making; minority nurse retention; asthma and public health; injustice, suffering, difference: Linking Them to Us; adolescent health.

University of Wisconsin–Eau Claire, College of Nursing and Health Sciences, Program in Nursing, Eau Claire, WI 54702-4004. Offers adult-gerontological administration (DNP); adult-gerontological clinical nurse specialist (DNP); adult-gerontological education (MSN); adult-gerontological primary care nurse practitioner

(DNP); family health administration (DNP); family health in education (MSN); family health nurse practitioner (DNP); nursing (MSN); nursing practice (DNP). *Accreditation:* AACN. *Program availability:* Part-time. Terminal master's awarded for partial completion of doctoral program. *Degree requirements:* For master's, thesis optional, 500-600 hours clinical practicum, oral and written exams. *Entrance requirements:* For master's, Wisconsin RN license, minimum GPA of 3.0, undergraduate statistics, course work in health assessment. Additional exam requirements/recommendations for international students: Required—TOEFL (minimum score 79 IBT). *Expenses:* Contact institution.

University of Wisconsin–Green Bay, Graduate Studies, Program in Nursing Leadership and Management in Health Systems, Green Bay, WI 54311-7001. Offers health and wellness management (MS); nursing (MSN). *Program availability:* Part-time, evening/weekend, online only, 100% online. *Degree requirements:* For master's, 9-credit practicum. *Entrance requirements:* For master's, baccalaureate degree in nursing with minimum GPA of 3.0; college-level inferential statistics course with minimum C grade (within past 5 years); statement of interest; official undergraduate and graduate transcripts; three letters of evaluation; curriculum vitae or resume; copy of current, unencumbered RN license; background check. Additional exam requirements/recommendations for international students: Required—TOEFL. Electronic applications accepted.

Vanderbilt University, Vanderbilt University School of Nursing, Nashville, TN 37240. Offers adult-gerontology acute care nurse practitioner (MSN), including hospitalist, intensivist; adult-gerontology primary care nurse practitioner (MSN); emergency nurse practitioner (MSN); family nurse practitioner (MSN); healthcare leadership (MSN); neonatal nurse practitioner (MSN); nurse midwifery (MSN); nurse midwifery/family nurse practitioner (MSN); nursing (Post-Master's Certificate); nursing informatics (MSN); nursing practice (DNP); nursing science (PhD); pediatric acute care nurse practitioner (MSN); pediatric primary care nurse practitioner (MSN); psychiatric-mental health nurse practitioner (MSN); women's health nurse practitioner (MSN); women's health nurse practitioner/adult gerontology primary care nurse practitioner (MSN); MSN/M Div; MSN/MTS. *Accreditation:* AACN; ACEN (one or more programs are accredited); ACNM/ACME. *Program availability:* Part-time, 100% online, blended/hybrid learning. *Faculty:* 292 full-time (267 women), 321 part-time/adjunct (253 women). *Students:* 501 full-time (435 women), 387 part-time (355 women); includes 153 minority (40 Black or African American, non-Hispanic/Latino; 1 American Indian or Alaska Native, non-Hispanic/Latino; 27 Asian, non-Hispanic/Latino; 48 Hispanic/Latino; 4 Native Hawaiian or other Pacific Islander, non-Hispanic/Latino; 33 Two or more races, non-Hispanic/Latino), 9 international. Average age 31. 1,210 applicants, 57% accepted, 473 enrolled. In 2017, 319 master's, 47 doctorates awarded. *Degree requirements:* For doctorate, comprehensive exam, thesis/dissertation. *Entrance requirements:* For master's, GRE General Test (taken within the past 5 years), minimum B average in undergraduate course work, 3 letters of recommendation; for doctorate, GRE General Test, interview, 3 letters of recommendation from doctorally-prepared faculty, MSN, essay. Additional exam requirements/recommendations for international students: Required—TOEFL (minimum score 570 paper-based), IELTS (minimum score 6.5). *Application deadline:* For fall admission, 11/1 priority date for domestic and international students. Applications are processed on a rolling basis. Application fee: $50. Electronic applications accepted. *Expenses:* Contact institution. *Financial support:* In 2017–18, 627 students received support. Scholarships/grants available. Financial award application deadline: 3/1; financial award applicants required to submit FAFSA. *Faculty research:* Lymphedema, palliative care and bereavement, health services research including workforce, safety and quality of care, gerontology, better birth outcomes including nutrition. *Total annual research expenditures:* $2 million. *Unit head:* Dr. Linda Norman, Dean, 615-343-8876, Fax: 615-343-7711, E-mail: linda.norman@vanderbilt.edu. *Application contact:* Patricia Peerman, Assistant Dean for Enrollment Management, 615-322-3800, Fax: 615-343-0333, E-mail: vusn-admissions@vanderbilt.edu.
Website: http://www.nursing.vanderbilt.edu

Virginia Commonwealth University, Graduate School, School of Nursing, Richmond, VA 23284-9005. Offers adult health acute nursing (MS); adult health primary nursing (MS); biobehavioral clinical research (PhD); child health nursing (MS); clinical nurse leader (MS); family health nursing (MS); nurse educator (MS); nurse practitioner (MS); nursing (Certificate); nursing administration (MS), including clinical nurse manager; psychiatric-mental health nursing (MS); quality and safety in health care (DNP); women's health nursing (MS). *Accreditation:* AACN; ACEN (one or more programs are accredited). *Program availability:* Part-time, evening/weekend, online learning. *Degree requirements:* For master's, thesis optional; for doctorate, thesis/dissertation. *Entrance requirements:* For master's, GRE General Test, BSN, minimum GPA of 2.8; for doctorate, GRE General Test. Additional exam requirements/recommendations for international students: Required—TOEFL (minimum score 600 paper-based; 100 iBT). Electronic applications accepted.

Walden University, Graduate Programs, School of Nursing, Minneapolis, MN 55401. Offers adult-gerontology acute care nurse practitioner (MSN); adult-gerontology nurse practitioner (MSN); education (MSN); family nurse practitioner (MSN); informatics (MSN); leadership and management (MSN); nursing (PhD, Post-Master's Certificate), including education (PhD), healthcare administration (PhD), interdisciplinary health (PhD), leadership (PhD), nursing education (Post-Master's Certificate), nursing informatics (Post-Master's Certificate), nursing leadership and management (Post-Master's Certificate), public health policy (PhD); nursing practice (DNP); psychiatric mental health (MSN). *Accreditation:* AACN. *Program availability:* Part-time, evening/weekend, online only, 100% online. *Degree requirements:* For doctorate, thesis/dissertation (for some programs), residency (for some programs), field experience (for some programs). *Entrance requirements:* For master's, bachelor's degree or equivalent in related field or RN; minimum GPA of 2.5; official transcripts; goal statement (for some programs); access to computer and Internet; for doctorate, master's degree or higher; RN; three years of related professional or academic experience; goal statement; access to computer and Internet; for Post-Master's Certificate, relevant work experience; access to computer and Internet. Additional exam requirements/recommendations for international students: Required—TOEFL (minimum score 550 paper-based, 79 iBT), IELTS (minimum score 6.5), Michigan English Language Assessment Battery (minimum score 82), or PTE (minimum score 53). Electronic applications accepted.

Walsh University, Graduate Programs, Gary and Linda Byers School of Nursing, North Canton, OH 44720-3396. Offers academic nurse educator (MSN); adult acute care nurse practitioner (MSN); clinical nurse leader (MSN); nursing practice (DNP). *Accreditation:* AACN. *Program availability:* Part-time, evening/weekend, online only, 100% online. *Degree requirements:* For doctorate, scholarly project; residency practicum. *Entrance requirements:* For master's, undergraduate nursing degree, current unencumbered RN license, completion of an undergraduate or graduate statistics course, essay, interview, recommendations; for doctorate, BSN; master's degree; statistics and research courses; essay; interview. Additional exam requirements/recommendations for international students: Required—TOEFL. Electronic applications accepted. *Expenses:* Contact institution. *Faculty research:* Self-efficacy, Newman theory, curriculum development and assessment on family nurse practitioner (FNP) practice, DNP online rubrics.

Washburn University, School of Nursing, Topeka, KS 66621. Offers clinical nurse leader (MSN); nursing (DNP); psychiatric mental health nurse practitioner (Post-Graduate Certificate). *Accreditation:* AACN. *Program availability:* Part-time. *Entrance requirements:* Additional exam requirements/recommendations for international students: Required—TOEFL (minimum score 550 paper-based).

Washington Adventist University, Program in Nursing - Business Leadership, Takoma Park, MD 20912. Offers MSN. *Program availability:* Part-time. *Students:* 5 full-time (1 woman), 3 part-time (all women); includes 4 minority (all Black or African American, non-Hispanic/Latino), 3 international. Average age 44. In 2017, 6 master's awarded. *Entrance requirements:* Additional exam requirements/recommendations for international students: Required—TOEFL (minimum score 550 paper-based), IELTS (minimum score 5). *Application deadline:* Applications are processed on a rolling basis. *Expenses: Tuition:* Part-time $625 per credit. *Financial support:* Applicants required to submit FAFSA. *Unit head:* Dr. Patrick Williams, Associate Provost, 301-891-4092, E-mail: jeedward@wau.edu. *Application contact:* Jessica Ritchie, Program Coordinator, 301-891-4086, Fax: 301-891-4023, E-mail: jritchie@wau.edu.
Website: http://www.wau.edu/index.php?option-com_content&view-article&id-408temid-965

Waynesburg University, Graduate and Professional Studies, Canonsburg, PA 15370. Offers business (MBA), including energy management, finance, health systems, human resources, leadership, market development; counseling (MA), including addictions counseling, clinical mental health; counselor education and supervision (PhD); criminal investigation (MA); education (M Ed), including autism, curriculum and instruction, educational leadership, online teaching; nursing (MSN), including administration, education, informatics; nursing practice (DNP); special education (M Ed); technology (M Ed); MSN/MBA. *Accreditation:* AACN. *Program availability:* Part-time, evening/weekend. *Degree requirements:* For doctorate, thesis/dissertation. *Entrance requirements:* Additional exam requirements/recommendations for international students: Required—TOEFL. Electronic applications accepted.

Weber State University, Dumke College of Health Professions, School of Nursing, Ogden, UT 84408-1001. Offers educator (MSN); executive (MSN); nurse practitioner (MSN). *Program availability:* Part-time, evening/weekend, 100% online. *Faculty:* 11 full-time (all women), 3 part-time/adjunct (all women). *Students:* 88 full-time (70 women), 5 part-time (all women); includes 2 minority (both Hispanic/Latino), 1 international. Average age 38. In 2017, 29 master's awarded. *Entrance requirements:* For master's, bachelor's degree in nursing from ACEN- or CCNE-accredited program. *Application deadline:* For fall admission, 4/1 priority date for domestic students. Application fee: $60 ($90 for international students). Electronic applications accepted. *Expenses:* Tuition, state resident: full-time $7283. Tuition, nonresident: full-time $17,166. *Required fees:* $898. Tuition and fees vary according to program. *Financial support:* In 2017–18, 26 students received support. Scholarships/grants available. Financial award application deadline: 4/1; financial award applicants required to submit FAFSA. *Unit head:* Dr. Melissa Neville, MSN Program Director, 801-626-6204, Fax: 801-626-6397, E-mail: mneville@weber.edu. *Application contact:* Robert Holt, Director of Enrollment, 801-626-7774, Fax: 801-626-6397, E-mail: rholt@weber.edu.
Website: http://www.weber.edu/nursing

Western Governors University, College of Health Professions, Salt Lake City, UT 84107. Offers healthcare management (MBA); leadership and management (MSN); nursing education (MSN); nursing informatics (MSN). *Program availability:* Evening/weekend, online learning. *Degree requirements:* For master's, capstone project. *Entrance requirements:* For master's, transcripts. Additional exam requirements/recommendations for international students: Required—TOEFL (minimum score 450 paper-based; 80 iBT). *Application deadline:* Applications are processed on a rolling basis. Application fee: $65. Electronic applications accepted. Application fee is waived when completed online. *Financial support:* Tuition waivers (partial) available. Financial award applicants required to submit FAFSA. *Unit head:* Dr. Jan Jones-Schenk, Director. *Application contact:* Enrollment Department, 866-225-5948, Fax: 801-274-3306, E-mail: info@wgu.edu.
Website: https://www.wgu.edu/online-nursing-health-degrees.html#

Western University of Health Sciences, College of Graduate Nursing, Master of Science in Nursing Program, Pomona, CA 91766-1854. Offers administrative nurse leader (MSN); clinical nurse leader (MSN); nursing (MSN). *Accreditation:* AACN. *Program availability:* Part-time, blended/hybrid learning. *Faculty:* 15 full-time (13 women), 20 part-time/adjunct (13 women). *Students:* 220 full-time (181 women), 15 part-time (all women); includes 164 minority (5 Black or African American, non-Hispanic/Latino; 1 American Indian or Alaska Native, non-Hispanic/Latino; 67 Asian, non-Hispanic/Latino; 64 Hispanic/Latino; 1 Native Hawaiian or other Pacific Islander, non-Hispanic/Latino; 26 Two or more races, non-Hispanic/Latino), 2 international. Average age 30. 454 applicants, 41% accepted, 129 enrolled. In 2017, 87 master's awarded. *Degree requirements:* For master's, comprehensive exam (for some programs), thesis (for some programs), project. *Entrance requirements:* For master's, personal statement, BSN, minimum GPA of 3.0, 3 letters of recommendation, resume/curriculum vitae, official transcripts of all schools attended. Additional exam requirements/recommendations for international students: Required—TOEFL (minimum score 80 iBT). *Application deadline:* For fall admission, 10/1 for domestic and international students. Application fee: $60. Electronic applications accepted. Application fee is waived when completed online. *Expenses:* $50,525 first year, $1,075 per unit. *Financial support:* In 2017–18, 25 students received support. Fellowships, research assistantships, teaching assistantships, and scholarships/grants available. Support available to part-time students. Financial award application deadline: 3/2; financial award applicants required to submit FAFSA. *Unit head:* Dr. Mary Lopez, Dean, 909-706-3860, Fax: 909-469-5521, E-mail: mlopez@westernu.edu. *Application contact:* Kathryn Ford, Director of Admissions/International Student Advisor, 909-469-5335, Fax: 909-469-5570, E-mail: admissions@westernu.edu.

West Virginia Wesleyan College, Department of Nursing, Buckhannon, WV 26201. Offers family nurse practitioner (MS, Post Master's Certificate); nurse administrator (MS); nurse educator (MS); nurse-midwifery (MS); nursing administration (Post Master's Certificate); nursing education (Post Master's Certificate); psychiatric mental health nurse practitioner (MS); MSN/MBA. *Accreditation:* ACEN.

Wilmington University, College of Health Professions, New Castle, DE 19720-6491. Offers adult nurse practitioner (MSN); family nurse practitioner (MSN); gerontology nurse practitioner (MSN); nursing (MSN); nursing leadership (MSN); nursing practice (DNP). *Accreditation:* AACN. *Program availability:* Part-time. *Faculty:* 10 full-time (9 women), 59 part-time/adjunct (50 women). *Students:* 164 full-time (154 women), 662 part-time (604 women); includes 178 minority (129 Black or African American, non-Hispanic/Latino; 5 American Indian or Alaska Native, non-Hispanic/Latino; 23 Asian, non-Hispanic/Latino; 7 Hispanic/Latino; 3 Native Hawaiian or other Pacific Islander, non-Hispanic/Latino; 11 Two or more races, non-Hispanic/Latino), 6 international. Average age 39. 770 applicants, 63% accepted, 361 enrolled. In 2017, 259 master's, 22 doctorates awarded. *Degree requirements:* For master's, thesis. *Entrance requirements:* For master's, BSN, RN license, interview, 3 letters of recommendation. Additional exam requirements/recommendations for international students: Required—TOEFL (minimum score 500 paper-based). *Application deadline:* For fall admission, 4/1 for domestic

students; for spring admission, 9/1 for domestic students. Applications are processed on a rolling basis. Application fee: $35. Electronic applications accepted. *Expenses: Tuition:* Part-time $466 per credit. *Required fees:* $25 per semester. Tuition and fees vary according to degree level and campus/location. *Financial support:* Fellowships with tuition reimbursements and traineeships available. Financial award applicants required to submit FAFSA. *Faculty research:* Outcomes assessment, student writing ability. *Unit head:* Denise Z. Westbrook, Dean, 302-356-6915. *Application contact:* Laura Morris, Director of Admissions, 877-967-5464, E-mail: infocenter@wilmu.edu.
Website: http://www.wilmu.edu/health/

Wilson College, Graduate Programs, Chambersburg, PA 17201-1285. Offers accounting (M Acc); choreography and visual art (MFA); education (M Ed); educational technology (MET); healthcare administration (MHA); humanities (MA), including art and culture, critical/cultural theory, English language and literature, women's studies; management (MSM); nursing (MSN), including nursing education, nursing leadership and management; special education (MSE). *Program availability:* Evening/weekend. *Degree requirements:* For master's, project. *Entrance requirements:* For master's, PRAXIS, minimum undergraduate cumulative GPA of 3.0, 2 letters of recommendation, current certification for eligibility to teach in grades K-12, resume, personal interview. Electronic applications accepted.

Winona State University, College of Nursing and Health Sciences, Winona, MN 55987. Offers adult-gerontology acute care nurse practitioner (MS, DNP, Post Master's Certificate); adult-gerontology clinical nurse specialist (MS, DNP, Post Master's Certificate); adult-gerontology primary care nurse practitioner (MS, DNP, Post Master's Certificate); family nurse practitioner (MS, DNP, Post Master's Certificate); nurse educator (MS); nursing and organizational leadership (MS, DNP, Post Master's Certificate); practice and leadership innovations (DNP, Post Master's Certificate). *Accreditation:* AACN. *Program availability:* Part-time, online learning. *Degree requirements:* For master's, thesis; for doctorate, capstone. *Entrance requirements:* For master's, GRE (if GPA less than 3.0). Additional exam requirements/recommendations for international students: Required—TOEFL (minimum score 550 paper-based).

Wright State University, Graduate School, College of Nursing and Health, Program in Nursing, Dayton, OH 45435. Offers administration of nursing and health care systems (MS); adult gerontology clinical nurse specialist (MS); adult-gerontology acute care nurse practitioner (MS); family nurse practitioner (MS); neonatal nurse practitioner (MS); pediatric nurse practitioner-acute care (MS); pediatric nurse practitioner-primary care (MS); psychiatric mental health nurse practitioner (MS); school nurse (MS). *Accreditation:* AACN. *Program availability:* Part-time, evening/weekend. *Degree requirements:* For master's, thesis or alternative. *Entrance requirements:* For master's, GRE General Test, BSN from ACEN-accredited college, Ohio RN license. Additional exam requirements/recommendations for international students: Required—TOEFL. *Faculty research:* Clinical nursing and health, teaching, caring, pain administration, informatics and technology.

Nursing Education

Abilene Christian University, College of Graduate and Professional Studies, Program in Nursing Practice, Abilene, TX 79699. Offers advanced practice nurse (DNP); executive nursing leadership (DNP); nursing education (DNP). *Program availability:* Part-time, online only, blended/hybrid learning. *Faculty:* 3 full-time (2 women), 3 part-time/adjunct (2 women). *Students:* 45 full-time (38 women), 3 part-time (all women); includes 17 minority (14 Black or African American, non-Hispanic/Latino; 3 Asian, non-Hispanic/Latino). 73 applicants, 59% accepted, 28 enrolled. *Entrance requirements:* For doctorate, master's degree in nursing, official transcripts, minimum graduate nursing cumulative GPA of 3.0, two recommendation letters, 500-word statement of purpose, professional curriculum vitae or resume. Additional exam requirements/recommendations for international students: Required—TOEFL (minimum score 80 iBT), IELTS (minimum score 6). *Application deadline:* For fall admission, 8/15 for domestic students; for winter admission, 10/1 for domestic students; for spring admission, 12/15 for domestic students; for summer admission, 4/1 for domestic students. Applications are processed on a rolling basis. Application fee: $50. Electronic applications accepted. *Expenses:* $1,000 per hour. *Financial support:* Application deadline: 4/1; applicants required to submit FAFSA. *Unit head:* Dr. Tonya Sawyer-McGee, Program Director, 214-305-9500, E-mail: tcs15b@acu.edu. *Application contact:* Graduate Advisor, 855-219-7300, E-mail: gradonline@acu.edu.
Website: http://www.acu.edu/online/academics/doctor-of-nursing-practice.html

Adelphi University, College of Nursing and Public Health, Program in Nursing Education, Garden City, NY 11530-0701. Offers MS, Certificate. *Students:* 12 part-time (10 women); includes 9 minority (5 Black or African American, non-Hispanic/Latino; 4 Asian, non-Hispanic/Latino). Average age 36. 24 applicants, 33% accepted, 3 enrolled. *Entrance requirements:* Additional exam requirements/recommendations for international students: Required—TOEFL (minimum score 550 paper-based; 80 iBT), IELTS (minimum score 6.5). Application fee: $50. *Expenses:* Contact institution. *Financial support:* Research assistantships, teaching assistantships, career-related internships or fieldwork, institutionally sponsored loans, scholarships/grants, traineeships, and unspecified assistantships available. Support available to part-time students. *Unit head:* Joan Valas, Director, 516-877-4571, E-mail: valas@adelphi.edu. *Application contact:* E-mail: graduateadmissions@adelphi.edu.

Albany State University, Darton College of Health Professions, Albany, GA 31705-2717. Offers nursing (MSN), including family nurse practitioner, nurse educator. *Accreditation:* ACEN. *Program availability:* Part-time, evening/weekend, online learning. *Degree requirements:* For master's, comprehensive exam, thesis. *Entrance requirements:* For master's, GRE or MAT, official transcript, letters of recommendation, pre-medical/certificate of immunizations. Electronic applications accepted.

Allen College, Graduate Programs, Waterloo, IA 50703. Offers adult-gerontology acute care nurse practitioner (MSN); community/public health nursing (MSN); education (MSN); family nurse practitioner (MSN); health sciences (Ed D); leadership in health care delivery (MSN); leadership in health care informatics (MSN); nursing (DNP); occupational therapy (MS); psychiatric mental health nurse practitioner (MSN). MSN in leadership in healthcare informatics offered in partnership with University of Minnesota. *Accreditation:* AACN; ACEN. *Program availability:* Part-time, 100% online, blended/hybrid learning. *Faculty:* 24 full-time (all women), 8 part-time/adjunct (7 women). *Students:* 106 full-time (91 women), 187 part-time (164 women); includes 22 minority (12 Black or African American, non-Hispanic/Latino; 1 American Indian or Alaska Native, non-Hispanic/Latino; 2 Asian, non-Hispanic/Latino; 3 Hispanic/Latino; 4 Two or more races, non-Hispanic/Latino), 2 international. Average age 33. 352 applicants, 56% accepted, 131 enrolled. In 2017, 73 master's, 2 doctorates awarded. *Entrance requirements:* For master's, minimum GPA of 3.0 in the last 60 hours of undergraduate coursework; for doctorate, minimum GPA of 3.25 in graduate coursework. *Application deadline:* For fall admission, 2/1 priority date for domestic students; for spring admission, 9/1 priority date for domestic students. Applications are processed on a rolling basis. Application fee: $50. Electronic applications accepted. *Expenses:* $17,860 per year. *Financial support:* In 2017–18, 97 students received support. Federal Work-Study, institutionally sponsored loans, scholarships/grants, and traineeships available. Support available to part-time students. Financial award application deadline: 8/1; financial award applicants required to submit FAFSA. *Faculty research:* Poverty. *Unit head:* Dr. Nancy Kramer, Vice Chancellor for Academic Affairs, 319-226-2040, Fax: 319-226-2070, E-mail: nancy.kramer@allencollege.edu. *Application contact:* Molly Quinn, Director of Admissions, 319-226-2001, Fax: 319-226-2010, E-mail: molly.quinn@allencollege.edu.
Website: http://www.allencollege.edu/

Alvernia University, School of Graduate Studies, Department of Nursing, Reading, PA 19607-1799. Offers adult gerontology nurse practitioner (DNP); family nurse practitioner (DNP); nursing education (MSN); nursing leadership (Graduate Certificate); nursing leadership and healthcare administration (MSN).

American International College, School of Health Sciences, Springfield, MA 01109-3189. Offers exercise science (MS); family nurse practitioner (MSN, Post-Master's Certificate); nursing administrator (MSN); nursing educator (MSN); occupational therapy (MSOT, OTD); physical therapy (DPT). *Program availability:* Part-time, 100% online. *Faculty:* 14 full-time (13 women), 10 part-time/adjunct (all women). *Students:* 286 full-time (220 women), 11 part-time (9 women); includes 75 minority (30 Black or African American, non-Hispanic/Latino; 21 Asian, non-Hispanic/Latino; 19 Hispanic/Latino; 5 Two or more races, non-Hispanic/Latino), 2 international. Average age 27. 652 applicants, 49% accepted, 109 enrolled. In 2017, 48 master's, 28 doctorates, 2 other advanced degrees awarded. *Degree requirements:* For master's, practicum; for doctorate, thesis/dissertation, practicum. *Entrance requirements:* For master's, 3 letters of recommendation, personal goal statement; minimum GPA of 3.2, interview, BS or BA, and 2 clinical PT observations (for DPT); minimum GPA of 3.0, MSOT, OT licensen, and 2 clinical OT observations (for OTD); for doctorate, personal goal statement, 2 letters of recommendation; minimum GPA of 3.0, BS or BA, 2 clinical OT observations (for MSOT); RN license and minimum GPA of 3.0 (for MSN). Additional exam requirements/recommendations for international students: Required—TOEFL (minimum score 577 paper-based; 91 iBT). *Application deadline:* For fall admission, 12/1 priority date for domestic and international students; for spring admission, 11/15 priority date for domestic and international students. Application fee: $50. Electronic applications accepted. *Expenses:* Contact institution. *Faculty research:* Teaching simulation, ergonomics, orthopedics, use of social media in health care. *Unit head:* Dr. Cesarina Thompson, Dean, 413-205-3056, Fax: 413-654-1430, E-mail: cesarina.thompson@aic.edu. *Application contact:* Kerry Barnes, Director of Graduate Admissions, 413-205-3703, Fax: 413-205-3051, E-mail: kerry.barnes@aic.edu.
Website: http://www.aic.edu/academics/hs

Anderson University, College of Health Professions, Anderson, SC 29621-4035. Offers advanced practice (DNP); executive leadership (MSN, DNP); family nurse practitioner (MSN, DNP); nurse educator (MSN); psychiatric mental health nurse practitioner (MSN, DNP). *Program availability:* Online learning. *Expenses: Tuition:* Full-time $24,290; part-time $650 per credit hour. Full-time tuition and fees vary according to degree level and program. *Unit head:* Dr. Donald M. Peace, Dean, 864-231-5513, E-mail: dpeace@andersonuniversity.edu. *Application contact:* Chris Woodlief, Associate Director of Adult and Graduate Programs, 864-231-5531, E-mail: cwoodlief@andersonuniversity.edu.
Website: http://www.andersonuniversity.edu/health-professions

Angelo State University, College of Graduate Studies and Research, Archer College of Health and Human Services, Department of Nursing, San Angelo, TX 76909. Offers family nurse practitioner (MSN); nurse educator (MSN). *Accreditation:* AACN; ACEN. *Program availability:* Part-time, evening/weekend, online learning. *Students:* 35 full-time (28 women), 55 part-time (49 women); includes 26 minority (4 Black or African American, non-Hispanic/Latino; 2 Asian, non-Hispanic/Latino; 18 Hispanic/Latino; 2 Two or more races, non-Hispanic/Latino). Average age 34. *Degree requirements:* For master's, comprehensive exam. *Entrance requirements:* For master's, essay, three letters of recommendation. Additional exam requirements/recommendations for international students: Required—TOEFL or IELTS. *Application deadline:* For fall admission, 4/1 priority date for domestic students, 6/10 for international students; for spring admission, 9/1 priority date for domestic students, 11/1 for international students. Applications are processed on a rolling basis. Application fee: $40 ($50 for international students). Electronic applications accepted. *Expenses:* Tuition, state resident: full-time $3856. Tuition, nonresident: full-time $11,324. *Required fees:* $2650. *Financial support:* Research assistantships, career-related internships or fieldwork, Federal Work-Study, and scholarships/grants available. Support available to part-time students. Financial award application deadline: 3/1. *Unit head:* Dr. Wrennah L. Gabbert, Chair, 325-942-2224, Fax: 325-942-2236, E-mail: wrennah.gabbert@angelo.edu. *Application contact:* Dr. Molly J. Walker, Graduate Advisor, 325-486-6872, Fax: 325-942-2236, E-mail: molly.walker@angelo.edu.
Website: http://www.angelo.edu/dept/nursing/

Arizona State University at the Tempe campus, College of Nursing and Health Innovation, Phoenix, AZ 85004. Offers advanced nursing practice (DNP); clinical research management (MS); community and public health practice (Graduate Certificate); family mental health nurse practitioner (Graduate Certificate); family nurse practitioner (Graduate Certificate); geriatric nursing (Graduate Certificate); healthcare innovation (MHI); nurse education in academic and practice settings (Graduate Certificate); nurse educator (MS); nursing and healthcare innovation (PhD). *Accreditation:* AACN. *Program availability:* Online learning. *Degree requirements:* For master's, comprehensive exam (for some programs), thesis (for some programs), interactive Program of Study (iPOS) submitted before completing 50 percent of required credit hours; for doctorate, comprehensive exam, thesis/dissertation, interactive Program of Study (iPOS) submitted before completing 50 percent of required credit hours. *Entrance requirements:* For master's and doctorate, GRE, minimum GPA of 3.0 or equivalent in last 2 years of work leading to bachelor's degree. Additional exam requirements/recommendations for international students: Required—TOEFL, IELTS, or PTE. Electronic applications accepted. *Expenses:* Contact institution.

Aspen University, Program in Nursing, Denver, CO 80246-1930. Offers forensic nursing (MSN); informatics (MSN); nursing (MSN); nursing administration and management (MSN); nursing education (MSN); public health (MSN).

Auburn University, Graduate School, School of Nursing, Auburn University, AL 36849. Offers nursing educator (MSN); primary care practitioner (MSN). *Accreditation:* AACN. *Faculty:* 26 full-time (24 women). *Students:* 9 full-time (all women), 116 part-time (105 women); includes 25 minority (18 Black or African American, non-Hispanic/Latino; 1 American Indian or Alaska Native, non-Hispanic/Latino; 3 Hispanic/Latino; 3 Two or more races, non-Hispanic/Latino). Average age 33. 67 applicants, 81% accepted, 43 enrolled. In 2017, 55 master's awarded. *Expenses:* Tuition, state resident: full-time $10,974; part-time $519 per credit hour. Tuition, nonresident: full-time $29,658; part-time $1557 per credit hour. *Required fees:* $816 per semester. Tuition and fees vary according to degree level and program. *Unit head:* Dr. Gregg Newschwander, Dean, 334-844-3658, E-mail: gen0002@auburn.edu. *Application contact:* Dr. George Flowers, Dean of the Graduate School, 334-844-4700, E-mail: gradadm@auburn.edu.
Website: https://cws.auburn.edu/nursing/

Auburn University at Montgomery, College of Nursing and Health Sciences, Montgomery, AL 36124-4023. Offers family nurse practitioner (MSN); nurse educator for interprofessional practice (MSN). Programs offered jointly with Auburn University. *Accreditation:* AACN. *Students:* 23 full-time (14 women), 19 part-time (9 women); includes 10 minority (9 Black or African American, non-Hispanic/Latino; 1 Hispanic/Latino), 2 international. *Entrance requirements:* Additional exam requirements/recommendations for international students: Recommended—TOEFL (minimum score 500 paper-based; 61 iBT), IELTS (minimum score 5.5), TSE (minimum score 44). *Application deadline:* For fall admission, 7/1 for domestic students; for spring admission, 10/1 for domestic students; for summer admission, 3/1 for domestic students. Applications are processed on a rolling basis. Application fee: $25 ($0 for international students). Electronic applications accepted. *Expenses:* Tuition, state resident: full-time $6930; part-time $385 per credit hour. Tuition, nonresident: full-time $15,588; part-time $866 per credit hour. *Required fees:* $640. *Unit head:* Dr. Jean Leuner, Dean, 334-244-3658, E-mail: jleuner@aum.edu. *Application contact:* Dr. Barbara Wilder, Graduate Program Director, 334-844-6766, E-mail: wildebf@auburn.edu.
Website: http://conhs.aum.edu/

Austin Peay State University, College of Graduate Studies, College of Behavioral and Health Sciences, School of Nursing, Clarksville, TN 37044. Offers family nurse practitioner (MSN); nursing administration (MSN); nursing education (MSN); nursing informatics (MSN). *Program availability:* Part-time, online learning. *Faculty:* 8 full-time (all women), 8 part-time/adjunct (all women). *Students:* 12 full-time (11 women), 139 part-time (128 women); includes 19 minority (11 Black or African American, non-Hispanic/Latino; 1 Asian, non-Hispanic/Latino; 5 Hispanic/Latino; 2 Two or more races, non-Hispanic/Latino). Average age 35. 36 applicants, 86% accepted, 20 enrolled. In 2017, 67 master's awarded. *Degree requirements:* For master's, comprehensive exam. *Entrance requirements:* For master's, minimum GPA of 3.0, RN license eligibility, 3 letters of recommendation. Additional exam requirements/recommendations for international students: Required—TOEFL (minimum score 500 paper-based). *Application deadline:* For fall admission, 8/8 priority date for domestic students. Applications are processed on a rolling basis. Application fee: $45 ($55 for international students). Electronic applications accepted. *Expenses:* Tuition, state resident: full-time $7686; part-time $427 per credit hour. Tuition, nonresident: full-time $20,268; part-time $1126 per credit hour. *Required fees:* $1529; $76.45 per credit hour. *Financial support:* Research assistantships with full tuition reimbursements, career-related internships or fieldwork, Federal Work-Study, institutionally sponsored loans, scholarships/grants, and unspecified assistantships available. Support available to part-time students. Financial award application deadline: 4/1; financial award applicants required to submit FAFSA. *Unit head:* Dr. Rebecca Corvey, Director of Nursing, 931-221-7710, Fax: 931-221-7595, E-mail: corveyr@apsu.edu. *Application contact:* Megan Mitchell, Coordinator of Graduate Admissions, 931-221-6189, Fax: 931-221-7641, E-mail: mitchellm@apsu.edu.
Website: http://www.apsu.edu/nursing

Azusa Pacific University, School of Nursing, Azusa, CA 91702-7000. Offers adult clinical nurse specialist (MSN); adult-gerontology nurse practitioner (MSN); family nurse practitioner (MSN); healthcare administration and leadership (MSN); nursing (MSN, DNP, PhD); nursing education (MSN); parent-child clinical nurse specialist (MSN); psychiatric mental health nurse practitioner (MSN). *Accreditation:* AACN. *Program availability:* Part-time, evening/weekend. *Degree requirements:* For master's, thesis optional. *Entrance requirements:* For master's, BSN.

Ball State University, Graduate School, College of Health, School of Nursing, Muncie, IN 47304. Offers adult/gerontology nurse practitioner (Post Master's Certificate); evidence-based clinical practice (Postbaccalaureate Certificate); family nurse practitioner (Post Master's Certificate); nurse educator (Post Master's Certificate); nursing (MS), including family nurse practitioner, nurse administrator, nurse educator; nursing education (Postbaccalaureate Certificate); nursing practice (DNP). *Accreditation:* AACN. *Program availability:* Part-time-only, online only, 100% online. *Faculty:* 10 full-time (all women), 9 part-time/adjunct (all women). *Students:* 9 full-time (8 women), 325 part-time (299 women); includes 26 minority (13 Black or African American, non-Hispanic/Latino; 3 Asian, non-Hispanic/Latino; 7 Hispanic/Latino; 3 Two or more races, non-Hispanic/Latino). Average age 33. 190 applicants, 37% accepted, 66 enrolled. In 2017, 88 master's, 2 doctorates awarded. *Entrance requirements:* For master's, bachelor's degree in nursing, minimum GPA of 3.0, minimum C grade in at least 2 quarter or semester hours in an undergraduate research course, unencumbered license as a registered nurse in state of practice; for doctorate, advanced practice nurse (nurse practitioner, clinical nurse specialist, nurse midwife); master's degree in nursing from accredited program with minimum GPA of 3.2; graduate-level statistics, nursing research, and health assessment courses; unencumbered license as registered nurse in state of practice. Additional exam requirements/recommendations for international students: Required—TOEFL (minimum score 550 paper-based; 79 iBT), IELTS (minimum score 6.5). *Application deadline:* For fall admission, 2/9 for domestic students; for spring admission, 8/9 for domestic students. Applications are processed on a rolling basis. Application fee: $60. Electronic applications accepted. *Expenses:* Contact institution. *Financial support:* Application deadline: 3/1; applicants required to submit FAFSA. *Unit head:* Dr. Linda Siktberg, Director, 765-285-8718, Fax: 765-285-2169, E-mail: lsiktberg@bsu.edu. *Application contact:* Shantelle Estes, Graduate Advisor, 765-285-9130, Fax: 765-285-2169, E-mail: smestes@bsu.edu.
Website: http://www.bsu.edu/nursing/

Barry University, School of Adult and Continuing Education, Division of Nursing, Program in Nursing Education, Miami Shores, FL 33161-6695. Offers MSN, Certificate. *Accreditation:* AACN. *Program availability:* Part-time, evening/weekend. *Degree requirements:* For master's, research project or thesis. *Entrance requirements:* For master's, GRE General Test or MAT, BSN, minimum GPA of 3.0, course work in statistics. Electronic applications accepted. *Faculty research:* HIV/AIDS, gerontology.

Bellarmine University, College of Health Professions, Donna and Allan Lansing School of Nursing and Clinical Sciences, Louisville, KY 40205. Offers family nurse practitioner (MSN); health science (MHS); nursing administration (MSN); nursing education (MSN); nursing practice (DNP). *Accreditation:* AACN; APTA. *Program availability:* Part-time, evening/weekend. *Faculty:* 20 full-time (17 women), 7 part-time/adjunct (6 women). *Students:* 10 full-time (6 women), 101 part-time (89 women); includes 10 minority (5 Black or African American, non-Hispanic/Latino; 2 Asian, non-Hispanic/Latino; 1 Hispanic/Latino; 2 Two or more races, non-Hispanic/Latino), 1 international. Average age 34. In 2017, 42 master's, 5 doctorates awarded. *Degree requirements:* For master's, comprehensive exam, thesis (for some programs); for doctorate, comprehensive exam, thesis/dissertation. *Entrance requirements:* For master's, GRE General Test, minimum GPA of 3.0, interview, resume; BSN from CCNE- or ACEN-accredited program, professional references, goal statement, and RN license (for MSN); bachelor's degree with exposure to health issues and grade of C or better in math/science courses (for MHS); for doctorate, GRE General Test, MSN from CCNE- or ACEN-accredited program; minimum GPA of 3.5 in graduate coursework; professional references; goal statement; current curriculum vitae or resume; RN license; verification of post-baccalaureate clinical and practice hours. Additional exam requirements/recommendations for international students: Required—TOEFL (minimum iBT score of 83, 26 on speaking test), IELTS (minimum score 7, speaking band score of 8), or language training at an approved center. *Application deadline:* Applications are processed on a rolling basis. Application fee: $40. Electronic applications accepted. *Expenses:* Contact institution. *Financial support:* Career-related internships or fieldwork and scholarships/grants available. Financial award applicants required to submit FAFSA. *Faculty research:* Nursing: pain, empathy, leadership styles, control; physical therapy: service-learning; exercise in chronic and pre-operative conditions, athletes; women's health; aging. *Unit head:* Dr. Nancy York, Dean, 502-272-8639, E-mail: nyork@bellarmine.edu. *Application contact:* Julie Armstrong-Binnix, Health Science Recruiter, 800-274-4723 Ext. 8364, E-mail: julieab@bellarmine.edu.
Website: http://www.bellarmine.edu/lansing

Bellin College, School of Nursing, Green Bay, WI 54305. Offers family nurse practitioner (MSN); nurse educator (MSN). *Accreditation:* AACN. *Faculty:* 10 part-time/adjunct (all women). *Students:* 13 full-time (12 women), 29 part-time (27 women). *Expenses: Tuition:* Part-time $728 per credit. *Unit head:* Dr. Amber B. Carriveau, Graduate Program Director, 920-433-6694, Fax: 920-433-1921, E-mail: amber.carriveau@bellincollege.edu.

Bethel University, Graduate School, St. Paul, MN 55112-6999. Offers business administration (MBA); classroom management (Certificate); counseling (MA); K-12 education (MA); leadership (Ed D); leadership foundations (Certificate); nurse educator (MS, Certificate); nurse-midwifery (MS); physician assistant (MS); special education (MA); strategic leadership (MA); teaching (MA); teaching and learning (Certificate). *Program availability:* Part-time, evening/weekend, 100% online, blended/hybrid learning. *Faculty:* 22 full-time (16 women), 70 part-time/adjunct (44 women). *Students:* 611 full-time (431 women), 393 part-time (249 women); includes 176 minority (82 Black or African American, non-Hispanic/Latino; 4 American Indian or Alaska Native, non-Hispanic/Latino; 31 Asian, non-Hispanic/Latino; 39 Hispanic/Latino; 2 Native Hawaiian or other Pacific Islander, non-Hispanic/Latino; 18 Two or more races, non-Hispanic/Latino), 9 international. Average age 36. 668 applicants, 42% accepted, 223 enrolled. In 2017, 287 master's, 30 doctorates, 172 other advanced degrees awarded. *Degree requirements:* For master's, comprehensive exam (for some programs), thesis (for some programs); for doctorate, comprehensive exam, thesis/dissertation. *Entrance requirements:* Additional exam requirements/recommendations for international students: Required—TOEFL (minimum score 550 paper-based, 80 iBT) or IELTS. *Application deadline:* Applications are processed on a rolling basis. Application fee: $0. Electronic applications accepted. *Expenses:* Contact institution. *Financial support:* Teaching assistantships, career-related internships or fieldwork, and scholarships/grants available. Support available to part-time students. Financial award applicants required to submit FAFSA. *Unit head:* Dr. Randy Bergen, Associate Provost, 651-635-8000, Fax: 651-635-8004, E-mail: r-bergen@bethel.edu. *Application contact:* Director of Admissions, 651-635-8000, Fax: 651-635-8004, E-mail: gs@bethel.edu.
Website: https://www.bethel.edu/graduate/

Blessing-Rieman College of Nursing & Health Sciences, Master of Science in Nursing Program, Quincy, IL 62305-7005. Offers nursing education (MSN); nursing leadership (MSN). *Program availability:* Part-time-only, evening/weekend, online only, 100% online. *Faculty:* 7 full-time (all women). *Students:* 16 part-time (14 women). Average age 35. *Degree requirements:* For master's, thesis or project. *Entrance requirements:* Additional exam requirements/recommendations for international students: Required—TOEFL (minimum score 500 paper-based; 80 iBT). *Application deadline:* Applications are processed on a rolling basis. Electronic applications accepted. *Expenses: Tuition:* Part-time $500 per credit hour. *Required fees:* $300 per unit. $150 per semester. One-time fee: $20 part-time. *Financial support:* Scholarships/grants available. Financial award application deadline: 4/30; financial award applicants required to submit FAFSA. *Unit head:* Dr. Karen Mayville, Administrative Coordinator, Assessment, 217-228-5520 Ext. 6968, Fax: 217-223-1781, E-mail: kmayville@brcn.edu. *Application contact:* Heather Mutter, Admissions Counselor, 217-228-5520 Ext. 6964, Fax: 217-223-4661, E-mail: hmutter@brcn.edu.
Website: https://www.brcn.edu/programs/msn-online

Bowie State University, Graduate Programs, Department of Nursing, Bowie, MD 20715-9465. Offers administration of nursing services (MS); family nurse practitioner (MS); nursing education (MS). *Accreditation:* ACEN. *Program availability:* Part-time. *Faculty:* 7 full-time (4 women), 15 part-time/adjunct (10 women). *Students:* 29 full-time (25 women), 30 part-time (24 women); includes 42 minority (35 Black or African American, non-Hispanic/Latino; 1 Asian, non-Hispanic/Latino; 6 Hispanic/Latino), 8 international. Average age 42. 9 applicants, 89% accepted, 7 enrolled. In 2017, 30 master's awarded. *Degree requirements:* For master's, comprehensive exam, thesis, research paper. *Entrance requirements:* For master's, minimum GPA of 2.5. *Application deadline:* For fall admission, 5/15 for domestic students. Applications are processed on a rolling basis. Application fee: $40. Electronic applications accepted. *Financial support:* Institutionally sponsored loans and traineeships available. Financial award application deadline: 4/1. *Faculty research:* Minority health, women's health, gerontology, leadership management. *Unit head:* Dr. Bonita Jenkins, Acting Chairperson, 301-860-3210, E-mail: mccaskill@bowiestate.edu. *Application contact:* Angela Issac, Information Contact, 301-860-4000.

Bradley University, The Graduate School, College of Education and Health Sciences, Department of Nursing, Peoria, IL 61625-0002. Offers family nurse practitioner (MSN, DNP, Certificate); leadership (DNP); nursing administration (MSN); nursing education (MSN, Certificate). *Accreditation:* AACN; ACEN. *Program availability:* Part-time, evening/weekend. *Degree requirements:* For master's, comprehensive exam, thesis optional. *Entrance requirements:* For master's, GRE General Test or MAT, interview, Illinois RN license, advanced cardiac life support certification, pediatric advanced life support certification, 3 letters of recommendation. Additional exam requirements/recommendations for international students: Required—TOEFL (minimum score 550 paper-based; 79 iBT), IELTS (minimum score 6.5). Electronic applications accepted.

Brenau University, Sydney O. Smith Graduate School, College of Health Sciences, Gainesville, GA 30501. Offers family nurse practitioner (MSN); nurse educator (MSN); nursing management (MSN); occupational therapy (MS); psychology (MS). *Accreditation:* AOTA. *Program availability:* Part-time, evening/weekend. *Degree* *requirements:* For master's, comprehensive exam (for some programs), thesis (for some programs), clinical practicum hours. *Entrance requirements:* For master's, GRE General Test or MAT (for some programs), interview, writing sample, references (for some programs). Additional exam requirements/recommendations for international students: Required—TOEFL (minimum score 500 paper-based; 61 iBT); Recommended—IELTS (minimum score 5). Electronic applications accepted. *Expenses:* Contact institution.

California Baptist University, Program in Nursing, Riverside, CA 92504-3206. Offers clinical nurse specialist (MSN); family nurse practitioner (MSN); healthcare systems management (MSN); teaching-learning (MSN). *Accreditation:* AACN. *Program availability:* Part-time. *Faculty:* 19 full-time (18 women), 12 part-time/adjunct (11 women). *Students:* 78 full-time (59 women), 130 part-time (106 women); includes 114 minority (25 Black or African American, non-Hispanic/Latino; 3 American Indian or Alaska Native, non-Hispanic/Latino; 34 Asian, non-Hispanic/Latino; 47 Hispanic/Latino; 2 Native Hawaiian or other Pacific Islander, non-Hispanic/Latino; 3 Two or more races, non-Hispanic/Latino), 2 international. Average age 32. 25 applicants, 84% accepted, 14 enrolled. In 2017, 49 master's awarded. *Degree requirements:* For master's, comprehensive exam or directed project thesis; capstone practicum. *Entrance requirements:* For master's, GRE or California Critical Thinking Skills Test; Test of Essential Academic Skills (TEAS), minimum undergraduate GPA of 3.0; completion of prerequisite courses with minimum grade of C; CPR certification; background check clearance; health clearance; drug testing; proof of health insurance; proof of motor vehicle insurance; three letters of recommendation; 1000-word essay; interview. Additional exam requirements/recommendations for international students: Required—TOEFL (minimum score 80 iBT). *Application deadline:* For fall admission, 8/1 priority date for domestic students, 7/1 for international students; for spring admission, 12/1 priority date for domestic students, 11/1 for international students. Applications are processed on a rolling basis. Application fee: $45. Electronic applications accepted. *Expenses:* Contact institution. *Financial support:* In 2017–18, 38 students received support. Federal Work-Study and scholarships/grants available. Financial award applicants required to submit CSS PROFILE or FAFSA. *Faculty research:* Qualitative research using Parse methodology, gerontology, disaster preparedness, medical-surgical nursing, maternal-child nursing. *Unit head:* Dr. Geneva Oaks, Dean, School of Nursing, 951-343-4702, E-mail: goaks@calbaptist.edu. *Application contact:* Tamakia King, Graduate Admissions Counselor, 951-552-8138, Fax: 951-343-5095, E-mail: tking@calbaptist.edu.
Website: http://www.calbaptist.edu/explore-cbu/schools-colleges/school-nursing/master-science-nursing/

California State University, Fullerton, Graduate Studies, College of Health and Human Development, School of Nursing, Fullerton, CA 92831-3599. Offers leadership (MS); nurse anesthesia (MS); nurse educator (MS); nursing (DNP); school nursing (MS); women's health care (MS). *Accreditation:* AACN. *Program availability:* Part-time. *Faculty:* 27 full-time (23 women), 11 part-time/adjunct (all women). *Students:* 136 full-time (107 women), 116 part-time (96 women); includes 142 minority (9 Black or African American, non-Hispanic/Latino; 81 Asian, non-Hispanic/Latino; 37 Hispanic/Latino; 1 Native Hawaiian or other Pacific Islander, non-Hispanic/Latino; 14 Two or more races, non-Hispanic/Latino), 2 international. Average age 36. 235 applicants, 59% accepted, 117 enrolled. Application fee: $55. *Financial support:* Career-related internships or fieldwork, Federal Work-Study, institutionally sponsored loans, scholarships/grants, and traineeships available. Support available to part-time students. Financial award application deadline: 3/1; financial award applicants required to submit FAFSA. *Unit head:* Dr. Cindy Greenberg, Chair, 657-278-3336. *Application contact:* Admissions/Applications, 657-278-2371.
Website: http://nursing.fullerton.edu/

California State University, San Marcos, College of Education, Health and Human Services, School of Nursing, San Marcos, CA 92096-0001. Offers advanced practice nursing (MSN), including clinical nurse specialist, family nurse practitioner, psychiatric mental health nurse practitioner; clinical nurse leader (MSN); nursing education (MSN). *Expenses:* Tuition, state resident: full-time $7176. Tuition, nonresident: full-time $9504. *Unit head:* Lorna Kendrick, Director, 760-750-7580, E-mail: lkendrick@csusm.edu.
Website: http://www.csusm.edu/nursing/

California State University, Stanislaus, College of Science, Master's in Nursing Program, Turlock, CA 95382. Offers gerontological nursing (MS); nursing education (MS). *Accreditation:* AACN. *Program availability:* Part-time. *Degree requirements:* For master's, comprehensive exam, thesis or alternative. *Entrance requirements:* For master's, GRE or MAT, minimum GPA of 3.0, 3 letters of reference, RN. Additional exam requirements/recommendations for international students: Required—TOEFL (minimum score 550 paper-based). Electronic applications accepted.

California University of Pennsylvania, School of Graduate Studies and Research, Eberly College of Science and Technology, Department of Nursing, California, PA 15419-1394. Offers nursing administration and leadership (MSN); nursing education (MSN).

Capella University, School of Public Service Leadership, Doctoral Programs in Nursing, Minneapolis, MN 55402. Offers nursing education (PhD); nursing practice (DNP).

Capella University, School of Public Service Leadership, Master's Programs in Nursing, Minneapolis, MN 55402. Offers diabetes nursing (MSN); general nursing (MSN); gerontology nursing (MSN); health information management (MS); nurse educator (MSN); nursing leadership and administration (MSN). *Accreditation:* AACN.

Carlow University, College of Health and Wellness, Program in Nursing Leadership and Education, Pittsburgh, PA 15213-3165. Offers MSN. *Program availability:* Part-time, evening/weekend, 100% online, blended/hybrid learning. *Students:* 35 full-time (34 women), 17 part-time (all women); includes 3 minority (1 Black or African American, non-Hispanic/Latino; 2 Hispanic/Latino). Average age 36. 12 applicants, 92% accepted, 6 enrolled. In 2017, 20 master's awarded. *Degree requirements:* For master's, internship. *Entrance requirements:* For master's, minimum undergraduate GPA of 3.0 from accredited BSN program; current license as RN in Pennsylvania; statistics class within past 6 years with minimum C grade; two professional recommendations; reflective essay of 300 words or less describing career goals and expectations for education. Additional exam requirements/recommendations for international students: Required—TOEFL (minimum score 550 paper-based). *Application deadline:* Applications are processed on a rolling basis. Electronic applications accepted. *Expenses: Tuition:* Full-time $12,103; part-time $825 per credit hour. Tuition and fees vary according to program. *Financial support:* Application deadline: 4/1; applicants required to submit FAFSA. *Unit head:* Dr. Renee Ingel, Director, Nursing Leadership and DNP Programs, 412-578-6103, Fax: 412-578-6114, E-mail: rmingel@carlow.edu.
Website: http://www.carlow.edu/Master_of_Science_in_Nursing_Concentration_in_Education_and_Leadership.aspx

Carson-Newman University, Department of Nursing, Jefferson City, TN 37760. Offers family nurse practitioner (MSN); nurse educator (MSN). *Accreditation:* AACN. *Program availability:* Part-time. *Faculty:* 4 full-time (3 women). *Students:* 7 full-time (6 women), 33 part-time (30 women), 2 international. Average age 33. 18 applicants, 100% accepted, 13 enrolled. In 2017, 14 master's awarded. *Degree requirements:* For master's, comprehensive exam, thesis optional. *Entrance requirements:* For master's, GRE (minimum score of 290 within ten years of application), minimum GPA of 3.0 for all undergraduate work. Additional exam requirements/recommendations for international students: Recommended—TOEFL (minimum score 79 iBT), IELTS (minimum score 6.5), TSE (minimum score 53). *Application deadline:* For fall admission, 3/15 for domestic students; for spring admission, 10/15 for domestic students. Applications are processed on a rolling basis. Application fee: $50. *Expenses: Tuition:* Full-time $10,516; part-time $478 per credit hour. *Required fees:* $240; $120 per semester. One-time fee: $150. *Financial support:* Federal Work-Study and tuition waivers (full and partial) available. Financial award applicants required to submit FAFSA. *Unit head:* Dr. Kimberly Bolton, Director, 865-471-4056, E-mail: kbolton@cn.edu. *Application contact:* Nilma Stewart, Graduate Admissions and Services Adviser, 865-471-3230, Fax: 865-471-3875, E-mail: adults@cn.edu.
Website: http://www.cn.edu/adult-graduate-studies/programs/new/nursing

Case Western Reserve University, Frances Payne Bolton School of Nursing, Master's Programs in Nursing, Cleveland, OH 44106. Offers nurse anesthesia (MSN); nurse education (MSN); nurse midwifery (MSN); nurse practitioner (MSN), including acute care pediatric nurse practitioner, acute care/cardiovascular nursing, acute care/flight nurse, adult gerontology acute care nurse practitioner, adult gerontology nurse practitioner, adult gerontology primary care nurse practitioner, family nurse practitioner, family systems psychiatric mental health nursing, neonatal nurse practitioner, palliative care, pediatric nurse practitioner, women's health nurse practitioner; nursing (MN). *Accreditation:* ACEN. *Program availability:* Part-time. *Faculty:* 67 full-time (60 women), 29 part-time/adjunct (26 women). *Students:* 140 full-time (108 women), 155 part-time (124 women); includes 62 minority (24 Black or African American, non-Hispanic/Latino; 20 Asian, non-Hispanic/Latino; 9 Hispanic/Latino; 1 Native Hawaiian or other Pacific Islander, non-Hispanic/Latino; 8 Two or more races, non-Hispanic/Latino), 9 international. Average age 33. 250 applicants, 63% accepted, 94 enrolled. In 2017, 134 master's awarded. *Degree requirements:* For master's, thesis optional, minimum GPA of 3.0, Typhon log of clinical hours corresponding to requirements to sit for certification exam. *Entrance requirements:* For master's, GRE General Test or MAT, CCRN certification (for nurse anesthesia). Additional exam requirements/recommendations for international students: Required—TOEFL (minimum score 577 paper-based; 90 iBT), IELTS (minimum score 7). *Application deadline:* For fall admission, 3/1 for domestic and international students; for spring admission, 10/1 for domestic and international students; for summer admission, 3/1 for domestic and international students. Applications are processed on a rolling basis. Application fee: $75. Electronic applications accepted. *Expenses:* $2,011 per credit hour; $215 lab fee; $15 activity fee. *Financial support:* In 2017–18, 22 students received support. Scholarships/grants available. Financial award application deadline: 5/15; financial award applicants required to submit FAFSA. *Faculty research:* Symptom science, family/community care, aging across the lifespan, self-management of health and illness, neuroscience. *Unit head:* Dr. Latina Brooks, Director, 216-368-1196, Fax: 215-368-3542, E-mail: lmb3@case.edu. *Application contact:* Jackie Tepale, Admissions Coordinator, 216-368-5253, Fax: 216-368-0124, E-mail: yyd@case.edu.
Website: https://case.edu/nursing/msn/

Cedar Crest College, Program in Nursing, Allentown, PA 18104-6196. Offers nursing administration (MS); nursing education (MS). *Program availability:* Part-time. *Faculty:* 4 full-time (3 women), 2 part-time/adjunct (1 woman). *Students:* 25 part-time (23 women); includes 7 minority (2 Black or African American, non-Hispanic/Latino; 2 Asian, non-Hispanic/Latino; 3 Hispanic/Latino). Average age 36. In 2017, 8 master's awarded. *Application deadline:* Applications are processed on a rolling basis. Electronic applications accepted. *Expenses:* Contact institution. *Unit head:* Dr. Wendy Robb, Director, 610-606-4666, E-mail: wjrobb@cedarcrest.edu. *Application contact:* Nancy Wunderly, Director of School of Adult and Graduate Education, 610-606-4666, E-mail: sage@cedarcrest.edu.
Website: http://sage.cedarcrest.edu/degrees/graduate/nursing-science/

Cedarville University, Graduate Programs, Cedarville, OH 45314. Offers business administration (MBA); family nurse practitioner (MSN); global ministry (M Div); global public health nursing (MSN); healthcare administration (MBA); ministry (M Min); nurse educator (MSN); operations management (MBA); pharmacy (Pharm D). *Program availability:* Part-time, evening/weekend, 100% online, blended/hybrid learning. *Faculty:* 23 full-time (9 women), 48 part-time/adjunct (21 women). *Students:* 202 full-time (123 women), 146 part-time (96 women); includes 63 minority (39 Black or African American, non-Hispanic/Latino; 3 American Indian or Alaska Native, non-Hispanic/Latino; 15 Asian, non-Hispanic/Latino; 2 Hispanic/Latino; 1 Native Hawaiian or other Pacific Islander, non-Hispanic/Latino; 3 Two or more races, non-Hispanic/Latino), 3 international. Average age 24. 345 applicants, 37% accepted, 91 enrolled. In 2017, 53 master's, 47 doctorates awarded. *Degree requirements:* For master's, portfolio; for doctorate, comprehensive exam. *Entrance requirements:* For master's, GRE, 2 professional recommendations; for doctorate, PCAT, professional recommendation from a practicing pharmacist or current employer/supervisor, resume, essay, interview. Additional exam requirements/recommendations for international students: Required—TOEFL (minimum score 550 paper-based; 80 iBT). *Application deadline:* For fall admission, 5/1 priority date for domestic and international students; for spring admission, 11/1 priority date for domestic and international students. Applications are processed on a rolling basis. Application fee: $0. Electronic applications accepted. *Expenses: Tuition:* Full-time $12,594; part-time $566 per credit. One-time fee: $100 full-time. Tuition and fees vary according to degree level and program. *Financial support:* Scholarships/grants and unspecified assistantships available. Support available to part-time students. Financial award application deadline: 1/30; financial award applicants required to submit FAFSA. *Faculty research:* Establishing competencies of clinical reasoning for nursing students in Taiwan, social determinants of health in pediatric primary care, meeting needs of palliative care populations, natural product utility in cancer, monoclonal antibodies directed at angiogenesis regulation. *Total annual research expenditures:* $3,800. *Unit head:* Dr. Janice Supplee, Dean of Graduate Studies, 937-766-7700, E-mail: suppleej@cedarville.edu. *Application contact:* Jim Amstutz, Director of Graduate Admissions, 937-766-7878, Fax: 937-766-7575, E-mail: amstutzj@cedarville.edu.
Website: https://www.cedarville.edu/Admissions/Graduate/Graduate-Programs.aspx

Central Methodist University, College of Graduate and Extended Studies, Fayette, MO 65248-1198. Offers clinical counseling (MS); clinical nurse leader (MSN); education (M Ed); music education (MME); nurse educator (MSN). *Program availability:* Part-time, evening/weekend, online learning. *Degree requirements:* For master's, thesis. *Entrance requirements:* For master's, GRE General Test, minimum GPA of 2.75. Electronic applications accepted.

Chatham University, Nursing Programs, Pittsburgh, PA 15232-2826. Offers education/leadership (MSN); nursing (DNP). *Accreditation:* AACN. *Program availability:* Online learning. *Faculty:* 12 full-time (all women), 12 part-time/adjunct (10 women). *Students:* 49 full-time (41 women), 95 part-time (80 women); includes 68 minority (51 Black or African American, non-Hispanic/Latino; 7 Asian, non-Hispanic/Latino; 8 Hispanic/Latino; 2 Two or more races, non-Hispanic/Latino), 11 international. Average age 42. 209 applicants, 51% accepted, 76 enrolled. In 2017, 13 master's, 82 doctorates awarded.

Entrance requirements: For master's, RN license, BSN, minimum GPA of 3.0; for doctorate, RN license, MSN. Additional exam requirements/recommendations for international students: Required—TOEFL (minimum score 600 paper-based; 100 iBT), IELTS (minimum score 6.5), TWE. *Application deadline:* For fall admission, 5/1 priority date for domestic and international students. Applications are processed on a rolling basis. Application fee: $35. Electronic applications accepted. Application fee is waived when completed online. *Expenses:* Contact institution. *Financial support:* Application deadline: 8/1; applicants required to submit FAFSA. *Unit head:* Dr. Diane Hunker, Director, 412-365-1738, E-mail: dhunker@chatham.edu. *Application contact:* Patricia Golla, Assistant Director of Graduate Admissions, 412-365-1386, Fax: 412-365-1720, E-mail: pgolla@chatham.edu.
Website: http://www.chatham.edu/nursing

Clarkson College, Master of Science in Nursing Program, Omaha, NE 68131. Offers adult nurse practitioner (MSN, Post-Master's Certificate); family nurse practitioner (MSN, Post-Master's Certificate); nursing education (MSN, Post-Master's Certificate); nursing health care leadership (MSN, Post-Master's Certificate). *Accreditation:* AANA/CANAEP; ACEN. *Program availability:* Part-time, evening/weekend, online learning. *Degree requirements:* For master's, on-campus skills assessment (family nurse practitioner, adult nurse practitioner), comprehensive exam or thesis. *Entrance requirements:* For master's, minimum GPA of 3.0, 2 references, resume. Additional exam requirements/recommendations for international students: Required—TOEFL (minimum score 600 paper-based; 100 iBT). Electronic applications accepted.

Cleveland State University, College of Graduate Studies, College of Education and Human Services, Program in Urban Education, Specialization in Nursing Education, Cleveland, OH 44115. Offers PhD. *Program availability:* Part-time. *Faculty:* 6 full-time (all women). *Students:* 2 part-time (both women); includes 1 minority (Asian, non-Hispanic/Latino). Average age 42. *Entrance requirements:* For doctorate, GRE General Test (minimum score of 297 for combined Verbal and Quantitative exams, 4.0 preferred for Analytical Writing), MSN with minimum GPA of 3.25, curriculum vitae or resume, personal statement, 2 letters of recommendation. Additional exam requirements/recommendations for international students: Required—TOEFL (minimum score 550 paper-based; 78 iBT), IELTS (minimum score 6). Application fee: $40. Electronic applications accepted. *Faculty research:* Aspects of educating individuals to function in a complex applied discipline, educating nurses. *Unit head:* Dr. Graham Stead, Program Coordinator, 216-875-9869, E-mail: g.b.stead@csuohio.edu. *Application contact:* Rita M. Grabowski, Administrative Coordinator, 216-687-4697, Fax: 216-875-9697, E-mail: r.grabowski@csuohio.edu.
Website: http://www.csuohio.edu/cehs/doc/specializations-nursing-education

College of Mount Saint Vincent, School of Professional and Graduate Studies, Department of Nursing, Riverdale, NY 10471-1093. Offers family nurse practitioner (MSN, PMC); nurse educator (PMC); nursing administration (MSN); nursing education (MSN). *Accreditation:* AACN. *Program availability:* Part-time. *Entrance requirements:* For master's, BSN, interview, RN license, minimum GPA of 3.0, letters of reference. Additional exam requirements/recommendations for international students: Required—TOEFL. *Expenses:* Contact institution.

The College of New Rochelle, Graduate School, Program in Nursing, New Rochelle, NY 10805-2308. Offers acute care nurse practitioner (MS, Certificate); clinical specialist in holistic nursing (MS, Certificate); family nurse practitioner (MS, Certificate); nursing and health care management (MS); nursing education (Certificate). *Accreditation:* AACN. *Program availability:* Part-time. *Entrance requirements:* For master's, GRE General Test or MAT, BSN, malpractice insurance, minimum GPA of 3.0, RN license. Electronic applications accepted. *Expenses: Tuition:* Full-time $17,406. *Required fees:* $1120.

Colorado Mesa University, Department of Health Sciences, Grand Junction, CO 81501-3122. Offers advanced nursing practice (MSN); family nurse practitioner (DNP); health information technology systems (Graduate Certificate); nursing education (MSN). *Accreditation:* AACN. *Program availability:* Part-time, evening/weekend, 100% online, blended/hybrid learning. *Degree requirements:* For master's and doctorate, capstone. *Entrance requirements:* For master's and doctorate, minimum GPA of 3.0 in BSN program. Additional exam requirements/recommendations for international students: Required—TOEFL (minimum score 550 paper-based). Electronic applications accepted.

Columbus State University, Graduate Studies, College of Education and Health Professions, School of Nursing, Columbus, GA 31907-5645. Offers family nurse practitioner (MSN); nursing (MSN), including nurse educator, nurse informatics, nurse leader. Program offered in collaboration with Georgia Southwestern StateUniversity. *Program availability:* Part-time, online only, 100% online. *Faculty:* 7 full-time (all women), 2 part-time/adjunct (both women). *Students:* 43 full-time (40 women), 134 part-time (121 women); includes 88 minority (65 Black or African American, non-Hispanic/Latino; 7 Asian, non-Hispanic/Latino; 10 Hispanic/Latino; 6 Two or more races, non-Hispanic/Latino). Average age 35. 141 applicants, 49% accepted, 12 enrolled. In 2017, 28 master's awarded. *Entrance requirements:* For master's, GRE, BSN, minimum undergraduate GPA of 3.0. Additional exam requirements/recommendations for international students: Required—TOEFL (minimum score 550 paper-based; 79 iBT). *Application deadline:* For fall admission, 5/1 for domestic and international students; for spring admission, 11/1 for domestic and international students; for summer admission, 3/1 for domestic and international students. Applications are processed on a rolling basis. Application fee: $50. Electronic applications accepted. *Expenses:* Contact institution. *Financial support:* In 2017–18, 3 students received support. Institutionally sponsored loans available. Financial award application deadline: 5/1; financial award applicants required to submit FAFSA. *Unit head:* Latonya Santo, Director, 706-507-8576, E-mail: santo_latonya@columbusstate.edu. *Application contact:* Catrina Smith-Edmond, Assistant Director for Graduate and Global Admission, 706-507-8824, Fax: 706-568-5091, E-mail: smithedmond_catrina@columbusstate.edu.
Website: http://nursing.columbusstate.edu/

Cox College, Programs in Nursing, Springfield, MO 65802. Offers clinical nurse leader (MSN); family nurse practitioner (MSN); nurse educator (MSN). *Accreditation:* AACN. *Entrance requirements:* For master's, RN license, essay, 2 letters of recommendation, official transcripts. Electronic applications accepted.

Daemen College, Department of Nursing, Amherst, NY 14226-3592. Offers adult nurse practitioner (MS, Post Master's Certificate); nurse executive leadership (Post Master's Certificate); nursing education (MS, Post Master's Certificate); nursing executive leadership (MS); nursing practice (DNP); palliative care nursing (Post Master's Certificate). *Accreditation:* ACEN. *Program availability:* Part-time. *Degree requirements:* For master's, thesis or alternative, degree completed in 4 years; minimum GPA of 3.0; for doctorate, degree completed in 5 years; 500 post-master's clinical hours. *Entrance requirements:* For master's, BN, 1 year medical/surgical experience, RN license and state registration, statistics course with minimum C grade, 3 letters of recommendation, minimum GPA of 3.25, interview; for doctorate, MS in advance nursing practice; New York state RN license; goal statement; resume; interview; statistics course with minimum grade of 'C'; for Post Master's Certificate, master's degree in clinical area; RN license and current registration; one year of clinical experience; statistics course with minimum grade of 'C'; 3 letters of recommendation; interview; letter of intent. Additional exam requirements/recommendations for international students: Required—TOEFL (minimum score 500 paper-based; 63 iBT), IELTS (minimum score 5.5). Electronic applications accepted. *Faculty research:* Professional stress, client behavior, drug therapy, treatment modalities and pulmonary cancers, chemical dependency.

Delta State University, Graduate Programs, Robert E. Smith School of Nursing, Cleveland, MS 38733. Offers family nurse practitioner (MSN); nurse administrator (MSN); nurse educator (MSN). *Accreditation:* AACN. *Program availability:* Part-time. *Degree requirements:* For master's, thesis optional. *Entrance requirements:* For master's, GRE General Test. Electronic applications accepted.

DeSales University, Division of Healthcare, Center Valley, PA 18034-9568. Offers adult-gerontology acute care (Post Master's Certificate); adult-gerontology acute care nurse practitioner (MSN); adult-gerontology acute certified nurse practitioner (Post Master's Certificate); adult-gerontology clinical nurse specialist (MSN, Post Master's Certificate); clinical leadership (DNP); family nurse practitioner (MSN, Post Master's Certificate); general nursing practice (DNP); nurse anesthetist (MSN); nurse educator (Post Master's Certificate, Postbaccalaureate Certificate); nurse midwife (MSN); nurse practitioner (MSN); psychiatric-mental health nurse practitioner (MSN, Post Master's Certificate); DNP/MBA. *Accreditation:* ACEN. *Program availability:* Part-time. *Faculty:* 26 full-time (20 women), 30 part-time/adjunct (19 women). *Students:* 282 full-time (210 women), 101 part-time (85 women); includes 39 minority (12 Black or African American, non-Hispanic/Latino; 11 Asian, non-Hispanic/Latino; 12 Hispanic/Latino; 4 Two or more races, non-Hispanic/Latino), 1 international. Average age 29. 2,884 applicants, 5% accepted, 114 enrolled. In 2017, 76 master's, 6 doctorates awarded. *Degree requirements:* For master's, minimum GPA of 3.0, portfolio; for doctorate, minimum GPA of 3.0, scholarly capstone project. *Entrance requirements:* For master's, GRE or MAT (waived if applicant has an undergraduate GPA of 3.0 or higher), BSN from ACEN- or CCNE-accredited program, minimum undergraduate GPA of 3.0, active RN license or eligibility, two letters of recommendation, essay, health care experience, personal interview; for doctorate, BSN or MSN from ACEN- or CCNE-accredited institution, minimum GPA of 3.3 in graduate program, current licensure as an RN. Additional exam requirements/recommendations for international students: Required—TOEFL (minimum score 104 iBT). *Application deadline:* Applications are processed on a rolling basis. Application fee: $50. Electronic applications accepted. *Expenses:* Contact institution. *Financial support:* Applicants required to submit FAFSA. *Unit head:* Ronald Nordone, Dean of Graduate Education, 610-282-1100 Ext. 1289, E-mail: ronald.nordone@desales.edu. *Application contact:* Julia Ferraro, Director of Graduate Admissions, 610-282-1100 Ext. 1768, E-mail: gradadmissions@desales.edu.

Drexel University, College of Nursing and Health Professions, Division of Graduate Nursing, Philadelphia, PA 19104-2875. Offers adult acute care (MSN); adult psychiatric/mental health (MSN); advanced practice nursing (MSN); clinical trials research (MSN); family nurse practitioner (MSN); leadership in health systems management (MSN); nursing education (MSN); pediatric primary care (MSN); women's health (MSN). *Accreditation:* AACN. Electronic applications accepted.

Duke University, School of Nursing, Durham, NC 27708-0586. Offers acute care pediatric nurse practitioner (MSN, Post-Graduate Certificate); adult-gerontology nurse practitioner (MSN, Post-Graduate Certificate), including acute care, primary care; family nurse practitioner (MSN, Post-Graduate Certificate); neonatal nurse practitioner (MSN, Post-Graduate Certificate); nurse anesthesia (DNP); nurse practitioner (DNP); nursing (PhD); nursing and health care leadership (MSN, Post-Graduate Certificate); nursing education (MSN, Post-Graduate Certificate); nursing informatics (MSN, Post-Graduate Certificate); pediatric nurse practitioner (MSN, Post-Graduate Certificate), including primary care; psychiatric mental health nurse practitioner (MSN, Post-Graduate Certificate); women's health nurse practitioner (MSN, Post-Graduate Certificate). *Accreditation:* AACN; AANA/CANAEP. *Program availability:* Part-time, evening/weekend, online with on-campus intensives. *Faculty:* 72 full-time (61 women). *Students:* 155 full-time (137 women), 613 part-time (548 women); includes 177 minority (64 Black or African American, non-Hispanic/Latino; 2 American Indian or Alaska Native, non-Hispanic/Latino; 47 Asian, non-Hispanic/Latino; 34 Hispanic/Latino; 30 Two or more races, non-Hispanic/Latino), 10 international. Average age 34. 631 applicants, 47% accepted, 211 enrolled. In 2017, 221 master's, 71 doctorates, 26 other advanced degrees awarded. Terminal master's awarded for partial completion of doctoral program. *Degree requirements:* For master's, thesis optional; for doctorate, capstone project. *Entrance requirements:* For master's, GRE General Test (waived if undergraduate GPA of 3.4 or higher), 1 year of nursing experience (recommended), BSN, minimum GPA of 3.0, previous course work in statistics; for doctorate, GRE General Test (waived if undergraduate GPA of 3.4 or higher), BSN or MSN, minimum GPA of 3.0, resume, personal statement, undergraduate statistics course, current licensure as a registered nurse, transcripts from all post-secondary institutions; for Post-Graduate Certificate, MSN, licensure or eligibility as a professional nurse, transcripts from all post-secondary institutions, previous course work in statistics. Additional exam requirements/recommendations for international students: Required—TOEFL (minimum score 100 iBT), IELTS (minimum score 7). *Application deadline:* For fall admission, 12/1 for domestic and international students; for spring admission, 5/1 for domestic and international students. Application fee: $50. Electronic applications accepted. *Expenses:* Contact institution. *Financial support:* Institutionally sponsored loans, scholarships/grants, and traineeships available. Support available to part-time students. Financial award applicants required to submit FAFSA. *Faculty research:* Cardiovascular disease, caregiver skill training, data mining, prostate cancer, neonatal immune system. *Unit head:* Dr. Marion E. Broome, Dean/Vice Chancellor for Nursing Affairs/Associate Vice President for Academic Affairs for Nursing, 919-684-9446, Fax: 919-684-9414, E-mail: marion.broome@duke.edu. *Application contact:* Dr. Ernie Rushing, Director of Admissions and Recruitment, 919-668-6274, Fax: 919-668-4693, E-mail: ernie.rushing@dm.duke.edu.
Website: http://www.nursing.duke.edu/

Duquesne University, School of Nursing, Master of Science in Nursing Program, Pittsburgh, PA 15282-0001. Offers family (individual across the life span) nurse practitioner (MSN); forensic nursing (MSN); nursing education and faculty role (MSN). *Accreditation:* AACN. *Program availability:* Part-time, evening/weekend, minimal on-campus study. *Faculty:* 26 full-time (21 women), 3 part-time/adjunct (all women). *Students:* 132 full-time (118 women), 54 part-time (49 women); includes 25 minority (7 Black or African American, non-Hispanic/Latino; 2 American Indian or Alaska Native, non-Hispanic/Latino; 5 Asian, non-Hispanic/Latino; 7 Hispanic/Latino; 4 Two or more races, non-Hispanic/Latino), 1 international. Average age 33. 160 applicants, 73% accepted, 87 enrolled. In 2017, 50 master's awarded. *Entrance requirements:* For master's, current RN license; BSN with minimum GPA of 3.0; minimum of 1 year of full-time work experience as RN prior to registration in clinical or specialty course. Additional exam requirements/recommendations for international students: Required—TOEFL (minimum score 600 paper-based; 100 iBT). *Application deadline:* For fall admission, 7/16 for domestic and international students; for spring admission, 11/29 for domestic and international students; for summer admission, 4/1 for domestic and international students. Application fee: $0. Electronic applications accepted. *Expenses:* $1,312 per credit. *Financial support:* In 2017–18, 10 students received support, including 10 teaching assistantships with partial tuition reimbursements available (averaging $3,297

per year); institutionally sponsored loans, scholarships/grants, traineeships, tuition waivers (partial), and unspecified assistantships also available. Support available to part-time students. Financial award application deadline: 5/1; financial award applicants required to submit FAFSA. *Faculty research:* Vulnerable populations, cultural competence, health disparities, wellness, technology. *Total annual research expenditures:* $650,096. *Unit head:* Dr. Alison Colbert, Associate Professor/Associate Dean of Academic Affairs, 412-396-1511, Fax: 412-396-1821, E-mail: colberta@duq.edu. *Application contact:* Susan Hardner, Nurse Recruiter, 412-396-4945, Fax: 412-396-6346, E-mail: nursing@duq.edu.
Website: http://www.duq.edu/academics/schools/nursing/graduate-programs/master-science-nursing

Duquesne University, School of Nursing, Post Master's Certificate Program, Pittsburgh, PA 15282-0001. Offers family (individual across the life span) nurse practitioner (Post-Master's Certificate); forensic nursing (Post-Master's Certificate); nursing education and faculty role (Post-Master's Certificate). *Program availability:* Part-time, evening/weekend, minimal on-campus study. *Faculty:* 8 full-time (6 women), 2 part-time/adjunct (both women). *Students:* 14 full-time (all women), 6 part-time (all women); includes 3 minority (2 Black or African American, non-Hispanic/Latino; 1 American Indian or Alaska Native, non-Hispanic/Latino). Average age 43. 27 applicants, 78% accepted, 10 enrolled. In 2017, 6 Post-Master's Certificates awarded. *Entrance requirements:* For degree, current RN license, BSN, MSN. Additional exam requirements/recommendations for international students: Required—TOEFL (minimum score 600 paper-based; 100 iBT). *Application deadline:* For fall admission, 7/16 for domestic and international students; for spring admission, 11/29 for domestic and international students; for summer admission, 4/1 for domestic and international students. Application fee: $0. Electronic applications accepted. *Expenses:* $1,312 per credit. *Financial support:* Teaching assistantships with partial tuition reimbursements, institutionally sponsored loans, scholarships/grants, traineeships, and tuition waivers (partial) available. Support available to part-time students. Financial award application deadline: 5/1; financial award applicants required to submit FAFSA. *Faculty research:* Vulnerable populations, cultural competence, health disparities, wellness, technology. *Total annual research expenditures:* $650,096. *Unit head:* Dr. Alison Colbert, Associate Professor/Associate Dean of Academic Affairs, 412-396-1511, Fax: 412-396-1821, E-mail: colberta@duq.edu. *Application contact:* Susan Hardner, Nurse Recruiter, 412-396-4945, Fax: 412-396-6346, E-mail: nursing@duq.edu.
Website: http://www.duq.edu/academics/schools/nursing/graduate-programs/post-masters-certificates

Eastern Michigan University, Graduate School, College of Health and Human Services, School of Nursing, Ypsilanti, MI 48197. Offers nursing (MSN); teaching in health care systems (MSN, Graduate Certificate). *Accreditation:* AACN. *Program availability:* Part-time, evening/weekend, online learning. *Faculty:* 25 full-time (22 women). *Students:* 20 full-time (18 women), 21 part-time (17 women); includes 12 minority (8 Black or African American, non-Hispanic/Latino; 2 Asian, non-Hispanic/Latino; 2 Hispanic/Latino), 1 international. Average age 38. 20 applicants, 55% accepted, 1 enrolled. In 2017, 12 master's, 1 other advanced degree awarded. *Degree requirements:* For master's, thesis optional. *Entrance requirements:* For master's, GRE General Test, Michigan RN license. Additional exam requirements/recommendations for international students: Required—TOEFL. *Application deadline:* Applications are processed on a rolling basis. Application fee: $45. *Financial support:* Fellowships, research assistantships with full tuition reimbursements, teaching assistantships with full tuition reimbursements, career-related internships or fieldwork, Federal Work-Study, institutionally sponsored loans, scholarships/grants, tuition waivers (partial), and unspecified assistantships available. Support available to part-time students. Financial award applicants required to submit FAFSA. *Unit head:* Dr. Michael Williams, Director, 734-487-2310, Fax: 734-487-6946, E-mail: mwilliams@emich.edu. *Application contact:* Roberta Towne, Coordinator, School of Nursing, 734-487-2340, Fax: 734-487-6946, E-mail: rtowne1@emich.edu.
Website: http://www.emich.edu/nursing

East Tennessee State University, School of Graduate Studies, College of Nursing, Johnson City, TN 37614. Offers acute care nurse practitioner (DNP); adult-gerontology primary care nurse practitioner (DNP); adult/gerontological nurse practitioner (Postbaccalaureate Certificate); executive leadership in nursing (DNP, Postbaccalaureate Certificate); family nurse practitioner (MSN, DNP, Post-Master's Certificate, Postbaccalaureate Certificate); nursing (PhD); nursing administration (MSN); nursing education (MSN); pediatric primary care nurse practitioner (DNP); psychiatric mental health nurse practitioner (Postbaccalaureate Certificate); psychiatric/mental health nurse practitioner (MSN, DNP, Post-Master's Certificate); women's health care nurse practitioner (DNP). *Accreditation:* AACN. *Program availability:* Part-time, evening/weekend, online learning. In 2017, 126 master's, 30 doctorates, 4 other advanced degrees awarded. *Degree requirements:* For master's and other advanced degree, comprehensive exam, practicum; for doctorate, comprehensive exam, thesis/dissertation (for some programs), practicum, internship, evidence of professional malpractice insurance, CPR certification. *Entrance requirements:* For master's, bachelor's degree, minimum GPA of 3.0, current RN license and eligibility to practice, resume, three letters of recommendation; for doctorate, GRE General Test, MSN (for PhD), BSN or MSN (for DNP), current RN license and eligibility to practice, 2 years of full-time registered nurse work experience or equivalent, three letters of recommendation, resume or curriculum vitae, interview, writing sample; for other advanced degree, MSN, minimum GPA of 3.0, current RN license and eligibility to practice, three letters of recommendation, resume or curriculum vitae; DNP with designated concentration in advanced clinical practice or nursing administration (for select programs). Additional exam requirements/recommendations for international students: Required—TOEFL (minimum score 600 paper-based; 79 iBT). *Application deadline:* For fall admission, 4/15 priority date for domestic and international students; for spring admission, 10/15 priority date for domestic and international students; for summer admission, 2/1 for domestic and international students. Application fee: $55 ($65 for international students). Electronic applications accepted. *Financial support:* Research assistantships with tuition reimbursements, teaching assistantships, career-related internships or fieldwork, institutionally sponsored loans, scholarships/grants, and unspecified assistantships available. Financial award application deadline: 7/1; financial award applicants required to submit FAFSA. *Faculty research:* Improving health of rural and underserved populations (low income elders living in public housing, rural caregivers, Hispanic populations), health services and systems research (quality outcomes of nurse-managed primary care, in-home, and rural health care), nursing education (experiences of second-degree BSN students, well-being of BSN students). *Unit head:* Dr. Wendy Nehring, Dean, 423-439-7051, Fax: 423-439-4543, E-mail: nursing@etsu.edu. *Application contact:* Dr. Myra Clark, Director of Graduate Programs, 423-439-4396, Fax: 423-439-4100, E-mail: clarkml2@etsu.edu.
Website: http://www.etsu.edu/nursing/

Edinboro University of Pennsylvania, Department of Nursing, Edinboro, PA 16444. Offers advanced practice nursing (DNP); family nurse practitioner (MSN); nurse educator (MSN). *Program availability:* Part-time, evening/weekend. *Degree requirements:* For master's, thesis, competency exam. *Entrance requirements:* For master's, GRE or MAT, minimum QPA of 2.5. Electronic applications accepted.

Elms College, School of Nursing, Chicopee, MA 01013-2839. Offers adult-gerontology acute care nurse practitioner (DNP); family nurse practitioner (DNP); health systems innovation and leadership (DNP); nursing and health services management (MSN); nursing education (MSN). *Accreditation:* AACN. *Program availability:* Part-time, evening/weekend. *Faculty:* 5 full-time (all women), 9 part-time/adjunct (6 women). *Students:* 20 full-time (16 women), 79 part-time (70 women); includes 12 minority (2 Black or African American, non-Hispanic/Latino; 2 American Indian or Alaska Native, non-Hispanic/Latino; 8 Hispanic/Latino). Average age 40. 33 applicants, 94% accepted, 28 enrolled. In 2017, 14 master's, 30 doctorates awarded. *Entrance requirements:* Additional exam requirements/recommendations for international students: Required—TOEFL. *Application deadline:* For fall admission, 7/1 priority date for domestic students; for spring admission, 11/1 priority date for domestic students. Applications are processed on a rolling basis. Application fee: $30. *Expenses: Tuition:* Full-time $13,860; part-time $770 per credit hour. *Required fees:* $200. Tuition and fees vary according to degree level and program. *Financial support:* Applicants required to submit FAFSA. *Unit head:* Dr. Kathleen Scoble, Dean, School of Nursing, 413-265-2204, E-mail: scoblek@elms.edu. *Application contact:* Dr. Cynthia L. Dakin, Director of Graduate Nursing Studies, 413-265-2455, Fax: 413-265-2335, E-mail: dakinc@elms.edu.

Emmanuel College, Graduate and Professional Programs, Graduate Program in Nursing, Boston, MA 02115. Offers education (MSN, Graduate Certificate); management (MSN, Graduate Certificate). *Accreditation:* AACN. *Program availability:* Part-time, evening/weekend. *Faculty:* 3 full-time (all women), 4 part-time/adjunct (all women). *Students:* 35 part-time (33 women); includes 6 minority (3 Black or African American, non-Hispanic/Latino; 3 Hispanic/Latino). Average age 42. 26 applicants, 27% accepted, 3 enrolled. In 2017, 7 master's awarded. *Degree requirements:* For master's, 36 credits, including 6-credit practicum. *Entrance requirements:* For master's, transcripts from all regionally-accredited institutions attended (showing proof of bachelor's degree completion), proof of RN license, 2 letters of recommendation, essay, resume; for Graduate Certificate, transcripts from all regionally-accredited institutions attended (showing proof of master's degree completion), proof of RN license, 2 letters of recommendation, essay, resume. Additional exam requirements/recommendations for international students: Required—TOEFL. *Application deadline:* Applications are processed on a rolling basis. Electronic applications accepted. *Expenses:* $28,391 (for MSN); $10,324 (for Graduate Certificate). *Financial support:* Application deadline: 2/15; applicants required to submit FAFSA. *Unit head:* Diane Shea, Associate Dean for Nursing/Professor of Nursing Practice, 617-732-1604, E-mail: shead@emmanuel.edu. *Application contact:* Helen Muterperl, Director of Graduate and Professional Programs, 617-735-9700, Fax: 617-507-0434, E-mail: gpp@emmanuel.edu.
Website: http://www.emmanuel.edu/graduate-professional-programs/academics/nursing.html

Endicott College, Van Loan School of Graduate and Professional Studies, Program in Nursing, Beverly, MA 01915-2096. Offers family nurse practitioner (MSN, Post-Master's Certificate); global health (MSN); nursing administration (MSN); nursing administrator (Post-Master's Certificate); nursing educator (MSN, Post-Master's Certificate). *Program availability:* Part-time, evening/weekend. *Faculty:* 5 full-time (4 women), 14 part-time/adjunct (12 women). *Students:* 43 full-time (41 women), 57 part-time (51 women); includes 8 minority (5 Black or African American, non-Hispanic/Latino; 3 Hispanic/Latino), 1 international. Average age 37. 41 applicants, 100% accepted, 38 enrolled. In 2017, 33 master's awarded. *Degree requirements:* For master's, thesis, practicum. *Entrance requirements:* For master's, MAT or GRE, statement of professional goals, official transcripts of all undergraduate and graduate course work, two letters of recommendation, photocopy of current and unrestricted RN license, basic statistics course, interview. Additional exam requirements/recommendations for international students: Required—TOEFL. *Application deadline:* Applications are processed on a rolling basis. Application fee: $50. Electronic applications accepted. *Expenses:* Contact institution. *Financial support:* Applicants required to submit FAFSA. *Unit head:* Dr. Kelly Fisher, Dean, 978-232-2328, Fax: 978-232-3000, E-mail: kfisher@endicott.edu. *Application contact:* Ian Menchini, Director, Graduate Enrollment and Advising, 978-232-5292, Fax: 978-232-3000, E-mail: imenchin@endicott.edu.
Website: https://vanloan.endicott.edu/programs-of-study/masters-programs/nursing-programs

Excelsior College, School of Nursing, Albany, NY 12203-5159. Offers nursing (MS); nursing education (MS); nursing informatics (MS); nursing leadership and administration of health care systems (MS). *Accreditation:* ACEN. *Program availability:* Part-time, evening/weekend, online learning. *Faculty:* 12 part-time/adjunct (9 women). *Students:* 388 part-time (313 women); includes 122 minority (63 Black or African American, non-Hispanic/Latino; 4 American Indian or Alaska Native, non-Hispanic/Latino; 18 Asian, non-Hispanic/Latino; 28 Hispanic/Latino; 2 Native Hawaiian or other Pacific Islander, non-Hispanic/Latino; 7 Two or more races, non-Hispanic/Latino). Average age 44. In 2017, 173 master's awarded. *Entrance requirements:* For master's, RN license. *Application deadline:* Applications are processed on a rolling basis. Application fee: $50. Electronic applications accepted. *Expenses: Tuition:* Part-time $645 per credit. *Required fees:* $265 per credit. *Financial support:* Scholarships/grants available. *Unit head:* Dr. Mary Lee Pollard, Dean, School of Nursing, 518-464-8500, Fax: 518-464-8777, E-mail: msn@excelsior.edu. *Application contact:* Admissions Counselor, 888-647-2388, Fax: 518-464-8777, E-mail: gradadmissions@excelsior.edu.
Website: http://www.excelsior.edu/programs/nursing

Felician University, Master of Science in Nursing Program, Lodi, NJ 07644-2117. Offers adult-gerontology nurse practitioner (MSN, PMC); executive leadership (MSN, PMC); family nurse practitioner (MSN, PMC); nursing education (MSN, PMC). *Accreditation:* AACN. *Program availability:* Evening/weekend, online only, 100% online, blended/hybrid learning. *Faculty:* 9 full-time (8 women), 1 (woman) part-time/adjunct. *Students:* 96 part-time (90 women); includes 48 minority (17 Black or African American, non-Hispanic/Latino; 1 American Indian or Alaska Native, non-Hispanic/Latino; 16 Asian, non-Hispanic/Latino; 12 Hispanic/Latino; 1 Native Hawaiian or other Pacific Islander, non-Hispanic/Latino; 1 Two or more races, non-Hispanic/Latino). Average age 37. 49 applicants, 86% accepted, 23 enrolled. In 2017, 35 master's, 3 other advanced degrees awarded. *Degree requirements:* For master's, thesis, clinical presentation; for PMC, thesis, education project. *Entrance requirements:* For master's, BSN; minimum GPA of 3.0; 2 letters of recommendation; NJ RN license; personal statement; for PMC, RN license, minimum GPA of 3.0. Additional exam requirements/recommendations for international students: Required—TOEFL (minimum score 550 paper-based; 79 iBT), IELTS (minimum score 6.5), PTE (minimum score 56). *Application deadline:* Applications are processed on a rolling basis. Application fee: $40. Electronic applications accepted. Application fee is waived when completed online. *Expenses:* Contact institution. *Financial support:* Federal Work-Study, scholarships/grants, and traineeships available. Financial award applicants required to submit FAFSA. *Faculty research:* Anxiety and fear, curriculum innovation, health promotion and populations, attitudes of college students towards aging. *Unit head:* Dr. Ann Tritak, Associate Dean of Graduate Nursing, 201-559-6151, E-mail: tritaka@felician.edu. *Application contact:* Michael Szarek, Assistant Vice-President, Graduate Admissions, 201-355-1450, E-mail: szarekm@felician.edu.

Ferris State University, College of Health Professions, School of Nursing, Big Rapids, MI 49307. Offers nursing (MSN); nursing administration (MSN); nursing education (MSN); nursing informatics (MSN). *Accreditation:* ACEN. *Program availability:* Part-time, evening/weekend, online only, 100% online. *Faculty:* 7 full-time (all women), 2 part-time/adjunct (both women). *Students:* 3 full-time (all women), 104 part-time (95 women); includes 15 minority (3 Black or African American, non-Hispanic/Latino; 5 American Indian or Alaska Native, non-Hispanic/Latino; 2 Asian, non-Hispanic/Latino; 3 Hispanic/Latino; 1 Native Hawaiian or other Pacific Islander, non-Hispanic/Latino; 1 Two or more races, non-Hispanic/Latino). Average age 40. 36 applicants, 92% accepted, 31 enrolled. In 2017, 25 master's awarded. *Degree requirements:* For master's, practicum, practicum project. *Entrance requirements:* For master's, BS in nursing (for nursing education track); BS in nursing or related field (for nursing administration and nursing informatics tracks); registered nurse license, writing sample, letters of reference, 2 years' clinical experience (recommended). Additional exam requirements/recommendations for international students: Required—TOEFL (minimum score 550 paper-based; 61 iBT). *Application deadline:* For fall admission, 4/15 priority date for domestic students; for spring admission, 10/15 for domestic students. Application fee: $0. Electronic applications accepted. *Financial support:* In 2017–18, 3 students received support. Career-related internships or fieldwork and scholarships/grants available. Financial award application deadline: 4/15; financial award applicants required to submit FAFSA. *Faculty research:* Nursing education, end of life, leadership/education introverts in nursing, complementary and alternative medicine therapies. *Unit head:* Dr. Susan Owens, Chair, School of Nursing, 231-591-2267, Fax: 231-591-2325, E-mail: owenss3@ferris.edu. *Application contact:* Sharon Colley, MSN Program Coordinator, 231-591-2288, Fax: 231-591-2325, E-mail: colleys@ferris.edu.
Website: http://www.ferris.edu/htmls/colleges/alliedhe/Nursing/homepage.htm

Florida Gulf Coast University, Elaine Nicpon Marieb College of Health and Human Services, Program in Nurse Educator, Fort Myers, FL 33965-6565. Offers MSN. *Program availability:* Online learning. *Faculty:* 71 full-time (49 women), 49 part-time/adjunct (32 women). *Students:* 4 part-time (all women); includes 1 minority (Hispanic/Latino). Average age 42. 2 applicants, 50% accepted. *Entrance requirements:* Additional exam requirements/recommendations for international students: Required—TOEFL (minimum score 550 paper-based). *Application deadline:* For fall admission, 5/1 priority date for domestic students. Applications are processed on a rolling basis. Application fee: $30. Electronic applications accepted. *Expenses:* Tuition, state resident: part-time $290 per credit hour. Tuition, nonresident: part-time $1173 per credit hour. *Required fees:* $127 per credit hour. Tuition and fees vary according to course load. *Financial support:* Application deadline: 6/30; applicants required to submit FAFSA. *Unit head:* Dr. Gretchen Warn, Graduate Program Assistant, E-mail: gwarn@fgcu.edu. *Application contact:* Susan Baurer, Administrative Assistant, 239-590-7451, Fax: 239-590-7474, E-mail: sbaurer@fgcu.edu.

Florida National University, Program in Nursing, Hialeah, FL 33012. Offers family nurse practitioner (MSN); nurse educator (MSN); nurse leadership and management (MSN). *Program availability:* 100% online, blended/hybrid learning. *Degree requirements:* For master's, practicum. *Entrance requirements:* For master's, active registered nurse license, BSN from accredited institution. *Expenses: Tuition:* Full-time $15,600. *Required fees:* $650.
Website: https://www.fnu.edu/prospective-students/our-programs/select-a-program/master-of-business-administration/nursing-msn-master/

Florida Southern College, Program in Nursing, Lakeland, FL 33801-5698. Offers adult gerontology clinical nurse specialist (MSN); adult gerontology primary care nurse practitioner (MSN); family nurse practitioner (MSN); nurse educator (MSN); nursing administration (MSN). *Accreditation:* AACN. *Program availability:* Part-time. *Faculty:* 5 full-time (all women), 2 part-time/adjunct (both women). *Students:* 142 full-time (126 women), 9 part-time (all women); includes 70 minority (39 Black or African American, non-Hispanic/Latino; 1 American Indian or Alaska Native, non-Hispanic/Latino; 11 Asian, non-Hispanic/Latino; 13 Hispanic/Latino; 1 Native Hawaiian or other Pacific Islander, non-Hispanic/Latino; 5 Two or more races, non-Hispanic/Latino), 1 international. Average age 40. 83 applicants, 93% accepted, 72 enrolled. In 2017, 41 master's awarded. *Degree requirements:* For master's, 780 clinical practice hours. *Entrance requirements:* For master's, GMAT or GRE General Test, Florida RN license, 3 letters of recommendation, personal statement, minimum GPA of 3.0, resume. Additional exam requirements/recommendations for international students: Required—TOEFL (minimum score 550 paper-based; 79 iBT), IELTS (minimum score 6.5). *Application deadline:* For fall admission, 6/1 for domestic and international students; for spring admission, 10/1 for domestic and international students. Applications are processed on a rolling basis. Application fee: $30. Electronic applications accepted. *Expenses:* $585 per credit hour, $100 required fees. *Financial support:* In 2017–18, 1 student received support. Scholarships/grants and traineeships available. Support available to part-time students. Financial award applicants required to submit FAFSA. *Faculty research:* End of life care, dementia, health promotion. *Unit head:* Dr. Linda Comer, Dean, 863-680-4310, Fax: 863-680-3872, E-mail: lcomer@flsouthern.edu. *Application contact:* Kathy Connelly, Evening Program Assistant Director, 863-680-4205, Fax: 863-680-3872, E-mail: kconnelly@flsouthern.edu.

Framingham State University, Graduate Studies, Program in Nursing, Framingham, MA 01701-9101. Offers nursing education (MSN); nursing leadership (MSN). *Accreditation:* AACN. *Entrance requirements:* For master's, BSN; minimum cumulative undergraduate GPA of 3.0, 3.25 in nursing courses; coursework in statistics; 2 letters of recommendation; interview. *Application deadline:* For fall admission, 7/1 for domestic students. Application fee: $50. Electronic applications accepted. *Unit head:* Dr. Cynthia Bechtel, Program Coordinator, 508-626-4997, Fax: 508-626-4030, E-mail: cbechtel@framingham.edu. *Application contact:* Dr. Scott Greenberg, Associate Vice President of Academic Affairs and Dean of Continuing Education, 508-626-4603, E-mail: sgreenberg@framingham.edu.

Francis Marion University, Graduate Programs, Department of Nursing, Florence, SC 29502-0547. Offers family nurse practitioner (MSN); family nurse practitioner with nurse educator certificate (MSN); nurse educator (MSN). *Program availability:* Part-time. *Entrance requirements:* For master's, GRE, official transcripts, two letters of recommendation from professional associates or former professors, written statement of applicant's career goals, current nursing license. Additional exam requirements/recommendations for international students: Required—TOEFL (minimum score 550 paper-based; 79 iBT). Electronic applications accepted. *Expenses:* Contact institution.

Franklin Pierce University, Graduate and Professional Studies, Rindge, NH 03461-0060. Offers curriculum and instruction (M Ed); elementary education (MS Ed); emerging network technologies (Graduate Certificate); energy and sustainability studies (MBA, Graduate Certificate); health administration (MBA, Graduate Certificate); human resource management (MBA, Graduate Certificate); information technology (MBA); leadership (MBA); nursing education (MS); nursing leadership (MS); physical therapy (DPT); physician assistant studies (MPAS); special education (M Ed); sports management (MBA). *Accreditation:* APTA. *Program availability:* Part-time, 100% online, blended/hybrid learning. *Degree requirements:* For master's, concentrated original research projects; student teaching; fieldwork and/or internship; leadership project; PRAXIS I and II (for M Ed); for doctorate, concentrated original research projects, clinical fieldwork and/or internship, leadership project. *Entrance requirements:* For master's, minimum GPA of 2.5, 3 letters of recommendation; competencies in accounting, economics, statistics, and computer skills through life experience or undergraduate coursework (for MBA); certification/e-portfolio, minimum C grade in all education courses (for M Ed); license to practice as RN (for MS); for doctorate, GRE, 80 hours of observation/work in PT settings; completion of anatomy, chemistry, physics, and statistics; minimum GPA of 3.0. Additional exam requirements/recommendations for international students: Required—TOEFL (minimum score 550 paper-based; 61 iBT). Electronic applications accepted. *Faculty research:* Evidence-based practice in sports physical therapy, human resource management in economic crisis, leadership in nursing, innovation in sports facility management, differentiated learning and understanding by design.

Frostburg State University, College of Liberal Arts and Sciences, Department of Nursing, Frostburg, MD 21532. Offers nursing administration (MSN); nursing education (MSN). *Program availability:* Part-time, online learning. *Faculty:* 6 full-time (all women). *Students:* 1 (woman) full-time, 22 part-time (all women); includes 3 minority (2 Black or African American, non-Hispanic/Latino; 1 Hispanic/Latino). Average age 35. 10 applicants, 80% accepted, 5 enrolled. In 2017, 12 master's awarded. *Entrance requirements:* For master's, current unrestricted RN license; BSN from a nursing program accredited by CCNE or ACEN. Additional exam requirements/recommendations for international students: Required—TOEFL. *Application deadline:* For spring admission, 11/1 for domestic students. Application fee: $45. *Expenses:* Tuition, state resident: part-time $433 per credit hour. Tuition, nonresident: part-time $557 per credit hour. *Required fees:* $121 per credit hour. $27 per term. *Financial support:* Unspecified assistantships available. Financial award application deadline: 4/1. *Unit head:* Dr. Heather Gable, Department Chair, 301-687-4894, E-mail: hagable@frostburg.edu. *Application contact:* Vickie Mazer, Director, Graduate Services, 301-687-7053, Fax: 301-687-4597, E-mail: vmmazer@frostburg.edu.
Website: http://www.frostburg.edu/nursing/

George Mason University, College of Health and Human Services, School of Nursing, Fairfax, VA 22030. Offers adult gerontology (DNP); adult/gerontological nurse practitioner (MSN); family nurse practitioner (MSN, DNP); nurse educator (MSN); nursing (PhD); nursing administration (MSN, DNP); nursing education (Certificate); psychiatric mental health (DNP). *Accreditation:* AACN. *Program availability:* Part-time, evening/weekend, blended/hybrid learning. *Faculty:* 28 full-time (27 women), 51 part-time/adjunct (47 women). *Students:* 51 full-time (40 women), 182 part-time (162 women); includes 110 minority (59 Black or African American, non-Hispanic/Latino; 1 American Indian or Alaska Native, non-Hispanic/Latino; 36 Asian, non-Hispanic/Latino; 10 Hispanic/Latino; 4 Two or more races, non-Hispanic/Latino), 8 international. Average age 37. 159 applicants, 70% accepted, 73 enrolled. In 2017, 33 master's, 24 doctorates, 1 other advanced degree awarded. *Degree requirements:* For master's, comprehensive exam (for some programs), thesis in clinical classes; for doctorate, comprehensive exam (for some programs), thesis/dissertation (for some programs). *Entrance requirements:* For master's, 2 official transcripts; expanded goals statement; resume; BSN from accredited institution; minimum GPA of 3.0 in last 60 credits of undergraduate work; 2 letters of recommendation; completion of undergraduate statistics and graduate-level bivariate statistics; certification in professional CPR; for doctorate, GRE, 2 official transcripts; expanded goals statement; resume; 2 recommendation letters; nursing license; at least 1 year of work experience as an RN; interview; writing sample; evidence of graduate-level course in applied statistics; master's degree in nursing with minimum GPA of 3.5; for Certificate, 2 official transcripts; expanded goals statement; resume; master's degree from accredited institution or currently enrolled with minimum GPA of 3.0. Additional exam requirements/recommendations for international students: Required—TOEFL (minimum score 570 paper-based; 88 iBT), IELTS (minimum score 6.5), PTE (minimum score 59). *Application deadline:* For fall admission, 2/1 for domestic and international students. Application fee: $75 ($80 for international students). Electronic applications accepted. *Expenses:* Contact institution. *Financial support:* In 2017–18, 7 students received support, including 5 research assistantships with tuition reimbursements available (averaging $20,500 per year), 2 teaching assistantships; career-related internships or fieldwork, Federal Work-Study, scholarships/grants, unspecified assistantships, and health care benefits (for full-time research or teaching assistantship recipients) also available. Financial award application deadline: 3/1; financial award applicants required to submit FAFSA. *Faculty research:* Health care, nursing science. *Total annual research expenditures:* $1.6 million. *Unit head:* Carol Urban, Director, 703-993-2991, Fax: 703-993-1949, E-mail: curban@gmu.edu. *Application contact:* Susan Eckis, Office Manager, 703-993-1938, Fax: 703-993-1949, E-mail: seckis@gmu.edu.
Website: http://chhs.gmu.edu/nursing

Georgetown University, Graduate School of Arts and Sciences, School of Nursing and Health Studies, Washington, DC 20057. Offers acute care nurse practitioner (MS); clinical nurse specialist (MS); family nurse practitioner (MS); nurse anesthesia (MS); nurse-midwifery (MS); nursing (DNP); nursing education (MS). *Accreditation:* AACN; AANA/CANAEP (one or more programs are accredited); ACNM/ACME (one or more programs are accredited). *Degree requirements:* For master's, thesis optional. *Entrance requirements:* For master's, GRE General Test or MAT, bachelor's degree in nursing from ACEN-accredited school, minimum undergraduate GPA of 3.0. Additional exam requirements/recommendations for international students: Required—TOEFL.

The George Washington University, School of Nursing, Washington, DC 20052. Offers adult nurse practitioner (MSN, DNP, Post-Master's Certificate); clinical research administration (MSN); family nurse practitioner (MSN, Post-Master's Certificate); health care quality (MSN, Post-Master's Certificate); nursing leadership and management (MSN); nursing practice (DNP), including nursing education; palliative care nurse practitioner (Post-Master's Certificate). *Accreditation:* AACN. *Faculty:* 58 full-time (56 women), 119 part-time/adjunct (111 women). *Students:* 38 full-time (34 women), 570 part-time (510 women); includes 197 minority (92 Black or African American, non-Hispanic/Latino; 2 American Indian or Alaska Native, non-Hispanic/Latino; 63 Asian, non-Hispanic/Latino; 28 Hispanic/Latino; 1 Native Hawaiian or other Pacific Islander, non-Hispanic/Latino; 11 Two or more races, non-Hispanic/Latino), 2 international. Average age 31. 507 applicants, 76% accepted, 185 enrolled. In 2017, 155 master's, 32 doctorates awarded. *Expenses: Tuition:* Full-time $28,800; part-time $1655 per credit hour. *Required fees:* $45; $2.75 per credit hour. *Unit head:* Pamela R. Jeffries, Dean, 202-994-3725, E-mail: pjeffries@gwu.edu. *Application contact:* Kristin Williams, Associate Provost for Graduate Enrollment Management, 202-994-0467, Fax: 202-994-0371, E-mail: ksw@gwu.edu.
Website: http://nursing.gwumc.edu/

Georgia Southern University, Jack N. Averitt College of Graduate Studies, College of Health and Human Sciences, School of Nursing, Nurse Educator Certificate Program, Statesboro, GA 30458. Offers Certificate. *Students:* 1 (woman) part-time. Average age 60. 1 applicant, 100% accepted. *Entrance requirements:* For degree, master's degree in nursing, minimum GPA of 3.0, current RN license. Additional exam requirements/recommendations for international students: Required—TOEFL (minimum score 80 iBT). *Application deadline:* For fall admission, 7/31 for domestic students; for spring admission, 11/30 for domestic students; for summer admission, 3/31 for domestic students. *Expenses:* Tuition, state resident: full-time $4986; part-time $3324 per year. Tuition, nonresident: full-time $21,982; part-time $15,352 per year. *Required fees:* $2092; $1802 per credit hour. $901 per semester. Tuition and fees vary according to course load, campus/location and program. *Financial support:* In 2017–18, 1 student received support. *Faculty research:* Promotion of health and quality of life for individuals, families, and communities within a global society. *Unit head:* Dr. Sharon Radzyminski, Department Chair, 912-478-5455, Fax: 912-478-0536, E-mail: sradzyminski@georgiasouthern.edu.

Georgia Southwestern State University, College of Nursing and Health Sciences, Americus, GA 31709-4693. Offers family nurse practitioner (MSN); health informatics (Postbaccalaureate Certificate); nurse educator (Post Master's Certificate); nursing educator (MSN); nursing informatics (MSN); nursing leadership (MSN). MSN program offered by the Georgia Intercollegiate Consortium for Graduate Nursing Education, a partnership with Columbus State University. *Program availability:* Part-time, online only, all theory courses are offered online. *Faculty:* 10 full-time, 5 part-time/adjunct. *Students:* 23 full-time (22 women), 106 part-time (92 women); includes 41 minority (all Black or African American, non-Hispanic/Latino). Average age 35. 95 applicants, 63% accepted, 30 enrolled. In 2017, 17 master's awarded. *Degree requirements:* For master's, comprehensive exam (for some programs), thesis (for some programs), minimum cumulative GPA of 3.0; maximum of 6 credit hours with C grade and no D grades; degree completed within 7 calendar years from initial enrollment date in graduate courses; for other advanced degree, minimum cumulative GPA of 3.0; maximum of 6 credit hours with C grade and no D grades; degree completed within 7 calendar years from initial enrollment date in graduate courses. *Entrance requirements:* For master's and other advanced degree, baccalaureate degree in nursing from regionally-accredited institution and nationally-accredited nursing program with minimum GPA of 3.0; three professional letters of recommendation; current unencumbered RN license in state where clinical course requirements will be met; background check/drug test; proof of immunizations. *Application deadline:* For fall admission, 1/15 for domestic students; for spring admission, 10/15 for domestic students. Application fee: $25. Electronic applications accepted. *Expenses:* $385 per credit hour, plus fees, which vary according to enrolled credit hours. *Financial support:* Application deadline: 6/1; applicants required to submit FAFSA. *Unit head:* Dr. Sandra Daniel, Dean, 229-931-2275. *Application contact:* Whitney Ford, Admissions Specialist, Office of Graduate Admissions, 800-338-0082, Fax: 229-931-2983, E-mail: graduateadmissions@gsw.edu.
Website: https://gsw.edu/Academics/Schools-and-Departments/School-of-Nursing/index

Graceland University, School of Nursing, Independence, MO 64050-3434. Offers adult and gerontology acute care (MSN, PMC); family nurse practitioner (MSN, PMC); nurse educator (MSN, PMC); organizational leadership (DNP). *Accreditation:* AACN. *Program availability:* Part-time, online learning. *Faculty:* 13 full-time (11 women), 24 part-time/adjunct (all women). *Students:* 338 full-time (294 women), 311 part-time (282 women); includes 102 minority (33 Black or African American, non-Hispanic/Latino; 8 American Indian or Alaska Native, non-Hispanic/Latino; 18 Asian, non-Hispanic/Latino; 29 Hispanic/Latino; 1 Native Hawaiian or other Pacific Islander, non-Hispanic/Latino; 13 Two or more races, non-Hispanic/Latino), 2 international. Average age 36. 119 applicants, 86% accepted, 95 enrolled. In 2017, 158 master's, 2 doctorates awarded. *Degree requirements:* For master's, comprehensive exam (for some programs), thesis optional, scholarly project; for doctorate, capstone project. *Entrance requirements:* For master's, BSN from nationally-accredited program, RN license, minimum GPA of 3.0, satisfactory criminal background check, three professional reference letters, professional goals statement of 150 words or less; for doctorate, MSN from nationally-accredited program, RN license, minimum GPA of 3.2, criminal background check. Additional exam requirements/recommendations for international students: Required—TOEFL (minimum score 550 paper-based; 79 iBT). *Application deadline:* For fall admission, 6/1 priority date for domestic students; for winter admission, 10/1 priority date for domestic students; for spring admission, 10/1 priority date for domestic students; for summer admission, 2/1 for domestic students. Application fee: $50. Electronic applications accepted. *Expenses:* $775 per credit hour tuition, $1,800 practicum fees, $480 research fees, $846 university technology fees, $655 lab fees, $300 program support fees. *Financial support:* In 2017–18, 14 students received support. Institutionally sponsored loans available. Support available to part-time students. Financial award application deadline: 6/1; financial award applicants required to submit FAFSA. *Faculty research:* International nursing, family care-giving, health promotion, mental health nursing. *Unit head:* Dr. Claudia D. Horton, Interim Vice President for Independence Campus/Dean, 816-423-4670, Fax: 816-423-4753, E-mail: horton@graceland.edu. *Application contact:* Admissions Representative, 816-423-4717, Fax: 816-833-2990, E-mail: distancelearning@graceland.edu.
Website: http://www.graceland.edu/nursing

Grand Canyon University, College of Nursing and Health Care Professions, Phoenix, AZ 85017-1097. Offers acute care nurse practitioner (MSN, PMC); family nurse practitioner (MSN, PMC); health care administration (MS); health care informatics (MS, MSN); leadership in health care systems (MSN); nursing (DNP); nursing education (MSN, PMC); public health (MPH, MSN); MBA/MSN. *Accreditation:* AACN. *Program availability:* Part-time, evening/weekend, online learning. *Degree requirements:* For master's and PMC, comprehensive exam (for some programs). *Entrance requirements:* For master's, minimum cumulative and science course undergraduate GPA of 3.0. Additional exam requirements/recommendations for international students: Required—TOEFL (minimum score 575 paper-based; 90 iBT), IELTS (minimum score 7).

Grand Valley State University, Kirkhof College of Nursing, Allendale, MI 49503-3314. Offers advanced practice (MSN); case management (MSN); nursing administration (MSN); nursing education (MSN); nursing practice (DNP); MSN/MBA. *Accreditation:* AACN. *Program availability:* Part-time. *Faculty:* 17 full-time (all women), 5 part-time/adjunct (4 women). *Students:* 44 full-time (40 women), 74 part-time (63 women); includes 15 minority (7 Black or African American, non-Hispanic/Latino; 4 Asian, non-Hispanic/Latino; 3 Hispanic/Latino; 1 Two or more races, non-Hispanic/Latino), 4 international. Average age 33. 34 applicants, 100% accepted, 23 enrolled. In 2017, 8 master's, 22 doctorates awarded. *Degree requirements:* For master's, thesis optional; for doctorate, thesis/dissertation optional. *Entrance requirements:* For master's, GRE, minimum upper-division GPA of 3.0, course work in statistics, Michigan RN license, writing sample, interview, criminal background check and drug screen, health records; for doctorate, minimum GPA of 3.0 in master's-level coursework, writing sample, interview, RN in Michigan, criminal background check and drug screen, health records. Additional exam requirements/recommendations for international students: Required—TOEFL (minimum iBT score of 80), IELTS (6.5), or Michigan English Language Assessment Battery (77). *Application deadline:* For fall admission, 3/15 priority date for domestic students. Applications are processed on a rolling basis. Application fee: $30. Electronic applications accepted. *Expenses:* $686 per credit hour (for MSN); $770 per credit hour (for DNP). *Financial support:* In 2017–18, 34 students received support, including 10 fellowships, 30 research assistantships with partial tuition reimbursements available (averaging $4,000 per year); career-related internships or fieldwork, Federal Work-Study, institutionally sponsored loans, and traineeships also available. Financial award application deadline: 2/15. *Faculty research:* Multigenerational health promotion, chronic disease prevention, end-of-life issues, nursing workload, family caregiver health. *Total annual research expenditures:* $36,000. *Unit head:* Dr. Cynthia McCurren, Dean, 616-331-3558, Fax: 616-331-2510, E-mail: mccurrec@gvsu.edu. *Application contact:* Dr. Karen Burritt, Associate Dean for Graduate Programs, 616-331-5585, Fax: 616-331-2510, E-mail: burritka@gvsu.edu.
Website: http://www.gvsu.edu/kcon/

Grand View University, Graduate Studies, Des Moines, IA 50316-1599. Offers athletic training (MS); clinical nurse leader (MSN, Post Master's Certificate); nursing education (MSN, Post Master's Certificate); organizational leadership (MS); sport management (MS); teacher leadership (M Ed); urban education (M Ed). *Program availability:* Part-time, evening/weekend. *Degree requirements:* For master's, completion of all required coursework in common core and selected track with minimum cumulative GPA of 3.0 and no more than two grades of C. *Entrance requirements:* For master's, GRE, GMAT, or essay, minimum undergraduate GPA of 3.0, professional resume, 3 letters of recommendation, interview. Additional exam requirements/recommendations for international students: Required—TOEFL (minimum score 550 paper-based). Electronic applications accepted.

Grantham University, College of Nursing and Allied Health, Lenexa, KS 66219. Offers case management (MSN); health systems management (MS); healthcare administration (MHA); nursing education (MSN); nursing informatics (MSN); nursing management and organizational leadership (MSN). *Program availability:* Part-time, evening/weekend, online only, 100% online. *Faculty:* 2 full-time, 34 part-time/adjunct. *Students:* 198 full-time (144 women), 113 part-time (83 women); includes 170 minority (118 Black or African American, non-Hispanic/Latino; 3 American Indian or Alaska Native, non-Hispanic/Latino; 27 Asian, non-Hispanic/Latino; 11 Hispanic/Latino; 2 Native Hawaiian or other Pacific Islander, non-Hispanic/Latino; 9 Two or more races, non-Hispanic/Latino). Average age 41. 95 applicants, 89% accepted, 72 enrolled. In 2017, 123 master's awarded. *Entrance requirements:* For master's, BSN from state-approved nursing program with minimum cumulative GPA of 2.5 from institution accredited by agency recognized by U.S. DOE or foreign equivalent; unencumbered and current RN license. Additional exam requirements/recommendations for international students: Required—TOEFL (minimum score 530 paper-based; 71 iBT), IELTS (minimum score 6.5), PTE (minimum score 50). *Application deadline:* Applications are processed on a rolling basis. Application fee: $0. Electronic applications accepted. *Expenses:* $325 per credit hour. *Financial support:* Scholarships/grants available. Financial award applicants required to submit FAFSA. *Faculty research:* Compassion in caring improving incivility in the ICU setting, get well network technology in enhancing patient education, opioid use and abuse in postpartum women. *Unit head:* Dr. Cheryl Rules, Dean of the College of Nursing and Allied Health, 913-309-4783, Fax: 844-897-6490, E-mail: crules@grantham.edu. *Application contact:* Jared Parlette, Vice President of Student Enrollment, 800-955-2527 Ext. 803, Fax: 866-914-4557, E-mail: admissions@grantham.edu.
Website: http://www.grantham.edu/nursing-and-allied-health/

Gwynedd Mercy University, Frances M. Maguire School of Nursing and Health Professions, Gwynedd Valley, PA 19437-0901. Offers clinical nurse specialist (MSN), including gerontology, oncology, pediatrics; nurse educator (MSN); nurse practitioner (MSN), including adult health, pediatric health; nursing (DNP). *Accreditation:* ACEN. *Program availability:* Part-time, blended/hybrid learning. *Faculty:* 4 full-time (all women), 1 (woman) part-time/adjunct. *Students:* 28 full-time (25 women), 48 part-time (43 women); includes 28 minority (15 Black or African American, non-Hispanic/Latino; 11 Asian, non-Hispanic/Latino; 1 Hispanic/Latino; 1 Two or more races, non-Hispanic/Latino). Average age 37. 72 applicants, 25% accepted, 16 enrolled. In 2017, 7 master's awarded. *Degree requirements:* For master's, thesis optional; for doctorate, evidence-based scholarly project. *Entrance requirements:* For master's, GRE General Test or MAT, current nursing experience, physical assessment, course work in statistics, BSN from ACEN-accredited program, 2 letters of recommendation, personal interview. Additional exam requirements/recommendations for international students: Required—TOEFL (minimum score 575 paper-based). *Application deadline:* For fall admission, 8/1 priority date for domestic students; for winter admission, 12/1 priority date for domestic students. Applications are processed on a rolling basis. Electronic applications accepted. *Expenses:* $825 per credit (non-doctoral degrees), $930 per credit (doctoral); $17 part-time fee, $165 graduation fee. *Financial support:* In 2017–18, 5 students received support. Scholarships/grants, traineeships, and unspecified assistantships available. Financial award application deadline: 8/30. *Faculty research:* Critical thinking, primary care, domestic violence, multiculturalism, nursing centers. *Unit head:* Dr. Andrea D. Hollingsworth, Dean, 215-646-7300 Ext. 539, Fax: 215-641-5517, E-mail: hollingsworth.a@gmc.edu. *Application contact:* Dr. Barbara A. Jones, Director, 215-646-7300 Ext. 407, Fax: 215-641-5564, E-mail: jones.b@gmc.edu.
Website: http://www.gmercyu.edu/academics/graduate-programs/nursing

Hampton University, School of Nursing, Hampton, VA 23668. Offers community health nursing (MS); family nurse practitioner (MS); family research (PhD); nursing administration (MS); nursing education (MS). *Accreditation:* AACN. *Program availability:* Part-time, online learning. *Students:* 6 full-time (all women), 28 part-time (25 women); includes 31 minority (29 Black or African American, non-Hispanic/Latino; 2 Hispanic/Latino). Average age 48. 7 applicants, 14% accepted. In 2017, 3 master's, 4 doctorates awarded. *Degree requirements:* For master's, comprehensive exam, thesis optional; for doctorate, comprehensive exam, thesis/dissertation. *Entrance requirements:* For master's, GRE General Test. *Application deadline:* For fall admission, 6/1 priority date for domestic students, 4/1 priority date for international students; for spring admission, 11/1 priority date for domestic students, 9/1 priority date for international students; for summer admission, 4/1 priority date for domestic students, 2/1 priority date for international students. Applications are processed on a rolling basis. Application fee: $35. Electronic applications accepted. *Expenses: Tuition:* Full-time $22,630; part-time $575 per semester hour. *Required fees:* $70. Tuition and fees vary according to program. *Financial support:* In 2017–18, 2 students received support. Fellowships, research assistantships, teaching assistantships, career-related internships or fieldwork, Federal Work-Study, institutionally sponsored loans, and scholarships/grants available. Support available to part-time students. Financial award application deadline: 6/30; financial award applicants required to submit FAFSA. *Faculty research:* African-American stress, HIV education, pediatric obesity, hypertension, breast cancer. *Unit head:* Dr. Shevallanie Lott, Dean, 757-727-5654, E-mail: shevellanie.lott@hamptonu.edu.
Website: http://nursing.hamptonu.edu

Hardin-Simmons University, Graduate School, Patty Hanks Shelton School of Nursing, Abilene, TX 79698-0001. Offers education (MSN); family nurse practitioner (MSN). Programs offered jointly with McMurry University. *Accreditation:* AACN. *Program availability:* Part-time. *Faculty:* 2 full-time (both women), 1 (woman) part-time/adjunct. *Students:* 17 part-time (8 women); includes 5 minority (1 Black or African American, non-Hispanic/Latino; 1 Asian, non-Hispanic/Latino; 3 Hispanic/Latino), 1 international. Average age 36. In 2017, 7 master's awarded. *Degree requirements:* For master's, comprehensive exam, thesis or alternative. *Entrance requirements:* For master's, GRE, minimum undergraduate GPA of 3.0; interview; upper-level course work in statistics; CPR certification; letters of recommendation. Additional exam requirements/recommendations for international students: Required—TOEFL (minimum score 550 paper-based; 75 iBT). *Application deadline:* For fall admission, 8/15 priority date for

domestic students, 4/1 for international students; for spring admission, 1/5 priority date for domestic students, 9/1 for international students. Applications are processed on a rolling basis. Application fee: $50 ($150 for international students). Electronic applications accepted. *Expenses:* Contact institution. *Financial support:* In 2017–18, 10 students received support. Career-related internships or fieldwork and scholarships/grants available. Support available to part-time students. Financial award application deadline: 6/30; financial award applicants required to submit FAFSA. *Faculty research:* Child abuse, alternative medicine, pediatric chronic disease, health promotion. *Unit head:* Dr. Nina Ouimette, Dean, 325-671-2357, Fax: 325-671-2386, E-mail: nouimette@phssn.edu. *Application contact:* Dr. Nancy Kucinski, Dean of Graduate Studies, 325-670-1298, Fax: 325-670-1564, E-mail: gradoff@hsutx.edu.
Website: http://www.phssn.edu/

Herzing University Online, Program in Nursing, Menomonee Falls, WI 53051. Offers nursing (MSN); nursing education (MSN); nursing management (MSN). *Accreditation:* AACN. *Program availability:* Online learning.

Holy Family University, Graduate and Professional Programs, School of Nursing and Allied Health Professions, Philadelphia, PA 19114. Offers nursing administration (MSN); nursing education (MSN). *Accreditation:* AACN. *Program availability:* Part-time, evening/weekend. *Degree requirements:* For master's, thesis or alternative, comprehensive portfolio, clinical practicum. *Entrance requirements:* For master's, BSN or RN from appropriately-accredited program, minimum GPA of 3.0, professional references, official transcripts of all college or university work, essay/personal statement, current resume, completion of one undergraduate statistics course with minimum grade of C. Additional exam requirements/recommendations for international students: Required—TOEFL (minimum score 550 paper-based; 79 iBT), IELTS (minimum score 6), or PTE (minimum score 54). Electronic applications accepted. *Expenses: Tuition:* Full-time $13,518; part-time $9012 per credit hour. Tuition and fees vary according to degree level and program.

Howard University, College of Nursing and Allied Health Sciences, Division of Nursing, Washington, DC 20059-0002. Offers family nurse practitioner (MSN); nurse educator (MSN). *Accreditation:* AACN. *Program availability:* Part-time. *Degree requirements:* For master's, comprehensive exam, thesis optional. *Entrance requirements:* For master's, RN license, minimum GPA of 3.0, BS in nursing. *Faculty research:* Urinary incontinence, breast cancer prevention, depression in the elderly, adolescent pregnancy.

Immaculata University, College of Graduate Studies, Division of Nursing, Immaculata, PA 19345. Offers nursing administration (MSN); nursing education (MSN). *Accreditation:* AACN. *Program availability:* Part-time, evening/weekend. *Entrance requirements:* For master's, MAT or GRE, BSN, minimum undergraduate GPA of 3.0. Additional exam requirements/recommendations for international students: Required—TOEFL.

Indiana State University, College of Graduate and Professional Studies, College of Health and Human Services, Department of Advanced Practice Nursing, Terre Haute, IN 47809. Offers advanced practice nursing (DNP); family nurse practitioner (MS); nursing administration (MS); nursing education (MS). *Accreditation:* ACEN. *Program availability:* Part-time. *Degree requirements:* For master's, thesis or alternative. *Entrance requirements:* For master's, BSN, RN license, minimum undergraduate GPA of 3.0. Electronic applications accepted. *Faculty research:* Nursing faculty-student interactions, clinical evaluation, program evaluation, sexual dysfunction, faculty attitudes.

Indiana University Kokomo, School of Nursing, Kokomo, IN 46904. Offers family nurse practitioner (MSN); nurse administrator (MSN); nurse educator (MSN). Electronic applications accepted. *Expenses:* Contact institution.

Indiana University of Pennsylvania, School of Graduate Studies and Research, College of Health and Human Services, Department of Nursing and Allied Health Professions, Program in Nursing Education, Indiana, PA 15705. Offers MS. *Program availability:* Part-time. *Faculty:* 12 full-time (11 women), 1 (woman) part-time/adjunct. *Students:* 7 full-time (all women), 27 part-time (25 women), 7 international. Average age 36. 17 applicants, 88% accepted, 8 enrolled. In 2017, 14 master's awarded. *Degree requirements:* For master's, thesis optional, practicum. *Entrance requirements:* Additional exam requirements/recommendations for international students: Required—TOEFL (minimum score 540 paper-based). *Application deadline:* Applications are processed on a rolling basis. Application fee: $50. Electronic applications accepted. *Expenses:* Contact institution. *Financial support:* In 2017–18, 5 research assistantships with tuition reimbursements (averaging $2,720 per year) were awarded; career-related internships or fieldwork, Federal Work-Study, scholarships/grants, and unspecified assistantships also available. Financial award application deadline: 4/15; financial award applicants required to submit FAFSA. *Unit head:* Dr. Nashat Zuraikat, Graduate Coordinator, 724-357-3262, E-mail: zuraikat@iup.edu.
Website: http://www.iup.edu/grad/nursing/default.aspx

Indiana University–Purdue University Fort Wayne, College of Health and Human Services, Department of Nursing, Fort Wayne, IN 46805-1499. Offers adult-gerontology primary care nurse practitioner (MS); family nurse practitioner (MS); nurse executive (MS); nursing administration (Certificate); nursing education (MS). *Accreditation:* ACEN. *Program availability:* Part-time. *Entrance requirements:* For master's, GRE Writing Test (if GPA below 3.0), BS in nursing, eligibility for Indiana RN license, minimum GPA of 3.0, essay, copy of resume, three references, undergraduate course work in research and statistics within last 5 years. Additional exam requirements/recommendations for international students: Required—TOEFL (minimum score 550 paper-based; 79 iBT); Recommended—TWE. Electronic applications accepted. *Faculty research:* Community engagement, cervical screening, evidence-based practice.

Indiana University–Purdue University Indianapolis, School of Nursing, MSN Program in Nursing, Indianapolis, IN 46202. Offers adult/gerontology acute care nurse practitioner (MSN); adult/gerontology clinical nurse specialist (MSN); adult/gerontology primary care nurse practitioner (MSN); family nurse practitioner (MSN); nursing education (MSN); nursing leadership in health systems (MSN); pediatric clinical nurse specialist (MSN); pediatric nurse practitioner (MSN). *Accreditation:* AACN. *Program availability:* Part-time, blended/hybrid learning. *Degree requirements:* For master's, thesis. *Entrance requirements:* For master's, BSN from ACEN- or CCNE-accredited program, minimum undergraduate GPA of 3.0 (preferred), professional resume or curriculum vitae, essay stating career goals and objectives, current unencumbered RN license, three references from individuals with knowledge of ability to succeed in graduate program. Additional exam requirements/recommendations for international students: Required—TOEFL (minimum score 550 paper-based; 79 iBT). Electronic applications accepted. *Expenses:* Contact institution. *Faculty research:* Quality of life, symptom management, cancer prevention and control, heart failure, pediatric oncology.

Indiana Wesleyan University, Graduate School, School of Nursing, Marion, IN 46953-4974. Offers nursing administration (MS); nursing education (MS); primary care nursing (MS); MSN/MBA. *Accreditation:* AACN. *Program availability:* Part-time, online learning. *Degree requirements:* For master's, capstone project or thesis. *Entrance requirements:* For master's, writing sample, RN license, 1 year of related experience, graduate statistics course. Additional exam requirements/recommendations for international students: Required—TOEFL. *Expenses:* Contact institution. *Faculty research:* Primary health care with international emphasis, international nursing.

Jacksonville University, Brooks Rehabilitation College of Healthcare Sciences, Keigwin School of Nursing, Master of Science in Nursing Program, Jacksonville, FL 32211. Offers clinical nurse educator (MSN); family nurse practitioner (MSN); family nurse practitioner/emergency nurse practitioner (MSN); leadership in the healthcare system (MSN); nursing informatics (MSN); psychiatric nurse practitioner (MSN); MSN/MBA. *Program availability:* Part-time, 100% online, blended/hybrid learning. *Faculty:* 8 full-time (all women), 8 part-time/adjunct (6 women). *Students:* 41 full-time (36 women), 456 part-time (415 women); includes 169 minority (102 Black or African American, non-Hispanic/Latino; 4 American Indian or Alaska Native, non-Hispanic/Latino; 24 Asian, non-Hispanic/Latino; 33 Hispanic/Latino; 1 Native Hawaiian or other Pacific Islander, non-Hispanic/Latino; 5 Two or more races, non-Hispanic/Latino), 1 international. Average age 39. 232 applicants, 59% accepted, 110 enrolled. In 2017, 87 master's awarded. *Degree requirements:* For master's, thesis. *Entrance requirements:* For master's, GRE General Test or undergraduate GPA above 3.0, BSN from ACEN- or CCNE-accredited program; course work in statistics and physical assessment within last 5 years; Florida nursing license; CPR/BLS certification; 3 recommendations, 2 of which are professional references; statement of intent; resume. Additional exam requirements/recommendations for international students: Required—TOEFL (minimum score 650 paper-based; 114 iBT), IELTS (minimum score 8). *Application deadline:* For fall admission, 2/1 for domestic and international students. Applications are processed on a rolling basis. Application fee: $50. Electronic applications accepted. *Expenses:* $620 per credit hour, $455 per credit hour off-campus, $720 per credit hour online. *Financial support:* Federal Work-Study, institutionally sponsored loans, scholarships/grants, and health care benefits available. Support available to part-time students. Financial award application deadline: 3/15; financial award applicants required to submit FAFSA. *Faculty research:* Treatment of anxiety. *Unit head:* Dr. Hilary Morgan, Director, Graduate Nursing Programs/Associate Professor, 904-256-7601, E-mail: hmorgan@ju.edu. *Application contact:* Stephanie Bloom, Assistant Director, Enrollment and Advanced Graduate Nursing, 904-256-7286, E-mail: sstrick4@ju.edu.
Website: https://www.ju.edu/nursing/graduate/master-science-nursing/index.php

Jefferson College of Health Sciences, Program in Nursing, Roanoke, VA 24013. Offers nursing education (MSN); nursing management (MSN). *Accreditation:* AACN. *Program availability:* Part-time. *Degree requirements:* For master's, project. *Entrance requirements:* For master's, MAT. Additional exam requirements/recommendations for international students: Required—TOEFL (minimum score 550 paper-based; 80 iBT). Electronic applications accepted. *Faculty research:* Nursing, teaching and learning techniques, cultural competence, spirituality and nursing.

Johns Hopkins University, School of Nursing, Certificate Programs in Nursing, Baltimore, MD 21205. Offers nursing education (Certificate); pediatric acute care nurse practitioner (Certificate); psychiatric mental health nurse practitioner (Certificate). *Program availability:* Part-time-only, online only, 100% online. *Faculty:* 62 full-time (46 women), 160 part-time/adjunct (all women). *Students:* 39 part-time (35 women); includes 14 minority (5 Black or African American, non-Hispanic/Latino; 2 Asian, non-Hispanic/Latino; 4 Hispanic/Latino; 3 Two or more races, non-Hispanic/Latino). Average age 44. 159 applicants, 33% accepted, 45 enrolled. In 2017, 18 Certificates awarded. *Entrance requirements:* For degree, minimum GPA of 3.0, goal statement/essay, resume, letters of recommendation, official transcripts from all post-secondary institutions, MSN, RN license, NP license. Additional exam requirements/recommendations for international students: Required—TOEFL (minimum score 600 paper-based; 100 iBT), IELTS (minimum score 7). *Application deadline:* For fall admission, 1/1 priority date for domestic students; for spring admission, 11/1 priority date for domestic students. Application fee: $70. Electronic applications accepted. *Expenses:* $1,591 per credit. *Financial support:* Application deadline: 3/1; applicants required to submit FAFSA. *Faculty research:* Palliative care, cardiovascular health, disease prevention and risk reduction, women's health, palliative and end-of-life care. *Unit head:* Dr. Patricia M. Davidson, Dean, 410-955-7544, Fax: 410-955-4890, E-mail: sondeansoffice@jhu.edu. *Application contact:* Cathy Wilson, Director of Admissions, 410-955-7548, Fax: 410-614-7086, E-mail: jhuson@jhu.edu.
Website: http://nursing.jhu.edu/

See Display on page 576 and Close-Up on page 763.

Kennesaw State University, WellStar College of Health and Human Services, Program in Leadership in Nursing, Kennesaw, GA 30144. Offers nursing administration (MSN); nursing education (MSN). *Program availability:* Part-time, evening/weekend, online learning. *Entrance requirements:* For master's, GRE General Test, minimum GPA of 3.0, RN license. Additional exam requirements/recommendations for international students: Required—TOEFL (minimum score 550 paper-based; 80 iBT), IELTS (minimum score 6.5). *Application deadline:* For fall admission, 6/1 for domestic and international students. Application fee: $60. Electronic applications accepted. *Financial support:* Research assistantships with tuition reimbursements and unspecified assistantships available. Financial award application deadline: 4/1; financial award applicants required to submit FAFSA. *Unit head:* Yvonne Eaves, Director, 470-578-6061, E-mail: yeaves@kennesaw.edu. *Application contact:* Jerryl Morris, Admissions Counselor, 470-578-2030, Fax: 470-578-9172, E-mail: ksugrad@kennesaw.edu.
Website: http://wellstarcollege.kennesaw.edu/nursing/master-science-nursing/leadership-in-nursing.php

Kent State University, College of Nursing, Kent, OH 44242. Offers advanced nursing practice (DNP), including adult/gerontology acute care nurse practitioner (MSN, DNP); nursing (MSN, PhD), including adult/gerontology acute care nurse practitioner (MSN, DNP), adult/gerontology clinical nurse specialist (MSN), adult/gerontology primary care nurse practitioner (MSN), family nurse practitioner (MSN), nurse educator (MSN), nursing and healthcare management (MSN), pediatric primary care nurse practitioner (MSN), psychiatric/mental health nurse practitioner (MSN); MBA/MSN. PhD program offered jointly with The University of Akron. *Accreditation:* AACN. *Program availability:* Part-time, online learning. *Faculty:* 29 full-time (28 women), 15 part-time/adjunct (12 women). *Students:* 167 full-time (142 women), 405 part-time (359 women); includes 70 minority (39 Black or African American, non-Hispanic/Latino; 11 Asian, non-Hispanic/Latino; 18 Hispanic/Latino; 2 Two or more races, non-Hispanic/Latino), 13 international. Average age 35. 272 applicants, 74% accepted, 166 enrolled. In 2017, 144 master's, 8 doctorates awarded. *Degree requirements:* For master's, thesis optional; for doctorate, comprehensive exam, thesis/dissertation. *Entrance requirements:* For master's, GRE or GMAT, minimum GPA of 3.0, active RN license, statement of purpose, 3 letters of reference, undergraduate level statistics class, baccalaureate or graduate-level nursing degree, curriculum vitae/resume; for doctorate, GRE, minimum GPA of 3.0, transcripts, 3 letters of reference, interview, active unrestricted Ohio RN license, statement of purpose, writing sample, curriculum vitae/resume, baccalaureate and master's degrees in nursing or DNP. Additional exam requirements/recommendations for international students: Required—TOEFL (minimum score 560 paper-based; 83 iBT), IELTS (minimum score 6.5), PTE (minimum score 55), Michigan English Language Assessment Battery (minimum score 78). *Application deadline:* For fall admission, 3/1 for domestic and international students; for spring admission, 10/1 for domestic and international students. Applications are processed on a rolling basis. Application fee: $45 ($70 for international students). Electronic applications accepted. *Expenses:* Tuition, state resident: full-time $11,310; part-time $515 per credit hour. Tuition,

nonresident: full-time $20,396; part-time $928 per credit hour. *International tuition:* $18,544 full-time. *Financial support:* Scholarships/grants available. Financial award application deadline: 5/4. *Unit head:* Dr. Barbara Broome, Dean, 330-672-3777, E-mail: bbroome1@kent.edu. *Application contact:* Dr. Wendy A. Umberger, Associate Dean for Graduate Programs/Professor, 330-672-8813, E-mail: wlewando@kent.edu.
Website: http://www.kent.edu/nursing/

Keuka College, Program in Nursing, Keuka Park, NY 14478. Offers adult gerontology (MS); nursing education (MS). *Accreditation:* AACN. *Degree requirements:* For master's, exam or thesis. *Entrance requirements:* For master's, bachelor's degree from accredited institution, minimum GPA of 3.0, unencumbered NY State license, and current registration as RN (for nursing); currently full-time or part-time working RN and 2 clinical letters of recommendation (for adult gerontology nurse practitioner). Additional exam requirements/recommendations for international students: Required—TOEFL (minimum score 550 paper-based). Electronic applications accepted. *Expenses:* Contact institution. *Faculty research:* Endocrinology and diabetes management of adults, insulin pump efficacy in those with type 2 diabetes; primary care for all ages, addiction, and substance abuse prevention and treatment; music therapy for those with chronic lung disease; maternal child health nursing; parish nursing; nursing education; homeopathy and wellness, pediatric health; effects of infant feeding experiences.

King University, School of Nursing, Bristol, TN 37620-2699. Offers family nurse practitioner (MSN); nurse educator (MSN); nursing (DNP); nursing administration (MSN); pediatric nurse practitioner (MSN).

Lamar University, College of Graduate Studies, College of Arts and Sciences, JoAnne Gay Dishman Department of Nursing, Beaumont, TX 77701. Offers nursing administration (MSN); nursing education (MSN); MSN/MBA. *Accreditation:* ACEN. *Program availability:* Part-time, evening/weekend, online learning. *Faculty:* 35 full-time (33 women), 3 part-time/adjunct (2 women). *Students:* 92 part-time (85 women); includes 43 minority (27 Black or African American, non-Hispanic/Latino; 7 Asian, non-Hispanic/Latino; 9 Hispanic/Latino). Average age 38. 68 applicants, 88% accepted, 18 enrolled. In 2017, 15 master's awarded. *Degree requirements:* For master's, comprehensive exam, practicum project presentation, evidence-based project. *Entrance requirements:* For master's, GRE General Test, MAT, criminal background check, RN license, ACEN-accredited BSN, college course work in statistics in past 5 years, letters of recommendation, minimum undergraduate GPA of 3.0. Additional exam requirements/recommendations for international students: Required—TOEFL (minimum score 550 paper-based; 79 iBT), IELTS (minimum score 6.5). *Application deadline:* For fall admission, 8/10 for domestic students, 7/1 for international students; for spring admission, 1/5 for domestic students, 12/1 for international students. Applications are processed on a rolling basis. Application fee: $25 ($50 for international students). Electronic applications accepted. *Expenses:* Contact institution. *Financial support:* In 2017–18, 2 teaching assistantships (averaging $24,000 per year) were awarded; scholarships/grants and traineeships also available. Financial award application deadline: 4/1; financial award applicants required to submit FAFSA. *Faculty research:* Student retention, theory, care giving, online course and research. *Unit head:* Cynthia Stinson, Interim Chair, 409-880-8817, Fax: 409-880-8698. *Application contact:* Deidre Mayer, Interim Director, Admissions and Academic Services, 409-880-8888, Fax: 409-880-7419, E-mail: gradmissions@lamar.edu.
Website: http://artssciences.lamar.edu/nursing

La Roche College, School of Graduate Studies and Adult Education, Program in Nursing, Pittsburgh, PA 15237-5898. Offers clinical nurse leader (MSN); nursing education (MSN); nursing management (MSN). *Accreditation:* ACEN. *Program availability:* Part-time, evening/weekend, online only, 100% online. *Faculty:* 3 full-time (all women), 2 part-time/adjunct (1 woman). *Students:* 17 full-time (15 women), 9 part-time (all women), 1 international. Average age 35. 16 applicants, 75% accepted, 10 enrolled. In 2017, 11 master's awarded. *Degree requirements:* For master's, thesis optional, internship, practicum. *Entrance requirements:* For master's, GRE General Test, BSN, nursing license, work experience. Additional exam requirements/recommendations for international students: Recommended—TOEFL (minimum score 550 paper-based). *Application deadline:* For fall admission, 8/15 priority date for domestic students, 8/15 for international students; for spring admission, 12/15 priority date for domestic students, 12/15 for international students. Applications are processed on a rolling basis. Application fee: $50. Electronic applications accepted. *Expenses:* Contact institution. *Financial support:* Application deadline: 3/31; applicants required to submit FAFSA. *Faculty research:* Patient education, perception. *Unit head:* Dr. Terri Liberto, Division Chair, 412-847-1813, Fax: 412-536-1175, E-mail: terri.liberto@laroche.edu. *Application contact:* Hope Schiffgens, Director of Graduate Studies and Adult Education, 412-536-1266, Fax: 412-536-1283, E-mail: schombh1@laroche.edu.

La Salle University, School of Nursing and Health Sciences, Program in Nursing, Philadelphia, PA 19141-1199. Offers adult gerontology primary care nurse practitioner (MSN, Certificate); adult health and illness clinical nurse specialist (MSN); adult-gerontology clinical nurse specialist (MSN, Certificate); clinical nurse leader (MSN); family primary care nurse practitioner (MSN, Certificate); gerontology (Certificate); nurse anesthetist (MSN, Certificate); nursing (MSN, Certificate); nursing administration (MSN, Certificate); nursing education (Certificate); nursing practice (DNP); nursing service administration (MSN); public health nursing (MSN, Certificate); school nursing (Certificate); MSN/MBA; MSN/MPH. *Accreditation:* AACN. *Program availability:* Part-time, evening/weekend, 100% online. *Faculty:* 12 full-time (11 women), 14 part-time/adjunct (11 women). *Students:* 1 (woman) full-time, 277 part-time (220 women); includes 72 minority (36 Black or African American, non-Hispanic/Latino; 1 American Indian or Alaska Native, non-Hispanic/Latino; 18 Asian, non-Hispanic/Latino; 10 Hispanic/Latino; 1 Native Hawaiian or other Pacific Islander, non-Hispanic/Latino; 6 Two or more races, non-Hispanic/Latino), 1 international. Average age 36. 70 applicants, 56% accepted, 24 enrolled. In 2017, 81 master's, 4 doctorates, 13 other advanced degrees awarded. *Degree requirements:* For doctorate, minimum of 1,000 hours of post baccalaureate clinical practice supervised by preceptors. *Entrance requirements:* For master's, GRE, MAT, or GMAT (for students with BSN GPA of less than 3.2), baccalaureate degree in nursing from ACEN- or CCNE-accredited program or an MSN Bridge program; Pennsylvania RN license; 2 letters of reference; resume; statement of philosophy articulating professional values and future educational goal; 1 year of work experience as a registered nurse; for doctorate, GRE (waived for applicants with MSN cumulative GPA of 3.7 or above), MSN, master's degree, MBA or MHA from nationally-accredited program; resume or curriculum vitae; 2 letters of reference; interview; for Certificate, GRE, MAT, or GMAT (for students with BSN GPA of less than 3.2, baccalaureate degree in nursing from ACEN- or CCNE-accredited program or an MSN Bridge program; Pennsylvania RN license; 2 letters of reference; resume; statement of philosophy articulating professional values and future educational goal; 1 year of work experience as a registered nurse. Additional exam requirements/recommendations for international students: Required—TOEFL. *Application deadline:* For fall admission, 8/15 priority date for domestic students, 7/15 for international students; for spring admission, 12/15 priority date for domestic students, 11/15 for international students; for summer admission, 4/15 priority date for domestic students, 3/15 for international students. Applications are processed on a rolling basis. Application fee: $35. Electronic applications accepted. Application fee is waived when completed online. *Expenses:* Contact institution. *Financial support:* In 2017–18, 7 students received support. Scholarships/grants and traineeships available. Support available to part-time students. Financial award application deadline: 8/31; financial award applicants required to submit FAFSA. *Unit head:* Dr. Patricia M. Dillon, Director, 215-951-1322, Fax: 215-951-1896, E-mail: msnapn@lasalle.edu. *Application contact:* Elizabeth Heenan, Director, Graduate and Adult Enrollment, 215-951-1100, Fax: 215-951-1462, E-mail: heenan@lasalle.edu.
Website: http://www.lasalle.edu/nursing/program-options/

Le Moyne College, Department of Nursing, Syracuse, NY 13214. Offers family nurse practitioner (MS, CAS); informatics (MS, CAS); nursing administration (MS, CAS); nursing education (MS, CAS). *Accreditation:* AACN. *Program availability:* Part-time, evening/weekend. *Faculty:* 3 full-time (all women), 5 part-time/adjunct (all women). *Students:* 27 full-time (20 women), 51 part-time (47 women); includes 10 minority (4 Black or African American, non-Hispanic/Latino; 1 Asian, non-Hispanic/Latino; 4 Hispanic/Latino; 1 Two or more races, non-Hispanic/Latino). Average age 32. 39 applicants, 95% accepted, 31 enrolled. In 2017, 20 master's, 2 other advanced degrees awarded. *Degree requirements:* For master's, scholarly project. *Entrance requirements:* For master's, bachelor's degree, interview, minimum GPA of 3.0, New York RN license, 2 letters of recommendation, writing sample, transcripts. *Application deadline:* For fall admission, 8/1 priority date for domestic students, 8/1 for international students; for spring admission, 12/15 priority date for domestic students, 12/15 for international students; for summer admission, 5/1 priority date for domestic students, 5/1 for international students. Applications are processed on a rolling basis. Application fee: $50. Electronic applications accepted. *Expenses:* $700 per credit hour. *Financial support:* In 2017–18, 2 students received support. Career-related internships or fieldwork, scholarships/grants, health care benefits, and unspecified assistantships available. Support available to part-time students. Financial award applicants required to submit FAFSA. *Faculty research:* Inter-profession education, gerontology, utilization of free healthcare services by the insured, health promotion education, innovative undergraduate nursing education models, patient and family education, horizontal violence. *Unit head:* Dr. Margaret M. Wells, Professor/Chair of Nursing, 315-445-5435, Fax: 315-445-6024, E-mail: wellsmm@lemoyne.edu. *Application contact:* Kristen P. Richards, Senior Director of Enrollment Management, 315-445-5444, Fax: 315-445-6092, E-mail: trapaskp@lemoyne.edu.
Website: http://www.lemoyne.edu/nursing

Lenoir-Rhyne University, Graduate Programs, School of Nursing, Program in Nursing, Hickory, NC 28601. Offers nursing administration (MSN); nursing education (MSN). *Accreditation:* AACN. *Program availability:* Online learning. *Degree requirements:* For master's, comprehensive exam, thesis optional. *Entrance requirements:* For master's, official transcripts, two recommendations, essay, resume, unrestricted RN license, criminal background check. Additional exam requirements/recommendations for international students: Required—TOEFL (minimum score 600 paper-based). Electronic applications accepted. *Expenses:* Contact institution.

Lewis University, College of Nursing and Health Professions, Program in Nursing, Romeoville, IL 60446. Offers adult gerontology acute care nurse practitioner (MSN); adult gerontology clinical nurse specialist (MSN); adult gerontology primary care nurse practitioner (MSN); family nurse practitioner (MSN); healthcare systems leadership (MSN); nursing (DNP); nursing education (MSN); school nurse (MSN). *Accreditation:* AACN. *Program availability:* Part-time, evening/weekend, 100% online, blended/hybrid learning. *Students:* 14 full-time (11 women), 361 part-time (336 women); includes 100 minority (27 Black or African American, non-Hispanic/Latino; 33 Asian, non-Hispanic/Latino; 35 Hispanic/Latino; 5 Two or more races, non-Hispanic/Latino), 1 international. Average age 37. *Degree requirements:* For master's, clinical practicum. *Entrance requirements:* For master's, minimum undergraduate GPA of 3.0, degree in nursing, RN license, letter of recommendation, interview, resume or curriculum vitae. Additional exam requirements/recommendations for international students: Required—TOEFL (minimum score 550 paper-based; 80 iBT). *Application deadline:* For fall admission, 5/1 priority date for international students; for spring admission, 11/15 priority date for international students. Applications are processed on a rolling basis. Application fee: $40. Electronic applications accepted. Tuition and fees vary according to program. *Financial support:* Federal Work-Study, scholarships/grants, tuition waivers (full and partial), and unspecified assistantships available. Financial award application deadline: 5/1; financial award applicants required to submit FAFSA. *Faculty research:* Cancer prevention, phenomenological methods, public policy analysis. *Total annual research expenditures:* $1,000. *Unit head:* 815-836-5610. *Application contact:* Nancy Wiksten, Adult Admission Counselor, 815-836-5628, Fax: 815-836-5578, E-mail: wikstena@lewisu.edu.

Liberty University, School of Nursing, Lynchburg, VA 24515. Offers family nurse practitioner (DNP); nurse educator (MSN); nursing administration (MSN); nursing informatics (MSN). *Accreditation:* AACN. *Program availability:* Part-time, online learning. *Students:* 148 full-time (131 women), 461 part-time (421 women); includes 103 minority (58 Black or African American, non-Hispanic/Latino; 4 American Indian or Alaska Native, non-Hispanic/Latino; 15 Asian, non-Hispanic/Latino; 11 Hispanic/Latino; 3 Native Hawaiian or other Pacific Islander, non-Hispanic/Latino; 12 Two or more races, non-Hispanic/Latino), 8 international. Average age 39. 536 applicants, 30% accepted, 105 enrolled. In 2017, 100 master's, 13 doctorates awarded. *Entrance requirements:* For master's, minimum cumulative undergraduate GPA of 3.0; for doctorate, minimum GPA of 3.25 in most current nursing program completed. Additional exam requirements/recommendations for international students: Recommended—TOEFL. *Application deadline:* Applications are processed on a rolling basis. Application fee: $50. Electronic applications accepted. *Financial support:* Applicants required to submit FAFSA. *Unit head:* Dr. Deanna Britt, Dean, 434-582-2519, E-mail: dbritt@liberty.edu. *Application contact:* Jay Bridge, Director of Admissions, 800-424-9595, Fax: 800-628-7977, E-mail: gradadmissions@liberty.edu.

Loma Linda University, School of Nursing, Program in Nurse Educator, Loma Linda, CA 92350. Offers adult/gerontology (MS); obstetrics-pediatrics (MS). *Accreditation:* AACN. *Program availability:* Part-time. *Degree requirements:* For master's, thesis or alternative. *Entrance requirements:* For master's, GRE General Test, BSN, minimum GPA of 3.0, RN license. Additional exam requirements/recommendations for international students: Required—TOEFL. Electronic applications accepted. *Faculty research:* Coping, integration of research.

Long Island University–LIU Brooklyn, Harriet Rothkopf Heilbrunn School of Nursing, Brooklyn, NY 11201. Offers adult nurse practitioner (MS, Advanced Certificate); family nurse practitioner (MS, Advanced Certificate); nurse educator (MS). *Accreditation:* AACN. *Program availability:* Part-time, evening/weekend, blended/hybrid learning. *Faculty:* 9 full-time (7 women), 6 part-time/adjunct (4 women). *Students:* 5 full-time (all women), 195 part-time (174 women); includes 117 minority (70 Black or African American, non-Hispanic/Latino; 28 Asian, non-Hispanic/Latino; 17 Hispanic/Latino; 2 Two or more races, non-Hispanic/Latino), 1 international. Average age 37. 168 applicants, 60% accepted, 73 enrolled. In 2017, 69 master's, 2 other advanced degrees awarded. *Entrance requirements:* Additional exam requirements/recommendations for international students: Required—TOEFL or IELTS. *Application deadline:* Applications are processed on a rolling basis. Application fee: $50. Electronic applications accepted. *Expenses: Tuition:* Full-time $21,618; part-time $1201 per credit. *Required fees:* $1840;

$920 per term. Tuition and fees vary according to course load. *Financial support:* In 2017–18, 15 students received support. Career-related internships or fieldwork, Federal Work-Study, scholarships/grants, and unspecified assistantships available. Support available to part-time students. Financial award application deadline: 2/15; financial award applicants required to submit FAFSA. *Faculty research:* Clinical and health outcomes in managed care; attitudes of nurses towards people with disabilities; adherence to CPAP in obstructive sleep apnea; diabetes and treatment compliance; chronic neurological disease management outside facilities. *Unit head:* Peggy Tallier, Interim Dean, 718-780-3367, E-mail: peggy.tallier@liu.edu. *Application contact:* Luis Santiago, Dean of Admissions, 718-488-1011, Fax: 718-780-6110, E-mail: bkln-admissions@liu.edu.
Website: http://www.liu.edu/Brooklyn/Academics/Harriet-Rothkopf-Heilbrunn-School-of-Nursing

Long Island University–LIU Post, School of Health Professions and Nursing, Brookville, NY 11548-1300. Offers biomedical science (MS); cardiovascular perfusion (MS); clinical lab sciences (MS); clinical laboratory management (MS); dietetic internship (Advanced Certificate); family nurse practitioner (MS, Advanced Certificate); forensic social work (Advanced Certificate); gerontology (Advanced Certificate); health administration (MPA); non-profit management (Advanced Certificate); nursing education (MS); nutrition (MS); public administration (MPA); social work (MSW). *Program availability:* Part-time, blended/hybrid learning. *Faculty:* 23 full-time (17 women), 33 part-time/adjunct (19 women). *Students:* 228 full-time (174 women), 227 part-time (185 women); includes 172 minority (76 Black or African American, non-Hispanic/Latino; 1 American Indian or Alaska Native, non-Hispanic/Latino; 44 Asian, non-Hispanic/Latino; 48 Hispanic/Latino; 3 Two or more races, non-Hispanic/Latino), 60 international. Average age 31. 392 applicants, 67% accepted, 138 enrolled. In 2017, 180 master's, 26 other advanced degrees awarded. *Degree requirements:* For master's, comprehensive exam (for some programs), thesis (for some programs). *Entrance requirements:* Additional exam requirements/recommendations for international students: Required—TOEFL (minimum score 85 iBT) or IELTS (7.5). *Application deadline:* Applications are processed on a rolling basis. Application fee: $50. Electronic applications accepted. *Expenses: Tuition:* Full-time $21,618; part-time $1201 per credit. *Required fees:* $1840; $920 per term. Tuition and fees vary according to course load. *Financial support:* In 2017–18, 102 students received support. Research assistantships, teaching assistantships, career-related internships or fieldwork, Federal Work-Study, scholarships/grants, and unspecified assistantships available. Support available to part-time students. Financial award application deadline: 2/15; financial award applicants required to submit FAFSA. *Faculty research:* Antibiotic resistance, evidence-based practice, family care, interprofessional learning, simulation learning. *Unit head:* Dr. Stacy Gropack, Dean, 516-299-2485, Fax: 516-299-2527, E-mail: post-shpn@liu.edu. *Application contact:* Kathy Riley, Associate Director of Graduate Admissions, 516-299-2900, Fax: 516-299-2137, E-mail: post-enroll@liu.edu.
Website: http://liu.edu/post/health

Louisiana State University Health Sciences Center, School of Nursing, New Orleans, LA 70112. Offers adult gerontology acute care nurse practitioner (DNP, Post-Master's Certificate); adult gerontology clinical nurse specialist (DNP, Post-Master's Certificate); adult gerontology primary care nurse practitioner (DNP, Post-Master's Certificate); clinical nurse leader (MSN); executive nurse leader (DNP, Post-Master's Certificate); neonatal nurse practitioner (DNP, Post-Master's Certificate); nurse anesthesia (DNP, Post-Master's Certificate); nurse educator (MSN); nursing (DNS); primary care family nurse practitioner (DNP, Post-Master's Certificate); public/community health nursing (DNP, Post-Master's Certificate). *Accreditation:* AACN; AANA/CANAEP (one or more programs are accredited). *Program availability:* Part-time. *Faculty:* 29 full-time (26 women), 20 part-time/adjunct (8 women). *Students:* 184 full-time (132 women), 41 part-time (35 women); includes 69 minority (45 Black or African American, non-Hispanic/Latino; 11 Asian, non-Hispanic/Latino; 12 Hispanic/Latino; 1 Two or more races, non-Hispanic/Latino), 1 international. Average age 30. 162 applicants, 42% accepted, 68 enrolled. In 2017, 52 master's, 46 doctorates awarded. *Degree requirements:* For master's, thesis optional; for doctorate, thesis/dissertation. *Entrance requirements:* For master's, GRE, minimum GPA of 3.0; for doctorate, GRE, minimum GPA of 3.0 (for DNP), 3.5 (for DNS). Additional exam requirements/recommendations for international students: Required—TOEFL (minimum score 550 paper-based; 79 iBT). *Application deadline:* Applications are processed on a rolling basis. Application fee: $100. Electronic applications accepted. *Expenses:* Contact institution. *Financial support:* Federal Work-Study, institutionally sponsored loans, scholarships/grants, and traineeships available. Financial award applicants required to submit FAFSA. *Faculty research:* Advanced clinical practice, nursing education, interprofessional education, nursing administration, culturally competent care. *Unit head:* Dr. Demetrius James Porche, Dean, 504-568-4106, Fax: 504-599-0573, E-mail: dporch@lsuhsc.edu. *Application contact:* Tracie Gravolet, Director, Office of Student Affairs, 504-568-4114, Fax: 504-568-5711, E-mail: tgravo@lsuhsc.edu.
Website: http://nursing.lsuhsc.edu/

Lourdes University, Graduate School, Sylvania, OH 43560-2898. Offers business (MBA); leadership (M Ed); nurse anesthesia (MSN); nurse educator (MSN); nurse leader (MSN); organizational leadership (MOL); reading (M Ed); teaching and curriculum (M Ed); theology (MA). *Program availability:* Evening/weekend. *Entrance requirements:* Additional exam requirements/recommendations for international students: Required—TOEFL.

Marian University, Leighton School of Nursing, Indianapolis, IN 46222-1997. Offers family nurse practitioner (DNP); nurse anesthesia (DNP); nursing education (MSN). *Program availability:* Part-time. *Faculty:* 6 full-time (all women), 2 part-time/adjunct (both women). *Students:* 23 full-time (20 women), 1 (woman) part-time; includes 7 minority (5 Black or African American, non-Hispanic/Latino; 1 Asian, non-Hispanic/Latino; 1 Hispanic/Latino). Average age 36. 69 applicants, 35% accepted, 5 enrolled. *Degree requirements:* For master's, 38 credits, designed to be completed in 2 years; 225-hour practicum including a culminating project; for doctorate, 70 credit hours (for family nurse practitioner track); 85 credits (for nurse anesthesia track); minimum of 1000 hours of supervised practice. *Entrance requirements:* For master's, degree in nursing from NLNAC- or CCNE-accredited program; current, valid RN license in State of Indiana; minimum undergraduate GPA of 3.0, 3 recommendations, interview with admissions committee; current resume; 500-word essay describing career goals; for doctorate, BSN from NSNAC- or CCNE-accredited program; minimum undergraduate GPA of 3.0; cureent, valid RN license; current resume or curriculum vitae; 500-word essay addressing career goals; 3 letters of recommendation; interview with Admissions Committee. Additional exam requirements/recommendations for international students: Required—TOEFL (minimum score 550 paper-based; 79 iBT). *Application deadline:* For fall admission, 2/15 for domestic and international students. Applications are processed on a rolling basis. Application fee: $40. Electronic applications accepted. Application fee is waived when completed online. *Expenses:* Contact institution. *Financial support:* Application deadline: 4/15; applicants required to submit FAFSA. *Unit head:* Dr. Dorothy A. Gomez, RN, Dean, 317-955-6159, E-mail: dgomez@marian.edu. *Application contact:* Bryan Moody, Executive Director of Graduate Admission, 317-955-6284, E-mail: bmoody@marian.edu.
Website: http://www.marian.edu/school-of-nursing

Marian University, School of Nursing and Health Professions, Fond du Lac, WI 54935-4699. Offers adult nurse practitioner (MSN); nurse educator (MSN); thanatology (MS). *Accreditation:* AACN. *Program availability:* Part-time, evening/weekend. *Degree requirements:* For master's, thesis, 675 clinical practicum hours. *Entrance requirements:* For master's, 3 letters of professional recommendation; undergraduate work in nursing research, statistics, health assessment. Additional exam requirements/recommendations for international students: Required—TOEFL (minimum score 525 paper-based; 70 iBT). Electronic applications accepted. *Expenses:* Contact institution.

McKendree University, Graduate Programs, Master of Science in Nursing Program, Lebanon, IL 62254-1299. Offers nursing education (MSN); nursing management/administration (MSN). *Accreditation:* AACN. *Program availability:* Part-time, evening/weekend, online learning. *Degree requirements:* For master's, research project or thesis. *Entrance requirements:* For master's, resume, references, valid Professional Registered Nurse license. Additional exam requirements/recommendations for international students: Required—TOEFL. Electronic applications accepted.

McMurry University, Graduate Studies, Abilene, TX 79697. Offers education (MSN); family nurse practitioner (MSN).

McNeese State University, Doré School of Graduate Studies, College of Nursing and Health Professions, MSN Program, Lake Charles, LA 70609. Offers family nurse practitioner (MSN); nurse educator (MSN); psychiatric/mental health nurse practitioner (MSN). *Entrance requirements:* For master's, GRE, baccalaureate degree in nursing, minimum overall GPA of 2.7 for all undergraduate coursework, eligibility for unencumbered licensure as Registered Nurse in Louisiana or Texas, course in introductory statistics with minimum C grade, physical assessment skills, two letters of professional reference, 500-word essay, current resume. *Application deadline:* For fall admission, 5/15 priority date for domestic and international students; for spring admission, 10/15 priority date for domestic and international students. Applications are processed on a rolling basis. Application fee: $20 ($30 for international students). *Financial support:* Application deadline: 5/1. *Unit head:* Dr. Sattaria Dilks, Co-Coordinator, 337-475-5840, Fax: 337-475-5924, E-mail: tdilks@mcneese.edu. *Application contact:* Dr. Ann Warner, Co-Coordinator, 337-475-5831, Fax: 337-475-5702, E-mail: awarner@mcneese.edu.
Website: http://www.mcneese.edu/nursing/graduate

Medical University of South Carolina, College of Nursing, Nurse Educator Program, Charleston, SC 29425. Offers MSN. *Program availability:* Part-time, evening/weekend, online learning. *Degree requirements:* For master's, thesis optional. *Entrance requirements:* For master's, BSN, course work in statistics, nursing license, minimum GPA of 3.0, current curriculum vitae, essay, three references. Additional exam requirements/recommendations for international students: Required—TOEFL (minimum score 600 paper-based). Electronic applications accepted. *Faculty research:* Prenatal care outcomes, perinatal wellness in Hispanic women, use of personal digital assistants (PDAs) in clinical practice.

Mercy College, School of Health and Natural Sciences, Programs in Nursing, Dobbs Ferry, NY 10522-1189. Offers nursing administration (MS); nursing education (MS). *Accreditation:* AACN. *Program availability:* Part-time, evening/weekend, blended/hybrid learning. *Students:* 4 full-time (all women), 136 part-time (128 women); includes 83 minority (54 Black or African American, non-Hispanic/Latino; 14 Asian, non-Hispanic/Latino; 12 Hispanic/Latino; 3 Native Hawaiian or other Pacific Islander, non-Hispanic/Latino). Average age 33. 80 applicants, 70% accepted, 38 enrolled. In 2017, 42 master's awarded. *Degree requirements:* For master's, comprehensive exam (for some programs), written comprehensive exam or the production of a comprehensive project. *Entrance requirements:* For master's, interview, two letters of reference, bachelor's degree, RN registration in the U.S. Additional exam requirements/recommendations for international students: Required—TOEFL (minimum score 600 paper-based; 100 iBT), IELTS (minimum score 8). *Application deadline:* For fall admission, 8/1 for international students. Applications are processed on a rolling basis. Application fee: $62. Electronic applications accepted. *Expenses: Tuition:* Full-time $15,426; part-time $857 per credit hour. *Required fees:* $630; $158 per term. Tuition and fees vary according to course load, degree level and program. *Financial support:* Career-related internships or fieldwork, Federal Work-Study, scholarships/grants, and unspecified assistantships available. Support available to part-time students. Financial award applicants required to submit FAFSA. *Unit head:* Dr. Joan Toglia, Dean, School of Health and Natural Sciences, 914-674-7837, E-mail: jtoglia@mercy.edu. *Application contact:* Allison Gurdineer, Senior Director of Admissions, 877-637-2946, Fax: 914-674-7382, E-mail: admissions@mercy.edu.
Website: https://www.mercy.edu/health-and-natural-sciences/graduate

Messiah College, Program in Nursing, Mechanicsburg, PA 17055. Offers nurse educator (MSN).

Metropolitan State University, College of Nursing and Health Sciences, St. Paul, MN 55106-5000. Offers advanced dental therapy (MS); leadership and management (MSN); nurse educator (MSN); nursing (DNP). *Accreditation:* AACN. *Program availability:* Part-time. *Degree requirements:* For master's, thesis or alternative; for doctorate, thesis/dissertation or alternative. *Entrance requirements:* For master's, GRE General Test, minimum GPA of 3.0, RN license, BS/BA; for doctorate, minimum GPA of 3.0, RN license, MSN. Additional exam requirements/recommendations for international students: Required—TOEFL (minimum score 550 paper-based). *Application deadline:* For fall admission, 1/15 for domestic and international students; for winter admission, 1/15 for international students. Application fee: $20. *Expenses:* Tuition, state resident: part-time $388.55 per credit. Tuition, nonresident: part-time $777.11 per credit. *Required fees:* $35.11 per credit. Part-time tuition and fees vary according to campus/location and program. *Financial support:* Fellowships, career-related internships or fieldwork, Federal Work-Study, institutionally sponsored loans, and traineeships available. Financial award applicants required to submit FAFSA. *Faculty research:* Women's health, gerontology.
Website: https://www.metrostate.edu/academics/nursing-and-health-sciences

MGH Institute of Health Professions, School of Nursing, Boston, MA 02129. Offers advanced practice nursing (MSN); gerontological nursing (MSN); nursing (DNP); pediatric nursing (MSN); psychiatric nursing (MSN); teaching and learning for health care education (Certificate); women's health nursing (MSN). *Accreditation:* AACN. *Degree requirements:* For master's, thesis or alternative. *Entrance requirements:* For master's, GRE General Test, bachelor's degree from regionally-accredited college or university. Additional exam requirements/recommendations for international students: Required—TOEFL (minimum score 550 paper-based; 80 iBT). Electronic applications accepted. *Faculty research:* Biobehavioral nursing, HIV/AIDS, gerontological nursing, women's health, vulnerable populations, health systems.

Miami Regional University, School of Nursing and Health Sciences, Miami Springs, FL 33166. Offers nursing (MSN); nursing education (MSN); nursing leadership (MSN).

MidAmerica Nazarene University, School of Nursing and Health Science, Olathe, KS 66062. Offers healthcare administration (MSN); healthcare quality management (MSN); nursing education (MSN); public health (MSN); MSN/MBA. *Accreditation:* AACN. *Program availability:* Part-time, evening/weekend, 100% online, blended/hybrid learning. *Entrance requirements:* For master's, BSN, minimum GPA of 3.0, active unencumbered

RN license, undergraduate statistics course. Additional exam requirements/recommendations for international students: Required—TOEFL. Electronic applications accepted. *Expenses:* Contact institution. *Faculty research:* Technology in education, minority recruitment and retention in nursing programs, faculty views and attitudes on culturally competency, innovative nursing program development, spirituality and holistic health.

Middle Tennessee State University, College of Graduate Studies, University College, Murfreesboro, TN 37132. Offers advanced studies in teaching and learning (M Ed); human resources leadership (MPS); nursing administration (MSN); nursing education (MSN); strategic leadership (MPS); training and development (MPS). *Program availability:* Part-time, evening/weekend, online learning. *Entrance requirements:* Additional exam requirements/recommendations for international students: Required—TOEFL (minimum score 525 paper-based; 71 iBT) or IELTS (minimum score 6).

Midwestern State University, Billie Doris McAda Graduate School, Robert D. and Carol Gunn College of Health Sciences and Human Services, Wilson School of Nursing, Wichita Falls, TX 76308. Offers family nurse practitioner (MSN); family psychiatric mental health nurse practitioner (MSN); nurse educator (MSN). *Accreditation:* AACN. *Program availability:* Part-time, evening/weekend. *Degree requirements:* For master's, comprehensive exam, thesis optional. *Entrance requirements:* For master's, GRE General Test or MAT. Additional exam requirements/recommendations for international students: Required—TOEFL (minimum score 550 paper-based). Electronic applications accepted. *Faculty research:* Infant feeding, musculoskeletal disorders, diabetes, community health education, water quality reporting.

Millersville University of Pennsylvania, College of Graduate Studies and Adult Learning, College of Science and Technology, Department of Nursing, Program in Nursing Education, Millersville, PA 17551-0302. Offers MSN, Post-Master's Certificate. *Program availability:* Part-time, evening/weekend. *Faculty:* 5 full-time (all women), 8 part-time/adjunct (7 women). *Students:* 6 part-time (all women), 1 international. Average age 42. In 2017, 3 master's awarded. *Degree requirements:* For master's, internship, scholarly project. *Entrance requirements:* For master's, resume, copy of RN license, minimum GPA of 3.0, all transfer transcripts, interview, three academic and/or professional references, completion of undergraduate statistics and health assessment course, minimum one year of clinical experience in nursing. Additional exam requirements/recommendations for international students: Required—TOEFL (minimum score 80 iBT), IELTS (minimum score 6.5), PTE (minimum score 60). *Application deadline:* Applications are processed on a rolling basis. Application fee: $40. Electronic applications accepted. *Expenses:* $500 per credit resident tuition and fees; $750 per credit non-resident tuition and fees; $114.75 per credit general fee (maximum of 12 credits); technology fee $27 per credit (resident), $39 per credit (non-resident). *Financial support:* In 2017–18, 1 student received support. Unspecified assistantships available. Financial award application deadline: 3/15; financial award applicants required to submit FAFSA. *Faculty research:* Nursing education, program evaluation, faculty professional development. *Unit head:* Dr. Kelly A. Kuhns, Chairperson, 717-871-5276, Fax: 717-871-4877, E-mail: kelly.kuhns@millersville.edu. *Application contact:* Dr. Victor S. DeSantis, Dean of College of Graduate Studies and Adult Learning/Associate Provost for Civic and Community Engagement, 717-871-7619, Fax: 717-871-7954, E-mail: victor.desantis@millersville.edu.
Website: http://www.millersville.edu/nursing/msn/nursing-education.php

Millikin University, School of Nursing, Decatur, IL 62522-2084. Offers entry into nursing practice (MSN); family nurse practitioner (DNP); nurse anesthesia (DNP); nurse educator (MSN). *Accreditation:* AACN. *Program availability:* Part-time. *Faculty:* 19 full-time (17 women), 7 part-time/adjunct (6 women). *Students:* 42 full-time (30 women), 20 part-time (17 women); includes 12 minority (8 Black or African American, non-Hispanic/Latino; 2 Asian, non-Hispanic/Latino; 2 Hispanic/Latino). Average age 30. 114 applicants, 36% accepted, 23 enrolled. In 2017, 3 master's, 13 doctorates awarded. *Degree requirements:* For master's, thesis or alternative, scholarly project; for doctorate, thesis/dissertation or alternative, scholarly project. *Entrance requirements:* For master's, GRE (if undergraduate cumulative GPA is below 3.0 for nurse educator, 3.25 for entry into nursing practice), official academic transcript(s), written statement, resume/vitae, 3 letters of recommendation, RN license; for doctorate, GRE (if undergraduate cumulative GPA is below 3.0), official academic transcript(s), written statement, resume/vitae, 3 letters of recommendation, RN or APRN license. Additional exam requirements/recommendations for international students: Required—TOEFL (minimum score 550 paper-based; 79 iBT), IELTS (minimum score 6.5). *Application deadline:* For spring admission, 7/1 priority date for domestic and international students; for summer admission, 11/1 priority date for domestic and international students. Applications are processed on a rolling basis. Application fee: $0. Electronic applications accepted. *Expenses:* $832 per credit hour (for MSN); $950 per credit hour (for DNP). *Financial support:* Traineeships and unspecified assistantships available. Financial award applicants required to submit FAFSA. *Faculty research:* Quality of life, teaching/learning strategies, clinical simulation. *Unit head:* Dr. Pamela Lindsey, Director, 217-424-6348, Fax: 217-420-6731, E-mail: plindsey@millikin.edu. *Application contact:* Bonnie Niemeyer, Administrative Assistant, 800-373-7733 Ext. 5034, Fax: 217-420-6731, E-mail: bniemeyer@millikin.edu.
Website: http://www.millikin.edu/grad-nursing

Minnesota State University Mankato, College of Graduate Studies and Research, College of Allied Health and Nursing, School of Nursing, Mankato, MN 56001. Offers family nurse practitioner (MSN), including family nurse practitioner; nurse educator (MSN); nursing (DNP). *Accreditation:* AACN. *Degree requirements:* For master's, comprehensive exam, internships, research project or thesis; for doctorate, capstone project. *Entrance requirements:* For master's, GRE General Test or on-campus essay, minimum GPA of 3.0 during previous 2 years, BSN or equivalent references; for doctorate, master's degree in nursing. Additional exam requirements/recommendations for international students: Required—TOEFL. Electronic applications accepted. *Faculty research:* Psychosocial nursing, computers in nursing, family adaptation.

Missouri State University, Graduate College, College of Health and Human Services, Department of Nursing, Springfield, MO 65897. Offers nursing (MSN), including family nurse practitioner, nurse educator; nursing practice (DNP). *Accreditation:* AACN. *Program availability:* 100% online, blended/hybrid learning. *Faculty:* 9 full-time (all women), 16 part-time/adjunct (13 women). *Students:* 30 full-time (26 women), 47 part-time (41 women); includes 13 minority (6 Black or African American, non-Hispanic/Latino; 1 American Indian or Alaska Native, non-Hispanic/Latino; 3 Asian, non-Hispanic/Latino; 1 Native Hawaiian or other Pacific Islander, non-Hispanic/Latino; 2 Two or more races, non-Hispanic/Latino). Average age 27. 12 applicants, 33% accepted, 1 enrolled. In 2017, 6 master's, 16 doctorates awarded. *Degree requirements:* For master's, comprehensive exam, thesis or alternative. *Entrance requirements:* For master's, GRE General Test, minimum GPA of 3.0, RN license (for MSN), 1 year of work experience (for MPH). Additional exam requirements/recommendations for international students: Required—TOEFL (minimum score 550 paper-based; 79 iBT), IELTS (minimum score 6). *Application deadline:* For fall admission, 12/1 priority date for domestic students, 5/1 for international students. Applications are processed on a rolling basis. Application fee: $35 ($50 for international students). Electronic applications accepted. *Expenses:* Tuition, state resident: full-time $2915; part-time $2021 per credit hour. Tuition, nonresident: full-time $5354; part-time $3647 per credit hour. *International tuition:* $11,992 full-time. *Required fees:* $173; $173 per credit hour. Tuition and fees vary according to class time, course level, course load, degree level, campus/location and program. *Financial support:* In 2017–18, 2 teaching assistantships with partial tuition reimbursements (averaging $8,772 per year) were awarded; Federal Work-Study, institutionally sponsored loans, scholarships/grants, and unspecified assistantships also available. Financial award application deadline: 3/31; financial award applicants required to submit FAFSA. *Faculty research:* Preconceptual health, women's health, nursing satisfaction, nursing education. *Unit head:* Dr. Stephen Stapleton, Department Head, 417-836-5310, Fax: 417-836-5484, E-mail: nursing@missouristate.edu. *Application contact:* Stephanie Praschan, Director, Graduate Enrollment Management, 417-836-5330, Fax: 417-836-6200, E-mail: stephaniepraschan@missouristate.edu.
Website: http://www.missouristate.edu/nursing/

Missouri Western State University, Program in Nursing, St. Joseph, MO 64507-2294. Offers health care leadership (MSN); nurse educator (MSN, Graduate Certificate). *Program availability:* Part-time. *Students:* 1 (woman) full-time, 40 part-time (38 women); includes 2 minority (1 Black or African American, non-Hispanic/Latino; 1 Hispanic/Latino), 2 international. Average age 36. 9 applicants, 100% accepted, 9 enrolled. In 2017, 8 master's awarded. *Entrance requirements:* For master's, minimum cumulative GPA of 2.75, statement of interest, current and unencumbered RN license. Additional exam requirements/recommendations for international students: Recommended—TOEFL (minimum score 79 iBT), IELTS (minimum score 6). *Application deadline:* For fall admission, 7/15 for domestic and international students; for spring admission, 10/1 for domestic and international students; for summer admission, 3/15 for domestic students. Applications are processed on a rolling basis. Application fee: $45 ($50 for international students). Electronic applications accepted. *Expenses:* Tuition, state resident: full-time $6391; part-time $336 per credit hour. Tuition, nonresident: full-time $11,483; part-time $604 per credit hour. *Required fees:* $542; $99 per credit hour. $176 per semester. One-time fee: $45. Tuition and fees vary according to course load and program. *Financial support:* Scholarships/grants and unspecified assistantships available. Support available to part-time students. *Unit head:* Dr. Carolyn Brose, Associate Professor, 816-271-5912, E-mail: brose@missouriwestern.edu. *Application contact:* Dr. Benjamin D. Caldwell, Dean of the Graduate School, 816-271-4394, Fax: 816-271-4525, E-mail: graduate@missouriwestern.edu.
Website: https://www.missouriwestern.edu/nursing/msn/

Molloy College, The Barbara H. Hagan School of Nursing, Rockville Centre, NY 11571-5002. Offers adult - gerontology nurse practitioner (MS); adult-gerontology clinical nurse specialist (DNP); adult-gerontology nurse practitioner (DNP); clinical nurse specialist: adult - gerontology (MS); family nurse practitioner (MS, DNP); family psychiatric/mental health nurse practitioner (MS, DNP); nursing (PhD, Advanced Certificate); nursing administration with informatics (MS); nursing education (MS); pediatric nurse practitioner (MS, DNP). *Accreditation:* AACN. *Program availability:* Part-time, evening/weekend. *Faculty:* 28 full-time (all women), 7 part-time/adjunct (6 women). *Students:* 19 full-time (14 women), 574 part-time (527 women); includes 336 minority (179 Black or African American, non-Hispanic/Latino; 2 American Indian or Alaska Native, non-Hispanic/Latino; 107 Asian, non-Hispanic/Latino; 42 Hispanic/Latino; 1 Native Hawaiian or other Pacific Islander, non-Hispanic/Latino; 5 Two or more races, non-Hispanic/Latino), 4 international. Average age 44. 292 applicants, 65% accepted, 147 enrolled. In 2017, 135 master's, 9 doctorates, 5 other advanced degrees awarded. *Degree requirements:* For master's, thesis optional. *Entrance requirements:* For master's, 3 letters of reference, BS in nursing, minimum undergraduate GPA of 3.0; for Advanced Certificate, 3 letters of reference, master's degree in nursing. Additional exam requirements/recommendations for international students: Required—TOEFL (minimum score 550 paper-based; 79 iBT). *Application deadline:* For fall admission, 9/2 priority date for domestic students; for spring admission, 1/20 priority date for domestic students. Applications are processed on a rolling basis. Application fee: $60. Electronic applications accepted. *Expenses:* *Tuition:* Full-time $19,980; part-time $1110 per credit. *Required fees:* $1040. Tuition and fees vary according to course load and degree level. *Financial support:* Research assistantships with partial tuition reimbursements, teaching assistantships with partial tuition reimbursements, institutionally sponsored loans, scholarships/grants, and unspecified assistantships available. Support available to part-time students. Financial award application deadline: 3/1; financial award applicants required to submit FAFSA. *Faculty research:* Workplace violence involving nurses and psychiatric patients; moral distress in nursing; primary care of veterans; the role of service immersion programs in graduate nursing education; academic integrity. *Unit head:* Dr. Marcia R. Gardner, Dean, The Barbara H. Hagan School of Nursing, 516-323-3651, E-mail: mgardner@molloy.edu. *Application contact:* Jaclyn Machowicz, Assistant Director for Admissions, 516-323-4010, E-mail: jmachowicz@molloy.edu.

Monmouth University, Graduate Studies, Marjorie K. Unterberg School of Nursing and Health Studies, West Long Branch, NJ 07764-1898. Offers adult-gerontological primary care nurse practitioner (MSN, Post-Master's Certificate); family nurse practitioner (MSN, Post-Master's Certificate); forensic nursing (MSN, Certificate); nursing (MSN); nursing administration (MSN); nursing education (MSN, Post-Master's Certificate); nursing practice (DNP); physician assistant (MS); psychiatric and mental health nurse practitioner (MSN, Post-Master's Certificate); school nursing (MSN, Certificate). *Accreditation:* AACN. *Program availability:* Part-time, evening/weekend, 100% online, blended/hybrid learning. *Faculty:* 12 full-time (all women), 20 part-time/adjunct (12 women). *Students:* 90 full-time (66 women), 329 part-time (302 women); includes 129 minority (51 Black or African American, non-Hispanic/Latino; 43 Asian, non-Hispanic/Latino; 31 Hispanic/Latino; 1 Native Hawaiian or other Pacific Islander, non-Hispanic/Latino; 3 Two or more races, non-Hispanic/Latino), 1 international. Average age 36. In 2017, 85 master's, 4 other advanced degrees awarded. *Degree requirements:* For master's, practicum (for some tracks); for doctorate, practicum, capstone course. *Entrance requirements:* For master's, GRE General Test (waived for MSN applicants with minimum B grade in each of the first four courses and for MS applicants with master's degree), BSN with minimum GPA of 2.75, current RN license, proof of liability and malpractice policy, personal statement, two letters of recommendation, college course work in health assessment, resume; CASPA application (for MS); for doctorate, accredited master's nursing program degree with minimum GPA of 3.2, active RN license, national certification as nurse practitioner or nurse administrator, working knowledge of statistics, statement of goals and vision for change, 2 letters of recommendation (professional or academic), resume, interview. Additional exam requirements/recommendations for international students: Required—TOEFL (minimum score 550 paper-based; 79 iBT), IELTS (minimum score 6) or Michigan English Language Assessment Battery (minimum score 77). *Application deadline:* For fall admission, 7/15 priority date for domestic students, 6/1 for international students; for spring admission, 12/1 priority date for domestic students, 11/1 for international students; for summer admission, 5/1 for domestic students. Applications are processed on a rolling basis. Application fee: $50. Electronic applications accepted. *Expenses:* Contact institution. *Financial support:* In 2017–18, 197 students received support. Institutionally sponsored loans, scholarships/grants, and unspecified assistantships available. Support available to part-time students. Financial award applicants required to submit FAFSA. *Faculty research:* School nursing, health policy, and smoking cessation in teens; Multiple Sclerosis; adherence and self-efficacy; aging issues and geriatric care.

Unit head: Dr. Janet Mahoney, Dean, 732-571-3443, Fax: 732-263-5131, E-mail: jmahoney@monmouth.edu. *Application contact:* Lucia Fedele, Graduate Admission Counselor, 732-571-3452, Fax: 732-263-5123, E-mail: gradadm@monmouth.edu.
Website: https://www.monmouth.edu/graduate/nursing-programs-of-study/

Montana State University, The Graduate School, College of Nursing, Bozeman, MT 59717. Offers clinical nurse leader (MN); family and individual nurse practitioner (DNP); family nurse practitioner (MN, Post-Master's Certificate); nursing education (Certificate, Post-Master's Certificate); psychiatric mental health nurse practitioner (MN); psychiatric/mental health nurse practitioner (DNP). *Accreditation:* AACN. *Program availability:* Part-time, online learning. *Degree requirements:* For master's, comprehensive exam, thesis (for some programs); for doctorate, thesis/dissertation, 1,125 hours in clinical settings. *Entrance requirements:* For master's, GRE General Test, minimum GPA of 3.0 for undergraduate and post-baccalaureate work. Additional exam requirements/recommendations for international students: Required—TOEFL (minimum score 580 paper-based). Electronic applications accepted. *Faculty research:* Rural nursing, health disparities, environmental/public health, oral health, resilience.

Moravian College, Graduate and Continuing Studies, Helen S. Breidegam School of Nursing, Bethlehem, PA 18018-6650. Offers clinical nurse leader (MS); nurse administrator (MS); nurse educator (MS); nurse practitioner - acute care (MS); nurse practitioner - primary care (MS). *Accreditation:* AACN. *Program availability:* Part-time, evening/weekend. *Faculty:* 5 full-time (all women), 4 part-time/adjunct (2 women). *Students:* 4 full-time (all women), 64 part-time (60 women); includes 9 minority (3 Black or African American, non-Hispanic/Latino; 2 Asian, non-Hispanic/Latino; 4 Hispanic/Latino), 1 international. Average age 38. 34 applicants, 85% accepted, 20 enrolled. In 2017, 24 master's awarded. *Degree requirements:* For master's, comprehensive exam (for some programs), evidence-based practice project. *Entrance requirements:* For master's, BSN with minimum GPA of 3.0, active RN license, statistics course with minimum C grade, 2 professional references, written statement of goals, professional resume, interview, official transcripts. Additional exam requirements/recommendations for international students: Required—TOEFL (minimum score 550 paper-based; 90 iBT), IELTS (minimum score 6.5). *Application deadline:* For fall admission, 8/1 priority date for domestic and international students; for spring admission, 1/1 priority date for domestic and international students; for summer admission, 5/1 priority date for domestic and international students. Applications are processed on a rolling basis. Electronic applications accepted. *Expenses:* Contact institution. *Financial support:* Applicants required to submit FAFSA. *Faculty research:* College binge drinking, obesity, underrepresented minorities in nursing, education needs of nursing preceptors, delirium superimposed on dementia. *Unit head:* Dr. Kerry Cheever, Professor/Chairperson, 610-861-1412, Fax: 610-861-1466, E-mail: nursing@moravian.edu. *Application contact:* Caroline Febbo, Student Experience Mentor, 610-861-1400, Fax: 610-861-1466, E-mail: graduate@moravian.edu.

Mount Carmel College of Nursing, Nursing Program, Columbus, OH 43222. Offers adult gerontology acute care nurse practitioner (MS); adult health clinical nurse specialist (MS); family nurse practitioner (MS); nursing (DNP); nursing administration (MS); nursing education (MS). *Accreditation:* AACN. *Program availability:* Part-time. *Faculty:* 11 full-time (all women), 5 part-time/adjunct (4 women). *Students:* 112 full-time (93 women), 72 part-time (65 women); includes 35 minority (20 Black or African American, non-Hispanic/Latino; 4 Asian, non-Hispanic/Latino; 3 Hispanic/Latino; 8 Two or more races, non-Hispanic/Latino). Average age 35. 135 applicants, 65% accepted, 68 enrolled. In 2017, 64 master's awarded. *Degree requirements:* For master's, professional manuscript; for doctorate, practicum. *Entrance requirements:* For master's, letters of recommendation, statement of purpose, current resume, baccalaureate degree in nursing, current Ohio RN license, minimum cumulative GPA of 3.0; for doctorate, master's degree in nursing from program accredited by either ACEN or CCNE. Additional exam requirements/recommendations for international students: Required—TOEFL (minimum score 550 paper-based; 80 iBT). *Application deadline:* For fall admission, 2/1 priority date for domestic students; for spring admission, 11/1 priority date for domestic students. Applications are processed on a rolling basis. Application fee: $30. Electronic applications accepted. *Expenses: Tuition:* Full-time $11,403; part-time $543 per credit. *Required fees:* $50; $50 per year. *Financial support:* In 2017–18, 3 students received support. Institutionally sponsored loans and scholarships/grants available. Financial award application deadline: 3/1; financial award applicants required to submit FAFSA. *Unit head:* Dr. Jill Kilanowski, Associate Dean, 614-234-5237, Fax: 614-234-2875, E-mail: jkilanowski@mccn.edu. *Application contact:* Dr. Kim Campbell, Director of Recruitment and Admissions, 614-234-5144, Fax: 614-234-5427, E-mail: kcampbell@mccn.edu.

Mount Mercy University, Program in Nursing, Cedar Rapids, IA 52402-4797. Offers health advocacy (MSN); nurse administration (MSN); nurse education (MSN). *Accreditation:* AACN. *Program availability:* Evening/weekend. *Degree requirements:* For master's, project/practicum.

Mount St. Joseph University, Master of Science in Nursing Program, Cincinnati, OH 45233-1670. Offers administration (MSN); clinical nurse leader (MSN); education (MSN). *Accreditation:* AACN. *Program availability:* Part-time. *Faculty:* 9 full-time (all women), 15 part-time/adjunct (all women). *Students:* 122 part-time (113 women); includes 3 minority (2 Black or African American, non-Hispanic/Latino; 1 Two or more races, non-Hispanic/Latino). Average age 40. In 2017, 8 master's awarded. *Entrance requirements:* For master's, essay; BSN from regionally-accredited university; minimum undergraduate GPA of 3.25 or GRE; professional resume; three professional references; interview; 2 years of clinical nursing experience; active RN license; criminal background check. Additional exam requirements/recommendations for international students: Required—TOEFL (minimum score 560 paper-based; 83 iBT). *Application deadline:* Applications are processed on a rolling basis. Application fee: $50. Electronic applications accepted. *Expenses:* $610 per credit hour. *Financial support:* Applicants required to submit FAFSA. *Unit head:* Dr. Nancy Hinzman, MSN/DNP Director, 513-244-4325, E-mail: nancy.hinzman@msj.edu. *Application contact:* Mary Brigham, Assistant Director for Graduate Recruitment, 513-244-4233, Fax: 513-244-4629, E-mail: mary.brigham@msj.edu.
Website: http://www.msj.edu/academics/graduate-programs/master-of-science-in-nursing/

Mount Saint Mary College, School of Nursing, Newburgh, NY 12550-3494. Offers adult nurse practitioner (MS, Advanced Certificate), including nursing education (MS), nursing management (MS); family nurse practitioner (Advanced Certificate); nursing education (Advanced Certificate). *Accreditation:* AACN. *Program availability:* Part-time, evening/weekend, blended/hybrid learning. *Faculty:* 7 full-time (all women), 5 part-time/adjunct (all women). *Students:* 3 full-time (1 woman), 153 part-time (143 women); includes 42 minority (22 Black or African American, non-Hispanic/Latino; 1 American Indian or Alaska Native, non-Hispanic/Latino; 6 Asian, non-Hispanic/Latino; 11 Hispanic/Latino; 1 Native Hawaiian or other Pacific Islander, non-Hispanic/Latino; 1 Two or more races, non-Hispanic/Latino). Average age 38. 34 applicants, 91% accepted, 28 enrolled. In 2017, 30 master's, 5 other advanced degrees awarded. *Degree requirements:* For master's, research utilization project. *Entrance requirements:* For master's, BSN, minimum GPA of 3.0, RN license. Additional exam requirements/recommendations for international students: Required—TOEFL (minimum score 80 iBT). *Application deadline:* For fall admission, 6/3 priority date for domestic students; for spring admission, 10/31 priority date for domestic students. Applications are processed on a rolling basis. Application fee: $45. Electronic applications accepted. Application fee is waived when completed online. *Expenses: Tuition:* Full-time $14,454; part-time $803 per credit. *Required fees:* $172; $86 per semester. *Financial support:* In 2017–18, 8 students received support. Unspecified assistantships available. Financial award application deadline: 4/15; financial award applicants required to submit FAFSA. *Unit head:* Christine Berte, Graduate Coordinator, 845-569-3141, Fax: 845-562-6762, E-mail: christine.berte@msmc.edu. *Application contact:* Lisa Alvarez, Director of Admissions for Graduate Programs and Adult Degree Completion, 845-569-3166, Fax: 845-569-3450, E-mail: lisa.gallina@msmc.edu.
Website: http://www.msmc.edu/Academics/Graduate_Programs/Master_of_Science_in_Nursing

National American University, Roueche Graduate Center, Austin, TX 78731. Offers accounting (MBA); aviation management (MBA, MM); care coordination (MSN); community college leadership (Ed D); criminal justice (MM); e-marketing (MBA, MM); health care administration (MBA, MM); higher education (MM); human resources management (MBA, MM); information technology management (MBA, MM); international business (MBA); leadership (EMBA); management (MBA); nursing administration (MSN); nursing education (MSN); nursing informatics (MSN); operations and configuration management (MBA, MM); project and process management (MBA, MM). Master's programs offered online through the Harold D. Buckingham Graduate School. *Program availability:* Part-time, evening/weekend, online learning. *Entrance requirements:* For master's, minimum undergraduate GPA of 2.75. Additional exam requirements/recommendations for international students: Required—TOEFL, TWE. Electronic applications accepted. *Faculty research:* Tourism, finance, marketing.

Nebraska Methodist College, Program in Nursing, Omaha, NE 68114. Offers nurse educator (MSN); nurse executive (MSN). *Accreditation:* AACN. *Program availability:* Evening/weekend, online learning. *Degree requirements:* For master's, thesis or alternative, Evidence Based Practice (EBP) project. *Entrance requirements:* For master's, interview. Additional exam requirements/recommendations for international students: Required—TOEFL (minimum score 550 paper-based; 80 iBT). *Faculty research:* Spirituality, student outcomes, service-learning, leadership and administration, women's issues.

New York University, Rory Meyers College of Nursing, Programs in Advanced Practice Nursing, New York, NY 10012-1019. Offers adult-gerontology acute care nurse practitioner (MS, Advanced Certificate); adult-gerontology primary care nurse practitioner (MS, Advanced Certificate); family nurse practitioner (MS, Advanced Certificate), gerontology nurse practitioner (Advanced Certificate); nurse midwifery (MS, Advanced Certificate); nursing administration (MS, Advanced Certificate); nursing education (MS, Advanced Certificate); nursing informatics (MS, Advanced Certificate); pediatrics nurse practitioner (MS, Advanced Certificate); psychiatric-mental health nurse practitioner (MS, Advanced Certificate); MS/MPH. *Accreditation:* AACN; ACNM/ACME. *Program availability:* Part-time, evening/weekend. *Faculty:* 23 full-time (all women), 62 part-time/adjunct (56 women). *Students:* 50 full-time (46 women), 557 part-time (509 women); includes 234 minority (58 Black or African American, non-Hispanic/Latino; 1 American Indian or Alaska Native, non-Hispanic/Latino; 116 Asian, non-Hispanic/Latino; 43 Hispanic/Latino; 1 Native Hawaiian or other Pacific Islander, non-Hispanic/Latino; 15 Two or more races, non-Hispanic/Latino), 23 international. Average age 32. 391 applicants, 59% accepted, 149 enrolled. In 2017, 187 master's, 5 other advanced degrees awarded. *Degree requirements:* For master's, thesis (for some programs), capstone. *Entrance requirements:* For master's, BS in nursing, AS in nursing with another BS/BA, interview, RN license, 1 year of clinical experience (3 for the MS in nursing education program); for Advanced Certificate, master's degree in nursing. Additional exam requirements/recommendations for international students: Required—TOEFL (minimum score 100 iBT), IELTS (minimum score 7). *Application deadline:* For fall admission, 3/1 priority date for domestic and international students; for spring admission, 11/1 priority date for domestic and international students; for summer admission, 3/1 for domestic and international students. Application fee: $80. Electronic applications accepted. *Expenses:* Contact institution. *Financial support:* In 2017–18, 130 students received support. Career-related internships or fieldwork, Federal Work-Study, and scholarships/grants available. Support available to part-time students. Financial award application deadline: 3/1; financial award applicants required to submit FAFSA. *Faculty research:* Vaccine hesitancy in pregnant women and mothers, palliative care and midwifery, diabetes education, curriculum development, workforce training, education and development, geriatrics. *Unit head:* Dr. James Pace, Senior Associate Dean for Academic Programs, 212-992-7343, E-mail: james.pace@nyu.edu. *Application contact:* Matthew Burke, Assistant Director, Graduate Student Affairs and Admissions, 212-998-7397, Fax: 212-995-4302, E-mail: mb6060@nyu.edu.

Nicholls State University, Graduate Studies, College of Nursing and Allied Health, Thibodaux, LA 70310. Offers family nurse practitioner (MSN); nurse executive (MSN); nursing education (MSN); psychiatric/mental health nurse practitioner (MSN).

Northeastern State University, College of Science and Health Professions, Department of Health Professions, Program in Nursing Education, Muskogee, OK 74401. Offers nursing (MSN). *Faculty:* 1 (woman) full-time. *Students:* 7 part-time (all women); includes 2 minority (1 American Indian or Alaska Native, non-Hispanic/Latino; 1 Two or more races, non-Hispanic/Latino). Average age 40. In 2017, 9 master's awarded. *Application deadline:* Applications are processed on a rolling basis. Application fee: $25. Electronic applications accepted. *Expenses:* Tuition, state resident: part-time $222 per credit hour. Tuition, nonresident: part-time $501.75 per credit hour. *Required fees:* $37.40 per credit hour. Tuition and fees vary according to degree level. *Unit head:* Dr. Heather Fenton, Program Coordinator, 918-444-5221, E-mail: fentonh@nsuok.edu. *Application contact:* Josh McCollum, Graduate Coordinator, 918-444-2093, E-mail: mccolluj@nsuok.edu.
Website: http://academics.nsuok.edu/healthprofessions/DegreePrograms/Graduate/NursingEducationMSN.aspx

Norwich University, College of Graduate and Continuing Studies, Master of Science in Nursing Program, Northfield, VT 05663. Offers nursing administration (MSN); nursing education (MSN). *Accreditation:* AACN. *Program availability:* Evening/weekend, online only, mostly all online with a week-long residency requirement. *Entrance requirements:* For master's, minimum undergraduate GPA of 3.0. Additional exam requirements/recommendations for international students: Required—TOEFL (minimum score 550 paper-based; 80 iBT), IELTS (minimum score 6.5). Electronic applications accepted. *Expenses:* Contact institution.

Nova Southeastern University, Ron and Kathy Assaf College of Nursing, Fort Lauderdale, FL 33314-7796. Offers advanced practice registered nurse (MSN), including adult-gerontology acute care nurse practitioner, family nurse practitioner, psychiatric mental health nurse practitioner; executive nurse leadership (MSN); nursing (PhD), including nursing education; nursing education (MSN); nursing informatics (MSN); nursing practice (DNP). *Accreditation:* AACN. *Program availability:* Part-time, evening/weekend, 100% online, blended/hybrid learning, annual one-week summer institute delivered face-to-face on main campus. *Faculty:* 9 full-time (all women), 47 part-time/adjunct (43 women). *Students:* 658 full-time (599 women); includes 414 minority (175 Black or African American, non-Hispanic/Latino; 37 Asian, non-Hispanic/Latino; 179 Hispanic/Latino; 1 Native Hawaiian or other Pacific Islander, non-Hispanic/Latino;

22 Two or more races, non-Hispanic/Latino), 3 international. Average age 38. 179 applicants, 100% accepted, 163 enrolled. In 2017, 161 master's, 16 doctorates awarded. *Degree requirements:* For doctorate, comprehensive exam, thesis/dissertation. *Entrance requirements:* For master's, minimum GPA of 3.0, RN, BSN, BS or BA; for doctorate, minimum GPA of 3.5, MSN, RN. Additional exam requirements/recommendations for international students: Recommended—TOEFL. *Application deadline:* For fall admission, 3/1 priority date for domestic students, 3/1 for international students; for winter admission, 11/1 for domestic and international students. Applications are processed on a rolling basis. Application fee: $50. Electronic applications accepted. *Expenses:* Contact institution. *Financial support:* Application deadline: 4/15; applicants required to submit FAFSA. *Faculty research:* Nursing education, curriculum, clinical research, interdisciplinary research. *Total annual research expenditures:* $9,500. *Unit head:* Dr. Marcella M. Rutherford, Dean, 954-262-1963, E-mail: rmarcell@nova.edu. *Application contact:* Dianna Murphey, Director of Operations, 954-262-1975, E-mail: dgardner1@nova.edu.
Website: http://www.nova.edu/nursing/

Ohio University, Graduate College, College of Health Sciences and Professions, School of Nursing, Athens, OH 45701-2979. Offers advanced clinical practice (DNP); executive practice (DNP); family nurse practitioner (MSN); nurse educator (MSN). *Accreditation:* AACN. *Degree requirements:* For master's, capstone project. *Entrance requirements:* For master's, GRE, bachelor's degree in nursing from accredited college or university, minimum overall undergraduate GPA of 3.0, official transcripts, statement of goals and objectives, resume, 3 letters of recommendation. Additional exam requirements/recommendations for international students: Required—TOEFL (minimum score 550 paper-based; 80 iBT) or IELTS (minimum score 6.5). Electronic applications accepted.

Oklahoma Baptist University, Program in Nursing, Shawnee, OK 74804. Offers global nursing (MSN); nursing education (MSN). *Accreditation:* AACN.

Oklahoma City University, Kramer School of Nursing, Oklahoma City, OK 73106-1402. Offers clinical nurse leader (MSN); nursing (DNP, PhD); nursing education (MSN). *Accreditation:* ACEN. *Program availability:* Part-time, evening/weekend, online learning. *Faculty:* 10 full-time (all women), 8 part-time/adjunct (all women). *Students:* 111 full-time (100 women), 25 part-time (all women); includes 48 minority (16 Black or African American, non-Hispanic/Latino; 9 American Indian or Alaska Native, non-Hispanic/Latino; 9 Asian, non-Hispanic/Latino; 4 Hispanic/Latino; 10 Two or more races, non-Hispanic/Latino), 8 international. Average age 37. 68 applicants, 72% accepted, 35 enrolled. In 2017, 10 master's, 34 doctorates awarded. *Degree requirements:* For master's, thesis, minimum GPA of 3.0; for doctorate, comprehensive exam, thesis/dissertation, minimum GPA of 3.0. *Entrance requirements:* For master's, registered nurse licensure, minimum undergraduate GPA of 3.0, BSN from nationally-accredited nursing program, completion of courses in health assessment and statistics; for doctorate, GRE, current RN licensure; bachelor's and master's degrees from accredited programs (at least one of which must be in nursing); minimum graduate GPA of 3.5; personal essay; approved scholarly paper or published article/paper in a refereed journal. Additional exam requirements/recommendations for international students: Required—TOEFL (minimum score 550 paper-based; 80 iBT), IELTS (minimum score 6). *Application deadline:* Applications are processed on a rolling basis. Application fee: $50. Electronic applications accepted. *Expenses:* $13,320. *Financial support:* In 2017–18, 89 students received support. Federal Work-Study, institutionally sponsored loans, scholarships/grants, and tuition waivers (full and partial) available. Support available to part-time students. Financial award application deadline: 3/1; financial award applicants required to submit FAFSA. *Unit head:* Dr. Lois Salmeron, Dean, Kramer School of Nursing, 405-208-5900, Fax: 405-208-5914, E-mail: lsalmeron@okcu.edu. *Application contact:* Michael Harrington, Director of Graduate Admissions, 800-633-7242, Fax: 405-208-5916, E-mail: gadmissions@okcu.edu.
Website: http://www.okcu.edu/nursing/

Oklahoma Wesleyan University, Professional Studies Division, Bartlesville, OK 74006-6299. Offers nursing administration (MSN); nursing education (MSN); strategic leadership (MS); theology and apologetics (MA).

Old Dominion University, College of Health Sciences, School of Nursing, Adult Gerontology Nursing Emphasis, Norfolk, VA 23529. Offers adult gerontology clinical nurse specialist/administrator (MSN); adult gerontology clinical nurse specialist/educator (MSN); advanced practice (DNP); neonatal clinical nurse specialist (MSN); pediatric clinical nurse specialist (MSN). *Program availability:* Part-time, online only, blended/hybrid learning. *Faculty:* 2 full-time (both women), 2 part-time/adjunct (both women). *Students:* 9 full-time (all women), 10 part-time (9 women); includes 10 minority (8 Black or African American, non-Hispanic/Latino; 2 Asian, non-Hispanic/Latino). Average age 37. 27 applicants, 96% accepted, 12 enrolled. In 2017, 5 master's awarded. *Degree requirements:* For master's, comprehensive exam, internship, practicum. *Entrance requirements:* For master's, GRE or MAT (waived with a GPA above 3.5), undergraduate health/physical assessment course, statistics, 3 letters of recommendation, essay, resume, transcripts. Additional exam requirements/recommendations for international students: Required—TOEFL. *Application deadline:* For fall admission, 6/1 priority date for domestic students, 4/15 priority date for international students. Applications are processed on a rolling basis. Application fee: $50. Electronic applications accepted. *Expenses:* $469 per credit; $450 School of Nursing fee per semester. *Financial support:* Unspecified assistantships available. Financial award applicants required to submit FAFSA. *Unit head:* Dr. Tina Haney, Program Director, 757-683-5428, Fax: 757-683-5253, E-mail: thaney@odu.edu. *Application contact:* Sue Parker, Graduate Program Coordinator, 757-683-4298, Fax: 757-683-5253, E-mail: sparker@odu.edu.

Oregon Health & Science University, School of Nursing, Program in Nursing Education, Portland, OR 97239-3098. Offers MN, Post Master's Certificate. *Program availability:* Part-time, online only, 100% online. *Entrance requirements:* For master's, minimum cumulative GPA of 3.0, 3 letters of recommendation, essay, RN license or eligibility, BS with major in nursing or BSN, statistics taken in last 5 years with minimum B- grade; for Post Master's Certificate, minimum cumulative GPA of 3.0, 3 letters of recommendation, essay, RN license or eligibility, master's degree in nursing, statistics taken in last 5 years with minimum B- grade. Additional exam requirements/recommendations for international students: Required—TOEFL (minimum score 83 iBT). Electronic applications accepted. *Expenses:* Contact institution. *Faculty research:* Quality of end-of-life care in long-term settings, ethical issues in studying dying people and their families, strategies for improving clinical judgement.

Otterbein University, Department of Nursing, Westerville, OH 43081. Offers advanced practice nurse educator (Certificate); clinical nurse leader (MSN); family nurse practitioner (MSN, Certificate); nurse anesthesia (MSN, Certificate); nursing (DNP); nursing service administration (MSN). *Accreditation:* AACN; AANA/CANAEP; ACEN. *Program availability:* Part-time, evening/weekend, online learning. *Degree requirements:* For master's, comprehensive exam (for some programs), thesis (for some programs). *Entrance requirements:* For master's, 2 reference forms, resume; for Certificate, official transcripts, 2 reference forms, essay, resumé. Additional exam requirements/recommendations for international students: Required—TOEFL (minimum score 550 paper-based; 79 iBT). *Faculty research:* Patient education, women's health, trauma curriculum development, administration.

Pennsylvania College of Health Sciences, Graduate Programs, Lancaster, PA 17601. Offers administration (MSN); education (MSHS, MSN); healthcare administration (MHA). *Degree requirements:* For master's, internship (for MHA, MSN in administration); practicum (for MSHS, MSN in education).

Pittsburg State University, Graduate School, College of Arts and Sciences, Irene Ransom Bailey School of Nursing, Pittsburg, KS 66762. Offers nursing (DNP); nursing education (MSN). *Accreditation:* AACN. *Program availability:* Part-time. *Students:* 48 (42 women); includes 11 minority (1 American Indian or Alaska Native, non-Hispanic/Latino; 2 Hispanic/Latino; 8 Two or more races, non-Hispanic/Latino). In 2017, 7 master's, 13 doctorates awarded. *Degree requirements:* For master's, thesis optional; for doctorate, thesis/dissertation optional. *Entrance requirements:* For master's, GRE General Test. Additional exam requirements/recommendations for international students: Required—TOEFL (minimum score 550 paper-based; 79 iBT), IELTS (minimum score 6.5), PTE (minimum score 53). *Application deadline:* For fall admission, 7/15 for domestic students, 6/1 for international students; for spring admission, 12/15 for domestic students, 10/15 for international students; for summer admission, 5/15 for domestic students, 4/1 for international students. Applications are processed on a rolling basis. Application fee: $35 ($60 for international students). Electronic applications accepted. *Expenses:* Contact institution. *Financial support:* In 2017–18, 3 teaching assistantships with full tuition reimbursements (averaging $5,500 per year) were awarded. Financial award application deadline: 2/1; financial award applicants required to submit FAFSA. *Unit head:* Dr. Chyerl Giefer, Chairperson, 620-235-4438, E-mail: cgiefer@pittstate.edu. *Application contact:* Lisa Allen, Assistant Director of Graduate and Continuing Studies, 620-235-4223, Fax: 620-235-4219, E-mail: lallen@pittstate.edu.

Purdue University Global, School of Nursing, Davenport, IA 52807. Offers nurse administrator (MS); nurse educator (MS). *Program availability:* Part-time, evening/weekend, online learning. *Entrance requirements:* For master's, RN. Additional exam requirements/recommendations for international students: Required—TOEFL (minimum score 550 paper-based).

Queens University of Charlotte, Presbyterian School of Nursing, Charlotte, NC 28274-0002. Offers clinical nurse leader (MSN); nurse educator (MSN); nursing administrator (MSN). *Accreditation:* AACN. *Degree requirements:* For master's, research project. *Entrance requirements:* For master's, minimum GPA of 3.0. Additional exam requirements/recommendations for international students: Required—TOEFL. Electronic applications accepted. *Expenses:* Contact institution.

Ramapo College of New Jersey, Master of Science in Nursing Program, Mahwah, NJ 07430-1680. Offers family nurse practitioner (MSN); nursing administrator (MSN); nursing education (MSN). *Accreditation:* ACEN. *Program availability:* Part-time. *Faculty:* 4 full-time (all women), 2 part-time/adjunct (1 woman). *Students:* 79 part-time (70 women); includes 28 minority (4 Black or African American, non-Hispanic/Latino; 18 Asian, non-Hispanic/Latino; 5 Hispanic/Latino; 1 Two or more races, non-Hispanic/Latino). Average age 33. 84 applicants, 67% accepted, 37 enrolled. In 2017, 9 master's awarded. *Entrance requirements:* For master's, official transcript; personal statement; 2 letters of recommendation; resume; current licensure as a Registered Nurse, or eligibility for licensure; evidence of one year of recent experience as RN prior to entry into clinical practicum courses; evidence of undergraduate statistics course; criminal background check. Additional exam requirements/recommendations for international students: Required—TOEFL (minimum score 550 paper-based; 90 iBT); Recommended—IELTS (minimum score 6). *Application deadline:* For fall admission, 5/1 for domestic and international students; for spring admission, 12/1 for domestic and international students. Applications are processed on a rolling basis. Application fee: $65. Electronic applications accepted. *Expenses:* $690.60 per credit tuition, $56.95 per credit fees. *Financial support:* Career-related internships or fieldwork available. Financial award application deadline: 3/1; financial award applicants required to submit FAFSA. *Faculty research:* Learning styles and critical thinking, evidence-based education, outcomes measurement. *Unit head:* Dr. Kathleen M. Burke, Assistant Dean of Nursing Programs/Professor, 201-684-7737, Fax: 201-684-7954, E-mail: kmburke@ramapo.edu. *Application contact:* Anthony Dovi, Associate Director of Admissions, Adult Learners and Graduate Programs, 201-684-7305, Fax: 201-684-7964, E-mail: adovi@ramapo.edu.
Website: http://www.ramapo.edu/msn/

Regis College, Nursing and Health Sciences School, Weston, MA 02493. Offers applied behavior analysis (MS); counseling psychology (MA); health administration (MS); nurse practitioner (Certificate); nursing (MS, DNP); nursing education (Certificate); occupational therapy (MS). *Accreditation:* ACEN. *Program availability:* Part-time, evening/weekend, 100% online, blended/hybrid learning. *Degree requirements:* For doctorate, thesis/dissertation. *Entrance requirements:* For master's, GRE General Test or MAT, minimum GPA of 3.0, official transcripts, recommendations, personal statement, resume/curriculum vitae, interview; for doctorate, MAT or GRE if GPA from master's lower than 3.5. Additional exam requirements/recommendations for international students: Required—TOEFL (minimum score 560 paper-based; 79 iBT); Recommended—IELTS (minimum score 6.5). *Application deadline:* Applications are processed on a rolling basis. Application fee: $75. Electronic applications accepted. *Financial support:* Federal Work-Study, scholarships/grants, traineeships, and unspecified assistantships available. Support available to part-time students. Financial award applicants required to submit FAFSA. *Faculty research:* Global public health, health policy, education, aging, job satisfaction, psychiatric nursing, critical thinking. *Application contact:* Hillary Lyons, Graduate Admission Counselor, 781-768-7746, E-mail: hillary.lyons@regiscollege.edu.

Regis University, Rueckert-Hartman College for Health Professions, Denver, CO 80221-1099. Offers advanced practice nurse (DNP); counseling (MA); counseling children and adolescents (Post-Graduate Certificate); counseling military families (Post-Graduate Certificate); depth psychotherapy (Post-Graduate Certificate); fellowship in orthopedic manual physical therapy (Certificate); health care business management (Certificate); health care quality and patient safety (Certificate); health industry leadership (MBA); health services administration (MS); marriage and family therapy (MA, Post-Graduate Certificate); neonatal nurse practitioner (MSN); nursing education (MSN); nursing leadership (MSN); occupational therapy (OTD); pharmacy (Pharm D); physical therapy (DPT). *Program availability:* Part-time, evening/weekend, 100% online, blended/hybrid learning. *Degree requirements:* For master's, thesis (for some programs), internship. *Entrance requirements:* For master's, official transcript reflecting baccalaureate degree awarded from regionally-accredited college or university. Additional exam requirements/recommendations for international students: Required—TOEFL (minimum score 550 paper-based; 82 iBT). Electronic applications accepted. *Expenses:* Contact institution. *Faculty research:* Normal and pathological balance and gait research, normal/pathological upper limb motor control/biomechanics, exercise energy/metabolism research, optical treatment protocols for therapeutic modalities.

Rivier University, School of Graduate Studies, Division of Nursing and Health Professions, Nashua, NH 03060. Offers family nurse practitioner (MS); leadership in health systems management (MS); nursing education (MS); nursing practice (DNP); psychiatric/mental health nurse practitioner (MS); public health (MPH). *Accreditation:* ACEN. *Program availability:* Part-time, evening/weekend. *Entrance requirements:* For master's, GRE, MAT. Electronic applications accepted.

Roberts Wesleyan College, Department of Nursing, Rochester, NY 14624-1997. Offers nursing education (MSN); nursing informatics (MSN); nursing leadership and administration (MSN). *Accreditation:* AACN. *Program availability:* Evening/weekend, online learning. *Degree requirements:* For master's, thesis. *Entrance requirements:* For master's, minimum GPA of 3.0; BS in nursing; interview; RN license; resume; course work in statistics. Additional exam requirements/recommendations for international students: Required—TOEFL (minimum score 90 iBT), IELTS (minimum score 6.5). Electronic applications accepted.

Sacred Heart University, Graduate Programs, College of Nursing, Fairfield, CT 06825. Offers clinical (DNP); clinical nurse leader (MSN); family nurse practitioner (MSN, Post-Master's Certificate); leadership (DNP); nursing education (MSN); nursing management and executive leadership (MSN). *Accreditation:* AACN. *Program availability:* Part-time, evening/weekend, 100% online, blended/hybrid learning. *Faculty:* 17 full-time (all women), 29 part-time/adjunct (26 women). *Students:* 21 full-time (20 women), 692 part-time (650 women); includes 136 minority (52 Black or African American, non-Hispanic/Latino; 2 American Indian or Alaska Native, non-Hispanic/Latino; 29 Asian, non-Hispanic/Latino; 46 Hispanic/Latino; 7 Two or more races, non-Hispanic/Latino). Average age 37. 70 applicants, 69% accepted, 32 enrolled. In 2017, 260 master's, 16 doctorates awarded. *Degree requirements:* For master's, thesis, 500 clinical hours; for doctorate, capstone. *Entrance requirements:* For master's, minimum GPA of 3.0, BSN or RN plus BS (for MSN); for doctorate, minimum GPA of 3.0, MSN or BSN plus MS in related field (for DNP). Additional exam requirements/recommendations for international students: Required—TOEFL (minimum score 570 paper-based, 80 iBT), TWE, or IELTS (6.5). *Application deadline:* For fall admission, 2/15 for domestic and international students. Applications are processed on a rolling basis. Application fee: $75. Electronic applications accepted. *Expenses:* Contact institution. *Financial support:* Unspecified assistantships available. Financial award applicants required to submit FAFSA. *Unit head:* Mary Alice Donius, Dean of Nursing, 203-365-4508, E-mail: donium@sacredheart.edu. *Application contact:* Tara Chudy, Executive Director of Graduate Admissions, 203-365-4735, Fax: 203-365-4732, E-mail: chudyt@sacredheart.edu.
Website: http://www.sacredheart.edu/academics/collegeofhealthprofessions/academicprograms/nursing/nursingprograms/graduateprograms/

Sage Graduate School, School of Health Sciences, Department of Nursing, Program in Education and Leadership, Troy, NY 12180-4115. Offers DNS. *Program availability:* Part-time-only. *Faculty:* 6 full-time (all women), 11 part-time/adjunct (10 women). *Students:* 1 (woman) full-time, 22 part-time (21 women); includes 2 minority (1 Hispanic/Latino; 1 Two or more races, non-Hispanic/Latino), 2 international. Average age 52. 0 applicants, 11% accepted. In 2017, 5 doctorates awarded. *Degree requirements:* For doctorate, thesis/dissertation. *Entrance requirements:* For doctorate, master's degree in nursing from accredited institution; minimum GPA of 3.5; official transcripts; academic curriculum vitae; 3 letters of recommendation; 1-2 page personal essay; interview; current registered nurse license. Additional exam requirements/recommendations for international students: Required—TOEFL (minimum score 550 paper-based). Application fee: $30. Electronic applications accepted. *Expenses:* Contact institution. *Financial support:* Fellowships, research assistantships, scholarships/grants, and unspecified assistantships available. *Unit head:* Dr. Theresa Hand, Dean, School of Health Sciences, 518-200-2264, Fax: 518-244-4571, E-mail: handt@sage.edu. *Application contact:* Dr. Kathleen A. Kelly, Associate Professor/Director, Doctor of Nursing Science Program, 518-244-2030, Fax: 518-244-2009, E-mail: kelly5@sage.edu.

St. Catherine University, Graduate Programs, Program in Nursing, St. Paul, MN 55105. Offers adult-gerontological nurse practitioner (MS); nurse educator (MS); nursing (DNP); nursing: entry-level (MS); pediatric nurse practitioner (MS). *Accreditation:* ACEN. *Program availability:* Part-time, evening/weekend. *Degree requirements:* For master's, thesis; for doctorate, portfolio, systems change project. *Entrance requirements:* For master's, GRE General Test, bachelor's degree in nursing, current nursing license, 2 years of recent clinical practice; for doctorate, master's degree in nursing, RN license, advanced nursing position. Additional exam requirements/recommendations for international students: Required—TOEFL (minimum score 600 paper-based; 100 iBT). *Application deadline:* For fall admission, 1/15 priority date for domestic students. Application fee: $35. *Expenses:* Contact institution. *Financial support:* Career-related internships or fieldwork and institutionally sponsored loans available. Support available to part-time students. Financial award application deadline: 4/1; financial award applicants required to submit FAFSA. *Unit head:* Margaret Dexheimer-Pharris, Professor/Associate Dean for Nursing, 651-690-6572, Fax: 651-690-6941, E-mail: mdpharris@stkate.edu. *Application contact:* Kristin Chalberg, Associate Director of Non-Traditional Admissions, 651-690-6868, Fax: 651-690-6064.

Saint Francis Medical Center College of Nursing, Graduate Programs, Peoria, IL 61603-3783. Offers adult gerontology (MSN); clinical nurse leader (MSN); family nurse practitioner (MSN, Post-Graduate Certificate); family psychiatric mental health nurse practitioner (MSN); neonatal nurse practitioner (MSN); nurse clinician (Post-Graduate Certificate); nurse educator (MSN, Post-Graduate Certificate); nursing (DNP); nursing management leadership (MSN). *Accreditation:* ACEN. *Program availability:* Part-time, online only, 100% online, blended/hybrid learning. *Faculty:* 11 full-time (all women), 7 part-time/adjunct (all women). *Students:* 4 full-time (all women), 239 part-time (209 women); includes 24 minority (12 Black or African American, non-Hispanic/Latino; 3 Asian, non-Hispanic/Latino; 4 Hispanic/Latino; 5 Two or more races, non-Hispanic/Latino). Average age 37. 105 applicants, 83% accepted, 60 enrolled. In 2017, 52 master's, 8 doctorates awarded. *Degree requirements:* For master's, research experience, portfolio, practicum; for doctorate, practicum. *Entrance requirements:* For master's, nursing research, health assessment, graduate course work in statistics, RN license; for doctorate, master's degree in nursing, professional portfolio, graduate statistics, transcripts, RN license. Additional exam requirements/recommendations for international students: Required—TOEFL (minimum score 550 paper-based; 79 iBT). *Application deadline:* For fall admission, 6/1 priority date for domestic and international students; for spring admission, 11/15 priority date for domestic and international students. Applications are processed on a rolling basis. Application fee: $50. *Expenses:* Contact institution. *Financial support:* In 2017–18, 13 students received support. Scholarships/grants and tuition waivers (partial) available. Support available to part-time students. Financial award application deadline: 6/15; financial award applicants required to submit FAFSA. *Faculty research:* Outcome and curriculum planning, health promotion, NCLEX-RN results, decision-making program evaluation. *Unit head:* Dr. Patti A. Stockert, President of the College, 309-655-4124, Fax: 309-624-8973, E-mail: patricia.a.stockert@osfhealthcare.org. *Application contact:* Dr. Kim A. Mitchell, Dean, Graduate Program, 309-655-2201, Fax: 309-624-8973, E-mail: kim.a.mitchell@osfhealthcare.org.
Website: http://www.sfmccon.edu/graduate-programs/

Saint Francis University, Nursing Program, Loretto, PA 15940-0600. Offers leadership/education (MSN). *Program availability:* Part-time, online only, blended/hybrid learning. *Faculty:* 2 full-time (both women), 4 part-time/adjunct (all women). *Students:* 12 part-time (all women). Average age 37. 5 applicants, 100% accepted, 4 enrolled. *Entrance requirements:* Additional exam requirements/recommendations for international students: Required—TOEFL. Application fee: $30. Electronic applications accepted. *Expenses:* $2,572.50 per course, $857.50 per credit, $55 technology fee per semester part-time, $111 technology fee per semester full-time. *Financial support:* Applicants required to submit FAFSA. *Unit head:* Dr. Camille Wendekier, RN, Coordinator, E-mail: cwendekier@francis.edu. *Application contact:* Dr. Peter Raymond Skoner, Associate Provost, 814-472-3085, Fax: 814-472-3365, E-mail: pskoner@francis.edu.
Website: https://www.francis.edu/Nursing-Masters/

St. Joseph's College, Long Island Campus, Program in Nursing, Patchogue, NY 11772-2399. Offers adult-gerontology clinical nurse specialist (MS); adult-gerontology primary care nurse practitioner (MS); nursing education (MS). *Program availability:* Part-time, evening/weekend. *Faculty:* 4 full-time (all women), 1 (woman) part-time/adjunct. *Students:* 1 (woman) full-time, 40 part-time (36 women); includes 15 minority (7 Black or African American, non-Hispanic/Latino; 3 Asian, non-Hispanic/Latino; 5 Hispanic/Latino). Average age 41. 39 applicants, 69% accepted, 21 enrolled. In 2017, 6 master's awarded. *Entrance requirements:* For master's, one year of professional clinical practice prior to admission, proof of New York State RN license and current professional registration, curriculum vitae, personal statement, two letters of reference, official college transcripts, proof of malpractice insurance. Additional exam requirements/recommendations for international students: Required—TOEFL (minimum score 550 paper-based; 80 iBT). *Application deadline:* Applications are processed on a rolling basis. Application fee: $25. Electronic applications accepted. *Expenses: Tuition:* Full-time $17,550; part-time $975 per credit. *Required fees:* $362. *Financial support:* In 2017–18, 23 students received support. *Unit head:* Dr. Maria Fletcher, RN, Director/Associate Professor, 631-687-5180, E-mail: mfletcher@sjcny.edu.
Website: http://www.sjcny.edu/long-island

St. Joseph's College, New York, Program in Nursing, Brooklyn, NY 11205-3688. Offers adult-gerontology clinical nurse specialist (MS); adult-gerontology primary care nurse practitioner (MS); nursing education (MS). *Accreditation:* ACEN. *Program availability:* Part-time, evening/weekend. *Faculty:* 4 full-time (all women), 1 (woman) part-time/adjunct. *Students:* 47 part-time (46 women); includes 38 minority (35 Black or African American, non-Hispanic/Latino; 1 Asian, non-Hispanic/Latino; 2 Two or more races, non-Hispanic/Latino). Average age 45. 51 applicants, 71% accepted, 20 enrolled. In 2017, 7 master's awarded. *Entrance requirements:* For master's, one year of professional clinical practice, proof of NY State RN license and current professional registration, curriculum vitae, personal statement, 2 letters of reference, official transcripts, malpractice insurance. Additional exam requirements/recommendations for international students: Required—TOEFL (minimum score 80 iBT). *Application deadline:* Applications are processed on a rolling basis. Application fee: $25. Electronic applications accepted. *Expenses: Tuition:* Full-time $17,550; part-time $975 per credit. *Required fees:* $362. *Financial support:* In 2017–18, 7 students received support. *Unit head:* Maria Fletcher, Associate Professor/Director, 718-940-5891, E-mail: mfletcher@sjcny.edu.
Website: http://www.sjcny.edu

Saint Joseph's College of Maine, Master of Science in Nursing Program, Standish, ME 04084. Offers administration (MSN); education (MSN); family nurse practitioner (MSN); nursing administration and leadership (Certificate); nursing and health care education (Certificate). *Accreditation:* AACN. *Program availability:* Part-time, online learning. *Entrance requirements:* For master's, MAT. Electronic applications accepted.

Salem State University, School of Graduate Studies, Program in Nursing, Salem, MA 01970-5353. Offers adult-gerontology primary care nursing (MSN); nursing administration (MSN); nursing education (MSN); MBA/MSN. *Accreditation:* AACN. *Program availability:* Part-time, evening/weekend. *Entrance requirements:* For master's, GRE or MAT. Additional exam requirements/recommendations for international students: Required—TOEFL (minimum score 550 paper-based; 80 iBT) or IELTS (minimum score 5.5).

Salisbury University, MS in Nursing Program, Salisbury, MD 21801-6837. Offers nursing (MS), including clinical nurse educator, health care leadership. *Accreditation:* AACN. *Program availability:* Part-time. *Faculty:* 4 full-time (3 women), 2 part-time/adjunct (both women). *Students:* 3 part-time (all women); includes 1 minority (Black or African American, non-Hispanic/Latino). Average age 40. In 2017, 1 master's awarded. *Degree requirements:* For master's, thesis. *Entrance requirements:* For master's, two letters of recommendation; transcripts from colleges and universities attended; BSN with minimum cumulative GPA of 3.0; personal statement; current U.S. RN license; resume. Additional exam requirements/recommendations for international students: Required—TOEFL (minimum score 550 paper-based; 79 iBT), IELTS (minimum score 6.5). *Application deadline:* For fall admission, 3/1 for domestic and international students. Application fee: $65. Electronic applications accepted. *Expenses:* $640 per credit hour resident; $807 per credit hour non-resident; $92 per credit hour fees. *Financial support:* Career-related internships or fieldwork and scholarships/grants available. Support available to part-time students. Financial award application deadline: 3/1; financial award applicants required to submit FAFSA. *Faculty research:* Gerontology; simulation education; palliative care; chronic disease management; mental illness. *Unit head:* Dr. Lisa Seldomridge, Graduate Program Director, Nursing MS, 410-543-6413, E-mail: laseldomridge@salisbury.edu.
Website: http://www.salisbury.edu/gsr/gradstudies/MSNpage.html

Seattle Pacific University, MS in Nursing Program, Seattle, WA 98119-1997. Offers administration (MSN); adult/gerontology nurse practitioner (MSN); clinical nurse specialist (MSN); family nurse practitioner (MSN, Certificate); informatics (MSN); nurse educator (MSN). *Accreditation:* AACN. *Program availability:* Part-time. *Students:* 22 full-time (17 women), 40 part-time (35 women); includes 13 minority (4 Black or African American, non-Hispanic/Latino; 1 American Indian or Alaska Native, non-Hispanic/Latino; 7 Asian, non-Hispanic/Latino; 1 Two or more races, non-Hispanic/Latino). Average age 36. 52 applicants, 73% accepted, 22 enrolled. In 2017, 23 master's awarded. *Degree requirements:* For master's, thesis. *Entrance requirements:* For master's, personal statement, transcripts, undergraduate nursing degree, proof of undergraduate statistics course with minimum GPA of 2.0, 2 recommendations. *Application deadline:* For fall admission, 1/15 priority date for domestic students; for spring admission, 1/15 for domestic students. Applications are processed on a rolling basis. Application fee: $50. Electronic applications accepted. *Expenses:* Contact institution. *Financial support:* Fellowships and scholarships/grants available. Financial award applicants required to submit FAFSA. *Unit head:* Dr. Christine Hoyle, Associate Dean, 206-281-2469, E-mail: hoylec@spu.edu.
Website: http://spu.edu/academics/school-of-health-sciences/undergraduate-programs/nursing

Seton Hall University, College of Nursing, South Orange, NJ 07079-2697. Offers advanced practice in primary health care (MSN, DNP), including adult/gerontological nurse practitioner, pediatric nurse practitioner; entry into practice (MSN); health systems administration (MSN, DNP); nursing (PhD); nursing case management (MSN); nursing education (MA); school nurse (MSN); MSN/MA. *Accreditation:* AACN. *Program availability:* Part-time, online learning. *Degree requirements:* For master's, research project; for doctorate, dissertation or scholarly project. *Entrance requirements:* For doctorate, GRE (waived for students with GPA of 3.5 or higher). Additional exam requirements/recommendations for international students: Required—TOEFL. Electronic applications accepted. *Faculty research:* Parent/child, adult, and gerontological nursing; breast cancer; families of children with HIV; parish nursing.

Nursing Education

Shenandoah University, Eleanor Wade Custer School of Nursing, Winchester, VA 22601. Offers adult gerontology primary care nurse practitioner (Graduate Certificate); adult-gerontology primary care nurse practitioner (MSN); family nurse practitioner (MSN, DNP, Graduate Certificate); general (MSN); health systems leadership (DNP); health systems management (MSN, Graduate Certificate); nurse midwifery (MSN); nurse-midwifery (Graduate Certificate); nursing education (Graduate Certificate); nursing practice (DNP); psychiatric mental health nurse practitioner (MSN, DNP, Graduate Certificate). *Accreditation:* AACN; ACNM/ACME. *Faculty:* 17 full-time (all women), 6 part-time/adjunct (all women). *Students:* 30 full-time (26 women), 51 part-time (48 women); includes 19 minority (13 Black or African American, non-Hispanic/Latino; 3 Asian, non-Hispanic/Latino; 2 Hispanic/Latino; 1 Two or more races, non-Hispanic/Latino), 3 international. Average age 37. 52 applicants, 88% accepted, 34 enrolled. In 2017, 18 master's, 1 doctorate, 28 other advanced degrees awarded. *Degree requirements:* For master's, research project, clinical hours; for doctorate, scholarly project, clinical hours; for Graduate Certificate, clinical hours. *Entrance requirements:* For master's, United States RN license; minimum GPA of 3.0; 2080 hours of clinical experience; curriculum vitae; 3 letters of recommendation from former dean, faculty member, or advisor familiar with the applicant, and a former or current supervisor; two-to-three-page essay on a specified topic; for doctorate, MSN, minimum GPA of 3.0, 3 letters of recommendation, interview, BSN, two-to-three page essay on a specific topic, 500-word statement of clinical practice research interest, resume, current U.S. RN license, 2080 clinical hours; for Graduate Certificate, MSN, minimum GPA of 3.0, 2 letters of recommendation, minimum of one year (2080 hours) of clinical nursing experience, interview, two-to-three page essay on a specific topic, resume, current United States RN license. Additional exam requirements/recommendations for international students: Required—TOEFL (minimum score 558 paper-based; 83 iBT). *Application deadline:* For fall admission, 4/15 priority date for domestic and international students; for spring admission, 11/1 for domestic and international students; for summer admission, 3/1 for domestic and international students. Application fee: $30. Electronic applications accepted. *Expenses:* $22,451 tuition, plus $3,579 fees (student services fee, technology fee, and clinical fee). *Financial support:* In 2017–18, 32 students received support. Scholarships/grants and unspecified assistantships available. Financial award applicants required to submit FAFSA. *Faculty research:* Emergency preparedness, workplace environment, maternal child, inter-professional education, health policy. *Total annual research expenditures:* $30,000. *Unit head:* Dr. Kathleen LaSala, RN, Dean, 540-678-4381, Fax: 540-665-5519, E-mail: klasala@su.edu. *Application contact:* Andrew Woodall, Executive Director of Recruitment and Admissions, 540-665-4581, Fax: 540-665-4627, E-mail: admit@su.edu.
Website: http://www.su.edu/nursing/

Southern Adventist University, School of Nursing, Collegedale, TN 37315-0370. Offers adult/gerontology acute care nurse practitioner (MSN, DNP); adult/gerontology nurse practitioner (MSN); family nurse practitioner (MSN, DNP); lifestyle therapeutics (DNP); nurse educator (MSN, DNP); psychiatric mental health nurse practitioner (MSN, DNP); MSN/MBA. *Accreditation:* ACEN. *Program availability:* Part-time. *Degree requirements:* For master's, thesis or project. *Entrance requirements:* For master's, RN license. Additional exam requirements/recommendations for international students: Required—TOEFL (minimum score 600 paper-based). *Application deadline:* For fall admission, 7/1 for domestic and international students; for winter admission, 12/1 for domestic and international students. Applications are processed on a rolling basis. Application fee: $40. Electronic applications accepted. *Expenses: Tuition:* Full-time $11,430; part-time $635 per credit hour. Tuition and fees vary according to degree level and program. *Financial support:* Teaching assistantships with partial tuition reimbursements available. *Faculty research:* Pain management, ethics, corporate wellness, caring spirituality, stress. *Unit head:* Dr. Barbara James, Dean, 423-236-2942, Fax: 423-236-1940, E-mail: bjames@southern.edu. *Application contact:* Sylvia Mayer, RN, Director of Nursing Admissions, 423-236-2941, Fax: 423-236-1940, E-mail: smayer@southern.edu.
Website: https://www.southern.edu/academics/nursing.html

Southern Connecticut State University, School of Graduate Studies, School of Health and Human Services, Department of Nursing, New Haven, CT 06515-1355. Offers family nurse practitioner (MSN); nursing (Ed D); nursing education (MSN). *Accreditation:* AACN. *Program availability:* Part-time, evening/weekend. *Degree requirements:* For master's, thesis. *Entrance requirements:* For master's, GRE, MAT, interview, minimum QPA of 2.8, RN license, minimum 1 year of professional nursing experience. Electronic applications accepted.

Southern Illinois University Edwardsville, Graduate School, School of Nursing, Program in Nurse Educator, Edwardsville, IL 62026. Offers MS, Post-Master's Certificate. *Program availability:* Part-time, evening/weekend. *Degree requirements:* For master's, comprehensive exam. *Entrance requirements:* For master's, RN licensure, minimum undergraduate nursing GPA of 3.0. Additional exam requirements/recommendations for international students: Required—TOEFL (minimum score 550 paper-based; 79 iBT), IELTS (minimum score 6.5). Electronic applications accepted.

Southern Nazarene University, College of Professional and Graduate Studies, School of Nursing, Bethany, OK 73008. Offers nursing education (MS); nursing leadership (MS). *Accreditation:* AACN. *Program availability:* Part-time, evening/weekend. *Degree requirements:* For master's, thesis. *Entrance requirements:* For master's, minimum undergraduate cumulative GPA of 3.0; baccalaureate degree in nursing from nationally-accredited program; current unencumbered registered nurse licensure in Oklahoma or eligibility for same; documentation of basic computer skills; basic statistics course; statement of professional goals; three letters of recommendation. Additional exam requirements/recommendations for international students: Required—TOEFL (minimum score 550 paper-based).

Southern New Hampshire University, Program in Nursing, Manchester, NH 03106-1045. Offers clinical nurse leader (MSN); nurse educator (MSN); nursing (MSN); patient safety and quality (MSN, Post Master's Certificate). *Program availability:* Online only, 100% online. *Entrance requirements:* For master's, undergraduate transcripts, active unencumbered license, bachelor's degree with minimum cumulative GPA of 3.0. *Application deadline:* Applications are processed on a rolling basis. Application fee: $40. Electronic applications accepted. *Expenses: Tuition:* Part-time $627 per credit hour. Part-time tuition and fees vary according to campus/location and program. *Application contact:* Office of Graduate Admission, 888-327-SNHU, Fax: 603-644-3144, E-mail: enroll@snhu.edu.
Website: https://www.snhu.edu/online-degrees/nursing

Southern University and Agricultural and Mechanical College, College of Nursing and Allied Health, School of Nursing, Baton Rouge, LA 70813. Offers educator/administrator (PhD); family health nursing (MSN); family nurse practitioner (Post Master's Certificate); geriatric nurse practitioner/gerontology (PhD); nursing (DNP). *Accreditation:* AACN. *Program availability:* Part-time. *Degree requirements:* For master's, comprehensive exam, thesis; for doctorate, comprehensive exam, thesis/dissertation. *Entrance requirements:* For master's, GRE General Test, BSN, minimum GPA of 2.7; for doctorate, GRE General Test; for Post Master's Certificate, MSN. Additional exam requirements/recommendations for international students: Required—TOEFL (minimum score 525 paper-based). *Faculty research:* Health promotions, vulnerable populations, (community-based) cardiovascular participating research, health disparities chronic diseases, care of the elderly.

South University, Graduate Programs, College of Nursing, Savannah, GA 31406. Offers nurse educator (MS). *Accreditation:* AACN.

South University, Program in Nursing, Tampa, FL 33614. Offers adult health nurse practitioner (MS); family nurse practitioner (MS); nurse educator (MS).

Spalding University, Graduate Studies, Kosair College of Health and Natural Sciences, School of Nursing, Louisville, KY 40203-2188. Offers adult nurse practitioner (MSN); family nurse practitioner (MSN); leadership in nursing and healthcare (MSN); nurse educator (Post-Master's Certificate); nurse practitioner (Post-Master's Certificate); pediatric nurse practitioner (MSN). *Accreditation:* AACN. *Program availability:* Part-time, evening/weekend. *Degree requirements:* For master's, comprehensive exam (for some programs), thesis. *Entrance requirements:* For master's, GRE General Test, BSN or bachelor's degree in related field, RN licensure, autobiographical statement, transcripts, letters of recommendation. Additional exam requirements/recommendations for international students: Required—TOEFL (minimum score 535 paper-based). *Faculty research:* Nurse educational administration, gerontology, bioterrorism, healthcare ethics, leadership.

State University of New York College of Technology at Delhi, Program in Nursing, Delhi, NY 13753. Offers nursing administration (MS); nursing education (MS). *Program availability:* Online only, 100% online. *Faculty:* 6 full-time (all women), 1 (woman) part-time/adjunct. *Students:* 6 full-time (all women), 35 part-time (32 women). *Expenses:* $462 per credit hour in-state tuition, $944 per credit hour out-of-state, $555 online. *Application contact:* Misty Fields, Associate Director of Admission, 607-746-4546, E-mail: fieldsmr@delhi.edu.

State University of New York Empire State College, School for Graduate Studies, Program in Nursing Education, Saratoga Springs, NY 12866-4391. Offers MSN. *Accreditation:* AACN. *Program availability:* Online learning. *Degree requirements:* For master's, capstone.

State University of New York Polytechnic Institute, Program in Nursing Education, Utica, NY 13502. Offers MS, CAS. *Program availability:* Part-time, 100% online. *Faculty:* 2 full-time (both women), 2 part-time/adjunct (both women). *Students:* 4 full-time (2 women), 57 part-time (52 women); includes 7 minority (3 Black or African American, non-Hispanic/Latino; 2 Asian, non-Hispanic/Latino; 2 Hispanic/Latino). Average age 40. 25 applicants, 60% accepted, 13 enrolled. In 2017, 17 master's awarded. *Degree requirements:* For master's and CAS, project/internship. *Entrance requirements:* For master's, minimum GPA of 3.0 in last 30 hours of undergraduate work, bachelor's degree in nursing, 1 year of RN experience, RN license, 2 letters of reference, resume; for CAS, master's degree in nursing. *Application deadline:* For fall admission, 7/1 for domestic and international students; for spring admission, 12/1 for domestic students, 11/1 for international students. Applications are processed on a rolling basis. Application fee: $60. Electronic applications accepted. *Expenses:* Tuition, state resident: full-time $8154; part-time $2718 per year. Tuition, nonresident: full-time $16,650; part-time $5550 per year. *Required fees:* $993; $331 per unit. Tuition and fees vary according to course load, degree level, campus/location and program. *Financial support:* Scholarships/grants available. Financial award application deadline: 6/1; financial award applicants required to submit FAFSA. *Faculty research:* Innovation in nursing education, nutrition education in nursing. *Unit head:* Dr. Esther Bankert, Program Coordinator, E-mail: esther.bankert@sunyit.edu. *Application contact:* Alicia Foster, Director of Graduate Admissions, E-mail: alicia.foster@sunyit.edu.
Website: https://sunypoly.edu/academics/majors-and-programs/ms-nursing-education.html

Stevenson University, Program in Nursing, Owings Mills, MD 21153. Offers nursing education (MS); nursing leadership/management (MS); population-based care coordination (MS). *Accreditation:* AACN. *Program availability:* Part-time, blended/hybrid learning. *Faculty:* 4 full-time (all women), 12 part-time/adjunct (all women). *Students:* 174 part-time (167 women); includes 53 minority (40 Black or African American, non-Hispanic/Latino; 5 Asian, non-Hispanic/Latino; 8 Two or more races, non-Hispanic/Latino). Average age 40. 45 applicants, 100% accepted, 38 enrolled. In 2017, 47 master's awarded. *Degree requirements:* For master's, capstone course. *Entrance requirements:* For master's, bachelor's degree from regionally-accredited institution, current registered nurse's license in good standing, official college transcripts from all previous academic work, minimum cumulative GPA of 3.0 in past academic work, personal statement (250-350 words), two professional letters of recommendation, resume. *Application deadline:* Applications are processed on a rolling basis. Application fee: $0. Electronic applications accepted. *Expenses:* Contact institution. *Financial support:* Unspecified assistantships available. Financial award applicants required to submit FAFSA. *Unit head:* Judith Feustle, PhD, Associate Dean, 443-352-4292, Fax: 443-394-0538, E-mail: jfeustle@stevenson.edu. *Application contact:* Amanda Courter, Enrollment Counselor, 443-352-4243, Fax: 443-394-0538, E-mail: acourter@stevenson.edu.
Website: http://www.stevenson.edu

Stony Brook University, State University of New York, Stony Brook Medicine, School of Nursing, Program in Nursing Education, Stony Brook, NY 11794. Offers MS, Certificate. *Program availability:* Part-time, blended/hybrid learning. *Students:* 1 (woman) full-time, 63 part-time (59 women); includes 26 minority (13 Black or African American, non-Hispanic/Latino; 1 American Indian or Alaska Native, non-Hispanic/Latino; 6 Asian, non-Hispanic/Latino; 5 Hispanic/Latino; 1 Two or more races, non-Hispanic/Latino). 35 applicants, 100% accepted, 24 enrolled. In 2017, 18 master's awarded. *Degree requirements:* For master's, thesis. *Entrance requirements:* For master's, baccalaureate degree with major in nursing, minimum cumulative GPA of 3.0, current professional RN license, three letters of recommendation. Additional exam requirements/recommendations for international students: Required—TOEFL (minimum score 90 iBT). *Application deadline:* For fall admission, 3/8 for domestic students. Application fee: $100. Electronic applications accepted. *Expenses:* Contact institution. *Unit head:* Lenore Lamanna, Program Director, 631-444-7640, Fax: 631-444-3136, E-mail: lenore.lamanna@stonybrook.edu. *Application contact:* Silvana Jara, Staff Assistant, 631-444-3392, Fax: 631-444-3136, E-mail: silvana.jara@stonybrook.edu.
Website: http://www.nursing.stonybrookmedicine.edu/nursingeducationmaster

Tarleton State University, College of Graduate Studies, College of Health Sciences and Human Services, Department of Nursing, Stephenville, TX 76402. Offers nursing administration (MSN); nursing education (MSN). *Accreditation:* AACN. *Program availability:* Part-time, evening/weekend. *Faculty:* 5 full-time (all women), 1 (woman) part-time/adjunct. *Students:* 1 (woman) full-time, 19 part-time (16 women); includes 6 minority (5 Black or African American, non-Hispanic/Latino; 1 Hispanic/Latino), 1 international. Average age 38. 15 applicants, 87% accepted, 10 enrolled. *Degree requirements:* For master's, comprehensive exam. *Entrance requirements:* For master's, GRE General Test, minimum GPA of 3.0. Additional exam requirements/recommendations for international students: Required—TOEFL (minimum score 550 paper-based; 80 iBT), IELTS (minimum score 6). *Application deadline:* For fall admission, 8/15 priority date for domestic students; for spring admission, 1/7 for domestic students. Applications are processed on a rolling basis. Application fee: $45 ($145 for international students). Electronic applications accepted. *Expenses:* Contact institution. *Financial support:* Career-related internships or fieldwork, Federal Work-

Study, and institutionally sponsored loans available. Support available to part-time students. Financial award applicants required to submit FAFSA. *Unit head:* Dr. Mary Winton, Department Head, 254-968-9139, E-mail: mwinton@tarleton.edu. *Application contact:* Information Contact, 254-968-9104, Fax: 254-968-9670, E-mail: gradoffice@tarleton.edu.
Website: http://www.tarleton.edu/nursing/degrees_grad.html

Teachers College, Columbia University, Department of Health and Behavior Studies, New York, NY 10027-6696. Offers applied behavior analysis (MA, PhD); applied educational psychology: school psychology (Ed M, PhD); behavioral nutrition (PhD), including nutrition (Ed D, PhD); community health education (MS); community nutrition education (Ed M), including community nutrition education; education of deaf and hard of hearing (MA, PhD); health education (MA, Ed D); hearing impairment (Ed D); intellectual disability/autism (MA, Ed D, PhD); nursing education (Ed D, Advanced Certificate); nutrition and education (MS); nutrition and exercise physiology (MS); nutrition and public health (MS); nutrition education (Ed D), including nutrition (Ed D, PhD); physical disabilities (Ed D); reading specialist (MA); severe or multiple disabilities (MA); special education (Ed M, MA, Ed D); teaching of sign language (MA). *Program availability:* Part-time, evening/weekend. *Students:* 245 full-time (226 women), 242 part-time (219 women); includes 167 minority (52 Black or African American, non-Hispanic/Latino; 2 American Indian or Alaska Native, non-Hispanic/Latino; 55 Asian, non-Hispanic/Latino; 48 Hispanic/Latino; 1 Native Hawaiian or other Pacific Islander, non-Hispanic/Latino; 9 Two or more races, non-Hispanic/Latino), 60 international. Average age 30. 480 applicants, 59% accepted, 157 enrolled. Terminal master's awarded for partial completion of doctoral program. *Unit head:* Prof. Dolores Perin, Chair, E-mail: dp111@tc.columbia.edu. *Application contact:* David Estrella, Director of Admission, 212-678-3305, E-mail: estrella@tc.columbia.edu.
Website: http://www.tc.columbia.edu/health-and-behavior-studies/

Tennessee Technological University, Whitson-Hester School of Nursing, MSN Programs, Cookeville, TN 38505. Offers family nurse practitioner (MSN); nursing administration (MSN); nursing education (MSN). *Program availability:* Part-time. *Students:* 22 full-time (17 women), 78 part-time (64 women); includes 5 minority (2 Black or African American, non-Hispanic/Latino; 2 Hispanic/Latino; 1 Two or more races, non-Hispanic/Latino). 48 applicants, 50% accepted, 20 enrolled. In 2017, 41 master's awarded. *Application deadline:* For fall admission, 7/1 for domestic students, 5/1 for international students; for spring admission, 12/1 for domestic students, 10/1 for international students; for summer admission, 5/1 for domestic students, 2/1 for international students. Applications are processed on a rolling basis. Application fee: $35 ($40 for international students). Electronic applications accepted. *Expenses:* Tuition, state resident: full-time $9925; part-time $565 per credit hour. Tuition, nonresident: full-time $22,993; part-time $1291 per credit hour. *Financial support:* Application deadline: 4/1; applicants required to submit FAFSA. *Unit head:* Dr. Kim Hanna, Interim Dean, Fax: 931-372-6244, E-mail: khanna@tntech.edu. *Application contact:* Shelia K. Kendrick, Coordinator of Graduate Studies, 931-372-3808, Fax: 931-372-3497, E-mail: skendrick@tntech.edu.
Website: https://www.tntech.edu/nursing/masters/

Texas A&M University, College of Nursing, Bryan, TX 77807. Offers family nurse practitioner (MSN); forensic nursing (MSN); nursing education (MSN). *Faculty:* 19. *Students:* 9 full-time (all women), 47 part-time (all women); includes 14 minority (2 Asian, non-Hispanic/Latino; 12 Hispanic/Latino). Average age 34. In 2017, 27 master's awarded. *Expenses:* Contact institution. *Financial support:* In 2017–18, 8 students received support, including 2 fellowships (averaging $4,300 per year); career-related internships or fieldwork, institutionally sponsored loans, scholarships/grants, traineeships, health care benefits, tuition waivers (full and partial), and unspecified assistantships also available. Support available to part-time students. Financial award applicants required to submit FAFSA. *Unit head:* Dr. Sharon A. Wilkerson, Founding Dean, 979-436-0111, Fax: 979-436-0098, E-mail: wilkerson@tamhsc.edu. *Application contact:* Jennifer Frank, Program Coordinator for Recruitment and Admission, 979-436-0110, E-mail: conadmissions@tamhsc.edu.
Website: http://nursing.tamhsc.edu/

Texas A&M University–Corpus Christi, College of Graduate Studies, College of Nursing and Health Sciences, Corpus Christi, TX 78412. Offers family nurse practitioner (MSN); leadership in nursing systems (MSN); nurse educator (MSN); nursing practice (DNP). *Accreditation:* AACN. *Program availability:* Part-time, evening/weekend, online only, 100% online. *Faculty:* 17 full-time (16 women), 21 part-time/adjunct (15 women). *Students:* 7 full-time (all women), 364 part-time (307 women); includes 194 minority (25 Black or African American, non-Hispanic/Latino; 26 Asian, non-Hispanic/Latino; 134 Hispanic/Latino; 9 Two or more races, non-Hispanic/Latino). Average age 38. 360 applicants, 33% accepted, 112 enrolled. In 2017, 98 master's awarded. *Degree requirements:* For master's, clinical capstone; for doctorate, capstone/scholarly project. *Entrance requirements:* For master's, essay, resume, 3 letters of recommendation, minimum GPA of 3.0, current valid unencumbered Texas nursing license. Additional exam requirements/recommendations for international students: Required—TOEFL (minimum score 550 paper-based; 79 iBT), IELTS (minimum score 6.5). *Application deadline:* For fall admission, 4/15 for domestic and international students; for spring admission, 1/7 for domestic and international students; for summer admission, 5/27 for domestic and international students. Applications are processed on a rolling basis. Application fee: $50 ($70 for international students). Electronic applications accepted. *Expenses:* Tuition, state resident: full-time $3568; part-time $198.24 per credit hour. Tuition, nonresident: full-time $11,038; part-time $613.24 per credit hour. *Required fees:* $2129; $1422.58 per semester. Tuition and fees vary according to program. *Financial support:* Research assistantships, teaching assistantships, career-related internships or fieldwork, Federal Work-Study, institutionally sponsored loans, scholarships/grants, health care benefits, and unspecified assistantships available. Support available to part-time students. Financial award application deadline: 3/15; financial award applicants required to submit FAFSA. *Unit head:* Dr. Julie Anne Hoff, Dean, 361-825-2275, E-mail: julie.hoff@tamucc.edu. *Application contact:* Graduate Admissions Coordinator, 361-825-2177, Fax: 361-825-2755, E-mail: gradweb@tamucc.edu.
Website: http://conhs.tamucc.edu/

Texas Christian University, Harris College of Nursing and Health Sciences, Master's Program in Nursing, Fort Worth, TX 76129. Offers administration (MSN); clinical nurse leader (MSN, Certificate); clinical nurse specialist (MSN), including adult/gerontology nursing, pediatrics; nursing education (MSN). *Accreditation:* AACN. *Program availability:* Part-time, online only, 100% online. *Faculty:* 29 full-time (26 women), 2 part-time/adjunct (both women). *Students:* 17 full-time (15 women), 7 part-time (all women); includes 6 minority (1 Black or African American, non-Hispanic/Latino; 2 Asian, non-Hispanic/Latino; 2 Hispanic/Latino; 1 Two or more races, non-Hispanic/Latino). Average age 36. 41 applicants, 49% accepted, 6 enrolled. In 2017, 41 master's awarded. *Degree requirements:* For master's, thesis or alternative, practicum. *Entrance requirements:* For master's, 3 letters of reference, essay, resume, two official transcripts from every institution attended. Additional exam requirements/recommendations for international students: Required—TOEFL. *Application deadline:* For spring admission, 9/1 for domestic and international students; for summer admission, 2/1 for domestic and international students. Application fee: $60. Electronic applications accepted. *Expenses:* $1,555 per credit hour, $125 per course fee, $500 lab fee. *Financial support:* In 2017–18, 20 students received support. Scholarships/grants available. Financial award application deadline: 2/15; financial award applicants required to submit FAFSA. *Faculty research:* Geriatrics, cancer survivorship, health literacy, endothelial cells, clinical simulation outcomes. *Unit head:* Dr. Kathy Ellis, Division Director, Graduate Nursing, 817-257-6726, Fax: 817-257-7944, E-mail: kathryn.ellis@tcu.edu. *Application contact:* Heather Lyon, Academic Program Specialist, 817-257-6726, Fax: 817-257-7944, E-mail: graduatenursing@tcu.edu.
Website: http://www.nursing.tcu.edu/graduate.asp

Texas Tech University Health Sciences Center, School of Nursing, Lubbock, TX 79430. Offers acute care nurse practitioner (MSN, Certificate); administration (MSN); advanced practice (DNP); education (MSN); executive leadership (DNP); family nurse practitioner (MSN, Certificate); geriatric nurse practitioner (MSN, Certificate); pediatric nurse practitioner (MSN, Certificate). *Accreditation:* AACN. *Program availability:* Part-time, online learning. *Degree requirements:* For master's, thesis optional. *Entrance requirements:* For master's, minimum GPA of 3.0, 3 letters of reference, BSN, RN license; for Certificate, minimum GPA of 3.0, 3 letters of reference, RN license. Additional exam requirements/recommendations for international students: Required—TOEFL (minimum score 550 paper-based). *Faculty research:* Diabetes/obesity, nurse competency, disease management, intervention and measurements, health disparities.

Texas Woman's University, Graduate School, College of Nursing, Denton, TX 76204. Offers adult health clinical nurse specialist (MS); adult health nurse practitioner (MS); adult/gerontology acute care nurse practitioner (MS); child health clinical nurse specialist (MS); clinical nurse leader (MS); family nurse practitioner (MS); health systems management (MS); nursing education (MS); nursing practice (DNP); nursing science (PhD); pediatric nurse practitioner (MS); women's health clinical nurse specialist (MS); women's health nurse practitioner (MS). *Accreditation:* AACN. *Program availability:* Part-time, 100% online, blended/hybrid learning. *Faculty:* 48 full-time (47 women), 44 part-time/adjunct (37 women). *Students:* 23 full-time (22 women), 816 part-time (750 women); includes 475 minority (188 Black or African American, non-Hispanic/Latino; 4 American Indian or Alaska Native, non-Hispanic/Latino; 171 Asian, non-Hispanic/Latino; 83 Hispanic/Latino; 3 Native Hawaiian or other Pacific Islander, non-Hispanic/Latino; 26 Two or more races, non-Hispanic/Latino), 12 international. Average age 37. 201 applicants, 88% accepted, 123 enrolled. In 2017, 232 master's, 17 doctorates awarded. *Degree requirements:* For master's, comprehensive exam, thesis or alternative, 6-year time limit for completion of degree, professional or clinical project; for doctorate, comprehensive exam, thesis/dissertation, 10-year time limit for completion of degree. *Entrance requirements:* For master's, GRE or MAT, minimum GPA of 3.0 on last 60 hours in undergraduate nursing degree and overall, RN license, BS in nursing, basic statistics course, 1 year of clinical experience; for doctorate, GRE (preferred minimum score 153 [500 old version] Verbal, 144 [500 old version] Quantitative, 4 Analytical), MS in nursing, minimum preferred GPA of 3.5, RN license, statistics course, 2 letters of reference, curriculum vitae, graduate nursing-theory course, graduate research course, statement of professional goals and research interests. Additional exam requirements/recommendations for international students: Required—TOEFL (minimum score 550 paper-based; 79 iBT); Recommended—IELTS (minimum score 6.5), TSE (minimum score 53). *Application deadline:* For fall admission, 5/1 for domestic students, 3/1 priority date for international students; for spring admission, 9/15 for domestic students, 7/1 priority date for international students; for summer admission, 2/1 for domestic and international students. Applications are processed on a rolling basis. Application fee: $50 ($75 for international students). Electronic applications accepted. *Expenses:* $8,510 per year full-time in-state, $17,810 per year full-time out-of-state. *Financial support:* In 2017–18, 146 students received support, including 7 teaching assistantships (averaging $28,195 per year); research assistantships, career-related internships or fieldwork, Federal Work-Study, institutionally sponsored loans, scholarships/grants, traineeships, health care benefits, and unspecified assistantships also available. Support available to part-time students. Financial award application deadline: 3/1; financial award applicants required to submit FAFSA. *Faculty research:* Women's health, nurse staffing and satisfaction in health systems, perinatal safety, chronic illness, pediatric health. *Total annual research expenditures:* $380,388. *Unit head:* Dr. Anita G. Hufft, Dean, 940-898-2401, Fax: 940-898-2437, E-mail: nursing@twu.edu. *Application contact:* Korie Hawkins, Associate Director of Admissions, Graduate Recruitment, 940-898-3188, Fax: 940-898-3081, E-mail: admissions@twu.edu.
Website: http://www.twu.edu/nursing/

Thomas Edison State University, W. Cary Edwards School of Nursing, Master of Science in Nursing Program, Trenton, NJ 08608. Offers nurse educator (MSN); nursing administration (MSN); nursing informatics (MSN). *Accreditation:* AACN; ACEN. *Program availability:* Part-time, online learning. *Degree requirements:* For master's, nursing education seminar, onground practicum, online practicum. *Entrance requirements:* For master's, BSN. Additional exam requirements/recommendations for international students: Required—TOEFL (minimum score 550 paper-based; 79 iBT). Electronic applications accepted.

Towson University, College of Health Professions, Program in Nursing, Towson, MD 21252-0001. Offers nursing education (Postbaccalaureate Certificate). *Accreditation:* AACN. *Program availability:* Part-time. *Students:* 3 full-time (2 women), 30 part-time (26 women); includes 11 minority (9 Black or African American, non-Hispanic/Latino; 1 Asian, non-Hispanic/Latino; 1 Hispanic/Latino), 1 international. *Entrance requirements:* For degree, minimum GPA of 3.0, copy of current nursing license, current resume or curriculum vitae, bachelor's degree, completion of an elementary statistics and/or nursing research course, completion of an approved physical assessment course, personal statement. *Application deadline:* For fall admission, 1/17 for domestic students, 5/15 for international students; for spring admission, 10/15 for domestic students, 12/1 for international students. Applications are processed on a rolling basis. Application fee: $45. Electronic applications accepted. *Expenses:* Tuition, state resident: full-time $7960; part-time $398 per unit. Tuition, nonresident: full-time $16,480; part-time $824 per unit. *Required fees:* $2600; $130 per year. $390 per term. *Financial support:* Application deadline: 4/1. *Unit head:* Dr. Kathy Ogle, Graduate Program Director, 410-704-4389, E-mail: nursinggradprogram@towson.edu. *Application contact:* Coverley Beidleman, Assistant Director of Graduate Admissions, 410-704-5000, Fax: 410-704-3030, E-mail: cbeidleman@towson.edu.
Website: http://www.towson.edu/chp/departments/nursing/grad/

Union University, School of Nursing, Jackson, TN 38305-3697. Offers executive leadership (DNP); nurse anesthesia (DNP); nurse practitioner (DNP); nursing education (MSN, PMC). *Accreditation:* AACN; AANA/CANAEP. *Degree requirements:* For master's, thesis or alternative. *Entrance requirements:* For master's, GRE, 3 letters of reference, bachelor's degree in nursing, minimum GPA of 3.0. Additional exam requirements/recommendations for international students: Required—TOEFL (minimum score 560 paper-based). Electronic applications accepted. *Faculty research:* Children's health, occupational rehabilitation, informatics, health promotion.

The University of Alabama in Huntsville, School of Graduate Studies, College of Nursing, Huntsville, AL 35899. Offers family nurse practitioner (Certificate); nursing (MSN, DNP), including adult-gerontology acute care nurse practitioner (MSN), adult-gerontology clinical nurse specialist (MSN), family nurse practitioner (MSN), leadership in health care systems (MSN); nursing education (Certificate). DNP offered jointly with The University of Alabama at Birmingham. *Accreditation:* AACN. *Program availability:* Part-time, evening/weekend, online learning. *Degree requirements:* For master's, comprehensive exam, thesis or alternative, oral and written exams. *Entrance requirements:* For master's, MAT or GRE, Alabama RN license, BSN, minimum GPA of 3.0; for doctorate, master's degree in nursing in an advanced practice area; for Certificate, MAT or GRE, minimum GPA of 3.0. Additional exam requirements/recommendations for international students: Required—TOEFL (minimum score 500 paper-based; 80 iBT), IELTS (minimum score 6.5). Electronic applications accepted. *Faculty research:* Health care informatics, chronic illness management, maternal and child health, genetics/genomics, technology and health care.

University of Central Arkansas, Graduate School, College of Health and Behavioral Sciences, Department of Nursing, Conway, AR 72035-0001. Offers adult nurse practitioner (PMC); clinical nurse leader (PMC); clinical nurse specialist (MSN); family nurse practitioner (PMC); nurse educator (PMC); nurse practitioner (MSN). *Accreditation:* AACN. *Program availability:* Part-time, evening/weekend, online learning. *Degree requirements:* For master's, comprehensive exam, thesis optional, clinicals. *Entrance requirements:* For master's, GRE General Test, minimum GPA of 2.7. Additional exam requirements/recommendations for international students: Required—TOEFL (minimum score 550 paper-based; 80 iBT). *Application deadline:* For fall admission, 3/1 priority date for domestic students; for spring admission, 10/1 for domestic students. Applications are processed on a rolling basis. Application fee: $25 ($50 for international students). Electronic applications accepted. *Expenses:* Contact institution. *Financial support:* Federal Work-Study, traineeships, and unspecified assistantships available. Financial award application deadline: 2/15; financial award applicants required to submit FAFSA.
Website: http://www.uca.edu/divisions/academic/chas/nurse2ab.asp

University of Central Florida, College of Nursing, Orlando, FL 32816. Offers adult-gerontology acute care nurse practitioner (Certificate); adult-gerontology primary care nurse practitioner (Certificate); family nurse practitioner (Certificate); nursing (MSN, PhD); nursing education (Post-Master's Certificate); nursing practice (DNP). *Accreditation:* AACN. *Program availability:* Part-time, evening/weekend. *Faculty:* 57 full-time (49 women), 70 part-time/adjunct (68 women). *Students:* 63 full-time (58 women), 327 part-time (297 women); includes 131 minority (40 Black or African American, non-Hispanic/Latino; 1 American Indian or Alaska Native, non-Hispanic/Latino; 16 Asian, non-Hispanic/Latino; 62 Hispanic/Latino; 12 Two or more races, non-Hispanic/Latino), 1 international. Average age 38. 303 applicants, 64% accepted, 129 enrolled. In 2017, 87 master's, 5 doctorates, 4 other advanced degrees awarded. *Degree requirements:* For master's, thesis or alternative; for doctorate, comprehensive exam, thesis/dissertation. *Entrance requirements:* For master's, essay, curriculum vitae; for doctorate, GRE General Test, letters of recommendation, resume, essay. Additional exam requirements/recommendations for international students: Required—TOEFL. *Application deadline:* For fall admission, 3/15 for domestic students; for spring admission, 10/15 for domestic students. Application fee: $30. Electronic applications accepted. *Expenses:* Tuition, state resident: part-time $288.16 per credit hour. Tuition, nonresident: part-time $1073.31 per credit hour. Tuition and fees vary according to program. *Financial support:* In 2017–18, 3 students received support, including 2 fellowships with partial tuition reimbursements available (averaging $7,377 per year), 1 research assistantship with partial tuition reimbursement available (averaging $11,952 per year); career-related internships or fieldwork, Federal Work-Study, institutionally sponsored loans, traineeships, and unspecified assistantships also available. Financial award application deadline: 3/1; financial award applicants required to submit FAFSA. *Unit head:* Dr. Mary Lou Sole, Dean, 407-823-5496, Fax: 407-823-5675, E-mail: mary.sole@ucf.edu. *Application contact:* Associate Director, Graduate Admissions, 407-823-2766, Fax: 407-823-6442, E-mail: gradadmissions@ucf.edu.
Website: http://nursing.ucf.edu/

University of Detroit Mercy, College of Health Professions, Detroit, MI 48221. Offers clinical nurse leader (MSN); family nurse practitioner (MSN); health services administration (MHSA); health systems management (MSN); nurse anesthesia (MS); nursing (DNP); nursing education (MSN, Certificate); nursing leadership and financial management (Certificate); outcomes performance management (Certificate); physician assistant (MS). *Entrance requirements:* For master's, GRE General Test, minimum GPA of 3.0. *Faculty research:* Research design, respiratory physiology, AIDS prevention, adolescent health, community, low income health education.

University of Hartford, College of Education, Nursing, and Health Professions, Program in Nursing, West Hartford, CT 06117-1599. Offers community/public health nursing (MSN); nursing education (MSN); nursing management (MSN). *Accreditation:* AACN. *Program availability:* Part-time, evening/weekend. *Degree requirements:* For master's, research project. *Entrance requirements:* For master's, BSN, Connecticut RN license. Additional exam requirements/recommendations for international students: Required—TOEFL (minimum score 550 paper-based). Electronic applications accepted. *Expenses:* Contact institution. *Faculty research:* Child development, women in doctoral study, applying feminist theory in teaching methods, near death experience, grandmothers as primary care providers.

University of Houston, College of Nursing, Sugar Land, TX 77479. Offers family nurse practitioner (MSN); nursing administration (MSN); nursing education (MSN). *Accreditation:* AACN. *Faculty:* 13 full-time (12 women). *Students:* 29 full-time (24 women); includes 15 minority (6 Black or African American, non-Hispanic/Latino; 5 Asian, non-Hispanic/Latino; 4 Hispanic/Latino), 3 international. Average age 37. 36 applicants, 61% accepted, 15 enrolled. In 2017, 14 master's awarded. *Entrance requirements:* For master's, GRE or MAT, minimum GPA of 3.0 in last 60 hours of academic course work, valid Texas RN licensure, 2 letters of recommendation, essay, resume, interview. Additional exam requirements/recommendations for international students: Required—TOEFL. *Application deadline:* For fall admission, 7/1 for domestic students, 6/1 for international students; for spring admission, 12/1 for domestic students, 10/1 for international students. Application fee: $75. Electronic applications accepted. *Financial support:* In 2017–18, 19 students received support. Federal Work-Study, scholarships/grants, and unspecified assistantships available. Support available to part-time students. Financial award application deadline: 5/1; financial award applicants required to submit FAFSA. *Unit head:* Dr. Kathryn Tart, Dean, 832-842-8200, E-mail: kmtart@uh.edu. *Application contact:* Tammy N. Whatley, Student Affairs Director, 832-842-8220, E-mail: tnwhatley@uh.edu.
Website: http://www.uh.edu/nursing

University of Indianapolis, Graduate Programs, School of Nursing, Indianapolis, IN 46227-3697. Offers advanced practice nursing (DNP); family nurse practitioner (MSN); gerontological nurse practitioner (MSN); neonatal nurse practitioner (MSN); nurse-midwifery (MSN); nursing (MSN); nursing and health systems leadership (MSN); nursing education (MSN); women's health nurse practitioner (MSN); MBA/MSN. *Accreditation:* AACN. *Entrance requirements:* For master's, minimum GPA of 3.0, interview, letters of recommendation, resume, IN nursing license, 1 year of professional practice; for doctorate, graduate of ACEN- or CCNE-accredited nursing program; MSN or MA with nursing major and minimum cumulative GPA of 3.25; unencumbered RN license with eligibility for licensure in Indiana; completion of graduate-level statistics course within last 5 years with minimum grade of B; resume; essay; official transcripts from all academic institutions. Additional exam requirements/recommendations for international students: Required—TOEFL (minimum score 550 paper-based). Electronic applications accepted.

University of Louisiana at Lafayette, College of Nursing and Allied Health Professions, Lafayette, LA 70504. Offers family nurse practitioner (MSN); nurse executive curriculum (MSN); nursing and allied health professions (DNP). Program offered jointly with Southern Louisiana University, McNeese State University, Southern University and Agricultural and Mechanical College. *Accreditation:* AACN. *Entrance requirements:* For master's, GRE General Test, minimum GPA of 2.75. Additional exam requirements/recommendations for international students: Required—TOEFL (minimum score 550 paper-based). *Application deadline:* For fall admission, 5/15 for domestic and international students; for spring admission, 10/1 for domestic students. Applications are processed on a rolling basis. Application fee: $25 ($30 for international students). Electronic applications accepted. *Unit head:* Dr. Lisa Broussard, Department Head, 337-482-5654, E-mail: lisabroussard@louisiana.edu. *Application contact:* Dr. Carolyn P. Delahoussaye, Graduate Coordinator, 337-482-5617, Fax: 337-482-5649, E-mail: cgp6303@louisiana.edu.
Website: http://nursing.louisiana.edu

University of Louisville, Graduate School, School of Nursing, Louisville, KY 40202. Offers adult gerontology nurse practitioner (MSN, DNP); education and administration (MSN); family nurse practitioner (MSN, DNP); neonatal nurse practitioner (MSN, DNP); nursing research (PhD); psychiatric/mental health nurse practitioner (MSN, DNP); women's health nurse practitioner (MSN). *Accreditation:* AACN. *Program availability:* Part-time. *Faculty:* 44 full-time (40 women), 45 part-time/adjunct (41 women). *Students:* 130 full-time (107 women), 30 part-time (25 women); includes 33 minority (16 Black or African American, non-Hispanic/Latino; 7 Asian, non-Hispanic/Latino; 5 Hispanic/Latino; 5 Two or more races, non-Hispanic/Latino), 2 international. Average age 33. 61 applicants, 67% accepted, 36 enrolled. In 2017, 54 master's awarded. *Degree requirements:* For doctorate, comprehensive exam (for some programs), thesis/dissertation (for some programs). *Entrance requirements:* For master's, bachelor's degree from nationally-accredited college, completion of 6 prerequisite courses, minimum undergraduate GPA of 3.0; for doctorate, GRE with minimum score of 156 Verbal, 146 Quantitative, 4.0 Analytic (for PhD), 3 letters of professional reference; minimum GPA of 3.0 with BSN, 3.25 with MSN; written statement of career goals, areas of expertise, and reasons for pursuing doctoral degree; resume including RN license. Additional exam requirements/recommendations for international students: Recommended—TOEFL (minimum score 560 paper-based), IELTS (minimum score 6.5). *Application deadline:* For fall admission, 1/15 priority date for domestic students, 1/15 for international students; for summer admission, 10/15 priority date for domestic students. Application fee: $65. Electronic applications accepted. *Expenses:* Tuition, state resident: full-time $12,246; part-time $681 per credit hour. Tuition, nonresident: full-time $25,486; part-time $1417 per credit hour. *Required fees:* $196. Tuition and fees vary according to course load, program and reciprocity agreements. *Financial support:* In 2017–18, 8 research assistantships with full tuition reimbursements (averaging $20,000 per year), 4 teaching assistantships with full tuition reimbursements (averaging $15,000 per year) were awarded; fellowships with full tuition reimbursements, scholarships/grants, and unspecified assistantships also available. Financial award application deadline: 10/1; financial award applicants required to submit FAFSA. *Faculty research:* Environmental health, health services research, women's mental health, self-management of chronic illness in adults and children, health disparities. *Total annual research expenditures:* $762,266. *Unit head:* Dr. Marcia J. Hern, RN, Dean and Professor, 502-852-8300, Fax: 502-852-8783, E-mail: m.hern@louisville.edu. *Application contact:* Trish Hart, Assistant Dean for Student Affairs, 502-852-5825, Fax: 502-852-8783, E-mail: trish.hart@louisville.edu.
Website: http://www.louisville.edu/nursing/

University of Maine, Graduate School, College of Natural Sciences, Forestry, and Agriculture, School of Nursing, Orono, ME 04469. Offers individualized (MS); nursing education (CGS); rural health family nurse practitioner (MS, CAS). *Accreditation:* AACN. *Faculty:* 6 full-time (all women), 6 part-time/adjunct (4 women). *Students:* 22 full-time (19 women), 14 part-time (12 women); includes 3 minority (1 American Indian or Alaska Native, non-Hispanic/Latino; 1 Asian, non-Hispanic/Latino; 1 Two or more races, non-Hispanic/Latino), 1 international. Average age 35. 22 applicants, 100% accepted, 17 enrolled. In 2017, 10 master's, 2 other advanced degrees awarded. *Entrance requirements:* For master's, GRE General Test; for other advanced degree, master's degree. Additional exam requirements/recommendations for international students: Required—TOEFL. *Application deadline:* For fall admission, 7/1 for domestic students; for spring admission, 12/15 for domestic students; for summer admission, 4/15 for domestic students. Applications are processed on a rolling basis. Application fee: $65. Electronic applications accepted. *Expenses:* Tuition, state resident: full-time $7722; part-time $429 per credit hour. Tuition, nonresident: full-time $25,146; part-time $1397 per credit hour. *Required fees:* $1162; $581 per credit hour. *Financial support:* Career-related internships or fieldwork, Federal Work-Study, institutionally sponsored loans, tuition waivers (full and partial), and unspecified assistantships available. Support available to part-time students. Financial award application deadline: 3/1. *Faculty research:* Population health, health disparities, infectious waste management, domestic violence older adults. *Total annual research expenditures:* $249,000. *Unit head:* Dr. Nancy Fishwick, Director, 207-581-2505, Fax: 207-581-2585. *Application contact:* Scott G. Delcourt, Assistant Vice President for Graduate Studies and Senior Associate Dean, 207-581-3291, Fax: 207-581-3232, E-mail: graduate@maine.edu.
Website: http://umaine.edu/nursing/

University of Mary, School of Health Sciences, Division of Nursing, Bismarck, ND 58504-9652. Offers family nurse practitioner (DNP); nurse administrator (MSN); nursing educator (MSN); MSN/MBA. *Accreditation:* AACN. *Program availability:* Part-time, evening/weekend, online learning. *Degree requirements:* For master's, comprehensive exam (for some programs), thesis (for some programs), internship (family nurse practitioner), teaching practice. *Entrance requirements:* For master's, minimum GPA of 2.75 in nursing, interview, letters of recommendation, criminal background check, immunizations, statement of professional goals. Additional exam requirements/recommendations for international students: Required—TOEFL (minimum score 500 paper-based; 71 iBT). Electronic applications accepted. *Faculty research:* Gerontology issues, rural nursing, health policy, primary care, women's health.

University of Mary Hardin-Baylor, Graduate Studies in Education, Belton, TX 76513. Offers curriculum and instruction (M Ed); educational administration (M Ed, Ed D), including higher education (Ed D), leadership in nursing education (Ed D), P-12 (Ed D). *Program availability:* Part-time, evening/weekend. *Faculty:* 12 full-time (8 women), 5 part-time/adjunct (2 women). *Students:* 29 full-time (20 women), 79 part-time (55 women); includes 53 minority (35 Black or African American, non-Hispanic/Latino; 17 Hispanic/Latino; 1 Two or more races, non-Hispanic/Latino), 1 international. Average age 39. 15 applicants, 80% accepted, 10 enrolled. In 2017, 47 master's, 16 doctorates awarded. *Degree requirements:* For master's, comprehensive exam; for doctorate, thesis/dissertation. *Entrance requirements:* For master's, minimum GPA of 3.0,

interview; for doctorate, minimum GPA of 3.5, interview, essay, resume, employment verification, 3 letters of recommendation. Additional exam requirements/recommendations for international students: Required—TOEFL (minimum score 60 iBT), IELTS (minimum score 4.5). *Application deadline:* For fall admission, 6/1 for domestic students, 4/30 priority date for international students; for spring admission, 11/1 for domestic students, 9/30 priority date for international students. Applications are processed on a rolling basis. Application fee: $35 ($135 for international students). Electronic applications accepted. *Expenses:* $920 per credit hour. *Financial support:* In 2017–18, 90 students received support. Federal Work-Study and scholarships for some active duty military personnel available. Support available to part-time students. Financial award application deadline: 6/1; financial award applicants required to submit FAFSA. *Faculty research:* Motivational orientation of preservice teachers. *Unit head:* Dr. Craig Hammonds, Director, Graduate Programs in Education, 254-295-4189, E-mail: rhammonds@umhb.edu. *Application contact:* Sharon Aguilera, Assistant Director, Graduate Admissions, 254-295-4835, E-mail: saguilera@umhb.edu.
Website: https://go.umhb.edu/graduate/education/home

University of Mary Hardin-Baylor, Graduate Studies in Nursing, Belton, TX 76513. Offers family nurse practitioner (MSN, Post-Master's Certificate); nursing education (MSN); nursing practice (DNP). *Accreditation:* AACN. *Program availability:* Evening/weekend. *Faculty:* 6 full-time (all women), 8 part-time/adjunct (7 women). *Students:* 44 full-time (40 women), 10 part-time (9 women); includes 19 minority (10 Black or African American, non-Hispanic/Latino; 7 Hispanic/Latino; 2 Two or more races, non-Hispanic/Latino). Average age 34. 47 applicants, 83% accepted, 31 enrolled. In 2017, 44 master's, 2 other advanced degrees awarded. *Degree requirements:* For master's, comprehensive exam, practicum; for doctorate, scholarly project. *Entrance requirements:* For master's, baccalaureate degree in nursing, current licensure as Registered Nurse in the state of Texas, minimum GPA of 3.0 in last 60 hours of undergraduate program, two letters of recommendation, full-time RN for 1 year, personal interview with director of MSN program; for doctorate, master's degree as an advanced practice nurse, nurse leader or nurse educator; three letters of recommendation; current RN license and approval to practice as an advanced practice nurse; essay; curriculum vitae; interview. Additional exam requirements/recommendations for international students: Required—TOEFL (minimum score 60 iBT), IELTS (minimum score 4.5). *Application deadline:* For fall admission, 6/1 for domestic students, 4/30 priority date for international students; for spring admission, 11/1 for domestic students, 9/30 priority date for international students. Applications are processed on a rolling basis. Application fee: $35 ($135 for international students). Electronic applications accepted. *Expenses:* $920 per credit hour. *Financial support:* In 2017–18, 34 students received support. Federal Work-Study, unspecified assistantships, and scholarships for some active duty military personnel available. Support available to part-time students. Financial award applicants required to submit FAFSA. *Faculty research:* Grief counseling, identifying escalating patients. *Unit head:* Dr. Sharon Souter, Dean, College of Nursing/MSN and DNP Programs Director, 254-295-4662, E-mail: ssouter@umhb.edu. *Application contact:* Sharon Aguilera, Assistant Director, Graduate Admissions, 254-295-4835, E-mail: saguilera@umhb.edu.
Website: https://go.umhb.edu/graduate/nursing/home

University of Maryland, Baltimore, School of Nursing, Baltimore, MD 21201. Offers adult-gerontology acute care nurse practitioner (DNP); adult-gerontology primary care nurse practitioner (DNP); clinical nurse leader (MS); community/public health nursing (MS); family nurse practitioner (DNP); global health (Postbaccalaureate Certificate); health services leadership and management (MS); neonatal nurse practitioner (DNP); nurse anesthesia (DNP); nursing (PhD); nursing informatics (MS, Postbaccalaureate Certificate); pediatric acute/primary care nurse practitioner (DNP); psychiatric mental health nurse practitioner (DNP); teaching in nursing and health professions (Postbaccalaureate Certificate); MS/MBA. MS/MBA offered jointly with University of Baltimore. *Program availability:* Part-time. *Faculty:* 130 full-time (117 women), 125 part-time/adjunct (114 women). *Students:* 504 full-time (442 women), 532 part-time (482 women); includes 443 minority (249 Black or African American, non-Hispanic/Latino; 1 American Indian or Alaska Native, non-Hispanic/Latino; 115 Asian, non-Hispanic/Latino; 48 Hispanic/Latino; 2 Native Hawaiian or other Pacific Islander, non-Hispanic/Latino; 28 Two or more races, non-Hispanic/Latino), 15 international. Average age 33. 935 applicants, 62% accepted, 394 enrolled. In 2017, 182 master's, 57 doctorates awarded. *Degree requirements:* For master's and Postbaccalaureate Certificate, thesis (for some programs); for doctorate, comprehensive exam, thesis/dissertation. *Entrance requirements:* Additional exam requirements/recommendations for international students: Required—TOEFL (minimum score 550 paper-based; 79 iBT); Recommended—IELTS (minimum score 7). *Application deadline:* For fall admission, 11/1 for domestic and international students; for spring admission, 8/1 for domestic and international students. Application fee: $75. Electronic applications accepted. *Expenses:* Contact institution. *Financial support:* In 2017–18, 22 research assistantships with full and partial tuition reimbursements (averaging $21,523 per year), 41 teaching assistantships with full and partial tuition reimbursements (averaging $13,439 per year) were awarded; fellowships and scholarships/grants also available. Financial award application deadline: 3/1; financial award applicants required to submit FAFSA. *Unit head:* Dr. Jane Kirschling, Dean, 410-706-4359, E-mail: kirschling@umaryland.edu. *Application contact:* Larry Fillian, Associate Dean of Student and Academic Services, 410-706-6298, E-mail: lfillian@umaryland.edu.
Website: http://www.nursing.umaryland.edu/

University of Massachusetts Medical School, Graduate School of Nursing, Worcester, MA 01655-0115. Offers adult gerontological acute care nurse practitioner (DNP, Post Master's Certificate); adult gerontological primary care nurse practitioner (DNP, Post Master's Certificate); family nursing practitioner (DNP); nurse administrator (DNP); nurse educator (MS, Post Master's Certificate); nursing (PhD). *Accreditation:* AACN. *Faculty:* 31 full-time (28 women), 39 part-time/adjunct (34 women). *Students:* 129 full-time (111 women), 31 part-time (30 women); includes 35 minority (17 Black or African American, non-Hispanic/Latino; 10 Asian, non-Hispanic/Latino; 7 Hispanic/Latino; 1 Native Hawaiian or other Pacific Islander, non-Hispanic/Latino), 1 international. Average age 32. 124 applicants, 55% accepted, 59 enrolled. In 2017, 48 master's, 10 doctorates, 2 other advanced degrees awarded. *Degree requirements:* For doctorate, thesis/dissertation (for some programs), comprehensive exam and manuscript (for PhD); capstone project and manuscript (for DNP). *Entrance requirements:* For master's, GRE General Test, bachelor's degree in nursing, course work in statistics, unrestricted Massachusetts license as registered nurse; for doctorate, GRE General Test, bachelor's or master's degree; for Post Master's Certificate, GRE General Test, MS in nursing. Additional exam requirements/recommendations for international students: Required—TOEFL (minimum score 400 paper-based; 81 iBT). *Application deadline:* For fall admission, 12/1 priority date for domestic students. Applications are processed on a rolling basis. Application fee: $60. Electronic applications accepted. *Expenses:* $14,778 in-state tuition and mandatory fees; $19,728 out-of-state. *Financial support:* In 2017–18, 6 students received support. Scholarships/grants available. Support available to part-time students. Financial award application deadline: 5/15; financial award applicants required to submit FAFSA. *Faculty research:* Health literacy, social justice, HIV prevention, cancer-related decision making, nursing education, diabetes care and education, family-focused interventions for children with type 1 diabetes. *Total annual research expenditures:* $874,000. *Unit head:* Dr. Joan Vitello-Cicciu, Dean, 508-856-5081, Fax: 508-856-6552, E-mail: joan.vitello@umassmed.edu. *Application contact:* Diane Brescia, Admissions Coordinator, 508-856-3488, Fax: 508-856-5851, E-mail: diane.brescia@umassmed.edu.
Website: http://www.umassmed.edu/gsn/

University of Memphis, Loewenberg College of Nursing, Memphis, TN 38152. Offers advanced practice nursing (Graduate Certificate); executive leadership (MSN); family nurse practitioner (MSN); nursing administration (MSN, Graduate Certificate); nursing education (MSN, Graduate Certificate). *Accreditation:* AACN. *Program availability:* Part-time, evening/weekend, online learning. *Faculty:* 15 full-time (14 women), 3 part-time/adjunct (all women). *Students:* 16 full-time (15 women), 225 part-time (201 women); includes 90 minority (72 Black or African American, non-Hispanic/Latino; 1 American Indian or Alaska Native, non-Hispanic/Latino; 9 Asian, non-Hispanic/Latino; 5 Hispanic/Latino; 1 Native Hawaiian or other Pacific Islander, non-Hispanic/Latino; 2 Two or more races, non-Hispanic/Latino). Average age 35. 168 applicants, 53% accepted, 55 enrolled. In 2017, 120 master's, 6 other advanced degrees awarded. *Degree requirements:* For master's, comprehensive exam, thesis optional, scholarly project; clinical practicum hours. *Entrance requirements:* For master's, NCLEX exam, minimum undergraduate GPA of 2.8, letter of interest, letters of recommendation, interview, resume, nursing licensure; for Graduate Certificate, unrestricted license to practice as RN in TN, current CPR certification, evidence of vaccination, annual flu shot, evidence of current professional malpractice insurance, letters of recommendation, letter of intent, resume. Additional exam requirements/recommendations for international students: Required—TOEFL (minimum score 550 paper-based; 79 iBT). *Application deadline:* For fall admission, 2/15 for domestic and international students; for spring admission, 10/1 for domestic and international students. Application fee: $35 ($60 for international students). *Expenses:* Contact institution. *Financial support:* In 2017–18, 147 students received support. Federal Work-Study and scholarships/grants available. Financial award application deadline: 2/1; financial award applicants required to submit FAFSA. *Faculty research:* Technology in nursing, nurse retention, cultural competence, health policy, health access. *Total annual research expenditures:* $560,619. *Unit head:* Dr. Lin Zhan, Dean, 901-678-2003, Fax: 901-678-4907, E-mail: lzhan@memphis.edu. *Application contact:* Dr. Shirleatha Lee, Associate Dean for Academic Programs, 901-678-2036, Fax: 901-678-5023, E-mail: sntaylr1@memphis.edu.
Website: http://www.memphis.edu/nursing

University of Missouri–Kansas City, School of Nursing and Health Studies, Kansas City, MO 64110-2499. Offers adult clinical nurse specialist (MSN), including adult nurse practitioner, women's health nurse practitioner (MSN, DNP); adult clinical nursing practice (DNP), including adult gerontology nurse practitioner, women's health nurse practitioner (MSN, DNP); clinical nursing practice (DNP), including family nurse practitioner; neonatal nurse practitioner (MSN); nurse educator (MSN); nurse executive (MSN); nursing practice (DNP); pediatric clinical nursing practice (DNP), including pediatric nurse practitioner; pediatric nurse practitioner (MSN). *Accreditation:* AACN. *Program availability:* Part-time, online learning. *Degree requirements:* For master's, thesis or alternative. *Entrance requirements:* For master's, minimum undergraduate GPA of 3.2; for doctorate, GRE, 3 letters of reference. Additional exam requirements/recommendations for international students: Required—TOEFL (minimum score 550 paper-based; 80 iBT). *Faculty research:* Geriatrics/gerontology, children's pain, neonatology, Alzheimer's care, cancer caregivers.

University of Mobile, Graduate Studies, Program in Nursing, Mobile, AL 36613. Offers education/administration (MSN); nurse practitioner (DNP). *Accreditation:* AACN. *Program availability:* Part-time, evening/weekend. *Degree requirements:* For master's, comprehensive exam, thesis or alternative. *Entrance requirements:* For master's, GRE. Additional exam requirements/recommendations for international students: Required—TOEFL (minimum score 550 paper-based; 80 iBT). *Application deadline:* For fall admission, 8/3 priority date for domestic and international students; for spring admission, 12/23 priority date for domestic and international students. Applications are processed on a rolling basis. Application fee: $40 ($50 for international students). Electronic applications accepted. *Financial support:* Application deadline: 8/1; applicants required to submit FAFSA. *Faculty research:* Nursing management, transcultural nursing, spiritual aspects, educational expectations. *Unit head:* Dr. Kathryn Sheppard, Dean, School of Nursing, 251-442-2343, Fax: 251-442-2520, E-mail: ksheppard@umobile.edu. *Application contact:* Brian Boyle, Director of Recruitment, 251-442-2727, Fax: 251-442-2523.

University of Nevada, Las Vegas, Graduate College, School of Nursing, Las Vegas, NV 89154-3018. Offers biobehavioral nursing (Advanced Certificate); family nurse practitioner (Advanced Certificate); nursing (MS, DNP, PhD); nursing education (Advanced Certificate). *Accreditation:* AACN. *Program availability:* Part-time, 100% online, blended/hybrid learning. *Faculty:* 11 full-time (9 women), 10 part-time/adjunct (all women). *Students:* 46 full-time (40 women), 78 part-time (73 women); includes 43 minority (6 Black or African American, non-Hispanic/Latino; 16 Asian, non-Hispanic/Latino; 12 Hispanic/Latino; 9 Two or more races, non-Hispanic/Latino). Average age 37. 185 applicants, 38% accepted, 54 enrolled. In 2017, 35 master's, 9 doctorates, 3 other advanced degrees awarded. *Degree requirements:* For master's, comprehensive exam, thesis; for doctorate, comprehensive exam (for some programs), thesis/dissertation, project defense (for DNP). *Entrance requirements:* For master's, bachelor's degree with minimum GPA 3.0; 2 letters of recommendation; valid RN license; statement of purpose; for doctorate, GRE General Test, bachelor's degree; statement of purpose; 3 letters of recommendation; for Advanced Certificate, 2 letters of recommendation; statement of purpose; valid RN license. Additional exam requirements/recommendations for international students: Recommended—TOEFL (minimum score 550 paper-based; 80 iBT), IELTS (minimum score 7). *Application deadline:* For fall admission, 2/1 for domestic students. Application fee: $60 ($95 for international students). Electronic applications accepted. *Expenses:* Contact institution. *Financial support:* In 2017–18, 3 students received support, including 1 research assistantship with partial tuition reimbursement available (averaging $20,250 per year), 2 teaching assistantships with partial tuition reimbursements available (averaging $20,250 per year); institutionally sponsored loans, scholarships/grants, health care benefits, and unspecified assistantships also available. Financial award application deadline: 3/15; financial award applicants required to submit FAFSA. *Faculty research:* Skeletal muscle injury; chronic diseases and health promotion in diabetes, cardiovascular disease, pain, trauma, and obesity; nursing education; sexual assault. *Total annual research expenditures:* $500,875. *Unit head:* Dr. Carolyn Yucha, Dean, 702-895-3906, Fax: 702-895-4807, E-mail: carolyn.yucha@unlv.edu.
Website: http://nursing.unlv.edu/

University of New Brunswick Fredericton, School of Graduate Studies, Faculty of Nursing, Fredericton, NB E3B 5A3, Canada. Offers nurse educator (MN); nurse practitioner (MN); nursing (MN). *Program availability:* Part-time, online learning. *Degree requirements:* For master's, comprehensive exam (for some programs), thesis (for some programs). *Entrance requirements:* For master's, undergraduate coursework in statistics and nursing research, minimum GPA of 3.3, registration as a nurse (or eligibility) in New Brunswick. Additional exam requirements/recommendations for international students: Required—TOEFL (minimum score 600 paper-based). Electronic applications accepted.

Faculty research: Intimate partner violence; abuse; healthy child development, chronic illness and addiction; rural populations' access to health care and primary healthcare; teaching and learning in the classroom, clinical lab, and by distance; Aboriginal nursing; workplace bullying; eating disorders; women's health; lesbian health; nurse managed primary care clinics; HIV/AIDS; returning to work after depression; adolescent mental health; cancer survivorship.

The University of North Carolina at Chapel Hill, School of Nursing, Chapel Hill, NC 27599-7460. Offers advanced practice registered nurse (DNP); nursing (MSN, PhD, PMC), including administration (MSN), adult gerontology primary care nurse practitioner (MSN), clinical nurse leader (MSN), education (MSN), health care systems (PMC), informatics (MSN, PMC), nursing leadership (PMC), outcomes management (MSN), primary care family nurse practitioner (MSN), primary care pediatric nurse practitioner (MSN), psychiatric/mental health nurse practitioner (MSN, PMC). *Accreditation:* AACN; ACEN (one or more programs are accredited). *Program availability:* Part-time. *Faculty:* 86 full-time (78 women), 44 part-time/adjunct (40 women). *Students:* 208 full-time (186 women), 128 part-time (116 women); includes 100 minority (49 Black or African American, non-Hispanic/Latino; 4 American Indian or Alaska Native, non-Hispanic/Latino; 23 Asian, non-Hispanic/Latino; 7 Hispanic/Latino; 17 Two or more races, non-Hispanic/Latino), 17 international. Average age 33. 624 applicants, 25% accepted, 150 enrolled. In 2017, 91 master's, 14 doctorates awarded. *Degree requirements:* For master's, comprehensive exam, thesis; for doctorate, thesis/dissertation, 3 exams; for PMC, thesis. *Entrance requirements:* Additional exam requirements/recommendations for international students: Required—TOEFL (minimum score 575 paper-based; 89 iBT), IELTS (minimum score 8). *Application deadline:* For fall admission, 12/15 for domestic and international students. Application fee: $88. Electronic applications accepted. *Financial support:* In 2017–18, 8 fellowships with full tuition reimbursements, 6 research assistantships with partial tuition reimbursements (averaging $8,000 per year), 10 teaching assistantships with partial tuition reimbursements (averaging $8,000 per year) were awarded; scholarships/grants, traineeships, health care benefits, and unspecified assistantships also available. Support available to part-time students. Financial award application deadline: 3/1; financial award applicants required to submit FAFSA. *Faculty research:* Preventing and managing chronic illness, reducing health disparities, Improving healthcare quality and patient outcomes, understanding biobehavioral and genetic bases of health and illness, developing innovative ways to enhance science and its clinical translation. *Unit head:* Dr. Nilda Peragallo Montano, Dean/Professor, 919-966-3731, Fax: 919-966-3540, E-mail: npm@email.unc.edu. *Application contact:* Emily Sayed, Assistant Director, Graduate Admissions, 919-966-4260, Fax: 919-966-3540, E-mail: sayed@unc.edu.
Website: http://nursing.unc.edu

The University of North Carolina at Charlotte, College of Health and Human Services, School of Nursing, Charlotte, NC 28223-0001. Offers adult-gerontology acute care nurse practitioner (Post-Master's Certificate); advanced clinical nursing (MSN), including adult psychiatric mental health, adult-gerontology acute care nurse practitioner, family nurse practitioner across the lifespan; family nurse practitioner across the lifespan (Post-Master's Certificate); nurse anesthesia (MSN), including nurse anesthesia across the lifespan; nurse anesthesia across the lifespan (Post-Master's Certificate); nursing (DNP); nursing administration (Graduate Certificate); nursing education (Graduate Certificate); systems/population nursing (MSN), including community/public health nursing, nurse administrator, nurse educator. *Accreditation:* AACN; AANA/CANAEP. *Program availability:* Part-time, blended/hybrid learning. *Faculty:* 24 full-time (22 women), 6 part-time/adjunct (4 women). *Students:* 113 full-time (84 women), 163 part-time (150 women); includes 63 minority (47 Black or African American, non-Hispanic/Latino; 2 American Indian or Alaska Native, non-Hispanic/Latino; 6 Asian, non-Hispanic/Latino; 3 Hispanic/Latino; 5 Two or more races, non-Hispanic/Latino). Average age 37. 443 applicants, 31% accepted, 113 enrolled. In 2017, 83 master's, 8 doctorates, 8 other advanced degrees awarded. Terminal master's awarded for partial completion of doctoral program. *Degree requirements:* For doctorate, thesis/dissertation or alternative, residency; for other advanced degree, practicum. *Entrance requirements:* For master's, GRE General Test, current unrestricted license as Registered Nurse in North Carolina; BSN from nationally-accredited program; one year of professional nursing practice in acute/critical care; minimum overall GPA of 3.0 in last degree; completion of undergraduate statistics course with minimum grade of C; statement of purpose; for doctorate, GRE or MAT, master's degree in nursing in an advanced nursing practice specialty from nationally-accredited program; minimum overall GPA of 3.5 in MSN program; current RN licensure in U.S. at time of application with eligibility for NC licensure; essay; resume/curriculum vitae; professional recommendations; clinical hours; for other advanced degree, GRE. Additional exam requirements/recommendations for international students: Required—TOEFL (minimum score 523 paper-based, 70 iBT) or IELTS (6.5). *Application deadline:* For fall admission, 1/10 for domestic and international students; for spring admission, 9/10 for domestic and international students; for summer admission, 4/1 for domestic and international students. Applications are processed on a rolling basis. Application fee: $75. Electronic applications accepted. *Expenses:* Contact institution. *Financial support:* In 2017–18, 6 students received support, including 4 research assistantships (averaging $6,338 per year), 2 teaching assistantships (averaging $6,250 per year); career-related internships or fieldwork, institutionally sponsored loans, scholarships/grants, traineeships, and unspecified assistantships also available. Support available to part-time students. Financial award application deadline: 3/1; financial award applicants required to submit FAFSA. *Total annual research expenditures:* $800,072. *Unit head:* Dr. Dena Evans, Director, 704-687-7974, E-mail: devans37@uncc.edu. *Application contact:* Kathy B. Giddings, Director of Graduate Admissions, 704-687-5503, Fax: 704-687-1668, E-mail: gradadm@uncc.edu.
Website: http://nursing.uncc.edu/

The University of North Carolina at Greensboro, Graduate School, School of Nursing, Greensboro, NC 27412-5001. Offers adult clinical nurse specialist (MSN, PMC); adult/gerontological nurse practitioner (MSN, PMC); nurse anesthesia (MSN, PMC); nursing (PhD); nursing administration (MSN); nursing education (MSN); MSN/MBA. *Accreditation:* ACEN. *Degree requirements:* For master's, thesis or alternative. *Entrance requirements:* For master's, GRE General Test or MAT, BSN, clinical experience, liability insurance, RN license; for PMC, liability insurance, MSN, RN license. Additional exam requirements/recommendations for international students: Required—TOEFL. Electronic applications accepted.

The University of North Carolina at Pembroke, The Graduate School, Department of Nursing, Pembroke, NC 28372-1510. Offers clinical nurse leader (MSN); nurse educator (MSN); rural case manager (MSN). *Accreditation:* AACN. *Program availability:* Part-time. Application fee: $45 ($60 for international students). *Unit head:* Julie Harrison-Swartz, Director of Graduate Programs, 910-775-4509, E-mail: julie.harrison-swartz@uncp.edu.
Website: http://www.uncp.edu/nursing/

The University of North Carolina Wilmington, School of Nursing, Wilmington, NC 28403-3297. Offers clinical research and product development (MS); family nurse practitioner (Post-Master's Certificate); nurse educator (Post-Master's Certificate); nursing (MSN); nursing practice (DNP). *Accreditation:* AACN; ACEN. *Program availability:* Part-time, 100% online. *Faculty:* 44 full-time (38 women). *Students:* 160 full-time (148 women), 237 part-time (213 women); includes 79 minority (55 Black or African American, non-Hispanic/Latino; 3 American Indian or Alaska Native, non-Hispanic/Latino; 6 Asian, non-Hispanic/Latino; 9 Hispanic/Latino; 6 Two or more races, non-Hispanic/Latino). Average age 36. 287 applicants, 71% accepted, 167 enrolled. In 2017, 40 master's awarded. *Degree requirements:* For master's, thesis or alternative, research project, presentation; for doctorate, clinical scholarly project, 1000 clinical hours. *Entrance requirements:* For master's, GRE General Test, 3 recommendations, statement of interest, resume, writing sample, RN experience, RN license (for MSN), bachelor's degree in related field; for doctorate, 3 recommendations, Advanced Practice Registered Nurse with current unrestricted RN license in state in which practice will occur, minimum GPA of 3.0, essay, resume or curriculum vitae, interview, criminal background check and 12-panel drug screening. Additional exam requirements/recommendations for international students: Required—TOEFL (minimum score 550 paper-based; 79 iBT), IELTS (minimum score 6.5). *Application deadline:* For fall admission, 3/1 for domestic students. Applications are processed on a rolling basis. Application fee: $75. Electronic applications accepted. *Expenses:* $318.15 per credit hour in-state, $965.60 per credit hour out-of-state (for DNP). *Financial support:* Application deadline: 1/1; applicants required to submit FAFSA. *Unit head:* Dr. Laurie Badzek, Director, 910-962-7410, Fax: 910-962-3723, E-mail: badzekl@uncw.edu. *Application contact:* Dr. Micah Scott, MSN Graduate Coordinator, 910-962-7534, E-mail: scottmi@uncw.edu.
Website: https://www.uncw.edu/son/academicprograms.html

University of North Dakota, Graduate School, College of Nursing and Professional Disciplines, Department of Nursing, Grand Forks, ND 58202. Offers adult-gerontological nurse practitioner (MS); advanced public health nurse (MS); family nurse practitioner (MS); nurse anesthesia (MS); nurse educator (MS); nursing (PhD, Post-Master's Certificate); nursing practice (DNP); psychiatric and mental health nurse practitioner (MS).

University of Northern Colorado, Graduate School, College of Natural and Health Sciences, School of Nursing, Greeley, CO 80639. Offers adult-gerontology acute care nurse practitioner (MSN, DNP); family nurse practitioner (MSN, DNP); nursing education (PhD); nursing practice (DNP). *Accreditation:* AACN. *Program availability:* Online learning. *Degree requirements:* For master's, comprehensive exam, thesis or alternative; for doctorate, comprehensive exam, thesis/dissertation. *Entrance requirements:* For master's and doctorate, GRE General Test, minimum GPA of 3.0 in last 60 hours, BS in nursing, 2 letters of recommendation. Electronic applications accepted.

University of North Georgia, Program in Nursing Education, Dahlonega, GA 30597. Offers MS. *Program availability:* Part-time, evening/weekend, online only, 100% online. *Students:* 3 part-time (all women). Average age 43. *Degree requirements:* For master's, practicum. *Entrance requirements:* For master's, BSN. Additional exam requirements/recommendations for international students: Required—TOEFL (minimum score 550 paper-based; 79 iBT), IELTS (minimum score 6.5). *Application deadline:* For summer admission, 2/28 for domestic students. Application fee: $40. Electronic applications accepted. *Expenses:* Contact institution. *Financial support:* Application deadline: 3/17; applicants required to submit FAFSA. *Unit head:* Dr. Kim Hudson-Gallogly, Department Head, 706-864-1934, E-mail: kim.hudson-gallogly@ung.edu. *Application contact:* Melinda Maxwell, Director of Graduate Admissions, 706-867-2077, E-mail: melinda.maxwell@ung.edu.
Website: https://ung.edu/nursing/graduate/ms-nursing-education.php

University of Phoenix–Bay Area Campus, College of Nursing, San Jose, CA 95134-1805. Offers education (MHA); gerontology (MHA); health administration (MHA, DHA); informatics (MHA, MSN); nursing (MSN, PhD); nursing/health care education (MSN); MSN/MBA. *Program availability:* Evening/weekend, online learning. *Degree requirements:* For master's, thesis (for some programs). *Entrance requirements:* For master's, minimum undergraduate GPA of 2.5, 3 years of work experience, RN license. Additional exam requirements/recommendations for international students: Required—TOEFL (minimum score 550 paper-based; 79 iBT). Electronic applications accepted.

University of Phoenix–Hawaii Campus, College of Nursing, Honolulu, HI 96813-3800. Offers education (MHA); family nurse practitioner (MSN); gerontology (MHA); health administration (MHA); nursing (MSN); nursing/health care education (MSN); MSN/MBA. *Program availability:* Evening/weekend. *Degree requirements:* For master's, thesis (for some programs). *Entrance requirements:* For master's, minimum undergraduate GPA of 2.5, 3 years of work experience, RN license. Additional exam requirements/recommendations for international students: Required—TOEFL (minimum score 550 paper-based; 79 iBT). Electronic applications accepted.

University of Phoenix–Online Campus, College of Health Sciences and Nursing, Phoenix, AZ 85034-7209. Offers family nurse practitioner (Certificate); health care (Certificate); health care education (Certificate); health care informatics (Certificate); informatics (MSN); nursing (MSN); nursing and health care education (MSN); MSN/MBA; MSN/MHA. *Accreditation:* AACN. *Program availability:* Evening/weekend, online learning. *Entrance requirements:* Additional exam requirements/recommendations for international students: Required—TOEFL, TOEIC (Test of English as an International Communication), Berlitz Online English Proficiency Exam, PTE, or IELTS. Electronic applications accepted. *Expenses:* Contact institution.

University of Phoenix–Phoenix Campus, College of Health Sciences and Nursing, Tempe, AZ 85282-2371. Offers family nurse practitioner (MSN, Certificate); gerontology health care (Certificate); health care education (MSN, Certificate); health care informatics (Certificate); informatics (MSN); nursing (MSN); MSN/MHA. *Program availability:* Evening/weekend, online learning. *Entrance requirements:* Additional exam requirements/recommendations for international students: Required—TOEFL, TOEIC (Test of English as an International Communication), Berlitz Online English Proficiency Exam, PTE, or IELTS. Electronic applications accepted. *Expenses:* Contact institution.

University of Phoenix–Sacramento Valley Campus, College of Nursing, Sacramento, CA 95833-4334. Offers family nurse practitioner (MSN); health administration (MHA); health care education (MSN); nursing (MSN); MSN/MBA. *Program availability:* Evening/weekend. *Degree requirements:* For master's, thesis (for some programs). *Entrance requirements:* For master's, RN license, minimum undergraduate GPA of 2.5, 3 years work experience. Additional exam requirements/recommendations for international students: Required—TOEFL (minimum score 550 paper-based; 79 iBT). Electronic applications accepted.

University of Phoenix–San Diego Campus, College of Nursing, San Diego, CA 92123. Offers health care education (MSN); nursing (MSN); MSN/MBA. *Program availability:* Evening/weekend. *Degree requirements:* For master's, thesis (for some programs). *Entrance requirements:* For master's, minimum undergraduate GPA of 2.5, 3 years work experience, RN license. Additional exam requirements/recommendations for international students: Required—TOEFL (minimum score 550 paper-based; 79 iBT). Electronic applications accepted.

University of Portland, School of Nursing, Portland, OR 97203. Offers clinical nurse leader (MS); family nurse practitioner (DNP); nurse educator (MS). *Accreditation:* AACN. *Program availability:* Part-time, evening/weekend, online learning. *Entrance requirements:* For master's, GRE General Test or MAT, Oregon RN license, BSN, course work in statistics, resume, letters of recommendation, writing sample; for doctorate, GRE General Test or MAT, Oregon RN license, BSN or MSN, 2 letters of recommendation, resume, writing sample, official transcripts. Additional exam requirements/recommendations for international students: Required—TOEFL (minimum score 550 paper-based; 80 iBT), IELTS (minimum score 7). *Expenses:* Contact institution.

University of Rhode Island, Graduate School, College of Nursing, Kingston, RI 02881. Offers acute care nurse practitioner (adult-gerontology focus) (Post Master's Certificate); adult gerontology nurse practitioner/clinical nurse specialist (Post Master's Certificate); adult-gerontological acute care nurse practitioner (MS); adult-gerontological nurse practitioner/clinical nurse specialist (MS); family nurse practitioner (MS, Post Master's Certificate); nursing (DNP, PhD); nursing education (MS, Post Master's Certificate). *Accreditation:* AACN; ACNM/ACME (one or more programs are accredited). *Program availability:* Part-time, evening/weekend, 100% online, blended/hybrid learning. *Faculty:* 31 full-time (30 women). *Students:* 42 full-time (36 women), 86 part-time (79 women); includes 12 minority (3 Black or African American, non-Hispanic/Latino; 3 Asian, non-Hispanic/Latino; 3 Hispanic/Latino; 1 Native Hawaiian or other Pacific Islander, non-Hispanic/Latino; 2 Two or more races, non-Hispanic/Latino), 3 international. 33 applicants, 79% accepted, 23 enrolled. In 2017, 25 master's, 8 doctorates, 2 other advanced degrees awarded. *Entrance requirements:* For master's, GRE or MAT, 2 letters of recommendation, scholarly papers; for doctorate, GRE, 3 letters of recommendation, scholarly papers. Additional exam requirements/recommendations for international students: Required—TOEFL. *Application deadline:* For fall admission, 2/15 for domestic students, 2/1 for international students; for spring admission, 10/15 for domestic students, 7/15 for international students. Application fee: $65. Electronic applications accepted. *Expenses:* Tuition, state resident: full-time $12,706; part-time $786 per credit. Tuition, nonresident: full-time $25,216; part-time $1401 per credit. *Required fees:* $1598; $45 per credit. One-time fee: $30 part-time. *Financial support:* In 2017–18, 1 research assistantship with tuition reimbursement (averaging $18,080 per year), 5 teaching assistantships with tuition reimbursements (averaging $10,133 per year) were awarded. Financial award application deadline: 2/1; financial award applicants required to submit FAFSA. *Unit head:* Dr. Barbara Wolfe, Dean, 401-874-5324, E-mail: bwolfe@uri.edu. *Application contact:* Dr. Denise Coppa, Associate Professor/Interim Associate Dean for Graduate Programs, 401-874-5036, E-mail: dcoppa@uri.edu.
Website: http://www.uri.edu/nursing/

University of Rochester, School of Nursing, Rochester, NY 14642. Offers adult gerontological acute care nurse practitioner (MS); adult gerontological primary care nurse practitioner (MS); clinical nurse leader (MS); family nurse practitioner (MS); family psychiatric mental health nurse practitioner (MS); health care organization management and leadership (MS); nursing (DNP); nursing and health science (PhD); nursing education (MS); pediatric nurse practitioner (MS); pediatric nurse practitioner/neonatal nurse practitioner (MS). *Accreditation:* AACN. *Program availability:* Part-time, 100% online, blended/hybrid learning. *Faculty:* 62 full-time (51 women), 73 part-time/adjunct (63 women). *Students:* 17 full-time (12 women), 306 part-time (252 women); includes 46 minority (16 Black or African American, non-Hispanic/Latino; 1 American Indian or Alaska Native, non-Hispanic/Latino; 7 Asian, non-Hispanic/Latino; 17 Hispanic/Latino; 5 Two or more races, non-Hispanic/Latino), 3 international. Average age 34. 143 applicants, 71% accepted, 87 enrolled. In 2017, 48 master's, 8 doctorates awarded. Terminal master's awarded for partial completion of doctoral program. *Degree requirements:* For master's, comprehensive exam; for doctorate, thesis/dissertation. *Entrance requirements:* For master's, BS in nursing, minimum GPA of 3.0, course work in statistics; for doctorate, GRE General Test (for PhD), MS in nursing, minimum GPA of 3.5. Additional exam requirements/recommendations for international students: Required—TOEFL (minimum score 560 paper-based; 88 iBT) or IELTS (minimum score 6.5) recommended. *Application deadline:* For fall admission, 4/1 for domestic and international students; for spring admission, 9/1 for domestic and international students; for summer admission, 1/2 for domestic and international students. Application fee: $50. Electronic applications accepted. *Financial support:* In 2017–18, 63 students received support, including 2 fellowships with full and partial tuition reimbursements available (averaging $16,000 per year); scholarships/grants, traineeships, health care benefits, tuition waivers (full and partial), and unspecified assistantships also available. Support available to part-time students. Financial award application deadline: 6/30; financial award applicants required to submit CSS PROFILE or FAFSA. *Faculty research:* Symptom science, systems of care, innovations in health technology, promoting healthy behaviors. *Total annual research expenditures:* $2.6 million. *Unit head:* Dr. Kathy H. Rideout, Dean, 585-273-8902, Fax: 585-273-1268, E-mail: kathy_rideout@urmc.rochester.edu. *Application contact:* Elaine Andolina, Director of Admissions, 585-275-2375, Fax: 585-756-8299, E-mail: elaine_andolina@urmc.rochester.edu.
Website: http://www.son.rochester.edu

University of St. Augustine for Health Sciences, Graduate Programs, Master of Science in Nursing Program, San Marcos, CA 92069. Offers nurse educator (MSN); nurse executive (MSN); nurse informatics (MSN). *Program availability:* Part-time, online learning.

University of St. Francis, Leach College of Nursing, Joliet, IL 60435-6169. Offers family nurse practitioner (MSN, Post-Master's Certificate); nursing administration (MSN); nursing education (MSN); nursing practice (DNP); psychology/mental health nurse practitioner (MSN, Post-Master's Certificate); teaching in nursing (Certificate). *Accreditation:* AACN. *Program availability:* Part-time, evening/weekend, 100% online. *Faculty:* 9 full-time (all women), 12 part-time/adjunct (11 women). *Students:* 66 full-time (61 women), 292 part-time (262 women); includes 136 minority (67 Black or African American, non-Hispanic/Latino; 2 American Indian or Alaska Native, non-Hispanic/Latino; 25 Asian, non-Hispanic/Latino; 29 Hispanic/Latino; 3 Native Hawaiian or other Pacific Islander, non-Hispanic/Latino; 10 Two or more races, non-Hispanic/Latino). Average age 40. 280 applicants, 34% accepted, 81 enrolled. In 2017, 117 master's, 5 doctorates, 12 other advanced degrees awarded. *Degree requirements:* For master's, comprehensive exam. *Entrance requirements:* Additional exam requirements/recommendations for international students: Required—TOEFL (minimum score 550 paper-based; 79 iBT), IELTS (minimum score 6). *Application deadline:* Applications are processed on a rolling basis. Application fee: $30. Electronic applications accepted. Application fee is waived when completed online. *Expenses:* $775 per credit hour. *Financial support:* In 2017–18, 115 students received support. Scholarships/grants available. Support available to part-time students. Financial award applicants required to submit FAFSA. *Unit head:* Dr. Carol Wilson, Dean, 815-740-3840, Fax: 815-740-4243, E-mail: cwilson@stfrancis.edu. *Application contact:* Sandra Sloka, Director of Admissions for Graduate and Degree Completion Programs, 800-735-7500, Fax: 815-740-3431, E-mail: ssloka@stfrancis.edu.
Website: http://www.stfrancis.edu/academics/college-of-nursing/

University of Saint Joseph, Department of Nursing, West Hartford, CT 06117-2700. Offers family nurse practitioner (MS); nurse educator (MS); nursing practice (DNP); psychiatric/mental health nurse practitioner (MS). *Accreditation:* AACN. *Program availability:* Part-time, evening/weekend. *Degree requirements:* For master's, thesis. *Entrance requirements:* For master's, 2 letters of recommendation. *Application deadline:* Applications are processed on a rolling basis. Application fee: $50. Electronic applications accepted. Application fee is waived when completed online. *Financial support:* Career-related internships or fieldwork and unspecified assistantships available. Support available to part-time students. Financial award applicants required to submit FAFSA.
Website: http://www.usj.edu/academics/schools/school-of-health-natural-sciences/nursing/

University of Saint Mary, Graduate Programs, Program in Nursing, Leavenworth, KS 66048-5082. Offers nurse administrator (MSN); nurse educator (MSN). *Accreditation:* AACN. *Program availability:* Part-time, online only, 100% online. *Degree requirements:* For master's, practicum. *Entrance requirements:* For master's, BSN from CCNE- or ACEN-accredited baccalaureate nursing program at regionally-accredited institution. Electronic applications accepted. *Expenses:* Contact institution.

University of South Alabama, College of Nursing, Mobile, AL 36688. Offers nursing (MSN, DNP); nursing administration (Certificate); nursing education (Certificate); nursing practice (Certificate). *Accreditation:* AACN. *Program availability:* Part-time, online learning. *Faculty:* 73 full-time (67 women), 112 part-time/adjunct (103 women). *Students:* 2,163 full-time (1,905 women), 714 part-time (619 women); includes 882 minority (566 Black or African American, non-Hispanic/Latino; 26 American Indian or Alaska Native, non-Hispanic/Latino; 117 Asian, non-Hispanic/Latino; 102 Hispanic/Latino; 7 Native Hawaiian or other Pacific Islander, non-Hispanic/Latino; 64 Two or more races, non-Hispanic/Latino), 6 international. Average age 35. 918 applicants, 77% accepted, 522 enrolled. In 2017, 791 master's, 96 doctorates, 95 other advanced degrees awarded. *Degree requirements:* For master's, thesis optional; for doctorate, final project. *Entrance requirements:* For master's, BSN, RN licensure, minimum GPA of 3.0, resume documenting clinical experience, background check, drug screening; for doctorate, MSN, RN licensure, minimum GPA of 3.0; for Certificate, MSN/DN/DNP, RN licensure, minimum GPA of 3.0, resume documenting clinical experience, background check, drug screening. Additional exam requirements/recommendations for international students: Required—TOEFL. *Application deadline:* For fall admission, 2/15 for domestic students; for spring admission, 7/15 priority date for domestic students; for summer admission, 11/15 priority date for domestic students. Applications are processed on a rolling basis. Application fee: $100. Electronic applications accepted. *Expenses:* Tuition, state resident: full-time $10,104; part-time $421 per semester hour. Tuition, nonresident: full-time $20,208; part-time $842 per semester hour. *Financial support:* Fellowships, research assistantships, teaching assistantships, career-related internships or fieldwork, Federal Work-Study, institutionally sponsored loans, scholarships/grants, and unspecified assistantships available. Support available to part-time students. Financial award application deadline: 3/31; financial award applicants required to submit FAFSA. *Unit head:* Dr. Heather Hall, Interim Dean, College of Nursing, 251-445-9400, Fax: 251-445-9416, E-mail: heatherhall@southalabama.edu. *Application contact:* Brenda Mosley, Academic Advisor II, 251-445-9400, Fax: 251-445-9416, E-mail: bmosley@southalabama.edu.
Website: http://www.southalabama.edu/colleges/con/index.html

University of Southern Indiana, Graduate Studies, College of Nursing and Health Professions, Program in Nursing, Evansville, IN 47712-3590. Offers adult-gerontology acute care nurse practitioner (MSN, PMC); adult-gerontology clinical nurse specialist (MSN, PMC); adult-gerontology primary care nurse practitioner (MSN, PMC); advanced nursing practice (DNP); family nurse practiioner (MSN); family nurse practitioner (PMC); nursing education (MSN, PMC); nursing management and leadership (MSN, PMC); organizational and systems leadership (DNP); psychiatric mental health nurse practitioner (MSN, PMC). *Accreditation:* AACN. *Program availability:* Part-time, online learning. *Faculty:* 9 full-time (8 women), 2 part-time/adjunct (both women). *Students:* 73 full-time (59 women), 370 part-time (314 women); includes 47 minority (18 Black or African American, non-Hispanic/Latino; 2 American Indian or Alaska Native, non-Hispanic/Latino; 10 Asian, non-Hispanic/Latino; 12 Hispanic/Latino; 1 Native Hawaiian or other Pacific Islander, non-Hispanic/Latino; 4 Two or more races, non-Hispanic/Latino), 1 international. Average age 36. In 2017, 91 master's, 10 doctorates, 18 other advanced degrees awarded. *Entrance requirements:* For master's, BSN from nationally-accredited school; minimum cumulative GPA of 3.0; satisfactory completion of a course in undergraduate statistics (minimum grade C); one year of full-time experience or 2,000 hours of clinical practice as an RN (recommended); unencumbered U.S. RN license; for doctorate, minimum GPA of 3.0, completion of graduate research course with minimum B grade, unencumbered RN license, resume/curriculum vitae, three professional references, 1-2 page narrative of practice experience and professional goals, Capstone Project Information form. Additional exam requirements/recommendations for international students: Required—TOEFL (minimum score 550 paper-based; 79 iBT), IELTS (minimum score 6). *Application deadline:* For fall admission, 2/1 for domestic students, 1/1 priority date for international students. Applications are processed on a rolling basis. Application fee: $40. Electronic applications accepted. *Expenses:* Contact institution. *Financial support:* In 2017–18, 1 student received support. Federal Work-Study, scholarships/grants, tuition waivers (full and partial), and unspecified assistantships available. Financial award application deadline: 3/1; financial award applicants required to submit FAFSA. *Unit head:* Dr. Mellisa A. Hall, Chair of the Master of Science in Nursing Program, 812-465-1168, E-mail: mhall@usi.edu. *Application contact:* Dr. Mayola Rowser, Director, Graduate Studies, 812-465-7015, Fax: 812-464-1956, E-mail: mrowser@usi.edu.
Website: https://www.usi.edu/health/nursing/

University of Southern Maine, College of Science, Technology, and Health, School of Nursing, Portland, ME 04103. Offers adult-gerontology primary care nurse practitioner (MS, PMC); education (MS); family nurse practitioner (MS, PMC); family psychiatric/mental health nurse practitioner (MS); management (MS); nursing (CAS, CGS); psychiatric-mental health nurse practitioner (PMC). *Accreditation:* AACN. *Program availability:* Part-time. *Degree requirements:* For master's, thesis optional. *Entrance requirements:* For master's, GRE General Test or MAT, minimum GPA of 3.0; for doctorate, GRE. Additional exam requirements/recommendations for international students: Required—TOEFL (minimum score 550 paper-based). Electronic applications accepted. *Faculty research:* Women's health, nursing history, weight control, community services, substance abuse.

University of South Florida, College of Nursing, Tampa, FL 33612. Offers nurse anesthesia (DNP); nursing (MS, DNP), including adult-gerontology acute care nursing, adult-gerontology primary care nursing, family health nursing, nurse anesthesia (MS), nursing education (MS), occupational health nursing/adult-gerontology primary care nursing, oncology nursing/adult-gerontology primary care nursing (DNP), pediatric health nursing; nursing education (Post Master's Certificate); nursing science (PhD); simulation based academic fellowship in advanced pain management (Graduate Certificate). *Accreditation:* AACN; AANA/CANAEP. *Program availability:* Part-time. *Faculty:* 37 full-time (32 women), 2 part-time/adjunct (1 woman). *Students:* 224 full-time (178 women), 669 part-time (577 women); includes 309 minority (105 Black or African American, non-Hispanic/Latino; 2 American Indian or Alaska Native, non-Hispanic/Latino; 53 Asian, non-Hispanic/Latino; 122 Hispanic/Latino; 1 Native Hawaiian or other Pacific Islander, non-Hispanic/Latino; 26 Two or more races, non-Hispanic/Latino), 6 international. Average age 32. 949 applicants, 47% accepted, 382 enrolled. In 2017, 264

master's, 39 doctorates awarded. *Degree requirements:* For master's, comprehensive exam, thesis optional; for doctorate, comprehensive exam, thesis/dissertation. *Entrance requirements:* For master's, GRE General Test, bachelor's degree from accredited program with minimum GPA of 3.0 in all upper-division coursework; current license as Registered Nurse; 3 letters of recommendation; personal statement of goals; resume or curriculum vitae; personal interview; for doctorate, GRE General Test (recommended), bachelor's degree in nursing from ACEN or CCNE regionally-accredited institution with minimum GPA of 3.0 in all coursework or in all upper-division coursework; current license as Registered Nurse in Florida; undergraduate statistics course with minimum B grade; 3 letters of recommendation; statement of goals; resume; interview. Additional exam requirements/recommendations for international students: Required—TOEFL (minimum score 550 paper-based; 79 iBT). *Application deadline:* For fall admission, 12/15 for domestic and international students; for spring admission, 10/1 for domestic students, 9/15 for international students. Application fee: $30. Electronic applications accepted. *Financial support:* In 2017–18, 132 students received support, including 7 research assistantships with tuition reimbursements available (averaging $18,935 per year), 29 teaching assistantships with tuition reimbursements available (averaging $30,814 per year); tuition waivers (partial) and unspecified assistantships also available. Financial award application deadline: 2/1; financial award applicants required to submit FAFSA. *Faculty research:* Women's health, palliative and end-of-life care, cardiac rehabilitation, complementary therapies for chronic illness and cancer. *Total annual research expenditures:* $3.2 million. *Unit head:* Dr. Victoria Rich, Dean, College of Nursing, 813-974-8939, Fax: 813-974-5418, E-mail: victoriarich@health.usf.edu. *Application contact:* Dr. Brian Graves, Assistant Professor/Assistant Dean, 813-974-8054, Fax: 813-974-5418, E-mail: bgraves1@health.usf.edu.
Website: http://health.usf.edu/nursing/index.htm

The University of Tennessee at Chattanooga, School of Nursing, Chattanooga, TN 37403. Offers certified nurse anesthetist (Post-Master's Certificate); family nurse practitioner (MSN, Post-Master's Certificate); gerontology acute care (MSN, Post-Master's Certificate); nurse anesthesia (MSN); nurse education (Post-Master's Certificate); nursing (DNP). *Accreditation:* AACN; AANA/CANAEP (one or more programs are accredited). *Students:* 62 full-time (33 women), 69 part-time (61 women); includes 24 minority (11 Black or African American, non-Hispanic/Latino; 1 American Indian or Alaska Native, non-Hispanic/Latino; 5 Asian, non-Hispanic/Latino; 3 Hispanic/Latino; 4 Two or more races, non-Hispanic/Latino). Average age 34. 47 applicants, 100% accepted, 45 enrolled. In 2017, 33 master's, 14 doctorates, 7 other advanced degrees awarded. *Degree requirements:* For master's, thesis optional, qualifying exams, professional project; for doctorate, professional project; for Post-Master's Certificate, thesis or alternative, practicum, seminar. *Entrance requirements:* For master's, GRE General Test, MAT, BSN, minimum GPA of 3.0, eligibility for Tennessee RN license, 1 year of direct patient care experience; for doctorate, GRE General Test or MAT (if applicant does not have MSN), minimum GPA of 3.0 for highest degree earned; for Post-Master's Certificate, GRE General Test, MAT, MSN, minimum GPA of 3.0, eligibility for Tennessee RN license, one year of direct patient care experience. Additional exam requirements/recommendations for international students: Required—TOEFL (minimum score 550 paper-based; 79 iBT), IELTS (minimum score 6). *Application deadline:* For fall admission, 6/15 priority date for domestic students, 7/1 for international students; for spring admission, 11/1 priority date for domestic students, 11/1 for international students. Applications are processed on a rolling basis. Application fee: $35 ($40 for international students). Electronic applications accepted. *Expenses:* Contact institution. *Financial support:* Teaching assistantships, career-related internships or fieldwork, and scholarships/grants available. Support available to part-time students. Financial award application deadline: 7/1; financial award applicants required to submit FAFSA. *Faculty research:* Diabetes in women, health care for elderly, alternative medicine, hypertension, nurse anesthesia. *Total annual research expenditures:* $985,388. *Unit head:* Dr. Chris Smith, Director, 423-425-1741, Fax: 423-425-4668, E-mail: chris-smith@utc.edu. *Application contact:* Dr. Joanne Romagni, Dean of the Graduate School, 423-425-4478, Fax: 423-425-5223, E-mail: joanne-romagni@utc.edu.
Website: http://www.utc.edu/nursing/

The University of Texas at Arlington, Graduate School, College of Nursing and Health Innovation, Arlington, TX 76019. Offers athletic training (MS); exercise science (MS); kinesiology (PhD); nurse practitioner (MSN); nursing (PhD); nursing administration (MSN); nursing education (MSN); nursing practice (DNP). *Accreditation:* AACN. *Program availability:* Part-time, evening/weekend, online learning. *Degree requirements:* For master's, practicum course; for doctorate, comprehensive exam (for some programs), thesis/dissertation (for some programs), proposal defense dissertation (for PhD); scholarship project (for DNP). *Entrance requirements:* For master's, GRE General Test if GPA less than 3.0, minimum GPA of 3.0, Texas nursing license, minimum C grade in undergraduate statistics course; for doctorate, GRE General Test (waived for MSN-to-PhD applicants), minimum undergraduate, graduate and statistics GPA of 3.0; Texas RN license; interview; written statement of goals. Additional exam requirements/recommendations for international students: Required—TOEFL (minimum score 550 paper-based), IELTS (minimum score 7). *Faculty research:* Simulation in clinical education and practice, cultural diversity, vulnerable populations, substance abuse.

The University of Texas at Austin, Graduate School, School of Nursing, Austin, TX 78712-1111. Offers adult - gerontology clinical nurse specialist (MSN); child health (MSN), including administration, public health nursing, teaching; family nurse practitioner (MSN); family psychiatric/mental health nurse practitioner (MSN); holistic adult health (MSN), including administration, teaching; maternity (MSN), including administration, public health nursing, teaching; nursing (PhD); nursing administration and healthcare systems management (MSN); nursing practice (DNP); pediatric nurse practitioner (MSN); public health nursing (MSN). *Accreditation:* AACN. *Program availability:* Part-time. *Degree requirements:* For master's, thesis optional; for doctorate, thesis/dissertation. *Entrance requirements:* For master's and doctorate, GRE General Test. Additional exam requirements/recommendations for international students: Required—TOEFL (minimum score 550 paper-based). Electronic applications accepted. *Faculty research:* Chronic illness management, memory and aging, health promotion, women's health, adolescent health.

The University of Texas at El Paso, Graduate School, School of Nursing, El Paso, TX 79968-0001. Offers family nurse practitioner (MSN); health care leadership and management (Certificate); interdisciplinary health sciences (PhD); nursing (DNP); nursing education (MSN, Certificate); nursing systems management (MSN). *Accreditation:* AACN. *Program availability:* Online learning. *Degree requirements:* For master's, thesis optional; for doctorate, thesis/dissertation. *Entrance requirements:* For master's, minimum GPA of 3.0, resume; for doctorate, GRE, letters of reference, relevant personal/professional experience; master's degree in nursing (for DNP); for Certificate, bachelor's degree in nursing. Additional exam requirements/recommendations for international students: Required—TOEFL; Recommended—IELTS. *Application deadline:* For fall admission, 8/1 for domestic students, 3/1 for international students; for spring admission, 11/1 for domestic students, 9/1 for international students. Applications are processed on a rolling basis. Application fee: $45 ($80 for international students). Electronic applications accepted. *Financial support:* Fellowships with partial tuition reimbursements, research assistantships with partial tuition reimbursements, teaching assistantships with partial tuition reimbursements, institutionally sponsored loans, scholarships/grants, health care benefits, tuition waivers (partial), and unspecified assistantships available. Support available to part-time students. Financial award application deadline: 3/15; financial award applicants required to submit FAFSA. *Unit head:* Dr. Elias Provencio-Vasquez, Dean, 915-747-8194, Fax: 915-747-8266, E-mail: eprovenciovasquez@utep.edu. *Application contact:* Dr. Benjamin Flores, Interim Dean of the Graduate School, 915-747-5491, Fax: 915-747-5788, E-mail: bflores@utep.edu.
Website: http://nursing.utep.edu/

The University of Texas at Tyler, College of Nursing and Health Sciences, Program in Nursing, Tyler, TX 75799-0001. Offers nurse practitioner (MSN); nursing (PhD); nursing administration (MSN); nursing education (MSN); MSN/MBA. *Accreditation:* AACN. *Program availability:* Part-time, evening/weekend, online learning. *Degree requirements:* For master's, comprehensive exam (for some programs), thesis (for some programs); for doctorate, thesis/dissertation. *Entrance requirements:* For master's, GRE General Test or MAT, GMAT, minimum undergraduate GPA of 3.0, course work in statistics, RN license, BSN. Additional exam requirements/recommendations for international students: Required—TOEFL. Electronic applications accepted. *Faculty research:* Psychosocial adjustment, aging, support/commitment of caregivers, psychological abuse and violence, hope/hopelessness, professional values, end of life care, suicidology, clinical supervision, workforce retention and issues, global health issues, health promotion.

The University of Texas Health Science Center at San Antonio, School of Nursing, San Antonio, TX 78229-3900. Offers administrative management (MSN); adult-gerontology acute care nurse practitioner (PGC); advanced practice leadership (DNP); clinical nurse leader (MSN); executive administrative management (DNP); family nurse practitioner (MSN, PGC); nursing (MSN, PhD); nursing education (MSN, PGC); pediatric nurse practitioner primary care (PGC); psychiatric mental health nurse practitioner (PGC); public health nurse leader (DNP). *Accreditation:* AACN. *Program availability:* Part-time. Terminal master's awarded for partial completion of doctoral program. *Degree requirements:* For master's, thesis optional; for doctorate, comprehensive exam, thesis/dissertation.

The University of Texas Rio Grande Valley, College of Health Affairs, School of Nursing, Edinburg, TX 78539. Offers adult health nursing (MSN); family nurse practitioner (MSN); nursing administration (MSN); nursing education (MSN); psychiatric mental health nursing (Post Master's Certificate). *Accreditation:* AACN. *Program availability:* Part-time, evening/weekend. *Faculty:* 7 full-time (all women), 5 part-time/adjunct (3 women). *Students:* 48 full-time, 5 part-time; includes 43 minority (5 Black or African American, non-Hispanic/Latino; 38 Hispanic/Latino). Average age 31. 61 applicants. In 2017, 46 master's awarded. *Degree requirements:* For master's, thesis optional. *Entrance requirements:* For master's, Texas RN licensure, undergraduate physical statistic course. Additional exam requirements/recommendations for international students: Required—TOEFL (minimum score 550 paper-based). *Application deadline:* For fall admission, 7/1 priority date for domestic and international students; for spring admission, 10/1 priority date for domestic and international students. Applications are processed on a rolling basis. Application fee: $50. Electronic applications accepted. *Expenses:* Contact institution. *Financial support:* Scholarships/grants and traineeships available. Financial award application deadline: 9/1; financial award applicants required to submit FAFSA. *Faculty research:* Health promotion, adolescent pregnancy, herbal and nontraditional approaches, healing touch stress. *Unit head:* Dr. Eloisa G. Tamez, Professor/Chief Nursing Administrator, 956-665-3616, Fax: 956-665-5252, E-mail: eloisa.tamez@utrgv.edu. *Application contact:* Dr. Beatriz Bautista, Clinical Professor, 956-665-3497, Fax: 956-665-3491, E-mail: beatriz.bautista@utrgv.edu.
Website: http://www.utrgv.edu/nursing/

The University of Toledo, College of Graduate Studies, College of Nursing, Department of Population and Community Care, Toledo, OH 43606-3390. Offers clinical nurse leader (MSN); family nurse practitioner (MSN, Certificate); nurse educator (MSN, Certificate); pediatric nurse practitioner (MSN, Certificate). *Program availability:* Part-time. *Degree requirements:* For master's, thesis or alternative. *Entrance requirements:* For master's, GRE, BS in nursing, minimum undergraduate GPA of 3.0, statement of purpose, three letters of recommendation, transcripts from all prior institutions attended, Nursing CAS application, UT supplemental application; for Certificate, BS in nursing, minimum undergraduate GPA of 3.0, statement of purpose, three letters of recommendation, transcripts from all prior institutions attended. Additional exam requirements/recommendations for international students: Required—TOEFL (minimum score 550 paper-based; 80 iBT). Electronic applications accepted.

University of Victoria, Faculty of Graduate Studies, Faculty of Human and Social Development, School of Nursing, Victoria, BC V8W 2Y2, Canada. Offers advanced nursing practice (advanced practice leadership option) (MN); advanced nursing practice (nurse educator option) (MN); advanced nursing practice (nurse practitioner option) (MN); nursing (PhD). *Program availability:* Part-time, online learning. *Entrance requirements:* Additional exam requirements/recommendations for international students: Required—TOEFL (minimum score 575 paper-based), IELTS (minimum score 7). Electronic applications accepted.

University of Washington, Tacoma, Graduate Programs, Program in Nursing, Tacoma, WA 98402-3100. Offers communities, populations and health (MN); leadership in healthcare (MN); nurse educator (MN). *Program availability:* Part-time. *Degree requirements:* For master's, thesis (for some programs), advance fieldwork. *Entrance requirements:* For master's, Washington State NCLEX exam, minimum GPA of 3.0. Additional exam requirements/recommendations for international students: Required—TOEFL (minimum score 580 paper-based; 70 iBT); Recommended—IELTS (minimum score 7). *Faculty research:* Hospice and palliative care; clinical trial decision-making; minority nurse retention; asthma and public health; injustice, suffering, difference: Linking Them to Us; adolescent health.

University of West Georgia, Tanner Health System School of Nursing, Carrollton, GA 30118. Offers health systems leadership (Post-Master's Certificate); nursing (MSN); nursing education (Ed D, Post-Master's Certificate). *Accreditation:* AACN. *Program availability:* Part-time, evening/weekend, 100% online, blended/hybrid learning. *Faculty:* 13 full-time (all women). *Students:* 64 full-time (63 women), 78 part-time (74 women); includes 34 minority (27 Black or African American, non-Hispanic/Latino; 1 Asian, non-Hispanic/Latino; 5 Hispanic/Latino; 1 Two or more races, non-Hispanic/Latino). Average age 41. 92 applicants, 88% accepted, 61 enrolled. In 2017, 36 master's, 7 doctorates, 1 other advanced degree awarded. *Entrance requirements:* Additional exam requirements/recommendations for international students: Required—TOEFL (minimum score 523 paper-based; 69 iBT); Recommended—IELTS (minimum score 6.5). *Application deadline:* For fall admission, 2/1 priority date for domestic and international students. Applications are processed on a rolling basis. Application fee: $40. Electronic applications accepted. *Expenses:* Contact institution. *Financial support:* Fellowships, research assistantships, teaching assistantships, career-related internships or fieldwork, Federal Work-Study, institutionally sponsored loans, scholarships/grants, and unspecified assistantships available. Support available to part-time students. Financial award application deadline: 4/1; financial award applicants required to submit FAFSA.

Unit head: Dr. Jennifer Schuessler, Dean of the School of Nursing, 678-839-5640, Fax: 678-839-6553, E-mail: jschuess@westga.edu. *Application contact:* Dr. Toby Ziglar, Assistant Dean of the Graduate School, 678-839-1390, Fax: 678-839-1395, E-mail: graduate@westga.edu.
Website: https://www.westga.edu/nursing

University of Wisconsin–Eau Claire, College of Nursing and Health Sciences, Program in Nursing, Eau Claire, WI 54702-4004. Offers adult-gerontological administration (DNP); adult-gerontological clinical nurse specialist (DNP); adult-gerontological education (MSN); adult-gerontological primary care nurse practitioner (DNP); family health administration (DNP); family health in education (MSN); family health nurse practitioner (DNP); nursing (MSN); nursing practice (DNP). *Accreditation:* AACN. *Program availability:* Part-time. Terminal master's awarded for partial completion of doctoral program. *Degree requirements:* For master's, thesis optional, 500-600 hours clinical practicum, oral and written exams. *Entrance requirements:* For master's, Wisconsin RN license, minimum GPA of 3.0, undergraduate statistics, course work in health assessment. Additional exam requirements/recommendations for international students: Required—TOEFL (minimum score 79 iBT). *Expenses:* Contact institution.

Ursuline College, School of Graduate and Professional Studies, Programs in Nursing, Pepper Pike, OH 44124-4398. Offers acute-care nurse practitioner (MSN); adult nurse practitioner (MSN); adult-gerontology acute care nurse practitioner (MSN); adult-gerontology clinical nurse specialist (MSN); adult-gerontology nurse practitioner (MSN); care management (MSN); clinical nurse specialist (MSN); family nurse practitioner (MSN); nursing (DNP); nursing education (MSN); palliative care (MSN). *Accreditation:* AACN. *Program availability:* Part-time. *Faculty:* 6 full-time (all women), 25 part-time/adjunct (23 women). *Students:* 136 applicants, 89% accepted, 85 enrolled. In 2017, 85 master's, 6 doctorates awarded. *Degree requirements:* For master's, comprehensive exam; for doctorate, thesis/dissertation. *Entrance requirements:* For master's, minimum undergraduate GPA of 3.0, bachelor's degree in nursing, eligibility for or current Ohio RN license. Additional exam requirements/recommendations for international students: Required—TOEFL (minimum score 500 paper-based). *Application deadline:* For fall admission, 8/1 priority date for domestic students. Applications are processed on a rolling basis. Application fee: $25. Electronic applications accepted. *Expenses:* $1,094 per credit hour. *Financial support:* In 2017–18, 6 students received support. Scholarships/grants available. Financial award application deadline: 3/1; financial award applicants required to submit FAFSA. *Faculty research:* Core Determinants of Health (CDH) screening tool and accompanying education, academic-practice partnerships, active learning/teaching strategies, innovative clinical education models, competency development and testing, health care policy and cultural competence. *Total annual research expenditures:* $864,511. *Unit head:* Dr. Janet Baker, Associate Dean of Graduate Nursing, 440-864-8172, Fax: 440-684-6053, E-mail: jbaker@ursuline.edu. *Application contact:* Melanie Steele, Director, Graduate Admission, 440-646-8119, Fax: 440-684-6138, E-mail: graduateadmissions@ursuline.edu.

Valparaiso University, Graduate School and Continuing Education, College of Nursing and Health Professions, Valparaiso, IN 46383. Offers nursing (DNP); nursing education (MSN, Certificate); physician assistant (MSPA); public health (MPH); MSN/MHA. *Accreditation:* AACN. *Program availability:* Part-time, evening/weekend, online learning. *Entrance requirements:* For master's, minimum GPA of 3.0, undergraduate major in nursing, Indiana registered nursing license, undergraduate courses in research and statistics. Additional exam requirements/recommendations for international students: Required—TOEFL (minimum score 550 paper-based; 80 iBT), IELTS (minimum score 6). Electronic applications accepted. *Expenses:* Contact institution.

Villanova University, M. Louise Fitzpatrick College of Nursing, Villanova, PA 19085. Offers adult gerontology primary care nurse practitioner (MSN, Post Master's Certificate); family primary care nurse practitioner (MSN, Post Master's Certificate); nurse anesthesia (DNP); nursing (PhD); nursing education (MSN, Post Master's Certificate); nursing practice (DNP); pediatric primary care nurse practitioner (MSN, Post Master's Certificate). *Accreditation:* AACN; AANA/CANAEP. *Program availability:* Part-time, online learning. *Students:* 151 full-time, 199 part-time; includes 42 minority (18 Black or African American, non-Hispanic/Latino; 12 Asian, non-Hispanic/Latino; 8 Hispanic/Latino; 4 Two or more races, non-Hispanic/Latino), 10 international. 274 applicants, 43% accepted, 92 enrolled. In 2017, 70 master's, 15 doctorates awarded. *Entrance requirements:* Additional exam requirements/recommendations for international students: Required—TOEFL, IELTS. *Application deadline:* For fall admission, 7/1 for domestic and international students; for spring admission, 10/1 for domestic and international students; for summer admission, 4/1 for domestic and international students. Application fee: $50. Electronic applications accepted. *Financial support:* Fellowships, research assistantships, teaching assistantships, scholarships/grants, traineeships, and tuition waivers available. *Unit head:* Dr. Marguerite K. Schlag, Associate Professor, Assistant Dean and Director of Graduate Nursing Program, 610-519-4907, Fax: 610-519-7650, E-mail: marguerite.schlag@villanova.edu. *Application contact:* Kathleen Geibel, Assistant to Graduate Program, 610-519-4934, Fax: 610-519-7650, E-mail: kathleen.geibel@villanova.edu.
Website: http://www.nursing.villanova.edu

Virginia Commonwealth University, Graduate School, School of Nursing, Richmond, VA 23284-9005. Offers adult health acute nursing (MS); adult health primary nursing (MS); biobehavioral clinical research (PhD); child health nursing (MS); clinical nurse leader (MS); family health nursing (MS); nurse educator (MS); nurse practitioner (MS); nursing (Certificate); nursing administration (MS), including clinical nurse manager; psychiatric-mental health nursing (MS); quality and safety in health care (DNP); women's health nursing (MS). *Accreditation:* AACN; ACEN (one or more programs are accredited). *Program availability:* Part-time, evening/weekend, online learning. *Degree requirements:* For master's, thesis optional; for doctorate, thesis/dissertation. *Entrance requirements:* For master's, GRE General Test, BSN, minimum GPA of 2.8; for doctorate, GRE General Test. Additional exam requirements/recommendations for international students: Required—TOEFL (minimum score 600 paper-based; 100 iBT). Electronic applications accepted.

Wagner College, Division of Graduate Studies, Evelyn L. Spiro School of Nursing, Staten Island, NY 10301-4495. Offers family nurse practitioner (MS, Certificate); nurse educator (MS); nursing (DNP). *Accreditation:* ACEN (one or more programs are accredited). *Program availability:* Part-time, evening/weekend. *Faculty:* 6 full-time (all women), 6 part-time/adjunct (5 women). *Students:* 15 full-time (13 women), 223 part-time (197 women); includes 75 minority (20 Black or African American, non-Hispanic/Latino; 29 Asian, non-Hispanic/Latino; 21 Hispanic/Latino; 5 Two or more races, non-Hispanic/Latino). Average age 35. 126 applicants, 75% accepted, 69 enrolled. In 2017, 52 master's, 11 doctorates, 2 other advanced degrees awarded. *Degree requirements:* For master's, thesis optional. *Entrance requirements:* For master's, BS in nursing, current clinical experience, minimum GPA of 3.3; for Certificate, master's degree in nursing from an NLN-accredited program, minimum GPA of 3.0. Additional exam requirements/recommendations for international students: Required—TOEFL (minimum score 550 paper-based; 79 iBT), IELTS (minimum score 6.5). *Application deadline:* For fall admission, 2/1 priority date for domestic students, 2/1 for international students. Application fee: $60. Electronic applications accepted. *Financial support:* In 2017–18, 62 students received support. Traineeships, unspecified assistantships, and alumni fellowship grants available. Financial award application deadline: 2/15; financial award applicants required to submit FAFSA. *Unit head:* Dr. Patricia Tooker, Dean, 718-390-3452, Fax: 718-420-4009, E-mail: ptooker@wagner.edu. *Application contact:* Patricia Clancy, Assistant Director, 718-420-4464, Fax: 718-390-3105, E-mail: patricia.clancy@wagner.edu.
Website: http://wagner.edu/nursing/

Walden University, Graduate Programs, School of Nursing, Minneapolis, MN 55401. Offers adult-gerontology acute care nurse practitioner (MSN); adult-gerontology nurse practitioner (MSN); education (MSN); family nurse practitioner (MSN); informatics (MSN); leadership and management (MSN); nursing (PhD, Post-Master's Certificate), including education (PhD), healthcare administration (PhD), interdisciplinary health (PhD), leadership (PhD), nursing education (Post-Master's Certificate), nursing informatics (Post-Master's Certificate), nursing leadership and management (Post-Master's Certificate), public health policy (PhD); nursing practice (DNP); psychiatric mental health (MSN). *Accreditation:* AACN. *Program availability:* Part-time, evening/weekend, online only, 100% online. *Degree requirements:* For doctorate, thesis/dissertation (for some programs), residency (for some programs), field experience (for some programs). *Entrance requirements:* For master's, bachelor's degree or equivalent in related field or RN; minimum GPA of 2.5; official transcripts; goal statement (for some programs); access to computer and Internet; for doctorate, master's degree or higher; RN; three years of related professional or academic experience; goal statement; access to computer and Internet; for Post-Master's Certificate, relevant work experience; access to computer and Internet. Additional exam requirements/recommendations for international students: Required—TOEFL (minimum score 550 paper-based, 79 iBT), IELTS (minimum score 6.5), Michigan English Language Assessment Battery (minimum score 82), or PTE (minimum score 53). Electronic applications accepted.

Walsh University, Graduate Programs, Gary and Linda Byers School of Nursing, North Canton, OH 44720-3396. Offers academic nurse educator (MSN); adult acute care nurse practitioner (MSN); clinical nurse leader (MSN); nursing practice (DNP). *Accreditation:* AACN. *Program availability:* Part-time, evening/weekend, online only, 100% online. *Degree requirements:* For doctorate, scholarly project; residency practicum. *Entrance requirements:* For master's, undergraduate nursing degree, current unencumbered RN license, completion of an undergraduate or graduate statistics course, essay, interview, recommendations; for doctorate, BSN; master's degree; statistics and research courses; essay; interview. Additional exam requirements/recommendations for international students: Required—TOEFL. Electronic applications accepted. *Expenses:* Contact institution. *Faculty research:* Self-efficacy, Newman theory, curriculum development and assessment on family nurse practitioner (FNP) practice, DNP online rubrics.

Washington Adventist University, Program in Nursing - Education, Takoma Park, MD 20912. Offers MS. *Program availability:* Part-time. *Students:* 13 full-time (12 women), 5 part-time (all women); includes 13 minority (9 Black or African American, non-Hispanic/Latino; 2 Asian, non-Hispanic/Latino; 1 Hispanic/Latino; 1 Two or more races, non-Hispanic/Latino), 5 international. Average age 46. In 2017, 1 master's awarded. *Entrance requirements:* Additional exam requirements/recommendations for international students: Required—TOEFL (minimum score 550 paper-based), IELTS (minimum score 5). *Application deadline:* Applications are processed on a rolling basis. *Expenses: Tuition:* Part-time $625 per credit. *Financial support:* Applicants required to submit FAFSA. *Unit head:* Dr. Patrick Williams, Associate Provost, 301-891-4116, E-mail: pawillia@wau.edu. *Application contact:* Jessica Ritchie, Program Coordinator, 301-891-4086, Fax: 301-891-4023, E-mail: jritchie@wau.edu.
Website: http://www.wau.edu/index.php?option-com_content&view-article&id-408temid-965

Waynesburg University, Graduate and Professional Studies, Canonsburg, PA 15370. Offers business (MBA), including energy management, finance, health systems, human resources, leadership, market development; counseling (MA), including addictions counseling, clinical mental health; counselor education and supervision (PhD); criminal investigation (MA); education (M Ed), including autism, curriculum and instruction, educational leadership, online teaching; nursing (MSN), including administration, education, informatics; nursing practice (DNP); special education (M Ed); technology (M Ed); MSN/MBA. *Accreditation:* AACN. *Program availability:* Part-time, evening/weekend. *Degree requirements:* For doctorate, thesis/dissertation. *Entrance requirements:* Additional exam requirements/recommendations for international students: Required—TOEFL. Electronic applications accepted.

Weber State University, Dumke College of Health Professions, School of Nursing, Ogden, UT 84408-1001. Offers educator (MSN); executive (MSN); nurse practitioner (MSN). *Program availability:* Part-time, evening/weekend, 100% online. *Faculty:* 11 full-time (all women), 3 part-time/adjunct (all women). *Students:* 88 full-time (70 women), 5 part-time (all women); includes 2 minority (both Hispanic/Latino), 1 international. Average age 38. In 2017, 29 master's awarded. *Entrance requirements:* For master's, bachelor's degree in nursing from ACEN- or CCNE-accredited program. *Application deadline:* For fall admission, 4/1 priority date for domestic students. Application fee: $60 ($90 for international students). Electronic applications accepted. *Expenses:* Tuition, state resident: full-time $7283. Tuition, nonresident: full-time $17,166. *Required fees:* $898. Tuition and fees vary according to program. *Financial support:* In 2017–18, 26 students received support. Scholarships/grants available. Financial award application deadline: 4/1; financial award applicants required to submit FAFSA. *Unit head:* Dr. Melissa Neville, MSN Program Director, 801-626-6204, Fax: 801-626-6397, E-mail: mneville@weber.edu. *Application contact:* Robert Holt, Director of Enrollment, 801-626-7774, Fax: 801-626-6397, E-mail: rholt@weber.edu.
Website: http://www.weber.edu/nursing

Webster University, College of Arts and Sciences, Department of Nursing, St. Louis, MO 63119-3194. Offers nurse educator (MSN). *Accreditation:* ACEN. *Degree requirements:* For master's, comprehensive exam. *Entrance requirements:* For master's, 1 year of clinical experience, BSN, interview, minimum C+ average in statistics and physical assessment, minimum GPA of 3.0, RN license. Additional exam requirements/recommendations for international students: Required—TOEFL. *Faculty research:* Health teaching.

West Chester University of Pennsylvania, College of Health Sciences, Department of Nursing, West Chester, PA 19383. Offers adult-gerontology clinical nurse specialist (MSN); nursing (DNP); nursing education (MSN); school nurse (Certificate). *Accreditation:* AACN. *Program availability:* Part-time, evening/weekend, 2-day on-campus residency requirement (for DNP). *Students:* 1 full-time (0 women), 102 part-time (94 women); includes 16 minority (12 Black or African American, non-Hispanic/Latino; 1 Asian, non-Hispanic/Latino; 2 Hispanic/Latino; 1 Two or more races, non-Hispanic/Latino). Average age 42. 57 applicants, 82% accepted, 38 enrolled. In 2017, 1 master's, 21 doctorates, 9 other advanced degrees awarded. *Entrance requirements:* For master's, goals statement; official academic transcript(s) from all colleges and universities attended, demonstrating minimum cumulative undergraduate GPA of 2.8, with successful completion of BSN and courses in statistics and physical assessment; documentation of current clinical experience and current RN; for doctorate, master's degree in nursing in an advanced nursing specialty, minimum master's GPA of 3.0, licensed Registered Nurse in state of practice, prerequisite graduate-level research

course and statistics course, two letters of reference, telephone or in-person interview with program coordinator. Additional exam requirements/recommendations for international students: Required—TOEFL or IELTS. *Application deadline:* For fall admission, 5/15 for international students; for spring admission, 10/15 for international students. Applications are processed on a rolling basis. Application fee: $50. Electronic applications accepted. *Expenses:* Tuition, state resident: full-time $9000; part-time $500 per credit. Tuition, nonresident: full-time $13,500; part-time $750 per credit. *Required fees:* $2959; $149.79 per credit. *Financial support:* Scholarships/grants and unspecified assistantships available. Financial award application deadline: 2/15; financial award applicants required to submit FAFSA. *Unit head:* Dr. Megan Infanti Mraz, Chair, 610-436-2219, Fax: 610-436-3083, E-mail: mmraz@wcupa.edu. *Application contact:* Dr. Cheryl Schlamb, Graduate Coordinator, 610-436-2219, E-mail: cschlamb@wcupa.edu.
Website: http://www.wcupa.edu/healthsciences/nursing/

Western Connecticut State University, Division of Graduate Studies, School of Professional Studies, Nursing Department, Ed D in Nursing Education Program, Danbury, CT 06810-6885. Offers Ed D. Offered in collaboration with Southern Connecticut State University. *Program availability:* Online learning. *Degree requirements:* For doctorate, thesis/dissertation. *Entrance requirements:* For doctorate, GRE or MAT, official transcripts, current copy of RN license, three letters of reference, curriculum vitae or resume, personal statement. *Expenses:* Tuition, state resident: full-time $6757; part-time $374 per credit hour. Tuition, nonresident: full-time $18,102; part-time $374 per credit hour. *Required fees:* $4994; $190 per credit hour. $60 per term. Tuition and fees vary according to degree level and program.

Western Governors University, College of Health Professions, Salt Lake City, UT 84107. Offers healthcare management (MBA); leadership and management (MSN); nursing education (MSN); nursing informatics (MSN). *Program availability:* Evening/weekend, online learning. *Degree requirements:* For master's, capstone project. *Entrance requirements:* For master's, transcripts. Additional exam requirements/recommendations for international students: Required—TOEFL (minimum score 450 paper-based; 80 iBT). *Application deadline:* Applications are processed on a rolling basis. Application fee: $65. Electronic applications accepted. Application fee is waived when completed online. *Financial support:* Tuition waivers (partial) available. Financial award applicants required to submit FAFSA. *Unit head:* Dr. Jan Jones-Schenk, Director. *Application contact:* Enrollment Department, 866-225-5948, Fax: 801-274-3306, E-mail: info@wgu.edu.
Website: https://www.wgu.edu/online-nursing-health-degrees.html#

West Virginia Wesleyan College, Department of Nursing, Buckhannon, WV 26201. Offers family nurse practitioner (MS, Post Master's Certificate); nurse administrator (MS); nurse educator (MS); nurse-midwifery (MS); nursing administration (Post Master's Certificate); nursing education (Post Master's Certificate); psychiatric mental health nurse practitioner (MS); MSN/MBA. *Accreditation:* ACEN.

William Paterson University of New Jersey, College of Science and Health, Wayne, NJ 07470-8420. Offers adult gerontology nurse practitioner (Certificate); biology (MS); biotechnology (MS); communication disorders (MS); exercise and sport studies (MS); materials chemistry (MS); nurse practitioner (Certificate); nursing (MSN); nursing education (Certificate); nursing practice (DNP); school nurse (Certificate). *Program availability:* Part-time. *Faculty:* 29 full-time (15 women), 25 part-time/adjunct (24 women). *Students:* 66 full-time (56 women), 197 part-time (163 women); includes 104 minority (15 Black or African American, non-Hispanic/Latino; 45 Asian, non-Hispanic/Latino; 38 Hispanic/Latino; 6 Two or more races, non-Hispanic/Latino), 3 international. Average age 33. 387 applicants, 34% accepted, 77 enrolled. In 2017, 87 master's, 5 doctorates awarded. *Degree requirements:* For master's, comprehensive exam (for some programs), thesis (for some programs), non-thesis internship/practicum (for some programs). *Entrance requirements:* For master's, GRE/MAT, minimum GPA of 3.0; 2-3 letters of recommendation; personal statement; work experience (for some programs); for doctorate, GRE/MAT, minimum GPA of 3.3; work experience; 3 letters of recommendation; interview; master's degree in nursing. Additional exam requirements/recommendations for international students: Required—TOEFL (minimum score 550 paper-based; 79 iBT), IELTS (minimum score 6). *Application deadline:* For fall admission, 6/1 for domestic students, 3/1 for international students; for spring admission, 11/1 for domestic students, 10/1 for international students. Applications are processed on a rolling basis. Application fee: $50. Electronic applications accepted. *Expenses:* Tuition, state resident: full-time $13,920; part-time $6264 per year. Tuition, nonresident: full-time $21,700; part-time $9765 per year. *Required fees:* $80; $36 per year. Tuition and fees vary according to course load, degree level and program. *Financial support:* In 2017–18, 9,800 students received support. Career-related internships or fieldwork, Federal Work-Study, scholarships/grants, and unspecified assistantships available. Support available to part-time students. Financial award application deadline: 3/15; financial award applicants required to submit FAFSA. *Faculty research:* Behaviors of American long-eared bats, postpartum fatigue, methodologies for coating carbon nano-tubes, paleoclimatology, and pre-linguistic gestures in children with language disorders. *Total annual research expenditures:* $291,600. *Unit head:* Dr. Venkat Sharma, Dean, 973-720-2194, Fax: 973-720-3414, E-mail: sharmav@wpunj.edu. *Application contact:* Christina Aiello, Assistant Director, Graduate Admissions, 973-720-2506, Fax: 973-720-2035, E-mail: aielloc@wpunj.edu.
Website: http://www.wpunj.edu/cosh

Wilson College, Graduate Programs, Chambersburg, PA 17201-1285. Offers accounting (M Acc); choreography and visual art (MFA); education (M Ed); educational technology (MET); healthcare administration (MHA); humanities (MA), including art and culture, critical/cultural theory, English language and literature, women's studies; management (MSM); nursing (MSN), including nursing education, nursing leadership and management; special education (MSE). *Program availability:* Evening/weekend. *Degree requirements:* For master's, project. *Entrance requirements:* For master's, PRAXIS, minimum undergraduate cumulative GPA of 3.0, 2 letters of recommendation, current certification for eligibility to teach in grades K-12, resume, personal interview. Electronic applications accepted.

Winona State University, College of Nursing and Health Sciences, Winona, MN 55987. Offers adult-gerontology acute care nurse practitioner (MS, DNP, Post Master's Certificate); adult-gerontology clinical nurse specialist (MS, DNP, Post Master's Certificate); adult-gerontology primary care nurse practitioner (MS, DNP, Post Master's Certificate); family nurse practitioner (MS, DNP, Post Master's Certificate); nurse educator (MS); nursing and organizational leadership (MS, DNP, Post Master's Certificate); practice and leadership innovations (DNP, Post Master's Certificate). *Accreditation:* AACN. *Program availability:* Part-time, online learning. *Degree requirements:* For master's, thesis; for doctorate, capstone. *Entrance requirements:* For master's, GRE (if GPA less than 3.0). Additional exam requirements/recommendations for international students: Required—TOEFL (minimum score 550 paper-based).

Winston-Salem State University, Program in Nursing, Winston-Salem, NC 27110-0003. Offers advanced nurse educator (MSN); family nurse practitioner (MSN); nursing (DNP). *Accreditation:* AACN. *Program availability:* Part-time, evening/weekend, online learning. *Entrance requirements:* For master's, GRE, MAT, resume, NC or state compact license, 3 letters of recommendation. Electronic applications accepted. *Faculty research:* Elimination of health care disparities.

Worcester State University, Graduate School, Department of Nursing, Program in Nurse Educator, Worcester, MA 01602-2597. Offers MSN. *Accreditation:* AACN. *Program availability:* Part-time. *Students:* 39 part-time (37 women); includes 8 minority (4 Black or African American, non-Hispanic/Latino; 3 Hispanic/Latino; 1 Two or more races, non-Hispanic/Latino). Average age 42. 14 applicants, 79% accepted, 5 enrolled. In 2017, 7 master's awarded. *Degree requirements:* For master's, practicum. *Entrance requirements:* For master's, unencumbered license to practice as a Registered Nurse in Massachusetts. Additional exam requirements/recommendations for international students: Required—TOEFL (minimum score 550 paper-based; 79 iBT). *Application deadline:* For fall admission, 6/15 for domestic and international students; for spring admission, 11/1 for domestic and international students; for summer admission, 4/1 for domestic and international students. Applications are processed on a rolling basis. Application fee: $50. Electronic applications accepted. *Expenses:* Tuition, state resident: full-time $3042; part-time $169 per credit hour. Tuition, nonresident: full-time $3042; part-time $169 per credit hour. *Required fees:* $2754; $153 per credit hour. *Financial support:* Career-related internships or fieldwork, scholarships/grants, and unspecified assistantships available. Financial award application deadline: 3/1; financial award applicants required to submit FAFSA. *Unit head:* Dr. Stephanie Chalupka, Program Coordinator, 508-929-8680, E-mail: schalupka@worcester.edu. *Application contact:* Sara Grady, Associate Dean of Graduate Studies and Professional Development, 508-929-8130, Fax: 508-929-8100, E-mail: sara.grady@worcester.edu.

Nursing Informatics

Allen College, Graduate Programs, Waterloo, IA 50703. Offers adult-gerontology acute care nurse practitioner (MSN); community/public health nursing (MSN); education (MSN); family nurse practitioner (MSN); health sciences (Ed D); leadership in health care delivery (MSN); leadership in health care informatics (MSN); nursing (DNP); occupational therapy (MS); psychiatric mental health nurse practitioner (MSN). MSN in leadership in healthcare informatics offered in partnership with University of Minnesota. *Accreditation:* AACN; ACEN. *Program availability:* Part-time, 100% online, blended/hybrid learning. *Faculty:* 24 full-time (all women), 8 part-time/adjunct (7 women). *Students:* 106 full-time (91 women), 187 part-time (164 women); includes 22 minority (12 Black or African American, non-Hispanic/Latino; 1 American Indian or Alaska Native, non-Hispanic/Latino; 2 Asian, non-Hispanic/Latino; 3 Hispanic/Latino; 4 Two or more races, non-Hispanic/Latino), 2 international. Average age 33. 352 applicants, 56% accepted, 131 enrolled. In 2017, 73 master's, 2 doctorates awarded. *Entrance requirements:* For master's, minimum GPA of 3.0 in the last 60 hours of undergraduate coursework; for doctorate, minimum GPA of 3.25 in graduate coursework. *Application deadline:* For fall admission, 2/1 priority date for domestic students; for spring admission, 9/1 priority date for domestic students. Applications are processed on a rolling basis. Application fee: $50. Electronic applications accepted. *Expenses:* $17,860 per year. *Financial support:* In 2017–18, 97 students received support. Federal Work-Study, institutionally sponsored loans, scholarships/grants, and traineeships available. Support available to part-time students. Financial award application deadline: 8/1; financial award applicants required to submit FAFSA. *Faculty research:* Poverty. *Unit head:* Dr. Nancy Kramer, Vice Chancellor for Academic Affairs, 319-226-2040, Fax: 319-226-2070, E-mail: nancy.kramer@allencollege.edu. *Application contact:* Molly Quinn, Director of Admissions, 319-226-2001, Fax: 319-226-2010, E-mail: molly.quinn@allencollege.edu.
Website: http://www.allencollege.edu/

Aspen University, Program in Nursing, Denver, CO 80246-1930. Offers forensic nursing (MSN); informatics (MSN); nursing (MSN); nursing administration and management (MSN); nursing education (MSN); public health (MSN).

Austin Peay State University, College of Graduate Studies, College of Behavioral and Health Sciences, School of Nursing, Clarksville, TN 37044. Offers family nurse practitioner (MSN); nursing administration (MSN); nursing education (MSN); nursing informatics (MSN). *Program availability:* Part-time, online learning. *Faculty:* 8 full-time (all women), 8 part-time/adjunct (all women). *Students:* 12 full-time (11 women), 139 part-time (128 women); includes 19 minority (11 Black or African American, non-Hispanic/Latino; 1 Asian, non-Hispanic/Latino; 5 Hispanic/Latino; 2 Two or more races, non-Hispanic/Latino). Average age 35. 36 applicants, 86% accepted, 20 enrolled. In 2017, 67 master's awarded. *Degree requirements:* For master's, comprehensive exam. *Entrance requirements:* For master's, minimum GPA of 3.0, RN license eligibility, 3 letters of recommendation. Additional exam requirements/recommendations for international students: Required—TOEFL (minimum score 500 paper-based). *Application deadline:* For fall admission, 8/8 priority date for domestic students. Applications are processed on a rolling basis. Application fee: $45 ($55 for international students). Electronic applications accepted. *Expenses:* Tuition, state resident: full-time $7686; part-time $427 per credit hour. Tuition, nonresident: full-time $20,268; part-time $1126 per credit hour. *Required fees:* $1529; $76.45 per credit hour. *Financial support:* Research assistantships with full tuition reimbursements, career-related internships or fieldwork, Federal Work-Study, institutionally sponsored loans, scholarships/grants, and unspecified assistantships available. Support available to part-time students. Financial award application deadline: 4/1; financial award applicants required to submit FAFSA. *Unit head:* Dr. Rebecca Corvey, Director of Nursing, 931-221-7710, Fax: 931-221-7595, E-mail: corveyr@apsu.edu. *Application contact:* Megan Mitchell, Coordinator of Graduate Admissions, 931-221-6189, Fax: 931-221-7641, E-mail: mitchellm@apsu.edu.
Website: http://www.apsu.edu/nursing

Columbus State University, Graduate Studies, College of Education and Health Professions, School of Nursing, Columbus, GA 31907-5645. Offers family nurse practitioner (MSN); nursing (MSN), including nurse educator, nurse informatics, nurse leader. Program offered in collaboration with Georgia Southwestern StateUniversity. *Program availability:* Part-time, online only, 100% online. *Faculty:* 7 full-time (all women), 2 part-time/adjunct (both women). *Students:* 43 full-time (40 women), 134 part-time (121

women); includes 88 minority (65 Black or African American, non-Hispanic/Latino; 7 Asian, non-Hispanic/Latino; 10 Hispanic/Latino; 6 Two or more races, non-Hispanic/Latino). Average age 35. 141 applicants, 49% accepted, 12 enrolled. In 2017, 28 master's awarded. *Entrance requirements:* For master's, GRE, BSN, minimum undergraduate GPA of 3.0. Additional exam requirements/recommendations for international students: Required—TOEFL (minimum score 550 paper-based; 79 iBT). *Application deadline:* For fall admission, 5/1 for domestic and international students; for spring admission, 11/1 for domestic and international students; for summer admission, 3/1 for domestic and international students. Applications are processed on a rolling basis. Application fee: $50. Electronic applications accepted. *Expenses:* Contact institution. *Financial support:* In 2017–18, 3 students received support. Institutionally sponsored loans available. Financial award application deadline: 5/1; financial award applicants required to submit FAFSA. *Unit head:* Latonya Santo, Director, 706-507-8576, E-mail: santo_latonya@columbusstate.edu. *Application contact:* Catrina Smith-Edmond, Assistant Director for Graduate and Global Admission, 706-507-8824, Fax: 706-568-5091, E-mail: smithedmond_catrina@columbusstate.edu.
Website: http://nursing.columbusstate.edu/

Duke University, School of Nursing, Durham, NC 27708-0586. Offers acute care pediatric nurse practitioner (MSN, Post-Graduate Certificate); adult-gerontology nurse practitioner (MSN, Post-Graduate Certificate), including acute care, primary care; family nurse practitioner (MSN, Post-Graduate Certificate); neonatal nurse practitioner (MSN, Post-Graduate Certificate); nurse anesthesia (DNP); nurse practitioner (DNP); nursing (PhD); nursing and health care leadership (MSN, Post-Graduate Certificate); nursing education (MSN, Post-Graduate Certificate); nursing informatics (MSN, Post-Graduate Certificate); pediatric nurse practitioner (MSN, Post-Graduate Certificate), including primary care; psychiatric mental health nurse practitioner (MSN, Post-Graduate Certificate); women's health nurse practitioner (MSN, Post-Graduate Certificate). *Accreditation:* AACN; AANA/CANAEP. *Program availability:* Part-time, evening/weekend, online with on-campus intensives. *Faculty:* 72 full-time (61 women). *Students:* 155 full-time (137 women), 613 part-time (548 women); includes 177 minority (64 Black or African American, non-Hispanic/Latino; 2 American Indian or Alaska Native, non-Hispanic/Latino; 47 Asian, non-Hispanic/Latino; 34 Hispanic/Latino; 30 Two or more races, non-Hispanic/Latino), 10 international. Average age 34. 631 applicants, 47% accepted, 211 enrolled. In 2017, 221 master's, 71 doctorates, 26 other advanced degrees awarded. Terminal master's awarded for partial completion of doctoral program. *Degree requirements:* For master's, thesis optional; for doctorate, capstone project. *Entrance requirements:* For master's, GRE General Test (waived if undergraduate GPA of 3.4 or higher), 1 year of nursing experience (recommended), BSN, minimum GPA of 3.0, previous course work in statistics; for doctorate, GRE General Test (waived if undergraduate GPA of 3.4 or higher), BSN or MSN, minimum GPA of 3.0, resume, personal statement, undergraduate statistics course, current licensure as a registered nurse, transcripts from all post-secondary institutions; for Post-Graduate Certificate, MSN, licensure or eligibility as a professional nurse, transcripts from all post-secondary institutions, previous course work in statistics. Additional exam requirements/recommendations for international students: Required—TOEFL (minimum score 100 iBT), IELTS (minimum score 7). *Application deadline:* For fall admission, 12/1 for domestic and international students; for spring admission, 5/1 for domestic and international students. Application fee: $50. Electronic applications accepted. *Expenses:* Contact institution. *Financial support:* Institutionally sponsored loans, scholarships/grants, and traineeships available. Support available to part-time students. Financial award applicants required to submit FAFSA. *Faculty research:* Cardiovascular disease, caregiver skill training, data mining, prostate cancer, neonatal immune system. *Unit head:* Dr. Marion E. Broome, Dean/Vice Chancellor for Nursing Affairs/Associate Vice President for Academic Affairs for Nursing, 919-684-9446, Fax: 919-684-9414, E-mail: marion.broome@duke.edu. *Application contact:* Dr. Ernie Rushing, Director of Admissions and Recruitment, 919-668-6274, Fax: 919-668-4693, E-mail: ernie.rushing@dm.duke.edu.
Website: http://www.nursing.duke.edu/

Excelsior College, School of Nursing, Albany, NY 12203-5159. Offers nursing (MS); nursing education (MS); nursing informatics (MS); nursing leadership and administration of health care systems (MS). *Accreditation:* ACEN. *Program availability:* Part-time, evening/weekend, online learning. *Faculty:* 12 part-time/adjunct (9 women). *Students:* 388 part-time (313 women); includes 122 minority (63 Black or African American, non-Hispanic/Latino; 4 American Indian or Alaska Native, non-Hispanic/Latino; 18 Asian, non-Hispanic/Latino; 28 Hispanic/Latino; 2 Native Hawaiian or other Pacific Islander, non-Hispanic/Latino; 7 Two or more races, non-Hispanic/Latino). Average age 44. In 2017, 173 master's awarded. *Entrance requirements:* For master's, RN license. *Application deadline:* Applications are processed on a rolling basis. Application fee: $50. Electronic applications accepted. *Expenses: Tuition:* Part-time $645 per credit. *Required fees:* $265 per credit. *Financial support:* Scholarships/grants available. *Unit head:* Dr. Mary Lee Pollard, Dean, School of Nursing, 518-464-8500, Fax: 518-464-8777, E-mail: msn@excelsior.edu. *Application contact:* Admissions Counselor, 888-647-2388, Fax: 518-464-8777, E-mail: gradadmissions@excelsior.edu.
Website: http://www.excelsior.edu/programs/nursing

Ferris State University, College of Health Professions, School of Nursing, Big Rapids, MI 49307. Offers nursing (MSN); nursing administration (MSN); nursing education (MSN); nursing informatics (MSN). *Accreditation:* ACEN. *Program availability:* Part-time, evening/weekend, online only, 100% online. *Faculty:* 7 full-time (all women), 2 part-time/adjunct (both women). *Students:* 3 full-time (all women), 104 part-time (95 women); includes 15 minority (3 Black or African American, non-Hispanic/Latino; 5 American Indian or Alaska Native, non-Hispanic/Latino; 2 Asian, non-Hispanic/Latino; 3 Hispanic/Latino; 1 Native Hawaiian or other Pacific Islander, non-Hispanic/Latino; 1 Two or more races, non-Hispanic/Latino). Average age 40. 36 applicants, 92% accepted, 31 enrolled. In 2017, 25 master's awarded. *Degree requirements:* For master's, practicum, practicum project. *Entrance requirements:* For master's, BS in nursing (for nursing education track); BS in nursing or related field (for nursing administration and nursing informatics tracks); registered nurse license, writing sample, letters of reference, 2 years' clinical experience (recommended). Additional exam requirements/recommendations for international students: Required—TOEFL (minimum score 550 paper-based; 61 iBT). *Application deadline:* For fall admission, 4/15 priority date for domestic students; for spring admission, 10/15 for domestic students. Application fee: $0. Electronic applications accepted. *Financial support:* In 2017–18, 3 students received support. Career-related internships or fieldwork and scholarships/grants available. Financial award application deadline: 4/15; financial award applicants required to submit FAFSA. *Faculty research:* Nursing education, end of life, leadership/education introverts in nursing, complementary and alternative medicine therapies. *Unit head:* Dr. Susan Owens, Chair, School of Nursing, 231-591-2267, Fax: 231-591-2325, E-mail: owenss3@ferris.edu. *Application contact:* Sharon Colley, MSN Program Coordinator, 231-591-2288, Fax: 231-591-2325, E-mail: colleys@ferris.edu.
Website: http://www.ferris.edu/htmls/colleges/alliedhe/Nursing/homepage.htm

Georgia Southwestern State University, College of Nursing and Health Sciences, Americus, GA 31709-4693. Offers family nurse practitioner (MSN); health informatics (Postbaccalaureate Certificate); nurse educator (Post Master's Certificate); nursing educator (MSN); nursing informatics (MSN); nursing leadership (MSN). MSN program offered by the Georgia Intercollegiate Consortium for Graduate Nursing Education, a partnership with Columbus State University. *Program availability:* Part-time, online only, all theory courses are offered online. *Faculty:* 10 full-time, 5 part-time/adjunct. *Students:* 23 full-time (22 women), 106 part-time (92 women); includes 41 minority (all Black or African American, non-Hispanic/Latino). Average age 35. 95 applicants, 63% accepted, 30 enrolled. In 2017, 17 master's awarded. *Degree requirements:* For master's, comprehensive exam (for some programs), thesis (for some programs), minimum cumulative GPA of 3.0; maximum of 6 credit hours with C grade and no D grades; degree completed within 7 calendar years from initial enrollment date in graduate courses; for other advanced degree, minimum cumulative GPA of 3.0; maximum of 6 credit hours with C grade and no D grades; degree completed within 7 calendar years from initial enrollment date in graduate courses. *Entrance requirements:* For master's and other advanced degree, baccalaureate degree in nursing from regionally-accredited institution and nationally-accredited nursing program with minimum GPA of 3.0; three professional letters of recommendation; current unencumbered RN license in state where clinical course requirements will be met; background check/drug test; proof of immunizations. *Application deadline:* For fall admission, 1/15 for domestic students; for spring admission, 10/15 for domestic students. Application fee: $25. Electronic applications accepted. *Expenses:* $385 per credit hour, plus fees, which vary according to enrolled credit hours. *Financial support:* Application deadline: 6/1; applicants required to submit FAFSA. *Unit head:* Dr. Sandra Daniel, Dean, 229-931-2275. *Application contact:* Whitney Ford, Admissions Specialist, Office of Graduate Admissions, 800-338-0082, Fax: 229-931-2983, E-mail: graduateadmissions@gsw.edu.
Website: https://gsw.edu/Academics/Schools-and-Departments/School-of-Nursing/index

Georgia State University, Byrdine F. Lewis School of Nursing, Atlanta, GA 30303. Offers adult health clinical nurse specialist/nurse practitioner (MS, Certificate); child health clinical nurse specialist/pediatric nurse practitioner (MS, Certificate); family nurse practitioner (MS, Certificate); family psychiatric mental health nurse practitioner (MS, Certificate); nursing (PhD); nursing leadership in healthcare innovations (MS), including nursing administration, nursing informatics; nutrition (MS); perinatal clinical nurse specialist/women's health nurse practitioner (MS, Certificate); physical therapy (DPT); respiratory therapy (MS). *Accreditation:* AACN. *Program availability:* Part-time, blended/hybrid learning. *Faculty:* 69 full-time (52 women). *Students:* 322 full-time (248 women), 481 part-time (466 women); includes 186 minority (112 Black or African American, non-Hispanic/Latino; 44 Asian, non-Hispanic/Latino; 20 Hispanic/Latino; 10 Two or more races, non-Hispanic/Latino), 18 international. Average age 31. 370 applicants, 56% accepted, 148 enrolled. In 2017, 131 master's, 49 doctorates, 11 other advanced degrees awarded. *Degree requirements:* For doctorate, comprehensive exam, thesis/dissertation. *Entrance requirements:* For doctorate, GRE. Additional exam requirements/recommendations for international students: Required—TOEFL. *Application deadline:* For fall admission, 2/1 priority date for domestic and international students; for spring admission, 9/15 for domestic and international students. Applications are processed on a rolling basis. Application fee: $50. Electronic applications accepted. *Expenses:* Contact institution. *Financial support:* In 2017–18, research assistantships with tuition reimbursements (averaging $1,666 per year), teaching assistantships with tuition reimbursements (averaging $1,920 per year) were awarded; scholarships/grants, tuition waivers (full and partial), and unspecified assistantships also available. Support available to part-time students. Financial award application deadline: 8/1; financial award applicants required to submit FAFSA. *Faculty research:* Stroke intervention for caregivers, stroke prevention in African-Americans; relationships between psychological distress and health outcomes in parents with a medically ill infant; medically fragile children; nursing expertise and patient outcomes. *Unit head:* Nancy Kropf, Dean of Nursing, 404-413-1101, Fax: 404-413-1090, E-mail: nkropf@gsu.edu.
Website: http://nursing.gsu.edu/

Grantham University, College of Nursing and Allied Health, Lenexa, KS 66219. Offers case management (MSN); health systems management (MS); healthcare administration (MHA); nursing education (MSN); nursing informatics (MSN); nursing management and organizational leadership (MSN). *Program availability:* Part-time, evening/weekend, online only, 100% online. *Faculty:* 2 full-time, 34 part-time/adjunct. *Students:* 198 full-time (144 women), 113 part-time (83 women); includes 170 minority (118 Black or African American, non-Hispanic/Latino; 3 American Indian or Alaska Native, non-Hispanic/Latino; 27 Asian, non-Hispanic/Latino; 11 Hispanic/Latino; 2 Native Hawaiian or other Pacific Islander, non-Hispanic/Latino; 9 Two or more races, non-Hispanic/Latino). Average age 41. 95 applicants, 89% accepted, 72 enrolled. In 2017, 123 master's awarded. *Entrance requirements:* For master's, BSN from state-approved nursing program with minimum cumulative GPA of 2.5 from institution accredited by agency recognized by U.S. DOE or foreign equivalent; unencumbered and current RN license. Additional exam requirements/recommendations for international students: Required—TOEFL (minimum score 530 paper-based; 71 iBT), IELTS (minimum score 6.5), PTE (minimum score 50). *Application deadline:* Applications are processed on a rolling basis. Application fee: $0. Electronic applications accepted. *Expenses:* $325 per credit hour. *Financial support:* Scholarships/grants available. Financial award applicants required to submit FAFSA. *Faculty research:* Compassion in caring improving incivility in the ICU setting, get well network technology in enhancing patient education, opioid use and abuse in postpartum women. *Unit head:* Dr. Cheryl Rules, Dean of the College of Nursing and Allied Health, 913-309-4783, Fax: 844-897-6490, E-mail: crules@grantham.edu. *Application contact:* Jared Parlette, Vice President of Student Enrollment, 800-955-2527 Ext. 803, Fax: 866-914-4557, E-mail: admissions@grantham.edu.
Website: http://www.grantham.edu/nursing-and-allied-health/

Holy Names University, Graduate Division, Department of Nursing, Oakland, CA 94619-1699. Offers administration/management (MSN, PMC); care transition management (MSN); family nurse practitioner (MSN, PMC); informatics (MSN); nurse educator (PMC); MSN/MBA. *Accreditation:* AACN. *Program availability:* Part-time, evening/weekend. *Entrance requirements:* For master's, bachelor's degree in nursing or related field; California RN license or eligibility; minimum cumulative GPA of 2.8, 3.0 in nursing courses from baccalaureate program; courses in pathophysiology, statistics, and research at the undergraduate level. Additional exam requirements/recommendations for international students: Required—TOEFL (minimum score 500 paper-based; 79 iBT). Electronic applications accepted. Application fee is waived when completed online. *Faculty research:* Women's reproductive health, gerontology, attitudes about aging, schizophrenic families, international health issues.

Jacksonville University, Brooks Rehabilitation College of Healthcare Sciences, Keigwin School of Nursing, Master of Science in Nursing Program, Jacksonville, FL 32211. Offers clinical nurse educator (MSN); family nurse practitioner (MSN); family nurse practitioner/emergency nurse practitioner (MSN); leadership in the healthcare system (MSN); nursing informatics (MSN); psychiatric nurse practitioner (MSN); MSN/MBA. *Program availability:* Part-time, 100% online, blended/hybrid learning. *Faculty:* 8 full-time (all women), 8 part-time/adjunct (6 women). *Students:* 41 full-time (36 women), 456 part-time (415 women); includes 169 minority (102 Black or African American, non-Hispanic/Latino; 4 American Indian or Alaska Native, non-Hispanic/Latino; 24 Asian, non-Hispanic/Latino; 33 Hispanic/Latino; 1 Native Hawaiian or other Pacific Islander, non-Hispanic/Latino; 5 Two or more races, non-Hispanic/Latino), 1 international.

Average age 39. 232 applicants, 59% accepted, 110 enrolled. In 2017, 87 master's awarded. *Degree requirements:* For master's, thesis. *Entrance requirements:* For master's, GRE General Test or undergraduate GPA above 3.0, BSN from ACEN- or CCNE-accredited program; course work in statistics and physical assessment within last 5 years; Florida nursing license; CPR/BLS certification; 3 recommendations, 2 of which are professional references; statement of intent; resume. Additional exam requirements/ recommendations for international students: Required—TOEFL (minimum score 650 paper-based; 114 iBT), IELTS (minimum score 8). *Application deadline:* For fall admission, 2/1 for domestic and international students. Applications are processed on a rolling basis. Application fee: $50. Electronic applications accepted. *Expenses:* $620 per credit hour, $455 per credit hour off-campus, $720 per credit hour online. *Financial support:* Federal Work-Study, institutionally sponsored loans, scholarships/grants, and health care benefits available. Support available to part-time students. Financial award application deadline: 3/15; financial award applicants required to submit FAFSA. *Faculty research:* Treatment of anxiety. *Unit head:* Dr. Hilary Morgan, Director, Graduate Nursing Programs/Associate Professor, 904-256-7601, E-mail: hmorgan@ju.edu. *Application contact:* Stephanie Bloom, Assistant Director, Enrollment and Advanced Graduate Nursing, 904-256-7286, E-mail: sstrick4@ju.edu.
Website: https://www.ju.edu/nursing/graduate/master-science-nursing/index.php

Le Moyne College, Department of Nursing, Syracuse, NY 13214. Offers family nurse practitioner (MS, CAS); informatics (MS, CAS); nursing administration (MS, CAS); nursing education (MS, CAS). *Accreditation:* AACN. *Program availability:* Part-time, evening/weekend. *Faculty:* 3 full-time (all women), 5 part-time/adjunct (all women). *Students:* 27 full-time (20 women), 51 part-time (47 women); includes 10 minority (4 Black or African American, non-Hispanic/Latino; 1 Asian, non-Hispanic/Latino; 4 Hispanic/Latino; 1 Two or more races, non-Hispanic/Latino). Average age 32. 39 applicants, 95% accepted, 31 enrolled. In 2017, 20 master's, 2 other advanced degrees awarded. *Degree requirements:* For master's, scholarly project. *Entrance requirements:* For master's, bachelor's degree, interview, minimum GPA of 3.0, New York RN license, 2 letters of recommendation, writing sample, transcripts. *Application deadline:* For fall admission, 8/1 priority date for domestic students, 8/1 for international students; for spring admission, 12/15 priority date for domestic students, 12/15 for international students; for summer admission, 5/1 priority date for domestic students, 5/1 for international students. Applications are processed on a rolling basis. Application fee: $50. Electronic applications accepted. *Expenses:* $700 per credit hour. *Financial support:* In 2017–18, 2 students received support. Career-related internships or fieldwork, scholarships/grants, health care benefits, and unspecified assistantships available. Support available to part-time students. Financial award applicants required to submit FAFSA. *Faculty research:* Inter-profession education, gerontology, utilization of free healthcare services by the insured, health promotion education, innovative undergraduate nursing education models, patient and family education, horizontal violence. *Unit head:* Dr. Margaret M. Wells, Professor/Chair of Nursing, 315-445-5435, Fax: 315-445-6024, E-mail: wellsmm@lemoyne.edu. *Application contact:* Kristen P. Richards, Senior Director of Enrollment Management, 315-445-5444, Fax: 315-445-6092, E-mail: trapaskp@lemoyne.edu.
Website: http://www.lemoyne.edu/nursing

Liberty University, School of Nursing, Lynchburg, VA 24515. Offers family nurse practitioner (DNP); nurse educator (MSN); nursing administration (MSN); nursing informatics (MSN). *Accreditation:* AACN. *Program availability:* Part-time, online learning. *Students:* 148 full-time (131 women), 461 part-time (421 women); includes 103 minority (58 Black or African American, non-Hispanic/Latino; 4 American Indian or Alaska Native, non-Hispanic/Latino; 15 Asian, non-Hispanic/Latino; 11 Hispanic/Latino; 3 Native Hawaiian or other Pacific Islander, non-Hispanic/Latino; 12 Two or more races, non-Hispanic/Latino), 8 international. Average age 39. 536 applicants, 30% accepted, 105 enrolled. In 2017, 100 master's, 13 doctorates awarded. *Entrance requirements:* For master's, minimum cumulative undergraduate GPA of 3.0; for doctorate, minimum GPA of 3.25 in most current nursing program completed. Additional exam requirements/ recommendations for international students: Recommended—TOEFL. *Application deadline:* Applications are processed on a rolling basis. Application fee: $50. Electronic applications accepted. *Financial support:* Applicants required to submit FAFSA. *Unit head:* Dr. Deanna Britt, Dean, 434-582-2519, E-mail: dbritt@liberty.edu. *Application contact:* Jay Bridge, Director of Admissions, 800-424-9595, Fax: 800-628-7977, E-mail: gradadmissions@liberty.edu.

National American University, Roueche Graduate Center, Austin, TX 78731. Offers accounting (MBA); aviation management (MBA, MM); care coordination (MSN); community college leadership (Ed D); criminal justice (MM); e-marketing (MBA, MM); health care administration (MBA, MM); higher education (MM); human resources management (MBA, MM); information technology management (MBA, MM); international business (MBA); leadership (EMBA); management (MBA); nursing administration (MSN); nursing education (MSN); nursing informatics (MSN); operations and configuration management (MBA, MM); project and process management (MBA, MM). Master's programs offered online through the Harold D. Buckingham Graduate School. *Program availability:* Part-time, evening/weekend, online learning. *Entrance requirements:* For master's, minimum undergraduate GPA of 2.75. Additional exam requirements/recommendations for international students: Required—TOEFL, TWE. Electronic applications accepted. *Faculty research:* Tourism, finance, marketing.

National University, School of Health and Human Services, La Jolla, CA 92037-1011. Offers clinical affairs (MS); clinical regulatory affairs (MS); complementary and integrative healthcare (MS); family nurse practitioner (MSN); health and life science analytics (MS); health informatics (MS, Certificate); healthcare administration (MHA); nurse anesthesia (MSNA); nursing administration (MSN); nursing informatics (MSN); psychiatric-mental health nurse practitioner (MSN); public health (MPH), including health promotion, healthcare administration, mental health. *Program availability:* Part-time, evening/weekend, 100% online, blended/hybrid learning. *Degree requirements:* For master's, thesis (for some programs). *Entrance requirements:* For master's, interview, minimum GPA of 2.5. Additional exam requirements/recommendations for international students: Required—TOEFL (minimum score 550 paper-based; 79 iBT), IELTS (minimum score 6). *Application deadline:* Applications are processed on a rolling basis. Application fee: $60 ($65 for international students). Electronic applications accepted. *Expenses: Tuition:* Part-time $430 per quarter hour. *Financial support:* Career-related internships or fieldwork, institutionally sponsored loans, scholarships/grants, and tuition waivers (partial) available. Support available to part-time students. Financial award application deadline: 6/30; financial award applicants required to submit FAFSA. *Faculty research:* Nursing education, obesity prevention, workforce diversity. *Unit head:* Dr. Gloria J. McNeal, Dean, 858-309-3473, E-mail: shhs@nu.edu. *Application contact:* Brandon Jouganatos, Vice President for Enrollment Services, 800-628-8648, E-mail: advisor@nu.edu.
Website: http://www.nu.edu/OurPrograms/SchoolOfHealthAndHumanServices.html

New York University, Rory Meyers College of Nursing, Programs in Advanced Practice Nursing, New York, NY 10012-1019. Offers adult-gerontology acute care nurse practitioner (MS, Advanced Certificate); adult-gerontology primary care nurse practitioner (MS, Advanced Certificate); family nurse practitioner (MS, Advanced Certificate); gerontology nurse practitioner (Advanced Certificate); nurse-midwifery (MS, Advanced Certificate); nursing administration (MS, Advanced Certificate); nursing education (MS, Advanced Certificate); nursing informatics (MS, Advanced Certificate); pediatrics nurse practitioner (MS, Advanced Certificate); psychiatric-mental health nurse practitioner (MS, Advanced Certificate); MS/MPH. *Accreditation:* AACN; ACNM/ACME. *Program availability:* Part-time, evening/weekend. *Faculty:* 23 full-time (all women), 62 part-time/adjunct (56 women). *Students:* 50 full-time (46 women), 557 part-time (509 women); includes 234 minority (58 Black or African American, non-Hispanic/Latino; 1 American Indian or Alaska Native, non-Hispanic/Latino; 116 Asian, non-Hispanic/Latino; 43 Hispanic/Latino; 1 Native Hawaiian or other Pacific Islander, non-Hispanic/Latino; 15 Two or more races, non-Hispanic/Latino), 23 international. Average age 32. 391 applicants, 59% accepted, 149 enrolled. In 2017, 187 master's, 5 other advanced degrees awarded. *Degree requirements:* For master's, thesis (for some programs), capstone. *Entrance requirements:* For master's, BS in nursing, AS in nursing with another BS/BA, interview, RN license, 1 year of clinical experience (3 for the MS in nursing education program); for Advanced Certificate, master's degree in nursing. Additional exam requirements/recommendations for international students: Required—TOEFL (minimum score 100 iBT), IELTS (minimum score 7). *Application deadline:* For fall admission, 3/1 priority date for domestic and international students; for spring admission, 11/1 priority date for domestic and international students; for summer admission, 3/1 for domestic and international students. Application fee: $80. Electronic applications accepted. *Expenses:* Contact institution. *Financial support:* In 2017–18, 130 students received support. Career-related internships or fieldwork, Federal Work-Study, and scholarships/grants available. Support available to part-time students. Financial award application deadline: 3/1; financial award applicants required to submit FAFSA. *Faculty research:* Vaccine hesitancy in pregnant women and mothers, palliative care and midwifery, diabetes education, curriculum development, workforce training, education and development, geriatrics. *Unit head:* Dr. James Pace, Senior Associate Dean for Academic Programs, 212-992-7343, E-mail: james.pace@nyu.edu. *Application contact:* Matthew Burke, Assistant Director, Graduate Student Affairs and Admissions, 212-998-7397, Fax: 212-995-4302, E-mail: mb6060@nyu.edu.

Nova Southeastern University, Ron and Kathy Assaf College of Nursing, Fort Lauderdale, FL 33314-7796. Offers advanced practice registered nurse (MSN), including adult-gerontology acute care nurse practitioner, family nurse practitioner, psychiatric mental health nurse practitioner; executive nurse leadership (MSN); nursing (PhD), including nursing education; nursing education (MSN); nursing informatics (MSN); nursing practice (DNP). *Accreditation:* AACN. *Program availability:* Part-time, evening/weekend, 100% online, blended/hybrid learning, annual one-week summer institute delivered face-to-face on main campus. *Faculty:* 9 full-time (all women), 47 part-time/adjunct (43 women). *Students:* 658 full-time (599 women); includes 414 minority (175 Black or African American, non-Hispanic/Latino; 37 Asian, non-Hispanic/Latino; 179 Hispanic/Latino; 1 Native Hawaiian or other Pacific Islander, non-Hispanic/Latino; 22 Two or more races, non-Hispanic/Latino), 3 international. Average age 38. 179 applicants, 100% accepted, 163 enrolled. In 2017, 161 master's, 16 doctorates awarded. *Degree requirements:* For doctorate, comprehensive exam, thesis/ dissertation. *Entrance requirements:* For master's, minimum GPA of 3.0, RN, BSN, BS or BA; for doctorate, minimum GPA of 3.5, MSN, RN. Additional exam requirements/ recommendations for international students: Recommended—TOEFL. *Application deadline:* For fall admission, 3/1 priority date for domestic students, 3/1 for international students; for winter admission, 11/1 for domestic and international students. Applications are processed on a rolling basis. Application fee: $50. Electronic applications accepted. *Expenses:* Contact institution. *Financial support:* Application deadline: 4/15; applicants required to submit FAFSA. *Faculty research:* Nursing education, curriculum, clinical research, interdisciplinary research. *Total annual research expenditures:* $9,500. *Unit head:* Dr. Marcella M. Rutherford, Dean, 954-262-1963, E-mail: rmarcell@nova.edu. *Application contact:* Dianna Murphey, Director of Operations, 954-262-1975, E-mail: dgardner1@nova.edu.
Website: http://www.nova.edu/nursing/

Roberts Wesleyan College, Department of Nursing, Rochester, NY 14624-1997. Offers nursing education (MSN); nursing informatics (MSN); nursing leadership and administration (MSN). *Accreditation:* AACN. *Program availability:* Evening/weekend, online learning. *Degree requirements:* For master's, thesis. *Entrance requirements:* For master's, minimum GPA of 3.0; BS in nursing; interview; RN license; resume; course work in statistics. Additional exam requirements/recommendations for international students: Required—TOEFL (minimum score 90 iBT), IELTS (minimum score 6.5). Electronic applications accepted.

Rutgers University–Newark, Rutgers School of Nursing, Program in Nursing Informatics - Newark, Newark, NJ 07102. Offers MSN. Program offered jointly with New Jersey Institute of Technology. *Entrance requirements:* Additional exam requirements/ recommendations for international students: Required—TOEFL. Electronic applications accepted.

Rutgers University–Newark, Rutgers School of Nursing, Program in Nursing Informatics - Stratford, Newark, NJ 07102. Offers MSN. Program offered jointly with New Jersey Institute of Technology. *Entrance requirements:* Additional exam requirements/ recommendations for international students: Required—TOEFL. Electronic applications accepted.

Samford University, Ida Moffett School of Nursing, Birmingham, AL 35229. Offers administration (DNP); advanced practice (DNP); dual nurse practitioner (family/emergency) (DNP); family nurse practitioner (MSN, DNP); nurse anesthesia (MSN, DNP); nursing administration (DNP), including health systems and administration, informatics, transformation of care. *Accreditation:* AACN; AANA/CANAEP. *Program availability:* Part-time, evening/weekend, blended/hybrid learning. *Faculty:* 20 full-time (19 women), 3 part-time/adjunct (0 women). *Students:* 296 full-time (240 women), 41 part-time (38 women); includes 67 minority (43 Black or African American, non-Hispanic/Latino; 2 American Indian or Alaska Native, non-Hispanic/Latino; 6 Asian, non-Hispanic/Latino; 8 Hispanic/Latino; 8 Two or more races, non-Hispanic/Latino). Average age 35. 79 applicants, 71% accepted, 29 enrolled. In 2017, 117 master's, 39 doctorates awarded. *Degree requirements:* For doctorate, project with poster presentation. *Entrance requirements:* For master's, GRE within the past five years (for nurse anesthesia), RN, minimum nursing GPA of 3.0, undergraduate course in nursing research with minimum C grade, undergraduate health assessment course with minimum B grade; interview, 1 year full-time critical care as RN, 3 letters of recommendation, undergraduate courses in general chemistry and research with minimum B grade for both (for nurse anesthesia); for doctorate, unencumbered licensure as registered nurse; master's degree from CCNE-, CNEA-, or ACEN-accredited program in the area of advanced practice or administration; minimum master's degree cumulative GPA of 3.5; video interview submission. Additional exam requirements/recommendations for international students: Required—TOEFL (minimum score 575 paper-based; 90 iBT); Recommended—IELTS (minimum score 6.5). *Application deadline:* For fall admission, 4/1 for domestic and international students; for spring admission, 8/1 for domestic and international students; for summer admission, 1/1 for domestic and international students. Application fee: $50. Electronic applications accepted. *Expenses:* $809 per credit (for DNP and MSN); $9,737 per semester (for MSN in nurse anesthesia). *Financial support:* In 2017–18, 63 students received support. Application deadline: 2/15; applicants required to submit FAFSA. *Unit head:* Dr. Nena F. Sanders, Vice Provost, College of Health Sciences/

Ida Moffett School of Nursing Dean/Professor, 205-726-2612, E-mail: nfsander@samford.edu. *Application contact:* Allyson Maddox, Director of Graduate Student Services, 205-726-2047, E-mail: amaddox@samford.edu.
Website: http://samford.edu/nursing

Seattle Pacific University, MS in Nursing Program, Seattle, WA 98119-1997. Offers administration (MSN); adult/gerontology nurse practitioner (MSN); clinical nurse specialist (MSN); family nurse practitioner (MSN, Certificate); informatics (MSN); nurse educator (MSN). *Accreditation:* AACN. *Program availability:* Part-time. *Students:* 22 full-time (17 women), 40 part-time (35 women); includes 13 minority (4 Black or African American, non-Hispanic/Latino; 1 American Indian or Alaska Native, non-Hispanic/Latino; 7 Asian, non-Hispanic/Latino; 1 Two or more races, non-Hispanic/Latino). Average age 36. 52 applicants, 73% accepted, 22 enrolled. In 2017, 23 master's awarded. *Degree requirements:* For master's, thesis. *Entrance requirements:* For master's, personal statement, transcripts, undergraduate nursing degree, proof of undergraduate statistics course with minimum GPA of 2.0, 2 recommendations. *Application deadline:* For fall admission, 1/15 priority date for domestic students; for spring admission, 1/15 for domestic students. Applications are processed on a rolling basis. Application fee: $50. Electronic applications accepted. *Expenses:* Contact institution. *Financial support:* Fellowships and scholarships/grants available. Financial award applicants required to submit FAFSA. *Unit head:* Dr. Christine Hoyle, Associate Dean, 206-281-2469, E-mail: hoylec@spu.edu.
Website: http://spu.edu/academics/school-of-health-sciences/undergraduate-programs/nursing

Thomas Edison State University, W. Cary Edwards School of Nursing, Master of Science in Nursing Program, Trenton, NJ 08608. Offers nurse educator (MSN); nursing administration (MSN); nursing informatics (MSN). *Accreditation:* AACN; ACEN. *Program availability:* Part-time, online learning. *Degree requirements:* For master's, nursing education seminar, onground practicum, online practicum. *Entrance requirements:* For master's, BSN. Additional exam requirements/recommendations for international students: Required—TOEFL (minimum score 550 paper-based; 79 iBT). Electronic applications accepted.

Troy University, Graduate School, College of Health and Human Services, Program in Nursing, Troy, AL 36082. Offers adult health (MSN); family nurse practitioner (DNP); maternal infant (MSN); nursing informatics specialist (MSN). *Accreditation:* ACEN. *Program availability:* Part-time, evening/weekend. *Faculty:* 15 full-time (14 women), 8 part-time/adjunct (all women). *Students:* 58 full-time (52 women), 207 part-time (184 women); includes 53 minority (40 Black or African American, non-Hispanic/Latino; 1 American Indian or Alaska Native, non-Hispanic/Latino; 1 Asian, non-Hispanic/Latino; 6 Hispanic/Latino; 5 Two or more races, non-Hispanic/Latino). Average age 36. 66 applicants, 100% accepted, 49 enrolled. In 2017, 113 master's, 14 doctorates awarded. *Degree requirements:* For master's, comprehensive exam, minimum GPA of 3.0, candidacy; for doctorate, minimum GPA of 3.0, submission of approved comprehensive e-portfolio, completion of residency synthesis project, minimum of 1000 hours of clinical practice, qualifying exam. *Entrance requirements:* For master's, GRE (minimum score of 850 on old exam or 290 on new exam) or MAT (minimum score of 396), minimum GPA of 3.0, BSN, current RN licensure, 2 letters of reference, undergraduate health assessment course; for doctorate, GRE (minimum score of 850 on old exam or 294 on new exam), BSN or MSN, minimum GPA of 3.0, 2 letters of reference, current RN licensure, essay. Additional exam requirements/recommendations for international students: Required—TOEFL (minimum score 523 paper-based; 70 iBT), IELTS (minimum score 6). *Application deadline:* Applications are processed on a rolling basis. Application fee: $50. Electronic applications accepted. *Expenses:* Tuition, state resident: part-time $417 per credit hour. Tuition, nonresident: part-time $834 per credit hour. *Required fees:* $42 per credit hour. $50 per semester. Tuition and fees vary according to campus/location. *Financial support:* Fellowships, career-related internships or fieldwork, and scholarships/grants available. Support available to part-time students. Financial award applicants required to submit FAFSA. *Unit head:* Dr. Denise Green, Director, School of Nursing, 334-670-5864, Fax: 334-670-3745, E-mail: dmgreen@troy.edu. *Application contact:* Crystal G. Bishop, Director of Graduate Admissions, School of Nursing, 334-241-8631, E-mail: cdgodwin@troy.edu.

The University of Alabama at Birmingham, School of Nursing, Birmingham, AL 35294-1210. Offers clinical nurse leader (MSN); nurse anesthesia (DNP); nurse practitioner (MSN, DNP), including adult-gerontology acute care (MSN), adult-gerontology primary care (MSN), family (MSN), pediatric (MSN), psychiatric/mental health (MSN), women's health (MSN); nursing (MSN, DNP, PhD); nursing health systems administration (MSN); nursing informatics (MSN). *Accreditation:* AACN; AANA/CANAEP. *Program availability:* Part-time, online only, blended/hybrid learning. Terminal master's awarded for partial completion of doctoral program. *Degree requirements:* For master's, comprehensive exam; for doctorate, comprehensive exam, thesis/dissertation, research mentorship experience (for PhD), scholarly project (for DNP). *Entrance requirements:* For master's, GRE, GMAT, or MAT, minimum cumulative undergraduate GPA of 3.0 or on last 60 semesters hours; letters of recommendation; for doctorate, GRE General Test, computer literacy, course work in statistics, interview, minimum GPA of 3.0, MS in nursing, references, writing sample. Additional exam requirements/recommendations for international students: Required—TOEFL (minimum score 500 paper-based, 80 iBT) or IELTS (5.5). Electronic applications accepted. *Expenses:* Contact institution. *Faculty research:* Palliative care; oncology; aging; HIV/AIDS; nursing work environments.

University of Maryland, Baltimore, School of Nursing, Baltimore, MD 21201. Offers adult-gerontology acute care nurse practitioner (DNP); adult-gerontology primary care nurse practitioner (DNP); clinical nurse leader (MS); community/public health nursing (MS); family nurse practitioner (DNP); global health (Postbaccalaureate Certificate); health services leadership and management (MS); neonatal nurse practitioner (DNP); nurse anesthesia (DNP); nursing (PhD); nursing informatics (MS, Postbaccalaureate Certificate); pediatric acute/primary care nurse practitioner (DNP); psychiatric mental health nurse practitioner (DNP); teaching in nursing and health professions (Postbaccalaureate Certificate); MS/MBA. MS/MBA offered jointly with University of Baltimore. *Program availability:* Part-time. *Faculty:* 130 full-time (117 women), 125 part-time/adjunct (114 women). *Students:* 504 full-time (442 women), 532 part-time (482 women); includes 443 minority (249 Black or African American, non-Hispanic/Latino; 1 American Indian or Alaska Native, non-Hispanic/Latino; 115 Asian, non-Hispanic/Latino; 48 Hispanic/Latino; 2 Native Hawaiian or other Pacific Islander, non-Hispanic/Latino; 28 Two or more races, non-Hispanic/Latino), 15 international. Average age 33. 935 applicants, 62% accepted, 394 enrolled. In 2017, 182 master's, 57 doctorates awarded. *Degree requirements:* For master's and Postbaccalaureate Certificate, thesis (for some programs); for doctorate, comprehensive exam, thesis/dissertation. *Entrance requirements:* Additional exam requirements/recommendations for international students: Required—TOEFL (minimum score 550 paper-based; 79 iBT); Recommended—IELTS (minimum score 7). *Application deadline:* For fall admission, 11/1 for domestic and international students; for spring admission, 8/1 for domestic and international students. Application fee: $75. Electronic applications accepted. *Expenses:* Contact institution. *Financial support:* In 2017–18, 22 research assistantships with full and partial tuition reimbursements (averaging $21,523 per year), 41 teaching assistantships with full and partial tuition reimbursements (averaging $13,439 per year) were awarded; fellowships and scholarships/grants also available. Financial award application deadline: 3/1; financial award applicants required to submit FAFSA. *Unit head:* Dr. Jane Kirschling, Dean, 410-706-4359, E-mail: kirschling@umaryland.edu. *Application contact:* Larry Fillian, Associate Dean of Student and Academic Services, 410-706-6298, E-mail: lfillian@umaryland.edu.
Website: http://www.nursing.umaryland.edu/

University of Minnesota, Twin Cities Campus, Graduate School, School of Nursing, Minneapolis, MN 55455-0213. Offers adult/gerontological clinical nurse specialist (DNP); adult/gerontological primary care nurse practitioner (DNP); family nurse practitioner (DNP); health innovation and leadership (DNP); integrative health and healing (DNP); nurse anesthesia (DNP); nurse midwifery (DNP); nursing (MN, PhD); nursing informatics (DNP); pediatric clinical nurse specialist (DNP); primary care certified pediatric nurse practitioner (DNP); psychiatric/mental health nurse practitioner (DNP); women's health nurse practitioner (DNP). *Accreditation:* AACN; AANA/CANAEP; ACNM/ACME (one or more programs are accredited). *Program availability:* Part-time, online learning. Terminal master's awarded for partial completion of doctoral program. *Degree requirements:* For master's, final oral exam, project or thesis; for doctorate, thesis/dissertation. *Entrance requirements:* For master's and doctorate, GRE General Test. Additional exam requirements/recommendations for international students: Required—TOEFL (minimum score 586 paper-based). *Expenses:* Contact institution. *Faculty research:* Child and family health promotion, nursing research on elders.

The University of North Carolina at Chapel Hill, School of Nursing, Chapel Hill, NC 27599-7460. Offers advanced practice registered nurse (DNP); nursing (MSN, PhD, PMC), including administration (MSN), adult gerontology primary care nurse practitioner (MSN), clinical nurse leader (MSN), education (MSN), health care systems (PMC), informatics (MSN, PMC), nursing leadership (PMC), outcomes management (MSN), primary care family nurse practitioner (MSN), primary care pediatric nurse practitioner (MSN), psychiatric/mental health nurse practitioner (MSN, PMC). *Accreditation:* AACN; ACEN (one or more programs are accredited). *Program availability:* Part-time. *Faculty:* 86 full-time (78 women), 44 part-time/adjunct (40 women). *Students:* 208 full-time (186 women), 128 part-time (116 women); includes 100 minority (49 Black or African American, non-Hispanic/Latino; 4 American Indian or Alaska Native, non-Hispanic/Latino; 23 Asian, non-Hispanic/Latino; 7 Hispanic/Latino; 17 Two or more races, non-Hispanic/Latino), 17 international. Average age 33. 624 applicants, 25% accepted, 150 enrolled. In 2017, 91 master's, 14 doctorates awarded. *Degree requirements:* For master's, comprehensive exam, thesis; for doctorate, thesis/dissertation, 3 exams; for PMC, thesis. *Entrance requirements:* Additional exam requirements/recommendations for international students: Required—TOEFL (minimum score 575 paper-based; 89 iBT), IELTS (minimum score 8). *Application deadline:* For fall admission, 12/15 for domestic and international students. Application fee: $88. Electronic applications accepted. *Financial support:* In 2017–18, 8 fellowships with full tuition reimbursements, 6 research assistantships with partial tuition reimbursements (averaging $8,000 per year), 10 teaching assistantships with partial tuition reimbursements (averaging $8,000 per year) were awarded; scholarships/grants, traineeships, health care benefits, and unspecified assistantships also available. Support available to part-time students. Financial award application deadline: 3/1; financial award applicants required to submit FAFSA. *Faculty research:* Preventing and managing chronic illness, reducing health disparities, improving healthcare quality and patient outcomes, understanding biobehavioral and genetic bases of health and illness, developing innovative ways to enhance science and its clinical translation. *Unit head:* Dr. Nilda Peragallo Montano, Dean/Professor, 919-966-3731, Fax: 919-966-3540, E-mail: npm@email.unc.edu. *Application contact:* Emily Sayed, Assistant Director, Graduate Admissions, 919-966-4260, Fax: 919-966-3540, E-mail: sayed@unc.edu.
Website: http://nursing.unc.edu

University of Phoenix–Bay Area Campus, College of Nursing, San Jose, CA 95134-1805. Offers education (MHA); gerontology (MHA); health administration (MHA, DHA); informatics (MHA, MSN); nursing (MSN, PhD); nursing/health care education (MSN); MSN/MBA. *Program availability:* Evening/weekend, online learning. *Degree requirements:* For master's, thesis (for some programs). *Entrance requirements:* For master's, minimum undergraduate GPA of 2.5, 3 years of work experience, RN license. Additional exam requirements/recommendations for international students: Required—TOEFL (minimum score 550 paper-based; 79 iBT). Electronic applications accepted.

University of Phoenix–Phoenix Campus, College of Health Sciences and Nursing, Tempe, AZ 85282-2371. Offers family nurse practitioner (MSN, Certificate); gerontology health care (Certificate); health care education (MSN, Certificate); health care informatics (Certificate); informatics (MSN); nursing (MSN); MSN/MHA. *Program availability:* Evening/weekend, online learning. *Entrance requirements:* Additional exam requirements/recommendations for international students: Required—TOEFL, TOEIC (Test of English as an International Communication), Berlitz Online English Proficiency Exam, PTE, or IELTS. Electronic applications accepted. *Expenses:* Contact institution.

University of Pittsburgh, School of Nursing, Nurse Specialty Role Program, Pittsburgh, PA 15260. Offers clinical nurse leader (MSN); health systems executive leadership (DNP); nursing informatics (MSN). *Accreditation:* AACN. *Program availability:* Part-time. *Faculty:* 9 full-time (8 women), 1 (woman) part-time/adjunct. *Students:* 5 full-time (4 women), 60 part-time (53 women); includes 8 minority (3 Black or African American, non-Hispanic/Latino; 5 Asian, non-Hispanic/Latino), 1 international. Average age 37. 43 applicants, 72% accepted, 26 enrolled. In 2017, 15 master's, 4 doctorates awarded. *Degree requirements:* For master's, comprehensive exam, thesis optional. *Entrance requirements:* For master's, GRE, BSN, RN license, 3 letters of recommendation, personal essay, resume, course work in statistics, relevant nursing experience; for doctorate, GRE, BSN/MSN, RN license, minimum GPA of 3.5, 3 letters of recommendation, personal essay, resume, course work in statistics, relevant nursing experience. Additional exam requirements/recommendations for international students: Required—TOEFL (minimum score 600 paper-based; 100 IBT) or IELTS (minimum score 7.0). *Application deadline:* For fall admission, 5/1 priority date for domestic students, 2/15 priority date for international students. Application fee: $50. Electronic applications accepted. *Expenses:* $13,068 per term full-time resident tuition, $1,064 per credit part-time; $15,270 per term full-time non-resident tuition, $1,247 per credit part-time; $437 per term full-time fees; $282 per term part-time fees. *Financial support:* In 2017–18, 37 students received support. Scholarships/grants and tuition waivers available. Financial award applicants required to submit FAFSA. *Faculty research:* Behavioral management of chronic disorders, patient management in critical care, consumer informatics, genetic applications (molecular genetics and psychosocial implications), technology for nurses and patients to improve care. *Unit head:* Dr. Sandra Engberg, Associate Dean for Clinical Education, 412-624-3835, Fax: 412-624-8521, E-mail: sje1@pitt.edu. *Application contact:* Laurie Lapsley, Graduate Administrator, 412-624-9670, Fax: 412-624-2409, E-mail: lapsleyl@pitt.edu.
Website: http://www.nursing.pitt.edu/

University of St. Augustine for Health Sciences, Graduate Programs, Master of Science in Nursing Program, San Marcos, CA 92069. Offers nurse educator (MSN); nurse executive (MSN); nurse informatics (MSN). *Program availability:* Part-time, online learning.

Vanderbilt University, Vanderbilt University School of Nursing, Nashville, TN 37240. Offers adult-gerontology acute care nurse practitioner (MSN), including hospitalist, intensivist; adult-gerontology primary care nurse practitioner (MSN); emergency nurse practitioner (MSN); family nurse practitioner (MSN); healthcare leadership (MSN); neonatal nurse practitioner (MSN); nurse midwifery (MSN); nurse midwifery/family nurse practitioner (MSN); nursing (Post-Master's Certificate); nursing informatics (MSN); nursing practice (DNP); nursing science (PhD); pediatric acute care nurse practitioner (MSN); pediatric primary care nurse practitioner (MSN); psychiatric-mental health nurse practitioner (MSN); women's health nurse practitioner (MSN); women's health nurse practitioner/adult gerontology primary care nurse practitioner (MSN); MSN/M Div; MSN/MTS. *Accreditation:* AACN; ACEN (one or more programs are accredited); ACNM/ACME. *Program availability:* Part-time, 100% online, blended/hybrid learning. *Faculty:* 292 full-time (267 women), 321 part-time/adjunct (253 women). *Students:* 501 full-time (435 women), 387 part-time (355 women); includes 153 minority (40 Black or African American, non-Hispanic/Latino; 1 American Indian or Alaska Native, non-Hispanic/Latino; 27 Asian, non-Hispanic/Latino; 48 Hispanic/Latino; 4 Native Hawaiian or other Pacific Islander, non-Hispanic/Latino; 33 Two or more races, non-Hispanic/Latino), 9 international. Average age 31. 1,210 applicants, 57% accepted, 473 enrolled. In 2017, 319 master's, 47 doctorates awarded. *Degree requirements:* For doctorate, comprehensive exam, thesis/dissertation. *Entrance requirements:* For master's, GRE General Test (taken within the past 5 years), minimum B average in undergraduate course work, 3 letters of recommendation; for doctorate, GRE General Test, interview, 3 letters of recommendation from doctorally-prepared faculty, MSN, essay. Additional exam requirements/recommendations for international students: Required—TOEFL (minimum score 570 paper-based), IELTS (minimum score 6.5). *Application deadline:* For fall admission, 11/1 priority date for domestic and international students. Applications are processed on a rolling basis. Application fee: $50. Electronic applications accepted. *Expenses:* Contact institution. *Financial support:* In 2017–18, 627 students received support. Scholarships/grants available. Financial award application deadline: 3/1; financial award applicants required to submit FAFSA. *Faculty research:* Lymphedema, palliative care and bereavement, health services research including workforce, safety and quality of care, gerontology, better birth outcomes including nutrition. *Total annual research expenditures:* $2 million. *Unit head:* Dr. Linda Norman, Dean, 615-343-8876, Fax: 615-343-7711, E-mail: linda.norman@vanderbilt.edu. *Application contact:* Patricia Peerman, Assistant Dean for Enrollment Management, 615-322-3800, Fax: 615-343-0333, E-mail: vusn-admissions@vanderbilt.edu.
Website: http://www.nursing.vanderbilt.edu

Walden University, Graduate Programs, School of Nursing, Minneapolis, MN 55401. Offers adult-gerontology acute care nurse practitioner (MSN); adult-gerontology nurse practitioner (MSN); education (MSN); family nurse practitioner (MSN); informatics (MSN); leadership and management (MSN); nursing (PhD, Post-Master's Certificate), including education (PhD), healthcare administration (PhD), interdisciplinary health (PhD), leadership (PhD), nursing education (Post-Master's Certificate), nursing informatics (Post-Master's Certificate), nursing leadership and management (Post-Master's Certificate), public health policy (PhD); nursing practice (DNP); psychiatric mental health (MSN). *Accreditation:* AACN. *Program availability:* Part-time, evening/weekend, online only, 100% online. *Degree requirements:* For doctorate, thesis/dissertation (for some programs), residency (for some programs), field experience (for some programs). *Entrance requirements:* For master's, bachelor's degree or equivalent in related field or RN; minimum GPA of 2.5; official transcripts; goal statement (for some programs); access to computer and Internet; for doctorate, master's degree or higher; RN; three years of related professional or academic experience; goal statement; access to computer and Internet; for Post-Master's Certificate, relevant work experience; access to computer and Internet. Additional exam requirements/recommendations for international students: Required—TOEFL (minimum score 550 paper-based, 79 iBT), IELTS (minimum score 6.5), Michigan English Language Assessment Battery (minimum score 82), or PTE (minimum score 53). Electronic applications accepted.

Waynesburg University, Graduate and Professional Studies, Canonsburg, PA 15370. Offers business (MBA), including energy management, finance, health systems, human resources, leadership, market development; counseling (MA), including addictions counseling, clinical mental health; counselor education and supervision (PhD); criminal investigation (MA); education (M Ed), including autism, curriculum and instruction, educational leadership, online teaching; nursing (MSN), including administration, education, informatics; nursing practice (DNP); special education (M Ed); technology (M Ed); MSN/MBA. *Accreditation:* AACN. *Program availability:* Part-time, evening/weekend. *Degree requirements:* For doctorate, thesis/dissertation. *Entrance requirements:* Additional exam requirements/recommendations for international students: Required—TOEFL. Electronic applications accepted.

Western Governors University, College of Health Professions, Salt Lake City, UT 84107. Offers healthcare management (MBA); leadership and management (MSN); nursing education (MSN); nursing informatics (MSN). *Program availability:* Evening/weekend, online learning. *Degree requirements:* For master's, capstone project. *Entrance requirements:* For master's, transcripts. Additional exam requirements/recommendations for international students: Required—TOEFL (minimum score 450 paper-based; 80 iBT). *Application deadline:* Applications are processed on a rolling basis. Application fee: $65. Electronic applications accepted. Application fee is waived when completed online. *Financial support:* Tuition waivers (partial) available. Financial award applicants required to submit FAFSA. *Unit head:* Dr. Jan Jones-Schenk, Director. *Application contact:* Enrollment Department, 866-225-5948, Fax: 801-274-3306, E-mail: info@wgu.edu.
Website: https://www.wgu.edu/online-nursing-health-degrees.html#

Occupational Health Nursing

Rutgers University–Newark, Rutgers School of Nursing, Newark, NJ 07107-3001. Offers adult health (MSN); adult occupational health (MSN); advanced practice nursing (MSN, Post Master's Certificate); family nurse practitioner (MSN); nurse anesthesia (MSN); nursing (MSN); nursing informatics (MSN); urban health (PhD); women's health practitioner (MSN). *Accreditation:* AANA/CANAEP. *Program availability:* Part-time. *Entrance requirements:* For master's, GRE, RN license; basic life support, statistics, and health assessment experience. Additional exam requirements/recommendations for international students: Required—TOEFL. Electronic applications accepted. *Expenses:* Contact institution. *Faculty research:* HIV/AIDS, diabetes education, learned helplessness, nursing science, psychoeducation.

University of Cincinnati, Graduate School, College of Nursing, Cincinnati, OH 45221-0038. Offers nurse midwifery (MSN); nurse practitioner (MSN, DNP), including acute care pediatrics (DNP), adult-gerontology acute care, adult-gerontology primary care, anesthesia (DNP), family (MSN), leadership (DNP), neonatal (MSN), women's health (MSN); nursing (MSN, PhD), including occupational health (MSN). *Accreditation:* AACN; AANA/CANAEP (one or more programs are accredited); ACNM/ACME. *Program availability:* Part-time, 100% online, blended/hybrid learning. *Faculty:* 74 full-time (69 women), 112 part-time/adjunct (105 women). *Students:* 323 full-time (261 women), 1,084 part-time (949 women); includes 311 minority (113 Black or African American, non-Hispanic/Latino; 4 American Indian or Alaska Native, non-Hispanic/Latino; 56 Asian, non-Hispanic/Latino; 108 Hispanic/Latino; 1 Native Hawaiian or other Pacific Islander, non-Hispanic/Latino; 29 Two or more races, non-Hispanic/Latino), 12 international. Average age 34. 582 applicants, 64% accepted, 314 enrolled. In 2017, 579 master's, 18 doctorates awarded. *Degree requirements:* For master's, thesis or alternative; for doctorate, comprehensive exam (for some programs), thesis/dissertation (for some programs). *Entrance requirements:* For doctorate, GRE General Test. Additional exam requirements/recommendations for international students: Required—TOEFL (minimum score 600 paper-based; 100 iBT); Recommended—IELTS (minimum score 7). *Application deadline:* For fall admission, 5/1 priority date for domestic students, 5/1 for international students; for spring admission, 10/1 for domestic students; for summer admission, 3/1 priority date for domestic students. Applications are processed on a rolling basis. Application fee: $130 ($70 for international students). Electronic applications accepted. *Expenses:* $14,668 annual full-time in-state tuition, $707 annual fees. *Financial support:* In 2017–18, 123 students received support, including 8 fellowships with full tuition reimbursements available (averaging $30,423 per year), 7 research assistantships with full tuition reimbursements available (averaging $17,971 per year), 5 teaching assistantships with full tuition reimbursements available (averaging $17,971 per year); Federal Work-Study, institutionally sponsored loans, scholarships/grants, traineeships, health care benefits, tuition waivers (partial), and unspecified assistantships also available. Support available to part-time students. Financial award application deadline: 5/1; financial award applicants required to submit FAFSA. *Faculty research:* Vulnerable populations, education, violence, chronicity/aging, cancer. *Total annual research expenditures:* $575,576. *Unit head:* Dr. Greer Glazer, Dean, 513-558-5330, Fax: 513-558-9030, E-mail: greer.glazer@uc.edu. *Application contact:* Office of Student Recruitment, 513-558-8400, Fax: 513-558-5012, E-mail: nursingbearcats@uc.edu.
Website: https://nursing.uc.edu/

University of Illinois at Chicago, College of Nursing, Program in Nursing, Chicago, IL 60607-7128. Offers acute care clinical nurse specialist (MS); administrative nursing leadership (Certificate); adult nurse practitioner (MS); adult/geriatric nurse practitioner (MS); advanced community health nurse specialist (MS); family nurse practitioner (MS); geriatric clinical nurse specialist (MS); geriatric nurse practitioner (MS); nurse midwifery (MS); occupational health/advanced community health nurse specialist (MS); occupational health/family nurse practitioner (MS); pediatric nurse practitioner (MS); perinatal clinical nurse specialist (MS); school/advanced community health nurse specialist (MS); school/family nurse practitioner (MS); women's health nurse practitioner (MS). *Accreditation:* AACN. *Program availability:* Part-time. *Degree requirements:* For master's, thesis or alternative. *Entrance requirements:* For master's, GRE General Test, minimum GPA of 2.75. Additional exam requirements/recommendations for international students: Required—TOEFL. Electronic applications accepted.

University of Minnesota, Twin Cities Campus, School of Public Health, Division of Environmental Health Sciences, Area in Occupational Health Nursing, Minneapolis, MN 55455-0213. Offers MPH, MS, PhD, MPH/MS. *Accreditation:* AACN. *Degree requirements:* For doctorate, thesis/dissertation. *Entrance requirements:* For master's and doctorate, GRE General Test. Electronic applications accepted.

The University of North Carolina at Chapel Hill, Graduate School, Gillings School of Global Public Health, Public Health Leadership Program, Chapel Hill, NC 27599. Offers health care and prevention (MPH); leadership (MPH); occupational health nursing (MPH). *Program availability:* Part-time, 100% online, blended/hybrid learning. *Faculty:* 12 full-time (10 women), 37 part-time/adjunct (25 women). *Students:* 89 full-time (61 women), 66 part-time (47 women); includes 56 minority (17 Black or African American, non-Hispanic/Latino; 16 Asian, non-Hispanic/Latino; 11 Hispanic/Latino; 12 Two or more races, non-Hispanic/Latino), 9 international. Average age 34. 111 applicants, 93% accepted, 68 enrolled. In 2017, 73 master's awarded. *Degree requirements:* For master's, comprehensive exam, thesis (MS), paper (MPH). *Entrance requirements:* For master's, GRE General Test or MCAT, three years of public health experience (recommended), three letters of recommendation (academic and/or professional; academic preferred). Additional exam requirements/recommendations for international students: Required—TOEFL (minimum score 90 iBT), IELTS (minimum score 7). *Application deadline:* For fall admission, 2/2 for domestic and international students. Applications are processed on a rolling basis. Application fee: $85. Electronic applications accepted. *Financial support:* Career-related internships or fieldwork, institutionally sponsored loans, traineeships, and health care benefits available. Financial award application deadline: 12/10; financial award applicants required to submit FAFSA. *Faculty research:* Occupational health issues, clinical outcomes, prenatal and early childcare, adolescent health, effectiveness of home visiting, issues in occupational health nursing, community-based interventions. *Unit head:* Dr. Anna P. Schenck, Director, 919-843-8580, E-mail: anna.schenck@unc.edu. *Application contact:* Kristen Hurdle, Student Services Specialist, 919-843-7629, E-mail: kristen_hurdle@unc.edu.
Website: http://sph.unc.edu/phlp/phlp/

University of South Florida, College of Nursing, Tampa, FL 33612. Offers nurse anesthesia (DNP); nursing (MS, DNP), including adult-gerontology acute care nursing, adult-gerontology primary care nursing, family health nursing, nurse anesthesia (MS), nursing education (MS), occupational health nursing/adult-gerontology primary care nursing, oncology nursing/adult-gerontology primary care nursing (DNP), pediatric health nursing; nursing education (Post Master's Certificate); nursing science (PhD); simulation based academic fellowship in advanced pain management (Graduate Certificate). *Accreditation:* AACN; AANA/CANAEP. *Program availability:* Part-time. *Faculty:* 37 full-time (32 women), 2 part-time/adjunct (1 woman). *Students:* 224 full-time (178 women), 669 part-time (577 women); includes 309 minority (105 Black or African American, non-Hispanic/Latino; 2 American Indian or Alaska Native, non-Hispanic/Latino; 53 Asian, non-Hispanic/Latino; 122 Hispanic/Latino; 1 Native Hawaiian or other Pacific Islander, non-Hispanic/Latino; 26 Two or more races, non-Hispanic/Latino), 6 international. Average age 32. 949 applicants, 47% accepted, 382 enrolled. In 2017, 264

master's, 39 doctorates awarded. *Degree requirements:* For master's, comprehensive exam, thesis optional; for doctorate, comprehensive exam, thesis/dissertation. *Entrance requirements:* For master's, GRE General Test, bachelor's degree from accredited program with minimum GPA of 3.0 in all upper-division coursework; current license as Registered Nurse; 3 letters of recommendation; personal statement of goals; resume or curriculum vitae; personal interview; for doctorate, GRE General Test (recommended), bachelor's degree in nursing from ACEN or CCNE regionally-accredited institution with minimum GPA of 3.0 in all coursework or in all upper-division coursework; current license as Registered Nurse in Florida; undergraduate statistics course with minimum B grade; 3 letters of recommendation; statement of goals; resume; interview. Additional exam requirements/recommendations for international students: Required—TOEFL (minimum score 550 paper-based; 79 iBT). *Application deadline:* For fall admission, 12/15 for domestic and international students; for spring admission, 10/1 for domestic students, 9/15 for international students. Application fee: $30. Electronic applications accepted. *Financial support:* In 2017–18, 132 students received support, including 7 research assistantships with tuition reimbursements available (averaging $18,935 per year), 29 teaching assistantships with tuition reimbursements available (averaging $30,814 per year); tuition waivers (partial) and unspecified assistantships also available. Financial award application deadline: 2/1; financial award applicants required to submit FAFSA. *Faculty research:* Women's health, palliative and end-of-life care, cardiac rehabilitation, complementary therapies for chronic illness and cancer. *Total annual research expenditures:* $3.2 million. *Unit head:* Dr. Victoria Rich, Dean, College of Nursing, 813-974-8939, Fax: 813-974-5418, E-mail: victoriarich@health.usf.edu. *Application contact:* Dr. Brian Graves, Assistant Professor/Assistant Dean, 813-974-8054, Fax: 813-974-5418, E-mail: bgraves1@health.usf.edu.
Website: http://health.usf.edu/nursing/index.htm

University of the Sacred Heart, Graduate Programs, Department of Natural Sciences, San Juan, PR 00914-0383. Offers occupational health and safety (MS); occupational nursing (MSN). *Program availability:* Part-time, evening/weekend.

Oncology Nursing

Gwynedd Mercy University, Frances M. Maguire School of Nursing and Health Professions, Gwynedd Valley, PA 19437-0901. Offers clinical nurse specialist (MSN), including gerontology, oncology, pediatrics; nurse educator (MSN); nurse practitioner (MSN), including adult health, pediatric health; nursing (DNP). *Accreditation:* ACEN. *Program availability:* Part-time, blended/hybrid learning. *Faculty:* 4 full-time (all women), 1 (woman) part-time/adjunct. *Students:* 28 full-time (25 women), 48 part-time (43 women); includes 28 minority (15 Black or African American, non-Hispanic/Latino; 11 Asian, non-Hispanic/Latino; 1 Hispanic/Latino; 1 Two or more races, non-Hispanic/Latino). Average age 37. 72 applicants, 25% accepted, 16 enrolled. In 2017, 7 master's awarded. *Degree requirements:* For master's, thesis optional; for doctorate, evidence-based scholarly project. *Entrance requirements:* For master's, GRE General Test or MAT, current nursing experience, physical assessment, course work in statistics, BSN from ACEN-accredited program, 2 letters of recommendation, personal interview. Additional exam requirements/recommendations for international students: Required—TOEFL (minimum score 575 paper-based). *Application deadline:* For fall admission, 8/1 priority date for domestic students; for winter admission, 12/1 priority date for domestic students. Applications are processed on a rolling basis. Electronic applications accepted. *Expenses:* $825 per credit (non-doctoral degrees), $930 per credit (doctoral); $17 part-time fee, $165 graduation fee. *Financial support:* In 2017–18, 5 students received support. Scholarships/grants, traineeships, and unspecified assistantships available. Financial award application deadline: 8/30. *Faculty research:* Critical thinking, primary care, domestic violence, multiculturalism, nursing centers. *Unit head:* Dr. Andrea D. Hollingsworth, Dean, 215-646-7300 Ext. 539, Fax: 215-641-5517, E-mail: hollingsworth.a@gmc.edu. *Application contact:* Dr. Barbara A. Jones, Director, 215-646-7300 Ext. 407, Fax: 215-641-5564, E-mail: jones.b@gmc.edu.
Website: http://www.gmercyu.edu/academics/graduate-programs/nursing

Universidad Metropolitana, School of Health Sciences, Department of Nursing, San Juan, PR 00928-1150. Offers case management (Certificate); nursing (MSN); oncology nursing (Certificate). *Accreditation:* ACEN.

University of Delaware, College of Health Sciences, School of Nursing, Newark, DE 19716. Offers adult nurse practitioner (MSN, PMC); cardiopulmonary clinical nurse specialist (MSN, PMC); cardiopulmonary clinical nurse specialist/adult nurse practitioner (MSN, PMC); family nurse practitioner (MSN, PMC); gerontology clinical nurse specialist (MSN, PMC); gerontology clinical nurse specialist geriatric nurse practitioner (PMC); gerontology clinical nurse specialist/geriatric nurse practitioner (MSN); health services administration (MSN, PMC); nursing of children clinical nurse specialist (MSN, PMC); nursing of children clinical nurse specialist/pediatric nurse practitioner (MSN, PMC); oncology/immune deficiency clinical nurse specialist (MSN, PMC); oncology/immune deficiency clinical nurse specialist/adult nurse practitioner (MSN, PMC); perinatal/women's health clinical nurse specialist (MSN, PMC); perinatal/women's health clinical nurse specialist/women's health nurse practitioner (MSN, PMC); psychiatric nursing clinical nurse specialist (MSN, PMC). *Accreditation:* AACN. *Program availability:* Part-time, evening/weekend, online learning. *Degree requirements:* For master's, thesis optional. *Entrance requirements:* For master's, BSN, interview, RN license. Electronic applications accepted. *Faculty research:* Marriage and chronic illness, health promotion, congestive heart failure patient outcomes, school nursing, diabetes in children, culture, health disparities, cardiovascular, prison nursing, oncology, public policy, child obesity, smoking and teen pregnancy, blood pressure measurements, men's health.

University of South Florida, College of Nursing, Tampa, FL 33612. Offers nurse anesthesia (DNP); nursing (MS, DNP), including adult-gerontology acute care nursing, adult-gerontology primary care nursing, family health nursing, nurse anesthesia (MS), nursing education (MS), occupational health nursing/adult-gerontology primary care nursing, oncology nursing/adult-gerontology primary care nursing (DNP), pediatric health nursing; nursing education (Post Master's Certificate); nursing science (PhD); simulation based academic fellowship in advanced pain management (Graduate Certificate). *Accreditation:* AACN; AANA/CANAEP. *Program availability:* Part-time. *Faculty:* 37 full-time (32 women), 2 part-time/adjunct (1 woman). *Students:* 224 full-time (178 women), 669 part-time (577 women); includes 309 minority (105 Black or African American, non-Hispanic/Latino; 2 American Indian or Alaska Native, non-Hispanic/Latino; 53 Asian, non-Hispanic/Latino; 122 Hispanic/Latino; 1 Native Hawaiian or other Pacific Islander, non-Hispanic/Latino; 26 Two or more races, non-Hispanic/Latino), 6 international. Average age 32. 949 applicants, 47% accepted, 382 enrolled. In 2017, 264 master's, 39 doctorates awarded. *Degree requirements:* For master's, comprehensive exam, thesis optional; for doctorate, comprehensive exam, thesis/dissertation. *Entrance requirements:* For master's, GRE General Test, bachelor's degree from accredited program with minimum GPA of 3.0 in all upper-division coursework; current license as Registered Nurse; 3 letters of recommendation; personal statement of goals; resume or curriculum vitae; personal interview; for doctorate, GRE General Test (recommended), bachelor's degree in nursing from ACEN or CCNE regionally-accredited institution with minimum GPA of 3.0 in all coursework or in all upper-division coursework; current license as Registered Nurse in Florida; undergraduate statistics course with minimum B grade; 3 letters of recommendation; statement of goals; resume; interview. Additional exam requirements/recommendations for international students: Required—TOEFL (minimum score 550 paper-based; 79 iBT). *Application deadline:* For fall admission, 12/15 for domestic and international students; for spring admission, 10/1 for domestic students, 9/15 for international students. Application fee: $30. Electronic applications accepted. *Financial support:* In 2017–18, 132 students received support, including 7 research assistantships with tuition reimbursements available (averaging $18,935 per year), 29 teaching assistantships with tuition reimbursements available (averaging $30,814 per year); tuition waivers (partial) and unspecified assistantships also available. Financial award application deadline: 2/1; financial award applicants required to submit FAFSA. *Faculty research:* Women's health, palliative and end-of-life care, cardiac rehabilitation, complementary therapies for chronic illness and cancer. *Total annual research expenditures:* $3.2 million. *Unit head:* Dr. Victoria Rich, Dean, College of Nursing, 813-974-8939, Fax: 813-974-5418, E-mail: victoriarich@health.usf.edu. *Application contact:* Dr. Brian Graves, Assistant Professor/Assistant Dean, 813-974-8054, Fax: 813-974-5418, E-mail: bgraves1@health.usf.edu.
Website: http://health.usf.edu/nursing/index.htm

Pediatric Nursing

Augusta University, College of Nursing, Doctor of Nursing Practice Program, Augusta, GA 30912. Offers adult gerontology acute care nurse practitioner (DNP); family nurse practitioner (DNP); nurse executive (DNP); nursing (DNP); nursing anesthesia (DNP); pediatric nurse practitioner (DNP); psychiatric mental health nurse practitioner (DNP). *Accreditation:* AACN; AANA/CANAEP. *Degree requirements:* For doctorate, thesis/dissertation or alternative. *Entrance requirements:* For doctorate, GRE General Test or MAT, master's degree in nursing or related field, current professional nurse licensure. Additional exam requirements/recommendations for international students: Required—TOEFL (minimum score 600 paper-based; 100 iBT). Electronic applications accepted.

Azusa Pacific University, School of Nursing, Azusa, CA 91702-7000. Offers adult clinical nurse specialist (MSN); adult-gerontology nurse practitioner (MSN); family nurse practitioner (MSN); healthcare administration and leadership (MSN); nursing (MSN, DNP, PhD); nursing education (MSN); parent-child clinical nurse specialist (MSN); psychiatric mental health nurse practitioner (MSN). *Accreditation:* AACN. *Program availability:* Part-time, evening/weekend. *Degree requirements:* For master's, thesis optional. *Entrance requirements:* For master's, BSN.

Boston College, William F. Connell School of Nursing, Chestnut Hill, MA 02467. Offers adult-gerontology primary care nurse practitioner (MS); family health nursing (MS); nurse anesthesia (MS); nursing (PhD); pediatric primary care nurse practitioner (MS), including pediatric and women's health; psychiatric-mental health nursing (MS); women's health nursing (MS); MBA/MS; MS/MA; MS/PhD. MS/MBA offered jointly with Carroll School of Management, MS/MA with School of Theology and Ministry. *Accreditation:* AACN; AANA/CANAEP (one or more programs are accredited). *Program availability:* Part-time. *Faculty:* 54 full-time (48 women). *Students:* 170 full-time (153 women), 90 part-time (83 women); includes 39 minority (8 Black or African American, non-Hispanic/Latino; 10 Asian, non-Hispanic/Latino; 12 Hispanic/Latino; 9 Two or more races, non-Hispanic/Latino), 3 international. Average age 28. 360 applicants, 56% accepted, 94 enrolled. In 2017, 104 master's, 5 doctorates awarded. *Degree requirements:* For master's, comprehensive exam; for doctorate, comprehensive exam, thesis/dissertation, computer literacy exam or foreign language. *Entrance requirements:* For master's, bachelor's degree in nursing; for doctorate, GRE General Test, MS in nursing. Additional exam requirements/recommendations for international students: Required—TOEFL (minimum score 600 paper-based; 100 iBT), IELTS (minimum score 7.5). *Application deadline:* For fall admission, 9/30 for domestic and international students; for winter admission, 1/15 for domestic and international students; for spring admission, 3/15 for domestic and international students. Application fee: $40. Electronic applications accepted. *Expenses:* $1,350 per credit tuition. *Financial support:* In 2017–18, 152 students received support, including 11 fellowships with full tuition reimbursements available (averaging $24,504 per year), 29 teaching assistantships (averaging $3,768 per year); scholarships/grants, health care benefits, tuition waivers (partial), and unspecified assistantships also available. Support available to part-time students. Financial award application deadline: 4/18; financial award applicants required to submit FAFSA. *Faculty research:* Sexual and reproductive health, health promotion/illness prevention, aging, eating disorders, symptom management. *Total annual research expenditures:* $879,812. *Unit head:* Dr. Susan Gennaro, Dean, 617-552-4251, Fax: 617-552-0931, E-mail: susan.gennaro@bc.edu. *Application contact:* Sean Sendall, Assistant Dean, Graduate Enrollment and Data Analytics, 617-552-4745, Fax: 617-552-2121, E-mail: sean.sendall@bc.edu.
Website: http://www.bc.edu/cson

Pediatric Nursing

Caribbean University, Graduate School, Bayamón, PR 00960-0493. Offers administration and supervision (MA Ed); criminal justice (MA); curriculum and instruction (MA Ed, PhD), including elementary education (MA Ed), English education (MA Ed), history education (MA Ed), mathematics education (MA Ed), primary education (MA Ed), science education (MA Ed), Spanish education (MA Ed); educational technology in instructional systems (MA Ed); gerontology (MSN); human resources (MBA); museology, archiving and art history (MA Ed); neonatal pediatrics (MSN); physical education (MA Ed); special education (MA Ed). *Entrance requirements:* For master's, interview, minimum GPA of 2.5.

Case Western Reserve University, Frances Payne Bolton School of Nursing, Master's Programs in Nursing, Nurse Practitioner Program, Cleveland, OH 44106. Offers acute care pediatric nurse practitioner (MSN); acute care/cardiovascular nursing (MSN); acute care/flight nurse (MSN); adult gerontology acute care nurse practitioner (MSN); adult gerontology primary care nurse practitioner (MSN); family nurse practitioner (MSN); family systems psychiatric mental health nursing (MSN); neonatal nurse practitioner (MSN); palliative care (MSN); pediatric nurse practitioner (MSN); women's health nurse practitioner (MSN). *Accreditation:* ACEN. *Program availability:* Part-time. *Faculty:* 30 full-time (26 women), 5 part-time/adjunct (3 women). *Students:* 34 full-time (28 women), 97 part-time (73 women); includes 24 minority (5 Black or African American, non-Hispanic/Latino; 9 Asian, non-Hispanic/Latino; 6 Hispanic/Latino; 4 Two or more races, non-Hispanic/Latino), 4 international. Average age 33. 56 applicants, 82% accepted, 29 enrolled. In 2017, 68 master's awarded. *Degree requirements:* For master's, minimum GPA of 3.0, clinical hours corresponding to requirements to sit for certification exam, portfolio. *Entrance requirements:* For master's, GRE General Test or MAT. Additional exam requirements/recommendations for international students: Required—TOEFL (minimum score 577 paper-based; 90 iBT), IELTS (minimum score 7). *Application deadline:* For fall admission, 5/1 for domestic and international students; for spring admission, 10/1 for domestic and international students; for summer admission, 3/1 for domestic and international students. Applications are processed on a rolling basis. Application fee: $75. Electronic applications accepted. *Expenses:* $2,011 per credit tuition; $15 nursing activity fee; $17 activity fee. *Financial support:* In 2017–18, 86 students received support, including 19 teaching assistantships with partial tuition reimbursements available (averaging $18,100 per year); scholarships/grants and traineeships also available. Support available to part-time students. Financial award application deadline: 5/15; financial award applicants required to submit FAFSA. *Faculty research:* Symptom science, family/community care, aging across the lifespan, self-management of health and illness, neuroscience. *Unit head:* Dr. Latina Brooks, Director, 216-368-1196, Fax: 216-368-3542, E-mail: lmb3@case.edu. *Application contact:* Jackie Tepale, Admissions Coordinator, 216-368-5253, Fax: 216-368-0124, E-mail: yyd@case.edu.
Website: http://fpb.cwru.edu/MSN/majors.shtm

Columbia University, School of Nursing, Program in Pediatric Nurse Practitioner, New York, NY 10032. Offers MS, Adv C. *Accreditation:* AACN. *Program availability:* Part-time. *Entrance requirements:* For master's, GRE General Test, NCLEX, BSN, 1 year of clinical experience (preferred); for Adv C, MSN. Additional exam requirements/recommendations for international students: Required—TOEFL. Electronic applications accepted. *Expenses: Tuition:* Full-time $44,864; part-time $1704 per credit. *Required fees:* $2370 per semester. One-time fee: $105.

Creighton University, College of Nursing, Omaha, NE 68178-0001. Offers adult gerontology acute care nurse practitioner (DNP, Post-Master's Certificate); adult gerontology nurse practitioner (DNP); clinical nurse leader (MSN, Post-Graduate Certificate); clinical systems administration (MSN, DNP); family nurse practitioner (DNP, Post-Master's Certificate); neonatal nurse practitioner (DNP, Post-Master's Certificate); nursing (Post-Graduate Certificate); pediatric acute care nurse practitioner (DNP, Post-Master's Certificate); psychiatric mental health nurse practitioner (DNP). *Accreditation:* AACN. *Program availability:* Part-time, blended/hybrid learning. *Degree requirements:* For master's, capstone project; for doctorate, scholarly project. *Entrance requirements:* For master's and doctorate, BSN from ACEN- or CCNE-accredited nursing school, minimum cumulative GPA of 3.0, personal statement, active unencumbered RN license with NE eligibility, undergraduate statistics course, physical assessment course or equivalent, three recommendation letters; for other advanced degree, MSN or MS in nursing from ACEN- or CCNE-accredited nursing school, minimum cumulative GPA of 3.0, active unencumbered RN license with NE eligibility. Additional exam requirements/recommendations for international students: Required—TOEFL (minimum score 600 paper-based, 100 iBT) or IELTS. Electronic applications accepted. *Expenses:* Contact institution. *Faculty research:* School health report card, obesity prevention in children, simulated clinical experience evaluation, vitamin D3 and calcium and cancer risk reduction education, online support and education to reduce stress for prenatal patients on bed rest, health literacy, immunization research.

Drexel University, College of Nursing and Health Professions, Division of Graduate Nursing, Philadelphia, PA 19104-2875. Offers adult acute care (MSN); adult psychiatric/mental health (MSN); advanced practice nursing (MSN); clinical trials research (MSN); family nurse practitioner (MSN); leadership in health systems management (MSN); nursing education (MSN); pediatric primary care (MSN); women's health (MSN). *Accreditation:* AACN. Electronic applications accepted.

Duke University, School of Nursing, Durham, NC 27708-0586. Offers acute care pediatric nurse practitioner (MSN, Post-Graduate Certificate); adult-gerontology nurse practitioner (MSN, Post-Graduate Certificate), including acute care, primary care; family nurse practitioner (MSN, Post-Graduate Certificate); neonatal nurse practitioner (MSN, Post-Graduate Certificate); nurse anesthesia (DNP); nurse practitioner (DNP); nursing (PhD); nursing and health care leadership (MSN, Post-Graduate Certificate); nursing education (MSN, Post-Graduate Certificate); nursing informatics (MSN, Post-Graduate Certificate); pediatric nurse practitioner (MSN, Post-Graduate Certificate), including primary care; psychiatric mental health nurse practitioner (MSN, Post-Graduate Certificate); women's health nurse practitioner (MSN, Post-Graduate Certificate). *Accreditation:* AACN; AANA/CANAEP. *Program availability:* Part-time, evening/weekend, online with on-campus intensives. *Faculty:* 72 full-time (61 women). *Students:* 155 full-time (137 women), 613 part-time (548 women); includes 177 minority (64 Black or African American, non-Hispanic/Latino; 2 American Indian or Alaska Native, non-Hispanic/Latino; 47 Asian, non-Hispanic/Latino; 34 Hispanic/Latino; 30 Two or more races, non-Hispanic/Latino), 10 international. Average age 34. 631 applicants, 47% accepted, 211 enrolled. In 2017, 221 master's, 71 doctorates, 26 other advanced degrees awarded. Terminal master's awarded for partial completion of doctoral program. *Degree requirements:* For master's, thesis optional; for doctorate, capstone project. *Entrance requirements:* For master's, GRE General Test (waived if undergraduate GPA of 3.4 or higher), 1 year of nursing experience (recommended), BSN, minimum GPA of 3.0, previous course work in statistics; for doctorate, GRE General Test (waived if undergraduate GPA of 3.4 or higher), BSN or MSN, minimum GPA of 3.0, resume, personal statement, undergraduate statistics course, current licensure as a registered nurse, transcripts from all post-secondary institutions; for Post-Graduate Certificate, MSN, licensure or eligibility as a professional nurse, transcripts from all post-secondary institutions, previous course work in statistics. Additional exam requirements/recommendations for international students: Required—TOEFL (minimum score 100 iBT), IELTS (minimum score 7). *Application deadline:* For fall admission, 12/1 for domestic and international students; for spring admission, 5/1 for domestic and international students. Application fee: $50. Electronic applications accepted. *Expenses:* Contact institution. *Financial support:* Institutionally sponsored loans, scholarships/grants, and traineeships available. Support available to part-time students. Financial award applicants required to submit FAFSA. *Faculty research:* Cardiovascular disease, caregiver skill training, data mining, prostate cancer, neonatal immune system. *Unit head:* Dr. Marion E. Broome, Dean/Vice Chancellor for Nursing Affairs/Associate Vice President for Academic Affairs for Nursing, 919-684-9446, Fax: 919-684-9414, E-mail: marion.broome@duke.edu. *Application contact:* Dr. Ernie Rushing, Director of Admissions and Recruitment, 919-668-6274, Fax: 919-668-4693, E-mail: ernie.rushing@dm.duke.edu.
Website: http://www.nursing.duke.edu/

East Tennessee State University, School of Graduate Studies, College of Nursing, Johnson City, TN 37614. Offers acute care nurse practitioner (DNP); adult-gerontology primary care nurse practitioner (DNP); adult/gerontological nurse practitioner (Postbaccalaureate Certificate); executive leadership in nursing (DNP, Postbaccalaureate Certificate); family nurse practitioner (MSN, DNP, Post-Master's Certificate, Postbaccalaureate Certificate); nursing (PhD); nursing administration (MSN); nursing education (MSN); pediatric primary care nurse practitioner (DNP); psychiatric mental health nurse practitioner (Postbaccalaureate Certificate); psychiatric/mental health nurse practitioner (MSN, DNP, Post-Master's Certificate); women's health care nurse practitioner (DNP). *Accreditation:* AACN. *Program availability:* Part-time, evening/weekend, online learning. In 2017, 126 master's, 30 doctorates, 4 other advanced degrees awarded. *Degree requirements:* For master's and other advanced degree, comprehensive exam, practicum; for doctorate, comprehensive exam, thesis/dissertation (for some programs), practicum, internship, evidence of professional malpractice insurance, CPR certification. *Entrance requirements:* For master's, bachelor's degree, minimum GPA of 3.0, current RN license and eligibility to practice, resume, three letters of recommendation; for doctorate, GRE General Test, MSN (for PhD), BSN or MSN (for DNP), current RN license and eligibility to practice, 2 years of full-time registered nurse work experience or equivalent, three letters of recommendation, resume or curriculum vitae, interview, writing sample; for other advanced degree, MSN, minimum GPA of 3.0, current RN license and eligibility to practice, three letters of recommendation, resume or curriculum vitae; DNP with designated concentration in advanced clinical practice or nursing administration (for select programs). Additional exam requirements/recommendations for international students: Required—TOEFL (minimum score 600 paper-based; 79 iBT). *Application deadline:* For fall admission, 4/15 priority date for domestic and international students; for spring admission, 10/15 priority date for domestic and international students; for summer admission, 2/1 for domestic and international students. Application fee: $55 ($65 for international students). Electronic applications accepted. *Financial support:* Research assistantships with tuition reimbursements, teaching assistantships, career-related internships or fieldwork, institutionally sponsored loans, scholarships/grants, and unspecified assistantships available. Financial award application deadline: 7/1; financial award applicants required to submit FAFSA. *Faculty research:* Improving health of rural and underserved populations (low income elders living in public housing, rural caregivers, Hispanic populations), health services and systems research (quality outcomes of nurse-managed primary care, in-home, and rural health care), nursing education (experiences of second-degree BSN students, well-being of BSN students). *Unit head:* Dr. Wendy Nehring, Dean, 423-439-7051, Fax: 423-439-4543, E-mail: nursing@etsu.edu. *Application contact:* Dr. Myra Clark, Director of Graduate Programs, 423-439-4396, Fax: 423-439-4100, E-mail: clarkml2@etsu.edu.
Website: http://www.etsu.edu/nursing/

Emory University, Nell Hodgson Woodruff School of Nursing, Atlanta, GA 30322-1100. Offers adult nurse practitioner (MSN); emergency nurse practitioner (MSN); family nurse practitioner (MSN); family nurse-midwife (MSN); health systems leadership (MSN); nurse-midwifery (MSN); pediatric nurse practitioner acute and primary care (MSN); women's health care (Title X) (MSN); women's health nurse practitioner (MSN); MSN/MPH. *Accreditation:* AACN; ACNM/ACME (one or more programs are accredited). *Program availability:* Part-time. *Entrance requirements:* For master's, GRE General Test or MAT, minimum GPA of 3.0, BS in nursing from an accredited institution, RN license and additional course work, 3 letters of recommendation. Additional exam requirements/recommendations for international students: Required—TOEFL (minimum score 600 paper-based; 100 iBT). Electronic applications accepted. *Expenses:* Contact institution. *Faculty research:* Older adult falls and injuries, minority health issues, cardiac symptoms and quality of life, bio-ethics and decision-making, menopausal issues.

Florida International University, Nicole Wertheim College of Nursing and Health Sciences, Nursing Program, Miami, FL 33199. Offers adult health nursing (MSN); family health (MSN); nurse anesthetist (MSN); nursing practice (DNP); nursing science research (PhD); pediatric nurse (MSN); psychiatric and mental health nursing (MSN); registered nurse (MSN). *Accreditation:* AACN; AANA/CANAEP. *Program availability:* Part-time, evening/weekend. *Faculty:* 40 full-time (33 women), 79 part-time/adjunct (69 women). *Students:* 330 full-time (233 women), 89 part-time (73 women); includes 326 minority (92 Black or African American, non-Hispanic/Latino; 1 American Indian or Alaska Native, non-Hispanic/Latino; 33 Asian, non-Hispanic/Latino; 195 Hispanic/Latino; 2 Native Hawaiian or other Pacific Islander, non-Hispanic/Latino; 3 Two or more races, non-Hispanic/Latino), 9 international. Average age 33. 304 applicants, 50% accepted, 148 enrolled. In 2017, 144 master's, 8 doctorates awarded. *Degree requirements:* For master's, thesis or alternative; for doctorate, comprehensive exam, thesis/dissertation. *Entrance requirements:* For master's, bachelor's degree in nursing, minimum undergraduate GPA of 3.0 in upper-level coursework, letters of recommendation; for doctorate, GRE, letters of recommendation, minimum undergraduate GPA of 3.0 in upper-level coursework, interview. Additional exam requirements/recommendations for international students: Required—TOEFL (minimum score 550 paper-based; 80 iBT). *Application deadline:* For fall admission, 6/1 for domestic students, 4/1 for international students; for spring admission, 10/1 for domestic students, 9/1 for international students. Applications are processed on a rolling basis. Application fee: $30. Electronic applications accepted. *Expenses:* Tuition, state resident: full-time $8912; part-time $446 per credit hour. Tuition, nonresident: full-time $21,393; part-time $992 per credit hour. *Required fees:* $390; $195 per semester. *Financial support:* Institutionally sponsored loans and scholarships/grants available. Financial award application deadline: 3/1; financial award applicants required to submit FAFSA. *Faculty research:* Adult health nursing. *Unit head:* Dr. Yhovana Gordon, Chair, 305-348-7733, Fax: 305-348-7051, E-mail: gordony@fiu.edu. *Application contact:* Nanett Rojas, Manager, Admissions Operations, 305-348-7464, Fax: 305-348-7441, E-mail: gradadm@fiu.edu.
Website: http://cnhs.fiu.edu/

Georgia State University, Byrdine F. Lewis School of Nursing, Atlanta, GA 30303. Offers adult health clinical nurse specialist/nurse practitioner (MS, Certificate); child health clinical nurse specialist/pediatric nurse practitioner (MS, Certificate); family nurse practitioner (MS, Certificate); family psychiatric mental health nurse practitioner (MS, Certificate); nursing (PhD); nursing leadership in healthcare innovations (MS), including nursing administration, nursing informatics; nutrition (MS); perinatal clinical nurse specialist/women's health nurse practitioner (MS, Certificate); physical therapy (DPT);

respiratory therapy (MS). *Accreditation:* AACN. *Program availability:* Part-time, blended/hybrid learning. *Faculty:* 69 full-time (52 women). *Students:* 322 full-time (248 women), 481 part-time (466 women); includes 186 minority (112 Black or African American, non-Hispanic/Latino; 44 Asian, non-Hispanic/Latino; 20 Hispanic/Latino; 10 Two or more races, non-Hispanic/Latino), 18 international. Average age 31. 370 applicants, 56% accepted, 148 enrolled. In 2017, 131 master's, 49 doctorates, 11 other advanced degrees awarded. *Degree requirements:* For doctorate, comprehensive exam, thesis/dissertation. *Entrance requirements:* For doctorate, GRE. Additional exam requirements/recommendations for international students: Required—TOEFL. *Application deadline:* For fall admission, 2/1 priority date for domestic and international students; for spring admission, 9/15 for domestic and international students. Applications are processed on a rolling basis. Application fee: $50. Electronic applications accepted. *Expenses:* Contact institution. *Financial support:* In 2017–18, research assistantships with tuition reimbursements (averaging $1,666 per year), teaching assistantships with tuition reimbursements (averaging $1,920 per year) were awarded; scholarships/grants, tuition waivers (full and partial), and unspecified assistantships also available. Support available to part-time students. Financial award application deadline: 8/1; financial award applicants required to submit FAFSA. *Faculty research:* Stroke intervention for caregivers, stroke prevention in African Americans; relationships between psychological distress and health outcomes in parents with a medically ill infant; medically fragile children; nursing expertise and patient outcomes. *Unit head:* Nancy Kropf, Dean of Nursing, 404-413-1101, Fax: 404-413-1090, E-mail: nkropf@gsu.edu.
Website: http://nursing.gsu.edu/

Gwynedd Mercy University, Frances M. Maguire School of Nursing and Health Professions, Gwynedd Valley, PA 19437-0901. Offers clinical nurse specialist (MSN), including gerontology, oncology, pediatrics; nurse educator (MSN); nurse practitioner (MSN), including adult health, pediatric health; nursing (DNP). *Accreditation:* ACEN. *Program availability:* Part-time, blended/hybrid learning. *Faculty:* 4 full-time (all women), 1 (woman) part-time/adjunct. *Students:* 28 full-time (25 women), 48 part-time (43 women); includes 28 minority (15 Black or African American, non-Hispanic/Latino; 11 Asian, non-Hispanic/Latino; 1 Hispanic/Latino; 1 Two or more races, non-Hispanic/Latino). Average age 37. 72 applicants, 25% accepted, 16 enrolled. In 2017, 7 master's awarded. *Degree requirements:* For master's, thesis optional; for doctorate, evidence-based scholarly project. *Entrance requirements:* For master's, GRE General Test or MAT, current nursing experience, physical assessment, course work in statistics, BSN from ACEN-accredited program, 2 letters of recommendation, personal interview. Additional exam requirements/recommendations for international students: Required—TOEFL (minimum score 575 paper-based). *Application deadline:* For fall admission, 8/1 priority date for domestic students; for winter admission, 12/1 priority date for domestic students. Applications are processed on a rolling basis. Electronic applications accepted. *Expenses:* $825 per credit (non-doctoral degrees), $930 per credit (doctoral); $17 part-time fee, $165 graduation fee. *Financial support:* In 2017–18, 5 students received support. Scholarships/grants, traineeships, and unspecified assistantships available. Financial award application deadline: 8/30. *Faculty research:* Critical thinking, primary care, domestic violence, multiculturalism, nursing centers. *Unit head:* Dr. Andrea D. Hollingsworth, Dean, 215-646-7300 Ext. 539, Fax: 215-641-5517, E-mail: hollingsworth.a@gmc.edu. *Application contact:* Dr. Barbara A. Jones, Director, 215-646-7300 Ext. 407, Fax: 215-641-5564, E-mail: jones.b@gmc.edu.
Website: http://www.gmercyu.edu/academics/graduate-programs/nursing

Indiana University–Purdue University Indianapolis, School of Nursing, MSN Program in Nursing, Indianapolis, IN 46202. Offers adult/gerontology acute care nurse practitioner (MSN); adult/gerontology clinical nurse specialist (MSN); adult/gerontology primary care nurse practitioner (MSN); family nurse practitioner (MSN); nursing education (MSN); nursing leadership in health systems (MSN); pediatric clinical nurse specialist (MSN); pediatric nurse practitioner (MSN). *Accreditation:* AACN. *Program availability:* Part-time, blended/hybrid learning. *Degree requirements:* For master's, thesis. *Entrance requirements:* For master's, BSN from ACEN- or CCNE-accredited program, minimum undergraduate GPA of 3.0 (preferred), professional resume or curriculum vitae, essay stating career goals and objectives, current unencumbered RN license, three references from individuals with knowledge of ability to succeed in graduate program. Additional exam requirements/recommendations for international students: Required—TOEFL (minimum score 550 paper-based; 79 iBT). Electronic applications accepted. *Expenses:* Contact institution. *Faculty research:* Quality of life, symptom management, cancer prevention and control, heart failure, pediatric oncology.

Johns Hopkins University, School of Nursing, Certificate Programs in Nursing, Baltimore, MD 21205. Offers nursing education (Certificate); pediatric acute care nurse practitioner (Certificate); psychiatric mental health nurse practitioner (Certificate). *Program availability:* Part-time-only, online only, 100% online. *Faculty:* 62 full-time (46 women), 160 part-time/adjunct (all women). *Students:* 39 part-time (35 women); includes 14 minority (5 Black or African American, non-Hispanic/Latino; 2 Asian, non-Hispanic/Latino; 4 Hispanic/Latino; 3 Two or more races, non-Hispanic/Latino). Average age 44. 159 applicants, 33% accepted, 45 enrolled. In 2017, 18 Certificates awarded. *Entrance requirements:* For degree, minimum GPA of 3.0, goal statement/essay, resume, letters of recommendation, official transcripts from all post-secondary institutions, MSN, RN license, NP license. Additional exam requirements/recommendations for international students: Required—TOEFL (minimum score 600 paper-based; 100 iBT), IELTS (minimum score 7). *Application deadline:* For fall admission, 1/1 priority date for domestic students; for spring admission, 11/1 priority date for domestic students. Application fee: $70. Electronic applications accepted. *Expenses:* $1,591 per credit. *Financial support:* Application deadline: 3/1; applicants required to submit FAFSA. *Faculty research:* Palliative care, cardiovascular health, disease prevention and risk reduction, women's health, palliative and end-of-life care. *Unit head:* Dr. Patricia M. Davidson, Dean, 410-955-7544, Fax: 410-955-4890, E-mail: sondeansoffice@jhu.edu. *Application contact:* Cathy Wilson, Director of Admissions, 410-955-7548, Fax: 410-614-7086, E-mail: jhuson@jhu.edu.
Website: http://nursing.jhu.edu/

See Display on page 576 and Close-Up on page 763.

Johns Hopkins University, School of Nursing, Nurse Practitioner Program, Baltimore, MD 21205. Offers adult/gerontological acute care nurse practitioner (DNP); adult/gerontological primary care nurse practitioner (DNP); family primary care nurse practitioner (DNP); pediatric primary care nurse practitioner (DNP). *Accreditation:* AACN. *Program availability:* Part-time. *Faculty:* 9 full-time (all women), 10 part-time/adjunct (all women). *Students:* 52 full-time (46 women), 173 part-time (160 women); includes 77 minority (28 Black or African American, non-Hispanic/Latino; 26 Asian, non-Hispanic/Latino; 18 Hispanic/Latino; 5 Two or more races, non-Hispanic/Latino), 2 international. Average age 33. 157 applicants, 55% accepted, 52 enrolled. *Entrance requirements:* For doctorate, GRE, minimum GPA of 3.0, goal statement/essay, resume, letters of recommendation, official transcripts from all post-secondary institutions attended; BSN; RN license; writing sample. Additional exam requirements/recommendations for international students: Required—TOEFL (minimum score 600 paper-based; 100 iBT), IELTS (minimum score 7). *Application deadline:* For fall admission, 11/1 priority date for domestic and international students. Application fee: $70. Electronic applications accepted. *Expenses:* $1,671 per credit. *Financial support:* In 2017–18, 28 students received support. Federal Work-Study and scholarships/grants available. Support available to part-time students. Financial award application deadline: 3/1; financial award applicants required to submit FAFSA. *Faculty research:* Community outreach, primary care of underserved populations, substance-abusing individuals, childhood violence, women's health. *Unit head:* Dr. Patricia M. Davidson, Dean, 410-955-7544, Fax: 410-955-4890, E-mail: sondeansoffice@jhu.edu. *Application contact:* Cathy Wilson, Director of Admissions, 410-955-7548, Fax: 410-614-7086, E-mail: jhuson@jhu.edu.
Website: http://www.nursing.jhu.edu

See Display on page 576 and Close-Up on page 763.

Johns Hopkins University, School of Nursing, Program in Clinical Nurse Specialist, Baltimore, MD 21205. Offers adult/gerontological critical care clinical nurse specialist (DNP); adult/gerontological health clinical nurse specialist (DNP); pediatric critical care clinical nurse specialist (DNP). *Accreditation:* AACN. *Program availability:* Part-time, 100% online, blended/hybrid learning. *Faculty:* 3 full-time (2 women). *Students:* 13 full-time (all women), 15 part-time (13 women); includes 11 minority (1 Black or African American, non-Hispanic/Latino; 1 American Indian or Alaska Native, non-Hispanic/Latino; 2 Asian, non-Hispanic/Latino; 6 Hispanic/Latino; 1 Two or more races, non-Hispanic/Latino). Average age 32. 32 applicants, 63% accepted, 14 enrolled. *Entrance requirements:* For doctorate, GRE, minimum GPA of 3.0, goal statement/essay, resume, letters of recommendation, official transcripts from all post-secondary institutions attended; BSN; RN license; writing sample. Additional exam requirements/recommendations for international students: Required—TOEFL (minimum score 600 paper-based; 100 iBT), IELTS (minimum score 7). *Application deadline:* For fall admission, 11/1 priority date for domestic and international students. Application fee: $70. Electronic applications accepted. *Expenses:* $1,671 per credit. *Financial support:* In 2017–18, 8 students received support. Federal Work-Study and scholarships/grants available. Support available to part-time students. Financial award application deadline: 3/1; financial award applicants required to submit FAFSA. *Faculty research:* Maternal child health, symptom management, cardiovascular risk reduction, asthma, hypertension. *Unit head:* Dr. Patricia M. Davidson, Dean, 410-955-7544, Fax: 410-955-4890, E-mail: sondeansoffice@jhu.edu. *Application contact:* Cathy Wilson, Director of Admissions, 410-955-7548, Fax: 410-614-7086, E-mail: jhuson@jhu.edu.
Website: http://www.nursing.jhu.edu

See Display on page 576 and Close-Up on page 763.

Kent State University, College of Nursing, Kent, OH 44242. Offers advanced nursing practice (DNP), including adult/gerontology acute care nurse practitioner (MSN, DNP); nursing (MSN, PhD), including adult/gerontology acute care nurse practitioner (MSN, DNP), adult/gerontology clinical nurse specialist (MSN), adult/gerontology primary care nurse practitioner (MSN), family nurse practitioner (MSN), nurse educator (MSN), nursing and healthcare management (MSN), pediatric primary care nurse practitioner (MSN), psychiatric/mental health nurse practitioner (MSN); MBA/MSN. PhD program offered jointly with The University of Akron. *Accreditation:* AACN. *Program availability:* Part-time, online learning. *Faculty:* 29 full-time (28 women), 15 part-time/adjunct (12 women). *Students:* 167 full-time (142 women), 405 part-time (359 women); includes 70 minority (39 Black or African American, non-Hispanic/Latino; 11 Asian, non-Hispanic/Latino; 18 Hispanic/Latino; 2 Two or more races, non-Hispanic/Latino), 13 international. Average age 35. 272 applicants, 74% accepted, 166 enrolled. In 2017, 144 master's, 8 doctorates awarded. *Degree requirements:* For master's, thesis optional; for doctorate, comprehensive exam, thesis/dissertation. *Entrance requirements:* For master's, GRE or GMAT, minimum GPA of 3.0, active RN license, statement of purpose, 3 letters of reference, undergraduate level statistics class, baccalaureate or graduate-level nursing degree, curriculum vitae/resume; for doctorate, GRE, minimum GPA of 3.0, transcripts, 3 letters of reference, interview, active unrestricted Ohio RN license, statement of purpose, writing sample, curriculum vitae/resume, baccalaureate and master's degrees in nursing or DNP. Additional exam requirements/recommendations for international students: Required—TOEFL (minimum score 560 paper-based; 83 iBT), IELTS (minimum score 6.5), PTE (minimum score 55), Michigan English Language Assessment Battery (minimum score 78). *Application deadline:* For fall admission, 3/1 for domestic and international students; for spring admission, 10/1 for domestic and international students. Applications are processed on a rolling basis. Application fee: $45 ($70 for international students). Electronic applications accepted. *Expenses:* Tuition, state resident: full-time $11,310; part-time $515 per credit hour. Tuition, nonresident: full-time $20,396; part-time $928 per credit hour. *International tuition:* $18,544 full-time. *Financial support:* Scholarships/grants available. Financial award application deadline: 5/4. *Unit head:* Dr. Barbara Broome, Dean, 330-672-3777, E-mail: bbroome1@kent.edu. *Application contact:* Dr. Wendy A. Umberger, Associate Dean for Graduate Programs/Professor, 330-672-8813, E-mail: wlewando@kent.edu.
Website: http://www.kent.edu/nursing/

King University, School of Nursing, Bristol, TN 37620-2699. Offers family nurse practitioner (MSN); nurse educator (MSN); nursing (DNP); nursing administration (MSN); pediatric nurse practitioner (MSN).

Lehman College of the City University of New York, School of Health Sciences, Human Services and Nursing, Department of Nursing, Bronx, NY 10468-1589. Offers adult health nursing (MS); nursing of older adults (MS); parent-child nursing (MS); pediatric nurse practitioner (MS). *Accreditation:* AACN. *Program availability:* Part-time, evening/weekend. *Entrance requirements:* For master's, bachelor's degree in nursing, New York RN license.

Loma Linda University, School of Nursing, Program in Nurse Educator, Loma Linda, CA 92350. Offers adult/gerontology (MS); obstetrics-pediatrics (MS). *Accreditation:* AACN. *Program availability:* Part-time. *Degree requirements:* For master's, thesis or alternative. *Entrance requirements:* For master's, GRE General Test, BSN, minimum GPA of 3.0, RN license. Additional exam requirements/recommendations for international students: Required—TOEFL. Electronic applications accepted. *Faculty research:* Coping, integration of research.

Marquette University, Graduate School, College of Nursing, Milwaukee, WI 53201-1881. Offers acute care nurse practitioner (Certificate); adult clinical nurse specialist (Certificate); adult nurse practitioner (Certificate); advanced practice nursing (MSN, DNP), including adult-older adult acute care (DNP), adults (MSN), adults-older adults (DNP), clinical nurse leader (MSN), health care systems leadership (DNP), nurse-midwifery (MSN), older adults (MSN), pediatrics-acute care, pediatrics-primary care, primary care (DNP), systems leadership and healthcare quality (MSN); family nurse practitioner (Certificate); nurse-midwifery (Certificate); nursing (PhD); pediatric acute care (Certificate); pediatric primary care (Certificate); systems leadership and healthcare quality (Certificate). *Accreditation:* AACN. Terminal master's awarded for partial completion of doctoral program. *Degree requirements:* For master's, comprehensive exam, thesis or alternative. *Entrance requirements:* For master's, GRE General Test, BSN, Wisconsin RN license, official transcripts from all current and previous colleges/universities except Marquette, three completed recommendation forms, resume, written statement of professional goals; for doctorate, GRE General Test, official transcripts from all current and previous colleges/universities except Marquette, three letters of recommendation, resume, written statement of professional goals, sample of scholarly writing. Additional exam requirements/recommendations for international students: Required—TOEFL (minimum score 530 paper-based). Electronic applications accepted. *Faculty research:* Psychosocial adjustment to chronic illness, gerontology, reminiscence, health policy: uninsured and access, hospital care delivery systems.

Maryville University of Saint Louis, Myrtle E. and Earl E. Walker College of Health Professions, The Catherine McAuley School of Nursing, St. Louis, MO 63141-7299. Offers acute care nurse practitioner (MSN); adult gerontology nurse practitioner (MSN); advanced practice nursing (DNP); family nurse practitioner (MSN); pediatric nurse practitioner (MSN). *Accreditation:* AACN. *Program availability:* 100% online, blended/hybrid learning. *Faculty:* 15 full-time (all women), 142 part-time/adjunct (123 women). *Students:* 49 full-time (42 women), 2,999 part-time (2,645 women); includes 773 minority (375 Black or African American, non-Hispanic/Latino; 51 American Indian or Alaska Native, non-Hispanic/Latino; 135 Asian, non-Hispanic/Latino; 149 Hispanic/Latino; 63 Two or more races, non-Hispanic/Latino), 21 international. Average age 36. In 2017, 843 master's, 42 doctorates awarded. *Degree requirements:* For master's, practicum. *Entrance requirements:* For master's, BSN, current licensure, minimum GPA of 3.0, 3 letters of recommendation, curriculum vitae. Additional exam requirements/recommendations for international students: Required—TOEFL (minimum score 550 paper-based). *Application deadline:* Applications are processed on a rolling basis. Electronic applications accepted. *Expenses:* Contact institution. *Financial support:* Federal Work-Study and campus employment available. Support available to part-time students. Financial award application deadline: 4/1; financial award applicants required to submit FAFSA. *Unit head:* Dr. Elizabeth Buck, Assistant Dean/Director of Online Nursing, 314-529-9453, Fax: 314-529-9139, E-mail: ebuck@maryville.edu. *Application contact:* Jeannie DeLuca, Director of Admissions and Advising, 314-929-9355, Fax: 314-529-9927, E-mail: cjacobsmeyer@maryville.edu.
Website: http://www.maryville.edu/hp/nursing/

MGH Institute of Health Professions, School of Nursing, Boston, MA 02129. Offers advanced practice nursing (MSN); gerontological nursing (MSN); nursing (DNP); pediatric nursing (MSN); psychiatric nursing (MSN); teaching and learning for health care education (Certificate); women's health nursing (MSN). *Accreditation:* AACN. *Degree requirements:* For master's, thesis or alternative. *Entrance requirements:* For master's, GRE General Test, bachelor's degree from regionally-accredited college or university. Additional exam requirements/recommendations for international students: Required—TOEFL (minimum score 550 paper-based; 80 iBT). Electronic applications accepted. *Faculty research:* Biobehavioral nursing, HIV/AIDS, gerontological nursing, women's health, vulnerable populations, health systems.

Molloy College, The Barbara H. Hagan School of Nursing, Rockville Centre, NY 11571-5002. Offers adult - gerontology nurse practitioner (MS); adult-gerontology clinical nurse specialist (DNP); adult-gerontology nurse practitioner (DNP); clinical nurse specialist: adult - gerontology (MS); family nurse practitioner (MS, DNP); family psychiatric/mental health nurse practitioner (MS, DNP); nursing (PhD, Advanced Certificate); nursing administration with informatics (MS); nursing education (MS); pediatric nurse practitioner (MS, DNP). *Accreditation:* AACN. *Program availability:* Part-time, evening/weekend. *Faculty:* 28 full-time (all women), 7 part-time/adjunct (6 women). *Students:* 19 full-time (14 women), 574 part-time (527 women); includes 336 minority (179 Black or African American, non-Hispanic/Latino; 2 American Indian or Alaska Native, non-Hispanic/Latino; 107 Asian, non-Hispanic/Latino; 42 Hispanic/Latino; 1 Native Hawaiian or other Pacific Islander, non-Hispanic/Latino; 5 Two or more races, non-Hispanic/Latino), 4 international. Average age 44. 292 applicants, 65% accepted, 147 enrolled. In 2017, 135 master's, 9 doctorates, 5 other advanced degrees awarded. *Degree requirements:* For master's, thesis optional. *Entrance requirements:* For master's, 3 letters of reference, BS in nursing, minimum undergraduate GPA of 3.0; for Advanced Certificate, 3 letters of reference, master's degree in nursing. Additional exam requirements/recommendations for international students: Required—TOEFL (minimum score 550 paper-based; 79 iBT). *Application deadline:* For fall admission, 9/2 priority date for domestic students; for spring admission, 1/20 priority date for domestic students. Applications are processed on a rolling basis. Application fee: $60. Electronic applications accepted. *Expenses: Tuition:* Full-time $19,980; part-time $1110 per credit. *Required fees:* $1040. Tuition and fees vary according to course load and degree level. *Financial support:* Research assistantships with partial tuition reimbursements, teaching assistantships with partial tuition reimbursements, institutionally sponsored loans, scholarships/grants, and unspecified assistantships available. Support available to part-time students. Financial award application deadline: 3/1; financial award applicants required to submit FAFSA. *Faculty research:* Workplace violence involving nurses and psychiatric patients; moral distress in nursing; primary care of veterans; the role of service immersion programs in graduate nursing education; academic integrity. *Unit head:* Dr. Marcia R. Gardner, Dean, The Barbara H. Hagan School of Nursing, 516-323-3651, E-mail: mgardner@molloy.edu. *Application contact:* Jaclyn Machowicz, Assistant Director for Admissions, 516-323-4010, E-mail: jmachowicz@molloy.edu.

New York University, Rory Meyers College of Nursing, Doctor of Nursing Practice Program, New York, NY 10012-1019. Offers nursing (DNP), including adult-gerontology acute care nurse practitioner, adult-gerontology primary care nurse practitioner, family nurse practitioner, nurse-midwifery, pediatrics nurse practitioner, psychiatric-mental health nurse practitioner. *Accreditation:* AACN. *Program availability:* Part-time, evening/weekend. *Faculty:* 16 full-time (all women), 1 (woman) part-time/adjunct. *Students:* 48 part-time (43 women); includes 11 minority (5 Black or African American, non-Hispanic/Latino; 5 Asian, non-Hispanic/Latino; 1 Hispanic/Latino). Average age 28. 20 applicants, 75% accepted, 10 enrolled. In 2017, 8 doctorates awarded. *Degree requirements:* For doctorate, thesis/dissertation, project. *Entrance requirements:* For doctorate, MS, RN license, interview, Nurse Practitioner Certification, writing sample. Additional exam requirements/recommendations for international students: Required—TOEFL (minimum score 100 iBT), IELTS (minimum score 7). *Application deadline:* For fall admission, 3/1 priority date for domestic and international students. Applications are processed on a rolling basis. Application fee: $80. Electronic applications accepted. *Expenses:* Contact institution. *Financial support:* In 2017–18, 13 students received support. Scholarships/grants available. Support available to part-time students. Financial award application deadline: 2/1; financial award applicants required to submit FAFSA. *Faculty research:* Workforce determinants of healthcare quality, genomics, health literacy and health outcomes, health policy. *Unit head:* Dr. Mary Jo Vetter, Director, DNP Program, 212-998-5165, E-mail: mjv5@nyu.edu. *Application contact:* Matthew Burke, Assistant Director, Graduate Student Affairs and Admissions, 212-998-7397, E-mail: mb6060@nyu.edu.

New York University, Rory Meyers College of Nursing, Programs in Advanced Practice Nursing, New York, NY 10012-1019. Offers adult-gerontology acute care nurse practitioner (MS, Advanced Certificate); adult-gerontology primary care nurse practitioner (MS, Advanced Certificate); family nurse practitioner (MS, Advanced Certificate); gerontology nurse practitioner (Advanced Certificate); nurse-midwifery (MS, Advanced Certificate); nursing administration (MS, Advanced Certificate); nursing education (MS, Advanced Certificate); nursing informatics (MS, Advanced Certificate); pediatrics nurse practitioner (MS, Advanced Certificate); psychiatric-mental health nurse practitioner (MS, Advanced Certificate); MS/MPH. *Accreditation:* AACN; ACNM/ACME. *Program availability:* Part-time, evening/weekend. *Faculty:* 23 full-time (all women), 62 part-time/adjunct (56 women). *Students:* 50 full-time (46 women), 557 part-time (509 women); includes 234 minority (58 Black or African American, non-Hispanic/Latino; 1 American Indian or Alaska Native, non-Hispanic/Latino; 116 Asian, non-Hispanic/Latino; 43 Hispanic/Latino; 1 Native Hawaiian or other Pacific Islander, non-Hispanic/Latino; 15 Two or more races, non-Hispanic/Latino), 23 international. Average age 32. 391 applicants, 59% accepted, 149 enrolled. In 2017, 187 master's, 5 other advanced degrees awarded. *Degree requirements:* For master's, thesis (for some programs), capstone. *Entrance requirements:* For master's, BS in nursing, AS in nursing with another BS/BA, interview, RN license, 1 year of clinical experience (3 for the MS in nursing education program); for Advanced Certificate, master's degree in nursing. Additional exam requirements/recommendations for international students: Required—TOEFL (minimum score 100 iBT), IELTS (minimum score 7). *Application deadline:* For fall admission, 3/1 priority date for domestic and international students; for spring admission, 11/1 priority date for domestic and international students; for summer admission, 3/1 for domestic and international students. Application fee: $80. Electronic applications accepted. *Expenses:* Contact institution. *Financial support:* In 2017–18, 130 students received support. Career-related internships or fieldwork, Federal Work-Study, and scholarships/grants available. Support available to part-time students. Financial award application deadline: 3/1; financial award applicants required to submit FAFSA. *Faculty research:* Vaccine hesitancy in pregnant women and mothers, palliative care and midwifery, diabetes education, curriculum development, workforce training, education and development, geriatrics. *Unit head:* Dr. James Pace, Senior Associate Dean for Academic Programs, 212-992-7343, E-mail: james.pace@nyu.edu. *Application contact:* Matthew Burke, Assistant Director, Graduate Student Affairs and Admissions, 212-998-7397, Fax: 212-995-4302, E-mail: mb6060@nyu.edu.

Northeastern University, Bouvé College of Health Sciences, Boston, MA 02115-5096. Offers applied behavior analysis (MS); audiology (Au D); counseling psychology (MS, PhD, CAGS); exercise science (MS); nursing (MS, PhD, CAGS), including administration (MS), adult-gerontology acute care nurse practitioner (MS, CAGS), adult-gerontology primary care nurse practitioner (MS, CAGS), anesthesia (MS), family nurse practitioner (MS, CAGS), neonatal nurse practitioner (MS, CAGS), pediatric nurse practitioner (MS, CAGS), psychiatric mental health nurse practitioner (MS, CAGS); nursing practice (DNP); pharmaceutical sciences (MS, PhD), including interdisciplinary concentration, pharmaceutics and drug delivery systems; pharmacology (MS); pharmacy (Pharm D); school psychology (PhD); speech-language pathology (MS); urban health (MPH); MS/MBA. *Accreditation:* ACPE (one or more programs are accredited). *Program availability:* Part-time, evening/weekend, online learning. *Faculty:* 192 full-time. *Students:* 1,685. In 2017, 352 master's, 312 doctorates, 25 other advanced degrees awarded. *Degree requirements:* For doctorate, thesis/dissertation (for some programs); for CAGS, comprehensive exam. Application fee: $75. Electronic applications accepted. *Expenses:* Contact institution. *Financial support:* Fellowships, research assistantships, teaching assistantships, career-related internships or fieldwork, scholarships/grants, health care benefits, tuition waivers, and unspecified assistantships available. Support available to part-time students. Financial award applicants required to submit FAFSA. *Unit head:* Susan L. Parish, Dean, Bouve College of Health Sciences, 617-373-3321, Fax: 617-373-3030, E-mail: s.parish@northeastern.edu. *Application contact:* 617-373-2708, Fax: 617-373-4701, E-mail: bouvegrad@northeastern.edu.
Website: https://www.northeastern.edu/bouve/

Old Dominion University, College of Health Sciences, School of Nursing, Adult Gerontology Nursing Emphasis, Norfolk, VA 23529. Offers adult gerontology clinical nurse specialist/administrator (MSN); adult gerontology clinical nurse specialist/educator (MSN); advanced practice (DNP); neonatal clinical nurse specialist (MSN); pediatric clinical nurse specialist (MSN). *Program availability:* Part-time, online only, blended/hybrid learning. *Faculty:* 2 full-time (both women), 2 part-time/adjunct (both women). *Students:* 9 full-time (all women), 10 part-time (9 women); includes 10 minority (8 Black or African American, non-Hispanic/Latino; 2 Asian, non-Hispanic/Latino). Average age 37. 27 applicants, 96% accepted, 12 enrolled. In 2017, 5 master's awarded. *Degree requirements:* For master's, comprehensive exam, internship, practicum. *Entrance requirements:* For master's, GRE or MAT (waived with a GPA above 3.5), undergraduate health/physical assessment course, statistics, 3 letters of recommendation, essay, resume, transcripts. Additional exam requirements/recommendations for international students: Required—TOEFL. *Application deadline:* For fall admission, 6/1 priority date for domestic students, 4/15 priority date for international students. Applications are processed on a rolling basis. Application fee: $50. Electronic applications accepted. *Expenses:* $469 per credit; $450 School of Nursing fee per semester. *Financial support:* Unspecified assistantships available. Financial award applicants required to submit FAFSA. *Unit head:* Dr. Tina Haney, Program Director, 757-683-5428, Fax: 757-683-5253, E-mail: thaney@odu.edu. *Application contact:* Sue Parker, Graduate Program Coordinator, 757-683-4298, Fax: 757-683-5253, E-mail: sparker@odu.edu.

Old Dominion University, College of Health Sciences, School of Nursing, Pediatric Nursing Emphasis, Norfolk, VA 23529. Offers advanced practice (DNP); pediatric clinical nurse specialist (MSN); pediatric nurse practitioner (MSN). *Program availability:* Part-time, blended/hybrid learning. *Faculty:* 2 full-time (both women), 2 part-time/adjunct (both women). *Students:* 21 full-time (20 women); includes 5 minority (2 Black or African American, non-Hispanic/Latino; 1 Asian, non-Hispanic/Latino; 2 Two or more races, non-Hispanic/Latino). Average age 32. 12 applicants, 75% accepted, 8 enrolled. *Degree requirements:* For master's, comprehensive exam; for doctorate, capstone project. *Entrance requirements:* For master's, GRE or MAT if the undergraduate GPA is below 3.5, current unencumbered license as a registered nurse (RN) with 1 year of current experience in the role; undergraduate physical/health assessment course; undergraduate statistics course; baccalaureate degree in nursing or related science field with minimum GPA of 3.0; three letters of recommendation. Additional exam requirements/recommendations for international students: Required—TOEFL. *Application deadline:* For fall admission, 3/1 for domestic students, 4/15 for international students. Application fee: $50. Electronic applications accepted. *Expenses:* $469 per credit; $450 School of Nursing fee per semester. *Financial support:* Traineeships available. *Unit head:* Dr. Karen Karlowicz, Chair, School of Nursing, 757-683-4297, Fax: 757-683-5253, E-mail: kkarlowic@odu.edu. *Application contact:* Sue Parker, Graduate Program Coordinator, 757-683-4298, Fax: 757-683-5253, E-mail: sparker@odu.edu.

Oregon Health & Science University, School of Nursing, Program in Pediatric Nurse Practitioner, Portland, OR 97239-3098. Offers MN. *Program availability:* Blended/hybrid learning. *Entrance requirements:* For master's, GRE General Test, bachelor's degree in nursing, minimum cumulative and science GPA of 3.0, 3 letters of recommendation, essay, statistics within last 5 years. Additional exam requirements/recommendations for international students: Required—TOEFL (minimum score 83 iBT). Electronic applications accepted. *Expenses:* Contact institution. *Faculty research:* Pediatric nursing, pediatric neurological/neurosurgical population, global health, pediatric pain and pain management.

Point Loma Nazarene University, School of Nursing, MS in Nursing Program, San Diego, CA 92106-2899. Offers adult-gerontology (MSN); family individual health (MSN); pediatrics (MSN). *Program availability:* Part-time. *Students:* 59 part-time (49 women); includes 28 minority (4 Black or African American, non-Hispanic/Latino; 1 American

Indian or Alaska Native, non-Hispanic/Latino; 4 Asian, non-Hispanic/Latino; 9 Hispanic/Latino; 4 Native Hawaiian or other Pacific Islander, non-Hispanic/Latino; 6 Two or more races, non-Hispanic/Latino), 1 international. Average age 36. 23 applicants, 96% accepted, 18 enrolled. In 2017, 21 master's awarded. *Entrance requirements:* For master's, NCLEX exam, ADN or BSN in nursing, interview, RN license, essay, letters of recommendation, interview. *Application deadline:* For fall admission, 7/5 priority date for domestic students; for spring admission, 11/1 priority date for domestic students; for summer admission, 3/22 priority date for domestic students. Applications are processed on a rolling basis. Electronic applications accepted. *Expenses:* Contact institution. *Financial support:* Scholarships/grants available. Financial award applicants required to submit FAFSA. *Unit head:* Dr. Barb Taylor, Dean of the School of Nursing, 619-849-2766, E-mail: bataylor@pointloma.edu. *Application contact:* Joanie Joy, Senior Director of Enrollment Management, 619-329-6785, E-mail: gradinfo@pointloma.edu.
Website: https://www.pointloma.edu/graduate-studies/programs/nursing-ms

Purdue University, Graduate School, College of Health and Human Sciences, School of Nursing, West Lafayette, IN 47907. Offers adult gerontology primary care nurse practitioner (MS, Post Master's Certificate); nursing (DNP, PhD); primary care family nurse practitioner (MS, Post Master's Certificate); primary care pediatric nurse practitioner (MS, Post Master's Certificate). *Faculty:* 31 full-time (30 women), 2 part-time/adjunct (both women). *Students:* 41 full-time (39 women), 33 part-time (32 women); includes 10 minority (5 Black or African American, non-Hispanic/Latino; 1 American Indian or Alaska Native, non-Hispanic/Latino; 1 Asian, non-Hispanic/Latino; 2 Hispanic/Latino; 1 Two or more races, non-Hispanic/Latino), 2 international. Average age 35. 36 applicants, 78% accepted, 16 enrolled. In 2017, 13 master's, 5 doctorates, 2 other advanced degrees awarded. *Unit head:* Jane M. Kirkpatrick, Head of the Graduate Program, 765-494-6644, E-mail: jmkirk@purdue.edu. *Application contact:* Reanne Hall, Graduate Contact, 765-494-9248, E-mail: gradnursing@purdue.edu.
Website: http://www.purdue.edu/hhs/nur/

Queen's University at Kingston, School of Graduate Studies, Faculty of Health Sciences, School of Nursing, Kingston, ON K7L 3N6, Canada. Offers health and chronic illness (M Sc); nurse scientist (PhD); primary health care nurse practitioner (Certificate); women's and children's health (M Sc). *Degree requirements:* For master's, thesis. *Entrance requirements:* For master's, RN license. Additional exam requirements/recommendations for international students: Required—TOEFL. *Faculty research:* Women and children's health, health and chronic illness.

Rush University, College of Nursing, Department of Women, Children, and Family Nursing, Chicago, IL 60612. Offers neonatal clinical nurse specialist (DNP); neonatal nurse practitioner (DNP, Post-Graduate Certificate); pediatric acute care nurse practitioner (DNP, Post-Graduate Certificate); pediatric clinical nurse specialist (DNP); pediatric primary care nurse practitioner (DNP); transformative leadership: systems (DNP). *Accreditation:* AACN. *Program availability:* Part-time, 100% online. *Students:* 3 full-time (all women), 219 part-time (208 women); includes 35 minority (7 Black or African American, non-Hispanic/Latino; 8 Asian, non-Hispanic/Latino; 18 Hispanic/Latino; 2 Two or more races, non-Hispanic/Latino). 119 applicants, 69% accepted, 59 enrolled. In 2017, 71 doctorates, 12 Post-Graduate Certificates awarded. *Degree requirements:* For doctorate, scholarly project. *Entrance requirements:* For doctorate, GRE General Test (waived for DNP if cumulative GPA is 3.25 or greater, nursing GPA is 3.0 or greater, or a completed graduate program GPA is 3.5 or greater), interview, 3 letters of recommendation, personal statement, current resume; for Post-Graduate Certificate, MSN in a clinical discipline, 3 letters of recommendation, personal statement, current resume, interview. Additional exam requirements/recommendations for international students: Required—TOEFL (minimum score 94 iBT). *Application deadline:* For fall admission, 1/2 for domestic students; for spring admission, 8/1 for domestic students; for summer admission, 12/1 for domestic students. Applications are processed on a rolling basis. Application fee: $110. Electronic applications accepted. *Expenses:* Contact institution. *Financial support:* Research assistantships, teaching assistantships with tuition reimbursements, Federal Work-Study, scholarships/grants, traineeships, and health care benefits available. Support available to part-time students. Financial award application deadline: 3/1; financial award applicants required to submit FAFSA. *Faculty research:* Health disparities; parenting and grandparenting; child and adolescent health; women's health, fatherhood and men's health. *Unit head:* Dr. Wrenetha Julion, Chairperson, 312-942-7117, E-mail: wrenetha_a_julion@rush.edu. *Application contact:* Jennifer Thorndyke, Director of Admissions, 312-563-7526, E-mail: jennifer_thorndyke@rush.edu.
Website: https://www.rushu.rush.edu/college-nursing/departments-college-nursing/department-women-children-and-family-nursing

St. Catherine University, Graduate Programs, Program in Nursing, St. Paul, MN 55105. Offers adult-gerontological nurse practitioner (MS); nurse educator (MS); nursing (DNP); nursing: entry-level (MS); pediatric nurse practitioner (MS). *Accreditation:* ACEN. *Program availability:* Part-time, evening/weekend. *Degree requirements:* For master's, thesis; for doctorate, portfolio, systems change project. *Entrance requirements:* For master's, GRE General Test, bachelor's degree in nursing, current nursing license, 2 years of recent clinical practice; for doctorate, master's degree in nursing, RN license, advanced nursing position. Additional exam requirements/recommendations for international students: Required—TOEFL (minimum score 600 paper-based; 100 iBT). *Application deadline:* For fall admission, 1/15 priority date for domestic students. Application fee: $35. *Expenses:* Contact institution. *Financial support:* Career-related internships or fieldwork and institutionally sponsored loans available. Support available to part-time students. Financial award application deadline: 4/1; financial award applicants required to submit FAFSA. *Unit head:* Margaret Dexheimer-Pharris, Professor/Associate Dean for Nursing, 651-690-6572, Fax: 651-690-6941, E-mail: mdpharris@stkate.edu. *Application contact:* Kristin Chalberg, Associate Director of Non-Traditional Admissions, 651-690-6868, Fax: 651-690-6064.

San Francisco State University, Division of Graduate Studies, College of Health and Social Sciences, School of Nursing, San Francisco, CA 94132-1722. Offers adult acute care (MS); clinical nurse specialist (MS); community/public health nursing (MS); family nurse practitioner (Certificate); nursing administration (MS); pediatrics (MS); women's health (MS). *Accreditation:* AACN. *Program availability:* Part-time. *Application deadline:* Applications are processed on a rolling basis. *Financial support:* Career-related internships or fieldwork available. *Unit head:* Connie Carr, Assistant Director of Graduate Programs, 415-338-6856, Fax: 415-338-0555, E-mail: ccarr@sfsu.edu.
Website: http://nursing.sfsu.edu

Seton Hall University, College of Nursing, South Orange, NJ 07079-2697. Offers advanced practice in primary health care (MSN, DNP), including adult/gerontological nurse practitioner, pediatric nurse practitioner; entry into practice (MSN); health systems administration (MSN, DNP); nursing (PhD); nursing case management (MSN); nursing education (MA); school nurse (MSN); MSN/MA. *Accreditation:* AACN. *Program availability:* Part-time, online learning. *Degree requirements:* For master's, research project; for doctorate, dissertation or scholarly project. *Entrance requirements:* For doctorate, GRE (waived for students with GPA of 3.5 or higher). Additional exam requirements/recommendations for international students: Required—TOEFL. Electronic applications accepted. *Faculty research:* Parent/child, adult, and gerontological nursing; breast cancer; families of children with HIV; parish nursing.

Spalding University, Graduate Studies, Kosair College of Health and Natural Sciences, School of Nursing, Louisville, KY 40203-2188. Offers adult nurse practitioner (MSN); family nurse practitioner (MSN); leadership in nursing and healthcare (MSN); nurse educator (Post-Master's Certificate); nurse practitioner (Post-Master's Certificate); pediatric nurse practitioner (MSN). *Accreditation:* AACN. *Program availability:* Part-time, evening/weekend. *Degree requirements:* For master's, comprehensive exam (for some programs), thesis. *Entrance requirements:* For master's, GRE General Test, BSN or bachelor's degree in related field, RN licensure, autobiographical statement, transcripts, letters of recommendation. Additional exam requirements/recommendations for international students: Required—TOEFL (minimum score 535 paper-based). *Faculty research:* Nurse educational administration, gerontology, bioterrorism, healthcare ethics, leadership.

Stony Brook University, State University of New York, Stony Brook Medicine, School of Nursing, Pediatric Primary Care Nurse Practitioner Program, Stony Brook, NY 11794. Offers child health nurse practitioner (Certificate); child health nursing (MS, DNP). *Accreditation:* AACN. *Program availability:* Part-time, blended/hybrid learning. *Students:* 10 full-time (9 women), 116 part-time (115 women); includes 41 minority (18 Black or African American, non-Hispanic/Latino; 11 Asian, non-Hispanic/Latino; 12 Hispanic/Latino). 57 applicants, 100% accepted, 53 enrolled. In 2017, 28 master's, 2 doctorates awarded. *Degree requirements:* For master's, thesis; for doctorate, thesis/dissertation. *Entrance requirements:* For master's, BSN, minimum GPA of 3.0, course work in statistics. Additional exam requirements/recommendations for international students: Required—TOEFL (minimum score 90 iBT). *Application deadline:* For fall admission, 1/18 for domestic students. Application fee: $100. *Expenses:* Contact institution. *Financial support:* Application deadline: 3/15. *Unit head:* Dr. Kammy McLoughlin, Program Director, 631-444-3264, Fax: 631-444-3136, E-mail: kammy.mcloughlin@stonybrook.edu. *Application contact:* Pamela Criscuolo, Staff Assistant, 631-444-3549, Fax: 631-444-3136, E-mail: pamela.criscuolo@stonybrook.edu.
Website: https://nursing.stonybrookmedicine.edu/graduate

Texas Christian University, Harris College of Nursing and Health Sciences, Doctor of Nursing Practice Program, Fort Worth, TX 76129. Offers clinical nurse specialist - adult/gerontology nursing (DNP); clinical nurse specialist - pediatrics (DNP); family nurse practitioner (DNP); general (DNP); nursing administration (DNP). *Accreditation:* AACN. *Program availability:* Part-time. *Faculty:* 29 full-time (26 women), 2 part-time/adjunct (both women). *Students:* 51 full-time (45 women), 10 part-time (9 women); includes 16 minority (6 Black or African American, non-Hispanic/Latino; 2 Asian, non-Hispanic/Latino; 6 Hispanic/Latino; 2 Two or more races, non-Hispanic/Latino). Average age 41. 59 applicants, 64% accepted, 24 enrolled. In 2017, 23 doctorates awarded. *Degree requirements:* For doctorate, thesis/dissertation or alternative, practicum. *Entrance requirements:* For doctorate, three reference letters, essay, resume, two official transcripts from each institution attended, APRN recognition or MSN with experience in nursing administration. Additional exam requirements/recommendations for international students: Required—TOEFL. *Application deadline:* For summer admission, 11/15 for domestic and international students. Application fee: $60. Electronic applications accepted. *Expenses:* $1,555 per credit hour, $125 per course fee, $500 lab fee. *Financial support:* In 2017–18, 14 students received support. Scholarships/grants available. Financial award application deadline: 2/15; financial award applicants required to submit FAFSA. *Faculty research:* Geriatrics, cancer survivorship, health literacy, endothelial cells, clinical simulation outcomes. *Unit head:* Dr. Kathy Ellis, Division Director, Graduate Nursing, 817-257-6726, Fax: 817-257-7944, E-mail: kathryn.ellis@tcu.edu. *Application contact:* Heather Lyon, Academic Program Specialist, 817-257-6726, Fax: 817-257-7944, E-mail: graduatenursing@tcu.edu.
Website: http://dnp.tcu.edu/

Texas Christian University, Harris College of Nursing and Health Sciences, Master's Program in Nursing, Fort Worth, TX 76129. Offers administration (MSN); clinical nurse leader (MSN, Certificate); clinical nurse specialist (MSN), including adult/gerontology nursing, pediatrics; nursing education (MSN). *Accreditation:* AACN. *Program availability:* Part-time, online only, 100% online. *Faculty:* 29 full-time (26 women), 2 part-time/adjunct (both women). *Students:* 17 full-time (15 women), 7 part-time (all women); includes 6 minority (1 Black or African American, non-Hispanic/Latino; 2 Asian, non-Hispanic/Latino; 2 Hispanic/Latino; 1 Two or more races, non-Hispanic/Latino). Average age 36. 41 applicants, 49% accepted, 6 enrolled. In 2017, 41 master's awarded. *Degree requirements:* For master's, thesis or alternative, practicum. *Entrance requirements:* For master's, 3 letters of reference, essay, resume, two official transcripts from every institution attended. Additional exam requirements/recommendations for international students: Required—TOEFL. *Application deadline:* For spring admission, 9/1 for domestic and international students; for summer admission, 2/1 for domestic and international students. Application fee: $60. Electronic applications accepted. *Expenses:* $1,555 per credit hour, $125 per course fee, $500 lab fee. *Financial support:* In 2017–18, 20 students received support. Scholarships/grants available. Financial award application deadline: 2/15; financial award applicants required to submit FAFSA. *Faculty research:* Geriatrics, cancer survivorship, health literacy, endothelial cells, clinical simulation outcomes. *Unit head:* Dr. Kathy Ellis, Division Director, Graduate Nursing, 817-257-6726, Fax: 817-257-7944, E-mail: kathryn.ellis@tcu.edu. *Application contact:* Heather Lyon, Academic Program Specialist, 817-257-6726, Fax: 817-257-7944, E-mail: graduatenursing@tcu.edu.
Website: http://www.nursing.tcu.edu/graduate.asp

Texas Tech University Health Sciences Center, School of Nursing, Lubbock, TX 79430. Offers acute care nurse practitioner (MSN, Certificate); administration (MSN); advanced practice (DNP); education (MSN); executive leadership (DNP); family nurse practitioner (MSN, Certificate); geriatric nurse practitioner (MSN, Certificate); pediatric nurse practitioner (MSN, Certificate). *Accreditation:* AACN. *Program availability:* Part-time, online learning. *Degree requirements:* For master's, thesis optional. *Entrance requirements:* For master's, minimum GPA of 3.0, 3 letters of reference, BSN, RN license; for Certificate, minimum GPA of 3.0, 3 letters of reference, RN license. Additional exam requirements/recommendations for international students: Required—TOEFL (minimum score 550 paper-based). *Faculty research:* Diabetes/obesity, nurse competency, disease management, intervention and measurements, health disparities.

Texas Woman's University, Graduate School, College of Nursing, Denton, TX 76204. Offers adult health clinical nurse specialist (MS); adult health nurse practitioner (MS); adult/gerontology acute care nurse practitioner (MS); child health clinical nurse specialist (MS); clinical nurse leader (MS); family nurse practitioner (MS); health systems management (MS); nursing education (MS); nursing practice (DNP); nursing science (PhD); pediatric nurse practitioner (MS); women's health clinical nurse specialist (MS); women's health nurse practitioner (MS). *Accreditation:* AACN. *Program availability:* Part-time, 100% online, blended/hybrid learning. *Faculty:* 48 full-time (47 women), 44 part-time/adjunct (37 women). *Students:* 23 full-time (22 women), 816 part-time (750 women); includes 475 minority (188 Black or African American, non-Hispanic/Latino; 4 American Indian or Alaska Native, non-Hispanic/Latino; 171 Asian, non-Hispanic/Latino; 83 Hispanic/Latino; 3 Native Hawaiian or other Pacific Islander, non-Hispanic/Latino; 26 Two or more races, non-Hispanic/Latino), 12 international. Average age 37. 201 applicants, 88% accepted, 123 enrolled. In 2017, 232 master's, 17 doctorates awarded. *Degree requirements:* For master's, comprehensive exam, thesis

or alternative, 6-year time limit for completion of degree, professional or clinical project; for doctorate, comprehensive exam, thesis/dissertation, 10-year time limit for completion of degree. *Entrance requirements:* For master's, GRE or MAT, minimum GPA of 3.0 on last 60 hours in undergraduate nursing degree and overall, RN license, BS in nursing, basic statistics course, 1 year of clinical experience; for doctorate, GRE (preferred minimum score 153 [500 old version] Verbal, 144 [500 old version] Quantitative, 4 Analytical), MS in nursing, minimum preferred GPA of 3.5, RN license, statistics course, 2 letters of reference, curriculum vitae, graduate nursing-theory course, graduate research course, statement of professional goals and research interests. Additional exam requirements/recommendations for international students: Required—TOEFL (minimum score 550 paper-based; 79 iBT); Recommended—IELTS (minimum score 6.5), TSE (minimum score 53). *Application deadline:* For fall admission, 5/1 for domestic students, 3/1 priority date for international students; for spring admission, 9/15 for domestic students, 7/1 priority date for international students; for summer admission, 2/1 for domestic and international students. Applications are processed on a rolling basis. Application fee: $50 ($75 for international students). Electronic applications accepted. *Expenses:* $8,510 per year full-time in-state, $17,810 per year full-time out-of-state. *Financial support:* In 2017–18, 146 students received support, including 7 teaching assistantships (averaging $28,195 per year); research assistantships, career-related internships or fieldwork, Federal Work-Study, institutionally sponsored loans, scholarships/grants, traineeships, health care benefits, and unspecified assistantships also available. Support available to part-time students. Financial award application deadline: 3/1; financial award applicants required to submit FAFSA. *Faculty research:* Women's health, nurse staffing and satisfaction in health systems, perinatal safety, chronic illness, pediatric health. *Total annual research expenditures:* $380,388. *Unit head:* Dr. Anita G. Hufft, Dean, 940-898-2401, Fax: 940-898-2437, E-mail: nursing@twu.edu. *Application contact:* Korie Hawkins, Associate Director of Admissions, Graduate Recruitment, 940-898-3188, Fax: 940-898-3081, E-mail: admissions@twu.edu.
Website: http://www.twu.edu/nursing/

The University of Alabama at Birmingham, School of Nursing, Birmingham, AL 35294-1210. Offers clinical nurse leader (MSN); nurse anesthesia (DNP); nurse practitioner (MSN, DNP), including adult-gerontology acute care (MSN), adult-gerontology primary care (MSN), family (MSN), pediatric (MSN), psychiatric/mental health (MSN), women's health (MSN); nursing (MSN, DNP, PhD); nursing health systems administration (MSN); nursing informatics (MSN). *Accreditation:* AACN; AANA/CANAEP. *Program availability:* Part-time, online only, blended/hybrid learning. Terminal master's awarded for partial completion of doctoral program. *Degree requirements:* For master's, comprehensive exam; for doctorate, comprehensive exam, thesis/dissertation, research mentorship experience (for PhD); scholarly project (for DNP). *Entrance requirements:* For master's, GRE, GMAT, or MAT, minimum cumulative undergraduate GPA of 3.0 or on last 60 semesters hours; letters of recommendation; for doctorate, GRE General Test, computer literacy, course work in statistics, interview, minimum GPA of 3.0, MS in nursing, references, writing sample. Additional exam requirements/recommendations for international students: Required—TOEFL (minimum score 500 paper-based, 80 iBT) or IELTS (5.5). Electronic applications accepted. *Expenses:* Contact institution. *Faculty research:* Palliative care; oncology; aging; HIV/AIDS; nursing work environments.

University of Cincinnati, Graduate School, College of Nursing, Cincinnati, OH 45221-0038. Offers nurse midwifery (MSN); nurse practitioner (MSN, DNP), including acute care pediatrics (DNP), adult-gerontology acute care, adult-gerontology primary care, anesthesia (DNP), family (MSN), leadership (DNP), neonatal (MSN), women's health (MSN); nursing (MSN, PhD), including occupational health (MSN). *Accreditation:* AACN; AANA/CANAEP (one or more programs are accredited); ACNM/ACME. *Program availability:* Part-time, 100% online, blended/hybrid learning. *Faculty:* 74 full-time (69 women), 112 part-time/adjunct (105 women). *Students:* 323 full-time (261 women), 1,084 part-time (949 women); includes 311 minority (113 Black or African American, non-Hispanic/Latino; 4 American Indian or Alaska Native, non-Hispanic/Latino; 56 Asian, non-Hispanic/Latino; 108 Hispanic/Latino; 1 Native Hawaiian or other Pacific Islander, non-Hispanic/Latino; 29 Two or more races, non-Hispanic/Latino), 12 international. Average age 34. 582 applicants, 64% accepted, 314 enrolled. In 2017, 579 master's, 18 doctorates awarded. *Degree requirements:* For master's, thesis or alternative; for doctorate, comprehensive exam (for some programs), thesis/dissertation (for some programs). *Entrance requirements:* For doctorate, GRE General Test. Additional exam requirements/recommendations for international students: Required—TOEFL (minimum score 600 paper-based; 100 iBT); Recommended—IELTS (minimum score 7). *Application deadline:* For fall admission, 5/1 priority date for domestic students, 5/1 for international students; for spring admission, 10/1 for domestic students; for summer admission, 3/1 priority date for domestic students. Applications are processed on a rolling basis. Application fee: $130 ($70 for international students). Electronic applications accepted. *Expenses:* $14,668 annual full-time in-state tuition, $707 annual fees. *Financial support:* In 2017–18, 123 students received support, including 8 fellowships with full tuition reimbursements available (averaging $30,423 per year), 7 research assistantships with full tuition reimbursements available (averaging $17,971 per year), 5 teaching assistantships with full tuition reimbursements available (averaging $17,971 per year); Federal Work-Study, institutionally sponsored loans, scholarships/grants, traineeships, health care benefits, tuition waivers (partial), and unspecified assistantships also available. Support available to part-time students. Financial award application deadline: 5/1; financial award applicants required to submit FAFSA. *Faculty research:* Vulnerable populations, education, violence, chronicity/aging, cancer. *Total annual research expenditures:* $575,576. *Unit head:* Dr. Greer Glazer, Dean, 513-558-5330, Fax: 513-558-9030, E-mail: greer.glazer@uc.edu. *Application contact:* Office of Student Recruitment, 513-558-8400, Fax: 513-558-5012, E-mail: nursingbearcats@uc.edu.
Website: https://nursing.uc.edu/

University of Colorado Denver, College of Nursing, Aurora, CO 80045. Offers adult clinical nurse specialist (MS); adult nurse practitioner (MS); family nurse practitioner (MS); family psychiatric mental health nurse practitioner (MS); health care informatics (MS); nurse-midwifery (MS); nursing (DNP, PhD); nursing leadership and health care systems (MS); pediatric nurse practitioner (MS); women's health (MS); MS/PhD. *Accreditation:* ACNM/ACME (one or more programs are accredited). *Program availability:* Part-time, evening/weekend, online learning. *Students:* 297 applicants, 55% accepted, 141 enrolled. In 2017, 138 master's, 18 doctorates awarded. Terminal master's awarded for partial completion of doctoral program. *Degree requirements:* For master's, thesis optional; for doctorate, comprehensive exam, thesis/dissertation, 42 credits of coursework. *Entrance requirements:* For master's, GRE if cumulative undergraduate GPA is less than 3.0, undergraduate nursing degree from ACEN- or CCNE-accredited school or university; completion of research and statistics courses with minimum grade of C; copy of current and unencumbered nursing license; for doctorate, GRE, bachelor's and/or master's degrees in nursing from ACEN- or CCNE-accredited institution; portfolio; minimum undergraduate GPA of 3.0, graduate 3.5; graduate-level intermediate statistics and master's-level nursing theory courses with minimum B grade; interview. Additional exam requirements/recommendations for international students: Required—TOEFL (minimum score 560 paper-based; 83 iBT). *Application deadline:* For fall admission, 2/15 for domestic students, 1/15 for international students; for spring admission, 7/1 for domestic students, 6/1 for international students. Application fee: $50 ($75 for international students). Electronic applications accepted. *Unit head:* Dr. Sarah Thompson, Dean, 303-724-1679, E-mail: sarah.a.thompson@ucdenver.edu. *Application contact:* Judy Campbell, Graduate Programs Coordinator, 303-724-8503, E-mail: judy.campbell@ucdenver.edu.
Website: http://www.ucdenver.edu/academics/colleges/nursing/Pages/default.aspx

University of Delaware, College of Health Sciences, School of Nursing, Newark, DE 19716. Offers adult nurse practitioner (MSN, PMC); cardiopulmonary clinical nurse specialist (MSN, PMC); cardiopulmonary clinical nurse specialist/adult nurse practitioner (MSN, PMC); family nurse practitioner (MSN, PMC); gerontology clinical nurse specialist (MSN, PMC); gerontology clinical nurse specialist geriatric nurse practitioner (PMC); gerontology clinical nurse specialist/geriatric nurse practitioner (MSN); health services administration (MSN, PMC); nursing of children clinical nurse specialist (MSN, PMC); nursing of children clinical nurse specialist/pediatric nurse practitioner (MSN, PMC); oncology/immune deficiency clinical nurse specialist (MSN, PMC); oncology/immune deficiency clinical nurse specialist/adult nurse practitioner (MSN, PMC); perinatal/women's health clinical nurse specialist (MSN, PMC); perinatal/women's health clinical nurse specialist/women's health nurse practitioner (MSN, PMC); psychiatric nursing clinical nurse specialist (MSN, PMC). *Accreditation:* AACN. *Program availability:* Part-time, evening/weekend, online learning. *Degree requirements:* For master's, thesis optional. *Entrance requirements:* For master's, BSN, interview, RN license. Electronic applications accepted. *Faculty research:* Marriage and chronic illness, health promotion, congestive heart failure patient outcomes, school nursing, diabetes in children, culture, health disparities, cardiovascular, prison nursing, oncology, public policy, child obesity, smoking and teen pregnancy, blood pressure measurements, men's health.

University of Illinois at Chicago, College of Nursing, Program in Nursing, Chicago, IL 60607-7128. Offers acute care clinical nurse specialist (MS); administrative nursing leadership (Certificate); adult nurse practitioner (MS); adult/geriatric nurse practitioner (MS); advanced community health nurse specialist (MS); family nurse practitioner (MS); geriatric clinical nurse specialist (MS); geriatric nurse practitioner (MS); nurse midwifery (MS); occupational health/advanced community health nurse specialist (MS); occupational health/family nurse practitioner (MS); pediatric nurse practitioner (MS); perinatal clinical nurse specialist (MS); school/advanced community health nurse specialist (MS); school/family nurse practitioner (MS); women's health nurse practitioner (MS). *Accreditation:* AACN. *Program availability:* Part-time. *Degree requirements:* For master's, thesis or alternative. *Entrance requirements:* For master's, GRE General Test, minimum GPA of 2.75. Additional exam requirements/recommendations for international students: Required—TOEFL. Electronic applications accepted.

University of Maryland, Baltimore, School of Nursing, Baltimore, MD 21201. Offers adult-gerontology acute care nurse practitioner (DNP); adult-gerontology primary care nurse practitioner (DNP); clinical nurse leader (MS); community/public health nursing (MS); family nurse practitioner (DNP); global health (Postbaccalaureate Certificate); health services leadership and management (MS); neonatal nurse practitioner (DNP); nurse anesthesia (DNP); nursing (PhD); nursing informatics (MS, Postbaccalaureate Certificate); pediatric acute/primary care nurse practitioner (DNP); psychiatric mental health nurse practitioner (DNP); teaching in nursing and health professions (Postbaccalaureate Certificate); MS/MBA. MS/MBA offered jointly with University of Baltimore. *Program availability:* Part-time. *Faculty:* 130 full-time (117 women), 125 part-time/adjunct (114 women). *Students:* 504 full-time (442 women), 532 part-time (482 women); includes 443 minority (249 Black or African American, non-Hispanic/Latino; 1 American Indian or Alaska Native, non-Hispanic/Latino; 115 Asian, non-Hispanic/Latino; 48 Hispanic/Latino; 2 Native Hawaiian or other Pacific Islander, non-Hispanic/Latino; 28 Two or more races, non-Hispanic/Latino), 15 international. Average age 33. 935 applicants, 62% accepted, 394 enrolled. In 2017, 182 master's, 57 doctorates awarded. *Degree requirements:* For master's and Postbaccalaureate Certificate, thesis (for some programs); for doctorate, comprehensive exam, thesis/dissertation. *Entrance requirements:* Additional exam requirements/recommendations for international students: Required—TOEFL (minimum score 550 paper-based; 79 iBT); Recommended—IELTS (minimum score 7). *Application deadline:* For fall admission, 11/1 for domestic and international students; for spring admission, 8/1 for domestic and international students. Application fee: $75. Electronic applications accepted. *Expenses:* Contact institution. *Financial support:* In 2017–18, 22 research assistantships with full and partial tuition reimbursements (averaging $21,523 per year), 41 teaching assistantships with full and partial tuition reimbursements (averaging $13,439 per year) were awarded; fellowships and scholarships/grants also available. Financial award application deadline: 3/1; financial award applicants required to submit FAFSA. *Unit head:* Dr. Jane Kirschling, Dean, 410-706-4359, E-mail: kirschling@umaryland.edu. *Application contact:* Larry Fillian, Associate Dean of Student and Academic Services, 410-706-6298, E-mail: lfillian@umaryland.edu.
Website: http://www.nursing.umaryland.edu/

University of Michigan, Rackham Graduate School, School of Nursing, Ann Arbor, MI 48109. Offers acute care pediatric nurse practitioner (MS); nursing (DNP, PhD, Post Master's Certificate). *Accreditation:* AACN; ACNM/ACME (one or more programs are accredited). *Program availability:* Part-time, online learning. Terminal master's awarded for partial completion of doctoral program. *Degree requirements:* For doctorate, thesis/dissertation. *Expenses:* Tuition, state resident: full-time $22,368; part-time $1201 per credit hour. Tuition, nonresident: full-time $45,156; part-time $2467 per credit hour. *Required fees:* $376 per term. Tuition and fees vary according to course load, degree level and program. *Faculty research:* Preparation of clinical nurse researchers, biobehavior, women's health, health promotion, substance abuse, psychobiology of menopause, fertility, obesity, health care systems.

University of Minnesota, Twin Cities Campus, Graduate School, School of Nursing, Minneapolis, MN 55455-0213. Offers adult/gerontological clinical nurse specialist (DNP); adult/gerontological primary care nurse practitioner (DNP); family nurse practitioner (DNP); health innovation and leadership (DNP); integrative health and healing (DNP); nurse anesthesia (DNP); nurse midwifery (DNP); nursing (MN, PhD); nursing informatics (DNP); pediatric clinical nurse specialist (DNP); primary care certified pediatric nurse practitioner (DNP); psychiatric/mental health nurse practitioner (DNP); women's health nurse practitioner (DNP). *Accreditation:* AACN; AANA/CANAEP; ACNM/ACME (one or more programs are accredited). *Program availability:* Part-time, online learning. Terminal master's awarded for partial completion of doctoral program. *Degree requirements:* For master's, final oral exam, project or thesis; for doctorate, thesis/dissertation. *Entrance requirements:* For master's and doctorate, GRE General Test. Additional exam requirements/recommendations for international students: Required—TOEFL (minimum score 586 paper-based). *Expenses:* Contact institution. *Faculty research:* Child and family health promotion, nursing research on elders.

University of Missouri, Office of Research and Graduate Studies, Sinclair School of Nursing, Columbia, MO 65211. Offers adult-gerontology clinical nurse specialist (DNP, Certificate); family nurse practitioner (DNP); family psychiatric and mental health nurse practitioner (DNP); nursing (MS, PhD); nursing leadership and innovations in health care (DNP); pediatric clinical nurse specialist (DNP, Certificate); pediatric nurse practitioner (DNP). *Accreditation:* AACN. *Program availability:* Part-time. *Degree requirements:* For

master's, thesis optional, oral exam; for doctorate, thesis/dissertation. *Entrance requirements:* For master's, GRE General Test, BSN, minimum GPA of 3.0 during last 60 hours, nursing license. Additional exam requirements/recommendations for international students: Required—TOEFL, IELTS. *Application deadline:* Applications are processed on a rolling basis. Electronic applications accepted. *Expenses:* Tuition, state resident: full-time $6480. Tuition, nonresident: full-time $17,744. *Required fees:* $1108. Tuition and fees vary according to course load, campus/location and program. *Financial support:* Fellowships, research assistantships, teaching assistantships, career-related internships or fieldwork, institutionally sponsored loans, scholarships/grants, traineeships, health care benefits, tuition waivers (full), and unspecified assistantships available. Support available to part-time students.
Website: http://nursing.missouri.edu/

University of Missouri–Kansas City, School of Nursing and Health Studies, Kansas City, MO 64110-2499. Offers adult clinical nurse specialist (MSN), including adult nurse practitioner, women's health nurse practitioner (MSN, DNP); adult clinical nursing practice (DNP), including adult gerontology nurse practitioner, women's health nurse practitioner (MSN, DNP); clinical nursing practice (DNP), including family nurse practitioner; neonatal nurse practitioner (MSN); nurse educator (MSN); nurse executive (MSN); nursing practice (DNP); pediatric clinical nursing practice (DNP), including pediatric nurse practitioner; pediatric nurse practitioner (MSN). *Accreditation:* AACN. *Program availability:* Part-time, online learning. *Degree requirements:* For master's, thesis or alternative. *Entrance requirements:* For master's, minimum undergraduate GPA of 3.2; for doctorate, GRE, 3 letters of reference. Additional exam requirements/recommendations for international students: Required—TOEFL (minimum score 550 paper-based; 80 iBT). *Faculty research:* Geriatrics/gerontology, children's pain, neonatology, Alzheimer's care, cancer caregivers.

University of Missouri–St. Louis, College of Nursing, St. Louis, MO 63121. Offers adult/geriatric nurse practitioner (Post Master's Certificate); family nurse practitioner (Post Master's Certificate); nursing (DNP, PhD); pediatric acute care nurse practitioner (Post Master's Certificate); pediatric nurse practitioner (Post Master's Certificate); psychiatric-mental health nurse practitioner (Post Master's Certificate); women's health nurse practitioner (Post Master's Certificate). *Accreditation:* AACN. *Program availability:* Part-time. *Faculty:* 24 full-time (22 women), 12 part-time/adjunct (11 women). *Students:* 47 full-time (44 women), 162 part-time (152 women); includes 53 minority (37 Black or African American, non-Hispanic/Latino; 10 Asian, non-Hispanic/Latino; 4 Hispanic/Latino; 2 Two or more races, non-Hispanic/Latino), 3 international. 112 applicants, 93% accepted, 70 enrolled. *Degree requirements:* For doctorate, comprehensive exam, thesis/dissertation; for Post Master's Certificate, thesis. *Entrance requirements:* For doctorate, GRE, 2 letters of recommendation, MSN, minimum GPA of 3.2, course in differential/inferential statistics; for Post Master's Certificate, 2 recommendation letters; MSN; advanced practice certificate; minimum GPA of 3.0; essay. Additional exam requirements/recommendations for international students: Recommended—TOEFL (minimum score 550 paper-based; 79 iBT), IELTS (minimum score 6.5). *Application deadline:* For fall admission, 2/15 for domestic and international students. Application fee: $50 ($40 for international students). Electronic applications accepted. *Expenses:* Tuition, state resident: part-time $476.50 per credit hour. Tuition, nonresident: part-time $1169.70 per credit hour. *Financial support:* Research assistantships with tuition reimbursements available. Financial award application deadline: 4/1; financial award applicants required to submit FAFSA. *Faculty research:* Health promotion and restoration, family disruption, violence, abuse, battered women, health survey methods. *Unit head:* Sue Dean-Baar, Dean, 314-516-6066. *Application contact:* 314-516-5458, Fax: 314-516-6996, E-mail: gradadm@umsl.edu.
Website: http://www.umsl.edu/divisions/nursing/

The University of North Carolina at Chapel Hill, School of Nursing, Chapel Hill, NC 27599-7460. Offers advanced practice registered nurse (DNP); nursing (MSN, PhD, PMC), including administration (MSN), adult gerontology primary care nurse practitioner (MSN), clinical nurse leader (MSN), education (MSN), health care systems (PMC), informatics (MSN, PMC), nursing leadership (PMC), outcomes management (MSN), primary care family nurse practitioner (MSN), primary care pediatric nurse practitioner (MSN), psychiatric/mental health nurse practitioner (MSN, PMC). *Accreditation:* AACN; ACEN (one or more programs are accredited). *Program availability:* Part-time. *Faculty:* 86 full-time (78 women), 44 part-time/adjunct (40 women). *Students:* 208 full-time (186 women), 128 part-time (116 women); includes 100 minority (49 Black or African American, non-Hispanic/Latino; 4 American Indian or Alaska Native, non-Hispanic/Latino; 23 Asian, non-Hispanic/Latino; 7 Hispanic/Latino; 17 Two or more races, non-Hispanic/Latino), 17 international. Average age 33. 624 applicants, 25% accepted, 150 enrolled. In 2017, 91 master's, 14 doctorates awarded. *Degree requirements:* For master's, comprehensive exam, thesis; for doctorate, thesis/dissertation, 3 exams; for PMC, thesis. *Entrance requirements:* Additional exam requirements/recommendations for international students: Required—TOEFL (minimum score 575 paper-based; 89 iBT), IELTS (minimum score 8). *Application deadline:* For fall admission, 12/15 for domestic and international students. Application fee: $88. Electronic applications accepted. *Financial support:* In 2017–18, 8 fellowships with full tuition reimbursements, 6 research assistantships with partial tuition reimbursements (averaging $8,000 per year), 10 teaching assistantships with partial tuition reimbursements (averaging $8,000 per year) were awarded; scholarships/grants, traineeships, health care benefits, and unspecified assistantships also available. Support available to part-time students. Financial award application deadline: 3/1; financial award applicants required to submit FAFSA. *Faculty research:* Preventing and managing chronic illness, reducing health disparities, Improving healthcare quality and patient outcomes, understanding biobehavioral and genetic bases of health and illness, developing innovative ways to enhance science and its clinical translation. *Unit head:* Dr. Nilda Peragallo Montano, Dean/Professor, 919-966-3731, Fax: 919-966-3540, E-mail: npm@email.unc.edu. *Application contact:* Emily Sayed, Assistant Director, Graduate Admissions, 919-966-4260, Fax: 919-966-3540, E-mail: sayed@unc.edu.
Website: http://nursing.unc.edu

University of Pennsylvania, School of Nursing, Pediatric Acute Care Nurse Practitioner Program, Philadelphia, PA 19104. Offers MSN. *Accreditation:* AACN. *Program availability:* Part-time, online learning. *Students:* 15 full-time (all women), 41 part-time (all women); includes 10 minority (1 Black or African American, non-Hispanic/Latino; 7 Asian, non-Hispanic/Latino; 2 Two or more races, non-Hispanic/Latino). Average age 27. 49 applicants, 67% accepted, 33 enrolled. In 2017, 31 master's awarded. Application fee: $80.

University of Pennsylvania, School of Nursing, Pediatric Clinical Nurse Specialist Program, Philadelphia, PA 19104. Offers MSN. *Accreditation:* AACN. *Students:* 2 full-time (both women), 4 part-time (3 women); includes 2 minority (1 Asian, non-Hispanic/Latino; 1 Hispanic/Latino). Average age 32. 10 applicants, 70% accepted, 6 enrolled. In 2017, 2 master's awarded. Application fee: $80. *Financial support:* Application deadline: 4/1. *Unit head:* Assistant Dean of Admissions and Financial Aid, 866-867-6877, Fax: 215-573-8439, E-mail: admissions@nursing.upenn.edu. *Application contact:* Judy Verger, Senior Lecturer, 215-898-4271, E-mail: jtv@nursing.upenn.edu.
Website: http://www.nursing.upenn.edu/peds/

University of Pennsylvania, School of Nursing, Pediatric Primary Care Nurse Practitioner Program, Philadelphia, PA 19104. Offers MSN. *Accreditation:* AACN. *Program availability:* Part-time. *Students:* 14 full-time (all women), 25 part-time (all women); includes 3 minority (2 Asian, non-Hispanic/Latino; 1 Two or more races, non-Hispanic/Latino). Average age 28. 33 applicants, 79% accepted, 22 enrolled. In 2017, 23 master's awarded. Application fee: $80.

University of Pittsburgh, School of Nursing, Nurse Practitioner Program, Pittsburgh, PA 15261. Offers adult-gerontology acute care (DNP), adult-gerontology primary care (DNP); family (individual across the lifespan) (DNP); neonatal (MSN, DNP); pediatric primary care (DNP); psychiatric mental health (DNP). *Accreditation:* AACN. *Program availability:* Part-time. *Faculty:* 17 full-time (14 women), 3 part-time/adjunct (2 women). *Students:* 50 full-time (47 women), 43 part-time (36 women); includes 9 minority (1 Black or African American, non-Hispanic/Latino; 1 American Indian or Alaska Native, non-Hispanic/Latino; 7 Asian, non-Hispanic/Latino), 1 international. Average age 31. 77 applicants, 40% accepted, 25 enrolled. In 2017, 6 master's, 35 doctorates awarded. *Degree requirements:* For master's, comprehensive exam, thesis optional. *Entrance requirements:* For master's, GRE General Test, BSN, RN license, 3 letters of recommendation, resume, course work in statistics, relevant nursing experience; for doctorate, GRE General Test, BSN, RN license, minimum GPA of 3.5, 3 letters of recommendation, relevant nursing experience, resume, course work in statistics. Additional exam requirements/recommendations for international students: Required—TOEFL (minimum score 600 paper-based; 100 IBT) or IELTS (minimum score 7.0). *Application deadline:* For fall admission, 5/1 priority date for domestic students, 2/15 priority date for international students. Application fee: $50. Electronic applications accepted. *Expenses:* $13,068 per term full-time resident tuition, $1,064 per credit part-time; $15,270 per term full-time non-resident tuition, $1,247 per credit part-time; $437 per term full-time fees; $282 per term part-time fees. *Financial support:* In 2017–18, 58 students received support, including 7 fellowships (averaging $15,755 per year), 15 teaching assistantships (averaging $12,454 per year); scholarships/grants, tuition waivers, and unspecified assistantships also available. Financial award applicants required to submit FAFSA. *Faculty research:* Behavioral management of chronic disorders, patient management in critical care, consumer informatics, genetic applications (molecular genetics and psychosocial implications), technology for nurses and patients to improve care. *Unit head:* Dr. Sandra Engberg, Associate Dean for Clinical Education, 412-624-3835, Fax: 412-624-8521, E-mail: sje1@pitt.edu. *Application contact:* Laurie Lapsley, Graduate Administrator, 412-624-9670, Fax: 412-624-2409, E-mail: lapsleyl@pitt.edu.
Website: http://www.nursing.pitt.edu

University of Puerto Rico–Medical Sciences Campus, School of Nursing, San Juan, PR 00936-5067. Offers adult and elderly nursing (MSN); child and adolescent nursing (MSN); critical care nursing (MSN); family and community nursing (MSN); family nurse practitioner (MSN); maternity nursing (MSN); mental health and psychiatric nursing (MSN). *Accreditation:* AACN; AANA/CANAEP. *Entrance requirements:* For master's, GRE or EXADEP, interview, Puerto Rico RN license or professional license for international students, general and specific point average, article analysis. Electronic applications accepted. *Faculty research:* HIV, health disparities, teen violence, women and violence, neurological disorders.

University of Rochester, School of Nursing, Rochester, NY 14642. Offers adult gerontological acute care nurse practitioner (MS); adult gerontological primary care nurse practitioner (MS); clinical nurse leader (MS); family nurse practitioner (MS); family psychiatric mental health nurse practitioner (MS); health care organization management and leadership (MS); nursing (DNP); nursing and health science (PhD); nursing education (MS); pediatric nurse practitioner (MS); pediatric nurse practitioner/neonatal nurse practitioner (MS). *Accreditation:* AACN. *Program availability:* Part-time, 100% online, blended/hybrid learning. *Faculty:* 62 full-time (51 women), 73 part-time/adjunct (63 women). *Students:* 17 full-time (12 women), 306 part-time (252 women); includes 46 minority (16 Black or African American, non-Hispanic/Latino; 1 American Indian or Alaska Native, non-Hispanic/Latino; 7 Asian, non-Hispanic/Latino; 17 Hispanic/Latino; 5 Two or more races, non-Hispanic/Latino), 3 international. Average age 34. 143 applicants, 71% accepted, 87 enrolled. In 2017, 48 master's, 8 doctorates awarded. Terminal master's awarded for partial completion of doctoral program. *Degree requirements:* For master's, comprehensive exam; for doctorate, thesis/dissertation. *Entrance requirements:* For master's, BS in nursing, minimum GPA of 3.0, course work in statistics; for doctorate, GRE General Test (for PhD), MS in nursing, minimum GPA of 3.5. Additional exam requirements/recommendations for international students: Required—TOEFL (minimum score 560 paper-based; 88 iBT) or IELTS (minimum score 6.5) recommended. *Application deadline:* For fall admission, 4/1 for domestic and international students; for spring admission, 9/1 for domestic and international students; for summer admission, 1/2 for domestic and international students. Application fee: $50. Electronic applications accepted. *Financial support:* In 2017–18, 63 students received support, including 2 fellowships with full and partial tuition reimbursements available (averaging $16,000 per year); scholarships/grants, traineeships, health care benefits, tuition waivers (full and partial), and unspecified assistantships also available. Support available to part-time students. Financial award application deadline: 6/30; financial award applicants required to submit CSS PROFILE or FAFSA. *Faculty research:* Symptom science, systems of care, innovations in health technology, promoting healthy behaviors. *Total annual research expenditures:* $2.6 million. *Unit head:* Dr. Kathy H. Rideout, Dean, 585-273-8902, Fax: 585-273-1268, E-mail: kathy_rideout@urmc.rochester.edu. *Application contact:* Elaine Andolina, Director of Admissions, 585-275-2375, Fax: 585-756-8299, E-mail: elaine_andolina@urmc.rochester.edu.
Website: http://www.son.rochester.edu

University of San Diego, Hahn School of Nursing and Health Science, San Diego, CA 92110-2492. Offers adult-gerontology clinical nurse specialist (MSN); adult-gerontology nurse practitioner/family nurse practitioner (MSN); clinical nurse leader (MSN); executive nurse leader (MSN); family nurse practitioner (MSN); healthcare informatics (MS, MSN); nursing (PhD); nursing practice (DNP); pediatric/family nurse practitioner (MSN); psychiatric-mental health nurse practitioner (MSN). *Accreditation:* AACN. *Program availability:* Part-time, evening/weekend. *Faculty:* 26 full-time (21 women), 36 part-time/adjunct (29 women). *Students:* 238 full-time (198 women), 230 part-time (167 women); includes 230 minority (32 Black or African American, non-Hispanic/Latino; 104 Asian, non-Hispanic/Latino; 75 Hispanic/Latino; 19 Two or more races, non-Hispanic/Latino), 12 international. Average age 35. In 2017, 93 master's, 44 doctorates awarded. *Degree requirements:* For doctorate, thesis/dissertation (for some programs), residency (DNP). *Entrance requirements:* For master's, GRE General Test (for entry-level nursing), BSN, current California RN licensure (except for entry-level nursing), minimum GPA of 3.0; for doctorate, minimum GPA of 3.5, MSN, current California RN licensure. Additional exam requirements/recommendations for international students: Required—TOEFL (minimum score 580 paper-based; 83 iBT), TWE. *Application deadline:* Applications are processed on a rolling basis. Application fee: $45. Electronic applications accepted. *Financial support:* In 2017–18, 242 students received support. Scholarships/grants and traineeships available. Support available to part-time students. Financial award application deadline: 4/1; financial award applicants required to submit FAFSA. *Faculty research:* Maternal/neonatal health, palliative and end of life care, adolescent obesity, health disparities, cognitive dysfunction. *Unit head:* Dr. Janes

Georges, Interim Dean, 619-260-4550, Fax: 619-260-6814, E-mail: nursing@sandiego.edu. *Application contact:* Monica Mahon, Associate Director of Graduate Admissions, 619-260-4524, Fax: 619-260-4158, E-mail: grads@sandiego.edu.
Website: http://www.sandiego.edu/nursing/

University of South Carolina, The Graduate School, College of Nursing, Program in Health Nursing, Columbia, SC 29208. Offers adult nurse practitioner (MSN); community/public health clinical nurse specialist (MSN); family nurse practitioner (MSN); pediatric nurse practitioner (MSN). *Accreditation:* AACN. *Program availability:* Part-time. *Degree requirements:* For master's, thesis or alternative. *Entrance requirements:* For master's, GRE General Test or MAT, BS in nursing, nursing license. Additional exam requirements/recommendations for international students: Required—TOEFL (minimum score 570 paper-based). Electronic applications accepted. *Faculty research:* System research, evidence based practice, breast cancer, violence.

University of South Florida, College of Nursing, Tampa, FL 33612. Offers nurse anesthesia (DNP); nursing (MS, DNP), including adult-gerontology acute care nursing, adult-gerontology primary care nursing, family health nursing, nurse anesthesia (MS), nursing education (MS), occupational health nursing/adult-gerontology primary care nursing, oncology nursing/adult-gerontology primary care nursing (DNP), pediatric health nursing; nursing education (Post Master's Certificate); nursing science (PhD); simulation based academic fellowship in advanced pain management (Graduate Certificate). *Accreditation:* AACN; AANA/CANAEP. *Program availability:* Part-time. *Faculty:* 37 full-time (32 women), 2 part-time/adjunct (1 woman). *Students:* 224 full-time (178 women), 669 part-time (577 women); includes 309 minority (105 Black or African American, non-Hispanic/Latino; 2 American Indian or Alaska Native, non-Hispanic/Latino; 53 Asian, non-Hispanic/Latino; 122 Hispanic/Latino; 1 Native Hawaiian or other Pacific Islander, non-Hispanic/Latino; 26 Two or more races, non-Hispanic/Latino), 6 international. Average age 32. 949 applicants, 47% accepted, 382 enrolled. In 2017, 264 master's, 39 doctorates awarded. *Degree requirements:* For master's, comprehensive exam, thesis optional; for doctorate, comprehensive exam, thesis/dissertation. *Entrance requirements:* For master's, GRE General Test, bachelor's degree from accredited program with minimum GPA of 3.0 in all upper-division coursework; current license as Registered Nurse; 3 letters of recommendation; personal statement of goals; resume or curriculum vitae; personal interview; for doctorate, GRE General Test (recommended), bachelor's degree in nursing from ACEN or CCNE regionally-accredited institution with minimum GPA of 3.0 in all coursework or in all upper-division coursework; current license as Registered Nurse in Florida; undergraduate statistics course with minimum B grade; 3 letters of recommendation; statement of goals; resume; interview. Additional exam requirements/recommendations for international students: Required—TOEFL (minimum score 550 paper-based; 79 iBT). *Application deadline:* For fall admission, 12/15 for domestic and international students; for spring admission, 10/1 for domestic students, 9/15 for international students. Application fee: $30. Electronic applications accepted. *Financial support:* In 2017–18, 132 students received support, including 7 research assistantships with tuition reimbursements available (averaging $18,935 per year), 29 teaching assistantships with tuition reimbursements available (averaging $30,814 per year); tuition waivers (partial) and unspecified assistantships also available. Financial award application deadline: 2/1; financial award applicants required to submit FAFSA. *Faculty research:* Women's health, palliative and end-of-life care, cardiac rehabilitation, complementary therapies for chronic illness and cancer. *Total annual research expenditures:* $3.2 million. *Unit head:* Dr. Victoria Rich, Dean, College of Nursing, 813-974-8939, Fax: 813-974-5418, E-mail: victoriarich@health.usf.edu. *Application contact:* Dr. Brian Graves, Assistant Professor/Assistant Dean, 813-974-8054, Fax: 813-974-5418, E-mail: bgraves1@health.usf.edu.
Website: http://health.usf.edu/nursing/index.htm

The University of Tennessee Health Science Center, College of Nursing, Memphis, TN 38163. Offers adult-gerontology acute care nurse practitioner (Post Master's Certificate); advance practice nursing (DNP); family nurse practitioner (Post-Doctoral Certificate); pediatric acute care nurse practitioner (Post-Doctoral Certificate); pediatric primary care nurse practitioner (Post-Doctoral Certificate); psychiatric/mental health nurse practitioner (Post-Doctoral Certificate); registered nurse first assistant (Certificate). *Accreditation:* AACN; AANA/CANAEP. *Program availability:* Part-time, blended/hybrid learning. *Faculty:* 52 full-time (47 women), 11 part-time/adjunct (4 women). *Students:* 262 full-time (228 women), 13 part-time (12 women); includes 83 minority (71 Black or African American, non-Hispanic/Latino; 6 Asian, non-Hispanic/Latino; 6 Hispanic/Latino). Average age 32. 215 applicants, 49% accepted, 79 enrolled. In 2017, 78 doctorates, 2 Certificates awarded. *Degree requirements:* For doctorate, project. *Entrance requirements:* For doctorate, RN license, minimum GPA of 3.0; for other advanced degree, MSN, APN license, minimum GPA of 3.0. Additional exam requirements/recommendations for international students: Required—TOEFL (minimum score 550 paper-based; 80 iBT). *Application deadline:* For fall admission, 1/15 for domestic students; for spring admission, 8/15 for domestic students. Application fee: $70. Electronic applications accepted. *Expenses:* $13,420 in-state tuition and fees; $17,222 out-of-state tuition and fees. *Financial support:* In 2017–18, 112 students received support, including 9 research assistantships (averaging $24,783 per year); Federal Work-Study, institutionally sponsored loans, scholarships/grants, and tuition waivers (partial) also available. Financial award application deadline: 3/15; financial award applicants required to submit FAFSA. *Faculty research:* Efficacy of a cognitive behavioral group intervention and its influence on symptoms of depression and anxiety as well as caregiver function; quality of life and sexual function in women who undergo vulvar surgeries; influence of prenatal and early childhood environments on health and developmental trajectories across childhood; interaction between physical activity, diet, genetics, insulin resistance, and obesity. *Total annual research expenditures:* $1.2 million. *Unit head:* Dr. Wendy Likes, Dean, 901-448-6135, Fax: 901-448-4121, E-mail: wlikes@uthsc.edu. *Application contact:* Jamie Overton, Director, Student Affairs, 901-448-6139, Fax: 901-448-4121, E-mail: joverton@uthsc.edu.
Website: http://uthsc.edu/nursing/

The University of Texas at Austin, Graduate School, School of Nursing, Austin, TX 78712-1111. Offers adult - gerontology clinical nurse specialist (MSN); child health (MSN), including administration, public health nursing, teaching; family nurse practitioner (MSN); family psychiatric/mental health nurse practitioner (MSN); holistic adult health (MSN), including administration, teaching; maternity (MSN), including administration, public health nursing, teaching; nursing (PhD); nursing administration and healthcare systems management (MSN); nursing practice (DNP); pediatric nurse practitioner (MSN); public health nursing (MSN). *Accreditation:* AACN. *Program availability:* Part-time. *Degree requirements:* For master's, thesis optional; for doctorate, thesis/dissertation. *Entrance requirements:* For master's and doctorate, GRE General Test. Additional exam requirements/recommendations for international students: Required—TOEFL (minimum score 550 paper-based). Electronic applications accepted. *Faculty research:* Chronic illness management, memory and aging, health promotion, women's health, adolescent health.

The University of Texas Health Science Center at San Antonio, School of Nursing, San Antonio, TX 78229-3900. Offers administrative management (MSN); adult-gerontology acute care nurse practitioner (PGC); advanced practice leadership (DNP); clinical nurse leader (MSN); executive administrative management (DNP); family nurse practitioner (MSN, PGC); nursing (MSN, PhD); nursing education (MSN, PGC); pediatric nurse practitioner primary care (PGC); psychiatric mental health nurse practitioner (PGC); public health nurse leader (DNP). *Accreditation:* AACN. *Program availability:* Part-time. Terminal master's awarded for partial completion of doctoral program. *Degree requirements:* For master's, thesis optional; for doctorate, comprehensive exam, thesis/dissertation.

The University of Toledo, College of Graduate Studies, College of Nursing, Department of Population and Community Care, Toledo, OH 43606-3390. Offers clinical nurse leader (MSN); family nurse practitioner (MSN, Certificate); nurse educator (MSN, Certificate); pediatric nurse practitioner (MSN, Certificate). *Program availability:* Part-time. *Degree requirements:* For master's, thesis or alternative. *Entrance requirements:* For master's, GRE, BS in nursing, minimum undergraduate GPA of 3.0, statement of purpose, three letters of recommendation, transcripts from all prior institutions attended, Nursing CAS application, UT supplemental application; for Certificate, BS in nursing, minimum undergraduate GPA of 3.0, statement of purpose, three letters of recommendation, transcripts from all prior institutions attended. Additional exam requirements/recommendations for international students: Required—TOEFL (minimum score 550 paper-based; 80 iBT). Electronic applications accepted.

University of Wisconsin–Madison, School of Nursing, Madison, WI 53706-1380. Offers adult/gerontology (DNP); nursing (PhD); pediatrics (DNP); psychiatric mental health (DNP); MS/MPH. *Accreditation:* AACN. *Program availability:* Part-time. *Degree requirements:* For doctorate, comprehensive exam, thesis/dissertation. *Entrance requirements:* For doctorate, GRE General Test, 2 samples of scholarly written work, BS in nursing from an accredited program, minimum undergraduate GPA of 3.0 in last 60 credits (for PhD); licensure as professional nurse (for DNP). Additional exam requirements/recommendations for international students: Required—TOEFL (minimum score 600 paper-based; 100 iBT). Electronic applications accepted. *Faculty research:* Nursing informatics to promote self-care and disease management skills among patients and caregivers; quality of care to frail, vulnerable, and chronically ill populations; study of health-related and health-seeking behaviors; eliminating health disparities; pain and symptom management for patients with cancer.

Vanderbilt University, Vanderbilt University School of Nursing, Nashville, TN 37240. Offers adult-gerontology acute care nurse practitioner (MSN), including hospitalist, intensivist; adult-gerontology primary care nurse practitioner (MSN); emergency nurse practitioner (MSN); family nurse practitioner (MSN); healthcare leadership (MSN); neonatal nurse practitioner (MSN); nurse midwifery (MSN); nurse midwifery/family nurse practitioner (MSN); nursing (Post-Master's Certificate); nursing informatics (MSN); nursing practice (DNP); nursing science (PhD); pediatric acute care nurse practitioner (MSN); pediatric primary care nurse practitioner (MSN); psychiatric-mental health nurse practitioner (MSN); women's health nurse practitioner (MSN); women's health nurse practitioner/adult gerontology primary care nurse practitioner (MSN); MSN/M Div; MSN/MTS. *Accreditation:* AACN; ACEN (one or more programs are accredited); ACNM/ACME. *Program availability:* Part-time, 100% online, blended/hybrid learning. *Faculty:* 292 full-time (267 women), 321 part-time/adjunct (253 women). *Students:* 501 full-time (435 women), 387 part-time (355 women); includes 153 minority (40 Black or African American, non-Hispanic/Latino; 1 American Indian or Alaska Native, non-Hispanic/Latino; 27 Asian, non-Hispanic/Latino; 48 Hispanic/Latino; 4 Native Hawaiian or other Pacific Islander, non-Hispanic/Latino; 33 Two or more races, non-Hispanic/Latino), 9 international. Average age 31. 1,210 applicants, 57% accepted, 473 enrolled. In 2017, 319 master's, 47 doctorates awarded. *Degree requirements:* For doctorate, comprehensive exam, thesis/dissertation. *Entrance requirements:* For master's, GRE General Test (taken within the past 5 years), minimum B average in undergraduate course work, 3 letters of recommendation; for doctorate, GRE General Test, interview, 3 letters of recommendation from doctorally-prepared faculty, MSN, essay. Additional exam requirements/recommendations for international students: Required—TOEFL (minimum score 570 paper-based), IELTS (minimum score 6.5). *Application deadline:* For fall admission, 11/1 priority date for domestic and international students. Applications are processed on a rolling basis. Application fee: $50. Electronic applications accepted. *Expenses:* Contact institution. *Financial support:* In 2017–18, 627 students received support. Scholarships/grants available. Financial award application deadline: 3/1; financial award applicants required to submit FAFSA. *Faculty research:* Lymphedema, palliative care and bereavement, health services research including workforce, safety and quality of care, gerontology, better birth outcomes including nutrition. *Total annual research expenditures:* $2 million. *Unit head:* Dr. Linda Norman, Dean, 615-343-8876, Fax: 615-343-7711, E-mail: linda.norman@vanderbilt.edu. *Application contact:* Patricia Peerman, Assistant Dean for Enrollment Management, 615-322-3800, Fax: 615-343-0333, E-mail: vusn-admissions@vanderbilt.edu.
Website: http://www.nursing.vanderbilt.edu

Villanova University, M. Louise Fitzpatrick College of Nursing, Villanova, PA 19085. Offers adult-gerontology primary care nurse practitioner (MSN, Post Master's Certificate); family primary care nurse practitioner (MSN, Post Master's Certificate); nurse anesthesia (DNP); nursing (PhD); nursing education (MSN, Post Master's Certificate); nursing practice (DNP); pediatric primary care nurse practitioner (MSN, Post Master's Certificate). *Accreditation:* AACN; AANA/CANAEP. *Program availability:* Part-time, online learning. *Students:* 151 full-time, 199 part-time; includes 42 minority (18 Black or African American, non-Hispanic/Latino; 12 Asian, non-Hispanic/Latino; 8 Hispanic/Latino; 4 Two or more races, non-Hispanic/Latino), 10 international. 274 applicants, 43% accepted, 92 enrolled. In 2017, 70 master's, 15 doctorates awarded. *Entrance requirements:* Additional exam requirements/recommendations for international students: Required—TOEFL, IELTS. *Application deadline:* For fall admission, 7/1 for domestic and international students; for spring admission, 10/1 for domestic and international students; for summer admission, 4/1 for domestic and international students. Application fee: $50. Electronic applications accepted. *Financial support:* Fellowships, research assistantships, teaching assistantships, scholarships/grants, traineeships, and tuition waivers available. *Unit head:* Dr. Marguerite K. Schlag, Associate Professor, Assistant Dean and Director of Graduate Nursing Program, 610-519-4907, Fax: 610-519-7650, E-mail: marguerite.schlag@villanova.edu. *Application contact:* Kathleen Geibel, Assistant to Graduate Program, 610-519-4934, Fax: 610-519-7650, E-mail: kathleen.geibel@villanova.edu.
Website: http://www.nursing.villanova.edu

Virginia Commonwealth University, Graduate School, School of Nursing, Richmond, VA 23284-9005. Offers adult health acute nursing (MS); adult health primary nursing (MS); biobehavioral clinical research (PhD); child health nursing (MS); clinical nurse leader (MS); family health nursing (MS); nurse educator (MS); nurse practitioner (MS); nursing (Certificate); nursing administration (MS), including clinical nurse manager; psychiatric-mental health nursing (MS); quality and safety in health care (DNP); women's health nursing (MS). *Accreditation:* AACN; ACEN (one or more programs are accredited). *Program availability:* Part-time, evening/weekend, online learning. *Degree requirements:* For master's, thesis optional; for doctorate, thesis/dissertation. *Entrance requirements:* For master's, GRE General Test, BSN, minimum GPA of 2.8; for doctorate, GRE General Test. Additional exam requirements/recommendations for international students: Required—TOEFL (minimum score 600 paper-based; 100 iBT). Electronic applications accepted.

Wayne State University, College of Nursing, Detroit, MI 48202. Offers adult gerontology acute care nurse practitioner (MSN); adult gerontology primary care nurse practitioner (MSN); advanced public health nursing (MSN); infant and mental health (DNP, PhD); neonatal nurse practitioner (MSN); nurse-midwifery (MSN); pediatric acute care nurse practitioner (MSN); pediatric primary care nurse practitioner (MSN); psychiatric mental health nurse practitioner (MSN); women's health nurse practitioner (MSN). Doctoral program admits for fall only. *Accreditation:* AACN. *Program availability:* Part-time. *Faculty:* 30. *Students:* 133 full-time (120 women), 184 part-time (167 women); includes 85 minority (57 Black or African American, non-Hispanic/Latino; 16 Asian, non-Hispanic/Latino; 4 Hispanic/Latino; 8 Two or more races, non-Hispanic/Latino), 22 international. Average age 34. 318 applicants, 39% accepted, 94 enrolled. In 2017, 51 master's, 29 doctorates awarded. *Degree requirements:* For doctorate, thesis/dissertation (for some programs). *Entrance requirements:* For master's, BSN from ACEN- or CCNE-accredited program with minimum GPA of 3.0; three references; current RN license; personal statement; for doctorate, resume or curriculum vitae; goals statement; bachelor's or master's degree in nursing from ACEN- or CCNE-accredited program with minimum GPA of 3.0; current RN license, writing sample and interview (for DNP); reference letters (3 for PhD, 2 for DNP). Additional exam requirements/recommendations for international students: Required—TOEFL (minimum score 101 iBT), TWE (minimum score 6), Michigan English Language Assessment Battery (minimum score 85); Recommended—IELTS (minimum score 7). Application fee: $50. Electronic applications accepted. *Expenses:* Contact institution. *Financial support:* In 2017–18, 92 students received support, including 16 fellowships with tuition reimbursements available (averaging $8,285 per year), 5 teaching assistantships with tuition reimbursements available (averaging $25,000 per year); scholarships/grants, health care benefits, and unspecified assistantships also available. Support available to part-time students. Financial award applicants required to submit FAFSA. *Faculty research:* Bridging transitions and technology to promote asthma care in the community, chronic wound care for persons who injected drugs, decreasing at-risk parenting to reduce child maltreatment and trauma, dementia symptoms (cognition, behavior, function), determining readiness to engage in end of life/palliative care conversations with adolescents and young adults living with advanced cancer, dyspnea assessment and treatment at the end of life. *Unit head:* Dr. Laurie Lauzon Clabo, Dean, College of Nursing, 313-577-4082, E-mail: laurie.lauzon.clabo@wayne.edu. *Application contact:* 313-577-4082, Fax: 313-577-6949, E-mail: nursinginfo@wayne.edu.
Website: http://nursing.wayne.edu/

Wayne State University, Eugene Applebaum College of Pharmacy and Health Sciences, Department of Health Care Sciences, Program in Nurse Anesthesia, Detroit, MI 48202. Offers anesthesia (MS); nurse anesthesia practice (DNP-A); pediatric anesthesia (Certificate). *Accreditation:* AACN; AANA/CANAEP. *Faculty:* 7. *Students:* 38 full-time (27 women); includes 7 minority (3 Black or African American, non-Hispanic/Latino; 3 Asian, non-Hispanic/Latino; 1 Hispanic/Latino). Average age 30. In 2017, 20 master's awarded. *Entrance requirements:* For master's, bachelor's degree in nursing or related science with minimum GPA of 3.0 overall and in science, current RN license, CCRN certification, one year of full-time experience in adult ICU, ACLS certification, PALS certification, hospital shadow experience (arranged by department); for Certificate, MS in anesthesia from accredited program, meeting with course coordinators from Children's Hospital of Michigan. Additional exam requirements/recommendations for international students: Required—TOEFL (minimum score 550 paper-based; 79 iBT), Michigan English Language Assessment Battery (minimum score 85); Recommended—IELTS (minimum score 6.5), TWE (minimum score 5.5). *Application deadline:* For fall admission, 7/1 for domestic and international students. Application fee: $50. Electronic applications accepted. *Expenses:* Contact institution. *Financial support:* In 2017–18, 17 students received support. Scholarships/grants available. Financial award applicants required to submit FAFSA. *Faculty research:* Music therapy in pain management, student success/students perspective, pacemaker management-safety, airway devices. *Unit head:* Dr. Prudentia A. Worth, Program Director, 313-993-7168, E-mail: aa1635@wayne.edu.
Website: http://cphs.wayne.edu/nurse-anesthesia/

Wright State University, Graduate School, College of Nursing and Health, Program in Nursing, Dayton, OH 45435. Offers administration of nursing and health care systems (MS); adult gerontology clinical nurse specialist (MS); adult-gerontology acute care nurse practitioner (MS); family nurse practitioner (MS); neonatal nurse practitioner (MS); pediatric nurse practitioner-acute care (MS); pediatric nurse practitioner-primary care (MS); psychiatric mental health nurse practitioner (MS); school nurse (MS). *Accreditation:* AACN. *Program availability:* Part-time, evening/weekend. *Degree requirements:* For master's, thesis or alternative. *Entrance requirements:* For master's, GRE General Test, BSN from ACEN-accredited college, Ohio RN license. Additional exam requirements/recommendations for international students: Required—TOEFL. *Faculty research:* Clinical nursing and health, teaching, caring, pain administration, informatics and technology.

Psychiatric Nursing

Allen College, Graduate Programs, Waterloo, IA 50703. Offers adult-gerontology acute care nurse practitioner (MSN); community/public health nursing (MSN); education (MSN); family nurse practitioner (MSN); health sciences (Ed D); leadership in health care delivery (MSN); leadership in health care informatics (MSN); nursing (DNP); occupational therapy (MS); psychiatric mental health nurse practitioner (MSN). MSN in leadership in healthcare informatics offered in partnership with University of Minnesota. *Accreditation:* AACN; ACEN. *Program availability:* Part-time, 100% online, blended/hybrid learning. *Faculty:* 24 full-time (all women), 8 part-time/adjunct (7 women). *Students:* 106 full-time (91 women), 187 part-time (164 women); includes 22 minority (12 Black or African American, non-Hispanic/Latino; 1 American Indian or Alaska Native, non-Hispanic/Latino; 2 Asian, non-Hispanic/Latino; 3 Hispanic/Latino; 4 Two or more races, non-Hispanic/Latino), 2 international. Average age 33. 352 applicants, 56% accepted, 131 enrolled. In 2017, 73 master's, 2 doctorates awarded. *Entrance requirements:* For master's, minimum GPA of 3.0 in the last 60 hours of undergraduate coursework; for doctorate, minimum GPA of 3.25 in graduate coursework. *Application deadline:* For fall admission, 2/1 priority date for domestic students; for spring admission, 9/1 priority date for domestic students. Applications are processed on a rolling basis. Application fee: $50. Electronic applications accepted. *Expenses:* $17,860 per year. *Financial support:* In 2017–18, 97 students received support. Federal Work-Study, institutionally sponsored loans, scholarships/grants, and traineeships available. Support available to part-time students. Financial award application deadline: 8/1; financial award applicants required to submit FAFSA. *Faculty research:* Poverty. *Unit head:* Dr. Nancy Kramer, Vice Chancellor for Academic Affairs, 319-226-2040, Fax: 319-226-2070, E-mail: nancy.kramer@allencollege.edu. *Application contact:* Molly Quinn, Director of Admissions, 319-226-2001, Fax: 319-226-2010, E-mail: molly.quinn@allencollege.edu.
Website: http://www.allencollege.edu/

Alverno College, JoAnn McGrath School of Nursing and Health Professions, Milwaukee, WI 53234-3922. Offers clinical nurse specialist (MSN); family nurse practitioner (MSN); nursing practice (DNP); psychiatric mental health nurse practitioner (MSN). *Accreditation:* AACN. *Program availability:* Part-time, evening/weekend. *Faculty:* 10 full-time (all women), 7 part-time/adjunct (4 women). *Students:* 119 full-time (107 women), 103 part-time (101 women); includes 53 minority (22 Black or African American, non-Hispanic/Latino; 1 American Indian or Alaska Native, non-Hispanic/Latino; 11 Asian, non-Hispanic/Latino; 15 Hispanic/Latino; 4 Two or more races, non-Hispanic/Latino), 1 international. Average age 35. 80 applicants, 99% accepted, 56 enrolled. In 2017, 47 master's awarded. *Degree requirements:* For master's, 500 clinical hours, capstone; for doctorate, 1,000 post-BSN clinical hours. *Entrance requirements:* For master's, BSN, current license; for doctorate, MSN, nursing license. Additional exam requirements/recommendations for international students: Required—TOEFL. *Application deadline:* For fall admission, 7/15 priority date for domestic and international students; for spring admission, 12/15 priority date for domestic and international students. Applications are processed on a rolling basis. Application fee: $0. Electronic applications accepted. *Expenses:* Contact institution. *Financial support:* Federal Work-Study and scholarships/grants available. Support available to part-time students. Financial award applicants required to submit FAFSA. *Faculty research:* International practicum experience and impact on future practice decision-making of family nurse practitioners; comparative health policy; improvement of HPV vaccination rates; use of language/words by healthcare practitioners and their effect on health outcomes. *Unit head:* Margaret Rauschenberger, Dean, 414-382-6276, Fax: 414-382-6354, E-mail: margaret.rauschenberger@alverno.edu. *Application contact:* Karin Wasiullah, Associate Dean, Master of Science in Nursing, 414-382-6275, Fax: 414-382-6354, E-mail: karin.wasiullah@alverno.edu.
Website: http://www.alverno.edu/academics/academicdepartments/joannmcgrathschoolofnursing/

American University of Beirut, Graduate Programs, Rafic Hariri School of Nursing, Beirut, Lebanon. Offers adult gerontology clinical nurse specialist (MSN); community and public health nursing (MSN); nursing administration and management (MSN); psychiatric mental health clinical nurse specialist (MSN). *Accreditation:* AACN. *Faculty:* 13 full-time (12 women), 23 part-time/adjunct (18 women). *Students:* 4 full-time (3 women), 40 part-time (34 women). Average age 28. 32 applicants, 81% accepted, 9 enrolled. In 2017, 18 master's awarded. *Degree requirements:* For master's, comprehensive exam, residency and project or thesis. *Entrance requirements:* For master's, minimum cumulative average of 80, minimum of 1 year of work experience. Additional exam requirements/recommendations for international students: Required—TOEFL (minimum score 583 paper-based; 97 iBT); Recommended—IELTS (minimum score 7). *Application deadline:* For fall admission, 4/4 for domestic students. Applications are processed on a rolling basis. Application fee: $50. Electronic applications accepted. *Expenses:* $810 per credit. *Financial support:* In 2017–18, 7 students received support. Teaching assistantships, scholarships/grants, traineeships, and unspecified assistantships available. Financial award application deadline: 12/20. *Faculty research:* Pain management and palliative care, postwar PTSD, depression, anxiety, and social support, cardiovascular care, vitamin D and cognitive function, nursing workforce and health systems research. *Total annual research expenditures:* $305,241. *Unit head:* Dr. Huda Abu-Saad Huijer, Director of the Hariri School of Nursing, 961-1-350000 Ext. 5953, Fax: 961-1-744476, E-mail: hh35@aub.edu.lb. *Application contact:* Nisreen Ghalayini, Administrative Assistant, 961-1-350000 Ext. 5951, E-mail: ng28@aub.edu.lb.
Website: http://www.aub.edu.lb/hson

Anderson University, College of Health Professions, Anderson, SC 29621-4035. Offers advanced practice (DNP); executive leadership (MSN, DNP); family nurse practitioner (MSN, DNP); nurse educator (MSN); psychiatric mental health nurse practitioner (MSN, DNP). *Program availability:* Online learning. *Expenses: Tuition:* Full-time $24,290; part-time $650 per credit hour. Full-time tuition and fees vary according to degree level and program. *Unit head:* Dr. Donald M. Peace, Dean, 864-231-5513, E-mail: dpeace@andersonuniversity.edu. *Application contact:* Chris Woodlief, Associate Director of Adult and Graduate Programs, 864-231-5531, E-mail: cwoodlief@andersonuniversity.edu.
Website: http://www.andersonuniversity.edu/health-professions

Arizona State University at the Tempe campus, College of Nursing and Health Innovation, Phoenix, AZ 85004. Offers advanced nursing practice (DNP); clinical research management (MS); community and public health practice (Graduate Certificate); family mental health nurse practitioner (Graduate Certificate); family nurse practitioner (Graduate Certificate); geriatric nursing (Graduate Certificate); healthcare innovation (MHI); nurse education in academic and practice settings (Graduate Certificate); nurse educator (MS); nursing and healthcare innovation (PhD). *Accreditation:* AACN. *Program availability:* Online learning. *Degree requirements:* For master's, comprehensive exam (for some programs), thesis (for some programs), interactive Program of Study (iPOS) submitted before completing 50 percent of required credit hours; for doctorate, comprehensive exam, thesis/dissertation, interactive Program of Study (iPOS) submitted before completing 50 percent of required credit hours. *Entrance requirements:* For master's and doctorate, GRE, minimum GPA of 3.0 or equivalent in last 2 years of work leading to bachelor's degree. Additional exam requirements/recommendations for international students: Required—TOEFL, IELTS, or PTE. Electronic applications accepted. *Expenses:* Contact institution.

Augusta University, College of Nursing, Doctor of Nursing Practice Program, Augusta, GA 30912. Offers adult gerontology acute care nurse practitioner (DNP); family nurse practitioner (DNP); nurse executive (DNP); nursing (DNP); nursing anesthesia (DNP); pediatric nurse practitioner (DNP); psychiatric mental health nurse practitioner (DNP). *Accreditation:* AACN; AANA/CANAEP. *Degree requirements:* For doctorate, thesis/dissertation or alternative. *Entrance requirements:* For doctorate, GRE General Test or MAT, master's degree in nursing or related field, current professional nurse licensure. Additional exam requirements/recommendations for international students: Required—TOEFL (minimum score 600 paper-based; 100 iBT). Electronic applications accepted.

Psychiatric Nursing

Azusa Pacific University, School of Nursing, Azusa, CA 91702-7000. Offers adult clinical nurse specialist (MSN); adult-gerontology nurse practitioner (MSN); family nurse practitioner (MSN); healthcare administration and leadership (MSN); nursing (MSN, DNP, PhD); nursing education (MSN); parent-child clinical nurse specialist (MSN); psychiatric mental health nurse practitioner (MSN). *Accreditation:* AACN. *Program availability:* Part-time, evening/weekend. *Degree requirements:* For master's, thesis optional. *Entrance requirements:* For master's, BSN.

Binghamton University, State University of New York, Graduate School, Decker School of Nursing, Binghamton, NY 13902-6000. Offers adult-gerontological nursing (MS, DNP, Certificate); community health nursing (MS, DNP, Certificate); family health nursing (MS, DNP, Certificate); family psychiatric mental health nursing (MS, DNP, Certificate); nursing (PhD). *Accreditation:* AACN. *Program availability:* Part-time, evening/weekend. *Faculty:* 52 full-time (45 women). *Students:* 94 full-time (79 women), 109 part-time (94 women); includes 43 minority (21 Black or African American, non-Hispanic/Latino; 10 Asian, non-Hispanic/Latino; 7 Hispanic/Latino; 5 Two or more races, non-Hispanic/Latino), 13 international. Average age 36. 111 applicants, 95% accepted, 63 enrolled. In 2017, 53 master's, 5 doctorates, 20 other advanced degrees awarded. Terminal master's awarded for partial completion of doctoral program. *Degree requirements:* For master's, comprehensive exam, thesis; for doctorate, comprehensive exam (for some programs), thesis/dissertation. *Entrance requirements:* For master's and doctorate, GRE General Test, nursing licensure. Additional exam requirements/recommendations for international students: Required—TOEFL (minimum score 90 iBT). Application fee: $75. Electronic applications accepted. *Expenses:* Contact institution. *Financial support:* In 2017–18, 33 students received support, including 1 fellowship with partial tuition reimbursement available (averaging $16,500 per year), research assistantships with full tuition reimbursements available (averaging $12,500 per year), 1 teaching assistantship with full tuition reimbursement available (averaging $16,500 per year); career-related internships or fieldwork, Federal Work-Study, institutionally sponsored loans, traineeships, health care benefits, tuition waivers (full and partial), and unspecified assistantships also available. Financial award applicants required to submit FAFSA. *Unit head:* Dr. Mario R. Ortiz, Dean, 607-777-2311, E-mail: mortiz@binghamton.edu. *Application contact:* Ben Balkaya, Assistant Dean and Director, 607-777-2151, Fax: 607-777-2501, E-mail: balkaya@binghamton.edu.
Website: http://www.binghamton.edu/dson/

Boston College, William F. Connell School of Nursing, Chestnut Hill, MA 02467. Offers adult-gerontology primary care nurse practitioner (MS); family health nursing (MS); nurse anesthesia (MS); nursing (PhD); pediatric primary care nurse practitioner (MS), including pediatric and women's health; psychiatric-mental health nursing (MS); women's health nursing (MS); MBA/MS; MS/MA; MS/PhD. MS/MBA offered jointly with Carroll School of Management, MS/MA with School of Theology and Ministry. *Accreditation:* AACN; AANA/CANAEP (one or more programs are accredited). *Program availability:* Part-time. *Faculty:* 54 full-time (48 women). *Students:* 170 full-time (153 women), 90 part-time (83 women); includes 39 minority (8 Black or African American, non-Hispanic/Latino; 10 Asian, non-Hispanic/Latino; 12 Hispanic/Latino; 9 Two or more races, non-Hispanic/Latino), 3 international. Average age 28. 360 applicants, 56% accepted, 94 enrolled. In 2017, 104 master's, 5 doctorates awarded. *Degree requirements:* For master's, comprehensive exam; for doctorate, comprehensive exam, thesis/dissertation, computer literacy exam or foreign language. *Entrance requirements:* For master's, bachelor's degree in nursing; for doctorate, GRE General Test, MS in nursing. Additional exam requirements/recommendations for international students: Required—TOEFL (minimum score 600 paper-based; 100 iBT), IELTS (minimum score 7.5). *Application deadline:* For fall admission, 9/30 for domestic and international students; for winter admission, 1/15 for domestic and international students; for spring admission, 3/15 for domestic and international students. Application fee: $40. Electronic applications accepted. *Expenses:* $1,350 per credit tuition. *Financial support:* In 2017–18, 152 students received support, including 11 fellowships with full tuition reimbursements available (averaging $24,504 per year), 29 teaching assistantships (averaging $3,768 per year); scholarships/grants, health care benefits, tuition waivers (partial), and unspecified assistantships also available. Support available to part-time students. Financial award application deadline: 4/18; financial award applicants required to submit FAFSA. *Faculty research:* Sexual and reproductive health, health promotion/illness prevention, aging, eating disorders, symptom management. *Total annual research expenditures:* $879,812. *Unit head:* Dr. Susan Gennaro, Dean, 617-552-4251, Fax: 617-552-0931, E-mail: susan.gennaro@bc.edu. *Application contact:* Sean Sendall, Assistant Dean, Graduate Enrollment and Data Analytics, 617-552-4745, Fax: 617-552-2121, E-mail: sean.sendall@bc.edu.
Website: http://www.bc.edu/cson

California State University, San Marcos, College of Education, Health and Human Services, School of Nursing, San Marcos, CA 92096-0001. Offers advanced practice nursing (MSN), including clinical nurse specialist, family nurse practitioner, psychiatric mental health nurse practitioner; clinical nurse leader (MSN); nursing education (MSN). *Expenses:* Tuition, state resident: full-time $7176. Tuition, nonresident: full-time $9504. *Unit head:* Lorna Kendrick, Director, 760-750-7580, E-mail: lkendrick@csusm.edu.
Website: http://www.csusm.edu/nursing/

Case Western Reserve University, Frances Payne Bolton School of Nursing, Master's Programs in Nursing, Nurse Practitioner Program, Cleveland, OH 44106. Offers acute care pediatric nurse practitioner (MSN); acute care/cardiovascular nursing (MSN); acute care/flight nurse (MSN); adult gerontology acute care nurse practitioner (MSN); adult gerontology primary care nurse practitioner (MSN); family nurse practitioner (MSN); family systems psychiatric mental health nursing (MSN); neonatal nurse practitioner (MSN); palliative care (MSN); pediatric nurse practitioner (MSN); women's health nurse practitioner (MSN). *Accreditation:* ACEN. *Program availability:* Part-time. *Faculty:* 30 full-time (26 women), 5 part-time/adjunct (3 women). *Students:* 34 full-time (28 women), 97 part-time (73 women); includes 24 minority (5 Black or African American, non-Hispanic/Latino; 9 Asian, non-Hispanic/Latino; 6 Hispanic/Latino; 4 Two or more races, non-Hispanic/Latino), 4 international. Average age 33. 56 applicants, 82% accepted, 29 enrolled. In 2017, 68 master's awarded. *Degree requirements:* For master's, minimum GPA of 3.0, clinical hours corresponding to requirements to sit for certification exam, portfolio. *Entrance requirements:* For master's, GRE General Test or MAT. Additional exam requirements/recommendations for international students: Required—TOEFL (minimum score 577 paper-based; 90 iBT), IELTS (minimum score 7). *Application deadline:* For fall admission, 5/1 for domestic and international students; for spring admission, 10/1 for domestic and international students; for summer admission, 3/1 for domestic and international students. Applications are processed on a rolling basis. Application fee: $75. Electronic applications accepted. *Expenses:* $2,011 per credit tuition; $15 nursing activity fee; $17 activity fee. *Financial support:* In 2017–18, 86 students received support, including 19 teaching assistantships with partial tuition reimbursements available (averaging $18,100 per year); scholarships/grants and traineeships also available. Support available to part-time students. Financial award application deadline: 5/15; financial award applicants required to submit FAFSA. *Faculty research:* Symptom science, family/community care, aging across the lifespan, self-management of health and illness, neuroscience. *Unit head:* Dr. Latina Brooks, Director, 216-368-1196, Fax: 216-368-3542, E-mail: lmb3@case.edu. *Application contact:* Jackie Tepale, Admissions Coordinator, 216-368-5253, Fax: 216-368-0124, E-mail: yyd@case.edu.
Website: http://fpb.cwru.edu/MSN/majors.shtm

Clarke University, Department of Nursing and Health, Dubuque, IA 52001-3198. Offers family nurse practitioner (DNP); health leadership and practice (DNP); psychiatric mental health nurse practitioner (DNP). *Accreditation:* AACN. *Program availability:* Part-time. *Faculty:* 6 full-time (all women). *Students:* 55 full-time (54 women), 11 part-time (10 women); includes 3 minority (1 Black or African American, non-Hispanic/Latino; 1 Asian, non-Hispanic/Latino; 1 Two or more races, non-Hispanic/Latino). Average age 32. 62 applicants, 40% accepted, 22 enrolled. In 2017, 36 doctorates awarded. *Degree requirements:* For doctorate, comprehensive exam, thesis/dissertation. *Entrance requirements:* For doctorate, GRE (if GPA under 3.0), bachelor's degree from accredited nursing program and accredited college or university; minimum GPA of 3.0; minimum C grade on undergraduate prerequisite courses; three recommendation forms; curriculum vitae; statement of goals; transcripts; copy of nursing license; proof of health insurance; interview. Additional exam requirements/recommendations for international students: Required—TOEFL (minimum score 550 paper-based; 80 iBT), IELTS (minimum score 6.5). *Application deadline:* For fall admission, 2/1 priority date for domestic students. Application fee: $35. Electronic applications accepted. *Expenses:* $850 per credit. *Financial support:* Applicants required to submit FAFSA. *Faculty research:* Narrative pedagogy, ethics, end-of-life care, pedagogy, family systems, simulation. *Unit head:* Dr. Jan Lee, Chair, 563-588-6339, E-mail: jan.lee@clarke.edu. *Application contact:* Kimberly Roush, Director of Admission, Graduate and Adult Programs, 563-588-6539, Fax: 563-552-7994, E-mail: graduate@clarke.edu.
Website: https://www.clarke.edu/academics/doctor-of-nursing-practice/

Columbia University, School of Nursing, Program in Psychiatric Mental Health Nursing, New York, NY 10032. Offers MS, Adv C. *Accreditation:* AACN. *Program availability:* Part-time. *Entrance requirements:* For master's, GRE General Test, NCLEX, BSN, 1 year of clinical experience (preferred); for Adv C, MSN. Additional exam requirements/recommendations for international students: Required—TOEFL (minimum score 100 iBT). Electronic applications accepted. *Expenses: Tuition:* Full-time $44,864; part-time $1704 per credit. *Required fees:* $2370 per semester. One-time fee: $105.

Creighton University, College of Nursing, Omaha, NE 68178-0001. Offers adult gerontology acute care nurse practitioner (DNP, Post-Master's Certificate); adult gerontology nurse practitioner (DNP); clinical nurse leader (MSN, Post-Graduate Certificate); clinical systems administration (MSN, DNP); family nurse practitioner (DNP, Post-Master's Certificate); neonatal nurse practitioner (DNP, Post-Master's Certificate); nursing (Post-Graduate Certificate); pediatric acute care nurse practitioner (DNP, Post-Master's Certificate); psychiatric mental health nurse practitioner (DNP). *Accreditation:* AACN. *Program availability:* Part-time, blended/hybrid learning. *Degree requirements:* For master's, capstone project; for doctorate, scholarly project. *Entrance requirements:* For master's and doctorate, BSN from ACEN- or CCNE-accredited nursing school, minimum cumulative GPA of 3.0, personal statement, active unencumbered RN license with NE eligibility, undergraduate statistics course, physical assessment course or equivalent, three recommendation letters; for other advanced degree, MSN or MS in nursing from ACEN- or CCNE-accredited nursing school, minimum cumulative GPA of 3.0, active unencumbered RN license with NE eligibility. Additional exam requirements/recommendations for international students: Required—TOEFL (minimum score 600 paper-based, 100 iBT) or IELTS. Electronic applications accepted. *Expenses:* Contact institution. *Faculty research:* School health report card, obesity prevention in children, simulated clinical experience evaluation, vitamin D3 and calcium and cancer risk reduction education, online support and education to reduce stress for prenatal patients on bed rest, health literacy, immunization research.

Drexel University, College of Nursing and Health Professions, Division of Graduate Nursing, Philadelphia, PA 19104-2875. Offers adult acute care (MSN); adult psychiatric/mental health (MSN); advanced practice nursing (MSN); clinical trials research (MSN); family nurse practitioner (MSN); leadership in health systems management (MSN); nursing education (MSN); pediatric primary care (MSN); women's health (MSN). *Accreditation:* AACN. Electronic applications accepted.

East Tennessee State University, School of Graduate Studies, College of Nursing, Johnson City, TN 37614. Offers acute care nurse practitioner (DNP); adult-gerontology primary care nurse practitioner (DNP); adult/gerontological nurse practitioner (Postbaccalaureate Certificate); executive leadership in nursing (DNP, Postbaccalaureate Certificate); family nurse practitioner (MSN, DNP, Post-Master's Certificate, Postbaccalaureate Certificate); nursing (PhD); nursing administration (MSN); nursing education (MSN); pediatric primary care nurse practitioner (DNP); psychiatric mental health nurse practitioner (Postbaccalaureate Certificate); psychiatric/mental health nurse practitioner (MSN, DNP, Post-Master's Certificate); women's health care nurse practitioner (DNP). *Accreditation:* AACN. *Program availability:* Part-time, evening/weekend, online learning. In 2017, 126 master's, 30 doctorates, 4 other advanced degrees awarded. *Degree requirements:* For master's and other advanced degree, comprehensive exam, practicum; for doctorate, comprehensive exam, thesis/dissertation (for some programs), practicum, internship, evidence of professional malpractice insurance, CPR certification. *Entrance requirements:* For master's, bachelor's degree, minimum GPA of 3.0, current RN license and eligibility to practice, resume, three letters of recommendation; for doctorate, GRE General Test, MSN (for PhD), BSN or MSN (for DNP), current RN license and eligibility to practice, 2 years of full-time registered nurse work experience or equivalent, three letters of recommendation, resume or curriculum vitae, interview, writing sample; for other advanced degree, MSN, minimum GPA of 3.0, current RN license and eligibility to practice, three letters of recommendation, resume or curriculum vitae; DNP with designated concentration in advanced clinical practice or nursing administration (for select programs). Additional exam requirements/recommendations for international students: Required—TOEFL (minimum score 600 paper-based; 79 iBT). *Application deadline:* For fall admission, 4/15 priority date for domestic and international students; for spring admission, 10/15 priority date for domestic and international students; for summer admission, 2/1 for domestic and international students. Application fee: $55 ($65 for international students). Electronic applications accepted. *Financial support:* Research assistantships with tuition reimbursements, teaching assistantships, career-related internships or fieldwork, institutionally sponsored loans, scholarships/grants, and unspecified assistantships available. Financial award application deadline: 7/1; financial award applicants required to submit FAFSA. *Faculty research:* Improving health of rural and underserved populations (low income elders living in public housing, rural caregivers, Hispanic populations), health services and systems research (quality outcomes of nurse-managed primary care, in-home, and rural health care), nursing education (experiences of second-degree BSN students, well-being of BSN students). *Unit head:* Dr. Wendy Nehring, Dean, 423-439-7051, Fax: 423-439-4543, E-mail: nursing@etsu.edu. *Application contact:* Dr. Myra Clark, Director of Graduate Programs, 423-439-4396, Fax: 423-439-4100, E-mail: clarkml2@etsu.edu.
Website: http://www.etsu.edu/nursing/

Fairfield University, Marion Peckham Egan School of Nursing and Health Studies, Fairfield, CT 06824. Offers advanced practice (DNP); family nurse practitioner (MSN, DNP); nurse anesthesia (DNP); nursing leadership (MSN); psychiatric nurse practitioner (MSN, DNP). *Accreditation:* AACN; AANA/CANAEP. *Program availability:* Part-time, evening/weekend. *Faculty:* 9 full-time (all women), 11 part-time/adjunct (8 women). *Students:* 50 full-time (42 women), 153 part-time (140 women); includes 48 minority (15

Black or African American, non-Hispanic/Latino; 1 American Indian or Alaska Native, non-Hispanic/Latino; 10 Asian, non-Hispanic/Latino; 19 Hispanic/Latino; 3 Two or more races, non-Hispanic/Latino), 2 international. Average age 34. 160 applicants, 50% accepted, 55 enrolled. In 2017, 26 master's, 36 doctorates awarded. *Degree requirements:* For master's, capstone project. *Entrance requirements:* For master's, minimum QPA of 3.0, RN license, resume, 2 recommendations; for doctorate, MSN (minimum QPA of 3.2) or BSN (minimum QPA of 3.0); critical care nursing experience (for nurse anesthesia DNP candidates). Additional exam requirements/recommendations for international students: Required—TOEFL (minimum score 550 paper-based; 80 iBT) or IELTS (minimum score 6.5). *Application deadline:* For fall admission, 5/15 for international students; for spring admission, 10/15 for international students. Applications are processed on a rolling basis. Application fee: $60. Electronic applications accepted. *Expenses:* $850 per credit hour (for MSN); $1,000 per credit hour (for DNP). *Financial support:* In 2017–18, 45 students received support. Scholarships/grants and unspecified assistantships available. Financial award applicants required to submit FAFSA. *Faculty research:* Aging, spiritual care, palliative and end of life care, psychiatric mental health, pediatric trauma. *Unit head:* Dr. Meredith Wallace Kazer, Dean, 203-254-4000 Ext. 2701, Fax: 203-254-4126, E-mail: mkazer@fairfield.edu. *Application contact:* Marianne Gumpper, Director of Graduate and Continuing Studies Admission, 203-254-4184, Fax: 203-254-4073, E-mail: gradadmis@fairfield.edu.
Website: http://fairfield.edu/son

Fairleigh Dickinson University, Florham Campus, University College: Arts, Sciences, and Professional Studies, The Henry P. Becton School of Nursing and Allied Health, Madison, NJ 07940-1099. Offers adult gerontology primary care nurse practitioner (MSN); family psychiatric/mental health nurse practitioner (MSN). *Program availability:* Part-time, evening/weekend. *Entrance requirements:* For master's, BSN, minimum undergraduate GPA of 3.0, courses in statistics and nursing research at the undergraduate level, NJ Registered Nurse licensure, minimum of 1 year of clinical nursing experience, two letters of recommendation. *Expenses: Tuition:* Full-time $22,410; part-time $1245 per credit. *Required fees:* $888; $414 per unit. Tuition and fees vary according to course load, degree level and program.

Florida International University, Nicole Wertheim College of Nursing and Health Sciences, Nursing Program, Miami, FL 33199. Offers adult health nursing (MSN); family health (MSN); nurse anesthetist (MSN); nursing practice (DNP); nursing science research (PhD); pediatric nurse (MSN); psychiatric and mental health nursing (MSN); registered nurse (MSN). *Accreditation:* AACN; AANA/CANAEP. *Program availability:* Part-time, evening/weekend. *Faculty:* 40 full-time (33 women), 70 part-time/adjunct (69 women). *Students:* 330 full-time (233 women), 89 part-time (73 women); includes 326 minority (92 Black or African American, non-Hispanic/Latino; 1 American Indian or Alaska Native, non-Hispanic/Latino; 33 Asian, non-Hispanic/Latino; 195 Hispanic/Latino; 2 Native Hawaiian or other Pacific Islander, non-Hispanic/Latino; 3 Two or more races, non-Hispanic/Latino), 9 international. Average age 33. 304 applicants, 50% accepted, 148 enrolled. In 2017, 144 master's, 8 doctorates awarded. *Degree requirements:* For master's, thesis or alternative; for doctorate, comprehensive exam, thesis/dissertation. *Entrance requirements:* For master's, bachelor's degree in nursing, minimum undergraduate GPA of 3.0 in upper-level coursework, letters of recommendation; for doctorate, GRE, letters of recommendation, minimum undergraduate GPA of 3.0 in upper-level coursework, interview. Additional exam requirements/recommendations for international students: Required—TOEFL (minimum score 550 paper-based; 80 iBT). *Application deadline:* For fall admission, 6/1 for domestic students, 4/1 for international students; for spring admission, 10/1 for domestic students, 9/1 for international students. Applications are processed on a rolling basis. Application fee: $30. Electronic applications accepted. *Expenses:* Tuition, state resident: full-time $8912; part-time $446 per credit hour. Tuition, nonresident: full-time $21,393; part-time $992 per credit hour. *Required fees:* $390; $195 per semester. *Financial support:* Institutionally sponsored loans and scholarships/grants available. Financial award application deadline: 3/1; financial award applicants required to submit FAFSA. *Faculty research:* Adult health nursing. *Unit head:* Dr. Yhovana Gordon, Chair, 305-348-7733, Fax: 305-348-7051, E-mail: gordony@fiu.edu. *Application contact:* Nanett Rojas, Manager, Admissions Operations, 305-348-7464, Fax: 305-348-7441, E-mail: gradadm@fiu.edu.
Website: http://cnhs.fiu.edu/

Florida State University, The Graduate School, College of Nursing, Tallahassee, FL 32306-4310. Offers family nurse practitioner (DNP); psychiatric mental health (Certificate). *Accreditation:* AACN; AANA/CANAEP. *Program availability:* Part-time, 100% online. *Faculty:* 20 full-time (19 women), 3 part-time/adjunct (all women). *Students:* 82 full-time (72 women), 26 part-time (25 women); includes 29 minority (9 Black or African American, non-Hispanic/Latino; 8 Asian, non-Hispanic/Latino; 10 Hispanic/Latino; 2 Two or more races, non-Hispanic/Latino). Average age 38. 123 applicants, 48% accepted, 41 enrolled. In 2017, 20 doctorates awarded. *Degree requirements:* For doctorate, thesis/dissertation, evidence-based project. *Entrance requirements:* For doctorate, GRE General Test, MAT, minimum GPA of 3.0, BSN or MSN, Florida RN license. Additional exam requirements/recommendations for international students: Required—TOEFL (minimum score 550 paper-based). *Application deadline:* For fall admission, 4/1 for domestic and international students. Application fee: $30. Electronic applications accepted. *Expenses:* Contact institution. *Financial support:* In 2017–18, 29 students received support, including fellowships with partial tuition reimbursements available (averaging $6,300 per year), research assistantships with partial tuition reimbursements available (averaging $3,000 per year), 3 teaching assistantships with partial tuition reimbursements available (averaging $3,000 per year); career-related internships or fieldwork, Federal Work-Study, institutionally sponsored loans, scholarships/grants, traineeships, and tuition waivers (partial) also available. Financial award application deadline: 4/1; financial award applicants required to submit FAFSA. *Faculty research:* Cardiac, women's health, health promotion and prevention, educational strategies, infectious diseases, health disparities. *Unit head:* Dr. Judith McFetridge-Durdle, Dean, 850-644-6846, Fax: 850-644-7660, E-mail: jdurdle@nursing.fsu.edu. *Application contact:* Carlos Urrutia, Assistant Director for Student Services, 850-644-5638, Fax: 850-645-7249, E-mail: currutia@fsu.edu.
Website: http://nursing.fsu.edu/

Frontier Nursing University, Graduate Programs, Hyden, KY 41749. Offers family nurse practitioner (MSN, DNP, Post Master's Certificate); nurse-midwifery (MSN, DNP, Post Master's Certificate); psychiatric-mental health nurse practitioner (MSN, DNP, Post Master's Certificate); women's health care nurse practitioner (MSN, DNP, Post Master's Certificate). *Accreditation:* ACEN. *Degree requirements:* For doctorate, capstone project, practicum.

See Display on page 570 and Close-Up on page 761.

George Mason University, College of Health and Human Services, School of Nursing, Fairfax, VA 22030. Offers adult gerontology (DNP); adult/gerontological nurse practitioner (MSN); family nurse practitioner (MSN, DNP); nurse educator (MSN); nursing (PhD); nursing administration (MSN, DNP); nursing education (Certificate); psychiatric mental health (DNP). *Accreditation:* AACN. *Program availability:* Part-time, evening/weekend, blended/hybrid learning. *Faculty:* 28 full-time (27 women), 51 part-time/adjunct (47 women). *Students:* 51 full-time (40 women), 182 part-time (162 women); includes 110 minority (59 Black or African American, non-Hispanic/Latino; 1 American Indian or Alaska Native, non-Hispanic/Latino; 36 Asian, non-Hispanic/Latino; 10 Hispanic/Latino; 4 Two or more races, non-Hispanic/Latino), 8 international. Average age 37. 159 applicants, 70% accepted, 73 enrolled. In 2017, 33 master's, 24 doctorates, 1 other advanced degree awarded. *Degree requirements:* For master's, comprehensive exam (for some programs), thesis in clinical classes; for doctorate, comprehensive exam (for some programs), thesis/dissertation (for some programs). *Entrance requirements:* For master's, 2 official transcripts; expanded goals statement; resume; BSN from accredited institution; minimum GPA of 3.0 in last 60 credits of undergraduate work; 2 letters of recommendation; completion of undergraduate statistics and graduate-level bivariate statistics; certification in professional CPR; for doctorate, GRE, 2 official transcripts; expanded goals statement; resume; 2 recommendation letters; nursing license; at least 1 year of work experience as an RN; interview; writing sample; evidence of graduate-level course in applied statistics; master's degree in nursing with minimum GPA of 3.5; for Certificate, 2 official transcripts; expanded goals statement; resume; master's degree from accredited institution or currently enrolled with minimum GPA of 3.0. Additional exam requirements/recommendations for international students: Required—TOEFL (minimum score 570 paper-based; 88 iBT), IELTS (minimum score 6.5), PTE (minimum score 59). *Application deadline:* For fall admission, 2/1 for domestic and international students. Application fee: $75 ($80 for international students). Electronic applications accepted. *Expenses:* Contact institution. *Financial support:* In 2017–18, 7 students received support, including 5 research assistantships with tuition reimbursements available (averaging $20,500 per year), 2 teaching assistantships; career-related internships or fieldwork, Federal Work-Study, scholarships/grants, unspecified assistantships, and health care benefits (for full-time research or teaching assistantship recipients) also available. Financial award application deadline: 3/1; financial award applicants required to submit FAFSA. *Faculty research:* Health care, nursing science. *Total annual research expenditures:* $1.6 million. *Unit head:* Carol Urban, Director, 703-993-2991, Fax: 703-993-1949, E-mail: curban@gmu.edu. *Application contact:* Susan Eckis, Office Manager, 703-993-1938, Fax: 703-993-1949, E-mail: seckis@gmu.edu.
Website: http://chhs.gmu.edu/nursing

Georgia Southern University, Jack N. Averitt College of Graduate Studies, College of Health and Human Sciences, School of Nursing, Program in Nurse Practitioner, Statesboro, GA 30458. Offers family nurse practitioner (MSN); psychiatric mental health nurse practitioner (MSN). *Program availability:* Part-time, blended/hybrid learning. *Students:* 2 part-time (both women); includes 1 minority (Black or African American, non-Hispanic/Latino). Average age 43. 3 applicants, 33% accepted. In 2017, 12 master's awarded. *Entrance requirements:* For master's, minimum GPA of 3.0, Georgia nursing license, 2 years of clinical experience, CPR certification. Additional exam requirements/recommendations for international students: Required—TOEFL (minimum score 550 paper-based; 80 iBT), IELTS (minimum score 6). *Application deadline:* For fall admission, 7/31 priority date for domestic and international students; for spring admission, 11/30 priority date for domestic students, 11/30 for international students; for summer admission, 3/31 for domestic and international students. Applications are processed on a rolling basis. Application fee: $50. Electronic applications accepted. *Expenses:* Tuition, state resident: full-time $4986; part-time $3324 per year. Tuition, nonresident: full-time $21,982; part-time $15,352 per year. *Required fees:* $2092; $1802 per credit hour. $901 per semester. Tuition and fees vary according to course load, campus/location and program. *Financial support:* In 2017–18, 1 student received support, including 5 fellowships with full tuition reimbursements available (averaging $7,750 per year); career-related internships or fieldwork, Federal Work-Study, scholarships/grants, traineeships, tuition waivers (full), and unspecified assistantships also available. Support available to part-time students. Financial award application deadline: 4/15; financial award applicants required to submit FAFSA. *Faculty research:* Vulnerable populations, breast cancer, diabetes, mellitus, advanced practice nursing issues. *Unit head:* Dr. Sharon Radzyminski, Department Chair, 912-478-5455, Fax: 912-478-5036, E-mail: sradzyminski@georgiasouthern.edu.

Georgia State University, Byrdine F. Lewis School of Nursing, Atlanta, GA 30303. Offers adult health clinical nurse specialist/nurse practitioner (MS, Certificate); child health clinical nurse specialist/pediatric nurse practitioner (MS, Certificate); family nurse practitioner (MS, Certificate); family psychiatric mental health nurse practitioner (MS, Certificate); nursing (PhD); nursing leadership in healthcare innovations (MS), including nursing administration, nursing informatics; nutrition (MS); perinatal clinical nurse specialist/women's health nurse practitioner (MS, Certificate); physical therapy (DPT); respiratory therapy (MS). *Accreditation:* AACN. *Program availability:* Part-time, blended/hybrid learning. *Faculty:* 69 full-time (52 women). *Students:* 322 full-time (248 women), 481 part-time (466 women); includes 186 minority (112 Black or African American, non-Hispanic/Latino; 44 Asian, non-Hispanic/Latino; 20 Hispanic/Latino; 10 Two or more races, non-Hispanic/Latino), 18 international. Average age 31. 370 applicants, 56% accepted, 148 enrolled. In 2017, 131 master's, 49 doctorates, 11 other advanced degrees awarded. *Degree requirements:* For doctorate, comprehensive exam, thesis/dissertation. *Entrance requirements:* For doctorate, GRE. Additional exam requirements/recommendations for international students: Required—TOEFL. *Application deadline:* For fall admission, 2/1 priority date for domestic and international students; for spring admission, 9/15 for domestic and international students. Applications are processed on a rolling basis. Application fee: $50. Electronic applications accepted. *Expenses:* Contact institution. *Financial support:* In 2017–18, research assistantships with tuition reimbursements (averaging $1,666 per year), teaching assistantships with tuition reimbursements (averaging $1,920 per year) were awarded; scholarships/grants, tuition waivers (full and partial), and unspecified assistantships also available. Support available to part-time students. Financial award application deadline: 8/1; financial award applicants required to submit FAFSA. *Faculty research:* Stroke intervention for caregivers, stroke prevention in African-Americans; relationships between psychological distress and health outcomes in parents with a medically ill infant; medically fragile children; nursing expertise and patient outcomes. *Unit head:* Nancy Kropf, Dean of Nursing, 404-413-1101, Fax: 404-413-1090, E-mail: nkropf@gsu.edu.
Website: http://nursing.gsu.edu/

Hofstra University, Hofstra Northwell School of Graduate Nursing and Physician Assistant Studies, Programs in Nursing, Hempstead, NY 11549. Offers adult-gerontology acute care nurse practitioner (MS); family nurse practitioner (MS); psychiatric-mental health nurse practitioner (MS). *Students:* 29 full-time (23 women), 107 part-time (89 women); includes 62 minority (16 Black or African American, non-Hispanic/Latino; 21 Asian, non-Hispanic/Latino; 25 Hispanic/Latino). Average age 35. 122 applicants, 62% accepted, 62 enrolled. *Degree requirements:* For master's, comprehensive exam, minimum GPA of 3.0. *Entrance requirements:* For master's, bachelor's degree in biology or equivalent, 2 letters of recommendation, essay, minimum GPA of 3.0. Additional exam requirements/recommendations for international students: Required—TOEFL (minimum score 550 paper-based; 80 iBT). *Application deadline:* For fall admission, 11/1 for domestic students. Application fee: $75. Electronic applications accepted. *Expenses: Tuition:* Full-time $1292. *Required fees:* $970. Tuition and fees vary according to program. *Financial support:* In 2017–18, 4 students received support, including 4 fellowships with full and partial tuition reimbursements available (averaging $16,205 per year); research assistantships with full and partial tuition reimbursements available, career-related internships or fieldwork, Federal Work-Study, institutionally sponsored loans, scholarships/grants, traineeships, tuition waivers (full and partial), and unspecified assistantships also available. Support available to part-time students. Financial award applicants required to submit FAFSA. *Faculty research:* Innovative educational pedagogies; simulation science; problem (case) based learning; chronic disease management; evidence based practice. *Unit head:* Dr. Kathleen Gallo, Dean, 516-463-7475, Fax: 516-463-7495, E-mail: kathleen.gallo@hofstra.edu. *Application contact:* Sunil Samuel, Assistant Vice President of Admissions, 516-463-4723, Fax: 516-463-4664, E-mail: graduateadmission@hofstra.edu.

Hunter College of the City University of New York, Graduate School, Hunter-Bellevue School of Nursing, Doctor of Nursing Practice Program, New York, NY 10065-5085. Offers adult-gerontology nurse practitioner (DNP); family nurse practitioner (DNP); psychiatric-mental health nurse practitioner (DNP).

Hunter College of the City University of New York, Graduate School, Hunter-Bellevue School of Nursing, Program in Psychiatric-Mental Health Nurse Practitioner, New York, NY 10065-5085. Offers MS, AC. *Accreditation:* AACN. *Program availability:* Part-time. *Degree requirements:* For master's, practicum. *Entrance requirements:* For master's, minimum GPA of 3.0, New York RN license, BSN. Additional exam requirements/recommendations for international students: Required—TOEFL. *Faculty research:* Nursing approaches with the homeless, chronic mentally ill, and depressed; power and empathy.

Husson University, Graduate Nursing Program, Bangor, ME 04401-2999. Offers educational leadership (MSN); family and community nurse practitioner (MSN, PMC); psychiatric mental health nurse practitioner (MSN, PMC). *Accreditation:* AACN. *Program availability:* Part-time, evening/weekend. *Faculty:* 4 full-time (all women), 4 part-time/adjunct (all women). *Students:* 1 full-time (0 women), 62 part-time (54 women); includes 3 minority (2 Black or African American, non-Hispanic/Latino; 1 Hispanic/Latino), 1 international. Average age 36. 62 applicants, 55% accepted, 26 enrolled. In 2017, 9 master's awarded. *Degree requirements:* For master's, comprehensive exam (for some programs), research project. *Entrance requirements:* For master's, proof of RN licensure. Additional exam requirements/recommendations for international students: Required—TOEFL (minimum score 550 paper-based; 80 iBT), IELTS (minimum score 6.5). *Application deadline:* For fall admission, 7/15 for domestic students; for spring admission, 10/30 for domestic students. Application fee: $50. Electronic applications accepted. *Expenses:* $577 per credit; $110 to $480 yearly fee depending on credit load. *Financial support:* In 2017–18, 1 student received support. Federal Work-Study, institutionally sponsored loans, traineeships, and unspecified assistantships available. Financial award application deadline: 3/31; financial award applicants required to submit FAFSA. *Faculty research:* Health disparities and methods to better identify and provide healthcare services to those most in need. *Unit head:* Prof. Mary Jude, Director, Graduate Nursing, 207-941-7769, Fax: 207-941-7198, E-mail: judem@husson.edu. *Application contact:* Kristen Card, Director of Graduate Admissions, 207-404-5660, Fax: 207-941-7935, E-mail: cardk@husson.edu.
Website: http://www.husson.edu/college-of-health-and-education/school-of-nursing/graduate-nursing/

Jacksonville University, Brooks Rehabilitation College of Healthcare Sciences, Keigwin School of Nursing, Master of Science in Nursing Program, Jacksonville, FL 32211. Offers clinical nurse educator (MSN); family nurse practitioner (MSN); family nurse practitioner/emergency nurse practitioner (MSN); leadership in the healthcare system (MSN); nursing informatics (MSN); psychiatric nurse practitioner (MSN); MSN/MBA. *Program availability:* Part-time, 100% online, blended/hybrid learning. *Faculty:* 8 full-time (all women), 8 part-time/adjunct (6 women). *Students:* 41 full-time (36 women), 456 part-time (415 women); includes 169 minority (102 Black or African American, non-Hispanic/Latino; 4 American Indian or Alaska Native, non-Hispanic/Latino; 24 Asian, non-Hispanic/Latino; 33 Hispanic/Latino; 1 Native Hawaiian or other Pacific Islander, non-Hispanic/Latino; 5 Two or more races, non-Hispanic/Latino), 1 international. Average age 39. 232 applicants, 59% accepted, 110 enrolled. In 2017, 87 master's awarded. *Degree requirements:* For master's, thesis. *Entrance requirements:* For master's, GRE General Test or undergraduate GPA above 3.0, BSN from ACEN- or CCNE-accredited program; course work in statistics and physical assessment within last 5 years; Florida nursing license; CPR/BLS certification; 3 recommendations, 2 of which are professional references; statement of intent; resume. Additional exam requirements/recommendations for international students: Required—TOEFL (minimum score 650 paper-based; 114 iBT), IELTS (minimum score 8). *Application deadline:* For fall admission, 2/1 for domestic and international students. Applications are processed on a rolling basis. Application fee: $50. Electronic applications accepted. *Expenses:* $620 per credit hour, $455 per credit hour off-campus, $720 per credit hour online. *Financial support:* Federal Work-Study, institutionally sponsored loans, scholarships/grants, and health care benefits available. Support available to part-time students. Financial award application deadline: 3/15; financial award applicants required to submit FAFSA. *Faculty research:* Treatment of anxiety. *Unit head:* Dr. Hilary Morgan, Director, Graduate Nursing Programs/Associate Professor, 904-256-7601, E-mail: hmorgan@ju.edu. *Application contact:* Stephanie Bloom, Assistant Director, Enrollment and Advanced Graduate Nursing, 904-256-7286, E-mail: sstrick4@ju.edu.
Website: https://www.ju.edu/nursing/graduate/master-science-nursing/index.php

James Madison University, The Graduate School, College of Health and Behavioral Studies, Program in Nursing, Harrisonburg, VA 22807. Offers adult/gerontology primary care nurse practitioner (MSN); clinical nurse leader (MSN); family nurse practitioner (MSN); nurse administrator (MSN); nurse midwifery (MSN); nursing (MSN, DNP); psychiatric mental health nurse practitioner (MSN). *Accreditation:* AACN. *Program availability:* Part-time, 100% online, blended/hybrid learning. *Students:* 10 full-time (9 women), 77 part-time (71 women); includes 10 minority (2 Black or African American, non-Hispanic/Latino; 5 Asian, non-Hispanic/Latino; 1 Hispanic/Latino; 2 Two or more races, non-Hispanic/Latino). Average age 30. In 2017, 27 master's awarded. Application fee: $55. Electronic applications accepted. *Expenses:* Tuition, state resident: full-time $10,512; part-time $438 per credit hour. Tuition, nonresident: full-time $28,358; part-time $1162 per credit hour. *Required fees:* $1128. *Financial support:* In 2017–18, 2 students received support. Federal Work-Study and 2 assistantships (averaging $7911) available. Financial award application deadline: 3/1; financial award applicants required to submit FAFSA. *Unit head:* Dr. Julie T. Sanford, Department Head, 540-568-6314, E-mail: sanforjt@jmu.edu. *Application contact:* Lynette D. Michael, Director of Graduate Admissions, 540-568-6131 Ext. 6395, Fax: 540-568-7860, E-mail: michaeld@jmu.edu.
Website: http://www.nursing.jmu.edu

Johns Hopkins University, School of Nursing, Certificate Programs in Nursing, Baltimore, MD 21205. Offers nursing education (Certificate); pediatric acute care nurse practitioner (Certificate); psychiatric mental health nurse practitioner (Certificate). *Program availability:* Part-time-only, online only, 100% online. *Faculty:* 62 full-time (46 women), 160 part-time/adjunct (all women). *Students:* 39 part-time (35 women); includes 14 minority (5 Black or African American, non-Hispanic/Latino; 2 Asian, non-Hispanic/Latino; 4 Hispanic/Latino; 3 Two or more races, non-Hispanic/Latino). Average age 44. 159 applicants, 33% accepted, 45 enrolled. In 2017, 18 Certificates awarded. *Entrance requirements:* For degree, minimum GPA of 3.0, goal statement/essay, resume, letters of recommendation, official transcripts from all post-secondary institutions, MSN, RN license, NP license. Additional exam requirements/recommendations for international students: Required—TOEFL (minimum score 600 paper-based; 100 iBT), IELTS (minimum score 7). *Application deadline:* For fall admission, 1/1 priority date for domestic students; for spring admission, 11/1 priority date for domestic students. Application fee: $70. Electronic applications accepted. *Expenses:* $1,591 per credit. *Financial support:* Application deadline: 3/1; applicants required to submit FAFSA. *Faculty research:* Palliative care, cardiovascular health, disease prevention and risk reduction, women's health, palliative and end-of-life care. *Unit head:* Dr. Patricia M. Davidson, Dean, 410-955-7544, Fax: 410-955-4890, E-mail: sondeansoffice@jhu.edu. *Application contact:* Cathy Wilson, Director of Admissions, 410-955-7548, Fax: 410-614-7086, E-mail: jhuson@jhu.edu.
Website: http://nursing.jhu.edu/

See Display on page 576 and Close-Up on page 763.

Kent State University, College of Nursing, Kent, OH 44242. Offers advanced nursing practice (DNP), including adult/gerontology acute care nurse practitioner (MSN, DNP); nursing (MSN, PhD), including adult/gerontology acute care nurse practitioner (MSN, DNP), adult/gerontology clinical nurse specialist (MSN), adult/gerontology primary care nurse practitioner (MSN), family nurse practitioner (MSN), nurse educator (MSN), nursing and healthcare management (MSN), pediatric primary care nurse practitioner (MSN), psychiatric/mental health nurse practitioner (MSN); MBA/MSN. PhD program offered jointly with The University of Akron. *Accreditation:* AACN. *Program availability:* Part-time, online learning. *Faculty:* 29 full-time (28 women), 15 part-time/adjunct (12 women). *Students:* 167 full-time (142 women), 405 part-time (359 women); includes 70 minority (39 Black or African American, non-Hispanic/Latino; 11 Asian, non-Hispanic/Latino; 18 Hispanic/Latino; 2 Two or more races, non-Hispanic/Latino), 13 international. Average age 35. 272 applicants, 74% accepted, 166 enrolled. In 2017, 144 master's, 8 doctorates awarded. *Degree requirements:* For master's, thesis optional; for doctorate, comprehensive exam, thesis/dissertation. *Entrance requirements:* For master's, GRE or GMAT, minimum GPA of 3.0, active RN license, statement of purpose, 3 letters of reference, undergraduate level statistics class, baccalaureate or graduate-level nursing degree, curriculum vitae/resume; for doctorate, GRE, minimum GPA of 3.0, transcripts, 3 letters of reference, interview, active unrestricted Ohio RN license, statement of purpose, writing sample, curriculum vitae/resume, baccalaureate and master's degrees in nursing or DNP. Additional exam requirements/recommendations for international students: Required—TOEFL (minimum score 560 paper-based; 83 iBT), IELTS (minimum score 6.5), PTE (minimum score 55), Michigan English Language Assessment Battery (minimum score 78). *Application deadline:* For fall admission, 3/1 for domestic and international students; for spring admission, 10/1 for domestic and international students. Applications are processed on a rolling basis. Application fee: $45 ($70 for international students). Electronic applications accepted. *Expenses:* Tuition, state resident: full-time $11,310; part-time $515 per credit hour. Tuition, nonresident: full-time $20,396; part-time $928 per credit hour. *International tuition:* $18,544 full-time. *Financial support:* Scholarships/grants available. Financial award application deadline: 5/4. *Unit head:* Dr. Barbara Broome, Dean, 330-672-3777, E-mail: bbroome1@kent.edu. *Application contact:* Dr. Wendy A. Umberger, Associate Dean for Graduate Programs/Professor, 330-672-8813, E-mail: wlewando@kent.edu.
Website: http://www.kent.edu/nursing/

Lincoln Memorial University, Caylor School of Nursing, Harrogate, TN 37752-1901. Offers family nurse practitioner (MSN); nurse anesthesia (MSN); psychiatric mental health nurse practitioner (MSN). *Accreditation:* AANA/CANAEP; ACEN. *Program availability:* Part-time. *Entrance requirements:* For master's, GRE.

McNeese State University, Doré School of Graduate Studies, College of Nursing and Health Professions, MSN Program, Lake Charles, LA 70609. Offers family nurse practitioner (MSN); nurse educator (MSN); psychiatric/mental health nurse practitioner (MSN). *Entrance requirements:* For master's, GRE, baccalaureate degree in nursing, minimum overall GPA of 2.7 for all undergraduate coursework, eligibility for unencumbered licensure as Registered Nurse in Louisiana or Texas, course in introductory statistics with minimum C grade, physical assessment skills, two letters of professional reference, 500-word essay, current resume. *Application deadline:* For fall admission, 5/15 priority date for domestic and international students; for spring admission, 10/15 priority date for domestic and international students. Applications are processed on a rolling basis. Application fee: $20 ($30 for international students). *Financial support:* Application deadline: 5/1. *Unit head:* Dr. Sattaria Dilks, Co-Coordinator, 337-475-5840, Fax: 337-475-5924, E-mail: tdilks@mcneese.edu. *Application contact:* Dr. Ann Warner, Co-Coordinator, 337-475-5831, Fax: 337-475-5702, E-mail: awarner@mcneese.edu.
Website: http://www.mcneese.edu/nursing/graduate

McNeese State University, Doré School of Graduate Studies, College of Nursing and Health Professions, Post Master's Psychiatric/Mental Health Nurse Practitioner Program, Lake Charles, LA 70609. Offers PMC. *Entrance requirements:* For degree, GRE, MSN, eligible for unencumbered licensure as RN in Louisiana. *Application deadline:* For fall admission, 5/15 priority date for domestic and international students; for spring admission, 10/15 priority date for domestic and international students. Applications are processed on a rolling basis. Application fee: $20 ($30 for international students). *Financial support:* Application deadline: 5/1. *Unit head:* Dr. Ann Warner, Co-Coordinator, 337-475-5831, Fax: 337-475-5702, E-mail: awarner@mcneese.edu.

MGH Institute of Health Professions, School of Nursing, Boston, MA 02129. Offers advanced practice nursing (MSN); gerontological nursing (MSN); nursing (DNP); pediatric nursing (MSN); psychiatric nursing (MSN); teaching and learning for health care education (Certificate); women's health nursing (MSN). *Accreditation:* AACN. *Degree requirements:* For master's, thesis or alternative. *Entrance requirements:* For master's, GRE General Test, bachelor's degree from regionally-accredited college or university. Additional exam requirements/recommendations for international students: Required—TOEFL (minimum score 550 paper-based; 80 iBT). Electronic applications accepted. *Faculty research:* Biobehavioral nursing, HIV/AIDS, gerontological nursing, women's health, vulnerable populations, health systems.

Midwestern State University, Billie Doris McAda Graduate School, Robert D. and Carol Gunn College of Health Sciences and Human Services, Wilson School of Nursing, Wichita Falls, TX 76308. Offers family nurse practitioner (MSN); family psychiatric mental health nurse practitioner (MSN); nurse educator (MSN). *Accreditation:* AACN. *Program availability:* Part-time, evening/weekend. *Degree requirements:* For master's, comprehensive exam, thesis optional. *Entrance requirements:* For master's, GRE General Test or MAT. Additional exam requirements/recommendations for international students: Required—TOEFL (minimum score 550 paper-based). Electronic applications accepted. *Faculty research:* Infant feeding, musculoskeletal disorders, diabetes, community health education, water quality reporting.

Molloy College, The Barbara H. Hagan School of Nursing, Rockville Centre, NY 11571-5002. Offers adult - gerontology nurse practitioner (MS); adult-gerontology clinical nurse specialist (DNP); adult-gerontology nurse practitioner (DNP); clinical nurse specialist: adult - gerontology (MS); family nurse practitioner (MS, DNP); family psychiatric/mental health nurse practitioner (MS, DNP); nursing (PhD, Advanced Certificate); nursing administration with informatics (MS); nursing education (MS); pediatric nurse practitioner

(MS, DNP). *Accreditation:* AACN. *Program availability:* Part-time, evening/weekend. *Faculty:* 28 full-time (all women), 7 part-time/adjunct (6 women). *Students:* 19 full-time (14 women), 574 part-time (527 women); includes 336 minority (179 Black or African American, non-Hispanic/Latino; 2 American Indian or Alaska Native, non-Hispanic/Latino; 107 Asian, non-Hispanic/Latino; 42 Hispanic/Latino; 1 Native Hawaiian or other Pacific Islander, non-Hispanic/Latino; 5 Two or more races, non-Hispanic/Latino), 4 international. Average age 44. 292 applicants, 65% accepted, 147 enrolled. In 2017, 135 master's, 9 doctorates, 5 other advanced degrees awarded. *Degree requirements:* For master's, thesis optional. *Entrance requirements:* For master's, 3 letters of reference, BS in nursing, minimum undergraduate GPA of 3.0; for Advanced Certificate, 3 letters of reference, master's degree in nursing. Additional exam requirements/recommendations for international students: Required—TOEFL (minimum score 550 paper-based; 79 iBT). *Application deadline:* For fall admission, 9/2 priority date for domestic students; for spring admission, 1/20 priority date for domestic students. Applications are processed on a rolling basis. Application fee: $60. Electronic applications accepted. *Expenses: Tuition:* Full-time $19,980; part-time $1110 per credit. *Required fees:* $1040. Tuition and fees vary according to course load and degree level. *Financial support:* Research assistantships with partial tuition reimbursements, teaching assistantships with partial tuition reimbursements, institutionally sponsored loans, scholarships/grants, and unspecified assistantships available. Support available to part-time students. Financial award application deadline: 3/1; financial award applicants required to submit FAFSA. *Faculty research:* Workplace violence involving nurses and psychiatric patients; moral distress in nursing; primary care of veterans; the role of service immersion programs in graduate nursing education; academic integrity. *Unit head:* Dr. Marcia R. Gardner, Dean, The Barbara H. Hagan School of Nursing, 516-323-3651, E-mail: mgardner@molloy.edu. *Application contact:* Jaclyn Machowicz, Assistant Director for Admissions, 516-323-4010, E-mail: jmachowicz@molloy.edu.

Monmouth University, Graduate Studies, Marjorie K. Unterberg School of Nursing and Health Studies, West Long Branch, NJ 07764-1898. Offers adult-gerontological primary care nurse practitioner (MSN, Post-Master's Certificate); family nurse practitioner (MSN, Post-Master's Certificate); forensic nursing (MSN, Certificate); nursing (MSN); nursing administration (MSN); nursing education (MSN, Post-Master's Certificate); nursing practice (DNP); physician assistant (MS); psychiatric and mental health nurse practitioner (MSN, Post-Master's Certificate); school nursing (MSN, Certificate). *Accreditation:* AACN. *Program availability:* Part-time, evening/weekend, 100% online, blended/hybrid learning. *Faculty:* 12 full-time (all women), 20 part-time/adjunct (12 women). *Students:* 90 full-time (66 women), 329 part-time (302 women); includes 129 minority (51 Black or African American, non-Hispanic/Latino; 43 Asian, non-Hispanic/Latino; 31 Hispanic/Latino; 1 Native Hawaiian or other Pacific Islander, non-Hispanic/Latino; 3 Two or more races, non-Hispanic/Latino), 1 international. Average age 36. In 2017, 85 master's, 4 other advanced degrees awarded. *Degree requirements:* For master's, practicum (for some tracks); for doctorate, practicum, capstone course. *Entrance requirements:* For master's, GRE General Test (waived for MSN applicants with minimum B grade in each of the first four courses and for MS applicants with master's degree), BSN with minimum GPA of 2.75, current RN license, proof of liability and malpractice policy, personal statement, two letters of recommendation, college course work in health assessment, resume; CASPA application (for MS); for doctorate, accredited master's nursing program degree with minimum GPA of 3.2, active RN license, national certification as nurse practitioner or nurse administrator, working knowledge of statistics, statement of goals and vision for change, 2 letters of recommendation (professional or academic), resume, interview. Additional exam requirements/recommendations for international students: Required—TOEFL (minimum score 550 paper-based; 79 iBT), IELTS (minimum score 6) or Michigan English Language Assessment Battery (minimum score 77). *Application deadline:* For fall admission, 7/15 priority date for domestic students, 6/1 for international students; for spring admission, 12/1 priority date for domestic students, 11/1 for international students; for summer admission, 5/1 for domestic students. Applications are processed on a rolling basis. Application fee: $50. Electronic applications accepted. *Expenses:* Contact institution. *Financial support:* In 2017–18, 197 students received support. Institutionally sponsored loans, scholarships/grants, and unspecified assistantships available. Support available to part-time students. Financial award applicants required to submit FAFSA. *Faculty research:* School nursing, health policy, and smoking cessation in teens; Multiple Sclerosis; adherence and self-efficacy; aging issues and geriatric care. *Unit head:* Dr. Janet Mahoney, Dean, 732-571-3443, Fax: 732-263-5131, E-mail: jmahoney@monmouth.edu. *Application contact:* Lucia Fedele, Graduate Admission Counselor, 732-571-3452, Fax: 732-263-5123, E-mail: gradadm@monmouth.edu.
Website: https://www.monmouth.edu/graduate/nursing-programs-of-study/

Montana State University, The Graduate School, College of Nursing, Bozeman, MT 59717. Offers clinical nurse leader (MN); family and individual nurse practitioner (DNP); family nurse practitioner (MN, Post-Master's Certificate); nursing education (Certificate, Post-Master's Certificate); psychiatric mental health nurse practitioner (MN); psychiatric/mental health nurse practitioner (DNP). *Accreditation:* AACN. *Program availability:* Part-time, online learning. *Degree requirements:* For master's, comprehensive exam, thesis (for some programs); for doctorate, thesis/dissertation, 1,125 hours in clinical settings. *Entrance requirements:* For master's, GRE General Test, minimum GPA of 3.0 for undergraduate and post-baccalaureate work. Additional exam requirements/recommendations for international students: Required—TOEFL (minimum score 580 paper-based). Electronic applications accepted. *Faculty research:* Rural nursing, health disparities, environmental/public health, oral health, resilience.

National University, School of Health and Human Services, La Jolla, CA 92037-1011. Offers clinical affairs (MS); clinical regulatory affairs (MS); complementary and integrative healthcare (MS); family nurse practitioner (MSN); health and life science analytics (MS); health informatics (MS, Certificate); healthcare administration (MHA); nurse anesthesia (MSNA); nursing administration (MSN); nursing informatics (MSN); psychiatric-mental health nurse practitioner (MSN); public health (MPH), including health promotion, healthcare administration, mental health. *Program availability:* Part-time, evening/weekend, 100% online, blended/hybrid learning. *Degree requirements:* For master's, thesis (for some programs). *Entrance requirements:* For master's, interview, minimum GPA of 2.5. Additional exam requirements/recommendations for international students: Required—TOEFL (minimum score 550 paper-based; 79 iBT), IELTS (minimum score 6). *Application deadline:* Applications are processed on a rolling basis. Application fee: $60 ($65 for international students). Electronic applications accepted. *Expenses: Tuition:* Part-time $430 per quarter hour. *Financial support:* Career-related internships or fieldwork, institutionally sponsored loans, scholarships/grants, and tuition waivers (partial) available. Support available to part-time students. Financial award application deadline: 6/30; financial award applicants required to submit FAFSA. *Faculty research:* Nursing education, obesity prevention, workforce diversity. *Unit head:* Dr. Gloria J. McNeal, Dean, 858-309-3473, E-mail: shhs@nu.edu. *Application contact:* Brandon Jouganatos, Vice President for Enrollment Services, 800-628-8648, E-mail: advisor@nu.edu.
Website: http://www.nu.edu/OurPrograms/SchoolOfHealthAndHumanServices.html

New Mexico State University, College of Health and Social Services, School of Nursing, Las Cruces, NM 88003. Offers family nurse practitioner (DNP, Graduate Certificate); nursing administration (MSN); nursing science (PhD); psychiatric/mental health nurse practitioner (DNP, Graduate Certificate). *Accreditation:* AACN. *Program availability:* Part-time, blended/hybrid learning. *Faculty:* 11 full-time (all women). *Students:* 29 full-time (26 women), 68 part-time (57 women); includes 46 minority (10 Black or African American, non-Hispanic/Latino; 6 Asian, non-Hispanic/Latino; 29 Hispanic/Latino; 1 Two or more races, non-Hispanic/Latino), 1 international. Average age 42. 47 applicants, 81% accepted, 25 enrolled. In 2017, 3 master's, 9 doctorates, 5 other advanced degrees awarded. *Degree requirements:* For master's, comprehensive exam, thesis optional, clinical practicum; for doctorate, comprehensive exam, thesis/dissertation. *Entrance requirements:* For master's, NCLEX exam, BSN, minimum GPA of 3.0, course work in statistics, 3 letters of reference, writing sample, RN license, CPR certification, proof of liability, immunizations, criminal background check; for doctorate, NCLEX exam, MSN, minimum GPA of 3.0, 3 letters of reference, writing sample, RN license, CPR certification, proof of liability, immunizations, criminal background check, statistics course. Additional exam requirements/recommendations for international students: Required—TOEFL (minimum score 550 paper-based; 79 iBT), IELTS (minimum score 6.5). *Application deadline:* For fall admission, 2/1 priority date for domestic students, 2/1 for international students. Application fee: $40 ($50 for international students). Electronic applications accepted. *Expenses:* Tuition, state resident: full-time $4390. Tuition, nonresident: full-time $15,309. *Required fees:* $853. *Financial support:* In 2017–18, 22 students received support, including 5 teaching assistantships (averaging $11,249 per year); career-related internships or fieldwork, Federal Work-Study, scholarships/grants, traineeships, health care benefits, and unspecified assistantships also available. Support available to part-time students. Financial award application deadline: 3/1. *Faculty research:* Women's health, community health, health disparities, nursing informatics and health care technologies, health care and nursing administration, nursing education, adolescent mental health, addiction and substance abuse. *Total annual research expenditures:* $1,321. *Unit head:* Dr. Alexa Doig, Director, 575-646-3812, Fax: 575-646-2167, E-mail: adoig@nmsu.edu. *Application contact:* Alyce Kolenovsky, 575-646-3812, Fax: 575-646-2167, E-mail: nursing@nmsu.edu.
Website: http://schoolofnursing.nmsu.edu

New York University, Rory Meyers College of Nursing, Doctor of Nursing Practice Program, New York, NY 10012-1019. Offers nursing (DNP), including adult-gerontology acute care nurse practitioner, adult-gerontology primary care nurse practitioner, family nurse practitioner, nurse-midwifery, pediatrics nurse practitioner, psychiatric-mental health nurse practitioner. *Accreditation:* AACN. *Program availability:* Part-time, evening/weekend. *Faculty:* 16 full-time (all women), 1 (woman) part-time/adjunct. *Students:* 48 part-time (43 women); includes 11 minority (5 Black or African American, non-Hispanic/Latino; 5 Asian, non-Hispanic/Latino; 1 Hispanic/Latino). Average age 28. 20 applicants, 75% accepted, 10 enrolled. In 2017, 8 doctorates awarded. *Degree requirements:* For doctorate, thesis/dissertation, project. *Entrance requirements:* For doctorate, MS, RN license, interview, Nurse Practitioner Certification, writing sample. Additional exam requirements/recommendations for international students: Required—TOEFL (minimum score 100 iBT), IELTS (minimum score 7). *Application deadline:* For fall admission, 3/1 priority date for domestic and international students. Applications are processed on a rolling basis. Application fee: $80. Electronic applications accepted. *Expenses:* Contact institution. *Financial support:* In 2017–18, 13 students received support. Scholarships/grants available. Support available to part-time students. Financial award application deadline: 2/1; financial award applicants required to submit FAFSA. *Faculty research:* Workforce determinants of healthcare quality, genomics, health literacy and health outcomes, health policy. *Unit head:* Dr. Mary Jo Vetter, Director, DNP Program, 212-998-5165, E-mail: mjv5@nyu.edu. *Application contact:* Matthew Burke, Assistant Director, Graduate Student Affairs and Admissions, 212-998-7397, E-mail: mb6060@nyu.edu.

New York University, Rory Meyers College of Nursing, Programs in Advanced Practice Nursing, New York, NY 10012-1019. Offers adult-gerontology acute care nurse practitioner (MS, Advanced Certificate); adult-gerontology primary care nurse practitioner (MS, Advanced Certificate); family nurse practitioner (MS, Advanced Certificate); gerontology nurse practitioner (Advanced Certificate); nurse-midwifery (MS, Advanced Certificate); nursing administration (MS, Advanced Certificate); nursing education (MS, Advanced Certificate); nursing informatics (MS, Advanced Certificate); pediatrics nurse practitioner (MS, Advanced Certificate); psychiatric-mental health nurse practitioner (MS, Advanced Certificate); MS/MPH. *Accreditation:* AACN; ACNM/ACME. *Program availability:* Part-time, evening/weekend. *Faculty:* 23 full-time (all women), 62 part-time/adjunct (56 women). *Students:* 50 full-time (46 women), 557 part-time (509 women); includes 234 minority (58 Black or African American, non-Hispanic/Latino; 1 American Indian or Alaska Native, non-Hispanic/Latino; 116 Asian, non-Hispanic/Latino; 43 Hispanic/Latino; 1 Native Hawaiian or other Pacific Islander, non-Hispanic/Latino; 15 Two or more races, non-Hispanic/Latino), 23 international. Average age 32. 391 applicants, 59% accepted, 149 enrolled. In 2017, 187 master's, 5 other advanced degrees awarded. *Degree requirements:* For master's, thesis (for some programs), capstone. *Entrance requirements:* For master's, BS in nursing, AS in nursing with another BS/BA, interview, RN license, 1 year of clinical experience (3 for the MS in nursing education program); for Advanced Certificate, master's degree in nursing. Additional exam requirements/recommendations for international students: Required—TOEFL (minimum score 100 iBT), IELTS (minimum score 7). *Application deadline:* For fall admission, 3/1 priority date for domestic and international students; for spring admission, 11/1 priority date for domestic and international students; for summer admission, 3/1 for domestic and international students. Application fee: $80. Electronic applications accepted. *Expenses:* Contact institution. *Financial support:* In 2017–18, 130 students received support. Career-related internships or fieldwork, Federal Work-Study, and scholarships/grants available. Support available to part-time students. Financial award application deadline: 3/1; financial award applicants required to submit FAFSA. *Faculty research:* Vaccine hesitancy in pregnant women and mothers, palliative care and midwifery, diabetes education, curriculum development, workforce training, education and development, geriatrics. *Unit head:* Dr. James Pace, Senior Associate Dean for Academic Programs, 212-992-7343, E-mail: james.pace@nyu.edu. *Application contact:* Matthew Burke, Assistant Director, Graduate Student Affairs and Admissions, 212-998-7397, Fax: 212-995-4302, E-mail: mb6060@nyu.edu.

Nicholls State University, Graduate Studies, College of Nursing and Allied Health, Thibodaux, LA 70310. Offers family nurse practitioner (MSN); nurse executive (MSN); nursing education (MSN); psychiatric/mental health nurse practitioner (MSN).

Northeastern University, Bouvé College of Health Sciences, Boston, MA 02115-5096. Offers applied behavior analysis (MS); audiology (Au D); counseling psychology (MS, PhD, CAGS); exercise science (MS); nursing (MS, PhD, CAGS), including administration (MS), adult-gerontology acute care nurse practitioner (MS, CAGS), adult-gerontology primary care nurse practitioner (MS, CAGS), anesthesia (MS), family nurse practitioner (MS, CAGS), neonatal nurse practitioner (MS, CAGS), pediatric nurse practitioner (MS, CAGS), psychiatric mental health nurse practitioner (MS, CAGS); nursing practice (DNP); pharmaceutical sciences (MS, PhD), including interdisciplinary concentration, pharmaceutics and drug delivery systems; pharmacology (MS); pharmacy (Pharm D); school psychology (PhD); speech-language pathology (MS); urban health (MPH); MS/MBA. *Accreditation:* ACPE (one or more programs are accredited). *Program availability:* Part-time, evening/weekend, online learning. *Faculty:* 192 full-time. *Students:* 1,685. In 2017, 352 master's, 312 doctorates, 25 other

advanced degrees awarded. *Degree requirements:* For doctorate, thesis/dissertation (for some programs); for CAGS, comprehensive exam. Application fee: $75. Electronic applications accepted. *Expenses:* Contact institution. *Financial support:* Fellowships, research assistantships, teaching assistantships, career-related internships or fieldwork, scholarships/grants, health care benefits, tuition waivers, and unspecified assistantships available. Support available to part-time students. Financial award applicants required to submit FAFSA. *Unit head:* Susan L. Parish, Dean, Bouve College of Health Sciences, 617-373-3321, Fax: 617-373-3030, E-mail: s.parish@northeastern.edu. *Application contact:* 617-373-2708, Fax: 617-373-4701, E-mail: bouvegrad@northeastern.edu.
Website: https://www.northeastern.edu/bouve/

Nova Southeastern University, Ron and Kathy Assaf College of Nursing, Fort Lauderdale, FL 33314-7796. Offers advanced practice registered nurse (MSN), including adult-gerontology acute care nurse practitioner, family nurse practitioner, psychiatric mental health nurse practitioner; executive nurse leadership (MSN); nursing (PhD), including nursing education; nursing education (MSN); nursing informatics (MSN); nursing practice (DNP). *Accreditation:* AACN. *Program availability:* Part-time, evening/weekend, 100% online, blended/hybrid learning, annual one-week summer institute delivered face-to-face on main campus. *Faculty:* 9 full-time (all women), 47 part-time/adjunct (43 women). *Students:* 658 full-time (599 women); includes 414 minority (175 Black or African American, non-Hispanic/Latino; 37 Asian, non-Hispanic/Latino; 179 Hispanic/Latino; 1 Native Hawaiian or other Pacific Islander, non-Hispanic/Latino; 22 Two or more races, non-Hispanic/Latino), 3 international. Average age 38. 179 applicants, 100% accepted, 163 enrolled. In 2017, 161 master's, 16 doctorates awarded. *Degree requirements:* For doctorate, comprehensive exam, thesis/dissertation. *Entrance requirements:* For master's, minimum GPA of 3.0, RN, BSN, BS or BA; for doctorate, minimum GPA of 3.5, MSN, RN. Additional exam requirements/recommendations for international students: Recommended—TOEFL. *Application deadline:* For fall admission, 3/1 priority date for domestic students, 3/1 for international students; for winter admission, 11/1 for domestic and international students. Applications are processed on a rolling basis. Application fee: $50. Electronic applications accepted. *Expenses:* Contact institution. *Financial support:* Application deadline: 4/15; applicants required to submit FAFSA. *Faculty research:* Nursing education, curriculum, clinical research, interdisciplinary research. *Total annual research expenditures:* $9,500. *Unit head:* Dr. Marcella M. Rutherford, Dean, 954-262-1963, E-mail: rmarcell@nova.edu. *Application contact:* Dianna Murphey, Director of Operations, 954-262-1975, E-mail: dgardner1@nova.edu.
Website: http://www.nova.edu/nursing/

Oregon Health & Science University, School of Nursing, Program in Psychiatric Mental Health Nurse Practitioner, Portland, OR 97239-3098. Offers MN. *Accreditation:* AACN. *Degree requirements:* For master's, thesis optional. *Entrance requirements:* For master's, GRE General Test, bachelor's degree in nursing, minimum cumulative and science GPA of 3.0, 3 letters of recommendation, essays, statistics within last 5 years. Additional exam requirements/recommendations for international students: Required—TOEFL (minimum score 83 iBT). Electronic applications accepted. *Expenses:* Contact institution.

Pontifical Catholic University of Puerto Rico, College of Sciences, Department of Nursing, Program in Mental Health and Psychiatric Nursing, Ponce, PR 00717-0777. Offers MSN. *Program availability:* Part-time, evening/weekend. *Degree requirements:* For master's, comprehensive exam (for some programs), thesis, clinical research paper. *Entrance requirements:* For master's, GRE General Test, 2 letters of recommendation, interview, minimum GPA of 2.75. Electronic applications accepted.

Rivier University, School of Graduate Studies, Division of Nursing and Health Professions, Nashua, NH 03060. Offers family nurse practitioner (MS); leadership in health systems management (MS); nursing education (MS); nursing practice (DNP); psychiatric/mental health nurse practitioner (MS); public health (MPH). *Accreditation:* ACEN. *Program availability:* Part-time, evening/weekend. *Entrance requirements:* For master's, GRE, MAT. Electronic applications accepted.

Rush University, College of Nursing, Department of Community, Systems, and Mental Health Nursing, Chicago, IL 60612. Offers advanced public health nursing (DNP); family nurse practitioner (DNP); psychiatric mental health nurse practitioner (DNP); transformative leadership: population health (DNP). *Accreditation:* AACN. *Program availability:* Part-time, 100% online, blended/hybrid learning. *Students:* 23 full-time (21 women), 264 part-time (245 women); includes 83 minority (36 Black or African American, non-Hispanic/Latino; 1 American Indian or Alaska Native, non-Hispanic/Latino; 16 Asian, non-Hispanic/Latino; 24 Hispanic/Latino; 6 Two or more races, non-Hispanic/Latino). 176 applicants, 56% accepted, 79 enrolled. In 2017, 64 doctorates awarded. *Degree requirements:* For doctorate, scholarly project. *Entrance requirements:* For doctorate, GRE General Test (waived for DNP if cumulative GPA is 3.25 or greater, nursing GPA is 3.0 or greater, or a completed graduate program GPA is 3.5 or greater), interview, 3 letters of recommendation, personal statement, current resume. Additional exam requirements/recommendations for international students: Required—TOEFL (minimum score 94 iBT). *Application deadline:* For fall admission, 1/2 for domestic students; for spring admission, 8/1 for domestic students; for summer admission, 12/1 for domestic students. Applications are processed on a rolling basis. Application fee: $110. Electronic applications accepted. *Expenses:* Contact institution. *Financial support:* Research assistantships, teaching assistantships, Federal Work-Study, scholarships/grants, traineeships, and health care benefits available. Support available to part-time students. Financial award application deadline: 3/1; financial award applicants required to submit FAFSA. *Faculty research:* Health behaviors; caregivers; psychiatric services; disabilities; population health. *Unit head:* Dr. Mona Shattell, Chairperson, 312-942-7117, E-mail: mona_shattell@rush.edu. *Application contact:* Jennifer Thorndyke, Director of Admissions, 312-563-7526, E-mail: jennifer_thorndyke@rush.edu.
Website: https://www.rushu.rush.edu/college-nursing/departments-college-nursing/department-community-systems-and-mental-health-nursing

Sage Graduate School, School of Health Sciences, Department of Nursing, Program in Psychiatric Mental Health Nurse Practitioner, Troy, NY 12180-4115. Offers MS, Post Master's Certificate. *Accreditation:* AACN. *Program availability:* Part-time, evening/weekend. *Faculty:* 6 full-time (all women), 11 part-time/adjunct (10 women). *Students:* 11 full-time (8 women), 53 part-time (47 women); includes 10 minority (8 Black or African American, non-Hispanic/Latino; 1 Asian, non-Hispanic/Latino; 1 Two or more races, non-Hispanic/Latino). Average age 41. 78 applicants, 45% accepted, 25 enrolled. In 2017, 11 master's awarded. *Degree requirements:* For master's, thesis or alternative. *Entrance requirements:* For master's, currently licensed as registered professional nurse in state of practice; baccalaureate degree in nursing from nationally-accredited program or its international equivalent. Additional exam requirements/recommendations for international students: Required—TOEFL (minimum score 550 paper-based). *Application deadline:* Applications are processed on a rolling basis. Application fee: $30. Electronic applications accepted. Tuition and fees vary according to degree level and program. *Financial support:* Fellowships, research assistantships, scholarships/grants, and unspecified assistantships available. Financial award application deadline: 3/1; financial award applicants required to submit FAFSA. *Unit head:* Dr. Theresa Hand, Dean, School of Health Sciences, 518-244-2264, Fax: 518-244-4571, E-mail: handt@sage.edu. *Application contact:* Dr. Carol Braungart, Co-Director, Graduate Nursing Program, 518-244-2459, Fax: 518-244-2009, E-mail: braunc@sage.edu.

Saint Francis Medical Center College of Nursing, Graduate Programs, Peoria, IL 61603-3783. Offers adult gerontology (MSN); clinical nurse leader (MSN); family nurse practitioner (MSN, Post-Graduate Certificate); family psychiatric mental health nurse practitioner (MSN); neonatal nurse practitioner (MSN); nurse clinician (Post-Graduate Certificate); nurse educator (MSN, Post-Graduate Certificate); nursing (DNP); nursing management leadership (MSN). *Accreditation:* ACEN. *Program availability:* Part-time, online only, 100% online, blended/hybrid learning. *Faculty:* 11 full-time (all women), 7 part-time/adjunct (all women). *Students:* 4 full-time (all women), 239 part-time (209 women); includes 24 minority (12 Black or African American, non-Hispanic/Latino; 3 Asian, non-Hispanic/Latino; 4 Hispanic/Latino; 5 Two or more races, non-Hispanic/Latino). Average age 37. 105 applicants, 83% accepted, 60 enrolled. In 2017, 52 master's, 8 doctorates awarded. *Degree requirements:* For master's, research experience, portfolio, practicum; for doctorate, practicum. *Entrance requirements:* For master's, nursing research, health assessment, graduate course work in statistics, RN license; for doctorate, master's degree in nursing, professional portfolio, graduate statistics, transcripts, RN license. Additional exam requirements/recommendations for international students: Required—TOEFL (minimum score 550 paper-based; 79 iBT). *Application deadline:* For fall admission, 6/1 priority date for domestic and international students; for spring admission, 11/15 priority date for domestic and international students. Applications are processed on a rolling basis. Application fee: $50. *Expenses:* Contact institution. *Financial support:* In 2017–18, 13 students received support. Scholarships/grants and tuition waivers (partial) available. Support available to part-time students. Financial award application deadline: 6/15; financial award applicants required to submit FAFSA. *Faculty research:* Outcome and curriculum planning, health promotion, NCLEX-RN results, decision-making program evaluation. *Unit head:* Dr. Patti A. Stockert, President of the College, 309-655-4124, Fax: 309-624-8973, E-mail: patricia.a.stockert@osfhealthcare.org. *Application contact:* Dr. Kim A. Mitchell, Dean, Graduate Program, 309-655-2201, Fax: 309-624-8973, E-mail: kim.a.mitchell@osfhealthcare.org.
Website: http://www.sfmccon.edu/graduate-programs/

Shenandoah University, Eleanor Wade Custer School of Nursing, Winchester, VA 22601. Offers adult gerontology primary care nurse practitioner (Graduate Certificate); adult-gerontology primary care nurse practitioner (MSN); family nurse practitioner (MSN, DNP, Graduate Certificate); general (MSN); health systems leadership (DNP); health systems management (MSN, Graduate Certificate); nurse midwifery (MSN); nurse-midwifery (Graduate Certificate); nursing education (Graduate Certificate); nursing practice (DNP); psychiatric mental health nurse practitioner (MSN, DNP, Graduate Certificate). *Accreditation:* AACN; ACNM/ACME. *Faculty:* 17 full-time (all women), 6 part-time/adjunct (all women). *Students:* 30 full-time (26 women), 51 part-time (48 women); includes 19 minority (13 Black or African American, non-Hispanic/Latino; 3 Asian, non-Hispanic/Latino; 2 Hispanic/Latino; 1 Two or more races, non-Hispanic/Latino), 3 international. Average age 37. 52 applicants, 88% accepted, 34 enrolled. In 2017, 18 master's, 1 doctorate, 28 other advanced degrees awarded. *Degree requirements:* For master's, research project, clinical hours; for doctorate, scholarly project, clinical hours; for Graduate Certificate, clinical hours. *Entrance requirements:* For master's, United States RN license; minimum GPA of 3.0; 2080 hours of clinical experience; curriculum vitae; 3 letters of recommendation from former dean, faculty member, or advisor familiar with the applicant, and a former or current supervisor; two-to-three-page essay on a specified topic; for doctorate, MSN, minimum GPA of 3.0, 3 letters of recommendation, interview, BSN, two-to-three page essay on a specific topic, 500-word statement of clinical practice research interest, resume, current U.S. RN license, 2080 clinical hours; for Graduate Certificate, MSN, minimum GPA of 3.0, 2 letters of recommendation, minimum of one year (2080 hours) of clinical nursing experience, interview, two-to-three page essay on a specific topic, resume, current United States RN license. Additional exam requirements/recommendations for international students: Required—TOEFL (minimum score 558 paper-based; 83 iBT). *Application deadline:* For fall admission, 4/15 priority date for domestic and international students; for spring admission, 11/1 for domestic and international students; for summer admission, 3/1 for domestic and international students. Application fee: $30. Electronic applications accepted. *Expenses:* $22,451 tuition, plus $3,579 fees (student services fee, technology fee, and clinical fee). *Financial support:* In 2017–18, 32 students received support. Scholarships/grants and unspecified assistantships available. Financial award applicants required to submit FAFSA. *Faculty research:* Emergency preparedness, workplace environment, maternal child, inter-professional education, health policy. *Total annual research expenditures:* $30,000. *Unit head:* Dr. Kathleen LaSala, RN, Dean, 540-678-4381, Fax: 540-665-5519, E-mail: klasala@su.edu. *Application contact:* Andrew Woodall, Executive Director of Recruitment and Admissions, 540-665-4581, Fax: 540-665-4627, E-mail: admit@su.edu.
Website: http://www.su.edu/nursing/

Southern Adventist University, School of Nursing, Collegedale, TN 37315-0370. Offers adult/gerontology acute care nurse practitioner (MSN, DNP); adult/gerontology nurse practitioner (MSN); family nurse practitioner (MSN, DNP); lifestyle therapeutics (DNP); nurse educator (MSN, DNP); psychiatric mental health nurse practitioner (MSN, DNP); MSN/MBA. *Accreditation:* ACEN. *Program availability:* Part-time. *Degree requirements:* For master's, thesis or project. *Entrance requirements:* For master's, RN license. Additional exam requirements/recommendations for international students: Required—TOEFL (minimum score 600 paper-based). *Application deadline:* For fall admission, 7/1 for domestic and international students; for winter admission, 12/1 for domestic and international students. Applications are processed on a rolling basis. Application fee: $40. Electronic applications accepted. *Expenses: Tuition:* Full-time $11,430; part-time $635 per credit hour. Tuition and fees vary according to degree level and program. *Financial support:* Teaching assistantships with partial tuition reimbursements available. *Faculty research:* Pain management, ethics, corporate wellness, caring spirituality, stress. *Unit head:* Dr. Barbara James, Dean, 423-236-2942, Fax: 423-236-1940, E-mail: bjames@southern.edu. *Application contact:* Sylvia Mayer, RN, Director of Nursing Admissions, 423-236-2941, Fax: 423-236-1940, E-mail: smayer@southern.edu.
Website: https://www.southern.edu/academics/nursing.html

Southern Arkansas University–Magnolia, School of Graduate Studies, Magnolia, AR 71753. Offers agriculture (MS); business administration (MBA), including agribusiness, social entrepreneurship, supply chain management; clinical and mental health counseling (MS); computer and information sciences (MS), including cyber security and privacy, data science, information technology; gifted and talented (M Ed), including curriculum and instruction, educational administration and supervision, gifted and talented P-8/7-12, instructional specialist P-4; higher, adult and lifelong education (M Ed); kinesiology (M Ed), including coaching; library media and information specialist (M Ed); public administration (MPA); school counseling K-12 (M Ed); student affairs and college counseling (M Ed); teaching (MAT). *Accreditation:* NCATE. *Program availability:* Part-time, 100% online, blended/hybrid learning. *Faculty:* 36 full-time (20 women), 31 part-time/adjunct (12 women). *Students:* 242 full-time (89 women), 889 part-time (459 women); includes 167 minority (143 Black or African American, non-Hispanic/Latino; 7 American Indian or Alaska Native, non-Hispanic/Latino; 7 Asian, non-Hispanic/Latino; 3 Hispanic/Latino; 7 Two or more races, non-Hispanic/Latino), 562 international. Average age 28. 400 applicants, 100% accepted, 239 enrolled. In 2017, 875 master's awarded.

Degree requirements: For master's, comprehensive exam (for some programs), thesis optional. *Entrance requirements:* For master's, GRE, MAT or GMAT, minimum GPA of 2.5. Additional exam requirements/recommendations for international students: Required—TOEFL (minimum score 550 paper-based), IELTS (minimum score 6). *Application deadline:* For fall admission, 7/20 for domestic students, 7/10 for international students; for spring admission, 12/1 for domestic students, 11/15 for international students; for summer admission, 4/1 for domestic students, 5/1 for international students. Applications are processed on a rolling basis. Application fee: $25 ($50 for international students). Electronic applications accepted. *Expenses:* Tuition, state resident: full-time $6038. Tuition, nonresident: full-time $8558. *Required fees:* $804. One-time fee: $110 full-time. Tuition and fees vary according to course load. *Financial support:* Career-related internships or fieldwork, Federal Work-Study, scholarships/grants, tuition waivers (full), and unspecified assistantships available. Financial award applicants required to submit FAFSA. *Faculty research:* Alternative certification for teachers, supervision of instruction, instructional leadership, counseling. *Unit head:* Dr. Kim Bloss, Dean, School of Graduate Studies, 870-235-4150, Fax: 870-235-5227, E-mail: kkbloss@saumag.edu. *Application contact:* Shrijana Malakar, Admissions Specialist, 870-235-4150, Fax: 870-235-5227, E-mail: smalakar@saumag.edu.
Website: http://www.saumag.edu/graduate

Stony Brook University, State University of New York, Stony Brook Medicine, School of Nursing, Psychiatric-Mental Health Nurse Practitioner Program, Stony Brook, NY 11794. Offers MS, DNP, Certificate. *Accreditation:* AACN. *Program availability:* Part-time, blended/hybrid learning. *Students:* 4 full-time (2 women), 124 part-time (98 women); includes 50 minority (24 Black or African American, non-Hispanic/Latino; 11 Asian, non-Hispanic/Latino; 9 Hispanic/Latino; 6 Two or more races, non-Hispanic/Latino). 154 applicants, 43% accepted, 57 enrolled. In 2017, 24 master's, 1 doctorate, 11 other advanced degrees awarded. *Degree requirements:* For master's, thesis; for doctorate, thesis/dissertation. *Entrance requirements:* For master's, BSN, minimum GPA of 3.0, course work in statistics. Additional exam requirements/recommendations for international students: Required—TOEFL (minimum score 90 iBT). *Application deadline:* For fall admission, 1/18 for domestic students. Application fee: $100. Electronic applications accepted. *Expenses:* Contact institution. *Financial support:* Application deadline: 3/15. *Unit head:* Dr. Barbara Sprung, Program Director, 631-444-3292, Fax: 631-444-3136, E-mail: barbara.sprung@stonybrook.edu. *Application contact:* Anita Defranco, Staff Assistant, 631-444-3276, Fax: 631-444-3136, E-mail: pmhnp_nursing@stonybrook.edu.
Website: http://www.nursing.stonybrookmedicine.edu/

Tennessee Technological University, Whitson-Hester School of Nursing, DNP Program, Cookeville, TN 38505. Offers adult-gerontology acute care nurse practitioner (DNP); executive leadership in nursing (DNP); family nurse practitioner (DNP); pediatric nurse practitioner-primary care (DNP); psychiatric/mental health nurse practitioner (DNP); women's health care nurse practitioner (DNP). *Program availability:* Part-time. *Students:* 10 part-time (all women). 14 applicants, 86% accepted, 10 enrolled. *Application deadline:* For fall admission, 7/1 for domestic students, 5/1 for international students; for spring admission, 12/1 for domestic students, 10/1 for international students; for summer admission, 5/1 for domestic students, 2/1 for international students. Applications are processed on a rolling basis. Application fee: $35 ($40 for international students). Electronic applications accepted. *Expenses:* Tuition, state resident: full-time $9925; part-time $565 per credit hour. Tuition, nonresident: full-time $22,993; part-time $1291 per credit hour. *Financial support:* Application deadline: 4/1; applicants required to submit FAFSA. *Unit head:* Dr. Bedelia Russell, Program Director, Fax: 931-372-6244, E-mail: bhrussell@tntech.edu. *Application contact:* Shelia K. Kendrick, Coordinator of Graduate Studies, 931-372-3808, Fax: 931-372-3497, E-mail: skendrick@tntech.edu.
Website: https://www.tntech.edu/nursing/doctor-of-nursing-practice/

Uniformed Services University of the Health Sciences, Daniel K. Inouye Graduate School of Nursing, Bethesda, MD 20814. Offers adult-gerontology clinical nurse specialist (MSN, DNP); family nurse practitioner (DNP); nurse anesthesia (DNP); nursing science (PhD); psychiatric mental health nurse practitioner (DNP); women's health nurse practitioner (DNP). *Accreditation:* AACN; AANA/CANAEP. *Faculty:* 42 full-time (28 women), 2 part-time/adjunct (1 woman). *Students:* 170 full-time (98 women); includes 51 minority (21 Black or African American, non-Hispanic/Latino; 17 Asian, non-Hispanic/Latino; 11 Hispanic/Latino; 2 Native Hawaiian or other Pacific Islander, non-Hispanic/Latino). Average age 34. 88 applicants, 75% accepted, 66 enrolled. In 2017, 55 doctorates awarded. *Degree requirements:* For master's, thesis, scholarly project; for doctorate, dissertation (for PhD); project (for DNP). *Entrance requirements:* For master's, GRE, BSN, clinical experience, minimum GPA of 3.0, previous course work in science; for doctorate, GRE, BSN, minimum GPA of 3.0, undergraduate/graduate science course within past 5 years, writing example, interview (for some programs), and 3 letters of reference (for DNP); master's degree, minimum GPA of 3.0 in nursing or related field, personal statement, 3 references, and interview (for PhD). *Application deadline:* For winter admission, 2/15 for domestic students; for summer admission, 8/15 for domestic students. Application fee: $0. Electronic applications accepted. *Expenses:* There are no tuition costs or fees; students incur obligated service according to the requirements of their sponsoring organization. *Faculty research:* Military health care, military readiness, women's health, family, behavioral health. *Total annual research expenditures:* $100,000. *Unit head:* Dr. Diane C. Seibert, Associate Dean for Academic Affairs, 301-295-1080, Fax: 301-295-1707, E-mail: diane.seibert@usuhs.edu. *Application contact:* Maureen Jackson, Registrar, 301-295-1055, Fax: 301-295-1707, E-mail: maureen.jackson.ctr@usuhs.edu.
Website: http://www.usuhs.edu/gsn/

University at Buffalo, the State University of New York, Graduate School, School of Nursing, Buffalo, NY 14260. Offers adult gerontology nurse practitioner (DNP); family nurse practitioner (DNP); health care systems and leadership (MS); nurse anesthetist (DNP); nursing (PhD); nursing education (Certificate); psychiatric/mental health nurse practitioner (DNP). *Accreditation:* AACN; AANA/CANAEP (one or more programs are accredited). *Program availability:* Part-time, 100% online. *Faculty:* 41 full-time (36 women), 15 part-time/adjunct (all women). *Students:* 64 full-time (39 women), 136 part-time (120 women); includes 32 minority (13 Black or African American, non-Hispanic/Latino; 1 American Indian or Alaska Native, non-Hispanic/Latino; 18 Asian, non-Hispanic/Latino). Average age 34. 182 applicants, 39% accepted, 50 enrolled. In 2017, 3 master's, 32 doctorates, 2 other advanced degrees awarded. *Degree requirements:* For master's, thesis optional; for doctorate, comprehensive exam (for some programs), capstone (for DNP), dissertation (for PhD). *Entrance requirements:* For master's, GRE or MAT; for doctorate, GRE or MAT, minimum GPA of 3.0 (for DNP), 3.25 (for PhD); RN license; BS or MS in nursing; 3 references; writing sample; resume; personal statement; for Certificate, interview, minimum GPA of 3.0 or GRE General Test, RN license, MS in nursing, professional certification. Additional exam requirements/recommendations for international students: Required—TOEFL (minimum score 550 paper-based; 79 iBT), IELTS (minimum score 6.5). *Application deadline:* For fall admission, 4/1 for domestic students, 2/1 for international students; for spring admission, 1/15 for domestic students, 10/1 for international students; for summer admission, 4/1 for domestic students. Applications are processed on a rolling basis. Application fee: $75. Electronic applications accepted. *Expenses:* Contact institution. *Financial support:* In 2017–18, 80 students received support, including 2 fellowships with tuition reimbursements available (averaging $17,000 per year), 4 research assistantships with tuition reimbursements available (averaging $10,600 per year), 7 teaching assistantships with tuition reimbursements available (averaging $10,600 per year); scholarships/grants, traineeships, health care benefits, and unspecified assistantships also available. Financial award application deadline: 4/1; financial award applicants required to submit FAFSA. *Faculty research:* Oncology, palliative care, gerontology, addictions, mental health, community wellness, sleep, workforce, care of underserved populations, quality and safety, person-centered care, adolescent health. *Total annual research expenditures:* $1.4 million. *Unit head:* Dr. Marsha L. Lewis, Dean and Professor, 716-829-2533, Fax: 716-829-2566, E-mail: ubnursingdean@buffalo.edu. *Application contact:* Jennifer H. Schreier, Director of Graduate Student Services, 716-829-3311, Fax: 716-829-2067, E-mail: jhv2@buffalo.edu.
Website: http://nursing.buffalo.edu/

The University of Alabama at Birmingham, School of Nursing, Birmingham, AL 35294-1210. Offers clinical nurse leader (MSN); nurse anesthesia (DNP); nurse practitioner (MSN, DNP), including adult-gerontology acute care (MSN), adult-gerontology primary care (MSN), family (MSN), pediatric (MSN), psychiatric/mental health (MSN), women's health (MSN); nursing (MSN, DNP, PhD); nursing health systems administration (MSN); nursing informatics (MSN). *Accreditation:* AACN; AANA/CANAEP. *Program availability:* Part-time, online only, blended/hybrid learning. Terminal master's awarded for partial completion of doctoral program. *Degree requirements:* For master's, comprehensive exam; for doctorate, comprehensive exam, thesis/dissertation, research mentorship experience (for PhD); scholarly project (for DNP). *Entrance requirements:* For master's, GRE, GMAT, or MAT, minimum cumulative undergraduate GPA of 3.0 or on last 60 semesters hours; letters of recommendation; for doctorate, GRE General Test, computer literacy, course work in statistics, interview, minimum GPA of 3.0, MS in nursing, references, writing sample. Additional exam requirements/recommendations for international students: Required—TOEFL (minimum score 500 paper-based, 80 iBT) or IELTS (5.5). Electronic applications accepted. *Expenses:* Contact institution. *Faculty research:* Palliative care; oncology; aging; HIV/AIDS; nursing work environments.

University of Colorado Denver, College of Nursing, Aurora, CO 80045. Offers adult clinical nurse specialist (MS); adult nurse practitioner (MS); family nurse practitioner (MS); family psychiatric mental health nurse practitioner (MS); health care informatics (MS); nurse-midwifery (MS); nursing (DNP, PhD); nursing leadership and health care systems (MS); pediatric nurse practitioner (MS); women's health (MS); MS/PhD. *Accreditation:* ACNM/ACME (one or more programs are accredited). *Program availability:* Part-time, evening/weekend, online learning. *Students:* 297 applicants, 55% accepted, 141 enrolled. In 2017, 138 master's, 18 doctorates awarded. Terminal master's awarded for partial completion of doctoral program. *Degree requirements:* For master's, thesis optional; for doctorate, comprehensive exam, thesis/dissertation, 42 credits of coursework. *Entrance requirements:* For master's, GRE if cumulative undergraduate GPA is less than 3.0, undergraduate nursing degree from ACEN- or CCNE-accredited school or university; completion of research and statistics courses with minimum grade of C; copy of current and unencumbered nursing license; for doctorate, GRE, bachelor's and/or master's degrees in nursing from ACEN- or CCNE-accredited institution; portfolio; minimum undergraduate GPA of 3.0, graduate 3.5; graduate-level intermediate statistics and master's-level nursing theory courses with minimum B grade; interview. Additional exam requirements/recommendations for international students: Required—TOEFL (minimum score 560 paper-based; 83 iBT). *Application deadline:* For fall admission, 2/15 for domestic students, 1/15 for international students; for spring admission, 7/1 for domestic students, 6/1 for international students. Application fee: $50 ($75 for international students). Electronic applications accepted. *Unit head:* Dr. Sarah Thompson, Dean, 303-724-1679, E-mail: sarah.a.thompson@ucdenver.edu. *Application contact:* Judy Campbell, Graduate Programs Coordinator, 303-724-8503, E-mail: judy.campbell@ucdenver.edu.
Website: http://www.ucdenver.edu/academics/colleges/nursing/Pages/default.aspx

University of Delaware, College of Health Sciences, School of Nursing, Newark, DE 19716. Offers adult nurse practitioner (MSN, PMC); cardiopulmonary clinical nurse specialist (MSN, PMC); cardiopulmonary clinical nurse specialist/adult nurse practitioner (MSN, PMC); family nurse practitioner (MSN, PMC); gerontology clinical nurse specialist (MSN, PMC); gerontology clinical nurse specialist geriatric nurse practitioner (PMC); gerontology clinical nurse specialist/geriatric nurse practitioner (MSN); health services administration (MSN, PMC); nursing of children clinical nurse specialist (MSN, PMC); nursing of children clinical nurse specialist/pediatric nurse practitioner (MSN, PMC); oncology/immune deficiency clinical nurse specialist (MSN, PMC); oncology/immune deficiency clinical nurse specialist/adult nurse practitioner (MSN, PMC); perinatal/women's health clinical nurse specialist (MSN, PMC); perinatal/women's health clinical nurse specialist/women's health nurse practitioner (MSN, PMC); psychiatric nursing clinical nurse specialist (MSN, PMC). *Accreditation:* AACN. *Program availability:* Part-time, evening/weekend, online learning. *Degree requirements:* For master's, thesis optional. *Entrance requirements:* For master's, BSN, interview, RN license. Electronic applications accepted. *Faculty research:* Marriage and chronic illness, health promotion, congestive heart failure patient outcomes, school nursing, diabetes in children, culture, health disparities, cardiovascular, prison nursing, oncology, public policy, child obesity, smoking and teen pregnancy, blood pressure measurements, men's health.

The University of Kansas, University of Kansas Medical Center, School of Nursing, Kansas City, KS 66160. Offers adult/gerontological clinical nurse specialist (PMC); adult/gerontological nurse practitioner (PMC); health care informatics (PMC); health professions educator (PMC); nurse midwife (PMC); nursing (MS, DNP, PhD); organizational leadership (PMC); psychiatric/mental health nurse practitioner (PMC); public health nursing (PMC). *Accreditation:* AACN; ACNM/ACME. *Program availability:* Part-time, 100% online, blended/hybrid learning. *Faculty:* 56. *Students:* 48 full-time (44 women), 260 part-time (235 women); includes 50 minority (12 Black or African American, non-Hispanic/Latino; 2 American Indian or Alaska Native, non-Hispanic/Latino; 16 Asian, non-Hispanic/Latino; 8 Hispanic/Latino; 12 Two or more races, non-Hispanic/Latino). Average age 36. 87 applicants, 95% accepted, 61 enrolled. In 2017, 37 master's, 10 doctorates, 0 other advanced degrees awarded. Terminal master's awarded for partial completion of doctoral program. *Degree requirements:* For master's, comprehensive exam, thesis (for some programs), general oral exam; for doctorate, thesis/dissertation or alternative, comprehensive oral exam (for DNP); comprehensive written and oral exam, or three publications (for PhD). *Entrance requirements:* For master's, bachelor's degree in nursing, minimum GPA of 3.0, 1 year of clinical experience, RN license in KS and MO; for doctorate, GRE General Test (for PhD only), bachelor's degree in nursing, minimum GPA of 3.5, RN license in KS and MO. Additional exam requirements/recommendations for international students: Required—TOEFL. *Application deadline:* For fall admission, 4/1 for domestic and international students; for spring admission, 9/1 for domestic and international students. Application fee: $75. Electronic applications accepted. *Financial support:* In 2017–18, 5 research assistantships with tuition reimbursements (averaging $20,000 per year), 30 teaching assistantships with tuition reimbursements (averaging $20,000 per year) were awarded; scholarships/grants and traineeships also available. Financial award application

deadline: 3/1; financial award applicants required to submit FAFSA. *Faculty research:* Breastfeeding practices of teen mothers, national database of nursing quality indicators, caregiving of families of patients using technology in the home, simulation in nursing education, diaphragm fatigue. *Total annual research expenditures:* $1.4 million. *Unit head:* Dr. Sally Maliski, Dean, 913-588-1601, Fax: 913-588-1660, E-mail: smaliski@kumc.edu. *Application contact:* Dr. Pamela K. Barnes, Associate Dean, Student Affairs, 913-588-1619, Fax: 913-588-1615, E-mail: pbarnes2@kumc.edu.
Website: http://nursing.kumc.edu

University of Louisville, Graduate School, School of Nursing, Louisville, KY 40202. Offers adult gerontology nurse practitioner (MSN, DNP); education and administration (MSN); family nurse practitioner (MSN, DNP); neonatal nurse practitioner (MSN, DNP); nursing research (PhD); psychiatric/mental health nurse practitioner (MSN, DNP); women's health nurse practitioner (MSN). *Accreditation:* AACN. *Program availability:* Part-time. *Faculty:* 44 full-time (40 women), 45 part-time/adjunct (41 women). *Students:* 130 full-time (107 women), 30 part-time (25 women); includes 33 minority (16 Black or African American, non-Hispanic/Latino; 7 Asian, non-Hispanic/Latino; 5 Hispanic/Latino; 5 Two or more races, non-Hispanic/Latino), 2 international. Average age 33. 61 applicants, 67% accepted, 36 enrolled. In 2017, 54 master's awarded. *Degree requirements:* For doctorate, comprehensive exam (for some programs), thesis/dissertation (for some programs). *Entrance requirements:* For master's, bachelor's degree from nationally-accredited college, completion of 6 prerequisite courses, minimum undergraduate GPA of 3.0; for doctorate, GRE with minimum score of 156 Verbal, 146 Quantitative, 4.0 Analytic (for PhD), 3 letters of professional reference; minimum GPA of 3.0 with BSN, 3.25 with MSN; written statement of career goals, areas of expertise, and reasons for pursuing doctoral degree; resume including RN license. Additional exam requirements/recommendations for international students: Recommended—TOEFL (minimum score 560 paper-based), IELTS (minimum score 6.5). *Application deadline:* For fall admission, 1/15 priority date for domestic students, 1/15 for international students; for summer admission, 10/15 priority date for domestic students. Application fee: $65. Electronic applications accepted. *Expenses:* Tuition, state resident: full-time $12,246; part-time $681 per credit hour. Tuition, nonresident: full-time $25,486; part-time $1417 per credit hour. *Required fees:* $196. Tuition and fees vary according to course load, program and reciprocity agreements. *Financial support:* In 2017–18, 8 research assistantships with full tuition reimbursements (averaging $20,000 per year), 4 teaching assistantships with full tuition reimbursements (averaging $15,000 per year) were awarded; fellowships with full tuition reimbursements, scholarships/grants, and unspecified assistantships also available. Financial award application deadline: 10/1; financial award applicants required to submit FAFSA. *Faculty research:* Environmental health, health services research, women's mental health, self-management of chronic illness in adults and children, health disparities. *Total annual research expenditures:* $762,266. *Unit head:* Dr. Marcia J. Hern, RN, Dean and Professor, 502-852-8300, Fax: 502-852-8783, E-mail: m.hern@louisville.edu. *Application contact:* Trish Hart, Assistant Dean for Student Affairs, 502-852-5825, Fax: 502-852-8783, E-mail: trish.hart@louisville.edu.
Website: http://www.louisville.edu/nursing/

University of Maryland, Baltimore, School of Nursing, Baltimore, MD 21201. Offers adult-gerontology acute care nurse practitioner (DNP); adult-gerontology primary care nurse practitioner (DNP); clinical nurse leader (MS); community/public health nursing (MS); family nurse practitioner (DNP); global health (Postbaccalaureate Certificate); health services leadership and management (MS); neonatal nurse practitioner (DNP); nurse anesthesia (DNP); nursing (PhD); nursing informatics (MS, Postbaccalaureate Certificate); pediatric acute/primary care nurse practitioner (DNP); psychiatric mental health nurse practitioner (DNP); teaching in nursing and health professions (Postbaccalaureate Certificate); MS/MBA. MS/MBA offered jointly with University of Baltimore. *Program availability:* Part-time. *Faculty:* 130 full-time (117 women), 125 part-time/adjunct (114 women). *Students:* 504 full-time (442 women), 532 part-time (482 women); includes 443 minority (249 Black or African American, non-Hispanic/Latino; 1 American Indian or Alaska Native, non-Hispanic/Latino; 115 Asian, non-Hispanic/Latino; 48 Hispanic/Latino; 2 Native Hawaiian or other Pacific Islander, non-Hispanic/Latino; 28 Two or more races, non-Hispanic/Latino), 15 international. Average age 33. 935 applicants, 62% accepted, 394 enrolled. In 2017, 182 master's, 57 doctorates awarded. *Degree requirements:* For master's and Postbaccalaureate Certificate, thesis (for some programs); for doctorate, comprehensive exam, thesis/dissertation. *Entrance requirements:* Additional exam requirements/recommendations for international students: Required—TOEFL (minimum score 550 paper-based; 79 iBT); Recommended—IELTS (minimum score 7). *Application deadline:* For fall admission, 11/1 for domestic and international students; for spring admission, 8/1 for domestic and international students. Application fee: $75. Electronic applications accepted. *Expenses:* Contact institution. *Financial support:* In 2017–18, 22 research assistantships with full and partial tuition reimbursements (averaging $21,523 per year), 41 teaching assistantships with full and partial tuition reimbursements (averaging $13,439 per year) were awarded; fellowships and scholarships/grants also available. Financial award application deadline: 3/1; financial award applicants required to submit FAFSA. *Unit head:* Dr. Jane Kirschling, Dean, 410-706-4359, E-mail: kirschling@umaryland.edu. *Application contact:* Larry Fillian, Associate Dean of Student and Academic Services, 410-706-6298, E-mail: lfillian@umaryland.edu.
Website: http://www.nursing.umaryland.edu/

University of Michigan–Flint, School of Nursing, Flint, MI 48502-1950. Offers adult-gerontology acute care (DNP); adult-gerontology primary care (DNP); family nurse practitioner (DNP); nursing (MSN); psychiatric mental health (DNP); psychiatric mental health nurse practitioner (Certificate). *Accreditation:* AACN. *Program availability:* Part-time, evening/weekend, 100% online. *Faculty:* 36 full-time (35 women), 66 part-time/adjunct (61 women). *Students:* 159 full-time (143 women), 148 part-time (126 women); includes 80 minority (36 Black or African American, non-Hispanic/Latino; 5 American Indian or Alaska Native, non-Hispanic/Latino; 14 Asian, non-Hispanic/Latino; 14 Hispanic/Latino; 2 Native Hawaiian or other Pacific Islander, non-Hispanic/Latino; 9 Two or more races, non-Hispanic/Latino), 3 international. Average age 37. 86 applicants, 78% accepted, 41 enrolled. In 2017, 12 master's, 42 doctorates, 9 other advanced degrees awarded. *Entrance requirements:* For master's, BSN from regionally-accredited college; minimum GPA of 3.2; current unencumbered RN license in the United States; three or more credits in college-level chemistry or statistics with minimum C grade; for doctorate, BSN or MSN (with APRN certification) from regionally-accredited college or university with minimum overall undergraduate GPA of 3.2; college-level statistics with minimum C grade; for Certificate, completion of nurse practitioner program with MS from regionally-accredited college or university with minimum overall GPA of 3.2; current unencumbered RN license in the United States; current unencumbered license as nurse practitioner; current certification as nurse practitioner in specialty other than discipline of study. Additional exam requirements/recommendations for international students: Required—TOEFL (minimum score 84 iBT), IELTS (minimum score 6.5). *Application deadline:* For fall admission, 7/1 for domestic students, 5/1 for international students; for winter admission, 11/1 for domestic students, 9/1 for international students; for spring admission, 3/15 for domestic students, 1/1 for international students. Applications are processed on a rolling basis. Application fee: $55. Electronic applications accepted. *Expenses:* Contact institution. *Financial support:* Federal Work-Study, scholarships/grants, and unspecified assistantships available. Support available to part-time students. Financial award application deadline: 3/1; financial award applicants required to submit FAFSA. *Faculty research:* Family system stress, self breast exam, family roads evaluation, causal model testing for psycho social development, basic needs, nurse preparation training. *Unit head:* Dr. Constance J. Creech, Director, 810-762-3420, Fax: 810-766-6851, E-mail: ccreech@umflint.edu. *Application contact:* Bradley T. Maki, Director of Graduate Admissions, 810-762-3171, Fax: 810-766-6789, E-mail: bmaki@umflint.edu.
Website: https://www.umflint.edu/nursing/graduate-nursing-programs

University of Minnesota, Twin Cities Campus, Graduate School, School of Nursing, Minneapolis, MN 55455-0213. Offers adult/gerontological clinical nurse specialist (DNP); adult/gerontological primary care nurse practitioner (DNP); family nurse practitioner (DNP); health innovation and leadership (DNP); integrative health and healing (DNP); nurse anesthesia (DNP); nurse midwifery (DNP); nursing (MN, PhD); nursing informatics (DNP); pediatric clinical nurse specialist (DNP); primary care certified pediatric nurse practitioner (DNP); psychiatric/mental health nurse practitioner (DNP); women's health nurse practitioner (DNP). *Accreditation:* AACN; AANA/CANAEP; ACNM/ACME (one or more programs are accredited). *Program availability:* Part-time, online learning. Terminal master's awarded for partial completion of doctoral program. *Degree requirements:* For master's, final oral exam, project or thesis; for doctorate, thesis/dissertation. *Entrance requirements:* For master's and doctorate, GRE General Test. Additional exam requirements/recommendations for international students: Required—TOEFL (minimum score 586 paper-based). *Expenses:* Contact institution. *Faculty research:* Child and family health promotion, nursing research on elders.

University of Missouri, Office of Research and Graduate Studies, Sinclair School of Nursing, Columbia, MO 65211. Offers adult-gerontology clinical nurse specialist (DNP, Certificate); family nurse practitioner (DNP); family psychiatric and mental health nurse practitioner (DNP); nursing (MS, PhD); nursing leadership and innovations in health care (DNP); pediatric clinical nurse specialist (DNP, Certificate); pediatric nurse practitioner (DNP). *Accreditation:* AACN. *Program availability:* Part-time. *Degree requirements:* For master's, thesis optional, oral exam; for doctorate, thesis/dissertation. *Entrance requirements:* For master's, GRE General Test, BSN, minimum GPA of 3.0 during last 60 hours, nursing license. Additional exam requirements/recommendations for international students: Required—TOEFL, IELTS. *Application deadline:* Applications are processed on a rolling basis. Electronic applications accepted. *Expenses:* Tuition, state resident: full-time $6480. Tuition, nonresident: full-time $17,744. *Required fees:* $1108. Tuition and fees vary according to course load, campus/location and program. *Financial support:* Fellowships, research assistantships, teaching assistantships, career-related internships or fieldwork, institutionally sponsored loans, scholarships/grants, traineeships, health care benefits, tuition waivers (full), and unspecified assistantships available. Support available to part-time students.
Website: http://nursing.missouri.edu/

University of Missouri–St. Louis, College of Nursing, St. Louis, MO 63121. Offers adult/geriatric nurse practitioner (Post Master's Certificate); family nurse practitioner (Post Master's Certificate); nursing (DNP, PhD); pediatric acute care nurse practitioner (Post Master's Certificate); pediatric nurse practitioner (Post Master's Certificate); psychiatric-mental health nurse practitioner (Post Master's Certificate); women's health nurse practitioner (Post Master's Certificate). *Accreditation:* AACN. *Program availability:* Part-time. *Faculty:* 24 full-time (22 women), 12 part-time/adjunct (11 women). *Students:* 47 full-time (44 women), 162 part-time (152 women); includes 53 minority (37 Black or African American, non-Hispanic/Latino; 10 Asian, non-Hispanic/Latino; 4 Hispanic/Latino; 2 Two or more races, non-Hispanic/Latino), 3 international. 112 applicants, 93% accepted, 70 enrolled. *Degree requirements:* For doctorate, comprehensive exam, thesis/dissertation; for Post Master's Certificate, thesis. *Entrance requirements:* For doctorate, GRE, 2 letters of recommendation, MSN, minimum GPA of 3.2, course in differential/inferential statistics; for Post Master's Certificate, 2 recommendation letters; MSN; advanced practice certificate; minimum GPA of 3.0; essay. Additional exam requirements/recommendations for international students: Recommended—TOEFL (minimum score 550 paper-based; 79 iBT), IELTS (minimum score 6.5). *Application deadline:* For fall admission, 2/15 for domestic and international students. Application fee: $50 ($40 for international students). Electronic applications accepted. *Expenses:* Tuition, state resident: part-time $476.50 per credit hour. Tuition, nonresident: part-time $1169.70 per credit hour. *Financial support:* Research assistantships with tuition reimbursements available. Financial award application deadline: 4/1; financial award applicants required to submit FAFSA. *Faculty research:* Health promotion and restoration, family disruption, violence, abuse, battered women, health survey methods. *Unit head:* Sue Dean-Baar, Dean, 314-516-6066. *Application contact:* 314-516-5458, Fax: 314-516-6996, E-mail: gradadm@umsl.edu.
Website: http://www.umsl.edu/divisions/nursing/

University of New Hampshire, Graduate School, College of Health and Human Services, Department of Nursing, Durham, NH 03824. Offers family nurse practitioner (Postbaccalaureate Certificate); nursing (MS, DNP); psychiatric mental health (Postbaccalaureate Certificate). *Accreditation:* AACN. *Program availability:* Part-time, online learning. *Students:* 40 full-time (32 women), 107 part-time (91 women); includes 8 minority (2 Black or African American, non-Hispanic/Latino; 2 Asian, non-Hispanic/Latino; 2 Hispanic/Latino; 2 Two or more races, non-Hispanic/Latino). Average age 35. 83 applicants, 58% accepted, 30 enrolled. In 2017, 38 master's, 1 doctorate, 5 other advanced degrees awarded. *Entrance requirements:* Additional exam requirements/recommendations for international students: Required—TOEFL (minimum score 550 paper-based; 80 iBT). *Application deadline:* For fall admission, 4/1 priority date for domestic students, 4/1 for international students; for spring admission, 11/1 for domestic students. Application fee: $65. Electronic applications accepted. *Financial support:* In 2017–18, 15 students received support, including 2 teaching assistantships; fellowships, research assistantships, Federal Work-Study, scholarships/grants, and tuition waivers (full and partial) also available. Financial award application deadline: 2/15. *Unit head:* Dr. Gene Harkless, Chair, 603-862-2285. *Application contact:* Jane Dufresne, Administrative Assistant, 603-862-2299, E-mail: nursing.department@unh.edu.
Website: https://chhs.unh.edu/nursing/graduate-program-nursing

The University of North Carolina at Chapel Hill, School of Nursing, Chapel Hill, NC 27599-7460. Offers advanced practice registered nurse (DNP); nursing (MSN, PhD, PMC), including administration (MSN), adult gerontology primary care nurse practitioner (MSN), clinical nurse leader (MSN), education (MSN), health care systems (PMC), informatics (MSN, PMC), nursing leadership (PMC), outcomes management (MSN), primary care family nurse practitioner (MSN), primary care pediatric nurse practitioner (MSN), psychiatric/mental health nurse practitioner (MSN, PMC). *Accreditation:* AACN; ACEN (one or more programs are accredited). *Program availability:* Part-time. *Faculty:* 86 full-time (78 women), 44 part-time/adjunct (40 women). *Students:* 208 full-time (186 women), 128 part-time (116 women); includes 100 minority (49 Black or African American, non-Hispanic/Latino; 4 American Indian or Alaska Native, non-Hispanic/Latino; 23 Asian, non-Hispanic/Latino; 7 Hispanic/Latino; 17 Two or more races, non-Hispanic/Latino), 17 international. Average age 33. 624 applicants, 25% accepted, 150 enrolled. In 2017, 91 master's, 14 doctorates awarded. *Degree requirements:* For master's, comprehensive exam, thesis; for doctorate, thesis/dissertation, 3 exams; for

PMC, thesis. *Entrance requirements:* Additional exam requirements/recommendations for international students: Required—TOEFL (minimum score 575 paper-based; 89 iBT), IELTS (minimum score 8). *Application deadline:* For fall admission, 12/15 for domestic and international students. Application fee: $88. Electronic applications accepted. *Financial support:* In 2017–18, 8 fellowships with full tuition reimbursements, 6 research assistantships with partial tuition reimbursements (averaging $8,000 per year), 10 teaching assistantships with partial tuition reimbursements (averaging $8,000 per year) were awarded; scholarships/grants, traineeships, health care benefits, and unspecified assistantships also available. Support available to part-time students. Financial award application deadline: 3/1; financial award applicants required to submit FAFSA. *Faculty research:* Preventing and managing chronic illness, reducing health disparities, Improving healthcare quality and patient outcomes, understanding biobehavioral and genetic bases of health and illness, developing innovative ways to enhance science and its clinical translation. *Unit head:* Dr. Nilda Peragallo Montano, Dean/Professor, 919-966-3731, Fax: 919-966-3540, E-mail: npm@email.unc.edu. *Application contact:* Emily Sayed, Assistant Director, Graduate Admissions, 919-966-4260, Fax: 919-966-3540, E-mail: sayed@unc.edu.
Website: http://nursing.unc.edu

University of North Dakota, Graduate School, College of Nursing and Professional Disciplines, Department of Nursing, Grand Forks, ND 58202. Offers adult-gerontological nurse practitioner (MS); advanced public health nurse (MS); family nurse practitioner (MS); nurse anesthesia (MS); nurse educator (MS); nursing (PhD, Post-Master's Certificate); nursing practice (DNP); psychiatric and mental health nurse practitioner (MS).

University of Pennsylvania, School of Nursing, Psychiatric Mental Health Advanced Practice Nurse Program, Philadelphia, PA 19104. Offers adult and special populations (MSN); child and family (MSN); geropsychiatrics (MSN). *Accreditation:* AACN. *Program availability:* Part-time. *Students:* 14 full-time (7 women), 22 part-time (16 women); includes 14 minority (8 Black or African American, non-Hispanic/Latino; 4 Hispanic/Latino; 2 Two or more races, non-Hispanic/Latino). Average age 35. 57 applicants, 63% accepted, 31 enrolled. In 2017, 18 master's awarded. Application fee: $80. *Financial support:* Application deadline: 4/1.

University of Pittsburgh, School of Nursing, Nurse Practitioner Program, Pittsburgh, PA 15261. Offers adult-gerontology acute care (DNP); adult-gerontology primary care (DNP); family (individual across the lifespan) (DNP); neonatal (MSN, DNP); pediatric primary care (DNP); psychiatric mental health (DNP). *Accreditation:* AACN. *Program availability:* Part-time. *Faculty:* 17 full-time (14 women), 3 part-time/adjunct (2 women). *Students:* 50 full-time (47 women), 43 part-time (36 women); includes 9 minority (1 Black or African American, non-Hispanic/Latino; 1 American Indian or Alaska Native, non-Hispanic/Latino; 7 Asian, non-Hispanic/Latino), 1 international. Average age 31. 77 applicants, 40% accepted, 25 enrolled. In 2017, 6 master's, 35 doctorates awarded. *Degree requirements:* For master's, comprehensive exam, thesis optional. *Entrance requirements:* For master's, GRE General Test, BSN, RN license, 3 letters of recommendation, resume, course work in statistics, relevant nursing experience; for doctorate, GRE General Test, BSN, RN license, minimum GPA of 3.5, 3 letters of recommendation, relevant nursing experience, resume, course work in statistics. Additional exam requirements/recommendations for international students: Required—TOEFL (minimum score 600 paper-based; 100 IBT) or IELTS (minimum score 7.0). *Application deadline:* For fall admission, 5/1 priority date for domestic students, 2/15 priority date for international students. Application fee: $50. Electronic applications accepted. *Expenses:* $13,068 per term full-time resident tuition, $1,064 per credit part-time; $15,270 per term full-time non-resident tuition, $1,247 per credit part-time; $437 per term full time fees; $282 per term part-time fees. *Financial support:* In 2017–18, 58 students received support, including 7 fellowships (averaging $15,755 per year), 15 teaching assistantships (averaging $12,454 per year); scholarships/grants, tuition waivers, and unspecified assistantships also available. Financial award applicants required to submit FAFSA. *Faculty research:* Behavioral management of chronic disorders, patient management in critical care, consumer informatics, genetic applications (molecular genetics and psychosocial implications), technology for nurses and patients to improve care. *Unit head:* Dr. Sandra Engberg, Associate Dean for Clinical Education, 412-624-3835, Fax: 412-624-8521, E-mail: sje1@pitt.edu. *Application contact:* Laurie Lapsley, Graduate Administrator, 412-624-9670, Fax: 412-624-2409, E-mail: lapsleyl@pitt.edu.
Website: http://www.nursing.pitt.edu

University of Puerto Rico–Medical Sciences Campus, School of Nursing, San Juan, PR 00936-5067. Offers adult and elderly nursing (MSN); child and adolescent nursing (MSN); critical care nursing (MSN); family and community nursing (MSN); family nurse practitioner (MSN); maternity nursing (MSN); mental health and psychiatric nursing (MSN). *Accreditation:* AACN; AANA/CANAEP. *Entrance requirements:* For master's, GRE or EXADEP, interview, Puerto Rico RN license or professional license for international students, general and specific point average, article analysis. Electronic applications accepted. *Faculty research:* HIV, health disparities, teen violence, women and violence, neurological disorders.

University of Rochester, School of Nursing, Rochester, NY 14642. Offers adult gerontological acute care nurse practitioner (MS); adult gerontological primary care nurse practitioner (MS); clinical nurse leader (MS); family nurse practitioner (MS); family psychiatric mental health nurse practitioner (MS); health care organization management and leadership (MS); nursing (DNP); nursing and health science (PhD); nursing education (MS); pediatric nurse practitioner (MS); pediatric nurse practitioner/neonatal nurse practitioner (MS). *Accreditation:* AACN. *Program availability:* Part-time, 100% online, blended/hybrid learning. *Faculty:* 62 full-time (51 women), 73 part-time/adjunct (63 women). *Students:* 17 full-time (12 women), 306 part-time (252 women); includes 46 minority (16 Black or African American, non-Hispanic/Latino; 1 American Indian or Alaska Native, non-Hispanic/Latino; 7 Asian, non-Hispanic/Latino; 17 Hispanic/Latino; 5 Two or more races, non-Hispanic/Latino), 3 international. Average age 34. 143 applicants, 71% accepted, 87 enrolled. In 2017, 48 master's, 8 doctorates awarded. Terminal master's awarded for partial completion of doctoral program. *Degree requirements:* For master's, comprehensive exam; for doctorate, thesis/dissertation. *Entrance requirements:* For master's, BS in nursing, minimum GPA of 3.0, course work in statistics; for doctorate, GRE General Test (for PhD), MS in nursing, minimum GPA of 3.5. Additional exam requirements/recommendations for international students: Required—TOEFL (minimum score 560 paper-based; 88 iBT) or IELTS (minimum score 6.5) recommended. *Application deadline:* For fall admission, 4/1 for domestic and international students; for spring admission, 9/1 for domestic and international students; for summer admission, 1/2 for domestic and international students. Application fee: $50. Electronic applications accepted. *Financial support:* In 2017–18, 63 students received support, including 2 fellowships with full and partial tuition reimbursements available (averaging $16,000 per year); scholarships/grants, traineeships, health care benefits, tuition waivers (full and partial), and unspecified assistantships also available. Support available to part-time students. Financial award application deadline: 6/30; financial award applicants required to submit CSS PROFILE or FAFSA. *Faculty research:* Symptom science, systems of care, innovations in health technology, promoting healthy behaviors. *Total annual research expenditures:* $2.6 million. *Unit head:* Dr. Kathy H. Rideout, Dean, 585-273-8902, Fax: 585-273-1268, E-mail: kathy_rideout@urmc.rochester.edu. *Application contact:* Elaine Andolina, Director of Admissions, 585-275-2375, Fax: 585-756-8299, E-mail: elaine_andolina@urmc.rochester.edu.
Website: http://www.son.rochester.edu

University of St. Francis, Leach College of Nursing, Joliet, IL 60435-6169. Offers family nurse practitioner (MSN, Post-Master's Certificate); nursing administration (MSN); nursing education (MSN); nursing practice (DNP); psychology/mental health nurse practitioner (MSN, Post-Master's Certificate); teaching in nursing (Certificate). *Accreditation:* AACN. *Program availability:* Part-time, evening/weekend, 100% online. *Faculty:* 9 full-time (all women), 12 part-time/adjunct (11 women). *Students:* 66 full-time (61 women), 292 part-time (262 women); includes 136 minority (67 Black or African American, non-Hispanic/Latino; 2 American Indian or Alaska Native, non-Hispanic/Latino; 25 Asian, non-Hispanic/Latino; 29 Hispanic/Latino; 3 Native Hawaiian or other Pacific Islander, non-Hispanic/Latino; 10 Two or more races, non-Hispanic/Latino). Average age 40. 280 applicants, 34% accepted, 81 enrolled. In 2017, 117 master's, 5 doctorates, 12 other advanced degrees awarded. *Degree requirements:* For master's, comprehensive exam. *Entrance requirements:* Additional exam requirements/recommendations for international students: Required—TOEFL (minimum score 550 paper-based; 79 iBT), IELTS (minimum score 6). *Application deadline:* Applications are processed on a rolling basis. Application fee: $30. Electronic applications accepted. Application fee is waived when completed online. *Expenses:* $775 per credit hour. *Financial support:* In 2017–18, 115 students received support. Scholarships/grants available. Support available to part-time students. Financial award applicants required to submit FAFSA. *Unit head:* Dr. Carol Wilson, Dean, 815-740-3840, Fax: 815-740-4243, E-mail: cwilson@stfrancis.edu. *Application contact:* Sandra Sloka, Director of Admissions for Graduate and Degree Completion Programs, 800-735-7500, Fax: 815-740-3431, E-mail: ssloka@stfrancis.edu.
Website: http://www.stfrancis.edu/academics/college-of-nursing/

University of Saint Joseph, Department of Nursing, West Hartford, CT 06117-2700. Offers family nurse practitioner (MS); nurse educator (MS); nursing practice (DNP); psychiatric/mental health nurse practitioner (MS). *Accreditation:* AACN. *Program availability:* Part-time, evening/weekend. *Degree requirements:* For master's, thesis. *Entrance requirements:* For master's, 2 letters of recommendation. *Application deadline:* Applications are processed on a rolling basis. Application fee: $50. Electronic applications accepted. Application fee is waived when completed online. *Financial support:* Career-related internships or fieldwork and unspecified assistantships available. Support available to part-time students. Financial award applicants required to submit FAFSA.
Website: http://www.usj.edu/academics/schools/school-of-health-natural-sciences/nursing/

University of San Diego, Hahn School of Nursing and Health Science, San Diego, CA 92110-2492. Offers adult-gerontology clinical nurse specialist (MSN); adult-gerontology nurse practitioner/family nurse practitioner (MSN); clinical nurse leader (MSN); executive nurse leader (MSN); family nurse practitioner (MSN); healthcare informatics (MS, MSN); nursing (PhD); nursing practice (DNP); pediatric/family nurse practitioner (MSN); psychiatric-mental health nurse practitioner (MSN). *Accreditation:* AACN. *Program availability:* Part-time, evening/weekend. *Faculty:* 26 full-time (21 women), 36 part-time/adjunct (29 women). *Students:* 238 full-time (198 women), 230 part-time (167 women); includes 230 minority (32 Black or African American, non-Hispanic/Latino; 104 Asian, non-Hispanic/Latino; 75 Hispanic/Latino; 19 Two or more races, non-Hispanic/Latino), 12 international. Average age 35. In 2017, 93 master's, 44 doctorates awarded. *Degree requirements:* For doctorate, thesis/dissertation (for some programs), residency (DNP). *Entrance requirements:* For master's, GRE General Test (for entry-level nursing), BSN, current California RN licensure (except for entry-level nursing), minimum GPA of 3.0; for doctorate, minimum GPA of 3.5, MSN, current California RN licensure. Additional exam requirements/recommendations for international students: Required—TOEFL (minimum score 580 paper-based; 83 iBT), TWE. *Application deadline:* Applications are processed on a rolling basis. Application fee: $45. Electronic applications accepted. *Financial support:* In 2017–18, 242 students received support. Scholarships/grants and traineeships available. Support available to part-time students. Financial award application deadline: 4/1; financial award applicants required to submit FAFSA. *Faculty research:* Maternal/neonatal health, palliative and end of life care, adolescent obesity, health disparities, cognitive dysfunction. *Unit head:* Dr. Janes Georges, Interim Dean, 619-260-4550, Fax: 619-260-6814, E-mail: nursing@sandiego.edu. *Application contact:* Monica Mahon, Associate Director of Graduate Admissions, 619-260-4524, Fax: 619-260-4158, E-mail: grads@sandiego.edu.
Website: http://www.sandiego.edu/nursing/

University of South Carolina, The Graduate School, College of Nursing, Program in Advanced Practice Nursing in Psychiatric Mental Health, Columbia, SC 29208. Offers MSN, Certificate. *Program availability:* Part-time, online learning. *Entrance requirements:* For master's, master's degree in nursing, RN license; for Certificate, MSN. Additional exam requirements/recommendations for international students: Required—TOEFL (minimum score 570 paper-based). Electronic applications accepted. *Faculty research:* Systems research, evidence based practice, breast cancer, violence.

University of South Carolina, The Graduate School, College of Nursing, Program in Community Mental Health and Psychiatric Health Nursing, Columbia, SC 29208. Offers psychiatric/mental health nurse practitioner (MSN); psychiatric/mental health specialist (MSN). *Accreditation:* AACN. *Program availability:* Part-time. *Degree requirements:* For master's, thesis or alternative. *Entrance requirements:* For master's, GRE General Test, MAT, BS in nursing, nursing license. Additional exam requirements/recommendations for international students: Required—TOEFL (minimum score 570 paper-based). Electronic applications accepted. *Faculty research:* Systems research, evidence based practice, breast cancer, violence.

University of Southern Indiana, Graduate Studies, College of Nursing and Health Professions, Program in Nursing, Evansville, IN 47712-3590. Offers adult-gerontology acute care nurse practitioner (MSN, PMC); adult-gerontology clinical nurse specialist (MSN, PMC); adult-gerontology primary care nurse practitioner (MSN, PMC); advanced nursing practice (DNP); family nurse practiioner (MSN); family nurse practitioner (PMC); nursing education (MSN, PMC); nursing management and leadership (MSN, PMC); organizational and systems leadership (DNP); psychiatric mental health nurse practitioner (MSN, PMC). *Accreditation:* AACN. *Program availability:* Part-time, online learning. *Faculty:* 9 full-time (8 women), 2 part-time/adjunct (both women). *Students:* 73 full-time (59 women), 370 part-time (314 women); includes 47 minority (18 Black or African American, non-Hispanic/Latino; 2 American Indian or Alaska Native, non-Hispanic/Latino; 10 Asian, non-Hispanic/Latino; 12 Hispanic/Latino; 1 Native Hawaiian or other Pacific Islander, non-Hispanic/Latino; 4 Two or more races, non-Hispanic/Latino), 1 international. Average age 36. In 2017, 91 master's, 10 doctorates, 18 other advanced degrees awarded. *Entrance requirements:* For master's, BSN from nationally-accredited school; minimum cumulative GPA of 3.0; satisfactory completion of a course in undergraduate statistics (minimum grade C); one year of full-time experience or 2,000 hours of clinical practice as an RN (recommended); unencumbered U.S. RN license; for doctorate, minimum GPA of 3.0, completion of graduate research course with minimum B grade, unencumbered RN license, resume/curriculum vitae, three professional

references, 1-2 page narrative of practice experience and professional goals, Capstone Project Information form. Additional exam requirements/recommendations for international students: Required—TOEFL (minimum score 550 paper-based; 79 iBT), IELTS (minimum score 6). *Application deadline:* For fall admission, 2/1 for domestic students, 1/1 priority date for international students. Applications are processed on a rolling basis. Application fee: $40. Electronic applications accepted. *Expenses:* Contact institution. *Financial support:* In 2017–18, 1 student received support. Federal Work-Study, scholarships/grants, tuition waivers (full and partial), and unspecified assistantships available. Financial award application deadline: 3/1; financial award applicants required to submit FAFSA. *Unit head:* Dr. Mellisa A. Hall, Chair of the Master of Science in Nursing Program, 812-465-1168, E-mail: mhall@usi.edu. *Application contact:* Dr. Mayola Rowser, Director, Graduate Studies, 812-465-7015, Fax: 812-464-1956, E-mail: mrowser@usi.edu.
Website: https://www.usi.edu/health/nursing/

University of Southern Maine, College of Science, Technology, and Health, School of Nursing, Portland, ME 04103. Offers adult-gerontology primary care nurse practitioner (MS, PMC); education (MS); family nurse practitioner (MS, PMC); family psychiatric/mental health nurse practitioner (MS); management (MS); nursing (CAS, CGS); psychiatric-mental health nurse practitioner (PMC). *Accreditation:* AACN. *Program availability:* Part-time. *Degree requirements:* For master's, thesis optional. *Entrance requirements:* For master's, GRE General Test or MAT, minimum GPA of 3.0; for doctorate, GRE. Additional exam requirements/recommendations for international students: Required—TOEFL (minimum score 550 paper-based). Electronic applications accepted. *Faculty research:* Women's health, nursing history, weight control, community services, substance abuse.

The University of Tennessee Health Science Center, College of Nursing, Memphis, TN 38163. Offers adult-gerontology acute care nurse practitioner (Post Master's Certificate); advance practice nursing (DNP); family nurse practitioner (Post-Doctoral Certificate); pediatric acute care nurse practitioner (Post-Doctoral Certificate); pediatric primary care nurse practitioner (Post-Doctoral Certificate); psychiatric/mental health nurse practitioner (Post-Doctoral Certificate); registered nurse first assistant (Certificate). *Accreditation:* AACN; AANA/CANAEP. *Program availability:* Part-time, blended/hybrid learning. *Faculty:* 52 full-time (47 women), 11 part-time/adjunct (4 women). *Students:* 262 full-time (228 women), 13 part-time (12 women); includes 83 minority (71 Black or African American, non-Hispanic/Latino; 6 Asian, non-Hispanic/Latino; 6 Hispanic/Latino). Average age 32. 215 applicants, 49% accepted, 79 enrolled. In 2017, 78 doctorates, 2 Certificates awarded. *Degree requirements:* For doctorate, project. *Entrance requirements:* For doctorate, RN license, minimum GPA of 3.0; for other advanced degree, MSN, APN license, minimum GPA of 3.0. Additional exam requirements/recommendations for international students: Required—TOEFL (minimum score 550 paper-based; 80 iBT). *Application deadline:* For fall admission, 1/15 for domestic students; for spring admission, 8/15 for domestic students. Application fee: $70. Electronic applications accepted. *Expenses:* $13,420 in-state tuition and fees; $17,222 out-of-state tuition and fees. *Financial support:* In 2017–18, 112 students received support, including 9 research assistantships (averaging $24,783 per year); Federal Work-Study, institutionally sponsored loans, scholarships/grants, and tuition waivers (partial) also available. Financial award application deadline: 3/15; financial award applicants required to submit FAFSA. *Faculty research:* Efficacy of a cognitive behavioral group intervention and its influence on symptoms of depression and anxiety as well as caregiver function; quality of life and sexual function in women who undergo vulvar surgeries; influence of prenatal and early childhood environments on health and developmental trajectories across childhood; interaction between physical activity, diet, genetics, insulin resistance, and obesity. *Total annual research expenditures:* $1.2 million. *Unit head:* Dr. Wendy Likes, Dean, 901-448-6135, Fax: 901-448-4121, E-mail: wlikes@uthsc.edu. *Application contact:* Jamie Overton, Director, Student Affairs, 901-448-6139, Fax: 901-448-4121, E-mail: joverton@uthsc.edu.
Website: http://uthsc.edu/nursing/

The University of Texas at Austin, Graduate School, School of Nursing, Austin, TX 78712-1111. Offers adult - gerontology clinical nurse specialist (MSN); child health (MSN), including administration, public health nursing, teaching; family nurse practitioner (MSN); family psychiatric/mental health nurse practitioner (MSN); holistic adult health (MSN), including administration, teaching; maternity (MSN), including administration, public health nursing, teaching; nursing (PhD); nursing administration and healthcare systems management (MSN); nursing practice (DNP); pediatric nurse practitioner (MSN); public health nursing (MSN). *Accreditation:* AACN. *Program availability:* Part-time. *Degree requirements:* For master's, thesis optional; for doctorate, thesis/dissertation. *Entrance requirements:* For master's and doctorate, GRE General Test. Additional exam requirements/recommendations for international students: Required—TOEFL (minimum score 550 paper-based). Electronic applications accepted. *Faculty research:* Chronic illness management, memory and aging, health promotion, women's health, adolescent health.

The University of Texas Health Science Center at San Antonio, School of Nursing, San Antonio, TX 78229-3900. Offers administrative management (MSN); adult-gerontology acute care nurse practitioner (PGC); advanced practice leadership (DNP); clinical nurse leader (MSN); executive administrative management (DNP); family nurse practitioner (MSN, PGC); nursing (MSN, PhD); nursing education (MSN, PGC); pediatric nurse practitioner primary care (PGC); psychiatric mental health nurse practitioner (PGC); public health nurse leader (DNP). *Accreditation:* AACN. *Program availability:* Part-time. Terminal master's awarded for partial completion of doctoral program. *Degree requirements:* For master's, thesis optional; for doctorate, comprehensive exam, thesis/dissertation.

The University of Texas Rio Grande Valley, College of Health Affairs, School of Nursing, Edinburg, TX 78539. Offers adult health nursing (MSN); family nurse practitioner (MSN); nursing administration (MSN); nursing education (MSN); psychiatric mental health nursing (Post Master's Certificate). *Accreditation:* AACN. *Program availability:* Part-time, evening/weekend. *Faculty:* 7 full-time (all women), 5 part-time/adjunct (3 women). *Students:* 48 full-time, 5 part-time; includes 43 minority (5 Black or African American, non-Hispanic/Latino; 38 Hispanic/Latino). Average age 31. 61 applicants. In 2017, 46 master's awarded. *Degree requirements:* For master's, thesis optional. *Entrance requirements:* For master's, Texas RN licensure, undergraduate physical statistic course. Additional exam requirements/recommendations for international students: Required—TOEFL (minimum score 550 paper-based). *Application deadline:* For fall admission, 7/1 priority date for domestic and international students; for spring admission, 10/1 priority date for domestic and international students. Applications are processed on a rolling basis. Application fee: $50. Electronic applications accepted. *Expenses:* Contact institution. *Financial support:* Scholarships/grants and traineeships available. Financial award application deadline: 9/1; financial award applicants required to submit FAFSA. *Faculty research:* Health promotion, adolescent pregnancy, herbal and nontraditional approaches, healing touch stress. *Unit head:* Dr. Eloisa G. Tamez, Professor/Chief Nursing Administrator, 956-665-3616, Fax: 956-665-5252, E-mail: eloisa.tamez@utrgv.edu. *Application contact:* Dr. Beatriz Bautista, Clinical Professor, 956-665-3497, Fax: 956-665-3491, E-mail: beatriz.bautista@utrgv.edu.
Website: http://www.utrgv.edu/nursing/

University of Virginia, School of Nursing, Charlottesville, VA 22903. Offers acute and specialty care (MSN); acute care nurse practitioner (MSN); clinical nurse leadership (MSN); community-public health leadership (MSN); nursing (DNP, PhD); psychiatric mental health counseling (MSN); MSN/MBA. *Accreditation:* AACN. *Program availability:* Part-time. *Faculty:* 51 full-time (44 women), 17 part-time/adjunct (16 women). *Students:* 202 full-time (168 women), 139 part-time (114 women); includes 78 minority (32 Black or African American, non-Hispanic/Latino; 2 American Indian or Alaska Native, non-Hispanic/Latino; 14 Asian, non-Hispanic/Latino; 17 Hispanic/Latino; 1 Native Hawaiian or other Pacific Islander, non-Hispanic/Latino; 12 Two or more races, non-Hispanic/Latino), 9 international. Average age 34. 183 applicants, 68% accepted, 98 enrolled. In 2017, 105 master's, 27 doctorates awarded. *Degree requirements:* For doctorate, comprehensive exam (for some programs), capstone project (DNP), dissertation (PhD). *Entrance requirements:* For master's, GRE General Test, MAT; for doctorate, GRE General Test. Additional exam requirements/recommendations for international students: Required—TOEFL, IELTS. *Application deadline:* Applications are processed on a rolling basis. Application fee: $60. Electronic applications accepted. *Financial support:* Fellowships, research assistantships, teaching assistantships, Federal Work-Study, and scholarships/grants available. Financial award applicants required to submit FAFSA. *Unit head:* Dorrie K. Fontaine, Dean, 434-924-0141, Fax: 434-982-1809, E-mail: dkf2u@virginia.edu. *Application contact:* Teresa Carroll, Senior Assistant Dean for Academic and Student Services, 434-924-0141, Fax: 434-982-1809, E-mail: nur-osa@virginia.edu.
Website: http://www.nursing.virginia.edu/

University of Wisconsin–Madison, School of Nursing, Madison, WI 53706-1380. Offers adult/gerontology (DNP); nursing (PhD); pediatrics (DNP); psychiatric mental health (DNP); MS/MPH. *Accreditation:* AACN. *Program availability:* Part-time. *Degree requirements:* For doctorate, comprehensive exam, thesis/dissertation. *Entrance requirements:* For doctorate, GRE General Test, 2 samples of scholarly written work, BS in nursing from an accredited program, minimum undergraduate GPA of 3.0 in last 60 credits (for PhD); licensure as professional nurse (for DNP). Additional exam requirements/recommendations for international students: Required—TOEFL (minimum score 600 paper-based; 100 iBT). Electronic applications accepted. *Faculty research:* Nursing informatics to promote self-care and disease management skills among patients and caregivers; quality of care to frail, vulnerable, and chronically ill populations; study of health-related and health-seeking behaviors; eliminating health disparities; pain and symptom management for patients with cancer.

Valdosta State University, College of Nursing and Health Sciences, Valdosta, GA 31698. Offers adult gerontology nurse practitioner (MSN); exercise physiology (MS); family nurse practitioner (MSN); family psychiatric mental health nurse practitioner (MSN). *Accreditation:* AACN. *Program availability:* Part-time, online learning. *Degree requirements:* For master's, thesis (for some programs), comprehensive written and/or oral exams. *Entrance requirements:* For master's, minimum GPA of 2.8. Additional exam requirements/recommendations for international students: Required—TOEFL (minimum score 523 paper-based). *Application deadline:* For fall admission, 7/1 for domestic and international students; for spring admission, 11/15 for domestic and international students. Applications are processed on a rolling basis. Application fee: $45. Electronic applications accepted. *Financial support:* Research assistantships with full tuition reimbursements, institutionally sponsored loans, scholarships/grants, and unspecified assistantships available. Support available to part-time students. Financial award application deadline: 7/1; financial award applicants required to submit FAFSA. *Faculty research:* Nutrition, children's health beliefs, alternative treatment modalities, job satisfaction, leadership. *Unit head:* Sheri Noviello, Dean, 229-333-5959, E-mail: srnoviello@valdosta.edu. *Application contact:* Sheri Noviello, Dean, 229-333-5959, E-mail: srnoviello@valdosta.edu.
Website: https://www.valdosta.edu/colleges/nursing-and-health-sciences/

Vanderbilt University, Vanderbilt University School of Nursing, Nashville, TN 37240. Offers adult-gerontology acute care nurse practitioner (MSN), including hospitalist, intensivist; adult-gerontology primary care nurse practitioner (MSN); emergency nurse practitioner (MSN); family nurse practitioner (MSN); healthcare leadership (MSN); neonatal nurse practitioner (MSN); nurse midwifery (MSN); nurse midwifery/family nurse practitioner (MSN); nursing (Post-Master's Certificate); nursing informatics (MSN); nursing practice (DNP); nursing science (PhD); pediatric acute care nurse practitioner (MSN); pediatric primary care nurse practitioner (MSN); psychiatric-mental health nurse practitioner (MSN); women's health nurse practitioner (MSN); women's health nurse practitioner/adult gerontology primary care nurse practitioner (MSN); MSN/M Div; MSN/MTS. *Accreditation:* AACN; ACEN (one or more programs are accredited); ACNM/ACME. *Program availability:* Part-time, 100% online, blended/hybrid learning. *Faculty:* 292 full-time (267 women), 321 part-time/adjunct (253 women). *Students:* 501 full-time (435 women), 387 part-time (355 women); includes 153 minority (40 Black or African American, non-Hispanic/Latino; 1 American Indian or Alaska Native, non-Hispanic/Latino; 27 Asian, non-Hispanic/Latino; 48 Hispanic/Latino; 4 Native Hawaiian or other Pacific Islander, non-Hispanic/Latino; 33 Two or more races, non-Hispanic/Latino), 9 international. Average age 31. 1,210 applicants, 57% accepted, 473 enrolled. In 2017, 319 master's, 47 doctorates awarded. *Degree requirements:* For doctorate, comprehensive exam, thesis/dissertation. *Entrance requirements:* For master's, GRE General Test (taken within the past 5 years), minimum B average in undergraduate course work, 3 letters of recommendation; for doctorate, GRE General Test, interview, 3 letters of recommendation from doctorally-prepared faculty, MSN, essay. Additional exam requirements/recommendations for international students: Required—TOEFL (minimum score 570 paper-based), IELTS (minimum score 6.5). *Application deadline:* For fall admission, 11/1 priority date for domestic and international students. Applications are processed on a rolling basis. Application fee: $50. Electronic applications accepted. *Expenses:* Contact institution. *Financial support:* In 2017–18, 627 students received support. Scholarships/grants available. Financial award application deadline: 3/1; financial award applicants required to submit FAFSA. *Faculty research:* Lymphedema, palliative care and bereavement, health services research including workforce, safety and quality of care, gerontology, better birth outcomes including nutrition. *Total annual research expenditures:* $2 million. *Unit head:* Dr. Linda Norman, Dean, 615-343-8876, Fax: 615-343-7711, E-mail: linda.norman@vanderbilt.edu. *Application contact:* Patricia Peerman, Assistant Dean for Enrollment Management, 615-322-3800, Fax: 615-343-0333, E-mail: vusn-admissions@vanderbilt.edu.
Website: http://www.nursing.vanderbilt.edu

Virginia Commonwealth University, Graduate School, School of Nursing, Richmond, VA 23284-9005. Offers adult health acute nursing (MS); adult health primary nursing (MS); biobehavioral clinical research (PhD); child health nursing (MS); clinical nurse leader (MS); family health nursing (MS); nurse educator (MS); nurse practitioner (MS); nursing (Certificate); nursing administration (MS), including clinical nurse manager; psychiatric-mental health nursing (MS); quality and safety in health care (DNP); women's health nursing (MS). *Accreditation:* AACN; ACEN (one or more programs are accredited). *Program availability:* Part-time, evening/weekend, online learning. *Degree requirements:* For master's, thesis optional; for doctorate, thesis/dissertation. *Entrance requirements:* For master's, GRE General Test, BSN, minimum GPA of 2.8; for doctorate, GRE General Test. Additional exam requirements/recommendations for international students: Required—TOEFL (minimum score 600 paper-based; 100 iBT). Electronic applications accepted.

Washington State University, College of Nursing, Spokane, WA 99210. Offers advanced population health (MN, DNP); family nurse practitioner (MN, DNP); nursing (PhD); psychiatric/mental health nurse practitioner (DNP); psychiatric/mental health practitioner (MN). Programs offered at the Spokane, Tri-Cities, and Vancouver campuses. *Accreditation:* AACN. *Degree requirements:* For master's, comprehensive exam (for some programs), thesis (for some programs), oral exam, research project. *Entrance requirements:* For master's, minimum GPA of 3.0, Washington state RN license, physical assessment skills, course work in statistics, recommendations, written interview (for nurse practitioner). *Faculty research:* Cardiovascular and Type 2 diabetes in children, evaluation of strategies to increase physical activity in sedentary people.

Wayne State University, College of Nursing, Detroit, MI 48202. Offers adult gerontology acute care nurse practitioner (MSN); adult gerontology primary care nurse practitioner (MSN); advanced public health nursing (MSN); infant and mental health (DNP, PhD); neonatal nurse practitioner (MSN); nurse-midwifery (MSN); pediatric acute care nurse practitioner (MSN); pediatric primary care nurse practitioner (MSN); psychiatric mental health nurse practitioner (MSN); women's health nurse practitioner (MSN). Doctoral program admits for fall only. *Accreditation:* AACN. *Program availability:* Part-time. *Faculty:* 30. *Students:* 133 full-time (120 women), 184 part-time (167 women); includes 85 minority (57 Black or African American, non-Hispanic/Latino; 16 Asian, non-Hispanic/Latino; 4 Hispanic/Latino; 8 Two or more races, non-Hispanic/Latino), 22 international. Average age 34. 318 applicants, 39% accepted, 94 enrolled. In 2017, 51 master's, 29 doctorates awarded. *Degree requirements:* For doctorate, thesis/dissertation (for some programs). *Entrance requirements:* For master's, BSN from ACEN- or CCNE-accredited program with minimum GPA of 3.0; three references; current RN license; personal statement; for doctorate, resume or curriculum vitae; goals statement; bachelor's or master's degree in nursing from ACEN- or CCNE-accredited program with minimum GPA of 3.0; current RN license, writing sample and interview (for DNP); reference letters (3 for PhD, 2 for DNP). Additional exam requirements/recommendations for international students: Required—TOEFL (minimum score 101 iBT), TWE (minimum score 6), Michigan English Language Assessment Battery (minimum score 85); Recommended—IELTS (minimum score 7). Application fee: $50. Electronic applications accepted. *Expenses:* Contact institution. *Financial support:* In 2017–18, 92 students received support, including 16 fellowships with tuition reimbursements available (averaging $8,285 per year), 5 teaching assistantships with tuition reimbursements available (averaging $25,000 per year); scholarships/grants, health care benefits, and unspecified assistantships also available. Support available to part-time students. Financial award applicants required to submit FAFSA. *Faculty research:* Bridging transitions and technology to promote asthma care in the community, chronic wound care for persons who injected drugs, decreasing at-risk parenting to reduce child maltreatment and trauma, dementia symptoms (cognition, behavior, function), determining readiness to engage in end of life/palliative care conversations with adolescents and young adults living with advanced cancer, dyspnea assessment and treatment at the end of life. *Unit head:* Dr. Laurie Lauzon Clabo, Dean, College of Nursing, 313-577-4082, E-mail: laurie.lauzon.clabo@wayne.edu. *Application contact:* 313-577-4082, Fax: 313-577-6949, E-mail: nursinginfo@wayne.edu.
Website: http://nursing.wayne.edu/

West Virginia Wesleyan College, Department of Nursing, Buckhannon, WV 26201. Offers family nurse practitioner (MS, Post Master's Certificate); nurse administrator (MS); nurse educator (MS); nurse-midwifery (MS); nursing administration (Post Master's Certificate); nursing education (Post Master's Certificate); psychiatric mental health nurse practitioner (MS); MSN/MBA. *Accreditation:* ACEN.

Wright State University, Graduate School, College of Nursing and Health, Program in Nursing, Dayton, OH 45435. Offers administration of nursing and health care systems (MS); adult gerontology clinical nurse specialist (MS); adult-gerontology acute care nurse practitioner (MS); family nurse practitioner (MS); neonatal nurse practitioner (MS); pediatric nurse practitioner-acute care (MS); pediatric nurse practitioner-primary care (MS); psychiatric mental health nurse practitioner (MS); school nurse (MS). *Accreditation:* AACN. *Program availability:* Part-time, evening/weekend. *Degree requirements:* For master's, thesis or alternative. *Entrance requirements:* For master's, GRE General Test, BSN from ACEN-accredited college, Ohio RN license. Additional exam requirements/recommendations for international students: Required—TOEFL. *Faculty research:* Clinical nursing and health, teaching, caring, pain administration, informatics and technology.

School Nursing

California State University, Fullerton, Graduate Studies, College of Health and Human Development, School of Nursing, Fullerton, CA 92831-3599. Offers leadership (MS); nurse anesthesia (MS); nurse educator (MS); nursing (DNP); school nursing (MS); women's health care (MS). *Accreditation:* AACN. *Program availability:* Part-time. *Faculty:* 27 full-time (23 women), 11 part-time/adjunct (all women). *Students:* 136 full-time (107 women), 116 part-time (96 women); includes 142 minority (9 Black or African American, non-Hispanic/Latino; 81 Asian, non-Hispanic/Latino; 37 Hispanic/Latino; 1 Native Hawaiian or other Pacific Islander, non-Hispanic/Latino; 14 Two or more races, non-Hispanic/Latino), 2 international. Average age 36. 235 applicants, 59% accepted, 117 enrolled. Application fee: $55. *Financial support:* Career-related internships or fieldwork, Federal Work-Study, institutionally sponsored loans, scholarships/grants, and traineeships available. Support available to part-time students. Financial award application deadline: 3/1; financial award applicants required to submit FAFSA. *Unit head:* Dr. Cindy Greenberg, Chair, 657-278-3336. *Application contact:* Admissions/Applications, 657-278-2371.
Website: http://nursing.fullerton.edu/

Cambridge College, School of Education, Boston, MA 02129. Offers autism specialist (M Ed); autism/behavior analyst (M Ed); behavior analyst (Post-Master's Certificate); curriculum and instruction (CAGS); early childhood teacher (M Ed); educational leadership (M Ed, Ed D); elementary teacher (M Ed); English as a second language (M Ed, Certificate); general science (M Ed); health education (Post-Master's Certificate); interdisciplinary studies (M Ed); library teacher (M Ed); mathematics education (M Ed); mathematics specialist (Certificate); school administration (M Ed, CAGS); school nurse education (M Ed); teacher of students with moderate disabilities (M Ed); teaching skills and methodologies (M Ed). *Program availability:* Part-time, evening/weekend, online learning. *Degree requirements:* For master's, thesis, internship/practicum (licensure program only); for doctorate, thesis/dissertation; for other advanced degree, thesis. *Entrance requirements:* For master's, interview, resume, documentation of licensure, 2 professional references; for doctorate, official transcripts, interview, resume, written personal statement/essay, portfolio of scholarly and professional work, 2 professional references, health insurance, immunizations form; for other advanced degree, official transcripts, interview, resume, written personal statement/essay, 2 professional references, health insurance, immunizations form. Additional exam requirements/recommendations for international students: Required—TOEFL (minimum score 550 paper-based; 79 iBT), Michigan English Language Assessment Battery (minimum score 85); Recommended—IELTS (minimum score 6). *Application deadline:* Applications are processed on a rolling basis. Application fee: $30. Electronic applications accepted. *Expenses:* Contact institution. *Financial support:* Career-related internships or fieldwork, Federal Work-Study, and scholarships/grants available. Financial award applicants required to submit FAFSA. *Faculty research:* Adult education, accelerated learning, mathematics education, brain compatible learning, special education and law. *Unit head:* Dr. Mary Garrity, Interim Dean, 617-873-0168, E-mail: mary.garrity@cambridgecollege.edu. *Application contact:* Robyn Shahid-Bellot, Interim Director of Admissions, 800-877-4723 Ext. 1191, Fax: 617-349-3561, E-mail: robyn.shahid-bellot@cambridgecollege.edu.
Website: https://www.cambridgecollege.edu/school/school-education

Eastern Mennonite University, Program in Nursing, Harrisonburg, VA 22802-2462. Offers leadership and management (MSN); leadership and school nursing (MSN); nursing management (DNP). *Accreditation:* AACN. *Program availability:* Part-time, online learning. *Degree requirements:* For master's, leadership project. *Entrance requirements:* For master's, RN license, one year of full-time work experience as RN, minimum GPA of 3.0. Additional exam requirements/recommendations for international students: Required—TOEFL. *Application deadline:* For fall admission, 6/1 for domestic students. Applications are processed on a rolling basis. Application fee: $25. Application fee is waived when completed online. *Financial support:* Federal Work-Study and scholarships/grants available. Financial award applicants required to submit FAFSA. *Faculty research:* Community health, international health, effectiveness of the nursing school environment, development of caring ability in nursing students, international nursing students. *Unit head:* Ann Hershberger, Coordinator, 540-432-4192, E-mail: hershbea@emu.edu. *Application contact:* Don A. Yoder, Director of Seminary and Graduate Admissions, 540-432-4257, Fax: 540-432-4598, E-mail: yoderda@emu.edu.

Eastern University, Department of Nursing, St. Davids, PA 19087-3696. Offers nursing (MSN); school health services (M Ed); school health supervisor (K-12) (Certificate); school nurse (K-12) (Certificate). *Students:* 1 (woman) full-time, 41 part-time (40 women); includes 5 minority (4 Black or African American, non-Hispanic/Latino; 1 Asian, non-Hispanic/Latino). Average age 43. In 2017, 8 master's awarded. *Application deadline:* Applications are processed on a rolling basis. Application fee: $35. Electronic applications accepted. Application fee is waived when completed online. *Expenses:* Contact institution. *Unit head:* Michael Dziedziak, Executive Director of Enrollment, 800-452-0996, E-mail: gpsadmissions@eastern.edu.
Website: https://www.eastern.edu/academics/programs/department-nursing-adult-undergraduate-graduate

La Salle University, School of Nursing and Health Sciences, Program in Nursing, Philadelphia, PA 19141-1199. Offers adult gerontology primary care nurse practitioner (MSN, Certificate); adult health and illness clinical nurse specialist (MSN); adult-gerontology clinical nurse specialist (MSN, Certificate); clinical nurse leader (MSN); family primary care nurse practitioner (MSN, Certificate); gerontology (Certificate); nurse anesthetist (MSN, Certificate); nursing (MSN, Certificate); nursing administration (MSN, Certificate); nursing education (Certificate); nursing practice (DNP); nursing service administration (MSN); public health nursing (MSN, Certificate); school nursing (Certificate); MSN/MBA; MSN/MPH. *Accreditation:* AACN. *Program availability:* Part-time, evening/weekend, 100% online. *Faculty:* 12 full-time (11 women), 14 part-time/adjunct (11 women). *Students:* 1 (woman) full-time, 277 part-time (220 women); includes 72 minority (36 Black or African American, non-Hispanic/Latino; 1 American Indian or Alaska Native, non-Hispanic/Latino; 18 Asian, non-Hispanic/Latino; 10 Hispanic/Latino; 1 Native Hawaiian or other Pacific Islander, non-Hispanic/Latino; 6 Two or more races, non-Hispanic/Latino), 1 international. Average age 36. 70 applicants, 56% accepted, 24 enrolled. In 2017, 81 master's, 4 doctorates, 13 other advanced degrees awarded. *Degree requirements:* For doctorate, minimum of 1,000 hours of post baccalaureate clinical practice supervised by preceptors. *Entrance requirements:* For master's, GRE, MAT, or GMAT (for students with BSN GPA of less than 3.2), baccalaureate degree in nursing from ACEN- or CCNE-accredited program or an MSN Bridge program; Pennsylvania RN license; 2 letters of reference; resume; statement of philosophy articulating professional values and future educational goal; 1 year of work experience as a registered nurse; for doctorate, GRE (waived for applicants with MSN cumulative GPA of 3.7 or above), MSN, master's degree, MBA or MHA from nationally-accredited program; resume or curriculum vitae; 2 letters of reference; interview; for Certificate, GRE, MAT, or GMAT (for students with BSN GPA of less than 3.2, baccalaureate degree in nursing from ACEN- or CCNE-accredited program or an MSN Bridge program; Pennsylvania RN license; 2 letters of reference; resume; statement of philosophy articulating professional values and future educational goal; 1 year of work experience as a registered nurse. Additional exam requirements/recommendations for international students: Required—TOEFL. *Application deadline:* For fall admission, 8/15 priority date for domestic students, 7/15 for international students; for spring admission, 12/15 priority date for domestic students, 11/15 for international students; for summer admission, 4/15 priority date for domestic students, 3/15 for international students. Applications are processed on a rolling basis. Application fee: $35. Electronic applications accepted. Application fee is waived when completed online. *Expenses:* Contact institution. *Financial support:* In 2017–18, 7 students received support. Scholarships/grants and traineeships available. Support available to part-time students. Financial award application deadline: 8/31; financial award applicants required to submit FAFSA. *Unit head:* Dr. Patricia M. Dillon, Director, 215-951-1322, Fax: 215-951-1896, E-mail: msnapn@lasalle.edu. *Application contact:* Elizabeth Heenan, Director, Graduate and Adult Enrollment, 215-951-1100, Fax: 215-951-1462, E-mail: heenan@lasalle.edu.
Website: http://www.lasalle.edu/nursing/program-options/

Lewis University, College of Nursing and Health Professions, Program in Nursing, Romeoville, IL 60446. Offers adult gerontology acute care nurse practitioner (MSN); adult gerontology clinical nurse specialist (MSN); adult gerontology primary care nurse practitioner (MSN); family nurse practitioner (MSN); healthcare systems leadership (MSN); nursing (DNP); nursing education (MSN); school nurse (MSN). *Accreditation:* AACN. *Program availability:* Part-time, evening/weekend, 100% online, blended/hybrid learning. *Students:* 14 full-time (11 women), 361 part-time (336 women); includes 100 minority (27 Black or African American, non-Hispanic/Latino; 33 Asian, non-Hispanic/

Latino; 35 Hispanic/Latino; 5 Two or more races, non-Hispanic/Latino), 1 international. Average age 37. *Degree requirements:* For master's, clinical practicum. *Entrance requirements:* For master's, minimum undergraduate GPA of 3.0, degree in nursing, RN license, letter of recommendation, interview, resume or curriculum vitae. Additional exam requirements/recommendations for international students: Required—TOEFL (minimum score 550 paper-based; 80 iBT). *Application deadline:* For fall admission, 5/1 priority date for international students; for spring admission, 11/15 priority date for international students. Applications are processed on a rolling basis. Application fee: $40. Electronic applications accepted. Tuition and fees vary according to program. *Financial support:* Federal Work-Study, scholarships/grants, tuition waivers (full and partial), and unspecified assistantships available. Financial award application deadline: 5/1; financial award applicants required to submit FAFSA. *Faculty research:* Cancer prevention, phenomenological methods, public policy analysis. *Total annual research expenditures:* $1,000. *Unit head:* 815-836-5610. *Application contact:* Nancy Wiksten, Adult Admission Counselor, 815-836-5628, Fax: 815-836-5578, E-mail: wikstena@lewisu.edu.

Monmouth University, Graduate Studies, Marjorie K. Unterberg School of Nursing and Health Studies, West Long Branch, NJ 07764-1898. Offers adult-gerontological primary care nurse practitioner (MSN, Post-Master's Certificate); family nurse practitioner (MSN, Post-Master's Certificate); forensic nursing (MSN, Certificate); nursing (MSN); nursing administration (MSN); nursing education (MSN, Post-Master's Certificate); nursing practice (DNP); physician assistant (MS); psychiatric and mental health nurse practitioner (MSN, Post-Master's Certificate); school nursing (MSN, Certificate). *Accreditation:* AACN. *Program availability:* Part-time, evening/weekend, 100% online, blended/hybrid learning. *Faculty:* 12 full-time (all women), 20 part-time/adjunct (12 women). *Students:* 90 full-time (66 women), 329 part-time (302 women); includes 129 minority (51 Black or African American, non-Hispanic/Latino; 43 Asian, non-Hispanic/Latino; 31 Hispanic/Latino; 1 Native Hawaiian or other Pacific Islander, non-Hispanic/Latino; 3 Two or more races, non-Hispanic/Latino), 1 international. Average age 36. In 2017, 85 master's, 4 other advanced degrees awarded. *Degree requirements:* For master's, practicum (for some tracks); for doctorate, practicum, capstone course. *Entrance requirements:* For master's, GRE General Test (waived for MSN applicants with minimum B grade in each of the first four courses and for MS applicants with master's degree), BSN with minimum GPA of 2.75, current RN license, proof of liability and malpractice policy, personal statement, two letters of recommendation, college course work in health assessment, resume; CASPA application (for MS); for doctorate, accredited master's nursing program degree with minimum GPA of 3.2, active RN license, national certification as nurse practitioner or nurse administrator, working knowledge of statistics, statement of goals and vision for change, 2 letters of recommendation (professional or academic), resume, interview. Additional exam requirements/recommendations for international students: Required—TOEFL (minimum score 550 paper-based; 79 iBT), IELTS (minimum score 6) or Michigan English Language Assessment Battery (minimum score 77). *Application deadline:* For fall admission, 7/15 priority date for domestic students, 6/1 for international students; for spring admission, 12/1 priority date for domestic students, 11/1 for international students; for summer admission, 5/1 for domestic students. Applications are processed on a rolling basis. Application fee: $50. Electronic applications accepted. *Expenses:* Contact institution. *Financial support:* In 2017–18, 197 students received support. Institutionally sponsored loans, scholarships/grants, and unspecified assistantships available. Support available to part-time students. Financial award applicants required to submit FAFSA. *Faculty research:* School nursing, health policy, and smoking cessation in teens; Multiple Sclerosis; adherence and self-efficacy; aging issues and geriatric care. *Unit head:* Dr. Janet Mahoney, Dean, 732-571-3443, Fax: 732-263-5131, E-mail: jmahoney@monmouth.edu. *Application contact:* Lucia Fedele, Graduate Admission Counselor, 732-571-3452, Fax: 732-263-5123, E-mail: gradadm@monmouth.edu. Website: https://www.monmouth.edu/graduate/nursing-programs-of-study/

Rowan University, Graduate School, College of Education, Department of Educational Services and Leadership, Glassboro, NJ 08028-1701. Offers counseling in educational settings (MA); educational leadership (Ed D, CAGS); higher education administration (MA); principal preparation (CAGS); school administration (MA); school and public librarianship (MA); school nursing (Postbaccalaureate Certificate); school psychology (MA, Ed S); supervisor (CAGS). *Accreditation:* NCATE. *Program availability:* Part-time, evening/weekend. *Degree requirements:* For master's, comprehensive exam, thesis; for other advanced degree, thesis or alternative. *Entrance requirements:* For master's and other advanced degree, GRE General Test. Additional exam requirements/recommendations for international students: Required—TOEFL. Electronic applications accepted. *Expenses:* Tuition, state resident: full-time $15,020; part-time $751 per semester hour. Tuition, nonresident: full-time $15,020; part-time $751 per semester hour. *Required fees:* $3158; $157.90 per semester hour. Tuition and fees vary according to course load, campus/location and program.

Seton Hall University, College of Nursing, South Orange, NJ 07079-2697. Offers advanced practice in primary health care (MSN, DNP), including adult/gerontological nurse practitioner, pediatric nurse practitioner; entry into practice (MSN); health systems administration (MSN, DNP); nursing (PhD); nursing case management (MSN); nursing education (MA); school nurse (MSN); MSN/MA. *Accreditation:* AACN. *Program availability:* Part-time, online learning. *Degree requirements:* For master's, research project; for doctorate, dissertation or scholarly project. *Entrance requirements:* For doctorate, GRE (waived for students with GPA of 3.5 or higher). Additional exam requirements/recommendations for international students: Required—TOEFL. Electronic applications accepted. *Faculty research:* Parent/child, adult, and gerontological nursing; breast cancer; families of children with HIV; parish nursing.

University of Illinois at Chicago, College of Nursing, Program in Nursing, Chicago, IL 60607-7128. Offers acute care clinical nurse specialist (MS); administrative nursing leadership (Certificate); adult nurse practitioner (MS); adult/geriatric nurse practitioner (MS); advanced community health nurse specialist (MS); family nurse practitioner (MS); geriatric clinical nurse specialist (MS); geriatric nurse practitioner (MS); nurse midwifery (MS); occupational health/advanced community health nurse specialist (MS); occupational health/family nurse practitioner (MS); pediatric nurse practitioner (MS); perinatal clinical nurse specialist (MS); school/advanced community health nurse specialist (MS); school/family nurse practitioner (MS); women's health nurse practitioner (MS). *Accreditation:* AACN. *Program availability:* Part-time. *Degree requirements:* For master's, thesis or alternative. *Entrance requirements:* For master's, GRE General Test, minimum GPA of 2.75. Additional exam requirements/recommendations for international students: Required—TOEFL. Electronic applications accepted.

West Chester University of Pennsylvania, College of Health Sciences, Department of Nursing, West Chester, PA 19383. Offers adult-gerontology clinical nurse specialist (MSN); nursing (DNP); nursing education (MSN); school nurse (Certificate). *Accreditation:* AACN. *Program availability:* Part-time, evening/weekend, 2-day on-campus residency requirement (for DNP). *Students:* 1 full-time (0 women), 102 part-time (94 women); includes 16 minority (12 Black or African American, non-Hispanic/Latino; 1 Asian, non-Hispanic/Latino; 2 Hispanic/Latino; 1 Two or more races, non-Hispanic/Latino). Average age 42. 57 applicants, 82% accepted, 38 enrolled. In 2017, 1 master's, 21 doctorates, 9 other advanced degrees awarded. *Entrance requirements:* For master's, goals statement; official academic transcript(s) from all colleges and universities attended, demonstrating minimum cumulative undergraduate GPA of 2.8, with successful completion of BSN and courses in statistics and physical assessment; documentation of current clinical experience and current RN; for doctorate, master's degree in nursing in an advanced nursing specialty, minimum master's GPA of 3.0, licensed Registered Nurse in state of practice, prerequisite graduate-level research course and statistics course, two letters of reference, telephone or in-person interview with program coordinator. Additional exam requirements/recommendations for international students: Required—TOEFL or IELTS. *Application deadline:* For fall admission, 5/15 for international students; for spring admission, 10/15 for international students. Applications are processed on a rolling basis. Application fee: $50. Electronic applications accepted. *Expenses:* Tuition, state resident: full-time $9000; part-time $500 per credit. Tuition, nonresident: full-time $13,500; part-time $750 per credit. *Required fees:* $2959; $149.79 per credit. *Financial support:* Scholarships/grants and unspecified assistantships available. Financial award application deadline: 2/15; financial award applicants required to submit FAFSA. *Unit head:* Dr. Megan Infanti Mraz, Chair, 610-436-2219, Fax: 610-436-3083, E-mail: mmraz@wcupa.edu. *Application contact:* Dr. Cheryl Schlamb, Graduate Coordinator, 610-436-2219, E-mail: cschlamb@wcupa.edu. Website: http://www.wcupa.edu/healthsciences/nursing/

William Paterson University of New Jersey, College of Science and Health, Wayne, NJ 07470-8420. Offers adult gerontology nurse practitioner (Certificate); biology (MS); biotechnology (MS); communication disorders (MS); exercise and sport studies (MS); materials chemistry (MS); nurse practitioner (Certificate); nursing (MSN); nursing education (Certificate); nursing practice (DNP); school nurse (Certificate). *Program availability:* Part-time. *Faculty:* 29 full-time (15 women), 25 part-time/adjunct (24 women). *Students:* 66 full-time (56 women), 197 part-time (163 women); includes 104 minority (15 Black or African American, non-Hispanic/Latino; 45 Asian, non-Hispanic/Latino; 38 Hispanic/Latino; 6 Two or more races, non-Hispanic/Latino), 3 international. Average age 33. 387 applicants, 34% accepted, 77 enrolled. In 2017, 87 master's, 5 doctorates awarded. *Degree requirements:* For master's, comprehensive exam (for some programs), thesis (for some programs), non-thesis internship/practicum (for some programs). *Entrance requirements:* For master's, GRE/MAT, minimum GPA of 3.0; 2-3 letters of recommendation; personal statement; work experience (for some programs); for doctorate, GRE/MAT, minimum GPA of 3.3; work experience; 3 letters of recommendation; interview; master's degree in nursing. Additional exam requirements/recommendations for international students: Required—TOEFL (minimum score 550 paper-based; 79 iBT), IELTS (minimum score 6). *Application deadline:* For fall admission, 6/1 for domestic students, 3/1 for international students; for spring admission, 11/1 for domestic students, 10/1 for international students. Applications are processed on a rolling basis. Application fee: $50. Electronic applications accepted. *Expenses:* Tuition, state resident: full-time $13,920; part-time $6264 per year. Tuition, nonresident: full-time $21,700; part-time $9765 per year. *Required fees:* $80; $36 per year. Tuition and fees vary according to course load, degree level and program. *Financial support:* In 2017–18, 9,800 students received support. Career-related internships or fieldwork, Federal Work-Study, scholarships/grants, and unspecified assistantships available. Support available to part-time students. Financial award application deadline: 3/15; financial award applicants required to submit FAFSA. *Faculty research:* Behaviors of American long-eared bats, postpartum fatigue, methodologies for coating carbon nano-tubes, paleoclimatology, and pre-linguistic gestures in children with language disorders. *Total annual research expenditures:* $291,600. *Unit head:* Dr. Venkat Sharma, Dean, 973-720-2194, Fax: 973-720-3414, E-mail: sharmav@wpunj.edu. *Application contact:* Christina Aiello, Assistant Director, Graduate Admissions, 973-720-2506, Fax: 973-720-2035, E-mail: aielloc@wpunj.edu. Website: http://www.wpunj.edu/cosh

Wright State University, Graduate School, College of Nursing and Health, Program in Nursing, Dayton, OH 45435. Offers administration of nursing and health care systems (MS); adult gerontology clinical nurse specialist (MS); adult-gerontology acute care nurse practitioner (MS); family nurse practitioner (MS); neonatal nurse practitioner (MS); pediatric nurse practitioner-acute care (MS); pediatric nurse practitioner-primary care (MS); psychiatric mental health nurse practitioner (MS); school nurse (MS). *Accreditation:* AACN. *Program availability:* Part-time, evening/weekend. *Degree requirements:* For master's, thesis or alternative. *Entrance requirements:* For master's, GRE General Test, BSN from ACEN-accredited college, Ohio RN license. Additional exam requirements/recommendations for international students: Required—TOEFL. *Faculty research:* Clinical nursing and health, teaching, caring, pain administration, informatics and technology.

Transcultural Nursing

Augsburg University, Programs in Nursing, Minneapolis, MN 55454-1351. Offers MA, DNP. *Accreditation:* AACN. *Degree requirements:* For master's, thesis or alternative.

Rutgers University–Newark, Rutgers School of Nursing, Newark, NJ 07107-3001. Offers adult health (MSN); adult occupational health (MSN); advanced practice nursing (MSN, Post Master's Certificate); family nurse practitioner (MSN); nurse anesthesia (MSN); nursing (MSN); nursing informatics (MSN); urban health (PhD); women's health practitioner (MSN). *Accreditation:* AANA/CANAEP. *Program availability:* Part-time. *Entrance requirements:* For master's, GRE, RN license; basic life support, statistics, and health assessment experience. Additional exam requirements/recommendations for international students: Required—TOEFL. Electronic applications accepted. *Expenses:* Contact institution. *Faculty research:* HIV/AIDS, diabetes education, learned helplessness, nursing science, psychoeducation.

Women's Health Nursing

Boston College, William F. Connell School of Nursing, Chestnut Hill, MA 02467. Offers adult-gerontology primary care nurse practitioner (MS); family health nursing (MS); nurse anesthesia (MS); nursing (PhD); pediatric primary care nurse practitioner (MS), including pediatric and women's health; psychiatric-mental health nursing (MS); women's health nursing (MS); MBA/MS; MS/MA; MS/PhD. MS/MBA offered jointly with Carroll School of Management, MS/MA with School of Theology and Ministry. *Accreditation:* AACN; AANA/CANAEP (one or more programs are accredited). *Program availability:* Part-time. *Faculty:* 54 full-time (48 women). *Students:* 170 full-time (153 women), 90 part-time (83 women); includes 39 minority (8 Black or African American, non-Hispanic/Latino; 10 Asian, non-Hispanic/Latino; 12 Hispanic/Latino; 9 Two or more races, non-Hispanic/Latino), 3 international. Average age 28. 360 applicants, 56% accepted, 94 enrolled. In 2017, 104 master's, 5 doctorates awarded. *Degree requirements:* For master's, comprehensive exam; for doctorate, comprehensive exam, thesis/dissertation, computer literacy exam or foreign language. *Entrance requirements:* For master's, bachelor's degree in nursing; for doctorate, GRE General Test, MS in nursing. Additional exam requirements/recommendations for international students: Required—TOEFL (minimum score 600 paper-based; 100 iBT), IELTS (minimum score 7.5). *Application deadline:* For fall admission, 9/30 for domestic and international students; for winter admission, 1/15 for domestic and international students; for spring admission, 3/15 for domestic and international students. Application fee: $40. Electronic applications accepted. *Expenses:* $1,350 per credit tuition. *Financial support:* In 2017–18, 152 students received support, including 11 fellowships with full tuition reimbursements available (averaging $24,504 per year), 29 teaching assistantships (averaging $3,768 per year); scholarships/grants, health care benefits, tuition waivers (partial), and unspecified assistantships also available. Support available to part-time students. Financial award application deadline: 4/18; financial award applicants required to submit FAFSA. *Faculty research:* Sexual and reproductive health, health promotion/illness prevention, aging, eating disorders, symptom management. *Total annual research expenditures:* $879,812. *Unit head:* Dr. Susan Gennaro, Dean, 617-552-4251, Fax: 617-552-0931, E-mail: susan.gennaro@bc.edu. *Application contact:* Sean Sendall, Assistant Dean, Graduate Enrollment and Data Analytics, 617-552-4745, Fax: 617-552-2121, E-mail: sean.sendall@bc.edu.
Website: http://www.bc.edu/cson

California State University, Fullerton, Graduate Studies, College of Health and Human Development, School of Nursing, Fullerton, CA 92831-3599. Offers leadership (MS); nurse anesthesia (MS); nurse educator (MS); nursing (DNP); school nursing (MS); women's health care (MS). *Accreditation:* AACN. *Program availability:* Part-time. *Faculty:* 27 full-time (23 women), 11 part-time/adjunct (all women). *Students:* 136 full-time (107 women), 116 part-time (96 women); includes 142 minority (9 Black or African American, non-Hispanic/Latino; 81 Asian, non-Hispanic/Latino; 37 Hispanic/Latino; 1 Native Hawaiian or other Pacific Islander, non-Hispanic/Latino; 14 Two or more races, non-Hispanic/Latino), 2 international. Average age 36. 235 applicants, 59% accepted, 117 enrolled. Application fee: $55. *Financial support:* Career-related internships or fieldwork, Federal Work-Study, institutionally sponsored loans, scholarships/grants, and traineeships available. Support available to part-time students. Financial award application deadline: 3/1; financial award applicants required to submit FAFSA. *Unit head:* Dr. Cindy Greenberg, Chair, 657-278-3336. *Application contact:* Admissions/Applications, 657-278-2371.
Website: http://nursing.fullerton.edu/

Carlow University, College of Health and Wellness, Program in Women's Health Nurse Practitioner, Pittsburgh, PA 15213-3165. Offers MSN, Certificate. *Program availability:* Part-time, evening/weekend. *Students:* 6 full-time (all women), 1 (woman) part-time. Average age 33. 9 applicants, 100% accepted, 7 enrolled. *Entrance requirements:* For master's, minimum undergraduate GPA of 3.0 from accredited BSN program; current license as RN in Pennsylvania; course in statistics with minimum C grade in past 6 years; two recommendations; personal statement; personal interview. Additional exam requirements/recommendations for international students: Required—TOEFL (minimum score 550 paper-based). *Application deadline:* Applications are processed on a rolling basis. *Expenses: Tuition:* Full-time $12,103; part-time $825 per credit hour. Tuition and fees vary according to program. *Financial support:* Application deadline: 4/1; applicants required to submit FAFSA. *Unit head:* Dr. Lynn George, Dean, Fax: 412-578-6114. *Application contact:* E-mail: gradstudies@carlow.edu.
Website: http://www.carlow.edu/Master_of_Science_in_Nursing_Womens_Health_Nurse_Practitioner.aspx

Case Western Reserve University, Frances Payne Bolton School of Nursing, Master's Programs in Nursing, Nurse Practitioner Program, Cleveland, OH 44106. Offers acute care pediatric nurse practitioner (MSN); acute care/cardiovascular nursing (MSN); acute care/flight nurse (MSN); adult gerontology acute care nurse practitioner (MSN); adult gerontology primary care nurse practitioner (MSN); family nurse practitioner (MSN); family systems psychiatric mental health nursing (MSN); neonatal nurse practitioner (MSN); palliative care (MSN); pediatric nurse practitioner (MSN); women's health nurse practitioner (MSN). *Accreditation:* ACEN. *Program availability:* Part-time. *Faculty:* 30 full-time (26 women), 5 part-time/adjunct (3 women). *Students:* 34 full-time (28 women), 97 part-time (73 women); includes 24 minority (5 Black or African American, non-Hispanic/Latino; 9 Asian, non-Hispanic/Latino; 6 Hispanic/Latino; 4 Two or more races, non-Hispanic/Latino), 4 international. Average age 33. 56 applicants, 82% accepted, 29 enrolled. In 2017, 68 master's awarded. *Degree requirements:* For master's, minimum GPA of 3.0, clinical hours corresponding to requirements to sit for certification exam, portfolio. *Entrance requirements:* For master's, GRE General Test or MAT. Additional exam requirements/recommendations for international students: Required—TOEFL (minimum score 577 paper-based; 90 iBT), IELTS (minimum score 7). *Application deadline:* For fall admission, 5/1 for domestic and international students; for spring admission, 10/1 for domestic and international students; for summer admission, 3/1 for domestic and international students. Applications are processed on a rolling basis. Application fee: $75. Electronic applications accepted. *Expenses:* $2,011 per credit tuition; $15 nursing activity fee; $17 activity fee. *Financial support:* In 2017–18, 86 students received support, including 19 teaching assistantships with partial tuition reimbursements available (averaging $18,100 per year); scholarships/grants and traineeships also available. Support available to part-time students. Financial award application deadline: 5/15; financial award applicants required to submit FAFSA. *Faculty research:* Symptom science, family/community care, aging across the lifespan, self-management of health and illness, neuroscience. *Unit head:* Dr. Latina Brooks, Director, 216-368-1196, Fax: 216-368-3542, E-mail: lmb3@case.edu. *Application contact:* Jackie Tepale, Admissions Coordinator, 216-368-5253, Fax: 216-368-0124, E-mail: yyd@case.edu.
Website: http://fpb.cwru.edu/MSN/majors.shtm

Drexel University, College of Nursing and Health Professions, Division of Graduate Nursing, Philadelphia, PA 19104-2875. Offers adult acute care (MSN); adult psychiatric/mental health (MSN); advanced practice nursing (MSN); clinical trials research (MSN); family nurse practitioner (MSN); leadership in health systems management (MSN); nursing education (MSN); pediatric primary care (MSN); women's health (MSN). *Accreditation:* AACN. Electronic applications accepted.

Duke University, School of Nursing, Durham, NC 27708-0586. Offers acute care pediatric nurse practitioner (MSN, Post-Graduate Certificate); adult-gerontology nurse practitioner (MSN, Post-Graduate Certificate), including acute care, primary care; family nurse practitioner (MSN, Post-Graduate Certificate); neonatal nurse practitioner (MSN, Post-Graduate Certificate); nurse anesthesia (DNP); nurse practitioner (DNP); nursing (PhD); nursing and health care leadership (MSN, Post-Graduate Certificate); nursing education (MSN, Post-Graduate Certificate); nursing informatics (MSN, Post-Graduate Certificate); pediatric nurse practitioner (MSN, Post-Graduate Certificate), including primary care; psychiatric mental health nurse practitioner (MSN, Post-Graduate Certificate); women's health nurse practitioner (MSN, Post-Graduate Certificate). *Accreditation:* AACN; AANA/CANAEP. *Program availability:* Part-time, evening/weekend, online with on-campus intensives. *Faculty:* 72 full-time (61 women). *Students:* 155 full-time (137 women), 613 part-time (548 women); includes 177 minority (64 Black or African American, non-Hispanic/Latino; 2 American Indian or Alaska Native, non-Hispanic/Latino; 47 Asian, non-Hispanic/Latino; 34 Hispanic/Latino; 30 Two or more races, non-Hispanic/Latino), 10 international. Average age 34. 631 applicants, 47% accepted, 211 enrolled. In 2017, 221 master's, 71 doctorates, 26 other advanced degrees awarded. Terminal master's awarded for partial completion of doctoral program. *Degree requirements:* For master's, thesis optional; for doctorate, capstone project. *Entrance requirements:* For master's, GRE General Test (waived if undergraduate GPA of 3.4 or higher), 1 year of nursing experience (recommended), BSN, minimum GPA of 3.0, previous course work in statistics; for doctorate, GRE General Test (waived if undergraduate GPA of 3.4 or higher), BSN or MSN, minimum GPA of 3.0, resume, personal statement, undergraduate statistics course, current licensure as a registered nurse, transcripts from all post-secondary institutions; for Post-Graduate Certificate, MSN, licensure or eligibility as a professional nurse, transcripts from all post-secondary institutions, previous course work in statistics. Additional exam requirements/recommendations for international students: Required—TOEFL (minimum score 100 iBT), IELTS (minimum score 7). *Application deadline:* For fall admission, 12/1 for domestic and international students; for spring admission, 5/1 for domestic and international students. Application fee: $50. Electronic applications accepted. *Expenses:* Contact institution. *Financial support:* Institutionally sponsored loans, scholarships/grants, and traineeships available. Support available to part-time students. Financial award applicants required to submit FAFSA. *Faculty research:* Cardiovascular disease, caregiver skill training, data mining, prostate cancer, neonatal immune system. *Unit head:* Dr. Marion E. Broome, Dean/Vice Chancellor for Nursing Affairs/Associate Vice President for Academic Affairs for Nursing, 919-684-9446, Fax: 919-684-9414, E-mail: marion.broome@duke.edu. *Application contact:* Dr. Ernie Rushing, Director of Admissions and Recruitment, 919-668-6274, Fax: 919-668-4693, E-mail: ernie.rushing@dm.duke.edu.
Website: http://www.nursing.duke.edu/

East Tennessee State University, School of Graduate Studies, College of Nursing, Johnson City, TN 37614. Offers acute care nurse practitioner (DNP); adult-gerontology primary care nurse practitioner (DNP); adult/gerontological nurse practitioner (Postbaccalaureate Certificate); executive leadership in nursing (DNP, Postbaccalaureate Certificate); family nurse practitioner (MSN, DNP, Post-Master's Certificate, Postbaccalaureate Certificate); nursing (PhD); nursing administration (MSN); nursing education (MSN); pediatric primary care nurse practitioner (DNP); psychiatric mental health nurse practitioner (Postbaccalaureate Certificate); psychiatric/mental health nurse practitioner (MSN, DNP, Post-Master's Certificate); women's health care nurse practitioner (DNP). *Accreditation:* AACN. *Program availability:* Part-time, evening/weekend, online learning. In 2017, 126 master's, 30 doctorates, 4 other advanced degrees awarded. *Degree requirements:* For master's and other advanced degree, comprehensive exam, practicum; for doctorate, comprehensive exam, thesis/dissertation (for some programs), practicum, internship, evidence of professional malpractice insurance, CPR certification. *Entrance requirements:* For master's, bachelor's degree, minimum GPA of 3.0, current RN license and eligibility to practice, resume, three letters of recommendation; for doctorate, GRE General Test, MSN (for PhD), BSN or MSN (for DNP), current RN license and eligibility to practice, 2 years of full-time registered nurse work experience or equivalent, three letters of recommendation, resume or curriculum vitae, interview, writing sample; for other advanced degree, MSN, minimum GPA of 3.0, current RN license and eligibility to practice, three letters of recommendation, resume or curriculum vitae; DNP with designated concentration in advanced clinical practice or nursing administration (for select programs). Additional exam requirements/recommendations for international students: Required—TOEFL (minimum score 600 paper-based; 79 iBT). *Application deadline:* For fall admission, 4/15 priority date for domestic and international students; for spring admission, 10/15 priority date for domestic and international students; for summer admission, 2/1 for domestic and international students. Application fee: $55 ($65 for international students). Electronic applications accepted. *Financial support:* Research assistantships with tuition reimbursements, teaching assistantships, career-related internships or fieldwork, institutionally sponsored loans, scholarships/grants, and unspecified assistantships available. Financial award application deadline: 7/1; financial award applicants required to submit FAFSA. *Faculty research:* Improving health of rural and underserved populations (low income elders living in public housing, rural caregivers, Hispanic populations), health services and systems research (quality outcomes of nurse-managed primary care, in-home, and rural health care), nursing education (experiences of second-degree BSN students, well-being of BSN students). *Unit head:* Dr. Wendy Nehring, Dean, 423-439-7051, Fax: 423-439-4543, E-mail: nursing@etsu.edu. *Application contact:* Dr. Myra Clark, Director of Graduate Programs, 423-439-4396, Fax: 423-439-4100, E-mail: clarkml2@etsu.edu.
Website: http://www.etsu.edu/nursing/

Emory University, Nell Hodgson Woodruff School of Nursing, Atlanta, GA 30322-1100. Offers adult nurse practitioner (MSN); emergency nurse practitioner (MSN); family nurse practitioner (MSN); family nurse-midwife (MSN); health systems leadership (MSN); nurse-midwifery (MSN); pediatric nurse practitioner acute and primary care (MSN); women's health care (Title X) (MSN); women's health nurse practitioner (MSN); MSN/MPH. *Accreditation:* AACN; ACNM/ACME (one or more programs are accredited). *Program availability:* Part-time. *Entrance requirements:* For master's, GRE General Test or MAT, minimum GPA of 3.0, BS in nursing from an accredited institution, RN license and additional course work, 3 letters of recommendation. Additional exam requirements/

recommendations for international students: Required—TOEFL (minimum score 600 paper-based; 100 iBT). Electronic applications accepted. *Expenses:* Contact institution. *Faculty research:* Older adult falls and injuries, minority health issues, cardiac symptoms and quality of life, bio-ethics and decision-making, menopausal issues.

Frontier Nursing University, Graduate Programs, Hyden, KY 41749. Offers family nurse practitioner (MSN, DNP, Post Master's Certificate); nurse-midwifery (MSN, DNP, Post Master's Certificate); psychiatric-mental health nurse practitioner (MSN, DNP, Post Master's Certificate); women's health care nurse practitioner (MSN, DNP, Post Master's Certificate). *Accreditation:* ACEN. *Degree requirements:* For doctorate, capstone project, practicum.

See Display on page 570 and Close-Up on page 761.

Georgia State University, Byrdine F. Lewis School of Nursing, Atlanta, GA 30303. Offers adult health clinical nurse specialist/nurse practitioner (MS, Certificate); child health clinical nurse specialist/pediatric nurse practitioner (MS, Certificate); family nurse practitioner (MS, Certificate); family psychiatric mental health nurse practitioner (MS, Certificate); nursing (PhD); nursing leadership in healthcare innovations (MS), including nursing administration, nursing informatics; nutrition (MS); perinatal clinical nurse specialist/women's health nurse practitioner (MS, Certificate); physical therapy (DPT); respiratory therapy (MS). *Accreditation:* AACN. *Program availability:* Part-time, blended/hybrid learning. *Faculty:* 69 full-time (52 women). *Students:* 322 full-time (248 women), 481 part-time (466 women); includes 186 minority (112 Black or African American, non-Hispanic/Latino; 44 Asian, non-Hispanic/Latino; 20 Hispanic/Latino; 10 Two or more races, non-Hispanic/Latino), 18 international. Average age 31. 370 applicants, 56% accepted, 148 enrolled. In 2017, 131 master's, 49 doctorates, 11 other advanced degrees awarded. *Degree requirements:* For doctorate, comprehensive exam, thesis/dissertation. *Entrance requirements:* For doctorate, GRE. Additional exam requirements/recommendations for international students: Required—TOEFL. *Application deadline:* For fall admission, 2/1 priority date for domestic and international students; for spring admission, 9/15 for domestic and international students. Applications are processed on a rolling basis. Application fee: $50. Electronic applications accepted. *Expenses:* Contact institution. *Financial support:* In 2017–18, research assistantships with tuition reimbursements (averaging $1,666 per year), teaching assistantships with tuition reimbursements (averaging $1,920 per year) were awarded; scholarships/grants, tuition waivers (full and partial), and unspecified assistantships also available. Support available to part-time students. Financial award application deadline: 8/1; financial award applicants required to submit FAFSA. *Faculty research:* Stroke intervention for caregivers, stroke prevention in African-Americans; relationships between psychological distress and health outcomes in parents with a medically ill infant; medically fragile children; nursing expertise and patient outcomes. *Unit head:* Nancy Kropf, Dean of Nursing, 404-413-1101, Fax: 404-413-1090, E-mail: nkropf@gsu.edu.
Website: http://nursing.gsu.edu/

Loyola University Chicago, Graduate School, Marcella Niehoff School of Nursing, Maywood, IL 60141. Offers adult clinical nurse specialist (MSN, Certificate); adult nurse practitioner (Certificate); dietetics (MS); family nurse practitioner (Certificate); family, adult, and women's health nurse practitioner (MSN); health systems leadership (MSN); healthcare quality using education in safety and technology (DNP); infection prevention (MSN, DNP); nursing science (PhD); women's health clinical nurse specialist (Certificate). *Accreditation:* AACN. *Program availability:* Part-time, blended/hybrid learning. *Faculty:* 24 full-time (22 women), 21 part-time/adjunct (19 women). *Students:* 188 full-time (178 women), 222 part-time (208 women); includes 105 minority (23 Black or African American, non-Hispanic/Latino; 40 Asian, non-Hispanic/Latino; 30 Hispanic/Latino; 2 Native Hawaiian or other Pacific Islander, non-Hispanic/Latino; 10 Two or more races, non-Hispanic/Latino), 4 international. Average age 36. 197 applicants, 55% accepted, 80 enrolled. In 2017, 94 master's, 17 doctorates, 26 other advanced degrees awarded. *Degree requirements:* For master's, comprehensive exam; for doctorate, thesis/dissertation, qualifying examination (for PhD); capstone project (for DNP). *Entrance requirements:* For master's, BSN, minimum nursing GPA of 3.0, Illinois RN license, 3 letters of recommendation, 1000 hours of experience in area of specialty prior to starting clinical rotations, personal statement; for doctorate, BSN or MSN, minimum GPA of 3.0, professional nursing license, 3 letters of recommendation, personal statement. Additional exam requirements/recommendations for international students: Required—TOEFL (minimum score 550 paper-based; 79 iBT), IELTS (minimum score 6.5). *Application deadline:* For fall admission, 6/1 priority date for domestic and international students; for spring admission, 11/15 priority date for domestic and international students; for summer admission, 3/15 priority date for domestic and international students. Applications are processed on a rolling basis. Application fee: $50. Electronic applications accepted. Application fee is waived when completed online. *Expenses:* Contact institution. *Financial support:* In 2017–18, 10 students received support, including 3 research assistantships with full tuition reimbursements available (averaging $18,000 per year), 1 teaching assistantship with full tuition reimbursement available (averaging $18,000 per year); scholarships/grants, unspecified assistantships, and nurse faculty loan program also available. Financial award application deadline: 5/1; financial award applicants required to submit FAFSA. *Faculty research:* Epigenetics and social determinants of health; women's health; vitamin D; health equity; interprofessional education; prevention and self-management of chronic disease; body mass in oncology patients. *Total annual research expenditures:* $1.4 million. *Unit head:* Dr. Vickie Keough, Dean, 708-216-5448, Fax: 708-216-9555, E-mail: vkeough@luc.edu. *Application contact:* Toni Topalova, Enrollment Advisor, 708-216-3751, Fax: 708-216-9555, E-mail: atopalova@luc.edu.
Website: http://www.luc.edu/nursing/

MGH Institute of Health Professions, School of Nursing, Boston, MA 02129. Offers advanced practice nursing (MSN); gerontological nursing (MSN); nursing (DNP); pediatric nursing (MSN); psychiatric nursing (MSN); teaching and learning for health care education (Certificate); women's health nursing (MSN). *Accreditation:* AACN. *Degree requirements:* For master's, thesis or alternative. *Entrance requirements:* For master's, GRE General Test, bachelor's degree from regionally-accredited college or university. Additional exam requirements/recommendations for international students: Required—TOEFL (minimum score 550 paper-based; 80 iBT). Electronic applications accepted. *Faculty research:* Biobehavioral nursing, HIV/AIDS, gerontological nursing, women's health, vulnerable populations, health systems.

Queen's University at Kingston, School of Graduate Studies, Faculty of Health Sciences, School of Nursing, Kingston, ON K7L 3N6, Canada. Offers health and chronic illness (M Sc); nurse scientist (PhD); primary health care nurse practitioner (Certificate); women's and children's health (M Sc). *Degree requirements:* For master's, thesis. *Entrance requirements:* For master's, RN license. Additional exam requirements/recommendations for international students: Required—TOEFL. *Faculty research:* Women and children's health, health and chronic illness.

Rutgers University–Newark, Rutgers School of Nursing, Newark, NJ 07107-3001. Offers adult health (MSN); adult occupational health (MSN); advanced practice nursing (MSN, Post Master's Certificate); family nurse practitioner (MSN); nurse anesthesia (MSN); nursing (MSN); nursing informatics (MSN); urban health (PhD); women's health practitioner (MSN). *Accreditation:* AANA/CANAEP. *Program availability:* Part-time. *Entrance requirements:* For master's, GRE, RN license; basic life support, statistics, and health assessment experience. Additional exam requirements/recommendations for international students: Required—TOEFL. Electronic applications accepted. *Expenses:* Contact institution. *Faculty research:* HIV/AIDS, diabetes education, learned helplessness, nursing science, psychoeducation.

San Francisco State University, Division of Graduate Studies, College of Health and Social Sciences, School of Nursing, San Francisco, CA 94132-1722. Offers adult acute care (MS); clinical nurse specialist (MS); community/public health nursing (MS); family nurse practitioner (Certificate); nursing administration (MS); pediatrics (MS); women's health (MS). *Accreditation:* AACN. *Program availability:* Part-time. *Application deadline:* Applications are processed on a rolling basis. *Financial support:* Career-related internships or fieldwork available. *Unit head:* Connie Carr, Assistant Director of Graduate Programs, 415-338-6856, Fax: 415-338-0555, E-mail: ccarr@sfsu.edu.
Website: http://nursing.sfsu.edu

Stony Brook University, State University of New York, Stony Brook Medicine, School of Nursing, Program in Perinatal Women's Health Nursing, Stony Brook, NY 11794. Offers MS, DNP, Certificate. *Accreditation:* AACN. *Program availability:* Blended/hybrid learning. *Students:* 7 part-time (all women); includes 1 minority (American Indian or Alaska Native, non-Hispanic/Latino). In 2017, 4 master's, 1 other advanced degree awarded. *Degree requirements:* For master's, thesis; for doctorate, thesis/dissertation. *Entrance requirements:* For master's, BSN, minimum GPA of 3.0, course work in statistics. Additional exam requirements/recommendations for international students: Required—TOEFL (minimum score 90 iBT). *Application deadline:* For fall admission, 3/8 for domestic students. Application fee: $100. *Expenses:* Contact institution. *Financial support:* Application deadline: 3/15. *Unit head:* Dr. Elizabeth Collins, Program Director, 631-444-3296, Fax: 631-444-3136, E-mail: elizabeth.collins@stonybrook.edu. *Application contact:* Linda Sacino, Staff Assistant, 631-632-3262, Fax: 631-444-3136, E-mail: elizabeth.collins@stonybrook.edu.
Website: http://www.nursing.stonybrookmedicine.edu/

Tennessee Technological University, Whitson-Hester School of Nursing, DNP Program, Cookeville, TN 38505. Offers adult-gerontology acute care nurse practitioner (DNP); executive leadership in nursing (DNP); family nurse practitioner (DNP); pediatric nurse practitioner-primary care (DNP); psychiatric/mental health nurse practitioner (DNP); women's health care nurse practitioner (DNP). *Program availability:* Part-time. *Students:* 10 part-time (all women). 14 applicants, 86% accepted, 10 enrolled. *Application deadline:* For fall admission, 7/1 for domestic students, 5/1 for international students; for spring admission, 12/1 for domestic students, 10/1 for international students; for summer admission, 5/1 for domestic students, 2/1 for international students. Applications are processed on a rolling basis. Application fee: $35 ($40 for international students). Electronic applications accepted. *Expenses:* Tuition, state resident: full-time $9925; part-time $565 per credit hour. Tuition, nonresident: full-time $22,993; part-time $1291 per credit hour. *Financial support:* Application deadline: 4/1; applicants required to submit FAFSA. *Unit head:* Dr. Bedelia Russell, Program Director, Fax: 931-372-6244, E-mail: bhrussell@tntech.edu. *Application contact:* Shelia K. Kendrick, Coordinator of Graduate Studies, 931-372-3808, Fax: 931-372-3497, E-mail: skendrick@tntech.edu.
Website: https://www.tntech.edu/nursing/doctor-of-nursing-practice/

Texas Woman's University, Graduate School, College of Nursing, Denton, TX 76204. Offers adult health clinical nurse specialist (MS); adult health nurse practitioner (MS); adult/gerontology acute care nurse practitioner (MS); child health clinical nurse specialist (MS); clinical nurse leader (MS); family nurse practitioner (MS); health systems management (MS); nursing education (MS); nursing practice (DNP); nursing science (PhD); pediatric nurse practitioner (MS); women's health clinical nurse specialist (MS); women's health nurse practitioner (MS). *Accreditation:* AACN. *Program availability:* Part-time, 100% online, blended/hybrid learning. *Faculty:* 48 full-time (47 women), 44 part-time/adjunct (37 women). *Students:* 23 full-time (22 women), 816 part-time (750 women); includes 475 minority (188 Black or African American, non-Hispanic/Latino; 4 American Indian or Alaska Native, non-Hispanic/Latino; 171 Asian, non-Hispanic/Latino; 83 Hispanic/Latino; 3 Native Hawaiian or other Pacific Islander, non-Hispanic/Latino; 26 Two or more races, non-Hispanic/Latino), 12 international. Average age 37. 201 applicants, 88% accepted, 123 enrolled. In 2017, 232 master's, 17 doctorates awarded. *Degree requirements:* For master's, comprehensive exam, thesis or alternative, 6-year time limit for completion of degree, professional or clinical project; for doctorate, comprehensive exam, thesis/dissertation, 10-year time limit for completion of degree. *Entrance requirements:* For master's, GRE or MAT, minimum GPA of 3.0 on last 60 hours in undergraduate nursing degree and overall, RN license, BS in nursing, basic statistics course, 1 year of clinical experience; for doctorate, GRE (preferred minimum score 153 [500 old version] Verbal, 144 [500 old version] Quantitative, 4 Analytical), MS in nursing, minimum preferred GPA of 3.5, RN license, statistics course, 2 letters of reference, curriculum vitae, graduate nursing-theory course, graduate research course, statement of professional goals and research interests. Additional exam requirements/recommendations for international students: Required—TOEFL (minimum score 550 paper-based; 79 iBT); Recommended—IELTS (minimum score 6.5), TSE (minimum score 53). *Application deadline:* For fall admission, 5/1 for domestic students, 3/1 priority date for international students; for spring admission, 9/15 for domestic students, 7/1 priority date for international students; for summer admission, 2/1 for domestic and international students. Applications are processed on a rolling basis. Application fee: $50 ($75 for international students). Electronic applications accepted. *Expenses:* $8,510 per year full-time in-state, $17,810 per year full-time out-of-state. *Financial support:* In 2017–18, 146 students received support, including 7 teaching assistantships (averaging $28,195 per year); research assistantships, career-related internships or fieldwork, Federal Work-Study, institutionally sponsored loans, scholarships/grants, traineeships, health care benefits, and unspecified assistantships also available. Support available to part-time students. Financial award application deadline: 3/1; financial award applicants required to submit FAFSA. *Faculty research:* Women's health, nurse staffing and satisfaction in health systems, perinatal safety, chronic illness, pediatric health. *Total annual research expenditures:* $380,388. *Unit head:* Dr. Anita G. Hufft, Dean, 940-898-2401, Fax: 940-898-2437, E-mail: nursing@twu.edu. *Application contact:* Korie Hawkins, Associate Director of Admissions, Graduate Recruitment, 940-898-3188, Fax: 940-898-3081, E-mail: admissions@twu.edu.
Website: http://www.twu.edu/nursing/

Uniformed Services University of the Health Sciences, Daniel K. Inouye Graduate School of Nursing, Bethesda, MD 20814. Offers adult-gerontology clinical nurse specialist (MSN, DNP); family nurse practitioner (DNP); nurse anesthesia (DNP); nursing science (PhD); psychiatric mental health nurse practitioner (DNP); women's health nurse practitioner (DNP). *Accreditation:* AACN; AANA/CANAEP. *Faculty:* 42 full-time (28 women), 2 part-time/adjunct (1 woman). *Students:* 170 full-time (98 women); includes 51 minority (21 Black or African American, non-Hispanic/Latino; 17 Asian, non-Hispanic/Latino; 11 Hispanic/Latino; 2 Native Hawaiian or other Pacific Islander, non-Hispanic/Latino). Average age 34. 88 applicants, 75% accepted, 66 enrolled. In 2017, 55 doctorates awarded. *Degree requirements:* For master's, thesis, scholarly project; for

doctorate, dissertation (for PhD); project (for DNP). *Entrance requirements:* For master's, GRE, BSN, clinical experience, minimum GPA of 3.0, previous course work in science; for doctorate, GRE, BSN, minimum GPA of 3.0, undergraduate/graduate science course within past 5 years, writing example, interview (for some programs), and 3 letters of reference (for DNP); master's degree, minimum GPA of 3.0 in nursing or related field, personal statement, 3 references, and interview (for PhD). *Application deadline:* For winter admission, 2/15 for domestic students; for summer admission, 8/15 for domestic students. Application fee: $0. Electronic applications accepted. *Expenses:* There are no tuition costs or fees; students incur obligated service according to the requirements of their sponsoring organization. *Faculty research:* Military health care, military readiness, women's health, family, behavioral health. *Total annual research expenditures:* $100,000. *Unit head:* Dr. Diane C. Seibert, Associate Dean for Academic Affairs, 301-295-1080, Fax: 301-295-1707, E-mail: diane.seibert@usuhs.edu. *Application contact:* Maureen Jackson, Registrar, 301-295-1055, Fax: 301-295-1707, E-mail: maureen.jackson.ctr@usuhs.edu.
Website: http://www.usuhs.edu/gsn/

The University of Alabama at Birmingham, School of Nursing, Birmingham, AL 35294-1210. Offers clinical nurse leader (MSN); nurse anesthesia (DNP); nurse practitioner (MSN, DNP), including adult-gerontology acute care, adult-gerontology primary care (MSN), family (MSN), pediatric (MSN), psychiatric/mental health (MSN), women's health (MSN); nursing (MSN, DNP, PhD); nursing health systems administration (MSN); nursing informatics (MSN). *Accreditation:* AACN; AANA/CANAEP. *Program availability:* Part-time, online only, blended/hybrid learning. Terminal master's awarded for partial completion of doctoral program. *Degree requirements:* For master's, comprehensive exam; for doctorate, comprehensive exam, thesis/dissertation, research mentorship experience (for PhD); scholarly project (for DNP). *Entrance requirements:* For master's, GRE, GMAT, or MAT, minimum cumulative undergraduate GPA of 3.0 or on last 60 semesters hours; letters of recommendation; for doctorate, GRE General Test, computer literacy, course work in statistics, interview, minimum GPA of 3.0, MS in nursing, references, writing sample. Additional exam requirements/recommendations for international students: Required—TOEFL (minimum score 500 paper-based, 80 iBT) or IELTS (5.5). Electronic applications accepted. *Expenses:* Contact institution. *Faculty research:* Palliative care; oncology; aging; HIV/AIDS; nursing work environments.

University of Cincinnati, Graduate School, College of Nursing, Cincinnati, OH 45221-0038. Offers nurse midwifery (MSN); nurse practitioner (MSN, DNP), including acute care pediatrics (DNP), adult-gerontology acute care, adult-gerontology primary care, anesthesia (DNP), family (MSN), leadership (DNP), neonatal (MSN), women's health (MSN); nursing (MSN, PhD), including occupational health (MSN). *Accreditation:* AACN; AANA/CANAEP (one or more programs are accredited); ACNM/ACME. *Program availability:* Part-time, 100% online, blended/hybrid learning. *Faculty:* 74 full-time (69 women), 112 part-time/adjunct (105 women). *Students:* 323 full-time (261 women), 1,084 part-time (949 women); includes 311 minority (113 Black or African American, non-Hispanic/Latino; 4 American Indian or Alaska Native, non-Hispanic/Latino; 56 Asian, non-Hispanic/Latino; 108 Hispanic/Latino; 1 Native Hawaiian or other Pacific Islander, non-Hispanic/Latino; 29 Two or more races, non-Hispanic/Latino), 12 international. Average age 34. 582 applicants, 64% accepted, 314 enrolled. In 2017, 579 master's, 18 doctorates awarded. *Degree requirements:* For master's, thesis or alternative; for doctorate, comprehensive exam (for some programs), thesis/dissertation (for some programs). *Entrance requirements:* For doctorate, GRE General Test. Additional exam requirements/recommendations for international students: Required—TOEFL (minimum score 600 paper-based; 100 iBT); Recommended—IELTS (minimum score 7). *Application deadline:* For fall admission, 5/1 priority date for domestic students, 5/1 for international students; for spring admission, 10/1 for domestic students; for summer admission, 3/1 priority date for domestic students. Applications are processed on a rolling basis. Application fee: $130 ($70 for international students). Electronic applications accepted. *Expenses:* $14,668 annual full-time in-state tuition, $707 annual fees. *Financial support:* In 2017–18, 123 students received support, including 8 fellowships with full tuition reimbursements available (averaging $30,423 per year), 7 research assistantships with full tuition reimbursements available (averaging $17,971 per year), 5 teaching assistantships with full tuition reimbursements available (averaging $17,971 per year); Federal Work-Study, institutionally sponsored loans, scholarships/grants, traineeships, health care benefits, tuition waivers (partial), and unspecified assistantships also available. Support available to part-time students. Financial award application deadline: 5/1; financial award applicants required to submit FAFSA. *Faculty research:* Vulnerable populations, education, violence, chronicity/aging, cancer. *Total annual research expenditures:* $575,576. *Unit head:* Dr. Greer Glazer, Dean, 513-558-5330, Fax: 513-558-9030, E-mail: greer.glazer@uc.edu. *Application contact:* Office of Student Recruitment, 513-558-8400, Fax: 513-558-5012, E-mail: nursingbearcats@uc.edu.
Website: https://nursing.uc.edu/

University of Colorado Denver, College of Nursing, Aurora, CO 80045. Offers adult clinical nurse specialist (MS); adult nurse practitioner (MS); family nurse practitioner (MS); family psychiatric mental health nurse practitioner (MS); health care informatics (MS); nurse-midwifery (MS); nursing (DNP, PhD); nursing leadership and health care systems (MS); pediatric nurse practitioner (MS); women's health (MS); MS/PhD. *Accreditation:* ACNM/ACME (one or more programs are accredited). *Program availability:* Part-time, evening/weekend, online learning. *Students:* 297 applicants, 55% accepted, 141 enrolled. In 2017, 138 master's, 18 doctorates awarded. Terminal master's awarded for partial completion of doctoral program. *Degree requirements:* For master's, thesis optional; for doctorate, comprehensive exam, thesis/dissertation, 42 credits of coursework. *Entrance requirements:* For master's, GRE if cumulative undergraduate GPA is less than 3.0, undergraduate nursing degree from ACEN- or CCNE-accredited school or university; completion of research and statistics courses with minimum grade of C; copy of current and unencumbered nursing license; for doctorate, GRE, bachelor's and/or master's degrees in nursing from ACEN- or CCNE-accredited institution; portfolio; minimum undergraduate GPA of 3.0, graduate 3.5; graduate-level intermediate statistics and master's-level nursing theory courses with minimum B grade; interview. Additional exam requirements/recommendations for international students: Required—TOEFL (minimum score 560 paper-based; 83 iBT). *Application deadline:* For fall admission, 2/15 for domestic students, 1/15 for international students; for spring admission, 7/1 for domestic students, 6/1 for international students. Application fee: $50 ($75 for international students). Electronic applications accepted. *Unit head:* Dr. Sarah Thompson, Dean, 303-724-1679, E-mail: sarah.a.thompson@ucdenver.edu. *Application contact:* Judy Campbell, Graduate Programs Coordinator, 303-724-8503, E-mail: judy.campbell@ucdenver.edu.
Website: http://www.ucdenver.edu/academics/colleges/nursing/Pages/default.aspx

University of Delaware, College of Health Sciences, School of Nursing, Newark, DE 19716. Offers adult nurse practitioner (MSN, PMC); cardiopulmonary clinical nurse specialist (MSN, PMC); cardiopulmonary clinical nurse specialist/adult nurse practitioner (MSN, PMC); family nurse practitioner (MSN, PMC); gerontology clinical nurse specialist (MSN, PMC); gerontology clinical nurse specialist geriatric nurse practitioner (PMC); gerontology clinical nurse specialist/geriatric nurse practitioner (MSN); health services administration (MSN, PMC); nursing of children clinical nurse specialist (MSN, PMC); nursing of children clinical nurse specialist/pediatric nurse practitioner (MSN, PMC); oncology/immune deficiency clinical nurse specialist (MSN, PMC); oncology/immune deficiency clinical nurse specialist/adult nurse practitioner (MSN, PMC); perinatal/women's health clinical nurse specialist (MSN, PMC); perinatal/women's health clinical nurse specialist/women's health nurse practitioner (MSN, PMC); psychiatric nursing clinical nurse specialist (MSN, PMC). *Accreditation:* AACN. *Program availability:* Part-time, evening/weekend, online learning. *Degree requirements:* For master's, thesis optional. *Entrance requirements:* For master's, BSN, interview, RN license. Electronic applications accepted. *Faculty research:* Marriage and chronic illness, health promotion, congestive heart failure patient outcomes, school nursing, diabetes in children, culture, health disparities, cardiovascular, prison nursing, oncology, public policy, child obesity, smoking and teen pregnancy, blood pressure measurements, men's health.

University of Illinois at Chicago, College of Nursing, Program in Nursing, Chicago, IL 60607-7128. Offers acute care clinical nurse specialist (MS); administrative nursing leadership (Certificate); adult nurse practitioner (MS); adult/geriatric nurse practitioner (MS); advanced community health nurse specialist (MS); family nurse practitioner (MS); geriatric clinical nurse specialist (MS); geriatric nurse practitioner (MS); nurse midwifery (MS); occupational health/advanced community health nurse specialist (MS); occupational health/family nurse practitioner (MS); pediatric nurse practitioner (MS); perinatal clinical nurse specialist (MS); school/advanced community health nurse specialist (MS); school/family nurse practitioner (MS); women's health nurse practitioner (MS). *Accreditation:* AACN. *Program availability:* Part-time. *Degree requirements:* For master's, thesis or alternative. *Entrance requirements:* For master's, GRE General Test, minimum GPA of 2.75. Additional exam requirements/recommendations for international students: Required—TOEFL. Electronic applications accepted.

University of Indianapolis, Graduate Programs, School of Nursing, Indianapolis, IN 46227-3697. Offers advanced practice nursing (DNP); family nurse practitioner (MSN); gerontological nurse practitioner (MSN); neonatal nurse practitioner (MSN); nurse-midwifery (MSN); nursing (MSN); nursing and health systems leadership (MSN); nursing education (MSN); women's health nurse practitioner (MSN); MBA/MSN. *Accreditation:* AACN. *Entrance requirements:* For master's, minimum GPA of 3.0, interview, letters of recommendation, resume, IN nursing license, 1 year of professional practice; for doctorate, graduate of ACEN- or CCNE-accredited nursing program; MSN or MA with nursing major and minimum cumulative GPA of 3.25; unencumbered RN license with eligibility for licensure in Indiana; completion of graduate-level statistics course within last 5 years with minimum grade of B; resume; essay; official transcripts from all academic institutions. Additional exam requirements/recommendations for international students: Required—TOEFL (minimum score 550 paper-based). Electronic applications accepted.

University of Louisville, Graduate School, School of Nursing, Louisville, KY 40202. Offers adult gerontology nurse practitioner (MSN, DNP); education and administration (MSN); family nurse practitioner (MSN, DNP); neonatal nurse practitioner (MSN, DNP); nursing research (PhD); psychiatric/mental health nurse practitioner (MSN, DNP); women's health nurse practitioner (MSN). *Accreditation:* AACN. *Program availability:* Part-time. *Faculty:* 44 full-time (40 women), 45 part-time/adjunct (41 women). *Students:* 130 full-time (107 women), 30 part-time (25 women); includes 33 minority (16 Black or African American, non-Hispanic/Latino; 7 Asian, non-Hispanic/Latino; 5 Hispanic/Latino; 5 Two or more races, non-Hispanic/Latino), 2 international. Average age 33. 61 applicants, 67% accepted, 36 enrolled. In 2017, 54 master's awarded. *Degree requirements:* For doctorate, comprehensive exam (for some programs), thesis/dissertation (for some programs). *Entrance requirements:* For master's, bachelor's degree from nationally-accredited college, completion of 6 prerequisite courses, minimum undergraduate GPA of 3.0; for doctorate, GRE with minimum score of 156 Verbal, 146 Quantitative, 4.0 Analytic (for PhD), 3 letters of professional reference; minimum GPA of 3.0 with BSN, 3.25 with MSN; written statement of career goals, areas of expertise, and reasons for pursuing doctoral degree; resume including RN license. Additional exam requirements/recommendations for international students: Recommended—TOEFL (minimum score 560 paper-based), IELTS (minimum score 6.5). *Application deadline:* For fall admission, 1/15 priority date for domestic students, 1/15 for international students; for summer admission, 10/15 priority date for domestic students. Application fee: $65. Electronic applications accepted. *Expenses:* Tuition, state resident: full-time $12,246; part-time $681 per credit hour. Tuition, nonresident: full-time $25,486; part-time $1417 per credit hour. *Required fees:* $196. Tuition and fees vary according to course load, program and reciprocity agreements. *Financial support:* In 2017–18, 8 research assistantships with full tuition reimbursements (averaging $20,000 per year), 4 teaching assistantships with full tuition reimbursements (averaging $15,000 per year) were awarded; fellowships with full tuition reimbursements, scholarships/grants, and unspecified assistantships also available. Financial award application deadline: 10/1; financial award applicants required to submit FAFSA. *Faculty research:* Environmental health, health services research, women's mental health, self-management of chronic illness in adults and children, health disparities. *Total annual research expenditures:* $762,266. *Unit head:* Dr. Marcia J. Hern, RN, Dean and Professor, 502-852-8300, Fax: 502-852-8783, E-mail: m.hern@louisville.edu. *Application contact:* Trish Hart, Assistant Dean for Student Affairs, 502-852-5825, Fax: 502-852-8783, E-mail: trish.hart@louisville.edu.
Website: http://www.louisville.edu/nursing/

University of Minnesota, Twin Cities Campus, Graduate School, School of Nursing, Minneapolis, MN 55455-0213. Offers adult/gerontological clinical nurse specialist (DNP); adult/gerontological primary care nurse practitioner (DNP); family nurse practitioner (DNP); health innovation and leadership (DNP); integrative health and healing (DNP); nurse anesthesia (DNP); nurse midwifery (DNP); nursing (MN, PhD); nursing informatics (DNP); pediatric clinical nurse specialist (DNP); primary care certified pediatric nurse practitioner (DNP); psychiatric/mental health nurse practitioner (DNP); women's health nurse practitioner (DNP). *Accreditation:* AACN; AANA/CANAEP; ACNM/ACME (one or more programs are accredited). *Program availability:* Part-time, online learning. Terminal master's awarded for partial completion of doctoral program. *Degree requirements:* For master's, final oral exam, project or thesis; for doctorate, thesis/dissertation. *Entrance requirements:* For master's and doctorate, GRE General Test. Additional exam requirements/recommendations for international students: Required—TOEFL (minimum score 586 paper-based). *Expenses:* Contact institution. *Faculty research:* Child and family health promotion, nursing research on elders.

University of Missouri–Kansas City, School of Nursing and Health Studies, Kansas City, MO 64110-2499. Offers adult clinical nurse specialist (MSN), including adult nurse practitioner, women's health nurse practitioner (MSN, DNP); adult clinical nursing practice (DNP), including adult gerontology nurse practitioner, women's health nurse practitioner (MSN, DNP); clinical nursing practice (DNP), including family nurse practitioner; neonatal nurse practitioner (MSN); nurse educator (MSN); nurse executive (MSN); nursing practice (DNP); pediatric clinical nursing practice (DNP), including pediatric nurse practitioner; pediatric nurse practitioner (MSN). *Accreditation:* AACN. *Program availability:* Part-time, online learning. *Degree requirements:* For master's, thesis or alternative. *Entrance requirements:* For master's, minimum undergraduate GPA of 3.2; for doctorate, GRE, 3 letters of reference. Additional exam requirements/recommendations for international students: Required—TOEFL (minimum score 550 paper-based; 80 iBT). *Faculty research:* Geriatrics/gerontology, children's pain, neonatology, Alzheimer's care, cancer caregivers.

University of Missouri–St. Louis, College of Nursing, St. Louis, MO 63121. Offers adult/geriatric nurse practitioner (Post Master's Certificate); family nurse practitioner (Post Master's Certificate); nursing (DNP, PhD); pediatric acute care nurse practitioner (Post Master's Certificate); pediatric nurse practitioner (Post Master's Certificate); psychiatric-mental health nurse practitioner (Post Master's Certificate); women's health nurse practitioner (Post Master's Certificate). *Accreditation:* AACN. *Program availability:* Part-time. *Faculty:* 24 full-time (22 women), 12 part-time/adjunct (11 women). *Students:* 47 full-time (44 women), 162 part-time (152 women); includes 53 minority (37 Black or African American, non-Hispanic/Latino; 10 Asian, non-Hispanic/Latino; 4 Hispanic/Latino; 2 Two or more races, non-Hispanic/Latino), 3 international. 112 applicants, 93% accepted, 70 enrolled. *Degree requirements:* For doctorate, comprehensive exam, thesis/dissertation; for Post Master's Certificate, thesis. *Entrance requirements:* For doctorate, GRE, 2 letters of recommendation, MSN, minimum GPA of 3.2, course in differential/inferential statistics; for Post Master's Certificate, 2 recommendation letters; MSN; advanced practice certificate; minimum GPA of 3.0; essay. Additional exam requirements/recommendations for international students: Recommended—TOEFL (minimum score 550 paper-based; 79 iBT), IELTS (minimum score 6.5). *Application deadline:* For fall admission, 2/15 for domestic and international students. Application fee: $50 ($40 for international students). Electronic applications accepted. *Expenses:* Tuition, state resident: part-time $476.50 per credit hour. Tuition, nonresident: part-time $1169.70 per credit hour. *Financial support:* Research assistantships with tuition reimbursements available. Financial award application deadline: 4/1; financial award applicants required to submit FAFSA. *Faculty research:* Health promotion and restoration, family disruption, violence, abuse, battered women, health survey methods. *Unit head:* Sue Dean-Baar, Dean, 314-516-6066. *Application contact:* 314-516-5458, Fax: 314-516-6996, E-mail: gradadm@umsl.edu.
Website: http://www.umsl.edu/divisions/nursing/

University of Pennsylvania, School of Nursing, Women's Health/Gender Related Nurse Practitioner Program, Philadelphia, PA 19104. Offers MSN. *Accreditation:* AACN. *Program availability:* Part-time, online learning. *Students:* 8 full-time (all women), 20 part-time (all women); includes 10 minority (5 Black or African American, non-Hispanic/Latino; 4 Hispanic/Latino; 1 Two or more races, non-Hispanic/Latino). Average age 28. In 2017, 18 master's awarded. *Financial support:* Application deadline: 4/1.

University of South Carolina, The Graduate School, College of Nursing, Program in Clinical Nursing, Columbia, SC 29208. Offers acute care clinical specialist (MSN); acute care nurse practitioner (MSN); women's health nurse practitioner (MSN). *Accreditation:* AACN. *Program availability:* Part-time. *Degree requirements:* For master's, thesis or alternative. *Entrance requirements:* For master's, GRE General Test or MAT, BS in nursing, RN licensure. Additional exam requirements/recommendations for international students: Required—TOEFL (minimum score 570 paper-based). Electronic applications accepted. *Faculty research:* Systems research, evidence based practice, breast cancer, violence.

Vanderbilt University, Vanderbilt University School of Nursing, Nashville, TN 37240. Offers adult-gerontology acute care nurse practitioner (MSN), including hospitalist, intensivist; adult-gerontology primary care nurse practitioner (MSN); emergency nurse practitioner (MSN); family nurse practitioner (MSN); healthcare leadership (MSN); neonatal nurse practitioner (MSN); nurse midwifery (MSN); nurse midwifery/family nurse practitioner (MSN); nursing (Post-Master's Certificate); nursing informatics (MSN); nursing practice (DNP); nursing science (PhD); pediatric acute care nurse practitioner (MSN); pediatric primary care nurse practitioner (MSN); psychiatric-mental health nurse practitioner (MSN); women's health nurse practitioner (MSN); women's health nurse practitioner/adult gerontology primary care nurse practitioner (MSN); MSN/M Div; MSN/MTS. *Accreditation:* AACN; ACEN (one or more programs are accredited); ACNM/ACME. *Program availability:* Part-time, 100% online, blended/hybrid learning. *Faculty:* 292 full-time (267 women), 321 part-time/adjunct (253 women). *Students:* 501 full-time (435 women), 387 part-time (355 women); includes 153 minority (40 Black or African American, non-Hispanic/Latino; 1 American Indian or Alaska Native, non-Hispanic/Latino; 27 Asian, non-Hispanic/Latino; 48 Hispanic/Latino; 4 Native Hawaiian or other Pacific Islander, non-Hispanic/Latino; 33 Two or more races, non-Hispanic/Latino), 9 international. Average age 31. 1,210 applicants, 57% accepted, 473 enrolled. In 2017, 319 master's, 47 doctorates awarded. *Degree requirements:* For doctorate, comprehensive exam, thesis/dissertation. *Entrance requirements:* For master's, GRE General Test (taken within the past 5 years), minimum B average in undergraduate course work, 3 letters of recommendation; for doctorate, GRE General Test, interview, 3 letters of recommendation from doctorally-prepared faculty, MSN, essay. Additional exam requirements/recommendations for international students: Required—TOEFL (minimum score 570 paper-based), IELTS (minimum score 6.5). *Application deadline:* For fall admission, 11/1 priority date for domestic and international students. Applications are processed on a rolling basis. Application fee: $50. Electronic applications accepted. *Expenses:* Contact institution. *Financial support:* In 2017–18, 627 students received support. Scholarships/grants available. Financial award application deadline: 3/1; financial award applicants required to submit FAFSA. *Faculty research:* Lymphedema, palliative care and bereavement, health services research including workforce, safety and quality of care, gerontology, better birth outcomes including nutrition. *Total annual research expenditures:* $2 million. *Unit head:* Dr. Linda Norman, Dean, 615-343-8876, Fax: 615-343-7711, E-mail: linda.norman@vanderbilt.edu. *Application contact:* Patricia Peerman, Assistant Dean for Enrollment Management, 615-322-3800, Fax: 615-343-0333, E-mail: vusn-admissions@vanderbilt.edu.
Website: http://www.nursing.vanderbilt.edu

Virginia Commonwealth University, Graduate School, School of Nursing, Richmond, VA 23284-9005. Offers adult health acute nursing (MS); adult health primary nursing (MS); biobehavioral clinical research (PhD); child health nursing (MS); clinical nurse leader (MS); family health nursing (MS); nurse educator (MS); nurse practitioner (MS); nursing (Certificate); nursing administration (MS), including clinical nurse manager; psychiatric-mental health nursing (MS); quality and safety in health care (DNP); women's health nursing (MS). *Accreditation:* AACN; ACEN (one or more programs are accredited). *Program availability:* Part-time, evening/weekend, online learning. *Degree requirements:* For master's, thesis optional; for doctorate, thesis/dissertation. *Entrance requirements:* For master's, GRE General Test, BSN, minimum GPA of 2.8; for doctorate, GRE General Test. Additional exam requirements/recommendations for international students: Required—TOEFL (minimum score 600 paper-based; 100 iBT). Electronic applications accepted.

Wayne State University, College of Nursing, Detroit, MI 48202. Offers adult gerontology acute care nurse practitioner (MSN); adult gerontology primary care nurse practitioner (MSN); advanced public health nursing (MSN); infant and mental health (DNP, PhD); neonatal nurse practitioner (MSN); nurse-midwifery (MSN); pediatric acute care nurse practitioner (MSN); pediatric primary care nurse practitioner (MSN); psychiatric mental health nurse practitioner (MSN); women's health nurse practitioner (MSN). Doctoral program admits for fall only. *Accreditation:* AACN. *Program availability:* Part-time. *Faculty:* 30. *Students:* 133 full-time (120 women), 184 part-time (167 women); includes 85 minority (57 Black or African American, non-Hispanic/Latino; 16 Asian, non-Hispanic/Latino; 4 Hispanic/Latino; 8 Two or more races, non-Hispanic/Latino), 22 international. Average age 34. 318 applicants, 39% accepted, 94 enrolled. In 2017, 51 master's, 29 doctorates awarded. *Degree requirements:* For doctorate, thesis/dissertation (for some programs). *Entrance requirements:* For master's, BSN from ACEN- or CCNE-accredited program with minimum GPA of 3.0; three references; current RN license; personal statement; for doctorate, resume or curriculum vitae; goals statement; bachelor's or master's degree in nursing from ACEN- or CCNE-accredited program with minimum GPA of 3.0; current RN license, writing sample and interview (for DNP); reference letters (3 for PhD, 2 for DNP). Additional exam requirements/recommendations for international students: Required—TOEFL (minimum score 101 iBT), TWE (minimum score 6), Michigan English Language Assessment Battery (minimum score 85); Recommended—IELTS (minimum score 7). Application fee: $50. Electronic applications accepted. *Expenses:* Contact institution. *Financial support:* In 2017–18, 92 students received support, including 16 fellowships with tuition reimbursements available (averaging $8,285 per year), 5 teaching assistantships with tuition reimbursements available (averaging $25,000 per year); scholarships/grants, health care benefits, and unspecified assistantships also available. Support available to part-time students. Financial award applicants required to submit FAFSA. *Faculty research:* Bridging transitions and technology to promote asthma care in the community, chronic wound care for persons who injected drugs, decreasing at-risk parenting to reduce child maltreatment and trauma, dementia symptoms (cognition, behavior, function), determining readiness to engage in end of life/palliative care conversations with adolescents and young adults living with advanced cancer, dyspnea assessment and treatment at the end of life. *Unit head:* Dr. Laurie Lauzon Clabo, Dean, College of Nursing, 313-577-4082, E-mail: laurie.lauzon.clabo@wayne.edu. *Application contact:* 313-577-4082, Fax: 313-577-6949, E-mail: nursinginfo@wayne.edu.
Website: http://nursing.wayne.edu/

FRONTIER NURSING UNIVERSITY

School of Nursing

FRONTIER NURSING UNIVERSITY

Programs of Study

Established in 1939, Frontier Nursing University is a pioneer in graduate-level nursing and midwifery education. Today, with more than 2,000 enrolled students, it provides innovative distance education that allows students from around the world to complete didactic courses online and receive clinical education in their communities. The university has received national recognition for its long tradition of providing innovation and excellence in education. *U.S. News & World Report* ranks Frontier Nursing University in the top 100 online graduate nursing programs.

Frontier Nursing University offers evidence-based Master of Science in Nursing (M.S.N.) degree programs, post-graduate certificates, and Doctor of Nursing Practice (D.N.P.) programs. Its curriculum includes four specialties: nurse-midwife, family nurse practitioner, women's health care nurse practitioner and psychiatric-mental health nurse practitioner.

The M.S.N. degree program allows students to complete a Master of Science in Nursing degree with the option to continue on and seamlessly complete a Doctor of Nursing Practice degree without reapplying. The program begins with a four-day "Frontier Bound" orientation that takes place on FNU's campus, then all coursework and clinicals are completed in the student's own community. The M.S.N. program takes approximately two years to complete full-time (a part-time option is also available) with the optional D.N.P. consisting of 19 additional credit hours. Levels I and II consist of online coursework that involves frequent interaction between faculty members and students via e-mail, forums, and telephone. Level III consists of a five-day "Clinical Bound" session at FNU where students demonstrate their ability to begin community-based clinical practice. Level IV consists of a 675-hour Clinical Practicum in students' communities. Finally, Level V, which takes place after the M.S.N. degree is conferred, involves completing three to five additional terms of D.N.P. coursework and clinical education if the student chooses to continue on to complete the D.N.P.

The practice-focused Post-Master's Doctor of Nursing (D.N.P.) degree program is for current nurse-midwives and nurse practitioners and builds on the M.S.N. curriculum by providing additional training in evidence-based practice, quality improvement, systems leadership, and other essential areas of advanced practice. The curriculum also includes 360 hours planning, implementing, and disseminating the results of a rapid cycle quality improvement project. Students become highly-skilled clinicians with competencies in evaluating evidence, translating research into practice, and using research findings in decision-making. They also become adept at using clinical innovations to change practice.

The Nurse-Midwife Specialty curriculum trains students to become outstanding clinicians as well as leaders and entrepreneurs in maternal and infant health care. The program's strong primary care component ensures that students also gain the skills needed to care for women across their life spans. The M.S.N. program consists of 49 didactic credits and 15 clinical credits. It can be completed in about two years full-time (a part-time option is also available). Students also have the option to exit the program once the M.S.N. is conferred.

Students who choose the Family Nurse Practitioner Specialty receive the training needed to become well-rounded clinicians, leaders, and entrepreneurs in primary health care. The M.S.N. program contains 46 didactic credits and 15 clinical credits. It can be completed in about two years full-time (a part-time option is also available). Students also have the option to exit the program once the M.S.N. is conferred.

The Women's Health Care Nurse Practitioner Specialty program prepares students for advanced nursing practice as well as leadership and entrepreneurial roles in women's health care. The curriculum's solid primary care component ensures that students receive the skills needed to care for women in all stages of life. The complete M.S.N. program consists of 43 didactic credits and 15 clinical credits. It can be completed in about two years full-time (a part-time option is also available). Students also have the option to exit the program once the M.S.N. is conferred.

The Psychiatric-Mental Health Nurse Practitioner Specialty program educates students for advanced practice to improve mental health care and overall health status of communities with a focus on individuals across the lifespan. The M.S.N. program consist of 45 didactic credits and 15 clinical credits. It can be completed in about two years full time (a part-time option is also available). Students have the option to exit the program once the M.S.N. is conferred.

Frontier Nursing University also offers the Associate Degree in Nursing (A.D.N.) Bridge Entry Option that allows nurses with associate degrees in nursing (but no bachelor's degrees in any field) to enroll in the M.S.N. program with either nurse-midwifery, family nurse practitioner, or psychiatric-mental health nurse practitioner specialties. The curriculum includes approximately one year to complete the required Bridge coursework, followed by approximately two years full-time to complete the M.S.N. (a part-time option is also available), and the optional D.N.P. consisting of 19 additional credit hours. The program begins with "Bridge Bound," an on-campus orientation that allows students to connect with fellow students and faculty members and learn more about the bridge program. Then, students go back to their communities to complete bridge courses online. During the fourth term, students return to FNU to participate in "Crossing the Bridge," an event that enables them to reconnect with FNU's community and present their community health projects. Upon successful completion of the bridge courses, students begin the M.S.N. curriculum in the nurse-midwife or family nurse practitioner specialty, and they can opt to complete the D.N.P. program once they earn their M.S.N. degrees.

How Distance Education Works

After attending an orientation session on the FNU campus in Kentucky, students return to their communities to study online. FNU courses are taught in eleven-week terms. All courses are taught each term and designed with flexibility that allows adult learners to develop their own study schedule. Students can choose the number of credits to take based on their other life responsibilities. Advisers assist students in developing individualized timelines that will meet their specific needs.

Faculty teach and guide using a variety of modalities such as computer forums, e-mail, chats, video or audio lectures, interactive sessions using Blackboard Collaborate, and the telephone. Assignments are designed to promote student engagement in the courses and within the community in which the student lives. Interaction with the school community is fostered through a dynamic web portal and Frontier Community Connection forums. Support, explanations, and information are readily available.

Frontier Nursing University

After completing the majority of their didactic course work, students begin their clinical learning experience. Clinical preceptors are sought within the student's own community whenever possible, allowing students to learn in their home area. While the goal is to keep the student as close to their home as possible, if appropriate clinical practice sites are not available, students may be required to travel to a clinical site for part or all of their clinical experiences.

Financial Aid

FNU students may qualify for Federal Stafford Unsubsidized Loans, private loans, and external scholarships. In addition, Frontier offers several scholarships including the Kitty Ernst Scholarship, Alumni Scholarship, Family Nurse Practitioner Scholarship, and Student Scholarship.

Cost of Study

Tuition is $580 per credit hour for all programs of study. The most current information regarding tuition and other fees associated with each program is available at https://www.frontier.edu/tuition.

The University

Frontier Nursing University is located in Kentucky in the southeastern region of the United States. Its campus provides a tranquil, picturesque environment in which to learn and connect with faculty and fellow students during the brief two to three brief required visits to campus.

Faculty

FNU has more than 100 faculty members who are accomplished teachers, expert clinicians, and dedicated mentors. They create mutually respectful relationships with students and support them in achieving their academic and professional goals.

They are also pioneers in distance nursing education who are highly accessible and skilled at supporting students in a virtual learning environment.

Applying

Frontier strives to make the admissions process easy. Complete admissions criteria and application forms for each program are available online at https://www.frontier.edu/admissions. Application deadlines and admission calendars for each program can be found at https://www.frontier.edu/admissions/admissions-calendar.

Frontier Nursing University
195 School Street
Hyden, Kentucky 41749
Phone: 606-672-2312
Fax: 606-672-3776
E-mail: FNU@frontier.edu
Website: https://www.frontier.edu

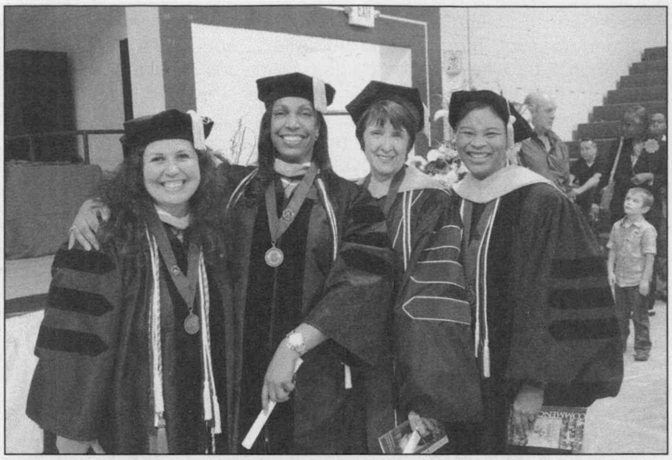

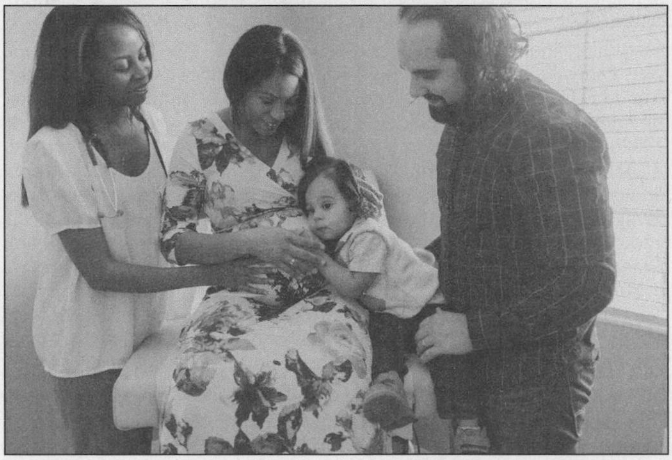

JOHNS HOPKINS

School of Nursing

Programs of Study

The Johns Hopkins School of Nursing offers a wide range of academic programs tailored to students' specialized needs, interests, and strengths.

Master of Science in Nursing (M.S.N.) Programs

M.S.N. Entry into Nursing Practice: This accelerated program gives students enhanced bedside nursing education and training and the necessary tools to work toward a leadership role or pursue a doctoral degree. It is meant for students with a bachelor's degree in another discipline who want to pursue a nursing career.

M.S.N. Health Services Management Track: This M.S.N. specialty track prepares students to lead health care systems by learning evidence-based decision making and outcomes. This degree opens doors to leadership positions in health education, program development, consultation, and administration.

M.S.N. Health Systems Management Track/MBA Dual Degree: In partnership with the Johns Hopkins Carey Business School, this dual degree will allow nurses to provide patient-centered care while also leading health organizations towards policies that preserve budgets even as they save lives.

M.S.N. Public Health/MPH Joint Degree: This specialty track, jointly offered through the Johns Hopkins School of Nursing and the Bloomberg School of Public Health, prepares the student to integrate advanced nursing practice with population-based public health perspectives.

M.S.N./MBA: This specialty track, offered through the Johns Hopkins School of Nursing and Carey Business School, prepares graduates who are exceptional at patient care and safety as well as effecting change at the health care leadership and corporate levels.

Doctor of Nursing Practice (D.N.P.) and Doctor of Philosophy (Ph.D.) Programs

D.N.P. Advanced Practice Tracks: This program offers multiple online options. It is designed for those with a Bachelor of Science in Nursing or entry-level nursing master's degree who wish to prepare for the doctoral-level role of nurse practitioner or clinical nurse specialist.

D.N.P. Advanced Practice Track/Ph.D.: This dual-degree program gives students the credentials, knowledge, skills, and seasoning to lead breakthroughs in research, health care practice, or both.

D.N.P. Executive Track: This is a two-year online program for nurses who have an M.S.N. degree in an advanced practice area and are actively practicing in a health care setting.

D.N.P. Executive Track/MBA Dual Degree: This dual-degree program, offered through the Johns Hopkins School of Nursing and Carey Business School, prepares graduates who are exceptional at patient care and safety as well as effecting change at the health care leadership and corporate levels.

Ph.D. in Nursing: This program advances the theoretical foundation of nursing practice and health care delivery. By graduation, most Hopkins nurse scholars have been awarded grants that continue their research and put them well on their way to a successful career.

Post-Master's Degree Certificates: Post-degree certificates are designed for M.S.N.-prepared nurses seeking further specialization in a field. Students are able to gain the knowledge and skills to prepare for certification in only a year.

A full listing of the school's programs can be found online at nursing.jhu.edu/academics.

Research Facilities

The School of Nursing is located adjacent to the highly-ranked Johns Hopkins School of Medicine, Bloomberg School of Public Health, and The Johns Hopkins Hospital. The school has an excellent research reputation and received 56 new grants and over $12 million dollars in grant funding in fiscal year 2018. Specialized facilities include the Office for Science and Innovation, incorporating the Center for Cardiovascular and Chronic Care, Center for Global Initiatives, Center for Innovative Care in Aging, and Center for Sleep-Related Symptom Science.

The school offers fellowships in violence, pain, psychiatric and mental health, health disparities, and cardiovascular research. Areas of excellence include aging and dementia care, cardiovascular/chronic care and symptom management, community/global/public health, mental health/behavioral intervention, quality and safety/health systems management

Students serve Baltimore's most vulnerable populations through school-sponsored centers: Wald Community Nursing Center, House of Ruth, and Isaiah Wellness Center. Faculty and students volunteer more than 12,000 hours annually in over 40 community-based service organizations.

In addition, the School has collaborations with more than 30 nursing and medical schools in more than 19 countries and seeks to address worldwide nursing advocacy, innovation, and capacity building through the Center for Global Initiatives.

Current initiatives include a focus on ethical care through curriculum, symposiums, and involvement with national nursing associations. The School also advises schools of nursing, healthcare providers, and government agencies in the areas of curriculum and program development, research, and policy reform—nationally and internationally. Online learning modules serve to develop and improve teaching and mentoring of clinical faculty and preceptors.

Financial Aid

The Johns Hopkins School of Nursing offers a range of financial aid programs within each degree, including grants, fellowships, scholarships, loans, and work-study. All returned Peace Corps Volunteers are offered the Coverdell Fellows scholarship. Qualified students interested in the Ph.D. program may be eligible for 100 percent funding for their first three years. Federal and supplemental (private) student loans are available to assist students in meeting their educational expenses.

Cost of Study

Costs for the 2018–19 academic year vary by program and are as follows:

M.S.N. Entry Into Nursing: Tuition, $59,594 (full-time); $1,639 per credit (full-time); and books/supplies, $1,224.

M.S.N. Health Systems Management Track: Tuition, $45,942 (full-time); $1,639 per credit (full-time); and books/supplies, $1,224.

M.S.N. Health Systems Management Track/MBA Dual Degree Tuition, $59,594 (full-time); $1,639 per credit (full-time); and books/supplies, $1,224.

M.S.N. Public Health/MPH Joint Degree: Tuition, $67,680 (full-time); $1,692 per credit (full-time); and books/supplies, $1,224.

D.N.P. Advanced Practice Tracks: Tuition, $46,935 (full-time), $1,721 per credit (full-time); and books/supplies, $1,224.

D.N.P. Executive Track: Tuition, $37,483 (full-time); $1,721 per credit (full-time); and books/supplies, $1,224.

D.N.P. Executive Track/MBA Dual Degree Executive: Tuition, $32,561 (full-time); $1,721 per credit (full-time); and books/supplies, $1,224.

Ph.D. in Nursing Tuition, $41,796 (full-time); $2,322 per credit (full-time); and books/supplies, $1,224.

D.N.P. Advanced Practice Track/PhD Dual Degree: Tuition, $54,621 (full-time); $2,322 per credit (full-time); and books/supplies, $1,224.

Living and Housing Costs

The University offers information about housing to all students through the Johns Hopkins Medical Institutions Off-Campus Housing Office. Although on-campus housing is not available to nursing students, the off-campus housing office offers many resources for finding a place to live in Baltimore and the surrounding counties. There is also a message board section to post requests for roommates, as well as a section for furniture for sale. More information about housing and moving to Baltimore is available through the Office of Student Affairs (410-955-7545). The University also has a Guide for Moving to Baltimore so students can learn more about the neighborhoods where many School of Nursing students live and the amenities that they enjoy in their area.

Johns Hopkins

Student Group

There are approximately 1,200 students in the School of Nursing. More than 30 percent are racial or ethnic minorities and more than 11 percent are male. There is a low student/faculty ratio in both labs and clinical courses. There are more than 25 extracurricular clubs and organizations specifically related to nursing.

Location

In many ways, Baltimore is the heart of American healthcare education and opportunity. Home to the world-class Johns Hopkins institutions, the city is the site of two rapidly developing biotechnology centers and several nationally ranked hospitals.

A unique combination of the old and the new, Baltimore is a national showcase for urban renewal and ethnic tradition. The city's most popular attraction is the Inner Harbor, which includes enclosed food and shopping pavilions, the National Aquarium, the Maryland Science Center, and the acclaimed Oriole Park Baseball Stadium at Camden Yards, as well as the Baltimore Ravens football stadium. Its cultural centers include the Walters Art Museum, the Peabody Conservatory of Music, and the Baltimore Museum of Art. The city also hosts major ballet, theater, and opera companies, as well as the Baltimore Symphony Orchestra. Baltimore is also geographically convenient to many areas along the mid-Atlantic region, including Washington, D.C., New York and Philadelphia.

The School

Standing with the top-ranked Johns Hopkins Schools of Medicine and Public Health and the internationally renowned Johns Hopkins Hospital, the Johns Hopkins School of Nursing offers an unmatched interprofessional environment to students and faculty.

The Johns Hopkins School of Nursing a globally-recognized leader in nursing education, research and practice and ranks No. 1 nationally among graduate schools of nursing and No. 2 for D.N.P. programs in the *U.S. News & World Report* 2019 rankings. In addition, the school is ranked by QS World University as the No. 3 nursing school in the world and is No.1 by College Choice for its master's program. The Johns Hopkins School of Nursing is also recognized as a Center of Excellence in Nursing Education by the National League of Nursing.

Johns Hopkins University is accredited by the Middle States Commission on Higher Education (MSCHE). The master's degree in nursing and Doctor of Nursing Practice at Johns Hopkins School of Nursing are accredited by the Commission on Collegiate Nursing Education. Additionally, the master's programs are approved by the Maryland State Board of Examiners of Nurses. The master's and doctoral programs are endorsed by the Maryland State Board for Higher Education.

Faculty

The outstanding faculty are nationally and internationally recognized for their contributions to nursing research and practice. The School has approximately 80 full-time faculty; 89 percent have doctoral degrees and 40 percent are Fellows in the American Academy of Nursing. Additional information regarding the nursing faculty can be found at nursing.jhu.edu/faculty

Applying

All program applications are via NursingCAS, the centralized application service for nursing, at nursingcas.org. In general, applicants to the School of Nursing are required to submit official transcripts from all post-secondary schools attended, academic and professional letters of recommendation, essay(s) or a goal statement, and a resume or CV through NursingCAS. The M.S.N./M.P.H., and Ph.D. programs require submission of the GRE. The Test of English as a Foreign Language is required if English is not the applicant's first language. A grade point average above 3.0 (on a 4.0 scale) is recommended. Personal interviews may be requested. Application requirements vary by program (see below). Applicants are encouraged to visit nursing.jhu.edu/academics to review specific program information and admissions requirements.

Priority application deadlines are as follows:

M.S.N. Entry into Nursing: Fall start, November 1 and January 1; spring start, July 1.

M.S.N. Health Systems Management Track: Fall start, June 15 (full-time), July 1 (part-time); spring start, November 15 (part-time).

M.S.N. Health Systems Management Track/MBA Dual Degree :Fall start, July 1.

M.S.N. Public Health/MPH Joint Degree: Summer start, November 1.

D.N.P. Advanced Practice Tracks: Fall start, November 1 and January 1.

D.N.P. Executive Track: Summer start: November 1 and January 1.

D.N.P. Executive Track/MBA Dual Degree: Summer start, November 1 and January 1.

Ph.D. in Nursing: Fall start: January 1.

D.N.P. Advanced Practice Track/Ph.D. Dual Degree: Summer start, January 1.

Post-Degree Certificates: Application deadliness vary, please visit nursing.jhu.edu/deadlines.

The most complete and up-to-date list of priority application deadlines by degree and specialty is available at nursing.jhu.edu/deadlines.

Additional information is available by contacting:

Johns Hopkins School of Nursing
525 North Wolfe Street
Baltimore, Maryland 21205
Phone: 410-955-7548
Fax: 410-614-7086
E-mail: jhuson@jhu.edu
Website: nursing.jhu.edu
youtube.com/hopkinsnursing

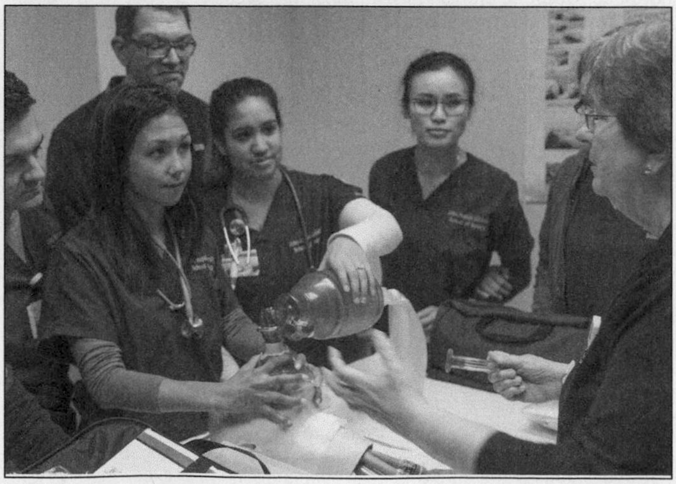

UNIVERSITY OF CONNECTICUT

Doctoral Programs in Nursing

★ For more information, visit http://petersons.to/uconnnursing

UCONN
SCHOOL OF NURSING

Programs of Study

The University of Connecticut (UConn) in Storrs, near Hartford, offers two doctoral degree programs in nursing: the Doctor of Philosophy in Nursing and the Doctorate of Nursing Practice. UConn's Doctorate of Nursing Practice degree program is recognized as one of the country's best by *U.S. News & World Report*, which also ranks UConn among the Top 20 Public Colleges. *Forbes* ranks the university among America's Best Public Colleges and Best Research Universities, as well.

Doctorate of Nursing Practice (D.N.P.): Graduates of this program are prepared to take on leadership roles in specialized practice or as clinical nurse leaders. The D.N.P. degree program at the UConn School of Nursing is open to applicants with a master's degree and any nursing specialty, including: clinical nurse leader, clinical nurse specialist, nurse anesthetist, nurse midwife, nurse practitioner, or nurse executive.

The post-master's D.N.P. plan of study is available for full- and part-time students. It includes 32 total hours of didactic and practice credits plus any post-B.S. clinical hours needed to reach 1,000. Students research and implement a project for evaluation during the residency portion of the program.

B.S. in Nursing or B.S.N. degree holders who want to earn the Master of Science degree in Nursing, an advanced practice certificate, and their doctoral degree in the same program can do so through UConn's B.S.-D.N.P. program. Students in this program may choose among four tracks of specialized study:

- Adult-Gerontology Nurse Practitioner: Acute Care
- Adult-Gerontology Nurse Practitioner: Primary Care
- Family Nurse Practitioner
- Neonatal Nurse Practitioner

Total credit requirements for these B.S.-D.N.P. tracks range from 72 to 75 hours.

Doctor of Philosophy (Ph.D.) in Nursing: The university's Ph.D. degree program in nursing is geared toward students who want to further their careers in basic or clinical research and health policy development. The School of Nursing offers full- and part-time B.S. to Ph.D. programs as well as part- and full-time Ph.D. programs for students with M.S. or M.S.N. degrees. Topics covered in the program are research methods and statistics, nursing theory and science, and specialized clinical study. Some courses in the program include: Philosophy of Science in Nursing, Responsible Conduct in Research, Introduction to Grantsmanship, and Advanced Nursing Knowledge Development.

Additional specialty courses in a concentrated area provides students with a focused program of research. The Ph.D. in Nursing program for students who already have an M.S./M.S.N. degree requires 52 credit hours, including the dissertation. The B.S.-Ph.D. program requires 72 credit hours, dissertation included.

Graduates of UConn's nursing doctoral programs include Dr. Millicent Malcolm, D.N.P., a gerontological nurse practitioner who practices at Middlesex Hospital, serves on the School of Nursing faculty, and was instrumental in acquiring federal funds for the interprofessional GOT Care! Program for senior health. Desiree Diaz, Ph.D., earned her bachelor's, master's, and doctoral nursing degrees from UConn and now directs the simulation center in the School of Nursing. Other graduates of the Ph.D. in Nursing program have published research in areas including breastfeeding and supplemental feeding tubes, pathogen identification tools for intestinal illnesses, adolescent healthcare outreach in schools, and neonatal health.

Research Resources and Interprofessional Opportunities

The university operates a number of programs that combine research opportunities and community outreach in such areas as correctional health for prison inmates, pain management improvements, neonatal and pediatric wellness, self-management Interventions, biobehavioral symptom science research, interprofessional education, and geriatric care. Among the resources available to doctoral candidates at UConn are nurse researchers with well-developed programs of research, federally funded projects ,and clinical expertise; and the biobehavioral research labs at the School of Nursing and UConn Health, including shared lab space and resources across the university to integrate genomics, proteomics, transcriptomics, metabolomics, and microbiomics. In addition, UConn's clinical partners across the University of Connecticut Health Center in Farmington and healthcare systems across the state provide students access to practical clinical experience and instruction, as well as offer ample opportunities for conducting research and implementing quality improvement projects. The nurse scholar archives in the Thomas Dodd Research Center and the nursing and sciences collections in the Homer Babbidge Library are among the best in the nation in terms of use for historical nursing research purposes.

The School of Nursing prides itself on providing interprofessional learning opportunities for its nursing students at every level. The interprofessional approach is widely accepted as a way to help students in a variety of health-related fields to understand various professional roles, learn to work collaboratively, and gain insights from other disciplines such as pharmacy, medicine, dentistry, and social work. UConn's CAMP (Center for Advancement in Managing Pain) is a nationally recognized center for collaborative, interdisciplinary research on pain research and treatment.

The School of Nursing's Center for Nursing Scholarship provides support from faculty members for students who are undertaking research projects. Some of the school's other opportunities for research and collaboration are available through:

- Conn AIMS (Analytics and Information Management Solutions), which uses patient data to improve care
- The annual ATHENA Research Conference on the Storrs campus, with presentations on a variety of nursing topics
- GOT Care! Geriatric Outreach and Training with Care, which provides interprofessional collaborative practice experiences in senior care as a partnership with Middlesex Hospital
- Center for Correctional Health Networks, which researches inmate healthcare issues and works to bring evidence-based care to prison populations
- Center for Advancement in Managing Pain, providing regular meeting and workshops for clinicians, researchers and educators across disciplines who work together on identifying better ways to manage pain and addiction

Each program includes input from researchers, practitioners, students, and patients.

Financial Aid

The Robert Wood Johnson Foundation funds two scholarships for UConn nursing PhD program students, and there are more than a dozen other University of Connecticut scholarship programs open to graduate nursing students. Research and teaching assistantships and federal nurse traineeships may be available to full-time students. Interested students should ask the School of Nursing's Admission and Enrollment Services office for a current list of financial aid options.

University of Connecticut

Cost of Study

Graduate tuition for the 2018–19 academic year is $853 per credit for Connecticut residents, $1,442 per credit for regional students, and $20,054 per credit for out-of-state students. Including fees, costs per semester range from $1,360 to $8,830 for in-state students, $1,949 to $14,128 for regional students, and $2,561 to $19,636 for out-of-state students.

Location

The D.N.P. program is primarily online, with intensive format courses on campus in August and in January.

The University

The University of Connecticut is one of the top public research universities in the nation, with more than 30,000 students pursuing answers to critical questions in labs, lecture halls, and the community. Knowledge exploration throughout the University's network of campuses is united by a culture of innovation. An unprecedented commitment from the state of Connecticut ensures UConn attracts internationally renowned faculty and the world's brightest students. As a vibrant, progressive leader, UConn fosters a diverse and dynamic culture that meets the challenges of a changing global society.

While the main campus is in Storrs, UConn expands beyond just that Storrs campus. With four regional campuses around the state, access to UConn is readily available throughout Connecticut. Small classes, access to talented faculty, and exclusive internships and majors allow students unique opportunities while still providing the benefit of a UConn education.

Faculty

The D.N.P. program at the University of Connecticut is directed by associate professor Joy Elwell, D.N.P., FNP-BC, FAANP, FAAN. She is a Fellow of the American Academy of Nursing whose experience includes private practice, parish practice, school district medical leadership, and academia.

The Ph.D. in Nursing program's interim director is professor E. Carol Polifroni, Ed.D., NEA-BC, CNE RN, ANEF. Her research has focused on medication errors, interdisciplinary education, and health policy.

Applying

Graduate School regulations and policies will govern admission to this program. These regulations require:

- An earned master's degree from an accredited college or university.
- Current licensure as a registered professional nurse.
- Master's degree level certification required in the applicant's area of specialty.
- A minimum grade point average of 3.0 in all courses of record.
- A personal statement from the applicant addressing his or her reasons for applying and his or her plans for the future.
- A personal Statement (reason for pursuing advanced practice nursing, reason for selecting the specialty track, and goals upon graduation)
- Three letters of reference from faculty or others who can address the candidate's potential for success in the graduate program.
- If not a native speaker of English, a TOEFL score of 550 or better.

In addition to Graduate School requirements, the following additional criteria will be used to evaluate students:

- Evidence of demonstrated competence in the discipline, including but not limited to undergraduate and graduate research experience or clinical experience.
- Personal interview by a potential graduate advisor, whenever possible.

Application forms and specific requirements and instructions are available online.

Contact

School of Nursing
Augustus Storrs Hall, Room WW17
231 Glenbrook Road, Unit 4026
University of Connecticut
Storrs, Connecticut 06269-4026
Phone: 860-486-1968
Fax: 860-486-0906
E-mail: Heatherspo@uconn.edu
Website: https://nursing.uconn.edu

UNIVERSITY OF CONNECTICUT

School of Nursing

★ For more information, visit http://petersons.to/uconnnursing

UCONN
SCHOOL OF NURSING

The University of Connecticut is a public research university located in Storrs, between Hartford and Providence. The university is among the top twenty public schools in the U.S., according to *US News & World Report*, and UConn's School of Nursing is home to top-rated graduate degree programs as well. *US News& World Report* rates UConn among its Best Nursing Schools for its master's and doctor of nursing practice degree programs. *Forbes* rates UConn among America's Best Research Universities and America's Best Public Colleges.

UConn's School of Nursing offers master's level, post-master's, and doctoral nursing programs, with flexibility to accommodate a variety of career goals and workloads.

There are two pathways to the Master of Science (M.S.) in Nursing in addition to the traditional B.S./B.S.N. to M.S./M.S.N. sequence. The RN to M.S. program gives NLN-accredited diploma- and associate degree–holders the opportunity to complete their bachelor's and master's degrees in nursing. The RN to M.S. program at UConn is also available with a slightly different course plan for registered nurses who have a bachelor's degree in a field other than nursing.

Master of Science (M.S.): This program is available part- or full-time and online. Students also work with a diverse group of medical mannequins in the Clinical Resource Center's Simulation Lab and undertake clinical practica for hands-on experience. Students in the M.S. degree program may choose from concentrations including:

- Adult-gerontology primary care nurse practitioner
- Adult-gerontology acute care nurse practitioner
- Family nurse practitioner, and
- Neonatal nurse practitioner

The master's degree program at UConn is fully accredited by the Commission on Collegiate Nursing Education. (CCNE).

Post-Master's Certificates: Registered nurses with an M.S. in Nursing or M.S.N. and a grade point average of at least 3.0 are eligible to apply for the University of Connecticut's post-master's certificate programs. Areas of clinical concentration include:

- Adult-Gerontology Acute Care Nurse Practitioner
- Adult-Gerontology Primary Care Nurse Practitioner
- Neonatal Nurse Practitioner

Each certificate program requires completion of 26 to 30 credit hours over the course of five semesters.

Doctoral Degrees: Nurses seeking a doctoral degree have two programs to choose from at the University of Connecticut. The Doctorate of Nursing Practice (D.N.P.) is open to students with a master's degree in nursing with a wide range of specialties, including: clinical nurse leader, clinical nurse specialist, nurse anesthetist, nurse midwife, nurse practitioner, or nurse executive.

The D.N.P. program is also open to B.S./B.S.N. degree holders who want to earn a master's degree and advanced practice certificate while pursuing their doctoral degree. The goal of the D.N.P. program is to prepare students for leadership and expert practice.

The Ph.D. in Nursing at UConn prepares students for research and health policy development roles. The pathways to a Ph.D. in Nursing at the school include full-time and part-time B.S. to Ph.D. programs as well as part- and full-time Ph.D. programs for students who already have a master's degree in nursing.

The School of Nursing has graduated many students who have gone on to be leaders in their fields. Among them are Christine Meehan, a 1974 graduate whose career has taken her from ICU nurse to medical device company founder to angel investor for medical tech companies run by women. Other UConn nursing students have built careers in clinical practice, hospital administration, healthcare training services, the federal government, and universities including Yale and the University of California, San Francisco.

The master's degree in nursing, Doctor of Nursing Practice program and post-graduate APRN certificate programs at the UConn School of Nursing are accredited by the Commission on Collegiate Nursing Education.

Facilities and Research Opportunities

UConn's affiliation with the University of Connecticut Health Center in Farmington, as well as other clinical partners across the state, expands students' practical learning opportunities. Among the school's on-campus resources for nursing graduate students are the nationally known Thomas Dodd Research Center and the Homer Babbidge Library. The School of Nursing's Josephine Dolan Collection focuses on the history of nursing.

Students can learn alongside professional nurses and researchers at UConn's yearly ATHENA Research Conference, where presentation topics range from critical care to professional ethics. Students wishing to pursue their own research projects can get guidance and support from the School of Nursing's Center for Nursing Scholarship. UConn AIMS (Analytics and Information Management Solutions) uses patient data to find ways to make healthcare more collaborative and to give patients better information for decision-making.

The School of Nursing at the University of Connecticut offers students interprofessional learning opportunities alongside students of pharmacy, social work, dentistry, and medicine. This interprofessional approach helps nursing students gain experience and develop skill in collaborating with teams of healthcare professionals. One example is UConn's nationally known Urban Service Track. It brings students in all these disciplines together with physician assistant students from Quinnipiac University to work with patients in under-served city neighborhoods.

UConn's School of Nursing also runs three programs designed to address specific care needs and best practices: GOT Care! Geriatric Outreach and Training with Care; the Center for Correctional Health Networks; and the Center for Advancement in Managing Pain. Each program involves interprofessional collaboration with researchers, practitioners, students, and patients in the community.

Financial Aid

There are more than a dozen University of Connecticut scholarship programs that are open to graduate nursing students, as well as two scholarships exclusively for students in the nursing Ph.D. program, funded by the Robert Wood Johnson Foundation. Full-time graduate students may be eligible for research and teaching assistantships and federal nurse traineeships that provide tuition support. Interested students should contact the School of Nursing's Admission and Enrollment Services office for a complete list of financial aid options.

Cost of Study

Graduate tuition for the 2018–19 academic year is $853 per credit for Connecticut residents, $1,442 per credit for regional students, and $20,054 per credit for out of state students. Including fees, costs per semester range from $1,360 to $8,830 for in-state students, $1,949 to $14,128 for regional students, and $2,561 to $19,636 for out-of-state students.

Location

Lecture courses usually meet once a week for three to four hours. Courses are primarily offered on the Storrs Campus in either morning, afternoon or evening time slots. Core courses are offered via distance technology to Hartford, UConn Health Center and/or Avery Point in either afternoon or evening time slots. Clinical practicums are offered in a variety of sites throughout Connecticut and nationally when appropriate.

The University

The University of Connecticut is one of the top public research universities in the nation, with more than 30,000 students pursuing answers to critical questions in labs, lecture halls, and the community. Knowledge exploration throughout the University's network of campuses is united by a culture of innovation. An unprecedented commitment from the state of Connecticut ensures UConn attracts internationally renowned faculty and the world's brightest students. As a vibrant, progressive leader, UConn fosters a diverse and dynamic culture that meets the challenges of a changing global society.

While the main campus is in Storrs, UConn expands beyond just that Storrs campus. With four regional campuses around the state, access to UConn is readily available throughout Connecticut. Small classes, access to talented faculty, and exclusive internships and majors allow students unique opportunities while still providing the benefit of a UConn education.

Faculty

UConn's School of Nursing has several dozen faculty members, some of whom have dual appointments in the University of Connecticut School of Medicine. Among the faculty members who direct programs within the nursing school is Sandra Bellini, D.N.P., APRN, NNP-BC, CNE, who directs the Neonatal Advance Practice Program and who helped to develop and launch the Doctorate of Nursing Practice degree program at UConn. Denise Bourassa, M.S.N., RN, CNL, contributes to the Interprofessional Education mission across the university and has received multiple awards for academics and the application of nursing research in practice. Joy Elwell, D.N.P., FNP-BC, FAANP, FAAN, is a practicing family nurse practitioner who directs the D.N.P. program, serves on the School of Medicine Faculty, and has earned national acclaim for her legislative efforts on behalf of the nurse practitioner profession.

Xiaomei Cong, Ph.D., RN, leads the Center for Advancement in Pain Management. Her areas of research include neonatal stress, pain responses, and the impact of stress and pain on infant development. She also leads a program of research to examine genetic vulnerabilities to chronic symptoms and alterations in the gut microbiome that influence health outcomes in adolescents and young adults. Cheryl Beck, D.N.Sc., CNM, FAAN, is Board of Trustees distinguished professor and acclaimed author of several nursing textbooks. Her program of research is focused on postpartum depression and traumatic birth. Angela Starkweather is Professor directs the National Institute of Health-funded P20 Center for Accelerating Precision Pain Self-Management. As a Fellow of the American Academy of Nursing she has served as Chair of the Genomic Nursing and Health Care Expert Panel, and serves on various professional committees including as an Ambassador of the Friends of the National Institute of Nursing, Council for Advancement of Nursing Science, and the American Association of Neuroscience Nurses Clinical Practice Guidelines Board.

Applying

General admission requirements for the M.S. program are:

- a bachelor's degree in nursing from an accredited college or university
- a cumulative grade point average of 3.0 or better for the entire undergraduate record, or 3.0 or better for the last two years of a bachelor's degree program
- a current Connecticut RN license
- a three-credit undergraduate statistics courses completed with a grade of C or better
- a three-credit undergraduate research course completed with a grade of C or better
- comprehensive health assessment knowledge for professional nursing praxis documented by a three-credit course or its equivalent for students enrolling in individual specialty tracks
- contemporary nursing and related science knowledge in order to be successful in the advanced courses within the graduate program.

The following application materials must be submitted online to the Graduate School:

- Official transcripts from all previous undergraduate and graduate coursework
- Graduate School Application
- Application fee
- Photocopy of the Connecticut RN license
- Three letters of reference (professional, employer/supervisor, academic)
- Copy of your curriculum vitae or resume
- Residency affidavit until May 1st
- Personal Statement (describe rationale for graduate nursing education and for specific track selected)

Applications are accepted through January 15. Rolling admissions will be available thereafter for programs with space available. For financial aid consideration application deadline for fall enrollment is March 1.

Contact

School of Nursing
Augustus Storrs Hall, Room WW17
231 Glenbrook Road, Unit 4026
University of Connecticut
Storrs, Connecticut 06269-4026
Phone: 860-486-1968
Fax: 860-486-0906
E-mail: Heatherspo@uconn.edu
Website: https://nursing.uconn.edu

UNIVERSITY OF WISCONSIN MILWAUKEE

College of Nursing

UNIVERSITY of WISCONSIN
UWMILWAUKEE
College of Nursing

Program of Study

An innovative, academic nursing community, the University of Wisconsin-Milwaukee College of Nursing faculty, staff, students and alumni are renowned leaders in creating bold and effective solutions for advancing local, national and global health.

UW-Milwaukee's nursing program is valued for its ability to prepare science-based, compassionate nurse leaders through innovative, superior educational programs. The College is a vibrant, innovative environment for teaching, research, practice, and service to the community and the profession. The College is one of three universities in the state to offer students the full range of nursing degrees including: Bachelor of Science in Nursing, Master of Nursing, Doctor of Philosophy in Nursing, and Doctor of Nursing Practice.

The College offers a Master in Nursing (M.N.) program with two entry options. The Master of Nursing degree is for nurses and non-nurses who hold a bachelor's degree and wish to pursue an advanced degree in nursing. The program provides the framework for practice as a clinical nurse leader, public health nurse, clinical research manager, health informatics specialist or nurse manager. The M.N. Direct Entry option admits students as a cohort which allows relationships among peers and faculty to develop through the program. After 16 months, students are eligible to sit for the NCLEX-RN examination, allowing students to work as Registered Nurses while completing the remaining MN credits. Through the curriculum and time spent in the Nursing Learning Resource Center (NLRC), students will have a variety of clinical experiences providing a broad overview of all of the major specialties in which nurses work, as well as a variety of settings across the health care. Students also have volunteer opportunities to expand their education.

The Master of Sustainable Peacebuilding (M.S.P.) is new to the College of Nursing and prepares practitioners, from any academic background, with skills and concepts required to engage and change issues at a global or local level. The interacting forces of urbanization, climate change, economic inequity and ideological polarization intertwine to generate complex pressures on the environment, society, and culture. Figuring out where to start requires transdisciplinary systems-based approaches and new ways of thinking about solutions and fixes. The M.S.P. provides the conceptual foundation and instills the practical skills for engaging complex problems with methods for building peace. The M.S.P.'s premise is that healthy and sustainable communities lead to long-term positive change. M.S.P. students learn techniques for grappling with complexity and developing strategies for effective change, while building critical leadership skills in facilitation, strategic planning, and evaluation. These skills can be applied across diverse employment sectors, such as population and community health, natural resources stewardship, conflict transformation, global security, education and nonprofit management.

In addition to the Masters programs, the College offers two doctoral programs: Doctor of Nursing Practice (D.N.P.) and Doctor of Philosophy in Nursing (Ph.D.) in face-to-face and online formats. Students in the doctoral programs work closely with faculty mentors to define success early and develop into key clinical and research partners.

The D.N.P. is a practice-focused doctoral program that prepares advanced-practice nurses for the highest level of clinical nursing practice beyond the initial preparation in the discipline. The program prepares students to develop clinical, organizational, economic, and leadership skills to design and implement programs of care delivery that will significantly impact health care outcomes and transform health care delivery. Graduates with this terminal practice degree will be prepared for roles in direct care or indirect, systems-focused care. Students who enter from a bachelor's degree to D.N.P. can specialize as: family nurse practitioner, clinical nurse specialist, leadership/systems, and community/public health.

The College of Nursing's Ph.D. program integrates science, theory, and research to educate the next generation of nurse scientists and educators. Students strive to advance nursing knowledge and translate research into practice that promotes the health and care of patients. This research-intensive program prepares doctoral students as scientists who generate knowledge to advance nursing. For maximum flexibility, the program is offered in-person and online, both full-time (9 credits) and part-time (6 credits), and structured so that the required courses are offered only one day per week. What students accomplish in the college's traditional Ph.D. program depends on their focus area, personal interests and long-term research and career preferences. Faculty mentors help Ph.D. candidates define their success early, and plan and conduct cutting-edge research. These research and mentorship experiences prepare doctoral students for successful careers as scientists, as educators and for other opportunities in the rapidly evolving nursing professions.

Research Facilities

UW-Milwaukee is designated as one of only 115 universities (out of 4,600) in the country as an R-1 doctoral research university by the Carnegie Classification of Institutions of Higher Education. The College of Nursing is one of the most robust scientific research ventures on campus. The global and national perspectives expand the reach of the College's work in key areas, including community-engaged health research, geriatric health care, global health, healthcare delivery and system development and self-management.

The College pioneered and is home to two nurse-managed Community Nursing Centers, serving the uninsured and underinsured communities and providing healthcare solutions aligned with their needs. The Self-Management Science Center, funded by the National Institutes of Health (P20NR015339), expands research aimed at enhancing the science of self-management in individuals and families. Faculty members and students have also extended the scope of international research to health care in rural Malawi, Thailand, and Kenya. The College also maintains a 15-year partnership with two sister nursing schools in South Korea.

Research support is provided through the Harriet H. Werley Center for Nursing Research and Evaluation (WCNRE). The WCNRE was established in 1977 under a federal Faculty Research Development Grant and continues to offer support to faculty and nursing community.

Financial Aid

A variety of options are available to help students finance their education, including over $500,000 in scholarships annually, as well as loans, grants, student employment, fellowships, military education benefits, and more.

Cost of Study

Graduate-level tuition and fees for the 2017–18 academic year were $11,830 for Wisconsin residents, $17,024 for Midwest Student Exchange Rate students, and $24,868 for nonresidents.

Location

As the seventh-most exciting city in America (Movoto.com), Milwaukee offers students a vibrant city on the shores of beautiful Lake Michigan, just 90 minutes north of Chicago. Milwaukee boasts a beautiful lakefront, a world-class art museum, hundreds of parks and recreational opportunities, major-league sports, a range of unique restaurants, and exciting events all year round. Big enough to offer urban amenities, small enough that it's possible to get most places within 20 minutes.

University of Wisconsin Milwaukee

UW–Milwaukee students can use UPASS for unlimited free rides on the county bus system.

The University and The College

As Wisconsin's largest nursing program, the University of Wisconsin–Milwaukee College of Nursing has made its home in the commercial, cultural, and economic capital of Wisconsin for over 50 years. The College of Nursing has an enrollment of over 1,200 undergraduate and 300 graduate students. The College of Nursing is a premier, urban, academic, collegial, nursing community that acts collaboratively with partners to:

- Prepare a diverse population of students to become science based, compassionate, nurse leaders through innovative, quality, educational programs for all settings and levels of practice.
- Conduct research and scholarship that advance science in nursing and health.
- Address emerging health needs through evidence based practice and consultation; and
- Develop leaders who transform health care delivery.

UW-Milwaukee is a community inspired by history and motivated by vision. It offers a uniquely relevant learning experience, educating more Wisconsin residents than any university in the world and recruiting a growing population of international students and faculty. As the most diverse institution in the University of Wisconsin System, it's a learning destination for more than 25,000 students. The campus occupies 104 acres and offers 193 degree programs.

Faculty

The College of Nursing faculty challenges students, creating innovative classroom environments using the latest technology while maintaining over 130 clinical and research partnerships throughout Southeast Wisconsin. Faculty members embrace practice by engaging regional and global communities in the development of solutions to improve health care. The College is consistently ranked in the top 15 percent for academic excellence among colleges with graduate nursing programs by *U.S. News & World Report.* Faculty members embrace practice by engaging regional and global communities in the development of solutions to improve health care.

Applying

The UW–Milwaukee College of Nursing offers a priority deadline for application to its programs. For fall admission, February 1 is the priority deadline for master's-level programs and January 1 is the priority deadline for Ph.D. programs. For spring admission, October 1 is the priority deadline for master's-level programs and September 1 is the priority deadline for Ph.D. programs. All materials should be sent in by the deadline for full consideration of admission and funding opportunities. After the priority deadline has passed, admission of applicants to the graduate programs will be made on a space available basis.

More information about the UW–Milwaukee College of Nursing can be found at www.nursing.uwm.edu.

Correspondence and Information

Office of Student Affairs
University of Wisconsin—Milwaukee College of Nursing
1921 East Hartford Avenue
Milwaukee, Wisconsin 53201
Phone: 414-229-5047
Fax: 414-229-5554
E-mail: uwmnurse@uwm.edu

Ph.D. in Nursing students discuss complex issues facing nursing science.

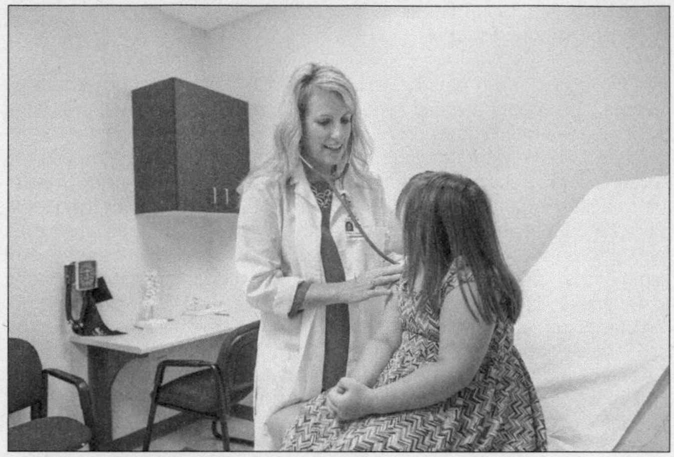

DNP students apply evidence-based research to practice.

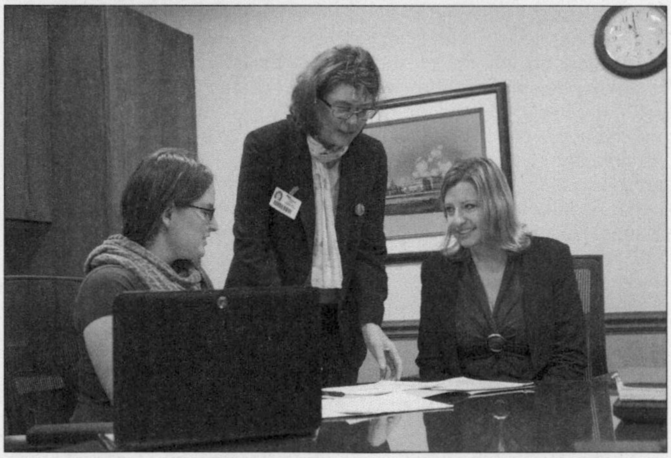

Students and faculty work together to impact health care quality and delivery.

Section 24
Public Health

This section contains a directory of institutions offering graduate work in public health, followed by an in-depth entry submitted by an institution that chose to prepare a detailed program description. Additional information about programs listed in the directory but not augmented by an in-depth entry may be obtained by writing directly to the dean of a graduate school or chair of a department at the address given in the directory.

For programs offering related work, see also in this book *Allied Health; Biological and Biomedical Sciences; Ecology, Environmental Biology, and Evolutionary Biology; Health Services; Microbiological Sciences; Nursing;* and *Nutrition.* In the other guides in this series:

Graduate Programs in the Humanities, Arts & Social Sciences

See *Family and Consumer Sciences (Gerontology)* and *Sociology, Anthropology, and Archaeology (Demography and Population Studies)*

Graduate Programs in the Physical Sciences, Mathematics, Agricultural Sciences, the Environment & Natural Resources

See *Mathematical Sciences* and *Environmental Sciences and Management*

Graduate Programs in Engineering & Applied Sciences

See *Biomedical Engineering and Biotechnology, Civil and Environmental Engineering, Industrial Engineering, Energy and Power Engineering (Nuclear Engineering),* and *Management of Engineering and Technology*

Graduate Programs in Business, Education, Information Studies, Law & Social Work

See *Education.*

CONTENTS

Program Directories

Featured Schools: Displays and Close-Ups

Public Health—General

Adelphi University, College of Nursing and Public Health, Program in Public Health, Garden City, NY 11530-0701. Offers MPH. *Students:* 20 full-time (14 women), 46 part-time (42 women); includes 32 minority (18 Black or African American, non-Hispanic/Latino; 8 Asian, non-Hispanic/Latino; 5 Hispanic/Latino; 1 Two or more races, non-Hispanic/Latino), 8 international. Average age 31. 87 applicants, 46% accepted, 22 enrolled. In 2017, 7 master's awarded. *Entrance requirements:* Additional exam requirements/recommendations for international students: Required—TOEFL (minimum score 550 paper-based; 80 iBT), IELTS (minimum score 6.5). Application fee: $50. *Expenses:* Contact institution. *Financial support:* Research assistantships, teaching assistantships, career-related internships or fieldwork, institutionally sponsored loans, scholarships/grants, traineeships, and unspecified assistantships available. Support available to part-time students. *Unit head:* Philip Alcabes, Director, 516-237-8668, E-mail: palcabes@adelphi.edu.

Allen College, Graduate Programs, Waterloo, IA 50703. Offers adult-gerontology acute care nurse practitioner (MSN); community/public health nursing (MSN); education (MSN); family nurse practitioner (MSN); health sciences (Ed D); leadership in health care delivery (MSN); leadership in health care informatics (MSN); nursing (DNP); occupational therapy (MS); psychiatric mental health nurse practitioner (MSN). MSN in leadership in healthcare informatics offered in partnership with University of Minnesota. *Accreditation:* AACN; ACEN. *Program availability:* Part-time, 100% online, blended/hybrid learning. *Faculty:* 24 full-time (all women), 8 part-time/adjunct (7 women). *Students:* 106 full-time (91 women), 187 part-time (164 women); includes 22 minority (12 Black or African American, non-Hispanic/Latino; 1 American Indian or Alaska Native, non-Hispanic/Latino; 2 Asian, non-Hispanic/Latino; 3 Hispanic/Latino; 4 Two or more races, non-Hispanic/Latino), 2 international. Average age 33. 352 applicants, 56% accepted, 131 enrolled. In 2017, 73 master's, 2 doctorates awarded. *Entrance requirements:* For master's, minimum GPA of 3.0 in the last 60 hours of undergraduate coursework; for doctorate, minimum GPA of 3.25 in graduate coursework. *Application deadline:* For fall admission, 2/1 priority date for domestic students; for spring admission, 9/1 priority date for domestic students. Applications are processed on a rolling basis. Application fee: $50. Electronic applications accepted. *Expenses:* $17,860 per year. *Financial support:* In 2017–18, 97 students received support. Federal Work-Study, institutionally sponsored loans, scholarships/grants, and traineeships available. Support available to part-time students. Financial award application deadline: 8/1; financial award applicants required to submit FAFSA. *Faculty research:* Poverty. *Unit head:* Dr. Nancy Kramer, Vice Chancellor for Academic Affairs, 319-226-2040, Fax: 319-226-2070, E-mail: nancy.kramer@allencollege.edu. *Application contact:* Molly Quinn, Director of Admissions, 319-226-2001, Fax: 319-226-2010, E-mail: molly.quinn@allencollege.edu.
Website: http://www.allencollege.edu/

American University of Armenia, Graduate Programs, Yerevan, Armenia. Offers business administration (MBA); computer and information science (MS), including business management, design and manufacturing, energy (ME, MS), industrial engineering and systems management; economics (MS); industrial engineering and systems management (ME), including business, computer aided design/manufacturing, energy (ME, MS), information technology; law (LL M); political science and international affairs (MPSIA); public health (MPH); teaching English as a foreign language (MA). *Program availability:* Part-time, evening/weekend. *Degree requirements:* For master's, thesis (for some programs), capstone/project. *Entrance requirements:* For master's, GRE, GMAT, or LSAT. Additional exam requirements/recommendations for international students: Recommended—TOEFL (minimum score 79 iBT), IELTS (minimum score 6.5). *Faculty research:* Microfinance, finance (rural/development, international, corporate), firm life cycle theory, TESOL, language proficiency testing, public policy, administrative law, economic development, cryptography, artificial intelligence, energy efficiency/renewable energy, computer-aided design/manufacturing, health financing, tuberculosis control, mother/child health, preventive ophthalmology, post-earthquake psychopathological investigations, tobacco control, environmental health risk assessments.

American University of Beirut, Graduate Programs, Faculty of Agricultural and Food Sciences, Beirut, Lebanon. Offers agricultural economics (MS); animal science (MS); ecosystem management (MSES); food safety (MS); food security (MS); food technology (MS); irrigation (MS); nutrition (MS); plant protection (MS); plant science (MS); poultry science (MS); public health nutrition (MS); rural community development (MS). *Program availability:* Part-time. *Faculty:* 16 full-time (4 women), 1 part-time/adjunct (0 women). *Students:* 76 full-time (58 women), 19 part-time (13 women); includes 6 minority (all Black or African American, non-Hispanic/Latino). Average age 25. 142 applicants, 72% accepted, 32 enrolled. In 2017, 20 master's awarded. *Degree requirements:* For master's, one foreign language, comprehensive exam, thesis (for some programs). *Entrance requirements:* Additional exam requirements/recommendations for international students: Required—TOEFL (minimum score 600 paper-based; 100 iBT), IELTS (minimum score 7.5). *Application deadline:* For fall admission, 2/10 for domestic and international students; for spring admission, 11/2 for domestic and international students. Application fee: $50. Electronic applications accepted. *Expenses: Tuition:* Full-time $17,244; part-time $958 per credit. *Required fees:* $740. Tuition and fees vary according to course load and program. *Financial support:* In 2017–18, 9 research assistantships with partial tuition reimbursements (averaging $1,800 per year), 47 teaching assistantships with full and partial tuition reimbursements (averaging $1,400 per year) were awarded; scholarships/grants, health care benefits, and unspecified assistantships also available. Financial award application deadline: 2/2. *Faculty research:* Refugee socio-economic vulnerability, nutrition in emergencies, forest and landscape restoration, broiler immunological response, vegetated infrastructure in deserts. *Total annual research expenditures:* $600,000. *Unit head:* Rabi Hassan Mohtar, Dean of Faculty of Agricultural and Food Sciences, 961-1-350000 Ext. 4400, Fax: 961-1-744460, E-mail: mohtar@aub.edu.lb. *Application contact:* Prof. Zaher Dawy, Graduate Council Chairperson, 961-1-374374 Ext. 4386, Fax: 961-1-374376, E-mail: graduate.council@aub.edu.lb.
Website: http://www.aub.edu.lb/fafs/Pages/default.aspx

American University of Beirut, Graduate Programs, Faculty of Health Sciences, 1107 2020, Lebanon. Offers environmental sciences (MS), including environmental health; epidemiology (MS, PhD); epidemiology and biostatistics (MPH); health care leadership (EMHCL); health management and policy (MPH), including health service administration; health promotion and community health (MPH); health research (MS); public health nutrition (MS). *Program availability:* Part-time. *Faculty:* 33 full-time (22 women), 5 part-time/adjunct (2 women). *Students:* 75 full-time (60 women), 78 part-time (67 women). Average age 27. 274 applicants, 56% accepted, 47 enrolled. In 2017, 63 master's awarded. *Degree requirements:* For master's, one foreign language, comprehensive exam (for some programs), thesis (for MS); for doctorate, one foreign language, comprehensive exam, thesis/dissertation. *Entrance requirements:* For master's, 2 letters of recommendations, personal statement, transcript; for doctorate, GRE, 3 letters of recommendations, personal statement, interview. Additional exam requirements/recommendations for international students: Required—TOEFL (minimum score 583 paper-based; 97 iBT), IELTS (minimum score 7). *Application deadline:* For fall admission, 4/4 for domestic and international students; for spring admission, 11/3 for domestic and international students. Application fee: $50. Electronic applications accepted. *Expenses:* Contact institution. *Financial support:* In 2017–18, 75 students received support. Scholarships/grants, health care benefits, and unspecified assistantships available. Financial award application deadline: 4/4. *Faculty research:* Reproductive and sexual health; occupational and environmental health; conflict and health; mental health; quality in health care delivery, tobacco control. *Total annual research expenditures:* $2 million. *Unit head:* Prof. Iman Adel Nuwayhid, Dean/Professor, 961-1-759683 Ext. 4600, Fax: 961-1-744470, E-mail: nuwayhid@aub.edu.lb. *Application contact:* Mitra Tauk, Administrative Coordinator, 961-1-350000 Ext. 4687, E-mail: mt12@aub.edu.lb.
Website: http://www.aub.edu.lb/fhs/fhs_home/Pages/index.aspx

Andrews University, School of Health Professions, Department of Nutrition, Berrien Springs, MI 49104. Offers nutrition (MS); nutrition and dietetics (Certificate); public health (MPH). *Program availability:* Part-time. *Faculty:* 1 (woman) full-time, 7 part-time/adjunct (2 women). *Students:* 1 (woman) full-time, 22 part-time (20 women); includes 13 minority (8 Black or African American, non-Hispanic/Latino; 1 Asian, non-Hispanic/Latino; 4 Hispanic/Latino), 5 international. Average age 35. 59 applicants, 78% accepted, 14 enrolled. In 2017, 10 master's, 14 other advanced degrees awarded. *Entrance requirements:* For master's, GRE. Additional exam requirements/recommendations for international students: Required—TOEFL (minimum score 550 paper-based). *Application deadline:* Applications are processed on a rolling basis. Application fee: $40. *Faculty research:* Exercise education. *Unit head:* Dr. Sherine Brown-Fraser, Chairperson, 269-471-3370. *Application contact:* Justina Clayburn, Supervisor of Graduate Admission, 800-253-2874, Fax: 269-471-6321, E-mail: graduate@andrews.edu.
Website: http://www.andrews.edu/shp/nutrition/

Arcadia University, College of Health Sciences, Department of Public Health, Program in Public Health, Glenside, PA 19038-3295. Offers MPH. *Accreditation:* CEPH. *Expenses:* Contact institution.

Argosy University, Atlanta, College of Health Sciences, Atlanta, GA 30328. Offers public health (MPH).

Argosy University, Chicago, College of Health Sciences, Chicago, IL 60601. Offers public health (MPH).

Argosy University, Hawai`i, College of Health Sciences, Honolulu, HI 96813. Offers public health (MPH).

Argosy University, Los Angeles, College of Health Sciences, Los Angeles, CA 90045. Offers public health (MPH).

Argosy University, Northern Virginia, College of Health Sciences, Arlington, VA 22209. Offers public health (MPH).

Argosy University, Orange County, College of Health Sciences, Orange, CA 92868. Offers public health (MPH).

Argosy University, Phoenix, College of Health Sciences, Phoenix, AZ 85021. Offers public health (MPH).

Argosy University, Seattle, College of Health Sciences, Seattle, WA 98121. Offers public health (MPH).

Argosy University, Tampa, College of Health Sciences, Tampa, FL 33607. Offers public health (MPH).

Argosy University, Twin Cities, College of Health Sciences, Eagan, MN 55121. Offers health services management (MS); public health (MPH).

Arizona State University at the Tempe campus, College of Nursing and Health Innovation, Phoenix, AZ 85004. Offers advanced nursing practice (DNP); clinical research management (MS); community and public health practice (Graduate Certificate); family mental health nurse practitioner (Graduate Certificate); family nurse practitioner (Graduate Certificate); geriatric nursing (Graduate Certificate); healthcare innovation (MHI); nurse education in academic and practice settings (Graduate Certificate); nurse educator (MS); nursing and healthcare innovation (PhD). *Accreditation:* AACN. *Program availability:* Online learning. *Degree requirements:* For master's, comprehensive exam (for some programs), thesis (for some programs), interactive Program of Study (iPOS) submitted before completing 50 percent of required credit hours; for doctorate, comprehensive exam, thesis/dissertation, interactive Program of Study (iPOS) submitted before completing 50 percent of required credit hours. *Entrance requirements:* For master's and doctorate, GRE, minimum GPA of 3.0 or equivalent in last 2 years of work leading to bachelor's degree. Additional exam requirements/recommendations for international students: Required—TOEFL, IELTS, or PTE. Electronic applications accepted. *Expenses:* Contact institution.

A.T. Still University, College of Graduate Health Studies, Kirksville, MO 63501. Offers dental public health (MPH); exercise and sport psychology (Certificate); fundamentals of education (Certificate); geriatric exercise science (Certificate); global health (Certificate); health administration (MHA, DHA); health professions (Ed D); health sciences (DH Sc); kinesiology (MS); leadership and organizational behavior (Certificate); public health (MPH); sports conditioning (Certificate). *Program availability:* Part-time, evening/weekend, online only, 100% online, blended/hybrid learning. *Faculty:* 28 full-time (18 women), 83 part-time/adjunct (43 women). *Students:* 537 full-time (334 women), 516 part-time (316 women); includes 397 minority (171 Black or African American, non-Hispanic/Latino; 14 American Indian or Alaska Native, non-Hispanic/Latino; 84 Asian, non-Hispanic/Latino; 106 Hispanic/Latino; 1 Native Hawaiian or other Pacific Islander, non-Hispanic/Latino; 21 Two or more races, non-Hispanic/Latino), 43 international. Average age 36. 392 applicants, 84% accepted, 270 enrolled. In 2017, 138 master's, 102 doctorates, 116 other advanced degrees awarded. *Degree requirements:* For master's, thesis, integrated terminal project, practicum; for doctorate, thesis/dissertation. *Entrance requirements:* For master's, minimum GPA of 2.5, bachelor's degree or equivalent, essay, resume, English proficiency; for doctorate, minimum GPA of 2.5, master's or terminal degree, essay, past experience in relevant field, resume, English proficiency. Additional exam requirements/recommendations for international students: Required—TOEFL (minimum score 550 paper-based; 80 iBT). *Application deadline:* For fall admission, 6/26 for domestic students, 5/20 for international students; for winter admission, 9/11 for domestic students, 9/12 for international students; for spring admission, 12/11 for domestic students, 12/12 for international students; for summer

admission, 3/5 for domestic students, 3/6 for international students. Applications are processed on a rolling basis. Application fee: $70. Electronic applications accepted. *Financial support:* In 2017–18, 18 students received support. Scholarships/grants available. Financial award applicants required to submit FAFSA. *Faculty research:* Public health: influence of availability of comprehensive wellness resources online, student wellness, oral health care needs assessment of community, oral health knowledge and behaviors of Medicaid-eligible pregnant women and mothers of young children in relations to early childhood caries and tooth decay, alcohol use and alcohol related problems among college students. *Unit head:* Dr. Donald Altman, Dean, 480-219-6008, Fax: 660-626-2826, E-mail: daltman@atsu.edu. *Application contact:* Amie Waldemer, Associate Director, Online Admissions, 480-219-6146, E-mail: awaldemer@atsu.edu.
Website: http://www.atsu.edu/college-of-graduate-health-studies

Augusta University, College of Allied Health Sciences, Program in Public Health, Augusta, GA 30912. Offers environmental health (MPH); health informatics (MPH); health management (MPH); social and behavioral sciences (MPH). *Accreditation:* CEPH. *Program availability:* Part-time. *Degree requirements:* For master's, thesis (for some programs). *Entrance requirements:* For master's, GRE General Test, three letters of recommendation. Additional exam requirements/recommendations for international students: Required—TOEFL. Electronic applications accepted.

Austin Peay State University, College of Graduate Studies, College of Behavioral and Health Sciences, Department of Health and Human Performance, Clarksville, TN 37044. Offers public health education (MS); sports and wellness leadership (MS). *Program availability:* Part-time, evening/weekend, online learning. *Faculty:* 8 full-time (4 women). *Students:* 14 full-time (7 women), 38 part-time (27 women); includes 15 minority (10 Black or African American, non-Hispanic/Latino; 1 Asian, non-Hispanic/Latino; 2 Hispanic/Latino; 2 Two or more races, non-Hispanic/Latino), 1 international. Average age 29. 66 applicants, 67% accepted, 33 enrolled. In 2017, 34 master's awarded. *Degree requirements:* For master's, comprehensive exam, thesis optional. *Entrance requirements:* For master's, GRE General Test, 3 letters of recommendation, minimum undergraduate GPA of 2.5. Additional exam requirements/recommendations for international students: Required—TOEFL (minimum score 500 paper-based). *Application deadline:* For fall admission, 8/8 priority date for domestic students. Applications are processed on a rolling basis. Application fee: $45 ($55 for international students). Electronic applications accepted. *Expenses:* Tuition, state resident: full-time $7686; part-time $427 per credit hour. Tuition, nonresident: full-time $20,268; part-time $1126 per credit hour. *Required fees:* $1529; $76.45 per credit hour. *Financial support:* Research assistantships with full tuition reimbursements, career-related internships or fieldwork, Federal Work-Study, institutionally sponsored loans, scholarships/grants, and unspecified assistantships available. Support available to part-time students. Financial award application deadline: 4/1; financial award applicants required to submit FAFSA. *Unit head:* Dr. Marcy Maurer, Chair, 931-221-6105, Fax: 931-221-7040, E-mail: maurerm@apsu.edu. *Application contact:* Megan Mitchell, Coordinator of Graduate Admissions, 931-221-6189, Fax: 931-221-7641, E-mail: mitchellm@apsu.edu.
Website: http://www.apsu.edu/hhp/index.php

Azusa Pacific University, University College, Azusa, CA 91702-7000. Offers leadership and organizational studies (MA); public health (MPH). *Program availability:* Online learning.

Baldwin Wallace University, Graduate Programs, Public Health Program, Berea, OH 44017-2088. Offers health education and disease prevention (MPH); population health leadership and management (MPH). Program offered in partnership with The MetroHealth System. *Program availability:* Part-time, evening/weekend, online learning. *Faculty:* 1 full-time (0 women), 1 part-time/adjunct (0 women). *Students:* 23 full-time (18 women), 1 (woman) part-time; includes 9 minority (2 Black or African American, non-Hispanic/Latino; 3 Asian, non-Hispanic/Latino; 2 Hispanic/Latino; 2 Two or more races, non-Hispanic/Latino), 1 international. Average age 39. 30 applicants, 57% accepted, 13 enrolled. *Entrance requirements:* For master's, GRE. Additional exam requirements/recommendations for international students: Required—TOEFL (minimum score 550 paper-based; 100 iBT). *Application deadline:* For fall admission, 7/15 for domestic students. Applications are processed on a rolling basis. *Expenses:* $921 per credit hour. *Financial support:* Applicants required to submit FAFSA. *Unit head:* Stephen D. Stahl, Provost, Academic Affairs, 440-826-2251, Fax: 440-826-2329, E-mail: sstahl@bw.edu. *Application contact:* Winnie W. Gerhardt, Director of Transfer, Adult and Graduate Admission, 440-826-8002, E-mail: wgerhard@bw.edu.
Website: http://www.bw.edu/academics/master-public-health/

Barry University, School of Podiatric Medicine, Podiatric Medicine and Surgery Program, Podiatric Medicine/Public Health Option, Miami Shores, FL 33161-6695. Offers DPM/MPH.

Belmont University, College of Pharmacy, Nashville, TN 37212. Offers advanced pharmacotherapy (Pharm D); health care informatics (Pharm D); management (Pharm D); missions/public health (Pharm D); Pharm D/MBA. Pharm D/MBA offered in collaboration with Jack C. Massey Graduate School of Business. *Accreditation:* ACPE. *Faculty:* 25 full-time (16 women), 3 part-time/adjunct (2 women). *Students:* 323 full-time (216 women); includes 90 minority (37 Black or African American, non-Hispanic/Latino; 38 Asian, non-Hispanic/Latino; 10 Hispanic/Latino; 5 Two or more races, non-Hispanic/Latino), 1 international. Average age 25. 638 applicants, 34% accepted, 94 enrolled. In 2017, 65 doctorates awarded. *Degree requirements:* For doctorate, comprehensive exam. *Entrance requirements:* For doctorate, PCAT. Additional exam requirements/recommendations for international students: Required—TOEFL. *Application deadline:* For fall admission, 8/31 priority date for domestic students; for spring admission, 3/1 for domestic students. Applications are processed on a rolling basis. Application fee: $50. Electronic applications accepted. *Expenses:* $18,670 tuition per semester. *Financial support:* In 2017–18, 112 students received support. Career-related internships or fieldwork and scholarships/grants available. Financial award applicants required to submit FAFSA. *Faculty research:* Academic innovation, cultural competency, medication errors, patient safety. *Unit head:* Dr. David Gregory, Dean, 615-460-6746, Fax: 615-460-6741, E-mail: david.gregory@belmont.edu.
Website: http://www.belmont.edu/pharmacy/index.html

Benedictine University, Graduate Programs, Program in Public Health, Lisle, IL 60532. Offers administration of health care institutions (MPH); dietetics (MPH); disaster management (MPH); health education (MPH); health information systems (MPH); MBA/MPH; MPH/MS. *Accreditation:* CEPH. *Program availability:* Part-time, evening/weekend, online learning. *Entrance requirements:* For master's, MAT, GRE, or GMAT. Additional exam requirements/recommendations for international students: Required—TOEFL (minimum score 550 paper-based).

Boise State University, College of Health Sciences, Boise, ID 83725-0399. Offers MAL, MHS, MK, MS, MSN, MSW, DNP, Graduate Certificate. *Program availability:* Part-time, 100% online. *Faculty:* 72. *Students:* 221 full-time (174 women), 183 part-time (138 women); includes 42 minority (11 Black or African American, non-Hispanic/Latino; 3 Asian, non-Hispanic/Latino; 24 Hispanic/Latino; 1 Native Hawaiian or other Pacific Islander, non-Hispanic/Latino; 3 Two or more races, non-Hispanic/Latino). Average age 35. 246 applicants, 49% accepted, 85 enrolled. In 2017, 151 master's, 13 other advanced degrees awarded. *Degree requirements:* For master's, comprehensive exam (for some programs), thesis (for some programs); for doctorate, thesis/dissertation. *Entrance requirements:* For master's, GRE General Test, GMAT or MAT, minimum GPA of 3.0. Additional exam requirements/recommendations for international students: Required—TOEFL (minimum score 550 paper-based; 80 iBT), IELTS (minimum score 6). *Application deadline:* Applications are processed on a rolling basis. Application fee: $65 ($95 for international students). Electronic applications accepted. *Expenses:* Tuition, state resident: full-time $6471; part-time $390 per credit. Tuition, nonresident: full-time $21,787; part-time $685 per credit. *Required fees:* $2283; $100 per term. Part-time tuition and fees vary according to course load and program. *Financial support:* Research assistantships, scholarships/grants, and unspecified assistantships available. Financial award applicants required to submit FAFSA. *Unit head:* Dr. Tim Dunnagan, Dean, 208-426-4150, E-mail: timdunnagan@boisestate.edu. *Application contact:* Alicia Anderson, Project Director, 208-426-2425, E-mail: aliciaanderson@boisestate.edu.
Website: http://hs.boisestate.edu/

Boston University, School of Public Health, Boston, MA 02118. Offers MA, MPH, MS, Dr PH, PhD, JD/MPH, MBA/MPH, MD/MPH, MPH/MS, MSW/MPH. *Program availability:* Part-time, evening/weekend. *Faculty:* 153 full-time, 271 part-time/adjunct. *Students:* 688 full-time (560 women), 318 part-time (271 women); includes 296 minority (66 Black or African American, non-Hispanic/Latino; 2 American Indian or Alaska Native, non-Hispanic/Latino; 124 Asian, non-Hispanic/Latino; 78 Hispanic/Latino; 1 Native Hawaiian or other Pacific Islander, non-Hispanic/Latino; 25 Two or more races, non-Hispanic/Latino), 125 international. Average age 26. 2,594 applicants, 43% accepted, 396 enrolled. In 2017, 489 master's, 22 doctorates awarded. *Degree requirements:* For master's, comprehensive exam (for some programs), thesis optional, practicum, integrative learning experience; for doctorate, comprehensive exam (for some programs), thesis/dissertation, comprehensive written and oral exams. *Entrance requirements:* For master's, GRE, GMAT, U.S. bachelor's degree or international equivalent; for doctorate, GRE, GMAT, MPH or equivalent. Additional exam requirements/recommendations for international students: Required—TOEFL (minimum score 600 paper-based; 100 iBT), IELTS (minimum score 7). *Application deadline:* For fall admission, 1/1 priority date for domestic and international students; for spring admission, 10/1 priority date for domestic and international students. Applications are processed on a rolling basis. Application fee: $120. Electronic applications accepted. *Financial support:* In 2017–18, 421 students received support. Fellowships, teaching assistantships, career-related internships or fieldwork, Federal Work-Study, institutionally sponsored loans, scholarships/grants, traineeships, and tuition waivers (partial) available. Support available to part-time students. Financial award application deadline: 5/31; financial award applicants required to submit FAFSA. *Faculty research:* Clinical trials, observational studies, environmental epidemiology, global ecology, environmental sustainability, community health, environmental justice, infectious disease, non-infectious disease, research methods, pharmaceutical assessment, bioethics, health law, human rights, health policy, management, finance and management, family health, disease control in developing countries, child and adolescent health, women's health, health disparities. *Unit head:* Dr. Sandro Galea, Dean, 617-638-4640, Fax: 617-638-5299, E-mail: asksph@bu.edu. *Application contact:* LePhan Quan, Associate Director of Admissions, 617-638-4640, Fax: 617-638-5299, E-mail: asksph@bu.edu.
Website: http://www.bu.edu/sph

Bowling Green State University, Graduate College, College of Health and Human Services, Program in Public Health, Bowling Green, OH 43403. Offers MPH. *Program availability:* Part-time. *Degree requirements:* For master's, thesis or alternative. *Entrance requirements:* For master's, GRE General Test, minimum GPA of 3.0. Additional exam requirements/recommendations for international students: Required—TOEFL. Electronic applications accepted.

Brigham Young University, Graduate Studies, College of Life Sciences, Department of Public Health, Provo, UT 84602. Offers MPH. *Faculty:* 19 full-time (6 women). *Students:* 25 full-time (20 women), 1 part-time (0 women); includes 8 minority (2 Black or African American, non-Hispanic/Latino; 2 American Indian or Alaska Native, non-Hispanic/Latino; 2 Hispanic/Latino; 2 Native Hawaiian or other Pacific Islander, non-Hispanic/Latino). Average age 24. 23 applicants, 65% accepted, 14 enrolled. In 2017, 16 master's awarded. *Degree requirements:* For master's, comprehensive exam, thesis or alternative, CPH exam. *Entrance requirements:* For master's, GRE General Test (minimum score of 300), minimum cumulative GPA of 3.2. Additional exam requirements/recommendations for international students: Required—TOEFL (minimum score 580 paper-based; 85 iBT), IELTS (minimum score 7). *Application deadline:* For fall admission, 2/1 for domestic and international students. Application fee: $50. Electronic applications accepted. *Expenses:* $14,160 tuition. *Financial support:* In 2017–18, 26 students received support, including 26 fellowships with partial tuition reimbursements available (averaging $1,250 per year), 10 research assistantships (averaging $1,645 per year), 3 teaching assistantships (averaging $595 per year); career-related internships or fieldwork, scholarships/grants, tuition waivers (partial), and unspecified assistantships also available. Financial award application deadline: 3/1. *Faculty research:* Social marketing, health communication, cancer, substance abuse. *Total annual research expenditures:* $39,334. *Unit head:* Carl Lee Hanson, Chair, 801-422-9103, Fax: 801-422-0004, E-mail: carl_hanson@byu.edu. *Application contact:* Benjamin T. Crookston, MPH Director, 801-422-3143, Fax: 801-422-0004, E-mail: benjamin_crookston@byu.edu.
Website: http://healthscience.byu.edu/

Brooklyn College of the City University of New York, School of Natural and Behavioral Sciences, Department of Health and Nutrition Sciences, Program in Public Health, Brooklyn, NY 11210-2889. Offers general public health (MPH); health care policy and administration (MPH). *Degree requirements:* For master's, thesis or alternative, 46 credits. *Entrance requirements:* For master's, GRE, 2 letters of recommendation, essay, interview. Electronic applications accepted.

Brown University, Graduate School, Division of Biology and Medicine, School of Public Health, Program in Public Health, Providence, RI 02912. Offers MPH. *Entrance requirements:* For master's, GRE General Test or MCAT. Additional exam requirements/recommendations for international students: Required—TOEFL.

California Baptist University, Program in Public Health, Riverside, CA 92504-3206. Offers health education and promotion (MPH); health policy and administration (MPH). *Program availability:* Part-time, evening/weekend. *Faculty:* 9 full-time (5 women), 4 part-time/adjunct (2 women). *Students:* 56 full-time (47 women), 37 part-time (30 women); includes 72 minority (18 Black or African American, non-Hispanic/Latino; 8 Asian, non-Hispanic/Latino; 38 Hispanic/Latino; 8 Two or more races, non-Hispanic/Latino), 4 international. Average age 28. 83 applicants, 64% accepted, 39 enrolled. In 2017, 4 master's awarded. *Degree requirements:* For master's, capstone project; practicum. *Entrance requirements:* For master's, minimum undergraduate GPA of 2.75, two recommendations, 500-word essay, resume. Additional exam requirements/recommendations for international students: Required—TOEFL (minimum score 80 iBT). *Application deadline:* For fall admission, 8/1 priority date for domestic students, 7/1 for international students; for spring admission, 12/1 priority date for domestic students, 11/1 for international students. Applications are processed on a rolling basis. Application

fee: $45. Electronic applications accepted. *Expenses:* Contact institution. *Financial support:* In 2017–18, 22 students received support. Federal Work-Study and scholarships/grants available. Financial award applicants required to submit CSS PROFILE or FAFSA. *Faculty research:* Epidemiology, statistical education, exercise and immunity, obesity and chronic disease. *Unit head:* Dr. David Pearson, Dean, College of Health Science, 951-343-4298, E-mail: dpearson@calbaptist.edu. *Application contact:* Tamakia King, Graduate Admissions Counselor, 951-552-8138, E-mail: tking@calbaptist.edu.
Website: http://www.calbaptist.edu/explore-cbu/schools-colleges/college-allied-health/health-sciences/master-public-health/

California State University, Fresno, Division of Research and Graduate Studies, College of Health and Human Services, Department of Public Health, Fresno, CA 93740-8027. Offers health policy and management (MPH); health promotion (MPH). *Accreditation:* CEPH. *Program availability:* Part-time, evening/weekend. *Degree requirements:* For master's, thesis or alternative. *Entrance requirements:* For master's, GRE General Test, minimum GPA of 2.5. Additional exam requirements/recommendations for international students: Required—TOEFL. Electronic applications accepted. *Faculty research:* Foster parent training, geriatrics, tobacco control.

California State University, Fullerton, Graduate Studies, College of Health and Human Development, Department of Public Health, Fullerton, CA 92831-3599. Offers environmental and occupational health and safety (MPH); gerontological health (MPH); health promotion and disease (MPH). *Accreditation:* CEPH. *Program availability:* Part-time. *Students:* 37 full-time (31 women), 29 part-time (21 women); includes 41 minority (2 Black or African American, non-Hispanic/Latino; 14 Asian, non-Hispanic/Latino; 23 Hispanic/Latino; 1 Native Hawaiian or other Pacific Islander, non-Hispanic/Latino; 1 Two or more races, non-Hispanic/Latino), 2 international. Average age 30. 105 applicants, 47% accepted, 21 enrolled. In 2017, 26 master's awarded. *Entrance requirements:* For master's, minimum GPA of 3.0 in last 60 units attempted. Application fee: $55. *Financial support:* Career-related internships or fieldwork, Federal Work-Study, institutionally sponsored loans, and scholarships/grants available. Support available to part-time students. Financial award application deadline: 3/1; financial award applicants required to submit FAFSA. *Unit head:* Head, 657-278-2620. *Application contact:* Admissions/Applications, 657-278-2371.
Website: http://hhd.fullerton.edu/hesc/

California State University, Long Beach, Graduate Studies, College of Health and Human Services, Department of Health Science, Long Beach, CA 90840. Offers MPH. *Accreditation:* CEPH; NCATE. *Program availability:* Part-time. *Degree requirements:* For master's, thesis optional. *Entrance requirements:* For master's, GRE, minimum GPA of 3.0 in last 60 units. Electronic applications accepted.

California State University, Northridge, Graduate Studies, College of Health and Human Development, Department of Health Sciences, Northridge, CA 91330. Offers health administration (MS); public health (MPH), including applied epidemiology, community health education. *Accreditation:* CEPH. *Students:* 128 full-time (96 women), 53 part-time (45 women); includes 96 minority (10 Black or African American, non-Hispanic/Latino; 21 Asian, non-Hispanic/Latino; 53 Hispanic/Latino; 1 Native Hawaiian or other Pacific Islander, non-Hispanic/Latino; 11 Two or more races, non-Hispanic/Latino), 6 international. Average age 30. 323 applicants, 38% accepted, 68 enrolled. In 2017, 70 master's awarded. *Entrance requirements:* For master's, GRE General Test or minimum GPA of 3.0. Additional exam requirements/recommendations for international students: Required—TOEFL. *Application deadline:* For fall admission, 11/30 for domestic students. Application fee: $55. *Financial support:* Teaching assistantships available. Financial award application deadline: 3/1. *Faculty research:* Labor market needs assessment, health education products, dental hygiene, independent practice prototype. *Unit head:* Louis Rubino, Chair, 818-677-3101.
Website: http://www.csun.edu/hhd/hsci/

California State University, San Bernardino, Graduate Studies, College of Natural Sciences, Program in Public Health, San Bernardino, CA 92407. Offers MPH. *Students:* 15 full-time (11 women), 30 part-time (25 women); includes 26 minority (1 Black or African American, non-Hispanic/Latino; 3 Asian, non-Hispanic/Latino; 20 Hispanic/Latino; 1 Native Hawaiian or other Pacific Islander, non-Hispanic/Latino; 1 Two or more races, non-Hispanic/Latino), 1 international. Average age 31. 54 applicants, 52% accepted, 18 enrolled. In 2017, 7 master's awarded. *Entrance requirements:* Additional exam requirements/recommendations for international students: Required—TOEFL. *Application deadline:* For fall admission, 5/5 for domestic students. Application fee: $55. *Unit head:* Dr. Monideepa Becerra, Program Coordinator, 909-537-5969, E-mail: mbecerra@csusb.edu. *Application contact:* Dr. Dorota Huizinga, Dean of Graduate Studies, 909-537-3064, E-mail: dorota.huizinga@csusb.edu.

California State University, San Marcos, College of Education, Health and Human Services, Program in Public Health, San Marcos, CA 92096-0001. Offers MPH. *Expenses:* Tuition, state resident: full-time $7176. Tuition, nonresident: full-time $9504.

Case Western Reserve University, School of Medicine and School of Graduate Studies, Graduate Programs in Medicine, Department of Population and Quantitative Health Sciences, Program in Public Health, Cleveland, OH 44106. Offers MPH. *Accreditation:* CEPH. *Program availability:* Part-time. *Degree requirements:* For master's, essay, field experience, presentation. *Entrance requirements:* For master's, GRE General Test or MCAT, 3 letters of recommendation. Additional exam requirements/recommendations for international students: Required—TOEFL. Electronic applications accepted. *Expenses: Tuition:* Full-time $43,854; part-time $1827 per credit hour. *Required fees:* $50; $50 per credit hour. Tuition and fees vary according to course load and program. *Faculty research:* Public policy and aging, statistical modeling, behavioral medicine and evaluation, continuous quality improvement; tobacco cessation and prevention.

Charles R. Drew University of Medicine and Science, College of Science and Health, Los Angeles, CA 90059. Offers urban public health (MPH). *Accreditation:* CEPH.

Chicago State University, School of Graduate and Professional Studies, College of Health Sciences, Department of Health Studies, Chicago, IL 60628. Offers public health (MPH). *Unit head:* Dr. Thomas Britt, Chairperson, 773-821-2201, Fax: 773-995-3284, E-mail: tbritt@csu.edu. *Application contact:* Daphne G. Townsend, Admissions and Records Officer II, 773-995-2404, Fax: 773-995-3671, E-mail: g-studies1@csu.edu.
Website: http://www.csu.edu/collegeofhealthsciences/healthstudies/

Claremont Graduate University, Graduate Programs, School of Community and Global Health, Claremont, CA 91773. Offers health promotion science (PhD); public health (MPH). *Accreditation:* CEPH. *Entrance requirements:* For master's and doctorate, GRE. Additional exam requirements/recommendations for international students: Required—TOEFL (minimum score 75 iBT). Electronic applications accepted.

Clemson University, Graduate School, College of Behavioral, Social and Health Sciences, Department of Public Health Sciences, Clemson, SC 29634. Offers applied health research and evaluation (MS, PhD); biomedical data science and informatics (PhD); clinical and translational research (Certificate). *Program availability:* Part-time, 100% online. *Faculty:* 22 full-time (13 women). *Students:* 13 full-time (9 women), 25 part-time (17 women); includes 3 minority (1 Black or African American, non-Hispanic/Latino; 1 Asian, non-Hispanic/Latino; 1 Hispanic/Latino), 4 international. Average age 36. 25 applicants, 68% accepted, 11 enrolled. In 2017, 1 master's, 10 other advanced degrees awarded. *Degree requirements:* For doctorate, comprehensive exam, thesis/dissertation. *Entrance requirements:* For master's and Certificate, GRE General Test, curriculum vitae, statement of career goals, letters of recommendation, unofficial transcripts; for doctorate, GRE General Test, MS/MA thesis or publications, curriculum vitae, statement of career goals, letters of recommendation, unofficial transcripts. Additional exam requirements/recommendations for international students: Required—TOEFL (minimum score 80 iBT), IELTS (minimum score 6.5), PTE (minimum score 54). *Application deadline:* For fall admission, 4/15 for international students; for spring admission, 10/15 for international students. Applications are processed on a rolling basis. Application fee: $80 ($90 for international students). Electronic applications accepted. *Expenses:* $6,564 per semester full-time resident, $12,538 per semester full-time non-resident, $743 per credit hour part-time resident, $1,486 per credit hour part-time non-resident, $1,203 per credit hour online, other fees may apply per session. *Financial support:* In 2017–18, 7 students received support, including 2 research assistantships with partial tuition reimbursements available (averaging $16,596 per year), 5 teaching assistantships with partial tuition reimbursements available (averaging $14,400 per year); career-related internships or fieldwork also available. *Faculty research:* Health promotion and behavior, epidemiology and outcomes research, public health informatics, health policy and health services research, global health, evaluation. *Total annual research expenditures:* $1.2 million. *Unit head:* Dr. Ronald Gimbel, Department Chair, 864-656-1969, E-mail: rgimbel@clemson.edu. *Application contact:* Dr. Joel Williams, Graduate Program Coordinator, 864-656-1017, E-mail: joel2@clemson.edu.
Website: http://www.clemson.edu/cbshs/departments/public-health/index.html

Cleveland State University, College of Graduate Studies, College of Education and Human Services, Department of Health and Human Performance, Cleveland, OH 44115. Offers physical education pedagogy (M Ed); public health (MPH). *Program availability:* Part-time. *Faculty:* 7 full-time (4 women), 3 part-time/adjunct (2 women). *Students:* 30 full-time (16 women), 60 part-time (36 women); includes 43 minority (33 Black or African American, non-Hispanic/Latino; 4 Asian, non-Hispanic/Latino; 2 Hispanic/Latino; 1 Native Hawaiian or other Pacific Islander, non-Hispanic/Latino; 3 Two or more races, non-Hispanic/Latino), 5 international. Average age 29. 103 applicants, 72% accepted, 43 enrolled. In 2017, 44 master's awarded. *Degree requirements:* For master's, comprehensive exam, thesis optional. *Entrance requirements:* For master's, GRE General Test or MAT (if undergraduate GPA less than 2.75), minimum undergraduate GPA of 2.75. Additional exam requirements/recommendations for international students: Required—TOEFL (minimum score 550 paper-based; 78 iBT), IELTS (minimum score 6). *Application deadline:* For fall admission, 7/15 priority date for domestic students; for spring admission, 12/15 priority date for domestic students. Applications are processed on a rolling basis. Application fee: $30. Electronic applications accepted. *Financial support:* In 2017–18, 6 research assistantships with tuition reimbursements (averaging $3,480 per year), 1 teaching assistantship with tuition reimbursement (averaging $3,480 per year) were awarded; career-related internships or fieldwork, tuition waivers (full), and unspecified assistantships also available. Financial award application deadline: 3/15; financial award applicants required to submit FAFSA. *Faculty research:* Bone density, marketing fitness centers, motor development of disabled, online learning and survey research. *Unit head:* Dr. Mike Loovis, Associate Professor/Department Chairperson, 216-687-3665, Fax: 216-687-5410, E-mail: e.loovis@csuohio.edu. *Application contact:* David Easler, Director, Graduate Recruitment, 216-687-5047, Fax: 216-687-5400, E-mail: d.easler@csuohio.edu.
Website: http://www.csuohio.edu/cehs/departments/HPERD/hperd_dept.html

The College at Brockport, State University of New York, School of Education, Health, and Human Services, Department of Public Health and Health Education, Brockport, NY 14420-2997. Offers community health education (MS Ed); health education (MS Ed), including health education K-12. *Faculty:* 2 full-time (0 women), 3 part-time/adjunct (2 women). *Students:* 5 full-time (3 women), 26 part-time (11 women); includes 2 minority (1 Black or African American, non-Hispanic/Latino; 1 Hispanic/Latino). 11 applicants, 82% accepted, 7 enrolled. In 2017, 7 master's awarded. *Degree requirements:* For master's, thesis or alternative. *Entrance requirements:* For master's, minimum GPA of 3.0, letters of recommendation. Additional exam requirements/recommendations for international students: Required—TOEFL (minimum score 550 paper-based; 79 iBT), IELTS (minimum score 6.5). *Application deadline:* For fall admission, 3/1 priority date for domestic and international students; for spring admission, 10/1 priority date for domestic and international students; for summer admission, 3/1 priority date for domestic and international students. Application fee: $80. Electronic applications accepted. *Expenses:* Tuition, state resident: full-time $10,870; part-time $453 per credit hour. Tuition, nonresident: full-time $22,210. *Required fees:* $988; $246 per semester. *Financial support:* In 2017–18, 1 teaching assistantship with full tuition reimbursement (averaging $6,000 per year) was awarded; Federal Work-Study, scholarships/grants, and unspecified assistantships also available. Support available to part-time students. Financial award application deadline: 3/15; financial award applicants required to submit FAFSA. *Faculty research:* Nutrition, substance use, HIV/AIDS, bioethics, worksite health. *Unit head:* Dr. Darson Rhodes, Graduate Director, 585-395-5901, Fax: 585-395-5246, E-mail: drhodes@brockport.edu. *Application contact:* Danielle A. Welch, Graduate Admissions Counselor, 585-395-5465, Fax: 585-395-2515.
Website: https://www.brockport.edu/academics/public_health/

The College of New Jersey, Office of Graduate and Advancing Education, School of Nursing, Health, and Exercise Science, Program in Public Health, Ewing, NJ 08628. Offers global health (MPH); health communications (MPH); precision health (MPH).

College of Saint Elizabeth, Program in Public Health, Morristown, NJ 07960-6989. Offers MPH. *Program availability:* Part-time. *Faculty:* 1 (woman) part-time/adjunct. *Students:* 5 part-time (all women); includes 4 minority (2 Black or African American, non-Hispanic/Latino; 2 Hispanic/Latino). Average age 34. 5 applicants, 100% accepted, 5 enrolled. *Degree requirements:* For master's, thesis. *Entrance requirements:* Additional exam requirements/recommendations for international students: Required—TOEFL (minimum score 550 paper-based; 79 iBT), IELTS (minimum score 6.5). *Application deadline:* For fall admission, 5/1 for international students. Applications are processed on a rolling basis. Application fee: $35. Electronic applications accepted. Application fee is waived when completed online. *Financial support:* Career-related internships or fieldwork, scholarships/grants, and unspecified assistantships available. Financial award applicants required to submit FAFSA. *Unit head:* Dr. Regina Riccioni, Chair, 973-290-4271, E-mail: rriccioni@cse.edu. *Application contact:* Lori J. Fragoso, Director of Graduate and Continuing Studies Admissions, 973-290-4194, Fax: 973-290-4710, E-mail: apply@cse.edu.
Website: http://www.cse.edu/academics/prof-studies/public-health/master-of-public-health

Columbia University, Columbia University Mailman School of Public Health, New York, NY 10032. Offers Exec MHA, Exec MPH, MHA, MPH, MS, Dr PH, PhD, DDS/MPH, MBA/MPH, MD/MPH, MPA/MPH, MPH/MIA, MPH/MOT, MPH/MS, MPH/MSN, MPH/MSSW. PhD offered in cooperation with the Graduate School of Arts and Sciences.

Accreditation: CEPH (one or more programs are accredited). *Program availability:* Part-time, evening/weekend. *Students:* 913 full-time (707 women), 483 part-time (346 women); includes 518 minority (91 Black or African American, non-Hispanic/Latino; 3 American Indian or Alaska Native, non-Hispanic/Latino; 272 Asian, non-Hispanic/Latino; 111 Hispanic/Latino; 41 Two or more races, non-Hispanic/Latino), 282 international. Average age 28. 3,146 applicants, 55% accepted, 644 enrolled. In 2017, 601 master's, 22 doctorates awarded. *Degree requirements:* For master's, thesis (for some programs); for doctorate, comprehensive exam, thesis/dissertation. *Entrance requirements:* For master's, GRE General Test; for doctorate, GRE General Test, MPH or equivalent (for Dr PH). Additional exam requirements/recommendations for international students: Required—TOEFL (minimum score 600 paper-based; 100 iBT). *Application deadline:* For fall admission, 12/1 priority date for domestic and international students. Application fee: $120. Electronic applications accepted. *Expenses:* Contact institution. *Financial support:* Fellowships, research assistantships, teaching assistantships, career-related internships or fieldwork, Federal Work-Study, and traineeships available. Support available to part-time students. Financial award application deadline: 2/1; financial award applicants required to submit FAFSA. *Unit head:* Dr. Linda P. Fried, Dean/Professor, 212-305-9300, Fax: 212-305-9342, E-mail: lpfried@columbia.edu. *Application contact:* Clare Norton, Associate Dean for Enrollment Management, 212-305-8698, Fax: 212-342-1861, E-mail: ph-admit@columbia.edu.
Website: https://www.mailman.columbia.edu/

Creighton University, Graduate School, Department of Interdisciplinary Studies, Master of Public Health Program, Omaha, NE 68178-0001. Offers MPH. *Program availability:* Part-time. *Faculty:* 4 full-time (all women). *Students:* 4 full-time (3 women), 82 part-time (66 women); includes 9 minority (3 Black or African American, non-Hispanic/Latino; 5 Asian, non-Hispanic/Latino; 1 Hispanic/Latino), 3 international. Average age 33. 15 applicants, 100% accepted, 10 enrolled. In 2017, 55 master's awarded. *Degree requirements:* For master's, practicum. *Entrance requirements:* For master's, resume, essay. Additional exam requirements/recommendations for international students: Required—TOEFL (minimum score 90 iBT), IELTS (minimum score 6.5). *Application deadline:* For fall admission, 7/1 for domestic and international students; for spring admission, 12/1 for domestic and international students. Applications are processed on a rolling basis. Application fee: $50. Electronic applications accepted. *Expenses:* $980 per credit. *Financial support:* Scholarships/grants available. Financial award applicants required to submit FAFSA. *Unit head:* Dr. Tanya Benedict, Director. *Application contact:* Lindsay Johnson, Director of Graduate and Adult Recruitment, 402-280-2703, Fax: 402-280-2423, E-mail: gradschool@creighton.edu.
Website: https://online.creighton.edu/mph/masters-in-public-health

Daemen College, Program in Public Health, Amherst, NY 14226-3592. Offers community health education (MPH); epidemiology (MPH); generalist (MPH). *Program availability:* Part-time, online learning. *Degree requirements:* For master's, practicum.

Dartmouth College, The Dartmouth Institute, Program in Public Health, Hanover, NH 03755. Offers MPH. *Accreditation:* CEPH. *Program availability:* Part-time. *Students:* 64 full-time (33 women), 49 part-time (35 women); includes 20 minority (3 Black or African American, non-Hispanic/Latino; 2 American Indian or Alaska Native, non-Hispanic/Latino; 11 Asian, non-Hispanic/Latino; 1 Hispanic/Latino; 3 Two or more races, non-Hispanic/Latino), 6 international. Average age 33. 307 applicants, 57% accepted, 83 enrolled. In 2017, 48 master's awarded. *Degree requirements:* For master's, research project or practicum. *Entrance requirements:* For master's, GRE or MCAT, 3 letters of recommendation. Additional exam requirements/recommendations for international students: Required—TOEFL. *Application deadline:* For fall admission, 1/15 for domestic students. Applications are processed on a rolling basis. Application fee: $135. *Unit head:* Dr. Elliot S. Fisher, Director, 603-653-0802. *Application contact:* Marc Aquila, Senior Director of Recruitment and Admissions, 603-650-1539, E-mail: marc.l.aquila@dartmouth.edu.
Website: http://tdi.dartmouth.edu/education/degree-programs/mph-ms

Davenport University, Sneden Graduate School, Grand Rapids, MI 49512. Offers accounting (MBA); business administration (EMBA); finance (MBA); health care management (MBA); human resources (MBA); information assurance (MS); public health (MPH); strategic management (MBA). *Program availability:* Evening/weekend. *Entrance requirements:* For master's, GMAT, minimum undergraduate GPA of 2.75. Additional exam requirements/recommendations for international students: Required—TOEFL. Electronic applications accepted. *Faculty research:* Leadership, management, marketing, organizational culture.

DePaul University, College of Liberal Arts and Social Sciences, Chicago, IL 60614. Offers Arabic (MA); Chinese (MA); critical ethnic studies (MA); English (MA); French (MA); German (MA); history (MA); interdisciplinary studies (MA, MS); international public service (MS); international studies (MA); Italian (MA); Japanese (MA); liberal studies (MA); nonprofit management (MNM); public administration (MPA); public health (MPH); public policy (MPP); public service management (MS); refugee and forced migration studies (MS); social work (MSW); sociology (MA); Spanish (MA); sustainable urban development (MA); women's and gender studies (MA); writing and publishing (MA); writing, rhetoric and discourse (MA); MA/PhD. *Program availability:* Part-time, evening/weekend, online learning. Terminal master's awarded for partial completion of doctoral program. *Degree requirements:* For master's, variable foreign language requirement, comprehensive exam (for some programs), thesis (for some programs). *Application deadline:* Applications are processed on a rolling basis. Application fee: $40. Electronic applications accepted. *Financial support:* Applicants required to submit FAFSA. *Unit head:* Dr. Guillermo Vasquez de Velasco, Dean, 773-325-7305. *Application contact:* Ann Spittle, Director of Graduate Admission, 773-325-8369, Fax: 312-476-3244, E-mail: graddepaul@depaul.edu.
Website: http://las.depaul.edu/

Des Moines University, College of Health Sciences, Program in Public Health, Des Moines, IA 50312-4104. Offers MPH. *Accreditation:* CEPH. *Program availability:* Part-time, evening/weekend. *Entrance requirements:* For master's, minimum GPA of 3.0. Additional exam requirements/recommendations for international students: Required—TOEFL (minimum score 600 paper-based). Electronic applications accepted. *Expenses:* Contact institution. *Faculty research:* Quality improvement, women's health, health promotion, patient education.

Drexel University, Dornsife School of Public Health, Philadelphia, PA 19104-2875. Offers MPH, MS, PhD, Certificate. *Entrance requirements:* For master's, GMAT, GRE, LSAT, or MCAT, previous course work in statistics and word processing. Additional exam requirements/recommendations for international students: Required—TOEFL. Electronic applications accepted. *Expenses:* Contact institution. *Faculty research:* Epidemiology, behavioral and social sciences, problem-based learning.

East Carolina University, Brody School of Medicine, Department of Public Health, Greenville, NC 27858-4353. Offers public health (Dr PH); MD/MPH. *Accreditation:* CEPH. *Program availability:* Part-time, online learning. *Students:* 75 full-time (56 women), 22 part-time (18 women); includes 46 minority (25 Black or African American, non-Hispanic/Latino; 4 American Indian or Alaska Native, non-Hispanic/Latino; 8 Asian, non-Hispanic/Latino; 6 Hispanic/Latino; 3 Two or more races, non-Hispanic/Latino), 2 international. Average age 26. 59 applicants, 90% accepted, 31 enrolled. In 2017, 41 master's awarded. *Degree requirements:* For master's, capstone courses (internship and professional paper). *Entrance requirements:* For master's, GRE. Additional exam requirements/recommendations for international students: Recommended—TOEFL (minimum score 550 paper-based; 78 iBT), IELTS (minimum score 6.5). *Application deadline:* For fall admission, 4/15 for domestic and international students; for spring admission, 10/15 for domestic and international students. Application fee: $75. Electronic applications accepted. *Expenses:* Tuition, state resident: full-time $4749; part-time $297 per credit hour. Tuition, nonresident: full-time $17,898; part-time $1119 per credit hour. *Required fees:* $2691; $224 per credit hour. Part-time tuition and fees vary according to course load and program. *Financial support:* Research assistantships and unspecified assistantships available. Financial award applicants required to submit FAFSA. *Faculty research:* Public health, disparities in public health. *Unit head:* Dr. Maria C. Clay, Chairman, Bioethics, 252-744-1290, E-mail: clayma@ecu.edu.

East Carolina University, Graduate School, College of Fine Arts and Communication, School of Communication, Greenville, NC 27858-4353. Offers communication (MA); health communication (Certificate). *Students:* 12 full-time (11 women), 32 part-time (25 women); includes 14 minority (11 Black or African American, non-Hispanic/Latino; 1 Asian, non-Hispanic/Latino; 1 Hispanic/Latino; 1 Two or more races, non-Hispanic/Latino), 1 international. Average age 32. 19 applicants, 84% accepted, 13 enrolled. In 2017, 12 master's, 3 other advanced degrees awarded. *Degree requirements:* For master's, thesis or alternative. *Entrance requirements:* For master's, GRE. Additional exam requirements/recommendations for international students: Required—TOEFL. *Application deadline:* For fall admission, 6/1 priority date for domestic students; for spring admission, 10/15 for domestic students. Applications are processed on a rolling basis. Electronic applications accepted. *Expenses:* Tuition, state resident: full-time $4749; part-time $297 per credit hour. Tuition, nonresident: full-time $17,898; part-time $1119 per credit hour. *Required fees:* $2691; $224 per credit hour. Part-time tuition and fees vary according to course load and program. *Financial support:* Teaching assistantships available. *Unit head:* Dr. Linda Kean, Director, 252-328-4227, E-mail: keanl@ecu.edu.
Website: http://www.ecu.edu/comm/

Eastern Virginia Medical School, Master of Public Health Program, Norfolk, VA 23501-1980. Offers MPH. Program offered jointly with Old Dominion University. *Accreditation:* CEPH. *Program availability:* Evening/weekend. *Degree requirements:* For master's, field practicum. *Entrance requirements:* For master's, GRE General Test. Additional exam requirements/recommendations for international students: Required—TOEFL (minimum score 650 paper-based). Electronic applications accepted. *Expenses:* Contact institution.

Eastern Washington University, Graduate Studies, College of Health Science and Public Health, Program in Public Health, Cheney, WA 99004-2431. Offers MPH. *Faculty:* 7. *Students:* 32 full-time (20 women), 22 part-time (14 women); includes 7 minority (2 Black or African American, non-Hispanic/Latino; 1 American Indian or Alaska Native, non-Hispanic/Latino; 1 Asian, non-Hispanic/Latino; 3 Hispanic/Latino), 1 international. Average age 31. 25 applicants, 84% accepted, 21 enrolled. In 2017, 6 master's awarded. *Degree requirements:* For master's, comprehensive exam (for some programs), thesis (for some programs). *Entrance requirements:* For master's, minimum cumulative GPA of 3.0 in last 90 quarter or 60 semester credits of post-secondary coursework; current resume; three short career plan essays. Additional exam requirements/recommendations for international students: Required—TOEFL (minimum score 580 paper-based; 92 iBT), IELTS (minimum score 7), PTE (minimum score 6). *Application deadline:* For fall admission, 8/1 for domestic students; for spring admission, 12/15 for domestic students. Application fee: $75. Electronic applications accepted. *Expenses:* Tuition, state resident: full-time $11,191; part-time $373.06 per credit. Tuition, nonresident: full-time $25,995; part-time $866.52 per credit. *Financial support:* Application deadline: 2/15; applicants required to submit FAFSA. *Unit head:* Dr. Anna Foucek Tresidder, 509-828-1490, E-mail: atressider1@ewu.edu. *Application contact:* Kathy White, Advisor/Recruiter for Graduate Studies, 509-359-2491, Fax: 509-359-6044, E-mail: gradprograms@ewu.edu.
Website: http://www.ewu.edu/chsph/programs/public-health

East Stroudsburg University of Pennsylvania, Graduate and Extended Studies, College of Health Sciences, Department of Health Studies, East Stroudsburg, PA 18301-2999. Offers MPH, MS. *Accreditation:* CEPH (one or more programs are accredited). *Program availability:* Part-time, evening/weekend, online learning. *Faculty:* 5 full-time (all women). *Students:* 19 full-time (14 women), 29 part-time (25 women); includes 9 minority (3 Black or African American, non-Hispanic/Latino; 1 Asian, non-Hispanic/Latino; 3 Hispanic/Latino; 2 Two or more races, non-Hispanic/Latino), 2 international. Average age 31. 39 applicants, 67% accepted, 20 enrolled. In 2017, 17 master's awarded. *Degree requirements:* For master's, oral comprehensive exam. *Entrance requirements:* For master's, GRE General Test, minimum GPA of 3.0 in major, 2.8 overall; undergraduate prerequisites in anatomy and physiology; 3 verifiable letters of recommendation; professional resume. Additional exam requirements/recommendations for international students: Recommended—TOEFL (minimum score 560 paper-based; 83 iBT), IELTS. *Application deadline:* For fall admission, 7/31 priority date for domestic students, 6/30 priority date for international students; for spring admission, 11/30 for domestic students, 10/31 for international students. Applications are processed on a rolling basis. Application fee: $50. Electronic applications accepted. *Expenses:* Tuition, state resident: full-time $4500; part-time $3000 per credit. Tuition, nonresident: full-time $6750; part-time $4500 per credit. *Required fees:* $2642; $1756 per credit. $878 per semester. Tuition and fees vary according to course load, campus/location and program. *Financial support:* Research assistantships with tuition reimbursements, Federal Work-Study, and unspecified assistantships available. Support available to part-time students. Financial award application deadline: 3/1; financial award applicants required to submit FAFSA. *Faculty research:* HIV prevention, wellness, international health issues. *Unit head:* Dr. Kim Razzano, Chair, 570-422-3693, Fax: 570-422-3848, E-mail: krazzano@esu.edu. *Application contact:* Kevin Quintero, Associate Director, Graduate and Extended Studies, 570-422-3890, Fax: 570-422-2711, E-mail: kquintero@esu.edu.

East Tennessee State University, School of Graduate Studies, College of Public Health, Johnson City, TN 37614. Offers MPH, MSEH, DPH, PhD, Postbaccalaureate Certificate. *Program availability:* Part-time, online learning. In 2017, 48 master's, 9 doctorates, 20 other advanced degrees awarded. *Degree requirements:* For master's, comprehensive exam, field experience; research project or thesis; environmental health practice; seminar; for doctorate, comprehensive exam, thesis/dissertation, practicum; seminar. *Entrance requirements:* For master's, GRE General Test, SOPHAS application, three letters of recommendation; for doctorate, GRE General Test, SOPHAS application, three letters of recommendation, curriculum vitae or resume; for Postbaccalaureate Certificate, minimum GPA of 2.5, three letters of recommendation, resume. Additional exam requirements/recommendations for international students: Required—TOEFL (minimum score 550 paper-based; 79 iBT), IELTS (minimum score 6.5). Application fee: $55 ($65 for international students). Electronic applications accepted. *Financial support:* Research assistantships with tuition reimbursements, teaching assistantships with tuition reimbursements, career-related internships or

fieldwork, institutionally sponsored loans, scholarships/grants, and unspecified assistantships available. Financial award application deadline: 7/1; financial award applicants required to submit FAFSA. *Faculty research:* Cancer prevention, obesity and diabetes prevention, prescription drug abuse, tobacco policy, women's health. *Unit head:* Dr. Randy Wykoff, Dean, 423-439-4243, Fax: 423-439-5238, E-mail: wykoff@etsu.edu. *Application contact:* Dr. Randy Wykoff, Dean, 423-439-4243, Fax: 423-439-5238, E-mail: wykoff@etsu.edu.
Website: http://www.etsu.edu/cph/

Elmhurst College, Graduate Programs, Program in Public Health, Elmhurst, IL 60126-3296. Offers MPH. *Program availability:* Part-time, evening/weekend, online learning. *Faculty:* 1 full-time (0 women), 5 part-time/adjunct (4 women). *Students:* 2 full-time (both women), 25 part-time (22 women); includes 12 minority (9 Black or African American, non-Hispanic/Latino; 2 Asian, non-Hispanic/Latino; 1 Hispanic/Latino), 1 international. Average age 31. 2 applicants. In 2017, 12 master's awarded. *Degree requirements:* For master's, practicum. *Entrance requirements:* For master's, 3 recommendations, resume, statement of purpose. Additional exam requirements/recommendations for international students: Required—TOEFL (minimum score 550 paper-based; 79 iBT). *Application deadline:* Applications are processed on a rolling basis. Application fee: $0. Electronic applications accepted. *Expenses:* Contact institution. *Financial support:* In 2017–18, 15 students received support. Scholarships/grants available. Support available to part-time students. Financial award application deadline: 3/1; financial award applicants required to submit FAFSA. *Unit head:* Dr. Terry Johnson, Associate Professor, 630-617-3510, E-mail: terryj@elmhurst.edu. *Application contact:* Timothy J. Panfil, Director of Enrollment Management, 630-617-3300 Ext. 3256, Fax: 630-617-6471, E-mail: panfilt@elmhurst.edu.

Emory University, Rollins School of Public Health, Atlanta, GA 30322. Offers MPH, MSPH, PhD, JD/MPH, MBA/MPH, MD/MPH, MM Sc/MPH, MSN/MPH. *Accreditation:* CEPH (one or more programs are accredited). *Program availability:* Part-time, evening/weekend, online learning. *Degree requirements:* For master's, variable foreign language requirement, comprehensive exam (for some programs), thesis (for some programs), practicum. *Entrance requirements:* For master's, GRE General Test. Additional exam requirements/recommendations for international students: Required—TOEFL (minimum score 550 paper-based; 80 iBT). Electronic applications accepted. *Expenses:* Contact institution. *Faculty research:* HIV/AIDS prevention, infectious disease, minority health, health disparities, bioterrorism.

Everglades University, Graduate Programs, Program in Public Health Administration, Boca Raton, FL 33431. Offers complementary and alternative medicine (MPH). *Program availability:* Part-time, evening/weekend, 100% online. *Degree requirements:* For master's, capstone course. *Entrance requirements:* For master's, GMAT (minimum score of 400) or GRE (minimum score of 290), bachelor's or graduate degree from college accredited by an agency recognized by the U.S. Department of Education; minimum cumulative GPA of 2.0 at the baccalaureate level, 3.0 at the master's level. Additional exam requirements/recommendations for international students: Recommended—TOEFL (minimum score 500 paper-based). Electronic applications accepted. *Expenses:* Contact institution.

Excelsior College, School of Health Sciences, Albany, NY 12203-5159. Offers health care administration (MS); health professions education (MSHS); healthcare informatics (MS); organizational development (MS); public health (MSHS). *Program availability:* Part-time, evening/weekend, online learning. *Faculty:* 4 part-time/adjunct (all women). *Students:* 133 part-time (92 women); includes 84 minority (49 Black or African American, non-Hispanic/Latino; 4 American Indian or Alaska Native, non-Hispanic/Latino; 8 Asian, non-Hispanic/Latino; 13 Hispanic/Latino; 2 Native Hawaiian or other Pacific Islander, non-Hispanic/Latino; 8 Two or more races, non-Hispanic/Latino). Average age 40. In 2017, 38 master's awarded. *Application deadline:* Applications are processed on a rolling basis. Application fee: $50. Electronic applications accepted. *Expenses: Tuition:* Part-time $645 per credit. *Required fees:* $265 per credit. *Financial support:* Scholarships/grants available. *Unit head:* Dr. Barbara Pieper, Dean, 518-464-8500, Fax: 518-464-8777. *Application contact:* Admissions Counselor, 518-464-8500, Fax: 518-464-8777, E-mail: gradadmissions@excelsior.edu.

Ferris State University, College of Health Professions, Program in Public Health, Big Rapids, MI 49307. Offers MPH. *Program availability:* Part-time, evening/weekend, online learning. *Faculty:* 5 full-time (3 women). *Students:* 5 full-time (2 women), 14 part-time (13 women); includes 2 minority (both Two or more races, non-Hispanic/Latino). Average age 32. 3 applicants, 100% accepted, 3 enrolled. *Degree requirements:* For master's, comprehensive exam, capstone project. *Entrance requirements:* For master's, GRE, minimum GPA of 3.0. Additional exam requirements/recommendations for international students: Recommended—TOEFL (minimum score 550 paper-based), TWE (minimum score 4). *Application deadline:* For fall admission, 7/18 for domestic students; for spring admission, 12/8 for domestic students. Electronic applications accepted. *Financial support:* Application deadline: 4/15; applicants required to submit FAFSA. *Faculty research:* Nutritional and chronic disease epidemiology; financing public health services; community-based health promotion and disease prevention; racial/ethnic disparities in maternal and child health; environmental policies and programs. *Unit head:* Dr. Michael Reger, Coordinator, 231-591-3132, E-mail: michaelreger@ferris.edu.
Website: https://ferris.edu/HTMLS/colleges/alliedhe/PublicHealth/MSPH/homepage.htm

Florida Agricultural and Mechanical University, Division of Graduate Studies, Research, and Continuing Education, College of Pharmacy and Pharmaceutical Sciences, Institute of Public Health, Tallahassee, FL 32307-3200. Offers MPH, DPH. *Accreditation:* CEPH. *Entrance requirements:* Additional exam requirements/recommendations for international students: Required—TOEFL.

Florida International University, Robert Stempel College of Public Health and Social Work, Programs in Public Health, Miami, FL 33199. Offers biostatistics (MPH); environmental and occupational health (MPH, PhD); epidemiology (MPH, PhD); health policy and management (MPH); health promotion and disease prevention (MPH, PhD). PhD program has fall admissions only; MPH offered jointly with University of Miami. *Program availability:* Part-time, evening/weekend, online learning. *Faculty:* 34 full-time (18 women), 2 part-time/adjunct (both women). *Students:* 132 full-time (88 women), 63 part-time (49 women); includes 133 minority (50 Black or African American, non-Hispanic/Latino; 17 Asian, non-Hispanic/Latino; 60 Hispanic/Latino; 6 Two or more races, non-Hispanic/Latino), 30 international. Average age 29. 249 applicants, 54% accepted, 65 enrolled. In 2017, 37 master's, 14 doctorates awarded. *Degree requirements:* For master's, thesis optional; for doctorate, comprehensive exam, thesis/dissertation. *Entrance requirements:* For master's, minimum GPA of 3.0, letters of recommendation; for doctorate, GRE, resume, minimum GPA of 3.0, letters of recommendation, letter of intent. Additional exam requirements/recommendations for international students: Required—TOEFL (minimum score 550 paper-based; 80 iBT). *Application deadline:* For fall admission, 6/1 for domestic students, 4/1 for international students; for spring admission, 10/1 for domestic students, 9/1 for international students. Applications are processed on a rolling basis. Application fee: $30. Electronic applications accepted. *Expenses:* Contact institution. *Financial support:* Institutionally sponsored loans, scholarships/grants, and tuition waivers (full) available. Financial award application deadline: 3/1; financial award applicants required to submit FAFSA. *Faculty research:* Drugs/AIDS intervention among migrant workers, provision of services for active/recovering drug users with HIV. *Unit head:* Dr. Benjamin C. Amick, III, Chair, 305-348-7527, E-mail: benjamin.amickiii@fiu.edu. *Application contact:* Nanett Rojas, Assistant Director, Graduate Admissions, 305-348-7464, Fax: 305-348-7441, E-mail: gradadm@fiu.edu.

Florida State University, The Graduate School, College of Social Sciences and Public Policy, Public Health Program, Tallahassee, FL 32306. Offers MPH, MPH/MSP. *Accreditation:* CEPH. *Program availability:* Part-time. *Faculty:* 9 full-time (2 women). *Students:* 57 full-time (41 women), 23 part-time (20 women); includes 37 minority (15 Black or African American, non-Hispanic/Latino; 1 American Indian or Alaska Native, non-Hispanic/Latino; 2 Asian, non-Hispanic/Latino; 11 Hispanic/Latino; 8 Two or more races, non-Hispanic/Latino), 5 international. Average age 26. 67 applicants, 70% accepted, 28 enrolled. In 2017, 26 master's awarded. *Degree requirements:* For master's, internship, research paper. *Entrance requirements:* For master's, GRE General Test, minimum GPA of 3.0. Additional exam requirements/recommendations for international students: Required—TOEFL (minimum score 550 paper-based; 80 iBT). *Application deadline:* For fall admission, 7/1 priority date for domestic students, 7/1 for international students; for spring admission, 11/1 for domestic and international students. Applications are processed on a rolling basis. Application fee: $30. Electronic applications accepted. *Financial support:* In 2017–18, 3 students received support, including 3 research assistantships with full tuition reimbursements available (averaging $5,000 per year); fellowships with tuition reimbursements available, career-related internships or fieldwork, Federal Work-Study, institutionally sponsored loans, and unspecified assistantships also available. Financial award application deadline: 2/15. *Faculty research:* Health behavior surveillance, long term care policy, long term care evaluation, HMOs, Medicaid. *Total annual research expenditures:* $1 million. *Unit head:* Dr. William G. Weissert, Director, 850-644-4418, Fax: 850-644-1367, E-mail: wweissert@fsu.edu. *Application contact:* Sabrina Smith, Academic Program Specialist, 850-644-4418, E-mail: ssmith9@fsu.edu.
Website: http://www.coss.fsu.edu/publichealth/

Fort Valley State University, College of Graduate Studies and Extended Education, Program in Public Health, Fort Valley, GA 31030. Offers environmental health (MPH). *Degree requirements:* For master's, thesis. *Entrance requirements:* For master's, GRE General Test. Additional exam requirements/recommendations for international students: Recommended—TOEFL.

George Mason University, College of Health and Human Services, Department of Global and Community Health, Fairfax, VA 22030. Offers global and community health (Certificate); global health (MS); public health (MPH, Certificate), including epidemiology (MPH), leadership and management (Certificate). *Accreditation:* CEPH. *Program availability:* Part-time, evening/weekend. *Faculty:* 18 full-time (13 women), 16 part-time/adjunct (13 women). *Students:* 70 full-time (63 women), 61 part-time (53 women); includes 62 minority (21 Black or African American, non-Hispanic/Latino; 21 Asian, non-Hispanic/Latino; 14 Hispanic/Latino; 1 Native Hawaiian or other Pacific Islander, non-Hispanic/Latino; 5 Two or more races, non-Hispanic/Latino), 8 international. Average age 29. 246 applicants, 71% accepted, 60 enrolled. In 2017, 46 master's, 2 other advanced degrees awarded. *Degree requirements:* For master's, thesis, 200-hour practicum. *Entrance requirements:* For master's, GRE, GMAT (depending on program), 2 official transcripts; expanded goals statement; 3 letters of recommendation; resume; 1 completed course in health science, statistics, natural sciences and social science (for MPH); 6 credits of foreign language if not fluent (for MS); minimum undergraduate GPA of 3.0; for Certificate, 2 official transcripts; expanded goals statement; 3 letters of recommendation; resume; bachelor's degree from regionally-accredited institution with minimum GPA of 3.0. Additional exam requirements/recommendations for international students: Required—TOEFL (minimum score 570 paper-based; 88 iBT), IELTS (minimum score 6.5), PTE (minimum score 59). *Application deadline:* For fall admission, 3/1 for domestic and international students. Application fee: $75 ($80 for international students). Electronic applications accepted. *Expenses:* Contact institution. *Financial support:* In 2017–18, 15 students received support, including 12 research assistantships with tuition reimbursements available (averaging $16,616 per year), 3 teaching assistantships with tuition reimbursements available (averaging $6,966 per year); career-related internships or fieldwork, Federal Work-Study, scholarships/grants, unspecified assistantships, and health care benefits (for full-time research or teaching assistantship recipients) also available. Financial award application deadline: 3/1; financial award applicants required to submit FAFSA. *Faculty research:* Environmental and infectious disease epidemiology; global health; health risk behaviors; social determinants of health; stress, well-being and chronic disease. *Total annual research expenditures:* $69,343. *Unit head:* Robert Weiler, Chair, 703-993-1920, E-mail: rweiler@gmu.edu. *Application contact:* Allan Weiss, Department Manager, 703-993-3126, E-mail: aweiss2@gmu.edu.
Website: http://chhs.gmu.edu/gch/index

Georgetown University, Graduate School of Arts and Sciences, Department of Microbiology and Immunology, Washington, DC 20057. Offers biohazardous threat agents and emerging infectious diseases (MS); biomedical science policy and advocacy (MS); general microbiology and immunology (MS); global infectious diseases (PhD); microbiology and immunology (PhD). *Program availability:* Part-time. *Degree requirements:* For master's, 30 credit hours of coursework; for doctorate, comprehensive exam, thesis/dissertation. *Entrance requirements:* For master's, GRE General Test, 3 letters of reference, bachelor's degree in related field; for doctorate, GRE General Test, 3 letters of reference, MS/BS in related field. Additional exam requirements/recommendations for international students: Required—TOEFL (minimum score 505 paper-based). Electronic applications accepted. *Faculty research:* Pathogenesis and basic biology of the fungus Candida albicans, molecular biology of viral immunopathological mechanisms in Multiple Sclerosis.

The George Washington University, Milken Institute School of Public Health, Department of Global Health, Washington, DC 20052. Offers global health (Dr PH); global health communication (MPH). *Students:* 16 full-time (15 women), 21 part-time (12 women); includes 16 minority (6 Black or African American, non-Hispanic/Latino; 7 Asian, non-Hispanic/Latino; 2 Hispanic/Latino; 1 Two or more races, non-Hispanic/Latino), 4 international. Average age 37. 126 applicants, 61% accepted, 14 enrolled. In 2017, 6 master's awarded. *Entrance requirements:* For master's, GMAT, GRE General Test, or MCAT. Additional exam requirements/recommendations for international students: Required—TOEFL. *Application deadline:* For fall admission, 4/15 priority date for domestic students, 4/15 for international students; for spring admission, 11/1 for domestic and international students. Applications are processed on a rolling basis. Application fee: $75. *Expenses: Tuition:* Full-time $28,800; part-time $1655 per credit hour. *Required fees:* $45; $2.75 per credit hour. *Financial support:* In 2017–18, 24 students received support. Tuition waivers available. Financial award application deadline: 2/15. *Unit head:* Prof. James Tielsch, Chair, 202-994-4124, Fax: 202-994-1955, E-mail: jtielsch@gwu.edu. *Application contact:* Jane Smith, Director of Admissions, 202-994-0248, Fax: 202-994-1860, E-mail: sphhsinfo@gwumc.edu.

Georgia Southern University, Jack N. Averitt College of Graduate Studies, Jiann-Ping Hsu College of Public Health, Program in Public Health, Statesboro, GA 30460. Offers biostatistics (MPH, Dr PH); community health behavior and education (Dr PH);

community health education (MPH); environmental health sciences (MPH); epidemiology (MPH); health policy and management (MPH, Dr PH). *Program availability:* Part-time. *Faculty:* 11 full-time (5 women). *Students:* 146 full-time (90 women), 70 part-time (57 women); includes 112 minority (95 Black or African American, non-Hispanic/Latino; 9 Asian, non-Hispanic/Latino; 5 Hispanic/Latino; 3 Two or more races, non-Hispanic/Latino), 47 international. Average age 32. 190 applicants, 78% accepted, 89 enrolled. In 2017, 34 master's, 13 doctorates awarded. *Degree requirements:* For master's, thesis optional, practicum; for doctorate, comprehensive exam, thesis/dissertation, preceptorship. *Entrance requirements:* For master's, GRE General Test, minimum GPA of 2.75, 3 letters of recommendation, statement of purpose, resume or curriculum vitae; for doctorate, GRE, GMAT, MCAT, LSAT, minimum GPA of 3.0, 3 letters of recommendation, statement of purpose, resume or curriculum vitae. Additional exam requirements/recommendations for international students: Required—TOEFL (minimum score 537 paper-based; 75 iBT), IELTS (minimum score 6). *Application deadline:* For fall admission, 6/1 for domestic students, 5/1 for international students. Applications are processed on a rolling basis. Application fee: $135. Electronic applications accepted. *Expenses:* $3,949 in-state, $13,929 out-of-state (for MPH); $4,014 in-state, $14,159 out-of-state (for Dr PH). *Financial support:* In 2017–18, 106 students received support, including 1 research assistantship with full tuition reimbursement available (averaging $12,350 per year), 6 teaching assistantships with full tuition reimbursements available (averaging $12,350 per year); scholarships/grants, tuition waivers (full), and unspecified assistantships also available. Financial award application deadline: 4/15; financial award applicants required to submit FAFSA. *Faculty research:* Rural public health best practices, health disparity elimination, community initiatives to enhance public health, cost effectiveness analysis, epidemiology of rural public health, environmental health issues, health care system assessment, rural health care, health policy and healthcare financing, survival analysis, nonparametric statistics and resampling methods, micro-arrays and genomics, data imputation techniques and clinical trial methodology. *Total annual research expenditures:* $415,747. *Unit head:* Dr. Robert Greg Evans, Dean, 912-478-2674, E-mail: rgevans@georgiasouthern.edu. *Application contact:* Shamia Garrett, Coordinator, Office of Student Services, 912-478-2674, Fax: 912-478-5811, E-mail: jphcoph-gradadvisor@georgiasouthern.edu.
Website: http://jphcoph.georgiasouthern.edu/

Georgia Southern University–Armstrong Campus, College of Graduate Studies, Program in Public Health, Savannah, GA 31419-1997. Offers MPH. *Accreditation:* CEPH. *Program availability:* Part-time, evening/weekend, online learning. *Faculty:* 5 full-time (4 women), 1 (woman) part-time/adjunct. *Students:* [illegible] full-time (27 women), 10 part-time (7 women); includes 30 minority (23 Black or African American, non-Hispanic/Latino; 4 Asian, non-Hispanic/Latino; 2 Hispanic/Latino; 1 Two or more races, non-Hispanic/Latino), 2 international. Average age 29. 66 applicants, 24% accepted, 12 enrolled. In 2017, 28 master's awarded. *Degree requirements:* For master's, comprehensive exam, thesis optional, internship. *Entrance requirements:* For master's, GMAT or GRE General Test, MAT, letters of recommendation, letter of intent, minimum undergraduate GPA of 2.8. Additional exam requirements/recommendations for international students: Required—TOEFL (minimum score 70 iBT). *Application deadline:* For fall admission, 6/1 priority date for domestic students, 5/1 priority date for international students; for spring admission, 11/15 priority date for domestic students, 9/15 priority date for international students; for summer admission, 4/15 for domestic students, 9/15 priority date for international students. Applications are processed on a rolling basis. Application fee: $30. Electronic applications accepted. *Expenses:* Tuition, state resident: part-time $211 per credit hour. Tuition, nonresident: part-time $782 per credit hour. *Required fees:* $737 per semester. Tuition and fees vary according to course load, degree level, campus/location and program. *Financial support:* In 2017–18, research assistantships with full tuition reimbursements (averaging $5,000 per year) were awarded; career-related internships or fieldwork, Federal Work-Study, scholarships/grants, tuition waivers (full), and unspecified assistantships also available. Support available to part-time students. Financial award application deadline: 3/15; financial award applicants required to submit FAFSA. *Unit head:* Dr. Robert LeFavi, Department Head, 912-344-3208, Fax: 912-344-3477, E-mail: robert.lefavi@armstrong.edu. *Application contact:* McKenzie Peterman, Graduate Admissions Specialist, 912-478-5678, Fax: 912-478-0740, E-mail: mpeterman@georgiasouthern.edu.
Website: http://www.armstrong.edu/Health_Professions/Health_Sciences/healthsciences_master_of_public_health

Georgia State University, Andrew Young School of Policy Studies, Department of Public Management and Policy, Atlanta, GA 30303. Offers criminal justice (MPA); disaster management (Certificate); disaster policy (MPA); environmental policy (PhD); health policy (PhD); management and finance (MPA); nonprofit management (MPA, Certificate); nonprofit policy (MPA); planning and economic development (MPP, Certificate); policy analysis and evaluation (MPA), including planning and economic development; public and nonprofit management (PhD); public finance and budgeting (PhD), including science and technology policy, urban and regional economic development; public finance policy (MPA), including social policy; public health (MPA). *Accreditation:* NASPAA (one or more programs are accredited). *Program availability:* Part-time. *Faculty:* 17 full-time (9 women). *Students:* 125 full-time (75 women), 78 part-time (51 women); includes 90 minority (67 Black or African American, non-Hispanic/Latino; 5 Asian, non-Hispanic/Latino; 9 Hispanic/Latino; 9 Two or more races, non-Hispanic/Latino), 34 international. Average age 30. 275 applicants, 62% accepted, 88 enrolled. In 2017, 71 master's, 5 doctorates, 12 other advanced degrees awarded. Terminal master's awarded for partial completion of doctoral program. *Degree requirements:* For master's, thesis optional; for doctorate, comprehensive exam, thesis/dissertation. *Entrance requirements:* For master's and doctorate, GRE. Additional exam requirements/recommendations for international students: Required—TOEFL (minimum score 603 paper-based; 100 iBT) or IELTS (minimum score 7). *Application deadline:* For fall admission, 1/15 for domestic and international students. Application fee: $50. Electronic applications accepted. *Expenses:* Tuition, state resident: full-time $7020. Tuition, nonresident: full-time $22,518. *Required fees:* $2128. Tuition and fees vary according to degree level and program. *Financial support:* In 2017–18, fellowships (averaging $8,194 per year), research assistantships (averaging $8,068 per year), teaching assistantships (averaging $3,600 per year) were awarded; institutionally sponsored loans, scholarships/grants, health care benefits, and unspecified assistantships also available. Financial award application deadline: 2/1. *Faculty research:* Public budgeting and finance, public management, nonprofit management, performance measurement and management, urban development. *Unit head:* Dr. Carolyn Bourdeaux, Chair and Professor, 404-413-0013, Fax: 404-413-0104, E-mail: cbourdeaux@gsu.edu.
Website: http://aysps.gsu.edu/pmap/

Georgia State University, School of Public Health, Atlanta, GA 30302-3995. Offers MPH, PhD, Certificate. *Program availability:* Part-time. *Faculty:* 21 full-time (12 women). *Students:* 224 full-time (166 women), 121 part-time (97 women); includes 192 minority (141 Black or African American, non-Hispanic/Latino; 1 American Indian or Alaska Native, non-Hispanic/Latino; 35 Asian, non-Hispanic/Latino; 8 Hispanic/Latino; 7 Two or more races, non-Hispanic/Latino), 36 international. Average age 29. 509 applicants, 59% accepted, 96 enrolled. In 2017, 104 master's, 5 doctorates, 8 other advanced degrees awarded. *Degree requirements:* For master's, thesis, applied practicum; for doctorate, comprehensive exam, thesis/dissertation, applied, research or teaching practicum. *Entrance requirements:* For master's, doctorate, and Certificate, GRE or GMAT. Additional exam requirements/recommendations for international students: Required—TOEFL (minimum score 550 paper-based; 80 iBT). *Application deadline:* For fall admission, 2/1 for domestic and international students; for spring admission, 10/1 for domestic and international students. Application fee: $50. Electronic applications accepted. *Expenses:* Contact institution. *Financial support:* In 2017–18, fellowships (averaging $2,500 per year), research assistantships with full tuition reimbursements (averaging $22,000 per year), teaching assistantships with full tuition reimbursements (averaging $22,000 per year) were awarded; career-related internships or fieldwork, scholarships/grants, health care benefits, unspecified assistantships, and out-of-state tuition waivers also available. *Faculty research:* Infectious and chronic disease epidemiology; environmental health and the built environment; adolescent risk behaviors: tobacco use, alcohol and drug use, and risky sexual behaviors; reduction of health disparities especially among minority populations in urban areas; program evaluation, evidence-based interventions and implementation. *Unit head:* Dr. Michael P. Eriksen, Dean, 404-413-1132, Fax: 404-413-1140, E-mail: meriksen@gsu.edu. *Application contact:* Courtney M. Burton, Graduate Coordinator, 404-413-1143, E-mail: cmburton@gsu.edu.
Website: http://publichealth.gsu.edu/

Grand Canyon University, College of Nursing and Health Care Professions, Phoenix, AZ 85017-1097. Offers acute care nurse practitioner (MSN, PMC); family nurse practitioner (MSN, PMC); health care administration (MS); health care informatics (MS, MSN); leadership in health care systems (MSN); nursing (DNP); nursing education (MSN, PMC); public health (MPH, MSN); MBA/MSN. *Accreditation:* AACN. *Program availability:* Part-time, evening/weekend, online learning. *Degree requirements:* For master's and PMC, comprehensive exam (for some programs). *Entrance requirements:* For master's, minimum cumulative and science course undergraduate GPA of 3.0. Additional exam requirements/recommendations for international students: Required—TOEFL (minimum score 575 paper-based; 90 iBT), IELTS (minimum score 7).

Grand Valley State University, College of Health Professions, Public Health Program, Allendale, MI 49401-9403. Offers MPH. *Program availability:* Part-time. *Faculty:* 9 full-time (7 women). *Students:* 80 full-time (68 women), 26 part-time (17 women); includes 16 minority (8 Black or African American, non-Hispanic/Latino; 1 American Indian or Alaska Native, non-Hispanic/Latino; 2 Asian, non-Hispanic/Latino; 5 Hispanic/Latino), 7 international. Average age 26. 85 applicants, 86% accepted, 46 enrolled. In 2017, 47 master's awarded. *Degree requirements:* For master's, practicum, project, or thesis. *Entrance requirements:* For master's, baccalaureate degree and official transcripts with minimum GPA of 3.0, 2 letters of recommendation, personal essay. Additional exam requirements/recommendations for international students: Required—TOEFL (minimum iBT score of 80), IELTS (6.5), or Michigan English Language Assessment Battery (77). *Application deadline:* For fall admission, 2/1 for domestic students. Application fee: $30. *Expenses:* $686 per credit hour. *Financial support:* In 2017–18, 14 students received support, including 9 fellowships, 1 research assistantship with full and partial tuition reimbursement available (averaging $8,000 per year); unspecified assistantships also available. *Unit head:* Dr. Ranelle Brew, Director, 616-331-5570, Fax: 616-331-5550, E-mail: brewr@gvsu.edu. *Application contact:* Darlene Zwart, Student Services Coordinator, 616-331-3958, Fax: 616-331-5643, E-mail: zwartda@gvsu.edu.
Website: http://www.gvsu.edu/grad/mph/

Harvard University, Cyprus International Institute for the Environment and Public Health in Association with Harvard School of Public Health, Cambridge, MA 02138. Offers environmental health (MS); environmental/public health (PhD); epidemiology and biostatistics (MS). *Entrance requirements:* For master's and doctorate, GRE, resume/curriculum vitae, 3 letters of recommendation, BA or BS (including diploma and official transcripts). Additional exam requirements/recommendations for international students: Required—TOEFL, IELTS (minimum score 7). Electronic applications accepted. *Faculty research:* Air pollution, climate change, biostatistics, sustainable development, environmental management.

Harvard University, Harvard T.H. Chan School of Public Health, Doctor of Public Health Program, Cambridge, MA 02138. Offers Dr PH. *Students:* 71 full-time (47 women); includes 22 minority (8 Black or African American, non-Hispanic/Latino; 1 American Indian or Alaska Native, non-Hispanic/Latino; 8 Asian, non-Hispanic/Latino; 4 Hispanic/Latino; 1 Two or more races, non-Hispanic/Latino), 32 international. Average age 29. 194 applicants, 11% accepted, 18 enrolled. In 2017, 8 doctorates awarded. *Entrance requirements:* Additional exam requirements/recommendations for international students: Recommended—TOEFL (minimum score 600 paper-based; 100 iBT), IELTS (minimum score 7). *Application deadline:* For fall admission, 12/1 for domestic students. Application fee: $120. Electronic applications accepted. *Unit head:* Richard Siegrist, Director. *Application contact:* Vincent W. James, Director of Admissions, 617-432-1031, Fax: 617-432-7080, E-mail: admissions@hsph.harvard.edu.
Website: http://www.hsph.harvard.edu/drph/

Harvard University, Harvard T.H. Chan School of Public Health, Master of Public Health Program, Boston, MA 02115-6096. Offers clinical effectiveness (MPH); global health (MPH); health and social behavior (MPH); health management (MPH); health policy (MPH); occupational and environmental health (MPH); quantitative methods (MPH); JD/MPH; MD/MPH. *Program availability:* Part-time. *Students:* 366 full-time (206 women), 194 part-time (110 women); includes 189 minority (35 Black or African American, non-Hispanic/Latino; 100 Asian, non-Hispanic/Latino; 35 Hispanic/Latino; 19 Two or more races, non-Hispanic/Latino), 126 international. Average age 29. 912 applicants, 65% accepted, 402 enrolled. In 2017, 369 master's awarded. *Entrance requirements:* For master's, GRE, MCAT, GMAT, DAT, LSAT. Additional exam requirements/recommendations for international students: Recommended—TOEFL (minimum score 600 paper-based; 100 iBT), IELTS (minimum score 7). *Application deadline:* For fall admission, 12/1 priority date for domestic and international students. Application fee: $120. Electronic applications accepted. *Financial support:* Federal Work-Study, scholarships/grants, and unspecified assistantships available. Support available to part-time students. Financial award application deadline: 2/15; financial award applicants required to submit FAFSA. *Faculty research:* Clinical effectiveness, global health, health and social behavior, health care management and policy, law and public health, occupational and environmental health, quantitative methods. *Unit head:* Dr. Murray Mittleman, Chair of the MPH Steering Committee, 617-432-0090, Fax: 617-432-3365, E-mail: mmittlem@hsph.harvard.edu. *Application contact:* Vincent W. James, Director of Admissions, 617-432-1031, Fax: 617-432-7080, E-mail: admissions@hsph.harvard.edu.
Website: http://www.hsph.harvard.edu/master-of-public-health-program/

See Display on the next page and Close-Up on page 841.

Harvard University, Harvard T.H. Chan School of Public Health, PhD Program in Biological Sciences in Public Health, Boston, MA 02115. Offers PhD. *Students:* 53 full-time (33 women); includes 17 minority (5 Black or African American, non-Hispanic/Latino; 7 Asian, non-Hispanic/Latino; 4 Hispanic/Latino; 1 Two or more races, non-

Hispanic/Latino), 6 international. Average age 29. 112 applicants, 11% accepted, 9 enrolled. In 2017, 8 doctorates awarded. *Degree requirements:* For doctorate, qualifying examination, dissertation/defense. *Entrance requirements:* For doctorate, GRE General Test. Additional exam requirements/recommendations for international students: Recommended—TOEFL (minimum score 600 paper-based; 100 iBT), IELTS (minimum score 7). Electronic applications accepted. *Financial support:* Fellowships, research assistantships, teaching assistantships, institutionally sponsored loans, health care benefits, and tuition waivers (full) available. Financial award application deadline: 1/1. *Faculty research:* Nutrition biochemistry, molecular and cellular toxicology, cardiovascular disease, cancer biology, immunology and infectious diseases, environmental health physiology. *Unit head:* Deirdre Duckett, Assistant Director, E-mail: bph@hsph.harvard.edu.
Website: http://www.hsph.harvard.edu/admissions/degree-programs/doctor-of-philosophy/phd-in-biological-sciences-and-public-health/

See Display below and Close-Up on page 841.

Hawai`i Pacific University, College of Health and Society, Program in Public Health, Honolulu, HI 96813. Offers MPH. *Program availability:* Part-time, evening/weekend, 100% online, blended/hybrid learning. *Faculty:* 1 full-time (0 women). *Students:* 11 full-time (6 women), 2 part-time (1 woman); includes 10 minority (3 Asian, non-Hispanic/Latino; 1 Hispanic/Latino; 6 Two or more races, non-Hispanic/Latino). Average age 26. 11 applicants, 91% accepted, 7 enrolled. *Entrance requirements:* For master's, transcripts; baccalaureate degree; personal statement; minimum overall GPA of 3.0; 3 letters of reference; current curriculum vitae/resume; one college-level course in each of the following areas: general biology, statistics, and a health-related science course (anatomy, physiology, nutrition, microbiology). Additional exam requirements/recommendations for international students: Recommended—TOEFL (minimum score 550 paper-based; 80 iBT), IELTS (minimum score 6), TWE (minimum score 5). *Application deadline:* For fall admission, 1/15 priority date for domestic students; for spring admission, 10/15 priority date for domestic students. Applications are processed on a rolling basis. Application fee: $50. Electronic applications accepted. *Expenses: Tuition:* Full-time $18,000; part-time $1000 per credit. *Required fees:* $200; $26 per credit. Tuition and fees vary according to course load and program. *Financial support:* In 2017–18, 5 students received support. Career-related internships or fieldwork, Federal Work-Study, scholarships/grants, tuition waivers (partial), and unspecified assistantships available. Financial award application deadline: 3/1; financial award applicants required to submit FAFSA. *Unit head:* Dr. Lyndall Ellingson, Department Chair and Professor, 808-236-5833, E-mail: lellingson@hpu.edu. *Application contact:* Danny Lam, Assistant Director of Graduate Admissions, 808-544-1135, E-mail: graduate@hpu.edu.
Website: https://www.hpu.edu/chs/public-health/ma-ph.html

Hofstra University, School of Health Professions and Human Services, Programs in Health, Hempstead, NY 11549. Offers foundations of public health (Advanced Certificate); health administration (MHA); health informatics (MS); occupational therapy (MS); public health (MPH); security and privacy in health information systems (Advanced Certificate); sports science (MS), including exercise physiology, strength and conditioning; teacher of students with speech-language disabilities (Advanced Certificate). *Program availability:* Part-time, evening/weekend. *Students:* 257 full-time (176 women), 128 part-time (95 women); includes 197 minority (76 Black or African American, non-Hispanic/Latino; 2 American Indian or Alaska Native, non-Hispanic/Latino; 70 Asian, non-Hispanic/Latino; 42 Hispanic/Latino; 6 Native Hawaiian or other Pacific Islander, non-Hispanic/Latino; 1 Two or more races, non-Hispanic/Latino), 25 international. Average age 28. 620 applicants, 50% accepted, 151 enrolled. In 2017, 87 master's awarded. *Degree requirements:* For master's, internship, minimum GPA of 3.0. *Entrance requirements:* For master's, interview, 2 letters of recommendation, essay, resume. Additional exam requirements/recommendations for international students: Required—TOEFL (minimum score 550 paper-based; 80 iBT). *Application deadline:* Applications are processed on a rolling basis. Application fee: $75. Electronic applications accepted. *Expenses: Tuition:* Full-time $1292. *Required fees:* $970. Tuition and fees vary according to program. *Financial support:* In 2017–18, 148 students received support, including 88 fellowships with full and partial tuition reimbursements available (averaging $3,026 per year), 4 research assistantships with full and partial tuition reimbursements available (averaging $5,619 per year); career-related internships or fieldwork, Federal Work-Study, institutionally sponsored loans, scholarships/grants, traineeships, tuition waivers (full and partial), and unspecified assistantships also available. Support available to part-time students. Financial award applicants required to submit FAFSA. *Faculty research:* Hand and upper extremity rehabilitation; orthotic fabrication; palliative care; neurorehabilitation; public health and health inequities, particularly in the American suburbs and minority communities; obesity; physical activity; social justice in physical education pedagogy. *Unit head:* Dr. Corinne Kyriacou, Chairperson, 516-463-4553, E-mail: corinne.m.kyriacou@hofstra.edu. *Application contact:* Sunil Samuel, Assistant Vice President of Admissions, 516-463-4723, Fax: 516-463-4664, E-mail: graduateadmission@hofstra.edu.
Website: http://www.hofstra.edu/academics/colleges/healthscienceshumanservices/

Howard University, College of Medicine, Program in Public Health, Washington, DC 20059-0002. Offers MPH.

Hunter College of the City University of New York, Graduate School, Hunter-Bellevue School of Nursing, Community/Public Health Nursing Program, New York, NY 10065-5085. Offers MS. *Accreditation:* AACN. *Program availability:* Part-time. *Degree requirements:* For master's, practicum. *Entrance requirements:* For master's, minimum GPA of 3.0, New York RN license, BSN. Additional exam requirements/recommendations for international students: Required—TOEFL. *Faculty research:* HIV/AIDS, health promotion with vulnerable populations.

Hunter College of the City University of New York, Graduate School, School of Urban Public Health, New York, NY 10065-5085. Offers nutrition (MS). *Program availability:* Part-time. *Degree requirements:* For master's, comprehensive exam. *Entrance requirements:* For master's, GRE General Test. Additional exam requirements/recommendations for international students: Required—TOEFL.

Icahn School of Medicine at Mount Sinai, Graduate School of Biomedical Sciences, New York, NY 10029-6504. Offers biomedical sciences (MS, PhD); clinical research education (MS, PhD); community medicine (MPH); genetic counseling (MS); neurosciences (PhD); MD/PhD. Terminal master's awarded for partial completion of doctoral program. *Degree requirements:* For master's, thesis; for doctorate, comprehensive exam, thesis/dissertation. *Entrance requirements:* For master's, GRE General Test; for doctorate, GRE General Test, GRE Subject Test, 3 years of college pre-med course work. Additional exam requirements/recommendations for international students: Required—TOEFL. Electronic applications accepted. *Faculty research:* Cancer, genetics and genomics, immunology, neuroscience, developmental and stem cell biology, translational research.

Idaho State University, Office of Graduate Studies, School of Health Professions, Department of Community and Public Health, Program in Public Health, Pocatello, ID 83209-8109. Offers MPH. *Accreditation:* CEPH. *Program availability:* Part-time. *Degree requirements:* For master's, comprehensive exam, thesis. *Entrance requirements:* For master's, GRE General Test, minimum GPA of 3.0 for upper division classes, 2 letters of recommendation. Additional exam requirements/recommendations for international students: Required—TOEFL (minimum score 600 paper-based). Electronic applications accepted.

Independence University, Program in Public Health, Salt Lake City, UT 84107. Offers MPH. *Program availability:* Part-time, evening/weekend, online learning. *Degree requirements:* For master's, final project or thesis.

Indiana University Bloomington, School of Public Health, Department of Applied Health Science, Bloomington, IN 47405. Offers behavioral, social, and community health (MPH); family health (MPH); health behavior (PhD); nutrition science (MS); professional health education (MPH); public health administration (MPH); safety management (MS); school and college health education (MS). *Degree requirements:* For master's, thesis optional; for doctorate, comprehensive exam, thesis/dissertation. *Entrance requirements:* For master's, GRE (for MS in nutrition science), 3 recommendations; for doctorate, GRE, 3 recommendations. Additional exam requirements/recommendations for international students: Required—TOEFL (minimum score 550 paper-based; 80 iBT). Electronic applications accepted. *Faculty research:* Cancer education, HIV/AIDS and drug education, public health, parent-child interactions, safety education, obesity, public health policy, public health administration, school health, health education, human development, nutrition, human sexuality, chronic disease, early childhood health.

Indiana University–Purdue University Indianapolis, Richard M. Fairbanks School of Public Health, Indianapolis, IN 46202. Offers biostatistics (MS, PhD); environmental health (MPH); epidemiology (MPH, PhD); global health leadership (Dr PH); health administration (MHA); health policy (Graduate Certificate); health policy and management (MPH, PhD); health systems management (Graduate Certificate); product stewardship (MS); public health (Graduate Certificate); social and behavioral sciences (MPH). *Expenses:* Contact institution.

Indiana University–Purdue University Indianapolis, School of Physical Education and Tourism Management, Indianapolis, IN 46202-5193. Offers event tourism (MS), including sport event tourism; kinesiology (MS), including clinical exercise science; public health (Graduate Certificate). *Degree requirements:* For master's, comprehensive exam (for some programs), thesis (for some programs). *Entrance requirements:* For master's, GRE. Additional exam requirements/recommendations for international students: Required—TOEFL. Electronic applications accepted. *Expenses:* Contact institution. *Faculty research:* Physical activity, exercise and diseases; human movement science; sport performance; sport event tourism; destination marketing and event management.

Jackson State University, Graduate School, School of Public Health, Public Health Program, Jackson, MS 39217. Offers MPH, Dr PH. *Accreditation:* CEPH.

Johns Hopkins University, Bloomberg School of Public Health, Baltimore, MD 21205. Offers MBE, MHA, MHS, MHS, MPH, MPP, MSPH, Sc M, Dr PH, PhD, Sc D, JD/MPH, MBA/MPH, MHS/MA, MSN/MPH, MSW/MPH. *Program availability:* Part-time, 100% online, blended/hybrid learning. *Faculty:* 670 full-time, 709 part-time/adjunct. *Students:* 1,340 full-time (946 women), 932 part-time (605 women); includes 649 minority (134 Black or African American, non-Hispanic/Latino; 4 American Indian or Alaska Native, non-Hispanic/Latino; 319 Asian, non-Hispanic/Latino; 128 Hispanic/Latino; 64 Two or more races, non-Hispanic/Latino), 636 international. Average age 30. 4,234 applicants, 49% accepted, 1085 enrolled. In 2017, 712 master's, 123 doctorates awarded. *Degree requirements:* For master's, comprehensive exam (for some programs), thesis (for some programs); for doctorate, comprehensive exam, thesis/dissertation. *Entrance requirements:* For master's and doctorate, official transcripts from every college-level institution attended (academic records from institutions outside the U.S. must undergo a credentials evaluation). Additional exam requirements/recommendations for international students: Required—TOEFL (minimum score 100 iBT), IELTS (minimum score 7). Application fee: $135. Electronic applications accepted. *Expenses:* Contact institution. *Financial support:* In 2017–18, 1,605 students received support. Fellowships, research assistantships, teaching assistantships, career-related internships or fieldwork, Federal Work-Study, scholarships/grants, traineeships, health care benefits, and unspecified assistantships available. Support available to part-time students. Financial award application deadline: 3/15; financial award applicants required to submit FAFSA. *Faculty research:* Biomedical research, environmental health, biostatistics, epidemiology, social science and health. *Unit head:* Dr. Ellen J. MacKenzie, Dean, 410-955-3540, Fax: 410-955-0121, E-mail: jhsph.deansoffice@jhu.edu. *Application contact:* Office of Admissions, 410-955-3543, Fax: 410-955-0464, E-mail: jhsph.admiss@jhu.edu.
Website: http://www.jhsph.edu/

Kansas State University, Graduate School, College of Human Ecology, Department of Food, Nutrition, Dietetics and Health, Manhattan, KS 66506. Offers dietetics (MS); human nutrition (PhD); nutrition, dietetics and sensory sciences (MS); nutritional sciences (PhD); public health nutrition (PhD); public health physical activity (PhD); sensory analysis and consumer behavior (PhD). *Program availability:* Part-time. *Degree requirements:* For master's, thesis or alternative, residency; for doctorate, thesis/dissertation, residency. *Entrance requirements:* For master's, GRE General Test, minimum undergraduate GPA of 3.0; for doctorate, GRE General Test, minimum graduate GPA of 3.0. Additional exam requirements/recommendations for international students: Required—TOEFL (minimum score 550 paper-based; 79 iBT), IELTS (minimum score 6.5). Electronic applications accepted. *Faculty research:* Cancer and immunology, obesity, sensory analysis and consumer behavior, nutrient metabolism, clinical and community interventions.

Kansas State University, Graduate School, College of Veterinary Medicine, Department of Clinical Sciences, Manhattan, KS 66506. Offers MPH, Graduate Certificate. *Degree requirements:* For master's, thesis. *Entrance requirements:* For master's, GRE, DVM. Additional exam requirements/recommendations for international students: Required—TOEFL (minimum score 550 paper-based). Electronic applications accepted. *Expenses:* Contact institution. *Faculty research:* Clinical trials, equine gastrointestinal ulceration, leptospirosis, food animal pharmacology, equine immunology, diabetes.

Kent State University, College of Public Health, Kent, OH 44242-0001. Offers public health (MPH, PhD), including biostatistics (MPH), environmental health sciences (MPH), epidemiology, health policy and management, prevention science (PhD), social and behavioral sciences (MPH). *Accreditation:* CEPH. *Program availability:* Part-time, online learning. *Faculty:* 23 full-time (14 women), 12 part-time/adjunct (3 women). *Students:* 123 full-time (87 women), 152 part-time (120 women); includes 57 minority (37 Black or African American, non-Hispanic/Latino; 1 American Indian or Alaska Native, non-Hispanic/Latino; 8 Asian, non-Hispanic/Latino; 6 Hispanic/Latino; 5 Two or more races, non-Hispanic/Latino), 40 international. Average age 31. 176 applicants, 76% accepted, 81 enrolled. In 2017, 79 master's, 5 doctorates awarded. *Degree requirements:* For master's, comprehensive exam, 300 hours' placement at public health agency, final portfolio and presentation; for doctorate, comprehensive exam, thesis/dissertation. *Entrance requirements:* For master's, GRE, minimum GPA of 3.0, transcripts, goal statement, 3 letters of recommendation; for doctorate, GRE, minimum GPA of 3.0, personal statement, resume, interview, 3 letters of recommendation. Additional exam requirements/recommendations for international students: Required—TOEFL (minimum score 550 paper-based; 79 iBT), IELTS (minimum score 6.5), PTE (minimum score 58), Michigan English Language Assessment Battery. *Application deadline:* For fall admission, 6/15 for domestic and international students; for spring admission, 10/15 for domestic and international students; for summer admission, 3/15 for domestic and international students. Applications are processed on a rolling basis. Application fee: $45 ($70 for international students). Electronic applications accepted. *Expenses:* Tuition, state resident: full-time $11,310; part-time $515 per credit hour. Tuition, nonresident: full-time $20,396; part-time $928 per credit hour. *International tuition:* $18,544 full-time. *Financial support:* Unspecified assistantships available. *Unit head:* Dr. Sonia Alemagno, Dean and Professor of Health Policy and Management, 330-672-6500, E-mail: salemagn@kent.edu. *Application contact:* Dr. Mark A. James, Professor/Chair/Graduate Advisor, 330-672-6506, E-mail: mjames22@kent.edu.
Website: http://www.kent.edu/publichealth/

Lamar University, College of Graduate Studies, College of Education and Human Development, Department of Health and Kinesiology, Beaumont, TX 77701. Offers public health (MS); science of kinesiology promotion (MS). *Faculty:* 16 full-time (7 women), 5 part-time/adjunct (3 women). *Students:* 26 full-time (8 women), 42 part-time (35 women); includes 36 minority (29 Black or African American, non-Hispanic/Latino; 1 Asian, non-Hispanic/Latino; 5 Hispanic/Latino; 1 Two or more races, non-Hispanic/Latino), 4 international. Average age 29. 55 applicants, 100% accepted, 23 enrolled. In 2017, 23 master's awarded. *Degree requirements:* For master's, comprehensive exam (for some programs), thesis optional. *Entrance requirements:* For master's, GRE General Test, minimum GPA of 2.5. Additional exam requirements/recommendations for international students: Required—TOEFL (minimum score 550 paper-based; 79 iBT), IELTS (minimum score 6.5). *Application deadline:* For fall admission, 8/10 for domestic students, 7/1 for international students; for spring admission, 1/5 for domestic students, 12/1 for international students. Applications are processed on a rolling basis. Application fee: $25. Electronic applications accepted. *Expenses:* Contact institution. *Financial support:* In 2017–18, 4 teaching assistantships (averaging $7,500 per year) were awarded. Financial award application deadline: 4/1; financial award applicants required to submit FAFSA. *Faculty research:* Motor learning, exercise physiology, pedagogy. *Unit head:* Dr. Bill Holmes, Interim Chair, 409-880-8724, Fax: 409-880-1761. *Application contact:* Deidre Mayer, Interim Director, Admissions and Academic Services, 409-880-8888, Fax: 409-880-7419, E-mail: gradmissions@lamar.edu.
Website: http://education.lamar.edu/health-and-kinesiology

La Salle University, School of Nursing and Health Sciences, Program in Public Health, Philadelphia, PA 19141-1199. Offers MPH, MPH/MSN. *Program availability:* Part-time, evening/weekend. *Faculty:* 3 full-time (2 women), 1 (woman) part-time/adjunct. *Students:* 23 part-time (22 women); includes 18 minority (15 Black or African American, non-Hispanic/Latino; 2 Asian, non-Hispanic/Latino; 1 Hispanic/Latino), 1 international. Average age 33. 11 applicants, 10% accepted, 0 enrolled. In 2017, 17 master's awarded. *Degree requirements:* For master's, capstone project. *Entrance requirements:* For master's, minimum undergraduate GPA of 3.0; curriculum vitae/resume; personal statement; 2 letters of reference; interview; prior academic and professional experience in healthcare (recommended). Additional exam requirements/recommendations for international students: Required—TOEFL. *Application deadline:* For fall admission, 8/15 priority date for domestic students, 8/15 for international students; for spring admission, 12/15 priority date for domestic students, 11/15 for international students; for summer admission, 4/14 priority date for domestic students, 3/15 for international students. Application fee: $35. Electronic applications accepted. Application fee is waived when completed online. *Expenses:* Contact institution. *Financial support:* In 2017–18, 3 students received support. Scholarships/grants available. Support available to part-time students. Financial award applicants required to submit FAFSA. *Unit head:* Dr. Candace Robertson-James, Director, 215-951-5032, Fax: 215-951-1896, E-mail: mph@lasalle.edu. *Application contact:* Elizabeth Heenan, Director, Graduate and Adult Enrollment, 215-951-1100, Fax: 215-951-1462, E-mail: heenan@lasalle.edu.
Website: http://www.lasalle.edu/master-public-health/

Laurentian University, School of Graduate Studies and Research, Interdisciplinary Program in Rural and Northern Health, Sudbury, ON P3E 2C6, Canada. Offers PhD.

Lenoir-Rhyne University, Graduate Programs, School of Health, Exercise and Sport Science, Program in Public Health, Hickory, NC 28601. Offers MPH. *Entrance requirements:* For master's, GRE General Test or MAT, essay; resume; minimum GPA of 2.7 undergraduate, 3.0 graduate. Additional exam requirements/recommendations for international students: Required—TOEFL (minimum score 600 paper-based). Electronic applications accepted. *Expenses:* Contact institution.

Liberty University, School of Health Sciences, Lynchburg, VA 24515. Offers anatomy and cell biology (PhD); biomedical sciences (MS); epidemiology (MPH); exercise science (MS), including clinical, community physical activity, human performance, nutrition; global health (MPH); health promotion (MPH); medical sciences (MA), including biopsychology, business management, health informatics, molecular medicine, public health; nutrition (MPH). *Program availability:* Part-time, online learning. *Students:* 542 full-time (394 women), 696 part-time (541 women); includes 402 minority (286 Black or African American, non-Hispanic/Latino; 10 American Indian or Alaska Native, non-Hispanic/Latino; 34 Asian, non-Hispanic/Latino; 46 Hispanic/Latino; 1 Native Hawaiian or other Pacific Islander, non-Hispanic/Latino; 25 Two or more races, non-Hispanic/Latino), 59 international. Average age 32. 1,592 applicants, 40% accepted, 297 enrolled. In 2017, 204 master's awarded. *Degree requirements:* For master's, thesis (for some programs); for doctorate, thesis/dissertation. *Entrance requirements:* For doctorate, MAT or GRE, minimum GPA of 3.25 in master's program, 2-3 recommendations, writing samples (for some programs), letter of intent, professional vitae. Additional exam requirements/recommendations for international students: Required—TOEFL (minimum score 600 paper-based; 100 iBT). Application fee: $50. *Financial support:* Applicants required to submit FAFSA. *Unit head:* Dr. Ralph Linstra, Dean. *Application contact:* Jay Bridge, Director of Admissions, 800-424-9595, Fax: 800-628-7977, E-mail: gradadmissions@liberty.edu.

Loma Linda University, School of Public Health, Loma Linda, CA 92350. Offers MBA, MPH, MS, Dr PH, PhD. *Program availability:* Part-time. *Degree requirements:* For doctorate, thesis/dissertation. *Entrance requirements:* For master's, GRE General Test, baccalaureate degree, minimum GPA of 3.0; for doctorate, GRE General Test, minimum GPA of 3.2. Additional exam requirements/recommendations for international students: Required—TOEFL (minimum score 550 paper-based) or Michigan English Language Assessment Battery. Electronic applications accepted. *Faculty research:* Lifestyle and health, nutrition and cancer, nutrition and cardiovascular disease, smoking and health, aging and longevity.

London Metropolitan University, Graduate Programs, London, United Kingdom. Offers applied psychology (M Sc); architecture (MA); biomedical science (M Sc); blood science (M Sc); cancer pharmacology (M Sc); computer networking and cyber security (M Sc); computing and information systems (M Sc); conference interpreting (MA); counter-terrorism studies (M Sc); creative, digital and professional writing (MA); crime, violence and prevention (M Sc); criminology (M Sc); curating contemporary art (MA); data analytics (M Sc); digital media (MA); early childhood studies (MA); education (MA, Ed D); financial services law, regulation and compliance (LL M); food science (M Sc); forensic psychology (M Sc); health and social care management and policy (M Sc); human nutrition (M Sc); human resource management (MA); human rights and international conflict (MA); information technology (M Sc); intelligence and security studies (M Sc); international oil, gas and energy law (LL M); international relations (MA);

interpreting (MA); learning and teaching in higher education (MA); legal practice (LL M); media and entertainment law (LL M); organizational and consumer psychology (M Sc); psychological therapy (M Sc); psychology of mental health (M Sc); public health (M Sc); public policy and management (MPA); security studies (M Sc); social work (M Sc); spatial planning and urban design (MA); sports therapy (M Sc); supporting older children and young people with dyslexia (MA); teaching languages (MA), including Arabic, English; translation (MA); woman and child abuse (MA).

Long Island University–LIU Brooklyn, School of Health Professions, Brooklyn, NY 11201-8423. Offers athletic training and sport sciences (MS); community health (MS Ed); exercise science (MS); forensic social work (Advanced Certificate); occupational therapy (MS); physical therapy (DPT); physician assistant (MS); public health (MPH); social work (MSW); speech-language pathology (MS). *Faculty:* 33 full-time (23 women), 82 part-time/adjunct (55 women). *Students:* 690 full-time (508 women), 86 part-time (74 women); includes 259 minority (120 Black or African American, non-Hispanic/Latino; 1 American Indian or Alaska Native, non-Hispanic/ Latino; 52 Asian, non-Hispanic/Latino; 76 Hispanic/Latino; 10 Two or more races, non-Hispanic/Latino), 65 international. Average age 27. 1,241 applicants, 45% accepted, 255 enrolled. In 2017, 249 master's, 42 doctorates, 8 other advanced degrees awarded. *Degree requirements:* For master's, comprehensive exam (for some programs), thesis (for some programs); for doctorate, comprehensive exam (for some programs). *Entrance requirements:* For master's and doctorate, GRE. Additional exam requirements/recommendations for international students: Required—TOEFL (minimum score 550 paper-based; 79 iBT). *Application deadline:* Applications are processed on a rolling basis. Application fee: $50. Electronic applications accepted. *Expenses: Tuition:* Full-time $21,618; part-time $1201 per credit. *Required fees:* $1840; $920 per term. Tuition and fees vary according to course load. *Financial support:* In 2017–18, 187 students received support. Research assistantships, teaching assistantships, career-related internships or fieldwork, Federal Work-Study, scholarships/grants, and unspecified assistantships available. Support available to part-time students. Financial award application deadline: 2/15; financial award applicants required to submit FAFSA. *Faculty research:* Pediatric physical therapy, complementary and alternative medicine, global health and human rights, sport leadership and entrepreneurship, feminist sport psychology. *Unit head:* Dr. Barry S. Eckert, Dean, 718-780-6578, Fax: 718-780-4561, E-mail: barry.eckert@liu.edu. *Application contact:* Dr. Dominick Fortugno, Associate Dean, 718-488-1496, Fax: 718-780-4561, E-mail: dominick.fortugno@liu.edu.
Website: http://liu.edu/brooklyn/academics/school-of-health-professions

Louisiana State University Health Sciences Center, School of Public Health, New Orleans, LA 70112. Offers behavioral and community health sciences (MPH); biostatistics (MPH, MS, PhD); community health sciences (PhD); environmental and occupational health sciences (MPH); epidemiology (MPH, PhD); health policy and systems management (MPH). *Accreditation:* CEPH. *Program availability:* Part-time. *Faculty:* 51 full-time (23 women), 41 part-time/adjunct (12 women). *Students:* 98 full-time (77 women), 24 part-time (18 women); includes 55 minority (26 Black or African American, non-Hispanic/Latino; 1 American Indian or Alaska Native, non-Hispanic/ Latino; 13 Asian, non-Hispanic/Latino; 13 Hispanic/Latino; 2 Two or more races, non-Hispanic/Latino), 16 international. Average age 24. 208 applicants, 67% accepted, 54 enrolled. *Degree requirements:* For doctorate, thesis/dissertation. *Entrance requirements:* For master's, GRE General Test. Additional exam requirements/ recommendations for international students: Recommended—TOEFL (minimum score 550 paper-based; 79 iBT), IELTS. *Application deadline:* Applications are processed on a rolling basis. Application fee: $30. Electronic applications accepted. *Expenses:* Tuition, state resident: full-time $11,835; part-time $518 per hour. Tuition, nonresident: full-time $24,108; part-time $1079 per hour. *Required fees:* $1254; $55 per hour. *Unit head:* Dr. Dean Smith, Dean, 504-568-5700, E-mail: dgsmith@lsuhsc.edu. *Application contact:* Isabel Billiot, Director of Admissions and Student Affairs, 504-568-5773, E-mail: ibilli@lsuhsc.edu.
Website: http://publichealth.lsuhsc.edu/

Louisiana State University in Shreveport, College of Business, Education, and Human Development, Program in Public Health, Shreveport, LA 71115-2399. Offers MPH. Program offered jointly with Louisiana State University Health Sciences Center at Shreveport. *Accreditation:* CEPH. *Program availability:* Part-time, evening/weekend. *Students:* 17 full-time (15 women), 12 part-time (11 women); includes 9 minority (8 Black or African American, non-Hispanic/Latino; 1 Hispanic/Latino), 3 international. Average age 36. 26 applicants, 100% accepted, 12 enrolled. In 2017, 14 master's awarded. *Degree requirements:* For master's, thesis optional, practicum. *Entrance requirements:* For master's, GRE or MCAT, 3 letters of recommendation, personal interview. Additional exam requirements/recommendations for international students: Required—TOEFL (minimum score 550 paper-based; 61 iBT). *Application deadline:* For fall admission, 6/30 for domestic and international students; for spring admission, 11/30 for domestic and international students; for summer admission, 4/30 for domestic and international students. Applications are processed on a rolling basis. Application fee: $20 ($30 for international students). Electronic applications accepted. *Expenses:* Tuition, state resident: full-time $3098; part-time $344 per credit hour. Tuition, nonresident: full-time $9923; part-time $1103 per credit hour. *Required fees:* $384 per semester. Tuition and fees vary according to program. *Financial support:* Applicants required to submit FAFSA. *Unit head:* Dr. Jill Rush-Kolodzey, MD, Program Director, 318-797-5218, E-mail: jill.rush-kolodzey@lsus.edu. *Application contact:* Mary Catherine Harvison, Director of Admissions, 318-797-2400, Fax: 318-797-5286, E-mail: mary.harvison@lsus.edu.

Loyola University Chicago, Graduate School, Public Health Program, Chicago, IL 60660. Offers MPH, Certificate. *Accreditation:* CEPH. *Program availability:* Part-time, online learning. *Faculty:* 7 full-time (3 women), 1 part-time/adjunct (0 women). *Students:* 50 full-time (32 women), 26 part-time (19 women); includes 39 minority (10 Black or African American, non-Hispanic/Latino; 13 Asian, non-Hispanic/Latino; 13 Hispanic/ Latino; 3 Two or more races, non-Hispanic/Latino), 4 international. Average age 29. 128 applicants, 73% accepted, 32 enrolled. In 2017, 24 master's, 10 other advanced degrees awarded. *Entrance requirements:* For master's, GRE, MCAT. Additional exam requirements/recommendations for international students: Required—TOEFL (minimum score 79 iBT). *Application deadline:* For fall admission, 5/15 for domestic and international students; for spring admission, 11/15 for domestic and international students. *Expenses:* $1,069 per credit hour tuition, $432 per semester mandatory fees. *Financial support:* Research assistantships and teaching assistantships available. Financial award applicants required to submit FAFSA. *Faculty research:* Genetics of hypertension and obesity, vitamin D metabolism, kidney diseases. *Unit head:* Dr. Ilze Berzina-Galbreath, MPH Director, 708-327-9224, E-mail: iberzin@luc.edu.

Marshall University, Academic Affairs Division, College of Health Professions, Department of Public Health, Huntington, WV 25755. Offers MPH. *Faculty:* 1 full-time (0 women). *Students:* 3 full-time (1 woman), 2 part-time (1 woman). Average age 31. In 2017, 14 master's awarded. *Unit head:* William Pewen, Chair, 304-696-3743, E-mail: pewen@marshall.edu. *Application contact:* Information Contact, 304-746-1900, Fax: 304-746-1902, E-mail: services@marshall.edu.
Website: http://www.marshall.edu/cohp/index.php/departments/public-health/

Medical College of Wisconsin, Graduate School, Program in Public and Community Health, Milwaukee, WI 53226-0509. Offers PhD, MD/PhD. *Accreditation:* CEPH. *Degree requirements:* For doctorate, comprehensive exam, thesis/dissertation. *Entrance requirements:* For doctorate, GRE, official transcripts, three letters of recommendation. Additional exam requirements/recommendations for international students: Required—TOEFL (minimum score 580 paper-based; 100 iBT). *Application deadline:* For fall admission, 12/1 for domestic and international students. Application fee: $50. Electronic applications accepted. *Expenses:* Contact institution. *Financial support:* Fellowships with full tuition reimbursements, scholarships/grants, health care benefits, and tuition waivers (full) available. Financial award application deadline: 2/15. *Faculty research:* Community-academic partnerships, community-based participatory research, injury prevention, health policy, women's health, emergency medical services. *Unit head:* Dr. Laura D. Cassidy, Director, 414-955-4517, Fax: 414-955-6555, E-mail: phdpch@mcw.edu. *Application contact:* Recruitment Office, 414-955-4402, Fax: 414-955-6555, E-mail: gradschoolrecruit@mcw.edu.
Website: http://www.mcw.edu/Graduate-School/Programs/Public-Health/Public-and-Community-Health.htm

Medical College of Wisconsin, Graduate School, Program in Public Health, Milwaukee, WI 53226-0509. Offers MPH, Graduate Certificate. *Accreditation:* CEPH. *Entrance requirements:* For master's and Graduate Certificate, GRE, official transcripts, three letters of recommendation. Additional exam requirements/recommendations for international students: Required—TOEFL. *Application deadline:* For fall admission, 7/1 for domestic and international students; for spring admission, 11/1 for domestic and international students; for summer admission, 4/1 for domestic and international students. Application fee: $50. *Unit head:* Terry Brandenburg, Director, 414-955-8218, Fax: 414-955-6555, E-mail: gradschool@mcw.edu. *Application contact:* Recruitment Office, 414-955-4402, Fax: 414-955-6555, E-mail: gradschoolrecruit@mcw.edu.
Website: https://www.mcw.edu/MPH-Program.htm

Meharry Medical College, School of Graduate Studies, Division of Public Health Practice, Nashville, TN 37208-9989. Offers occupational medicine (MSPH); public health administration (MSPH). *Accreditation:* CEPH. *Program availability:* Part-time, evening/weekend. *Degree requirements:* For master's, thesis, externship. *Entrance requirements:* For master's, GRE General Test, GMAT. *Expenses:* Contact institution.

Mercer University, Graduate Studies, Cecil B. Day Campus, College of Health Professions, Atlanta, GA 30341. Offers athletic training (MAT); clinical medical psychology (Psy D); physical therapy (DPT); physician assistant studies (MM Sc); public health (MPH); DPT/MBA; DPT/MPH; MM Sc/MPH; Pharm D/MPH. *Faculty:* 23 full-time (14 women), 10 part-time/adjunct (7 women). *Students:* 345 full-time (261 women), 67 part-time (55 women); includes 167 minority (116 Black or African American, non-Hispanic/Latino; 28 Asian, non-Hispanic/Latino; 21 Hispanic/Latino; 2 Two or more races, non-Hispanic/Latino), 2 international. Average age 26. In 2017, 83 master's, 37 doctorates awarded. *Expenses:* Contact institution. *Financial support:* Federal Work-Study, traineeships, and unspecified assistantships available. *Faculty research:* Scholarship of teaching and learning, health disparities, clinical outcomes, health promotion. *Unit head:* Dr. Lisa Lundquist, Dean/Clinical Professor, 678-547-6308, E-mail: lundquist_lm@mercer.edu. *Application contact:* Laura Ellison, Director of Admissions and Student Affairs, 678-547-6391, E-mail: ellison_la@mercer.edu.
Website: http://chp.mercer.edu/

Michigan State University, College of Human Medicine and The Graduate School, Graduate Programs in Human Medicine, Program in Public Health, East Lansing, MI 48824. Offers MPH.

MidAmerica Nazarene University, School of Nursing and Health Science, Olathe, KS 66062. Offers healthcare administration (MSN); healthcare quality management (MSN); nursing education (MSN); public health (MSN); MSN/MBA. *Accreditation:* AACN. *Program availability:* Part-time, evening/weekend, 100% online, blended/hybrid learning. *Entrance requirements:* For master's, BSN, minimum GPA of 3.0, active unencumbered RN license, undergraduate statistics course. Additional exam requirements/ recommendations for international students: Required—TOEFL. Electronic applications accepted. *Expenses:* Contact institution. *Faculty research:* Technology in education, minority recruitment and retention in nursing programs, faculty views and attitudes on culturally competency, innovative nursing program development, spirituality and holistic health.

Mississippi University for Women, Graduate School, College of Nursing and Health Sciences, Columbus, MS 39701-9998. Offers nursing (MSN, DNP, PMC); public health education (MPH); speech-language pathology (MS). *Accreditation:* AACN; ASHA. *Program availability:* Part-time. *Degree requirements:* For master's, comprehensive exam, thesis. *Entrance requirements:* For master's, GRE General Test, bachelor's degree in nursing, previous course work in statistics, proficiency in English.

Missouri State University, Graduate College, College of Health and Human Services, Program in Public Health, Springfield, MO 65897. Offers MPH. *Accreditation:* CEPH. *Faculty:* 3 full-time (1 woman). *Students:* 16 full-time (14 women), 17 part-time (10 women), 14 international. Average age 30. 24 applicants, 50% accepted, 5 enrolled. In 2017, 17 master's awarded. *Degree requirements:* For master's, comprehensive exam, thesis or alternative. *Entrance requirements:* For master's, GRE, minimum GPA of 3.0, 1 year of work experience. Additional exam requirements/recommendations for international students: Required—TOEFL (minimum score 550 paper-based; 79 iBT), IELTS (minimum score 6). *Application deadline:* For fall admission, 4/1 priority date for domestic students, 4/1 for international students; for spring admission, 10/1 priority date for domestic students, 10/1 for international students. Applications are processed on a rolling basis. Application fee: $35 ($50 for international students). Electronic applications accepted. *Expenses:* Tuition, state resident: full-time $2915; part-time $2021 per credit hour. Tuition, nonresident: full-time $5354; part-time $3647 per credit hour. *International tuition:* $11,992 full-time. *Required fees:* $173; $173 per credit hour. Tuition and fees vary according to class time, course level, course load, degree level, campus/location and program. *Financial support:* Federal Work-Study, institutionally sponsored loans, scholarships/grants, and unspecified assistantships available. Financial award application deadline: 3/31; financial award applicants required to submit FAFSA. *Unit head:* Dr. David Claborn, Department Head, 417-836-8850, E-mail: davidclaborn@missouristate.edu. *Application contact:* Stephanie Praschan, Director, Graduate Enrollment Management, 417-836-5033, Fax: 417-836-6200, E-mail: stephaniepraschan@missouristate.edu.
Website: http://www.missouristate.edu/mph/

Monroe College, King Graduate School, Bronx, NY 10468. Offers accounting (MS); business administration (MBA), including entrepreneurship, finance, general business administration, healthcare management, human resources, information technology, marketing; computer science (MS); criminal justice (MS); hospitality management (MS); public health (MPH), including biostatistics and epidemiology, community health, health administration and leadership. *Program availability:* Online learning. Application fee: $50.
Website: https://www.monroecollege.edu/Degrees/King-Graduate-School/

Montclair State University, The Graduate School, College of Education and Human Services, Program in Public Health, Montclair, NJ 07043-1624. Offers MPH.

Accreditation: CEPH. *Program availability:* Part-time, evening/weekend. *Degree requirements:* For master's, comprehensive exam, thesis or alternative. *Entrance requirements:* For master's, GRE General Test, essay, 2 letters of recommendation. Additional exam requirements/recommendations for international students: Required—TOEFL (minimum score 83 iBT), IELTS (minimum score 6.5). Electronic applications accepted.

Morehouse School of Medicine, Master of Public Health Program, Atlanta, GA 30310-1495. Offers MPH. *Accreditation:* CEPH. *Program availability:* Part-time. *Degree requirements:* For master's, thesis, practicum, public health leadership seminar. *Entrance requirements:* For master's, GRE General Test, writing test, public health or human service experience. Additional exam requirements/recommendations for international students: Required—TOEFL (minimum score 550 paper-based). Electronic applications accepted. *Expenses:* Contact institution. *Faculty research:* Women's and adolescent health, violence prevention, cancer epidemiology/disparities, substance abuse prevention.

Morgan State University, School of Graduate Studies, School of Community Health and Policy, Baltimore, MD 21251. Offers behavioral health sciences (MPH, Dr PH); nursing (MS, PhD). *Accreditation:* CEPH. *Entrance requirements:* For doctorate, GRE, minimum GPA of 3.0. Additional exam requirements/recommendations for international students: Required—TOEFL (minimum score 550 paper-based). *Application deadline:* For fall admission, 2/1 priority date for domestic students; for spring admission, 10/1 priority date for domestic students. Applications are processed on a rolling basis. Application fee: $0. *Expenses:* Tuition, state resident: part-time $433 per credit. Tuition, nonresident: part-time $851 per credit. *Required fees:* $81.50 per credit. *Financial support:* Application deadline: 2/1. *Unit head:* Dr. Kim Dobson Sydnor, Dean, 443-885-3560, E-mail: kim.sydnor@morgan.edu. *Application contact:* Dr. Dean Campbell, Graduate Recruitment Specialist, 443-885-3185, Fax: 443-885-8226, E-mail: dean.campbell@morgan.edu.
Website: http://php.morgan.edu

National University, School of Health and Human Services, La Jolla, CA 92037-1011. Offers clinical affairs (MS); clinical regulatory affairs (MS); complementary and integrative healthcare (MS); family nurse practitioner (MSN); health and life science analytics (MS); health informatics (MS, Certificate); healthcare administration (MHA); nurse anesthesia (MSNA); nursing administration (MSN); nursing informatics (MSN); psychiatric-mental health nurse practitioner (MSN); public health (MPH), including health promotion, healthcare administration, mental health. *Program availability:* Part-time, evening/weekend, 100% online, blended/hybrid learning. *Degree requirements:* For master's, thesis (for some programs). *Entrance requirements:* For master's, interview, minimum GPA of 2.5. Additional exam requirements/recommendations for international students: Required—TOEFL (minimum score 550 paper-based; 79 iBT), IELTS (minimum score 6). *Application deadline:* Applications are processed on a rolling basis. Application fee: $60 ($65 for international students). Electronic applications accepted. *Expenses: Tuition:* Part-time $430 per quarter hour. *Financial support:* Career-related internships or fieldwork, institutionally sponsored loans, scholarships/grants, and tuition waivers (partial) available. Support available to part-time students. Financial award application deadline: 6/30; financial award applicants required to submit FAFSA. *Faculty research:* Nursing education, obesity prevention, workforce diversity. *Unit head:* Dr. Gloria J. McNeal, Dean, 858-309-3473, E-mail: shhs@nu.edu. *Application contact:* Brandon Jouganatos, Vice President for Enrollment Services, 800-628-8648, E-mail: advisor@nu.edu.
Website: http://www.nu.edu/OurPrograms/SchoolOfHealthAndHumanServices.html

New England Institute of Technology, Program in Public Health, East Greenwich, RI 02818. Offers MPH. *Program availability:* Part-time-only, evening/weekend, online only, 100% online. *Entrance requirements:* For master's, minimum GPA of 2.5; bachelor's degree in health-related field (health care, community health, health sciences, management, nursing, psychology, wellness, etc.) from accredited institution or in any other field along with 3+ years' public health experience. Additional exam requirements/recommendations for international students: Required—TOEFL. *Application deadline:* Applications are processed on a rolling basis. Application fee: $25. Electronic applications accepted. *Expenses:* $375 per credit. *Unit head:* Douglas H. Sherman, Senior Vice President and Provost, 401-739-5000 Ext. 3481, Fax: 401-886-0859, E-mail: dsherman@neit.edu. *Application contact:* Michael Caruso, Director of Admissions, 800-736-7744 Ext. 3411, Fax: 401-886-0868, E-mail: mcaruso@neit.edu.
Website: https://www.neit.edu/Programs/Online-and-Hybrid-Degree-Programs/Master-of-Public-Health-Degree-Online

New Mexico State University, College of Health and Social Services, Department of Public Health Sciences, Las Cruces, NM 88003. Offers public health (MPH, Graduate Certificate). *Accreditation:* CEPH. *Program availability:* Part-time, blended/hybrid learning. *Faculty:* 10 full-time (6 women), 3 part-time/adjunct (1 woman). *Students:* 38 full-time (33 women), 51 part-time (33 women); includes 40 minority (3 Black or African American, non-Hispanic/Latino; 2 American Indian or Alaska Native, non-Hispanic/Latino; 2 Asian, non-Hispanic/Latino; 31 Hispanic/Latino; 2 Two or more races, non-Hispanic/Latino), 5 international. Average age 36. 59 applicants, 63% accepted, 3 enrolled. In 2017, 19 master's, 5 other advanced degrees awarded. *Degree requirements:* For master's, thesis optional. *Entrance requirements:* For master's, GRE. Additional exam requirements/recommendations for international students: Required—TOEFL (minimum score 550 paper-based; 79 iBT), IELTS (minimum score 6.5). *Application deadline:* For fall admission, 2/15 for domestic and international students. Application fee: $40 ($50 for international students). Electronic applications accepted. *Expenses:* Tuition, state resident: full-time $4390. Tuition, nonresident: full-time $15,309. *Required fees:* $853. *Financial support:* In 2017–18, 15 students received support, including 8 research assistantships (averaging $13,527 per year), 4 teaching assistantships (averaging $6,232 per year); career-related internships or fieldwork, Federal Work-Study, health care benefits, and unspecified assistantships also available. Financial award application deadline: 3/1. *Faculty research:* Community health education, health issues of U.S.-Mexico border, health policy and management, victims of violence, environmental and occupational health issues. *Total annual research expenditures:* $375,591. *Unit head:* Dr. Karen Kipera-Frye, Interim Department Head, 575-646-4300, Fax: 575-646-4343, E-mail: kfrye@nmsu.edu. *Application contact:* Dr. Joe Tomaka, Graduate Coordinator, 575-646-7431, Fax: 575-646-4343, E-mail: tomaka@nmsu.edu.
Website: http://publichealth.nmsu.edu

New York Medical College, School of Health Sciences and Practice, Valhalla, NY 10595. Offers behavioral sciences and health promotion (MPH); biostatistics (MS); children with special health care (Graduate Certificate); emergency preparedness (Graduate Certificate); environmental health science (MPH); epidemiology (MPH, MS); global health (Graduate Certificate); health education (Graduate Certificate); health policy and management (MPH, Dr PH); industrial hygiene (Graduate Certificate); pediatric dysphagia (Post-Graduate Certificate); physical therapy (DPT); public health (Graduate Certificate); speech-language pathology (MS). *Accreditation:* CEPH. *Program availability:* Part-time, evening/weekend, 100% online, blended/hybrid learning. *Faculty:* 48 full-time (33 women), 235 part-time/adjunct (141 women). *Students:* 221 full-time (153 women), 270 part-time (194 women); includes 202 minority (83 Black or African American, non-Hispanic/Latino; 2 American Indian or Alaska Native, non-Hispanic/Latino; 64 Asian, non-Hispanic/Latino; 47 Hispanic/Latino; 1 Native Hawaiian or other Pacific Islander, non-Hispanic/Latino; 5 Two or more races, non-Hispanic/Latino), 19 international. Average age 29. 1,118 applicants, 38% accepted, 169 enrolled. In 2017, 110 master's, 41 doctorates awarded. *Degree requirements:* For master's, comprehensive exam (for some programs), thesis (for some programs); for doctorate, thesis/dissertation. *Entrance requirements:* For master's, GRE (for MS in speech-language pathology); for doctorate, GRE. Additional exam requirements/recommendations for international students: Required—TOEFL, IELTS. *Application deadline:* For fall admission, 8/1 for domestic students, 4/15 for international students; for spring admission, 12/1 for domestic students; for summer admission, 5/1 for domestic students, 4/15 for international students. Application fee: $125. Electronic applications accepted. *Expenses:* $1,125 per credit, $245 fees. *Financial support:* In 2017–18, 10,000 students received support. Scholarships/grants and unspecified assistantships available. Financial award application deadline: 4/30; financial award applicants required to submit FAFSA. *Unit head:* Ben Watson, PhD, Vice Dean, 914-594-4531, E-mail: ben_watson@nymc.edu. *Application contact:* Irene Bundziak, Assistant to Director of Admissions, 914-594-4905, E-mail: irene_bundziak@nymc.edu.
Website: http://www.nymc.edu/school-of-health-sciences-and-practice-shsp/

New York University, College of Global Public Health, New York, NY 10012. Offers biological basis of public health (PhD); community and international health (MPH); global health leadership (MPH); health systems and health services research (PhD); population and community health (PhD); public health nutrition (MPH); social and behavioral sciences (MPH); socio-behavioral health (PhD). *Accreditation:* CEPH. *Program availability:* Part-time, online learning. *Faculty:* 26 full-time (20 women), 104 part-time/adjunct (53 women). *Students:* 161 full-time (136 women), 70 part-time (54 women); includes 74 minority (24 Black or African American, non-Hispanic/Latino; 1 American Indian or Alaska Native, non-Hispanic/Latino; 27 Asian, non-Hispanic/Latino; 11 Hispanic/Latino; 4 Native Hawaiian or other Pacific Islander, non-Hispanic/Latino; 7 Two or more races, non-Hispanic/Latino), 39 international. Average age 29. 802 applicants, 70% accepted, 97 enrolled. In 2017, 1 master's awarded. *Degree requirements:* For master's, thesis (for some programs); for doctorate, thesis/dissertation. *Entrance requirements:* For master's and doctorate, GRE. Additional exam requirements/recommendations for international students: Required—TOEFL. *Application deadline:* For fall admission, 2/1 for domestic and international students. Applications are processed on a rolling basis. Electronic applications accepted. *Expenses:* Contact institution. *Financial support:* Federal Work-Study and scholarships/grants available. *Unit head:* Dr. Cheryl G. Healton, Director, 212-992-6741. *Application contact:* New York University Information, 212-998-1212.
Website: http://publichealth.nyu.edu/

★ **North Dakota State University,** College of Graduate and Interdisciplinary Studies, College of Health Professions, Department of Public Health, Fargo, ND 58102. Offers American Indian public health (MPH); community health sciences (MPH); management of infectious diseases (MPH); Pharm D/MPH. *Accreditation:* CEPH. *Program availability:* Online learning. *Expenses:* Tuition, state resident: full-time $4323; part-time $360.21 per credit. Tuition, nonresident: full-time $6484; part-time $540.31 per credit. *Required fees:* $668; $55.70 per credit. Part-time tuition and fees vary according to degree level, program and reciprocity agreements. *Unit head:* Stefanie Meyer, Program Coordinator, 701-231-6549, E-mail: stefanie.meyer@ndsu.edu. *Application contact:* Stefanie Meyer, Program Coordinator, 701-231-6549, E-mail: stefanie.meyer@ndsu.edu.
Website: http://www.ndsu.edu/publichealth/

See Display on the next page and Close-Up on page 845.

Northeast Ohio Medical University, College of Graduate Studies, Rootstown, OH 44272-0095. Offers bioethics (Certificate); health-system pharmacy administration (MS); integrated pharmaceutical medicine (MS, PhD); medical ethics and humanities (MS); public health (MPH). MPH offered as part of consortium with The University of Akron, Youngstown State University, Ohio University, and Cleveland State University. *Program availability:* Part-time, evening/weekend. *Faculty:* 23 part-time/adjunct (14 women). *Students:* 22 full-time (13 women), 21 part-time (13 women); includes 10 minority (1 Black or African American, non-Hispanic/Latino; 8 Asian, non-Hispanic/Latino; 1 Two or more races, non-Hispanic/Latino). In 2017, 3 master's, 1 doctorate awarded. *Degree requirements:* For master's, thesis (for MS in medical ethics and humanities, integrated pharmaceutical medicine); for doctorate, thesis/dissertation. *Application deadline:* For fall admission, 5/1 priority date for domestic students; for winter admission, 1/5 priority date for domestic students. Applications are processed on a rolling basis. Application fee: $95. Electronic applications accepted. *Expenses:* Contact institution. *Financial support:* Institutionally sponsored loans and tuition waivers available. Financial award application deadline: 3/15; financial award applicants required to submit FAFSA. *Unit head:* Dr. Steven Schmidt, Dean, 330-325-6290. *Application contact:* Heidi Terry, Executive Director, Enrollment Services, 330-325-6479, E-mail: hterry@neomed.edu.
Website: https://www.neomed.edu/graduatestudies/

Northern Illinois University, Graduate School, College of Health and Human Sciences, School of Health Studies, De Kalb, IL 60115-2854. Offers nutrition and dietetics (MS); public health (MPH). *Students:* 15 full-time (11 women), 33 part-time (24 women); includes 13 minority (6 Black or African American, non-Hispanic/Latino; 6 Asian, non-Hispanic/Latino; 1 Hispanic/Latino), 4 international. Average age 33. 37 applicants, 49% accepted, 5 enrolled. *Unit head:* Jim Ciesla, Interim Chair, 815-753-1384. *Application contact:* Graduate School Office, 815-753-0395, E-mail: gradsch@niu.edu.
Website: http://chhs.niu.edu/health-studies/

Northwestern University, Feinberg School of Medicine, Program in Public Health, Evanston, IL 60208. Offers MPH. *Accreditation:* CEPH. *Program availability:* Part-time, evening/weekend. *Entrance requirements:* For master's, GRE General Test. Additional exam requirements/recommendations for international students: Required—TOEFL. *Faculty research:* Cardiovascular epidemiology, cancer epidemiology, nutritional interventions for the prevention of cardiovascular disease and cancer, women's health, outcomes research.

Nova Southeastern University, Dr. Kiran C. Patel College of Osteopathic Medicine, Fort Lauderdale, FL 33328. Offers biomedical informatics (MS, Graduate Certificate), including biomedical informatics (MS), clinical informatics (Graduate Certificate), public health informatics (Graduate Certificate); disaster and emergency management (MS); medical education (MS); nutrition (MS, Graduate Certificate), including functional nutrition and herbal therapy (Graduate Certificate); osteopathic medicine (DO); public health (MPH, Graduate Certificate), including health education (Graduate Certificate); social medicine (Graduate Certificate); DO/DMD. *Accreditation:* AOsA. *Faculty:* 98 full-time (58 women), 1,484 part-time/adjunct (401 women). *Students:* 1,032 full-time (479 women), 197 part-time (129 women); includes 656 minority (97 Black or African American, non-Hispanic/Latino; 308 Asian, non-Hispanic/Latino; 215 Hispanic/Latino; 1 Native Hawaiian or other Pacific Islander, non-Hispanic/Latino; 35 Two or more races, non-Hispanic/Latino), 67 international. Average age 26. 5,226 applicants, 9% accepted, 248 enrolled. In 2017, 110 master's, 239 doctorates, 7 other advanced degrees

awarded. *Degree requirements:* For master's, comprehensive exam (for MPH); field/special projects; for doctorate, comprehensive exam, COMLEX Board Exams; for Graduate Certificate, thesis or alternative. *Entrance requirements:* For master's, GRE; for doctorate, MCAT, coursework in biology, chemistry, organic chemistry, physics (all with labs), biochemistry, and English. *Application deadline:* For fall admission, 1/15 for domestic students. Applications are processed on a rolling basis. Application fee: $50. Electronic applications accepted. *Expenses:* Contact institution. *Financial support:* In 2017–18, 83 students received support, including 24 fellowships with tuition reimbursements available; Federal Work-Study and scholarships/grants also available. Financial award application deadline: 6/1; financial award applicants required to submit FAFSA. *Faculty research:* Teaching strategies, simulated patient use, HIV/AIDS education, minority health issues, immune disorders. *Unit head:* Elaine M. Wallace, Dean, 954-262-1457, Fax: 954-262-2250, E-mail: ewallace@nova.edu. *Application contact:* HPD Admissions, 877-640-0218, E-mail: hpdinfo@nova.edu.
Website: https://www.osteopathic.nova.edu/

The Ohio State University, College of Public Health, Columbus, OH 43210. Offers MHA, MPH, MS, PhD, DVM/MPH, JD/MHA, MHA/MBA, MHA/MD, MHA/MPA, MHA/MS, MPH/MBA, MPH/MD, MPH/MSW. *Accreditation:* CAHME. *Program availability:* Part-time. *Faculty:* 57. *Students:* 241 full-time (177 women), 77 part-time (57 women); includes 75 minority (25 Black or African American, non-Hispanic/Latino; 25 Asian, non-Hispanic/Latino; 15 Hispanic/Latino; 10 Two or more races, non-Hispanic/Latino), 18 international. Average age 27. In 2017, 123 master's, 7 doctorates awarded. Terminal master's awarded for partial completion of doctoral program. *Degree requirements:* For master's, thesis optional, practicum; for doctorate, thesis/dissertation. *Entrance requirements:* For master's and doctorate, GRE. Additional exam requirements/recommendations for international students: Required—TOEFL (minimum score 550 paper-based; 79 iBT); Recommended—IELTS (minimum score 7). *Application deadline:* For fall admission, 12/1 priority date for domestic students, 11/1 priority date for international students. Applications are processed on a rolling basis. Application fee: $60 ($70 for international students). Electronic applications accepted. *Financial support:* Fellowships with tuition reimbursements and research assistantships with tuition reimbursements available. *Unit head:* Dr. William J. Martin, II, Dean and Professor, 614-292-8350, E-mail: martin.3047@osu.edu. *Application contact:* 614-292-8350, Fax: 614-247-1846, E-mail: cph@cph.osu.edu.
Website: http://cph.osu.edu/

Ohio University, Graduate College, College of Health Sciences and Professions, Department of Social and Public Health, Athens, OH 45701-2979. Offers early child development and family life (MS); family studies (MS); health administration (MHA); public health (MPH); social work (MSW). *Program availability:* Part-time, evening/weekend, online learning. *Degree requirements:* For master's, capstone (MPH). *Entrance requirements:* For master's, GMAT, GRE General Test, previous course work in accounting, management, and statistics; previous public health background (MHA, MPH). Additional exam requirements/recommendations for international students: Required—TOEFL (minimum score 550 paper-based; 80 iBT) or IELTS (minimum score 6.5). Electronic applications accepted. *Expenses:* Contact institution. *Faculty research:* Health care management, health policy, managed care, health behavior, disease prevention.

Old Dominion University, College of Health Sciences, School of Dental Hygiene, Norfolk, VA 23529. Offers dental hygiene (MS), including community/public health, education, generalist, global health, marketing, modeling and simulation, research. *Program availability:* Part-time, evening/weekend, blended/hybrid learning. *Faculty:* 10 full-time (9 women). *Students:* 3 full-time (1 woman), 22 part-time (21 women); includes 5 minority (3 Black or African American, non-Hispanic/Latino; 1 Asian, non-Hispanic/Latino; 1 Hispanic/Latino), 3 international. Average age 38. 12 applicants, 25% accepted, 2 enrolled. In 2017, 8 master's awarded. *Degree requirements:* For master's, comprehensive exam, thesis optional, writing proficiency exam, responsible conduct of research training. *Entrance requirements:* For master's, Dental Hygiene National Board Examination or copy of license to practice dental hygiene, BS or certificate in dental hygiene or related area, minimum GPA of 2.8 (3.0 in major), 4 letters of recommendation. Additional exam requirements/recommendations for international students: Required—TOEFL (minimum score 550 paper-based, 79 iBT) or IELTS (minimum score 6.5). *Application deadline:* For fall admission, 7/1 for domestic students, 4/15 for international students; for spring admission, 12/1 for domestic students, 10/1 for international students; for summer admission, 3/1 for domestic students, 2/1 for international students. Applications are processed on a rolling basis. Application fee: $50. Electronic applications accepted. *Expenses:* Contact institution. *Financial support:* In 2017–18, 4 students received support, including 4 teaching assistantships with partial tuition reimbursements available (averaging $13,000 per year); scholarships/grants and health care benefits also available. Support available to part-time students. Financial award application deadline: 2/15; financial award applicants required to submit CSS PROFILE or FAFSA. *Faculty research:* Clinical dental hygiene, dental hygiene client health behaviors, dental hygiene education interventions, oral product testing, cold plasma. *Total annual research expenditures:* $43,581. *Unit head:* Dr. Denise M. Claiborne, Assistant Professor/Graduate Program Director, 757-683-5949, Fax: 757-683-5239, E-mail: dclaibor@odu.edu. *Application contact:* William Heffelfinger, Director of Graduate Admissions, 757-683-5554, Fax: 757-683-3255, E-mail: gradadmit@odu.edu.
Website: http://www.odu.edu/academics/programs/masters/dental-hygiene

Oregon State University, College of Public Health and Human Sciences, Program in Public Health, Corvallis, OR 97331. Offers biostatistics (MPH); environmental and occupational health (MPH, PhD); epidemiology (MPH, PhD); global health (MPH, PhD). Terminal master's awarded for partial completion of doctoral program. *Entrance requirements:* For master's and doctorate, GRE, minimum GPA of 3.0 in last 90 hours. Additional exam requirements/recommendations for international students: Required—TOEFL (minimum score 80 iBT), IELTS (minimum score 6.5). *Application deadline:* For fall admission, 12/1 priority date for domestic and international students. Applications are processed on a rolling basis. Electronic applications accepted. *Expenses:* Contact institution. *Financial support:* Application deadline: 12/1. *Unit head:* Amanda Armington, MPH Program Manager, 541-737-3825, E-mail: amanda.armington@oregonstate.edu.

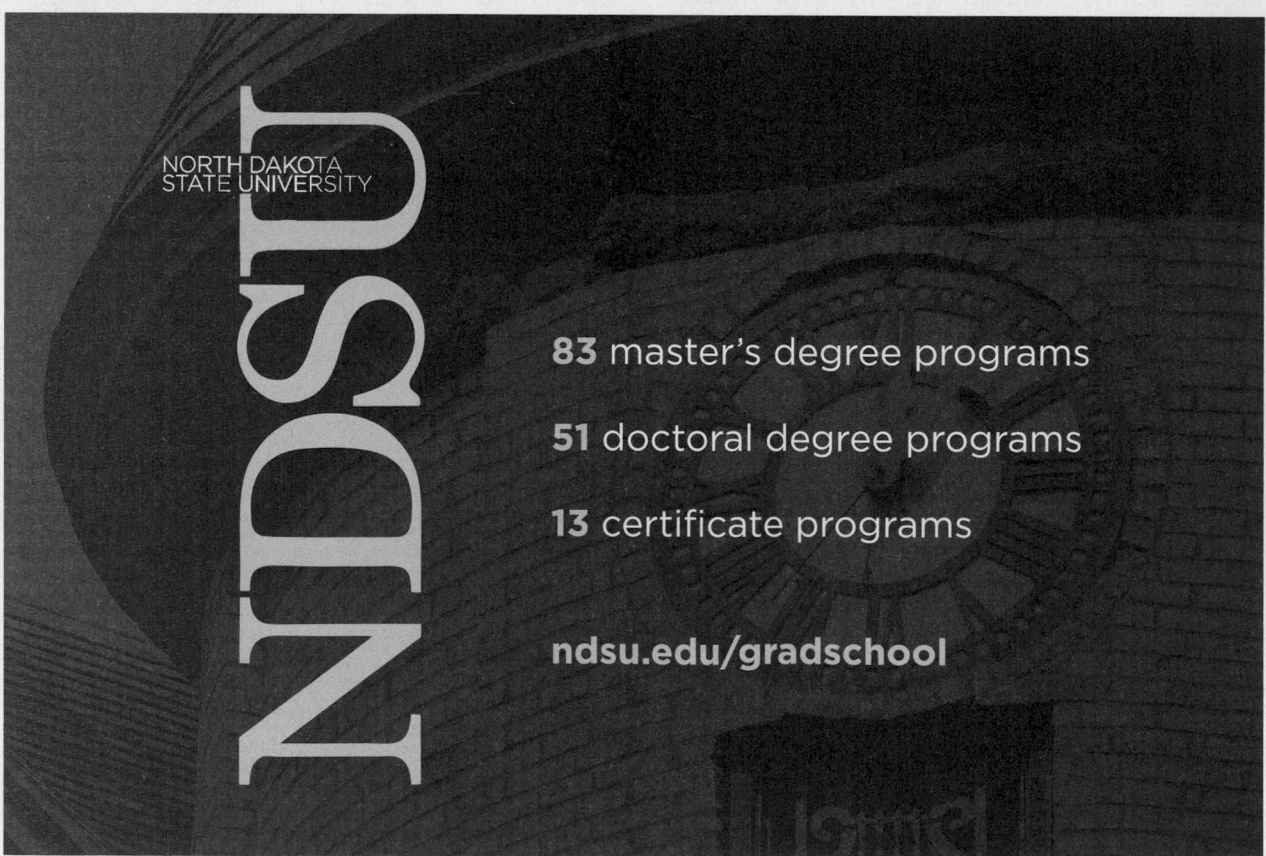

Penn State Hershey Medical Center, College of Medicine, Graduate School Programs in the Biomedical Sciences, Graduate Program in Public Health, Hershey, PA 17033. Offers MPH, Dr PH. *Accreditation:* CEPH. *Program availability:* Part-time, evening/weekend. *Students:* 32 full-time (23 women); includes 9 minority (3 Black or African American, non-Hispanic/Latino; 5 Asian, non-Hispanic/Latino; 1 Hispanic/Latino), 3 international. 56 applicants, 73% accepted, 22 enrolled. *Degree requirements:* For master's, thesis or alternative; for doctorate, comprehensive exam, thesis/dissertation. *Entrance requirements:* For master's, GRE General Test; for doctorate, GRE General Test, master's degree. Additional exam requirements/recommendations for international students: Required—TOEFL (minimum score 81 iBT). *Application deadline:* For fall admission, 2/1 for domestic students, 1/15 for international students. Applications are processed on a rolling basis. Application fee: $65. Electronic applications accepted. *Financial support:* In 2017–18, research assistantships with full tuition reimbursements (averaging $26,982 per year) were awarded. Financial award applicants required to submit FAFSA. *Unit head:* Dr. Wenke Hwang, Director, 717-531-1502, E-mail: whwang@phs.psu.edu. *Application contact:* Shannon Bowman-Tuninga, Program Coordinator, 717-531-1502, E-mail: pennstatepublichealth@phs.psu.edu.
Website: http://med.psu.edu

Penn State Hershey Medical Center, College of Medicine, Graduate School Programs in the Biomedical Sciences, Graduate Program in Public Health Sciences, Hershey, PA 17033. Offers MS. *Program availability:* Part-time. *Students:* 26 applicants, 12% accepted, 3 enrolled. *Entrance requirements:* For master's, GRE General Test. Additional exam requirements/recommendations for international students: Required—TOEFL (minimum score 81 iBT). *Application deadline:* For fall admission, 1/31 priority date for domestic students, 2/1 priority date for international students. Applications are processed on a rolling basis. Application fee: $65. Electronic applications accepted. *Financial support:* Applicants required to submit FAFSA. *Faculty research:* Clinical trials, statistical methods in genetic epidemiology, genetic factors in nicotine dependence and dementia syndromes, health economics, cancer. *Unit head:* Dr. Kristen Kjerulff, Chair, 717-531-7178, Fax: 717-531-5779, E-mail: hes-grad-hmc@psu.edu. *Application contact:* Mardi Sawyer, Program Administrator, 717-531-7178, Fax: 717-531-5779, E-mail: hes-grad-hmc@psu.edu.
Website: http://med.psu.edu

Philadelphia College of Osteopathic Medicine, Graduate and Professional Programs, Department of Psychology, Philadelphia, PA 19131-1694. Offers applied behavior analysis (Certificate); clinical health psychology (Post-Doctoral Certificate); clinical neuropsychology (Post-Doctoral Certificate); clinical psychology (Psy D); educational psychology (PhD); mental health counseling (MS); organizational development and leadership (MS); psychology (Certificate); public health management and administration (MS); school psychology (MS, Psy D, Ed S). *Accreditation:* APA. *Faculty:* 19 full-time (11 women), 122 part-time/adjunct (58 women). *Students:* 487 (335 women); includes 138 minority (89 Black or African American, non-Hispanic/Latino; 4 American Indian or Alaska Native, non-Hispanic/Latino; 11 Asian, non-Hispanic/Latino; 12 Hispanic/Latino; 22 Two or more races, non-Hispanic/Latino). 298 applicants, 44% accepted, 100 enrolled. In 2017, 50 master's, 43 doctorates, 10 other advanced degrees awarded. Terminal master's awarded for partial completion of doctoral program. *Degree requirements:* For master's, comprehensive exam (for some programs), thesis (for some programs); for doctorate, comprehensive exam, thesis/dissertation. *Entrance requirements:* For master's, GRE or MAT, minimum GPA of 3.0; bachelor's degree from regionally-accredited college or university; for doctorate, PRAXIS II (for Psy D in school psychology), minimum undergraduate GPA of 3.0; for other advanced degree, GRE (for Ed S). Additional exam requirements/recommendations for international students: Required—TOEFL (minimum score 79 iBT). *Application deadline:* Applications are processed on a rolling basis. Application fee: $50. Electronic applications accepted. *Financial support:* In 2017–18, 28 teaching assistantships were awarded; Federal Work-Study, institutionally sponsored loans, and scholarships/grants also available. Financial award application deadline: 3/15; financial award applicants required to submit FAFSA. *Faculty research:* Adult and childhood anxiety and ADHD; coping with chronic illness; primary care psychology/integrated health care; applied behavior analysis; psychological, educational, and neuropsychological assessment. *Total annual research expenditures:* $533,489. *Unit head:* Dr. Robert DiTomasso, Chairman, 215-871-6442, Fax: 215-871-6458, E-mail: robertd@pcom.edu. *Application contact:* Johnathan Cox, Associate Director of Admissions, 215-871-6700, Fax: 215-871-6719, E-mail: johnathancox@pcom.edu.

Ponce Health Sciences University, Program in Public Health, Ponce, PR 00732-7004. Offers epidemiology (Dr PH); public health (MPH). *Accreditation:* CEPH. *Degree requirements:* For master's, one foreign language, comprehensive exam, thesis. *Entrance requirements:* For master's, GRE General Test or EXADEP, proficiency in Spanish and English, minimum GPA of 2.7, 3 letters of recommendation; for doctorate, GRE, proficiency in Spanish and English, minimum GPA of 3.0, letter of recommendation.

Portland State University, Graduate Studies, OHSU-PSU School of Public Health, Portland, OR 97207-0751. Offers MA, MPH, PhD. *Program availability:* Part-time. *Faculty:* 20 full-time (16 women), 4 part-time/adjunct (2 women). *Students:* 18 full-time (16 women), 183 part-time (150 women); includes 51 minority (6 Black or African American, non-Hispanic/Latino; 4 American Indian or Alaska Native, non-Hispanic/Latino; 10 Asian, non-Hispanic/Latino; 18 Hispanic/Latino; 13 Two or more races, non-Hispanic/Latino), 2 international. Average age 32. In 2017, 41 master's, 1 doctorate awarded. *Degree requirements:* For master's, comprehensive exam, field experience, CPH exam (for MPH); for doctorate, thesis/dissertation. *Entrance requirements:* For master's, GRE General Test, SOPHAS application, background check, personal statement, 3 letters of recommendation, curriculum vitae/resume. Additional exam requirements/recommendations for international students: Required—TOEFL (minimum score 550 paper-based; 90 iBT). *Application deadline:* For fall admission, 4/1 for domestic students. Application fee: $165. *Expenses:* Tuition, state resident: full-time $14,436; part-time $401 per credit. Tuition, nonresident: full-time $21,780; part-time $605 per credit. *Required fees:* $1380; $22 per credit. $119 per quarter. One-time fee: $325. Tuition and fees vary according to program. *Financial support:* In 2017–18, 15 students received support, including 9 research assistantships with full and partial tuition reimbursements available (averaging $7,038 per year), 2 teaching assistantships with full and partial tuition reimbursements available (averaging $10,584 per year); Federal Work-Study and unspecified assistantships also available. Financial award applicants required to submit FAFSA. *Unit head:* Dr. David Bangsberg, Dean, 503-494-8257. *Application contact:* Kelly Doherty, Director of Graduate Admissions, 503-725-5391, Fax: 503-725-3416, E-mail: dohertyk@pdx.edu.
Website: http://ohsu-psu-sph.org/

Purdue University, Graduate School, College of Health and Human Sciences, Department of Nutrition Science, West Lafayette, IN 47907. Offers animal health (MS, PhD); biochemical and molecular nutrition (MS, PhD); growth and development (MS, PhD); human and clinical nutrition (MS, PhD); public health and education (MS, PhD). *Faculty:* 21 full-time (15 women), 1 part-time/adjunct (0 women). *Students:* 40 full-time (29 women), 9 part-time (7 women); includes 5 minority (3 Black or African American, non-Hispanic/Latino; 1 Asian, non-Hispanic/Latino; 1 Two or more races, non-Hispanic/Latino), 20 international. Average age 28. 66 applicants, 33% accepted, 13 enrolled. In 2017, 2 master's, 6 doctorates awarded. *Degree requirements:* For master's, thesis; for doctorate, thesis/dissertation. *Entrance requirements:* For master's and doctorate, GRE General Test (minimum scores in verbal and quantitative areas of 1000 or 300 on new scoring), minimum undergraduate GPA of 3.0 or equivalent. Additional exam requirements/recommendations for international students: Required—TOEFL (minimum score 600 paper-based; 77 iBT). *Application deadline:* For fall admission, 1/10 for domestic and international students. Applications are processed on a rolling basis. Application fee: $60 ($75 for international students). Electronic applications accepted. *Financial support:* Fellowships, research assistantships, and teaching assistantships available. Support available to part-time students. Financial award applicants required to submit FAFSA. *Faculty research:* Nutrient requirements, nutrient metabolism, nutrition and disease prevention. *Unit head:* Michele R. Forman, Head, 765-494-9921, E-mail: mforman@purdue.edu. *Application contact:* Jon A. Story, Graduate Contact for Admissions, 765-494-6843, E-mail: jastory@purdue.edu.
Website: http://www.cfs.purdue.edu/fn/

Purdue University, School of Veterinary Medicine and Graduate School, Graduate Programs in Veterinary Medicine, Department of Comparative Pathobiology, West Lafayette, IN 47907-2027. Offers comparative epidemiology and public health (MS); comparative epidemiology and public heath (PhD); comparative microbiology and immunology (MS, PhD); comparative pathobiology (MS, PhD); interdisciplinary studies (PhD), including microbial pathogenesis, molecular signaling and cancer biology, molecular virology; lab animal medicine (MS); veterinary anatomic pathology (MS); veterinary clinical pathology (MS). Terminal master's awarded for partial completion of doctoral program. *Degree requirements:* For master's, thesis (for some programs); for doctorate, thesis/dissertation. *Entrance requirements:* For master's and doctorate, GRE General Test. Additional exam requirements/recommendations for international students: Required—TOEFL (minimum score 575 paper-based), IELTS (minimum score 6.5), TWE (minimum score 4). Electronic applications accepted.

Queen's University at Kingston, School of Graduate Studies, Faculty of Health Sciences, Department of Community Health and Epidemiology, Kingston, ON K7L 3N6, Canada. Offers epidemiology (PhD); epidemiology and population health (M Sc); health services (M Sc); policy research and clinical epidemiology (M Sc); public health (MPH). *Program availability:* Part-time. *Degree requirements:* For master's, thesis. *Entrance requirements:* For master's, GRE General Test (strongly recommended). Additional exam requirements/recommendations for international students: Required—TOEFL (minimum score 600 paper-based). *Faculty research:* Cancer epidemiology, clinical trials, biostatistics health services research, health policy.

Rivier University, School of Graduate Studies, Division of Nursing and Health Professions, Nashua, NH 03060. Offers family nurse practitioner (MS); leadership in health systems management (MS); nursing education (MS); nursing practice (DNP); psychiatric/mental health nurse practitioner (MS); public health (MPH). *Accreditation:* ACEN. *Program availability:* Part-time, evening/weekend. *Entrance requirements:* For master's, GRE, MAT. Electronic applications accepted.

Rollins College, Hamilton Holt School, Master of Public Health Program, Winter Park, FL 32789-4499. Offers MPH. *Expenses: Tuition:* Full-time $15,000; part-time $2500 per credit hour.

Rutgers University–Camden, School of Public Health, Stratford, NJ 08084. Offers general public health (Certificate); health systems and policy (MPH); DO/MPH. *Program availability:* Part-time, evening/weekend. *Degree requirements:* For master's, thesis, internship. *Entrance requirements:* For master's, GRE General Test. Additional exam requirements/recommendations for international students: Required—TOEFL. Electronic applications accepted.

Rutgers University–Newark, School of Public Health, Newark, NJ 07107-1709. Offers clinical epidemiology (Certificate); dental public health (MPH); general public health (Certificate); public policy and oral health services administration (Certificate); quantitative methods (MPH); urban health (MPH); DMD/MPH; MD/MPH; MS/MPH. *Program availability:* Part-time, evening/weekend. *Degree requirements:* For master's, thesis, internship. *Entrance requirements:* For master's, GRE General Test. Additional exam requirements/recommendations for international students: Required—TOEFL. Electronic applications accepted.

Rutgers University–New Brunswick, School of Public Health, Program in Public Health, Piscataway, NJ 08854-8097. Offers MPH, Dr PH, PhD, MBA/MPH, MD/MPH. *Program availability:* Part-time, evening/weekend. *Degree requirements:* For master's, internship; for doctorate, thesis/dissertation. *Entrance requirements:* For master's, GMAT, GRE General Test; for doctorate, GRE General Test, MPH (for Dr PH). Additional exam requirements/recommendations for international students: Required—TOEFL. *Expenses:* Contact institution. *Faculty research:* Epidemiology, risk perception, statistical research design, health care utilization, health promotion.

Sacred Heart University, Graduate Programs, College of Health Professions, Department of Public Health, Fairfield, CT 06825. Offers MPH. *Program availability:* Part-time. *Entrance requirements:* For master's, bachelor's degree with minimum cumulative GPA of 3.0. *Expenses: Tuition:* Full-time $28,114; part-time $739 per credit. *Unit head:* Dr. Anna E. Greer, Director, 203-416-3936, E-mail: greera@sacredheart.edu. *Application contact:* Tara Chudy, Executive Director of Graduate Admissions, 203-365-4735, Fax: 203-365-4732, E-mail: chudyt@sacredheart.edu.
Website: http://www.sacredheart.edu/academics/collegeofhealthprofessions/academicprograms/publichealth/

St. Ambrose University, College of Health and Human Services, Program in Public Health, Davenport, IA 52803-2898. Offers MPH. *Program availability:* Online learning.

St. Catherine University, Graduate Programs, Program in Holistic Health Studies, St. Paul, MN 55105. Offers MA. *Program availability:* Part-time. *Students:* 1 (woman) full-time, 84 part-time (81 women); includes 15 minority (1 Black or African American, non-Hispanic/Latino; 4 American Indian or Alaska Native, non-Hispanic/Latino; 2 Asian, non-Hispanic/Latino; 5 Hispanic/Latino; 3 Two or more races, non-Hispanic/Latino). Average age 40. In 2017, 17 master's awarded. *Degree requirements:* For master's, thesis optional. *Entrance requirements:* For master's, 1 course in anatomy, physiology and psychology. Additional exam requirements/recommendations for international students: Required—TOEFL (minimum score 600 paper-based; 100 iBT). *Application deadline:* For fall admission, 7/1 priority date for domestic students. Application fee: $35. *Expenses:* Contact institution. *Financial support:* In 2017–18, 48 students received support. *Unit head:* Laurie Sathe, Director, 651-690-8118, Fax: 651-690-7849. *Application contact:* Anita Cline-Cole, Office of Admission, 651-690-6030, Fax: 651-690-6064.

St. John's University, College of Pharmacy and Health Sciences, Graduate Programs in Pharmaceutical Sciences and Division of Library and Information Science, Master of Public Health Program, Queens, NY 11439. Offers MPH. *Students:* 17 full-time (11 women), 4 part-time (2 women); includes 9 minority (5 Black or African American, non-Hispanic/Latino; 2 Asian, non-Hispanic/Latino; 2 Hispanic/Latino), 8 international. Average age 30. 38 applicants, 45% accepted, 1 enrolled. *Entrance requirements:* For master's, GRE General Test, letters of recommendation, transcripts, resume, personal statement. Additional exam requirements/recommendations for international students: Required—TOEFL (minimum score 100 iBT), IELTS (minimum score 7). *Application deadline:* For fall admission, 3/1 for domestic students; for spring admission, 11/1 for domestic students. Applications are processed on a rolling basis. Application fee: $70. Electronic applications accepted. *Expenses: Tuition:* Full-time $44,280; part-time $1230 per credit. *Required fees:* $340; $340 per credit. Tuition and fees vary according to course load, degree level and program. *Financial support:* Fellowships, teaching assistantships, career-related internships or fieldwork, scholarships/grants, and unspecified assistantships available. Support available to part-time students. Financial award application deadline: 2/1; financial award applicants required to submit FAFSA. *Unit head:* Dr. Wenchen Wu, Chair, 718-990-5690, E-mail: wuw@stjohns.edu. *Application contact:* Robert Medrano, Director of Graduate Admissions, 718-990-1601, Fax: 718-990-5686, E-mail: gradhelp@stjohns.edu.
Website: http://www.stjohns.edu/academics/schools-and-colleges/college-pharmacy-and-health-sciences/programs-and-majors/public-health-master-public-health

Saint Louis University, Graduate Programs, College for Public Health and Social Justice and Graduate Programs, Department of Health Management and Policy, St. Louis, MO 63103. Offers health administration (MHA); health policy (MPH); public health studies (PhD). *Accreditation:* CAHME. *Program availability:* Part-time. *Degree requirements:* For master's, comprehensive exam, internship. *Entrance requirements:* For master's, GMAT or GRE General Test, LSAT, MCAT, letters of recommendation, resume. Additional exam requirements/recommendations for international students: Required—TOEFL (minimum score 525 paper-based). *Faculty research:* Management of HIV/AIDS, rural health services, prevention of asthma, genetics and health services use, health insurance and access to care.

Salus University, College of Health Sciences, Elkins Park, PA 19027-1598. Offers physician assistant (MMS); public health (MPH). *Accreditation:* ARC-PA. *Entrance requirements:* For master's, GRE (recommended). Additional exam requirements/recommendations for international students: Required—TOEFL. Electronic applications accepted.

Samford University, School of Public Health, Birmingham, AL 35229. Offers health informatics (MSHI); healthcare administration (MHA); nutrition (MS); public health (MPH); social work (MSW). *Program availability:* Part-time, 100% online. *Faculty:* 17 full-time (12 women), 4 part-time/adjunct (2 women). *Students:* 93 full-time (87 women), 5 part-time (all women); includes 20 minority (14 Black or African American, non-Hispanic/Latino; 2 Asian, non-Hispanic/Latino; 2 Hispanic/Latino; 2 Two or more races, non-Hispanic/Latino), 1 international. Average age 27. 90 applicants, 44% accepted, 32 enrolled. In 2017, 34 master's awarded. *Degree requirements:* For master's, capstone course. *Entrance requirements:* For master's, GRE, MAT, recommendations, resume, personal statement. Additional exam requirements/recommendations for international students: Required—TOEFL (minimum score 550 paper-based); Recommended—IELTS. *Application deadline:* For fall admission, 10/1 for domestic students; for spring admission, 5/1 for domestic students. Application fee: $75. Electronic applications accepted. *Expenses:* $813 per credit hour. *Financial support:* In 2017–18, 32 students received support. Scholarships/grants available. Financial award application deadline: 2/15; financial award applicants required to submit FAFSA. *Faculty research:* Chronic kidney disease, disasters and vulnerable populations, children's health, obesity, metabolism and diabetes, health policy and health care delivery. *Unit head:* Dr. Keith Elder, Dean, School of Public Health, 205-726-4655, E-mail: kelder@samford.edu. *Application contact:* Dr. Marian Carter, Assistant Dean of Enrollment Management and Student Services, 205-726-2611, E-mail: mwcarter@samford.edu.
Website: http://www.samford.edu/publichealth/

San Diego State University, Graduate and Research Affairs, College of Health and Human Services, Graduate School of Public Health, San Diego, CA 92182. Offers environmental health (MPH); epidemiology (MPH, PhD), including biostatistics (MPH); global emergency preparedness and response (MS); global health (PhD); health behavior (PhD); health promotion (MPH); health services administration (MPH); toxicology (MS); MPH/MA; MSW/MPH. *Accreditation:* CAHME (one or more programs are accredited). *Program availability:* Part-time. *Degree requirements:* For master's, comprehensive exam (for some programs), thesis (for some programs); for doctorate, thesis/dissertation. *Entrance requirements:* For master's, GMAT (MPH in health services administration), GRE General Test; for doctorate, GRE General Test. Additional exam requirements/recommendations for international students: Required—TOEFL. *Faculty research:* Evaluation of tobacco, AIDS prevalence and prevention, mammography, infant death project, Alzheimer's in elderly Chinese.

San Francisco State University, Division of Graduate Studies, College of Health and Social Sciences, Department of Health Education, San Francisco, CA 94132-1722. Offers community health education (MPH). *Accreditation:* CEPH. *Program availability:* Part-time. *Students:* Average age 36. *Application deadline:* Applications are processed on a rolling basis. *Unit head:* Dr. Mary Beth Love, Chair, 415-338-1413, Fax: 415-338-0570, E-mail: love@sfsu.edu. *Application contact:* Vincent Lam, Graduate Coordinator, 415-338-1413, Fax: 415-338-0570, E-mail: vlam@sfsu.edu.
Website: http://healthed.sfsu.edu/graduate

San Jose State University, Graduate Studies and Research, College of Health and Human Sciences, San Jose, CA 95192-0049. Offers criminology (MS), including global criminology, law and justice; justice studies (MS); kinesiology (MA), including athletic training, exercise physiology, interdisciplinary, sport studies, sports management; library and information science (MLIS); mass communications (MS); nursing (MS), including family nurse practitioner; nutritional science (MS); occupational therapy (MS); public health (MPH); social work (MSW); MD/M Div. *Program availability:* Part-time, 100% online, blended/hybrid learning. *Faculty:* 15 full-time (7 women), 6 part-time/adjunct (3 women). *Students:* 517 full-time (407 women), 405 part-time (302 women); includes 523 minority (39 Black or African American, non-Hispanic/Latino; 2 American Indian or Alaska Native, non-Hispanic/Latino; 141 Asian, non-Hispanic/Latino; 226 Hispanic/Latino; 2 Native Hawaiian or other Pacific Islander, non-Hispanic/Latino; 113 Two or more races, non-Hispanic/Latino), 14 international. Average age 32. 1,250 applicants, 45% accepted, 375 enrolled. In 2017, 808 master's awarded. *Degree requirements:* For master's, thesis (for some programs), graduate writing assessment. *Entrance requirements:* Additional exam requirements/recommendations for international students: Required—TOEFL (minimum score 550 paper-based; 80 iBT), IELTS (minimum score 6.5), PTE (minimum score 53). *Application deadline:* For fall admission, 2/1 for domestic and international students. Applications are processed on a rolling basis. Application fee: $55. Electronic applications accepted. *Expenses:* Tuition, state resident: full-time $7176. Tuition, nonresident: full-time $16,680. Tuition and fees vary according to course load and program. *Financial support:* Fellowships, research assistantships, teaching assistantships, career-related internships or fieldwork, Federal Work-Study, scholarships/grants, and tuition waivers (full and partial) available. Support available to part-time students. Financial award application deadline: 4/24; financial award applicants required to submit FAFSA. *Unit head:* Dr. Mary Schutten, Dean, College of Health and Human Sciences, 408-924-2900, Fax: 408-924-2901, E-mail: mary.schutten@sjsu.edu.
Website: http://www.sjsu.edu/casa/

San Juan Bautista School of Medicine, Graduate and Professional Programs, Caguas, PR 00726-4968. Offers MPH, MD. *Accreditation:* LCME/AMA. *Degree requirements:* For doctorate, comprehensive exam, United States Medical Licensing Exam Steps I and II. *Entrance requirements:* For master's, bachelor's degree from university or college accredited by the Council of Higher Education of Puerto Rico or by a renowned accrediting agency that is registered at the Federal Education Department; minimum GPA of 2.5; for doctorate, MCAT, interview. *Faculty research:* Protein structure, CI tissue inflammations, bacterial metabolism, human hormone.

Sarah Lawrence College, Graduate Studies, Program in Health Advocacy, Bronxville, NY 10708-5999. Offers MA. *Program availability:* Part-time. *Degree requirements:* For master's, thesis, fieldwork. *Entrance requirements:* For master's, previous course work in biology and microeconomics, minimum B average in undergraduate course work. Additional exam requirements/recommendations for international students: Required—TOEFL (minimum score 600 paper-based). Electronic applications accepted.

Shenandoah University, School of Health Professions, Winchester, VA 22601. Offers athletic training (MSAT); non-traditional physical therapy (MS); occupational training (MS); performing arts medicine (Certificate); physician assistant studies (MS); public health (MPH, Certificate); transitional physical therapy (DPT). *Program availability:* Part-time, all online except for two on-site weekend sessions (for DPT). *Faculty:* 35 full-time (27 women), 18 part-time/adjunct (13 women). *Students:* 446 full-time (355 women), 134 part-time (112 women); includes 78 minority (14 Black or African American, non-Hispanic/Latino; 28 Asian, non-Hispanic/Latino; 25 Hispanic/Latino; 11 Two or more races, non-Hispanic/Latino), 22 international. Average age 28. 839 applicants, 31% accepted, 166 enrolled. In 2017, 100 master's, 75 doctorates, 4 other advanced degrees awarded. *Degree requirements:* For master's and Certificate, thesis; for doctorate, comprehensive exam. *Entrance requirements:* For master's, GRE; for doctorate, GRE, minimum cumulative and prerequisite GPA of 2.8. Additional exam requirements/recommendations for international students: Required—TOEFL (minimum score 558 paper-based; 83 iBT). *Application deadline:* For fall admission, 10/1 for domestic and international students; for summer admission, 4/1 for domestic and international students. Application fee: $30. Electronic applications accepted. *Expenses:* Contact institution. *Financial support:* In 2017–18, 53 students received support. Scholarships/grants and unspecified assistantships available. Financial award applicants required to submit FAFSA. *Faculty research:* 3D motion analysis of running mechanics; quality improvement in clinical practice; functional movement screen to predict injury in professional athletes and dancers; sensory integration for children with autism; chronic ankle instability. *Total annual research expenditures:* $15,000. *Unit head:* Dr. Karen Elizabeth Abraham, Dean of School of Health Professions, 540-545.6209, Fax: 540-665.5530, E-mail: kabraham@su.edu. *Application contact:* Jon Brannon, Graduate Admissions Specialist, Office of Admissions, 540-545-7394, Fax: 540-665-4627, E-mail: jbannan09@su.edu.
Website: http://www.health.su.edu

Simmons College, College of Arts and Sciences, Boston, MA 02115. Offers English (MA); gender/cultural studies (MA); history (MA); public health (MPH); public policy (MPP). *Program availability:* Part-time. *Faculty:* 19 full-time (13 women), 2 part-time/adjunct (both women). *Students:* 4 full-time (3 women), 39 part-time (34 women); includes 11 minority (7 Black or African American, non-Hispanic/Latino; 1 Hispanic/Latino; 3 Two or more races, non-Hispanic/Latino). Average age 26. 99 applicants, 57% accepted, 27 enrolled. In 2017, 23 master's awarded. Terminal master's awarded for partial completion of doctoral program. *Degree requirements:* For master's, thesis optional. *Entrance requirements:* For master's, GRE, bachelor's degree from accredited college or university; minimum B average (preferred). Additional exam requirements/recommendations for international students: Required—TOEFL (minimum score 600 paper-based; 100 iBT). *Application deadline:* For fall admission, 8/1 for domestic and international students; for spring admission, 12/15 for domestic and international students; for summer admission, 5/1 for domestic and international students. Applications are processed on a rolling basis. Application fee: $35. Electronic applications accepted. *Expenses:* $1,052 per credit, $55 activity fee per semester. *Financial support:* In 2017–18, 4 fellowships with partial tuition reimbursements, 22 teaching assistantships with partial tuition reimbursements were awarded; scholarships/grants and unspecified assistantships also available. Support available to part-time students. Financial award applicants required to submit FAFSA. *Faculty research:* Film and media studies, postcolonial literature, critical theory, arts and culture. *Unit head:* Dr. Leanne Doherty, Dean, 617-521-2581, E-mail: leanne.doherty@simmons.edu. *Application contact:* Patricia Flaherty, Director, Graduate Studies Admission, 617-521-3902, Fax: 617-521-3058, E-mail: gsa@simmons.edu.
Website: http://www.simmons.edu/gradstudies/

Simon Fraser University, Office of Graduate Studies and Postdoctoral Fellows, Faculty of Health Sciences, Burnaby, BC V5A 1S6, Canada. Offers global health (Graduate Diploma); health sciences (M Sc, PhD); public health (MPH). *Accreditation:* CEPH. *Degree requirements:* For master's, thesis (for some programs); for doctorate, comprehensive exam, thesis/dissertation. *Entrance requirements:* For master's, minimum GPA of 3.0 (on scale of 4.33) or 3.33 based on last 60 credits of undergraduate courses; for doctorate, minimum GPA of 3.5 (on scale of 4.33); for Graduate Diploma, minimum GPA of 2.5 (on scale of 4.33) or 2.67 based on last 60 credits of undergraduate courses. Additional exam requirements/recommendations for international students: Recommended—TOEFL (minimum score 580 paper-based; 93 iBT), IELTS (minimum score 7), TWE (minimum score 5). Electronic applications accepted.

Slippery Rock University of Pennsylvania, Graduate Studies (Recruitment), College of Health, Environment, and Science, Department of Public Health and Social Work, Slippery Rock, PA 16057-1383. Offers public health (MPH). *Program availability:* Part-time, blended/hybrid learning. *Degree requirements:* For master's, thesis. *Entrance requirements:* For master's, personal statement, letter of recommendation, official transcripts, minimum GPA of 3.0, statistics course, natural or social science course. Additional exam requirements/recommendations for international students: Required—TOEFL (minimum score 550 paper-based; 80 iBT). Electronic applications accepted. *Expenses:* Contact institution.

Southern Connecticut State University, School of Graduate Studies, School of Health and Human Services, Department of Public Health, New Haven, CT 06515-1355. Offers MPH. *Accreditation:* CEPH. *Program availability:* Part-time, evening/weekend. *Degree requirements:* For master's, thesis or alternative. *Entrance requirements:* For master's, minimum undergraduate QPA of 3.0 in graduate major field or 2.5 overall, interview. Electronic applications accepted.

State University of New York Downstate Medical Center, College of Medicine, Program in Public Health, Brooklyn, NY 11203-2098. Offers urban and immigrant health (MPH); MD/MPH. *Program availability:* Part-time. *Degree requirements:* For master's, practicum. *Entrance requirements:* For master's, GRE, MCAT or OAT, 2 letters of recommendation, minimum undergraduate GPA of 3.0. Additional exam requirements/recommendations for international students: Required—TOEFL (minimum score 550 paper-based).

Stony Brook University, State University of New York, Stony Brook Medicine, School of Medicine, Program in Public Health, Stony Brook, NY 11794. Offers community health (MPH); evaluation sciences (MPH); family violence (MPH); health communication (Certificate); health economics (MPH); health education and promotion (Certificate); population health (MPH); substance abuse (MPH). *Accreditation:* CEPH. *Program availability:* Part-time, evening/weekend. *Students:* 32 full-time (24 women), 11 part-time (10 women); includes 18 minority (4 Black or African American, non-Hispanic/Latino; 10 Asian, non-Hispanic/Latino; 4 Hispanic/Latino), 2 international. Average age 29. 128 applicants, 71% accepted, 29 enrolled. In 2017, 25 master's, 1 other advanced degree awarded. *Entrance requirements:* For master's, GRE, 3 references, bachelor's degree from accredited college or university with minimum GPA of 3.0, essays, interview. Additional exam requirements/recommendations for international students: Required—TOEFL (minimum score 90 iBT). *Application deadline:* For fall admission, 7/15 for domestic students, 3/15 for international students. Application fee: $100. Electronic applications accepted. *Expenses:* Contact institution. *Financial support:* Fellowships available. *Faculty research:* Abnormal psychology, academic achievement, broadcast media, communications, communications systems, public health. *Total annual research expenditures:* $422,408. *Unit head:* Dr. Lisa A. Benz Scott, Director, 631-444-8811, E-mail: lisa.benzscott@stonybrook.edu. *Application contact:* Joanie Maniaci, Assistant Director for Student Affairs, 631-444-2074, Fax: 631-444-6035, E-mail: joanmarie.maniaci@stonybrook.edu.
Website: http://publichealth.stonybrookmedicine.edu/

Tarleton State University, College of Graduate Studies, College of Health Sciences and Human Services, Department of Medical Laboratory Sciences and Public Health, Fort Worth, TX 76104. Offers medical laboratory sciences (MS). *Program availability:* Part-time, evening/weekend. *Faculty:* 5 full-time (4 women), 2 part-time/adjunct (both women). *Students:* 7 full-time (3 women), 5 part-time (all women); includes 6 minority (2 Black or African American, non-Hispanic/Latino; 1 American Indian or Alaska Native, non-Hispanic/Latino; 3 Asian, non-Hispanic/Latino), 2 international. Average age 30. 14 applicants, 79% accepted, 10 enrolled. In 2017, 1 master's awarded. *Degree requirements:* For master's, comprehensive exam, thesis optional. *Entrance requirements:* For master's, GRE, minimum GPA of 3.0. Additional exam requirements/recommendations for international students: Required—TOEFL (minimum score 550 paper-based; 80 iBT), IELTS (minimum score 6). *Application deadline:* For fall admission, 8/15 for domestic students; for spring admission, 1/7 for domestic students. Applications are processed on a rolling basis. Application fee: $45 ($145 for international students). Electronic applications accepted. *Expenses:* Contact institution. *Financial support:* Career-related internships or fieldwork, Federal Work-Study, and scholarships/grants available. Support available to part-time students. Financial award application deadline: 5/1; financial award applicants required to submit FAFSA. *Unit head:* Sally Lewis, Head, 817-926-1101, E-mail: slewis@tarleton.edu. *Application contact:* Information Contact, 254-968-9104, Fax: 254-968-9670, E-mail: gradoffice@tarleton.edu.
Website: http://www.tarleton.edu/degrees/masters/ms-medical-laboratory-science/

Temple University, College of Public Health, Department of Social and Behavioral Sciences, Philadelphia, PA 19122. Offers MPH, PhD. *Accreditation:* CEPH (one or more programs are accredited). *Program availability:* Part-time, evening/weekend. *Faculty:* 16 full-time (11 women). *Students:* 53 full-time (42 women), 88 part-time (67 women); includes 44 minority (29 Black or African American, non-Hispanic/Latino; 4 Asian, non-Hispanic/Latino; 9 Hispanic/Latino; 2 Two or more races, non-Hispanic/Latino), 13 international. 262 applicants, 56% accepted, 45 enrolled. In 2017, 23 master's, 4 doctorates awarded. Terminal master's awarded for partial completion of doctoral program. *Degree requirements:* For master's, thesis (for some programs), capstone project; for doctorate, comprehensive exam, thesis/dissertation. *Entrance requirements:* For master's, GRE General Test (for MS only); DAT, GMAT, MCAT, OAT, or PCAT (for MPH, Ed M), minimum undergraduate GPA of 3.0, letters of reference, statement of goals, writing sample, resume, interview (for MS only); for doctorate, GRE General Test, minimum undergraduate GPA of 3.0, 3 letters of reference, statement of goals, writing sample, resume. Additional exam requirements/recommendations for international students: Required—TOEFL (minimum score 550 paper-based; 79 iBT). *Application deadline:* For fall admission, 3/1 for domestic students, 2/1 for international students; for spring admission, 10/15 for domestic students, 8/1 for international students. Applications are processed on a rolling basis. Application fee: $60. Electronic applications accepted. *Expenses:* Contact institution. *Financial support:* Fellowships with tuition reimbursements, research assistantships with tuition reimbursements, teaching assistantships with tuition reimbursements, career-related internships or fieldwork, Federal Work-Study, scholarships/grants, tuition waivers (partial), and unspecified assistantships available. Financial award application deadline: 1/15. *Faculty research:* Smoking cessation, obesity prevention, tobacco policy, community engagement, health communication. *Unit head:* Dr. Stephen Lepore, Department Chair/Professor, 215-204-8726, Fax: 215-204-1854, E-mail: slepore@temple.edu. *Application contact:* Theresa White, Senior Graduate Advisor/Admissions, 215-204-5105, E-mail: theresawhite@temple.edu.
Website: https://cph.temple.edu/socialbehavioral/home

Tennessee State University, The School of Graduate Studies and Research, College of Health Sciences, Department of Public Health, Health Administration and Health Sciences, Nashville, TN 37209-1561. Offers public health (MPH). *Accreditation:* CEPH. *Degree requirements:* For master's, capstone project.

Texas A&M University, College of Dentistry, Dallas, TX 75266-0677. Offers advanced education in general dentistry (Certificate); biomedical sciences (MS); dental hygiene (MS); dental public health (Certificate); endodontics (Certificate); maxillofacial surgery (Certificate); oral and maxillofacial pathology (Certificate); oral and maxillofacial radiology (Certificate); oral and maxillofacial surgery (Certificate); oral biology (MS, PhD); orthodontics (Certificate); pediatric dentistry (Certificate); periodontics (Certificate); prosthodontics (Certificate). *Accreditation:* ADA; SACS/CC. *Faculty:* 44. *Enrollment:* 499 full-time matriculated graduate/professional students (251 women), 37 part-time matriculated graduate/professional students (12 women). *Students:* 499 full-time (251 women), 37 part-time (12 women); includes 275 minority (54 Black or African American, non-Hispanic/Latino; 2 American Indian or Alaska Native, non-Hispanic/Latino; 100 Asian, non-Hispanic/Latino; 109 Hispanic/Latino; 10 Two or more races, non-Hispanic/Latino), 30 international. Average age 27. In 2017, 18 master's, 2 doctorates, 101 other advanced degrees awarded. *Entrance requirements:* Additional exam requirements/recommendations for international students: Required—TOEFL (minimum score 550 paper-based; 79 iBT). Application fee: $35. Electronic applications accepted. *Expenses:* Contact institution. *Financial support:* In 2017–18, 235 students received support, including 32 research assistantships with tuition reimbursements available (averaging $8,712 per year), 43 teaching assistantships with tuition reimbursements available (averaging $14,231 per year); career-related internships or fieldwork, institutionally sponsored loans, scholarships/grants, traineeships, health care benefits, tuition waivers (full and partial), and unspecified assistantships also available. Support available to part-time students. Financial award applicants required to submit FAFSA. *Unit head:* Dr. Lawrence E. Wolinsky, Dean, 214-828-8300, E-mail: wolinsky@tamhsc.edu. *Application contact:* Ernestine S. Lacy, Associate Dean for Student Affairs and Student Diversity, 214-828-8374, Fax: 214-874-4572, E-mail: eslacy@tamhsc.edu.
Website: http://www.dentistry.tamhsc.edu/

Texas A&M University, School of Public Health, College Station, TX 77845. Offers biostatistics (MPH, MSPH); environmental health (MPH, MSPH); epidemiology (MPH, MSPH); executive health administration (MHA); health administration (MHA); health policy and management (MPH, MSPH); health promotion and community health sciences (MPH); health services research (PhD); occupational safety and health (MPH). *Program availability:* Part-time, blended/hybrid learning. *Faculty:* 56. *Students:* 279 full-time (196 women), 86 part-time (56 women); includes 153 minority (48 Black or African American, non-Hispanic/Latino; 36 Asian, non-Hispanic/Latino; 62 Hispanic/Latino; 7 Two or more races, non-Hispanic/Latino), 77 international. Average age 29. 179 applicants, 96% accepted, 148 enrolled. In 2017, 124 master's, 8 doctorates awarded. *Entrance requirements:* For master's, GRE General Test, 3 letters of recommendation; statement of purpose; current curriculum vitae or resume; official transcripts; for doctorate, GRE General Test, 3 letters of recommendation; statement of purpose; current curriculum vitae or resume; official transcripts; interview (in some cases). Additional exam requirements/recommendations for international students: Required—TOEFL (minimum score 597 paper-based, 95 iBT) or GRE (minimum verbal score 153). Application fee: $120. Electronic applications accepted. *Expenses:* Contact institution. *Financial support:* In 2017–18, 203 students received support, including 62 research assistantships with tuition reimbursements available (averaging $10,041 per year), 25 teaching assistantships with tuition reimbursements available (averaging $12,913 per year); career-related internships or fieldwork, institutionally sponsored loans, scholarships/grants, traineeships, health care benefits, tuition waivers (full and partial), and unspecified assistantships also available. Support available to part-time students. Financial award applicants required to submit FAFSA. *Unit head:* Dr. Jay Maddock, Dean, 979-436-9322, Fax: 979-458-1878, E-mail: maddock@tamhsc.edu. *Application contact:* Erin E. Schneider, Associate Director of Admissions and Recruitment, 979-436-9380, E-mail: eschneider@sph.tamhsc.edu.
Website: http://sph.tamhsc.edu/

Thomas Edison State University, John S. Watson School of Public Service and Continuing Studies, Trenton, NJ 08608. Offers community and economic development (MSM); environmental policy/environmental justice (MSM); homeland security (MSHS, MSM); information and technology for public service (MSM); nonprofit management (MSM); public and municipal finance (MSM); public health (MSM); public service administration and leadership (MSM); public service leadership (MPSL). *Program availability:* Part-time, online learning. *Entrance requirements:* Additional exam requirements/recommendations for international students: Required—TOEFL (minimum score 550 paper-based; 79 iBT). Electronic applications accepted.

Thomas Jefferson University, Jefferson College of Population Health, Program in Public Health, Philadelphia, PA 19107. Offers MPH, Certificate. *Accreditation:* CEPH. *Program availability:* Part-time, evening/weekend, online learning. Terminal master's awarded for partial completion of doctoral program. *Degree requirements:* For master's, capstone project or thesis. *Entrance requirements:* For master's, GRE or other graduate examination, 2 letters of recommendation, interview, curriculum vitae. Additional exam requirements/recommendations for international students: Required—TOEFL (minimum score 100 iBT). Electronic applications accepted.

Touro University California, Graduate Programs, Vallejo, CA 94592. Offers education (MA); medical health sciences (MS); osteopathic medicine (DO); pharmacy (Pharm D); public health (MPH). *Accreditation:* AOsA; ARC-PA. *Program availability:* Part-time, evening/weekend. *Degree requirements:* For master's, comprehensive exam, thesis; for doctorate, comprehensive exam. *Entrance requirements:* For doctorate, BS/BA. Electronic applications accepted. *Faculty research:* Cancer, heart disease.

Trident University International, College of Health Sciences, Cypress, CA 90630. Offers MS, PhD, Certificate. *Program availability:* Part-time, evening/weekend, online learning. *Degree requirements:* For doctorate, comprehensive exam, thesis/dissertation. *Entrance requirements:* For master's, minimum GPA of 2.5 (students with GPA 3.0 or greater may transfer up to 30% of graduate level credits); for doctorate, minimum GPA of 3.4. Additional exam requirements/recommendations for international students: Required—TOEFL. Electronic applications accepted.

Trinity Washington University, School of Business and Graduate Studies, Washington, DC 20017-1094. Offers business administration (MBA); communication (MA); international security studies (MA); organizational management (MSA), including federal program management, human resource management, nonprofit management, organizational development, public and community health. *Program availability:* Part-time, evening/weekend. *Degree requirements:* For master's, thesis (for some programs), capstone project (MSA). *Entrance requirements:* For master's, minimum GPA of 2.5. Additional exam requirements/recommendations for international students: Required—TOEFL (minimum score 550 paper-based).

Tufts University, School of Medicine, Public Health and Professional Degree Programs, Boston, MA 02111. Offers biomedical sciences (MS); health communication (MS, Certificate); pain research, education and policy (MS, Certificate); physician assistant (MS); public health (MPH, Dr PH), including behavioral science (MPH), biostatistics (MPH), epidemiology (MPH), health communication (MPH), health services (MPH), management and policy (MPH), nutrition (MPH); DMD/MPH; DVM/MPH; JD/MPH; MD/MPH; MMS/MPH; MS/MBA; MS/MPH. *Accreditation:* CEPH (one or more programs are accredited). *Program availability:* Part-time, evening/weekend. *Faculty:* 62 full-time (25 women), 50 part-time/adjunct (25 women). *Students:* 449 full-time (280 women), 60 part-time (46 women); includes 188 minority (23 Black or African American, non-Hispanic/Latino; 112 Asian, non-Hispanic/Latino; 35 Hispanic/Latino; 18 Two or more races, non-Hispanic/Latino), 23 international. Average age 27. 1,750 applicants, 46% accepted, 252 enrolled. In 2017, 283 master's awarded. Terminal master's awarded for partial completion of doctoral program. *Degree requirements:* For master's, thesis (for some programs); for doctorate, thesis/dissertation. *Entrance requirements:* For master's, GRE General Test, MCAT, or GMAT; for doctorate, GRE General Test or MCAT. Additional exam requirements/recommendations for international students: Required—TOEFL (minimum score 100 iBT); Recommended—IELTS (minimum score 7). *Application deadline:* For fall admission, 1/15 priority date for domestic and international students; for spring admission, 10/25 priority date for domestic and international students. Applications are processed on a rolling basis. Application fee: $70. Electronic applications accepted. *Expenses:* Contact institution. *Financial support:* In 2017–18, 13 students received support, including 1 fellowship (averaging $3,000 per year), 50 research assistantships (averaging $1,000 per year), 65 teaching assistantships (averaging $2,000 per year); Federal Work-Study and scholarships/grants also available. Financial award application deadline: 2/23; financial award applicants required to submit FAFSA. *Faculty research:* Environmental and occupational health, nutrition, epidemiology, health communication, biostatics, obesity/chronic disease, health policy and health care delivery, global health, health inequality and social determinants of health. *Unit head:* Dr. Aviva Must, Dean, 617-636-0935, Fax: 617-636-0898, E-mail: aviva.must@tufts.edu. *Application contact:* Emily Keily, Director of Admissions, 617-636-0935, Fax: 617-636-0898, E-mail: med-phpd@tufts.edu.
Website: http://publichealth.tufts.edu

Tulane University, School of Public Health and Tropical Medicine, New Orleans, LA 70112. Offers MHA, MPH, MPHTM, MS, MSPH, Dr PH, PhD, JD/MHA, JD/MPH, MBA/MHA, MD/MPH, MD/MPHTM, MD/MSPH, MSW/MPH. *Accreditation:* CAHME (one or more programs are accredited). *Program availability:* Part-time, evening/weekend, 100% online, synchronous sessions. *Faculty:* 117 full-time (61 women), 25 part-time/adjunct (16 women). *Students:* 487 full-time (352 women), 134 part-time (97 women); includes 183 minority (73 Black or African American, non-Hispanic/Latino; 2 American Indian or Alaska Native, non-Hispanic/Latino; 48 Asian, non-Hispanic/Latino; 42 Hispanic/Latino; 18 Two or more races, non-Hispanic/Latino), 127 international. Average age 24. 1,341 applicants, 74% accepted, 240 enrolled. *Degree requirements:* For master's, comprehensive exam (for some programs); for doctorate, comprehensive exam, thesis/dissertation. *Entrance requirements:* For master's and doctorate, GRE General Test, career statement; letters of recommendation. Additional exam requirements/recommendations for international students: Required—TOEFL, IELTS. *Application deadline:* For fall admission, 7/15 priority date for domestic students, 6/15 priority date for international students; for winter admission, 11/15 priority date for domestic students, 10/15 priority date for international students; for spring admission, 11/15 for domestic students, 10/15 for international students; for summer admission, 5/15 for domestic students, 4/15 for international students. Applications are processed on a rolling basis. Application fee: $135. Electronic applications accepted. *Expenses:* $1,260 per credit tuition; $100 per credit academic support fee; $120 per year student activity fee; $100 per semester technology fee. *Financial support:* In 2017–18, 188 students received support, including 10 fellowships with full and partial tuition reimbursements available (averaging $25,000 per year), 149 research assistantships

(averaging $1,870 per year), 39 teaching assistantships (averaging $1,612 per year); Federal Work-Study, scholarships/grants, traineeships, and unspecified assistantships also available. Financial award application deadline: 4/15; financial award applicants required to submit FAFSA. *Faculty research:* Global health; cardiovascular epidemiology; emerging infectious tropical diseases; maternal and child health; health outcomes. *Total annual research expenditures:* $50 million. *Unit head:* Pierre Buekens, Dean, 504-988-5388, Fax: 504-988-5718, E-mail: sphtmdo@tulane.edu. *Application contact:* Ian Shirt, Admissions Counselor, 504-988-0908, E-mail: sphtmadmissions@tulane.edu.
Website: http://www.sph.tulane.edu/

Uniformed Services University of the Health Sciences, F. Edward Hebert School of Medicine, Graduate Programs in the Biomedical Sciences and Public Health, Bethesda, MD 20814. Offers emerging infectious diseases (PhD); medical and clinical psychology (PhD), including clinical psychology, medical psychology; medicine (MS, PhD), including health professions education; molecular and cell biology (MS, PhD); neuroscience (PhD); preventive medicine and biometrics (MPH, MS, MSPH, MTMH, PhD), including environmental health sciences (PhD), healthcare administration and policy (MS), medical zoology (PhD), public health (MPH, MSPH), tropical medicine and hygiene (MTMH). *Students:* Average age 25. 598 applicants, 17% accepted, 77 enrolled. In 2017, 19 master's, 50 doctorates awarded. Terminal master's awarded for partial completion of doctoral program. *Degree requirements:* For master's, comprehensive exam, thesis or alternative; for doctorate, comprehensive exam, thesis/dissertation, qualifying exam. *Entrance requirements:* For master's, GRE General Test; for doctorate, GRE General Test, minimum GPA of 3.0. *Application deadline:* For fall admission, 12/1 priority date for domestic students. Application fee: $0. Electronic applications accepted. *Expenses:* There are no tuition charges or fees for graduate students at USU. *Financial support:* In 2017–18, 50 fellowships (averaging $43,000 per year) were awarded; research assistantships, career-related internships or fieldwork, scholarships/grants, and health care benefits also available. *Unit head:* Dr. Gregory Mueller, Associate Dean, 301-295-3507, E-mail: gregory.mueller@usuhs.edu. *Application contact:* Tina Finley, Administrative Officer, 301-295-3642, Fax: 301-295-6772, E-mail: netina.finley@usuhs.edu.
Website: http://www.usuhs.mil/graded

Uniformed Services University of the Health Sciences, F. Edward Hebert School of Medicine, Graduate Programs in the Biomedical Sciences and Public Health, Department of Preventive Medicine and Biometrics, Program in Public Health, Bethesda, MD 20814-4799. Offers MPH, MSPH. *Accreditation:* CEPH (one or more programs are accredited). *Degree requirements:* For master's, comprehensive exam. *Entrance requirements:* For master's, GRE General Test. Additional exam requirements/recommendations for international students: Required—TOEFL. *Faculty research:* Epidemiology, biostatistics, health services administration, environmental and occupational health, tropical public health.

Université de Montréal, Faculty of Arts and Sciences, Program in Societies, Public Policies and Health, Montréal, QC H3C 3J7, Canada. Offers DESS.

Université de Montréal, Faculty of Medicine, Program in Communal and Public Health, Montréal, QC H3C 3J7, Canada. Offers community health (M Sc, DESS); public health (PhD). *Accreditation:* CEPH. *Program availability:* Part-time. Terminal master's awarded for partial completion of doctoral program. *Degree requirements:* For master's, thesis; for doctorate, thesis/dissertation, general exam. *Entrance requirements:* For master's and doctorate, proficiency in French, knowledge of English; for DESS, proficiency in French. Electronic applications accepted. *Faculty research:* Epidemiology, health services utilization, health promotion and education, health behaviors, poverty and child health.

University at Albany, State University of New York, School of Public Health, Program in Public Health, Rensselaer, NY 12144. Offers MPH, Dr PH. *Accreditation:* CEPH. *Program availability:* Part-time, evening/weekend, 100% online, blended/hybrid learning. *Students:* 377 applicants, 76% accepted, 145 enrolled. In 2017, 79 master's, 4 doctorates awarded. *Entrance requirements:* For master's and doctorate, GRE General Test. Additional exam requirements/recommendations for international students: Required—TOEFL (minimum score 550 paper-based). *Application deadline:* For fall admission, 4/1 for domestic students, 5/1 for international students; for spring admission, 10/31 for domestic students, 11/1 for international students. Applications are processed on a rolling basis. Application fee: $75. Electronic applications accepted. *Expenses:* Tuition, state resident: full-time $10,870; part-time $453 per credit hour. Tuition, nonresident: full-time $22,210; part-time $925 per credit hour. *Required fees:* $84.68 per credit hour. $508.06 per semester. Part-time tuition and fees vary according to course load and program. *Financial support:* Application deadline: 5/30. *Faculty research:* Methodological issues in public health research and prevention research, adverse health effects of environmental and occupational exposures to toxic agents, non-parametric and semi-parametric statistical methods for model selection in longitudinal studies with missing data. *Total annual research expenditures:* $244,442. *Unit head:* Dr. Gregory DiRienzo, Chair, 518-402-0394, Fax: 518-402-0380, E-mail: gdirienzo@albany.edu. *Application contact:* Michael DeRensis, Director, Graduate Admissions, 518-442-3980, Fax: 518-442-3922, E-mail: graduate@albany.edu.

University at Buffalo, the State University of New York, Graduate School, School of Public Health and Health Professions, Department of Epidemiology and Environmental Health, Buffalo, NY 14214. Offers epidemiology (MS, PhD); public health (MPH). *Accreditation:* CEPH. *Program availability:* Part-time. *Faculty:* 13 full-time (10 women), 5 part-time/adjunct (2 women). *Students:* 50 full-time (32 women), 21 part-time (15 women); includes 12 minority (2 Black or African American, non-Hispanic/Latino; 1 American Indian or Alaska Native, non-Hispanic/Latino; 9 Asian, non-Hispanic/Latino), 9 international. Average age 27. 124 applicants, 25% accepted, 23 enrolled. In 2017, 25 master's, 2 doctorates awarded. Terminal master's awarded for partial completion of doctoral program. *Entrance requirements:* For master's and doctorate, GRE General Test. Additional exam requirements/recommendations for international students: Required—TOEFL (minimum score 600 paper-based; 100 iBT). *Application deadline:* For fall admission, 1/15 priority date for domestic and international students. Applications are processed on a rolling basis. Application fee: $50. Electronic applications accepted. *Financial support:* In 2017–18, 17 students received support, including 4 fellowships with full tuition reimbursements available (averaging $22,000 per year), 5 research assistantships with full tuition reimbursements available (averaging $20,000 per year); teaching assistantships with full tuition reimbursements available, career-related internships or fieldwork, Federal Work-Study, institutionally sponsored loans, health care benefits, and unspecified assistantships also available. Financial award application deadline: 2/1; financial award applicants required to submit FAFSA. *Faculty research:* Epidemiology of cancer, nutrition, infectious diseases, epidemiology of environmental, women's health and cardiovascular disease research. *Total annual research expenditures:* $2.2 million. *Unit head:* Dr. Jo Freudenheim, Interim Chair, 716-829-5375, Fax: 716-829-2979, E-mail: phhpadv@buffalo.edu. *Application contact:* Dr. Carl Li, Director of Graduate Studies, 716-829-5382, Fax: 716-829-2979, E-mail: carlli@buffalo.edu.
Website: http://sphhp.buffalo.edu/epidemiology-and-environmental-health.html

The University of Akron, Graduate School, College of Health Professions, School of Nursing, Akron, OH 44325-3701. Offers nursing (MSN, PhD); nursing practice (DNP); public health (MPH). PhD offered jointly with Kent State University. *Accreditation:* AACN; AANA/CANAEP (one or more programs are accredited). *Program availability:* Part-time. *Faculty:* 14 full-time (all women), 15 part-time/adjunct (13 women). *Students:* 39 full-time (22 women), 246 part-time (179 women); includes 29 minority (12 Black or African American, non-Hispanic/Latino; 8 Asian, non-Hispanic/Latino; 6 Hispanic/Latino; 3 Two or more races, non-Hispanic/Latino), 6 international. Average age 31. 110 applicants, 75% accepted, 70 enrolled. In 2017, 90 master's, 6 doctorates awarded. *Degree requirements:* For doctorate, one foreign language, thesis/dissertation, qualifying exam. *Entrance requirements:* For master's, current Ohio state license as registered nurse, three letters of reference, 300-word essay, interview with program coordinator; for doctorate, GRE, minimum GPA of 3.0, MSN, nursing license or eligibility for licensure, writing sample, letters of recommendation, interview, resume, personal statement of research interests and career goals. Additional exam requirements/recommendations for international students: Required—TOEFL (minimum score 79 iBT), IELTS (minimum score 6.5). *Application deadline:* For fall admission, 7/15 for domestic and international students. Applications are processed on a rolling basis. Application fee: $45 ($70 for international students). Electronic applications accepted. *Financial support:* In 2017–18, 3 teaching assistantships with full tuition reimbursements were awarded. *Faculty research:* Health promotion and chronic disease prevention, mental health and psychosocial resilience, erotological health, trauma and violence, gut oxygenation during shock and trauma, simulation and the pedagogy of teaching and learning. *Total annual research expenditures:* $476,886. *Unit head:* Dr. Marlene Huff, Director, 330-972-5930, E-mail: mhuff@uakron.edu. *Application contact:* Dr. Linda Shanks, Assistant Director, Graduate Programs, 330-972-6699, E-mail: shanks@uakron.edu.
Website: http://www.uakron.edu/nursing/

The University of Alabama at Birmingham, School of Public Health, Program in Public Health, Birmingham, AL 35294. Offers applied epidemiology and pharmacoepidemiology (MSPH); biostatistics (MPH); clinical and translational science (MSPH); environmental health (MPH); environmental health and toxicology (MSPH); epidemiology (MPH); general theory and practice (MPH); health behavior (MPH); health care organization (MPH); health policy quantitative policy analysis (MPH); industrial hygiene (MPH, MSPH); maternal and child health policy (Dr PH); maternal and child health policy and leadership (MPH); occupational health and safety (MPH); outcomes research (MSPH, Dr PH); public health (PhD); public health management (Dr PH); public health preparedness management (MPH). *Program availability:* Part-time, online learning. *Degree requirements:* For doctorate, comprehensive exam, thesis/dissertation. *Entrance requirements:* For master's and doctorate, GRE. Additional exam requirements/recommendations for international students: Recommended—TOEFL (minimum score 550 paper-based; 79 iBT), IELTS (minimum score 6.5). Electronic applications accepted.

University of Alaska Anchorage, College of Health, Department of Health Sciences, Anchorage, AK 99508. Offers health administration (MPA); physicians assistant (MS); public health practice (MPH); MSW/MPH. *Accreditation:* CEPH. *Program availability:* Part-time. *Degree requirements:* For master's, comprehensive exam, thesis. *Entrance requirements:* For master's, writing sample. Additional exam requirements/recommendations for international students: Required—TOEFL (minimum score 550 paper-based). *Application deadline:* For fall admission, 3/1 for domestic and international students; for spring admission, 10/1 for domestic and international students. Application fee: $45. *Expenses:* Tuition, state resident: part-time $489 per credit hour. Tuition, nonresident: part-time $1028 per credit hour. *Unit head:* Dr. Rhonda Johnson, Chair, 907-786-6565, E-mail: rhonda.johnson@uaa.alaska.edu. *Application contact:* Elisa Mattison, Director, Graduate School, 907-786-1096, Fax: 907-786-1791, E-mail: esmattison@uaa.alaska.edu.
Website: http://www.uaa.alaska.edu/healthsciences/

University of Alberta, School of Public Health, Department of Public Health Sciences, Edmonton, AB T6G 2E1, Canada. Offers clinical epidemiology (M Sc, MPH); environmental and occupational health (MPH); environmental health sciences (M Sc); epidemiology (M Sc); global health (M Sc, MPH); health policy and management (MPH); health policy research (M Sc); health technology assessment (MPH); occupational health (M Sc); population health (M Sc); public health leadership (MPH); public health sciences (PhD); quantitative methods (MPH). Terminal master's awarded for partial completion of doctoral program. *Degree requirements:* For master's, thesis (for some programs); for doctorate, thesis/dissertation. *Entrance requirements:* For master's, GMAT or GRE General Test. Additional exam requirements/recommendations for international students: Required—TOEFL (minimum score 550 paper-based) or IELTS (minimum score 6). Electronic applications accepted. *Faculty research:* Biostatistics, health promotion and socio-behavioral health science.

The University of Arizona, Mel and Enid Zuckerman College of Public Health, Program in Public Health, Tucson, AZ 85721. Offers MPH, Dr PH, PhD. *Entrance requirements:* Additional exam requirements/recommendations for international students: Required—TOEFL (minimum score 550 paper-based; 79 iBT). Electronic applications accepted.

University of Arkansas for Medical Sciences, College of Public Health, Little Rock, AR 72205-7199. Offers biostatistics (MPH); environmental and occupational health (MPH, Certificate); epidemiology (MPH, PhD); health behavior and health education (MPH); health policy and management (MPH); health promotion and prevention research (PhD); health services administration (MHSA); health systems research (PhD); public health (Certificate); public health leadership (Dr PH). *Accreditation:* CEPH. *Program availability:* Part-time. *Degree requirements:* For master's, preceptorship, culminating experience, internship; for doctorate, comprehensive exam, capstone. *Entrance requirements:* For master's, GRE, GMAT, LSAT, PCAT, MCAT, DAT; for doctorate, GRE. Additional exam requirements/recommendations for international students: Required—TOEFL (minimum score 80 iBT), IELTS. Electronic applications accepted. *Expenses:* Contact institution. *Faculty research:* Health systems, tobacco prevention control, obesity prevention, environmental and occupational exposure, cancer prevention.

The University of British Columbia, Faculty of Medicine, School of Population and Public Health, Vancouver, BC V6T 1Z3, Canada. Offers health administration (MHA); health sciences (MH Sc); occupational and environmental hygiene (M Sc); population and public health (M Sc, MPH, PhD); MPH/MSN. *Program availability:* Online learning. *Degree requirements:* For master's, thesis (for some programs), major paper (MH Sc), research project (MHA); for doctorate, thesis/dissertation. *Entrance requirements:* For master's, GRE General Test or GMAT, PCAT, MCAT (for MHA), MD or equivalent (for MH Sc); 4-year undergraduate degree from accredited university with minimum B+ overall academic average and in math or statistics course at undergraduate level (for MPH); 4-year undergraduate degree from accredited university with minimum B+ overall academic average plus work experience (for MHA); for doctorate, master's degree from accredited university with minimum B+ overall academic average and in math or statistics course at undergraduate level. Additional exam requirements/recommendations for international students: Required—TOEFL. Electronic applications accepted. *Expenses:* Contact institution. *Faculty research:* Population and public health, clinical epidemiology, epidemiology and biostatistics, global health and vulnerable populations, health care services and systems, occupational and environmental health, public health emerging threats and rapid response, social and life course determinants of health, health administration.

University of California, Berkeley, Graduate Division, Haas School of Business and School of Public Health, Concurrent MBA/MPH Program, Berkeley, CA 94720-1500. Offers MBA/MPH. *Accreditation:* AACSB. *Students:* 45 full-time (23 women); includes 14 minority (1 Black or African American, non-Hispanic/Latino; 9 Asian, non-Hispanic/Latino; 2 Hispanic/Latino; 2 Two or more races, non-Hispanic/Latino). Average age 29. *Entrance requirements:* Additional exam requirements/recommendations for international students: Required—TOEFL (minimum score 570 paper-based; 90 iBT); Recommended—IELTS (minimum score 7). *Application deadline:* For fall admission, 10/1 for domestic and international students; for winter admission, 1/7 for domestic and international students; for spring admission, 3/31 for domestic students, 3/11 for international students. Application fee: $200. Electronic applications accepted. *Expenses:* Contact institution. *Financial support:* Fellowships, research assistantships with partial tuition reimbursements, teaching assistantships with partial tuition reimbursements, career-related internships or fieldwork, institutionally sponsored loans, scholarships/grants, and non-resident tuition waivers for some students, such as veterans available. *Faculty research:* Accounting, business and public policy, economic analysis and public policy, entrepreneurship, finance, management of organizations, marketing, operations and information technology management, real estate. *Unit head:* Prof. Kim MacPherson, Associate Director, Health Services Management Program, 510-642-9175, Fax: 510-643-6659, E-mail: kmacpherson@haas.berkeley.edu. *Application contact:* Morgan Bernstein, Executive Director of Admissions, 510-642-1405, Fax: 510-643-6659, E-mail: mbaadm@haas.berkeley.edu.
Website: http://www.haas.berkeley.edu/

University of California, Berkeley, Graduate Division, School of Public Health, Programs in Public Health, Berkeley, CA 94720-1500. Offers MPH, Dr PH. *Program availability:* Blended/hybrid learning. *Degree requirements:* For doctorate, thesis/dissertation, exam. *Entrance requirements:* For doctorate, GRE General Test, minimum GPA of 3.0. Electronic applications accepted.

University of California, Irvine, Programs in Health Sciences, Program in Public Health, Irvine, CA 92697. Offers MPH, PhD. *Accreditation:* CEPH. *Students:* 65 full-time (49 women), 13 part-time (10 women); includes 45 minority (4 Black or African American, non-Hispanic/Latino; 24 Asian, non-Hispanic/Latino; 9 Hispanic/Latino; 8 Two or more races, non-Hispanic/Latino), 6 international. Average age 28. 247 applicants, 50% accepted, 31 enrolled. In 2017, 20 master's, 1 doctorate awarded. Application fee: $105 ($125 for international students). *Unit head:* Oladele A. Ogunseitan, Chair, 949-824-6350, Fax: 949-824-2056, E-mail: oladele.ogunseitan@uci.edu. *Application contact:* Stephanie Leonard, Director of Student Affairs, 949-824-0546, E-mail: stephapl@uci.edu.
Website: http://publichealth.uci.edu/

University of California, Irvine, School of Social Ecology, Programs in Social Ecology, Irvine, CA 92697. Offers environmental analysis and design (PhD); epidemiology and public health (PhD); social ecology (PhD). *Students:* 9 full-time (8 women), 1 (woman) part-time; includes 1 minority (Hispanic/Latino), 1 international. Average age 30. 14 applicants, 43% accepted, 3 enrolled. In 2017, 2 doctorates awarded. Application fee: $105 ($125 for international students). *Unit head:* Tim-Allen Bruckner, Professor, 949-824-5797, Fax: 949-824-1845, E-mail: tim.bruckner@uci.edu. *Application contact:* Jennifer Craig, Director of Graduate Student Services, 949-824-5918, Fax: 949-824-1845, E-mail: craigj@uci.edu.
Website: http://socialecology.uci.edu/core/graduate-se-core-programs

University of California, Los Angeles, Graduate Division, School of Public Health, Los Angeles, CA 90095. Offers MPH, MS, D Env, Dr PH, PhD, JD/MPH, MA/MPH, MBA/MPH, MD/MPH, MD/PhD, MSW/MPH. *Accreditation:* CEPH (one or more programs are accredited). *Degree requirements:* For doctorate, thesis/dissertation, oral and written qualifying exams. *Entrance requirements:* For master's, GRE General Test, minimum GPA of 3.0; for doctorate, GRE General Test, minimum undergraduate GPA of 3.0. Electronic applications accepted.

University of California, San Diego, Graduate Division, Program in Public Health, La Jolla, CA 92093. Offers epidemiology (PhD); global health (PhD); health behavior (PhD). Program offered jointly with San Diego State University. *Students:* 21 full-time (17 women), 15 part-time (11 women). In 2017, 14 doctorates awarded. *Degree requirements:* For doctorate, thesis/dissertation, 2 semesters/quarters of teaching assistantship. *Entrance requirements:* For doctorate, GRE General Test, minimum GPA of 3.0, curriculum vitae or resume, letters of recommendation, statement of purpose. Additional exam requirements/recommendations for international students: Required—TOEFL (minimum score 550 paper-based; 80 iBT), IELTS (minimum score 7). Electronic applications accepted. *Financial support:* Teaching assistantships available. Financial award applicants required to submit FAFSA. *Faculty research:* Maternal and pediatric HIV/AIDS; healthy aging and gender differences; non-parametric and semi-parametric regression, resampling, and the analysis of high-dimensional data; neighborhood correlates of physical activity in children, teens, adults and older adults; medication safety and medication therapy management through practice-based research networks. *Unit head:* David Strong, Faculty Director, 858-657-5241, E-mail: dstrong@ucsd.edu. *Application contact:* Hollie Ward, Graduate Coordinator, 858-822-2382, E-mail: hward@ucsd.edu.
Website: http://publichealth.ucsd.edu/jdp/

University of Cincinnati, Graduate School, College of Education, Criminal Justice, and Human Services, School of Human Services, Health Promotion and Education Program, Cincinnati, OH 45221. Offers exercise and fitness (MS); health education (PhD); public and community health (MS); public health (MPH). *Accreditation:* NCATE. *Program availability:* Part-time, evening/weekend. *Degree requirements:* For master's, thesis or alternative; for doctorate, thesis/dissertation. *Entrance requirements:* For master's and doctorate, GRE General Test. Additional exam requirements/recommendations for international students: Required—TOEFL (minimum score 580 paper-based). Electronic applications accepted. *Expenses: Tuition, area resident:* Full-time $14,468. Tuition, state resident: full-time $14,968; part-time $754 per credit hour. Tuition, nonresident: full-time $24,210; part-time $1311 per credit hour. *International tuition:* $26,460 full-time. *Required fees:* $3958; $84 per credit hour. One-time fee: $85 full-time. Tuition and fees vary according to course load, degree level and program.

University of Colorado Denver, Colorado School of Public Health, Program in Public Health, Aurora, CO 80045. Offers community and behavioral health (MPH, Dr PH). *Program availability:* Part-time, evening/weekend. In 2017, 200 master's, 0 doctorates awarded. *Degree requirements:* For master's, thesis or alternative, 42 credit hours; for doctorate, comprehensive exam, thesis/dissertation, 67 credit hours. *Entrance requirements:* For master's, GRE, MCAT, DAT, LSAT, PCAT, GMAT or master's degree from accredited institution, baccalaureate degree or equivalent; minimum GPA of 3.0; transcripts; references; resume; essay; for doctorate, GRE, MCAT, DAT, LSAT, PCAT or GMAT, MPH or master's or higher degree in related field or equivalent; 2 years of previous work experience in public health; essay; resume. Additional exam requirements/recommendations for international students: Required—TOEFL (minimum score 550 paper-based; 80 iBT). Application fee: $0. *Faculty research:* Cancer prevention by nutrition, cancer survivorship outcomes, social and cultural factors related to health. *Unit head:* Dr. Lori Crane, Chair, 303-724-4385, E-mail: lori.crane@ucdenver.edu. *Application contact:* Dr. Lori Crane, Chair, 303-724-4385, E-mail: lori.crane@ucdenver.edu.
Website: http://www.ucdenver.edu/academics/colleges/PublicHealth/Academics/degreesandprograms/Pages/index.aspx

University of Connecticut Health Center, Graduate School, Program in Public Health, Farmington, CT 06030. Offers MPH, DMD/MPH, MD/MPH. *Accreditation:* CEPH. *Program availability:* Part-time, evening/weekend. *Degree requirements:* For master's, thesis optional. *Entrance requirements:* For master's, GRE. Additional exam requirements/recommendations for international students: Required—TOEFL (minimum score 600 paper-based). Electronic applications accepted. *Faculty research:* Cancer epidemiology, birth defects, gerontology, health manpower, health services.

University of Florida, College of Medicine, Program in Clinical Investigation, Gainesville, FL 32611. Offers clinical investigation (MS); epidemiology (MS); public health (MPH). *Program availability:* Part-time. *Entrance requirements:* For master's, GRE, MD, PhD, DMD/DDS or Pharm D.

University of Florida, Graduate School, College of Public Health and Health Professions, Programs in Public Health, Gainesville, FL 32611. Offers biostatistics (MPH); clinical and translational science (PhD); environmental health (MPH); epidemiology (MPH); health management and policy (MPH); public health (MPH, PhD, Certificate); public health practice (MPH); rehabilitation science (PhD); social and behavioral sciences (MPH); DPT/MPH; DVM/MPH; JD/MPH; MD/MPH; Pharm D/MPH. *Accreditation:* CEPH. *Program availability:* Online learning. *Degree requirements:* For master's, internship. *Entrance requirements:* For master's, GRE General Test, minimum GPA of 3.0. Additional exam requirements/recommendations for international students: Required—TOEFL (minimum score 550 paper-based; 80 iBT), IELTS (minimum score 6).

University of Georgia, College of Public Health, Doctor of Public Health Program, Athens, GA 30602. Offers Dr PH.

University of Hawaii at Manoa, John A. Burns School of Medicine, Department of Public Health Sciences and Epidemiology, Honolulu, HI 96822. Offers epidemiology (PhD); global health and population studies (Graduate Certificate); public health (MPH, MS, Dr PH). *Accreditation:* CEPH. *Program availability:* Part-time. *Entrance requirements:* Additional exam requirements/recommendations for international students: Required—TOEFL (minimum score 550 paper-based; 79 iBT), IELTS (minimum score 5).

University of Illinois at Chicago, School of Public Health, Chicago, IL 60607-7128. Offers MHA, MPH, MS, Dr PH, PhD, DDS/MPH, MBA/MPH, MD/PhD, MPH/MS. *Program availability:* Part-time. Terminal master's awarded for partial completion of doctoral program. *Degree requirements:* For master's, thesis, field practicum; for doctorate, thesis/dissertation, independent research, internship. *Entrance requirements:* For master's and doctorate, GRE General Test, minimum GPA of 2.75. Additional exam requirements/recommendations for international students: Required—TOEFL. Electronic applications accepted. *Expenses:* Contact institution. *Faculty research:* Global health, community health, environmental and occupational health, epidemiology and biostatistics, health policy and administration.

University of Illinois at Springfield, Graduate Programs, College of Public Affairs and Administration, Program in Public Health, Springfield, IL 62703-5407. Offers community health education (Graduate Certificate); emergency preparedness and homeland security (Graduate Certificate); environmental health (MPH, Graduate Certificate); environmental risk assessment (Graduate Certificate); epidemiology (Graduate Certificate); public health (MPH). *Program availability:* Part-time, evening/weekend, 100% online. *Faculty:* 7 full-time (4 women). *Students:* 38 full-time (23 women), 46 part-time (34 women); includes 27 minority (16 Black or African American, non-Hispanic/Latino; 4 Asian, non-Hispanic/Latino; 5 Hispanic/Latino; 2 Two or more races, non-Hispanic/Latino), 22 international. Average age 32. 47 applicants, 51% accepted, 18 enrolled. In 2017, 28 master's, 17 other advanced degrees awarded. *Degree requirements:* For master's, comprehensive exam, internship. *Entrance requirements:* For master's, GRE, minimum undergraduate GPA of 3.0, 3 letters of recommendation, statement of personal goals. Additional exam requirements/recommendations for international students: Required—TOEFL (minimum score 500 paper-based; 61 iBT). *Application deadline:* Applications are processed on a rolling basis. Application fee: $60 ($75 for international students). Electronic applications accepted. *Expenses:* Tuition, state resident: full-time $7896; part-time $329 per credit hour. Tuition, nonresident: full-time $16,200; part-time $675 per credit hour. Tuition and fees vary according to program. *Financial support:* In 2017–18, research assistantships with full tuition reimbursements (averaging $10,249 per year), teaching assistantships with full tuition reimbursements (averaging $10,303 per year) were awarded; fellowships, career-related internships or fieldwork, Federal Work-Study, scholarships/grants, health care benefits, and unspecified assistantships also available. Support available to part-time students. Financial award application deadline: 11/15; financial award applicants required to submit FAFSA. *Unit head:* Dr. Josiah Alamu, Program Administrator, 217-206-7874, Fax: 217-206-7279, E-mail: jalam3@uis.edu.
Website: http://www.uis.edu/publichealth/

University of Illinois at Urbana–Champaign, Graduate College, College of Applied Health Sciences, Department of Kinesiology and Community Health, Champaign, IL 61820. Offers community health (MS, MSPH, PhD); kinesiology (MS, PhD); public health (MPH); rehabilitation (MS); PhD/MPH.

University of Indianapolis, Graduate Programs, College of Health Sciences, Program in Public Health, Indianapolis, IN 46227-3697. Offers MPH. *Degree requirements:* For master's, capstone.

The University of Iowa, College of Dentistry and Graduate College, Graduate Programs in Dentistry, Department of Preventive and Community Dentistry, Iowa City, IA 52242-1316. Offers dental public health (MS). *Degree requirements:* For master's, thesis. *Entrance requirements:* For master's, GRE, DDS. Additional exam requirements/recommendations for international students: Required—TOEFL.

The University of Iowa, Graduate College, College of Public Health, Iowa City, IA 52242-1316. Offers MHA, MPH, MS, PhD, Certificate, DVM/MPH, JD/MHA, JD/MPH, MBA/MHA, MD/MPH, MHA/MA, MS/MA, MS/MS, Pharm D/MPH. *Degree requirements:* For master's, exam; for doctorate, comprehensive exam, thesis/dissertation. *Entrance requirements:* For master's and doctorate, GRE General Test, minimum GPA of 3.0. Additional exam requirements/recommendations for international students: Required—TOEFL. Electronic applications accepted. *Expenses:* Contact institution.

The University of Kansas, University of Kansas Medical Center, School of Medicine, Department of Preventive Medicine and Public Health, Kansas City, KS 66160. Offers clinical research (MS); epidemiology (MPH); public health management (MPH); social and behavioral health (MPH); MD/MPH; PhD/MPH. *Accreditation:* CEPH. *Program availability:* Part-time. *Faculty:* 71. *Students:* 39 full-time (30 women), 40 part-time (28 women); includes 21 minority (10 Black or African American, non-Hispanic/Latino; 1 American Indian or Alaska Native, non-Hispanic/Latino; 4 Asian, non-Hispanic/Latino; 3 Hispanic/Latino; 3 Two or more races, non-Hispanic/Latino), 7 international. Average age 30. 66 applicants, 68% accepted, 32 enrolled. In 2017, 33 master's awarded. *Degree requirements:* For master's, thesis, capstone practicum defense. *Entrance requirements:* For master's, GRE, MCAT, LSAT, GMAT or other equivalent graduate professional exam. Additional exam requirements/recommendations for international students: Required—TOEFL. *Application deadline:* For fall admission, 3/1 for domestic and international students. Applications are processed on a rolling basis. Application

fee: $60. Electronic applications accepted. *Financial support:* In 2017–18, 9 research assistantships (averaging $15,000 per year) were awarded; career-related internships or fieldwork, Federal Work-Study, scholarships/grants, and unspecified assistantships also available. Support available to part-time students. Financial award application deadline: 3/1; financial award applicants required to submit FAFSA. *Faculty research:* Cancer screening and prevention, smoking cessation, obesity and physical activity, health services/outcomes research, health disparities. *Total annual research expenditures:* $8.4 million. *Unit head:* Dr. Edward F. Ellerbeck, Chairman, 913-588-2774, Fax: 913-588-2780, E-mail: eellerbe@kumc.edu. *Application contact:* Tanya Honderick, MPH Director, 913-588-2720, Fax: 913-588-8505, E-mail: thonderick@kumc.edu.
Website: http://www.kumc.edu/school-of-medicine/preventive-medicine-and-public-health.html

University of Kentucky, Graduate School, College of Public Health, Program in Public Health, Lexington, KY 40506-0032. Offers MPH, Dr PH. *Entrance requirements:* For master's, GRE General Test, minimum undergraduate GPA of 2.75. Additional exam requirements/recommendations for international students: Required—TOEFL (minimum score 550 paper-based). Electronic applications accepted.

University of La Verne, College of Business and Public Management, Master's Program in Public Administration, La Verne, CA 91750-4443. Offers gerontology (MPA); nonprofit (MPA); public health (MPA); urban management and affairs (MPA). *Accreditation:* NASPAA. *Program availability:* Part-time. *Faculty:* 11 full-time (5 women), 1 part-time/adjunct (0 women). *Students:* 33 full-time (18 women), 21 part-time (15 women); includes 40 minority (3 Black or African American, non-Hispanic/Latino; 2 Asian, non-Hispanic/Latino; 35 Hispanic/Latino), 1 international. Average age 33. *Entrance requirements:* For master's, minimum undergraduate GPA of 3.0, statement of purpose, 2 letters of recommendation, resume. Additional exam requirements/recommendations for international students: Required—TOEFL (minimum score 550 paper-based). *Application deadline:* Applications are processed on a rolling basis. Application fee: $50. *Expenses:* Contact institution. *Financial support:* Institutionally sponsored loans and scholarships/grants available. Financial award application deadline: 3/2; financial award applicants required to submit FAFSA. *Unit head:* Marcia Godwin, Chairperson, 909-448-4103, E-mail: mgodwin@laverne.edu. *Application contact:* Cathy Cook, Associate Director of Graduate Admissions, 909-448-4719, Fax: 909-971-2295, E-mail: ccook2@laverne.edu.
Website: https://business.laverne.edu/mpa/

University of Louisville, Graduate School, School of Public Health and Information Sciences, Department of Epidemiology and Population Health, Louisville, KY 40292-0001. Offers epidemiology (MPH, MS); public health sciences (PhD), including epidemiology. *Program availability:* Evening/weekend. *Faculty:* 9 full-time (5 women). *Students:* 4 full-time (2 women), 18 part-time (15 women); includes 6 minority (2 Asian, non-Hispanic/Latino; 2 Hispanic/Latino; 2 Two or more races, non-Hispanic/Latino), 2 international. Average age 31. 12 applicants, 92% accepted, 8 enrolled. In 2017, 7 master's awarded. *Degree requirements:* For master's, thesis; for doctorate, comprehensive exam, thesis/dissertation. *Entrance requirements:* For master's and doctorate, GRE (taken within past 5 years), bachelor's degree from accredited institution or its equivalent; minimum GPA of 3.0 (recommended); two letters of recommendation written within last twelve months; official transcripts of all degrees; one-page personal statement. Additional exam requirements/recommendations for international students: Required—TOEFL (minimum score 90 iBT). *Application deadline:* For fall admission, 4/1 for domestic students, 1/2 priority date for international students. Applications are processed on a rolling basis. Application fee: $65. Electronic applications accepted. *Expenses:* Tuition, state resident: full-time $12,246; part-time $681 per credit hour. Tuition, nonresident: full-time $25,486; part-time $1417 per credit hour. *Required fees:* $196. Tuition and fees vary according to course load, program and reciprocity agreements. *Financial support:* In 2017–18, 3 fellowships with full tuition reimbursements (averaging $20,000 per year), 3 research assistantships with full tuition reimbursements (averaging $20,000 per year) were awarded; scholarships/grants, traineeships, and tuition waivers (full) also available. Financial award application deadline: 3/1; financial award applicants required to submit FAFSA. *Faculty research:* Breast cancer, health disparities along the cancer continuum, childhood leukemia, genetic epidemiology of cardiovascular diseases, developmental disorders associated with environmental exposure to lead and metals, global health. *Total annual research expenditures:* $386,400. *Unit head:* Dr. Richard Baumgartner, Professor and Chair, 502-852-3003, Fax: 502-852-3291, E-mail: mbaum01@gwise.louisville.edu. *Application contact:* Robin Newlon, Administrative Specialist, 502-852-3003, Fax: 502-852-3294, E-mail: robin.newlon@louisville.edu.
Website: http://louisville.edu/sphis/departments/epidemiology-population-health

University of Louisville, Graduate School, School of Public Health and Information Sciences, Department of Health Management and Systems Sciences, Louisville, KY 40202. Offers health policy (MPH); population health management (MPH); public health sciences (PhD), including health management and policy. *Program availability:* Part-time. *Students:* 109 full-time (74 women), 36 part-time (21 women); includes 47 minority (31 Black or African American, non-Hispanic/Latino; 12 Asian, non-Hispanic/Latino; 2 Hispanic/Latino; 2 Two or more races, non-Hispanic/Latino), 26 international. Average age 32. 135 applicants, 76% accepted, 59 enrolled. In 2017, 25 master's, 4 doctorates awarded. *Degree requirements:* For master's, thesis optional; for doctorate, comprehensive exam, thesis/dissertation. *Entrance requirements:* For master's, GRE, GMAT, MCAT, LSAT, or DAT, bachelor's degree from accredited institution or its equivalent; minimum GPA of 3.0 (recommended); three letters of recommendation written within last twelve months; official transcripts of all degrees; one-page personal statement; for doctorate, GRE, MCAT, DAT, bachelor's degree from accredited institution or its equivalent; relevant master's degree (e.g. MPH); minimum GPA of 3.0 (recommended); three letters of recommendation written within last twelve months; official transcripts of all degrees; one-page personal statement. Additional exam requirements/recommendations for international students: Required—TOEFL (minimum score 90 iBT). *Application deadline:* For fall admission, 5/15 for domestic students, 4/15 for international students. Applications are processed on a rolling basis. Application fee: $65. Electronic applications accepted. *Expenses:* Tuition, state resident: full-time $12,246; part-time $681 per credit hour. Tuition, nonresident: full-time $25,486; part-time $1417 per credit hour. *Required fees:* $196. Tuition and fees vary according to course load, program and reciprocity agreements. *Financial support:* In 2017–18, 1 fellowship with full tuition reimbursement (averaging $20,000 per year), 2 research assistantships with full tuition reimbursements (averaging $20,000 per year), 1 teaching assistantship with full tuition reimbursement (averaging $20,000 per year) were awarded; health care benefits and unspecified assistantships also available. Support available to part-time students. Financial award application deadline: 5/15; financial award applicants required to submit FAFSA. *Faculty research:* Policy development in public health, complex adaptive networks in health transaction cost economics, strengthening the safety net and improving health care access for the uninsured, healthy communities approach to improving quality of life, public health management and administration. *Total annual research expenditures:* $2 million. *Unit head:* Dr. Christopher Johnson, Professor and Chair, 502-852-3987, Fax: 502-852-3294, E-mail: cejohn23@louisville.edu. *Application contact:* Vicki Lewis, Administrative Assistant, 502-852-1798, E-mail: vicki.lewis@louisville.edu.
Website: http://louisville.edu/sphis/departments/health-management-systems-science

University of Lynchburg, Graduate Studies, Master of Public Health Program, Lynchburg, VA 24501-3199. Offers public health (MPH), including health promotion. *Program availability:* Part-time. *Faculty:* 5 full-time (4 women). *Students:* 20 full-time (18 women), 7 part-time (4 women); includes 10 minority (8 Black or African American, non-Hispanic/Latino; 2 Hispanic/Latino), 3 international. Average age 27. 34 applicants, 100% accepted, 17 enrolled. In 2017, 14 master's awarded. *Degree requirements:* For master's, internship, capstone project. *Entrance requirements:* For master's, GRE. Additional exam requirements/recommendations for international students: Required—TOEFL (minimum score 550 paper-based; 80 iBT), IELTS (minimum score 6). *Application deadline:* For fall admission, 7/31 for domestic and international students; for spring admission, 11/30 for domestic and international students. Applications are processed on a rolling basis. Application fee: $30. Electronic applications accepted. Application fee is waived when completed online. *Expenses:* $510 per credit hour tuition, $100 fees. *Financial support:* Scholarships/grants and unspecified assistantships available. Financial award applicants required to submit FAFSA. *Unit head:* Dr. Charlotte Guynes, Director, 434-544-8644, E-mail: guynes@lynchburg.edu. *Application contact:* Ellen Thompson, Graduate Admissions Counselor, 434-544-8841, E-mail: thompson_e@lynchburg.edu.
Website: https://www.lynchburg.edu/graduate/master-of-public-health/

The University of Manchester, School of Dentistry, Manchester, United Kingdom. Offers basic dental sciences (cancer studies) (M Phil, PhD); basic dental sciences (molecular genetics) (M Phil, PhD); basic dental sciences (stem cell biology) (M Phil, PhD); biomaterials sciences and dental technology (M Phil, PhD); dental public health/community dentistry (M Phil, PhD); dental science (clinical) (PhD); endodontology (M Phil, PhD); fixed and removable prosthodontics (M Phil, PhD); operative dentistry (M Phil, PhD); oral and maxillofacial surgery (M Phil, PhD); oral radiology (M Phil, PhD); orthodontics (M Phil, PhD); restorative dentistry (M Phil, PhD).

University of Maryland, College Park, Academic Affairs, School of Public Health, College Park, MD 20742. Offers MA, MHA, MPH, MS, PhD. *Program availability:* Part-time, evening/weekend. *Degree requirements:* For doctorate, thesis/dissertation. *Entrance requirements:* For master's and doctorate, GRE General Test, minimum GPA of 3.0, 3 letters of recommendation. Additional exam requirements/recommendations for international students: Required—TOEFL. Electronic applications accepted.

University of Massachusetts Amherst, Graduate School, Interdisciplinary Programs, Dual Degree Program in Public Policy and Administration and Public Health, Amherst, MA 01003. Offers MPH/MPPA. *Entrance requirements:* Additional exam requirements/recommendations for international students: Required—TOEFL (minimum score 550 paper-based; 80 iBT), IELTS (minimum score 6.5). Electronic applications accepted.

University of Massachusetts Amherst, Graduate School, School of Public Health and Health Sciences, Department of Public Health, Amherst, MA 01003. Offers biostatistics (MPH, MS, PhD); community health education (MPH, MS, PhD); environmental health sciences (MPH, MS, PhD); epidemiology (MPH, MS, PhD); health policy and management (MPH, MS, PhD); nutrition (MPH, PhD); public health practice (MPH); MPH/MPPA. *Program availability:* Part-time, evening/weekend, online learning. Terminal master's awarded for partial completion of doctoral program. *Degree requirements:* For master's, thesis (for some programs); for doctorate, comprehensive exam, thesis/dissertation. *Entrance requirements:* For master's and doctorate, GRE General Test. Additional exam requirements/recommendations for international students: Required—TOEFL (minimum score 550 paper-based; 80 iBT), IELTS (minimum score 6.5). Electronic applications accepted.

University of Memphis, Graduate School, School of Public Health, Memphis, TN 38152. Offers biostatistics (MPH); environmental health (MPH); epidemiology (MPH, PhD); health systems and policy (PhD); health systems management (MPH); public health (MHA); social and behavioral sciences (MPH, PhD). *Program availability:* Part-time, evening/weekend. *Faculty:* 20 full-time (7 women), 4 part-time/adjunct (1 woman). *Students:* 111 full-time (76 women), 59 part-time (45 women); includes 77 minority (48 Black or African American, non-Hispanic/Latino; 18 Asian, non-Hispanic/Latino; 6 Hispanic/Latino; 5 Two or more races, non-Hispanic/Latino), 23 international. Average age 31. 100 applicants, 91% accepted, 60 enrolled. In 2017, 56 master's, 4 doctorates awarded. *Degree requirements:* For master's, comprehensive exam, thesis (for some programs), practicum/field experience; for doctorate, comprehensive exam, thesis/dissertation, residency. *Entrance requirements:* For master's, GRE or GMAT, letters of recommendation; letter of intent; for doctorate, GRE, letters of recommendation; personal statement. Additional exam requirements/recommendations for international students: Required—TOEFL (minimum score 550 paper-based; 79 iBT). *Application deadline:* For fall admission, 4/1 for domestic students; for spring admission, 11/1 for domestic students. Application fee: $35 ($60 for international students). Electronic applications accepted. *Expenses:* Contact institution. *Financial support:* In 2017–18, 46 students received support, including 8 research assistantships with full tuition reimbursements available (averaging $8,950 per year); Federal Work-Study, scholarships/grants, and unspecified assistantships also available. Financial award application deadline: 2/1; financial award applicants required to submit FAFSA. *Faculty research:* Health and medical savings accounts, adoption rates, health informatics, Telehealth technologies, biostatistics, environmental health, epidemiology, health systems management, social and behavioral sciences. *Unit head:* Dr. Lisa M. Klesges, Dean, 901-678-4501, E-mail: lmklsges@memphis.edu. *Application contact:* Dr. Marian Levy, Assistant Dean, 901-678-4514, Fax: 901-678-5023, E-mail: sph-admin@memphis.edu.
Website: http://www.memphis.edu/sph/

University of Miami, Graduate School, Miller School of Medicine, Graduate Programs in Medicine, Department of Epidemiology and Public Health, Coral Gables, FL 33124. Offers epidemiology (PhD); public health (MPH, MSPH); JD/MPH; MD/MPH; MD/PhD; MPA/MPH; MPH/MAIA. *Accreditation:* CEPH (one or more programs are accredited). *Program availability:* Part-time. *Degree requirements:* For master's, thesis (for some programs), project, practicum; for doctorate, comprehensive exam, thesis/dissertation. *Entrance requirements:* For master's, GRE General Test, minimum GPA of 3.0, 3 letters of recommendation; for doctorate, GRE General Test, minimum GPA of 3.0, course work in epidemiology and statistics, 3 letters of recommendation. Additional exam requirements/recommendations for international students: Required—TOEFL (minimum score 550 paper-based; 59 iBT). Electronic applications accepted. *Faculty research:* Behavioral epidemiology, substance abuse, AIDS, cardiovascular diseases, women's health.

University of Michigan, School of Public Health, Ann Arbor, MI 48109. Offers MHSA, MPH, MS, PhD, JD/MHSA, MD/MPH, MHSA/MBA, MHSA/MPP, MHSA/MSIOE, MPH/JD, MPH/MA, MPH/MBA, MPH/MPP, MPH/MS, MPH/MSW. MS and PhD offered through the Rackham Graduate School. *Accreditation:* CAHME (one or more programs are accredited); CEPH (one or more programs are accredited). *Program availability:* Evening/weekend. Terminal master's awarded for partial completion of doctoral program. *Degree requirements:* For master's, internship; for doctorate, oral defense of dissertation, preliminary exam. *Entrance requirements:* For master's and doctorate, GRE General Test. Additional exam requirements/recommendations for international students: Required—TOEFL (minimum score 100 iBT). Electronic applications accepted. *Expenses:* Tuition, state resident: full-time $22,368; part-time $1201 per credit hour. Tuition, nonresident: full-time $45,156; part-time $2467 per credit hour. *Required fees:* $376 per term. Tuition and fees vary according to course load, degree level and program.

University of Michigan–Flint, School of Health Professions and Studies, Program in Public Health, Flint, MI 48502-1950. Offers health administration (MPH); health education (MPH). *Program availability:* Part-time. *Faculty:* 16 full-time (11 women), 36 part-time/adjunct (19 women). *Students:* 14 full-time (11 women), 37 part-time (32 women); includes 15 minority (9 Black or African American, non-Hispanic/Latino; 2 American Indian or Alaska Native, non-Hispanic/Latino; 2 Asian, non-Hispanic/Latino; 2 Two or more races, non-Hispanic/Latino), 7 international. Average age 31. 38 applicants, 50% accepted, 9 enrolled. In 2017, 18 master's awarded. *Degree requirements:* For master's, thesis, public health capstone. *Entrance requirements:* For master's, GRE, bachelor's degree from accredited institution with sufficient preparation in algebra to succeed in epidemiology and biostatistics; minimum overall undergraduate GPA of 3.0. Additional exam requirements/recommendations for international students: Required—TOEFL (minimum score 84 iBT), IELTS (minimum score 6.5). *Application deadline:* For fall admission, 8/1 for domestic students, 5/1 for international students; for winter admission, 11/15 for domestic students, 9/1 for international students; for spring admission, 3/15 for domestic students, 1/1 for international students. Applications are processed on a rolling basis. Application fee: $55. Electronic applications accepted. *Expenses:* Contact institution. *Financial support:* Federal Work-Study, institutionally sponsored loans, scholarships/grants, and unspecified assistantships available. Support available to part-time students. Financial award application deadline: 3/1; financial award applicants required to submit FAFSA. *Unit head:* Dr. Shan Parker, Director, 810-762-3172, E-mail: shanpark@umflint.edu. *Application contact:* Bradley T. Maki, Director of Graduate Admissions, 810-762-3171, Fax: 810-766-6789, E-mail: bmaki@umflint.edu.
Website: http://www.umflint.edu/graduateprograms/public-health-mph

University of Minnesota, Twin Cities Campus, School of Public Health, Minneapolis, MN 55455. Offers MHA, MPH, MS, PhD, Certificate, DVM/MPH, JD/MS, JD/PhD, MD/MPH, MD/PhD, MPH/JD, MPH/MS, MPH/MSN, MPP/MS. *Accreditation:* CEPH (one or more programs are accredited). *Program availability:* Part-time, online learning. Terminal master's awarded for partial completion of doctoral program. *Degree requirements:* For doctorate, thesis/dissertation. *Entrance requirements:* For master's and doctorate, GRE General Test. Additional exam requirements/recommendations for international students: Required—TOEFL. Electronic applications accepted. *Expenses:* Contact institution.

University of Montana, Graduate School, College of Health Professions and Biomedical Sciences, School of Public and Community Health Sciences, Missoula, MT 59812. Offers public health (MPH, CPH). *Program availability:* Part-time, online learning.

University of Nebraska Medical Center, College of Public Health, Omaha, NE 68198-4355. Offers MPH. *Accreditation:* CEPH. *Program availability:* Part-time, online learning. *Degree requirements:* For master's, service-learning capstone course. *Entrance requirements:* Additional exam requirements/recommendations for international students: Required—TOEFL (minimum score 550 paper-based). Electronic applications accepted. *Expenses:* Tuition, state resident: full-time $8451; part-time $4225 per semester. Tuition, nonresident: full-time $24,219; part-time $11,295 per semester. *Required fees:* $589; $117 per term. *Faculty research:* Ethics, environmental health, cultural influence on health, rural health policy, cancer prevention.

University of Nevada, Las Vegas, Graduate College, School of Community Health Sciences, Department of Environmental and Occupational Health, Las Vegas, NV 89154-3064. Offers infection prevention (Certificate); public health (MPH, PhD, Certificate). *Program availability:* Part-time. *Faculty:* 7 full-time (4 women), 1 part-time/adjunct (0 women). *Students:* 47 full-time (34 women), 54 part-time (39 women); includes 44 minority (7 Black or African American, non-Hispanic/Latino; 2 American Indian or Alaska Native, non-Hispanic/Latino; 13 Asian, non-Hispanic/Latino; 15 Hispanic/Latino; 1 Native Hawaiian or other Pacific Islander, non-Hispanic/Latino; 6 Two or more races, non-Hispanic/Latino), 10 international. Average age 31. 68 applicants, 78% accepted, 31 enrolled. In 2017, 28 master's, 3 doctorates, 1 other advanced degree awarded. *Degree requirements:* For master's, thesis; for doctorate, comprehensive exam, thesis/dissertation. *Entrance requirements:* For master's, GRE General Test, bachelor's degree with minimum GPA 3.0; personal essay; 3 letters of recommendation; for doctorate, GRE General Test, bachelor's degree; master's degree with minimum GPA of 3.0; 3 letters of recommendation; personal interview. Additional exam requirements/recommendations for international students: Required—TOEFL (minimum score 550 paper-based; 85 iBT), IELTS (minimum score 7). *Application deadline:* For fall admission, 4/1 for domestic and international students; for spring admission, 11/1 for domestic and international students. Application fee: $60 ($95 for international students). Electronic applications accepted. *Expenses:* $275 per credit, $850 per course, $7,969 per year resident, $22,157 per year non-resident, $7,094 non-resident fee (7 credits or more), $1,307 annual health insurance fee. *Financial support:* In 2017–18, 33 students received support, including 28 research assistantships with full and partial tuition reimbursements available (averaging $14,246 per year), 5 teaching assistantships with full and partial tuition reimbursements available (averaging $12,957 per year); institutionally sponsored loans, scholarships/grants, health care benefits, and unspecified assistantships also available. Financial award application deadline: 3/15; financial award applicants required to submit FAFSA. *Faculty research:* Environmental health: micro (mold) to macro (Lake Mead ecosystem). *Total annual research expenditures:* $1.5 million. *Unit head:* Dr. Francisco Sy, Chair, 702-895-5420, Fax: 702-895-5184, E-mail: francisco.sy@unlv.edu. *Application contact:* Dr. Mark Buttner, Interim Dean, 702-895-1418, Fax: 702-895-5184, E-mail: mark.buttner@unlv.edu.

University of Nevada, Reno, Graduate School, Division of Health Sciences, Department of Public Health, Reno, NV 89557. Offers MPH, PhD, MPH/MSN. Terminal master's awarded for partial completion of doctoral program. *Degree requirements:* For master's, thesis optional, culminating experience; for doctorate, thesis/dissertation. *Entrance requirements:* For master's, GRE General Test, GMAT, LSAT, MCAT or DAT, minimum GPA of 2.75; for doctorate, GRE General Test, GMAT, LSAT, MCAT or DAT, minimum GPA of 3.0. Additional exam requirements/recommendations for international students: Required—TOEFL (minimum score 500 paper-based; 61 iBT), IELTS (minimum score 6). Electronic applications accepted. *Faculty research:* Biomechanics and basic fundamentals of skiing, social psychology in sports and recreation, fitness and aging, elementary physical education, body fat evaluation.

University of New England, College of Graduate and Professional Studies, Portland, ME 04005-9526. Offers advanced educational leadership (CAGS); applied nutrition (MS); career and technical education (MS Ed); curriculum and instruction (MS Ed); education (CAGS, Post-Master's Certificate); educational leadership (MS Ed, Ed D); generalist (MS Ed); health informatics (MS, Graduate Certificate); inclusion education (MS Ed); literacy K-12 (MS Ed); medical education leadership (MMEL); public health (MPH); public health (Graduate Certificate); reading specialist (MS Ed); social work (MSW). *Program availability:* Part-time, evening/weekend, online only, 100% online. *Faculty:* 125 part-time/adjunct (94 women). *Students:* 1,403 full-time (1,128 women), 594 part-time (475 women); includes 474 minority (332 Black or African American, non-Hispanic/Latino; 13 American Indian or Alaska Native, non-Hispanic/Latino; 83 Asian, non-Hispanic/Latino; 27 Hispanic/Latino; 11 Native Hawaiian or other Pacific Islander, non-Hispanic/Latino; 8 Two or more races, non-Hispanic/Latino). Average age 35. 3,153 applicants, 41% accepted, 990 enrolled. In 2017, 307 master's, 59 doctorates, 124 other advanced degrees awarded. *Application deadline:* Applications are processed on a rolling basis. Electronic applications accepted. Tuition and fees vary according to degree level, program and student level. *Financial support:* Application deadline: 5/1; applicants required to submit FAFSA. *Unit head:* Dr. Martha Wilson, Associate Provost for Online Worldwide Learning/Dean of the College of Graduate and Professional Studies, 207-221-4985, E-mail: mwilson13@une.edu.
Website: http://online.une.edu

University of New Hampshire, Graduate School, College of Health and Human Services, Department of Health Management and Policy, Durham, NH 03824. Offers public health (MPH, Postbaccalaureate Certificate). *Program availability:* Part-time, evening/weekend. *Students:* 9 full-time (6 women), 6 part-time (5 women); includes 1 minority (Asian, non-Hispanic/Latino). Average age 30. 11 applicants, 45% accepted, 2 enrolled. In 2017, 7 master's, 1 other advanced degree awarded. *Entrance requirements:* Additional exam requirements/recommendations for international students: Required—TOEFL (minimum score 550 paper-based; 80 iBT). *Application deadline:* For fall admission, 7/1 priority date for domestic students, 4/1 for international students; for spring admission, 12/1 for domestic students. Application fee: $65. Electronic applications accepted. *Financial support:* Fellowships, research assistantships, teaching assistantships, and scholarships/grants available. Financial award application deadline: 2/15. *Unit head:* Rosemary M. Caron, Chair, 603-862-3653. *Application contact:* Ann-Marie Matteucci, Academic Coordinator, 603-862-1570, E-mail: ann-marie.matteucci@unh.edu.
Website: http://chhs.unh.edu/hmp

University of New Hampshire, Graduate School Manchester Campus, Manchester, NH 03101. Offers business administration (MBA); cybersecurity policy and risk management (MS); educational administration and supervision (Ed S); educational studies (M Ed); elementary education (M Ed); information technology (MS); public administration (MPA); public health (MPH, Certificate); secondary education (M Ed, MAT); social work (MSW); substance use disorders (Certificate). *Program availability:* Part-time, evening/weekend. *Students:* 13 full-time (6 women), 17 part-time (0 women); includes 7 minority (1 Black or African American, non-Hispanic/Latino; 4 Asian, non-Hispanic/Latino; 1 Hispanic/Latino; 1 Two or more races, non-Hispanic/Latino), 10 international. Average age 33. 42 applicants, 71% accepted, 8 enrolled. In 2017, 4 master's awarded. *Entrance requirements:* Additional exam requirements/recommendations for international students: Required—TOEFL (minimum score 550 paper-based; 80 iBT). *Application deadline:* For fall admission, 6/1 for domestic students, 4/1 for international students; for spring admission, 12/1 for domestic students. Application fee: $65. Electronic applications accepted. *Financial support:* Fellowships, research assistantships, teaching assistantships, Federal Work-Study, scholarships/grants, health care benefits, and unspecified assistantships available. Support available to part-time students. Financial award application deadline: 2/15; financial award applicants required to submit FAFSA. *Unit head:* Candice Morey, Educational Programs Coordinator, 603-641-4313, E-mail: unhm.gradcenter@unh.edu.
Website: http://www.gradschool.unh.edu/manchester/

University of New Mexico, Graduate Studies, Health Sciences Center, Program in Public Health, Albuquerque, NM 87131-5196. Offers community health (MPH); epidemiology (MPH); health systems, services and policy (MPH). *Program availability:* Part-time, online learning. *Faculty:* 9 full-time (6 women), 1 (woman) part-time/adjunct. *Students:* 23 full-time (20 women), 20 part-time (14 women); includes 15 minority (1 Black or African American, non-Hispanic/Latino; 1 American Indian or Alaska Native, non-Hispanic/Latino; 1 Asian, non-Hispanic/Latino; 12 Hispanic/Latino), 2 international. Average age 32. 34 applicants, 53% accepted, 18 enrolled. In 2017, 13 master's awarded. *Entrance requirements:* For master's, GRE, MCAT, 2 years of experience in health field. Additional exam requirements/recommendations for international students: Required—TOEFL. *Application deadline:* For fall admission, 2/1 for domestic students. Application fee: $50. *Financial support:* Fellowships, research assistantships, and Federal Work-Study available. Financial award application deadline: 12/15; financial award applicants required to submit FAFSA. *Faculty research:* Epidemiology, rural health, environmental health, Native American health issues. *Unit head:* Dr. Kristine Tollestrup, Director, 505-272-4173, Fax: 505-272-4494, E-mail: ktollestrup@salud.unm.edu. *Application contact:* Gayle Garcia, Education Coordinator, 505-272-3982, Fax: 505-272-4494, E-mail: garciag@salud.unm.edu.
Website: http://fcm.unm.edu/

The University of North Carolina at Chapel Hill, Graduate School, Gillings School of Global Public Health, Chapel Hill, NC 27599. Offers MHA, MPH, MS, MSCR, MSEE, MSPH, Dr PH, PhD, JD/MPH, MBA/MSPH, MD/MPH, MD/MSPH, MHA/MBA, MHA/MCRP, MHA/MSIS, MHA/MSLS, MPH/MCRP, MPH/MSW, MS/MCRP, MSPH/M Ed, MSPH/MCRP, MSPH/MSIS, MSPH/MSLS, MSPH/MSW, MSPH/PhD, PhD/MD, Pharm D/MPH. *Accreditation:* CAHME (one or more programs are accredited). *Program availability:* Part-time, 100% online, blended/hybrid learning. *Faculty:* 240 full-time (139 women), 514 part-time/adjunct (257 women). *Students:* 1,116 full-time (808 women), 132 part-time (81 women); includes 382 minority (106 Black or African American, non-Hispanic/Latino; 2 American Indian or Alaska Native, non-Hispanic/Latino; 111 Asian, non-Hispanic/Latino; 81 Hispanic/Latino; 1 Native Hawaiian or other Pacific Islander, non-Hispanic/Latino; 81 Two or more races, non-Hispanic/Latino), 163 international. Average age 30. 1,969 applicants, 41% accepted, 423 enrolled. In 2017, 300 master's, 94 doctorates awarded. Terminal master's awarded for partial completion of doctoral program. *Degree requirements:* For master's, comprehensive exam, thesis; for doctorate, comprehensive exam, thesis/dissertation. *Entrance requirements:* For master's and doctorate, GRE General Test. Additional exam requirements/recommendations for international students: Required—TOEFL (minimum score 90 iBT), IELTS (minimum score 7). *Application deadline:* For fall admission, 1/10 for domestic and international students. Applications are processed on a rolling basis. Application fee: $85. Electronic applications accepted. *Financial support:* Fellowships, research assistantships, teaching assistantships, career-related internships or fieldwork, Federal Work-Study, scholarships/grants, traineeships, health care benefits, and unspecified assistantships available. Financial award application deadline: 12/11; financial award applicants required to submit FAFSA. *Faculty research:* Infectious disease, health promotion and disease prevention, injury prevention, international health, environmental studies, occupational health studies. *Unit head:* Dr. Barbara K. Rimer, Dean, 919-966-3245, Fax: 919-966-7678. *Application contact:* Johnston King, Enrollment Management Coordinator, 919-962-6314, Fax: 919-966-6352, E-mail: sph-osa@unc.edu.
Website: http://www.sph.unc.edu/

The University of North Carolina at Charlotte, College of Health and Human Services, Department of Public Health Sciences, Charlotte, NC 28223-0001. Offers community health (Certificate); health administration (MHA); public health (MPH); public health core concepts (Graduate Certificate); public health sciences (PhD). *Accreditation:* CAHME; CEPH. *Program availability:* Part-time. *Faculty:* 23 full-time (12 women), 3 part-time/adjunct (2 women). *Students:* 94 full-time (74 women), 17 part-time (15 women); includes 49 minority (28 Black or African American, non-Hispanic/Latino; 3 American Indian or Alaska Native, non-Hispanic/Latino; 5 Asian, non-Hispanic/Latino; 6 Hispanic/Latino; 7 Two or more races, non-Hispanic/Latino), 7 international. Average age 25. 169 applicants, 60% accepted, 51 enrolled. In 2017, 44 master's, 2 other advanced degrees

awarded. *Degree requirements:* For master's, thesis (for some programs), thesis or project; internship; capstone; for doctorate, thesis/dissertation. *Entrance requirements:* For master's, GRE or MCAT (for MSPH); GRE or GMAT (for MHA), career goal statement, current resume, letters of recommendation; for doctorate, GRE, master's degree in public health or a related field with minimum GPA of 3.5 in all graduate work; statement of purpose detailing why applicant wants to pursue a PhD in public health sciences in the specified concentration at UNC Charlotte; three letters of recommendation (including at least two letters from former professors); for other advanced degree, bachelor's degree from regionally-accredited university; minimum GPA of 2.75 on all post-secondary work attempted; transcripts; personal statement outlining why the applicant seeks admission to the program. Additional exam requirements/recommendations for international students: Required—TOEFL (minimum score 523 paper-based, 70 iBT) or IELTS (6.5). *Application deadline:* For fall admission, 1/10 priority date for domestic and international students; for spring admission, 9/15 priority date for domestic and international students; for summer admission, 4/1 priority date for domestic and international students. Applications are processed on a rolling basis. Application fee: $75. Electronic applications accepted. *Expenses:* Contact institution. *Financial support:* In 2017–18, 26 students received support, including 1 fellowship (averaging $11,869 per year), 22 research assistantships (averaging $7,008 per year), 3 teaching assistantships (averaging $5,176 per year); career-related internships or fieldwork, Federal Work-Study, institutionally sponsored loans, scholarships/grants, and unspecified assistantships also available. Support available to part-time students. Financial award application deadline: 3/1; financial award applicants required to submit FAFSA. *Total annual research expenditures:* $704,999. *Unit head:* Dr. Melinda Forthofer, Chair, 704-687-5682, Fax: 704-687-1644, E-mail: forthofer@uncc.edu. *Application contact:* Kathy B. Giddings, Director of Graduate Admissions, 704-687-5503, Fax: 704-687-1668, E-mail: gradadm@uncc.edu.
Website: http://publichealth.uncc.edu/

University of North Dakota, School of Medicine and Health Sciences, Program in Public Health, Grand Forks, ND 58202. Offers MPH.

University of Northern Colorado, Graduate School, College of Natural and Health Sciences, School of Human Sciences, Program in Public Health, Greeley, CO 80639. Offers community health education (MPH); global health and community health education (MPH); healthy aging and community health education (MPH). *Degree requirements:* For master's, comprehensive exam, thesis or alternative. *Entrance requirements:* For master's, GRE General Test, 2 letters of recommendation. Electronic applications accepted.

University of North Florida, Brooks College of Health, Department of Public Health, Jacksonville, FL 32224. Offers aging services (Certificate); community health (MPH). *Program availability:* Part-time, evening/weekend. *Degree requirements:* For master's, thesis optional. *Entrance requirements:* For master's, GRE General Test (MSH, MS, MPH); GMAT or GRE General Test (MHA), minimum GPA of 3.0 in last 60 hours. Additional exam requirements/recommendations for international students: Required—TOEFL (minimum score 500 paper-based). Electronic applications accepted. *Faculty research:* Dietary supplements; alcohol, tobacco, and other drug use prevention; turnover among health professionals; aging; psychosocial aspects of disabilities.

University of North Texas Health Science Center at Fort Worth, School of Public Health, Fort Worth, TX 76107-2699. Offers biostatistics (MS); epidemiology (MPH, MS, PhD); food security and public health (Graduate Certificate); GIS in public health (Graduate Certificate); global health (Graduate Certificate); global health for medical professionals (Graduate Certificate); health administration (MHA); health behavior research (MS, PhD); maternal and child health (MPH); public health (Graduate Certificate); public health practice (MPH); DO/MPH; MS/MPH. *Accreditation:* CEPH. *Program availability:* Part-time, evening/weekend, 100% online. *Degree requirements:* For master's, thesis or alternative, supervised internship; for doctorate, thesis/dissertation, supervised internship. *Entrance requirements:* For master's, GRE General Test. Additional exam requirements/recommendations for international students: Required—TOEFL. Electronic applications accepted. *Expenses:* Contact institution.

University of Oklahoma Health Sciences Center, Graduate College, College of Public Health, Program in General Public Health, Oklahoma City, OK 73190. Offers MPH, Dr PH. *Accreditation:* CEPH.

University of Oklahoma Health Sciences Center, Graduate College, College of Public Health, Program in Preparedness and Terrorism, Oklahoma City, OK 73190. Offers MPH.

University of Ottawa, Faculty of Graduate and Postdoctoral Studies, Interdisciplinary Programs, Program in Population Health, Ottawa, ON K1N 6N5, Canada. Offers PhD. *Degree requirements:* For doctorate, comprehensive exam, thesis/dissertation. Electronic applications accepted. *Faculty research:* Population health.

University of Pennsylvania, Perelman School of Medicine, Master of Public Health Program, Philadelphia, PA 19104. Offers environmental health (MPH); generalist (MPH); global health (MPH); DMD/MPH; JD/MPH; MD/MPH; MES/MPH; MPH/MBE; MPH/MPA; MPH/MS; MSN/MPH; MSSP/MPH; MSW/MPH; PhD/MPH. *Accreditation:* CEPH. *Program availability:* Part-time, evening/weekend. *Faculty:* 12 full-time (10 women), 36 part-time/adjunct (27 women). *Students:* 130 full-time (102 women), 61 part-time (50 women); includes 85 minority (29 Black or African American, non-Hispanic/Latino; 33 Asian, non-Hispanic/Latino; 4 Hispanic/Latino; 19 Two or more races, non-Hispanic/Latino), 12 international. Average age 29. 385 applicants, 47% accepted, 62 enrolled. In 2017, 50 master's awarded. *Degree requirements:* For master's, thesis. *Entrance requirements:* For master's, GRE. Additional exam requirements/recommendations for international students: Required—TOEFL (minimum score 100 iBT), IELTS (minimum score 7). *Application deadline:* For fall admission, 4/15 for domestic and international students. Applications are processed on a rolling basis. Electronic applications accepted. *Expenses:* $31,682 tuition, $4,066 fees. *Financial support:* In 2017–18, 27 students received support, including 6 research assistantships with partial tuition reimbursements available (averaging $18,104 per year), 21 teaching assistantships with partial tuition reimbursements available (averaging $4,526 per year); fellowships and tuition waivers (partial) also available. Financial award application deadline: 4/15; financial award applicants required to submit FAFSA. *Faculty research:* Health disparities, health behaviors, obesity, global health, epidemiology and prevention research. *Unit head:* Dr. Jennifer Pinto-Martin, Director, 215-898-4726, E-mail: pinto@nursing.upenn.edu. *Application contact:* Moriah Hall, Associate Director, MPH Program, 215-573-8841, E-mail: moriahh@mail.med.upenn.edu.
Website: http://www.cphi.upenn.edu/mph

University of Pittsburgh, Graduate School of Public Health, Pittsburgh, PA 15260. Offers MHA, MPH, MS, Dr PH, PhD, Certificate, JD/MPH, MD/MPH, MD/PhD, MID/MPH, MPH/MPA, MPH/MSW, MPH/PhD, MS/MPH. *Accreditation:* CEPH (one or more programs are accredited). *Program availability:* Part-time. *Faculty:* 158 full-time (75 women), 179 part-time/adjunct (92 women). *Students:* 486 full-time (341 women), 104 part-time (77 women); includes 121 minority (32 Black or African American, non-Hispanic/Latino; 44 Asian, non-Hispanic/Latino; 24 Hispanic/Latino; 2 Native Hawaiian or other Pacific Islander, non-Hispanic/Latino; 19 Two or more races, non-Hispanic/Latino), 134 international. Average age 28. 1,496 applicants, 54% accepted, 231 enrolled. In 2017, 163 master's, 40 doctorates awarded. Terminal master's awarded for partial completion of doctoral program. *Degree requirements:* For master's, final paper; comprehensive exam (MS); for doctorate, comprehensive exam, thesis/dissertation, preliminary exam, dissertation defense. *Entrance requirements:* For master's and Certificate, GRE, U.S. bachelor's or equivalent foreign degree; for doctorate, GRE, U.S. graduate, bachelor's, or equivalent foreign degree; MPH (for Dr PH); courses in mathematics and the biological and social sciences (for PhD). Additional exam requirements/recommendations for international students: Required—TOEFL (minimum score 550 paper-based, 80 iBT) or IELTS (minimum score 6.5). *Application deadline:* For fall admission, 1/15 for domestic and international students; for spring admission, 10/15 for domestic students, 8/1 for international students; for summer admission, 3/15 for domestic students, 12/1 for international students. Applications are processed on a rolling basis. Application fee: $135. Electronic applications accepted. *Expenses:* $13,068 per term full-time in-state, $21,696 out-of-state, $425 per term fees; $1,064 per credit part-time in-state, $1,777 out-of-state, $270 per term fees. *Financial support:* In 2017–18, 131 students received support, including 80 fellowships (averaging $10,000 per year), 118 research assistantships (averaging $20,500 per year), 5 teaching assistantships (averaging $18,500 per year); career-related internships or fieldwork, scholarships/grants, traineeships, health care benefits, and unspecified assistantships also available. Financial award applicants required to submit FAFSA. *Faculty research:* Aging epidemiology, enhanced detection system for infection, violence prevention, genomics of acute lung disease. *Total annual research expenditures:* $61.1 million. *Unit head:* Dr. Donald S. Burke, MD, Dean, 412-624-3001, Fax: 412-624-3013, E-mail: bradym1@pitt.edu. *Application contact:* Karrie A. Lukin, Admissions Manager, 412-624-3003, Fax: 412-624-3755, E-mail: presutti@pitt.edu.
Website: http://www.publichealth.pitt.edu/

University of Rochester, School of Medicine and Dentistry, Graduate Programs in Medicine and Dentistry, Department of Community and Preventive Medicine, Programs in Public Health and Clinical Investigation, Rochester, NY 14627. Offers clinical investigation (MS); public health (MPH); MBA/MPH; MD/MPH; MPH/MS; MPH/PhD. *Entrance requirements:* For master's, GRE General Test.

University of Saint Joseph, Department of Nutrition and Public Health, West Hartford, CT 06117-2700. Offers nutrition (MS); public health (MPH). *Program availability:* Part-time, evening/weekend, online learning. *Entrance requirements:* For master's, 2 letters of recommendation, letter of intent. *Application deadline:* Applications are processed on a rolling basis. Application fee: $50. Electronic applications accepted. Application fee is waived when completed online. *Financial support:* Career-related internships or fieldwork and unspecified assistantships available. Support available to part-time students. Financial award applicants required to submit FAFSA.
Website: https://www.usj.edu/academics/schools/sihs/nutrition-public-health/

University of San Francisco, School of Nursing and Health Professions, Program in Public Health, San Francisco, CA 94117-1080. Offers MPH.

University of South Africa, College of Human Sciences, Pretoria, South Africa. Offers adult education (M Ed); African languages (MA, PhD); African politics (MA, PhD); Afrikaans (MA, PhD); ancient history (MA, PhD); ancient Near Eastern studies (MA, PhD); anthropology (MA, PhD); applied linguistics (MA); Arabic (MA, PhD); archaeology (MA); art history (MA); Biblical archaeology (MA); Biblical studies (M Th, D Th, PhD); Christian spirituality (M Th, D Th); church history (M Th, D Th); classical studies (MA, PhD); clinical psychology (MA); communication (MA, PhD); comparative education (M Ed, Ed D); consulting psychology (D Admin, D Com, PhD); curriculum studies (M Ed, Ed D); development studies (M Admin, MA, D Admin, PhD); didactics (M Ed, Ed D); education (M Tech); education management (M Ed, Ed D); educational psychology (M Ed); English (MA); environmental education (M Ed); French (MA, PhD); German (MA, PhD); Greek (MA); guidance and counseling (M Ed); health studies (MA, PhD), including health sciences education (MA), health services management (MA), medical and surgical nursing science (critical care general) (MA), midwifery and neonatal nursing science (MA), trauma and emergency care (MA); history (MA, PhD); history of education (Ed D); inclusive education (M Ed, Ed D); information and communications technology policy and regulation (MA); information science (MA, MIS, PhD); international politics (MA, PhD); Islamic studies (MA, PhD); Italian (MA, PhD); Judaica (MA, PhD); linguistics (MA, PhD); mathematical education (M Ed); mathematics education (MA); missiology (M Th, D Th); modern Hebrew (MA, PhD); musicology (MA, MMus, D Mus, PhD); natural science education (M Ed); New Testament (M Th, D Th); Old Testament (D Th); pastoral therapy (M Th, D Th); philosophy (MA); philosophy of education (M Ed, Ed D); politics (MA, PhD); Portuguese (MA, PhD); practical theology (M Th, D Th); psychology (MA, MS, PhD); psychology of education (M Ed, Ed D); public health (MA); religious studies (MA, D Th, PhD); Romance languages (MA); Russian (MA, PhD); Semitic languages (MA, PhD); social behavior studies in HIV/AIDS (MA); social science (mental health) (MA); social science in development studies (MA); social science in psychology (MA); social science in social work (MA); social science in sociology (MA); social work (MSW, DSW, PhD); socio-education (M Ed, Ed D); sociolinguistics (MA); sociology (MA, PhD); Spanish (MA, PhD); systematic theology (M Th, D Th); TESOL (teaching English to speakers of other languages) (MA); theological ethics (M Th, D Th); theory of literature (MA, PhD); urban ministries (D Th); urban ministry (M Th).

University of South Carolina, The Graduate School, Arnold School of Public Health, Program in General Public Health, Columbia, SC 29208. Offers MPH. *Accreditation:* CEPH. *Program availability:* Part-time. *Degree requirements:* For master's, comprehensive exam, practicum. *Entrance requirements:* For master's, DAT or MCAT, GRE General Test, previously earned MD or doctoral degree. Additional exam requirements/recommendations for international students: Required—TOEFL (minimum score 570 paper-based). Electronic applications accepted.

University of South Carolina, The Graduate School, Arnold School of Public Health, Program in Physical Activity and Public Health, Columbia, SC 29208. Offers MPH. *Accreditation:* CEPH. *Program availability:* Part-time. *Degree requirements:* For master's, comprehensive exam, practicum. *Entrance requirements:* For master's, GRE. Additional exam requirements/recommendations for international students: Required—TOEFL (minimum score 570 paper-based). Electronic applications accepted.

University of South Carolina, The Graduate School, College of Nursing, Program in Nursing and Public Health, Columbia, SC 29208. Offers MPH/MSN. *Accreditation:* AACN; CEPH. *Program availability:* Part-time. *Entrance requirements:* Additional exam requirements/recommendations for international students: Required—TOEFL (minimum score 570 paper-based). Electronic applications accepted. *Faculty research:* System research, evidence based practice, breast cancer, violence.

University of South Dakota, Graduate School, School of Health Sciences, Program in Public Health, Vermillion, SD 57069. Offers MPH. *Program availability:* Part-time, evening/weekend, 100% online. *Entrance requirements:* For master's, official transcript, two letters of recommendation, statement of purpose, criminal background check. Additional exam requirements/recommendations for international students: Required—TOEFL (minimum score 550 paper-based; 79 iBT), IELTS (minimum score 6). *Application deadline:* For fall admission, 6/15 for domestic students; for spring admission, 10/15 for domestic students; for summer admission, 3/15 for domestic students. Application fee: $35. *Application contact:* Graduate School, 605-658-6140, Fax: 605-677-6118, E-mail: grad@usd.edu.
Website: http://www.usd.edu/health-sciences

University of Southern California, Keck School of Medicine and Graduate School, Graduate Programs in Medicine, Department of Preventive Medicine, Master of Public Health Program, Los Angeles, CA 90032. Offers biostatistics and epidemiology (MPH); child and family health (MPH); environmental health (MPH); geohealth (MPH); global health leadership (MPH); health communication (MPH); health education and promotion (MPH); public health policy (MPH). *Accreditation:* CEPH. *Program availability:* Part-time, evening/weekend. *Faculty:* 47 full-time (35 women), 13 part-time/adjunct (8 women). *Students:* 258 full-time (204 women), 61 part-time (50 women); includes 167 minority (28 Black or African American, non-Hispanic/Latino; 1 American Indian or Alaska Native, non-Hispanic/Latino; 61 Asian, non-Hispanic/Latino; 64 Hispanic/Latino; 4 Native Hawaiian or other Pacific Islander, non-Hispanic/Latino; 9 Two or more races, non-Hispanic/Latino), 28 international. Average age 26. 378 applicants, 53% accepted, 87 enrolled. In 2017, 91 master's awarded. *Degree requirements:* For master's, practicum, final report, oral presentation. *Entrance requirements:* For master's, GRE General Test, MCAT, GMAT, minimum GPA of 3.0. Additional exam requirements/recommendations for international students: Required—TOEFL (minimum score 600 paper-based; 90 iBT). *Application deadline:* For fall admission, 12/1 priority date for domestic students, 5/1 priority date for international students; for spring admission, 9/1 priority date for domestic and international students; for summer admission, 3/1 for domestic and international students. Applications are processed on a rolling basis. Application fee: $90. Electronic applications accepted. *Expenses:* Contact institution. *Financial support:* Career-related internships or fieldwork, Federal Work-Study, institutionally sponsored loans, and scholarships/grants available. Support available to part-time students. Financial award application deadline: 5/4; financial award applicants required to submit CSS PROFILE or FAFSA. *Faculty research:* Cancer and heart disease epidemiology and prevention, mass media and health communication research, effects of air pollution on health, tobacco control, global health. *Total annual research expenditures:* $7 million. *Unit head:* Dr. Louise A. Rohrbach, Director, 323-442-8237, Fax: 323-442-8297, E-mail: rohrbac@usc.edu. *Application contact:* Valerie Burris, Admissions Counselor, 323-442-7257, Fax: 323-442-8297, E-mail: valeriem@usc.edu.
Website: http://mph.usc.edu/

University of Southern Maine, College of Management and Human Service, Muskie School of Public Service, Program in Health Policy and Management, Portland, ME 04103. Offers MPH, CGS, MBA/MPH. *Program availability:* Part-time, evening/weekend, online learning. *Degree requirements:* For master's, thesis, capstone project, field experience. *Entrance requirements:* For master's, GRE General Test. Additional exam requirements/recommendations for international students: Required—TOEFL. Electronic applications accepted. *Faculty research:* Public health systems, population health and health policy, rural health, patient safety, health services research, aging and disability policy, Medicare and Medicaid policy, mental health policy.

University of Southern Mississippi, College of Health, Department of Public Health, Hattiesburg, MS 39406-0001. Offers epidemiology and biostatistics (MPH); health policy and administration (MPH). *Program availability:* Part-time, evening/weekend. *Students:* 17 full-time (6 women). 42 applicants, 88% accepted, 17 enrolled. In 2017, 2 master's awarded. *Degree requirements:* For master's, comprehensive exam, thesis (for some programs). *Entrance requirements:* For master's, GRE General Test, minimum GPA of 2.75 in last 60 hours. Additional exam requirements/recommendations for international students: Required—TOEFL, IELTS. *Application deadline:* For fall admission, 3/1 priority date for domestic and international students; for spring admission, 1/10 priority date for domestic and international students. Applications are processed on a rolling basis. Application fee: $60. Electronic applications accepted. *Expenses:* Tuition, state resident: full-time $3830. *Financial support:* Research assistantships with full tuition reimbursements, teaching assistantships with full tuition reimbursements, career-related internships or fieldwork, Federal Work-Study, institutionally sponsored loans, scholarships/grants, health care benefits, and unspecified assistantships available. Financial award application deadline: 3/15; financial award applicants required to submit FAFSA. *Faculty research:* Rural health care delivery, school health, nutrition of pregnant teens, risk factor reduction, sexually transmitted diseases. *Unit head:* Charkarra Anderson-Lewis, Interim Chair, 601-266-5435, Fax: 601-266-5043, E-mail: charkarra.andersonlewis@usm.edu.
Website: http://www.usm.edu/community-public-health-sciences

★ **University of South Florida,** College of Public Health, Tampa, FL 33612. Offers MHA, MPH, MSPH, Dr PH, PhD. *Accreditation:* CEPH (one or more programs are accredited). *Program availability:* Part-time, evening/weekend, 100% online, blended/hybrid learning. *Faculty:* 60 full-time (27 women), 34 part-time/adjunct (13 women). *Students:* 399 full-time (278 women), 399 part-time (298 women); includes 237 minority (122 Black or African American, non-Hispanic/Latino; 3 American Indian or Alaska Native, non-Hispanic/Latino; 48 Asian, non-Hispanic/Latino; 64 Hispanic/Latino), 94 international. Average age 33. 1,200 applicants, 54% accepted, 400 enrolled. In 2017, 136 master's, 6 doctorates awarded. *Degree requirements:* For master's, comprehensive exam, thesis (for some programs); for doctorate, comprehensive exam, thesis/dissertation. *Entrance requirements:* For master's, GRE General Test, minimum GPA of 3.0 in upper-level course work, 3 professional letters of recommendation, resume/curriculum vitae; for doctorate, GRE General Test, minimum GPA of 3.0 in upper-level course work, goal statement, three professional letters of recommendation, resume/curriculum vitae, writing sample. Additional exam requirements/recommendations for international students: Required—TOEFL (minimum score 550 paper-based; 79 iBT). *Application deadline:* For fall admission, 5/1 for domestic and international students; for spring admission, 6/15 for domestic and international students; for summer admission, 11/15 for domestic and international students. Applications are processed on a rolling basis. Application fee: $30. Electronic applications accepted. *Expenses:* $470 per credit hour in-state; $855 for credit hour out-of-state. *Financial support:* In 2017–18, 46 students received support, including 18 fellowships with full tuition reimbursements available (averaging $32,033 per year), 135 research assistantships with full and partial tuition reimbursements available (averaging $19,597 per year), 66 teaching assistantships (averaging $19,296 per year); career-related internships or fieldwork, Federal Work-Study, institutionally sponsored loans, scholarships/grants, traineeships, and unspecified assistantships also available. Support available to part-time students. Financial award application deadline: 11/15; financial award applicants required to submit FAFSA. *Total annual research expenditures:* $17.3 million. *Unit head:* Dr. Donna J. Petersen, Dean, 813-974-3623, Fax: 813-974-7350. *Application contact:* Kamala Dontamsetti, Assistant Director of Graduate Admissions, 813-974-8874, Fax: 813-974-8121, E-mail: kamalad@health.usf.edu.
Website: http://www.publichealth.usf.edu/

See Display below and Close-Up on page 847.

University of South Florida, Innovative Education, Tampa, FL 33620-9951. Offers adult, career and higher education (Graduate Certificate), including college teaching, leadership in developing human resources, leadership in higher education; Africana studies (Graduate Certificate), including diasporas and health disparities, genocide and human rights; aging studies (Graduate Certificate), including gerontology; art research (Graduate Certificate), including museum studies; business foundations (Graduate Certificate); chemical and biomedical engineering (Graduate Certificate), including materials science and engineering, water, health and sustainability; child and family studies (Graduate Certificate), including positive behavior support; civil and industrial engineering (Graduate Certificate), including transportation systems analysis; community and family health (Graduate Certificate), including maternal and child health,

social marketing and public health, violence and injury: prevention and intervention, women's health; criminology (Graduate Certificate), including criminal justice administration; data science for public administration (Graduate Certificate); digital humanities (Graduate Certificate); educational measurement and research (Graduate Certificate), including evaluation; English (Graduate Certificate), including comparative literary studies, creative writing, professional and technical communication; entrepreneurship (Graduate Certificate); environmental health (Graduate Certificate), including safety management; epidemiology and biostatistics (Graduate Certificate), including applied biostatistics, biostatistics, concepts and tools of epidemiology, epidemiology, epidemiology of infectious diseases; geography, environment and planning (Graduate Certificate), including community development, environmental policy and management, geographical information systems; geology (Graduate Certificate), including hydrogeology; global health (Graduate Certificate), including disaster management, global health and Latin American and Caribbean studies, global health practice, humanitarian assistance, infection control; government and international affairs (Graduate Certificate), including Cuban studies, globalization studies; health policy and management (Graduate Certificate), including health management and leadership, public health policy and programs; hearing specialist: early intervention (Graduate Certificate); industrial and management systems engineering (Graduate Certificate), including systems engineering, technology management; information studies (Graduate Certificate), including school library media specialist; information systems/decision sciences (Graduate Certificate), including analytics and business intelligence; instructional technology (Graduate Certificate), including distance education, Florida digital/virtual educator, instructional design, multimedia design, Web design; internal medicine, bioethics and medical humanities (Graduate Certificate), including biomedical ethics; Latin American and Caribbean studies (Graduate Certificate); leadership for coastal resiliency planning (Graduate Certificate); mass communications (Graduate Certificate), including multimedia journalism; mathematics and statistics (Graduate Certificate), including mathematics; medicine (Graduate Certificate), including aging and neuroscience, bioinformatics, biotechnology, brain fitness and memory management, clinical investigation, hand and upper limb rehabilitation, health informatics, health sciences, integrative weight management, intellectual property, medicine and gender, metabolic and nutritional medicine, metabolic cardiology, pharmacy sciences; national and competitive intelligence (Graduate Certificate); nursing (Graduate Certificate), including simulation based academic fellowship in advanced pain management; psychological and social foundations (Graduate Certificate), including career counseling, college teaching, diversity in education, mental health counseling, school counseling; public affairs (Graduate Certificate), including nonprofit management, public management, research administration; public health (Graduate Certificate), including assessing chemical toxicity and public health risks, health equity, pharmacoepidemiology, public health generalist, toxicology, translational research in adolescent behavioral health; public health practices (Graduate Certificate), including planning for healthy communities; rehabilitation and mental health counseling (Graduate Certificate), including integrative mental health care, marriage and family therapy, rehabilitation technology; secondary education (Graduate Certificate), including ESOL, foreign language education: culture and content, foreign language education: professional; social work (Graduate Certificate), including geriatric social work/clinical gerontology; special education (Graduate Certificate), including autism spectrum disorder, disabilities education: severe/profound; world languages (Graduate Certificate), including teaching English as a second language (TESL) or foreign language. *Unit head:* Dr. Cynthia DeLuca, Associate Vice President and Assistant Vice Provost, 813-974-3077, Fax: 813-974-7061, E-mail: deluca@usf.edu. *Application contact:* Owen Hooper, Director, Summer and Alternative Calendar Programs, 813-974-6917, E-mail: hooper@usf.edu.
Website: http://www.usf.edu/innovative-education/

The University of Tennessee, Graduate School, College of Education, Health and Human Sciences, Program in Public Health, Knoxville, TN 37996. Offers community health education (MPH); gerontology (MPH); health planning/administration (MPH); MS/MPH. *Accreditation:* CEPH. *Degree requirements:* For master's, thesis optional. *Entrance requirements:* For master's, minimum GPA of 2.7. Additional exam requirements/recommendations for international students: Required—TOEFL. Electronic applications accepted.

The University of Texas at El Paso, Graduate School, College of Health Sciences, Department of Public Health Sciences, El Paso, TX 79968-0001. Offers MPH, Graduate Certificate. *Accreditation:* CEPH. *Program availability:* Part-time, evening/weekend. *Degree requirements:* For master's, thesis optional. *Entrance requirements:* For master's, GRE, minimum GPA of 3.0, resume, letters of recommendation. Additional exam requirements/recommendations for international students: Required—TOEFL; Recommended—IELTS. *Application deadline:* For fall admission, 8/1 priority date for domestic students, 3/1 for international students; for spring admission, 11/1 priority date for domestic students, 9/1 for international students. Applications are processed on a rolling basis. Application fee: $45 ($80 for international students). Electronic applications accepted. *Financial support:* Fellowships with partial tuition reimbursements, research assistantships, teaching assistantships with partial tuition reimbursements, institutionally sponsored loans, scholarships/grants, health care benefits, tuition waivers (partial), and unspecified assistantships available. Support available to part-time students. Financial award application deadline: 3/15; financial award applicants required to submit FAFSA.
Website: http://www.utep.edu/chs/phs/

The University of Texas Health Science Center at Houston, School of Public Health, Houston, TX 77030. Offers behavioral science (PhD); biostatistics (MPH, MS, PhD); environmental health (MPH); epidemiology (MPH, MS, PhD); general public health (Certificate); genomics and bioinformatics (Certificate); health disparities (Certificate); health promotion/health education (MPH, Dr PH); healthcare management (Certificate); management, policy and community health (MPH, Dr PH, PhD); maternal and child health (Certificate); public health informatics (Certificate); DDS/MPH; JD/MPH; MBA/MPH; MD/MPH; MGPS/MPH; MP Aff/MPH; MS/MPH; MSN/MPH; MSW/MPH; PhD/MPH. Specific programs are offered at each of our six campuses in Texas (Austin, Brownsville, Dallas, El Paso, Houston, and San Antonio). *Accreditation:* CEPH. *Program availability:* Part-time. *Faculty:* 140 full-time (74 women), 23 part-time/adjunct (14 women). *Students:* 604 full-time (446 women), 534 part-time (384 women); includes 504 minority (106 Black or African American, non-Hispanic/Latino; 177 Asian, non-Hispanic/Latino; 88 Hispanic/Latino; 1 Native Hawaiian or other Pacific Islander, non-Hispanic/Latino; 132 Two or more races, non-Hispanic/Latino). Average age 31. 1,425 applicants, 58% accepted, 423 enrolled. In 2017, 315 master's, 68 doctorates awarded. *Degree requirements:* For master's, thesis (for some programs); for doctorate, comprehensive exam, thesis/dissertation. *Entrance requirements:* For master's and doctorate, GRE General Test. Additional exam requirements/recommendations for international students: Required—TOEFL (minimum score 600 paper-based, 100 iBT) or IELTS (7.5). *Application deadline:* For fall admission, 3/1 for domestic and international students; for spring admission, 10/1 for domestic and international students; for summer admission, 3/1 for domestic students. Applications are processed on a rolling basis. Application fee: $135. Electronic applications accepted. *Expenses:* $233 per semester credit hour resident tuition, $980 per semester credit hour non-resident tuition. *Financial support:* Fellowships, research assistantships, teaching assistantships, career-related internships or fieldwork, institutionally sponsored loans, scholarships/grants, traineeships, health care benefits, and unspecified assistantships available. Support available to part-time students. Financial award application deadline: 5/5; financial award applicants required to submit FAFSA. *Faculty research:* Chronic and infectious disease epidemiology; health promotion and health education; applied and theoretical biostatistics; healthcare management, policy and economics; environmental and occupational health. *Total annual research expenditures:* $47.8 million. *Unit head:* Dr. Susan Emery, Senior Associate Dean of Academic and Research Affairs. *Application contact:* Elvis Parada, Manager of Admissions and Recruitment, 713-500-9028, Fax: 713-500-9068, E-mail: elvis.a.parada@uth.tmc.edu.
Website: https://sph.uth.edu

The University of Texas Medical Branch, Graduate School of Biomedical Sciences, Program in Public Health, Galveston, TX 77555. Offers MPH. *Accreditation:* CEPH. *Degree requirements:* For master's, thesis. *Entrance requirements:* For master's, GRE, United States Medical Licensing Exam (USMLE) or NBE, preventive medicine residency. Additional exam requirements/recommendations for international students: Required—TOEFL (minimum score 550 paper-based). Electronic applications accepted.

University of the Sciences, Program in Public Health, Philadelphia, PA 19104-4495. Offers MPH. *Program availability:* Part-time, evening/weekend, online learning. *Entrance requirements:* Additional exam requirements/recommendations for international students: Required—TOEFL, TWE.

The University of Toledo, College of Graduate Studies, College of Health and Human Services, School of Population Health, Toledo, OH 43606-3390. Offers health education (PhD); occupational health-industrial hygiene (MS); public health (MPH).

The University of Toledo, College of Graduate Studies, College of Medicine and Life Sciences, Department of Public Health and Preventative Medicine, Toledo, OH 43606-3390. Offers biostatistics and epidemiology (Certificate); contemporary gerontological practice (Certificate); environmental and occupational health and safety (MPH); epidemiology (Certificate); global public health (Certificate); health promotion and education (MPH); industrial hygiene (MSOH); medical and health science teaching and learning (Certificate); occupational health (Certificate); public health administration (MPH); public health and emergency response (Certificate); public health epidemiology (MPH); public health nutrition (MPH); MD/MPH. *Program availability:* Part-time, evening/weekend. *Degree requirements:* For master's, thesis or alternative. *Entrance requirements:* For master's, GRE, minimum undergraduate GPA of 3.0, three letters of recommendation, statement of purpose, transcripts from all prior institutions attended, resume; for Certificate, minimum undergraduate GPA of 3.0, three letters of recommendation, statement of purpose, transcripts from all prior institutions attended, resume. Additional exam requirements/recommendations for international students: Required—TOEFL (minimum score 550 paper-based; 80 iBT), IELTS (minimum score 6.5). Electronic applications accepted.

University of Toronto, School of Graduate Studies, Department of Public Health Sciences, Toronto, ON M5S 1A1, Canada. Offers biostatistics (M Sc, PhD); community health (M Sc); community nutrition (MPH), including nutrition and dietetics; epidemiology (MPH, PhD); family and community medicine (MPH); occupational and environmental health (MPH); social and behavioral health science (PhD); social and behavioral health sciences (MPH), including health promotion. *Accreditation:* CAHME (one or more programs are accredited). *Program availability:* Part-time. *Degree requirements:* For master's, thesis (for some programs), practicum; for doctorate, comprehensive exam, thesis/dissertation, oral thesis defense. *Entrance requirements:* For master's, 2 letters of reference, relevant professional/research experience, minimum B average in final year; for doctorate, 2 letters of reference, relevant professional/research experience, minimum B+ average. Additional exam requirements/recommendations for international students: Required—TOEFL (minimum score 580 paper-based; 93 iBT), TWE (minimum score 5). Electronic applications accepted. *Expenses:* Contact institution.

University of Utah, School of Medicine and Graduate School, Graduate Programs in Medicine, Programs in Public Health, Salt Lake City, UT 84112-1107. Offers biostatistics (M Stat); public health (MPH, MSPH, PhD). *Accreditation:* CEPH (one or more programs are accredited). *Program availability:* Part-time. *Degree requirements:* For master's, comprehensive exam, thesis or project (MSPH); for doctorate, comprehensive exam, thesis/dissertation. *Entrance requirements:* For master's and doctorate, GRE General Test, 3 letters of reference, in-person interviews, minimum GPA of 3.0. Additional exam requirements/recommendations for international students: Required—TOEFL (minimum score 550 paper-based). Electronic applications accepted. *Faculty research:* Health services, health policy, epidemiology of chronic disease, infectious disease epidemiology, cancer epidemiology.

University of Vermont, The Robert Larner, MD College of Medicine and Graduate College, Graduate Programs in Medicine, Program in Public Health, Burlington, VT 05405. Offers epidemiology (Graduate Certificate); global and environmental health (Graduate Certificate); healthcare management and policy (Graduate Certificate); public health (MPH). *Program availability:* Online only, 100% online. *Students:* 96. 73 applicants, 88% accepted, 41 enrolled. In 2017, 6 master's, 6 other advanced degrees awarded. *Entrance requirements:* For master's and Graduate Certificate, resume/curriculum vitae. Additional exam requirements/recommendations for international students: Required—TOEFL (minimum iBT score of 90) or IELTS (6.5). *Application deadline:* For fall admission, 7/1 for domestic and international students; for spring admission, 11/15 for domestic and international students; for summer admission, 4/1 for domestic and international students. Application fee: $65. Electronic applications accepted. *Expenses:* $646 per credit in-state, $970 per credit out-of-state. *Unit head:* Dr. Jan Carney, Coordinator, 802-656-2085, E-mail: public.health@uvm.edu.
Website: https://learn.uvm.edu/program/master-of-public-health/

University of Virginia, School of Medicine, Department of Public Health Sciences, Program in Public Health, Charlottesville, VA 22903. Offers MPH, MPP/MPH. *Students:* 54 full-time (38 women), 10 part-time (8 women); includes 24 minority (9 Black or African American, non-Hispanic/Latino; 8 Asian, non-Hispanic/Latino; 5 Hispanic/Latino; 2 Two or more races, non-Hispanic/Latino), 5 international. Average age 25. 131 applicants, 78% accepted, 39 enrolled. In 2017, 47 master's awarded. *Degree requirements:* For master's, written or oral comprehensive exam or thesis. *Entrance requirements:* For master's, GRE, MCAT, LSAT or GMAT, 2 letters of recommendation. Additional exam requirements/recommendations for international students: Required—TOEFL. *Application deadline:* For fall admission, 3/30 for domestic and international students. Applications are processed on a rolling basis. Application fee: $60. Electronic applications accepted. *Financial support:* Applicants required to submit FAFSA. *Unit head:* Ruth Gaare Bernheim, Chair, 434-924-8430, Fax: 434-924-8437, E-mail: rg3r@virginia.edu. *Application contact:* Tracey C. Brookman, Academic Programs Administrator, 434-924-8430, Fax: 434-924-8437, E-mail: phsdegrees@virginia.edu.
Website: http://www.medicine.virginia.edu/clinical/departments/phs/degree_programs/mph

University of Virginia, School of Nursing, Charlottesville, VA 22903. Offers acute and specialty care (MSN); acute care nurse practitioner (MSN); clinical nurse leadership (MSN); community-public health leadership (MSN); nursing (DNP, PhD); psychiatric mental health counseling (MSN); MSN/MBA. *Accreditation:* AACN. *Program availability:*

Part-time. *Faculty:* 51 full-time (44 women), 17 part-time/adjunct (16 women). *Students:* 202 full-time (168 women), 139 part-time (114 women); includes 78 minority (32 Black or African American, non-Hispanic/Latino; 2 American Indian or Alaska Native, non-Hispanic/Latino; 14 Asian, non-Hispanic/Latino; 17 Hispanic/Latino; 1 Native Hawaiian or other Pacific Islander, non-Hispanic/Latino; 12 Two or more races, non-Hispanic/Latino), 9 international. Average age 34. 183 applicants, 68% accepted, 98 enrolled. In 2017, 105 master's, 27 doctorates awarded. *Degree requirements:* For doctorate, comprehensive exam (for some programs), capstone project (DNP), dissertation (PhD). *Entrance requirements:* For master's, GRE General Test, MAT; for doctorate, GRE General Test. Additional exam requirements/recommendations for international students: Required—TOEFL, IELTS. *Application deadline:* Applications are processed on a rolling basis. Application fee: $60. Electronic applications accepted. *Financial support:* Fellowships, research assistantships, teaching assistantships, Federal Work-Study, and scholarships/grants available. Financial award applicants required to submit FAFSA. *Unit head:* Dorrie K. Fontaine, Dean, 434-924-0141, Fax: 434-982-1809, E-mail: dkf2u@virginia.edu. *Application contact:* Teresa Carroll, Senior Assistant Dean for Academic and Student Services, 434-924-0141, Fax: 434-982-1809, E-mail: nur-osa@virginia.edu.
Website: http://www.nursing.virginia.edu/

University of Washington, Graduate School, School of Public Health, Executive MPH Program, Seattle, WA 98195. Offers MPH. *Program availability:* Evening/weekend, online learning. *Students:* 28 full-time (22 women), 28 part-time (19 women); includes 23 minority (6 Black or African American, non-Hispanic/Latino; 13 Asian, non-Hispanic/Latino; 3 Hispanic/Latino; 1 Native Hawaiian or other Pacific Islander, non-Hispanic/Latino), 1 international. Average age 36. 39 applicants, 90% accepted, 28 enrolled. *Entrance requirements:* Additional exam requirements/recommendations for international students: Required—TOEFL. Electronic applications accepted. *Expenses:* Contact institution. *Unit head:* Dr. Branko Kopjar, Director, 206-221-3349, E-mail: brankok@uw.edu. *Application contact:* Angela Cross, Student Services Coordinator, 206-685-7580, Fax: 206-543-3964, E-mail: uwemph@uw.edu.
Website: https://www.executivemph.uw.edu/

University of Waterloo, Graduate Studies, Faculty of Applied Health Sciences, School of Public Health and Health Systems, Waterloo, ON N2L 3G1, Canada. Offers health evaluation (MHE); health informatics (MHI); health studies and gerontology (M Sc, PhD); public health (MPH). *Program availability:* Part-time. *Degree requirements:* For master's, thesis; for doctorate, comprehensive exam, thesis/dissertation. *Entrance requirements:* For master's, honors degree, minimum B average, resume, writing sample; for doctorate, GRE (recommended), master's degree, minimum B average, resume, writing sample. Additional exam requirements/recommendations for international students: Required—TOEFL, IELTS, PTE. Electronic applications accepted. *Faculty research:* Population health, health promotion and disease prevention, healthy aging, health policy, planning and evaluation, health information management and health informatics, aging, health and well-being, work and health.

University of West Florida, Usha Kundu, MD College of Health, Department of Public Health, Pensacola, FL 32514-5750. Offers MPH. *Program availability:* Part-time, evening/weekend. *Entrance requirements:* For master's, GRE (minimum score: verbal 450, quantitative 550), GMAT (minimum score 465), or MCAT (minimum score 25), official transcripts; two personal writing samples (e.g., written reports completed by applicant or other representative samples of professional writing skills); basic computer competency; three letters of recommendation. Additional exam requirements/recommendations for international students: Required—TOEFL (minimum score 550 paper-based).

University of Wisconsin–La Crosse, College of Science and Health, Department of Health Education and Health Promotion, Program in Community Health Education, La Crosse, WI 54601-3742. Offers community health education (MS); public health (MPH). *Students:* 16 full-time (11 women), 9 part-time (7 women); includes 4 minority (2 Asian, non-Hispanic/Latino; 2 Two or more races, non-Hispanic/Latino). Average age 31. 15 applicants, 93% accepted, 10 enrolled. In 2017, 8 master's awarded. *Degree requirements:* For master's, thesis. *Entrance requirements:* For master's, GRE General Test, GRE Subject Test (for MPH), 3 letters of recommendation. Additional exam requirements/recommendations for international students: Required—TOEFL (minimum score 550 paper-based; 79 iBT). Electronic applications accepted. *Financial support:* Research assistantships with partial tuition reimbursements, Federal Work-Study, scholarships/grants, health care benefits, and tuition waivers (partial) available. Support available to part-time students. Financial award applicants required to submit FAFSA. *Unit head:* Dr. Gary Gilmore, Director, 608-785-8163, E-mail: gilmore.gary@uwlax.edu. *Application contact:* Brandon Schaller, Senior Graduate Student Status Examiner, 608-785-8941, E-mail: admissions@uwlax.edu.

University of Wisconsin–Madison, School of Medicine and Public Health, Master of Public Health Program, Madison, WI 53706-1380. Offers MPH. *Application contact:* 608-263-4889, E-mail: mph@mailplus.wisc.edu.
Website: http://mph.wisc.edu/

University of Wisconsin–Milwaukee, Graduate School, Joseph J. Zilber School of Public Health, Milwaukee, WI 53201-0413. Offers MPH, PhD, Graduate Certificate. *Accreditation:* CEPH. *Program availability:* Part-time. *Students:* 64 full-time (54 women), 24 part-time (18 women); includes 24 minority (5 Black or African American, non-Hispanic/Latino; 11 Asian, non-Hispanic/Latino; 8 Two or more races, non-Hispanic/Latino), 10 international. Average age 31. 66 applicants, 74% accepted, 34 enrolled. In 2017, 28 master's, 2 doctorates awarded. Electronic applications accepted. *Financial support:* Fellowships and scholarships/grants available. *Unit head:* Ronald Perez, Interim Dean, 414-229-4587, E-mail: perez@uwm.edu. *Application contact:* Advisor, 414-227-3001, Fax: 414-227-3002, E-mail: applyph@uwm.edu.
Website: http://uwm.edu/publichealth/

Utah State University, School of Graduate Studies, Emma Eccles Jones College of Education and Human Services, Department of Kinesiology and Health Science, Logan, UT 84322. Offers fitness promotion (MS); health and human movement (MS); pathokinesiology (PhD); physical and sport eductaion (M Ed); public health (MPH). *Program availability:* Part-time, evening/weekend, online learning. *Degree requirements:* For master's, thesis (for some programs). *Entrance requirements:* For master's, GRE General Test or MAT, minimum GPA of 3.0. Additional exam requirements/recommendations for international students: Required—TOEFL. *Faculty research:* Sport psychology intervention, motor learning biomechanics, pedagogy, physiology.

Valparaiso University, Graduate School and Continuing Education, College of Nursing and Health Professions, Valparaiso, IN 46383. Offers nursing (DNP); nursing education (MSN, Certificate); physician assistant (MSPA); public health (MPH); MSN/MHA. *Accreditation:* AACN. *Program availability:* Part-time, evening/weekend, online learning. *Entrance requirements:* For master's, minimum GPA of 3.0, undergraduate major in nursing, Indiana registered nursing license, undergraduate courses in research and statistics. Additional exam requirements/recommendations for international students: Required—TOEFL (minimum score 550 paper-based; 80 iBT), IELTS (minimum score 6). Electronic applications accepted. *Expenses:* Contact institution.

Vanderbilt University, Center for Medicine, Health, and Society, Nashville, TN 37240-1001. Offers MA. *Students:* Average age 23. 22 applicants, 77% accepted, 12 enrolled. In 2017, 10 master's awarded. *Degree requirements:* For master's, comprehensive exam (for some programs), thesis (for some programs). *Entrance requirements:* Additional exam requirements/recommendations for international students: Required—TOEFL (minimum score 570 paper-based; 88 iBT). *Application deadline:* For fall admission, 1/15 for domestic and international students. Electronic applications accepted. *Financial support:* Federal Work-Study, scholarships/grants, and health care benefits available. Financial award application deadline: 1/15; financial award applicants required to submit CSS PROFILE or FAFSA. *Faculty research:* Cultural history of health and disease, the rise of scientific medicine, scientific and medical constructions of gender and sexuality, integrative medicine, domestic and international public health, healthcare administration. *Unit head:* Dr. Jonathan Metzl, Director, 615-343-2504, Fax: 615-343-8889, E-mail: jonathan.metzl@vanderbilt.edu. *Application contact:* Dominique Behague, Acting Director/Director of Graduate Studies, 615-322-0919, Fax: 615-322-2731, E-mail: dominique.behague@vanderbilt.edu.
Website: http://www.vanderbilt.edu/mhs/

Virginia Polytechnic Institute and State University, Virginia-Maryland Regional College of Veterinary Medicine, Blacksburg, VA 24061. Offers biomedical and veterinary sciences (MS, PhD); public health (MPH); veterinary medicine (DVM). *Accreditation:* AVMA (one or more programs are accredited). *Faculty:* 100 full-time (49 women), 2 part-time/adjunct (both women). *Students:* 580 full-time (407 women), 40 part-time (31 women); includes 120 minority (21 Black or African American, non-Hispanic/Latino; 1 American Indian or Alaska Native, non-Hispanic/Latino; 33 Asian, non-Hispanic/Latino; 36 Hispanic/Latino; 29 Two or more races, non-Hispanic/Latino), 27 international. Average age 26. 66 applicants, 68% accepted, 36 enrolled. In 2017, 53 master's, 129 doctorates awarded. *Degree requirements:* For master's, comprehensive exam (for some programs), thesis (for some programs); for doctorate, comprehensive exam (for some programs), thesis/dissertation (for some programs). *Entrance requirements:* For master's and doctorate, GRE/GMAT. Additional exam requirements/recommendations for international students: Required—TOEFL (minimum score 80 iBT). *Application deadline:* For fall admission, 8/1 for domestic students, 4/1 for international students; for spring admission, 1/1 for domestic students, 9/1 for international students. Applications are processed on a rolling basis. Application fee: $75. Electronic applications accepted. *Expenses:* Contact institution. *Financial support:* In 2017–18, 4 fellowships with full and partial tuition reimbursements (averaging $30,618 per year), 16 research assistantships with full tuition reimbursements (averaging $24,872 per year), 18 teaching assistantships with full tuition reimbursements (averaging $26,904 per year) were awarded. Financial award application deadline: 3/1; financial award applicants required to submit FAFSA. *Total annual research expenditures:* $6.4 million. *Unit head:* Dr. Gregory B. Daniel, Interim Dean, 540-231-7910, Fax: 540-231-3505, E-mail: gdaniel@vt.edu. *Application contact:* Sheila Steele, Executive Assistant, 540-231-7910, Fax: 540-231-3505, E-mail: ssteele@vt.edu.
Website: http://www.vetmed.vt.edu

Walden University, Graduate Programs, School of Counseling, Minneapolis, MN 55401. Offers addiction counseling (MS), including addictions and public health, child and adolescent counseling, family studies and interventions, forensic counseling, general program, military families and culture, trauma and crisis counseling; clinical mental health counseling (MS), including addiction counseling, forensic counseling, military families and culture, trauma and crisis counseling; counselor education and supervision (PhD), including consultation, counseling and social change, forensic mental health counseling, leadership and program evaluation, trauma and crisis; marriage, couple, and family counseling (MS), including addiction counseling, career counseling, forensic counseling, military families and culture, trauma and crisis counseling; school counseling (MS), including addiction counseling, career counseling, crisis and trauma, military families and culture. *Accreditation:* ACA. *Program availability:* Part-time, evening/weekend, online only, 100% online. *Degree requirements:* For master's, residency, field experience, professional development plan, licensure plan; for doctorate, thesis/dissertation, residency, practicum, internship. *Entrance requirements:* For master's, bachelor's degree or higher; minimum GPA of 2.5; official transcripts; goal statement (for some programs); access to computer and Internet; for doctorate, master's degree or higher; three years of related professional or academic experience (preferred); minimum GPA of 3.0; goal statement and current resume (for select programs); official transcripts; access to computer and Internet. Additional exam requirements/recommendations for international students: Required—TOEFL (minimum score 550 paper-based, 79 iBT), IELTS (minimum score 6.5), Michigan English Language Assessment Battery (minimum score 82), or PTE (minimum score 53). Electronic applications accepted.

Walden University, Graduate Programs, School of Health Sciences, Minneapolis, MN 55401. Offers clinical research administration (MS, Graduate Certificate); health education and promotion (MS, PhD), including behavioral health (PhD), disease surveillance (PhD), emergency preparedness (MS), general (MHA, MS), global health (PhD), health policy (PhD), health policy and advocacy (MS), population health (PhD); health informatics (MS); health services (PhD), including community health, healthcare administration, leadership, public health policy, self-designed; healthcare administration (MHA, DHA), including general (MHA, MS); leadership and organizational development (MHA); public health (MPH, Dr PH, PhD, Graduate Certificate), including community health education (PhD), epidemiology (PhD); systems policy (MHA). *Program availability:* Part-time, evening/weekend, online only, 100% online. *Degree requirements:* For doctorate, thesis/dissertation, residency. *Entrance requirements:* For master's, bachelor's degree or higher; minimum GPA of 2.5; official transcripts; goal statement (for some programs); access to computer and Internet; for doctorate, master's degree or higher; three years of related professional or academic experience (preferred); minimum GPA of 3.0; goal statement and current resume (for select programs); official transcripts; access to computer and Internet; for Graduate Certificate, relevant work experience; access to computer and Internet. Additional exam requirements/recommendations for international students: Required—TOEFL (minimum score 550 paper-based, 79 iBT), IELTS (minimum score 6.5), Michigan English Language Assessment Battery (minimum score 82), or PTE (minimum score 53). Electronic applications accepted.

Walden University, Graduate Programs, School of Nursing, Minneapolis, MN 55401. Offers adult-gerontology acute care nurse practitioner (MSN); adult-gerontology nurse practitioner (MSN); education (MSN); family nurse practitioner (MSN); informatics (MSN); leadership and management (MSN); nursing (PhD, Post-Master's Certificate), including education (PhD), healthcare administration (PhD), interdisciplinary health (PhD), leadership (PhD), nursing education (Post-Master's Certificate), nursing informatics (Post-Master's Certificate), nursing leadership and management (Post-Master's Certificate), public health policy (PhD); nursing practice (DNP); psychiatric mental health (MSN). *Accreditation:* AACN. *Program availability:* Part-time, evening/weekend, online only, 100% online. *Degree requirements:* For doctorate, thesis/dissertation (for some programs), residency (for some programs), field experience (for some programs). *Entrance requirements:* For master's, bachelor's degree or equivalent in related field or RN; minimum GPA of 2.5; official transcripts; goal statement (for some programs); access to computer and Internet; for doctorate, master's degree or higher;

RN; three years of related professional or academic experience; goal statement; access to computer and Internet; for Post-Master's Certificate, relevant work experience; access to computer and Internet. Additional exam requirements/recommendations for international students: Required—TOEFL (minimum score 550 paper-based, 79 iBT), IELTS (minimum score 6.5), Michigan English Language Assessment Battery (minimum score 82), or PTE (minimum score 53). Electronic applications accepted.

Washington University in St. Louis, Brown School, St. Louis, MO 63110. Offers American Indian/Alaska native (MSW); children, youth and families (MSW); epidemiology/biostatistics (MPH); generalist (MPH); global health (MPH); health (MSW); health policy analysis (MPH); individualized (MSW), including health; mental health (MSW); older adults and aging societies (MSW); public health sciences (PhD); social and economic development (MSW), including domestic, international; social work (PhD); urban design (MPH); violence and injury prevention (MSW); JD/MSW; M Arch/MSW; MPH/MBA; MSW/M Div; MSW/M Ed; MSW/MAPS; MSW/MBA; MSW/MPH; MUD/MSW. MSW/M Div and MSW/MAPS offered in partnership with Eden Theological Seminary. *Accreditation:* CSWE (one or more programs are accredited). *Faculty:* 54 full-time (31 women), 87 part-time/adjunct (61 women). *Students:* 294 full-time (254 women); includes 114 minority (56 Black or African American, non-Hispanic/Latino; 8 American Indian or Alaska Native, non-Hispanic/Latino; 17 Asian, non-Hispanic/Latino; 10 Hispanic/Latino; 1 Native Hawaiian or other Pacific Islander, non-Hispanic/Latino; 22 Two or more races, non-Hispanic/Latino). Average age 26. *Degree requirements:* For master's, 60 credit hours (for MSW); 52 credit hours (for MPH); practicum; for doctorate, comprehensive exam, thesis/dissertation. *Entrance requirements:* For master's, GRE (preferred), GMAT, LSAT, MCAT, PCAT, or United States Medical Licensing Exam (for MPH); for doctorate, GRE. Additional exam requirements/recommendations for international students: Required—TOEFL (minimum score 100 iBT), IELTS (minimum score 7). *Application deadline:* For fall admission, 12/15 priority date for domestic and international students; for winter admission, 3/1 priority date for domestic and international students. Applications are processed on a rolling basis. Electronic applications accepted. *Expenses:* Contact institution. *Financial support:* In 2017–18, 30 fellowships, 60 research assistantships were awarded; career-related internships or fieldwork, Federal Work-Study, scholarships/grants, and unspecified assistantships also available. Support available to part-time students. Financial award applicants required to submit FAFSA. *Faculty research:* Mental health, social policy, health policy, epidemiology, social and economic development. *Total annual research expenditures:* $14.5 million. *Unit head:* Jamie L. Adkisson-Hennessey, Director of Admissions and Recruitment, 314-935-3524, Fax: 314-935-4859, E-mail: jadkisson@wustl.edu. *Application contact:* Office of Admissions and Recruitment, 314-935-6676, Fax: 314-935-4859, E-mail: brownadmissions@wustl.edu.
Website: http://brownschool.wustl.edu

Washington University in St. Louis, School of Medicine, Master of Population Health Sciences Program, St. Louis, MO 63110. Offers clinical epidemiology (MPHS); health services (MPHS); psychiatric and behavioral health sciences (MPHS); quantitative methods (MPHS). *Program availability:* Part-time. *Entrance requirements:* For master's, possess or currently be in pursuit of a clinical doctorate degree (including but not limited to: MD, PhD, PharmD, DPH, DO, DPT, DNP, OTD, etc.). Additional exam requirements/recommendations for international students: Required—TOEFL. *Faculty research:* Clinical epidemiology, population health, biostatistics, clinical outcomes research and comparative effectiveness research.

Wayne State University, School of Medicine, Office of Biomedical Graduate Programs, Detroit, MI 48202. Offers anatomy and cell biology (MS, PhD); basic medical sciences (MS); biochemistry and molecular biology (MS, PhD); cancer biology (MS, PhD); clinical and translational science (Graduate Certificate); family medicine and public health sciences (MPH, Graduate Certificate), including public health practice; genetic counseling (MS); immunology and microbiology (MS, PhD); medical physics (MS, PhD, Graduate Certificate); medical research (MS); molecular medicine and genomics (MS, PhD), including molecular genetics and genomics; pathology (PhD); pharmacology (MS, PhD); physiology (MS, PhD), including physiology, reproductive sciences (PhD); psychiatry and behavioral neurosciences (PhD), including translational neuroscience; MD/MPH; MD/PhD; MPH/MA; MSW/MPH. *Program availability:* Part-time, evening/weekend. *Students:* 268 full-time (152 women), 117 part-time (59 women); includes 108 minority (19 Black or African American, non-Hispanic/Latino; 1 American Indian or Alaska Native, non-Hispanic/Latino; 62 Asian, non-Hispanic/Latino; 9 Hispanic/Latino; 17 Two or more races, non-Hispanic/Latino), 48 international. Average age 26. 1,133 applicants, 21% accepted, 151 enrolled. In 2017, 70 master's, 25 doctorates, 10 other advanced degrees awarded. Terminal master's awarded for partial completion of doctoral program. *Degree requirements:* For master's, thesis (for some programs); for doctorate, thesis/dissertation. *Entrance requirements:* For master's, doctorate, and Graduate Certificate, GRE. Additional exam requirements/recommendations for international students: Required—TOEFL (minimum score 550 paper-based; 100 iBT), Michigan English Language Assessment Battery (minimum score 85); Recommended—IELTS (minimum score 6.5), TWE (minimum score 5.5). *Application deadline:* For fall admission, 2/1 for domestic and international students. Applications are processed on a rolling basis. Application fee: $50. Electronic applications accepted. *Expenses:* Contact institution. *Financial support:* In 2017–18, 177 students received support, including 64 fellowships with full tuition reimbursements available (averaging $24,388 per year), 79 research assistantships with full tuition reimbursements available (averaging $26,894 per year); scholarships/grants, traineeships, and health care benefits also available. *Faculty research:* Cancer biology, neurosciences, vision sciences, molecular biology, pathology, physiology, pharmacology, public health, medical physics. *Unit head:* Dr. Daniel A. Walz, Associate Dean for Biomedical Graduate Programs, 313-577-1455, Fax: 313-577-8796, E-mail: gradprogs@med.wayne.edu.
Website: https://www.med.wayne.edu/biomedical-graduate-programs/

West Chester University of Pennsylvania, College of Health Sciences, Department of Health, West Chester, PA 19383. Offers health care management (Certificate); integrative health (Certificate); public health (MPH). *Accreditation:* CEPH. *Program availability:* Part-time, evening/weekend, 100% online. *Students:* 99 full-time (78 women), 72 part-time (57 women); includes 78 minority (60 Black or African American, non-Hispanic/Latino; 11 Asian, non-Hispanic/Latino; 5 Hispanic/Latino; 2 Two or more races, non-Hispanic/Latino), 11 international. Average age 29. 108 applicants, 90% accepted, 63 enrolled. In 2017, 75 master's, 13 other advanced degrees awarded. *Degree requirements:* For master's, minimum GPA of 3.0, completion of major project and practicum (for MPH). *Entrance requirements:* For master's, undergraduate introduction to statistics course. Additional exam requirements/recommendations for international students: Required—TOEFL or IELTS. *Application deadline:* For fall admission, 5/15 for international students; for spring admission, 10/15 for international students. Applications are processed on a rolling basis. Application fee: $50. Electronic applications accepted. *Expenses:* Tuition, state resident: full-time $9000; part-time $500 per credit. Tuition, nonresident: full-time $13,500; part-time $750 per credit. *Required fees:* $2959; $149.79 per credit. *Financial support:* Scholarships/grants and unspecified assistantships available. Financial award application deadline: 2/15; financial award applicants required to submit FAFSA. *Faculty research:* Healthy communities, community health issues and evidence-based programs, environment and health, current issues in health care management and integrative health. *Unit head:* Dr. James W. Brenner, Chair, 610-436-2931, E-mail: jbrenner@wcupa.edu. *Application contact:* Dr. Lynn Carson, Graduate Coordinator, 610-436-2138, E-mail: lcarson@wcupa.edu.
Website: http://www.wcupa.edu/HealthSciences/health/

Western Illinois University, School of Graduate Studies, College of Education and Human Services, Department of Health Sciences and Social Work, Macomb, IL 61455-1390. Offers health sciences (MS), including public health, school health. *Accreditation:* NCATE. *Program availability:* Part-time. *Degree requirements:* For master's, comprehensive exam, thesis or alternative. *Entrance requirements:* Additional exam requirements/recommendations for international students: Required—TOEFL (minimum score 550 paper-based; 80 iBT). *Application deadline:* Applications are processed on a rolling basis. Application fee: $30. Electronic applications accepted. *Financial support:* Unspecified assistantships available. Financial award applicants required to submit FAFSA. *Unit head:* Dr. Lorette Oden, Chairperson, 309-298-1076. *Application contact:* Dr. Nancy Parsons, Associate Provost and Director of Graduate Studies, 309-298-1806, Fax: 309-298-2345, E-mail: grad-office@wiu.edu.
Website: http://www.wiu.edu/coehs/health_sciences/

Western Kentucky University, Graduate Studies, College of Health and Human Services, Department of Public Health, Bowling Green, KY 42101. Offers healthcare administration (MHA); public health (MPH). *Program availability:* Part-time, evening/weekend. *Degree requirements:* For master's, comprehensive exam, thesis or alternative. *Entrance requirements:* For master's, GRE General Test, minimum GPA of 2.75. Additional exam requirements/recommendations for international students: Required—TOEFL (minimum score 555 paper-based; 79 iBT). *Faculty research:* Health education training, driver traffic safety, community readiness, occupational injuries, local health departments.

Westminster College, School of Nursing and Health Sciences, Salt Lake City, UT 84105-3697. Offers family nurse practitioner (MSN); nurse anesthesia (MSNA); public health (MPH). *Accreditation:* AACN; AANA/CANAEP. *Faculty:* 9 full-time (5 women), 10 part-time/adjunct (5 women). *Students:* 130 full-time (81 women), 1 (woman) part-time; includes 18 minority (2 Black or African American, non-Hispanic/Latino; 1 American Indian or Alaska Native, non-Hispanic/Latino; 5 Asian, non-Hispanic/Latino; 4 Hispanic/Latino; 2 Native Hawaiian or other Pacific Islander, non-Hispanic/Latino; 4 Two or more races, non-Hispanic/Latino), 3 international. Average age 33. 149 applicants, 51% accepted, 62 enrolled. In 2017, 49 master's awarded. *Degree requirements:* For master's, clinical practicum, 504 clinical practice hours. *Entrance requirements:* For master's, GRE (can be waived in select cases), personal statement, resume, 3 professional recommendations, copy of unrestricted Utah license to practice professional nursing, background check, minimum cumulative GPA of 3.0, documentation of current immunizations, physical and mental health certificate signed by primary care provider. Additional exam requirements/recommendations for international students: Required—TOEFL (minimum score 84 iBT), IELTS (minimum score 7). Application fee: $50. Electronic applications accepted. *Expenses:* Contact institution. *Financial support:* In 2017–18, 7 students received support. Career-related internships or fieldwork, scholarships/grants, unspecified assistantships, and tuition remission available. Financial award applicants required to submit FAFSA. *Faculty research:* Intellectual empathy, professional boundaries, learned optimism, collaborative testing in nursing: student outcomes and perspectives, implementing new educational paradigms into pre-licensure nursing curricula. *Unit head:* Dr. Sheryl Steadman, Dean, 801-832-2164, Fax: 801-832-3110, E-mail: ssteadman@westminstercollege.edu. *Application contact:* Collin Bess, Enrollment Coordinator/Admissions Recruiter, 801-832-2207, Fax: 801-832-3101, E-mail: cbess@westminstercollege.edu.
Website: https://www.westminstercollege.edu/graduate/programs

West Virginia University, School of Public Health, Morgantown, WV 26506-9190. Offers biostatistics (MPH, MS, PhD); epidemiology (MPH, PhD); health policy (MPH); occupational and environmental health sciences (MPH, PhD); public health (MPH); school health education (MS); social and behavioral science (MPH, PhD). *Accreditation:* CEPH. *Program availability:* Part-time, online learning. *Students:* 69 full-time (48 women), 27 part-time (15 women); includes 14 minority (5 Black or African American, non-Hispanic/Latino; 4 Asian, non-Hispanic/Latino; 1 Hispanic/Latino; 4 Two or more races, non-Hispanic/Latino), 11 international. *Degree requirements:* For master's, practicum, project. *Entrance requirements:* For master's, GRE General Test, MCAT, medical degree, medical internship. Additional exam requirements/recommendations for international students: Required—TOEFL (minimum score 550 paper-based; 80 iBT). *Application deadline:* For fall admission, 4/15 priority date for domestic students; for spring admission, 12/1 for domestic students. Applications are processed on a rolling basis. Application fee: $60. *Expenses:* Contact institution. *Financial support:* Research assistantships, teaching assistantships, scholarships/grants, and health care benefits available. Financial award application deadline: 2/1; financial award applicants required to submit FAFSA. *Faculty research:* Occupational health, environmental health, clinical epidemiology, health care management, prevention. *Unit head:* Leah Adkins, Senior Program Coordinator, 304-293-1097, E-mail: leadkins@hsc.wvu.edu.
Website: http://publichealth.hsc.wvu.edu/

Wright State University, Boonshoft School of Medicine, Department of Population and Public Health Sciences, Dayton, OH 45435. Offers health promotion and education (MPH).

Yale University, Yale School of Medicine, Yale School of Public Health, New Haven, CT 06520. Offers applied biostatistics and epidemiology (APMPH); biostatistics (MPH, MS, PhD), including global health (MPH); chronic disease epidemiology (MPH, PhD), including global health (MPH); environmental health sciences (MPH, PhD), including global health (MPH); epidemiology of microbial diseases (MPH, PhD), including global health (MPH); global health (APMPH); health management (MPH), including global health; health policy (MPH), including global health; health policy and administration (APMPH, PhD); occupational and environmental medicine (APMPH); preventive medicine (APMPH); social and behavioral sciences (APMPH, MPH), including global health (MPH); JD/MPH; M Div/MPH; MBA/MPH; MD/MPH; MEM/MPH; MFS/MPH; MM Sc/MPH; MPH/MA; MSN/MPH. MS and PhD offered through the Graduate School. *Accreditation:* CEPH. *Program availability:* Part-time. Terminal master's awarded for partial completion of doctoral program. *Degree requirements:* For master's, thesis, summer internship; for doctorate, comprehensive exam, thesis/dissertation, residency. *Entrance requirements:* For master's, GMAT, GRE, or MCAT, two years of undergraduate coursework in math and science; for doctorate, GRE General Test. Additional exam requirements/recommendations for international students: Required—TOEFL (minimum score 100 iBT). Electronic applications accepted. *Expenses:* Contact institution. *Faculty research:* Genetic and emerging infections epidemiology, virology, cost/quality, vector biology, quantitative methods, aging, asthma, cancer.

Community Health

Adelphi University, Ruth S. Ammon School of Education, Program in Health Studies, Garden City, NY 11530-0701. Offers community health education (MA, Certificate); school health education (MA). *Program availability:* Part-time, evening/weekend. *Students:* 10 full-time (7 women), 17 part-time (9 women); includes 2 minority (1 Black or African American, non-Hispanic/Latino; 1 Hispanic/Latino), 1 international. Average age 30. 17 applicants, 65% accepted, 7 enrolled. In 2017, 9 master's awarded. *Degree requirements:* For master's, internship. *Entrance requirements:* For master's, 3 letters of recommendation, resume, minimum cumulative GPA of 2.75. Additional exam requirements/recommendations for international students: Required—TOEFL (minimum score 550 paper-based; 80 iBT), IELTS (minimum score 6.5). *Application deadline:* For fall admission, 4/1 for international students; for spring admission, 11/1 for international students. Applications are processed on a rolling basis. Application fee: $50. Electronic applications accepted. *Expenses:* Contact institution. *Financial support:* Research assistantships with partial tuition reimbursements, teaching assistantships, career-related internships or fieldwork, institutionally sponsored loans, scholarships/grants, traineeships, and unspecified assistantships available. Support available to part-time students. Financial award application deadline: 2/15; financial award applicants required to submit FAFSA. *Faculty research:* Alcohol abuse, tobacco cessation, drug abuse, healthy family lives, healthy personal living. *Unit head:* Dr. Ronald Feingold, Director, 516-877-4764, E-mail: feingold@adelphi.edu. *Application contact:* E-mail: graduateadmissions@adelphi.edu.

Adler University, Graduate Programs, Master of Public Policy Program, Chicago, IL 60602. Offers community health (MPP); human rights advocacy (MPP). *Program availability:* Part-time, evening/weekend.

American University of Beirut, Graduate Programs, Faculty of Health Sciences, 1107 2020, Lebanon. Offers environmental sciences (MS), including environmental health; epidemiology (MS, PhD); epidemiology and biostatistics (MPH); health care leadership (EMHCL); health management and policy (MPH), including health service administration; health promotion and community health (MPH); health research (MS); public health nutrition (MS). *Program availability:* Part-time. *Faculty:* 33 full-time (22 women), 5 part-time/adjunct (2 women). *Students:* 75 full-time (60 women), 78 part-time (67 women). Average age 27. 274 applicants, 56% accepted, 47 enrolled. In 2017, 63 master's awarded. *Degree requirements:* For master's, one foreign language, comprehensive exam (for some programs), thesis (for MS); for doctorate, one foreign language, comprehensive exam, thesis/dissertation. *Entrance requirements:* For master's, 2 letters of recommendations, personal statement, transcript; for doctorate, GRE, 3 letters of recommendations, personal statement, interview. Additional exam requirements/recommendations for international students: Required—TOEFL (minimum score 583 paper-based; 97 iBT), IELTS (minimum score 7). *Application deadline:* For fall admission, 4/4 for domestic and international students; for spring admission, 11/3 for domestic and international students. Application fee: $50. Electronic applications accepted. *Expenses:* Contact institution. *Financial support:* In 2017–18, 75 students received support. Scholarships/grants, health care benefits, and unspecified assistantships available. Financial award application deadline: 4/4. *Faculty research:* Reproductive and sexual health; occupational and environmental health; conflict and health; mental health; quality in health care delivery, tobacco control. *Total annual research expenditures:* $2 million. *Unit head:* Prof. Iman Adel Nuwayhid, Dean/Professor, 961-1-759683 Ext. 4600, Fax: 961-1-744470, E-mail: nuwayhid@aub.edu.lb. *Application contact:* Mitra Tauk, Administrative Coordinator, 961-1-350000 Ext. 4687, E-mail: mt12@aub.edu.lb.
Website: http://www.aub.edu.lb/fhs/fhs_home/Pages/index.aspx

Arizona State University at the Tempe campus, College of Nursing and Health Innovation, Phoenix, AZ 85004. Offers advanced nursing practice (DNP); clinical research management (MS); community and public health practice (Graduate Certificate); family mental health nurse practitioner (Graduate Certificate); family nurse practitioner (Graduate Certificate); geriatric nursing (Graduate Certificate); healthcare innovation (MHI); nurse education in academic and practice settings (Graduate Certificate); nurse educator (MS); nursing and healthcare innovation (PhD). *Accreditation:* AACN. *Program availability:* Online learning. *Degree requirements:* For master's, comprehensive exam (for some programs), thesis (for some programs), interactive Program of Study (iPOS) submitted before completing 50 percent of required credit hours; for doctorate, comprehensive exam, thesis/dissertation, interactive Program of Study (iPOS) submitted before completing 50 percent of required credit hours. *Entrance requirements:* For master's and doctorate, GRE, minimum GPA of 3.0 or equivalent in last 2 years of work leading to bachelor's degree. Additional exam requirements/recommendations for international students: Required—TOEFL, IELTS, or PTE. Electronic applications accepted. *Expenses:* Contact institution.

Baylor University, Graduate School, Robbins College of Health and Human Sciences, Department of Health, Human Performance and Recreation, Waco, TX 76798. Offers athletic training (MS); community health (MPH); exercise physiology (MS); kinesiology, exercise nutrition, and health promotion (PhD); sport pedagogy (MS). *Accreditation:* NCATE. *Program availability:* Part-time. *Faculty:* 24 full-time (11 women). *Students:* 86 full-time (52 women), 9 part-time (6 women); includes 24 minority (7 Black or African American, non-Hispanic/Latino; 3 Asian, non-Hispanic/Latino; 10 Hispanic/Latino; 1 Native Hawaiian or other Pacific Islander, non-Hispanic/Latino; 3 Two or more races, non-Hispanic/Latino), 8 international. 109 applicants, 59% accepted, 44 enrolled. In 2017, 30 master's, 3 doctorates awarded. *Degree requirements:* For master's, comprehensive exam, thesis optional; for doctorate, comprehensive exam, thesis/dissertation. *Entrance requirements:* For master's and doctorate, GRE General Test. Additional exam requirements/recommendations for international students: Required—TOEFL (minimum score 550 paper-based; 80 iBT). *Application deadline:* For fall admission, 2/1 priority date for domestic students, 2/1 for international students; for spring admission, 10/1 for domestic and international students. Applications are processed on a rolling basis. Application fee: $25. Electronic applications accepted. *Financial support:* In 2017–18, 60 students received support, including 1 research assistantship with full tuition reimbursement available (averaging $12,700 per year), 33 teaching assistantships with full tuition reimbursements available (averaging $7,650 per year); career-related internships or fieldwork, Federal Work-Study, institutionally sponsored loans, scholarships/grants, tuition waivers (full), and unspecified assistantships also available. Financial award application deadline: 2/1. *Faculty research:* Exercise testing, cardio-metabolic health, resistance exercise and training, nutritional intervention, population health, health promotion, global health epidemiology, coaching, natural resource management, stimulant misuse, diet, microbiome and colon cancer etiology. *Total annual research expenditures:* $250,118. *Unit head:* Dr. Jaeho Shim, Graduate Program Director, 254-710-4009, Fax: 254-710-3527, E-mail: joe_shim@baylor.edu. *Application contact:* Deepa Morris, Graduate Program Coordinator, 254-710-3526, Fax: 254-710-3527, E-mail: deepa_morris@baylor.edu.
Website: http://www.baylor.edu/HHPR/

Bloomsburg University of Pennsylvania, School of Graduate Studies, College of Science and Technology, Department of Nursing, Bloomsburg, PA 17815-1301. Offers adult and family nurse practitioner (MSN); community health (MSN); nurse anesthesia (MSN); nursing (MSN, DNP); nursing administration (MSN). *Accreditation:* AACN. *Degree requirements:* For master's, thesis (for some programs), clinical experience. *Entrance requirements:* For master's, minimum QPA of 3.0, personal statement, 2 letters of recommendation, nursing license. Additional exam requirements/recommendations for international students: Required—TOEFL, IELTS. Electronic applications accepted. *Expenses:* Contact institution.

Boston University, School of Public Health, Community Health Sciences Department, Boston, MA 02215. Offers MPH, Dr PH. *Program availability:* Part-time, evening/weekend. *Degree requirements:* For doctorate, thesis/dissertation. *Entrance requirements:* For master's, GRE, MCAT, GMAT; for doctorate, GRE, GMAT. Additional exam requirements/recommendations for international students: Required—TOEFL (minimum score 600 paper-based; 100 iBT), IELTS (minimum score 7). Electronic applications accepted. *Faculty research:* Sexual and reproductive health, substance use, mental health, community health, maternal and child health.

Brooklyn College of the City University of New York, School of Natural and Behavioral Sciences, Department of Health and Nutrition Sciences, Program in Community Health, Brooklyn, NY 11210-2889. Offers community health education (MA); thanatology (MA). *Accreditation:* CEPH. *Degree requirements:* For master's, thesis or alternative. *Entrance requirements:* For master's, 2 letters of recommendation, essay. Additional exam requirements/recommendations for international students: Required—TOEFL. Electronic applications accepted. *Faculty research:* Diet restriction, religious practices in bereavement, diabetes, stress management, palliative care.

Brown University, Graduate School, Division of Biology and Medicine, School of Public Health, Providence, RI 02912. Offers behavioral and social sciences intervention (M Sc); biostatistics (AM, Sc M, PhD); epidemiology (Sc M); health services, policy and practice (PhD); public health (MPH); MD/PhD. *Degree requirements:* For doctorate, thesis/dissertation, preliminary exam. *Entrance requirements:* For master's and doctorate, GRE General Test. Additional exam requirements/recommendations for international students: Required—TOEFL.

Canisius College, Graduate Division, School of Education and Human Services, Office of Professional Studies, Buffalo, NY 14208-1098. Offers applied nutrition (MS, Certificate); community and school health (MS); health and human performance (MS); health information technology (MS); respiratory care (MS). *Program availability:* Part-time, evening/weekend, 100% online, blended/hybrid learning. *Faculty:* 2 full-time (0 women), 8 part-time/adjunct (6 women). *Students:* 21 full-time (11 women), 40 part-time (34 women); includes 9 minority (7 Black or African American, non-Hispanic/Latino; 1 Hispanic/Latino; 1 Two or more races, non-Hispanic/Latino), 1 international. Average age 36. 18 applicants, 94% accepted, 17 enrolled. In 2017, 31 master's awarded. *Entrance requirements:* For master's, GRE (recommended), bachelor's degree transcript, two letters of recommendation, current licensure (for applied nutrition), minimum GPA of 2.7, current resume. Additional exam requirements/recommendations for international students: Required—TOEFL (minimum score 550 paper-based, 79 iBT), IELTS (minimum score 6.5), or CAEL (minimum score 70). *Application deadline:* Applications are processed on a rolling basis. Application fee: $0. Electronic applications accepted. *Expenses: Tuition:* Full-time $22,860; part-time $820 per credit. *Required fees:* $720; $25 per credit. $65 per semester. One-time fee: $425. *Financial support:* Career-related internships or fieldwork, Federal Work-Study, scholarships/grants, tuition waivers (partial), and unspecified assistantships available. Support available to part-time students. Financial award application deadline: 4/30; financial award applicants required to submit FAFSA. *Faculty research:* Nutrition, community and school health; community and health; health and human performance applied; nutrition and respiratory care. *Unit head:* Dennis W. Koch, Director, Office of Professional Studies, 716-888-8292, E-mail: koch5@canisius.edu.
Website: http://www.canisius.edu/graduate/

Clark University, Graduate School, Department of International Development, Community, and Environment, Program in Community and Global Health, Worcester, MA 01610-1477. Offers MHS. *Students:* 16 full-time (10 women); includes 3 minority (1 Black or African American, non-Hispanic/Latino; 1 Hispanic/Latino; 1 Two or more races, non-Hispanic/Latino), 8 international. Average age 32. 33 applicants, 52% accepted, 16 enrolled. *Degree requirements:* For master's, project; capstone, practicum, or internship. *Entrance requirements:* Additional exam requirements/recommendations for international students: Required—TOEFL (minimum score 90 iBT), IELTS (minimum score 6.5). *Application deadline:* For fall admission, 4/15 for domestic and international students. Application fee: $75. Electronic applications accepted. *Expenses:* $5,685 tuition per unit, $490 fees. *Financial support:* Fellowships, research assistantships, teaching assistantships, institutionally sponsored loans, and health care benefits available. *Unit head:* Dr. Ed Carr, 508-421-3895, Fax: 508-793-8820, E-mail: edcarr@clarku.edu. *Application contact:* Erika Paradis, Student and Academic Services Director, 508-793-7201, Fax: 508-793-8820, E-mail: eparadis@clarku.edu.
Website: http://www.clarku.edu/master-health-science-community-global-health

The College at Brockport, State University of New York, School of Education, Health, and Human Services, Department of Public Health and Health Education, Brockport, NY 14420-2997. Offers community health education (MS Ed); health education (MS Ed), including health education K-12. *Faculty:* 2 full-time (0 women), 3 part-time/adjunct (2 women). *Students:* 5 full-time (3 women), 26 part-time (11 women); includes 2 minority (1 Black or African American, non-Hispanic/Latino; 1 Hispanic/Latino). 11 applicants, 82% accepted, 7 enrolled. In 2017, 7 master's awarded. *Degree requirements:* For master's, thesis or alternative. *Entrance requirements:* For master's, minimum GPA of 3.0, letters of recommendation. Additional exam requirements/recommendations for international students: Required—TOEFL (minimum score 550 paper-based; 79 iBT), IELTS (minimum score 6.5). *Application deadline:* For fall admission, 3/1 priority date for domestic and international students; for spring admission, 10/1 priority date for domestic and international students; for summer admission, 3/1 priority date for domestic and international students. Application fee: $80. Electronic applications accepted. *Expenses:* Tuition, state resident: full-time $10,870; part-time $453 per credit hour. Tuition, nonresident: full-time $22,210. *Required fees:* $988; $246 per semester. *Financial support:* In 2017–18, 1 teaching assistantship with full tuition reimbursement (averaging $6,000 per year) was awarded; Federal Work-Study, scholarships/grants, and unspecified assistantships also available. Support available to part-time students. Financial award application deadline: 3/15; financial award applicants required to submit FAFSA. *Faculty research:* Nutrition, substance use, HIV/AIDS, bioethics, worksite health. *Unit head:* Dr. Darson Rhodes, Graduate Director, 585-395-5901, Fax: 585-395-5246, E-mail: drhodes@brockport.edu. *Application contact:* Danielle A. Welch, Graduate Admissions Counselor, 585-395-5465, Fax: 585-395-2515.
Website: https://www.brockport.edu/academics/public_health/

Community Health

Columbia University, Columbia University Mailman School of Public Health, Department of Sociomedical Sciences, New York, NY 10032. Offers MPH, MS, Dr PH, PhD. PhD offered in cooperation with the Graduate School of Arts and Sciences. *Accreditation:* CEPH (one or more programs are accredited). *Program availability:* Part-time. *Students:* 158 full-time (140 women), 52 part-time (41 women); includes 85 minority (25 Black or African American, non-Hispanic/Latino; 1 American Indian or Alaska Native, non-Hispanic/Latino; 30 Asian, non-Hispanic/Latino; 24 Hispanic/Latino; 5 Two or more races, non-Hispanic/Latino), 13 international. Average age 27. 549 applicants, 49% accepted, 89 enrolled. In 2017, 99 master's, 5 doctorates awarded. *Degree requirements:* For master's, thesis; for doctorate, thesis/dissertation. *Entrance requirements:* For master's, GRE General Test; for doctorate, GRE General Test, MPH or equivalent (for Dr PH). Additional exam requirements/recommendations for international students: Required—TOEFL (minimum score 600 paper-based; 100 iBT). *Application deadline:* For fall admission, 12/1 priority date for domestic and international students. Application fee: $120. Electronic applications accepted. *Expenses: Tuition:* Full-time $44,864; part-time $1704 per credit. *Required fees:* $2370 per semester. One-time fee: $105. *Financial support:* Research assistantships, teaching assistantships, career-related internships or fieldwork, and Federal Work-Study available. Support available to part-time students. Financial award application deadline: 2/1; financial award applicants required to submit FAFSA. *Faculty research:* Social and cultural factors in health and health care, health services delivery and utilization, health promotion and disease prevention, AIDS. *Unit head:* Dr. James Colgrove, Professor and Interim Chair. *Application contact:* Clare Norton, Associate Dean for Enrollment Management, 212-305-8698, Fax: 212-342-1861, E-mail: ph-admit@columbia.edu.
Website: https://www.mailman.columbia.edu/become-student/departments/sociomedical-sciences

Daemen College, Program in Public Health, Amherst, NY 14226-3592. Offers community health education (MPH); epidemiology (MPH); generalist (MPH). *Program availability:* Part-time, online learning. *Degree requirements:* For master's, practicum.

Dalhousie University, Faculty of Medicine, Department of Community Health and Epidemiology, Halifax, NS B3H 4R2, Canada. Offers M Sc. *Degree requirements:* For master's, thesis. *Entrance requirements:* Additional exam requirements/recommendations for international students: Required—1 of 5 approved tests: TOEFL, IELTS, CANTEST, CAEL, Michigan English Language Assessment Battery. Electronic applications accepted. *Expenses:* Contact institution. *Faculty research:* Population health, health promotion and disease prevention, health services utilization, chronic disease epidemiology.

Eastern Kentucky University, The Graduate School, College of Health Sciences, Program in Public Health, Richmond, KY 40475-3102. Offers community health education (MPH); environmental health science (MPH); industrial hygiene (MPH); public health nutrition (MPH). *Accreditation:* CEPH. *Degree requirements:* For master's, comprehensive exam, thesis optional, practicum, capstone course. *Entrance requirements:* For master's, GRE. *Faculty research:* Water quality, food safety, occupational health, air quality.

East Tennessee State University, School of Graduate Studies, College of Public Health, Program in Public Health, Johnson City, TN 37614. Offers biostatistics (MPH, Postbaccalaureate Certificate); community health (MPH, DPH); environmental health (MPH); epidemiology (MPH, DPH, Postbaccalaureate Certificate); gerontology (Postbaccalaureate Certificate); global health (Postbaccalaureate Certificate); health care management (Postbaccalaureate Certificate); health management and policy (DPH); public health (Postbaccalaureate Certificate); public health services administration (MPH); rural health (Postbaccalaureate Certificate). *Accreditation:* CEPH. *Program availability:* Part-time, online learning. *Degree requirements:* For master's, comprehensive exam, field experience; for doctorate, thesis/dissertation, practicum. *Entrance requirements:* For master's, GRE General Test, minimum GPA of 2.75, SOPHAS application, three letters of recommendation; for doctorate, GRE General Test, SOPHAS application, three letters of recommendation; for Postbaccalaureate Certificate, minimum GPA of 2.5, three letters of recommendation, resume. Additional exam requirements/recommendations for international students: Required—TOEFL (minimum score 550 paper-based; 79 iBT), IELTS (minimum score 6.5). *Application deadline:* For fall admission, 3/1 for domestic and international students. Application fee: $35 ($45 for international students). Electronic applications accepted. *Financial support:* Research assistantships with tuition reimbursements, teaching assistantships with full tuition reimbursements, career-related internships or fieldwork, institutionally sponsored loans, scholarships/grants, and unspecified assistantships available. Financial award application deadline: 7/1; financial award applicants required to submit FAFSA. *Unit head:* Dr. Randy Wykoff, Dean, 423-439-4243, Fax: 423-439-5238, E-mail: wykoff@etsu.edu. *Application contact:* Dr. Randy Wykoff, Dean, 423-439-4243, Fax: 423-439-5238, E-mail: wykoff@etsu.edu.
Website: http://www.etsu.edu/cph/

George Mason University, College of Health and Human Services, Department of Global and Community Health, Fairfax, VA 22030. Offers global and community health (Certificate); global health (MS); public health (MPH, Certificate), including epidemiology (MPH), leadership and management (Certificate). *Accreditation:* CEPH. *Program availability:* Part-time, evening/weekend. *Faculty:* 18 full-time (13 women), 16 part-time/adjunct (13 women). *Students:* 70 full-time (63 women), 61 part-time (53 women); includes 62 minority (21 Black or African American, non-Hispanic/Latino; 21 Asian, non-Hispanic/Latino; 14 Hispanic/Latino; 1 Native Hawaiian or other Pacific Islander, non-Hispanic/Latino; 5 Two or more races, non-Hispanic/Latino), 8 international. Average age 29. 246 applicants, 71% accepted, 60 enrolled. In 2017, 46 master's, 2 other advanced degrees awarded. *Degree requirements:* For master's, thesis, 200-hour practicum. *Entrance requirements:* For master's, GRE, GMAT (depending on program), 2 official transcripts; expanded goals statement; 3 letters of recommendation; resume; 1 completed course in health science, statistics, natural sciences and social science (for MPH); 6 credits of foreign language if not fluent (for MS); minimum undergraduate GPA of 3.0; for Certificate, 2 official transcripts; expanded goals statement; 3 letters of recommendation; resume; bachelor's degree from regionally-accredited institution with minimum GPA of 3.0. Additional exam requirements/recommendations for international students: Required—TOEFL (minimum score 570 paper-based; 88 iBT), IELTS (minimum score 6.5), PTE (minimum score 59). *Application deadline:* For fall admission, 3/1 for domestic and international students. Application fee: $75 ($80 for international students). Electronic applications accepted. *Expenses:* Contact institution. *Financial support:* In 2017–18, 15 students received support, including 12 research assistantships with tuition reimbursements available (averaging $16,616 per year), 3 teaching assistantships with tuition reimbursements available (averaging $6,966 per year); career-related internships or fieldwork, Federal Work-Study, scholarships/grants, unspecified assistantships, and health care benefits (for full-time research or teaching assistantship recipients) also available. Financial award application deadline: 3/1; financial award applicants required to submit FAFSA. *Faculty research:* Environmental and infectious disease epidemiology; global health; health risk behaviors; social determinants of health; stress, well-being and chronic disease. *Total annual research expenditures:* $69,343. *Unit head:* Robert Weiler, Chair, 703-993-1920, E-mail: rweiler@gmu.edu. *Application contact:* Allan Weiss, Department Manager, 703-993-3126, E-mail: aweiss2@gmu.edu.
Website: http://chhs.gmu.edu/gch/index

The George Washington University, Milken Institute School of Public Health, Department of Prevention and Community Health, Washington, DC 20052. Offers MPH, Dr PH. *Students:* 28 full-time (18 women), 20 part-time (15 women); includes 11 minority (3 Black or African American, non-Hispanic/Latino; 4 Asian, non-Hispanic/Latino; 1 Hispanic/Latino; 3 Two or more races, non-Hispanic/Latino). Average age 27. 105 applicants, 70% accepted, 25 enrolled. In 2017, 28 master's awarded. *Expenses: Tuition:* Full-time $28,800; part-time $1655 per credit hour. *Required fees:* $45; $2.75 per credit hour. *Unit head:* Dr. Lynn Goldman, Dean, 202-994-5179, E-mail: goldmanl@gwu.edu. *Application contact:* Director of Admissions, 202-994-2160, Fax: 202-994-1860, E-mail: sphhsinfo@gwumc.edu.

Georgia Southern University, Jack N. Averitt College of Graduate Studies, Jiann-Ping Hsu College of Public Health, Program in Public Health, Statesboro, GA 30460. Offers biostatistics (MPH, Dr PH); community health behavior and education (Dr PH); community health education (MPH); environmental health sciences (MPH); epidemiology (MPH); health policy and management (MPH, Dr PH). *Program availability:* Part-time. *Faculty:* 11 full-time (5 women). *Students:* 146 full-time (90 women), 70 part-time (57 women); includes 112 minority (95 Black or African American, non-Hispanic/Latino; 9 Asian, non-Hispanic/Latino; 5 Hispanic/Latino; 3 Two or more races, non-Hispanic/Latino), 47 international. Average age 32. 190 applicants, 78% accepted, 89 enrolled. In 2017, 34 master's, 13 doctorates awarded. *Degree requirements:* For master's, thesis optional, practicum; for doctorate, comprehensive exam, thesis/dissertation, preceptorship. *Entrance requirements:* For master's, GRE General Test, minimum GPA of 2.75, 3 letters of recommendation, statement of purpose, resume or curriculum vitae; for doctorate, GRE, GMAT, MCAT, LSAT, minimum GPA of 3.0, 3 letters of recommendation, statement of purpose, resume or curriculum vitae. Additional exam requirements/recommendations for international students: Required—TOEFL (minimum score 537 paper-based; 75 iBT), IELTS (minimum score 6). *Application deadline:* For fall admission, 6/1 for domestic students, 5/1 for international students. Applications are processed on a rolling basis. Application fee: $135. Electronic applications accepted. *Expenses:* $3,949 in-state, $13,929 out-of-state (for MPH); $4,014 in-state, $14,159 out-of-state (for Dr PH). *Financial support:* In 2017–18, 106 students received support, including 1 research assistantship with full tuition reimbursement available (averaging $12,350 per year), 6 teaching assistantships with full tuition reimbursements available (averaging $12,350 per year); scholarships/grants, tuition waivers (full), and unspecified assistantships also available. Financial award application deadline: 4/15; financial award applicants required to submit FAFSA. *Faculty research:* Rural public health best practices, health disparity elimination, community initiatives to enhance public health, cost effectiveness analysis, epidemiology of rural public health, environmental health issues, health care system assessment, rural health care, health policy and healthcare financing, survival analysis, nonparametric statistics and resampling methods, micro-arrays and genomics, data imputation techniques and clinical trial methodology. *Total annual research expenditures:* $415,747. *Unit head:* Dr. Robert Greg Evans, Dean, 912-478-2674, E-mail: rgevans@georgiasouthern.edu. *Application contact:* Shamia Garrett, Coordinator, Office of Student Services, 912-478-2674, Fax: 912-478-5811, E-mail: jphcoph-gradadvisor@georgiasouthern.edu.
Website: http://jphcoph.georgiasouthern.edu/

Icahn School of Medicine at Mount Sinai, Graduate School of Biomedical Sciences, New York, NY 10029-6504. Offers biomedical sciences (MS, PhD); clinical research education (MS, PhD); community medicine (MPH); genetic counseling (MS); neurosciences (PhD); MD/PhD. Terminal master's awarded for partial completion of doctoral program. *Degree requirements:* For master's, thesis; for doctorate, comprehensive exam, thesis/dissertation. *Entrance requirements:* For master's, GRE General Test; for doctorate, GRE General Test, GRE Subject Test, 3 years of college pre-med course work. Additional exam requirements/recommendations for international students: Required—TOEFL. Electronic applications accepted. *Faculty research:* Cancer, genetics and genomics, immunology, neuroscience, developmental and stem cell biology, translational research.

Idaho State University, Office of Graduate Studies, Office of Medical and Oral Health, Department of Family Medicine, Pocatello, ID 83209-8357. Offers Post-Master's Certificate. *Degree requirements:* For Post-Master's Certificate, comprehensive exam, thesis optional, 3 year residency program. *Entrance requirements:* For degree, GRE General Test, MD or DO. Additional exam requirements/recommendations for international students: Required—TOEFL (minimum score 600 paper-based). Electronic applications accepted. *Faculty research:* Health disparities in primary care, cardiovascular risk reduction (particularly in dyslipidemia, diabetes, hypertension), health application of geographic information systems, mechanisms for increasing quality in primary care, collaborative care models for improving health.

Independence University, Program in Health Services, Salt Lake City, UT 84107. Offers community health (MSHS); wellness promotion (MSHS). *Program availability:* Part-time, evening/weekend, online learning. *Degree requirements:* For master's, fieldwork, internship, final project (wellness promotion). *Entrance requirements:* For master's, previous course work in psychology.

Indiana University Bloomington, School of Public Health, Department of Applied Health Science, Bloomington, IN 47405. Offers behavioral, social, and community health (MPH); family health (MPH); health behavior (PhD); nutrition science (MS); professional health education (MPH); public health administration (MPH); safety management (MS); school and college health education (MS). *Degree requirements:* For master's, thesis optional; for doctorate, comprehensive exam, thesis/dissertation. *Entrance requirements:* For master's, GRE (for MS in nutrition science), 3 recommendations; for doctorate, GRE, 3 recommendations. Additional exam requirements/recommendations for international students: Required—TOEFL (minimum score 550 paper-based; 80 iBT). Electronic applications accepted. *Faculty research:* Cancer education, HIV/AIDS and drug education, public health, parent-child interactions, safety education, obesity, public health policy, public health administration, school health, health education, human development, nutrition, human sexuality, chronic disease, early childhood health.

Indiana University–Purdue University Indianapolis, Richard M. Fairbanks School of Public Health, Indianapolis, IN 46202. Offers biostatistics (MS, PhD); environmental health (MPH); epidemiology (MPH, PhD); global health leadership (Dr PH); health administration (MHA); health policy (Graduate Certificate); health policy and management (MPH, PhD); health systems management (Graduate Certificate); product stewardship (MS); public health (Graduate Certificate); social and behavioral sciences (MPH). *Expenses:* Contact institution.

Johns Hopkins University, Bloomberg School of Public Health, Department of Health, Behavior and Society, Baltimore, MD 21218. Offers genetic counseling (Sc M); health education and health communication (MSPH); social and behavioral sciences (PhD); social factors in health (MHS). *Students:* 86 full-time (76 women), 5 part-time (4 women); includes 33 minority (8 Black or African American, non-Hispanic/Latino; 13 Asian, non-Hispanic/Latino; 7 Hispanic/Latino; 5 Two or more races, non-Hispanic/Latino), 13 international. Average age 28. 312 applicants, 29% accepted, 28 enrolled. In 2017, 27 master's, 10 doctorates awarded. *Degree requirements:* For master's, comprehensive exam (for some programs), thesis (for some programs); for doctorate, comprehensive exam, thesis/dissertation. *Entrance requirements:* For master's, GRE, curriculum vitae, 3 letters of

recommendation; for doctorate, GRE, transcripts, curriculum vitae, 3 recommendation letters. Additional exam requirements/recommendations for international students: Required—TOEFL (minimum score 100 iBT), IELTS (minimum score 7). *Application deadline:* Applications are processed on a rolling basis. Application fee: $135. Electronic applications accepted. *Financial support:* Fellowships with tuition reimbursements, research assistantships, teaching assistantships, career-related internships or fieldwork, Federal Work-Study, scholarships/grants, traineeships, health care benefits, unspecified assistantships, and stipends available. *Faculty research:* Social determinants of health and structural and community-level inventions to improve health, communication and health education, behavioral and social aspects of genetic counseling. *Unit head:* Margaret Ensminger, Interim Chair, 410-502-4076, Fax: 410-502-4080. *Application contact:* Shenay Johnson, Academic Program Administrator, 410-502-4415, E-mail: shejohns@jhu.edu.
Website: http://jhsph.edu/dept/hbs

Long Island University–LIU Brooklyn, School of Health Professions, Brooklyn, NY 11201-8423. Offers athletic training and sport sciences (MS); community health (MS Ed); exercise science (MS); forensic social work (Advanced Certificate); occupational therapy (MS); physical therapy (DPT); physician assistant (MS); public health (MPH); social work (MSW); speech-language pathology (MS). *Faculty:* 33 full-time (23 women), 82 part-time/adjunct (55 women). *Students:* 690 full-time (508 women), 86 part-time (74 women); includes 259 minority (120 Black or African American, non-Hispanic/Latino; 1 American Indian or Alaska Native, non-Hispanic/Latino; 52 Asian, non-Hispanic/Latino; 76 Hispanic/Latino; 10 Two or more races, non-Hispanic/Latino), 65 international. Average age 27. 1,241 applicants, 45% accepted, 255 enrolled. In 2017, 249 master's, 42 doctorates, 8 other advanced degrees awarded. *Degree requirements:* For master's, comprehensive exam (for some programs), thesis (for some programs); for doctorate, comprehensive exam (for some programs). *Entrance requirements:* For master's and doctorate, GRE. Additional exam requirements/recommendations for international students: Required—TOEFL (minimum score 550 paper-based; 79 iBT). *Application deadline:* Applications are processed on a rolling basis. Application fee: $50. Electronic applications accepted. *Expenses: Tuition:* Full-time $21,618; part-time $1201 per credit. *Required fees:* $1840; $920 per term. Tuition and fees vary according to course load. *Financial support:* In 2017–18, 187 students received support. Research assistantships, teaching assistantships, career-related internships or fieldwork, Federal Work-Study, scholarships/grants, and unspecified assistantships available. Support available to part-time students. Financial award application deadline: 2/15; financial award applicants required to submit FAFSA. *Faculty research:* Pediatric physical therapy, complementary and alternative medicine, global health and human rights, sport leadership and entrepreneurship, feminist sport psychology. *Unit head:* Dr. Barry S. Eckert, Dean, 718-780-6578, Fax: 718-780-4561, E-mail: barry.eckert@liu.edu. *Application contact:* Dr. Dominick Fortugno, Associate Dean, 718-488-1496, Fax: 718-780-4561, E-mail: dominick.fortugno@liu.edu.
Website: http://liu.edu/brooklyn/academics/school-of-health-professions

Louisiana State University Health Sciences Center, School of Public Health, New Orleans, LA 70112. Offers behavioral and community health sciences (MPH); biostatistics (MPH, MS, PhD); community health sciences (PhD); environmental and occupational health sciences (MPH); epidemiology (MPH, PhD); health policy and systems management (MPH). *Accreditation:* CEPH. *Program availability:* Part-time. *Faculty:* 51 full-time (23 women), 41 part-time/adjunct (12 women). *Students:* 98 full-time (77 women), 24 part-time (18 women); includes 55 minority (26 Black or African American, non-Hispanic/Latino; 1 American Indian or Alaska Native, non-Hispanic/Latino; 13 Asian, non-Hispanic/Latino; 13 Hispanic/Latino; 2 Two or more races, non-Hispanic/Latino), 16 international. Average age 24. 208 applicants, 67% accepted, 54 enrolled. *Degree requirements:* For doctorate, thesis/dissertation. *Entrance requirements:* For master's, GRE General Test. Additional exam requirements/recommendations for international students: Recommended—TOEFL (minimum score 550 paper-based; 79 iBT), IELTS. *Application deadline:* Applications are processed on a rolling basis. Application fee: $30. Electronic applications accepted. *Expenses:* Tuition, state resident: full-time $11,835; part-time $518 per hour. Tuition, nonresident: full-time $24,108; part-time $1079 per hour. *Required fees:* $1254; $55 per hour. *Unit head:* Dr. Dean Smith, Dean, 504-568-5700, E-mail: dgsmith@lsuhsc.edu. *Application contact:* Isabel Billiot, Director of Admissions and Student Affairs, 504-568-5773, E-mail: ibilli@lsuhsc.edu.
Website: http://publichealth.lsuhsc.edu/

McGill University, Faculty of Graduate and Postdoctoral Studies, Faculty of Medicine, Department of Epidemiology and Biostatistics, Montréal, QC H3A 2T5, Canada. Offers community health (M Sc); environmental health (M Sc); epidemiology and biostatistics (M Sc, PhD, Diploma); health care evaluation (M Sc); medical statistics (M Sc).

Medical College of Wisconsin, Graduate School, Program in Public and Community Health, Milwaukee, WI 53226-0509. Offers PhD, MD/PhD. *Accreditation:* CEPH. *Degree requirements:* For doctorate, comprehensive exam, thesis/dissertation. *Entrance requirements:* For doctorate, GRE, official transcripts, three letters of recommendation. Additional exam requirements/recommendations for international students: Required—TOEFL (minimum score 580 paper-based; 100 iBT). *Application deadline:* For fall admission, 12/1 for domestic and international students. Application fee: $50. Electronic applications accepted. *Expenses:* Contact institution. *Financial support:* Fellowships with full tuition reimbursements, scholarships/grants, health care benefits, and tuition waivers (full) available. Financial award application deadline: 2/15. *Faculty research:* Community-academic partnerships, community-based participatory research, injury prevention, health policy, women's health, emergency medical services. *Unit head:* Dr. Laura D. Cassidy, Director, 414-955-4517, Fax: 414-955-6555, E-mail: phdpch@mcw.edu. *Application contact:* Recruitment Office, 414-955-4402, Fax: 414-955-6555, E-mail: gradschoolrecruit@mcw.edu.
Website: http://www.mcw.edu/Graduate-School/Programs/Public-Health/Public-and-Community-Health.htm

Memorial University of Newfoundland, Faculty of Medicine and School of Graduate Studies, Graduate Programs in Medicine, Division of Community Health and Humanities, St. John's, NL A1C 5S7, Canada. Offers community health (M Sc, PhD, Diploma). *Program availability:* Part-time. *Degree requirements:* For master's, thesis; for doctorate, comprehensive exam, thesis/dissertation, oral defense of thesis. *Entrance requirements:* For master's, MD or B Sc; for doctorate, MD or M Sc; for Diploma, bachelor's degree in health-related field. Additional exam requirements/recommendations for international students: Required—TOEFL. *Faculty research:* Health care delivery and administration, health services, psychosocial, aging.

Midwestern State University, Billie Doris McAda Graduate School, Robert D. and Carol Gunn College of Health Sciences and Human Services, Department of Criminal Justice and Health Services Administration, Wichita Falls, TX 76308. Offers criminal justice (MA); health information management (MHA); health services administration (Graduate Certificate); medical practice management (MHA); public and community sector health care management (MHA); rural and urban hospital management (MHA). *Program availability:* Part-time, evening/weekend. *Degree requirements:* For master's, comprehensive exam, thesis. *Entrance requirements:* For master's, GRE. Additional exam requirements/recommendations for international students: Required—TOEFL (minimum score 550 paper-based). Electronic applications accepted. *Faculty research:* Universal service policy, telehealth, bullying, healthcare financial management, public health ethics.

Minnesota State University Mankato, College of Graduate Studies and Research, College of Allied Health and Nursing, Department of Health Science, Mankato, MN 56001. Offers community health education (MS); public health education (Postbaccalaureate Certificate); school health education (MS, Postbaccalaureate Certificate). *Program availability:* Part-time. *Degree requirements:* For master's, comprehensive exam, thesis or alternative. *Entrance requirements:* For master's, minimum GPA of 3.0 during previous 2 years; for Postbaccalaureate Certificate, teaching license. Additional exam requirements/recommendations for international students: Required—TOEFL (minimum score 500 paper-based; 61 iBT). Electronic applications accepted.

Monroe College, King Graduate School, Bronx, NY 10468. Offers accounting (MS); business administration (MBA), including entrepreneurship, finance, general business administration, healthcare management, human resources, information technology, marketing; computer science (MS); criminal justice (MS); hospitality management (MS); public health (MPH), including biostatistics and epidemiology, community health, health administration and leadership. *Program availability:* Online learning. Application fee: $50.
Website: https://www.monroecollege.edu/Degrees/King-Graduate-School/

New Jersey City University, College of Professional Studies, Department of Health Sciences, Jersey City, NJ 07305-1597. Offers community health education (MS); health administration (MS); school health education (MS). *Program availability:* Part-time, evening/weekend. *Degree requirements:* For master's, thesis or alternative, internship. *Entrance requirements:* Additional exam requirements/recommendations for international students: Required—TOEFL (minimum score 79 iBT).

New York University, College of Global Public Health, New York, NY 10012. Offers biological basis of public health (PhD); community and international health (MPH); global health leadership (MPH); health systems and health services research (PhD); population and community health (PhD); public health nutrition (MPH); social and behavioral sciences (MPH); socio-behavioral health (PhD). *Accreditation:* CEPH. *Program availability:* Part-time, online learning. *Faculty:* 26 full-time (20 women), 104 part-time/adjunct (53 women). *Students:* 161 full-time (136 women), 70 part-time (54 women); includes 74 minority (24 Black or African American, non-Hispanic/Latino; 1 American Indian or Alaska Native, non-Hispanic/Latino; 27 Asian, non-Hispanic/Latino; 11 Hispanic/Latino; 4 Native Hawaiian or other Pacific Islander, non-Hispanic/Latino; 7 Two or more races, non-Hispanic/Latino), 39 international. Average age 29. 802 applicants, 70% accepted, 97 enrolled. In 2017, 1 master's awarded. *Degree requirements:* For master's, thesis (for some programs); for doctorate, thesis/dissertation. *Entrance requirements:* For master's and doctorate, GRE. Additional exam requirements/recommendations for international students: Required—TOEFL. *Application deadline:* For fall admission, 2/1 for domestic and international students. Applications are processed on a rolling basis. Electronic applications accepted. *Expenses:* Contact institution. *Financial support:* Federal Work-Study and scholarships/grants available. *Unit head:* Dr. Cheryl G. Healton, Director, 212-992-6741. *Application contact:* New York University Information, 212-998-1212.
Website: http://publichealth.nyu.edu/

★ **North Dakota State University,** College of Graduate and Interdisciplinary Studies, College of Health Professions, Department of Public Health, Fargo, ND 58102. Offers American Indian public health (MPH); community health sciences (MPH); management of infectious diseases (MPH); Pharm D/MPH. *Accreditation:* CEPH. *Program availability:* Online learning. *Expenses:* Tuition, state resident: full-time $4323; part-time $360.21 per credit. Tuition, nonresident: full-time $6484; part-time $540.31 per credit. *Required fees:* $668; $55.70 per credit. Part-time tuition and fees vary according to degree level, program and reciprocity agreements. *Unit head:* Stefanie Meyer, Program Coordinator, 701-231-6549, E-mail: stefanie.meyer@ndsu.edu. *Application contact:* Stefanie Meyer, Program Coordinator, 701-231-6549, E-mail: stefanie.meyer@ndsu.edu.
Website: http://www.ndsu.edu/publichealth/

See Display on page 781 and Close-Up on page 845.

Old Dominion University, College of Health Sciences, School of Community and Environmental Health, Norfolk, VA 23529. Offers general environmental health (MS); industrial hygiene (MS). *Faculty:* 5 full-time (2 women), 4 part-time/adjunct (2 women). *Students:* 9 full-time (7 women), 12 part-time (5 women); includes 9 minority (7 Black or African American, non-Hispanic/Latino; 1 Hispanic/Latino; 1 Two or more races, non-Hispanic/Latino), 1 international. Average age 28. 15 applicants, 67% accepted, 8 enrolled. In 2017, 9 master's awarded. *Degree requirements:* For master's, comprehensive exam, oral exam, written exam, practicum or thesis. *Entrance requirements:* For master's, GRE General Test, minimum GPA of 2.75. Additional exam requirements/recommendations for international students: Required—TOEFL (minimum score 650 paper-based). *Application deadline:* For fall admission, 8/1 priority date for domestic students, 7/1 priority date for international students; for winter admission, 11/1 priority date for domestic students, 10/1 priority date for international students; for spring admission, 4/1 priority date for domestic students, 3/1 priority date for international students. Applications are processed on a rolling basis. Application fee: $50. Electronic applications accepted. *Expenses:* Contact institution. *Financial support:* In 2017–18, 4 students received support, including 4 teaching assistantships with partial tuition reimbursements available (averaging $10,000 per year); scholarships/grants and tuition waivers (partial) also available. Financial award application deadline: 6/30; financial award applicants required to submit FAFSA. *Faculty research:* Toxicology, occupational health, environmental hazards. *Total annual research expenditures:* $150,133. *Unit head:* Dr. Anna Jeng, Graduate Program Director, 757-683-4594, Fax: 757-683-4410, E-mail: hjeng@odu.edu. *Application contact:* William Heffelfinger, Director of Graduate Admissions, 757-683-5554, Fax: 757-683-3255, E-mail: gradadmit@odu.edu.
Website: http://www.odu.edu/commhealth

Old Dominion University, College of Health Sciences, School of Dental Hygiene, Norfolk, VA 23529. Offers dental hygiene (MS), including community/public health, education, generalist, global health, marketing, modeling and simulation, research. *Program availability:* Part-time, evening/weekend, blended/hybrid learning. *Faculty:* 10 full-time (9 women). *Students:* 3 full-time (1 woman), 22 part-time (21 women); includes 5 minority (3 Black or African American, non-Hispanic/Latino; 1 Asian, non-Hispanic/Latino; 1 Hispanic/Latino), 3 international. Average age 38. 12 applicants, 25% accepted, 2 enrolled. In 2017, 8 master's awarded. *Degree requirements:* For master's, comprehensive exam, thesis optional, writing proficiency exam, responsible conduct of research training. *Entrance requirements:* For master's, Dental Hygiene National Board Examination or copy of license to practice dental hygiene, BS or certificate in dental hygiene or related area, minimum GPA of 2.8 (3.0 in major), 4 letters of recommendation. Additional exam requirements/recommendations for international students: Required—TOEFL (minimum score 550 paper-based, 79 iBT) or IELTS (minimum score 6.5). *Application deadline:* For fall admission, 7/1 for domestic students, 4/15 for international students; for spring admission, 12/1 for domestic students, 10/1 for international students; for summer admission, 3/1 for domestic students, 2/1 for international students. Applications are processed on a rolling basis. Application fee: $50. Electronic applications accepted. *Expenses:* Contact institution. *Financial support:*

In 2017–18, 4 students received support, including 4 teaching assistantships with partial tuition reimbursements available (averaging $13,000 per year); scholarships/grants and health care benefits also available. Support available to part-time students. Financial award application deadline: 2/15; financial award applicants required to submit CSS PROFILE or FAFSA. *Faculty research:* Clinical dental hygiene, dental hygiene client health behaviors, dental hygiene education interventions, oral product testing, cold plasma. *Total annual research expenditures:* $43,581. *Unit head:* Dr. Denise M. Claiborne, Assistant Professor/Graduate Program Director, 757-683-5949, Fax: 757-683-5239, E-mail: dclaibor@odu.edu. *Application contact:* William Heffelfinger, Director of Graduate Admissions, 757-683-5554, Fax: 757-683-3255, E-mail: gradadmit@odu.edu.
Website: http://www.odu.edu/academics/programs/masters/dental-hygiene

Quinnipiac University, School of Nursing, Care of Populations Track, Hamden, CT 06518-1940. Offers DNP. *Program availability:* Part-time-only, evening/weekend, online only. *Faculty:* 17 full-time (16 women), 10 part-time/adjunct (6 women). *Students:* 38 part-time (36 women); includes 14 minority (10 Black or African American, non-Hispanic/Latino; 1 American Indian or Alaska Native, non-Hispanic/Latino; 1 Asian, non-Hispanic/Latino; 1 Hispanic/Latino; 1 Two or more races, non-Hispanic/Latino). 24 applicants, 100% accepted, 19 enrolled. In 2017, 9 doctorates awarded. *Entrance requirements:* For doctorate, minimum GPA of 3.0; RN or NCLEX-eligible nurse with bachelor's degree in nursing or another field; master's degree in relevant field; minimum of 1000 hours of field work observation. Additional exam requirements/recommendations for international students: Required—TOEFL (minimum score 575 paper-based; 90 iBT), IELTS (minimum score 6.5). *Application deadline:* Applications are processed on a rolling basis. Application fee: $45. Electronic applications accepted. *Expenses:* Contact institution. *Financial support:* Scholarships/grants and unspecified assistantships available. Financial award application deadline: 6/1; financial award applicants required to submit FAFSA. *Application contact:* Quinnipiac University Online Admissions Office, 203-582-3918, E-mail: quonlineadmissions@qu.edu.
Website: https://quonline.quinnipiac.edu/online-programs/online-doctorate-programs/doctor-of-nursing-practice/care-of-populations-track.php

Saint Louis University, Graduate Programs, College for Public Health and Social Justice and Graduate Programs, Department of Community Health, St. Louis, MO 63103. Offers MPH, MS, MSPH. *Program availability:* Part-time, online learning. *Degree requirements:* For master's, comprehensive exam. *Entrance requirements:* For master's, GRE General Test, LSAT, GMAT or MCAT, letters of recommendation, resume. Additional exam requirements/recommendations for international students: Required—TOEFL (minimum score 525 paper-based). Electronic applications accepted. *Faculty research:* Obesity prevention, health disparities, health policy, child health.

San Francisco State University, Division of Graduate Studies, College of Health and Social Sciences, Department of Health Education, San Francisco, CA 94132-1722. Offers community health education (MPH). *Accreditation:* CEPH. *Program availability:* Part-time. *Students:* Average age 36. *Application deadline:* Applications are processed on a rolling basis. *Unit head:* Dr. Mary Beth Love, Chair, 415-338-1413, Fax: 415-338-0570, E-mail: love@sfsu.edu. *Application contact:* Vincent Lam, Graduate Coordinator, 415-338-1413, Fax: 415-338-0570, E-mail: vlam@sfsu.edu.
Website: http://healthed.sfsu.edu/graduate

Southern Illinois University Carbondale, Graduate School, College of Education and Human Services, Department of Health Education and Recreation, Program in Community Health Education, Carbondale, IL 62901-4701. Offers MPH, MD/MPH, PhD/MPH. *Accreditation:* CEPH. *Entrance requirements:* Additional exam requirements/recommendations for international students: Required—TOEFL (minimum score 550 paper-based; 80 iBT).

State University of New York College at Cortland, Graduate Studies, School of Professional Studies, Department of Health, Cortland, NY 13045. Offers community health (MS); health education (MST). *Accreditation:* NCATE. *Program availability:* Part-time, evening/weekend. *Entrance requirements:* Additional exam requirements/recommendations for international students: Required—TOEFL.

State University of New York College at Potsdam, School of Education and Professional Studies, Program in Community Health, Potsdam, NY 13676. Offers MS. *Entrance requirements:* For master's, baccalaureate degree from accredited institution, minimum GPA of 3.0 for final 60 credits of baccalaureate work, statement of professional and educational goals, three letters of recommendation, resume or curriculum vitae. *Application deadline:* For fall admission, 2/1 priority date for domestic students. Applications are processed on a rolling basis. *Expenses:* Tuition, state resident: full-time $11,090; part-time $462 per credit hour. Tuition, nonresident: full-time $22,650; part-time $944 per credit hour. *Required fees:* $58 per credit hour. $684 per semester. *Unit head:* Janelle Jacobson, Coordinator, 315-267-3136, E-mail: jacobsjj@potsdam.edu. *Application contact:* Graduate Admissions Counselor, 315-267-2165, Fax: 315-267-2544, E-mail: graduate@potsdam.edu.
Website: http://www.potsdam.edu/academics/SOEPS/CommunityHealth/msincommunityhealth

State University of New York Downstate Medical Center, College of Medicine, Program in Public Health, Brooklyn, NY 11203-2098. Offers urban and immigrant health (MPH); MD/MPH. *Program availability:* Part-time. *Degree requirements:* For master's, practicum. *Entrance requirements:* For master's, GRE, MCAT or OAT, 2 letters of recommendation, minimum undergraduate GPA of 3.0. Additional exam requirements/recommendations for international students: Required—TOEFL (minimum score 550 paper-based).

Stony Brook University, State University of New York, Stony Brook Medicine, School of Medicine, Program in Population Health and Clinical Outcomes Research, Stony Brook, NY 11794. Offers PhD. *Students:* 3 full-time (all women), 1 (woman) part-time, 2 international. 25 applicants, 28% accepted, 4 enrolled. *Degree requirements:* For doctorate, thesis/dissertation. *Entrance requirements:* For doctorate, GRE (verbal, quantitative, and analytical), personal or telephone interview, minimum GPA of 3.0 in undergraduate work. Additional exam requirements/recommendations for international students: Required—TOEFL (minimum score 600 paper-based; 90 iBT). *Application deadline:* For fall admission, 1/15 for domestic students, 3/15 for international students. Electronic applications accepted. *Expenses:* Contact institution. *Unit head:* Dr. Norman H. Edelman, Director, 631-444-3484, E-mail: norman.edelman@stonybrookmedicine.edu. *Application contact:* Joanie Maniaci, Assistant Director for Student Affairs, 631-632-2074, Fax: 631-444-6035, E-mail: joanmarie.maniaci@stonybrook.edu.
Website: https://publichealth.stonybrookmedicine.edu/phcor

Stony Brook University, State University of New York, Stony Brook Medicine, School of Medicine, Program in Public Health, Stony Brook, NY 11794. Offers community health (MPH); evaluation sciences (MPH); family violence (MPH); health communication (Certificate); health economics (MPH); health education and promotion (Certificate); population health (MPH); substance abuse (MPH). *Accreditation:* CEPH. *Program availability:* Part-time, evening/weekend. *Students:* 32 full-time (24 women), 11 part-time (10 women); includes 18 minority (4 Black or African American, non-Hispanic/Latino; 10 Asian, non-Hispanic/Latino; 4 Hispanic/Latino), 2 international. Average age 29. 128 applicants, 71% accepted, 29 enrolled. In 2017, 25 master's, 1 other advanced degree awarded. *Entrance requirements:* For master's, GRE, 3 references, bachelor's degree from accredited college or university with minimum GPA of 3.0, essays, interview. Additional exam requirements/recommendations for international students: Required—TOEFL (minimum score 90 iBT). *Application deadline:* For fall admission, 7/15 for domestic students, 3/15 for international students. Application fee: $100. Electronic applications accepted. *Expenses:* Contact institution. *Financial support:* Fellowships available. *Faculty research:* Abnormal psychology, academic achievement, broadcast media, communications, communications systems, public health. *Total annual research expenditures:* $422,408. *Unit head:* Dr. Lisa A. Benz Scott, Director, 631-444-8811, E-mail: lisa.benzscott@stonybrook.edu. *Application contact:* Joanie Maniaci, Assistant Director for Student Affairs, 631-444-2074, Fax: 631-444-6035, E-mail: joanmarie.maniaci@stonybrook.edu.
Website: http://publichealth.stonybrookmedicine.edu/

Suffolk University, Sawyer Business School, Department of Public Administration, Boston, MA 02108-2770. Offers community health (MPA); information systems, performance management, and big data analytics (MPA); nonprofit management (MPA); state and local government (MPA); JD/MPA; MPA/MS; MPA/MSCJ; MPA/MSMHC; MPA/MSPS. *Accreditation:* NASPAA (one or more programs are accredited). *Program availability:* Part-time, evening/weekend. *Faculty:* 6 full-time (3 women), 8 part-time/adjunct (6 women). *Students:* 25 full-time (12 women), 90 part-time (56 women); includes 43 minority (20 Black or African American, non-Hispanic/Latino; 7 Asian, non-Hispanic/Latino; 14 Hispanic/Latino; 2 Two or more races, non-Hispanic/Latino), 2 international. Average age 34. 134 applicants, 38% accepted, 5 enrolled. In 2017, 44 master's awarded. *Entrance requirements:* Additional exam requirements/recommendations for international students: Required—TOEFL (minimum score 550 paper-based; 80 iBT). *Application deadline:* For fall admission, 3/15 priority date for domestic and international students; for spring admission, 10/15 priority date for domestic and international students. Applications are processed on a rolling basis. Application fee: $50. Electronic applications accepted. *Expenses:* $35,130 per year full-time tuition; $1,171 per credit part-time. *Financial support:* In 2017–18, 76 students received support, including 2 fellowships (averaging $4,650 per year); career-related internships or fieldwork, Federal Work-Study, institutionally sponsored loans, and scholarships/grants also available. Support available to part-time students. Financial award application deadline: 4/1; financial award applicants required to submit FAFSA. *Faculty research:* Local government, health care, federal policy, mental health, HIV/AIDS. *Unit head:* Brenda Bond, Director/Department Chair, 617-305-1768, E-mail: bbond@suffolk.edu. *Application contact:* Mara Marzocchi, Associate Director of Graduate Admissions, 617-573-8302, Fax: 617-305-1733, E-mail: grad.admission@suffolk.edu.
Website: http://www.suffolk.edu/mpa

Suffolk University, Sawyer Business School, Program in Healthcare Administration, Boston, MA 02108-2770. Offers community health (MPA); health (MBAH); healthcare administration (MHA). *Program availability:* Part-time, evening/weekend. *Faculty:* 5 full-time (1 woman), 6 part-time/adjunct (3 women). *Students:* 32 full-time (24 women), 40 part-time (30 women); includes 23 minority (16 Black or African American, non-Hispanic/Latino; 2 Asian, non-Hispanic/Latino; 5 Hispanic/Latino), 7 international. Average age 30. 47 applicants, 77% accepted, 18 enrolled. In 2017, 32 master's awarded. *Entrance requirements:* Additional exam requirements/recommendations for international students: Required—TOEFL (minimum score 550 paper-based; 80 iBT). *Application deadline:* For fall admission, 3/15 priority date for domestic and international students; for spring admission, 10/15 priority date for domestic and international students. Applications are processed on a rolling basis. Application fee: $50. Electronic applications accepted. *Expenses:* $35,130 per year full-time tuition; $1,171 per credit part-time. *Financial support:* In 2017–18, 46 students received support, including 1 fellowship (averaging $6,200 per year); career-related internships or fieldwork, Federal Work-Study, institutionally sponsored loans, scholarships/grants, and health care benefits also available. Support available to part-time students. Financial award application deadline: 4/1; financial award applicants required to submit FAFSA. *Faculty research:* Mental health, federal policy, health care. *Unit head:* Richard Gregg, Director of Programs in Healthcare Administration/Chair of Healthcare Department, 617-994-4246, E-mail: rgregg@suffolk.edu. *Application contact:* Mara Marzocchi, Associate Director of Graduate Admissions, 617-573-8302, Fax: 617-305-1733, E-mail: grad.admission@suffolk.edu.
Website: http://www.suffolk.edu/business/graduate/62398.php

Teachers College, Columbia University, Department of Health and Behavior Studies, New York, NY 10027-6696. Offers applied behavior analysis (MA, PhD); applied educational psychology: school psychology (Ed M, PhD); behavioral nutrition (PhD), including nutrition (Ed D, PhD); community health education (MS); community nutrition education (Ed M), including community nutrition education; education of deaf and hard of hearing (MA, PhD); health education (MA, Ed D); hearing impairment (Ed D); intellectual disability/autism (MA, Ed D, PhD); nursing education (Ed D, Advanced Certificate); nutrition and education (MS); nutrition and exercise physiology (MS); nutrition and public health (MS); nutrition education (Ed D), including nutrition (Ed D, PhD); physical disabilities (Ed D); reading specialist (MA); severe or multiple disabilities (MA); special education (Ed M, MA, Ed D); teaching of sign language (MA). *Program availability:* Part-time, evening/weekend. *Students:* 245 full-time (226 women), 242 part-time (219 women); includes 167 minority (52 Black or African American, non-Hispanic/Latino; 2 American Indian or Alaska Native, non-Hispanic/Latino; 55 Asian, non-Hispanic/Latino; 48 Hispanic/Latino; 1 Native Hawaiian or other Pacific Islander, non-Hispanic/Latino; 9 Two or more races, non-Hispanic/Latino), 60 international. Average age 30. 480 applicants, 59% accepted, 157 enrolled. Terminal master's awarded for partial completion of doctoral program. *Unit head:* Prof. Dolores Perin, Chair, E-mail: dp111@tc.columbia.edu. *Application contact:* David Estrella, Director of Admission, 212-678-3305, E-mail: estrella@tc.columbia.edu.
Website: http://www.tc.columbia.edu/health-and-behavior-studies/

Texas A&M University, School of Public Health, College Station, TX 77845. Offers biostatistics (MPH, MSPH); environmental health (MPH, MSPH); epidemiology (MPH, MSPH); executive health administration (MHA); health administration (MHA); health policy and management (MPH, MSPH); health promotion and community health sciences (MPH); health services research (PhD); occupational safety and health (MPH). *Program availability:* Part-time, blended/hybrid learning. *Faculty:* 56. *Students:* 279 full-time (196 women), 86 part-time (56 women); includes 153 minority (48 Black or African American, non-Hispanic/Latino; 36 Asian, non-Hispanic/Latino; 62 Hispanic/Latino; 7 Two or more races, non-Hispanic/Latino), 77 international. Average age 29. 179 applicants, 96% accepted, 148 enrolled. In 2017, 124 master's, 8 doctorates awarded. *Entrance requirements:* For master's, GRE General Test, 3 letters of recommendation; statement of purpose; current curriculum vitae or resume; official transcripts; for doctorate, GRE General Test, 3 letters of recommendation; statement of purpose; current curriculum vitae or resume; official transcripts; interview (in some cases). Additional exam requirements/recommendations for international students: Required—TOEFL (minimum score 597 paper-based, 95 iBT) or GRE (minimum verbal score 153). Application fee: $120. Electronic applications accepted. *Expenses:* Contact institution. *Financial support:* In 2017–18, 203 students received support, including 62 research

assistantships with tuition reimbursements available (averaging $10,041 per year), 25 teaching assistantships with tuition reimbursements available (averaging $12,913 per year); career-related internships or fieldwork, institutionally sponsored loans, scholarships/grants, traineeships, health care benefits, tuition waivers (full and partial), and unspecified assistantships also available. Support available to part-time students. Financial award applicants required to submit FAFSA. *Unit head:* Dr. Jay Maddock, Dean, 979-436-9322, Fax: 979-458-1878, E-mail: maddock@tamhsc.edu. *Application contact:* Erin E. Schneider, Associate Director of Admissions and Recruitment, 979-436-9380, E-mail: eschneider@sph.tamhsc.edu.
Website: http://sph.tamhsc.edu/

Tulane University, School of Public Health and Tropical Medicine, Department of Global Community Health and Behavioral Sciences, New Orleans, LA 70118-5669. Offers community health sciences (MPH); global community health and behavioral sciences (Dr PH, PhD); JD/MPH; MD/MPH; MSW/MPH. *Program availability:* Part-time. *Degree requirements:* For doctorate, comprehensive exam, thesis/dissertation. *Entrance requirements:* For master's and doctorate, GRE General Test. Additional exam requirements/recommendations for international students: Required—TOEFL. Electronic applications accepted. *Expenses: Tuition:* Full-time $50,920; part-time $2829 per credit hour. *Required fees:* $2040; $44.50 per credit hour. $580 per term. Tuition and fees vary according to course load, degree level and program.

Universidad de Ciencias Medicas, Graduate Programs, San Jose, Costa Rica. Offers dermatology (SP); family health (MS); health service center administration (MHA); human anatomy (MS); medical and surgery (MD); occupational medicine (MS); pharmacy (Pharm D). *Program availability:* Part-time. *Degree requirements:* For master's, thesis; for doctorate and SP, comprehensive exam. *Entrance requirements:* For master's, MD or bachelor's degree; for doctorate, admissions test; for SP, admissions test, MD.

Université de Montréal, Faculty of Medicine, Program in Communal and Public Health, Montréal, QC H3C 3J7, Canada. Offers community health (M Sc, DESS); public health (PhD). *Accreditation:* CEPH. *Program availability:* Part-time. Terminal master's awarded for partial completion of doctoral program. *Degree requirements:* For master's, thesis; for doctorate, thesis/dissertation, general exam. *Entrance requirements:* For master's and doctorate, proficiency in French, knowledge of English; for DESS, proficiency in French. Electronic applications accepted. *Faculty research:* Epidemiology, health services utilization, health promotion and education, health behaviors, poverty and child health.

Université Laval, Faculty of Medicine, Graduate Programs in Medicine, Department of Social and Preventive Medicine, Program in Community Health, Québec, QC G1K 7P4, Canada. Offers M Sc, PhD. *Program availability:* Part-time. Terminal master's awarded for partial completion of doctoral program. *Degree requirements:* For master's, thesis (for some programs); for doctorate, comprehensive exam, thesis/dissertation. *Entrance requirements:* For master's, knowledge of French, comprehension of written English; for doctorate, French exam, comprehension of French, written comprehension of English. Electronic applications accepted.

Université Laval, Faculty of Medicine, Post-Professional Programs in Medical Studies, Québec, QC G1K 7P4, Canada. Offers anatomy–pathology (DESS); anesthesiology (DESS); cardiology (DESS); care of older people (Diploma); clinical research (DESS); community health (DESS); dermatology (DESS); diagnostic radiology (DESS); emergency medicine (Diploma); family medicine (DESS); general surgery (DESS); geriatrics (DESS); hematology (DESS); internal medicine (DESS); maternal and fetal medicine (Diploma); medical biochemistry (DESS); medical microbiology and infectious diseases (DESS); medical oncology (DESS); nephrology (DESS); neurology (DESS); neurosurgery (DESS); obstetrics and gynecology (DESS); ophthalmology (DESS); orthopedic surgery (DESS); oto-rhino-laryngology (DESS); palliative medicine (Diploma); pediatrics (DESS); plastic surgery (DESS); psychiatry (DESS); pulmonary medicine (DESS); radiology–oncology (DESS); thoracic surgery (DESS); urology (DESS). *Degree requirements:* For other advanced degree, comprehensive exam. *Entrance requirements:* For degree, knowledge of French. Electronic applications accepted.

University at Buffalo, the State University of New York, Graduate School, School of Architecture and Planning, Department of Urban and Regional Planning, Buffalo, NY 12414. Offers community health and food systems (MUP); economic development (MUP); environment/land use (MUP); historic preservation (MUP, Certificate); neighborhood/community development (MUP); real estate development (MSRED); urban and regional planning (PhD); urban design (MUP); JD/MUP; M Arch/MUP. *Accreditation:* ACSP. *Program availability:* Part-time. *Faculty:* 13 full-time (6 women), 12 part-time/adjunct (3 women). *Students:* 76 full-time (27 women), 20 part-time (9 women); includes 17 minority (9 Black or African American, non-Hispanic/Latino; 5 Hispanic/Latino; 3 Two or more races, non-Hispanic/Latino), 20 international. Average age 27. 196 applicants, 20% accepted, 32 enrolled. In 2017, 35 master's, 1 doctorate, 5 other advanced degrees awarded. *Degree requirements:* For master's, thesis or alternative, project; for doctorate, comprehensive exam, thesis/dissertation. *Entrance requirements:* For master's, resume, three letters of recommendation, personal statement, transcripts; for doctorate, GRE, transcripts, three letters of recommendation, resume, research statement, writing sample. Additional exam requirements/recommendations for international students: Required—TOEFL (minimum score 79 iBT), IELTS (minimum score 6.5). *Application deadline:* For fall admission, 3/1 priority date for domestic and international students; for spring admission, 10/31 priority date for domestic students, 10/1 priority date for international students. Applications are processed on a rolling basis. Application fee: $75. Electronic applications accepted. *Expenses:* $13,382. *Financial support:* In 2017–18, 45 students received support, including 3 fellowships with full tuition reimbursements available (averaging $15,600 per year), 2 research assistantships with partial tuition reimbursements available (averaging $13,390 per year), 15 teaching assistantships with partial tuition reimbursements available (averaging $4,800 per year); career-related internships or fieldwork, Federal Work-Study, institutionally sponsored loans, scholarships/grants, health care benefits, and unspecified assistantships also available. Financial award application deadline: 3/1; financial award applicants required to submit FAFSA. *Faculty research:* Economic and international development, environmental and land use planning, GIS and spatial analysis, urban design and physical planning, neighborhood planning and community development, historic preservation. *Total annual research expenditures:* $1.3 million. *Unit head:* Dr. Daniel B. Hess, Professor and Chair, 716-829-3671 Ext. 109, Fax: 716-829-3256, E-mail: dbhess@buffalo.edu. *Application contact:* Donna Rogalski, Department Secretary, 716-829-3671, Fax: 716-829-3256, E-mail: dmr1@buffalo.edu.
Website: http://www.ap.buffalo.edu/planning/

University at Buffalo, the State University of New York, Graduate School, School of Public Health and Health Professions, Department of Community Health and Health Behavior, Buffalo, NY 14260. Offers MPH, PhD. *Accreditation:* CEPH. *Program availability:* Part-time. *Faculty:* 9 full-time (5 women), 2 part-time/adjunct (1 woman). *Students:* 25 full-time (23 women), 7 part-time (5 women); includes 4 minority (all Black or African American, non-Hispanic/Latino). Average age 30. 57 applicants, 18% accepted, 10 enrolled. In 2017, 12 master's, 3 doctorates awarded. *Entrance requirements:* For master's and doctorate, GRE. Additional exam requirements/recommendations for international students: Required—TOEFL (minimum score 79 iBT). *Application deadline:* For fall admission, 1/15 priority date for domestic students, 2/1 priority date for international students. Applications are processed on a rolling basis. Application fee: $50. Electronic applications accepted. *Financial support:* In 2017–18, 6 students received support, including 2 fellowships with full tuition reimbursements available (averaging $4,000 per year), 2 research assistantships with full tuition reimbursements available (averaging $21,000 per year). Financial award application deadline: 3/15; financial award applicants required to submit FAFSA. *Total annual research expenditures:* $679,170. *Unit head:* Dr. Gary A. Giovino, Chair, 716-829-6952, E-mail: ggiovino@buffalo.edu. *Application contact:* Barbara L. Sen, Graduate Program Coordinator, 716-829-6956, Fax: 716-829-6040, E-mail: bsen@buffalo.edu.
Website: http://sphhp.buffalo.edu/community-health-and-health-behavior.html

The University of Alabama, Graduate School, College of Human Environmental Sciences, Program in Human Environmental Science, Tuscaloosa, AL 35487. Offers interactive technology (MS); quality management (MS); restaurant and meeting management (MS); rural community health (MS); sport management (MS). *Program availability:* Part-time, evening/weekend, online learning. *Students:* 90 full-time (44 women), 158 part-time (86 women); includes 60 minority (42 Black or African American, non-Hispanic/Latino; 1 American Indian or Alaska Native, non-Hispanic/Latino; 2 Asian, non-Hispanic/Latino; 7 Hispanic/Latino; 3 Native Hawaiian or other Pacific Islander, non-Hispanic/Latino; 5 Two or more races, non-Hispanic/Latino). Average age 34. 147 applicants, 84% accepted, 110 enrolled. In 2017, 108 master's awarded. *Degree requirements:* For master's, comprehensive exam. *Entrance requirements:* For master's, GRE (for some specializations), minimum GPA of 3.0. Additional exam requirements/recommendations for international students: Required—TOEFL. *Application deadline:* For fall admission, 7/1 for domestic students; for spring admission, 11/1 for domestic students; for summer admission, 4/15 for domestic students. Applications are processed on a rolling basis. Application fee: $50 ($60 for international students). Electronic applications accepted. *Financial support:* Teaching assistantships with full tuition reimbursements available. Financial award application deadline: 7/1. *Faculty research:* Rural health, hospitality management, sport management, interactive technology, consumer quality management, environmental health and safety. *Unit head:* Dr. Milla D. Boschung, Dean, 205-348-6250, Fax: 205-348-1786, E-mail: mboschun@ches.ua.edu. *Application contact:* Dr. Stuart Usdan, Associate Dean, 205-348-6150, Fax: 205-348-3789, E-mail: susdan@ches.ua.edu.
Website: http://www.ches.ua.edu/programs-of-study.html

The University of Alabama at Birmingham, School of Education, Community Health and Human Services Program, Birmingham, AL 35294. Offers MA Ed. *Accreditation:* NCATE. *Degree requirements:* For master's, comprehensive exam (for some programs), thesis optional. *Entrance requirements:* For master's, GRE General Test or MAT, minimum GPA of 3.0, references. Electronic applications accepted. *Faculty research:* College student health, minority health disparities/disease, health eating.

University of Alberta, School of Public Health, Department of Public Health Sciences, Edmonton, AB T6G 2E1, Canada. Offers clinical epidemiology (M Sc, MPH); environmental and occupational health (MPH); environmental health sciences (M Sc); epidemiology (M Sc); global health (M Sc, MPH); health policy and management (MPH); health policy research (M Sc); health technology assessment (MPH); occupational health (M Sc); population health (M Sc); public health leadership (MPH); public health sciences (PhD); quantitative methods (MPH). Terminal master's awarded for partial completion of doctoral program. *Degree requirements:* For master's, thesis (for some programs); for doctorate, thesis/dissertation. *Entrance requirements:* For master's, GMAT or GRE General Test. Additional exam requirements/recommendations for international students: Required—TOEFL (minimum score 550 paper-based) or IELTS (minimum score 6). Electronic applications accepted. *Faculty research:* Biostatistics, health promotion and socio-behavioral health science.

University of Arkansas, Graduate School, College of Education and Health Professions, Department of Health, Human Performance and Recreation, Program in Community Health Promotion, Fayetteville, AR 72701. Offers MS, PhD. In 2017, 2 master's, 3 doctorates awarded. *Application deadline:* For fall admission, 8/1 for domestic students, 4/1 for international students; for spring admission, 12/1 for domestic students, 10/1 for international students; for summer admission, 4/15 for domestic students, 3/1 for international students. Application fee: $60. *Expenses:* Tuition, state resident: full-time $3782. Tuition, nonresident: full-time $10,238. *Unit head:* Dr. Matthew Stueck Ganio, Department Head, 479-575-2956, Fax: 479-575-5778, E-mail: msganio@uark.edu. *Application contact:* Dr. Stephen Dittmore, Coordinator of Graduate Studies, 479-575-6625, E-mail: dittmore@uark.edu.
Website: https://hhpr.uark.edu

University of Calgary, Cumming School of Medicine and Faculty of Graduate Studies, Department of Community Health Sciences, Calgary, AB T2N 1N4, Canada. Offers M Sc, PhD. *Degree requirements:* For master's, thesis; for doctorate, thesis/dissertation, candidacy exam. *Entrance requirements:* For master's and doctorate, minimum GPA of 3.2. Additional exam requirements/recommendations for international students: Required—TOEFL (minimum score 600 paper-based). Electronic applications accepted. *Faculty research:* Epidemiology, health research, biostatistics, health economics, health policy.

University of California, Los Angeles, Graduate Division, School of Public Health, Department of Community Health Sciences, Los Angeles, CA 90095. Offers public health (MPH, MS, Dr PH, PhD); JD/MPH; MA/MPH; MD/MPH; MSW/MPH. *Accreditation:* CEPH. *Degree requirements:* For master's, comprehensive exam or thesis; for doctorate, thesis/dissertation, oral and written qualifying exams. *Entrance requirements:* For master's, GRE General Test, minimum GPA of 3.0; for doctorate, GRE General Test, minimum undergraduate GPA of 3.0. Electronic applications accepted.

University of Colorado Denver, College of Liberal Arts and Sciences, Program in Humanities, Denver, CO 80217. Offers community health (MSS); ethnic studies (MH, MSS); humanities (MH, Graduate Certificate); international studies (MSS); philosophy and theory (MH); social justice (MH, MSS); society and the environment (MSS); visual studies (MH); women's and gender studies (MH, MSS). *Program availability:* Part-time, evening/weekend. *Faculty:* 3 full-time (1 woman), 1 (woman) part-time/adjunct. *Students:* 9 full-time (6 women), 7 part-time (6 women); includes 2 minority (both Hispanic/Latino). Average age 38. 8 applicants, 63% accepted, 5 enrolled. In 2017, 9 master's awarded. *Degree requirements:* For master's, 36 credit hours, project or thesis. *Entrance requirements:* For master's, writing sample, statement of purpose/letter of intent, three letters of recommendation. Additional exam requirements/recommendations for international students: Required—TOEFL (minimum score 537 paper-based; 75 iBT); Recommended—IELTS (minimum score 6.5). *Application deadline:* For fall admission, 5/15 for domestic students, 5/15 priority date for international students; for spring admission, 10/15 for domestic students, 10/15 priority date for international students; for summer admission, 3/15 for domestic and international students. Application fee: $50 ($75 for international students). Electronic applications accepted. *Faculty research:* Women and gender in the classical Mediterranean, communication theory and democracy, relationship between psychology and philosophy. *Unit head:* Margaret Woodhull, Director of Humanities, 303-315-3568, E-mail: margaret.woodhull@ucdenver.edu. *Application contact:* Angela Beale, Program Assistant, 303-315-3565, E-mail: mastershs@ucdenver.edu.
Website: http://www.ucdenver.edu/academics/colleges/CLAS/Programs/HumanitiesSocialSciences/Programs/Pages/MasterofHumanities.aspx

Community Health

University of Colorado Denver, Colorado School of Public Health, Program in Public Health, Aurora, CO 80045. Offers community and behavioral health (MPH, Dr PH). *Program availability:* Part-time, evening/weekend. In 2017, 203 master's, 6 doctorates awarded. *Degree requirements:* For master's, thesis or alternative, 42 credit hours; for doctorate, comprehensive exam, thesis/dissertation, 67 credit hours. *Entrance requirements:* For master's, GRE, MCAT, DAT, LSAT, PCAT, GMAT or master's degree from accredited institution, baccalaureate degree or equivalent; minimum GPA of 3.0; transcripts; references; resume; essay; for doctorate, GRE, MCAT, DAT, LSAT, PCAT or GMAT, MPH or master's or higher degree in related field or equivalent; 2 years of previous work experience in public health; essay; resume. Additional exam requirements/recommendations for international students: Required—TOEFL (minimum score 550 paper-based; 80 iBT). Application fee: $0. *Faculty research:* Cancer prevention by nutrition, cancer survivorship outcomes, social and cultural factors related to health. *Unit head:* Dr. Lori Crane, Chair, 303-724-4385, E-mail: lori.crane@ucdenver.edu. *Application contact:* Dr. Lori Crane, Chair, 303-724-4385, E-mail: lori.crane@ucdenver.edu.
Website: http://www.ucdenver.edu/academics/colleges/PublicHealth/Academics/degreesandprograms/Pages/index.aspx

University of Colorado Denver, School of Medicine, Physician Assistant Program, Aurora, CO 80045. Offers child health associate (MPAS), including global health, leadership, education, advocacy, development, and scholarship, pediatric critical and acute care, rural health, urban/underserved populations. *Accreditation:* ARC-PA. *Students:* 130 full-time (108 women); includes 21 minority (4 Black or African American, non-Hispanic/Latino; 4 Asian, non-Hispanic/Latino; 8 Hispanic/Latino; 5 Two or more races, non-Hispanic/Latino). Average age 27. 57 applicants, 96% accepted, 44 enrolled. *Degree requirements:* For master's, comprehensive exam. *Entrance requirements:* For master's, GRE General Test, minimum GPA of 2.8; 3 letters of recommendation; prerequisite courses in chemistry, biology, general genetics, psychology and statistics; interview. Additional exam requirements/recommendations for international students: Required—TOEFL (minimum score 550 paper-based; 80 iBT). *Application deadline:* For fall admission, 9/1 for domestic students, 8/15 for international students. Application fee: $170. Electronic applications accepted. *Faculty research:* Clinical genetics and genetic counseling, evidence-based medicine, pediatric allergy and asthma, childhood diabetes, standardized patient assessment. *Unit head:* Jonathan Bowser, Program Director, 303-724-1349, E-mail: jonathan.bowser@ucdenver.edu. *Application contact:* Kay Denler, Academic Services Program Manager, 303-724-7963, E-mail: kay.denler@ucdenver.edu.
Website: http://www.ucdenver.edu/academics/colleges/medicalschool/education/degree_programs/PAProgram/Pages/Home.aspx

University of Illinois at Chicago, School of Public Health, Division of Community Health Sciences, Chicago, IL 60607-7128. Offers MPH, MS, Dr PH, PhD. *Program availability:* Part-time. Terminal master's awarded for partial completion of doctoral program. *Degree requirements:* For master's, thesis, field practicum; for doctorate, thesis/dissertation, independent research, internship. *Entrance requirements:* For master's and doctorate, GRE General Test, minimum GPA of 2.75. Additional exam requirements/recommendations for international students: Required—TOEFL. Electronic applications accepted. *Expenses:* Contact institution. *Faculty research:* Promoting wellness, disease prevention; public health preparedness; public health security capabilities.

University of Illinois at Springfield, Graduate Programs, College of Public Affairs and Administration, Program in Public Health, Springfield, IL 62703-5407. Offers community health education (Graduate Certificate); emergency preparedness and homeland security (Graduate Certificate); environmental health (MPH, Graduate Certificate); environmental risk assessment (Graduate Certificate); epidemiology (Graduate Certificate); public health (MPH). *Program availability:* Part-time, evening/weekend, 100% online. *Faculty:* 7 full-time (4 women). *Students:* 38 full-time (23 women), 46 part-time (34 women); includes 27 minority (16 Black or African American, non-Hispanic/Latino; 4 Asian, non-Hispanic/Latino; 5 Hispanic/Latino; 2 Two or more races, non-Hispanic/Latino), 22 international. Average age 32. 47 applicants, 51% accepted, 18 enrolled. In 2017, 28 master's, 17 other advanced degrees awarded. *Degree requirements:* For master's, comprehensive exam, internship. *Entrance requirements:* For master's, GRE, minimum undergraduate GPA of 3.0, 3 letters of recommendation, statement of personal goals. Additional exam requirements/recommendations for international students: Required—TOEFL (minimum score 500 paper-based; 61 iBT). *Application deadline:* Applications are processed on a rolling basis. Application fee: $60 ($75 for international students). Electronic applications accepted. *Expenses:* Tuition, state resident: full-time $7896; part-time $329 per credit hour. Tuition, nonresident: full-time $16,200; part-time $675 per credit hour. Tuition and fees vary according to program. *Financial support:* In 2017–18, research assistantships with full tuition reimbursements (averaging $10,249 per year), teaching assistantships with full tuition reimbursements (averaging $10,303 per year) were awarded; fellowships, career-related internships or fieldwork, Federal Work-Study, scholarships/grants, health care benefits, and unspecified assistantships also available. Support available to part-time students. Financial award application deadline: 11/15; financial award applicants required to submit FAFSA. *Unit head:* Dr. Josiah Alamu, Program Administrator, 217-206-7874, Fax: 217-206-7279, E-mail: jalam3@uis.edu.
Website: http://www.uis.edu/publichealth/

University of Illinois at Urbana–Champaign, Graduate College, College of Applied Health Sciences, Department of Kinesiology and Community Health, Champaign, IL 61820. Offers community health (MS, MSPH, PhD); kinesiology (MS, PhD); public health (MPH); rehabilitation (MS); PhD/MPH.

The University of Iowa, Graduate College, College of Public Health, Department of Community and Behavioral Health, Iowa City, IA 52242-1316. Offers MPH, MS, PhD. *Degree requirements:* For master's, thesis; for doctorate, comprehensive exam, thesis/dissertation. *Entrance requirements:* For master's and doctorate, GRE General Test, minimum GPA of 3.0. Additional exam requirements/recommendations for international students: Required—TOEFL (minimum score 600 paper-based; 100 iBT). Electronic applications accepted.

The University of Kansas, Graduate Studies, College of Liberal Arts and Sciences, Department of Applied Behavioral Science, Lawrence, KS 66045. Offers applied behavioral science (MA); behavioral psychology (PhD); community health and development (Graduate Certificate); PhD/MPH. *Program availability:* Part-time. *Students:* 46 full-time (33 women), 15 part-time (12 women); includes 5 minority (3 Black or African American, non-Hispanic/Latino; 1 Asian, non-Hispanic/Latino; 1 Two or more races, non-Hispanic/Latino), 3 international. Average age 29. 79 applicants, 43% accepted, 30 enrolled. In 2017, 8 master's, 5 doctorates awarded. Terminal master's awarded for partial completion of doctoral program. *Entrance requirements:* For master's, curriculum vitae; 3 letters of recommendation; personal statement; all academic transcripts; copies of pertinent written work, published or not, as well as presented papers; for doctorate, curriculum vitae; 3 letters of recommendation; personal statement; copies of pertinent written work, published or not, as well as presented papers. Additional exam requirements/recommendations for international students: Required—TOEFL. *Application deadline:* For fall admission, 12/15 priority date for domestic students, 12/15 for international students. Application fee: $65 ($85 for international students). Electronic applications accepted. *Financial support:* Fellowships, research assistantships, teaching assistantships, career-related internships or fieldwork, traineeships, tuition waivers (full), and unspecified assistantships available. Financial award application deadline: 12/15; financial award applicants required to submit CSS PROFILE or FAFSA. *Faculty research:* Organizational behavioral management, community health and development, early childhood education and intervention, developmental disabilities, behavioral economics of choice. *Unit head:* Dr. Florence DiGennaro Reed, Chairperson, 785-864-0521, E-mail: fdreed@ku.edu. *Application contact:* Andrea Noltner, Office Manager, 785-864-0503, E-mail: anoltner@ku.edu.
Website: http://absc.ku.edu

University of Louisville, Graduate School, College of Education and Human Development, Department of Health and Sport Sciences, Louisville, KY 40292-0001. Offers community health education (M Ed); exercise physiology (MS), including health and sport sciences, strength and conditioning; health and physical education (MAT); sport administration (MS). *Program availability:* Part-time, evening/weekend. *Students:* 35 full-time (11 women), 6 part-time (4 women); includes 10 minority (5 Black or African American, non-Hispanic/Latino; 4 Hispanic/Latino; 1 Two or more races, non-Hispanic/Latino), 1 international. Average age 28. 46 applicants, 67% accepted, 20 enrolled. In 2017, 21 master's awarded. Application fee: $65. *Expenses:* Tuition, state resident: full-time $12,246; part-time $681 per credit hour. Tuition, nonresident: full-time $25,486; part-time $1417 per credit hour. *Required fees:* $196. Tuition and fees vary according to course load, program and reciprocity agreements. *Financial support:* Applicants required to submit FAFSA. *Faculty research:* Sport administration, exercise physiology, exercise science, physical education, health education. *Total annual research expenditures:* $91,688. *Unit head:* Dr. Margaret Hancock, Interim Chair/Assistant Professor, 502-852-6645, E-mail: meg.hancock@louisville.edu. *Application contact:* Betty Hampton, Director of Graduate Student Services, 502-852-5597, Fax: 502-852-1465, E-mail: edadvise@louisville.edu.
Website: http://www.louisville.edu/education/departments/hss

University of Manitoba, Max Rady College of Medicine and Faculty of Graduate Studies, Graduate Programs in Medicine, Department of Community Health Sciences, Winnipeg, MB R3T 2N2, Canada. Offers M Sc, MPH, PhD, G Dip. *Program availability:* Part-time. *Degree requirements:* For master's, thesis; for doctorate, thesis/dissertation. *Entrance requirements:* For master's and doctorate, minimum GPA of 3.0. *Faculty research:* Health services, aboriginal health, health policy, epidemiology, international health.

University of Massachusetts Amherst, Graduate School, School of Public Health and Health Sciences, Department of Public Health, Amherst, MA 01003. Offers biostatistics (MPH, MS, PhD); community health education (MPH, MS, PhD); environmental health sciences (MPH, MS, PhD); epidemiology (MPH, MS, PhD); health policy and management (MPH, MS, PhD); nutrition (MPH, PhD); public health practice (MPH); MPH/MPPA. *Program availability:* Part-time, evening/weekend, online learning. Terminal master's awarded for partial completion of doctoral program. *Degree requirements:* For master's, thesis (for some programs); for doctorate, comprehensive exam, thesis/dissertation. *Entrance requirements:* For master's and doctorate, GRE General Test. Additional exam requirements/recommendations for international students: Required—TOEFL (minimum score 550 paper-based; 80 iBT), IELTS (minimum score 6.5). Electronic applications accepted.

University of Miami, Graduate School, School of Education and Human Development, Department of Educational and Psychological Studies, Program in Community Well-Being, Coral Gables, FL 33124. Offers PhD. *Degree requirements:* For doctorate, thesis/dissertation, qualifying exam. *Entrance requirements:* For doctorate, GRE General Test. Additional exam requirements/recommendations for international students: Required—TOEFL (minimum score 550 paper-based; 80 iBT); Recommended—IELTS (minimum score 6.5). Electronic applications accepted.

University of Minnesota, Twin Cities Campus, School of Public Health, Major in Community Health Education, Minneapolis, MN 55455-0213. Offers MPH. *Accreditation:* CEPH. *Program availability:* Part-time. *Degree requirements:* For master's, fieldwork, project. *Entrance requirements:* For master's, GRE General Test. Additional exam requirements/recommendations for international students: Required—TOEFL. Electronic applications accepted. *Faculty research:* Assessing population behavior, designing community-wide prevention and treatment, preventing alcohol and drug abuse, influencing health policies.

University of Missouri, School of Medicine and Office of Research and Graduate Studies, Graduate Programs in Medicine, Columbia, MO 65211. Offers family and community medicine (MS); health administration (MS); medical pharmacology and physiology (MS, PhD); molecular microbiology and immunology (MS, PhD); pathology and anatomical sciences (MS, PhD). *Program availability:* Part-time. *Degree requirements:* For doctorate, thesis/dissertation. *Entrance requirements:* For master's and doctorate, GRE General Test, minimum GPA of 3.0. Additional exam requirements/recommendations for international students: Required—TOEFL. *Application deadline:* Applications are processed on a rolling basis. *Expenses:* Contact institution. *Financial support:* Fellowships, research assistantships, teaching assistantships, career-related internships or fieldwork, and institutionally sponsored loans available.
Website: http://som.missouri.edu/departments.shtml

University of Montana, Graduate School, Phyllis J. Washington College of Education and Human Sciences, Department of Health and Human Performance, Missoula, MT 59812. Offers community health (MS); exercise science (MS); health and human performance generalist (MS). *Program availability:* Part-time. *Entrance requirements:* For master's, GRE General Test. Additional exam requirements/recommendations for international students: Required—TOEFL. *Faculty research:* Exercise physiology, performance psychology, nutrition, pre-employment physical screening, program evaluation.

University of Nevada, Las Vegas, Graduate College, School of Community Health Sciences, Las Vegas, NV 89154-3063. Offers Exec MHA, MHA, MPH, PhD, Certificate. *Program availability:* Part-time. *Faculty:* 23 full-time (10 women), 8 part-time/adjunct (6 women). *Students:* 82 full-time (58 women), 70 part-time (48 women); includes 66 minority (12 Black or African American, non-Hispanic/Latino; 2 American Indian or Alaska Native, non-Hispanic/Latino; 19 Asian, non-Hispanic/Latino; 22 Hispanic/Latino; 1 Native Hawaiian or other Pacific Islander, non-Hispanic/Latino; 10 Two or more races, non-Hispanic/Latino), 15 international. Average age 32. 97 applicants, 81% accepted, 47 enrolled. In 2017, 39 master's, 3 doctorates, 1 other advanced degree awarded. *Degree requirements:* For master's, thesis (for some programs); for doctorate, comprehensive exam, thesis/dissertation. *Entrance requirements:* For master's and doctorate, GRE General Test. Additional exam requirements/recommendations for international students: Required—TOEFL (minimum score 550 paper-based; 85 iBT), IELTS (minimum score 7). Application fee: $60 ($95 for international students). Electronic applications accepted. *Expenses:* $275 per credit, $850 per course, $7,969 per year resident, $22,157 per year non-resident, $7,094 non-resident fee (7 credits or more), $1,307 annual health insurance fee. *Financial support:* In 2017–18, 40 students

received support, including 35 research assistantships with full and partial tuition reimbursements available (averaging $13,724 per year), 5 teaching assistantships with full and partial tuition reimbursements available (averaging $12,957 per year); institutionally sponsored loans, scholarships/grants, health care benefits, and unspecified assistantships also available. Financial award application deadline: 3/15; financial award applicants required to submit FAFSA. *Faculty research:* Environmental health: micro (mold), hospital-acquired infections; health care: health services research, patient-centered outcome research, comparative effectiveness research, health management and policy/ health information technology, healthcare disparities; social and behavioral health disease prevention: health equity, asthma, diabetes, cancer, HIV/AIDS, substance abuse, injury; biostatistics and epidemiology: big data, health data analysis and disease patterns among minority populations. *Total annual research expenditures:* $5 million. *Unit head:* Dr. Shawn Gerstenberger, Dean, 702-895-1565, Fax: 702-895-5184, E-mail: shawn.gerstenberger@unlv.edu.
Website: http://publichealth.unlv.edu/

University of New Mexico, Graduate Studies, College of Education, Program in Health Education, Albuquerque, NM 87131-2039. Offers community health education (MS). *Accreditation:* NCATE. *Program availability:* Part-time. *Faculty:* 4 full-time (3 women), 1 (woman) part-time/adjunct. *Students:* 10 full-time (all women), 8 part-time (7 women); includes 12 minority (2 Black or African American, non-Hispanic/Latino; 5 American Indian or Alaska Native, non-Hispanic/Latino; 5 Hispanic/Latino), 1 international. Average age 32. 8 applicants, 75% accepted, 6 enrolled. In 2017, 11 master's awarded. *Degree requirements:* For master's, comprehensive exam, thesis optional. *Entrance requirements:* For master's, 3 letters of reference, resume, minimum cumulative GPA of 3.0 in last 2 years of bachelor's degree, letter of intent. Additional exam requirements/recommendations for international students: Required—TOEFL (minimum score 550 paper-based). *Application deadline:* For fall admission, 6/15 priority date for domestic students; for spring admission, 11/1 priority date for domestic students. Applications are processed on a rolling basis. Application fee: $50. Electronic applications accepted. *Financial support:* Fellowships, teaching assistantships with full tuition reimbursements, career-related internships or fieldwork, institutionally sponsored loans, scholarships/grants, and health care benefits available. Financial award application deadline: 3/1; financial award applicants required to submit FAFSA. *Faculty research:* Alcohol and families, health behaviors and sexuality, multicultural health behavior, health promotion policy, school/community-based prevention, health and aging. *Unit head:* Dr. Elias Duryea, Coordinator, 505-277-5151, Fax: 505-277-6227, E-mail: duryea@unm.edu. *Application contact:* Carol Catania, Graduate Coordinator, 505-277-5151, Fax: 505-277-6227, E-mail: catania@unm.edu.

University of New Mexico, Graduate Studies, Health Sciences Center, Program in Public Health, Albuquerque, NM 87131-5196. Offers community health (MPH); epidemiology (MPH); health systems, services and policy (MPH). *Program availability:* Part-time, online learning. *Faculty:* 9 full-time (6 women), 1 (woman) part-time/adjunct. *Students:* 23 full-time (20 women), 20 part-time (14 women); includes 15 minority (1 Black or African American, non-Hispanic/Latino; 1 American Indian or Alaska Native, non-Hispanic/Latino; 1 Asian, non-Hispanic/Latino; 12 Hispanic/Latino), 2 international. Average age 32. 34 applicants, 53% accepted, 18 enrolled. In 2017, 13 master's awarded. *Entrance requirements:* For master's, GRE, MCAT, 2 years of experience in health field. Additional exam requirements/recommendations for international students: Required—TOEFL. *Application deadline:* For fall admission, 2/1 for domestic students. Application fee: $50. *Financial support:* Fellowships, research assistantships, and Federal Work-Study available. Financial award application deadline: 12/15; financial award applicants required to submit FAFSA. *Faculty research:* Epidemiology, rural health, environmental health, Native American health issues. *Unit head:* Dr. Kristine Tollestrup, Director, 505-272-4173, Fax: 505-272-4494, E-mail: ktollestrup@salud.unm.edu. *Application contact:* Gayle Garcia, Education Coordinator, 505-272-3982, Fax: 505-272-4494, E-mail: garciag@salud.unm.edu.
Website: http://fcm.unm.edu/

The University of North Carolina at Charlotte, College of Health and Human Services, Department of Public Health Sciences, Charlotte, NC 28223-0001. Offers community health (Certificate); health administration (MHA); public health (MPH); public health core concepts (Graduate Certificate); public health sciences (PhD). *Accreditation:* CAHME; CEPH. *Program availability:* Part-time. *Faculty:* 23 full-time (12 women), 3 part-time/adjunct (2 women). *Students:* 94 full-time (74 women), 17 part-time (15 women); includes 49 minority (28 Black or African American, non-Hispanic/Latino; 3 American Indian or Alaska Native, non-Hispanic/Latino; 5 Asian, non-Hispanic/Latino; 6 Hispanic/Latino; 7 Two or more races, non-Hispanic/Latino), 7 international. Average age 25. 169 applicants, 60% accepted, 51 enrolled. In 2017, 44 master's, 2 other advanced degrees awarded. *Degree requirements:* For master's, thesis (for some programs), thesis or project; internship; capstone; for doctorate, thesis/dissertation. *Entrance requirements:* For master's, GRE or MCAT (for MSPH); GRE or GMAT (for MHA), career goal statement, current resume, letters of recommendation; for doctorate, GRE, master's degree in public health or a related field with minimum GPA of 3.5 in all graduate work; statement of purpose detailing why applicant wants to pursue a PhD in public health sciences in the specified concentration at UNC Charlotte; three letters of recommendation (including at least two letters from former professors); for other advanced degree, bachelor's degree from regionally-accredited university; minimum GPA of 2.75 on all post-secondary work attempted; transcripts; personal statement outlining why the applicant seeks admission to the program. Additional exam requirements/recommendations for international students: Required—TOEFL (minimum score 523 paper-based, 70 iBT) or IELTS (6.5). *Application deadline:* For fall admission, 1/10 priority date for domestic and international students; for spring admission, 9/15 priority date for domestic and international students; for summer admission, 4/1 priority date for domestic and international students. Applications are processed on a rolling basis. Application fee: $75. Electronic applications accepted. *Expenses:* Contact institution. *Financial support:* In 2017–18, 26 students received support, including 1 fellowship (averaging $11,869 per year), 22 research assistantships (averaging $7,008 per year), 3 teaching assistantships (averaging $5,176 per year); career-related internships or fieldwork, Federal Work-Study, institutionally sponsored loans, scholarships/grants, and unspecified assistantships also available. Support available to part-time students. Financial award application deadline: 3/1; financial award applicants required to submit FAFSA. *Total annual research expenditures:* $704,999. *Unit head:* Dr. Melinda Forthofer, Chair, 704-687-5682, Fax: 704-687-1644, E-mail: forthofer@uncc.edu. *Application contact:* Kathy B. Giddings, Director of Graduate Admissions, 704-687-5503, Fax: 704-687-1668, E-mail: gradadm@uncc.edu.
Website: http://publichealth.uncc.edu/

The University of North Carolina at Greensboro, Graduate School, School of Health and Human Sciences, Department of Public Health Education, Greensboro, NC 27412-5001. Offers community health education (MPH, Dr PH). *Accreditation:* CEPH; NCATE. *Degree requirements:* For master's, comprehensive exam, thesis or alternative. *Entrance requirements:* For master's, GRE General Test or MAT. Additional exam requirements/recommendations for international students: Required—TOEFL. Electronic applications accepted. *Faculty research:* Peer facilitator training, innovative health education approaches.

University of Northern British Columbia, Office of Graduate Studies, Prince George, BC V2N 4Z9, Canada. Offers business administration (Diploma); community health science (M Sc); disability management (MA); education (M Ed); first nations studies (MA); gender studies (MA); history (MA); interdisciplinary studies (MA); international studies (MA); mathematical, computer and physical sciences (M Sc); natural resources and environmental studies (M Sc, MA, MNRES, PhD); political science (MA); psychology (M Sc, PhD); social work (MSW). *Program availability:* Part-time, evening/weekend, online learning. *Degree requirements:* For master's, thesis; for doctorate, thesis/dissertation. *Entrance requirements:* For master's, GRE, minimum B average in undergraduate course work; for doctorate, candidacy exam, minimum A average in graduate course work.

University of Northern Colorado, Graduate School, College of Natural and Health Sciences, School of Human Sciences, Program in Public Health, Greeley, CO 80639. Offers community health education (MPH); global health and community health education (MPH); healthy aging and community health education (MPH). *Degree requirements:* For master's, comprehensive exam, thesis or alternative. *Entrance requirements:* For master's, GRE General Test, 2 letters of recommendation. Electronic applications accepted.

University of Northern Iowa, Graduate College, College of Education, School of Kinesiology, Allied Health and Human Services, MA Program in Health Education, Cedar Falls, IA 50614. Offers community health education (MA); health promotion/fitness management (MA); school health education (MA). *Program availability:* Part-time, evening/weekend. *Degree requirements:* For master's, comprehensive exam, thesis or alternative. *Entrance requirements:* For master's, minimum GPA of 3.0. Additional exam requirements/recommendations for international students: Required—TOEFL (minimum score 500 paper-based; 61 iBT). Electronic applications accepted.

University of North Florida, Brooks College of Health, Department of Public Health, Jacksonville, FL 32224. Offers aging services (Certificate); community health (MPH). *Program availability:* Part-time, evening/weekend. *Degree requirements:* For master's, thesis optional. *Entrance requirements:* For master's, GRE General Test (MSH, MS, MPH); GMAT or GRE General Test (MHA), minimum GPA of 3.0 in last 60 hours. Additional exam requirements/recommendations for international students: Required—TOEFL (minimum score 500 paper-based). Electronic applications accepted. *Faculty research:* Dietary supplements; alcohol, tobacco, and other drug use prevention; turnover among health professionals; aging; psychosocial aspects of disabilities.

University of Ottawa, Faculty of Graduate and Postdoctoral Studies, Interdisciplinary Programs, Ottawa, ON K1N 6N5, Canada. Offers e-business (Certificate); e-commerce (Certificate); finance (Certificate); health services and policies research (Diploma); population health (PhD); population health risk assessment and management (Certificate); public management and governance (Certificate); systems science (Certificate).

University of Phoenix–Central Valley Campus, College of Nursing, Fresno, CA 93720-1552. Offers education (MHA); gerontology (MHA); health administration (MHA); nursing (MSN); MSN/MBA.

University of Phoenix–Hawaii Campus, College of Nursing, Honolulu, HI 96813-3800. Offers education (MHA); family nurse practitioner (MSN); gerontology (MHA); health administration (MHA); nursing (MSN); nursing/health care education (MSN); MSN/MBA. *Program availability:* Evening/weekend. *Degree requirements:* For master's, thesis (for some programs). *Entrance requirements:* For master's, minimum undergraduate GPA of 2.5, 3 years of work experience, RN license. Additional exam requirements/recommendations for international students: Required—TOEFL (minimum score 550 paper-based; 79 iBT). Electronic applications accepted.

University of Pittsburgh, Graduate School of Public Health, Department of Behavioral and Community Health Sciences, Pittsburgh, PA 15261. Offers applied research and leadership in behavioral and community health sciences (Dr PH); applied social and behavioral concepts in public health (MPH); community-based participatory research (Certificate); evaluation of public health programs (Certificate); global health (Certificate); health equity (Certificate); LGBT health and wellness (Certificate); maternal and child health (MPH); MID/MPH; MPH/MPA; MPH/MSW; MPH/PhD. *Accreditation:* CEPH. *Program availability:* Part-time, online learning. *Faculty:* 17 full-time (10 women), 1 (woman) part-time/adjunct. *Students:* 89 full-time (68 women), 22 part-time (17 women); includes 22 minority (12 Black or African American, non-Hispanic/Latino; 7 Hispanic/Latino; 3 Two or more races, non-Hispanic/Latino), 9 international. Average age 29. 186 applicants, 71% accepted, 33 enrolled. In 2017, 32 master's, 7 doctorates awarded. *Degree requirements:* For master's, thesis, 200-contact hour practicum, final paper; for doctorate, comprehensive exam, thesis/dissertation, preliminary exam, dissertation defense. *Entrance requirements:* For master's, GRE, bachelor's degree; for doctorate, GRE, master's degree in public health or related field; for Certificate, GRE. Additional exam requirements/recommendations for international students: Required—TOEFL (minimum score 550 paper-based, 80 iBT) or IELTS (6.5). *Application deadline:* For fall admission, 1/15 for domestic and international students; for winter admission, 9/1 for international students; for spring admission, 10/15 for domestic students, 9/1 for international students; for summer admission, 12/1 for international students. Applications are processed on a rolling basis. Application fee: $135. Electronic applications accepted. *Expenses:* $13,068 per term full-time resident, $21,696 nonresident, $425 per term fees. *Financial support:* In 2017–18, 21 students received support, including 19 fellowships with full tuition reimbursements available (averaging $14,620 per year), 8 research assistantships with full tuition reimbursements available (averaging $14,620 per year). Financial award applicants required to submit FAFSA. *Faculty research:* Health disparities, HIV/AIDS, healthy aging, violence prevention, substance abuse. *Total annual research expenditures:* $4 million. *Unit head:* Dr. Steven M. Albert, Chairman, 412-383-8693, Fax: 412-624-5510, E-mail: smalbert@pitt.edu. *Application contact:* Paul J. Markgraf, Recruitment and Academic Affairs Administrator, 412-624-3107, Fax: 412-624-5510, E-mail: pjm111@pitt.edu.
Website: http://www.bchs.pitt.edu/

University of Pittsburgh, Graduate School of Public Health, Department of Infectious Diseases and Microbiology, Pittsburgh, PA 15261. Offers infectious diseases and microbiology (MS, PhD); management, intervention, and community practice (MPH); pathogenesis, eradication, and laboratory practice (MPH). *Program availability:* Part-time. *Faculty:* 21 full-time (7 women), 5 part-time/adjunct (2 women). *Students:* 55 full-time (34 women), 19 part-time (12 women); includes 17 minority (2 Black or African American, non-Hispanic/Latino; 8 Asian, non-Hispanic/Latino; 1 Hispanic/Latino; 6 Two or more races, non-Hispanic/Latino), 8 international. Average age 26. 152 applicants, 51% accepted, 27 enrolled. In 2017, 34 master's, 2 doctorates awarded. Terminal master's awarded for partial completion of doctoral program. *Degree requirements:* For master's, thesis, comprehensive exam (for MS); for doctorate, comprehensive exam, thesis/dissertation, preliminary exam, dissertation defense. *Entrance requirements:* For master's, GRE General Test, MCAT, or DAT, minimum GPA of 3.0, 6 credits of behavioral science; for doctorate, GRE General Test, MCAT, DAT, minimum GPA of 3.0; research experience; knowledge of biology or microbiology, chemistry, and algebra. Additional exam requirements/recommendations for international students: Required—TOEFL (minimum score 550 paper-based, 80 iBT) or IELTS (minimum score 6.5).

Application deadline: For fall admission, 1/15 priority date for domestic students, 3/15 priority date for international students. Applications are processed on a rolling basis. Application fee: $135. Electronic applications accepted. *Expenses:* $26,136 per year in-state tuition, $43,392 out-of-state, $850 fees. *Financial support:* In 2017–18, 38 students received support, including 19 research assistantships with full tuition reimbursements available; fellowships, teaching assistantships, scholarships/grants, and tuition waivers (full) also available. Financial award applicants required to submit FAFSA. *Faculty research:* Development of HIV vaccines, complications of antiretroviral therapy, emerging infections, herpes viruses. *Unit head:* Robin Tierno, Department Administrator, 412-624-3105, Fax: 412-624-4953, E-mail: rtierno@pitt.edu. *Application contact:* Abby Kincaid, Student Services Coordinator, 412-624-3331, E-mail: abbykincaid@pitt.edu.
Website: http://www.publichealth.pitt.edu/idm

University of Saskatchewan, College of Medicine, Department of Community Health and Epidemiology, Saskatoon, SK S7N 5A2, Canada. Offers M Sc, PhD. *Degree requirements:* For master's, thesis; for doctorate, thesis/dissertation. *Entrance requirements:* Additional exam requirements/recommendations for international students: Required—TOEFL.

University of South Florida, College of Public Health, Department of Community and Family Health, Tampa, FL 33620-9951. Offers MPH, MSPH, Dr PH, PhD. *Accreditation:* CEPH (one or more programs are accredited). *Program availability:* Part-time, evening/weekend. *Degree requirements:* For master's, comprehensive exam, thesis (for some programs); for doctorate, comprehensive exam, thesis/dissertation. *Entrance requirements:* For master's, GRE General Test, minimum GPA of 3.0 in upper-level course work, goal statement letter, two professional letters of recommendation, resume/curriculum vitae; for doctorate, GRE General Test, minimum GPA of 3.0 in upper-level course work, goal statement letter, three professional letters of recommendation, resume/curriculum vitae, writing sample. Additional exam requirements/recommendations for international students: Required—TOEFL (minimum score 550 paper-based; 79 iBT). Electronic applications accepted. *Faculty research:* Family violence, high-risk infants, medical material and child health, healthy start, social marketing, adolescent health, high-risk behaviors.

University of South Florida, Innovative Education, Tampa, FL 33620-9951. Offers adult, career and higher education (Graduate Certificate), including college teaching, leadership in developing human resources, leadership in higher education; Africana studies (Graduate Certificate), including diasporas and health disparities, genocide and human rights; aging studies (Graduate Certificate), including gerontology; art research (Graduate Certificate), including museum studies; business foundations (Graduate Certificate); chemical and biomedical engineering (Graduate Certificate), including materials science and engineering, water, health and sustainability; child and family studies (Graduate Certificate), including positive behavior support; civil and industrial engineering (Graduate Certificate), including transportation systems analysis; community and family health (Graduate Certificate), including maternal and child health, social marketing and public health, violence and injury: prevention and intervention, women's health; criminology (Graduate Certificate), including criminal justice administration; data science for public administration (Graduate Certificate); digital humanities (Graduate Certificate); educational measurement and research (Graduate Certificate), including evaluation; English (Graduate Certificate), including comparative literary studies, creative writing, professional and technical communication; entrepreneurship (Graduate Certificate); environmental health (Graduate Certificate), including safety management; epidemiology and biostatistics (Graduate Certificate), including applied biostatistics, biostatistics, concepts and tools of epidemiology, epidemiology, epidemiology of infectious diseases; geography, environment and planning (Graduate Certificate), including community development, environmental policy and management, geographical information systems; geology (Graduate Certificate), including hydrogeology; global health (Graduate Certificate), including disaster management, global health and Latin American and Caribbean studies, global health practice, humanitarian assistance, infection control; government and international affairs (Graduate Certificate), including Cuban studies, globalization studies; health policy and management (Graduate Certificate), including health management and leadership, public health policy and programs; hearing specialist: early intervention (Graduate Certificate); industrial and management systems engineering (Graduate Certificate), including systems engineering, technology management; information studies (Graduate Certificate), including school library media specialist; information systems/decision sciences (Graduate Certificate), including analytics and business intelligence; instructional technology (Graduate Certificate), including distance education, Florida digital/virtual educator, instructional design, multimedia design, Web design; internal medicine, bioethics and medical humanities (Graduate Certificate), including biomedical ethics; Latin American and Caribbean studies (Graduate Certificate); leadership for coastal resiliency planning (Graduate Certificate); mass communications (Graduate Certificate), including multimedia journalism; mathematics and statistics (Graduate Certificate), including mathematics; medicine (Graduate Certificate), including aging and neuroscience, bioinformatics, biotechnology, brain fitness and memory management, clinical investigation, hand and upper limb rehabilitation, health informatics, health sciences, integrative weight management, intellectual property, medicine and gender, metabolic and nutritional medicine, metabolic cardiology, pharmacy sciences; national and competitive intelligence (Graduate Certificate); nursing (Graduate Certificate), including simulation based academic fellowship in advanced pain management; psychological and social foundations (Graduate Certificate), including career counseling, college teaching, diversity in education, mental health counseling, school counseling; public affairs (Graduate Certificate), including nonprofit management, public management, research administration; public health (Graduate Certificate), including assessing chemical toxicity and public health risks, health equity, pharmacoepidemiology, public health generalist, toxicology, translational research in adolescent behavioral health; public health practices (Graduate Certificate), including planning for healthy communities; rehabilitation and mental health counseling (Graduate Certificate), including integrative mental health care, marriage and family therapy, rehabilitation technology; secondary education (Graduate Certificate), including ESOL, foreign language education: culture and content, foreign language education: professional; social work (Graduate Certificate), including geriatric social work/clinical gerontology; special education (Graduate Certificate), including autism spectrum disorder, disabilities education: severe/profound; world languages (Graduate Certificate), including teaching English as a second language (TESL) or foreign language. *Unit head:* Dr. Cynthia DeLuca, Associate Vice President and Assistant Vice Provost, 813-974-3077, Fax: 813-974-7061, E-mail: deluca@usf.edu. *Application contact:* Owen Hooper, Director, Summer and Alternative Calendar Programs, 813-974-6917, E-mail: hooper@usf.edu.
Website: http://www.usf.edu/innovative-education/

The University of Tennessee, Graduate School, College of Education, Health and Human Sciences, Program in Human Ecology, Knoxville, TN 37996. Offers child and family studies (PhD); community health (PhD); nutrition science (PhD); retailing and consumer sciences (PhD); textile science (PhD). *Degree requirements:* For doctorate, thesis/dissertation. *Entrance requirements:* For doctorate, GRE General Test, minimum GPA of 2.7. Additional exam requirements/recommendations for international students: Required—TOEFL. Electronic applications accepted.

The University of Tennessee, Graduate School, College of Education, Health and Human Sciences, Program in Public Health, Knoxville, TN 37996. Offers community health education (MPH); gerontology (MPH); health planning/administration (MPH); MS/MPH. *Accreditation:* CEPH. *Degree requirements:* For master's, thesis optional. *Entrance requirements:* For master's, minimum GPA of 2.7. Additional exam requirements/recommendations for international students: Required—TOEFL. Electronic applications accepted.

The University of Texas Health Science Center at Houston, School of Public Health, Houston, TX 77030. Offers behavioral science (PhD); biostatistics (MPH, MS, PhD); environmental health (MPH); epidemiology (MPH, MS, PhD); general public health (Certificate); genomics and bioinformatics (Certificate); health disparities (Certificate); health promotion/health education (MPH, Dr PH); healthcare management (Certificate); management, policy and community health (MPH, Dr PH, PhD); maternal and child health (Certificate); public health informatics (Certificate); DDS/MPH; JD/MPH; MBA/MPH; MD/MPH; MGPS/MPH; MP Aff/MPH; MS/MPH; MSN/MPH; MSW/MPH; PhD/MPH. Specific programs are offered at each of our six campuses in Texas (Austin, Brownsville, Dallas, El Paso, Houston, and San Antonio). *Accreditation:* CEPH. *Program availability:* Part-time. *Faculty:* 140 full-time (74 women), 23 part-time/adjunct (14 women). *Students:* 604 full-time (446 women), 534 part-time (384 women); includes 504 minority (106 Black or African American, non-Hispanic/Latino; 177 Asian, non-Hispanic/Latino; 88 Hispanic/Latino; 1 Native Hawaiian or other Pacific Islander, non-Hispanic/Latino; 132 Two or more races, non-Hispanic/Latino). Average age 31. 1,425 applicants, 58% accepted, 423 enrolled. In 2017, 315 master's, 68 doctorates awarded. *Degree requirements:* For master's, thesis (for some programs); for doctorate, comprehensive exam, thesis/dissertation. *Entrance requirements:* For master's and doctorate, GRE General Test. Additional exam requirements/recommendations for international students: Required—TOEFL (minimum score 600 paper-based, 100 iBT) or IELTS (7.5). *Application deadline:* For fall admission, 3/1 for domestic and international students; for spring admission, 10/1 for domestic and international students; for summer admission, 3/1 for domestic students. Applications are processed on a rolling basis. Application fee: $135. Electronic applications accepted. *Expenses:* $233 per semester credit hour resident tuition, $980 per semester credit hour non-resident tuition. *Financial support:* Fellowships, research assistantships, teaching assistantships, career-related internships or fieldwork, institutionally sponsored loans, scholarships/grants, traineeships, health care benefits, and unspecified assistantships available. Support available to part-time students. Financial award application deadline: 5/5; financial award applicants required to submit FAFSA. *Faculty research:* Chronic and infectious disease epidemiology; health promotion and health education; applied and theoretical biostatistics; healthcare management, policy and economics; environmental and occupational health. *Total annual research expenditures:* $47.8 million. *Unit head:* Dr. Susan Emery, Senior Associate Dean of Academic and Research Affairs. *Application contact:* Elvis Parada, Manager of Admissions and Recruitment, 713-500-9028, Fax: 713-500-9068, E-mail: elvis.a.parada@uth.tmc.edu.
Website: https://sph.uth.edu

University of Toronto, School of Graduate Studies, Department of Public Health Sciences, Toronto, ON M5S 1A1, Canada. Offers biostatistics (M Sc, PhD); community health (M Sc); community nutrition (MPH), including nutrition and dietetics; epidemiology (MPH, PhD); family and community medicine (MPH); occupational and environmental health (MPH); social and behavioral health science (PhD); social and behavioral health sciences (MPH), including health promotion. *Accreditation:* CAHME (one or more programs are accredited). *Program availability:* Part-time. *Degree requirements:* For master's, thesis (for some programs), practicum; for doctorate, comprehensive exam, thesis/dissertation, oral thesis defense. *Entrance requirements:* For master's, 2 letters of reference, relevant professional/research experience, minimum B average in final year; for doctorate, 2 letters of reference, relevant professional/research experience, minimum B+ average. Additional exam requirements/recommendations for international students: Required—TOEFL (minimum score 580 paper-based; 93 iBT), TWE (minimum score 5). Electronic applications accepted. *Expenses:* Contact institution.

University of Vermont, Graduate College, College of Agriculture and Life Sciences, Program in Dietetics, Burlington, VT 05405-0086. Offers dietetics (MS), including community health and nutrition. *Students:* 12 full-time (10 women). Average age 26. 18 applicants, 50% accepted, 6 enrolled. In 2017, 5 master's awarded. *Entrance requirements:* For master's, GRE General Test. Additional exam requirements/recommendations for international students: Required—TOEFL (minimum score 550 paper-based, 90 iBT) or IELTS (6.5). *Application deadline:* For fall admission, 2/15 for domestic students, 12/15 for international students. Application fee: $65. Electronic applications accepted. *Expenses:* Tuition, state resident: full-time $11,628; part-time $646 per credit. Tuition, nonresident: full-time $29,340; part-time $1630 per credit. *Required fees:* $1994; $10 per credit. Tuition and fees vary according to course load and program. *Unit head:* Amy Nickerson, Director, 802-656-0670, E-mail: uvmmsd@uvm.edu.
Website: https://www.uvm.edu/cals/nfs/ms_dietetics

University of Virginia, School of Nursing, Charlottesville, VA 22903. Offers acute and specialty care (MSN); acute care nurse practitioner (MSN); clinical nurse leadership (MSN); community-public health leadership (MSN); nursing (DNP, PhD); psychiatric mental health counseling (MSN); MSN/MBA. *Accreditation:* AACN. *Program availability:* Part-time. *Faculty:* 51 full-time (44 women), 17 part-time/adjunct (16 women). *Students:* 202 full-time (168 women), 139 part-time (114 women); includes 78 minority (32 Black or African American, non-Hispanic/Latino; 2 American Indian or Alaska Native, non-Hispanic/Latino; 14 Asian, non-Hispanic/Latino; 17 Hispanic/Latino; 1 Native Hawaiian or other Pacific Islander, non-Hispanic/Latino; 12 Two or more races, non-Hispanic/Latino), 9 international. Average age 34. 183 applicants, 68% accepted, 98 enrolled. In 2017, 105 master's, 27 doctorates awarded. *Degree requirements:* For doctorate, comprehensive exam (for some programs), capstone project (DNP), dissertation (PhD). *Entrance requirements:* For master's, GRE General Test, MAT; for doctorate, GRE General Test. Additional exam requirements/recommendations for international students: Required—TOEFL, IELTS. *Application deadline:* Applications are processed on a rolling basis. Application fee: $60. Electronic applications accepted. *Financial support:* Fellowships, research assistantships, teaching assistantships, Federal Work-Study, and scholarships/grants available. Financial award applicants required to submit FAFSA. *Unit head:* Dorrie K. Fontaine, Dean, 434-924-0141, Fax: 434-982-1809, E-mail: dkf2u@virginia.edu. *Application contact:* Teresa Carroll, Senior Assistant Dean for Academic and Student Services, 434-924-0141, Fax: 434-982-1809, E-mail: nur-osa@virginia.edu.
Website: http://www.nursing.virginia.edu/

University of Washington, Graduate School, School of Public Health, Department of Health Services, Seattle, WA 98195. Offers community-oriented public health practice (MPH); health services (MPH, MS, PhD); health systems and policy (MPH); maternal and child health (MPH); social and behavioral sciences (MPH); MPH/JD; MPH/MD; MPH/MN; MPH/MPA; MPH/MS; MPH/MSD; MPH/MSW; MPH/PhD. *Program availability:* Online learning. *Faculty:* 51 full-time (24 women), 69 part-time/adjunct (36 women). *Students:* 156 full-time (133 women), 9 part-time (all women); includes 58 minority (12 Black or African American, non-Hispanic/Latino; 4 American Indian or

Alaska Native, non-Hispanic/Latino; 25 Asian, non-Hispanic/Latino; 16 Hispanic/Latino; 1 Native Hawaiian or other Pacific Islander, non-Hispanic/Latino), 5 international. Average age 30. 288 applicants, 64% accepted, 82 enrolled. In 2017, 69 master's, 5 doctorates awarded. Terminal master's awarded for partial completion of doctoral program. Electronic applications accepted. *Expenses:* Contact institution. *Financial support:* Fellowships, research assistantships, teaching assistantships, institutionally sponsored loans, traineeships, and health care benefits available. Financial award applicants required to submit FAFSA. *Faculty research:* Public health practice, health promotion and disease prevention, maternal and child health, organizational behavior and culture, health policy. *Unit head:* Dr. Larry Kessler, Chair, 206-543-2703. *Application contact:* Programs Manager, 206-616-2926, Fax: 206-543-3964, E-mail: hservmph@u.washington.edu.
Website: http://depts.washington.edu/hserv/

University of Wisconsin–La Crosse, College of Science and Health, Department of Health Education and Health Promotion, Program in Community Health Education, La Crosse, WI 54601-3742. Offers community health education (MS); public health (MPH). *Students:* 16 full-time (11 women), 9 part-time (7 women); includes 4 minority (2 Asian, non-Hispanic/Latino; 2 Two or more races, non-Hispanic/Latino). Average age 31. 15 applicants, 93% accepted, 10 enrolled. In 2017, 8 master's awarded. *Degree requirements:* For master's, thesis. *Entrance requirements:* For master's, GRE General Test, GRE Subject Test (for MPH), 3 letters of recommendation. Additional exam requirements/recommendations for international students: Required—TOEFL (minimum score 550 paper-based; 79 iBT). Electronic applications accepted. *Financial support:* Research assistantships with partial tuition reimbursements, Federal Work-Study, scholarships/grants, health care benefits, and tuition waivers (partial) available. Support available to part-time students. Financial award applicants required to submit FAFSA. *Unit head:* Dr. Gary Gilmore, Director, 608-785-8163, E-mail: gilmore.gary@uwlax.edu. *Application contact:* Brandon Schaller, Senior Graduate Student Status Examiner, 608-785-8941, E-mail: admissions@uwlax.edu.

University of Wisconsin–Milwaukee, Graduate School, College of Health Sciences, Program in Health Sciences, Milwaukee, WI 53201-0413. Offers health sciences (PhD), including diagnostic and biomedical sciences, disability and rehabilitation, health administration and policy, human movement sciences, population health. *Students:* 17 full-time (10 women), 7 part-time (4 women); includes 6 minority (1 Black or African American, non-Hispanic/Latino; 3 Asian, non-Hispanic/Latino; 2 Two or more races, non-Hispanic/Latino), 11 international. Average age 33. 7 applicants, 43% accepted, 3 enrolled. In 2017, 1 doctorate awarded. *Degree requirements:* For doctorate, comprehensive exam, thesis/dissertation. *Entrance requirements:* For doctorate, GRE. Additional exam requirements/recommendations for international students: Required—TOEFL (minimum score 600 paper-based), IELTS (minimum score 6.5). Application fee: $56 ($96 for international students). *Financial support:* Fellowships, research assistantships, teaching assistantships, and project assistantships available. *Application contact:* Susan Cashin, PhD, Assistant Dean, 414-229-3303, E-mail: scashin@uwm.edu.
Website: http://uwm.edu/healthsciences/academics/phd-health-sciences/

University of Wyoming, College of Education, Programs in Counselor Education, Laramie, WY 82071. Offers community mental health (MS); counselor education and supervision (PhD); school counseling (MS); student affairs (MS). *Accreditation:* ACA (one or more programs are accredited). *Degree requirements:* For master's, comprehensive exam (for some programs), thesis optional; for doctorate, thesis/dissertation, video demonstration. *Entrance requirements:* For master's, interview, background check; for doctorate, video tape session, interview, writing sample, master's degree, background check. Additional exam requirements/recommendations for international students: Required—TOEFL. *Faculty research:* Wyoming SAGE photovoice project; accountable school counseling programs; GLBT issues; addictions; play therapy-early childhood mental health.

Virginia State University, College of Graduate Studies, College of Natural and Health Sciences, Department of Psychology, Petersburg, VA 23806-0001. Offers behavioral and community health sciences (PhD); clinical health psychology (PhD); clinical psychology (MS); general psychology (MS). *Degree requirements:* For master's, one foreign language, thesis. *Entrance requirements:* For master's, GRE General Test.

Walden University, Graduate Programs, School of Health Sciences, Minneapolis, MN 55401. Offers clinical research administration (MS, Graduate Certificate); health education and promotion (MS, PhD), including behavioral health (PhD), disease surveillance (PhD), emergency preparedness (MS), general (MHA, MS), global health (PhD), health policy (PhD), health policy and advocacy (MS), population health (PhD); health informatics (MS); health services (PhD), including community health, healthcare administration, leadership, public health policy, self-designed; healthcare administration (MHA, DHA), including general (MHA, MS); leadership and organizational development (MHA); public health (MPH, Dr PH, PhD, Graduate Certificate), including community health education (PhD), epidemiology (PhD); systems policy (MHA). *Program availability:* Part-time, evening/weekend, online only, 100% online. *Degree requirements:* For doctorate, thesis/dissertation, residency. *Entrance requirements:* For master's, bachelor's degree or higher; minimum GPA of 2.5; official transcripts; goal statement (for some programs); access to computer and Internet; for doctorate, master's degree or higher; three years of related professional or academic experience (preferred); minimum GPA of 3.0; goal statement and current resume (for select programs); official transcripts; access to computer and Internet; for Graduate Certificate, relevant work experience; access to computer and Internet. Additional exam requirements/recommendations for international students: Required—TOEFL (minimum score 550 paper-based, 79 iBT), IELTS (minimum score 6.5), Michigan English Language Assessment Battery (minimum score 82), or PTE (minimum score 53). Electronic applications accepted.

Washington State University, College of Nursing, Spokane, WA 99210. Offers advanced population health (MN, DNP); family nurse practitioner (MN, DNP); nursing (PhD); psychiatric/mental health nurse practitioner (DNP); psychiatric/mental health practitioner (MN). Programs offered at the Spokane, Tri-Cities, and Vancouver campuses. *Accreditation:* AACN. *Degree requirements:* For master's, comprehensive exam (for some programs), thesis (for some programs), oral exam, research project. *Entrance requirements:* For master's, minimum GPA of 3.0, Washington state RN license, physical assessment skills, course work in statistics, recommendations, written interview (for nurse practitioner). *Faculty research:* Cardiovascular and Type 2 diabetes in children, evaluation of strategies to increase physical activity in sedentary people.

William James College, Graduate Programs, Newton, MA 02459. Offers applied psychology in higher education student personnel administration (MA); clinical psychology (Psy D); counseling psychology (MA); counseling psychology and community mental health (MA); counseling psychology and global mental health (MA); executive coaching (Graduate Certificate); forensic and counseling psychology (MA); leadership psychology (Psy D); organizational psychology (MA); primary care psychology (MA); respecialization in clinical psychology (Certificate); school psychology (Psy D); MA/CAGS. *Accreditation:* APA. *Degree requirements:* For master's, comprehensive exam (for some programs); for doctorate, thesis/dissertation (for some programs). Electronic applications accepted.

Environmental and Occupational Health

American University of Beirut, Graduate Programs, Faculty of Health Sciences, 1107 2020, Lebanon. Offers environmental sciences (MS), including environmental health; epidemiology (MS, PhD); epidemiology and biostatistics (MPH); health care leadership (EMHCL); health management and policy (MPH), including health service administration; health promotion and community health (MPH); health research (MS); public health nutrition (MS). *Program availability:* Part-time. *Faculty:* 33 full-time (22 women), 5 part-time/adjunct (2 women). *Students:* 75 full-time (60 women), 78 part-time (67 women). Average age 27. 274 applicants, 56% accepted, 47 enrolled. In 2017, 63 master's awarded. *Degree requirements:* For master's, one foreign language, comprehensive exam (for some programs), thesis (for MS); for doctorate, one foreign language, comprehensive exam, thesis/dissertation. *Entrance requirements:* For master's, 2 letters of recommendations, personal statement, transcript; for doctorate, GRE, 3 letters of recommendations, personal statement, interview. Additional exam requirements/recommendations for international students: Required—TOEFL (minimum score 583 paper-based; 97 iBT), IELTS (minimum score 7). *Application deadline:* For fall admission, 4/4 for domestic and international students; for spring admission, 11/3 for domestic and international students. Application fee: $50. Electronic applications accepted. *Expenses:* Contact institution. *Financial support:* In 2017–18, 75 students received support. Scholarships/grants, health care benefits, and unspecified assistantships available. Financial award application deadline: 4/4. *Faculty research:* Reproductive and sexual health; occupational and environmental health; conflict and health; mental health; quality in health care delivery, tobacco control. *Total annual research expenditures:* $2 million. *Unit head:* Prof. Iman Adel Nuwayhid, Dean/Professor, 961-1-759683 Ext. 4600, Fax: 961-1-744470, E-mail: nuwayhid@aub.edu.lb. *Application contact:* Mitra Tauk, Administrative Coordinator, 961-1-350000 Ext. 4687, E-mail: mt12@aub.edu.lb.
Website: http://www.aub.edu.lb/fhs/fhs_home/Pages/index.aspx

Augusta University, College of Allied Health Sciences, Program in Public Health, Augusta, GA 30912. Offers environmental health (MPH); health informatics (MPH); health management (MPH); social and behavioral sciences (MPH). *Accreditation:* CEPH. *Program availability:* Part-time. *Degree requirements:* For master's, thesis (for some programs). *Entrance requirements:* For master's, GRE General Test, three letters of recommendation. Additional exam requirements/recommendations for international students: Required—TOEFL. Electronic applications accepted.

Boise State University, College of Health Sciences, Department of Community and Environmental Health, Boise, ID 83725-0399. Offers community and environmental health (MHS); health science (MHS), including health policy, health promotion, health services leadership; health services leadership (Graduate Certificate). *Faculty:* 11. *Students:* 20 full-time (18 women), 38 part-time (33 women); includes 7 minority (1 Asian, non-Hispanic/Latino; 5 Hispanic/Latino; 1 Two or more races, non-Hispanic/Latino). Average age 36. 38 applicants, 50% accepted, 11 enrolled. In 2017, 21 master's, 13 Graduate Certificates awarded. *Entrance requirements:* For master's, writing assessment, minimum GPA of 3.0. Additional exam requirements/recommendations for international students: Required—TOEFL (minimum score 550 paper-based; 80 iBT), IELTS (minimum score 6). *Application deadline:* For fall admission, 3/15 for domestic and international students; for spring admission, 10/15 for domestic and international students. Application fee: $65 ($95 for international students). Electronic applications accepted. *Expenses:* Tuition, state resident: full-time $6471; part-time $390 per credit. Tuition, nonresident: full-time $21,787; part-time $685 per credit. *Required fees:* $2283; $100 per term. Part-time tuition and fees vary according to course load and program. *Financial support:* Research assistantships, scholarships/grants, and unspecified assistantships available. Financial award application deadline: 3/15; financial award applicants required to submit FAFSA. *Unit head:* Dr. Lillian Smith, Department Head, 208-426-3795, E-mail: lilliansmith@boisestate.edu. *Application contact:* Dr. Sarah Toevs, Director, Master of Health Science Program, 208-426-2452, E-mail: stoevs@boisestate.edu.
Website: http://hs.boisestate.edu/ceh/

Boston University, School of Public Health, Environmental Health Department, Boston, MA 02215. Offers MPH, MS, PhD. *Program availability:* Part-time, evening/weekend. *Degree requirements:* For master's, comprehensive exam (for some programs), thesis (for some programs); for doctorate, one foreign language, thesis/dissertation, comprehensive written and oral exams. *Entrance requirements:* For master's, GRE, GMAT, or MCAT, U.S. bachelor's degree or foreign equivalent; for doctorate, GRE, MPH or equivalent. Additional exam requirements/recommendations for international students: Required—TOEFL (minimum score 600 paper-based; 100 iBT) or IELTS (minimum score 6). Electronic applications accepted. *Faculty research:* Exposure assessment, GIS, toxicology.

California State University, Fullerton, Graduate Studies, College of Health and Human Development, Department of Public Health, Fullerton, CA 92831-3599. Offers environmental and occupational health and safety (MPH); gerontological health (MPH); health promotion and disease (MPH). *Accreditation:* CEPH. *Program availability:* Part-time. *Students:* 37 full-time (31 women), 29 part-time (21 women); includes 41 minority (2 Black or African American, non-Hispanic/Latino; 14 Asian, non-Hispanic/Latino; 23 Hispanic/Latino; 1 Native Hawaiian or other Pacific Islander, non-Hispanic/Latino; 1 Two or more races, non-Hispanic/Latino), 2 international. Average age 30. 105 applicants, 47% accepted, 21 enrolled. In 2017, 26 master's awarded. *Entrance requirements:* For master's, minimum GPA of 3.0 in last 60 units attempted. Application fee: $55. *Financial support:* Career-related internships or fieldwork, Federal Work-Study, institutionally sponsored loans, and scholarships/grants available. Support available to part-time students. Financial award application deadline: 3/1; financial award applicants required to submit FAFSA. *Unit head:* Head, 657-278-2620. *Application contact:* Admissions/Applications, 657-278-2371.
Website: http://hhd.fullerton.edu/hesc/

Environmental and Occupational Health

California State University, Northridge, Graduate Studies, College of Health and Human Development, Department of Environmental and Occupational Health, Northridge, CA 91330. Offers environmental and occupational health (MS); industrial hygiene (MS). *Accreditation:* CEPH. *Faculty:* 6. *Students:* 25 full-time (10 women), 34 part-time (18 women); includes 29 minority (2 Black or African American, non-Hispanic/Latino; 9 Asian, non-Hispanic/Latino; 16 Hispanic/Latino; 2 Two or more races, non-Hispanic/Latino), 7 international. Average age 29. 39 applicants, 67% accepted, 19 enrolled. In 2017, 18 master's awarded. *Degree requirements:* For master's, seminar, field experience, comprehensive exam or thesis. *Entrance requirements:* For master's, GRE General Test or minimum GPA of 3.0. Additional exam requirements/recommendations for international students: Required—TOEFL. *Application deadline:* For fall admission, 11/30 for domestic students. Application fee: $55. *Financial support:* Application deadline: 3/1. *Unit head:* Frankline Augustin, Chair, 818-677-7476.
Website: http://www.csun.edu/hhd/eoh/

Capella University, School of Public Service Leadership, Doctoral Programs in Healthcare, Minneapolis, MN 55402. Offers criminal justice (PhD); emergency management (PhD); epidemiology (Dr PH); general health administration (DHA); general public administration (DPA); health advocacy and leadership (Dr PH); health care administration (PhD); health care leadership (DHA); health policy advocacy (DHA); multidisciplinary human services (PhD); nonprofit management and leadership (PhD); public safety leadership (PhD); social and community services (PhD).

Capella University, School of Public Service Leadership, Master's Programs in Healthcare, Minneapolis, MN 55402. Offers criminal justice (MS); emergency management (MS); general public health (MPH); gerontology (MS); health administration (MHA); health care operations (MHA); health management policy (MPH); health policy (MHA); homeland security (MS); multidisciplinary human services (MS); public administration (MPA); public safety leadership (MS); social and community services (MS); social behavioral sciences (MPH); MS/MPA.

Clemson University, Graduate School, College of Engineering, Computing and Applied Sciences, Department of Environmental Engineering and Earth Sciences, Anderson, SC 29625. Offers biosystems engineering (MS, PhD); environmental engineering and science (MS, PhD); environmental health physics (MS); hydrogeology (MS). *Program availability:* Part-time. *Faculty:* 32 full-time (9 women), 4 part-time/adjunct (2 women). *Students:* 112 full-time (39 women), 21 part-time (14 women); includes 9 minority (4 Black or African American, non-Hispanic/Latino; 1 Asian, non-Hispanic/Latino; 4 Two or more races, non-Hispanic/Latino), 39 international. Average age 27. 675 applicants, 40% accepted, 98 enrolled. In 2017, 26 master's, 6 doctorates awarded. *Degree requirements:* For master's, thesis or alternative; for doctorate, comprehensive exam, thesis/dissertation. *Entrance requirements:* For master's and doctorate, GRE General Test, unofficial transcripts, letters of recommendation. Additional exam requirements/recommendations for international students: Required—TOEFL (minimum score 80 iBT), IELTS (minimum score 6.5), PTE (minimum score 54). *Application deadline:* For fall admission, 2/15 for domestic and international students. Applications are processed on a rolling basis. Application fee: $80 ($90 for international students). Electronic applications accepted. *Expenses:* $5,767 per semester full-time resident, $10,918 per semester full-time non-resident, $656 per credit hour part-time resident, $1,310 per credit hour part-time non-resident, $915 per credit hour online; other fees may apply per session. *Financial support:* In 2017–18, 37 students received support, including 10 fellowships with partial tuition reimbursements available (averaging $14,106 per year), 17 research assistantships with partial tuition reimbursements available (averaging $22,015 per year), 9 teaching assistantships with partial tuition reimbursements available (averaging $22,142 per year); career-related internships or fieldwork and unspecified assistantships also available. Financial award application deadline: 2/15. *Faculty research:* Environmental engineering, bioprocess and ecological engineering, nuclear environmental engineering and science, hydrogeology, environmental chemistry and microbiology. *Total annual research expenditures:* $5.2 million. *Unit head:* Dr. David Freedman, Department Chair, 864-656-5566, E-mail: dfreedm@clemson.edu. *Application contact:* Dr. Kevin Finneran, Graduate Program Coordinator, 864-656-5019, E-mail: ktf@clemson.edu.
Website: https://www.clemson.edu/cecas/departments/eees/

Colorado State University, College of Veterinary Medicine and Biomedical Sciences, Department of Environmental and Radiological Health Sciences, Fort Collins, CO 80523-1681. Offers environmental health (MS, PhD), including environmental health and safety (MS), epidemiology (PhD). *Faculty:* 33 full-time (14 women), 5 part-time/adjunct (3 women). *Students:* 91 full-time (45 women), 52 part-time (29 women); includes 34 minority (9 Black or African American, non-Hispanic/Latino; 6 Asian, non-Hispanic/Latino; 14 Hispanic/Latino; 5 Two or more races, non-Hispanic/Latino), 14 international. Average age 29. 87 applicants, 75% accepted, 44 enrolled. In 2017, 59 master's, 3 doctorates awarded. Terminal master's awarded for partial completion of doctoral program. *Degree requirements:* For master's, comprehensive exam (for some programs), thesis (for some programs); for doctorate, comprehensive exam (for some programs), thesis/dissertation (for some programs). *Entrance requirements:* For master's, GRE, minimum GPA of 3.0, bachelor's degree, resume or curriculum vitae, official transcripts, written statement, 3 letters of recommendation; for doctorate, GRE, minimum GPA of 3.0, MS or proof of research, resume or curriculum vitae, official transcripts, written statement, 3 letters of recommendation. Additional exam requirements/recommendations for international students: Required—TOEFL (minimum score 80 iBT), IELTS (minimum score 6.5). *Application deadline:* For fall admission, 7/1 for domestic students, 5/1 for international students; for spring admission, 11/1 for domestic students, 9/1 for international students. Application fee: $60 ($70 for international students). Electronic applications accepted. *Expenses:* $120 per credit hour. *Financial support:* In 2017–18, 32 students received support, including 22 research assistantships with tuition reimbursements available (averaging $22,859 per year), 2 teaching assistantships with tuition reimbursements available (averaging $14,256 per year); fellowships with tuition reimbursements available and traineeships also available. Financial award applicants required to submit FAFSA. *Faculty research:* Air pollution, radiation physics, treatment of occupational illnesses and injuries, DNA damage and repair. *Total annual research expenditures:* $10.6 million. *Unit head:* Dr. Jac Nickoloff, Department Head, 970-491-6674, E-mail: j.nickoloff@colostate.edu. *Application contact:* Toni Brown, Graduate Coordinator, 970-491-5003, E-mail: toni.m.brown@colostate.edu.
Website: http://csu-cvmbs.colostate.edu/academics/erhs/Pages/graduate-studies.aspx

Columbia Southern University, College of Safety and Emergency Services, Orange Beach, AL 36561. Offers criminal justice administration (MS); emergency services management (MS); occupational safety and health (MS), including environmental management. *Program availability:* Part-time, evening/weekend, online learning. *Entrance requirements:* For master's, bachelor's degree from accredited/approved institution. Additional exam requirements/recommendations for international students: Required—TOEFL. Electronic applications accepted.

Columbia University, Columbia University Mailman School of Public Health, Department of Environmental Health Sciences, New York, NY 10032. Offers environmental health sciences (MPH, Dr PH, PhD); radiological sciences (MS); toxicology (MS). PhD offered in cooperation with the Graduate School of Arts and Sciences. *Accreditation:* CEPH (one or more programs are accredited). *Program availability:* Part-time. *Students:* 54 full-time (43 women), 25 part-time (16 women); includes 28 minority (3 Black or African American, non-Hispanic/Latino; 15 Asian, non-Hispanic/Latino; 8 Hispanic/Latino; 2 Two or more races, non-Hispanic/Latino), 10 international. Average age 28. 173 applicants, 55% accepted, 38 enrolled. In 2017, 30 master's, 7 doctorates awarded. *Degree requirements:* For master's, thesis optional; for doctorate, thesis/dissertation. *Entrance requirements:* For master's, GRE General Test, 1 year of course work in biology, general chemistry, organic chemistry, and mathematics; for doctorate, GRE General Test, MPH or equivalent (for Dr PH). Additional exam requirements/recommendations for international students: Required—TOEFL (minimum score 600 paper-based; 100 iBT). *Application deadline:* For fall admission, 12/1 priority date for domestic and international students. Applications are processed on a rolling basis. Application fee: $120. Electronic applications accepted. *Expenses: Tuition:* Full-time $44,864; part-time $1704 per credit. *Required fees:* $2370 per semester. One-time fee: $105. *Financial support:* Research assistantships, teaching assistantships, career-related internships or fieldwork, and Federal Work-Study available. Support available to part-time students. Financial award application deadline: 2/1; financial award applicants required to submit FAFSA. *Faculty research:* Laboratory science, field research, and community-based efforts to understand the impact of environmental exposures on human health, including areas of molecular epidemiology, environmental toxicology, environmental health policy, global health, air pollution, children's health, climate and health, epigenetics, radiological sciences, and health physics. *Unit head:* Dr. Andrea Baccarelli, Chair, 212-305-3466, Fax: 212-305-4012. *Application contact:* Clare Norton, Associate Dean for Enrollment Management, 212-305-8698, Fax: 212-342-1861, E-mail: ph-admit@columbia.edu.
Website: https://www.mailman.columbia.edu/become-student/departments/environmental-health-sciences

Duke University, Graduate School, Integrated Toxicology and Environmental Health Program, Durham, NC 27708. Offers Certificate. *Entrance requirements:* Additional exam requirements/recommendations for international students: Required—TOEFL (minimum score 577 paper-based; 90 iBT) or IELTS (minimum score 7). Electronic applications accepted.

East Carolina University, Graduate School, College of Health and Human Performance, Department of Health Education and Promotion, Greenville, NC 27858-4353. Offers environmental health (MS); health education (MA Ed); health education and promotion (MA). *Accreditation:* CEPH; NCATE. *Students:* 18 full-time (15 women), 54 part-time (42 women); includes 18 minority (11 Black or African American, non-Hispanic/Latino; 2 Asian, non-Hispanic/Latino; 4 Hispanic/Latino; 1 Two or more races, non-Hispanic/Latino). Average age 31. 25 applicants, 80% accepted, 18 enrolled. In 2017, 31 master's awarded. *Degree requirements:* For master's, comprehensive exam, thesis optional. *Entrance requirements:* For master's, GRE General Test or MAT. Additional exam requirements/recommendations for international students: Recommended—TOEFL (minimum score 78 iBT), IELTS (minimum score 6.5). *Application deadline:* For fall admission, 6/1 priority date for domestic students. Applications are processed on a rolling basis. Application fee: $75. *Expenses:* Tuition, state resident: full-time $4749; part-time $297 per credit hour. Tuition, nonresident: full-time $17,898; part-time $1119 per credit hour. *Required fees:* $2691; $224 per credit hour. Part-time tuition and fees vary according to course load and program. *Financial support:* Fellowships, research assistantships, teaching assistantships, and career-related internships or fieldwork available. Support available to part-time students. Financial award application deadline: 6/1. *Faculty research:* Community health education, worksite health promotion, school health education, environmental health. *Unit head:* Dr. J. Don Chaney, Chair, 252-737-4942, E-mail: chaneyj@ecu.edu.
Website: https://hhp.ecu.edu/hep/

East Carolina University, Graduate School, Thomas Harriot College of Arts and Sciences, Department of Psychology, Greenville, NC 27858-4353. Offers health psychology (PhD), including clinical health psychology, occupational health psychology, pediatric school psychology; industrial and organizational psychology (MA); quantitative methods for the social and behavioral sciences (Certificate); MA/CAS. *Program availability:* Part-time, evening/weekend. *Students:* 77 full-time (52 women), 17 part-time (15 women); includes 12 minority (8 Black or African American, non-Hispanic/Latino; 3 Hispanic/Latino; 1 Two or more races, non-Hispanic/Latino). Average age 26. 221 applicants, 31% accepted, 22 enrolled. In 2017, 31 master's, 7 doctorates, 21 other advanced degrees awarded. *Degree requirements:* For doctorate, comprehensive exam, thesis/dissertation or alternative. *Entrance requirements:* For master's and doctorate, GRE General Test. Additional exam requirements/recommendations for international students: Recommended—TOEFL (minimum score 78 iBT), IELTS (minimum score 6.5). *Application deadline:* For fall admission, 12/1 priority date for domestic and international students. Applications are processed on a rolling basis. Application fee: $75. Electronic applications accepted. *Expenses:* Tuition, state resident: full-time $4749; part-time $297 per credit hour. Tuition, nonresident: full-time $17,898; part-time $1119 per credit hour. *Required fees:* $2691; $224 per credit hour. Part-time tuition and fees vary according to course load and program. *Financial support:* Research assistantships with partial tuition reimbursements, teaching assistantships with partial tuition reimbursements, Federal Work-Study, and traineeships available. Support available to part-time students. Financial award application deadline: 6/1. *Unit head:* Dr. Susan L. McCammon, Chair, 252-328-6357, E-mail: mccammons@ecu.edu. *Application contact:* Dean of Graduate School, 252-328-6012, Fax: 252-328-6071, E-mail: gradschool@ecu.edu.
Website: http://www.ecu.edu/psyc/

Eastern Kentucky University, The Graduate School, College of Health Sciences, Program in Public Health, Richmond, KY 40475-3102. Offers community health education (MPH); environmental health science (MPH); industrial hygiene (MPH); public health nutrition (MPH). *Accreditation:* CEPH. *Degree requirements:* For master's, comprehensive exam, thesis optional, practicum, capstone course. *Entrance requirements:* For master's, GRE. *Faculty research:* Water quality, food safety, occupational health, air quality.

East Tennessee State University, School of Graduate Studies, College of Public Health, Department of Environmental Health, Johnson City, TN 37614. Offers MSEH, PhD. *Program availability:* Part-time. *Degree requirements:* For master's, comprehensive exam, research project or thesis; environmental health practice; seminar; for doctorate, comprehensive exam, thesis/dissertation, environmental health practice, seminar. *Entrance requirements:* For master's, GRE General Test, 30 hours of course work in natural and physical sciences, minimum GPA of 2.75, SOPHAS application, three letters of recommendation; for doctorate, GRE General Test, MPH or MS in related field of study with research-based thesis, SOPHAS application, three letters of recommendation, curriculum vitae or resume. Additional exam requirements/recommendations for international students: Required—TOEFL (minimum score 550 paper-based; 79 iBT). *Application deadline:* For fall admission, 6/1 for domestic students, 4/29 for international students; for spring admission, 11/1 for domestic students, 9/29 for international students. Application fee: $55 ($65 for international students). Electronic applications accepted. *Financial support:* Research assistantships with full tuition reimbursements, career-related internships or fieldwork, institutionally

sponsored loans, scholarships/grants, and unspecified assistantships available. Financial award application deadline: 7/1; financial award applicants required to submit FAFSA. *Faculty research:* Water quality, ecotoxicology, occupational health, indoor air quality, community-focused environmental health. *Unit head:* Dr. Kurt Maier, Chair, 423-439-5251, Fax: 423-439-5230, E-mail: maier@etsu.edu. *Application contact:* Dr. Kurt Maier, Chair, 423-439-5251, Fax: 423-439-5230, E-mail: maier@etsu.edu.
Website: http://www.etsu.edu/cph/eh/

East Tennessee State University, School of Graduate Studies, College of Public Health, Program in Public Health, Johnson City, TN 37614. Offers biostatistics (MPH, Postbaccalaureate Certificate); community health (MPH, DPH); environmental health (MPH); epidemiology (MPH, DPH, Postbaccalaureate Certificate); gerontology (Postbaccalaureate Certificate); global health (Postbaccalaureate Certificate); health care management (Postbaccalaureate Certificate); health management and policy (DPH); public health (Postbaccalaureate Certificate); public health services administration (MPH); rural health (Postbaccalaureate Certificate). *Accreditation:* CEPH. *Program availability:* Part-time, online learning. *Degree requirements:* For master's, comprehensive exam, field experience; for doctorate, thesis/dissertation, practicum. *Entrance requirements:* For master's, GRE General Test, minimum GPA of 2.75, SOPHAS application, three letters of recommendation; for doctorate, GRE General Test, SOPHAS application, three letters of recommendation; for Postbaccalaureate Certificate, minimum GPA of 2.5, three letters of recommendation, resume. Additional exam requirements/recommendations for international students: Required—TOEFL (minimum score 550 paper-based; 79 iBT), IELTS (minimum score 6.5). *Application deadline:* For fall admission, 3/1 for domestic and international students. Application fee: $35 ($45 for international students). Electronic applications accepted. *Financial support:* Research assistantships with tuition reimbursements, teaching assistantships with full tuition reimbursements, career-related internships or fieldwork, institutionally sponsored loans, scholarships/grants, and unspecified assistantships available. Financial award application deadline: 7/1; financial award applicants required to submit FAFSA. *Unit head:* Dr. Randy Wykoff, Dean, 423-439-4243, Fax: 423-439-5238, E-mail: wykoff@etsu.edu. *Application contact:* Dr. Randy Wykoff, Dean, 423-439-4243, Fax: 423-439-5238, E-mail: wykoff@etsu.edu.
Website: http://www.etsu.edu/cph/

Embry-Riddle Aeronautical University–Worldwide, Department of Aeronautics, Graduate Studies, Daytona Beach, FL 32114-3900. Offers aeronautics (MSA); aeronautics and design (MS); aviation maintenance (MAM); aviation/aerospace management (MS); aviation/aerospace research (MS); education (MS); human factors (MSHFS), including aerospace, systems engineering; occupational safety management (MS); operations (MS); safety/emergency response (MS); space systems (MS); unmanned systems (MS). *Program availability:* Part-time, evening/weekend. *Faculty:* 31 full-time (9 women), 145 part-time/adjunct (18 women). *Students:* 821 full-time (175 women), 972 part-time (146 women); includes 403 minority (136 Black or African American, non-Hispanic/Latino; 5 American Indian or Alaska Native, non-Hispanic/Latino; 65 Asian, non-Hispanic/Latino; 90 Hispanic/Latino; 8 Native Hawaiian or other Pacific Islander, non-Hispanic/Latino; 99 Two or more races, non-Hispanic/Latino), 128 international. Average age 37. 515 applicants, 75% accepted, 329 enrolled. In 2017, 514 master's awarded. *Degree requirements:* For master's, comprehensive exam, thesis or capstone project. *Entrance requirements:* For master's, GRE (for MSHFS). Additional exam requirements/recommendations for international students: Required—TOEFL (minimum score 550 paper-based, 79 iBT) or IELTS (6). *Application deadline:* Applications are processed on a rolling basis. Application fee: $50. Electronic applications accepted. *Expenses: Tuition:* Full-time $7680; part-time $640 per credit hour. Tuition and fees vary according to program. *Financial support:* Career-related internships or fieldwork and scholarships/grants available. Financial award applicants required to submit FAFSA. *Unit head:* Kenneth Witcher, PhD, Associate Professor and Dean, College of Aeronautics, E-mail: kenneth.witcher@erau.edu. *Application contact:* Worldwide Campus, 800-522-6787, E-mail: worldwide@erau.edu.
Website: http://worldwide.erau.edu/colleges/aeronautics/department-aeronautics-graduate-studies/

Emory University, Rollins School of Public Health, Department of Environmental Health, Atlanta, GA 30322-1100. Offers environmental health (MPH); environmental health and epidemiology (MSPH); environmental health sciences (PhD); global environmental health (MPH). *Program availability:* Part-time. *Degree requirements:* For master's, thesis, practicum. *Entrance requirements:* For master's, GRE General Test. Additional exam requirements/recommendations for international students: Required—TOEFL. Electronic applications accepted.

Florida International University, Robert Stempel College of Public Health and Social Work, Programs in Public Health, Miami, FL 33199. Offers biostatistics (MPH); environmental and occupational health (MPH, PhD); epidemiology (MPH, PhD); health policy and management (MPH); health promotion and disease prevention (MPH, PhD). PhD program has fall admissions only; MPH offered jointly with University of Miami. *Program availability:* Part-time, evening/weekend, online learning. *Faculty:* 34 full-time (18 women), 2 part-time/adjunct (both women). *Students:* 132 full-time (88 women), 63 part-time (49 women); includes 133 minority (50 Black or African American, non-Hispanic/Latino; 17 Asian, non-Hispanic/Latino; 60 Hispanic/Latino; 6 Two or more races, non-Hispanic/Latino), 30 international. Average age 29. 249 applicants, 54% accepted, 65 enrolled. In 2017, 37 master's, 14 doctorates awarded. *Degree requirements:* For master's, thesis optional; for doctorate, comprehensive exam, thesis/dissertation. *Entrance requirements:* For master's, minimum GPA of 3.0, letters of recommendation; for doctorate, GRE, resume, minimum GPA of 3.0, letters of recommendation, letter of intent. Additional exam requirements/recommendations for international students: Required—TOEFL (minimum score 550 paper-based; 80 iBT). *Application deadline:* For fall admission, 6/1 for domestic students, 4/1 for international students; for spring admission, 10/1 for domestic students, 9/1 for international students. Applications are processed on a rolling basis. Application fee: $30. Electronic applications accepted. *Expenses:* Contact institution. *Financial support:* Institutionally sponsored loans, scholarships/grants, and tuition waivers (full) available. Financial award application deadline: 3/1; financial award applicants required to submit FAFSA. *Faculty research:* Drugs/AIDS intervention among migrant workers, provision of services for active/recovering drug users with HIV. *Unit head:* Dr. Benjamin C. Amick, III, Chair, 305-348-7527, E-mail: benjamin.amickiii@fiu.edu. *Application contact:* Nanett Rojas, Assistant Director, Graduate Admissions, 305-348-7464, Fax: 305-348-7441, E-mail: gradadm@fiu.edu.

Fort Valley State University, College of Graduate Studies and Extended Education, Program in Public Health, Fort Valley, GA 31030. Offers environmental health (MPH). *Degree requirements:* For master's, thesis. *Entrance requirements:* For master's, GRE General Test. Additional exam requirements/recommendations for international students: Recommended—TOEFL.

Gannon University, School of Graduate Studies, College of Engineering and Business, School of Engineering and Computer Science, Program in Environmental Science and Engineering, Erie, PA 16541-0001. Offers environmental health (MSEH); environmental health and engineering (MS). *Program availability:* Part-time, evening/weekend. *Degree requirements:* For master's, thesis (for some programs), research paper or project (for some programs). *Entrance requirements:* For master's, GRE, bachelor's degree in science or engineering from an accredited college or university. Additional exam requirements/recommendations for international students: Required—TOEFL (minimum score 79 iBT), GRE. Electronic applications accepted. Application fee is waived when completed online.

The George Washington University, Milken Institute School of Public Health, Department of Environmental and Occupational Health, Washington, DC 20052. Offers Dr PH. *Students:* 1 (woman) full-time, 10 part-time (7 women); includes 6 minority (3 Black or African American, non-Hispanic/Latino; 2 Asian, non-Hispanic/Latino; 1 Hispanic/Latino), 1 international. Average age 37. 43 applicants, 91% accepted, 9 enrolled. In 2017, 2 doctorates awarded. *Entrance requirements:* Additional exam requirements/recommendations for international students: Required—TOEFL. *Application deadline:* For fall admission, 4/15 priority date for domestic students, 4/15 for international students; for spring admission, 11/1 for domestic and international students. Applications are processed on a rolling basis. Application fee: $75. *Expenses: Tuition:* Full-time $28,800; part-time $1655 per credit hour. *Required fees:* $45; $2.75 per credit hour. *Financial support:* In 2017–18, 7 students received support. Tuition waivers available. Financial award application deadline: 2/15. *Unit head:* Dr. Melissa Perry, Director, 202-994-1731, E-mail: mperry@gwu.edu. *Application contact:* Jane Smith, Director of Admissions, 202-994-0248, Fax: 202-994-1860, E-mail: sphhsinfo@gwumc.edu.

Georgia Southern University, Jack N. Averitt College of Graduate Studies, Allen E. Paulson College of Engineering and Information Technology, Department of Mechanical Engineering, Program in Occupational Safety and Environmental Compliance, Statesboro, GA 30458. Offers Graduate Certificate. *Students:* 6 applicants, 100% accepted. *Entrance requirements:* Additional exam requirements/recommendations for international students: Required—TOEFL (minimum score 550 paper-based; 80 iBT), IELTS (minimum score 6). *Application deadline:* For fall admission, 3/1 priority date for domestic and international students. Applications are processed on a rolling basis. Application fee: $50. Electronic applications accepted. *Expenses:* Tuition, state resident: full-time $4986; part-time $3324 per year. Tuition, nonresident: full-time $21,982; part-time $15,352 per year. *Required fees:* $2092; $1802 per credit hour. $901 per semester. Tuition and fees vary according to course load, campus/location and program. *Financial support:* Applicants required to submit FAFSA. *Faculty research:* Mechatronics, mechanical engineering, electronic systems, electrical systems, energy science. *Unit head:* Dr. Biswanath Samanta, Program Coordinator, 912-478-0334, E-mail: bsamanta@georgiasouthern.edu.

Georgia Southern University, Jack N. Averitt College of Graduate Studies, Jiann-Ping Hsu College of Public Health, Program in Public Health, Statesboro, GA 30460. Offers biostatistics (MPH, Dr PH); community health behavior and education (Dr PH); community health education (MPH); environmental health sciences (MPH); epidemiology (MPH); health policy and management (MPH, Dr PH). *Program availability:* Part-time. *Faculty:* 11 full-time (5 women). *Students:* 146 full-time (90 women), 70 part-time (57 women); includes 112 minority (95 Black or African American, non-Hispanic/Latino; 9 Asian, non-Hispanic/Latino; 5 Hispanic/Latino; 3 Two or more races, non-Hispanic/Latino), 47 international. Average age 32. 190 applicants, 78% accepted, 89 enrolled. In 2017, 34 master's, 13 doctorates awarded. *Degree requirements:* For master's, thesis optional, practicum; for doctorate, comprehensive exam, thesis/dissertation, preceptorship. *Entrance requirements:* For master's, GRE General Test, minimum GPA of 2.75, 3 letters of recommendation, statement of purpose, resume or curriculum vitae; for doctorate, GRE, GMAT, MCAT, LSAT, minimum GPA of 3.0, 3 letters of recommendation, statement of purpose, resume or curriculum vitae. Additional exam requirements/recommendations for international students: Required—TOEFL (minimum score 537 paper-based; 75 iBT), IELTS (minimum score 6). *Application deadline:* For fall admission, 6/1 for domestic students, 5/1 for international students. Applications are processed on a rolling basis. Application fee: $135. Electronic applications accepted. *Expenses:* $3,949 in-state, $13,929 out-of-state (for MPH); $4,014 in-state, $14,159 out-of-state (for Dr PH). *Financial support:* In 2017–18, 106 students received support, including 1 research assistantship with full tuition reimbursement available (averaging $12,350 per year), 6 teaching assistantships with full tuition reimbursements available (averaging $12,350 per year); scholarships/grants, tuition waivers (full), and unspecified assistantships also available. Financial award application deadline: 4/15; financial award applicants required to submit FAFSA. *Faculty research:* Rural public health best practices, health disparity elimination, community initiatives to enhance public health, cost effectiveness analysis, epidemiology of rural public health, environmental health issues, health care system assessment, rural health care, health policy and healthcare financing, survival analysis, nonparametric statistics and resampling methods, micro-arrays and genomics, data imputation techniques and clinical trial methodology. *Total annual research expenditures:* $415,747. *Unit head:* Dr. Robert Greg Evans, Dean, 912-478-2674, E-mail: rgevans@georgiasouthern.edu. *Application contact:* Shamia Garrett, Coordinator, Office of Student Services, 912-478-2674, Fax: 912-478-5811, E-mail: jphcoph-gradadvisor@georgiasouthern.edu.
Website: http://jphcoph.georgiasouthern.edu/

Harvard University, Cyprus International Institute for the Environment and Public Health in Association with Harvard School of Public Health, Cambridge, MA 02138. Offers environmental health (MS); environmental/public health (PhD); epidemiology and biostatistics (MS). *Entrance requirements:* For master's and doctorate, GRE, resume/curriculum vitae, 3 letters of recommendation, BA or BS (including diploma and official transcripts). Additional exam requirements/recommendations for international students: Required—TOEFL, IELTS (minimum score 7). Electronic applications accepted. *Faculty research:* Air pollution, climate change, biostatistics, sustainable development, environmental management.

Harvard University, Harvard T.H. Chan School of Public Health, Department of Environmental Health, Boston, MA 02115-6096. Offers environmental epidemiology (SM); environmental exposure assessment (SM); ergonomics and safety (SM); occupational health (SM); occupational hygiene (SM); population health sciences (PhD); risk and decision science (SM). *Program availability:* Part-time. *Faculty:* 41 full-time (9 women), 18 part-time/adjunct (4 women). *Students:* 49 full-time (33 women); includes 14 minority (2 Black or African American, non-Hispanic/Latino; 7 Asian, non-Hispanic/Latino; 3 Hispanic/Latino; 2 Two or more races, non-Hispanic/Latino), 25 international. Average age 29. 48 applicants, 67% accepted, 19 enrolled. In 2017, 15 master's, 14 doctorates awarded. *Degree requirements:* For doctorate, thesis/dissertation, qualifying exam. *Entrance requirements:* For master's, GRE, MCAT; for doctorate, GRE. Additional exam requirements/recommendations for international students: Recommended—TOEFL (minimum score 600 paper-based; 100 iBT), IELTS (minimum score 7). *Application deadline:* For fall admission, 12/1 for domestic and international students. Application fee: $120. Electronic applications accepted. *Financial support:* Fellowships, research assistantships, teaching assistantships, career-related internships or fieldwork, Federal Work-Study, scholarships/grants, traineeships, and unspecified assistantships available. Support available to part-time students. Financial award application deadline: 2/15; financial award applicants required to submit FAFSA. *Faculty research:* Exposure assessment, epidemiology, risk assessment, environmental

epidemiology, ergonomics and safety, environmental exposure assessment, occupational hygiene, industrial hygiene and occupational safety, population genetics, indoor and outdoor air pollution, cell and molecular biology of the lungs, infectious diseases. *Unit head:* Dr. Russ Hauser, Chairman, 617-432-1270, Fax: 617-432-6913. *Application contact:* Vincent W. James, Director of Admissions, 617-432-1031, Fax: 617-432-7080, E-mail: admissions@hsph.harvard.edu.
Website: http://www.hsph.harvard.edu/environmental-health/

Harvard University, Harvard T.H. Chan School of Public Health, PhD Program in Population Health Sciences, Boston, MA 02115. Offers environmental health (PhD); epidemiology (PhD); global health and population (PhD); nutrition (PhD); social and behavioral sciences (PhD). *Students:* 80 full-time (56 women); includes 23 minority (5 Black or African American, non-Hispanic/Latino; 7 Asian, non-Hispanic/Latino; 6 Hispanic/Latino; 5 Two or more races, non-Hispanic/Latino), 26 international. Average age 29. 469 applicants, 11% accepted, 42 enrolled. *Entrance requirements:* Additional exam requirements/recommendations for international students: Recommended—TOEFL, IELTS. *Application deadline:* For fall admission, 12/1 for domestic and international students. Electronic applications accepted. *Financial support:* Application deadline: 2/15; applicants required to submit FAFSA. *Unit head:* Bruce Villineau, Assistant Director, E-mail: phdphs@hsph.harvard.edu. *Application contact:* Vincent W. James, Director of Admissions, 617-432-1031, Fax: 617-432-7080, E-mail: admissions@hsph.harvard.edu.

Indiana State University, College of Graduate and Professional Studies, College of Technology, Department of Built Environment, Terre Haute, IN 47809. Offers occupational safety management (MS).

Indiana University Bloomington, School of Public Health, Department of Environmental Health, Bloomington, IN 47405. Offers MPH, PhD. *Degree requirements:* For doctorate, comprehensive exam, thesis/dissertation. *Entrance requirements:* For master's, GRE if cumulative GPA less than 2.8; for doctorate, GRE. Additional exam requirements/recommendations for international students: Required—TOEFL (minimum score 550 paper-based; 80 iBT). Electronic applications accepted. *Faculty research:* Toxicology, environmental health, oxidative stress, cancer biology.

Indiana University of Pennsylvania, School of Graduate Studies and Research, College of Health and Human Services, Department of Safety Sciences, MS Program in Safety Sciences, Indiana, PA 15705. Offers MS. *Program availability:* Part-time, online learning. *Faculty:* 7 full-time (3 women). *Students:* 16 full-time (3 women), 38 part-time (9 women); includes 5 minority (2 Black or African American, non-Hispanic/Latino; 1 American Indian or Alaska Native, non-Hispanic/Latino; 1 Hispanic/Latino; 1 Two or more races, non-Hispanic/Latino), 9 international. Average age 31. 52 applicants, 71% accepted, 19 enrolled. In 2017, 20 master's awarded. *Degree requirements:* For master's, thesis optional. *Entrance requirements:* For master's, 2 letters of recommendation. Additional exam requirements/recommendations for international students: Required—TOEFL (minimum score 540 paper-based). *Application deadline:* For fall admission, 4/1 priority date for domestic students. Applications are processed on a rolling basis. Application fee: $50. Electronic applications accepted. *Expenses:* Contact institution. *Financial support:* In 2017–18, 4 research assistantships with tuition reimbursements (averaging $3,180 per year) were awarded; fellowships with full tuition reimbursements, teaching assistantships, career-related internships or fieldwork, Federal Work-Study, scholarships/grants, and unspecified assistantships also available. Financial award application deadline: 4/15; financial award applicants required to submit FAFSA. *Unit head:* Dr. Chris Janicak, Graduate Coordinator, 724-357-3274, E-mail: cjanicak@iup.edu.
Website: http://www.iup.edu/grad/safety/default.aspx

Indiana University of Pennsylvania, School of Graduate Studies and Research, College of Health and Human Services, Department of Safety Sciences, PhD Program in Safety Sciences, Indiana, PA 15705. Offers PhD. *Program availability:* Online learning. *Faculty:* 7 full-time (3 women). *Students:* 46 part-time (17 women); includes 10 minority (7 Black or African American, non-Hispanic/Latino; 1 American Indian or Alaska Native, non-Hispanic/Latino; 2 Hispanic/Latino), 1 international. Average age 45. 64 applicants, 41% accepted, 13 enrolled. In 2017, 4 doctorates awarded. *Degree requirements:* For doctorate, thesis/dissertation. *Entrance requirements:* For doctorate, GRE, master's degree in safety sciences or closely-related field such as industrial hygiene, environmental health, or ergonomics; minimum graduate GPA of 3.0; official transcripts; three letters of recommendation; statement of goals; resume; sample of written work. Additional exam requirements/recommendations for international students: Required—TOEFL (minimum score 540 paper-based). Application fee: $50. *Expenses:* Contact institution. *Financial support:* In 2017–18, 1 teaching assistantship with partial tuition reimbursement (averaging $23,305 per year) was awarded; fellowships with full tuition reimbursements, research assistantships with tuition reimbursements, and unspecified assistantships also available. *Unit head:* Dr. Chris Janicak, Coordinator, 724-357-3274, E-mail: cjanicak@iup.edu.
Website: http://www.iup.edu/safetysciences/grad/safety-sciences-phd/

Indiana University–Purdue University Indianapolis, Richard M. Fairbanks School of Public Health, Indianapolis, IN 46202. Offers biostatistics (MS, PhD); environmental health (MPH); epidemiology (MPH, PhD); global health leadership (Dr PH); health administration (MHA); health policy (Graduate Certificate); health policy and management (MPH, PhD); health systems management (Graduate Certificate); product stewardship (MS); public health (Graduate Certificate); social and behavioral sciences (MPH). *Expenses:* Contact institution.

Indiana University–Purdue University Indianapolis, School of Public and Environmental Affairs, Indianapolis, IN 46202. Offers criminal justice and public safety (MS); homeland security and emergency management (Graduate Certificate); library management (Graduate Certificate); nonprofit management (Graduate Certificate); public affairs (MPA); public management (Graduate Certificate); social entrepreneurship: nonprofit and public benefit organizations (Graduate Certificate); JD/MPA; MLS/NMC; MLS/PMC; MPA/MA. *Accreditation:* CAHME (one or more programs are accredited); NASPAA. *Program availability:* Part-time, evening/weekend, online learning. *Entrance requirements:* For master's, GRE General Test, GMAT or LSAT, minimum GPA of 3.0 (preferred). Additional exam requirements/recommendations for international students: Required—TOEFL (minimum score 93 iBT), IELTS (minimum score 6.5). Electronic applications accepted. *Faculty research:* Nonprofit and public management, public policy, urban policy, sustainability policy, disaster preparedness and recovery, vehicular safety, homicide, offender rehabilitation and re-entry.

Johns Hopkins University, Bloomberg School of Public Health, Department of Environmental Health and Engineering, Baltimore, MD 21218. Offers environmental health (MHS, Sc M, Dr PH, PhD); occupational and environmental hygiene (MSPH); toxicity testing and human health risk assessment of environmental agents (MSPH). *Students:* 63 full-time (38 women), 23 part-time (15 women); includes 24 minority (5 Black or African American, non-Hispanic/Latino; 10 Asian, non-Hispanic/Latino; 7 Hispanic/Latino; 2 Two or more races, non-Hispanic/Latino), 12 international. Average age 29. 180 applicants, 44% accepted, 47 enrolled. In 2017, 20 master's, 6 doctorates awarded. *Degree requirements:* For master's, essay, presentation; for doctorate, comprehensive exam, thesis/dissertation, 1-year full-time residency, oral and written exams. *Entrance requirements:* For master's, GRE General Test or MCAT, 3 letters of recommendation, transcripts; for doctorate, GRE General Test or MCAT, 3 letters of recommendation. Additional exam requirements/recommendations for international students: Required—TOEFL (minimum score 100 iBT), IELTS (minimum score 7). *Application deadline:* For fall admission, 12/1 for domestic students. Application fee: $135. Electronic applications accepted. *Financial support:* Fellowships with full tuition reimbursements, Federal Work-Study, institutionally sponsored loans, scholarships/grants, traineeships, health care benefits, and stipends available. Support available to part-time students. *Faculty research:* Chemical carcinogenesis/toxicology, lung disease, occupational and environmental health, nuclear imaging, molecular epidemiology. *Unit head:* Dr. Marsha Wills-Karp, Chair, 410-955-2452. *Application contact:* Katie Phipps, Academic Program Administrator, 410-955-2212, E-mail: kphipps4@jhu.edu.
Website: http://ehe.jhu.edu/

Johns Hopkins University, G. W. C. Whiting School of Engineering, Department of Environmental Health and Engineering, Baltimore, MD 21218. Offers MA, MS, MSE, PhD. Terminal master's awarded for partial completion of doctoral program. *Degree requirements:* For master's, thesis optional, 1-year full-time residency; for doctorate, comprehensive exam, thesis/dissertation, oral exam, 2-year full-time residency. *Entrance requirements:* For master's and doctorate, GRE General Test, 3 letters of recommendation, statement of purpose, transcripts. Additional exam requirements/recommendations for international students: Required—TOEFL (minimum score 600 paper-based, 100 iBT) or IELTS (7). Electronic applications accepted. *Faculty research:* Environmental engineering and science; water and air resources engineering; geomorphology, hydrology and ecology; systems analysis and economics for public decision making; human geography.

Kent State University, College of Public Health, Kent, OH 44242-0001. Offers public health (MPH, PhD), including biostatistics (MPH), environmental health sciences (MPH), epidemiology, health policy and management, prevention science (PhD), social and behavioral sciences (MPH). *Accreditation:* CEPH. *Program availability:* Part-time, online learning. *Faculty:* 23 full-time (14 women), 12 part-time/adjunct (3 women). *Students:* 123 full-time (87 women), 152 part-time (120 women); includes 57 minority (37 Black or African American, non-Hispanic/Latino; 1 American Indian or Alaska Native, non-Hispanic/Latino; 8 Asian, non-Hispanic/Latino; 6 Hispanic/Latino; 5 Two or more races, non-Hispanic/Latino), 40 international. Average age 31. 176 applicants, 76% accepted, 81 enrolled. In 2017, 79 master's, 5 doctorates awarded. *Degree requirements:* For master's, comprehensive exam, 300 hours' placement at public health agency, final portfolio and presentation; for doctorate, comprehensive exam, thesis/dissertation. *Entrance requirements:* For master's, GRE, minimum GPA of 3.0, transcripts, goal statement, 3 letters of recommendation; for doctorate, GRE, minimum GPA of 3.0, personal statement, resume, interview, 3 letters of recommendation. Additional exam requirements/recommendations for international students: Required—TOEFL (minimum score 550 paper-based; 79 iBT), IELTS (minimum score 6.5), PTE (minimum score 58), Michigan English Language Assessment Battery. *Application deadline:* For fall admission, 6/15 for domestic and international students; for spring admission, 10/15 for domestic and international students; for summer admission, 3/15 for domestic and international students. Applications are processed on a rolling basis. Application fee: $45 ($70 for international students). Electronic applications accepted. *Expenses:* Tuition, state resident: full-time $11,310; part-time $515 per credit hour. Tuition, nonresident: full-time $20,396; part-time $928 per credit hour. *International tuition:* $18,544 full-time. *Financial support:* Unspecified assistantships available. *Unit head:* Dr. Sonia Alemagno, Dean and Professor of Health Policy and Management, 330-672-6500, E-mail: salemagn@kent.edu. *Application contact:* Dr. Mark A. James, Professor/Chair/Graduate Advisor, 330-672-6506, E-mail: mjames22@kent.edu.
Website: http://www.kent.edu/publichealth/

Lehigh University, College of Arts and Sciences, Environmental Policy Program, Bethlehem, PA 18015. Offers environmental health (Graduate Certificate); environmental justice (Graduate Certificate); environmental policy and law (Graduate Certificate); environmental policy design (MA); sustainable development (Graduate Certificate); urban environmental policy (Graduate Certificate). *Faculty:* 6 full-time (2 women). *Students:* 6 full-time (3 women), 1 (woman) part-time; includes 1 minority (Black or African American, non-Hispanic/Latino). Average age 28. 6 applicants, 83% accepted, 3 enrolled. In 2017, 3 master's awarded. *Degree requirements:* For master's, thesis or additional course work. *Entrance requirements:* For master's, GRE, minimum GPA of 2.75, 3.0 for last two undergraduate semesters; essay; 2 letters of recommendation. Additional exam requirements/recommendations for international students: Required—TOEFL (minimum score 85 iBT), IELTS (minimum score 6.5). *Application deadline:* For fall admission, 1/1 for domestic and international students; for spring admission, 12/1 for domestic and international students. Applications are processed on a rolling basis. Application fee: $75. Electronic applications accepted. *Expenses:* $1,460 per credit. *Financial support:* In 2017–18, 6 students received support. Teaching assistantships and community fellowship and tuition remission available. Financial award application deadline: 1/1. *Faculty research:* Environmental policy, environmental law, urban policy, urban politics, urban environmental policy, sustainability, sustainable development, international environmental law, international environmental policy, environmental justice, social justice. *Unit head:* Dr. Karen B. Pooley, Director, 610-758-1238, E-mail: kbp312@lehigh.edu. *Application contact:* Gary Burgess, Academic Coordinator, 610-758-4281, Fax: 610-758-6232, E-mail: glb215@lehigh.edu.
Website: http://ei.cas2.lehigh.edu/

Lewis University, College of Arts and Sciences, Program in Public Safety Administration, Romeoville, IL 60446. Offers MS. *Program availability:* Part-time, evening/weekend, 100% online, blended/hybrid learning. *Students:* 3 full-time (0 women), 78 part-time (20 women); includes 12 minority (3 Black or African American, non-Hispanic/Latino; 2 Asian, non-Hispanic/Latino; 7 Hispanic/Latino), 1 international. Average age 35. *Entrance requirements:* For master's, bachelor's degree, 2 letters of recommendation, personal statement. Additional exam requirements/recommendations for international students: Required—TOEFL (minimum score 550 paper-based; 79 iBT), IELTS (minimum score 6). *Application deadline:* For fall admission, 5/1 priority date for international students; for spring admission, 11/15 priority date for international students. Applications are processed on a rolling basis. Application fee: $40. Electronic applications accepted. Tuition and fees vary according to program. *Financial support:* Federal Work-Study and unspecified assistantships available. Financial award application deadline: 5/1; financial award applicants required to submit FAFSA. *Unit head:* Dr. Raymond Garritano, Director of the Public Safety Administration Graduate Program, Fax: 815-836-5949, E-mail: garritra@lewisu.edu. *Application contact:* Linda Campbell, Graduate Admission Counselor, 815-838-5610, E-mail: grad@lewisu.edu.

Loma Linda University, School of Public Health, Program in Environmental and Occupational Health, Loma Linda, CA 92350. Offers MPH. *Entrance requirements:* Additional exam requirements/recommendations for international students: Required—Michigan English Language Assessment Battery or TOEFL. *Faculty research:* Human exposure to toxins, smog.

Louisiana State University Health Sciences Center, School of Public Health, New Orleans, LA 70112. Offers behavioral and community health sciences (MPH); biostatistics (MPH, MS, PhD); community health sciences (PhD); environmental and occupational health sciences (MPH); epidemiology (MPH, PhD); health policy and systems management (MPH). *Accreditation:* CEPH. *Program availability:* Part-time. *Faculty:* 51 full-time (23 women), 41 part-time/adjunct (12 women). *Students:* 98 full-time (77 women), 24 part-time (18 women); includes 55 minority (26 Black or African American, non-Hispanic/Latino; 1 American Indian or Alaska Native, non-Hispanic/Latino; 13 Asian, non-Hispanic/Latino; 13 Hispanic/Latino; 2 Two or more races, non-Hispanic/Latino), 16 international. Average age 24. 208 applicants, 67% accepted, 54 enrolled. *Degree requirements:* For doctorate, thesis/dissertation. *Entrance requirements:* For master's, GRE General Test. Additional exam requirements/recommendations for international students: Recommended—TOEFL (minimum score 550 paper-based; 79 iBT), IELTS. *Application deadline:* Applications are processed on a rolling basis. Application fee: $30. Electronic applications accepted. *Expenses:* Tuition, state resident: full-time $11,835; part-time $518 per hour. Tuition, nonresident: full-time $24,108; part-time $1079 per hour. *Required fees:* $1254; $55 per hour. *Unit head:* Dr. Dean Smith, Dean, 504-568-5700, E-mail: dgsmith@lsuhsc.edu. *Application contact:* Isabel Billiot, Director of Admissions and Student Affairs, 504-568-5773, E-mail: ibilli@lsuhsc.edu.
Website: http://publichealth.lsuhsc.edu/

McGill University, Faculty of Graduate and Postdoctoral Studies, Faculty of Medicine, Department of Epidemiology and Biostatistics, Montréal, QC H3A 2T5, Canada. Offers community health (M Sc); environmental health (M Sc); epidemiology and biostatistics (M Sc, PhD, Diploma); health care evaluation (M Sc); medical statistics (M Sc).

McGill University, Faculty of Graduate and Postdoctoral Studies, Faculty of Medicine and Department of Epidemiology and Biostatistics, Department of Occupational Health, Montréal, QC H3A 2T5, Canada. Offers M Sc, PhD.

Meharry Medical College, School of Graduate Studies, Division of Public Health Practice, Nashville, TN 37208-9989. Offers occupational medicine (MSPH); public health administration (MSPH). *Accreditation:* CEPH. *Program availability:* Part-time, evening/weekend. *Degree requirements:* For master's, thesis, externship. *Entrance requirements:* For master's, GRE General Test, GMAT. *Expenses:* Contact institution.

Mercer University, Graduate Studies, Cecil B. Day Campus, Penfield College, Atlanta, GA 30341. Offers certified rehabilitation counseling (MS); clinical mental health (MS); counselor education and supervision (PhD); criminal justice and public safety leadership (MS); health informatics (MS); human services (MS), including child and adolescent services, gerontology services; organizational leadership (MS), including leadership for the health care professional, leadership for the nonprofit organization, organizational development and change; school counseling (MS). *Program availability:* Part-time, evening/weekend, 100% online, blended/hybrid learning. *Faculty:* 17 full-time (10 women), 27 part-time/adjunct (24 women). *Students:* 199 full-time (165 women), 266 part-time (218 women); includes 268 minority (226 Black or African American, non-Hispanic/Latino; 1 American Indian or Alaska Native, non-Hispanic/Latino; 19 Asian, non-Hispanic/Latino; 19 Hispanic/Latino; 3 Two or more races, non-Hispanic/Latino). Average age 32. 300 applicants, 45% accepted, 114 enrolled. In 2017, 101 master's, 5 doctorates awarded. *Degree requirements:* For master's, comprehensive exam (for some programs), thesis (for some programs); for doctorate, thesis/dissertation. *Entrance requirements:* For master's, GRE or MAT, Georgia Professional Standards Commission (GPSC) Certification at the SC-5 level; for doctorate, GRE or MAT. Additional exam requirements/recommendations for international students: Recommended—TOEFL (minimum score 550 paper-based; 80 iBT), IELTS (minimum score 6.5). *Application deadline:* For fall admission, 7/1 priority date for domestic and international students; for spring admission, 11/1 priority date for domestic and international students; for summer admission, 4/1 priority date for domestic and international students. Application fee: $35. Electronic applications accepted. Application fee is waived when completed online. *Expenses:* $637 per credit. *Financial support:* In 2017–18, 32 students received support. Federal Work-Study, scholarships/grants, and unspecified assistantships available. Financial award applicants required to submit FAFSA. *Faculty research:* Marriage and families issues, leadership and ethics, cyber-bullying, trauma, narrative counseling and theory. *Total annual research expenditures:* $85,000. *Unit head:* Dr. Priscilla R. Danheiser, Dean, 678-547-6028, Fax: 678-547-6008, E-mail: danheiser_p@mercer.edu. *Application contact:* Dr. Melissa McCants Cruz, Director of Graduate Admissions, 678-547-6024, E-mail: penfield.admissions@mercer.edu.
Website: http://penfield.mercer.edu/programs/graduate-professional/

Mississippi Valley State University, Department of Natural Sciences and Environmental Health, Itta Bena, MS 38941-1400. Offers environmental health (MS). *Program availability:* Part-time, evening/weekend. *Degree requirements:* For master's, comprehensive exam, thesis optional. *Entrance requirements:* For master's, GRE, minimum GPA of 3.0. Additional exam requirements/recommendations for international students: Recommended—TOEFL (minimum score 525 paper-based). *Expenses:* Contact institution. *Faculty research:* Toxicology, water equality, microbiology, ecology.

Murray State University, Jesse D. Jones College of Science, Engineering and Technology, Department of Occupational Safety and Health, Murray, KY 42071. Offers environmental science (MS). *Program availability:* Part-time, evening/weekend, 100% online, blended/hybrid learning. *Faculty:* 8 full-time (3 women), 1 part-time/adjunct (0 women). *Students:* 35 full-time (7 women), 34 part-time (8 women); includes 5 minority (4 Black or African American, non-Hispanic/Latino; 1 Two or more races, non-Hispanic/Latino), 9 international. Average age 30. 47 applicants, 72% accepted, 21 enrolled. In 2017, 18 master's awarded. *Entrance requirements:* For master's, GRE or GMAT, minimum university GPA of 2.75. Additional exam requirements/recommendations for international students: Required—TOEFL (minimum score 527 paper-based; 71 iBT). *Application deadline:* Applications are processed on a rolling basis. Application fee: $40 ($50 for international students). Electronic applications accepted. *Expenses:* Tuition, state resident: full-time $9504. Tuition, nonresident: full-time $26,811. *International tuition:* $14,400 full-time. Tuition and fees vary according to course load, degree level and reciprocity agreements. *Financial support:* Federal Work-Study and unspecified assistantships available. Financial award applicants required to submit FAFSA. *Unit head:* Dr. Tracey Wortham, Chair, Department of Occupational Safety and Health, 270-809-6654, Fax: 270-809-3630, E-mail: tworthman@murraystate.edu. *Application contact:* Kaitlyn Burzynski, Interim Assistant Director for Graduate Admission and Records, 270-809-5732, Fax: 270-809-3780, E-mail: msu.graduateadmissions@murraystate.edu.
Website: http://murraystate.edu/academics/CollegesDepartments/CollegeOfScienceEngineeringandTechnology/CollegeOfSciencePrograms/OSH/index.aspx

New York Medical College, School of Health Sciences and Practice, Valhalla, NY 10595. Offers behavioral sciences and health promotion (MPH); biostatistics (MS); children with special health care (Graduate Certificate); emergency preparedness (Graduate Certificate); environmental health science (MPH); epidemiology (MPH, MS); global health (Graduate Certificate); health education (Graduate Certificate); health policy and management (MPH, Dr PH); industrial hygiene (Graduate Certificate); pediatric dysphagia (Post-Graduate Certificate); physical therapy (DPT); public health (Graduate Certificate); speech-language pathology (MS). *Accreditation:* CEPH. *Program availability:* Part-time, evening/weekend, 100% online, blended/hybrid learning. *Faculty:* 48 full-time (33 women), 235 part-time/adjunct (141 women). *Students:* 221 full-time (153 women), 270 part-time (194 women); includes 202 minority (83 Black or African American, non-Hispanic/Latino; 2 American Indian or Alaska Native, non-Hispanic/Latino; 64 Asian, non-Hispanic/Latino; 47 Hispanic/Latino; 1 Native Hawaiian or other Pacific Islander, non-Hispanic/Latino; 5 Two or more races, non-Hispanic/Latino), 19 international. Average age 29. 1,118 applicants, 38% accepted, 169 enrolled. In 2017, 110 master's, 41 doctorates awarded. *Degree requirements:* For master's, comprehensive exam (for some programs), thesis (for some programs); for doctorate, thesis/dissertation. *Entrance requirements:* For master's, GRE (for MS in speech-language pathology); for doctorate, GRE. Additional exam requirements/recommendations for international students: Required—TOEFL, IELTS. *Application deadline:* For fall admission, 8/1 for domestic students, 4/15 for international students; for spring admission, 12/1 for domestic students; for summer admission, 5/1 for domestic students, 4/15 for international students. Application fee: $125. Electronic applications accepted. *Expenses:* $1,125 per credit, $245 fees. *Financial support:* In 2017–18, 10,000 students received support. Scholarships/grants and unspecified assistantships available. Financial award application deadline: 4/30; financial award applicants required to submit FAFSA. *Unit head:* Ben Watson, PhD, Vice Dean, 914-594-4531, E-mail: ben_watson@nymc.edu. *Application contact:* Irene Bundziak, Assistant to Director of Admissions, 914-594-4905, E-mail: irene_bundziak@nymc.edu.
Website: http://www.nymc.edu/school-of-health-sciences-and-practice-shsp/

★ **New York University,** Graduate School of Arts and Science, Department of Environmental Medicine, New York, NY 10012-1019. Offers environmental health sciences (MS, PhD), including biostatistics (PhD), environmental hygiene (MS), epidemiology (PhD), ergonomics and biomechanics (PhD), exposure assessment and health effects (PhD), molecular toxicology/carcinogenesis (PhD), toxicology. *Program availability:* Part-time. *Students:* Average age 30. 79 applicants, 44% accepted, 20 enrolled. In 2017, 8 master's, 6 doctorates awarded. Terminal master's awarded for partial completion of doctoral program. *Degree requirements:* For master's, thesis or alternative; for doctorate, one foreign language, thesis/dissertation, oral and written exams. *Entrance requirements:* For master's and doctorate, GRE General Test, minimum GPA of 3.0; bachelor's degree in biological, physical, or engineering science. Additional exam requirements/recommendations for international students: Required—TOEFL. *Application deadline:* For fall admission, 12/18 for domestic and international students. Application fee: $100. *Expenses: Tuition:* Full-time $41,352; part-time $19,968 per year. *Required fees:* $2496; $1628 per unit. $814 per term. Tuition and fees vary according to course load and program. *Financial support:* Fellowships, teaching assistantships, career-related internships or fieldwork, Federal Work-Study, institutionally sponsored loans, and health care benefits available. Financial award application deadline: 12/18; financial award applicants required to submit FAFSA. *Unit head:* Dr. Max Costa, Chair, 845-731-3661, Fax: 845-351-4510, E-mail: ehs@env.med.nyu.edu. *Application contact:* Dr. Jerome J. Solomon, Director of Graduate Studies, 845-731-3661, Fax: 845-351-4510, E-mail: ehs@env.med.nyu.edu.
Website: http://environmental-medicine.med.nyu.edu/

See Close-Up on page 843.

North Carolina Agricultural and Technical State University, School of Graduate Studies, School of Technology, Department of Construction Management and Occupational Safety and Health, Greensboro, NC 27411. Offers construction management (MSTM); environmental and occupational safety (MSTM); occupational safety and health (MSTM).

Oakland University, Graduate Study and Lifelong Learning, School of Health Sciences, Environmental Health and Safety Program, Rochester, MI 48309-4401. Offers safety management (MS). *Expenses:* Tuition, state resident: full-time $16,950; part-time $706.25 per credit. Tuition, nonresident: full-time $24,648; part-time $1027 per credit.

Oregon State University, College of Public Health and Human Sciences, Program in Public Health, Corvallis, OR 97331. Offers biostatistics (MPH); environmental and occupational health (MPH, PhD); epidemiology (MPH, PhD); global health (MPH, PhD). Terminal master's awarded for partial completion of doctoral program. *Entrance requirements:* For master's and doctorate, GRE, minimum GPA of 3.0 in last 90 hours. Additional exam requirements/recommendations for international students: Required—TOEFL (minimum score 80 iBT), IELTS (minimum score 6.5). *Application deadline:* For fall admission, 12/1 priority date for domestic and international students. Applications are processed on a rolling basis. Electronic applications accepted. *Expenses:* Contact institution. *Financial support:* Application deadline: 12/1. *Unit head:* Amanda Armington, MPH Program Manager, 541-737-3825, E-mail: amanda.armington@oregonstate.edu.

Purdue University, Graduate School, College of Health and Human Sciences, School of Health Sciences, West Lafayette, IN 47907. Offers health physics (MS, PhD); medical physics (MS, PhD); occupational and environmental health science (MS, PhD), including aerosol deposition and lung disease, ergonomics, exposure and risk assessment, indoor air quality and bioaerosols (PhD), liver/lung toxicology; radiation biology (PhD); toxicology (PhD); MS/PhD. *Program availability:* Part-time. *Faculty:* 12 full-time (4 women), 1 part-time/adjunct (0 women). *Students:* 37 full-time (16 women), 5 part-time (1 woman); includes 6 minority (2 Black or African American, non-Hispanic/Latino; 2 Asian, non-Hispanic/Latino; 1 Hispanic/Latino; 1 Two or more races, non-Hispanic/Latino), 9 international. Average age 28. 57 applicants, 65% accepted, 15 enrolled. In 2017, 10 master's, 4 doctorates awarded. *Degree requirements:* For master's, thesis optional; for doctorate, one foreign language, thesis/dissertation. *Entrance requirements:* For master's and doctorate, GRE General Test, minimum undergraduate GPA of 3.0 or equivalent. Additional exam requirements/recommendations for international students: Required—TOEFL (minimum score 550 paper-based; 77 iBT); Recommended—TWE. *Application deadline:* For fall admission, 5/15 for domestic and international students; for spring admission, 10/15 for domestic and international students. Applications are processed on a rolling basis. Application fee: $60 ($75 for international students). Electronic applications accepted. *Financial support:* In 2017–18, fellowships with tuition reimbursements (averaging $14,400 per year), research assistantships with tuition reimbursements (averaging $12,000 per year), teaching assistantships with tuition reimbursements (averaging $12,000 per year) were awarded; career-related internships or fieldwork and traineeships also available. Support available to part-time students. Financial award applicants required to submit FAFSA. *Faculty research:* Environmental toxicology, industrial hygiene, radiation dosimetry. *Unit head:* Jason T. Harris, Interim Head of the Graduate Program, 765-496-1271, E-mail: jtharris@purdue.edu. *Application contact:* Karen E. Walker, Graduate Contact, 765-494-1419, E-mail: kwalker@purdue.edu.
Website: https://www.purdue.edu/hhs/hsci/

Rochester Institute of Technology, Graduate Enrollment Services, College of Applied Science and Technology, School of Engineering Technology, MS Program in Environmental, Health and Safety Management, Rochester, NY 14623. Offers MS. *Program availability:* Part-time, evening/weekend, 100% online, blended/hybrid learning. *Students:* 19 full-time (11 women), 20 part-time (5 women); includes 5 minority (2 Black or African American, non-Hispanic/Latino; 1 Asian, non-Hispanic/Latino; 2 Hispanic/

Latino), 12 international. Average age 30. 47 applicants, 43% accepted, 9 enrolled. In 2017, 16 master's awarded. *Degree requirements:* For master's, thesis or alternative. *Entrance requirements:* For master's, minimum GPA of 3.0 (recommended). Additional exam requirements/recommendations for international students: Required—TOEFL (minimum score 88 iBT), IELTS (minimum score 6.5), PTE (minimum score 61). *Application deadline:* Applications are processed on a rolling basis. Application fee: $65. Electronic applications accepted. *Expenses:* $1,035 per credit hour (online study). *Financial support:* In 2017–18, 20 students received support. Research assistantships with partial tuition reimbursements available, teaching assistantships with partial tuition reimbursements available, career-related internships or fieldwork, scholarships/grants, and unspecified assistantships available. Support available to part-time students. Financial award applicants required to submit FAFSA. *Faculty research:* Design and implementation of integrated management systems for environmental sustainability, health and safety (ESHS); multidimensional corporate sustainability; global resilience and disaster science. *Unit head:* Joseph Rosenbeck, Graduate Program Director, 585-475-6469, E-mail: jmrcem@rit.edu. *Application contact:* Diane Ellison, Senior Associate Vice President, Graduate Enrollment Services, 585-475-2229, Fax: 585-475-7164, E-mail: gradinfo@rit.edu.
Website: https://www.rit.edu/cast/cetems/ms-environmental-health-safety-management

Rutgers University–New Brunswick, School of Public Health, Piscataway, NJ 08854. Offers biostatistics (MPH, MS, Dr PH, PhD); clinical epidemiology (Certificate); environmental and occupational health (MPH, Dr PH, PhD, Certificate); epidemiology (MPH, Dr PH, PhD); general public health (Certificate); health education and behavioral science (MPH, Dr PH, PhD); health systems and policy (MPH, PhD); public health (MPH, Dr PH, PhD); public health preparedness (Certificate); DO/MPH; JD/MPH; MBA/MPH; MD/MPH; MPH/MBA; MPH/MSPA; MS/MPH; Psy D/MPH. *Accreditation:* CEPH. *Program availability:* Part-time, evening/weekend. *Degree requirements:* For master's, thesis, internship; for doctorate, comprehensive exam, thesis/dissertation. *Entrance requirements:* For master's, GRE General Test; for doctorate, GRE General Test, MPH (Dr PH); MA, MPH, or MS (PhD). Additional exam requirements/recommendations for international students: Required—TOEFL. Electronic applications accepted.

San Diego State University, Graduate and Research Affairs, College of Health and Human Services, Graduate School of Public Health, San Diego, CA 92182. Offers environmental health (MPH); epidemiology (MPH, PhD), including biostatistics (MPH); global emergency preparedness and response (MS); global health (PhD); health behavior (PhD); health promotion (MPH); health services administration (MPH); toxicology (MS); MPH/MA; MSW/MPH. *Accreditation:* CAHME (one or more programs are accredited). *Program availability:* Part-time. *Degree requirements:* For master's, comprehensive exam (for some programs), thesis (for some programs); for doctorate, thesis/dissertation. *Entrance requirements:* For master's, GMAT (MPH in health services administration), GRE General Test; for doctorate, GRE General Test. Additional exam requirements/recommendations for international students: Required—TOEFL. *Faculty research:* Evaluation of tobacco, AIDS prevalence and prevention, mammography, infant death project, Alzheimer's in elderly Chinese.

Southeastern Oklahoma State University, School of Arts and Sciences, Durant, OK 74701-0609. Offers biology (MT); computer information systems (MT); occupational safety and health (MT). *Program availability:* Part-time, evening/weekend. *Degree requirements:* For master's, thesis optional. *Entrance requirements:* For master's, minimum GPA of 3.0 in last 60 hours or 2.75 overall. Additional exam requirements/recommendations for international students: Required—TOEFL (minimum score 550 paper-based; 79 iBT). Electronic applications accepted.

Syracuse University, College of Engineering and Computer Science, CAS Program in Environmental Health, Syracuse, NY 13244. Offers CAS. *Program availability:* Part-time. *Entrance requirements:* For degree, three letters of recommendation, resume, personal statement, official transcripts. *Application deadline:* For fall admission, 7/1 for domestic students, 6/1 for international students; for spring admission, 11/15 for domestic students, 10/15 for international students. Applications are processed on a rolling basis. Application fee: $75. Electronic applications accepted. *Financial support:* Fellowships, research assistantships, teaching assistantships, and tuition waivers available. Financial award application deadline: 1/1. *Faculty research:* Environmental health engineering, hazardous waste management, industrial hygiene, risk assessment, toxicology. *Unit head:* Dr. Sam Salem, Department Chair, 315-443-2311, E-mail: omsalem@syr.edu. *Application contact:* Kathleen Joyce, Assistant Dean, 315-443-2219, E-mail: topgrads@syr.edu.
Website: http://eng-cs.syr.edu/program/environmental-health/?degree=graduate_certificate

Temple University, College of Public Health, Department of Epidemiology and Biostatistics, Philadelphia, PA 19122. Offers applied biostatistics (MPH); environmental health (MPH); epidemiology (MPH, MS, PhD). *Accreditation:* CEPH. *Program availability:* Part-time, evening/weekend. *Faculty:* 9 full-time (5 women). *Students:* 20 full-time (11 women), 7 part-time (5 women); includes 8 minority (5 Black or African American, non-Hispanic/Latino; 1 Asian, non-Hispanic/Latino; 2 Hispanic/Latino), 8 international. 136 applicants, 54% accepted, 20 enrolled. In 2017, 6 master's awarded. *Entrance requirements:* For master's, GRE or MCAT. Additional exam requirements/recommendations for international students: Required—TOEFL (minimum score 550 paper-based; 79 iBT). *Application deadline:* For fall admission, 2/15 for domestic students, 12/15 for international students. Applications are processed on a rolling basis. Application fee: $50. Electronic applications accepted. *Expenses:* Contact institution. *Financial support:* Application deadline: 1/15; applicants required to submit FAFSA. *Unit head:* Dr. Adam Davey, Chair, 215-204-8726, E-mail: adam.davey@temple.edu. *Application contact:* Theresa White, Senior Graduate Advisor/Admissions, 215-204-5105, E-mail: theresawhite@temple.edu.
Website: https://cph.temple.edu/epibio/

Texas A&M University, School of Public Health, College Station, TX 77845. Offers biostatistics (MPH, MSPH); environmental health (MPH, MSPH); epidemiology (MPH, MSPH); executive health administration (MHA); health administration (MHA); health policy and management (MPH, MSPH); health promotion and community health sciences (MPH); health services research (PhD); occupational safety and health (MPH). *Program availability:* Part-time, blended/hybrid learning. *Faculty:* 56. *Students:* 279 full-time (196 women), 86 part-time (56 women); includes 153 minority (48 Black or African American, non-Hispanic/Latino; 36 Asian, non-Hispanic/Latino; 62 Hispanic/Latino; 7 Two or more races, non-Hispanic/Latino), 77 international. Average age 29. 179 applicants, 96% accepted, 148 enrolled. In 2017, 124 master's, 8 doctorates awarded. *Entrance requirements:* For master's, GRE General Test, 3 letters of recommendation; statement of purpose; current curriculum vitae or resume; official transcripts; for doctorate, GRE General Test, 3 letters of recommendation; statement of purpose; current curriculum vitae or resume; official transcripts; interview (in some cases). Additional exam requirements/recommendations for international students: Required—TOEFL (minimum score 597 paper-based, 95 iBT) or GRE (minimum verbal score 153). Application fee: $120. Electronic applications accepted. *Expenses:* Contact institution. *Financial support:* In 2017–18, 203 students received support, including 62 research assistantships with tuition reimbursements available (averaging $10,041 per year), 25 teaching assistantships with tuition reimbursements available (averaging $12,913 per year); career-related internships or fieldwork, institutionally sponsored loans, scholarships/grants, traineeships, health care benefits, tuition waivers (full and partial), and unspecified assistantships also available. Support available to part-time students. Financial award applicants required to submit FAFSA. *Unit head:* Dr. Jay Maddock, Dean, 979-436-9322, Fax: 979-458-1878, E-mail: maddock@tamhsc.edu. *Application contact:* Erin E. Schneider, Associate Director of Admissions and Recruitment, 979-436-9380, E-mail: eschneider@sph.tamhsc.edu.
Website: http://sph.tamhsc.edu/

Towson University, College of Health Professions, Program in Occupational Science, Towson, MD 21252-0001. Offers Sc D. *Program availability:* Part-time, evening/weekend. *Students:* 4 full-time (all women), 6 part-time (5 women); includes 3 minority (2 Black or African American, non-Hispanic/Latino; 1 Two or more races, non-Hispanic/Latino). *Degree requirements:* For doctorate, thesis/dissertation. *Entrance requirements:* For doctorate, master's degree with minimum GPA of 3.25, interview, 3 letters of recommendation, letter of intent. Additional exam requirements/recommendations for international students: Required—TOEFL (minimum score 600 paper-based). *Application deadline:* For fall admission, 1/17 for domestic students, 5/15 for international students; for spring admission, 10/15 for domestic students, 12/1 for international students. Applications are processed on a rolling basis. Application fee: $45. Electronic applications accepted. *Expenses:* Tuition, state resident: full-time $7960; part-time $398 per unit. Tuition, nonresident: full-time $16,480; part-time $824 per unit. *Required fees:* $2600; $130 per year. $390 per term. *Financial support:* Application deadline: 4/1. *Unit head:* Dr. Beth Merryman, Department Chair, 410-704-3499, E-mail: bmerryman@towson.edu. *Application contact:* Coverley Beidleman, Assistant Director of Graduate Admissions, 410-704-5630, Fax: 410-704-3030, E-mail: cbeidleman@towson.edu.
Website: http://www.towson.edu/chp/departments/occutherapy/programs/gradoccusci/

Trident University International, College of Health Sciences, Program in Health Sciences, Cypress, CA 90630. Offers clinical research administration (MS, Certificate); emergency and disaster management (MS, Certificate); environmental health science (Certificate); health care administration (PhD); health care management (MS), including health informatics; health education (MS, Certificate); health informatics (Certificate); health sciences (PhD); international health (MS); international health: educator or researcher option (PhD); international health: practitioner option (PhD); law and expert witness studies (MS, Certificate); public health (MS); quality assurance (Certificate). *Program availability:* Part-time, evening/weekend, online learning. *Degree requirements:* For doctorate, comprehensive exam, thesis/dissertation, defense of dissertation. *Entrance requirements:* For master's, minimum GPA of 2.5 (students with GPA 3.0 or greater may transfer up to 30% of graduate level credits); for doctorate, minimum GPA of 3.4, curriculum vitae, course work in research methods or statistics. Additional exam requirements/recommendations for international students: Required—TOEFL. Electronic applications accepted.

Tufts University, Cummings School of Veterinary Medicine, Program in Conservation Medicine, Medford, MA 02155. Offers MS. *Degree requirements:* For master's, case study, preceptorship. *Entrance requirements:* For master's, GRE, official transcripts, curriculum vitae. Additional exam requirements/recommendations for international students: Required—TOEFL or IELTS. Electronic applications accepted. *Expenses: Tuition:* Full-time $49,892. *Required fees:* $874. Full-time tuition and fees vary according to degree level, program and student level. Part-time tuition and fees vary according to course load. *Faculty research:* Non-invasive saliva collection techniques for free-ranging mountain gorillas and captive eastern gorillas, animal sentinels for infectious diseases.

Tufts University, School of Engineering, Department of Civil and Environmental Engineering, Medford, MA 02155. Offers bioengineering (MS), including environmental biotechnology; civil and environmental engineering (MS, PhD), including applied data science, environmental and water resources engineering, environmental health, geosystems engineering, structural engineering and mechanics; PhD/PhD. *Program availability:* Part-time. *Faculty:* 23 full-time, 10 part-time/adjunct. *Students:* 56 full-time (27 women), 2 part-time (0 women); includes 3 minority (2 Asian, non-Hispanic/Latino; 1 Hispanic/Latino), 26 international. Average age 29. 166 applicants, 42% accepted, 27 enrolled. In 2017, 21 master's, 6 doctorates awarded. Terminal master's awarded for partial completion of doctoral program. *Degree requirements:* For master's, thesis (for some programs); for doctorate, thesis/dissertation. *Entrance requirements:* For master's and doctorate, GRE General Test. Additional exam requirements/recommendations for international students: Required—TOEFL (minimum score 550 paper-based; 80 iBT), IELTS (minimum score 6.5). *Application deadline:* For fall admission, 1/15 priority date for domestic students, 1/15 for international students; for spring admission, 9/15 for domestic and international students. Applications are processed on a rolling basis. Application fee: $85. Electronic applications accepted. *Expenses: Tuition:* Full-time $49,892. *Required fees:* $874. Full-time tuition and fees vary according to degree level, program and student level. Part-time tuition and fees vary according to course load. *Financial support:* Fellowships with full tuition reimbursements, research assistantships with full and partial tuition reimbursements, teaching assistantships with full and partial tuition reimbursements, Federal Work-Study, scholarships/grants, tuition waivers (partial), and unspecified assistantships available. Financial award application deadline: 5/15; financial award applicants required to submit FAFSA. *Faculty research:* Environmental and water resources engineering, environmental health, geotechnical and geoenvironmental engineering, structural engineering and mechanics, water diplomacy. *Unit head:* Dr. Helen Suh, Graduate Program Chair. *Application contact:* Office of Graduate Admissions, 617-627-3395, E-mail: gradadmissions@tufts.edu.
Website: http://engineering.tufts.edu/cee/

Tulane University, School of Public Health and Tropical Medicine, Department of Global Environmental Health Sciences, New Orleans, LA 70118-5669. Offers MPH, MSPH, PhD, JD/MPH, MD/MPH, MSW/MPH. *Accreditation:* ABET (one or more programs are accredited). *Degree requirements:* For doctorate, comprehensive exam, thesis/dissertation. *Entrance requirements:* For master's and doctorate, GRE General Test. Additional exam requirements/recommendations for international students: Required—TOEFL. Electronic applications accepted. *Expenses: Tuition:* Full-time $50,920; part-time $2829 per credit hour. *Required fees:* $2040; $44.50 per credit hour. $580 per term. Tuition and fees vary according to course load, degree level and program.

Uniformed Services University of the Health Sciences, F. Edward Hebert School of Medicine, Graduate Programs in the Biomedical Sciences and Public Health, Bethesda, MD 20814. Offers emerging infectious diseases (PhD); medical and clinical psychology (PhD), including clinical psychology, medical psychology; medicine (MS, PhD), including health professions education; molecular and cell biology (MS, PhD); neuroscience (PhD); preventive medicine and biometrics (MPH, MS, MSPH, MTMH, PhD), including environmental health sciences (PhD), healthcare administration and policy (MS), medical zoology (PhD), public health (MPH, MSPH), tropical medicine and hygiene (MTMH). *Students:* Average age 25. 598 applicants, 17% accepted, 77 enrolled. In 2017, 19 master's, 50 doctorates awarded. Terminal master's awarded for partial completion of doctoral program. *Degree requirements:* For master's, comprehensive exam, thesis or alternative; for doctorate, comprehensive exam, thesis/dissertation, qualifying exam. *Entrance requirements:* For master's, GRE General Test; for doctorate,

GRE General Test, minimum GPA of 3.0. *Application deadline:* For fall admission, 12/1 priority date for domestic students. Application fee: $0. Electronic applications accepted. *Expenses:* There are no tuition charges or fees for graduate students at USU. *Financial support:* In 2017–18, 50 fellowships (averaging $43,000 per year) were awarded; research assistantships, career-related internships or fieldwork, scholarships/grants, and health care benefits also available. *Unit head:* Dr. Gregory Mueller, Associate Dean, 301-295-3507, E-mail: gregory.mueller@usuhs.edu. *Application contact:* Tina Finley, Administrative Officer, 301-295-3642, Fax: 301-295-6772, E-mail: netina.finley@usuhs.edu.
Website: http://www.usuhs.mil/graded

Uniformed Services University of the Health Sciences, F. Edward Hebert School of Medicine, Graduate Programs in the Biomedical Sciences and Public Health, Department of Preventive Medicine and Biometrics, Program in Environmental Health Sciences, Bethesda, MD 20814-4799. Offers PhD. *Accreditation:* CEPH. *Degree requirements:* For doctorate, comprehensive exam, thesis/dissertation, qualifying exam. *Entrance requirements:* For doctorate, GRE, minimum GPA of 3.0. Additional exam requirements/recommendations for international students: Required—TOEFL.

Universidad Autonoma de Guadalajara, Graduate Programs, Guadalajara, Mexico. Offers administrative law and justice (LL M); advertising and corporate communications (MA); architecture (M Arch); business (MBA); computational science (MCC); education (Ed M, Ed D); English-Spanish translation (MA); entrepreneurship and management (MBA); integrated management of digital animation (MA); international business (MIB); international corporate law (LL M); internet technologies (MS); manufacturing systems (MMS); occupational health (MS); philosophy (MA, PhD); power electronics (MS); quality systems (MQS); renewable energy (MS); social evaluation of projects (MBA); strategic market research (MBA); tax law (MA); teaching mathematics (MA).

Universidad de Ciencias Medicas, Graduate Programs, San Jose, Costa Rica. Offers dermatology (SP); family health (MS); health service center administration (MHA); human anatomy (MS); medical and surgery (MD); occupational medicine (MS); pharmacy (Pharm D). *Program availability:* Part-time. *Degree requirements:* For master's, thesis; for doctorate and SP, comprehensive exam. *Entrance requirements:* For master's, MD or bachelor's degree; for doctorate, admissions test; for SP, admissions test, MD.

Université de Montréal, Faculty of Medicine, Department of Environmental and Occupational Health, Montréal, QC H3C 3J7, Canada. Offers M Sc. *Accreditation:* CEPH. *Degree requirements:* For master's, thesis. *Entrance requirements:* For master's, proficiency in French, knowledge of English. Electronic applications accepted. *Faculty research:* Metabolism of chemical substances, toxicity, biological surveillance, risk analysis.

Université du Québec à Montréal, Graduate Programs, Program in Ergonomics in Occupational Health and Safety, Montréal, QC H3C 3P8, Canada. Offers Diploma. *Program availability:* Part-time. *Entrance requirements:* For degree, appropriate bachelor's degree or equivalent, proficiency in French.

Université Laval, Faculty of Medicine, Graduate Programs in Medicine, Department of Social and Preventive Medicine, Program in Accident Prevention and Occupational Health and Safety Management, Québec, QC G1K 7P4, Canada. Offers Diploma. *Program availability:* Part-time. *Entrance requirements:* For degree, knowledge of French. Electronic applications accepted.

University at Albany, State University of New York, School of Public Health, Department of Environmental Health Sciences, Albany, NY 12222-0001. Offers environmental and occupational health (MS, PhD); environmental chemistry (MS, PhD); toxicology (MS, PhD). *Accreditation:* CEPH. *Faculty:* 15 full-time (8 women), 2 part-time/adjunct (1 woman). *Students:* 7 full-time (5 women), 8 part-time (all women); includes 4 minority (3 Black or African American, non-Hispanic/Latino; 1 Asian, non-Hispanic/Latino), 5 international. 16 applicants, 75% accepted, 3 enrolled. In 2017, 2 doctorates awarded. *Degree requirements:* For master's, thesis; for doctorate, comprehensive exam, thesis/dissertation. *Entrance requirements:* For master's and doctorate, GRE General Test, GRE Subject Test, 3 letters of reference. Additional exam requirements/recommendations for international students: Required—TOEFL (minimum score 600 paper-based). *Application deadline:* For fall admission, 1/15 for domestic and international students; for winter admission, 4/1 for domestic and international students; for spring admission, 10/1 for domestic students, 11/1 for international students. Applications are processed on a rolling basis. Application fee: $75. Electronic applications accepted. *Expenses:* Tuition, state resident: full-time $10,870; part-time $453 per credit hour. Tuition, nonresident: full-time $22,210; part-time $925 per credit hour. *Required fees:* $84.68 per credit hour. $508.06 per semester. Part-time tuition and fees vary according to course load and program. *Financial support:* Fellowships, research assistantships with full tuition reimbursements, teaching assistantships with full tuition reimbursements, scholarships/grants, health care benefits, tuition waivers (partial), and unspecified assistantships available. Financial award application deadline: 1/15. *Faculty research:* Xenobiotic metabolism, neurotoxicity of halogenated hydrocarbons, pharmacy/toxic genomics, environmental analytical chemistry. *Unit head:* Dr. David Lawrence, Chair, 518-474-7161, E-mail: dalawrence@albany.edu.
Website: http://www.albany.edu/sph/eht/index.html

The University of Alabama at Birmingham, School of Public Health, Program in Environmental Health Sciences, Birmingham, AL 35294. Offers environmental health sciences research (PhD); industrial hygiene (PhD). *Degree requirements:* For doctorate, comprehensive exam, thesis/dissertation. *Entrance requirements:* For doctorate, GRE General Test. Additional exam requirements/recommendations for international students: Recommended—TOEFL, IELTS. Electronic applications accepted. *Faculty research:* Aquatic toxicology, virology.

The University of Alabama at Birmingham, School of Public Health, Program in Public Health, Birmingham, AL 35294. Offers applied epidemiology and pharmacoepidemiology (MSPH); biostatistics (MPH); clinical and translational science (MSPH); environmental health (MPH); environmental health and toxicology (MSPH); epidemiology (MPH); general theory and practice (MPH); health behavior (MPH); health care organization (MPH); health policy quantitative policy analysis (MPH); industrial hygiene (MPH, MSPH); maternal and child health policy (Dr PH); maternal and child health policy and leadership (MPH); occupational health and safety (MPH); outcomes research (MSPH, Dr PH); public health (PhD); public health management (Dr PH); public health preparedness management (MPH). *Program availability:* Part-time, online learning. *Degree requirements:* For doctorate, comprehensive exam, thesis/dissertation. *Entrance requirements:* For master's and doctorate, GRE. Additional exam requirements/recommendations for international students: Recommended—TOEFL (minimum score 550 paper-based; 79 iBT), IELTS (minimum score 6.5). Electronic applications accepted.

University of Alberta, School of Public Health, Department of Public Health Sciences, Edmonton, AB T6G 2E1, Canada. Offers clinical epidemiology (M Sc, MPH); environmental and occupational health (MPH); environmental health sciences (M Sc); epidemiology (M Sc); global health (M Sc, MPH); health policy and management (MPH); health policy research (M Sc); health technology assessment (MPH); occupational health (M Sc); population health (M Sc); public health leadership (MPH); public health sciences (PhD); quantitative methods (MPH). Terminal master's awarded for partial completion of doctoral program. *Degree requirements:* For master's, thesis (for some programs); for doctorate, thesis/dissertation. *Entrance requirements:* For master's, GMAT or GRE General Test. Additional exam requirements/recommendations for international students: Required—TOEFL (minimum score 550 paper-based) or IELTS (minimum score 6). Electronic applications accepted. *Faculty research:* Biostatistics, health promotion and socio-behavioral health science.

University of Arkansas for Medical Sciences, College of Public Health, Little Rock, AR 72205-7199. Offers biostatistics (MPH); environmental and occupational health (MPH, Certificate); epidemiology (MPH, PhD); health behavior and health education (MPH); health policy and management (MPH); health promotion and prevention research (PhD); health services administration (MHSA); health systems research (PhD); public health (Certificate); public health leadership (Dr PH). *Accreditation:* CEPH. *Program availability:* Part-time. *Degree requirements:* For master's, preceptorship, culminating experience, internship; for doctorate, comprehensive exam, capstone. *Entrance requirements:* For master's, GRE, GMAT, LSAT, PCAT, MCAT, DAT; for doctorate, GRE. Additional exam requirements/recommendations for international students: Required—TOEFL (minimum score 80 iBT), IELTS. Electronic applications accepted. *Expenses:* Contact institution. *Faculty research:* Health systems, tobacco prevention control, obesity prevention, environmental and occupational exposure, cancer prevention.

University of California, Berkeley, Graduate Division, School of Public Health, Group in Environmental Health Sciences, Berkeley, CA 94720-1500. Offers MS, PhD. *Degree requirements:* For master's, comprehensive exam (MPH), project or thesis (MS); for doctorate, thesis/dissertation, departmental and qualifying exams. *Entrance requirements:* For master's, GRE General Test, minimum GPA of 3.0; previous course work in biology, calculus, and chemistry; 3 letters of recommendation; for doctorate, GRE General Test, master's degree in relevant scientific discipline or engineering; minimum GPA of 3.0; previous course work in biology, calculus, and chemistry; 3 letters of recommendation. Additional exam requirements/recommendations for international students: Required—TOEFL (minimum score 570 paper-based; 90 iBT). Electronic applications accepted. *Faculty research:* Toxicology, industrial hygiene, exposure assessment, risk assessment, ergonomics.

University of California, Irvine, School of Medicine, Program in Environmental Health Sciences, Irvine, CA 92697. Offers environmental health sciences (MS); environmental toxicology (PhD); exposure sciences and risk assessment (PhD). *Students:* 16 full-time (11 women); includes 6 minority (3 Asian, non-Hispanic/Latino; 2 Hispanic/Latino; 1 Two or more races, non-Hispanic/Latino), 2 international. Average age 30. 19 applicants, 32% accepted, 4 enrolled. In 2017, 2 master's, 1 doctorate awarded. Terminal master's awarded for partial completion of doctoral program. *Degree requirements:* For master's, comprehensive exam; for doctorate, comprehensive exam, thesis/dissertation. *Entrance requirements:* For master's and doctorate, GRE General Test, GRE Subject Test, minimum GPA of 3.0. Additional exam requirements/recommendations for international students: Required—TOEFL (minimum score 550 paper-based). *Application deadline:* For fall admission, 1/15 for domestic students. Applications are processed on a rolling basis. Application fee: $105 ($125 for international students). Electronic applications accepted. *Financial support:* Fellowships, research assistantships with full tuition reimbursements, teaching assistantships, institutionally sponsored loans, traineeships, health care benefits, and unspecified assistantships available. Financial award application deadline: 12/15; financial award applicants required to submit FAFSA. *Faculty research:* Inhalation/pulmonary toxicology, environmental carcinogenesis, biochemical neurotoxicology, toxic kinetics, chemical pathology. *Unit head:* Dr. Ulrike Luderer, Director, 949-824-8848, E-mail: uluderer@uci.edu. *Application contact:* Armando Villalpando, Student Affairs Officer, 949-824-8848, E-mail: afvillal@uci.edu.
Website: http://www.medicine.uci.edu/occupational/graduate.asp

University of California, Los Angeles, Graduate Division, School of Public Health, Department of Environmental Health Sciences, Los Angeles, CA 90095. Offers environmental health sciences (MS, PhD); environmental science and engineering (D Env); molecular toxicology (PhD); JD/MPH. *Accreditation:* ABET (one or more programs are accredited); CEPH. *Degree requirements:* For master's, comprehensive exam or thesis; for doctorate, thesis/dissertation, oral and written qualifying exams. *Entrance requirements:* For master's, GRE General Test, minimum GPA of 3.0; for doctorate, GRE General Test, minimum undergraduate GPA of 3.0. Electronic applications accepted.

University of Central Missouri, The Graduate School, Warrensburg, MO 64093. Offers accountancy (MA); accounting (MBA); applied mathematics (MS); aviation safety (MA); biology (MS); business administration (MBA); career and technical education leadership (MS); college student personnel administration (MS); communication (MA); computer science (MS); counseling (MS); criminal justice (MS); educational leadership (Ed D); educational technology (MS); elementary and early childhood education (MSE); English (MA); environmental studies (MA); finance (MBA); history (MA); human services/educational technology (Ed S); human services/learning resources (Ed S); human services/professional counseling (Ed S); industrial hygiene (MS); industrial management (MS); information systems (MBA); information technology (MS); kinesiology (MS); library science and information services (MS); literacy education (MSE); marketing (MBA); mathematics (MS); music (MA); occupational safety management (MS); psychology (MS); rural family nursing (MS); school administration (MSE); social gerontology (MS); sociology (MA); special education (MSE); speech language pathology (MS); superintendency (Ed S); teaching (MAT); teaching English as a second language (MA); technology (MS); technology management (PhD); theatre (MA). *Program availability:* Part-time, 100% online, blended/hybrid learning. *Faculty:* 337 full-time (145 women), 41 part-time/adjunct (28 women). *Students:* 785 full-time (398 women), 1,633 part-time (1,063 women); includes 231 minority (102 Black or African American, non-Hispanic/Latino; 4 American Indian or Alaska Native, non-Hispanic/Latino; 16 Asian, non-Hispanic/Latino; 52 Hispanic/Latino; 57 Two or more races, non-Hispanic/Latino), 692 international. Average age 30. In 2017, 2,605 master's, 122 other advanced degrees awarded. *Degree requirements:* For master's and Ed S, comprehensive exam (for some programs), thesis (for some programs). *Entrance requirements:* Additional exam requirements/recommendations for international students: Required—TOEFL (minimum score 550 paper-based; 79 iBT). *Application deadline:* For fall admission, 6/1 priority date for domestic and international students; for spring admission, 10/1 priority date for domestic and international students; for summer admission, 4/1 priority date for domestic and international students. Applications are processed on a rolling basis. Application fee: $30 ($75 for international students). Electronic applications accepted. *Expenses:* Tuition, state resident: full-time $8771; part-time $292.35 per credit hour. Tuition, nonresident: full-time $17,541; part-time $584.70 per credit hour. *Required fees:* $372; $24.78 per credit hour. *Financial support:* In 2017–18, 99 students received support. Research assistantships, teaching assistantships, career-related internships or fieldwork, Federal Work-Study, scholarships/grants, and administrative and laboratory assistantships available. Support available to part-time students. Financial award application deadline: 3/1; financial award applicants required to submit FAFSA. *Unit head:* Shellie Hewitt, Director of Graduate and International Student Services, 660-543-4621, Fax: 660-543-4778, E-mail: hewitt@ucmo.edu. *Application contact:* 660-543-4621, E-mail: admit_intl@ucmo.edu.
Website: http://www.ucmo.edu/graduate/

Environmental and Occupational Health

University of Cincinnati, Graduate School, College of Medicine, Graduate Programs in Biomedical Sciences, Department of Environmental Health, Cincinnati, OH 45221. Offers environmental and industrial hygiene (MS, PhD); environmental and occupational medicine (MS); environmental genetics and molecular toxicology (MS, PhD); epidemiology and biostatistics (MS, PhD); occupational safety and ergonomics (MS, PhD). *Accreditation:* ABET (one or more programs are accredited); CEPH. Terminal master's awarded for partial completion of doctoral program. *Degree requirements:* For master's, thesis; for doctorate, thesis/dissertation, qualifying exam. *Entrance requirements:* For master's, GRE General Test, bachelor's degree in science; for doctorate, GRE General Test. Additional exam requirements/recommendations for international students: Required—TOEFL (minimum score 600 paper-based; 100 iBT). Electronic applications accepted. *Expenses: Tuition, area resident:* Full-time $14,468. Tuition, state resident: full-time $14,968; part-time $754 per credit hour. Tuition, nonresident: full-time $24,210; part-time $1311 per credit hour. *International tuition:* $26,460 full-time. *Required fees:* $3958; $84 per credit hour. One-time fee: $85 full-time. Tuition and fees vary according to course load, degree level and program. *Faculty research:* Carcinogens and mutagenesis, pulmonary studies, reproduction and development.

University of Colorado Denver, College of Liberal Arts and Sciences, Department of Geography and Environmental Sciences, Denver, CO 80217. Offers environmental sciences (MS), including air quality, ecosystems, environmental health, geospatial analysis, hazardous waste, water quality. *Program availability:* Part-time, evening/weekend. *Faculty:* 13 full-time (4 women), 5 part-time/adjunct (2 women). *Students:* 58 applicants, 76% accepted, 21 enrolled. In 2017, 17 master's awarded. *Degree requirements:* For master's, thesis or alternative, 30 credits including 21 of core requirements and 9 of environmental science electives. *Entrance requirements:* For master's, GRE General Test, BA in one of the natural/physical sciences or engineering (or equivalent background); prerequisite coursework in calculus and physics (one semester each); general chemistry with lab and general biology with lab (two semesters each); three letters of recommendation. Additional exam requirements/recommendations for international students: Required—TOEFL (minimum score 537 paper-based; 75 iBT); Recommended—IELTS (minimum score 6.5). *Application deadline:* For fall admission, 1/20 for domestic and international students; for spring admission, 10/1 for domestic and international students. Application fee: $50 ($75 for international students). Electronic applications accepted. *Faculty research:* Air quality, environmental health, ecosystems, hazardous waste, water quality, geospatial analysis and environmental science education. *Unit head:* Anne Chinn, Director of MS in Environmental Sciences Program, 303-556-3958, E-mail: ges@ucdenver.edu. *Application contact:* Sue Eddleman, Program Assistant, 303-352-3698, E-mail: sue.eddleman@ucdenver.edu.
Website: http://www.ucdenver.edu/academics/colleges/CLAS/Departments/ges/Programs/MasterofScience/Pages/MasterofScience.aspx

University of Connecticut, Graduate School, eCampus, Program in Occupational Safety and Health Management, Storrs, CT 06269. Offers Certificate.

University of Florida, Graduate School, College of Public Health and Health Professions, Department of Environmental and Global Health, Gainesville, FL 32611. Offers environmental health (PhD); one health (MHS, PhD). *Entrance requirements:* For master's and doctorate, GRE, minimum GPA of 3.0. Additional exam requirements/recommendations for international students: Required—TOEFL (minimum score 550 paper-based; 80 iBT), IELTS (minimum score 6).

University of Florida, Graduate School, College of Public Health and Health Professions, Programs in Public Health, Gainesville, FL 32611. Offers biostatistics (MPH); clinical and translational science (PhD); environmental health (MPH); epidemiology (MPH); health management and policy (MPH); public health (MPH, PhD, Certificate); public health practice (MPH); rehabilitation science (PhD); social and behavioral sciences (MPH); DPT/MPH; DVM/MPH; JD/MPH; MD/MPH; Pharm D/MPH. *Accreditation:* CEPH. *Program availability:* Online learning. *Degree requirements:* For master's, internship. *Entrance requirements:* For master's, GRE General Test, minimum GPA of 3.0. Additional exam requirements/recommendations for international students: Required—TOEFL (minimum score 550 paper-based; 80 iBT), IELTS (minimum score 6).

University of Georgia, College of Public Health, Department of Environmental Health Science, Athens, GA 30602. Offers MPH, MS, PhD. Terminal master's awarded for partial completion of doctoral program. *Degree requirements:* For master's, thesis; for doctorate, comprehensive exam, thesis/dissertation. *Entrance requirements:* For master's and doctorate, GRE General Test. Additional exam requirements/recommendations for international students: Required—TOEFL. Electronic applications accepted. *Faculty research:* Risk assessment, environmental toxicology, water quality, air quality.

University of Illinois at Chicago, School of Public Health, Division of Environmental and Occupational Health Sciences, Chicago, IL 60607-7128. Offers MPH, MS, Dr PH, PhD. *Accreditation:* ABET (one or more programs are accredited). *Program availability:* Part-time. Terminal master's awarded for partial completion of doctoral program. *Degree requirements:* For master's, thesis, field practicum; for doctorate, thesis/dissertation, independent research, internship. *Entrance requirements:* For master's and doctorate, GRE General Test, minimum GPA of 2.75. Additional exam requirements/recommendations for international students: Required—TOEFL. Electronic applications accepted. *Expenses:* Contact institution. *Faculty research:* Workers compensation, injury and illness surveillance, and disparities in occupational health; emergency/disaster management and continuity planning; water quality; air pollution; environmental chemistry; industrial hygiene; occupational medicine; hazardous substances management; toxicology; occupational safety, environmental epidemiology, and policy.

University of Illinois at Springfield, Graduate Programs, College of Public Affairs and Administration, Program in Public Health, Springfield, IL 62703-5407. Offers community health education (Graduate Certificate); emergency preparedness and homeland security (Graduate Certificate); environmental health (MPH, Graduate Certificate); environmental risk assessment (Graduate Certificate); epidemiology (Graduate Certificate); public health (MPH). *Program availability:* Part-time, evening/weekend, 100% online. *Faculty:* 7 full-time (4 women). *Students:* 38 full-time (23 women), 46 part-time (34 women); includes 27 minority (16 Black or African American, non-Hispanic/Latino; 4 Asian, non-Hispanic/Latino; 5 Hispanic/Latino; 2 Two or more races, non-Hispanic/Latino), 22 international. Average age 32. 47 applicants, 51% accepted, 18 enrolled. In 2017, 28 master's, 17 other advanced degrees awarded. *Degree requirements:* For master's, comprehensive exam, internship. *Entrance requirements:* For master's, GRE, minimum undergraduate GPA of 3.0, 3 letters of recommendation, statement of personal goals. Additional exam requirements/recommendations for international students: Required—TOEFL (minimum score 500 paper-based; 61 iBT). *Application deadline:* Applications are processed on a rolling basis. Application fee: $60 ($75 for international students). Electronic applications accepted. *Expenses:* Tuition, state resident: full-time $7896; part-time $329 per credit hour. Tuition, nonresident: full-time $16,200; part-time $675 per credit hour. Tuition and fees vary according to program. *Financial support:* In 2017–18, research assistantships with full tuition reimbursements (averaging $10,249 per year), teaching assistantships with full tuition reimbursements (averaging $10,303 per year) were awarded; fellowships, career-related internships or fieldwork, Federal Work-Study, scholarships/grants, health care benefits, and unspecified assistantships also available. Support available to part-time students. Financial award application deadline: 11/15; financial award applicants required to submit FAFSA. *Unit head:* Dr. Josiah Alamu, Program Administrator, 217-206-7874, Fax: 217-206-7279, E-mail: jalam3@uis.edu.
Website: http://www.uis.edu/publichealth/

The University of Iowa, Graduate College, College of Public Health, Department of Occupational and Environmental Health, Iowa City, IA 52242-1316. Offers agricultural safety and health (MS, PhD); ergonomics (MPH); industrial hygiene (MS, PhD); occupational and environmental health (MPH, MS, PhD, Certificate); MS/MA; MS/MS. *Accreditation:* ABET (one or more programs are accredited). *Degree requirements:* For master's, thesis optional, exam; for doctorate, comprehensive exam, thesis/dissertation. *Entrance requirements:* For master's and doctorate, GRE General Test, minimum GPA of 3.0. Additional exam requirements/recommendations for international students: Required—TOEFL (minimum score 600 paper-based; 100 iBT). Electronic applications accepted.

University of Maryland, College Park, Academic Affairs, School of Public Health, Maryland Institute for Applied Environmental Health, College Park, MD 20742. Offers environmental health sciences (MPH). *Entrance requirements:* For master's, GRE General Test, 3 letters of recommendation, minimum undergraduate GPA of 3.0, undergraduate transcripts, statement of goals and interests. Electronic applications accepted.

University of Massachusetts Amherst, Graduate School, School of Public Health and Health Sciences, Department of Public Health, Amherst, MA 01003. Offers biostatistics (MPH, MS, PhD); community health education (MPH, MS, PhD); environmental health sciences (MPH, MS, PhD); epidemiology (MPH, MS, PhD); health policy and management (MPH, MS, PhD); nutrition (MPH, PhD); public health practice (MPH); MPH/MPPA. *Program availability:* Part-time, evening/weekend, online learning. Terminal master's awarded for partial completion of doctoral program. *Degree requirements:* For master's, thesis (for some programs); for doctorate, comprehensive exam, thesis/dissertation. *Entrance requirements:* For master's and doctorate, GRE General Test. Additional exam requirements/recommendations for international students: Required—TOEFL (minimum score 550 paper-based; 80 iBT), IELTS (minimum score 6.5). Electronic applications accepted.

University of Memphis, Graduate School, School of Public Health, Memphis, TN 38152. Offers biostatistics (MPH); environmental health (MPH); epidemiology (MPH, PhD); health systems and policy (PhD); health systems management (MPH); public health (MHA); social and behavioral sciences (MPH, PhD). *Program availability:* Part-time, evening/weekend. *Faculty:* 20 full-time (7 women), 4 part-time/adjunct (1 woman). *Students:* 111 full-time (76 women), 59 part-time (45 women); includes 77 minority (48 Black or African American, non-Hispanic/Latino; 18 Asian, non-Hispanic/Latino; 6 Hispanic/Latino; 5 Two or more races, non-Hispanic/Latino), 23 international. Average age 31. 100 applicants, 91% accepted, 60 enrolled. In 2017, 56 master's, 4 doctorates awarded. *Degree requirements:* For master's, comprehensive exam, thesis (for some programs), practicum/field experience; for doctorate, comprehensive exam, thesis/dissertation, residency. *Entrance requirements:* For master's, GRE or GMAT, letters of recommendation; letter of intent; for doctorate, GRE, letters of recommendation; personal statement. Additional exam requirements/recommendations for international students: Required—TOEFL (minimum score 550 paper-based; 79 iBT). *Application deadline:* For fall admission, 4/1 for domestic students; for spring admission, 11/1 for domestic students. Application fee: $35 ($60 for international students). Electronic applications accepted. *Expenses:* Contact institution. *Financial support:* In 2017–18, 46 students received support, including 8 research assistantships with full tuition reimbursements available (averaging $8,950 per year); Federal Work-Study, scholarships/grants, and unspecified assistantships also available. Financial award application deadline: 2/1; financial award applicants required to submit FAFSA. *Faculty research:* Health and medical savings accounts, adoption rates, health informatics, Telehealth technologies, biostatistics, environmental health, epidemiology, health systems management, social and behavioral sciences. *Unit head:* Dr. Lisa M. Klesges, Dean, 901-678-4501, E-mail: lmklsges@memphis.edu. *Application contact:* Dr. Marian Levy, Assistant Dean, 901-678-4514, Fax: 901-678-5023, E-mail: sph-admin@memphis.edu.
Website: http://www.memphis.edu/sph/

University of Miami, Graduate School, College of Engineering, Department of Industrial Engineering, Program in Occupational Ergonomics and Safety, Coral Gables, FL 33124. Offers environmental health and safety (MS); occupational ergonomics and safety (MSOES). *Program availability:* Part-time. *Degree requirements:* For master's, thesis optional. *Entrance requirements:* For master's, GRE General Test, minimum GPA of 3.0. Additional exam requirements/recommendations for international students: Required—TOEFL (minimum score 550 paper-based). Electronic applications accepted. *Faculty research:* Noise, heat stress, water pollution.

University of Michigan, School of Public Health, Department of Environmental Health Sciences, Ann Arbor, MI 48109. Offers environmental health policy and promotion (MPH); environmental health sciences (MS, PhD); environmental quality, sustainability and health (MPH); industrial hygiene (MPH, MS); occupational and environmental epidemiology (MPH); toxicology (MPH, MS, PhD). *Accreditation:* CEPH (one or more programs are accredited). Terminal master's awarded for partial completion of doctoral program. *Degree requirements:* For master's, thesis (for some programs); for doctorate, thesis/dissertation, preliminary exam, oral defense of dissertation. *Entrance requirements:* For master's and doctorate, GRE General Test and/or MCAT. Additional exam requirements/recommendations for international students: Required—TOEFL (minimum score 100 iBT). Electronic applications accepted. *Expenses:* Tuition, state resident: full-time $22,368; part-time $1201 per credit hour. Tuition, nonresident: full-time $45,156; part-time $2467 per credit hour. *Required fees:* $376 per term. Tuition and fees vary according to course load, degree level and program. *Faculty research:* Toxicology, occupational hygiene, environmental exposure sciences, environmental epidemiology.

University of Minnesota, Twin Cities Campus, School of Public Health, Division of Environmental Health Sciences, Area in Environmental Health Policy, Minneapolis, MN 55455-0213. Offers MPH, MS, PhD. *Accreditation:* CEPH (one or more programs are accredited). *Degree requirements:* For doctorate, thesis/dissertation. *Entrance requirements:* For master's and doctorate, GRE General Test. Electronic applications accepted.

University of Minnesota, Twin Cities Campus, School of Public Health, Division of Environmental Health Sciences, Area in Occupational Medicine, Minneapolis, MN 55455-0213. Offers MPH. *Accreditation:* CEPH. *Entrance requirements:* For master's, GRE General Test. Electronic applications accepted.

University of Minnesota, Twin Cities Campus, School of Public Health, Major in Public Health Practice, Minneapolis, MN 55455-0213. Offers core concepts (Certificate); food safety and biosecurity (Certificate); occupational health and safety (Certificate); preparedness, response and recovery (Certificate); public health practice (MPH); DVM/

MPH; MD/MPH. *Program availability:* Part-time, online learning. *Degree requirements:* For master's, thesis. *Entrance requirements:* For master's, GRE, MCAT, United States Medical Licensing Exam. Additional exam requirements/recommendations for international students: Required—TOEFL (minimum score 600 paper-based). Electronic applications accepted.

University of Nebraska Medical Center, Environmental Health, Occupational Health and Toxicology Graduate Program, Omaha, NE 68198-4388. Offers PhD. *Degree requirements:* For doctorate, comprehensive exam, thesis/dissertation. *Entrance requirements:* For doctorate, GRE General Test, BS in chemistry, biology, biochemistry or related area. Additional exam requirements/recommendations for international students: Required—TOEFL (minimum score 550 paper-based; 80 iBT). Electronic applications accepted. *Expenses:* Tuition, state resident: full-time $8451; part-time $4225 per semester. Tuition, nonresident: full-time $24,219; part-time $11,295 per semester. *Required fees:* $589; $117 per term. *Faculty research:* Mechanisms of carcinogenesis, alcohol and metal toxicity, DNA damage, human molecular genetics, agrochemicals in soil and water.

University of Nevada, Reno, Graduate School, Interdisciplinary Program in Environmental Sciences and Health, Reno, NV 89557. Offers MS, PhD. Terminal master's awarded for partial completion of doctoral program. *Degree requirements:* For master's, thesis; for doctorate, thesis/dissertation. *Entrance requirements:* For master's, GRE General Test, minimum GPA of 2.75; for doctorate, GRE General Test, minimum GPA of 3.0. Additional exam requirements/recommendations for international students: Required—TOEFL (minimum score 500 paper-based; 61 iBT), IELTS (minimum score 6). Electronic applications accepted. *Faculty research:* Environmental chemistry, environmental toxicology, ecological toxicology.

University of New Haven, Graduate School, College of Arts and Sciences, Program in Environmental Science, West Haven, CT 06516. Offers environmental ecology (MS); environmental geoscience (MS); environmental health and management (MS); environmental science (MS); geographical information systems (MS). *Program availability:* Part-time, evening/weekend. *Students:* 27 full-time (17 women), 8 part-time (3 women); includes 3 minority (2 Black or African American, non-Hispanic/Latino; 1 Hispanic/Latino), 6 international. Average age 25. 46 applicants, 87% accepted, 19 enrolled. In 2017, 11 master's awarded. *Entrance requirements:* Additional exam requirements/recommendations for international students: Required—TOEFL (minimum score 80 iBT), IELTS, PTE. *Application deadline:* Applications are processed on a rolling basis. Application fee: $50. Electronic applications accepted. Application fee is waived when completed online. *Expenses: Tuition:* Full-time $16,020; part-time $890 per credit hour. *Required fees:* $220; $90 per term. *Financial support:* Research assistantships with partial tuition reimbursements, teaching assistantships with partial tuition reimbursements, Federal Work-Study, scholarships/grants, and unspecified assistantships available. Support available to part-time students. Financial award applicants required to submit FAFSA. *Unit head:* Dr. Roman Zajac, Coordinator, 203-932-7114, E-mail: rzajac@newhaven.edu. *Application contact:* Michelle Mason, Director of Graduate Enrollment, 203-932-7067, E-mail: mmason@newhaven.edu.
Website: http://www.newhaven.edu/4728/

The University of North Carolina at Chapel Hill, Graduate School, Gillings School of Global Public Health, Department of Environmental Sciences and Engineering, Chapel Hill, NC 27599. Offers environmental engineering (MPH, MS, MSEE, MSPH); environmental health sciences (MPH, MS, MSPH, PhD); MPH/MCRP; MS/MCRP; MSPH/MCRP. *Faculty:* 25 full-time (8 women), 30 part-time/adjunct (6 women). *Students:* 94 full-time (51 women), 4 part-time (2 women); includes 19 minority (1 Black or African American, non-Hispanic/Latino; 4 Asian, non-Hispanic/Latino; 5 Hispanic/Latino; 9 Two or more races, non-Hispanic/Latino), 23 international. Average age 28. 157 applicants, 32% accepted, 20 enrolled. In 2017, 18 master's, 11 doctorates awarded. Terminal master's awarded for partial completion of doctoral program. *Degree requirements:* For master's, comprehensive exam, thesis (for some programs), research paper; for doctorate, comprehensive exam, thesis/dissertation. *Entrance requirements:* For master's and doctorate, GRE General Test, 3 letters of recommendation (academic and/or professional; at least one academic). Additional exam requirements/recommendations for international students: Required—TOEFL (minimum score 90 iBT), IELTS (minimum score 7). *Application deadline:* For fall admission, 4/10 for domestic and international students. Applications are processed on a rolling basis. Application fee: $85. Electronic applications accepted. *Financial support:* Fellowships with tuition reimbursements, research assistantships with tuition reimbursements, teaching assistantships with tuition reimbursements, career-related internships or fieldwork, Federal Work-Study, traineeships, health care benefits, and unspecified assistantships available. Support available to part-time students. Financial award application deadline: 12/10; financial award applicants required to submit FAFSA. *Faculty research:* Air, radiation and industrial hygiene, aquatic and atmospheric sciences, environmental health sciences, environmental management and policy, water resources engineering. *Unit head:* Dr. Barbara J. Turpin, Professor and Chair, 919-966-1024, Fax: 919-966-7911, E-mail: esechair@unc.edu. *Application contact:* Karla Townley-Tilson, Academic Coordinator, 919-966-4818, Fax: 919-966-7911, E-mail: kttilson@unc.edu.
Website: http://sph.unc.edu/envr/environmental-sciences-and-engineering-home/

University of Oklahoma Health Sciences Center, Graduate College, College of Public Health, Department of Occupational and Environmental Health, Oklahoma City, OK 73190. Offers MPH, MS, Dr PH, PhD, JD/MPH, JD/MS. JD/MPH, JD/MS offered jointly with University of Oklahoma. *Accreditation:* ABET (one or more programs are accredited); CEPH (one or more programs are accredited). *Program availability:* Part-time. *Degree requirements:* For master's, comprehensive exam, thesis (for some programs); for doctorate, comprehensive exam, thesis/dissertation. *Entrance requirements:* For master's, GRE General Test (for all except occupational medicine), 3 letters of recommendation, resume; for doctorate, GRE (for all except occupational medicine), 3 letters of recommendation, resume. Additional exam requirements/recommendations for international students: Required—TOEFL (minimum score 570 paper-based). *Faculty research:* Environmental safety, accident prevention and injury control.

University of Pennsylvania, Perelman School of Medicine, Master of Public Health Program, Philadelphia, PA 19104. Offers environmental health (MPH); generalist (MPH); global health (MPH); DMD/MPH; JD/MPH; MD/MPH; MES/MPH; MPH/MBE; MPH/MPA; MPH/MS; MSN/MPH; MSSP/MPH; MSW/MPH; PhD/MPH. *Accreditation:* CEPH. *Program availability:* Part-time, evening/weekend. *Faculty:* 12 full-time (10 women), 36 part-time/adjunct (27 women). *Students:* 130 full-time (102 women), 61 part-time (50 women); includes 85 minority (29 Black or African American, non-Hispanic/Latino; 33 Asian, non-Hispanic/Latino; 4 Hispanic/Latino; 19 Two or more races, non-Hispanic/Latino), 12 international. Average age 29. 385 applicants, 47% accepted, 62 enrolled. In 2017, 50 master's awarded. *Degree requirements:* For master's, thesis. *Entrance requirements:* For master's, GRE. Additional exam requirements/recommendations for international students: Required—TOEFL (minimum score 100 iBT), IELTS (minimum score 7). *Application deadline:* For fall admission, 4/15 for domestic and international students. Applications are processed on a rolling basis. Electronic applications accepted. *Expenses:* $31,682 tuition, $4,066 fees. *Financial support:* In 2017–18, 27 students received support, including 6 research assistantships with partial tuition reimbursements available (averaging $18,104 per year), 21 teaching assistantships with partial tuition reimbursements available (averaging $4,526 per year); fellowships and tuition waivers (partial) also available. Financial award application deadline: 4/15; financial award applicants required to submit FAFSA. *Faculty research:* Health disparities, health behaviors, obesity, global health, epidemiology and prevention research. *Unit head:* Dr. Jennifer Pinto-Martin, Director, 215-898-4726, E-mail: pinto@nursing.upenn.edu. *Application contact:* Moriah Hall, Associate Director, MPH Program, 215-573-8841, E-mail: moriahh@mail.med.upenn.edu.
Website: http://www.cphi.upenn.edu/mph

University of Pittsburgh, Graduate School of Public Health, Department of Environmental and Occupational Health, Pittsburgh, PA 15261. Offers MPH, MS, PhD. *Accreditation:* CEPH (one or more programs are accredited). *Program availability:* Part-time. *Faculty:* 16 full-time (4 women), 1 part-time/adjunct (0 women). *Students:* 31 full-time (16 women), 3 part-time (all women); includes 7 minority (2 Black or African American, non-Hispanic/Latino; 2 Asian, non-Hispanic/Latino; 3 Hispanic/Latino), 15 international. Average age 31. 40 applicants, 73% accepted, 5 enrolled. Terminal master's awarded for partial completion of doctoral program. *Degree requirements:* For master's, thesis, practica; essay (for MPH); comprehensive exam (for MS); for doctorate, comprehensive exam, thesis/dissertation, preliminary exams, journal club. *Entrance requirements:* For master's, GRE General Test, transcripts, recommendation letters, personal statement, bachelor's degree; for doctorate, GRE General Test, minimum GPA of 3.4; 2 courses each in physics, chemistry and math; bachelor's or master's degree. Additional exam requirements/recommendations for international students: Required—TOEFL (minimum score 550 paper-based, 80 iBT) or IELTS (minimum score 6.5). *Application deadline:* For fall admission, 4/15 for domestic students, 3/15 for international students; for winter admission, 10/15 for domestic students, 9/15 for international students; for summer admission, 5/15 for domestic students, 4/15 for international students. Application fee: $135. Electronic applications accepted. *Expenses:* $25,500 per year in-state, $42,130 out-of-state. *Financial support:* In 2017–18, 13 students received support, including 12 research assistantships with full tuition reimbursements available (averaging $28,800 per year), 1 teaching assistantship with full tuition reimbursement available (averaging $9,600 per year); fellowships, scholarships/grants, and tuition waivers also available. Financial award applicants required to submit FAFSA. *Faculty research:* DNA damage and repair, free radical biology, genomics of acute lung disease, exposure to metals, lipid-associated genes in pathogenesis in Alzheimer's disease. *Total annual research expenditures:* $8 million. *Unit head:* Dr. Sally E. Wenzel, Chair, 412-624-8300. *Application contact:* Eileen Penny Weiss, Student Affairs Coordinator, 412-383-7297, E-mail: pweiss@pitt.edu.
Website: https://www.publichealth.pitt.edu/eoh/_rdr

University of Puerto Rico–Medical Sciences Campus, Graduate School of Public Health, Department of Environmental Health, Doctoral Program in Environmental Health, San Juan, PR 00936-5067. Offers MS, Dr PH. *Program availability:* Part-time. *Expenses:* Contact institution.

University of Saint Francis, Graduate School, Keith Busse School of Business and Entrepreneurial Leadership, Fort Wayne, IN 46808-3994. Offers business administration (MBA), including sustainability; environmental health (MEH); healthcare administration (MHA); organizational leadership (MOL). *Accreditation:* ACBSP. *Program availability:* Part-time, evening/weekend, online only, 100% online. *Faculty:* 4 full-time (3 women), 11 part-time/adjunct (1 woman). *Students:* 75 full-time (43 women), 108 part-time (59 women); includes 37 minority (21 Black or African American, non-Hispanic/Latino; 1 Asian, non-Hispanic/Latino; 11 Hispanic/Latino; 1 Native Hawaiian or other Pacific Islander, non-Hispanic/Latino; 3 Two or more races, non-Hispanic/Latino). Average age 34. 101 applicants, 98% accepted, 75 enrolled. In 2017, 133 master's awarded. *Entrance requirements:* For master's, GMAT (if cumulative GPA is below 2.75 with less than five years' professional work experience), minimum undergraduate GPA of 2.75; statement of professional goals; resume. Additional exam requirements/recommendations for international students: Required—TOEFL (minimum score 550 paper-based) or IELTS (minimum score 6.5). *Application deadline:* For fall admission, 7/1 for international students; for spring admission, 11/1 for international students; for summer admission, 3/1 for international students. Applications are processed on a rolling basis. Application fee: $0. Electronic applications accepted. *Expenses:* $475 per hour. *Financial support:* Application deadline: 4/15; applicants required to submit FAFSA. *Unit head:* Dr. Robert Lee, Dean, 260-399-7700 Ext. 8304, Fax: 260-399-8174, E-mail: rlee@sf.edu. *Application contact:* Kyle Richardson, Associate Director of Enrollment Services for Adult Learning, 260-399-7700 Ext. 6310, Fax: 260-399-8152, E-mail: krichardson@sf.edu.
Website: https://business.sf.edu/graduate/

University of South Alabama, Graduate School, Program in Environmental Toxicology, Mobile, AL 36688. Offers basic medical sciences (MS); biology (MS); chemistry (MS); environmental toxicology (MS); exposure route and chemical transport (MS). *Faculty:* 3 full-time (0 women), 1 (woman) part-time/adjunct. *Students:* 9 full-time (2 women), 2 part-time (both women); includes 1 minority (Black or African American, non-Hispanic/Latino). Average age 26. 7 applicants, 29% accepted, 2 enrolled. In 2017, 3 master's awarded. *Degree requirements:* For master's, comprehensive exam, research project or thesis. *Entrance requirements:* For master's, GRE, BA/BS in related discipline, minimum undergraduate GPA of 3.0. Additional exam requirements/recommendations for international students: Required—TOEFL (minimum score 525 paper-based; 71 iBT). *Application deadline:* For fall admission, 7/15 for domestic students, 6/15 for international students; for spring admission, 12/1 for domestic students, 11/1 for international students. Application fee: $35. Electronic applications accepted. *Expenses:* Tuition, state resident: full-time $10,104; part-time $421 per semester hour. Tuition, nonresident: full-time $20,208; part-time $842 per semester hour. *Financial support:* Fellowships, research assistantships, teaching assistantships, career-related internships or fieldwork, Federal Work-Study, institutionally sponsored loans, scholarships/grants, and unspecified assistantships available. Support available to part-time students. Financial award application deadline: 3/31; financial award applicants required to submit FAFSA. *Unit head:* Dr. Harold Pardue, Dean of the Graduate School, 251-460-6310, E-mail: hpardue@southalabama.edu. *Application contact:* Dr. David Forbes, Chair, Chemistry, 251-460-6181, E-mail: dforbes@southalabama.edu.
Website: http://www.southalabama.edu/graduatemajors/etox/index.html

University of South Carolina, The Graduate School, Arnold School of Public Health, Department of Environmental Health Sciences, Program in Environmental Quality, Columbia, SC 29208. Offers MPH, MS, MSPH, PhD. *Accreditation:* CEPH (one or more programs are accredited). *Program availability:* Part-time. *Degree requirements:* For master's, comprehensive exam, thesis (for some programs), practicum (MPH); for doctorate, one foreign language, comprehensive exam, thesis/dissertation. *Entrance requirements:* For master's and doctorate, GRE General Test. Additional exam requirements/recommendations for international students: Required—TOEFL (minimum score 570 paper-based). Electronic applications accepted. *Faculty research:* Environmental assessment and planning; environmental toxicology; ecosystems analysis; air quality monitoring and modeling.

Environmental and Occupational Health

University of Southern California, Keck School of Medicine and Graduate School, Graduate Programs in Medicine, Department of Preventive Medicine, Master of Public Health Program, Los Angeles, CA 90032. Offers biostatistics and epidemiology (MPH); child and family health (MPH); environmental health (MPH); geohealth (MPH); global health leadership (MPH); health communication (MPH); health education and promotion (MPH); public health policy (MPH). *Accreditation:* CEPH. *Program availability:* Part-time, evening/weekend. *Faculty:* 47 full-time (35 women), 13 part-time/adjunct (8 women). *Students:* 258 full-time (204 women), 61 part-time (50 women); includes 167 minority (28 Black or African American, non-Hispanic/Latino; 1 American Indian or Alaska Native, non-Hispanic/Latino; 61 Asian, non-Hispanic/Latino; 64 Hispanic/Latino; 4 Native Hawaiian or other Pacific Islander, non-Hispanic/Latino; 9 Two or more races, non-Hispanic/Latino), 28 international. Average age 26. 378 applicants, 53% accepted, 87 enrolled. In 2017, 91 master's awarded. *Degree requirements:* For master's, practicum, final report, oral presentation. *Entrance requirements:* For master's, GRE General Test, MCAT, GMAT, minimum GPA of 3.0. Additional exam requirements/recommendations for international students: Required—TOEFL (minimum score 600 paper-based; 90 iBT). *Application deadline:* For fall admission, 12/1 priority date for domestic students, 5/1 priority date for international students; for spring admission, 9/1 priority date for domestic and international students; for summer admission, 3/1 for domestic and international students. Applications are processed on a rolling basis. Application fee: $90. Electronic applications accepted. *Expenses:* Contact institution. *Financial support:* Career-related internships or fieldwork, Federal Work-Study, institutionally sponsored loans, and scholarships/grants available. Support available to part-time students. Financial award application deadline: 5/4; financial award applicants required to submit CSS PROFILE or FAFSA. *Faculty research:* Cancer and heart disease epidemiology and prevention, mass media and health communication research, effects of air pollution on health, tobacco control, global health. *Total annual research expenditures:* $7 million. *Unit head:* Dr. Louise A. Rohrbach, Director, 323-442-8237, Fax: 323-442-8297, E-mail: rohrbac@usc.edu. *Application contact:* Valerie Burris, Admissions Counselor, 323-442-7257, Fax: 323-442-8297, E-mail: valeriem@usc.edu.
Website: http://mph.usc.edu/

University of South Florida, College of Public Health, Department of Environmental and Occupational Health, Tampa, FL 33620-9951. Offers MPH, MSPH, PhD. *Accreditation:* ABET (one or more programs are accredited); CEPH (one or more programs are accredited). *Program availability:* Part-time, evening/weekend. *Degree requirements:* For master's, comprehensive exam, thesis (for some programs); for doctorate, comprehensive exam, thesis/dissertation. *Entrance requirements:* For master's, GRE General Test, minimum GPA of 3.0 in upper-level course work, goal statement letter, two professional letters of recommendation, resume/curriculum vitae; for doctorate, GRE General Test, minimum GPA of 3.0 in upper-level course work, goal statement letter, three professional letters of recommendation, resume/curriculum vitae, writing sample. Additional exam requirements/recommendations for international students: Required—TOEFL (minimum score 550 paper-based; 79 iBT). Electronic applications accepted. *Faculty research:* Biomedical assessment/stress test, risk impact, nitrobenzes on mammalism glutathion transferases, lysimeter research management, independent hygiene development.

University of South Florida, Innovative Education, Tampa, FL 33620-9951. Offers adult, career and higher education (Graduate Certificate), including college teaching, leadership in developing human resources, leadership in higher education; Africana studies (Graduate Certificate), including diasporas and health disparities, genocide and human rights; aging studies (Graduate Certificate), including gerontology; art research (Graduate Certificate), including museum studies; business foundations (Graduate Certificate); chemical and biomedical engineering (Graduate Certificate), including materials science and engineering, water, health and sustainability; child and family studies (Graduate Certificate), including positive behavior support; civil and industrial engineering (Graduate Certificate), including transportation systems analysis; community and family health (Graduate Certificate), including maternal and child health, social marketing and public health, violence and injury: prevention and intervention, women's health; criminology (Graduate Certificate), including criminal justice administration; data science for public administration (Graduate Certificate); digital humanities (Graduate Certificate); educational measurement and research (Graduate Certificate), including evaluation; English (Graduate Certificate), including comparative literary studies, creative writing, professional and technical communication; entrepreneurship (Graduate Certificate); environmental health (Graduate Certificate), including safety management; epidemiology and biostatistics (Graduate Certificate), including applied biostatistics, biostatistics, concepts and tools of epidemiology, epidemiology, epidemiology of infectious diseases; geography, environment and planning (Graduate Certificate), including community development, environmental policy and management, geographical information systems; geology (Graduate Certificate), including hydrogeology; global health (Graduate Certificate), including disaster management, global health and Latin American and Caribbean studies, global health practice, humanitarian assistance, infection control; government and international affairs (Graduate Certificate), including Cuban studies, globalization studies; health policy and management (Graduate Certificate), including health management and leadership, public health policy and programs; hearing specialist: early intervention (Graduate Certificate); industrial and management systems engineering (Graduate Certificate), including systems engineering, technology management; information studies (Graduate Certificate), including school library media specialist; information systems/decision sciences (Graduate Certificate), including analytics and business intelligence; instructional technology (Graduate Certificate), including distance education, Florida digital/virtual educator, instructional design, multimedia design, Web design; internal medicine, bioethics and medical humanities (Graduate Certificate), including biomedical ethics; Latin American and Caribbean studies (Graduate Certificate); leadership for coastal resiliency planning (Graduate Certificate); mass communications (Graduate Certificate), including multimedia journalism; mathematics and statistics (Graduate Certificate), including mathematics; medicine (Graduate Certificate), including aging and neuroscience, bioinformatics, biotechnology, brain fitness and memory management, clinical investigation, hand and upper limb rehabilitation, health informatics, health sciences, integrative weight management, intellectual property, medicine and gender, metabolic and nutritional medicine, metabolic cardiology, pharmacy sciences; national and competitive intelligence (Graduate Certificate); nursing (Graduate Certificate), including simulation based academic fellowship in advanced pain management; psychological and social foundations (Graduate Certificate), including career counseling, college teaching, diversity in education, mental health counseling, school counseling; public affairs (Graduate Certificate), including nonprofit management, public management, research administration; public health (Graduate Certificate), including assessing chemical toxicity and public health risks, health equity, pharmacoepidemiology, public health generalist, toxicology, translational research in adolescent behavioral health; public health practices (Graduate Certificate), including planning for healthy communities; rehabilitation and mental health counseling (Graduate Certificate), including integrative mental health care, marriage and family therapy, rehabilitation technology; secondary education (Graduate Certificate), including ESOL, foreign language education: culture and content, foreign language education: professional; social work (Graduate Certificate), including geriatric social work/clinical gerontology; special education (Graduate Certificate), including autism spectrum disorder, disabilities education: severe/profound; world languages (Graduate Certificate), including teaching English as a second language (TESL) or foreign language. *Unit head:* Dr. Cynthia DeLuca, Associate Vice President and Assistant Vice Provost, 813-974-3077, Fax: 813-974-7061, E-mail: deluca@usf.edu. *Application contact:* Owen Hooper, Director, Summer and Alternative Calendar Programs, 813-974-6917, E-mail: hooper@usf.edu.
Website: http://www.usf.edu/innovative-education/

The University of Texas at Tyler, College of Engineering, Department of Civil Engineering, Tyler, TX 75799-0001. Offers environmental engineering (MS); industrial safety (MS); structural engineering (MS); transportation engineering (MS); water resources engineering (MS). *Program availability:* Part-time, evening/weekend. *Degree requirements:* For master's, thesis optional. *Entrance requirements:* For master's, GRE General Test, bachelor's degree in engineering, associated science degree. Additional exam requirements/recommendations for international students: Required—TOEFL. *Faculty research:* Non-destructive strength testing, indoor air quality, transportation routing and signaling, pavement replacement criteria, flood water routing, construction and long-term behavior of innovative geotechnical foundation and embankment construction used in highway construction, engineering education.

The University of Texas Health Science Center at Houston, School of Public Health, Houston, TX 77030. Offers behavioral science (PhD); biostatistics (MPH, MS, PhD); environmental health (MPH); epidemiology (MPH, MS, PhD); general public health (Certificate); genomics and bioinformatics (Certificate); health disparities (Certificate); health promotion/health education (MPH, Dr PH); healthcare management (Certificate); management, policy and community health (MPH, Dr PH, PhD); maternal and child health (Certificate); public health informatics (Certificate); DDS/MPH; JD/MPH; MBA/MPH; MD/MPH; MGPS/MPH; MP Aff/MPH; MS/MPH; MSN/MPH; MSW/MPH; PhD/MPH. Specific programs are offered at each of our six campuses in Texas (Austin, Brownsville, Dallas, El Paso, Houston, and San Antonio). *Accreditation:* CEPH. *Program availability:* Part-time. *Faculty:* 140 full-time (74 women), 23 part-time/adjunct (14 women). *Students:* 604 full-time (446 women), 534 part-time (384 women); includes 504 minority (106 Black or African American, non-Hispanic/Latino; 177 Asian, non-Hispanic/Latino; 88 Hispanic/Latino; 1 Native Hawaiian or other Pacific Islander, non-Hispanic/Latino; 132 Two or more races, non-Hispanic/Latino). Average age 31. 1,425 applicants, 58% accepted, 423 enrolled. In 2017, 315 master's, 68 doctorates awarded. *Degree requirements:* For master's, thesis (for some programs); for doctorate, comprehensive exam, thesis/dissertation. *Entrance requirements:* For master's and doctorate, GRE General Test. Additional exam requirements/recommendations for international students: Required—TOEFL (minimum score 600 paper-based, 100 iBT) or IELTS (7.5). *Application deadline:* For fall admission, 3/1 for domestic and international students; for spring admission, 10/1 for domestic and international students; for summer admission, 3/1 for domestic students. Applications are processed on a rolling basis. Application fee: $135. Electronic applications accepted. *Expenses:* $233 per semester credit hour resident tuition, $980 per semester credit hour non-resident tuition. *Financial support:* Fellowships, research assistantships, teaching assistantships, career-related internships or fieldwork, institutionally sponsored loans, scholarships/grants, traineeships, health care benefits, and unspecified assistantships available. Support available to part-time students. Financial award application deadline: 5/5; financial award applicants required to submit FAFSA. *Faculty research:* Chronic and infectious disease epidemiology; health promotion and health education; applied and theoretical biostatistics; healthcare management, policy and economics; environmental and occupational health. *Total annual research expenditures:* $47.8 million. *Unit head:* Dr. Susan Emery, Senior Associate Dean of Academic and Research Affairs. *Application contact:* Elvis Parada, Manager of Admissions and Recruitment, 713-500-9028, Fax: 713-500-9068, E-mail: elvis.a.parada@uth.tmc.edu.
Website: https://sph.uth.edu

University of the Sacred Heart, Graduate Programs, Department of Natural Sciences, Program in Occupational Health and Safety, San Juan, PR 00914-0383. Offers MS.

The University of Toledo, College of Graduate Studies, College of Health and Human Services, School of Population Health, Toledo, OH 43606-3390. Offers health education (PhD); occupational health-industrial hygiene (MS); public health (MPH).

The University of Toledo, College of Graduate Studies, College of Medicine and Life Sciences, Department of Public Health and Preventative Medicine, Toledo, OH 43606-3390. Offers biostatistics and epidemiology (Certificate); contemporary gerontological practice (Certificate); environmental and occupational health and safety (MPH); epidemiology (Certificate); global public health (Certificate); health promotion and education (MPH); industrial hygiene (MSOH); medical and health science teaching and learning (Certificate); occupational health (Certificate); public health administration (MPH); public health and emergency response (Certificate); public health epidemiology (MPH); public health nutrition (MPH); MD/MPH. *Program availability:* Part-time, evening/weekend. *Degree requirements:* For master's, thesis or alternative. *Entrance requirements:* For master's, GRE, minimum undergraduate GPA of 3.0, three letters of recommendation, statement of purpose, transcripts from all prior institutions attended, resume; for Certificate, minimum undergraduate GPA of 3.0, three letters of recommendation, statement of purpose, transcripts from all prior institutions attended, resume. Additional exam requirements/recommendations for international students: Required—TOEFL (minimum score 550 paper-based; 80 iBT), IELTS (minimum score 6.5). Electronic applications accepted.

University of Toronto, School of Graduate Studies, Department of Public Health Sciences, Toronto, ON M5S 1A1, Canada. Offers biostatistics (M Sc, PhD); community health (M Sc); community nutrition (MPH), including nutrition and dietetics; epidemiology (MPH, PhD); family and community medicine (MPH); occupational and environmental health (MPH); social and behavioral health science (PhD); social and behavioral health sciences (MPH), including health promotion. *Accreditation:* CAHME (one or more programs are accredited). *Program availability:* Part-time. *Degree requirements:* For master's, thesis (for some programs), practicum; for doctorate, comprehensive exam, thesis/dissertation, oral thesis defense. *Entrance requirements:* For master's, 2 letters of reference, relevant professional/research experience, minimum B average in final year; for doctorate, 2 letters of reference, relevant professional/research experience, minimum B+ average. Additional exam requirements/recommendations for international students: Required—TOEFL (minimum score 580 paper-based; 93 iBT), TWE (minimum score 5). Electronic applications accepted. *Expenses:* Contact institution.

University of Vermont, The Robert Larner, MD College of Medicine and Graduate College, Graduate Programs in Medicine, Program in Public Health, Burlington, VT 05405. Offers epidemiology (Graduate Certificate); global and environmental health (Graduate Certificate); healthcare management and policy (Graduate Certificate); public health (MPH). *Program availability:* Online only, 100% online. *Students:* 96. 73 applicants, 88% accepted, 41 enrolled. In 2017, 6 master's, 6 other advanced degrees awarded. *Entrance requirements:* For master's and Graduate Certificate, resume/curriculum vitae. Additional exam requirements/recommendations for international students: Required—TOEFL (minimum iBT score of 90) or IELTS (6.5). *Application deadline:* For fall admission, 7/1 for domestic and international students; for spring admission, 11/15 for domestic and international students; for summer admission, 4/1 for domestic and international students. Application fee: $65. Electronic applications accepted. *Expenses:* $646 per credit in-state, $970 per credit out-of-state. *Unit head:* Dr. Jan Carney, Coordinator, 802-656-2085, E-mail: public.health@uvm.edu.
Website: https://learn.uvm.edu/program/master-of-public-health/

University of Washington, Graduate School, School of Public Health, Department of Environmental and Occupational Health Sciences, Seattle, WA 98195. Offers applied toxicology (MS); environmental and occupational health (MPH); environmental and occupational hygiene (PhD); environmental health (MS); environmental toxicology (MS, PhD); occupational and environmental exposure sciences (MS); occupational and environmental medicine (MPH). *Accreditation:* CEPH. *Program availability:* Part-time. *Faculty:* 38 full-time (14 women), 17 part-time/adjunct (8 women). *Students:* 68 full-time (51 women), 9 part-time (3 women); includes 21 minority (2 Black or African American, non-Hispanic/Latino; 1 American Indian or Alaska Native, non-Hispanic/Latino; 11 Asian, non-Hispanic/Latino; 6 Hispanic/Latino; 1 Native Hawaiian or other Pacific Islander, non-Hispanic/Latino), 9 international. Average age 31. 121 applicants, 50% accepted, 33 enrolled. In 2017, 20 master's, 10 doctorates awarded. Terminal master's awarded for partial completion of doctoral program. *Entrance requirements:* For master's and doctorate, GRE General Test. Additional exam requirements/recommendations for international students: Required—TOEFL. Electronic applications accepted. *Expenses:* Contact institution. *Financial support:* Fellowships, research assistantships, teaching assistantships, career-related internships or fieldwork, institutionally sponsored loans, scholarships/grants, traineeships, health care benefits, and unspecified assistantships available. *Faculty research:* Developmental and behavioral toxicology, biochemical toxicology, exposure assessment, hazardous waste, industrial chemistry. *Unit head:* Dr. Michael Yost, Chair, 206-543-3199, Fax: 206-543-9616. *Application contact:* Trina Sterry, Manager of Student and Academic Services, 206-543-3199, E-mail: ehgrad@uw.edu.
Website: http://deohs.washington.edu/

University of Wisconsin–Milwaukee, Graduate School, Joseph J. Zilber School of Public Health, Program in Environmental Health Sciences, Milwaukee, WI 53201-0413. Offers PhD. *Students:* 2 full-time (1 woman), 1 (woman) part-time. Average age 44. 1 applicant, 100% accepted. In 2017, 1 doctorate awarded. Electronic applications accepted. *Unit head:* Ronald Perez, Interim Dean, 414-229-6543. *Application contact:* Darcie K. G. Warren, Graduate Program Manager, 414-229-5633, E-mail: darcie@uwm.edu.

University of Wisconsin–Milwaukee, Graduate School, Joseph J. Zilber School of Public Health, Program in Public Health, Milwaukee, WI 53201-0413. Offers biostatistics (MPH); community and behavioral health promotion (MPH); environmental health sciences (MPH); epidemiology (MPH, PhD); public and population health (Graduate Certificate); public health policy and administration (MPH); public health: biostatistics (PhD); public health: community and behavioral health promotion (PhD). *Students:* 62 full-time (53 women), 23 part-time (17 women); includes 24 minority (5 Black or African American, non-Hispanic/Latino; 11 Asian, non-Hispanic/Latino; 8 Two or more races, non-Hispanic/Latino), 10 international. Average age 31. 65 applicants, 74% accepted, 34 enrolled. In 2017, 28 master's, 1 doctorate awarded. Electronic applications accepted. *Application contact:* Darcie K. G. Warren, Graduate Program Manager, 414-229-5633, E-mail: darcie@uwm.edu.

University of Wisconsin–Whitewater, School of Graduate Studies, College of Education and Professional Studies, Department of Occupational and Environmental Safety, Whitewater, WI 53190-1790. Offers safety (MS). *Program availability:* Part-time, evening/weekend, online learning. *Degree requirements:* For master's, thesis or alternative. *Entrance requirements:* For master's, 2 letters of recommendation. Additional exam requirements/recommendations for international students: Required—TOEFL (minimum score 550 paper-based; 80 iBT), IELTS (minimum score 6). Electronic applications accepted.

West Virginia University, School of Public Health, Morgantown, WV 26506-9190. Offers biostatistics (MPH, MS, PhD); epidemiology (MPH, PhD); health policy (MPH); occupational and environmental health sciences (MPH, PhD); public health (MPH); school health education (MS); social and behavioral science (MPH, PhD). *Accreditation:* CEPH. *Program availability:* Part-time, online learning. *Students:* 69 full-time (48 women), 27 part-time (15 women); includes 14 minority (5 Black or African American, non-Hispanic/Latino; 4 Asian, non-Hispanic/Latino; 1 Hispanic/Latino; 4 Two or more races, non-Hispanic/Latino), 11 international. *Degree requirements:* For master's, practicum, project. *Entrance requirements:* For master's, GRE General Test, MCAT, medical degree, medical internship. Additional exam requirements/recommendations for international students: Required—TOEFL (minimum score 550 paper-based; 80 iBT). *Application deadline:* For fall admission, 4/15 priority date for domestic students; for spring admission, 12/1 for domestic students. Applications are processed on a rolling basis. Application fee: $60. *Expenses:* Contact institution. *Financial support:* Research assistantships, teaching assistantships, scholarships/grants, and health care benefits available. Financial award application deadline: 2/1; financial award applicants required to submit FAFSA. *Faculty research:* Occupational health, environmental health, clinical epidemiology, health care management, prevention. *Unit head:* Leah Adkins, Senior Program Coordinator, 304-293-1097, E-mail: leadkins@hsc.wvu.edu.
Website: http://publichealth.hsc.wvu.edu/

Yale University, Yale School of Medicine, Yale School of Public Health, New Haven, CT 06520. Offers applied biostatistics and epidemiology (APMPH); biostatistics (MPH, MS, PhD), including global health (MPH); chronic disease epidemiology (MPH, PhD), including global health (MPH); environmental health sciences (MPH, PhD), including global health (MPH); epidemiology of microbial diseases (MPH, PhD), including global health (MPH); global health (APMPH); health management (MPH), including global health; health policy (MPH), including global health; health policy and administration (APMPH, PhD); occupational and environmental medicine (APMPH); preventive medicine (APMPH); social and behavioral sciences (APMPH, MPH), including global health (MPH); JD/MPH; M Div/MPH; MBA/MPH; MD/MPH; MEM/MPH; MFS/MPH; MM Sc/MPH; MPH/MA; MSN/MPH. MS and PhD offered through the Graduate School. *Accreditation:* CEPH. *Program availability:* Part-time. Terminal master's awarded for partial completion of doctoral program. *Degree requirements:* For master's, thesis, summer internship; for doctorate, comprehensive exam, thesis/dissertation, residency. *Entrance requirements:* For master's, GMAT, GRE, or MCAT, two years of undergraduate coursework in math and science; for doctorate, GRE General Test. Additional exam requirements/recommendations for international students: Required—TOEFL (minimum score 100 iBT). Electronic applications accepted. *Expenses:* Contact institution. *Faculty research:* Genetic and emerging infections epidemiology, virology, cost/quality, vector biology, quantitative methods, aging, asthma, cancer.

Epidemiology

American University of Beirut, Graduate Programs, Faculty of Health Sciences, 1107 2020, Lebanon. Offers environmental sciences (MS), including environmental health; epidemiology (MS, PhD); epidemiology and biostatistics (MPH); health care leadership (EMHCL); health management and policy (MPH), including health service administration; health promotion and community health (MPH); health research (MS); public health nutrition (MS). *Program availability:* Part-time. *Faculty:* 33 full-time (22 women), 5 part-time/adjunct (2 women). *Students:* 75 full-time (60 women), 78 part-time (67 women). Average age 27. 274 applicants, 56% accepted, 47 enrolled. In 2017, 63 master's awarded. *Degree requirements:* For master's, one foreign language, comprehensive exam (for some programs), thesis (for MS); for doctorate, one foreign language, comprehensive exam, thesis/dissertation. *Entrance requirements:* For master's, 2 letters of recommendations, personal statement, transcript; for doctorate, GRE, 3 letters of recommendations, personal statement, interview. Additional exam requirements/recommendations for international students: Required—TOEFL (minimum score 583 paper-based; 97 iBT), IELTS (minimum score 7). *Application deadline:* For fall admission, 4/4 for domestic and international students; for spring admission, 11/3 for domestic and international students. Application fee: $50. Electronic applications accepted. *Expenses:* Contact institution. *Financial support:* In 2017–18, 75 students received support. Scholarships/grants, health care benefits, and unspecified assistantships available. Financial award application deadline: 4/4. *Faculty research:* Reproductive and sexual health; occupational and environmental health; conflict and health; mental health; quality in health care delivery, tobacco control. *Total annual research expenditures:* $2 million. *Unit head:* Prof. Iman Adel Nuwayhid, Dean/Professor, 961-1-759683 Ext. 4600, Fax: 961-1-744470, E-mail: nuwayhid@aub.edu.lb. *Application contact:* Mitra Tauk, Administrative Coordinator, 961-1-350000 Ext. 4687, E-mail: mt12@aub.edu.lb.
Website: http://www.aub.edu.lb/fhs/fhs_home/Pages/index.aspx

Boston University, School of Public Health, Epidemiology Department, Boston, MA 02215. Offers MPH, MS, PhD. *Program availability:* Part-time, evening/weekend. *Degree requirements:* For master's, comprehensive exam (for some programs), thesis (for some programs); for doctorate, comprehensive exam, thesis/dissertation. *Entrance requirements:* For master's, GRE, GMAT, or MCAT, U.S. bachelor's degree or foreign equivalent; for doctorate, GRE, MPH or equivalent. Additional exam requirements/recommendations for international students: Required—TOEFL (minimum score 600 paper-based; 100 iBT), IELTS (minimum score 7). Electronic applications accepted. *Faculty research:* Infectious disease, chronic disease, reproductive epidemiology, social epidemiology, research methods.

Brown University, Graduate School, Division of Biology and Medicine, School of Public Health, Department of Epidemiology, Providence, RI 02912. Offers Sc M, PhD. *Degree requirements:* For doctorate, thesis/dissertation, preliminary exam. *Entrance requirements:* For master's and doctorate, GRE General Test.

California State University, Northridge, Graduate Studies, College of Health and Human Development, Department of Health Sciences, Northridge, CA 91330. Offers health administration (MS); public health (MPH), including applied epidemiology, community health education. *Accreditation:* CEPH. *Students:* 128 full-time (96 women), 53 part-time (45 women); includes 96 minority (10 Black or African American, non-Hispanic/Latino; 21 Asian, non-Hispanic/Latino; 53 Hispanic/Latino; 1 Native Hawaiian or other Pacific Islander, non-Hispanic/Latino; 11 Two or more races, non-Hispanic/Latino), 6 international. Average age 30. 323 applicants, 38% accepted, 68 enrolled. In 2017, 70 master's awarded. *Entrance requirements:* For master's, GRE General Test or minimum GPA of 3.0. Additional exam requirements/recommendations for international students: Required—TOEFL. *Application deadline:* For fall admission, 11/30 for domestic students. Application fee: $55. *Financial support:* Teaching assistantships available. Financial award application deadline: 3/1. *Faculty research:* Labor market needs assessment, health education products, dental hygiene, independent practice prototype. *Unit head:* Louis Rubino, Chair, 818-677-3101.
Website: http://www.csun.edu/hhd/hsci/

Capella University, School of Public Service Leadership, Doctoral Programs in Healthcare, Minneapolis, MN 55402. Offers criminal justice (PhD); emergency management (PhD); epidemiology (Dr PH); general health administration (DHA); general public administration (DPA); health advocacy and leadership (Dr PH); health care administration (PhD); health care leadership (DHA); health policy advocacy (DHA); multidisciplinary human services (PhD); nonprofit management and leadership (PhD); public safety leadership (PhD); social and community services (PhD).

Case Western Reserve University, School of Medicine and School of Graduate Studies, Graduate Programs in Medicine, Department of Population and Quantitative Health Sciences, Program in Epidemiology and Biostatistics, Cleveland, OH 44106. Offers PhD. *Accreditation:* CEPH. *Program availability:* Part-time. Terminal master's awarded for partial completion of doctoral program. *Degree requirements:* For doctorate, comprehensive exam, thesis/dissertation. *Entrance requirements:* For doctorate, GRE General Test, 3 recommendations. Additional exam requirements/recommendations for international students: Required—TOEFL (minimum score 550 paper-based). Electronic applications accepted. *Expenses: Tuition:* Full-time $43,854; part-time $1827 per credit hour. *Required fees:* $50; $50 per credit hour. Tuition and fees vary according to course load and program. *Faculty research:* Cardiovascular epidemiology, cancer risk factors, HIV in underserved populations, effectiveness studies in Medicare patients.

Colorado State University, College of Veterinary Medicine and Biomedical Sciences, Department of Environmental and Radiological Health Sciences, Fort Collins, CO 80523-1681. Offers environmental health (MS, PhD), including environmental health and safety (MS), epidemiology (PhD). *Faculty:* 33 full-time (14 women), 5 part-time/adjunct (3 women). *Students:* 91 full-time (45 women), 52 part-time (29 women); includes 34 minority (9 Black or African American, non-Hispanic/Latino; 6 Asian, non-Hispanic/Latino; 14 Hispanic/Latino; 5 Two or more races, non-Hispanic/Latino), 14 international. Average age 29. 87 applicants, 75% accepted, 44 enrolled. In 2017, 59 master's, 3 doctorates awarded. Terminal master's awarded for partial completion of doctoral program. *Degree requirements:* For master's, comprehensive exam (for some programs), thesis (for some programs); for doctorate, comprehensive exam (for some programs), thesis/dissertation (for some programs). *Entrance requirements:* For master's, GRE, minimum GPA of 3.0, bachelor's degree, resume or curriculum vitae, official transcripts, written statement, 3 letters of recommendation; for doctorate, GRE, minimum GPA of 3.0, MS or proof of research, resume or curriculum vitae, official transcripts, written statement, 3 letters of recommendation. Additional exam requirements/recommendations for international students: Required—TOEFL (minimum score 80 iBT), IELTS (minimum score 6.5). *Application deadline:* For fall admission, 7/1

for domestic students, 5/1 for international students; for spring admission, 11/1 for domestic students, 9/1 for international students. Application fee: $60 ($70 for international students). Electronic applications accepted. *Expenses:* $120 per credit hour. *Financial support:* In 2017–18, 32 students received support, including 22 research assistantships with tuition reimbursements available (averaging $22,859 per year), 2 teaching assistantships with tuition reimbursements available (averaging $14,256 per year); fellowships with tuition reimbursements available and traineeships also available. Financial award applicants required to submit FAFSA. *Faculty research:* Air pollution, radiation physics, treatment of occupational illnesses and injuries, DNA damage and repair. *Total annual research expenditures:* $10.6 million. *Unit head:* Dr. Jac Nickoloff, Department Head, 970-491-6674, E-mail: j.nickoloff@colostate.edu. *Application contact:* Toni Brown, Graduate Coordinator, 970-491-5003, E-mail: toni.m.brown@colostate.edu.
Website: http://csu-cvmbs.colostate.edu/academics/erhs/Pages/graduate-studies.aspx

Columbia University, Columbia University Mailman School of Public Health, Department of Epidemiology, New York, NY 10032. Offers MPH, MS, Dr PH, PhD. PhD offered in cooperation with the Graduate School of Arts and Sciences. *Accreditation:* CEPH (one or more programs are accredited). *Program availability:* Part-time, evening/ weekend. *Students:* 216 full-time (163 women), 141 part-time (103 women); includes 152 minority (23 Black or African American, non-Hispanic/Latino; 1 American Indian or Alaska Native, non-Hispanic/Latino; 86 Asian, non-Hispanic/Latino; 31 Hispanic/Latino; 11 Two or more races, non-Hispanic/Latino), 58 international. Average age 28. 757 applicants, 57% accepted, 137 enrolled. In 2017, 146 master's, 8 doctorates awarded. *Degree requirements:* For master's, thesis; for doctorate, thesis/dissertation. *Entrance requirements:* For master's, GRE General Test; for doctorate, GRE General Test, MPH or equivalent (for Dr PH). Additional exam requirements/recommendations for international students: Required—TOEFL (minimum score 600 paper-based; 100 iBT). *Application deadline:* For fall admission, 12/1 priority date for domestic and international students. Application fee: $120. Electronic applications accepted. *Expenses: Tuition:* Full-time $44,864; part-time $1704 per credit. *Required fees:* $2370 per semester. One-time fee: $105. *Financial support:* Research assistantships, teaching assistantships, career-related internships or fieldwork, and Federal Work-Study available. Support available to part-time students. Financial award application deadline: 2/1; financial award applicants required to submit FAFSA. *Faculty research:* Infectious disease epidemiology, chronic disease epidemiology, social epidemiology, psychiatric epidemiology, neurological epidemiology. *Unit head:* Dr. Charles Branas, Chairperson, 212-305-8755. *Application contact:* Clare Norton, Associate Dean for Enrollment Management, 212-305-8698, Fax: 212-342-1861, E-mail: ph-admit@columbia.edu.
Website: https://www.mailman.columbia.edu/become-student/departments/epidemiology

Daemen College, Program in Public Health, Amherst, NY 14226-3592. Offers community health education (MPH); epidemiology (MPH); generalist (MPH). *Program availability:* Part-time, online learning. *Degree requirements:* For master's, practicum.

Dalhousie University, Faculty of Medicine, Department of Community Health and Epidemiology, Halifax, NS B3H 4R2, Canada. Offers M Sc. *Degree requirements:* For master's, thesis. *Entrance requirements:* Additional exam requirements/ recommendations for international students: Required—1 of 5 approved tests: TOEFL, IELTS, CANTEST, CAEL, Michigan English Language Assessment Battery. Electronic applications accepted. *Expenses:* Contact institution. *Faculty research:* Population health, health promotion and disease prevention, health services utilization, chronic disease epidemiology.

Dartmouth College, School of Graduate and Advanced Studies, Institute for Quantitative Biomedical Sciences, Hanover, NH 03755. Offers epidemiology (MS); health data science (MS); quantitative biomedical sciences (PhD). PhD offered in collaboration with the Department of Genetics and the Department of Community and Family Medicine. *Students:* 30 full-time (18 women); includes 7 minority (1 Black or African American, non-Hispanic/Latino; 4 Asian, non-Hispanic/Latino; 2 Hispanic/ Latino), 12 international. Average age 27. 40 applicants, 35% accepted, 9 enrolled. In 2017, 1 doctorate awarded. *Entrance requirements:* For doctorate, GRE (minimum scores: 1200 old scoring, 308 new scoring verbal and quantitative; analytical writing 4.5; verbal 500 old scoring, 153 new scoring). *Application deadline:* For fall admission, 3/1 for domestic students. Applications are processed on a rolling basis. Application fee: $75. Electronic applications accepted. *Financial support:* Fellowships available. *Unit head:* Dr. Micheal Whitfield, Director, 603-650-1109. *Application contact:* Gary Hutchins, Assistant Dean, School of Arts and Sciences, 603-646-2107, Fax: 603-646-3488, E-mail: g.hutchins@dartmouth.edu.
Website: https://www.dartmouth.edu/~qbs/index.html

Drexel University, Dornsife School of Public Health, Department of Epidemiology and Biostatistics, Philadelphia, PA 19104-2875. Offers biostatistics (MS); epidemiology (PhD); epidemiology and biostatistics (Certificate).

East Tennessee State University, School of Graduate Studies, College of Public Health, Program in Public Health, Johnson City, TN 37614. Offers biostatistics (MPH, Postbaccalaureate Certificate); community health (MPH, DPH); environmental health (MPH); epidemiology (MPH, DPH, Postbaccalaureate Certificate); gerontology (Postbaccalaureate Certificate); global health (Postbaccalaureate Certificate); health care management (Postbaccalaureate Certificate); health management and policy (DPH); public health (Postbaccalaureate Certificate); public health services administration (MPH); rural health (Postbaccalaureate Certificate). *Accreditation:* CEPH. *Program availability:* Part-time, online learning. *Degree requirements:* For master's, comprehensive exam, field experience; for doctorate, thesis/dissertation, practicum. *Entrance requirements:* For master's, GRE General Test, minimum GPA of 2.75, SOPHAS application, three letters of recommendation; for doctorate, GRE General Test, SOPHAS application, three letters of recommendation; for Postbaccalaureate Certificate, minimum GPA of 2.5, three letters of recommendation, resume. Additional exam requirements/recommendations for international students: Required—TOEFL (minimum score 550 paper-based; 79 iBT), IELTS (minimum score 6.5). *Application deadline:* For fall admission, 3/1 for domestic and international students. Application fee: $35 ($45 for international students). Electronic applications accepted. *Financial support:* Research assistantships with tuition reimbursements, teaching assistantships with full tuition reimbursements, career-related internships or fieldwork, institutionally sponsored loans, scholarships/grants, and unspecified assistantships available. Financial award application deadline: 7/1; financial award applicants required to submit FAFSA. *Unit head:* Dr. Randy Wykoff, Dean, 423-439-4243, Fax: 423-439-5238, E-mail: wykoff@etsu.edu. *Application contact:* Dr. Randy Wykoff, Dean, 423-439-4243, Fax: 423-439-5238, E-mail: wykoff@etsu.edu.
Website: http://www.etsu.edu/cph/

Emory University, Rollins School of Public Health, Department of Environmental Health, Atlanta, GA 30322-1100. Offers environmental health (MPH); environmental health and epidemiology (MSPH); environmental health sciences (PhD); global environmental health (MPH). *Program availability:* Part-time. *Degree requirements:* For master's, thesis, practicum. *Entrance requirements:* For master's, GRE General Test. Additional exam requirements/recommendations for international students: Required—TOEFL. Electronic applications accepted.

Emory University, Rollins School of Public Health, Department of Epidemiology, Atlanta, GA 30322-1100. Offers MPH, MSPH, PhD. *Program availability:* Part-time. *Degree requirements:* For master's, thesis, practicum. *Entrance requirements:* For master's, GRE General Test. Additional exam requirements/recommendations for international students: Required—TOEFL (minimum score 550 paper-based; 80 iBT). Electronic applications accepted. *Expenses:* Contact institution. *Faculty research:* Cancer, infectious diseases, epidemiological methods, environmental/occupational health, women's and children's health.

Emory University, Rollins School of Public Health, Online Program in Public Health, Atlanta, GA 30322-1100. Offers applied epidemiology (MPH); applied public health informatics (MPH); prevention science (MPH). *Program availability:* Part-time, evening/ weekend, online learning. *Degree requirements:* For master's, thesis, practicum. *Entrance requirements:* For master's, GRE. Additional exam requirements/ recommendations for international students: Required—TOEFL (minimum score 550 paper-based; 80 iBT). Electronic applications accepted.

Florida International University, Robert Stempel College of Public Health and Social Work, Programs in Public Health, Miami, FL 33199. Offers biostatistics (MPH); environmental and occupational health (MPH, PhD); epidemiology (MPH, PhD); health policy and management (MPH); health promotion and disease prevention (MPH, PhD). PhD program has fall admissions only; MPH offered jointly with University of Miami. *Program availability:* Part-time, evening/weekend, online learning. *Faculty:* 34 full-time (18 women), 2 part-time/adjunct (both women). *Students:* 132 full-time (88 women), 63 part-time (49 women); includes 133 minority (50 Black or African American, non-Hispanic/Latino; 17 Asian, non-Hispanic/Latino; 60 Hispanic/Latino; 6 Two or more races, non-Hispanic/Latino), 30 international. Average age 29. 249 applicants, 54% accepted, 65 enrolled. In 2017, 37 master's, 14 doctorates awarded. *Degree requirements:* For master's, thesis optional; for doctorate, comprehensive exam, thesis/ dissertation. *Entrance requirements:* For master's, minimum GPA of 3.0, letters of recommendation; for doctorate, GRE, resume, minimum GPA of 3.0, letters of recommendation, letter of intent. Additional exam requirements/recommendations for international students: Required—TOEFL (minimum score 550 paper-based; 80 iBT). *Application deadline:* For fall admission, 6/1 for domestic students, 4/1 for international students; for spring admission, 10/1 for domestic students, 9/1 for international students. Applications are processed on a rolling basis. Application fee: $30. Electronic applications accepted. *Expenses:* Contact institution. *Financial support:* Institutionally sponsored loans, scholarships/grants, and tuition waivers (full) available. Financial award application deadline: 3/1; financial award applicants required to submit FAFSA. *Faculty research:* Drugs/AIDS intervention among migrant workers, provision of services for active/recovering drug users with HIV. *Unit head:* Dr. Benjamin C. Amick, III, Chair, 305-348-7527, E-mail: benjamin.amickiii@fiu.edu. *Application contact:* Nanett Rojas, Assistant Director, Graduate Admissions, 305-348-7464, Fax: 305-348-7441, E-mail: gradadm@fiu.edu.

George Mason University, College of Health and Human Services, Department of Global and Community Health, Fairfax, VA 22030. Offers global and community health (Certificate); global health (MS); public health (MPH, Certificate), including epidemiology (MPH), leadership and management (Certificate). *Accreditation:* CEPH. *Program availability:* Part-time, evening/weekend. *Faculty:* 18 full-time (13 women), 16 part-time/ adjunct (13 women). *Students:* 70 full-time (63 women), 61 part-time (53 women); includes 62 minority (21 Black or African American, non-Hispanic/Latino; 21 Asian, non-Hispanic/Latino; 14 Hispanic/Latino; 1 Native Hawaiian or other Pacific Islander, non-Hispanic/Latino; 5 Two or more races, non-Hispanic/Latino), 8 international. Average age 29. 246 applicants, 71% accepted, 60 enrolled. In 2017, 46 master's, 2 other advanced degrees awarded. *Degree requirements:* For master's, thesis, 200-hour practicum. *Entrance requirements:* For master's, GRE, GMAT (depending on program), 2 official transcripts; expanded goals statement; 3 letters of recommendation; resume; 1 completed course in health science, statistics, natural sciences and social science (for MPH); 6 credits of foreign language if not fluent (for MS); minimum undergraduate GPA of 3.0; for Certificate, 2 official transcripts; expanded goals statement; 3 letters of recommendation; resume; bachelor's degree from regionally-accredited institution with minimum GPA of 3.0. Additional exam requirements/recommendations for international students: Required—TOEFL (minimum score 570 paper-based; 88 iBT), IELTS (minimum score 6.5), PTE (minimum score 59). *Application deadline:* For fall admission, 3/1 for domestic and international students. Application fee: $75 ($80 for international students). Electronic applications accepted. *Expenses:* Contact institution. *Financial support:* In 2017–18, 15 students received support, including 12 research assistantships with tuition reimbursements available (averaging $16,616 per year), 3 teaching assistantships with tuition reimbursements available (averaging $6,966 per year); career-related internships or fieldwork, Federal Work-Study, scholarships/grants, unspecified assistantships, and health care benefits (for full-time research or teaching assistantship recipients) also available. Financial award application deadline: 3/1; financial award applicants required to submit FAFSA. *Faculty research:* Environmental and infectious disease epidemiology; global health; health risk behaviors; social determinants of health; stress, well-being and chronic disease. *Total annual research expenditures:* $69,343. *Unit head:* Robert Weiler, Chair, 703-993-1920, E-mail: rweiler@gmu.edu. *Application contact:* Allan Weiss, Department Manager, 703-993-3126, E-mail: aweiss2@gmu.edu.
Website: http://chhs.gmu.edu/gch/index

Georgetown University, Graduate School of Arts and Sciences, Department of Biostatistics, Bioinformatics and Biomathematics, Washington, DC 20057-1484. Offers biostatistics (MS, Certificate), including bioinformatics (MS), epidemiology (MS); epidemiology (Certificate). *Entrance requirements:* For master's, GRE General Test. Additional exam requirements/recommendations for international students: Required—TOEFL. *Faculty research:* Occupation epidemiology, cancer.

The George Washington University, Milken Institute School of Public Health, Department of Epidemiology and Biostatistics, Washington, DC 20052. Offers biostatistics (MPH); epidemiology (MPH); microbiology and emerging infectious diseases (MSPH). *Students:* 75 full-time (58 women), 78 part-time (62 women); includes 62 minority (14 Black or African American, non-Hispanic/Latino; 32 Asian, non-Hispanic/ Latino; 12 Hispanic/Latino; 1 Native Hawaiian or other Pacific Islander, non-Hispanic/ Latino; 3 Two or more races, non-Hispanic/Latino), 14 international. Average age 28. 521 applicants, 59% accepted, 48 enrolled. In 2017, 51 master's awarded. *Entrance requirements:* For master's, GMAT, GRE General Test, or MCAT. Additional exam requirements/recommendations for international students: Required—TOEFL. *Application deadline:* For fall admission, 4/15 priority date for domestic students, 4/15 for international students; for spring admission, 11/1 for domestic and international students. Applications are processed on a rolling basis. Application fee: $75. *Expenses: Tuition:* Full-time $28,800; part-time $1655 per credit hour. *Required fees:* $45; $2.75 per credit hour. *Financial support:* In 2017–18, 6 students received support. Tuition waivers available. Financial award application deadline: 2/15. *Unit head:* Dr. Alan E. Greenberg, Chair, 202-994-0612, E-mail: aeg1@gwu.edu. *Application contact:* Jane Smith, Director of Admissions, 202-994-0248, Fax: 202-994-1860, E-mail: sphhsinfo@gwumc.edu.

Georgia Southern University, Jack N. Averitt College of Graduate Studies, Jiann-Ping Hsu College of Public Health, Program in Public Health, Statesboro, GA 30460. Offers biostatistics (MPH, Dr PH); community health behavior and education (Dr PH); community health education (MPH); environmental health sciences (MPH); epidemiology (MPH); health policy and management (MPH, Dr PH). *Program availability:* Part-time. *Faculty:* 11 full-time (5 women). *Students:* 146 full-time (90 women), 70 part-time (57 women); includes 112 minority (95 Black or African American, non-Hispanic/Latino; 9 Asian, non-Hispanic/Latino; 5 Hispanic/Latino; 3 Two or more races, non-Hispanic/Latino), 47 international. Average age 32. 190 applicants, 78% accepted, 89 enrolled. In 2017, 34 master's, 13 doctorates awarded. *Degree requirements:* For master's, thesis optional, practicum; for doctorate, comprehensive exam, thesis/dissertation, preceptorship. *Entrance requirements:* For master's, GRE General Test, minimum GPA of 2.75, 3 letters of recommendation, statement of purpose, resume or curriculum vitae; for doctorate, GRE, GMAT, MCAT, LSAT, minimum GPA of 3.0, 3 letters of recommendation, statement of purpose, resume or curriculum vitae. Additional exam requirements/recommendations for international students: Required—TOEFL (minimum score 537 paper-based; 75 iBT), IELTS (minimum score 6). *Application deadline:* For fall admission, 6/1 for domestic students, 5/1 for international students. Applications are processed on a rolling basis. Application fee: $135. Electronic applications accepted. *Expenses:* $3,949 in-state, $13,929 out-of-state (for MPH); $4,014 in-state, $14,159 out-of-state (for Dr PH). *Financial support:* In 2017–18, 106 students received support, including 1 research assistantship with full tuition reimbursement available (averaging $12,350 per year), 6 teaching assistantships with full tuition reimbursements available (averaging $12,350 per year); scholarships/grants, tuition waivers (full), and unspecified assistantships also available. Financial award application deadline: 4/15; financial award applicants required to submit FAFSA. *Faculty research:* Rural public health best practices, health disparity elimination, community initiatives to enhance public health, cost effectiveness analysis, epidemiology of rural public health, environmental health issues, health care system assessment, rural health care, health policy and healthcare financing, survival analysis, nonparametric statistics and resampling methods, micro-arrays and genomics, data imputation techniques and clinical trial methodology. *Total annual research expenditures:* $415,747. *Unit head:* Dr. Robert Greg Evans, Dean, 912-478-2674, E-mail: rgevans@georgiasouthern.edu. *Application contact:* Shamia Garrett, Coordinator, Office of Student Services, 912-478-2674, Fax: 912-478-5811, E-mail: jphcoph-gradadvisor@georgiasouthern.edu.
Website: http://jphcoph.georgiasouthern.edu/

Harvard University, Cyprus International Institute for the Environment and Public Health in Association with Harvard School of Public Health, Cambridge, MA 02138. Offers environmental health (MS); environmental/public health (PhD); epidemiology and biostatistics (MS). *Entrance requirements:* For master's and doctorate, GRE, resume/curriculum vitae, 3 letters of recommendation, BA or BS (including diploma and official transcripts). Additional exam requirements/recommendations for international students: Required—TOEFL, IELTS (minimum score 7). Electronic applications accepted. *Faculty research:* Air pollution, climate change, biostatistics, sustainable development, environmental management.

Harvard University, Harvard T.H. Chan School of Public Health, Department of Epidemiology, Boston, MA 02115-6096. Offers cancer epidemiology (SM); cardiovascular epidemiology (SM); clinical epidemiology (SM); environmental and occupational epidemiology (SM); epidemiologic methods (SM); epidemiology of aging (SM); genetic epidemiology and statistical genetics (SM); infectious disease epidemiology (SM); neuro-psychiatric epidemiology (SM); nutritional epidemiology (SM); pharmacoepidemiology (SM); population health sciences (PhD); reproductive epidemiology (SM). *Program availability:* Part-time. *Faculty:* 84 full-time (37 women), 44 part-time/adjunct (20 women). *Students:* 107 full-time (68 women), 27 part-time (7 women); includes 30 minority (4 Black or African American, non-Hispanic/Latino; 18 Asian, non-Hispanic/Latino; 5 Hispanic/Latino; 3 Two or more races, non-Hispanic/Latino), 68 international. Average age 29. 192 applicants, 40% accepted, 64 enrolled. In 2017, 50 master's, 19 doctorates awarded. *Entrance requirements:* For master's, GRE, MCAT. Additional exam requirements/recommendations for international students: Recommended—TOEFL (minimum score 600 paper-based; 100 iBT), IELTS (minimum score 7). *Application deadline:* For fall admission, 12/1 for domestic and international students. Application fee: $120. Electronic applications accepted. *Financial support:* Fellowships, research assistantships, teaching assistantships, Federal Work-Study, scholarships/grants, traineeships, and unspecified assistantships available. Support available to part-time students. Financial award application deadline: 2/15; financial award applicants required to submit FAFSA. *Faculty research:* Cancer prevention and epidemiology; epidemiologic methods; epidemiology of aging; infectious diseases; pharmacoepidemiology; cardiovascular, clinical, environmental and occupational, molecular/genetic, neuropsychiatric, nutritional, psychiatric, reproductive, perinatal, and pediatric epidemiology. *Unit head:* Dr. Albert Hofman, Chair, 617-432-6477. *Application contact:* Vincent W. James, Director of Admissions, 617-432-1031, Fax: 617-432-7080, E-mail: admissions@hsph.harvard.edu.
Website: http://www.hsph.harvard.edu/epidemiology/

Harvard University, Harvard T.H. Chan School of Public Health, PhD Program in Population Health Sciences, Boston, MA 02115. Offers environmental health (PhD); epidemiology (PhD); global health and population (PhD); nutrition (PhD); social and behavioral sciences (PhD). *Students:* 80 full-time (56 women); includes 23 minority (5 Black or African American, non-Hispanic/Latino; 7 Asian, non-Hispanic/Latino; 6 Hispanic/Latino; 5 Two or more races, non-Hispanic/Latino), 26 international. Average age 29. 469 applicants, 11% accepted, 42 enrolled. *Entrance requirements:* Additional exam requirements/recommendations for international students: Recommended—TOEFL, IELTS. *Application deadline:* For fall admission, 12/1 for domestic and international students. Electronic applications accepted. *Financial support:* Application deadline: 2/15; applicants required to submit FAFSA. *Unit head:* Bruce Villineau, Assistant Director, E-mail: phdphs@hsph.harvard.edu. *Application contact:* Vincent W. James, Director of Admissions, 617-432-1031, Fax: 617-432-7080, E-mail: admissions@hsph.harvard.edu.

Indiana University Bloomington, School of Public Health, Department of Epidemiology and Biostatistics, Bloomington, IN 47405. Offers biostatistics (MPH); epidemiology (MPH, PhD). *Degree requirements:* For master's, thesis or alternative; for doctorate, comprehensive exam, thesis/dissertation. *Entrance requirements:* For master's, GRE (for applicants with cumulative undergraduate GPA less than 2.8); for doctorate, GRE. Additional exam requirements/recommendations for international students: Required—TOEFL (minimum score 550 paper-based; 80 iBT). Electronic applications accepted. *Faculty research:* Nutritional epidemiology, cancer epidemiology, global health, biostatistics.

Indiana University–Purdue University Indianapolis, Richard M. Fairbanks School of Public Health, Indianapolis, IN 46202. Offers biostatistics (MS, PhD); environmental health (MPH); epidemiology (MPH, PhD); global health leadership (Dr PH); health administration (MHA); health policy (Graduate Certificate); health policy and management (MPH, PhD); health systems management (Graduate Certificate); product stewardship (MS); public health (Graduate Certificate); social and behavioral sciences (MPH). *Expenses:* Contact institution.

Johns Hopkins University, Bloomberg School of Public Health, Department of Epidemiology, Baltimore, MD 21205. Offers cancer epidemiology (MHS, Sc M, PhD, Sc D); cardiovascular disease and clinical epidemiology (MHS, Sc M, PhD, Sc D); clinical trials (PhD, Sc D); clinical trials and evidence synthesis (MHS, Sc M, PhD, Sc D); environmental epidemiology (MHS, Sc M, PhD, Sc D); epidemiology of aging (MHS, Sc M, PhD, Sc D); general epidemiology and methodology (MHS, Sc M); genetic epidemiology (MHS, Sc M, PhD, Sc D); infectious disease epidemiology (MHS, Sc M, PhD, Sc D). *Students:* 160 full-time (111 women), 14 part-time (9 women); includes 44 minority (9 Black or African American, non-Hispanic/Latino; 1 American Indian or Alaska Native, non-Hispanic/Latino; 20 Asian, non-Hispanic/Latino; 9 Hispanic/Latino; 1 Native Hawaiian or other Pacific Islander, non-Hispanic/Latino; 4 Two or more races, non-Hispanic/Latino), 64 international. Average age 29. 408 applicants, 29% accepted, 61 enrolled. In 2017, 36 master's, 16 doctorates awarded. *Degree requirements:* For master's, comprehensive exam, thesis, 1-year full-time residency; for doctorate, comprehensive exam, thesis/dissertation, 2 years' full-time residency, oral and written exams, student teaching. *Entrance requirements:* For master's, GRE General Test or MCAT, 3 letters of recommendation, curriculum vitae; for doctorate, GRE General Test, minimum 1 year of work experience, 3 letters of recommendation, curriculum vitae, academic records from all schools. Additional exam requirements/recommendations for international students: Required—TOEFL (minimum score 100 iBT), IELTS (minimum score 7.5). *Application deadline:* Applications are processed on a rolling basis. Application fee: $135. Electronic applications accepted. *Financial support:* Fellowships, Federal Work-Study, institutionally sponsored loans, scholarships/grants, traineeships, and stipends available. Support available to part-time students. Financial award application deadline: 3/15. *Faculty research:* Cancer and congenital malformations, nutritional epidemiology, AIDS, tuberculosis, cardiovascular disease, risk assessment. *Unit head:* Dr. David D. Celentano, Chair, 410-955-3286, Fax: 410-955-0863. *Application contact:* Frances S. Burman, Academic Program Manager, 410-955-3926, Fax: 410-955-0863, E-mail: fburman@jhsph.edu.
Website: http://www.jhsph.edu/dept/epi/index.html

Johns Hopkins University, Bloomberg School of Public Health, Department of International Health, Baltimore, MD 21205. Offers global disease epidemiology and control (MSPH, PhD); global health economics (MHS); health systems (MSPH, PhD); human nutrition (MSPH, PhD); social and behavioral interventions (MSPH, PhD). *Students:* 270 full-time (216 women); includes 80 minority (8 Black or African American, non-Hispanic/Latino; 1 American Indian or Alaska Native, non-Hispanic/Latino; 52 Asian, non-Hispanic/Latino; 8 Hispanic/Latino; 11 Two or more races, non-Hispanic/Latino), 70 international. Average age 28. 562 applicants, 40% accepted, 82 enrolled. *Degree requirements:* For master's, comprehensive exam, thesis (for some programs), 1-year full-time residency, 4-9 month internship; for doctorate, comprehensive exam, thesis/dissertation or alternative, 1.5 years' full-time residency, oral and written exams. *Entrance requirements:* For master's, GRE General Test or MCAT, 3 letters of recommendation, resume; for doctorate, GRE General Test or MCAT, 3 letters of recommendation, resume, transcripts. Additional exam requirements/recommendations for international students: Required—TOEFL (minimum score 600 paper-based; 100 iBT); Recommended—IELTS (minimum score 7). Electronic applications accepted. *Financial support:* Fellowships, Federal Work-Study, scholarships/grants, traineeships, and stipends available. *Faculty research:* Nutrition, infectious diseases, health systems, health economics, humanitarian emergencies. *Unit head:* Dr. David Peters, Chair, 410-955-3928, Fax: 410-955-7159, E-mail: dpeters@jhsph.edu. *Application contact:* Cristina G. Salazar, Academic Program Manager, 410-955-3734, Fax: 410-955-7159, E-mail: csalazar@jhsph.edu.
Website: http://www.jhsph.edu/dept/IH/

Kent State University, College of Public Health, Kent, OH 44242-0001. Offers public health (MPH, PhD), including biostatistics (MPH), environmental health sciences (MPH), epidemiology, health policy and management, prevention science (PhD), social and behavioral sciences (MPH). *Accreditation:* CEPH. *Program availability:* Part-time, online learning. *Faculty:* 23 full-time (14 women), 12 part-time/adjunct (3 women). *Students:* 123 full-time (87 women), 152 part-time (120 women); includes 57 minority (37 Black or African American, non-Hispanic/Latino; 1 American Indian or Alaska Native, non-Hispanic/Latino; 8 Asian, non-Hispanic/Latino; 6 Hispanic/Latino; 5 Two or more races, non-Hispanic/Latino), 40 international. Average age 31. 176 applicants, 76% accepted, 81 enrolled. In 2017, 79 master's, 5 doctorates awarded. *Degree requirements:* For master's, comprehensive exam, 300 hours' placement at public health agency, final portfolio and presentation; for doctorate, comprehensive exam, thesis/dissertation. *Entrance requirements:* For master's, GRE, minimum GPA of 3.0, transcripts, goal statement, 3 letters of recommendation; for doctorate, GRE, minimum GPA of 3.0, personal statement, resume, interview, 3 letters of recommendation. Additional exam requirements/recommendations for international students: Required—TOEFL (minimum score 550 paper-based; 79 iBT), IELTS (minimum score 6.5), PTE (minimum score 58), Michigan English Language Assessment Battery. *Application deadline:* For fall admission, 6/15 for domestic and international students; for spring admission, 10/15 for domestic and international students; for summer admission, 3/15 for domestic and international students. Applications are processed on a rolling basis. Application fee: $45 ($70 for international students). Electronic applications accepted. *Expenses:* Tuition, state resident: full-time $11,310; part-time $515 per credit hour. Tuition, nonresident: full-time $20,396; part-time $928 per credit hour. *International tuition:* $18,544 full-time. *Financial support:* Unspecified assistantships available. *Unit head:* Dr. Sonia Alemagno, Dean and Professor of Health Policy and Management, 330-672-6500, E-mail: salemagn@kent.edu. *Application contact:* Dr. Mark A. James, Professor/Chair/Graduate Advisor, 330-672-6506, E-mail: mjames22@kent.edu.
Website: http://www.kent.edu/publichealth/

Liberty University, School of Health Sciences, Lynchburg, VA 24515. Offers anatomy and cell biology (PhD); biomedical sciences (MS); epidemiology (MPH); exercise science (MS), including clinical, community physical activity, human performance, nutrition; global health (MPH); health promotion (MPH); medical sciences (MA), including biopsychology, business management, health informatics, molecular medicine, public health; nutrition (MPH). *Program availability:* Part-time, online learning. *Students:* 542 full-time (394 women), 696 part-time (541 women); includes 402 minority (286 Black or African American, non-Hispanic/Latino; 10 American Indian or Alaska Native, non-Hispanic/Latino; 34 Asian, non-Hispanic/Latino; 46 Hispanic/Latino; 1 Native Hawaiian or other Pacific Islander, non-Hispanic/Latino; 25 Two or more races, non-Hispanic/Latino), 59 international. Average age 32. 1,592 applicants, 40% accepted, 297 enrolled. In 2017, 204 master's awarded. *Degree requirements:* For master's, thesis (for some programs); for doctorate, thesis/dissertation. *Entrance requirements:* For doctorate, MAT or GRE, minimum GPA of 3.25 in master's program, 2-3 recommendations, writing samples (for some programs), letter of intent, professional vitae. Additional exam requirements/recommendations for international students: Required—TOEFL (minimum score 600 paper-based; 100 iBT). Application fee: $50. *Financial support:* Applicants required to submit FAFSA. *Unit head:* Dr. Ralph Linstra, Dean. *Application contact:* Jay Bridge, Director of Admissions, 800-424-9595, Fax: 800-628-7977, E-mail: gradadmissions@liberty.edu.

Loma Linda University, School of Public Health, Programs in Epidemiology and Biostatistics, Loma Linda, CA 92350. Offers biostatistics (MPH); epidemiology (MPH, Dr PH, PhD). *Entrance requirements:* Additional exam requirements/recommendations for international students: Required—Michigan English Language Assessment Battery or TOEFL.

Louisiana State University Health Sciences Center, School of Public Health, New Orleans, LA 70112. Offers behavioral and community health sciences (MPH); biostatistics

(MPH, MS, PhD); community health sciences (PhD); environmental and occupational health sciences (MPH); epidemiology (MPH, PhD); health policy and systems management (MPH). *Accreditation:* CEPH. *Program availability:* Part-time. *Faculty:* 51 full-time (23 women), 41 part-time/adjunct (12 women). *Students:* 98 full-time (77 women), 24 part-time (18 women); includes 55 minority (26 Black or African American, non-Hispanic/Latino; 1 American Indian or Alaska Native, non-Hispanic/Latino; 13 Asian, non-Hispanic/Latino; 13 Hispanic/Latino; 2 Two or more races, non-Hispanic/Latino), 16 international. Average age 24. 208 applicants, 67% accepted, 54 enrolled. *Degree requirements:* For doctorate, thesis/dissertation. *Entrance requirements:* For master's, GRE General Test. Additional exam requirements/recommendations for international students: Recommended—TOEFL (minimum score 550 paper-based; 79 iBT), IELTS. *Application deadline:* Applications are processed on a rolling basis. Application fee: $30. Electronic applications accepted. *Expenses:* Tuition, state resident: full-time $11,835; part-time $518 per hour. Tuition, nonresident: full-time $24,108; part-time $1079 per hour. *Required fees:* $1254; $55 per hour. *Unit head:* Dr. Dean Smith, Dean, 504-568-5700, E-mail: dgsmith@lsuhsc.edu. *Application contact:* Isabel Billiot, Director of Admissions and Student Affairs, 504-568-5773, E-mail: ibilli@lsuhsc.edu.
Website: http://publichealth.lsuhsc.edu/

McGill University, Faculty of Graduate and Postdoctoral Studies, Faculty of Medicine, Department of Epidemiology and Biostatistics, Montréal, QC H3A 2T5, Canada. Offers community health (M Sc); environmental health (M Sc); epidemiology and biostatistics (M Sc, PhD, Diploma); health care evaluation (M Sc); medical statistics (M Sc).

Medical University of South Carolina, College of Graduate Studies, Division of Biostatistics and Epidemiology, Charleston, SC 29425. Offers biostatistics (MS, PhD); epidemiology (MS, PhD); DMD/PhD; MD/PhD. Terminal master's awarded for partial completion of doctoral program. *Degree requirements:* For master's, comprehensive exam, thesis (for some programs); for doctorate, comprehensive exam, oral and written exams. *Entrance requirements:* For master's, GRE General Test, two semesters of college-level calculus; for doctorate, GRE General Test, interview, minimum GPA of 3.0, two semesters of college-level calculus. Additional exam requirements/recommendations for international students: Required—TOEFL (minimum score 600 paper-based; 100 iBT). Electronic applications accepted. *Faculty research:* Health disparities, central nervous system injuries, radiation exposure, analysis of clinical trial data, biomedical information.

Memorial University of Newfoundland, Faculty of Medicine and School of Graduate Studies, Graduate Programs in Medicine, Division of Clinical Epidemiology, St. John's, NL A1C 5S7, Canada. Offers M Sc, PhD, Diploma.

Michigan State University, College of Human Medicine and The Graduate School, Graduate Programs in Human Medicine, Department of Epidemiology, East Lansing, MI 48824. Offers MS, PhD. *Degree requirements:* For master's, oral thesis defense. *Entrance requirements:* Additional exam requirements/recommendations for international students: Required—TOEFL. Electronic applications accepted.

Monroe College, King Graduate School, Bronx, NY 10468. Offers accounting (MS); business administration (MBA), including entrepreneurship, finance, general business administration, healthcare management, human resources, information technology, marketing; computer science (MS); criminal justice (MS); hospitality management (MS); public health (MPH), including biostatistics and epidemiology, community health, health administration and leadership. *Program availability:* Online learning. Application fee: $50.
Website: https://www.monroecollege.edu/Degrees/King-Graduate-School/

New York Medical College, School of Health Sciences and Practice, Valhalla, NY 10595. Offers behavioral sciences and health promotion (MPH); biostatistics (MS); children with special health care (Graduate Certificate); emergency preparedness (Graduate Certificate); environmental health science (MPH); epidemiology (MPH, MS); global health (Graduate Certificate); health education (Graduate Certificate); health policy and management (MPH, Dr PH); industrial hygiene (Graduate Certificate); pediatric dysphagia (Post-Graduate Certificate); physical therapy (DPT); public health (Graduate Certificate); speech-language pathology (MS). *Accreditation:* CEPH. *Program availability:* Part-time, evening/weekend, 100% online, blended/hybrid learning. *Faculty:* 48 full-time (33 women), 235 part-time/adjunct (141 women). *Students:* 221 full-time (153 women), 270 part-time (194 women); includes 202 minority (83 Black or African American, non-Hispanic/Latino; 2 American Indian or Alaska Native, non-Hispanic/Latino; 64 Asian, non-Hispanic/Latino; 47 Hispanic/Latino; 1 Native Hawaiian or other Pacific Islander, non-Hispanic/Latino; 5 Two or more races, non-Hispanic/Latino), 19 international. Average age 29. 1,118 applicants, 38% accepted, 169 enrolled. In 2017, 110 master's, 41 doctorates awarded. *Degree requirements:* For master's, comprehensive exam (for some programs), thesis (for some programs); for doctorate, thesis/dissertation. *Entrance requirements:* For master's, GRE (for MS in speech-language pathology); for doctorate, GRE. Additional exam requirements/recommendations for international students: Required—TOEFL, IELTS. *Application deadline:* For fall admission, 8/1 for domestic students, 4/15 for international students; for spring admission, 12/1 for domestic students; for summer admission, 5/1 for domestic students, 4/15 for international students. Application fee: $125. Electronic applications accepted. *Expenses:* $1,125 per credit, $245 fees. *Financial support:* In 2017–18, 10,000 students received support. Scholarships/grants and unspecified assistantships available. Financial award application deadline: 4/30; financial award applicants required to submit FAFSA. *Unit head:* Ben Watson, PhD, Vice Dean, 914-594-4531, E-mail: ben_watson@nymc.edu. *Application contact:* Irene Bundziak, Assistant to Director of Admissions, 914-594-4905, E-mail: irene_bundziak@nymc.edu.
Website: http://www.nymc.edu/school-of-health-sciences-and-practice-shsp/

★ **New York University,** Graduate School of Arts and Science, Department of Environmental Medicine, New York, NY 10012-1019. Offers environmental health sciences (MS, PhD), including biostatistics (PhD), environmental hygiene (MS), epidemiology (PhD), ergonomics and biomechanics (PhD), exposure assessment and health effects (PhD), molecular toxicology/carcinogenesis (PhD), toxicology. *Program availability:* Part-time. *Students:* Average age 30. 79 applicants, 44% accepted, 20 enrolled. In 2017, 8 master's, 6 doctorates awarded. Terminal master's awarded for partial completion of doctoral program. *Degree requirements:* For master's, thesis or alternative; for doctorate, one foreign language, thesis/dissertation, oral and written exams. *Entrance requirements:* For master's and doctorate, GRE General Test, minimum GPA of 3.0; bachelor's degree in biological, physical, or engineering science. Additional exam requirements/recommendations for international students: Required—TOEFL. *Application deadline:* For fall admission, 12/18 for domestic and international students. Application fee: $100. *Expenses:* Tuition: Full-time $41,352; part-time $19,968 per year. *Required fees:* $2496; $1628 per unit. $814 per term. Tuition and fees vary according to course load and program. *Financial support:* Fellowships, teaching assistantships, career-related internships or fieldwork, Federal Work-Study, institutionally sponsored loans, and health care benefits available. Financial award application deadline: 12/18; financial award applicants required to submit FAFSA. *Unit head:* Dr. Max Costa, Chair, 845-731-3661, Fax: 845-351-4510, E-mail: ehs@env.med.nyu.edu. *Application contact:* Dr. Jerome J. Solomon, Director of Graduate Studies, 845-731-3661, Fax: 845-351-4510, E-mail: ehs@env.med.nyu.edu.
Website: http://environmental-medicine.med.nyu.edu/

See Close-Up on page 843.

New York University, School of Medicine and Graduate School of Arts and Science, Sackler Institute of Graduate Biomedical Sciences, New York, NY 10016. Offers biomedical imaging and technology (PhD); biostatistics (PhD); cellular and molecular biology (PhD); developmental genetics (PhD); epidemiology (PhD); genome integrity (PhD); immunology and inflammation (PhD); microbiology (PhD); molecular biophysics (PhD); molecular oncology and tumor immunology (PhD); molecular pharmacology (PhD); neuroscience and physiology (PhD), including immunology, molecular oncology; stem cell biology (PhD); systems and computational biomedicine (PhD); MD/PhD. *Faculty:* 207 full-time (51 women). *Students:* 236 full-time (138 women), 1 part-time (0 women); includes 68 minority (13 Black or African American, non-Hispanic/Latino; 26 Asian, non-Hispanic/Latino; 28 Hispanic/Latino; 1 Native Hawaiian or other Pacific Islander, non-Hispanic/Latino), 79 international. Average age 27. 761 applicants, 18% accepted, 59 enrolled. In 2017, 35 doctorates awarded. *Degree requirements:* For doctorate, comprehensive exam, thesis/dissertation, qualifying exam; thesis defense. *Entrance requirements:* For doctorate, GRE. Additional exam requirements/recommendations for international students: Required—TOEFL, IELTS. *Application deadline:* For fall admission, 12/1 for domestic and international students. Applications are processed on a rolling basis. Application fee: $100. Electronic applications accepted. Application fee is waived when completed online. *Expenses:* Contact institution. *Financial support:* Health care benefits, tuition waivers (full), and unspecified assistantships available. *Faculty research:* Biomedical sciences. *Unit head:* Dr. Naoko Tanese, Associate Dean for Biomedical Sciences/Director, Sackler Institute, 212-263-8945, E-mail: naoko.tanese@nyumc.org. *Application contact:* Jessica Dong, Program Manager, 212-263-5648, E-mail: sackler-info@nyumc.org.
Website: https://med.nyu.edu/research/sackler-institute-graduate-biomedical-sciences/

North Carolina State University, College of Veterinary Medicine, Program in Comparative Biomedical Sciences, Raleigh, NC 27695. Offers cell biology (MS, PhD); infectious disease (MS, PhD); pathology (MS, PhD); pharmacology (MS, PhD); population medicine (MS, PhD). *Program availability:* Part-time. *Degree requirements:* For master's, thesis; for doctorate, thesis/dissertation. *Entrance requirements:* For master's and doctorate, GRE General Test. Additional exam requirements/recommendations for international students: Required—TOEFL (minimum score 550 paper-based). Electronic applications accepted. *Expenses:* Contact institution. *Faculty research:* Infectious diseases, cell biology, pharmacology and toxicology, genomics, pathology and population medicine.

Northwestern University, Feinberg School of Medicine and Interdepartmental Programs, Driskill Graduate Program in Life Sciences, Chicago, IL 60611. Offers biostatistics (PhD); epidemiology (PhD); health and biomedical informatics (PhD); health services and outcomes research (PhD); healthcare quality and patient safety (PhD); translational outcomes in science (PhD). *Degree requirements:* For doctorate, comprehensive exam, thesis/dissertation, written and oral qualifying exams. *Entrance requirements:* For doctorate, GRE General Test. Additional exam requirements/recommendations for international students: Required—TOEFL (minimum score 600 paper-based). Electronic applications accepted.

Oregon State University, College of Public Health and Human Sciences, Program in Public Health, Corvallis, OR 97331. Offers biostatistics (MPH); environmental and occupational health (MPH, PhD); epidemiology (MPH, PhD); global health (MPH, PhD). Terminal master's awarded for partial completion of doctoral program. *Entrance requirements:* For master's and doctorate, GRE, minimum GPA of 3.0 in last 90 hours. Additional exam requirements/recommendations for international students: Required—TOEFL (minimum score 80 iBT), IELTS (minimum score 6.5). *Application deadline:* For fall admission, 12/1 priority date for domestic and international students. Applications are processed on a rolling basis. Electronic applications accepted. *Expenses:* Contact institution. *Financial support:* Application deadline: 12/1. *Unit head:* Amanda Armington, MPH Program Manager, 541-737-3825, E-mail: amanda.armington@oregonstate.edu.

Ponce Health Sciences University, Program in Public Health, Ponce, PR 00732-7004. Offers epidemiology (Dr PH); public health (MPH). *Accreditation:* CEPH. *Degree requirements:* For master's, one foreign language, comprehensive exam, thesis. *Entrance requirements:* For master's, GRE General Test or EXADEP, proficiency in Spanish and English, minimum GPA of 2.7, 3 letters of recommendation; for doctorate, GRE, proficiency in Spanish and English, minimum GPA of 3.0, letter of recommendation.

Purdue University, School of Veterinary Medicine and Graduate School, Graduate Programs in Veterinary Medicine, Department of Comparative Pathobiology, West Lafayette, IN 47907-2027. Offers comparative epidemiology and public health (MS); comparative epidemiology and public heath (PhD); comparative microbiology and immunology (MS, PhD); comparative pathobiology (MS, PhD); interdisciplinary studies (PhD), including microbial pathogenesis, molecular signaling and cancer biology, molecular virology; lab animal medicine (MS); veterinary anatomic pathology (MS); veterinary clinical pathology (MS). Terminal master's awarded for partial completion of doctoral program. *Degree requirements:* For master's, thesis (for some programs); for doctorate, thesis/dissertation. *Entrance requirements:* For master's and doctorate, GRE General Test. Additional exam requirements/recommendations for international students: Required—TOEFL (minimum score 575 paper-based), IELTS (minimum score 6.5), TWE (minimum score 4). Electronic applications accepted.

Queen's University at Kingston, School of Graduate Studies, Faculty of Health Sciences, Department of Community Health and Epidemiology, Kingston, ON K7L 3N6, Canada. Offers epidemiology (PhD); epidemiology and population health (M Sc); health services (M Sc); policy research and clinical epidemiology (M Sc); public health (MPH). *Program availability:* Part-time. *Degree requirements:* For master's, thesis. *Entrance requirements:* For master's, GRE General Test (strongly recommended). Additional exam requirements/recommendations for international students: Required—TOEFL (minimum score 600 paper-based). *Faculty research:* Cancer epidemiology, clinical trials, biostatistics health services research, health policy.

Rutgers University–Newark, School of Public Health, Newark, NJ 07107-1709. Offers clinical epidemiology (Certificate); dental public health (MPH); general public health (Certificate); public policy and oral health services administration (Certificate); quantitative methods (MPH); urban health (MPH); DMD/MPH; MD/MPH; MS/MPH. *Program availability:* Part-time, evening/weekend. *Degree requirements:* For master's, thesis, internship. *Entrance requirements:* For master's, GRE General Test. Additional exam requirements/recommendations for international students: Required—TOEFL. Electronic applications accepted.

Rutgers University–New Brunswick, School of Public Health, Piscataway, NJ 08854. Offers biostatistics (MPH, MS, Dr PH, PhD); clinical epidemiology (Certificate); environmental and occupational health (MPH, Dr PH, PhD, Certificate); epidemiology (MPH, Dr PH, PhD); general public health (Certificate); health education and behavioral science (MPH, Dr PH, PhD); health systems and policy (MPH, PhD); public health (MPH, Dr PH, PhD); public health preparedness (Certificate); DO/MPH; JD/MPH; MBA/MPH; MD/MPH; MPH/MBA; MPH/MSPA; MS/MPH; Psy D/MPH. *Accreditation:* CEPH. *Program availability:* Part-time, evening/weekend. *Degree requirements:* For master's, thesis, internship; for doctorate, comprehensive exam, thesis/dissertation. *Entrance requirements:* For master's, GRE General Test; for doctorate, GRE General Test, MPH (Dr PH); MA, MPH, or MS (PhD). Additional exam requirements/recommendations for international students: Required—TOEFL. Electronic applications accepted.

San Diego State University, Graduate and Research Affairs, College of Health and Human Services, Graduate School of Public Health, San Diego, CA 92182. Offers environmental health (MPH); epidemiology (MPH, PhD), including biostatistics (MPH); global emergency preparedness and response (MS); global health (PhD); health behavior (PhD); health promotion (MPH); health services administration (MPH); toxicology (MS); MPH/MA; MSW/MPH. *Accreditation:* CAHME (one or more programs are accredited). *Program availability:* Part-time. *Degree requirements:* For master's, comprehensive exam (for some programs), thesis (for some programs); for doctorate, thesis/dissertation. *Entrance requirements:* For master's, GMAT (MPH in health services administration), GRE General Test; for doctorate, GRE General Test. Additional exam requirements/recommendations for international students: Required—TOEFL. *Faculty research:* Evaluation of tobacco, AIDS prevalence and prevention, mammography, infant death project, Alzheimer's in elderly Chinese.

Stanford University, School of Medicine, Graduate Programs in Medicine, Department of Health Research and Policy, Program in Epidemiology and Clinical Research, Stanford, CA 94305-2004. Offers MS, PhD. *Degree requirements:* For master's, thesis; for doctorate, thesis/dissertation, qualifying examinations. *Entrance requirements:* For doctorate, GRE General Test or MCAT. Additional exam requirements/recommendations for international students: Required—TOEFL. Electronic applications accepted. *Expenses: Tuition:* Full-time $48,987; part-time $10,620 per quarter. One-time fee: $400. Tuition and fees vary according to program.

Temple University, College of Public Health, Department of Epidemiology and Biostatistics, Philadelphia, PA 19122. Offers applied biostatistics (MPH); environmental health (MPH); epidemiology (MPH, MS, PhD). *Accreditation:* CEPH. *Program availability:* Part-time, evening/weekend. *Faculty:* 9 full-time (5 women). *Students:* 20 full-time (11 women), 7 part-time (5 women); includes 8 minority (5 Black or African American, non-Hispanic/Latino; 1 Asian, non-Hispanic/Latino; 2 Hispanic/Latino), 8 international. 136 applicants, 54% accepted, 20 enrolled. In 2017, 6 master's awarded. *Entrance requirements:* For master's, GRE or MCAT. Additional exam requirements/recommendations for international students: Required—TOEFL (minimum score 550 paper-based; 79 iBT). *Application deadline:* For fall admission, 2/15 for domestic students, 12/15 for international students. Applications are processed on a rolling basis. Application fee: $50. Electronic applications accepted. *Expenses:* Contact institution. *Financial support:* Application deadline: 1/15; applicants required to submit FAFSA. *Unit head:* Dr. Adam Davey, Chair, 215-204-8726, E-mail: adam.davey@temple.edu. *Application contact:* Theresa White, Senior Graduate Advisor/Admissions, 215-204-5105, E-mail: theresawhite@temple.edu.
Website: https://cph.temple.edu/epibio/

Texas A&M University, School of Public Health, College Station, TX 77845. Offers biostatistics (MPH, MSPH); environmental health (MPH, MSPH); epidemiology (MPH, MSPH); executive health administration (MHA); health administration (MHA); health policy and management (MPH, MSPH); health promotion and community health sciences (MPH); health services research (PhD); occupational safety and health (MPH). *Program availability:* Part-time, blended/hybrid learning. *Faculty:* 56. *Students:* 279 full-time (196 women), 86 part-time (56 women); includes 153 minority (48 Black or African American, non-Hispanic/Latino; 36 Asian, non-Hispanic/Latino; 62 Hispanic/Latino; 7 Two or more races, non-Hispanic/Latino), 77 international. Average age 29. 179 applicants, 96% accepted, 148 enrolled. In 2017, 124 master's, 8 doctorates awarded. *Entrance requirements:* For master's, GRE General Test, 3 letters of recommendation; statement of purpose; current curriculum vitae or resume; official transcripts; for doctorate, GRE General Test, 3 letters of recommendation; statement of purpose; current curriculum vitae or resume; official transcripts; interview (in some cases). Additional exam requirements/recommendations for international students: Required—TOEFL (minimum score 597 paper-based, 95 iBT) or GRE (minimum verbal score 153). Application fee: $120. Electronic applications accepted. *Expenses:* Contact institution. *Financial support:* In 2017–18, 203 students received support, including 62 research assistantships with tuition reimbursements available (averaging $10,041 per year), 25 teaching assistantships with tuition reimbursements available (averaging $12,913 per year); career-related internships or fieldwork, institutionally sponsored loans, scholarships/grants, traineeships, health care benefits, tuition waivers (full and partial), and unspecified assistantships also available. Support available to part-time students. Financial award applicants required to submit FAFSA. *Unit head:* Dr. Jay Maddock, Dean, 979-436-9322, Fax: 979-458-1878, E-mail: maddock@tamhsc.edu. *Application contact:* Erin E. Schneider, Associate Director of Admissions and Recruitment, 979-436-9380, E-mail: eschneider@sph.tamhsc.edu.
Website: http://sph.tamhsc.edu/

Tufts University, Graduate School of Arts and Sciences, Graduate Certificate Programs, Program in Epidemiology, Medford, MA 02155. Offers Certificate. Electronic applications accepted. *Expenses: Tuition:* Full-time $49,892. *Required fees:* $874. Full-time tuition and fees vary according to degree level, program and student level. Part-time tuition and fees vary according to course load.

Tufts University, School of Medicine, Public Health and Professional Degree Programs, Boston, MA 02111. Offers biomedical sciences (MS); health communication (MS, Certificate); pain research, education and policy (MS, Certificate); physician assistant (MS); public health (MPH, Dr PH), including behavioral science (MPH), biostatistics (MPH), epidemiology (MPH), health communication (MPH), health services (MPH), management and policy (MPH), nutrition (MPH); DMD/MPH; DVM/MPH; JD/MPH; MD/MPH; MMS/MPH; MS/MBA; MS/MPH. *Accreditation:* CEPH (one or more programs are accredited). *Program availability:* Part-time, evening/weekend. *Faculty:* 62 full-time (25 women), 50 part-time/adjunct (25 women). *Students:* 449 full-time (280 women), 60 part-time (46 women); includes 188 minority (23 Black or African American, non-Hispanic/Latino; 112 Asian, non-Hispanic/Latino; 35 Hispanic/Latino; 18 Two or more races, non-Hispanic/Latino), 23 international. Average age 27. 1,750 applicants, 46% accepted, 252 enrolled. In 2017, 283 master's awarded. Terminal master's awarded for partial completion of doctoral program. *Degree requirements:* For master's, thesis (for some programs); for doctorate, thesis/dissertation. *Entrance requirements:* For master's, GRE General Test, MCAT, or GMAT; for doctorate, GRE General Test or MCAT. Additional exam requirements/recommendations for international students: Required—TOEFL (minimum score 100 iBT); Recommended—IELTS (minimum score 7). *Application deadline:* For fall admission, 1/15 priority date for domestic and international students; for spring admission, 10/25 priority date for domestic and international students. Applications are processed on a rolling basis. Application fee: $70. Electronic applications accepted. *Expenses:* Contact institution. *Financial support:* In 2017–18, 13 students received support, including 1 fellowship (averaging $3,000 per year), 50 research assistantships (averaging $1,000 per year), 65 teaching assistantships (averaging $2,000 per year); Federal Work-Study and scholarships/grants also available. Financial award application deadline: 2/23; financial award applicants required to submit FAFSA. *Faculty research:* Environmental and occupational health, nutrition, epidemiology, health communication, biostatics, obesity/chronic disease, health policy and health care delivery, global health, health inequality and social determinants of health. *Unit head:* Dr. Aviva Must, Dean, 617-636-0935, Fax: 617-636-0898, E-mail: aviva.must@tufts.edu. *Application contact:* Emily Keily, Director of Admissions, 617-636-0935, Fax: 617-636-0898, E-mail: med-phpd@tufts.edu.
Website: http://publichealth.tufts.edu

Tulane University, School of Public Health and Tropical Medicine, Department of Epidemiology, New Orleans, LA 70118-5669. Offers MPH, MS, Dr PH, PhD, MD/MPH. MS and PhD offered through the Graduate School. *Program availability:* Part-time. *Degree requirements:* For doctorate, comprehensive exam, thesis/dissertation. *Entrance requirements:* For master's and doctorate, GRE General Test. Additional exam requirements/recommendations for international students: Required—TOEFL. Electronic applications accepted. *Expenses: Tuition:* Full-time $50,920; part-time $2829 per credit hour. *Required fees:* $2040; $44.50 per credit hour. $580 per term. Tuition and fees vary according to course load, degree level and program. *Faculty research:* Environment, cancer, cardiovascular epidemiology, women's health.

Université Laval, Faculty of Medicine, Graduate Programs in Medicine, Department of Medicine, Programs in Epidemiology, Québec, QC G1K 7P4, Canada. Offers M Sc, PhD. Terminal master's awarded for partial completion of doctoral program. *Degree requirements:* For master's, thesis; for doctorate, comprehensive exam, thesis/dissertation. *Entrance requirements:* For master's and doctorate, knowledge of French, comprehension of written English. Electronic applications accepted.

University at Albany, State University of New York, School of Public Health, Department of Epidemiology and Biostatistics, Albany, NY 12222-0001. Offers epidemiology and biostatistics (MS, PhD). *Accreditation:* CEPH. *Faculty:* 18 full-time (9 women), 4 part-time/adjunct (3 women). *Students:* 14 full-time (9 women), 34 part-time (15 women); includes 15 minority (1 Black or African American, non-Hispanic/Latino; 1 American Indian or Alaska Native, non-Hispanic/Latino; 9 Asian, non-Hispanic/Latino; 3 Hispanic/Latino; 1 Two or more races, non-Hispanic/Latino), 12 international. 75 applicants, 31% accepted, 12 enrolled. In 2017, 10 master's, 2 doctorates awarded. *Degree requirements:* For master's, thesis; for doctorate, thesis/dissertation. *Entrance requirements:* For master's and doctorate, GRE General Test. Additional exam requirements/recommendations for international students: Required—TOEFL (minimum score 550 paper-based). *Application deadline:* For fall admission, 6/30 for domestic students, 5/1 for international students; for spring admission, 11/30 for domestic students, 11/1 for international students. Applications are processed on a rolling basis. Application fee: $75. Electronic applications accepted. *Expenses:* Tuition, state resident: full-time $10,870; part-time $453 per credit hour. Tuition, nonresident: full-time $22,210; part-time $925 per credit hour. *Required fees:* $84.68 per credit hour. $508.06 per semester. Part-time tuition and fees vary according to course load and program. *Financial support:* Application deadline: 4/1. *Faculty research:* Developmental origins of disease, psychosocial adversity, epigenetics, cardiovascular epidemiology, non-parametric and semi parametric statistical methods, Bayesian computational algorithms, adverse health effects of environmental and occupational exposures to toxic agents, diabetes and chronic disease epidemiology and others. *Unit head:* Dr. Recai Ycel, Chair, 518-402-0372.
Website: http://www.albany.edu/sph/epi/index.html

University at Buffalo, the State University of New York, Graduate School, School of Public Health and Health Professions, Department of Epidemiology and Environmental Health, Buffalo, NY 14214. Offers epidemiology (MS, PhD); public health (MPH). *Accreditation:* CEPH. *Program availability:* Part-time. *Faculty:* 13 full-time (10 women), 5 part-time/adjunct (2 women). *Students:* 50 full-time (32 women), 21 part-time (15 women); includes 12 minority (2 Black or African American, non-Hispanic/Latino; 1 American Indian or Alaska Native, non-Hispanic/Latino; 9 Asian, non-Hispanic/Latino), 9 international. Average age 27. 124 applicants, 25% accepted, 23 enrolled. In 2017, 25 master's, 2 doctorates awarded. Terminal master's awarded for partial completion of doctoral program. *Entrance requirements:* For master's and doctorate, GRE General Test. Additional exam requirements/recommendations for international students: Required—TOEFL (minimum score 600 paper-based; 100 iBT). *Application deadline:* For fall admission, 1/15 priority date for domestic and international students. Applications are processed on a rolling basis. Application fee: $50. Electronic applications accepted. *Financial support:* In 2017–18, 17 students received support, including 4 fellowships with full tuition reimbursements available (averaging $22,000 per year), 5 research assistantships with full tuition reimbursements available (averaging $20,000 per year); teaching assistantships with full tuition reimbursements available, career-related internships or fieldwork, Federal Work-Study, institutionally sponsored loans, health care benefits, and unspecified assistantships also available. Financial award application deadline: 2/1; financial award applicants required to submit FAFSA. *Faculty research:* Epidemiology of cancer, nutrition, infectious diseases, epidemiology of environmental, women's health and cardiovascular disease research. *Total annual research expenditures:* $2.2 million. *Unit head:* Dr. Jo Freudenheim, Interim Chair, 716-829-5375, Fax: 716-829-2979, E-mail: phhpadv@buffalo.edu. *Application contact:* Dr. Carl Li, Director of Graduate Studies, 716-829-5382, Fax: 716-829-2979, E-mail: carlli@buffalo.edu.
Website: http://sphhp.buffalo.edu/epidemiology-and-environmental-health.html

The University of Alabama at Birmingham, School of Public Health, Program in Epidemiology, Birmingham, AL 35294. Offers PhD. *Degree requirements:* For doctorate, comprehensive exam, thesis/dissertation, teaching practicum. *Entrance requirements:* For doctorate, GRE General Test, MPH or MSPH. Additional exam requirements/recommendations for international students: Recommended—TOEFL, IELTS. *Faculty research:* Biometry.

The University of Alabama at Birmingham, School of Public Health, Program in Public Health, Birmingham, AL 35294. Offers applied epidemiology and pharmacoepidemiology (MSPH); biostatistics (MPH); clinical and translational science (MSPH); environmental health (MPH); environmental health and toxicology (MSPH); epidemiology (MPH); general theory and practice (MPH); health behavior (MPH); health care organization (MPH); health policy quantitative policy analysis (MPH); industrial hygiene (MPH, MSPH); maternal and child health policy (Dr PH); maternal and child health policy and leadership (MPH); occupational health and safety (MPH); outcomes research (MSPH, Dr PH); public health (PhD); public health management (Dr PH); public health preparedness management (MPH). *Program availability:* Part-time, online learning. *Degree requirements:* For doctorate, comprehensive exam, thesis/dissertation. *Entrance requirements:* For master's and doctorate, GRE. Additional exam requirements/recommendations for international students: Recommended—TOEFL (minimum score 550 paper-based; 70 iBT), IELTS (minimum score 6.5). Electronic applications accepted.

University of Alberta, School of Public Health, Department of Public Health Sciences, Edmonton, AB T6G 2E1, Canada. Offers clinical epidemiology (M Sc, MPH); environmental and occupational health (MPH); environmental health sciences (M Sc); epidemiology (M Sc); global health (M Sc, MPH); health policy and management (MPH); health policy research (M Sc); health technology assessment (MPH); occupational health (M Sc); population health (M Sc); public health leadership (MPH); public health sciences (PhD); quantitative methods (MPH). Terminal master's awarded for partial completion of doctoral program. *Degree requirements:* For master's, thesis (for some programs); for doctorate, thesis/dissertation. *Entrance requirements:* For master's, GMAT or GRE General Test. Additional exam requirements/recommendations for international students: Required—TOEFL (minimum score 550 paper-based) or IELTS (minimum score 6). Electronic applications accepted. *Faculty research:* Biostatistics, health promotion and socio-behavioral health science.

Epidemiology

The University of Arizona, Mel and Enid Zuckerman College of Public Health, Program in Epidemiology, Tucson, AZ 85721. Offers MS, PhD. *Entrance requirements:* Additional exam requirements/recommendations for international students: Required—TOEFL (minimum score 550 paper-based; 79 iBT). Electronic applications accepted.

University of Arkansas for Medical Sciences, College of Public Health, Little Rock, AR 72205-7199. Offers biostatistics (MPH); environmental and occupational health (MPH, Certificate); epidemiology (MPH, PhD); health behavior and health education (MPH); health policy and management (MPH); health promotion and prevention research (PhD); health services administration (MHSA); health systems research (PhD); public health (Certificate); public health leadership (Dr PH). *Accreditation:* CEPH. *Program availability:* Part-time. *Degree requirements:* For master's, preceptorship, culminating experience, internship; for doctorate, comprehensive exam, capstone. *Entrance requirements:* For master's, GRE, GMAT, LSAT, PCAT, MCAT, DAT; for doctorate, GRE. Additional exam requirements/recommendations for international students: Required—TOEFL (minimum score 80 iBT), IELTS. Electronic applications accepted. *Expenses:* Contact institution. *Faculty research:* Health systems, tobacco prevention control, obesity prevention, environmental and occupational exposure, cancer prevention.

University of California, Berkeley, Graduate Division, School of Public Health, Group in Epidemiology, Berkeley, CA 94720-1500. Offers epidemiology (MS, PhD); infectious diseases (PhD). *Degree requirements:* For master's, comprehensive exam; for doctorate, thesis/dissertation, oral and written exam. *Entrance requirements:* For master's, GRE General Test, minimum GPA of 3.0; MD, DDS, DVM, or PhD in biomedical science (MPH); for doctorate, GRE General Test, minimum GPA of 3.0. Electronic applications accepted.

University of California, Davis, Graduate Studies, Graduate Group in Epidemiology, Davis, CA 95616. Offers MS, PhD. *Accreditation:* CEPH. Terminal master's awarded for partial completion of doctoral program. *Degree requirements:* For master's, comprehensive exam (for some programs), thesis (for some programs); for doctorate, thesis/dissertation. *Entrance requirements:* For master's and doctorate, GRE General Test, GRE Subject Test (biology), minimum GPA of 3.25. Additional exam requirements/recommendations for international students: Required—TOEFL (minimum score 550 paper-based). Electronic applications accepted. *Faculty research:* Environmental/occupational wildlife, reproductive and veterinary epidemiology, infectious/chronic disease epidemiology, public health.

University of California, Irvine, School of Medicine, Department of Epidemiology, Irvine, CA 92697. Offers MS, PhD. *Accreditation:* CEPH. *Students:* 16 full-time (13 women), 1 (woman) part-time; includes 7 minority (3 Black or African American, non-Hispanic/Latino; 1 Asian, non-Hispanic/Latino; 2 Hispanic/Latino; 1 Two or more races, non-Hispanic/Latino), 3 international. Average age 29. 29 applicants, 17% accepted, 2 enrolled. In 2017, 1 master's, 2 doctorates awarded. Terminal master's awarded for partial completion of doctoral program. *Degree requirements:* For master's, comprehensive exam, thesis; for doctorate, comprehensive exam, thesis/dissertation, 72 quarter units. *Entrance requirements:* For master's, GRE, minimum GPA of 3.0, letters of recommendation; for doctorate, GRE, minimum GPA of 3.0, personal statement, letters of recommendation. Additional exam requirements/recommendations for international students: Required—TOEFL (minimum score 550 paper-based; 80 iBT), IELTS (minimum score 7). *Application deadline:* For fall admission, 1/15 priority date for domestic and international students. Application fee: $105 ($125 for international students). Electronic applications accepted. *Financial support:* In 2017–18, fellowships with full tuition reimbursements (averaging $25,000 per year), research assistantships with full tuition reimbursements (averaging $46,000 per year), teaching assistantships with full tuition reimbursements (averaging $33,000 per year) were awarded; Federal Work-Study, institutionally sponsored loans, scholarships/grants, traineeships, health care benefits, and unspecified assistantships also available. Financial award application deadline: 1/15; financial award applicants required to submit FAFSA. *Faculty research:* Genetic/molecular epidemiology, cancer epidemiology, biostatistics, environmental health, occupational health. *Total annual research expenditures:* $15 million. *Unit head:* Dr. Hoda Anton-Culver, Chair, 949-824-7401, Fax: 949-824-4773, E-mail: hantoncu@uci.edu. *Application contact:* Julie Strope, Departmental Administrator, 949-824-0306, Fax: 949-824-4773, E-mail: jstrope@uci.edu.
Website: http://www.epi.uci.edu/

University of California, Irvine, School of Social Ecology, Programs in Social Ecology, Irvine, CA 92697. Offers environmental analysis and design (PhD); epidemiology and public health (PhD); social ecology (PhD). *Students:* 9 full-time (8 women), 1 (woman) part-time; includes 1 minority (Hispanic/Latino), 1 international. Average age 30. 14 applicants, 43% accepted, 3 enrolled. In 2017, 2 doctorates awarded. Application fee: $105 ($125 for international students). *Unit head:* Tim-Allen Bruckner, Professor, 949-824-5797, Fax: 949-824-1845, E-mail: tim.bruckner@uci.edu. *Application contact:* Jennifer Craig, Director of Graduate Student Services, 949-824-5918, Fax: 949-824-1845, E-mail: craigj@uci.edu.
Website: http://socialecology.uci.edu/core/graduate-se-core-programs

University of California, Los Angeles, Graduate Division, School of Public Health, Department of Epidemiology, Los Angeles, CA 90095. Offers MPH, MS, Dr PH, PhD, MD/MPH. *Accreditation:* CEPH. *Degree requirements:* For master's, comprehensive exam or thesis; for doctorate, thesis/dissertation, oral and written qualifying exams. *Entrance requirements:* For master's, GRE General Test, minimum GPA of 3.0; for doctorate, GRE General Test, minimum undergraduate GPA of 3.0. Electronic applications accepted.

University of California, San Diego, Graduate Division, Program in Public Health, La Jolla, CA 92093. Offers epidemiology (PhD); global health (PhD); health behavior (PhD). Program offered jointly with San Diego State University. *Students:* 21 full-time (17 women), 15 part-time (11 women). In 2017, 14 doctorates awarded. *Degree requirements:* For doctorate, thesis/dissertation, 2 semesters/quarters of teaching assistantship. *Entrance requirements:* For doctorate, GRE General Test, minimum GPA of 3.0, curriculum vitae or resume, letters of recommendation, statement of purpose. Additional exam requirements/recommendations for international students: Required—TOEFL (minimum score 550 paper-based; 80 iBT), IELTS (minimum score 7). Electronic applications accepted. *Financial support:* Teaching assistantships available. Financial award applicants required to submit FAFSA. *Faculty research:* Maternal and pediatric HIV/AIDS; healthy aging and gender differences; non-parametric and semi-parametric regression, resampling, and the analysis of high-dimensional data; neighborhood correlates of physical activity in children, teens, adults and older adults; medication safety and medication therapy management through practice-based research networks. *Unit head:* David Strong, Faculty Director, 858-657-5241, E-mail: dstrong@ucsd.edu. *Application contact:* Hollie Ward, Graduate Coordinator, 858-822-2382, E-mail: hward@ucsd.edu.
Website: http://publichealth.ucsd.edu/jdp/

University of Cincinnati, Graduate School, College of Medicine, Graduate Programs in Biomedical Sciences, Department of Environmental Health, Cincinnati, OH 45221. Offers environmental and industrial hygiene (MS, PhD); environmental and occupational medicine (MS); environmental genetics and molecular toxicology (MS, PhD); epidemiology and biostatistics (MS, PhD); occupational safety and ergonomics (MS, PhD). *Accreditation:* ABET (one or more programs are accredited); CEPH. Terminal master's awarded for partial completion of doctoral program. *Degree requirements:* For master's, thesis; for doctorate, thesis/dissertation, qualifying exam. *Entrance requirements:* For master's, GRE General Test, bachelor's degree in science; for doctorate, GRE General Test. Additional exam requirements/recommendations for international students: Required—TOEFL (minimum score 600 paper-based; 100 iBT). Electronic applications accepted. *Expenses: Tuition, area resident:* Full-time $14,468. Tuition, state resident: full-time $14,968; part-time $754 per credit hour. Tuition, nonresident: full-time $24,210; part-time $1311 per credit hour. *International tuition:* $26,460 full-time. *Required fees:* $3958; $84 per credit hour. One-time fee: $85 full-time. Tuition and fees vary according to course load, degree level and program. *Faculty research:* Carcinogens and mutagenesis, pulmonary studies, reproduction and development.

University of Colorado Denver, Colorado School of Public Health, Department of Epidemiology, Aurora, CO 80045. Offers MS, PhD. *Program availability:* Part-time. *Faculty:* 15 full-time (11 women), 1 part-time/adjunct (0 women). *Students:* 25 full-time (18 women), 2 part-time (both women); includes 6 minority (1 Black or African American, non-Hispanic/Latino; 1 American Indian or Alaska Native, non-Hispanic/Latino; 2 Asian, non-Hispanic/Latino; 2 Two or more races, non-Hispanic/Latino), 1 international. Average age 29. 54 applicants, 17% accepted, 8 enrolled. In 2017, 1 master's, 4 doctorates awarded. *Degree requirements:* For master's, thesis, 38 credit hours; for doctorate, comprehensive exam, thesis/dissertation, 67 credit hours. *Entrance requirements:* For master's, GRE General Test, baccalaureate degree in scientific field, minimum GPA of 3.0, math course work through integral calculus, two official copies of all academic transcripts, four letters of recommendation/reference, essays describing the applicant's career goals and reasons for applying to the program, resume; for doctorate, GRE or MCAT, bachelor's, master's, or higher degree; minimum undergraduate and graduate GPA of 3.0; coursework in calculus, organic chemistry, epidemiology, biological sciences, and public health; 2 official copies of all academic transcripts; 4 letters of reference; essays. Additional exam requirements/recommendations for international students: Required—TOEFL (minimum score 550 paper-based; 80 iBT). *Application deadline:* For fall admission, 2/1 priority date for domestic students, 1/15 priority date for international students. Application fee: $65. Electronic applications accepted. *Faculty research:* Public health practice and practice-based research, reproductive and perinatal epidemiology, obesity, infectious disease epidemiology, diabetes. *Unit head:* Dr. Jill Norris, Chair, 303-724-4428, E-mail: jill.norris@ucdenver.edu. *Application contact:* Melodie Proffitt, Department Assistant, 303-724-4488, E-mail: melodie.proffitt@ucdenver.edu.
Website: http://www.ucdenver.edu/academics/colleges/PublicHealth/departments/Epidemiology/Pages/welcome.aspx

University of Florida, College of Medicine, Program in Clinical Investigation, Gainesville, FL 32611. Offers clinical investigation (MS); epidemiology (MS); public health (MPH). *Program availability:* Part-time. *Entrance requirements:* For master's, GRE, MD, PhD, DMD/DDS or Pharm D.

University of Florida, Graduate School, College of Public Health and Health Professions, Department of Epidemiology, Gainesville, FL 32611. Offers clinical and translational science (PhD); epidemiology (MS, PhD). *Degree requirements:* For master's, thesis; for doctorate, thesis/dissertation. *Entrance requirements:* For master's and doctorate, GRE (minimum score verbal/quantitative combined 300), minimum GPA of 3.0. Additional exam requirements/recommendations for international students: Required—TOEFL (minimum score 550 paper-based; 80 iBT), IELTS (minimum score 6). *Faculty research:* Substance abuse, psychiatric epidemiology, cancer epidemiology, infectious disease epidemiology, bioinformatics.

University of Florida, Graduate School, College of Public Health and Health Professions, Programs in Public Health, Gainesville, FL 32611. Offers biostatistics (MPH); clinical and translational science (PhD); environmental health (MPH); epidemiology (MPH); health management and policy (MPH); public health (MPH, PhD, Certificate); public health practice (MPH); rehabilitation science (PhD); social and behavioral sciences (MPH); DPT/MPH; DVM/MPH; JD/MPH; MD/MPH; Pharm D/MPH. *Accreditation:* CEPH. *Program availability:* Online learning. *Degree requirements:* For master's, internship. *Entrance requirements:* For master's, GRE General Test, minimum GPA of 3.0. Additional exam requirements/recommendations for international students: Required—TOEFL (minimum score 550 paper-based; 80 iBT), IELTS (minimum score 6).

University of Guelph, Ontario Veterinary College and Graduate Studies, Graduate Programs in Veterinary Sciences, Department of Population Medicine, Guelph, ON N1G 2W1, Canada. Offers epidemiology (M Sc, DV Sc, PhD); health management (DV Sc); population medicine and health management (M Sc); swine health management (M Sc); theriogenology (M Sc, DV Sc). *Degree requirements:* For master's, thesis; for doctorate, comprehensive exam, thesis/dissertation. *Entrance requirements:* Additional exam requirements/recommendations for international students: Required—TOEFL.

University of Hawaii at Manoa, John A. Burns School of Medicine, Department of Public Health Sciences and Epidemiology, Program in Epidemiology, Honolulu, HI 96822. Offers PhD. *Program availability:* Part-time. *Degree requirements:* For doctorate, comprehensive exam, thesis/dissertation. *Entrance requirements:* For doctorate, GRE General Test. Additional exam requirements/recommendations for international students: Required—TOEFL (minimum score 600 paper-based; 100 iBT), IELTS (minimum score 7).

University of Illinois at Chicago, School of Public Health, Epidemiology and Biostatistics Division, Chicago, IL 60607-7128. Offers biostatistics (MPH, MS, PhD); epidemiology (MPH, MS, PhD). *Program availability:* Part-time. Terminal master's awarded for partial completion of doctoral program. *Degree requirements:* For master's, thesis, field practicum; for doctorate, thesis/dissertation, independent research, internship. *Entrance requirements:* For master's and doctorate, GRE General Test, minimum GPA of 2.75. Additional exam requirements/recommendations for international students: Required—TOEFL. Electronic applications accepted. *Expenses:* Contact institution. *Faculty research:* Quantitative methods.

University of Illinois at Springfield, Graduate Programs, College of Public Affairs and Administration, Program in Public Health, Springfield, IL 62703-5407. Offers community health education (Graduate Certificate); emergency preparedness and homeland security (Graduate Certificate); environmental health (MPH, Graduate Certificate); environmental risk assessment (Graduate Certificate); epidemiology (Graduate Certificate); public health (MPH). *Program availability:* Part-time, evening/weekend, 100% online. *Faculty:* 7 full-time (4 women). *Students:* 38 full-time (23 women), 46 part-time (34 women); includes 27 minority (16 Black or African American, non-Hispanic/Latino; 4 Asian, non-Hispanic/Latino; 5 Hispanic/Latino; 2 Two or more races, non-Hispanic/Latino), 22 international. Average age 32. 47 applicants, 51% accepted, 18 enrolled. In 2017, 28 master's, 17 other advanced degrees awarded. *Degree requirements:* For master's, comprehensive exam, internship. *Entrance requirements:* For master's, GRE, minimum undergraduate GPA of 3.0, 3 letters of recommendation, statement of personal goals. Additional exam requirements/recommendations for

international students: Required—TOEFL (minimum score 500 paper-based; 61 iBT). *Application deadline:* Applications are processed on a rolling basis. Application fee: $60 ($75 for international students). Electronic applications accepted. *Expenses:* Tuition, state resident: full-time $7896; part-time $329 per credit hour. Tuition, nonresident: full-time $16,200; part-time $675 per credit hour. Tuition and fees vary according to program. *Financial support:* In 2017–18, research assistantships with full tuition reimbursements (averaging $10,249 per year), teaching assistantships with full tuition reimbursements (averaging $10,303 per year) were awarded; fellowships, career-related internships or fieldwork, Federal Work-Study, scholarships/grants, health care benefits, and unspecified assistantships also available. Support available to part-time students. Financial award application deadline: 11/15; financial award applicants required to submit FAFSA. *Unit head:* Dr. Josiah Alamu, Program Administrator, 217-206-7874, Fax: 217-206-7279, E-mail: jalam3@uis.edu.
Website: http://www.uis.edu/publichealth/

The University of Iowa, Graduate College, College of Public Health, Department of Epidemiology, Iowa City, IA 52242-1316. Offers clinical investigation (MS); epidemiology (MPH, MS, PhD). *Degree requirements:* For master's, thesis optional, exam; for doctorate, comprehensive exam, thesis/dissertation. *Entrance requirements:* For master's and doctorate, GRE General Test, minimum GPA of 3.0. Additional exam requirements/recommendations for international students: Required—TOEFL (minimum score 600 paper-based; 100 iBT). Electronic applications accepted.

The University of Kansas, University of Kansas Medical Center, School of Medicine, Department of Preventive Medicine and Public Health, Kansas City, KS 66160. Offers clinical research (MS); epidemiology (MPH); public health management (MPH); social and behavioral health (MPH); MD/MPH; PhD/MPH. *Accreditation:* CEPH. *Program availability:* Part-time. *Faculty:* 71. *Students:* 39 full-time (30 women), 40 part-time (28 women); includes 21 minority (10 Black or African American, non-Hispanic/Latino; 1 American Indian or Alaska Native, non-Hispanic/Latino; 4 Asian, non-Hispanic/Latino; 3 Hispanic/Latino; 3 Two or more races, non-Hispanic/Latino), 7 international. Average age 30. 66 applicants, 68% accepted, 32 enrolled. In 2017, 33 master's awarded. *Degree requirements:* For master's, thesis, capstone practicum defense. *Entrance requirements:* For master's, GRE, MCAT, LSAT, GMAT or other equivalent graduate professional exam. Additional exam requirements/recommendations for international students: Required—TOEFL. *Application deadline:* For fall admission, 3/1 for domestic and international students. Applications are processed on a rolling basis. Application fee: $60. Electronic applications accepted. *Financial support:* In 2017–18, 9 research assistantships (averaging $15,000 per year) were awarded; career-related internships or fieldwork, Federal Work-Study, scholarships/grants, and unspecified assistantships also available. Support available to part-time students. Financial award application deadline: 3/1; financial award applicants required to submit FAFSA. *Faculty research:* Cancer screening and prevention, smoking cessation, obesity and physical activity, health services/outcomes research, health disparities. *Total annual research expenditures:* $8.4 million. *Unit head:* Dr. Edward F. Ellerbeck, Chairman, 913-588-2774, Fax: 913-588-2780, E-mail: eellerbe@kumc.edu. *Application contact:* Tanya Honderick, MPH Director, 913-588-2720, Fax: 913-588-8505, E-mail: thonderick@kumc.edu.
Website: http://www.kumc.edu/school-of-medicine/preventive-medicine-and-public-health.html

University of Kentucky, Graduate School, College of Public Health, Program in Epidemiology and Biostatistics, Lexington, KY 40506-0032. Offers PhD.

University of Louisville, Graduate School, School of Public Health and Information Sciences, Department of Epidemiology and Population Health, Louisville, KY 40292-0001. Offers epidemiology (MPH, MS); public health sciences (PhD), including epidemiology. *Program availability:* Evening/weekend. *Faculty:* 9 full-time (5 women). *Students:* 4 full-time (2 women), 18 part-time (15 women); includes 6 minority (2 Asian, non-Hispanic/Latino; 2 Hispanic/Latino; 2 Two or more races, non-Hispanic/Latino), 2 international. Average age 31. 12 applicants, 92% accepted, 8 enrolled. In 2017, 7 master's awarded. *Degree requirements:* For master's, thesis; for doctorate, comprehensive exam, thesis/dissertation. *Entrance requirements:* For master's and doctorate, GRE (taken within past 5 years), bachelor's degree from accredited institution or its equivalent; minimum GPA of 3.0 (recommended); two letters of recommendation written within last twelve months; official transcripts of all degrees; one-page personal statement. Additional exam requirements/recommendations for international students: Required—TOEFL (minimum score 90 iBT). *Application deadline:* For fall admission, 4/1 for domestic students, 1/2 priority date for international students. Applications are processed on a rolling basis. Application fee: $65. Electronic applications accepted. *Expenses:* Tuition, state resident: full-time $12,246; part-time $681 per credit hour. Tuition, nonresident: full-time $25,486; part-time $1417 per credit hour. *Required fees:* $196. Tuition and fees vary according to course load, program and reciprocity agreements. *Financial support:* In 2017–18, 3 fellowships with full tuition reimbursements (averaging $20,000 per year), 3 research assistantships with full tuition reimbursements (averaging $20,000 per year) were awarded; scholarships/grants, traineeships, and tuition waivers (full) also available. Financial award application deadline: 3/1; financial award applicants required to submit FAFSA. *Faculty research:* Breast cancer, health disparities along the cancer continuum, childhood leukemia, genetic epidemiology of cardiovascular diseases, developmental disorders associated with environmental exposure to lead and metals, global health. *Total annual research expenditures:* $386,400. *Unit head:* Dr. Richard Baumgartner, Professor and Chair, 502-852-3003, Fax: 502-852-3291, E-mail: rnbaum01@gwise.louisville.edu. *Application contact:* Robin Newlon, Administrative Specialist, 502-852-3003, Fax: 502-852-3294, E-mail: robin.newlon@louisville.edu.
Website: http://louisville.edu/sphis/departments/epidemiology-population-health

University of Maryland, Baltimore, Graduate School, Graduate Program in Life Sciences, Baltimore, MD 21201. Offers biochemistry and molecular biology (MS, PhD), including biochemistry; cellular and molecular biomedical science (MS); clinical research (Postbaccalaureate Certificate); epidemiology (PhD); gerontology (PhD); molecular medicine (PhD), including cancer biology, cell and molecular physiology, human genetics and genomic medicine, molecular toxicology and pharmacology; molecular microbiology and immunology (PhD); neuroscience (PhD); physical rehabilitation science (PhD); toxicology (MS, PhD); MD/MS; MD/PhD. *Students:* 251 full-time (153 women), 53 part-time (37 women); includes 88 minority (29 Black or African American, non-Hispanic/Latino; 34 Asian, non-Hispanic/Latino; 16 Hispanic/Latino; 9 Two or more races, non-Hispanic/Latino), 47 international. Average age 29. 579 applicants, 23% accepted, 46 enrolled. In 2017, 22 master's, 52 doctorates awarded. *Degree requirements:* For master's, comprehensive exam (for some programs), thesis (for some programs); for doctorate, comprehensive exam, thesis/dissertation. *Entrance requirements:* For master's and doctorate, GRE. Additional exam requirements/recommendations for international students: Required—TOEFL (minimum score 80 iBT); Recommended—IELTS (minimum score 7). *Application deadline:* For fall admission, 12/15 for domestic students, 1/15 for international students. Application fee: $75. Electronic applications accepted. *Expenses:* Tuition, state resident: full-time $13,990; part-time $661 per credit. Tuition, nonresident: full-time $30,484; part-time $1310 per credit. *Required fees:* $1894; $94 per credit. $415 per semester. Part-time tuition and fees vary according to course load, degree level and program. *Financial support:* In 2017–18, research assistantships with partial tuition reimbursements (averaging $26,000 per year) were awarded; fellowships, scholarships/grants, health care benefits, and unspecified assistantships also available. Financial award application deadline: 3/1; financial award applicants required to submit FAFSA. *Faculty research:* Cancer, reproduction, cardiovascular, immunology. *Unit head:* Dr. Dudley Strickland, Assistant Dean for Graduate Studies, 410-706-8010. *Application contact:* Keith T. Brooks, Assistant Dean, 410-706-7131, Fax: 410-706-3473, E-mail: kbrooks@umaryland.edu.
Website: http://lifesciences.umaryland.edu

University of Maryland, Baltimore, Graduate School, Graduate Programs in Pharmacy, Department of Pharmaceutical Health Service Research, Baltimore, MD 21201. Offers epidemiology (MS); pharmacy administration (PhD); Pharm D/PhD. *Degree requirements:* For doctorate, comprehensive exam, thesis/dissertation. *Entrance requirements:* For doctorate, GRE General Test. Additional exam requirements/recommendations for international students: Required—TOEFL, IELTS. Electronic applications accepted. *Expenses:* Tuition, state resident: full-time $13,990; part-time $661 per credit. Tuition, nonresident: full-time $30,484; part-time $1310 per credit. *Required fees:* $1894; $94 per credit. $415 per semester. Part-time tuition and fees vary according to course load, degree level and program. *Faculty research:* Pharmacoeconomics, outcomes research, public health policy, drug therapy and aging.

University of Maryland, Baltimore, School of Medicine, Department of Epidemiology and Public Health, Baltimore, MD 21201. Offers biostatistics (MS); clinical research (MS); epidemiology and preventive medicine (MPH, MS, PhD); gerontology (PhD); human genetics and genomic medicine (MS, PhD); molecular epidemiology (MS, PhD); toxicology (MS, PhD); JD/MS; MD/PhD; MS/PhD. *Accreditation:* CEPH. *Program availability:* Part-time. *Students:* 88 full-time (72 women), 53 part-time (38 women); includes 51 minority (21 Black or African American, non-Hispanic/Latino; 20 Asian, non-Hispanic/Latino; 7 Hispanic/Latino; 3 Two or more races, non-Hispanic/Latino), 29 international. Average age 30. In 2017, 24 master's, 14 doctorates awarded. *Degree requirements:* For doctorate, comprehensive exam, thesis/dissertation. *Entrance requirements:* For master's and doctorate, GRE General Test. Additional exam requirements/recommendations for international students: Required—TOEFL (minimum score 550 paper-based; 80 iBT); Recommended—IELTS (minimum score 7). *Application deadline:* For fall admission, 1/15 for domestic and international students. Application fee: $75. Electronic applications accepted. *Expenses:* Contact institution. *Financial support:* In 2017–18, research assistantships with partial tuition reimbursements (averaging $26,000 per year) were awarded; fellowships, Federal Work-Study, scholarships/grants, and unspecified assistantships also available. Financial award application deadline: 3/1; financial award applicants required to submit FAFSA. *Unit head:* Dr. Laura Hungerford, Program Director, 410-706-8492, Fax: 410-706-4225. *Application contact:* Jessica Kelley, Program Coordinator, 410-706-8492, Fax: 410-706-4225, E-mail: jkelley@som.umaryland.edu.
Website: http://lifesciences.umaryland.edu/epidemiology/

University of Maryland, Baltimore County, The Graduate School, College of Arts, Humanities and Social Sciences, Department of Emergency Health Services, Baltimore, MD 21250. Offers emergency health services (MS), including administration, planning, and policy, preventive medicine and epidemiology; emergency management (Postbaccalaureate Certificate); public policy (PhD), including emergency health, emergency management. Some of the required/elective courses within the Preventative Medicine and Epidemiology track are offered in collaboration with the University of Maryland, Baltimore (UMB) and other University System Schools. *Program availability:* Part-time, evening/weekend, 100% online, blended/hybrid learning. *Faculty:* 4 full-time (2 women), 8 part-time/adjunct (3 women). *Students:* 18 full-time (11 women), 4 part-time (3 women); includes 9 minority (6 Black or African American, non-Hispanic/Latino; 1 Asian, non-Hispanic/Latino; 1 Hispanic/Latino; 1 Two or more races, non-Hispanic/Latino). Average age 28. 22 applicants, 91% accepted, 18 enrolled. In 2017, 12 master's awarded. Terminal master's awarded for partial completion of doctoral program. *Degree requirements:* For master's, comprehensive exam (for some programs), capstone project or thesis. *Entrance requirements:* For master's, GRE General Test if GPA is below 3.2, minimum GPA of 3.2. Additional exam requirements/recommendations for international students: Required—TOEFL (minimum score 80 iBT), IELTS, or PTE. *Application deadline:* For fall admission, 6/15 for domestic students, 3/1 for international students; for spring admission, 12/1 for domestic students, 10/1 for international students. Applications are processed on a rolling basis. Application fee: $50. Electronic applications accepted. *Expenses:* $753 per credit hour. *Financial support:* In 2017–18, 6 students received support, including 7 research assistantships with full tuition reimbursements available (averaging $16,875 per year); career-related internships or fieldwork, Federal Work-Study, scholarships/grants, health care benefits, and unspecified assistantships also available. Financial award application deadline: 5/30; financial award applicants required to submit FAFSA. *Faculty research:* EMS management, disaster health services, emergency management, epidemiology, risk profiles, infectious disease control, stress management for care providers, climate change and public health. *Total annual research expenditures:* $715,419. *Unit head:* Dr. J. Lee Jenkins, Department Chair, 410-455-3216, Fax: 410-455-3045, E-mail: jleejenkins@umbc.edu. *Application contact:* Dr. Rick Bissell, Program Director, 410-455-3776, Fax: 410-455-3045, E-mail: bissell@umbc.edu.
Website: http://ehs.umbc.edu/

University of Maryland, College Park, Academic Affairs, School of Public Health, Department of Epidemiology and Biostatistics, College Park, MD 20742. Offers biostatistics (MPH); epidemiology (MPH, PhD).

University of Massachusetts Amherst, Graduate School, School of Public Health and Health Sciences, Department of Public Health, Amherst, MA 01003. Offers biostatistics (MPH, MS, PhD); community health education (MPH, MS, PhD); environmental health sciences (MPH, MS, PhD); epidemiology (MPH, MS, PhD); health policy and management (MPH, MS, PhD); nutrition (MPH, PhD); public health practice (MPH); MPH/MPPA. *Program availability:* Part-time, evening/weekend, online learning. Terminal master's awarded for partial completion of doctoral program. *Degree requirements:* For master's, thesis (for some programs); for doctorate, comprehensive exam, thesis/dissertation. *Entrance requirements:* For master's and doctorate, GRE General Test. Additional exam requirements/recommendations for international students: Required—TOEFL (minimum score 550 paper-based; 80 iBT), IELTS (minimum score 6.5). Electronic applications accepted.

University of Memphis, Graduate School, School of Public Health, Memphis, TN 38152. Offers biostatistics (MPH); environmental health (MPH); epidemiology (MPH, PhD); health systems and policy (PhD); health systems management (MPH); public health (MHA); social and behavioral sciences (MPH, PhD). *Program availability:* Part-time, evening/weekend. *Faculty:* 20 full-time (7 women), 4 part-time/adjunct (1 woman). *Students:* 111 full-time (76 women), 59 part-time (45 women); includes 77 minority (48 Black or African American, non-Hispanic/Latino; 18 Asian, non-Hispanic/Latino; 6 Hispanic/Latino; 5 Two or more races, non-Hispanic/Latino), 23 international. Average age 31. 100 applicants, 91% accepted, 60 enrolled. In 2017, 56 master's, 4 doctorates awarded. *Degree requirements:* For master's, comprehensive exam, thesis (for some programs), practicum/field experience; for doctorate, comprehensive exam, thesis/

dissertation, residency. *Entrance requirements:* For master's, GRE or GMAT, letters of recommendation; letter of intent; for doctorate, GRE, letters of recommendation; personal statement. Additional exam requirements/recommendations for international students: Required—TOEFL (minimum score 550 paper-based; 79 iBT). *Application deadline:* For fall admission, 4/1 for domestic students; for spring admission, 11/1 for domestic students. Application fee: $35 ($60 for international students). Electronic applications accepted. *Expenses:* Contact institution. *Financial support:* In 2017–18, 46 students received support, including 8 research assistantships with full tuition reimbursements available (averaging $8,950 per year); Federal Work-Study, scholarships/grants, and unspecified assistantships also available. Financial award application deadline: 2/1; financial award applicants required to submit FAFSA. *Faculty research:* Health and medical savings accounts, adoption rates, health informatics, Telehealth technologies, biostatistics, environmental health, epidemiology, health systems management, social and behavioral sciences. *Unit head:* Dr. Lisa M. Klesges, Dean, 901-678-4501, E-mail: lmklsges@memphis.edu. *Application contact:* Dr. Marian Levy, Assistant Dean, 901-678-4514, Fax: 901-678-5023, E-mail: sph-admin@memphis.edu.
Website: http://www.memphis.edu/sph/

University of Miami, Graduate School, Miller School of Medicine, Graduate Programs in Medicine, Department of Epidemiology and Public Health, Coral Gables, FL 33124. Offers epidemiology (PhD); public health (MPH, MSPH); JD/MPH; MD/MPH; MD/PhD; MPA/MPH; MPH/MAIA. *Accreditation:* CEPH (one or more programs are accredited). *Program availability:* Part-time. *Degree requirements:* For master's, thesis (for some programs), project, practicum; for doctorate, comprehensive exam, thesis/dissertation. *Entrance requirements:* For master's, GRE General Test, minimum GPA of 3.0, 3 letters of recommendation; for doctorate, GRE General Test, minimum GPA of 3.0, course work in epidemiology and statistics, 3 letters of recommendation. Additional exam requirements/recommendations for international students: Required—TOEFL (minimum score 550 paper-based; 59 iBT). Electronic applications accepted. *Faculty research:* Behavioral epidemiology, substance abuse, AIDS, cardiovascular diseases, women's health.

University of Michigan, School of Public Health, Department of Epidemiology, Ann Arbor, MI 48109-2029. Offers epidemiological science (PhD); general epidemiology (MPH); global health epidemiology (MPH); hospital and molecular epidemiology (MPH); occupational and environmental epidemiology (MPH). PhD and MS offered through the Rackham Graduate School. *Accreditation:* CEPH (one or more programs are accredited). Terminal master's awarded for partial completion of doctoral program. *Degree requirements:* For master's, thesis (for some programs); for doctorate, comprehensive exam, thesis/dissertation, oral defense of dissertation, preliminary exam. *Entrance requirements:* For master's and doctorate, GRE General Test, MCAT. Additional exam requirements/recommendations for international students: Required—TOEFL (minimum score 100 iBT). Electronic applications accepted. *Expenses:* Tuition, state resident: full-time $22,368; part-time $1201 per credit hour. Tuition, nonresident: full-time $45,156; part-time $2467 per credit hour. *Required fees:* $376 per term. Tuition and fees vary according to course load, degree level and program. *Faculty research:* Molecular virology, infectious diseases, women's health, genetics, social epidemiology.

University of Minnesota, Twin Cities Campus, School of Public Health, Division of Environmental Health Sciences, Area in Environmental and Occupational Epidemiology, Minneapolis, MN 55455-0213. Offers MPH, MS, PhD. *Accreditation:* CEPH (one or more programs are accredited). *Degree requirements:* For doctorate, thesis/dissertation. *Entrance requirements:* For master's and doctorate, GRE General Test. Electronic applications accepted.

University of Minnesota, Twin Cities Campus, School of Public Health, Major in Epidemiology, Minneapolis, MN 55455-0213. Offers MPH, PhD. *Accreditation:* CEPH (one or more programs are accredited). *Program availability:* Part-time. Terminal master's awarded for partial completion of doctoral program. *Degree requirements:* For master's, fieldwork, project; for doctorate, comprehensive exam, thesis/dissertation. *Entrance requirements:* For master's, GRE General Test; for doctorate, GRE General Test, master's degree in related field. Additional exam requirements/recommendations for international students: Required—TOEFL. Electronic applications accepted. *Expenses:* Contact institution. *Faculty research:* Prevention of cardiovascular disease, nutrition, genetic epidemiology, behavioral interventions, research methods.

University of Nebraska Medical Center, Department of Epidemiology, Omaha, NE 68198-4395. Offers PhD. *Accreditation:* CEPH. *Program availability:* Part-time. *Degree requirements:* For doctorate, comprehensive exam, thesis/dissertation. *Entrance requirements:* For doctorate, GRE, master's degree in epidemiology or related field. Additional exam requirements/recommendations for international students: Required—TOEFL (minimum score 550 paper-based; 80 iBT). Electronic applications accepted. *Expenses:* Tuition, state resident: full-time $8451; part-time $4225 per semester. Tuition, nonresident: full-time $24,219; part-time $11,295 per semester. *Required fees:* $589; $117 per term. *Faculty research:* Arsenic in drinking water and diabetes, environmental tobacco smoke exposure, injuries in pork processing, cancer-related disparities in Northern Plains American Indian communities, pandemic flu preparedness in Nebraska nursing homes.

University of New Mexico, Graduate Studies, Health Sciences Center, Program in Public Health, Albuquerque, NM 87131-5196. Offers community health (MPH); epidemiology (MPH); health systems, services and policy (MPH). *Program availability:* Part-time, online learning. *Faculty:* 9 full-time (6 women), 1 (woman) part-time/adjunct. *Students:* 23 full-time (20 women), 20 part-time (14 women); includes 15 minority (1 Black or African American, non-Hispanic/Latino; 1 American Indian or Alaska Native, non-Hispanic/Latino; 1 Asian, non-Hispanic/Latino; 12 Hispanic/Latino), 2 international. Average age 32. 34 applicants, 53% accepted, 18 enrolled. In 2017, 13 master's awarded. *Entrance requirements:* For master's, GRE, MCAT, 2 years of experience in health field. Additional exam requirements/recommendations for international students: Required—TOEFL. *Application deadline:* For fall admission, 2/1 for domestic students. Application fee: $50. *Financial support:* Fellowships, research assistantships, and Federal Work-Study available. Financial award application deadline: 12/15; financial award applicants required to submit FAFSA. *Faculty research:* Epidemiology, rural health, environmental health, Native American health issues. *Unit head:* Dr. Kristine Tollestrup, Director, 505-272-4173, Fax: 505-272-4494, E-mail: ktollestrup@salud.unm.edu. *Application contact:* Gayle Garcia, Education Coordinator, 505-272-3982, Fax: 505-272-4494, E-mail: garciag@salud.unm.edu.
Website: http://fcm.unm.edu/

The University of North Carolina at Chapel Hill, Graduate School, Gillings School of Global Public Health, Department of Epidemiology, Chapel Hill, NC 27599. Offers clinical research (MSCR); epidemiology (MPH, PhD); veterinary epidemiology (MPH); Pharm D/MPH. *Faculty:* 56 full-time (36 women), 93 part-time/adjunct (52 women). *Students:* 180 full-time (137 women), 11 part-time (6 women); includes 59 minority (13 Black or African American, non-Hispanic/Latino; 1 American Indian or Alaska Native, non-Hispanic/Latino; 21 Asian, non-Hispanic/Latino; 11 Hispanic/Latino; 13 Two or more races, non-Hispanic/Latino), 21 international. Average age 31. 259 applicants, 31% accepted, 43 enrolled. In 2017, 12 master's, 36 doctorates awarded. Terminal master's awarded for partial completion of doctoral program. *Degree requirements:* For master's, comprehensive exam, major paper; for doctorate, comprehensive exam, thesis/dissertation. *Entrance requirements:* For master's, GRE General Test or MCAT, doctoral degree (completed or in-progress); for doctorate, GRE General Test, strong quantitative and biological preparation, 3 letters of recommendation (academic and/or professional). Additional exam requirements/recommendations for international students: Required—TOEFL (minimum score 90 iBT), IELTS (minimum score 7). *Application deadline:* For fall admission, 1/10 for domestic and international students. Applications are processed on a rolling basis. Application fee: $85. Electronic applications accepted. *Financial support:* Fellowships with tuition reimbursements, research assistantships with tuition reimbursements, teaching assistantships with tuition reimbursements, career-related internships or fieldwork, Federal Work-Study, institutionally sponsored loans, scholarships/grants, traineeships, and health care benefits available. Support available to part-time students. Financial award application deadline: 12/10; financial award applicants required to submit FAFSA. *Faculty research:* Chronic disease: cancer, cardiovascular, nutritional; environmental/occupational injury; infectious diseases; reproductive diseases; healthcare. *Unit head:* Dr. Andrew Olshan, Chair, 919-966-7424, Fax: 919-966-2089, E-mail: andy_olshan@unc.edu. *Application contact:* Jennifer Joyce Moore, Student Services Specialist, 919-966-7458, Fax: 919-966-2089, E-mail: jenjoyce@email.unc.edu.
Website: https://sph.unc.edu/epid/epidemiology-landing/

The University of North Carolina at Chapel Hill, School of Dentistry and Graduate School, Graduate Programs in Dentistry, Chapel Hill, NC 27599. Offers dental hygiene (MS); endodontics (MS); epidemiology (PhD); operative dentistry (MS); oral and maxillofacial pathology (MS); oral and maxillofacial radiology (MS); oral biology (PhD); orthodontics (MS); pediatric dentistry (MS); periodontology (MS); prosthodontics (MS). *Degree requirements:* For master's, thesis; for doctorate, thesis/dissertation. *Entrance requirements:* For master's, GRE General Test (for orthodontics and oral biology only); National Dental Board Part I (Part II if available), dental degree (for all except dental hygiene); for doctorate, GRE General Test. Additional exam requirements/recommendations for international students: Required—TOEFL (minimum score 550 paper-based; 79 iBT). Electronic applications accepted. *Expenses:* Contact institution. *Faculty research:* Clinical research, inflammation, immunology, neuroscience, molecular biology.

University of North Texas Health Science Center at Fort Worth, School of Public Health, Fort Worth, TX 76107-2699. Offers biostatistics (MS); epidemiology (MPH, MS, PhD); food security and public health (Graduate Certificate); GIS in public health (Graduate Certificate); global health (Graduate Certificate); global health for medical professionals (Graduate Certificate); health administration (MHA); health behavior research (MS, PhD); maternal and child health (MPH); public health (Graduate Certificate); public health practice (MPH); DO/MPH; MS/MPH. *Accreditation:* CEPH. *Program availability:* Part-time, evening/weekend, 100% online. *Degree requirements:* For master's, thesis or alternative, supervised internship; for doctorate, thesis/dissertation, supervised internship. *Entrance requirements:* For master's, GRE General Test. Additional exam requirements/recommendations for international students: Required—TOEFL. Electronic applications accepted. *Expenses:* Contact institution.

University of Oklahoma Health Sciences Center, Graduate College, College of Public Health, Program in Biostatistics and Epidemiology, Oklahoma City, OK 73190. Offers biostatistics (MPH, MS, Dr PH, PhD); epidemiology (MPH, MS, Dr PH, PhD). *Accreditation:* CEPH (one or more programs are accredited). *Program availability:* Part-time. *Degree requirements:* For master's, comprehensive exam, thesis (for some programs); for doctorate, comprehensive exam, thesis/dissertation. *Entrance requirements:* For master's, 3 letters of recommendation, resume; for doctorate, GRE General Test, letters of recommendation. Additional exam requirements/recommendations for international students: Required—TOEFL (minimum score 570 paper-based), TWE. *Faculty research:* Statistical methodology, applied statistics, acute and chronic disease epidemiology.

University of Ottawa, Faculty of Graduate and Postdoctoral Studies, Faculty of Medicine, Department of Epidemiology and Community Medicine, Ottawa, ON K1N 6N5, Canada. Offers epidemiology (M Sc), including health technology assessment. *Degree requirements:* For master's, thesis. *Entrance requirements:* For master's, honors degree or equivalent, minimum B average. Electronic applications accepted. *Faculty research:* Epidemiologic concepts and methods, health technology assessment.

University of Pennsylvania, Perelman School of Medicine, Center for Clinical Epidemiology and Biostatistics, Philadelphia, PA 19104. Offers clinical epidemiology (MSCE), including bioethics, clinical trials, human genetics, patient centered outcome research, pharmacoepidemiology. *Program availability:* Part-time. *Faculty:* 102 full-time (49 women), 69 part-time/adjunct (25 women). *Students:* 92 full-time (61 women), 3 part-time (2 women); includes 35 minority (11 Black or African American, non-Hispanic/Latino; 18 Asian, non-Hispanic/Latino; 6 Hispanic/Latino). Average age 35. 45 applicants, 87% accepted, 30 enrolled. In 2017, 23 master's awarded. *Degree requirements:* For master's, comprehensive exam, thesis. *Entrance requirements:* For master's, GRE General Test or MCAT, advanced degree, clinical experience. Additional exam requirements/recommendations for international students: Required—TOEFL. *Application deadline:* For fall admission, 12/1 priority date for domestic students, 12/1 for international students. Application fee: $0. Electronic applications accepted. *Expenses:* Contact institution. *Financial support:* In 2017–18, 50 students received support, including 50 fellowships with tuition reimbursements available (averaging $45,500 per year); research assistantships, teaching assistantships, and tuition waivers also available. Financial award application deadline: 12/1. *Faculty research:* Patient-centered outcomes, pharmacoepidemiology, women's health, cancer epidemiology, genetic epidemiology. *Total annual research expenditures:* $38.7 million. *Unit head:* Dr. Harold I. Feldman, Director, 215-573-0901, E-mail: hfeldman@mail.med.upenn.edu. *Application contact:* Jennifer Kuklinski, Program Coordinator, 215-573-2382, E-mail: jkuklins@mail.med.upenn.edu.
Website: http://www.cceb.med.upenn.edu/

University of Pittsburgh, Graduate School of Public Health, Department of Epidemiology, Pittsburgh, PA 15261. Offers epidemiology (MPH, MS, PhD); theory and research methods (Dr PH); MD/PhD. *Accreditation:* CEPH (one or more programs are accredited). *Program availability:* Part-time. *Faculty:* 43. *Students:* 86 full-time (66 women), 21 part-time (15 women); includes 15 minority (2 Black or African American, non-Hispanic/Latino; 3 Asian, non-Hispanic/Latino; 5 Hispanic/Latino; 5 Two or more races, non-Hispanic/Latino), 30 international. Average age 29. 416 applicants, 46% accepted, 47 enrolled. *Degree requirements:* For master's, internship and essay (for MPH); comprehensive exam and thesis (for MS); for doctorate, comprehensive exam, thesis/dissertation, practicum (for Dr PH). *Entrance requirements:* For master's, GRE General Test, DAT, or MCAT, 3 credits each of course work in human biology and algebra or higher mathematics, 6 in behavioral science (MPH); for doctorate, GRE General Test, DAT, or MCAT, 3 credits of course work in biology and math. Additional exam requirements/recommendations for international students: Required—TOEFL (minimum score 550 paper-based, 80 iBT) or IELTS (minimum score 6.5). *Application deadline:* For fall admission, 4/15 for domestic students, 3/15 for international students. Applications are processed on a rolling basis. Application fee: $135. Electronic applications accepted. *Expenses:* $13,068 full-time resident per semester, $21,696 non-

resident; $425 full-time fees per semester. *Financial support:* Fellowships, research assistantships, and teaching assistantships available. Financial award applicants required to submit FAFSA. *Faculty research:* Cardiovascular and diabetes epidemiology; clinical trials and methods; molecular and genetic epidemiology; aging epidemiology; women's health epidemiology. *Total annual research expenditures:* $24.9 million. *Unit head:* Dr. Anne B. Newman, Chair, 412-624-3056, Fax: 412-624-3737, E-mail: newmana@edc.pitt.edu. *Application contact:* Lori Sarracino Smith, Student Services Manager/Program Administrator, 412-383-5260, Fax: 412 383-5325, E-mail: smithl@edc.pitt.edu.
Website: http://www.epidemiology.pitt.edu/

University of Prince Edward Island, Atlantic Veterinary College, Graduate Program in Veterinary Medicine, Charlottetown, PE C1A 4P3, Canada. Offers anatomy (M Sc, PhD); bacteriology (M Sc, PhD); clinical pharmacology (M Sc, PhD); clinical sciences (M Sc, PhD); epidemiology (M Sc, PhD), including reproduction; fish health (M Sc, PhD); food animal nutrition (M Sc, PhD); immunology (M Sc, PhD); microanatomy (M Sc, PhD); parasitology (M Sc, PhD); pathology (M Sc, PhD); pharmacology (M Sc, PhD); physiology (M Sc, PhD); toxicology (M Sc, PhD); veterinary science (M Vet Sc); virology (M Sc, PhD). *Program availability:* Part-time. *Degree requirements:* For master's, thesis; for doctorate, thesis/dissertation. *Entrance requirements:* For master's, DVM, B Sc honors degree, or equivalent; for doctorate, M Sc. Additional exam requirements/recommendations for international students: Required—TOEFL (minimum score 550 paper-based; 80 iBT). *Expenses:* Contact institution. *Faculty research:* Animal health management, infectious diseases, fin fish and shellfish health, basic biomedical sciences, ecosystem health.

University of Puerto Rico–Medical Sciences Campus, Graduate School of Public Health, Department of Social Sciences, Program in Epidemiology, San Juan, PR 00936-5067. Offers MPH, MS. *Accreditation:* CEPH (one or more programs are accredited). *Program availability:* Part-time. *Entrance requirements:* For master's, GRE, previous course work in biology, chemistry, physics, mathematics, and social sciences. *Expenses:* Contact institution.

University of Rochester, School of Medicine and Dentistry, Graduate Programs in Medicine and Dentistry, Department of Community and Preventive Medicine, Program in Epidemiology, Rochester, NY 14627. Offers PhD. *Degree requirements:* For doctorate, thesis/dissertation, qualifying exam. *Entrance requirements:* For doctorate, GRE General Test.

University of Saskatchewan, College of Medicine, Department of Community Health and Epidemiology, Saskatoon, SK S7N 5A2, Canada. Offers M Sc, PhD. *Degree requirements:* For master's, thesis; for doctorate, thesis/dissertation. *Entrance requirements:* Additional exam requirements/recommendations for international students: Required—TOEFL.

University of South Carolina, The Graduate School, Arnold School of Public Health, Department of Epidemiology and Biostatistics, Program in Epidemiology, Columbia, SC 29208. Offers MPH, MSPH, Dr PH, PhD. *Accreditation:* CEPH (one or more programs are accredited). *Program availability:* Part-time. *Degree requirements:* For master's, comprehensive exam, thesis (for some programs), practicum (MPH); for doctorate, comprehensive exam, thesis/dissertation (for some programs), practicum. *Entrance requirements:* For master's, GRE General Test; for doctorate, GRE General Test, master's degree. Additional exam requirements/recommendations for international students: Required—TOEFL (minimum score 570 paper-based; 88 iBT). Electronic applications accepted. *Faculty research:* Cancer epidemiology, mental health epidemiology, health effects of physical activity, environmental epidemiology, genetic epidemiology, asthma epidemiology.

University of Southern California, Keck School of Medicine and Graduate School, Graduate Programs in Medicine, Department of Preventive Medicine, Division of Biostatistics, Los Angeles, CA 90032. Offers applied biostatistics and epidemiology (MS); biostatistics (MS, PhD); epidemiology (PhD); molecular epidemiology (MS). *Program availability:* Part-time. *Faculty:* 47 full-time (8 women), 7 part-time/adjunct (3 women). *Students:* 93 full-time (59 women); includes 23 minority (3 Black or African American, non-Hispanic/Latino; 1 American Indian or Alaska Native, non-Hispanic/Latino; 17 Asian, non-Hispanic/Latino; 2 Native Hawaiian or other Pacific Islander, non-Hispanic/Latino), 55 international. Average age 30. 108 applicants, 55% accepted, 22 enrolled. In 2017, 15 master's, 12 doctorates awarded. Terminal master's awarded for partial completion of doctoral program. *Degree requirements:* For master's, thesis; for doctorate, thesis/dissertation. *Entrance requirements:* For master's, GRE General Test (minimum scores of 150 each on Verbal and Quantitative sections), minimum GPA of 3.0; for doctorate, GRE General Test (minimum scores of 160 each on Verbal and Quantitative sections), minimum GPA of 3.5. Additional exam requirements/recommendations for international students: Required—TOEFL (minimum score 600 paper-based; 100 iBT), IELTS (minimum score 7). *Application deadline:* For fall admission, 12/1 priority date for domestic and international students; for winter admission, 5/15 priority date for domestic and international students; for spring admission, 11/1 priority date for domestic and international students; for summer admission, 3/1 priority date for domestic and international students. Applications are processed on a rolling basis. Application fee: $85. Electronic applications accepted. *Expenses:* Contact institution. *Financial support:* In 2017–18, 38 students received support, including 10 fellowships with full tuition reimbursements available (averaging $32,000 per year), 36 research assistantships with tuition reimbursements available (averaging $32,000 per year), 15 teaching assistantships with tuition reimbursements available (averaging $32,000 per year); career-related internships or fieldwork, Federal Work-Study, institutionally sponsored loans, scholarships/grants, traineeships, health care benefits, and unspecified assistantships also available. Financial award application deadline: 12/1; financial award applicants required to submit CSS PROFILE or FAFSA. *Faculty research:* Clinical trials in ophthalmology and cancer research, methods of analysis for epidemiological studies, genetic epidemiology. *Total annual research expenditures:* $1.3 million. *Unit head:* Dr. Kiros Berhane, Director, Graduate Programs in Biostatistics and Epidemiology, 323-442-1994, Fax: 323-442-2993, E-mail: kiros@usc.edu. *Application contact:* Mary L. Trujillo, Student Advisor/Program Manager, 323-442-2633, Fax: 323-442-2993, E-mail: mtrujill@usc.edu.
Website: https://biostatspi.usc.edu/

University of Southern California, Keck School of Medicine and Graduate School, Graduate Programs in Medicine, Department of Preventive Medicine, Master of Public Health Program, Los Angeles, CA 90032. Offers biostatistics and epidemiology (MPH); child and family health (MPH); environmental health (MPH); geohealth (MPH); global health leadership (MPH); health communication (MPH); health education and promotion (MPH); public health policy (MPH). *Accreditation:* CEPH. *Program availability:* Part-time, evening/weekend. *Faculty:* 47 full-time (35 women), 13 part-time/adjunct (8 women). *Students:* 258 full-time (204 women), 61 part-time (50 women); includes 167 minority (28 Black or African American, non-Hispanic/Latino; 1 American Indian or Alaska Native, non-Hispanic/Latino; 61 Asian, non-Hispanic/Latino; 64 Hispanic/Latino; 4 Native Hawaiian or other Pacific Islander, non-Hispanic/Latino; 9 Two or more races, non-Hispanic/Latino), 28 international. Average age 26. 378 applicants, 53% accepted, 87 enrolled. In 2017, 91 master's awarded. *Degree requirements:* For master's, practicum, final report, oral presentation. *Entrance requirements:* For master's, GRE General Test, MCAT, GMAT, minimum GPA of 3.0. Additional exam requirements/recommendations for international students: Required—TOEFL (minimum score 600 paper-based; 90 iBT). *Application deadline:* For fall admission, 12/1 priority date for domestic students, 5/1 priority date for international students; for spring admission, 9/1 priority date for domestic and international students; for summer admission, 3/1 for domestic and international students. Applications are processed on a rolling basis. Application fee: $90. Electronic applications accepted. *Expenses:* Contact institution. *Financial support:* Career-related internships or fieldwork, Federal Work-Study, institutionally sponsored loans, and scholarships/grants available. Support available to part-time students. Financial award application deadline: 5/4; financial award applicants required to submit CSS PROFILE or FAFSA. *Faculty research:* Cancer and heart disease epidemiology and prevention, mass media and health communication research, effects of air pollution on health, tobacco control, global health. *Total annual research expenditures:* $7 million. *Unit head:* Dr. Louise A. Rohrbach, Director, 323-442-8237, Fax: 323-442-8297, E-mail: rohrbac@usc.edu. *Application contact:* Valerie Burris, Admissions Counselor, 323-442-7257, Fax: 323-442-8297, E-mail: valeriem@usc.edu.
Website: http://mph.usc.edu/

University of Southern Mississippi, College of Health, Department of Public Health, Hattiesburg, MS 39406-0001. Offers epidemiology and biostatistics (MPH); health policy and administration (MPH). *Program availability:* Part-time, evening/weekend. *Students:* 17 full-time (6 women). 42 applicants, 88% accepted, 17 enrolled. In 2017, 2 master's awarded. *Degree requirements:* For master's, comprehensive exam, thesis (for some programs). *Entrance requirements:* For master's, GRE General Test, minimum GPA of 2.75 in last 60 hours. Additional exam requirements/recommendations for international students: Required—TOEFL, IELTS. *Application deadline:* For fall admission, 3/1 priority date for domestic and international students; for spring admission, 1/10 priority date for domestic and international students. Applications are processed on a rolling basis. Application fee: $60. Electronic applications accepted. *Expenses:* Tuition, state resident: full-time $3830. *Financial support:* Research assistantships with full tuition reimbursements, teaching assistantships with full tuition reimbursements, career-related internships or fieldwork, Federal Work-Study, institutionally sponsored loans, scholarships/grants, health care benefits, and unspecified assistantships available. Financial award application deadline: 3/15; financial award applicants required to submit FAFSA. *Faculty research:* Rural health care delivery, school health, nutrition of pregnant teens, risk factor reduction, sexually transmitted diseases. *Unit head:* Charkarra Anderson-Lewis, Interim Chair, 601-266-5435, Fax: 601-266-5043, E-mail: charkarra.andersonlewis@usm.edu.
Website: http://www.usm.edu/community-public-health-sciences

University of South Florida, College of Public Health, Department of Epidemiology and Biostatistics, Tampa, FL 33620-9951. Offers MPH, MSPH, PhD. *Accreditation:* CEPH (one or more programs are accredited). *Program availability:* Part-time, evening/weekend. *Degree requirements:* For master's, comprehensive exam, thesis (for some programs); for doctorate, comprehensive exam, thesis/dissertation. *Entrance requirements:* For master's, GRE General Test, minimum GPA of 3.0 in upper-level course work, goal statement letter, two professional letters of recommendation, resume/curriculum vitae; for doctorate, GRE General Test, minimum GPA of 3.0 in upper-level course work, 3 professional letters of recommendation, resume/curriculum vitae, writing sample. Additional exam requirements/recommendations for international students: Required—TOEFL (minimum score 550 paper-based; 79 iBT). Electronic applications accepted. *Faculty research:* Dementia, mental illness, mental health preventative trails, rural health outreach, clinical and administrative studies.

University of South Florida, Innovative Education, Tampa, FL 33620-9951. Offers adult, career and higher education (Graduate Certificate), including college teaching, leadership in developing human resources, leadership in higher education; Africana studies (Graduate Certificate), including diasporas and health disparities, genocide and human rights; aging studies (Graduate Certificate), including gerontology; art research (Graduate Certificate), including museum studies; business foundations (Graduate Certificate); chemical and biomedical engineering (Graduate Certificate), including materials science and engineering, water, health and sustainability; child and family studies (Graduate Certificate), including positive behavior support; civil and industrial engineering (Graduate Certificate), including transportation systems analysis; community and family health (Graduate Certificate), including maternal and child health, social marketing and public health, violence and injury: prevention and intervention, women's health; criminology (Graduate Certificate), including criminal justice administration; data science for public administration (Graduate Certificate); digital humanities (Graduate Certificate); educational measurement and research (Graduate Certificate), including evaluation; English (Graduate Certificate), including comparative literary studies, creative writing, professional and technical communication; entrepreneurship (Graduate Certificate); environmental health (Graduate Certificate), including safety management; epidemiology and biostatistics (Graduate Certificate), including applied biostatistics, biostatistics, concepts and tools of epidemiology, epidemiology, epidemiology of infectious diseases; geography, environment and planning (Graduate Certificate), including community development, environmental policy and management, geographical information systems; geology (Graduate Certificate), including hydrogeology; global health (Graduate Certificate), including disaster management, global health and Latin American and Caribbean studies, global health practice, humanitarian assistance, infection control; government and international affairs (Graduate Certificate), including Cuban studies, globalization studies; health policy and management (Graduate Certificate), including health management and leadership, public health policy and programs; hearing specialist: early intervention (Graduate Certificate); industrial and management systems engineering (Graduate Certificate), including systems engineering, technology management; information studies (Graduate Certificate), including school library media specialist; information systems/decision sciences (Graduate Certificate), including analytics and business intelligence; instructional technology (Graduate Certificate), including distance education, Florida digital/virtual educator, instructional design, multimedia design, Web design; internal medicine, bioethics and medical humanities (Graduate Certificate), including biomedical ethics; Latin American and Caribbean studies (Graduate Certificate); leadership for coastal resiliency planning (Graduate Certificate); mass communications (Graduate Certificate), including multimedia journalism; mathematics and statistics (Graduate Certificate), including mathematics; medicine (Graduate Certificate), including aging and neuroscience, bioinformatics, biotechnology, brain fitness and memory management, clinical investigation, hand and upper limb rehabilitation, health informatics, health sciences, integrative weight management, intellectual property, medicine and gender, metabolic and nutritional medicine, metabolic cardiology, pharmacy sciences; national and competitive intelligence (Graduate Certificate); nursing (Graduate Certificate), including simulation based academic fellowship in advanced pain management; psychological and social foundations (Graduate Certificate), including career counseling, college teaching, diversity in education, mental health counseling, school counseling; public affairs (Graduate Certificate), including nonprofit management, public management, research administration; public health (Graduate Certificate), including assessing chemical toxicity and public health risks, health equity, pharmacoepidemiology, public health generalist, toxicology, translational research in adolescent behavioral health; public health practices (Graduate Certificate), including planning for healthy communities; rehabilitation and mental health counseling (Graduate Certificate), including integrative mental health care, marriage and family therapy,

rehabilitation technology; secondary education (Graduate Certificate), including ESOL, foreign language education: culture and content, foreign language education: professional; social work (Graduate Certificate), including geriatric social work/clinical gerontology; special education (Graduate Certificate), including autism spectrum disorder, disabilities education: severe/profound; world languages (Graduate Certificate), including teaching English as a second language (TESL) or foreign language. *Unit head:* Dr. Cynthia DeLuca, Associate Vice President and Assistant Vice Provost, 813-974-3077, Fax: 813-974-7061, E-mail: deluca@usf.edu. *Application contact:* Owen Hooper, Director, Summer and Alternative Calendar Programs, 813-974-6917, E-mail: hooper@usf.edu.
Website: http://www.usf.edu/innovative-education/

The University of Tennessee Health Science Center, College of Graduate Health Sciences, Memphis, TN 38163. Offers biomedical engineering (MS, PhD); biomedical sciences (PhD); dental sciences (MDS); epidemiology (MS); health outcomes and policy research (PhD); laboratory research and management (MS); nursing science (PhD); pharmaceutical sciences (PhD); pharmacology (MS); speech and hearing science (PhD); DDS/PhD; DNP/PhD; MD/PhD; Pharm D/PhD. MS and PhD programs in biomedical engineering offered jointly with University of Memphis. *Faculty:* 528 full-time (176 women). *Students:* 258 full-time (130 women); includes 87 minority (14 Black or African American, non-Hispanic/Latino; 68 Asian, non-Hispanic/Latino; 5 Hispanic/Latino). Average age 28. 673 applicants, 17% accepted, 102 enrolled. In 2017, 23 master's, 30 doctorates awarded. Terminal master's awarded for partial completion of doctoral program. *Degree requirements:* For master's, comprehensive exam, thesis; for doctorate, thesis/dissertation, oral and written preliminary and comprehensive exams. *Entrance requirements:* For master's and doctorate, GRE General Test, minimum GPA of 3.0. Additional exam requirements/recommendations for international students: Recommended—TOEFL (minimum score 79 iBT), IELTS (minimum score 6.5). *Application deadline:* For winter admission, 1/1 for domestic and international students; for spring admission, 3/1 for domestic and international students. Applications are processed on a rolling basis. Application fee: $0. Electronic applications accepted. *Expenses:* Contact institution. *Financial support:* In 2017–18, 150 students received support, including 150 research assistantships (averaging $25,000 per year); fellowships, institutionally sponsored loans, scholarships/grants, health care benefits, and tuition waivers (full and partial) also available. Support available to part-time students. *Faculty research:* Cell biology, epidemiology, biomedical engineering, speech and hearing science, health policy, pharmaceutical sciences, dental sciences, nursing science, pharmacology. *Unit head:* Dr. Donald B. Thomason, Dean, 901-448-5538, E-mail: dthomaso@uthsc.edu. *Application contact:* Dr. Isaac O. Donkor, Associate Dean for Student Affairs, 901-448-5538, E-mail: idonkor@uthsc.edu.
Website: http://grad.uthsc.edu/

The University of Texas Health Science Center at Houston, School of Public Health, Houston, TX 77030. Offers behavioral science (PhD); biostatistics (MPH, MS, PhD); environmental health (MPH); epidemiology (MPH, MS, PhD); general public health (Certificate); genomics and bioinformatics (Certificate); health disparities (Certificate); health promotion/health education (MPH, Dr PH); healthcare management (Certificate); management, policy and community health (MPH, Dr PH, PhD); maternal and child health (Certificate); public health informatics (Certificate); DDS/MPH; JD/MPH; MBA/MPH; MD/MPH; MGPS/MPH; MP Aff/MPH; MS/MPH; MSN/MPH; MSW/MPH; PhD/MPH. Specific programs are offered at each of our six campuses in Texas (Austin, Brownsville, Dallas, El Paso, Houston, and San Antonio). *Accreditation:* CEPH. *Program availability:* Part-time. *Faculty:* 140 full-time (74 women), 23 part-time/adjunct (14 women). *Students:* 604 full-time (446 women), 534 part-time (384 women); includes 504 minority (106 Black or African American, non-Hispanic/Latino; 177 Asian, non-Hispanic/Latino; 88 Hispanic/Latino; 1 Native Hawaiian or other Pacific Islander, non-Hispanic/Latino; 132 Two or more races, non-Hispanic/Latino). Average age 31. 1,425 applicants, 58% accepted, 423 enrolled. In 2017, 315 master's, 68 doctorates awarded. *Degree requirements:* For master's, thesis (for some programs); for doctorate, comprehensive exam, thesis/dissertation. *Entrance requirements:* For master's and doctorate, GRE General Test. Additional exam requirements/recommendations for international students: Required—TOEFL (minimum score 600 paper-based, 100 iBT) or IELTS (7.5). *Application deadline:* For fall admission, 3/1 for domestic and international students; for spring admission, 10/1 for domestic and international students; for summer admission, 3/1 for domestic students. Applications are processed on a rolling basis. Application fee: $135. Electronic applications accepted. *Expenses:* $233 per semester credit hour resident tuition, $980 per semester credit hour non-resident tuition. *Financial support:* Fellowships, research assistantships, teaching assistantships, career-related internships or fieldwork, institutionally sponsored loans, scholarships/grants, traineeships, health care benefits, and unspecified assistantships available. Support available to part-time students. Financial award application deadline: 5/5; financial award applicants required to submit FAFSA. *Faculty research:* Chronic and infectious disease epidemiology; health promotion and health education; applied and theoretical biostatistics; healthcare management, policy and economics; environmental and occupational health. *Total annual research expenditures:* $47.8 million. *Unit head:* Dr. Susan Emery, Senior Associate Dean of Academic and Research Affairs. *Application contact:* Elvis Parada, Manager of Admissions and Recruitment, 713-500-9028, Fax: 713-500-9068, E-mail: elvis.a.parada@uth.tmc.edu.
Website: https://sph.uth.edu

The University of Toledo, College of Graduate Studies, College of Medicine and Life Sciences, Department of Public Health and Preventative Medicine, Toledo, OH 43606-3390. Offers biostatistics and epidemiology (Certificate); contemporary gerontological practice (Certificate); environmental and occupational health and safety (MPH); epidemiology (Certificate); global public health (Certificate); health promotion and education (MPH); industrial hygiene (MSOH); medical and health science teaching and learning (Certificate); occupational health (Certificate); public health administration (MPH); public health and emergency response (Certificate); public health epidemiology (MPH); public health nutrition (MPH); MD/MPH. *Program availability:* Part-time, evening/weekend. *Degree requirements:* For master's, thesis or alternative. *Entrance requirements:* For master's, GRE, minimum undergraduate GPA of 3.0, three letters of recommendation, statement of purpose, transcripts from all prior institutions attended, resume; for Certificate, minimum undergraduate GPA of 3.0, three letters of recommendation, statement of purpose, transcripts from all prior institutions attended, resume. Additional exam requirements/recommendations for international students: Required—TOEFL (minimum score 550 paper-based; 80 iBT), IELTS (minimum score 6.5). Electronic applications accepted.

University of Toronto, School of Graduate Studies, Department of Public Health Sciences, Toronto, ON M5S 1A1, Canada. Offers biostatistics (M Sc, PhD); community health (M Sc); community nutrition (MPH), including nutrition and dietetics; epidemiology (MPH, PhD); family and community medicine (MPH); occupational and environmental health (MPH); social and behavioral health science (PhD); social and behavioral health sciences (MPH), including health promotion. *Accreditation:* CAHME (one or more programs are accredited). *Program availability:* Part-time. *Degree requirements:* For master's, thesis (for some programs), practicum; for doctorate, comprehensive exam, thesis/dissertation, oral thesis defense. *Entrance requirements:* For master's, 2 letters of reference, relevant professional/research experience, minimum B average in final year; for doctorate, 2 letters of reference, relevant professional/research experience, minimum B+ average. Additional exam requirements/recommendations for international students: Required—TOEFL (minimum score 580 paper-based; 93 iBT), TWE (minimum score 5). Electronic applications accepted. *Expenses:* Contact institution.

University of Vermont, The Robert Larner, MD College of Medicine and Graduate College, Graduate Programs in Medicine, Program in Public Health, Burlington, VT 05405. Offers epidemiology (Graduate Certificate); global and environmental health (Graduate Certificate); healthcare management and policy (Graduate Certificate); public health (MPH). *Program availability:* Online only, 100% online. *Students:* 96. 73 applicants, 88% accepted, 41 enrolled. In 2017, 6 master's, 6 other advanced degrees awarded. *Entrance requirements:* For master's and Graduate Certificate, resume/curriculum vitae. Additional exam requirements/recommendations for international students: Required—TOEFL (minimum iBT score of 90) or IELTS (6.5). *Application deadline:* For fall admission, 7/1 for domestic and international students; for spring admission, 11/15 for domestic and international students; for summer admission, 4/1 for domestic and international students. Application fee: $65. Electronic applications accepted. *Expenses:* $646 per credit in-state, $970 per credit out-of-state. *Unit head:* Dr. Jan Carney, Coordinator, 802-656-2085, E-mail: public.health@uvm.edu.
Website: https://learn.uvm.edu/program/master-of-public-health/

University of Washington, Graduate School, School of Public Health, Department of Epidemiology, Seattle, WA 98195. Offers clinical research methods (MS); epidemiology (PhD); general epidemiology (MPH, MS); global health (MPH); maternal and child health (MPH); MPH/MPA. *Accreditation:* CEPH (one or more programs are accredited). *Faculty:* 51 full-time (30 women), 40 part-time/adjunct (20 women). *Students:* 145 full-time (104 women), 30 part-time (23 women); includes 54 minority (6 Black or African American, non-Hispanic/Latino; 2 American Indian or Alaska Native, non-Hispanic/Latino; 32 Asian, non-Hispanic/Latino; 13 Hispanic/Latino; 1 Native Hawaiian or other Pacific Islander, non-Hispanic/Latino), 17 international. Average age 31. 395 applicants, 43% accepted, 58 enrolled. In 2017, 40 master's, 9 doctorates awarded. *Entrance requirements:* For master's, GRE (except for those MD/DO from U.S. institutions); for doctorate, GRE. Additional exam requirements/recommendations for international students: Required—TOEFL. Electronic applications accepted. *Financial support:* Fellowships, research assistantships, teaching assistantships, career-related internships or fieldwork, scholarships/grants, traineeships, health care benefits, and tuition waivers (full and partial) available. Support available to part-time students. Financial award applicants required to submit FAFSA. *Faculty research:* Chronic disease, health disparities and social determinants of health, aging and neuroepidemiology, maternal and child health, molecular and genetic epidemiology. *Unit head:* E-mail: epiadmin@uw.edu. *Application contact:* John Paulson, Assistant Director of Student Academic Services, 206-685-1762, E-mail: epi@uw.edu.
Website: https://epi.washington.edu/

The University of Western Ontario, Faculty of Graduate Studies, Biosciences Division, Department of Epidemiology and Biostatistics, London, ON N6A 5B8, Canada. Offers M Sc, PhD. *Program availability:* Part-time. *Degree requirements:* For master's, thesis; for doctorate, comprehensive exam, thesis proposal defense. *Entrance requirements:* For master's, BA or B Sc honors degree, minimum B+ average in last 10 courses; for doctorate, M Sc or equivalent, minimum B+ average in last 10 courses. *Faculty research:* Chronic disease epidemiology, clinical epidemiology.

University of Wisconsin–Madison, School of Medicine and Public Health, Population Health and Epidemiology Program, Madison, WI 53726. Offers epidemiology (MS, PhD); population health (MS, PhD), including epidemiology. *Program availability:* Part-time. *Faculty:* 21 full-time (10 women). *Students:* 36 full-time (31 women), 11 part-time (7 women); includes 8 minority (2 Black or African American, non-Hispanic/Latino; 3 Asian, non-Hispanic/Latino; 2 Hispanic/Latino; 1 Two or more races, non-Hispanic/Latino), 6 international. Average age 29. 45 applicants, 44% accepted, 10 enrolled. In 2017, 9 master's, 5 doctorates awarded. Terminal master's awarded for partial completion of doctoral program. *Degree requirements:* For master's, thesis, thesis defense; for doctorate, comprehensive exam, thesis/dissertation, qualifying exam, preliminary exam, dissertation defense. *Entrance requirements:* For master's and doctorate, GRE taken within the last 5 years (MCAT or LSAT acceptable for those with doctoral degrees), minimum GPA of 3.0, quantitative preparation (calculus, statistics, or other) with minimum B average. Additional exam requirements/recommendations for international students: Required—TOEFL (minimum score 580 paper-based; 92 iBT). *Application deadline:* For fall admission, 1/15 for domestic and international students. Application fee: $75. Electronic applications accepted. *Expenses:* $5,993 full-time resident per semster; $12,657 full-time nonresident per semester. *Financial support:* In 2017–18, 31 students received support, including 5 research assistantships with full tuition reimbursements available (averaging $25,000 per year), 2 teaching assistantships with full tuition reimbursements available (averaging $18,000 per year); fellowships, scholarships/grants, traineeships, health care benefits, and unspecified assistantships also available. Support available to part-time students. Financial award application deadline: 4/15; financial award applicants required to submit FAFSA. *Faculty research:* Epidemiology (cancer, environmental, aging, infectious and genetic disease), determinants of population health, health services research, social and behavioral health sciences, biostatistics. *Total annual research expenditures:* $16.6 million. *Unit head:* Mari Palta, Graduate Program Chair, 608-263-4029, Fax: 608-263-2820, E-mail: mpalta@wisc.edu. *Application contact:* Quinn H. Fullenkamp, Graduate Program Coordinator, 608-265-8108, Fax: 608-263-2820, E-mail: pophealth@mailplus.wisc.edu.
Website: https://pophealth.wisc.edu/grad

University of Wisconsin–Milwaukee, Graduate School, Joseph J. Zilber School of Public Health, Program in Public Health, Milwaukee, WI 53201-0413. Offers biostatistics (MPH); community and behavioral health promotion (MPH); environmental health sciences (MPH); epidemiology (MPH, PhD); public and population health (Graduate Certificate); public health policy and administration (MPH); public health: biostatistics (PhD); public health: community and behavioral health promotion (PhD). *Students:* 62 full-time (53 women), 23 part-time (17 women); includes 24 minority (5 Black or African American, non-Hispanic/Latino; 11 Asian, non-Hispanic/Latino; 8 Two or more races, non-Hispanic/Latino), 10 international. Average age 31. 65 applicants, 74% accepted, 34 enrolled. In 2017, 28 master's, 1 doctorate awarded. Electronic applications accepted. *Application contact:* Darcie K. G. Warren, Graduate Program Manager, 414-229-5633, E-mail: darcie@uwm.edu.

Walden University, Graduate Programs, School of Health Sciences, Minneapolis, MN 55401. Offers clinical research administration (MS, Graduate Certificate); health education and promotion (MS, PhD), including behavioral health (PhD), disease surveillance (PhD), emergency preparedness (MS), general (MHA, MS), global health (PhD), health policy (PhD), health policy and advocacy (MS), population health (PhD); health informatics (MS); health services (PhD), including community health, healthcare administration, leadership, public health policy, self-designed; healthcare administration (MHA, DHA), including general (MHA, MS); leadership and organizational development (MHA); public health (MPH, Dr PH, PhD, Graduate Certificate), including community health education (PhD), epidemiology (PhD); systems policy (MHA). *Program availability:* Part-time, evening/weekend, online only, 100% online. *Degree requirements:* For doctorate, thesis/dissertation, residency. *Entrance requirements:* For master's, bachelor's degree or higher; minimum GPA of 2.5; official transcripts; goal statement (for some programs); access to computer and Internet; for doctorate, master's degree or higher; three years of related professional or academic experience (preferred); minimum GPA of 3.0; goal statement and current resume (for select programs); official transcripts; access to computer and Internet; for Graduate Certificate, relevant work experience; access to computer and Internet. Additional exam requirements/recommendations for international students: Required—TOEFL (minimum score 550 paper-based, 79 iBT), IELTS (minimum score 6.5), Michigan English Language Assessment Battery (minimum score 82), or PTE (minimum score 53). Electronic applications accepted.

Washington University in St. Louis, Brown School, St. Louis, MO 63110. Offers American Indian/Alaska native (MSW); children, youth and families (MSW); epidemiology/biostatistics (MPH); generalist (MPH); global health (MPH); health (MSW); health policy analysis (MPH); individualized (MSW), including health; mental health (MSW); older adults and aging societies (MSW); public health sciences (PhD); social and economic development (MSW), including domestic, international; social work (PhD); urban design (MPH); violence and injury prevention (MSW); JD/MSW; M Arch/MSW; MPH/MBA; MSW/M Div; MSW/M Ed; MSW/MAPS; MSW/MBA; MSW/MPH; MUD/MSW. MSW/M Div and MSW/MAPS offered in partnership with Eden Theological Seminary. *Accreditation:* CSWE (one or more programs are accredited). *Faculty:* 54 full-time (31 women), 87 part-time/adjunct (61 women). *Students:* 294 full-time (254 women); includes 114 minority (56 Black or African American, non-Hispanic/Latino; 8 American Indian or Alaska Native, non-Hispanic/Latino; 17 Asian, non-Hispanic/Latino; 10 Hispanic/Latino; 1 Native Hawaiian or other Pacific Islander, non-Hispanic/Latino; 22 Two or more races, non-Hispanic/Latino). Average age 26. *Degree requirements:* For master's, 60 credit hours (for MSW); 52 credit hours (for MPH); practicum; for doctorate, comprehensive exam, thesis/dissertation. *Entrance requirements:* For master's, GRE (preferred), GMAT, LSAT, MCAT, PCAT, or United States Medical Licensing Exam (for MPH); for doctorate, GRE. Additional exam requirements/recommendations for international students: Required—TOEFL (minimum score 100 iBT), IELTS (minimum score 7). *Application deadline:* For fall admission, 12/15 priority date for domestic and international students; for winter admission, 3/1 priority date for domestic and international students. Applications are processed on a rolling basis. Electronic applications accepted. *Expenses:* Contact institution. *Financial support:* In 2017–18, 30 fellowships, 60 research assistantships were awarded; career-related internships or fieldwork, Federal Work-Study, scholarships/grants, and unspecified assistantships also available. Support available to part-time students. Financial award applicants required to submit FAFSA. *Faculty research:* Mental health, social policy, health policy, epidemiology, social and economic development. *Total annual research expenditures:* $14.5 million. *Unit head:* Jamie L. Adkisson-Hennessey, Director of Admissions and Recruitment, 314-935-3524, Fax: 314-935-4859, E-mail: jadkisson@wustl.edu. *Application contact:* Office of Admissions and Recruitment, 314-935-6676, Fax: 314-935-4859, E-mail: brownadmissions@wustl.edu.
Website: http://brownschool.wustl.edu

Weill Cornell Medicine, Weill Cornell Graduate School of Medical Sciences, Program in Clinical Epidemiology and Health Services Research, New York, NY 10021. Offers MS. *Degree requirements:* For master's, thesis. *Entrance requirements:* For master's, 3 years of work experience, MD or RN certificate. *Faculty research:* Research methodology, biostatistical techniques, data management, decision analysis, health economics.

West Virginia University, School of Public Health, Morgantown, WV 26506-9190. Offers biostatistics (MPH, MS, PhD); epidemiology (MPH, PhD); health policy (MPH); occupational and environmental health sciences (MPH, PhD); public health (MPH); school health education (MS); social and behavioral science (MPH, PhD). *Accreditation:* CEPH. *Program availability:* Part-time, online learning. *Students:* 69 full-time (48 women), 27 part-time (15 women); includes 14 minority (5 Black or African American, non-Hispanic/Latino; 4 Asian, non-Hispanic/Latino; 1 Hispanic/Latino; 4 Two or more races, non-Hispanic/Latino), 11 international. *Degree requirements:* For master's, practicum, project. *Entrance requirements:* For master's, GRE General Test, MCAT, medical degree, medical internship. Additional exam requirements/recommendations for international students: Required—TOEFL (minimum score 550 paper-based; 80 iBT). *Application deadline:* For fall admission, 4/15 priority date for domestic students; for spring admission, 12/1 for domestic students. Applications are processed on a rolling basis. Application fee: $60. *Expenses:* Contact institution. *Financial support:* Research assistantships, teaching assistantships, scholarships/grants, and health care benefits available. Financial award application deadline: 2/1; financial award applicants required to submit FAFSA. *Faculty research:* Occupational health, environmental health, clinical epidemiology, health care management, prevention. *Unit head:* Leah Adkins, Senior Program Coordinator, 304-293-1097, E-mail: leadkins@hsc.wvu.edu.
Website: http://publichealth.hsc.wvu.edu/

Yale University, Yale School of Medicine, Yale School of Public Health, New Haven, CT 06520. Offers applied biostatistics and epidemiology (APMPH); biostatistics (MPH, MS, PhD), including global health (MPH); chronic disease epidemiology (MPH, PhD), including global health (MPH); environmental health sciences (MPH, PhD), including global health (MPH); epidemiology of microbial diseases (MPH, PhD), including global health (MPH); global health (APMPH); health management (MPH), including global health; health policy (MPH), including global health; health policy and administration (APMPH, PhD); occupational and environmental medicine (APMPH); preventive medicine (APMPH); social and behavioral sciences (APMPH, MPH), including global health (MPH); JD/MPH; M Div/MPH; MBA/MPH; MD/MPH; MEM/MPH; MFS/MPH; MM Sc/MPH; MPH/MA; MSN/MPH. MS and PhD offered through the Graduate School. *Accreditation:* CEPH. *Program availability:* Part-time. Terminal master's awarded for partial completion of doctoral program. *Degree requirements:* For master's, thesis, summer internship; for doctorate, comprehensive exam, thesis/dissertation, residency. *Entrance requirements:* For master's, GMAT, GRE, or MCAT, two years of undergraduate coursework in math and science; for doctorate, GRE General Test. Additional exam requirements/recommendations for international students: Required—TOEFL (minimum score 100 iBT). Electronic applications accepted. *Expenses:* Contact institution. *Faculty research:* Genetic and emerging infections epidemiology, virology, cost/quality, vector biology, quantitative methods, aging, asthma, cancer.

Health Promotion

American College of Healthcare Sciences, Graduate Programs, Portland, OR 97239-3719. Offers anatomy and physiology (Graduate Certificate); aromatherapy (MS, Graduate Certificate); botanical safety (Graduate Certificate); complementary alternative medicine (MS, Graduate Certificate); health and wellness (MS); herbal medicine (MS, Graduate Certificate); holistic nutrition (MS, Graduate Certificate); wellness coaching (Graduate Certificate). *Program availability:* Part-time, evening/weekend, online learning. *Degree requirements:* For master's, capstone project. *Entrance requirements:* For master's, interview, letters of recommendation, essay.

American University, College of Arts and Sciences, Department of Health Studies, Program in Health Promotion Management, Washington, DC 22016-8030. Offers MS. *Students:* 6 full-time (all women), 9 part-time (6 women); includes 5 minority (3 Black or African American, non-Hispanic/Latino; 1 Asian, non-Hispanic/Latino; 1 Two or more races, non-Hispanic/Latino), 1 international. Average age 27. 12 applicants, 83% accepted, 6 enrolled. In 2017, 27 master's awarded. *Degree requirements:* For master's, comprehensive exam, thesis or alternative. *Entrance requirements:* For master's, GRE, interview (recommended), statement of purpose, transcripts, 2 letters of recommendation, resume. Additional exam requirements/recommendations for international students: Required—TOEFL (minimum score 600 paper-based; 100 iBT). *Application deadline:* For fall admission, 2/1 priority date for domestic students; for spring admission, 11/1 for domestic students. Application fee: $55. *Expenses: Tuition:* Full-time $29,556. *Required fees:* $690. Tuition and fees vary according to course load and program. *Financial support:* Unspecified assistantships available. Financial award applicants required to submit FAFSA. *Unit head:* Dr. Anastasia Snelling, Chair, Department of Health Studies, 202-885-6278, Fax: 202-885-1187, E-mail: stacey@american.edu. *Application contact:* Laurel Semple, Assistant Director, Graduate Enrollment Management, E-mail: semple@american.edu.
Website: http://www.american.edu/cas/seth/health/index.cfm

American University of Beirut, Graduate Programs, Faculty of Health Sciences, 1107 2020, Lebanon. Offers environmental sciences (MS), including environmental health; epidemiology (MS, PhD); epidemiology and biostatistics (MPH); health care leadership (EMHCL); health management and policy (MPH), including health service administration; health promotion and community health (MPH); health research (MS); public health nutrition (MS). *Program availability:* Part-time. *Faculty:* 33 full-time (22 women), 5 part-time/adjunct (2 women). *Students:* 75 full-time (60 women), 78 part-time (67 women). Average age 27. 274 applicants, 56% accepted, 47 enrolled. In 2017, 63 master's awarded. *Degree requirements:* For master's, one foreign language, comprehensive exam (for some programs), thesis (for MS); for doctorate, one foreign language, comprehensive exam, thesis/dissertation. *Entrance requirements:* For master's, 2 letters of recommendations, personal statement, transcript; for doctorate, GRE, 3 letters of recommendations, personal statement, interview. Additional exam requirements/recommendations for international students: Required—TOEFL (minimum score 583 paper-based; 97 iBT), IELTS (minimum score 7). *Application deadline:* For fall admission, 4/4 for domestic and international students; for spring admission, 11/3 for domestic and international students. Application fee: $50. Electronic applications accepted. *Expenses:* Contact institution. *Financial support:* In 2017–18, 75 students received support. Scholarships/grants, health care benefits, and unspecified assistantships available. Financial award application deadline: 4/4. *Faculty research:* Reproductive and sexual health; occupational and environmental health; conflict and health; mental health; quality in health care delivery, tobacco control. *Total annual research expenditures:* $2 million. *Unit head:* Prof. Iman Adel Nuwayhid, Dean/Professor, 961-1-759683 Ext. 4600, Fax: 961-1-744470, E-mail: nuwayhid@aub.edu.lb. *Application contact:* Mitra Tauk, Administrative Coordinator, 961-1-350000 Ext. 4687, E-mail: mt12@aub.edu.lb.
Website: http://www.aub.edu.lb/fhs/fhs_home/Pages/index.aspx

Arizona State University at the Tempe campus, College of Health Solutions, School of Nutrition and Health Promotion, Tempe, AZ 85287. Offers clinical exercise physiology (MS); exercise and wellness (MS); nutrition (MS), including dietetics, human nutrition; obesity prevention and management (MS); physical activity, nutrition and wellness (PhD).

Ball State University, Graduate School, College of Health, School of Kinesiology, Interdepartmental Program in Wellness Management, Muncie, IN 47306. Offers MA, MS. *Students:* 3 part-time (1 woman), 1 international. Average age 30. In 2017, 7 master's awarded. *Entrance requirements:* For master's, GRE General Test, interview. Application fee: $60 ($35 for international students). *Financial support:* Research assistantships with partial tuition reimbursements, teaching assistantships with partial tuition reimbursements, and unspecified assistantships available. Financial award application deadline: 3/1. *Unit head:* Dr. Tom Weidner, Chairperson, 765-285-5039, E-mail: tweidner@bsu.edu.
Website: http://www.bsu.edu/wellness/

Benedictine University, Graduate Programs, Program in Nutrition and Wellness, Lisle, IL 60532. Offers MS. *Entrance requirements:* Additional exam requirements/recommendations for international students: Required—TOEFL (minimum score 550 paper-based). Electronic applications accepted. *Faculty research:* Community and corporate wellness risk assessment, health behavior change, self-efficacy, evaluation of health program impact and effectiveness.

Boise State University, College of Health Sciences, Department of Community and Environmental Health, Boise, ID 83725-0399. Offers community and environmental health (MHS); health science (MHS), including health policy, health promotion, health services leadership; health services leadership (Graduate Certificate). *Faculty:* 11. *Students:* 20 full-time (18 women), 38 part-time (33 women); includes 7 minority (1 Asian, non-Hispanic/Latino; 5 Hispanic/Latino; 1 Two or more races, non-Hispanic/Latino). Average age 36. 38 applicants, 50% accepted, 11 enrolled. In 2017, 21 master's, 13 Graduate Certificates awarded. *Entrance requirements:* For master's, writing assessment, minimum GPA of 3.0. Additional exam requirements/recommendations for international students: Required—TOEFL (minimum score 550 paper-based; 80 iBT), IELTS (minimum score 6). *Application deadline:* For fall admission, 3/15 for domestic and international students; for spring admission, 10/15 for domestic and international students. Application fee: $65 ($95 for international students). Electronic applications accepted. *Expenses:* Tuition, state resident: full-time $6471; part-time $390 per credit. Tuition, nonresident: full-time $21,787; part-time $685 per credit. *Required fees:* $2283; $100 per term. Part-time tuition and fees vary according to course load and program. *Financial support:* Research assistantships, scholarships/grants, and unspecified assistantships available. Financial award application deadline: 3/15; financial award applicants required to submit FAFSA. *Unit head:* Dr. Lillian Smith, Department Head, 208-426-3795, E-mail: lilliansmith@boisestate.edu. *Application contact:* Dr. Sarah Toevs, Director, Master of Health Science Program, 208-426-2452, E-mail: stoevs@boisestate.edu.
Website: http://hs.boisestate.edu/ceh/

Health Promotion

Bridgewater State University, College of Graduate Studies, College of Education and Allied Studies, Department of Movement Arts, Health Promotion, and Leisure Studies, Program in Health Promotion, Bridgewater, MA 02325. Offers M Ed. *Program availability:* Part-time, evening/weekend. *Entrance requirements:* For master's, GRE General Test.

Brigham Young University, Graduate Studies, College of Life Sciences, Department of Exercise Sciences, Provo, UT 84602. Offers athletic training (MS); exercise physiology (MS, PhD); exercise sciences (MS); health promotion (MS, PhD); physical medicine and rehabilitation (PhD). *Faculty:* 21 full-time (2 women). *Students:* 12 full-time (4 women), 18 part-time (11 women); includes 4 minority (3 Asian, non-Hispanic/Latino; 1 Hispanic/Latino). Average age 32. 21 applicants, 48% accepted, 6 enrolled. In 2017, 7 master's awarded. *Degree requirements:* For master's, thesis, oral defense; for doctorate, comprehensive exam, thesis/dissertation, oral defense, oral and written exams. *Entrance requirements:* For master's, GRE General Test (minimum score of 300, 4.0 on analytic writing portion), minimum GPA of 3.2 in last 60 hours of course work; for doctorate, GRE General Test (minimum score of 300, 4.0 on analytic writing portion), minimum GPA of 3.5 in last 60 hours of course work. Additional exam requirements/recommendations for international students: Required—TOEFL (minimum score 580 paper-based; 85 iBT), IELTS (minimum score 7). *Application deadline:* For fall admission, 2/1 for domestic and international students. Application fee: $50. Electronic applications accepted. *Expenses:* $5,160 per year. *Financial support:* In 2017–18, 40 students received support, including 19 research assistantships (averaging $69,400 per year), 21 teaching assistantships (averaging $38,500 per year); career-related internships or fieldwork, scholarships/grants, unspecified assistantships, and 8 PhD full-tuition scholarships also available. Financial award application deadline: 4/15. *Faculty research:* Injury prevention and rehabilitation, human skeletal muscle adaptation, cardiovascular health and fitness, lifestyle modification and health promotion. *Total annual research expenditures:* $107,348. *Unit head:* Dr. Allen Parcell, Chair, 801-422-4450, Fax: 801-422-0555, E-mail: allenparcell@gmail.com. *Application contact:* Dr. J. Ty Hopkins, Graduate Coordinator, 801-422-1573, Fax: 801-422-0555, E-mail: tyhopkins@byu.edu.
Website: http://exsc.byu.edu/

California Baptist University, Program in Public Health, Riverside, CA 92504-3206. Offers health education and promotion (MPH); health policy and administration (MPH). *Program availability:* Part-time, evening/weekend. *Faculty:* 9 full-time (5 women), 4 part-time/adjunct (2 women). *Students:* 56 full-time (47 women), 37 part-time (30 women); includes 72 minority (18 Black or African American, non-Hispanic/Latino; 8 Asian, non-Hispanic/Latino; 38 Hispanic/Latino; 8 Two or more races, non-Hispanic/Latino), 4 international. Average age 28. 83 applicants, 64% accepted, 39 enrolled. In 2017, 4 master's awarded. *Degree requirements:* For master's, capstone project; practicum. *Entrance requirements:* For master's, minimum undergraduate GPA of 2.75, two recommendations, 500-word essay, resume. Additional exam requirements/recommendations for international students: Required—TOEFL (minimum score 80 iBT). *Application deadline:* For fall admission, 8/1 priority date for domestic students, 7/1 for international students; for spring admission, 12/1 priority date for domestic students, 11/1 for international students. Applications are processed on a rolling basis. Application fee: $45. Electronic applications accepted. *Expenses:* Contact institution. *Financial support:* In 2017–18, 22 students received support. Federal Work-Study and scholarships/grants available. Financial award applicants required to submit CSS PROFILE or FAFSA. *Faculty research:* Epidemiology, statistical education, exercise and immunity, obesity and chronic disease. *Unit head:* Dr. David Pearson, Dean, College of Health Science, 951-343-4298, E-mail: dpearson@calbaptist.edu. *Application contact:* Tamakia King, Graduate Admissions Counselor, 951-552-8138, E-mail: tking@calbaptist.edu.
Website: http://www.calbaptist.edu/explore-cbu/schools-colleges/college-allied-health/health-sciences/master-public-health/

California State University, Fresno, Division of Research and Graduate Studies, College of Health and Human Services, Department of Public Health, Fresno, CA 93740-8027. Offers health policy and management (MPH); health promotion (MPH). *Accreditation:* CEPH. *Program availability:* Part-time, evening/weekend. *Degree requirements:* For master's, thesis or alternative. *Entrance requirements:* For master's, GRE General Test, minimum GPA of 2.5. Additional exam requirements/recommendations for international students: Required—TOEFL. Electronic applications accepted. *Faculty research:* Foster parent training, geriatrics, tobacco control.

California State University, Fullerton, Graduate Studies, College of Health and Human Development, Department of Public Health, Fullerton, CA 92831-3599. Offers environmental and occupational health and safety (MPH); gerontological health (MPH); health promotion and disease (MPH). *Accreditation:* CEPH. *Program availability:* Part-time. *Students:* 37 full-time (31 women), 29 part-time (21 women); includes 41 minority (2 Black or African American, non-Hispanic/Latino; 14 Asian, non-Hispanic/Latino; 23 Hispanic/Latino; 1 Native Hawaiian or other Pacific Islander, non-Hispanic/Latino; 1 Two or more races, non-Hispanic/Latino), 2 international. Average age 30. 105 applicants, 47% accepted, 21 enrolled. In 2017, 26 master's awarded. *Entrance requirements:* For master's, minimum GPA of 3.0 in last 60 units attempted. Application fee: $55. *Financial support:* Career-related internships or fieldwork, Federal Work-Study, institutionally sponsored loans, and scholarships/grants available. Support available to part-time students. Financial award application deadline: 3/1; financial award applicants required to submit FAFSA. *Unit head:* Head, 657-278-2620. *Application contact:* Admissions/Applications, 657-278-2371.
Website: http://hhd.fullerton.edu/hesc/

Claremont Graduate University, Graduate Programs, School of Community and Global Health, Claremont, CA 91773. Offers health promotion science (PhD); public health (MPH). *Accreditation:* CEPH. *Entrance requirements:* For master's and doctorate, GRE. Additional exam requirements/recommendations for international students: Required—TOEFL (minimum score 75 iBT). Electronic applications accepted.

Cleveland University–Kansas City, Program in Health Education and Promotion, Overland Park, KS 66210. Offers MS. *Program availability:* Part-time. *Entrance requirements:* For master's, professional statement. Additional exam requirements/recommendations for international students: Required—TOEFL (minimum score 550 paper-based; 79 iBT). *Application deadline:* For fall admission, 7/1 for domestic and international students; for winter admission, 10/1 for domestic and international students. Applications are processed on a rolling basis. Electronic applications accepted. *Expenses:* Contact institution. *Financial support:* Applicants required to submit FAFSA. *Application contact:* Melissa Denton, Director of Admissions, 913-234-0744, Fax: 913-234-0906, E-mail: kc.admissions@cleveland.edu.
Website: https://www.cleveland.edu/academics/college-of-health-sciences/ms-in-health-promotion

Concord University, Graduate Studies, Athens, WV 24712-1000. Offers educational leadership and supervision (M Ed); health promotion (MA); reading specialist (M Ed); social work (MSW); special education (M Ed); teaching (MAT). *Program availability:* Part-time, evening/weekend, 100% online. *Faculty:* 16 full-time (10 women), 7 part-time/adjunct (4 women). *Students:* 146 full-time (117 women), 195 part-time (161 women); includes 26 minority (15 Black or African American, non-Hispanic/Latino; 1 American Indian or Alaska Native, non-Hispanic/Latino; 4 Asian, non-Hispanic/Latino; 1 Hispanic/Latino; 5 Two or more races, non-Hispanic/Latino). Average age 34. 591 applicants, 99% accepted, 144 enrolled. In 2017, 114 master's awarded. *Degree requirements:* For master's, thesis (for some programs). *Entrance requirements:* For master's, GRE or MAT, baccalaureate degree with minimum GPA of 2.5 from regionally-accredited institution; teaching license; 2 letters of recommendation; completed disposition assessment form. *Application deadline:* Applications are processed on a rolling basis. Application fee: $30. Electronic applications accepted. *Expenses:* Tuition, state resident: full-time $8132; part-time $453 per semester hour. Tuition, nonresident: full-time $14,180; part-time $788 per semester hour. *Financial support:* Tuition waivers and unspecified assistantships available. Financial award applicants required to submit FAFSA. *Unit head:* Dr. Cheryl Barnes, Director, 304-384-6306, E-mail: cbarnes@concord.edu. *Application contact:* Debra Moore, Special Events Assistant, 304-384-5113, E-mail: dlm@concord.edu.
Website: http://www.concord.edu/graduate

Creighton University, Graduate School, Department of Interdisciplinary Studies, MS Program in Health and Wellness Coaching, Omaha, NE 68178-0001. Offers MS. *Program availability:* Part-time, online only, 100% online. *Faculty:* 2 full-time (1 woman). *Students:* 8 full-time (6 women), 50 part-time (39 women); includes 5 minority (3 Black or African American, non-Hispanic/Latino; 1 American Indian or Alaska Native, non-Hispanic/Latino; 1 Asian, non-Hispanic/Latino), 1 international. Average age 35. 38 applicants, 89% accepted, 17 enrolled. In 2017, 4 master's awarded. *Entrance requirements:* Additional exam requirements/recommendations for international students: Required—TOEFL (minimum score 90 iBT). *Application deadline:* Applications are processed on a rolling basis. Application fee: $50. Electronic applications accepted. *Expenses:* Contact institution. *Financial support:* Scholarships/grants available. *Unit head:* Dr. Tom Lenz, Professor, 402-280-3144, E-mail: thomaslenz@creighton.edu. *Application contact:* Lindsay Johnson, Director of Graduate and Adult Recruitment, 402-280-2703, Fax: 402-280-2423, E-mail: gradschool@creighton.edu.
Website: http://gradschool.creighton.edu/program/Health-and-Wellness-Coaching-MS

East Carolina University, Graduate School, College of Health and Human Performance, Department of Health Education and Promotion, Greenville, NC 27858-4353. Offers environmental health (MS); health education (MA Ed); health education and promotion (MA). *Accreditation:* CEPH; NCATE. *Students:* 18 full-time (15 women), 54 part-time (42 women); includes 18 minority (11 Black or African American, non-Hispanic/Latino; 2 Asian, non-Hispanic/Latino; 4 Hispanic/Latino; 1 Two or more races, non-Hispanic/Latino). Average age 31. 25 applicants, 80% accepted, 18 enrolled. In 2017, 31 master's awarded. *Degree requirements:* For master's, comprehensive exam, thesis optional. *Entrance requirements:* For master's, GRE General Test or MAT. Additional exam requirements/recommendations for international students: Recommended—TOEFL (minimum score 78 iBT), IELTS (minimum score 6.5). *Application deadline:* For fall admission, 6/1 priority date for domestic students. Applications are processed on a rolling basis. Application fee: $75. *Expenses:* Tuition, state resident: full-time $4749; part-time $297 per credit hour. Tuition, nonresident: full-time $17,898; part-time $1119 per credit hour. *Required fees:* $2691; $224 per credit hour. Part-time tuition and fees vary according to course load and program. *Financial support:* Fellowships, research assistantships, teaching assistantships, and career-related internships or fieldwork available. Support available to part-time students. Financial award application deadline: 6/1. *Faculty research:* Community health education, worksite health promotion, school health education, environmental health. *Unit head:* Dr. J. Don Chaney, Chair, 252-737-4942, E-mail: chaneyj@ecu.edu.
Website: https://hhp.ecu.edu/hep/

Eastern Kentucky University, The Graduate School, College of Health Sciences, Department of Exercise and Sport Science, Richmond, KY 40475-3102. Offers exercise and sport science (MS); exercise and wellness (MS); sports administration (MS). *Program availability:* Part-time. *Entrance requirements:* For master's, GRE General Test (minimum score 700 verbal and quantitative), minimum GPA of 2.5 (for most), minimum GPA of 3.0 (analytical writing). *Faculty research:* Nutrition and exercise.

Eastern Michigan University, Graduate School, College of Health and Human Services, School of Health Promotion and Human Performance, Ypsilanti, MI 48197. Offers MS, Graduate Certificate. *Program availability:* Part-time, evening/weekend, online learning. *Faculty:* 34 full-time (16 women). *Students:* 128 full-time (85 women), 44 part-time (23 women); includes 19 minority (5 Black or African American, non-Hispanic/Latino; 4 Asian, non-Hispanic/Latino; 5 Hispanic/Latino; 5 Two or more races, non-Hispanic/Latino), 3 international. Average age 27. 214 applicants, 42% accepted, 45 enrolled. In 2017, 92 master's awarded. *Entrance requirements:* For master's, MAT (for orthotics and prosthetics). Additional exam requirements/recommendations for international students: Required—TOEFL. *Application deadline:* For fall admission, 8/1 for domestic students, 5/1 for international students; for winter admission, 12/1 for domestic students, 10/1 for international students; for spring admission, 4/15 for domestic students, 3/1 for international students. Applications are processed on a rolling basis. Application fee: $45. *Financial support:* Fellowships, research assistantships with full tuition reimbursements, teaching assistantships with full tuition reimbursements, career-related internships or fieldwork, Federal Work-Study, institutionally sponsored loans, scholarships/grants, tuition waivers (partial), and unspecified assistantships available. Support available to part-time students. Financial award applicants required to submit FAFSA. *Unit head:* Dr. Christopher Herman, Director, 734-487-2185, Fax: 734-487-2024, E-mail: cherman2@emich.edu. *Application contact:* Linda Jermone, Academic Advisor, 734-487-0092, Fax: 734-487-2024, E-mail: ljerme@emich.edu.

Emory University, Rollins School of Public Health, Online Program in Public Health, Atlanta, GA 30322-1100. Offers applied epidemiology (MPH); applied public health informatics (MPH); prevention science (MPH). *Program availability:* Part-time, evening/weekend, online learning. *Degree requirements:* For master's, thesis, practicum. *Entrance requirements:* For master's, GRE. Additional exam requirements/recommendations for international students: Required—TOEFL (minimum score 550 paper-based; 80 iBT). Electronic applications accepted.

Fairmont State University, Programs in Education, Fairmont, WV 26554. Offers digital media, new literacies and learning (M Ed); education (MAT); exercise science, fitness and wellness (M Ed); professional studies (M Ed); reading (M Ed); special education (M Ed). *Accreditation:* NCATE. *Program availability:* Part-time, evening/weekend, 100% online. *Entrance requirements:* For master's, GRE. Additional exam requirements/recommendations for international students: Required—TOEFL (minimum score 80 iBT), IELTS (minimum score 6.5). Electronic applications accepted.

Florida Atlantic University, College of Education, Department of Exercise Science and Health Promotion, Boca Raton, FL 33431-0991. Offers MS. *Program availability:* Part-time, evening/weekend. *Faculty:* 6 full-time (2 women). *Students:* 40 full-time (16 women), 10 part-time (6 women); includes 13 minority (5 Black or African American, non-Hispanic/Latino; 7 Hispanic/Latino; 1 Two or more races, non-Hispanic/Latino), 2 international. Average age 26. 73 applicants, 52% accepted, 20 enrolled. In 2017, 29 master's awarded. *Degree requirements:* For master's, comprehensive exam, thesis optional. *Entrance requirements:* For master's, GRE General Test, minimum GPA of 3.0 during last 60 hours of course work. Additional exam requirements/recommendations for international students: Required—TOEFL (minimum score 500 paper-based; 61 iBT),

IELTS (minimum score 6). *Application deadline:* For fall admission, 7/1 priority date for domestic students, 2/15 for international students; for spring admission, 11/1 priority date for domestic students, 7/15 for international students. Applications are processed on a rolling basis. Application fee: $30. *Expenses:* Tuition, state resident: full-time $7400; part-time $369.82 per credit. Tuition, nonresident: full-time $20,496; part-time $1042.81 per credit. *Financial support:* Research assistantships with partial tuition reimbursements, teaching assistantships with partial tuition reimbursements, and career-related internships or fieldwork available. *Faculty research:* Pulmonary limitations during exercise, metabolism regulation, determinants of performance, age-related change in functional mobility and geriatric exercise, behavioral change aimed at promoting active lifestyles. *Unit head:* Dr. Michael Whitehurst, 561-297-2938, E-mail: eshpinfo@fau.edu.
Website: http://www.coe.fau.edu/academicdepartments/eshp/

Florida International University, Robert Stempel College of Public Health and Social Work, Programs in Public Health, Miami, FL 33199. Offers biostatistics (MPH); environmental and occupational health (MPH, PhD); epidemiology (MPH, PhD); health policy and management (MPH); health promotion and disease prevention (MPH, PhD). PhD program has fall admissions only; MPH offered jointly with University of Miami. *Program availability:* Part-time, evening/weekend, online learning. *Faculty:* 34 full-time (18 women), 2 part-time/adjunct (both women). *Students:* 132 full-time (88 women), 63 part-time (49 women); includes 133 minority (50 Black or African American, non-Hispanic/Latino; 17 Asian, non-Hispanic/Latino; 60 Hispanic/Latino; 6 Two or more races, non-Hispanic/Latino), 30 international. Average age 29. 249 applicants, 54% accepted, 65 enrolled. In 2017, 37 master's, 14 doctorates awarded. *Degree requirements:* For master's, thesis optional; for doctorate, comprehensive exam, thesis/dissertation. *Entrance requirements:* For master's, minimum GPA of 3.0, letters of recommendation; for doctorate, GRE, resume, minimum GPA of 3.0, letters of recommendation, letter of intent. Additional exam requirements/recommendations for international students: Required—TOEFL (minimum score 550 paper-based; 80 iBT). *Application deadline:* For fall admission, 6/1 for domestic students, 4/1 for international students; for spring admission, 10/1 for domestic students, 9/1 for international students. Applications are processed on a rolling basis. Application fee: $30. Electronic applications accepted. *Expenses:* Contact institution. *Financial support:* Institutionally sponsored loans, scholarships/grants, and tuition waivers (full) available. Financial award application deadline: 3/1; financial award applicants required to submit FAFSA. *Faculty research:* Drugs/AIDS intervention among migrant workers, provision of services for active/recovering drug users with HIV. *Unit head:* Dr. Benjamin C. Amick, III, Chair, 305-348-7527, E-mail: benjamin.amickiii@fiu.edu. *Application contact:* Nanett Rojas, Assistant Director, Graduate Admissions, 305-348-7464, Fax: 305-348-7441, E-mail: gradadm@fiu.edu.

George Mason University, College of Education and Human Development, School of Recreation, Health and Tourism, Manassas, VA 20110. Offers athletic training (MS); exercise, fitness, and health promotion (MS), including advanced practitioner, wellness practitioner; international sport management (Certificate); recreation, health and tourism (Certificate); sport management (MS), including sport and recreation studies. *Program availability:* Part-time, evening/weekend. *Faculty:* 29 full-time (13 women), 87 part-time/adjunct (48 women). *Students:* 62 full-time (24 women), 23 part-time (11 women); includes 27 minority (20 Black or African American, non-Hispanic/Latino; 1 Asian, non-Hispanic/Latino; 3 Hispanic/Latino; 1 Native Hawaiian or other Pacific Islander, non-Hispanic/Latino; 2 Two or more races, non-Hispanic/Latino), 8 international. Average age 26. 74 applicants, 93% accepted, 46 enrolled. In 2017, 20 master's awarded. *Degree requirements:* For master's, thesis optional. *Entrance requirements:* For master's, 3 letters of recommendation; official transcripts; expanded goals statement; undergraduate course in statistics and minimum GPA of 3.0 in last 60 credit hours and overall (for MS in sport and recreation studies); baccalaureate degree related to kinesiology, exercise science or athletic training (for MS in exercise, fitness and health promotion). Additional exam requirements/recommendations for international students: Required—TOEFL (minimum score 575 paper-based; 88 iBT), IELTS (minimum score 6.5), PTE (minimum score 59). *Application deadline:* For fall admission, 4/2 priority date for domestic and international students; for spring admission, 11/1 for domestic and international students. Application fee: $75 ($80 for international students). Electronic applications accepted. *Expenses:* Tuition, state resident: full-time $11,228; part-time $459.50 per credit. Tuition, nonresident: full-time $30,932; part-time $1280.50 per credit. *Required fees:* $3252; $135.50 per credit. Part-time tuition and fees vary according to course load and program. *Financial support:* In 2017–18, 1 student received support, including 1 research assistantship with tuition reimbursement available; career-related internships or fieldwork, Federal Work-Study, scholarships/grants, unspecified assistantships, and health care benefits (for full-time research or teaching assistantship recipients) also available. Support available to part-time students. Financial award application deadline: 3/1; financial award applicants required to submit FAFSA. *Faculty research:* Sport for development and peace, sport analytics, leadership and coaching, diversity and inclusion in sport, sport communication. *Total annual research expenditures:* $826,386. *Unit head:* Martin Ford, Senior Associate Dean, 703-993-2004, E-mail: mford@gmu.edu. *Application contact:* Lindsey Olson, Office Assistant, 703-993-2098, Fax: 703-993-2025, E-mail: lolson7@gmu.edu.
Website: http://rht.gmu.edu/

Georgetown University, Graduate School of Arts and Sciences, Department of Microbiology and Immunology, Washington, DC 20057. Offers biohazardous threat agents and emerging infectious diseases (MS); biomedical science policy and advocacy (MS); general microbiology and immunology (MS); global infectious diseases (PhD); microbiology and immunology (PhD). *Program availability:* Part-time. *Degree requirements:* For master's, 30 credit hours of coursework; for doctorate, comprehensive exam, thesis/dissertation. *Entrance requirements:* For master's, GRE General Test, 3 letters of reference, bachelor's degree in related field; for doctorate, GRE General Test, 3 letters of reference, MS/BS in related field. Additional exam requirements/recommendations for international students: Required—TOEFL (minimum score 505 paper-based). Electronic applications accepted. *Faculty research:* Pathogenesis and basic biology of the fungus Candida albicans, molecular biology of viral immunopathological mechanisms in Multiple Sclerosis.

Georgia College & State University, Graduate School, College of Health Sciences, School of Health and Human Performance, Milledgeville, GA 31061. Offers health and human performance (MS), including health performance, health promotion; kinesiology/health education (MAT). *Accreditation:* NCATE (one or more programs are accredited). *Program availability:* Part-time, 100% online. *Faculty:* 19 full-time (9 women). *Students:* 35 full-time (20 women), 17 part-time (10 women); includes 9 minority (3 Black or African American, non-Hispanic/Latino; 5 Hispanic/Latino; 1 Two or more races, non-Hispanic/Latino), 2 international. Average age 27. 21 applicants, 100% accepted, 19 enrolled. In 2017, 21 master's awarded. *Degree requirements:* For master's, thesis (for some programs), completed in 6 years with minimum GPA of 3.0 (for MS); minimum GPA of 3.0 and electronic teaching portfolio (for MAT). *Entrance requirements:* For master's, GRE with minimum score of 297 or MAT with minimum score of 385 (for MS); GRE with minimum score of 297, MAT 385, SAT 1000, ACT 43, or GACE with 250 on each section (for MAT), resume, 3 professional references; minimum GPA of 2.75 in upper-level undergraduate courses and undergraduate statistics course (for MS); minimum GPA of 2.75 on upper-division major courses (for MAT). *Application deadline:* For fall admission, 7/15 priority date for domestic students, 4/1 for international students; for spring admission, 11/15 priority date for domestic students, 9/1 for international students; for summer admission, 4/15 priority date for domestic students. Applications are processed on a rolling basis. Application fee: $40. Electronic applications accepted. *Expenses:* Contact institution. *Financial support:* In 2017–18, 22 students received support. Unspecified assistantships available. Support available to part-time students. Financial award application deadline: 3/1; financial award applicants required to submit FAFSA. *Unit head:* Dr. Lisa Griffin, Director, School of Health and Human Performance, 478-445-4072, Fax: 478-445-4074, E-mail: lisa.griffin@gcsu.edu.
Website: http://www.gcsu.edu/health/shhp

Goddard College, Graduate Division, Master of Arts in Health Arts and Sciences Program, Plainfield, VT 05667-9432. Offers MA. *Degree requirements:* For master's, thesis. *Entrance requirements:* For master's, 3 letters of recommendation, interview. Electronic applications accepted.

Harvard University, Harvard T.H. Chan School of Public Health, Department of Social and Behavioral Sciences, Boston, MA 02115-6096. Offers population health sciences (PhD). *Program availability:* Part-time. *Faculty:* 30 full-time (17 women), 12 part-time/adjunct (4 women). *Students:* 28 full-time (20 women), 3 part-time (2 women); includes 11 minority (2 Black or African American, non-Hispanic/Latino; 4 Asian, non-Hispanic/Latino; 2 Hispanic/Latino; 3 Two or more races, non-Hispanic/Latino), 7 international. Average age 29. In 2017, 4 master's, 14 doctorates awarded. *Entrance requirements:* For master's, GRE, MCAT. Additional exam requirements/recommendations for international students: Recommended—TOEFL (minimum score 600 paper-based; 100 iBT), IELTS (minimum score 7). *Application deadline:* For fall admission, 12/1 for domestic and international students. Application fee: $120. Electronic applications accepted. *Financial support:* Fellowships, research assistantships, teaching assistantships, Federal Work-Study, scholarships/grants, traineeships, and unspecified assistantships available. Support available to part-time students. Financial award application deadline: 2/15; financial award applicants required to submit FAFSA. *Faculty research:* Social determinants of health, program design and planned social change, health and social policy, heath care and community-based interventions, health effects and prevention of gender-based violence. *Unit head:* Dr. Ichiro Kawachi, Chair, 617-432-1135, Fax: 617-432-3123, E-mail: ikawachi@hsph.harvard.edu. *Application contact:* Vincent W. James, Director of Admissions, 617-432-1031, Fax: 617-432-7080, E-mail: admissions@hsph.harvard.edu.
Website: http://www.hsph.harvard.edu/social-and-behavioral-sciences/

Immaculata University, College of Graduate Studies, Program in Nutrition Education, Immaculata, PA 19345. Offers nutrition education for the registered dietitian (MA); nutrition education with dietetic internship (MA); nutrition education with wellness promotion (MA). *Program availability:* Part-time, evening/weekend. *Degree requirements:* For master's, comprehensive exam, thesis optional. *Entrance requirements:* For master's, GRE or MAT, minimum GPA of 3.0. Additional exam requirements/recommendations for international students: Required—TOEFL. Electronic applications accepted. *Faculty research:* Sports nutrition, pediatric nutrition, changes in food consumption patterns in weight loss, nutritional counseling.

Independence University, Program in Health Services, Salt Lake City, UT 84107. Offers community health (MSHS); wellness promotion (MSHS). *Program availability:* Part-time, evening/weekend, online learning. *Degree requirements:* For master's, fieldwork, internship, final project (wellness promotion). *Entrance requirements:* For master's, previous course work in psychology.

Independence University, Program in Nursing, Salt Lake City, UT 84107. Offers community health (MSN); gerontology (MSN); nursing administration (MSN); wellness promotion (MSN).

Indiana University Bloomington, School of Public Health, Department of Kinesiology, Bloomington, IN 47405. Offers applied sport science (MS); athletic administration/sport management (MS); athletic training (MS); biomechanics (MS); ergonomics (MS); exercise physiology (MS); human performance (PhD), including biomechanics, exercise physiology, motor learning/control, sport management; motor learning/control (MS); physical activity (MPH); physical activity, fitness and wellness (MS). *Program availability:* Part-time. Terminal master's awarded for partial completion of doctoral program. *Degree requirements:* For master's, thesis optional; for doctorate, variable foreign language requirement, comprehensive exam, thesis/dissertation. *Entrance requirements:* For master's, GRE General Test, minimum GPA of 2.8; for doctorate, GRE General Test, minimum graduate GPA of 3.5, undergraduate 3.0. Additional exam requirements/recommendations for international students: Required—TOEFL (minimum score 80 iBT). *Faculty research:* Exercise physiology and biochemistry, sports biomechanics, human motor control, adaptation of fitness and exercise to special populations.

Instituto Tecnologico de Santo Domingo, Graduate School, Area of Health Sciences, Santo Domingo, Dominican Republic. Offers bioethics (M Bioethics); clinical bioethics (Certificate); clinical nutrition (Certificate); comprehensive health and the adolescent (Certificate); comrehensive adloescent health (MS); health and social security (M Mgmt).

Kent State University, College of Education, Health and Human Services, School of Health Sciences, Program in Health Education and Promotion, Kent, OH 44242-0001. Offers M Ed, PhD. *Accreditation:* NCATE. *Degree requirements:* For doctorate, comprehensive exam, thesis/dissertation. *Entrance requirements:* For master's, 2 letters of reference, goals statement; for doctorate, GRE General Test, goals statement, resume, interview. Additional exam requirements/recommendations for international students: Required—TOEFL (minimum score 550 paper-based; 80 iBT). Electronic applications accepted. *Expenses:* Tuition, state resident: full-time $11,310; part-time $515 per credit hour. Tuition, nonresident: full-time $20,396; part-time $928 per credit hour. *International tuition:* $18,544 full-time. *Faculty research:* Substance use/abuse, sexuality, community health assessment, epidemiology, HIV/AIDS.

Lehman College of the City University of New York, School of Health Sciences, Human Services and Nursing, Department of Health Sciences, Program in Health Education and Promotion, Bronx, NY 10468-1589. Offers MA. *Accreditation:* NCATE. *Program availability:* Part-time, evening/weekend. *Degree requirements:* For master's, thesis or alternative. *Entrance requirements:* For master's, minimum GPA of 2.7.

Liberty University, School of Behavioral Sciences, Lynchburg, VA 24515. Offers applied psychology (MA), including developmental psychology (MA, MS), industrial/organizational psychology (MA, MS); clinical mental health counseling (MA); community care and counseling (Ed D), including marriage and family counseling, pastoral care and counseling, traumatology; counselor education and supervision (PhD); human services counseling (MA), including addictions and recovery, business, child and family law, Christian ministries, criminal justice, crisis response and trauma, executive leadership, health and wellness, life coaching, marriage and family, military resilience; marriage and family counseling (MA); marriage and family therapy (MA); military resilience (Certificate); pastoral counseling (MA), including addictions and recovery, community chaplaincy, crisis response and trauma, discipleship and church ministry, leadership, life coaching, marriage and family, marriage and family studies, military resilience, parenting and child/adolescent, pastoral counseling, theology; professional counseling (MA); psychology (MS), including developmental psychology (MA, MS), industrial/ organizational psychology (MA, MS); school counseling (M Ed). *Program availability:* Part-time, online learning. *Students:* 2,649 full-time (2,085 women), 5,086 part-time (4,015 women); includes 2,275 minority (1,784 Black or African American, non-Hispanic/ Latino; 44 American Indian or Alaska Native, non-Hispanic/Latino; 67 Asian, non-Hispanic/Latino; 200 Hispanic/Latino; 11 Native Hawaiian or other Pacific Islander, non-Hispanic/Latino; 169 Two or more races, non-Hispanic/Latino), 145 international. Average age 39. 5,839 applicants, 51% accepted, 1710 enrolled. In 2017, 1,626 master's, 7 doctorates, 61 other advanced degrees awarded. *Application deadline:* Applications are processed on a rolling basis. Application fee: $50. Electronic applications accepted. *Financial support:* Applicants required to submit FAFSA. *Unit head:* Dr. Ronald Hawkins, Founding Dean, School of Behavioral Sciences. *Application contact:* Jay Bridge, Director of Admissions, 800-424-9595, Fax: 800-628-7977, E-mail: gradadmissions@liberty.edu.

Liberty University, School of Health Sciences, Lynchburg, VA 24515. Offers anatomy and cell biology (PhD); biomedical sciences (MS); epidemiology (MPH); exercise science (MS), including clinical, community physical activity, human performance, nutrition; global health (MPH); health promotion (MPH); medical sciences (MA), including biopsychology, business management, health informatics, molecular medicine, public health; nutrition (MPH). *Program availability:* Part-time, online learning. *Students:* 542 full-time (394 women), 696 part-time (541 women); includes 402 minority (286 Black or African American, non-Hispanic/Latino; 10 American Indian or Alaska Native, non-Hispanic/Latino; 34 Asian, non-Hispanic/Latino; 46 Hispanic/Latino; 1 Native Hawaiian or other Pacific Islander, non-Hispanic/Latino; 25 Two or more races, non-Hispanic/ Latino), 59 international. Average age 32. 1,592 applicants, 40% accepted, 297 enrolled. In 2017, 204 master's awarded. *Degree requirements:* For master's, thesis (for some programs); for doctorate, thesis/dissertation. *Entrance requirements:* For doctorate, MAT or GRE, minimum GPA of 3.25 in master's program, 2-3 recommendations, writing samples (for some programs), letter of intent, professional vitae. Additional exam requirements/recommendations for international students: Required—TOEFL (minimum score 600 paper-based; 100 iBT). Application fee: $50. *Financial support:* Applicants required to submit FAFSA. *Unit head:* Dr. Ralph Linstra, Dean. *Application contact:* Jay Bridge, Director of Admissions, 800-424-9595, Fax: 800-628-7977, E-mail: gradadmissions@liberty.edu.

Lindenwood University, Graduate Programs, School of Health Sciences, St. Charles, MO 63301-1695. Offers human performance (MS); nursing (MS). *Program availability:* Part-time, blended/hybrid learning. *Faculty:* 9 full-time (4 women), 4 part-time/adjunct (3 women). *Students:* 24 full-time (12 women), 57 part-time (51 women); includes 13 minority (7 Black or African American, non-Hispanic/Latino; 5 Hispanic/Latino; 1 Two or more races, non-Hispanic/Latino), 4 international. Average age 35. 65 applicants, 49% accepted, 22 enrolled. In 2017, 24 master's awarded. *Degree requirements:* For master's, minimum cumulative GPA of 3.0. *Entrance requirements:* For master's, BSN with 1 year of clinical experience as an RN, minimum cumulative GPA of 3.0. Additional exam requirements/recommendations for international students: Required—TOEFL (minimum score 550 paper-based; 80 iBT); Recommended—IELTS (minimum score 6.5). *Application deadline:* For fall admission, 8/27 priority date for domestic and international students; for spring admission, 1/14 priority date for domestic and international students; for summer admission, 6/4 priority date for domestic and international students. Applications are processed on a rolling basis. Application fee: $30 ($100 for international students). Electronic applications accepted. *Expenses: Tuition:* Full-time $16,300; part-time $460 per credit. *Required fees:* $660; $330 per credit. Tuition and fees vary according to degree level and program. *Financial support:* In 2017–18, 79 students received support. Career-related internships or fieldwork, Federal Work-Study, institutionally sponsored loans, scholarships/grants, tuition waivers (partial), and unspecified assistantships available. Financial award application deadline: 6/30; financial award applicants required to submit FAFSA. *Unit head:* Dr. Cynthia Schroeder, Dean, School of Health Sciences, 636-949-4318, E-mail: cschroeder@lindenwood.edu. *Application contact:* Kara Schilli, Director, Evening and Graduate Admissions, 636-949-4349, Fax: 636-949-4109, E-mail: adultadmissions@lindenwood.edu.
Website: http://www.lindenwood.edu/academics/academic-schools/school-of-health-sciences/

Lock Haven University of Pennsylvania, College of Natural, Behavioral and Health Sciences, Lock Haven, PA 17745-2390. Offers actuarial science (PSM); athletic training (MS); health promotion/education (MHS); healthcare management (MHS); physician assistant (MHS). Program also offered at the Clearfield, Coudersport, and Harrisburg campuses. *Accreditation:* ARC-PA. *Entrance requirements:* For master's, minimum undergraduate GPA of 3.0. Additional exam requirements/recommendations for international students: Required—TOEFL. Electronic applications accepted.

Manhattanville College, School of Education, Program in Physical Education and Sports Pedagogy, Purchase, NY 10577-2132. Offers health and wellness specialist (Advanced Certificate); physical education and sport pedagogy (MAT). *Program availability:* Part-time, evening/weekend. *Faculty:* 3 full-time (2 women), 7 part-time/ adjunct (2 women). *Students:* 39 full-time (10 women), 45 part-time (10 women); includes 15 minority (4 Black or African American, non-Hispanic/Latino; 11 Hispanic/ Latino). Average age 28. 9 applicants, 89% accepted, 8 enrolled. In 2017, 42 master's awarded. *Degree requirements:* For master's, comprehensive exam (for some programs), thesis (for some programs), student teaching, research seminars, portfolios, internships, writing assessment; for Advanced Certificate, comprehensive exam (for some programs). *Entrance requirements:* For master's, GRE or MAT (for programs leading to certification), minimum GPA of 3.0, 2 letters of recommendation, interview, essay (2-3 page personal statement that describes reasons for choosing teaching or educational leadership as profession and philosophy of education), proof of immunization (for those born after 1957). Additional exam requirements/ recommendations for international students: Required—TOEFL (minimum score 600 paper-based; 110 iBT); Recommended—IELTS (minimum score 8). *Application deadline:* Applications are processed on a rolling basis. Application fee: $75. Electronic applications accepted. *Expenses:* $915 per credit. *Financial support:* Teaching assistantships, career-related internships or fieldwork, Federal Work-Study, institutionally sponsored loans, scholarships/grants, and unspecified assistantships available. Financial award application deadline: 3/15; financial award applicants required to submit FAFSA. *Faculty research:* Early childhood and physical education. *Unit head:* Dr. Shelly Wepner, Dean, 914-323-3153, Fax: 914-323-5493, E-mail: shelly.wepner@mville.edu. *Application contact:* Alissa Wilson, Director, Graduate Admissions, 914-323-3150, Fax: 914-694-1732, E-mail: edschool@mville.edu.
Website: http://www.mville.edu/programs/physical-education-and-sports-pedagogy

Maryland University of Integrative Health, Programs in Health and Wellness Coaching, Laurel, MD 20723. Offers MA, Postbaccalaureate Certificate.

Maryland University of Integrative Health, Programs in Health Promotion and Yoga Therapy, Laurel, MD 20723. Offers health promotion (MS); yoga therapy (MS).

Marymount University, Malek School of Health Professions, Program in Health Education and Promotion, Arlington, VA 22207-4299. Offers MS. *Program availability:* Part-time, evening/weekend. *Faculty:* 4 full-time (3 women). *Students:* 10 full-time (5 women), 5 part-time (all women); includes 3 minority (1 Black or African American, non-Hispanic/Latino; 2 Asian, non-Hispanic/Latino), 3 international. Average age 29. 15 applicants, 100% accepted, 10 enrolled. In 2017, 4 master's awarded. *Degree requirements:* For master's, internship. *Entrance requirements:* For master's, GRE, MAT, minimum cumulative GPA of 3.0, or significant related experience, 2 letters of recommendation, interview, resume, personal statement. Additional exam requirements/ recommendations for international students: Required—TOEFL (minimum score 600 paper-based; 96 iBT), IELTS (minimum score 6.5). *Application deadline:* Applications are processed on a rolling basis. Application fee: $40. Electronic applications accepted. *Expenses: Tuition:* Full-time $17,550; part-time $975 per credit hour. *Required fees:* $198; $11 per credit hour. One-time fee: $250. Tuition and fees vary according to program. *Financial support:* In 2017–18, 5 students received support, including 3 teaching assistantships with full and partial tuition reimbursements available (averaging $11,700 per year); research assistantships with full and partial tuition reimbursements available, career-related internships or fieldwork, Federal Work-Study, scholarships/ grants, and unspecified assistantships also available. Support available to part-time students. Financial award application deadline: 3/1; financial award applicants required to submit FAFSA. *Unit head:* Dr. Jennifer Tripken, Chair, Health and Human Performance, 703-526-1597, Fax: 703-284-3819, E-mail: jennifer.tripken@marymount.edu. *Application contact:* Francesca Reed, Director, Graduate Admissions, 703-284-5901, Fax: 703-527-3815, E-mail: grad.admissions@marymount.edu.
Website: http://www.marymount.edu/Academics/Malek-School-of-Health-Professions/Graduate-Programs/Health-Education-Promotion-(M-S-)

McNeese State University, Doré School of Graduate Studies, Burton College of Education, Department of Health and Human Performance, Lake Charles, LA 70609. Offers exercise physiology (MS); health promotion (MS); nutrition and wellness (MS). *Accreditation:* NCATE. *Program availability:* Evening/weekend. *Entrance requirements:* For master's, GRE, undergraduate major or minor in health and human performance or related field of study. *Application deadline:* For fall admission, 5/15 priority date for domestic and international students; for spring admission, 10/15 priority date for domestic and international students. Applications are processed on a rolling basis. Application fee: $20 ($30 for international students). *Financial support:* Application deadline: 5/1. *Unit head:* Dr. Michael Soileau, Department Head, 337-475-5274, Fax: 337-475-5947, E-mail: msoileau@mcneese.edu. *Application contact:* Dr. Dustin M. Hebert, Director of Dore' School of Graduate Studies, 337-475-5396, Fax: 337-475-5397, E-mail: admissions@mcneese.edu.

Merrimack College, School of Health Sciences, North Andover, MA 01845-5800. Offers athletic training (MS); community health education (MS); exercise and sport science (MS); health and wellness management (MS). *Program availability:* Part-time, evening/ weekend. *Faculty:* 8 full-time, 6 part-time/adjunct. *Students:* 87 full-time (58 women), 4 part-time (all women); includes 10 minority (2 Black or African American, non-Hispanic/ Latino; 7 Hispanic/Latino; 1 Two or more races, non-Hispanic/Latino), 3 international. Average age 25. 147 applicants, 90% accepted, 83 enrolled. In 2017, 47 master's awarded. *Degree requirements:* For master's, capstone (for community health education, exercise and sport science, and health and wellness management). *Entrance requirements:* For master's, resume, official college transcripts, personal statement, 2 recommendations. Additional exam requirements/recommendations for international students: Required—TOEFL (minimum score 84 iBT), IELTS (minimum score 6.5), PTE (minimum score 56). *Application deadline:* For fall admission, 8/24 for domestic students, 7/30 for international students; for summer admission, 5/10 for domestic students, 4/10 for international students. Applications are processed on a rolling basis. Electronic applications accepted. *Expenses:* $865 per credit hour tuition; $670 per credit hour (for MAT); comprehensive fees are $165 per semester for 1-8 credit hours and $320 per semester for 9+ credit hours. *Financial support:* Fellowships with partial tuition reimbursements, career-related internships or fieldwork, scholarships/grants, and health care benefits available. Support available to part-time students. Financial award application deadline: 5/1; financial award applicants required to submit FAFSA. *Unit head:* Kyle McInnis, Dean, 978-837-3590, E-mail: mcinnisk@merrimack.edu. *Application contact:* Allison Pena, Office of Graduate Studies, 978-837-3563, E-mail: graduate@merrimack.edu.
Website: http://www.merrimack.edu/academics/health-sciences/

Mount St. Joseph University, Graduate Program in Religious Studies, Cincinnati, OH 45233-1670. Offers religious studies (MA); spirituality and wellness (Certificate). *Program availability:* Part-time, evening/weekend. *Faculty:* 1 (woman) full-time. *Students:* 1 (woman) full-time, 8 part-time (7 women); includes 4 minority (3 Black or African American, non-Hispanic/Latino; 1 Hispanic/Latino). Average age 45. In 2017, 1 master's awarded. *Degree requirements:* For master's, comprehensive exam, 36 hours of credit, pastoral PRAXIS component (3 credit hours), integrating project (3 credit hours). *Entrance requirements:* For master's, undergraduate transcript with minimum overall GPA of 3.0, 3 letters of recommendation from professional colleagues, 3-page essay, interview with the Graduate Admissions Committee, current work resume. Additional exam requirements/recommendations for international students: Required—TOEFL (minimum score 560 paper-based; 83 iBT). *Application deadline:* Applications are processed on a rolling basis. Application fee: $50. Electronic applications accepted. *Expenses:* $600 per credit hour. *Financial support:* In 2017–18, 7 students received support. Scholarships/grants available. Financial award applicants required to submit FAFSA. *Faculty research:* Contextual/cultural/systematic theology, historical/spiritual theology, business/economics ethics, social justice, Biblical/cultural/pastoral theology. *Unit head:* Dr. John Trokan, Associate Professor of Religious and Pastoral Studies/ Director of Graduate Program, 513-244-4272, Fax: 513-244-4222, E-mail: john.trokan@msj.edu. *Application contact:* Mary Brigham, Assistant Director of Graduate Recruitment, 513-244-4233, Fax: 513-244-4629, E-mail: mary.brigham@msj.edu.
Website: http://www.msj.edu/academics/graduate-programs/religious-studies-programs/

National University, School of Health and Human Services, La Jolla, CA 92037-1011. Offers clinical affairs (MS); clinical regulatory affairs (MS); complementary and integrative healthcare (MS); family nurse practitioner (MSN); health and life science analytics (MS); health informatics (MS, Certificate); healthcare administration (MHA); nurse anesthesia (MSNA); nursing administration (MSN); nursing informatics (MSN); psychiatric-mental health nurse practitioner (MSN); public health (MPH), including health promotion, healthcare administration, mental health. *Program availability:* Part-time, evening/ weekend, 100% online, blended/hybrid learning. *Degree requirements:* For master's, thesis (for some programs). *Entrance requirements:* For master's, interview, minimum GPA of 2.5. Additional exam requirements/recommendations for international students: Required—TOEFL (minimum score 550 paper-based; 79 iBT), IELTS (minimum score 6). *Application deadline:* Applications are processed on a rolling basis. Application fee: $60 ($65 for international students). Electronic applications accepted. *Expenses: Tuition:* Part-time $430 per quarter hour. *Financial support:* Career-related internships or fieldwork, institutionally sponsored loans, scholarships/grants, and tuition waivers (partial) available. Support available to part-time students. Financial award application deadline: 6/30; financial award applicants required to submit FAFSA. *Faculty research:* Nursing education, obesity prevention, workforce diversity. *Unit head:* Dr. Gloria J. McNeal, Dean, 858-309-3473, E-mail: shhs@nu.edu. *Application contact:* Brandon Jouganatos, Vice President for Enrollment Services, 800-628-8648, E-mail: advisor@nu.edu.
Website: http://www.nu.edu/OurPrograms/SchoolOfHealthAndHumanServices.html

Nebraska Methodist College, Program in Health Promotion Management, Omaha, NE 68114. Offers MS. *Program availability:* Part-time, evening/weekend, online learning. *Degree requirements:* For master's, thesis or alternative, capstone project. *Entrance requirements:* For master's, interview. Additional exam requirements/recommendations for international students: Required—TOEFL (minimum score 550 paper-based; 80 iBT). *Faculty research:* Congregational health promotion, fitness testing with elderly, educational assessment, statistics instruction, resilience.

New York University, Steinhardt School of Culture, Education, and Human Development, Department of Applied Psychology, Programs in Counseling, New York, NY 10012. Offers counseling and guidance (MA, Advanced Certificate), including bilingual school counseling K-12 (MA), school counseling K-12 (MA); counseling for mental health and wellness (MA); counseling psychology (PhD); LGBT health, education, and social services (Advanced Certificate); Advanced Certificate/MPH; MA/Advanced Certificate. *Accreditation:* APA (one or more programs are accredited). *Program availability:* Part-time. *Students:* Average age 29. 663 applicants, 33% accepted, 74 enrolled. In 2017, 87 master's, 7 doctorates awarded. *Entrance requirements:* For doctorate, GRE General Test, interview. Additional exam requirements/recommendations for international students: Required—TOEFL (minimum score 100 iBT). *Application deadline:* For fall admission, 12/1 priority date for domestic and international students. Applications are processed on a rolling basis. Application fee: $75. Electronic applications accepted. *Expenses: Tuition:* Full-time $41,352; part-time $19,968 per year. *Required fees:* $2496; $1628 per unit. $814 per term. Tuition and fees vary according to course load and program. *Financial support:* Fellowships with full and partial tuition reimbursements, research assistantships, teaching assistantships with partial tuition reimbursements, career-related internships or fieldwork, Federal Work-Study, institutionally sponsored loans, scholarships/grants, tuition waivers (partial), and unspecified assistantships available. Support available to part-time students. Financial award application deadline: 2/1; financial award applicants required to submit FAFSA. *Faculty research:* Sexual and gender identities, group dynamics, psychopathy and personality, multicultural assessment, working people's lives. *Unit head:* Dr. Randolph Mowry, Co-Director, 212-998-5222, Fax: 212-995-4358, E-mail: randolph.mowry@nyu.edu. *Application contact:* 212-998-5030, Fax: 212-995-4328, E-mail: steinhardt.gradadmissions@nyu.edu.
Website: http://steinhardt.nyu.edu/appsych/counseling

Old Dominion University, Darden College of Education, Program in Physical Education, Exercise Science and Wellness Emphasis, Norfolk, VA 23529. Offers physical education (MS Ed), including exercise science and wellness. *Program availability:* Part-time, evening/weekend. *Faculty:* 7 full-time (3 women). *Students:* 14 full-time (9 women), 3 part-time (1 woman); includes 6 minority (3 Black or African American, non-Hispanic/Latino; 1 Asian, non-Hispanic/Latino; 1 Hispanic/Latino; 1 Two or more races, non-Hispanic/Latino). Average age 26. 16 applicants, 88% accepted, 8 enrolled. In 2017, 9 master's awarded. *Degree requirements:* For master's, comprehensive exam, thesis or alternative, internship, research project. *Entrance requirements:* For master's, GRE (minimum score of 291 for combined verbal and quantitative), minimum GPA of 2.8 overall, 3.0 in major. Additional exam requirements/recommendations for international students: Required—TOEFL (minimum score 550 paper-based; 79 iBT). *Application deadline:* For fall admission, 3/1 for domestic and international students. Applications are processed on a rolling basis. Application fee: $50. Electronic applications accepted. *Expenses:* Tuition, state resident: full-time $8928; part-time $496 per credit. Tuition, nonresident: full-time $22,482; part-time $1249 per credit. *Required fees:* $66 per semester. *Financial support:* In 2017–18, 7 students received support, including 4 research assistantships (averaging $10,000 per year), 3 teaching assistantships (averaging $10,000 per year); unspecified assistantships also available. Financial award application deadline: 3/1. *Faculty research:* Cardiovascular response to exercise, exercise prescription, nutrition, lower extremity biomechanics, metabolic responses in special populations. *Total annual research expenditures:* $104,000. *Unit head:* Dr. Lynn Ridinger, Chair, 757-683-4353, E-mail: lridinge@odu.edu. *Application contact:* William Heffelfinger, Director of Graduate Admissions, 757-683-5554, Fax: 757-683-3255, E-mail: gradadmit@odu.edu.
Website: http://www.odu.edu/hms/academics/exercise/graduate#.Wr0u402otrQ

Oregon State University, College of Public Health and Human Sciences, Program in Public Health, Corvallis, OR 97331. Offers biostatistics (MPH); environmental and occupational health (MPH, PhD); epidemiology (MPH, PhD); global health (MPH, PhD). Terminal master's awarded for partial completion of doctoral program. *Entrance requirements:* For master's and doctorate, GRE, minimum GPA of 3.0 in last 90 hours. Additional exam requirements/recommendations for international students: Required—TOEFL (minimum score 80 iBT), IELTS (minimum score 6.5). *Application deadline:* For fall admission, 12/1 priority date for domestic and international students. Applications are processed on a rolling basis. Electronic applications accepted. *Expenses:* Contact institution. *Financial support:* Application deadline: 12/1. *Unit head:* Amanda Armington, MPH Program Manager, 541-737-3825, E-mail: amanda.armington@oregonstate.edu.

Plymouth State University, College of Graduate Studies, Graduate Studies in Education, Program in Health Education, Plymouth, NH 03264-1595. Offers eating disorders (M Ed); health education (M Ed); health promotion (MS). *Program availability:* Part-time, evening/weekend. *Entrance requirements:* For master's, MAT, minimum GPA of 3.0. *Application deadline:* Applications are processed on a rolling basis. Application fee: $75. *Expenses:* Tuition, state resident: part-time $525 per credit. Tuition, nonresident: part-time $605 per credit. *Required fees:* $38 per credit. Part-time tuition and fees vary according to course level and program. *Financial support:* Applicants required to submit FAFSA. *Unit head:* Dr. Irene Cucina, Program Coordinator/Advisor, 603-535-2517, E-mail: icucina@plymouth.edu. *Application contact:* Cheryl B. Baker, Director of Recruitment and Outreach, 603-535-2737, Fax: 603-535-2572, E-mail: cbaker@plymouth.edu.

Plymouth State University, Program in Personal and Organizational Wellness, Plymouth, NH 03264-1595. Offers MA, Graduate Certificate. *Expenses:* Tuition, state resident: part-time $525 per credit. Tuition, nonresident: part-time $605 per credit. *Required fees:* $38 per credit. Part-time tuition and fees vary according to course level and program. *Unit head:* Dr. Nancy Puglisi, Program Coordinator/Advisor, 603-862-3116, E-mail: npuglisi@plymouth.edu. *Application contact:* Cheryl B. Baker, Director of Recruitment and Outreach, 603-535-2737, Fax: 603-535-2572, E-mail: cbaker@plymouth.edu.
Website: http://www.plymouth.edu/graduate/academics/degrees/masters/ma/personal-organizational-wellness/

Portland State University, Graduate Studies, OHSU-PSU School of Public Health, Health Promotion Program, Portland, OR 97207-0751. Offers community health (PhD); health promotion (MPH); health studies (MA). MPH offered jointly with Oregon Health and Science University. *Program availability:* Part-time. *Faculty:* 25 full-time (19 women), 4 part-time/adjunct (2 women). *Students:* 11 full-time (10 women), 12 part-time (9 women); includes 5 minority (2 American Indian or Alaska Native, non-Hispanic/Latino; 1 Asian, non-Hispanic/Latino; 2 Hispanic/Latino). Average age 33. In 2017, 21 master's awarded. *Degree requirements:* For master's, comprehensive exam (for some programs), thesis (for some programs), internship/practicum, oral and written exams (depending on program); for doctorate, comprehensive exam, thesis/dissertation. *Entrance requirements:* For master's, GRE General Test (minimum scores: Verbal 153; Quantitative 148; Analytic Writing 4.5), personal statement, 3 letters of recommendation, minimum GPA of 3.0, resume, background check; for doctorate, GRE General Test (minimum scores: Verbal 153; Quantitative 148; Analytic Writing 4.5), transcripts, personal statement, resume, writing sample, 3 letters of recommendation, background check. Additional exam requirements/recommendations for international students: Required—TOEFL (minimum score 550 paper-based; 80 iBT). *Application deadline:* For fall admission, 2/1 for domestic and international students. Applications are processed on a rolling basis. Application fee: $65. *Expenses:* Tuition, state resident: full-time $14,436; part-time $401 per credit. Tuition, nonresident: full-time $21,780; part-time $605 per credit. *Required fees:* $1380; $22 per credit. $119 per quarter. One-time fee: $325. Tuition and fees vary according to program. *Financial support:* In 2017–18, 9 research assistantships with full and partial tuition reimbursements (averaging $7,556 per year) were awarded; teaching assistantships, career-related internships or fieldwork, Federal Work-Study, scholarships/grants, and unspecified assistantships also available. Support available to part-time students. Financial award application deadline: 3/1; financial award applicants required to submit FAFSA. *Unit head:* Dr. David Bangsberg, Founding Dean, 503-282-7537. *Application contact:* Dr. Jill Rissi, Associate Dean for Academic Affairs, 503-725-8217, E-mail: jrissi@pdx.edu.
Website: https://ohsu-psu-sph.org/

Rosalind Franklin University of Medicine and Science, College of Health Professions, Department of Nutrition, North Chicago, IL 60064-3095. Offers clinical nutrition (MS); health promotion and wellness (MS); nutrition education (MS). *Program availability:* Part-time, evening/weekend, online learning. *Degree requirements:* For master's, thesis optional, portfolio. *Entrance requirements:* For master's, minimum GPA of 2.75, registered dietitian (RD), professional certificate or license. Additional exam requirements/recommendations for international students: Required—TOEFL. *Expenses:* Contact institution. *Faculty research:* Nutrition education, distance learning, computer-based graduate education, childhood obesity, nutrition medical education.

Rowan University, Graduate School, School of Biomedical Science and Health Professions, Department of Health and Exercise Science, Glassboro, NJ 08028-1701. Offers wellness and lifestyle management (MA). *Degree requirements:* For master's, comprehensive exam, thesis. *Entrance requirements:* For master's, GRE General Test, GRE Subject Test, interview, minimum GPA of 2.8. Additional exam requirements/recommendations for international students: Required—TOEFL. Electronic applications accepted. *Expenses:* Tuition, state resident: full-time $15,020; part-time $751 per semester hour. Tuition, nonresident: full-time $15,020; part-time $751 per semester hour. *Required fees:* $3158; $157.90 per semester hour. Tuition and fees vary according to course load, campus/location and program.

San Diego State University, Graduate and Research Affairs, College of Health and Human Services, Graduate School of Public Health, San Diego, CA 92182. Offers environmental health (MPH); epidemiology (MPH, PhD), including biostatistics (MPH); global emergency preparedness and response (MS); global health (PhD); health behavior (PhD); health promotion (MPH); health services administration (MPH); toxicology (MS); MPH/MA; MSW/MPH. *Accreditation:* CAHME (one or more programs are accredited). *Program availability:* Part-time. *Degree requirements:* For master's, comprehensive exam (for some programs), thesis (for some programs); for doctorate, thesis/dissertation. *Entrance requirements:* For master's, GMAT (MPH in health services administration), GRE General Test; for doctorate, GRE General Test. Additional exam requirements/recommendations for international students: Required—TOEFL. *Faculty research:* Evaluation of tobacco, AIDS prevalence and prevention, mammography, infant death project, Alzheimer's in elderly Chinese.

Simmons College, School of Nursing and Health Sciences, Boston, MA 02115. Offers didactic dietetics (Certificate); dietetic internship (Certificate); health professions education (PhD, CAGS); nursing (MS, MSN), including family nurse practitioner (MS); nursing practice (DNP); nutrition and health promotion (MS); physical therapy (DPT); sports nutrition (Certificate). *Accreditation:* AACN. *Program availability:* Part-time, 100% online, blended/hybrid learning. *Faculty:* 34 full-time (28 women), 44 part-time/adjunct (40 women). *Students:* 390 full-time (350 women), 1,286 part-time (1,169 women); includes 346 minority (131 Black or African American, non-Hispanic/Latino; 6 American Indian or Alaska Native, non-Hispanic/Latino; 75 Asian, non-Hispanic/Latino; 91 Hispanic/Latino; 3 Native Hawaiian or other Pacific Islander, non-Hispanic/Latino; 40 Two or more races, non-Hispanic/Latino), 9 international. Average age 34. 1,219 applicants, 74% accepted, 481 enrolled. In 2017, 423 master's, 39 doctorates, 55 other advanced degrees awarded. *Entrance requirements:* For doctorate, GRE. Additional exam requirements/recommendations for international students: Required—TOEFL (minimum score 570 paper-based; 88 iBT). *Application deadline:* For fall admission, 6/1 for international students. Application fee: $50. Electronic applications accepted. *Expenses:* $1,278 per credit, $116 activity fee per semester. *Financial support:* In 2017–18, 15 research assistantships with partial tuition reimbursements were awarded; scholarships/grants and unspecified assistantships also available. Financial award applicants required to submit FAFSA. *Unit head:* Dr. Judy Beal, Dean, 617-521-2139. *Application contact:* Brett DiMarzo, Director of Graduate Admission, 617-521-2651, Fax: 617-521-3137, E-mail: brett.dimarzo@simmons.edu.
Website: http://www.simmons.edu/snhs/

Sonoma State University, School of Science and Technology, Department of Kinesiology, Rohnert Park, CA 94928. Offers exercise science/pre-physical therapy (MA); interdisciplinary (MA); interdisciplinary pre-occupational therapy (MA); lifetime physical activity (MA), including coach education, fitness and wellness. *Program availability:* Part-time. *Degree requirements:* For master's, thesis, oral exam. *Entrance requirements:* For master's, minimum GPA of 2.8. Additional exam requirements/recommendations for international students: Required—TOEFL (minimum score 500 paper-based). *Application deadline:* For fall admission, 11/30 for domestic students; for spring admission, 9/1 for domestic students. Applications are processed on a rolling basis. Application fee: $55. *Financial support:* Career-related internships or fieldwork available. Financial award application deadline: 3/2; financial award applicants required to submit FAFSA. *Unit head:* Dr. Steven Winter, Chair, 707-664-2188, E-mail: steven.winter@sonoma.edu. *Application contact:* Dr. Bulent Sokmen, Graduate Coordinator, 707-664-2789, E-mail: sokmen@sonoma.edu.
Website: http://www.sonoma.edu/kinesiology/

Southern Methodist University, Simmons School of Education and Human Development, Department of Allied Physiology and Wellness, Dallas, TX 75275. Offers applied physiology (PhD); health promotion management (MS); sport management (MS). Program offered jointly with Cox School of Business. *Entrance requirements:* For master's, GMAT, resume, essays, transcripts from all colleges and universities attended, two references. Additional exam requirements/recommendations for international students: Required—TOEFL or PTE. *Unit head:* Dr. Lynn Romejko Jacobs, Department Chair, 214-768-1811, E-mail: lromejko@smu.edu. *Application contact:* Michael Lysko, Program Director, 214-768-7834, E-mail: mlysko@smu.edu.
Website: http://smu.edu/education/APW/

Springfield College, Graduate Programs, Programs in Physical Education, Springfield, MA 01109-3797. Offers adapted physical education (MS); advanced-level coaching (M Ed); athletic administration (MS); exercise physiology (PhD); health promotion and

disease prevention (MS); physical education initial licensure (CAGS); sport and exercise psychology (PhD); teaching and administration (PhD). *Program availability:* Part-time. *Students:* 82 applicants, 73% accepted, 37 enrolled. *Degree requirements:* For master's, comprehensive exam, thesis (for some programs). *Entrance requirements:* For master's and doctorate, GRE General Test. Additional exam requirements/recommendations for international students: Required—TOEFL (minimum score 550 paper-based); Recommended—IELTS (minimum score 7). *Application deadline:* For fall admission, 1/15 priority date for domestic students, 1/15 for international students; for winter admission, 11/1 for domestic and international students; for spring admission, 11/1 for domestic and international students. Applications are processed on a rolling basis. Application fee: $50. Electronic applications accepted. *Financial support:* Fellowships with partial tuition reimbursements, teaching assistantships with partial tuition reimbursements, career-related internships or fieldwork, Federal Work-Study, institutionally sponsored loans, scholarships/grants, and unspecified assistantships available. Financial award application deadline: 3/1; financial award applicants required to submit FAFSA. *Unit head:* Dr. Michelle Moosbrugger, Graduate Coordinator, 413-748-3486, E-mail: mmoosbrugger@springfield.edu. *Application contact:* Anne Griffin, Director of Graduate Admissions, 413-748-3225, Fax: 413-748-3694, E-mail: agriffin2@springfield.edu.
Website: http://springfield.edu/gradpe

Stony Brook University, State University of New York, Stony Brook Medicine, School of Medicine, Program in Public Health, Stony Brook, NY 11794. Offers community health (MPH); evaluation sciences (MPH); family violence (MPH); health communication (Certificate); health economics (MPH); health education and promotion (Certificate); population health (MPH); substance abuse (MPH). *Accreditation:* CEPH. *Program availability:* Part-time, evening/weekend. *Students:* 32 full-time (24 women), 11 part-time (10 women); includes 18 minority (4 Black or African American, non-Hispanic/Latino; 10 Asian, non-Hispanic/Latino; 4 Hispanic/Latino), 2 international. Average age 29. 128 applicants, 71% accepted, 29 enrolled. In 2017, 25 master's, 1 other advanced degree awarded. *Entrance requirements:* For master's, GRE, 3 references, bachelor's degree from accredited college or university with minimum GPA of 3.0, essays, interview. Additional exam requirements/recommendations for international students: Required—TOEFL (minimum score 90 iBT). *Application deadline:* For fall admission, 7/15 for domestic students, 3/15 for international students. Application fee: $100. Electronic applications accepted. *Expenses:* Contact institution. *Financial support:* Fellowships available. *Faculty research:* Abnormal psychology, academic achievement, broadcast media, communications, communications systems, public health. *Total annual research expenditures:* $422,408. *Unit head:* Dr. Lisa A. Benz Scott, Director, 631-444-8811, E-mail: lisa.benzscott@stonybrook.edu. *Application contact:* Joanie Maniaci, Assistant Director for Student Affairs, 631-444-2074, Fax: 631-444-6035, E-mail: joanmarie.maniaci@stonybrook.edu.
Website: http://publichealth.stonybrookmedicine.edu/

Tennessee Technological University, College of Graduate Studies, College of Education, Department of Exercise Science, Physical Education and Wellness, Cookeville, TN 38505. Offers adapted physical education (MA); elementary/middle school physical education (MA); lifetime wellness (MA); sport management (MA). *Accreditation:* NCATE. *Program availability:* Part-time, online learning. *Faculty:* 7 full-time (0 women). *Students:* 17 full-time (8 women), 34 part-time (14 women); includes 10 minority (5 Black or African American, non-Hispanic/Latino; 1 Asian, non-Hispanic/Latino; 2 Hispanic/Latino; 2 Two or more races, non-Hispanic/Latino). 35 applicants, 71% accepted, 23 enrolled. In 2017, 28 master's awarded. *Degree requirements:* For master's, comprehensive exam, thesis or alternative. *Entrance requirements:* For master's, MAT or GRE. Additional exam requirements/recommendations for international students: Required—TOEFL (minimum score 527 paper-based; 71 iBT), IELTS (minimum score 5.5), PTE (minimum score 48), or TOEIC (Test of English as an International Communication). *Application deadline:* For fall admission, 8/1 for domestic students, 5/1 for international students; for spring admission, 12/1 for domestic students, 10/1 for international students; for summer admission, 5/1 for domestic students, 2/1 for international students. Applications are processed on a rolling basis. Application fee: $35 ($40 for international students). Electronic applications accepted. *Expenses:* Tuition, state resident: full-time $9925; part-time $565 per credit hour. Tuition, nonresident: full-time $22,993; part-time $1291 per credit hour. *Financial support:* Fellowships, research assistantships, teaching assistantships, and career-related internships or fieldwork available. Financial award application deadline: 4/1. *Unit head:* Dr. Christy Killman, Chairperson, 931-372-3467, Fax: 931-372-6319, E-mail: ckillman@tntech.edu. *Application contact:* Shelia K. Kendrick, Coordinator of Graduate Studies, 931-372-3808, Fax: 931-372-3497, E-mail: skendrick@tntech.edu.

Texas A&M University, School of Public Health, College Station, TX 77845. Offers biostatistics (MPH, MSPH); environmental health (MPH, MSPH); epidemiology (MPH, MSPH); executive health administration (MHA); health administration (MHA); health policy and management (MPH, MSPH); health promotion and community health sciences (MPH); health services research (PhD); occupational safety and health (MPH). *Program availability:* Part-time, blended/hybrid learning. *Faculty:* 56. *Students:* 279 full-time (196 women), 86 part-time (56 women); includes 153 minority (48 Black or African American, non-Hispanic/Latino; 36 Asian, non-Hispanic/Latino; 62 Hispanic/Latino; 7 Two or more races, non-Hispanic/Latino), 77 international. Average age 29. 179 applicants, 96% accepted, 148 enrolled. In 2017, 124 master's, 8 doctorates awarded. *Entrance requirements:* For master's, GRE General Test, 3 letters of recommendation; statement of purpose; current curriculum vitae or resume; official transcripts; for doctorate, GRE General Test, 3 letters of recommendation; statement of purpose; current curriculum vitae or resume; official transcripts; interview (in some cases). Additional exam requirements/recommendations for international students: Required—TOEFL (minimum score 597 paper-based, 95 iBT) or GRE (minimum verbal score 153). Application fee: $120. Electronic applications accepted. *Expenses:* Contact institution. *Financial support:* In 2017–18, 203 students received support, including 62 research assistantships with tuition reimbursements available (averaging $10,041 per year), 25 teaching assistantships with tuition reimbursements available (averaging $12,913 per year); career-related internships or fieldwork, institutionally sponsored loans, scholarships/grants, traineeships, health care benefits, tuition waivers (full and partial), and unspecified assistantships also available. Support available to part-time students. Financial award applicants required to submit FAFSA. *Unit head:* Dr. Jay Maddock, Dean, 979-436-9322, Fax: 979-458-1878, E-mail: maddock@tamhsc.edu. *Application contact:* Erin E. Schneider, Associate Director of Admissions and Recruitment, 979-436-9380, E-mail: eschneider@sph.tamhsc.edu.
Website: http://sph.tamhsc.edu/

Tulane University, School of Professional Advancement, New Orleans, LA 70118-5669. Offers health and wellness management (MPS); homeland security studies (MPS); information technology management (MPS); liberal arts (MLA). *Program availability:* Part-time. *Degree requirements:* For master's, thesis. *Entrance requirements:* For master's, GRE General Test, minimum B average in undergraduate course work. Additional exam requirements/recommendations for international students: Required—TOEFL. *Expenses: Tuition:* Full-time $50,920; part-time $2829 per credit hour. *Required fees:* $2040; $44.50 per credit hour. $580 per term. Tuition and fees vary according to course load, degree level and program.

Union Institute & University, Master of Arts Program, Cincinnati, OH 45206-1925. Offers creativity studies (MA); health and wellness (MA); history and culture (MA); leadership, public policy, and social issues (MA); literature and writing (MA). *Program availability:* Part-time, online only, 100% online. *Students:* 9 full-time (7 women), 70 part-time (56 women); includes 33 minority (22 Black or African American, non-Hispanic/Latino; 1 American Indian or Alaska Native, non-Hispanic/Latino; 6 Hispanic/Latino; 4 Two or more races, non-Hispanic/Latino). Average age 40. *Degree requirements:* For master's, thesis. *Entrance requirements:* For master's, transcript, essay, 3 letters of recommendation, resume. Additional exam requirements/recommendations for international students: Recommended—TOEFL. *Application deadline:* For spring admission, 3/13 for domestic students. Applications are processed on a rolling basis. Application fee: $50. Electronic applications accepted. *Expenses:* Contact institution. *Financial support:* Career-related internships or fieldwork and tuition waivers available. Financial award applicants required to submit FAFSA. *Unit head:* Elden Golden, Director, 513-487-1153, E-mail: elden.golden@myunion.edu. *Application contact:* Director of Admissions, 800-861-6400.

Universidad del Turabo, Graduate Programs, Programs in Education, Program in Wellness, Gurabo, PR 00778-3030. Offers MPHE. *Entrance requirements:* For master's, GRE, EXADEP, GMAT, interview, official transcript, essay, recommendation letters. Electronic applications accepted.

The University of Alabama, Graduate School, College of Human Environmental Sciences, Department of Health Science, Tuscaloosa, AL 35487-0311. Offers health education and promotion (PhD); health studies (MA). *Program availability:* Part-time, online learning. *Faculty:* 11 full-time (7 women). *Students:* 53 full-time (44 women), 102 part-time (86 women); includes 55 minority (40 Black or African American, non-Hispanic/Latino; 2 American Indian or Alaska Native, non-Hispanic/Latino; 2 Asian, non-Hispanic/Latino; 7 Hispanic/Latino; 4 Two or more races, non-Hispanic/Latino), 2 international. Average age 33. 87 applicants, 74% accepted, 46 enrolled. In 2017, 74 master's, 8 doctorates awarded. *Degree requirements:* For master's, comprehensive exam, thesis optional; for doctorate, one foreign language, comprehensive exam, thesis/dissertation. *Entrance requirements:* For master's, minimum GPA of 3.0; for doctorate, GRE General Test, minimum GPA of 3.0, prerequisites in health education. Additional exam requirements/recommendations for international students: Required—TOEFL. *Application deadline:* For fall admission, 3/15 priority date for domestic students, 3/15 for international students. Applications are processed on a rolling basis. Application fee: $50 ($60 for international students). Electronic applications accepted. *Financial support:* In 2017–18, 10 students received support, including research assistantships with full tuition reimbursements available (averaging $10,500 per year), teaching assistantships with full tuition reimbursements available (averaging $10,500 per year); career-related internships or fieldwork, Federal Work-Study, institutionally sponsored loans, health care benefits, and unspecified assistantships also available. Financial award application deadline: 4/14. *Faculty research:* Program planning, substance abuse prevention, obesity prevention, nutrition, physical activity, athletic training, osteoporosis, health behavior. *Unit head:* Dr. David Birch, Department Head and Professor, 205-348-4751, E-mail: dabirch@ches.ua.edu. *Application contact:* Dr. Stuart Usdan, Associate Professor and Doctoral Program Coordinator, 205-348-8373, Fax: 205-348-7568, E-mail: susdan@ches.ua.edu.
Website: http://ches.ua.edu/

The University of Alabama at Birmingham, School of Public Health, Program in Health Education and Health Promotion, Birmingham, AL 35294-0022. Offers PhD. Program offered jointly with the School of Education and The University of Alabama (Tuscaloosa). *Program availability:* Part-time. *Faculty:* 9 full-time (6 women), 4 part-time/adjunct (1 woman). *Students:* 7 full-time (5 women), 19 part-time (15 women); includes 10 minority (all Black or African American, non-Hispanic/Latino), 3 international. Average age 37. 11 applicants, 73% accepted, 6 enrolled. In 2017, 3 doctorates awarded. *Degree requirements:* For doctorate, comprehensive exam, thesis/dissertation, research internship. *Entrance requirements:* For doctorate, GRE, 3 letters of recommendation, transcripts, personal statement, curriculum vitae/resume. Additional exam requirements/recommendations for international students: Required—TOEFL (minimum score 550 paper-based; 80 iBT), IELTS (minimum score 6.5). *Application deadline:* For fall admission, 2/15 priority date for domestic and international students. Applications are processed on a rolling basis. Application fee: $50 ($60 for international students). Electronic applications accepted. *Expenses:* $451 per semester hour in-state; $1,025 per semester hour out-of-state; $250 per online course fee. *Financial support:* In 2017–18, 23 students received support, including 1 fellowship with full tuition reimbursement available (averaging $26,400 per year), 1 research assistantship with full tuition reimbursement available (averaging $20,424 per year), 5 teaching assistantships (averaging $3,000 per year); career-related internships or fieldwork, Federal Work-Study, scholarships/grants, traineeships, health care benefits, and full-time employee tuition coverage also available. Financial award application deadline: 2/15. *Faculty research:* Obesity prevention including lifestyle interventions, family and adolescent health issues, prevention and control of addictive behaviors, sexual health risks including HIV/AIDS prevention and treatment, and mental health issues including issues of homelessness. *Total annual research expenditures:* $574,000. *Unit head:* Dr. Robin G. Lanzi, Graduate Program Director, 205-975-8071, Fax: 205-934-9325, E-mail: rlanzi@uab.edu. *Application contact:* Hannah VanSlambrouck, Director, Enrollment Management, 205-975-8688, E-mail: hannahv@uab.edu.
Website: http://www.soph.uab.edu/hb

University of Alberta, School of Public Health, Centre for Health Promotion Studies, Edmonton, AB T6G 2E1, Canada. Offers health promotion (M Sc, Postgraduate Diploma). *Program availability:* Part-time, online learning.

University of Arkansas, Graduate School, College of Education and Health Professions, Department of Health, Human Performance and Recreation, Program in Community Health Promotion, Fayetteville, AR 72701. Offers MS, PhD. In 2017, 2 master's, 3 doctorates awarded. *Application deadline:* For fall admission, 8/1 for domestic students, 4/1 for international students; for spring admission, 12/1 for domestic students, 10/1 for international students; for summer admission, 4/15 for domestic students, 3/1 for international students. Application fee: $60. *Expenses:* Tuition, state resident: full-time $3782. Tuition, nonresident: full-time $10,238. *Unit head:* Dr. Matthew Stueck Ganio, Department Head, 479-575-2956, Fax: 479-575-5778, E-mail: msganio@uark.edu. *Application contact:* Dr. Stephen Dittmore, Coordinator of Graduate Studies, 479-575-6625, E-mail: dittmore@uark.edu.
Website: https://hhpr.uark.edu

University of Arkansas for Medical Sciences, College of Public Health, Little Rock, AR 72205-7199. Offers biostatistics (MPH); environmental and occupational health (MPH, Certificate); epidemiology (MPH, PhD); health behavior and health education (MPH); health policy and management (MPH); health promotion and prevention research (PhD); health services administration (MHSA); health systems research (PhD); public health (Certificate); public health leadership (Dr PH). *Accreditation:* CEPH. *Program availability:* Part-time. *Degree requirements:* For master's, preceptorship, culminating experience, internship; for doctorate, comprehensive exam, capstone. *Entrance requirements:* For master's, GRE, GMAT, LSAT, PCAT, MCAT, DAT; for doctorate, GRE. Additional exam requirements/recommendations for international students: Required—TOEFL (minimum score 80 iBT), IELTS. Electronic applications accepted. *Expenses:* Contact institution. *Faculty research:* Health systems, tobacco prevention control, obesity prevention, environmental and occupational exposure, cancer prevention.

University of Central Oklahoma, The Jackson College of Graduate Studies, College of Education and Professional Studies, Department of Kinesiology and Health Studies, Edmond, OK 73034-5209. Offers athletic training (MS); wellness management (MS), including exercise science, health promotion. *Faculty:* 7 full-time (4 women), 1 (woman) part-time/adjunct. *Students:* 31 full-time (20 women), 32 part-time (18 women); includes 19 minority (8 Black or African American, non-Hispanic/Latino; 2 American Indian or Alaska Native, non-Hispanic/Latino; 6 Hispanic/Latino; 3 Two or more races, non-Hispanic/Latino), 5 international. Average age 29. 41 applicants, 71% accepted, 13 enrolled. In 2017, 19 master's awarded. *Degree requirements:* For master's, comprehensive exam (for some programs), thesis (for some programs). *Entrance requirements:* Additional exam requirements/recommendations for international students: Required—TOEFL (minimum score 550 paper-based; 79 iBT), IELTS (minimum score 6.5). *Application deadline:* For fall admission, 12/15 priority date for domestic students, 7/15 for international students; for spring admission, 11/15 for international students; for summer admission, 3/1 for domestic and international students. Application fee: $60. Electronic applications accepted. *Expenses:* Tuition, state resident: full-time $5375; part-time $268.75 per credit hour. Tuition, nonresident: full-time $13,295; part-time $664.75 per credit hour. *Required fees:* $626; $31.30 per credit hour. One-time fee: $50. Tuition and fees vary according to program. *Financial support:* In 2017–18, 15 students received support, including 2 research assistantships with partial tuition reimbursements available (averaging $4,436 per year), 1 teaching assistantship with partial tuition reimbursement available (averaging $2,958 per year); career-related internships or fieldwork, scholarships/grants, tuition waivers (partial), and unspecified assistantships also available. Financial award application deadline: 3/31; financial award applicants required to submit FAFSA. *Unit head:* Dr. Debra Traywick, Chair, 405-974-5230, Fax: 405-974-3805. *Application contact:* Carlie Wellington, Assistant Director, CEPS Graduate Enrollment, 405-974-5105, Fax: 405-974-3851, E-mail: gradcoll@uco.edu.
Website: http://sites.uco.edu/ceps/dept/Professional-Studies-Programs/khs/index.asp

University of Chicago, Division of the Biological Sciences, Department of Public Health Sciences, Chicago, IL 60637. Offers MS, PhD. *Program availability:* Part-time. *Faculty:* 21. *Students:* 14 full-time (8 women), 11 part-time (5 women); includes 9 minority (1 Black or African American, non-Hispanic/Latino; 5 Asian, non-Hispanic/Latino; 3 Hispanic/Latino), 5 international. Average age 30. 75 applicants, 24% accepted, 11 enrolled. In 2017, 10 master's, 4 doctorates awarded. Terminal master's awarded for partial completion of doctoral program. *Degree requirements:* For master's, thesis; for doctorate, comprehensive exam, thesis/dissertation, ethics class, 2 teaching assistantships. *Entrance requirements:* For master's, MCAT or GRE, doctoral-level clinical degree or completed pre-clinical training at accredited medical school, transcripts, statement of purpose, 3 letters of recommendation; for doctorate, GRE General Test, transcripts, statement of purpose, 3 letters of recommendation. Additional exam requirements/recommendations for international students: Required—TOEFL (minimum score 600 paper-based; 104 iBT), IELTS (minimum score 7). *Application deadline:* For fall admission, 12/1 for domestic and international students. Application fee: $90. Electronic applications accepted. *Financial support:* In 2017–18, 13 students received support, including fellowships with full tuition reimbursements available (averaging $31,000 per year), research assistantships with full tuition reimbursements available (averaging $31,000 per year); institutionally sponsored loans, scholarships/grants, traineeships, and health care benefits also available. Financial award application deadline: 12/1. *Faculty research:* Biostatistics, epidemiology, health services research. *Unit head:* Diane Sperling Lauderdale, PhD, Chair, E-mail: dlauderd@uchicago.edu. *Application contact:* Michele Thompson, Graduate Student Affairs Administrator, 773-834-1836, E-mail: mthompso@uchicago.edu.
Website: http://health.bsd.uchicago.edu/

University of Cincinnati, Graduate School, College of Education, Criminal Justice, and Human Services, School of Human Services, Health Promotion and Education Program, Cincinnati, OH 45221. Offers exercise and fitness (MS); health education (PhD); public and community health (MS); public health (MPH). *Accreditation:* NCATE. *Program availability:* Part-time, evening/weekend. *Degree requirements:* For master's, thesis or alternative; for doctorate, thesis/dissertation. *Entrance requirements:* For master's and doctorate, GRE General Test. Additional exam requirements/recommendations for international students: Required—TOEFL (minimum score 580 paper-based). Electronic applications accepted. *Expenses: Tuition, area resident:* Full-time $14,468. Tuition, state resident: full-time $14,968; part-time $754 per credit hour. Tuition, nonresident: full-time $24,210; part-time $1311 per credit hour. *International tuition:* $26,460 full-time. *Required fees:* $3958; $84 per credit hour. One-time fee: $85 full-time. Tuition and fees vary according to course load, degree level and program.

University of Delaware, College of Health Sciences, Department of Behavioral Health and Nutrition, Newark, DE 19716. Offers health promotion (MS); human nutrition (MS). *Program availability:* Part-time. *Degree requirements:* For master's, thesis. *Entrance requirements:* For master's, GRE General Test, interview, minimum GPA of 3.0. Additional exam requirements/recommendations for international students: Required—TOEFL (minimum score 550 paper-based). Electronic applications accepted. *Faculty research:* Sport biomechanics, rehabilitation biomechanics, vascular dynamics.

University of Georgia, College of Public Health, Department of Health Promotion and Behavior, Athens, GA 30602. Offers MA, MPH, Dr PH, PhD. *Accreditation:* NCATE (one or more programs are accredited). *Degree requirements:* For master's, thesis (MA); for doctorate, thesis/dissertation. *Entrance requirements:* For master's, GRE General Test or MAT; for doctorate, GRE General Test. Electronic applications accepted.

The University of Kansas, Graduate Studies, School of Architecture and Design, Department of Architecture, Lawrence, KS 66045. Offers architectural acoustics (Certificate); architecture (M Arch, PhD); health and wellness (Certificate); historic preservation (Certificate); urban design (Certificate). *Students:* 91 full-time (43 women), 14 part-time (6 women); includes 14 minority (3 Black or African American, non-Hispanic/Latino; 4 Asian, non-Hispanic/Latino; 4 Hispanic/Latino; 3 Two or more races, non-Hispanic/Latino), 21 international. Average age 25. 100 applicants, 52% accepted, 20 enrolled. In 2017, 77 master's, 7 doctorates, 5 other advanced degrees awarded. Terminal master's awarded for partial completion of doctoral program. *Entrance requirements:* For master's, GRE, transcript; resume; minimum GPA of 3.0; statement of purpose; letters of recommendation; portfolio of design work, or samples of written work or other creative artifacts produced if previous degree was not in a design-related discipline; for doctorate, GRE, transcript, resume, minimum GPA of 3.0, statement of purpose, letters of recommendation, research-informed writing sample, exhibit of work illustrating applicant's interests and abilities in areas related to the design disciplines. Additional exam requirements/recommendations for international students: Required—TOEFL, IELTS. *Application deadline:* For fall admission, 1/15 priority date for domestic and international students; for summer admission, 1/15 priority date for domestic and international students. Application fee: $65 ($85 for international students). Electronic applications accepted. *Financial support:* Fellowships, research assistantships, teaching assistantships, scholarships/grants, health care benefits, and unspecified assistantships available. Financial award application deadline: 1/15; financial award applicants required to submit FAFSA. *Faculty research:* Design build, sustainability, emergent technology, healthy places, urban design. *Unit head:* Prof. Jae Chang, Chair, 785-864-1446, E-mail: jdchang@ku.edu. *Application contact:* Gera Elliott, Admissions Coordinator, 785-864-3167, Fax: 785-864-5185, E-mail: archku@ku.edu.
Website: http://architecture.ku.edu/

University of Kentucky, Graduate School, College of Education, Program in Kinesiology and Health Promotion, Lexington, KY 40506-0032. Offers biomechanics (MS); exercise physiology (MS, PhD); exercise science (PhD); health promotion (MS, Ed D); physical education training (Ed D); sport leadership (MS); teaching and coaching (MS). Terminal master's awarded for partial completion of doctoral program. *Degree requirements:* For master's, comprehensive exam, thesis optional; for doctorate, comprehensive exam, thesis/dissertation. *Entrance requirements:* For master's, GRE General Test, minimum undergraduate GPA of 2.75; for doctorate, GRE General Test, minimum graduate GPA of 3.0. Additional exam requirements/recommendations for international students: Required—TOEFL (minimum score 550 paper-based). Electronic applications accepted.

University of Lynchburg, Graduate Studies, Master of Public Health Program, Lynchburg, VA 24501-3199. Offers public health (MPH), including health promotion. *Program availability:* Part-time. *Faculty:* 5 full-time (4 women). *Students:* 20 full-time (18 women), 7 part-time (4 women); includes 10 minority (8 Black or African American, non-Hispanic/Latino; 2 Hispanic/Latino), 3 international. Average age 27. 34 applicants, 100% accepted, 17 enrolled. In 2017, 14 master's awarded. *Degree requirements:* For master's, internship, capstone project. *Entrance requirements:* For master's, GRE. Additional exam requirements/recommendations for international students: Required—TOEFL (minimum score 550 paper-based; 80 iBT), IELTS (minimum score 6). *Application deadline:* For fall admission, 7/31 for domestic and international students; for spring admission, 11/30 for domestic and international students. Applications are processed on a rolling basis. Application fee: $30. Electronic applications accepted. Application fee is waived when completed online. *Expenses:* $510 per credit hour tuition, $100 fees. *Financial support:* Scholarships/grants and unspecified assistantships available. Financial award applicants required to submit FAFSA. *Unit head:* Dr. Charlotte Guynes, Director, 434-544-8644, E-mail: guynes@lynchburg.edu. *Application contact:* Ellen Thompson, Graduate Admissions Counselor, 434-544-8841, E-mail: thompson_e@lynchburg.edu.
Website: https://www.lynchburg.edu/graduate/master-of-public-health/

University of Massachusetts Lowell, College of Health Sciences, School of Nursing, PhD Program in Nursing, Lowell, MA 01854. Offers PhD. *Accreditation:* AACN. *Degree requirements:* For doctorate, thesis/dissertation, qualifying examination. *Entrance requirements:* For doctorate, GRE General Test, master's degree in nursing with minimum GPA of 3.3, current MA RN license, 2 years of professional nursing experience, 3 letters of recommendation.

University of Memphis, Graduate School, School of Health Studies, Memphis, TN 38152. Offers faith and health (Graduate Certificate); health studies (MS), including exercise, sport and movement sciences, health promotion, physical education teacher education; nutrition (MS), including clinical nutrition, environmental nutrition, nutrition science; sport nutrition and dietary supplementation (Graduate Certificate). *Program availability:* 100% online. *Faculty:* 19 full-time (10 women), 2 part-time/adjunct (both women). In 2017, 42 master's awarded. *Degree requirements:* For master's, comprehensive exam, thesis or alternative, culminating experience; for Graduate Certificate, practicum. *Entrance requirements:* For master's, GRE or PRAXIS II, letters of recommendation, statement of goals, minimum undergraduate GPA of 2.5; for Graduate Certificate, minimum undergraduate GPA of 2.5. Additional exam requirements/recommendations for international students: Required—TOEFL (minimum score 550 paper-based; 79 iBT). *Application deadline:* For fall admission, 4/15 priority date for domestic students; for spring admission, 10/15 priority date for domestic students; for summer admission, 4/15 priority date for domestic students. Application fee: $35 ($60 for international students). *Expenses:* Contact institution. *Financial support:* In 2017–18, 33 research assistantships (averaging $11,930 per year), 4 teaching assistantships (averaging $10,000 per year) were awarded; career-related internships or fieldwork, Federal Work-Study, scholarships/grants, and unspecified assistantships also available. Financial award application deadline: 2/1; financial award applicants required to submit FAFSA. *Unit head:* Dr. Richard J. Bloomer, Director, 901-678-4316, Fax: 901-678-3591, E-mail: rbloomer@memphis.edu. *Application contact:* Dr. Lawrence Weiss, Director of Graduate Programs, 901-678-5037, E-mail: lweiss@memphis.edu.
Website: http://www.memphis.edu/shs/

University of Michigan, School of Public Health, Department of Health Behavior and Health Education, Ann Arbor, MI 48109. Offers MPH, PhD, MPH/MSW. PhD offered through the Rackham Graduate School. *Accreditation:* CEPH (one or more programs are accredited). Terminal master's awarded for partial completion of doctoral program. *Degree requirements:* For doctorate, oral defense of dissertation, preliminary exam. *Entrance requirements:* For master's, GRE General Test (preferred); MCAT; for doctorate, GRE General Test. Additional exam requirements/recommendations for international students: Required—TOEFL (minimum score 100 iBT). Electronic applications accepted. *Expenses:* Tuition, state resident: full-time $22,368; part-time $1201 per credit hour. Tuition, nonresident: full-time $45,156; part-time $2467 per credit hour. *Required fees:* $376 per term. Tuition and fees vary according to course load, degree level and program. *Faculty research:* Empowerment theory; structure, culture, and health; health disparities; community-based participatory research; health and medical decision-making.

University of Mississippi, Graduate School, School of Applied Sciences, University, MS 38677. Offers communicative disorders (MS); criminal justice (MCJ); exercise science (MS); food and nutrition services (MS); health and kinesiology (PhD); health promotion (MS); nutrition and hospitality management (PhD); park and recreation management (MA); social welfare (PhD); social work (MSW). *Faculty:* 66 full-time (38 women), 33 part-time/adjunct (14 women). *Students:* 182 full-time (139 women), 41 part-time (27 women); includes 49 minority (41 Black or African American, non-Hispanic/Latino; 1 American Indian or Alaska Native, non-Hispanic/Latino; 3 Asian, non-Hispanic/Latino; 3 Hispanic/Latino; 1 Two or more races, non-Hispanic/Latino), 13 international. Average age 26. *Entrance requirements:* For master's, GRE General Test, minimum GPA of 3.0. Additional exam requirements/recommendations for international students: Required—TOEFL. *Application deadline:* For fall admission, 4/1 for domestic students; for spring admission, 10/1 for domestic students. Applications are processed on a rolling basis. Application fee: $50. Electronic applications accepted. *Financial support:* Scholarships/grants available. Financial award application deadline: 3/1; financial award applicants required to submit FAFSA. *Unit head:* Dr. Teresa C. Carithers, Dean, 662-915-1081, Fax: 662-915-5717, E-mail: applsci@olemiss.edu.

University of Nebraska–Lincoln, Graduate College, College of Education and Human Sciences, Department of Nutrition and Health Sciences, Lincoln, NE 68588. Offers community nutrition and health promotion (MS); nutrition (MS, PhD); nutrition and exercise (MS); nutrition and health sciences (MS, PhD). *Degree requirements:* For master's, thesis optional. *Entrance requirements:* For master's, GRE General Test. Additional exam requirements/recommendations for international students: Required—TOEFL (minimum score 550 paper-based). Electronic applications accepted. *Faculty research:* Foods/food service administration, community nutrition science, diet-health relationships.

University of Nebraska Medical Center, Department of Health Promotion, Social and Behavioral Health, Omaha, NE 68198. Offers health promotion and disease prevention research (PhD). *Program availability:* Part-time. *Degree requirements:* For doctorate, comprehensive exam, thesis/dissertation, teaching experience. *Entrance requirements:* For doctorate, GRE, official transcripts, master's or other advanced degree, written statement of career goals, three letters of recommendation. Additional exam requirements/recommendations for international students: Required—TOEFL (minimum score 550 paper-based; 80 iBT). Electronic applications accepted. *Expenses:* Tuition, state resident: full-time $8451; part-time $4225 per semester. Tuition, nonresident: full-time $24,219; part-time $11,295 per semester. *Required fees:* $589; $117 per term.

University of North Alabama, College of Education, Department of Health, Physical Education, and Recreation, Florence, AL 35632-0001. Offers health and human performance (MS), including exercise science, kinesiology, wellness and health promotion. *Program availability:* Part-time. *Faculty:* 7 full-time (2 women), 1 part-time/adjunct (0 women). *Students:* 14 full-time (10 women), 14 part-time (6 women); includes 4 minority (all Black or African American, non-Hispanic/Latino), 3 international. Average age 25. 22 applicants, 82% accepted, 9 enrolled. In 2017, 7 master's awarded. *Degree requirements:* For master's, comprehensive exam (for some programs), thesis optional. *Entrance requirements:* For master's, MAT or GRE, 3 letters of recommendation, essay. Additional exam requirements/recommendations for international students: Required—TOEFL (minimum score 79 iBT), IELTS (minimum score 6), PTE (minimum score 54). *Application deadline:* Applications are processed on a rolling basis. Application fee: $50 ($100 for international students). Electronic applications accepted. *Expenses:* Tuition, state resident: full-time $7824; part-time $5943 per year. Tuition, nonresident: full-time $15,648; part-time $11,736 per year. *Required fees:* $3064; $2298 per unit. Tuition and fees vary according to course load and reciprocity agreements. *Financial support:* In 2017–18, 19 students received support. Federal Work-Study, scholarships/grants, and unspecified assistantships available. Financial award application deadline: 2/1; financial award applicants required to submit FAFSA. *Total annual research expenditures:* $13,976. *Unit head:* Dr. Thomas E. Coates, Chair, 256-765-4377. *Application contact:* Hillary N. Coats, Graduate Admissions Coordinator, 256-765-4447, E-mail: graduate@una.edu.
Website: https://www.una.edu/hper/index.html

The University of North Carolina at Chapel Hill, Graduate School, Gillings School of Global Public Health, Public Health Leadership Program, Chapel Hill, NC 27599. Offers health care and prevention (MPH); leadership (MPH); occupational health nursing (MPH). *Program availability:* Part-time, 100% online, blended/hybrid learning. *Faculty:* 12 full-time (10 women), 37 part-time/adjunct (25 women). *Students:* 89 full-time (61 women), 66 part-time (47 women); includes 56 minority (17 Black or African American, non-Hispanic/Latino; 16 Asian, non-Hispanic/Latino; 11 Hispanic/Latino; 12 Two or more races, non-Hispanic/Latino), 9 international. Average age 34. 111 applicants, 93% accepted, 68 enrolled. In 2017, 73 master's awarded. *Degree requirements:* For master's, comprehensive exam, thesis (MS), paper (MPH). *Entrance requirements:* For master's, GRE General Test or MCAT, three years of public health experience (recommended), three letters of recommendation (academic and/or professional; academic preferred). Additional exam requirements/recommendations for international students: Required—TOEFL (minimum score 90 iBT), IELTS (minimum score 7). *Application deadline:* For fall admission, 2/2 for domestic and international students. Applications are processed on a rolling basis. Application fee: $85. Electronic applications accepted. *Financial support:* Career-related internships or fieldwork, institutionally sponsored loans, traineeships, and health care benefits available. Financial award application deadline: 12/10; financial award applicants required to submit FAFSA. *Faculty research:* Occupational health issues, clinical outcomes, prenatal and early childcare, adolescent health, effectiveness of home visiting, issues in occupational health nursing, community-based interventions. *Unit head:* Dr. Anna P. Schenck, Director, 919-843-8580, E-mail: anna.schenck@unc.edu. *Application contact:* Kristen Hurdle, Student Services Specialist, 919-843-7629, E-mail: kristen_hurdle@unc.edu.
Website: http://sph.unc.edu/phlp/phlp/

University of Northern Iowa, Graduate College, College of Education, School of Kinesiology, Allied Health and Human Services, MA Program in Health Education, Cedar Falls, IA 50614. Offers community health education (MA); health promotion/fitness management (MA); school health education (MA). *Program availability:* Part-time, evening/weekend. *Degree requirements:* For master's, comprehensive exam, thesis or alternative. *Entrance requirements:* For master's, minimum GPA of 3.0. Additional exam requirements/recommendations for international students: Required—TOEFL (minimum score 500 paper-based; 61 iBT). Electronic applications accepted.

University of Oklahoma, College of Arts and Sciences, Department of Health and Exercise Science, Norman, OK 73019. Offers exercise physiology (MS, PhD); health and exercise science (MS); health promotion (MS, PhD). *Faculty:* 10 full-time (5 women), 1 part-time/adjunct (0 women). *Students:* 36 full-time (13 women), 16 part-time (8 women); includes 15 minority (2 Black or African American, non-Hispanic/Latino; 2 Asian, non-Hispanic/Latino; 5 Hispanic/Latino; 1 Native Hawaiian or other Pacific Islander, non-Hispanic/Latino; 5 Two or more races, non-Hispanic/Latino), 7 international. Average age 26. 28 applicants, 50% accepted, 14 enrolled. In 2017, 12 master's, 4 doctorates awarded. *Degree requirements:* For master's, comprehensive exam (for some programs), thesis; for doctorate, comprehensive exam, thesis/dissertation. *Entrance requirements:* For master's and doctorate, GRE. Additional exam requirements/recommendations for international students: Required—TOEFL (minimum score 79 iBT) or IELTS (minimum score 6.5). *Application deadline:* For fall admission, 2/1 priority date for domestic and international students. Applications are processed on a rolling basis. Application fee: $50 ($100 for international students). Electronic applications accepted. *Expenses:* Tuition, state resident: full-time $5119; part-time $213.30 per credit hour. Tuition, nonresident: full-time $19,778; part-time $824.10 per credit hour. *Required fees:* $3458; $133.55 per credit hour. $126.50 per semester. *Financial support:* In 2017–18, 51 students received support, including 46 teaching assistantships with full tuition reimbursements available (averaging $12,396 per year); health care benefits, tuition waivers (full), and unspecified assistantships also available. Financial award application deadline: 6/1; financial award applicants required to submit FAFSA. *Faculty research:* Health promotion, neuromuscular exercise physiology, aging, endocrine and bone metabolism, behavioral science. *Unit head:* Dr. Michael G. Bemben, Professor/Chair, 405-325-2717, Fax: 405-325-0594, E-mail: mgbemben@ou.edu. *Application contact:* Dr. Marshall Cheney, Assistant Professor/Graduate Liaison, 405-325-6322, Fax: 405-325-0594, E-mail: marshall@ou.edu.
Website: http://www.ou.edu/cas/hes

University of Oklahoma Health Sciences Center, Graduate College, College of Public Health, Department of Health Promotion Sciences, Oklahoma City, OK 73190. Offers MPH, MS, Dr PH, PhD. *Accreditation:* CEPH (one or more programs are accredited). *Program availability:* Part-time. *Degree requirements:* For master's, comprehensive exam, thesis (for some programs); for doctorate, 2 foreign languages, comprehensive exam, thesis/dissertation. *Entrance requirements:* For master's, letters of recommendation, resume; for doctorate, GRE, letters of recommendation. Additional exam requirements/recommendations for international students: Required—TOEFL (minimum score 570 paper-based). *Faculty research:* Health education, school health, health behavior, American Indian health.

University of Puerto Rico–Medical Sciences Campus, Graduate School of Public Health, Department of Human Development, Program in School Health Promotion, San Juan, PR 00936-5067. Offers Certificate.

University of South Carolina, The Graduate School, Arnold School of Public Health, Department of Health Promotion, Education, and Behavior, Columbia, SC 29208. Offers health education (MAT); health promotion, education, and behavior (MPH, MS, MSPH, Dr PH, PhD); school health education (Certificate); MSW/MPH. MAT offered in cooperation with the College of Education. *Accreditation:* CEPH (one or more programs are accredited); NCATE (one or more programs are accredited). *Program availability:* Part-time. *Degree requirements:* For master's, comprehensive exam, thesis or alternative, practicum (MPH), project (MS); for doctorate, comprehensive exam, thesis/dissertation. *Entrance requirements:* For master's and doctorate, GRE General Test. Additional exam requirements/recommendations for international students: Required—TOEFL (minimum score 570 paper-based; 75 iBT). Electronic applications accepted. *Faculty research:* Health disparities and inequalities in communities, global health and nutrition, cancer and HIV/AIDS prevention, health communication, policy and program design.

University of South Carolina, The Graduate School, Arnold School of Public Health, Program in Physical Activity and Public Health, Columbia, SC 29208. Offers MPH. *Accreditation:* CEPH. *Program availability:* Part-time. *Degree requirements:* For master's, comprehensive exam, practicum. *Entrance requirements:* For master's, GRE. Additional exam requirements/recommendations for international students: Required—TOEFL (minimum score 570 paper-based). Electronic applications accepted.

University of Southern California, Keck School of Medicine and Graduate School, Graduate Programs in Medicine, Department of Preventive Medicine, Master of Public Health Program, Los Angeles, CA 90032. Offers biostatistics and epidemiology (MPH); child and family health (MPH); environmental health (MPH); geohealth (MPH); global health leadership (MPH); health communication (MPH); health education and promotion (MPH); public health policy (MPH). *Accreditation:* CEPH. *Program availability:* Part-time, evening/weekend. *Faculty:* 47 full-time (35 women), 13 part-time/adjunct (8 women). *Students:* 258 full-time (204 women), 61 part-time (50 women); includes 167 minority (28 Black or African American, non-Hispanic/Latino; 1 American Indian or Alaska Native, non-Hispanic/Latino; 61 Asian, non-Hispanic/Latino; 64 Hispanic/Latino; 4 Native Hawaiian or other Pacific Islander, non-Hispanic/Latino; 9 Two or more races, non-Hispanic/Latino), 28 international. Average age 26. 378 applicants, 53% accepted, 87 enrolled. In 2017, 91 master's awarded. *Degree requirements:* For master's, practicum, final report, oral presentation. *Entrance requirements:* For master's, GRE General Test, MCAT, GMAT, minimum GPA of 3.0. Additional exam requirements/recommendations for international students: Required—TOEFL (minimum score 600 paper-based; 90 iBT). *Application deadline:* For fall admission, 12/1 priority date for domestic students, 5/1 priority date for international students; for spring admission, 9/1 priority date for domestic and international students; for summer admission, 3/1 for domestic and international students. Applications are processed on a rolling basis. Application fee: $90. Electronic applications accepted. *Expenses:* Contact institution. *Financial support:* Career-related internships or fieldwork, Federal Work-Study, institutionally sponsored loans, and scholarships/grants available. Support available to part-time students. Financial award application deadline: 5/4; financial award applicants required to submit CSS PROFILE or FAFSA. *Faculty research:* Cancer and heart disease epidemiology and prevention, mass media and health communication research, effects of air pollution on health, tobacco control, global health. *Total annual research expenditures:* $7 million. *Unit head:* Dr. Louise A. Rohrbach, Director, 323-442-8237, Fax: 323-442-8297, E-mail: rohrbac@usc.edu. *Application contact:* Valerie Burris, Admissions Counselor, 323-442-7257, Fax: 323-442-8297, E-mail: valeriem@usc.edu.
Website: http://mph.usc.edu/

The University of Tennessee, Graduate School, College of Education, Health and Human Sciences, Program in Health Promotion and Health Education, Knoxville, TN 37996. Offers MS. *Program availability:* Part-time. *Degree requirements:* For master's, thesis optional. *Entrance requirements:* For master's, minimum GPA of 2.7. Additional exam requirements/recommendations for international students: Required—TOEFL. Electronic applications accepted.

The University of Texas Health Science Center at Houston, School of Public Health, Houston, TX 77030. Offers behavioral science (PhD); biostatistics (MPH, MS, PhD); environmental health (MPH); epidemiology (MPH, MS, PhD); general public health (Certificate); genomics and bioinformatics (Certificate); health disparities (Certificate); health promotion/health education (MPH, Dr PH); healthcare management (Certificate); management, policy and community health (MPH, Dr PH, PhD); maternal and child health (Certificate); public health informatics (Certificate); DDS/MPH; JD/MPH; MBA/MPH; MD/MPH; MGPS/MPH; MP Aff/MPH; MS/MPH; MSN/MPH; MSW/MPH; PhD/MPH. Specific programs are offered at each of our six campuses in Texas (Austin, Brownsville, Dallas, El Paso, Houston, and San Antonio). *Accreditation:* CEPH. *Program availability:* Part-time. *Faculty:* 140 full-time (74 women), 23 part-time/adjunct (14 women). *Students:* 604 full-time (446 women), 534 part-time (384 women); includes 504 minority (106 Black or African American, non-Hispanic/Latino; 177 Asian, non-Hispanic/Latino; 88 Hispanic/Latino; 1 Native Hawaiian or other Pacific Islander, non-Hispanic/Latino; 132 Two or more races, non-Hispanic/Latino). Average age 31. 1,425 applicants, 58% accepted, 423 enrolled. In 2017, 315 master's, 68 doctorates awarded. *Degree requirements:* For master's, thesis (for some programs); for doctorate, comprehensive exam, thesis/dissertation. *Entrance requirements:* For master's and doctorate, GRE General Test. Additional exam requirements/recommendations for international students: Required—TOEFL (minimum score 600 paper-based, 100 iBT) or IELTS (7.5). *Application deadline:* For fall admission, 3/1 for domestic and international students; for spring admission, 10/1 for domestic and international students; for summer admission, 3/1 for domestic students. Applications are processed on a rolling basis. Application fee: $135. Electronic applications accepted. *Expenses:* $233 per semester credit hour resident tuition, $980 per semester credit hour non-resident tuition. *Financial support:* Fellowships, research assistantships, teaching assistantships, career-related internships or fieldwork, institutionally sponsored loans, scholarships/grants, traineeships, health care benefits, and unspecified assistantships available. Support available to part-time students. Financial award application deadline: 5/5; financial award applicants required to submit FAFSA. *Faculty research:* Chronic and infectious disease epidemiology; health promotion and health education; applied and theoretical biostatistics; healthcare management, policy and economics; environmental and occupational health. *Total annual research expenditures:* $47.8 million. *Unit head:* Dr. Susan Emery, Senior Associate Dean of Academic and Research Affairs. *Application contact:* Elvis Parada, Manager of Admissions and Recruitment, 713-500-9028, Fax: 713-500-9068, E-mail: elvis.a.parada@uth.tmc.edu.
Website: https://sph.uth.edu

The University of Toledo, College of Graduate Studies, College of Medicine and Life Sciences, Department of Public Health and Preventative Medicine, Toledo, OH 43606-3390. Offers biostatistics and epidemiology (Certificate); contemporary gerontological practice (Certificate); environmental and occupational health and safety (MPH); epidemiology (Certificate); global public health (Certificate); health promotion and education (MPH); industrial hygiene (MSOH); medical and health science teaching and learning (Certificate); occupational health (Certificate); public health administration (MPH); public health and emergency response (Certificate); public health epidemiology (MPH); public health nutrition (MPH); MD/MPH. *Program availability:* Part-time, evening/weekend. *Degree requirements:* For master's, thesis or alternative. *Entrance requirements:* For master's, GRE, minimum undergraduate GPA of 3.0, three letters of recommendation, statement of purpose, transcripts from all prior institutions attended, resume; for Certificate, minimum undergraduate GPA of 3.0, three letters of recommendation, statement of purpose, transcripts from all prior institutions attended, resume. Additional exam requirements/recommendations for international students: Required—TOEFL (minimum score 550 paper-based; 80 iBT), IELTS (minimum score 6.5). Electronic applications accepted.

The University of Toledo, College of Graduate Studies, College of Nursing, Department of Health Promotions, Outcomes, Systems, and Policy, Toledo, OH 43606-3390. Offers MSN, DNP. *Program availability:* Online learning. *Degree requirements:* For doctorate, thesis/dissertation or alternative, evidence-based project. *Entrance requirements:* For doctorate, GRE (taken within the past 5 years), personal statement, resume/curriculum vitae, letters of recommendation, documented supervised clinical hours in master's program, Nursing CAS application, UT supplemental application. Additional exam requirements/recommendations for international students: Required—TOEFL (minimum score 550 paper-based; 80 iBT). Electronic applications accepted.

University of Toronto, School of Graduate Studies, Department of Public Health Sciences, Toronto, ON M5S 1A1, Canada. Offers biostatistics (M Sc, PhD); community health (M Sc); community nutrition (MPH), including nutrition and dietetics; epidemiology (MPH, PhD); family and community medicine (MPH); occupational and environmental health (MPH); social and behavioral health science (PhD); social and behavioral health sciences (MPH), including health promotion. *Accreditation:* CAHME (one or more programs are accredited). *Program availability:* Part-time. *Degree requirements:* For master's, thesis (for some programs), practicum; for doctorate, comprehensive exam, thesis/dissertation, oral thesis defense. *Entrance requirements:* For master's, 2 letters of reference, relevant professional/research experience, minimum B average in final year; for doctorate, 2 letters of reference, relevant professional/research experience, minimum B+ average. Additional exam requirements/recommendations for international students: Required—TOEFL (minimum score 580 paper-based; 93 iBT), TWE (minimum score 5). Electronic applications accepted. *Expenses:* Contact institution.

University of Utah, Graduate School, College of Health, Health Promotion and Education Program, Salt Lake City, UT 84112. Offers M Phil, MS, PhD. *Program availability:* Part-time. *Faculty:* 5 full-time (2 women), 9 part-time/adjunct (5 women). *Students:* 38 full-time (32 women), 3 part-time (1 woman); includes 5 minority (1 Black or African American, non-Hispanic/Latino; 1 American Indian or Alaska Native, non-Hispanic/Latino; 2 Asian, non-Hispanic/Latino; 1 Hispanic/Latino), 2 international. Average age 29. 26 applicants, 69% accepted, 16 enrolled. In 2017, 24 master's, 3 doctorates awarded. *Degree requirements:* For master's, comprehensive exam, thesis or alternative, field experience; for doctorate, comprehensive exam, thesis/dissertation, field experience. *Entrance requirements:* For master's, GRE, minimum GPA of 3.0; for doctorate, GRE, minimum GPA of 3.2. Additional exam requirements/recommendations for international students: Required—TOEFL (minimum score 550 paper-based; 80 iBT). *Application deadline:* For fall admission, 1/15 for domestic and international students. Application fee: $55 ($65 for international students). Electronic applications accepted. *Financial support:* In 2017–18, 11 students received support, including 3 research assistantships with full tuition reimbursements available (averaging $14,500 per year), 6 teaching assistantships with full tuition reimbursements available (averaging $14,500 per year); health care benefits and unspecified assistantships also available. Financial award application deadline: 3/1; financial award applicants required to submit FAFSA. *Faculty research:* Health behavior and counseling, health service administration, evaluation of health programs. *Unit head:* Dr. Tim Brusseau, Program Director, 801-581-7558, Fax: 801-585-3992, E-mail: tim.brusseau@utah.edu. *Application contact:* Dr. Maria Newton, Director of Graduate Studies, 801-581-7558, Fax: 801-585-3992, E-mail: maria.newton@health.utah.edu.
Website: http://www.health.utah.edu/healthed/index.htm

University of Vermont, Graduate College, College of Nursing and Health Sciences, Program in Physical Activity and Wellness Science, Burlington, VT 05405. Offers MS. *Entrance requirements:* Additional exam requirements/recommendations for international students: Required—TOEFL (minimum iBT score of 90) or IELTS (6.5). *Application deadline:* For fall admission, 4/1 for domestic and international students. Application fee: $65. Electronic applications accepted. *Expenses:* Tuition, state resident: full-time $11,628; part-time $646 per credit. Tuition, nonresident: full-time $29,340; part-time $1630 per credit. *Required fees:* $1994; $10 per credit. Tuition and fees vary according to course load and program. *Financial support:* Federal Work-Study and scholarships/grants available. *Application contact:* Kristen Cella, Admissions Specialist, 802-656-3858, E-mail: cnhsgrad@uvm.edu.
Website: https://www.uvm.edu/cnhs/rms/master-science-physical-activity-and-wellness-science-0

University of West Florida, Usha Kundu, MD College of Health, Department of Exercise Science and Community Health, Pensacola, FL 32514-5750. Offers health promotion (MS); health, leisure, and exercise science (MS), including exercise science, physical education. *Program availability:* Part-time, evening/weekend. *Degree requirements:* For master's, thesis or alternative. *Entrance requirements:* For master's, GRE or MAT, official transcripts; minimum GPA of 3.0; letter of intent; three personal references; work experience as reflected in resume. Additional exam requirements/recommendations for international students: Required—TOEFL (minimum score 550 paper-based).

University of Wisconsin–Milwaukee, Graduate School, Joseph J. Zilber School of Public Health, Program in Public Health, Milwaukee, WI 53201-0413. Offers biostatistics (MPH); community and behavioral health promotion (MPH); environmental health sciences (MPH); epidemiology (MPH, PhD); public and population health (Graduate Certificate); public health policy and administration (MPH); public health: biostatistics (PhD); public health: community and behavioral health promotion (PhD). *Students:* 62 full-time (53 women), 23 part-time (17 women); includes 24 minority (5 Black or African American, non-Hispanic/Latino; 11 Asian, non-Hispanic/Latino; 8 Two or more races, non-Hispanic/Latino), 10 international. Average age 31. 65 applicants, 74% accepted, 34 enrolled. In 2017, 28 master's, 1 doctorate awarded. Electronic applications accepted. *Application contact:* Darcie K. G. Warren, Graduate Program Manager, 414-229-5633, E-mail: darcie@uwm.edu.

University of Wisconsin–Parkside, College of Natural and Health Sciences, Program in Health and Wellness Management, Kenosha, WI 53141-2000. Offers MS. *Program availability:* Online learning. *Entrance requirements:* For master's, bachelor's degree with minimum GPA of 3.0.

University of Wisconsin–Stevens Point, College of Professional Studies, School of Health Promotion and Human Development, Stevens Point, WI 54481-3897. Offers human and community resources (MS); nutritional sciences (MS). *Program availability:* Part-time. *Degree requirements:* For master's, thesis or alternative. *Entrance requirements:* For master's, minimum GPA of 2.75. *Application deadline:* For fall admission, 5/1 priority date for domestic students. Applications are processed on a rolling basis. Application fee: $45. *Expenses:* Tuition, state resident: part-time $562.55 per credit. Tuition, nonresident: part-time $1085.04 per credit. Part-time tuition and fees vary according to course load, program and reciprocity agreements. *Financial support:* Research assistantships, teaching assistantships, career-related internships or fieldwork, Federal Work-Study, and unspecified assistantships available. Support available to part-time students. Financial award application deadline: 5/1; financial award applicants required to submit FAFSA.
Website: http://www.uwsp.edu/hphd/

University of Wyoming, College of Health Sciences, Division of Kinesiology and Health, Laramie, WY 82071. Offers MS. *Accreditation:* NCATE. *Program availability:* Part-time, online learning. *Degree requirements:* For master's, comprehensive exam (for some programs), thesis (for some programs). *Entrance requirements:* For master's, GRE General Test, minimum GPA of 3.0. Additional exam requirements/recommendations for international students: Required—TOEFL. Electronic applications accepted. *Faculty research:* Teacher effectiveness, effects of exercising on heart function, physiological responses of overtraining, psychological benefits of physical activity, health behavior.

Utah State University, School of Graduate Studies, Emma Eccles Jones College of Education and Human Services, Department of Kinesiology and Health Science, Logan, UT 84322. Offers fitness promotion (MS); health and human movement (MS); pathokinesiology (PhD); physical and sport eductaion (M Ed); public health (MPH). *Program availability:* Part-time, evening/weekend, online learning. *Degree requirements:* For master's, thesis (for some programs). *Entrance requirements:* For master's, GRE General Test or MAT, minimum GPA of 3.0. Additional exam requirements/recommendations for international students: Required—TOEFL. *Faculty research:* Sport psychology intervention, motor learning biomechanics, pedagogy, physiology.

Walden University, Graduate Programs, School of Health Sciences, Minneapolis, MN 55401. Offers clinical research administration (MS, Graduate Certificate); health education and promotion (MS, PhD), including behavioral health (PhD), disease surveillance (PhD), emergency preparedness (MS), general (MHA, MS), global health (PhD), health policy (PhD), health policy and advocacy (MS), population health (PhD); health informatics (MS); health services (PhD), including community health, healthcare administration, leadership, public health policy, self-designed; healthcare administration (MHA, DHA), including general (MHA, MS); leadership and organizational development (MHA); public health (MPH, Dr PH, PhD, Graduate Certificate), including community health education (PhD), epidemiology (PhD); systems policy (MHA). *Program availability:* Part-time, evening/weekend, online only, 100% online. *Degree requirements:* For doctorate, thesis/dissertation, residency. *Entrance requirements:* For master's, bachelor's degree or higher; minimum GPA of 2.5; official transcripts; goal statement (for some programs); access to computer and Internet; for doctorate, master's degree or higher; three years of related professional or academic experience (preferred); minimum GPA of 3.0; goal statement and current resume (for select programs); official transcripts; access to computer and Internet; for Graduate Certificate, relevant work experience; access to computer and Internet. Additional exam requirements/recommendations for international students: Required—TOEFL (minimum score 550 paper-based, 79 iBT), IELTS (minimum score 6.5), Michigan English Language Assessment Battery (minimum score 82), or PTE (minimum score 53). Electronic applications accepted.

Wilfrid Laurier University, Faculty of Graduate and Postdoctoral Studies, Faculty of Science, Department of Kinesiology and Physical Education, Waterloo, ON N2L 3C5, Canada. Offers physical activity and health (M Sc). *Degree requirements:* For master's, thesis. *Entrance requirements:* For master's, honours degree in kinesiology, health, physical education with a minimum B+ in kinesiology and health-related courses. Additional exam requirements/recommendations for international students: Required—TOEFL (minimum score 89 iBT). Electronic applications accepted. *Faculty research:* Biomechanics, health, exercise physiology, motor control, sport psychology.

Wright State University, Boonshoft School of Medicine, Department of Population and Public Health Sciences, Dayton, OH 45435. Offers health promotion and education (MPH).

Industrial Hygiene

California State University, Northridge, Graduate Studies, College of Health and Human Development, Department of Environmental and Occupational Health, Northridge, CA 91330. Offers environmental and occupational health (MS); industrial hygiene (MS). *Accreditation:* CEPH. *Faculty:* 6. *Students:* 25 full-time (10 women), 34 part-time (18 women); includes 29 minority (2 Black or African American, non-Hispanic/Latino; 9 Asian, non-Hispanic/Latino; 16 Hispanic/Latino; 2 Two or more races, non-Hispanic/Latino), 7 international. Average age 29. 39 applicants, 67% accepted, 19 enrolled. In 2017, 18 master's awarded. *Degree requirements:* For master's, seminar, field experience, comprehensive exam or thesis. *Entrance requirements:* For master's, GRE General Test or minimum GPA of 3.0. Additional exam requirements/recommendations for international students: Required—TOEFL. *Application deadline:* For fall admission, 11/30 for domestic students. Application fee: $55. *Financial support:* Application deadline: 3/1. *Unit head:* Frankline Augustin, Chair, 818-677-7476.
Website: http://www.csun.edu/hhd/eoh/

Eastern Kentucky University, The Graduate School, College of Health Sciences, Program in Public Health, Richmond, KY 40475-3102. Offers community health education (MPH); environmental health science (MPH); industrial hygiene (MPH); public health nutrition (MPH). *Accreditation:* CEPH. *Degree requirements:* For master's, comprehensive exam, thesis optional, practicum, capstone course. *Entrance requirements:* For master's, GRE. *Faculty research:* Water quality, food safety, occupational health, air quality.

Industrial Hygiene

Montana Tech of The University of Montana, Department of Industrial Hygiene, Butte, MT 59701-8997. Offers MS. *Accreditation:* ABET. *Program availability:* Part-time, online learning. *Degree requirements:* For master's, comprehensive exam (for some programs), thesis. *Entrance requirements:* For master's, GRE or 5 years' work experience (for online program), minimum GPA of 3.0. Additional exam requirements/recommendations for international students: Required—TOEFL (minimum score 545 paper-based; 78 iBT), IELTS (minimum score 6.5). Electronic applications accepted. *Faculty research:* Ergonomics, metal bioavailability, aerosols, particulate sizing, respiration protection.

New York Medical College, School of Health Sciences and Practice, Valhalla, NY 10595. Offers behavioral sciences and health promotion (MPH); biostatistics (MS); children with special health care (Graduate Certificate); emergency preparedness (Graduate Certificate); environmental health science (MPH); epidemiology (MPH, MS); global health (Graduate Certificate); health education (Graduate Certificate); health policy and management (MPH, Dr PH); industrial hygiene (Graduate Certificate); pediatric dysphagia (Post-Graduate Certificate); physical therapy (DPT); public health (Graduate Certificate); speech-language pathology (MS). *Accreditation:* CEPH. *Program availability:* Part-time, evening/weekend, 100% online, blended/hybrid learning. *Faculty:* 48 full-time (33 women), 235 part-time/adjunct (141 women). *Students:* 221 full-time (153 women), 270 part-time (194 women); includes 202 minority (83 Black or African American, non-Hispanic/Latino; 2 American Indian or Alaska Native, non-Hispanic/Latino; 64 Asian, non-Hispanic/Latino; 47 Hispanic/Latino; 1 Native Hawaiian or other Pacific Islander, non-Hispanic/Latino; 5 Two or more races, non-Hispanic/Latino), 19 international. Average age 29. 1,118 applicants, 38% accepted, 169 enrolled. In 2017, 110 master's, 41 doctorates awarded. *Degree requirements:* For master's, comprehensive exam (for some programs), thesis (for some programs); for doctorate, thesis/dissertation. *Entrance requirements:* For master's, GRE (for MS in speech-language pathology); for doctorate, GRE. Additional exam requirements/recommendations for international students: Required—TOEFL, IELTS. *Application deadline:* For fall admission, 8/1 for domestic students, 4/15 for international students; for spring admission, 12/1 for domestic students; for summer admission, 5/1 for domestic students, 4/15 for international students. Application fee: $125. Electronic applications accepted. *Expenses:* $1,125 per credit, $245 fees. *Financial support:* In 2017–18, 10,000 students received support. Scholarships/grants and unspecified assistantships available. Financial award application deadline: 4/30; financial award applicants required to submit FAFSA. *Unit head:* Ben Watson, PhD, Vice Dean, 914-594-4531, E-mail: ben_watson@nymc.edu. *Application contact:* Irene Bundziak, Assistant to Director of Admissions, 914-594-4905, E-mail: irene_bundziak@nymc.edu.
Website: http://www.nymc.edu/school-of-health-sciences-and-practice-shsp/

Old Dominion University, College of Health Sciences, School of Community and Environmental Health, Norfolk, VA 23529. Offers general environmental health (MS); industrial hygiene (MS). *Faculty:* 5 full-time (2 women), 4 part-time/adjunct (2 women). *Students:* 9 full-time (7 women), 12 part-time (5 women); includes 9 minority (7 Black or African American, non-Hispanic/Latino; 1 Hispanic/Latino; 1 Two or more races, non-Hispanic/Latino), 1 international. Average age 28. 15 applicants, 67% accepted, 8 enrolled. In 2017, 9 master's awarded. *Degree requirements:* For master's, comprehensive exam, oral exam, written exam, practicum or thesis. *Entrance requirements:* For master's, GRE General Test, minimum GPA of 2.75. Additional exam requirements/recommendations for international students: Required—TOEFL (minimum score 650 paper-based). *Application deadline:* For fall admission, 8/1 priority date for domestic students, 7/1 priority date for international students; for winter admission, 11/1 priority date for domestic students, 10/1 priority date for international students; for spring admission, 4/1 priority date for domestic students, 3/1 priority date for international students. Applications are processed on a rolling basis. Application fee: $50. Electronic applications accepted. *Expenses:* Contact institution. *Financial support:* In 2017–18, 4 students received support, including 4 teaching assistantships with partial tuition reimbursements available (averaging $10,000 per year); scholarships/grants and tuition waivers (partial) also available. Financial award application deadline: 6/30; financial award applicants required to submit FAFSA. *Faculty research:* Toxicology, occupational health, environmental hazards. *Total annual research expenditures:* $150,133. *Unit head:* Dr. Anna Jeng, Graduate Program Director, 757-683-4594, Fax: 757-683-4410, E-mail: hjeng@odu.edu. *Application contact:* William Heffelfinger, Director of Graduate Admissions, 757-683-5554, Fax: 757-683-3255, E-mail: gradadmit@odu.edu.
Website: http://www.odu.edu/commhealth

The University of Alabama at Birmingham, School of Public Health, Program in Environmental Health Sciences, Birmingham, AL 35294. Offers environmental health sciences research (PhD); industrial hygiene (PhD). *Degree requirements:* For doctorate, comprehensive exam, thesis/dissertation. *Entrance requirements:* For doctorate, GRE General Test. Additional exam requirements/recommendations for international students: Recommended—TOEFL, IELTS. Electronic applications accepted. *Faculty research:* Aquatic toxicology, virology.

The University of Alabama at Birmingham, School of Public Health, Program in Public Health, Birmingham, AL 35294. Offers applied epidemiology and pharmacoepidemiology (MSPH); biostatistics (MPH); clinical and translational science (MSPH); environmental health (MPH); environmental health and toxicology (MSPH); epidemiology (MPH); general theory and practice (MPH); health behavior (MPH); health care organization (MPH); health policy quantitative policy analysis (MPH); industrial hygiene (MPH, MSPH); maternal and child health policy (Dr PH); maternal and child health policy and leadership (MPH); occupational health and safety (MPH); outcomes research (MSPH, Dr PH); public health (PhD); public health management (Dr PH); public health preparedness management (MPH). *Program availability:* Part-time, online learning. *Degree requirements:* For doctorate, comprehensive exam, thesis/dissertation. *Entrance requirements:* For master's and doctorate, GRE. Additional exam requirements/recommendations for international students: Recommended—TOEFL (minimum score 550 paper-based; 79 iBT), IELTS (minimum score 6.5). Electronic applications accepted.

University of Central Missouri, The Graduate School, Warrensburg, MO 64093. Offers accountancy (MA); accounting (MBA); applied mathematics (MS); aviation safety (MA); biology (MS); business administration (MBA); career and technical education leadership (MS); college student personnel administration (MS); communication (MA); computer science (MS); counseling (MS); criminal justice (MS); educational leadership (Ed D); educational technology (MS); elementary and early childhood education (MSE); English (MA); environmental studies (MA); finance (MBA); history (MA); human services/educational technology (Ed S); human services/learning resources (Ed S); human services/professional counseling (Ed S); industrial hygiene (MS); industrial management (MS); information systems (MBA); information technology (MS); kinesiology (MS); library science and information services (MS); literacy education (MSE); marketing (MBA); mathematics (MS); music (MA); occupational safety management (MS); psychology (MS); rural family nursing (MS); school administration (MSE); social gerontology (MS); sociology (MA); special education (MSE); speech language pathology (MS); superintendency (Ed S); teaching (MAT); teaching English as a second language (MA); technology (MS); technology management (PhD); theatre (MA). *Program availability:* Part-time, 100% online, blended/hybrid learning. *Faculty:* 337 full-time (145 women), 41 part-time/adjunct (28 women). *Students:* 785 full-time (398 women), 1,633 part-time (1,063 women); includes 231 minority (102 Black or African American, non-Hispanic/Latino; 4 American Indian or Alaska Native, non-Hispanic/Latino; 16 Asian, non-Hispanic/Latino; 52 Hispanic/Latino; 57 Two or more races, non-Hispanic/Latino), 692 international. Average age 30. In 2017, 2,605 master's, 122 other advanced degrees awarded. *Degree requirements:* For master's and Ed S, comprehensive exam (for some programs), thesis (for some programs). *Entrance requirements:* Additional exam requirements/recommendations for international students: Required—TOEFL (minimum score 550 paper-based; 79 iBT). *Application deadline:* For fall admission, 6/1 priority date for domestic and international students; for spring admission, 10/1 priority date for domestic and international students; for summer admission, 4/1 priority date for domestic and international students. Applications are processed on a rolling basis. Application fee: $30 ($75 for international students). Electronic applications accepted. *Expenses:* Tuition, state resident: full-time $8771; part-time $292.35 per credit hour. Tuition, nonresident: full-time $17,541; part-time $584.70 per credit hour. *Required fees:* $372; $24.78 per credit hour. *Financial support:* In 2017–18, 99 students received support. Research assistantships, teaching assistantships, career-related internships or fieldwork, Federal Work-Study, scholarships/grants, and administrative and laboratory assistantships available. Support available to part-time students. Financial award application deadline: 3/1; financial award applicants required to submit FAFSA. *Unit head:* Shellie Hewitt, Director of Graduate and International Student Services, 660-543-4621, Fax: 660-543-4778, E-mail: hewitt@ucmo.edu. *Application contact:* 660-543-4621, E-mail: admit_intl@ucmo.edu.
Website: http://www.ucmo.edu/graduate/

University of Cincinnati, Graduate School, College of Medicine, Graduate Programs in Biomedical Sciences, Department of Environmental Health, Cincinnati, OH 45221. Offers environmental and industrial hygiene (MS, PhD); environmental and occupational medicine (MS); environmental genetics and molecular toxicology (MS, PhD); epidemiology and biostatistics (MS, PhD); occupational safety and ergonomics (MS, PhD). *Accreditation:* ABET (one or more programs are accredited); CEPH. Terminal master's awarded for partial completion of doctoral program. *Degree requirements:* For master's, thesis; for doctorate, thesis/dissertation, qualifying exam. *Entrance requirements:* For master's, GRE General Test, bachelor's degree in science; for doctorate, GRE General Test. Additional exam requirements/recommendations for international students: Required—TOEFL (minimum score 600 paper-based; 100 iBT). Electronic applications accepted. *Expenses: Tuition, area resident:* Full-time $14,468. Tuition, state resident: full-time $14,968; part-time $754 per credit hour. Tuition, nonresident: full-time $24,210; part-time $1311 per credit hour. *International tuition:* $26,460 full-time. *Required fees:* $3958; $84 per credit hour. One-time fee: $85 full-time. Tuition and fees vary according to course load, degree level and program. *Faculty research:* Carcinogens and mutagenesis, pulmonary studies, reproduction and development.

The University of Iowa, Graduate College, College of Public Health, Department of Occupational and Environmental Health, Iowa City, IA 52242-1316. Offers agricultural safety and health (MS, PhD); ergonomics (MPH); industrial hygiene (MS, PhD); occupational and environmental health (MPH, MS, PhD, Certificate); MS/MA; MS/MS. *Accreditation:* ABET (one or more programs are accredited). *Degree requirements:* For master's, thesis optional, exam; for doctorate, comprehensive exam, thesis/dissertation. *Entrance requirements:* For master's and doctorate, GRE General Test, minimum GPA of 3.0. Additional exam requirements/recommendations for international students: Required—TOEFL (minimum score 600 paper-based; 100 iBT). Electronic applications accepted.

University of Michigan, School of Public Health, Department of Environmental Health Sciences, Ann Arbor, MI 48109. Offers environmental health policy and promotion (MPH); environmental health sciences (MS, PhD); environmental quality, sustainability and health (MPH); industrial hygiene (MPH, MS); occupational and environmental epidemiology (MPH); toxicology (MPH, MS, PhD). *Accreditation:* CEPH (one or more programs are accredited). Terminal master's awarded for partial completion of doctoral program. *Degree requirements:* For master's, thesis (for some programs); for doctorate, thesis/dissertation, preliminary exam, oral defense of dissertation. *Entrance requirements:* For master's and doctorate, GRE General Test and/or MCAT. Additional exam requirements/recommendations for international students: Required—TOEFL (minimum score 100 iBT). Electronic applications accepted. *Expenses:* Tuition, state resident: full-time $22,368; part-time $1201 per credit hour. Tuition, nonresident: full-time $45,156; part-time $2467 per credit hour. *Required fees:* $376 per term. Tuition and fees vary according to course load, degree level and program. *Faculty research:* Toxicology, occupational hygiene, environmental exposure sciences, environmental epidemiology.

University of Minnesota, Twin Cities Campus, School of Public Health, Division of Environmental Health Sciences, Area in Industrial Hygiene, Minneapolis, MN 55455-0213. Offers MPH, MS, PhD. *Accreditation:* ABET (one or more programs are accredited); CEPH (one or more programs are accredited). *Degree requirements:* For doctorate, thesis/dissertation. *Entrance requirements:* For master's and doctorate, GRE General Test. Electronic applications accepted.

University of Puerto Rico–Medical Sciences Campus, Graduate School of Public Health, Department of Environmental Health, Program in Industrial Hygiene, San Juan, PR 00936-5067. Offers MS. *Program availability:* Part-time. *Degree requirements:* For master's, thesis. *Entrance requirements:* For master's, GRE, previous course work in biology, chemistry, mathematics, and physics. *Expenses:* Contact institution.

University of South Carolina, The Graduate School, Arnold School of Public Health, Department of Environmental Health Sciences, Program in Industrial Hygiene, Columbia, SC 29208. Offers MPH, MSPH, PhD. *Accreditation:* CEPH (one or more programs are accredited). *Degree requirements:* For master's, comprehensive exam, thesis (for some programs), practicum (MPH); for doctorate, one foreign language, comprehensive exam, thesis/dissertation. *Entrance requirements:* Additional exam requirements/recommendations for international students: Required—TOEFL (minimum score 570 paper-based). Electronic applications accepted. *Faculty research:* Sampling and calibration method development, exposure and risk assessment, respirator and dermal protective equipment, ergonomics, air cleaning methods and devices.

The University of Toledo, College of Graduate Studies, College of Health and Human Services, School of Population Health, Toledo, OH 43606-3390. Offers health education (PhD); occupational health-industrial hygiene (MS); public health (MPH).

The University of Toledo, College of Graduate Studies, College of Medicine and Life Sciences, Department of Public Health and Preventative Medicine, Toledo, OH 43606-3390. Offers biostatistics and epidemiology (Certificate); contemporary gerontological practice (Certificate); environmental and occupational health and safety (MPH); epidemiology (Certificate); global public health (Certificate); health promotion and education (MPH); industrial hygiene (MSOH); medical and health science teaching and learning (Certificate); occupational health (Certificate); public health administration (MPH); public health and emergency response (Certificate); public health epidemiology (MPH); public health nutrition (MPH); MD/MPH. *Program availability:* Part-time, evening/weekend. *Degree requirements:* For master's, thesis or alternative. *Entrance* *requirements:* For master's, GRE, minimum undergraduate GPA of 3.0, three letters of recommendation, statement of purpose, transcripts from all prior institutions attended, resume; for Certificate, minimum undergraduate GPA of 3.0, three letters of recommendation, statement of purpose, transcripts from all prior institutions attended, resume. Additional exam requirements/recommendations for international students: Required—TOEFL (minimum score 550 paper-based; 80 iBT), IELTS (minimum score 6.5). Electronic applications accepted.

University of Wisconsin–Stout, Graduate School, College of Management, Program in Risk Control, Menomonie, WI 54751. Offers MS. *Program availability:* Part-time. *Degree requirements:* For master's, thesis. *Entrance requirements:* For master's, minimum GPA of 3.0. Additional exam requirements/recommendations for international students: Required—TOEFL (minimum score 500 paper-based; 61 iBT). Electronic applications accepted. *Faculty research:* Environmental microbiology, water supply safety, facilities planning, industrial ventilation, bioterrorist.

West Virginia University, Statler College of Engineering and Mineral Resources, Morgantown, WV 26506-6070. Offers aerospace engineering (MSAE, PhD); chemical engineering (MS Ch E, PhD); civil engineering (MSCE, PhD); computer engineering (PhD); computer science (MSCS, PhD); electrical engineering (MSEE, PhD); energy systems engineering (MSESE); engineering (MSE); industrial engineering (MSIE, PhD); industrial hygiene (MS); material science and engineering (MSMSE, PhD); mechanical engineering (MSME, PhD); mining engineering (MS Min E, PhD); petroleum and natural gas engineering (MSPNGE, PhD); safety engineering (MS); software engineering (MSSE). *Program availability:* Part-time. *Students:* 522 full-time (110 women), 131 part-time (23 women); includes 56 minority (22 Black or African American, non-Hispanic/Latino; 2 American Indian or Alaska Native, non-Hispanic/Latino; 14 Asian, non-Hispanic/Latino; 11 Hispanic/Latino; 7 Two or more races, non-Hispanic/Latino), 305 international. Terminal master's awarded for partial completion of doctoral program. *Degree requirements:* For master's, thesis optional; for doctorate, comprehensive exam, thesis/dissertation. *Entrance requirements:* Additional exam requirements/recommendations for international students: Required—TOEFL (minimum score 550 paper-based). *Application deadline:* For fall admission, 4/1 for international students; for winter admission, 4/1 for international students; for spring admission, 10/1 for international students. Applications are processed on a rolling basis. Application fee: $60. Electronic applications accepted. *Expenses:* Contact institution. *Financial support:* Fellowships, research assistantships, teaching assistantships, career-related internships or fieldwork, Federal Work-Study, institutionally sponsored loans, health care benefits, tuition waivers (full and partial), unspecified assistantships, and administrative assistantships available. Financial award application deadline: 2/1; financial award applicants required to submit FAFSA. *Faculty research:* Composite materials, software engineering, information systems, aerodynamics, vehicle propulsion and emission. *Unit head:* Dr. Eugene V. Cilento, Dean, 304-293-4821 Ext. 2237, Fax: 304-293-2037, E-mail: gene.cilento@mail.wvu.edu. *Application contact:* Dr. David A. Wyrick, Associate Dean, Academic Affairs, 304-293-4334, Fax: 304-293-5024, E-mail: david.wyrick@mail.wvu.edu.
Website: https://www.statler.wvu.edu

International Health

Arizona State University at the Tempe campus, College of Liberal Arts and Sciences, School of Human Evolution and Social Change, Tempe, AZ 85287-2402. Offers anthropology (MA, PhD), including anthropology (PhD), archaeology (PhD), bioarchaeology (PhD), evolutionary (PhD), museum studies (MA), sociocultural (PhD); applied mathematics for the life and social sciences (PhD); environmental social science (PhD), including environmental social science, urbanism; global health (MA, PhD), including complex adaptive systems science (PhD), evolutionary global health sciences (PhD), health and culture (PhD), urbanism (PhD); immigration studies (Graduate Certificate). Terminal master's awarded for partial completion of doctoral program. *Degree requirements:* For master's, thesis or alternative, interactive Program of Study (iPOS) submitted before completing 50 percent of required credit hours; for doctorate, comprehensive exam, thesis/dissertation, interactive Program of Study (iPOS) submitted before completing 50 percent of required credit hours. *Entrance requirements:* For master's and doctorate, GRE, minimum GPA of 3.0 or equivalent in last 2 years of work leading to bachelor's degree. Additional exam requirements/recommendations for international students: Required—TOEFL, IELTS, or PTE. Electronic applications accepted.

A.T. Still University, College of Graduate Health Studies, Kirksville, MO 63501. Offers dental public health (MPH); exercise and sport psychology (Certificate); fundamentals of education (Certificate); geriatric exercise science (Certificate); global health (Certificate); health administration (MHA, DHA); health professions (Ed D); health sciences (DH Sc); kinesiology (MS); leadership and organizational behavior (Certificate); public health (MPH); sports conditioning (Certificate). *Program availability:* Part-time, evening/weekend, online only, 100% online, blended/hybrid learning. *Faculty:* 28 full-time (18 women), 83 part-time/adjunct (43 women). *Students:* 537 full-time (334 women), 516 part-time (316 women); includes 397 minority (171 Black or African American, non-Hispanic/Latino; 14 American Indian or Alaska Native, non-Hispanic/Latino; 84 Asian, non-Hispanic/Latino; 106 Hispanic/Latino; 1 Native Hawaiian or other Pacific Islander, non-Hispanic/Latino; 21 Two or more races, non-Hispanic/Latino), 43 international. Average age 36. 392 applicants, 84% accepted, 270 enrolled. In 2017, 138 master's, 102 doctorates, 116 other advanced degrees awarded. *Degree requirements:* For master's, thesis, integrated terminal project, practicum; for doctorate, thesis/dissertation. *Entrance requirements:* For master's, minimum GPA of 2.5, bachelor's degree or equivalent, essay, resume, English proficiency; for doctorate, minimum GPA of 2.5, master's or terminal degree, essay, past experience in relevant field, resume, English proficiency. Additional exam requirements/recommendations for international students: Required—TOEFL (minimum score 550 paper-based; 80 iBT). *Application deadline:* For fall admission, 6/26 for domestic students, 5/20 for international students; for winter admission, 9/11 for domestic students, 9/12 for international students; for spring admission, 12/11 for domestic students, 12/12 for international students; for summer admission, 3/5 for domestic students, 3/6 for international students. Applications are processed on a rolling basis. Application fee: $70. Electronic applications accepted. *Financial support:* In 2017–18, 18 students received support. Scholarships/grants available. Financial award applicants required to submit FAFSA. *Faculty research:* Public health: influence of availability of comprehensive wellness resources online, student wellness, oral health care needs assessment of community, oral health knowledge and behaviors of Medicaid-eligible pregnant women and mothers of young children in relations to early childhood caries and tooth decay, alcohol use and alcohol related problems among college students. *Unit head:* Dr. Donald Altman, Dean, 480-219-6008, Fax: 660-626-2826, E-mail: daltman@atsu.edu. *Application contact:* Amie Waldemer, Associate Director, Online Admissions, 480-219-6146, E-mail: awaldemer@atsu.edu.
Website: http://www.atsu.edu/college-of-graduate-health-studies

Boston University, School of Public Health, Global Health Department, Boston, MA 02215. Offers MPH, Dr PH. *Program availability:* Part-time, evening/weekend. *Degree requirements:* For doctorate, thesis/dissertation. *Entrance requirements:* For master's, GRE, MCAT, GMAT; for doctorate, GRE, GMAT. Additional exam requirements/recommendations for international students: Required—TOEFL (minimum score 600 paper-based; 100 iBT), IELTS (minimum score 7). Electronic applications accepted. *Faculty research:* Pharmaceutical assessment, monitoring and evaluation, program management, capacity building, program assessment.

Brandeis University, The Heller School for Social Policy and Management, Program in International Health Policy and Management, Waltham, MA 02454-9110. Offers MS. *Entrance requirements:* For master's, 3 letters of recommendation, curriculum vitae or resume, 5 years of international health experience. Additional exam requirements/recommendations for international students: Required—TOEFL (minimum score 600 paper-based; 100 iBT). Electronic applications accepted. *Expenses: Tuition:* Full-time $48,720. *Required fees:* $88. Tuition and fees vary according to course load, degree level, program and student level. *Faculty research:* International development, health financing, and health systems.

Brandeis University, The Heller School for Social Policy and Management, Program in Social Policy, Waltham, MA 02454-9110. Offers assets and inequalities (PhD); children, youth and families (PhD); global health and development (PhD); health and behavioral health (PhD). *Degree requirements:* For doctorate, comprehensive exam, thesis/dissertation, qualifying paper, 2-year residency. *Entrance requirements:* For doctorate, GRE General Test, 3 letters of recommendation, statement of purpose, writing sample, at least 3-5 years of professional experience. Additional exam requirements/recommendations for international students: Required—TOEFL (minimum score 600 paper-based; 100 iBT). Electronic applications accepted. *Expenses: Tuition:* Full-time $48,720. *Required fees:* $88. Tuition and fees vary according to course load, degree level, program and student level. *Faculty research:* Health; mental health; substance abuse; children, youth, and families; aging; international and community development; disabilities; work and inequality; hunger and poverty.

Cedarville University, Graduate Programs, Cedarville, OH 45314. Offers business administration (MBA); family nurse practitioner (MSN); global ministry (M Div); global public health nursing (MSN); healthcare administration (MBA); ministry (M Min); nurse educator (MSN); operations management (MBA); pharmacy (Pharm D). *Program availability:* Part-time, evening/weekend, 100% online, blended/hybrid learning. *Faculty:* 23 full-time (9 women), 48 part-time/adjunct (21 women). *Students:* 202 full-time (123 women), 146 part-time (96 women); includes 63 minority (39 Black or African American, non-Hispanic/Latino; 3 American Indian or Alaska Native, non-Hispanic/Latino; 15 Asian, non-Hispanic/Latino; 2 Hispanic/Latino; 1 Native Hawaiian or other Pacific Islander, non-Hispanic/Latino; 3 Two or more races, non-Hispanic/Latino), 3 international. Average age 24. 345 applicants, 37% accepted, 91 enrolled. In 2017, 53 master's, 47 doctorates awarded. *Degree requirements:* For master's, portfolio; for doctorate, comprehensive exam. *Entrance requirements:* For master's, GRE, 2 professional recommendations; for doctorate, PCAT, professional recommendation from a practicing pharmacist or current employer/supervisor, resume, essay, interview. Additional exam requirements/recommendations for international students: Required—TOEFL (minimum score 550 paper-based; 80 iBT). *Application deadline:* For fall admission, 5/1 priority date for domestic and international students; for spring admission, 11/1 priority date for domestic and international students. Applications are processed on a rolling basis. Application fee: $0. Electronic applications accepted. *Expenses: Tuition:* Full-time $12,594; part-time $566 per credit. One-time fee: $100 full-time. Tuition and fees vary according to degree level and program. *Financial support:* Scholarships/grants and unspecified assistantships available. Support available to part-time students. Financial award application deadline: 1/30; financial award applicants required to submit FAFSA. *Faculty research:* Establishing competencies of clinical reasoning for nursing students in Taiwan, social determinants of health in pediatric primary care, meeting needs of palliative care populations, natural product utility in cancer, monoclonal antibodies directed at angiogenesis regulation. *Total annual research expenditures:* $3,800. *Unit head:* Dr. Janice Supplee, Dean of Graduate Studies, 937-766-7700, E-mail: suppleej@cedarville.edu. *Application contact:* Jim Amstutz, Director of Graduate Admissions, 937-766-7878, Fax: 937-766-7575, E-mail: amstutzj@cedarville.edu.
Website: https://www.cedarville.edu/Admissions/Graduate/Graduate-Programs.aspx

Central Michigan University, Central Michigan University Global Campus, Program in Health Administration, Mount Pleasant, MI 48859. Offers health administration (DHA); international health (Certificate); nutrition and dietetics (MS). *Program availability:* Part-time, evening/weekend, online learning. Electronic applications accepted.

Clark University, Graduate School, Department of International Development, Community, and Environment, Program in Community and Global Health, Worcester, MA 01610-1477. Offers MHS. *Students:* 16 full-time (10 women); includes 3 minority (1 Black or African American, non-Hispanic/Latino; 1 Hispanic/Latino; 1 Two or more races, non-Hispanic/Latino), 8 international. Average age 32. 33 applicants, 52% accepted, 16 enrolled. *Degree requirements:* For master's, project; capstone, practicum, or internship. *Entrance requirements:* Additional exam requirements/recommendations for international students: Required—TOEFL (minimum score 90 iBT), IELTS (minimum score 6.5). *Application deadline:* For fall admission, 4/15 for domestic and international students. Application fee: $75. Electronic applications accepted. *Expenses:* $5,685 tuition per unit, $490 fees. *Financial support:* Fellowships, research assistantships, teaching assistantships, institutionally sponsored loans, and health care benefits available. *Unit head:* Dr. Ed Carr, 508-421-3895, Fax: 508-793-8820, E-mail: edcarr@clarku.edu. *Application contact:* Erika Paradis, Student and Academic Services Director, 508-793-7201, Fax: 508-793-8820, E-mail: eparadis@clarku.edu.
Website: http://www.clarku.edu/master-health-science-community-global-health

Clemson University, Graduate School, College of Behavioral, Social and Health Sciences, School of Nursing, Clemson, SC 29634. Offers clinical and translational research (PhD); global health (Certificate), including low resource countries; healthcare genetics (PhD); nursing (MS, DNP), including adult/gerontology nurse practitioner (MS),

family nurse practitioner (MS). *Accreditation:* AACN. *Program availability:* Part-time, 100% online, blended/hybrid learning. *Faculty:* 37 full-time (35 women). *Students:* 130 full-time (118 women), 195 part-time (170 women); includes 50 minority (23 Black or African American, non-Hispanic/Latino; 5 Asian, non-Hispanic/Latino; 16 Hispanic/Latino; 6 Two or more races, non-Hispanic/Latino), 14 international. Average age 34. 71 applicants, 66% accepted, 33 enrolled. In 2017, 88 master's, 2 doctorates, 10 other advanced degrees awarded. *Degree requirements:* For master's, comprehensive exam, thesis or alternative; for doctorate, comprehensive exam, thesis/dissertation. *Entrance requirements:* For master's, GRE General Test, South Carolina RN license, unofficial transcripts, resume, letters of recommendation; for doctorate, GRE General Test, unofficial transcripts, MS/MA thesis or publications, curriculum vitae, statement of career goals, letters of recommendation. Additional exam requirements/recommendations for international students: Required—TOEFL (minimum score 80 iBT), IELTS (minimum score 6.5), PTE (minimum score 54). *Application deadline:* For fall admission, 3/1 priority date for domestic and international students; for spring admission, 10/1 priority date for domestic and international students. Application fee: $80 ($90 for international students). Electronic applications accepted. *Expenses:* Contact institution. *Financial support:* In 2017–18, 41 students received support, including 46 teaching assistantships with partial tuition reimbursements available (averaging $4,919 per year); career-related internships or fieldwork and unspecified assistantships also available. Financial award application deadline: 3/1. *Faculty research:* Breast cancer, healthcare, genetics, international healthcare, educational innovation and technology. *Total annual research expenditures:* $371,674. *Unit head:* Dr. Kathleen Valentine, Director and Associate College Dean, 864-656-4758, E-mail: klvalen@clemson.edu. *Application contact:* Dr. Stephanie Davis, Graduate Studies Coordinator, 864-656-2588, E-mail: stephad@clemson.edu.
Website: http://www.clemson.edu/cbshs/departments/nursing/

The College of New Jersey, Office of Graduate and Advancing Education, School of Nursing, Health, and Exercise Science, Program in Public Health, Ewing, NJ 08628. Offers global health (MPH); health communications (MPH); precision health (MPH).

Duke University, Graduate School, Duke Global Health Institute, Durham, NC 27708. Offers MS. *Degree requirements:* For master's, thesis. *Entrance requirements:* For master's, GRE General Test or MCAT. Additional exam requirements/recommendations for international students: Required—TOEFL (minimum score 577 paper-based; 90 iBT) or IELTS (minimum score 7).

East Tennessee State University, School of Graduate Studies, College of Public Health, Program in Public Health, Johnson City, TN 37614. Offers biostatistics (MPH, Postbaccalaureate Certificate); community health (MPH, DPH); environmental health (MPH); epidemiology (MPH, DPH, Postbaccalaureate Certificate); gerontology (Postbaccalaureate Certificate); global health (Postbaccalaureate Certificate); health care management (Postbaccalaureate Certificate); health management and policy (DPH); public health (Postbaccalaureate Certificate); public health services administration (MPH); rural health (Postbaccalaureate Certificate). *Accreditation:* CEPH. *Program availability:* Part-time, online learning. *Degree requirements:* For master's, comprehensive exam, field experience; for doctorate, thesis/dissertation, practicum. *Entrance requirements:* For master's, GRE General Test, minimum GPA of 2.75, SOPHAS application, three letters of recommendation; for doctorate, GRE General Test, SOPHAS application, three letters of recommendation; for Postbaccalaureate Certificate, minimum GPA of 2.5, three letters of recommendation, resume. Additional exam requirements/recommendations for international students: Required—TOEFL (minimum score 550 paper-based; 79 iBT), IELTS (minimum score 6.5). *Application deadline:* For fall admission, 3/1 for domestic and international students. Application fee: $35 ($45 for international students). Electronic applications accepted. *Financial support:* Research assistantships with tuition reimbursements, teaching assistantships with full tuition reimbursements, career-related internships or fieldwork, institutionally sponsored loans, scholarships/grants, and unspecified assistantships available. Financial award application deadline: 7/1; financial award applicants required to submit FAFSA. *Unit head:* Dr. Randy Wykoff, Dean, 423-439-4243, Fax: 423-439-5238, E-mail: wykoff@etsu.edu. *Application contact:* Dr. Randy Wykoff, Dean, 423-439-4243, Fax: 423-439-5238, E-mail: wykoff@etsu.edu.
Website: http://www.etsu.edu/cph/

Emory University, Rollins School of Public Health, Hubert Department of Global Health, Atlanta, GA 30322-1100. Offers global health (MPH); public nutrition (MSPH). *Degree requirements:* For master's, thesis, practicum. *Entrance requirements:* For master's, GRE General Test. Additional exam requirements/recommendations for international students: Required—TOEFL (minimum score 550 paper-based; 80 iBT). Electronic applications accepted.

Endicott College, Van Loan School of Graduate and Professional Studies, Program in Nursing, Beverly, MA 01915-2096. Offers family nurse practitioner (MSN, Post-Master's Certificate); global health (MSN); nursing administration (MSN); nursing administrator (Post-Master's Certificate); nursing educator (MSN, Post-Master's Certificate). *Program availability:* Part-time, evening/weekend. *Faculty:* 5 full-time (4 women), 14 part-time/adjunct (12 women). *Students:* 43 full-time (41 women), 57 part-time (51 women); includes 8 minority (5 Black or African American, non-Hispanic/Latino; 3 Hispanic/Latino), 1 international. Average age 37. 41 applicants, 100% accepted, 38 enrolled. In 2017, 33 master's awarded. *Degree requirements:* For master's, thesis, practicum. *Entrance requirements:* For master's, MAT or GRE, statement of professional goals, official transcripts of all undergraduate and graduate course work, two letters of recommendation, photocopy of current and unrestricted RN license, basic statistics course, interview. Additional exam requirements/recommendations for international students: Required—TOEFL. *Application deadline:* Applications are processed on a rolling basis. Application fee: $50. Electronic applications accepted. *Expenses:* Contact institution. *Financial support:* Applicants required to submit FAFSA. *Unit head:* Dr. Kelly Fisher, Dean, 978-232-2328, Fax: 978-232-3000, E-mail: kfisher@endicott.edu. *Application contact:* Ian Menchini, Director, Graduate Enrollment and Advising, 978-232-5292, Fax: 978-232-3000, E-mail: imenchin@endicott.edu.
Website: https://vanloan.endicott.edu/programs-of-study/masters-programs/nursing-programs

George Mason University, College of Health and Human Services, Department of Global and Community Health, Fairfax, VA 22030. Offers global and community health (Certificate); global health (MS); public health (MPH, Certificate), including epidemiology (MPH), leadership and management (Certificate). *Accreditation:* CEPH. *Program availability:* Part-time, evening/weekend. *Faculty:* 18 full-time (13 women), 16 part-time/adjunct (13 women). *Students:* 70 full-time (63 women), 61 part-time (53 women); includes 62 minority (21 Black or African American, non-Hispanic/Latino; 21 Asian, non-Hispanic/Latino; 14 Hispanic/Latino; 1 Native Hawaiian or other Pacific Islander, non-Hispanic/Latino; 5 Two or more races, non-Hispanic/Latino), 8 international. Average age 29. 246 applicants, 71% accepted, 60 enrolled. In 2017, 46 master's, 2 other advanced degrees awarded. *Degree requirements:* For master's, thesis, 200-hour practicum. *Entrance requirements:* For master's, GRE, GMAT (depending on program), 2 official transcripts; expanded goals statement; 3 letters of recommendation; resume; 1 completed course in health science, statistics, natural sciences and social science (for MPH); 6 credits of foreign language if not fluent (for MS); minimum undergraduate GPA of 3.0; for Certificate, 2 official transcripts; expanded goals statement; 3 letters of recommendation; resume; bachelor's degree from regionally-accredited institution with minimum GPA of 3.0. Additional exam requirements/recommendations for international students: Required—TOEFL (minimum score 570 paper-based; 88 iBT), IELTS (minimum score 6.5), PTE (minimum score 59). *Application deadline:* For fall admission, 3/1 for domestic and international students. Application fee: $75 ($80 for international students). Electronic applications accepted. *Expenses:* Contact institution. *Financial support:* In 2017–18, 15 students received support, including 12 research assistantships with tuition reimbursements available (averaging $16,616 per year), 3 teaching assistantships with tuition reimbursements available (averaging $6,966 per year); career-related internships or fieldwork, Federal Work-Study, scholarships/grants, unspecified assistantships, and health care benefits (for full-time research or teaching assistantship recipients) also available. Financial award application deadline: 3/1; financial award applicants required to submit FAFSA. *Faculty research:* Environmental and infectious disease epidemiology; global health; health risk behaviors; social determinants of health; stress, well-being and chronic disease. *Total annual research expenditures:* $69,343. *Unit head:* Robert Weiler, Chair, 703-993-1920, E-mail: rweiler@gmu.edu. *Application contact:* Allan Weiss, Department Manager, 703-993-3126, E-mail: aweiss2@gmu.edu.
Website: http://chhs.gmu.edu/gch/index

Georgetown University, Law Center, Washington, DC 20001. Offers environmental law (LL M); global health law (LL M); global health law and international institutions (LL M); individualized study (LL M); international business and economic law (LL M); law (JD, SJD); national security law (LL M); securities and financial regulation (LL M); taxation (LL M); JD/LL M; JD/MA; JD/MBA; JD/MPH; JD/PhD. *Accreditation:* ABA. *Program availability:* Part-time, evening/weekend. *Degree requirements:* For master's, thesis; for doctorate, thesis/dissertation (for some programs). *Entrance requirements:* For master's, JD, LL B, or first law degree earned in country of origin; for doctorate, LSAT (for JD). Additional exam requirements/recommendations for international students: Required—TOEFL. *Expenses:* Contact institution. *Faculty research:* Constitutional law, legal history, jurisprudence.

The George Washington University, Milken Institute School of Public Health, Department of Global Health, Washington, DC 20052. Offers global health (Dr PH); global health communication (MPH). *Students:* 16 full-time (15 women), 21 part-time (12 women); includes 16 minority (6 Black or African American, non-Hispanic/Latino; 7 Asian, non-Hispanic/Latino; 2 Hispanic/Latino; 1 Two or more races, non-Hispanic/Latino), 4 international. Average age 37. 126 applicants, 61% accepted, 14 enrolled. In 2017, 6 master's awarded. *Entrance requirements:* For master's, GMAT, GRE General Test, or MCAT. Additional exam requirements/recommendations for international students: Required—TOEFL. *Application deadline:* For fall admission, 4/15 priority date for domestic students, 4/15 for international students; for spring admission, 11/1 for domestic and international students. Applications are processed on a rolling basis. Application fee: $75. *Expenses: Tuition:* Full-time $28,800; part-time $1655 per credit hour. *Required fees:* $45; $2.75 per credit hour. *Financial support:* In 2017–18, 24 students received support. Tuition waivers available. Financial award application deadline: 2/15. *Unit head:* Prof. James Tielsch, Chair, 202-994-4124, Fax: 202-994-1955, E-mail: jtielsch@gwu.edu. *Application contact:* Jane Smith, Director of Admissions, 202-994-0248, Fax: 202-994-1860, E-mail: sphhsinfo@gwumc.edu.

Harvard University, Harvard T.H. Chan School of Public Health, Department of Global Health and Population, Boston, MA 02115-6096. Offers global health and population (SM); population health sciences (PhD). *Program availability:* Part-time. *Faculty:* 47 full-time (18 women), 22 part-time/adjunct (7 women). *Students:* 121 full-time (87 women), 9 part-time (8 women); includes 9 minority (2 Black or African American, non-Hispanic/Latino; 6 Asian, non-Hispanic/Latino; 1 Hispanic/Latino), 27 international. Average age 29. 51 applicants, 55% accepted, 15 enrolled. In 2017, 28 master's, 10 doctorates awarded. *Degree requirements:* For master's, thesis; for doctorate, thesis/dissertation, qualifying exam. *Entrance requirements:* For master's, GRE, MCAT; for doctorate, GRE. Additional exam requirements/recommendations for international students: Recommended—TOEFL (minimum score 600 paper-based; 100 iBT), IELTS (minimum score 7). *Application deadline:* For fall admission, 12/1 for domestic and international students. Application fee: $120. Electronic applications accepted. *Financial support:* Fellowships, research assistantships, teaching assistantships, Federal Work-Study, scholarships/grants, traineeships, and unspecified assistantships available. Support available to part-time students. Financial award application deadline: 2/15; financial award applicants required to submit FAFSA. *Faculty research:* Health systems, international health policy, economics, population and reproductive health, ecology. *Unit head:* Dr. Wafaie W. Fawzi, Chair, 617-432-1232, Fax: 617-432-2435, E-mail: mina@hsph.harvard.edu. *Application contact:* Vincent W. James, Director of Admissions, 617-432-1031, Fax: 617-432-7080, E-mail: admissions@hsph.harvard.edu.
Website: http://www.hsph.harvard.edu/global-health-and-population/

Harvard University, Harvard T.H. Chan School of Public Health, PhD Program in Population Health Sciences, Boston, MA 02115. Offers environmental health (PhD); epidemiology (PhD); global health and population (PhD); nutrition (PhD); social and behavioral sciences (PhD). *Students:* 80 full-time (56 women); includes 23 minority (5 Black or African American, non-Hispanic/Latino; 7 Asian, non-Hispanic/Latino; 6 Hispanic/Latino; 5 Two or more races, non-Hispanic/Latino), 26 international. Average age 29. 469 applicants, 11% accepted, 42 enrolled. *Entrance requirements:* Additional exam requirements/recommendations for international students: Recommended—TOEFL, IELTS. *Application deadline:* For fall admission, 12/1 for domestic and international students. Electronic applications accepted. *Financial support:* Application deadline: 2/15; applicants required to submit FAFSA. *Unit head:* Bruce Villineau, Assistant Director, E-mail: phdphs@hsph.harvard.edu. *Application contact:* Vincent W. James, Director of Admissions, 617-432-1031, Fax: 617-432-7080, E-mail: admissions@hsph.harvard.edu.

Indiana University–Purdue University Indianapolis, Richard M. Fairbanks School of Public Health, Indianapolis, IN 46202. Offers biostatistics (MS, PhD); environmental health (MPH); epidemiology (MPH, PhD); global health leadership (Dr PH); health administration (MHA); health policy (Graduate Certificate); health policy and management (MPH, PhD); health systems management (Graduate Certificate); product stewardship (MS); public health (Graduate Certificate); social and behavioral sciences (MPH). *Expenses:* Contact institution.

Johns Hopkins University, Bloomberg School of Public Health, Department of International Health, Baltimore, MD 21205. Offers global disease epidemiology and control (MSPH, PhD); global health economics (MHS); health systems (MSPH, PhD); human nutrition (MSPH, PhD); social and behavioral interventions (MSPH, PhD). *Students:* 270 full-time (216 women); includes 80 minority (8 Black or African American, non-Hispanic/Latino; 1 American Indian or Alaska Native, non-Hispanic/Latino; 52 Asian, non-Hispanic/Latino; 8 Hispanic/Latino; 11 Two or more races, non-Hispanic/Latino), 70 international. Average age 28. 562 applicants, 40% accepted, 82 enrolled. *Degree requirements:* For master's, comprehensive exam, thesis (for some programs), 1-year full-time residency, 4-9 month internship; for doctorate, comprehensive exam, thesis/dissertation or alternative, 1.5 years' full-time residency, oral and written exams. *Entrance requirements:* For master's, GRE General Test or MCAT, 3 letters of

recommendation, resume; for doctorate, GRE General Test or MCAT, 3 letters of recommendation, resume, transcripts. Additional exam requirements/recommendations for international students: Required—TOEFL (minimum score 600 paper-based; 100 iBT); Recommended—IELTS (minimum score 7). Electronic applications accepted. *Financial support:* Fellowships, Federal Work-Study, scholarships/grants, traineeships, and stipends available. *Faculty research:* Nutrition, infectious diseases, health systems, health economics, humanitarian emergencies. *Unit head:* Dr. David Peters, Chair, 410-955-3928, Fax: 410-955-7159, E-mail: dpeters@jhsph.edu. *Application contact:* Cristina G. Salazar, Academic Program Manager, 410-955-3734, Fax: 410-955-7159, E-mail: csalazar@jhsph.edu.
Website: http://www.jhsph.edu/dept/IH/

Liberty University, School of Health Sciences, Lynchburg, VA 24515. Offers anatomy and cell biology (PhD); biomedical sciences (MS); epidemiology (MPH); exercise science (MS), including clinical, community physical activity, human performance, nutrition; global health (MPH); health promotion (MPH); medical sciences (MA), including biopsychology, business management, health informatics, molecular medicine, public health; nutrition (MPH). *Program availability:* Part-time, online learning. *Students:* 542 full-time (394 women), 696 part-time (541 women); includes 402 minority (286 Black or African American, non-Hispanic/Latino; 10 American Indian or Alaska Native, non-Hispanic/Latino; 34 Asian, non-Hispanic/Latino; 46 Hispanic/Latino; 1 Native Hawaiian or other Pacific Islander, non-Hispanic/Latino; 25 Two or more races, non-Hispanic/Latino), 59 international. Average age 32. 1,592 applicants, 40% accepted, 297 enrolled. In 2017, 204 master's awarded. *Degree requirements:* For master's, thesis (for some programs); for doctorate, thesis/dissertation. *Entrance requirements:* For doctorate, MAT or GRE, minimum GPA of 3.25 in master's program, 2-3 recommendations, writing samples (for some programs), letter of intent, professional vitae. Additional exam requirements/recommendations for international students: Required—TOEFL (minimum score 600 paper-based; 100 iBT). Application fee: $50. *Financial support:* Applicants required to submit FAFSA. *Unit head:* Dr. Ralph Linstra, Dean. *Application contact:* Jay Bridge, Director of Admissions, 800-424-9595, Fax: 800-628-7977, E-mail: gradadmissions@liberty.edu.

Loma Linda University, School of Public Health, Program in Global Health, Loma Linda, CA 92350. Offers MPH. *Entrance requirements:* Additional exam requirements/recommendations for international students: Required—Michigan English Language Assessment Battery or TOEFL. *Expenses:* Contact institution.

Medical University of South Carolina, College of Health Professions, Program in Health Administration-Global, Charleston, SC 29425. Offers MHA. *Entrance requirements:* Additional exam requirements/recommendations for international students: Required—TOEFL.

National University of Natural Medicine, School of Graduate Studies, Portland, OR 97201. Offers Ayurveda (MS); global health (MS); integrative medicine research (MS); integrative mental health (MS); nutrition (MS). *Faculty:* 7 full-time (5 women), 35 part-time/adjunct (25 women). *Students:* 184 (161 women). Average age 31. In 2017, 67 master's awarded. *Entrance requirements:* Additional exam requirements/recommendations for international students: Recommended—TOEFL, IELTS, TSE. *Application deadline:* For fall and winter admission, 5/1 for domestic and international students. Applications are processed on a rolling basis. Application fee: $75. Electronic applications accepted. *Expenses: Tuition:* Full-time $23,979. *Financial support:* Federal Work-Study and scholarships/grants available. Financial award application deadline: 2/15; financial award applicants required to submit FAFSA. *Faculty research:* Reliability of three constitutional questionnaires in Ayurveda diagnosis; mindfulness-based stress reduction for MS: feasibility, durability, and clinical outcomes; meditative neuroplasticity: the effect of qigong meditation on brain-derived neurotrophic factor and cortisol levels; food as medicine everyday research (FAMER): evaluating physiological changes associated with a shift toward a whole-foods diet. *Unit head:* Dr. Charles Kunert, Dean, 503-552-1742, Fax: 503-499-0027, E-mail: admission@nunm.edu. *Application contact:* Ryan Hollister, Associate Director of Admissions and Operations, 503-552-1665, Fax: 503-499-0027, E-mail: admissions@numn.edu.
Website: http://nunm.edu/academics/school-of-research-graduate-studies/

New York Institute of Technology, College of Osteopathic Medicine, Old Westbury, NY 11568-8000. Offers global health (Certificate); DO/MS. *Accreditation:* AOsA. *Faculty:* 91 full-time, 33 part-time/adjunct. *Students:* 1,484 full-time (707 women); includes 649 minority (47 Black or African American, non-Hispanic/Latino; 540 Asian, non-Hispanic/Latino; 44 Hispanic/Latino; 18 Two or more races, non-Hispanic/Latino). Average age 27. 7,036 applicants, 13% accepted, 436 enrolled. In 2017, 16 Certificates awarded. *Entrance requirements:* Additional exam requirements/recommendations for international students: Required—TOEFL (minimum score 79 iBT), IELTS (minimum score 6). *Application deadline:* For fall admission, 2/1 for domestic students. Application fee: $80. Electronic applications accepted. *Expenses:* $58,345 per year plus $1,500 fees. *Financial support:* Federal Work-Study and scholarships/grants available. Financial award application deadline: 2/15; financial award applicants required to submit FAFSA. *Faculty research:* Cancer biology; computational biomechanics and motor control; neurobiology and sensory evolution; degenerative diseases; sports medicine and osteopathic manipulative medicine; cardiovascular biology; evolution and development. *Unit head:* Dr. Wolfgang Gilliar, Dean, 516-686-3722, Fax: 516-686-3830, E-mail: wgilliar@nyit.edu. *Application contact:* Gina Moses, Director, Admissions, 516-686-3997, E-mail: gmoses@nyit.edu.
Website: http://www.nyit.edu/medicine

New York Medical College, School of Health Sciences and Practice, Valhalla, NY 10595. Offers behavioral sciences and health promotion (MPH); biostatistics (MS); children with special health care (Graduate Certificate); emergency preparedness (Graduate Certificate); environmental health science (MPH); epidemiology (MPH, MS); global health (Graduate Certificate); health education (Graduate Certificate); health policy and management (MPH, Dr PH); industrial hygiene (Graduate Certificate); pediatric dysphagia (Post-Graduate Certificate); physical therapy (DPT); public health (Graduate Certificate); speech-language pathology (MS). *Accreditation:* CEPH. *Program availability:* Part-time, evening/weekend, 100% online, blended/hybrid learning. *Faculty:* 48 full-time (33 women), 235 part-time/adjunct (141 women). *Students:* 221 full-time (153 women), 270 part-time (194 women); includes 202 minority (83 Black or African American, non-Hispanic/Latino; 2 American Indian or Alaska Native, non-Hispanic/Latino; 64 Asian, non-Hispanic/Latino; 47 Hispanic/Latino; 1 Native Hawaiian or other Pacific Islander, non-Hispanic/Latino; 5 Two or more races, non-Hispanic/Latino), 19 international. Average age 29. 1,118 applicants, 38% accepted, 169 enrolled. In 2017, 110 master's, 41 doctorates awarded. *Degree requirements:* For master's, comprehensive exam (for some programs), thesis (for some programs); for doctorate, thesis/dissertation. *Entrance requirements:* For master's, GRE (for MS in speech-language pathology); for doctorate, GRE. Additional exam requirements/recommendations for international students: Required—TOEFL, IELTS. *Application deadline:* For fall admission, 8/1 for domestic students, 4/15 for international students; for spring admission, 12/1 for domestic students; for summer admission, 5/1 for domestic students, 4/15 for international students. Application fee: $125. Electronic applications accepted. *Expenses:* $1,125 per credit, $245 fees. *Financial support:* In 2017–18, 10,000 students received support. Scholarships/grants and unspecified assistantships available. Financial award application deadline: 4/30; financial award applicants required to submit FAFSA. *Unit head:* Ben Watson, PhD, Vice Dean, 914-594-4531, E-mail: ben_watson@nymc.edu. *Application contact:* Irene Bundziak, Assistant to Director of Admissions, 914-594-4905, E-mail: irene_bundziak@nymc.edu.
Website: http://www.nymc.edu/school-of-health-sciences-and-practice-shsp/

New York University, College of Global Public Health, New York, NY 10012. Offers biological basis of public health (PhD); community and international health (MPH); global health leadership (MPH); health systems and health services research (PhD); population and community health (PhD); public health nutrition (MPH); social and behavioral sciences (MPH); socio-behavioral health (PhD). *Accreditation:* CEPH. *Program availability:* Part-time, online learning. *Faculty:* 26 full-time (20 women), 104 part-time/adjunct (53 women). *Students:* 161 full-time (136 women), 70 part-time (54 women); includes 74 minority (24 Black or African American, non-Hispanic/Latino; 1 American Indian or Alaska Native, non-Hispanic/Latino; 27 Asian, non-Hispanic/Latino; 11 Hispanic/Latino; 4 Native Hawaiian or other Pacific Islander, non-Hispanic/Latino; 7 Two or more races, non-Hispanic/Latino), 39 international. Average age 29. 802 applicants, 70% accepted, 97 enrolled. In 2017, 1 master's awarded. *Degree requirements:* For master's, thesis (for some programs); for doctorate, thesis/dissertation. *Entrance requirements:* For master's and doctorate, GRE. Additional exam requirements/recommendations for international students: Required—TOEFL. *Application deadline:* For fall admission, 2/1 for domestic and international students. Applications are processed on a rolling basis. Electronic applications accepted. *Expenses:* Contact institution. *Financial support:* Federal Work-Study and scholarships/grants available. *Unit head:* Dr. Cheryl G. Healton, Director, 212-992-6741. *Application contact:* New York University Information, 212-998-1212.
Website: http://publichealth.nyu.edu/

Northwestern University, School of Professional Studies, Program in Global Health, Evanston, IL 60208. Offers MS. Program offered in partnership with Northwestern University Feinberg School of Medicine's Center for Global Health. *Program availability:* Part-time, evening/weekend, online learning. *Degree requirements:* For master's, practicum.
Website: https://sps.northwestern.edu/masters/global-health/index.php

Oregon State University, College of Public Health and Human Sciences, Program in Public Health, Corvallis, OR 97331. Offers biostatistics (MPH); environmental and occupational health (MPH, PhD); epidemiology (MPH, PhD); global health (MPH, PhD). Terminal master's awarded for partial completion of doctoral program. *Entrance requirements:* For master's and doctorate, GRE, minimum GPA of 3.0 in last 90 hours. Additional exam requirements/recommendations for international students: Required—TOEFL (minimum score 80 iBT), IELTS (minimum score 6.5). *Application deadline:* For fall admission, 12/1 priority date for domestic and international students. Applications are processed on a rolling basis. Electronic applications accepted. *Expenses:* Contact institution. *Financial support:* Application deadline: 12/1. *Unit head:* Amanda Armington, MPH Program Manager, 541-737-3825, E-mail: amanda.armington@oregonstate.edu.

Park University, School of Graduate and Professional Studies, Kansas City, MO 54105. Offers adult education (M Ed); business and government leadership (Graduate Certificate); business, government, and global society (MPA); communication and leadership (MA); creative and life writing (Graduate Certificate); disaster and emergency management (MPA, Graduate Certificate); educational leadership (M Ed); finance (MBA, Graduate Certificate); general business (MBA); global business (Graduate Certificate); healthcare administration (MHA); healthcare services management and leadership (Graduate Certificate); international business (MBA); language and literacy (M Ed), including English for speakers of other languages, special reading teacher/literacy coach; leadership of international healthcare organizations (Graduate Certificate); management information systems (MBA, Graduate Certificate); music performance (ADP, Graduate Certificate), including cello (MM, ADP), piano (MM, ADP), viola (MM, ADP), violin (MM, ADP); nonprofit and community services management (MPA); nonprofit leadership (Graduate Certificate); performance (MM), including cello (MM, ADP), piano (MM, ADP), viola (MM, ADP), violin (MM, ADP); public management (MPA); social work (MSW); teacher leadership (M Ed), including curriculum and assessment, instructional leader. *Program availability:* Part-time, evening/weekend, online learning. *Degree requirements:* For master's, comprehensive exam (for some programs), thesis (for some programs), internship (for some programs); exam (for some programs). *Entrance requirements:* For master's, GRE or GMAT (for some programs), teacher certification (for some M Ed programs), letters of recommendation, essay, resume (for some programs). Additional exam requirements/recommendations for international students: Required—TOEFL (minimum score 550 paper-based; 79 iBT), IELTS (minimum score 6). Electronic applications accepted.

St. Catherine University, Graduate Programs, Program in Global Health, St. Paul, MN 55105. Offers MPH. *Students:* 32 full-time (30 women), 16 part-time (all women); includes 14 minority (9 Black or African American, non-Hispanic/Latino; 5 Asian, non-Hispanic/Latino), 4 international. Average age 29. Tuition and fees vary according to program. *Unit head:* Mary Hearst, Director, 651-690-6157, E-mail: mohearst@stkate.edu.
Website: https://www.stkate.edu/academics/graduate-degrees/academic-programs/mph

San Diego State University, Graduate and Research Affairs, College of Health and Human Services, Graduate School of Public Health, San Diego, CA 92182. Offers environmental health (MPH); epidemiology (MPH, PhD), including biostatistics (MPH); global emergency preparedness and response (MS); global health (PhD); health behavior (PhD); health promotion (MPH); health services administration (MPH); toxicology (MS); MPH/MA; MSW/MPH. *Accreditation:* CAHME (one or more programs are accredited). *Program availability:* Part-time. *Degree requirements:* For master's, comprehensive exam (for some programs), thesis (for some programs); for doctorate, thesis/dissertation. *Entrance requirements:* For master's, GMAT (MPH in health services administration), GRE General Test; for doctorate, GRE General Test. Additional exam requirements/recommendations for international students: Required—TOEFL. *Faculty research:* Evaluation of tobacco, AIDS prevalence and prevention, mammography, infant death project, Alzheimer's in elderly Chinese.

Seton Hall University, School of Diplomacy and International Relations, South Orange, NJ 07079-2697. Offers diplomacy and international relations (MA); global health management (Graduate Certificate); post-conflict state reconstruction and sustainability (Graduate Certificate); United Nations studies (Graduate Certificate); JD/MA; MA/MA; MBA/MA; MPA/MA. *Program availability:* Part-time, evening/weekend, 100% online, blended/hybrid learning. *Degree requirements:* For master's, thesis (for some programs), 45 credits; for Graduate Certificate, 15 credits. *Entrance requirements:* For master's, GRE, GMAT, or LSAT. Additional exam requirements/recommendations for international students: Required—TOEFL. Electronic applications accepted. *Expenses:* Contact institution. *Faculty research:* International economics and development, global health, United Nations, conflict negotiation, foreign policy analysis, international security, energy politics, Eastern and Central Europe, Latin America, Africa, peacemaking, genocide prevention, international organizations, international political economy, U.S.-China relations, democratization, international law, research methods.

International Health

Simon Fraser University, Office of Graduate Studies and Postdoctoral Fellows, Faculty of Health Sciences, Burnaby, BC V5A 1S6, Canada. Offers global health (Graduate Diploma); health sciences (M Sc, PhD); public health (MPH). *Accreditation:* CEPH. *Degree requirements:* For master's, thesis (for some programs); for doctorate, comprehensive exam, thesis/dissertation. *Entrance requirements:* For master's, minimum GPA of 3.0 (on scale of 4.33) or 3.33 based on last 60 credits of undergraduate courses; for doctorate, minimum GPA of 3.5 (on scale of 4.33); for Graduate Diploma, minimum GPA of 2.5 (on scale of 4.33) or 2.67 based on last 60 credits of undergraduate courses. Additional exam requirements/recommendations for international students: Recommended—TOEFL (minimum score 580 paper-based; 93 iBT), IELTS (minimum score 7), TWE (minimum score 5). Electronic applications accepted.

Syracuse University, David B. Falk College of Sport and Human Dynamics, MS Program in Global Health, Syracuse, NY 13244. Offers MS. *Program availability:* Part-time. *Entrance requirements:* For master's, GRE, personal statement, official transcripts, three letters of recommendation, resume. Additional exam requirements/recommendations for international students: Required—TOEFL (minimum score 100 iBT). *Application deadline:* For fall admission, 2/15 priority date for domestic and international students; for spring admission, 11/15 priority date for domestic and international students. Electronic applications accepted. *Financial support:* Fellowships, research assistantships, teaching assistantships, and career-related internships or fieldwork available. Financial award application deadline: 1/1. *Faculty research:* Cardiovascular disease risk in children, environmental toxicants, health disparities and socioeconomic status, stress and health. *Unit head:* Dr. Brooks Gump, Graduate Program Director, 315-443-2208, E-mail: bbgump@syr.edu. *Application contact:* Felicia Otero, Director of College Admissions, 315-443-5555, Fax: 315-443-2562, E-mail: falk@syr.edu.
Website: https://falk.syr.edu/public-health/academic-programs/#msgh

Trident University International, College of Health Sciences, Program in Health Sciences, Cypress, CA 90630. Offers clinical research administration (MS, Certificate); emergency and disaster management (MS, Certificate); environmental health science (Certificate); health care administration (PhD); health care management (MS), including health informatics; health education (MS, Certificate); health informatics (Certificate); health sciences (PhD); international health (MS); international health: educator or researcher option (PhD); international health: practitioner option (PhD); law and expert witness studies (MS, Certificate); public health (MS); quality assurance (Certificate). *Program availability:* Part-time, evening/weekend, online learning. *Degree requirements:* For doctorate, comprehensive exam, thesis/dissertation, defense of dissertation. *Entrance requirements:* For master's, minimum GPA of 2.5 (students with GPA 3.0 or greater may transfer up to 30% of graduate level credits); for doctorate, minimum GPA of 3.4, curriculum vitae, course work in research methods or statistics. Additional exam requirements/recommendations for international students: Required—TOEFL. Electronic applications accepted.

Tulane University, School of Public Health and Tropical Medicine, Department of Global Community Health and Behavioral Sciences, New Orleans, LA 70118-5669. Offers community health sciences (MPH); global community health and behavioral sciences (Dr PH, PhD); JD/MPH; MD/MPH; MSW/MPH. *Program availability:* Part-time. *Degree requirements:* For doctorate, comprehensive exam, thesis/dissertation. *Entrance requirements:* For master's and doctorate, GRE General Test. Additional exam requirements/recommendations for international students: Required—TOEFL. Electronic applications accepted. *Expenses: Tuition:* Full-time $50,920; part-time $2829 per credit hour. *Required fees:* $2040; $44.50 per credit hour. $580 per term. Tuition and fees vary according to course load, degree level and program.

Tulane University, School of Public Health and Tropical Medicine, Department of Global Environmental Health Sciences, New Orleans, LA 70118-5669. Offers MPH, MSPH, PhD, JD/MPH, MD/MPH, MSW/MPH. *Accreditation:* ABET (one or more programs are accredited). *Degree requirements:* For doctorate, comprehensive exam, thesis/dissertation. *Entrance requirements:* For master's and doctorate, GRE General Test. Additional exam requirements/recommendations for international students: Required—TOEFL. Electronic applications accepted. *Expenses: Tuition:* Full-time $50,920; part-time $2829 per credit hour. *Required fees:* $2040; $44.50 per credit hour. $580 per term. Tuition and fees vary according to course load, degree level and program.

Tulane University, School of Public Health and Tropical Medicine, Department of Global Health Management and Policy, New Orleans, LA 70118-5669. Offers MHA, MPH, PhD, Sc D, JD/MHA, MBA/MHA, MD/MPH, MSW/MPH. *Accreditation:* CAHME (one or more programs are accredited). *Degree requirements:* For doctorate, comprehensive exam, thesis/dissertation. *Entrance requirements:* For master's, GMAT, GRE General Test; for doctorate, GRE General Test. Additional exam requirements/recommendations for international students: Required—TOEFL. Electronic applications accepted. *Expenses: Tuition:* Full-time $50,920; part-time $2829 per credit hour. *Required fees:* $2040; $44.50 per credit hour. $580 per term. Tuition and fees vary according to course load, degree level and program. *Faculty research:* Health policy, organizational governance, international health administration.

Uniformed Services University of the Health Sciences, F. Edward Hebert School of Medicine, Graduate Programs in the Biomedical Sciences and Public Health, Bethesda, MD 20814. Offers emerging infectious diseases (PhD); medical and clinical psychology (PhD), including clinical psychology, medical psychology; medicine (MS, PhD), including health professions education; molecular and cell biology (MS, PhD); neuroscience (PhD); preventive medicine and biometrics (MPH, MS, MSPH, MTMH, PhD), including environmental health sciences (PhD), healthcare administration and policy (MS), medical zoology (PhD), public health (MPH, MSPH), tropical medicine and hygiene (MTMH). *Students:* Average age 25. 598 applicants, 17% accepted, 77 enrolled. In 2017, 19 master's, 50 doctorates awarded. Terminal master's awarded for partial completion of doctoral program. *Degree requirements:* For master's, comprehensive exam, thesis or alternative; for doctorate, comprehensive exam, thesis/dissertation, qualifying exam. *Entrance requirements:* For master's, GRE General Test; for doctorate, GRE General Test, minimum GPA of 3.0. *Application deadline:* For fall admission, 12/1 priority date for domestic students. Application fee: $0. Electronic applications accepted. *Expenses:* There are no tuition charges or fees for graduate students at USU. *Financial support:* In 2017–18, 50 fellowships (averaging $43,000 per year) were awarded; research assistantships, career-related internships or fieldwork, scholarships/grants, and health care benefits also available. *Unit head:* Dr. Gregory Mueller, Associate Dean, 301-295-3507, E-mail: gregory.mueller@usuhs.edu. *Application contact:* Tina Finley, Administrative Officer, 301-295-3642, Fax: 301-295-6772, E-mail: netina.finley@usuhs.edu.
Website: http://www.usuhs.mil/graded

Uniformed Services University of the Health Sciences, F. Edward Hebert School of Medicine, Graduate Programs in the Biomedical Sciences and Public Health, Department of Preventive Medicine and Biometrics, Program in Tropical Medicine and Hygiene, Bethesda, MD 20814-4799. Offers MTMH. *Accreditation:* CEPH. *Degree requirements:* For master's, comprehensive exam. *Entrance requirements:* For master's, GRE General Test, MD, U.S. citizenship. *Faculty research:* Epidemiology, biostatistics, tropical public health.

University of Alberta, School of Public Health, Department of Public Health Sciences, Edmonton, AB T6G 2E1, Canada. Offers clinical epidemiology (M Sc, MPH); environmental and occupational health (MPH); environmental health sciences (M Sc); epidemiology (M Sc); global health (M Sc, MPH); health policy and management (MPH); health policy research (M Sc); health technology assessment (MPH); occupational health (M Sc); population health (M Sc); public health leadership (MPH); public health sciences (PhD); quantitative methods (MPH). Terminal master's awarded for partial completion of doctoral program. *Degree requirements:* For master's, thesis (for some programs); for doctorate, thesis/dissertation. *Entrance requirements:* For master's, GMAT or GRE General Test. Additional exam requirements/recommendations for international students: Required—TOEFL (minimum score 550 paper-based) or IELTS (minimum score 6). Electronic applications accepted. *Faculty research:* Biostatistics, health promotion and socio-behavioral health science.

University of California, Riverside, Graduate Division, School of Public Policy, Riverside, CA 92521-0102. Offers global health (MS); public policy (MPP, PhD); MD/MPP. MD/MPP offered in partnership with School of Medicine. *Expenses:* Tuition, state resident: full-time $5746. Tuition, nonresident: full-time $10,780. Tuition and fees vary according to campus/location and program.

University of California, San Diego, Graduate Division, Program in Public Health, La Jolla, CA 92093. Offers epidemiology (PhD); global health (PhD); health behavior (PhD). Program offered jointly with San Diego State University. *Students:* 21 full-time (17 women), 15 part-time (11 women). In 2017, 14 doctorates awarded. *Degree requirements:* For doctorate, thesis/dissertation, 2 semesters/quarters of teaching assistantship. *Entrance requirements:* For doctorate, GRE General Test, minimum GPA of 3.0, curriculum vitae or resume, letters of recommendation, statement of purpose. Additional exam requirements/recommendations for international students: Required—TOEFL (minimum score 550 paper-based; 80 iBT), IELTS (minimum score 7). Electronic applications accepted. *Financial support:* Teaching assistantships available. Financial award applicants required to submit FAFSA. *Faculty research:* Maternal and pediatric HIV/AIDS; healthy aging and gender differences; non-parametric and semi-parametric regression, resampling, and the analysis of high-dimensional data; neighborhood correlates of physical activity in children, teens, adults and older adults; medication safety and medication therapy management through practice-based research networks. *Unit head:* David Strong, Faculty Director, 858-657-5241, E-mail: dstrong@ucsd.edu. *Application contact:* Hollie Ward, Graduate Coordinator, 858-822-2382, E-mail: hward@ucsd.edu.
Website: http://publichealth.ucsd.edu/jdp/

University of Colorado Denver, School of Medicine, Physician Assistant Program, Aurora, CO 80045. Offers child health associate (MPAS), including global health, leadership, education, advocacy, development, and scholarship, pediatric critical and acute care, rural health, urban/underserved populations. *Accreditation:* ARC-PA. *Students:* 130 full-time (108 women); includes 21 minority (4 Black or African American, non-Hispanic/Latino; 4 Asian, non-Hispanic/Latino; 8 Hispanic/Latino; 5 Two or more races, non-Hispanic/Latino). Average age 27. 57 applicants, 96% accepted, 44 enrolled. *Degree requirements:* For master's, comprehensive exam. *Entrance requirements:* For master's, GRE General Test, minimum GPA of 2.8; 3 letters of recommendation; prerequisite courses in chemistry, biology, general genetics, psychology and statistics; interview. Additional exam requirements/recommendations for international students: Required—TOEFL (minimum score 550 paper-based; 80 iBT). *Application deadline:* For fall admission, 9/1 for domestic students, 8/15 for international students. Application fee: $170. Electronic applications accepted. *Faculty research:* Clinical genetics and genetic counseling, evidence-based medicine, pediatric allergy and asthma, childhood diabetes, standardized patient assessment. *Unit head:* Jonathan Bowser, Program Director, 303-724-1349, E-mail: jonathan.bowser@ucdenver.edu. *Application contact:* Kay Denler, Academic Services Program Manager, 303-724-7963, E-mail: kay.denler@ucdenver.edu.
Website: http://www.ucdenver.edu/academics/colleges/medicalschool/education/degree_programs/PAProgram/Pages/Home.aspx

University of Denver, Josef Korbel School of International Studies, Denver, CO 80208. Offers conflict resolution (MA); global business and corporate social responsibility (Certificate); global finance, trade and economic integration (MA); global health affairs (Certificate); homeland security (Certificate); humanitarian assistance (Certificate); international administration (MA); international development (MA); international human rights (MA); international security (MA); international studies (MA, PhD); public policy studies (MPP); religion and international affairs (Certificate). *Program availability:* Part-time. *Faculty:* 46 full-time (16 women), 28 part-time/adjunct (8 women). *Students:* 245 full-time (132 women), 40 part-time (21 women); includes 58 minority (8 Black or African American, non-Hispanic/Latino; 2 American Indian or Alaska Native, non-Hispanic/Latino; 11 Asian, non-Hispanic/Latino; 27 Hispanic/Latino; 10 Two or more races, non-Hispanic/Latino), 22 international. Average age 27. 627 applicants, 74% accepted, 106 enrolled. In 2017, 218 master's, 6 doctorates, 25 other advanced degrees awarded. *Degree requirements:* For master's, one foreign language, thesis (for some programs); for doctorate, one foreign language, comprehensive exam, thesis/dissertation, two extended research papers. *Entrance requirements:* For master's, GRE General Test, bachelor's degree, transcripts, two letters of recommendation, statement of purpose, resume or curriculum vitae; for doctorate, GRE General Test, master's degree, transcripts, three letters of recommendation, statement of purpose, resume or curriculum vitae, writing sample; for Certificate, bachelor's degree, transcripts, two letters of recommendation, statement of purpose, resume or curriculum vitae. Additional exam requirements/recommendations for international students: Required—TOEFL (minimum score 587 paper-based; 95 iBT). *Application deadline:* For fall admission, 1/15 priority date for domestic and international students; for winter admission, 11/1 for domestic and international students. Applications are processed on a rolling basis. Application fee: $65. Electronic applications accepted. *Expenses:* $47,823 per year full-time. *Financial support:* In 2017–18, 225 students received support, including 1 teaching assistantship with tuition reimbursement available (averaging $2,236 per year); research assistantships with tuition reimbursements available, career-related internships or fieldwork, Federal Work-Study, institutionally sponsored loans, scholarships/grants, and unspecified assistantships also available. Support available to part-time students. Financial award application deadline: 2/15; financial award applicants required to submit FAFSA. *Faculty research:* Human rights and international security, international politics and economics, economic-social and political development, international technology analysis and management. *Unit head:* Dr. Pardis Mahdavi, Dean, 303-871-6338, E-mail: pardis.mahdavi@du.edu. *Application contact:* Admissions Contact, E-mail: korbeladm@du.edu.
Website: http://www.du.edu/korbel

University of Florida, Graduate School, College of Public Health and Health Professions, Department of Environmental and Global Health, Gainesville, FL 32611. Offers environmental health (PhD); one health (MHS, PhD). *Entrance requirements:* For master's and doctorate, GRE, minimum GPA of 3.0. Additional exam requirements/recommendations for international students: Required—TOEFL (minimum score 550 paper-based; 80 iBT), IELTS (minimum score 6).

University of Maryland, Baltimore, School of Nursing, Baltimore, MD 21201. Offers adult-gerontology acute care nurse practitioner (DNP); adult-gerontology primary care nurse practitioner (DNP); clinical nurse leader (MS); community/public health nursing (MS); family nurse practitioner (DNP); global health (Postbaccalaureate Certificate); health services leadership and management (MS); neonatal nurse practitioner (DNP); nurse anesthesia (DNP); nursing (PhD); nursing informatics (MS, Postbaccalaureate Certificate); pediatric acute/primary care nurse practitioner (DNP); psychiatric mental health nurse practitioner (DNP); teaching in nursing and health professions (Postbaccalaureate Certificate); MS/MBA. MS/MBA offered jointly with University of Baltimore. *Program availability:* Part-time. *Faculty:* 130 full-time (117 women), 125 part-time/adjunct (114 women). *Students:* 504 full-time (442 women), 532 part-time (482 women); includes 443 minority (249 Black or African American, non-Hispanic/Latino; 1 American Indian or Alaska Native, non-Hispanic/Latino; 115 Asian, non-Hispanic/Latino; 48 Hispanic/Latino; 2 Native Hawaiian or other Pacific Islander, non-Hispanic/Latino; 28 Two or more races, non-Hispanic/Latino), 15 international. Average age 33. 935 applicants, 62% accepted, 394 enrolled. In 2017, 182 master's, 57 doctorates awarded. *Degree requirements:* For master's and Postbaccalaureate Certificate, thesis (for some programs); for doctorate, comprehensive exam, thesis/dissertation. *Entrance requirements:* Additional exam requirements/recommendations for international students: Required—TOEFL (minimum score 550 paper-based; 79 iBT); Recommended—IELTS (minimum score 7). *Application deadline:* For fall admission, 11/1 for domestic and international students; for spring admission, 8/1 for domestic and international students. Application fee: $75. Electronic applications accepted. *Expenses:* Contact institution. *Financial support:* In 2017–18, 22 research assistantships with full and partial tuition reimbursements (averaging $21,523 per year), 41 teaching assistantships with full and partial tuition reimbursements (averaging $13,439 per year) were awarded; fellowships and scholarships/grants also available. Financial award application deadline: 3/1; financial award applicants required to submit FAFSA. *Unit head:* Dr. Jane Kirschling, Dean, 410-706-4359, E-mail: kirschling@umaryland.edu. *Application contact:* Larry Fillian, Associate Dean of Student and Academic Services, 410-706-6298, E-mail: lfillian@umaryland.edu.
Website: http://www.nursing.umaryland.edu/

University of Michigan, School of Public Health, Department of Epidemiology, Ann Arbor, MI 48109-2029. Offers epidemiological science (PhD); general epidemiology (MPH); global health epidemiology (MPH); hospital and molecular epidemiology (MPH); occupational and environmental epidemiology (MPH). PhD and MS offered through the Rackham Graduate School. *Accreditation:* CEPH (one or more programs are accredited). Terminal master's awarded for partial completion of doctoral program. *Degree requirements:* For master's, thesis (for some programs); for doctorate, comprehensive exam, thesis/dissertation, oral defense of dissertation, preliminary exam. *Entrance requirements:* For master's and doctorate, GRE General Test, MCAT. Additional exam requirements/recommendations for international students: Required—TOEFL (minimum score 100 iBT). Electronic applications accepted. *Expenses:* Tuition, state resident: full-time $22,368; part-time $1201 per credit hour. Tuition, nonresident: full-time $45,156; part-time $2467 per credit hour. *Required fees:* $376 per term. Tuition and fees vary according to course load, degree level and program. *Faculty research:* Molecular virology, infectious diseases, women's health, genetics, social epidemiology.

University of Minnesota, Twin Cities Campus, School of Public Health, Division of Environmental Health Sciences, Minneapolis, MN 55455-0213. Offers environmental and occupational epidemiology (MPH, MS, PhD); environmental chemistry (MS, PhD); environmental health policy (MPH, MS, PhD); environmental infectious diseases (MPH, MS, PhD); environmental toxicology (MPH, MS, PhD); exposure sciences (MS); general environmental health (MPH, MS); global environmental health (MPH, MS, PhD); industrial hygiene (MPH, MS, PhD); occupational health nursing (MPH, MS, PhD); occupational medicine (MPH); MPH/MS. *Accreditation:* CEPH (one or more programs are accredited). *Program availability:* Part-time. *Degree requirements:* For master's, thesis optional; for doctorate, thesis/dissertation. *Entrance requirements:* For master's and doctorate, GRE General Test. Additional exam requirements/recommendations for international students: Required—TOEFL (minimum score 600 paper-based; 100 iBT). Electronic applications accepted. *Faculty research:* Behavior/measurement of airborne particles, toxicity mechanisms of environmental contaminants, health and safety interventions, foodborne disease surveillance, measuring pesticide exposures in children.

University of Northern Colorado, Graduate School, College of Natural and Health Sciences, School of Human Sciences, Program in Public Health, Greeley, CO 80639. Offers community health education (MPH); global health and community health education (MPH); healthy aging and community health education (MPH). *Degree requirements:* For master's, comprehensive exam, thesis or alternative. *Entrance requirements:* For master's, GRE General Test, 2 letters of recommendation. Electronic applications accepted.

University of North Texas Health Science Center at Fort Worth, School of Public Health, Fort Worth, TX 76107-2699. Offers biostatistics (MS); epidemiology (MPH, MS, PhD); food security and public health (Graduate Certificate); GIS in public health (Graduate Certificate); global health (Graduate Certificate); global health for medical professionals (Graduate Certificate); health administration (MHA); health behavior research (MS, PhD); maternal and child health (MPH); public health (Graduate Certificate); public health practice (MPH); DO/MPH; MS/MPH. *Accreditation:* CEPH. *Program availability:* Part-time, evening/weekend, 100% online. *Degree requirements:* For master's, thesis or alternative, supervised internship; for doctorate, thesis/dissertation, supervised internship. *Entrance requirements:* For master's, GRE General Test. Additional exam requirements/recommendations for international students: Required—TOEFL. Electronic applications accepted. *Expenses:* Contact institution.

University of Pennsylvania, Perelman School of Medicine, Master of Public Health Program, Philadelphia, PA 19104. Offers environmental health (MPH); generalist (MPH); global health (MPH); DMD/MPH; JD/MPH; MD/MPH; MES/MPH; MPH/MBE; MPH/MPA; MPH/MS; MSN/MPH; MSSP/MPH; MSW/MPH; PhD/MPH. *Accreditation:* CEPH. *Program availability:* Part-time, evening/weekend. *Faculty:* 12 full-time (10 women), 36 part-time/adjunct (27 women). *Students:* 130 full-time (102 women), 61 part-time (50 women); includes 85 minority (29 Black or African American, non-Hispanic/Latino; 33 Asian, non-Hispanic/Latino; 4 Hispanic/Latino; 19 Two or more races, non-Hispanic/Latino), 12 international. Average age 29. 385 applicants, 47% accepted, 62 enrolled. In 2017, 50 master's awarded. *Degree requirements:* For master's, thesis. *Entrance requirements:* For master's, GRE. Additional exam requirements/recommendations for international students: Required—TOEFL (minimum score 100 iBT), IELTS (minimum score 7). *Application deadline:* For fall admission, 4/15 for domestic and international students. Applications are processed on a rolling basis. Electronic applications accepted. *Expenses:* $31,682 tuition, $4,066 fees. *Financial support:* In 2017–18, 27 students received support, including 6 research assistantships with partial tuition reimbursements available (averaging $18,104 per year), 21 teaching assistantships with partial tuition reimbursements available (averaging $4,526 per year); fellowships and tuition waivers (partial) also available. Financial award application deadline: 4/15; financial award applicants required to submit FAFSA. *Faculty research:* Health disparities, health behaviors, obesity, global health, epidemiology and prevention research. *Unit head:* Dr. Jennifer Pinto-Martin, Director, 215-898-4726, E-mail: pinto@nursing.upenn.edu. *Application contact:* Moriah Hall, Associate Director, MPH Program, 215-573-8841, E-mail: moriahh@mail.med.upenn.edu.
Website: http://www.cphi.upenn.edu/mph

University of Pittsburgh, Graduate School of Public Health, Department of Behavioral and Community Health Sciences, Pittsburgh, PA 15261. Offers applied research and leadership in behavioral and community health sciences (Dr PH); applied social and behavioral concepts in public health (MPH); community-based participatory research (Certificate); evaluation of public health programs (Certificate); global health (Certificate); health equity (Certificate); LGBT health and wellness (Certificate); maternal and child health (MPH); MID/MPH; MPH/MPA; MPH/MSW; MPH/PhD. *Accreditation:* CEPH. *Program availability:* Part-time, online learning. *Faculty:* 17 full-time (10 women), 1 (woman) part-time/adjunct. *Students:* 89 full-time (68 women), 22 part-time (17 women); includes 22 minority (12 Black or African American, non-Hispanic/Latino; 7 Hispanic/Latino; 3 Two or more races, non-Hispanic/Latino), 9 international. Average age 29. 186 applicants, 71% accepted, 33 enrolled. In 2017, 32 master's, 7 doctorates awarded. *Degree requirements:* For master's, thesis, 200-contact hour practicum, final paper; for doctorate, comprehensive exam, thesis/dissertation, preliminary exam, dissertation defense. *Entrance requirements:* For master's, GRE, bachelor's degree; for doctorate, GRE, master's degree in public health or related field; for Certificate, GRE. Additional exam requirements/recommendations for international students: Required—TOEFL (minimum score 550 paper-based, 80 iBT) or IELTS (6.5). *Application deadline:* For fall admission, 1/15 for domestic and international students; for winter admission, 9/1 for international students; for spring admission, 10/15 for domestic students, 9/1 for international students; for summer admission, 12/1 for international students. Applications are processed on a rolling basis. Application fee: $135. Electronic applications accepted. *Expenses:* $13,068 per term full-time resident, $21,696 nonresident, $425 per term fees. *Financial support:* In 2017–18, 21 students received support, including 19 fellowships with full tuition reimbursements available (averaging $14,620 per year), 8 research assistantships with full tuition reimbursements available (averaging $14,620 per year). Financial award applicants required to submit FAFSA. *Faculty research:* Health disparities, HIV/AIDS, healthy aging, violence prevention, substance abuse. *Total annual research expenditures:* $4 million. *Unit head:* Dr. Steven M. Albert, Chairman, 412-383-8693, Fax: 412-624-5510, E-mail: smalbert@pitt.edu. *Application contact:* Paul J. Markgraf, Recruitment and Academic Affairs Administrator, 412-624-3107, Fax: 412-624-5510, E-mail: pjm111@pitt.edu.
Website: http://www.bchs.pitt.edu/

University of Pittsburgh, School of Pharmacy, Professional Program in Pharmacy, Pittsburgh, PA 15261. Offers community, leadership, innovation, and practice (Pharm D); global health (Pharm D); pediatrics (Pharm D); pharmacotherapy (Pharm D); pharmacy business administration (Pharm D). *Accreditation:* ACPE. *Faculty:* 70 full-time (37 women), 7 part-time/adjunct (0 women). *Students:* 457 full-time (300 women); includes 115 minority (14 Black or African American, non-Hispanic/Latino; 1 American Indian or Alaska Native, non-Hispanic/Latino; 81 Asian, non-Hispanic/Latino; 7 Hispanic/Latino; 12 Two or more races, non-Hispanic/Latino), 7 international. Average age 23. 435 applicants, 33% accepted, 115 enrolled. In 2017, 110 doctorates awarded. *Entrance requirements:* For doctorate, PCAT. *Application deadline:* For fall admission, 12/1 for domestic students. Application fee: $175. Electronic applications accepted. *Expenses:* $31,040 in-state tuition per year; $34,924 out-of-state tuition per year; $1,534 fees per year. *Financial support:* In 2017–18, 125 students received support. Scholarships/grants available. Financial award application deadline: 3/31. *Faculty research:* Pharmacy practice, patient care models, clinical outcomes, healthcare policy, clinical and translational focusing on identifying genetic predictors of clinically-relevant drug-related outcomes, role of transporters in drug disposition and pathophysiology in critical care, clinical importance of pharmacogenomics in drug response. *Total annual research expenditures:* $5.8 million. *Unit head:* Dr. Patricia Dowley Kroboth, Dean, 412-624-2400, Fax: 412-648-1086, E-mail: pkroboth@pitt.edu. *Application contact:* Marcia Borrelli, Director of Student Services, 412-648-1120, Fax: 412-383-9996, E-mail: borrelli@pitt.edu.
Website: http://www.pharmacy.pitt.edu

University of Southern California, Keck School of Medicine and Graduate School, Graduate Programs in Medicine, Department of Preventive Medicine, Master of Public Health Program, Los Angeles, CA 90032. Offers biostatistics and epidemiology (MPH); child and family health (MPH); environmental health (MPH); geohealth (MPH); global health leadership (MPH); health communication (MPH); health education and promotion (MPH); public health policy (MPH). *Accreditation:* CEPH. *Program availability:* Part-time, evening/weekend. *Faculty:* 47 full-time (35 women), 13 part-time/adjunct (8 women). *Students:* 258 full-time (204 women), 61 part-time (50 women); includes 167 minority (28 Black or African American, non-Hispanic/Latino; 1 American Indian or Alaska Native, non-Hispanic/Latino; 61 Asian, non-Hispanic/Latino; 64 Hispanic/Latino; 4 Native Hawaiian or other Pacific Islander, non-Hispanic/Latino; 9 Two or more races, non-Hispanic/Latino), 28 international. Average age 26. 378 applicants, 53% accepted, 87 enrolled. In 2017, 91 master's awarded. *Degree requirements:* For master's, practicum, final report, oral presentation. *Entrance requirements:* For master's, GRE General Test, MCAT, GMAT, minimum GPA of 3.0. Additional exam requirements/recommendations for international students: Required—TOEFL (minimum score 600 paper-based; 90 iBT). *Application deadline:* For fall admission, 12/1 priority date for domestic students, 5/1 priority date for international students; for spring admission, 9/1 priority date for domestic and international students; for summer admission, 3/1 for domestic and international students. Applications are processed on a rolling basis. Application fee: $90. Electronic applications accepted. *Expenses:* Contact institution. *Financial support:* Career-related internships or fieldwork, Federal Work-Study, institutionally sponsored loans, and scholarships/grants available. Support available to part-time students. Financial award application deadline: 5/4; financial award applicants required to submit CSS PROFILE or FAFSA. *Faculty research:* Cancer and heart disease epidemiology and prevention, mass media and health communication research, effects of air pollution on health, tobacco control, global health. *Total annual research expenditures:* $7 million. *Unit head:* Dr. Louise A. Rohrbach, Director, 323-442-8237, Fax: 323-442-8297, E-mail: rohrbac@usc.edu. *Application contact:* Valerie Burris, Admissions Counselor, 323-442-7257, Fax: 323-442-8297, E-mail: valeriem@usc.edu.
Website: http://mph.usc.edu/

University of Southern California, Keck School of Medicine and Graduate School, Graduate Programs in Medicine, Master of Science Program in Global Medicine, Los Angeles, CA 90033. Offers MS, Certificate. *Program availability:* Part-time. *Faculty:* 10 part-time/adjunct (4 women). *Students:* 121 full-time (84 women), 2 part-time (1 woman); includes 60 minority (5 Black or African American, non-Hispanic/Latino; 38 Asian, non-Hispanic/Latino; 15 Hispanic/Latino; 2 Two or more races, non-Hispanic/Latino), 5 international. Average age 24. 144 applicants, 60% accepted, 68 enrolled. In 2017, 93 master's awarded. *Entrance requirements:* For master's and Certificate, GRE, MCAT, or DAT. Additional exam requirements/recommendations for international students: Required—TOEFL (minimum score 100 iBT), IELTS (6.5), or PTE. *Application deadline:* For fall admission, 6/15 for domestic and international students; for spring admission, 10/31 for domestic and international students; for summer admission, 4/7 for domestic and international students. Applications are processed on a rolling basis. Application

fee: $90. Electronic applications accepted. *Expenses:* Contact institution. *Financial support:* Application deadline: 5/10; applicants required to submit FAFSA. *Faculty research:* Global health; infectious diseases; anatomy, physiology, and pathology; mental health; interprofessional health; palliative care. *Unit head:* Dr. Elahe Nezami, Program Director, 323-442-3141, E-mail: nezami@usc.edu. *Application contact:* Caroline Cristal, Student Services Advisor, 323-442-3141, E-mail: ccristal@usc.edu.
Website: http://msgm.usc.edu

University of South Florida, College of Public Health, Department of Global Health, Tampa, FL 33620-9951. Offers MPH, MSPH, Dr PH, PhD. *Program availability:* Part-time, evening/weekend. *Degree requirements:* For master's, comprehensive exam, thesis (for some programs), minimum GPA of 3.0; for doctorate, comprehensive exam, thesis/dissertation. *Entrance requirements:* For master's, GRE General Test, minimum GPA of 3.0 in upper-level course work, goal statement letter, two professional letters of recommendation, resume/curriculum vitae; for doctorate, GRE General Test, minimum GPA of 3.0 in upper-level course work, goal statement letter, three professional letters of recommendation, resume/curriculum vitae, writing sample. Additional exam requirements/recommendations for international students: Required—TOEFL (minimum score 550 paper-based; 79 iBT). Electronic applications accepted.

University of South Florida, Innovative Education, Tampa, FL 33620-9951. Offers adult, career and higher education (Graduate Certificate), including college teaching, leadership in developing human resources, leadership in higher education; Africana studies (Graduate Certificate), including diasporas and health disparities, genocide and human rights; aging studies (Graduate Certificate), including gerontology; art research (Graduate Certificate), including museum studies; business foundations (Graduate Certificate); chemical and biomedical engineering (Graduate Certificate), including materials science and engineering, water, health and sustainability; child and family studies (Graduate Certificate), including positive behavior support; civil and industrial engineering (Graduate Certificate), including transportation systems analysis; community and family health (Graduate Certificate), including maternal and child health, social marketing and public health, violence and injury: prevention and intervention, women's health; criminology (Graduate Certificate), including criminal justice administration; data science for public administration (Graduate Certificate); digital humanities (Graduate Certificate); educational measurement and research (Graduate Certificate), including evaluation; English (Graduate Certificate), including comparative literary studies, creative writing, professional and technical communication; entrepreneurship (Graduate Certificate); environmental health (Graduate Certificate), including safety management; epidemiology and biostatistics (Graduate Certificate), including applied biostatistics, biostatistics, concepts and tools of epidemiology, epidemiology, epidemiology of infectious diseases; geography, environment and planning (Graduate Certificate), including community development, environmental policy and management, geographical information systems; geology (Graduate Certificate), including hydrogeology; global health (Graduate Certificate), including disaster management, global health and Latin American and Caribbean studies, global health practice, humanitarian assistance, infection control; government and international affairs (Graduate Certificate), including Cuban studies, globalization studies; health policy and management (Graduate Certificate), including health management and leadership, public health policy and programs; hearing specialist: early intervention (Graduate Certificate); industrial and management systems engineering (Graduate Certificate), including systems engineering, technology management; information studies (Graduate Certificate), including school library media specialist; information systems/decision sciences (Graduate Certificate), including analytics and business intelligence; instructional technology (Graduate Certificate), including distance education, Florida digital/virtual educator, instructional design, multimedia design, Web design; internal medicine, bioethics and medical humanities (Graduate Certificate), including biomedical ethics; Latin American and Caribbean studies (Graduate Certificate); leadership for coastal resiliency planning (Graduate Certificate); mass communications (Graduate Certificate), including multimedia journalism; mathematics and statistics (Graduate Certificate), including mathematics; medicine (Graduate Certificate), including aging and neuroscience, bioinformatics, biotechnology, brain fitness and memory management, clinical investigation, hand and upper limb rehabilitation, health informatics, health sciences, integrative weight management, intellectual property, medicine and gender, metabolic and nutritional medicine, metabolic cardiology, pharmacy sciences; national and competitive intelligence (Graduate Certificate); nursing (Graduate Certificate), including simulation based academic fellowship in advanced pain management; psychological and social foundations (Graduate Certificate), including career counseling, college teaching, diversity in education, mental health counseling, school counseling; public affairs (Graduate Certificate), including nonprofit management, public management, research administration; public health (Graduate Certificate), including assessing chemical toxicity and public health risks, health equity, pharmacoepidemiology, public health generalist, toxicology, translational research in adolescent behavioral health; public health practices (Graduate Certificate), including planning for healthy communities; rehabilitation and mental health counseling (Graduate Certificate), including integrative mental health care, marriage and family therapy, rehabilitation technology; secondary education (Graduate Certificate), including ESOL, foreign language education: culture and content, foreign language education: professional; social work (Graduate Certificate), including geriatric social work/clinical gerontology; special education (Graduate Certificate), including autism spectrum disorder, disabilities education: severe/profound; world languages (Graduate Certificate), including teaching English as a second language (TESL) or foreign language. *Unit head:* Dr. Cynthia DeLuca, Associate Vice President and Assistant Vice Provost, 813-974-3077, Fax: 813-974-7061, E-mail: deluca@usf.edu. *Application contact:* Owen Hooper, Director, Summer and Alternative Calendar Programs, 813-974-6917, E-mail: hooper@usf.edu.
Website: http://www.usf.edu/innovative-education/

The University of Toledo, College of Graduate Studies, College of Medicine and Life Sciences, Department of Public Health and Preventative Medicine, Toledo, OH 43606-3390. Offers biostatistics and epidemiology (Certificate); contemporary gerontological practice (Certificate); environmental and occupational health and safety (MPH); epidemiology (Certificate); global public health (Certificate); health promotion and education (MPH); industrial hygiene (MSOH); medical and health science teaching and learning (Certificate); occupational health (Certificate); public health administration (MPH); public health and emergency response (Certificate); public health epidemiology (MPH); public health nutrition (MPH); MD/MPH. *Program availability:* Part-time, evening/weekend. *Degree requirements:* For master's, thesis or alternative. *Entrance requirements:* For master's, GRE, minimum undergraduate GPA of 3.0, three letters of recommendation, statement of purpose, transcripts from all prior institutions attended, resume; for Certificate, minimum undergraduate GPA of 3.0, three letters of recommendation, statement of purpose, transcripts from all prior institutions attended, resume. Additional exam requirements/recommendations for international students: Required—TOEFL (minimum score 550 paper-based; 80 iBT), IELTS (minimum score 6.5). Electronic applications accepted.

University of Vermont, The Robert Larner, MD College of Medicine and Graduate College, Graduate Programs in Medicine, Program in Public Health, Burlington, VT 05405. Offers epidemiology (Graduate Certificate); global and environmental health (Graduate Certificate); healthcare management and policy (Graduate Certificate); public health (MPH). *Program availability:* Online only, 100% online. *Students:* 96. 73 applicants, 88% accepted, 41 enrolled. In 2017, 6 master's, 6 other advanced degrees awarded. *Entrance requirements:* For master's and Graduate Certificate, resume/curriculum vitae. Additional exam requirements/recommendations for international students: Required—TOEFL (minimum iBT score of 90) or IELTS (6.5). *Application deadline:* For fall admission, 7/1 for domestic and international students; for spring admission, 11/15 for domestic and international students; for summer admission, 4/1 for domestic and international students. Application fee: $65. Electronic applications accepted. *Expenses:* $646 per credit in-state, $970 per credit out-of-state. *Unit head:* Dr. Jan Carney, Coordinator, 802-656-2085, E-mail: public.health@uvm.edu.
Website: https://learn.uvm.edu/program/master-of-public-health/

University of Washington, Graduate School, School of Public Health, Department of Epidemiology, Seattle, WA 98195. Offers clinical research methods (MS); epidemiology (PhD); general epidemiology (MPH, MS); global health (MPH); maternal and child health (MPH); MPH/MPA. *Accreditation:* CEPH (one or more programs are accredited). *Faculty:* 51 full-time (30 women), 40 part-time/adjunct (20 women). *Students:* 145 full-time (104 women), 30 part-time (23 women); includes 54 minority (6 Black or African American, non-Hispanic/Latino; 2 American Indian or Alaska Native, non-Hispanic/Latino; 32 Asian, non-Hispanic/Latino; 13 Hispanic/Latino; 1 Native Hawaiian or other Pacific Islander, non-Hispanic/Latino), 17 international. Average age 31. 395 applicants, 43% accepted, 58 enrolled. In 2017, 40 master's, 9 doctorates awarded. *Entrance requirements:* For master's, GRE (except for those MD/DO from U.S. institutions); for doctorate, GRE. Additional exam requirements/recommendations for international students: Required—TOEFL. Electronic applications accepted. *Financial support:* Fellowships, research assistantships, teaching assistantships, career-related internships or fieldwork, scholarships/grants, traineeships, health care benefits, and tuition waivers (full and partial) available. Support available to part-time students. Financial award applicants required to submit FAFSA. *Faculty research:* Chronic disease, health disparities and social determinants of health, aging and neuroepidemiology, maternal and child health, molecular and genetic epidemiology. *Unit head:* E-mail: epiadmin@uw.edu. *Application contact:* John Paulson, Assistant Director of Student Academic Services, 206-685-1762, E-mail: epi@uw.edu.
Website: https://epi.washington.edu/

University of Washington, Graduate School, School of Public Health, Department of Global Health, Seattle, WA 98195. Offers global health (MPH); global health metrics and implementation science (PhD); health metrics and evaluation (MPH); leadership, policy and management (MPH); pathobiology (PhD). *Accreditation:* CEPH. *Program availability:* Part-time, online learning. *Faculty:* 84 full-time (37 women), 71 part-time/adjunct (33 women). *Students:* 100 full-time (75 women), 52 part-time (28 women); includes 42 minority (8 Black or African American, non-Hispanic/Latino; 1 American Indian or Alaska Native, non-Hispanic/Latino; 22 Asian, non-Hispanic/Latino; 10 Hispanic/Latino; 1 Native Hawaiian or other Pacific Islander, non-Hispanic/Latino), 29 international. Average age 29. 286 applicants, 43% accepted, 71 enrolled. In 2017, 46 master's, 2 doctorates awarded. Terminal master's awarded for partial completion of doctoral program. Electronic applications accepted. *Financial support:* Fellowships, research assistantships, teaching assistantships, career-related internships or fieldwork, scholarships/grants, tuition waivers (full and partial), and unspecified assistantships available. Financial award applicants required to submit FAFSA. *Unit head:* Dr. Judith Wasserheit, Chair, 206-221-4970, Fax: 206-685-8519, E-mail: jwasserh@uw.edu. *Application contact:* Noura Youssoufa, Academic Program Coordinator, 206-685-1292, E-mail: ghprog@uw.edu.
Website: http://globalhealth.washington.edu/

Walden University, Graduate Programs, School of Health Sciences, Minneapolis, MN 55401. Offers clinical research administration (MS, Graduate Certificate); health education and promotion (MS, PhD), including behavioral health (PhD), disease surveillance (PhD), emergency preparedness (MS), general (MHA, MS), global health (PhD), health policy (PhD), health policy and advocacy (MS), population health (PhD); health informatics (MS); health services (PhD), including community health, healthcare administration, leadership, public health policy, self-designed; healthcare administration (MHA, DHA), including general (MHA, MS); leadership and organizational development (MHA); public health (MPH, Dr PH, PhD, Graduate Certificate), including community health education (PhD), epidemiology (PhD); systems policy (MHA). *Program availability:* Part-time, evening/weekend, online only, 100% online. *Degree requirements:* For doctorate, thesis/dissertation, residency. *Entrance requirements:* For master's, bachelor's degree or higher; minimum GPA of 2.5; official transcripts; goal statement (for some programs); access to computer and Internet; for doctorate, master's degree or higher; three years of related professional or academic experience (preferred); minimum GPA of 3.0; goal statement and current resume (for select programs); official transcripts; access to computer and Internet; for Graduate Certificate, relevant work experience; access to computer and Internet. Additional exam requirements/recommendations for international students: Required—TOEFL (minimum score 550 paper-based, 79 iBT), IELTS (minimum score 6.5), Michigan English Language Assessment Battery (minimum score 82), or PTE (minimum score 53). Electronic applications accepted.

Washington University in St. Louis, Brown School, St. Louis, MO 63110. Offers American Indian/Alaska native (MSW); children, youth and families (MSW); epidemiology/biostatistics (MPH); generalist (MPH); global health (MPH); health (MSW); health policy analysis (MPH); individualized (MSW), including health; mental health (MSW); older adults and aging societies (MSW); public health sciences (PhD); social and economic development (MSW), including domestic, international; social work (PhD); urban design (MPH); violence and injury prevention (MSW); JD/MSW; M Arch/MSW; MPH/MBA; MSW/M Div; MSW/M Ed; MSW/MAPS; MSW/MBA; MSW/MPH; MUD/MSW. MSW/M Div and MSW/MAPS offered in partnership with Eden Theological Seminary. *Accreditation:* CSWE (one or more programs are accredited). *Faculty:* 54 full-time (31 women), 87 part-time/adjunct (61 women). *Students:* 294 full-time (254 women); includes 114 minority (56 Black or African American, non-Hispanic/Latino; 8 American Indian or Alaska Native, non-Hispanic/Latino; 17 Asian, non-Hispanic/Latino; 10 Hispanic/Latino; 1 Native Hawaiian or other Pacific Islander, non-Hispanic/Latino; 22 Two or more races, non-Hispanic/Latino). Average age 26. *Degree requirements:* For master's, 60 credit hours (for MSW); 52 credit hours (for MPH); practicum; for doctorate, comprehensive exam, thesis/dissertation. *Entrance requirements:* For master's, GRE (preferred), GMAT, LSAT, MCAT, PCAT, or United States Medical Licensing Exam (for MPH); for doctorate, GRE. Additional exam requirements/recommendations for international students: Required—TOEFL (minimum score 100 iBT), IELTS (minimum score 7). *Application deadline:* For fall admission, 12/15 priority date for domestic and international students; for winter admission, 3/1 priority date for domestic and international students. Applications are processed on a rolling basis. Electronic applications accepted. *Expenses:* Contact institution. *Financial support:* In 2017–18, 30 fellowships, 60 research assistantships were awarded; career-related internships or fieldwork, Federal Work-Study, scholarships/grants, and unspecified assistantships also available. Support available to part-time students. Financial award applicants required to submit FAFSA. *Faculty research:* Mental health, social policy, health policy, epidemiology, social and economic development. *Total annual research expenditures:*

$14.5 million. *Unit head:* Jamie L. Adkisson-Hennessey, Director of Admissions and Recruitment, 314-935-3524, Fax: 314-935-4859, E-mail: jadkisson@wustl.edu. *Application contact:* Office of Admissions and Recruitment, 314-935-6676, Fax: 314-935-4859, E-mail: brownadmissions@wustl.edu.
Website: http://brownschool.wustl.edu

William James College, Graduate Programs, Newton, MA 02459. Offers applied psychology in higher education student personnel administration (MA); clinical psychology (Psy D); counseling psychology (MA); counseling psychology and community mental health (MA); counseling psychology and global mental health (MA); executive coaching (Graduate Certificate); forensic and counseling psychology (MA); leadership psychology (Psy D); organizational psychology (MA); primary care psychology (MA); respecialization in clinical psychology (Certificate); school psychology (Psy D); MA/CAGS. *Accreditation:* APA. *Degree requirements:* For master's, comprehensive exam (for some programs); for doctorate, thesis/dissertation (for some programs). Electronic applications accepted.

Yale University, Yale School of Medicine, Yale School of Public Health, New Haven, CT 06520. Offers applied biostatistics and epidemiology (APMPH); biostatistics (MPH, MS, PhD), including global health (MPH); chronic disease epidemiology (MPH, PhD), including global health (MPH); environmental health sciences (MPH, PhD), including global health (MPH); epidemiology of microbial diseases (MPH, PhD), including global health (MPH); global health (APMPH); health management (MPH), including global health; health policy (MPH), including global health; health policy and administration (APMPH, PhD); occupational and environmental medicine (APMPH); preventive medicine (APMPH); social and behavioral sciences (APMPH, MPH), including global health (MPH); JD/MPH; M Div/MPH; MBA/MPH; MD/MPH; MEM/MPH; MFS/MPH; MM Sc/MPH; MPH/MA; MSN/MPH. MS and PhD offered through the Graduate School. *Accreditation:* CEPH. *Program availability:* Part-time. Terminal master's awarded for partial completion of doctoral program. *Degree requirements:* For master's, thesis, summer internship; for doctorate, comprehensive exam, thesis/dissertation, residency. *Entrance requirements:* For master's, GMAT, GRE, or MCAT, two years of undergraduate coursework in math and science; for doctorate, GRE General Test. Additional exam requirements/recommendations for international students: Required—TOEFL (minimum score 100 iBT). Electronic applications accepted. *Expenses:* Contact institution. *Faculty research:* Genetic and emerging infections epidemiology, virology, cost/quality, vector biology, quantitative methods, aging, asthma, cancer.

Maternal and Child Health

Bank Street College of Education, Graduate School, Program in Child Life, New York, NY 10025. Offers MS. *Degree requirements:* For master's, thesis. *Entrance requirements:* For master's, interview, essays, 100 hours of volunteer experience in a child life setting. Additional exam requirements/recommendations for international students: Required—TOEFL (minimum score 600 paper-based; 100 iBT), IELTS (minimum score 7). *Faculty research:* Therapeutic play in child life setting, child advocacy, psychosocial and educational intervention with care of sick children.

Bank Street College of Education, Graduate School, Program in Infant and Family Development and Early Intervention, New York, NY 10025. Offers infant and family development (MS Ed); infant and family early childhood special and general education (MS Ed); infant and family/early childhood special education (Ed M). *Degree requirements:* For master's, thesis. *Entrance requirements:* For master's, interview, essays. Additional exam requirements/recommendations for international students: Required—TOEFL (minimum score 600 paper-based; 100 iBT), IELTS (minimum score 7). Electronic applications accepted. *Faculty research:* Early intervention, early attachment practice in infant and toddler childcare, parenting skills in adolescents.

Bastyr University, School of Natural Health Arts and Sciences, Kenmore, WA 98028-4966. Offers counseling psychology (MA); maternal-child health systems (MA); midwifery (MS); nutrition (Certificate); nutrition and clinical health psychology (MS); nutrition and wellness (MS). *Accreditation:* AND. *Program availability:* Part-time. *Degree requirements:* For master's, thesis optional. *Entrance requirements:* For master's, 1-2 years' basic sciences course work (depending on program). Additional exam requirements/recommendations for international students: Required—TOEFL (minimum score 550 paper-based; 79 iBT). *Application deadline:* For fall admission, 3/15 priority date for domestic and international students. Applications are processed on a rolling basis. Application fee: $75. *Expenses: Tuition:* Part-time $714 per credit hour. *Required fees:* $75. *Financial support:* Career-related internships or fieldwork, Federal Work-Study, and scholarships/grants available. Support available to part-time students. Financial award application deadline: 4/15; financial award applicants required to submit FAFSA. *Faculty research:* Whole-food nutrition for type 2 diabetes; meditation in end-of-life care; stress management; Qi Gong, Tai Chi and yoga for older adults; Echinacea and immunology. *Unit head:* Dr. Lynelle Golden, Dean, 425-602-3110, Fax: 425-823-6222, E-mail: lgolden@bastyr.edu. *Application contact:* Admissions Office, 425-602-3330, Fax: 425-602-3090, E-mail: admissions@bastyr.edu.
Website: http://www.bastyr.edu/academics/schools-departments/school-natural-health-arts-sciences

Columbia University, Columbia University Mailman School of Public Health, Department of Population and Family Health, New York, NY 10032. Offers MPH, Dr PH. *Accreditation:* CEPH (one or more programs are accredited). *Program availability:* Part-time. *Students:* 100 full-time (92 women), 20 part-time (18 women); includes 40 minority (6 Black or African American, non-Hispanic/Latino; 21 Asian, non-Hispanic/Latino; 6 Hispanic/Latino; 7 Two or more races, non-Hispanic/Latino), 15 international. Average age 28. 288 applicants, 60% accepted, 53 enrolled. In 2017, 66 master's, 1 doctorate awarded. *Entrance requirements:* For master's, GRE General Test; for doctorate, GRE General Test, MPH or equivalent (for Dr PH). Additional exam requirements/recommendations for international students: Required—TOEFL (minimum score 600 paper-based; 100 iBT). *Application deadline:* For fall admission, 12/1 priority date for domestic and international students. Application fee: $120. *Expenses: Tuition:* Full-time $44,864; part-time $1704 per credit. *Required fees:* $2370 per semester. One-time fee: $105. *Financial support:* Research assistantships, career-related internships or fieldwork, and Federal Work-Study available. Financial award application deadline: 2/1; financial award applicants required to submit FAFSA. *Faculty research:* Child and adolescent health, global health systems, health and human rights, humanitarian disasters, sexual and reproductive health. *Unit head:* Terry McGovern, Professor and Interim Chairperson, 212-304-5200. *Application contact:* Clare Norton, Associate Dean for Enrollment Management, 212-305-8698, Fax: 212-342-1861, E-mail: ph-admit@columbia.edu.
Website: https://www.mailman.columbia.edu/become-student/departments/population-and-family-health

East Carolina University, Graduate School, Thomas Harriot College of Arts and Sciences, Department of Psychology, Greenville, NC 27858-4353. Offers health psychology (PhD), including clinical health psychology, occupational health psychology, pediatric school psychology; industrial and organizational psychology (MA); quantitative methods for the social and behavioral sciences (Certificate); MA/CAS. *Program availability:* Part-time, evening/weekend. *Students:* 77 full-time (52 women), 17 part-time (15 women); includes 12 minority (8 Black or African American, non-Hispanic/Latino; 3 Hispanic/Latino; 1 Two or more races, non-Hispanic/Latino). Average age 26. 221 applicants, 31% accepted, 22 enrolled. In 2017, 31 master's, 7 doctorates, 21 other advanced degrees awarded. *Degree requirements:* For doctorate, comprehensive exam, thesis/dissertation or alternative. *Entrance requirements:* For master's and doctorate, GRE General Test. Additional exam requirements/recommendations for international students: Recommended—TOEFL (minimum score 78 iBT), IELTS (minimum score 6.5). *Application deadline:* For fall admission, 12/1 priority date for domestic and international students. Applications are processed on a rolling basis. Application fee: $75. Electronic applications accepted. *Expenses:* Tuition, state resident: full-time $4749; part-time $297 per credit hour. Tuition, nonresident: full-time $17,898; part-time $1119 per credit hour. *Required fees:* $2691; $224 per credit hour. Part-time tuition and fees vary according to course load and program. *Financial support:* Research assistantships with partial tuition reimbursements, teaching assistantships with partial tuition reimbursements, Federal Work-Study, and traineeships available. Support available to part-time students. Financial award application deadline: 6/1. *Unit head:* Dr. Susan L. McCammon, Chair, 252-328-6357, E-mail: mccammons@ecu.edu. *Application contact:* Dean of Graduate School, 252-328-6012, Fax: 252-328-6071, E-mail: gradschool@ecu.edu.
Website: http://www.ecu.edu/psyc/

Instituto Tecnologico de Santo Domingo, Graduate School, Area of Health Sciences, Santo Domingo, Dominican Republic. Offers bioethics (M Bioethics); clinical bioethics (Certificate); clinical nutrition (Certificate); comprehensive health and the adolescent (Certificate); comrehensive adloescent health (MS); health and social security (M Mgmt).

Oakland University, Graduate Study and Lifelong Learning, School of Health Sciences, Program in Physical Therapy, Rochester, MI 48309-4401. Offers clinical exercise science (Dr Sc PT); complementary medicine and wellness (Dr Sc PT); corporate worksite wellness (Dr Sc PT); exercise science (Dr Sc PT); neurological rehabilitation (Dr Sc PT, TDPT); orthopedic manual physical therapy (Dr Sc PT, TDPT, Graduate Certificate); orthopedic physical therapy (Graduate Certificate); orthopedics (Dr Sc PT, TDPT); pediatric rehabilitation (Dr Sc PT, TDPT); physical therapy (DPT); teaching and learning for rehabilitation professionals (Dr Sc PT, TDPT). *Accreditation:* APTA. *Entrance requirements:* For doctorate, GRE General Test. Additional exam requirements/recommendations for international students: Required—TOEFL (minimum score 550 paper-based). *Expenses:* Contact institution.

Troy University, Graduate School, College of Health and Human Services, Program in Nursing, Troy, AL 36082. Offers adult health (MSN); family nurse practitioner (DNP); maternal infant (MSN); nursing informatics specialist (MSN). *Accreditation:* ACEN. *Program availability:* Part-time, evening/weekend. *Faculty:* 15 full-time (14 women), 8 part-time/adjunct (all women). *Students:* 58 full-time (52 women), 207 part-time (184 women); includes 53 minority (40 Black or African American, non-Hispanic/Latino; 1 American Indian or Alaska Native, non-Hispanic/Latino; 1 Asian, non-Hispanic/Latino; 6 Hispanic/Latino; 5 Two or more races, non-Hispanic/Latino). Average age 36. 66 applicants, 100% accepted, 49 enrolled. In 2017, 113 master's, 14 doctorates awarded. *Degree requirements:* For master's, comprehensive exam, minimum GPA of 3.0, candidacy; for doctorate, minimum GPA of 3.0, submission of approved comprehensive e-portfolio, completion of residency synthesis project, minimum of 1000 hours of clinical practice, qualifying exam. *Entrance requirements:* For master's, GRE (minimum score of 850 on old exam or 290 on new exam) or MAT (minimum score of 396), minimum GPA of 3.0, BSN, current RN licensure, 2 letters of reference, undergraduate health assessment course; for doctorate, GRE (minimum score of 850 on old exam or 294 on new exam), BSN or MSN, minimum GPA of 3.0, 2 letters of reference, current RN licensure, essay. Additional exam requirements/recommendations for international students: Required—TOEFL (minimum score 523 paper-based; 70 iBT), IELTS (minimum score 6). *Application deadline:* Applications are processed on a rolling basis. Application fee: $50. Electronic applications accepted. *Expenses:* Tuition, state resident: part-time $417 per credit hour. Tuition, nonresident: part-time $834 per credit hour. *Required fees:* $42 per credit hour. $50 per semester. Tuition and fees vary according to campus/location. *Financial support:* Fellowships, career-related internships or fieldwork, and scholarships/grants available. Support available to part-time students. Financial award applicants required to submit FAFSA. *Unit head:* Dr. Denise Green, Director, School of Nursing, 334-670-5864, Fax: 334-670-3745, E-mail: dmgreen@troy.edu. *Application contact:* Crystal G. Bishop, Director of Graduate Admissions, School of Nursing, 334-241-8631, E-mail: cdgodwin@troy.edu.

The University of Alabama at Birmingham, School of Public Health, Program in Public Health, Birmingham, AL 35294. Offers applied epidemiology and pharmacoepidemiology (MSPH); biostatistics (MPH); clinical and translational science (MSPH); environmental health (MPH); environmental health and toxicology (MSPH); epidemiology (MPH); general theory and practice (MPH); health behavior (MPH); health care organization (MPH); health policy quantitative policy analysis (MPH); industrial hygiene (MPH, MSPH); maternal and child health policy (Dr PH); maternal and child health policy and leadership (MPH); occupational health and safety (MPH); outcomes research (MSPH, Dr PH); public health (PhD); public health management (Dr PH); public health preparedness management (MPH). *Program availability:* Part-time, online learning. *Degree requirements:* For doctorate, comprehensive exam, thesis/dissertation. *Entrance requirements:* For master's and doctorate, GRE. Additional exam requirements/recommendations for international students: Recommended—TOEFL (minimum score 550 paper-based; 79 iBT), IELTS (minimum score 6.5). Electronic applications accepted.

University of California, Davis, Graduate Studies, Program in Maternal and Child Nutrition, Davis, CA 95616. Offers MAS. *Degree requirements:* For master's, comprehensive exam. *Entrance requirements:* Additional exam requirements/recommendations for international students: Required—TOEFL (minimum score 550 paper-based).

Maternal and Child Health

University of Manitoba, Max Rady College of Medicine and Faculty of Graduate Studies, Graduate Programs in Medicine, Department of Pediatrics and Child Health, Winnipeg, MB R3T 2N2, Canada. Offers M Sc.

University of Maryland, College Park, Academic Affairs, School of Public Health, Department of Family Science, College Park, MD 20742. Offers family studies (PhD); marriage and family therapy (MS); maternal and child health (PhD). *Accreditation:* AAMFT/COAMFTE. *Program availability:* Part-time, evening/weekend. *Degree requirements:* For master's, thesis or alternative; for doctorate, comprehensive exam, thesis/dissertation, oral defense. *Entrance requirements:* For master's, GRE General Test, minimum GPA of 3.0, 3 letters of recommendation; for doctorate, GRE General Test, minimum GPA of 3.0, 3 letters of recommendation, research sample. Electronic applications accepted. *Faculty research:* Family life quality, interracial couples, child support, homeless families, family and child well-being.

University of Minnesota, Twin Cities Campus, School of Public Health, Major in Maternal and Child Health, Minneapolis, MN 55455-0213. Offers MPH. *Accreditation:* CEPH. *Program availability:* Part-time. *Degree requirements:* For master's, fieldwork, project. *Entrance requirements:* For master's, GRE General Test, 1 year of relevant experience. Additional exam requirements/recommendations for international students: Required—TOEFL. Electronic applications accepted. *Expenses:* Contact institution. *Faculty research:* Reproductive and perinatal health, family planning, child adolescent and family health, risk reduction and resiliency, child and family adaptation to chronic health conditions.

The University of North Carolina at Chapel Hill, Graduate School, Gillings School of Global Public Health, Department of Maternal and Child Health, Chapel Hill, NC 27599. Offers MPH, MSPH, Dr PH, PhD, MD/MSPH, MPH/MSW, MSPH/M Ed, MSPH/MSW. *Faculty:* 18 full-time (14 women), 59 part-time/adjunct (43 women). *Students:* 101 full-time (95 women); includes 30 minority (9 Black or African American, non-Hispanic/Latino; 1 American Indian or Alaska Native, non-Hispanic/Latino; 6 Asian, non-Hispanic/Latino; 7 Hispanic/Latino; 7 Two or more races, non-Hispanic/Latino), 7 international. Average age 28. 135 applicants, 56% accepted, 39 enrolled. In 2017, 39 master's, 5 doctorates awarded. *Degree requirements:* For master's, comprehensive exam, major paper; for doctorate, comprehensive exam, thesis/dissertation. *Entrance requirements:* For master's, GRE General Test or MCAT, at least one year of post-BA maternal health/child health-related work experience, interview, 3 letters of recommendation (academic and/or professional; academic preferred); for doctorate, GRE General Test, graduate-level degree, at least one year of post-BA maternal health/child health-related work experience, interview, 3 letters of recommendation (academic and/or professional; academic preferred). Additional exam requirements/recommendations for international students: Required—TOEFL (minimum score 90 iBT), IELTS (minimum score 7). *Application deadline:* For fall admission, 1/9 for domestic and international students. Applications are processed on a rolling basis. Application fee: $85. Electronic applications accepted. *Financial support:* Fellowships with tuition reimbursements, research assistantships with tuition reimbursements, teaching assistantships with tuition reimbursements, career-related internships or fieldwork, Federal Work-Study, institutionally sponsored loans, scholarships/grants, traineeships, health care benefits, and unspecified assistantships available. Financial award application deadline: 12/10; financial award applicants required to submit FAFSA. *Faculty research:* Women's health, prenatal health, family planning, program evaluation, child health policy and priorities. *Unit head:* Dr. Carolyn Halpern, Chair, 919-966-5981, E-mail: carolyn_halpern@unc.edu. *Application contact:* Carrie Aldrich, Student Services Manager, 919-966-2018, Fax: 919-966-0458, E-mail: carrie_aldrich@unc.edu.
Website: https://sph.unc.edu/mch/maternal-and-child-health/

University of Puerto Rico–Medical Sciences Campus, Graduate School of Public Health, Department of Human Development, Program in Maternal and Child Health, San Juan, PR 00936-5067. Offers MPH. *Accreditation:* CEPH. *Program availability:* Part-time, evening/weekend. *Entrance requirements:* For master's, GRE, previous course work in algebra.

University of South Florida, Innovative Education, Tampa, FL 33620-9951. Offers adult, career and higher education (Graduate Certificate), including college teaching, leadership in developing human resources, leadership in higher education; Africana studies (Graduate Certificate), including diasporas and health disparities, genocide and human rights; aging studies (Graduate Certificate), including gerontology; art research (Graduate Certificate), including museum studies; business foundations (Graduate Certificate); chemical and biomedical engineering (Graduate Certificate), including materials science and engineering, water, health and sustainability; child and family studies (Graduate Certificate), including positive behavior support; civil and industrial engineering (Graduate Certificate), including transportation systems analysis; community and family health (Graduate Certificate), including maternal and child health, social marketing and public health, violence and injury: prevention and intervention, women's health; criminology (Graduate Certificate), including criminal justice administration; data science for public administration (Graduate Certificate); digital humanities (Graduate Certificate); educational measurement and research (Graduate Certificate), including evaluation; English (Graduate Certificate), including comparative literary studies, creative writing, professional and technical communication; entrepreneurship (Graduate Certificate); environmental health (Graduate Certificate), including safety management; epidemiology and biostatistics (Graduate Certificate), including applied biostatistics, biostatistics, concepts and tools of epidemiology, epidemiology, epidemiology of infectious diseases; geography, environment and planning (Graduate Certificate), including community development, environmental policy and management, geographical information systems; geology (Graduate Certificate), including hydrogeology; global health (Graduate Certificate), including disaster management, global health and Latin American and Caribbean studies, global health practice, humanitarian assistance, infection control; government and international affairs (Graduate Certificate), including Cuban studies, globalization studies; health policy and management (Graduate Certificate), including health management and leadership, public health policy and programs; hearing specialist: early intervention (Graduate Certificate); industrial and management systems engineering (Graduate Certificate), including systems engineering, technology management; information studies (Graduate Certificate), including school library media specialist; information systems/decision sciences (Graduate Certificate), including analytics and business intelligence; instructional technology (Graduate Certificate), including distance education, Florida digital/virtual educator, instructional design, multimedia design, Web design; internal medicine, bioethics and medical humanities (Graduate Certificate), including biomedical ethics; Latin American and Caribbean studies (Graduate Certificate); leadership for coastal resiliency planning (Graduate Certificate); mass communications (Graduate Certificate), including multimedia journalism; mathematics and statistics (Graduate Certificate), including mathematics; medicine (Graduate Certificate), including aging and neuroscience, bioinformatics, biotechnology, brain fitness and memory management, clinical investigation, hand and upper limb rehabilitation, health informatics, health sciences, integrative weight management, intellectual property, medicine and gender, metabolic and nutritional medicine, metabolic cardiology, pharmacy sciences; national and competitive intelligence (Graduate Certificate); nursing (Graduate Certificate), including simulation based academic fellowship in advanced pain management; psychological and social foundations (Graduate Certificate), including career counseling, college teaching, diversity in education, mental health counseling, school counseling; public affairs (Graduate Certificate), including nonprofit management, public management, research administration; public health (Graduate Certificate), including assessing chemical toxicity and public health risks, health equity, pharmacoepidemiology, public health generalist, toxicology, translational research in adolescent behavioral health; public health practices (Graduate Certificate), including planning for healthy communities; rehabilitation and mental health counseling (Graduate Certificate), including integrative mental health care, marriage and family therapy, rehabilitation technology; secondary education (Graduate Certificate), including ESOL, foreign language education: culture and content, foreign language education: professional; social work (Graduate Certificate), including geriatric social work/clinical gerontology; special education (Graduate Certificate), including autism spectrum disorder, disabilities education: severe/profound; world languages (Graduate Certificate), including teaching English as a second language (TESL) or foreign language. *Unit head:* Dr. Cynthia DeLuca, Associate Vice President and Assistant Vice Provost, 813-974-3077, Fax: 813-974-7061, E-mail: deluca@usf.edu. *Application contact:* Owen Hooper, Director, Summer and Alternative Calendar Programs, 813-974-6917, E-mail: hooper@usf.edu.
Website: http://www.usf.edu/innovative-education/

The University of Texas Health Science Center at Houston, School of Public Health, Houston, TX 77030. Offers behavioral science (PhD); biostatistics (MPH, MS, PhD); environmental health (MPH); epidemiology (MPH, MS, PhD); general public health (Certificate); genomics and bioinformatics (Certificate); health disparities (Certificate); health promotion/health education (MPH, Dr PH); healthcare management (Certificate); management, policy and community health (MPH, Dr PH, PhD); maternal and child health (Certificate); public health informatics (Certificate); DDS/MPH; JD/MPH; MBA/MPH; MD/MPH; MGPS/MPH; MP Aff/MPH; MS/MPH; MSN/MPH; MSW/MPH; PhD/MPH. Specific programs are offered at each of our six campuses in Texas (Austin, Brownsville, Dallas, El Paso, Houston, and San Antonio). *Accreditation:* CEPH. *Program availability:* Part-time. *Faculty:* 140 full-time (74 women), 23 part-time/adjunct (14 women). *Students:* 604 full-time (446 women), 534 part-time (384 women); includes 504 minority (106 Black or African American, non-Hispanic/Latino; 177 Asian, non-Hispanic/Latino; 88 Hispanic/Latino; 1 Native Hawaiian or other Pacific Islander, non-Hispanic/Latino; 132 Two or more races, non-Hispanic/Latino). Average age 31. 1,425 applicants, 58% accepted, 423 enrolled. In 2017, 315 master's, 68 doctorates awarded. *Degree requirements:* For master's, thesis (for some programs); for doctorate, comprehensive exam, thesis/dissertation. *Entrance requirements:* For master's and doctorate, GRE General Test. Additional exam requirements/recommendations for international students: Required—TOEFL (minimum score 600 paper-based, 100 iBT) or IELTS (7.5). *Application deadline:* For fall admission, 3/1 for domestic and international students; for spring admission, 10/1 for domestic and international students; for summer admission, 3/1 for domestic students. Applications are processed on a rolling basis. Application fee: $135. Electronic applications accepted. *Expenses:* $233 per semester credit hour resident tuition, $980 per semester credit hour non-resident tuition. *Financial support:* Fellowships, research assistantships, teaching assistantships, career-related internships or fieldwork, institutionally sponsored loans, scholarships/grants, traineeships, health care benefits, and unspecified assistantships available. Support available to part-time students. Financial award application deadline: 5/5; financial award applicants required to submit FAFSA. *Faculty research:* Chronic and infectious disease epidemiology; health promotion and health education; applied and theoretical biostatistics; healthcare management, policy and economics; environmental and occupational health. *Total annual research expenditures:* $47.8 million. *Unit head:* Dr. Susan Emery, Senior Associate Dean of Academic and Research Affairs. *Application contact:* Elvis Parada, Manager of Admissions and Recruitment, 713-500-9028, Fax: 713-500-9068, E-mail: elvis.a.parada@uth.tmc.edu.
Website: https://sph.uth.edu

University of Washington, Graduate School, School of Public Health, Department of Epidemiology, Seattle, WA 98195. Offers clinical research methods (MS); epidemiology (PhD); general epidemiology (MPH, MS); global health (MPH); maternal and child health (MPH); MPH/MPA. *Accreditation:* CEPH (one or more programs are accredited). *Faculty:* 51 full-time (30 women), 40 part-time/adjunct (20 women). *Students:* 145 full-time (104 women), 30 part-time (23 women); includes 54 minority (6 Black or African American, non-Hispanic/Latino; 2 American Indian or Alaska Native, non-Hispanic/Latino; 32 Asian, non-Hispanic/Latino; 13 Hispanic/Latino; 1 Native Hawaiian or other Pacific Islander, non-Hispanic/Latino), 17 international. Average age 31. 395 applicants, 43% accepted, 58 enrolled. In 2017, 40 master's, 9 doctorates awarded. *Entrance requirements:* For master's, GRE (except for those MD/DO from U.S. institutions); for doctorate, GRE. Additional exam requirements/recommendations for international students: Required—TOEFL. Electronic applications accepted. *Financial support:* Fellowships, research assistantships, teaching assistantships, career-related internships or fieldwork, scholarships/grants, traineeships, health care benefits, and tuition waivers (full and partial) available. Support available to part-time students. Financial award applicants required to submit FAFSA. *Faculty research:* Chronic disease, health disparities and social determinants of health, aging and neuroepidemiology, maternal and child health, molecular and genetic epidemiology. *Unit head:* E-mail: epiadmin@uw.edu. *Application contact:* John Paulson, Assistant Director of Student Academic Services, 206-685-1762, E-mail: epi@uw.edu.
Website: https://epi.washington.edu/

University of Washington, Graduate School, School of Public Health, Department of Health Services, Seattle, WA 98195. Offers community-oriented public health practice (MPH); health services (MPH, MS, PhD); health systems and policy (MPH); maternal and child health (MPH); social and behavioral sciences (MPH); MPH/JD; MPH/MD; MPH/MN; MPH/MPA; MPH/MS; MPH/MSD; MPH/MSW; MPH/PhD. *Program availability:* Online learning. *Faculty:* 51 full-time (24 women), 69 part-time/adjunct (36 women). *Students:* 156 full-time (133 women), 9 part-time (all women); includes 58 minority (12 Black or African American, non-Hispanic/Latino; 4 American Indian or Alaska Native, non-Hispanic/Latino; 25 Asian, non-Hispanic/Latino; 16 Hispanic/Latino; 1 Native Hawaiian or other Pacific Islander, non-Hispanic/Latino), 5 international. Average age 30. 288 applicants, 64% accepted, 82 enrolled. In 2017, 69 master's, 5 doctorates awarded. Terminal master's awarded for partial completion of doctoral program. Electronic applications accepted. *Expenses:* Contact institution. *Financial support:* Fellowships, research assistantships, teaching assistantships, institutionally sponsored loans, traineeships, and health care benefits available. Financial award applicants required to submit FAFSA. *Faculty research:* Public health practice, health promotion and disease prevention, maternal and child health, organizational behavior and culture, health policy. *Unit head:* Dr. Larry Kessler, Chair, 206-543-2703. *Application contact:* Programs Manager, 206-616-2926, Fax: 206-543-3964, E-mail: hservmph@u.washington.edu.
Website: http://depts.washington.edu/hserv/

HARVARD UNIVERSITY

T. H. Chan School of Public Health

HARVARD T.H. CHAN | SCHOOL OF PUBLIC HEALTH
Powerful ideas for a healthier world

Programs of Study

The Harvard T. H. Chan School of Public Health offers programs leading to the graduate degrees of Master of Public Health (M.P.H.), Master in Health Care Management (M.H.C.M.), Doctor of Public Health (Dr.P.H.), and Master of Science in a specified field (S.M. in that field). Doctor of Philosophy (Ph.D.) degrees are offered in specific fields of study through the Harvard Graduate School of Arts and Sciences. Programs are offered in biostatistics; computational biology and quantitative genetics; environmental health; epidemiology; genetics and complex diseases; global health and population; health data science; health policy and management; immunology and infectious diseases; nutrition; population health sciences, and social and behavioral sciences. Some programs are designed for physicians, lawyers, managers, and other health-care professionals; some for college graduates who wish to train for health careers; and others for individuals who hold graduate degrees in medicine, law, business, government, education, and other fields who wish to apply their special skills to public health problems. Degrees offered jointly with other Harvard University Schools include the M.U.P. (Master of Urban Planning)/M.P.H. with Harvard Graduate School of Design, the M.D. or D.M.D./M.P.H. for Harvard Medical School and Harvard School of Dental Medicine students post-primary clinical year, and the J.D./M.P.H. for Harvard Law School students. Degrees offered jointly with other institutions include the M.S.N. (Master of Science in Nursing)/M.P.H. with Simmons College School of Nursing and Health Sciences and the M.D., D.O., D.M.D., or D.D.S/M.P.H. for medical and dental students enrolled in U.S.-based programs post-primary clinical year. The School offers residency training leading to certification by the American Board of Preventive Medicine in occupational medicine.

Research Facilities

The main buildings of the School are the Sebastian S. Kresge Educational Facilities Building at 677 Huntington Avenue, the François-Xavier Bagnoud Building at 651 Huntington Avenue, and the Health Sciences Laboratories at 665 Huntington Avenue. The School maintains well-equipped research laboratories containing sophisticated instrumentation and supporting animal facilities. Computing and data processing resources are also available to students through the Instructional Computing Facility. The Francis A. Countway Library serves the library needs of the School. It holds more than 630,000 volumes, subscribes to 3,500 current journal titles, and houses over 10,000 noncurrent biomedical journal titles in addition to its extensive collection of historical materials, making it the largest library in the country serving a medical and health-related school.

Financial Aid

Financial aid at the Harvard Chan School can come from a variety of sources. Some departments have training grants that offer students full tuition plus a stipend. Through need-based and merit-based programs at the School and University levels, other students are offered grants that range from quarter to full tuition. To supplement other aid, many students borrow through one or more of the federal student loan programs and work at part-time jobs at Harvard and in the community.

Cost of Study

Master's program students are assessed a program-specific flat tuition rate. The full-time rate for the Master of Public Health 45 Credit (1 year) Program is $60,400. The full-time rate for the Master of Public Health 65 Credit (1.5 year) program is $53,040. The full-time rate for the Master of Science 42.5 Credit (1 year) program is $57,060. The full-time rate for both the Master of Science 80 Credit (2 year) and 60 Credit (1.5 year) program is $45,540.

Doctoral students are assessed a flat tuition rate. The full-time rate for 2018–19 for students in their first or second year is $45,540.

Health insurance and health services fee are required, which total $4,542. Books and supplies are estimated to be $1,386 in 2018–19.

Living and Housing Costs

For the academic year 2018–19, it is estimated that a single student in a master's program needs a minimum of $22,464 for housing and living costs: $13,230 for rent and utilities and $9,234 for other expenses. If a master's student elects to start their program in the summer, an additional $5,377 should be added to that estimate.

Limited housing is available in the Shattuck International House, with preference given to international students. Most students arrange for housing in the adjacent communities.

Student Group

There were 1,130 graduate students (670 women and 460 men) enrolled in 2017–18. Sixty-nine nations are represented.

Student Outcomes

Graduates of the Harvard T. H. Chan School of Public Health find employment in a variety of settings. It depends in part upon their previous experience and in part upon department and degree programs from which they graduate. Recent graduates have found positions in research institutes, with pharmaceutical companies and governmental and nongovernmental agencies, within the health-care industry, and as faculty members of universities.

Location

Boston is a heterogeneous metropolis rich in history and charm. Athletic, cultural, and recreational activities are abundant. The School is within walking distance of museums, colleges and universities, waterways, and parks.

The University and The School

Harvard College was founded in 1636; until the establishment of professorships in medicine in 1782, it composed the whole of the institution now called Harvard University. In addition to the college, eleven graduate schools are now part of the University.

The Harvard T. H. Chan School of Public Health traces its roots to public health activism at the beginning of the last century, a time of energetic social reform. The School began as the Harvard-MIT School for Health Officers, founded in 1913 as the first professional public health training program in the United States. In 1922, the School split off from MIT; in 1946, the Harvard School of Public Health became an independent, degree-granting body. In 2014, the Harvard School of Public Health was renamed the Harvard T. H. Chan School of Public Health in recognition of an extraordinary gift from The Morningside Foundation. The primary mission of the School is to carry out teaching and research aimed at improving the health of population groups throughout the world. The School emphasizes not only the development and implementation of disease prevention and treatment programs but also the planning and management of systems involved in the delivery of health services in this country and abroad. The School cooperates with the Medical School in teaching and research and has close ties with other Harvard faculties. The School has more than 480 full-time and part-time faculty members and nine academic departments representing major biomedical and social disciplines.

Applying

Harvard Chan School participates in SOPHAS, which is the centralized application service for schools and programs of public health. Students should visit the SOPHAS website at http://www.sophas.org for more specific information and for access to the application for admission. All applicants to the School are required to submit scores from the GRE (ETS school code: 3456); applicants are urged to take the test no later than November, since applications are not considered without the scores. Applicants may submit the DAT, GMAT, LSAT, or MCAT, as appropriate to the applicant's background, in lieu of the GRE. In addition, applicants must persuade the Committee on Admissions and Degrees of their ability to meet academic standards and of their overall qualifications to undertake advanced study at a graduate level. Students should visit the School's website (http://www.hsph.harvard.edu/admissions) for information concerning the deadline to apply for admission and to apply online.

As a matter of policy, law, and commitment, the Harvard Chan School does not discriminate against any person on the basis of race, color, sex, sexual orientation, gender identity, religion, age, national or ethnic origin, political beliefs, veteran status, or disability in admission to, access to, treatment in, or employment in its programs and activities. Members of minority groups are strongly encouraged to apply.

Correspondence and Information

Harvard T. H. Chan School of Public Health Admissions Office
158 Longwood Avenue
Boston, Massachusetts 02115-5810
United States
Phone: 617-432-1031
Fax: 617-432-7080
E-mail: admissions@hsph.harvard.edu
Website: http://www.hsph.harvard.edu/admissions

Counseling and program information:

Vincent W. James, Director
Kerri Noonan, Associate Director
Charlie Dill, Assistant Director
Kelly Latendresse, Assistant Director
Priti Thareja, Admissions Coordinator
Ruth Thompson, Admissions Coordinator

Harvard University

FACULTY CHAIRS AND DEPARTMENTAL ACTIVITIES

Biostatistics
(617-432-1056, biostat_admissions@hsph.harvard.edu)
Chair: John Quackenbush, Ph.D., M.S. Advancing health science research, education, and practice by turning data into knowledge to address the greatest public health challenges of the 21st century. The program combines both theory and application of statistical science to analyze public health problems and further biomedical research. Students are prepared for academic and private-sector research careers. Current departmental research on statistical and computing methods for observational studies and clinical trials includes survival analysis, missing-data problems, and causal inference. Other areas of investigation include environmental research; statistical aspects of the study of AIDS and cancer; quantitative problems in health-risk analysis, technology assessment, and clinical decision making; statistical methodology in psychiatric research and in genetic studies; and statistical genetics and computational biology.

Environmental Health
(617-432-1270, envhlth@hsph.harvard.edu)
Chair: Russ Hauser, M.D., Sc.D., M.P.H. The mission of the Department of Environmental Health is to address critical environmental and public health challenges through national and global leadership in research and training. The department emphasizes the role of air, water, the built environment, and the workplace as critical determinants of health. Teaching and research activities of the department are carried out through three concentrations: exposure, epidemiology, and risk; occupational health; and molecular and integrative physiological sciences.

Epidemiology
(617-432-1055, elfurxhi@hsph.harvard.edu)
Chair: Albert Hofman, M.D., Ph.D. Epidemiology, the study of the frequency, distribution, and determinants of disease in humans, is a fundamental science of public health. Epidemiologists use many approaches, but the ultimate aim of epidemiologic research is the prevention or effective control of human disease. The department has a long tradition of teaching and research in the epidemiology of cancer, cardiovascular disease, and other chronic diseases as well as in epidemiologic methodology. Areas of interest include: cancer epidemiology; cardiovascular epidemiology; clinical epidemiology; environmental and occupational epidemiology; epidemiologic methods; epidemiology of aging; infectious disease epidemiology; genetic epidemiology and statistical genetics; neuro-psychiatric epidemiology; nutritional epidemiology; pharmacoepidemiology; and reproductive, perinatal, and pediatric epidemiology.

Genetics and Complex Diseases
(617-432-0054, aepshtei@hsph.harvard.edu)
Chair: Gökhan Hotamisligil, M.D., Ph.D. The complex interplay of biological processes with environmental factors as they apply to chronic, multigenic, and multifactorial diseases, with special attention to metabolism, is the emphasis of the Department of Genetics and Complex Diseases. Research programs in the department focus on molecular mechanisms of adaptive responses to environmental signals to elucidate the mechanisms underlying the intricate interaction between genetic determinants and their divergent responses to stress signals.

Global Health and Population
(617-432-2253, bheil@hsph.harvard.edu)
Chair: Wafaie Fawzi, M.B.B.S., M.P.H., S.M., Dr.P.H. The department seeks to improve global health through education, research, and service from a population-based perspective. Research interests span a wide spectrum of topics, including social and economic development, health policy, and demography; design and financing of health care systems; women's and children's health; global nutritional epidemiology and practice; prevention and control of infectious and chronic diseases; program evaluation; and humanitarian assistance and ethics. The department has a special concern with questions of health equity and human rights, particularly in relation to health and population issues in developing countries.

Health Policy and Management
(617-432-4324, jmoltoni@hsph.harvard.edu)
Chair: Arnold Epstein, M.D. The department is committed to training and inspiring the next generation of health care leaders. Academic programs focus on developing the critical thinking and applied problem-solving skills needed to address a wide variety of challenges throughout the health care delivery, public policy, and public health systems.

Immunology and Infectious Diseases
(617-432-1023, asabarof@hsph.harvard.edu)
Chair: Eric Rubin, M.D., Ph.D. The department focuses on the biological, immunological, epidemiological, and ecological aspects of viral, bacterial, and protozoan diseases, primarily in developing countries. Emphasis is on research identifying basic pathogenic mechanisms that may lead to better diagnostic tools and the development of vaccines as well as the identification of new targets for antiviral and antiparasitic drugs.

Nutrition
(617-432-1528, sdean@hsph.harvard.edu)
Chair: Frank B. Hu, M.D., M.P.H., Ph.D. The department's mission is to improve human health through better nutrition and lifestyle. The department strives to accomplish this goal through research aimed at an increased understanding of how diet influences health at molecular and population levels, the development of nutritional strategies, informing policy, the education of researchers and practitioners, and the dissemination of nutrition information to health professionals and the public. Department research ranges from molecular biology to human studies of cancer and heart disease, including the conduct of population-based intervention trials.

Social and Behavioral Sciences
(617-432-3761, esolomon@hsph.harvard.edu)
Chair: Ichiro Kawachi, MB.ChB., Ph.D. The mission of the Department of Social and Behavioral Sciences is to understand and intervene on the social determinants of health and health equity across the life-course. This mission is achieved through research to identify the social and behavioral determinants of health, development and evaluation of interventions and policies leading to the improvement of population health, and the preparation of professionals and researchers who fill leadership positions in advocacy and public service.

Master of Public Health Program
(617-432-0090, mph@hsph.harvard.edu)
Director: Murray Mittleman, M.D.C.M., M.P.H., D.P.H. The program is designed to provide both a general background and flexibility of specialization in public health. The fields of study are clinical effectiveness, global health, health and social behavior, health management, health policy, nutrition, occupational and environmental health, and quantitative methods. There is also an online and on-campus M.P.H. in Epidemiology.

Doctor of Public Health Program
(617-432-5008, drph@hsph.harvard.edu)
Director: Rick Siegrist, M.B.A., M.S., CPA. The Doctor of Public Health degree is for exceptional individuals with proven potential who want to accelerate their careers, lead organizations, and have an important impact on people's health and lives. Students will enjoy unique opportunities to engage with Harvard's world-renowned faculty through rigorous teaching, interactive learning, case discussions, simulations, and field experiences in a variety of major public health organizations. This innovative, transformative educational experience has been designed so that no prior public health degree is required.

Division of Biological Sciences
(617-432-4470, bph@hsph.harvard.edu)
Director: Brendan Manning, Ph.D. The Division of Biological Sciences is an umbrella organization encompassing the Harvard Chan School Departments of Environmental Health, Genetics and Complex Diseases, Immunology and Infectious Diseases, and Nutrition. The Ph.D. program in Biological Sciences in Public Health trains students in individual fields of biological research with a focus on understanding, preventing, and treating diseases affecting large populations. The Ph.D. programs are offered under the aegis of the Harvard Graduate School of Arts and Sciences and administered by the Harvard Chan School Division of Biological Sciences.

Population Health Sciences
(phdphs@hsph.harvard.edu)
Director: Lisa Berkman, Ph.D. The program offers advanced doctoral-level research training that builds on multiple disciplinary perspectives to understand origins and determinants of health and disease across populations. Population Health Sciences is an umbrella organization encompassing the Departments of Environmental Health, Epidemiology, Global Health and Population, Nutrition, and Social and Behavioral Sciences. In these departments, the doctoral degree offered is the Doctor of Philosophy (Ph.D.). The Ph.D. programs are offered under the aegis of the Harvard Graduate School of Arts and Sciences and administered by the Harvard Chan School Program in Population Health Sciences.

NEW YORK UNIVERSITY

Department of Environmental Medicine

★ For more information, visit http://petersons.to/nyu_environmentalsciences

NYU Langone Health

Programs of Study

The Department of Environmental Medicine at New York University (NYU) offers both Master of Science (M.S.) and Doctor of Philosophy (Ph.D.) degrees in environmental health sciences. These programs provide students with advanced training in scientific disciplines related to environmental health, focusing on major health problems such as cancer, respiratory illness, and cardiovascular diseases.

Students also acquire specialized knowledge in several environmental health areas including biostatistics, epidemiology, ergonomics and biomechanics, exposure assessment and health effects, molecular toxicology/carcinogenesis, and toxicology.

The **Master of Science (M.S.) in Environmental Health Sciences program** is ideal for individuals who are seeking career opportunities in occupational health and safety, health hazard communication, health risk assessment, and environmental analysis of toxicants. It has two main areas of study: environmental toxicology and occupational and environmental hygiene.

The program, which can be pursued on a full- or part-time basis, focuses on teaching students how to use scientific methodology to find solutions to real-world environmental problems. Students acquire fundamental knowledge about environmental pollution, toxicology, and biostatistics and gain the ability to present scientific data and interpret scientific reports.

Because the program gives students the opportunity to develop individualized courses of study, they may take relevant courses in other schools within New York University such as environment management and planning, environmental law, and risk assessment.

Graduates of the program complete 36 points of course work, at least 24 of which are to be accumulated while in residence at the Graduate School of Arts and Sciences. They must also complete a special project that is either a research or library thesis that is based on a faculty-supervised laboratory project.

Students also attend departmental seminars and participate in journal clubs.

Additional information about the M.S. degree program can be found online at http://www.med.nyu.edu/environmentalmedicine/graduate-program/ms-program.

The **Ph.D. in Environmental Health Sciences program** prepares students for active and productive careers in research and professional service. The instructive component of the program focuses on providing students with a solid foundation in basic sciences. In addition, a research component gives students hands-on experience designing, conducting, and interpreting studies that address scientific issues in environmental health. Areas of study include Molecular Toxicology/Carcinogenesis, Toxicology (Inhalation or Aquatic), and Exposure Assessment and Health Effects.

Doctoral students earn 72 credits that include at least 48 credits of didactic courses. They also attend department seminars and journal clubs as well as write and defend a doctoral dissertation.

First-year students also participate in laboratory rotations that are based on their interests. Students can choose specific courses of study that reflect their educational and career backgrounds, interests, and career goals.

More information about the Ph.D. program is available at http://www.med.nyu.edu/environmentalmedicine/graduate-program/phd-program.

Training Program in Environmental Toxicology: Predoctoral students and post-doctoral fellows in the environmental toxicology program at New York University may be eligible to receive training grant support from the National Institute of Environmental Health Sciences. Grant recipients receive research training in pulmonary or molecular toxicology.

Research

The major mission of the Department of Environmental Medicine is to conduct cutting edge research in Environmental Health Sciences. This is accomplished by obtaining funded grants from The National Institute of Health, The United States EPA, and other government and non-government funding agencies. Some major areas of research include chemical carcinogenesis, epigenetics, health effects of particulate air pollution, epidemiology of cancer susceptibility and causation, and environmental etiology of cardiovascular disease and diabetes. Students have access to more than 14 labs associated with NYU.

The NYU Department of Environmental Medicine is a designated center of excellence supported by the National Institutes of Health, National Institute of Environmental Health Sciences. This designation is through a funded Center Grant from NIH that supports facility cores and is the engine that drives Environmental Health Sciences research at NYU.

Many members of the department are also members of the NCI-funded NYU cancer center. Research programs include exposure assessment and health effects, molecular toxicology/carcinogenesis, and pulmonary toxicology.

The department's Community Outreach and Education Core (COEC) is designed to help the public understand more about environmental health issues and to reduce misconceptions about toxic chemicals in the air, water, and homes. Once accurately informed, individuals can make better decisions regarding prevention and unintentional exposures. Students who are interested in getting more involved in COEC activities in environmental health science can also participate community-based programs, youth education, and laboratory mentoring initiatives.

Financial Aid

Full-time M.S. applicants who are planning laboratory research-based thesis projects are considered for graduate assistantships that cover tuition and fees and supplement living costs while studying at New York University.

All full-time predoctoral trainees receive tuition and fees waivers and a generous annual stipend during their years of study and research in the program.

In the 2018–19 academic year, stipends are $33,000 for Ph.D. students and $17,750 for M.S. students.

New York University

The Faculty

Faculty members are dedicated to providing comprehensive education in environmental health sciences and conducting cutting-edge research in the field. They conduct research in a wide variety of areas including chemical carcinogenesis, epigenetics, health effects of particulate air pollution, and epidemiology of cancer susceptibility.

The chair of the Department of Environmental Medicine, Dr. Max Costa's current research interests include molecular and epigenetic mechanisms of metal carcinogenesis. He holds a Ph.D. in pharmacology and began his extensive research and publishing career in 1976.

More information on the department's faculty members and their areas of research can be found online at http://www.med.nyu.edu/environmentalmedicine/graduate-program/faculty-research.

Student Outcomes

Graduates of the Environmental Health Sciences program are well-regarded in the government, business, and education sectors. They have acquired top-tier positions in numerous businesses, private and non-profit organizations, governmental agencies, pharmaceutical corporations, and academic institutions, including the New York City Department of Health, the U.S. EPA, U.S. FDA, and U.S. Army Corps of Engineers.

Location

Located in New York City in the northeastern region of the United States, NYU is one of the largest private universities in the country. Diverse in nature, it educates more than 40,000 students per year and consists of 18 schools and colleges located at five major centers in Manhattan (a borough of New York City) as well as sites in Africa, Asia, Europe, and South America.

The university's location in vibrant and culturally-diverse New York City offers students a wealth of work, entertainment, and cultural options such as the American Museum of Natural History, Broadway, Central Park, and Times Square.

The University

Founded in 1831, the prestigious New York University is ranked 30th on *U.S. News & World Report*'s "Best Colleges 2019" list. It is also one of only 60 colleges and universities in the United States to become a member of the distinguished Association of American Universities.

Admissions Requirements and Applying

The admissions process for the Environmental Health Sciences programs at New York University is by application that requests academic transcripts from undergraduate and graduate schools attended, personal statements of career interests, goals and accomplishments, as well as three letters of recommendations. A wholistic approach to the evaluation of applications takes into account all prior experiences, future goals and supporting documents.

Applicants to the M.S. and Ph.D. Graduate Programs in Environmental Health Sciences must use the online admissions application that is available at gsas.nyu.edu/page/grad.admissionsapplication.

International students must submit scores on the TOEFL.

Applications and supporting documents must be received by December 12 of each year. Decisions on GSAS admissions are made by April 15.

Correspondence and Information

Dr. Max Costa, Chair
Dr. Jerome Solomon, Director of Graduate Studies
Dr. Catherine B. Klein, Director of Masters Program
Department of Environmental Medicine
Graduate School of Arts and Science
New York University
70 Washington Square South
New York, New York 10012-1019
United States
Phone: 646-754-9462
Fax: 646-754-9465
E-mail: ehs@env.med.nyu.edu
Website: http://www.med.nyu.edu/environmentalmedicine/graduate-program

NORTH DAKOTA STATE UNIVERSITY

College of Health Professions

NDSU GRADUATE SCHOOL

★ For more information, visit http://petersons.to/ndsu-healthprofs

Program of Study

The College of Health Professions at North Dakota State University provides education, patient care, research, and public service that advance health care in the state, region, and country. Its programs in allied sciences, nursing, pharmaceutical sciences, pharmacy practice, and public health help students become competent, compassionate, and ethical professionals, as well as lifelong learners.

Graduate Programs in Public Health: Graduate programs in public health include the Master of Public Health (M.P.H.) and Pharm.D./M.P.H. The 42-credit M.P.H. program focuses on disease state management, health promotion and prevention, and rural health. It has specializations in American Indian public health, community health sciences, and management of infectious diseases. The Pharm.D./M.P.H. program trains students to provide pharmaceutical care within a public health context. Pharm.D. students can complete this dual program in one year of additional study.

Bachelor of Nursing Science (B.S.N.) to Doctor of Nursing Practice (D.N.P.): The B.S.N. to D.N.P. program is ideal for baccalaureate-prepared registered nurses who want to become family nurse practitioners. Its 86-credit curriculum focuses on nursing leadership, clinical expertise, evidence-based methods in healthcare, and strategic problem-solving skills.

Graduate Programs in Pharmaceutical Sciences: North Dakota State University offers a Ph.D. in Pharmaceutical Sciences program consisting of core and elective courses, with advanced work in medicinal chemistry, pharmaceutics, pharmacokinetics, and pharmacology. The program focuses on research, leadership, and critical thinking skills to prepare students for leadership roles in the academic, government, and industrial sectors.

Research

With research expenditures of more than $150 million annually, North Dakota State University is a leading research institution. It offers faculty members and student researchers an exceptional research infrastructure.

The College of Health Professions is an important part of the university's research endeavors. For example, science researchers obtain key federally-funded grants from the National Institutes of Health, Department of Defense, Environmental Protection Agency, National Science Foundation, and Experimental Program to Stimulate Competitive Research. Furthermore, faculty members conduct research that advances health care theory and practice and contributes to curriculum development. Their research interests include the following:

- internal medicine
- diabetes mellitus
- health promotion/disease prevention
- hospital epidemiology
- drug-resistant micro-organisms
- antimicrobial stewardship
- West Nile Virus infection
- gerontology throughout the nursing curriculum
- use of simulations in classroom
- alternative delivery of clinical experiences

Students conduct research that enhances learning and examines relevant issues in health care, health sciences, nursing, pharmaceutical sciences, and public health. They also assist faculty members with their research projects.

Financial Aid

The College of Health Professions provides graduate assistantships and scholarships for students who qualify. Students can also pursue loans through federal programs or private lenders and participate in employer tuition reimbursement programs.

Cost of Study

The most current information on tuition and fees can be found online at https://www.ndsu.edu/onestop/accounts/tuition/.

Living and Housing Costs

Information about on-campus housing for graduate students can be found at www.ndsu.edu/reslife/general_apartment_information.

While there is no specific residence hall for graduate students, they are able to live in the University apartments. There are also numerous housing options in the Fargo community.

Faculty

Faculty members in the College of Health Professions are highly-skilled teachers, researchers, and practitioners. They are committed to helping students achieve academic success and providing health services to people and communities.

For example, Dr. Amanda Brooks is a professor in pharmaceutical sciences. Her research interests are antimicrobial biomaterial surfaces, combination hemo-compatible and antimicrobial biomaterial surface coating, and combination polymers pertaining to advanced drug delivery.

Dean Gross, Ph.D., FNP-C is an assistant professor of practice in the School of Nursing and director of the D.N.P. program. He is also a clinical specialist and preceptor. His research interests include clinical practice guidelines, community health, health literacy, and problem-based learning.

Student Life

The College of Health Professions provides a vibrant and welcoming community where students excel academically, professionally, and socially. It offers student organizations, community service projects, symposia, workshops, research opportunities, and special events. The larger campus community also provides many supportive services and recreational options such as the Career Center, Counseling Center, Disability Services, intercollegiate athletics, military and veteran services, multicultural student services, performing and fine arts, and the Wallman Wellness Center.

Location

North Dakota State University is located on the eastern edge of North Dakota in Fargo, the state's largest community. With its sister city, Moorhead, Minnesota, directly across the Red River, Fargo is one of the largest metropolitan centers between Minneapolis and Seattle and offers a family-friendly environment with excellent schools, safe neighborhoods, and a low crime rate; an active arts and cultural scene, including a symphony, civic opera company, art museums, and community theater; and many places to shop and eat, including numerous restaurants, coffee shops, and a newly refurbished downtown district.

The University

Established in 1890, North Dakota State University is a student-focused, land-grant, research institution located in Fargo, North Dakota in the Midwestern region of the United States. It enrolls more than 14,300 students (including more than 2,000 graduate students). The Graduate School at North Dakota State University offers 86 master's programs, 53 doctoral programs, and 15 graduate certificate programs.

The National Science Foundation has designated several of the university's programs within the top 100 in the country.

Correspondence and Information

College of Health Professions
Graduate School
North Dakota State University
Dept. 2820, P.O. Box 6050
Fargo, North Dakota 58108-6050
Phone: 701-231-7033
800-608-6378 (toll-free)
E-mail: ndsu.grad.school@ndsu.edu
Website: www.ndsu.edu/gradschool
facebook.com/ndsugradschool (Facebook)
@NDSUGradSchool (Twitter)

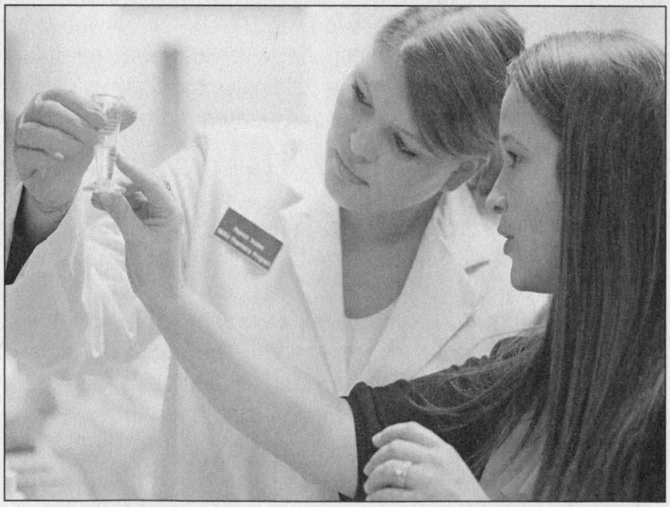

For more than 100 years, North Dakota State University College of Health Professions has led the advancement of healthcare for the benefit of society through innovation, growth, and excellence in teaching, research, and practice. NDSU aims to educate students and advance research and professional service in pharmacy, nursing, and allied sciences fields.

UNIVERSITY OF SOUTH FLORIDA

College of Public Health

★ For more information, visit http://petersons.to/usf-public-health

our practice is our passion.
University of South Florida
College of Public Health

Programs of Study

A founding member of the Association of Schools and Programs of Public Health, the University of South Florida (USF) College of Public Health (COPH) is ranked by *U.S. News & World Report* at #1 in the state of Florida, #2 public institution in the southeast, and #16 nationally among Council on Education for Public Health accredited public health schools and colleges.

The College offers Master of Public Health (M.P.H.), Master of Science in Public Health (M.S.P.H.), Master of Health Administration (M.H.A.), Doctor of Philosophy (Ph.D.), and Doctor of Public Health (Dr.P.H.) degrees. Depending on the degree program, graduate students may choose from more than 20 concentrations including:

- Advanced practice leadership in public health
- Applied biostatistics
- Behavioral health
- Biostatistics
- Community and family health
- Environmental and occupational health
- Epidemiology
- Epidemiology (online)
- Epidemiology and global communicable disease
- Epidemiology and global health
- Epidemiology and maternal and child health
- Genetic counseling
- Genomics (coming soon)
- Global communicable disease
- Global disaster management, humanitarian relief, and homeland security (online)
- Global health practice
- Health care organizations and management
- Health policies and programs
- Health services research
- Health, safety and environment (online)
- Infection control (online)
- Maternal and child health
- Nutrition and dietetics (online)
- Occupational exposure science
- Public health and clinical laboratory science and practice
- Public health education
- Public health practice (online)
- Social marketing (online)

Concurrent degrees include the M.P.H. or Ph.D. and anthropology (M.A. or Ph.D.), M.P.H. and health administration (M.H.A.), M.P.H. and medicine (M.D.), M.P.H. and nursing (M.S.), and the M.P.H. and social work (M.S.W.).

In addition, COPH offers more than 20 certificate options, including some offered fully online.

The average duration to complete the master's degree is two years and three to five years for the doctoral degree.

The COPH curriculum prepares students to improve the health of communities locally and globally. Service-learning opportunities are woven throughout the curriculum at the undergraduate and graduate level. This, paired with opportunities to practice what they've learned in the field, provides the foundation for students to improve the public's health as practitioners, researchers, analysts and policymakers with hospitals and health care providers; NGOs and other nonprofits; academia; military; consulting firms; health insurance companies; and, of course, local, state, and federal government.

Research is encouraged, if not expected, of all students. Under the mentorship of faculty, students conduct research on the major public health challenges and engage in active community-based research and service learning—recognizing that it is not only through discovery and learning, but through the direct translation and application of that knowledge to policies and programs that one succeeds in improving the public's health.

Students continually present their award-winning research and practice at local, state, national, and international professional meetings, and are published in numerous peer-reviewed journals.

Research Facilities

The COPH is home to 12 internationally recognized centers and institutes addressing areas of public health importance. Within the primary COPH building there are labs that support research and training in environmental health, industrial hygiene, physiology, water and air quality, immunology, toxicology, parasitology, risk management, ergonomics, heat stress, occupational safety, infectious diseases, and microbiology.

USF's Interdisciplinary Research Building is home to the Center for Global Health Infectious Disease with approximately 26,000 square feet of BSL-2 and BSL-3 laboratories. Neglected diseases are researched using drug and vaccine discovery methods with functional genomics and computational biology analysis.

The USF Library provides access to more than 1.3 million books and print and electronic resources including 52,000 e-journal subscriptions, 443,000 e-books, and over 800 databases. Additional facilities include the Shimberg Health Sciences Library, Louis de la Parte Florida Mental Health Institute Research Library, and libraries on the USF St. Petersburg and Sarasota-Manatee campuses.

Financial Aid

Students are the COPH's greatest strength and inspiration. As such, the College makes a variety of funding vehicles available to degree-seeking students. In 2015–16, COPH provided more than $2.7 million in student financial support via scholarships, graduate assistantships, and tuition waivers. For this same time period, 80 percent of COPH undergraduates and graduate students reported receiving some sort of financial aid. In addition, the College participates in the federal work-study program. Additional information is available at http://health.usf.edu/publichealth/academicaffairs/FinAid.

Cost of Study

For the 2017–18 academic year, Florida residents paid $431.43 and non-residents $877.17 per graduate credit hour in tuition and fees. For up-to-date information on costs, visit http://www.usf.edu/business-finance/controller/student-services/tuition-rates.aspx.

Other considerations include a reduced-rate program for out-of-state online students and the Academic Common Market tuition-savings program. More details on these programs can be found at http://health.usf.edu/publichealth/academicaffairs/FinAid.

Living and Housing Costs

USF offers three building styles: traditional college halls, suite-style halls, and full-kitchen apartments. Graduate students may live in any hall open to upper-classmen. The local area offers a variety of communal living arrangements.

Living expenses for graduate students were estimated $16,158 for the 2018–19 academic year. This estimate includes housing, meals, entertainment, health care, clothing, etc. Additional information on housing costs is available online at http://www.usf.edu/student-affairs/housing.

Student Group

Prospective students should view themselves as a catalyst for health and plan to be fully engaged in research, volunteer in the community, and hone skills via service-learning. Applicants with insufficient training in health/science may need prerequisites. Basic computer competency is expected.

In the spring 2018 semester, the 1,602 students in the COPH broke down as follows: 729 bachelor's degree students, 873 graduates; 73 percent women; 46 percent underrepresented minorities; 74 percent Florida residents; 10 percent international students; and 25 percent online students.

Student Outcomes

More than 6,800 COPH alumni are improving the public's health as practitioners, researchers, analysts, and policymakers with hospitals and health care providers, NGOs and other nonprofits, academia, military, consulting firms, health insurance companies, and, of course, local, state and federal government.

Alumni practice public health throughout the U.S. and in remote areas around the world. Outside of Florida, the largest concentrations of alumni work in metro Atlanta with CDC-related organizations and in metro Washington, D.C.

Location

Students can enjoy the outdoors year-round in this major metropolis on Florida's west coast. The region offers plenty of sunshine, arts and entertainment, shopping and dining, professional sports, and an annual average temperature of 73 degrees. Tampa International Airport is only 17 miles from campus and provides service from more than 15 major airlines. Students ride free on the campus and regional buses.

The University and The College

"Our practice is our passion" is more than a tagline for the COPH. Every day students, faculty, alumni, and staff work tirelessly to improve the health of the population in Tampa and around the world. By experiencing public health first-hand, students help find solutions to pressing health issues and understand the human, financial, and other resources needed to make it happen.

University of South Florida

The COPH joins the Colleges of Medicine, Nursing, and Pharmacy to form USF Health, whose mission is to envision and implement the future of health.

The COPH was founded in statute by the Florida Legislature in 1984 as the first school of public health in the state. A nationally recognized leader in community health, online education, maternal and child health, social marketing, and global infectious disease research, the COPH is leading a national movement that transforms the M.P.H. curriculum to meet today's public health needs.

The University of South Florida System is a high-impact global research system dedicated to student success. The USF System includes three institutions: USF, USF St. Petersburg, and USF Sarasota-Manatee. Serving over 50,000 students, the USF System has an annual budget of $1.8 billion and an annual economic impact of $4.4 billion. USF is a member of the American Athletic Conference.

The University and College are accredited by the Commission on Colleges of the Southern Association of Colleges and Schools (USF), the Council on Education for Public Health (COPH), the Commission on Accreditation Healthcare Management Education (M.H.A.), the Accreditation Council for Genetic Counseling (M.S.P.H. in genetic counseling), the Applied Science Accreditation Commission of ABET (M.P.H. in occupational exposure science), and the Accreditation Council for Education in Nutrition and Dietetics (ACEND) of The Academy of Nutrition and Dietetics (M.P.H. in nutrition and dietetics).

The Faculty and Their Research

Committed to the college's mission to improve the public's health through advancing discovery, learning, and service, COPH faculty as a whole are:

- Dedicated to excellence in teaching, scholarship, and mentoring of students
- Developing leaders in health sciences who meet the needs of diverse populations
- Involved in active funded research and are engaged in nationally recognized research programs
- United around improving the health and lives of the poorest people on the planet
- Preparing managers and researchers for leadership positions in health-related organizations

The COPH has 176 faculty members with regular, adjunct, and affiliate appointments, including six who earned the designation of Distinguished University Professor or Distinguished University Health Professor. In fiscal year 2016–2017, the college's faculty generated more than $25.7 million in external grants and contracts.

Applying

Graduate applicants are required to submit the SOPHAS application and fee. Once verified by SOPHAS, COPH emails applicant with USF application link and the applicant then submits the completed USF application and fee and COPH reviews the applications for the desired term. More details are available at http://health.usf.edu/publichealth/apply/graduate-admissions.

Correspondence and Information

To learn more about programs of study and a community who commits to passionately solve problems and create conditions that allow every person the universal right to health and well-being, interested applicants are encouraged to contact a COPH admissions representative.

College of Public Health
University of South Florida
13201 Bruce B. Downs Blvd, MDC 56 (mailing address)
3010 USF Banyan Circle (physical address)
Tampa, Florida 33612
Phone: 813-974-6505 or 888-USF-COPH (toll-free)
Website: www.publichealth.usf.edu

Kamala Dontamsetti, MBA, M.A., Assistant Director of Graduate Admissions
Phone: 813-974-8874
Fax: 813-974-8121
E-mail: cophinfo@health.usf.edu
Website: http://health.usf.edu/publichealth/apply/graduate-admissions

COPH students strike a bullish pose with Dean Donna Petersen.

Students with a passion for public health find the USF College of Public Health a great place to build their future.

ACADEMIC AND PROFESSIONAL PROGRAMS IN THE MEDICAL PROFESSIONS AND SCIENCES

Section 25
Acupuncture and Oriental Medicine

This section contains a directory of institutions offering graduate work in acupuncture and oriental medicine. Additional information about programs listed in the directory but not augmented by an in-depth entry may be obtained by writing directly to the dean of a graduate school or chair of a department at the address given in the directory.

CONTENTS

Program Directory

Acupuncture and Oriental Medicine

Academy for Five Element Acupuncture, Graduate Program, Gainesville, FL 32601. Offers M Ac. *Accreditation:* ACAOM.

Academy of Chinese Culture and Health Sciences, Program in Traditional Chinese Medicine, Oakland, CA 94612. Offers MS. *Accreditation:* ACAOM. *Program availability:* Part-time, evening/weekend. *Degree requirements:* For master's, comprehensive exam, thesis. *Entrance requirements:* Additional exam requirements/recommendations for international students: Required—TOEFL (minimum score 500 paper-based). *Faculty research:* Herbs, acupuncture.

Acupuncture & Integrative Medicine College, Berkeley, Master of Science in Oriental Medicine Program, Berkeley, CA 94704. Offers MS. *Accreditation:* ACAOM. *Program availability:* Part-time. *Faculty:* 24 part-time/adjunct (15 women). *Students:* 58 full-time (44 women), 28 part-time (23 women); includes 27 minority (3 Black or African American, non-Hispanic/Latino; 10 Asian, non-Hispanic/Latino; 6 Hispanic/Latino; 8 Two or more races, non-Hispanic/Latino), 3 international. Average age 37. 40 applicants, 85% accepted, 29 enrolled. In 2017, 33 master's awarded. *Degree requirements:* For master's, comprehensive exam, 350 clinic treatments. *Entrance requirements:* For master's, interview, minimum GPA of 3.0, 60 semester units of course work at the baccalaureate level. Additional exam requirements/recommendations for international students: Required—TOEFL (minimum score 61 iBT). *Application deadline:* For fall admission, 3/15 priority date for domestic and international students; for winter admission, 7/15 priority date for domestic and international students; for spring admission, 11/15 priority date for domestic and international students. Applications are processed on a rolling basis. Application fee: $100. Electronic applications accepted. *Expenses:* Contact institution. *Financial support:* Federal Work-Study available. Support available to part-time students. Financial award application deadline: 7/31; financial award applicants required to submit FAFSA. *Faculty research:* Stimulus therapy, oxygen hemoglobin, acupuncture needling, classical Chinese medicine. *Unit head:* Yasou Tanaka, President, 510-666-8248, Fax: 510-666-0111, E-mail: ytanaka@aimc.edu. *Application contact:* Rain Jordan, E-mail: admissions@aimc.edu.

Acupuncture and Massage College, Program in Oriental Medicine, Miami, FL 33176. Offers MOM. *Accreditation:* ACAOM.

American Academy of Acupuncture and Oriental Medicine, Graduate Programs, Roseville, MN 55113. Offers MAOM, DAOM.

American College of Acupuncture and Oriental Medicine, Graduate Studies, Houston, TX 77063. Offers MAOM. *Accreditation:* ACAOM. *Program availability:* Part-time. *Entrance requirements:* For master's, 60 undergraduate credit hours. Additional exam requirements/recommendations for international students: Required—TOEFL.

AOMA Graduate School of Integrative Medicine, Doctor of Acupuncture and Oriental Medicine Program, Austin, TX 78757. Offers DAOM. *Faculty:* 2 full-time (1 woman), 7 part-time/adjunct (3 women). *Students:* 19 full-time (7 women), 12 part-time (9 women); includes 9 minority (4 Black or African American, non-Hispanic/Latino; 1 Asian, non-Hispanic/Latino; 4 Hispanic/Latino). Average age 39. In 2017, 3 doctorates awarded. *Degree requirements:* For doctorate, comprehensive exam, clinical internship, clinical externship, capstone research project, portfolio. *Entrance requirements:* For doctorate, master's degree from ACAOM-accredited program in acupuncture and Oriental medicine; minimum GPA of 3.0 in master's studies; current license or eligibility to obtain a license to practice acupuncture in the state of Texas. Additional exam requirements/recommendations for international students: Required—TOEFL (minimum score 508 paper-based; 87 iBT), IELTS (minimum score 6.5). *Application deadline:* For fall admission, 8/25 for domestic students; for winter admission, 12/9 for domestic students; for spring admission, 3/17 for domestic students; for summer admission, 5/15 priority date for domestic students, 5/23 priority date for international students. Applications are processed on a rolling basis. Application fee: $75. Electronic applications accepted. *Financial support:* In 2017–18, 1 student received support. Application deadline: 6/30; applicants required to submit FAFSA. *Faculty research:* Allergy, cancer, women's health. *Unit head:* Dr. John S. Finnell, Director, Doctoral Program and Research, 512-492-3057, Fax: 512-454-7001, E-mail: jfinnell@aoma.edu. *Application contact:* Jessica Du, Director of Admissions, 512-492-3017, Fax: 512-454-7001, E-mail: admissions@aoma.edu.
Website: http://aoma.edu/doctoral-program/

AOMA Graduate School of Integrative Medicine, Master of Acupuncture and Oriental Medicine Program, Austin, TX 78757. Offers MAcOM. *Accreditation:* ACAOM. *Faculty:* 11 full-time (4 women), 20 part-time/adjunct (12 women). *Students:* 100 full-time (81 women), 27 part-time (22 women); includes 19 minority (1 Black or African American, non-Hispanic/Latino; 16 Asian, non-Hispanic/Latino; 2 Hispanic/Latino). Average age 35. 39 applicants, 67% accepted, 24 enrolled. In 2017, 37 master's awarded. *Degree requirements:* For master's, comprehensive exam, clinical rotations (40.5 credits), portfolio. *Entrance requirements:* For master's, BA or higher or minimum of 90 credits at baccalaureate level from regionally-accredited institution with 30 credits of general education coursework; minimum GPA of 2.5. Additional exam requirements/recommendations for international students: Required—TOEFL (minimum score 508 paper-based; 87 iBT), IELTS. *Application deadline:* For fall admission, 8/25 priority date for domestic students; for winter admission, 12/9 priority date for domestic students; for spring admission, 3/17 priority date for domestic students; for summer admission, 6/23 priority date for domestic students, 5/23 priority date for international students. Applications are processed on a rolling basis. Application fee: $75. Electronic applications accepted. *Financial support:* In 2017–18, 21 students received support. Federal Work-Study and scholarships/grants available. Financial award application deadline: 6/30; financial award applicants required to submit FAFSA. *Faculty research:* Acupuncture, Chinese herbal medicine, integrative medicine, pulse diagnosis. *Unit head:* Lesley Hamilton, Program Director, 512-454-3040, Fax: 512-454-7001, E-mail: lhamilton@aoma.edu. *Application contact:* Jessica Du, Director of Admissions, 512-492-3017, Fax: 512-454-7001, E-mail: admissions@aoma.edu.
Website: https://aoma.edu/admissions

Arizona School of Acupuncture and Oriental Medicine, Graduate Programs, Tucson, AZ 85712. Offers M Ac, M Ac OM. *Accreditation:* ACAOM.

Atlantic Institute of Oriental Medicine, Graduate Program, Fort Lauderdale, FL 33301. Offers MS, DAOM. *Accreditation:* ACAOM. *Program availability:* Evening/weekend. *Faculty:* 7 full-time (1 woman), 15 part-time/adjunct (6 women). *Students:* 145 full-time (103 women); includes 66 minority (8 Black or African American, non-Hispanic/Latino; 13 Asian, non-Hispanic/Latino; 45 Hispanic/Latino), 8 international. Average age 37. 30 applicants, 53% accepted, 16 enrolled. In 2017, 29 master's, 15 doctorates awarded. *Degree requirements:* For master's, comprehensive exam; for doctorate, comprehensive exam, thesis/dissertation. *Entrance requirements:* For master's, official transcripts, professional resume, essay, two letters of reference. Additional exam requirements/recommendations for international students: Required—TOEFL (minimum score 500 paper-based). *Application deadline:* For fall admission, 7/1 for domestic students, 5/1 for international students; for spring admission, 11/30 for domestic students, 2/28 for international students. Applications are processed on a rolling basis. Application fee: $20 ($30 for international students). *Expenses: Tuition:* Full-time $17,000. *Required fees:* $250. One-time fee: $250 full-time. *Financial support:* Applicants required to submit FAFSA. *Unit head:* Dr. Johanna C. Yen, President, 954-763-9840 Ext. 202, Fax: 954-763-9844, E-mail: president@atom.edu. *Application contact:* Karen Gemignani, Admissions Counselor, 954-763-9840 Ext. 213, Fax: 954-763-9844, E-mail: admissions@atom.edu.

Bastyr University, School of Traditional World Medicines, Kenmore, WA 98028-4966. Offers acupuncture and Oriental medicine (MS, DAOM); Ayurvedic sciences (MS). *Accreditation:* ACAOM. *Program availability:* Evening/weekend. *Entrance requirements:* For master's, course work in biology, chemistry, intermediate algebra and psychology; for doctorate, MS in acupuncture or certificate and 10 years of clinical experience. Additional exam requirements/recommendations for international students: Required—TOEFL (minimum score 550 paper-based; 79 iBT). *Application deadline:* For fall admission, 3/15 priority date for domestic and international students. Applications are processed on a rolling basis. Application fee: $75. Electronic applications accepted. *Expenses: Tuition:* Part-time $714 per credit hour. *Required fees:* $75. *Financial support:* Career-related internships or fieldwork, Federal Work-Study, and scholarships/grants available. Support available to part-time students. Financial award application deadline: 4/15; financial award applicants required to submit FAFSA. *Faculty research:* Integrative oncology, acupuncture and chemotherapy-induced peripheral neuropathy (CIPN), traditional Chinese medicine and stroke rehabilitation, acupuncture and prevention and wellness, electroacupuncture. *Unit head:* Dean, 425-602-3151, Fax: 425-823-6222. *Application contact:* Admissions Office, 425-602-3330, Fax: 425-602-3090, E-mail: admissions@bastyr.edu.
Website: https://bastyr.edu/academics/schools-departments/school-traditional-world-medicines

California Institute of Integral Studies, American College of Traditional Chinese Medicine, San Francisco, CA 94103. Offers acupuncture and Chinese medicine (DACM, tDACM); acupuncture and Oriental medicine (DAOM); traditional Chinese medicine (MSTCM). *Students:* 157 full-time (118 women), 68 part-time (53 women); includes 84 minority (3 Black or African American, non-Hispanic/Latino; 54 Asian, non-Hispanic/Latino; 13 Hispanic/Latino; 3 Native Hawaiian or other Pacific Islander, non-Hispanic/Latino; 11 Two or more races, non-Hispanic/Latino), 9 international. Average age 37. 56 applicants, 100% accepted, 44 enrolled. In 2017, 33 master's, 29 doctorates awarded. *Entrance requirements:* Additional exam requirements/recommendations for international students: Required—TOEFL (minimum score 550 paper-based). *Application deadline:* For fall admission, 8/1 priority date for domestic students; for spring admission, 12/1 priority date for domestic students; for summer admission, 4/1 priority date for domestic students. Application fee: $65. Electronic applications accepted. *Expenses:* Contact institution. *Unit head:* Dr. Bingzen Zou, Academic Dean, 415-828-7600, E-mail: bingzou@actcm.edu. *Application contact:* Yuwen Chiu, Associate Director of Admissions, 415-828-7600, E-mail: yuwenchiu@actcm.edu.
Website: https://www.actcm.edu

Canadian Memorial Chiropractic College, Certificate Programs, Toronto, ON M2H 3J1, Canada. Offers chiropractic clinical sciences (Certificate); chiropractic radiology (Certificate); chiropractic sports sciences (Certificate); clinical acupuncture (Certificate). *Degree requirements:* For Certificate, thesis. *Entrance requirements:* For degree, DC, board certification. *Faculty research:* Theories and concepts of chiropractic, sciences related to chiropractic, assessments of the efficacy and efficiency of chiropractic.

Colorado School of Traditional Chinese Medicine, Graduate Programs, Denver, CO 80206-2127. Offers acupuncture (MS); traditional Chinese medicine (MS). *Accreditation:* ACAOM. *Faculty:* 52 part-time/adjunct (20 women). *Students:* 96 full-time (77 women). Average age 33. 50 applicants, 54% accepted, 23 enrolled. In 2017, 61 master's awarded. *Entrance requirements:* Additional exam requirements/recommendations for international students: Required—TOEFL (minimum score 80 iBT), IELTS (minimum score 6.5). *Application deadline:* For fall admission, 8/18 for domestic students, 8/19 for international students; for winter admission, 12/29 for domestic and international students; for summer admission, 4/21 for domestic and international students. Applications are processed on a rolling basis. Application fee: $50. *Expenses:* Contact institution. *Financial support:* Scholarships/grants available. Financial award applicants required to submit FAFSA. *Unit head:* Vladimir Dibrigida, Administrative Director, 303-329-6355 Ext. 11, Fax: 303-388-8165, E-mail: director@cstcm.edu. *Application contact:* Chris Duxbury-Edwards, Recruiting Director, 303-329-6355 Ext. 21, Fax: 303-388-8165, E-mail: recruiting@cstcm.edu.
Website: http://www.cstcm.edu

Dongguk University Los Angeles, Program in Oriental Medicine, Los Angeles, CA 90020. Offers MS. *Accreditation:* ACAOM. *Program availability:* Part-time, evening/weekend.

Dragon Rises College of Oriental Medicine, Graduate Program, Gainesville, FL 32601. Offers MAOM. *Accreditation:* ACAOM. *Faculty:* 2 full-time (0 women), 12 part-time/adjunct (7 women). *Students:* 45 full-time (35 women). *Entrance requirements:* For master's, two letters of recommendation, official transcripts. Application fee: $50. Electronic applications accepted. *Expenses: Tuition:* Full-time $11,000. *Required fees:* $365. One-time fee: $75 full-time. *Application contact:* Chantay Moxley, Director of Admissions, 352-371-2833 Ext. 27, Fax: 352-244-0003, E-mail: admissions@dragonrises.edu.
Website: https://www.dragonrises.edu/program/the-masters-program/

East West College of Natural Medicine, Graduate Programs, Sarasota, FL 34234. Offers MSOM. *Accreditation:* ACAOM.

Emperor's College of Traditional Oriental Medicine, Graduate Programs, Santa Monica, CA 90403. Offers MTOM, DAOM. *Accreditation:* ACAOM. *Program availability:* Part-time, evening/weekend. *Entrance requirements:* For master's, minimum 2 years of undergraduate course work, interview; for doctorate, CA acupuncture licensure. *Faculty research:* Menopause, dysmenorrhea.

Five Branches University, Graduate School of Traditional Chinese Medicine, Santa Cruz, CA 95062. Offers acupuncture (M Ac); acupuncture and Oriental medicine (DAOM); traditional Chinese medicine (MTCM, PhD). *Accreditation:* ACAOM. *Degree requirements:* For master's, comprehensive exam. *Entrance requirements:* For master's, 6 units in anatomy and physiology, 9 units in basic sciences, minimum GPA of 2.5. Additional exam requirements/recommendations for international students: Required—TOEFL, IELTS. Electronic applications accepted.

Florida College of Integrative Medicine, Graduate Program, Orlando, FL 32809. Offers MSOM. *Accreditation:* ACAOM. *Program availability:* Evening/weekend. *Entrance requirements:* For master's, minimum 60 semester hours of undergraduate coursework. Electronic applications accepted.

Institute of Clinical Acupuncture and Oriental Medicine, Program in Oriental Medicine, Honolulu, HI 96817. Offers MSOM. *Accreditation:* ACAOM.

Institute of Taoist Education and Acupuncture, Graduate Program, Louisville, CO 80027. Offers classical five-element acupuncture (M Ac).

Maryland University of Integrative Health, Program in Herbal Medicine, Laurel, MD 20723. Offers clinical herbalism (Certificate); herbal studies (Certificate); therapeutic herbalism (MS). *Entrance requirements:* Additional exam requirements/recommendations for international students: Required—TOEFL. *Faculty research:* Philosophical roots of holistic healing, botany, herbal pharmacology; materia medica, holistic healing.

Maryland University of Integrative Health, Programs in Acupuncture and Oriental Medicine, Laurel, MD 20723. Offers acupuncture (M Ac, D Ac); Chinese herbs (Certificate); Oriental medicine (MOM, DOM). *Accreditation:* ACAOM. *Degree requirements:* For master's, comprehensive exam, 500 clinical hours, oral exams. *Entrance requirements:* Additional exam requirements/recommendations for international students: Required—TOEFL. *Faculty research:* Philosophical roots of oriental medicine, meridian pathways, points, pulses.

MCPHS University, New England School of Acupuncture, Boston, MA 02115-5896. Offers acupuncture (M Ac); acupuncture and Oriental medicine (MAOM). *Accreditation:* ACAOM (one or more programs are accredited). *Program availability:* Part-time. *Degree requirements:* For master's, comprehensive exam. *Entrance requirements:* For master's, previous course work in anatomy, biology, physiology, and psychology. Additional exam requirements/recommendations for international students: Required—TOEFL (minimum score 550 paper-based). *Faculty research:* Acupuncture and women's health, acupuncture and stroke rehabilitation, tai chi and cardiovascular health, tai chi and balance, cancer.

Midwest College of Oriental Medicine, Graduate Programs, Racine, WI 53403-9747. Offers acupuncture (Certificate); Oriental medicine (MSOM). *Accreditation:* ACAOM. *Program availability:* Part-time, evening/weekend. *Degree requirements:* For master's and Certificate, comprehensive exam, thesis. *Entrance requirements:* For master's and Certificate, 60 semester credit hours from accredited school, 2 letters of recommendation, interview. Additional exam requirements/recommendations for international students: Required—TOEFL. *Faculty research:* Pharmacology.

Midwest College of Oriental Medicine, Graduate Programs-Chicago, Chicago, IL 60613. Offers acupuncture (Certificate); oriental medicine (MSOM). *Accreditation:* ACAOM. *Program availability:* Part-time, evening/weekend. *Degree requirements:* For master's and Certificate, comprehensive exam, thesis. *Entrance requirements:* For master's and Certificate, 60 semester credit hours from accredited school, 2 letters of recommendation, interview. Additional exam requirements/recommendations for international students: Required—TOEFL.

National University of Health Sciences, Graduate Programs, Lombard, IL 60148-4583. Offers acupuncture (MSAC); chiropractic (DC); diagnostic imaging (MS); naturopathic medicine (ND); Oriental medicine (MSOM).

National University of Natural Medicine, College of Classical Chinese Medicine, Portland, OR 97201. Offers M Ac, MSOM, DOM. *Accreditation:* ACAOM. *Faculty:* 14 full-time (3 women), 22 part-time/adjunct (10 women). *Students:* 167 full-time (123 women). Average age 33. In 2017, 29 master's, 7 doctorates awarded. *Degree requirements:* For master's, thesis. *Entrance requirements:* Additional exam requirements/recommendations for international students: Recommended—TOEFL, IELTS, TSE. *Application deadline:* For fall and winter admission, 5/1 priority date for domestic and international students. Applications are processed on a rolling basis. Application fee: $75. Electronic applications accepted. *Expenses: Tuition:* Full-time $23,979. *Financial support:* Federal Work-Study and scholarships/grants available. Financial award application deadline: 2/15; financial award applicants required to submit FAFSA. *Faculty research:* Cases on herbs and acupuncture for asthma, diabetes, depression associated with menopause; qigong to maintain weight loss; qigong for multiple sclerosis: a feasibility study; patient perspectives on care received at community acupuncture clinics: A qualitative thematic analysis. *Unit head:* Dr. Laurie Regan, Dean, 503-552-1775, Fax: 503-499-0027, E-mail: admissions@nunm.edu. *Application contact:* Ryan Hollister, Associate Director of Admissions and Operations, 503-552-1665, Fax: 503-499-0027, E-mail: admissions@numn.edu.
Website: http://nunm.edu/academics/school-of-classical-chinese-medicine/

New York Chiropractic College, Finger Lakes School of Acupuncture and Oriental Medicine, Seneca Falls, NY 13148-0800. Offers acupuncture (MS); acupuncture and Oriental medicine (MS). *Accreditation:* ACAOM. *Degree requirements:* For master's, clinical internship. *Entrance requirements:* For master's, interview, three written references. Additional exam requirements/recommendations for international students: Recommended—TOEFL (minimum score 550 paper-based). Electronic applications accepted. *Faculty research:* Chinese herbal medicine, traditional Chinese medicine, cancer, gait and posture, obesity.

New York College of Health Professions, Graduate School of Oriental Medicine, Syosset, NY 11791-4413. Offers acupuncture (MS); Oriental medicine (MS). *Accreditation:* ACAOM. *Program availability:* Part-time. *Degree requirements:* For master's, thesis. *Entrance requirements:* For master's, minimum GPA of 2.5, 60 semester credits in undergraduate course work. Additional exam requirements/recommendations for international students: Required—TOEFL. *Faculty research:* Breast cancer, diabetic neuropathy hemolysis.

New York College of Traditional Chinese Medicine, Graduate Programs, Mineola, NY 11501. Offers Oriental medicine (MAOM). *Accreditation:* ACAOM. *Entrance requirements:* For master's, statement of purpose, official transcript, three recommendation letters, immunizations. Additional exam requirements/recommendations for international students: Required—TOEFL (minimum score 61 iBT), IELTS (minimum score 6).

Northwestern Health Sciences University, College of Health and Wellness, Bloomington, MN 55431-1599. Offers acupuncture (M Ac); applied clinical nutrition (MHS); Oriental medicine (MOM). *Accreditation:* ACAOM. *Entrance requirements:* For master's, 60 semester credits of course work with minimum GPA of 2.5. Additional exam requirements/recommendations for international students: Required—TOEFL (minimum score 540 paper-based; 76 iBT). Electronic applications accepted.

Oregon College of Oriental Medicine, Graduate Program in Acupuncture and Oriental Medicine, Portland, OR 97216. Offers M Ac OM, MAcOM, DAOM. *Accreditation:* ACAOM. *Program availability:* Part-time. *Entrance requirements:* For master's, minimum 3 years of college; course work in chemistry, biology, and psychology; for doctorate, documentation of clinical practice, 3 years of clinical experience. Additional exam requirements/recommendations for international students: Required—TOEFL (minimum score 550 paper-based).

Pacific College of Oriental Medicine, Graduate Program, San Diego, CA 92108. Offers MSTOM, DAOM. *Accreditation:* ACAOM. *Program availability:* Part-time, evening/weekend. *Entrance requirements:* For master's, 2 letters of reference, interviews, minimum GPA of 3.0. *Faculty research:* PMS, acupuncture, herbs, Tai Ji Quan, sports medicine.

Pacific College of Oriental Medicine–Chicago, Graduate Program, Chicago, IL 60601. Offers MTOM. *Accreditation:* ACAOM. *Program availability:* Part-time, evening/weekend. *Entrance requirements:* For master's, 2 letters of reference, interview, minimum GPA of 3.0. *Faculty research:* AIDS, cancer, mental health, clinical counseling.

Pacific College of Oriental Medicine-New York, Graduate Program, New York, NY 10010. Offers MSTOM. *Accreditation:* ACAOM. *Program availability:* Part-time, evening/weekend. *Entrance requirements:* For master's, 2 letters of reference, interview, minimum GPA of 3.0. *Faculty research:* Energy medicine, acupuncture in the treatment of neurological disorders.

Phoenix Institute of Herbal Medicine & Acupuncture, Graduate Programs, Phoenix, AZ 85018. Offers acupuncture (MSAC); Oriental medicine (MSOM). *Accreditation:* ACAOM. *Entrance requirements:* For master's, baccalaureate degree, personal statement, resume, 2 letters of recommendation, official transcripts.

Seattle Institute of Oriental Medicine, Graduate Program, Seattle, WA 98115. Offers M Ac OM. *Accreditation:* ACAOM. *Degree requirements:* For master's, one foreign language, comprehensive exam. *Entrance requirements:* For master's, course work in biology, psychology, chemistry, anatomy, physiology; CPR/first aid certification; 3 years (90 semester credits) post secondary coursework. Additional exam requirements/recommendations for international students: Recommended—TOEFL (minimum score 500 paper-based).

South Baylo University, Program in Oriental Medicine and Acupuncture, Anaheim, CA 92801-1701. Offers MS. *Accreditation:* ACAOM. *Program availability:* Evening/weekend. *Degree requirements:* For master's, 3 foreign languages, comprehensive exam. *Entrance requirements:* Additional exam requirements/recommendations for international students: Required—TOEFL (minimum score 500 paper-based). Electronic applications accepted. *Faculty research:* Effectiveness of acupuncture therapy.

Southern California University of Health Sciences, College of Eastern Medicine, Whittier, CA 90609-1166. Offers MAOM, DAOM. *Accreditation:* ACAOM. *Program availability:* Part-time, evening/weekend. *Degree requirements:* For master's and doctorate, comprehensive exam. *Entrance requirements:* For master's, 60 semester hours or 90 quarter credits of undergraduate course work, interview. Additional exam requirements/recommendations for international students: Required—TOEFL (minimum score 500 paper-based). Electronic applications accepted. *Faculty research:* Stress study.

Southwest Acupuncture College, Program in Oriental Medicine, Boulder Campus, Boulder, CO 80301. Offers MS. *Accreditation:* ACAOM. *Program availability:* Part-time. *Entrance requirements:* For master's, minimum 2 years of college general education.

Southwest Acupuncture College, Program in Oriental Medicine, Santa Fe Campus, Santa Fe, NM 87505. Offers MS. *Accreditation:* ACAOM. *Program availability:* Part-time. *Entrance requirements:* For master's, minimum 2 years of college general education. Additional exam requirements/recommendations for international students: Required—TOEFL (minimum score 500 paper-based). Electronic applications accepted.

Swedish Institute, College of Health Sciences, Graduate Program, New York, NY 10001-6700. Offers acupuncture (MS). *Program availability:* Part-time, evening/weekend. *Entrance requirements:* Additional exam requirements/recommendations for international students: Required—TOEFL (minimum score 72 iBT).

Texas Health and Science University, Graduate Programs, Austin, TX 78704. Offers acupuncture and Oriental medicine (MS, DAOM); business administration (MBA); healthcare management (MBA). *Accreditation:* ACAOM. *Faculty:* 8 full-time (3 women), 7 part-time/adjunct (5 women). *Students:* 102 full-time (64 women), 9 part-time (8 women); includes 43 minority (1 Black or African American, non-Hispanic/Latino; 1 American Indian or Alaska Native, non-Hispanic/Latino; 35 Asian, non-Hispanic/Latino; 6 Hispanic/Latino). Average age 34. *Entrance requirements:* For master's, 60 hours applicable to bachelor's degree. Additional exam requirements/recommendations for international students: Required—TOEFL (minimum score 500 paper-based), TWE. *Application deadline:* For fall admission, 8/25 priority date for domestic and international students; for spring admission, 12/22 priority date for domestic and international students. Applications are processed on a rolling basis. Application fee: $75 ($300 for international students). Electronic applications accepted. *Expenses: Tuition:* Full-time $11,460. *Required fees:* $600. Tuition and fees vary according to course load, degree level and program. *Financial support:* Teaching assistantships with partial tuition reimbursements, career-related internships or fieldwork, Federal Work-Study, institutionally sponsored loans, scholarships/grants, and tuition waivers (partial) available. Financial award applicants required to submit FAFSA. *Unit head:* Dr. David G. Vequist, IV, Vice President of Academic Affairs, 512-444-8082. *Application contact:* Caleb Li, Admissions Coordinator, 512-444-8082, Fax: 512-444-6345, E-mail: admissions@thsu.edu.

Tri-State College of Acupuncture, Graduate Programs, New York, NY 10011. Offers acupuncture (MS); Chinese herbology (Certificate); Oriental medicine (MS). *Accreditation:* ACAOM. *Program availability:* Evening/weekend. *Entrance requirements:* For master's, interview, essay. Additional exam requirements/recommendations for international students: Required—TOEFL (minimum score 61 iBT), IELTS (minimum score 6). Electronic applications accepted.

University of Bridgeport, Acupuncture Institute, Bridgeport, CT 06604. Offers MS. *Accreditation:* ACAOM. *Program availability:* Part-time. *Entrance requirements:* Additional exam requirements/recommendations for international students: Recommended—TOEFL (minimum score 550 paper-based; 80 iBT), IELTS (minimum score 6.5). Electronic applications accepted. *Expenses:* Contact institution.

University of East-West Medicine, Graduate Programs, Sunnyvale, CA 94085-3922. Offers acupuncture and Oriental medicine (DAOM); Tai Chi (MS); traditional Chinese medicine (MSTCM). *Accreditation:* ACAOM.

WON Institute of Graduate Studies, Acupuncture Studies Program, Glenside, PA 19038. Offers M Ac. *Accreditation:* ACAOM. *Students:* 37 full-time (30 women); includes 6 minority (2 Black or African American, non-Hispanic/Latino; 2 Asian, non-Hispanic/Latino; 2 Native Hawaiian or other Pacific Islander, non-Hispanic/Latino), 2 international. Average age 38. *Entrance requirements:* For master's, 6 prerequisite credits in anatomy and physiology, 2 letters of recommendation, essay, bachelor's degree, 3 credits of basic science (chemistry, biology, physics or botany). Additional exam requirements/recommendations for international students: Required—TOEFL (minimum score 550 paper-based; 79 iBT). *Application deadline:* For fall admission, 6/15 for domestic students. Applications are processed on a rolling basis. Application fee: $75. Electronic applications accepted. *Faculty research:* Meditation and pulse taking, acupuncture and apprehension. *Unit head:* Ben Griffith, Chair, 215-884-8942, Fax: 215-884-8942, E-mail: ben.griffith@woninstitute.edu. *Application contact:* Jennifer Cake, Lead Enrollment Management Counselor, 215-884-8942 Ext. 212, E-mail: jennifer.cake@woninstitute.edu.
Website: https://www.woninstitute.edu/academics/master-of-acupuncture-studies-degree/

Acupuncture and Oriental Medicine

WON Institute of Graduate Studies, Program in Chinese Herbal Medicine, Glenside, PA 19038. Offers Certificate. *Students:* 34 full-time (27 women); includes 9 minority (1 Black or African American, non-Hispanic/Latino; 6 Asian, non-Hispanic/Latino; 2 Two or more races, non-Hispanic/Latino). Average age 42. *Entrance requirements:* For degree, licensed acupuncturist with bachelor's degree, graduate of ACAOM-approved acupuncture program, or currently enrolled in ACAOM-approved acupuncture program. Additional exam requirements/recommendations for international students: Required—TOEFL (minimum score 550 paper-based; 79 iBT). *Application deadline:* For fall admission, 8/1 for domestic students. Applications are processed on a rolling basis. Application fee: $75. Electronic applications accepted. *Financial support:* Scholarships/grants available. *Unit head:* Jacqueline Lacava, Acupuncture and Chinese Herbal Medicine Chair, 215-884-8942, Fax: 215-884-9002, E-mail: chp.director@woninstitute.edu. *Application contact:* Jennifer Cake, Enrollment Management Counselor, 215-884-8942 Ext. 219, Fax: 215-884-9002, E-mail: jennifer.cake@woninstitute.edu.
Website: https://www.woninstitute.edu/academics/certificate-in-chinese-herbal-medicine/

World Medicine Institute, Program in Acupuncture and Oriental Medicine, Honolulu, HI 96821. Offers M Ac OM. *Accreditation:* ACAOM. *Program availability:* Part-time, evening/weekend. *Entrance requirements:* For master's, minimum 60 college credits.

Yo San University of Traditional Chinese Medicine, Program in Acupuncture and Traditional Chinese Medicine, Los Angeles, CA 90066. Offers MATCM. *Accreditation:* ACAOM. *Program availability:* Part-time, online learning. *Degree requirements:* For master's, observation and practice internships, exam. *Entrance requirements:* For master's, minimum 2 years of college, interview, minimum GPA of 2.5.

Section 26
Chiropractic

This section contains a directory of institutions offering graduate work in chiropractic. Additional information about programs listed in the directory but not augmented by an in-depth entry may be obtained by writing directly to the dean of a graduate school or chair of a department at the address given in the directory.

CONTENTS

Chiropractic

Canadian Memorial Chiropractic College, Certificate Programs, Toronto, ON M2H 3J1, Canada. Offers chiropractic clinical sciences (Certificate); chiropractic radiology (Certificate); chiropractic sports sciences (Certificate); clinical acupuncture (Certificate). *Degree requirements:* For Certificate, thesis. *Entrance requirements:* For degree, DC, board certification. *Faculty research:* Theories and concepts of chiropractic, sciences related to chiropractic, assessments of the efficacy and efficiency of chiropractic.

Canadian Memorial Chiropractic College, Professional Program, Toronto, ON M2H 3J1, Canada. Offers DC. *Entrance requirements:* For doctorate, 3 full years of university (15 full courses or 90 hours). *Faculty research:* Theories and concepts of chiropractic, sciences related to chiropractic, assessment of the efficacy and efficiency of chiropractic.

Cleveland University–Kansas City, Doctor of Chiropractic Program, Overland Park, KS 66210. Offers DC. *Accreditation:* CCE. *Program availability:* Part-time. *Degree requirements:* For doctorate, comprehensive exam. *Entrance requirements:* For doctorate, 90 semester hours of pre-professional study, college transcripts, minimum cumulative college GPA of 3.0. Additional exam requirements/recommendations for international students: Required—TOEFL (minimum score 550 paper-based; 79 iBT). *Application deadline:* For fall admission, 7/1 priority date for domestic and international students; for winter admission, 11/1 priority date for domestic and international students; for spring admission, 3/1 priority date for domestic and international students. Applications are processed on a rolling basis. Electronic applications accepted. *Financial support:* Federal Work-Study and scholarships/grants available. Financial award applicants required to submit FAFSA. *Faculty research:* Effectiveness and efficacy of chiropractic care. *Application contact:* Melissa Denton, Director of Admissions, 913-234-0744, Fax: 913-234-0906, E-mail: kc.admissions@cleveland.edu.
Website: https://www.cleveland.edu/academics/college-of-chiropractic

D'Youville College, Department of Chiropractic, Buffalo, NY 14201-1084. Offers DC. *Accreditation:* CCE. *Entrance requirements:* For doctorate, minimum GPA of 2.5, 90 undergraduate credits. Electronic applications accepted. *Expenses:* Contact institution. *Faculty research:* Radiology diagnosis, chiropractic treatment and diagnosis.

Institut Franco-EuropÃ©en de Chiropraxie, Professional Program, Ivry-sur-Seine, France. Offers DC.

Life Chiropractic College West, Professional Program, Hayward, CA 94545. Offers DC. *Accreditation:* CCE. *Entrance requirements:* For doctorate, minimum GPA of 3.0. Additional exam requirements/recommendations for international students: Required—TOEFL (minimum score 550 paper-based). Electronic applications accepted. *Faculty research:* Imaging, ergonomics, upper cervical adjusting, academics.

Life University, College of Chiropractic, Marietta, GA 30060-2903. Offers DC. *Accreditation:* CCE. *Faculty:* 83 full-time (32 women), 22 part-time/adjunct (6 women). *Students:* 1,552 full-time (712 women), 99 part-time (50 women); includes 576 minority (207 Black or African American, non-Hispanic/Latino; 17 American Indian or Alaska Native, non-Hispanic/Latino; 62 Asian, non-Hispanic/Latino; 290 Hispanic/Latino), 66 international. Average age 28. In 2017, 353 doctorates awarded. *Degree requirements:* For doctorate, comprehensive exam, thesis/dissertation or alternative. *Entrance requirements:* For doctorate, minimum of 3 years of college; course work in biology, chemistry, physics, humanities, psychology, and English; minimum GPA of 2.75. Additional exam requirements/recommendations for international students: Required—TOEFL (minimum score 500 paper-based). *Application deadline:* For fall admission, 8/1 for domestic students; for winter admission, 11/1 for domestic students; for spring admission, 3/1 for domestic students; for summer admission, 7/1 for domestic students. Applications are processed on a rolling basis. Application fee: $50. Electronic applications accepted. *Expenses:* $30,181 annual tuition, $1,050 fees. *Financial support:* Research assistantships, Federal Work-Study, institutionally sponsored loans, scholarships/grants, and tuition waivers (partial) available. Support available to part-time students. Financial award application deadline: 9/1; financial award applicants required to submit FAFSA. *Faculty research:* Chiropractic clinical trial, spinal modeling, biomechanics, clinical evaluation studies, chiropractic technique development, sports performance. *Unit head:* Dr. Leslie King, Dean, 770-426-2713, E-mail: lesliek@life.edu. *Application contact:* Robyn Stanley, Director of Enrollment, 770-426-2877, Fax: 770-426-2895, E-mail: roby.stanley@life.edu.
Website: http://www.life.edu/academics/chiropractic/

Logan University, College of Chiropractic, Chesterfield, MO 63017. Offers DC. *Accreditation:* CCE. *Faculty:* 39 full-time (15 women), 7 part-time/adjunct (4 women). *Students:* 744 full-time (302 women); includes 90 minority (29 Black or African American, non-Hispanic/Latino; 4 American Indian or Alaska Native, non-Hispanic/Latino; 19 Asian, non-Hispanic/Latino; 23 Hispanic/Latino; 1 Native Hawaiian or other Pacific Islander, non-Hispanic/Latino; 14 Two or more races, non-Hispanic/Latino), 13 international. Average age 26. 267 applicants, 58% accepted, 141 enrolled. In 2017, 81 doctorates awarded. *Degree requirements:* For doctorate, comprehensive exam, preceptorship. *Entrance requirements:* For doctorate, 90 hours of pre-chiropractic including biology, chemistry, physics, and social sciences; minimum GPA of 3.0. Additional exam requirements/recommendations for international students: Required—TOEFL (minimum score 500 paper-based; 79 iBT); Recommended—IELTS. *Application deadline:* Applications are processed on a rolling basis. Application fee: $50. Electronic applications accepted. *Expenses:* $10,832 tuition, $140 per trimester fees. *Financial support:* In 2017–18, 129 students received support. Federal Work-Study and scholarships/grants available. Support available to part-time students. Financial award applicants required to submit FAFSA. *Faculty research:* Effects of injury on proprioception as measured by joint position sense, interventions for older adults with low back pain, interventions affecting heart rate variability, finite element computer modeling of spinal biomechanics, electrophysiological diagnosis of common neuromusculoskeletal conditions, the effects of spinal manipulation on posture and postural control. *Unit head:* Dr. Vincent DeBono, Dean of the College of Chiropractic, 636-227-2100 Ext. 2701, Fax: 636-207-2431, E-mail: vincent.debono@logan.edu. *Application contact:* Natacha Douglas, Executive Director of Admissions, 636-227-2100 Ext. 1718, Fax: 636-207-2425, E-mail: admissions@logan.edu.
Website: http://www.logan.edu/academics/doctor-of-chiropractic

National University of Health Sciences, Graduate Programs, Lombard, IL 60148-4583. Offers acupuncture (MSAC); chiropractic (DC); diagnostic imaging (MS); naturopathic medicine (ND); Oriental medicine (MSOM).

New York Chiropractic College, Doctor of Chiropractic Program, Seneca Falls, NY 13148-0800. Offers DC. *Accreditation:* CCE. *Degree requirements:* For doctorate, internship in health center. *Entrance requirements:* For doctorate, 24 credit hours of course work in science; 90 credit hours with minimum GPA of 2.5; references; interview. Additional exam requirements/recommendations for international students: Recommended—TOEFL (minimum score 550 paper-based). Electronic applications accepted. *Faculty research:* Anatomy, pathophysiology, neurophysiology biomechanics, musculoskeletal pain syndrome, nutrition.

See Display on the next page and Close-Up on page 859.

Northwestern Health Sciences University, College of Chiropractic, Bloomington, MN 55431-1599. Offers DC. *Accreditation:* CCE. *Entrance requirements:* For doctorate, 90 semester hours of course work in health or science, minimum GPA of 2.75. Additional exam requirements/recommendations for international students: Required—TOEFL (minimum score 540 paper-based; 76 iBT). Electronic applications accepted. *Faculty research:* Headache, low back pain, neck pain, sciatica, rehabilitative exercise.

Palmer College of Chiropractic, Professional Program, Davenport, IA 52803-5287. Offers DC. *Accreditation:* CCE. *Program availability:* Part-time. *Entrance requirements:* For doctorate, minimum GPA of 2.5, 90 hours of prerequisite coursework. Additional exam requirements/recommendations for international students: Required—TOEFL (minimum score 500 paper-based; 61 iBT). Electronic applications accepted. *Expenses:* Contact institution. *Faculty research:* Studies to advance the understanding of chiropractic.

Palmer College of Chiropractic, Professional Program–Florida Campus, Port Orange, FL 32129. Offers DC. *Program availability:* Part-time. *Degree requirements:* For doctorate, clinical internship. *Entrance requirements:* For doctorate, minimum GPA of 2.5, 90 hours of prerequisite coursework. Additional exam requirements/recommendations for international students: Recommended—TOEFL (minimum score 500 paper-based; 61 iBT). *Expenses:* Contact institution.

Palmer College of Chiropractic, Professional Program–West Campus, San Jose, CA 95134-1617. Offers DC. *Accreditation:* CCE. *Program availability:* Part-time. *Degree requirements:* For doctorate, clinical internship. *Entrance requirements:* For doctorate, minimum GPA of 2.5. Additional exam requirements/recommendations for international students: Required—TOEFL. Electronic applications accepted. *Expenses:* Contact institution. *Faculty research:* Low back pain complaints, spinal manipulation therapy, cervical biomechanics, clinical trials, practice guidelines.

Parker University, Doctor of Chiropractic Program, Dallas, TX 75229-5668. Offers DC. *Accreditation:* CCE. *Program availability:* Part-time. *Entrance requirements:* For doctorate, minimum GPA of 2.65. Additional exam requirements/recommendations for international students: Required—TOEFL (minimum score 550 paper-based). Electronic applications accepted. *Faculty research:* Arterial tonometry, bioenergetics, outcome assessment for clinical care.

Sherman College of Chiropractic, Professional Program, Spartanburg, SC 29304-1452. Offers DC. *Accreditation:* CCE. *Entrance requirements:* For doctorate, two letters of recommendation, official transcripts. Electronic applications accepted. *Faculty research:* Chiropractic effect of immune response, biomechanics, video fluoroscopy, dynamic motion.

Southern California University of Health Sciences, Los Angeles College of Chiropractic, Whittier, CA 90609-1166. Offers DC. *Accreditation:* CCE. *Degree requirements:* For doctorate, comprehensive exam, clinical internship. *Entrance requirements:* For doctorate, minimum GPA of 2.5, 90 incoming units in prerequisite coursework. Additional exam requirements/recommendations for international students: Required—TOEFL (minimum score 500 paper-based). Electronic applications accepted. *Faculty research:* Sports medicine.

Texas Chiropractic College, Professional Program, Pasadena, TX 77505-1699. Offers DC. *Accreditation:* CCE. *Entrance requirements:* For doctorate, 90 semester hours at regionally-accredited college or university, minimum GPA of 3.0 (24 hours of life and physical sciences, half of which have a lab component). Additional exam requirements/recommendations for international students: Required—TOEFL. *Faculty research:* Range of motion comparison male vs. female student stress levels.

Université du Québec à Trois-Rivières, Graduate Programs, Program in Chiropractic, Trois-Rivières, QC G9A 5H7, Canada. Offers DC.

University of Bridgeport, College of Chiropractic, Bridgeport, CT 06604. Offers DC. *Accreditation:* CCE. *Degree requirements:* For doctorate, thesis/dissertation, National Board of Chiropractic Exam Parts I and II. *Entrance requirements:* Additional exam requirements/recommendations for international students: Recommended—TOEFL (minimum score 550 paper-based; 80 iBT), IELTS (minimum score 6.5). Electronic applications accepted. *Expenses:* Contact institution.

University of Western States, Professional Program, Portland, OR 97230-3099. Offers DC. *Accreditation:* CCE. *Degree requirements:* For doctorate, comprehensive exam, internship. *Entrance requirements:* For doctorate, 3 years of pre-chiropractic study in biological sciences, minimum GPA of 2.5. *Faculty research:* Low back pain.

Academic Excellence.
Professional Success.

NEW YORK CHIROPRACTIC COLLEGE

Doctor of Chiropractic Program

Programs of Study

New York Chiropractic College (NYCC) offers a rigorous but highly rewarding program leading to the degree of Doctor of Chiropractic (D.C.) and prepares students for a professional career in chiropractic health care as well as in related research and teaching. The program is ten trimesters in length and takes five academic years to complete. New York Chiropractic College offers classes year-round, and students generally complete the program in forty months of continuous study. The program is open only to full-time students. It includes three trimesters of internship at one of the College's three health centers.

Several 3+1 joint-degree B.S./D.C. programs, which enable the student to save a year in the completion of the two degrees, are offered. NYCC's Postgraduate Division offers continuing education for chiropractors to further their professional development and to satisfy the license renewal requirements of various states.

Research Facilities

NYCC research department activity encompasses a wide variety of research interests. The research programs incorporate sports medicine and chiropractic geriatric studies, biomechanics, nutrition, and pathophysiology. The College supports three primary research laboratories: a biochemistry laboratory; a biodynamics laboratory, where sports chiropractic and related ergonomic and neurophysiology research is conducted; and a biomechanical/gait research laboratory. All laboratories are equipped with state-of-the-art technology capable of supporting extensive research activity in those respective areas. The laboratories are housed in an 8,000-square-foot research facility that contains administrative offices as well as a bone histology and microscopy laboratory and several computer graphics and data analysis workstations.

Financial Aid

Financial aid is generally available on the basis of need, as evidenced by information supplied on the FAFSA as well as an institutional application. Federal sources of aid include Federal Perkins Loans, Federal Work-Study, and veterans' benefits to eligible students. Limited grants are available under New York State's Tuition Assistance Program (TAP). Students may obtain Federal Stafford Student Loans and may compete for scholarships offered by chiropractic associations, private foundations, and NYCC.

Cost of Study

Only full-time students are admitted into the doctoral program. For 2017–18, tuition was $12,241 per trimester; tuition and fees for the calendar year (three trimesters) from September 2017 through summer 2018 are estimated at $36,723. The estimated cost of textbooks, equipment, and supplies is an additional $750 per trimester.

Living and Housing Costs

NYCC offers excellent on-campus housing in eight residence halls. The cost of a suite for married students is $3,692 (these are trimester rates). Meal plans are additional and range from $450 to $950 per trimester. Off-campus housing is available and comparatively priced. The cost of living in the area is substantially lower than that of urban areas.

Student Group

New York Chiropractic College's 700 students (including senior interns) come from more than twenty states and several other countries. The majority are residents of the Northeast. Students range in age from 21 to over 55, with the largest age group consisting of those in their mid-20s. Thirty percent of the students are women, and 80 percent of all students hold a baccalaureate or higher degree. Many students participate in intramural sports and student government as well as in the more than thirty student organizations that include special interests such as nutrition, sports injuries, publications, and research. Numerous technique clubs (e.g., Applied Kinesiology, Gonstead) are active on campus.

Location

New York Chiropractic College is located in Seneca Falls, New York, in the scenic wine-growing region of the Finger Lakes, a popular vacation spot less than a 45-minute drive from Syracuse, Rochester, and Ithaca. Outpatient clinics are located in Buffalo, Seneca Falls, and Levittown (Long Island). The 286-acre campus has 250 feet of frontage property on Cayuga Lake, the largest of the Finger Lakes. The College borders a state park and has a nine-hole, par 3 golf course on the campus.

The College

Established in 1919 in New York City as Columbia Institute of Chiropractic, the College is the oldest chiropractic institution in the Northeast. In 1976, it moved to Nassau County on suburban Long Island and moved again to a larger campus in upstate New York in 1991. The College is accredited by the Middle States Association of Colleges and Schools and by the Council on Chiropractic Education. It holds an Absolute Charter from the Board of Regents of the University of the State of New York.

Applying

Applications for admission should be submitted via the online application Information and application forms may be obtained by visiting NYCC's website or by calling 800-234-6922 (toll-free). Admission is a continuous process; there are entering classes in September, January, and May of each year. Approximately 300 students are admitted for each year, and applicants are encouraged to apply ten to twelve months in advance of their desired entrance date. Reference forms are supplied upon receipt of an application.

Correspondence and Information

Admissions Office
New York Chiropractic College
2360 Route 89
Seneca Falls, New York 13148-0800
United States
Phone: 315-568-3040
800-234-6922 (toll-free)
E-mail: Enrollnow@nycc.edu
Website: http://www.nycc.edu

THE FACULTY

Anatomy

M. Elizabeth Bedford, Ph.D., Kent State, 1994.
Andrew S. Choi, D.C., New York Chiropractic, 2000.
Michael L. Lentini, D.C., National Chiropractic, 1991.
Raj J. Philomin, Ph.D., Madras Medical College (India), 1986.

New York Chiropractic College

Maria Thomadaki, D.C., New York Chiropractic, 1994.
Robert A. Walker, Ph.D., Kent State, 1989.
Michael P. Zumpano, Ph.D., SUNY at Buffalo, 1997.

Physiopathology
David S. Aberant, M.S., LIU, C.W. Post, 1970.
Mary E. Balliett, D.C., New York Chiropractic, 1988.
Deborah A. Barr, Sc.D., Boston University, 1988.
Scott Coon, D.C., New York Chiropractic, 1994.
Chithambaram S. Philomin, M.B.B.S., Stanley Medical College, 1989.
Carolyn M. Pover, Ph.D., Bristol, 1986.
Veronica M. Sciotti, Ph.D., SUNY at Buffalo, 1988.
Lee C. VanDusen, D.C., National Chiropractic, 1985.

Diagnosis and Clinical Practice
Lisa K. Bloom, D.C., New York Chiropractic, 1990.
Susan E. Conley, D.C., New York Chiropractic, 1995.
Christine M. Cunningham, M.S., SUNY at Stony Brook, 1988.
Paul E. Dougherty, D.C., Logan Chiropractic, 1990.
Margaret M. Finn, D.C., New York Chiropractic, 1992.
Fiona Jarrett-Thelwell, D.C., New York Chiropractic, 1994.
Stephen J. Mesiti, D.C., New York Chiropractic, 1997.
Joseph A. Miller, D.C., National Chiropractic, 1991.
Michael J. O'Connor, D.C., New York Chiropractic, 1982.
Julie A. Plezbert, D.C., National Chiropractic, 1986.
Robert Ruddy, D.C., New York Chiropractic, 1996.
Fred L. SanFilipo, D.C., New York Chiropractic, 1982.
Judy M. Silvestrone, D.C., Palmer Chiropractic, 1984.
John A. M. Taylor, D.C., Canadian Memorial Chiropractic, 1979.
Meghan B. VanLoon, D.C., Northwestern Chiropractic, 1991.
Jeneen L. Wallace, D.C., New York Chiropractic, 1997.

Technique and Principles
Karen A. Bobak, D.C., National Chiropractic, 1986.
Brian M. Cunningham, D.C., New York Chiropractic, 1986.
John L. DeCicco, D.C., New York Chiropractic, 1982.
James R. Ebbets, D.C., New York Chiropractic, 1992.
Lillian M. Ford, D.C., New York Chiropractic, 1985.
Christopher J. Good, D.C., Palmer Chiropractic, 1982.
Sandra Hartwell-Ford, D.C., New York Chiropractic, 1996.
Lloyd E. Henby, D.C., National Chiropractic, 1952.
Michael E. Howard, D.C., Life Chiropractic, 1981.
Thomas McCloughan, D.C., New York Chiropractic, 1993.
Hunter A. Mollin, D.C., New York Chiropractic, 1980.
David F. Petters, D.C., New York Chiropractic, 1986.
Christopher P. Ryan, D.C., New York Chiropractic, 1987.
Paul W. Ryan, D.C., New York Chiropractic, 1989.
Eileen C. Santipadri, D.C., Palmer Chiropractic, 1981.
David A. Shinherr, D.C., New York Chiropractic, 1995.
Edward J. Sullivan, D.C., Northwestern Chiropractic, 1991.
Michael S. Young, D.C., New York Chiropractic, 1996.

Research
JeanMarie Burke, Ph.D., Indiana, 1991.

Depew Health Center
Margaret M. Anticola, D.C., Life Chiropractic, 1986.
Charles D. Coyle, D.C., National Chiropractic, 1988.
Mark A. Dux, D.C., Western States Chiropractic, 1980.
Daniel R. Johnson, D.C., Logan Chiropractic, 1981.
Sherri L. LaShomb, D.C., Palmer Chiropractic, 1988.
David L. Ribakove, D.C., New York Chiropractic, 1992.
Mark D. Sokolowski, D.C., Palmer Chiropractic, 1985.
Mercedes M. Trzcinski, D.C., Palmer Chiropractic, 1981.

Levittown Health Center
Patricia M. Flynn, D.C., National Chiropractic, 1996.
Charles A. Hemsey, D.C., Life Chiropractic, 1981.
Lloyd H. Kupferman, D.C., New York Chiropractic, 1981.
Frank S. Lizzio, D.C., New York Chiropractic, 1980.
Mariangela Penna, D.C., New York Chiropractic, 1986.
Michael G. Perillo, D.C., National Chiropractic, 1978.
Joseph E. Pfeifer, D.C., New York Chiropractic, 1984.
Lana K. Slinkard, D.C., National Chiropractic, 1985.
Veronica A. Wicks, D.C., New York Chiropractic, 1988.

Seneca Falls Health Center
Steven Feldman, D.C., New York Chiropractic, 1981.
Dennis M. Homack, D.C., New York Chiropractic, 1997.
Wendy L. Maneri, D.C., New York Chiropractic, 1999.
William H. Sherwood, D.C., National Chiropractic, 1990.

Dr. Chris Marchese instructing students in an active care class.

An NYCC student working on adjusting skills in an open lab class.

Section 27
Dentistry and Dental Sciences

This section contains a directory of institutions offering graduate work in dentistry and dental sciences, followed by an in-depth entry submitted by an institution that chose to prepare a detailed program description. Additional information about programs listed in the directory but not augmented by an in-depth entry may be obtained by writing directly to the dean of a graduate school or chair of a department at the address given in the directory.

For programs offering related work, see also in this book *Allied Health.*

CONTENTS

Program Directories

Dentistry

A.T. Still University, Arizona School of Dentistry & Oral Health, Mesa, AZ 85206. Offers dental medicine (DMD); orthodontics (MS, Certificate). *Accreditation:* ADA. *Faculty:* 50 full-time (26 women), 101 part-time/adjunct (36 women). *Students:* 311 full-time (164 women); includes 129 minority (5 Black or African American, non-Hispanic/Latino; 4 American Indian or Alaska Native, non-Hispanic/Latino; 83 Asian, non-Hispanic/Latino; 20 Hispanic/Latino; 17 Two or more races, non-Hispanic/Latino), 1 international. Average age 28. 2,433 applicants, 6% accepted, 76 enrolled. In 2017, 74 doctorates, 4 other advanced degrees awarded. *Degree requirements:* For doctorate, National Board Exams I and II. *Entrance requirements:* For doctorate, DAT, minimum GPA of 2.5 overall and in science. Additional exam requirements/recommendations for international students: Recommended—TOEFL. *Application deadline:* For fall admission, 11/15 for domestic and international students; for summer admission, 11/15 for domestic and international students. Applications are processed on a rolling basis. Application fee: $70. Electronic applications accepted. Application fee is waived when completed online. *Financial support:* In 2017–18, 49 students received support. Federal Work-Study and scholarships/grants available. Financial award application deadline: 6/1; financial award applicants required to submit FAFSA. *Faculty research:* Evidence-based dentistry in clinical practice; xerostomia and malnutrition in assisted living settings; medical screenings in the dental office: patient attitudes; rapid oral HIV screening in the dental setting; dental public health: early childhood caries, self-efficacy and oral health. *Total annual research expenditures:* $20,692. *Unit head:* Dr. Robert Trombly, Dean, 480-248-8105, Fax: 623-223-7063, E-mail: rtrombly@atsu.edu. *Application contact:* Donna Sparks, Director, Admissions Processing, 660-626-2117, Fax: 660-626-2969, E-mail: admissions@atsu.edu.
Website: http://www.atsu.edu/asdoh

A.T. Still University, Missouri School of Dentistry & Oral Health, Kirksville, MO 63501. Offers dental medicine (DMD). *Faculty:* 17 full-time (4 women), 42 part-time/adjunct (12 women). *Students:* 167 full-time (88 women); includes 43 minority (1 American Indian or Alaska Native, non-Hispanic/Latino; 29 Asian, non-Hispanic/Latino; 11 Hispanic/Latino; 2 Two or more races, non-Hispanic/Latino). Average age 27. 1,430 applicants, 8% accepted, 42 enrolled. In 2017, 42 doctorates awarded. *Degree requirements:* For doctorate, National Board exams 1 and 2. *Entrance requirements:* For doctorate, DAT, minimum GPA of 2.5 overall and in science. *Application deadline:* For fall admission, 12/1 for domestic students; for summer admission, 12/1 for domestic students. Applications are processed on a rolling basis. Application fee: $70. Electronic applications accepted. Application fee is waived when completed online. *Financial support:* In 2017–18, 33 students received support. Federal Work-Study and scholarships/grants available. Financial award application deadline: 6/1; financial award applicants required to submit FAFSA. *Faculty research:* Oral perception, dental education assessments, dental ethics, practice-based research, adverse events of dentistry, maxillary arterial variation in the dental anesthesia. *Unit head:* Dr. Dwight McLeod, Dean, 660-626-2969, Fax: 660-626-2969, E-mail: dmcleod@atsu.edu. *Application contact:* Donna Sparks, Director, Admissions Processing, 660-626-2237, Fax: 660-626-2969, E-mail: admissions@atsu.edu.
Website: http://www.atsu.edu/mosdoh/

Augusta University, The Dental College of Georgia, Augusta, GA 30912. Offers DMD, DMD/MS, DMD/PhD. *Accreditation:* ADA. *Degree requirements:* For doctorate, comprehensive exam. *Entrance requirements:* For doctorate, DAT, previous course work in biology, English, organic chemistry, and general chemistry; 1 semester of course work in physics. Additional exam requirements/recommendations for international students: Required—TOEFL (minimum score 100 iBT). Electronic applications accepted. *Expenses:* Contact institution.

Boston University, Henry M. Goldman School of Dental Medicine, Boston, MA 02118. Offers MS, MSD, D Sc, D Sc D, DMD, CAGS. *Accreditation:* ADA (one or more programs are accredited). *Faculty:* 137 full-time (58 women), 91 part-time/adjunct (36 women). *Students:* 770 full-time (371 women); includes 273 minority (12 Black or African American, non-Hispanic/Latino; 3 American Indian or Alaska Native, non-Hispanic/Latino; 178 Asian, non-Hispanic/Latino; 65 Hispanic/Latino; 15 Two or more races, non-Hispanic/Latino), 231 international. Average age 28. 6,401 applicants, 8% accepted, 259 enrolled. In 2017, 18 master's, 209 doctorates, 62 other advanced degrees awarded. Terminal master's awarded for partial completion of doctoral program. *Degree requirements:* For master's, thesis; for doctorate, thesis/dissertation (for some programs), National Board Dental Exam (for DMD). *Entrance requirements:* For master's, National Board Dental Exam Part 1; for doctorate, DAT (for DMD), minimum recommended GPA of 3.2 (for DMD); for CAGS, National Board Dental Exam Part 1, dental degree (DMD, DDS or international BDS or equivalent). Additional exam requirements/recommendations for international students: Required—TOEFL (minimum score 550 paper-based; 90 iBT). *Application deadline:* For fall admission, 12/15 for domestic and international students. Applications are processed on a rolling basis. Application fee: $75. Electronic applications accepted. *Expenses:* Contact institution. *Financial support:* In 2017–18, 91 students received support. Institutionally sponsored loans, scholarships/grants, and stipends (for oral surgery residents) available. Financial award application deadline: 4/15; financial award applicants required to submit FAFSA. *Faculty research:* Salivary biochemistry, epithelial cell biology, oral cancer treatment, mechanisms of pancreatitis, gene regulation. *Total annual research expenditures:* $9.3 million. *Unit head:* Dr. Jeffrey W. Hutter, Dean, 617-638-4780, E-mail: jhutter@bu.edu. *Application contact:* Admissions Representative, 617-638-4787, Fax: 617-638-4798, E-mail: applydmd@bu.edu.
Website: http://www.bu.edu/dental

Case Western Reserve University, School of Dental Medicine, Professional Program in Dentistry, Cleveland, OH 44106. Offers DMD. *Accreditation:* ADA. *Degree requirements:* For doctorate, thesis/dissertation. *Entrance requirements:* For doctorate, DAT. Additional exam requirements/recommendations for international students: Required—TOEFL (minimum score 550 paper-based). *Expenses:* Contact institution. *Faculty research:* Periodontal disease; overall health; natural antibodies; obesity and periodontal disease; 3D cone beam computerized tomography.

Columbia University, College of Dental Medicine, Professional Program in Dental and Oral Surgery, New York, NY 10032. Offers DDS, DDS/MBA, DDS/MPH. *Accreditation:* ADA. *Entrance requirements:* For doctorate, DAT, previous course work in biology, organic chemistry, inorganic chemistry, physics, and English. *Expenses: Tuition:* Full-time $44,864; part-time $1704 per credit. *Required fees:* $2370 per semester. One-time fee: $105.

Creighton University, School of Dentistry, Omaha, NE 68178-0001. Offers DDS. *Accreditation:* ADA. *Entrance requirements:* For doctorate, DAT. *Expenses:* Contact institution. *Faculty research:* Dental implants, bone calcification, dental materials, laser usage in dentistry.

East Carolina University, School of Dental Medicine, Greenville, NC 27834. Offers DMD. *Accreditation:* ADA. *Students:* 213 full-time (115 women); includes 81 minority (41 Black or African American, non-Hispanic/Latino; 4 American Indian or Alaska Native, non-Hispanic/Latino; 16 Asian, non-Hispanic/Latino; 14 Hispanic/Latino; 6 Two or more races, non-Hispanic/Latino). Average age 26. 94 applicants, 81% accepted, 52 enrolled. In 2017, 46 doctorates awarded. *Entrance requirements:* For doctorate, DAT. *Application deadline:* For fall admission, 6/30 for domestic students. Applications are processed on a rolling basis. Application fee: $80. Electronic applications accepted. *Expenses:* $36,405 per year. *Unit head:* Dr. Greg Chadwick, Dean, 252-737-7703.
Website: http://www.ecu.edu/dental/

Harvard University, School of Dental Medicine, Advanced Graduate Programs in Dentistry, Cambridge, MA 02138. Offers advanced general dentistry (Certificate); dental public health (Certificate); endodontics (Certificate); general practice residency (Certificate); oral biology (M Med Sc, D Med Sc); oral implantology (Certificate); oral medicine (Certificate); oral pathology (Certificate); oral surgery (Certificate); orthodontics (Certificate); pediatric dentistry (Certificate); periodontics (Certificate); prosthodontics (Certificate). *Faculty:* 90 full-time. *Students:* 105 full-time (59 women); includes 44 minority (8 Black or African American, non-Hispanic/Latino; 28 Asian, non-Hispanic/Latino; 2 Hispanic/Latino; 6 Two or more races, non-Hispanic/Latino), 26 international. Average age 27. In 2017, 17 master's, 9 doctorates awarded. *Degree requirements:* For master's, comprehensive exam, thesis optional; for doctorate, comprehensive exam, thesis/dissertation. *Entrance requirements:* Additional exam requirements/recommendations for international students: Required—TOEFL (minimum iBT score of 95; subcategory score minimums of Reading 21, Listening 17, Speaking 24, and Writing 25). *Application deadline:* Applications are processed on a rolling basis. Application fee: $80. *Financial support:* In 2017–18, 15 students received support. Scholarships/grants available. Financial award application deadline: 5/15; financial award applicants required to submit FAFSA. *Unit head:* Dr. Sang Lee, Director, 617-432-3064, E-mail: sang_lee@hsdm.harvard.edu. *Application contact:* Sarah M. Troy-Petrakos, Director of Admissions, 617-432-1443, Fax: 617-432-3881, E-mail: sarah_petrakos@hsdm.harvard.edu.

Harvard University, School of Dental Medicine, Professional Program in Dental Medicine, Cambridge, MA 02138. Offers DMD. *Accreditation:* ADA. *Students:* 135 full-time (77 women); includes 71 minority (4 Black or African American, non-Hispanic/Latino; 1 American Indian or Alaska Native, non-Hispanic/Latino; 49 Asian, non-Hispanic/Latino; 4 Hispanic/Latino; 1 Native Hawaiian or other Pacific Islander, non-Hispanic/Latino; 12 Two or more races, non-Hispanic/Latino), 14 international. Average age 24. 1,013 applicants, 35 enrolled. In 2017, 35 doctorates awarded. *Degree requirements:* For doctorate, comprehensive exam, thesis/dissertation. *Entrance requirements:* For doctorate, DAT, 1 semester of biochemistry; 2 semesters each of biology, inorganic/general chemistry, organic chemistry, physics, English, and calculus or one semester each of calculus and statistics, preferably biostatistics. *Application deadline:* For winter admission, 12/15 for domestic and international students. Applications are processed on a rolling basis. Application fee: $80. Electronic applications accepted. *Financial support:* In 2017–18, 87 students received support. Federal Work-Study, institutionally sponsored loans, and scholarships/grants available. Financial award application deadline: 2/15; financial award applicants required to submit CSS PROFILE or FAFSA. *Unit head:* Dr. Sang Park, Associate Dean for Dental Education, 617-432-1447, Fax: 617-432-3881, E-mail: sang_park@hsdm.harvard.edu. *Application contact:* Sarah M. Troy-Petrakos, Director of Admissions, 617-432-1443, Fax: 617-432-3881, E-mail: sarah_petrakos@hsdm.harvard.edu.
Website: http://www.hsdm.harvard.edu/

Howard University, College of Dentistry, Washington, DC 20059-0002. Offers advanced education in general dentistry (Certificate); dentistry (DDS); general dentistry practice (Certificate); oral and maxillofacial surgery (Certificate); orthodontics (Certificate); pediatric dentistry (Certificate). *Accreditation:* ADA (one or more programs are accredited). *Degree requirements:* For doctorate, comprehensive exam, didactic and clinical exams. *Entrance requirements:* For doctorate, DAT, 8 semester hours of course work each in biology, inorganic chemistry, and organic chemistry. *Expenses:* Contact institution. *Faculty research:* Epidemiological, biomaterial, molecular genetic, behavioral modification, and clinical trial studies.

Idaho State University, Office of Graduate Studies, Office of Medical and Oral Health, Department of Dental Sciences, Pocatello, ID 83209-8088. Offers advanced general dentistry (Post-Doctoral Certificate). First year of Idaho Dental Education Program available in conjunction with Creighton University's School of Dentistry. *Degree requirements:* For Post-Doctoral Certificate, comprehensive exam, thesis optional, 1-year residency. *Entrance requirements:* For degree, DAT, 3 dental application forms. Additional exam requirements/recommendations for international students: Required—TOEFL (minimum score 600 paper-based). Electronic applications accepted. *Expenses:* Contact institution.

Indiana University–Purdue University Indianapolis, School of Dentistry, Indianapolis, IN 46202. Offers cariology and operative dentistry (MSD); dental materials (MS, MSD); dental sciences (PhD); dentistry (DDS, Certificate); endodontics (MSD); oral and maxillofacial surgery (MSD); orthodontics (MSD); pediatric dentistry (MSD); periodontics (MSD); prosthodontics (MSD). *Accreditation:* ADA (one or more programs are accredited). *Degree requirements:* For master's, thesis or manuscript, qualifying exam; for doctorate, thesis/dissertation, minimum GPA of 3.0 and qualifying examination (for PhD); minimum GPA of 2.0 and Part I and II of National Board of Dental Examinations (for DDS); for Certificate, thesis, minimum GPA of 3.0. *Entrance requirements:* For master's, GRE (orthodontics); National Board Dental Exam Part I (periodontics), Parts I and II (endodontics); ADAT (pediatric dentistry); for doctorate, GRE (for PhD); DAT (for DDS). Additional exam requirements/recommendations for international students: Required—TOEFL (minimum iBT score 90; 79 for MDS) or IELTS (6.5). Electronic applications accepted. *Expenses:* Contact institution. *Faculty research:* Caries research: early caries detection and management, secondary caries, remineralization, oral biofilms, fluoride, dental erosion; oral biology: molecular biology and immunobiology of streptococcus mutans, oral biofilms, infection control, actinobaccillus actinomycetemcomitans; orthodontics and oral facial genetics: orthodontics biomechanics; oral pathology and immunology: chronic inflammation and autoimmunity, innate immunity in oral pathology; periodontal disease and implants.

Jacksonville University, Brooks Rehabilitation College of Healthcare Sciences, School of Orthodontics, Jacksonville, FL 32211. Offers dentistry (MS); orthodontics (Certificate). *Faculty:* 15 full-time (5 women), 2 part-time/adjunct (both women). *Students:* 37 full-time (12 women), 6 part-time (2 women); includes 12 minority (6 Asian, non-Hispanic/Latino; 5 Hispanic/Latino; 1 Two or more races, non-Hispanic/Latino), 10 international. Average age 30. 201 applicants, 10% accepted, 20 enrolled. In 2017, 15 other advanced degrees awarded. *Degree requirements:* For master's and Certificate, thesis. *Entrance*

requirements: For master's, DDS/DMD or equivalent; for Certificate, American Board of Orthodontics written exam; U.S. National Dental Boards (part 1 and 2), curriculum vitae, official transcripts, 3 professional evaluations, 3 professional recommendations (dean of dental school or faculty, or other professional colleagues), statement of intent, clinical competencies through delivering evidence-based patient care, DDS/DMD or equivalent. Additional exam requirements/recommendations for international students: Required—TOEFL (minimum score 610 paper-based). *Application deadline:* For fall admission, 9/14 priority date for domestic students, 9/14 for international students. Applications are processed on a rolling basis. Application fee: $175. Electronic applications accepted. *Expenses:* $95,000 per year ($140,000 international). *Financial support:* In 2017–18, 5 fellowships (averaging $35,000 per year) were awarded; scholarships/grants and health care benefits also available. Financial award application deadline: 3/15; financial award applicants required to submit FAFSA. *Faculty research:* Orthodontics and dentofacial orthopedics with emphasis on pre-adjusted appliances and related techniques. *Unit head:* Dr. Eman Othman, Interim Department Chair, Clinical Assistant Professor, and Director of Fellowship in Clinical Research, 904-256-7803, E-mail: eothman1@ju.edu. *Application contact:* Sharon Frazier, Executive Operations Coordinator, 904-256-7847, Fax: 904-256-7847, E-mail: juorthoadmissions@ju.edu.
Website: https://www.ju.edu/orthodontics/index.php

Loma Linda University, School of Dentistry, Loma Linda, CA 92350. Offers MS, DDS, Certificate, DDS/MS, DDS/PhD, MS/Certificate. *Accreditation:* ADA. *Entrance requirements:* For master's, GRE, minimum GPA of 3.0; for doctorate, DAT. Additional exam requirements/recommendations for international students: Required—TOEFL (minimum score 550 paper-based). *Expenses:* Contact institution.

Louisiana State University Health Sciences Center, School of Dentistry, New Orleans, LA 70112-2223. Offers DDS. *Accreditation:* ADA. *Entrance requirements:* For doctorate, DAT, interview. *Expenses:* Contact institution. *Faculty research:* HIV/AIDS, implants, metallurgy, lipids, DNA.

Marquette University, School of Dentistry, Professional Program in Dentistry, Milwaukee, WI 53201-1881. Offers DDS. *Accreditation:* ADA. *Degree requirements:* For doctorate, National Board Dental Exam Part 1 and 2, regional licensure exam. *Entrance requirements:* For doctorate, DAT, 1 year of course work each in biology, inorganic chemistry, organic chemistry, physics, and English. Additional exam requirements/recommendations for international students: Required—TOEFL. *Expenses:* Contact institution. *Faculty research:* Biomaterials, wound healing, diabetes, biocompatibility, cancer, aging, lasers.

McGill University, Faculty of Graduate and Postdoctoral Studies, Faculty of Dentistry, Montréal, QC H3A 2T5, Canada. Offers forensic dentistry (Certificate); oral and maxillofacial surgery (M Sc, PhD).

McGill University, Professional Program in Dentistry, Montréal, QC H3A 2T5, Canada. Offers DMD. *Accreditation:* ADA. Electronic applications accepted.

Medical University of South Carolina, College of Dental Medicine, Charleston, SC 29425. Offers DMD, DMD/PhD. *Accreditation:* ADA. *Degree requirements:* For doctorate, National Board of Dental Examinations Part I and II. *Entrance requirements:* For doctorate, DAT, interview, 52 hours of specific pre-dental course work. Additional exam requirements/recommendations for international students: Required—TOEFL (minimum score 600 paper-based). Electronic applications accepted. *Expenses:* Contact institution. *Faculty research:* South Carolina oral health, genetics, health disparities, chlamydia, oral cancer.

Meharry Medical College, School of Dentistry, Nashville, TN 37208-9989. Offers DDS, PhD. *Accreditation:* ADA. *Entrance requirements:* For doctorate, DAT.

Midwestern University, Downers Grove Campus, College of Dental Medicine-Illinois, Downers Grove, IL 60515-1235. Offers DMD. *Accreditation:* ADA. *Entrance requirements:* For doctorate, DAT, bachelor's degree, minimum overall GPA of 2.75, three letters of recommendation.
Website: http://www.midwestern.edu/Programs_and_Admission/IL_Dental_Medicine.html

Midwestern University, Glendale Campus, College of Dental Medicine, Glendale, AZ 85308. Offers DMD. *Accreditation:* ADA.

New York University, College of Dentistry, Advanced Standing DDS Program, New York, NY 10010. Offers DDS. *Accreditation:* ADA. *Faculty:* 275 full-time (118 women), 573 part-time/adjunct (204 women). *Students:* 20 full-time (14 women); includes 16 minority (10 Asian, non-Hispanic/Latino; 6 Hispanic/Latino). Average age 31. 364 applicants, 3% accepted, 10 enrolled. In 2017, 15 doctorates awarded. *Degree requirements:* For doctorate, one foreign language. *Entrance requirements:* For doctorate, National Board Dental Exam Parts I and II, official ECE course-by-course evaluation, notarized copies of dental diploma, three letters of evaluation, letter of evaluation from dean of dental school from which applicant graduated, two other letters of evaluation from faculty members. Additional exam requirements/recommendations for international students: Required—TOEFL (minimum score 603 paper-based; 100 iBT). *Application deadline:* For fall admission, 12/15 for domestic and international students. Application fee: $100. Electronic applications accepted. *Expenses:* Contact institution. *Financial support:* Application deadline: 4/1; applicants required to submit FAFSA. *Faculty research:* Clinical research, HIV/AIDS, skeletal and craniofacial biology, oral cancer research, family translational research. *Unit head:* Dr. Charles Bertolami, Dean, 212-998-9898, Fax: 212-995-4240, E-mail: charles.bertolami@nyu.edu. *Application contact:* Dr. Eugenia E. Mejia, Assistant Dean, Admissions and Enrollment Management, 212-998-9918, Fax: 212-995-4240, E-mail: dental.admissions@nyu.edu.
Website: https://dental.nyu.edu/

Nova Southeastern University, College of Dental Medicine, Fort Lauderdale, FL 33328. Offers dental medicine (DMD); dentistry (MS). *Accreditation:* ADA. *Faculty:* 106 full-time (38 women), 163 part-time/adjunct (31 women). *Students:* 604 full-time (293 women), 7 part-time (3 women); includes 278 minority (4 Black or African American, non-Hispanic/Latino; 105 Asian, non-Hispanic/Latino; 155 Hispanic/Latino; 14 Two or more races, non-Hispanic/Latino), 77 international. Average age 28. 2,274 applicants, 11% accepted, 124 enrolled. In 2017, 16 master's, 129 doctorates awarded. *Degree requirements:* For master's, thesis. *Entrance requirements:* For doctorate, DAT, minimum GPA of 3.25. Additional exam requirements/recommendations for international students: Required—TOEFL (minimum score 550 paper-based), IELTS (minimum score 6), PTE (minimum score 54). *Application deadline:* For fall admission, 12/31 for domestic students, 1/1 for international students. Applications are processed on a rolling basis. Application fee: $50. Electronic applications accepted. *Expenses:* Contact institution. *Financial support:* Application deadline: 4/15; applicants required to submit FAFSA. *Faculty research:* Tissue engineering, dental materials, clinical trials for oral health care products, school-based preventive dental programs. *Unit head:* Dr. Linda C. Niessen, Dean, 954-262-7334, Fax: 954-262-3293, E-mail: lniessen@nova.edu. *Application contact:* Su-Ann Zarrett, Associate Director of Admissions, 954-262-1108, Fax: 954-262-2282, E-mail: zarrett@nsu.nova.edu.
Website: http://dental.nova.edu/

The Ohio State University, College of Dentistry, Columbus, OH 43210. Offers dental anesthesiology (MS); dental hygiene (MDH); dentistry (DDS); endodontics (MS); oral and maxillofacial pathology (MS); oral and maxillofacial surgery (MS); oral biology (PhD); orthodontics (MS); pediatric dentistry (MS); periodontology (MS); prosthodontics (MS); DDS/PhD. *Accreditation:* ADA (one or more programs are accredited). *Faculty:* 86. *Students:* 506 full-time (213 women), 11 part-time (8 women). Average age 26. In 2017, 34 master's, 109 doctorates awarded. Terminal master's awarded for partial completion of doctoral program. *Degree requirements:* For master's, thesis; for doctorate, thesis/dissertation (for some programs). *Entrance requirements:* For master's, GRE General Test (for all applicants with cumulative GPA below 3.0); for doctorate, DAT (for DDS); GRE General Test, GRE Subject Test in biology recommended (for PhD). Additional exam requirements/recommendations for international students: Required—TOEFL (minimum score 550 paper-based; 79 iBT), IELTS (minimum score 7), Michigan English Language Assessment Battery (minimum score 82). *Application deadline:* For fall admission, 10/1 for domestic and international students; for summer admission, 4/11 for domestic students, 3/10 for international students. Applications are processed on a rolling basis. Electronic applications accepted. *Expenses:* Contact institution. *Financial support:* Fellowships with tuition reimbursements, research assistantships with tuition reimbursements, teaching assistantships with tuition reimbursements, Federal Work-Study, institutionally sponsored loans, and health care benefits available. Financial award application deadline: 2/15. *Faculty research:* Neurobiology, inflammation and immunity, materials science, bone biology. *Unit head:* Dr. Patrick M. Lloyd, Dean, 614-292-9755, E-mail: lloyd.256@osu.edu. *Application contact:* Graduate and Professional Admissions, 614-292-9444, Fax: 614-292-3895, E-mail: gpadmissions@osu.edu.
Website: http://www.dentistry.osu.edu/

Oregon Health & Science University, School of Dentistry, Professional Program in Dentistry, Portland, OR 97239-3098. Offers dentistry (DMD); oral and maxillofacial surgery (Certificate); MD/DMD. *Accreditation:* ADA. *Entrance requirements:* For doctorate, DAT. Electronic applications accepted. *Faculty research:* Dentin permeability, tooth sensations, fluoride metabolism, immunology of periodontal disease, craniofacial growth.

Roseman University of Health Sciences, College of Dental Medicine - Henderson Campus, Henderson, NV 89014. Offers business administration (MBA); dental medicine (Post-Doctoral Certificate). *Faculty:* 6 full-time (2 women), 6 part-time/adjunct (1 woman). *Students:* 30 full-time (12 women); includes 19 minority (18 Asian, non-Hispanic/Latino; 1 Hispanic/Latino). Average age 30. 92 applicants, 16% accepted, 10 enrolled. In 2017, 12 other advanced degrees awarded. *Degree requirements:* For master's, comprehensive exam, thesis or alternative. *Entrance requirements:* For master's, National Board Dental Examination 1 and 2, graduation from U.S. or Canadian dental school, Nevada dental license. *Application deadline:* For fall admission, 1/31 for domestic and international students. Application fee: $50. *Expenses:* Contact institution. *Financial support:* In 2017–18, 10 students received support. Scholarships/grants available. Financial award application deadline: 6/15; financial award applicants required to submit FAFSA. *Faculty research:* Oral cancer; CBCT (Cone Beam Computed Tomography) 3D scan data related projects; in-vitro biomaterial testing such as orthodontic bond strength studies using Instron; nanotechnology and orthodontic practice management research. *Unit head:* Dr. Prashanti Bollu, Program Director, 702-968-5690, Fax: 702-968-5277, E-mail: pbollu@roseman.edu. *Application contact:* Carol Shannon, Administrative Assistant to the Program Director, 702-968-1682, E-mail: cshannon@roseman.edu.
Website: http://www.roseman.edu

Roseman University of Health Sciences, College of Dental Medicine - South Jordan, Utah Campus, South Jordan, UT 84095. Offers DMD. *Accreditation:* ADA. *Faculty:* 43 full-time (8 women), 41 part-time/adjunct (5 women). *Students:* 330 full-time (149 women); includes 109 minority (2 Black or African American, non-Hispanic/Latino; 1 American Indian or Alaska Native, non-Hispanic/Latino; 81 Asian, non-Hispanic/Latino; 17 Hispanic/Latino; 4 Native Hawaiian or other Pacific Islander, non-Hispanic/Latino; 4 Two or more races, non-Hispanic/Latino), 3 international. Average age 28. 2,270 applicants, 8% accepted, 84 enrolled. In 2017, 77 doctorates awarded. *Degree requirements:* For doctorate, comprehensive exam, thesis/dissertation or alternative, National Board Dental Examinations (NBDE). *Entrance requirements:* For doctorate, DAT. Additional exam requirements/recommendations for international students: Recommended—TOEFL. *Application deadline:* For fall admission, 12/1 for domestic and international students. Applications are processed on a rolling basis. Application fee: $75. Electronic applications accepted. *Expenses:* Contact institution. *Financial support:* In 2017–18, 32 students received support. Federal Work-Study and tuition waivers (partial) available. Financial award application deadline: 6/15; financial award applicants required to submit FAFSA. *Faculty research:* Targeting inflammatory signaling pathways in the treatment of periodontal disease and oral cancers; impact of e-cigarette vapors on oral and systemic health; early authentic patient-centered learning in dental education; team-based mastery learning in dental education; determining clinical efficiency to improve patient-centered care. *Unit head:* Dr. Frank W. Licari, Dean, College of Dental Medicine, 801-878-1400, E-mail: flicari@roseman.edu. *Application contact:* Alicia Spittle, Admissions Coordinator, 801-878-1429, E-mail: aspittle@roseman.edu.

Rutgers University–Newark, Rutgers School of Dental Medicine, Newark, NJ 07101-1709. Offers dental science (MS); dentistry (DMD); endodontics (Certificate); oral medicine (Certificate); orthodontics (Certificate); pediatric dentistry (Certificate); periodontics (Certificate); prosthodontics (Certificate); DMD/MPH; DMD/PhD; MD/Certificate; MS/Certificate. DMD/MPH offered jointly with New Jersey Institute of Technology, Rutgers, The State University of New Jersey, Camden. *Accreditation:* ADA (one or more programs are accredited). *Entrance requirements:* For doctorate, DAT. Electronic applications accepted. *Expenses:* Contact institution.

Saint Louis University, Graduate Programs, Center for Advanced Dental Education, St. Louis, MO 63103. Offers endodontics (MSD); orthodontics (MSD); periodontics (MSD). *Degree requirements:* For master's, comprehensive exam, thesis, teaching practicum. *Entrance requirements:* For master's, GRE General Test, NBDE (National Board Dental Exam), DDS or DMD, interview, letters of recommendation. Additional exam requirements/recommendations for international students: Required—TOEFL (minimum score 525 paper-based). Electronic applications accepted. *Faculty research:* Craniofacial growth.

Southern Illinois University Edwardsville, School of Dental Medicine, Alton, IL 62002. Offers DMD. *Accreditation:* ADA. *Entrance requirements:* For doctorate, DAT. Electronic applications accepted. *Expenses:* Contact institution.

Stony Brook University, State University of New York, Stony Brook Medicine, School of Dental Medicine, Professional Program in Dental Medicine, Stony Brook, NY 11794. Offers dental medicine (DDS); endodontics (Certificate); orthodontics (Certificate); periodontics (Certificate). *Accreditation:* ADA (one or more programs are accredited). *Faculty:* 32 full-time (14 women), 82 part-time/adjunct (24 women). *Students:* 197 full-time (102 women); includes 63 minority (2 Black or African American, non-Hispanic/Latino; 50 Asian, non-Hispanic/Latino; 8 Hispanic/Latino; 3 Two or more races, non-Hispanic/Latino), 2 international. Average age 26. 1,435 applicants, 7% accepted, 52 enrolled. In 2017, 41 doctorates, 9 Certificates awarded. *Entrance requirements:* For doctorate, DAT (minimum score of 17 preferred in all subsections), minimum GPA of 3.0 (preferred). Additional exam requirements/recommendations for international students: Required—TOEFL. *Application deadline:* For fall admission, 12/1 for domestic students. Application fee: $100. *Expenses:*

Contact institution. *Financial support:* Research assistantships, teaching assistantships, and Federal Work-Study available. Support available to part-time students. *Faculty research:* Dentistry, oral diseases, oral or maxillofacial surgery. *Unit head:* Dr. Mary R. Truhlar, Dean, 631-632-6985, Fax: 631-632-6621, E-mail: mary.truhlar@stonybrook.edu. *Application contact:* Patricia Berry, Acting Director of Admissions, 631-632-8871, Fax: 631-632-7130, E-mail: patricia.berry@stonybrook.edu.
Website: http://dentistry.stonybrookmedicine.edu/

Temple University, Maurice H. Kornberg School of Dentistry, Professional Program in Dentistry, Philadelphia, PA 19122-6096. Offers DMD, DMD/MBA. *Accreditation:* ADA. *Entrance requirements:* For doctorate, DAT, 6 credits of course work in each biology, chemistry, organic chemistry, physics, and English. *Expenses:* Contact institution.

Texas A&M University, College of Dentistry, Dallas, TX 75266-0677. Offers advanced education in general dentistry (Certificate); biomedical sciences (MS); dental hygiene (MS); dental public health (Certificate); endodontics (Certificate); maxillofacial surgery (Certificate); oral and maxillofacial pathology (Certificate); oral and maxillofacial radiology (Certificate); oral and maxillofacial surgery (Certificate); oral biology (MS, PhD); orthodontics (Certificate); pediatric dentistry (Certificate); periodontics (Certificate); prosthodontics (Certificate). *Accreditation:* ADA; SACS/CC. *Faculty:* 44. *Enrollment:* 499 full-time matriculated graduate/professional students (251 women), 37 part-time matriculated graduate/professional students (12 women). *Students:* 499 full-time (251 women), 37 part-time (12 women); includes 275 minority (54 Black or African American, non-Hispanic/Latino; 2 American Indian or Alaska Native, non-Hispanic/Latino; 100 Asian, non-Hispanic/Latino; 109 Hispanic/Latino; 10 Two or more races, non-Hispanic/Latino), 30 international. Average age 27. In 2017, 18 master's, 2 doctorates, 101 other advanced degrees awarded. *Entrance requirements:* Additional exam requirements/recommendations for international students: Required—TOEFL (minimum score 550 paper-based; 79 iBT). Application fee: $35. Electronic applications accepted. *Expenses:* Contact institution. *Financial support:* In 2017–18, 235 students received support, including 32 research assistantships with tuition reimbursements available (averaging $8,712 per year), 43 teaching assistantships with tuition reimbursements available (averaging $14,231 per year); career-related internships or fieldwork, institutionally sponsored loans, scholarships/grants, traineeships, health care benefits, tuition waivers (full and partial), and unspecified assistantships also available. Support available to part-time students. Financial award applicants required to submit FAFSA. *Unit head:* Dr. Lawrence E. Wolinsky, Dean, 214-828-8300, E-mail: wolinsky@tamhsc.edu. *Application contact:* Ernestine S. Lacy, Associate Dean for Student Affairs and Student Diversity, 214-828-8374, Fax: 214-874-4572, E-mail: eslacy@tamhsc.edu.
Website: http://www.dentistry.tamhsc.edu/

Tufts University, School of Dental Medicine, International Student Program in Dental Medicine, Medford, MA 02155. Offers DMD. *Accreditation:* ADA. *Entrance requirements:* For doctorate, National Dental Hygiene Board Exam Part I, BDS, DDS, or equivalent. Additional exam requirements/recommendations for international students: Required—TOEFL. *Expenses: Tuition:* Full-time $49,892. *Required fees:* $874. Full-time tuition and fees vary according to degree level, program and student level. Part-time tuition and fees vary according to course load.

Tufts University, School of Dental Medicine, Professional Program in Dental Medicine, Medford, MA 02155. Offers DMD, DMD/PhD. *Accreditation:* ADA. *Entrance requirements:* For doctorate, DAT. *Expenses: Tuition:* Full-time $49,892. *Required fees:* $874. Full-time tuition and fees vary according to degree level, program and student level. Part-time tuition and fees vary according to course load.

Universidad Central del Este, School of Dentistry, San Pedro de Macoris, Dominican Republic. Offers DMD.

Universidad Iberoamericana, Graduate School, Santo Domingo D.N., Dominican Republic. Offers business administration (MBA, PMBA); constitutional law (LL M); dentistry (DMD); educational management (MA); integrated marketing communication (MA); psychopedagogical intervention (M Ed); real estate law (LL M); strategic management of human talent (MM).

Universidad Nacional Pedro Henriquez Urena, School of Dentistry, Santo Domingo, Dominican Republic. Offers DDS.

Université Laval, Faculty of Dentistry, Professional Programs in Dentistry, Québec, QC G1K 7P4, Canada. Offers DMD. *Accreditation:* ADA. *Entrance requirements:* For doctorate, visual perception exam, manual dexterity exam, interview, knowledge of French. Electronic applications accepted.

University at Buffalo, the State University of New York, Graduate School, School of Dental Medicine, Professional Program in Dental Medicine, Buffalo, NY 14260. Offers DDS. *Accreditation:* ADA. *Degree requirements:* For doctorate, National Dental Board Exams. *Entrance requirements:* For doctorate, DAT, GRE. Additional exam requirements/recommendations for international students: Required—TOEFL (minimum score 550 paper-based; 79 iBT).

The University of Alabama at Birmingham, School of Dentistry, Professional Program in Dentistry, Birmingham, AL 35294. Offers DMD. *Accreditation:* ADA. *Degree requirements:* For doctorate, comprehensive exam. *Entrance requirements:* For doctorate, DAT, letters of recommendation, interview. Additional exam requirements/recommendations for international students: Required—TOEFL (minimum score 94 iBT), National Boards Part I. Electronic applications accepted. *Expenses:* Contact institution. *Faculty research:* Etiology and pathogenesis of dental diseases, dental biomaterials, therapy of dental diseases, practice-based dental, dental implantology.

University of Alberta, Faculty of Medicine and Dentistry, Department of Dentistry, Professional Program in Dentistry, Edmonton, AB T6G 2E1, Canada. Offers DDS. *Accreditation:* ADA. *Entrance requirements:* For doctorate, DAT (Canadian version), interview. Additional exam requirements/recommendations for international students: Required—TOEFL. Electronic applications accepted. *Faculty research:* Oral biology, biochemistry of connective tissues, preventive dentistry, applied clinical orthodontics, biomaterials.

The University of British Columbia, Faculty of Dentistry, Professional Program in Dentistry, Vancouver, BC V6T 1Z1, Canada. Offers DMD. *Accreditation:* ADA. *Entrance requirements:* For doctorate, DAT, ACFD Eligibility Exam, interview, psychomotor assessment. Additional exam requirements/recommendations for international students: Required—IELTS. Electronic applications accepted. *Expenses:* Contact institution.

University of California, Los Angeles, School of Dentistry, Professional Program in Dentistry, Los Angeles, CA 90095. Offers DDS, Certificate, DDS/MS, DDS/PhD, MS/Certificate, PhD/Certificate. *Accreditation:* ADA (one or more programs are accredited). *Entrance requirements:* For doctorate, DAT, interview. Additional exam requirements/recommendations for international students: Required—TOEFL. Electronic applications accepted. *Expenses:* Contact institution.

University of California, San Francisco, School of Dentistry, San Francisco, CA 94143-0150. Offers DDS. *Accreditation:* ADA. *Entrance requirements:* For doctorate, DAT. *Expenses:* Contact institution.

University of Colorado Denver, School of Dental Medicine, Aurora, CO 80045. Offers dental surgery (DDS); orthodontics (Certificate); periodontics (Certificate). *Accreditation:* ADA. In 2017, 118 doctorates awarded. *Entrance requirements:* For doctorate, DAT, prerequisite courses in microbiology, general biochemistry and English composition (1 semester each); general chemistry/lab, organic chemistry/lab, general biology/lab and general physics/lab (2 semesters each); interview; letters of recommendation; essay. Additional exam requirements/recommendations for international students: Required—TOEFL (minimum score 580 paper-based; 80 iBT); Recommended—IELTS (minimum score 6.8). Application fee: $0. *Faculty research:* Pain control, materials research, geriatric dentistry, restorative dentistry, periodontics. *Unit head:* Dr. Denise K. Kassebaum, Dean, 303-724-7100, Fax: 303-724-7109, E-mail: denise.kassebaum@ucdenver.edu. *Application contact:* Graduate Student Admissions, 303-724-7122, Fax: 303-724-7109, E-mail: ddsadmissioninquiries@ucdenver.edu.
Website: http://www.ucdenver.edu/academics/colleges/dentalmedicine/Pages/DentalMedicine.aspx

University of Connecticut Health Center, School of Dental Medicine, Professional Program in Dental Medicine, Farmington, CT 06030. Offers DMD, Certificate. *Accreditation:* ADA. *Entrance requirements:* For doctorate, National Board Dental Examination. Additional exam requirements/recommendations for international students: Required—TOEFL (minimum score 550 paper-based).

University of Detroit Mercy, School of Dentistry, Detroit, MI 48208. Offers MS, DDS, Certificate. *Accreditation:* ADA (one or more programs are accredited). *Degree requirements:* For master's, thesis. *Entrance requirements:* For master's, DDS or DMD; for doctorate, DAT; for Certificate, DAT, DDS or DMD. *Expenses:* Contact institution. *Faculty research:* HIV and periodontal disease, chemotherapeutic management of periodontal disease, oral analgesics, sterilization/disinfection, prosthodontic materials.

University of Florida, College of Dentistry, Professional Programs in Dentistry, Gainesville, FL 32611. Offers dentistry (DMD); foreign trained dentistry (Certificate). *Accreditation:* ADA. *Degree requirements:* For Certificate, National Dental Boards Parts I and II. *Entrance requirements:* For doctorate, DAT, interview; for Certificate, interview. Additional exam requirements/recommendations for international students: Required—TOEFL (minimum score 550 paper-based). *Faculty research:* Actinobacillus, critical thinking, DNA adenine, methylase, LJP.

University of Illinois at Chicago, College of Dentistry, Professional Program in Dentistry, Chicago, IL 60607-7128. Offers DDS, DDS/MPH, DDS/PhD. *Accreditation:* ADA. *Entrance requirements:* For doctorate, DAT. Additional exam requirements/recommendations for international students: Required—TOEFL. Electronic applications accepted. *Expenses:* Contact institution. *Faculty research:* Oral cancer, wound healing, public health, craniofacial and oral heath, cariology.

The University of Iowa, College of Dentistry and Graduate College, Graduate Programs in Dentistry, Iowa City, IA 52242-1316. Offers endodontics (MS, Certificate); operative dentistry (MS, Certificate); oral and maxillofacial surgery (MS, PhD, Certificate); oral pathology, radiology and medicine (MS, PhD, Certificate); oral science (MS, PhD); orthodontics (MS, Certificate); pediatric dentistry (Certificate); periodontics (MS, Certificate); preventive and community dentistry (MS), including dental public health; prosthodontics (MS, Certificate). *Accreditation:* ADA. *Degree requirements:* For master's, thesis; for doctorate, thesis/dissertation. *Entrance requirements:* For master's, GRE, DDS; for Certificate, DDS. Additional exam requirements/recommendations for international students: Required—TOEFL. *Expenses:* Contact institution.

The University of Iowa, College of Dentistry, Professional Program in Dentistry, Iowa City, IA 52242-1316. Offers DDS. *Accreditation:* ADA. *Entrance requirements:* For doctorate, DAT, minimum 90 semester hours with minimum GPA of 2.5.

University of Kentucky, College of Dentistry, Lexington, KY 40536. Offers DMD. *Accreditation:* ADA. *Faculty:* 66 full-time (20 women), 45 part-time/adjunct (13 women). *Students:* 260 full-time (135 women); includes 93 minority (25 Black or African American, non-Hispanic/Latino; 1 American Indian or Alaska Native, non-Hispanic/Latino; 35 Asian, non-Hispanic/Latino; 16 Hispanic/Latino; 16 Two or more races, non-Hispanic/Latino), 3 international. Average age 27. 1,838 applicants, 7% accepted, 65 enrolled. In 2017, 66 doctorates awarded. *Degree requirements:* For doctorate, comprehensive exam. *Entrance requirements:* For doctorate, DAT. *Application deadline:* For fall admission, 12/1 priority date for domestic students. Applications are processed on a rolling basis. Application fee: $75. Electronic applications accepted. *Expenses:* Contact institution. *Financial support:* In 2017–18, 158 students received support. Institutionally sponsored loans and scholarships/grants available. Financial award application deadline: 3/1; financial award applicants required to submit FAFSA. *Faculty research:* Effects of diabetes and methotrexate anti-inflammatory therapy; international, multicenter registry to collect data of treatment patterns in patients with bilateral condylar fracture (BCFx) of the mandible; quality and quantity of bone regeneration in maxillary sinus using Osteocel, radiographic and histomorphometrically randomized controlled clinical study. *Total annual research expenditures:* $1.3 million. *Unit head:* Dr. Stephanos Kyrkanides, Dean, 859-323-1884, Fax: 859-323-1042, E-mail: stephanos@uky.edu. *Application contact:* Rebekah Huff, Student Affairs Officer, 859-323-6071, Fax: 859-257-5550, E-mail: rebekah.huff@uky.edu.
Website: https://dentistry.uky.edu/

University of Louisville, School of Dentistry, Louisville, KY 40202. Offers dentistry (DMD); oral biology (MS). *Accreditation:* ADA (one or more programs are accredited). *Program availability:* Part-time. *Faculty:* 77 full-time (32 women), 70 part-time/adjunct (18 women). *Students:* 507 full-time (228 women), 15 part-time (11 women); includes 122 minority (20 Black or African American, non-Hispanic/Latino; 60 Asian, non-Hispanic/Latino; 26 Hispanic/Latino; 16 Two or more races, non-Hispanic/Latino), 16 international. Average age 26. 183 applicants, 93% accepted, 137 enrolled. In 2017, 7 master's, 113 doctorates awarded. *Degree requirements:* For master's, thesis; for doctorate, National Board exams. *Entrance requirements:* For master's, DAT, GRE General Test, or National Board Dental Exam, minimum GPA of 2.75; for doctorate, DAT, 32 hours of course work in science. Additional exam requirements/recommendations for international students: Required—TOEFL (minimum score 100 iBT). *Application deadline:* For fall admission, 1/1 for domestic and international students. Applications are processed on a rolling basis. Application fee: $65. Electronic applications accepted. *Expenses:* Contact institution. *Financial support:* In 2017–18, 1 research assistantship with full tuition reimbursement (averaging $20,000 per year) was awarded. Financial award application deadline: 3/15; financial award applicants required to submit FAFSA. *Faculty research:* Inflammation and periodontitis, birth defects and developmental biology, biomaterials, oral infections, digital imaging. *Total annual research expenditures:* $5.9 million. *Unit head:* Dr. T. Gerry Bradley, Dean, 502-852-5295, E-mail: t0brad03@exchange.louisville.edu. *Application contact:* Robin Benningfield, Admissions Counselor, 502-852-5081, Fax: 502-852-1210, E-mail: dmdadms@louisville.edu.
Website: http://louisville.edu/dental/

The University of Manchester, School of Dentistry, Manchester, United Kingdom. Offers basic dental sciences (cancer studies) (M Phil, PhD); basic dental sciences (molecular genetics) (M Phil, PhD); basic dental sciences (stem cell biology) (M Phil, PhD); biomaterials sciences and dental technology (M Phil, PhD); dental public health/community dentistry (M Phil, PhD); dental science (clinical) (PhD); endodontology (M Phil, PhD); fixed and removable prosthodontics (M Phil, PhD); operative dentistry (M Phil, PhD); oral and maxillofacial surgery (M Phil, PhD); oral radiology (M Phil, PhD); orthodontics (M Phil, PhD); restorative dentistry (M Phil, PhD).

University of Manitoba, Dr. Gerald Niznick College of Dentistry, Professional Program in Dentistry, Winnipeg, MB R3T 2N2, Canada. Offers DMD. *Accreditation:* ADA. *Entrance requirements:* For doctorate, DAT, interview. *Faculty research:* Oral physiology, microbiology, and biochemistry of the oral cavity in health and disease; application of clinical research.

University of Maryland, Baltimore, Professional and Advanced Education Programs in Dentistry, Baltimore, MD 21201-1627. Offers advanced general dentistry (Certificate); dentistry (DDS); endodontics (Certificate); oral-maxillofacial surgery (Certificate); orthodontics (Certificate); pediatric dentistry (Certificate); periodontics (Certificate); prosthodontics (Certificate); DDS/MBA; DDS/PhD. *Accreditation:* ADA. *Students:* 583 full-time (311 women), 2 part-time (1 woman); includes 255 minority (58 Black or African American, non-Hispanic/Latino; 126 Asian, non-Hispanic/Latino; 44 Hispanic/Latino; 27 Two or more races, non-Hispanic/Latino), 23 international. Average age 26. 799 applicants, 72% accepted, 133 enrolled. In 2017, 131 doctorates, 22 Certificates awarded. *Entrance requirements:* For doctorate, DAT, coursework in science; for Certificate, National Dental Board Exams, DDS. Additional exam requirements/recommendations for international students: Required—TOEFL (minimum score 550 paper-based; 80 iBT). *Application deadline:* Applications are processed on a rolling basis. Application fee: $85. Electronic applications accepted. *Expenses:* Contact institution. *Financial support:* Career-related internships or fieldwork, Federal Work-Study, scholarships/grants, and traineeships available. Financial award application deadline: 3/1; financial award applicants required to submit FAFSA. *Faculty research:* Pain/neuroscience, oncology/molecular and cell biology, infectious disease/microbiology, bio-material studies, health promotion and disparities. *Unit head:* Dr. Mark A. Reynolds, Dean, 410-706-7461. *Application contact:* Dr. Judith A. Porter, Assistant Dean for Admissions and Recruitment, 410-706-7472, Fax: 410-706-0945, E-mail: ddsadmissions@umaryland.edu.
Website: http://www.dental.umaryland.edu/

University of Michigan, School of Dentistry, Professional Program in Dentistry, Ann Arbor, MI 48109. Offers DDS. *Accreditation:* ADA. *Students:* 494 full-time (253 women); includes 158 minority (19 Black or African American, non-Hispanic/Latino; 2 American Indian or Alaska Native, non-Hispanic/Latino; 110 Asian, non-Hispanic/Latino; 16 Hispanic/Latino; 11 Two or more races, non-Hispanic/Latino). Average age 23. 2,179 applicants, 13% accepted, 108 enrolled. In 2017, 117 doctorates awarded. *Entrance requirements:* For doctorate, DAT, 6 credits of course work in English; 8 credits of course work each in chemistry, organic chemistry, biology, and physics; 3 credits each of biochemistry, microbiology, psychology, and sociology. *Application deadline:* For fall admission, 10/15 for domestic and international students. Applications are processed on a rolling basis. Application fee: $75. Electronic applications accepted. *Expenses:* Contact institution. *Unit head:* Dr. Renee Duff, Assistant Dean for Student Services, 734-763-3313, Fax: 734-764-1922, E-mail: ddsadmissions@umich.edu. *Application contact:* Patricia Katcher, Associate Director of Admissions, 734-763-3316, Fax: 734-764-1922, E-mail: ddsadmissions@umich.edu.
Website: http://www.dent.umich.edu/admissions/admissions

University of Minnesota, Twin Cities Campus, School of Dentistry, Professional Program in Dentistry, Minneapolis, MN 55455-0213. Offers DDS. *Accreditation:* ADA. *Entrance requirements:* For doctorate, DAT. Additional exam requirements/recommendations for international students: Required—TOEFL.

University of Mississippi Medical Center, School of Dentistry, Jackson, MS 39216-4505. Offers MS, DMD, PhD. *Accreditation:* ADA. *Entrance requirements:* For doctorate, DAT (for DMD). *Expenses:* Contact institution. *Faculty research:* Bone growth factors, salivary markers of disease, biomaterial synthesis and evaluation, metabolic bone disease, periodontal disease.

University of Missouri–Kansas City, School of Dentistry, Kansas City, MO 64110-2499. Offers advanced education in dentistry (Graduate Dental Certificate); dental hygiene education (MS); endodontics (Graduate Dental Certificate); oral and maxillofacial surgery (Graduate Dental Certificate); oral biology (MS, PhD); orthodontics and dentofacial orthopedics (Graduate Dental Certificate); periodontics (Graduate Dental Certificate). PhD (interdisciplinary) offered through the School of Graduate Studies. *Accreditation:* ADA (one or more programs are accredited). *Degree requirements:* For master's, thesis; for doctorate, thesis/dissertation (for some programs). *Entrance requirements:* For master's, DAT, letters of evaluation, personal interview; for doctorate, DAT (for DDS); for Graduate Dental Certificate, DDS. Additional exam requirements/recommendations for international students: Required—TOEFL (minimum score 550 paper-based; 80 iBT). *Expenses:* Contact institution. *Faculty research:* Biomaterials, dental use of lasers, effectiveness of periodontal treatments, temporomandibular joint dysfunction.

University of Nebraska Medical Center, College of Dentistry, Lincoln, NE 68583-0740. Offers MS, DDS, PhD, Certificate. *Accreditation:* ADA (one or more programs are accredited). *Degree requirements:* For Certificate, thesis or alternative. *Entrance requirements:* For doctorate, DAT (for DDS). Additional exam requirements/recommendations for international students: Required—TOEFL. Electronic applications accepted. *Expenses:* Contact institution.

University of Nevada, Las Vegas, School of Dental Medicine, Las Vegas, NV 89106. Offers dental medicine (DMD); dental surgery (DDS); dentistry (DMD); oral biology (MS); orthodontics and dentofacial orthopedics (Certificate). *Accreditation:* ADA. *Program availability:* Part-time, evening/weekend, online learning. *Faculty:* 67 full-time (28 women), 57 part-time/adjunct (17 women). *Students:* 356 full-time (152 women); includes 118 minority (3 Black or African American, non-Hispanic/Latino; 2 American Indian or Alaska Native, non-Hispanic/Latino; 71 Asian, non-Hispanic/Latino; 23 Hispanic/Latino; 2 Native Hawaiian or other Pacific Islander, non-Hispanic/Latino; 17 Two or more races, non-Hispanic/Latino), 3 international. Average age 28. 1,754 applicants, 7% accepted, 88 enrolled. In 2017, 5 master's, 75 doctorates, 6 other advanced degrees awarded. *Entrance requirements:* For doctorate, DAT; for Certificate, National Board Dental Exam part 1 and 2. Additional exam requirements/recommendations for international students: Required—TOEFL (minimum score 550 paper-based; 80 iBT), IELTS (minimum score 7). *Application deadline:* For fall admission, 1/1 for domestic and international students; for summer admission, 3/1 for domestic students. Applications are processed on a rolling basis. Application fee: $75. Electronic applications accepted. *Expenses:* Contact institution. *Financial support:* In 2017–18, 28 students received support. Federal Work-Study, institutionally sponsored loans, scholarships/grants, health care benefits, and unspecified assistantships available. Support available to part-time students. Financial award application deadline: 3/15; financial award applicants required to submit FAFSA. *Faculty research:* HPV, oral cancer, flouridtion, microbiology, virology in oral infectious disease, oral-systemic linkages to periodontal disease. *Total annual research expenditures:* $941,448. *Unit head:* Dr. Christine C. Ancajas, Assistant Dean of Admissions and Student Affairs, 702-774-2522, Fax: 702-774-2521, E-mail: christine.ancajas@unlv.edu. *Application contact:* Kamber Davoren, Admissions and Records Assistant, 702-774-2520, Fax: 702-774-2520, E-mail: kamber.davoren@unlv.edu.
Website: http://www.unlv.edu/dental

University of New England, College of Dental Medicine, Biddeford, ME 04005-9526. Offers DMD. *Accreditation:* ADA. *Faculty:* 23 full-time (12 women), 29 part-time/adjunct (9 women). *Students:* 252 full-time (127 women); includes 50 minority (2 Black or African American, non-Hispanic/Latino; 1 American Indian or Alaska Native, non-Hispanic/Latino; 33 Asian, non-Hispanic/Latino; 9 Hispanic/Latino; 5 Two or more races, non-Hispanic/Latino), 10 international. Average age 27. 1,912 applicants, 6% accepted, 49 enrolled. In 2017, 62 doctorates awarded. *Entrance requirements:* For doctorate, DAT, minimum 30 hours of clinical experience in dental setting. *Application deadline:* For fall admission, 11/1 for domestic and international students. Electronic applications accepted. Tuition and fees vary according to degree level, program and student level. *Financial support:* Application deadline: 5/1; applicants required to submit FAFSA. *Unit head:* Dr. Jon Ryder, Dean, College of Dental Medicine, 207-221-4707, Fax: 207-523-1915, E-mail: jryder2@une.edu. *Application contact:* Scott Steinberg, Dean of University Admissions, 207-221-4225, Fax: 207-523-1925, E-mail: ssteinberg@une.edu.
Website: http://www.une.edu/dentalmedicine/

The University of North Carolina at Chapel Hill, School of Dentistry, Professional Program in Dentistry, Chapel Hill, NC 27599-7450. Offers DDS, DDS/PhD. *Accreditation:* ADA. *Entrance requirements:* For doctorate, DAT, interview. Additional exam requirements/recommendations for international students: Required—TOEFL (minimum score 550 paper-based). Electronic applications accepted. *Expenses:* Contact institution.

University of Oklahoma Health Sciences Center, College of Dentistry, Advanced Education in General Dentistry Program, Oklahoma City, OK 73190. Offers Certificate. *Accreditation:* ADA. Electronic applications accepted.

University of Oklahoma Health Sciences Center, College of Dentistry, Professional Program in Dentistry, Oklahoma City, OK 73190. Offers DDS. *Accreditation:* ADA. *Degree requirements:* For doctorate, National Board Dental Exam Part I and Part II. *Entrance requirements:* For doctorate, DAT, minimum GPA of 2.5; course work in English, general psychology, biology, general chemistry, organic chemistry, physics, and biochemistry. Additional exam requirements/recommendations for international students: Required—TOEFL (minimum score 570 paper-based). Electronic applications accepted. *Faculty research:* Dental caries, microwave sterilization, dental care delivery systems, dental materials, oral health of Native Americans.

University of Pennsylvania, School of Dental Medicine, Philadelphia, PA 19104. Offers DMD, DMD/MS Ed. *Accreditation:* ADA. *Entrance requirements:* For doctorate, DAT. *Expenses:* Contact institution. *Faculty research:* Bone, teeth and extracellular matrix; craniofacial genetic anomalies, infection and host response, periodonatal diseases; stem cells; improvement of tempormandibular function.

University of Pittsburgh, School of Dental Medicine, Advanced Education Program in General Dentistry, Pittsburgh, PA 15260. Offers Certificate. *Accreditation:* ADA. *Faculty:* 3 part-time/adjunct (1 woman). *Students:* 2 full-time (1 woman); includes 1 minority (Asian, non-Hispanic/Latino). Average age 27. 30 applicants, 13% accepted, 2 enrolled. In 2017, 2 Certificates awarded. *Entrance requirements:* For degree, National Dental Boards Parts I and II, U.S. or Canadian dental degree. *Application deadline:* For summer admission, 12/1 for domestic and international students. Applications are processed on a rolling basis. Application fee: $50. Electronic applications accepted. *Expenses:* No tuition; $1,200 university fees. *Financial support:* In 2017–18, 2 fellowships (averaging $40,000 per year) were awarded. *Unit head:* Dr. Maribeth Krzesinski, Director, 412-648-8093.
Website: http://www.dental.pitt.edu/students/residencyprogram.php

University of Pittsburgh, School of Dental Medicine, Advanced Education Program in General Practice, Pittsburgh, PA 15213. Offers Certificate. *Accreditation:* ADA. *Faculty:* 1 full-time (0 women), 4 part-time/adjunct (1 woman). *Students:* 3 full-time (1 woman); includes 1 minority (Asian, non-Hispanic/Latino). Average age 29. 25 applicants, 12% accepted, 3 enrolled. *Entrance requirements:* For degree, DMD or DDS. *Application deadline:* For fall admission, 10/15 for domestic students. Application fee: $0. Electronic applications accepted. *Unit head:* Dr. Keith Scott Richmond, Program Director, 412-648-6730, Fax: 412-648-6505, E-mail: ksr31@pitt.edu. *Application contact:* Andrea M. Ford, Residency Coordinator, 412-648-6801, Fax: 412-648-6835, E-mail: fordam@upmc.edu.
Website: http://www.dental.pitt.edu/students/general-practice-residency-program

University of Pittsburgh, School of Dental Medicine, Department of Pediatric Dentistry, Pittsburgh, PA 15260. Offers dental science (MDS); multidisciplinary public health (MPH); pediatric dentistry (Certificate). *Accreditation:* ADA. *Faculty:* 3 full-time (all women), 10 part-time/adjunct (6 women). *Students:* 6 full-time (5 women); includes 2 minority (1 Asian, non-Hispanic/Latino; 1 Native Hawaiian or other Pacific Islander, non-Hispanic/Latino). Average age 34. 45 applicants, 9% accepted, 4 enrolled. *Degree requirements:* For master's, thesis. *Entrance requirements:* For degree, National Dental Board Examinations Parts I and II, DDS or DMD from U.S. or Canadian dental school. *Application deadline:* For fall admission, 10/1 for domestic students. Electronic applications accepted. *Expenses:* $49,280 per year in-state, $59,774 out-of-state; $850 mandatory fees. *Financial support:* In 2017–18, 6 students received support. Traineeships and stipends (averaging $24,000 per year) available. *Faculty research:* Behavior management techniques, mouth guard use, obesity and dental development, non-nutritive sucking habits, infant oral health. *Unit head:* Dr. Deborah Studen-Pavlovich, Program Director, 412-648-8183, Fax: 412-648-8435, E-mail: das12@pitt.edu. *Application contact:* Sharon A. Hohman, Departmental Secretary, 412-648-8416, Fax: 412-648-8435.
Website: http://www.dental.pitt.edu

University of Pittsburgh, School of Dental Medicine, Predoctoral Program in Dental Medicine, Pittsburgh, PA 15261. Offers DMD. *Accreditation:* ADA. *Faculty:* 90 full-time (36 women), 103 part-time/adjunct (28 women). *Students:* 327 full-time (175 women); includes 118 minority (6 Black or African American, non-Hispanic/Latino; 8 American Indian or Alaska Native, non-Hispanic/Latino; 79 Asian, non-Hispanic/Latino; 17 Hispanic/Latino; 1 Native Hawaiian or other Pacific Islander, non-Hispanic/Latino; 7 Two or more races, non-Hispanic/Latino). Average age 25. 1,904 applicants, 80 enrolled. *Entrance requirements:* For doctorate, DAT, minimum GPA of 3.2 (science and non-science). Additional exam requirements/recommendations for international students: Required—TOEFL (minimum score 100 iBT). *Application deadline:* For fall admission, 11/1 for domestic students. Applications are processed on a rolling basis. Application fee: $75. Electronic applications accepted. *Expenses:* $46,270 in-state tuition, $54,264 out-of-state; $1,228 university fees; $9,782 instruments and fees. *Financial support:* In 2017–18, 141 students received support. Scholarships/grants available. Financial award application deadline: 4/30; financial award applicants required to submit FAFSA. *Faculty research:* Human genetics, tissue engineering, public health, periodontal disease, cardiology. *Unit head:* Dr. Christine Rebecca Wankiiri-Hale, Associate Dean for Student Affairs, 412-383-9975, Fax: 412-648-9571, E-mail: chwst11@pitt.edu. *Application contact:* Molly Kunzman, Admissions Manager, 412-648-7375, Fax: 412-648-9571, E-mail: molly.kunzman@pitt.edu.
Website: http://www.dental.pitt.edu

University of Puerto Rico–Medical Sciences Campus, School of Dental Medicine, Professional Program in Dentistry, San Juan, PR 00936-5067. Offers DMD. *Accreditation:* ADA. *Entrance requirements:* For doctorate, DAT, interview. *Expenses:* Contact institution. *Faculty research:* Analgesic drugs, anti-inflammatory drugs, saliva cytoanalysis, dental material and cariology, oral health condition of school-age population.

University of Saskatchewan, College of Dentistry, Saskatoon, SK S7N 5A2, Canada. Offers DMD. *Accreditation:* ADA. *Entrance requirements:* For doctorate, DAT. Additional exam requirements/recommendations for international students: Required—TOEFL (minimum score 550 paper-based; 80 iBT), IELTS (minimum score 6.5), Michigan English Language Assessment Battery (85); CanTEST (4.0); CAEL (60); CPE (C). Electronic applications accepted. *Expenses:* Contact institution. *Faculty research:* Protein structure, oral cavity, immunology, bone densitometry, biological sciences.

University of Southern California, Graduate School, Herman Ostrow School of Dentistry, Professional Program in Dentistry, Los Angeles, CA 90089. Offers DDS, DDS/MBA, DDS/MS. *Accreditation:* ADA (one or more programs are accredited).

The University of Tennessee Health Science Center, College of Dentistry, Memphis, TN 38163-0002. Offers DDS. *Accreditation:* ADA. *Entrance requirements:* For doctorate, DAT, interview, pre-professional evaluation. Additional exam requirements/recommendations for international students: Required—TOEFL. Electronic applications accepted. *Expenses:* Contact institution. *Faculty research:* Oral cancer, proteomics, inflammation mechanisms, defensins, periopathogens, dental material.

The University of Texas Health Science Center at Houston, School of Dentistry, Houston, TX 77225-0036. Offers MS, DDS. *Accreditation:* ADA. *Entrance requirements:* For doctorate, DAT, 90 semester hours of prerequisite courses. Electronic applications accepted. *Faculty research:* Salivary diagnostics, autoimmune disease, mucosal immunity, craniofacial anomalies, molecular imaging, bioengineering.

The University of Texas Health Science Center at San Antonio, Graduate School of Biomedical Sciences, Program in Dental Science, San Antonio, TX 78229-3900. Offers MS. *Degree requirements:* For master's, thesis.

The University of Texas Health Science Center at San Antonio, School of Dentistry, San Antonio, TX 78229-3900. Offers MS, DDS, Certificate, DDS/PhD. *Accreditation:* ADA (one or more programs are accredited). *Faculty:* 103 full-time (37 women), 81 part-time/adjunct (18 women). *Students:* 514 full-time (273 women), 42 part-time (19 women); includes 254 minority (22 Black or African American, non-Hispanic/Latino; 91 Asian, non-Hispanic/Latino; 126 Hispanic/Latino; 15 Two or more races, non-Hispanic/Latino), 33 international. Average age 27. 1,417 applicants, 15% accepted, 100 enrolled. In 2017, 20 master's, 104 doctorates, 43 other advanced degrees awarded. *Degree requirements:* For master's, thesis; for doctorate, comprehensive exam. *Entrance requirements:* For master's, GRE General Test, DDS; for doctorate, DAT; for Certificate, National Board Part 1 and Part 2, DDS. Additional exam requirements/recommendations for international students: Required—TOEFL (minimum score 92 iBT). *Application deadline:* For fall admission, 10/1 for domestic students. Applications are processed on a rolling basis. Application fee: $150. Electronic applications accepted. *Expenses:* Contact institution. *Financial support:* In 2017–18, 86 students received support, including 4 research assistantships (averaging $2,624 per year), 81 teaching assistantships (averaging $14,050 per year); Federal Work-Study and institutionally sponsored loans also available. Financial award application deadline: 3/1; financial award applicants required to submit FAFSA. *Faculty research:* Neuropharmacology, periodontal disease, biomaterials, bone mineralization. *Total annual research expenditures:* $5.1 million. *Unit head:* Dr. Kay Malone, Director of Admissions, 210-567-3180, Fax: 210-567-6721, E-mail: malonek@uthscsa.edu. *Application contact:* E-mail: dsadmissions@uthscsa.edu.
Website: http://dental.uthscsa.edu/

University of the Pacific, Arthur A. Dugoni School of Dentistry, Stockton, CA 95211-0197. Offers MSD, DDS, Certificate. *Accreditation:* ADA (one or more programs are accredited). *Faculty:* 66 full-time (21 women), 171 part-time/adjunct (67 women). *Students:* 568 full-time (255 women); includes 329 minority (6 Black or African American, non-Hispanic/Latino; 1 American Indian or Alaska Native, non-Hispanic/Latino; 247 Asian, non-Hispanic/Latino; 39 Hispanic/Latino; 36 Two or more races, non-Hispanic/Latino), 51 international. Average age 26. 3,197 applicants, 9% accepted, 179 enrolled. In 2017, 8 master's, 156 doctorates awarded. *Degree requirements:* For master's, comprehensive exam, thesis. *Entrance requirements:* For master's, GRE General Test; for doctorate, National Board Dental Exam Part I, DAT, foreign dental degree (for international students); for Certificate, DDS/DMD. Additional exam requirements/recommendations for international students: Required—TOEFL. *Application deadline:* For fall admission, 9/15 priority date for international students. Applications are processed on a rolling basis. Electronic applications accepted. *Expenses:* Contact institution. *Financial support:* Institutionally sponsored loans, scholarships/grants, and stipends available. Support available to part-time students. Financial award application deadline: 3/2; financial award applicants required to submit FAFSA. *Faculty research:* Cell kinetics, cell membrane transport, orthodontics, virus cell membrane fusion, bioenergy transduction. *Unit head:* Nader Nadershahi, Dean, 415-929-6425, E-mail: nnadershahi@pacific.edu. *Application contact:* Dr. Craig S. Yarborough, Associate Professor, 415-929-6430, E-mail: cyarborough@pacific.edu.
Website: http://dental.pacific.edu/

University of Toronto, School of Graduate Studies, Faculty of Dentistry, Professional Program in Dentistry, Toronto, ON M5S 1A1, Canada. Offers DDS. *Accreditation:* ADA. *Entrance requirements:* For doctorate, Canadian DAT or equivalent, minimum GPA of 3.0; completion of at least 2 courses in life sciences and 1 course in humanities or social sciences. Additional exam requirements/recommendations for international students: Required—TOEFL (minimum score 600 paper-based; 100 iBT), TWE (minimum score 5). Electronic applications accepted. *Expenses:* Contact institution.

University of Utah, School of Dentistry, Salt Lake City, UT 84108. Offers DDS. *Accreditation:* ADA. *Students:* 148 full-time (41 women); includes 30 minority (1 Black or African American, non-Hispanic/Latino; 8 Asian, non-Hispanic/Latino; 17 Hispanic/Latino; 4 Two or more races, non-Hispanic/Latino). Average age 27. In 2017, 20 doctorates awarded. *Degree requirements:* For doctorate, comprehensive exam. *Entrance requirements:* For doctorate, DAT, minimum overall and science GPA of 3.3. *Application deadline:* For fall admission, 10/1 priority date for domestic students. Application fee: $75. Electronic applications accepted. *Expenses:* Contact institution. *Financial support:* Scholarships/grants available. Financial award application deadline: 4/1; financial award applicants required to submit FAFSA. *Faculty research:* Fibrin hydrogels salivary glands, synthetic cathinone's, Sjogren's syndrome, tooth agenesis, neurotensin methamphetamine, tooth development, oral health sustainability for substance use disorder patients and families. *Unit head:* Dr. Wyatt R. Hume, DDS, Dean, 801-587-1208, Fax: 801-585-6485, E-mail: wyatt.hume@hsc.utah.edu. *Application contact:* Gary W. Lowder, DDS, Office of Admissions, 801-213-3506, Fax: 801-585-6485, E-mail: dental.admissions@hsc.utah.edu.
Website: http://dentistry.utah.edu/

University of Washington, Graduate School, School of Dentistry and Graduate School, Graduate Programs in Dentistry, Department of Pediatric Dentistry, Seattle, WA 98195. Offers MSD, Certificate.

University of Washington, Graduate School, School of Dentistry and Graduate School, Graduate Programs in Dentistry, Department of Restorative Dentistry, Seattle, WA 98195. Offers prosthodontics (MSD, Certificate).

University of Washington, Graduate School, School of Dentistry, Program in Dental Surgery, Seattle, WA 98195. Offers DDS. *Accreditation:* ADA. *Entrance requirements:* For doctorate, DAT.

The University of Western Ontario, Schulich School of Medicine and Dentistry, Graduate and Professional Programs in Dentistry, Professional Program in Dentistry, London, ON N6A 5B8, Canada. Offers DDS. *Accreditation:* ADA. *Entrance requirements:* For doctorate, DAT (Canadian version), minimum B average.

Virginia Commonwealth University, Medical College of Virginia-Professional Programs, School of Dentistry, Richmond, VA 23284-9005. Offers MS, DDS. *Accreditation:* ADA. *Entrance requirements:* For master's, National Board Dental Exam; for doctorate, DAT. Electronic applications accepted. *Expenses:* Contact institution.

Western University of Health Sciences, College of Dental Medicine, Pomona, CA 91766-1854. Offers DMD. *Accreditation:* ADA. *Faculty:* 39 full-time (18 women), 18 part-time/adjunct (7 women). *Students:* 274 full-time (138 women); includes 174 minority (7 Black or African American, non-Hispanic/Latino; 2 American Indian or Alaska Native, non-Hispanic/Latino; 103 Asian, non-Hispanic/Latino; 42 Hispanic/Latino; 20 Two or more races, non-Hispanic/Latino), 4 international. Average age 28. 2,559 applicants, 7% accepted, 67 enrolled. In 2017, 67 doctorates awarded. *Degree requirements:* For doctorate, comprehensive exam. *Entrance requirements:* For doctorate, DAT, minimum of 90 semester or 135 quarter units of undergraduate/graduate course work; minimum 30 hours of dental-related work experience; complete all prerequisite coursework with minimum grade of C; letters of recommendation. Additional exam requirements/recommendations for international students: Required—TOEFL (minimum score 79 iBT). *Application deadline:* For fall admission, 12/1 for domestic and international students. Applications are processed on a rolling basis. Application fee: $60. Electronic applications accepted. Application fee is waived when completed online. *Expenses:* Contact institution. *Financial support:* In 2017–18, 19 students received support. Scholarships/grants available. Financial award application deadline: 3/2; financial award applicants required to submit FAFSA. *Unit head:* Dr. Steven Friedrichsen, Dean, 909-706-3911, E-mail: sfriedrichsen@westernu.edu. *Application contact:* Marie Anderson, Director of Admissions, 909-469-5335, Fax: 909-469-5570, E-mail: admissions@westernu.edu.
Website: http://www.westernu.edu/dentistry/

West Virginia University, School of Dentistry, Morgantown, WV 26506-9400. Offers dental hygiene (MS); dentistry (DDS); endodontics (MS); orthodontics (MS); periodontics (MS); prosthodontics (MS). *Accreditation:* ADA (one or more programs are accredited). *Students:* 223 full-time (109 women), 1 part-time (0 women); includes 22 minority (1 Black or African American, non-Hispanic/Latino; 16 Asian, non-Hispanic/Latino; 3 Hispanic/Latino; 2 Two or more races, non-Hispanic/Latino), 12 international. *Degree requirements:* For master's, thesis; for doctorate, comprehensive exam. *Entrance requirements:* For doctorate, DAT, letters of recommendation, interview, minimum of 50 semester credit hours. Additional exam requirements/recommendations for international students: Required—TOEFL (minimum score 500 paper-based). *Application deadline:* For fall admission, 11/1 for domestic and international students. Applications are processed on a rolling basis. Application fee: $60. Electronic applications accepted. *Expenses:* Contact institution. *Financial support:* Research assistantships, teaching assistantships, Federal Work-Study, institutionally sponsored loans, scholarships/grants, health care benefits, and tuition waivers (partial) available. Financial award application deadline: 3/1; financial award applicants required to submit FAFSA. *Faculty research:* Growth and development, cephalography, endodontic interpretation and therapy, basic biological and clinical sciences, genetics and oral health. *Unit head:* Dr. Tom Borgia, Dean, 304-293-2521, E-mail: aborgia@hsc.wvu.edu. *Application contact:* Dr. Sheila Price, Associate Dean for Admissions, Recruitment, and Access, 304-293-1980, E-mail: sprice@hsc.wvu.edu.
Website: http://www.dentistry.hsc.wvu.edu

Oral and Dental Sciences

American University of Beirut, Graduate Programs, Faculty of Medicine, Beirut, Lebanon. Offers biochemistry (MS); biomedical engineering (MS); biomedical sciences (PhD); health research (MS); human morphology (MS); medicine (MD); microbiology and immunology (MS); neuroscience (MS); orthodontics (clinical) (MS); pharmacology and therapeutics (MS); physiology (MS). *Program availability:* Part-time. *Faculty:* 335 full-time (117 women), 54 part-time/adjunct (5 women). *Students:* 513 full-time (274 women). Average age 23. 527 applicants, 47% accepted, 169 enrolled. In 2017, 18 master's, 98 doctorates awarded. *Degree requirements:* For master's, one foreign language, comprehensive exam, thesis (for some programs); for doctorate, one foreign language, comprehensive exam, thesis/dissertation. *Entrance requirements:* For doctorate, MCAT (for MD); GRE (for PhD). Additional exam requirements/recommendations for international students: Required—TOEFL (minimum score 600 paper-based; 100 iBT), IELTS (minimum score 7.5). *Application deadline:* Applications are processed on a rolling basis. Application fee: $75. Electronic applications accepted. *Expenses:* Contact institution. *Financial support:* In 2017–18, 302 students received support. Fellowships, research assistantships, teaching assistantships, institutionally sponsored loans, scholarships/grants, tuition waivers, and unspecified assistantships available. *Unit head:* Dr. Mohamed Sayegh, Dean, 961-1-135000 Ext. 4700, Fax: 961-1-744489, E-mail: msayegh@aub.edu.lb. *Application contact:* Dr. Salim Kanaan, Director, Admission's Office, 961-1-350000 Ext. 2594, Fax: 961-1-750775, E-mail: sk00@aub.edu.lb.

A.T. Still University, Arizona School of Dentistry & Oral Health, Mesa, AZ 85206. Offers dental medicine (DMD); orthodontics (MS, Certificate). *Accreditation:* ADA. *Faculty:* 50 full-time (26 women), 101 part-time/adjunct (36 women). *Students:* 311 full-time (164 women); includes 129 minority (5 Black or African American, non-Hispanic/Latino; 4 American Indian or Alaska Native, non-Hispanic/Latino; 83 Asian, non-Hispanic/Latino; 20 Hispanic/Latino; 17 Two or more races, non-Hispanic/Latino), 1 international. Average age 28. 2,433 applicants, 6% accepted, 76 enrolled. In 2017, 74 doctorates, 4

other advanced degrees awarded. *Degree requirements:* For doctorate, National Board Exams I and II. *Entrance requirements:* For doctorate, DAT, minimum GPA of 2.5 overall and in science. Additional exam requirements/recommendations for international students: Recommended—TOEFL. *Application deadline:* For fall admission, 11/15 for domestic and international students; for summer admission, 11/15 for domestic and international students. Applications are processed on a rolling basis. Application fee: $70. Electronic applications accepted. Application fee is waived when completed online. *Financial support:* In 2017–18, 49 students received support. Federal Work-Study and scholarships/grants available. Financial award application deadline: 6/1; financial award applicants required to submit FAFSA. *Faculty research:* Evidence-based dentistry in clinical practice; xerostomia and malnutrition in assisted living settings; medical screenings in the dental office: patient attitudes; rapid oral HIV screening in the dental setting; dental public health: early childhood caries, self-efficacy and oral health. *Total annual research expenditures:* $20,692. *Unit head:* Dr. Robert Trombly, Dean, 480-248-8105, Fax: 623-223-7063, E-mail: rtrombly@atsu.edu. *Application contact:* Donna Sparks, Director, Admissions Processing, 660-626-2117, Fax: 660-626-2969, E-mail: admissions@atsu.edu.
Website: http://www.atsu.edu/asdoh

A.T. Still University, College of Graduate Health Studies, Kirksville, MO 63501. Offers dental public health (MPH); exercise and sport psychology (Certificate); fundamentals of education (Certificate); geriatric exercise science (Certificate); global health (Certificate); health administration (MHA, DHA); health professions (Ed D); health sciences (DH Sc); kinesiology (MS); leadership and organizational behavior (Certificate); public health (MPH); sports conditioning (Certificate). *Program availability:* Part-time, evening/weekend, online only, 100% online, blended/hybrid learning. *Faculty:* 28 full-time (18 women), 83 part-time/adjunct (43 women). *Students:* 537 full-time (334 women), 516 part-time (316 women); includes 397 minority (171 Black or African American, non-Hispanic/Latino; 14 American Indian or Alaska Native, non-Hispanic/Latino; 84 Asian, non-Hispanic/Latino; 106 Hispanic/Latino; 1 Native Hawaiian or other Pacific Islander, non-Hispanic/Latino; 21 Two or more races, non-Hispanic/Latino), 43 international. Average age 36. 392 applicants, 84% accepted, 270 enrolled. In 2017, 138 master's, 102 doctorates, 116 other advanced degrees awarded. *Degree requirements:* For master's, thesis, integrated terminal project, practicum; for doctorate, thesis/dissertation. *Entrance requirements:* For master's, minimum GPA of 2.5, bachelor's degree or equivalent, essay, resume, English proficiency; for doctorate, minimum GPA of 2.5, master's or terminal degree, essay, past experience in relevant field, resume, English proficiency. Additional exam requirements/recommendations for international students: Required—TOEFL (minimum score 550 paper-based; 80 iBT). *Application deadline:* For fall admission, 6/26 for domestic students, 5/20 for international students; for winter admission, 9/11 for domestic students, 9/12 for international students; for spring admission, 12/11 for domestic students, 12/12 for international students; for summer admission, 3/5 for domestic students, 3/6 for international students. Applications are processed on a rolling basis. Application fee: $70. Electronic applications accepted. *Financial support:* In 2017–18, 18 students received support. Scholarships/grants available. Financial award applicants required to submit FAFSA. *Faculty research:* Public health: influence of availability of comprehensive wellness resources online, student wellness, oral health care needs assessment of community, oral health knowledge and behaviors of Medicaid-eligible pregnant women and mothers of young children in relations to early childhood caries and tooth decay, alcohol use and alcohol related problems among college students. *Unit head:* Dr. Donald Altman, Dean, 480-219-6008, Fax: 660-626-2826, E-mail: daltman@atsu.edu. *Application contact:* Amie Waldemer, Associate Director, Online Admissions, 480-219-6146, E-mail: awaldemer@atsu.edu.
Website: http://www.atsu.edu/college-of-graduate-health-studies

Augusta University, Program in Oral Biology, Augusta, GA 30912. Offers MS, PhD. *Program availability:* Part-time. *Degree requirements:* For master's, thesis; for doctorate, thesis/dissertation. *Entrance requirements:* For master's and doctorate, GRE General Test or DAT, DDS, DMD, or equivalent degree. Additional exam requirements/recommendations for international students: Required—TOEFL (minimum score 550 paper-based; 79 iBT). Electronic applications accepted. *Faculty research:* Oral cancer and chemoprevention, properties of biomaterials including oxidative stress, mechanical stress and shear stress responses, taurine and blood pressure in diabetes, bone and dentin biology, induction of periodontal regeneration.

Boston University, School of Medicine, Division of Graduate Medical Sciences, Program in Oral Biology, Boston, MA 02215. Offers PhD. *Degree requirements:* For doctorate, thesis/dissertation. *Application deadline:* For fall admission, 1/15 priority date for domestic students; for spring admission, 10/15 for domestic students. *Unit head:* Dr. Phillip Trackman, Director, 617-638-4942, E-mail: trackman@bu.edu. *Application contact:* GMS Admissions Office, 617-638-5255, Fax: 617-638-5740, E-mail: askgms@bu.edu.
Website: http://www.bu.edu/dental-research/student-research/phd-in-oral-biology/

Boston University, School of Medicine, Division of Graduate Medical Sciences, Program in Oral Health Sciences, Boston, MA 02118. Offers MS. *Degree requirements:* For master's, capstone project or thesis. *Entrance requirements:* For master's, DAT. Electronic applications accepted. *Unit head:* Dr. Theresa A. Davies, Director, 618-638-5242, E-mail: tdavies@bu.edu. *Application contact:* GMS Office of Admissions, 617-638-5255, E-mail: askgms@bu.edu.
Website: http://www.bumc.bu.edu/gms/oral-health-masters/

Case Western Reserve University, School of Dental Medicine and School of Graduate Studies, Advanced Specialty Education Programs in Dentistry, Cleveland, OH 44106. Offers advanced general dentistry (Certificate); endodontics (MSD, Certificate); oral surgery (Certificate); orthodontics (MSD, Certificate); pedodontics (MSD, Certificate); periodontics (MSD, Certificate). *Degree requirements:* For master's, thesis. *Entrance requirements:* For master's, National Dental Board Exam, DDS, minimum GPA of 3.0; for Certificate, DDS. Additional exam requirements/recommendations for international students: Required—TOEFL (minimum score 550 paper-based; 79 iBT). *Expenses:* Contact institution. *Faculty research:* Natural antibiotics, obesity and periodontal disease, perioninfection and CV disease, periodontal disease and overall health, 3D cone beam computerized tomography.

Columbia University, College of Dental Medicine and Graduate School of Arts and Sciences, Programs in Dental Specialties, New York, NY 10027. Offers advanced education in general dentistry (Certificate); biomedical informatics (MA, PhD); endodontics (Certificate); orthodontics (MS, Certificate); periodontics (MS, Certificate); prosthodontics (MS, Certificate); science education (MA). *Degree requirements:* For master's, thesis, presentation of seminar. *Entrance requirements:* For master's, GRE General Test, DDS or equivalent. *Expenses:* Contact institution. *Faculty research:* Analysis of growth/form, pulpal microcirculation, implants, microbiology of oral environment, calcified tissues.

Dalhousie University, Faculty of Dentistry, Department of Oral and Maxillofacial Surgery, Halifax, NS B3H 3J5, Canada. Offers MD/M Sc. Electronic applications accepted. *Expenses:* Contact institution. *Faculty research:* Cleft lip/palate, jaw biomechanics.

Harvard University, Graduate School of Arts and Sciences, Program in Biological Sciences in Dental Medicine, Cambridge, MA 02138. Offers PhD.

Harvard University, School of Dental Medicine, Advanced Graduate Programs in Dentistry, Cambridge, MA 02138. Offers advanced general dentistry (Certificate); dental public health (Certificate); endodontics (Certificate); general practice residency (Certificate); oral biology (M Med Sc, D Med Sc); oral implantology (Certificate); oral medicine (Certificate); oral pathology (Certificate); oral surgery (Certificate); orthodontics (Certificate); pediatric dentistry (Certificate); periodontics (Certificate); prosthodontics (Certificate). *Faculty:* 90 full-time. *Students:* 105 full-time (59 women); includes 44 minority (8 Black or African American, non-Hispanic/Latino; 28 Asian, non-Hispanic/Latino; 2 Hispanic/Latino; 6 Two or more races, non-Hispanic/Latino), 26 international. Average age 27. In 2017, 17 master's, 9 doctorates awarded. *Degree requirements:* For master's, comprehensive exam, thesis optional; for doctorate, comprehensive exam, thesis/dissertation. *Entrance requirements:* Additional exam requirements/recommendations for international students: Required—TOEFL (minimum iBT score of 95; subcategory score minimums of Reading 21, Listening 17, Speaking 24, and Writing 25). *Application deadline:* Applications are processed on a rolling basis. Application fee: $80. *Financial support:* In 2017–18, 15 students received support. Scholarships/grants available. Financial award application deadline: 5/15; financial award applicants required to submit FAFSA. *Unit head:* Dr. Sang Lee, Director, 617-432-3064, E-mail: sang_lee@hsdm.harvard.edu. *Application contact:* Sarah M. Troy-Petrakos, Director of Admissions, 617-432-1443, Fax: 617-432-3881, E-mail: sarah_petrakos@hsdm.harvard.edu.

Howard University, College of Dentistry, Washington, DC 20059-0002. Offers advanced education in general dentistry (Certificate); dentistry (DDS); general dentistry practice (Certificate); oral and maxillofacial surgery (Certificate); orthodontics (Certificate); pediatric dentistry (Certificate). *Accreditation:* ADA (one or more programs are accredited). *Degree requirements:* For doctorate, comprehensive exam, didactic and clinical exams. *Entrance requirements:* For doctorate, DAT, 8 semester hours of course work each in biology, inorganic chemistry, and organic chemistry. *Expenses:* Contact institution. *Faculty research:* Epidemiological, biomaterial, molecular genetic, behavioral modification, and clinical trial studies.

Idaho State University, Office of Graduate Studies, Office of Medical and Oral Health, Department of Dental Sciences, Pocatello, ID 83209-8088. Offers advanced general dentistry (Post-Doctoral Certificate). First year of Idaho Dental Education Program available in conjunction with Creighton University's School of Dentistry. *Degree requirements:* For Post-Doctoral Certificate, comprehensive exam, thesis optional, 1-year residency. *Entrance requirements:* For degree, DAT, 3 dental application forms. Additional exam requirements/recommendations for international students: Required—TOEFL (minimum score 600 paper-based). Electronic applications accepted. *Expenses:* Contact institution.

Jacksonville University, Brooks Rehabilitation College of Healthcare Sciences, School of Orthodontics, Jacksonville, FL 32211. Offers dentistry (MS); orthodontics (Certificate). *Faculty:* 15 full-time (5 women), 2 part-time/adjunct (both women). *Students:* 37 full-time (12 women), 6 part-time (2 women); includes 12 minority (6 Asian, non-Hispanic/Latino; 5 Hispanic/Latino; 1 Two or more races, non-Hispanic/Latino), 10 international. Average age 30. 201 applicants, 10% accepted, 20 enrolled. In 2017, 15 other advanced degrees awarded. *Degree requirements:* For master's and Certificate, thesis. *Entrance requirements:* For master's, DDS/DMD or equivalent; for Certificate, American Board of Orthodontics written exam; U.S. National Dental Boards (part 1 and 2), curriculum vitae, official transcripts, 3 professional evaluations, 3 professional recommendations (dean of dental school or faculty, or other professional colleagues), statement of intent, clinical competencies through delivering evidence-based patient care, DDS/DMD or equivalent. Additional exam requirements/recommendations for international students: Required—TOEFL (minimum score 610 paper-based). *Application deadline:* For fall admission, 9/14 priority date for domestic students, 9/14 for international students. Applications are processed on a rolling basis. Application fee: $175. Electronic applications accepted. *Expenses:* $95,000 per year ($140,000 international). *Financial support:* In 2017–18, 5 fellowships (averaging $35,000 per year) were awarded; scholarships/grants and health care benefits also available. Financial award application deadline: 3/15; financial award applicants required to submit FAFSA. *Faculty research:* Orthodontics and dentofacial orthopedics with emphasis on pre-adjusted appliances and related techniques. *Unit head:* Dr. Eman Othman, Interim Department Chair, Clinical Assistant Professor, and Director of Fellowship in Clinical Research, 904-256-7803, E-mail: eothman1@ju.edu. *Application contact:* Sharon Frazier, Executive Operations Coordinator, 904-256-7847, Fax: 904-256-7847, E-mail: juorthoadmissions@ju.edu.
Website: https://www.ju.edu/orthodontics/index.php

Loma Linda University, School of Dentistry, Program in Endodontics, Loma Linda, CA 92350. Offers MS, Certificate, MS/Certificate. *Degree requirements:* For master's, thesis. *Entrance requirements:* For master's, GRE General Test, DDS or DMD, minimum GPA of 3.0, National Boards. Additional exam requirements/recommendations for international students: Required—TOEFL (minimum score 550 paper-based).

Loma Linda University, School of Dentistry, Program in Implant Dentistry, Loma Linda, CA 92350. Offers MS, Certificate, MS/Certificate. *Degree requirements:* For master's, thesis. *Entrance requirements:* For master's, GRE General Test, DDS or DMD, minimum GPA of 3.0.

Loma Linda University, School of Dentistry, Program in Oral and Maxillofacial Surgery, Loma Linda, CA 92350. Offers MS, Certificate, MS/Certificate. *Degree requirements:* For master's, thesis. *Entrance requirements:* For master's, GRE General Test, DDS or DMD, minimum GPA of 3.0.

Loma Linda University, School of Dentistry, Program in Orthodontics and Dentofacial Orthopedics, Loma Linda, CA 92350. Offers MS, Certificate, MS/Certificate. *Degree requirements:* For master's, thesis. *Entrance requirements:* For master's, GRE General Test, DDS or DMD, minimum GPA of 3.0. Additional exam requirements/recommendations for international students: Required—TOEFL (minimum score 550 paper-based).

Loma Linda University, School of Dentistry, Program in Periodontics, Loma Linda, CA 92350. Offers MS. *Degree requirements:* For master's, thesis. *Entrance requirements:* For master's, GRE General Test, DDS or DMD, minimum GPA of 3.0. Additional exam requirements/recommendations for international students: Required—TOEFL (minimum score 550 paper-based).

Marquette University, School of Dentistry and Graduate School, Graduate Programs in Dentistry, Program in Advanced Training in General Dentistry, Milwaukee, WI 53201-1881. Offers MS, Certificate. *Entrance requirements:* For master's, National Board Dental Exams I and II, DDS or equivalent. Additional exam requirements/recommendations for international students: Required—TOEFL.

Marquette University, School of Dentistry and Graduate School, Graduate Programs in Dentistry, Program in Dental Biomaterials, Milwaukee, WI 53201-1881. Offers MS. *Program availability:* Part-time. *Degree requirements:* For master's, thesis. *Entrance requirements:* For master's, GRE General Test. Additional exam requirements/recommendations for international students: Required—TOEFL. *Faculty research:* Metallurgy, ceramics, polymers, mechanical behavior, cements.

Oral and Dental Sciences

Marquette University, School of Dentistry and Graduate School, Graduate Programs in Dentistry, Program in Endodontics, Milwaukee, WI 53201-1881. Offers MS, Certificate. *Degree requirements:* For master's, research thesis or acceptance of a paper in a peer-reviewed journal. *Entrance requirements:* For master's, National Board Dental Exams I and II, DDS or equivalent. Additional exam requirements/recommendations for international students: Required—TOEFL. *Expenses:* Contact institution. *Faculty research:* Properties of NiTi files, prevention of post-endodontic pain.

Marquette University, School of Dentistry and Graduate School, Graduate Programs in Dentistry, Program in Orthodontics, Milwaukee, WI 53201-1881. Offers MS, Certificate. *Degree requirements:* For master's, thesis. *Entrance requirements:* For master's, National Board Dental Exams I and II, DDS or equivalent. Additional exam requirements/recommendations for international students: Required—TOEFL. *Expenses:* Contact institution. *Faculty research:* In vitro and in vivo behavior of orthodontic wires, effect of orthodontic treatment on facial esthetics.

Marquette University, School of Dentistry and Graduate School, Graduate Programs in Dentistry, Program in Periodontics, Milwaukee, WI 53201-1881. Offers MS, Certificate.

Marquette University, School of Dentistry and Graduate School, Graduate Programs in Dentistry, Program in Prosthodontics, Milwaukee, WI 53201-1881. Offers MS, Certificate. *Degree requirements:* For master's, thesis or alternative. *Entrance requirements:* For master's, National Board Dental Exams I and II, DDS or equivalent. Additional exam requirements/recommendations for international students: Required—TOEFL. *Faculty research:* Properties of ceramic materials.

McGill University, Faculty of Graduate and Postdoctoral Studies, Faculty of Dentistry, Montréal, QC H3A 2T5, Canada. Offers forensic dentistry (Certificate); oral and maxillofacial surgery (M Sc, PhD).

Metropolitan State University, College of Nursing and Health Sciences, St. Paul, MN 55106-5000. Offers advanced dental therapy (MS); leadership and management (MSN); nurse educator (MSN); nursing (DNP). *Accreditation:* AACN. *Program availability:* Part-time. *Degree requirements:* For master's, thesis or alternative; for doctorate, thesis/dissertation or alternative. *Entrance requirements:* For master's, GRE General Test, minimum GPA of 3.0, RN license, BS/BA; for doctorate, minimum GPA of 3.0, RN license, MSN. Additional exam requirements/recommendations for international students: Required—TOEFL (minimum score 550 paper-based). *Application deadline:* For fall admission, 1/15 for domestic and international students; for winter admission, 1/15 for international students. Application fee: $20. *Expenses:* Tuition, state resident: part-time $388.55 per credit. Tuition, nonresident: part-time $777.11 per credit. *Required fees:* $35.11 per credit. Part-time tuition and fees vary according to campus/location and program. *Financial support:* Fellowships, career-related internships or fieldwork, Federal Work-Study, institutionally sponsored loans, and traineeships available. Financial award applicants required to submit FAFSA. *Faculty research:* Women's health, gerontology.
Website: https://www.metrostate.edu/academics/nursing-and-health-sciences

New York University, College of Dentistry and College of Dentistry, Department of Biomaterials, New York, NY 10012-1019. Offers biomaterials science (MS). *Faculty:* 5 full-time (2 women). *Students:* 18 full-time (11 women); includes 13 minority (8 Asian, non-Hispanic/Latino; 4 Hispanic/Latino; 1 Native Hawaiian or other Pacific Islander, non-Hispanic/Latino). Average age 29. 30 applicants, 53% accepted, 12 enrolled. In 2017, 14 master's awarded. *Degree requirements:* For master's, thesis optional. *Entrance requirements:* For master's, GRE or another standardized test (such as DAT, CDAT, National Dental Board Part I and National Dental Board Part II), academic transcripts, personal statement, resume or curriculum vitae, three letters of recommendation. Additional exam requirements/recommendations for international students: Required—TOEFL (minimum score 600 paper-based; 100 iBT). *Application deadline:* For fall admission, 7/1 for domestic and international students. Applications are processed on a rolling basis. Application fee: $100. Electronic applications accepted. *Expenses:* $1,664 per credit. *Financial support:* Application deadline: 7/1; applicants required to submit FAFSA. *Faculty research:* Calcium phosphate, composite restoratives, surfactants, dental metallurgy, impression materials and craniofacial research. *Unit head:* Dr. John L. Ricci, Director of Graduate Studies, 212-998-9623, Fax: 212-995-4244, E-mail: john.ricci@nyu.edu. *Application contact:* Champa Chonzom, Department Manager, 212-998-9703, Fax: 212-995-4244, E-mail: champa.chonzom@nyu.edu.
Website: https://dental.nyu.edu/academicprograms/masters-degree-programs/biomaterials.html

New York University, College of Dentistry, Post-Graduate Programs, New York, NY 10010. Offers endodontics (Advanced Certificate); oral and maxillofacial surgery (Advanced Certificate); orthodontics (Advanced Certificate); pediatric dentistry (Advanced Certificate); periodontics (Advanced Certificate); prosthodontics (Advanced Certificate). *Faculty:* 275 full-time (118 women), 573 part-time/adjunct (204 women). *Students:* 100 full-time (57 women); includes 52 minority (46 Asian, non-Hispanic/Latino; 6 Hispanic/Latino). Average age 28. 694 applicants, 8% accepted, 50 enrolled. In 2017, 43 Advanced Certificates awarded. *Degree requirements:* For Advanced Certificate, one foreign language. *Entrance requirements:* For degree, National Dental Board Exam Part I and II, three sealed letters of recommendation, including the dean's letter; official dental school transcript noting degree; personal essay. Additional exam requirements/recommendations for international students: Required—TOEFL (minimum score 603 paper-based; 100 iBT). *Application deadline:* For fall admission, 8/1 for domestic and international students. Application fee: $100. Electronic applications accepted. *Expenses:* Contact institution. *Financial support:* Scholarships/grants and unspecified assistantships available. Financial award application deadline: 4/1; financial award applicants required to submit FAFSA. *Faculty research:* Clinical research, HIV/AIDS, skeletal and craniofacial biology, oral cancer research, family translational research. *Unit head:* Dr. Andrea Schreiber, Senior Associate Dean for Education, 212-998-9624, Fax: 212-995-4240, E-mail: andrea.schreiber@nyu.edu. *Application contact:* Dr. Eugenia E. Mejia, Assistant Dean, Admissions and Enrollment Management, 212-998-9818, Fax: 212-995-4240, E-mail: dental.admissions@nyu.edu.
Website: https://dental.nyu.edu/

New York University, Graduate School of Arts and Science, Department of Biology, New York, NY 10012-1019. Offers biology (PhD); biomedical journalism (MS); cancer and molecular biology (PhD); computational biology (PhD); computers in biological research (MS); developmental genetics (PhD); general biology (MS); immunology and microbiology (PhD); molecular genetics (PhD); neurobiology (PhD); oral biology (MS); plant biology (PhD); recombinant DNA technology (MS); MS/MBA. *Program availability:* Part-time. *Students:* Average age 27. 394 applicants, 56% accepted, 77 enrolled. In 2017, 68 master's, 9 doctorates awarded. Terminal master's awarded for partial completion of doctoral program. *Degree requirements:* For master's, thesis or alternative, qualifying paper; for doctorate, comprehensive exam, thesis/dissertation. *Entrance requirements:* For master's and doctorate, GRE General Test. Additional exam requirements/recommendations for international students: Required—TOEFL. *Application deadline:* For fall admission, 12/1 priority date for domestic students, 12/1 for international students. Application fee: $100. *Expenses: Tuition:* Full-time $41,352; part-time $19,968 per year. *Required fees:* $2496; $1628 per unit. $814 per term. Tuition and fees vary according to course load and program. *Financial support:* Fellowships, research assistantships, teaching assistantships, career-related internships or fieldwork, Federal Work-Study, institutionally sponsored loans, scholarships/grants, health care benefits, and unspecified assistantships available. Financial award application deadline: 12/1; financial award applicants required to submit FAFSA. *Faculty research:* Genomics, molecular and cell biology, development and molecular genetics, molecular evolution of plants and animals. *Unit head:* Stephen Small, Chair, 212-998-8200, Fax: 212-995-4015, E-mail: biology.admissions@nyu.edu. *Application contact:* Ken Birnbaum, Director of Graduate Studies, PhD Programs, 212-998-8200, Fax: 212-995-4015, E-mail: biology.admissions@nyu.edu.
Website: http://biology.as.nyu.edu/

The Ohio State University, College of Dentistry, Columbus, OH 43210. Offers dental anesthesiology (MS); dental hygiene (MDH); dentistry (DDS); endodontics (MS); oral and maxillofacial pathology (MS); oral and maxillofacial surgery (MS); oral biology (PhD); orthodontics (MS); pediatric dentistry (MS); periodontology (MS); prosthodontics (MS); DDS/PhD. *Accreditation:* ADA (one or more programs are accredited). *Faculty:* 86. *Students:* 506 full-time (213 women), 11 part-time (8 women). Average age 26. In 2017, 34 master's, 109 doctorates awarded. Terminal master's awarded for partial completion of doctoral program. *Degree requirements:* For master's, thesis; for doctorate, thesis/dissertation (for some programs). *Entrance requirements:* For master's, GRE General Test (for all applicants with cumulative GPA below 3.0); for doctorate, DAT (for DDS); GRE General Test, GRE Subject Test in biology recommended (for PhD). Additional exam requirements/recommendations for international students: Required—TOEFL (minimum score 550 paper-based; 79 iBT), IELTS (minimum score 7), Michigan English Language Assessment Battery (minimum score 82). *Application deadline:* For fall admission, 10/1 for domestic and international students; for summer admission, 4/11 for domestic students, 3/10 for international students. Applications are processed on a rolling basis. Electronic applications accepted. *Expenses:* Contact institution. *Financial support:* Fellowships with tuition reimbursements, research assistantships with tuition reimbursements, teaching assistantships with tuition reimbursements, Federal Work-Study, institutionally sponsored loans, and health care benefits available. Financial award application deadline: 2/15. *Faculty research:* Neurobiology, inflammation and immunity, materials science, bone biology. *Unit head:* Dr. Patrick M. Lloyd, Dean, 614-292-9755, E-mail: lloyd.256@osu.edu. *Application contact:* Graduate and Professional Admissions, 614-292-9444, Fax: 614-292-3895, E-mail: gpadmissions@osu.edu.
Website: http://www.dentistry.osu.edu/

Oregon Health & Science University, School of Dentistry, Graduate Programs in Dentistry, Department of Endodontics, Portland, OR 97239-3098. Offers Certificate. *Entrance requirements:* For degree, GRE General Test. Additional exam requirements/recommendations for international students: Required—TOEFL.

Oregon Health & Science University, School of Dentistry, Graduate Programs in Dentistry, Department of Orthodontics, Portland, OR 97239-3098. Offers MS, Certificate. *Degree requirements:* For master's, thesis. *Entrance requirements:* For master's and Certificate, GRE General Test, DMD/DDS. Additional exam requirements/recommendations for international students: Required—TOEFL.

Oregon Health & Science University, School of Dentistry, Graduate Programs in Dentistry, Department of Pediatric Dentistry, Portland, OR 97239-3098. Offers Certificate.

Oregon Health & Science University, School of Dentistry, Graduate Programs in Dentistry, Department of Periodontology, Portland, OR 97239-3098. Offers MS, Certificate. *Degree requirements:* For master's, thesis. *Entrance requirements:* For master's and Certificate, GRE General Test, DMD/DDS. Additional exam requirements/recommendations for international students: Required—TOEFL.

Oregon Health & Science University, School of Dentistry, Graduate Programs in Dentistry, Department of Restorative Dentistry, Division of Biomaterials and Biomechanics, Portland, OR 97239-3098. Offers MS.

Oregon Health & Science University, School of Dentistry, Graduate Programs in Dentistry, Program in Oral Molecular Biology, Portland, OR 97239-3098. Offers MS.

Oregon Health & Science University, School of Dentistry, Professional Program in Dentistry, Portland, OR 97239-3098. Offers dentistry (DMD); oral and maxillofacial surgery (Certificate); MD/DMD. *Accreditation:* ADA. *Entrance requirements:* For doctorate, DAT. Electronic applications accepted. *Faculty research:* Dentin permeability, tooth sensations, fluoride metabolism, immunology of periodontal disease, craniofacial growth.

Rutgers University–Newark, Rutgers School of Dental Medicine, Newark, NJ 07101-1709. Offers dental science (MS); dentistry (DMD); endodontics (Certificate); oral medicine (Certificate); orthodontics (Certificate); pediatric dentistry (Certificate); periodontics (Certificate); prosthodontics (Certificate); DMD/MPH; DMD/PhD; MD/Certificate; MS/Certificate. DMD/MPH offered jointly with New Jersey Institute of Technology, Rutgers, The State University of New Jersey, Camden. *Accreditation:* ADA (one or more programs are accredited). *Entrance requirements:* For doctorate, DAT. Electronic applications accepted. *Expenses:* Contact institution.

Saint Louis University, Graduate Programs, Center for Advanced Dental Education, St. Louis, MO 63103. Offers endodontics (MSD); orthodontics (MSD); periodontics (MSD). *Degree requirements:* For master's, comprehensive exam, thesis, teaching practicum. *Entrance requirements:* For master's, GRE General Test, NBDE (National Board Dental Exam), DDS or DMD, interview, letters of recommendation. Additional exam requirements/recommendations for international students: Required—TOEFL (minimum score 525 paper-based). Electronic applications accepted. *Faculty research:* Craniofacial growth.

Seton Hill University, Master's and Certificate Program in Orthodontics, Greensburg, PA 15601. Offers MS, Certificate. *Entrance requirements:* For degree, U.S. National Dental Board Exams (Part 1 and Part 2), eligibility for PA licensure, DDS/DMD, minimum GPA of 3.0, transcripts, personal statement. Additional exam requirements/recommendations for international students: Required—TOEFL (minimum score 650 paper-based; 114 iBT), IELTS (minimum score 7). *Application deadline:* Applications are processed on a rolling basis. Electronic applications accepted. *Expenses: Tuition:* Part-time $734 per credit. Tuition and fees vary according to class time, course level, course load and program. *Financial support:* Application deadline: 5/15; applicants required to submit FAFSA.
Website: http://www.setonhill.edu/academics/graduate_programs/orthodontics

Stony Brook University, State University of New York, Stony Brook Medicine, School of Dental Medicine and Graduate School, Department of Oral Biology and Pathology, Stony Brook, NY 11794. Offers MS, PhD. *Faculty:* 8 full-time (3 women), 1 (woman) part-time/adjunct. *Students:* 3 full-time (1 woman), 4 part-time (all women); includes 2 minority (both Asian, non-Hispanic/Latino), 2 international. Average age 35. 1 applicant, 100% accepted. Terminal master's awarded for partial completion of doctoral program. *Degree requirements:* For master's, thesis; for doctorate, thesis/dissertation. *Entrance requirements:* For doctorate, GRE General Test. Additional exam requirements/recommendations for international students: Required—TOEFL. *Application deadline:* For fall admission, 1/15 for domestic students; for spring admission, 10/1 for domestic students. Application fee: $100. *Expenses:* Contact institution. *Financial support:* Fellowships, research assistantships, teaching assistantships, and Federal Work-Study

available. Financial award application deadline: 3/15. *Faculty research:* Oral biology, oral diseases, dentistry, pathology, dental health and hygiene. *Total annual research expenditures:* $921,069. *Unit head:* Dr. Maria Ryan, Chair, 631-632-9529. *Application contact:* Marguerite Baldwin, Graduate Program Coordinator, 631-632-9189, Fax: 631-632-9704, E-mail: marguerite.baldwin@stonybrook.edu.
Website: https://dentistry.stonybrookmedicine.edu/oralbiology

Stony Brook University, State University of New York, Stony Brook Medicine, School of Dental Medicine, Professional Program in Dental Medicine, Stony Brook, NY 11794. Offers dental medicine (DDS); endodontics (Certificate); orthodontics (Certificate); periodontics (Certificate). *Accreditation:* ADA (one or more programs are accredited). *Faculty:* 32 full-time (14 women), 82 part-time/adjunct (24 women). *Students:* 197 full-time (102 women); includes 63 minority (2 Black or African American, non-Hispanic/Latino; 50 Asian, non-Hispanic/Latino; 8 Hispanic/Latino; 3 Two or more races, non-Hispanic/Latino), 2 international. Average age 26. 1,435 applicants, 7% accepted, 52 enrolled. In 2017, 41 doctorates, 9 Certificates awarded. *Entrance requirements:* For doctorate, DAT (minimum score of 17 preferred in all subsections), minimum GPA of 3.0 (preferred). Additional exam requirements/recommendations for international students: Required—TOEFL. *Application deadline:* For fall admission, 12/1 for domestic students. Application fee: $100. *Expenses:* Contact institution. *Financial support:* Research assistantships, teaching assistantships, and Federal Work-Study available. Support available to part-time students. *Faculty research:* Dentistry, oral diseases, oral or maxillofacial surgery. *Unit head:* Dr. Mary R. Truhlar, Dean, 631-632-6985, Fax: 631-632-6621, E-mail: mary.truhlar@stonybrook.edu. *Application contact:* Patricia Berry, Acting Director of Admissions, 631-632-8871, Fax: 631-632-7130, E-mail: patricia.berry@stonybrook.edu.
Website: http://dentistry.stonybrookmedicine.edu/

Temple University, Maurice H. Kornberg School of Dentistry and Graduate School, Graduate Programs in Dentistry, Philadelphia, PA 19122-6096. Offers advanced education in general dentistry (Certificate); endodontology (Certificate); oral biology (MS); orthodontics (Certificate); periodontology (Certificate). *Degree requirements:* For master's, thesis; for Certificate, comprehensive exam. *Entrance requirements:* For master's, GRE; for Certificate, National Boards Parts I and II, DMD or DDS, 3 letters of recommendation. Additional exam requirements/recommendations for international students: Required—TOEFL (minimum score 650 paper-based). *Expenses:* Contact institution. *Faculty research:* Saliva and salivary glands, implantology, material science, periodontal disease, geriatric dentistry.

Texas A&M University, College of Dentistry, Dallas, TX 75266-0677. Offers advanced education in general dentistry (Certificate); biomedical sciences (MS); dental hygiene (MS); dental public health (Certificate); endodontics (Certificate); maxillofacial surgery (Certificate); oral and maxillofacial pathology (Certificate); oral and maxillofacial radiology (Certificate); oral and maxillofacial surgery (Certificate); oral biology (MS, PhD); orthodontics (Certificate); pediatric dentistry (Certificate); periodontics (Certificate); prosthodontics (Certificate). *Accreditation:* ADA; SACS/CC. *Faculty:* 44. *Enrollment:* 499 full-time matriculated graduate/professional students (251 women), 37 part-time matriculated graduate/professional students (12 women). *Students:* 499 full-time (251 women), 37 part-time (12 women); includes 275 minority (54 Black or African American, non-Hispanic/Latino; 2 American Indian or Alaska Native, non-Hispanic/Latino; 100 Asian, non-Hispanic/Latino; 109 Hispanic/Latino; 10 Two or more races, non-Hispanic/Latino), 30 international. Average age 27. In 2017, 18 master's, 2 doctorates, 101 other advanced degrees awarded. *Entrance requirements:* Additional exam requirements/recommendations for international students: Required—TOEFL (minimum score 550 paper-based; 79 iBT). Application fee: $35. Electronic applications accepted. *Expenses:* Contact institution. *Financial support:* In 2017–18, 235 students received support, including 32 research assistantships with tuition reimbursements available (averaging $8,712 per year), 43 teaching assistantships with tuition reimbursements available (averaging $14,231 per year); career-related internships or fieldwork, institutionally sponsored loans, scholarships/grants, traineeships, health care benefits, tuition waivers (full and partial), and unspecified assistantships also available. Support available to part-time students. Financial award applicants required to submit FAFSA. *Unit head:* Dr. Lawrence E. Wolinsky, Dean, 214-828-8300, E-mail: wolinsky@tamhsc.edu. *Application contact:* Ernestine S. Lacy, Associate Dean for Student Affairs and Student Diversity, 214-828-8374, Fax: 214-874-4572, E-mail: eslacy@tamhsc.edu.
Website: http://www.dentistry.tamhsc.edu/

Tufts University, School of Dental Medicine, Advanced Education Programs in Dental Medicine, Medford, MA 02155. Offers dentistry (Certificate), including endodontics, oral and maxillofacial surgery, orthodontics, pediatric dentistry, periodontology, prosthodontics. *Entrance requirements:* Additional exam requirements/recommendations for international students: Required—TOEFL. *Expenses:* Contact institution.

Tufts University, School of Dental Medicine, Graduate Programs in Dental Medicine, Medford, MA 02155. Offers MS. *Degree requirements:* For master's, thesis. *Entrance requirements:* For master's, DDS, DMD, or equivalent; minimum B average. Additional exam requirements/recommendations for international students: Required—TOEFL. *Expenses:* Contact institution. *Faculty research:* Periodontal research, dental materials, salivary research, epidemiology, bone biology.

Université de Montréal, Faculty of Dental Medicine, Program in Multidisciplinary Residency, Montréal, QC H3C 3J7, Canada. Offers Certificate. Electronic applications accepted.

Université de Montréal, Faculty of Dental Medicine, Program in Oral and Dental Sciences, Montréal, QC H3C 3J7, Canada. Offers M Sc. Electronic applications accepted.

Université de Montréal, Faculty of Dental Medicine, Program in Orthodontics, Montréal, QC H3C 3J7, Canada. Offers M Sc. Electronic applications accepted.

Université de Montréal, Faculty of Dental Medicine, Program in Pediatric Dentistry, Montréal, QC H3C 3J7, Canada. Offers M Sc. Electronic applications accepted.

Université de Montréal, Faculty of Dental Medicine, Program in Prosthodontics Rehabilitation, Montréal, QC H3C 3J7, Canada. Offers M Sc. Electronic applications accepted.

Université Laval, Faculty of Dentistry, Diploma Program in Buccal and Maxillofacial Surgery, Québec, QC G1K 7P4, Canada. Offers DESS. *Degree requirements:* For DESS, comprehensive exam. *Entrance requirements:* For degree, interview, knowledge of French. Electronic applications accepted.

Université Laval, Faculty of Dentistry, Diploma Program in Gerodontology, Québec, QC G1K 7P4, Canada. Offers DESS. *Program availability:* Part-time. *Entrance requirements:* For degree, interview, good knowledge of French. Electronic applications accepted.

Université Laval, Faculty of Dentistry, Diploma Program in Multidisciplinary Dentistry, Québec, QC G1K 7P4, Canada. Offers DESS. *Entrance requirements:* For degree, interview, knowledge of French. Electronic applications accepted.

Université Laval, Faculty of Dentistry, Diploma Program in Periodontics, Québec, QC G1K 7P4, Canada. Offers DESS. *Entrance requirements:* For degree, interview, knowledge of French. Electronic applications accepted.

Université Laval, Faculty of Dentistry, Graduate Program in Dentistry, Québec, QC G1K 7P4, Canada. Offers M Sc. *Degree requirements:* For master's, thesis (for some programs). Electronic applications accepted.

University at Buffalo, the State University of New York, Graduate School, School of Dental Medicine, Graduate Programs in Dental Medicine, Department of Oral Biology, Buffalo, NY 14260. Offers PhD. *Degree requirements:* For doctorate, thesis/dissertation. *Entrance requirements:* For doctorate, GRE General Test. Additional exam requirements/recommendations for international students: Required—TOEFL (minimum score 550 paper-based; 79 iBT). Electronic applications accepted. *Faculty research:* Oral immunology and microbiology, bone physiology, biochemistry, molecular genetics, neutrophil biology.

University at Buffalo, the State University of New York, Graduate School, School of Dental Medicine, Graduate Programs in Dental Medicine, Department of Orthodontics, Buffalo, NY 14260. Offers MS, Certificate. *Degree requirements:* For master's, thesis. *Entrance requirements:* For master's, GRE General Test, National Board Dental Exam, DDS or equivalent. Additional exam requirements/recommendations for international students: Required—TOEFL (minimum score 550 paper-based; 79 iBT). Electronic applications accepted. *Faculty research:* Stem cell, clinical respiration, growth and development.

University at Buffalo, the State University of New York, Graduate School, School of Dental Medicine, Graduate Programs in Dental Medicine, Program in Biomaterials, Buffalo, NY 14260. Offers MS. *Program availability:* Part-time. *Degree requirements:* For master's, thesis. *Entrance requirements:* For master's, GRE General Test. Additional exam requirements/recommendations for international students: Required—TOEFL (minimum score 550 paper-based; 79 iBT). Electronic applications accepted. *Faculty research:* Orofacial pain, surface science, bioadhesion, ontology, oral medicine.

University at Buffalo, the State University of New York, Graduate School, School of Dental Medicine, Graduate Programs in Dental Medicine, Program in Oral Sciences, Buffalo, NY 14260. Offers MS. *Degree requirements:* For master's, thesis. *Entrance requirements:* For master's, DDS, DMD or equivalent foreign degree. Additional exam requirements/recommendations for international students: Required—TOEFL (minimum score 550 paper-based; 79 iBT). Electronic applications accepted. *Faculty research:* Oral biology and pathology, behavioral sciences, neuromuscular physiology, facial pain, oral microbiology.

The University of Alabama at Birmingham, School of Dentistry, Graduate Programs in Dentistry, Birmingham, AL 35294. Offers MS. *Degree requirements:* For master's, thesis.

University of Alberta, Faculty of Medicine and Dentistry, Department of Dentistry, Program in Orthodontics, Edmonton, AB T6G 2E1, Canada. Offers M Sc, PhD. *Degree requirements:* For master's, thesis; for doctorate, thesis/dissertation. *Entrance requirements:* Additional exam requirements/recommendations for international students: Required—TOEFL (minimum score 580 paper-based). Electronic applications accepted.

The University of British Columbia, Faculty of Dentistry, Research Training Programs in Dentistry, Vancouver, BC V6T 1Z1, Canada. Offers craniofacial science (M Sc, PhD). *Degree requirements:* For master's, thesis; for doctorate, comprehensive exam, thesis/dissertation. *Entrance requirements:* Additional exam requirements/recommendations for international students: Required—TOEFL (minimum score 580 paper-based). Electronic applications accepted. *Expenses:* Contact institution. *Faculty research:* Cell biology, oral physiology, microbiology, immunology, biomaterials.

University of California, Los Angeles, Graduate Division, College of Letters and Science and David Geffen School of Medicine, UCLA ACCESS to Programs in the Molecular, Cellular and Integrative Life Sciences, Los Angeles, CA 90095. Offers biochemistry and molecular biology (PhD); biological chemistry (PhD); cellular and molecular pathology (PhD); human genetics (PhD); microbiology, immunology, and molecular genetics (PhD); molecular biology (PhD); molecular toxicology (PhD); molecular, cellular and integrative physiology (PhD); neurobiology (PhD); oral biology (PhD); physiology (PhD). *Degree requirements:* For doctorate, thesis/dissertation, oral and written qualifying exams. *Entrance requirements:* For doctorate, GRE General Test, bachelor's degree; minimum undergraduate GPA of 3.0 (or its equivalent if letter grade system not used). Additional exam requirements/recommendations for international students: Required—TOEFL. Electronic applications accepted.

University of California, Los Angeles, School of Dentistry and Graduate Division, Graduate Programs in Dentistry, Program in Oral Biology, Los Angeles, CA 90095. Offers MS, PhD, DDS/MS, DDS/PhD, MD/PhD, MS/Certificate, PhD/Certificate. *Degree requirements:* For master's, thesis; for doctorate, thesis/dissertation, oral and written qualifying exams; 1 quarter of teaching experience. *Entrance requirements:* For master's and doctorate, GRE General Test, bachelor's degree; minimum undergraduate GPA of 3.0 (or its equivalent if letter grade system not used). Additional exam requirements/recommendations for international students: Required—TOEFL. Electronic applications accepted.

University of California, San Francisco, Graduate Division, Program in Oral and Craniofacial Sciences, San Francisco, CA 94143. Offers MS, PhD. Terminal master's awarded for partial completion of doctoral program. *Degree requirements:* For master's, thesis; for doctorate, thesis/dissertation. *Entrance requirements:* For master's and doctorate, GRE General Test.

University of Colorado Denver, School of Dental Medicine, Aurora, CO 80045. Offers dental surgery (DDS); orthodontics (Certificate); periodontics (Certificate). *Accreditation:* ADA. In 2017, 118 doctorates awarded. *Entrance requirements:* For doctorate, DAT, prerequisite courses in microbiology, general biochemistry and English composition (1 semester each); general chemistry/lab, organic chemistry/lab, general biology/lab and general physics/lab (2 semesters each); interview; letters of recommendation; essay. Additional exam requirements/recommendations for international students: Required—TOEFL (minimum score 580 paper-based; 80 iBT); Recommended—IELTS (minimum score 6.8). Application fee: $0. *Faculty research:* Pain control, materials research, geriatric dentistry, restorative dentistry, periodontics. *Unit head:* Dr. Denise K. Kassebaum, Dean, 303-724-7100, Fax: 303-724-7109, E-mail: denise.kassebaum@ucdenver.edu. *Application contact:* Graduate Student Admissions, 303-724-7122, Fax: 303-724-7109, E-mail: ddsadmissioninquiries@ucdenver.edu.
Website: http://www.ucdenver.edu/academics/colleges/dentalmedicine/Pages/DentalMedicine.aspx

University of Connecticut Health Center, Graduate School, Programs in Biomedical Sciences, Combined Degree Programs in Oral Biology, Farmington, CT 06030. Offers DMD/PhD. *Entrance requirements:* Additional exam requirements/recommendations for international students: Required—TOEFL (minimum score 600 paper-based).

University of Connecticut Health Center, School of Dental Medicine, Program in Dental Science, Farmington, CT 06030. Offers MDS. *Program availability:* Part-time. *Degree requirements:* For master's, comprehensive exam, thesis. *Entrance requirements:* For master's, National Board Dental Examination Parts I and II. *Expenses:* Contact institution.

Oral and Dental Sciences

University of Detroit Mercy, School of Dentistry, Detroit, MI 48208. Offers MS, DDS, Certificate. *Accreditation:* ADA (one or more programs are accredited). *Degree requirements:* For master's, thesis. *Entrance requirements:* For master's, DDS or DMD; for doctorate, DAT; for Certificate, DAT, DDS or DMD. *Expenses:* Contact institution. *Faculty research:* HIV and periodontal disease, chemotherapeutic management of periodontal disease, oral analgesics, sterilization/disinfection, prosthodontic materials.

University of Florida, College of Dentistry and Graduate School, Graduate Programs in Dentistry, Department of Endodontics, Gainesville, FL 32611. Offers MS, Certificate. *Entrance requirements:* For master's, DAT, GRE General Test, National Board Dental Examination Parts I and II, minimum GPA of 3.0, interview; for Certificate, DAT. Additional exam requirements/recommendations for international students: Required—TOEFL (minimum score 550 paper-based). *Faculty research:* Canal cleanliness, antibiotics, resilon, lasers, microbes.

University of Florida, College of Dentistry and Graduate School, Graduate Programs in Dentistry, Department of Oral Biology, Gainesville, FL 32611. Offers PhD. *Degree requirements:* For doctorate, thesis/dissertation. *Entrance requirements:* For doctorate, GRE General Test, minimum GPA of 3.0. Additional exam requirements/recommendations for international students: Required—TOEFL. Electronic applications accepted. *Faculty research:* Bacterial genetics, cell adhesion, salivary glands, cell proliferation.

University of Florida, College of Dentistry and Graduate School, Graduate Programs in Dentistry, Department of Orthodontics, Gainesville, FL 32611. Offers MS, Certificate. *Degree requirements:* For master's, thesis. *Entrance requirements:* For master's, DAT, GRE General Test, National Board Dental Examination Parts I and II, minimum GPA of 3.0, interview. Additional exam requirements/recommendations for international students: Required—TOEFL (minimum score 550 paper-based). *Faculty research:* Bone biology, osteoclasts, clinical research, root resorption, pain control.

University of Florida, College of Dentistry and Graduate School, Graduate Programs in Dentistry, Department of Periodontology, Gainesville, FL 32611. Offers MS, Certificate. *Degree requirements:* For master's, thesis. *Entrance requirements:* For master's, DAT, GRE General Test, National Board Dental Examination Parts I and II, minimum GPA of 3.0, interview. Additional exam requirements/recommendations for international students: Required—TOEFL (minimum score 550 paper-based). *Faculty research:* Gingival grafting, periodontal plastic surgery, regenerative periodontal surgery, dental implant complications, osteogenic fibroma.

University of Florida, College of Dentistry and Graduate School, Graduate Programs in Dentistry, Department of Prosthodontics, Gainesville, FL 32611. Offers MS, Certificate. *Degree requirements:* For master's, thesis. *Entrance requirements:* For master's, DAT, GRE General Test, National Board Dental Examination Parts I and II, minimum GPA of 3.0, interview. Additional exam requirements/recommendations for international students: Required—TOEFL (minimum score 550 paper-based). *Faculty research:* Computer panograph, dental implants, resin provisional materials wear rate, implant surface variation, Sjorgen's Syndrome.

University of Illinois at Chicago, College of Dentistry and Graduate College, Graduate Programs in Oral Sciences, Chicago, IL 60607-7128. Offers MS, PhD. *Degree requirements:* For master's, thesis. *Entrance requirements:* For master's, GRE General Test, DDS, DVM, or MD. Additional exam requirements/recommendations for international students: Required—TOEFL. Electronic applications accepted. *Expenses:* Contact institution. *Faculty research:* Medical anthropology and ethnopharmacology research associated with plants and other natural products used for oral medicine conditions, pains and pathologies, craniofacial genetics, genomics, mechanisms of biomineralization, oral microbiology.

The University of Iowa, College of Dentistry and Graduate College, Graduate Programs in Dentistry, Department of Endodontics, Iowa City, IA 52242-1316. Offers MS, Certificate. *Degree requirements:* For master's, thesis. *Entrance requirements:* For master's, GRE, DDS; for Certificate, DDS. Additional exam requirements/recommendations for international students: Required—TOEFL.

The University of Iowa, College of Dentistry and Graduate College, Graduate Programs in Dentistry, Department of Operative Dentistry, Iowa City, IA 52242-1316. Offers MS, Certificate. *Degree requirements:* For master's, thesis. *Entrance requirements:* For master's, GRE, DDS; for Certificate, DDS. Additional exam requirements/recommendations for international students: Required—TOEFL.

The University of Iowa, College of Dentistry and Graduate College, Graduate Programs in Dentistry, Department of Oral and Maxillofacial Surgery, Iowa City, IA 52242-1316. Offers MS, PhD, Certificate. *Degree requirements:* For master's, thesis. *Entrance requirements:* For master's, GRE, DDS; for Certificate, DDS.

The University of Iowa, College of Dentistry and Graduate College, Graduate Programs in Dentistry, Department of Oral Pathology, Radiology and Medicine, Iowa City, IA 52242-1316. Offers MS, PhD, Certificate. *Degree requirements:* For master's, thesis. *Entrance requirements:* For master's, GRE, DDS, minimum GPA of 2.7. Additional exam requirements/recommendations for international students: Required—TOEFL.

The University of Iowa, College of Dentistry and Graduate College, Graduate Programs in Dentistry, Department of Orthodontics, Iowa City, IA 52242-1316. Offers MS, Certificate. *Degree requirements:* For master's, thesis. *Entrance requirements:* For master's, GRE, DDS; for Certificate, DDS. Additional exam requirements/recommendations for international students: Required—TOEFL.

The University of Iowa, College of Dentistry and Graduate College, Graduate Programs in Dentistry, Department of Pediatric Dentistry, Iowa City, IA 52242-1316. Offers Certificate. *Entrance requirements:* For degree, DDS. Additional exam requirements/recommendations for international students: Required—TOEFL.

The University of Iowa, College of Dentistry and Graduate College, Graduate Programs in Dentistry, Department of Periodontics, Iowa City, IA 52242-1316. Offers MS, Certificate. *Degree requirements:* For master's, thesis. *Entrance requirements:* For master's, GRE, DDS; for Certificate, DDS. Additional exam requirements/recommendations for international students: Required—TOEFL.

The University of Iowa, College of Dentistry and Graduate College, Graduate Programs in Dentistry, Department of Preventive and Community Dentistry, Iowa City, IA 52242-1316. Offers dental public health (MS). *Degree requirements:* For master's, thesis. *Entrance requirements:* For master's, GRE, DDS. Additional exam requirements/recommendations for international students: Required—TOEFL.

The University of Iowa, College of Dentistry and Graduate College, Graduate Programs in Dentistry, Department of Prosthodontics, Iowa City, IA 52242-1316. Offers MS, Certificate. *Degree requirements:* For master's, thesis. *Entrance requirements:* For master's, GRE, DDS; for Certificate, DDS. Additional exam requirements/recommendations for international students: Required—TOEFL.

The University of Iowa, College of Dentistry and Graduate College, Graduate Programs in Dentistry, Oral Science Graduate Program, Iowa City, IA 52242-1316. Offers MS, PhD. *Degree requirements:* For master's, thesis; for doctorate, thesis/dissertation. *Entrance requirements:* For master's, GRE, DDS. Additional exam requirements/recommendations for international students: Required—TOEFL.

University of Kentucky, Graduate School, Graduate Program in Dentistry, Lexington, KY 40506-0032. Offers MS. *Degree requirements:* For master's, comprehensive exam, thesis. *Entrance requirements:* For master's, GRE General Test, minimum undergraduate GPA of 2.5. Additional exam requirements/recommendations for international students: Required—TOEFL (minimum score 550 paper-based). Electronic applications accepted.

University of Louisville, School of Dentistry, Louisville, KY 40202. Offers dentistry (DMD); oral biology (MS). *Accreditation:* ADA (one or more programs are accredited). *Program availability:* Part-time. *Faculty:* 77 full-time (32 women), 70 part-time/adjunct (18 women). *Students:* 507 full-time (228 women), 15 part-time (11 women); includes 122 minority (20 Black or African American, non-Hispanic/Latino; 60 Asian, non-Hispanic/Latino; 26 Hispanic/Latino; 16 Two or more races, non-Hispanic/Latino), 16 international. Average age 26. 183 applicants, 93% accepted, 137 enrolled. In 2017, 7 master's, 113 doctorates awarded. *Degree requirements:* For master's, thesis; for doctorate, National Board exams. *Entrance requirements:* For master's, DAT, GRE General Test, or National Board Dental Exam, minimum GPA of 2.75; for doctorate, DAT, 32 hours of course work in science. Additional exam requirements/recommendations for international students: Required—TOEFL (minimum score 100 iBT). *Application deadline:* For fall admission, 1/1 for domestic and international students. Applications are processed on a rolling basis. Application fee: $65. Electronic applications accepted. *Expenses:* Contact institution. *Financial support:* In 2017–18, 1 research assistantship with full tuition reimbursement (averaging $20,000 per year) was awarded. Financial award application deadline: 3/15; financial award applicants required to submit FAFSA. *Faculty research:* Inflammation and periodontitis, birth defects and developmental biology, biomaterials, oral infections, digital imaging. *Total annual research expenditures:* $5.9 million. *Unit head:* Dr. T. Gerry Bradley, Dean, 502-852-5295, E-mail: t0brad03@exchange.louisville.edu. *Application contact:* Robin Benningfield, Admissions Counselor, 502-852-5081, Fax: 502-852-1210, E-mail: dmdadms@louisville.edu.
Website: http://louisville.edu/dental/

The University of Manchester, School of Dentistry, Manchester, United Kingdom. Offers basic dental sciences (cancer studies) (M Phil, PhD); basic dental sciences (molecular genetics) (M Phil, PhD); basic dental sciences (stem cell biology) (M Phil, PhD); biomaterials sciences and dental technology (M Phil, PhD); dental public health/community dentistry (M Phil, PhD); dental science (clinical) (PhD); endodontology (M Phil, PhD); fixed and removable prosthodontics (M Phil, PhD); operative dentistry (M Phil, PhD); oral and maxillofacial surgery (M Phil, PhD); oral radiology (M Phil, PhD); orthodontics (M Phil, PhD); restorative dentistry (M Phil, PhD).

University of Manitoba, Dr. Gerald Niznick College of Dentistry and Faculty of Graduate Studies, Graduate Programs in Dentistry, Department of Dental Diagnostic and Surgical Sciences, Winnipeg, MB R3T 2N2, Canada. Offers oral and maxillofacial surgery (M Dent); periodontology (M Dent). *Entrance requirements:* For master's, dental degree. *Faculty research:* Implantology, clinical trials, tobacco use, periodontal disease.

University of Manitoba, Dr. Gerald Niznick College of Dentistry and Faculty of Graduate Studies, Graduate Programs in Dentistry, Department of Oral Biology, Winnipeg, MB R3T 2N2, Canada. Offers M Sc, PhD. *Degree requirements:* For master's, thesis; for doctorate, comprehensive exam, thesis/dissertation. *Entrance requirements:* For master's, B Sc or pre-M Sc. Additional exam requirements/recommendations for international students: Required—TOEFL. *Faculty research:* Oral bacterial ecology and metabolism, biofilms, saliva and oral health, secretory mechanisms.

University of Manitoba, Dr. Gerald Niznick College of Dentistry and Faculty of Graduate Studies, Graduate Programs in Dentistry, Department of Preventive Dental Science, Winnipeg, MB R3T 2N2, Canada. Offers orthodontics (M Sc). *Degree requirements:* For master's, thesis. *Entrance requirements:* For master's, dental degree. Electronic applications accepted.

University of Maryland, Baltimore, Graduate School, Graduate Programs in Dentistry, Department of Oral Pathology, Baltimore, MD 21201. Offers PhD. *Students:* 3 full-time (1 woman), 2 part-time (1 woman), all international. Average age 32. 8 applicants, 13% accepted, 1 enrolled. *Degree requirements:* For doctorate, comprehensive exam, thesis/dissertation. *Entrance requirements:* For doctorate, GRE General Test, DDS, DMD, minimum GPA of 3.0, curriculum vitae, essay, 3 letters of recommendation. Additional exam requirements/recommendations for international students: Required—TOEFL (minimum score 80 iBT); Recommended—IELTS (minimum score 7). *Application deadline:* For fall admission, 5/1 for domestic students, 1/15 for international students; for spring admission, 10/1 for domestic students. Applications are processed on a rolling basis. Application fee: $75. Electronic applications accepted. *Expenses:* Tuition, state resident: full-time $13,990; part-time $661 per credit. Tuition, nonresident: full-time $30,484; part-time $1310 per credit. *Required fees:* $1894; $94 per credit. $415 per semester. Part-time tuition and fees vary according to course load, degree level and program. *Financial support:* Fellowships, research assistantships, and teaching assistantships available. Support available to part-time students. Financial award application deadline: 3/15; financial award applicants required to submit FAFSA. *Faculty research:* Histopathology, epidemiology of oral lesions, embryology. *Unit head:* Dr. Mark A. Reynolds, Dean and Professor, 410-706-7461, Fax: 410-706-0406, E-mail: mreynolds@umaryland.edu. *Application contact:* Dr. Rania Younis, Director, 410-706-7628, E-mail: ryounis@umaryland.edu.
Website: http://www.dental.umaryland.edu/ods/education/

University of Maryland, Baltimore, Graduate School, Graduate Programs in Dentistry, Graduate Program in Biomedical Sciences, Baltimore, MD 21201. Offers MS, PhD, DDS/PhD. *Students:* 10 full-time (5 women), all international. Average age 30. 12 applicants, 58% accepted, 4 enrolled. In 2017, 17 master's awarded. *Degree requirements:* For doctorate, comprehensive exam, thesis/dissertation. *Entrance requirements:* For doctorate, GRE General Test, minimum GPA of 3.0, curriculum vitae, essay, 3 letters of recommendation. Additional exam requirements/recommendations for international students: Required—TOEFL (minimum score 80 iBT); Recommended—IELTS (minimum score 7). *Application deadline:* For fall admission, 2/15 for domestic students, 1/15 for international students. Application fee: $75. Electronic applications accepted. *Expenses:* Tuition, state resident: full-time $13,990; part-time $661 per credit. Tuition, nonresident: full-time $30,484; part-time $1310 per credit. *Required fees:* $1894; $94 per credit. $415 per semester. Part-time tuition and fees vary according to course load, degree level and program. *Financial support:* In 2017–18, research assistantships with full tuition reimbursements (averaging $23,000 per year) were awarded; Federal Work-Study and health care benefits also available. Financial award application deadline: 3/1; financial award applicants required to submit FAFSA. *Faculty research:* Neuroscience, molecular and cell biology, infectious diseases. *Unit head:* Dr. Pei Feng, Graduate Program Director, 410-706-7340, Fax: 410-706-0865, E-mail: pfeng@umaryland.edu. *Application contact:* Nicki Mitchell, Graduate Program Coordinator, 410-706-6915, Fax: 410-706-0865, E-mail: nmitchell@umaryland.edu.

University of Maryland, Baltimore, Professional and Advanced Education Programs in Dentistry, Baltimore, MD 21201-1627. Offers advanced general dentistry (Certificate); dentistry (DDS); endodontics (Certificate); oral-maxillofacial surgery (Certificate);

orthodontics (Certificate); pediatric dentistry (Certificate); periodontics (Certificate); prosthodontics (Certificate); DDS/MBA; DDS/PhD. *Accreditation:* ADA. *Students:* 583 full-time (311 women), 2 part-time (1 woman); includes 255 minority (58 Black or African American, non-Hispanic/Latino; 126 Asian, non-Hispanic/Latino; 44 Hispanic/Latino; 27 Two or more races, non-Hispanic/Latino), 23 international. Average age 26. 799 applicants, 72% accepted, 133 enrolled. In 2017, 131 doctorates, 22 Certificates awarded. *Entrance requirements:* For doctorate, DAT, coursework in science; for Certificate, National Dental Board Exams, DDS. Additional exam requirements/recommendations for international students: Required—TOEFL (minimum score 550 paper-based; 80 iBT). *Application deadline:* Applications are processed on a rolling basis. Application fee: $85. Electronic applications accepted. *Expenses:* Contact institution. *Financial support:* Career-related internships or fieldwork, Federal Work-Study, scholarships/grants, and traineeships available. Financial award application deadline: 3/1; financial award applicants required to submit FAFSA. *Faculty research:* Pain/neuroscience, oncology/molecular and cell biology, infectious disease/microbiology, bio-material studies, health promotion and disparities. *Unit head:* Dr. Mark A. Reynolds, Dean, 410-706-7461. *Application contact:* Dr. Judith A. Porter, Assistant Dean for Admissions and Recruitment, 410-706-7472, Fax: 410-706-0945, E-mail: ddsadmissions@umaryland.edu.
Website: http://www.dental.umaryland.edu/

University of Michigan, School of Dentistry and Rackham Graduate School, Graduate Programs in Dentistry, Endodontics Program, Ann Arbor, MI 48109-1078. Offers MS. *Students:* 12 full-time (2 women); includes 2 minority (both Asian, non-Hispanic/Latino). 53 applicants, 8% accepted, 4 enrolled. In 2017, 4 master's awarded. *Degree requirements:* For master's, thesis. *Entrance requirements:* For master's, DDS. Additional exam requirements/recommendations for international students: Required—TOEFL (minimum score 84 iBT). *Application deadline:* For fall admission, 7/15 for domestic and international students. Applications are processed on a rolling basis. Application fee: $75 ($90 for international students). Electronic applications accepted. *Expenses:* Contact institution. *Unit head:* Dr. Neville McDonald, Program Director, 734-615-2811, E-mail: somerled@umich.edu. *Application contact:* Patricia Katcher, Associate Admissions Director, 734-763-3316, Fax: 734-764-1922, E-mail: graddentinquiry@umich.edu.
Website: http://www.dent.umich.edu/about-school/department/crse/graduate-endodontics-home

University of Michigan, School of Dentistry and Rackham Graduate School, Graduate Programs in Dentistry, Orthodontics Program, Ann Arbor, MI 48109-1078. Offers MS. *Students:* 21 full-time (11 women); includes 2 minority (1 Black or African American, non-Hispanic/Latino; 1 Asian, non-Hispanic/Latino), 1 international. 190 applicants, 4% accepted, 7 enrolled. In 2017, 7 master's awarded. *Degree requirements:* For master's, thesis. *Entrance requirements:* For master's, GRE, National Dental Board Exam, DDS. Additional exam requirements/recommendations for international students: Required—TOEFL (minimum score 84 iBT). *Application deadline:* For fall admission, 8/15 for domestic and international students. Application fee: $75 ($90 for international students). Electronic applications accepted. *Expenses:* Contact institution. *Unit head:* Dr. Hera Kim-Berman, Program Director, 734-764-1080, E-mail: bermanh@umich.edu. *Application contact:* Patricia Katcher, Associate Admissions Director, 734-763-3316, Fax: 734-764-1922, E-mail: graddentinquiry@umich.edu.
Website: http://www.dent.umich.edu/about-school/department/opd/graduate-program-orthodontics

University of Michigan, School of Dentistry and Rackham Graduate School, Graduate Programs in Dentistry, Pediatric Dentistry Program, Ann Arbor, MI 48109-1078. Offers MS. *Students:* 18 full-time (16 women); includes 10 minority (7 Asian, non-Hispanic/Latino; 2 Hispanic/Latino; 1 Two or more races, non-Hispanic/Latino), 2 international. 109 applicants, 6% accepted, 6 enrolled. In 2017, 6 master's awarded. *Degree requirements:* For master's, thesis. *Entrance requirements:* For master's, National Dental Board Exam, DDS. Additional exam requirements/recommendations for international students: Required—TOEFL (minimum score 84 iBT). *Application deadline:* For fall admission, 10/1 for domestic and international students. Application fee: $75 ($90 for international students). Electronic applications accepted. *Expenses:* Contact institution. *Unit head:* Dr. James Boynton, Program Director, 734-764-1522, E-mail: jboynton@umich.edu. *Application contact:* Patricia Katcher, Associate Admissions Director, 734-763-3316, Fax: 734-764-1922, E-mail: graddentinquiry@umich.edu.
Website: http://www.dent.umich.edu/about-school/department/opd/graduate-program-pediatric-dentistry

University of Michigan, School of Dentistry and Rackham Graduate School, Graduate Programs in Dentistry, Periodontics Program, Ann Arbor, MI 48109-1078. Offers MS. *Students:* 14 full-time (7 women); includes 4 minority (3 Asian, non-Hispanic/Latino; 1 Hispanic/Latino). 51 applicants, 10% accepted, 5 enrolled. In 2017, 3 master's awarded. *Degree requirements:* For master's, thesis. *Entrance requirements:* For master's, DDS. Additional exam requirements/recommendations for international students: Required—TOEFL (minimum score 84 iBT). *Application deadline:* For fall admission, 8/30 for domestic and international students. Applications are processed on a rolling basis. Application fee: $75 ($90 for international students). Electronic applications accepted. *Expenses:* Contact institution. *Unit head:* Dr. Hom-Lay Wang, Program Director, 734-764-1948, E-mail: homlay@umich.edu. *Application contact:* Patricia Katcher, Associate Admissions Director, 734-763-3316, Fax: 734-764-1922, E-mail: graddentinquiry@umich.edu.
Website: http://www.dent.umich.edu/about-school/department/pom/academic-programs-pom

University of Michigan, School of Dentistry and Rackham Graduate School, Graduate Programs in Dentistry, Prosthodontics Program, Ann Arbor, MI 48109-1078. Offers MS. *Students:* 13 full-time (6 women); includes 2 minority (1 Black or African American, non-Hispanic/Latino; 1 Asian, non-Hispanic/Latino), 9 international. 48 applicants, 15% accepted, 5 enrolled. In 2017, 4 master's awarded. *Degree requirements:* For master's, thesis. *Entrance requirements:* For master's, DDS. Additional exam requirements/recommendations for international students: Required—TOEFL (minimum score 84 iBT). *Application deadline:* For fall admission, 9/1 for domestic and international students. Applications are processed on a rolling basis. Application fee: $75 ($90 for international students). Electronic applications accepted. *Expenses:* Contact institution. *Unit head:* Dr. Michael Razzoog, Program Director, 734-763-5280, E-mail: merim@umich.edu. *Application contact:* Patricia Katcher, Associate Admissions Director, 734-763-3316, Fax: 734-764-1922, E-mail: graddentinquiry@umich.edu.
Website: http://www.dent.umich.edu/about-school/department/bms/prosthodontics/prosthodontic-graduate-program

University of Michigan, School of Dentistry and Rackham Graduate School, Graduate Programs in Dentistry, Restorative Dentistry Program, Ann Arbor, MI 48109-1078. Offers MS. *Students:* 19 full-time (5 women); includes 4 minority (2 Asian, non-Hispanic/Latino; 2 Hispanic/Latino). 47 applicants, 23% accepted, 7 enrolled. In 2017, 6 master's awarded. *Degree requirements:* For master's, thesis. *Entrance requirements:* For master's, DDS. Additional exam requirements/recommendations for international students: Required—TOEFL (minimum score 84 iBT). *Application deadline:* For fall admission, 9/1 for domestic and international students. Applications are processed on a rolling basis. Application fee: $75 ($90 for international students). Electronic applications accepted. *Expenses:* Contact institution. *Unit head:* Dr. Gisele Neiva, Program Director, 734-647-3722, E-mail: gisele@umich.edu. *Application contact:* Patricia Katcher, Associate Admissions Director, 734-763-3316, Fax: 734-764-1922, E-mail: graddentinquiry@umich.edu.
Website: http://www.dent.umich.edu/about-school/department/crse/graduate-restorative

University of Michigan, School of Dentistry, Oral Health Sciences PhD Program, Ann Arbor, MI 48109-1078. Offers PhD. *Faculty:* 33 full-time (9 women). *Students:* 17 full-time (10 women); includes 4 minority (3 Asian, non-Hispanic/Latino; 1 Two or more races, non-Hispanic/Latino), 5 international. Average age 29. 28 applicants, 18% accepted, 5 enrolled. In 2017, 2 doctorates awarded. *Degree requirements:* For doctorate, thesis/dissertation, preliminary exam, oral defense of dissertation. *Entrance requirements:* For doctorate, GRE. Additional exam requirements/recommendations for international students: Required—TOEFL (minimum score 560 paper-based, 84 iBT) or IELTS (6.5). *Application deadline:* For fall admission, 12/5 for domestic and international students. Applications are processed on a rolling basis. Application fee: $75 ($90 for international students). Electronic applications accepted. *Expenses:* Contact institution. *Financial support:* In 2017–18, 7 students received support, including fellowships with full tuition reimbursements available (averaging $29,000 per year), research assistantships with full tuition reimbursements available (averaging $29,000 per year); scholarships/grants and health care benefits also available. Financial award application deadline: 12/5. *Faculty research:* Craniofacial development, oral and pharyngeal cancer, mineralized tissue biology and musculoskeletal disorders, tissue engineering and regeneration, oral infectious and immunologic diseases, oral sensory systems and central circuits. *Total annual research expenditures:* $16.8 million. *Unit head:* Dr. Jan Hu, Director, 734-615-1970, E-mail: janhu@umich.edu. *Application contact:* Kimberly G. Smith, Project and Administrative Coordinator, 734-763-3388, E-mail: kimbsmit@umich.edu.
Website: http://dent.umich.edu/phd

University of Minnesota, Twin Cities Campus, School of Dentistry and Graduate School, Graduate Programs in Dentistry, Advanced Education Program in Periodontology, Minneapolis, MN 55455-0213. Offers MS. *Degree requirements:* For master's, comprehensive exam, thesis. *Entrance requirements:* For master's, DDS/DMD, letter from Dental Dean, specific GGP/class rank, two letters of recommendation. Additional exam requirements/recommendations for international students: Required—TOEFL (minimum score 590 paper-based). *Faculty research:* Periodontitis, risk factors, regenerating, diabetes immunology.

University of Minnesota, Twin Cities Campus, School of Dentistry and Graduate School, Graduate Programs in Dentistry, Division of Endodontics, Minneapolis, MN 55455-0213. Offers MS, Certificate. *Degree requirements:* For master's, thesis. *Entrance requirements:* Additional exam requirements/recommendations for international students: Required—TOEFL. *Faculty research:* Pain, inflammation, neuropharmacology, neuropeptides, cytokines.

University of Minnesota, Twin Cities Campus, School of Dentistry and Graduate School, Graduate Programs in Dentistry, Division of Orthodontics, Minneapolis, MN 55455-0213. Offers MS. *Degree requirements:* For master's, thesis. *Entrance requirements:* Additional exam requirements/recommendations for international students: Required—TOEFL (minimum score 587 paper-based). *Faculty research:* Bone biology, 3-D imaging.

University of Minnesota, Twin Cities Campus, School of Dentistry and Graduate School, Graduate Programs in Dentistry, Division of Pediatric Dentistry, Minneapolis, MN 55455-0213. Offers MS. *Degree requirements:* For master's, thesis. *Entrance requirements:* Additional exam requirements/recommendations for international students: Required—TOEFL. *Faculty research:* Molecular genetics of facial growth, dental material/adhesion, expanded functions dental auxiliary utilization.

University of Minnesota, Twin Cities Campus, School of Dentistry and Graduate School, Graduate Programs in Dentistry, Division of Prosthodontics, Minneapolis, MN 55455-0213. Offers MS. *Degree requirements:* For master's, thesis, clinical. *Entrance requirements:* Additional exam requirements/recommendations for international students: Required—TOEFL.

University of Minnesota, Twin Cities Campus, School of Dentistry and Graduate School, Graduate Programs in Dentistry, Program in Oral Biology, Minneapolis, MN 55455-0213. Offers MS, PhD. *Degree requirements:* For master's, thesis. *Faculty research:* Microbiology, neuroscience, biomaterials, biochemistry, cancer biology.

University of Minnesota, Twin Cities Campus, School of Dentistry and Graduate School, Graduate Programs in Dentistry, Program in Oral Health Services for Older Adults (Geriatrics), Minneapolis, MN 55455-0213. Offers MS, Certificate. *Degree requirements:* For master's, thesis (for some programs). *Entrance requirements:* For master's, DDS degree or equivalent. Additional exam requirements/recommendations for international students: Required—TOEFL (minimum score 560 paper-based). Electronic applications accepted. *Faculty research:* Geriatrics dental care, long-term care dental services, oral-systemic health relationships, utilization of care by older adults.

University of Minnesota, Twin Cities Campus, School of Dentistry and Graduate School, Graduate Programs in Dentistry, Program in Temporomandibular Joint Disorders, Minneapolis, MN 55455-0213. Offers MS. *Degree requirements:* For master's, comprehensive exam, thesis. *Entrance requirements:* Additional exam requirements/recommendations for international students: Required—TOEFL. Electronic applications accepted. *Faculty research:* Clinical trials, TMJ mechanicals, diagnostic criteria, biomarkers, genetics.

University of Mississippi Medical Center, School of Dentistry, Department of Craniofacial and Dental Research, Jackson, MS 39216-4505. Offers MS, PhD.

University of Missouri–Kansas City, School of Dentistry, Kansas City, MO 64110-2499. Offers advanced education in dentistry (Graduate Dental Certificate); dental hygiene education (MS); endodontics (Graduate Dental Certificate); oral and maxillofacial surgery (Graduate Dental Certificate); oral biology (MS, PhD); orthodontics and dentofacial orthopedics (Graduate Dental Certificate); periodontics (Graduate Dental Certificate). PhD (interdisciplinary) offered through the School of Graduate Studies. *Accreditation:* ADA (one or more programs are accredited). *Degree requirements:* For master's, thesis; for doctorate, thesis/dissertation (for some programs). *Entrance requirements:* For master's, DAT, letters of evaluation, personal interview; for doctorate, DAT (for DDS); for Graduate Dental Certificate, DDS. Additional exam requirements/recommendations for international students: Required—TOEFL (minimum score 550 paper-based; 80 iBT). *Expenses:* Contact institution. *Faculty research:* Biomaterials, dental use of lasers, effectiveness of periodontal treatments, temporomandibular joint dysfunction.

University of Missouri–Kansas City, School of Graduate Studies, Kansas City, MO 64110-2499. Offers interdisciplinary studies (PhD), including art history, cell biology and biophysics, chemistry, computer and electrical engineering, computer science and informatics, economics, education, engineering, English, entrepreneurship and innovation, geosciences, history, mathematics and statistics, molecular biology and biochemistry, music education, oral and craniofacial sciences, pharmaceutical sciences, pharmacology, physics, political science, public affairs and administration, religious studies, social science, telecommunications and computer networking; PMBA/MHA. *Degree requirements:* For doctorate, comprehensive exam, thesis/dissertation, residency. *Entrance requirements:* For doctorate, GRE General Test, minimum GPA of 2.75 (undergraduate), 3.0 (graduate). Additional exam requirements/recommendations for international students: Required—TOEFL (minimum score 550 paper-based; 80 iBT), TWE (minimum score 4). Electronic applications accepted.

University of Nebraska Medical Center, Medical Sciences Interdepartmental Area, Omaha, NE 68198-4000. Offers applied behavior analysis (PhD); clinical translational research (MS, PhD); health practice and medical education research (MS); oral biology (MS, PhD). *Program availability:* Part-time. *Faculty:* 170 full-time, 20 part-time/adjunct. *Students:* 48 full-time (31 women), 59 part-time (37 women); includes 34 minority (1 Black or African American, non-Hispanic/Latino; 30 Asian, non-Hispanic/Latino; 3 Hispanic/Latino). Average age 32. 68 applicants, 34% accepted, 23 enrolled. In 2017, 26 master's, 915 doctorates awarded. Terminal master's awarded for partial completion of doctoral program. *Degree requirements:* For master's, comprehensive exam, thesis; for doctorate, comprehensive exam, thesis/dissertation. *Entrance requirements:* For master's, GRE General Test; for doctorate, GRE General Test, MCAT, DAT, LSAT. Additional exam requirements/recommendations for international students: Required—TOEFL (minimum score 550 paper-based; 80 iBT). *Application deadline:* For fall admission, 6/1 for domestic students, 4/1 for international students; for spring admission, 10/1 for domestic students, 9/1 for international students. Applications are processed on a rolling basis. Application fee: $60. Electronic applications accepted. *Expenses:* Contact institution. *Financial support:* In 2017–18, 72 students received support, including 1 fellowship with full tuition reimbursement available (averaging $23,400 per year), 37 research assistantships with full tuition reimbursements available (averaging $23,400 per year), 2 teaching assistantships with full tuition reimbursements available (averaging $23,400 per year); scholarships/grants and health care benefits also available. Financial award application deadline: 2/15; financial award applicants required to submit FAFSA. *Faculty research:* Molecular genetics, oral biology, veterinary pathology, newborn medicine, immunology, clinical research. *Unit head:* Dr. Laura Bilek, Graduate Committee Chair, 402-559-6923, E-mail: lbilek@unmc.edu. *Application contact:* Rhonda Sheibal-Carver, Interdisciplinary Programs Coordinator, 402-559-5141, E-mail: rhonda.sheibalcarver@unmc.edu.
Website: https://www.unmc.edu/msia/index.html

University of Nevada, Las Vegas, School of Dental Medicine, Las Vegas, NV 89106. Offers dental medicine (DMD); dental surgery (DDS); dentistry (DMD); oral biology (MS); orthodontics and dentofacial orthopedics (Certificate). *Accreditation:* ADA. *Program availability:* Part-time, evening/weekend, online learning. *Faculty:* 67 full-time (28 women), 57 part-time/adjunct (17 women). *Students:* 356 full-time (152 women); includes 118 minority (3 Black or African American, non-Hispanic/Latino; 2 American Indian or Alaska Native, non-Hispanic/Latino; 71 Asian, non-Hispanic/Latino; 23 Hispanic/Latino; 2 Native Hawaiian or other Pacific Islander, non-Hispanic/Latino; 17 Two or more races, non-Hispanic/Latino), 3 international. Average age 28. 1,754 applicants, 7% accepted, 88 enrolled. In 2017, 5 master's, 75 doctorates, 6 other advanced degrees awarded. *Entrance requirements:* For doctorate, DAT; for Certificate, National Board Dental Exam part 1 and 2. Additional exam requirements/recommendations for international students: Required—TOEFL (minimum score 550 paper-based; 80 iBT), IELTS (minimum score 7). *Application deadline:* For fall admission, 1/1 for domestic and international students; for summer admission, 3/1 for domestic students. Applications are processed on a rolling basis. Application fee: $75. Electronic applications accepted. *Expenses:* Contact institution. *Financial support:* In 2017–18, 28 students received support. Federal Work-Study, institutionally sponsored loans, scholarships/grants, health care benefits, and unspecified assistantships available. Support available to part-time students. Financial award application deadline: 3/15; financial award applicants required to submit FAFSA. *Faculty research:* HPV, oral cancer, flouridtion, microbiology, virology in oral infectious disease, oral-systemic linkages to periodontal disease. *Total annual research expenditures:* $941,448. *Unit head:* Dr. Christine C. Ancajas, Assistant Dean of Admissions and Student Affairs, 702-774-2522, Fax: 702-774-2521, E-mail: christine.ancajas@unlv.edu. *Application contact:* Kamber Davoren, Admissions and Records Assistant, 702-774-2520, Fax: 702-774-2520, E-mail: kamber.davoren@unlv.edu.
Website: http://www.unlv.edu/dental

The University of North Carolina at Chapel Hill, School of Dentistry and Graduate School, Graduate Programs in Dentistry, Chapel Hill, NC 27599. Offers dental hygiene (MS); endodontics (MS); epidemiology (PhD); operative dentistry (MS); oral and maxillofacial pathology (MS); oral and maxillofacial radiology (MS); oral biology (PhD); orthodontics (MS); pediatric dentistry (MS); periodontology (MS); prosthodontics (MS). *Degree requirements:* For master's, thesis; for doctorate, thesis/dissertation. *Entrance requirements:* For master's, GRE General Test (for orthodontics and oral biology only); National Dental Board Part I (Part II if available), dental degree (for all except dental hygiene); for doctorate, GRE General Test. Additional exam requirements/recommendations for international students: Required—TOEFL (minimum score 550 paper-based; 79 iBT). Electronic applications accepted. *Expenses:* Contact institution. *Faculty research:* Clinical research, inflammation, immunology, neuroscience, molecular biology.

University of Oklahoma Health Sciences Center, College of Dentistry and Graduate College, Graduate Programs in Dentistry, Department of Orthodontics, Oklahoma City, OK 73190. Offers MS. *Degree requirements:* For master's, thesis. *Entrance requirements:* For master's, minimum GPA of 3.0, DDS/DMD. Additional exam requirements/recommendations for international students: Required—TOEFL. Electronic applications accepted. *Faculty research:* Craniofacial growth and development, biomechanical principles in orthodontics.

University of Oklahoma Health Sciences Center, College of Dentistry and Graduate College, Graduate Programs in Dentistry, Department of Periodontics, Oklahoma City, OK 73190. Offers MS. *Degree requirements:* For master's, thesis. *Entrance requirements:* For master's, DDS/DMD, minimum GPA of 3.0. Additional exam requirements/recommendations for international students: Required—TOEFL (minimum score 550 paper-based). Electronic applications accepted.

University of Pittsburgh, School of Dental Medicine, Advanced Education Program in Oral and Maxillofacial Pathology, Pittsburgh, PA 15260. Offers Certificate. *Faculty:* 2 full-time (1 woman), 1 (woman) part-time/adjunct. *Students:* 3 full-time (2 women); includes 1 minority (Asian, non-Hispanic/Latino). Average age 30. 2 applicants, 100% accepted, 1 enrolled. In 2017, 1 Certificate awarded. *Entrance requirements:* For degree, National Board Dental Exam Parts 1 and 2, three letters of recommendation, official transcripts, current curriculum vitae, one-page personal statement, DMD/DDS from U.S. or Canada. *Application deadline:* For fall admission, 10/1 for domestic students. Applications are processed on a rolling basis. Application fee: $50. Electronic applications accepted. Application fee is waived when completed online. *Expenses:* Contact institution. *Financial support:* Scholarships/grants, health care benefits, and stipends (averaging $56,000 per year) available. *Faculty research:* Quality assurance, odontogenic tumors, treatment outcomes. *Unit head:* Dr. Kurt F. Summersgill, Program Director, 412-648-8635, Fax: 412-383-9142, E-mail: kfs8@pitt.edu. *Application contact:* Erin King, Coordinator, 412-648-8636, Fax: 412-383-9142, E-mail: emk74@pitt.edu.
Website: https://www.dental.pitt.edu/residency-program-oral-and-maxillofacial-pathology

University of Pittsburgh, School of Dental Medicine, Department of Dental Anesthesiology, Pittsburgh, PA 15260. Offers Certificate. *Program availability:* Part-time, online learning. *Faculty:* 3 full-time (0 women), 9 part-time/adjunct (0 women). *Students:* 12 full-time (4 women); includes 3 minority (2 Black or African American, non-Hispanic/Latino; 1 Asian, non-Hispanic/Latino). Average age 29. 22 applicants, 18% accepted, 4 enrolled. *Entrance requirements:* Additional exam requirements/recommendations for international students: Required—TOEFL. *Application deadline:* For fall admission, 9/15 for domestic students. *Faculty research:* General anesthesia utilization trends by board certified pediatric dentists; practice patterns of dentist anesthesiologists in North America. *Unit head:* Dr. Michael A. Cuddy, Program Director, 412-648-9901, Fax: 412-648-2591, E-mail: mc2@pitt.edu. *Application contact:* Lisa Lehman, Department Administrator, 412-648-8609, Fax: 412-648-2591, E-mail: lrl12@pitt.edu.

University of Pittsburgh, School of Dental Medicine, Department of Endodontics, Pittsburgh, PA 15260. Offers Certificate. *Faculty:* 3 full-time (0 women), 9 part-time/adjunct (3 women). *Students:* 8 full-time (3 women). Average age 35. 120 applicants, 5% accepted, 4 enrolled. *Degree requirements:* For Certificate, thesis optional, 300 root canals, 15 surgery cases. *Entrance requirements:* For degree, DDS/DMD. Additional exam requirements/recommendations for international students: Required—TOEFL. *Application deadline:* For fall admission, 9/1 for domestic and international students. Application fee: $50. *Faculty research:* Pulpal regeneration, micro CT analysis of obturation methods, resistance to fracture, micro CT analysis of instrument techniques, access preparation and relation to fracture. *Unit head:* Dr. Herbert L. Ray, Chair, 412-648-8647, Fax: 412-383-9478. *Application contact:* Rosann Donahoe, Department Administrator, 412-648-8647, Fax: 412-383-9478, E-mail: rod8@pitt.edu.

University of Pittsburgh, School of Dental Medicine, Department of Oral and Maxillofacial Surgery, Pittsburgh, PA 15213. Offers oral and maxillofacial surgery (Certificate); pediatric cranio-maxillofacial surgery (Certificate). *Faculty:* 9 full-time (0 women), 3 part-time/adjunct (1 woman). *Students:* 18 full-time (2 women); includes 4 minority (all Asian, non-Hispanic/Latino). Average age 25. 256 applicants, 1% accepted, 3 enrolled. In 2017, 4 Certificates awarded. *Degree requirements:* For Certificate, comprehensive exam. *Entrance requirements:* For degree, National Boards Part I, U.S. or Canadian dental degree (DDS or DMD). Additional exam requirements/recommendations for international students: Required—TOEFL. *Application deadline:* For fall admission, 9/1 for domestic students. Applications are processed on a rolling basis. Application fee: $0. Electronic applications accepted. *Financial support:* In 2017–18, 4 fellowships with partial tuition reimbursements (averaging $36,000 per year) were awarded; scholarships/grants, health care benefits, and tuition waivers also available. *Faculty research:* Cleft craniofacial anomaly, facial trauma, TMJ, craniofacial tissue regeneration, dental implants. *Unit head:* Dr. Richard E. Bauer, Program Director, 412-648-6801, Fax: 412-648-6835, E-mail: bauerre@upmc.edu. *Application contact:* Andrea M. Ford, Residency Coordinator, 412-648-6801, Fax: 412-648-6835, E-mail: fordam@upmc.edu.
Website: http://www.dental.pitt.edu/

University of Pittsburgh, School of Dental Medicine, Department of Oral Biology, Pittsburgh, PA 15261. Offers oral biology (MS, PhD), including craniofacial genetics (PhD), craniofacial regeneration (PhD). *Program availability:* Part-time. *Faculty:* 15 full-time (5 women). *Students:* 15 full-time (8 women), 1 (woman) part-time; includes 6 minority (5 Asian, non-Hispanic/Latino; 1 Hispanic/Latino). Average age 24. 17 applicants, 35% accepted, 4 enrolled. In 2017, 2 master's awarded. Terminal master's awarded for partial completion of doctoral program. *Degree requirements:* For master's, thesis; for doctorate, comprehensive exam, thesis/dissertation. *Entrance requirements:* For master's and doctorate, GRE, BS or equivalent; minimum undergraduate GPA of 3.0. Additional exam requirements/recommendations for international students: Required—TOEFL (minimum score 100 iBT). *Application deadline:* For winter admission, 1/15 for domestic and international students. Application fee: $50. Electronic applications accepted. *Expenses:* $30,500 per year. *Financial support:* In 2017–18, 4 research assistantships with tuition reimbursements (averaging $31,000 per year) were awarded. Financial award application deadline: 1/15. *Faculty research:* Tissue engineering, craniofacial genetics, mineralized tissue, TMJ. *Unit head:* Dr. Elia Beniash, Professor/Chair, 412-648-0108, E-mail: ebeniash@pitt.edu. *Application contact:* Lynn Marendo, Program Administrator, 412-373-7695, E-mail: lmk55@pitt.edu.
Website: http://www.dental.pitt.edu/oral-biology-academic-programs

University of Pittsburgh, School of Dental Medicine, Department of Orthodontics and Dentofacial Orthopedics, Pittsburgh, PA 15261. Offers orthodontics (MDS, Certificate). *Faculty:* 2 full-time (0 women), 12 part-time/adjunct (2 women). *Students:* 12 full-time (7 women); includes 5 minority (all Asian, non-Hispanic/Latino). Average age 27. 174 applicants, 2% accepted, 4 enrolled. *Degree requirements:* For master's, comprehensive exam, thesis; for Certificate, comprehensive exam. *Entrance requirements:* For master's and Certificate, National Boards Parts I and II. *Application deadline:* For fall admission, 9/1 for domestic students. *Unit head:* Dr. Joseph F. A. Petrone, Chair, 412-648-8638, Fax: 412-648-8817, E-mail: jfap@pitt.edu. *Application contact:* Lauren B. Lagana, Department Administrator, 412-648-8419, Fax: 412-648-8817, E-mail: lmb111@pitt.edu.
Website: http://www.dental.pitt.edu/department/orthodontics-and-dentofacial-orthopedics

University of Pittsburgh, School of Dental Medicine, Department of Pediatric Dentistry, Pittsburgh, PA 15260. Offers dental science (MDS); multidisciplinary public health (MPH); pediatric dentistry (Certificate). *Accreditation:* ADA. *Faculty:* 3 full-time (all women), 10 part-time/adjunct (6 women). *Students:* 6 full-time (5 women); includes 2 minority (1 Asian, non-Hispanic/Latino; 1 Native Hawaiian or other Pacific Islander, non-Hispanic/Latino). Average age 34. 45 applicants, 9% accepted, 4 enrolled. *Degree requirements:* For master's, thesis. *Entrance requirements:* For degree, National Dental Board Examinations Parts I and II, DDS or DMD from U.S. or Canadian dental school. *Application deadline:* For fall admission, 10/1 for domestic students. Electronic applications accepted. *Expenses:* $49,280 per year in-state, $59,774 out-of-state; $850 mandatory fees. *Financial support:* In 2017–18, 6 students received support. Traineeships and stipends (averaging $24,000 per year) available. *Faculty research:* Behavior management techniques, mouth guard use, obesity and dental development, non-nutritive sucking habits, infant oral health. *Unit head:* Dr. Deborah Studen-Pavlovich, Program Director, 412-648-8183, Fax: 412-648-8435, E-mail: das12@pitt.edu. *Application contact:* Sharon A. Hohman, Departmental Secretary, 412-648-8416, Fax: 412-648-8435.
Website: http://www.dental.pitt.edu

University of Pittsburgh, School of Dental Medicine, Department of Periodontics and Preventive Dentistry, Pittsburgh, PA 15261. Offers periodontics (MDS, Certificate). *Faculty:* 6 full-time (2 women), 9 part-time/adjunct (1 woman). *Students:* 9 full-time (4 women); includes 4 minority (all Asian, non-Hispanic/Latino). Average age 30. 41 applicants, 7% accepted, 3 enrolled. *Entrance requirements:* For degree, DMD, DDS. *Application deadline:* For fall admission, 8/1 priority date for domestic students.

Application fee: $50. Electronic applications accepted. *Expenses:* $53,764 per year (for first two years), $4,040 (for third year). *Financial support:* Stipends (averaging $25,000 per year) available. *Faculty research:* Implantology, osteoporosis, periosystemic disease, regeneration. *Unit head:* Dr. Kelly Williams, Residency Director, 412-648-8837, Fax: 412-648-8594. *Application contact:* Alycia Maltony, Alumni Affairs/Development and Residency Education Administrator, 412-648-5096, Fax: 412-648-8637, E-mail: aam111@pitt.edu.
Website: http://www.dental.pitt.edu/department/periodontics-and-preventive-dentistry

University of Pittsburgh, School of Dental Medicine, Department of Prosthodontics, Pittsburgh, PA 15261. Offers MDS, Certificate. *Faculty:* 2 full-time (0 women), 2 part-time/adjunct (0 women). *Students:* 7 full-time (1 woman); includes 1 minority (Asian, non-Hispanic/Latino). Average age 29. 48 applicants, 21% accepted, 3 enrolled. *Degree requirements:* For master's, thesis. *Entrance requirements:* Additional exam requirements/recommendations for international students: Required—TOEFL (minimum score 95 iBT). *Application deadline:* For fall admission, 10/30 for domestic and international students. Application fee: $50. *Expenses:* $49,724 in-state tuition, $59,630 out-of-state. *Financial support:* Institutionally sponsored loans, scholarships/grants, and stipends available. *Faculty research:* Dental implants. *Unit head:* Dr. Robert L. Engelmeies, DMD, Graduate Program Director, 412-648-8675, Fax: 412-648-8850, E-mail: rle14@pitt.edu.

University of Puerto Rico–Medical Sciences Campus, School of Dental Medicine, Graduate Programs in Dentistry, San Juan, PR 00936-5067. Offers general dentistry (Certificate); oral and maxillofacial surgery (Certificate); orthodontics (Certificate); pediatric dentistry (Certificate); prosthodontics (Certificate). *Degree requirements:* For Certificate, comprehensive exam (for some programs). *Entrance requirements:* For degree, National Board Dental Exam I, National Board Dental Exam II, DDS or DMD, interview. Electronic applications accepted. *Expenses:* Contact institution. *Faculty research:* Analgesic drugs, anti-inflammatory drugs, saliva cytoanalysis, dental materials, oral epidemiology and dental caries.

University of Rochester, School of Medicine and Dentistry, Graduate Programs in Medicine and Dentistry, Center for Oral Biology, Rochester, NY 14627. Offers dental science (MS). *Degree requirements:* For master's, thesis. *Entrance requirements:* For master's, GRE General Test, DDS or equivalent.

University of Southern California, Graduate School, Herman Ostrow School of Dentistry and Graduate School, Department of Craniofacial Biology, Los Angeles, CA 90089. Offers MS, PhD, Graduate Certificate. Terminal master's awarded for partial completion of doctoral program. *Degree requirements:* For master's, comprehensive exam, thesis; for doctorate, comprehensive exam, thesis/dissertation. *Entrance requirements:* For master's and doctorate, GRE, undergraduate degree. Additional exam requirements/recommendations for international students: Required—TOEFL. Electronic applications accepted. *Faculty research:* Orthodontics, periodontics, tooth development, oral biology, stem cell biology.

The University of Tennessee Health Science Center, College of Graduate Health Sciences, Memphis, TN 38163. Offers biomedical engineering (MS, PhD); biomedical sciences (PhD); dental sciences (MDS); epidemiology (MS); health outcomes and policy research (PhD); laboratory research and management (MS); nursing science (PhD); pharmaceutical sciences (PhD); pharmacology (MS); speech and hearing science (PhD); DDS/PhD; DNP/PhD; MD/PhD; Pharm D/PhD. MS and PhD programs in biomedical engineering offered jointly with University of Memphis. *Faculty:* 528 full-time (176 women). *Students:* 258 full-time (130 women); includes 87 minority (14 Black or African American, non-Hispanic/Latino; 68 Asian, non-Hispanic/Latino; 5 Hispanic/Latino). Average age 28. 673 applicants, 17% accepted, 102 enrolled. In 2017, 23 master's, 30 doctorates awarded. Terminal master's awarded for partial completion of doctoral program. *Degree requirements:* For master's, comprehensive exam, thesis; for doctorate, thesis/dissertation, oral and written preliminary and comprehensive exams. *Entrance requirements:* For master's and doctorate, GRE General Test, minimum GPA of 3.0. Additional exam requirements/recommendations for international students: Recommended—TOEFL (minimum score 79 iBT), IELTS (minimum score 6.5). *Application deadline:* For winter admission, 1/1 for domestic and international students; for spring admission, 3/1 for domestic and international students. Applications are processed on a rolling basis. Application fee: $0. Electronic applications accepted. *Expenses:* Contact institution. *Financial support:* In 2017–18, 150 students received support, including 150 research assistantships (averaging $25,000 per year); fellowships, institutionally sponsored loans, scholarships/grants, health care benefits, and tuition waivers (full and partial) also available. Support available to part-time students. *Faculty research:* Cell biology, epidemiology, biomedical engineering, speech and hearing science, health policy, pharmaceutical sciences, dental sciences, nursing science, pharmacology. *Unit head:* Dr. Donald B. Thomason, Dean, 901-448-5538, E-mail: dthomaso@uthsc.edu. *Application contact:* Dr. Isaac O. Donkor, Associate Dean for Student Affairs, 901-448-5538, E-mail: idonkor@uthsc.edu.
Website: http://grad.uthsc.edu/

The University of Toledo, College of Graduate Studies, College of Medicine and Life Sciences, Department of Surgery, Toledo, OH 43606-3390. Offers oral biology (MSBS). *Degree requirements:* For master's, thesis or alternative. *Entrance requirements:* For master's, DAT, minimum undergraduate GPA of 3.0, three letters of recommendation, statement of purpose, transcripts from all prior institutions attended, acceptance into Pediatric Dental Residency Program at UT. Additional exam requirements/recommendations for international students: Required—TOEFL (minimum score 550 paper-based; 80 iBT). Electronic applications accepted. *Faculty research:* Oral biology-tissue cultures.

University of Toronto, School of Graduate Studies, Faculty of Dentistry, Graduate Programs in Dentistry, Toronto, ON M5S 1A1, Canada. Offers M Sc, PhD. *Program availability:* Part-time. Terminal master's awarded for partial completion of doctoral program. *Degree requirements:* For master's, thesis; for doctorate, thesis/dissertation. *Entrance requirements:* For master's, honors B Sc, minimum B average, 2 letters of reference; for doctorate, M Sc, minimum B+ average. Additional exam requirements/recommendations for international students: Required—Michigan English Language Assessment Battery, IELTS, TOEFL, or COPE. Electronic applications accepted. *Expenses:* Contact institution. *Faculty research:* Plaque, periodontal biology, biomaterials/dental implants, community dentistry, growth and development.

University of Toronto, School of Graduate Studies, Faculty of Dentistry, Specialty Master's Programs, Toronto, ON M5S 1A1, Canada. Offers dental public health (M Sc); endodontics (M Sc); oral and maxillofacial radiology (M Sc); oral and maxillofacial surgery (M Sc); oral medicine (M Sc); orthodontics and dentofacial orthopedics (M Sc); pediatric dentistry (M Sc); periodontology (M Sc). *Degree requirements:* For master's, thesis. *Entrance requirements:* For master's, completion of professional degree of DDS/BDS, DMD, minimum B average, 2 letters of reference. Additional exam requirements/recommendations for international students: Required—TOEFL (minimum score 600 paper-based; 100 iBT), TWE (minimum score 5). *Expenses:* Contact institution. *Faculty research:* Plaque and periodontal biology, biomaterials/dental implants, community dentistry, growth development, neurophysiology.

University of Washington, Graduate School, School of Dentistry and Graduate School, Graduate Programs in Dentistry, Department of Endodontics, Seattle, WA 98195. Offers MSD, Certificate.

University of Washington, Graduate School, School of Dentistry and Graduate School, Graduate Programs in Dentistry, Department of Oral Biology, Seattle, WA 98195. Offers MS, MSD, PhD.

University of Washington, Graduate School, School of Dentistry and Graduate School, Graduate Programs in Dentistry, Department of Oral Medicine, Seattle, WA 98195. Offers MSD.

University of Washington, Graduate School, School of Dentistry and Graduate School, Graduate Programs in Dentistry, Department of Orthodontics, Seattle, WA 98195. Offers MSD, Certificate.

University of Washington, Graduate School, School of Dentistry and Graduate School, Graduate Programs in Dentistry, Department of Periodontics, Seattle, WA 98195. Offers MSD, PhD, Certificate.

University of Washington, Graduate School, School of Dentistry, Program in Dental Surgery, Seattle, WA 98195. Offers DDS. *Accreditation:* ADA. *Entrance requirements:* For doctorate, DAT.

The University of Western Ontario, Schulich School of Medicine and Dentistry, Graduate and Professional Programs in Dentistry, Program in Graduate Orthodontics, London, ON N6A 5B8, Canada. Offers M Cl D. *Degree requirements:* For master's, thesis. *Entrance requirements:* For master's, GRE General Test, minimum B average, 1 year of general practice preferred. Additional exam requirements/recommendations for international students: Required—TOEFL (minimum score 600 paper-based).

West Virginia University, School of Dentistry, Morgantown, WV 26506-9400. Offers dental hygiene (MS); dentistry (DDS); endodontics (MS); orthodontics (MS); periodontics (MS); prosthodontics (MS). *Accreditation:* ADA (one or more programs are accredited). *Students:* 223 full-time (109 women), 1 part-time (0 women); includes 22 minority (1 Black or African American, non-Hispanic/Latino; 16 Asian, non-Hispanic/Latino; 3 Hispanic/Latino; 2 Two or more races, non-Hispanic/Latino), 12 international. *Degree requirements:* For master's, thesis; for doctorate, comprehensive exam. *Entrance requirements:* For doctorate, DAT, letters of recommendation, interview, minimum of 50 semester credit hours. Additional exam requirements/recommendations for international students: Required—TOEFL (minimum score 500 paper-based). *Application deadline:* For fall admission, 11/1 for domestic and international students. Applications are processed on a rolling basis. Application fee: $60. Electronic applications accepted. *Expenses:* Contact institution. *Financial support:* Research assistantships, teaching assistantships, Federal Work-Study, institutionally sponsored loans, scholarships/grants, health care benefits, and tuition waivers (partial) available. Financial award application deadline: 3/1; financial award applicants required to submit FAFSA. *Faculty research:* Growth and development, cephalography, endodontic interpretation and therapy, basic biological and clinical sciences, genetics and oral health. *Unit head:* Dr. Tom Borgia, Dean, 304-293-2521, E-mail: aborgia@hsc.wvu.edu. *Application contact:* Dr. Sheila Price, Associate Dean for Admissions, Recruitment, and Access, 304-293-1980, E-mail: sprice@hsc.wvu.edu.
Website: http://www.dentistry.hsc.wvu.edu

Section 28
Medicine

This section contains a directory of institutions offering graduate work in medicine, followed by an in-depth entry submitted by an institution that chose to prepare a detailed program description. Additional information about programs listed in the directory but not augmented by an in-depth entry may be obtained by writing directly to the dean of a graduate school or chair of a department at the address given in the directory.

CONTENTS

Program Directories

Featured School: Display and Close-Up

See:

Allopathic Medicine

Albany Medical College, Professional Program, Albany, NY 12208-3479. Offers MD. *Accreditation:* LCME/AMA. *Degree requirements:* For doctorate, United States Medical Licensing Exam Steps 1 and 2, clinical skills. *Entrance requirements:* For doctorate, MCAT, letters of recommendation, interview. Electronic applications accepted. *Expenses:* Contact institution.

Albert Einstein College of Medicine, Professional Program in Medicine, Bronx, NY 10461. Offers MD, MD/PhD. *Accreditation:* LCME/AMA. *Degree requirements:* For doctorate, independent scholars project. *Entrance requirements:* For doctorate, MCAT, interview. *Application deadline:* Applications are processed on a rolling basis. *Financial support:* Research assistantships, career-related internships or fieldwork, Federal Work-Study, institutionally sponsored loans, and scholarships/grants available. *Faculty research:* Cancer, diabetes mellitus, liver disease, infectious disease, neuroscience. *Unit head:* Dr. Joshua D. Nosanchuk, Senior Associate Dean for Medical Education, 718-430-2801. *Application contact:* Noreen Kerrigan, Associate Dean of Admissions, 718-430-2106, Fax: 718-430-8840, E-mail: noreen.kerrigan@einstein.yu.edu.
Website: http://www.einstein.yu.edu/education/md-program/

American University of Beirut, Graduate Programs, Faculty of Medicine, Beirut, Lebanon. Offers biochemistry (MS); biomedical engineering (MS); biomedical sciences (PhD); health research (MS); human morphology (MS); medicine (MD); microbiology and immunology (MS); neuroscience (MS); orthodontics (clinical) (MS); pharmacology and therapeutics (MS); physiology (MS). *Program availability:* Part-time. *Faculty:* 335 full-time (117 women), 54 part-time/adjunct (5 women). *Students:* 513 full-time (274 women). Average age 23. 527 applicants, 47% accepted, 169 enrolled. In 2017, 18 master's, 98 doctorates awarded. *Degree requirements:* For master's, one foreign language, comprehensive exam, thesis (for some programs); for doctorate, one foreign language, comprehensive exam, thesis/dissertation. *Entrance requirements:* For doctorate, MCAT (for MD); GRE (for PhD). Additional exam requirements/recommendations for international students: Required—TOEFL (minimum score 600 paper-based; 100 iBT), IELTS (minimum score 7.5). *Application deadline:* Applications are processed on a rolling basis. Application fee: $75. Electronic applications accepted. *Expenses:* Contact institution. *Financial support:* In 2017–18, 302 students received support. Fellowships, research assistantships, teaching assistantships, institutionally sponsored loans, scholarships/grants, tuition waivers, and unspecified assistantships available. *Unit head:* Dr. Mohamed Sayegh, Dean, 961-1-135000 Ext. 4700, Fax: 961-1-744489, E-mail: msayegh@aub.edu.lb. *Application contact:* Dr. Salim Kanaan, Director, Admission's Office, 961-1-350000 Ext. 2594, Fax: 961-1-750775, E-mail: sk00@aub.edu.lb.

Augusta University, Medical College of Georgia, Augusta, GA 30912. Offers MD, MD/PhD. *Degree requirements:* For doctorate, comprehensive exam. *Entrance requirements:* For doctorate, MCAT (minimum score of 509). *Expenses:* Contact institution.

Baylor College of Medicine, Medical School, Professional Program in Medicine, Houston, TX 77030-3498. Offers MD. *Entrance requirements:* For doctorate, MCAT, 90 hours of pre-med course work. Electronic applications accepted. *Expenses:* Contact institution.

Boston University, School of Medicine, Professional Program in Medicine, Boston, MA 02118. Offers MD, MD/Certificate, MD/JD, MD/MA, MD/MBA, MD/MPH, MD/MSCI, MD/PhD. *Accreditation:* LCME/AMA. *Faculty:* 1,645 full-time, 119 part-time/adjunct. *Students:* 674 full-time (353 women), 25 part-time (7 women); includes 333 minority (19 Black or African American, non-Hispanic/Latino; 191 Asian, non-Hispanic/Latino; 97 Hispanic/Latino; 2 Native Hawaiian or other Pacific Islander, non-Hispanic/Latino; 24 Two or more races, non-Hispanic/Latino), 43 international. Average age 24. In 2017, 159 doctorates awarded. *Entrance requirements:* For doctorate, MCAT, 1 year each of English literature/composition, humanities, biology with lab, and physics; 2 semesters of chemistry or biochemistry with lab; minimum 2 letters of recommendation. *Application deadline:* For fall admission, 11/1 for domestic students. Applications are processed on a rolling basis. Application fee: $110. Electronic applications accepted. *Expenses:* $85,531. *Financial support:* Federal Work-Study available. Support available to part-time students. *Unit head:* Dr. Karen H. Antman, Dean/Provost, 617-638-5300. *Application contact:* Dr. Kristen Goodell, Associate Dean for Admissions, 617-638-4631, E-mail: kgoodell@bu.edu.

Brown University, Graduate School, Division of Biology and Medicine, Program in Medicine, Providence, RI 02912. Offers MD, MD/PhD. *Accreditation:* LCME/AMA. *Expenses:* Contact institution.

California Northstate University, College of Medicine, Elk Grove, CA 95757. Offers MD. *Entrance requirements:* For doctorate, MCAT, three letters of recommendation.

Case Western Reserve University, School of Medicine, Professional Program in Medicine, Cleveland, OH 44106. Offers MD, MD/JD, MD/MA, MD/MBA, MD/MPH, MD/MS, MD/PhD. *Accreditation:* LCME/AMA. *Entrance requirements:* For doctorate, MCAT, interview. Electronic applications accepted. *Expenses: Tuition:* Full-time $43,854; part-time $1827 per credit hour. *Required fees:* $50; $50 per credit hour. Tuition and fees vary according to course load and program.

Charles R. Drew University of Medicine and Science, Professional Program in Medicine, Los Angeles, CA 90059. Offers MD. *Entrance requirements:* For doctorate, MCAT.

Columbia University, College of Physicians and Surgeons, Professional Program in Medicine, New York, NY 10032. Offers MD, MD/DDS, MD/MPH, MD/MS, MD/PhD. *Accreditation:* LCME/AMA. *Program availability:* Part-time. *Entrance requirements:* For doctorate, MCAT. *Expenses: Tuition:* Full-time $44,864; part-time $1704 per credit. *Required fees:* $2370 per semester. One-time fee: $105.

Columbia University, School of Professional Studies, Program in Narrative Medicine, New York, NY 10027. Offers MS. Electronic applications accepted. *Expenses: Tuition:* Full-time $44,864; part-time $1704 per credit. *Required fees:* $2370 per semester. One-time fee: $105.

Creighton University, School of Medicine, Professional Program in Medicine, Omaha, NE 68178-0001. Offers MD, MD/PhD. *Accreditation:* LCME/AMA. *Entrance requirements:* For doctorate, MCAT. Electronic applications accepted. Part-time tuition and fees vary according to course load, degree level, campus/location and program. *Faculty research:* Hereditary cancer, osteoporosis, diabetes, immunology, microbiology.

Dalhousie University, Faculty of Medicine, Halifax, NS B3H 4H7, Canada. Offers M Sc, MD, PhD, M Sc/PhD, MD/M Sc, MD/PhD. *Accreditation:* LCME/AMA. *Entrance requirements:* For master's, MCAT; for doctorate, MCAT (for MD). Electronic applications accepted.

Dartmouth College, Geisel School of Medicine, Hanover, NH 03755. Offers MD, MD/MBA, MD/MPH, MD/MS, MD/PhD. *Accreditation:* LCME/AMA. *Faculty:* 148 full-time (54 women), 40 part-time/adjunct (18 women). *Students:* 380 full-time (223 women), 4 part-time (3 women); includes 173 minority (27 Black or African American, non-Hispanic/Latino; 5 American Indian or Alaska Native, non-Hispanic/Latino; 79 Asian, non-Hispanic/Latino; 47 Hispanic/Latino; 15 Two or more races, non-Hispanic/Latino), 31 international. Average age 27. 6,781 applicants, 4% accepted, 92 enrolled. In 2017, 72 doctorates awarded. *Entrance requirements:* For doctorate, one year (8 semester hours or equivalent) of general biology and general physics; two years (16 semester hours or equivalent) of chemistry, which must include one semester each or equivalent of organic chemistry and biochemistry; one half-year (3 semester hours or equivalent) of college-level mathematics. *Application deadline:* For fall admission, 11/1 for domestic students. Application fee: $130. Electronic applications accepted. *Financial support:* Institutionally sponsored loans and scholarships/grants available. *Unit head:* Dr. Leslie Henderson, Senior Associate Dean for Faculty Affairs, 603-650-1574, E-mail: leslie.p.henderson@dartmouth.edu. *Application contact:* Rand S. Swenson, Chair, Geisel Admissions Committee, 603-650-1505, Fax: 603-650-1560, E-mail: geisel.admissions@dartmouth.edu.
Website: http://dms.dartmouth.edu/

Drexel University, College of Medicine, Professional Program in Medicine, Philadelphia, PA 19104-2875. Offers MD, MD/PhD. *Accreditation:* LCME/AMA. *Degree requirements:* For doctorate, National Board Exam Parts I and II. *Entrance requirements:* For doctorate, MCAT. Electronic applications accepted.

Duke University, School of Medicine, Professional Program in Medicine, Durham, NC 27708-0586. Offers MD, MD/JD, MD/MA, MD/MALS, MD/MBA, MD/MHS, MD/MLS, MD/MMCi, MD/MPH, MD/MPP, MD/MS, MD/MSE, MD/MSIS, MD/PhD. *Accreditation:* LCME/AMA. *Faculty:* 1,488 full-time (518 women). *Students:* 487 full-time; includes 223 minority (53 Black or African American, non-Hispanic/Latino; 11 American Indian or Alaska Native, non-Hispanic/Latino; 149 Asian, non-Hispanic/Latino; 10 Hispanic/Latino). Average age 26. 7,030 applicants, 4% accepted, 116 enrolled. In 2017, 108 doctorates awarded. *Degree requirements:* For doctorate, thesis for third-year scholarly experience. *Entrance requirements:* For doctorate, MCAT. *Application deadline:* For fall admission, 10/15 for domestic students. Application fee: $85. Electronic applications accepted. *Financial support:* In 2017–18, 319 students received support. Scholarships/grants available. Financial award application deadline: 5/1; financial award applicants required to submit CSS PROFILE or FAFSA. *Unit head:* Dr. Edward G. Buckley, Vice Dean of Medical Education, 919-668-3381, Fax: 919-660-7040, E-mail: buckl002@mc.duke.edu. *Application contact:* Andrea Liu, Director of Admissions, 919-684-2985, Fax: 919-684-8893, E-mail: medadm@mc.duke.edu.
Website: http://www.dukemed.duke.edu/

East Carolina University, Brody School of Medicine, Professional Program in Medicine, Greenville, NC 27858-4353. Offers MD. *Students:* 322 full-time (161 women); includes 93 minority (32 Black or African American, non-Hispanic/Latino; 3 American Indian or Alaska Native, non-Hispanic/Latino; 46 Asian, non-Hispanic/Latino; 11 Hispanic/Latino; 1 Two or more races, non-Hispanic/Latino). Average age 26. 958 applicants, 13% accepted, 83 enrolled. In 2017, 77 doctorates awarded. *Entrance requirements:* For doctorate, MCAT, pre-med courses, interviews, faculty evaluations. *Application deadline:* For fall admission, 11/1 for domestic students. Applications are processed on a rolling basis. Application fee: $70. Electronic applications accepted. *Expenses:* $23,137 per year. *Financial support:* Institutionally sponsored loans and scholarships/grants available. *Faculty research:* Diabetes, cardiovascular disease, cancer, neurological disorders. *Unit head:* Dr. Paul Cunningham, Dean, 252-744-2201, E-mail: cunninghamp@ecu.edu.
Website: http://www.ecu.edu/cs-dhs/med/md.cfm

Eastern Virginia Medical School, Professional Program in Medicine, Norfolk, VA 23501-1980. Offers MD, MD/MPH. *Accreditation:* LCME/AMA. *Entrance requirements:* For doctorate, MCAT, bachelor's degree or equivalent, course work in sciences. Electronic applications accepted.

East Tennessee State University, Quillen College of Medicine, Professional Program in Medicine, Johnson City, TN 37614. Offers MD. *Accreditation:* LCME/AMA. In 2017, 74 doctorates awarded. *Entrance requirements:* For doctorate, MCAT. Additional exam requirements/recommendations for international students: Required—TOEFL (minimum score 550 paper-based). *Application deadline:* For fall admission, 6/1 for domestic students, 4/29 for international students; for spring admission, 11/1 for domestic students, 9/29 for international students; for summer admission, 3/15 for domestic students, 2/1 for international students. Applications are processed on a rolling basis. Application fee: $55 ($65 for international students). *Financial support:* Career-related internships or fieldwork, Federal Work-Study, institutionally sponsored loans, and scholarships/grants available. Financial award application deadline: 5/10; financial award applicants required to submit FAFSA. *Unit head:* Dr. William A. Block, Jr., Dean, 423-439-6316, Fax: 423-439-8090, E-mail: deanofmedicine@etsu.edu. *Application contact:* Doug Taylor, Assistant Dean for Admissions and Records, 423-439-2033, Fax: 423-439-2110, E-mail: dougt@etsu.edu.

Emory University, School of Medicine, Professional Program in Medicine, Atlanta, GA 30322-4510. Offers MD, MD/MA, MD/MPH, MD/MSCR, MD/PhD. *Accreditation:* LCME/AMA. *Degree requirements:* For doctorate, United States Medical Licensing Exam Step 1 and 2. *Entrance requirements:* For doctorate, MCAT, AMCAS application, supplemental application, interview (by invitation only). Electronic applications accepted. *Expenses:* Contact institution. *Faculty research:* Immunology and pathogenesis of chronic viral infections, immunological memory and vaccine development, development of antiviral agents to treat infections caused by human immunodeficiency and hepatitis viruses, development of therapeutic and diagnostic approaches to improve outcomes after transplantation genetic mechanisms of neuropsychiatric disease, Fragile X Syndrome, immune system ontogeny and phylogeny.

Florida International University, Herbert Wertheim College of Medicine, Miami, FL 33199. Offers biomedical sciences (PhD); medicine (MD); physician assistant studies (MPAS). *Accreditation:* LCME/AMA. *Faculty:* 84 full-time (45 women), 83 part-time/adjunct (28 women). *Students:* 638 full-time (364 women); includes 418 minority (42 Black or African American, non-Hispanic/Latino; 124 Asian, non-Hispanic/Latino; 228 Hispanic/Latino; 24 Two or more races, non-Hispanic/Latino), 13 international. Average age 26. 5,410 applicants, 7% accepted, 170 enrolled. In 2017, 115 doctorates awarded. *Entrance requirements:* For doctorate, MCAT (minimum score of 25), minimum overall GPA of 3.0; 3 letters of recommendation, 2 from basic science faculty (biology, chemistry, physics, math) and 1 from any other faculty member. *Application deadline:* For fall admission, 12/15 for domestic students. Application fee: $160. Electronic applications accepted. *Expenses:* Contact institution. *Financial support:* Institutionally

sponsored loans and scholarships/grants available. Financial award application deadline: 3/1; financial award applicants required to submit FAFSA. *Unit head:* Dr. John Rock, Dean, 305-348-0570, E-mail: med.admissions@fiu.edu. *Application contact:* Cristina M. Arabatzis, Assistant Director of Admissions, 305-348-0639, Fax: 305-348-0650, E-mail: carabatz@fiu.edu.
Website: http://medicine.fiu.edu/

Florida State University, College of Medicine, Tallahassee, FL 32306. Offers MD, PhD. *Accreditation:* LCME/AMA. *Faculty:* 165 full time (83 women), 56 part-time/adjunct (19 women). *Students:* 480 full-time (250 women); includes 200 minority (53 Black or African American, non-Hispanic/Latino; 59 Asian, non-Hispanic/Latino; 80 Hispanic/Latino; 8 Two or more races, non-Hispanic/Latino). Average age 26. 5,866 applicants, 3% accepted, 120 enrolled. In 2017, 116 doctorates awarded. *Degree requirements:* For doctorate, comprehensive exam. *Entrance requirements:* For doctorate, MCAT (for MD), baccalaureate degree, letters of recommendation (for MD). *Application deadline:* Applications are processed on a rolling basis. Electronic applications accepted. *Expenses:* $26,311 per year in-state; $60,862 per year out-of-state. *Financial support:* In 2017–18, 123 students received support. Scholarships/grants and tuition waivers (partial) available. Financial award application deadline: 6/30; financial award applicants required to submit FAFSA. *Faculty research:* Geriatrics, women's health, autism, medical education, rural health, minority health, biomedical sciences. *Total annual research expenditures:* $9. *Unit head:* Dr. John Patrick Fogarty, MD, Dean, 850-644-1346, Fax: 850-645-1420, E-mail: john.fogarty@med.fsu.edu. *Application contact:* Dana Urrutia, Admissions Coordinator, 850-644-1857, Fax: 850-645-2846, E-mail: medadmissions@med.fsu.edu.
Website: http://www.med.fsu.edu/

Geisinger Commonwealth School of Medicine, Professional Program in Medicine, Scranton, PA 18509. Offers MD, MD/MHA, MD/MPH. *Entrance requirements:* For doctorate, MCAT, bachelor's degree.

Georgetown University, School of Medicine, Washington, DC 20057. Offers MD, MD/MBA, MD/PhD. *Accreditation:* LCME/AMA. *Entrance requirements:* For doctorate, MCAT, minimum 90 credit hours with 1 year of course work in biology, organic chemistry, inorganic chemistry, physics, mathematics, and English. *Expenses:* Contact institution.

The George Washington University, School of Medicine and Health Sciences, Professional Program in Medicine, Washington, DC 20052. Offers MD. *Accreditation:* LCME/AMA. *Students:* 705 full-time (422 women), 3 part-time (1 woman); includes 328 minority (51 Black or African American, non-Hispanic/Latino; 5 American Indian or Alaska Native, non-Hispanic/Latino; 186 Asian, non-Hispanic/Latino; 66 Hispanic/Latino; 3 Native Hawaiian or other Pacific Islander, non-Hispanic/Latino; 17 Two or more races, non-Hispanic/Latino), 17 international. Average age 26. *Entrance requirements:* For doctorate, MCAT, minimum of 90 undergraduate semester hours, specific pre-med courses equal to 38 semester hours. *Application deadline:* For fall admission, 12/1 for domestic students. Applications are processed on a rolling basis. Application fee: $80. *Expenses: Tuition:* Full-time $28,800; part-time $1655 per credit hour. *Required fees:* $45; $2.75 per credit hour. *Financial support:* Career-related internships or fieldwork, Federal Work-Study, and institutionally sponsored loans available. *Unit head:* Dr. Alan Wasserman, Chair, 202-741-2302. *Application contact:* Diane P. McQuail, Director of Admissions, 202-994-3507, E-mail: maeve@gwu.edu.

Harvard University, Harvard Medical School, Professional Program in Medicine, Cambridge, MA 02138. Offers MD, PhD, MD/MBA, MD/MM Sc, MD/MPH, MD/MPP, MD/PhD. *Accreditation:* LCME/AMA. Electronic applications accepted.

Hofstra University, Donald and Barbara Zucker School of Medicine at Hofstra/Northwell, Hempstead, NY 11549. Offers medicine (MD); molecular basis of medicine (PhD); MD/MPH; MD/PhD. *Accreditation:* LCME/AMA. *Faculty:* 19 full-time (13 women), 15 part-time/adjunct (7 women). *Students:* 417 full-time (196 women); includes 181 minority (20 Black or African American, non-Hispanic/Latino; 90 Asian, non-Hispanic/Latino; 56 Hispanic/Latino; 5 Native Hawaiian or other Pacific Islander, non-Hispanic/Latino; 10 Two or more races, non-Hispanic/Latino), 1 international. Average age 25. 6,088 applicants, 6% accepted, 100 enrolled. In 2017, 75 doctorates awarded. *Entrance requirements:* For doctorate, MCAT. Additional exam requirements/recommendations for international students: Required—TOEFL (for PhD students only). *Application deadline:* For fall admission, 12/1 priority date for domestic students. Application fee: $100. Electronic applications accepted. *Expenses:* $24,720 per term. *Financial support:* In 2017–18, 298 students received support, including 288 fellowships with full and partial tuition reimbursements available (averaging $24,461 per year), research assistantships with full and partial tuition reimbursements available (averaging $6,075 per year); career-related internships or fieldwork, Federal Work-Study, institutionally sponsored loans, scholarships/grants, tuition waivers (full and partial), and unspecified assistantships also available. Support available to part-time students. Financial award applicants required to submit FAFSA. *Faculty research:* Bioelectric medicine; immunology and inflammation; neuroscience; cancer biology; health services/outcomes. *Unit head:* Dr. Lawrence Smith, Dean, 516-463-7517, Fax: 516-463-7543, E-mail: lawrence.smith@hofstra.edu. *Application contact:* Sunil Samuel, Assistant Vice President of Admissions, 516-463-4723, Fax: 516-463-4664.
Website: http://medicine.hofstra.edu/index.html

Howard University, College of Medicine, Professional Program in Medicine, Washington, DC 20059-0002. Offers MD, PhD, MD/PhD. *Accreditation:* LCME/AMA. *Faculty research:* Infectious diseases, protein modeling, neuropsychopharmacology.

Icahn School of Medicine at Mount Sinai, Department of Medical Education, New York, NY 10029-6504. Offers MD, MD/PhD. *Accreditation:* LCME/AMA. *Degree requirements:* For doctorate, comprehensive exam, United States Medical Licensing Examination Steps 1 and 2. *Entrance requirements:* For doctorate, MCAT. Additional exam requirements/recommendations for international students: Required—TOEFL. Electronic applications accepted. *Expenses:* Contact institution. *Faculty research:* Academic medicine, translational research.

Indiana University–Purdue University Indianapolis, Indiana University School of Medicine, Indianapolis, IN 46202-5114. Offers MS, MD, PhD, MD/MA, MD/MBA, MD/MS, MD/PhD. *Accreditation:* LCME/AMA. *Degree requirements:* For doctorate, thesis/dissertation (for some programs). *Entrance requirements:* For master's, GRE General Test; for doctorate, GRE General Test (for PhD); MCAT (for MD). Additional exam requirements/recommendations for international students: Required—TOEFL. *Expenses:* Contact institution.

Instituto Tecnologico de Santo Domingo, School of Medicine, Santo Domingo, Dominican Republic. Offers M Bioethics, MD.

Johns Hopkins University, School of Medicine, Professional Program in Medicine, Baltimore, MD 21218. Offers MD, MD/PhD. *Accreditation:* LCME/AMA. *Entrance requirements:* For doctorate, MCAT. Electronic applications accepted.

Loma Linda University, School of Medicine, Loma Linda, CA 92350. Offers MS, MD, PhD. *Accreditation:* LCME/AMA. *Degree requirements:* For master's, thesis optional; for doctorate, thesis/dissertation (for some programs). *Entrance requirements:* For doctorate, MCAT (for MD). Additional exam requirements/recommendations for international students: Required—TOEFL (minimum score 550 paper-based). *Expenses:* Contact institution.

Louisiana State University Health Sciences Center, School of Medicine in New Orleans, New Orleans, LA 70112-2223. Offers MPH, MD, MD/PhD. Open only to Louisiana residents. *Accreditation:* LCME/AMA. *Entrance requirements:* For doctorate, MCAT. Electronic applications accepted. *Expenses:* Contact institution. *Faculty research:* Medical and basic sciences.

Louisiana State University Health Sciences Center at Shreveport, School of Medicine, Shreveport, LA 71130-3932. Offers MD, MD/PhD. *Accreditation:* LCME/AMA. *Entrance requirements:* For doctorate, MCAT. *Expenses:* Contact institution. *Faculty research:* Biomedical science, molecular biology, cardiovascular science.

Marshall University, Joan C. Edwards School of Medicine, MD Program, Huntington, WV 25701. Offers MD. *Accreditation:* LCME/AMA. *Faculty:* 291 full-time (109 women), 51 part-time/adjunct (21 women). *Students:* 309 full-time (124 women); includes 58 minority (15 Black or African American, non-Hispanic/Latino; 2 American Indian or Alaska Native, non-Hispanic/Latino; 32 Asian, non-Hispanic/Latino; 9 Hispanic/Latino). Average age 25. 1,960 applicants, 6% accepted, 75 enrolled. In 2017, 58 doctorates awarded. *Degree requirements:* For doctorate, U. S. Medical Licensing Exam, Steps 1 and 2. *Entrance requirements:* For doctorate, MCAT, 1 year of course work in biology, physics, chemistry, organic chemistry, English, and social or behavioral sciences; 1 semester of biochemistry. *Application deadline:* For fall admission, 11/1 for domestic students. Applications are processed on a rolling basis. Application fee: $75. Electronic applications accepted. *Expenses:* $23,084 per year resident tuition and fees, $54,772 per year nonresident tuition and fees. *Financial support:* Scholarships/grants available. Financial award application deadline: 5/1; financial award applicants required to submit FAFSA. *Unit head:* Dr. Joseph I. Shapiro, Dean, 304-691-1700, Fax: 304-691-1726. *Application contact:* Cynthia A. Warren, Assistant Dean for Admissions and Student Affairs, 304-691-1738, Fax: 304-691-1744, E-mail: warren@marshall.edu.
Website: http://www.musom.marshall.edu/

Mayo Clinic School of Medicine, Professional Program, Rochester, MN 55905. Offers MD, MD/Certificate, MD/PhD. MD offered through the Mayo Foundation's Division of Education; MD/PhD, MD/Certificate with Mayo Graduate School. *Accreditation:* LCME/AMA. *Entrance requirements:* For doctorate, MCAT, previous undergraduate course work in biology, chemistry, physics, and biochemistry. Electronic applications accepted.

McGill University, Faculty of Graduate and Postdoctoral Studies, Faculty of Medicine, Department of Surgery, Montréal, QC H3A 2T5, Canada. Offers M Sc, PhD.

McGill University, Professional Program in Medicine, Montréal, QC H3A 2T5, Canada. Offers MD/CM, MD/MBA, MD/PhD. *Accreditation:* LCME/AMA.

Medical College of Wisconsin, Medical School, Professional Program in Medicine, Milwaukee, WI 53226-0509. Offers MD, MD/MPH, MD/MS, MD/PhD. *Accreditation:* LCME/AMA. *Entrance requirements:* For doctorate, GRE, MCAT, official transcripts, three letters of recommendation. Additional exam requirements/recommendations for international students: Required—TOEFL. *Application deadline:* For fall admission, 12/3 for domestic students. Applications are processed on a rolling basis. Application fee: $50. *Financial support:* Fellowships available. *Unit head:* Joseph E. Kerschner, MD, Provost/Executive Vice President/Dean, 414-955-8739. *Application contact:* Registrar, 414-456-8733.

Medical University of South Carolina, College of Medicine, Charleston, SC 29425. Offers MD, MD/MBA, MD/MHA, MD/MPH, MD/MSCR, MD/PhD. *Accreditation:* LCME/AMA. *Degree requirements:* For doctorate, Steps 1 and 2 of Clinical Performance Exam and U.S. Medical Licensing Examination. *Entrance requirements:* For doctorate, MCAT, interview. Electronic applications accepted. *Expenses:* Contact institution. *Faculty research:* Cardiovascular proteomics, translational cancer research, diabetes mellitus, neurodegenerative diseases, addiction.

Meharry Medical College, School of Medicine, Nashville, TN 37208-9989. Offers MD. *Accreditation:* LCME/AMA. *Entrance requirements:* For doctorate, MCAT. Electronic applications accepted.

Mercer University, School of Medicine, Macon, GA 31207. Offers MFT, MPH, MSA, MD. *Accreditation:* AAMFT/COAMFTE; LCME/AMA (one or more programs are accredited). *Entrance requirements:* Additional exam requirements/recommendations for international students: Required—TOEFL. *Faculty research:* Anatomy, biochemistry/nutrition, genetics, microbiology/immunology, neuroscience.

Michigan State University, College of Human Medicine, Professional Program in Human Medicine, East Lansing, MI 48824. Offers human medicine (MD); human medicine/medical scientist training program (MD). *Accreditation:* LCME/AMA. *Entrance requirements:* Additional exam requirements/recommendations for international students: Required—TOEFL, Michigan State University ELT (minimum score 85), Michigan Michigan English Language Assessment Battery (minimum score 83). Electronic applications accepted.

Morehouse School of Medicine, Professional Program, Atlanta, GA 30310-1495. Offers MD, MD/MPH. *Accreditation:* LCME/AMA. *Degree requirements:* For doctorate, U.S. Medical Licensing Exam Steps 1 and 2. *Entrance requirements:* For doctorate, MCAT. Electronic applications accepted. *Expenses:* Contact institution. *Faculty research:* Cardiovascular disease and related sequela, infectious diseases/HIV-AIDS, neurological diseases, cancer.

New York Medical College, School of Medicine, Valhalla, NY 10595-1691. Offers MD, MD/MPH, MD/PhD. *Accreditation:* LCME/AMA. *Faculty:* 1,051 full-time (413 women), 1,299 part-time/adjunct (434 women). *Students:* 865 full-time (466 women); includes 403 minority (86 Black or African American, non-Hispanic/Latino; 1 American Indian or Alaska Native, non-Hispanic/Latino; 211 Asian, non-Hispanic/Latino; 90 Hispanic/Latino; 15 Two or more races, non-Hispanic/Latino), 7 international. Average age 26. 9,527 applicants, 7% accepted, 216 enrolled. In 2017, 204 doctorates awarded. *Entrance requirements:* For doctorate, MCAT, 2 semesters of course work in general biology, general chemistry, organic chemistry, physics, and English. *Application deadline:* For fall admission, 1/31 for domestic and international students. Applications are processed on a rolling basis. Application fee: $120. Electronic applications accepted. *Expenses:* $52,720 tuition, $3,427 fees. *Financial support:* In 2017–18, 324 students received support. Federal Work-Study, scholarships/grants, and health care benefits available. Support available to part-time students. Financial award application deadline: 4/30; financial award applicants required to submit FAFSA. *Faculty research:* Cardiovascular diseases, cancer, infectious diseases, neurosciences, renal diseases, pulmonary diseases. *Total annual research expenditures:* $15.6 million. *Unit head:* Jennifer Koestler, MD, Senior Associate Dean for Medical Education, 914-594-4500, E-mail: jennifer_koestler@nymc.edu. *Application contact:* Robin Baum, Assistant Dean of Admissions, 914-594-4882, Fax: 914-594-4613, E-mail: mdadmit@nymc.edu.
Website: http://www.nymc.edu/

New York University, School of Medicine, New York, NY 10012. Offers MS, MD, PhD, MD/MA, MD/MBA, MD/MPA, MD/MPH, MD/PhD. *Accreditation:* LCME/AMA (one or more programs are accredited). *Students:* Average age 24. 8,341 applicants, 6% accepted, 149 enrolled. In 2017, 11 master's awarded. *Entrance requirements:* For doctorate, MCAT (for MD). *Application deadline:* For fall admission, 10/15 for domestic students; for winter admission, 12/18 for domestic students, 12/15 for international students. Applications are processed on a rolling basis. Application fee: $110. Electronic applications accepted.

Expenses: Contact institution. *Financial support:* In 2017–18, 240 students received support. Fellowships, research assistantships, teaching assistantships, Federal Work-Study, institutionally sponsored loans, scholarships/grants, and health care benefits available. Financial award application deadline: 3/1; financial award applicants required to submit FAFSA. *Faculty research:* AIDS, cancer, neuroscience, molecular biology, neuroscience, cell biology and molecular genetics, structural biology, microbial pathogenesis and host defense, pharmacology, molecular oncology and immunology. *Total annual research expenditures:* $201.1 million. *Unit head:* Dr. Robert Grossman, Dean, 212-263-3269, Fax: 212-263-1828, E-mail: robert.grossman@nyumc.org. *Application contact:* Dr. Rafael Rivera, Associate Dean, Admissions and Financial Aid, 212-263-5290, Fax: 212-263-0720, E-mail: rafael.rivera@nyumc.org.
Website: http://school.med.nyu.edu/

Northeast Ohio Medical University, College of Medicine, Rootstown, OH 44272-0095. Offers MD. *Accreditation:* LCME/AMA. *Faculty:* 59 full-time (21 women), 1,977 part-time/adjunct (593 women). *Students:* 606 full-time (310 women); includes 276 minority (18 Black or African American, non-Hispanic/Latino; 1 American Indian or Alaska Native, non-Hispanic/Latino; 215 Asian, non-Hispanic/Latino; 14 Hispanic/Latino; 28 Two or more races, non-Hispanic/Latino). 3,401 applicants, 7% accepted, 153 enrolled. In 2017, 140 doctorates awarded. *Degree requirements:* For doctorate, U. S. Medical Licensing Exam Step 2. *Entrance requirements:* For doctorate, MCAT, two semesters each of organic chemistry and lab, physics and lab, and biology and lab; one semester of biochemistry. *Application deadline:* For fall admission, 8/1 priority date for domestic students; for winter admission, 10/1 for domestic students. Applications are processed on a rolling basis. Application fee: $95. Electronic applications accepted. *Expenses:* Contact institution. *Financial support:* Institutionally sponsored loans and scholarships/grants available. Financial award application deadline: 3/15; financial award applicants required to submit FAFSA. *Faculty research:* Auditory neuroscience, musculoskeletal biology, antiviral and immunomodulatory vaccine development, cellular and molecular mechanisms of thermogenesis associated with diabetes and obesity, cellular and molecular regulation of cardiac remodeling. *Total annual research expenditures:* $9.2 million. *Unit head:* Dr. Jeffrey L. Susman, Dean, 330-325-6101. *Application contact:* Heidi Terry, Executive Director, Enrollment Services, 330-325-6479, E-mail: hterry@neomed.edu.
Website: http://www.neomed.edu/academics/medicine

Northwestern University, Feinberg School of Medicine, Combined MD/PhD Medical Scientist Training Program, Evanston, IL 60208. Offers MD/PhD. Application must be made to both The Graduate School and the Medical School. *Accreditation:* LCME/AMA. Electronic applications accepted. *Faculty research:* Cardiovascular epidemiology, cancer epidemiology, nutritional interventions for the prevention of cardiovascular disease and cancer, women's health, outcomes research.

Nova Southeastern University, College of Allopathic Medicine, Fort Lauderdale, FL 33314-7796. Offers MD. Tuition and fees vary according to course load, degree level and program. *Unit head:* Dr. Johannes Vieweg, MD, Dean, 954-262-1501, E-mail: jvieweg@nova.edu. *Application contact:* Information Contact, 800-541-6682, E-mail: nsuinfo@nsu.nova.edu.
Website: http://md.nova.edu/

The Ohio State University, College of Medicine, Professional Program in Medicine, Columbus, OH 43210. Offers MD, MD/PhD. *Accreditation:* LCME/AMA. *Students:* 770 (400 women); includes 346 minority (79 Black or African American, non-Hispanic/Latino; 151 Asian, non-Hispanic/Latino; 74 Hispanic/Latino; 42 Two or more races, non-Hispanic/Latino). Average age 25. In 2017, 168 doctorates awarded. *Entrance requirements:* For doctorate, MCAT. *Application deadline:* For fall admission, 11/1 for domestic and international students. Applications are processed on a rolling basis. Application fee: $80. Electronic applications accepted. *Financial support:* Fellowships, research assistantships, teaching assistantships, Federal Work-Study, institutionally sponsored loans, and scholarships/grants available. Support available to part-time students. Financial award application deadline: 2/15; financial award applicants required to submit FAFSA. *Faculty research:* Molecular genetics, stress and the immune system, molecular cardiology, transplantation biology. *Unit head:* Dr. K. Craig Kent, MD, Dean, 614-292-2600, Fax: 614-292-1301. *Application contact:* Graduate and Professional Admissions, 614-292-9444, Fax: 614-292-3895, E-mail: gpadmissions@osu.edu.
Website: http://medicine.osu.edu/

Oregon Health & Science University, School of Medicine, Professional Program in Medicine, Portland, OR 97239-3098. Offers MD, MD/MPH, MD/PhD. MD/MPH offered with Portland State University. *Accreditation:* LCME/AMA. *Faculty:* 1,737. *Students:* 595 full-time (323 women); includes 164 minority (9 Black or African American, non-Hispanic/Latino; 3 American Indian or Alaska Native, non-Hispanic/Latino; 91 Asian, non-Hispanic/Latino; 25 Hispanic/Latino; 1 Native Hawaiian or other Pacific Islander, non-Hispanic/Latino; 35 Two or more races, non-Hispanic/Latino). Average age 28. 6,365 applicants, 4% accepted, 160 enrolled. In 2017, 135 doctorates awarded. *Degree requirements:* For doctorate, thesis/dissertation (for some programs), National Board Exam Parts I and II. *Entrance requirements:* For doctorate, MCAT, 1 year of course work in biology, English, social science and physics; 2 years of course work in chemistry and genetics. *Application deadline:* For fall admission, 10/15 for domestic students. Applications are processed on a rolling basis. Application fee: $100. Electronic applications accepted. *Financial support:* Fellowships, research assistantships, Federal Work-Study, institutionally sponsored loans, scholarships/grants, and health care benefits available. Financial award application deadline: 3/1; financial award applicants required to submit FAFSA. *Unit head:* Dr. Tracy Bumsted, Associate Dean for Medical Education. *Application contact:* Debbie Melton, Director of Admissions.
Website: http://www.ohsu.edu/som/

Penn State Hershey Medical Center, College of Medicine, Hershey, PA 17033. Offers MPAS, MPH, MS, Dr PH, MD, PhD, MD/PhD, PhD/MBA. *Accreditation:* LCME/AMA. Terminal master's awarded for partial completion of doctoral program. *Degree requirements:* For master's, thesis optional; for doctorate, comprehensive exam, thesis/dissertation, minimum GPA of 3.0 (for PhD). *Entrance requirements:* For master's, GRE; for doctorate, GRE (for PhD); MCAT (for MD). Additional exam requirements/recommendations for international students: Required—TOEFL (minimum score 560 paper-based; 81 iBT). *Application deadline:* Applications are processed on a rolling basis. Electronic applications accepted. *Expenses:* Contact institution. *Financial support:* In 2017–18, research assistantships with full tuition reimbursements (averaging $27,802 per year) were awarded; fellowships with full tuition reimbursements, career-related internships or fieldwork, scholarships/grants, health care benefits, and unspecified assistantships also available. *Unit head:* Dr. A. Craig Hillemeier, Dean, 717-531-8323, Fax: 717-531-0786, E-mail: grad-hmc@psu.edu. *Application contact:* Kristin E. Smith, Director of Graduate Admissions, 717-531-1045, Fax: 717-531-0786, E-mail: kec17@psu.edu.
Website: http://med.psu.edu

Ponce Health Sciences University, Professional Program, Ponce, PR 00732-7004. Offers MD. *Accreditation:* LCME/AMA. *Degree requirements:* For doctorate, one foreign language, comprehensive exam, United States Medical Licensing Exam. *Entrance requirements:* For doctorate, MCAT, coursework in Spanish language, proficiency in Spanish/English (highly recommended).

Pontificia Universidad Catolica Madre y Maestra, Department of Medicine, Santiago, Dominican Republic. Offers MD.

Queen's University at Kingston, School of Medicine, Professional Program in Medicine, Kingston, ON K7L 3N6, Canada. Offers MD. *Accreditation:* LCME/AMA. *Entrance requirements:* For doctorate, MCAT.

Quinnipiac University, Frank H. Netter MD School of Medicine, MD Program, Hamden, CT 06518-1940. Offers MD. *Faculty:* 28 full-time (12 women). *Students:* 358 full-time (172 women); includes 137 minority (23 Black or African American, non-Hispanic/Latino; 1 American Indian or Alaska Native, non-Hispanic/Latino; 88 Asian, non-Hispanic/Latino; 24 Hispanic/Latino; 1 Native Hawaiian or other Pacific Islander, non-Hispanic/Latino). Average age 27. 6,984 applicants, 5% accepted, 92 enrolled. *Degree requirements:* For doctorate, capstone project. *Entrance requirements:* For doctorate, MCAT. *Application deadline:* For fall admission, 12/1 for domestic students. Applications are processed on a rolling basis. Application fee: $100. Electronic applications accepted. *Expenses:* $58,900. *Financial support:* In 2017–18, 205 students received support. Institutionally sponsored loans and scholarships/grants available. Financial award application deadline: 3/1; financial award applicants required to submit FAFSA. *Unit head:* Dr. Bruce Koeppen, Dean, 203-582-5301, E-mail: brucedean.koeppen@quinnipiac.edu. *Application contact:* Michael Cole, Director of Admissions Operations, 203-582-6562, E-mail: michael.cole@quinnipiac.edu.
Website: https://www.qu.edu/schools/medicine/academics/md-program.html

Rosalind Franklin University of Medicine and Science, Chicago Medical School, North Chicago, IL 60064-3095. Offers MD, MD/MS, MD/PhD. *Accreditation:* LCME/AMA. *Degree requirements:* For doctorate, clerkship, step 1 and step 2 exams. *Entrance requirements:* For doctorate, MCAT, 3 years of course work with lab in biology, physics, inorganic chemistry, and organic chemistry. *Expenses:* Contact institution. *Faculty research:* Neurosciences, structural biology, cancer biology, cell biology, developmental biology.

Rowan University, Cooper Medical School, Glassboro, NJ 08028-1701. Offers MD. *Expenses:* Tuition, state resident: full-time $15,020; part-time $751 per semester hour. Tuition, nonresident: full-time $15,020; part-time $751 per semester hour. *Required fees:* $3158; $157.90 per semester hour. Tuition and fees vary according to course load, campus/location and program.

Rush University, Rush Medical College, Chicago, IL 60612. Offers MD. *Accreditation:* LCME/AMA. *Faculty:* 1,246 full-time (539 women), 239 part-time/adjunct (104 women). *Students:* 527 full-time (250 women); includes 195 minority (28 Black or African American, non-Hispanic/Latino; 114 Asian, non-Hispanic/Latino; 37 Hispanic/Latino; 16 Two or more races, non-Hispanic/Latino). Average age 26. 5,347 applicants, 6% accepted, 136 enrolled. In 2017, 116 doctorates awarded. *Degree requirements:* For doctorate, USMLE Step 1, Step 2 CK, Step 2 CS. *Entrance requirements:* For doctorate, MCAT, on-campus interview. *Application deadline:* For fall admission, 11/1 for domestic students. Applications are processed on a rolling basis. Application fee: $100. Electronic applications accepted. *Expenses:* Contact institution. *Financial support:* In 2017–18, 273 students received support. Federal Work-Study, institutionally sponsored loans, and scholarships/grants available. Financial award application deadline: 3/1; financial award applicants required to submit FAFSA. *Faculty research:* Neurodegenerative disease, glomerular disease, prevention of multi-drug resistant infections, total joint replacement performance, complications of HIV infection. *Total annual research expenditures:* $70.8 million. *Unit head:* Dr. Cynthia E. Boyd, Assistant Dean, Admissions and Recruitment, 312-942-6915, E-mail: rmc_admissions@rush.edu. *Application contact:* E-mail: rmc_admissions@rush.edu.
Website: https://www.rushu.rush.edu/rush-medical-college

Rutgers University–Newark, New Jersey Medical School, Newark, NJ 07101-1709. Offers MD, MD/Certificate, MD/JD, MD/MBA, MD/MPH, MD/PhD. *Accreditation:* LCME/AMA. *Entrance requirements:* For doctorate, MCAT. Additional exam requirements/recommendations for international students: Required—TOEFL. Electronic applications accepted. *Expenses:* Contact institution.

Rutgers University–New Brunswick, Robert Wood Johnson Medical School, Piscataway, NJ 08822. Offers MD, MD/JD, MD/MBA, MD/MPH, MD/MS, MD/MSJ, MD/PhD. *Accreditation:* LCME/AMA (one or more programs are accredited). *Entrance requirements:* For doctorate, MCAT. Additional exam requirements/recommendations for international students: Required—TOEFL. Electronic applications accepted. *Expenses:* Contact institution.

Saint Louis University, Graduate Programs, School of Medicine, Professional Program in Medicine, St. Louis, MO 63103. Offers MD. *Accreditation:* LCME/AMA. *Degree requirements:* For doctorate, U.S. Medical Licensing Exam Steps 1 and 2. *Entrance requirements:* For doctorate, MCAT, photograph, letters of recommendation, interview. Additional exam requirements/recommendations for international students: Required—TOEFL (minimum score 525 paper-based). Electronic applications accepted. *Expenses:* Contact institution. *Faculty research:* Geriatric medicine, organ transplantation, chronic disease prevention, vaccine research.

See Display on page 78 and Close-Up on page 113.

San Juan Bautista School of Medicine, Graduate and Professional Programs, Caguas, PR 00726-4968. Offers MPH, MD. *Accreditation:* LCME/AMA. *Degree requirements:* For doctorate, comprehensive exam, United States Medical Licensing Exam Steps I and II. *Entrance requirements:* For master's, bachelor's degree from university or college accredited by the Council of Higher Education of Puerto Rico or by a renowned accrediting agency that is registered at the Federal Education Department; minimum GPA of 2.5; for doctorate, MCAT, interview. *Faculty research:* Protein structure, CI tissue inflammations, bacterial metabolism, human hormone.

Seton Hall University, School of Medicine, Nutley, NJ 07110. Offers MD.

Stanford University, School of Medicine, Professional Program in Medicine, Stanford, CA 94305-2004. Offers MD, MD/PhD. *Accreditation:* LCME/AMA. *Entrance requirements:* For doctorate, MCAT. Electronic applications accepted. *Expenses:* Contact institution.

State University of New York Downstate Medical Center, College of Medicine, Brooklyn, NY 11203-2098. Offers MPH, MD, MD/MPH, MD/PhD. *Accreditation:* LCME/AMA. *Entrance requirements:* For doctorate, MCAT. *Expenses:* Contact institution. *Faculty research:* AIDS epidemiology, virus/host interaction, molecular genetics, developmental neurobiology, prostate cancer.

State University of New York Downstate Medical Center, School of Graduate Studies, MD/PhD Program, Brooklyn, NY 11203-2098. Offers MD/PhD. *Accreditation:* LCME/AMA. *Entrance requirements:* Additional exam requirements/recommendations for international students: Recommended—TOEFL.

State University of New York Upstate Medical University, College of Medicine, Syracuse, NY 13210. Offers MD, MD/PhD. *Accreditation:* LCME/AMA. *Degree requirements:* For doctorate, comprehensive exam. *Entrance requirements:* For doctorate, MCAT. Additional exam requirements/recommendations for international students: Required—TOEFL. Electronic applications accepted. *Expenses:* Contact institution.

Stony Brook University, State University of New York, Stony Brook Medicine, School of Medicine, Medical Scientist Training Program, Stony Brook, NY 11794. Offers MD/PhD. *Entrance requirements:* Additional exam requirements/recommendations for international students: Required—TOEFL. *Application deadline:* For fall admission, 12/1 for domestic students. *Expenses:* Tuition, state resident: full-time $10,870; part-time $453 per credit. Tuition, nonresident: full-time $22,210; part-time $925 per credit. *Financial support:* Tuition waivers (full) available. *Unit head:* Dr. Michael A. Frohman, Director, 631-444-3050, Fax: 631-444-9749, E-mail: michael.frohman@stonybrook.edu. *Application contact:* Carron Allen, Program Administrator, 631-444-3219, Fax: 631-444-3492, E-mail: carron.allen@stonybrook.edu.
Website: http://www.pharm.stonybrook.edu/mstp/

Stony Brook University, State University of New York, Stony Brook Medicine, School of Medicine, Professional Program in Medicine, Stony Brook, NY 11794. Offers MD, MD/PhD. *Accreditation:* LCME/AMA. *Faculty:* 820 full-time (349 women), 124 part-time/adjunct (80 women). *Students:* 536 full-time (248 women); includes 240 minority (26 Black or African American, non-Hispanic/Latino; 1 American Indian or Alaska Native, non-Hispanic/Latino; 171 Asian, non-Hispanic/Latino; 34 Hispanic/Latino; 8 Two or more races, non-Hispanic/Latino), 20 international. Average age 26. 5,505 applicants, 8% accepted, 136 enrolled. In 2017, 129 doctorates awarded. *Entrance requirements:* For doctorate, MCAT, interview. Additional exam requirements/recommendations for international students: Required—TOEFL. *Application deadline:* For fall admission, 12/1 for domestic students. Application fee: $100. Electronic applications accepted. *Expenses:* Contact institution. *Financial support:* Fellowships and teaching assistantships available. *Total annual research expenditures:* $44.2 million. *Unit head:* Dr. Kenneth Kaushansky, Dean, 631-444-2121, Fax: 631-444-6621, E-mail: kenneth.kaushansky@stonybrook.edu. *Application contact:* Committee on Admissions, 631-444-2113, Fax: 631-444-6032, E-mail: somadmissions@stonybrookmedicine.edu.
Website: https://medicine.stonybrookmedicine.edu/

Temple University, Lewis Katz School of Medicine, Doctor of Medicine Program, Philadelphia, PA 19140. Offers MD, MD/MA, MD/MBA, MD/MPH, MD/PhD. *Degree requirements:* For doctorate, United States Medical Licensing Exam Step 1, Step 2CK, Step 2CS. *Entrance requirements:* For doctorate, MCAT. Electronic applications accepted. *Expenses:* Contact institution. *Faculty research:* Translational medicine, molecular biology and immunology of autoimmune diseases and cancer, cardiovascular and pulmonary disease pathophysiology, biology of substance abuse, causes and consequences of obesity, molecular mechanisms of neurological dysfunction.

Texas A&M University, College of Medicine, Bryan, TX 77807. Offers education for healthcare professionals (MS); medical sciences (MS, PhD); medicine (MD). *Accreditation:* LCME/AMA. *Faculty:* 92. *Students:* 854 full-time (404 women), 15 part-time (13 women); includes 410 minority (28 Black or African American, non-Hispanic/Latino; 2 American Indian or Alaska Native, non-Hispanic/Latino; 268 Asian, non-Hispanic/Latino; 94 Hispanic/Latino; 1 Native Hawaiian or other Pacific Islander, non-Hispanic/Latino; 17 Two or more races, non-Hispanic/Latino), 67 international. Average age 27. 304 applicants, 82% accepted, 222 enrolled. In 2017, 4 master's, 11 doctorates awarded. *Degree requirements:* For doctorate, comprehensive exam (for some programs), thesis/dissertation (for some programs), United States Medical Licensing Exam Steps 1 and 2 (for MD). *Entrance requirements:* For doctorate, GRE General Test (for PhD); MCAT (for MD), TMDSAS Application; letters of recommendation; official transcripts. *Application deadline:* For fall admission, 9/30 for domestic students. Application fee: $200. Electronic applications accepted. *Expenses:* Contact institution. *Financial support:* In 2017–18, 329 students received support, including 124 research assistantships with tuition reimbursements available (averaging $15,092 per year), 2 teaching assistantships (averaging $9,721 per year); career related internships or fieldwork, institutionally sponsored loans, scholarships/grants, traineeships, health care benefits, tuition waivers (full and partial), and unspecified assistantships also available. Support available to part-time students. Financial award applicants required to submit FAFSA. *Faculty research:* Cardiovascular medicine, fetal alcohol syndrome, molecular pathogenesis, near science membrane structure and biology. *Unit head:* Dr. Paul E. Ogden, MD, Interim Senior Vice President and Chief Operating Officer, 979-436-0202, Fax: 979-436-0092, E-mail: ogden@medicine.tamhsc.edu. *Application contact:* Filomeno G. Maldonado, Associate Dean of Admissions, 979-436-0231, Fax: 979-436-0097, E-mail: fgmaldonado@medicine.tamhsc.edu.
Website: http://medicine.tamhsc.edu/

Texas Tech University Health Sciences Center, School of Medicine, Lubbock, TX 79430-0002. Offers MD, JD/MD, MD/MBA, MD/PhD. Open only to residents of Texas, eastern New Mexico, and southwestern Oklahoma; MD/PhD offered jointly with Texas Tech University; JD/MD with School of Law. *Accreditation:* LCME/AMA. *Entrance requirements:* For doctorate, MCAT. Additional exam requirements/recommendations for international students: Required—TOEFL. Electronic applications accepted. *Expenses:* Contact institution.

Texas Tech University Health Sciences Center El Paso, Paul L. Foster School of Medicine, El Paso, TX 79905. Offers MD.

Thomas Jefferson University, Jefferson College of Biomedical Sciences, MD/PhD Program, Philadelphia, PA 19107. Offers MD/PhD. *Entrance requirements:* Additional exam requirements/recommendations for international students: Required—TOEFL (minimum score 100 iBT) or IELTS (7.0). *Application deadline:* For fall admission, 11/1 for domestic and international students. Applications are processed on a rolling basis. Electronic applications accepted. *Financial support:* Fellowships with full tuition reimbursements, Federal Work-Study, and institutionally sponsored loans available. Financial award application deadline: 5/1; financial award applicants required to submit FAFSA. *Faculty research:* Signal transduction, tumorigenesis, apoptosis, molecular immunology, structural biology. *Unit head:* Dr. Scott A. Waldman, Academic Director, 215-955-6086, Fax: 215-955-5681, E-mail: scott.waldman@jefferson.edu. *Application contact:* Marc E. Stearns, Director of Admissions, 215-503-0155, Fax: 215-503-3433, E-mail: jgsbs-info@jefferson.edu.
Website: http://www.jefferson.edu/university/skmc/programs/md-phd.html

Thomas Jefferson University, Sidney Kimmel Medical College, Philadelphia, PA 19107. Offers MD, MD/PhD. *Accreditation:* LCME/AMA. *Faculty:* 1,219 full-time (449 women), 84 part-time/adjunct (41 women). *Students:* 1,086 full-time (539 women); includes 354 minority (24 Black or African American, non-Hispanic/Latino; 4 American Indian or Alaska Native, non-Hispanic/Latino; 257 Asian, non-Hispanic/Latino; 69 Hispanic/Latino), 38 international. Average age 23. 10,052 applicants, 5% accepted, 272 enrolled. In 2017, 251 doctorates awarded. *Entrance requirements:* For doctorate, MCAT. *Application deadline:* For fall admission, 11/15 for domestic and international students. Applications are processed on a rolling basis. Application fee: $80. Electronic applications accepted. *Expenses:* Contact institution. *Financial support:* In 2017–18, 553 students received support. Federal Work-Study, institutionally sponsored loans, and scholarships/grants available. Financial award application deadline: 3/1; financial award applicants required to submit FAFSA. *Faculty research:* Neuroscience, Alzheimer's research, pancreatic cancer, oncology and endocrinology. *Total annual research expenditures:* $80.2 million. *Unit head:* Dr. Mark Tykowcinski, Dean, 215-955-6980, Fax: 215-923-6939, E-mail: mark.tykowcinski@jefferson.edu. *Application contact:* Dr. Clara Callahan, Dean for Students and Admissions, 215-955-4077, Fax: 215-955-5151, E-mail: clara.callahan@jefferson.edu.
Website: http://www.jefferson.edu/university/skmc.html

Tufts University, School of Medicine, Professional Program in Medicine, Medford, MA 02155. Offers MD, MD/MA, MD/MBA, MD/MPH, MD/PhD. MD/PhD offered jointly with Sackler School of Graduate Biomedical Sciences; MD/MBA with Brandeis University. *Accreditation:* LCME/AMA. *Students:* 840 full-time (452 women), 1 part-time (0 women); includes 304 minority (51 Black or African American, non-Hispanic/Latino; 1 American Indian or Alaska Native, non-Hispanic/Latino; 151 Asian, non-Hispanic/Latino; 66 Hispanic/Latino; 1 Native Hawaiian or other Pacific Islander, non-Hispanic/Latino; 34 Two or more races, non-Hispanic/Latino), 1 international. Average age 26. 9,786 applicants, 6% accepted, 210 enrolled. In 2017, 216 doctorates awarded. *Entrance requirements:* For doctorate, MCAT. *Application deadline:* For fall admission, 1/15 for domestic students. Applications are processed on a rolling basis. Application fee: $105. Electronic applications accepted. *Expenses:* Contact institution. *Financial support:* Federal Work-Study, institutionally sponsored loans, and scholarships/grants available. Financial award application deadline: 3/25; financial award applicants required to submit FAFSA. *Unit head:* Dr. Harris Berman, Dean, 617-636-6565. *Application contact:* John Matias, Associate Dean of Admissions, 617-636-6571, E-mail: med-admissions@tufts.edu.
Website: http://medicine.tufts.edu/

Tulane University, School of Medicine, Professional Programs in Medicine, New Orleans, LA 70118-5669. Offers MD, MD/MBA, MD/MPH, MD/MPHTM, MD/MSPH, MD/PhD. *Accreditation:* LCME/AMA. *Entrance requirements:* For doctorate, MCAT. *Expenses: Tuition:* Full-time $50,920; part-time $2829 per credit hour. *Required fees:* $2040; $44.50 per credit hour. $580 per term. Tuition and fees vary according to course load, degree level and program.

Uniformed Services University of the Health Sciences, F. Edward Hebert School of Medicine, Bethesda, MD 20814. Offers MPH, MS, MSPH, MTMH, Dr PH, MD, PhD. Terminal master's awarded for partial completion of doctoral program. *Degree requirements:* For master's, comprehensive exam, thesis or alternative; for doctorate, comprehensive exam (for some programs), thesis/dissertation (for some programs). *Entrance requirements:* For master's, GRE General Test. Additional exam requirements/recommendations for international students: Required—TOEFL.

Universidad Autonoma de Guadalajara, School of Medicine, Guadalajara, Mexico. Offers MD.

Universidad Central del Caribe, School of Medicine, Bayamón, PR 00960-6032. Offers MA, MS, MD, PhD. *Accreditation:* LCME/AMA. *Degree requirements:* For doctorate, variable foreign language requirement. *Entrance requirements:* For doctorate, MCAT (for MD). *Faculty research:* Membrane neurotransmitter receptors, brain neurotransmission, cocaine toxicology, membrane transport, antimetabolite pharmacology.

Universidad Central del Este, Medical School, San Pedro de Macoris, Dominican Republic. Offers MD.

Universidad de Ciencias Medicas, Graduate Programs, San Jose, Costa Rica. Offers dermatology (SP); family health (MS); health service center administration (MHA); human anatomy (MS); medical and surgery (MD); occupational medicine (MS); pharmacy (Pharm D). *Program availability:* Part-time. *Degree requirements:* For master's, thesis; for doctorate and SP, comprehensive exam. *Entrance requirements:* For master's, MD or bachelor's degree; for doctorate, admissions test; for SP, admissions test, MD.

Universidad de Iberoamerica, Graduate School, San Jose, Costa Rica. Offers clinical neuropsychology (PhD); clinical psychology (M Psych); educational psychology (M Psych); forensic psychology (M Psych); hospital management (MHA); intensive care nursing (MN); medicine (MD).

Universidad Iberoamericana, School of Medicine, Santo Domingo D.N., Dominican Republic. Offers MD.

Universidad Nacional Pedro Henriquez Urena, School of Medicine, Santo Domingo, Dominican Republic. Offers MD.

Université de Montréal, Faculty of Medicine, Professional Program in Medicine, Montréal, QC H3C 3J7, Canada. Offers MD. Open only to Canadian residents. *Accreditation:* LCME/AMA. *Entrance requirements:* For doctorate, proficiency in French. Electronic applications accepted.

Université de Sherbrooke, Faculty of Medicine and Health Sciences, Professional Program in Medicine, Sherbrooke, QC J1K 2R1, Canada. Offers MD. *Accreditation:* LCME/AMA. Electronic applications accepted.

Université Laval, Faculty of Medicine, Post-Professional Programs in Medical Studies, Québec, QC G1K 7P4, Canada. Offers anatomy–pathology (DESS); anesthesiology (DESS); cardiology (DESS); care of older people (Diploma); clinical research (DESS); community health (DESS); dermatology (DESS); diagnostic radiology (DESS); emergency medicine (Diploma); family medicine (DESS); general surgery (DESS); geriatrics (DESS); hematology (DESS); internal medicine (DESS); maternal and fetal medicine (Diploma); medical biochemistry (DESS); medical microbiology and infectious diseases (DESS); medical oncology (DESS); nephrology (DESS); neurology (DESS); neurosurgery (DESS); obstetrics and gynecology (DESS); ophthalmology (DESS); orthopedic surgery (DESS); oto-rhino-laryngology (DESS); palliative medicine (Diploma); pediatrics (DESS); plastic surgery (DESS); psychiatry (DESS); pulmonary medicine (DESS); radiology–oncology (DESS); thoracic surgery (DESS); urology (DESS). *Degree requirements:* For other advanced degree, comprehensive exam. *Entrance requirements:* For degree, knowledge of French. Electronic applications accepted.

Université Laval, Faculty of Medicine, Professional Program in Medicine, Québec, QC G1K 7P4, Canada. Offers MD. *Accreditation:* LCME/AMA. *Entrance requirements:* For doctorate, interview, proficiency in French. Electronic applications accepted.

University at Buffalo, the State University of New York, Graduate School, Jacobs School of Medicine and Biomedical Sciences, Professional Program in Medicine, Buffalo, NY 14203. Offers MD, MD/MBA, MD/MPH, MD/PhD. *Accreditation:* LCME/AMA. *Students:* 619 full-time (308 women); includes 215 minority (15 Black or African American, non-Hispanic/Latino; 1 American Indian or Alaska Native, non-Hispanic/Latino; 110 Asian, non-Hispanic/Latino; 56 Hispanic/Latino; 33 Two or more races, non-Hispanic/Latino). Average age 25. 3,862 applicants, 11% accepted, 180 enrolled. In 2017, 140 doctorates awarded. *Entrance requirements:* For doctorate, MCAT. *Application deadline:* For fall admission, 11/15 for domestic students. Applications are processed on a rolling basis. Application fee: $65. Electronic applications accepted. *Unit head:* Dr. David A. Milling, Senior Associate Dean for Student and Academic Affairs, 716-829-2802 Ext. 2381, Fax: 716-829-2798, E-mail: dmilling@buffalo.edu.
Website: http://medicine.buffalo.edu/education/md.html

The University of Alabama at Birmingham, School of Medicine, Birmingham, AL 35294. Offers MD, MD/PhD. *Accreditation:* LCME/AMA (one or more programs are accredited). *Entrance requirements:* For doctorate, MCAT (minimum score of 24), AMCAS application, letters of recommendation, interview, U.S. citizenship or permanent residency. Electronic applications accepted. *Expenses:* Contact institution.

Allopathic Medicine

The University of Arizona, College of Medicine, Professional Programs in Medicine, Tucson, AZ 85721. Offers MD, PhD. MD program open only to state residents. *Accreditation:* LCME/AMA. *Entrance requirements:* For doctorate, MCAT, previous course work in general chemistry, organic chemistry, biology/zoology, physics, and English. *Faculty research:* Developmental biology, cellular structure and function, immunology, clinical cancer research, heart and respiratory disease.

The University of Arizona, College of Medicine, Program in Medical Sciences, Tucson, AZ 85721. Offers MS, PhD. *Accreditation:* LCME/AMA. *Degree requirements:* For doctorate, comprehensive exam, thesis/dissertation.

University of Arkansas for Medical Sciences, College of Medicine, Little Rock, AR 72205-7199. Offers MD, MD/PhD. *Accreditation:* LCME/AMA. *Entrance requirements:* For doctorate, MCAT. Electronic applications accepted. *Expenses:* Contact institution.

The University of British Columbia, Faculty of Medicine, Department of Surgery, Vancouver, BC V5Z 1M9, Canada. Offers M Sc. *Program availability:* Part-time. *Degree requirements:* For master's, thesis. *Entrance requirements:* Additional exam requirements/recommendations for international students: Required—TOEFL. Electronic applications accepted. *Expenses:* Contact institution. *Faculty research:* Photodynamic therapy, transplantation immunobiology, isolated cell culture, neurophysiology.

The University of British Columbia, Faculty of Medicine, MD/PhD Program, Vancouver, BC V6T 1Z3, Canada. Offers MD/PhD. *Entrance requirements:* Additional exam requirements/recommendations for international students: Required—TOEFL. Electronic applications accepted. *Expenses:* Contact institution.

The University of British Columbia, Faculty of Medicine, Professional Program in Medicine, Vancouver, BC V6T 1Z1, Canada. Offers MD, MD/PhD. *Accreditation:* LCME/AMA. *Entrance requirements:* For doctorate, MCAT.

University of Calgary, Cumming School of Medicine, MD Program, Calgary, AB T2N 4N1, Canada. Offers MD. *Accreditation:* LCME/AMA. *Entrance requirements:* For doctorate, MCAT. Electronic applications accepted.

University of California, Berkeley, Graduate Division, School of Public Health, Group in Health and Medical Sciences, Berkeley, CA 94720-1500. Offers MD/MS. Program offered jointly with University of California, San Francisco. Electronic applications accepted.

University of California, Davis, School of Medicine, Sacramento, CA 95817. Offers MD, MD/MBA, MD/MPH, MD/MS, MD/PhD. *Accreditation:* LCME/AMA. *Degree requirements:* For doctorate, comprehensive exam. *Entrance requirements:* For doctorate, MCAT, 1 year each of English, biological science (lower-division with lab), general chemistry (with lab), organic chemistry (with lab), physics, and college-level math, plus 1/2 year upper-division biology. Electronic applications accepted. *Expenses:* Contact institution. *Faculty research:* Cancer biology, cardiovascular disease, clinical and translational research, neuroscience, regenerative medicine.

University of California, Irvine, School of Medicine, Professional Program in Medicine, Irvine, CA 92697. Offers MD, MD/MBA, MD/MPH, MD/PhD. *Accreditation:* LCME/AMA. *Students:* 410 full-time (212 women), 44 part-time (19 women); includes 40 minority (3 Black or African American, non-Hispanic/Latino; 26 Asian, non-Hispanic/Latino; 11 Hispanic/Latino). Average age 26. In 2017, 94 doctorates awarded. *Entrance requirements:* For doctorate, MCAT. Additional exam requirements/recommendations for international students: Required—TOEFL (minimum score 550 paper-based). *Application deadline:* For fall admission, 11/1 for domestic students. Application fee: $105 ($125 for international students). Electronic applications accepted. *Financial support:* Fellowships, institutionally sponsored loans, traineeships, health care benefits, and unspecified assistantships available. Financial award application deadline: 3/1; financial award applicants required to submit FAFSA. *Unit head:* Ellena Peterson, Associate Dean, 949-824-4169, Fax: 949-824-2160, E-mail: ellena.peterson@uci.edu. *Application contact:* Frances Stephens, Admissions Counselor, 949-824-4614, E-mail: fran.stephens@uci.edu.
Website: http://www.som.uci.edu/graduate-studies/education/md-degree.asp

University of California, Los Angeles, David Geffen School of Medicine, Professional Program in Medicine, Los Angeles, CA 90095. Offers MD, MD/MBA, MD/PhD. *Entrance requirements:* For doctorate, MCAT, interview. *Expenses:* Contact institution.

University of California, Riverside, School of Medicine, Riverside, CA 92521-0102. Offers MD. *Expenses:* Tuition, state resident: full-time $5746. Tuition, nonresident: full-time $10,780. Tuition and fees vary according to campus/location and program.

University of California, San Diego, School of Medicine, Professional Program in Medicine, La Jolla, CA 92093. Offers MD, MD/PhD. *Accreditation:* LCME/AMA. *Students:* 502. *Entrance requirements:* For doctorate, MCAT. *Application deadline:* For fall admission, 11/2 for domestic students. Application fee: $90. *Expenses:* Contact institution. *Unit head:* Dr. Carolyn J. Kelly, MD, Associate Dean, Admissions and Student Affairs. *Application contact:* 858-534-3880, E-mail: somadmissions@ucsd.edu.

University of California, San Francisco, School of Medicine, San Francisco, CA 94143-0410. Offers MD, PhD, MD/MPH, MD/MS, MD/PhD. *Accreditation:* LCME/AMA (one or more programs are accredited). *Entrance requirements:* For doctorate, MCAT (for MD), interview (for MD). Electronic applications accepted. *Expenses:* Contact institution. *Faculty research:* Neurosciences, human genetics, developmental biology, social/behavioral/policy sciences, immunology.

University of Central Florida, College of Medicine, Orlando, FL 32816. Offers MS, MD, PhD. *Accreditation:* LCME/AMA. *Expenses:* Tuition, state resident: part-time $288.16 per credit hour. Tuition, nonresident: part-time $1073.31 per credit hour. Tuition and fees vary according to program. *Financial support:* Fellowships, research assistantships, and teaching assistantships available. *Unit head:* Dr. Deborah C. German, Vice President for Medical Affairs/Dean, 407-266-1000, E-mail: deb@ucf.edu. *Application contact:* Associate Director, Graduate Admissions, 407-823-2766, Fax: 407-823-6442, E-mail: gradadmissions@ucf.edu.
Website: http://www.med.ucf.edu

University of Chicago, Pritzker School of Medicine, Chicago, IL 60637. Offers MD, MD/PhD. *Faculty:* 911 full-time (366 women), 124 part-time/adjunct (67 women). *Students:* 364 full-time (183 women); includes 172 minority (54 Black or African American, non-Hispanic/Latino; 3 American Indian or Alaska Native, non-Hispanic/Latino; 73 Asian, non-Hispanic/Latino; 27 Hispanic/Latino; 2 Native Hawaiian or other Pacific Islander, non-Hispanic/Latino; 13 Two or more races, non-Hispanic/Latino), 1 international. Average age 26. 5,549 applicants, 5% accepted, 90 enrolled. In 2017, 89 doctorates awarded. *Entrance requirements:* For doctorate, MCAT, competency requirements in the following areas: biology, chemistry, physics, mathematics, humanities, writing and analysis, interpersonal skills, and clinical exploration. *Application deadline:* For fall admission, 10/15 for domestic and international students. Applications are processed on a rolling basis. Application fee: $85. Electronic applications accepted. *Expenses:* $55,514. *Financial support:* In 2017–18, 354 students received support. Career-related internships or fieldwork, Federal Work-Study, institutionally sponsored loans, and scholarships/grants available. Financial award application deadline: 8/2. *Faculty research:* Microbiome and immunology, cancer biology, neuroscience, genetics and genomics, cell and developmental biology. *Total annual research expenditures:* $263.6 million. *Unit head:* Dr. Holly J. Humphrey, Dean for Medical Education, 773-834-2138, E-mail: dean-for-meded@bsd.uchicago.edu. *Application contact:* Dr. Keme Carter, Assistant Dean for Admissions, 773-702-1937, Fax: 773-834-5412, E-mail: pritzkeradmissions@bsd.uchicago.edu.
Website: http://pritzker.uchicago.edu/

University of Cincinnati, Graduate School, College of Medicine, Physician Scientist Training Program, Cincinnati, OH 45221. Offers MD/PhD. *Entrance requirements:* Additional exam requirements/recommendations for international students: Required—TOEFL. Electronic applications accepted. *Expenses: Tuition, area resident:* Full-time $14,468. Tuition, state resident: full-time $14,968; part-time $754 per credit hour. Tuition, nonresident: full-time $24,210; part-time $1311 per credit hour. *International tuition:* $26,460 full-time. *Required fees:* $3958; $84 per credit hour. One-time fee: $85 full-time. Tuition and fees vary according to course load, degree level and program.

University of Cincinnati, Graduate School, College of Medicine, Professional Program in Medicine, Cincinnati, OH 45221. Offers MD. *Accreditation:* LCME/AMA. *Entrance requirements:* For doctorate, MCAT. Electronic applications accepted. *Expenses: Tuition, area resident:* Full-time $14,468. Tuition, state resident: full-time $14,968; part-time $754 per credit hour. Tuition, nonresident: full-time $24,210; part-time $1311 per credit hour. *International tuition:* $26,460 full-time. *Required fees:* $3958; $84 per credit hour. One-time fee: $85 full-time. Tuition and fees vary according to course load, degree level and program. *Faculty research:* Molecular genetics, environmental health, neuroscience and cell biology, cardiovascular science, developmental biology.

University of Colorado Denver, School of Medicine, Professional Program in Medicine, Aurora, CO 80045. Offers MD, MD/MBA, MD/PhD. *Accreditation:* LCME/AMA. *Students:* 287 applicants, 66% accepted, 184 enrolled. In 2017, 155 doctorates awarded. *Entrance requirements:* For doctorate, MCAT, AMCAS application, essay, interviews, prerequisite coursework in biology (with lab), general chemistry (with lab), organic chemistry (with lab), general physics (with lab), English literature/composition, college-level mathematics (algebra and above). Additional exam requirements/recommendations for international students: Required—TOEFL (minimum score 550 paper-based; 80 iBT). *Application deadline:* For fall admission, 11/1 for domestic students, 10/1 for international students. Application fee: $100 ($125 for international students). Electronic applications accepted.
Website: http://www.ucdenver.edu/academics/colleges/medicalschool/Pages/somWelcome.aspx

University of Connecticut Health Center, School of Medicine, Farmington, CT 06030. Offers MD, MD/MBA, MD/MPH, MD/PhD. *Accreditation:* LCME/AMA. *Entrance requirements:* For doctorate, MCAT. Electronic applications accepted. *Expenses:* Contact institution.

University of Florida, College of Medicine, Professional Program in Medicine, Gainesville, FL 32611. Offers MD, MD/PhD. *Accreditation:* LCME/AMA. *Entrance requirements:* For doctorate, MCAT, 8 semester hours of course work in biology, general chemistry, and general physics; 4 semester hours of course work in geochemistry and organic chemistry. Electronic applications accepted. *Faculty research:* Neurobiology, gene therapy and genetic imaging technologies, diabetes and autoimmune diseases, transplantation.

University of Hawaii at Manoa, John A. Burns School of Medicine, Professional Program in Medicine, Honolulu, HI 96822. Offers MD. *Accreditation:* LCME/AMA. *Entrance requirements:* For doctorate, MCAT. Electronic applications accepted. *Expenses:* Contact institution.

University of Illinois at Chicago, College of Medicine, Professional Program in Medicine, Chicago, IL 60607-7128. Offers MD, MD/MS, MD/PhD. *Program availability:* Part-time. *Entrance requirements:* For doctorate, MCAT. Electronic applications accepted. *Faculty research:* Biomedical and clinical sciences.

The University of Iowa, Roy J. and Lucille A. Carver College of Medicine and Graduate College, Medical Scientist Training Program, Iowa City, IA 52242-1316. Offers MD/PhD. Electronic applications accepted. Application fee is waived when completed online. *Faculty research:* Structure and function of ion channels, molecular genetics of human disease, neurobiology of pain, viral immunology and immunopathology, epidemiology of aging and cancer, human learning and memory, structural enzymology.

The University of Iowa, Roy J. and Lucille A. Carver College of Medicine, Professional Program in Medicine, Iowa City, IA 52242-1316. Offers MD, MD/JD, MD/MBA, MD/MPH, MD/PhD. *Accreditation:* LCME/AMA. *Degree requirements:* For doctorate, U.S. Medical Licensing Examination Steps 1 and 2. *Entrance requirements:* For doctorate, MCAT, course work in biology, chemistry, organic chemistry, biochemistry, physics, mathematics, English, and social sciences; bachelor's degree. Electronic applications accepted. Application fee is waived when completed online. *Expenses:* Contact institution.

The University of Kansas, University of Kansas Medical Center, School of Medicine, MD/PhD Program, Kansas City, KS 66160. Offers MD/PhD. *Students:* 25 full-time (11 women); includes 4 minority (2 Black or African American, non-Hispanic/Latino; 1 Asian, non-Hispanic/Latino; 1 Hispanic/Latino). Average age 28. 85 applicants, 6% accepted, 3 enrolled. *Application deadline:* For fall admission, 10/15 priority date for domestic students. Applications are processed on a rolling basis. Application fee: $50. Electronic applications accepted. *Expenses:* Contact institution. *Financial support:* Fellowships with full tuition reimbursements, research assistantships with full tuition reimbursements, and teaching assistantships with full tuition reimbursements available. Financial award application deadline: 3/1; financial award applicants required to submit FAFSA. *Unit head:* Dr. Timothy A. Fields, Director, 913-588-7169, E-mail: tfields@kumc.edu. *Application contact:* Janice Fletcher, Administrative Manager, 913-588-5241, Fax: 913-945-6848, E-mail: jfletcher@kumc.edu.
Website: http://www.kumc.edu/md-phd-program.html

The University of Kansas, University of Kansas Medical Center, School of Medicine, MD Program, Kansas City, KS 66160. Offers MD. *Accreditation:* LCME/AMA. *Students:* 858 full-time (405 women); includes 214 minority (14 Black or African American, non-Hispanic/Latino; 70 Asian, non-Hispanic/Latino; 59 Hispanic/Latino; 71 Two or more races, non-Hispanic/Latino). Average age 26. 3,557 applicants, 7% accepted, 209 enrolled. In 2017, 198 doctorates awarded. *Degree requirements:* For doctorate, comprehensive exam. *Entrance requirements:* For doctorate, MCAT, bachelor's degree. *Application deadline:* For fall admission, 10/15 for domestic students. Applications are processed on a rolling basis. Application fee: $50. Electronic applications accepted. *Expenses:* Contact institution. *Financial support:* Scholarships/grants available. Financial award application deadline: 3/1; financial award applicants required to submit FAFSA. *Faculty research:* Reproductive biology, multidisciplinary research on the basic mechanisms of cancer, renal research, neurological research, liver research. *Unit head:* Dr. Robert Simari, Executive Dean, 913-588-1440. *Application contact:* Jason Edwards, Director of Admissions and Premedical Programs, 913-588-5280, Fax: 913-588-5259, E-mail: premedinfo@kumc.edu.
Website: http://www.kumc.edu/school-of-medicine.html

University of Kentucky, College of Medicine, Lexington, KY 40536. Offers MD, MD/MBA, MD/MPH, MD/PhD. *Accreditation:* LCME/AMA. *Students:* 543 full-time (245 women). Average age 24. *Degree requirements:* For doctorate, comprehensive exam (for some programs), thesis/dissertation (for some programs). *Entrance requirements:* For doctorate, MCAT (for MD). *Application deadline:* For fall admission, 11/1 for domestic students. Applications are processed on a rolling basis. Application fee: $50. Electronic applications accepted. *Expenses:* Contact institution. *Financial support:* Institutionally sponsored loans available. Financial award applicants required to submit FAFSA. *Faculty research:* Aging, cancer, cardiovascular disease, infectious disease, women's maternal and child health. *Unit head:* Dr. Wendy L. Jackson, Associate Dean for Admissions, 859-323-6161. *Application contact:* Kimberly Scott, Assistant Director of Admissions, 859-323-6161, E-mail: kymedap@uky.edu.
Website: http://med.uky.edu/

University of Louisville, School of Medicine, Professional Programs in Medicine, Louisville, KY 40292-0001. Offers MD, MD/MBA, MD/MS, MD/PhD. *Accreditation:* LCME/AMA. *Faculty:* 62 full-time (22 women), 16 part-time/adjunct (7 women). *Students:* 636 full-time (283 women), 5 part-time (3 women); includes 136 minority (36 Black or African American, non-Hispanic/Latino; 64 Asian, non-Hispanic/Latino; 16 Hispanic/Latino; 20 Two or more races, non-Hispanic/Latino). Average age 26. 3,562 applicants, 9% accepted, 165 enrolled. In 2017, 144 doctorates awarded. *Entrance requirements:* For doctorate, MCAT. Additional exam requirements/recommendations for international students: Required—TOEFL (minimum score 550 paper-based; 79 iBT). *Application deadline:* For fall admission, 1/28 for domestic students. Applications are processed on a rolling basis. Application fee: $65. Electronic applications accepted. *Expenses:* Tuition, state resident: full-time $12,246; part-time $681 per credit hour. Tuition, nonresident: full-time $25,486; part-time $1417 per credit hour. *Required fees:* $196. Tuition and fees vary according to course load, program and reciprocity agreements. *Faculty research:* Environmental effects on the cardiovascular system, diabetes, obesity and metabolic, molecular targets for cancer chemotherapy, plasticity of neural tissue, stem cells in repair of damaged cardiovascular tissue. *Total annual research expenditures:* $30.3 million. *Unit head:* Dr. Toni M. Ganzel, Dean, 502-852-1499, Fax: 502-852-1484, E-mail: meddean@louisville.edu. *Application contact:* Director of Admissions, 502-852-5793, Fax: 502-852-6849.
Website: http://louisville.edu/medicine/departments

University of Lynchburg, Graduate Studies, Doctor of Medical Science Program, Lynchburg, VA 24501-3199. Offers physician assisted medicine (D Med Sc). *Program availability:* Online learning. *Faculty:* 9 full-time (3 women), 2 part-time/adjunct (0 women). *Students:* 63 full-time (33 women), 21 part-time (8 women); includes 17 minority (3 Black or African American, non-Hispanic/Latino; 4 Asian, non-Hispanic/Latino; 5 Hispanic/Latino; 5 Two or more races, non-Hispanic/Latino), 1 international. Average age 38. 91 applicants, 100% accepted, 84 enrolled. *Degree requirements:* For doctorate, scholarly project and practicum. *Entrance requirements:* For doctorate, graduate-level research course, minimum overall graduate cumulative GPA of 3.0; all official transcripts prior to matriculation; 300-word essay describing areas of interest and scholarly project; intended discipline and plan for completing clinical or PA education; master's or doctoral degree from regionally-accredited institution. Additional exam requirements/recommendations for international students: Required—TOEFL (minimum score 550 paper-based; 80 iBT), IELTS (minimum score 6). *Application deadline:* For fall admission, 6/1 for domestic and international students; for spring admission, 10/15 for domestic and international students; for summer admission, 3/1 for domestic and international students. Applications are processed on a rolling basis. Application fee: $100. Electronic applications accepted. *Expenses:* Contact institution. *Financial support:* Institutionally sponsored loans, scholarships/grants, unspecified assistantships, and tobacco fund awards available. *Faculty research:* Partnerships with: Central Regional Healthcare, Arrowhead Regional Medical Center, Johnson Health Center, Albemarle Orthopedics. *Unit head:* Dr. Jeremy Welsh, Associate Dean, Graduate Health Sciences/Program Director, Department of PA Medicine, E-mail: welsh.jm@lynchburg.edu. *Application contact:* Ellen Thompson, Graduate Admissions Counselor, 434-544-8841, E-mail: thompson_e@lynchburg.edu.
Website: https://www.lynchburg.edu/graduate/physician-assistant-medicine/doctor-of-medical-science/for-interested-students/

University of Manitoba, Max Rady College of Medicine and Faculty of Graduate Studies, Graduate Programs in Medicine, Department of Surgery, Winnipeg, MB R3T 2N2, Canada. Offers M Sc.

University of Maryland, Baltimore, School of Medicine, Professional Program in Medicine, Baltimore, MD 21201. Offers MD, MD/PhD. *Accreditation:* LCME/AMA. *Students:* 633 full-time (378 women), 4 part-time (0 women); includes 267 minority (36 Black or African American, non-Hispanic/Latino; 190 Asian, non-Hispanic/Latino; 26 Hispanic/Latino; 15 Two or more races, non-Hispanic/Latino), 8 international. Average age 25. 4,852 applicants, 7% accepted, 180 enrolled. In 2017, 161 doctorates awarded. *Entrance requirements:* For doctorate, MCAT, AMCAS application, science coursework. *Application deadline:* For fall admission, 11/1 for domestic students. Applications are processed on a rolling basis. Application fee: $70. Electronic applications accepted. *Expenses:* Contact institution. *Financial support:* Federal Work-Study and scholarships/grants available. Financial award application deadline: 3/15; financial award applicants required to submit FAFSA. *Unit head:* Dr. E. Albert Reece, Dean and Vice President for Medical Affairs, 410-706-7410, Fax: 410-706-0235, E-mail: deanmed@som.umaryland.edu. *Application contact:* Dr. Milford M. Foxwell, Jr., Associate Dean for Admissions, 410-706-7478, Fax: 410-706-0467, E-mail: admissions@som.umaryland.edu.

University of Massachusetts Medical School, School of Medicine, Worcester, MA 01655-0115. Offers MD. *Accreditation:* LCME/AMA. *Faculty:* 1,316 full-time (526 women), 357 part-time/adjunct (229 women). *Students:* 565 full-time (310 women); includes 178 minority (31 Black or African American, non-Hispanic/Latino; 3 American Indian or Alaska Native, non-Hispanic/Latino; 128 Asian, non-Hispanic/Latino; 15 Hispanic/Latino; 1 Native Hawaiian or other Pacific Islander, non-Hispanic/Latino), 1 international. Average age 26. 3,614 applicants, 9% accepted, 162 enrolled. In 2017, 132 doctorates awarded. *Degree requirements:* For doctorate, U.S. Medical Licensing Examination Step 1 and Step 2 (CS and CK). *Entrance requirements:* For doctorate, MCAT, bachelor's degree. *Application deadline:* For fall admission, 12/1 for domestic students. Applications are processed on a rolling basis. Application fee: $100. Electronic applications accepted. *Expenses:* $36,678 in-state tuition and mandatory fees; $61,478 out-of-state. *Financial support:* In 2017–18, 485 students received support, including 4 fellowships with partial tuition reimbursements available (averaging $29,000 per year), 31 research assistantships with full tuition reimbursements available (averaging $31,212 per year); institutionally sponsored loans, scholarships/grants, and tuition waivers (partial) also available. Financial award application deadline: 3/31; financial award applicants required to submit FAFSA. *Faculty research:* RNA interference, cell dynamics, immunology and virology, chemical biology, stem cell research. *Total annual research expenditures:* $279 million. *Unit head:* Dr. Terence R. Flotte, Dean/Provost/Executive Deputy Chancellor, 508-856-8000, E-mail: terry.flotte@umassmed.edu. *Application contact:* Jennifer Lee Shea, Admissions Coordinator, 508-856-2323, Fax: 508-856-3629, E-mail: admissions@umassmed.edu.
Website: http://www.umassmed.edu/som

University of Miami, Graduate School, Miller School of Medicine, Professional Program in Medicine, Coral Gables, FL 33124. Offers MD. *Accreditation:* LCME/AMA. *Entrance requirements:* For doctorate, MCAT, 90 pre-med semester hours. Electronic applications accepted. *Faculty research:* AIDS, cancer, diabetes, neuroscience, wound healing.

University of Michigan, Medical School, Ann Arbor, MI 48109. Offers MD, MD/MA Edu, MD/MBA, MD/MPH, MD/MPP, MD/MS, MD/MSI, MD/PhD. *Faculty:* 2,466 full-time (937 women), 1,357 part-time/adjunct (701 women). *Students:* 735 full-time (394 women); includes 224 minority (46 Black or African American, non-Hispanic/Latino; 124 Asian, non-Hispanic/Latino; 54 Hispanic/Latino). Average age 27. 5,991 applicants, 6% accepted, 170 enrolled. In 2017, 174 doctorates awarded. *Entrance requirements:* For doctorate, MCAT. *Application deadline:* For fall admission, 9/30 for domestic students. Applications are processed on a rolling basis. Electronic applications accepted. *Expenses:* Contact institution. *Financial support:* Institutionally sponsored loans and scholarships/grants available. Financial award application deadline: 9/30; financial award applicants required to submit FAFSA. *Unit head:* Dr. Marschall S. Runge, MD, Dean, 734-764-8175, E-mail: mrunge@umich.edu. *Application contact:* Carol Teener, Director of Admissions, 734-764-6317, Fax: 734-936-3510, E-mail: cteener@umich.edu.
Website: https://medicine.umich.edu/medschool/

University of Minnesota, Duluth, Medical School, Professional Program in Medicine, Duluth, MN 55812-2496. Offers MD. Program offered jointly with University of Minnesota, Twin Cities Campus. *Entrance requirements:* For doctorate, MCAT. Electronic applications accepted.

University of Minnesota, Twin Cities Campus, Medical School, Minneapolis, MN 55455-0213. Offers MA, MS, DPT, MD, PhD, JD/MD, MD/MBA, MD/MHI, MD/MPH, MD/MS, MD/PhD. *Accreditation:* LCME/AMA. *Program availability:* Part-time, evening/weekend. *Expenses:* Contact institution.

University of Mississippi Medical Center, School of Medicine, Jackson, MS 39216-4505. Offers MD, MD/PhD. *Accreditation:* LCME/AMA. *Program availability:* Part-time. *Entrance requirements:* For doctorate, MCAT. Electronic applications accepted.

University of Missouri, School of Medicine, Professional Program in Medicine, Columbia, MO 65211. Offers MD, MD/PhD. *Accreditation:* LCME/AMA. *Entrance requirements:* For doctorate, MCAT, minimum GPA of 3.49. *Application deadline:* Applications are processed on a rolling basis. *Expenses:* Tuition, state resident: full-time $6480. Tuition, nonresident: full-time $17,744. *Required fees:* $1108. Tuition and fees vary according to course load, campus/location and program. *Financial support:* Career-related internships or fieldwork, institutionally sponsored loans, and scholarships/grants available. Financial award applicants required to submit FAFSA. *Faculty research:* Basic and clinical biomedical sciences. *Unit head:* Dr. Edward Yeh, Chairman, 573-882-8280, E-mail: yehet@health.missouri.edu. *Application contact:* Dr. Edward Yeh, Chairman, 573-882-8280, E-mail: yehet@health.missouri.edu.
Website: http://som.missouri.edu/

University of Missouri–Kansas City, School of Medicine, Kansas City, MO 64110-2499. Offers health professions education (MS); MD/PhD. *Accreditation:* LCME/AMA. *Degree requirements:* For doctorate, one foreign language, United States Medical Licensing Exam Step 1 and 2. *Entrance requirements:* For doctorate, interview. *Expenses:* Contact institution. *Faculty research:* Cardiovascular disease, women's and children's health, trauma and infectious diseases, neurological, metabolic disease.

University of Nebraska Medical Center, College of Medicine, Omaha, NE 68198-5527. Offers MD, Certificate, MD/MPH, MD/PhD. *Accreditation:* LCME/AMA. *Entrance requirements:* For doctorate, MCAT. Electronic applications accepted. *Expenses:* Tuition, state resident: full-time $8451; part-time $4225 per semester. Tuition, nonresident: full-time $24,219; part-time $11,295 per semester. *Required fees:* $589; $117 per term.

University of Nevada, Reno, School of Medicine, Reno, NV 89557. Offers MD, MD/PhD. *Expenses:* Contact institution.

University of New Mexico, School of Medicine, Professional Program in Medicine, Albuquerque, NM 87131-2039. Offers MD. *Degree requirements:* For doctorate, comprehensive exam, research. *Entrance requirements:* For doctorate, MCAT, general biology, general chemistry, organic chemistry, biochemistry and physics; minimum GPA of 3.0. Electronic applications accepted. *Expenses:* Contact institution. *Faculty research:* Cancer, infectious disease, brain and behavioral illness, children's health, cardiovascular and metabolic disease.

The University of North Carolina at Chapel Hill, School of Medicine, Professional Program in Medicine, Chapel Hill, NC 27599. Offers MD, MD/MPH, MD/PhD. *Accreditation:* LCME/AMA. *Entrance requirements:* For doctorate, MCAT.

University of Oklahoma Health Sciences Center, College of Medicine, Professional Program in Medicine, Oklahoma City, OK 73190. Offers MD, MD/PhD. *Accreditation:* LCME/AMA. *Entrance requirements:* For doctorate, MCAT. *Faculty research:* Behavior and drugs, structure and function of endothelium, genetics and behavior, gene structure and function, action of antibiotics.

University of Ottawa, Faculty of Graduate and Postdoctoral Studies, Faculty of Medicine, Ottawa, ON K1N 6N5, Canada. Offers M Sc, MD, PhD. *Accreditation:* LCME/AMA. *Degree requirements:* For master's, thesis; for doctorate, thesis/dissertation (for some programs). *Entrance requirements:* For master's, honors degree or equivalent, minimum B average. Electronic applications accepted.

University of Pennsylvania, Perelman School of Medicine, Professional Program in Medicine, Philadelphia, PA 19104. Offers MD, MD/JD, MD/MBA, MD/MPH, MD/MSCE, MD/MSHP, MD/MSME, MD/MTR, MD/PhD. *Accreditation:* LCME/AMA. *Faculty:* 3,170 full-time (1,294 women), 1,251 part-time/adjunct (576 women). *Students:* 770 full-time (349 women); includes 373 minority (37 Black or African American, non-Hispanic/Latino; 178 Asian, non-Hispanic/Latino; 108 Hispanic/Latino; 50 Two or more races, non-Hispanic/Latino), 18 international. Average age 27. 6,200 applicants, 4% accepted, 159 enrolled. *Entrance requirements:* For doctorate, MCAT. Additional exam requirements/recommendations for international students: Required—TOEFL. *Application deadline:* For fall admission, 10/15 for domestic and international students. Application fee: $90. Electronic applications accepted. *Financial support:* In 2017–18, 373 students received support. Scholarships/grants available. Financial award application deadline: 5/1; financial award applicants required to submit FAFSA. *Unit head:* Dr. Gail Morrison, Senior Vice Dean for Education, 215-898-8034, E-mail: morrisog@mail.med.upenn.edu. *Application contact:* Gaye Sheffler, Director, Admissions, 215-898-8000, E-mail: sheffler@mail.med.upenn.edu.

University of Pittsburgh, School of Medicine, Professional Program in Medicine, Pittsburgh, PA 15261. Offers MD. *Accreditation:* LCME/AMA. *Faculty:* 2,300 full-time (889 women), 85 part-time/adjunct (38 women). *Students:* 591 full-time (300 women); includes 236 minority (52 Black or African American, non-Hispanic/Latino; 132 Asian, non-Hispanic/Latino; 31 Hispanic/Latino; 21 Two or more races, non-Hispanic/Latino), 11 international. Average age 26. 6,151 applicants, 6% accepted, 147 enrolled. In 2017, 163 doctorates awarded. *Entrance requirements:* For doctorate, MCAT, undergraduate degree including at least one year of post secondary education in the United States or Canada; one year of course work each in biology (with lab), general or inorganic

chemistry (with lab), organic chemistry (with lab), physics (with lab), and English. Additional exam requirements/recommendations for international students: Required—TOEFL (minimum score 600 paper-based; 100 iBT), IELTS (minimum score 7). *Application deadline:* For fall admission, 10/15 for domestic and international students. Applications are processed on a rolling basis. Application fee: $100. Electronic applications accepted. *Expenses:* $54,872 in-state, $56,410 out-of-state. *Financial support:* In 2017–18, 317 students received support. Institutionally sponsored loans and scholarships/grants available. Financial award application deadline: 3/1; financial award applicants required to submit CSS PROFILE or FAFSA. *Faculty research:* Organ transplantation/immunology; cancer research and therapy; biomedical informatics and computational biology; psychiatry/neurobiology/systems neuroscience. *Total annual research expenditures:* $512.6 million. *Unit head:* Dr. Beth Piraino, Associate Dean of Admissions and Financial Aid, 412-648-9891, Fax: 412-648-8768, E-mail: piraino@pitt.edu. *Application contact:* Cynthia May Bonetti, Executive Director for Admissions and Financial Aid, 412-648-9891, Fax: 412-648-8768, E-mail: cmb103@pitt.edu.
Website: http://www.medschool.pitt.edu/

University of Puerto Rico–Medical Sciences Campus, School of Medicine, Professional Program in Medicine, San Juan, PR 00936-5067. Offers MD. *Accreditation:* LCME/AMA. *Degree requirements:* For doctorate, one foreign language. *Entrance requirements:* For doctorate, MCAT, minimum GPA of 2.5, computer literacy.

University of Rochester, School of Medicine and Dentistry, Professional Program in Medicine, Rochester, NY 14627. Offers MD, MD/MPH, MD/MS, MD/PhD. *Accreditation:* LCME/AMA. *Entrance requirements:* For doctorate, MCAT.

University of Saskatchewan, College of Medicine, Professional Program in Medicine, Saskatoon, SK S7N 5A2, Canada. Offers MD. *Accreditation:* LCME/AMA.

University of South Alabama, College of Medicine, Doctor of Medicine Program, Mobile, AL 36688. Offers MD. *Accreditation:* LCME/AMA. *Faculty:* 165 full-time (51 women), 37 part-time/adjunct (11 women). *Students:* 297 full-time (123 women); includes 80 minority (33 Black or African American, non-Hispanic/Latino; 2 American Indian or Alaska Native, non-Hispanic/Latino; 39 Asian, non-Hispanic/Latino; 3 Hispanic/Latino; 3 Two or more races, non-Hispanic/Latino). Average age 25. In 2017, 70 doctorates awarded. *Degree requirements:* For doctorate, residency. *Entrance requirements:* For doctorate, MCAT, two semesters or three quarters in general chemistry with lab, general biology with lab, mathematics (calculus recommended), organic chemistry with lab, general physics with lab, humanities, English composition or literature; composite evaluation prepared by premedical committee of undergraduate college. Additional exam requirements/recommendations for international students: Required—TOEFL. *Application deadline:* For fall admission, 11/15 for domestic and international students. Application fee: $75. Electronic applications accepted. *Expenses:* Contact institution. *Financial support:* Fellowships, research assistantships, teaching assistantships, career-related internships or fieldwork, institutionally sponsored loans, scholarships/grants, and unspecified assistantships available. Support available to part-time students. Financial award application deadline: 3/31; financial award applicants required to submit FAFSA. *Unit head:* Mark Scott, Director, USA College of Medicine Admissions, 251-460-7176, Fax: 251-460-6278, E-mail: mscott@southalabama.edu. *Application contact:* Jonathan Scammell, Assistant Dean for Admissions, 251-460-7176, Fax: 251-460-6278, E-mail: jscammell@southalabama.edu.
Website: http://www.usahealthsystem.com/doctor-of-medicine

University of South Carolina, School of Medicine, Professional Program in Medicine, Columbia, SC 29208. Offers MD, MD/MPH, MD/PhD. *Accreditation:* LCME/AMA. *Entrance requirements:* For doctorate, MCAT. Electronic applications accepted. *Faculty research:* Cardiovascular diseases, oncology, reproductive biology, vision, neuroscience.

University of South Dakota, Graduate School, Sanford School of Medicine, Professional Program in Medicine, Vermillion, SD 57069. Offers bioethics (Certificate); medicine (MD). *Accreditation:* LCME/AMA. In 2017, 52 doctorates awarded. *Degree requirements:* For doctorate, U. S. Medical Licensing Exam-Step 1 and 2. *Entrance requirements:* For doctorate, MCAT, previous course work in biology, chemistry, organic chemistry, mathematics and physics. *Application deadline:* For fall admission, 11/15 for domestic and international students. Applications are processed on a rolling basis. Application fee: $35. Electronic applications accepted. *Financial support:* In 2017–18, 199 students received support. Institutionally sponsored loans and scholarships/grants available. *Unit head:* 605-658-6302, Fax: 605-375-1311, E-mail: md@usd.edu. *Application contact:* Graduate School, 605-658-6140, Fax: 605-677-6118.
Website: http://www.usd.edu/med/

University of Southern California, Keck School of Medicine, Professional Program in Medicine, Los Angeles, CA 90089. Offers MD, MD/MBA, MD/MPH, MD/PhD. *Students:* 720 full-time (339 women); includes 413 minority (45 Black or African American, non-Hispanic/Latino; 1 American Indian or Alaska Native, non-Hispanic/Latino; 258 Asian, non-Hispanic/Latino; 75 Hispanic/Latino; 1 Native Hawaiian or other Pacific Islander, non-Hispanic/Latino; 33 Two or more races, non-Hispanic/Latino), 1 international. Average age 24. 8,099 applicants, 5% accepted, 186 enrolled. In 2017, 199 doctorates awarded. *Entrance requirements:* For doctorate, MCAT, baccalaureate degree, or its equivalent, from accredited college or university. *Application deadline:* For fall admission, 11/1 for domestic and international students. Applications are processed on a rolling basis. Application fee: $100. Electronic applications accepted. *Expenses:* $62,258 tuition and mandatory fees. *Financial support:* In 2017–18, 241 students received support, including 24 research assistantships (averaging $27,500 per year); institutionally sponsored loans, scholarships/grants, and tuition waivers also available. Financial award application deadline: 4/15; financial award applicants required to submit FAFSA. *Unit head:* Dr. Raquel Arias, Associate Dean for Admissions, 323-442-2552, Fax: 323-442-2433, E-mail: medadmit@usc.edu. *Application contact:* Susan Wong, Admissions Coordinator, 323-442-2552, Fax: 323-442-2433, E-mail: medadmit@usc.edu.
Website: http://keck.usc.edu/

University of South Florida, Morsani College of Medicine, Tampa, FL 33620-9951. Offers MS, MSB, MSBCB, MSHI, MSMS, DPT, MD, PhD. *Program availability:* Part-time. *Faculty:* 181 full-time (73 women), 27 part-time/adjunct (12 women). *Students:* 1,271 full-time (650 women), 256 part-time (167 women); includes 582 minority (113 Black or African American, non-Hispanic/Latino; 8 American Indian or Alaska Native, non-Hispanic/Latino; 282 Asian, non-Hispanic/Latino; 154 Hispanic/Latino; 25 Two or more races, non-Hispanic/Latino), 66 international. Average age 26. 9,224 applicants, 10% accepted, 555 enrolled. In 2017, 441 master's, 268 doctorates awarded. Terminal master's awarded for partial completion of doctoral program. *Degree requirements:* For master's, comprehensive exam, thesis; for doctorate, comprehensive exam (for some programs), thesis/dissertation (for some programs). *Entrance requirements:* For master's, GRE General Test or GMAT, BA or equivalent degree from regionally-accredited university with minimum GPA of 3.0 in upper-division coursework; for doctorate, GRE General Test, BA or equivalent degree from regionally-accredited university with minimum GPA of 3.0 in upper-division sciences coursework; three letters of recommendation; personal interview; one- to two-page personal statement. Additional exam requirements/recommendations for international students: Required—TOEFL (minimum score 550 paper-based; 79 iBT). *Application deadline:* For fall admission, 2/1 priority date for domestic students, 2/1 for international students. Application fee: $30. Electronic applications accepted. *Financial support:* In 2017–18, 766 students received support. *Faculty research:* Allergy, immunology, and infectious diseases; cancer biology; cardiovascular research; neuroscience research; biomedical engineering; nanomedicine; neuromusculoskeletal disorders; pharmacogenomics; regenerative medicine; sport's medicine; women's health. *Total annual research expenditures:* $46.2 million. *Unit head:* Dr. Charles J. Lockwood, Dean, 813-974-0533, Fax: 813-974-4990, E-mail: cjlockwood@health.usf.edu. *Application contact:* Dr. Michael Barber, Associate Dean/Professor, 813-974-9702, Fax: 813-974-4990, E-mail: mbarber@health.usf.edu.
Website: http://health.usf.edu/medicine/index.htm

The University of Tennessee Health Science Center, College of Medicine, Memphis, TN 38163-0002. Offers MD, MD/PhD. *Accreditation:* LCME/AMA. *Entrance requirements:* For doctorate, MCAT. Electronic applications accepted. *Expenses:* Contact institution.

The University of Texas at Austin, Dell Medical School, Austin, TX 78712-1111. Offers MD.

The University of Texas Health Science Center at Houston, McGovern Medical School, Houston, TX 77225-0036. Offers MD, MD/MPH, MD/PhD. *Accreditation:* LCME/AMA. *Entrance requirements:* For doctorate, MCAT. Electronic applications accepted. *Expenses:* Contact institution. *Faculty research:* Stroke, infectious diseases, cardiovascular disease, neoplastic disease (cancer), molecular medicine for the prevention of diseases.

The University of Texas Health Science Center at San Antonio, Joe R. and Teresa Lozano Long School of Medicine, San Antonio, TX 78229-3900. Offers deaf education and hearing (MS); medicine (MD); MPH/MD. *Accreditation:* LCME/AMA. *Degree requirements:* For master's, comprehensive exam, practicum assignments. *Entrance requirements:* For master's, minimum GPA of 3.0, interview, 3 professional letters of recommendation; for doctorate, MCAT. Electronic applications accepted. *Expenses:* Contact institution. *Faculty research:* Geriatrics, diabetes, cancer, AIDS, obesity.

The University of Texas Medical Branch, School of Medicine, Galveston, TX 77555. Offers MD. *Accreditation:* LCME/AMA. *Entrance requirements:* For doctorate, MCAT. *Expenses:* Contact institution.

The University of Texas Rio Grande Valley, School of Medicine, Edinburg, TX 78539. Offers MD. *Accreditation:* LCME/AMA. *Program availability:* Part-time, evening/weekend, online learning. *Expenses:* Tuition, state resident: full-time $5550; part-time $417 per credit hour. Tuition, nonresident: full-time $13,020; part-time $832 per credit hour. *Required fees:* $1169.

The University of Texas Southwestern Medical Center, Southwestern Medical School, Dallas, TX 75390. Offers MD, MD/PhD. *Accreditation:* LCME/AMA. *Entrance requirements:* For doctorate, MCAT. Electronic applications accepted. *Expenses:* Contact institution. *Faculty research:* Endocrinology, molecular biology, immunology, cancer biology, neuroscience.

University of Toronto, Faculty of Medicine, Toronto, ON M5S 1A1, Canada. Offers M Sc, M Sc BMC, M Sc OT, M Sc PT, MH Sc, MD, PhD, MD/PhD. *Accreditation:* LCME/AMA. *Entrance requirements:* For doctorate, MCAT (for MD). Electronic applications accepted. *Expenses:* Contact institution.

University of Utah, School of Medicine, MD/PhD Program in Medicine, Salt Lake City, UT 84112-1107. Offers MD/PhD. *Program availability:* Part-time. Electronic applications accepted. *Faculty research:* Molecular biology, biochemistry, cell biology, immunology, bioengineering.

University of Utah, School of Medicine, Professional Program in Medicine, Salt Lake City, UT 84112-1107. Offers MD. *Accreditation:* LCME/AMA. *Entrance requirements:* For doctorate, MCAT, 2 years chemistry with lab, 1 year physics with lab, writing/speech, 2 courses biology, 1 course cell biology or biochemistry, 1 course humanities, 1 course diversity, 1 course social science. Electronic applications accepted. *Expenses:* Contact institution. *Faculty research:* Molecular biology, genetics, immunology, cardiology, endocrinology.

University of Vermont, The Robert Larner, MD College of Medicine, Burlington, VT 05405. Offers MPH, MS, MD, PhD, Certificate, Graduate Certificate, MD/MS, MD/PhD. *Students:* 615 (331 women). 5,857 applicants, 5% accepted, 119 enrolled. *Degree requirements:* For master's, thesis; for doctorate, thesis/dissertation (for some programs). *Entrance requirements:* For master's, GRE General Test; for doctorate, GRE General Test (for PhD); MCAT (for MD). *Application deadline:* For fall admission, 11/15 for domestic and international students. Applications are processed on a rolling basis. Electronic applications accepted. *Expenses:* $37,993 in-state, $63,873 out-of-state. *Financial support:* Fellowships, research assistantships, teaching assistantships, and Federal Work-Study available. *Faculty research:* Cardiovascular medicine, cancer, genetic toxicology, low-back pain, pulmonary medicine. *Unit head:* Dr. Frederick C. Morin, III, Dean, 802-656-2156, E-mail: rick.morin@med.uvm.edu. *Application contact:* Medical Admissions, 802-656-2154, E-mail: medadmissions@med.uvm.edu.
Website: http://www.med.uvm.edu/

University of Virginia, School of Medicine, Charlottesville, VA 22903. Offers MPH, MS, MD, PhD, JD/MD, JD/MPH, MD/JD, MD/MBA, MD/PhD, MPP/MPH. *Accreditation:* LCME/AMA. *Faculty:* 1,084 full-time (374 women), 77 part-time/adjunct (53 women). *Students:* 935 full-time (469 women), 22 part-time (15 women); includes 363 minority (86 Black or African American, non-Hispanic/Latino; 1 American Indian or Alaska Native, non-Hispanic/Latino; 150 Asian, non-Hispanic/Latino; 87 Hispanic/Latino; 1 Native Hawaiian or other Pacific Islander, non-Hispanic/Latino; 38 Two or more races, non-Hispanic/Latino), 57 international. Average age 26. 6,079 applicants, 11% accepted, 259 enrolled. In 2017, 71 master's, 188 doctorates awarded. *Entrance requirements:* For doctorate, MCAT (for MD). Additional exam requirements/recommendations for international students: Required—TOEFL. *Application deadline:* Applications are processed on a rolling basis. Application fee: $80. Electronic applications accepted. *Financial support:* Institutionally sponsored loans and scholarships/grants available. Financial award applicants required to submit FAFSA. *Unit head:* David S. Wilkes, Interim Dean, 434-924-4050, E-mail: dsw4n@virginia.edu. *Application contact:* Randolph J. Canterbury, Senior Associate Dean for Education, 434-243-2522, Fax: 434-982-2586, E-mail: rjc9s@virginia.edu.
Website: http://www.medicine.virginia.edu/

University of Washington, Graduate School, School of Medicine, Professional Program in Medicine, Seattle, WA 98195. Offers MD, MD/MPH, MD/PhD. *Accreditation:* LCME/AMA. *Entrance requirements:* For doctorate, MCAT or GRE, minimum 3 years of college. Electronic applications accepted.

The University of Western Ontario, Faculty of Graduate Studies, Biosciences Division, Department of Family Medicine, London, ON N6A 5B8, Canada. Offers M Cl Sc. *Accreditation:* LCME/AMA. *Program availability:* Part-time, online learning. *Degree requirements:* For master's, thesis. *Entrance requirements:* For master's, medical degree, minimum B average. Additional exam requirements/recommendations for international students: Required—TOEFL. *Faculty research:* Family medicine education, dietary counseling, alcohol problems, palliative care support, multicultural health care.

The University of Western Ontario, Schulich School of Medicine and Dentistry, Professional Program in Medicine, London, ON N6A 5B8, Canada. Offers MD. *Accreditation:* LCME/AMA.

University of Wisconsin–Madison, School of Medicine and Public Health, Doctor of Medicine Program, Madison, WI 53705. Offers MD, MD/MPH, MD/PhD. *Accreditation:* LCME/AMA. *Faculty:* 1,153 full-time, 469 part-time/adjunct. *Students:* 727 full-time (371 women); includes 153 minority (26 Black or African American, non-Hispanic/Latino; 120 Asian, non-Hispanic/Latino; 4 Hispanic/Latino; 3 Two or more races, non-Hispanic/Latino). Average age 25. 5,474 applicants, 5% accepted, 176 enrolled. In 2017, 171 doctorates awarded. *Degree requirements:* For doctorate, comprehensive exam. *Entrance requirements:* For doctorate, MCAT. *Application deadline:* For fall admission, 10/15 for domestic students. Applications are processed on a rolling basis. Application fee: $75. Electronic applications accepted. *Expenses:* $30,109 per year. *Financial support:* Fellowships with full and partial tuition reimbursements, research assistantships with full tuition reimbursements, teaching assistantships with full tuition reimbursements, career-related internships or fieldwork, Federal Work-Study, institutionally sponsored loans, scholarships/grants, traineeships, health care benefits, tuition waivers (full and partial), and unspecified assistantships available. Support available to part-time students. Financial award application deadline: 5/1; financial award applicants required to submit FAFSA. *Faculty research:* Alzheimer's disease, asthma and allergy, cancer, cardiovascular medicine, health services research. *Total annual research expenditures:* $258 million. *Unit head:* Dr. Robert N. Golden, Dean, 608-263-4910, Fax: 608-265-3286, E-mail: rngolden@wisc.edu. *Application contact:* Becky Duffy, MD Admissions Advisor, 608-263-8228, Fax: 608-262-4226, E-mail: rlduffy@wisc.edu.
Website: http://www.med.wisc.edu/education/main/100

Vanderbilt University, School of Medicine, Nashville, TN 37240-1001. Offers MDE, MMP, MS, MSCI, Au D, DMP, MD, PhD, MD/PhD. *Accreditation:* LCME/AMA (one or more programs are accredited). *Entrance requirements:* For doctorate, MCAT (for MD). *Application deadline:* For fall admission, 11/15 for domestic and international students. Application fee: $50. *Expenses:* Contact institution. *Financial support:* Institutionally sponsored loans and scholarships/grants available. Financial award application deadline: 3/1; financial award applicants required to submit FAFSA. *Unit head:* Dr. Jeffrey R. Balser, Dean, School of Medicine, 615-936-3030, E-mail: jeffrey.balser@vanderbilt.edu.
Website: http://www.mc.vanderbilt.edu/medschool/

Virginia Commonwealth University, Medical College of Virginia-Professional Programs, School of Medicine, Professional Program in Medicine, Richmond, VA 23284-9005. Offers MD, MD/MHA, MD/MPH, MD/PhD. *Accreditation:* LCME/AMA. *Entrance requirements:* For doctorate, MCAT. Electronic applications accepted. *Expenses:* Contact institution.

Wake Forest University, School of Medicine, Professional Program in Medicine, Winston-Salem, NC 27109. Offers MD, MD/MA, MD/MBA, MD/MS, MD/PhD. *Accreditation:* LCME/AMA. *Entrance requirements:* For doctorate, MCAT, 32 hours of course work in science. Electronic applications accepted. *Faculty research:* Cancer, stroke, infectious diseases, membrane biology, nutrition.

Washington State University, Elson S. Floyd College of Medicine, Pullman, WA 99164. Offers MS, MD.

Washington University in St. Louis, School of Medicine, Professional Program in Medicine, St. Louis, MO 63130-4899. Offers MD, MD/MA, MD/MS, MD/PhD. *Accreditation:* LCME/AMA. *Degree requirements:* For doctorate, thesis/dissertation (for some programs). *Entrance requirements:* For doctorate, MCAT (for MD). *Application deadline:* For fall admission, 12/31 for domestic and international students. Applications are processed on a rolling basis. Application fee: $80. Electronic applications accepted. *Financial support:* Career-related internships or fieldwork, institutionally sponsored loans, scholarships/grants, health care benefits, and unspecified assistantships available. Financial award application deadline: 4/1; financial award applicants required to submit FAFSA. *Unit head:* Dr. Larry Shapiro, Dean, 314-362-6827. *Application contact:* Dr. Valerie Ratts, Associate Dean, 314-362-6848, Fax: 314-362-4658, E-mail: wumscoa@msnotes.wustl.edu.

Wayne State University, School of Medicine, Professional Program in Medicine, Detroit, MI 48202. Offers MD, MD/PhD. *Accreditation:* LCME/AMA. *Students:* 1,174 full-time (512 women), 26 part-time (13 women); includes 404 minority (81 Black or African American, non-Hispanic/Latino; 9 American Indian or Alaska Native, non-Hispanic/Latino; 242 Asian, non-Hispanic/Latino; 56 Hispanic/Latino; 16 Two or more races, non-Hispanic/Latino), 80 international. Average age 25. 5,581 applicants, 9% accepted, 293 enrolled. In 2017, 268 doctorates awarded. *Degree requirements:* For doctorate, National Board examinations Step 1 and 2. *Entrance requirements:* For doctorate, MCAT, bachelor's degree or equivalent; strong background in basic sciences; 2 semesters each of inorganic chemistry with labs, biology/zoology with labs, college English, organic chemistry with labs, and physics with labs. Additional exam requirements/recommendations for international students: Required—TOEFL, TWE. *Application deadline:* For fall admission, 12/31 for domestic and international students. Application fee: $100. Electronic applications accepted. *Expenses:* Contact institution. *Financial support:* In 2017–18, 859 students received support. Scholarships/grants available. Financial award applicants required to submit FAFSA. *Unit head:* Dr. Jack Sobel, Dean, 313-577-1335, Fax: 313-577-8777, E-mail: officeofthedean@med.wayne.edu. *Application contact:* Dr. Kevin Sprague, Associate Dean for Admissions, 313-577-1466, Fax: 313-577-9420, E-mail: mdadmissions@wayne.edu.
Website: https://www.med.wayne.edu/

West Virginia University, School of Medicine, Morgantown, WV 26506-9600. Offers biochemistry and molecular biology (PhD); biomedical science (MS); cancer cell biology (PhD); cellular and integrative physiology (PhD); exercise physiology (MS, PhD); health sciences (MS); immunology (PhD); medicine (MD); occupational therapy (MOT); pathologists assistant (MHS); physical therapy (DPT). *Program availability:* Part-time, evening/weekend. *Students:* 781 full-time (440 women), 25 part-time (13 women); includes 140 minority (15 Black or African American, non-Hispanic/Latino; 1 American Indian or Alaska Native, non-Hispanic/Latino; 68 Asian, non-Hispanic/Latino; 37 Hispanic/Latino; 1 Native Hawaiian or other Pacific Islander, non-Hispanic/Latino; 18 Two or more races, non-Hispanic/Latino), 19 international. *Entrance requirements:* Additional exam requirements/recommendations for international students: Required—TOEFL. *Application deadline:* Applications are processed on a rolling basis. Application fee: $60. Electronic applications accepted. *Expenses:* Contact institution. *Financial support:* Fellowships, research assistantships, teaching assistantships, career-related internships or fieldwork, Federal Work-Study, institutionally sponsored loans, health care benefits, tuition waivers (full and partial), and administrative assistantships available. Financial award applicants required to submit FAFSA. *Unit head:* Dr. Clay Marsh, Executive Dean, 304-293-6607, Fax: 304-293-6627, E-mail: clay.marsh@hsc.wvu.edu. *Application contact:* Lisa M. Salati, Assistant Vice President, Graduate Education, 304-293-7759, Fax: 304-293-3080, E-mail: lsalati@hsc.wvu.edu.
Website: https://medicine.hsc.wvu.edu

Wright State University, Boonshoft School of Medicine, Professional Program in Medicine, Dayton, OH 45435. Offers MD. *Accreditation:* LCME/AMA. *Entrance requirements:* For doctorate, MCAT.

Yale University, Yale School of Medicine, Professional Program in Medicine, New Haven, CT 06510. Offers MD. *Accreditation:* LCME/AMA. *Degree requirements:* For doctorate, thesis/dissertation. *Entrance requirements:* For doctorate, MCAT. Electronic applications accepted.

Bioethics

Albany Medical College, Alden March Bioethics Institute, Albany, NY 12208. Offers bioethics (MS, DPS); clinical ethics (Certificate); clinical ethics consultation (Certificate). *Program availability:* Part-time, evening/weekend, online learning. *Degree requirements:* For master's, thesis. *Entrance requirements:* For master's and Certificate, GRE, GMAT, LSAT, or MCAT (if no graduate degree), essay, official transcripts, 2 letters of reference. Additional exam requirements/recommendations for international students: Recommended—TOEFL. Electronic applications accepted. *Expenses:* Contact institution. *Faculty research:* Ethics in nanotechnology, ethics in genetics, ethics in transplants, philosophy and bioethics, the states and bioethics.

Case Western Reserve University, School of Medicine and School of Graduate Studies, Graduate Programs in Medicine, Department of Bioethics, Cleveland, OH 44106. Offers MA, JD/MA, MA/MD, MA/MPH, MA/MSN, MSSA/MA. *Entrance requirements:* For master's, GRE General Test or MCAT or MAT or LSAT or GMAT. Additional exam requirements/recommendations for international students: Required—TOEFL (minimum score 550 paper-based). Electronic applications accepted. *Expenses: Tuition:* Full-time $43,854; part-time $1827 per credit hour. *Required fees:* $50; $50 per credit hour. Tuition and fees vary according to course load and program. *Faculty research:* Ethical issues in genetics, conflicts of interest, organ donation, end-of-life decision making, clinical ethics consultation.

Clarkson University, Department of Bioethics, Schenectady, NY 12308. Offers bioethics (MS, Advanced Certificate), including bioethics policy (MS), clinical ethics, health, policy, and law (Advanced Certificate), research ethics. Offered jointly with Icahn School of Medicine at Mount Sinai. *Program availability:* Part-time, evening/weekend, 100% online, blended/hybrid learning. *Faculty:* 1 full-time (0 women), 5 part-time/adjunct (4 women). *Students:* 10 full-time (7 women), 22 part-time (18 women); includes 5 minority (2 Black or African American, non-Hispanic/Latino; 1 Asian, non-Hispanic/Latino; 1 Hispanic/Latino; 1 Two or more races, non-Hispanic/Latino), 10 international. 26 applicants, 81% accepted, 16 enrolled. In 2017, 19 master's, 3 other advanced degrees awarded. *Degree requirements:* For master's, project. *Entrance requirements:* Additional exam requirements/recommendations for international students: Required—TOEFL (minimum score 550 paper-based, 80 iBT) or IELTS (6.5). *Application deadline:* Applications are processed on a rolling basis. Application fee: $50. Electronic applications accepted. *Expenses:* Contact institution. *Financial support:* Scholarships/grants available. *Unit head:* Dr. Sean Philpott, Chair of Bioethics, 518-631-9860, E-mail: sphilpott@clarkson.edu. *Application contact:* Ann Nolte, Assistant Chair of Bioethics, 518-631-9860, E-mail: anolte@clarkson.edu.
Website: https://www.clarkson.edu/academics/graduate

Cleveland State University, College of Graduate Studies, College of Liberal Arts and Social Sciences, Department of Philosophy and Comparative Religion, Cleveland, OH 44115. Offers bioethics (MA, Certificate), including bioethics (MA); philosophy (MA), including philosophy. *Program availability:* Part-time, evening/weekend. *Faculty:* 4 full-time (all women), 2 part-time/adjunct (1 woman). *Students:* 3 full-time (0 women), 2 part-time (1 woman); includes 1 minority (Asian, non-Hispanic/Latino). Average age 35. 11 applicants, 100% accepted, 4 enrolled. In 2017, 2 master's, 1 other advanced degree awarded. *Degree requirements:* For master's, comprehensive exam, thesis optional, 32 credit hours of coursework; for Certificate, 12 credit hours of coursework. *Entrance requirements:* For master's and Certificate, BA, BS, or equivalent degree with minimum GPA of 2.75. Additional exam requirements/recommendations for international students: Required—TOEFL (minimum score 550 paper-based; 78 iBT). *Application deadline:* For fall admission, 7/1 priority date for domestic students, 5/15 priority date for international students; for spring admission, 11/15 for domestic students, 11/1 for international students; for summer admission, 4/1 for domestic students, 3/15 for international students. Applications are processed on a rolling basis. Application fee: $40. Electronic applications accepted. *Financial support:* In 2017–18, 5 students received support, including 5 teaching assistantships with full tuition reimbursements available (averaging $4,000 per year); health care benefits, tuition waivers (full), and unspecified assistantships also available. Support available to part-time students. *Faculty research:* Ethics, early modern philosophy, bioethics, social and political philosophy, history of women philosophers. *Unit head:* Dr. Mary Ellen Waithe, Chairperson, 216-687-3900, Fax: 216-523-7482, E-mail: m.waithe@csuohio.edu. *Application contact:* Deborah L. Brown, Interim Assistant Director, Graduate Admissions, 216-523-7572, Fax: 216-687-5400, E-mail: d.l.brown@csuohio.edu.
Website: http://www.csuohio.edu/class/philosophy-religion/philosophy-religion

Columbia University, School of Professional Studies, Program in Bioethics, New York, NY 10027. Offers MS. *Program availability:* Part-time. *Degree requirements:* For master's, thesis. Electronic applications accepted. *Expenses: Tuition:* Full-time $44,864; part-time $1704 per credit. *Required fees:* $2370 per semester. One-time fee: $105.

Creighton University, Graduate School, Department of Interdisciplinary Studies, MS Program in Health Care Ethics, Omaha, NE 68178-0001. Offers MS. *Program availability:* Part-time. *Faculty:* 4 full-time (2 women). *Students:* 35 part-time (24 women); includes 3 minority (2 American Indian or Alaska Native, non-Hispanic/Latino; 1 Hispanic/Latino). Average age 42. 5 applicants, 80% accepted, 4 enrolled. In 2017, 21 master's awarded. *Degree requirements:* For master's, practicum, capstone. *Entrance requirements:* For master's, resume, essay. Additional exam requirements/recommendations for international students: Required—TOEFL (minimum score 90

iBT), IELTS (minimum score 6.5). *Application deadline:* For fall admission, 7/1 for domestic and international students; for spring admission, 12/1 for domestic and international students. Applications are processed on a rolling basis. Application fee: $50. Electronic applications accepted. Part-time tuition and fees vary according to course load, degree level, campus/location and program. *Financial support:* Scholarships/grants available. Financial award applicants required to submit FAFSA. *Unit head:* Dr. Sarah Lux, Graduate Program Director, 402-280-2639, E-mail: sarahlux@creighton.edu. *Application contact:* Lindsay Johnson, Director of Graduate and Adult Recruitment, 402-280-2703, Fax: 402-280-2423, E-mail: gradschool@creighton.edu.
Website: https://online.creighton.edu/mshce/masters-in-healthcare-ethics

Duke University, Graduate School, Program in Bioethics and Science Policy, Durham, NC 27708-0141. Offers MA. *Entrance requirements:* For master's, GRE General Test. Additional exam requirements/recommendations for international students: Required—TOEFL (minimum score 577 paper-based; 90 iBT) or IELTS (minimum score 7).

Duquesne University, Graduate School of Liberal Arts, Center for Healthcare Ethics, Pittsburgh, PA 15282-0001. Offers MA, DHCE, PhD, Certificate. *Program availability:* Part-time, 100% online. *Faculty:* 3 full-time (0 women). *Students:* 44 full-time (25 women), 1 (woman) part-time; includes 9 minority (4 Black or African American, non-Hispanic/Latino; 4 Asian, non-Hispanic/Latino; 1 Two or more races, non-Hispanic/Latino), 14 international. Average age 37. 18 applicants, 89% accepted, 8 enrolled. In 2017, 1 master's, 11 doctorates awarded. Terminal master's awarded for partial completion of doctoral program. *Degree requirements:* For doctorate, 2 foreign languages, comprehensive exam, thesis/dissertation. *Entrance requirements:* For master's, GRE General Test; for doctorate, GRE General Test, master's degree in health care ethics. Additional exam requirements/recommendations for international students: Required—TOEFL. *Application deadline:* For fall admission, 8/1 for domestic students, 5/1 for international students. Application fee: $0. Electronic applications accepted. *Expenses:* $1,284 per credit. *Financial support:* In 2017–18, 7 students received support, including 5 teaching assistantships with full and partial tuition reimbursements available (averaging $18,000 per year); Federal Work-Study and tuition waivers (full and partial) also available. Support available to part-time students. Financial award application deadline: 5/1. *Unit head:* Dr. Henk Ten Have, Director, 412-396-1585, E-mail: tenhaveh@duq.edu. *Application contact:* Linda Rendulic, Assistant to the Dean, 412-396-6400, Fax: 412-396-5265, E-mail: rendulic@duq.edu.
Website: http://www.duq.edu/academics/schools/liberal-arts/graduate-school/programs/healthcare-ethics

Emory University, Laney Graduate School, Emory Center for Ethics, Atlanta, GA 30322-1100. Offers bioethics (MA). Terminal master's awarded for partial completion of doctoral program. *Degree requirements:* For master's, practicum experience, capstone project. *Entrance requirements:* Additional exam requirements/recommendations for international students: Recommended—TOEFL. Electronic applications accepted.

Hofstra University, Maurice A. Deane School of Law, Hempstead, NY 11549. Offers alternative dispute resolution (JD); American legal studies (LL M); business law honors (JD); clinical bioethics (Certificate); corporate compliance (JD); criminal law and procedure (JD); family law (LL M, JD); health law (JD); health law and policy (LL M, MA); intellectual property law honors (JD); international law honors (JD); JD/MBA; JD/MPH. *Accreditation:* ABA. *Program availability:* Part-time, 100% online. *Faculty:* 41 full-time (23 women), 69 part-time/adjunct (20 women). *Students:* 698 full-time (382 women), 136 part-time (91 women); includes 201 minority (66 Black or African American, non-Hispanic/Latino; 3 American Indian or Alaska Native, non-Hispanic/Latino; 31 Asian, non-Hispanic/Latino; 90 Hispanic/Latino; 8 Native Hawaiian or other Pacific Islander, non-Hispanic/Latino; 3 Two or more races, non-Hispanic/Latino), 28 international. Average age 28. 3,212 applicants, 50% accepted, 317 enrolled. In 2017, 9 master's, 234 doctorates awarded. *Entrance requirements:* For doctorate, LSAT, letter of recommendation, personal statement, undergraduate transcripts; for Certificate, 2 letters of recommendation, JD or LL B, personal statement, law school transcripts. Additional exam requirements/recommendations for international students: Recommended—TOEFL (minimum score 600 paper-based; 100 iBT). *Application deadline:* For fall admission, 4/15 priority date for domestic and international students. Applications are processed on a rolling basis. Application fee: $75. Electronic applications accepted. *Expenses:* $28,397 per term. *Financial support:* In 2017–18, 506 students received support, including 493 fellowships with full and partial tuition reimbursements available (averaging $33,296 per year); research assistantships with full and partial tuition reimbursements available, career-related internships or fieldwork, Federal Work-Study, institutionally sponsored loans, scholarships/grants, tuition waivers (full and partial), and unspecified assistantships also available. Support available to part-time students. Financial award applicants required to submit FAFSA. *Faculty research:* Family law; international law; constitutional law; legal ethics; health law. *Unit head:* Gail Prudenti, Dean, 516-463-4068, E-mail: gail.prudenti@hofstra.edu. *Application contact:* Sunil Samuel, Assistant Vice President of Admissions, 516-463-4723, Fax: 516-463-4664.
Website: http://law.hofstra.edu/

Icahn School of Medicine at Mount Sinai, The Bioethics Program, New York, NY 10029-6504. Offers MS. Program offered jointly with Union Graduate College.

Indiana University–Purdue University Indianapolis, Robert H. McKinney School of Law, Indianapolis, IN 46202. Offers advocacy skills (Certificate); American law for foreign lawyers (LL M); civil and human rights (Certificate); corporate and commercial law (LL M, Certificate); criminal law (Certificate); environmental and natural resources (Certificate); health law (Certificate); health law, policy and bioethics (LL M); intellectual property law (LL M, Certificate); international and comparative law (LL M, Certificate); international human rights law (LL M); law (MJ, JD, SJD); JD/M Phil; JD/MBA; JD/MD; JD/MHA; JD/MLS; JD/MPA; JD/MPH; JD/MSW. *Accreditation:* ABA. *Program availability:* Part-time. *Entrance requirements:* For doctorate, LSAT. Additional exam requirements/recommendations for international students: Required—TOEFL (minimum score 79 iBT), IELTS (minimum score 6.5). Electronic applications accepted. *Expenses:* Contact institution.

Indiana University–Purdue University Indianapolis, School of Liberal Arts, Department of Philosophy, Indianapolis, IN 46202. Offers American philosophy (Certificate); bioethics (Certificate); philosophy (MA); philosophy/bioethics (MA); JD/MA; MD/MA. *Program availability:* Part-time. *Degree requirements:* For master's, thesis optional. *Entrance requirements:* For master's, GRE, writing sample, transcripts, three letters of recommendation, personal statement; for Certificate, letter of recommendation, transcripts, statement of purpose. Additional exam requirements/recommendations for international students: Required—TOEFL, PTE, IUPUI ESL Exam. Electronic applications accepted. *Expenses:* Contact institution. *Faculty research:* American philosophy, pierce bioethics, metaphysics, ethical theory, philosophy of science, early modern philosophy (esp. Kant).

Instituto Tecnologico de Santo Domingo, Graduate School, Area of Health Sciences, Santo Domingo, Dominican Republic. Offers bioethics (M Bioethics); clinical bioethics (Certificate); clinical nutrition (Certificate); comprehensive health and the adolescent (Certificate); comrehensive adloescent health (MS); health and social security (M Mgmt).

Johns Hopkins University, Bloomberg School of Public Health, Berman Institute of Bioethics, Baltimore, MD 21218. Offers MBE. *Students:* 20 applicants, 70% accepted, 8 enrolled. *Degree requirements:* For master's, thesis, practicum. *Application deadline:* For fall admission, 7/1 for domestic students. Applications are processed on a rolling basis. Application fee: $135. Electronic applications accepted. *Faculty research:* Public health and clinical ethics, science and bioethics, research ethics, global bioethics, practical ethics. *Unit head:* Dr. Jeffrey Kahn, Director of the Johns Hopkins Berman Institute of Bioethics, 410-614-5679, E-mail: jeffkahn@jhu.edu. *Application contact:* Office of Admissions, 410-955-3543, Fax: 410-955-0464, E-mail: jhsph.admiss@jhu.edu.
Website: http://www.bioethicsinstitute.org/

Johns Hopkins University, Bloomberg School of Public Health, Department of Health Policy and Management, Baltimore, MD 21205-1996. Offers bioethics and policy (PhD); health administration (MHA), health and public policy (PhD); health economics (MHS); health economics and policy (PhD); health finance and management (MHS); health policy (MSPH); health policy and management (Dr PH); health services research and policy (PhD); public policy (MPP). *Accreditation:* CAHME (one or more programs are accredited). *Program availability:* Part-time. *Students:* 190 full-time (123 women), 135 part-time (73 women); includes 90 minority (10 Black or African American, non-Hispanic/Latino; 53 Asian, non-Hispanic/Latino; 17 Hispanic/Latino; 1 Native Hawaiian or other Pacific Islander, non-Hispanic/Latino; 9 Two or more races, non-Hispanic/Latino), 107 international. Average age 31. 729 applicants, 31% accepted, 96 enrolled. In 2017, 80 master's, 26 doctorates awarded. *Degree requirements:* For master's, thesis (for some programs), internship (for some programs); for doctorate, comprehensive exam, thesis/dissertation, 1-year full-time residency (for some programs), oral and written exams. *Entrance requirements:* For master's, GRE General Test or GMAT, 3 letters of recommendation, curriculum vitae/resume; for doctorate, GRE General Test or GMAT, 3 letters of recommendation, curriculum vitae, transcripts. Additional exam requirements/recommendations for international students: Required—TOEFL (minimum score 100 iBT), IELTS (minimum score 7). *Application deadline:* Applications are processed on a rolling basis. Application fee: $135. Electronic applications accepted. *Financial support:* Fellowships, research assistantships, teaching assistantships, career-related internships or fieldwork, Federal Work-Study, scholarships/grants, traineeships, and stipends available. Support available to part-time students. *Faculty research:* Quality of care and health outcomes, health care finance and technology, health disparities and vulnerable populations, injury prevention, health policy and health care policy. *Unit head:* Dr. Colleen Barry, Chairman. *Application contact:* Mary Sewell, Coordinator, 410-955-2489, Fax: 410-614-9152, E-mail: msewell@jhsph.edu.

Kansas City University of Medicine and Biosciences, College of Biosciences, Kansas City, MO 64106-1453. Offers bioethics (MA); biomedical sciences (MS). *Program availability:* Part-time. *Degree requirements:* For master's, comprehensive exam, thesis (for some programs). *Entrance requirements:* For master's, MCAT, GRE.

Loma Linda University, School of Religion, Program in Bioethics, Loma Linda, CA 92350. Offers MA, Certificate. *Degree requirements:* For master's, comprehensive exam, thesis optional. *Entrance requirements:* For master's, GRE General Test, baccalaureate degree. Additional exam requirements/recommendations for international students: Required—TOEFL. Electronic applications accepted.

Loyola Marymount University, Bellarmine College of Liberal Arts, Program in Bioethics, Los Angeles, CA 90045-2659. Offers MA. *Unit head:* Dr. Roberto Dell'Oro, Director, Bioethics Institute, 310-338-2752, E-mail: rdelloro@lmu.edu. *Application contact:* Chake H. Kouyoumjian, Associate Dean of Graduate Studies, 310-338-2721, Fax: 310-338-6086, E-mail: graduateinfo@lmu.edu.
Website: http://bellarmine.lmu.edu/bioethics/academics/gradprograms

Loyola University Chicago, Graduate School, Neiswanger Institute for Bioethics, Maywood, IL 60141. Offers MA, D Be, Certificate, MD/MA. *Program availability:* Online learning. *Faculty:* 7 full-time (4 women), 6 part-time/adjunct (2 women). *Students:* 29 full-time (19 women), 95 part-time (58 women); includes 22 minority (5 Black or African American, non-Hispanic/Latino; 1 American Indian or Alaska Native, non-Hispanic/Latino; 5 Asian, non-Hispanic/Latino; 7 Hispanic/Latino; 1 Native Hawaiian or other Pacific Islander, non-Hispanic/Latino; 3 Two or more races, non-Hispanic/Latino). Average age 48. 42 applicants, 79% accepted, 28 enrolled. In 2017, 24 master's, 9 doctorates, 6 other advanced degrees awarded. *Degree requirements:* For master's, thesis; for doctorate, comprehensive exam, thesis/dissertation. *Entrance requirements:* For master's, advanced degree; for doctorate, master's degree in bioethics or health care ethics. Additional exam requirements/recommendations for international students: Required—TOEFL (minimum score 550 paper-based). *Expenses:* $1,069 per credit hour tuition, $527 per semester mandatory fees. *Financial support:* Scholarships/grants available. Financial award applicants required to submit FAFSA. *Faculty research:* Clinical ethics, research ethics, professional ethics, culture and spirituality in decision making, community health. *Unit head:* Dr. Mark Kuczewski, Director, Neiswanger Institute for Bioethics, 708-327-9200, Fax: 708-327-9209, E-mail: mkuczew@luc.edu. *Application contact:* Robbin Hiller, Coordinator, Bioethics Education, 708-321-9219, Fax: 708-327-9209, E-mail: rhiller@luc.edu.
Website: http://bioethics.luc.edu

McGill University, Faculty of Graduate and Postdoctoral Studies, Faculty of Arts, Department of Philosophy, Montréal, QC H3A 2T5, Canada. Offers bioethics (MA); philosophy (PhD).

McGill University, Faculty of Graduate and Postdoctoral Studies, Faculty of Law, Montréal, QC H3A 2T5, Canada. Offers air and space law (LL M, DCL, Graduate Certificate); bioethics (LL M); comparative law (LL M, DCL, Graduate Certificate); law (LL M, DCL). Applications for LL M with specialization in bioethics are made initially through the Biomedical Ethics Unit in the Faculty of Medicine.

McGill University, Faculty of Graduate and Postdoctoral Studies, Faculty of Medicine, Department of Medicine, Montréal, QC H3A 2T5, Canada. Offers experimental medicine (M Sc, PhD), including bioethics (M Sc), experimental medicine.

Medical College of Wisconsin, Graduate School, Center for Bioethics and Medical Humanities, Milwaukee, WI 53226-0509. Offers bioethics (MA); clinical bioethics (Graduate Certificate); research ethics (Graduate Certificate). *Program availability:* Part-time. *Degree requirements:* For master's, thesis. *Entrance requirements:* For master's and Graduate Certificate, GRE, official transcripts, three letters of recommendation. Additional exam requirements/recommendations for international students: Required—TOEFL. *Application deadline:* For fall admission, 1/15 priority date for domestic students. Applications are processed on a rolling basis. Application fee: $50. *Financial support:* Available to part-time students. Application deadline: 2/15; applicants required to submit FAFSA. *Faculty research:* Ethics committees and consultation, ethics of managed care, discussion of code status by physicians. *Application contact:* Recruitment Office, 414-955-4402, Fax: 414-955-6555, E-mail: gradschoolrecruit@mcw.edu.
Website: http://www.mcw.edu/Graduate-School/Programs/Bioethics.htm

New York University, Graduate School of Arts and Science, Program in Bioethics, New York, NY 10012-1019. Offers MA. *Program availability:* Part-time. *Students:* Average age 27. 27 applicants, 96% accepted, 19 enrolled. In 2017, 11 master's awarded.

Entrance requirements: For master's, GRE General Test. Additional exam requirements/recommendations for international students: Required—TOEFL. *Application deadline:* For fall admission, 5/1 for domestic and international students; for spring admission, 11/1 for domestic and international students. Application fee: $100. *Expenses: Tuition:* Full-time $41,352; part-time $19,968 per year. *Required fees:* $2496; $1628 per unit. $814 per term. Tuition and fees vary according to course load and program. *Financial support:* Application deadline: 5/1. *Unit head:* S. Matthew Liao, Director of Graduate Studies, 212-992-7999, Fax: 212-995-4157, E-mail: bioethics@nyu.edu. *Application contact:* Amanda Anjum, Graduate Program Administrator, 212-992-7999, Fax: 212-995-4157, E-mail: bioethics@nyu.edu.

Northeast Ohio Medical University, College of Graduate Studies, Rootstown, OH 44272-0095. Offers bioethics (Certificate); health-system pharmacy administration (MS); integrated pharmaceutical medicine (MS, PhD); medical ethics and humanities (MS); public health (MPH). MPH offered as part of consortium with The University of Akron, Youngstown State University, Ohio University, and Cleveland State University. *Program availability:* Part-time, evening/weekend. *Faculty:* 23 part-time/adjunct (14 women). *Students:* 22 full-time (13 women), 21 part-time (13 women); includes 10 minority (1 Black or African American, non-Hispanic/Latino; 8 Asian, non-Hispanic/Latino; 1 Two or more races, non-Hispanic/Latino). In 2017, 3 master's, 1 doctorate awarded. *Degree requirements:* For master's, thesis (for MS in medical ethics and humanities, integrated pharmaceutical medicine); for doctorate, thesis/dissertation. *Application deadline:* For fall admission, 5/1 priority date for domestic students; for winter admission, 1/5 priority date for domestic students. Applications are processed on a rolling basis. Application fee: $95. Electronic applications accepted. *Expenses:* Contact institution. *Financial support:* Institutionally sponsored loans and tuition waivers available. Financial award application deadline: 3/15; financial award applicants required to submit FAFSA. *Unit head:* Dr. Steven Schmidt, Dean, 330-325-6290. *Application contact:* Heidi Terry, Executive Director, Enrollment Services, 330-325-6479, E-mail: hterry@neomed.edu.
Website: https://www.neomed.edu/graduatestudies/

Saint Louis University, Graduate Programs, Center for Health Care Ethics, St. Louis, MO 63103. Offers clinical health care ethics (Certificate); health care ethics (PhD). *Degree requirements:* For doctorate, comprehensive exam, thesis/dissertation. *Entrance requirements:* For doctorate, GRE General Test, master's degree in ethics or a field related to health care, basic competencies in philosophical and applied ethics, transcripts. Additional exam requirements/recommendations for international students: Required—TOEFL (minimum score 525 paper-based). Electronic applications accepted. *Faculty research:* Health policy, clinical ethics, research ethics, empirical bioethics, ethics education and assessment.

Stony Brook University, State University of New York, Stony Brook Medicine, School of Medicine, Center for Medical Humanities, Compassionate Care, and Bioethics, Stony Brook, NY 11794. Offers MD/MA. *Students:* 9 full-time (8 women), 8 part-time (4 women); includes 7 minority (2 Black or African American, non-Hispanic/Latino; 4 Asian, non-Hispanic/Latino; 1 Hispanic/Latino). Average age 28. 25 applicants, 52% accepted, 8 enrolled. *Entrance requirements:* Additional exam requirements/recommendations for international students: Required—TOEFL. *Application deadline:* For fall admission, 7/15 for domestic students, 4/1 for international students; for spring admission, 10/1 for domestic and international students. Application fee: $100. *Expenses:* Contact institution. *Financial support:* Fellowships available. *Unit head:* Dr. Stephen G. Post, Director, 631-444-9797, E-mail: stephen.post@stonybrookmedicine.edu. *Application contact:* Michael Ortega, Master's Program Coordinator, 631-444-8029, Fax: 631-444-9744, E-mail: michael.ortega@stonybrookmedicine.edu.
Website: https://www.stonybrook.edu/bioethics/

Trinity International University, Trinity Graduate School, Deerfield, IL 60015-1284. Offers athletic training (MA); bioethics (MA); counseling psychology (MA); diverse learning (M Ed); leadership (MA); teaching (MA). *Program availability:* Part-time, evening/weekend, online learning. *Degree requirements:* For master's, comprehensive exam. *Entrance requirements:* For master's, GRE General Test or MAT, minimum undergraduate GPA of 3.0. Additional exam requirements/recommendations for international students: Required—TOEFL (minimum score 580 paper-based), TWE (minimum score 4). Electronic applications accepted.

Trinity International University, Trinity Law School, Santa Ana, CA 92705. Offers bioethics (MLS); church and ministry management (MLS); general legal studies (MLS); human resources management (MLS); human rights (MLS); law (JD); nonprofit organizations (MLS). *Program availability:* Part-time, evening/weekend. *Entrance requirements:* For doctorate, LSAT. Additional exam requirements/recommendations for international students: Required—TOEFL (minimum score 580 paper-based). *Expenses:* Contact institution.

Université de Montréal, Faculty of Medicine, Programs in Bioethics, Montréal, QC H3C 3J7, Canada. Offers MA, DESS. Electronic applications accepted.

Université de Montréal, Faculty of Theology and Sciences of Religions, Montréal, QC H3C 3J7, Canada. Offers health, spirituality and bioethics (DESS); practical theology (MA, PhD); religious sciences (MA, PhD); theology (MA, D Th, PhD, L Th); theology-Biblical studies (PhD). *Degree requirements:* For master's, one foreign language; for doctorate, 2 foreign languages, thesis/dissertation, general exam. Electronic applications accepted.

University of Louisville, School of Interdisciplinary and Graduate Studies, Louisville, KY 40292. Offers interdisciplinary studies (MA, MS, PhD), including bioethics and medical humanities (MA), bioinformatics (PhD), sustainability (MA, MS), translational bioengineering (PhD), translational neuroscience (PhD). *Program availability:* Part-time. *Students:* 26 full-time (17 women), 12 part-time (6 women); includes 5 minority (1 Black or African American, non-Hispanic/Latino; 2 Hispanic/Latino; 2 Two or more races, non-Hispanic/Latino), 9 international. Average age 31. 29 applicants, 38% accepted, 11 enrolled. *Degree requirements:* For master's, variable foreign language requirement, comprehensive exam (for some programs), thesis (for some programs); for doctorate, variable foreign language requirement, comprehensive exam, thesis/dissertation. *Entrance requirements:* For master's and doctorate, GRE General Test, 3 letters of recommendation, transcripts from previous post-secondary educational institutions. Additional exam requirements/recommendations for international students: Required—TOEFL (minimum score 550 paper-based; 79 iBT), IELTS (minimum score 6.5). *Application deadline:* For fall admission, 12/1 priority date for domestic and international students; for winter admission, 11/1 for domestic students, 6/1 for international students; for spring admission, 11/1 for domestic students, 6/1 for international students; for summer admission, 4/1 for domestic students, 1/1 for international students. Applications are processed on a rolling basis. Application fee: $65. Electronic applications accepted. *Expenses:* Tuition, state resident: full-time $12,246; part-time $681 per credit hour. Tuition, nonresident: full-time $25,486; part-time $1417 per credit hour. *Required fees:* $196. Tuition and fees vary according to course load, program and reciprocity agreements. *Financial support:* In 2017–18, 120 fellowships with full tuition reimbursements (averaging $20,000 per year) were awarded. Financial award application deadline: 1/15. *Unit head:* Dr. Beth A. Boehm, Dean and Vice Provost for Graduate Affairs, 502-852-6495, E-mail: beth.boehm@louisville.edu. *Application contact:* Dr. Paul DeMarco, Associate Dean, 502-852-6490, E-mail: gradadm@louisville.edu.
Website: http://www.graduate.louisville.edu

University of Mary, School of Health Sciences, Program in Bioethics, Bismarck, ND 58504-9652. Offers MS. *Degree requirements:* For master's, practicum, capstone project.

University of Pennsylvania, Perelman School of Medicine, Department of Medical Ethics and Health Policy, Philadelphia, PA 19104. Offers MBE, MSME, DMD/MBE, JD/MBE, LL M/MBE, MBE/MSME, MD/MBE, MPA/MBE, MRA/MBE, MS Ed/MBE, MSN/MBE, MSW/MBE, PhD/MBE. *Program availability:* Part-time, evening/weekend. *Faculty:* 20 full-time (8 women), 31 part-time/adjunct (16 women). *Students:* 51 full-time (28 women), 23 part-time (18 women); includes 21 minority (3 Black or African American, non-Hispanic/Latino; 6 Asian, non-Hispanic/Latino; 4 Hispanic/Latino; 8 Two or more races, non-Hispanic/Latino). Average age 28. 30 applicants, 83% accepted, 17 enrolled. In 2017, 45 master's awarded. *Degree requirements:* For master's, thesis. *Entrance requirements:* For master's, transcript, essay, 3 letters of recommendation. Additional exam requirements/recommendations for international students: Required—TOEFL (minimum score 600 paper-based; 100 iBT). *Application deadline:* Applications are processed on a rolling basis. Application fee: $75. *Expenses:* $5,193 tuition; $372 general fee; $181 technology fee. *Financial support:* In 2017–18, 5 students received support. Scholarships/grants available. *Faculty research:* LGBTQ bioethics, resource allocation/rationing, public health ethics, pediatric clinical ethics, mental healthcare ethics. *Unit head:* Dr. Autumn Fiester, Assistant Chair of Education and Training, 215-573-2602, E-mail: fiester@mail.med.upenn.edu. *Application contact:* AJ Roholt, Program Coordinator, 215-898-3837, E-mail: arroholt@upenn.edu.
Website: http://medicalethicshealthpolicy.med.upenn.edu

University of Pittsburgh, Kenneth P. Dietrich School of Arts and Sciences, Center for Bioethics and Health Law, Pittsburgh, PA 15213. Offers bioethics (MA). *Program availability:* Part-time. *Faculty:* 8 full-time (4 women), 1 (woman) part-time/adjunct. *Students:* 2 full-time (1 woman), 5 part-time (all women). Average age 27. 8 applicants, 88% accepted, 6 enrolled. *Entrance requirements:* For master's, GRE General Test, MCAT, LSAT, letters of recommendation, writing sample, personal statement. Additional exam requirements/recommendations for international students: Required—TOEFL (minimum score 550 paper-based), IELTS (minimum score 7). *Application deadline:* For fall admission, 3/1 priority date for domestic and international students. Applications are processed on a rolling basis. Application fee: $50. Electronic applications accepted. *Financial support:* In 2017–18, 7 students received support. Scholarships/grants and tuition waivers (partial) available. Financial award application deadline: 3/1. *Faculty research:* Genetics and genetic research, palliative care, clinical communication and informed consent, conscientious objection in health care and issues of professionalism, end-of-life decision-making, human subject research. *Unit head:* Dr. Lisa S. Parker, Director, 412-648-7007, Fax: 412-648-2649, E-mail: lisap@pitt.edu. *Application contact:* Beth Ann Pischke, Administrator, 412-648-7007, Fax: 412-648-2649, E-mail: pischke@pitt.edu.
Website: http://www.bioethics.pitt.edu

University of South Dakota, Graduate School, Sanford School of Medicine, Professional Program in Medicine, Vermillion, SD 57069. Offers bioethics (Certificate); medicine (MD). *Accreditation:* LCME/AMA. In 2017, 52 doctorates awarded. *Degree requirements:* For doctorate, U. S. Medical Licensing Exam-Step 1 and 2. *Entrance requirements:* For doctorate, MCAT, previous course work in biology, chemistry, organic chemistry, mathematics and physics. *Application deadline:* For fall admission, 11/15 for domestic and international students. Applications are processed on a rolling basis. Application fee: $35. Electronic applications accepted. *Financial support:* In 2017–18, 199 students received support. Institutionally sponsored loans and scholarships/grants available. *Unit head:* 605-658-6302, Fax: 605-375-1311, E-mail: md@usd.edu. *Application contact:* Graduate School, 605-658-6140, Fax: 605-677-6118.
Website: http://www.usd.edu/med/

University of South Florida, Innovative Education, Tampa, FL 33620-9951. Offers adult, career and higher education (Graduate Certificate), including college teaching, leadership in developing human resources, leadership in higher education; Africana studies (Graduate Certificate), including diasporas and health disparities, genocide and human rights; aging studies (Graduate Certificate), including gerontology; art research (Graduate Certificate), including museum studies; business foundations (Graduate Certificate); chemical and biomedical engineering (Graduate Certificate), including materials science and engineering, water, health and sustainability; child and family studies (Graduate Certificate), including positive behavior support; civil and industrial engineering (Graduate Certificate), including transportation systems analysis; community and family health (Graduate Certificate), including maternal and child health, social marketing and public health, violence and injury: prevention and intervention, women's health; criminology (Graduate Certificate), including criminal justice administration; data science for public administration (Graduate Certificate); digital humanities (Graduate Certificate); educational measurement and research (Graduate Certificate), including evaluation; English (Graduate Certificate), including comparative literary studies, creative writing, professional and technical communication; entrepreneurship (Graduate Certificate); environmental health (Graduate Certificate), including safety management; epidemiology and biostatistics (Graduate Certificate), including applied biostatistics, biostatistics, concepts and tools of epidemiology, epidemiology, epidemiology of infectious diseases; geography, environment and planning (Graduate Certificate), including community development, environmental policy and management, geographical information systems; geology (Graduate Certificate), including hydrogeology; global health (Graduate Certificate), including disaster management, global health and Latin American and Caribbean studies, global health practice, humanitarian assistance, infection control; government and international affairs (Graduate Certificate), including Cuban studies, globalization studies; health policy and management (Graduate Certificate), including health management and leadership, public health policy and programs; hearing specialist: early intervention (Graduate Certificate); industrial and management systems engineering (Graduate Certificate), including systems engineering, technology management; information studies (Graduate Certificate), including school library media specialist; information systems/decision sciences (Graduate Certificate), including analytics and business intelligence; instructional technology (Graduate Certificate), including distance education, Florida digital/virtual educator, instructional design, multimedia design, Web design; internal medicine, bioethics and medical humanities (Graduate Certificate), including biomedical ethics; Latin American and Caribbean studies (Graduate Certificate); leadership for coastal resiliency planning (Graduate Certificate); mass communications (Graduate Certificate), including multimedia journalism; mathematics and statistics (Graduate Certificate), including mathematics; medicine (Graduate Certificate), including aging and neuroscience, bioinformatics, biotechnology, brain fitness and memory management, clinical investigation, hand and upper limb rehabilitation, health informatics, health sciences, integrative weight management, intellectual property, medicine and gender, metabolic and nutritional medicine, metabolic cardiology, pharmacy sciences; national and competitive intelligence (Graduate Certificate); nursing (Graduate Certificate), including simulation based academic fellowship in advanced pain management; psychological and social foundations (Graduate Certificate), including career counseling, college teaching, diversity in education, mental health counseling, school counseling; public affairs (Graduate Certificate), including nonprofit management, public management, research administration; public health (Graduate Certificate), including assessing chemical toxicity and public health risks, health equity, pharmacoepidemiology, public health generalist,

toxicology, translational research in adolescent behavioral health; public health practices (Graduate Certificate), including planning for healthy communities; rehabilitation and mental health counseling (Graduate Certificate), including integrative mental health care, marriage and family therapy, rehabilitation technology; secondary education (Graduate Certificate), including ESOL, foreign language education: culture and content, foreign language education: professional; social work (Graduate Certificate), including geriatric social work/clinical gerontology; special education (Graduate Certificate), including autism spectrum disorder, disabilities education: severe/profound; world languages (Graduate Certificate), including teaching English as a second language (TESL) or foreign language. *Unit head:* Dr. Cynthia DeLuca, Associate Vice President and Assistant Vice Provost, 813-974-3077, Fax: 813-974-7061, E-mail: deluca@usf.edu. *Application contact:* Owen Hooper, Director, Summer and Alternative Calendar Programs, 813-974-6917, E-mail: hooper@usf.edu.
Website: http://www.usf.edu/innovative-education/

The University of Tennessee, Graduate School, College of Arts and Sciences, Department of Philosophy, Knoxville, TN 37996. Offers medical ethics (MA, PhD); philosophy (MA, PhD); religious studies (MA). *Program availability:* Part-time. *Degree requirements:* For master's, thesis or alternative; for doctorate, one foreign language, thesis/dissertation. *Entrance requirements:* For master's and doctorate, GRE General Test, minimum GPA of 2.7. Additional exam requirements/recommendations for international students: Required—TOEFL. Electronic applications accepted.

University of Toronto, Faculty of Medicine, Institute of Medical Science, Toronto, ON M5S 1A1, Canada. Offers bioethics (MH Sc); biomedical communications (M Sc BMC); medical radiation science (MH Sc); medical science (PhD). *Degree requirements:* For master's, thesis; for doctorate, thesis/dissertation, thesis defense. *Entrance requirements:* For master's, minimum GPA of 3.7 in 3 of 4 years (M Sc), interview; for doctorate, M Sc or equivalent, defended thesis, minimum A- average, interview. Additional exam requirements/recommendations for international students: Required—TOEFL (minimum score 600 paper-based; 93 iBT), TWE (minimum score 5). Electronic applications accepted.

University of Washington, Graduate School, School of Medicine, Graduate Programs in Medicine, Department of Medical History and Ethics, Seattle, WA 98195. Offers bioethics (MA).

Washington State University, College of Arts and Sciences, School of Politics, Philosophy and Public Affairs, Pullman, WA 99164-4880. Offers bioethics (Graduate Certificate); political science (MA, PhD); public affairs (MPA). MPA, MA, and PhD programs also offered at the Vancouver campus; Graduate Certificate offered through Global (online) campus. *Accreditation:* NASPAA. *Program availability:* Online learning. Terminal master's awarded for partial completion of doctoral program. *Degree requirements:* For master's, comprehensive exam (for some programs), thesis, oral exam; for doctorate, comprehensive exam, thesis/dissertation, oral exam, written exam. *Entrance requirements:* For master's, GRE General Test, minimum GPA of 3.0; for doctorate, GRE General Test, minimum GPA of 3.5. Additional exam requirements/recommendations for international students: Required—TOEFL. Electronic applications accepted. *Faculty research:* Political psychology and image theory, grass roots environmental policy, federal juvenile policy.

Washington University in St. Louis, School of Medicine, Program in Clinical Investigation, St. Louis, MO 63130-4899. Offers clinical investigation (MS), including bioethics, entrepreneurship, genetics/genomics, translational medicine. *Program availability:* Part-time, evening/weekend. *Degree requirements:* For master's, thesis. *Entrance requirements:* For master's, doctoral-level degree or in process of obtaining doctoral-level degree. Electronic applications accepted. *Faculty research:* Anesthesiology, infectious diseases, neurology, obstetrics and gynecology, orthopedic surgery.

Naturopathic Medicine

Bastyr University, School of Naturopathic Medicine, Kenmore, WA 98028-4966. Offers ND, Postbaccalaureate Certificate. *Accreditation:* CNME; MEAC. *Program availability:* Part-time. *Degree requirements:* For doctorate, comprehensive exam. *Entrance requirements:* For doctorate, 1 year of course work each in biology, chemistry, organic chemistry and physics; for Postbaccalaureate Certificate, BS or BA with 1 year of course work each in biology, chemistry, organic chemistry and physics. Additional exam requirements/recommendations for international students: Required—TOEFL (minimum score 550 paper-based; 79 iBT). *Application deadline:* For fall admission, 2/1 priority date for domestic and international students. Applications are processed on a rolling basis. Application fee: $75. Electronic applications accepted. *Expenses: Tuition:* Part-time $714 per credit hour. *Required fees:* $75. *Financial support:* Career-related internships or fieldwork, Federal Work-Study, and scholarships/grants available. Support available to part-time students. Financial award application deadline: 4/15; financial award applicants required to submit FAFSA. *Faculty research:* Integrative oncology, integrative care for neurodegenerative diseases, vitamin D supplementation, sauna (hyperthermia-based) detoxification, intranasal glutathione (nasal spray) for Parkinson's disease. *Unit head:* Dr. Jane Guiltinan, Dean, 425-823-1300, Fax: 425-823-6222, E-mail: jguiltin@bastyr.edu. *Application contact:* Alexis Rush, Associate Director of Admissions, 425-602-3330, Fax: 425-602-3090, E-mail: ndadvise@bastyr.edu.
Website: https://bastyr.edu/academics/schools-departments/school-naturopathic-medicine

Canadian College of Naturopathic Medicine, Bachelor of Naturopathy Program, Toronto, ON M2K 1E2, Canada. Offers BN. *Accreditation:* CNME. *Degree requirements:* For BN, 12-month internship. *Entrance requirements:* For degree, 1 year of course work in general biology, humanities and physiology; 1 semester of course work in organic chemistry and psychology. Additional exam requirements/recommendations for international students: Recommended—TOEFL (minimum score 580 paper-based; 86 iBT), IELTS (minimum score 6.5). Electronic applications accepted. *Faculty research:* Natural health products for lung cancer; the use of habanero chili pepper for cancer; melatonin as an anticancer agent with and without chemotherapy; interactions between natural health products and pharmaceuticals; the use of selenium for patients with HIV/AIDS.

Maryland University of Integrative Health, Program in Naturopathic Medicine, Laurel, MD 20723. Offers ND.

National University of Natural Medicine, College of Naturopathic Medicine, Portland, OR 97201. Offers integrative medicine research (MS); naturopathic medicine (ND). *Accreditation:* CNME. *Faculty:* 18 full-time (10 women), 56 part-time/adjunct (33 women). *Students:* 367 full-time (285 women). Average age 30. In 2017, 71 doctorates awarded. *Entrance requirements:* Additional exam requirements/recommendations for international students: Recommended—TOEFL, IELTS, TSE. *Application deadline:* For fall and winter admission, 5/1 priority date for domestic and international students. Applications are processed on a rolling basis. Application fee: $75. Electronic applications accepted. *Expenses: Tuition:* Full-time $23,979. *Financial support:* Federal Work-Study and scholarships/grants available. Financial award application deadline: 2/15; financial award applicants required to submit FAFSA. *Faculty research:* Secular trends in health-related quality of life among older women with breast cancer, 1998-2013; naturopathic medicine for the prevention of cardiovascular disease: a randomized clinical trial; adjunctive naturopathic care for type 2 diabetes: patient-reported and clinical outcomes after one year; naturopathic anti-inflammatory diet on inflammatory markers in type 2 diabetics; multi-biomarker exploration of SIBO: an observational study. *Unit head:* Dr. Shehab El-Hashemy, Dean, 503-552-1848, Fax: 503-499-0027, E-mail: admissions@nunm.edu. *Application contact:* Ryan Hollister, Associate Director of Admissions and Operations, 503-552-1665, Fax: 503-499-0027, E-mail: admissions@nunm.edu.
Website: http://nunm.edu/academics/school-of-naturopathic-medicine/

National University of Natural Medicine, School of Graduate Studies, Portland, OR 97201. Offers Ayurveda (MS); global health (MS); integrative medicine research (MS); integrative mental health (MS); nutrition (MS). *Faculty:* 7 full-time (5 women), 35 part-time/adjunct (25 women). *Students:* 184 (161 women). Average age 31. In 2017, 67 master's awarded. *Entrance requirements:* Additional exam requirements/recommendations for international students: Recommended—TOEFL, IELTS, TSE. *Application deadline:* For fall and winter admission, 5/1 for domestic and international students. Applications are processed on a rolling basis. Application fee: $75. Electronic applications accepted. *Expenses: Tuition:* Full-time $23,979. *Financial support:* Federal Work-Study and scholarships/grants available. Financial award application deadline: 2/15; financial award applicants required to submit FAFSA. *Faculty research:* Reliability of three constitutional questionnaires in Ayurveda diagnosis; mindfulness-based stress reduction for MS: feasibility, durability, and clinical outcomes; meditative neuroplasticity: the effect of qigong meditation on brain-derived neurotrophic factor and cortisol levels; food as medicine everyday research (FAMER): evaluating physiological changes associated with a shift toward a whole-foods diet. *Unit head:* Dr. Charles Kunert, Dean, 503-552-1742, Fax: 503-499-0027, E-mail: admission@nunm.edu. *Application contact:* Ryan Hollister, Associate Director of Admissions and Operations, 503-552-1665, Fax: 503-499-0027, E-mail: admissions@numn.edu.
Website: http://nunm.edu/academics/school-of-research-graduate-studies/

Southwest College of Naturopathic Medicine and Health Sciences, Doctor of Naturopathic Medicine Program, Tempe, AZ 85282. Offers ND. *Accreditation:* CNME. *Faculty:* 16 full-time (8 women), 50 part-time/adjunct (32 women). *Students:* 329 full-time (258 women), 31 part-time (24 women); includes 122 minority (33 Black or African American, non-Hispanic/Latino; 2 American Indian or Alaska Native, non-Hispanic/Latino; 26 Asian, non-Hispanic/Latino; 44 Hispanic/Latino; 1 Native Hawaiian or other Pacific Islander, non-Hispanic/Latino; 16 Two or more races, non-Hispanic/Latino), 13 international. Average age 30. 190 applicants, 80% accepted, 107 enrolled. In 2017, 83 doctorates awarded. *Entrance requirements:* For doctorate, minimum GPA of 3.0, letters of recommendation, in-person interview. Additional exam requirements/recommendations for international students: Required—TOEFL (minimum score 637 paper-based; 110 iBT). *Application deadline:* For fall admission, 4/1 priority date for domestic and international students; for spring admission, 12/1 priority date for domestic and international students. Applications are processed on a rolling basis. Application fee: $115. Electronic applications accepted. *Expenses:* $36,336 per year, $340 per credit. *Financial support:* In 2017–18, 132 students received support. Federal Work-Study and scholarships/grants available. Financial award application deadline: 5/1; financial award applicants required to submit FAFSA. *Faculty research:* Antimicrobials, anticancer, immune modulation, botanicals, diabetes. *Unit head:* Dr. Garrett Thompson, Dean of Academic Affairs, 480-858-9100 Ext. 207, E-mail: g.thompson@scnm.edu. *Application contact:* Eve Adams, Director of Admissions, 480-858-9100 Ext. 213, Fax: 480-222-9413, E-mail: e.adams@scnm.edu.
Website: http://www.scnm.edu

Universidad del Turabo, Graduate Programs, School of Health Sciences, Program in Naturopathy, Gurabo, PR 00778-3030. Offers ND. *Entrance requirements:* For doctorate, GRE, EXADEP or GMAT, official transcript, recommendation letters, essay, curriculum vitae, interview. Electronic applications accepted.

University of Bridgeport, College of Naturopathic Medicine, Bridgeport, CT 06604. Offers ND. *Accreditation:* CNME. *Degree requirements:* For doctorate, NPLEX Part I. *Entrance requirements:* For doctorate, minimum GPA of 2.5. Additional exam requirements/recommendations for international students: Recommended—TOEFL (minimum score 550 paper-based; 80 iBT), IELTS. Electronic applications accepted.

Osteopathic Medicine

Alabama College of Osteopathic Medicine, Graduate Program, Dothan, AL 36303. Offers DO.

A.T. Still University, Kirksville College of Osteopathic Medicine, Kirksville, MO 63501. Offers biomedical sciences (MS); osteopathic medicine (DO). *Accreditation:* AOsA. *Faculty:* 37 full-time (6 women), 30 part-time/adjunct (6 women). *Students:* 716 full-time (309 women), 10 part-time (5 women); includes 133 minority (18 Black or African American, non-Hispanic/Latino; 1 American Indian or Alaska Native, non-Hispanic/Latino; 43 Asian, non-Hispanic/Latino; 36 Hispanic/Latino; 35 Two or more races, non-Hispanic/Latino), 1 international. Average age 27. 4,481 applicants, 9% accepted, 183 enrolled. In 2017, 13 master's, 172 doctorates awarded. *Degree requirements:* For master's, thesis; for doctorate, Level 1 and 2 COMLEX-PE and CE exams. *Entrance requirements:* For master's, GRE, MCAT, or DAT, minimum undergraduate GPA of 2.65 (cumulative and science); for doctorate, MCAT, bachelor's degree with minimum GPA of 2.8 (cumulative and science) or 90 semester hours with minimum GPA of 3.5 (cumulative and science) and MCAT (minimum score 500). Additional exam requirements/recommendations for international students: Required—TOEFL. *Application deadline:* For fall admission, 2/1 for domestic students; for summer admission, 2/1 for domestic students. Applications are processed on a rolling basis. Application fee: $70. Electronic applications accepted. Application fee is waived when completed online. *Financial support:* In 2017–18, 142 students received support, including 22 fellowships with full tuition reimbursements available (averaging $55,455 per year); Federal Work-Study and scholarships/grants also available. Financial award application deadline: 6/1; financial award applicants required to submit FAFSA. *Faculty research:* Practice-based research network, antibiotic resistance, staphylococcus aureus, bacterial virulence and environmental survival, excitability of the exercise pressor reflex, clinical trials. *Total annual research expenditures:* $127,751. *Unit head:* Dr. Margaret Wilson, Dean, 660-626-2354, Fax: 660-626-2080, E-mail: mwilson@atsu.edu. *Application contact:* Donna Sparks, Director, Admissions Processing, 660-626-2117, Fax: 660-626-2969, E-mail: admissions@atsu.edu.
Website: http://www.atsu.edu/kcom/

A.T. Still University, School of Osteopathic Medicine in Arizona, Mesa, AZ 85206. Offers DO. *Accreditation:* AOsA. *Faculty:* 39 full-time (19 women), 27 part-time/adjunct (19 women). *Students:* 427 full-time (237 women); includes 212 minority (7 Black or African American, non-Hispanic/Latino; 1 American Indian or Alaska Native, non-Hispanic/Latino; 142 Asian, non-Hispanic/Latino; 32 Hispanic/Latino; 2 Native Hawaiian or other Pacific Islander, non-Hispanic/Latino; 28 Two or more races, non-Hispanic/Latino). Average age 28. 5,555 applicants, 5% accepted, 108 enrolled. In 2017, 103 doctorates awarded. *Degree requirements:* For doctorate, Level 1 and 2 COMLEX-PE and CE exams. *Entrance requirements:* For doctorate, MCAT, minimum undergraduate GPA of 2.8 (cumulative and science) with bachelor's degree. Additional exam requirements/recommendations for international students: Required—TOEFL. *Application deadline:* For fall admission, 3/1 for domestic students; for summer admission, 3/1 for domestic students. Applications are processed on a rolling basis. Application fee: $70. Electronic applications accepted. Application fee is waived when completed online. *Financial support:* In 2017–18, 50 students received support, including 3 fellowships with full tuition reimbursements available (averaging $55,972 per year); Federal Work-Study and scholarships/grants also available. Financial award application deadline: 6/1; financial award applicants required to submit FAFSA. *Faculty research:* Medical education research, osteopathic medicine research, practice-based research network, QI within community health centers. *Total annual research expenditures:* $291,686. *Unit head:* Dr. Jeffrey Morgan, Dean, 480-265-8017, Fax: 480-219-6159, E-mail: jeffreymorgan@atsu.edu. *Application contact:* Donna Sparks, Director, Admissions Processing, 660-626-2117, Fax: 660-626-2969, E-mail: admissions@atsu.edu.
Website: http://www.atsu.edu/soma

Campbell University, Graduate and Professional Programs, Jerry M. Wallace School of Osteopathic Medicine, Buies Creek, NC 27506. Offers DO.

Des Moines University, College of Osteopathic Medicine, Des Moines, IA 50312-4104. Offers DO. *Accreditation:* AOsA. *Degree requirements:* For doctorate, National Board of Osteopathic Medical Examiners Exam Level 1 and 2. *Entrance requirements:* For doctorate, MCAT, minimum GPA of 3.0; 8 hours of course work in biology, chemistry, organic chemistry, and physics; 3 hours of biochemistry; 6 hours of course work in English; interview. Electronic applications accepted. *Expenses:* Contact institution. *Faculty research:* Cardiovascular, infectious disease, cancer immunology, cell signaling nociception.

Edward Via College of Osteopathic Medicine–Carolinas Campus, Graduate Program, Spartanburg, SC 29303. Offers DO. *Accreditation:* AOsA.

Edward Via College of Osteopathic Medicine–Virginia Campus, Graduate Program, Blacksburg, VA 24060. Offers DO. *Accreditation:* AOsA. *Degree requirements:* For doctorate, thesis/dissertation. *Entrance requirements:* For doctorate, MCAT, 8 hours of biology, general chemistry, and organic chemistry; 6 hours each of additional science and English; minimum overall science GPA of 2.75. *Faculty research:* Nanobiology of aging, calcium transport regulation, prescription drug abuse, oxidative stress and inflammation, immune protection.

Georgia Campus–Philadelphia College of Osteopathic Medicine, Doctor of Osteopathic Medicine Program, Suwanee, GA 30024. Offers DO. *Accreditation:* AOsA. *Degree requirements:* For doctorate, comprehensive exam. *Entrance requirements:* For doctorate, MCAT. Additional exam requirements/recommendations for international students: Required—TOEFL (minimum score 79 iBT). Electronic applications accepted. *Expenses:* Contact institution.

Kansas City University of Medicine and Biosciences, College of Osteopathic Medicine, Kansas City, MO 64106-1453. Offers DO, DO/MA, DO/MBA. *Accreditation:* AOsA. *Degree requirements:* For doctorate, comprehensive exam, National Board Exam - COMLEX. *Entrance requirements:* For doctorate, MCAT, on-campus interview. *Faculty research:* 2-Chloroadenine in DNA use in controlling leukemia, dietary isoprenoids role in tumor cell control, preventive medicine and public health research of maternal and child health, nonenzymatic glycosylation in cardiac tissue.

Lake Erie College of Osteopathic Medicine, Professional Programs, Erie, PA 16509-1025. Offers biomedical sciences (Postbaccalaureate Certificate); medical education (MS); osteopathic medicine (DO); pharmacy (Pharm D). *Accreditation:* ACPE; AOsA. *Degree requirements:* For doctorate, comprehensive exam, National Osteopathic Medical Licensing Exam, Levels 1 and 2; for Postbaccalaureate Certificate, comprehensive exam, North American Pharmacist Licensure Examination (NAPLEX). *Entrance requirements:* For doctorate, MCAT, minimum GPA of 3.2, letters of recommendation; for Postbaccalaureate Certificate, PCAT, letters of recommendation, minimum GPA of 3.5. Electronic applications accepted. *Faculty research:* Cardiac smooth and skeletal muscle mechanics, chemotherapeutics and vitamins, osteopathic manipulation.

Liberty University, College of Osteopathic Medicine, Lynchburg, VA 24515. Offers DO. *Accreditation:* AOsA. *Students:* 593 full-time (276 women), 6 part-time (3 women); includes 67 minority (8 Black or African American, non-Hispanic/Latino; 39 Asian, non-Hispanic/Latino; 11 Hispanic/Latino; 9 Two or more races, non-Hispanic/Latino), 20 international. Average age 27. 1,428 applicants, 11% accepted, 153 enrolled. *Entrance requirements:* For doctorate, MCAT (minimum cumulative score of 22). *Application deadline:* Applications are processed on a rolling basis. Electronic applications accepted. *Expenses:* Contact institution. *Unit head:* Dr. Ronnie B. Martin, Dean, 434-592-6400. *Application contact:* Jay Bridge, Director of Admissions, 800-424-9595, Fax: 800-628-7977, E-mail: gradadmissions@liberty.edu.
Website: http://www.liberty.edu/lucom/

Lincoln Memorial University, DeBusk College of Osteopathic Medicine, Harrogate, TN 37752-1901. Offers DO. *Accreditation:* AOsA. *Entrance requirements:* For doctorate, MCAT. Additional exam requirements/recommendations for international students: Required—TOEFL (minimum score 600 paper-based; 100 iBT).

Marian University, College of Osteopathic Medicine, Indianapolis, IN 46222-1997. Offers MS, DO. *Accreditation:* AOsA. *Faculty:* 33 full-time (15 women), 2 part-time/adjunct (1 woman). *Students:* 715 full-time (334 women), 3 part-time (all women); includes 156 minority (19 Black or African American, non-Hispanic/Latino; 1 American Indian or Alaska Native, non-Hispanic/Latino; 88 Asian, non-Hispanic/Latino; 30 Hispanic/Latino; 1 Native Hawaiian or other Pacific Islander, non-Hispanic/Latino; 17 Two or more races, non-Hispanic/Latino), 27 international. Average age 25. 4,470 applicants, 10% accepted, 227 enrolled. In 2017, 134 doctorates awarded. *Degree requirements:* For master's, thesis; for doctorate, comprehensive exam, COMLEX licensing exam. *Entrance requirements:* For master's, MCAT or GRE; for doctorate, MCAT. Additional exam requirements/recommendations for international students: Required—TOEFL. *Application deadline:* For fall admission, 3/1 for domestic and international students. Applications are processed on a rolling basis. Application fee: $100. Electronic applications accepted. *Expenses:* $48,900 annual tuition, $1,500 annual student fees, plus total COMLEX examination fees (for DO); $11,400 tuition plus $750 fee per semester (for MS). *Financial support:* Application deadline: 4/15; applicants required to submit FAFSA. *Faculty research:* Somatic dysfunction and osteopathic manipulative treatment, anatomy and physiology, genetic and molecular analysis, pharmacology, pathogenesis. *Total annual research expenditures:* $19,000. *Unit head:* Dr. Donald Sefcik, Vice President of Health Professions/Dean of the College of Osteopathic Medicine, 317-955-6289, E-mail: dsefcik@marian.edu. *Application contact:* Bryan Moody, Executive Director of Graduate Admission, 317-955-6284, E-mail: bmoody@marian.edu.
Website: http://www.marian.edu/osteopathic-medical-school

Michigan State University, College of Osteopathic Medicine, Professional Program in Osteopathic Medicine, East Lansing, MI 48824. Offers DO. *Accreditation:* AOsA. Electronic applications accepted.

Midwestern University, Downers Grove Campus, Chicago College of Osteopathic Medicine, Downers Grove, IL 60515-1235. Offers DO. *Accreditation:* AOsA. *Entrance requirements:* For doctorate, MCAT, 1 year course work each in organic chemistry, general chemistry, biology, physics, and English. *Application deadline:* For fall admission, 1/1 for domestic students. Applications are processed on a rolling basis. Application fee: $50. *Expenses:* Contact institution. *Financial support:* Fellowships with partial tuition reimbursements, career-related internships or fieldwork, Federal Work-Study, institutionally sponsored loans, and tuition waivers (full and partial) available. Financial award application deadline: 6/1; financial award applicants required to submit FAFSA. *Faculty research:* Cadmium toxicity, amino acid transport, metabolic actions of vanadium, diabetes and obesity.
Website: http://www.midwestern.edu/Programs_and_Admission/IL_Osteopathic_Medicine.html

Midwestern University, Glendale Campus, Arizona College of Osteopathic Medicine, Glendale, AZ 85308. Offers DO. *Accreditation:* AOsA. *Entrance requirements:* For doctorate, MCAT. *Application deadline:* For fall admission, 11/1 priority date for domestic students; for winter admission, 2/1 for domestic students. Applications are processed on a rolling basis. Application fee: $50. Electronic applications accepted. *Expenses:* Contact institution. *Financial support:* Fellowships with partial tuition reimbursements, career-related internships or fieldwork, Federal Work-Study, institutionally sponsored loans, and tuition waivers (full and partial) available. Financial award application deadline: 6/12; financial award applicants required to submit FAFSA.

New York Institute of Technology, College of Osteopathic Medicine, Old Westbury, NY 11568-8000. Offers global health (Certificate); DO/MS. *Accreditation:* AOsA. *Faculty:* 91 full-time, 33 part-time/adjunct. *Students:* 1,484 full-time (707 women); includes 649 minority (47 Black or African American, non-Hispanic/Latino; 540 Asian, non-Hispanic/Latino; 44 Hispanic/Latino; 18 Two or more races, non-Hispanic/Latino). Average age 27. 7,036 applicants, 13% accepted, 436 enrolled. In 2017, 16 Certificates awarded. *Entrance requirements:* Additional exam requirements/recommendations for international students: Required—TOEFL (minimum score 79 iBT), IELTS (minimum score 6). *Application deadline:* For fall admission, 2/1 for domestic students. Application fee: $80. Electronic applications accepted. *Expenses:* $58,345 per year plus $1,500 fees. *Financial support:* Federal Work-Study and scholarships/grants available. Financial award application deadline: 2/15; financial award applicants required to submit FAFSA. *Faculty research:* Cancer biology; computational biomechanics and motor control; neurobiology and sensory evolution; degenerative diseases; sports medicine and osteopathic manipulative medicine; cardiovascular biology; evolution and development. *Unit head:* Dr. Wolfgang Gilliar, Dean, 516-686-3722, Fax: 516-686-3830, E-mail: wgilliar@nyit.edu. *Application contact:* Gina Moses, Director, Admissions, 516-686-3997, E-mail: gmoses@nyit.edu.
Website: http://www.nyit.edu/medicine

Nova Southeastern University, Dr. Kiran C. Patel College of Osteopathic Medicine, Fort Lauderdale, FL 33328. Offers biomedical informatics (MS, Graduate Certificate), including biomedical informatics (MS), clinical informatics (Graduate Certificate), public health informatics (Graduate Certificate); disaster and emergency management (MS); medical education (MS); nutrition (MS, Graduate Certificate), including functional nutrition and herbal therapy (Graduate Certificate); osteopathic medicine (DO); public health (MPH, Graduate Certificate), including health education (Graduate Certificate); social medicine (Graduate Certificate); DO/DMD. *Accreditation:* AOsA. *Faculty:* 98 full-time (58 women), 1,484 part-time/adjunct (401 women). *Students:* 1,032 full-time (479 women), 197 part-time (129 women); includes 656 minority (97 Black or African American, non-Hispanic/Latino; 308 Asian, non-Hispanic/Latino; 215 Hispanic/Latino; 1 Native Hawaiian or other Pacific Islander, non-Hispanic/Latino; 35 Two or more races, non-Hispanic/Latino), 67 international. Average age 26. 5,226 applicants, 9% accepted,

248 enrolled. In 2017, 110 master's, 239 doctorates, 7 other advanced degrees awarded. *Degree requirements:* For master's, comprehensive exam (for MPH); field/special projects; for doctorate, comprehensive exam, COMLEX Board Exams; for Graduate Certificate, thesis or alternative. *Entrance requirements:* For master's, GRE; for doctorate, MCAT, coursework in biology, chemistry, organic chemistry, physics (all with labs), biochemistry, and English. *Application deadline:* For fall admission, 1/15 for domestic students. Applications are processed on a rolling basis. Application fee: $50. Electronic applications accepted. *Expenses:* Contact institution. *Financial support:* In 2017–18, 83 students received support, including 24 fellowships with tuition reimbursements available; Federal Work-Study and scholarships/grants also available. Financial award application deadline: 6/1; financial award applicants required to submit FAFSA. *Faculty research:* Teaching strategies, simulated patient use, HIV/AIDS education, minority health issues, immune disorders. *Unit head:* Elaine M. Wallace, Dean, 954-262-1457, Fax: 954-262-2250, E-mail: ewallace@nova.edu. *Application contact:* HPD Admissions, 877-640-0218, E-mail: hpdinfo@nova.edu.
Website: https://www.osteopathic.nova.edu/

Ohio University, Heritage College of Osteopathic Medicine, Athens, OH 45701. Offers DO, DO/MBA, DO/MGH, DO/MPH, DO/MS, DO/PhD. Applicants must be U.S. residents to apply. *Accreditation:* AOsA. *Faculty:* 107 full-time (55 women), 38 part-time/adjunct (12 women). *Students:* 922 full-time; includes 225 minority (74 Black or African American, non-Hispanic/Latino; 4 American Indian or Alaska Native, non-Hispanic/Latino; 79 Asian, non-Hispanic/Latino; 38 Hispanic/Latino; 1 Native Hawaiian or other Pacific Islander, non-Hispanic/Latino; 29 Two or more races, non-Hispanic/Latino). Average age 26. 4,944 applicants, 7% accepted, 249 enrolled. In 2017, 128 doctorates awarded. *Degree requirements:* For doctorate, comprehensive exam, National Board Exam Parts I and II, COMLEX-PE. *Entrance requirements:* For doctorate, MCAT, interview; course work in English, physics, biology, general chemistry, organic chemistry, and behavioral sciences with minimum grade of C. *Application deadline:* For fall admission, 2/1 for domestic students. Applications are processed on a rolling basis. Application fee: $60. Electronic applications accepted. *Expenses:* $36,784 (first and second years each); $54,576 (third and fourth years each). *Financial support:* In 2017–18, 284 students received support, including 20 fellowships (averaging $25,439 per year); Federal Work-Study, institutionally sponsored loans, scholarships/grants, and tuition waivers (partial) also available. Financial award applicants required to submit FAFSA. *Faculty research:* Musculoskeletal rehabilitation in pain reduction, frailty and fractures in aging, diabetes and related cardio-metabolic diseases, tropical and infectious diseases, primary care and community research. *Total annual research expenditures:* $3.7 million. *Unit head:* Dr. Kenneth Johnson, Executive Dean, 740-593-9350, Fax: 740-593-0761, E-mail: wilcox@ohio.edu. *Application contact:* Jill Harman, Senior Director of Admissions and Recruitment, 740-593-2147, Fax: 740-593-2256, E-mail: harmanj@ohio.edu.
Website: https://www.ohio.edu/medicine/index.cfm

Oklahoma State University Center for Health Sciences, College of Osteopathic Medicine, Tulsa, OK 74114. Offers DO, DO/MBA, DO/MPH, DO/MS, DO/PhD. *Accreditation:* AOsA. *Degree requirements:* For doctorate, COMLEX Board exams. *Entrance requirements:* For doctorate, MCAT (minimum score 492), interview; minimum 90 hours of college course work; minimum cumulative GPA of 3.0, science 2.75. Electronic applications accepted. *Faculty research:* Neuroscience, artificial vision, mechanisms of hormone action, vaccines and immunotherapy, pathogenic free-living amoebae.

Pacific Northwest University of Health Sciences, College of Osteopathic Medicine, Yakima, WA 98901. Offers DO. *Accreditation:* AOsA. *Faculty:* 25 full-time (10 women), 28 part-time/adjunct (8 women). *Students:* 572 full-time (277 women), 1 (woman) part-time; includes 163 minority (9 Black or African American, non-Hispanic/Latino; 2 American Indian or Alaska Native, non-Hispanic/Latino; 74 Asian, non-Hispanic/Latino; 41 Hispanic/Latino; 1 Native Hawaiian or other Pacific Islander, non-Hispanic/Latino; 36 Two or more races, non-Hispanic/Latino). Average age 29. 3,999 applicants, 7% accepted, 142 enrolled. In 2017, 133 doctorates awarded. *Degree requirements:* For doctorate, COMLEX-USA licensure exams. *Entrance requirements:* For doctorate, MCAT. *Application deadline:* For fall admission, 2/1 for domestic and international students. Application fee: $85. Electronic applications accepted. *Expenses:* Contact institution. *Financial support:* In 2017–18, 10 students received support, including 1 research assistantship, 108 teaching assistantships; scholarships/grants, health care benefits, tuition waivers (full and partial), and unspecified assistantships also available. Financial award application deadline: 7/1; financial award applicants required to submit FAFSA. *Faculty research:* Community health and education, disparities, unique care models, simulation, interprofessional education and practice. *Total annual research expenditures:* $377,000. *Unit head:* Dr. Thomas Scandalis, Dean, 509-249-7803, E-mail: vkoch@pnwu.edu. *Application contact:* Hope Ennis, Assistant Director for Applications, 509-249-7888, Fax: 509-249-7909, E-mail: admission@pnwu.edu.
Website: http://www.pnwu.edu/

Philadelphia College of Osteopathic Medicine, Graduate and Professional Programs, Doctor of Osteopathic Medicine Program, Philadelphia, PA 19131-1694. Offers DO, DO/MA, DO/MBA, DO/MPH, DO/MS, DO/PhD. *Accreditation:* AOsA. *Faculty:* 77 full-time (38 women), 1,293 part-time/adjunct (257 women). *Students:* 1,084 full-time (532 women); includes 350 minority (91 Black or African American, non-Hispanic/Latino; 107 Asian, non-Hispanic/Latino; 22 Hispanic/Latino; 130 Two or more races, non-Hispanic/Latino), 4 international. Average age 28. 9,235 applicants, 5% accepted, 270 enrolled. In 2017, 256 doctorates awarded. *Entrance requirements:* For doctorate, MCAT, minimum GPA of 3.2; premedical prerequisite coursework; biochemistry (recommended). Additional exam requirements/recommendations for international students: Required—TOEFL (minimum score 79 iBT). *Application deadline:* For fall admission, 2/1 for domestic students. Applications are processed on a rolling basis. Application fee: $75. Electronic applications accepted. *Expenses:* $50,700. *Financial support:* In 2017–18, 870 students received support, including 14 fellowships with partial tuition reimbursements available; Federal Work-Study, institutionally sponsored loans, and scholarships/grants also available. Financial award application deadline: 3/15; financial award applicants required to submit FAFSA. *Faculty research:* Neuroscience and neurodegenerative disorders, inflammation and allergic response to food allergens, cardiovascular function and disease, bone and joint disorders, cancer biology. *Total annual research expenditures:* $533,489. *Unit head:* Dr. Kenneth J. Veit, Dean, 215-871-6770, Fax: 215-871-6781, E-mail: kenv@pcom.edu. *Application contact:* Kari A. Shotwell, Director of Admissions, 215-871-6700, Fax: 215-871-6719, E-mail: karis@pcom.edu.
Website: http://www.pcom.edu

Rocky Vista University, College of Osteopathic Medicine, Parker, CO 80134. Offers DO. *Accreditation:* AOsA. *Application deadline:* For fall admission, 3/15 priority date for domestic students. *Expenses:* $54,980 tuition. *Unit head:* Dr. Thomas N. Told, Dean. *Application contact:* Dr. Thomas N. Told, Dean.

Rowan University, School of Osteopathic Medicine, Stratford, NJ 08084-1501. Offers DO, DO/MA, DO/MBA, DO/MPH, DO/MS, DO/PhD, JD/DO. *Accreditation:* AOsA. *Degree requirements:* For doctorate, comprehensive exam. *Entrance requirements:* For doctorate, MCAT. Electronic applications accepted. *Expenses:* Contact institution.

Touro University California, Graduate Programs, Vallejo, CA 94592. Offers education (MA); medical health sciences (MS); osteopathic medicine (DO); pharmacy (Pharm D); public health (MPH). *Accreditation:* AOsA; ARC-PA. *Program availability:* Part-time, evening/weekend. *Degree requirements:* For master's, comprehensive exam, thesis; for doctorate, comprehensive exam. *Entrance requirements:* For doctorate, BS/BA. Electronic applications accepted. *Faculty research:* Cancer, heart disease.

University of New England, College of Osteopathic Medicine, Biddeford, ME 04005-9526. Offers DO, DO/MPH. *Accreditation:* AOsA. *Faculty:* 39 full-time (16 women), 36 part-time/adjunct (15 women). *Students:* 710 full-time (344 women); includes 114 minority (4 Black or African American, non-Hispanic/Latino; 2 American Indian or Alaska Native, non-Hispanic/Latino; 97 Asian, non-Hispanic/Latino; 5 Hispanic/Latino; 6 Two or more races, non-Hispanic/Latino), 24 international. Average age 27. 4,586 applicants, 10% accepted, 178 enrolled. In 2017, 161 doctorates awarded. *Entrance requirements:* For doctorate, MCAT. *Application deadline:* For fall admission, 3/1 for domestic students. Tuition and fees vary according to degree level, program and student level. *Financial support:* Application deadline: 5/1; applicants required to submit FAFSA. *Unit head:* Dr. Jane Carreiro, Dean, College of Osteopathic Medicine, 207-602-2898, E-mail: deanunecom@une.edu. *Application contact:* Scott Steinberg, Dean of University Admission, 207-221-4225, Fax: 207-523-1925, E-mail: ssteinberg@une.edu.
Website: http://www.une.edu/com/index.cfm

University of North Texas Health Science Center at Fort Worth, Texas College of Osteopathic Medicine, Fort Worth, TX 76107-2699. Offers DO, DO/MPH, DO/MS, DO/PhD. *Accreditation:* AOsA. *Entrance requirements:* For doctorate, MCAT, 1 year of course work each in biology, physics and English; 2 years' course work in chemistry. Electronic applications accepted. *Faculty research:* Tuberculosis, aging, cardiovascular disease, cancer.

University of Pikeville, Kentucky College of Osteopathic Medicine, Pikeville, KY 41501. Offers DO. *Accreditation:* AOsA. *Faculty:* 24 full-time (9 women), 35 part-time/adjunct (13 women). *Students:* 534 full-time (227 women); includes 50 minority (3 Black or African American, non-Hispanic/Latino; 1 American Indian or Alaska Native, non-Hispanic/Latino; 22 Asian, non-Hispanic/Latino; 21 Hispanic/Latino; 3 Native Hawaiian or other Pacific Islander, non-Hispanic/Latino). Average age 25. 3,262 applicants, 7% accepted, 135 enrolled. In 2017, 128 doctorates awarded. *Degree requirements:* For doctorate, COMLEX Level 1 and COMLEX Level 2CE and 2PE. *Entrance requirements:* For doctorate, MCAT. *Application deadline:* For fall admission, 5/1 for domestic students. Applications are processed on a rolling basis. Application fee: $75. *Expenses:* Contact institution. *Financial support:* In 2017–18, 11 students received support, including 11 fellowships with full and partial tuition reimbursements available (averaging $28,169 per year); scholarships/grants also available. Financial award application deadline: 8/1; financial award applicants required to submit FAFSA. *Faculty research:* Primary care in rural and medically underserved areas. *Unit head:* Dr. Boyd Buser, Dean, 606-218-5410, Fax: 606-218-8442, E-mail: boydbuser@upike.edu. *Application contact:* Dr. Linda Dunatov, Associate Dean for Student Affairs, 606-218-5408, Fax: 606-218-5442, E-mail: lindadunatov@upike.edu.
Website: http://www.upike.edu/College-of-Osteopathic-Medicine

University of the Incarnate Word, School of Osteopathic Medicine, San Antonio, TX 78209-6397. Offers MBS, DO. *Faculty:* 7 full-time (5 women), 3 part-time/adjunct (1 woman). *Students:* 200 full-time (113 women); includes 125 minority (14 Black or African American, non-Hispanic/Latino; 1 American Indian or Alaska Native, non-Hispanic/Latino; 43 Asian, non-Hispanic/Latino; 60 Hispanic/Latino; 7 Two or more races, non-Hispanic/Latino). *Degree requirements:* For master's, thesis or alternative; for doctorate, comprehensive exam. *Entrance requirements:* For master's, GRE or MCAT, courses in biology, general chemistry, anatomy and physiology, biochemistry, and mathematics; for doctorate, MCAT, courses in biology, inorganic chemistry, organic chemistry, physics, and English; three letters of recommendation. *Application deadline:* For fall admission, 9/1 for domestic students; for spring admission, 3/15 for domestic students. Applications are processed on a rolling basis. Application fee: $50. Electronic applications accepted. *Expenses:* $52,600 per year. *Financial support:* Research assistantships, career-related internships or fieldwork, scholarships/grants, and unspecified assistantships available. Financial award applicants required to submit FAFSA. *Unit head:* Dr. Robyn Phillips-Madson, Dean, E-mail: rmadson@uiwtx.edu. *Application contact:* Alexandra R. Shipley, Admissions Recruiter, 210-283-6998, E-mail: ashipley@uiwtx.edu.
Website: http://www.uiwtx.edu/som/

Western University of Health Sciences, College of Osteopathic Medicine of the Pacific, Pomona, CA 91766-1854. Offers DO. *Accreditation:* AOsA. *Faculty:* 72 full-time (32 women), 16 part-time/adjunct (5 women). *Students:* 1,349 full-time (636 women); includes 629 minority (14 Black or African American, non-Hispanic/Latino; 1 American Indian or Alaska Native, non-Hispanic/Latino; 405 Asian, non-Hispanic/Latino; 94 Hispanic/Latino; 3 Native Hawaiian or other Pacific Islander, non-Hispanic/Latino; 112 Two or more races, non-Hispanic/Latino), 13 international. Average age 27. 5,109 applicants, 13% accepted, 328 enrolled. In 2017, 309 doctorates awarded. *Degree requirements:* For doctorate, comprehensive exam (for some programs). *Entrance requirements:* For doctorate, MCAT, minimum GPA of 3.3, interview, two letters of recommendation. *Application deadline:* For fall admission, 2/15 for domestic and international students. Applications are processed on a rolling basis. Application fee: $65. Electronic applications accepted. *Expenses:* $56,290 first-year tuition and fees. *Financial support:* In 2017–18, 216 students received support. Scholarships/grants and unspecified assistantships available. Financial award application deadline: 3/2; financial award applicants required to submit FAFSA. *Faculty research:* Adaptive mechanisms of serotonergic 5-HT2 receptor functions; the role of delta-9-THC and synthetic cannabinoids on chemotherapy and radiotherapy-induced vomiting; examining the efficacy of osteopathic manipulative treatment in individuals with vertigo; therapy of lymphomas with immunotoxins comprised of soluble T-cell receptors conjugated to ricin A-chain. *Total annual research expenditures:* $1.4 million. *Unit head:* Dr. Paula Crone, Dean, 541-259-0206, Fax: 541-259-0201, E-mail: pcrone@westernu.edu. *Application contact:* Susan Hanson, Director of Admissions, 909-469-5335, Fax: 909-469-5570, E-mail: admissions@westernu.edu.
Website: http://www.westernu.edu/osteopathy/

West Virginia School of Osteopathic Medicine, Professional Program, Lewisburg, WV 24901-1196. Offers DO. *Accreditation:* AOsA. *Faculty:* 61 full-time (33 women). *Students:* 849 full-time (434 women); includes 217 minority (30 Black or African American, non-Hispanic/Latino; 1 American Indian or Alaska Native, non-Hispanic/Latino; 139 Asian, non-Hispanic/Latino; 32 Hispanic/Latino; 15 Native Hawaiian or other Pacific Islander, non-Hispanic/Latino). Average age 27. *Degree requirements:* For doctorate, comprehensive exam, Comlex Level 1 and 2 (PE and CE). *Entrance requirements:* For doctorate, MCAT, 6 semester hours each of biology/zoology, physics, English, and behavioral sciences; 9 semester hours in chemistry; 3 semester hours in biochemistry. *Application deadline:* For fall admission, 2/15 for domestic students. Applications are processed on a rolling basis. Application fee: $80. Electronic applications accepted. *Expenses:* Tuition, state resident: full-time $19,450. Tuition, nonresident: full-time $49,200. *Financial support:* Teaching assistantships with full tuition reimbursements, Federal Work-Study, scholarships/grants, tuition waivers (full), and unspecified assistantships available. Financial award application deadline: 4/1;

financial award applicants required to submit FAFSA. *Faculty research:* OMT response bio-markers, linking muscle energy use to power production in primates. *Unit head:* Dr. Michael D. Adelman, President, 304-645-6295, Fax: 304-645-4859, E-mail: madelman@osteo.wvsom.edu. *Application contact:* Gwen Byrd, Director of Admissions, 304-647-6336, Fax: 304-647-6384, E-mail: gbyrd@osteo.wvsom.edu. Website: http://www.wvsom.edu

William Carey University, College of Osteopathic Medicine, Hattiesburg, MS 39401. Offers DO. *Accreditation:* AOsA.

Podiatric Medicine

Barry University, School of Podiatric Medicine, Podiatric Medicine and Surgery Program, Miami Shores, FL 33161-6695. Offers DPM, DPM/MBA, DPM/MPH. *Accreditation:* APMA. *Entrance requirements:* For doctorate, MCAT, GRE General Test, previous course work in science and English. Additional exam requirements/ recommendations for international students: Required—TOEFL. Electronic applications accepted. *Expenses:* Contact institution.

Des Moines University, College of Podiatric Medicine and Surgery, Des Moines, IA 50312-4104. Offers DPM. *Accreditation:* APMA. *Entrance requirements:* For doctorate, MCAT, interview; minimum GPA of 2.5; 1 year of organic chemistry, inorganic chemistry, physics, biology, and English. Electronic applications accepted. *Expenses:* Contact institution. *Faculty research:* Physics of equines, gait analysis.

Kent State University, College of Podiatric Medicine, Kent, OH 44242-0001. Offers DPM. *Accreditation:* APMA. *Degree requirements:* For doctorate, comprehensive exam, clinical competencies; NBPME Boards 1 & 2. *Entrance requirements:* For doctorate, MCAT, satisfactory course work in biology, chemistry, English and physics; background check, drug test. Additional exam requirements/recommendations for international students: Recommended—TOEFL (minimum score 81 iBT). Electronic applications accepted. *Expenses:* Tuition, state resident: full-time $11,310; part-time $515 per credit hour. Tuition, nonresident: full-time $20,396; part-time $928 per credit hour. *International tuition:* $18,544 full-time. *Faculty research:* Diabetic foot ulcers, plantar shear stresses, nonvisual foot examinations, treatment modalities for onychomycosis.

Midwestern University, Glendale Campus, College of Health Sciences, Arizona Campus, Program in Podiatric Medicine, Glendale, AZ 85308. Offers DPM. *Accreditation:* APMA. *Entrance requirements:* For doctorate, MCAT or PCAT, 90 semester hours at an accredited college or university, minimum GPA of 2.75. *Application deadline:* For fall admission, 6/1 for domestic students. Applications are processed on a rolling basis. Application fee: $50. *Expenses:* Contact institution.

New York College of Podiatric Medicine, Professional Program, New York, NY 10035. Offers DPM, DPM/MPH. *Accreditation:* APMA. *Degree requirements:* For doctorate, comprehensive exam. *Entrance requirements:* For doctorate, MCAT or DAT, 1 year course work in biology, physics, English, and general and organic chemistry. Additional exam requirements/recommendations for international students: Required—TOEFL.

Rosalind Franklin University of Medicine and Science, Dr. William M. Scholl College of Podiatric Medicine, North Chicago, IL 60064-3095. Offers DPM. *Accreditation:* APMA. *Entrance requirements:* For doctorate, MCAT (or GRE on approval), 12 semester hours of biology; 8 semester hours of inorganic chemistry, organic chemistry and physics; 6 semester hours of English. Additional exam requirements/recommendations for international students: Required—TOEFL.

Samuel Merritt University, California School of Podiatric Medicine, Oakland, CA 94609-3108. Offers DPM. *Faculty:* 17 full-time (6 women), 5 part-time/adjunct (3 women). *Students:* 176 full-time (76 women), 1 part-time (0 women); includes 98 minority (2 Black or African American, non-Hispanic/Latino; 1 American Indian or Alaska Native, non-Hispanic/Latino; 62 Asian, non-Hispanic/Latino; 20 Hispanic/Latino; 13 Two or more races, non-Hispanic/Latino). 360 applicants, 31% accepted, 46 enrolled. In 2017, 51 doctorates awarded. *Entrance requirements:* For doctorate, MCAT (less than 3 years old), at least 90 semester hours of undergraduate course work; 1 year of course work in organic chemistry or biochemistry, inorganic chemistry, physics, biological sciences (all courses must come with a lab), and English/communications. Additional exam requirements/recommendations for international students: Required—TOEFL (minimum score 100 iBT). *Application deadline:* For fall admission, 4/1 priority date for domestic and international students. Applications are processed on a rolling basis. Application fee: $160. Electronic applications accepted. *Expenses:* $42,695 annual tuition (for first-year students). *Financial support:* Federal Work-Study, institutionally sponsored loans, and scholarships/grants available. Financial award applicants required to submit FAFSA. *Faculty research:* Glycation in diabetes and protein dysfunction, lower extremity biomechanics, diabetic wound care, plantar warts among HIV-infected patients, interdisciplinary equity and inclusion issues. *Unit head:* Irma Walker-Adame, Associate Dean for Administrative Affairs, 510-869-8742, E-mail: iadame@samuelmerritt.edu. *Application contact:* Dr. David Tran, Assistant Director of Admission, 510-869-6789, Fax: 510-869-6525, E-mail: dtran@samuelmerritt.edu.

Temple University, School of Podiatric Medicine, Philadelphia, PA 19107-2496. Offers DPM, DPM/MBA, DPM/PhD. DPM/PhD offered jointly with Drexel University, University of Pennsylvania. *Accreditation:* APMA. *Degree requirements:* For doctorate, National Board Exam. *Entrance requirements:* For doctorate, MCAT, GRE, or DAT, interview, 8 hours of organic chemistry, inorganic chemistry, physics, biology. *Expenses:* Tuition, state resident: full-time $16,164; part-time $898 per credit hour. Tuition, nonresident: full-time $22,158; part-time $1231 per credit hour. *Required fees:* $890; $445 per semester. Full-time tuition and fees vary according to course load, degree level, campus/location and program. *Faculty research:* Gait analysis, infectious diseases, diabetic neuropathy, peripheral vascular disease.

Western University of Health Sciences, College of Podiatric Medicine, Pomona, CA 91766-1854. Offers DPM. *Accreditation:* APMA. *Faculty:* 10 full-time (5 women), 6 part-time/adjunct (1 woman). *Students:* 147 full-time (51 women); includes 76 minority (4 Black or African American, non-Hispanic/Latino; 48 Asian, non-Hispanic/Latino; 12 Hispanic/Latino; 12 Two or more races, non-Hispanic/Latino), 2 international. Average age 27. 368 applicants, 28% accepted, 27 enrolled. In 2017, 35 doctorates awarded. *Degree requirements:* For doctorate, comprehensive exam (for some programs). *Entrance requirements:* For doctorate, MCAT, letters of recommendation; BS or BA (recommended); transcripts from all colleges, universities and professional schools attended. Additional exam requirements/recommendations for international students: Required—TOEFL (minimum score 79 iBT). *Application deadline:* For fall admission, 6/30 for domestic and international students. Applications are processed on a rolling basis. Application fee: $0. Electronic applications accepted. *Expenses:* $37,360 (first three years); $37,710 (fourth year). *Financial support:* In 2017–18, 40 students received support. Scholarships/grants available. Financial award application deadline: 3/2; financial award applicants required to submit FAFSA. *Total annual research expenditures:* $42,841. *Unit head:* Dr. Lawrence B. Harkless, Dean, 909-706-3933, E-mail: lharkless@westernu.edu. *Application contact:* Marie Anderson, Director of Admissions, 909-469-5335, Fax: 909-469-5570, E-mail: admissions@westernu.edu. Website: http://www.westernu.edu/podiatry/

Section 29
Optometry and Vision Sciences

This section contains a directory of institutions offering graduate work in optometry and vision sciences. Additional information about programs listed in the directory may be obtained by writing directly to the dean of a graduate school or chair of a department at the address given in the directory.

In the other guides in this series:

Graduate Programs in the Humanities, Arts & Social Sciences
See *Psychology and Counseling*

Graduate Programs in the Physical Sciences, Mathematics, Agricultural Sciences, the Environment & Natural Resources
See *Physics*

Graduate Programs in Engineering & Applied Sciences
See *Biomedical Engineering* and *Biotechnology*

CONTENTS

Program Directories

Optometry

Ferris State University, Michigan College of Optometry, Big Rapids, MI 49307. Offers OD. *Accreditation:* AOA. *Faculty:* 19 full-time (9 women), 115 part-time/adjunct (52 women). *Students:* 149 full-time (80 women); includes 4 minority (2 Asian, non-Hispanic/ Latino; 2 Hispanic/Latino), 5 international. Average age 24. 177 applicants, 31% accepted, 37 enrolled. In 2017, 35 doctorates awarded. *Degree requirements:* For doctorate, comprehensive exam, research project. *Entrance requirements:* For doctorate, OAT, OPTOMCAS application. Additional exam requirements/ recommendations for international students: Recommended—TOEFL (minimum score 550 paper-based; 80 iBT). *Application deadline:* For fall admission, 2/1 for domestic and international students. Applications are processed on a rolling basis. Application fee: $165. Electronic applications accepted. *Expenses:* $27,018 (first and second years each); $36,972 (third year); $31,284 (fourth year). *Financial support:* In 2017–18, 38 students received support. Career-related internships or fieldwork, Federal Work-Study, and scholarships/grants available. Financial award application deadline: 3/30; financial award applicants required to submit FAFSA. *Faculty research:* Corneal reshaping, spatial vision and vision science, reading disabilities, vision development, vision care access, contact lens studies. *Total annual research expenditures:* $4,247. *Unit head:* Dr. David Damari, Dean, 231-591-3706, Fax: 231-591-2394, E-mail: damarid@ferris.edu. *Application contact:* Amy Parks, Health College Administrative Specialist, 231-591-3703, Fax: 231-591-2394, E-mail: amyparks@ferris.edu.
Website: http://www.ferris.edu/mco/

Illinois College of Optometry, Professional Program, Chicago, IL 60616-3878. Offers OD. *Accreditation:* AOA. *Faculty:* 47 full-time (34 women), 40 part-time/adjunct (24 women). *Students:* 599 full-time (426 women); includes 170 minority (12 Black or African American, non-Hispanic/Latino; 5 American Indian or Alaska Native, non-Hispanic/ Latino; 140 Asian, non-Hispanic/Latino; 13 Hispanic/Latino), 94 international. *Entrance requirements:* For doctorate, OAT. *Application deadline:* For fall admission, 2/15 for domestic and international students. Applications are processed on a rolling basis. Application fee: $75. Electronic applications accepted. *Expenses: Tuition:* Full-time $40,410; part-time $842 per credit hour. *Required fees:* $355. *Financial support:* Federal Work-Study and scholarships/grants available. Support available to part-time students. Financial award application deadline: 4/15; financial award applicants required to submit FAFSA. *Faculty research:* Eye disease treatment, binocular vision, cataract development, pediatric vision, genetic eye disease. *Unit head:* Dr. Arol Augsburger, President, 312-949-7705, Fax: 312-949-7670, E-mail: aaugsburger@eyecare.ico.edu. *Application contact:* Teisha Johnson, Director of Admissions, 312-949-7400, Fax: 312-949-7680, E-mail: tjohnson@ico.edu.

Indiana University Bloomington, School of Optometry, Bloomington, IN 47405-3680. Offers MS, OD, PhD. *Accreditation:* AOA (one or more programs are accredited). Terminal master's awarded for partial completion of doctoral program. *Degree requirements:* For master's, thesis; for doctorate, comprehensive exam, thesis/ dissertation. *Entrance requirements:* For master's, GRE, BA in science; for doctorate, GRE; OAT (for OD), BA in science (master's degree preferred). Additional exam requirements/recommendations for international students: Required—TOEFL (minimum score 550 paper-based; 80 iBT). Electronic applications accepted. *Expenses:* Contact institution. *Faculty research:* Corneal physiology, contact lenses, adaptive optics, dry eye, low vision, refractive anomalies, ophthalmic imaging, glaucoma, ocular physiology, infant vision, retinal disease.

Inter American University of Puerto Rico School of Optometry, Professional Program, BayamÃ³n, PR 00957. Offers OD. *Accreditation:* AOA. *Degree requirements:* For doctorate, thesis/dissertation, research project. *Entrance requirements:* For doctorate, OAT, interview, minimum GPA of 2.5, 2 letters of recommendation. Electronic applications accepted. *Expenses:* Contact institution. *Faculty research:* Visual characteristics of special populations, contact lenses, refraction and diabetes.

Marshall B. Ketchum University, Graduate and Professional Programs, Fullerton, CA 92831-1615. Offers optometry (OD); pharmacy (Pharm D); vision science (MS). *Degree requirements:* For doctorate, thesis/dissertation. *Entrance requirements:* For doctorate, OAT. Electronic applications accepted. *Faculty research:* Structure and function of the human visual system.

MCPHS University, School of Optometry, Boston, MA 02115-5896. Offers OD. *Accreditation:* AOA.

Midwestern University, Downers Grove Campus, Chicago College of Optometry, Downers Grove, IL 60515-1235. Offers OD. *Entrance requirements:* For doctorate, OAT, bachelor's degree, minimum overall cumulative and science GPA of 2.75, two letters of recommendation.

Midwestern University, Glendale Campus, Arizona College of Optometry, Glendale, AZ 85308. Offers OD. *Accreditation:* AOA. *Entrance requirements:* For doctorate, OAT, bachelor's degree, minimum overall cumulative and science GPA of 2.75, 2 letters of recommendation.

New England College of Optometry, Graduate and Professional Programs, Boston, MA 02115-1100. Offers optometry (OD); vision science (MS). *Accreditation:* AOA. *Entrance requirements:* For doctorate, OAT. Electronic applications accepted.

Northeastern State University, Oklahoma College of Optometry, Tahlequah, OK 74464. Offers OD. *Accreditation:* AOA. *Faculty:* 14 full-time (4 women). *Students:* 110 full-time (58 women); includes 31 minority (3 Black or African American, non-Hispanic/ Latino; 10 American Indian or Alaska Native, non-Hispanic/Latino; 7 Asian, non-Hispanic/Latino; 5 Hispanic/Latino; 6 Two or more races, non-Hispanic/Latino). Average age 26. In 2017, 29 doctorates awarded. *Degree requirements:* For doctorate, research project. *Entrance requirements:* For doctorate, OAT. *Application deadline:* For fall admission, 2/1 for domestic students. Applications are processed on a rolling basis. Application fee: $45. Electronic applications accepted. *Expenses:* Contact institution. *Financial support:* Federal Work-Study, institutionally sponsored loans, scholarships/ grants, tuition waivers (partial), and residencies available. Financial award application deadline: 5/1; financial award applicants required to submit FAFSA. *Unit head:* Dr. Douglas Penisten, Dean of Oklahoma College of Optometry, 918-444-4025, E-mail: penisten@nsuok.edu. *Application contact:* Sandy Medearis, Optometric Student and Alumni Services Director, 918-444-4006, Fax: 918-458-2104, E-mail: medearis@ nsuok.edu.
Website: http://optometry.nsuok.edu

Nova Southeastern University, College of Optometry, Fort Lauderdale, FL 33328. Offers MS, OD. *Accreditation:* AOA. *Program availability:* Online learning. *Students:* 435 full-time (300 women), 10 part-time (7 women); includes 196 minority (33 Black or African American, non-Hispanic/Latino; 2 American Indian or Alaska Native, non-Hispanic/Latino; 74 Asian, non-Hispanic/Latino; 72 Hispanic/Latino; 15 Two or more races, non-Hispanic/Latino), 51 international. Average age 26. In 2017, 104 doctorates awarded. *Entrance requirements:* For master's, OAT or GRE, BA; for doctorate, OAT, minimum GPA of 3.0. Additional exam requirements/recommendations for international students: Required—TOEFL (minimum score 79 iBT). *Application deadline:* Applications are processed on a rolling basis. Application fee: $50. Electronic applications accepted. *Expenses:* Contact institution. *Financial support:* Federal Work-Study, institutionally sponsored loans, and scholarships/grants available. Support available to part-time students. Financial award application deadline: 4/15; financial award applicants required to submit FAFSA. *Faculty research:* Retinal disease, low vision, binocular vision, contact lenses, accommodation. *Unit head:* Dr. David Loshin, Dean, 954-262-1404, Fax: 954-262-1818, E-mail: loshin@nova.edu. *Application contact:* Juan Saavedra, Admissions Counselor, 954-262-1132, Fax: 954-262-2282, E-mail: jsaavedra@nova.edu.
Website: http://optometry.nova.edu/

The Ohio State University, College of Optometry, Columbus, OH 43210. Offers optometry (OD); vision science (MS, PhD); OD/MS. *Accreditation:* AOA (one or more programs are accredited). *Faculty:* 35. *Students:* 276 (187 women); includes 39 minority (10 Black or African American, non-Hispanic/Latino; 17 Asian, non-Hispanic/Latino; 6 Hispanic/Latino; 6 Two or more races, non-Hispanic/Latino), 2 international. Average age 25. In 2017, 9 master's, 57 doctorates awarded. *Degree requirements:* For master's, thesis; for doctorate, thesis/dissertation. *Entrance requirements:* For master's, GRE; for doctorate, GRE (for PhD); OAT (for OD). Additional exam requirements/ recommendations for international students: Required—TOEFL minimum score 550 paper-based, 79 iBT, Michigan English Language Assessment Battery minimum score 82, IELTS minimum score 7 (for MS and PhD); TOEFL minimum score 577 paper-based; 90 iBT, Michigan English Language Assessment Battery minimum score 84, IELTS minimum score 7.5 (for OD). *Application deadline:* For fall admission, 3/31 for domestic and international students; for spring admission, 12/1 for domestic students, 11/1 for international students. Applications are processed on a rolling basis. Application fee: $60 ($70 for international students). Electronic applications accepted. *Expenses:* Contact institution. *Financial support:* Research assistantships with full tuition reimbursements, teaching assistantships with full tuition reimbursements, institutionally sponsored loans, and scholarships/grants available. Financial award application deadline: 2/15; financial award applicants required to submit FAFSA. *Unit head:* Dr. Karla Zadnik, Dean, 614-292-6603, E-mail: zadnik.4@osu.edu. *Application contact:* Office of Student Affairs, College of Optometry, 614-292-2647, Fax: 614-292-7493, E-mail: admissions@optometry.osu.edu.
Website: http://www.optometry.osu.edu/

Pacific University, College of Optometry, Forest Grove, OR 97116-1797. Offers optometry (OD); vision science (MS, PhD). *Accreditation:* AOA (one or more programs are accredited). *Degree requirements:* For doctorate, thesis/dissertation optional. *Entrance requirements:* For master's, GRE General Test, course work in natural sciences; for doctorate, OAT, 30 hours OD observation; course work in natural sciences, math, psychology, English, letters of recommendation. Additional exam requirements/ recommendations for international students: Required—TOEFL (minimum score 600 paper-based). Electronic applications accepted. *Expenses:* Contact institution. *Faculty research:* Sports vision, infant vision care, visual training, contact lenses, ocular pathology.

Salus University, Pennsylvania College of Optometry, Elkins Park, PA 19027-1598. Offers OD, OD/MS. *Degree requirements:* For doctorate, comprehensive exam (for some programs). *Entrance requirements:* For doctorate, OAT, interview. Additional exam requirements/recommendations for international students: Required—TOEFL. Electronic applications accepted. *Faculty research:* Vision research, visual perception, ocular motility, electrodiagnosis, photobiology glaucoma, myopia, keratoconus.

Southern College of Optometry, Professional Program, Memphis, TN 38104-2222. Offers OD. *Accreditation:* AOA. *Degree requirements:* For doctorate, clinical experience. *Entrance requirements:* For doctorate, OAT, 3 years of undergraduate pre-optometry course work.

State University of New York College of Optometry, Professional Program, New York, NY 10036. Offers OD, OD/MS, OD/PhD. *Accreditation:* AOA. *Entrance requirements:* For doctorate, OAT. Additional exam requirements/recommendations for international students: Required—TOEFL (minimum score 550 paper-based; 80 iBT). Electronic applications accepted. *Faculty research:* Optometry, vision research.

Université de Montréal, School of Optometry, Professional Program in Optometry, Montréal, QC H3C 3J7, Canada. Offers OD. Open only to Canadian residents. *Accreditation:* AOA. *Degree requirements:* For doctorate, thesis/dissertation. Electronic applications accepted.

The University of Alabama at Birmingham, School of Optometry, Professional Program in Optometry, Birmingham, AL 35294. Offers OD. *Accreditation:* AOA. *Entrance requirements:* For doctorate, OAT, composite evaluation or letters of recommendation, interview. Additional exam requirements/recommendations for international students: Required—TOEFL. Electronic applications accepted.

University of California, Berkeley, School of Optometry, Berkeley, CA 94720-1500. Offers OD, Certificate. *Accreditation:* AOA. *Entrance requirements:* For doctorate, OAT. Additional exam requirements/recommendations for international students: Required—TOEFL (minimum score 570 paper-based; 90 iBT). Electronic applications accepted. *Faculty research:* Low vision, spatial vision, psychophysics of vision, clinical optics, patient care.

University of Houston, College of Optometry, Professional Program in Optometry, Houston, TX 77204. Offers OD. *Accreditation:* AOA. *Faculty research:* Refractive error development, corneal physiology, low vision, binocular vision.

The University of Manchester, School of Biological Sciences, Manchester, United Kingdom. Offers adaptive organismal biology (M Phil, PhD); animal biology (M Phil, PhD); biochemistry (M Phil, PhD); bioinformatics (M Phil, PhD); biomolecular sciences (M Phil, PhD); biotechnology (M Phil, PhD); cell biology (M Phil, PhD); cell matrix research (M Phil, PhD); channels and transporters (M Phil, PhD); developmental biology (M Phil, PhD); environmental biology (M Phil, PhD); evolutionary biology (M Phil, PhD); gene expression (M Phil, PhD); genetics (M Phil, PhD); history of science, technology and medicine (M Phil, PhD); immunology (M Phil, PhD); integrative neurobiology and behavior (M Phil, PhD); membrane trafficking (M Phil, PhD); microbiology (M Phil, PhD); molecular and cellular neuroscience (M Phil, PhD); molecular biology (M Phil, PhD); molecular cancer studies (M Phil, PhD); neuroscience (M Phil, PhD); ophthalmology (M Phil, PhD); optometry (M Phil, PhD); organelle function (M Phil, PhD); pharmacology (M Phil, PhD); physiology (M Phil, PhD); plant sciences (M Phil, PhD); stem cell research (M Phil, PhD); structural biology (M Phil, PhD); systems neuroscience (M Phil, PhD); toxicology (M Phil, PhD).

University of Missouri–St. Louis, College of Optometry, Professional Program in Optometry, St. Louis, MO 63121. Offers OD. *Accreditation:* AOA. *Faculty:* 19 full-time (12 women), 13 part-time/adjunct (5 women). *Students:* 172 full-time (103 women); includes 18 minority (2 Black or African American, non-Hispanic/Latino; 13 Asian, non-Hispanic/Latino; 3 Hispanic/Latino), 4 international. Average age 23. 403 applicants, 26% accepted, 49 enrolled. *Entrance requirements:* For doctorate, OAT, 90 hours of undergraduate course work. *Application deadline:* For fall admission, 2/15 for domestic and international students. Applications are processed on a rolling basis. Application fee: $50. Electronic applications accepted. *Expenses:* Contact institution. *Financial support:* In 2017–18, 131 students received support, including 35 teaching assistantships (averaging $1,200 per year); research assistantships, Federal Work-Study, and scholarships/grants also available. Financial award application deadline: 2/15; financial award applicants required to submit FAFSA. *Faculty research:* Visual psychophysics and perception, noninvasive assessment of visual processing, aging and Alzheimer's disease, orthokeratology. *Unit head:* Nick G. Palisch, Director, Student Services, 314-516-6263, Fax: 314-516-6708, E-mail: optstuaff@umsl.edu. *Application contact:* Linda Stein, Student Support Specialist, 314-516-5905, Fax: 314-516-6708, E-mail: linda_stein@umsl.edu.
Website: http://www.umsl.edu/divisions/optometry/Academic%20Programs/opt_curric.html

University of Pikeville, Kentucky College of Optometry, Pikeville, KY 41501. Offers OD. *Faculty:* 15 full-time (5 women). *Students:* 124 full-time (71 women); includes 20 minority (6 Black or African American, non-Hispanic/Latino; 2 American Indian or Alaska Native, non-Hispanic/Latino; 5 Asian, non-Hispanic/Latino; 7 Hispanic/Latino). Average age 24. 504 applicants, 44% accepted, 60 enrolled. *Degree requirements:* For doctorate, comprehensive exam. *Entrance requirements:* For doctorate, OAT. *Application deadline:* For fall admission, 4/15 for domestic students. *Expenses:* Contact institution. *Financial support:* Fellowships available. Financial award application deadline: 7/1; financial award applicants required to submit FAFSA. *Unit head:* Dr. Donnie Akers, Acting Dean, 606-218-5510, E-mail: andrewbuzzelli@upike.edu. *Application contact:* Casey Price, Coordinator of Admissions, 606-218-5517, E-mail: caseyprice@upike.edu.
Website: http://www.upike.edu/KYCO

University of the Incarnate Word, Rosenberg School of Optometry, San Antonio, TX 78209-6397. Offers OD. *Accreditation:* AOA. *Faculty:* 19 full-time (6 women), 1 (woman) part-time/adjunct. *Students:* 260 full-time (177 women), 1 (woman) part-time; includes 151 minority (8 Black or African American, non-Hispanic/Latino; 2 American Indian or Alaska Native, non-Hispanic/Latino; 89 Asian, non-Hispanic/Latino; 51 Hispanic/Latino; 1 Two or more races, non-Hispanic/Latino), 4 international. In 2017, 65 doctorates awarded. *Degree requirements:* For doctorate, clinical contact hours. *Entrance requirements:* For doctorate, OAT, 90 credit hours of prerequisite course work; letters of recommendation; interview. Additional exam requirements/recommendations for international students: Required—TOEFL (minimum score 560 paper-based; 83 iBT). *Application deadline:* For fall admission, 5/1 for domestic students. Application fee: $50. Electronic applications accepted. *Expenses:* $36,600 per year. *Financial support:* In 2017–18, 5 fellowships (averaging $4,000 per year) were awarded; Federal Work-Study and scholarships/grants also available. Financial award applicants required to submit FAFSA. *Faculty research:* Macular pigment and visual performance, normal and abnormal color vision with cone specific veps, binocular facilitation of cone specific visual evoked potentials for color deficiency, efficacy of mibo thermoflo in treatment of meibomian gland dysfunction. *Unit head:* Dr. Timothy Wingert, Dean, 210-883-1195, Fax: 210-283-6890, E-mail: twingert@uiwtx.edu. *Application contact:* Kristine Benne, Assistant Dean of Student Affairs, 210-883-1190, Fax: 210-883-1191, E-mail: benne@uiwtx.edu.
Website: http://optometry.uiw.edu/

University of Waterloo, Graduate Studies, Faculty of Science, School of Optometry and Vision Science, Waterloo, ON N2L 3G1, Canada. Offers optometry (OD); vision science (M Sc, PhD). *Accreditation:* AOA. *Program availability:* Part-time. *Degree requirements:* For master's, thesis; for doctorate, thesis/dissertation. *Entrance requirements:* For master's, honors degree, minimum B average; for doctorate, master's degree, minimum B average. Additional exam requirements/recommendations for international students: Required—TOEFL, IELTS, PTE. Electronic applications accepted. *Faculty research:* Vision science, fundamental and clinical vision, physiological optics, psycho-physics, perception.

Western University of Health Sciences, College of Optometry, Pomona, CA 91766-1854. Offers OD. *Accreditation:* AOA. *Faculty:* 31 full-time (15 women), 5 part-time/adjunct (3 women). *Students:* 320 full-time (233 women); includes 198 minority (9 Black or African American, non-Hispanic/Latino; 1 American Indian or Alaska Native, non-Hispanic/Latino; 113 Asian, non-Hispanic/Latino; 37 Hispanic/Latino; 2 Native Hawaiian or other Pacific Islander, non-Hispanic/Latino; 36 Two or more races, non-Hispanic/Latino), 18 international. Average age 27. 477 applicants, 32% accepted, 65 enrolled. In 2017, 85 doctorates awarded. *Degree requirements:* For doctorate, comprehensive exam (for some programs), thesis/dissertation (for some programs). *Entrance requirements:* For doctorate, OAT, 3 letters of recommendation; BS or BA (recommended). Additional exam requirements/recommendations for international students: Required—TOEFL (minimum score 79 iBT). *Application deadline:* For fall admission, 5/1 for domestic and international students. Applications are processed on a rolling basis. Application fee: $65. Electronic applications accepted. *Expenses:* $39,895 first-year tuition and fees. *Financial support:* In 2017–18, 37 students received support. Career-related internships or fieldwork, scholarships/grants, and traineeships available. Financial award application deadline: 3/2; financial award applicants required to submit FAFSA. *Unit head:* Dr. Elizabeth Hoppe, Dean, 909-706-3497, E-mail: ehoppe@westernu.edu. *Application contact:* Marie Anderson, Director of Admissions, 909-469-5335, Fax: 909-469-5570, E-mail: admissions@westernu.edu.
Website: http://www.westernu.edu/optometry/

Vision Sciences

Eastern Virginia Medical School, Ophthalmic Technology Program, Norfolk, VA 23501-1980. Offers Certificate. Electronic applications accepted. *Expenses:* Contact institution.

Marshall B. Ketchum University, Graduate and Professional Programs, Fullerton, CA 92831-1615. Offers optometry (OD); pharmacy (Pharm D); vision science (MS). *Degree requirements:* For doctorate, thesis/dissertation. *Entrance requirements:* For doctorate, OAT. Electronic applications accepted. *Faculty research:* Structure and function of the human visual system.

New England College of Optometry, Graduate and Professional Programs, Boston, MA 02115-1100. Offers optometry (OD); vision science (MS). *Accreditation:* AOA. *Entrance requirements:* For doctorate, OAT. Electronic applications accepted.

Pacific University, College of Optometry, Forest Grove, OR 97116-1797. Offers optometry (OD); vision science (MS, PhD). *Accreditation:* AOA (one or more programs are accredited). *Degree requirements:* For doctorate, thesis/dissertation optional. *Entrance requirements:* For master's, GRE General Test, course work in natural sciences; for doctorate, OAT, 30 hours OD observation; course work in natural sciences, math, psychology, English, letters of recommendation. Additional exam requirements/recommendations for international students: Required—TOEFL (minimum score 600 paper-based). Electronic applications accepted. *Expenses:* Contact institution. *Faculty research:* Sports vision, infant vision care, visual training, contact lenses, ocular pathology.

Salus University, College of Education and Rehabilitation, Elkins Park, PA 19027-1598. Offers education of children and youth with visual and multiple impairments (M Ed, Certificate); low vision rehabilitation (MS, Certificate); occupational therapy (MS); orientation and mobility therapy (MS, Certificate); speech-language pathology (MS); vision rehabilitation therapy (MS, Certificate); OD/MS. *Accreditation:* AOTA. *Program availability:* Part-time, online learning. *Entrance requirements:* For master's, GRE or MAT, letters of reference (3), interviews (2). Additional exam requirements/recommendations for international students: Required—TOEFL, TWE. *Expenses:* Contact institution. *Faculty research:* Knowledge utilization, technology transfer.

State University of New York College of Optometry, Graduate Programs, New York, NY 10036. Offers PhD, OD/MS, OD/PhD. *Program availability:* Part-time. Terminal master's awarded for partial completion of doctoral program. *Degree requirements:* For doctorate, comprehensive exam, thesis/dissertation, specialty exam. *Entrance requirements:* For doctorate, GRE General Test. Additional exam requirements/recommendations for international students: Required—TOEFL (minimum score 550 paper-based; 80 iBT). *Expenses:* Contact institution. *Faculty research:* Oculomotor systems, perception, physiological optics, ocular biochemistry, accommodation, color and motion.

Université de Montréal, School of Optometry, Graduate Programs in Optometry, Montréal, QC H3C 3J7, Canada. Offers vision sciences (M Sc); visual impairment intervention-orientation and mobility (DESS); visual impairment intervention-readaptation (DESS). *Program availability:* Part-time. *Degree requirements:* For master's, thesis. *Entrance requirements:* For master's, OD or appropriate bachelor's degree, minimum GPA of 2.7. Electronic applications accepted. *Faculty research:* Binocular vision, visual electrophysiology, eye movements, corneal metabolism, glare sensitivity.

The University of Alabama at Birmingham, School of Optometry, Graduate Program in Vision Science, Birmingham, AL 35294. Offers sensory impairment (PhD); vision science (MS, PhD). Terminal master's awarded for partial completion of doctoral program. *Degree requirements:* For master's, thesis; for doctorate, thesis/dissertation. *Entrance requirements:* For master's, GRE General Test (minimum combined verbal and quantitative score of 270), minimum GPA of 3.0, letters of recommendation, interview; for doctorate, GRE General Test (minimum combined verbal and quantitative score of 300), interview. Additional exam requirements/recommendations for international students: Required—TOEFL (minimum score 570 paper-based). Electronic applications accepted.

University of Alberta, Faculty of Medicine and Dentistry and Faculty of Graduate Studies and Research, Graduate Programs in Medicine, Department of Ophthalmology, Edmonton, AB T6G 2E1, Canada. Offers M Sc, PhD. *Program availability:* Part-time. Terminal master's awarded for partial completion of doctoral program. *Degree requirements:* For master's, thesis; for doctorate, comprehensive exam, thesis/dissertation. *Faculty research:* Ocular genetics.

University of California, Berkeley, Graduate Division, Group in Vision Science, Berkeley, CA 94720-1500. Offers MS, PhD. *Degree requirements:* For master's, thesis; for doctorate, thesis/dissertation. *Entrance requirements:* For master's and doctorate, GRE General Test, GRE Subject Test, minimum GPA of 3.0, 3 letters of recommendation. Electronic applications accepted. *Faculty research:* Visual neuroscience, bioengineering, computational vision, molecular cell biology, basic and clinical psychophysics.

University of Guelph, Ontario Veterinary College and Graduate Studies, Graduate Programs in Veterinary Sciences, Department of Clinical Studies, Guelph, ON N1G 2W1, Canada. Offers anesthesiology (M Sc, DV Sc); cardiology (DV Sc, Diploma); clinical studies (Diploma); dermatology (M Sc); diagnostic imaging (M Sc, DV Sc); emergency/critical care (M Sc, DV Sc, Diploma); medicine (M Sc, DV Sc); neurology (M Sc, DV Sc); ophthalmology (M Sc, DV Sc); surgery (M Sc, DV Sc). *Degree requirements:* For master's, thesis; for doctorate, comprehensive exam, thesis/dissertation. *Entrance requirements:* Additional exam requirements/recommendations for international students: Required—TOEFL (minimum score 550 paper-based), IELTS (minimum score 6.5). Electronic applications accepted. *Faculty research:* Orthopedics, respirology, oncology, exercise physiology, cardiology.

University of Houston, College of Optometry, Program in Physiological Optics/Vision Science, Houston, TX 77204. Offers physiological optics (MS, PhD). *Faculty research:* Space perception, amblyopia, binocular vision, development of visual skills, strabismus, visual cell biology, refractive error.

The University of Manchester, School of Biological Sciences, Manchester, United Kingdom. Offers adaptive organismal biology (M Phil, PhD); animal biology (M Phil, PhD); biochemistry (M Phil, PhD); bioinformatics (M Phil, PhD); biomolecular sciences (M Phil, PhD); biotechnology (M Phil, PhD); cell biology (M Phil, PhD); cell matrix research (M Phil, PhD); channels and transporters (M Phil, PhD); developmental biology (M Phil, PhD); environmental biology (M Phil, PhD); evolutionary biology (M Phil, PhD); gene expression (M Phil, PhD); genetics (M Phil, PhD); history of science, technology and medicine (M Phil, PhD); immunology (M Phil, PhD); integrative neurobiology and behavior (M Phil, PhD); membrane trafficking (M Phil, PhD); microbiology (M Phil, PhD); molecular and cellular neuroscience (M Phil, PhD); molecular biology (M Phil, PhD); molecular cancer studies (M Phil, PhD); neuroscience (M Phil, PhD); ophthalmology (M Phil, PhD); optometry (M Phil, PhD); organelle function (M Phil, PhD); pharmacology (M Phil, PhD); physiology (M Phil, PhD); plant sciences (M Phil, PhD); stem cell research (M Phil, PhD); structural biology (M Phil, PhD); systems neuroscience (M Phil, PhD); toxicology (M Phil, PhD).

Vision Sciences

University of Massachusetts Boston, Graduate School of Global Inclusion and Social Development, Program in Vision Studies, Boston, MA 02125-3393. Offers M Ed. *Students:* 1 (woman) full-time, 119 part-time (101 women); includes 19 minority (6 Black or African American, non-Hispanic/Latino; 2 Asian, non-Hispanic/Latino; 10 Hispanic/Latino; 1 Native Hawaiian or other Pacific Islander, non-Hispanic/Latino), 2 international. Average age 38. 43 applicants, 81% accepted, 32 enrolled. In 2017, 22 master's awarded. *Expenses:* Tuition, state resident: full-time $17,375. Tuition, nonresident: full-time $33,915. *Required fees:* $355. *Application contact:* Graduate Admissions Coordinator, 617-287-6400, Fax: 617-287-6236, E-mail: bos.gadm@dpc.umassp.edu.

University of Pittsburgh, School of Education, Department of Instruction and Learning, Program in Special Education, Pittsburgh, PA 15260. Offers applied behavior analysis (M Ed); early intervention (M Ed, PhD); general special education (M Ed, Ed D); special education teacher preparation (M Ed); vision studies (M Ed, PhD). *Program availability:* Part-time, evening/weekend. *Degree requirements:* For master's, thesis; for doctorate, thesis/dissertation. *Entrance requirements:* For master's, PRAXIS I; for doctorate, GRE General Test. Additional exam requirements/recommendations for international students: Required—TOEFL.

University of Waterloo, Graduate Studies, Faculty of Science, School of Optometry and Vision Science, Waterloo, ON N2L 3G1, Canada. Offers optometry (OD); vision science (M Sc, PhD). *Accreditation:* AOA. *Program availability:* Part-time. *Degree requirements:* For master's, thesis; for doctorate, thesis/dissertation. *Entrance requirements:* For master's, honors degree, minimum B average; for doctorate, master's degree, minimum B average. Additional exam requirements/recommendations for international students: Required—TOEFL, IELTS, PTE. Electronic applications accepted. *Faculty research:* Vision science, fundamental and clinical vision, physiological optics, psycho-physics, perception.

Section 30
Pharmacy and Pharmaceutical Sciences

This section contains a directory of institutions offering graduate work in pharmacy and pharmaceutical sciences, followed by in-depth entries submitted by institutions that chose to prepare detailed program descriptions. Additional information about programs listed in the directory but not augmented by an in-depth entry may be obtained by writing directly to the dean of a graduate school or chair of a department at the address given in the directory.

For programs offering related work, see also in this book *Allied Health, Biochemistry, Biological and Biomedical Sciences, Nutrition, Pharmacology and Toxicology,* and *Physiology.* In the other guides in this series:

Graduate Programs in the Physical Sciences, Mathematics, Agricultural Sciences, the Environment & Natural Resources

See *Chemistry*

Graduate Programs in Engineering & Applied Sciences

See *Biomedical Engineering and Biotechnology,* and *Chemical Engineering*

CONTENTS

Program Directories

Featured Schools: Displays and Close-Ups

See also:

Medicinal and Pharmaceutical Chemistry

Duquesne University, School of Pharmacy, Graduate School of Pharmaceutical Sciences, Program in Medicinal Chemistry, Pittsburgh, PA 15282-0001. Offers MS, PhD. *Faculty:* 5 full-time (0 women). *Students:* 19 full-time (10 women), 17 international. Average age 28. 12 applicants, 25% accepted, 1 enrolled. In 2017, 1 master's, 2 doctorates awarded. *Degree requirements:* For master's, thesis; for doctorate, comprehensive exam, thesis/dissertation. *Entrance requirements:* For master's and doctorate, GRE General Test. Additional exam requirements/recommendations for international students: Required—TOEFL (minimum score 100 iBT). *Application deadline:* For fall admission, 12/1 priority date for domestic and international students; for spring admission, 10/1 priority date for domestic and international students. Applications are processed on a rolling basis. Electronic applications accepted. *Expenses:* $1,542 per credit. *Financial support:* In 2017–18, 20 students received support, including 7 research assistantships with full tuition reimbursements available, 13 teaching assistantships with full tuition reimbursements available. *Unit head:* Dr. Aleem Gangjee, Head, 412-396-6070. *Application contact:* Information Contact, 412-396-1172, E-mail: gsps-adm@duq.edu.
Website: http://www.duq.edu/academics/schools/pharmacy/graduate-school-of-pharmaceutical-sciences

Florida Agricultural and Mechanical University, Division of Graduate Studies, Research, and Continuing Education, College of Pharmacy and Pharmaceutical Sciences, Graduate Programs in Pharmaceutical Sciences, Tallahassee, FL 32307-3200. Offers environmental toxicology (PhD); health outcomes research and pharmacoeconomics (PhD); medicinal chemistry (MS, PhD); pharmaceutics (MS, PhD); pharmacology/toxicology (MS, PhD); pharmacy administration (MS). *Accreditation:* CEPH. *Degree requirements:* For master's, comprehensive exam, thesis, publishable paper; for doctorate, comprehensive exam, thesis/dissertation, publishable paper. *Entrance requirements:* For master's and doctorate, GRE General Test, minimum GPA of 3.0 in last 60 hours. Additional exam requirements/recommendations for international students: Required—TOEFL. *Faculty research:* Anticancer agents, anti-inflammatory drugs, chronopharmacology, neuroendocrinology, microbiology.

Idaho State University, Office of Graduate Studies, College of Pharmacy, Department of Biomedical and Pharmaceutical Sciences, Pocatello, ID 83209-8334. Offers biopharmaceutical analysis (PhD); drug delivery (PhD); medicinal chemistry (PhD); pharmaceutical sciences (MS); pharmacology (PhD). *Program availability:* Part-time. *Degree requirements:* For master's, one foreign language, comprehensive exam, thesis, thesis research, classes in speech and technical writing; for doctorate, comprehensive exam, thesis/dissertation, written and oral exams, classes in speech and technical writing. *Entrance requirements:* For master's, GRE General Test, minimum GPA of 3.0, 3 letters of recommendation; for doctorate, GRE General Test, BS in pharmacy or related field, minimum GPA of 3.0, 3 letters of recommendation. Additional exam requirements/recommendations for international students: Required—TOEFL (minimum score 550 paper-based; 80 iBT). Electronic applications accepted. *Expenses:* Contact institution. *Faculty research:* Metabolic toxicity of heavy metals, neuroendocrine pharmacology, cardiovascular pharmacology, cancer biology, immunopharmacology.

Medical University of South Carolina, College of Graduate Studies, Department of Pharmaceutical and Biomedical Sciences, Charleston, SC 29425. Offers cell injury and repair (PhD); drug discovery (PhD); medicinal chemistry (PhD); toxicology (PhD); DMD/PhD; MD/PhD; Pharm D/PhD. *Degree requirements:* For doctorate, thesis/dissertation, oral and written exams, teaching and research seminar. *Entrance requirements:* For doctorate, GRE General Test, interview, minimum GPA of 3.0. Additional exam requirements/recommendations for international students: Required—TOEFL (minimum score 600 paper-based; 100 iBT). Electronic applications accepted. *Faculty research:* Drug discovery, toxicology, metabolomics, cell stress and injury.

New Jersey Institute of Technology, College of Science and Liberal Arts, Newark, NJ 07102. Offers applied mathematics (MS); applied physics (MS, PhD); applied statistics (MS, Certificate); biology (MS, PhD); biostatistics (MS); chemistry (MS, PhD); environmental and sustainability policy (MS); environmental science (MS, PhD); history (MA, MAT); materials science and engineering (MS, PhD); mathematical and computational finance (MS); mathematical sciences (PhD); pharmaceutical chemistry (MS); professional and technical communications (MS); technical communication essentials (Certificate). *Program availability:* Part-time, evening/weekend. *Students:* Average age 28. 504 applicants, 64% accepted, 65 enrolled. In 2017, 81 master's, 18 doctorates, 1 other advanced degree awarded. Terminal master's awarded for partial completion of doctoral program. *Entrance requirements:* For master's, GRE General Test; for doctorate, GRE General Test, minimum graduate GPA of 3.5. Additional exam requirements/recommendations for international students: Required—TOEFL (minimum score 550 paper-based; 79 iBT). *Application deadline:* For fall admission, 6/1 priority date for domestic students, 5/1 priority date for international students; for spring admission, 11/15 priority date for domestic and international students. Applications are processed on a rolling basis. Application fee: $75. Electronic applications accepted. *Expenses:* Contact institution. *Financial support:* In 2017–18, 106 students received support, including 8 fellowships (averaging $3,436 per year), 51 research assistantships (averaging $23,452 per year), 91 teaching assistantships (averaging $25,553 per year); scholarships/grants, traineeships, and unspecified assistantships also available. Financial award application deadline: 1/15. *Faculty research:* Biophotonics and bioimaging, morphogenetic patterning, embryogenesis, biological fluid dynamics, applied research in the mathematical sciences. *Unit head:* Dr. Kevin Belfield, Dean, 973-596-3676, Fax: 973-565-0586, E-mail: kevin.d.belfield@njit.edu. *Application contact:* Stephen Eck, Director of Admissions, 973-596-3300, Fax: 973-596-3461, E-mail: admissions@njit.edu.
Website: http://csla.njit.edu/

Purdue University, College of Pharmacy and Graduate School, Graduate Programs in Pharmacy and Pharmacal Sciences, Department of Medicinal Chemistry and Molecular Pharmacology, West Lafayette, IN 47907. Offers biophysical and computational chemistry (PhD); cancer research (PhD); immunology and infectious disease (PhD); medicinal biochemistry and molecular biology (PhD); medicinal chemistry and chemical biology (PhD); molecular pharmacology (PhD); neuropharmacology, neurodegeneration, and neurotoxicity (PhD); systems biology and functional genomics (PhD). *Faculty:* 26 full-time (5 women). *Students:* 52 full-time (22 women), 3 part-time (all women); includes 4 minority (1 Black or African American, non-Hispanic/Latino; 2 Asian, non-Hispanic/Latino; 1 Hispanic/Latino), 29 international. Average age 26. 151 applicants, 19% accepted, 13 enrolled. In 2017, 18 doctorates awarded. *Degree requirements:* For doctorate, thesis/dissertation. *Entrance requirements:* For doctorate, GRE General Test; GRE Subject Test in biology, biochemistry, and chemistry (recommended), minimum undergraduate GPA of 3.0. Additional exam requirements/recommendations for international students: Required—TOEFL (minimum score 550 paper-based; 77 iBT); Recommended—TWE. *Application deadline:* For fall admission, 2/1 for domestic and international students. Applications are processed on a rolling basis. Application fee: $60 ($75 for international students). Electronic applications accepted. *Financial support:* Fellowships, research assistantships, teaching assistantships, and traineeships available. Support available to part-time students. Financial award applicants required to submit FAFSA. *Faculty research:* Drug design and development, cancer research, drug synthesis and analysis, chemical pharmacology, environmental toxicology. *Unit head:* Zhong-Yin Zhang, Head, 765-494-1403, E-mail: zhang-yn@purdue.edu. *Application contact:* Delayne Graham, Graduate Contact, 765-494-1362, E-mail: dkgraham@purdue.edu.

Rutgers University–New Brunswick, Ernest Mario School of Pharmacy, Program in Medicinal Chemistry, Piscataway, NJ 08854-8097. Offers MS, PhD. *Program availability:* Part-time. *Degree requirements:* For master's, comprehensive exam, thesis; for doctorate, comprehensive exam, thesis/dissertation. *Entrance requirements:* For master's and doctorate, GRE General Test. Additional exam requirements/recommendations for international students: Required—TOEFL (minimum score 600 paper-based; 90 iBT). Electronic applications accepted. *Faculty research:* Synthesis and design of anticancer drugs, synthesis of pro-drugs for prostate cancer, natural product synthesis, natural product isolation and structure elucidation, computational chemistry.

Temple University, School of Pharmacy, Department of Pharmaceutical Sciences, Philadelphia, PA 19122. Offers medicinal chemistry (MS, PhD); pharmaceutics (MS, PhD); pharmacodynamics (MS, PhD); regulatory affairs and quality assurance (MS). *Program availability:* Part-time, online learning. *Faculty:* 13 full-time (4 women), 1 part-time/adjunct (0 women). *Students:* 29 full-time (11 women), 11 part-time (4 women); includes 2 minority (both Asian, non-Hispanic/Latino), 21 international. 51 applicants, 24% accepted, 4 enrolled. In 2017, 24 master's, 4 doctorates awarded. *Degree requirements:* For master's, comprehensive exam (for some programs), thesis (for some programs); for doctorate, 2 foreign languages, comprehensive exam, thesis/dissertation. *Entrance requirements:* For master's, GRE General Test, minimum undergraduate GPA of 3.0; for doctorate, GRE General Test, minimum GPA of 3.0. Additional exam requirements/recommendations for international students: Required—TOEFL (minimum score 550 paper-based; 82 iBT). *Application deadline:* For fall admission, 1/15 for domestic students, 12/15 for international students. Application fee: $60. Electronic applications accepted. *Expenses:* Contact institution. *Financial support:* Fellowships with full tuition reimbursements, research assistantships with full tuition reimbursements, and teaching assistantships with full tuition reimbursements available. Financial award application deadline: 1/15; financial award applicants required to submit FAFSA. *Faculty research:* Pharmacokinetics, synthesis of medicinals, protein research, biopharmaformulation. *Unit head:* Dr. Daniel Canney, Director of Graduate Studies, 215-707-6924, E-mail: phscgrad@temple.edu. *Application contact:* Sophon Din, Administrative Assistant, 215-204-4948, E-mail: tuspgrad@temple.edu.
Website: http://pharmacy.temple.edu/academics/department-pharmaceutical-science

University at Buffalo, the State University of New York, Graduate School, College of Arts and Sciences, Department of Chemistry, Buffalo, NY 14260. Offers chemistry (MA, PhD); medicinal chemistry (MS, PhD). *Program availability:* Part-time. *Faculty:* 29 full-time (5 women), 2 part-time/adjunct (both women). *Students:* 163 full-time (74 women); includes 23 minority (7 Black or African American, non-Hispanic/Latino; 4 Asian, non-Hispanic/Latino; 12 Hispanic/Latino), 51 international. Average age 26. 225 applicants, 28% accepted, 37 enrolled. In 2017, 10 master's, 17 doctorates awarded. Terminal master's awarded for partial completion of doctoral program. *Degree requirements:* For master's, thesis or alternative, project; for doctorate, thesis/dissertation, synopsis proposal. *Entrance requirements:* For master's and doctorate, GRE General Test. Additional exam requirements/recommendations for international students: Required—TOEFL (minimum score 550 paper-based; 79 iBT). *Application deadline:* For fall admission, 3/1 for domestic and international students; for spring admission, 11/1 for domestic students. Applications are processed on a rolling basis. Application fee: $75. Electronic applications accepted. *Expenses:* Contact institution. *Financial support:* In 2017–18, 11 students received support, including 3 fellowships with full tuition reimbursements available (averaging $23,000 per year), 46 research assistantships with full tuition reimbursements available (averaging $23,000 per year), 81 teaching assistantships with full tuition reimbursements available (averaging $23,000 per year); Federal Work-Study, institutionally sponsored loans, and unspecified assistantships also available. Financial award application deadline: 6/15; financial award applicants required to submit FAFSA. *Faculty research:* Synthesis, measurements, structure theory, translation. *Total annual research expenditures:* $6 million. *Unit head:* Dr. David F. Watson, Chairman, 716-645-6824, Fax: 716-645-6963, E-mail: chechair@buffalo.edu. *Application contact:* Dr. Diana S. Aga, Director of Graduate Studies, 716-645-4220, Fax: 716-645-6963, E-mail: dianaaga@buffalo.edu.
Website: http://www.chemistry.buffalo.edu/

University of California, Irvine, Programs in Health Sciences, Program in Medicinal Chemistry and Pharmacology, Irvine, CA 92697. Offers PhD. *Students:* 6 full-time (4 women); includes 3 minority (1 Asian, non-Hispanic/Latino; 2 Hispanic/Latino), 1 international. Average age 24. 45 applicants, 31% accepted, 6 enrolled. Application fee: $105 ($125 for international students). *Unit head:* Stephen Hanessian, Director, 949-824-5449, Fax: 949-824-9920, E-mail: shanessi@uci.edu. *Application contact:* Geneva Lopez-Sandoval, Student Affairs Office, 949-824-0878, E-mail: lopezg@uci.edu.
Website: http://www.pharmsci.uci.edu/graduate/index.php

University of California, San Francisco, School of Pharmacy and Graduate Division, Chemistry and Chemical Biology Graduate Program, San Francisco, CA 94143. Offers PhD. *Degree requirements:* For doctorate, thesis/dissertation. *Entrance requirements:* For doctorate, GRE General Test, minimum GPA of 3.0, bachelor's degree. Additional exam requirements/recommendations for international students: Required—TOEFL (minimum score 550 paper-based; 80 iBT). Electronic applications accepted. *Faculty research:* Macromolecular structure function and dynamics, computational chemistry and biology, biological chemistry and synthetic biology, chemical biology and molecular design, nanomolecular design.

University of Connecticut, Graduate School, School of Pharmacy, Department of Pharmaceutical Sciences, Program in Medicinal Chemistry, Storrs, CT 06269. Offers MS, PhD. Terminal master's awarded for partial completion of doctoral program. *Degree requirements:* For master's, comprehensive exam, thesis; for doctorate, thesis/dissertation. *Entrance requirements:* Additional exam requirements/recommendations for international students: Required—TOEFL (minimum score 550 paper-based). Electronic applications accepted.

University of Florida, Graduate School, College of Pharmacy, Graduate Programs in Pharmacy, Department of Medicinal Chemistry, Gainesville, FL 32611. Offers clinical toxicology (MSP); forensic DNA and serology (MSP); forensic drug chemistry (MSP); forensic science (MSP); medicinal chemistry (MSP, PhD); pharmaceutical chemistry

(MSP). *Program availability:* Part-time, evening/weekend, online learning. Terminal master's awarded for partial completion of doctoral program. *Degree requirements:* For master's, thesis optional; for doctorate, comprehensive exam, thesis/dissertation. *Entrance requirements:* For master's and doctorate, GRE General Test, minimum GPA of 3.0. Additional exam requirements/recommendations for international students: Required—TOEFL (minimum score 550 paper-based; 80 iBT), IELTS (minimum score 6). Electronic applications accepted. *Faculty research:* Drug metabolism and toxicology, discovery of biologically active natural products, chelator chemistry and biochemistry, anti-cancer drug and pro-drug discovery, discovery of anti-infective drugs and biosynthetic engineering.

University of Illinois at Chicago, College of Pharmacy and Graduate College, Graduate Programs in Pharmacy, Chicago, IL 60607-7128. Offers comparative effectiveness research (MS); forensic science (MS); forensic toxicology (MS); medicinal chemistry (MS, PhD); pharmacognosy (MS, PhD); pharmacy (PhD). Terminal master's awarded for partial completion of doctoral program. *Degree requirements:* For master's, variable foreign language requirement, thesis; for doctorate, variable foreign language requirement, thesis/dissertation. *Entrance requirements:* For master's and doctorate, GRE General Test. Additional exam requirements/recommendations for international students: Required—TOEFL. Electronic applications accepted. *Faculty research:* Biopharmaceutical science, forensic science, forensic toxicology, medicinal chemistry, pharmacognosy.

The University of Iowa, College of Pharmacy, Iowa City, IA 52242-1316. Offers clinical pharmaceutical sciences (PhD); medicinal and natural products chemistry (PhD); pharamaceutics (PhD); pharmaceutical socioeconomics (PhD); pharmaceutics (MS); pharmacy (Pharm D); Pharm D/MPH. *Accreditation:* ACPE (one or more programs are accredited). *Degree requirements:* For master's, thesis optional, exam; for doctorate, comprehensive exam, thesis/dissertation. *Entrance requirements:* For master's and doctorate, GRE General Test, minimum GPA of 3.0. Additional exam requirements/recommendations for international students: Required—TOEFL (minimum score 550 paper-based; 81 iBT). Electronic applications accepted.

The University of Kansas, Graduate Studies, School of Pharmacy, Department of Medicinal Chemistry, Lawrence, KS 66045. Offers MS, PhD. *Students:* 21 full-time (6 women); includes 1 minority (Asian, non-Hispanic/Latino), 7 international. Average age 27. 42 applicants, 33% accepted, 5 enrolled. In 2017, 2 master's, 6 doctorates awarded. Terminal master's awarded for partial completion of doctoral program. *Entrance requirements:* For master's, GRE General Test, BS in pharmacy, medicinal chemistry, chemistry, biochemistry, or closely-related field; minimum undergraduate GPA of 3.0; one year of organic chemistry with laboratory; for doctorate, GRE General Test, BS or MS in pharmacy, medicinal chemistry, chemistry, biochemistry, or closely-related field; minimum undergraduate GPA of 3.0; one year of organic chemistry with laboratory. Additional exam requirements/recommendations for international students: Required—TOEFL. *Application deadline:* For fall admission, 2/1 for domestic and international students. Application fee: $65 ($85 for international students). Electronic applications accepted. *Financial support:* Fellowships, research assistantships, teaching assistantships, health care benefits, and unspecified assistantships available. Financial award application deadline: 2/1. *Faculty research:* Cancer, neuroscience, synthetic methods, natural products, biochemistry. *Unit head:* Dr. Thomas Prisinzano, Chair, 785-864-3267, E-mail: prisinza@ku.edu. *Application contact:* Norma Henley, Administrative Associate, 785-864-4495, E-mail: medchem@ku.edu.
Website: http://www.medchem.ku.edu/

The University of Kansas, Graduate Studies, School of Pharmacy, Department of Pharmaceutical Chemistry, Lawrence, KS 66047. Offers MS, PhD. *Program availability:* Part-time, evening/weekend, online learning. *Students:* 38 full-time (13 women), 11 part-time (6 women); includes 7 minority (4 Asian, non-Hispanic/Latino; 1 Hispanic/Latino; 2 Two or more races, non-Hispanic/Latino), 22 international. Average age 28. 56 applicants, 25% accepted, 8 enrolled. In 2017, 10 master's, 5 doctorates awarded. Terminal master's awarded for partial completion of doctoral program. *Entrance requirements:* For master's, GRE General Test, bachelor's degree in biological sciences, chemical engineering, chemistry, or pharmacy; official transcripts from all universities/institutions in which the applicant has studied; personal statement; resume; three letters of recommendation; for doctorate, GRE General Test, official transcripts from all universities/institutions in which the applicant has studied, personal statement, resume, three letters of recommendation. Additional exam requirements/recommendations for international students: Required—TOEFL. *Application deadline:* For fall admission, 1/15 priority date for domestic and international students; for spring admission, 12/15 for domestic and international students; for summer admission, 5/15 for domestic and international students. Application fee: $65 ($85 for international students). Electronic applications accepted. *Financial support:* Fellowships, research assistantships, career-related internships or fieldwork, scholarships/grants, traineeships, and unspecified assistantships available. Financial award application deadline: 1/15. *Faculty research:* Physical pharmacy, biotechnology, bioanalytical chemistry, biopharmaceutics and pharmacokinetics, nanotechnology. *Unit head:* Dr. Christian Schoneich, Chair, 785-864-4880, E-mail: schoneic@ku.edu. *Application contact:* Nancy Helm, Administrative Associate, 785-864-4822, E-mail: nhelm@ku.edu.
Website: http://www.pharmchem.ku.edu/

University of Michigan, College of Pharmacy and University of Michigan, Department of Medicinal Chemistry, Ann Arbor, MI 48109. Offers PhD. *Faculty:* 11 full-time (4 women), 3 part-time/adjunct (0 women). *Students:* 39 full-time (19 women); includes 6 minority (2 Asian, non-Hispanic/Latino; 3 Hispanic/Latino; 1 Two or more races, non-Hispanic/Latino), 7 international. Average age 27. 84 applicants, 17% accepted, 6 enrolled. In 2017, 4 doctorates awarded. *Degree requirements:* For doctorate, thesis/dissertation, oral defense of dissertation, preliminary exam. *Entrance requirements:* For doctorate, GRE. Additional exam requirements/recommendations for international students: Required—TOEFL (minimum score 560 paper-based; 84 iBT) or IELTS (minimum score 6.5). *Application deadline:* For fall admission, 12/31 for domestic and international students. Applications are processed on a rolling basis. Application fee: $75 ($90 for international students). Electronic applications accepted. *Expenses:* Tuition, state resident: full-time $22,368; part-time $1201 per credit hour. Tuition, nonresident: full-time $45,156; part-time $2467 per credit hour. *Required fees:* $376 per term. Tuition and fees vary according to course load, degree level and program. *Financial support:* In 2017–18, 39 students received support, including 16 fellowships (averaging $48,037 per year), 13 research assistantships (averaging $48,037 per year), 10 teaching assistantships (averaging $48,037 per year); career-related internships or fieldwork, institutionally sponsored loans, scholarships/grants, traineeships, health care benefits, and unspecified assistantships also available. *Unit head:* Dr. George A. Garcia, Chair, 734-764-2202, Fax: 734-647-8430, E-mail: gagarcia@med.umich.edu. *Application contact:* Sarah Lloyd, Executive Secretary, 734-647-8429, Fax: 734-647-8430, E-mail: sarlloyd@med.umich.edu.
Website: https://pharmacy.umich.edu/medchem

University of Minnesota, Twin Cities Campus, College of Pharmacy and Graduate School, Graduate Programs in Pharmacy, Graduate Program in Medicinal Chemistry, Minneapolis, MN 55455. Offers MS, PhD. *Faculty:* 28 full-time (4 women), 8 part-time/adjunct (4 women). *Students:* 50 full-time (17 women); includes 4 minority (1 Black or African American, non-Hispanic/Latino; 1 Asian, non-Hispanic/Latino; 2 Two or more races, non-Hispanic/Latino), 7 international. Average age 26. 67 applicants, 34% accepted, 9 enrolled. In 2017, 1 master's, 7 doctorates awarded. Terminal master's awarded for partial completion of doctoral program. *Degree requirements:* For master's, comprehensive exam, thesis; for doctorate, comprehensive exam, thesis/dissertation. *Entrance requirements:* For doctorate, GRE General Test, BS in biology, chemistry, biochemistry or pharmacy. Additional exam requirements/recommendations for international students: Required—TOEFL (minimum score 550 paper-based; 100 iBT), IELTS (minimum score 7.5). *Application deadline:* For fall admission, 1/3 for domestic and international students. Application fee: $75 ($95 for international students). Electronic applications accepted. *Financial support:* In 2017–18, 30 students received support, including 36 fellowships with full tuition reimbursements available (averaging $9,500 per year), 28 research assistantships with full tuition reimbursements available (averaging $26,750 per year), 9 teaching assistantships with full tuition reimbursements available (averaging $16,669 per year); health care benefits and unspecified assistantships also available. Financial award application deadline: 1/3. *Faculty research:* Drug design and synthesis, molecular modeling, chemical aspects of drug metabolism and toxicity. *Total annual research expenditures:* $5.1 million. *Unit head:* Dr. Gunda I. Georg, Department Head of Medicinal Chemistry, 612-626-6320, Fax: 612-626-3114, E-mail: georg@umn.edu. *Application contact:* Information Contact, 612-625-3014, Fax: 612-625-6002, E-mail: gsquest@umn.edu.
Website: https://www.pharmacy.umn.edu/departments/medicinal-chemistry

University of Mississippi, Graduate School, School of Pharmacy, University, MS 38677. Offers environmental toxicology (MS, PhD); industrial pharmacy (MS); medicinal chemistry (MS, PhD); pharmaceutics (MS, PhD); pharmacognosy (MS, PhD); pharmacology (MS, PhD); pharmacy (Pharm D); pharmacy administration (MS, PhD). *Accreditation:* ACPE (one or more programs are accredited). *Program availability:* Part-time. *Faculty:* 71 full-time (32 women), 17 part-time/adjunct (6 women). *Students:* 417 full-time (256 women), 16 part-time (7 women); includes 71 minority (24 Black or African American, non-Hispanic/Latino; 1 American Indian or Alaska Native, non-Hispanic/Latino; 36 Asian, non-Hispanic/Latino; 4 Hispanic/Latino; 6 Two or more races, non-Hispanic/Latino), 88 international. Average age 25. In 2017, 22 master's, 49 doctorates awarded. Terminal master's awarded for partial completion of doctoral program. *Degree requirements:* For master's, thesis; for doctorate, thesis/dissertation (for some programs). *Entrance requirements:* For master's, GRE General Test, minimum GPA of 3.0; for doctorate, GRE General Test (for PhD). Additional exam requirements/recommendations for international students: Required—TOEFL. *Application deadline:* For fall admission, 2/1 priority date for domestic students; for spring admission, 10/1 priority date for domestic students. Applications are processed on a rolling basis. Application fee: $50. Electronic applications accepted. *Financial support:* Fellowships, research assistantships, teaching assistantships, career-related internships or fieldwork, Federal Work-Study, institutionally sponsored loans, scholarships/grants, tuition waivers (full), and unspecified assistantships available. Financial award application deadline: 3/1; financial award applicants required to submit FAFSA. *Unit head:* Dr. David D. Allen, II, Dean, 662-915-7265, Fax: 662-915-5118, E-mail: sopdean@olemiss.edu.
Website: http://www.pharmacy.olemiss.edu/

University of Montana, Graduate School, College of Health Professions and Biomedical Sciences, Skaggs School of Pharmacy, Department of Biomedical and Pharmaceutical Sciences, Missoula, MT 59812. Offers biomedical sciences (PhD); medicinal chemistry (MS, PhD); molecular and cellular toxicology (MS, PhD); neuroscience (PhD); pharmaceutical sciences (MS). *Accreditation:* ACPE. *Degree requirements:* For master's, oral defense of thesis; for doctorate, research dissertation defense. *Entrance requirements:* For master's and doctorate, GRE General Test. Additional exam requirements/recommendations for international students: Required—TOEFL (minimum score 540 paper-based). Electronic applications accepted. *Faculty research:* Cardiovascular pharmacology, medicinal chemistry, neurosciences, environmental toxicology, pharmacogenetics, cancer.

University of Rhode Island, Graduate School, College of Pharmacy, Department of Biomedical and Pharmaceutical Sciences, Kingston, RI 02881. Offers health outcomes (MS, PhD); medicinal chemistry and pharmacognosy (MS, PhD); pharmaceutics and pharmacokinetics (MS, PhD); pharmacology and toxicology (MS, PhD). *Program availability:* Part-time. *Faculty:* 23 full-time (11 women). *Students:* 36 full-time (14 women), 9 part-time (4 women); includes 4 minority (1 Black or African American, non-Hispanic/Latino; 1 American Indian or Alaska Native, non-Hispanic/Latino; 2 Asian, non-Hispanic/Latino), 22 international. 138 applicants, 18% accepted, 14 enrolled. In 2017, 3 master's, 6 doctorates awarded. *Entrance requirements:* Additional exam requirements/recommendations for international students: Required—TOEFL. *Application deadline:* For fall admission, 7/15 for domestic students, 2/1 for international students. Application fee: $65. Electronic applications accepted. *Expenses:* Tuition, state resident: full-time $12,706; part-time $786 per credit. Tuition, nonresident: full-time $25,216; part-time $1401 per credit. *Required fees:* $1598; $45 per credit. One-time fee: $30 part-time. *Financial support:* In 2017–18, 10 research assistantships with tuition reimbursements (averaging $13,958 per year), 10 teaching assistantships with tuition reimbursements (averaging $11,291 per year) were awarded. Financial award application deadline: 2/1; financial award applicants required to submit FAFSA. *Unit head:* Dr. David Rowley, Chair, 401-874-9228, E-mail: drowley@uri.edu.
Website: http://www.uri.edu/pharmacy/departments/bps/index.shtml

The University of Texas at Austin, Graduate School, College of Pharmacy, Graduate Programs in Pharmacy, Austin, TX 78712-1111. Offers health outcomes and pharmacy practice (PhD); health outcomes and pharmacy practice (MS); medicinal chemistry (PhD); pharmaceutics (PhD); pharmacology and toxicology (PhD); pharmacotherapy (MS, PhD); translational science (PhD). PhD in translational science offered jointly with The University of Texas Health Science Center at San Antonio and The University of Texas at San Antonio. *Degree requirements:* For master's, thesis; for doctorate, thesis/dissertation. *Entrance requirements:* For master's and doctorate, GRE General Test. Electronic applications accepted. *Faculty research:* Synthetic medical chemistry, synthetic molecular biology, bio-organic chemistry, pharmacoeconomics, pharmacy practice.

University of the Sciences, Program in Chemistry, Biochemistry and Pharmacognosy, Philadelphia, PA 19104-4495. Offers biochemistry (MS, PhD); chemistry (MS, PhD); pharmacognosy (MS, PhD). *Program availability:* Part-time. *Degree requirements:* For master's, thesis, qualifying exams; for doctorate, comprehensive exam, thesis/dissertation, qualifying exams. *Entrance requirements:* For master's and doctorate, GRE General Test, GRE Subject Test. Additional exam requirements/recommendations for international students: Required—TOEFL, TWE. *Expenses:* Contact institution.

The University of Toledo, College of Graduate Studies, College of Pharmacy and Pharmaceutical Sciences, Program in Medicinal and Biological Chemistry, Toledo, OH 43606-3390. Offers MS, PhD. Terminal master's awarded for partial completion of doctoral program. *Degree requirements:* For master's, thesis; for doctorate, thesis/dissertation. *Entrance requirements:* For master's and doctorate, GRE General Test. Additional exam requirements/recommendations for international students: Required—TOEFL (minimum score 550 paper-based; 80 iBT). Electronic applications accepted. *Faculty research:* Neuroscience, molecular modeling, immunotoxicology, organic synthesis, peptide biochemistry.

University of Utah, Graduate School, College of Pharmacy, Department of Medicinal Chemistry, Salt Lake City, UT 84112-5820. Offers MS, PhD. *Faculty:* 8 full-time (2 women), 6 part-time/adjunct (1 woman). *Students:* 11 full-time (7 women), 1 part-time (0 women); includes 1 minority (Asian, non-Hispanic/Latino), 6 international. 14 applicants, 7% accepted. In 2017, 3 doctorates awarded. Terminal master's awarded for partial completion of doctoral program. *Degree requirements:* For master's, comprehensive exam, thesis, end of first-year capstone exam; for doctorate, comprehensive exam, thesis/dissertation, end of first-year capstone exam. *Entrance requirements:* For doctorate, GRE, minimum GPA of 3.0. Additional exam requirements/recommendations for international students: Required—TOEFL (minimum score 550 paper-based; 80 iBT), IELTS (minimum score 6.5). *Application deadline:* For fall admission, 12/15 for domestic and international students. Application fee: $55 ($65 for international students). Electronic applications accepted. *Expenses:* Contact institution. *Financial support:* In 2017–18, 11 students received support. Fellowships, research assistantships, health care benefits, and tuition waivers (full) available. Financial award application deadline: 12/15. *Faculty research:* Anticancer and anti-infective drug discovery, assays for high-throughput screening, neuroactive peptides, bioinorganic chemistry, structure-based drug design and modeling. *Total annual research expenditures:* $3.5 million. *Unit head:* Dr. Darrell R. Davis, Chair, 801-581-7063, Fax: 801-585-6208, E-mail: darrell.davis@utah.edu. *Application contact:* Dr. Thomas E. Cheatham, Director of Graduate Studies, 801-587-9652, Fax: 801-585-6208, E-mail: tom.cheatham@pharm.utah.edu.
Website: http://www.pharmacy.utah.edu/medchem/

University of Utah, Graduate School, College of Pharmacy, Department of Pharmaceutics and Pharmaceutical Chemistry, Salt Lake City, UT 84112. Offers PhD. *Faculty:* 6 full-time (1 woman), 6 part-time/adjunct (3 women). *Students:* 11 full-time (5 women), 3 part-time (1 woman); includes 2 minority (1 Black or African American, non-Hispanic/Latino; 1 Asian, non-Hispanic/Latino), 7 international. Average age 27. 41 applicants, 7% accepted, 3 enrolled. In 2017, 1 doctorate awarded. Terminal master's awarded for partial completion of doctoral program. *Entrance requirements:* For doctorate, GRE. Additional exam requirements/recommendations for international students: Required—TOEFL (minimum score 550 paper-based). *Application deadline:* Applications are processed on a rolling basis. Application fee: $55 ($65 for international students). Electronic applications accepted. *Expenses:* Contact institution. *Financial support:* In 2017–18, 20 students received support, including 1 fellowship with full tuition reimbursement available (averaging $18,000 per year), 11 research assistantships with full tuition reimbursements available (averaging $26,000 per year); scholarships/grants, health care benefits, tuition waivers (full), and unspecified assistantships also available. Financial award application deadline: 1/1. *Faculty research:* Delivery of therapeutic genes, trafficking mechanisms for drugs within cells, combination devices and local drug release from implants, anti-cancer polymer-based therapeutics and vaccines, nanotechnology for drug carriers. *Total annual research expenditures:* $591,623. *Unit head:* Dr. Carol Lim, Interim Chairperson, 801-581-7831, Fax: 801-581-3674, E-mail: carol.lim@utah.edu. *Application contact:* Dalynn Bergund, Manager, Administration, 801-585-0070, E-mail: dalynn.berglund@utah.edu.
Website: http://www.pharmacy.utah.edu/pharmaceutics/

University of Washington, School of Pharmacy, Department of Medicinal Chemistry, Seattle, WA 98195. Offers PhD. *Faculty:* 9 full-time (1 woman). *Students:* 27 full-time (13 women); includes 5 minority (1 American Indian or Alaska Native, non-Hispanic/Latino; 4 Asian, non-Hispanic/Latino), 3 international. Average age 29. 94 applicants, 11% accepted, 6 enrolled. In 2017, 2 doctorates awarded. *Degree requirements:* For doctorate, thesis/dissertation, cumulative exams, general oral exam, final defense exam. *Entrance requirements:* For doctorate, GRE General Test, minimum GPA of 3.0, 3 letters of recommendation, statement of purpose, transcripts, resume. Additional exam requirements/recommendations for international students: Required—TOEFL (minimum score 580 paper-based; 92 iBT). *Application deadline:* For fall admission, 12/15 for domestic and international students. Electronic applications accepted. *Financial support:* Fellowships, research assistantships with full tuition reimbursement, and scholarships/grants available. *Faculty research:* Biomedical mass spectrometry, structural virology, protein structure and function, drug metabolism and pharmacogenomics, cardiac and neural toxicology. *Unit head:* Dr. Kent L. Kunze, Chairman, 206-543-2224, Fax: 206-685-3252, E-mail: kkunze@uw.edu. *Application contact:* Caryl Corsi, Graduate Program Operations Specialist, 206-543-2224, Fax: 206-685-3252, E-mail: medchem@uw.edu.
Website: https://sop.washington.edu/department-of-medicinal-chemistry/

Virginia Commonwealth University, Medical College of Virginia-Professional Programs, School of Pharmacy, Department of Pharmaceutics, Richmond, VA 23284-9005. Offers medicinal chemistry (MS); pharmaceutical sciences (PhD); pharmaceutics (MS); pharmacotherapy and pharmacy administration (MS). Terminal master's awarded for partial completion of doctoral program. *Degree requirements:* For master's, thesis; for doctorate, thesis/dissertation. *Entrance requirements:* For master's and doctorate, GRE General Test. Additional exam requirements/recommendations for international students: Required—TOEFL. Electronic applications accepted. *Faculty research:* Drug delivery systems, drug development.

Wayne State University, Eugene Applebaum College of Pharmacy and Health Sciences, Department of Pharmaceutical Sciences, Detroit, MI 48202. Offers medicinal chemistry (MS, PhD); pharmaceutics (MS, PhD), including medicinal chemistry (PhD); pharmacology and toxicology (MS, PhD). *Faculty:* 20. *Students:* 23 full-time (17 women), 1 (woman) part-time, 19 international. Average age 29. 119 applicants, 9% accepted, 7 enrolled. In 2017, 7 master's, 3 doctorates awarded. *Degree requirements:* For master's, thesis; for doctorate, thesis/dissertation. *Entrance requirements:* For master's, GRE General Test, bachelor's degree; adequate background in biology, physics, calculus, and chemistry; three letters of recommendation; personal statement; for doctorate, GRE General Test, bachelor's or master's degree in one of the behavioral, biological, pharmaceutical or physical sciences; three letters of recommendation. Additional exam requirements/recommendations for international students: Required—TOEFL (minimum score 550 paper-based; 79 iBT), Michigan English Language Assessment Battery (minimum score 85); Recommended—IELTS (minimum score 6.5), TWE (minimum score 5.5). *Application deadline:* For fall admission, 12/1 priority date for domestic and international students. Applications are processed on a rolling basis. Application fee: $50. Electronic applications accepted. *Expenses:* Contact institution. *Financial support:* In 2017–18, 16 students received support, including 2 fellowships with tuition reimbursements available (averaging $26,000 per year), 11 research assistantships with full tuition reimbursements available (averaging $25,182 per year); scholarships/grants, health care benefits, and unspecified assistantships also available. Financial award applicants required to submit FAFSA. *Faculty research:* Design of new anthracyclines, genetic and epigenetic effects of extracellular inducers, cellular injury and cell death, drug metabolism and nutrition, anti-infective agents, carcinogenesis, diabetes research, Thera gnostic nanomedicines, neurotoxicity, drug discovery, insulin resistance. *Unit head:* Dr. George Corcoran, Chair and Professor, 313-577-1737, E-mail: corcoran@wayne.edu. *Application contact:* 313-577-5415, Fax: 313-577-2033, E-mail: pscgrad@wayne.edu.
Website: http://cphs.wayne.edu/sciences/index.php

Pharmaceutical Administration

Belmont University, College of Pharmacy, Nashville, TN 37212. Offers advanced pharmacotherapy (Pharm D); health care informatics (Pharm D); management (Pharm D); missions/public health (Pharm D); Pharm D/MBA. Pharm D/MBA offered in collaboration with Jack C. Massey Graduate School of Business. *Accreditation:* ACPE. *Faculty:* 25 full-time (16 women), 3 part-time/adjunct (2 women). *Students:* 323 full-time (216 women); includes 90 minority (37 Black or African American, non-Hispanic/Latino; 38 Asian, non-Hispanic/Latino; 10 Hispanic/Latino; 5 Two or more races, non-Hispanic/Latino), 1 international. Average age 25. 638 applicants, 34% accepted, 94 enrolled. In 2017, 65 doctorates awarded. *Degree requirements:* For doctorate, comprehensive exam. *Entrance requirements:* For doctorate, PCAT. Additional exam requirements/recommendations for international students: Required—TOEFL. *Application deadline:* For fall admission, 8/31 priority date for domestic students; for spring admission, 3/1 for domestic students. Applications are processed on a rolling basis. Application fee: $50. Electronic applications accepted. *Expenses:* $18,670 tuition per semester. *Financial support:* In 2017–18, 112 students received support. Career-related internships or fieldwork and scholarships/grants available. Financial award applicants required to submit FAFSA. *Faculty research:* Academic innovation, cultural competency, medication errors, patient safety. *Unit head:* Dr. David Gregory, Dean, 615-460-6746, Fax: 615-460-6741, E-mail: david.gregory@belmont.edu.
Website: http://www.belmont.edu/pharmacy/index.html

Columbia University, Graduate School of Business, MBA Program, New York, NY 10027. Offers accounting (MBA); decision, risk, and operations (MBA); entrepreneurship (MBA); finance and economics (MBA); healthcare and pharmaceutical management (MBA); human resource management (MBA); international business (MBA); leadership and ethics (MBA); management (MBA); marketing (MBA); media (MBA); private equity (MBA); real estate (MBA); social enterprise (MBA); value investing (MBA); DDS/MBA; JD/MBA; MBA/MIA; MBA/MPH; MBA/MS; MD/MBA. *Entrance requirements:* For master's, GMAT, 2 letters of recommendation. Additional exam requirements/recommendations for international students: Required—TOEFL. Electronic applications accepted. *Expenses:* Contact institution. *Faculty research:* Human decision making and behavioral research; real estate market and mortgage defaults; financial crisis and corporate governance; international business; security analysis and accounting.

Duquesne University, School of Pharmacy, Graduate School of Pharmaceutical Sciences, Program in Pharmacy Administration, Pittsburgh, PA 15282-0001. Offers MS. *Faculty:* 5 full-time (2 women). *Students:* 6 full-time (5 women), 5 international. Average age 25. 3 applicants, 67% accepted, 2 enrolled. In 2017, 2 master's awarded. *Degree requirements:* For master's, thesis. *Entrance requirements:* For master's, GRE General Test. Additional exam requirements/recommendations for international students: Required—TOEFL (minimum score 100 iBT). *Application deadline:* For fall admission, 12/1 priority date for domestic and international students. Applications are processed on a rolling basis. Electronic applications accepted. *Expenses:* $1,542 per credit. *Financial support:* In 2017–18, 4 students received support, including 4 teaching assistantships with full tuition reimbursements available. *Unit head:* Dr. Khalid Kamal, Head, 412-396-1926. *Application contact:* Information Contact, 412-396-1172, E-mail: gsps-adm@duq.edu.
Website: http://www.duq.edu/academics/schools/pharmacy/graduate-school-of-pharmaceutical-sciences

Fairleigh Dickinson University, Metropolitan Campus, Silberman College of Business, Program in Pharmaceutical Studies, Teaneck, NJ 07666-1914. Offers chemical studies (Certificate); pharmaceutical studies (MBA, Certificate). *Expenses: Tuition:* Full-time $22,410; part-time $1245 per credit. *Required fees:* $888; $414 per unit. Tuition and fees vary according to course load, degree level and program.

Florida Agricultural and Mechanical University, Division of Graduate Studies, Research, and Continuing Education, College of Pharmacy and Pharmaceutical Sciences, Graduate Programs in Pharmaceutical Sciences, Tallahassee, FL 32307-3200. Offers environmental toxicology (PhD); health outcomes research and pharmacoeconomics (PhD); medicinal chemistry (MS, PhD); pharmaceutics (MS, PhD); pharmacology/toxicology (MS, PhD); pharmacy administration (MS). *Accreditation:* CEPH. *Degree requirements:* For master's, comprehensive exam, thesis, publishable paper; for doctorate, comprehensive exam, thesis/dissertation, publishable paper. *Entrance requirements:* For master's and doctorate, GRE General Test, minimum GPA of 3.0 in last 60 hours. Additional exam requirements/recommendations for international students: Required—TOEFL. *Faculty research:* Anticancer agents, anti-inflammatory drugs, chronopharmacology, neuroendocrinology, microbiology.

Idaho State University, Office of Graduate Studies, College of Pharmacy, Department of Pharmacy Practice and Administrative Sciences, Pocatello, ID 83209-8333. Offers pharmacy (Pharm D); pharmacy administration (MS, PhD). *Accreditation:* ACPE (one or more programs are accredited). *Program availability:* Part-time. *Degree requirements:* For master's, one foreign language, comprehensive exam, thesis, thesis research, speech and technical writing classes; for doctorate, comprehensive exam, thesis/dissertation, oral and written exams, speech and technical writing classes. *Entrance requirements:* For master's, GRE General Test, minimum GPA of 3.0, 3 letters of recommendation; for doctorate, GRE General Test, BS in pharmacy or related field, minimum GPA of 3.0, 3 letters of recommendation. Additional exam requirements/recommendations for international students: Required—TOEFL (minimum score 550 paper-based; 80 iBT). Electronic applications accepted. *Expenses:* Contact institution. *Faculty research:* Pharmaceutical care outcomes, drug use review, pharmacoeconomics.

New Jersey Institute of Technology, Newark College of Engineering, Newark, NJ 07102. Offers biomedical engineering (MS, PhD); chemical engineering (MS, PhD); computer engineering (MS, PhD); electrical engineering (MS, PhD); engineering management (MS); environmental engineering (PhD); healthcare systems management (MS); industrial engineering (MS, PhD); Internet engineering (MS); manufacturing engineering (MS); mechanical engineering (MS, PhD); occupational safety and health

engineering (MS); pharmaceutical bioprocessing (MS); pharmaceutical engineering (MS); pharmaceutical systems management (MS); power and energy systems (MS); telecommunications (MS); transportation (MS, PhD). *Program availability:* Part-time, evening/weekend. *Students:* Average age 27. 2,959 applicants, 51% accepted, 442 enrolled. In 2017, 595 master's, 29 doctorates awarded. Terminal master's awarded for partial completion of doctoral program. *Entrance requirements:* For master's, GRE General Test; for doctorate, GRE General Test, minimum graduate GPA of 3.5. Additional exam requirements/recommendations for international students: Required—TOEFL (minimum score 550 paper-based; 79 iBT). *Application deadline:* For fall admission, 6/1 priority date for domestic students, 5/1 priority date for international students; for spring admission, 11/15 priority date for domestic and international students. Applications are processed on a rolling basis. Application fee: $75. Electronic applications accepted. *Expenses:* Contact institution. *Financial support:* In 2017–18, 172 students received support, including 24 fellowships (averaging $7,124 per year), 112 research assistantships (averaging $19,407 per year), 101 teaching assistantships (averaging $24,173 per year); scholarships/grants also available. Financial award application deadline: 1/15. *Faculty research:* Nonlinear signal processing, intelligent medical image analysis, calibration issues in coherent localization, computer-aided design, neural network for tool wear measurement. *Total annual research expenditures:* $11.1 million. *Unit head:* Dr. Moshe Kam, Dean, 973-596-5534, E-mail: moshe.kam@njit.edu. *Application contact:* Stephen Eck, Director of Admissions, 973-596-3300, Fax: 973-596-3461, E-mail: admissions@njit.edu.
Website: http://engineering.njit.edu/

Northeast Ohio Medical University, College of Graduate Studies, Rootstown, OH 44272-0095. Offers bioethics (Certificate); health-system pharmacy administration (MS); integrated pharmaceutical medicine (MS, PhD); medical ethics and humanities (MS); public health (MPH). MPH offered as part of consortium with The University of Akron, Youngstown State University, Ohio University, and Cleveland State University. *Program availability:* Part-time, evening/weekend. *Faculty:* 23 part-time/adjunct (14 women). *Students:* 22 full-time (13 women), 21 part-time (13 women); includes 10 minority (1 Black or African American, non-Hispanic/Latino; 8 Asian, non-Hispanic/Latino; 1 Two or more races, non-Hispanic/Latino). In 2017, 3 master's, 1 doctorate awarded. *Degree requirements:* For master's, thesis (for MS in medical ethics and humanities, integrated pharmaceutical medicine); for doctorate, thesis/dissertation. *Application deadline:* For fall admission, 5/1 priority date for domestic students; for winter admission, 1/5 priority date for domestic students. Applications are processed on a rolling basis. Application fee: $95. Electronic applications accepted. *Expenses:* Contact institution. *Financial support:* Institutionally sponsored loans and tuition waivers available. Financial award application deadline: 3/15; financial award applicants required to submit FAFSA. *Unit head:* Dr. Steven Schmidt, Dean, 330-325-6290. *Application contact:* Heidi Terry, Executive Director, Enrollment Services, 330-325-6479, E-mail: hterry@neomed.edu.
Website: https://www.neomed.edu/graduatestudies/

The Ohio State University, College of Pharmacy, Columbus, OH 43210. Offers MS, PhD, Pharm D, Pharm D/MBA, Pharm D/MPH, Pharm D/PhD. *Accreditation:* ACPE (one or more programs are accredited). *Faculty:* 53. *Students:* 608 (331 women); includes 175 minority (42 Black or African American, non-Hispanic/Latino; 97 Asian, non-Hispanic/Latino; 22 Hispanic/Latino; 14 Two or more races, non-Hispanic/Latino), 61 international. Average age 25. In 2017, 15 master's, 127 doctorates awarded. Terminal master's awarded for partial completion of doctoral program. *Degree requirements:* For doctorate, comprehensive exam (for some programs), thesis/dissertation (for some programs). *Entrance requirements:* For master's, GRE General Test, minimum GPA of 3.0; for doctorate, GRE General Test; PCAT (for PharmD), minimum GPA of 3.0. Additional exam requirements/recommendations for international students: Required—TOEFL minimum score 600 paper-based, 100 iBT (for MS and PhD); TOEFL minimum score 577 paper-based; 90 iBT, Michigan English Language Assessment Battery minimum score 84, IELTS minimum score 7.5 (for PharmD). *Application deadline:* For fall admission, 12/15 for domestic and international students. Application fee: $60 ($70 for international students). Electronic applications accepted. *Expenses:* Contact institution. *Financial support:* Fellowships with full tuition reimbursements, research assistantships with full tuition reimbursements, teaching assistantships with full tuition reimbursements, career-related internships or fieldwork, Federal Work-Study, institutionally sponsored loans, scholarships/grants, and traineeships available. *Unit head:* Dr. Henry J. Mann, Dean and Professor, 614-292-5711, Fax: 614-292-2588, E-mail: mann.414@osu.edu. *Application contact:* E-mail: admissions@pharmacy.ohio-state.edu.
Website: http://www.pharmacy.osu.edu

Purdue University, College of Pharmacy and Graduate School, Graduate Programs in Pharmacy and Pharmacal Sciences, Department of Industrial and Physical Pharmacy, West Lafayette, IN 47907. Offers pharmaceutics (PhD); regulatory quality compliance (MS, Certificate). *Faculty:* 8 full-time (3 women), 1 part-time/adjunct (0 women). *Students:* 35 full-time (20 women), 2 part-time (0 women); includes 2 minority (1 Black or African American, non-Hispanic/Latino; 1 Asian, non-Hispanic/Latino), 30 international. Average age 28. 57 applicants, 14% accepted, 5 enrolled. In 2017, 8 master's, 7 doctorates awarded. *Degree requirements:* For doctorate, thesis/dissertation. *Entrance requirements:* For master's, minimum GPA of 3.0; for doctorate, GRE General Test, minimum GPA of 3.0. Additional exam requirements/recommendations for international students: Required—TOEFL (minimum score 580 paper-based; 77 iBT). *Application deadline:* For fall admission, 1/1 for domestic and international students. Applications are processed on a rolling basis. Application fee: $60 ($75 for international students). Electronic applications accepted. *Financial support:* Fellowships, research assistantships, teaching assistantships, and traineeships available. Support available to part-time students. Financial award applicants required to submit FAFSA. *Faculty research:* Controlled drug delivery systems, liposomes, antacids, coating technology. *Unit head:* Tonglei Li, Interim Head of the Graduate Program, 765-496-4145, E-mail: tonglei@purdue.edu. *Application contact:* Delayne Graham, Graduate Contact, 765-494-1362, E-mail: dkgraham@purdue.edu.

Rutgers University–Newark, Rutgers Business School–Newark and New Brunswick, Program in Pharmaceutical Management, Newark, NJ 07102. Offers MBA.

St. John's University, College of Pharmacy and Health Sciences, Graduate Programs in Pharmaceutical Sciences, Program in Pharmacy Administration, Queens, NY 11439. Offers MS. *Students:* 17 full-time (10 women), 8 part-time (2 women); includes 1 minority (Asian, non-Hispanic/Latino), 23 international. Average age 26. 29 applicants, 38% accepted, 2 enrolled. In 2017, 7 master's awarded. *Entrance requirements:* For master's, GRE General Test, letters of recommendation, transcripts, resume, personal statement. Additional exam requirements/recommendations for international students: Required—TOEFL (minimum score 100 iBT), IELTS (minimum score 7). *Application deadline:* For fall admission, 3/1 for domestic students; for spring admission, 11/1 for domestic students. Applications are processed on a rolling basis. Application fee: $70. Electronic applications accepted. *Expenses:* $1,420 per credit tuition, $170 per semester fees; tuition may vary by program. *Financial support:* Fellowships, teaching assistantships, career-related internships or fieldwork, scholarships/grants, and unspecified assistantships available. Support available to part-time students. Financial award application deadline: 2/1; financial award applicants required to submit FAFSA. *Unit head:* Dr. Wenchen Wu, Chair, 718-990-5690, E-mail: wuw@stjohns.edu. *Application contact:* Robert Medrano, Director of Graduate Admissions, 718-990-1601, Fax: 718-990-5686, E-mail: gradhelp@stjohns.edu.
Website: http://www.stjohns.edu/academics/schools-and-colleges/college-pharmacy-and-health-sciences/programs-and-majors/pharmacy-administration-master-science

San Diego State University, Graduate and Research Affairs, College of Sciences, Program in Regulatory Affairs, San Diego, CA 92182. Offers MS. *Degree requirements:* For master's, thesis. *Entrance requirements:* For master's, GRE General Test, 3 letters of recommendation, employment/volunteer experience list. Additional exam requirements/recommendations for international students: Required—TOEFL. Electronic applications accepted.

Temple University, Fox School of Business, MBA Programs, Philadelphia, PA 19122-6096. Offers accounting (MBA); business management (MBA); financial management (MBA); healthcare and life sciences innovation (MBA); human resource management (MBA); international business (IMBA); IT management (MBA); marketing management (MBA); pharmaceutical management (MBA); strategic management (EMBA, MBA). EMBA offered in Philadelphia, PA and Tokyo, Japan. *Accreditation:* AACSB. *Program availability:* Part-time, evening/weekend, online learning. *Entrance requirements:* For master's, GMAT, minimum undergraduate GPA of 3.0. Additional exam requirements/recommendations for international students: Required—TOEFL (minimum score 600 paper-based; 100 iBT), IELTS (minimum score 7.5). *Expenses:* Tuition, state resident: full-time $16,164; part-time $898 per credit hour. Tuition, nonresident: full-time $22,158; part-time $1231 per credit hour. *Required fees:* $890; $445 per semester. Full-time tuition and fees vary according to course load, degree level, campus/location and program.

University of Florida, Graduate School, College of Pharmacy, Graduate Programs in Pharmacy, Department of Pharmaceutical Outcomes and Policy, Gainesville, FL 32611. Offers MSP, PhD. *Program availability:* Part-time, online learning. *Degree requirements:* For doctorate, thesis/dissertation. *Entrance requirements:* For master's and doctorate, GRE General Test, minimum GPA of 3.0. Additional exam requirements/recommendations for international students: Required—TOEFL (minimum score 550 paper-based; 80 iBT), IELTS (minimum score 6). Electronic applications accepted. *Faculty research:* Phamacoepidemiology, patient safety and program evaluation, sociology-behavioral issues in medication use, medication safety, pharmacoeconomics, medication therapy management.

University of Georgia, College of Pharmacy, Department of Clinical and Administrative Pharmacy, Athens, GA 30602. Offers clinical and experimental therapeutics (PhD); pharmacy care administration (PhD).

University of Houston, College of Pharmacy, Houston, TX 77204. Offers pharmaceutics (MSPHR, PhD); pharmacology (MSPHR, PhD); pharmacy (Pharm D); pharmacy administration (MSPHR, PhD). *Accreditation:* ACPE. *Program availability:* Part-time. Terminal master's awarded for partial completion of doctoral program. *Entrance requirements:* For doctorate, PCAT (for Pharm D). Additional exam requirements/recommendations for international students: Required—TOEFL. Electronic applications accepted. *Faculty research:* Drug screening and design, cardiovascular pharmacology, infectious disease, asthma research, herbal medicine.

University of Illinois at Chicago, College of Pharmacy and Graduate College, Graduate Programs in Pharmacy, Chicago, IL 60607-7128. Offers comparative effectiveness research (MS); forensic science (MS); forensic toxicology (MS); medicinal chemistry (MS, PhD); pharmacognosy (MS, PhD); pharmacy (PhD). Terminal master's awarded for partial completion of doctoral program. *Degree requirements:* For master's, variable foreign language requirement, thesis; for doctorate, variable foreign language requirement, thesis/dissertation. *Entrance requirements:* For master's and doctorate, GRE General Test. Additional exam requirements/recommendations for international students: Required—TOEFL. Electronic applications accepted. *Faculty research:* Biopharmaceutical science, forensic science, forensic toxicology, medicinal chemistry, pharmacognosy.

University of Maryland, Baltimore, Graduate School, Graduate Programs in Pharmacy, Department of Pharmaceutical Health Service Research, Baltimore, MD 21201. Offers epidemiology (MS); pharmacy administration (PhD); Pharm D/PhD. *Degree requirements:* For doctorate, comprehensive exam, thesis/dissertation. *Entrance requirements:* For doctorate, GRE General Test. Additional exam requirements/recommendations for international students: Required—TOEFL, IELTS. Electronic applications accepted. *Expenses:* Tuition, state resident: full-time $13,990; part-time $661 per credit. Tuition, nonresident: full-time $30,484; part-time $1310 per credit. *Required fees:* $1894; $94 per credit. $415 per semester. Part-time tuition and fees vary according to course load, degree level and program. *Faculty research:* Pharmacoeconomics, outcomes research, public health policy, drug therapy and aging.

University of Maryland, Baltimore, Graduate School, Graduate Programs in Pharmacy, Program in Regulatory Science, Baltimore, MD 21201. Offers MS. *Expenses:* Tuition, state resident: full-time $13,990; part-time $661 per credit. Tuition, nonresident: full-time $30,484; part-time $1310 per credit. *Required fees:* $1894; $94 per credit. $415 per semester. Part-time tuition and fees vary according to course load, degree level and program.

University of Michigan, College of Pharmacy and Rackham Graduate School, Department of Clinical Pharmacy, Ann Arbor, MI 48109. Offers PhD. *Faculty:* 11 full-time (6 women), 3 part-time/adjunct (0 women). *Students:* 1 full-time (0 women), all international. Average age 28. In 2017, 2 doctorates awarded. Terminal master's awarded for partial completion of doctoral program. *Degree requirements:* For doctorate, thesis/dissertation, oral defense of dissertation, preliminary exam. *Entrance requirements:* For doctorate, GRE. Additional exam requirements/recommendations for international students: Required—TOEFL (minimum score 560 paper-based; 84 iBT) or IELTS (minimum score 6.5). Application fee: $75 ($90 for international students). *Expenses:* Contact institution. *Financial support:* In 2017–18, 1 student received support, including 1 fellowship (averaging $46,191 per year); research assistantships, teaching assistantships, career-related internships or fieldwork, institutionally sponsored loans, scholarships/grants, traineeships, health care benefits, tuition waivers, and unspecified assistantships also available. *Unit head:* Dr. Karen Farris, Chair, 734-763-6629, Fax: 734-763-4480, E-mail: kfarris@med.umich.edu. *Application contact:* Antoinette Hopper, Student Affairs Program Manager, 734-615-6326, Fax: 734-763-4480, E-mail: acast@med.umich.edu.
Website: https://pharmacy.umich.edu/cp

University of Minnesota, Twin Cities Campus, College of Pharmacy and Graduate School, Graduate Programs in Pharmacy, Graduate Program in Social and Administrative Pharmacy, Minneapolis, MN 55455-0213. Offers MS, PhD. *Program availability:* Part-time. *Faculty:* 29 full-time (10 women), 12 part-time/adjunct (6 women). *Students:* 23 full-time (15 women), 8 part-time (5 women); includes 10 minority (2 Black or African American, non-Hispanic/Latino; 8 Asian, non-Hispanic/Latino). Average age 28. 33 applicants, 27% accepted, 8 enrolled. In 2017, 2 master's, 3 doctorates awarded. Terminal master's awarded for partial completion of doctoral program. *Degree requirements:* For master's, thesis (for some programs); for doctorate, thesis/dissertation. *Entrance requirements:* For master's, GRE General Test, BS in science; for

doctorate, GRE General Test or Pharm D. Additional exam requirements/ recommendations for international students: Required—TOEFL (minimum score 100 iBT). *Application deadline:* For fall admission, 2/1 priority date for domestic and international students. Applications are processed on a rolling basis. Application fee: $75 ($95 for international students). Electronic applications accepted. *Financial support:* In 2017–18, 3 fellowships with full tuition reimbursements (averaging $15,000 per year), 3 research assistantships with full tuition reimbursements (averaging $15,000 per year), 7 teaching assistantships with full tuition reimbursements (averaging $15,000 per year) were awarded; career-related internships or fieldwork, scholarships/grants, traineeships, health care benefits, and unspecified assistantships also available. *Faculty research:* Pharmaceutical economics, pharmaceutical policy, pharmaceutical social/behavioral sciences. *Total annual research expenditures:* $507,493. *Unit head:* Dr. Jon C. Schommer, Director of Graduate Studies, 612-626-9915, Fax: 612-625-9931, E-mail: schom010@umn.edu. *Application contact:* Valorie Cremin, Graduate Program Coordinator, 612-624-2973, Fax: 612-625-9931, E-mail: cremi001@umn.edu.
Website: http://www.pharmacy.umn.edu/

University of Mississippi, Graduate School, School of Pharmacy, University, MS 38677. Offers environmental toxicology (MS, PhD); industrial pharmacy (MS); medicinal chemistry (MS, PhD); pharmaceutics (MS, PhD); pharmacognosy (MS, PhD); pharmacology (MS, PhD); pharmacy (Pharm D); pharmacy administration (MS, PhD). *Accreditation:* ACPE (one or more programs are accredited). *Program availability:* Part-time. *Faculty:* 71 full-time (32 women), 17 part-time/adjunct (6 women). *Students:* 417 full-time (256 women), 16 part-time (7 women); includes 71 minority (24 Black or African American, non-Hispanic/Latino; 1 American Indian or Alaska Native, non-Hispanic/ Latino; 36 Asian, non-Hispanic/Latino; 4 Hispanic/Latino; 6 Two or more races, non-Hispanic/Latino), 88 international. Average age 25. In 2017, 22 master's, 49 doctorates awarded. Terminal master's awarded for partial completion of doctoral program. *Degree requirements:* For master's, thesis; for doctorate, thesis/dissertation (for some programs). *Entrance requirements:* For master's, GRE General Test, minimum GPA of 3.0; for doctorate, GRE General Test (for PhD). Additional exam requirements/ recommendations for international students: Required—TOEFL. *Application deadline:* For fall admission, 2/1 priority date for domestic students; for spring admission, 10/1 priority date for domestic students. Applications are processed on a rolling basis. Application fee: $50. Electronic applications accepted. *Financial support:* Fellowships, research assistantships, teaching assistantships, career-related internships or fieldwork, Federal Work-Study, institutionally sponsored loans, scholarships/grants, tuition waivers (full), and unspecified assistantships available. Financial award application deadline: 3/ 1; financial award applicants required to submit FAFSA. *Unit head:* Dr. David D. Allen, II, Dean, 662-915-7265, Fax: 662-915-5118, E-mail: sopdean@olemiss.edu.
Website: http://www.pharmacy.olemiss.edu/

The University of North Carolina at Chapel Hill, Eshelman School of Pharmacy, Chapel Hill, NC 27599. Offers pharmaceutical sciences (PhD); pharmaceutical sciences - health system pharmacy administration (MS); pharmacy (Pharm D). *Accreditation:* ACPE (one or more programs are accredited). *Faculty:* 115 full-time (47 women), 362 part-time/adjunct (189 women). *Students:* 107 full-time (60 women); includes 27 minority (3 Black or African American, non-Hispanic/Latino; 17 Asian, non-Hispanic/Latino; 4 Hispanic/Latino; 3 Two or more races, non-Hispanic/Latino), 16 international. Average age 26. 229 applicants, 7% accepted, 16 enrolled. In 2017, 8 master's, 16 doctorates awarded. Terminal master's awarded for partial completion of doctoral program. *Degree requirements:* For master's, comprehensive exam, thesis; for doctorate, comprehensive exam, thesis/dissertation. *Entrance requirements:* For master's and doctorate, GRE General Test, minimum GPA of 3.0. Additional exam requirements/recommendations for international students: Required—TOEFL (minimum score 550 paper-based; 90 iBT), IELTS (minimum score 7). *Application deadline:* For fall admission, 12/12 for domestic students, 12/12 priority date for international students. Applications are processed on a rolling basis. Application fee: $90. Electronic applications accepted. *Expenses:* Contact institution. *Financial support:* In 2017–18, 107 students received support, including 18 fellowships with full tuition reimbursements available (averaging $30,000 per year), 56 research assistantships with full tuition reimbursements available (averaging $30,000 per year); career-related internships or fieldwork, Federal Work-Study, institutionally sponsored loans, scholarships/grants, traineeships, health care benefits, tuition waivers (full), and unspecified assistantships also available. Financial award application deadline: 12/12. *Faculty research:* Health services research, pharmacokinetics, molecular modeling, infectious disease, genomics and proteomics, translational research. *Total annual research expenditures:* $25 million. *Unit head:* Dr. Dhiren Thakker, Dean, 919-966-1122, Fax: 919-966-6919, E-mail: dhiren_thakker@unc.edu. *Application contact:* Olivia Hammill, Assistant Director of Recruitment and Admissions, 919-962-0097, Fax: 919-966-9428, E-mail: olivia_hammill@unc.edu.
Website: http://pharmacy.unc.edu/

University of Pittsburgh, School of Pharmacy, Program in Pharmacy Business Administration, Pittsburgh, PA 15261. Offers MS. *Program availability:* Part-time, evening/ weekend. *Faculty:* 15 full-time (6 women), 3 part-time/adjunct (0 women). *Students:* 6 full-time (2 women). Average age 34. 8 applicants, 88% accepted, 6 enrolled. *Entrance requirements:* For master's, GMAT (recommended), Pharm D, BS in pharmacy, or equivalent undergraduate degree from accredited U.S. institution; minimum of 2 years' professional experience; 2 professional letters of reference. Additional exam requirements/recommendations for international students: Required—TOEFL (minimum score 80 iBT) or IELTS (minimum score 6.5). *Application deadline:* Applications are processed on a rolling basis. Application fee: $0. *Expenses:* $19,350 per term. *Unit head:* Bridget T. Regan, Director, 412-648-8565, E-mail: bridget.regan@pitt.edu.
Website: http://www.mspba.pitt.edu

University of Southern California, Graduate School, School of Pharmacy, Program in Healthcare Decision Analysis, Los Angeles, CA 90089. Offers MS. *Program availability:* Part-time, online learning.

University of the Sciences, Program in Pharmaceutical and Healthcare Business, Philadelphia, PA 19104-4495. Offers MBA. *Program availability:* Part-time, evening/ weekend, online learning. *Entrance requirements:* Additional exam requirements/ recommendations for international students: Required—TOEFL, TWE. *Expenses:* Contact institution.

University of the Sciences, Program in Pharmacy Administration, Philadelphia, PA 19104-4495. Offers MS. *Program availability:* Part-time. *Entrance requirements:* Additional exam requirements/recommendations for international students: Required—TOEFL, TWE. *Expenses:* Contact institution.

The University of Toledo, College of Graduate Studies, College of Pharmacy and Pharmaceutical Sciences, Program in Pharmaceutical Sciences, Toledo, OH 43606-3390. Offers administrative pharmacy (MSPS); industrial pharmacy (MSPS); pharmacology toxicology (MSPS). *Degree requirements:* For master's, thesis. *Entrance requirements:* For master's, GRE General Test. Additional exam requirements/ recommendations for international students: Required—TOEFL (minimum score 550 paper-based; 80 iBT). Electronic applications accepted.

University of Utah, Graduate School, College of Pharmacy, Department of Pharmacotherapy, Salt Lake City, UT 84112. Offers health system pharmacy administration (MS); outcomes research and health policy (PhD). *Faculty:* 5 full-time (3 women), 18 part-time/adjunct (13 women). *Students:* 2 full-time (0 women), 4 part-time (3 women), 1 international. Average age 28. 26 applicants, 19% accepted, 4 enrolled. In 2017, 5 master's, 2 doctorates awarded. Terminal master's awarded for partial completion of doctoral program. *Degree requirements:* For master's, comprehensive exam, thesis or alternative, project; for doctorate, comprehensive exam, thesis/ dissertation. *Entrance requirements:* For doctorate, GRE. Additional exam requirements/recommendations for international students: Required—TOEFL (minimum score 550 paper-based; 80 iBT). *Application deadline:* For fall admission, 1/10 for domestic students, 12/15 for international students. Application fee: $55 ($65 for international students). *Financial support:* In 2017–18, 7 students received support, including 9 research assistantships with full tuition reimbursements available (averaging $21,400 per year); health care benefits also available. Financial award application deadline: 12/15. *Faculty research:* Outcomes in pharmacy, pharmacotherapy. *Total annual research expenditures:* $131,217. *Unit head:* Dr. Diana I. Brixner, Department Chair and Professor, 801-581-6731, E-mail: diana.brixner@utah.edu. *Application contact:* Ashley Weisman, Manager, Administration, 801-581-5984, Fax: 801-585-6160, E-mail: ashley.weisman@pharm.utah.edu.
Website: http://www.pharmacy.utah.edu/pharmacotherapy/

University of Wisconsin–Madison, School of Pharmacy and Graduate School, Graduate Programs in Pharmacy, Madison, WI 53706-1380. Offers pharmaceutical sciences (PhD); social and administrative sciences in pharmacy (MS, PhD). Terminal master's awarded for partial completion of doctoral program. *Degree requirements:* For master's, thesis (for some programs); for doctorate, comprehensive exam (for some programs), thesis/dissertation. *Entrance requirements:* For master's and doctorate, GRE. Additional exam requirements/recommendations for international students: Required—TOEFL. Electronic applications accepted. *Expenses:* Contact institution.

Virginia Commonwealth University, Medical College of Virginia-Professional Programs, School of Pharmacy, Department of Pharmaceutics, Richmond, VA 23284-9005. Offers medicinal chemistry (MS); pharmaceutical sciences (PhD); pharmaceutics (MS); pharmacotherapy and pharmacy administration (MS). Terminal master's awarded for partial completion of doctoral program. *Degree requirements:* For master's, thesis; for doctorate, thesis/dissertation. *Entrance requirements:* For master's and doctorate, GRE General Test. Additional exam requirements/recommendations for international students: Required—TOEFL. Electronic applications accepted. *Faculty research:* Drug delivery systems, drug development.

Pharmaceutical Sciences

Albany College of Pharmacy and Health Sciences, School of Pharmacy and Pharmaceutical Sciences, Albany, NY 12208. Offers health outcomes research (MS); pharmaceutical sciences (MS), including pharmaceutics, pharmacology; pharmacy (Pharm D). *Accreditation:* ACPE. *Degree requirements:* For master's, thesis; for doctorate, practice experience. *Entrance requirements:* For master's, GRE, minimum GPA of 3.0; for doctorate, PCAT, minimum GPA of 2.5. Additional exam requirements/ recommendations for international students: Required—TOEFL (minimum score 84 iBT). Electronic applications accepted. *Faculty research:* Therapeutic use of drugs, pharmacokinetics, drug delivery and design.

Auburn University, Harrison School of Pharmacy and Graduate School, Graduate Program in Pharmacy, Auburn University, AL 36849. Offers pharmacal sciences (MS, PhD); pharmaceutical sciences (PhD); pharmacy care systems (MS, PhD). *Program availability:* Part-time. *Faculty:* 58 full-time (33 women), 1 (woman) part-time/adjunct. *Students:* 47 full-time (19 women), 12 part-time (8 women); includes 4 minority (2 Black or African American, non-Hispanic/Latino; 1 Asian, non-Hispanic/Latino; 1 Two or more races, non-Hispanic/Latino), 42 international. Average age 29. 153 applicants, 10% accepted, 10 enrolled. In 2017, 4 master's, 6 doctorates awarded. *Degree requirements:* For master's, thesis; for doctorate, thesis/dissertation. *Entrance requirements:* For master's and doctorate, GRE General Test. *Application deadline:* Applications are processed on a rolling basis. Application fee: $50 ($60 for international students). Electronic applications accepted. *Expenses:* Tuition, state resident: full-time $10,974; part-time $519 per credit hour. Tuition, nonresident: full-time $29,658; part-time $1557 per credit hour. *Required fees:* $816 per semester. Tuition and fees vary according to degree level and program. *Financial support:* Fellowships, research assistantships, and teaching assistantships available. *Faculty research:* Communications, facilities design, substance abuse. *Unit head:* Dr. Richard Hansen, Dean/Professor, Harrison School of Pharmacy, 334-844-8348, Fax: 334-844-8307. *Application contact:* Dr. George Flowers, Dean of the Graduate School, 334-844-2125.

Boston University, School of Medicine, Division of Graduate Medical Sciences, Department of Pharmacology and Experimental Therapeutics, Boston, MA 02118. Offers PhD, MD/PhD. Terminal master's awarded for partial completion of doctoral program. *Degree requirements:* For doctorate, thesis/dissertation. *Application deadline:* For fall admission, 1/15 for domestic students; for spring admission, 10/15 for domestic students. *Unit head:* Dr. David H. Farb, Chairman, 617-638-4300, Fax: 617-638-4329, E-mail: dfarb@bu.edu. *Application contact:* GMS Admissions Office, 617-638-5255, E-mail: askgms@bu.edu.
Website: http://www.bumc.bu.edu/busm-pm/

Butler University, College of Pharmacy and Health Sciences, Indianapolis, IN 46208-3485. Offers pharmaceutical science (MS); pharmacy (Pharm D), including medical Spanish, research; physician assistant studies (MS). *Accreditation:* ACPE (one or more programs are accredited). *Faculty:* 62 full-time (42 women). *Students:* 390 full-time (302 women), 10 part-time (6 women); includes 35 minority (3 Black or African American, non-Hispanic/Latino; 21 Asian, non-Hispanic/Latino; 7 Hispanic/Latino; 4 Two or more races, non-Hispanic/Latino), 3 international. Average age 24. 581 applicants, 25% accepted, 131 enrolled. In 2017, 75 master's, 116 doctorates awarded. *Degree requirements:* For master's, comprehensive exam, research paper or thesis. *Entrance requirements:* For master's, GRE General Test, CASPA application, official transcripts, baccalaureate

degree from accredited institution (for physician assistant studies). Additional exam requirements/recommendations for international students: Required—TOEFL (minimum score 550 paper-based; 79 iBT), IELTS (minimum score 6). *Application deadline:* For fall admission, 4/1 for domestic and international students. Application fee: $0. Electronic applications accepted. *Expenses:* Contact institution. *Financial support:* In 2017–18, 8 students received support. Scholarships/grants, tuition waivers (full and partial), and unspecified assistantships available. Financial award application deadline: 7/15; financial award applicants required to submit FAFSA. *Faculty research:* Cancer research; targeted drug delivery and pharmacokinetics; neuropharmacology; gene regulation; next generation sequencing. *Unit head:* Dr. Robert Soltis, Dean, 317-940-8056, E-mail: rsoltis@butler.edu. *Application contact:* Diane Dubord, Graduate Student Services Specialist, 317-940-8107, E-mail: ddubord@butler.edu.
Website: https://www.butler.edu/pharmacy-pa/about

Campbell University, Graduate and Professional Programs, College of Pharmacy and Health Sciences, Buies Creek, NC 27506. Offers clinical research (MS); pharmaceutical sciences (MS); pharmacy (Pharm D); physician assistant (MPAP); public health (MS). *Accreditation:* ACPE. *Program availability:* Part-time, evening/weekend. *Entrance requirements:* For master's, MCAT, PCAT, GRE, bachelor's degree in health sciences or related field; for doctorate, PCAT. Additional exam requirements/recommendations for international students: Required—TOEFL (minimum score 550 paper-based; 79 iBT). Electronic applications accepted. *Expenses:* Contact institution. *Faculty research:* Immunology, medicinal chemistry, pharmaceutics, applied pharmacology.

Chapman University, School of Pharmacy, Orange, CA 92866. Offers pharmaceutical sciences (MS, PhD); pharmacy (Pharm D). *Faculty:* 37 full-time (17 women), 7 part-time/adjunct (1 woman). *Students:* 290 full-time (177 women), 1 part-time (0 women); includes 192 minority (12 Black or African American, non-Hispanic/Latino; 1 American Indian or Alaska Native, non-Hispanic/Latino; 146 Asian, non-Hispanic/Latino; 24 Hispanic/Latino; 1 Native Hawaiian or other Pacific Islander, non-Hispanic/Latino; 8 Two or more races, non-Hispanic/Latino), 24 international. Average age 27. 725 applicants, 26% accepted, 107 enrolled. In 2017, 5 master's awarded. *Degree requirements:* For master's, thesis; for doctorate, capstone project. *Entrance requirements:* For doctorate, PCAT. *Application deadline:* Applications are processed on a rolling basis. Electronic applications accepted. *Expenses:* Contact institution. *Financial support:* Fellowships, research assistantships, Federal Work-Study, and scholarships/grants available. *Unit head:* Ronald P. Jordan, Dean, 714-516-5486, E-mail: rpjordan@chapman.edu. *Application contact:* Dr. Lawrence Brown, Associate Dean of Student and Academic Affairs, 714-516-5000, E-mail: pharmacyadmissions@chapman.edu.
Website: https://www.chapman.edu/pharmacy/index.aspx

Creighton University, School of Medicine and Graduate School, Graduate Programs in Medicine, Department of Pharmacology, Omaha, NE 68178-0001. Offers pharmaceutical sciences (MS); pharmacology (MS, PhD); Pharm D/MS. Terminal master's awarded for partial completion of doctoral program. *Degree requirements:* For master's, comprehensive exam, thesis; for doctorate, comprehensive exam, thesis/dissertation, oral and written preliminary exams. *Entrance requirements:* For master's and doctorate, GRE General Test, minimum GPA of 3.0, undergraduate degree in sciences. Additional exam requirements/recommendations for international students: Required—TOEFL. Electronic applications accepted. Part-time tuition and fees vary according to course load, degree level, campus/location and program. *Faculty research:* Pharmacology secretion, cardiovascular-renal pharmacology, adrenergic receptors, signal transduction, genetic regulation of receptors.

Creighton University, School of Pharmacy and Health Professions and Department of Pharmacology, Program in Pharmaceutical Sciences, Omaha, NE 68178-0001. Offers MS, Pharm D/MS. *Degree requirements:* For master's, thesis. *Entrance requirements:* For master's, GRE, three recommendations. Additional exam requirements/recommendations for international students: Required—TOEFL (minimum score 550 paper-based; 80 iBT). Electronic applications accepted. Part-time tuition and fees vary according to course load, degree level, campus/location and program.

Drexel University, College of Medicine, Biomedical Graduate Programs, Program in Drug Discovery and Development, Philadelphia, PA 19104-2875. Offers MS. *Degree requirements:* For master's, thesis.

Duquesne University, School of Pharmacy, Graduate School of Pharmaceutical Sciences, Program in Pharmaceutics, Pittsburgh, PA 15282-0001. Offers MS, PhD, MBA/MS. *Faculty:* 6 full-time (1 woman). *Students:* 20 full-time (8 women), 1 part-time (0 women); includes 2 minority (1 Asian, non-Hispanic/Latino; 1 Hispanic/Latino), 15 international. Average age 28. 16 applicants, 13% accepted, 2 enrolled. In 2017, 1 doctorate awarded. *Degree requirements:* For master's, thesis; for doctorate, comprehensive exam, thesis/dissertation. *Entrance requirements:* For master's and doctorate, GRE General Test. Additional exam requirements/recommendations for international students: Required—TOEFL (minimum score 100 iBT). *Application deadline:* For fall admission, 12/1 priority date for domestic and international students; for spring admission, 10/1 priority date for domestic and international students. Applications are processed on a rolling basis. Electronic applications accepted. *Expenses:* $1,542 per credit. *Financial support:* In 2017–18, 21 students received support, including 5 research assistantships with full tuition reimbursements available, 16 teaching assistantships with full tuition reimbursements available; unspecified assistantships also available. *Unit head:* Dr. Wilson S. Meng, Head, 412-396-6366. *Application contact:* Information Contact, 412-396-1172, E-mail: gsps-adm@duq.edu.
Website: http://www.duq.edu/academics/schools/pharmacy/graduate-school-of-pharmaceutical-sciences

East Tennessee State University, Quillen College of Medicine, Department of Biomedical Sciences, Johnson City, TN 37614. Offers anatomy (PhD); biochemistry (PhD); microbiology (PhD); pharmaceutical sciences (PhD); pharmacology (PhD); physiology (PhD); quantitative biosciences (PhD). In 2017, 5 doctorates awarded. *Degree requirements:* For doctorate, comprehensive exam, thesis/dissertation, comprehensive qualifying exam; one-year residency. *Entrance requirements:* For doctorate, GRE General Test, GRE Subject Test, 3 letters of recommendation, minimum of 60 credit hours beyond the baccalaureate degree. Additional exam requirements/recommendations for international students: Required—TOEFL (minimum score 550 paper-based; 79 iBT). *Application deadline:* For fall admission, 6/1 priority date for domestic students, 4/29 for international students; for spring admission, 11/1 for domestic students, 9/29 for international students; for summer admission, 3/15 for domestic students, 2/1 for international students. Applications are processed on a rolling basis. Application fee: $55 ($65 for international students). Electronic applications accepted. *Expenses:* Contact institution. *Financial support:* Research assistantships with full tuition reimbursements, career-related internships or fieldwork, institutionally sponsored loans, scholarships/grants, and unspecified assistantships available. Financial award application deadline: 7/1; financial award applicants required to submit FAFSA. *Faculty research:* Cardiovascular, infectious disease, neurosciences, cancer, immunology. *Unit head:* Theo Hagg, Chair, 423-439-6294, Fax: 423-439-2140, E-mail: haggt1@etsu.edu. *Application contact:* Theo Hagg, Chair, 423-439-6294, Fax: 423-439-2140, E-mail: haggt1@etsu.edu.
Website: http://www.etsu.edu/com/dbms/

Florida Agricultural and Mechanical University, Division of Graduate Studies, Research, and Continuing Education, College of Pharmacy and Pharmaceutical Sciences, Graduate Programs in Pharmaceutical Sciences, Tallahassee, FL 32307-3200. Offers environmental toxicology (PhD); health outcomes research and pharmacoeconomics (PhD); medicinal chemistry (MS, PhD); pharmaceutics (MS, PhD); pharmacology/toxicology (MS, PhD); pharmacy administration (MS). *Accreditation:* CEPH. *Degree requirements:* For master's, comprehensive exam, thesis, publishable paper; for doctorate, comprehensive exam, thesis/dissertation, publishable paper. *Entrance requirements:* For master's and doctorate, GRE General Test, minimum GPA of 3.0 in last 60 hours. Additional exam requirements/recommendations for international students: Required—TOEFL. *Faculty research:* Anticancer agents, anti-inflammatory drugs, chronopharmacology, neuroendocrinology, microbiology.

Idaho State University, Office of Graduate Studies, College of Pharmacy, Department of Biomedical and Pharmaceutical Sciences, Pocatello, ID 83209-8334. Offers biopharmaceutical analysis (PhD); drug delivery (PhD); medicinal chemistry (PhD); pharmaceutical sciences (MS); pharmacology (PhD). *Program availability:* Part-time. *Degree requirements:* For master's, one foreign language, comprehensive exam, thesis, thesis research, classes in speech and technical writing; for doctorate, comprehensive exam, thesis/dissertation, written and oral exams, classes in speech and technical writing. *Entrance requirements:* For master's, GRE General Test, minimum GPA of 3.0, 3 letters of recommendation; for doctorate, GRE General Test, BS in pharmacy or related field, minimum GPA of 3.0, 3 letters of recommendation. Additional exam requirements/recommendations for international students: Required—TOEFL (minimum score 550 paper-based; 80 iBT). Electronic applications accepted. *Expenses:* Contact institution. *Faculty research:* Metabolic toxicity of heavy metals, neuroendocrine pharmacology, cardiovascular pharmacology, cancer biology, immunopharmacology.

Irell & Manella Graduate School of Biological Sciences, Graduate Program, Duarte, CA 91010. Offers brain metastatic cancer (PhD); cancer and stem cell metabolism (PhD); cancer biology (PhD); cancer biology and developmental therapeutics (PhD); cell biology (PhD); chemical biology (PhD); chromosomal break repair (PhD); diabetes and pancreatic progenitor cell biology (PhD); DNA repair and cancer biology (PhD); germline epigenetic remodeling and endocrine disruptors (PhD); hematology and hematopoietic cell transplantation (PhD); hematology and immunology (PhD); inflammation and cancer (PhD); micrornas and gene regulation in cardiovascular disease (PhD); mixed chimrism for reversal of autoimmunity (PhD); molecular and cellular biology (PhD); molecular biology and genetics (PhD); nanoparticle mediated twist1 silencing in metastatic cancer (PhD); neuro-oncology and stem cell biology (PhD); neuroscience (PhD); RNA directed therapies for HIV 1 (PhD); small RNA induced transcriptional gene activation (PhD); stem cell regulation by the microenvironment (PhD); translational oncology and pharmaceutical sciences (PhD); tumor biology (PhD). *Degree requirements:* For doctorate, comprehensive exam, thesis/dissertation, qualifying exams, two advanced courses. *Entrance requirements:* For doctorate, GRE General Test; GRE Subject Test (recommended), 2 years of course work in chemistry (general and organic); 1 year of course work each in biochemistry, general biology, and general physics; 2 semesters of course work in mathematics; significant research laboratory experience. Additional exam requirements/recommendations for international students: Required—TOEFL. Electronic applications accepted. *Faculty research:* Cancer biology, diabetes, stem cell biology, neuroscience, immunology.

See Display on page 65 and Close-Up on page 109.

Johns Hopkins University, Zanvyl Krieger School of Arts and Sciences, Advanced Academic Programs, Program in Regulatory Science, Washington, DC 20036. Offers MS. *Program availability:* Part-time, evening/weekend, online learning. *Degree requirements:* For master's, practicum. *Entrance requirements:* For master's, undergraduate degree in the life sciences or engineering with minimum GPA of 3.0 from a four-year college. Additional exam requirements/recommendations for international students: Required—TOEFL (minimum score 100 iBT).

Long Island University–Hudson, Graduate School, Purchase, NY 10577. Offers autism (Advanced Certificate); bilingual education (Advanced Certificate); childhood education (MS Ed); crisis management (Advanced Certificate); early childhood education (MS Ed); educational leadership (MS Ed); health administration (MPA); literacy (MS Ed); marriage and family therapy (MS); mental health counseling (MS, Advanced Certificate), including credentialed alcoholism and substance abuse counselor (MS); middle childhood and adolescence education (MS Ed); pharmaceutics (MS), including cosmetic science, industrial pharmacy; public administration (MPA); school counseling (MS Ed, Advanced Certificate); school psychology (MS Ed); special education (MS Ed); TESOL (MS Ed); TESOL (all grades) (Advanced Certificate). *Program availability:* Part-time, evening/weekend. *Faculty:* 8 full-time (6 women), 41 part-time/adjunct (24 women). *Students:* 69 full-time (54 women), 249 part-time (200 women); includes 102 minority (29 Black or African American, non-Hispanic/Latino; 1 American Indian or Alaska Native, non-Hispanic/Latino; 9 Asian, non-Hispanic/Latino; 62 Hispanic/Latino; 1 Native Hawaiian or other Pacific Islander, non-Hispanic/Latino). Average age 33. 153 applicants, 96% accepted, 103 enrolled. In 2017, 138 master's, 36 other advanced degrees awarded. *Entrance requirements:* Additional exam requirements/recommendations for international students: Required—TOEFL. *Application deadline:* Applications are processed on a rolling basis. Application fee: $50. Electronic applications accepted. *Expenses:* Contact institution. *Financial support:* In 2017–18, 32 students received support. Scholarships/grants available. Support available to part-time students. Financial award application deadline: 2/15; financial award applicants required to submit FAFSA. *Unit head:* Dr. Sylvia Blake, Dean and Chief Operating Officer, 914-831-2700, E-mail: westchester@liu.edu.

Long Island University–LIU Brooklyn, Arnold and Marie Schwartz College of Pharmacy and Health Sciences, Brooklyn, NY 11201-8423. Offers drug regulatory affairs (MS); pharmaceutics (MS, PhD), including cosmetic science (MS), industrial pharmacy (MS); pharmacology and toxicology (MS); pharmacy (Pharm D). *Accreditation:* ACPE. *Program availability:* Part-time. *Faculty:* 51 full-time (29 women), 33 part-time/adjunct (14 women). *Students:* 497 full-time (296 women), 77 part-time (42 women); includes 228 minority (26 Black or African American, non-Hispanic/Latino; 143 Asian, non-Hispanic/Latino; 31 Hispanic/Latino; 28 Two or more races, non-Hispanic/Latino), 137 international. Average age 25. 241 applicants, 62% accepted, 38 enrolled. In 2017, 57 master's, 183 doctorates awarded. Terminal master's awarded for partial completion of doctoral program. *Degree requirements:* For master's, comprehensive exam, thesis; for doctorate, comprehensive exam, thesis/dissertation. *Entrance requirements:* For master's and doctorate, GRE. Additional exam requirements/recommendations for international students: Required—TOEFL (minimum score 550 paper-based, 79 iBT) or IELTS. *Application deadline:* Applications are processed on a rolling basis. Application fee: $50. Electronic applications accepted. *Expenses:* Contact institution. *Financial support:* In 2017–18, 200 students received support. Research assistantships, teaching assistantships, career-related internships or fieldwork, Federal Work-Study, scholarships/grants, tuition waivers (full and partial), and unspecified assistantships available. Support available to part-time students. Financial award application deadline: 2/15; financial award applicants required to submit FAFSA. *Faculty research:* Preformulation, formulation and drug delivery; pharmacokinetics; pharmacology research; drug regulatory affairs; pharmaceutical analysis. *Total annual*

research expenditures: $100,000. *Unit head:* Dr. John M. Pezzuto, Dean, 718-488-1004, Fax: 718-488-0628, E-mail: john.pezzuto@liu.edu. *Application contact:* Michael Young, Senior Assistant Director of Admissions, 718-488-1000, E-mail: michael.young@liu.edu.
Website: http://liu.edu/Pharmacy

MCPHS University, Graduate Studies, Program in Pharmaceutics/Industrial Pharmacy, Boston, MA 02115-5896. Offers MS, PhD. Terminal master's awarded for partial completion of doctoral program. *Degree requirements:* For master's, thesis, oral defense of thesis; for doctorate, one foreign language, comprehensive exam, thesis/dissertation, oral defense of dissertation, qualifying exam. *Entrance requirements:* For master's and doctorate, GRE General Test, minimum QPA of 3.0. Additional exam requirements/recommendations for international students: Required—TOEFL (minimum score 550 paper-based; 79 iBT). *Faculty research:* Pharmacokinetics and drug metabolism, pharmaceutics and physical pharmacy, dosage forms.

Memorial University of Newfoundland, School of Graduate Studies, School of Pharmacy, St. John's, NL A1C 5S7, Canada. Offers MSCPharm, PhD. *Program availability:* Part-time. *Degree requirements:* For master's, thesis, seminar; for doctorate, comprehensive exam, thesis/dissertation, oral defense of thesis. *Entrance requirements:* For master's, B Sc in pharmacy or related area; for doctorate, master's degree in pharmacy or closely-related field. Electronic applications accepted. *Faculty research:* Pharmaceutics, medicinal chemistry, physical pharmacy, pharmacology, toxicology.

Mercer University, Graduate Studies, Cecil B. Day Campus, College of Pharmacy, Atlanta, GA 30341. Offers pharmaceutical sciences (PhD); pharmacy (Pharm D); Pharm D/MBA; Pharm D/MPH; Pharm D/PhD. PharmD/MBA offered jointly with Eugene W. Stetson School of Business and Economics; PharmD/MPH with College of Health Professions; PharmD/MSHI with Penfield College. *Accreditation:* ACPE (one or more programs are accredited). *Faculty:* 44 full-time (27 women), 1 part-time/adjunct (0 women). *Students:* 635 full-time (407 women), 6 part-time (4 women); includes 397 minority (150 Black or African American, non-Hispanic/Latino; 206 Asian, non-Hispanic/Latino; 27 Hispanic/Latino; 14 Two or more races, non-Hispanic/Latino), 43 international. Average age 26. 677 applicants, 48% accepted, 152 enrolled. In 2017, 166 doctorates awarded. *Degree requirements:* For doctorate, comprehensive exam (for some programs), thesis/dissertation (for some programs). *Entrance requirements:* For doctorate, GRE (for PhD); PCAT, MCAT, DAT, OAT, GRE (for Pharm D), Pharm D or BS in pharmacy or science and minimum GPA of 3.0 (for PhD); 66 hours of undergraduate pre-pharmacy coursework (for PharmD). Additional exam requirements/recommendations for international students: Required—TOEFL (minimum score 100 iBT). *Application deadline:* For fall admission, 6/3 for domestic and international students. Applications are processed on a rolling basis. Electronic applications accepted. *Expenses:* $35,606 per year tuition, $484 course fee in final year (for Pharm D). *Financial support:* In 2017–18, 238 students received support, including 10 research assistantships with full tuition reimbursements available (averaging $15,000 per year), 35 teaching assistantships with full tuition reimbursements available (averaging $15,000 per year); Federal Work-Study, scholarships/grants, and tuition waivers (full) also available. Financial award application deadline: 5/1; financial award applicants required to submit FAFSA. *Faculty research:* Nanosphere-based drug delivery, transdermal drug delivery, molecular pharmacology, behavioral pharmacology, cell signaling. *Total annual research expenditures:* $479,640. *Unit head:* Dr. Brian L. Crabtree, Dean, 678-547-6306, Fax: 678-547-6315, E-mail: crabtree_bl@mercer.edu. *Application contact:* Jordana S. Berry, Director of Admissions, 678-547-6182, Fax: 678-547-6518, E-mail: berry_js@mercer.edu.
Website: http://pharmacy.mercer.edu/

Northeastern University, Bouvé College of Health Sciences, Boston, MA 02115-5096. Offers applied behavior analysis (MS); audiology (Au D); counseling psychology (MS, PhD, CAGS); exercise science (MS); nursing (MS, PhD, CAGS), including administration (MS), adult-gerontology acute care nurse practitioner (MS, CAGS), adult-gerontology primary care nurse practitioner (MS, CAGS), anesthesia (MS), family nurse practitioner (MS, CAGS), neonatal nurse practitioner (MS, CAGS), pediatric nurse practitioner (MS, CAGS), psychiatric mental health nurse practitioner (MS, CAGS); nursing practice (DNP); pharmaceutical sciences (MS, PhD), including interdisciplinary concentration, pharmaceutics and drug delivery systems; pharmacology (MS); pharmacy (Pharm D); school psychology (PhD); speech-language pathology (MS); urban health (MPH); MS/MBA. *Accreditation:* ACPE (one or more programs are accredited). *Program availability:* Part-time, evening/weekend, online learning. *Faculty:* 192 full-time. *Students:* 1,685. In 2017, 352 master's, 312 doctorates, 25 other advanced degrees awarded. *Degree requirements:* For doctorate, thesis/dissertation (for some programs); for CAGS, comprehensive exam. Application fee: $75. Electronic applications accepted. *Expenses:* Contact institution. *Financial support:* Fellowships, research assistantships, teaching assistantships, career-related internships or fieldwork, scholarships/grants, health care benefits, tuition waivers, and unspecified assistantships available. Support available to part-time students. Financial award applicants required to submit FAFSA. *Unit head:* Susan L. Parish, Dean, Bouve College of Health Sciences, 617-373-3321, Fax: 617-373-3030, E-mail: s.parish@northeastern.edu. *Application contact:* 617-373-2708, Fax: 617-373-4701, E-mail: bouvegrad@northeastern.edu.
Website: https://www.northeastern.edu/bouve/

Northeast Ohio Medical University, College of Graduate Studies, Rootstown, OH 44272-0095. Offers bioethics (Certificate); health-system pharmacy administration (MS); integrated pharmaceutical medicine (MS, PhD); medical ethics and humanities (MS); public health (MPH). MPH offered as part of consortium with The University of Akron, Youngstown State University, Ohio University, and Cleveland State University. *Program availability:* Part-time, evening/weekend. *Faculty:* 23 part-time/adjunct (14 women). *Students:* 22 full-time (13 women), 21 part-time (13 women); includes 10 minority (1 Black or African American, non-Hispanic/Latino; 8 Asian, non-Hispanic/Latino; 1 Two or more races, non-Hispanic/Latino). In 2017, 3 master's, 1 doctorate awarded. *Degree requirements:* For master's, thesis (for MS in medical ethics and humanities, integrated pharmaceutical medicine); for doctorate, thesis/dissertation. *Application deadline:* For fall admission, 5/1 priority date for domestic students; for winter admission, 1/5 priority date for domestic students. Applications are processed on a rolling basis. Application fee: $95. Electronic applications accepted. *Expenses:* Contact institution. *Financial support:* Institutionally sponsored loans and tuition waivers available. Financial award application deadline: 3/15; financial award applicants required to submit FAFSA. *Unit head:* Dr. Steven Schmidt, Dean, 330-325-6290. *Application contact:* Heidi Terry, Executive Director, Enrollment Services, 330-325-6479, E-mail: hterry@neomed.edu.
Website: https://www.neomed.edu/graduatestudies/

Oregon State University, College of Pharmacy, Program in Pharmaceutical Sciences, Corvallis, OR 97331. Offers biopharmaceutics (MS, PhD). *Entrance requirements:* For master's and doctorate, GRE. Additional exam requirements/recommendations for international students: Required—TOEFL (minimum score 80 iBT), IELTS (minimum score 6.5). *Application deadline:* For fall admission, 1/1 for domestic and international students. Application fee: $75 ($85 for international students). *Application contact:* Debra Peters, Pharmacy Advisor, 541-737-8743, E-mail: debra.peters@oregonstate.edu.
Website: http://pharmacy.oregonstate.edu/

Purdue University, College of Pharmacy and Graduate School, Graduate Programs in Pharmacy and Pharmacal Sciences, Department of Pharmacy Practice, West Lafayette, IN 47907. Offers clinical pharmacy (MS, PhD); pharmacy administration (MS, PhD). *Faculty:* 36 full-time (21 women), 4 part-time/adjunct (3 women). *Students:* 12 full-time (7 women), 3 part-time (2 women); includes 4 minority (1 Asian, non-Hispanic/Latino; 2 Hispanic/Latino; 1 Two or more races, non-Hispanic/Latino), 7 international. Average age 29. 42 applicants, 14% accepted, 3 enrolled. In 2017, 1 master's, 4 doctorates awarded. Terminal master's awarded for partial completion of doctoral program. *Degree requirements:* For master's, thesis optional; for doctorate, thesis/dissertation. *Entrance requirements:* For master's, GRE General Test, minimum undergraduate GPA of 3.0 or equivalent; for doctorate, GRE General Test, minimum undergraduate GPA of 3.0 or equivalent; master's degree with minimum GPA of 3.0 or equivalent. Additional exam requirements/recommendations for international students: Required—TOEFL (minimum score 550 paper-based; 77 iBT), TWE (recommended for MS, required for PhD). *Application deadline:* Applications are processed on a rolling basis. Application fee: $60 ($75 for international students). Electronic applications accepted. *Financial support:* In 2017–18, teaching assistantships with tuition reimbursements (averaging $20,000 per year) were awarded; fellowships, research assistantships, career-related internships or fieldwork, and traineeships also available. Support available to part-time students. Financial award applicants required to submit FAFSA. *Faculty research:* Clinical drug studies, pharmacy education advancement, administrative studies. *Unit head:* Alan J. Zillich, Head of the Graduate Program, 317-880-5430, E-mail: azillich@purdue.edu. *Application contact:* Delayne Graham, Graduate Contact, 765-494-1362, E-mail: dkgraham@purdue.edu.

Queen's University at Kingston, School of Graduate Studies, Faculty of Health Sciences, Department of Anatomy and Cell Biology, Kingston, ON K7L 3N6, Canada. Offers biology of reproduction (M Sc, PhD); cancer (M Sc, PhD); cardiovascular pathophysiology (M Sc, PhD); cell and molecular biology (M Sc, PhD); drug metabolism (M Sc, PhD); endocrinology (M Sc, PhD); motor control (M Sc, PhD); neural regeneration (M Sc, PhD); neurophysiology (M Sc, PhD). *Program availability:* Part-time. *Degree requirements:* For master's, thesis; for doctorate, one foreign language, comprehensive exam, thesis/dissertation. *Entrance requirements:* Additional exam requirements/recommendations for international students: Required—TOEFL. Electronic applications accepted. *Faculty research:* Human kinetics, neuroscience, reproductive biology, cardiovascular.

Rowan University, Graduate School, College of Science and Mathematics, Program in Pharmaceutical Sciences, Glassboro, NJ 08028-1701. Offers MS. Electronic applications accepted. *Expenses:* Tuition, state resident: full-time $15,020; part-time $751 per semester hour. Tuition, nonresident: full-time $15,020; part-time $751 per semester hour. *Required fees:* $3158; $157.90 per semester hour. Tuition and fees vary according to course load, campus/location and program.

Rush University, Graduate College, Division of Pharmacology, Chicago, IL 60612-3832. Offers clinical research (MS); pharmacology (MS, PhD); MD/PhD. Terminal master's awarded for partial completion of doctoral program. *Degree requirements:* For master's, thesis; for doctorate, thesis/dissertation. *Entrance requirements:* For master's and doctorate, GRE General Test, interview. Additional exam requirements/recommendations for international students: Required—TOEFL (minimum score 550 paper-based). *Faculty research:* Dopamine neurobiology and Parkinson's disease; cardiac electrophysiology and clinical pharmacology; neutrophil motility, apoptosis, and adhesion; angiogenesis; pulmonary vascular physiology.

Rutgers University–New Brunswick, Ernest Mario School of Pharmacy, Program in Pharmaceutical Science, Piscataway, NJ 08854-8097. Offers MS, PhD. *Program availability:* Part-time. Terminal master's awarded for partial completion of doctoral program. *Degree requirements:* For master's, thesis; for doctorate, thesis/dissertation. *Entrance requirements:* For master's and doctorate, GRE General Test, 3 letters of recommendation. Additional exam requirements/recommendations for international students: Required—TOEFL (minimum score 550 paper-based; 83 iBT). Electronic applications accepted. *Faculty research:* Drug delivery, drug transport and drug metabolism; pharmacokinetics and pharmacodynamics; cancer chemoprevention and dietary phytochemicals; pharmacogenomics and personalized medicine; bioinformatics and computational pharmaceutical sciences.

St. John's University, College of Pharmacy and Health Sciences, Graduate Programs in Pharmaceutical Sciences, Program in Pharmaceutical Sciences, Queens, NY 11439. Offers MS, PhD. *Program availability:* Part-time. *Students:* 106 full-time (60 women), 19 part-time (7 women); includes 20 minority (5 Black or African American, non-Hispanic/Latino; 8 Asian, non-Hispanic/Latino; 7 Hispanic/Latino), 94 international. Average age 28. 215 applicants, 56% accepted, 29 enrolled. In 2017, 15 master's, 14 doctorates awarded. Terminal master's awarded for partial completion of doctoral program. *Degree requirements:* For master's, comprehensive exam (for some programs), thesis (for some programs); for doctorate, comprehensive exam, thesis/dissertation, residency requirement: 24 credits in first two academic years. *Entrance requirements:* For master's and doctorate, GRE General Test, letters of recommendation, transcripts, resume, personal statement. Additional exam requirements/recommendations for international students: Required—TOEFL (minimum score 100 iBT), IELTS (minimum score 7). *Application deadline:* For fall admission, 3/1 for domestic students; for spring admission, 11/1 for domestic students. Applications are processed on a rolling basis. Application fee: $70. Electronic applications accepted. *Expenses:* $25,270 per year. *Financial support:* Fellowships, teaching assistantships, career-related internships or fieldwork, scholarships/grants, and unspecified assistantships available. Support available to part-time students. Financial award application deadline: 2/1; financial award applicants required to submit FAFSA. *Faculty research:* Neurotoxicology, biochemical toxicology, molecular pharmacology, neuropharmacology, intermediary metabolism. *Unit head:* Dr. Vijaya L. Korlipara, Chair, 718-990-5369, Fax: 718-990-1877, E-mail: korlipav@stjohns.edu. *Application contact:* Robert Medrano, Director of Graduate Admission, 718-990-1601, Fax: 718-990-5686, E-mail: gradhelp@stjohns.edu.
Website: http://www.stjohns.edu/academics/schools-and-colleges/college-pharmacy-and-health-sciences/programs-and-majors/pharmaceutical-sciences-master-science

South Dakota State University, Graduate School, College of Pharmacy and Allied Health Professions, Department of Pharmaceutical Sciences, Brookings, SD 57007. Offers biological science (MS); pharmaceutical sciences (PhD). *Degree requirements:* For master's, thesis, oral exam; for doctorate, comprehensive exam, thesis/dissertation, oral exam. *Entrance requirements:* For master's and doctorate, GRE General Test. Additional exam requirements/recommendations for international students: Required—TOEFL (minimum score 550 paper-based). *Faculty research:* Drugs of abuse, anti-cancer drugs, sustained drug delivery, drug metabolism.

Stevens Institute of Technology, Graduate School, Charles V. Schaefer Jr. School of Engineering and Science, Department of Mechanical Engineering, Program in Pharmaceutical Manufacturing, Hoboken, NJ 07030. Offers M Eng, MS, Certificate. *Program availability:* Part-time, evening/weekend. *Students:* 21 full-time (8 women), 22 part-time (7 women); includes 11 minority (1 Black or African American, non-Hispanic/Latino; 9 Asian, non-Hispanic/Latino; 1 Hispanic/Latino), 12 international. Average age 29. 47 applicants, 62% accepted, 17 enrolled. In 2017, 29 master's, 29 other advanced degrees awarded. *Degree requirements:* For master's, thesis optional, minimum B average in major field and overall; for Certificate, minimum B average. *Entrance requirements:* Additional exam requirements/recommendations for international students: Required—TOEFL (minimum score 74 iBT), IELTS (minimum score 6). *Application deadline:* For fall admission, 7/1 for domestic students, 4/15 for international students; for spring admission, 12/1 for domestic and international students. Applications are processed on a rolling basis. Application fee: $60. Electronic applications accepted. *Expenses: Tuition:* Full-time $34,494; part-time $1554 per credit. *Required fees:* $291 per semester. *Financial support:* Fellowships, research assistantships, teaching assistantships, career-related internships or fieldwork, Federal Work-Study, scholarships/grants, and unspecified assistantships available. Financial award application deadline: 2/15; financial award applicants required to submit FAFSA. *Unit head:* Dr. Frank Fisher, Interim Department Director, 201-216-8913, Fax: 201-216-8315, E-mail: ffisher@stevens.edu. *Application contact:* Graduate Admissions, 888-783-8367, Fax: 888-511-1306, E-mail: graduate@stevens.edu.

Stevens Institute of Technology, Graduate School, School of Business, Program in Business Administration, Hoboken, NJ 07030. Offers business intelligence and analytics (MBA); engineering management (MBA); finance (MBA); information systems (MBA); innovation and entrepreneurship (MBA); marketing (MBA); pharmaceutical management (MBA); project management (MBA, Certificate); technology management (MBA); telecommunications management (MBA). *Accreditation:* AACSB. *Program availability:* Part-time, evening/weekend. *Students:* 46 full-time (19 women), 179 part-time (88 women); includes 46 minority (10 Black or African American, non-Hispanic/Latino; 2 American Indian or Alaska Native, non-Hispanic/Latino; 30 Asian, non-Hispanic/Latino; 4 Hispanic/Latino), 45 international. Average age 36. 218 applicants, 49% accepted, 53 enrolled. In 2017, 33 master's awarded. *Degree requirements:* For master's, thesis optional, minimum B average in major field and overall; for Certificate, minimum B average. *Entrance requirements:* Additional exam requirements/recommendations for international students: Required—TOEFL (minimum score 74 iBT), IELTS (minimum score 6). *Application deadline:* For fall admission, 7/1 for domestic students, 4/15 for international students; for spring admission, 12/1 for domestic and international students. Applications are processed on a rolling basis. Application fee: $60. Electronic applications accepted. *Expenses: Tuition:* Full-time $34,494; part-time $1554 per credit. *Required fees:* $291 per semester. *Financial support:* Fellowships, research assistantships, teaching assistantships, career-related internships or fieldwork, Federal Work-Study, scholarships/grants, and unspecified assistantships available. Financial award application deadline: 2/15; financial award applicants required to submit FAFSA. *Unit head:* Dr. Gregory Prastacos, Dean, 201-216-8366, E-mail: gprastac@stevens.edu. *Application contact:* Graduate Admissions, 888-783-8367, Fax: 888-511-1306, E-mail: graduate@stevens.edu.
Website: https://www.stevens.edu/school-business/masters-programs/mbaemba

Temple University, School of Pharmacy, Department of Pharmaceutical Sciences, Philadelphia, PA 19122. Offers medicinal chemistry (MS, PhD); pharmaceutics (MS, PhD); pharmacodynamics (MS, PhD); regulatory affairs and quality assurance (MS). *Program availability:* Part-time, online learning. *Faculty:* 13 full-time (4 women), 1 part-time/adjunct (0 women). *Students:* 29 full-time (11 women), 11 part-time (4 women); includes 2 minority (both Asian, non-Hispanic/Latino), 21 international. 51 applicants, 24% accepted, 4 enrolled. In 2017, 24 master's, 4 doctorates awarded. *Degree requirements:* For master's, comprehensive exam (for some programs), thesis (for some programs); for doctorate, 2 foreign languages, comprehensive exam, thesis/dissertation. *Entrance requirements:* For master's, GRE General Test, minimum undergraduate GPA of 3.0; for doctorate, GRE General Test, minimum GPA of 3.0. Additional exam requirements/recommendations for international students: Required—TOEFL (minimum score 550 paper-based; 82 iBT). *Application deadline:* For fall admission, 1/15 for domestic students, 12/15 for international students. Application fee: $60. Electronic applications accepted. *Expenses:* Contact institution. *Financial support:* Fellowships with full tuition reimbursements, research assistantships with full tuition reimbursements, and teaching assistantships with full tuition reimbursements available. Financial award application deadline: 1/15; financial award applicants required to submit FAFSA. *Faculty research:* Pharmacokinetics, synthesis of medicinals, protein research, biopharma-formulation. *Unit head:* Dr. Daniel Canney, Director of Graduate Studies, 215-707-6924, E-mail: phscgrad@temple.edu. *Application contact:* Sophon Din, Administrative Assistant, 215-204-4948, E-mail: tuspgrad@temple.edu.
Website: http://pharmacy.temple.edu/academics/department-pharmaceutical-science

Texas Southern University, College of Pharmacy and Health Sciences, Department of Pharmaceutical Sciences, Houston, TX 77004-4584. Offers MS, PhD. *Program availability:* Online learning. *Entrance requirements:* For master's, PCAT; for doctorate, GRE General Test. Electronic applications accepted.

Texas Tech University Health Sciences Center, Graduate School of Biomedical Sciences, Program in Pharmaceutical Sciences, Lubbock, TX 79430. Offers MS, PhD. *Accreditation:* ACPE. Terminal master's awarded for partial completion of doctoral program. *Degree requirements:* For master's, thesis; for doctorate, thesis/dissertation. *Entrance requirements:* For master's and doctorate, GRE General Test, minimum GPA of 3.0. Additional exam requirements/recommendations for international students: Required—TOEFL (minimum score 550 paper-based; 79 iBT). Electronic applications accepted. *Faculty research:* Drug design and delivery, pharmacology, pharmacokinetics, drug receptor modeling, molecular and reproductive biology.

Université de Montréal, Faculty of Pharmacy, Montréal, QC H3C 3J7, Canada. Offers drugs development (DESS); pharmaceutical care (DESS); pharmaceutical practice (M Sc, PhD); pharmaceutical sciences (M Sc, PhD); pharmacist-supervisor teacher (DESS). *Program availability:* Part-time. Terminal master's awarded for partial completion of doctoral program. *Degree requirements:* For master's, thesis; for doctorate, thesis/dissertation. *Entrance requirements:* For master's and doctorate, proficiency in French. Electronic applications accepted. *Faculty research:* Novel drug delivery systems, immunoassay development, medicinal chemistry of CNS compounds, pharmacokinetics and biopharmaceutical compounds.

Université Laval, Faculty of Pharmacy, Program in Hospital Pharmacy, Québec, QC G1K 7P4, Canada. Offers M Sc. *Entrance requirements:* For master's, knowledge of French, interview. Electronic applications accepted.

Université Laval, Faculty of Pharmacy, Programs in Community Pharmacy, Québec, QC G1K 7P4, Canada. Offers DESS. *Program availability:* Part-time. *Entrance requirements:* For degree, knowledge of French. Electronic applications accepted.

Université Laval, Faculty of Pharmacy, Programs in Pharmacy, Québec, QC G1K 7P4, Canada. Offers M Sc, PhD. *Program availability:* Part-time. Terminal master's awarded for partial completion of doctoral program. *Degree requirements:* For master's, thesis; for doctorate, comprehensive exam, thesis/dissertation. *Entrance requirements:* For master's and doctorate, knowledge of French. Electronic applications accepted.

University at Buffalo, the State University of New York, Graduate School, School of Pharmacy and Pharmaceutical Sciences, Department of Pharmaceutical Sciences, Buffalo, NY 14260. Offers MS, PhD, Pharm D/MS, Pharm D/PhD. *Faculty:* 16 full-time (4 women), 1 part-time/adjunct (0 women). *Students:* 69 full-time (35 women), 16 part-time (11 women); includes 19 minority (4 Black or African American, non-Hispanic/Latino; 14 Asian, non-Hispanic/Latino; 1 Hispanic/Latino), 29 international. Average age 27. 297 applicants, 8% accepted, 17 enrolled. In 2017, 13 master's, 8 doctorates awarded. Terminal master's awarded for partial completion of doctoral program. *Degree requirements:* For master's, comprehensive exam (for some programs), thesis optional, project; for doctorate, comprehensive exam, thesis/dissertation. *Entrance requirements:* For master's, GRE, BS, B Eng, or Pharm D; for doctorate, GRE, BS, MS, B Eng, M Eng, or Pharm D. Additional exam requirements/recommendations for international students: Required—TOEFL (minimum score 550 paper-based; 79 iBT); Recommended—IELTS, TSE. *Application deadline:* For fall admission, 2/15 for domestic and international students. Applications are processed on a rolling basis. Application fee: $50. Electronic applications accepted. *Expenses:* $10,870 in-state tuition, $24,723 out-of-state; $2,010.50 comprehensive fee; $128 student activity fee. *Financial support:* In 2017–18, 43 students received support, including 43 research assistantships with full tuition reimbursements available (averaging $23,994 per year); fellowships also available. Financial award application deadline: 3/1; financial award applicants required to submit FAFSA. *Faculty research:* Pharmacokinetics/pharmacodynamics, bioanalysis, pharmacogenomics, drug delivery, pharmacodynamics, drug metabolism and transport, cancer therapeutics, protein therapeutics. *Total annual research expenditures:* $5.3 million. *Unit head:* Dr. Marilyn E. Morris, Chair, 716-645-4839, Fax: 716-829-6569, E-mail: memorris@buffalo.edu. *Application contact:* Dr. Murali Ramanathan, Director of Graduate Studies, 716-645-4846, Fax: 716-645-3690, E-mail: murali@buffalo.edu.
Website: http://pharmacy.buffalo.edu/departments-offices/pharmaceutical-sciences.html

University of Alberta, Faculty of Graduate Studies and Research, Department of Pharmacy and Pharmaceutical Sciences, Edmonton, AB T6G 2E1, Canada. Offers M Sc, PhD. Terminal master's awarded for partial completion of doctoral program. *Degree requirements:* For master's, thesis; for doctorate, thesis/dissertation. *Entrance requirements:* Additional exam requirements/recommendations for international students: Required—Michigan English Language Assessment Battery or IELTS. Electronic applications accepted. *Faculty research:* Radiopharmacy, pharmacokinetics, bionucleonics, medicinal chemistry, microbiology.

The University of Arizona, College of Pharmacy, Program in Pharmaceutical Sciences, Tucson, AZ 85721. Offers medicinal and natural products chemistry (MS, PhD); pharmaceutical economics (MS, PhD); pharmaceutics and pharmacokinetics (MS, PhD). *Degree requirements:* For master's, thesis; for doctorate, one foreign language, thesis/dissertation. *Entrance requirements:* For master's, GRE General Test, 3 letters of recommendation, bachelor's degree in related field; for doctorate, GRE General Test, 3 letters of recommendation, statement of purpose, bachelor's degree in related field. Additional exam requirements/recommendations for international students: Required—TOEFL (minimum score 550 paper-based; 79 iBT). Electronic applications accepted. *Faculty research:* Drug design, natural products isolation, biological applications of NMR and mass spectrometry, drug formulation and delivery, pharmacokinetics.

The University of British Columbia, Faculty of Pharmaceutical Sciences, Vancouver, BC V6T 1Z3, Canada. Offers M Sc, PhD, Pharm D. *Degree requirements:* For master's, thesis, seminar; for doctorate, comprehensive exam, thesis/dissertation, seminar. *Entrance requirements:* Additional exam requirements/recommendations for international students: Required—TOEFL (minimum score 600 paper-based; 100 iBT), IELTS (minimum score 6.5). Electronic applications accepted. *Expenses:* Contact institution. *Faculty research:* Pharmacology and cellular pharmacology, neuropharmacology, toxicology, nanomedicines and drug delivery, pharmacogenomics and personalized medicine, health outcomes research and evaluation, pharmacoepidemiology, and medicinal chemistry.

University of California, Irvine, School of Medicine, Program in Pharmacological Sciences, Irvine, CA 92697. Offers PhD, MD/PhD. *Students:* 35 full-time (17 women); includes 19 minority (1 Black or African American, non-Hispanic/Latino; 13 Asian, non-Hispanic/Latino; 5 Hispanic/Latino), 7 international. Average age 28. 64 applicants, 22% accepted, 6 enrolled. In 2017, 7 doctorates awarded. *Entrance requirements:* For doctorate, GRE General Test, GRE Subject Test, minimum GPA of 3.0. Additional exam requirements/recommendations for international students: Required—TOEFL (minimum score 550 paper-based). *Application deadline:* For fall admission, 1/15 priority date for domestic students, 1/15 for international students. Applications are processed on a rolling basis. Application fee: $105 ($125 for international students). Electronic applications accepted. *Financial support:* Fellowships, research assistantships, teaching assistantships, institutionally sponsored loans, traineeships, and unspecified assistantships available. Financial award application deadline: 3/1; financial award applicants required to submit FAFSA. *Unit head:* Dr. Olivier Civelli, Chair, 949-924-2522, Fax: 949-824-4855, E-mail: ocivelli@uci.edu.
Website: http://www.pharmacology.uci.edu/graduate-program/

University of California, San Francisco, School of Pharmacy and Graduate Division, Pharmaceutical Sciences and Pharmacogenomics Program, San Francisco, CA 94158-0775. Offers PhD. *Degree requirements:* For doctorate, comprehensive exam, thesis/dissertation. *Entrance requirements:* For doctorate, GRE General Test, bachelor's degree, 3 letters of recommendation, personal statement. Additional exam requirements/recommendations for international students: Required—TOEFL. Electronic applications accepted. *Faculty research:* Drug development sciences, molecular pharmacology, therapeutic bioengineering, pharmacogenomics and functional genomics, quantitative and systems pharmacology, computational genomics.

University of Cincinnati, James L. Winkle College of Pharmacy, Division of Pharmaceutical Sciences, Cincinnati, OH 45237. Offers biomembrane science (MS), including cosmetic science (MS, PhD); biomembrane sciences (PhD), including cosmetic science (MS, PhD); experiential therapeutics (MS). *Program availability:* Part-time, evening/weekend, 100% online, blended/hybrid learning. *Faculty:* 15 full-time (2 women), 8 part-time/adjunct (3 women). *Students:* 36 full-time (18 women), 28 part-time (12 women); includes 9 minority (all Asian, non-Hispanic/Latino), 24 international. Average age 27. 197 applicants. In 2017, 3 master's, 5 doctorates awarded. *Degree requirements:* For master's, thesis; for doctorate, thesis/dissertation. *Entrance requirements:* For master's and doctorate, GRE General Test, minimum GPA of 3.0. Additional exam requirements/recommendations for international students: Required—TOEFL (minimum score 90 iBT); Recommended—IELTS (minimum score 6.5). *Application deadline:* For fall admission, 3/1 priority date for domestic students, 3/1 for international students. Application fee: $75. Electronic applications accepted. *Expenses: Tuition, area resident:* Full-time $14,468. Tuition, state resident: full-time $14,968; part-time $754 per credit hour. Tuition, nonresident: full-time $24,210; part-time $1311 per credit hour. *International tuition:* $26,460 full-time. *Required fees:* $3958; $84 per credit hour. One-time fee: $85 full-time. Tuition and fees vary according to course load, degree level and program. *Financial support:* In 2017–18, 29 students received support, including 29 fellowships with tuition reimbursements available (averaging $23,000 per year); research assistantships, tuition waivers (full), and unspecified assistantships also available. Support available to part-time students. Financial award application deadline: 3/1. *Unit head:* Dr. Bingfang Yan, Associate Dean of Research and Innovation, 513-558-6297, Fax: 513-558-3233, E-mail: bingfang.yan@uc.edu. *Application contact:* Karen Henry, Associate to the Director, 513-558-6172, Fax: 513-558-3233, E-mail: karen.henry@uc.edu.

University of Colorado Denver, Skaggs School of Pharmacy and Pharmaceutical Sciences, Program in Pharmaceutical Sciences, Aurora, CO 80045. Offers clinical

pharmaceutical sciences (PhD). *Entrance requirements:* For doctorate, GRE, minimum undergraduate GPA of 3.0; prior coursework in general chemistry, organic chemistry, calculus, biology, and physics. Application fee: $0.
Website: http://www.ucdenver.edu/academics/colleges/pharmacy/AcademicPrograms/PhDPrograms/PhDPharmaceuticalSciences/Pages/PhDPharmaceuticalSciences.aspx

University of Connecticut, Graduate School, School of Pharmacy, Department of Pharmaceutical Sciences, Program in Pharmaceutics, Storrs, CT 06269. Offers MS, PhD. Terminal master's awarded for partial completion of doctoral program. *Degree requirements:* For master's, comprehensive exam, thesis; for doctorate, thesis/dissertation. *Entrance requirements:* For master's and doctorate, GRE General Test. Additional exam requirements/recommendations for international students: Required—TOEFL (minimum score 550 paper-based). Electronic applications accepted.

University of Florida, Graduate School, College of Pharmacy, Graduate Programs in Pharmacy, Department of Pharmaceutics, Gainesville, FL 32611. Offers clinical and translational sciences (PhD); pharmaceutical sciences (MSP, PhD); pharmacy (MSP, PhD). *Degree requirements:* For doctorate, comprehensive exam, thesis/dissertation. *Entrance requirements:* For master's and doctorate, GRE General Test, minimum GPA of 3.0. Additional exam requirements/recommendations for international students: Required—TOEFL (minimum score 550 paper-based; 80 iBT), IELTS (minimum score 6). Electronic applications accepted. *Faculty research:* Basic, applied, and clinical investigations in pharmacokinetics/biopharmaceutics; pharmaceutical analysis, pharmaceutical biotechnology and drug delivery; herbal medicine.

University of Florida, Graduate School, College of Pharmacy, Graduate Programs in Pharmacy, Department of Pharmacotherapy and Translational Research, Gainesville, FL 32611. Offers clinical pharmaceutical sciences (PhD); clinical pharmacy (MSP). *Entrance requirements:* For master's and doctorate, GRE General Test, minimum GPA of 3.0. Additional exam requirements/recommendations for international students: Required—TOEFL (minimum score 550 paper-based; 80 iBT), IELTS (minimum score 6). Electronic applications accepted. *Faculty research:* Understanding genetic and non-genetic factors that contribute to variability in drug response in various therapeutic areas as cardiology, transplant/immunology, asthma/pulmonary, psychiatry, oncology, clinical pharmacology/drug metabolism.

University of Georgia, College of Pharmacy, Department of Pharmaceutical and Biomedical Sciences, Athens, GA 30602. Offers MS, PhD. *Degree requirements:* For master's, thesis; for doctorate, one foreign language, thesis/dissertation. *Entrance requirements:* For master's and doctorate, GRE General Test, minimum GPA of 3.0. Additional exam requirements/recommendations for international students: Required—TOEFL. Electronic applications accepted. *Faculty research:* Cancer and infectious diseases, drug delivery, neuropharmacology, cardiovascular pharmacology, bioanalytical chemistry, structural biology.

★ **University of Hawaii at Hilo,** Program in Pharmaceutical Sciences, Hilo, HI 96720-4091. Offers PhD. *Entrance requirements:* Additional exam requirements/recommendations for international students: Required—TOEFL. Electronic applications accepted.

See Display below and Close-Up on page 923.

University of Houston, College of Pharmacy, Houston, TX 77204. Offers pharmaceutics (MSPHR, PhD); pharmacology (MSPHR, PhD); pharmacy (Pharm D); pharmacy administration (MSPHR, PhD). *Accreditation:* ACPE. *Program availability:* Part-time. Terminal master's awarded for partial completion of doctoral program. *Entrance requirements:* For doctorate, PCAT (for Pharm D). Additional exam requirements/recommendations for international students: Required—TOEFL. Electronic applications accepted. *Faculty research:* Drug screening and design, cardiovascular pharmacology, infectious disease, asthma research, herbal medicine.

University of Illinois at Chicago, College of Pharmacy, Department of Biopharmaceutical Sciences, Chicago, IL 60607-7173. Offers PhD. *Faculty research:* Lipid and polymer-based drug delivery systems, targeted drug delivery, pharmacokinetic membrane transport and absorption, behavioral and cardiovascular pharmacology; neuropharmacology, environmental toxicology, cancer chemotherapy.

University of Illinois at Chicago, College of Pharmacy and Graduate College, Graduate Programs in Pharmacy, Chicago, IL 60607-7128. Offers comparative effectiveness research (MS); forensic science (MS); forensic toxicology (MS); medicinal chemistry (MS, PhD); pharmacognosy (MS, PhD); pharmacy (PhD). Terminal master's awarded for partial completion of doctoral program. *Degree requirements:* For master's, variable foreign language requirement, thesis; for doctorate, variable foreign language requirement, thesis/dissertation. *Entrance requirements:* For master's and doctorate, GRE General Test. Additional exam requirements/recommendations for international students: Required—TOEFL. Electronic applications accepted. *Faculty research:* Biopharmaceutical science, forensic science, forensic toxicology, medicinal chemistry, pharmacognosy.

The University of Iowa, College of Pharmacy, Iowa City, IA 52242-1316. Offers clinical pharmaceutical sciences (PhD); medicinal and natural products chemistry (PhD); pharamaceutics (PhD); pharmaceutical socioeconomics (PhD); pharmaceutics (MS); pharmacy (Pharm D); Pharm D/MPH. *Accreditation:* ACPE (one or more programs are accredited). *Degree requirements:* For master's, thesis optional, exam; for doctorate, comprehensive exam, thesis/dissertation. *Entrance requirements:* For master's and doctorate, GRE General Test, minimum GPA of 3.0. Additional exam requirements/recommendations for international students: Required—TOEFL (minimum score 550 paper-based; 81 iBT). Electronic applications accepted.

University of Kentucky, Graduate School, Graduate Programs in Pharmaceutical Sciences, Lexington, KY 40506-0032. Offers MS, PhD. Terminal master's awarded for partial completion of doctoral program. *Degree requirements:* For master's, thesis optional; for doctorate, comprehensive exam, thesis/dissertation. *Entrance requirements:* For master's, GRE General Test, minimum undergraduate GPA of 3.2; for doctorate, GRE General Test, minimum graduate GPA of 3.2. Additional exam requirements/recommendations for international students: Required—TOEFL (minimum score 550 paper-based; 79 iBT). Electronic applications accepted. *Faculty research:* Drug development, biotechnology, medicinal chemistry, cardiology, pharmacokinetics, CNS pharmacology, clinical pharmacology, pharmacotherapy and health outcomes, pharmaceutical policy.

The University of Manchester, School of Pharmacy and Pharmaceutical Sciences, Manchester, United Kingdom. Offers M Phil, PhD.

University of Manitoba, Faculty of Graduate Studies, College of Pharmacy, Winnipeg, MB R3T 2N2, Canada. Offers M Sc, PhD. *Degree requirements:* For master's, one foreign language, thesis.

University of Maryland, Baltimore, Graduate School, Graduate Programs in Pharmacy, Department of Pharmaceutical Sciences, Baltimore, MD 21201. Offers PhD. *Degree requirements:* For doctorate, comprehensive exam, thesis/dissertation. *Entrance requirements:* For doctorate, GRE General Test. Additional exam requirements/recommendations for international students: Required—TOEFL (minimum score 600 paper-based), IELTS. Electronic applications accepted. *Expenses:* Tuition, state resident: full-time $13,990; part-time $661 per credit. Tuition, nonresident: full-time $30,484; part-time $1310 per credit. *Required fees:* $1894; $94 per credit. $415 per semester. Part-time tuition and fees vary according to course load, degree level and program. *Faculty research:* Drug delivery, cellular and biological chemistry, clinical pharmaceutical sciences, biopharmaceutics, neuroscience.

University of Maryland Eastern Shore, Graduate Programs, School of Pharmacy, Princess Anne, MD 21853. Offers pharmaceutical sciences (MS, PhD); pharmacy (Pharm D). *Expenses:* Tuition, state resident: part-time $325 per credit hour. Tuition, nonresident: part-time $604 per credit hour. *Required fees:* $85 per credit hour. Part-time tuition and fees vary according to campus/location, program and reciprocity agreements. *Unit head:* Dr. Mark Simmons, 410-651-8327, E-mail: masimmons1@umes.edu. *Application contact:* Dr. Mark Simmons, 410-651-8327, E-mail: masimmons1@umes.edu. Website: http://www.umes.edu/pharmacy/

University of Michigan, College of Pharmacy and Rackham Graduate School, Department of Pharmaceutical Sciences, Ann Arbor, MI 48109. Offers PhD. *Faculty:* 16 full-time (4 women), 4 part-time/adjunct (0 women). *Students:* 43 full-time (14 women); includes 6 minority (1 Black or African American, non-Hispanic/Latino; 3 Asian, non-Hispanic/Latino; 1 Hispanic/Latino; 1 Two or more races, non-Hispanic/Latino), 16 international. Average age 25. 95 applicants, 14% accepted, 8 enrolled. In 2017, 5 doctorates awarded. Terminal master's awarded for partial completion of doctoral program. *Degree requirements:* For doctorate, thesis/dissertation, oral defense of dissertation, preliminary exam. *Entrance requirements:* For doctorate, GRE. Additional exam requirements/recommendations for international students: Required—TOEFL (minimum score 560 paper-based; 84 iBT) or IELTS (minimum score 6.5). *Application deadline:* For fall admission, 1/6 for domestic and international students. Applications are processed on a rolling basis. Application fee: $75 ($90 for international students). Electronic applications accepted. *Expenses:* Contact institution. *Financial support:* In 2017–18, 44 students received support, including 15 fellowships (averaging $48,037 per year), 17 research assistantships (averaging $48,037 per year), 8 teaching assistantships (averaging $48,037 per year); career-related internships or fieldwork, institutionally sponsored loans, scholarships/grants, traineeships, health care benefits, and unspecified assistantships also available. *Faculty research:* New drug design, new drug delivery systems, new biotechnology, pharmacy and the public sector. *Unit head:* Dr. Steven P. Schwedeman, Chair, 734-647-8339, Fax: 734-615-6162, E-mail: schwende@med.umich.edu. *Application contact:* Patrina Hardy, Executive Secretary, 734-615-3749, Fax: 734-615-6162, E-mail: thardy@med.umich.edu. Website: https://pharmacy.umich.edu/pharmsci

University of Minnesota, Twin Cities Campus, College of Pharmacy and Graduate School, Graduate Programs in Pharmacy, Graduate Program in Pharmaceutics, Minneapolis, MN 55455. Offers MS, PhD. *Faculty:* 10 full-time (1 woman), 19 part-time/adjunct (5 women). *Students:* 30 full-time (17 women); includes 1 minority (Asian, non-Hispanic/Latino), 25 international. Average age 26. 66 applicants, 24% accepted, 11 enrolled. In 2017, 2 master's, 4 doctorates awarded. Terminal master's awarded for partial completion of doctoral program. *Degree requirements:* For master's, comprehensive exam, thesis; for doctorate, comprehensive exam, thesis/dissertation. *Entrance requirements:* For master's and doctorate, GRE General Test (preferred minimum scores: Quantitative 80%, Analytical Writing 3.5), bachelor's degree. Additional exam requirements/recommendations for international students: Required—TOEFL (minimum score 100 iBT), IELTS (minimum score 6.5). *Application deadline:* For fall admission, 11/30 for domestic and international students. Application fee: $75 ($95 for international students). Electronic applications accepted. *Expenses:* Contact institution. *Financial support:* In 2017–18, 23 students received support, including 5 fellowships with full tuition reimbursements available (averaging $22,500 per year), 10 research assistantships with full tuition reimbursements available (averaging $22,500 per year), 7 teaching assistantships with full tuition reimbursements available (averaging $23,000 per year); career-related internships or fieldwork, health care benefits, unspecified assistantships, and summer internships with pharmaceutical companies also available. Financial award application deadline: 11/30. *Faculty research:* Drug delivery, drug metabolism, molecular biopharmaceutics, pharmacokinetics/pharmacodynamics, crystal engineering, biophysical chemistry. *Unit head:* Dr. Jayanth Panyam, Professor and Department Head, 612-624-0951, Fax: 612-626-2125, E-mail: jpanyam@umn.edu. *Application contact:* Katie M. James, Graduate Program Coordinator, 612-624-5153, Fax: 612-626-2125, E-mail: kmjames@umn.edu. Website: http://www.pharmacy.umn.edu/pharmaceutics/

University of Mississippi, Graduate School, School of Pharmacy, University, MS 38677. Offers environmental toxicology (MS, PhD); industrial pharmacy (MS); medicinal chemistry (MS, PhD); pharmaceutics (MS, PhD); pharmacognosy (MS, PhD); pharmacology (MS, PhD); pharmacy (Pharm D); pharmacy administration (MS, PhD). *Accreditation:* ACPE (one or more programs are accredited). *Program availability:* Part-time. *Faculty:* 71 full-time (32 women), 17 part-time/adjunct (6 women). *Students:* 417 full-time (256 women), 16 part-time (7 women); includes 71 minority (24 Black or African American, non-Hispanic/Latino; 1 American Indian or Alaska Native, non-Hispanic/Latino; 36 Asian, non-Hispanic/Latino; 4 Hispanic/Latino; 6 Two or more races, non-Hispanic/Latino), 88 international. Average age 25. In 2017, 22 master's, 49 doctorates awarded. Terminal master's awarded for partial completion of doctoral program. *Degree requirements:* For master's, thesis; for doctorate, thesis/dissertation (for some programs). *Entrance requirements:* For master's, GRE General Test, minimum GPA of 3.0; for doctorate, GRE General Test (for PhD). Additional exam requirements/recommendations for international students: Required—TOEFL. *Application deadline:* For fall admission, 2/1 priority date for domestic students; for spring admission, 10/1 priority date for domestic students. Applications are processed on a rolling basis. Application fee: $50. Electronic applications accepted. *Financial support:* Fellowships, research assistantships, teaching assistantships, career-related internships or fieldwork, Federal Work-Study, institutionally sponsored loans, scholarships/grants, tuition waivers (full), and unspecified assistantships available. Financial award application deadline: 3/1; financial award applicants required to submit FAFSA. *Unit head:* Dr. David D. Allen, II, Dean, 662-915-7265, Fax: 662-915-5118, E-mail: sopdean@olemiss.edu. Website: http://www.pharmacy.olemiss.edu/

University of Montana, Graduate School, College of Health Professions and Biomedical Sciences, Skaggs School of Pharmacy, Department of Biomedical and Pharmaceutical Sciences, Missoula, MT 59812. Offers biomedical sciences (PhD); medicinal chemistry (MS, PhD); molecular and cellular toxicology (MS, PhD); neuroscience (PhD); pharmaceutical sciences (MS). *Accreditation:* ACPE. *Degree requirements:* For master's, oral defense of thesis; for doctorate, research dissertation defense. *Entrance requirements:* For master's and doctorate, GRE General Test. Additional exam requirements/recommendations for international students: Required—TOEFL (minimum score 540 paper-based). Electronic applications accepted. *Faculty research:* Cardiovascular pharmacology, medicinal chemistry, neurosciences, environmental toxicology, pharmacogenetics, cancer.

University of Nebraska Medical Center, Department of Pharmaceutical Sciences, Omaha, NE 68198-6120. Offers MS, PhD, MD/PhD. *Faculty:* 20 full-time (3 women), 1 part-time/adjunct (0 women). *Students:* 57 full-time (24 women), 48 international. Average age 29. 72 applicants, 21% accepted, 13 enrolled. In 2017, 9 doctorates awarded. Terminal master's awarded for partial completion of doctoral program. *Degree requirements:* For master's, comprehensive exam, thesis; for doctorate, comprehensive exam, thesis/dissertation. *Entrance requirements:* For master's, GRE General Test; for doctorate, GRE. Additional exam requirements/recommendations for international students: Required—TOEFL (minimum score 550 paper-based; 80 iBT). *Application deadline:* For fall admission, 6/1 priority date for domestic students, 4/1 priority date for international students; for spring admission, 10/1 for domestic students, 8/1 for international students. Applications are processed on a rolling basis. Application fee: $60. Electronic applications accepted. *Expenses:* Contact institution. *Financial support:* In 2017–18, 95 students received support, including 10 fellowships with full tuition reimbursements available (averaging $25,000 per year), 35 research assistantships with full tuition reimbursements available (averaging $24,500 per year); scholarships/grants and unspecified assistantships also available. Financial award application deadline: 4/1. *Faculty research:* Pharmaceutics, medicinal chemistry, biophysical chemistry, nanomedicine, pharmacokinetics. *Total annual research expenditures:* $8.8 million. *Unit head:* Dr. Ram Mahato, Chair, Pharmaceutical Sciences Graduate Program Committee, 402-559-5422, E-mail: ram.mahato@unmc.edu. *Application contact:* Renee Kaszynski, Office Associate, 402-559-5320, E-mail: renee.kaszynski@unmc.edu. Website: http://www.unmc.edu/pharmacy/faculty/pharmaceutical-sciences/

University of New Mexico, Graduate Studies, College of Pharmacy, Graduate Programs in Pharmaceutical Sciences, Albuquerque, NM 87131-2039. Offers MS, PhD. *Program availability:* Part-time. *Degree requirements:* For master's, comprehensive exam, thesis; for doctorate, comprehensive exam, thesis/dissertation. *Entrance requirements:* For master's and doctorate, GRE General Test (for some concentrations), 3 letters of recommendation, letter of intent, resume. Additional exam requirements/recommendations for international students: Required—TOEFL (minimum score 580 paper-based; 93 iBT). Electronic applications accepted. *Faculty research:* Pharmaceutical research, cancer research, pharmacy administration, radiopharmacy, toxicology.

The University of North Carolina at Chapel Hill, Eshelman School of Pharmacy, Chapel Hill, NC 27599. Offers pharmaceutical sciences (PhD); pharmaceutical sciences - health system pharmacy administration (MS); pharmacy (Pharm D). *Accreditation:* ACPE (one or more programs are accredited). *Faculty:* 115 full-time (47 women), 362 part-time/adjunct (189 women). *Students:* 107 full-time (60 women); includes 27 minority (3 Black or African American, non-Hispanic/Latino; 17 Asian, non-Hispanic/Latino; 4 Hispanic/Latino; 3 Two or more races, non-Hispanic/Latino), 16 international. Average age 26. 229 applicants, 7% accepted, 16 enrolled. In 2017, 8 master's, 16 doctorates awarded. Terminal master's awarded for partial completion of doctoral program. *Degree requirements:* For master's, comprehensive exam, thesis; for doctorate, comprehensive exam, thesis/dissertation. *Entrance requirements:* For master's and doctorate, GRE General Test, minimum GPA of 3.0. Additional exam requirements/recommendations for international students: Required—TOEFL (minimum score 550 paper-based; 90 iBT), IELTS (minimum score 7). *Application deadline:* For fall admission, 12/12 for domestic students, 12/12 priority date for international students. Applications are processed on a rolling basis. Application fee: $90. Electronic applications accepted. *Expenses:* Contact institution. *Financial support:* In 2017–18, 107 students received support, including 18 fellowships with full tuition reimbursements available (averaging $30,000 per year), 56 research assistantships with full tuition reimbursements available (averaging $30,000 per year); career-related internships or fieldwork, Federal Work-Study, institutionally sponsored loans, scholarships/grants, traineeships, health care benefits, tuition waivers (full), and unspecified assistantships also available. Financial award application deadline: 12/12. *Faculty research:* Health services research, pharmacokinetics, molecular modeling, infectious disease, genomics and proteomics, translational research. *Total annual research expenditures:* $25 million. *Unit head:* Dr. Dhiren Thakker, Dean, 919-966-1122, Fax: 919-966-6919, E-mail: dhiren_thakker@unc.edu. *Application contact:* Olivia Hammill, Assistant Director of Recruitment and Admissions, 919-962-0097, Fax: 919-966-9428, E-mail: olivia_hammill@unc.edu. Website: http://pharmacy.unc.edu/

University of North Texas Health Science Center at Fort Worth, Graduate School of Biomedical Sciences, Fort Worth, TX 76107-2699. Offers biochemistry and cancer biology (MS, PhD); biotechnology (MS); cell biology, immunology and microbiology (MS, PhD); clinical research management (MS); forensic genetics (MS); genetics (MS, PhD); integrative physiology (MS, PhD); medical sciences (MS); pharmaceutical sciences and pharmacotherapy (MS, PhD); pharmacology and neuroscience (MS, PhD); structural anatomy and rehabilitation sciences (MS, PhD); DO/MS; DO/PhD. Terminal master's awarded for partial completion of doctoral program. *Degree requirements:* For master's, thesis; for doctorate, thesis/dissertation. *Entrance requirements:* For master's and doctorate, GRE General Test. Additional exam requirements/recommendations for international students: Required—TOEFL. *Expenses:* Contact institution. *Faculty research:* Alzheimer's disease, aging, eye diseases, cancer, cardiovascular disease.

University of Oklahoma Health Sciences Center, College of Pharmacy and Graduate College, Graduate Programs in Pharmacy, Oklahoma City, OK 73190. Offers MS, PhD, MS/MBA. MS/MBA offered jointly with Oklahoma State University and University of Oklahoma. Terminal master's awarded for partial completion of doctoral program. *Degree requirements:* For master's, comprehensive exam, thesis; for doctorate, comprehensive exam, thesis/dissertation. *Entrance requirements:* For master's and doctorate, GRE General Test. Additional exam requirements/recommendations for international students: Required—TOEFL. *Faculty research:* Medicinal chemistry, pharmacokinetics/biopharmaceutics, nuclear pharmacy, pharmacy administration, pharmacodynamics and toxicology.

University of Pittsburgh, School of Pharmacy, Graduate Programs in Pharmaceutical Sciences, Pittsburgh, PA 15261. Offers pharmaceutical sciences (MS, PhD), including biochemical pharmacology, clinical pharmaceutical scientist, medicinal chemistry, pharmaceutical outcomes and policy research, pharmaceutics. *Program availability:* Part-time. *Faculty:* 55 full-time (27 women), 2 part-time/adjunct (1 woman). *Students:* 73 full-time (41 women), 2 part-time (0 women); includes 2 minority (1 Black or African American, non-Hispanic/Latino; 1 Asian, non-Hispanic/Latino), 62 international. Average age 27. 166 applicants, 23% accepted, 25 enrolled. In 2017, 6 master's, 7 doctorates awarded. Terminal master's awarded for partial completion of doctoral program. *Degree requirements:* For master's, comprehensive exam (for some programs), thesis (for some programs), 34 credits (for non-thesis), 30 credits (for thesis); for doctorate, comprehensive exam, thesis/dissertation, 72 credits. *Entrance requirements:* For master's, GRE General Test, bachelor's degree; for doctorate, GRE General Test, bachelor's degree, research experience. Additional exam requirements/recommendations for international students: Required—TOEFL (minimum score 100 iBT), IELTS (minimum score 7). *Application deadline:* For fall admission, 1/5 for domestic and international students. Application fee: $75. Electronic applications accepted. *Expenses:* $26,136 tuition per year, $850 fees. *Financial support:* In 2017–18, 6 fellowships with full tuition reimbursements (averaging $30,700 per year), 27 research assistantships with full tuition reimbursements (averaging $30,700 per year), 12 teaching assistantships with full tuition reimbursements (averaging $27,400 per year) were awarded; scholarships/grants, health care benefits, and unspecified assistantships also available. *Faculty research:* Comparative effectiveness and outcomes; pharmacogenomics in drug response; chemogenomics; drug delivery systems for HIV prevention; small molecular design/development; cell instructive biomaterials for regenerative therapy. *Total annual research expenditures:* $5.8 million. *Unit head:* Dr. Patricia Dowley Kroboth, Dean, 412-624-2400, Fax: 412-648-1086, E-mail: pkroboth@pitt.edu. *Application contact:* Lori M. Altenbaugh, Program Coordinator, 412-648-1014, Fax: 412-383-9000, E-mail: altenbaughlm@pitt.edu. Website: http://www.pharmacy.pitt.edu/programs/grad/grad_index.php

Pharmaceutical Sciences

University of Puerto Rico–Medical Sciences Campus, School of Pharmacy, San Juan, PR 00936-5067. Offers industrial pharmacy (MS); pharmaceutical sciences (MS); pharmacy (Pharm D). *Accreditation:* ACPE. *Program availability:* Part-time, evening/weekend. *Degree requirements:* For master's, thesis; for doctorate, portfolio, research project. *Entrance requirements:* For master's, GRE, interview; for doctorate, PCAT, interview. Electronic applications accepted. *Expenses:* Contact institution. *Faculty research:* Controlled release, solid dosage form, screening of anti-HIV drugs, pharmacokinetic/pharmacodynamic of drugs.

University of Rhode Island, Graduate School, College of Pharmacy, Department of Biomedical and Pharmaceutical Sciences, Kingston, RI 02881. Offers health outcomes (MS, PhD); medicinal chemistry and pharmacognosy (MS, PhD); pharmaceutics and pharmacokinetics (MS, PhD); pharmacology and toxicology (MS, PhD). *Program availability:* Part-time. *Faculty:* 23 full-time (11 women). *Students:* 36 full-time (14 women), 9 part-time (4 women); includes 4 minority (1 Black or African American, non-Hispanic/Latino; 1 American Indian or Alaska Native, non-Hispanic/Latino; 2 Asian, non-Hispanic/Latino), 22 international. 138 applicants, 18% accepted, 14 enrolled. In 2017, 3 master's, 6 doctorates awarded. *Entrance requirements:* Additional exam requirements/recommendations for international students: Required—TOEFL. *Application deadline:* For fall admission, 7/15 for domestic students, 2/1 for international students. Application fee: $65. Electronic applications accepted. *Expenses:* Tuition, state resident: full-time $12,706; part-time $786 per credit. Tuition, nonresident: full-time $25,216; part-time $1401 per credit. *Required fees:* $1598; $45 per credit. One-time fee: $30 part-time. *Financial support:* In 2017–18, 10 research assistantships with tuition reimbursements (averaging $13,958 per year), 10 teaching assistantships with tuition reimbursements (averaging $11,291 per year) were awarded. Financial award application deadline: 2/1; financial award applicants required to submit FAFSA. *Unit head:* Dr. David Rowley, Chair, 401-874-9228, E-mail: drowley@uri.edu.
Website: http://www.uri.edu/pharmacy/departments/bps/index.shtml

University of Saskatchewan, College of Graduate Studies and Research, College of Pharmacy and Nutrition, Saskatoon, SK S7N 5A2, Canada. Offers M Sc, PhD. *Degree requirements:* For master's, thesis; for doctorate, thesis/dissertation. *Entrance requirements:* Additional exam requirements/recommendations for international students: Required—TOEFL.

University of South Carolina, South Carolina College of Pharmacy and The Graduate School, Department of Basic Pharmaceutical Sciences, Columbia, SC 29208. Offers MS, PhD. PhD offered jointly with Medical University of South Carolina. *Program availability:* Part-time. Terminal master's awarded for partial completion of doctoral program. *Degree requirements:* For master's, one foreign language, comprehensive exam, thesis; for doctorate, one foreign language, comprehensive exam, thesis/dissertation. *Entrance requirements:* For master's, GRE General Test, BS in biology, chemistry, pharmacy, or related field; for doctorate, GRE General Test, BS in biology, chemistry, or related field. Additional exam requirements/recommendations for international students: Required—TOEFL. Electronic applications accepted. *Faculty research:* Cancer treatment and prevention, Ion channels, DNA damage repair, inflammation.

University of Southern California, Graduate School, School of Pharmacy, Department of Pharmacology and Pharmaceutical Sciences, Los Angeles, CA 90089. Offers MS, PhD. Terminal master's awarded for partial completion of doctoral program. *Degree requirements:* For master's, comprehensive exam, thesis, 24 units of formal course work, excluding research and seminar courses; for doctorate, comprehensive exam, thesis/dissertation, 24 units of formal course work, excluding research and seminar courses. *Entrance requirements:* For master's and doctorate, GRE. Additional exam requirements/recommendations for international students: Required—TOEFL (minimum score 603 paper-based; 100 iBT). Electronic applications accepted. *Faculty research:* Drug design, drug delivery, pharmaceutical sciences.

University of Southern California, Graduate School, School of Pharmacy, Graduate Programs in Pharmaceutical Economics and Policy, Los Angeles, CA 90033. Offers MS, PhD. Terminal master's awarded for partial completion of doctoral program. *Degree requirements:* For master's, comprehensive exam, thesis, 24 units of formal course work, excluding research and seminar courses; for doctorate, comprehensive exam, thesis/dissertation, 24 units of formal course work, excluding research and seminar courses. *Entrance requirements:* For master's and doctorate, GRE. Additional exam requirements/recommendations for international students: Required—TOEFL (minimum score 603 paper-based; 100 iBT). Electronic applications accepted. *Faculty research:* Cost-effective analyses/modeling, retrospective data analysis of comparative effectiveness, quality of life measurement, competitive pricing systems in health care.

University of Southern California, Graduate School, School of Pharmacy, Program in Clinical and Experimental Therapeutics, Los Angeles, CA 90089. Offers PhD. Terminal master's awarded for partial completion of doctoral program. *Degree requirements:* For doctorate, comprehensive exam, thesis/dissertation, 24 units of course work, excluding research and dissertation courses. *Entrance requirements:* For doctorate, GRE, minimum overall GPA of 3.0, three letters of recommendation. Additional exam requirements/recommendations for international students: Required—TOEFL (minimum score 625 paper-based; 100 iBT). Electronic applications accepted. *Faculty research:* Pharmacology and therapeutics: inflammation, tissue regeneration, myelosuppression, bacterial resistance and virulence, alcoholism, CNS disorders, metabolomics and lipidomics.

University of Southern California, Graduate School, School of Pharmacy, Regulatory Science Programs, Los Angeles, CA 90089. Offers clinical research design and management (Graduate Certificate); food safety (Graduate Certificate); patient and product safety (Graduate Certificate); preclinical drug development (Graduate Certificate); regulatory and clinical affairs (Graduate Certificate); regulatory science (MS, DRSc). *Program availability:* Part-time, evening/weekend, online learning. Terminal master's awarded for partial completion of doctoral program. *Degree requirements:* For master's, thesis optional; for doctorate, comprehensive exam, thesis/dissertation. *Entrance requirements:* For master's, GRE. Additional exam requirements/recommendations for international students: Required—TOEFL (minimum score 603 paper-based; 100 iBT). Electronic applications accepted.

University of South Florida, College of Pharmacy, Tampa, FL 33620-9951. Offers pharmaceutical nanotechnology (MS), including biomedical engineering, drug discovery, delivery, development and manufacturing; pharmacy (Pharm D), including pharmacy and health education. *Accreditation:* ACPE. *Faculty:* 39 full-time (28 women), 1 part-time/adjunct (0 women). *Students:* 381 full-time (226 women), 3 part-time (1 woman); includes 172 minority (27 Black or African American, non-Hispanic/Latino; 70 Asian, non-Hispanic/Latino; 59 Hispanic/Latino; 4 Native Hawaiian or other Pacific Islander, non-Hispanic/Latino; 12 Two or more races, non-Hispanic/Latino), 4 international. Average age 25. 678 applicants, 31% accepted, 105 enrolled. In 2017, 111 doctorates awarded. *Degree requirements:* For master's, comprehensive exam, thesis optional. *Entrance requirements:* For master's, GRE, MCAT or DAT, minimum GPA of 3.0, letters of reference, resume; for doctorate, PCAT, minimum GPA of 2.75 overall (preferred); completion of 72 prerequisite credit hours; U.S. citizenship or permanent resident. Additional exam requirements/recommendations for international students: Required—TOEFL (minimum score 550 paper-based; 79 iBT), IELTS (minimum score 6.5). *Application deadline:* For fall admission, 2/1 priority date for domestic students, 2/1 for international students; for spring admission, 10/15 for domestic students, 9/15 for international students; for summer admission, 2/15 for domestic and international students. Electronic applications accepted. *Financial support:* In 2017–18, 91 students received support. *Total annual research expenditures:* $1.7 million. *Unit head:* Dr. Kevin Sneed, Dean, 813-974-5699, E-mail: ksneed@health.usf.edu. *Application contact:* Dr. Amy Schwartz, Associate Dean, 813-974-2251, E-mail: aschwar1@health.usf.edu.

The University of Tennessee Health Science Center, College of Graduate Health Sciences, Memphis, TN 38163. Offers biomedical engineering (MS, PhD); biomedical sciences (PhD); dental sciences (MDS); epidemiology (MS); health outcomes and policy research (PhD); laboratory research and management (MS); nursing science (PhD); pharmaceutical sciences (PhD); pharmacology (MS); speech and hearing science (PhD); DDS/PhD; DNP/PhD; MD/PhD; Pharm D/PhD. MS and PhD programs in biomedical engineering offered jointly with University of Memphis. *Faculty:* 528 full-time (176 women). *Students:* 258 full-time (130 women); includes 87 minority (14 Black or African American, non-Hispanic/Latino; 68 Asian, non-Hispanic/Latino; 5 Hispanic/Latino). Average age 28. 673 applicants, 17% accepted, 102 enrolled. In 2017, 23 master's, 30 doctorates awarded. Terminal master's awarded for partial completion of doctoral program. *Degree requirements:* For master's, comprehensive exam, thesis; for doctorate, thesis/dissertation, oral and written preliminary and comprehensive exams. *Entrance requirements:* For master's and doctorate, GRE General Test, minimum GPA of 3.0. Additional exam requirements/recommendations for international students: Recommended—TOEFL (minimum score 79 iBT), IELTS (minimum score 6.5). *Application deadline:* For winter admission, 1/1 for domestic and international students; for spring admission, 3/1 for domestic and international students. Applications are processed on a rolling basis. Application fee: $0. Electronic applications accepted. *Expenses:* Contact institution. *Financial support:* In 2017–18, 150 students received support, including 150 research assistantships (averaging $25,000 per year); fellowships, institutionally sponsored loans, scholarships/grants, health care benefits, and tuition waivers (full and partial) also available. Support available to part-time students. *Faculty research:* Cell biology, epidemiology, biomedical engineering, speech and hearing science, health policy, pharmaceutical sciences, dental sciences, nursing science, pharmacology. *Unit head:* Dr. Donald B. Thomason, Dean, 901-448-5538, E-mail: dthomaso@uthsc.edu. *Application contact:* Dr. Isaac O. Donkor, Associate Dean for Student Affairs, 901-448-5538, E-mail: idonkor@uthsc.edu.
Website: http://grad.uthsc.edu/

The University of Texas at Austin, Graduate School, College of Pharmacy, Graduate Programs in Pharmacy, Austin, TX 78712-1111. Offers health outcomes and pharmacy practice (PhD); health outcomes and pharmacy practice (MS); medicinal chemistry (PhD); pharmaceutics (PhD); pharmacology and toxicology (PhD); pharmacotherapy (MS, PhD); translational science (PhD). PhD in translational science offered jointly with The University of Texas Health Science Center at San Antonio and The University of Texas at San Antonio. *Degree requirements:* For master's, thesis; for doctorate, thesis/dissertation. *Entrance requirements:* For master's and doctorate, GRE General Test. Electronic applications accepted. *Faculty research:* Synthetic medical chemistry, synthetic molecular biology, bio-organic chemistry, pharmacoeconomics, pharmacy practice.

University of the Pacific, Thomas J. Long School of Pharmacy and Health Sciences, Pharmaceutical and Chemical Sciences Graduate Program, Stockton, CA 95211-0197. Offers MS, PhD. *Faculty:* 9 full-time (3 women). *Students:* 8 full-time (5 women), 53 part-time (21 women); includes 11 minority (2 Black or African American, non-Hispanic/Latino; 5 Asian, non-Hispanic/Latino; 3 Hispanic/Latino; 1 Two or more races, non-Hispanic/Latino), 39 international. Average age 28. 65 applicants, 23% accepted, 10 enrolled. In 2017, 7 master's, 4 doctorates awarded. *Entrance requirements:* Additional exam requirements/recommendations for international students: Required—TOEFL. Application fee: $75. *Financial support:* Teaching assistantships available. Financial award application deadline: 3/1; financial award applicants required to submit FAFSA. *Unit head:* Dr. Xiaolin Li, Head/Associate Dean, 209-946-3163, E-mail: xli@pacific.edu. *Application contact:* Ron Espejo, Recruitment Specialist, 209-946-3957, Fax: 209-946-3147, E-mail: respejo@pacific.edu.

University of the Sciences, Program in Pharmaceutics, Philadelphia, PA 19104-4495. Offers MS, PhD. *Program availability:* Part-time. Terminal master's awarded for partial completion of doctoral program. *Degree requirements:* For master's, thesis (for some programs); for doctorate, comprehensive exam, thesis/dissertation, oral defense. *Entrance requirements:* For master's and doctorate, GRE General Test. Additional exam requirements/recommendations for international students: Required—TOEFL, TWE.

The University of Toledo, College of Graduate Studies, College of Pharmacy and Pharmaceutical Sciences, Program in Pharmaceutical Sciences, Toledo, OH 43606-3390. Offers administrative pharmacy (MSPS); industrial pharmacy (MSPS); pharmacology toxicology (MSPS). *Degree requirements:* For master's, thesis. *Entrance requirements:* For master's, GRE General Test. Additional exam requirements/recommendations for international students: Required—TOEFL (minimum score 550 paper-based; 80 iBT). Electronic applications accepted.

University of Toronto, School of Graduate Studies, Leslie Dan Faculty of Pharmacy, Toronto, ON M5S 1A1, Canada. Offers M Sc, PhD, Pharm D. *Program availability:* Part-time. *Degree requirements:* For master's, thesis, poster presentation, oral thesis defense; for doctorate, thesis/dissertation (for some programs). *Entrance requirements:* For master's, minimum B average in last 2 years of full-time study, 3 letters of reference, resume. Additional exam requirements/recommendations for international students: Required—TOEFL (minimum score 600 paper-based), Michigan English Language Assessment Battery (minum score 88) or IELTS (minimum score 7). Electronic applications accepted.

University of Utah, Graduate School, College of Pharmacy, Department of Pharmacotherapy, Salt Lake City, UT 84112. Offers health system pharmacy administration (MS); outcomes research and health policy (PhD). *Faculty:* 5 full-time (3 women), 18 part-time/adjunct (13 women). *Students:* 2 full-time (0 women), 4 part-time (3 women), 1 international. Average age 28. 26 applicants, 19% accepted, 4 enrolled. In 2017, 5 master's, 2 doctorates awarded. Terminal master's awarded for partial completion of doctoral program. *Degree requirements:* For master's, comprehensive exam, thesis or alternative, project; for doctorate, comprehensive exam, thesis/dissertation. *Entrance requirements:* For doctorate, GRE. Additional exam requirements/recommendations for international students: Required—TOEFL (minimum score 550 paper-based; 80 iBT). *Application deadline:* For fall admission, 1/10 for domestic students, 12/15 for international students. Application fee: $55 ($65 for international students). *Financial support:* In 2017–18, 7 students received support, including 9 research assistantships with full tuition reimbursements available (averaging $21,400 per year); health care benefits also available. Financial award application deadline: 12/15. *Faculty research:* Outcomes in pharmacy, pharmacotherapy. *Total annual research expenditures:* $131,217. *Unit head:* Dr. Diana I. Brixner, Department Chair and Professor, 801-581-6731, E-mail: diana.brixner@utah.edu. *Application contact:* Ashley Weisman, Manager, Administration, 801-581-5984, Fax: 801-585-6160, E-mail: ashley.weisman@pharm.utah.edu.
Website: http://www.pharmacy.utah.edu/pharmacotherapy/

University of Washington, School of Pharmacy, Department of Pharmaceutics, Seattle, WA 98195. Offers MS, PhD, Pharm D/PhD. *Faculty:* 13 full-time (5 women). *Students:* 28 full-time (10 women); includes 11 minority (1 Black or African American, non-Hispanic/Latino; 7 Asian, non-Hispanic/Latino; 3 Hispanic/Latino), 6 international. Average age 30. 75 applicants, 11% accepted, 4 enrolled. In 2017, 6 doctorates awarded. Terminal master's awarded for partial completion of doctoral program. *Degree requirements:* For master's, thesis; for doctorate, thesis/dissertation. *Entrance requirements:* For master's and doctorate, GRE General Test. Additional exam requirements/recommendations for international students: Required—TOEFL. *Application deadline:* For fall admission, 12/31 for domestic and international students. Application fee: $85. Electronic applications accepted. *Financial support:* In 2017–18, 28 students received support, including 3 fellowships with full tuition reimbursements available (averaging $31,800 per year), 25 research assistantships with full tuition reimbursements available (averaging $31,800 per year); career-related internships or fieldwork, institutionally sponsored loans, scholarships/grants, traineeships, health care benefits, tuition waivers (full), and unspecified assistantships also available. *Faculty research:* Pharmacokinetics, drug delivery, drug metabolism, pharmacogenetics, transporters. *Unit head:* Dr. Kenneth E. Thummel, Chair, 206-543-9434, Fax: 206-543-3204, E-mail: thummel@u.washington.edu. *Application contact:* Kate Reinking, Graduate Program Advisor, 206-616-2797, Fax: 206-543-3204, E-mail: pceut@u.washington.edu.
Website: http://sop.washington.edu/pharmaceutics

University of Wisconsin–Madison, School of Pharmacy and Graduate School, Graduate Programs in Pharmacy, Pharmaceutical Sciences Division, Madison, WI 53705. Offers PhD. Terminal master's awarded for partial completion of doctoral program. *Degree requirements:* For doctorate, comprehensive exam, thesis/dissertation. *Entrance requirements:* For doctorate, GRE. Additional exam requirements/recommendations for international students: Required—TOEFL. Electronic applications accepted. *Faculty research:* Drug action, drug delivery, drug discovery.

University of Wisconsin–Madison, School of Pharmacy and Graduate School, Graduate Programs in Pharmacy, Social and Administrative Sciences in Pharmacy Division, Madison, WI 53706-1380. Offers MS, PhD. Terminal master's awarded for partial completion of doctoral program. *Degree requirements:* For master's, comprehensive exam (for some programs), thesis optional; for doctorate, comprehensive exam, thesis/dissertation. *Entrance requirements:* For master's and doctorate, GRE. Additional exam requirements/recommendations for international students: Required—TOEFL. Electronic applications accepted. *Faculty research:* Patient-provider communication, economics, patient care systems.

Virginia Commonwealth University, Medical College of Virginia-Professional Programs, School of Pharmacy, Department of Pharmaceutics, Richmond, VA 23284-9005. Offers medicinal chemistry (MS); pharmaceutical sciences (PhD); pharmaceutics (MS); pharmacotherapy and pharmacy administration (MS). Terminal master's awarded for partial completion of doctoral program. *Degree requirements:* For master's, thesis; for doctorate, thesis/dissertation. *Entrance requirements:* For master's and doctorate, GRE General Test. Additional exam requirements/recommendations for international students: Required—TOEFL. Electronic applications accepted. *Faculty research:* Drug delivery systems, drug development.

Wayne State University, Eugene Applebaum College of Pharmacy and Health Sciences, Department of Pharmaceutical Sciences, Detroit, MI 48202. Offers medicinal chemistry (MS, PhD); pharmaceutics (MS, PhD), including medicinal chemistry (PhD); pharmacology and toxicology (MS, PhD). *Faculty:* 20. *Students:* 23 full-time (17 women), 1 (woman) part-time, 19 international. Average age 29. 119 applicants, 9% accepted, 7 enrolled. In 2017, 7 master's, 3 doctorates awarded. *Degree requirements:* For master's, thesis; for doctorate, thesis/dissertation. *Entrance requirements:* For master's, GRE General Test, bachelor's degree; adequate background in biology, physics, calculus, and chemistry; three letters of recommendation; personal statement; for doctorate, GRE General Test, bachelor's or master's degree in one of the behavioral, biological, pharmaceutical or physical sciences; three letters of recommendation. Additional exam requirements/recommendations for international students: Required—TOEFL (minimum score 550 paper-based; 79 iBT), Michigan English Language Assessment Battery (minimum score 85); Recommended—IELTS (minimum score 6.5), TWE (minimum score 5.5). *Application deadline:* For fall admission, 12/1 priority date for domestic and international students. Applications are processed on a rolling basis. Application fee: $50. Electronic applications accepted. *Expenses:* Contact institution. *Financial support:* In 2017–18, 16 students received support, including 2 fellowships with tuition reimbursements available (averaging $26,000 per year), 11 research assistantships with full tuition reimbursements available (averaging $25,182 per year); scholarships/grants, health care benefits, and unspecified assistantships also available. Financial award applicants required to submit FAFSA. *Faculty research:* Design of new anthracyclines, genetic and epigenetic effects of extracellular inducers, cellular injury and cell death, drug metabolism and nutrition, anti-infective agents, carcinogenesis, diabetes research, Thera gnostic nanomedicines, neurotoxicity, drug discovery, insulin resistance. *Unit head:* Dr. George Corcoran, Chair and Professor, 313-577-1737, E-mail: corcoran@wayne.edu. *Application contact:* 313-577-5415, Fax: 313-577-2033, E-mail: pscgrad@wayne.edu.
Website: http://cphs.wayne.edu/sciences/index.php

Western University of Health Sciences, College of Pharmacy, Program in Pharmaceutical Sciences, Pomona, CA 91766-1854. Offers MS. *Faculty:* 12 full-time (4 women). *Students:* 11 full-time (7 women), 5 part-time (1 woman); includes 11 minority (1 Black or African American, non-Hispanic/Latino; 6 Asian, non-Hispanic/Latino; 2 Hispanic/Latino; 2 Two or more races, non-Hispanic/Latino), 3 international. Average age 25. 36 applicants, 22% accepted, 6 enrolled. In 2017, 8 master's awarded. *Degree requirements:* For master's, comprehensive exam. *Entrance requirements:* For master's, GRE, minimum overall GPA of 2.5; BS in pharmacy, chemistry, biology or related scientific area; letters of recommendation; curriculum vitae. Additional exam requirements/recommendations for international students: Required—TOEFL (minimum score 89 iBT), IELTS (minimum score 6.5). *Application deadline:* For fall admission, 4/1 for domestic and international students; for spring admission, 9/1 for domestic and international students. Applications are processed on a rolling basis. Application fee: $40. Electronic applications accepted. *Expenses:* $759 per unit. *Financial support:* In 2017–18, 14 students received support. Teaching assistantships with full and partial tuition reimbursements available and scholarships/grants available. Financial award application deadline: 3/2; financial award applicants required to submit FAFSA. *Faculty research:* The role of inflammation in acute and chronic conditions, zebrafish model of heart failure to study the quote; effect of e-cigarette vapor on inflammatory changes in oral and cardiovascular disease, formulation and drug delivery using lipids and liposomes, reversible lipidization of proteins and peptides. *Unit head:* Jeffrey Wang, Chair, 909-469-5413, Fax: 909-469-5539, E-mail: jwang@westernu.edu. *Application contact:* Kathryn Ford, Director of Admissions, 909-469-5335, Fax: 909-469-5570, E-mail: admissions@westernu.edu.
Website: http://www.westernu.edu/pharmacy-dpp_message

West Virginia University, School of Pharmacy, Morgantown, WV 26506-9500. Offers health services and outcomes research (PhD); pharmaceutical and pharmacological sciences (PhD); professional pharmacy (Pharm D). *Students:* 338 full-time (211 women), 3 part-time (2 women); includes 41 minority (10 Black or African American, non-Hispanic/Latino; 1 American Indian or Alaska Native, non-Hispanic/Latino; 15 Asian, non-Hispanic/Latino; 8 Hispanic/Latino; 7 Two or more races, non-Hispanic/Latino), 19 international. Terminal master's awarded for partial completion of doctoral program. *Degree requirements:* For doctorate, variable foreign language requirement, comprehensive exam (for some programs), thesis/dissertation (for some programs). *Entrance requirements:* For doctorate, GRE General Test (for PhD), minimum GPA of 2.75 (for PhD). Additional exam requirements/recommendations for international students: Required—TOEFL (minimum score 500 paper-based). *Application deadline:* For fall admission, 3/1 priority date for domestic and international students. Application fee: $60. Electronic applications accepted. *Expenses:* Contact institution. *Financial support:* Research assistantships, teaching assistantships, career-related internships or fieldwork, Federal Work-Study, institutionally sponsored loans, health care benefits, tuition waivers (full and partial), and unspecified assistantships available. Financial award application deadline: 3/1; financial award applicants required to submit FAFSA. *Faculty research:* Pharmaceutics, medicinal chemistry, biopharmaceutics/pharmacokinetics, health outcomes research. *Unit head:* Dr. Mary K. Stamatakis, Interim Dean, 304-293-5101, Fax: 304-293-5483, E-mail: mkstamatakis@hsc.wvu.edu. *Application contact:* Dr. Mary L. Euler, Associate Dean for Student Services, 304-293-7806, Fax: 304-293-5483, E-mail: mleuler@hsc.wvu.edu.
Website: https://pharmacy.hsc.wvu.edu

York College of the City University of New York, School of Arts and Sciences, Jamaica, NY 11451. Offers pharmaceutcial science and business (MS).

Pharmacy

Albany College of Pharmacy and Health Sciences, School of Pharmacy and Pharmaceutical Sciences, Albany, NY 12208. Offers health outcomes research (MS); pharmaceutical sciences (MS), including pharmaceutics, pharmacology; pharmacy (Pharm D). *Accreditation:* ACPE. *Degree requirements:* For master's, thesis; for doctorate, practice experience. *Entrance requirements:* For master's, GRE, minimum GPA of 3.0; for doctorate, PCAT, minimum GPA of 2.5. Additional exam requirements/recommendations for international students: Required—TOEFL (minimum score 84 iBT). Electronic applications accepted. *Faculty research:* Therapeutic use of drugs, pharmacokinetics, drug delivery and design.

Appalachian College of Pharmacy, Doctor of Pharmacy Program, Oakwood, VA 24631. Offers Pharm D. *Accreditation:* ACPE.

Auburn University, Harrison School of Pharmacy, Professional Program in Pharmacy, Auburn University, AL 36849. Offers Pharm D. *Accreditation:* ACPE. *Program availability:* Part-time. *Faculty:* 58 full-time (33 women), 1 (woman) part-time/adjunct. *Students:* 582 full-time (384 women), 1 part-time (0 women); includes 120 minority (51 Black or African American, non-Hispanic/Latino; 4 American Indian or Alaska Native, non-Hispanic/Latino; 45 Asian, non-Hispanic/Latino; 13 Hispanic/Latino; 1 Native Hawaiian or other Pacific Islander, non-Hispanic/Latino; 6 Two or more races, non-Hispanic/Latino), 4 international. Average age 25. 427 applicants, 70% accepted, 146 enrolled. In 2017, 153 doctorates awarded. *Expenses:* Contact institution. *Financial support:* Federal Work-Study available. Support available to part-time students. Financial award applicants required to submit FAFSA. *Unit head:* Dr. Richard Hansen, Dean/Professor, Harrison School of Pharmacy, 334-844-8348, Fax: 334-844-8307. *Application contact:* Dr. George Flowers, Dean of the Graduate School, 334-844-2125.

Belmont University, College of Pharmacy, Nashville, TN 37212. Offers advanced pharmacotherapy (Pharm D); health care informatics (Pharm D); management (Pharm D); missions/public health (Pharm D); Pharm D/MBA. Pharm D/MBA offered in collaboration with Jack C. Massey Graduate School of Business. *Accreditation:* ACPE. *Faculty:* 25 full-time (16 women), 3 part-time/adjunct (2 women). *Students:* 323 full-time (216 women); includes 90 minority (37 Black or African American, non-Hispanic/Latino; 38 Asian, non-Hispanic/Latino; 10 Hispanic/Latino; 5 Two or more races, non-Hispanic/Latino), 1 international. Average age 25. 638 applicants, 34% accepted, 94 enrolled. In 2017, 65 doctorates awarded. *Degree requirements:* For doctorate, comprehensive exam. *Entrance requirements:* For doctorate, PCAT. Additional exam requirements/recommendations for international students: Required—TOEFL. *Application deadline:* For fall admission, 8/31 priority date for domestic students; for spring admission, 3/1 for domestic students. Applications are processed on a rolling basis. Application fee: $50. Electronic applications accepted. *Expenses:* $18,670 tuition per semester. *Financial support:* In 2017–18, 112 students received support. Career-related internships or fieldwork and scholarships/grants available. Financial award applicants required to submit FAFSA. *Faculty research:* Academic innovation, cultural competency, medication errors, patient safety. *Unit head:* Dr. David Gregory, Dean, 615-460-6746, Fax: 615-460-6741, E-mail: david.gregory@belmont.edu.
Website: http://www.belmont.edu/pharmacy/index.html

Binghamton University, State University of New York, Graduate School, School of Pharmacy and Pharmaceutical Sciences, Binghamton, NY 13902-6000. Offers pharmacy (Pharm D). *Faculty:* 18 full-time (12 women). *Students:* 65 full-time (35 women); includes 44 minority (9 Black or African American, non-Hispanic/Latino; 30 Asian, non-Hispanic/Latino; 3 Hispanic/Latino; 2 Two or more races, non-Hispanic/Latino). Average age 24. 277 applicants, 52% accepted, 65 enrolled. *Application deadline:* For fall admission, 3/1 for domestic students. *Financial support:* In 2017–18, 2 students received support. *Unit head:* Dr. Gloria E. Meredith, Dean, 607-777-2761, E-mail: gmeredith@binghamton.edu. *Application contact:* Ben Balkaya, Assistant Dean and Director, 607-777-2151, Fax: 607-777-2501, E-mail: balkaya@binghamton.edu.
Website: http://www.binghamton.edu/pharmacy-and-pharmaceutical-sciences/

Butler University, College of Pharmacy and Health Sciences, Indianapolis, IN 46208-3485. Offers pharmaceutical science (MS); pharmacy (Pharm D), including medical

Spanish, research; physician assistant studies (MS). *Accreditation:* ACPE (one or more programs are accredited). *Faculty:* 62 full-time (42 women). *Students:* 390 full-time (302 women), 10 part-time (6 women); includes 35 minority (3 Black or African American, non-Hispanic/Latino; 21 Asian, non-Hispanic/Latino; 7 Hispanic/Latino; 4 Two or more races, non-Hispanic/Latino), 3 international. Average age 24. 581 applicants, 25% accepted, 131 enrolled. In 2017, 75 master's, 116 doctorates awarded. *Degree requirements:* For master's, comprehensive exam, research paper or thesis. *Entrance requirements:* For master's, GRE General Test, CASPA application, official transcripts, baccalaureate degree from accredited institution (for physician assistant studies). Additional exam requirements/recommendations for international students: Required—TOEFL (minimum score 550 paper-based; 79 iBT), IELTS (minimum score 6). *Application deadline:* For fall admission, 4/1 for domestic and international students. Application fee: $0. Electronic applications accepted. *Expenses:* Contact institution. *Financial support:* In 2017–18, 8 students received support. Scholarships/grants, tuition waivers (full and partial), and unspecified assistantships available. Financial award application deadline: 7/15; financial award applicants required to submit FAFSA. *Faculty research:* Cancer research; targeted drug delivery and pharmacokinetics; neuropharmacology; gene regulation; next generation sequencing. *Unit head:* Dr. Robert Soltis, Dean, 317-940-8056, E-mail: rsoltis@butler.edu. *Application contact:* Diane Dubord, Graduate Student Services Specialist, 317-940-8107, E-mail: ddubord@butler.edu.
Website: https://www.butler.edu/pharmacy-pa/about

California Health Sciences University, College of Pharmacy, Clovis, CA 93612. Offers Pharm D. *Accreditation:* ACPE.

California Northstate University, College of Pharmacy, Elk Grove, CA 95757. Offers Pharm D.

Campbell University, Graduate and Professional Programs, College of Pharmacy and Health Sciences, Buies Creek, NC 27506. Offers clinical research (MS); pharmaceutical sciences (MS); pharmacy (Pharm D); physician assistant (MPAP); public health (MS). *Accreditation:* ACPE. *Program availability:* Part-time, evening/weekend. *Entrance requirements:* For master's, MCAT, PCAT, GRE, bachelor's degree in health sciences or related field; for doctorate, PCAT. Additional exam requirements/recommendations for international students: Required—TOEFL (minimum score 550 paper-based; 79 iBT). Electronic applications accepted. *Expenses:* Contact institution. *Faculty research:* Immunology, medicinal chemistry, pharmaceutics, applied pharmacology.

Cedarville University, Graduate Programs, Cedarville, OH 45314. Offers business administration (MBA); family nurse practitioner (MSN); global ministry (M Div); global public health nursing (MSN); healthcare administration (MBA); ministry (M Min); nurse educator (MSN); operations management (MBA); pharmacy (Pharm D). *Program availability:* Part-time, evening/weekend, 100% online, blended/hybrid learning. *Faculty:* 23 full-time (9 women), 48 part-time/adjunct (21 women). *Students:* 202 full-time (123 women), 146 part-time (96 women); includes 63 minority (39 Black or African American, non-Hispanic/Latino; 3 American Indian or Alaska Native, non-Hispanic/Latino; 15 Asian, non-Hispanic/Latino; 2 Hispanic/Latino; 1 Native Hawaiian or other Pacific Islander, non-Hispanic/Latino; 3 Two or more races, non-Hispanic/Latino), 3 international. Average age 24. 345 applicants, 37% accepted, 91 enrolled. In 2017, 53 master's, 47 doctorates awarded. *Degree requirements:* For master's, portfolio; for doctorate, comprehensive exam. *Entrance requirements:* For master's, GRE, 2 professional recommendations; for doctorate, PCAT, professional recommendation from a practicing pharmacist or current employer/supervisor, resume, essay, interview. Additional exam requirements/recommendations for international students: Required—TOEFL (minimum score 550 paper-based; 80 iBT). *Application deadline:* For fall admission, 5/1 priority date for domestic and international students; for spring admission, 11/1 priority date for domestic and international students. Applications are processed on a rolling basis. Application fee: $0. Electronic applications accepted. *Expenses: Tuition:* Full-time $12,594; part-time $566 per credit. One-time fee: $100 full-time. Tuition and fees vary according to degree level and program. *Financial support:* Scholarships/grants and unspecified assistantships available. Support available to part-time students. Financial award application deadline: 1/30; financial award applicants required to submit FAFSA. *Faculty research:* Establishing competencies of clinical reasoning for nursing students in Taiwan, social determinants of health in pediatric primary care, meeting needs of palliative care populations, natural product utility in cancer, monoclonal antibodies directed at angiogenesis regulation. *Total annual research expenditures:* $3,800. *Unit head:* Dr. Janice Supplee, Dean of Graduate Studies, 937-766-7700, E-mail: suppleej@cedarville.edu. *Application contact:* Jim Amstutz, Director of Graduate Admissions, 937-766-7878, Fax: 937-766-7575, E-mail: amstutzj@cedarville.edu.
Website: https://www.cedarville.edu/Admissions/Graduate/Graduate-Programs.aspx

Chapman University, School of Pharmacy, Orange, CA 92866. Offers pharmaceutical sciences (MS, PhD); pharmacy (Pharm D). *Faculty:* 37 full-time (17 women), 7 part-time/adjunct (1 woman). *Students:* 290 full-time (177 women), 1 part-time (0 women); includes 192 minority (12 Black or African American, non-Hispanic/Latino; 1 American Indian or Alaska Native, non-Hispanic/Latino; 146 Asian, non-Hispanic/Latino; 24 Hispanic/Latino; 1 Native Hawaiian or other Pacific Islander, non-Hispanic/Latino; 8 Two or more races, non-Hispanic/Latino), 24 international. Average age 27. 725 applicants, 26% accepted, 107 enrolled. In 2017, 5 master's awarded. *Degree requirements:* For master's, thesis; for doctorate, capstone project. *Entrance requirements:* For doctorate, PCAT. *Application deadline:* Applications are processed on a rolling basis. Electronic applications accepted. *Expenses:* Contact institution. *Financial support:* Fellowships, research assistantships, Federal Work-Study, and scholarships/grants available. *Unit head:* Ronald P. Jordan, Dean, 714-516-5486, E-mail: rpjordan@chapman.edu. *Application contact:* Dr. Lawrence Brown, Associate Dean of Student and Academic Affairs, 714-516-5600, E-mail: pharmacyadmissions@chapman.edu.
Website: https://www.chapman.edu/pharmacy/index.aspx

Chicago State University, College of Pharmacy, Chicago, IL 60628. Offers Pharm D. *Accreditation:* ACPE. *Entrance requirements:* For doctorate, PCAT, minimum cumulative GPA of 2.5. *Application deadline:* For fall admission, 2/3 for domestic students. Application fee: $50. *Unit head:* Carmita A. Coleman, Interim Dean, E-mail: ccolem30@csu.edu. *Application contact:* Daphne G. Townsend, Admissions and Records Officer II, 773-995-2404, Fax: 773-995-3671, E-mail: g-studies1@csu.edu.
Website: http://www.csu.edu/pharmacy/

Concordia University Wisconsin, Graduate Programs, School of Pharmacy, Mequon, WI 53097-2402. Offers pharmaceutical/chemical product development (MPD); pharmacy (Pharm D).

Creighton University, School of Pharmacy and Health Professions, Professional Program in Pharmacy, Omaha, NE 68178-0001. Offers Pharm D. *Accreditation:* ACPE. *Program availability:* Online learning. *Entrance requirements:* For doctorate, PCAT. Additional exam requirements/recommendations for international students: Required—TOEFL. Electronic applications accepted. Part-time tuition and fees vary according to course load, degree level, campus/location and program. *Faculty research:* Patient safety in health services research, health information technology and health services research, nanotechnology and drug development, pharmacy practice outcomes research, cross-cultural care of patients in pharmacy practice.

Drake University, College of Pharmacy and Health Sciences, Des Moines, IA 50311-4516. Offers athletic training (MAT); occupational therapy (OTD); pharmacy (Pharm D); Pharm D/JD; Pharm D/MBA; Pharm D/MPA. *Accreditation:* ACPE. *Degree requirements:* For doctorate, rotations. *Entrance requirements:* For doctorate, PCAT, interview. Additional exam requirements/recommendations for international students: Required—TOEFL. *Application deadline:* For fall admission, 2/1 priority date for domestic students. Application fee: $135. Electronic applications accepted. *Expenses:* Contact institution. *Financial support:* Teaching assistantships, career-related internships or fieldwork, Federal Work-Study, institutionally sponsored loans, and scholarships/grants available. Support available to part-time students. Financial award application deadline: 3/1; financial award applicants required to submit FAFSA. *Faculty research:* Cost-benefit and cost-analysis of pharmaceutical products and services, patient satisfaction, community health planning and development, nutrition, ambulatory care. *Unit head:* Dr. Renae Chesnut, Dean, 515-271-3018, Fax: 515-271-4171, E-mail: renae.chesnut@drake.edu.
Website: http://www.drake.edu/cphs/

Duquesne University, School of Pharmacy, Pharm D Program, Pittsburgh, PA 15282. Offers Pharm D. *Accreditation:* ACPE. *Program availability:* Evening/weekend. *Faculty:* 48 full-time (21 women), 3 part-time/adjunct (0 women). *Students:* 662 full-time (418 women), 47 part-time (31 women); includes 81 minority (20 Black or African American, non-Hispanic/Latino; 33 Asian, non-Hispanic/Latino; 16 Hispanic/Latino; 12 Two or more races, non-Hispanic/Latino), 6 international. Average age 23. 368 applicants, 60% accepted, 200 enrolled. In 2017, 187 doctorates awarded. *Degree requirements:* For doctorate, comprehensive exam, Pharmacy Curriculum Outcomes Assessment Exam (PCOA). *Entrance requirements:* For doctorate, PCAT. Additional exam requirements/recommendations for international students: Required—TOEFL. *Application deadline:* For fall admission, 12/1 priority date for domestic and international students. Applications are processed on a rolling basis. Application fee: $0. Electronic applications accepted. *Expenses:* $1,440 per credit. *Financial support:* In 2017–18, 622 students received support. Federal Work-Study and scholarships/grants available. Financial award application deadline: 5/1; financial award applicants required to submit FAFSA. *Faculty research:* Synthesis of anti tumor agents, identification and management of asthma, Lewy body pathology in Parkinson's disease, design of drug delivery systems to modulate immune functions. *Total annual research expenditures:* $217,500. *Unit head:* Dr. Janet K. Astle, Assistant Dean for Student Services, 412-396-6393, Fax: 412-396-4375, E-mail: astle@duq.edu. *Application contact:* E-mail: pharmadmission@duq.edu.
Website: http://www.duq.edu/academics/schools/pharmacy/become-a-student/doctor-of-pharmacy

D'Youville College, School of Pharmacy, Buffalo, NY 14201-1084. Offers Pharm D. *Accreditation:* ACPE. *Entrance requirements:* For doctorate, PCAT, PharmCAS application, official transcripts from all colleges previously attended, three letters of recommendation. Electronic applications accepted. *Expenses:* Contact institution. *Faculty research:* Investigating anticancer properties of aspirin and other compounds; design, development, implementation and analysis of inter-professional educational programs, medication adherence and polypharmacy; geriatrics, medication reconciliation; buccal/transmucosal drug delivery, application of herbal medicine in cancer; acute care of internal medicine.

East Tennessee State University, Bill Gatton College of Pharmacy, Johnson City, TN 37614. Offers Pharm D. *Accreditation:* ACPE. *Program availability:* Part-time. *Faculty:* 52 full-time (30 women). *Students:* 311 full-time (178 women); includes 33 minority (14 Black or African American, non-Hispanic/Latino; 11 Asian, non-Hispanic/Latino; 5 Hispanic/Latino; 3 Two or more races, non-Hispanic/Latino), 6 international. Average age 25. 470 applicants, 37% accepted, 74 enrolled. In 2017, 76 doctorates awarded. *Degree requirements:* For doctorate, comprehensive exam. *Entrance requirements:* Additional exam requirements/recommendations for international students: Required—TOEFL (minimum score 550 paper-based; 79 iBT). *Application deadline:* For fall admission, 6/1 for domestic students, 4/29 for international students; for spring admission, 11/1 for domestic students, 9/29 for international students; for summer admission, 3/15 for domestic students, 2/1 for international students. Applications are processed on a rolling basis. Application fee: $55 ($65 for international students). Electronic applications accepted. *Unit head:* Dr. Debbie C. Byrd, Dean, 423-439-2068, Fax: 423-439-6310, E-mail: byrdc1@etsu.edu. *Application contact:* Admissions and Records Office, 423-439-6300, Fax: 423-439-6320, E-mail: pharmacy@etsu.edu.
Website: http://www.etsu.edu/pharmacy/

Fairleigh Dickinson University, Florham Campus, School of Pharmacy, Madison, NJ 07940-1099. Offers Pharm D. *Expenses: Tuition:* Full-time $22,410; part-time $1245 per credit. *Required fees:* $888; $414 per unit. Tuition and fees vary according to course load, degree level and program.

Ferris State University, College of Pharmacy, Big Rapids, MI 49307. Offers Pharm D. *Accreditation:* ACPE. *Program availability:* Part-time, evening/weekend, online learning. *Faculty:* 35 full-time (24 women), 4 part-time/adjunct (2 women). *Students:* 547 full-time (305 women), 18 part-time (8 women); includes 38 minority (5 Black or African American, non-Hispanic/Latino; 1 American Indian or Alaska Native, non-Hispanic/Latino; 12 Asian, non-Hispanic/Latino; 14 Hispanic/Latino; 6 Two or more races, non-Hispanic/Latino), 16 international. Average age 24. 404 applicants, 44% accepted, 143 enrolled. In 2017, 147 doctorates awarded. *Degree requirements:* For doctorate, 6 clerkships during 4th professional year which equals 1,740 hours of clerkship. *Entrance requirements:* For doctorate, PCAT, 3 years or more of pre-pharmacy course work. *Application deadline:* For fall admission, 2/1 for domestic and international students. Application fee: $150. *Expenses:* Contact institution. *Financial support:* Career-related internships or fieldwork, Federal Work-Study, institutionally sponsored loans, and scholarships/grants available. Financial award application deadline: 4/15; financial award applicants required to submit FAFSA. *Faculty research:* Diabetes, rural health education, managed care practice, antimicrobial pharmacotherapy, medicinal flora. *Unit head:* Dr. Stephen Durst, Dean, 231-591-2254, Fax: 231-591-3829, E-mail: dursts@ferris.edu. *Application contact:* Tara M. Lee, Director of Admissions, 231-591-2249, Fax: 231-591-3829, E-mail: leet@ferris.edu.
Website: http://www.ferris.edu/colleges/pharmacy/

Florida Agricultural and Mechanical University, Division of Graduate Studies, Research, and Continuing Education, College of Pharmacy and Pharmaceutical Sciences, Professional Program in Pharmacy and Pharmaceutical Sciences, Tallahassee, FL 32307-3200. Offers Pharm D. *Accreditation:* ACPE. *Entrance requirements:* Additional exam requirements/recommendations for international students: Required—TOEFL.

Georgia Campus–Philadelphia College of Osteopathic Medicine, School of Pharmacy, Suwanee, GA 30024. Offers Pharm D. *Accreditation:* ACPE. *Degree requirements:* For doctorate, capstone. *Entrance requirements:* For doctorate, PCAT. Additional exam requirements/recommendations for international students: Required—TOEFL (minimum score 79 iBT). Electronic applications accepted. *Expenses:* Contact institution.

See Display on the next page and Close-Up on page 919.

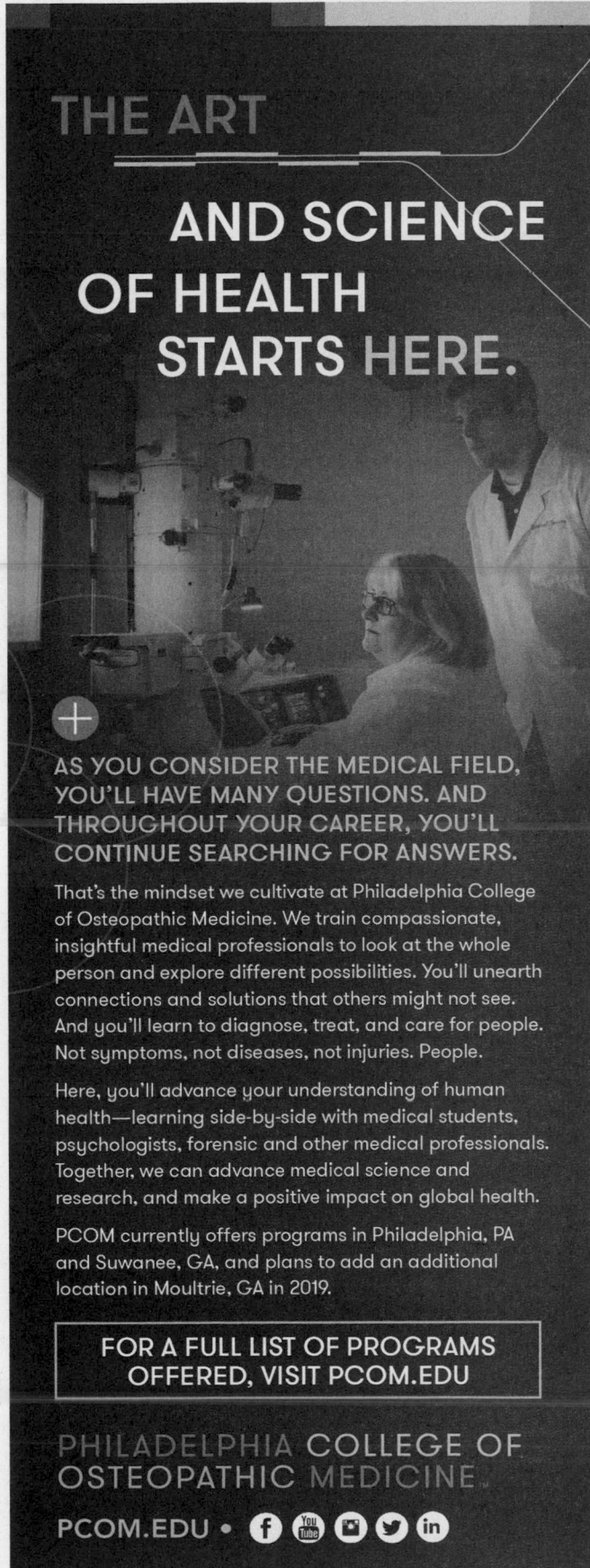

Harding University, College of Pharmacy, Searcy, AR 72147-2230. Offers Pharm D. *Accreditation:* ACPE. *Faculty:* 34 full-time (18 women), 1 part-time/adjunct (0 women). *Students:* 209 full-time (138 women), 4 part-time (3 women); includes 54 minority (21 Black or African American, non-Hispanic/Latino; 3 American Indian or Alaska Native, non-Hispanic/Latino; 25 Asian, non-Hispanic/Latino; 4 Hispanic/Latino; 1 Two or more races, non-Hispanic/Latino), 8 international. Average age 27. 293 applicants, 19% accepted, 36 enrolled. In 2017, 55 doctorates awarded. *Degree requirements:* For doctorate, licensure as a pharmacy intern in AR, completion of 300 hours of introductory pharmacy practice experience and 1,440 hours of advanced pharmacy practice experience. *Entrance requirements:* For doctorate, PCAT, 90 semester hours of undergraduate work. Additional exam requirements/recommendations for international students: Required—TOEFL (minimum score 550 paper-based). *Application deadline:* For fall admission, 3/1 priority date for domestic and international students. Applications are processed on a rolling basis. Application fee: $50. Electronic applications accepted. *Expenses:* Contact institution. *Financial support:* In 2017–18, 35 students received support. Scholarships/grants available. Financial award applicants required to submit FAFSA. *Faculty research:* Field stable molecular diagnostics reagent development; the impact of UGT2B17 genetic polymorphisms on the disposition and action exemestane in healthy volunteers; optimization of 5-FU cancer chemotherapy, evaluation of issues associated with pediatric dosing; exploration of the physiologic impact of salmonella toxins; clinical study evaluating a novel point of care device as compared to the current industry standard for measurement of prothrombin time. *Total annual research expenditures:* $53,000. *Unit head:* Dr. Jeff Mercer, Dean, 501-279-5205, Fax: 501-279-5525, E-mail: jmercer@harding.edu. *Application contact:* Carol Jones, Director of Admissions, 501-279-5523, Fax: 501-279-5525, E-mail: ccjones@harding.edu.
Website: http://www.harding.edu/pharmacy/

High Point University, Norcross Graduate School, High Point, NC 27268. Offers athletic training (MSAT); business administration (MBA); educational leadership (M Ed, Ed D); elementary education (M Ed, MAT); pharmacy (Pharm D); physical therapy (DPT); physician assistant studies (MPAS); secondary mathematics (M Ed, MAT); special education (M Ed); strategic communication (MA). *Accreditation:* NCATE. *Program availability:* Part-time, evening/weekend. *Degree requirements:* For master's, comprehensive exam (for some programs), thesis (for some programs). *Entrance requirements:* For master's, GMAT (MBA), GRE, MAT, minimum GPA of 3.0. Additional exam requirements/recommendations for international students: Required—TOEFL (minimum score 550 paper-based). Electronic applications accepted.

Howard University, College of Pharmacy, Washington, DC 20059-0002. Offers Pharm D, Pharm D/MBA. *Accreditation:* ACPE. *Program availability:* Online learning. *Degree requirements:* For doctorate, comprehensive exam. *Entrance requirements:* For doctorate, PCAT, minimum GPA of 2.5. Electronic applications accepted. *Expenses:* Contact institution. *Faculty research:* Kinetics of drug absorption, stealth liposomes, synthesis, opiate analgesics.

Husson University, School of Pharmacy, Bangor, ME 04401-2999. Offers pharmacology (MS); pharmacy (Pharm D). *Accreditation:* ACPE. *Faculty:* 24 full-time (7 women), 1 part-time/adjunct (0 women). *Students:* 189 full-time (109 women); includes 55 minority (26 Black or African American, non-Hispanic/Latino; 2 American Indian or Alaska Native, non-Hispanic/Latino; 20 Asian, non-Hispanic/Latino; 6 Hispanic/Latino; 1 Two or more races, non-Hispanic/Latino), 7 international. Average age 26. 158 applicants, 48% accepted, 46 enrolled. In 2017, 56 doctorates awarded. *Entrance requirements:* For doctorate, PCAT, PharmCAS application. Additional exam requirements/recommendations for international students: Required—TOEFL (minimum score 550 paper-based; 80 iBT), IELTS (minimum score 6.5). *Application deadline:* For fall admission, 3/1 for domestic students. Application fee: $50 ($0 for international students). Electronic applications accepted. *Expenses:* $968 per credit; $580 in fees per year. *Financial support:* In 2017–18, 112 students received support. Federal Work-Study, scholarships/grants, and unspecified assistantships available. Financial award application deadline: 3/1; financial award applicants required to submit FAFSA. *Faculty research:* Development of nanoparticles for noninvasive delivery of therapeutic agents; clinical implications in anti-infective resistance; using stochastic modeling to determine appropriate antibiotic selection, infectious diseases surveillance and epidemiology; impaired healing in individuals with diabetes; assessment of pharmaceutical needs in rural settings in the midst of the changing health care environment. *Total annual research expenditures:* $25,460. *Unit head:* Dr. Rodney A. Larson, Dean, 207-941-7122, E-mail: larsonr@husson.edu. *Application contact:* Kristen Card, Director of Graduate Admissions, 207-404-5660, E-mail: cardk@husson.edu.
Website: http://www.husson.edu/pharmacy

Idaho State University, Office of Graduate Studies, College of Pharmacy, Department of Pharmacy Practice and Administrative Sciences, Pocatello, ID 83209-8333. Offers pharmacy (Pharm D); pharmacy administration (MS, PhD). *Accreditation:* ACPE (one or more programs are accredited). *Program availability:* Part-time. *Degree requirements:* For master's, one foreign language, comprehensive exam, thesis, thesis research, speech and technical writing classes; for doctorate, comprehensive exam, thesis/dissertation, oral and written exams, speech and technical writing classes. *Entrance requirements:* For master's, GRE General Test, minimum GPA of 3.0, 3 letters of recommendation; for doctorate, GRE General Test, BS in pharmacy or related field, minimum GPA of 3.0, 3 letters of recommendation. Additional exam requirements/recommendations for international students: Required—TOEFL (minimum score 550 paper-based; 80 iBT). Electronic applications accepted. *Expenses:* Contact institution. *Faculty research:* Pharmaceutical care outcomes, drug use review, pharmacoeconomics.

Keck Graduate Institute, School of Pharmacy, Claremont, CA 91711. Offers Pharm D.

Lake Erie College of Osteopathic Medicine, Professional Programs, Erie, PA 16509-1025. Offers biomedical sciences (Postbaccalaureate Certificate); medical education (MS); osteopathic medicine (DO); pharmacy (Pharm D). *Accreditation:* ACPE; AOsA. *Degree requirements:* For doctorate, comprehensive exam, National Osteopathic Medical Licensing Exam, Levels 1 and 2; for Postbaccalaureate Certificate, comprehensive exam, North American Pharmacist Licensure Examination (NAPLEX). *Entrance requirements:* For doctorate, MCAT, minimum GPA of 3.2, letters of recommendation; for Postbaccalaureate Certificate, PCAT, letters of recommendation, minimum GPA of 3.5. Electronic applications accepted. *Faculty research:* Cardiac smooth and skeletal muscle mechanics, chemotherapeutics and vitamins, osteopathic manipulation.

Lebanese American University, School of Pharmacy, Beirut, Lebanon. Offers Pharm D. *Accreditation:* ACPE.

Lipscomb University, College of Pharmacy, Nashville, TN 37204-3951. Offers healthcare informatics (MS); pharmacy (Pharm D); Pharm D/MM; Pharm D/MS. *Accreditation:* ACPE. *Faculty:* 36 full-time (17 women), 1 (woman) part-time/adjunct. *Students:* 349 full-time (227 women), 20 part-time (15 women); includes 100 minority (42 Black or African American, non-Hispanic/Latino; 4 American Indian or Alaska Native, non-Hispanic/Latino; 34 Asian, non-Hispanic/Latino; 13 Hispanic/Latino; 7 Two or more races, non-Hispanic/Latino), 3 international. Average age 26. 550 applicants, 33% accepted, 99 enrolled. In 2017, 22 master's, 72 doctorates awarded. *Degree*

requirements: For master's, capstone project; for doctorate, comprehensive exam. *Entrance requirements:* For master's, GRE, 2 references, transcripts, resume, personal statement, eligibility documentation (degree and/or experience in related area); for doctorate, PCAT (minimum 45th percentile), 66 pre-professional semester hours, minimum GPA of 2.5, interview, PharmCAS application (for international students). Additional exam requirements/recommendations for international students: Required—TOEFL (minimum score 550 paper-based; 80 iBT). *Application deadline:* For fall admission, 2/7 for domestic students. Applications are processed on a rolling basis. Application fee: $50 ($75 for international students). Electronic applications accepted. *Expenses:* Contact institution. *Financial support:* Application deadline: 2/15; applicants required to submit FAFSA. *Total annual research expenditures:* $1.3 million. *Unit head:* Dr. Roger Davis, Dean/Professor of Pharmacy Practice, 615-966-7161. *Application contact:* Laura Ward, Director of Admissions and Student Affairs, 615-966-7173, E-mail: laura.ward@lipscomb.edu.
Website: http://lipscomb.edu/pharmacy

Loma Linda University, School of Pharmacy, Loma Linda, CA 92350. Offers Pharm D. *Accreditation:* ACPE. *Degree requirements:* For doctorate, intern pharmacist license.

Long Island University–Hudson, Graduate School, Purchase, NY 10577. Offers autism (Advanced Certificate); bilingual education (Advanced Certificate); childhood education (MS Ed); crisis management (Advanced Certificate); early childhood education (MS Ed); educational leadership (MS Ed); health administration (MPA); literacy (MS Ed); marriage and family therapy (MS); mental health counseling (MS, Advanced Certificate), including credentialed alcoholism and substance abuse counselor (MS); middle childhood and adolescence education (MS Ed); pharmaceutics (MS), including cosmetic science, industrial pharmacy; public administration (MPA); school counseling (MS Ed, Advanced Certificate); school psychology (MS Ed); special education (MS Ed); TESOL (MS Ed); TESOL (all grades) (Advanced Certificate). *Program availability:* Part-time, evening/weekend. *Faculty:* 8 full-time (6 women), 41 part-time/adjunct (24 women). *Students:* 69 full-time (54 women), 249 part-time (200 women); includes 102 minority (29 Black or African American, non-Hispanic/Latino; 1 American Indian or Alaska Native, non-Hispanic/Latino; 9 Asian, non-Hispanic/Latino; 62 Hispanic/Latino; 1 Native Hawaiian or other Pacific Islander, non-Hispanic/Latino). Average age 33. 153 applicants, 96% accepted, 103 enrolled. In 2017, 138 master's, 36 other advanced degrees awarded. *Entrance requirements:* Additional exam requirements/recommendations for international students: Required—TOEFL. *Application deadline:* Applications are processed on a rolling basis. Application fee: $50. Electronic applications accepted. *Expenses:* Contact institution. *Financial support:* In 2017–18, 32 students received support. Scholarships/grants available. Support available to part-time students. Financial award application deadline: 2/15; financial award applicants required to submit FAFSA. *Unit head:* Dr. Sylvia Blake, Dean and Chief Operating Officer, 914-831-2700, E-mail: westchester@liu.edu.

Long Island University–LIU Brooklyn, Arnold and Marie Schwartz College of Pharmacy and Health Sciences, Brooklyn, NY 11201-8423. Offers drug regulatory affairs (MS); pharmaceutics (MS, PhD), including cosmetic science (MS), industrial pharmacy (MS); pharmacology and toxicology (MS); pharmacy (Pharm D). *Accreditation:* ACPE. *Program availability:* Part-time. *Faculty:* 51 full-time (29 women), 33 part-time/adjunct (14 women). *Students:* 497 full-time (296 women), 77 part-time (42 women); includes 228 minority (26 Black or African American, non-Hispanic/Latino; 143 Asian, non-Hispanic/Latino; 31 Hispanic/Latino; 28 Two or more races, non-Hispanic/Latino), 137 international. Average age 25. 241 applicants, 62% accepted, 38 enrolled. In 2017, 57 master's, 183 doctorates awarded. Terminal master's awarded for partial completion of doctoral program. *Degree requirements:* For master's, comprehensive exam, thesis; for doctorate, comprehensive exam, thesis/dissertation. *Entrance requirements:* For master's and doctorate, GRE. Additional exam requirements/recommendations for international students: Required—TOEFL (minimum score 550 paper-based, 79 iBT) or IELTS. *Application deadline:* Applications are processed on a rolling basis. Application fee: $50. Electronic applications accepted. *Expenses:* Contact institution. *Financial support:* In 2017–18, 200 students received support. Research assistantships, teaching assistantships, career-related internships or fieldwork, Federal Work-Study, scholarships/grants, tuition waivers (full and partial), and unspecified assistantships available. Support available to part-time students. Financial award application deadline: 2/15; financial award applicants required to submit FAFSA. *Faculty research:* Preformulation, formulation and drug delivery; pharmacokinetics; pharmacology research; drug regulatory affairs; pharmaceutical analysis. *Total annual research expenditures:* $100,000. *Unit head:* Dr. John M. Pezzuto, Dean, 718-488-1004, Fax: 718-488-0628, E-mail: john.pezzuto@liu.edu. *Application contact:* Michael Young, Senior Assistant Director of Admissions, 718-488-1000, E-mail: michael.young@liu.edu.
Website: http://liu.edu/Pharmacy

Manchester University, Doctor of Pharmacy Program, Fort Wayne, IN 46845. Offers Pharm D. *Accreditation:* ACPE. *Faculty:* 33 full-time (17 women). *Students:* 281 full-time (168 women), 8 part-time (3 women); includes 95 minority (36 Black or African American, non-Hispanic/Latino; 1 American Indian or Alaska Native, non-Hispanic/Latino; 47 Asian, non-Hispanic/Latino; 9 Hispanic/Latino; 1 Native Hawaiian or other Pacific Islander, non-Hispanic/Latino; 1 Two or more races, non-Hispanic/Latino). Average age 24. 610 applicants, 18% accepted, 74 enrolled. *Degree requirements:* For doctorate, service learning, portfolio, competency assessments. *Entrance requirements:* For doctorate, minimum GPA of 2.5 (cumulative and prerequisites), minimum C grade on all prerequisite courses, U.S. citizenship or permanent residency, PharmCAS and supplemental application, 3 letters of recommendation. *Application deadline:* For fall admission, 3/1 for domestic students. Application fee: $175. Electronic applications accepted. *Expenses:* $39,300. *Faculty research:* Pharmacogenetics and pharmacogenomics, neuroprotection and neuroinflammation, drug formulation and delivery, health services research, infectious disease epidemiology. *Unit head:* W. Thomas Smith, Dean of Pharmacy Programs/Professor of Pharmaceutical Sciences, 260-470-2668, E-mail: wtsmith@manchester.edu. *Application contact:* Greg Hetrick, Director of Enrollment and Student Services, 260-470-2656, E-mail: gbhetrick@manchester.edu.
Website: https://www.manchester.edu/academics/colleges/college-of-pharmacy-natural-health-sciences/academic-programs/pharmacy

Marshall B. Ketchum University, Graduate and Professional Programs, Fullerton, CA 92831-1615. Offers optometry (OD); pharmacy (Pharm D); vision science (MS). *Degree requirements:* For doctorate, thesis/dissertation. *Entrance requirements:* For doctorate, OAT. Electronic applications accepted. *Faculty research:* Structure and function of the human visual system.

Marshall University, Academic Affairs Division, School of Pharmacy, Huntington, WV 25755. Offers Pharm D. *Accreditation:* ACPE. *Faculty:* 10 full-time (5 women). *Students:* 307 part-time (162 women); includes 50 minority (16 Black or African American, non-Hispanic/Latino; 1 American Indian or Alaska Native, non-Hispanic/Latino; 19 Asian, non-Hispanic/Latino; 8 Hispanic/Latino; 6 Two or more races, non-Hispanic/Latino). Average age 26. In 2017, 65 doctorates awarded. *Unit head:* Dr. Kevin W. Yingling, Founding Dean, 304-696-7302, E-mail: pharmacy@marshall.edu. *Application contact:* Dr. Tammy Johnson, Graduate Admissions, 304-746-1900, Fax: 304-746-1902, E-mail: services@marshall.edu.
Website: http://www.marshall.edu/wpmu/pharmacy/

MCPHS University, Graduate Studies, Doctoral Programs in Pharmacy–Boston, Doctor of Pharmacy Program - Boston, Boston, MA 02115-5896. Offers Pharm D. Students enter program as undergraduates. *Accreditation:* ACPE. *Program availability:* Online learning. *Entrance requirements:* For doctorate, SAT (if fewer than 30 semester hours completed), minimum GPA of 2.5, interview. Additional exam requirements/recommendations for international students: Required—TOEFL (minimum score 550 paper-based; 79 iBT). Electronic applications accepted.

MCPHS University, Graduate Studies, Doctoral Programs in Pharmacy–Boston, Postbaccalaureate Doctor of Pharmacy Pathway Program, Boston, MA 02115-5896. Offers Pharm D. *Program availability:* Part-time, online learning. *Entrance requirements:* For doctorate, registered pharmacist status in the U.S.; working at or have access to a site that provides opportunities to practice pharmaceutical care; curriculum vitae; letter of recommendation. Additional exam requirements/recommendations for international students: Required—TOEFL (minimum score 550 paper-based; 79 iBT). Electronic applications accepted.

MCPHS University, School of Pharmacy–Worcester/Manchester, Boston, MA 02115-5896. Offers Pharm D. *Accreditation:* ACPE. *Entrance requirements:* Additional exam requirements/recommendations for international students: Required—TOEFL (minimum score 550 paper-based; 79 iBT).

Medical College of Wisconsin, Pharmacy School, Milwaukee, WI 53226-0509. Offers Pharm D. *Entrance requirements:* For doctorate, interview. *Application deadline:* For fall admission, 5/1 for domestic students. *Unit head:* Dr. George E. MacKinnon, III, Dean, E-mail: gmackinnon@mcw.edu. *Application contact:* Dr. George E. MacKinnon, III, Dean, E-mail: gmackinnon@mcw.edu.
Website: http://www.mcw.edu/Pharmacy-School.htm

Medical University of South Carolina, South Carolina College of Pharmacy, Charleston, SC 29425. Offers Pharm D. *Accreditation:* ACPE. *Entrance requirements:* For doctorate, PCAT, 2 years of pre-professional course work, interview, minimum GPA of 2.5. Additional exam requirements/recommendations for international students: Required—TOEFL (minimum score 550 paper-based). Electronic applications accepted. *Expenses:* Contact institution. *Faculty research:* Rational and computer aided drug design; drug metabolism and transport; molecular immunology and cellular toxicology; cell injury, death and regeneration; outcome sciences.

Mercer University, Graduate Studies, Cecil B. Day Campus, College of Pharmacy, Atlanta, GA 30341. Offers pharmaceutical sciences (PhD); pharmacy (Pharm D); Pharm D/MBA; Pharm D/MPH; Pharm D/PhD. PharmD/MBA offered jointly with Eugene W. Stetson School of Business and Economics; PharmD/MPH with College of Health Professions; PharmD/MSHI with Penfield College. *Accreditation:* ACPE (one or more programs are accredited). *Faculty:* 44 full-time (27 women), 1 part-time/adjunct (0 women). *Students:* 635 full-time (407 women), 6 part-time (4 women); includes 397 minority (150 Black or African American, non-Hispanic/Latino; 206 Asian, non-Hispanic/Latino; 27 Hispanic/Latino; 14 Two or more races, non-Hispanic/Latino), 43 international. Average age 26. 677 applicants, 48% accepted, 152 enrolled. In 2017, 166 doctorates awarded. *Degree requirements:* For doctorate, comprehensive exam (for some programs), thesis/dissertation (for some programs). *Entrance requirements:* For doctorate, GRE (for PhD); PCAT, MCAT, DAT, OAT, GRE (for Pharm D), Pharm D or BS in pharmacy or science and minimum GPA of 3.0 (for PhD); 66 hours of undergraduate pre-pharmacy coursework (for PharmD). Additional exam requirements/recommendations for international students: Required—TOEFL (minimum score 100 iBT). *Application deadline:* For fall admission, 6/3 for domestic and international students. Applications are processed on a rolling basis. Electronic applications accepted. *Expenses:* $35,606 per year tuition, $484 course fee in final year (for Pharm D). *Financial support:* In 2017–18, 238 students received support, including 10 research assistantships with full tuition reimbursements available (averaging $15,000 per year), 35 teaching assistantships with full tuition reimbursements available (averaging $15,000 per year); Federal Work-Study, scholarships/grants, and tuition waivers (full) also available. Financial award application deadline: 5/1; financial award applicants required to submit FAFSA. *Faculty research:* Nanosphere-based drug delivery, transdermal drug delivery, molecular pharmacology, behavioral pharmacology, cell signaling. *Total annual research expenditures:* $479,640. *Unit head:* Dr. Brian L. Crabtree, Dean, 678-547-6306, Fax: 678-547-6315, E-mail: crabtree_bl@mercer.edu. *Application contact:* Jordana S. Berry, Director of Admissions, 678-547-6182, Fax: 678-547-6518, E-mail: berry_js@mercer.edu.
Website: http://pharmacy.mercer.edu/

Midwestern University, Downers Grove Campus, Chicago College of Pharmacy, Downers Grove, IL 60515-1235. Offers Pharm D. *Accreditation:* ACPE. *Program availability:* Part-time, online learning. *Entrance requirements:* For doctorate, PCAT. *Application deadline:* For fall admission, 2/3 for domestic students. Application fee: $50. *Expenses:* Contact institution. *Financial support:* Federal Work-Study and institutionally sponsored loans available. Support available to part-time students. Financial award applicants required to submit FAFSA.
Website: http://www.midwestern.edu/Programs_and_Admission/IL_Pharmacy.html

Midwestern University, Glendale Campus, College of Pharmacy-Glendale, Glendale, AZ 85308. Offers Pharm D. *Accreditation:* ACPE. *Entrance requirements:* For doctorate, PCAT. *Application deadline:* For fall admission, 2/1 for domestic students. Application fee: $50. *Expenses:* Contact institution. *Financial support:* Applicants required to submit FAFSA.
Website: http://www.midwestern.edu/Programs_and_Admission/AZ_Pharmacy.html

North Dakota State University, College of Graduate and Interdisciplinary Studies, College of Health Professions, School of Pharmacy, Fargo, ND 58102. Offers MS, PhD, Pharm D, Pharm D/MBA, Pharm D/MPH, Pharm D/PhD. *Accreditation:* ACPE. *Program availability:* Part-time. Terminal master's awarded for partial completion of doctoral program. *Entrance requirements:* For master's and doctorate, GRE General Test. Additional exam requirements/recommendations for international students: Required—TOEFL. *Application deadline:* For fall admission, 3/15 priority date for domestic students; for spring admission, 11/15 priority date for domestic students. Applications are processed on a rolling basis. Application fee: $35. Electronic applications accepted. *Expenses:* Tuition, state resident: full-time $4323; part-time $360.21 per credit. Tuition, nonresident: full-time $6484; part-time $540.31 per credit. *Required fees:* $668; $55.70 per credit. Part-time tuition and fees vary according to degree level, program and reciprocity agreements. *Financial support:* Application deadline: 4/15. *Faculty research:* Subcellular pharmacokinetics, cancer, cardiovascular drug design, iontophoresis, neuropharmacology. *Unit head:* Dr. Jagdish Singh, Chair, Department of Pharmaceutical Sciences, 701-231-7943, E-mail: jagdish.singh@ndsu.edu. *Application contact:* Dr. Jagdish Singh, Chair, Department of Pharmaceutical Sciences, 701-231-7943, E-mail: jagdish.singh@ndsu.edu.
Website: http://www.ndsu.edu/pharmacy/

Northeastern University, Bouvé College of Health Sciences, Boston, MA 02115-5096. Offers applied behavior analysis (MS); audiology (Au D); counseling psychology (MS, PhD, CAGS); exercise science (MS); nursing (MS, PhD, CAGS), including administration (MS), adult-gerontology acute care nurse practitioner (MS, CAGS), adult-gerontology primary care nurse practitioner (MS, CAGS), anesthesia (MS), family nurse

practitioner (MS, CAGS), neonatal nurse practitioner (MS, CAGS), pediatric nurse practitioner (MS, CAGS), psychiatric mental health nurse practitioner (MS, CAGS); nursing practice (DNP); pharmaceutical sciences (MS, PhD), including interdisciplinary concentration, pharmaceutics and drug delivery systems; pharmacology (MS); pharmacy (Pharm D); school psychology (PhD); speech-language pathology (MS); urban health (MPH); MS/MBA. *Accreditation:* ACPE (one or more programs are accredited). *Program availability:* Part-time, evening/weekend, online learning. *Faculty:* 192 full-time. *Students:* 1,685. In 2017, 352 master's, 312 doctorates, 25 other advanced degrees awarded. *Degree requirements:* For doctorate, thesis/dissertation (for some programs); for CAGS, comprehensive exam. Application fee: $75. Electronic applications accepted. *Expenses:* Contact institution. *Financial support:* Fellowships, research assistantships, teaching assistantships, career-related internships or fieldwork, scholarships/grants, health care benefits, tuition waivers, and unspecified assistantships available. Support available to part-time students. Financial award applicants required to submit FAFSA. *Unit head:* Susan L. Parish, Dean, Bouve College of Health Sciences, 617-373-3321, Fax: 617-373-3030, E-mail: s.parish@northeastern.edu. *Application contact:* 617-373-2708, Fax: 617-373-4701, E-mail: bouvegrad@northeastern.edu.
Website: https://www.northeastern.edu/bouve/

Northeast Ohio Medical University, College of Pharmacy, Rootstown, OH 44272-0095. Offers Pharm D. *Accreditation:* ACPE. *Faculty:* 24 full-time (11 women), 579 part-time/adjunct (320 women). *Students:* 302 full-time (168 women); includes 64 minority (21 Black or African American, non-Hispanic/Latino; 33 Asian, non-Hispanic/Latino; 7 Hispanic/Latino; 3 Two or more races, non-Hispanic/Latino). 400 applicants, 33% accepted, 75 enrolled. In 2017, 77 doctorates awarded. *Entrance requirements:* For doctorate, Pharmacy College Application Service (PharmCAS) application. *Application deadline:* For fall admission, 3/1 priority date for domestic students; for winter admission, 1/5 for domestic students. Applications are processed on a rolling basis. Application fee: $0. Electronic applications accepted. *Expenses:* Contact institution. *Financial support:* Institutionally sponsored loans and scholarships/grants available. Financial award application deadline: 3/15; financial award applicants required to submit FAFSA. *Faculty research:* Cancer, metabolic and liver disease, neurodegenerative diseases and psychiatric illness, drug delivery systems. *Total annual research expenditures:* $3.3 million. *Unit head:* Dr. Charles Taylor, Dean, 330-325-6461, Fax: 330-325-5930. *Application contact:* Heidi Terry, Executive Director, Enrollment Services, 330-325-6479, E-mail: hterry@neomed.edu.
Website: http://www.neomed.edu/academics/pharmacy

Notre Dame of Maryland University, Graduate Studies, Program in Pharmacy, Baltimore, MD 21210-2476. Offers Pharm D. *Accreditation:* ACPE.

Nova Southeastern University, College of Pharmacy, Fort Lauderdale, FL 33328. Offers pharmaceutical affairs (MS); pharmaceutical sciences (MS, PhD), including drug development, molecular medicine and pharmacogenomics, social and administrative pharmacy; pharmacy (Pharm D); Pharm D/MBA; Pharm D/MPH; Pharm D/MSBI. *Accreditation:* ACPE. *Faculty:* 115 full-time (38 women), 3 part-time/adjunct (1 woman). *Students:* 977 full-time (670 women), 48 part-time (28 women); includes 773 minority (71 Black or African American, non-Hispanic/Latino; 168 Asian, non-Hispanic/Latino; 518 Hispanic/Latino; 1 Native Hawaiian or other Pacific Islander, non-Hispanic/Latino; 15 Two or more races, non-Hispanic/Latino), 86 international. Average age 27. 1,047 applicants, 35% accepted, 248 enrolled. In 2017, 242 doctorates awarded. Terminal master's awarded for partial completion of doctoral program. *Degree requirements:* For master's, thesis or alternative; for doctorate, comprehensive exam, thesis/dissertation. *Entrance requirements:* For master's, PCAT or GRE (for pharmaceutical affairs); GRE (for pharmaceutical sciences); for doctorate, PCAT (for Pharm D); GRE (for PhD). *Application deadline:* For fall admission, 3/15 for domestic and international students. Applications are processed on a rolling basis. Application fee: $50. Electronic applications accepted. Tuition and fees vary according to course load, degree level and program. *Financial support:* In 2017–18, 62 students received support, including 12 teaching assistantships with full tuition reimbursements available (averaging $45,465 per year); career-related internships or fieldwork, Federal Work-Study, scholarships/grants, tuition waivers (full), and unspecified assistantships also available. Financial award application deadline: 4/15; financial award applicants required to submit FAFSA. *Faculty research:* Cancer, health care delivery, pharmacoeconomics, cardiovascular/metabolic diseases, autism, neuroscience. *Total annual research expenditures:* $344,728. *Unit head:* Dr. Lisa Deziel, Dean, 954-262-1304, Fax: 954-262-2278, E-mail: copdean@nova.edu. *Application contact:* Jennifer Gundersen, Admissions Counselor, 954-262-1112, Fax: 954-262-2282, E-mail: nsupharmacyinfo@nova.edu.
Website: http://pharmacy.nova.edu/

See Display below and Close-Up on page 921.

Ohio Northern University, Raabe College of Pharmacy, Ada, OH 45810-1599. Offers Pharm D. Students enter the program as undergraduates. *Accreditation:* ACPE. *Faculty:* 26 full-time (11 women), 2 part-time/adjunct (0 women). *Students:* 558 full-time (370 women), 9 part-time (8 women); includes 64 minority (11 Black or African American, non-Hispanic/Latino; 25 Asian, non-Hispanic/Latino; 5 Hispanic/Latino; 23 Two or more races, non-Hispanic/Latino), 22 international. Average age 22. 658 applicants, 50% accepted, 172 enrolled. In 2017, 153 doctorates awarded. *Degree requirements:* For doctorate, 9 clinical rotations, capstone course. *Entrance requirements:* For doctorate, ACT or SAT. Additional exam requirements/recommendations for international students: Required—TOEFL (minimum score 550 paper-based; 80 iBT). *Expenses:* Contact institution. *Financial support:* Federal Work-Study, institutionally sponsored loans, and scholarships/grants available. Financial award applicants required to submit FAFSA. *Faculty research:* Alcohol and substance abuse, women in pharmacy, non-traditional educations, continuing pharmaceutical education, medicinal chemistry. *Unit head:* Dr. Steve Martin, Interim Dean, 419-772-2277, Fax: 419-772-2282, E-mail: s-martin.11@onu.edu. *Application contact:* Dr. Kelly Shields, Assistant Dean of Student Services, 419-772-2752, Fax: 419-772-2752, E-mail: k-shields@onu.edu.
Website: http://www.onu.edu/pharmacy/

The Ohio State University, College of Pharmacy, Columbus, OH 43210. Offers MS, PhD, Pharm D, Pharm D/MBA, Pharm D/MPH, Pharm D/PhD. *Accreditation:* ACPE (one or more programs are accredited). *Faculty:* 53. *Students:* 608 (331 women); includes 175 minority (42 Black or African American, non-Hispanic/Latino; 97 Asian, non-Hispanic/Latino; 22 Hispanic/Latino; 14 Two or more races, non-Hispanic/Latino), 61 international. Average age 25. In 2017, 15 master's, 127 doctorates awarded. Terminal master's awarded for partial completion of doctoral program. *Degree requirements:* For doctorate, comprehensive exam (for some programs), thesis/dissertation (for some programs). *Entrance requirements:* For master's, GRE General Test, minimum GPA of 3.0; for doctorate, GRE General Test; PCAT (for PharmD), minimum GPA of 3.0. Additional exam requirements/recommendations for international students: Required—TOEFL minimum score 600 paper-based, 100 iBT (for MS and PhD); TOEFL minimum score 577 paper-based; 90 iBT, Michigan English Language Assessment Battery minimum score 84, IELTS minimum score 7.5 (for PharmD). *Application deadline:* For fall admission, 12/15 for domestic and international students. Application fee: $60 ($70 for international students). Electronic applications accepted. *Expenses:* Contact institution. *Financial support:* Fellowships with full tuition reimbursements, research assistantships with full tuition reimbursements, teaching assistantships with full tuition reimbursements, career-related internships or fieldwork, Federal Work-Study, institutionally sponsored loans, scholarships/grants, and traineeships available. *Unit head:* Dr. Henry J. Mann, Dean and Professor, 614-292-5711, Fax: 614-292-2588, E-mail: mann.414@osu.edu. *Application contact:* E-mail: admissions@pharmacy.ohio-state.edu.
Website: http://www.pharmacy.osu.edu

Pharmacy

Oregon State University, College of Pharmacy, Pharmacy Doctoral Program, Corvallis, OR 97331. Offers Pharm D. *Accreditation:* ACPE. *Application deadline:* For fall admission, 11/1 priority date for domestic and international students. Applications are processed on a rolling basis. *Expenses:* Contact institution. *Unit head:* Debra Peters, Pharmacy Advisor, 541-737-8743, E-mail: debra.peters@oregonstate.edu. *Application contact:* Angela Austin Haney, Director of Student Services/Head Advisor, 541-737-5784, E-mail: angela.austinhaney@oregonstate.edu.
Website: http://pharmacy.oregonstate.edu/

Pacific University, School of Pharmacy, Forest Grove, OR 97116-1797. Offers Pharm D. *Accreditation:* ACPE. *Entrance requirements:* Additional exam requirements/recommendations for international students: Required—TOEFL (minimum score 600 paper-based). Electronic applications accepted. *Expenses:* Contact institution. *Faculty research:* Informatics, enzyme metabolism, apostosis/cell cycle, neurophysiology of chronic pain, neurophysiology of Alzheimer's.

Palm Beach Atlantic University, Gregory School of Pharmacy, West Palm Beach, FL 33416-4708. Offers Pharm D, Pharm D/MBA. *Accreditation:* ACPE. *Entrance requirements:* For doctorate, PCAT, minimum GPA of 2.75. Additional exam requirements/recommendations for international students: Required—TOEFL (minimum score 550 paper-based; 79 iBT). Electronic applications accepted. *Expenses:* Contact institution. *Faculty research:* Heart disease and heart failure, asthma, medical missions, anticoagulants.

Presbyterian College, School of Pharmacy, Clinton, SC 29325. Offers Pharm D.

Purdue University, College of Pharmacy, Professional Program in Pharmacy and Pharmacal Sciences, West Lafayette, IN 47907. Offers Pharm D. *Accreditation:* ACPE. *Students:* 610 full-time (413 women), 1 part-time (0 women); includes 148 minority (27 Black or African American, non-Hispanic/Latino; 1 American Indian or Alaska Native, non-Hispanic/Latino; 86 Asian, non-Hispanic/Latino; 19 Hispanic/Latino; 15 Two or more races, non-Hispanic/Latino), 22 international. Average age 23. 498 applicants, 34% accepted, 152 enrolled. *Entrance requirements:* For doctorate, minimum 2 years of pre-pharmacy course work, interview. *Application deadline:* For fall admission, 12/2 for domestic and international students. Application fee: $60 ($75 for international students). *Expenses:* Contact institution. *Financial support:* Career-related internships or fieldwork, Federal Work-Study, and scholarships/grants available. Financial award application deadline: 3/15; financial award applicants required to submit FAFSA. *Faculty research:* Medicinal chemistry, pharmacology, pharmaceutics, clinical pharmacy, pharmacy administration. *Unit head:* Eric L. Barker, Dean, 765-494-1368, Fax: 765-494-7880, E-mail: barkerel@purdue.edu. *Application contact:* Danzhou Yang, Associate Dean for Research and Graduate Programs, 765-494-1362, E-mail: yangdz@purdue.edu.

Regis University, Rueckert-Hartman College for Health Professions, Denver, CO 80221-1099. Offers advanced practice nurse (DNP); counseling (MA); counseling children and adolescents (Post-Graduate Certificate); counseling military families (Post-Graduate Certificate); depth psychotherapy (Post-Graduate Certificate); fellowship in orthopedic manual physical therapy (Certificate); health care business management (Certificate); health care quality and patient safety (Certificate); health industry leadership (MBA); health services administration (MS); marriage and family therapy (MA, Post-Graduate Certificate); neonatal nurse practitioner (MSN); nursing education (MSN); nursing leadership (MSN); occupational therapy (OTD); pharmacy (Pharm D); physical therapy (DPT). *Program availability:* Part-time, evening/weekend, 100% online, blended/hybrid learning. *Degree requirements:* For master's, thesis (for some programs), internship. *Entrance requirements:* For master's, official transcript reflecting baccalaureate degree awarded from regionally-accredited college or university. Additional exam requirements/recommendations for international students: Required—TOEFL (minimum score 550 paper-based; 82 iBT). Electronic applications accepted. *Expenses:* Contact institution. *Faculty research:* Normal and pathological balance and gait research, normal/pathological upper limb motor control/biomechanics, exercise energy/metabolism research, optical treatment protocols for therapeutic modalities.

Roosevelt University, Graduate Division, College of Pharmacy, Chicago, IL 60605. Offers Pharm D. *Accreditation:* ACPE. *Students:* 177 full-time (106 women), 5 part-time (4 women); includes 83 minority (20 Black or African American, non-Hispanic/Latino; 41 Asian, non-Hispanic/Latino; 15 Hispanic/Latino; 7 Two or more races, non-Hispanic/Latino), 9 international. Average age 27. 181 applicants, 100% accepted, 54 enrolled. In 2017, 59 doctorates awarded. Electronic applications accepted. *Expenses:* $49,904 per year full-time. *Financial support:* Scholarships/grants available. *Unit head:* Melissa Hogan, Dean, 847-330-4503. *Application contact:* Angela Ryan, Associate Director of Enrollment, 847-330-4531, E-mail: aryan@roosevelt.edu.
Website: http://www.roosevelt.edu/pharmacy/

Rosalind Franklin University of Medicine and Science, College of Pharmacy, North Chicago, IL 60064-3095. Offers Pharm D. *Accreditation:* ACPE.

Roseman University of Health Sciences, College of Pharmacy, Henderson, NV 89014. Offers Pharm D. *Accreditation:* ACPE. *Faculty:* 41 full-time (18 women), 1 part-time/adjunct (0 women). *Students:* 697 full-time (382 women); includes 414 minority (49 Black or African American, non-Hispanic/Latino; 3 American Indian or Alaska Native, non-Hispanic/Latino; 313 Asian, non-Hispanic/Latino; 29 Hispanic/Latino; 5 Native Hawaiian or other Pacific Islander, non-Hispanic/Latino; 15 Two or more races, non-Hispanic/Latino), 2 international. Average age 29. 861 applicants, 41% accepted, 241 enrolled. In 2017, 251 doctorates awarded. *Degree requirements:* For doctorate, comprehensive exam. *Entrance requirements:* For doctorate, PCAT or bachelor's degree. *Application deadline:* For fall admission, 2/1 for domestic and international students. Applications are processed on a rolling basis. Application fee: $60. Electronic applications accepted. *Expenses:* Contact institution. *Financial support:* In 2017–18, 110 students received support. Federal Work-Study and scholarships/grants available. Financial award application deadline: 7/15; financial award applicants required to submit FAFSA. *Faculty research:* Adolescent drug abuse surveillance and prevention; intracellular signaling mechanisms in cardiovascular and neoplastic diseases; antidepressant and anxiolytic drug discovery; biopharmaceutical analysis of drug formulations; patient behaviors and attitudes toward medication adherence. *Total annual research expenditures:* $62,280. *Unit head:* Dr. Larry Fannin, Dean, 702-968-5944, Fax: 702-990-4435, E-mail: lfannin@roseman.edu. *Application contact:* Dr. Helen Park, Assistant Dean for Admissions and Student Affairs, 702-968-5248, Fax: 702-968-1644, E-mail: hpark@roseman.edu.
Website: http://www.roseman.edu

Rutgers University–New Brunswick, Ernest Mario School of Pharmacy, Piscataway, NJ 08854-8097. Offers medicinal chemistry (MS, PhD); pharmaceutical science (MS, PhD); pharmacy (Pharm D). *Accreditation:* ACPE. *Degree requirements:* For doctorate, variable foreign language requirement. *Entrance requirements:* For doctorate, SAT or PCAT (for Pharm D), interview, criminal background check (for Pharm D). Additional exam requirements/recommendations for international students: Recommended—TOEFL (minimum score 550 paper-based). Electronic applications accepted. *Expenses:* Contact institution. *Faculty research:* Pharmacokinetics, cancer prevention, cardiology, neurology, pharmacodynamics.

St. John Fisher College, Wegmans School of Pharmacy, Doctor of Pharmacy Program, Rochester, NY 14618-3597. Offers Pharm D. *Accreditation:* ACPE. *Faculty:* 20 full-time (12 women). *Students:* 329 full-time (201 women), 2 part-time (1 woman); includes 66 minority (12 Black or African American, non-Hispanic/Latino; 38 Asian, non-Hispanic/Latino; 10 Hispanic/Latino; 6 Two or more races, non-Hispanic/Latino), 5 international. Average age 24. 417 applicants, 32% accepted, 81 enrolled. In 2017, 80 doctorates awarded. *Degree requirements:* For doctorate, advanced pharmacy practice experience. *Entrance requirements:* For doctorate, PCAT, 2 letters of recommendation, interview, minimum of 62 credit hours of specific undergraduate courses. Additional exam requirements/recommendations for international students: Required—TOEFL (minimum score 575 paper-based; 80 iBT). *Application deadline:* For fall admission, 3/1 for domestic students. Applications are processed on a rolling basis. Electronic applications accepted. *Expenses:* Contact institution. *Financial support:* Scholarships/grants available. Financial award applicants required to submit FAFSA. *Faculty research:* Opioid pharmacology, heavy metal toxicology. *Unit head:* Dr. Christine Birnie, Dean of the School of Pharmacy, 585-385-7202, E-mail: cbirnie@sjfc.edu. *Application contact:* Michelle Gosier, Director of Transfer and Graduate Admissions, 585-385-8064, E-mail: mgosier@sjfc.edu.
Website: https://www.sjfc.edu/graduate-programs/doctor-of-pharmacy-pharmd/

St. John's University, College of Pharmacy and Health Sciences, Queens, NY 11439. Offers MPH, MS, PhD. *Accreditation:* ACPE (one or more programs are accredited). *Program availability:* Part-time, evening/weekend. *Faculty:* 100 full-time (58 women), 31 part-time/adjunct (12 women). *Students:* 627 full-time (397 women), 39 part-time (15 women); includes 384 minority (26 Black or African American, non-Hispanic/Latino; 320 Asian, non-Hispanic/Latino; 22 Hispanic/Latino; 1 Native Hawaiian or other Pacific Islander, non-Hispanic/Latino; 15 Two or more races, non-Hispanic/Latino), 142 international. Average age 24. 306 applicants, 53% accepted, 41 enrolled. In 2017, 36 master's, 285 doctorates awarded. Terminal master's awarded for partial completion of doctoral program. *Degree requirements:* For master's, comprehensive exam (for some programs), thesis (for some programs); for doctorate, comprehensive exam, thesis/dissertation, residency requirement: 24 credits in first two academic years. *Entrance requirements:* For master's and doctorate, GRE General Test, letters of recommendation, transcripts, resume, personal statement. Additional exam requirements/recommendations for international students: Required—TOEFL (minimum score 100 iBT), IELTS (minimum score 7). *Application deadline:* For fall admission, 3/1 priority date for domestic students, 5/1 priority date for international students; for spring admission, 11/1 priority date for domestic and international students. Applications are processed on a rolling basis. Application fee: $70. Electronic applications accepted. *Expenses:* $1,420 per credit tuition, $170 per semester fees; tuition may vary by program. *Financial support:* In 2017–18, 87 students received support, including 34 fellowships with full tuition reimbursements available (averaging $24,000 per year), 53 teaching assistantships with full tuition reimbursements available (averaging $12,000 per year); career-related internships or fieldwork, scholarships/grants, and unspecified assistantships also available. Support available to part-time students. Financial award application deadline: 2/1; financial award applicants required to submit FAFSA. *Faculty research:* Neurotoxicology, biochemical toxicology, molecular pharmacology, neurotoxicology, renal toxicology. *Total annual research expenditures:* $547,090. *Unit head:* Dr. Russell J. DiGate, Dean, 718-990-6411, Fax: 718-990-8070, E-mail: digate@stjohns.edu. *Application contact:* Robert Medrano, Director of Graduate Admission, 718-990-1601, Fax: 718-990-5686, E-mail: gradhelp@stjohns.edu.
Website: http://www.stjohns.edu/academics/schools-and-colleges/college-pharmacy-and-health-sciences

St. Louis College of Pharmacy, School of Pharmacy, St. Louis, MO 63110-1088. Offers Pharm D. *Accreditation:* ACPE. *Faculty:* 64 full-time (43 women), 30 part-time/adjunct (20 women). *Students:* 855 full-time (507 women), 6 part-time (2 women); includes 283 minority (62 Black or African American, non-Hispanic/Latino; 1 American Indian or Alaska Native, non-Hispanic/Latino; 194 Asian, non-Hispanic/Latino; 11 Hispanic/Latino; 2 Native Hawaiian or other Pacific Islander, non-Hispanic/Latino; 13 Two or more races, non-Hispanic/Latino), 30 international. Average age 24. 522 applicants, 56% accepted, 250 enrolled. In 2017, 218 doctorates awarded. *Entrance requirements:* For doctorate, PCAT. Additional exam requirements/recommendations for international students: Required—TOEFL (minimum score 550 paper-based); Recommended—IELTS. *Application deadline:* For fall admission, 3/1 for domestic and international students. Applications are processed on a rolling basis. Application fee: $55. Electronic applications accepted. *Expenses:* Contact institution. *Financial support:* In 2017–18, 392 students received support. Federal Work-Study and scholarships/grants available. Financial award application deadline: 3/15; financial award applicants required to submit FAFSA. *Faculty research:* Patient-oriented research, neuroscience and pain, medication outcomes. *Total annual research expenditures:* $369,072. *Unit head:* Dr. Bruce Canaday, Dean of Pharmacy, 314-446-8184. *Application contact:* Chase Davis, Director of Admissions, 314-446-8140, Fax: 314-446-8309, E-mail: chase.davis@stlcop.edu.

Samford University, McWhorter School of Pharmacy, Birmingham, AL 35229. Offers Pharm D, Pharm D/MBA, Pharm D/MPH. *Accreditation:* ACPE. *Faculty:* 34 full-time (23 women), 1 part-time/adjunct (0 women). *Students:* 469 full-time (301 women), 9 part-time (5 women); includes 93 minority (49 Black or African American, non-Hispanic/Latino; 3 American Indian or Alaska Native, non-Hispanic/Latino; 29 Asian, non-Hispanic/Latino; 5 Hispanic/Latino; 7 Two or more races, non-Hispanic/Latino), 7 international. Average age 24. 448 applicants, 28% accepted, 122 enrolled. In 2017, 134 doctorates awarded. *Entrance requirements:* For doctorate, PCAT, minimum GPA of 2.75. Additional exam requirements/recommendations for international students: Required—TOEFL (minimum score 550 paper-based; 80 iBT). *Application deadline:* For fall admission, 3/1 for domestic students. Applications are processed on a rolling basis. Electronic applications accepted. *Expenses: Tuition:* Full-time $19,058; part-time $813 per credit hour. *Required fees:* $550. Tuition and fees vary according to course load, degree level, program and student level. *Financial support:* In 2017–18, 217 students received support. Federal Work-Study and scholarships/grants available. Financial award application deadline: 2/15; financial award applicants required to submit FAFSA. *Unit head:* Dr. Michael Crouch, Dean/Professor, 205-726-4475, E-mail: mcrouch@samford.edu. *Application contact:* Jonathan Parker, Director of Pharmacy Admissions, 205-726-4242, Fax: 205-726-4141, E-mail: jmparker@samford.edu.
Website: https://www.samford.edu/pharmacy

Shenandoah University, Bernard J. Dunn School of Pharmacy, Winchester, VA 22601. Offers Pharm D. *Accreditation:* ACPE. *Program availability:* Part-time, evening/weekend, 100% online. *Faculty:* 38 full-time (24 women), 7 part-time/adjunct (5 women). *Students:* 317 full-time (218 women), 142 part-time (85 women); includes 156 minority (73 Black or African American, non-Hispanic/Latino; 70 Asian, non-Hispanic/Latino; 7 Hispanic/Latino; 1 Native Hawaiian or other Pacific Islander, non-Hispanic/Latino; 5 Two or more races, non-Hispanic/Latino), 17 international. Average age 32. 481 applicants, 56% accepted, 159 enrolled. In 2017, 153 doctorates awarded. *Degree requirements:* For doctorate, 149 credit hours in the didactic and experiential curriculum (not including prerequisite courses) with minimum cumulative GPA of 2.0. *Entrance requirements:* For doctorate, PCAT, 63 credits of prerequisites, essay, interview, minimum GPA of 2.5, three letters of recommendation. Additional exam requirements/recommendations for

international students: Required—TOEFL (minimum score 550 paper-based, 79 iBT) or IELTS (6.5). *Application deadline:* For fall admission, 6/1 for domestic and international students. Application fee: $30. Electronic applications accepted. *Expenses:* $135,330 tuition, plus $6,200 fees (technology fee, non-traditional pharmacy fee, pharmacy clinical fee, student services fee). *Financial support:* In 2017–18, 28 students received support. Scholarships/grants and unspecified assistantships available. Financial award applicants required to submit FAFSA. *Faculty research:* Scholarship of teaching and learning, pharmaceutical sciences, genomics, clinical pharmacology, clinical pharmacy. *Total annual research expenditures:* $293,860. *Unit head:* Robert DiCenzo, PhD, Dean, 540-665-1282, Fax: 540-665-1283, E-mail: rdicenzo@su.edu. *Application contact:* Andrew Woodall, Executive Director of Recruitment and Admissions, 540-665-4581, Fax: 540-665-4627, E-mail: admit@su.edu.
Website: http://www.pharmacy.su.edu

South College, Program in Pharmacy, Knoxville, TN 37917. Offers Pharm D. *Entrance requirements:* For doctorate, PharmCAS application.

South Dakota State University, Graduate School, College of Pharmacy and Allied Health Professions, Professional Program in Pharmacy, Brookings, SD 57007. Offers Pharm D. *Accreditation:* ACPE. *Entrance requirements:* For doctorate, ACT or PCAT, bachelor's degree in pharmacy. Additional exam requirements/recommendations for international students: Required—TOEFL (minimum score 550 paper-based). *Faculty research:* Geriatric medicine, drugs of abuse, anti-cancer drugs, drug metabolism, sustained drug delivery.

Southern Illinois University Edwardsville, School of Pharmacy, Edwardsville, IL 62026. Offers pharmacy education (Pharm D); pharmacy pediatrics (Pharm D). *Accreditation:* ACPE. *Entrance requirements:* For doctorate, PCAT. Electronic applications accepted.

South University, Graduate Programs, School of Pharmacy, Savannah, GA 31406. Offers Pharm D/MBA. *Accreditation:* ACPE.

South University, Program in Pharmacy, Columbia, SC 29203. Offers Pharm D.

Southwestern Oklahoma State University, College of Pharmacy, Weatherford, OK 73096-3098. Offers Pharm D. *Accreditation:* ACPE. *Entrance requirements:* For doctorate, PCAT.

Stony Brook University, State University of New York, Stony Brook Medicine, School of Medicine, School of Pharmacy and Pharmaceutical Sciences, Stony Brook, NY 11794. Offers Pharm D. *Entrance requirements:* For doctorate, PCAT (taken within previous three years). Additional exam requirements/recommendations for international students: Required—TOEFL. *Application deadline:* For fall admission, 6/1 for domestic students. Application fee: $100. *Expenses:* Tuition, state resident: full-time $10,870; part-time $453 per credit. Tuition, nonresident: full-time $22,210; part-time $925 per credit. *Unit head:* Dr. L. Douglas Ried, Founding Dean/Professor, 631-638-3738, E-mail: douglas.ried@stonybrookmedicine.edu. *Application contact:* Dr. Jack Fuhrer, Associate Dean of Admissions, 631-444-2113, Fax: 631-444-6032, E-mail: somadmissions@stonybrook.edu.
Website: https://pharmacy.stonybrookmedicine.edu/

Sullivan University, College of Pharmacy, Louisville, KY 40205. Offers Pharm D.

Temple University, School of Pharmacy, Philadelphia, PA 19122. Offers MS, PhD, Pharm D. *Accreditation:* ACPE (one or more programs are accredited). *Program availability:* Part-time, evening/weekend, online learning. *Faculty:* 40 full-time (22 women), 39 part-time/adjunct (15 women). *Students:* 595 full-time (329 women), 313 part-time (225 women); includes 344 minority (40 Black or African American, non-Hispanic/Latino; 136 Asian, non-Hispanic/Latino; 16 Hispanic/Latino; 152 Two or more races, non-Hispanic/Latino), 70 international. 100 applicants, 57% accepted, 41 enrolled. In 2017, 108 master's, 147 doctorates awarded. Terminal master's awarded for partial completion of doctoral program. *Entrance requirements:* For master's, GRE General Test, minimum undergraduate GPA of 3.0; for doctorate, GRE General Test, PCAT, minimum GPA of 3.0. Additional exam requirements/recommendations for international students: Required—TOEFL (minimum score 550 paper-based; 82 iBT). *Application deadline:* For fall admission, 2/1 priority date for domestic and international students. Application fee: $60. Electronic applications accepted. *Expenses:* Tuition, state resident: full-time $16,164; part-time $898 per credit hour. Tuition, nonresident: full-time $22,158; part-time $1231 per credit hour. *Required fees:* $890; $445 per semester. Full-time tuition and fees vary according to course load, degree level, campus/location and program. *Financial support:* Fellowships, research assistantships, teaching assistantships, career-related internships or fieldwork, Federal Work-Study, and institutionally sponsored loans available. Financial award application deadline: 1/15; financial award applicants required to submit FAFSA. *Faculty research:* Pharmacokinetics, synthesis of medicinals, industrial pharmacy, protein research, biopharma-formulation and clinical research. *Unit head:* Dr. Peter H. Doukas, Dean, 215-707-4990, Fax: 215-707-5620, E-mail: peter.doukas@temple.edu. *Application contact:* E-mail: phscgrad@temple.edu.
Website: http://www.temple.edu/pharmacy/

Texas A&M University, Irma Lerma Rangel College of Pharmacy, Kingsville, TX 78363. Offers Pharm D. *Accreditation:* ACPE. *Faculty:* 37. *Students:* 453 full-time (267 women), 2 part-time (1 woman); includes 343 minority (35 Black or African American, non-Hispanic/Latino; 155 Asian, non-Hispanic/Latino; 144 Hispanic/Latino; 1 Native Hawaiian or other Pacific Islander, non-Hispanic/Latino; 8 Two or more races, non-Hispanic/Latino), 7 international. Average age 27. *Entrance requirements:* For doctorate, PCAT, transcripts from each college/university attended; 3 PharmCAS recommendations. Additional exam requirements/recommendations for international students: Required—TOEFL (minimum score 550 paper-based; 80 iBT). *Application deadline:* For fall admission, 11/1 for domestic students. Application fee: $100. Electronic applications accepted. *Expenses:* Contact institution. *Financial support:* In 2017–18, 145 students received support. Career-related internships or fieldwork, institutionally sponsored loans, scholarships/grants, traineeships, health care benefits, tuition waivers (full and partial), and unspecified assistantships available. Support available to part-time students. Financial award applicants required to submit FAFSA. *Unit head:* Dr. Indra K. Reddy, Dean, 361-593-4273, Fax: 361-593-4929, E-mail: ireddy@pharmacy.tamhsc.edu. *Application contact:* Maria de Leon, Director of Admission, 361-221-0642, E-mail: mdeleon@tamhsc.edu.
Website: http://pharmacy.tamhsc.edu/

Texas Southern University, College of Pharmacy and Health Sciences, Department of Pharmacy Practice, Houston, TX 77004-4584. Offers Pharm D. *Accreditation:* ACPE. *Program availability:* Online learning. *Entrance requirements:* For doctorate, GRE General Test, PCAT. Electronic applications accepted.

Thomas Jefferson University, Jefferson College of Pharmacy, Philadelphia, PA 19107. Offers Pharm D. *Accreditation:* ACPE. *Degree requirements:* For doctorate, 141 semester credits. *Entrance requirements:* For doctorate, PCAT. Additional exam requirements/recommendations for international students: Required—TOEFL (minimum score 87 iBT), PCAT. Electronic applications accepted. *Faculty research:* Health outcomes and pharmacoeconomics; drug development - identification and synthesis of active molecules, in vitro and in vivo evaluation; drug delivery systems, stability, and formulations.

Touro University California, Graduate Programs, Vallejo, CA 94592. Offers education (MA); medical health sciences (MS); osteopathic medicine (DO); pharmacy (Pharm D); public health (MPH). *Accreditation:* AOsA; ARC-PA. *Program availability:* Part-time, evening/weekend. *Degree requirements:* For master's, comprehensive exam, thesis; for doctorate, comprehensive exam. *Entrance requirements:* For doctorate, BS/BA. Electronic applications accepted. *Faculty research:* Cancer, heart disease.

Union University, College of Pharmacy, Jackson, TN 38305-3697. Offers Pharm D. *Faculty:* 25 full-time (11 women), 3 part-time/adjunct (0 women). *Students:* 192 full-time (118 women); includes 46 minority (22 Black or African American, non-Hispanic/Latino; 1 American Indian or Alaska Native, non-Hispanic/Latino; 15 Asian, non-Hispanic/Latino; 6 Hispanic/Latino; 2 Two or more races, non-Hispanic/Latino). Average age 25. 218 applicants, 38% accepted, 46 enrolled. In 2017, 56 doctorates awarded. *Entrance requirements:* For doctorate, PCAT. Additional exam requirements/recommendations for international students: Required—TOEFL (minimum score 80 paper-based). *Application deadline:* For spring admission, 3/1 for domestic and international students. Applications are processed on a rolling basis. Electronic applications accepted. *Expenses:* $35,775 per year. *Financial support:* In 2017–18, 4 fellowships (averaging $45,000 per year) were awarded. Financial award application deadline: 8/1; financial award applicants required to submit FAFSA. *Faculty research:* Synthetic methodology; cancer pharmacology; drug stability; natural product synthesis; clinical research. *Total annual research expenditures:* $100,000. *Unit head:* Sheila Mitchell, Dean, 731-661-5953, E-mail: smitchell@uu.edu. *Application contact:* Stephen Hauss, Director of Admissions and Recruitment, 731-661-5979, E-mail: shauss@uu.edu.
Website: http://www.uu.edu/pharmacy/

Universidad de Ciencias Medicas, Graduate Programs, San Jose, Costa Rica. Offers dermatology (SP); family health (MS); health service center administration (MHA); human anatomy (MS); medical and surgery (MD); occupational medicine (MS); pharmacy (Pharm D). *Program availability:* Part-time. *Degree requirements:* For master's, thesis; for doctorate and SP, comprehensive exam. *Entrance requirements:* For master's, MD or bachelor's degree; for doctorate, admissions test; for SP, admissions test, MD.

University at Buffalo, the State University of New York, Graduate School, School of Pharmacy and Pharmaceutical Sciences, Professional Program in Pharmacy, Buffalo, NY 14260. Offers Pharm D, Pharm D/JD, Pharm D/MBA, Pharm D/MPH, Pharm D/MS, Pharm D/PhD. *Accreditation:* ACPE. *Faculty:* 22 full-time (8 women), 9 part-time/adjunct (5 women). *Students:* 532 full-time (304 women), 4 part-time (all women); includes 214 minority (23 Black or African American, non-Hispanic/Latino; 189 Asian, non-Hispanic/Latino; 2 Hispanic/Latino), 26 international. Average age 24. 650 applicants, [illegible] accepted, 131 enrolled. In 2017, 117 doctorates awarded. *Degree requirements:* For doctorate, project. *Entrance requirements:* For doctorate, PCAT. Additional exam requirements/recommendations for international students: Required—TOEFL (minimum score 550 paper-based; 79 iBT); Recommended—IELTS, TSE. *Application deadline:* For fall admission, 2/1 priority date for domestic and international students. Applications are processed on a rolling basis. Application fee: $50. Electronic applications accepted. *Expenses:* $25,840 in-state tuition, $36,450 out-of-state; $2,011 comprehensive fee; $110 student activity fee. *Financial support:* In 2017–18, 324 students received support. Scholarships/grants available. Financial award application deadline: 3/1; financial award applicants required to submit FAFSA. *Faculty research:* Pharmacokinetics/pharmacodynamics, HIV/AIDS, oncology, health outcomes research, translational research. *Total annual research expenditures:* $4.6 million. *Unit head:* Dr. William Prescott, Interim Chair, 716-645-4780, Fax: 716-829-6568, E-mail: prescott@buffalo.edu. *Application contact:* Dr. Jennifer M. Rosenberg, Associate Dean, 716-645-2825 Ext. 1, Fax: 716-829-6568, E-mail: prepharm@buffalo.edu.
Website: http://pharmacy.buffalo.edu/departments-offices/pharmacy-practice.html

University of Alberta, Faculty of Graduate Studies and Research, Department of Pharmacy and Pharmaceutical Sciences, Edmonton, AB T6G 2E1, Canada. Offers M Sc, PhD. Terminal master's awarded for partial completion of doctoral program. *Degree requirements:* For master's, thesis; for doctorate, thesis/dissertation. *Entrance requirements:* Additional exam requirements/recommendations for international students: Required—Michigan English Language Assessment Battery or IELTS. Electronic applications accepted. *Faculty research:* Radiopharmacy, pharmacokinetics, bionucleonics, medicinal chemistry, microbiology.

The University of Arizona, College of Pharmacy, Pharmacy Professional Program, Tucson, AZ 85721. Offers Pharm D. *Accreditation:* ACPE. *Program availability:* Part-time. *Entrance requirements:* For doctorate, PCAT, 4-6 months of pharmacy experience. Additional exam requirements/recommendations for international students: Required—TOEFL (minimum score 550 paper-based; 79 iBT). Electronic applications accepted. *Faculty research:* Health/service administrative pharmacy education, geriatric pharmacy, social and behavioral pharmacy management and economics.

University of Arkansas for Medical Sciences, College of Pharmacy, Little Rock, AR 72205-7199. Offers MS, Pharm D. *Accreditation:* ACPE (one or more programs are accredited). *Degree requirements:* For master's, thesis. *Entrance requirements:* For master's, GRE; for doctorate, PCAT. Additional exam requirements/recommendations for international students: Recommended—TOEFL. Electronic applications accepted. *Expenses:* Contact institution.

The University of British Columbia, Faculty of Pharmaceutical Sciences, Vancouver, BC V6T 1Z3, Canada. Offers M Sc, PhD, Pharm D. *Degree requirements:* For master's, thesis, seminar; for doctorate, comprehensive exam, thesis/dissertation, seminar. *Entrance requirements:* Additional exam requirements/recommendations for international students: Required—TOEFL (minimum score 600 paper-based; 100 iBT), IELTS (minimum score 6.5). Electronic applications accepted. *Expenses:* Contact institution. *Faculty research:* Pharmacology and cellular pharmacology, neuropharmacology, toxicology, nanomedicines and drug delivery, pharmacogenomics and personalized medicine, health outcomes research and evaluation, pharmacoepidemiology, and medicinal chemistry.

University of California, San Diego, Skaggs School of Pharmacy and Pharmaceutical Sciences, La Jolla, CA 92093. Offers Pharm D, Pharm D/PhD. *Accreditation:* ACPE. *Students:* 251. *Unit head:* Dr. James McKerrow, Dean. *Application contact:* 858-822-4900, Fax: 858-822-5591, E-mail: sppsadmissions@ucsd.edu.
Website: http://www.pharmacy.ucsd.edu/

University of California, San Francisco, School of Pharmacy, Program in Pharmacy, San Francisco, CA 94143. Offers Pharm D. *Accreditation:* ACPE. *Degree requirements:* For doctorate, comprehensive exam, supervised practice experience. *Entrance requirements:* For doctorate, 2 years of preparatory course work in basic sciences. Electronic applications accepted. *Faculty research:* Drug delivery, drug metabolism and chemical toxicology, macromolecular structure, molecular parasitology, pharmacokinetics.

University of Charleston, School of Pharmacy, Charleston, WV 25304-1099. Offers Pharm D. *Accreditation:* ACPE. *Degree requirements:* For doctorate, minimum cumulative GPA of 2.3 for all courses. *Entrance requirements:* For doctorate, PCAT (taken within 3 years of the date of application), criminal background check, proof of health insurance, immunizations and health clearance, minimum undergraduate GPA of 2.75, two letters of recommendation, interview. Additional exam requirements/recommendations for international students: Required—TOEFL. Electronic applications accepted.

Pharmacy

University of Cincinnati, James L. Winkle College of Pharmacy, Division of Pharmacy Practice, Cincinnati, OH 45221. Offers Pharm D. *Accreditation:* ACPE. *Entrance requirements:* For doctorate, GRE General Test, BS in pharmacy or equivalent, minimum GPA of 3.0. Additional exam requirements/recommendations for international students: Required—TOEFL. *Expenses: Tuition, area resident:* Full-time $14,468. Tuition, state resident: full-time $14,968; part-time $754 per credit hour. Tuition, nonresident: full-time $24,210; part-time $1311 per credit hour. *International tuition:* $26,460 full-time. *Required fees:* $3958; $84 per credit hour. One-time fee: $85 full-time. Tuition and fees vary according to course load, degree level and program.

University of Colorado Denver, Skaggs School of Pharmacy and Pharmaceutical Sciences, Doctor of Pharmacy Program, Aurora, CO 80045. Offers Pharm D. *Accreditation:* ACPE. *Program availability:* Online learning. Application fee: $0.
Website: http://www.ucdenver.edu/academics/colleges/pharmacy/AcademicPrograms/PharmDProgram/Pages/PharmDProgram.aspx

University of Connecticut, Graduate School, School of Pharmacy, Professional Program in Pharmacy, Storrs, CT 06269. Offers Pharm D. *Accreditation:* ACPE.

The University of Findlay, Office of Graduate Admissions, Findlay, OH 45840. Offers applied security and analytics (MSAS); athletic training (MAT); business (MBA), including certified management accountant, certified public accountant, health care management, hospitality management; education (MA Ed, Ed D), including children's literature (MA Ed), curriculum and teaching (MA Ed), education (MA Ed), educational administration (MA Ed), human resource development (MA Ed), mathematics (MA Ed), reading (MA Ed), science education (MA Ed), superintendent (Ed D), teaching (Ed D), technology (MA Ed); environmental, safety, and health management (MSEM); health informatics (MS); occupational therapy (MOT); pharmacy (Pharm D); physical therapy (DPT); physician assistant (MPA); rhetoric and writing (MA); teaching English to speakers of other languages (TESOL) and applied linguistics (MA). *Program availability:* Part-time, evening/weekend, 100% online, blended/hybrid learning. *Students:* 688 full-time (430 women), 553 part-time (308 women), 170 international. Average age 28. In 2017, 366 master's, 137 doctorates awarded. *Degree requirements:* For master's, comprehensive exam (for some programs), thesis (for some programs), cumulative project, capstone project; for doctorate, thesis/dissertation (for some programs). *Entrance requirements:* For master's, GRE/GMAT, bachelor's degree from accredited institution, minimum undergraduate GPA of 2.5 in last 64 hours of course work; for doctorate, GRE, MAT, minimum cumulative GPA of 3.0. Additional exam requirements/recommendations for international students: Required—TOEFL (minimum score 79 iBT), IELTS (minimum score 7), PTE (minimum score 61). *Application deadline:* Applications are processed on a rolling basis. Electronic applications accepted. *Financial support:* In 2017–18, 10 research assistantships with partial tuition reimbursements (averaging $7,200 per year), 35 teaching assistantships with partial tuition reimbursements (averaging $7,200 per year) were awarded; Federal Work-Study, institutionally sponsored loans, and unspecified assistantships also available. Financial award applicants required to submit FAFSA. *Unit head:* Christopher M. Harris, Director of Admissions, 419-434-4347, E-mail: harrisc1@findlay.edu. *Application contact:* Madeline Fauser Brennan, Graduate Admissions Counselor, 419-434-4636, Fax: 419-434-4898, E-mail: fauserbrennan@findlay.edu.
Website: http://www.findlay.edu/admissions/graduate/Pages/default.aspx

University of Florida, Graduate School, College of Pharmacy, Graduate Programs in Pharmacy, Department of Pharmaceutics, Gainesville, FL 32611. Offers clinical and translational sciences (PhD); pharmaceutical sciences (MSP, PhD); pharmacy (MSP, PhD). *Degree requirements:* For doctorate, comprehensive exam, thesis/dissertation. *Entrance requirements:* For master's and doctorate, GRE General Test, minimum GPA of 3.0. Additional exam requirements/recommendations for international students: Required—TOEFL (minimum score 550 paper-based; 80 iBT), IELTS (minimum score 6). Electronic applications accepted. *Faculty research:* Basic, applied, and clinical investigations in pharmacokinetics/biopharmaceutics; pharmaceutical analysis, pharmaceutical biotechnology and drug delivery; herbal medicine.

University of Florida, Graduate School, College of Pharmacy, Professional Program in Pharmacy, Gainesville, FL 32611. Offers Pharm D, MBA/Pharm D, Pharm D/MPH, Pharm D/PhD. *Accreditation:* ACPE. *Program availability:* Part-time, online learning. *Entrance requirements:* For doctorate, PCAT, minimum GPA of 2.5. Additional exam requirements/recommendations for international students: Required—TOEFL. Electronic applications accepted. *Faculty research:* Drug discovery, drug delivery, pharmacodynamics, socioeconomics of pharmacy, neurobiology of aging.

University of Georgia, College of Pharmacy, Athens, GA 30602. Offers MS, PhD, Pharm D, Certificate. *Accreditation:* ACPE (one or more programs are accredited). *Degree requirements:* For doctorate, variable foreign language requirement, thesis/dissertation (for some programs). *Entrance requirements:* For master's, GRE General Test, minimum GPA of 3.0; for doctorate, GRE General Test (for PhD), minimum GPA of 3.0 (for PhD). Additional exam requirements/recommendations for international students: Required—TOEFL (minimum score 80 iBT). Electronic applications accepted. *Expenses:* Contact institution.

University of Hawaii at Hilo, Program in Pharmacy, Hilo, HI 96720-4091. Offers Pharm D. *Accreditation:* ACPE. Electronic applications accepted.

University of Houston, College of Pharmacy, Houston, TX 77204. Offers pharmaceutics (MSPHR, PhD); pharmacology (MSPHR, PhD); pharmacy (Pharm D); pharmacy administration (MSPHR, PhD). *Accreditation:* ACPE. *Program availability:* Part-time. Terminal master's awarded for partial completion of doctoral program. *Entrance requirements:* For doctorate, PCAT (for Pharm D). Additional exam requirements/recommendations for international students: Required—TOEFL. Electronic applications accepted. *Faculty research:* Drug screening and design, cardiovascular pharmacology, infectious disease, asthma research, herbal medicine.

University of Illinois at Chicago, College of Pharmacy, Professional Program in Pharmacy, Chicago, IL 60607-7128. Offers Pharm D. *Accreditation:* ACPE. *Entrance requirements:* For doctorate, PCAT. *Expenses:* Contact institution.

The University of Iowa, College of Pharmacy, Iowa City, IA 52242-1316. Offers clinical pharmaceutical sciences (PhD); medicinal and natural products chemistry (PhD); pharamaceutics (PhD); pharmaceutical socioeconomics (PhD); pharmaceutics (MS); pharmacy (Pharm D); Pharm D/MPH. *Accreditation:* ACPE (one or more programs are accredited). *Degree requirements:* For master's, thesis optional, exam; for doctorate, comprehensive exam, thesis/dissertation. *Entrance requirements:* For master's and doctorate, GRE General Test, minimum GPA of 3.0. Additional exam requirements/recommendations for international students: Required—TOEFL (minimum score 550 paper-based; 81 iBT). Electronic applications accepted.

The University of Kansas, Graduate Studies, School of Pharmacy, Lawrence, KS 66045. Offers MS, PhD. *Accreditation:* ACPE (one or more programs are accredited). *Students:* 94 full-time (44 women), 15 part-time (8 women); includes 12 minority (1 American Indian or Alaska Native, non-Hispanic/Latino; 6 Asian, non-Hispanic/Latino; 3 Hispanic/Latino; 2 Two or more races, non-Hispanic/Latino), 43 international. Average age 28. 165 applicants, 25% accepted, 25 enrolled. In 2017, 23 master's, 15 doctorates awarded. *Entrance requirements:* For master's and doctorate, GRE General Test, curriculum vitae, personal statement, official transcripts. Additional exam requirements/recommendations for international students: Required—TOEFL or IELTS. Application fee: $65 ($85 for international students). Electronic applications accepted. *Financial support:* Fellowships, research assistantships, teaching assistantships, career-related internships or fieldwork, scholarships/grants, traineeships, and unspecified assistantships available. *Unit head:* Kenneth L. Audus, Dean, 785-864-3591, E-mail: audus@ku.edu. *Application contact:* Gina King, Senior Administrative Associate, 785-864-3592, E-mail: ginaking@ku.edu.
Website: http://www.pharm.ku.edu/

University of Kentucky, Graduate School, Professional Program in Pharmacy, Lexington, KY 40506-0032. Offers Pharm D. *Accreditation:* ACPE. *Entrance requirements:* For doctorate, PCAT, interview, minimum GPA of 2.5. Additional exam requirements/recommendations for international students: Required—TOEFL (minimum score 527 paper-based). Electronic applications accepted. *Expenses:* Contact institution. *Faculty research:* Innovations in pharmacy practice and education; policy and outcomes research; drug discovery and development; drug delivery and nanotechnology; natural products and computational chemistry.

University of Louisiana at Monroe, Graduate School, College of Health and Pharmaceutical Sciences, School of Pharmacy, Monroe, LA 71209-0001. Offers pharmacy (PhD); toxicology (PhD). *Accreditation:* ACPE. *Faculty:* 22 full-time (10 women). *Students:* 390 full-time (236 women), 5 part-time (2 women); includes 96 minority (41 Black or African American, non-Hispanic/Latino; 1 American Indian or Alaska Native, non-Hispanic/Latino; 39 Asian, non-Hispanic/Latino; 5 Hispanic/Latino; 10 Two or more races, non-Hispanic/Latino), 30 international. Average age 24. 48 applicants, 96% accepted, 45 enrolled. In 2017, 108 doctorates awarded. *Degree requirements:* For doctorate, comprehensive exam, thesis/dissertation. *Entrance requirements:* For doctorate, GRE General Test, minimum undergraduate GPA of 2.5. Additional exam requirements/recommendations for international students: Required—TOEFL (minimum score 500 paper-based; 61 iBT). *Application deadline:* For fall admission, 3/1 for domestic and international students; for winter admission, 12/14 for domestic students; for spring admission, 9/1 for domestic and international students. Applications are processed on a rolling basis. Application fee: $20 ($30 for international students). Electronic applications accepted. *Expenses:* $11,792 per semester tuition and fees. *Financial support:* In 2017–18, 63 students received support. Research assistantships, Federal Work-Study, and unspecified assistantships available. Financial award application deadline: 4/1; financial award applicants required to submit FAFSA. *Unit head:* Dr. Glenn Anderson, Dean, 318-342-1600, E-mail: ganderson@ulm.edu. *Application contact:* Dr. Paul W. Sylvester, Director, Research and Graduate Studies, 318-342-1958, Fax: 318-342-1606, E-mail: sylvester@ulm.edu.
Website: http://www.ulm.edu/pharmacy/

The University of Manchester, School of Pharmacy and Pharmaceutical Sciences, Manchester, United Kingdom. Offers M Phil, PhD.

University of Maryland, Baltimore, Graduate School, Graduate Programs in Pharmacy, Baltimore, MD 21201. Offers pharmaceutical health service research (MS, PhD), including epidemiology (MS), pharmacy administration (PhD); pharmaceutical sciences (PhD); Pharm D/PhD. *Degree requirements:* For doctorate, comprehensive exam, thesis/dissertation. *Entrance requirements:* For doctorate, GRE General Test. Additional exam requirements/recommendations for international students: Required—TOEFL (minimum score 550 paper-based), IELTS. Electronic applications accepted. *Expenses:* Tuition, state resident: full-time $13,990; part-time $661 per credit. Tuition, nonresident: full-time $30,484; part-time $1310 per credit. *Required fees:* $1894; $94 per credit. $415 per semester. Part-time tuition and fees vary according to course load, degree level and program. *Faculty research:* Drug discovery, pharmacokinetics, drug delivery, pharmaceutical outcomes and policy, pharmaceutical sciences.

University of Maryland, Baltimore, Professional Program in Pharmacy, Baltimore, MD 21201. Offers Pharm D, JD/Pharm D, Pharm D/MBA, Pharm D/MPH, Pharm D/PhD. *Accreditation:* ACPE. *Entrance requirements:* For doctorate, PCAT, 65 hours in pre-pharmacy course work, on-site interview. Additional exam requirements/recommendations for international students: Required—TOEFL (minimum score 550 paper-based; 80 iBT). Electronic applications accepted. *Expenses:* Tuition, state resident: full-time $13,990; part-time $661 per credit. Tuition, nonresident: full-time $30,484; part-time $1310 per credit. *Required fees:* $1894; $94 per credit. $415 per semester. Part-time tuition and fees vary according to course load, degree level and program. *Faculty research:* Pharmaceutics, molecular biology, pharmacology, pharmacoepidemiology, pharmacoeconomics.

University of Michigan, College of Pharmacy, Professional Program in Pharmacy, Ann Arbor, MI 48109. Offers Pharm D, Pharm D/PhD. *Accreditation:* ACPE. *Entrance requirements:* For doctorate, PCAT. *Application deadline:* For fall admission, 2/1 for domestic students. *Expenses:* Contact institution. *Financial support:* Applicants required to submit FAFSA. *Unit head:* James T. Dalton, Dean, 734-764-7144, Fax: 734-763-2022, E-mail: cop.deansoffice@med.umich.edu. *Application contact:* Mark S. Nelson, Director, Admissions and Student Counseling Services, 734-764-7312, E-mail: mnelson@med.umich.edu.
Website: https://pharmacy.umich.edu/pharmd

University of Minnesota, Duluth, Medical School, Department of Biochemistry, Molecular Biology and Biophysics, Duluth, MN 55812-2496. Offers biochemistry, molecular biology and biophysics (MS); biology and biophysics (PhD); social, administrative, and clinical pharmacy (MS, PhD); toxicology (MS, PhD). Terminal master's awarded for partial completion of doctoral program. *Degree requirements:* For master's, comprehensive exam, thesis; for doctorate, comprehensive exam, thesis/dissertation. *Entrance requirements:* For master's and doctorate, GRE General Test. Additional exam requirements/recommendations for international students: Required—TOEFL. Electronic applications accepted. *Faculty research:* Intestinal cancer biology; hepatotoxins and mitochondriopathies; toxicology; cell cycle regulation in stem cells; neurobiology of brain development, trace metal function and blood-brain barrier; hibernation biology.

University of Minnesota, Twin Cities Campus, College of Pharmacy, Professional Program in Pharmacy, Minneapolis, MN 55455-0213. Offers Pharm D. *Accreditation:* ACPE. *Degree requirements:* For doctorate, paper and seminar presentation. *Entrance requirements:* For doctorate, 2 years of pharmacy-related course work.

University of Mississippi, Graduate School, School of Pharmacy, University, MS 38677. Offers environmental toxicology (MS, PhD); industrial pharmacy (MS); medicinal chemistry (MS, PhD); pharmaceutics (MS, PhD); pharmacognosy (MS, PhD); pharmacology (MS, PhD); pharmacy (Pharm D); pharmacy administration (MS, PhD). *Accreditation:* ACPE (one or more programs are accredited). *Program availability:* Part-time. *Faculty:* 71 full-time (32 women), 17 part-time/adjunct (6 women). *Students:* 417 full-time (256 women), 16 part-time (7 women); includes 71 minority (24 Black or African American, non-Hispanic/Latino; 1 American Indian or Alaska Native, non-Hispanic/Latino; 36 Asian, non-Hispanic/Latino; 4 Hispanic/Latino; 6 Two or more races, non-Hispanic/Latino), 88 international. Average age 25. In 2017, 22 master's, 49 doctorates awarded. Terminal master's awarded for partial completion of doctoral program. *Degree requirements:* For master's, thesis; for doctorate, thesis/dissertation (for some

programs). *Entrance requirements:* For master's, GRE General Test, minimum GPA of 3.0; for doctorate, GRE General Test (for PhD). Additional exam requirements/recommendations for international students: Required—TOEFL. *Application deadline:* For fall admission, 2/1 priority date for domestic students; for spring admission, 10/1 priority date for domestic students. Applications are processed on a rolling basis. Application fee: $50. Electronic applications accepted. *Financial support:* Fellowships, research assistantships, teaching assistantships, career-related internships or fieldwork, Federal Work-Study, institutionally sponsored loans, scholarships/grants, tuition waivers (full), and unspecified assistantships available. Financial award application deadline: 3/1; financial award applicants required to submit FAFSA. *Unit head:* Dr. David D. Allen, II, Dean, 662-915-7265, Fax: 662-915-5118, E-mail: sopdean@olemiss.edu.
Website: http://www.pharmacy.olemiss.edu/

University of Missouri–Kansas City, School of Pharmacy, Kansas City, MO 64110-2499. Offers PhD, Pharm D. PhD offered through School of Graduate Studies. *Accreditation:* ACPE (one or more programs are accredited). *Program availability:* Online learning. *Degree requirements:* For doctorate, comprehensive exam (for some programs), thesis/dissertation (for some programs). *Entrance requirements:* For doctorate, PCAT (for Pharm D). Additional exam requirements/recommendations for international students: Required—TOEFL (minimum score 550 paper-based; 80 iBT). Electronic applications accepted. *Expenses:* Contact institution. *Faculty research:* Bio-organic and medicinal chemistry, drug delivery, pharmaceutics, molecular neurobiology, neurology.

University of Montana, Graduate School, College of Health Professions and Biomedical Sciences, Skaggs School of Pharmacy, Missoula, MT 59812. Offers biomedical and pharmaceutical sciences (MS, PhD), including biomedical sciences (PhD), medicinal chemistry, molecular and cellular toxicology, neuroscience (PhD), pharmaceutical sciences (MS); pharmacy (Pharm D). *Accreditation:* ACPE. Electronic applications accepted. *Faculty research:* Neuroendocrinology, neuropharmacology, molecular biochemistry, cardiovascular pharmacology, pharmacognosy.

University of Nebraska Medical Center, College of Pharmacy, Omaha, NE 68198-6000. Offers Pharm D. *Accreditation:* ACPE. *Entrance requirements:* For doctorate, PCAT, 90 semester hours of pre-pharmacy work. Electronic applications accepted. *Expenses:* Contact institution. *Faculty research:* Biopharmaceutics, nanomedicine, drug design, pharmaceutics, pharmacokinetics.

University of New England, College of Pharmacy, Portland, ME 04005-9526. Offers Pharm D. *Accreditation:* ACPE. *Faculty:* 24 full-time (11 women), 3 part-time/adjunct (1 woman). *Students:* 317 full-time (197 women); includes 102 minority (34 Black or African American, non-Hispanic/Latino; 2 American Indian or Alaska Native, non-Hispanic/Latino; 52 Asian, non-Hispanic/Latino; 8 Hispanic/Latino; 1 Native Hawaiian or other Pacific Islander, non-Hispanic/Latino; 5 Two or more races, non-Hispanic/Latino), 3 international. Average age 26. 351 applicants, 33% accepted, 49 enrolled. In 2017, 87 doctorates awarded. *Entrance requirements:* For doctorate, PCAT. *Application deadline:* For fall admission, 3/1 for domestic students. Applications are processed on a rolling basis. Electronic applications accepted. Tuition and fees vary according to degree level, program and student level. *Financial support:* Application deadline: 5/1; applicants required to submit FAFSA. *Unit head:* Dr. Gayle A. Brazeau, Dean, College of Pharmacy, 207-221-4500, Fax: 207-523-1927, E-mail: gbrazeau@une.edu. *Application contact:* Scott Steinberg, Dean of University Admission, 207-221-4225, Fax: 207-523-1925, E-mail: ssteinberg@une.edu.
Website: http://www.une.edu/pharmacy/

University of New Mexico, Graduate Studies, College of Pharmacy, Professional Program in Pharmacy, Albuquerque, NM 87131-2039. Offers Pharm D. *Accreditation:* ACPE. *Entrance requirements:* For doctorate, PCAT, 3 letters of recommendation, interview, 91 credit hours of prerequisites, letter of intent, Pharmcas application. Electronic applications accepted. *Expenses:* Contact institution.

The University of North Carolina at Chapel Hill, Eshelman School of Pharmacy, Chapel Hill, NC 27599. Offers pharmaceutical sciences (PhD); pharmaceutical sciences - health system pharmacy administration (MS); pharmacy (Pharm D). *Accreditation:* ACPE (one or more programs are accredited). *Faculty:* 115 full-time (47 women), 362 part-time/adjunct (189 women). *Students:* 107 full-time (60 women); includes 27 minority (3 Black or African American, non-Hispanic/Latino; 17 Asian, non-Hispanic/Latino; 4 Hispanic/Latino; 3 Two or more races, non-Hispanic/Latino), 16 international. Average age 26. 229 applicants, 7% accepted, 16 enrolled. In 2017, 8 master's, 16 doctorates awarded. Terminal master's awarded for partial completion of doctoral program. *Degree requirements:* For master's, comprehensive exam, thesis; for doctorate, comprehensive exam, thesis/dissertation. *Entrance requirements:* For master's and doctorate, GRE General Test, minimum GPA of 3.0. Additional exam requirements/recommendations for international students: Required—TOEFL (minimum score 550 paper-based; 90 iBT), IELTS (minimum score 7). *Application deadline:* For fall admission, 12/12 for domestic students, 12/12 priority date for international students. Applications are processed on a rolling basis. Application fee: $90. Electronic applications accepted. *Expenses:* Contact institution. *Financial support:* In 2017–18, 107 students received support, including 18 fellowships with full tuition reimbursements available (averaging $30,000 per year), 56 research assistantships with full tuition reimbursements available (averaging $30,000 per year); career-related internships or fieldwork, Federal Work-Study, institutionally sponsored loans, scholarships/grants, traineeships, health care benefits, tuition waivers (full), and unspecified assistantships also available. Financial award application deadline: 12/12. *Faculty research:* Health services research, pharmacokinetics, molecular modeling, infectious disease, genomics and proteomics, translational research. *Total annual research expenditures:* $25 million. *Unit head:* Dr. Dhiren Thakker, Dean, 919-966-1122, Fax: 919-966-6919, E-mail: dhiren_thakker@unc.edu. *Application contact:* Olivia Hammill, Assistant Director of Recruitment and Admissions, 919-962-0097, Fax: 919-966-9428, E-mail: olivia_hammill@unc.edu.
Website: http://pharmacy.unc.edu/

University of Oklahoma Health Sciences Center, College of Pharmacy, Professional Program in Pharmacy, Oklahoma City, OK 73190. Offers Pharm D. *Accreditation:* ACPE.

University of Pittsburgh, School of Pharmacy, Professional Program in Pharmacy, Pittsburgh, PA 15261. Offers community, leadership, innovation, and practice (Pharm D); global health (Pharm D); pediatrics (Pharm D); pharmacotherapy (Pharm D); pharmacy business administration (Pharm D). *Accreditation:* ACPE. *Faculty:* 70 full-time (37 women), 7 part-time/adjunct (0 women). *Students:* 457 full-time (300 women); includes 115 minority (14 Black or African American, non-Hispanic/Latino; 1 American Indian or Alaska Native, non-Hispanic/Latino; 81 Asian, non-Hispanic/Latino; 7 Hispanic/Latino; 12 Two or more races, non-Hispanic/Latino), 7 international. Average age 23. 435 applicants, 33% accepted, 115 enrolled. In 2017, 110 doctorates awarded. *Entrance requirements:* For doctorate, PCAT. *Application deadline:* For fall admission, 12/1 for domestic students. Application fee: $175. Electronic applications accepted. *Expenses:* $31,040 in-state tuition per year; $34,924 out-of-state tuition per year; $1,534 fees per year. *Financial support:* In 2017–18, 125 students received support. Scholarships/grants available. Financial award application deadline: 3/31. *Faculty research:* Pharmacy practice, patient care models, clinical outcomes, healthcare policy, clinical and translational focusing on identifying genetic predictors of clinically-relevant drug-related outcomes, role of transporters in drug disposition and pathophysiology in critical care, clinical importance of pharmacogenomics in drug response. *Total annual research expenditures:* $5.8 million. *Unit head:* Dr. Patricia Dowley Kroboth, Dean, 412-624-2400, Fax: 412-648-1086, E-mail: pkroboth@pitt.edu. *Application contact:* Marcia Borrelli, Director of Student Services, 412-648-1120, Fax: 412-383-9996, E-mail: borrelli@pitt.edu.
Website: http://www.pharmacy.pitt.edu

University of Puerto Rico–Medical Sciences Campus, School of Pharmacy, San Juan, PR 00936-5067. Offers industrial pharmacy (MS); pharmaceutical sciences (MS); pharmacy (Pharm D). *Accreditation:* ACPE. *Program availability:* Part-time, evening/weekend. *Degree requirements:* For master's, thesis; for doctorate, portfolio, research project. *Entrance requirements:* For master's, GRE, interview; for doctorate, PCAT, interview. Electronic applications accepted. *Expenses:* Contact institution. *Faculty research:* Controlled release, solid dosage form, screening of anti-HIV drugs, pharmacokinetic/pharmacodynamic of drugs.

University of Rhode Island, Graduate School, College of Pharmacy, Department of Pharmacy Practice, Kingston, RI 02881. Offers pharmacy practice (Pharm D); Pharm D/MBA; Pharm D/MPAS; Pharm D/MS. *Accreditation:* ACPE. *Faculty:* 30 full-time (25 women). *Students:* 732 full-time (494 women), 2 part-time (1 woman); includes 117 minority (6 Black or African American, non-Hispanic/Latino; 57 Asian, non-Hispanic/Latino; 37 Hispanic/Latino; 17 Two or more races, non-Hispanic/Latino), 39 international. 664 applicants, 53% accepted, 137 enrolled. In 2017, 116 doctorates awarded. *Entrance requirements:* Additional exam requirements/recommendations for international students: Required—TOEFL. *Application deadline:* For fall admission, 12/1 for domestic and international students. Application fee: $65. Electronic applications accepted. *Expenses:* Tuition, state resident: full-time $12,706; part-time $786 per credit. Tuition, nonresident: full-time $25,216; part-time $1401 per credit. *Required fees:* $1598; $45 per credit. One-time fee: $30 part-time. *Financial support:* Application deadline: 12/1; applicants required to submit FAFSA. *Unit head:* Dr. Marilyn Barbour, Chair, 401-874-5842, Fax: 401-874-2181, E-mail: mbarbourri@aol.com.
Website: http://www.uri.edu/pharmacy/departments/php/index.shtml

University of Saint Joseph, School of Pharmacy and Physician Assistant Studies, West Hartford, CT 06117-2700. Offers pharmacy (Pharm D). *Application deadline:* Applications are processed on a rolling basis. Application fee: $50. Electronic applications accepted. *Financial support:* Career-related internships or fieldwork available. *Unit head:* Dr. Joseph Ofosu, Dean, 860-231-5451, E-mail: jofosu@usj.edu.
Website: https://www.usj.edu/academics/schools/sppas/

University of South Carolina, South Carolina College of Pharmacy, Professional Program in Pharmacy, Columbia, SC 29208. Offers Pharm D. *Accreditation:* ACPE. *Degree requirements:* For doctorate, one foreign language. *Entrance requirements:* For doctorate, PCAT, 2 years of preprofessional study, interview. Electronic applications accepted. *Faculty research:* Cancer treatment and prevention, Ion channels, DNA damage repair, inflammation.

University of Southern California, Graduate School, School of Pharmacy, Professional Program in Pharmacy, Los Angeles, CA 90089. Offers Pharm D, Pharm D/MBA, Pharm D/MS, Pharm D/PhD. *Accreditation:* ACPE. Electronic applications accepted. *Faculty research:* Infectious diseases, health services research, geriatric pharmacology, clinical psychopharmacology.

University of South Florida, College of Engineering, Department of Chemical and Biomedical Engineering, Tampa, FL 33620. Offers biomedical engineering (MSBE), including pharmacy; chemical engineering (MSCH, PhD). *Program availability:* Part-time. *Faculty:* 15 full-time (2 women). *Students:* 47 full-time (13 women), 15 part-time (5 women); includes 7 minority (2 Black or African American, non-Hispanic/Latino; 2 Asian, non-Hispanic/Latino; 3 Hispanic/Latino), 40 international. Average age 27. 92 applicants, 43% accepted, 17 enrolled. In 2017, 36 master's, 12 doctorates awarded. Terminal master's awarded for partial completion of doctoral program. *Degree requirements:* For master's, comprehensive exam, thesis (for some programs); for doctorate, comprehensive exam, thesis/dissertation. *Entrance requirements:* For master's, GRE General Test, undergraduate degree in engineering, science, or chemical engineering with minimum GPA of 3.0; at least two letters of recommendation; current resume; statement of research interests (for students who wish to pursue thesis option); for doctorate, GRE General Test, undergraduate degree in engineering, science, or chemical engineering with minimum GPA of 3.0; three letters of recommendation; current resume; statement of research interests. Additional exam requirements/recommendations for international students: Required—TOEFL (minimum score 550 paper-based; 79 iBT) or IELTS (minimum score 6.5). *Application deadline:* For fall admission, 2/15 for domestic and international students; for spring admission, 10/15 for domestic students, 9/15 for international students; for summer admission, 2/15 for domestic students, 1/15 for international students. Application fee: $30. Electronic applications accepted. *Financial support:* In 2017–18, 13 students received support, including 29 research assistantships with tuition reimbursements available (averaging $13,171 per year), 12 teaching assistantships with tuition reimbursements available (averaging $14,017 per year); unspecified assistantships also available. Financial award applicants required to submit FAFSA. *Faculty research:* Neuroengineering, tissue engineering, biomedicine and biotechnology, engineering education, functional materials and nanotechnology, energy, environment/sustainability. *Total annual research expenditures:* $1 million. *Unit head:* Dr. Venkat R. Bhethanabotla, Professor and Department Chair, 813-974-3997, E-mail: bhethana@usf.edu. *Application contact:* Dr. Robert Frisina, Jr., Professor and Graduate Program Director, 813-974-4013, Fax: 813-974-3651, E-mail: rfrisina@usf.edu.
Website: http://che.eng.usf.edu/

University of South Florida, College of Pharmacy, Tampa, FL 33620-9951. Offers pharmaceutical nanotechnology (MS), including biomedical engineering, drug discovery, delivery, development and manufacturing; pharmacy (Pharm D), including pharmacy and health education. *Accreditation:* ACPE. *Faculty:* 39 full-time (28 women), 1 part-time/adjunct (0 women). *Students:* 381 full-time (226 women), 3 part-time (1 woman); includes 172 minority (27 Black or African American, non-Hispanic/Latino; 70 Asian, non-Hispanic/Latino; 59 Hispanic/Latino; 4 Native Hawaiian or other Pacific Islander, non-Hispanic/Latino; 12 Two or more races, non-Hispanic/Latino), 4 international. Average age 25. 678 applicants, 31% accepted, 105 enrolled. In 2017, 111 doctorates awarded. *Degree requirements:* For master's, comprehensive exam, thesis optional. *Entrance requirements:* For master's, GRE, MCAT or DAT, minimum GPA of 3.0, letters of reference, resume; for doctorate, PCAT, minimum GPA of 2.75 overall (preferred); completion of 72 prerequisite credit hours; U.S. citizenship or permanent resident. Additional exam requirements/recommendations for international students: Required—TOEFL (minimum score 550 paper-based; 79 iBT), IELTS (minimum score 6.5). *Application deadline:* For fall admission, 2/1 priority date for domestic students, 2/1 for international students; for spring admission, 10/15 for domestic students, 9/15 for international students; for summer admission, 2/15 for domestic and international students. Electronic applications accepted. *Financial support:* In 2017–18, 91 students received support. *Total annual research expenditures:* $1.7 million. *Unit head:* Dr. Kevin Sneed, Dean, 813-974-5699, E-mail: ksneed@health.usf.edu. *Application contact:* Dr. Amy Schwartz, Associate Dean, 813-974-2251, E-mail: aschwar1@health.usf.edu.

University of South Florida, Innovative Education, Tampa, FL 33620-9951. Offers adult, career and higher education (Graduate Certificate), including college teaching, leadership in developing human resources, leadership in higher education; Africana studies (Graduate Certificate), including diasporas and health disparities, genocide and human rights; aging studies (Graduate Certificate), including gerontology; art research (Graduate Certificate), including museum studies; business foundations (Graduate Certificate); chemical and biomedical engineering (Graduate Certificate), including materials science and engineering, water, health and sustainability; child and family studies (Graduate Certificate), including positive behavior support; civil and industrial engineering (Graduate Certificate), including transportation systems analysis; community and family health (Graduate Certificate), including maternal and child health, social marketing and public health, violence and injury: prevention and intervention, women's health; criminology (Graduate Certificate), including criminal justice administration; data science for public administration (Graduate Certificate); digital humanities (Graduate Certificate); educational measurement and research (Graduate Certificate), including evaluation; English (Graduate Certificate), including comparative literary studies, creative writing, professional and technical communication; entrepreneurship (Graduate Certificate); environmental health (Graduate Certificate), including safety management; epidemiology and biostatistics (Graduate Certificate), including applied biostatistics, biostatistics, concepts and tools of epidemiology, epidemiology, epidemiology of infectious diseases; geography, environment and planning (Graduate Certificate), including community development, environmental policy and management, geographical information systems; geology (Graduate Certificate), including hydrogeology; global health (Graduate Certificate), including disaster management, global health and Latin American and Caribbean studies, global health practice, humanitarian assistance, infection control; government and international affairs (Graduate Certificate), including Cuban studies, globalization studies; health policy and management (Graduate Certificate), including health management and leadership, public health policy and programs; hearing specialist: early intervention (Graduate Certificate); industrial and management systems engineering (Graduate Certificate), including systems engineering, technology management; information studies (Graduate Certificate), including school library media specialist; information systems/decision sciences (Graduate Certificate), including analytics and business intelligence; instructional technology (Graduate Certificate), including distance education, Florida digital/virtual educator, instructional design, multimedia design, Web design; internal medicine, bioethics and medical humanities (Graduate Certificate), including biomedical ethics; Latin American and Caribbean studies (Graduate Certificate); leadership for coastal resiliency planning (Graduate Certificate); mass communications (Graduate Certificate), including multimedia journalism; mathematics and statistics (Graduate Certificate), including mathematics; medicine (Graduate Certificate), including aging and neuroscience, bioinformatics, biotechnology, brain fitness and memory management, clinical investigation, hand and upper limb rehabilitation, health informatics, health sciences, integrative weight management, intellectual property, medicine and gender, metabolic and nutritional medicine, metabolic cardiology, pharmacy sciences; national and competitive intelligence (Graduate Certificate); nursing (Graduate Certificate), including simulation based academic fellowship in advanced pain management; psychological and social foundations (Graduate Certificate), including career counseling, college teaching, diversity in education, mental health counseling, school counseling; public affairs (Graduate Certificate), including nonprofit management, public management, research administration; public health (Graduate Certificate), including assessing chemical toxicity and public health risks, health equity, pharmacoepidemiology, public health generalist, toxicology, translational research in adolescent behavioral health; public health practices (Graduate Certificate), including planning for healthy communities; rehabilitation and mental health counseling (Graduate Certificate), including integrative mental health care, marriage and family therapy, rehabilitation technology; secondary education (Graduate Certificate), including ESOL, foreign language education: culture and content, foreign language education: professional; social work (Graduate Certificate), including geriatric social work/clinical gerontology; special education (Graduate Certificate), including autism spectrum disorder, disabilities education: severe/profound; world languages (Graduate Certificate), including teaching English as a second language (TESL) or foreign language. *Unit head:* Dr. Cynthia DeLuca, Associate Vice President and Assistant Vice Provost, 813-974-3077, Fax: 813-974-7061, E-mail: deluca@usf.edu. *Application contact:* Owen Hooper, Director, Summer and Alternative Calendar Programs, 813-974-6917, E-mail: hooper@usf.edu.
Website: http://www.usf.edu/innovative-education/

The University of Tennessee Health Science Center, College of Pharmacy, Memphis, TN 38163. Offers MS, PhD, Pharm D, Pharm D/PhD. *Accreditation:* ACPE (one or more programs are accredited). Terminal master's awarded for partial completion of doctoral program. *Degree requirements:* For master's, thesis; for doctorate, thesis/dissertation (for some programs). *Entrance requirements:* For master's, GRE; for doctorate, PCAT (for Pharm D); GRE (for PhD). Additional exam requirements/recommendations for international students: Required—TOEFL. Electronic applications accepted. *Expenses:* Contact institution. *Faculty research:* Detection and quantification of molecular entities of biological and pharmaceutical interest; design, synthesis, and biologic evaluation of new medications; quantitative assessment of drug disposition and effects using mathematical models; design, development, and evaluation of drug delivery systems.

The University of Texas at Austin, Graduate School, College of Pharmacy, Professional Program in Pharmacy, Austin, TX 78712-1111. Offers Pharm D, Pharm D/PhD. Program offered jointly with The University of Texas Health Science Center at San Antonio. *Accreditation:* ACPE. *Entrance requirements:* For doctorate, GRE General Test.

The University of Texas at Tyler, Ben and Maytee Fisch College of Pharmacy, Tyler, TX 75799-0001. Offers Pharm D.

University of the Incarnate Word, Feik School of Pharmacy, San Antonio, TX 78209-6397. Offers Pharm D. *Accreditation:* ACPE. *Faculty:* 24 full-time (14 women), 1 (woman) part-time/adjunct. *Students:* 354 full-time (242 women), 9 part-time (6 women); includes 248 minority (18 Black or African American, non-Hispanic/Latino; 68 Asian, non-Hispanic/Latino; 152 Hispanic/Latino; 1 Native Hawaiian or other Pacific Islander, non-Hispanic/Latino; 9 Two or more races, non-Hispanic/Latino), 5 international. In 2017, 91 doctorates awarded. *Entrance requirements:* For doctorate, PCAT, 80 hours of documented pharmacy observational experience; minimum GPA of 2.5; 64 hours (71 hours for financial aid) in accredited pre-pharmacy course. Additional exam requirements/recommendations for international students: Required—TOEFL (minimum score 560 paper-based; 83 iBT). *Application deadline:* For fall admission, 12/1 for domestic and international students. Application fee: $50. Electronic applications accepted. *Expenses:* $36,500 per year. *Financial support:* Research assistantships, Federal Work-Study, scholarships/grants, and unspecified assistantships available. Financial award applicants required to submit FAFSA. *Faculty research:* Enzymatic inhibitors against tropical diseases, natural products chemistry, development of methods for the identification and quantification of drugs and their metabolites in biological fluids, characterization of novel compounds to inhibit specific brain transporters and assess their effectiveness as new antidepressants. *Unit head:* Dr. David Maize, Dean, 210-883-1000, Fax: 210-822-1516, E-mail: maize@uiwtx.edu. *Application contact:* Dr. Amy Diepenbrock, Assistant Dean, Student Affairs, 210-883-1060, Fax: 210-822-1521, E-mail: diepenbr@uiwtx.edu.
Website: http://www.uiw.edu/pharmacy

University of the Pacific, Thomas J. Long School of Pharmacy and Health Sciences, Professional Program in Pharmacy, Stockton, CA 95211-0197. Offers Pharm D. *Accreditation:* ACPE. *Faculty:* 42 full-time (24 women), 7 part-time/adjunct (3 women). *Students:* 605 full-time (367 women), 15 part-time (6 women); includes 527 minority (5 Black or African American, non-Hispanic/Latino; 1 American Indian or Alaska Native, non-Hispanic/Latino; 460 Asian, non-Hispanic/Latino; 29 Hispanic/Latino; 6 Native Hawaiian or other Pacific Islander, non-Hispanic/Latino; 26 Two or more races, non-Hispanic/Latino), 1 international. Average age 24. 1,070 applicants, 38% accepted, 204 enrolled. In 2017, 207 doctorates awarded. *Entrance requirements:* Additional exam requirements/recommendations for international students: Required—TOEFL. *Application deadline:* For fall admission, 2/1 for domestic students. Application fee: $75. *Financial support:* In 2017–18, 27 teaching assistantships were awarded; career-related internships or fieldwork, Federal Work-Study, institutionally sponsored loans, and tuition waivers (partial) also available. Support available to part-time students. Financial award application deadline: 3/1; financial award applicants required to submit FAFSA. *Unit head:* Dr. Philip Oppenheimer, Dean, 209-946-2561, Fax: 209-946-2410. *Application contact:* Ron Espejo, Recruitment Specialist, 209-946-3957, Fax: 209-946-3147, E-mail: respejo@pacific.edu.
Website: http://www.pacific.edu/pharmacy/

University of the Sciences, Philadelphia College of Pharmacy, Philadelphia, PA 19104-4495. Offers Pharm D. *Accreditation:* ACPE. *Entrance requirements:* Additional exam requirements/recommendations for international students: Required—TOEFL, TWE.

The University of Toledo, College of Graduate Studies, College of Pharmacy and Pharmaceutical Sciences, Toledo, OH 43606-3390. Offers MS, MSPS, PhD, Pharm D. Terminal master's awarded for partial completion of doctoral program. *Degree requirements:* For master's, thesis; for doctorate, thesis/dissertation. *Entrance requirements:* For master's and doctorate, GRE General Test. Additional exam requirements/recommendations for international students: Required—TOEFL (minimum score 550 paper-based; 80 iBT). Electronic applications accepted.

University of Utah, Graduate School, College of Pharmacy, Professional Program in Pharmacy, Salt Lake City, UT 84112-5820. Offers Pharm D. *Accreditation:* ACPE. *Faculty:* 37 full-time (11 women), 46 part-time/adjunct (21 women). *Students:* 221 full-time (113 women), 5 part-time (4 women); includes 84 minority (3 Black or African American, non-Hispanic/Latino; 55 Asian, non-Hispanic/Latino; 13 Hispanic/Latino; 13 Two or more races, non-Hispanic/Latino), 1 international. Average age 26. 198 applicants, 39% accepted, 59 enrolled. In 2017, 59 doctorates awarded. *Entrance requirements:* For doctorate, PCAT. Additional exam requirements/recommendations for international students: Required—TOEFL (minimum score 80 iBT), IELTS (minimum score 6.5). Application fee: $55 ($65 for international students). Electronic applications accepted. *Expenses:* Contact institution. *Financial support:* In 2017–18, 96 students received support, including 31 teaching assistantships (averaging $1,500 per year); Federal Work-Study, institutionally sponsored loans, and scholarships/grants also available. Financial award application deadline: 2/4; financial award applicants required to submit FAFSA. *Faculty research:* Drug discovery, development, metabolism and toxicology; molecular and cellular neuroscience; nanomedicine; precision medicine; outcomes research. *Total annual research expenditures:* $15.9 million. *Unit head:* Dr. James N. Herron, Executive Associate Dean for Professional Education, 801-581-6731, E-mail: james.herron@utah.edu.
Website: http://www.pharmacy.utah.edu/

University of Washington, School of Pharmacy and Graduate School, Department of Pharmacy, Seattle, WA 98195-7630. Offers biomedical regulatory affairs (MS); pharmaceutical outcomes research and policy (PhD). *Degree requirements:* For master's, thesis; for doctorate, thesis/dissertation. *Entrance requirements:* For master's and doctorate, GRE General Test. Additional exam requirements/recommendations for international students: Required—TOEFL (minimum score 100 iBT). *Application deadline:* For fall admission, 12/31 priority date for domestic and international students; for winter admission, 1/1 for domestic and international students. Application fee: $75 ($100 for international students). Electronic applications accepted. *Expenses:* Contact institution. *Financial support:* Fellowships with full tuition reimbursements, research assistantships with full tuition reimbursements, teaching assistantships with full tuition reimbursements, institutionally sponsored loans, scholarships/grants, health care benefits, tuition waivers (full), and unspecified assistantships available. *Faculty research:* Pharmacoeconomics, pharmacoepidemiology, drug policy, outcomes research. *Unit head:* Dr. H. Steve White, Chair, 206-543-3782, Fax: 206-543-3835, E-mail: hswhite@uw.edu. *Application contact:* Dr. Beth Devine, Associate Professor, 206-221-5760, Fax: 206-543-3835, E-mail: bdevine@uw.edu.
Website: https://sop.washington.edu/department-of-pharmacy/

University of Washington, School of Pharmacy, Doctor of Pharmacy Program, Seattle, WA 98195-7631. Offers Pharm D, Pharm D/Certificate, Pharm D/MS. *Accreditation:* ACPE. *Students:* 366 applicants, 105 enrolled. In 2017, 82 doctorates awarded. *Entrance requirements:* For doctorate, PCAT. Additional exam requirements/recommendations for international students: Required—TOEFL (minimum score 100 iBT). *Application deadline:* For fall admission, 12/1 for domestic and international students. Applications are processed on a rolling basis. Electronic applications accepted. *Financial support:* In 2017–18, 168 students received support. Career-related internships or fieldwork and scholarships/grants available. Financial award application deadline: 6/30. *Unit head:* Dr. Peggy Odegard, Associate Dean, Office of Professional Pharmacy Education, 206-543-6100, Fax: 206-685-9297. *Application contact:* Cher Espina, Director of Admissions, 206-543-6100, Fax: 206-685-9297, E-mail: cherelyn@uw.edu.
Website: https://sop.washington.edu/pharmd/

University of Wisconsin–Madison, School of Pharmacy, Professional Program in Pharmacy, Madison, WI 53706-1380. Offers Pharm D. *Accreditation:* ACPE.

University of Wyoming, College of Health Sciences, School of Pharmacy, Laramie, WY 82071. Offers health services administration (MS); pharmacy (Pharm D). *Accreditation:* ACPE (one or more programs are accredited). *Program availability:* Online learning. *Entrance requirements:* For doctorate, PCAT. Additional exam requirements/recommendations for international students: Required—TOEFL.

Virginia Commonwealth University, Medical College of Virginia-Professional Programs, School of Pharmacy, Professional Program in Pharmacy, Richmond, VA 23284-9005. Offers Pharm D. *Accreditation:* ACPE. *Program availability:* Part-time. *Degree requirements:* For doctorate, research project. *Entrance requirements:* For doctorate, PCAT. Electronic applications accepted. *Faculty research:* Oncology, cardiology, infectious diseases, epilepsy, connective tissue.

Washington State University, College of Pharmacy, Spokane, WA 99210-1495. Offers health policy and administration (MHPA); nutrition and exercise physiology (MS); pharmacy (Pharm D). Programs offered at the Spokane campus. *Accreditation:* ACPE (one or more programs are accredited). *Degree requirements:* For master's, comprehensive exam, thesis, oral exam; for doctorate, comprehensive exam, thesis/dissertation, oral exam (for PhD). *Entrance requirements:* For master's, GRE General Test, minimum GPA of 3.0, interview; for doctorate, GRE General Test, minimum GPA of 3.0, interview, minimum 60 hours of documented pharmacy experience. *Faculty research:* Hormonal carcinogenesis, drug metabolism/transport, toxicology of chlorinated compounds, alcohol effects on immune system, effects of cocaine on neuronal function.

Wayne State University, Eugene Applebaum College of Pharmacy and Health Sciences, Doctor of Pharmacy Program, Detroit, MI 48202. Offers Pharm D, Pharm D/PhD. *Accreditation:* ACPE. *Faculty:* 20. *Students:* 409 full-time (250 women), 4 part-time (all women); includes 61 minority (7 Black or African American, non-Hispanic/Latino; 1 American Indian or Alaska Native, non-Hispanic/Latino; 42 Asian, non-Hispanic/Latino; 7 Hispanic/Latino; 1 Native Hawaiian or other Pacific Islander, non-Hispanic/Latino; 3 Two or more races, non-Hispanic/Latino), 32 international. Average age 24. 299 applicants, 54% accepted, 117 enrolled. In 2017, 92 doctorates awarded. *Degree requirements:* For doctorate, advanced practice rotations. *Entrance requirements:* For doctorate, PCAT, PharmCAS application, interview, criminal background check, minimum GPA of 3.0 in required preprofessional courses and overall, work experience, community service, leadership abilities. Additional exam requirements/recommendations for international students: Required—TOEFL (minimum score 550 paper-based; 79 iBT), Michigan English Language Assessment Battery (minimum score 85); Recommended—IELTS (minimum score 6.5), TWE (minimum score 5.5). *Application deadline:* For fall admission, 11/1 for domestic and international students. Applications are processed on a rolling basis. Electronic applications accepted. *Expenses:* Contact institution. *Financial support:* In 2017–18, 126 students received support. Scholarships/grants available. Financial award applicants required to submit FAFSA. *Unit head:* Dr. Richard L. Lucarotti, Associate Dean of Pharmacy, 313-577-8741, E-mail: rll@wayne.edu. *Application contact:* 313-577-6823, E-mail: cphsinfo@wayne.edu.
Website: http://cphs.wayne.edu/pharmd/index.php

West Coast University, Graduate Programs, North Hollywood, CA 91606. Offers advanced generalist (MSN); family nurse practitioner (MSN); health administration (MHA); occupational therapy (MS); pharmacy (Pharm D); physical therapy (DPT).

Western New England University, College of Pharmacy and Health Sciences, Pharm D Program, Springfield, MA 01119. Offers Pharm D, Pharm D/MBA, Pharm D/MS. *Faculty:* 33 full-time (17 women). *Students:* 272 full-time (174 women); includes 48 minority (16 Black or African American, non-Hispanic/Latino; 1 American Indian or Alaska Native, non-Hispanic/Latino; 16 Asian, non-Hispanic/Latino; 15 Hispanic/Latino), 2 international. Average age 21. 286 applicants, 36% accepted, 62 enrolled. In 2017, 71 doctorates awarded. *Entrance requirements:* For doctorate, PCAT, two letters of recommendation, completion of all pre-pharmacy course requirements at accredited college or university. Additional exam requirements/recommendations for international students: Required—TOEFL (minimum score 80 iBT). *Application deadline:* For fall admission, 5/1 for domestic students. Application fee: $150. Electronic applications accepted. *Expenses:* $41,236 tuition, $2,360 fees. *Financial support:* Scholarships/grants available. Financial award application deadline: 4/15; financial award applicants required to submit FAFSA. *Unit head:* Dr. Evan T. Robinson, Dean, 413-796-2323, E-mail: erobinson@wne.edu. *Application contact:* Lori Berg, Assistant Director of Pharmacy Admissions, 413-796-2073, Fax: 413-796-2266, E-mail: rxadmissions@wne.edu.
Website: http://www1.wne.edu/pharmacy-and-health-sciences/academics/pharmd/index.cfm

Western University of Health Sciences, College of Pharmacy, Program in Pharmacy, Pomona, CA 91766-1854. Offers Pharm D. *Accreditation:* ACPE. *Faculty:* 27 full-time (13 women), 3 part-time/adjunct (1 woman). *Students:* 534 full-time (350 women); includes 375 minority (19 Black or African American, non-Hispanic/Latino; 1 American Indian or Alaska Native, non-Hispanic/Latino; 279 Asian, non-Hispanic/Latino; 39 Hispanic/Latino; 37 Two or more races, non-Hispanic/Latino), 15 international. Average age 27. 869 applicants, 37% accepted, 137 enrolled. In 2017, 124 doctorates awarded. *Degree requirements:* For doctorate, comprehensive exam (for some programs). *Entrance requirements:* For doctorate, minimum GPA of 2.75, interview, PharmCAS letters of recommendation; BS in pharmacy or equivalent (recommended), official transcripts. Additional exam requirements/recommendations for international students: Required—TOEFL (minimum score 79 iBT). *Application deadline:* For fall admission, 9/8 priority date for domestic and international students. Application fee: $65. Electronic applications accepted. *Expenses:* $49,725 tuition and fees (first three years); $50,075 (fourth year). *Financial support:* In 2017–18, 42 students received support. Scholarships/grants available. Financial award application deadline: 3/2; financial award applicants required to submit FAFSA. *Faculty research:* Drug policy, international pharmacy education, formulation development of novel drug delivery systems, application of nanotechnology for controlled release system design, cancer chemoprevention. *Unit head:* Dr. Daniel Robinson, Dean, 909-469-5533, Fax: 909-469-5539, E-mail: drobinson@westernu.edu. *Application contact:* Kathryn Ford, Admission Director, 909-469-5335, Fax: 909-469-5570, E-mail: admissions@westernu.edu.
Website: http://www.westernu.edu/pharmacy-dpp_message

West Virginia University, School of Pharmacy, Morgantown, WV 26506-9500. Offers health services and outcomes research (PhD); pharmaceutical and pharmacological sciences (PhD); professional pharmacy (Pharm D). *Students:* 338 full-time (211 women), 3 part-time (2 women); includes 41 minority (10 Black or African American, non-Hispanic/Latino; 1 American Indian or Alaska Native, non-Hispanic/Latino; 15 Asian, non-Hispanic/Latino; 8 Hispanic/Latino; 7 Two or more races, non-Hispanic/Latino), 19 international. Terminal master's awarded for partial completion of doctoral program. *Degree requirements:* For doctorate, variable foreign language requirement, comprehensive exam (for some programs), thesis/dissertation (for some programs). *Entrance requirements:* For doctorate, GRE General Test (for PhD), minimum GPA of 2.75 (for PhD). Additional exam requirements/recommendations for international students: Required—TOEFL (minimum score 500 paper-based). *Application deadline:* For fall admission, 3/1 priority date for domestic and international students. Application fee: $60. Electronic applications accepted. *Expenses:* Contact institution. *Financial support:* Research assistantships, teaching assistantships, career-related internships or fieldwork, Federal Work-Study, institutionally sponsored loans, health care benefits, tuition waivers (full and partial), and unspecified assistantships available. Financial award application deadline: 3/1; financial award applicants required to submit FAFSA. *Faculty research:* Pharmaceutics, medicinal chemistry, biopharmaceutics/pharmacokinetics, health outcomes research. *Unit head:* Dr. Mary K. Stamatakis, Interim Dean, 304-293-5101, Fax: 304-293-5483, E-mail: mkstamatakis@hsc.wvu.edu. *Application contact:* Dr. Mary L. Euler, Associate Dean for Student Services, 304-293-7806, Fax: 304-293-5483, E-mail: mleuler@hsc.wvu.edu.
Website: https://pharmacy.hsc.wvu.edu

Wilkes University, College of Graduate and Professional Studies, Nesbitt School of Pharmacy, Wilkes-Barre, PA 18766-0002. Offers Pharm D. *Accreditation:* ACPE. *Students:* 285 full-time (190 women); includes 40 minority (4 Black or African American, non-Hispanic/Latino; 1 American Indian or Alaska Native, non-Hispanic/Latino; 17 Asian, non-Hispanic/Latino; 5 Hispanic/Latino; 13 Two or more races, non-Hispanic/Latino), 3 international. Average age 22. In 2017, 69 doctorates awarded. *Entrance requirements:* Additional exam requirements/recommendations for international students: Required—TOEFL (minimum score 550 paper-based; 79 iBT). *Application deadline:* Applications are processed on a rolling basis. *Expenses:* Contact institution. *Financial support:* Federal Work-Study and unspecified assistantships available. Financial award application deadline: 3/1; financial award applicants required to submit FAFSA. *Unit head:* Dr. Scott Stolte, Dean, 570-408-4280, Fax: 570-408-7828, E-mail: scott.stolte@wilkes.edu.
Website: http://www.wilkes.edu/academics/colleges/nesbitt-college-of-pharmacy/index.aspx

Wingate University, School of Pharmacy, Wingate, NC 28174. Offers Pharm D. *Accreditation:* ACPE. *Degree requirements:* For doctorate, comprehensive exam. *Entrance requirements:* For doctorate, PCAT. Electronic applications accepted. *Expenses:* Contact institution. *Faculty research:* Stress response in aging, arthritis therapy educational processes, professional development, sarcopenia in aging, geriatric-psych drug therapy.

Xavier University of Louisiana, College of Pharmacy, New Orleans, LA 70125. Offers Pharm D. *Accreditation:* ACPE. *Entrance requirements:* Additional exam requirements/recommendations for international students: Required—TOEFL. Electronic applications accepted. *Expenses:* Contact institution.

PHILADELPHIA COLLEGE OF OSTEOPATHIC MEDICINE

School of Pharmacy–Georgia Campus

Program of Study

The Philadelphia College of Osteopathic Medicine (PCOM) School of Pharmacy–Georgia Campus offers a four-year Doctor of Pharmacy (Pharm.D.) degree program. The program prepares generalist, entry-level pharmacists capable of delivering high-quality pharmaceutical care. The PCOM School of Pharmacy–Georgia Campus's mission is to educate caring, proactive pharmacists according to a model of patient-centered care, a practice of pharmacy in which the practitioner assumes responsibility for a patient's medication-related needs and is held accountable for this commitment.

While preparing pharmacy practitioners is the primary mission of the Pharm.D. program, it also provides an avenue by which students may explore a broad range of career opportunities. The program is designed to prepare a well-rounded student who is able to practice in many areas of pharmacy. The program also aspires to develop analytical and life-long learning skills to help students excel after graduation in the rapidly changing and evolving field of health care. Each student in the program is assigned to a group of peers for team- and case-based learning to foster team-building skills in clinical case discussions. Each student is also assigned a faculty adviser to assist with their academic needs and guide them as they progress through the curriculum and prepare for a career in pharmacy.

Research Facilities and Library Resources

Georgia Campus–Philadelphia College of Osteopathic Medicine (GA–PCOM) features teaching and research laboratories, and an Information Commons which integrates library and student computer lab functions.

Faculty members conduct research in basic, clinical, and administrative sciences, sharing their experience and scholarly expertise with students. GA–PCOM has more than 6,500 square feet of research space in addition to an animal-care facility research laboratory that houses shared common equipment such as -80° C freezers and centrifuges. There are multiple storage spaces outside of the labs for supplies and areas that store cell culture equipment and laboratory gases.

The PCOM Digital Library provides access to a wealth of licensed internet resources, including over 10,000 full-text e-journals, electronic textbooks, bibliographic databases, streaming videos, clinical simulations, diagnostic decision support programs, and evidence-based clinical information systems, as well as subject access to selected internet resources. Print subscriptions to a number of core journals are also available in the Information Commons. The PCOM library electronically provides articles from any print-only titles in its collection to GA–PCOM users. GA–PCOM and the School of Pharmacy are committed to the advancement of knowledge and intellectual growth through teaching and research, and to the well-being of the community through leadership and service.

Financial Aid

GA–PCOM's Office of Financial Aid provides comprehensive assistance to all admitted students. Financial assistance can be provided through the Federal Direct Loan program, institutional scholarships, and various alternative private loan programs.

Cost of Study

Tuition and fees for the Pharm.D. program for the 2018–19 academic year are $39,330.

Living and Housing Costs

Suwanee and the neighboring communities of Lawrenceville and Duluth offer a less hurried lifestyle with an abundance of amenities and easy access to all Atlanta has to offer: shopping, professional sports, the arts, and more. There is no on-campus housing so students live off-campus. Room and board costs vary based on each student's arrangements.

Student Group

For the 2017–18 academic year, the School of Pharmacy enrolled 85 new students with a diverse cultural makeup. Current enrollment projections call for approximately 80 new students to be admitted to the Pharm.D. program each year.

Location

The GA–PCOM campus is located in Gwinnett County, approximately 30 minutes north of Atlanta. A welcoming community with a nationally recognized public school system, an award-winning park and recreation department, and ample entertainment options, Gwinnett is home to a minor league sports team, and numerous shopping and dining opportunities. The campus is close to a myriad of outdoor recreational opportunities, including Stone Mountain Park, the North Georgia mountains, and scenic Lake Lanier which offers boating, fishing, water parks, canoeing, and horseback riding.

The College

PCOM is one of the largest of 34 osteopathic colleges in the United States, with campuses in Philadelphia, suburban Atlanta, and South Georgia. GA–PCOM was chartered in 2005, and is committed to educating responsive medical professionals prepared to practice in the 21st century. Supported by advanced medical and educational technology, Georgia Campus shares the PCOM mission and also seeks to improve the quality of life for residents of Georgia and the Southeast by preparing healthcare practitioners and professionals to address the social, economic, and healthcare needs of the region. Since joining the established community of students, faculty, and staff in Georgia in 2010, the School of Pharmacy's focus has been to train students for entry-level careers with the right combination of skills, knowledge, and attitudes to develop and grow in the ever-changing field.

Applying

Admission to the Pharm.D. program is competitive and selective. Students are evaluated on a variety of criteria. Academic performance in science courses, as well as overall academic performance as determined by grade point average (GPA), are the major criteria used by the Admissions Committee. Competitive scores on the Pharmacy College Admissions Test (PCAT) as well as the MCAT, DAT, OAT, and GRE are also considered. Professional preparedness, motivation, decision-making skills, and written and verbal communication skills are also evaluated. Prior degrees earned and previous pharmacy-related work experiences are additional considerations. Qualified applicants who have satisfactorily completed all prerequisite coursework, but have not earned a bachelor's degree can apply and enroll at PCOM School of Pharmacy–Georgia Campus. Qualified applicants may also apply and be offered admission without having completed all prerequisite course work. However, all applicants must successfully complete prerequisite coursework before matriculating to the School of Pharmacy in August. Note also, that while a bachelor's degree is not required, the Admissions Committee gives preference to those students who have earned a bachelor's degree.

PCOM School of Pharmacy–Georgia Campus participates in the PharmCAS application service (http://www.pharmcas.org). The School participates in the Early Decision Program, with a primary application deadline in early September. The application deadline for regular decision candidates is early March. Supplemental applications are due in early April.

Prospective students can find additional information about the application process, including prerequisite coursework requirements, at http://admissions.pcom.edu/app-process/pharmacy-pharmd/.

Correspondence and Information

Office of Admissions
Georgia Campus–Philadelphia College of Osteopathic Medicine
625 Old Peachtree Road NW
Suwanee, Georgia 30024
Phone: 678-225-7500
866-282-4544 (toll-free)
Fax: 678-225-7509
E-mail: pharmdadmissions@pcom.edu
Website: http://www.pcom.edu
Twitter: @PCOMAdmissions

THE FACULTY

Shari Allen, Pharm.D., Associate Professor of Pharmacy Practice.
Yun Bai, Ph.D., Associate Professor of Pharmaceutical Sciences.
Kimberly Barefield, Pharm.D., Associate Professor of Pharmacy Practice.
Vishakha Bhave, Ph.D., Assistant Professor of Pharmaceutical Sciences.
Drew Cates, Pharm.D., Assistant Professor of Pharmacy Practice.
Caroline Champion, Pharm.D., Assistant Professor of Pharmacy Practice.
Naushad Khan Ghilzai, Ph.D., Associate Dean for Academics, Professor of Pharmaceutical Sciences.
Christopher (Shawn) Holaway, Pharm.D., Assistant Professor of Pharmacy Practice.
Yue-Qiao (George) Huang, Ph.D., Assistant Professor of Pharmaceutical Sciences.
Samuel M. John, Pharm.D., Associate Professor of Pharmacy Practice.
Jiehyun Lee, Pharm.D., Assistant Professor of Pharmacy Practice.
Michael Lee, Ph.D., Assistant Dean of Professional and Student Affairs, Associate Professor of Pharmaceutical Sciences.
Hua Ling, Pharm.D., Assistant Professor of Pharmacy Practice.
Dusty Lisi, Pharm.D., Assistant Professor of Pharmacy Practice.
Shirin Madzhidova, Pharm.D., Assistant Professor of Pharmacy Practice.
Edo-abasi McGee, Pharm.D., Assistant Professor of Pharmacy Practice.
Candis McGraw, Pharm.D., Assistant Professor of Pharmacy Practice.
Vicky Mody, Ph.D., Associate Professor of Pharmaceutical Sciences.
Kumar Mukergee, Ph.D., Assistant Professor of Pharmacy Practice.
Harish S. Parihar, R.Ph., Ph.D., Associate Professor of Pharmacy Practice.
Sonia Patel, Pharm.D., Assistant Professor of Pharmacy Practice.
Srujana Rayalam, Ph.D., Assistant Professor of Pharmaceutical Sciences.
Mandy Reece, Pharm.D., BC-ADM, CDE, Associate Professor of Pharmacy Practice.
Brent Rollins, R.Ph., Ph.D., Assistant Professor of Pharmacy Administration.
Essie Samuel, Pharm.D., Assistant Professor of Pharmacy Practice.
Rangaiah Shashidharamurthy, Ph.D., Assistant Professor of Pharmaceutical Sciences.
Avadhesh C. Sharma, Pharm.D., Ph.D., Chair and Professor, Department of Pharmaceutical Science.
Gregory Smallwood, Pharm.D., Associate Professor of Pharmacy Practice.
Shawn Spencer, Ph.D., Dean and Chief Academic Officer.
LeAnne Honeycutt Varner, Pharm.D., Assistant Professor of Pharmacy Practice.
Desuo Wang, Ph.D., Associate Professor of Pharmaceutical Sciences.
Xinyu (Eric) Wang, Ph.D., Associate Professor of Pharmaceutical Sciences.
Julie Wickman, Pharm.D., Assistant Dean for Experiential and Clinical Education, Associate Professor of Pharmacy Practice.
Zhiqian (James) Wu, Ph.D., Associate Professor of Pharmaceutical Sciences.

The PCOM School of Pharmacy–Georgia Campus provides students with a collaborative learning environment.

Pharmacy students learn pharmaceutical and clinical skills in modern lab facilities.

NOVA SOUTHEASTERN UNIVERSITY

College of Pharmacy

NSU NOVA SOUTHEASTERN UNIVERSITY
College of Pharmacy

Programs of Study

Nova Southeastern University (NSU) offers an innovative program of graduate study and research leading to the Master of Science (M.S.) or Doctor of Philosophy degree (Ph.D.). Students can choose to pursue the M.S. or Ph.D. degree in one of three sequences: Molecular Medicine and Pharmacogenomics (Drug Discovery), Drug Development (Pharmaceutics), or Social and Administrative Pharmacy (Determinants of Drug Use). The first year of study involves course work and rotations through several research laboratories and selection of a major adviser. During the second year, area-specific course work will be taken and the student will begin their research. Subsequent years are devoted to research. A variety of research areas are available including cancer research, neuroscience, cardiovascular research, novel drug delivery systems, health outcomes, and pharmacoeconomics. The typical time to degree completion is five years. All of the graduates of the program have obtained employment in academic and industrial positions.

Research Facilities

The research laboratories in the COP occupy approximately 3,000 square feet in the Library/Research Building in the Health Professions Division (HPD) and an additional 2,000 square feet in the Center for Collaborative Research (CCR). Individual laboratory space ranges from 300 to 750 square feet and labs are equipped for biochemistry, molecular biology, or pharmacological research, and/or tissue culture equipment. There are also common laboratory facilities for chromatography, imaging, tissue culture, proteomics, and cell sorting. All common use laboratories are located in close proximity to the COP laboratories and are fully accessible to all of the College's researchers.

The animal facility is located in Rumbaugh-Goodwin Institute for Cancer Research (RGICR), which is housed in the CCR. They comply with the standards for use of mice, rats, and rabbits and are OLAW approved. They are maintained by a full-time caretaker and governed by an Institutional Animal Care and Use Committee. A veterinarian is responsible for oversight of the health of animals in the facility.

NSU maintains an extensive information technology network for research-based computing. Comprehensive fiber-optic and wireless networks provide connectivity for user access. A dedicated wide area network supports high-speed connections from all campuses. The research facilities have computers for data collection, processing, and analysis. All COP researchers have access to modern computers in their offices as well as in their laboratories, equipped with the necessary software for word processing, routine data analysis, and photo processing. High-performance computing, a wide range of research-related databases, and Internet support is available to all researchers. Local supercomputer facilities are under development.

Financial Aid

Top candidates are eligible for scholarships, which consist of a tuition waiver and teaching assistantships. Funded faculty may provide support in the form of research assistantships. Students can apply for a variety of loans. Work-study programs are also available.

Cost of Study

Tuition for 2018–19 is $27,465 (subject to change by the board of trustees without notice). A Health Professions Division general access fee of $145 is required each year. An NSU student services fee of $1,050 is also required annually.

Living and Housing Costs

The Rolling Hills Graduate Apartments are about one mile west of the NSU main campus and offer housing for approximately 373 students. Rooms are fully furnished and include a kitchen, bathroom, and living room. Married housing is also available. Costs are approximately $5,940 per semester (fall or winter); $14,500 for a twelve-month contract. Unlimited laundry, NSU-secured Wi-Fi, furnishings, utilities, air conditioning, cable TV, and local telephone service are included. More information about student housing is available at http://www.nova.edu/housing/.

Student Group

The current enrollment in all three sequences is approximately 40 students and roughly 96 percent of these students have scholarships or fellowships. The student population is comprised of about 40 percent women and about 80 percent are international students. The desired background of students is a degree in pharmacy or areas closely related to one of the three sequences.

Student Outcomes

Graduates of the program are prepared for employment by the pharmaceutical industry, governmental regulatory agencies, biomedical sciences profession, and academic positions. All of the graduates of the program have obtained employment in academic and industrial positions.

Location

Davie, a city of more than 95,000, maintains a sense of small-town intimacy while located near both an international airport and a seaport. The area is famous for its wide expanses of sandy beaches and its tropical climate. Nearby Fort Lauderdale is home to numerous museums, art galleries, and a performing arts center.

The College of Pharmacy also has branch campuses in Palm Beach, Florida and San Juan, Puerto Rico.

The University

Founded in 1964 as Nova University, the institution merged with Southeastern University of the Health Sciences in 1994, creating Nova Southeastern University. NSU offers a wide range of undergraduate, graduate, and professional degree programs to more than 29,000 students every year. It is the seventh-largest independent institution in the nation and the largest independent not-for-profit university in the Southeast. NSU is experiencing a sustained period of academic and fiscal growth and is committed to preparing students to meet the challenges of the twenty-first century.

Applying

Application materials that must be submitted include GRE results (NSU code 5522), proof of proficiency in English, transcripts received directly from the degree-granting institution (international applicants must have course work evaluated by World Education Services, Josef Silney & Associates, or Educational Credential Evaluators, Inc.), a formal application form, three letters of reference, and a brief written essay on the goals of the applicant.

Applications and a $50 nonrefundable fee must be submitted to Enrollment Processing Services (EPS), College of Pharmacy, Office of Admissions, 3301 College Ave, P.O. Box 299000, Ft. Lauderdale, Florida 33329-9905 prior to March 1. Applicants may also have an application mailed to them upon request.

Correspondence and Information

Dr. Peter M. Gannett
Associate Dean, Research and Graduate Education
Health Professions Division
College of Pharmacy
Nova Southeastern University
3200 South University Drive
Fort Lauderdale, Florida 33328
United States
E-mail: copphd@nova.edu

Health Professions Admissions Office
Attention: Thomas Bouchard, Jr.
Nova Southeastern University
Phone: 954-262-1112
877-640-0218 (toll-free)
Website: http://pharmacy.nova.edu

THE FACULTY AND THEIR RESEARCH

Drug Development and Molecular Medicine and Pharmacogenomics (Drug Discovery) Sequences

Michelle A. Clark, Professor and Interim Dean, College of Pharmacy; Ph.D., South Florida, 1996. Central signaling pathways for blood pressure regulation and control, role of the central renin angiotensin system in the regulation of cardiovascular and other diseases.

Rais A. Ansari, Associate Professor, Pharmaceutical Sciences; Ph.D., Kanpur (India), 1985. Mechanism of alcohol-mediated hypertension, transcriptional regulation of human angiotensinogen gene after ethanol and environmental toxicants exposure.

Ana Maria Castejon, Associate Professor and Interim Chair, Pharmaceutical Sciences; Ph.D., Central University (Venezuela), 1997. Oxidative stress and autism, diabetes mellitus, effects of statins in vascular smooth muscle cells, genetics of salt sensitivity in human subjects.

Luigi Cubeddu, Professor, Pharmaceutical Sciences; M.D., Central University (Venezuela); Ph.D., Colorado. Mechanisms and treatment of hypertension associated with obesity, salt-sensitive hypertension, early detection of insulin resistance and abnormalities in glucose metabolism, statin withdrawal syndrome.

Richard C. Deth, Professor, Pharmaceutical Sciences, Ph.D., Miami (Florida), 1975. Role of redox and methylation status in neurodevelopmental disorders.

Young M. Kwon, Associate Professor, Pharmaceutical Sciences, Ph.D., Utah, 2003. Targeted delivery and triggered release system for therapeutic macromolecules; bioconjugate chemistry and PEGylation; nonviral gene carriers and intracellular drug delivery; protein stability and release from biodegradable polymer.

Jean J. Latimer, Associate Professor, Pharmaceutical Sciences; Ph.D., Buffalo, SUNY, 1989. Loss of DNA repair as causative factor in cancer formation; breast tissue engineering; ancestral disparity in breast cancer development and pharmacogenomics; drug resistance (via cancer stem cells) in childhood leukemia.

Anastasios Lymperopoulos, Associate Professor, Pharmaceutical Sciences; Ph.D., Patras (Greece), 2004. Cardiovascular biology/pharmacology and gene therapy, with a focus on adrenergic system regulation in heart failure; novel roles of G-protein coupled receptor kinases and their cofactors, beta-arrestins, in regulation of various important cardiovascular G-protein coupled receptors; roles of G-protein coupled receptor kinases and their cofactors, beta-arrestins, in adrenal gland physiology and biology.

David J. Mastropietro, Assistant Professor, Pharmaceutical Sciences; Ph.D., Nova Southeastern, 2014. Formulation and laboratory assessment of abuse deterrent pharmaceutical dosage forms, personalized medicine through the art and science of pharmacy compounding.

Enrique A. Nieves, Assistant Professor, Pharmaceutical Sciences; Ph.D., Florida, 1982. Applications of nanotechnology in drug product development and pharmaceutical process designs, development of co-excipients for improved drug formulations, nanotechnology applications in the extraction and isolation of new drugs from natural sources.

Hamid Omidian, Professor, Pharmaceutical Sciences; Ph.D., Brunel (London), 1997. Hydrogels for pharmaceutical and biomedical applications, hydrogel-based controlled delivery systems and technologies, hydrogel-based gastroretentive drug delivery platforms, hydrogel-based platforms for cell culture and proliferation.

Mutasem Rawas-Qalaji, Associate Professor, Pharmaceutical Sciences; Ph.D., Manitoba (Canada), 2006. Enhancing the permeability and the relative bioavailability of poorly absorbed drugs by nanotechnology, formulation and delivery of drug-loaded nanoparticles through noninvasive and user-friendly routes of administration, formulation and evaluation of sublingual ODT tablets as an alternative noninvasive dosage form.

Robert C. Speth, Professor, Pharmaceutical Sciences; Ph.D., Vanderbilt, 1976. Brain renin-angiotensin system pharmacology and functionality.

Malav S. Trivedi, Assistant Professor, Pharmaceutical Sciences, Ph.D., Northeastern, 2013. Investigating the effect of environmental insults and dietary interventions on nuclear and mitochondrial epigenetic changes, and characterizing its contribution in neurodevelopmental and neurodegenerative diseases as well as tumor biology and drug targeting.

Social and Administrative Pharmacy (Determinants of Drug Use) Sequence

Barry A. Bleidt, Professor, Sociobehavioral and Administrative Pharmacy; Pharm.D., Xavier of Louisiana, 1994; Ph.D., Florida, 1982. Cultural competency/diversity/health disparities; assessment of student achievement; faculty workload and performance measures; peer teaching evaluation strategies; Internet, technology and medical information; and pharmacoeconomics.

Manuel J. Carvajal, Professor and Chairperson, Department of Sociobehavioral and Administrative Pharmacy; Ph.D., Florida, 1974. Applied econometrics geared to problem solving; various areas of human capital including fertility, migration, poverty, and discrimination; gender and ethnic differences in labor market outcomes and job satisfaction.

Nile M. Khanfar, Assistant Professor, Sociobehavioral and Administrative Pharmacy; Ph.D., Louisiana at Monroe, 2005; M.B.A., Louisiana at Monroe, 2001. Management leadership, strategic management/marketing business cases, direct-to-consumer advertising of prescription medication and its influence on consumer behavior.

L. Leanne Lai, Professor, Sociobehavioral and Administrative Pharmacy; Ph.D., Maryland, Baltimore, 1996. Pharmacoeconomics and outcomes research, pharmacoepidemiology and secondary data analysis, international education.

Ioana Popovici, Assistant Professor, Sociobehavioral and Administrative Pharmacy; Ph.D., Florida International, 2007. Economic evaluation of substance abuse treatment interventions, relationship between addictive substance use or abuse and its economic consequences.

Sylvia E. Rabionet, Associate Professor, Sociobehavioral and Administrative Pharmacy; Ed.D., Harvard, 2002. Health disparities, public health issues.

Jesus Sanchez, Associate Professor, Sociobehavioral and Administrative Pharmacy; Ph.D., Miami (Florida), 2001. HIV reduction among high-risk migrant workers; building capacity and infrastructure in the migrant farm worker communities in South Florida; prevalence of HIV, hepatitis B and C, and associated risk factors among Hispanic injection drug users.

Georgina Silva-Suárez, Assistant Professor, Sociobehavioral and Administrative Pharmacy; Ph.D., Florida International, 2014. Adherence to ART, HIV prevention, adolescent health, human sexuality and sex education.

Albert Wertheimer, Professor, Sociobehavioral and Administrative Pharmacy; MBA, 1967, SUNY-Buffalo, Ph.D., Purdue University, 1969. Current research interests include pharmaceutical counterfeiting, off-label prescribing, and cost-benefit studies.

UNIVERSITY OF HAWAI'I AT HILO

Daniel K. Inouye College of Pharmacy (DKICP)
Ph.D. in Pharmaceutical Sciences

★ For more information, visit http://petersons.to/uhawaii-hilo_pharm-phd

Programs of Study

The Daniel K. Inouye College of Pharmacy (DKICP) at the University of Hawai`i at Hilo (UH Hilo) is the only institution in the central Pacific to offer the Ph.D. in Pharmaceutical Sciences degree program.

The Ph.D. in Pharmaceutical Sciences degree program utilizes the extraordinary intellectual, biological, physical, and cultural diversity on the Island of Hawaii, and within both the State and Asia-Pacific Region, as a focus of investigation and study. The Ph.D. degree program provides graduate training in the pharmaceutical sciences, including medicinal chemistry, pharmacology, pharmaceutics, and pharmacognosy, with an emphasis on natural product drug discovery and development, and their importance in pharmacy and healthcare in general.

The Ph.D. degree program is aimed at students with B.S., M.S., or Pharm.D. degrees, and those currently working in the field. The program is designed to foster student development as critical thinkers, team players, self-directed interdisciplinary scholars, and communicators.

Students are prepared for senior leadership positions in the pharmaceutical sciences in academia, research, education, government, industry, and related fields. They are trained to become leaders who can identify, research, and solve problems related to the pharmaceutical sciences.

The University of Hawai`i at Hilo's Doctor of Pharmacy (Pharm.D.) program is accredited by the Accreditation Council for Pharmacy Education (ACPE).

Research Facilities

The research facilities are located on the main UH Hilo campus and at the Waiakea research facility a few miles away. These facilities house all the scientific equipment and instruments needed for natural product isolation and structural analyses, including 400 MHz multinuclear NMR spectrometers, LC-MC systems with ESI and APCI interfaces, LC-qTOF high mass accuracy mass spectrometer, GC-triple quadrupole mass spectrometer, X-ray diffractometer, polarimeter, FT-IR, several UV-VIS spectrophotometers, and HPLC systems (analytical and preparative). Pharmaceutics equipment includes a NiComp 380 particle analyzer and a Nano DeBEE homogenizer while a microwave reactor is available for chemical synthesis. Equipment for cellular analysis and molecular biology includes a Perkin Elmer Operetta high content imaging system, Leica confocal microscopes, flow cytometers, multiple research grade upright, inverted and stereo microscopes, centrifuges (high speed, ultra- and microcentrifuges), a GenePix microarray scanner, real-time qPCR cyclers, and a variety of microplate readers with state-of-the-art detection technologies based on photometry, fluorometry, luminometry, time-resolved fluorescence and fluorescence polarization. All of the University's BSL-2 labs are equipped for the culture of microbes and mammalian cells.

The Daniel K. Inouye College of Pharmacy also has strong research programs in cancer biology and natural product drug discovery.

In addition to the well-stocked and well-equipped Mookini Library on the main campus, UH Hilo DKICP students also have access to a specialized pharmacy library. Students utilize information systems that serve as a foundation for their ability to use concepts and evidence-based medicine to answer drug information questions and compare therapeutic alternatives.

Financial Aid

Qualified applicants are eligible to apply for a Graduate Assistantship. Students may also submit the free application for Federal Student Aid (FAFSA) in January and indicate the University of Hawai`i at Hilo (UH Hilo) code number 001611. However, applicants must be accepted for admission before a financial aid award can be issued.

More information can be found on the UH Hilo Financial Aid Office's website at http://hilo.hawaii.edu/financialaid/.

Cost of Study

Resident tuition for the Ph.D. in Pharmaceutical Sciences program is $484 per credit hour, or $5,808 per semester, for full-time students for the 2018–19 academic year. Tuition for nonresidents is $1,102 per credit hour, or $13,224 per semester, for full-time students.

The most recent information on tuition, fees, and living and housing costs can be found at http://hilo.hawaii.edu/uhh/bo/cashier/tuition_schedule.php.

The Faculty

The faculty includes cancer researchers, Dr. Linda Connelly (the role of inflammatory signaling and breast cancer), Dr. Aaron Jacobs (cell signaling molecules and their involvement in disease processes), Dr. Dana-Lynn Koomoa-Lange (calcium signaling changes in disease states), and Dr. Ingo Koomoa-Lange (calcium signaling in innate immune cell and neuroblastoma patho/physiology).

Faculty members who are medicinal chemists include Dr. Dianqing Sun (organic synthesis of anticancer and antimicrobial drugs) and Dr. Daniela Gündisch (organic synthesis of central nervous system drugs and development of *in vivo* tracers for imaging).

University of Hawai'i at Hilo

The research of Drs. Leng Chee Chang and Shugeng Cao centers on the isolation of novel molecules that possess anticancer and other biological activities from terrestrial and marine sources. Dr. Ghee Tan's multidisciplinary drug discovery work focuses on the identification and mechanistic elucidation of anticancer and antimalarial natural products from ethnomedicines and microorganisms, from both terrestrial and marine environments. Dr. Susan Jarvi is actively involved in rat lung worm disease. Dr. Abhijit Date focuses on targeted therapies utilizing nanoparticles as a drug delivery system. Dr. Supakit Wongwiwatthananukit is involved in mathematical analysis of health care outcomes.

A complete listing of DKICP faculty and their research interests is available online at http://pharmacy.uhh.hawaii.edu/academics/graduate/FacResInt.php.

Location

UH Hilo is located on the windward side of the Big Island of Hawai'i in the bayside town of Hilo. With a population of approximately 43,000, Hilo has small-town charm, but is large enough to support 5 shopping centers, and to provide needed services and amenities. The island of Hawai`i offers many natural attractions, including Hawai`i Volcanoes National Park, white sand beaches, plunging waterfalls, and scenic Waipio valley.

The University

The University of Hawai`i, with a student population of about 4,000, is a multicultural comprehensive university, offering a wide range of baccalaureate and graduate degrees in a few selected disciplines. While UH Hilo is a state university, the atmosphere is that of a private college, with small class sizes, a low faculty-to-student ratio, and opportunities for research, and hands-on learning.

As a public university, the University of Hawai`i at Hilo has a unique position in the State—and country—by offering a rigorous and engaging curriculum at an affordable tuition rate. The admission requirements are moderately selective, allowing above-average students the opportunity to enjoy the benefits of a small school experience.

UH Hilo is accredited by the Accrediting Commission for Senior Colleges and Universities of the Western Association of Schools and Colleges.

Applying

Acceptance is granted at the discretion of the Pharmaceutical Science Ph.D. Admissions Committee. Applicants must: 1) complete the application process; 2) hold a baccalaureate degree or graduate degree from a regionally accredited U.S. college or university, or its equivalent from a recognized non–U.S. institution of learning; 3) have a minimum GPA of 3.0 out of 4.0, or the equivalent in the last 60 semester credits of undergraduate and in all post-baccalaureate work; 4) submit a personal statement of objectives which includes applicant's background, professional goals, and academic and research interests; 5) submit a resume; 6) provide official GRE scores; 7) submit three letters of recommendation using the "Ph.D. Letter of Recommendation Form" from individuals who can attest to the applicant's educational ability, motivation, and character, and/or leadership experiences, including a professor of one of the natural or physical sciences; 8) complete a SKYPE or equivalent electronic interview; and 9) submit a $50 application fee.

Applicants are also recommended to have successfully completed the following courses with a grade of C or higher: General Biology I and II for science majors with labs, General Chemistry I and II for science majors with labs, Organic Chemistry I and II for science majors with labs, and Calculus 1 or Advanced Calculus. Students may have to take additional courses if proficiency cannot be demonstrated.

Foreign applicants must also submit an official TOEFL or IELTS score report and the International Graduate Student Supplemental Information form.

Further information on the details of fulfilling admissions requirements is available from the Ph.D. Program Admissions Office (pharmacy@hawaii.edu), and the DKICP Graduate Admissions website. All documents can be found online at http://pharmacy.uhh.hawaii.edu/academics/graduate/admissions.php.

Applications are accepted and reviewed on a rolling basis until all seats are filled for the following Fall semester. The final application deadline is May 15.

Correspondence and Information

Ph.D. Program Admissions
Office of Student Services
The Daniel K. Inouye College of Pharmacy (DKICP)
University of Hawaii at Hilo
200 W. Kawili Street
Hilo, Hawaii 96720
United States
Fax: 808-933-3889
E-mail: pharmacy@hawaii.edu
Website: http://pharmacy.uhh.hawaii.edu/academics/graduate/

Section 31
Veterinary Medicine and Sciences

This section contains a directory of institutions offering graduate work in veterinary medicine and sciences. Additional information about programs listed in the directory may be obtained by writing directly to the dean of a graduate school or chair of a department at the address given in the directory.

For programs offering related work, see also in this book *Biological and Biomedical Sciences* and *Zoology*. In the other guides in this series:

Graduate Programs in the Humanities, Arts & Social Sciences
See *Economics (Agricultural Economics and Agribusiness)*

Graduate Programs in the Physical Sciences, Mathematics, Agricultural Sciences, the Environment & Natural Resources
See *Agricultural and Food Sciences, Marine Sciences and Oceanography,* and *Natural Resources*

Graduate Programs in Engineering & Applied Sciences
See *Agricultural Engineering and Bioengineering* and *Biomedical Engineering and Biotechnology*

CONTENTS

Program Directories

Veterinary Medicine

Auburn University, College of Veterinary Medicine, Professional Program in Veterinary Medicine, Auburn University, AL 36849. Offers DVM, DVM/MS. *Accreditation:* AVMA. *Faculty:* 100 full-time (41 women), 3 part-time/adjunct (1 woman). *Students:* 482 full-time (397 women), 40 part-time (32 women); includes 41 minority (7 Black or African American, non-Hispanic/Latino; 5 Asian, non-Hispanic/Latino; 21 Hispanic/Latino; 1 Native Hawaiian or other Pacific Islander, non-Hispanic/Latino; 7 Two or more races, non-Hispanic/Latino). Average age 25. 980 applicants, 17% accepted, 120 enrolled. In 2017, 118 doctorates awarded. *Degree requirements:* For doctorate, preceptorship. *Application deadline:* Applications are processed on a rolling basis. Application fee: $50 ($60 for international students). *Expenses:* Contact institution. *Financial support:* Fellowships available. Financial award application deadline: 3/15; financial award applicants required to submit FAFSA. *Unit head:* Dr. Calvin Johnson, Dean, 334-844-4546. *Application contact:* Dr. George Flowers, Interim Dean of the Graduate School, 334-844-2125.

Colorado State University, College of Veterinary Medicine and Biomedical Sciences, Doctor of Veterinary Medicine Program, Fort Collins, CO 80523-1601. Offers DVM, DVM/MPH, DVM/MS, DVM/MST, DVM/PhD, MBA/DVM. *Accreditation:* AVMA. *Students:* 579 full-time (485 women); includes 120 minority (2 Black or African American, non-Hispanic/Latino; 36 Asian, non-Hispanic/Latino; 53 Hispanic/Latino; 29 Two or more races, non-Hispanic/Latino), 2 international. Average age 27. 2,140 applicants, 8% accepted, 156 enrolled. *Entrance requirements:* For doctorate, GRE, interview by invitation; CSA supplemental application; transcripts; VMCAS application; letters of recommendation. Additional exam requirements/recommendations for international students: Required—TOEFL (minimum score 550 paper-based; 80 iBT), IELTS (minimum score 6.5). *Application deadline:* For fall admission, 9/17 for domestic and international students. Application fee: $60 ($70 for international students). Electronic applications accepted. *Expenses:* Tuition, state resident: full-time $9917. Tuition, nonresident: full-time $24,312. *Required fees:* $2284. Tuition and fees vary according to course load and program. *Financial support:* Scholarships/grants available. *Total annual research expenditures:* $215,282. *Unit head:* Gretchen Delcambre, Director, Veterinary Admissions, 970-491-6163, E-mail: gh.delcambre@colostate.edu. *Application contact:* Janet Janke, Director, DVM Admissions Operations, 970-491-7052, E-mail: janet.janke@colostate.edu.
Website: http://csu-cvmbs.colostate.edu/dvm-program/Pages/default.aspx

Cornell University, College of Veterinary Medicine, Ithaca, NY 14853. Offers DVM. *Accreditation:* AVMA. *Faculty:* 202 full-time (96 women). *Students:* 413 full-time (321 women); includes 94 minority (8 Black or African American, non-Hispanic/Latino; 23 Asian, non-Hispanic/Latino; 17 Hispanic/Latino; 1 Native Hawaiian or other Pacific Islander, non-Hispanic/Latino; 45 Two or more races, non-Hispanic/Latino), 6 international. Average age 26. 1,205 applicants, 15% accepted, 116 enrolled. In 2017, 99 doctorates awarded. *Entrance requirements:* For doctorate, GRE General Test or MCAT, veterinary experience with letter(s) of recommendation. Additional exam requirements/recommendations for international students: Required—TOEFL (minimum score 600 paper-based; 100 iBT). *Application deadline:* For fall admission, 9/15 for domestic and international students. Electronic applications accepted. *Expenses:* Contact institution. *Financial support:* In 2017–18, 371 students received support. Federal Work-Study, institutionally sponsored loans, and scholarships/grants available. Financial award application deadline: 2/1; financial award applicants required to submit CSS PROFILE or FAFSA. *Faculty research:* Animal models of human disease, cancer biology, genetics and genomics, infection and pathobiology, regenerative and stem cell biology. *Total annual research expenditures:* $46.7 million. *Unit head:* Dr. Lorin Warnick, Dean, 607-253-3771, Fax: 607-253-3701. *Application contact:* Jennifer A. Mailey, Director of Admissions, 607-253-3700, Fax: 607-253-3709, E-mail: jam333@cornell.edu.
Website: http://www.vet.cornell.edu/

Iowa State University of Science and Technology, Department of Veterinary Diagnostic and Production Animal Medicine, Ames, IA 50011. Offers veterinary preventative medicine (MS). *Accreditation:* AVMA. *Degree requirements:* For master's, thesis or alternative. *Entrance requirements:* For master's, GRE General Test. Additional exam requirements/recommendations for international students: Required—TOEFL (minimum score 550 paper-based; 79 iBT), IELTS (minimum score 6.5). Electronic applications accepted.

Kansas State University, Graduate School, College of Veterinary Medicine, Professional Program in Veterinary Medicine, Manhattan, KS 66506. Offers DVM. *Accreditation:* AVMA. *Entrance requirements:* Additional exam requirements/recommendations for international students: Required—TOEFL. *Expenses:* Contact institution. *Faculty research:* Surgery and medicine, epithelial function, infectious disease of animals, neuroscience, analytical pharmacology.

Louisiana State University and Agricultural & Mechanical College, School of Veterinary Medicine, Professional Program in Veterinary Medicine, Baton Rouge, LA 70803. Offers DVM. *Accreditation:* AVMA. *Faculty:* 1 (woman) full-time. *Students:* 350 full-time (290 women); includes 44 minority (7 Black or African American, non-Hispanic/Latino; 6 Asian, non-Hispanic/Latino; 26 Hispanic/Latino; 5 Two or more races, non-Hispanic/Latino), 1 international. Average age 25. 94 applicants, 100% accepted, 89 enrolled. In 2017, 84 doctorates awarded. *Total annual research expenditures:* $4,924.

Michigan State University, College of Veterinary Medicine, Professional Program in Veterinary Medicine, East Lansing, MI 48824. Offers veterinary medicine (DVM); veterinary medicine/medical scientist training program (DVM). *Accreditation:* AVMA. *Entrance requirements:* Additional exam requirements/recommendations for international students: Required—TOEFL. Electronic applications accepted. *Expenses:* Contact institution.

Mississippi State University, College of Veterinary Medicine, Professional Program in Veterinary Medicine, Mississippi State, MS 39762. Offers DVM. *Accreditation:* AVMA. *Students:* 332 full-time (251 women); includes 26 minority (8 Black or African American, non-Hispanic/Latino; 3 American Indian or Alaska Native, non-Hispanic/Latino; 3 Asian, non-Hispanic/Latino; 10 Hispanic/Latino; 2 Two or more races, non-Hispanic/Latino). Average age 25. 92 applicants, 100% accepted, 88 enrolled. *Entrance requirements:* For doctorate, GRE, minimum overall GPA of 2.8. Additional exam requirements/recommendations for international students: Required—TOEFL. *Application deadline:* For fall admission, 10/1 for domestic students. Application fee: $60. Electronic applications accepted. *Expenses:* Contact institution. *Financial support:* Scholarships/grants available. Financial award applicants required to submit FAFSA. *Faculty research:* Veterinary education, advancing research in veterinary medicine and biomedical fields. *Unit head:* Dr. Margaret Kern, Associate Dean for Academic Affairs, 662-325-1326, Fax: 662-325-8714, E-mail: kern@cvm.msstate.edu. *Application contact:* Missy Hadaway, Admissions Coordinator, 662-325-9065, Fax: 662-325-8714, E-mail: hadaway@cvm.msstate.edu.
Website: http://www.cvm.msstate.edu/

North Carolina State University, College of Veterinary Medicine, Professional Program, Raleigh, NC 27695. Offers DVM. *Accreditation:* AVMA. *Entrance requirements:* For doctorate, GRE. Additional exam requirements/recommendations for international students: Required—TOEFL.

North Carolina State University, College of Veterinary Medicine, Program in Veterinary Public Health, Raleigh, NC 27695. Offers MVPH. *Degree requirements:* For master's, thesis optional. Electronic applications accepted.

Oklahoma State University, Center for Veterinary Health Sciences, Professional Program in Veterinary Medicine, Stillwater, OK 74078. Offers DVM. *Accreditation:* AVMA. *Entrance requirements:* For doctorate, GRE General Test, GRE Subject Test (biology). Electronic applications accepted. *Expenses:* Tuition, state resident: full-time $4019; part-time $2679.60 per year. Tuition, nonresident: full-time $15,286; part-time $10,190.40 per year. *Required fees:* $2129; $1419 per unit. Tuition and fees vary according to program. *Faculty research:* Infectious diseases, physiology, toxicology, biomedical lasers, clinical studies.

Oregon State University, College of Veterinary Medicine, Veterinary Medicine Professional Program, Corvallis, OR 97331. Offers DVM. Program admissions open only to residents of Oregon and other states participating in the Western Interstate Commission for Higher Education. *Accreditation:* AVMA. *Entrance requirements:* For doctorate, GRE. *Application deadline:* For fall admission, 9/15 for domestic and international students. *Expenses:* Contact institution. *Unit head:* Dr. Susan J. Tornquist, Dean, 541-737-6943, Fax: 541-737-4245, E-mail: vetmed@oregonstate.edu. *Application contact:* Admissions, 541-737-2098, E-mail: cvmproginfo@oregonstate.edu.
Website: http://vetmed.oregonstate.edu/

Purdue University, School of Veterinary Medicine, Professional Program in Veterinary Medicine, West Lafayette, IN 47907. Offers DVM, DVM/MS, DVM/PhD. *Accreditation:* AVMA. *Entrance requirements:* For doctorate, GRE General Test. Additional exam requirements/recommendations for international students: Required—TOEFL. Electronic applications accepted.

Texas A&M University, College of Veterinary Medicine and Biomedical Sciences, College Station, TX 77843. Offers biomedical sciences (MS, PhD); science and technology journalism (MS); veterinary medicine (DVM); veterinary pathobiology (MS); veterinary public health-epidemiology (MS). *Accreditation:* AVMA. *Program availability:* Part-time. *Faculty:* 137. *Students:* 789 full-time (598 women), 44 part-time (33 women); includes 199 minority (24 Black or African American, non-Hispanic/Latino; 48 Asian, non-Hispanic/Latino; 108 Hispanic/Latino; 19 Two or more races, non-Hispanic/Latino), 57 international. Average age 26. 268 applicants, 84% accepted, 203 enrolled. In 2017, 90 master's, 24 doctorates awarded. Terminal master's awarded for partial completion of doctoral program. *Entrance requirements:* For master's and doctorate, GRE General Test. Additional exam requirements/recommendations for international students: Required—TOEFL (minimum score 550 paper-based; 80 iBT), IELTS (minimum score 6), PTE (minimum score 53). *Application deadline:* For fall admission, 6/1 for domestic students, 3/1 for international students; for spring admission, 11/1 for domestic students, 8/1 for international students; for summer admission, 3/1 for domestic students, 12/1 for international students. Application fee: $50 ($90 for international students). *Expenses:* Contact institution. *Financial support:* In 2017–18, 706 students received support, including 18 fellowships with tuition reimbursements available (averaging $22,465 per year), 108 research assistantships with tuition reimbursements available (averaging $12,596 per year), 31 teaching assistantships with tuition reimbursements available (averaging $10,235 per year); career-related internships or fieldwork, institutionally sponsored loans, scholarships/grants, traineeships, health care benefits, tuition waivers (full and partial), unspecified assistantships, and clinical associateships also available. Support available to part-time students. Financial award application deadline: 3/15; financial award applicants required to submit FAFSA. *Faculty research:* Physiology, pharmacology, anatomy, microbiology, parasitology. *Unit head:* Dr. Eleanor M. Green, Dean, 979-845-5053, Fax: 979-845-5088, E-mail: emgreen@tamu.edu. *Application contact:* Graduate Admissions, 979-845-1044, E-mail: admissions@tamu.edu.
Website: http://vetmed.tamu.edu/

Tufts University, Cummings School of Veterinary Medicine, North Grafton, MA 01536. Offers animals and public policy (MS); biomedical sciences (PhD), including digestive diseases, infectious diseases, neuroscience and reproductive biology, pathology; conservation medicine (MS); veterinary medicine (DVM); DVM/MPH; DVM/MS. *Accreditation:* AVMA (one or more programs are accredited). *Degree requirements:* For master's, thesis (for some programs); for doctorate, comprehensive exam, thesis/dissertation (for some programs). *Entrance requirements:* For master's and doctorate, GRE General Test. Additional exam requirements/recommendations for international students: Required—TOEFL or IELTS. Electronic applications accepted. *Expenses:* Contact institution. *Faculty research:* Oncology, veterinary ethics, international veterinary medicine, veterinary genomics, pathogenesis of Clostridium difficile, wildlife fertility control.

Tuskegee University, Graduate Programs, College of Veterinary Medicine, Nursing and Allied Health, School of Veterinary Medicine, Tuskegee, AL 36088. Offers MS, DVM. *Degree requirements:* For master's, thesis. *Entrance requirements:* For master's, GRE General Test; for doctorate, VCAT. Additional exam requirements/recommendations for international students: Required—TOEFL (minimum score 500 paper-based).

Université de Montréal, Faculty of Veterinary Medicine, Professional Program in Veterinary Medicine, Montréal, QC H3C 3J7, Canada. Offers DES. Open only to Canadian residents. *Accreditation:* AVMA. *Program availability:* Part-time. Electronic applications accepted. *Faculty research:* Animal reproduction, infectious diseases of swine, physiology of exercise in horses, viral diseases of cattle, health management and epidemiology.

University of California, Davis, School of Veterinary Medicine, Program in Veterinary Medicine, Davis, CA 95616. Offers DVM, DVM/MPVM. *Accreditation:* AVMA. *Entrance requirements:* For doctorate, GRE General Test. Additional exam requirements/recommendations for international students: Required—TOEFL. Electronic applications accepted.

University of Florida, College of Veterinary Medicine, Professional Program in Veterinary Medicine, Gainesville, FL 32611. Offers DVM. *Accreditation:* AVMA. *Entrance requirements:* For doctorate, GRE General Test.

University of Georgia, College of Veterinary Medicine, Athens, GA 30602. Offers MS, DVM, PhD. *Accreditation:* AVMA (one or more programs are accredited). *Degree requirements:* For doctorate, variable foreign language requirement, thesis/dissertation (for some programs). *Entrance requirements:* For master's, GRE General Test; for doctorate, GRE General Test; GRE Subject Test in biology (for DVM). Electronic applications accepted. *Expenses:* Contact institution.

University of Guelph, Ontario Veterinary College and Graduate Studies, Graduate Programs in Veterinary Sciences, Department of Clinical Studies, Guelph, ON N1G 2W1, Canada. Offers anesthesiology (M Sc, DV Sc); cardiology (DV Sc, Diploma); clinical studies (Diploma); dermatology (M Sc); diagnostic imaging (M Sc, DV Sc); emergency/critical care (M Sc, DV Sc, Diploma); medicine (M Sc, DV Sc); neurology (M Sc, DV Sc); ophthalmology (M Sc, DV Sc); surgery (M Sc, DV Sc). *Degree requirements:* For master's, thesis; for doctorate, comprehensive exam, thesis/dissertation. *Entrance requirements:* Additional exam requirements/recommendations for international students: Required—TOEFL (minimum score 550 paper-based), IELTS (minimum score 6.5). Electronic applications accepted. *Faculty research:* Orthopedics, respirology, oncology, exercise physiology, cardiology.

University of Illinois at Urbana–Champaign, College of Veterinary Medicine, Professional Program in Veterinary Medicine, Champaign, IL 61820. Offers veterinary medical science (DVM). *Accreditation:* AVMA. *Expenses:* Contact institution.

University of Maryland, College Park, Academic Affairs, College of Agriculture and Natural Resources, Maryland Campus of VA/MD Regional College of Veterinary Medicine, Professional Program in Veterinary Medicine, College Park, MD 20742. Offers DVM. *Degree requirements:* For doctorate, thesis/dissertation, oral exam, public seminar.

University of Minnesota, Twin Cities Campus, College of Veterinary Medicine, Professional Program in Veterinary Medicine, Minneapolis, MN 55455-0213. Offers DVM, DVM/PhD. *Accreditation:* AVMA. *Entrance requirements:* For doctorate, GRE General Test. Electronic applications accepted. *Expenses:* Contact institution. *Faculty research:* Infectious toxic diseases of animals, zoonotic animal models of human disease, epidemiologic and preventive medicine.

University of Missouri, College of Veterinary Medicine and Office of Research and Graduate Studies, Graduate Programs in Veterinary Medicine, Department of Biomedical Sciences, Columbia, MO 65211. Offers biomedical sciences (MS, PhD); comparative medicine (MS); veterinary medicine and surgery (MS); DVM/PhD. *Entrance requirements:* For master's and doctorate, GRE General Test, minimum GPA of 3.0; 10 hours each of biology and chemistry; 3 hours each of physics, biochemistry, and calculus. *Expenses:* Tuition, state resident: full-time $6480. Tuition, nonresident: full-time $17,744. *Required fees:* $1108. Tuition and fees vary according to course load, campus/location and program. *Faculty research:* Anatomy (gross or microscopic); physiology/pharmacology (molecular, cellular and integrative); biochemistry/molecular biology; endocrinology; toxicology; exercise biology including cardiac, vascular and muscle biology; cardiovascular biology including neuroendocrine regulation; membrane transport biology including cystic fibrosis and cardiac disease; reproductive biology.
Website: http://biomed.missouri.edu/

University of Pennsylvania, School of Veterinary Medicine, Philadelphia, PA 19104. Offers VMD, VMD/MBA, VMD/PhD. *Accreditation:* AVMA. *Faculty:* 106 full-time (51 women), 63 part-time/adjunct (42 women). *Students:* 468 full-time (383 women), 8 part-time (all women); includes 61 minority (7 Black or African American, non-Hispanic/Latino; 24 Asian, non-Hispanic/Latino; 20 Hispanic/Latino; 10 Two or more races, non-Hispanic/Latino), 3 international. Average age 26. 1,093 applicants, 11% accepted, 113 enrolled. In 2017, 119 doctorates awarded.
Website: http://www.vet.upenn.edu/

University of Prince Edward Island, Atlantic Veterinary College, Professional Program in Veterinary Medicine, Charlottetown, PE C1A 4P3, Canada. Offers DVM. *Accreditation:* AVMA. *Entrance requirements:* For doctorate, GRE. Additional exam requirements/recommendations for international students: Required—TOEFL (minimum score 550 paper-based; 80 iBT), Canadian Academic English Language Assessment, Michigan English Language Assessment Battery, Canadian Test of English for Scholars and Trainees. *Faculty research:* Shellfish toxicology, animal nutrition, fish health, toxicology, animal health management.

University of Saskatchewan, Western College of Veterinary Medicine and College of Graduate Studies and Research, Graduate Programs in Veterinary Medicine, Department of Large Animal Clinical Sciences, Saskatoon, SK S7N 5A2, Canada. Offers M Sc, M Vet Sc, PhD. *Degree requirements:* For master's, thesis (for some programs); for doctorate, comprehensive exam (for some programs), thesis/dissertation. *Entrance requirements:* Additional exam requirements/recommendations for international students: Required—TOEFL (minimum score 80 iBT); Recommended—IELTS (minimum score 6.5). Electronic applications accepted. *Faculty research:* Reproduction, infectious diseases, epidemiology, food safety.

University of Saskatchewan, Western College of Veterinary Medicine and College of Graduate Studies and Research, Graduate Programs in Veterinary Medicine, Department of Small Animal Clinical Sciences, Saskatoon, SK S7N 5A2, Canada. Offers small animal clinical sciences (M Sc, PhD); veterinary anesthesiology, radiology and surgery (M Vet Sc); veterinary internal medicine (M Vet Sc). *Degree requirements:* For master's, thesis (for some programs); for doctorate, comprehensive exam (for some programs), thesis/dissertation. *Entrance requirements:* Additional exam requirements/recommendations for international students: Required—TOEFL (minimum score 80 iBT); Recommended—IELTS (minimum score 6.5). Electronic applications accepted. *Faculty research:* Orthopedics, wildlife, cardiovascular exercise/myelopathy, ophthalmology.

University of Saskatchewan, Western College of Veterinary Medicine, Professional Program in Veterinary Medicine, Saskatoon, SK S7N 5A2, Canada. Offers DVM. *Accreditation:* AVMA. *Degree requirements:* For doctorate, thesis/dissertation.

The University of Tennessee, Graduate School, College of Veterinary Medicine, Knoxville, TN 37996. Offers DVM. *Accreditation:* AVMA. *Entrance requirements:* For doctorate, VCAT, interview, minimum GPA of 2.7. Additional exam requirements/recommendations for international students: Required—TOEFL. *Expenses:* Contact institution.

University of Wisconsin–Madison, School of Veterinary Medicine, Madison, WI 53706-1380. Offers MS, DVM, PhD. *Accreditation:* AVMA (one or more programs are accredited). Terminal master's awarded for partial completion of doctoral program. *Degree requirements:* For master's, thesis; for doctorate, thesis/dissertation (for some programs). *Entrance requirements:* For doctorate, GRE General Test (for DVM). *Expenses:* Contact institution. *Faculty research:* Infectious disease, ophthalmology, orthopedics, food animal production, oncology, cardio-respiratory.

Virginia Polytechnic Institute and State University, Virginia-Maryland Regional College of Veterinary Medicine, Blacksburg, VA 24061. Offers biomedical and veterinary sciences (MS, PhD); public health (MPH); veterinary medicine (DVM). *Accreditation:* AVMA (one or more programs are accredited). *Faculty:* 100 full-time (49 women), 2 part-time/adjunct (both women). *Students:* 580 full-time (407 women), 40 part-time (31 women); includes 120 minority (21 Black or African American, non-Hispanic/Latino; 1 American Indian or Alaska Native, non-Hispanic/Latino; 33 Asian, non-Hispanic/Latino; 36 Hispanic/Latino; 29 Two or more races, non-Hispanic/Latino), 27 international. Average age 26. 66 applicants, 68% accepted, 36 enrolled. In 2017, 53 master's, 129 doctorates awarded. *Degree requirements:* For master's, comprehensive exam (for some programs), thesis (for some programs); for doctorate, comprehensive exam (for some programs), thesis/dissertation (for some programs). *Entrance requirements:* For master's and doctorate, GRE/GMAT. Additional exam requirements/recommendations for international students: Required—TOEFL (minimum score 80 iBT). *Application deadline:* For fall admission, 8/1 for domestic students, 4/1 for international students; for spring admission, 1/1 for domestic students, 9/1 for international students. Applications are processed on a rolling basis. Application fee: $75. Electronic applications accepted. *Expenses:* Contact institution. *Financial support:* In 2017–18, 4 fellowships with full and partial tuition reimbursements (averaging $30,618 per year), 16 research assistantships with full tuition reimbursements (averaging $24,872 per year), 18 teaching assistantships with full tuition reimbursements (averaging $26,904 per year) were awarded. Financial award application deadline: 3/1; financial award applicants required to submit FAFSA. *Total annual research expenditures:* $6.4 million. *Unit head:* Dr. Gregory B. Daniel, Interim Dean, 540-231-7910, Fax: 540-231-3505, E-mail: gdaniel@vt.edu. *Application contact:* Sheila Steele, Executive Assistant, 540-231-7910, Fax: 540-231-3505, E-mail: ssteele@vt.edu.
Website: http://www.vetmed.vt.edu

Washington State University, College of Veterinary Medicine, Professional Program in Veterinary Medicine, Pullman, WA 99164. Offers DVM, DVM/MS, DVM/PhD. *Accreditation:* AVMA. *Faculty:* 28 full-time (6 women), 48 part-time/adjunct (12 women). *Students:* 131 full-time (95 women); includes 28 minority (6 Asian, non-Hispanic/Latino; 2 Hispanic/Latino; 20 Two or more races, non-Hispanic/Latino), 13 international. Average age 27. 1,288 applicants, 16% accepted, 131 enrolled. In 2017, 124 doctorates awarded. Terminal master's awarded for partial completion of doctoral program. *Entrance requirements:* For doctorate, GRE General Test. Additional exam requirements/recommendations for international students: Required—TOEFL (minimum score 550 paper-based; 79 iBT). *Application deadline:* For fall admission, 9/15 for domestic and international students. Application fee: $75. Electronic applications accepted. *Expenses:* Contact institution. *Financial support:* In 2017–18, 446 students received support, including 28 fellowships with full tuition reimbursements available, 87 research assistantships with full tuition reimbursements available (averaging $23,000 per year), 34 teaching assistantships with full tuition reimbursements available (averaging $22,000 per year); career-related internships or fieldwork, Federal Work-Study, institutionally sponsored loans, scholarships/grants, traineeships, health care benefits, and unspecified assistantships also available. Support available to part-time students. Financial award application deadline: 1/15; financial award applicants required to submit FAFSA. *Faculty research:* Biotechnology, immunology, pathology, neurosciences, clinical sciences. *Total annual research expenditures:* $20.3 million. *Unit head:* Dr. Patricia Talcott, Director of Admissions, 509-355-1532. *Application contact:* Stacey Poler, Recruitment Officer, 509-335-1532, Fax: 509-335-6133, E-mail: s.poler@wsu.edu.
Website: http://www.vetmed.wsu.edu/

Western University of Health Sciences, College of Veterinary Medicine, Pomona, CA 91766-1854. Offers DVM. *Accreditation:* AVMA. *Faculty:* 53 full-time (25 women), 4 part-time/adjunct (1 woman). *Students:* 420 full-time (330 women); includes 204 minority (13 Black or African American, non-Hispanic/Latino; 60 Asian, non-Hispanic/Latino; 89 Hispanic/Latino; 1 Native Hawaiian or other Pacific Islander, non-Hispanic/Latino; 41 Two or more races, non-Hispanic/Latino), 6 international. Average age 27. 725 applicants, 37% accepted, 95 enrolled. In 2017, 105 doctorates awarded. *Degree requirements:* For doctorate, comprehensive exam (for some programs). *Entrance requirements:* For doctorate, MCAT or GRE General Test (within 5 years of matriculation), minimum GPA of 2.75, three letters of recommendation, BA or BS (recommended), 500 hours of hands-on animal-related experience, transcripts from all colleges or universities attended. Additional exam requirements/recommendations for international students: Required—TOEFL (minimum score 550 paper-based; 79 iBT). *Application deadline:* For fall admission, 9/15 for domestic and international students. Applications are processed on a rolling basis. Application fee: $50. Electronic applications accepted. *Expenses:* $54,220 first-year tuition and fees. *Financial support:* In 2017–18, 39 students received support. Institutionally sponsored loans, scholarships/grants, and veterans' educational benefits available. Financial award application deadline: 3/2; financial award applicants required to submit FAFSA. *Faculty research:* Diagnosing, managing and preventing complications related to small animal surgery; toxoplasmosis. *Unit head:* Dr. Phil Nelson, Dean, 909-469-5661, Fax: 909-469-5635, E-mail: pnelson@westernu.edu. *Application contact:* Karen Hutton-Lopez, Director of Admissions, 909-469-5650, Fax: 909-469-5570, E-mail: admissions@westernu.edu.
Website: http://www.westernu.edu/veterinary

Veterinary Sciences

Clemson University, Graduate School, College of Agriculture, Forestry and Life Sciences, Department of Animal and Veterinary Sciences, Clemson, SC 29634. Offers MS, PhD. *Program availability:* Part-time. *Faculty:* 18 full-time (9 women), 1 part-time/adjunct (0 women). *Students:* 19 full-time (14 women), 7 part-time (3 women); includes 3 minority (1 Black or African American, non-Hispanic/Latino; 1 Hispanic/Latino; 1 Two or more races, non-Hispanic/Latino), 1 international. Average age 28. 11 applicants, 82% accepted, 9 enrolled. In 2017, 2 master's awarded. *Degree requirements:* For master's, thesis optional; for doctorate, comprehensive exam, thesis/dissertation. *Entrance requirements:* For master's and doctorate, GRE General Test, unofficial transcripts, letters of recommendation. Additional exam requirements/recommendations for international students: Required—TOEFL (minimum score 80 iBT), IELTS (minimum score 6.5). *Application deadline:* For fall admission, 4/15 for domestic and international students; for spring admission, 10/15 for domestic students, 9/15 for international students. Applications are processed on a rolling basis. Application fee: $80 ($90 for international students). Electronic applications accepted. *Expenses:* $5,174 per semester full-time resident, $9,714 per semester full-time non-resident, $511 per credit

hour part-time resident, $1,017 per credit hour part-time non-resident; $741 per credit hour online; other fees may apply per session. *Financial support:* In 2017–18, 29 students received support, including 3 fellowships with partial tuition reimbursements available (averaging $6,667 per year), 12 research assistantships with partial tuition reimbursements available (averaging $11,927 per year), 14 teaching assistantships with partial tuition reimbursements available (averaging $10,884 per year); career-related internships or fieldwork also available. Financial award application deadline: 4/15. *Faculty research:* Reproduction, ruminant nutrition, muscle biology/biochemistry, fetal growth and development, immunology. *Total annual research expenditures:* $330,783. *Unit head:* Dr. James Strickland, Department Chair, 864-656-3138, E-mail: jrstric@clemson.edu. *Application contact:* Dr. Susan Duckett, Professor, 864-656-5151, E-mail: sducket@clemson.edu.
Website: http://www.clemson.edu/cafls/departments/animal_vet_science/

Colorado State University, College of Veterinary Medicine and Biomedical Sciences, Department of Clinical Sciences, Fort Collins, CO 80523-1678. Offers MS, PhD. *Faculty:* 85 full-time (47 women), 14 part-time/adjunct (7 women). *Students:* 13 full-time (11 women), 53 part-time (37 women); includes 3 minority (2 Hispanic/Latino; 1 Two or more races, non-Hispanic/Latino), 23 international. Average age 32. 16 applicants, 88% accepted, 13 enrolled. In 2017, 12 master's, 4 doctorates awarded. *Degree requirements:* For master's, comprehensive exam, thesis (for some programs); for doctorate, comprehensive exam, thesis/dissertation. *Entrance requirements:* For master's and doctorate, minimum overall GPA of 3.0; transcripts; 3 letters of recommendation; statement of purpose. Additional exam requirements/recommendations for international students: Required—TOEFL (minimum score 550 paper-based; 80 iBT), IELTS (minimum score 6.5). *Application deadline:* For fall admission, 4/1 for international students; for spring admission, 9/1 for international students. Applications are processed on a rolling basis. Application fee: $60 ($70 for international students). Electronic applications accepted. *Expenses:* Tuition, state resident: full-time $9917. Tuition, nonresident: full-time $24,312. *Required fees:* $2284. Tuition and fees vary according to course load and program. *Financial support:* In 2017–18, 2 students received support, including 9 research assistantships (averaging $24,296 per year); fellowships, career-related internships or fieldwork, institutionally sponsored loans, scholarships/grants, health care benefits, and unspecified assistantships also available. Financial award applicants required to submit FAFSA. *Faculty research:* Immunology, cancer biology, infectious disease, gene and stem cell therapies. *Total annual research expenditures:* $5.8 million. *Unit head:* Dr. Wayne Jensen, Professor and Department Head, 970-297-1274, Fax: 970-297-1275, E-mail: wayne.jensen@colostate.edu. *Application contact:* Morna Mynard, Graduate Coordinator, 970-297-4030, Fax: 970-297-1275, E-mail: mmynard@colostate.edu.
Website: http://csu-cvmbs.colostate.edu/academics/clinsci/graduate-programs/Pages/default.aspx

Drexel University, College of Medicine, Biomedical Graduate Programs, Program in Laboratory Animal Science, Philadelphia, PA 19104-2875. Offers MLAS. *Program availability:* Part-time. *Degree requirements:* For master's, comprehensive exam. *Entrance requirements:* For master's, GRE General Test, minimum GPA of 3.0. Additional exam requirements/recommendations for international students: Required—TOEFL. Electronic applications accepted. *Faculty research:* Laboratory animal medicine, experimental surgery, development of animal models for human diseases.

Iowa State University of Science and Technology, Department of Veterinary Clinical Sciences, Ames, IA 50011. Offers MS. *Degree requirements:* For master's, thesis or alternative. *Entrance requirements:* For master's, GRE. Additional exam requirements/recommendations for international students: Required—TOEFL (minimum score 550 paper-based; 79 iBT), IELTS (minimum score 6.5). Electronic applications accepted. *Faculty research:* Theriogenology, veterinary medicine, veterinary surgery, extracorporeal shock waves, therapy, orthopedic research in animals.

Iowa State University of Science and Technology, Department of Veterinary Microbiology and Preventive Medicine, Ames, IA 50011. Offers veterinary microbiology (MS, PhD). *Entrance requirements:* For master's and doctorate, GRE General Test. Additional exam requirements/recommendations for international students: Required—TOEFL (minimum score 550 paper-based; 79 iBT), IELTS (minimum score 6.5). Electronic applications accepted. *Faculty research:* Bacteriology, immunology, virology, public health and food safety.

Kansas State University, Graduate School, College of Veterinary Medicine, Department of Clinical Sciences, Manhattan, KS 66506. Offers MPH, Graduate Certificate. *Degree requirements:* For master's, thesis. *Entrance requirements:* For master's, GRE, DVM. Additional exam requirements/recommendations for international students: Required—TOEFL (minimum score 550 paper-based). Electronic applications accepted. *Expenses:* Contact institution. *Faculty research:* Clinical trials, equine gastrointestinal ulceration, leptospirosis, food animal pharmacology, equine immunology, diabetes.

Louisiana State University and Agricultural & Mechanical College, School of Veterinary Medicine and Graduate School, Department of Comparative Biomedical Sciences, Baton Rouge, LA 70803. Offers MS, PhD. *Faculty:* 24 full-time (10 women). *Students:* 12 full-time (7 women); includes 2 minority (1 Black or African American, non-Hispanic/Latino; 1 Asian, non-Hispanic/Latino), 6 international. Average age 29. 11 applicants, 18% accepted, 2 enrolled. In 2017, 2 master's, 2 doctorates awarded. *Financial support:* In 2017–18, 12 research assistantships (averaging $25,041 per year) were awarded. *Total annual research expenditures:* $1.1 million.

Louisiana State University and Agricultural & Mechanical College, School of Veterinary Medicine and Graduate School, Department of Pathobiological Sciences, Baton Rouge, LA 70803. Offers MS, PhD. *Faculty:* 26 full-time (7 women), 1 (woman) part-time/adjunct. *Students:* 25 full-time (15 women), 2 part-time (both women); includes 2 minority (both Asian, non-Hispanic/Latino), 6 international. Average age 29. 13 applicants, 62% accepted, 6 enrolled. In 2017, 3 master's, 3 doctorates awarded. *Financial support:* In 2017–18, 1 fellowship (averaging $50,006 per year), 23 research assistantships (averaging $27,128 per year) were awarded. *Total annual research expenditures:* $5.2 million.

Louisiana State University and Agricultural & Mechanical College, School of Veterinary Medicine and Graduate School, Department of Veterinary Clinical Sciences, Baton Rouge, LA 70803. Offers MS, PhD. *Faculty:* 24 full-time (10 women). *Students:* 7 full-time (3 women), 5 part-time (4 women), 6 international. Average age 30. 6 applicants, 67% accepted, 2 enrolled. In 2017, 3 doctorates awarded. *Financial support:* In 2017–18, 8 research assistantships (averaging $26,354 per year) were awarded. *Total annual research expenditures:* $801,474.

Michigan State University, College of Veterinary Medicine and The Graduate School, Graduate Programs in Veterinary Medicine, East Lansing, MI 48824. Offers comparative medicine and integrative biology (MS, PhD), including comparative medicine and integrative biology, comparative medicine and integrative biology–environmental toxicology (PhD); food safety and toxicology (MS), including food safety; integrative toxicology (PhD), including animal science–environmental toxicology, biochemistry and molecular biology–environmental toxicology, chemistry–environmental toxicology, crop and soil sciences–environmental toxicology, environmental engineering–environmental toxicology, environmental geosciences–environmental toxicology, fisheries and wildlife–environmental toxicology, food science–environmental toxicology, forestry–environmental toxicology, genetics–environmental toxicology, human nutrition–environmental toxicology, microbiology–environmental toxicology, pharmacology and toxicology–environmental toxicology, zoology–environmental toxicology; large animal clinical sciences (MS, PhD); microbiology and molecular genetics (MS, PhD), including industrial microbiology, microbiology, microbiology and molecular genetics, microbiology–environmental toxicology (PhD); pathobiology and diagnostic investigation (MS, PhD), including pathology, pathology–environmental toxicology (PhD); pharmacology and toxicology (MS, PhD); pharmacology and toxicology–environmental toxicology (PhD); physiology (MS, PhD); small animal clinical sciences (MS). Electronic applications accepted. *Faculty research:* Molecular genetics, food safety/toxicology, comparative orthopedics, airway disease, population medicine.

Mississippi State University, College of Veterinary Medicine, Office of Research and Graduate Studies, Mississippi State, MS 39762. Offers MS, PhD. *Program availability:* Part-time. *Faculty:* 85 full-time (30 women), 46 part-time/adjunct (16 women). *Students:* 33 full-time (18 women), 26 part-time (15 women); includes 5 minority (2 Black or African American, non-Hispanic/Latino; 1 Asian, non-Hispanic/Latino; 1 Native Hawaiian or other Pacific Islander, non-Hispanic/Latino; 1 Two or more races, non-Hispanic/Latino), 23 international. Average age 31. 15 applicants, 53% accepted, 8 enrolled. In 2017, 1 master's, 11 doctorates awarded. Terminal master's awarded for partial completion of doctoral program. *Degree requirements:* For master's, thesis (for some programs); for doctorate, thesis/dissertation. *Entrance requirements:* For master's, minimum undergraduate GPA of 3.0, bachelor's degree; for doctorate, minimum undergraduate GPA of 3.0. Additional exam requirements/recommendations for international students: Required—TOEFL (minimum score 550 paper-based; 79 iBT); Recommended—IELTS (minimum score 6.5). *Application deadline:* For fall admission, 7/1 priority date for domestic students, 5/1 priority date for international students; for spring admission, 11/1 priority date for domestic students, 10/1 priority date for international students; for summer admission, 5/1 priority date for domestic students, 3/1 priority date for international students. Applications are processed on a rolling basis. Application fee: $60. Electronic applications accepted. *Expenses:* Tuition, state resident: full-time $8318; part-time $462.12 per credit hour. Tuition, nonresident: full-time $22,358; part-time $1242.12 per credit hour. *Required fees:* $110; $12.24 per credit hour. $6.12 per semester. *Financial support:* In 2017–18, 30 students received support, including 28 research assistantships with full tuition reimbursements available (averaging $20,107 per year); career-related internships or fieldwork, institutionally sponsored loans, scholarships/grants, and unspecified assistantships also available. Financial award application deadline: 4/1; financial award applicants required to submit FAFSA. *Faculty research:* Food animal health (poultry and warm-water aquaculture) using immunology, microbiology, molecular biology, parasitology, pathology, pharmacology, and environmental toxicology. *Total annual research expenditures:* $13.1 million. *Unit head:* Dr. Mark L. Lawrence, Associate Dean of Research and Graduate Studies, 662-325-1205, Fax: 662-325-1193, E-mail: lawrence@cvm.msstate.edu. *Application contact:* Tia H. Perkins, Coordinator, Graduate Studies, 662-325-1417, Fax: 662-325-1193, E-mail: tia.perkins@msstate.edu.
Website: http://www.cvm.msstate.edu/index.php/academics/degree-programs-research/office-of-research-graduate-studies-orgs

North Carolina State University, College of Veterinary Medicine, Program in Comparative Biomedical Sciences, Raleigh, NC 27695. Offers cell biology (MS, PhD); infectious disease (MS, PhD); pathology (MS, PhD); pharmacology (MS, PhD); population medicine (MS, PhD). *Program availability:* Part-time. *Degree requirements:* For master's, thesis; for doctorate, thesis/dissertation. *Entrance requirements:* For master's and doctorate, GRE General Test. Additional exam requirements/recommendations for international students: Required—TOEFL (minimum score 550 paper-based). Electronic applications accepted. *Expenses:* Contact institution. *Faculty research:* Infectious diseases, cell biology, pharmacology and toxicology, genomics, pathology and population medicine.

The Ohio State University, College of Veterinary Medicine, Program in Comparative and Veterinary Medicine, Columbus, OH 43210. Offers MS, PhD. *Faculty:* 126. *Students:* 56 full-time (31 women), 40 part-time (29 women). Average age 30. In 2017, 21 master's, 10 doctorates awarded. *Entrance requirements:* For master's and doctorate, GRE. Additional exam requirements/recommendations for international students: Required—TOEFL (minimum score 550 paper-based; 79 iBT), Michigan English Language Assessment Battery (minimum score 82); Recommended—IELTS (minimum score 7). *Application deadline:* For fall admission, 12/15 priority date for domestic students, 11/30 priority date for international students; for spring admission, 10/15 for domestic students, 9/15 for international students; for summer admission, 3/15 for domestic students, 2/15 for international students. Applications are processed on a rolling basis. Application fee: $60 ($70 for international students). Electronic applications accepted. *Unit head:* Dr. Rustin M. Moore, Dean/Chair/Professor, 614-688-8749, Fax: 614-292-3544, E-mail: moore.66@osu.edu. *Application contact:* Graduate and Professional Admissions, 614-292-6031, Fax: 614-292-3656, E-mail: gpadmissions@osu.edu.
Website: http://vet.osu.edu/education/graduate-programs

Oklahoma State University, Center for Veterinary Health Sciences and Graduate College, Graduate Program in Veterinary Biomedical Sciences, Stillwater, OK 74078. Offers MS, PhD. *Program availability:* Online learning. Terminal master's awarded for partial completion of doctoral program. *Degree requirements:* For master's, thesis; for doctorate, comprehensive exam, thesis/dissertation. *Entrance requirements:* For master's and doctorate, GRE General Test. Additional exam requirements/recommendations for international students: Required—TOEFL (minimum score 80 iBT). Electronic applications accepted. *Expenses:* Contact institution. *Faculty research:* Infectious and parasitic diseases, physiology, toxicology, biomedical lasers, clinical studies.

Penn State Hershey Medical Center, College of Medicine, Graduate School Programs in the Biomedical Sciences, Graduate Program in Laboratory Animal Medicine, Hershey, PA 17033. Offers MS. *Students:* 4 full-time (3 women); includes 1 minority (Black or African American, non-Hispanic/Latino). 2 applicants, 100% accepted, 2 enrolled. In 2017, 1 master's awarded. *Degree requirements:* For master's, thesis or alternative. *Entrance requirements:* For master's, GRE, DVM. Additional exam requirements/recommendations for international students: Required—TOEFL (minimum score 550 paper-based). *Application deadline:* For fall admission, 1/31 priority date for domestic students, 2/1 priority date for international students. Applications are processed on a rolling basis. Application fee: $65. Electronic applications accepted. *Financial support:* In 2017–18, 2 students received support. Fellowships with full tuition reimbursements available, research assistantships with full tuition reimbursements available, scholarships/grants, traineeships, health care benefits, and unspecified assistantships available. Financial award applicants required to submit FAFSA. *Faculty research:* Veterinary pathology; pain, analgesia and anesthesia of lab animals; genetically modified animal models of cancer; transgenic animals. *Unit head:* Dr. Ronald P. Wilson, Chair, 717-531-8460, Fax: 717-531-5001, E-mail: grad-hmc@psu.edu. *Application contact:* Nannette Kirst, Program Aide, 717-531-8460, Fax: 717-531-5001, E-mail: nkirst@psu.edu.
Website: http://med.psu.edu

Purdue University, School of Veterinary Medicine and Graduate School, Graduate Programs in Veterinary Medicine, Department of Basic Medical Sciences, West Lafayette, IN 47907. Offers anatomy (MS, PhD); pharmacology (MS, PhD); physiology (MS, PhD). *Program availability:* Part-time. Terminal master's awarded for partial completion of doctoral program. *Degree requirements:* For master's, thesis; for doctorate, thesis/dissertation. *Entrance requirements:* For master's and doctorate, GRE General Test. Additional exam requirements/recommendations for international students: Required—TOEFL. Electronic applications accepted. *Faculty research:* Development and regeneration, tissue injury and shock, biomedical engineering, ovarian function, bone and cartilage biology, cell and molecular biology.

Purdue University, School of Veterinary Medicine and Graduate School, Graduate Programs in Veterinary Medicine, Department of Comparative Pathobiology, West Lafayette, IN 47907-2027. Offers comparative epidemiology and public health (MS); comparative epidemiology and public heath (PhD); comparative microbiology and immunology (MS, PhD); comparative pathobiology (MS, PhD); interdisciplinary studies (PhD), including microbial pathogenesis, molecular signaling and cancer biology, molecular virology; lab animal medicine (MS); veterinary anatomic pathology (MS); veterinary clinical pathology (MS). Terminal master's awarded for partial completion of doctoral program. *Degree requirements:* For master's, thesis (for some programs); for doctorate, thesis/dissertation. *Entrance requirements:* For master's and doctorate, GRE General Test. Additional exam requirements/recommendations for international students: Required—TOEFL (minimum score 575 paper-based), IELTS (minimum score 6.5), TWE (minimum score 4). Electronic applications accepted.

Purdue University, School of Veterinary Medicine and Graduate School, Graduate Programs in Veterinary Medicine, Department of Veterinary Clinical Sciences, West Lafayette, IN 47907. Offers MS, PhD. Degrees offered are post-DVM. Terminal master's awarded for partial completion of doctoral program. *Degree requirements:* For master's, thesis (for some programs); for doctorate, thesis/dissertation. *Entrance requirements:* For master's and doctorate, DVM. *Faculty research:* Flow cytometry, chemotherapy, biologic response modifiers, broncho-alveolar lavage, lithotripsy.

South Dakota State University, Graduate School, College of Agriculture and Biological Sciences, Department of Veterinary and Biomedical Sciences, Brookings, SD 57007. Offers biological sciences (MS, PhD). *Program availability:* Part-time, evening/weekend. *Degree requirements:* For master's, thesis (for some programs), oral exam; for doctorate, comprehensive exam, thesis/dissertation, preliminary oral and written exams. *Entrance requirements:* Additional exam requirements/recommendations for international students: Required—TOEFL (minimum score 525 paper-based; 71 iBT). *Faculty research:* Infectious disease, food animal, virology, immunology.

Texas A&M University, College of Veterinary Medicine and Biomedical Sciences, College Station, TX 77843. Offers biomedical sciences (MS, PhD); science and technology journalism (MS); veterinary medicine (DVM); veterinary pathobiology (MS); veterinary public health-epidemiology (MS). *Accreditation:* AVMA. *Program availability:* Part-time. *Faculty:* 137. *Students:* 789 full-time (598 women), 44 part-time (33 women); includes 199 minority (24 Black or African American, non-Hispanic/Latino; 48 Asian, non-Hispanic/Latino; 108 Hispanic/Latino; 19 Two or more races, non-Hispanic/Latino), 57 international. Average age 26. 268 applicants, 84% accepted, 203 enrolled. In 2017, 90 master's, 24 doctorates awarded. Terminal master's awarded for partial completion of doctoral program. *Entrance requirements:* For master's and doctorate, GRE General Test. Additional exam requirements/recommendations for international students: Required—TOEFL (minimum score 550 paper-based; 80 iBT), IELTS (minimum score 6), PTE (minimum score 53). *Application deadline:* For fall admission, 6/1 for domestic students, 3/1 for international students; for spring admission, 11/1 for domestic students, 8/1 for international students; for summer admission, 3/1 for domestic students, 12/1 for international students. Application fee: $50 ($90 for international students). *Expenses:* Contact institution. *Financial support:* In 2017–18, 706 students received support, including 18 fellowships with tuition reimbursements available (averaging $22,465 per year), 108 research assistantships with tuition reimbursements available (averaging $12,596 per year), 31 teaching assistantships with tuition reimbursements available (averaging $10,235 per year); career-related internships or fieldwork, institutionally sponsored loans, scholarships/grants, traineeships, health care benefits, tuition waivers (full and partial), unspecified assistantships, and clinical associateships also available. Support available to part-time students. Financial award application deadline: 3/15; financial award applicants required to submit FAFSA. *Faculty research:* Physiology, pharmacology, anatomy, microbiology, parasitology. *Unit head:* Dr. Eleanor M. Green, Dean, 979-845-5053, Fax: 979-845-5088, E-mail: emgreen@tamu.edu. *Application contact:* Graduate Admissions, 979-845-1044, E-mail: admissions@tamu.edu.
Website: http://vetmed.tamu.edu/

Tuskegee University, Graduate Programs, College of Veterinary Medicine, Nursing and Allied Health, School of Veterinary Medicine, Tuskegee, AL 36088. Offers MS, DVM. *Degree requirements:* For master's, thesis. *Entrance requirements:* For master's, GRE General Test; for doctorate, VCAT. Additional exam requirements/recommendations for international students: Required—TOEFL (minimum score 500 paper-based).

Université de Montréal, Faculty of Veterinary Medicine and Faculty of Graduate Studies, Graduate Programs in Veterinary Sciences, Montréal, QC H3C 3J7, Canada. Offers M Sc, PhD. *Degree requirements:* For master's, one foreign language, thesis optional. Electronic applications accepted. *Faculty research:* Animal reproduction, infectious diseases of swine, physiology of exercise in horses, viral diseases of cattle, health management and epidemiology.

University of California, Davis, School of Veterinary Medicine and Graduate Studies, Program in Preventive Veterinary Medicine, Davis, CA 95616. Offers MPVM, DVM/MPVM. *Program availability:* Part-time. *Degree requirements:* For master's, thesis. *Entrance requirements:* For master's, DVM or equivalent. Additional exam requirements/recommendations for international students: Required—TOEFL (minimum score 550 paper-based). *Faculty research:* Epidemiology, zoonoses, veterinary public health, wildlife and ecosystem health.

University of California, Davis, School of Veterinary Medicine, Residency Training Program, Davis, CA 95616. Offers Certificate. *Entrance requirements:* For degree, DVM or equivalent, 1 year of related experience. *Faculty research:* Small animal and large animal medicine, surgery, infectious diseases, pathology.

University of Florida, College of Veterinary Medicine, Graduate Program in Veterinary Medical Sciences, Gainesville, FL 32611. Offers forensic toxicology (Certificate); veterinary medical sciences (MS, PhD), including forensic toxicology (MS). *Program availability:* Online learning. Terminal master's awarded for partial completion of doctoral program. *Degree requirements:* For master's, thesis; for doctorate, thesis/dissertation. *Entrance requirements:* For master's and doctorate, GRE General Test, minimum GPA of 3.0. Additional exam requirements/recommendations for international students: Required—TOEFL (minimum score 550 paper-based). Electronic applications accepted. *Expenses:* Contact institution.

University of Guelph, Ontario Veterinary College and Graduate Studies, Graduate Programs in Veterinary Sciences, Guelph, ON N1G 2W1, Canada. Offers M Sc, DV Sc, PhD, Diploma. *Accreditation:* AVMA (one or more programs are accredited). *Degree requirements:* For master's, thesis; for doctorate, comprehensive exam, thesis/dissertation. *Entrance requirements:* Additional exam requirements/recommendations for international students: Required—TOEFL. *Faculty research:* Veterinary and comparative medicine, biomedical sciences, population medicine, pathology, microbiology.

University of Idaho, College of Graduate Studies, College of Agricultural and Life Sciences, Department of Animal and Veterinary Science, Moscow, ID 83844. Offers MS, PhD. *Faculty:* 4. *Students:* 16 full-time, 10 part-time. Average age 29. In 2017, 2 master's, 1 doctorate awarded. *Degree requirements:* For doctorate, thesis/dissertation. *Entrance requirements:* For master's and doctorate, minimum GPA of 3.0. Additional exam requirements/recommendations for international students: Required—TOEFL (minimum score 79 iBT). *Application deadline:* For fall admission, 8/1 for domestic students; for spring admission, 12/15 for domestic students. Applications are processed on a rolling basis. Application fee: $60. Electronic applications accepted. *Expenses:* Tuition, state resident: full-time $6722; part-time $430 per credit hour. Tuition, nonresident: full-time $23,046; part-time $1337 per credit hour. *Required fees:* $2142; $63 per credit hour. *Financial support:* Research assistantships and teaching assistantships available. Financial award applicants required to submit FAFSA. *Faculty research:* Reproductive biology, muscle and growth physiology, meat science, aquaculture, ruminant nutrition. *Unit head:* Dr. Amin Ahmadzadeh, Interim Department Co-Chair, 208-885-6345, E-mail: avs@uidaho.edu. *Application contact:* Sean Scoggin, Graduate Recruitment Coordinator, 208-885-4001, Fax: 208-885-4406, E-mail: graduateadmissions@uidaho.edu.
Website: http://www.uidaho.edu/cals/animal-and-veterinary-science

University of Illinois at Urbana–Champaign, College of Veterinary Medicine, Department of Comparative Biosciences, Urbana, IL 61802. Offers MS, PhD, DVM/PhD. *Degree requirements:* For doctorate, thesis/dissertation.

University of Illinois at Urbana–Champaign, College of Veterinary Medicine, Department of Pathobiology, Urbana, IL 61802. Offers MS, PhD, DVM/PhD. Terminal master's awarded for partial completion of doctoral program. *Degree requirements:* For doctorate, thesis/dissertation.

University of Illinois at Urbana–Champaign, College of Veterinary Medicine, Department of Veterinary Clinical Medicine, Urbana, IL 61801. Offers MS, PhD, DVM/PhD. *Degree requirements:* For doctorate, thesis/dissertation.

University of Kentucky, Graduate School, College of Agriculture, Food and Environment, Program in Veterinary Science, Lexington, KY 40506-0032. Offers MS, PhD. *Degree requirements:* For master's, comprehensive exam, thesis; for doctorate, comprehensive exam, thesis/dissertation. *Entrance requirements:* For master's, GRE General Test, minimum undergraduate GPA of 2.75; for doctorate, GRE General Test, minimum graduate GPA of 3.0. Additional exam requirements/recommendations for international students: Required—TOEFL (minimum score 550 paper-based). Electronic applications accepted. *Faculty research:* Microbiology, reproductive physiology, genetics, pharmacology/toxicology, parasitology.

University of Maryland, College Park, Academic Affairs, College of Agriculture and Natural Resources, Maryland Campus of VA/MD Regional College of Veterinary Medicine, Veterinary Medical Sciences Program, College Park, MD 20742. Offers MS, PhD. *Degree requirements:* For master's, thesis, oral exam; for doctorate, thesis/dissertation, oral exam, public seminar. *Entrance requirements:* For doctorate, GRE General Test. Electronic applications accepted.

University of Minnesota, Twin Cities Campus, College of Veterinary Medicine and Graduate School, Graduate Programs in Veterinary Medicine, Program in Comparative and Molecular Bioscience, Minneapolis, MN 55455-0213. Offers MS, PhD, DVM/PhD. Terminal master's awarded for partial completion of doctoral program. *Degree requirements:* For master's, comprehensive exam, thesis; for doctorate, comprehensive exam, thesis/dissertation. *Entrance requirements:* For master's and doctorate, GRE. Additional exam requirements/recommendations for international students: Required—TOEFL (minimum score 550 paper-based; 79 iBT). Electronic applications accepted. *Faculty research:* Molecular regulation of immunity; mechanisms of bacterial, viral, and parasite pathogenesis; structural and functional comparative physiology and pathology.

University of Minnesota, Twin Cities Campus, College of Veterinary Medicine and Graduate School, Graduate Programs in Veterinary Medicine, Program in Veterinary Medicine, Minneapolis, MN 55455-0213. Offers MS, PhD, DVM/PhD. Terminal master's awarded for partial completion of doctoral program. *Degree requirements:* For master's, comprehensive exam, thesis; for doctorate, comprehensive exam, thesis/dissertation. *Entrance requirements:* Additional exam requirements/recommendations for international students: Required—TOEFL (minimum score 550 paper-based; 79 iBT). Electronic applications accepted. *Faculty research:* Infectious diseases, internal medicine, population medicine, surgery/radiology/anesthesiology, theriogenology.

University of Missouri, College of Veterinary Medicine and Office of Research and Graduate Studies, Graduate Programs in Veterinary Medicine, Department of Veterinary Medicine and Surgery, Columbia, MO 65211. Offers MS. *Entrance requirements:* For master's, GRE General Test, minimum GPA of 3.0; 2 letters of recommendation. *Expenses:* Tuition, state resident: full-time $6480. Tuition, nonresident: full-time $17,744. *Required fees:* $1108. Tuition and fees vary according to course load, campus/location and program. *Faculty research:* Anesthesiology, comparative cardiology, equine, food animal and companion animal medicine and surgery, neurology, oncology, comparative ophthalmology, radiation oncology, radiology, nutrition, theriogenology.
Website: http://www.vms.missouri.edu/vmsgraduateprogram.html

University of Nebraska–Lincoln, Graduate College, College of Agricultural Sciences and Natural Resources, School of Veterinary Medicine and Biomedical Sciences, Lincoln, NE 68588. Offers veterinary science (MS). MS, PhD offered jointly with University of Nebraska Medical Center. *Program availability:* Online learning. *Degree requirements:* For master's, thesis optional; for doctorate, comprehensive exam, thesis/dissertation. *Entrance requirements:* For master's, GRE General Test; for doctorate, GRE General Test, MCAT, or VCAT. Additional exam requirements/recommendations for international students: Required—TOEFL (minimum score 550 paper-based). Electronic applications accepted. *Faculty research:* Virology, immunobiology, molecular biology, mycotoxins, ocular degeneration.

University of Prince Edward Island, Atlantic Veterinary College, Graduate Program in Veterinary Medicine, Charlottetown, PE C1A 4P3, Canada. Offers anatomy (M Sc, PhD); bacteriology (M Sc, PhD); clinical pharmacology (M Sc, PhD); clinical sciences (M Sc, PhD); epidemiology (M Sc, PhD), including reproduction; fish health (M Sc, PhD); food animal nutrition (M Sc, PhD); immunology (M Sc, PhD); microanatomy (M Sc, PhD); parasitology (M Sc, PhD); pathology (M Sc, PhD); pharmacology (M Sc, PhD); physiology (M Sc, PhD); toxicology (M Sc, PhD); veterinary science (M Vet Sc); virology (M Sc, PhD). *Program availability:* Part-time. *Degree requirements:* For master's, thesis; for doctorate, thesis/dissertation. *Entrance requirements:* For master's, DVM, B Sc honors degree, or equivalent; for doctorate, M Sc. Additional exam requirements/recommendations for international students: Required—TOEFL (minimum score 550 paper-based; 80 iBT). *Expenses:* Contact institution. *Faculty research:* Animal health management, infectious diseases, fin fish and shellfish health, basic biomedical sciences, ecosystem health.

Veterinary Sciences

University of Saskatchewan, Western College of Veterinary Medicine and College of Graduate Studies and Research, Graduate Programs in Veterinary Medicine, Saskatoon, SK S7N 5A2, Canada. Offers large animal clinical sciences (M Sc, M Vet Sc, PhD); small animal clinical sciences (M Sc, M Vet Sc, PhD), including small animal clinical sciences (M Sc, PhD), veterinary anesthesiology, radiology and surgery (M Vet Sc), veterinary internal medicine (M Vet Sc); veterinary biomedical sciences (M Sc, M Vet Sc, PhD), including veterinary anatomy (M Sc), veterinary biomedical sciences (M Vet Sc), veterinary physiological sciences (M Sc, PhD); veterinary medicine (M Sc, PhD); veterinary microbiology (M Sc, M Vet Sc, PhD); veterinary pathology (M Sc, M Vet Sc, PhD). *Degree requirements:* For master's, comprehensive exam, thesis (for some programs); for doctorate, comprehensive exam, thesis/dissertation. *Entrance requirements:* Additional exam requirements/recommendations for international students: Required—TOEFL (minimum score 80 iBT) or IELTS (minimum score 6.5). Electronic applications accepted. *Expenses:* Contact institution. *Faculty research:* Reproduction, toxicology, wildlife diseases, food animal medicine, equine health.

University of Vermont, Graduate College, College of Agriculture and Life Sciences, Department of Animal and Veterinary Sciences, Burlington, VT 05405-0148. Offers animal science (MS); animal, nutrition and food sciences (PhD). *Students:* 14 full-time (9 women). Average age 24. 11 applicants, 45% accepted, 3 enrolled. In 2017, 1 master's, 4 doctorates awarded. *Degree requirements:* For master's, thesis; for doctorate, one foreign language, thesis/dissertation. *Entrance requirements:* For master's and doctorate, GRE General Test. Additional exam requirements/recommendations for international students: Required—TOEFL (minimum score 550 paper-based, 90 iBT) or IELTS (6.5). *Application deadline:* For fall admission, 4/1 priority date for domestic and international students. Applications are processed on a rolling basis. Application fee: $65. Electronic applications accepted. *Expenses:* Tuition, state resident: full-time $11,628; part-time $646 per credit. Tuition, nonresident: full-time $29,340; part-time $1630 per credit. *Required fees:* $1994; $10 per credit. Tuition and fees vary according to course load and program. *Financial support:* In 2017–18, 9 students received support, including 1 research assistantship with full tuition reimbursement available (averaging $23,500 per year), 8 teaching assistantships with full tuition reimbursements available (averaging $25,000 per year); fellowships and health care benefits also available. Financial award application deadline: 4/1. *Faculty research:* Animal nutrition, dairy production. *Unit head:* Dr. David Townson, Chair, 802-656-1192, E-mail: dave.townson@uvm.edu. *Application contact:* Dr. Feng-Qi Zhao, Coordinator, 802-656-2070, E-mail: ascidept@uvm.edu.
Website: https://www.uvm.edu/cals/asci/graduate-program

University of Washington, Graduate School, School of Medicine, Graduate Programs in Medicine, Department of Comparative Medicine, Seattle, WA 98195. Offers MS.

University of Wisconsin–Madison, School of Veterinary Medicine, Madison, WI 53706-1380. Offers MS, DVM, PhD. *Accreditation:* AVMA (one or more programs are accredited). Terminal master's awarded for partial completion of doctoral program. *Degree requirements:* For master's, thesis; for doctorate, thesis/dissertation (for some programs). *Entrance requirements:* For doctorate, GRE General Test (for DVM). *Expenses:* Contact institution. *Faculty research:* Infectious disease, ophthalmology, orthopedics, food animal production, oncology, cardio-respiratory.

Utah State University, School of Graduate Studies, College of Agriculture and Applied Sciences, Department of Animal, Dairy and Veterinary Sciences, Logan, UT 84322. Offers animal science (MS, PhD); bioveterinary science (MS, PhD); dairy science (MS). *Program availability:* Part-time. *Degree requirements:* For master's, thesis (for some programs); for doctorate, comprehensive exam, thesis/dissertation. *Entrance requirements:* For master's and doctorate, GRE General Test, minimum GPA of 3.0. Additional exam requirements/recommendations for international students: Required—TOEFL. Electronic applications accepted. *Faculty research:* Monoclonal antibodies, antiviral chemotherapy, management systems, biotechnology, rumen fermentation manipulation.

Virginia Polytechnic Institute and State University, Virginia-Maryland Regional College of Veterinary Medicine, Blacksburg, VA 24061. Offers biomedical and veterinary sciences (MS, PhD); public health (MPH); veterinary medicine (DVM). *Accreditation:* AVMA (one or more programs are accredited). *Faculty:* 100 full-time (49 women), 2 part-time/adjunct (both women). *Students:* 580 full-time (407 women), 40 part-time (31 women); includes 120 minority (21 Black or African American, non-Hispanic/Latino; 1 American Indian or Alaska Native, non-Hispanic/Latino; 33 Asian, non-Hispanic/Latino; 36 Hispanic/Latino; 29 Two or more races, non-Hispanic/Latino), 27 international. Average age 26. 66 applicants, 68% accepted, 36 enrolled. In 2017, 53 master's, 129 doctorates awarded. *Degree requirements:* For master's, comprehensive exam (for some programs), thesis (for some programs); for doctorate, comprehensive exam (for some programs), thesis/dissertation (for some programs). *Entrance requirements:* For master's and doctorate, GRE/GMAT. Additional exam requirements/recommendations for international students: Required—TOEFL (minimum score 80 iBT). *Application deadline:* For fall admission, 8/1 for domestic students, 4/1 for international students; for spring admission, 1/1 for domestic students, 9/1 for international students. Applications are processed on a rolling basis. Application fee: $75. Electronic applications accepted. *Expenses:* Contact institution. *Financial support:* In 2017–18, 4 fellowships with full and partial tuition reimbursements (averaging $30,618 per year), 16 research assistantships with full tuition reimbursements (averaging $24,872 per year), 18 teaching assistantships with full tuition reimbursements (averaging $26,904 per year) were awarded. Financial award application deadline: 3/1; financial award applicants required to submit FAFSA. *Total annual research expenditures:* $6.4 million. *Unit head:* Dr. Gregory B. Daniel, Interim Dean, 540-231-7910, Fax: 540-231-3505, E-mail: gdaniel@vt.edu. *Application contact:* Sheila Steele, Executive Assistant, 540-231-7910, Fax: 540-231-3505, E-mail: ssteele@vt.edu.
Website: http://www.vetmed.vt.edu

Washington State University, College of Veterinary Medicine, Program in Veterinary Clinical Sciences, Pullman, WA 99164. Offers clinical and translational science (MS, PhD). *Program availability:* Part-time. *Faculty:* 49 full-time (28 women). *Students:* 9 full-time (5 women), 28 part-time (22 women); includes 11 minority (3 Asian, non-Hispanic/Latino; 8 Hispanic/Latino), 17 international. Average age 30. 11 applicants, 100% accepted, 11 enrolled. In 2017, 7 master's, 1 doctorate awarded. *Degree requirements:* For master's, thesis, oral exam; for doctorate, thesis/dissertation, oral exam. *Entrance requirements:* For master's and doctorate, minimum GPA of 3.0, DVM or equivalent. Additional exam requirements/recommendations for international students: Required—TOEFL (minimum score 550 paper-based; 80 iBT), IELTS (minimum score 7). *Application deadline:* For fall admission, 3/31 for domestic and international students. Application fee: $75. Electronic applications accepted. *Financial support:* In 2017–18, 34 students received support, including 1 fellowship with full tuition reimbursement available (averaging $41,430 per year), 33 research assistantships with full tuition reimbursements available (averaging $31,624 per year); health care benefits also available. Financial award application deadline: 3/1. *Faculty research:* Oncology, mastitis, nuclear medicine, neuroanesthesia, exercise physiology. *Total annual research expenditures:* $500,000. *Unit head:* Dr. Katrina Mealey, Chair, 509-335-0738, Fax: 509-335-0880, E-mail: kmealey@wsu.edu. *Application contact:* Kathy L. Dahmen, Administrative Manager, 509-335-4156, Fax: 509-335-0880, E-mail: dahmen@wsu.edu.
Website: http://graduate.vetmed.wsu.edu/

APPENDIXES

Institutional Changes Since the 2018 Edition

Following is an alphabetical listing of institutions that have recently closed, merged with other institutions, or changed their names or status. In the case of a name change, the former name appears first, followed by the new name.

Argosy University, Dallas (Farmers Branch, TX): *closed.*
Argosy University, Denver (Denver, CO): *closed.*
Argosy University, Inland Empire (Ontario, CA): *closed.*
Argosy University, Nashville (Nashville, TN): *closed.*
Argosy University, Salt Lake City (Draper, UT): *closed.*
Argosy University, San Diego (San Diego, CA): *closed.*
Argosy University, San Francisco Bay Area (Alameda, CA): *closed.*
Argosy University, Sarasota (Sarasota, FL): *closed.*
Argosy University, Schaumburg (Schaumburg, IL): *closed.*
Arlington Baptist College (Arlington, TX): *name changed to Arlington Baptist University.*
Armstrong State University (Savannah, GA): *name changed to Georgia Southern University-Armstrong Campus.*
Art Center College of Design (Pasadena, CA): *name changed to ArtCenter College of Design.*
The Art Institute of California-San Francisco, a campus of Argosy University (San Francisco, CA): *closed.*
Augsburg College (Minneapolis, MN): *name changed to Augsburg University.*
Bristol University (Anaheim, CA): *closed.*
Claremont McKenna College (Claremont, CA): *no longer profiled by request from the institution. Graduate program is for students attending the Claremont Colleges.*
Coleman University (San Diego, CA): *closed.*
Digital Media Arts College (Boca Raton, FL): *merged into Lynn University (Boca Raton, FL).*
Episcopal Divinity School (Cambridge, MA): *merged into Union Theological Seminary in the City of New York (New York, NY).*
Everest University (Tampa, FL): *name changed to Altierus Career College and no longer offers graduate degrees.*
Fairleigh Dickinson University, College at Florham (Madison, NJ): *name changed to Fairleigh Dickinson University, Florham Campus.*
Faith Evangelical College & Seminary (Tacoma, WA): *name changed to Faith International University.*
Frank Lloyd Wright School of Architecture (Scottsdale, AZ): *name changed to School of Architecture at Taliesin.*
Future Generations Graduate School (Franklin, WV): *name changed to Future Generations University.*
Grace University (Omaha, NE): *closed.*
Greenville College (Greenville, IL): *name changed to Greenville University.*
Hazelden Graduate School of Addiction Studies (Center City, MN): *name changed to Hazelden Betty Ford Graduate School of Addiction Studies.*
Henley-Putnam University (San Jose, CA): *name changed to Henley-Putnam School of Strategic Security.*
Huntington College of Health Sciences (Knoxville, TN): *name changed to Huntington University of Health Sciences.*
The Institute for the Psychological Sciences (Arlington, VA): *name changed to Divine Mercy University.*
International College of the Cayman Islands (Newlands, Cayman Islands): *no longer accredited by agency recognized by USDE or CHEA.*
Johnson State College (Johnson, VT): *name changed to Northern Vermont University-Johnson.*
John Wesley University (High Point, NC): *closed.*
Kaplan University, Davenport Campus (Davenport, IA): *name changed to Purdue University Global.*
Knowledge Systems Institute (Skokie, IL): *no longer degree granting.*
Long Island University-Hudson at Westchester (Purchase, NY): *name changed to Long Island University-Hudson.*
Lutheran Theological Seminary at Gettysburg (Gettysburg, PA): *name changed to United Lutheran Seminary.*
The Lutheran Theological Seminary at Philadelphia (Philadelphia, PA): *name changed to United Lutheran Seminary.*
Lynchburg College (Lynchburg, VA): *name changed to University of Lynchburg.*
Lyndon State College (Lyndonville, VT): *name changed to Northern Vermont University-Lyndon.*
Marylhurst University (Marylhurst, OR): *closed.*
McNally Smith College of Music (Saint Paul, MN): *closed.*
Memphis College of Art (Memphis, TN): *closed.*
Mirrer Yeshiva (Brooklyn, NY): *name changed to Mirrer Yeshiva Central Institute.*
Mount Ida College (Newton, MA): *merged into University of Massachusetts Amherst (Amherst, MA).*
National American University (Rapid City, SD): *graduate programs now listed under National American University (Austin, TX).*
The Ohio State University-Mansfield Campus (Mansfield, OH): *name changed to The Ohio State University at Mansfield.*
The Ohio State University-Newark Campus (Newark, OH): *name changed to The Ohio State University at Newark.*
Our Lady of the Lake College (Baton Rouge, LA): *name changed to Franciscan Missionaries of Our Lady University.*
Philadelphia University (Philadelphia, PA): *merged into Thomas Jefferson University (Philadelphia, PA).*
Sacred Heart School of Theology (Hales Corners, WI): *name changed to Sacred Heart Seminary and School of Theology.*
Sewanee: The University of the South (Sewanee, TN): *name changed to The University of the South.*
Shepherd University (Los Angeles, CA): *closed.*
Silicon Valley University (San Jose, CA): *closed.*
South University (Novi, MI): *closed.*
South University (High Point, NC): *closed.*
South University (Cleveland, OH): *closed.*
University of Great Falls (Great Falls, MT): *name changed to University of Providence.*
University of Phoenix-Atlanta Campus (Sandy Springs, GA): *closed.*
University of Phoenix-Augusta Campus (Augusta, GA): *closed.*
University of Phoenix-Central Florida Campus (Orlando, FL): *closed.*
University of Phoenix-Charlotte Campus (Charlotte, NC): *closed.*
University of Phoenix-Colorado Campus (Lone Tree, CO): *closed.*
University of Phoenix-Colorado Springs Downtown Campus (Colorado Springs, CO): *closed.*
University of Phoenix-Columbus Georgia Campus (Columbus, GA): *closed.*
University of Phoenix-Jersey City Campus (Jersey City, NJ): *closed.*
University of Phoenix-New Mexico Campus (Albuquerque, NM): *closed.*
University of Phoenix-North Florida Campus (Jacksonville, FL): *closed.*
University of Phoenix-Southern Arizona Campus (Tucson, AZ): *closed.*
University of Phoenix-Southern California Campus (Costa Mesa, CA): *closed.*
University of Phoenix-South Florida Campus (Miramar, FL): *closed.*
University of Phoenix-Utah Campus (Salt Lake City, UT): *closed.*
University of Phoenix-Washington D.C. Campus (Washington, DC): *closed.*
University of Phoenix-Western Washington Campus (Tukwila, WA): *closed.*
University of Puerto Rico, Mayagüez Campus (Mayagüez, PR): *name changed to University of Puerto Rico-Mayagüez.*
University of Puerto Rico, Medical Sciences Campus (San Juan, PR): *name changed to University of Puerto Rico-Medical Sciences Campus.*
University of Puerto Rico, Río Piedras Campus (San Juan, PR): *name changed to University of Puerto Rico-Río Piedras.*
The University of South Dakota (Vermillion, SD): *name changed to University of South Dakota.*
Urbana University (Urbana, OH): *name changed to Urbana University-A Branch Campus of Franklin University.*
Virginia College in Birmingham (Birmingham, AL): *no longer offers graduate degrees.*

Warner Pacific College (Portland, OR): *name changed to Warner Pacific University.*

Wheelock College (Boston, MA): *merged with Boston University's School of Education.*

Wright Institute (Berkeley, CA): *name changed to The Wright Institute.*

Yeshiva Karlin Stolin Rabbinical Institute (Brooklyn, NY): *name changed to Yeshiva Karlin Stolin.*

Abbreviations Used in the Guides

The following list includes abbreviations of degree names used in the profiles in the 2019 edition of the guides. Because some degrees (e.g., Doctor of Education) can be abbreviated in more than one way (e.g., D.Ed. or Ed.D.), and because the abbreviations used in the guides reflect the preferences of the individual colleges and universities, the list may include two or more abbreviations for a single degree.

DEGREES

A Mus D	Doctor of Musical Arts
AC	Advanced Certificate
AD	Artist's Diploma
	Doctor of Arts
ADP	Artist's Diploma
Adv C	Advanced Certificate
AGC	Advanced Graduate Certificate
AGSC	Advanced Graduate Specialist Certificate
ALM	Master of Liberal Arts
AM	Master of Arts
AMBA	Accelerated Master of Business Administration
APC	Advanced Professional Certificate
APMPH	Advanced Professional Master of Public Health
App Sc	Applied Scientist
App Sc D	Doctor of Applied Science
AstE	Astronautical Engineer
ATC	Advanced Training Certificate
Au D	Doctor of Audiology
B Th	Bachelor of Theology
BN	Bachelor of Naturopathy
CAES	Certificate of Advanced Educational Specialization
CAGS	Certificate of Advanced Graduate Studies
CAL	Certificate in Applied Linguistics
CAPS	Certificate of Advanced Professional Studies
CAS	Certificate of Advanced Studies
CATS	Certificate of Achievement in Theological Studies
CE	Civil Engineer
CEM	Certificate of Environmental Management
CET	Certificate in Educational Technologies
CGS	Certificate of Graduate Studies
Ch E	Chemical Engineer
Clin Sc D	Doctor of Clinical Science
CM	Certificate in Management
CMH	Certificate in Medical Humanities
CMM	Master of Church Ministries
CMS	Certificate in Ministerial Studies
CNM	Certificate in Nonprofit Management
CPC	Certificate in Publication and Communication
CPH	Certificate in Public Health
CPS	Certificate of Professional Studies
CScD	Doctor of Clinical Science
CSD	Certificate in Spiritual Direction
CSS	Certificate of Special Studies
CTS	Certificate of Theological Studies
D Ac	Doctor of Acupuncture
D Admin	Doctor of Administration
D Arch	Doctor of Architecture
D Be	Doctor in Bioethics
D Com	Doctor of Commerce
D Couns	Doctor of Counseling
D Des	Doctorate of Design
D Div	Doctor of Divinity
D Ed	Doctor of Education
D Ed Min	Doctor of Educational Ministry
D Eng	Doctor of Engineering
D Engr	Doctor of Engineering
D Ent	Doctor of Enterprise
D Env	Doctor of Environment
D Law	Doctor of Law
D Litt	Doctor of Letters
D Med Sc	Doctor of Medical Science
D Mgt	Doctor of Management
D Min	Doctor of Ministry
D Miss	Doctor of Missiology
D Mus	Doctor of Music
D Mus A	Doctor of Musical Arts
D Phil	Doctor of Philosophy
D Prof	Doctor of Professional Studies
D Ps	Doctor of Psychology
D Sc	Doctor of Science
D Sc D	Doctor of Science in Dentistry
D Sc IS	Doctor of Science in Information Systems
D Sc PA	Doctor of Science in Physician Assistant Studies
D Th	Doctor of Theology
D Th P	Doctor of Practical Theology
DA	Doctor of Accounting
	Doctor of Arts
DACM	Doctor of Acupuncture and Chinese Medicine
DAIS	Doctor of Applied Intercultural Studies
DAOM	Doctorate in Acupuncture and Oriental Medicine
DAT	Doctorate of Athletic Training
	Professional Doctor of Art Therapy
DBA	Doctor of Business Administration
DBH	Doctor of Behavioral Health
DBL	Doctor of Business Leadership
DC	Doctor of Chiropractic
DCC	Doctor of Computer Science
DCD	Doctor of Communications Design
DCE	Doctor of Computer Engineering
DCL	Doctor of Civil Law
	Doctor of Comparative Law
DCM	Doctor of Church Music
DCN	Doctor of Clinical Nutrition
DCS	Doctor of Computer Science
DDN	Diplôme du Droit Notarial
DDS	Doctor of Dental Surgery
DE	Doctor of Education
	Doctor of Engineering
DED	Doctor of Economic Development
DEIT	Doctor of Educational Innovation and Technology
DEL	Doctor of Executive Leadership
DEM	Doctor of Educational Ministry
DEPD	Diplôme Études Spécialisées
DES	Doctor of Engineering Science
DESS	Diplôme Études Supérieures Spécialisées
DET	Doctor of Educational Technology
DFA	Doctor of Fine Arts
DGP	Diploma in Graduate and Professional Studies
DGS	Doctor of Global Security
DH Sc	Doctor of Health Sciences
DHA	Doctor of Health Administration
DHCE	Doctor of Health Care Ethics
DHL	Doctor of Hebrew Letters
DHPE	Doctorate of Health Professionals Education
DHS	Doctor of Health Science
DHSc	Doctor of Health Science
DIT	Doctor of Industrial Technology

	Doctor of Information Technology
DJS	Doctor of Jewish Studies
DLS	Doctor of Liberal Studies
DM	Doctor of Management
	Doctor of Music
DMA	Doctor of Musical Arts
DMD	Doctor of Dental Medicine
DME	Doctor of Manufacturing Management
	Doctor of Music Education
DMFT	Doctor of Marital and Family Therapy
DMH	Doctor of Medical Humanities
DML	Doctor of Modern Languages
DMP	Doctorate in Medical Physics
DMPNA	Doctor of Management Practice in Nurse Anesthesia
DN Sc	Doctor of Nursing Science
DNAP	Doctor of Nurse Anesthesia Practice
DNP	Doctor of Nursing Practice
DNP-A	Doctor of Nursing Practice - Anesthesia
DNS	Doctor of Nursing Science
DO	Doctor of Osteopathy
DOL	Doctorate of Organizational Leadership
DOM	Doctor of Oriental Medicine
DOT	Doctor of Occupational Therapy
DPA	Diploma in Public Administration
	Doctor of Public Administration
DPDS	Doctor of Planning and Development Studies
DPH	Doctor of Public Health
DPM	Doctor of Plant Medicine
	Doctor of Podiatric Medicine
DPPD	Doctor of Policy, Planning, and Development
DPS	Doctor of Professional Studies
DPT	Doctor of Physical Therapy
DPTSc	Doctor of Physical Therapy Science
Dr DES	Doctor of Design
Dr NP	Doctor of Nursing Practice
Dr OT	Doctor of Occupational Therapy
Dr PH	Doctor of Public Health
Dr Sc PT	Doctor of Science in Physical Therapy
DRSc	Doctor of Regulatory Science
DS	Doctor of Science
DS Sc	Doctor of Social Science
DScPT	Doctor of Science in Physical Therapy
DSI	Doctor of Strategic Intelligence
DSJS	Doctor of Science in Jewish Studies
DSL	Doctor of Strategic Leadership
DSS	Doctor of Strategic Security
DSW	Doctor of Social Work
DTL	Doctor of Talmudic Law
	Doctor of Transformational Leadership
DV Sc	Doctor of Veterinary Science
DVM	Doctor of Veterinary Medicine
DWS	Doctor of Worship Studies
EAA	Engineer in Aeronautics and Astronautics
EASPh D	Engineering and Applied Science Doctor of Philosophy
ECS	Engineer in Computer Science
Ed D	Doctor of Education
Ed DCT	Doctor of Education in College Teaching
Ed L D	Doctor of Education Leadership
Ed M	Master of Education
Ed S	Specialist in Education
Ed Sp	Specialist in Education
EDB	Executive Doctorate in Business
EDM	Executive Doctorate in Management
EE	Electrical Engineer
EJD	Executive Juris Doctor
EMBA	Executive Master of Business Administration
EMFA	Executive Master of Forensic Accounting
EMHA	Executive Master of Health Administration
EMHCL	Executive Master in Healthcare Leadership
EMIB	Executive Master of International Business
EMIR	Executive Master in International Relations
EML	Executive Master of Leadership
EMPA	Executive Master of Public Administration
EMPL	Executive Master in Policy Leadership
	Executive Master in Public Leadership
EMS	Executive Master of Science
EMTM	Executive Master of Technology Management
Eng	Engineer
Eng Sc D	Doctor of Engineering Science
Engr	Engineer
Exec MHA	Executive Master of Health Administration
Exec Ed D	Executive Doctor of Education
Exec MBA	Executive Master of Business Administration
Exec MPA	Executive Master of Public Administration
Exec MPH	Executive Master of Public Health
Exec MS	Executive Master of Science
G Dip	Graduate Diploma
GBC	Graduate Business Certificate
GDM	Graduate Diploma in Management
GDPA	Graduate Diploma in Public Administration
GEMBA	Global Executive Master of Business Administration
GM Acc	Graduate Master of Accountancy
GMBA	Global Master of Business Administration
GP LL M	Global Professional Master of Laws
GPD	Graduate Performance Diploma
GSS	Graduate Special Certificate for Students in Special Situations
IEMBA	International Executive Master of Business Administration
IMA	Interdisciplinary Master of Arts
IMBA	International Master of Business Administration
IMES	International Master's in Environmental Studies
Ingeniero	Engineer
JCD	Doctor of Canon Law
JCL	Licentiate in Canon Law
JD	Juris Doctor
JM	Juris Master
JSD	Doctor of Juridical Science
	Doctor of Jurisprudence
	Doctor of the Science of Law
JSM	Master of the Science of Law
L Th	Licenciate in Theology
LL B	Bachelor of Laws
LL CM	Master of Comparative Law
LL D	Doctor of Laws
LL M	Master of Laws
LL M in Tax	Master of Laws in Taxation
LL M CL	Master of Laws in Common Law
M Ac	Master of Accountancy
	Master of Accounting
	Master of Acupuncture
M Ac OM	Master of Acupuncture and Oriental Medicine
M Acc	Master of Accountancy
	Master of Accounting
M Acct	Master of Accountancy
	Master of Accounting
M Accy	Master of Accountancy
M Actg	Master of Accounting
M Acy	Master of Accountancy
M Ad	Master of Administration
M Ad Ed	Master of Adult Education
M Adm	Master of Administration
M Adm Mgt	Master of Administrative Management
M Admin	Master of Administration

M ADU	Master of Architectural Design and Urbanism
M Adv	Master of Advertising
M AEST	Master of Applied Environmental Science and Technology
M Ag	Master of Agriculture
M Ag Ed	Master of Agricultural Education
M Agr	Master of Agriculture
M App Comp Sc	Master of Applied Computer Science
M App St	Master of Applied Statistics
M Appl Stat	Master of Applied Statistics
M Aq	Master of Aquaculture
M Ar	Master of Architecture
M Arc	Master of Architecture
M Arch	Master of Architecture
M Arch I	Master of Architecture I
M Arch II	Master of Architecture II
M Arch E	Master of Architectural Engineering
M Arch H	Master of Architectural History
M Bioethics	Master in Bioethics
M Biomath	Master of Biomathematics
M Cat	Master of Catechesis
M Ch E	Master of Chemical Engineering
M Cl D	Master of Clinical Dentistry
M Cl Sc	Master of Clinical Science
M Comm	Master of Communication
M Comp	Master of Computing
M Comp Sc	Master of Computer Science
M Coun	Master of Counseling
M Dent	Master of Dentistry
M Dent Sc	Master of Dental Sciences
M Des	Master of Design
M Des S	Master of Design Studies
M Div	Master of Divinity
M E Sci	Master of Earth Science
M Ec	Master of Economics
M Econ	Master of Economics
M Ed	Master of Education
M Ed T	Master of Education in Teaching
M En	Master of Engineering
M En S	Master of Environmental Sciences
M Eng	Master of Engineering
M Eng Mgt	Master of Engineering Management
M Engr	Master of Engineering
M Ent	Master of Enterprise
M Env	Master of Environment
M Env Des	Master of Environmental Design
M Env E	Master of Environmental Engineering
M Env Sc	Master of Environmental Science
M Ext Ed	Master of Extension Education
M Fin	Master of Finance
M Geo E	Master of Geological Engineering
M Geoenv E	Master of Geoenvironmental Engineering
M Geog	Master of Geography
M Hum	Master of Humanities
M IDST	Master's in Interdisciplinary Studies
M Jur	Master of Jurisprudence
M Kin	Master of Kinesiology
M Land Arch	Master of Landscape Architecture
M Litt	Master of Letters
M Mark	Master of Marketing
M Mat SE	Master of Material Science and Engineering
M Math	Master of Mathematics
M Mech E	Master of Mechanical Engineering
M Med Sc	Master of Medical Science
M Mgmt	Master of Management
M Mgt	Master of Management
M Min	Master of Ministries
M Mtl E	Master of Materials Engineering

M Mu	Master of Music
M Mus	Master of Music
M Mus Ed	Master of Music Education
M Music	Master of Music
M Pet E	Master of Petroleum Engineering
M Pharm	Master of Pharmacy
M Phil	Master of Philosophy
M Phil F	Master of Philosophical Foundations
M Pl	Master of Planning
M Plan	Master of Planning
M Pol	Master of Political Science
M Pr Met	Master of Professional Meteorology
M Prob S	Master of Probability and Statistics
M Psych	Master of Psychology
M Pub	Master of Publishing
M Rel	Master of Religion
M Sc	Master of Science
M Sc A	Master of Science (Applied)
M Sc AC	Master of Science in Applied Computing
M Sc AHN	Master of Science in Applied Human Nutrition
M Sc BMC	Master of Science in Biomedical Communications
M Sc CS	Master of Science in Computer Science
M Sc E	Master of Science in Engineering
M Sc Eng	Master of Science in Engineering
M Sc Engr	Master of Science in Engineering
M Sc F	Master of Science in Forestry
M Sc FE	Master of Science in Forest Engineering
M Sc Geogr	Master of Science in Geography
M Sc N	Master of Science in Nursing
M Sc OT	Master of Science in Occupational Therapy
M Sc P	Master of Science in Planning
M Sc Pl	Master of Science in Planning
M Sc PT	Master of Science in Physical Therapy
M Sc T	Master of Science in Teaching
M SEM	Master of Sustainable Environmental Management
M Serv Soc	Master of Social Service
M Soc	Master of Sociology
M Sp Ed	Master of Special Education
M Stat	Master of Statistics
M Sys E	Master of Systems Engineering
M Sys Sc	Master of Systems Science
M Tax	Master of Taxation
M Tech	Master of Technology
M Th	Master of Theology
M Tox	Master of Toxicology
M Trans E	Master of Transportation Engineering
M U Ed	Master of Urban Education
M Urb	Master of Urban Planning
M Vet Sc	Master of Veterinary Science
MA	Master of Accounting
	Master of Administration
	Master of Arts
MA Comm	Master of Arts in Communication
MA Ed	Master of Arts in Education
MA Ed/HD	Master of Arts in Education and Human Development
MA Ext	Master of Agricultural Extension
MA Islamic	Master of Arts in Islamic Studies
MA Min	Master of Arts in Ministry
MA Miss	Master of Arts in Missiology
MA Past St	Master of Arts in Pastoral Studies
MA Ph	Master of Arts in Philosophy
MA Psych	Master of Arts in Psychology
MA Sc	Master of Applied Science
MA Sp	Master of Arts (Spirituality)
MA Th	Master of Arts in Theology
MA-R	Master of Arts (Research)

MAA	Master of Applied Anthropology
	Master of Applied Arts
	Master of Arts in Administration
MAAA	Master of Arts in Arts Administration
MAAAP	Master of Arts Administration and Policy
MAAD	Master of Advanced Architectural Design
MAAE	Master of Arts in Art Education
MAAPPS	Master of Arts in Asia Pacific Policy Studies
MAAS	Master of Arts in Aging and Spirituality
MAASJ	Master of Arts in Applied Social Justice
MAAT	Master of Arts in Applied Theology
	Master of Arts in Art Therapy
MAB	Master of Agribusiness
	Master of Applied Bioengineering
MABA	Master's in Applied Behavior Analysis
MABC	Master of Arts in Biblical Counseling
MABE	Master of Arts in Bible Exposition
MABL	Master of Arts in Biblical Languages
MABM	Master of Agribusiness Management
MABS	Master of Arts in Biblical Studies
MABT	Master of Arts in Bible Teaching
MAC	Master of Accountancy
	Master of Accounting
	Master of Arts in Communication
	Master of Arts in Counseling
MACC	Master of Arts in Christian Counseling
MACCT	Master of Accounting
MACD	Master of Arts in Christian Doctrine
MACE	Master of Arts in Christian Education
MACH	Master of Arts in Church History
MACI	Master of Arts in Curriculum and Instruction
MACIS	Master of Accounting and Information Systems
MACJ	Master of Arts in Criminal Justice
MACL	Master of Arts in Christian Leadership
	Master of Arts in Community Leadership
MACM	Master of Arts in Christian Ministries
	Master of Arts in Christian Ministry
	Master of Arts in Church Music
	Master of Arts in Counseling Ministries
MACML	Master of Arts in Christian Ministry and Leadership
MACN	Master of Arts in Counseling
MACO	Master of Arts in Counseling
MAcOM	Master of Acupuncture and Oriental Medicine
MACP	Master of Arts in Christian Practice
	Master of Arts in Church Planting
	Master of Arts in Counseling Psychology
MACS	Master of Applied Computer Science
	Master of Arts in Catholic Studies
	Master of Arts in Christian Studies
MACSE	Master of Arts in Christian School Education
MACT	Master of Arts in Communications and Technology
MAD	Master in Educational Institution Administration
	Master of Applied Design
	Master of Art and Design
MADR	Master of Arts in Dispute Resolution
MADS	Master of Applied Disability Studies
MAE	Master of Aerospace Engineering
	Master of Agricultural Economics
	Master of Agricultural Education
	Master of Applied Economics
	Master of Architectural Engineering
	Master of Art Education
	Master of Arts in Education
	Master of Arts in English
MAEd	Master of Arts Education
MAEE	Master of Agricultural and Extension Education
MAEL	Master of Arts in Educational Leadership
MAEM	Master of Arts in Educational Ministries
MAEP	Master of Arts in Economic Policy
	Master of Arts in Educational Psychology
MAES	Master of Arts in Environmental Sciences
MAET	Master of Arts in English Teaching
MAF	Master of Arts in Finance
MAFE	Master of Arts in Financial Economics
MAFM	Master of Accounting and Financial Management
MAFS	Master of Arts in Family Studies
MAG	Master of Applied Geography
MAGU	Master of Urban Analysis and Management
MAH	Master of Arts in Humanities
MAHA	Master of Arts in Humanitarian Assistance
MAHCM	Master of Arts in Health Care Mission
MAHG	Master of American History and Government
MAHL	Master of Arts in Hebrew Letters
MAHN	Master of Applied Human Nutrition
MAHR	Master of Applied Historical Research
MAHS	Master of Arts in Human Services
MAHSR	Master in Applied Health Services Research
MAIA	Master of Arts in International Administration
	Master of Arts in International Affairs
MAICS	Master of Arts in Intercultural Studies
MAIDM	Master of Arts in Interior Design and Merchandising
MAIH	Master of Arts in Interdisciplinary Humanities
MAIOP	Master of Applied Industrial/Organizational Psychology
MAIS	Master of Arts in Intercultural Studies
	Master of Arts in Interdisciplinary Studies
	Master of Arts in International Studies
MAIT	Master of Administration in Information Technology
MAJ	Master of Arts in Journalism
MAJCS	Master of Arts in Jewish Communal Service
MAJPS	Master of Arts in Jewish Professional Studies
MAJS	Master of Arts in Jewish Studies
MAL	Master of Athletic Leadership
MALA	Master of Arts in Liberal Arts
MALCM	Master in Arts Leadership and Cultural Management
MALD	Master of Arts in Law and Diplomacy
MALER	Master of Arts in Labor and Employment Relations
MALL	Master of Arts in Language Learning
MALLT	Master of Arts in Language, Literature, and Translation
MALP	Master of Arts in Language Pedagogy
MALS	Master of Arts in Liberal Studies
MAM	Master of Acquisition Management
	Master of Agriculture and Management
	Master of Applied Mathematics
	Master of Arts in Management
	Master of Arts in Ministry
	Master of Arts Management
	Master of Aviation Management
MAMC	Master of Arts in Mass Communication
	Master of Arts in Ministry and Culture
	Master of Arts in Ministry for a Multicultural Church
MAME	Master of Arts in Missions/Evangelism
MAMFC	Master of Arts in Marriage and Family Counseling
MAMFT	Master of Arts in Marriage and Family Therapy
MAMHC	Master of Arts in Mental Health Counseling
MAMS	Master of Applied Mathematical Sciences
	Master of Arts in Ministerial Studies
	Master of Arts in Ministry and Spirituality

MAMT	Master of Arts in Mathematics Teaching
MAN	Master of Applied Nutrition
MANT	Master of Arts in New Testament
MAOL	Master of Arts in Organizational Leadership
MAOM	Master of Acupuncture and Oriental Medicine
	Master of Arts in Organizational Management
MAOT	Master of Arts in Old Testament
MAP	Master of Applied Politics
	Master of Applied Psychology
	Master of Arts in Planning
	Master of Psychology
	Master of Public Administration
MAP Min	Master of Arts in Pastoral Ministry
MAPA	Master of Arts in Public Administration
MAPC	Master of Arts in Pastoral Counseling
MAPE	Master of Arts in Physics Education
MAPM	Master of Arts in Pastoral Ministry
	Master of Arts in Pastoral Music
	Master of Arts in Practical Ministry
MAPP	Master of Arts in Public Policy
MAPS	Master of Applied Psychological Sciences
	Master of Arts in Pastoral Studies
	Master of Arts in Public Service
MAPW	Master of Arts in Professional Writing
MAQRM	Master's of Actuarial and Quantitative Risk Management
MAR	Master of Arts in Reading
	Master of Arts in Religion
Mar Eng	Marine Engineer
MARC	Master of Arts in Rehabilitation Counseling
MARE	Master of Arts in Religious Education
MARL	Master of Arts in Religious Leadership
MARS	Master of Arts in Religious Studies
MAS	Master of Accounting Science
	Master of Actuarial Science
	Master of Administrative Science
	Master of Advanced Study
	Master of American Studies
	Master of Animal Science
	Master of Applied Science
	Master of Applied Statistics
	Master of Archival Studies
MASA	Master of Advanced Studies in Architecture
MASC	Master of Arts in School Counseling
MASD	Master of Arts in Spiritual Direction
MASE	Master of Arts in Special Education
MASF	Master of Arts in Spiritual Formation
MASJ	Master of Arts in Systems of Justice
MASLA	Master of Advanced Studies in Landscape Architecture
MASM	Master of Aging Services Management
	Master of Arts in Specialized Ministries
MASP	Master of Arts in School Psychology
MASS	Master of Applied Social Science
MASW	Master of Aboriginal Social Work
MAT	Master of Arts in Teaching
	Master of Arts in Theology
	Master of Athletic Training
	Master's in Administration of Telecommunications
Mat E	Materials Engineer
MATCM	Master of Acupuncture and Traditional Chinese Medicine
MATDE	Master of Arts in Theology, Development, and Evangelism
MATDR	Master of Territorial Management and Regional Development
MATE	Master of Arts for the Teaching of English
MATESL	Master of Arts in Teaching English as a Second Language
MATESOL	Master of Arts in Teaching English to Speakers of Other Languages
MATF	Master of Arts in Teaching English as a Foreign Language/Intercultural Studies
MATFL	Master of Arts in Teaching Foreign Language
MATH	Master of Arts in Therapy
MATI	Master of Administration of Information Technology
MATL	Master of Arts in Teaching of Languages
	Master of Arts in Transformational Leadership
MATM	Master of Arts in Teaching of Mathematics
MATRN	Master of Athletic Training
MATS	Master of Arts in Theological Studies
	Master of Arts in Transforming Spirituality
MAUA	Master of Arts in Urban Affairs
MAUD	Master of Arts in Urban Design
MAURP	Master of Arts in Urban and Regional Planning
MAW	Master of Arts in Worship
MAWSHP	Master of Arts in Worship
MAYM	Master of Arts in Youth Ministry
MB	Master of Bioinformatics
MBA	Master of Business Administration
MBA-AM	Master of Business Administration in Aviation Management
MBA-EP	Master of Business Administration–Experienced Professionals
MBAA	Master of Business Administration in Aviation
MBAE	Master of Biological and Agricultural Engineering
	Master of Biosystems and Agricultural Engineering
MBAH	Master of Business Administration in Health
MBAi	Master of Business Administration–International
MBAICT	Master of Business Administration in Information and Communication Technology
MBC	Master of Building Construction
MBE	Master of Bilingual Education
	Master of Bioengineering
	Master of Bioethics
	Master of Biomedical Engineering
	Master of Business Economics
	Master of Business Education
MBEE	Master in Biotechnology Enterprise and Entrepreneurship
MBET	Master of Business, Entrepreneurship and Technology
MBI	Master in Business Informatics
MBIOT	Master of Biotechnology
MBiotech	Master of Biotechnology
MBL	Master of Business Leadership
MBLE	Master in Business Logistics Engineering
MBME	Master's in Biomedical Engineering
MBMSE	Master of Business Management and Software Engineering
MBOE	Master of Business Operational Excellence
MBS	Master of Biblical Studies
	Master of Biological Science
	Master of Biomedical Sciences
	Master of Bioscience
	Master of Building Science
	Master of Business and Science
	Master of Business Statistics
MBST	Master of Biostatistics
MBT	Master of Biomedical Technology
	Master of Biotechnology
	Master of Business Taxation
MBV	Master of Business for Veterans
MC	Master of Classics
	Master of Communication
	Master of Counseling

MC Ed	Master of Continuing Education
MC Sc	Master of Computer Science
MCA	Master of Commercial Aviation
	Master of Communication Arts
	Master of Criminology (Applied)
MCAM	Master of Computational and Applied Mathematics
MCC	Master of Computer Science
MCD	Master of Communications Disorders
	Master of Community Development
MCE	Master in Electronic Commerce
	Master of Chemistry Education
	Master of Christian Education
	Master of Civil Engineering
	Master of Control Engineering
MCEM	Master of Construction Engineering Management
MCEPA	Master of Chinese Economic and Political Affairs
MCHE	Master of Chemical Engineering
MCIS	Master of Communication and Information Studies
	Master of Computer and Information Science
	Master of Computer Information Systems
MCIT	Master of Computer and Information Technology
MCJ	Master of Criminal Justice
MCL	Master in Communication Leadership
	Master of Canon Law
	Master of Christian Leadership
	Master of Comparative Law
MCM	Master of Christian Ministry
	Master of Church Ministry
	Master of Church Music
	Master of Communication Management
	Master of Community Medicine
	Master of Construction Management
	Master of Contract Management
MCMin	Master of Christian Ministry
MCMM	Master in Communications and Media Management
MCMP	Master of City and Metropolitan Planning
MCMS	Master of Clinical Medical Science
MCN	Master of Clinical Nutrition
MCOL	Master of Arts in Community and Organizational Leadership
MCP	Master of City Planning
	Master of Community Planning
	Master of Counseling Psychology
	Master of Cytopathology Practice
	Master of Science in Quality Systems and Productivity
MCPD	Master of Community Planning and Development
MCR	Master in Clinical Research
MCRP	Master of City and Regional Planning
	Master of Community and Regional Planning
MCRS	Master of City and Regional Studies
MCS	Master of Chemical Sciences
	Master of Christian Studies
	Master of Clinical Science
	Master of Combined Sciences
	Master of Communication Studies
	Master of Computer Science
	Master of Consumer Science
MCSE	Master of Computer Science and Engineering
MCSL	Master of Catholic School Leadership
MCSM	Master of Construction Science and Management
MCT	Master of Commerce and Technology
MCTM	Master of Clinical Translation Management
MCTP	Master of Communication Technology and Policy
MCTS	Master of Clinical and Translational Science
MCVS	Master of Cardiovascular Science
MD	Doctor of Medicine
MDA	Master of Dietetic Administration
MDB	Master of Design-Build
MDE	Master in Design Engineering
	Master of Developmental Economics
	Master of Distance Education
	Master of the Education of the Deaf
MDH	Master of Dental Hygiene
MDI	Master of Disruptive Innovation
MDM	Master of Design Methods
	Master of Digital Media
MDP	Master in Sustainable Development Practice
	Master of Development Practice
MDR	Master of Dispute Resolution
MDS	Master in Data Science
	Master of Dental Surgery
	Master of Design Studies
	Master of Digital Sciences
MDSPP	Master in Data Science for Public Policy
ME	Master of Education
	Master of Engineering
	Master of Entrepreneurship
ME Sc	Master of Engineering Science
ME-PD	Master of Education–Professional Development
MEA	Master of Educational Administration
	Master of Engineering Administration
MEAE	Master of Entertainment Arts and Engineering
MEAP	Master of Environmental Administration and Planning
MEB	Master of Energy Business
MEBD	Master in Environmental Building Design
MEBT	Master in Electronic Business Technologies
MEC	Master of Electronic Commerce
Mech E	Mechanical Engineer
MEDS	Master of Environmental Design Studies
MEE	Master in Education
	Master of Electrical Engineering
	Master of Energy Engineering
	Master of Environmental Engineering
MEECON	Master of Energy Economics
MEEM	Master of Environmental Engineering and Management
MEENE	Master of Engineering in Environmental Engineering
MEEP	Master of Environmental and Energy Policy
MEERM	Master of Earth and Environmental Resource Management
MEH	Master in Humanistic Studies
	Master of Environmental Health
	Master of Environmental Horticulture
MEHS	Master of Environmental Health and Safety
MEIM	Master of Entertainment Industry Management
	Master of Equine Industry Management
MEL	Master of Educational Leadership
	Master of Engineering Leadership
	Master of English Literature
MELP	Master of Environmental Law and Policy
MEM	Master of Engineering Management
	Master of Environmental Management
	Master of Marketing
MEME	Master of Engineering in Manufacturing Engineering
	Master of Engineering in Mechanical Engineering
MENR	Master of Environment and Natural Resources

MENVEGR	Master of Environmental Engineering
MEP	Master of Engineering Physics
MEPC	Master of Environmental Pollution Control
MEPD	Master of Environmental Planning and Design
MER	Master of Employment Relations
MERE	Master of Entrepreneurial Real Estate
MERL	Master of Energy Regulation and Law
MES	Master of Education and Science
	Master of Engineering Science
	Master of Environment and Sustainability
	Master of Environmental Science
	Master of Environmental Studies
	Master of Environmental Systems
MESM	Master of Environmental Science and Management
MET	Master of Educational Technology
	Master of Engineering Technology
	Master of Entertainment Technology
	Master of Environmental Toxicology
METM	Master of Engineering and Technology Management
MEVE	Master of Environmental Engineering
MF	Master of Finance
	Master of Forestry
MFA	Master of Financial Administration
	Master of Fine Arts
MFALP	Master of Food and Agriculture Law and Policy
MFAS	Master of Fisheries and Aquatic Science
MFC	Master of Forest Conservation
MFCS	Master of Family and Consumer Sciences
MFE	Master of Financial Economics
	Master of Financial Engineering
	Master of Forest Engineering
MFES	Master of Fire and Emergency Services
MFG	Master of Functional Genomics
MFHD	Master of Family and Human Development
MFM	Master of Financial Management
	Master of Financial Mathematics
MFPE	Master of Food Process Engineering
MFR	Master of Forest Resources
MFRC	Master of Forest Resources and Conservation
MFRE	Master of Food and Resource Economics
MFS	Master of Food Science
	Master of Forensic Sciences
	Master of Forest Science
	Master of Forest Studies
	Master of French Studies
MFST	Master of Food Safety and Technology
MFT	Master of Family Therapy
MFWCB	Master of Fish, Wildlife and Conservation Biology
MFWS	Master of Fisheries and Wildlife Sciences
MFYCS	Master of Family, Youth and Community Sciences
MG	Master of Genetics
MGA	Master of Global Affairs
	Master of Government Administration
	Master of Governmental Administration
MGBA	Master of Global Business Administration
MGC	Master of Genetic Counseling
MGCS	Master of Genetic Counselor Studies
MGD	Master of Graphic Design
MGE	Master of Geotechnical Engineering
MGEM	Master of Geomatics for Environmental Management
	Master of Global Entrepreneurship and Management
MGIS	Master of Geographic Information Science
	Master of Geographic Information Systems
MGM	Master of Global Management
MGMA	Master of Greenhouse Gas Management and Accounting
MGP	Master of Gestion de Projet
MGPS	Master of Global Policy Studies
MGREM	Master of Global Real Estate Management
MGS	Master of Gender Studies
	Master of Gerontological Studies
	Master of Global Studies
MH	Master of Humanities
MH Sc	Master of Health Sciences
MHA	Master of Health Administration
	Master of Healthcare Administration
	Master of Hospital Administration
	Master of Hospitality Administration
MHB	Master of Human Behavior
MHC	Master of Mental Health Counseling
MHCA	Master of Health Care Administration
MHCD	Master of Health Care Design
MHCI	Master of Human-Computer Interaction
MHCL	Master of Health Care Leadership
MHCM	Master of Health Care Management
MHE	Master of Health Education
	Master of Human Ecology
MHE Ed	Master of Home Economics Education
MHEA	Master of Higher Education Administration
MHHS	Master of Health and Human Services
MHI	Master of Health Informatics
	Master of Healthcare Innovation
MHID	Master of Healthcare Interior Design
MHIHIM	Master of Health Informatics and Health Information Management
MHIIM	Master of Health Informatics and Information Management
MHK	Master of Human Kinetics
MHM	Master of Healthcare Management
MHMS	Master of Health Management Systems
MHP	Master of Health Physics
	Master of Heritage Preservation
	Master of Historic Preservation
MHPA	Master of Heath Policy and Administration
MHPCTL	Master of High Performance Coaching and Technical Leadership
MHPE	Master of Health Professions Education
MHR	Master of Human Resources
MHRD	Master in Human Resource Development
MHRIR	Master of Human Resources and Industrial Relations
MHRLR	Master of Human Resources and Labor Relations
MHRM	Master of Human Resources Management
MHS	Master of Health Science
	Master of Health Sciences
	Master of Health Studies
	Master of Hispanic Studies
	Master of Human Services
	Master of Humanistic Studies
MHSA	Master of Health Services Administration
MHSM	Master of Health Systems Management
MI	Master of Information
	Master of Instruction
MI Arch	Master of Interior Architecture
MIA	Master of Interior Architecture
	Master of International Affairs
MIAA	Master of International Affairs and Administration
MIAM	Master of International Agribusiness Management
MIAPD	Master of Interior Architecture and Product Design

MIB	Master of International Business
MIBS	Master of International Business Studies
MICLJ	Master of International Criminal Law and Justice
MICM	Master of International Construction Management
MID	Master of Industrial Design
	Master of Industrial Distribution
	Master of Innovation Design
	Master of Interior Design
	Master of International Development
MIDA	Master of International Development Administration
MIDP	Master of International Development Policy
MIDS	Master of Information and Data Science
MIE	Master of Industrial Engineering
MIF	Master of International Forestry
MIHTM	Master of International Hospitality and Tourism Management
MIJ	Master of International Journalism
MILR	Master of Industrial and Labor Relations
MIM	Master in Ministry
	Master of Information Management
	Master of International Management
	Master of International Marketing
MIMFA	Master of Investment Management and Financial Analysis
MIMLAE	Master of International Management for Latin American Executives
MIMS	Master of Information Management and Systems
	Master of Integrated Manufacturing Systems
MIP	Master of Infrastructure Planning
	Master of Intellectual Property
	Master of International Policy
MIPA	Master of International Public Affairs
MIPD	Master of Integrated Product Design
MIPER	Master of International Political Economy of Resources
MIPM	Master of International Policy Management
MIPP	Master of International Policy and Practice
	Master of International Public Policy
MIPS	Master of International Planning Studies
MIR	Master of Industrial Relations
	Master of International Relations
MIRD	Master of International Relations and Diplomacy
MIRHR	Master of Industrial Relations and Human Resources
MIS	Master of Imaging Science
	Master of Industrial Statistics
	Master of Information Science
	Master of Information Systems
	Master of Integrated Science
	Master of Interdisciplinary Studies
	Master of International Service
	Master of International Studies
MISE	Master of Industrial and Systems Engineering
MISKM	Master of Information Sciences and Knowledge Management
MISM	Master of Information Systems Management
MISW	Master of Indigenous Social Work
MIT	Master in Teaching
	Master of Industrial Technology
	Master of Information Technology
	Master of Initial Teaching
	Master of International Trade
MITA	Master of Information Technology Administration
MITM	Master of Information Technology and Management
MJ	Master of Journalism
	Master of Jurisprudence
MJ Ed	Master of Jewish Education
MJA	Master of Justice Administration
MJM	Master of Justice Management
MJS	Master of Judaic Studies
	Master of Judicial Studies
	Master of Juridical Studies
MK	Master of Kinesiology
MKM	Master of Knowledge Management
ML	Master of Latin
	Master's in Law
ML Arch	Master of Landscape Architecture
MLA	Master of Landscape Architecture
	Master of Liberal Arts
MLAS	Master of Laboratory Animal Science
	Master of Liberal Arts and Sciences
MLAUD	Master of Landscape Architecture in Urban Development
MLD	Master of Leadership Development
	Master of Leadership Studies
MLE	Master of Applied Linguistics and Exegesis
MLER	Master of Labor and Employment Relations
MLI Sc	Master of Library and Information Science
MLIS	Master of Library and Information Science
	Master of Library and Information Studies
MLM	Master of Leadership in Ministry
MLPD	Master of Land and Property Development
MLRHR	Master of Labor Relations and Human Resources
MLS	Master of Leadership Studies
	Master of Legal Studies
	Master of Liberal Studies
	Master of Library Science
	Master of Life Sciences
	Master of Medical Laboratory Sciences
MLSCM	Master of Logistics and Supply Chain Management
MLT	Master of Language Technologies
MLTCA	Master of Long Term Care Administration
MLW	Master of Studies in Law
MLWS	Master of Land and Water Systems
MM	Master of Management
	Master of Mediation
	Master of Ministry
	Master of Music
MM Ed	Master of Music Education
MM Sc	Master of Medical Science
MM St	Master of Museum Studies
MMA	Master of Marine Affairs
	Master of Media Arts
	Master of Ministry Administration
	Master of Musical Arts
MMAL	Master of Maritime Administration and Logistics
MMAS	Master of Military Art and Science
MMB	Master of Microbial Biotechnology
MMC	Master of Manufacturing Competitiveness
	Master of Mass Communications
MMCM	Master of Music in Church Music
MMCSS	Master of Mathematical Computational and Statistical Sciences
MME	Master of Management in Energy
	Master of Manufacturing Engineering
	Master of Mathematics for Educators
	Master of Mechanical Engineering
	Master of Mining Engineering
	Master of Music Education
MMEL	Master's in Medical Education Leadership

MMF	Master of Mathematical Finance
MMFC/T	Master of Marriage and Family Counseling/Therapy
MMFT	Master of Marriage and Family Therapy
MMG	Master of Management
MMH	Master of Management in Hospitality
	Master of Medical Humanities
MMI	Master of Management of Innovation
MMIS	Master of Management Information Systems
MML	Master of Managerial Logistics
MMM	Master of Manufacturing Management
	Master of Marine Management
	Master of Medical Management
MMP	Master of Marine Policy
	Master of Medical Physics
	Master of Music Performance
MMPA	Master of Management and Professional Accounting
MMQM	Master of Manufacturing Quality Management
MMR	Master of Marketing Research
MMRM	Master of Marine Resources Management
MMS	Master in Migration Studies
	Master of Management Science
	Master of Management Studies
	Master of Manufacturing Systems
	Master of Marine Studies
	Master of Materials Science
	Master of Mathematical Sciences
	Master of Medical Science
	Master of Medieval Studies
MMSE	Master of Manufacturing Systems Engineering
MMSM	Master of Music in Sacred Music
MMT	Master in Marketing
	Master of Math for Teaching
	Master of Music Therapy
	Master's in Marketing Technology
MMus	Master of Music
MN	Master of Nursing
	Master of Nutrition
MN NP	Master of Nursing in Nurse Practitioner
MNA	Master of Nonprofit Administration
	Master of Nurse Anesthesia
MNAL	Master of Nonprofit Administration and Leadership
MNAS	Master of Natural and Applied Science
MNCL	Master of Nonprofit and Civic Leadership
MNCM	Master of Network and Communications Management
MNE	Master of Nuclear Engineering
MNL	Master in International Business for Latin America
MNM	Master of Nonprofit Management
MNO	Master of Nonprofit Organization
MNPL	Master of Not-for-Profit Leadership
MNpS	Master of Nonprofit Studies
MNR	Master of Natural Resources
MNRD	Master of Natural Resources Development
MNRES	Master of Natural Resources and Environmental Studies
MNRM	Master of Natural Resource Management
MNRMG	Master of Natural Resource Management and Geography
MNRS	Master of Natural Resource Stewardship
MNS	Master of Natural Science
MNSE	Master of Natural Sciences Education
MO	Master of Oceanography
MOD	Master of Organizational Development
MOGS	Master of Oil and Gas Studies
MOL	Master of Organizational Leadership
MOM	Master of Organizational Management
	Master of Oriental Medicine
MOR	Master of Operations Research
MOT	Master of Occupational Therapy
MP	Master of Physiology
	Master of Planning
MP Ac	Master of Professional Accountancy
MP Acc	Master of Professional Accountancy
	Master of Professional Accounting
	Master of Public Accounting
MP Aff	Master of Public Affairs
MP Th	Master of Pastoral Theology
MPA	Master of Performing Arts
	Master of Physician Assistant
	Master of Professional Accountancy
	Master of Professional Accounting
	Master of Public Administration
	Master of Public Affairs
MPAC	Master of Professional Accounting
MPAID	Master of Public Administration and International Development
MPAP	Master of Physician Assistant Practice
	Master of Public Administration and Policy
	Master of Public Affairs and Politics
MPAS	Master of Physician Assistant Science
	Master of Physician Assistant Studies
MPC	Master of Professional Communication
MPD	Master of Product Development
	Master of Public Diplomacy
MPDS	Master of Planning and Development Studies
MPE	Master of Physical Education
MPEM	Master of Project Engineering and Management
MPFM	Master of Public Financial Management
MPH	Master of Public Health
MPHE	Master of Public Health Education
MPHM	Master in Plant Health Management
MPHS	Master of Population Health Sciences
MPHTM	Master of Public Health and Tropical Medicine
MPIA	Master of Public and International Affairs
MPL	Master of Pastoral Leadership
MPM	Master of Pastoral Ministry
	Master of Pest Management
	Master of Policy Management
	Master of Practical Ministries
	Master of Professional Management
	Master of Project Management
	Master of Public Management
MPNA	Master of Public and Nonprofit Administration
MPNL	Master of Philanthropy and Nonprofit Leadership
MPO	Master of Prosthetics and Orthotics
MPOD	Master of Positive Organizational Development
MPP	Master of Public Policy
MPPA	Master of Public Policy Administration
	Master of Public Policy and Administration
MPPAL	Master of Public Policy, Administration and Law
MPPGA	Master of Public Policy and Global Affairs
MPPM	Master of Public Policy and Management
MPRTM	Master of Parks, Recreation, and Tourism Management
MPS	Master of Pastoral Studies
	Master of Perfusion Science
	Master of Planning Studies
	Master of Political Science
	Master of Preservation Studies
	Master of Prevention Science
	Master of Professional Studies
	Master of Public Service
MPSA	Master of Public Service Administration

MPSG	Master of Population and Social Gerontology
MPSIA	Master of Political Science and International Affairs
MPSL	Master of Public Safety Leadership
MPT	Master of Pastoral Theology
	Master of Physical Therapy
	Master of Practical Theology
MPVM	Master of Preventive Veterinary Medicine
MPW	Master of Professional Writing
	Master of Public Works
MQF	Master of Quantitative Finance
MQM	Master of Quality Management
	Master of Quantitative Management
MQS	Master of Quality Systems
MR	Master of Recreation
	Master of Retailing
MRA	Master in Research Administration
	Master of Regulatory Affairs
MRC	Master of Rehabilitation Counseling
MRCP	Master of Regional and City Planning
	Master of Regional and Community Planning
MRD	Master of Rural Development
MRE	Master of Real Estate
	Master of Religious Education
MRED	Master of Real Estate Development
MREM	Master of Resource and Environmental Management
MRLS	Master of Resources Law Studies
MRM	Master of Resources Management
MRP	Master of Regional Planning
MRRD	Master in Recreation Resource Development
MRS	Master of Religious Studies
MRSc	Master of Rehabilitation Science
MRUD	Master of Resilient Design
MS	Master of Science
MS Cmp E	Master of Science in Computer Engineering
MS Kin	Master of Science in Kinesiology
MS Acct	Master of Science in Accounting
MS Accy	Master of Science in Accountancy
MS Aero E	Master of Science in Aerospace Engineering
MS Ag	Master of Science in Agriculture
MS Arch	Master of Science in Architecture
MS Arch St	Master of Science in Architectural Studies
MS Bio E	Master of Science in Bioengineering
MS Bm E	Master of Science in Biomedical Engineering
MS Ch E	Master of Science in Chemical Engineering
MS Cp E	Master of Science in Computer Engineering
MS Eco	Master of Science in Economics
MS Econ	Master of Science in Economics
MS Ed	Master of Science in Education
MS Ed Admin	Master of Science in Educational Administration
MS El	Master of Science in Educational Leadership and Administration
MS En E	Master of Science in Environmental Engineering
MS Eng	Master of Science in Engineering
MS Engr	Master of Science in Engineering
MS Env E	Master of Science in Environmental Engineering
MS Exp Surg	Master of Science in Experimental Surgery
MS Mat SE	Master of Science in Material Science and Engineering
MS Met E	Master of Science in Metallurgical Engineering
MS Mgt	Master of Science in Management
MS Min	Master of Science in Mining
MS Min E	Master of Science in Mining Engineering
MS Mt E	Master of Science in Materials Engineering
MS Otol	Master of Science in Otolaryngology
MS Pet E	Master of Science in Petroleum Engineering

MS Sc	Master of Social Science
MS Sp Ed	Master of Science in Special Education
MS Stat	Master of Science in Statistics
MS Surg	Master of Science in Surgery
MS Tax	Master of Science in Taxation
MS Tc E	Master of Science in Telecommunications Engineering
MS-R	Master of Science (Research)
MSA	Master of School Administration
	Master of Science in Accountancy
	Master of Science in Accounting
	Master of Science in Administration
	Master of Science in Aeronautics
	Master of Science in Agriculture
	Master of Science in Analytics
	Master of Science in Anesthesia
	Master of Science in Architecture
	Master of Science in Aviation
	Master of Sports Administration
	Master of Surgical Assisting
MSAA	Master of Science in Astronautics and Aeronautics
MSABE	Master of Science in Agricultural and Biological Engineering
MSAC	Master of Science in Acupuncture
MSACC	Master of Science in Accounting
MSACS	Master of Science in Applied Computer Science
MSAE	Master of Science in Aeronautical Engineering
	Master of Science in Aerospace Engineering
	Master of Science in Applied Economics
	Master of Science in Applied Engineering
	Master of Science in Architectural Engineering
MSAEM	Master of Science in Aerospace Engineering and Mechanics
MSAF	Master of Science in Aviation Finance
MSAG	Master of Science in Applied Geosciences
MSAH	Master of Science in Allied Health
MSAL	Master of Sport Administration and Leadership
MSAM	Master of Science in Applied Mathematics
MSANR	Master of Science in Agriculture and Natural Resources
MSAS	Master of Science in Administrative Studies
	Master of Science in Applied Statistics
	Master of Science in Architectural Studies
MSAT	Master of Science in Accounting and Taxation
	Master of Science in Advanced Technology
	Master of Science in Athletic Training
MSB	Master of Science in Biotechnology
MSBA	Master of Science in Business Administration
	Master of Science in Business Analysis
MSBAE	Master of Science in Biological and Agricultural Engineering
	Master of Science in Biosystems and Agricultural Engineering
MSBCB	Master's in Bioinformatics and Computational Biology
MSBE	Master of Science in Biological Engineering
	Master of Science in Biomedical Engineering
MSBENG	Master of Science in Bioengineering
MSBH	Master of Science in Behavioral Health
MSBM	Master of Sport Business Management
MSBME	Master of Science in Biomedical Engineering
MSBMS	Master of Science in Basic Medical Science
MSBS	Master of Science in Biomedical Sciences
MSBTM	Master of Science in Biotechnology and Management
MSC	Master of Science in Commerce
	Master of Science in Communication
	Master of Science in Counseling
	Master of Science in Criminology

	Master of Strategic Communication
MSCC	Master of Science in Community Counseling
MSCD	Master of Science in Communication Disorders
	Master of Science in Community Development
MSCE	Master of Science in Chemistry Education
	Master of Science in Civil Engineering
	Master of Science in Clinical Epidemiology
	Master of Science in Computer Engineering
	Master of Science in Continuing Education
MSCEE	Master of Science in Civil and Environmental Engineering
MSCF	Master of Science in Computational Finance
MSCH	Master of Science in Chemical Engineering
MSChE	Master of Science in Chemical Engineering
MSCI	Master of Science in Clinical Investigation
MSCID	Master of Science in Community and International Development
MSCIS	Master of Science in Computer and Information Science
	Master of Science in Computer and Information Systems
	Master of Science in Computer Information Science
	Master of Science in Computer Information Systems
MSCIT	Master of Science in Computer Information Technology
MSCJ	Master of Science in Criminal Justice
MSCJA	Master of Science in Criminal Justice Administration
MSCJS	Master of Science in Crime and Justice Studies
MSCLS	Master of Science in Clinical Laboratory Studies
MSCM	Master of Science in Church Management
	Master of Science in Conflict Management
	Master of Science in Construction Management
	Master of Supply Chain Management
MSCMP	Master of Science in Cybersecurity Management and Policy
MSCNU	Master of Science in Clinical Nutrition
MSCP	Master of Science in Clinical Psychology
	Master of Science in Community Psychology
	Master of Science in Computer Engineering
	Master of Science in Counseling Psychology
MSCPE	Master of Science in Computer Engineering
MSCPharm	Master of Science in Pharmacy
MSCR	Master of Science in Clinical Research
MSCRP	Master of Science in City and Regional Planning
	Master of Science in Community and Regional Planning
MSCS	Master of Science in Clinical Science
	Master of Science in Computer Science
	Master of Science in Cyber Security
MSCSD	Master of Science in Communication Sciences and Disorders
MSCSE	Master of Science in Computer Science and Engineering
MSCTE	Master of Science in Career and Technical Education
MSD	Master of Science in Dentistry
	Master of Science in Design
	Master of Science in Dietetics
MSDM	Master of Security and Disaster Management
MSE	Master of Science Education
	Master of Science in Education
	Master of Science in Engineering
	Master of Science in Engineering Management
	Master of Software Engineering
	Master of Special Education
	Master of Structural Engineering
MSECE	Master of Science in Electrical and Computer Engineering
MSED	Master of Sustainable Economic Development
MSEE	Master of Science in Electrical Engineering
	Master of Science in Environmental Engineering
MSEH	Master of Science in Environmental Health
MSEL	Master of Science in Educational Leadership
MSEM	Master of Science in Engineering and Management
	Master of Science in Engineering Management
	Master of Science in Engineering Mechanics
	Master of Science in Environmental Management
MSENE	Master of Science in Environmental Engineering
MSEO	Master of Science in Electro-Optics
MSES	Master of Science in Embedded Software Engineering
	Master of Science in Engineering Science
	Master of Science in Environmental Science
	Master of Science in Environmental Studies
	Master of Science in Exercise Science
MSESE	Master of Science in Energy Systems Engineering
MSET	Master of Science in Educational Technology
	Master of Science in Engineering Technology
MSEV	Master of Science in Environmental Engineering
MSF	Master of Science in Finance
	Master of Science in Forestry
MSFA	Master of Science in Financial Analysis
MSFCS	Master of Science in Family and Consumer Science
MSFE	Master of Science in Financial Engineering
MSFM	Master of Sustainable Forest Management
MSFOR	Master of Science in Forestry
MSFP	Master of Science in Financial Planning
MSFS	Master of Science in Financial Sciences
	Master of Science in Forensic Science
MSFSB	Master of Science in Financial Services and Banking
MSFT	Master of Science in Family Therapy
MSGC	Master of Science in Genetic Counseling
MSH	Master of Science in Health
	Master of Science in Hospice
MSHA	Master of Science in Health Administration
MSHCA	Master of Science in Health Care Administration
MSHCPM	Master of Science in Health Care Policy and Management
MSHE	Master of Science in Health Education
MSHES	Master of Science in Human Environmental Sciences
MSHFID	Master of Science in Human Factors in Information Design
MSHFS	Master of Science in Human Factors and Systems
MSHI	Master of Science in Health Informatics
MSHP	Master of Science in Health Professions
	Master of Science in Health Promotion
MSHR	Master of Science in Human Resources
MSHRL	Master of Science in Human Resource Leadership
MSHRM	Master of Science in Human Resource Management
MSHROD	Master of Science in Human Resources and Organizational Development
MSHS	Master of Science in Health Science
	Master of Science in Health Services
	Master of Science in Homeland Security

MSHSR	Master of Science in Human Security and Resilience
MSI	Master of Science in Information
	Master of Science in Instruction
	Master of System Integration
MSIA	Master of Science in Industrial Administration
	Master of Science in Information Assurance
MSIB	Master of Science in International Business
MSIDM	Master of Science in Interior Design and Merchandising
MSIE	Master of Science in Industrial Engineering
MSIEM	Master of Science in Information Engineering and Management
MSIM	Master of Science in Industrial Management
	Master of Science in Information Management
	Master of Science in International Management
MSIMC	Master of Science in Integrated Marketing Communications
MSIMS	Master of Science in Identity Management and Security
MSIS	Master of Science in Information Science
	Master of Science in Information Studies
	Master of Science in Information Systems
	Master of Science in Interdisciplinary Studies
MSISE	Master of Science in Infrastructure Systems Engineering
MSISM	Master of Science in Information Systems Management
MSISPM	Master of Science in Information Security Policy and Management
MSIST	Master of Science in Information Systems Technology
MSIT	Master of Science in Industrial Technology
	Master of Science in Information Technology
	Master of Science in Instructional Technology
MSITM	Master of Science in Information Technology Management
MSJ	Master of Science in Journalism
	Master of Science in Jurisprudence
MSJC	Master of Social Justice and Criminology
MSJFP	Master of Science in Juvenile Forensic Psychology
MSJJ	Master of Science in Juvenile Justice
MSJPS	Master of Science in Justice and Public Safety
MSK	Master of Science in Kinesiology
MSL	Master in the Study of Law
	Master of School Leadership
	Master of Science in Leadership
	Master of Science in Limnology
	Master of Sports Leadership
	Master of Strategic Leadership
	Master of Studies in Law
MSLA	Master of Science in Legal Administration
MSLB	Master of Sports Law and Business
MSLFS	Master of Science in Life Sciences
MSLP	Master of Speech-Language Pathology
MSLS	Master of Science in Library Science
MSLSCM	Master of Science in Logistics and Supply Chain Management
MSLT	Master of Second Language Teaching
MSM	Master of Sacred Ministry
	Master of Sacred Music
	Master of School Mathematics
	Master of Science in Management
	Master of Science in Medicine
	Master of Science in Organization Management
	Master of Security Management
	Master of Strategic Ministry
	Master of Supply Management
MSMA	Master of Science in Marketing Analysis
MSMAE	Master of Science in Materials Engineering
MSMC	Master of Science in Management and Communications
	Master of Science in Mass Communications
MSME	Master of Science in Mathematics Education
	Master of Science in Mechanical Engineering
	Master of Science in Medical Ethics
MSMHC	Master of Science in Mental Health Counseling
MSMIT	Master of Science in Management and Information Technology
MSMLS	Master of Science in Medical Laboratory Science
MSMOT	Master of Science in Management of Technology
MSMP	Master of Science in Medical Physics
	Master of Science in Molecular Pathology
MSMS	Master of Science in Management Science
	Master of Science in Marine Science
	Master of Science in Medical Sciences
MSMSE	Master of Science in Manufacturing Systems Engineering
	Master of Science in Material Science and Engineering
	Master of Science in Material Science Engineering
	Master of Science in Mathematics and Science Education
MSMus	Master of Sacred Music
MSN	Master of Science in Nursing
MSNA	Master of Science in Nurse Anesthesia
MSNE	Master of Science in Nuclear Engineering
MSNS	Master of Science in Natural Science
	Master of Science in Nutritional Science
MSOD	Master of Science in Organization Development
	Master of Science in Organizational Development
MSOEE	Master of Science in Outdoor and Environmental Education
MSOES	Master of Science in Occupational Ergonomics and Safety
MSOH	Master of Science in Occupational Health
MSOL	Master of Science in Organizational Leadership
MSOM	Master of Science in Oriental Medicine
MSOR	Master of Science in Operations Research
MSOT	Master of Science in Occupational Technology
	Master of Science in Occupational Therapy
MSP	Master of Science in Pharmacy
	Master of Science in Planning
	Master of Speech Pathology
	Master of Sustainable Peacebuilding
MSPA	Master of Science in Physician Assistant
MSPAS	Master of Science in Physician Assistant Studies
MSPC	Master of Science in Professional Communications
MSPE	Master of Science in Petroleum Engineering
MSPH	Master of Science in Public Health
MSPHR	Master of Science in Pharmacy
MSPM	Master of Science in Professional Management
	Master of Science in Project Management
MSPNGE	Master of Science in Petroleum and Natural Gas Engineering
MSPPM	Master of Science in Public Policy and Management
MSPS	Master of Science in Pharmaceutical Science
	Master of Science in Political Science
	Master of Science in Psychological Services
MSPT	Master of Science in Physical Therapy
MSpVM	Master of Specialized Veterinary Medicine
MSRA	Master of Science in Recreation Administration
MSRE	Master of Science in Real Estate
	Master of Science in Religious Education

MSRED	Master of Science in Real Estate Development
	Master of Sustainable Real Estate Development
MSRLS	Master of Science in Recreation and Leisure Studies
MSRM	Master of Science in Risk Management
MSRMP	Master of Science in Radiological Medical Physics
MSRS	Master of Science in Radiological Sciences
	Master of Science in Rehabilitation Science
MSS	Master of Security Studies
	Master of Social Science
	Master of Social Services
	Master of Sports Science
	Master of Strategic Studies
	Master's in Statistical Science
MSSA	Master of Science in Social Administration
MSSCM	Master of Science in Supply Chain Management
MSSD	Master of Arts in Software Driven Systems Design
	Master of Science in Sustainable Design
MSSE	Master of Science in Software Engineering
	Master of Science in Special Education
MSSEM	Master of Science in Systems and Engineering Management
MSSI	Master of Science in Security Informatics
	Master of Science in Strategic Intelligence
MSSIS	Master of Science in Security and Intelligence Studies
MSSL	Master of Science in School Leadership
MSSLP	Master of Science in Speech-Language Pathology
MSSM	Master of Science in Sports Medicine
	Master of Science in Systems Management
MSSP	Master of Science in Social Policy
MSSS	Master of Science in Safety Science
	Master of Science in Systems Science
MSST	Master of Science in Security Technologies
MSSW	Master of Science in Social Work
MSSWE	Master of Science in Software Engineering
MST	Master of Science and Technology
	Master of Science in Taxation
	Master of Science in Teaching
	Master of Science in Technology
	Master of Science in Telecommunications
	Master of Science Teaching
MSTC	Master of Science in Technical Communication
	Master of Science in Telecommunications
MSTCM	Master of Science in Traditional Chinese Medicine
MSTE	Master of Science in Telecommunications Engineering
	Master of Science in Transportation Engineering
MSTL	Master of Science in Teacher Leadership
MSTM	Master of Science in Technology Management
	Master of Science in Transfusion Medicine
MSTOM	Master of Science in Traditional Oriental Medicine
MSUASE	Master of Science in Unmanned and Autonomous Systems Engineering
MSUD	Master of Science in Urban Design
MSUS	Master of Science in Urban Studies
MSW	Master of Social Work
MSWE	Master of Software Engineering
MSWREE	Master of Science in Water Resources and Environmental Engineering
MT	Master of Taxation
	Master of Teaching
	Master of Technology
	Master of Textiles
MTA	Master of Tax Accounting
	Master of Teaching Arts
	Master of Tourism Administration
MTC	Master of Technical Communications
MTCM	Master of Traditional Chinese Medicine
MTD	Master of Training and Development
MTE	Master in Educational Technology
	Master of Technological Entrepreneurship
MTESOL	Master in Teaching English to Speakers of Other Languages
MTHM	Master of Tourism and Hospitality Management
MTI	Master of Information Technology
MTID	Master of Tangible Interaction Design
MTL	Master of Talmudic Law
MTM	Master of Technology Management
	Master of Telecommunications Management
	Master of the Teaching of Mathematics
	Master of Transformative Ministry
	Master of Translational Medicine
MTMH	Master of Tropical Medicine and Hygiene
MTMS	Master in Teaching Mathematics and Science
MTOM	Master of Traditional Oriental Medicine
MTPC	Master of Technical and Professional Communication
MTR	Master of Translational Research
MTS	Master of Theatre Studies
	Master of Theological Studies
MTW	Master of Teaching Writing
MTWM	Master of Trust and Wealth Management
MUA	Master of Urban Affairs
MUAP	Master's of Urban Affairs and Policy
MUCD	Master of Urban and Community Design
MUD	Master of Urban Design
MUDS	Master of Urban Design Studies
MUEP	Master of Urban and Environmental Planning
MUP	Master of Urban Planning
MUPD	Master of Urban Planning and Development
MUPP	Master of Urban Planning and Policy
MUPRED	Master of Urban Planning and Real Estate Development
MURP	Master of Urban and Regional Planning
	Master of Urban and Rural Planning
MURPL	Master of Urban and Regional Planning
MUS	Master of Urban Studies
Mus M	Master of Music
MUSA	Master of Urban Spatial Analytics
MVP	Master of Voice Pedagogy
MVPH	Master of Veterinary Public Health
MVS	Master of Visual Studies
MWBS	Master of Won Buddhist Studies
MWC	Master of Wildlife Conservation
MWPS	Master of Wood and Paper Science
MWR	Master of Water Resources
MWS	Master of Women's Studies
	Master of Worship Studies
MWSc	Master of Wildlife Science
MZS	Master of Zoological Science
Nav Arch	Naval Architecture
Naval E	Naval Engineer
ND	Doctor of Naturopathic Medicine
	Doctor of Nursing
NE	Nuclear Engineer
Nuc E	Nuclear Engineer
OD	Doctor of Optometry
OTD	Doctor of Occupational Therapy
PBME	Professional Master of Biomedical Engineering
PC	Performer's Certificate
PD	Professional Diploma
PGC	Post-Graduate Certificate
PGD	Postgraduate Diploma

Ph L	Licentiate of Philosophy
Pharm D	Doctor of Pharmacy
PhD	Doctor of Philosophy
PhD Otol	Doctor of Philosophy in Otolaryngology
PhD Surg	Doctor of Philosophy in Surgery
PhDEE	Doctor of Philosophy in Electrical Engineering
PMBA	Professional Master of Business Administration
PMC	Post Master Certificate
PMD	Post-Master's Diploma
PMS	Professional Master of Science Professional Master's
Post-Doctoral MS	Post-Doctoral Master of Science
Post-MSN Certificate	Post-Master of Science in Nursing Certificate
PPDPT	Postprofessional Doctor of Physical Therapy
Pro-MS	Professional Science Master's
Professional MA	Professional Master of Arts
Professional MBA	Professional Master of Business Administration
Professional MS	Professional Master of Science
PSM	Professional Master of Science Professional Science Master's
Psy D	Doctor of Psychology
Psy M	Master of Psychology
Psy S	Specialist in Psychology
Psya D	Doctor of Psychoanalysis
S Psy S	Specialist in Psychological Services
Sc D	Doctor of Science
Sc M	Master of Science
SCCT	Specialist in Community College Teaching
ScDPT	Doctor of Physical Therapy Science
SD	Specialist Degree
SJD	Doctor of Juridical Sciences
SLPD	Doctor of Speech-Language Pathology
SM	Master of Science
SM Arch S	Master of Science in Architectural Studies
SMACT	Master of Science in Art, Culture and Technology
SMBT	Master of Science in Building Technology
SP	Specialist Degree
Sp Ed	Specialist in Education
Sp LIS	Specialist in Library and Information Science
SPA	Specialist in Arts
Spec	Specialist's Certificate
Spec M	Specialist in Music
Spt	Specialist Degree
SSP	Specialist in School Psychology
STB	Bachelor of Sacred Theology
STD	Doctor of Sacred Theology
STL	Licentiate of Sacred Theology
STM	Master of Sacred Theology
tDACM	Transitional Doctor of Acupuncture and Chinese Medicine
TDPT	Transitional Doctor of Physical Therapy
Th D	Doctor of Theology
Th M	Master of Theology
TOTD	Transitional Doctor of Occupational Therapy
VMD	Doctor of Veterinary Medicine
WEMBA	Weekend Executive Master of Business Administration
XMA	Executive Master of Arts

INDEXES

Displays and Close-Ups

Directories and Subject Areas

Following is an alphabetical listing of directories and subject areas. Also listed are cross-references for subject area names not used in the directory structure of the guides, for example, "City and Regional Planning (*see* Urban and Regional Planning)"

Graduate Programs in the Humanities, Arts & Social Sciences

Addictions/Substance Abuse Counseling
Administration (*see* Arts Administration; Public Administration)
African-American Studies
African Languages and Literatures (*see* African Studies)
African Studies
Agribusiness (*see* Agricultural Economics and Agribusiness)
Agricultural Economics and Agribusiness
Alcohol Abuse Counseling (*see* Addictions/Substance Abuse Counseling)
American Indian/Native American Studies
American Studies
Anthropology
Applied Arts and Design—General
Applied Behavior Analysis
Applied Economics
Applied History (*see* Public History)
Applied Psychology
Applied Social Research
Arabic (*see* Near and Middle Eastern Languages)
Arab Studies (*see* Near and Middle Eastern Studies)
Archaeology
Architectural History
Architecture
Archives Administration (*see* Public History)
Area and Cultural Studies (*see* African-American Studies; African Studies; American Indian/Native American Studies; American Studies; Asian-American Studies; Asian Studies; Canadian Studies; Cultural Studies; East European and Russian Studies; Ethnic Studies; Folklore; Gender Studies; Hispanic Studies; Holocaust Studies; Jewish Studies; Latin American Studies; Near and Middle Eastern Studies; Northern Studies; Pacific Area/Pacific Rim Studies; Western European Studies; Women's Studies)
Art/Fine Arts
Art History
Arts Administration
Arts Journalism
Art Therapy
Asian-American Studies
Asian Languages
Asian Studies
Behavioral Sciences (*see* Psychology)
Bible Studies (*see* Religion; Theology)
Biological Anthropology
Black Studies (*see* African-American Studies)
Broadcasting (*see* Communication; Film, Television, and Video Production)
Broadcast Journalism
Building Science
Canadian Studies
Celtic Languages
Ceramics (*see* Art/Fine Arts)
Child and Family Studies
Child Development
Chinese
Chinese Studies (*see* Asian Languages; Asian Studies)
Christian Studies (*see* Missions and Missiology; Religion; Theology)
Cinema (*see* Film, Television, and Video Production)
City and Regional Planning (*see* Urban and Regional Planning)
Classical Languages and Literatures (*see* Classics)
Classics
Clinical Psychology
Clothing and Textiles
Cognitive Psychology (*see* Psychology—General; Cognitive Sciences)
Cognitive Sciences
Communication—General
Community Affairs (*see* Urban and Regional Planning; Urban Studies)
Community Planning (*see* Architecture; Environmental Design; Urban and Regional Planning; Urban Design; Urban Studies)
Community Psychology (*see* Social Psychology)
Comparative and Interdisciplinary Arts
Comparative Literature
Composition (*see* Music)
Computer Art and Design
Conflict Resolution and Mediation/Peace Studies
Consumer Economics
Corporate and Organizational Communication
Corrections (*see* Criminal Justice and Criminology)
Counseling (*see* Counseling Psychology; Pastoral Ministry and Counseling)
Counseling Psychology
Crafts (*see* Art/Fine Arts)
Creative Arts Therapies (*see* Art Therapy, Therapies—Dance, Drama, and Music)
Criminal Justice and Criminology
Cultural Anthropology
Cultural Studies
Dance
Decorative Arts
Demography and Population Studies
Design (*see* Applied Arts and Design; Architecture; Art/Fine Arts; Environmental Design; Graphic Design; Industrial Design; Interior Design; Textile Design; Urban Design)
Developmental Psychology
Diplomacy (*see* International Affairs)
Disability Studies
Drama Therapy (*see* Therapies—Dance, Drama, and Music)
Dramatic Arts (*see* Theater)
Drawing (*see* Art/Fine Arts)
Drug Abuse Counseling (*see* Addictions/Substance Abuse Counseling)
Drug and Alcohol Abuse Counseling (*see* Addictions/Substance Abuse Counseling)
East Asian Studies (*see* Asian Studies)
East European and Russian Studies
Economic Development
Economics
Educational Theater (*see* Theater; Therapies—Dance, Drama, and Music)
Emergency Management
English
Environmental Design
Ethics
Ethnic Studies
Ethnomusicology (*see* Music)
Experimental Psychology
Family and Consumer Sciences—General
Family Studies (*see* Child and Family Studies)
Family Therapy (*see* Child and Family Studies; Clinical Psychology; Counseling Psychology; Marriage and Family Therapy)
Filmmaking (*see* Film, Television, and Video Production)
Film Studies (*see* Film, Television, and Video Production)
Film, Television, and Video Production
Film, Television, and Video Theory and Criticism
Fine Arts (*see* Art/Fine Arts)
Folklore
Foreign Languages (*see* specific language)
Foreign Service (*see* International Affairs; International Development)
Forensic Psychology
Forensic Sciences
Forensics (*see* Speech and Interpersonal Communication)

Transpersonal and Humanistic Psychology
Urban and Regional Planning
Urban Design
Urban Planning (*see* Architecture; Urban and Regional Planning; Urban Design; Urban Studies)
Urban Studies
Video (*see* Film, Television, and Video Production)
Visual Arts (*see* Applied Arts and Design; Art/Fine Arts; Film, Television, and Video Production; Graphic Design; Illustration; Photography)
Western European Studies
Women's Studies
World Wide Web (*see* Internet and Interactive Multimedia)
Writing

Graduate Programs in the Biological/ Biomedical Sciences & Health-Related Medical Professions

Acupuncture and Oriental Medicine
Acute Care/Critical Care Nursing Administration (*see* Health Services Management and Hospital Administration; Nursing and Healthcare Administration; Pharmaceutical Administration)
Adult Nursing
Advanced Practice Nursing (*see* Family Nurse Practitioner Studies)
Allied Health—General
Allied Health Professions (*see* Clinical Laboratory Sciences/Medical Technology; Clinical Research; Communication Disorders; Dental Hygiene; Emergency Medical Services; Occupational Therapy; Physical Therapy; Physician Assistant Studies; Rehabilitation Sciences)
Allopathic Medicine
Anatomy
Anesthesiologist Assistant Studies
Animal Behavior
Bacteriology
Behavioral Sciences (*see* Biopsychology; Neuroscience; Zoology)
Biochemistry
Bioethics
Biological and Biomedical Sciences—General Biological Chemistry (*see* Biochemistry)
Biological Oceanography (*see* Marine Biology)
Biophysics
Biopsychology
Botany
Breeding (*see* Botany; Plant Biology; Genetics)
Cancer Biology/Oncology
Cardiovascular Sciences
Cell Biology
Cellular Physiology (*see* Cell Biology; Physiology)
Child-Care Nursing (*see* Maternal and Child/Neonatal Nursing)
Chiropractic
Clinical Laboratory Sciences/Medical Technology
Clinical Research
Community Health
Community Health Nursing
Computational Biology
Conservation (*see* Conservation Biology; Environmental Biology)
Conservation Biology
Crop Sciences (*see* Botany; Plant Biology)
Cytology (*see* Cell Biology)
Dental and Oral Surgery (*see* Oral and Dental Sciences)
Dental Assistant Studies (*see* Dental Hygiene)
Dental Hygiene
Dental Services (*see* Dental Hygiene)
Dentistry
Developmental Biology Dietetics (*see* Nutrition)
Ecology
Embryology (*see* Developmental Biology)
Emergency Medical Services
Endocrinology (*see* Physiology)
Entomology
Environmental Biology
Environmental and Occupational Health
Epidemiology
Evolutionary Biology
Family Nurse Practitioner Studies
Foods (*see* Nutrition)
Forensic Nursing
Genetics
Genomic Sciences
Gerontological Nursing
Health Physics/Radiological Health
Health Promotion
Health-Related Professions (*see* individual allied health professions)
Health Services Management and Hospital Administration
Health Services Research
Histology (*see* Anatomy; Cell Biology)
HIV/AIDS Nursing
Hospice Nursing
Hospital Administration (*see* Health Services Management and Hospital Administration)
Human Genetics
Immunology
Industrial Hygiene
Infectious Diseases
International Health
Laboratory Medicine (*see* Clinical Laboratory Sciences/Medical Technology; Immunology; Microbiology; Pathology)
Life Sciences (*see* Biological and Biomedical Sciences)
Marine Biology
Maternal and Child Health
Maternal and Child/Neonatal Nursing
Medical Imaging
Medical Microbiology
Medical Nursing (*see* Medical/Surgical Nursing)
Medical Physics
Medical/Surgical Nursing
Medical Technology (*see* Clinical Laboratory Sciences/Medical Technology)
Medical Sciences (*see* Biological and Biomedical Sciences)
Medical Science Training Programs (*see* Biological and Biomedical Sciences)
Medicinal and Pharmaceutical Chemistry
Medicinal Chemistry (*see* Medicinal and Pharmaceutical Chemistry)
Medicine (*see* Allopathic Medicine; Naturopathic Medicine; Osteopathic Medicine; Podiatric Medicine)
Microbiology
Midwifery (*see* Nurse Midwifery)
Molecular Biology
Molecular Biophysics
Molecular Genetics
Molecular Medicine
Molecular Pathogenesis
Molecular Pathology
Molecular Pharmacology
Molecular Physiology
Molecular Toxicology
Naturopathic Medicine
Neural Sciences (*see* Biopsychology; Neurobiology; Neuroscience)
Neurobiology
Neuroendocrinology (*see* Biopsychology; Neurobiology; Neuroscience; Physiology)
Neuropharmacology (*see* Biopsychology; Neurobiology; Neuroscience; Pharmacology)
Neurophysiology (*see* Biopsychology; Neurobiology; Neuroscience; Physiology)
Neuroscience
Nuclear Medical Technology (*see* Clinical Laboratory Sciences/ Medical Technology)
Nurse Anesthesia
Nurse Midwifery
Nurse Practitioner Studies (*see* Family Nurse Practitioner Studies)
Nursing Administration (*see* Nursing and Healthcare Administration)
Nursing and Healthcare Administration
Nursing Education
Nursing—General
Nursing Informatics

Graduate Programs in the Physical Sciences, Mathematics, Agricultural Sciences, the Environment & Natural Resources

Graduate Programs in Engineering & Applied Sciences

Graduate Programs in Business, Education, Information Studies, Law & Social Work

Directories and Subject Areas in This Book

NOTES

NOTES

NOTES

NOTES

NOTES

NOTES

NOTES

NOTES

NOTES

NOTES

NOTES

NOTES

NOTES

NOTES

NOTES